THE CIVIL WAR EXTRA

Rally round the Flag, boys!
Rally once again;
There are traitors in the camp, boys,
And pirates on the main;
There are rebels in the front, boys,
And foes across the sea,
Who hate the proud republican
And scoff at you and me.

Rally round the Flag, boys!
Rally in your might;
Let the nations see how freemen
Can battle for the right;
Make the throbbing mountains echo
With the thunder of your tread;
With music sweet of martial feet
Salute our gallant dead.

Rally round the Flag, boys!
Rally with a cheer;
For all you love and cherish most,
For all that hold you dear,
Defend the brave old banner,
Unsullied from the earth —
Within its folds enshrined it holds
All that this life is worth.

Then rally round the Flag, boys!
Rally, rally still!
Rally from the valley,
And rally from the hill;
Rally from the ship, boys,
And rally from the plow;
Now or never is the word —
Never! failing now.

THE CIVIL WAR EXTRA

FROM THE PAGES OF
The Charleston Mercury & The New York Times

Edited by
Eugene P. Moehring
and
Arleen Keylin

ARNO PRESS
New York • 1975

A Note to the Reader

In the interest of legibility, complete front pages of *The Charleston Mercury* could not be reproduced in this book. The editors, therefore, have included only the most important news articles and editorials from each front page. (See page viii for a facsimile of a complete *Mercury* front page.)

In addition, *The New York Times* editorials did not originally appear on page one. They have been included in this book on redesigned pages.

The illustrations that appear under the *Mercury* banner and with *Times* editorials were not originally published by the newspapers, but have now been added for the benefit of the reader.

The art of printing newspapers in the 1860s obviously was not what it is today and certainly original copies of the two newspapers were not available to the Publisher. This volume, therefore, was created from 35mm microfilm.

Library of Congress Cataloging in Publication Data
Main entry under title:

The Civil War extra.

1. United States—History—Civil War, 1861-1865—Sources. I. Moehring, Eugene P. II. Keylin, Arleen. III. Charleston mercury. IV. New York times.
E464.C48 973.7 75-20220
ISBN 0-405-06662-7

Manufactured in the United States of America

Contents

1863

1864

1865

The Charleston Mercury.

VOLUME LXXIX. | CHARLESTON, S. C., TUESDAY, JULY 23, 1861. | NUMBER 11,209

The Daily Mercury

The Tri-Weekly Mercury

THE MERCURY.

TUESDAY, JULY 23, 1861.

Obituary.

GEN. BARNARD E. BEE.

Upon the wings of shining Victory comes the dark shaft of Death.

Our Richmond Correspondence.

RICHMOND, July 18.

THE WAR ON THE SEAS.

The Tri-Weekly Mercury

TRAVELLER'S GUIDE.

CHARLESTON POST OFFICE.

WHY NOT
STOP THE NUISANCE?

DEATH
TO BED BUGS!
DEATH
TO COCKROACHES!
DEATH
TO ANTS, ETC.

A HOUSE CLEANING GUARANTEED BY THE USE, according to directions, of ADOLPH ISAACSEN'S ELECTRIC POWDER. Mr. I. visits Europe and selects the powder himself, thus securing a uniformly good article. It is not poisonous to the human family. We append "a few from many" certificates:

CHARLESTON HOTEL, January 21, 1860.

Mr. ADOLPH ISAACSEN has tested in my establishment of ELECTRIC POWDER for the destruction of Roaches, vermin, etc., TO MY ENTIRE SATISFACTION, and I cheerfully recommend his article as worthy of patronage, considering it the best vermin destroyer in market.

GEO. MIXER.

THIS IS TO CERTIFY THAT MR. ADOLPH ISAACSEN has used his Exterminator on board this steamer with every success, and I recommend his Powder to all who are troubled, as a very good article.

W. C. PECK, Steamer Cecile.

THIS IS TO CERTIFY THAT MR. A. ISAACSEN HAS used his Insect Powder on board this steamer with complete success, and I cheerfully recommend it to any who may be troubled with Roaches, Ants, and other insects.

ISAAC B. DAVIS, Agent Steamer Edisto.

ISAACSEN'S GENUINE ELECTRIC POWDER is sold in this city and State only by his duly appointed Agents,

Van Schaack & Grierson,

WHOLESALE AND RETAIL DRUGGISTS,
No. 221 KING-STREET,
AT THE SIGN OF THE NEGRO AND GOLDEN MORTAR.

SANFORD'S
LIVER
INVIGORATOR

NEVER DEBILITATES.

PRICE ONE DOLLAR PER BOTTLE.

SANFORD'S
FAMILY
Cathartic Pills!

PRICE THIRTY CENTS.

CHARLES'
LONDON CORDIAL GIN.

STOP IT!!

Introduction

The Civil War wounded America as no other event in its history. Four bloody years of fighting left 600,000 dead and many more injured. The conflict devastated the plantations, homes and cities of half the nation. It depleted treasuries north and south, left families homeless, children fatherless and, worst of all, saddled a generation with bitter memories and life-long hatreds.

Previous decades had seen men struggle to prevent the holocaust, but a thousand events propelled America to war. General causes were legion: slavery, the "failure of race adjustment," constitutional paralysis, a war-mongering press, fierce economic conflict between the sections and a "blundering generation" of leaders. Southerners postponed secession throughout the 1850s in hopes that moderates like Stephen Douglas might draw the North to compromise. But those dreams vanished in 1860 with the election of anti-slavery's champion, Abraham Lincoln; his victory made civil war inevitable.

Once fighting had begun, the North relied on its cities. They were the distribution points through which men and materiel flowed southward to the front. They were also the scene of mass, patriotic demonstrations and draft riots and the home of a thousand factories whose whirling wheels produced the uniforms, arms and ammunition for the great conflict. Then too, these towns served as information centers to which war news was hurried from the battlefields. In Boston, Chicago, Philadelphia and New York great metropolitan newspapers collected reports daily and fed them to a news-hungry public. Competition was stiff, as fledgling journals battled established sheets for circulation.

No city boasted more newspapers than New York. There *The New York Times, Sun, Herald, Tribune, Evening Post* and a score of others vied for readers. Yet, by 1861, the ten-year-old *Times* had won plaudits for crisp, objective reporting, and its coverage of the Civil War only enhanced that reputation. Every day the latest war news blanketed the *Times* front page. Important proclamations, detailed battle accounts, troop movements and strategy all greeted the reader. Maps, too, appeared in the midst of campaigns or as previews to fighting. During the first two years especially, the *Times* provided maps of the key war zones in Virginia, North Carolina, Tennessee, Kentucky and Missouri. The paper's in-depth approach dictated front page treatment for all significant events. In fact, during major battles — Bull Run, Antietam, Chancellorsville, Gettysburg, Chickamauga, the Wilderness — headline coverage often ran three to five days.

Accuracy usually improved with later editions, since facts rarely emerged from the confusion immediately following a skirmish. A glaring example of inaccuracy occurred in 1861 when the *Times* erroneously credited the Union Army with victory in the First Battle of Bull Run; the next day brought an embarrassing admission of a brilliant Confederate triumph. Nevertheless, misstatement was inevitable in an era devoid of telephones, radios and other modern communication. Editors constantly exercised judgment over the authenticity of stories and no doubt withheld many a tale from print. Verification might delay some news, but once in print, stories were clear though spiced with traces of Yankee patriotism.

With news columns covering the front page, editorials usually appeared further back. The paper took positions on every aspect of the war: it evaluated generals, reviewed strategy, scrutinized Lincoln and condemned Jefferson Davis. Victory brought praise for all, and defeat the searching questions so vital to recovery. Nothing escaped the purview of the *Times* editors. Space and other limitations have restricted us somewhat, but we have printed key editorials to illustrate their flavor. These combined with numerous front pages represent Northern war coverage at its best.

Yet, if reporting in the North was commendable, what of the South? In this region, too, cities served as information centers. At first, however, urban Dixie had opposed secession. Indeed, the Presidential election of 1860 had seen New Orleans, Memphis, Louisville, Augusta and even Richmond vote heavily for the moderates, John Bell and Stephen Douglas. John Breckenridge, the secessionist, failed in every city but Savannah and Charleston. Savannah, dependent upon regional trade for its growth, hoped secession would cut Southern ties to Northern ports. Charleston favored disunion for similar reasons. Though once the South's great metropolis, Charleston suffered decline after 1800 in the face of competition from Savannah, New Orleans and other river towns. As mid-century approached, Charlestonites surely viewed secession as the key to resurgence. Only a rebel Confederacy could exile New York, Chicago, Pittsburgh, Boston and other dangerous rivals.

The *Charleston Mercury* led the town in support of rebellion. The paper was rabidly pro-South, and in flaming language depicted the War as an economic conflict — a

"Second War of Independence." Written in a style often tinged with emotion, the *Mercury* teems with denunciations of Lincoln and the "Yankees." Moreover, this fierce anti-Yankee sentiment usually seeps into the news stories as well, adding a sparkle to the coverage. Sarcasm and levity seemed more inspired in the *Mercury* than *Times*.

Despite its colorful writing, the *Mercury's* handling of the war never approaches the in-depth style of the *Times*. On some occasions, one can compare their treatment of the same event. Unfortunately, however, only major battles won front page coverage from both papers. The *Mercury* rarely awarded an item more space than the *Times*. This points to another difference between the two, emphasis. In the *Mercury*, war news usually shared page one with advertisements and other narratives. Even the bombing of Ft. Sumter conceded space to local stories and commercial notes. But still, this style provides refreshing contrast to the *Times's* all-news approach.

Unlike its New York counterpart, the *Mercury* printed front page editorials. These columns are of particular importance, since every war forces a society both to define and reinforce the values it is fighting for. And newspapers, as opinion-makers, invariably reflect this societal introspection. Reading the *Mercury* puts us inside the Confederate Mind to reveal a compelling personality. The paper responds to such critical questions as: "Must We Have War?" and "For What Are We Contending?" In addition, a fierce democratic impulse provokes denunciations of the Richmond government for attacks on the South's free press and suspension of *habeas corpus*. Then too, a loyal devotion to the rebel cause results in continuous pillorying of Jefferson Davis and his policy of "defensive warfare." These and other questions fill the *Mercury's* columns from Sumter's first shots until the *Mercury* suspended publication with Charleston's fall in February 1865.

Besides newspapers, Americans looked to illustrations for war description. Indeed, the conflict not only inspired numerous paintings, sketches and cartoons, but was also the first recorded on film. Thousands of pictures translated reams of copy into visible action. These graphics satisfied various needs. Some pictures served to shock the public conscience. Many artists hoped their depiction of falling horses, dying soldiers, blood-tinged streams and hillside cemeteries would force the nation to realize how vicious and de-humanizing war could become. Also, in time of battle, art often descends to propaganda. In the 1860s, various periodicals used pictures to reinforce sectional preferences and sustain the crusading spirit. Important, too, were the biting cartoons which debunked the enemy. *Harper's Weekly*, in particular, employed this weapon to ridicule Jefferson Davis, Robert E. Lee and the rebel cause itself. And, on occasion, Lincoln, Grant and other "heroes" found themselves, too, the object of *Harper's* scorn. For, even in wartime, sarcasm and humor refuse the backseat.

This book, therefore, chronicles how the media presented the Civil War to America. In addition to typical illustrations, all the human elements of a newspaper — distortion, bias, emphasis, humor, elation and chagrin — are presented as they actually appeared on page one.

Eugene P. Moehring

1861

The New-York Times.

VOL. X....NO. 2903. NEW-YORK, THURSDAY, JANUARY 10, 1861. PRICE TWO CENTS.

THE NATIONAL CRISIS.

STARTLING NEWS FROM CHARLESTON.

The Star of the West Fired into from Morris Island and Fort Moultrie.

The First Gun Fired by South Carolina.

The Steamer Gone to Sea Again.

HIGHLY IMPORTANT FROM WASHINGTON.

The President's Special Message on the Southern Troubles.

MAJOR ANDERSON SUSTAINED.

Great Fluttering Among the Secessionists.

INTERESTING DISCUSSION IN THE SENATE.

Appointment of a Special Committee of Investigation by the House.

The Sloop-of-War Brooklyn Going to Sea with Sealed Orders.

THE NEWS FROM CHARLESTON.

CHARLESTON, Wednesday, Jan. 9.

The *Star of the West*, in endeavoring to enter our harbor about daylight this morning, was opened upon by the garrison on Morris Island, and also by Fort Moultrie. The steamer put about, and went to sea.

I have not been able to learn whether the steamer or any person on board was injured. The belief is that no injury was sustained by either the boat or those on board. Fort Sumter did not respond.

Lieut. HALL, of Fort Sumter, came over to the city about 11 o'clock with a flag of truce. He repaired to the quarters of the Governor, followed by a crowd of citizens. He was in secret communication with the Governor and Council for two hours. At 2 o'clock he was sent in a carriage with the Governor's Aids to the wharf, and returned to Fort Sumter. The object of his mission is not known. It is supposed that it relates to the firing on the *Star of the West*.

The people are intensely excited.

There were no demonstrations against Lieut. HALL. There is a great curiosity to know what Lieut. HALL came for.

Our citizens were drawn in crowds to our wharves early this morning, in consequence of the frequent reports of cannon from seaward. Some twelve or fifteen reports were heard; many of them proceeded from the works on Morris Island.

LATER.

Lieut. HALL closed his interview with the Governor and Council about 2 o'clock. The facts have not transpired. We learn from high authority that they are of a most threatening character.

AUGUSTA, Ga., Wednesday, Jan. 9.

A dispatch received here from Charleston states that the steamship *Star of the West* attempted to reinforce Fort Sumter this morning, when the batteries on Morris Island opened a fire upon her. Some ten shots were fired at the *Star of the West*, when she retired. Fort Sumter did not fire a gun.

THE BROOKLYN GONE TO SEA.

NORFOLK, Va., Wednesday, Jan. 9.

The *Brooklyn* has put to sea. She passed the Capes at 2 o'clock this afternoon.

WASHINGTON, Wednesday, Jan. 9.

The object of the departure of the *Brooklyn* for Charleston is supposed to be relating to the *Star of the West*. In case the authorities of South Carolina oppose the ingress of the latter into the harbor the *Brooklyn* will probably bring back the troops to Norfolk.

THE STAR OF THE WEST SPOKEN.

Capt. RAMSAY, of the steamer *Thomas Swann*, which arrived on Tuesday night, reports that he passed the steamer *Star of the West* off Cape Hatteras on Monday, the 7th, bound south. Observing that she was a California steamer, her position attracted his notice, remarking, as he did at the time, that she was out of her track, and he ran for her. As they passed the steamer, soldiers were seen on board, and the passengers inquired of Capt. RAMSAY where they could be going. He replied that he thought they were bound to Charleston. From her position, and the time of day, the *Star of the West* would not have arrived at Charleston Bar before Tuesday noon. There Capt. McGOWAN would meet with unlooked-for obstacles in crossing the Bar,—all the buoys having been removed, and the ranges by which vessels may safely enter having been destroyed. One of the most important of these is a shield set upon a wooden frame-work, by which the light, at night, is obscured at a given point of the channel, and which serves as a range by which to steer during the day. This would render it very unsafe to attempt the bar until the channel could be sounded out, or until circumstances would permit him to proceed slowly by the lead. He may thus have been detained outside the bar until Wednesday morning. These circumstances probably account for the delay in hearing of the arrival of the steamer in the harbor of Charleston. What may have occurred upon the attempt of Capt. McGOWAN to reach Fort Sumter must be left to conjecture. A prominent citizen of Charleston yesterday stated that the *Star of the West* would as certainly be fired into as that she came within range of South Carolina guns. The rumors prevailing yesterday to the effect that a collision had already occurred were, of course, premature. Several South Carolinians in town, on hearing that "the war had commenced," hurriedly left for home by the evening train South, and others took passage this morning for Charleston on board of the steamer *Nashville*, which sails at 9 o'clock A. M.

MILITARY MOVEMENTS.

CHICAGO, Wednesday, Jan. 9.

Troops from Fort Leavenworth, numbering 200 men, 28 officers and 27 horses, *en route* for Fort McHenry, arrived here this evening, and leave to-night, *via* Pittsburgh.

BALTIMORE, Wednesday, Jan. 9.

A company of marines, numbering forty muskets, under Lieut. HOWELL, came in a special train from Washington this morning, and took possession of Fort McHenry, and raised the Stars and Stripes.

OUR WASHINGTON DISPATCHES.

WASHINGTON, Wednesday, Jan. 9.

In the Senate the reading of the Message created a great fluttering on the secession side. The allusion in it to the gallant Major ANDERSON was greeted with hisses and applause. The attempt of Senator DAVIS, of Mississippi, to get the letter of the South Carolina Commissioners to the President placed on the Senate record, was admirably prevented by Senator KING, who denounced their acts as "worse treason than that of ARNOLD and BURR." The failure of Senator DAVIS' proposal to read them, is regarded as an indorsement of the President by the Senate.

The appointment of a Special Committee by the House to investigate the statements in the Message, and consider the whole subject, is regarded as a test on indorsing the Message in that branch. The Chairman, Mr. HOWARD, is a staunch Republican.

The whole message receives almost universal commendation from the Union men, and censure and repudiation from the Secessionists. The latter regard the declaration of the intention to defend and hold the Federal property as a declaration of war and coercion.

Rumor this evening announces that to-morrow's issue of the *Constitution* will make a formal break with the President, the fire-eaters who now control the columns of the late Government organ having decided to denounce Mr. BUCHANAN for having entrapped them, by false promises and encouragement, into their present miserable position. They will denounce him editorially as a betrayer of all his friendships, and threaten to give proofs of his former connivance with their plans. The *Constitution* is said to be now mainly supported on funds advanced by Ex-Secretaries COBB, FLOYD, and THOMPSON, who wish to keep it in existence, as an element of mischief and distraction, until after next 4th of March, when its support from these sources—and probably from all others—will be cut off, unless its nominal editor and proprietor should see fit to become a candidate for the public printing, under Mr. LINCOLN, and prove successful in his endeavors.

I am informed that the *Star of the West*, although positively under orders for Charleston, sailed sooner than was expected, and that subsequent orders changing her course were forwarded, but did not reach her in season. The President is said to have been somewhat disappointed at this.

Prominent gentlemen in Charleston sent advices here to-day to the effect that the *Star of the West*, or any other vessel, attempting to reach Fort Sumter, or enter the harbor under the American flag, would be fired upon by the batteries and troops.

It has been a question in doubt for some days whether the members of seceding States will retain their seats in Congress after their States pass ordinances of secession. Although Florida virtually went out on Saturday, Senator YULEE was in the Senate on Monday and to-day, voting as usual. No objection will be made, as it would be considered a recognition of actual secession, although many express indignation at their presence even now among the members. It is well known that they remain only for mischief.

I understand the President has determined to purge the Executive departments of every officer who preaches secession. This measure is highly important. It is to be hoped that it will be enforced with prompt rigor.

The Government has advices from Major ANDERSON that he has everything necessary in abundance for a long seige, including fuel, which it had been feared was short.

The Committee of Thirty-three did not meet to-day. It stands adjourned subject to the call of Mr. CORWIN, the Chairman, who is expected in the meantime to make up a report to be submitted when it next meets. Upon this is to come a test as to whether the Republicans will compromise. It is reported here to-night that two other prominent Republican members manifest a disposition to compromise. This is said to be the result of THURLOW WEED's efforts in favor of the modification of ADAMS' proposition. The non-compromising members are laboring with them to-night to prevent their acceptance of that compromise. It is generally understood that the mission of that Committee has already been performed as far as it can be.

The indications to-night are that the Pacific Railroad will be killed in the Senate altogether, or materially modified. Senator WILSON designs to propose a modification, adding a northern route, and giving more lands and less money to the Southern and Central routes than is provided for by the present bill, so that the total increase of money expenditure shall be only fourteen millions more than for the two routes. He thinks this will secure a decided majority in both Houses.

Mr. RUSSELL was released from jail to-day, half a million of dollars bail having been procured—his own jailers going bail sufficient to make up the amount. His release was entirely unexpected by Mr. RUSSELL. He was surrounded by a large number of friends at the time, was warmly congratulated, and went at once with his friends to his rooms.

LATER.—It is stated privately on the authority of a Democratic Senator that the war steamer *Brooklyn* sails from Norfolk to-night under sealed orders. The hour is too late to enable me to verify the statement. If it is true it is probable that she goes to support the *Star of the West*, in relation to which vessel great anxiety is felt here.

DISPATCH TO THE ASSOCIATED PRESS.

WASHINGTON, Wednesday, Jan. 9.

There seems to be a mistake or misapprehension somewhere. It is denied by gentlemen very intimately related to the Administration, that the recruits to Fort Sumter were ordered without the previous sanction of the President; and, further, that the subject was discussed in the Cabinet, and that Acting Secretary of War HOLT, as well as some other members of the Cabinet, clearly understood that it was the wish of the President that the recruits should at once be sent.

The War Department is in possession of information that the Governor of South Carolina has forbidden the United States Sub-Treasurer at Charleston from paying the drafts of the Paymaster in favor of Major ANDERSON and his command, and the Sub-Treasurer has refused accordingly.

Half-a-million of dollars are daily expected from New-York by the Treasury Department.

Commander HARTSTENE, of South Carolina, has resigned his position in the Navy.

Capt. KEARNEY, of New-Jersey, has written a letter recalling his letter of resignation, but it appears this was never received at the Navy Department.

Senator SEWARD has the floor for Saturday, to speak on the State of the Union.

It appears from an official report, that since April last the Government has sold to various parties 24,000 muskets, altered from flint to percussion locks at a cost of 22 cents a-piece. The amount realized was $60,000. They are almost worthless, and were previously condemned by the ordnance officers.

A telegraphic dispatch from the Navy Department to an officer at Key West was recently intercepted at Mobile by the authorities there.

Energetic measures are being made for the protection of public property in and about the city.

Mr. J. H. RUSSELL was bailed out to-day. His bail was qualified to over $1,000,000, but at the instance of the United States District-Attorney it was reduced to $500,000.

Owing to a typographical error in the list of yeas on the adoption of Mr. ADRAIN's resolution, laudatory of Major ANDERSON, &c., the name of Mr. JENKINS, of Virginia, was printed instead of that of Mr. JUNKIN, of Pennsylvania. The former was not then in the city.

The following has been obtained from an official source.

The excess of Post-office Department expenditures over the income is thus given:

State	Amount	State	Amount
Maine	$32,534 88	Tennessee	161,278 59
Vermont	21 635 61	Missouri	420,714 81
New-Jersey	15 548 51	Illinois	199,390 41
Maryland	109,135 60	Ohio	280,462 87
Virginia	255 330 26	Indiana	147,500 63
North Carolina	128,859 89	Arkansas	289 808 14
South Carolina	140,409 67	Iowa	123,788 25
Georgia	165,744 23	California	774,942 75
Florida	167,218 78	Oregon	24,360 52
Alabama	262,351 44	Minnesota	66,032 62
Mississippi	251,904 80	New-Mexico	13,789 15
Texas	578,103 29	Utah	102,149 00
Kentucky	196,042 28	Nebraska	23,703 33
Michigan	84,515 02	Washington Ter.	37,449 47
Wisconsin	44,240 01	Kansas	42,253 16
Louisiana	357,693 14		
Total			$5,577,815 26

EXCESS OF RECEIPTS OVER EXPENDITURES.

State	Amount	State	Amount
New-Hampshire	$1,664 87	New-York	$604,006 78
Massachusetts	182,126 13	Pennsylvania	77,015 23
Rhode Island	25,113 50	Delaware	14,013 87
Connecticut	3,748 65	District Colum.	11,263 43
Total			$820,759 46

It may be remarked that the largest amount of foreign postage also is collected in these States.

Commander MAURY says that the long passage of the *Levant* does not, in his judgment, justify the supposition of her loss. He gives the reasons for his belief.

CONGRESSIONAL PROCEEDINGS.

SENATE.

A message from the President was received.

To the Senate and House of Representatives:

At the opening of your present session, I called your attention to the dangers which threatened the existence of the Union. I expressed my opinion freely concerning the original causes of those dangers, and recommended such measures as I believed would have the effect of tranquilizing the country, saving it from the peril in which it had been needlessly and most unfortunately thrown.

Those opinions and recommendations I do not propose now to defeat. My own convictions upon the whole subject remain unchanged. The fact that a great calamity was impending over the nation was even at that time acknowledged by every intelligent citizen. It had already made itself felt throughout the length and breadth of the land. The necessary consequences of the alarm thus produced were most deplorable. The imports fell off with a rapidity never known before, except in time of war, in the history of our foreign commerce. The Treasury was unexpectedly left without means, which it had reasonably counted upon, to meet its public engagements. Trade was paralyzed, manufactures were stopped, the best public securities suddenly sunk in the market, every species of property depreciated more or less, and thousands of poor men who depended upon their daily labor for their daily bread, were turned out of employment. I deeply regret that I am not able to give you any information upon the state of the Union, which is more satisfactory than what I was then obliged to communicate. On the contrary, matters are still worse at present than they then were. When Congress met a strong hope pervaded the whole public mind that some amicable adjustment of the subject would be speedily made by the representatives of the States, which might restore peace between the conflicting sections of the country. That hope has been diminished by every hour of delay, and as the prospect of a bloodless settlement fades away, the public distress becomes more and more aggravated. As an evidence of this, it is only necessary to say the Treasury notes authorized by the act of the 17th December last, were advertised according to law, and that no responsible bidder offered to take any considerable sum at par at a lower rate of interest than twelve per cent. From these facts it appears that in a Government, organized like ours, domestic strife, or even a well-grounded fear of civil hostilities, is more destructive of our public and private interests than the most formidable foreign war.

In my Annual Message I expressed the conviction, which I have long deliberately held, and which recent reflection has only tended to deepen and confirm, that no State has the right by its own act to secede from the Union, or throw off its Federal obligations at pleasure. I also declare my opinion to be, that even if that right existed, and should be exercised by any State of the Confederacy, the Executive Department of this Government had no authority, under the Constitution, to recognize its validity, by acknowledging the independence of such State. This left me no alternative, as the chief executive officer under the Constitution of the United States, but to collect the public revenues and protect the public property, so far as this might be practicable under existing laws. This is still my purpose. My province is to execute, not to make the laws. It belongs to Congress exclusively to repeal, modify or enlarge their provisions to meet exigencies as they may occur. I possess no dispensing power. I certainly had no right to make aggressive war upon any State, and I am perfectly satisfied that the Constitution has wisely withheld that power, even from Congress.

But the right and the duty to use military force defensively against those who resist the Federal officers in the execution of their legal functions, and against those who assail the property of the Federal Government, is clear and undeniable. But the dangerous and hostile attitude of the States towards each other has already far transcended and cast into the shade the ordinary Executive duties already provided for by law, and has assumed such vast and alarming proportions as to place the subject entirely above and beyond Executive control. The fact cannot be disguised that we are in the midst of a great revolution. Therefore, I recommend the question to Congress as the only human tribunal under Providence possessing the power to meet the existing emergency. To them, exclusively, belongs the power to declare war or to authorize the employment of military force in all cases contemplated by the Constitution, and they alone possess the power to remove all the grievances which might lead to war, and to secure peace and union to this distracted country. On them, and on them alone, rests the responsibility. The Union is a sacred trust, left by our revolutionary fathers for their descendants, and never did any other people inherit so rich a legacy. It has rendered us prosperous in peace and triumphant in war. The national flag has floated in glory over every sea, and under its shadow American citizens have found protection and respect in all lands beneath the sun. If we descend to considerations of purely material interest, when in the history of all time has a Confederacy been bound together by such strong ties of mutual interest? Each portion of it is dependent upon all, and all upon each portion, for prosperity and domestic security. Free trade throughout the whole supplies the wants of one portion from the productions of another, and scatters wealth everywhere. The great planting and farming States require the aid of the commercial and navigating States to send their productions to domestic and foreign markets, and furnish the naval power to render their transportation secure against all hostile attacks.

Should the Union perish in the midst of the present excitement, we have already had a sad foretaste of the universal suffering which would result from its destruction. The calamity would be severe in every portion of the Union, and would be quite as great, to say the least, in the Southern as in the Northern States.

The greatest aggravation of the evil and that which would place us in the most unfavorable light, both before the world and posterity, is, as I am firmly convinced, that the secession movement has been chiefly based upon misapprehension at the South of the sentiments of the majority in several of the Northern States. Let the question be answered from the political assemblies to the ballot-box, and the people themselves would speedily redress the serious grievances which the South have suffered. But in Heaven's name let the trial be made before we plunge into armed conflict upon the mere assumption that there is no other alternative. Time is a great conservative power. Let us pause at the momentous point, and afford the people, both of the North and South, an opportunity for reflection. Would that South Carolina had been convinced of this truth before her precipitate action. I therefore appeal through you to the people of the country, to declare in their might that the Union must and shall be preserved by all constitutional means. I most earnestly recommend that you devote yourselves to the question how this can be accomplished in peace. All other questions, when compared with this, sink into insignificance. The present is no time for palliatives. Prompt action is required. A delay in Congress to prescribe or recommend a distinct and practical proposition for conciliation, may drive us to a point from which it will be almost impossible to recede. A common ground on which conciliation and harmony may be produced, is surely not unattainable.

The proposition to compromise, by letting the North have exclusive control of the territory above a certain line, and to give Southern institutions protection below that line, ought to receive universal approbation. In itself, indeed, it may not be entirely satisfactory, but when the alternative is between reasonable concession on both sides and the destruction of the Union, it is an imputation on the patriotism of Congress to assert that its members will hesitate a moment. Even now the danger is upon us. In several States which have not yet seceded, the forts, arsenals and magazines of the United States have been seized. This is by far the most serious step which has been taken since the commencement of the troubles. This public property has long been left without garrisons and troops for its protection, because no person doubted its security under the flag of the country in any State of the Union. Besides, our small army has scarcely been sufficient to guard our remote frontiers against Indian incursions. The seizure of this property, from all appearances has been purely aggressive, and not in resistance to any attempt to coerce a State or States to remain in the Union. At the beginning of these unhappy troubles, I determined that no act of mine should increase the excitement in either section of the country. If the political conflict were to end in civil war, it was my determined purpose not to commence it, nor to furnish an excuse for it by any act of this Government. My opinion remains unchanged, that justice as well as sound policy requires us still to seek a peaceful solution of the questions at issue between the North and the South. Entertaining this conviction, I refrained even from sending reinforcements to Major ANDERSON, who commanded the forts of Charleston harbor, until an absolute necessity for doing so should make itself apparent, lest it might be regarded as a menace of military coercion, and thus furnish a provocation, or at least a pretext for an outbreak on the part of South Carolina. No necessity for these reinforcements seemed to exist. I was assured by distinguished, upright gentlemen of South Carolina that no attack on Major ANDERSON was intended, but that on the contrary it was the desire of the State authorities as much as it was my own, to avoid the fatal consequences which must eventually follow a military collision. And here I deem it proper to submit for your information copies of a communication dated 28th December, 1860, addressed to me by R. W. BARNWELL, J. H. ADAMS, and JAMES L. ORR, Commissioners of South Carolina, with the accompanying documents and copies of my answer thereto, dated Dec. 31. In further explanation of Major ANDERSON's removal from Fort Moultrie to Fort Sumter, it is proper to state that after my answer to the South Carolina Commissioners, the War Department received a letter from that gallant officer, dated Dec. 27, 1860, the day after his movement, from which the following is an extract:

"I will add, as my opinion, that many things convinced me that the authorities of the State designed to proceed to an hostile act (evidently referring to the orders dated Dec. 11, of the late Secretary of War.) Under this impression I could not hesitate that it was my solemn duty to move my command from a fort which we could not probably have held longer than 48 or 60 hours, to this one, where my power of resistance is increased to a very great degree."

It will be recollected that the concluding part of the orders was in the following words:

"The smallness of your force will not permit you, perhaps, to occupy more than one of the three forts, but an attack on, or attempt to take possession of either one of them, will be regarded as an act of hostility, and you may then put your command into either of them which you may deem most proper to increase its power of resistance. You are also authorized to take similar defensive steps whenever you have tangible evidence of a design to proceed to an hostile act."

It is said that serious apprehensions are to some extent entertained, in which I do not share, that the peace of this District may be disturbed before the 4th of March next. In any event it will be my duty to preserve it, and this duty shall be performed.

In conclusion, it may be permitted to me to remark that I have often warned my countrymen of the dangers which now surround us. This may be the last time I shall refer to the subject officially. I feel that my duty has been faithfully, though it may be imperfectly, performed, and whatever the result may be, I shall carry to my grave the consciousness that I at least meant well for my country.

(Signed,) JAMES BUCHANAN.

WASHINGTON CITY, Jan. 8, 1861.

Mr. SEWARD, of New-York, (Rep.,) presented the memorial of the New-York Chamber of Commerce, asking the establishment of steam postal service between San Francisco and China. Referred to the Committee on Post-offices and Post-roads.

Mr. SEWARD also presented a memorial, signed by the most prominent citizens of New-York City, concerning the present state and future happiness of the Union.

Mr. SEWARD got the floor to express his views on the President's Message.

Mr. HUNTER, of Virginia, (Dem.,) asked that the resolutions offered by him be made the special order for Friday. Agreed to.

Mr. YULEE, of Florida, (Dem.,) presented a bill to adjust the present differences between the States, which was ordered to be printed.

Mr. SLIDELL, of Louisiana, (Dem.,) presented a resolution of inquiry—that the President inform the Senate whether JOHN B. FLOYD at present fills the office of Secretary of War? If not, who fills the office? and if the appointment of Acting or Provisional Secretary has been made? and when, and by what authority it was made? and why the fact of such appointment was not communicated to the Senate? Laid over.

Mr. BROWN, of Mississippi, (Dem.,) presented the petition of W. C. JEWITT, of Pike's Peak, praying that Congress authorize the election of delegates by the people to a Convention to form a new Constitution, and providing for a new President and Congressmen, the assumption of National and State debts, acknowledging the rights of property of the South, and acknowledging our reliance as a Nation in the Almighty Power for the perpetuity of the Union, and our prosperity, peace and happiness as a people.

Mr. CLARK, of Missouri, (Dem.,) presented a resolution which he said he should offer as an amendment to the resolutions of the Senator from Kentucky (Mr. CRITTENDEN) when it came up:

Resolved, That the provisions of the Constitution are ample for the preservation of the Union, and the protection of all the material interests of the country; that it needs to be obeyed rather than to be amended; and an extrication from our present difficulties is to be looked for in strenuous efforts to preserve and protect the public property, and enforce the laws, rather than in new guarantees for particular interests, or compromises or concessions to unreasonable demands.

Resolved, That all attempts to dissolve the Union or overthrow the Constitution, with the exception of constructing it anew, are dangerous and illusory, and in the opinion of the Senate no reconstruction is practicable, and therefore to the maintenance of the existing Union and Constitution should be directed all the energies of the Government.

The resolutions were ordered to be printed.

Mr. BIGLER, of Pennsylvania, (Dem.,) presented sixty-five memorials of citizens of Pennsylvania, asking that the Crittenden resolutions be submitted to the people.

Mr. SEWARD called for the reading of the President's Message, and it was read.

Mr. DAVIS, of Mississippi, (Dem.,) called for the reading of the accompanying papers. [The correspondence with the South Carolina Commissioners, already published.]

Mr. DAVIS, of Mississippi, (Dem.,) said: At this time, when the whole country was looking anxiously to South Carolina, and especially to the port of Charleston, the excitement was intensified by the arrival of Commissioners here from South Carolina, with an offer to make peace negotiations, and to adjust the difficulties between South Carolina and the United States. The high character of these Commissioners, which was well known—especially one of them was known to those who have served in this Senate for many years, for his urbanity and Christianity in all relations of life—gave assurances that this negotiation might be peaceable, and gave reason to hope they might be successful. They were, however, suddenly terminated, and the rumor went forth that notwithstanding the high character of these gentlemen, they had violated all the amenities of life, and had insulted the President, and the fact was known everywhere that the Commissioners had retired from Washington, and the negotiations were abruptly terminated. The President, in his Message here, does not even allude to the cause of the failure of these negotiations, and does not even tell us that the Commissioners have gone home. He stops with the letter which he sent to them, and which I must say, with all respect to the high office which he holds, was wanting in fairness, and was a perversion of the arguments which they had presented. They replied to him, and exposed the unfairness of his treatment of the facts which they stated, certainly in a manner most uncomfortable to him, and he returned their letter as one which he could not receive, and in his communication to us he does not even permit us to know that these Commissioners had attempted to reply to the position he had taken. But, with this great misstatement of his paper to them, he sends that paper to the world without even a reference to the fact that he was answered. I have an authentic copy of their answer, and I send it to the desk that it may be read.

Mr. KING, of New-York, (Rep.,) said the Senator talks of the high character of the Commissioners. BENEDICT ARNOLD and AARON BURR once also had high characters.

Mr. DAVIS, interrupting—The Senator from New-York once occupied a higher position than he does now. I call the Senator to order.

Mr. KING—These men were here with a treasonable purpose.

Mr. DAVIS—I call the Senator to order. I sent a paper to be read, Sir.

Mr. KING—I call the Senator to order. I object to the reading of the paper.

Mr. DAVIS—If the Senator has the meanness to object, let it come back.

Mr. KING said he objected to the reading. He did not want the papers read.

A long discussion ensued on a point of order, and the Yeas and Nays were called on the decision of the Chair that the paper was understood to be part of the Senate papers.

Mr. KING said he objected to the reception of the paper, as he supposed it was supposed to supply a defect in the President's Message.

Mr. DAVIS explained that he sent the paper simply to be read as part of his remarks, consequently he was much surprised to hear the objection; but if the Senate chose to take the paper as a paper of his own, he had no objection. As the Senate had taken charge of it, he wanted them to dispose of it.

Mr. KING said he simply objected to the reception, as he supposed it was intended to supply a defect in the message, and thought it would be a rebuke to the President. He was willing the Senator should read the paper, but he was not willing to disapprove the action of the President in saying nothing of that letter.

The decision of the Chair was sustained. Ayes 31, Nays 19.

The Ayes and Nays were called on reading the paper—Ayes 36, Nays 13.

The last letter of the Commissioners was then read. It has already been published.

Mr. DAVIS—A very long episode has been introduced into the remarks which I proposed to make, and it has changed the conclusions to which I would have arrived. I feel now, even more than before, pity for the Chief Executive of the United States. The proposition was made here to read a paper as a part of my remarks, when the Senator from New-York took upon himself the duty of protecting the Executive. Fallen indeed is that Executive, who so lately was borne into the high office which he holds, upon the shoulders of the Democracy of the land, when he comes down to depend upon the Senator from New-York for protection. I well know that new converts are zealous, and to that excess of zeal I am willing to attribute that discourtesy to which I made reply this morning. But I ask, while the peace of the country was at stake, when all men who loved the Government which we inherited from our fathers looked anxiously for peace, why did not this paper, harsh in some of its terms I admit, change the purposes of the President? Why did he not then call upon them for the means by which peace could be restored? Thus he would have initiated a measure which might have led to auspicious results, and might have turned civil war away. Then we should not have stood waiting hourly, as we do to-day, for what the telegraph may bring us to decide whether we are to have peace or war. In the time which I have occupied here to-day, I have verified the proverb that our curses sometimes prove blessings. What I intended to have read and incorporated in my remarks, the Senator has placed in a position it would never have found, and has brought it out to the broad light of the Senate journals.

Mr. DAVIS here yielded to the motion of Mr. BIGLER, that the consideration of the message be postponed till to-morrow.

Mr. CRITTENDEN, of Kentucky, (Am.,) moved that his resolutions to submit amendments of the Constitution to the people be taken up.

Mr. CLARK said he wished to amend by substituting the resolution he had offered.

Mr. WILSON, of Massachusetts, (Rep.,) moved to postpone it till to-morrow.

Mr. PUGH, of Ohio, (Dem.,) thought it better to decide the question at once.

Mr. BIGLER spoke in favor of voting on the resolution now. He thought they had neglected the question too long. He thought there was political power enough here to save the country. It was never too late to struggle for the Union.

Mr. SAULSBURY, of Del., (Dem.,) made an appeal for a vote now, that the country might know if there was patriotism enough here to save the country, by the adoption of the resolutions.

The resolutions were then postponed till to-morrow.

The Pacific Railroad bill was taken up.

Mr. WILKINSON, of Minnesota, (Rep.,) moved that the bill be referred to a Select Committee.

Mr. GWIN, of California, (Dem.,) said he thought it would destroy the bill if it were referred to a Committee.

Mr. LATHAM, of California, (Dem.,) entered his protest against any reference of the bill.

Mr. RICE, of Minnesota, (Dem.,) said that it was evident that the friends of the bill intended to pass it without giving the Northwest a fair show. He moved its indefinite postponement.

Mr. BAKER, of Oregon, (Rep.,) seconded the motion.

Mr. LATHAM demanded the ayes and noes on the motion.

Mr. LANE, of Oregon, (Dem.,) thought that this was not the time to pass such a bill. He thought it was better to say to the South that their rights should be protected. He (LANE) did not believe that this railroad would restore peace.

Adjourned.

HOUSE OF REPRESENTATIVES.

Mr. STRATTON, of New-Jersey, (Rep.,) asked leave to present a memorial of the citizens of Princeton, on the subject of national affairs, containing practical suggestions.

Mr. BURNETT, of Kentucky, (Dem.,) objected.

The Speaker laid before the House the message from the President, given in the Senate's proceedings.

Mr. HOWARD, of Michigan, (Dem.,) moved that the message be referred to a Special Committee of five, with instructions to inquire whether any executive officers of the United States have been or are now treating or holding communication with any person or persons for the transfer of forts and other property; whether any demand for their surrender has been made, and by whom, and what answer has been given; whether any officer or officers have entered into any pledge not to send reinforcements of troops to the harbor of Charleston, and if so, when and where, by whom, and on what considerations; whether the Custom-house, Post-office and Arsenal at Charleston have been seized, by whom held in possession; whether any revenue cutter has been seized, and whether any efforts have been made to recover it. The Committee have powers to send for persons and papers, and report from time to time such facts as may be required by the national honor, &c.

Mr. HOUSTON, of Alabama, (Dem.,) raised the point that such instructions were against the rules.

Mr. HOWARD replied, and moved the previous question.

Mr. CRAWFORD, of Ga., (Dem.,) said there was no cause for excitement. They had passed beyond that point.

VOICES—There is no excitement—we are calm.

Mr. CRAWFORD continued—Men should be cool and understand the line on which they are going. He ineffectually sought to offer a substitute for the resolution.

Mr. GARNETT, of Va., (Dem.,) desired to have the President's Message considered in the Committee of the Whole on the state of the Union.

Mr. PHELPS, of Mo., (Dem.,) remarked that the President informs them they were in the midst of a revolution, inviting the adoption of such measures as may avert civil war. The President appeals to Congress to make an effort to restore the fraternal relations which ought to exist. The recommendation made by the President is entitled to the respect of the American people; but the resolutions pending, instead of proposing a remedy, look to a Special Committee to indict somebody. He would vote against the resolution as it did not meet the emergency.

Mr. FLORENCE, of Pennsylvania, (Dem.,) believing the resolution productive of no good, opposed it.

Mr. HILL, of Georgia, (Dem.,) said the resolution was not based on a pacific plan to adjust the difficulties.

Mr. MARTIN, of Virginia, (Dem.,) looked on the resolution as a firebrand to be thrown into the country, which was already excited.

The resolution passed; yeas, 133; nays, 62.

YEAS—Adams of Massachusetts, Adams of Kentucky, Adrain, Aldrich, Allen, Alley, Anderson of Kentucky, Ashley, Babbit, Beale, Bingham, Blair, Blake, Brayton, Briggs, Bristow, Buffinton, Burch, Burlingame, Burnham, Butterfield, Campbell, Carey, Carter, Clemens, Coburn, John Cochrane, Colfax, Covode, Cox, Curtis, Davis of Indiana, Dawes, Delano, Duell, Dunn, Edgerton, Edwards, Elliot, Ely, Etheridge, Farnsworth, Fenton, Ferry, Foster, Fouke, Frank, French, Gilmer, Gooch, Grow, Gurley, Hale, Hall, Hamilton, Haskin, Helmick, Hickman, Hoard, Holman, Howard of Ohio, Howard of Michigan, Humphrey, Hutchins, Irvine, Junkin, Kellogg of Michigan, Kellogg of Illinois, Kenyon, Kilgour, Larrabee, Leach of Michigan, Lee, Logan, Longnecker, Loomis, Lovejoy, Maclay, Marston, McClernand, McKean, McKnight, McPherson, Millward, Montgomery, Moorhead, Morrill, Morris of Pennsylvania, Morse, Nelson, Nixon, Nixon, Olin, Palmer, Perry, Pettit, Porter, Pottle, Edwin R. Reynolds, John H. Reynolds, Rice, Riggs, Robinson of Rhode Island, Robinson of Illinois, Royce, Scranton, Sedgwick, Sherman, Somes, Spaulding, Spinner, Stanton, Stevens, Stewart of Pennsylvania, Stokes, Stratton, Tappan, Thayer, Theaker, Tompkins, Train, Trimble, Vandever, Wade, Waldron, Washburn of Wisconsin, Washburne of Illinois, Webster, Wells, Wilson, Windom, Wood, Woodruff.

NAYS—Messrs. Anderson of Missouri, Avery, Barksdale, Barrett, Bocock, Boteler, Bouligny, Branch, Brown, Burnett, Clark of Missouri, Clopton, Cobb, Crawford, Dejarnette, Dimmick, Edmundson, English, Florence, Garnett, Gartrell, Hardeman, Harris of Virginia, Hatton, Hawkins, Hill, Houston, Hughes, Jones, Kunkel, Landrum, Leach of North Carolina, Leake, Love, Mallory, Martin of Ohio, Martin of Virginia, Maynard, McClernand, McRae, Millson, Moore of Kentucky, Moore of Alabama, Niblack, Pendleton, Peyton, Phelps, Pryor, Quarles, Reagan, Rust, Sickles, Simms, Smith of Virginia, Smith of North Carolina, Taylor, Vallandigham, Vance, Whiteley, Winslow, Woodson, Wright.

Mr. MAYNARD, of Tennessee, (Am.,) asked consent to offer a resolution that the minority report might be made from the Committee of Thirty-three.

Mr. HINDMAN, of Arkansas, (Dem.,) called on the Chairman to state the number of members attending the meetings; whether there was any probability of making a report, and state such particulars as would be calculated to shed some light on the subject.

Mr. BURNETT, of Kentucky, (Dem.,) said he understood from the member from Arkansas that there was no probability of agreeing. A number of the members representing the Slave States had withdrawn from it. Was it therefore politic or wise to continue the Committee, when there was no prospect that they ever would report. He wanted to discharge them.

No action was taken on the resolution.

The House went into Committee of the Whole on the State of the Union on the Civil and Miscellaneous Appropriation bill.

The Committee rose without coming to a conclusion on the bill.

On motion of Mr. LEAKE, of Virginia, (Dem.,) the Select Committee on the President's Special Message were instructed to inquire whether any arms have recently been removed from Harper's Ferry to Pittsburgh, and if so, by whose authority, and for what reasons?

The resolution was amended so as to extend the inquiry as to the removal of arms from all the arsenals.

Mr. MORRIS, of Pennsylvania, (Ind.,) presented a memorial from citizens of Philadelphia, (signed by men of all parties,) in favor of Mr. CRITTENDEN's Compromise. Referred to the Committee of Thirty-three. Adjourned.

THE DISUNION MOVEMENT.

THE MISSISSIPPI STATE CONVENTION.

PASSAGE OF THE ORDINANCE OF SECESSION.

JACKSON, Miss., Wednesday, Jan. 9.

The Convention has been in secret session nearly all the morning.

LATER.

The ordinance for the immediate secession of the State has passed the Convention by a vote of 84 to 15.

The prominent places in the city are illuminated to-night, guns are being fired, and fireworks let off in honor of the event.

THE ALABAMA STATE CONVENTION.

MONTGOMERY, Wednesday, Jan. 9.

The Convention yesterday and to-day has mostly been in secret session.

A Committee of Thirteen, consisting of seven Secessionists and six Coöperationists, were appointed yesterday to draw up the ordinance of secession. The Committee will probable report to-morrow. Nothing of interest was determined to-day.

Five Volunteer companies departed for Pensacola, Florida, to-day. It is understood that they went on request of the Governor of Florida.

On a test vote the secession ordinance will probably be passed by a few majority.

AN ATTACK FROM ALABAMA UPON THE FORTS AT PENSACOLA.

Extract of a private Letter dated

MONTGOMERY, Ala., Friday, Jan. 4.

* * * I have no doubt but there is now on foot,—indeed I may say I *know* there is,—*a scheme to capture the forts and public works at Pensacola.* The plan has it's head-quarters at this place, no doubt, and preparations are now being made here to this end. The details are kept secret of course, but the preparations are going on and our military are to take a hand in it. *It is confidently expected that a considerable force will leave here in a few days.*

Now, you know that I am a loyal citizen of Alabama, and sufficiently opposed to all the schemes of the enemies of the South. But I look upon this movement as madness, just as I look upon the action of South Carolina in regard to the public property there. I consider it absolutely suicidal in every view of the case for the South to do anything to provoke hostilities. I do not despair of a final settlement. The trouble is with those who have got placed in the front rank by the force of circumstances, and are so far committed to extreme measures that they would sooner see their country ruined than yield their position. There are enough, however, in both sections to take care of the country, if they could only be heard.

UNION MILITARY MOVEMENTS.

A meeting of about fifty persons was held, last evening, at the Mercer House, for the purpose of taking the preliminary steps towards organizing a military *corps* to be held in reserve, at the call of the Government, to sustain the laws, and to assist in maintaining the Union. Persons representing all parties were present. There was a free interchange of views, and Committees were appointed to draft by-laws and prepare business. Many names were placed on the roll.

THE PROPOSED NATIONAL CONVENTION.

RICHMOND, Tuesday, Jan. 8.

Resolutions have been laid before the Senate for a call for a National Convention, to propose amendments to the Constitution.

THE VIRGINIA LEGISLATURE.

RICHMOND, Va., Wednesday, Jan. 9.

A joint resolution was introduced in the Senate to-day to appoint a Committee to represent to the President of the United States that, in the judgment of the General Assembly of the State of Virginia, any additional display of military power on the South will jeopardize the tranquillity of the Republic, and that the evacuation of Fort Sumter is the first step that should be taken towards the restoration of peace and harmony. Laid over.

The resolutions relating to a National Convention, with the amendment for a Convention of the Slaveholding States to produce concert of action, were referred to the Joint Committee on Federal Relations.

The House has passed the second section of the Convention bill, designating the 4th of February next for the election of delegates.

UNION MEETING AT ELKTON, MD.

ELKTON, Md., Tuesday, Jan. 8.

A very large County meeting assembled here to-day. Every one was taken by surprise at the hearty enthusiasm with which strong Union resolutions were adopted. The refusal of Gov. HICKS to summon an Extra Session of the Legislature was warmly indorsed. Hon. ALEXANDER EVANS made a very able speech in support of the Union. The meeting was also addressed by JOHN BROWN and JAMES T. McCULLOUGH, Esqs. It indicated unmistakably a feeling of strong attachment and devotion to the Union.

WORKINGMEN'S MASS MEETING AT NEWARK.

NEWARK, N. J., Wednesday, Jan. 9.

A rather intemperate call for a mass meeting, this evening, of workingmen out of employment, caused some apprehensions of a disturbance; but the ulterior designs, if any, were frustrated by the good sense of the meeting, under the instructions of temperate speakers. Union speeches were delivered by Judges PIERSON, WAUGH, and others. A majority of a Committee of five presented resolutions indorsing and recommending the Crittenden Compromise, and commending the action of the President in supporting the act of Major ANDERSON, which were passed.

CONVENTIONS AT LOUISVILLE, KY.

LOUISVILLE, Wednesday, Jan. 9.

Both the Union and Douglas Democratic Conventions unanimously recommended the adoption of the Crittenden resolutions.

AFFAIRS IN SOUTH CAROLINA.

The Auburn *Advertiser* publishes the following letter from a citizen of Charleston:

CHARLESTON, Jan. 3, 1861.

DEAR ——: Things remain pretty much the same as when I last wrote you, which was on the 1st. It

[*Continued on Eighth Page.*]

The New-York Times.

VOL. X....NO. 2908. NEW-YORK, WEDNESDAY, JANUARY 16, 1861. PRICE TWO CENTS.

THE NATIONAL TROUBLES.

IMPORTANT FROM THE FEDERAL CAPITAL.

Programme for the Establishment of a Southern Confederacy.

Bad News for the Secessionists from Louisiana and Texas.

Another Proposition for Pacification by Mr. Crittenden.

The Pacific Railroad Bill Before the Senate.

Debate on the Army Appropriation Bill in the House.

Brilliant Assemblage at the President's First Levee.

RETURN OF THE BROOKLYN TO HAMPTON ROADS

The Seizure of the Government Works at Pensacola.

An Offer of New-York Militia to the Government.

OUR WASHINGTON DISPATCHES.

WASHINGTON, Tuesday, Jan. 15.

The Post-office Department is making up the accounts of the Mail contractors in South Carolina for the fourth quarter of 1860. Some seventy thousand dollars of balances will be due contractors, for which it is proposed to *give orders on the Sub-Treasury of Charleston.*

The resolution of the New-York Bankers at their meeting on Saturday to sustain the Government with money, is hailed here as a most encouraging token of confidence in its stability, and chills the movers for the Southern Confederacy, for they foresee that the two Republics cannot borrow in the same market.

[illegible]

MR. SEWARD'S SPEECH.

[illegible]

DISPATCH TO THE ASSOCIATED PRESS.

[illegible]

THE DISUNION MOVEMENT.

THE UNITED STATES SLOOP-OF-WAR BROOKLYN IN HAMPTON ROADS.

[illegible]

FIRST DIVISION N. Y. S. M. TENDERED FOR SERVICE.

[illegible]

MEETING OF THE STATE MILITARY ASSOCIATION.

[illegible]

THE POSITION OF PENNSYLVANIA.

INAUGURATION AND MESSAGE OF GOV. CURTIN.

[illegible]

VIRGINIA LEGISLATURE.

[illegible]

NORTH CAROLINA LEGISLATURE.

[illegible]

MEETING OF THE ALABAMA LEGISLATURE.

[illegible]

MASSACHUSETTS LEGISLATURE.

[illegible]

MAINE LEGISLATURE.

[illegible]

THE GEORGIA CONVENTION.

[illegible]

KENTUCKY AND A SOUTHERN CONFEDERACY.

[illegible]

FROM CHARLESTON.

[illegible]

HOW THE PENSACOLA NAVY-YARD WAS SURRENDERED.

[illegible]

SYMPATHY FOR SECESSION.

MEETING AT BROOKES' HALL

SOUTH CAROLINIAN RESOLUTIONS.

Speeches by D. W. Groot, Hon. Levi S. Chatfield, Marshal Rynders, &c.

[illegible]

THE CHAIRMAN'S SPEECH.

[illegible]

VICE-PRESIDENTS.

[illegible]

RESOLUTIONS.

[illegible]

[Continued on Eighth Page.]

The New-York Times.

VOL. X.....NO 2925. NEW-YORK, TUESDAY, FEBRUARY 5, 1861. PRICE TWO CENTS.

THE NATIONAL TROUBLES.

Assembling of the Peace Congress at Washington.

THE SESSIONS TO BE SECRET.

Probable Ultimatum of the Border Slave States.

THE MONTGOMERY CONVENTION ORGANIZED

Farewell Speeches of Messrs. Benjamin and Slidell in the Senate.

Statement of the Objects of a Southern Confederacy.

LATEST DISPATCHES FROM THE SOUTH.

Seizure of the Cutter Lewis Cass by the Alabamians.

ARRIVAL OF THE U. S. SHIP SUPPLY.

CONDITION OF AFFAIRS AT PENSACOLA.

Statement of Mrs. Lieutenant Slemmer and Mrs. Lieutenant Gilman.

OUR WASHINGTON DISPATCHES.

THE PEACE CONVENTION.

WASHINGTON, Monday, Feb. 4.

The Virginia delegation in the Peace Convention are determined to demand the equality of the South in all the territory hereafter to be acquired, as well as in that now held by the United States in order they say, that the present settlement may stand forever. Temporary expedients they ignore. In this they are supported by the entire Kentucky delegation, and a majority from Maryland. Missouri it is understood will take the same position.

The South will press for speedy action, as their Commissioners insist on a showing of hands immediately. The Northern delegations say they cannot see the policy of hurrying things, and will aim to take time for deliberation. The adjournment to-day, without permanent organization, looked at delay. Adjournments hereafter will be strenuously resisted by Virginia and Kentucky.

Mr. TYLER will be reported by the Committee for the Presidency of the Convention, but he does not desire it. He would much prefer being left free in the Convention, but will not decline.

The North Carolina men have indicated no policy as yet, but seem to be awaiting the developments from Virginia.

The Convention will hold its sessions secret, in order that Commissioners may confer more freely without public commital. Some of the Northern Commissioners were desirous to have open sessions, but the Southern men opposed it. They said they could hope for no good result with their conferences public.

The straightout Republican Congressmen, who are opposed to any and all compromises, about forty in number, are now in caucus at the Capitol, to canvass their future course, in eiew of the possible action of the Convention.

The Republicans in the Convention generally express themselves against any compromise, and have no expectation that anything will be agreed upon that will satisfy both sections. The chances are that the Convention will be utterly fruitless. The Vermont delegation did not act in the Convention, but are waiting for Massachusetts.

JUDGE GREENWOOD AND THE DEPARTMENT OF THE INTERIOR.

A telegram to one of your cotemporaries, that Judge GREENWOOD's nomination to the Interior Department had been speedily confirmed, and that he had attended Cabinet meetings, took the Judge by surprise, as it was the first information he had of the fact. He has neither been nominated, nor confirmed, but is quietly discharging his duties as Commissioner of Indian Affairs.

INTERVIEW BETWEEN THE PRESIDENT AND SENATOR SUMNER.

Senator SUMNER, at the request of Gov. ANDREW, has had an interview with the President, to get his answer to the tender, by Massachusetts, of her militia to sustain the Government.

This business ended, SUMNER asked "Is there anything else Massachusetts can do?"

The President replied "Yes; no State can do more. She can adopt the Crittenden compromise."

Mr. SUMNER continued—"Is that necessary?"

PRESIDENT—"It is."

Mr. SUMNER—"Massachusetts has not acted directly on the Crittenden proposition, which seeks to give Constitutional protection to Slavery, and disfranchise a large number of her citizens."

He added his opinion in the strongest language, that such are the convictions of her people, that they never would consent to any such proposition.

The President said he was discouraged by this declaration.

Mr. SUMNER rejoined that they could all stand on the common ground of the Constitution as administered by GEORGE WASHINGTON, and that the verdict of the people last November should both be recognized and protected, without price or condition.

RETURN OF THE OFFICERS OF THE COAST SURVEY.

DORR, the chief of the Coast Survey party, and HEBERTON, his assistant, who were on board the surveying schooner which was seized some time since by the Secessionists, near San Agustine, Florida, reported themselves, to-day, at the Coast Survey Office, and gave the particulars of the seizure and subsequent release of the vessel. DORR, on returning from a triangulating expedition ashore, found the schooner in the hands of the rebels. He told them he didn't care; that he was sent by Government to perform certain duties, and intended to do so. He was permitted to continue to use the vessel as a dépôt. When his work there was completed, he found that a battery had been planted, and was told he would be blown out of the water if he attempted to leave. Subsequently the vessel was drawn up by the rebels, under the guns of the battery. DORR and HEBERTON were taken out of the schooner, and the sailing master and crew were left on board. On receiving the news of the capture of the Louisiana forts, the garrison had a spree and got drunk. DORR and HEBERTON, remaining sober, found the sailing-master and started him to sea, and in order not to break their parole, and not to attempt to run away with the vessel, they took the land route themselves and arrived here to-day. The schooner was to be expected in New-York within a day or two.

DORR and his [aid were detained at Charleston a day and a half. They report a large force of Georgians concentrated around Fort Moultrie, ready to assist in the assault upon Sumter.]

THE REINFORCEMENT OF FORT SUMTER.

Many doubts are expressed here about the accuracy of the reported reinforcements of Sumter, especially in view of BUCHANAN's letter to JOHN TYLER, on the 25th ult., in which he says, distinctly, that the movements of the steamer *Brooklyn* are in no way connected with South Carolina.

ENGINEERS WANTED.

Steam frigates *Colorado*, *Mississippi* and *Minnesota*, now at Boston, and *Roanoke*, at Brooklyn, are at once to be put in requisition for service connected with the collection of the revenue at certain ports where the same cannot be collected by the usual means. The Navy Department is embarrassed by a lack of Engineers for the service now necessary,—the corps of Chiefs lacking five or more of its full complement. Besides, neither the first nor second assistant-corps are more than half complete.

A RESOLUTION TO UNMASK THE AUTHORS OF THE TREASON.

A resolution has been prepared to offer in the House, probably to-morrow, empowering the Select Committee of five on the President's Special Message, to inquire, in addition to the matters heretofore referred to them, concerning any movements that have been initiated, instigated, advised, counseled, or in anywise encouraged or promoted, having for their object the transfer, seizure, possession, use or occupancy, of arms, arsenals, fortifications, Custom-houses, Navy-yards, vessels, mints, or other property of the United States, by any person or persons, or under any other than Federal authority, with power to send for persons and papers. The intention of this movement is to unmask the conspirators. Its result will be to exhibit what few master spirits have really devised and directed the entire secession programme.

NOMINATIONS FOR THE SUPREME COURT.

Judge PETTIT is about to be nominated as Judge of the Supreme Court for Kansas.

J. S. BLACK, Secretary of State, is soon to be nominated to the vacancy on the Supreme Court Bench, occasioned by the death of Judge DANIELS.

UNION TRIUMPH IN VIRGINIA.

The Virginians here united have partial returns of the election to-day, by telegraph. They say their advices indicate that the Secessionists are defeated in twenty five out of thirty Counties. These are the Southwestern and the Central Counties. If the accounts are true, they show that the Secessionists are overwhelmingly defeated.

DISPATCH TO THE ASSOCIATED PRESS.

WASHINGTON, Mondah, Feb. 4.

It appears from the returns received at the War Department that the militia force of South Carolina, Georgia, Alabama, Florida, Mississippi and Louisiana, combined, is 341,000. These returns were severally made from the years 1838 to 1859. The returns for 1860 were only from the following:

Massachusetts	161,200	Virginia	143,155
Rhode Island	19,541	Minnesota	24,480
Connecticut	51,576	New-York	419,000

The aggregate of the whole country from these imperfect returns, is 3,168,000, of which about two and a half millions are infantry, 20,000 artillery cavalry, 13,000 artillery, and between 19,000 and 20,000 riflemen.

Within the last two weeks fifty speeches have been delivered in the House of Representatives on the crisis, nearly all of them in connection with the report from the Committee of Thirty-three. A number of gentlemen, besides, have been making preparations for an expression of their views on the same subject. Among so many contestants for the floor, the struggle to obtain it is quite lively, though as much cannot be said of all the speeches.

The Secretary of State thus far, since his entrance upon the duties of that office, has performed them without the assistance of an assistant Secretary. He desired much to secure in that capacity F. BAYARD, of Delaware, owing to this gentleman's peculiar qualifications for the place; but overruling considerations led him to decline the proffered appointment.

Col. HAYNE intended to leave for Charleston to-day, but having been informed that the President is preparing a reply to his communication demanding the surrender of Fort Sumter, will delay his departure till Wednesday.

The Executive Department of South Carolina has defined the position of that State on the subject of commercial arrangements, regarding it probable that the payment of duties and the clearance of vessels will be interfered with by the Government at Washington in such a manner as to render the transaction of business at Charleston difficult and embarrassing. The exposition of the law of nations, as made by the former and the present Secretary of State in the Peru case affecting the vessels *Georgiana* and *Lizzie Thomson*, is regarded as a sound doctrine appliable to South Carolina, which will permit no interference by the Government of the United States with such regulations as it may adopt, nor will the authority of the latter be permitted to be exercised within the limits of the State. It will be for the United States to impose upon vessels of States still members of this Confederacy such penalties as it may choose to provide for, what it may consider violations of its municipal laws.

The revenue cutter *McClelland*, lately fallen into the hands of Louisiana, is one of the largest and best cutters in the revenue service, just rebuilt and refitted.

Senator WIGFALL and others have telegraphed to Montgomery urging the appointment of ALEXANDER H. STEPHENS as Provisional President of the Southern Confederacy, in order to conciliate Southern conservatives.

The nomination of Judge PETIT, for Judge of the District of Kansas has been determined on.

Secretary of State BLACK will probably soon be nominated as Associate Justice of the Supreme Court, in place of Justice DANIEL, deceased.

PROCEEDINGS OF THE PEACE CONVENTION.

WASHINGTON, Monday, Feb. 4.

The Convention is sitting with closed doors. Mr. WRIGHT, of Ohio, is in the chair. A Committee on Permanent Organization has been appointed. It is supposed that JOHN TYLER will be permanent President. The Convention has refused to admit the Press.

LATER.—The Convention adjourned at half-past one to meet at noon to-morrow. All the States are present that have elected Commissioners except New-York, Tennessee, Missouri and Illinois. Eleven are fully represented.

Mr. WRIGHT, of Ohio, was temporary Chairman, and A. E. WARD of Maryland, temporary Secretary. A motion was made to admit the representatives of the Press to the floor. Laid on the table, to proceed to a permanent organization. A Committee of one from each State was appointed on Permanent Organization. Adjourned.

Maj. BERRETT says the doors will be kept closed to the public Press, until the Convention shall order otherwise. It is understood that he entire proceedings will be conducted in secret session.

A Committee are here of Secessionists from Maryland, to protest against the admission of the delegates from that State.

OUR WASHINGTON CORRESPONDENCE.

POSITION OF THE REPRESENTATIVES FROM THE FREE STATES UPON THE QUESTION OF COMPROMISE.

WASHINGTON, D. C., Sunday, Feb. 3, 1861.

In connection with the Convention which meets in this city to-morrow, your readers will find much interest in a statement of the division of Representatives in Congress from the Free States upon the question of compromise. For the Crittenden scheme there is not a single Republican in Congress, so far as I know, and very few Northern men of any party. It is believed here that the most of Northern readers hold the mistaken view that Mr. CRITTENDEN's plan is simply a restoration of the old Missouri Compromise of 1820. This is far from true—for while the act of 1820 merely prohibited Slavery north of 36° 30', and was silent with respect to it south of that line, Mr. CRITTENDEN's plan distinctly recognizes the right of Slavery to all territory south of the parallel of 36° 30', and, in its present shape, applies the dont line to all territory which may be hereafter acquired—thus offering a heavy premium to war and fillibusterism for slave territory hereafter.

The "Border State proposition" is the old Missouri Compromise, with the addition of a stipulation that neither Congress nor the Territorial Legislatures shall ever either introduce or exclude Slavery south of 36° 30', but leave the institution to fight its own way in the courts, and before the people when they come to form State Governments. The proposition of Mr. ADAMS, of Massachusetts, looks to the immediate admission of New-Mexico as a State, with such Constitution as the people may frame at a Convention next Autumn; also to the incorporation into the Constitution of a guarantee that the Federal Government shall never interfere with Slavery in the States. There is little difference between the supporters of the Border State and the Adams propositions; and all who would sustain one of them would sustain the other, probably if necessary to provide an adjustment of the pending national issues.

The following is a statement, as nearly as can be ascertained, of the relative strength of the friends of amicable adjustment, upon the basis of either of the propositions last named, or some other which does not contribute practically to the extension of Slavery or the humiliation of the Republican Party:

	For Compromise.	Against Compromise.
Maine	3	3
New-Hampshire	—	3
Vermont	3	—
Massachusetts	4	7
Rhode Island	2	—
Connecticut	3	1
New-York	19	10
Pennsylvania	20	—
Ohio	16	4
Wisconsin	1	2
Illinois	7	2
Indiana	7	1
Michigan	2	2
Minnesota	—	2
New-Jersey	5	3
Iowa	2	—
Oregon	1	—
California	2	—
Kansas	1	—
Totals	98	40

Of course in this list some are left out whose political *status* never is known until they discover which course the majority will pursue. A few doubtful gentlemen are counted among those who are willing to make accommodating terms with the Border States, as they will undoubtedly be found voting thus when a vote upon the subject is reached. This class includes both Republicans and Democrats who are willing to accept some one or all the measures that have been proposed. Those who are set down as against compromise are those gentlemen who by their words and votes upon the few test questions that have arisen have thus far exhibited a disposition to yield nothing to the Southern States, or to "make concessions to the slave power," as they term it.

It is not to be presumed that this canvass is strictly correct, but the result stated is certainly not far from the present complexion of the House. What effect may be had upon members by events of the ensuing week, before the end of which a vote cannot probably be reached, cannot be foreseen. Should the Border States demand more than has been already offered them, the Anti-Compromisists will have a majority of the House at once. Should the same moderation prevail which has marked the past week in the House, almost any one of the present pending propositions, except Mr. CRITTENDEN's, will receive a large majority of the votes of the House.

The political complexion of the Senate is more doubtful and not so easily ascertained, but it is believed by the leaders that a large majority are now in favor of the adoption of any reasonable proposition for settlement of our national difficulties.

In consideration of the important action to which Congress will soon be called, with regard to the state of the Union, the Republicans have resolved to call to their posts all the absentees, and to attend more constantly to their duties, according to the resolution of the Republicans in caucus some weeks since.

A Union man, from Virginia and a Secessionist from Louisiana, got into violent words yesterday about political matters, when the Secessionist struck the Union man, who was off his guard, knocking him down, severely beating and injuring him, and the bystanders say would have killed him had they not interfered and separated them. This is the first blood drawn by secession in Washington.

THE MONTGOMERY CONVENTION.

PERMANENT ORGANIZATION EFFECTED.

HOWELL COBB SELECTED TO PRESIDE—HIS ADDRESS, ETC.

MONTGOMERY, Ala., Monday, Feb. 4.

The Convention met at noon, R. W. BARNWELL, temporary Chairman.

An impressive prayer was offered by Rev. BASIL MANLEY.

On motion of R. B. RHETT, HOWELL COBB was selected for permanent President by acclamation, and JOHNSON F. HOOPER was selected as permanent Secretary.

All the Delegates were present except Mr. F. MORTON, of Florida.

In the course of Mr. COBB's address, after taking the Chair, he said, the occasion which assembled us together was one of no ordinary character. We meet as the representatives of sovereign and independent States, who by a solemn judgment have dissolved all the political association which connected them with the Government of the United States. It is now a fixed irrevocable fact. The separation is perfect, complete and perpetual. The great duty now imposed is to provide a Government for our future security and protection. We can and should extend to our sister States, our late sister States, who are identified in interest and feeling and institutions, a cordial invitation to unite in a common destiny, and should be desirous at the same time of maintaining with our confederates friendly relations, political and commercial.

After the usual preliminary business was attended to, adjourned till to-morrow.

THE VIRGINIA ELECTION.

RICHMOND, Monday, Feb. 4.

This county elects one Secessionist and two Unionists. Henrico, Chesterfield, Diuwiddie, Prince George, Greenville, Surry, Alexandria, Petersburgh, Norfolk and Portsmouth elect Unionists.

WHEELING, Monday, Feb. 4.

The election, to-day, for delegates to the State Convention, resulted in the election of SHERRARD CLEMENS, and C. D. HUBBARD, Anti-Secessionists, by about 500 majority. The excitement was very great. Union candidates are elected in Marion, Taylor, Wood, Brooke and Hancock Counties. But very few votes were polled against referring the action of the Convention back to the people.

RICHMOND, Monday, Feb. 4.

Henrico elects three Unionists.

Augusta, three Unionists.

Campbell, two Unionists.

Charlotte County is for secession.

Amelia and Nottoway, probably so.

Pittsylvania and Halifax, Union.

Lynchburgh, Union.

The vote is generally in favor of a reference to the people.

HON. SHERRARD CLEMENS SUSTAINED.

WHEELING, Monday, Feb. 4.

Hon. SHERRARD CLEMENS and C. D. HUBBARD, anti-secession under any circumstances, were elected triumphantly to-day, to the State Convention, over their opponents, who refused to pledge themselves that they would not sign an ordinance of secession.

Reports from all the counties of the Pan Handle elect the anti-secession candidates by decided majorities.

A dead set was made at CLEMENS by the ultra-disunionists, reducing his majority somewhat, but he was triumphantly carried through. Thus was his position in Congress victoriously sustained.

THE NORTH CAROLINA LEGISLATURE.

RALEIGH, N. C., Monday, Feb. 4.

The House, to-day passed, unanimously, a resolution declaring that in case reconciliation fails, North Carolina goes with the other Slave States.

The Legislature will adjourn, perhaps, and await results.

FROM FORT PICKENS.

ARRIVAL OF THE UNITED STATES SHIP SUPPLY.

THE OFFICERS AND GARRISON OF THE WARRINGTON YARD ON BOARD.

The United States storeship *Supply* arrived here yesterday from Pensacola, Fla., which port she left on the 16th ult. She has on board the officers, marines and United States sailors who were on duty at the Warrington Yard when it was taken possession of by the Floridians.

The *Supply* is a staunch old ship, and was purchased for $10,000 during the Mexican war. She was taking in coal and stores for the home fleet, which they badly need at present, when necessity compelled her destination to be changed. Part of the stores and provisions which were on board the vessel were left at Fort Pickens, for the use of the garrison there.

The *Supply* reports that the old steamer *Fulton* was taken by the Secessionists, confirming our advices of the 6th ult. The only Government property on board is about 300 tons of coal and some provisions.

The Commander of the *Supply*, immediately on his arrival, telegraphed for instructions to Washington, pending the reply to which his command will remain as at present. The marines are in charge of Sergeant REYNOLDS, and will, it is believed, be immediately sent on to reinforce the Federal troops at the National Capital. Up to last evening they had not left the vessel. There are only about forty-eight of them altogether. Annexed is a correct list of the officers and others who came here in the *Supply*:

Captain—Henry Stalke.

Lieutenants—J. D. Daniels, Henry Erben, W. L. Bradford.

Master—W. N. Allen.

Paymaster—E. W. Dunne.

Captain's Clerk—John Van Dyke.

Purser's Clerk—A. C. Bowie.

Passengers—Mrs. Slemmer, wife of Lieut. Slemmer, nurse and child; Mrs. Gilman, wife of Lieut. Gilman, now at Fort Pickens; Boatswain Dixon, and family; Gunner Cooper, and family; Sailmaker Hunter; Carpenter Holmes, Lieut. Irwin lady, mother-in-law and two children and some mechanics from the Pensacola Yard.

The United States ship *Relief*, having taken in a heavy cargo of stores and provisions, left the Navy-yard yesterday, bound, it is said, for the coast of Africa. There is a rumor that her destination is located on this hemisphere.

WHAT HAS BEEN DONE AT PENSACOLA.

Correspondence by the Supply.

NAVY YARD, WARRINGTON, Fa., Monday, Jan. 14, 1861.

I propose giving to your readers a statement of facts, in reference to recent events connected with the Navy yard here, and the forts that protect and command the entrance of this harbor. At such times as these, facts that exhibit prominent political moves are interesting, even if they are not from the "pen of a ready writer."

Upon the right hand of the entrance of the Bay of Pensacola stands Fort Pickens; upon the left hand is Fort McCrea, and upon the same shore with the latter, one mile and a quarter further up the bay, is Fort Barrancas. These forts are nearly equidistant from each other, and so situated as to completely command the entrance to the harbor. Fort Pickens is an admirably constructed fortification at the extremity of a long, shallow sand-spit, that separates the Bay from the Gulf for some distance, and the fort is so situated as really to command the entrance to the Bay completely. It is approachable by land only along the narrow neck mentioned above, and its defences are so arranged that even a small force may defend it against vastly superior numbers. Fort McCrea is rather a dilapidated concern, but is nevertheless a strong water-battery. Fort Barrancas is well built, and a powerful defence of the entrance of the harbor, but neither its construction nor position is adapted to resist a strong land attack.

These three large fortifications, with all their guns, ammunition &c., were in charge of a single Company of Artillery, under the command at present of Lieut. A. J. SLEMMER.

The Navy-yard is situated upon the same shore of the Bay with the Forts McCrea and Barrancas, about one-and-a-half miles above the latter. It was under command of Commodore JAMES ARMSTRONG. The next officer in rank was Commander EBENEZER FARRAND. The disposable force at the yard consisted of about seventy sailors or ordinary men, as they are termed, and forty-eight marines, under Capt. JAMES WATSON; there was also at the yard, subject to the command of Commander ARMSTRONG, the United States store-ship *Supply*, with two thirty-pounders and thirty-eight men, and the steamer *Wyandotte*, with six thirty-twos and eighty men.

For a number of days rumors had been in circulation of an intention, on the part of the authorities of Florida and Alabama to take possession of the Navy-yard and forts at this point. On the night of the 9th, Lieut. SLEMMER stationed a guard at Fort Barrancas. On the morning of the 10th he received orders from the War Department, requiring him to use every means in his power to protect Government property, and especially to keep control of the entrance to the harbor. He was also informed, at the same time, that the Commander of the Navy-yard would be directed to coöperate with him.

On consultation with Commodore ARMSTRONG, and the promise of assistance from him, Lieut. SLEMMER decided on removing at once into Fort Pickens, that post being the most tenable position, and where he could more nearly obey the spirit of his instructions. The matter being decided upon, the Army officers went to work with a will, and during the next twenty-four hours had thrown their entire force, with all their provisions, camp equipage, &c., into the fort, and by the assistance of boats from the *Supply* and *Wyandotte*, had removed the ammunition from Fort Barrancas to the magazines of Fort Pickens.

To what extent Commodore ARMSTRONG was ordered to coöperate with the Army officers I do not know; but it is a fair presumption that it was to the extent of his power.

The Navy-yard itself is so situated that no military man would think of defending it against a large attacking force, with the means at the Commodore's command. In a military point of view, retaining possession of the Navy-yard was of small consequence, compared to a successful defence of the entrance of the harbor; and where it was necessary to make a choice, the available force ought by all means to have been concentrated in Fort Pickens. Taking this view of the case, not thinking he was asking too much from the Commodore, Lieut. SLEMMER urgently requested that the marines might be sent to assist his own company. The ordinary men of the yard, useless where they were, would also have been a not undesirable addition, and the two ships could have been so placed as to make their guns completely cover an enemy's advance by land. Lieut. SLEMMER asked in all good faith for this coöperation. Even after the Navy-yard was surrounded by armed men, and before it was taken, he wrote to the Commodore, repeating his request, that the marines might be sent him while there was yet time. This again met with no attention, and three hours later these men had all been taken prisoners without having made even a show of resistance, and the brave little band, already in Fort Pickens, were left to their own resources in carrying out their instructions.

Why such a course was pursued by the authorities at the Navy-yard, and by what and whose counsels it was brought about, may become a subject for official investigation; and it would be improper for me at this time to express my regret that while Lieut. SLEMMER, ably seconded by Lieut. GILMAN, has so far met a heavy responsibility with a degree of energy and decision worthy of very high praise, I cannot speak in terms of commendation of the way in which the authorities at the Navy-yard met the responsibilities that devolved upon them in this case. NEMO.

STATEMENT OF MRS. SLEMMER.

Mrs. Lieut. SLEMMER and Mrs. Lieut. J. H. GILMAN, the two ladies whose names have been most prominently connected with the late proceedings at Fort Pickens, took rooms at the Metropolitan Hotel. They are both ladies of much refinement and intelligence, and the events through which they have so lately passed have made a deep impression upon them. In addition to the leading facts embraced in the above narrative, they have related many things of interest to our reporters, who waited upon them shortly after they arrived.

The exodus from the Barrancas Fort was made necessarily in much haste, there being little time except to hurriedly pack up the most valuable of their articles of furniture and wardrobe. No personal violence was offered to these retreating women and children, but the sudden and peaceable breaking-up of so many peaceful households, and the violent separation of family ties, were cause of great distress. To many the parting of husband and wife was as if for the last time, and tears bedewed many a hardy cheek when the last "good-bye" was spoken.

The excitement produced upon the officers when they saw their flag at the Navy-yard hauled down, Mrs. SLEMMER says, was most intense. It was a sight they never expected to see, and they had never conceived of the deep feeling of humiliation and vexation that the spectacle excited in every breast.

During the day and night of the evacuation of Barrancas, and the transfer of the garrison to Fort Pickens, every person, men, the officers, and their wives, performed prodigies of labor, and never obtained a wink of sleep for nearly twenty-four hours; and the hard work fell about equally upon all, without regard to rank or sex. The ladies cheerfully performed their part throughout the trying ordeal. On the day following the embarkation of the families on board of the *Supply*, Mrs. GILMAN and Mrs. SLEMMER, accompanied by officers from the storeship, went on shore under a flag of truce, to obtain a last interview with their husbands.

Every step of their progress was met by armed officials. They were obliged, first, to obtain permission from the new Commandant of the Navy-yard—RANDOLPH, who ten days before had resigned his commission in the Navy. This was very reluctantly granted, after appeals had been made to him as a husband and father. They then had to pass the Barrancas forts, whose commander, after some hesitation, allowed them to pass. In this place, so lately deserted by these peaceful and happy families, all was now confusion. The undisciplined soldiers or their understrappers had broken open some of the trunks and boxes containing the wardrobes and household relics of Col. WINDER, late Commander, probably in pursuit of clothing for their own use, and they saw ladies' dresses, and family daguerreotypes, scattered about with little regard to their vaunted respect for the rights of personal property. In justice to the officers, these ladies wished to exonerate them, personally, from these acts of vandalism, and believe they were done by the baser sort upon whom discipline had as yet exerted no control.

Lieut. SLEMMER asserted that he could hold the place against five thousand men, and declared he would do it. It is needless to say that both these ladies exhorted their husbands to stand by their country's flag to the last, and never to haul it down except to an overpowering force.

All the prisoners in the Navy-yard were permitted to leave after giving their parole, and those who could get away left. Such as decided to remain were compelled to take the oath of allegiance to serve the State of Florida.

THE WYANDOTTE—RESIGNATION OF HER OFFICERS.

This vessel is kept constantly under steam, at a safe distance from the reach of enemies, and in readiness to coöperate in the defence of the fort. In case of an emergency she will be at hand ready to receive on board the garrison, should they be overpowered and obliged to abandon the fort to the enemy. There are arrangements by which the entire forces will be able to escape through a covered way to the beach, where they can take to boats and go on board any vessel that may be in waiting to receive them. In such an event it will probably be blown up.

It is stated that every one of the Lieutenants, and most of the other officers on board the *Wyandotte*, have resigned, and that with the exception of the Engineers, Capt. BERRYMAN has been left entirely alone. The Captain, however, is not one of those who betray his country's flag into the hands of enemies.

THE CUTTER LEWIS CASS SURRENDERED TO ALABAMA.

MOBILE, Saturday, Feb. 2.

The United States Revenue cutter *Lewis Cass* has been surrendered to the State of Alabama.

RUMORED ATTACK ON FORT PICKENS.

NEW-ORLEANS, Friday, Feb. 1.

There are flying reports that fighting has commenced at Pensacola, in consequence of the sloop-of-war *Brooklyn* trying to land troops at Fort Pickens, but no reliable authority can be found for them, though authoritatively stated by Alabamians.

[Dispatches of later date make no further mention of the matter, and the reports are doubtless unfounded.—EDS.]

A SOMEWHAT DIFFERENT REPORT.

BALTIMORE, Monday, Feb. 4.

The latest dates received here by mail from Pensacola, (27th ult.,) speak of the withdrawal of the troops. No mention is made of the *Brooklyn*.

The Montgomery and Milledgeville papers speak of the withdrawal of the troops from Pensacola as a thing fixed upon.

A Pensacola correspondent says it is deemed impossible to take Fort Pickens unsupported by a war vessel.

FROM LOUISIANA AND TEXAS.

NEW-ORLEANS, Saturday, Feb. 2.

The Convention has made the resolution to establish a standing army the special order for Tuesday.

The resolution conferring citizenship on persons residing in the State on the day of the passage of the ordinance of secession, was referred.

A resolution was referred to the Committee on Commerce that they report on the expediency of adopting an ordinance exempting from taxation for five years all property and capital employed in manufactures.

Adjourned till Monday.

Advices from Austin, Texas, state that the House has passed by a vote of 65 to 13, an act legalizing a Convention, under the bill of rights.

MASSACHUSETTS DELEGATES TO WASHINGTON.

BOSTON, Monday, Feb. 4.

The Senate this afternoon passed resolves for the appointment of seven Commissioners to confer with the General Government, with the separate States, or with any association of delegates from such States, and to report their doings to the Legislature at its present session. The House refused to suspend the rules to enable the resolves to go to the Governor to-night. The resolves will pass to-morrow and will receive the sanction of the Governor.

THE VIRGINIA LEGISLATURE.

RICHMOND, Monday, Feb. 4.

The Senate voted, to-day, to send back the Minnesota resolutions. A resolution was adopted that, in the opinion of the General Assembly, there is no just grounds for believing that the citizens of Virginia meditate an attack or seizure of the Federal property, or invasion of the District of Columbia, and all preparations are unnecessary, so far as this State is concerned.

THE RECENT SEIZURE OF ARMS.

ALBANY, Monday, Feb. 4.

The recent seizure of arms destined for Georgia, by Superintendent KENNEDY, is likely to create more trouble. It is said here to-night that Governor MORGAN has received a communication from Governor BROWN, of Georgia, demanding the instant surrender of the muskets and expressing a hope that a like outrage will not again be committed. A reply is desired. The Governor, it is understood, has not replied.

REPORTS FROM SPRINGFIELD.

SPRINGFIELD, Ill., Monday, Feb. 4.

Gov. KIRKWOOD, of Iowa, arrived here this evening. He says the Iowa delegates to Congress have been instructed to act as Commissioners from that State.

It is rumored that Gov. WASHBURNE, of Maine, not only refuses to send Commissioners to the Virginia Conference, but advises others to pursue the same course.

Part of the Illinois delegates to the Washington Convention, left here this evening.

SPRINGFIELD, Monday, Feb. 4.

Grave apprehensions prevail in Presidential circles of fatal dissensions in the Republican Party on the compromise question, and consequent embarrassments of the incoming Administration. The *Chicago Tribune* reads Mr. KELLOGG, of Illinois, out of the party on account of his compromise propositions. Much feeling is manifested here among the radical Republicans in view of the apparent discrepancy between his declarations during his late visit to this place and the position now occupied by him.

Mr. WASHBURNE, of Maine, telegraphed to Gov. YATES urging him not to appoint Commissioners to to Washington, as the appointment would demoralize the Republican Party. This, and other appeals of the same nature, prevented the departure of the Commissioners until this evening.

HORACE GREELEY arrived here this morning, and went west after a few hours' stay, without seeing Mr. LINCOLN. He is expected back to-morrow morning, when he will make his wishes known to the President elect. He is very severe on Mr. CAMERON and Mr. KELLOGG. A positive declaration, in reference to the compromise movement, will, doubtlessly, be elicited by him. Mr. LINCOLN received the news of GREELEY's defeat at Albany with his usual complacency.

A Pennsylvania delegation is here to urge Gov. READER in case of CAMERON's withdrawal.

Mr. LINCOLN has received and accepted an invitation from the State authorities and citizens of Albany to visit that city. The trip to New-York from Albany is now evidently determined upon. The Presidential party will stop at the Metropolitan Hotel while in New-York City.

STATE OF FEELING IN MARYLAND.

BALTIMORE, Monday, Feb. 4.

People here, excepting the extremists, discountenance the efforts making towards calling a State Convention or convening the Legislature. The primary meetings to-morrow night excite no interest. The Unionists will refuse to participate in them, as the movement is suspected to be inaugurated by the Democratic clique for specific partisan purposes.

If such a Convention should be called, its action will be resisted by the Minute Men and others, if any measures tending to secession are adopted.

Parties are emphatically divided. A large majority sustains Gov. HICKS, but all will eventually unite with the South, if Virginia goes out and no compromise is effected. Such is the prevailing sentiment.

CONGRESSIONAL PROCEEDINGS.

SENATE.

WASHINGTON, Monday, Feb. 4.

Mr. CRITTENDEN, of Kentucky, (Am.) presented several memorials from citizens of various States in favor of the Crittenden resolutions.

Mr. WILSON, of Massachusetts, (Rep.) offered a resolution of inquiry, asking the President to communicate to the Senate whether any arsenals, forts, arms, or munitions of war belonging to the United States have been seized by any persons in the State of Louisiana, and especially whether the Mint of the United States at New-Orleans has been taken possession of unlawfully by any persons, and if any money of the United States, and how much, has been unlawfully appropriated by any persons, and by whom. Laid over.

Mr. CHANDLER, of Michigan, (Rep.) presented a petition of the citizens of Michigan, remonstrating against any change in the Constitution.

Mr. BIGLER, of Pennsylvania, (Dem.) presented petitions in favor of the Crittenden resolutions.

Mr. FOSTER, of Connecticut, (Rep.) presented a memorial from the citizens of Connecticut, asking for the passage of the Border State resolutions.

Mr. FESSENDEN, of Maine, (Rep.) presented a petition in favor of restoring peace to the country, and preserving the bond of our fathers.

Mr. SLIDELL, of Louisiana, (Dem.) sent to be read by the Clerk, the ordinance of secession passed by Louisiana.

Mr. SLIDELL—Mr. President: The document which the Secretary has just read, and which places on the files of the Senate official information that Louisiana has ceased to be a component part of these once United States, terminates the connection of my colleague and myself with this body. The occasion, however, justifies, if it does not call for, some parting words to those whom we leave behind—some, forever—others, we trust, to meet again, to participate with them in the noble work of constructing and defending a new Confederacy, which, if it may want, at first, the grand proportions and vast resources of the old, will still possess the essential elements of greatness—a people, bold, hardy, homogeneous in interest and sentiments, a fertile soil an extensive territory, the capacity and the will to govern themselves through the forms and in the spirit of the Constitution under which they have been born and educated. Beside all these, they have an advantage which no other people seeking to change the Government under which they had before lived, have ever enjoyed—they have to pass through no intervening period of anarchy. They have in their several State Governments, already shaped to their hands, everything necessary for the preservation of order, the administration of justice, and the protection of the soil and their property from foreign or domestic policy. They can consult with calmness, and act with deliberation on every subject, either of immediate interest or future policy.

But if we do not greatly mistake the prevailing sentiment of the Southern mind, no attempt will be made to improve the Constitution. We shall take it, such as it is—such as has been found sufficient for our security and happiness so long as its true spirit lived in the hearts of a majority of the people of the Free States, and controlled the action, not only of the Federal, but of the State Legislatures. We will adopt all laws not locally inapplicable or incompatible with our new relations. We will recognize the obligations of all existing treaties—those respecting the African Slave-trade included. We shall be prepared to assume our just proportion of the national debt, to account for the cost of all the forts and other property of the United States which we have been compelled to seize in self-defence, if it should appear that our share of such expenditure has been greater than in other sections; and, above all we shall, as well from the dictates of natural justice and the principles of international law, as of political and geographical affinities and of mutual pecuniary interests, recognize the right of the inhabitants of the Valley of the Mississippi and its tributaries to its free navigation. We will guarantee to them a free interchange of all productions, without import tax duty, or toil of any kind, the free transit from foreign countries of every species of merchandise, subject only to such regulations as may be absolutely necessary for the protection of any revenue system we may establish, and for purposes of police.

As for such States of the Union as may not choose to unite their destinies with ours, we shall consider them as all other foreign nations—"Enemies in war—in peace, friends." We wish, and we hope, to part with them amicably, and so far as depends on us, they shall have no provocation to pursue a hostile course. But in this regard we, from the necessities of the case, can only be passive. It will be for the people of the Free States to decide this momentous question. This declaration, however, requires some qualification. Could the issue be fairly presented to the people of those States, we should have little doubt of a peaceful separation, with the possibility of a complete, and the probability of a partial reconstruction on a basis satisfactory to us and honorable to them. But with the present representations in either branch of Congress, we see nothing to justify our indulging any such expectation. We must be prepared to resist coercion, whether attempted by avowed enemies, or by a hand heretofore supposed friendly—by open war or under the more insidious, and, therefore, the more dangerous pretext of enforcing the laws, protecting public property, or collecting the revenue. We shall not cavil about words or discuss legal and technical distinctions. We shall consider the one as equivalent to the other, and shall be prepared to act accordingly,—*utroque arbitro parati*. you will find us ready to meet you with the outstretched hand of fellowship, or in the mailed panoply of war, as you may will it. Elect between these alternatives.

We have no idea that you will ever attempt to invade our soil with your armies. But we acknowledge your superiority on the sea at present, in some degree accidental, but in the main natural and permanent, until we shall have acquired better ports for our marine. You may, if you so will it, persist in considering us bound to you during your good pleasure. You may deny the sacred and indefeasible right, we will not say of secession, but of revolution, aye, of rebellion, if you choose thus to style our action—the right of every people to establish for itself that form of government which it may, even in its folly, if such you deem it, consider best calculated to secure its safety and promote its welfare. You may ignore the principles of our immortal Declaration of

[*Continued on Eighth Page.*]

The New-York Times.

VOL. X.....NO. 2950 | NEW-YORK, WEDNESDAY, MARCH 6, 1861. | PRICE TWO CENTS.

HIGHLY IMPORTANT NEWS.

THE NEW FEDERAL ADMINISTRATION.

The Cabinet and its Confirmation by the Senate.

What is Thought of the Inaugural Address

Visits of the State Delegations to the President, Secretary of State, and Others.

Speeches of Mr. Lincoln and Mr. Seward.

IMPORTANT DISPATCHES FROM THE SOUTH

Capt. Hill Prepared to Defend Fort Brown.

THE TEXANS CONCENTRATING TROOPS.

General Twiggs' Treason Indorsed in New-Orleans.

SEIZURE OF ANOTHER REVENUE CUTTER.

Excited Session of the Virginia Convention.

OUR WASHINGTON DISPATCHES.

WASHINGTON, Tuesday, March 5.

THE CABINET NOMINATIONS CONFIRMED.

The Cabinet appointments, as sent to the Senate, and immediately confirmed to-day, are as follows:

Secretary of State—WM. H. SEWARD.
Secretary of the Treasury—S. P. CHASE.
Secretary of the Interior—CALEB B. SMITH.
Postmaster-General—MONTGOMERY BLAIR.
Secretary of War—SIMON CAMERON.
Secretary of the Navy—GIDEON WELLES.
Attorney-General—EDWARD BATES.

The Cabinet nominations were all confirmed without objection except in the case of Messrs. BATES and BLAIR, against whom some Southern Senators voted. No other nominations came in, nor have any others been decided upon. The new Cabinet meets to-morrow.

As soon as the confirmation of the members of the Cabinet was made public, the office-seekers began a raid upon them, of course with no view but to pay their respects.

I hear again to-night, under circumstances which lead me to put some faith in it, that Mr. CHASE may resign the Treasury after all. The question is expected to be decided early to-morrow forenoon.

THE LOCAL APPOINTMENTS.

Some of the Congressional delegations met to-day to discuss and argue, as far as possible, upon the men for the important offices in their respective States. It is understood that Hon. J. Z. GOODRICH, the present Lieutenant Governor of Massachusetts, will be recommended for Collector of Boston. Mr. HUMPHRIES, ex-member of Congress from New-York, is strongly urged by his friends to apply for and accept the Surveyorship of New-York. He would prefer to go abroad.

In his reply to the Massachusetts Delegation, Mr. SEWARD said he could not speak for the Administration, but hoped and believed that before the close of the present Administration, Massachusetts and South Carolina would again grasp the right hand of fellowship.

The Treasury will not pay anything until Mr CHASE assumes his position. A large amount of claims have passed since Friday last, when Mr. DIX declined to pay anything more, and they have been accumulating. The claimants are exceedingly anxious to get their dues and leave the place.

It is probable that Mr. TUCK, of New-Hampshire, will be tendered the Chief Clerkship in the Treasury Department, by Mr. CHASE, if he will accept it. He would prefer a Foreign appointment. This is one of the first places that must be filled.

From remarks made by the President to-day, it is evident that he regards the departments as having become so corrupt that an entire change of officials, from first to last, is necessary.

Mr. LINCOLN wrote to Mr. CAMERON requesting him to appoint Col ELLSWORTH chief clerk of the War Department, if there was no reason why the present incumbent should not be changed. And it is apparently settled that Col. ELLSWORTH will be installed as such as soon as it can with propriety be done.

There was quite an animated discussion this morning at the White House as to the propriety of placing Mr. BATES on the Supreme Court Bench and Mr. GILMER in the Cabinet.

Mr. GREELEY and Mr. GRIMES, of Iowa, had a protracted interview with Mr. LINCOLN, to night on the questions of internal policy. Mr. GREELEY availed himself of the occasion to press Col. FREMONT for the French mission, and received assurances that there would be no trouble on that point.

MR. SEWARD AND THE ILLINOIS DELEGATION.

I happened in at Mr. SEWARD'S to-night, just as he was replying to the address from the Illinois citizens who are in town, who called to pay their respects. I could not get near enough to hear distinctly, but caught the following significant sentiment:

"GENTLEMEN: If you want to save this Administration, and have it successful and profitable to the country, I implore you to remember that the battle for Freedom has been fought and won. Henceforth forget that Freedom ever was in danger, and exert your best influence now to save the Union. Let it not be said that the Republican Party of the United States won its first, last and only victory over the dissolution of the Union."

The scene which followed when the delegation took its leave, was a touching demonstration of respect and affection entertained for Mr. SEWARD. Great, stalwart, gray-haired men, whose faces seemed of iron mould, gave way to tears as they shook him by the hand, and said "Farewell,"—each adding some peculiar expression of his hopes and wishes for the Administration.

One man, as he came up, said:

"Governor, I want the integrity of the Republican Party maintained."

Mr. SEWARD instantly responded: "Remember, that the way to maintain the integrity of the Republican Party is by maintaining the Union. Remember, the point at which the enemy strikes is always the point where you should defend."

Mr. LOVEJOY, of Illinois, standing near, interposed—"And remember that the Union is worth nothing except so long as there is freedom in it."

Mr. SEWARD responded: "Freedom is always in the Union."

During the day Mr. SEWARD was also visited by delegations from Pennsylvania, Massachusetts, New-Jersey and Iowa. He is quite hoarse from such constant speaking. The last few days have greatly increased the number of his warm friends, by means of his intercourse with so many strangers, for all who come within his influence, for ever so brief a period, go away captivated.

SOUTHERN POLITICIANS AND THE INAUGURAL.

The Inaugural Address is the subject of much excited comment among Southern politicians here. Hon JOHN BELL is said to pronounce it a declaration of war, and to declare that he shall urge Tennessee to prepare for conflict. This is very doubtful. Some Southern men consider it a hostile paper clothed in the most pacific and conciliatory language, or, in other words, that it presents a basis for either war or peace. Some contend that the declaration concerning the collection of the revenue and the defence of the forts was made to satisfy the ultra Republicans, while the pacific tone of the Inaugural would afford a basis on which Senator SEWARD could diplomatize through our national difficulties and finally restore harmony.

While the objectionable portion of the Inaugural was being delivered yesterday, several Southern gentlemen telegraphed to Gov. PICKENS advising against any attack on Fort Sumter until action could be had by the Confederated States.

ARRIVAL OF A SOUTHERN COMMISSIONER.

Hon. MARTIN J. CRAWFORD has arrived here and taken private lodgings. He is one of the Commissioners from the Southern Confederacy, who are to demand its recognition as announced in Monday's TIMES.

RUMORS.

Mr. SEWARD was summoned to the White House at a late hour to-night, and the impression outside is that the call relates to news from Fort Sumter; but nothing has yet transpired on the subject. Another surmise is that Commissioner CRAWFORD has indicated his demand. The hour is too late to verify the reports.

THE PRESIDENT AND HIS FAMILY.

Mr. LINCOLN is very well to-day. Mrs. LINCOLN has a severe cold. ROBERT returned to College this afternoon.

Col. and Mrs. BAKER, Miss EDWARDS, and others of the President's household, attended the promenade concert to-night, where the ladies were the recipients of marked attention.

Mr. LINCOLN'S first public reception will be given on Friday night.

THE DEPARTURE OF THE EX PRESIDENT.

Except for the quickstep music of the military band, one might have mistaken the procession escorting Mr. BUCHANAN to the cars to-day for a funeral. First came a corps of cavalry and sappers and miners; then several carriages, containing the Ex-President and suite, followed by the District Union Regiment Militia. No citizens joined the *cortege*.

CAPT. POPE'S COURT-MARTIAL DISCONTINUED BY MR. BUCHANAN.

Mr. BUCHANAN, yesterday, ordered the proceedings for the Court-martial of Capt. POPE to be discontinued. The reason he assigns for so doing is that he don't think the Captain's reflections upon him in the Cincinnati lecture did him any harm. That is pretty good.

THE COMMISSION OF CAPT. SCHAEFFER STILL WITHHELD.

The report that Capt. SCHAEFFER, of the District Militia, had received his commission, turns out to be untrue. Mr. BUCHANAN, on an appeal being made to him, ordered it to be delivered, but the Secretary still refused on account of Capt. SCHAEFFER'S refusal to say he would maintain his oath to support the Constitution under all circumstances. The President, not desiring to make an issue with a member of his Cabinet, allowed the commission to remain suspended. This resulted in the resignation of Hon. ROBERT OULD, who had just been appointed Brigadier General of the Militia, and the appointment of Mr. BOTELER, of this city, as his successor, has created such general dissatisfaction among the volunteer companies that serious difficulties are anticipated.

STRANGERS LEAVING.

It is estimated that four thousand persons left town by the cars to-day. Four heavy trains left this afternoon loaded to their utmost capacity, yet the hotel lobbies are so full that it is difficult to pass. The horde of office-seekers is remarkable for number and pertinacity.

OFFICIAL DISPATCHES FROM MEXICO.

Official dispatches from the City of Mexico, dated Feb. 18, say that Gen. URAGA has been appointed Envoy Extraordinary and Minister Plenipotentiary to Washington. Gen. URAGA was formerly the Mexican Minister to Prussia, and subsequently lost his leg at the battle of Guadalajara. Gens. ZUOLAGA and VICARIO, commanding remnants of the Church-party Army, were defeated at Cuautla. The difficulties with the English Minister had been settled. The *conducta* taken by Gen. DEGOLLADO, at Lagos, is to be paid back in four months, and the British bondholders' money, which was taken in the City of Mexico, is to be paid out of the property of the persons who authorized the seizure of these funds, the property being already attached for that purpose.

The difficulties with France have been satisfactorily arranged, and the best feeling exists between the French Minister and the Government. The affair with Spain for the expulsion of Senor PACHECO remains in an unsettled condition. The Presidential election will probably be determined by Congress, no one of the candidates having received a majority of the whole vote cast.

There came near being a serious difficulty in Mexico growing out of the convent question. The Government having determined to require the nuns to occupy only as many Convents in the city as might be necessary for their comfortable accommodation and retire from the others, some twenty in number, with a view to their sale on public account, the priests attempted to get up a revolt, but failed. Several of these Convents cover a square of ground each, and are occupied by less than a dozen nuns. The Government is taking active steps to encourage immigration, and the several departments are earnestly striving to restore prosperity to the country. Gen. URAGA may arrive in the *Tennessee* on her next trip from Vera Cruz.

DISPATCH TO THE ASSOCIATED PRESS.

WASHINGTON, Monday, March 4.

Several State delegations this morning, at different times, paid their respects to President LINCOLN. Prominent among them were those from Pennsylvania and Massachusetts. The latter, as did the former, assembled in the East room, when Mr. LINCOLN making his appearance. Mr. HANSCOMB, introduced Hon. CHARLES R. TRAIN, who, in briefly addressing Mr. LINCOLN, said Massachusetts had read his Inaugural, and would stand by it, and that from none would it meet with a more cordial support than from the old Bay State.

Mr. LINCOLN replying, said substantially:

"I am thankful for this renewed assurance of kind feeling and confidence and support of the old Bay State, in so far as you, Mr. Chairman, have expressed, in behalf of those whom you represent, your sanction of what I have enunciated in my inaugural address. This is very grateful to my feelings. The subject was one of great delicacy. In presenting my views at the opening of an Administration, under the peculiar circumstances attending my entrance upon the official duties connected with the Government, I studied all the points with great anxiety, and presented them with whatever of ability and sense of justice I could bring to bear. If it meet the approbation of our good friends in Massachusetts I shall be exceedingly gratified while I hope it will meet the approbation of friends everywhere. I am thankful for the expressions of those who have voted with us, and like every other man of you, I like them, certainly, as I do others (Laughter.) As President, in the administration of the Government, I hope to be man enough not to know one citizen of the United States from another, (cries of "Good,") nor one section from another. I shall be gratified to have the good friends of Massachusetts, and others who have thus far supported me in these national views, still to support me in carrying them out."

Mr. LINCOLN excused himself from further remarks on account of pressing business, and, therefore, retired without further ceremony than a farewell bow.

Gen. SCOTT and Secretary HOLT were also visited. To the greetings of the Pennsylvania Delegation, Gen. SCOTT made a brief, patriotic and friendly speech. Mr. HOLT expressed himself honored by the visit, and his regret that the brief time he had occupied in the War Department had not enabled him to do more for the country in this time of troubles.

Major ANDERSON, up to the 4th of March, has continued to speak of his condition as safe, and to express the opinion that reinforcements had better not be sent to him.

The point of difference between the two Houses on the bill reorganizing the Patent Office, was with reference to the extension of patents. The House had amended it, providing that no patent should be reissued when the Commissioner was satisfied that both the Inventor and assignee had netted one hundred thousand dollars. The Senate amended this by confining that amount of profit to the inventor alone. The Committee of Conference consisted of Messrs. Douglas, Cameron and Fitch, of the Senate, and Cox, Frank and Barr, of the House, who adopted, in place of what is above stated, the following: "All patents hereafter granted shall remain in force for seventeen years from the date of issue, and all extensions of such patents is hereby prohibited."

The bill was thus passed. It stops all the corruption and intrigue as to present patents in Congress, and all patents granted after its passage cannot be renewed at the patent office.

The drafts drawn by Ex Secretary DIX on the Assistant Treasurer at New Orleans, to pay for work done on the Custom house, and also the drafts by Ex-Postmaster General KING, on the same officer, in connection with the postal service, amounting to between two and three hundred thousand dollars, have been returned unpaid.

The resignations to Mr. BUCHANAN of his Cabinet officers were to take effect on the 4th of March, or not until their successors were appointed, consequently they have been attending to the business, until closing hours, of their respective departments, to-day.

Gen. DIX will return to New-York on Thursday.

Judge BLACK will not leave Washington for the present. He remains on private and professional business, and will probably continue to practice the law here.

Ex-President BUCHANAN departed on his journey to Wheatland this afternoon. He was escorted to the railroad station by two mounted and two infantry companies, together with the Committee from that locality and prominent citizens of Washington. He exchanged many farewell hand-shakings, appearing to be deeply affected by the manifestations of friendship; and when he bowed adieu to the large crowds, as the train was about to start, they further testified their respect by vigorous cheers.

The resignation of Mr. PRESTON, Minister to Spain, was this morning filed in the State Department.

Capt LAY, of Virginia, by local rank a Brevet Lieutenant Colonel, as an aid to Lieut.-Gen. SCOTT, has resigned.

The Republican Senators held a caucus this morning to arrange the Standing Committees.

A large number of citizens of Kentucky and Indiana are here urging the promotion of Major ROBERT ANDERSON, as Brigadier General, *vice* Gen. TWIGGS, stricken from the roll as recently officially published, for treachery.

State delegations have all day been calling on the President and Gen. SCOTT, and other distinguished gentlemen. Gen. SCOTT, in addressing the Illinoisans this afternoon, exhorted them to stand by the Union, and to cherish feelings of fraternity towards all citizens.

Representative LOVEJOY, who occupies apartments in the same house with Gen. SCOTT, was called out, and said, among other things, that SCOTT saved the Union in 1832 and 1860, paying an eloquent tribute to his bravery and patriotism.

The newly confirmed Cabinet are overcrowded to-night with visitors.

MARTIN J. CRAWFORD, one of the Commissioners from the Southern Confederacy, accredited to negotiate with the Administration, has arrived here.

The Border Slave States men almost generally condemn the Inaugural. There is, however, a difference of opinion among them, some saying it is capable of two constructions, war or peace, and that it remains to be seen what policy Mr. LINCOLN will pursue. The Republicans indorse the Inaugural nearly all enthusiastically. Other classes regard the Inaugural favorably.

THIRTY-SEVENTH CONGRESS.

UNITED STATES SENATE—EXTRA SESSION.

WASHINGTON, Tuesday, March 5.

The floor of the Senate chamber was densely crowded to-day before the members were called to order.

The utmost anxiety was everywhere expressed to learn the formation of the Cabinet.

The galleries were about two thirds filled.

The Senate met at 1 P. M.

A prayer was offered up by the Chaplain especially in behalf of the President of the United States.

On motion of Mr. HALE, of New-Hampshire, (Rep.,) a Committee of Two was appointed to wait on the President and inform him that the Senate was ready to receive any communication he might be pleased to make.

Messrs. HALE and DOUGLAS were appointed such Committee, and immediately proceeded to perform their duty.

The Senate here took a recess till 4¼ P. M.

On the Senate again coming to order, Mr. HALE reported that the Committee had performed their duty, and that the President had informed them that he would forthwith communicate a Message in writing.

After a short interview, Mr. NICOLAY, the Private Secretary of the President, appeared with the message, when, on motion of Mr. HALE, the Senate went into Executive session at 4¾ o'clock.

The following gentlemen were confirmed as members of Mr LINCOLN'S Cabinet:

Hon. WM. H. SEWARD, Secretary of State.
Hon. SALMON P. CHASE, Secretary of the Treasury.
Hon. SIMON CAMERON, Secretary of War.
Hon. GIDEON WELLES, Secretary of the Navy.
Hon MONTGOMERY BLAIR, Postmaster General.
Hon. CALEB B. SMITH, Secretary of the Interior.
Hon EDWARD BATES, Attorney-General.

The votes were unanimous for all except Messrs. BATES and BLAIR, four or five votes being cast against each of these gentlemen, that many objecting to them because they were unwilling that any one from the Slave States should go into the Cabinet.

A large crowd assembled around the doors, anxious to hear the result of the session.

MR. CRITTENDEN'S FAREWELL SPEECH.

The following is the latter portion of Mr. CRITTENDEN'S farewell speech, delivered on Sunday night, March 3:

Now, in regard to the South and the Border States, I would have them trust to the Union and to the people. The North has given assurances of their sympathy for them, and justice will be done. I believe it. There are assurances given of kindness and patriotism that will be redeemed; that sympathy and that kindness which exists in the North will attract others to it. Its standard of Liberty and Justice will be raised from one end of the country to the other, and the people will crowd around it until States shall come and make peace offerings to their brethren. That day will come, and it will be a happy day. I believe this, and I would have the South and the Border States believe it. Our Northern fellow-citizens have entitled themselves to confidence by their action upon these very resolutions; thousands and tens of thousands have come here with petitions in their favor; States have petitioned for them; and in all this I recognize a spirit of kindness which should bind the hearts of Southern men. I will say, I am for the Union; I am not for secession. No, Sir. And as to my native State, I will say to her, more than to others, I desire to see you stand by the Union of the country. Do not go off unless an imperious necessity forces you. You have given to the world long-continued evidences of your consistency, your patriotism, and your fidelity to the Union. Stand by it. You have stood there heretofore; why not now? You have literally founded your State upon a rock. Yes, Sir, upon a rock that State is founded, and you have engraven on a rock your testimony to the Union. The stone you sent to be a portion of the monument to WASHINGTON bore upon its Kentucky marble front these words: "Kentucky was the first to enter the Union after the adoption of the Constitution; she will be the last to leave it." That sentiment she has engraved upon marble, and it now stands sanctified still more by forming a portion of the monument to GEORGE WASHINGTON. I want to see her true to that great and noble sentiment. It swells the heart within me. There is nothing, it seems to me in all the hope of triumph—nothing of the manly and heart-swelling character of the feelings which this noble and patriotic sentiment has called forth! Let her stand there with us; and stand by those sentiments. Let her be the last to leave the Union which is covered with so much glory, so much of triumph and so much of blessing. This is the only Government on earth under which man can control his action, can speak his own thoughts, and where no man is imprisoned unlawfully from one end to the other—from San Francisco to Portland. What if our Treasury is empty and our money spent, and our Government badly administered? Still, with all these faults, it is the best Government in the world. It is here only, in the arms of this great and mighty Empire, that Liberty was presented to the world, in all her might and all her glory, and all her usefulness. In the little Republics in the Alpine hills of Europe, whose little territories are too small to attract the ambition or cupidity of imperial power, there Liberty is kept as a thing to be looked at and petted; but here she stands in all her majesty and might, with her arms stretching across a continent. Who does not love his great country, with its mighty benefits to every citizen? The name of his country goes before him like a host, and is a shield over him. The very name contains a charm and a spell which attaches to him in every region of the world; and its greatness and blessing is magnified still more every day. I say I hope Kentucky will stand for the Union. Try it, and try it again! If one Congress does not judge rightly and does not act rightly, another will; it is a principle of our Government that these frequent changes will give us justice, and every State in the Union should exercise patience and forbearance. Let us wait; and when, if it be our sad fate, rebellion and revolution shall have passed over the whole land, I want to see old Kentucky standing up, even in that day of dissolution—standing up with unwasted strength and with the Flag of our Union in her hand—standing up on her conquered fields like the last soldier of a brave and gallant band; and then, when the Union is no more, and she stands the image of patriotism, honor, freedom and fidelity to the Union to the last; then, and not till then, I would have her consider what next is to be done for herself. My principle is, take care of the Union; compromise—to constitute for it. It is the Palladium of Government. Take care of it, and it will take care of you.

Mr. President, I have occupied more of your time than I intended. I am about to part from all my friends here, whom I shall be sorry to leave. If I have offenced or grieved the heart of any man, I never so intended. I have spoken what in soberness and truth I believe, and what to some extent, coming from the region which I do, I may say I know as a fact. I have endeavored to give you warning, but not to threaten. I have long ago learned not to threaten. I may warn; it is one of the duties of brotherhood; it is one of the duties of my place in the Senate to warn you of any danger I see approaching our common country. I have endeavored to do so. To morrow, after to morrow, and each succeeding to-morrow, brings with it new fears and new apprehensions. To my mind, rebellion and revolution seem to be epidemic in the land, and some remedy must be devised.

Mr. CRITTENDEN closed with an appeal to the Senate to pass some measure, "not of compromise, but of policy," which should bring peace to the country and allow the sunshine once more to break through the clouds and make us once again the brethren of one common family.

THE VIRGINIA STATE CONVENTION.

RICHMOND, Tuesday, March 5.

Mr COX, of Chesterfield, introduced a resolution instructing the Committee on Federal Relations to report without delay, a plan for a Convention of the Border Slave States at the earliest practicable day; also to report on the subject of the coercion of the seceded States by the Government.

Mr. LEAK, of Goochland, offered a substitute, instructing the Committee, in view of the coercive policy indicated by the President, and a long list of aggressions, to report an ordinance for Virginia to reassume all the powers she delegated to the Government, and declare herself independent, and then call a Convention of the Slaveholding States to determine what new Constitution would be necessary for the protection of their rights in a Confederacy of Slave States, and such Free States as were willing to come in.

Mr. HARVIE, of Amelia, introduced an amendment instructing the Committee to report in effect, that,

Whereas, It is plain that it is Mr. LINCOLN'S purpose to plunge the country into civil war by his coercive policy, which Virginia will resist,

Resolved, That the Legislature be requested to make the needful appropriations of means, and provide the necessary forces to resist and repel every attempt of the Federal authorities to hold, occupy and possess the property and places of the United States in any of the seceded States or those that may withdraw, or collect duties on imports in the same.

Mr. GOODE read a series of resolutions against coercive measures for the collection of the Revenue, etc; that Virginia would repel such attempts; requesting the coöperation of the Border Slave States in effecting a plan for uniting with the South, with the hope of restoring harmony to the Union, and of reforming the United States upon the basis of the Constitution modified to protect the rights of person and property in the Territories for all time; that in the event of a separation of Virginia from the Union, the Government property in Virginia ought to be resumed by her, as well for the defence of her citizens and property in particular locations, as for purposes of general defence; that while Virginia remains a member of the Union she will assume no hostile attitude towards the Government, but be prepared to repel any assaults made upon her.

The debate exhibited the effect of the Inaugural to a nay extent. The Union men, including Messrs. Cox and Goode urged that some action was necessary, as all Virginia's previous efforts had failed. They want the opinion of the Border Slave States before determining, but contemplate no Union with the North on unequal terms.

Mr. DORMAN of Rockbridge, though regretting Mr. LINCOLN'S position thinks the Union men should work all the harder to oppose coercion.

The Secessionists are "death" on the Inaugural, and are for hard blows, and this feeling is apparent among the people; but the Union men will prevent hasty action in the Convention and perhaps prevent the passage of the Ordinance of Secession.

There was great excitement in the Convention all day, but an adjournment was had without taking action. The Secessionists are in better spirits.

INAUGURATION DAY.

A Brief Resume of its Happenings and a Briefer Account of the Highly Successful Inauguration Ball.

From Our Special Correspondent.

NATIONAL HOTEL, WASHINGTON, Tuesday, March 5, 1861—3 o'clock A. M.

Though the streets of the city are deserted, and no noise, save that of the occasional rapping of the watchman's club, is heard, the busy feet of the merry dancers still trip gaily on the floor of the Inauguration ball-room. Monday was, as you may imagine, an exciting day, and as well an interesting one, particularly to those who have sympathized with Republican movements, and who, being National men, were anxious that everything should pass off pleasantly and peaceably.

A brief resume of what has fallen under the eye of your correspondent may be of interest to the readers of the TIMES, who have not found all that they require under the telegraphic announcement of this evening.

For several days past the heat has been most extraordinary, the dust has been intolerably thick, and the wind remarkable for its stirring up proclivities and relentless persecution of the dust aforesaid. Old ladies versed in signs have prognosticated that on Monday the windows of heaven would be opened, and that the rain which for so long a time has been but a memory in the minds of the Washingtonians, would descend upon the head of ABRAHAM and scatter incontinently the hosts who would assemble at the Capitol to do him honor. This prophecy bid fair to eventuate in entire fulfillment, for on Monday morning clouds filled the air, dense masses of watery vapor sailed slowly across the sky, and it was very evident that a wet time might be expected. Umbrellas and overshoes were in great demand, and surtouts, which for weeks had been laid off as cumbersome articles of clothing, were hunted up, brushed up, and gotten ready for use and service. Thank Heaven the rain was withheld, the clouds are dispersed, and by nine o'clock the sun had so gained the bright ascendency as to render it certain that the day on which ABRAHAM LINCOLN was to be inaugurated President of the United States was to be bright, cheerful, sunny, and peaceful.

The two events of the day were, of course, the inauguration ceremonies and the ball in honor of the President, in the evening. Rumors of war, of insurrection, of conspiracy, of treason, of murder and assassination, had been rife for weeks. It was certain to the eyes of many a good old man and woman that he would certainly be shot or stabbed as he rode to the Senate Chamber, and it was equally certain to the eyes of the military chieftains here in charge, that trouble might be apprehended, so much so that soldiers clad in all the panoply of war, surrounded the city, promenaded the avenues, and aided greatly in keeping up the feelings of insecurity and danger that were so prevalent among the white residents of the city. It was certain also to the minds of others that of all times in the world, this was to be the jolliest kind of a time for a row of the first water. These three classes,—the timid, the warriors and the roughs had created a public sentiment here which was prepared for anything and everything disagreeable. Still, in spite of all this preparatory state, the storm of passion was blown over, even as was the storm of rain which early in the morning had brooded over the city.

After breakfast I sauntered up towards Willard's. On the road I met hundreds of people who were hastening toward the Capitol, anxious to get seats or standing places at the Capitol steps, where the inauguration was to take place some five hours after. All sorts of men—all kinds of people—all races, all colors, all tongues, were represented in the throngs of human beings who rushed frantically up the avenue. At Willard's there was a vast collection of individuals—specimens of all sorts and conditions of men—most of whom wanted office, and if they did not their friends did for them, which is just as bad and harder to manage. The ladies were there dressed in their prettiest, arrayed most gorgeously, and all on tip-toe for what was yet to happen.

Mr. LINCOLN, the object of all solicitude and the object of all curiosity, was in his room. To it no one was admitted save his immediate family, his particular friends, and Gov. SEWARD. The Senate had held over from Sunday night until Monday at noon. It was important that he should know what they had done concerning the matter at issue before the people ere he completed his Inaugural or appointed his Cabinet. At last word had been brought to him, that beyond the passing of a certain compromising measure, nothing would be done, and he at once proceeded to put the finishing touches to the Inaugural, which was looked for with much interest by thousands of people on both sides of the broad Atlantic, and which ere now has been flashed along the telegraphic wire to every hamlet in the Union, and has been read by every man, woman and child who is old enough to know the difference between Major ANDERSON and Gen TWIGGS.

Soon the sound of brass and leather announced that President BUCHANAN was approaching, and sure enough, looking from the window, we saw the old man in his barouche, surrounded by soldiers of a sanguinary appearance. In a few moments Mr. LINCOLN was with him, promptness and exact obedience to engagement being with him imperative rules of life. As he took his seat in the barouche, Mr. BUCHANAN occupying the seat of honor, Mr. LINCOLN was saluted with cheers of the most enthusiastic nature, which were continued the whole ride from the hotel to the Capitol.

The procession was like all other similar performances, gotten up for the delectation of some grand or chief marshal, and the prospective tickling of an indefinite number of assistant marshals and aids, and so on. There was a good band, a carload of pretty girls, thirty-four in all, each one of whom personated a State; militia-men, who walked like country paupers on a semi-diluted spree, and that climax of absurdities, "citizens in carriages." However, the road was lined with people, was crowded with people, and every place was occupied by some man more or less distinguished in the world of science, politics, learning, or nothing. The brass band exhausted its capabilities and the endurance of the throats of the musicians. Patriotic airs were generally played, though I noticed that "Way down South in Dixie" was a great favorite with anybody who knew what a good tune was, and, as the procession moved on, the President elect was obliged, in response to repeated calls, to rise and bow with hat in hand.

In the meantime I cut across lots, so to speak, and encountered a stern old codger at the doorway of an immense temporary corridor, built expressly for the admission of the biggest kind of bugs. I knew that I was not clearly entitled to a classification of that stamp, but I also knew that the readers of the TIMES would look to me for an account of the affair, so I "pitched in." I attempted to bribe the door keeper, but he was utterly incorruptible; and at last, as a forlorn hope, I went to the house of Senator FOOTE, the Chairman of the Committee, whose bell I had rung for the past hour. After a little coaxing, Mr FOOTE gave me a pass to no place, or any place, as I might prefer, and at once I dashed on, to the astonishment of sundry keepers, who are not accustomed to frolicsome oysters, or habits of individuals who are determined to get all that is properly within their reach. The result was, that in about five minutes I found myself on the floor of the Senate of the United States.

The Senate was in session for the last time. Many of the members were to leave their seats forever—others were ready to take them, and the Vice-President was ready to take his farewell, to resign the insignia of his office, and to reassume his position as Senator—a position to which Kentucky has just reëlected him for the term of six years. There were but few people there, few speeches, and dry ones at that, were made, until BRIGHT, of Indiana, commenced a long rigmarole about some gas company, located in some untraveled region, whose merits he argued at length, and until the striking of the noon-day hour announced that the moment of adjournment had arrived.

I will pass over the affecting scene that followed, when Mr. BRECKINRIDGE made his farewell speech, and swore in his successor, HAMLIN; an account of the jolly old coves, the animated mummies who compose the Supreme Tribunal of our land; the inauguration, so grand, so simple, so effective and so eminently gratifying, and the many pleasing and singular incidents of the day—that I may indulge for a few moments in a description of the Inauguration Ball.

The Inauguration Ball was a success, and not only a success, but a complete success. It was a victory achieved by a few hard-working and reliable Republicans over caste prejudice and scoffings on one side, and fear, forebodings and disinclination on the other. A large hall, capable of accommodating say three thousand people, was erected especially for the purpose, connecting conveniently with the City Hall, whose Committee-rooms and Council-chambers were of great service for dressing-apartments and sundry other domestic purposes. The hall, which was shaped like a parallelogram, was beautifully decorated with red and white muslin, while around the walls were a number of shields, bearing the arms of the United States. A ball is a ball, and but little can be said of one that is not equally true of another, save the mentioning of the *personnel* thereof, and a description of toilettes, elegant and rare, for the delight of the ladies.

At 5 o'clock in the morning after a hard day's work and an evening of telegraphing, I do not propose at any extended length to enter upon the details of the affair; but as the chief interest of the occasion centered upon Mr. and Mrs LINCOLN, and a few of their friends, I will give a short account of them and their appearance.

The hall was well filled by 11 o'clock with dancers impatient for the signal to commence "the mazy," but as Mr. LINCOLN had not yet arrived, it was not considered etiquette to begin. A little while longer and the youngsters impatient for the pastime, started the band and at it they went. Soon, however, it was noised about that the party had arrived. Dancing was for a moment suspended, and all eyes turned in the direction of the door. Presently the President appeared, leaning on the arms of Vice-President HAMLIN and Senator ANTHONY, of Rhode Island. His entrance was of course, the signal for applause, and the band struck up "Hail Columbia." Behind the President came a couple the sight of whom was singular and yet eminently gratifying; singular, because so wholly unexpected, and gratifying, because it was an indication of the beginning of an era of good feeling.

The parties were Mrs LINCOLN and Senator DOUGLAS. Mrs. LINCOLN appeared remarkably well. She wore a very tasteful and becoming head-dress, and a low-necked lavender silk, (I think,) of exquisite shade, perfect fit, and evident richness. Her lace was point, her jewelry was the simple diamond, and her attire such as commended itself to the good taste, the sense of propriety and the love of the beautiful of every person in the room. It was a general remark that LINCOLN was an infinitely better-looking man than he was represented, and that Mrs. LINCOLN was evidently a lady of refinement, of tact and of taste.

Of the ladies who were with her, Miss EDWARDS of Springfield, was the most noticeable. She dressed with great elegance and equal simplicity—what the name of the material is, I do not pretend to say or know. It was very thin, gauzy and white, looked as if it would burn very easily and had a long row of beautiful bouquets down the front of it. That's not a very technical description of a lady's ball-dress, but it may answer every purpose just as well.

Mrs. BAKER was also dressed very elegantly. She wore a white silk, in which were embroidered flowers of exquisite color. She wore a head-dress to match, and looked well.

Mrs. SEDGWICK and Miss BEAN of New-York; Miss WILLIAMS and Miss CAMERON, of Pennsylvania; Miss CHASE, of Ohio; Miss DIXON, of Connecticut, and Miss BLAIR, of Maryland, were also "bright, particular stars." There were many others there deserving of notice, but time forbids.

They danced, talked, flirted, chatted, supped most bounteously, had a splendid time, and all that sort of thing, affording a series of items unrivaled for sketches, but as the cars are soon to go, I must close by stating that this Inauguration Ball is considered to have been one of the pleasantest and most enjoyable of any ever given in this good City of Washington. HOWARD.

RECEPTION OF THE INAUGURAL ADDRESS.

IN RICHMOND.

RICHMOND, Va., Tuesday, March 5.

The *Whig* (conservative) says: The policy indicated towards the seceding States will meet the stern and unyielding resistance of the united South.

The *Enquirer* (secessionist) says: No action of our Convention can now maintain peace. Virginia must fight.

The *Dispatch* remarks: "Every Border State ought to go out of the Union in 24 hours."

Dispatches from Staunton state that the Inaugural was received with universal dissatisfaction. Resistance to coercion is the feeling of all parties.

The Inaugural creates intense excitement. The Secessionists regard it as equivalent to a declaration of war. The Union men say but little, but evidently are disappointed.

IN PETERSBURGH, VA.

PETERSBURGH, Tuesday, March 5.

There was intense excitement on the reception of the Inaugural. Hundreds, hitherto for the Union, avowed boldly for revolution, if the Convention does not immediately pass the secession ordinance.

IN ALEXANDRIA.

ALEXANDRIA, Va., Tuesday, March 5.

The *Gazette* (Union) says the Inaugural is not such a one as it wished, nor such as will probably conciliate or satisfy those whom Mr. LINCOLN speaks of as dissatisfied in the South.

The *Sentinel* (secession) says the positions taken are a declaration of war, having sown distrust which would reduce the Southern section to the conditioned dominion of the North as a vassal.

IN LOUISVILLE AND ELSEWHERE.

LOUISVILLE, Ky., Tuesday, March 5.

The opinions on the Inaugural at Nashville are unfavorable. It is believed that Mr. LINCOLN is determined to retake the forts and forcibly collect the revenue. Opinions are unsettled here, waiting for Washington. The people are awaiting the document in full.

At Jackson and Columbus, Miss., and Tuscaloosa, Ala., it is considered a declaration of war.

At Vicksburgh, it is regarded unfavorably, and is generally considered a silly production.

At New-Orleans, it is most generally condemned.

In this city, the Union men are rather favorably impressed.

[Continued on Eighth Page.]

The New-York Times.

VOL. X.....NO. 2976. NEW-YORK, FRIDAY, APRIL 5, 1861. PRICE TWO CENTS.

THE CRISIS APPROACHING.

A Policy Decided Upon by the Administration.

Meaning of the Extensive Military and Naval Preparations.

The Revenue Laws to be Enforced in the Whole Union.

Sympathy of the Foreign Diplomats with the Government.

IMPORTANT NEWS FROM CHARLESTON.

A Schooner Fired Into from Morris Island.

MAJ. ANDERSON DEMANDS AN EXPLANATION

A Special Messenger from Fort Sumpter to Washington.

THE SUPPLIES AND MAILS CUT OFF.

PREPARATIONS FOR AN ATTACK UPON THE FORT.

A GOVERNMENT POLICY AT LAST.

WASHINGTON, Thursday, April 4.

It is evident here that the policy of the Administration is rapidly crystallizing. The power of the Government is to be tested, or rather the will of the people to sustain the laws and enforce unity. The President has come slowly up to realize the necessity of decisive and vigorous action, and the Revenue laws are to be enforced in Louisiana, as in New-York, if the Army and Navy at the command of the Government can do it.

I am confident that in less than a week every port of importance, south of Charleston, which has inland communication, will be blockaded. It is for this purpose that vessels of war are being fitted for sea, and not for transport, as was supposed. Merchant vessels will be chartered for transport service. Suddenly, all our army officers that were quartered in this vicinity are missing, and the fact is ascertained that they have left under sealed orders, to be opened at sea. The distracted wives leak out this latter fact.

Capt. MEIGS was detailed from the Capitol buildings Wednesday night, and ordered away with only twelve hours' notice. About thirty artificers were sent with him on secret service, not knowing their destination beyond New-York. No visitors were admitted at the War Department to-day, except those connected with the service.

The article in the TIMES on Wednesday, on the necessity of developing the policy of the Government, has attracted profound attention in political and military circles. The only dissent which I have heard expressed, was a remark made by an official that "perhaps the charges it contained of inaction were unjust; that the Government would be found to have considered the subject, and already acted in the direction indicated." This was a significant remark, taken in connection with the preparations that are evidently being made for a warlike demonstration.

I have reason to believe that the Government is to be sustained in its efforts to perpetuate its authority by the sympathy of the Great Powers, whose representatives have decidedly, though unofficially, expressed a desire that the integrity of the Union shall be maintained. They dread the dissensions among themselves which our dissolution would be likely to engender.

The fact that Secretary CHASE accepted only a portion of the bids for the eight million loan, I see, is construed in Wall-street as an evidence of a peace policy. This is a mistake. The Government will not lower the standard of public credit by an act of its own. It will make such expenditures as are necessary to maintain its existence, and will rely upon the patriotism of the people to furnish the money. When it cannot obtain funds at fair rates, it will use Treasury notes. It is husbanding its resources. Every expenditure that can be delayed is stopped; only Army and Navy bills receive prompt dispatch.

I need not tell you that the supposed warlike action of the Administration is warmly commended. The hosts of Republicans that are still here have received the fact with the most intense satisfaction. One of the most noted Democrats in the city, known of all men, was the warmest in his rejoicings over the sudden activity which his experienced eye had detected in Army and Navy circles.

LEO.

GENERAL WASHINGTON NEWS.

RUMORS OF WAR.

The unusual activity at the War and Navy Departments, and news of orders to the vessels at the Brooklyn and Boston Navy Yards, give rise to innumerable, and some very ridiculous, stories. The local papers have it that the Navy is ordered to Southern ports, and that a blockade is to be commenced at once. Another rumor has it that the vessels go to carry reinforcements to the Forts, including Sumpter; and still another, that they are sent to resent the action of the Governor-General of Cuba. In reply to all this the Cabinet officers answer that everything will be amicably settled "in due time."

A dispatch was received here this noon, posted in the hotels, and published in the evening papers, that supplies were cut off from Major ANDERSON, and a dispatch had been sent by the forces at Charleston to Montgomery for orders to commence the attack on Sumpter, and that probably, ere night, hostilities would commence. It created intense anxiety. Subsequently the Administration received information, not authoritative, that ANDERSON had sent a flag of truce, with two lieutenants, to Gov. PICKENS. The same dispatch was given to the Associated Press.

WHAT THE PRESIDENT SAYS.

Mr. LINCOLN assured a Senator, to-day, that under no circumstances should he act hastily, or without carefully considering, himself, every step.

SOUTHERN SENTIMENT.

The Southern people who write here express strong hopes that LINCOLN will not attempt to enforce the laws of the United States. They say they will resist to the bitter end. I have seen communications to the Southern Commissioners, not of an official character, expressing this sentiment. The Commissioners declare that our Government can never enforce even the revenue laws by force of arms. They still anticipate a peaceable separation, and negotiations for a settlement.

Quite a sensation was created yesterday by a report which reached the Southern Commissioners, that President LINCOLN had ordered no further communication with or Government service in the seceding States. It, however, proved to be a "sell."

AN ERROR CORRECTED.

Parties arriving from the South deny *in toto* the reports that the seceded States are filling up with foreign merchandise, imported under the Confederate States' Tariff.

FALSE RUMOR.

The rumor that Forts Monroe and McHenry were to be evacuated, and the troops sent further South, is not correct. Many people have urged CAMERON and Gen. SCOTT to do so, upon the plea that it would do good in Virginia and Maryland.

THE FORCED REBELLION IN TEXAS.

Mr. BLAISDELL, the late constructor of the Custom-house at Galveston, Texas, has returned, and gives many strange incidents of the secession movement in that State. He says the action of Texas is clearly without the authority or sanction of the people, and, as stated heretofore, is nothing but a forced rebellion.

The Collector at Galveston was a strong Union man, and was therefore compelled to "evacuate" his office; but before doing so handed over the money in his possession, $9,000, belonging to the Government, to Mr. BLAISDELL. The latter has been much with members of the Cabinet, and had long interviews with the President and Secretaries CAMERON and WELLES.

THE ARMY OF TEXAS.

Advices from Texas tend to show that the treason of TWIGGS demoralized, to an alarming degree, the entire military force of the United States in Texas. For this reason it has become a military necessity to withdraw from that section all the troops now there, even though their place should be promptly supplied by new companies of picked and tried men. Certainly the Union men of Texas—who have been over-awed and overwhelmed by the Secessionists because TWIGGS' treason thoroughly armed the latter against them—ought not be left at the mercy of the Indians on one side, and marauding Mexicans on the other. It happens, unfortunately, that the section of the State most exposed to Indian depredations is precisely that in which the Union sentiment is very strong.

THE REGIMENT OF MOUNTED RANGERS.

Gen. HOUSTON has sufficiently indicated his disposition to resist the Disunionists if he only had the means,—and it would seem to be eminently proper that the Federal Government should supply him with the needed arms and ammunition. So, too, the President has it in his power to call out the regiment of Mounted Rangers for the defence of the frontier, authorized two or three years ago. True, there is no appropriation made for their pay; but any number of volunteers for this service can be supplied by the Union men of Texas, who will furnish their own horses and wait for their pay until a future Congress can act in the premises.

THE LONDON TIMES CORRESPONDENT ON HIS TRAVELS.

WM. H. RUSSELL, the correspondent of the London *Times*, is still here, but leaves for the South to-morrow or next day, accompanied by T. R. DAVIS, the young artist who sketched for *Leslie's Pictorial* scenes in connection with the Prince of Wales' sojourn in the United States. Mr. RUSSELL finds himself exceedingly puzzled by the complications of American politics—and no wonder. A campaign in the Crimea or in India was easily comprehensible to a gentleman of his intelligence. Military campaigns are conducted upon fixed principles and rules, and the base of operations once understood, the remarkable powers of description possessed by Mr. RUSSELL made his task in the East a comparatively easy one.

A TROUBLESOME AND PUZZLING TASK.

But, in the examination and consideration of the political troubles of America, his artistic "word-painting" is comparatively of little value; and even the most careful judgment which he brings to bear upon his new task may well be at fault. He seeks the society of gentlemen of intellect and character, representing different political interests, and in cases where he cannot doubt the honesty and *sincerity* of their respective views and facts, he finds each man has his individual story, quite at variance with all the rest. As a result, Mr. RUSSELL declares himself unable to find any solid ground to stand upon, and to accept as the basis of his reflection and study. In one interview he thinks he has fathomed the depth at last, and is ready to begin to erect his tower of argument, and the very next man he meets sweeps away his theory, and shows him the unsatisfactory character of the supposed facts.

SECTIONAL HATRED IN THE UNITED STATES.

On one point alone he is able to stick to a conclusion,—he has discovered that there is no nation on earth which hates another so cordially as the Southern Secessionists hate the people of the Free States, whom they seem to look upon as their bitter and uncompromising enemies. It is safe to assume that he finds no such spirit of hostility on the part of Northern men towards their Southern brethren. That the latter have been exasperated to their present condition of mind by the greatest misunderstandings and the grossest misrepresentations of the character and motive of Northern hostility to Slavery, Mr. RUSSELL will probably ascertain upon personal investigation. As an impartial and intelligent party, he may do much good to mankind by showing that the North opposes the *extension* of Slavery—under a Government for which they are responsible—upon principle, and not with the slightest disposition to interfere with Southern institutions, or to annoy those who look upon Slavery as a blessing instead of the curse of a nation, which all sound and unprejudiced statesmen have long understood it to be.

THE CALIFORNIA APPOINTMENTS.

IRA P. RANKIN was to-day appointed Collector of San Francisco. This is the best selection that possibly could have been made, on every score. I am assured, late to-night, from the highest source, that this is the only California appointment yet made. Nevertheless, I hear on the authority of intimate friends of Senator BAKER, that the latter's son-in-law, R. J. STEVENS, has been settled upon for Superintendent of the Mint. It is probably true. It is generally understood on the street, also, and is undoubtedly true, that S. H. PARKER was decided upon to-day for Postmaster of San Francisco, D. W. CHEESEMAN Sub-Treasurer, and B. W. MUDGE Appraiser-General. RANKIN's appointment is a glorious triumph for those who have battled against the effort to saddle improper men upon California, in the Federal offices. No objection ever has been urged against STEVENS' moral character, except that he is too weak a man to be subjected to the temptations by which he will be surrounded. The opposition to him is chiefly on the ground that he is a Breckinridge Democrat, which is so notorious in California, that his appointment will inevitably discourage and demoralize the Republican Party in that State, and lead to their defeat next Fall. It is due to the President, however, to state that BAKER pledged his honor that STEVENS was a sound Republican. CHEESEMAN, who is made Sub-Treasurer, was the leading Republican candidate for the Mint. It is uncertain whether he will accept the responsible position tendered him. Dr. JOHN HASTINGS, brother-in-law of Senator SUMNER, another Republican competitor, will probably be Visiting Physician to the Marine Hospital. Dr. RABE, Secretary of the Republican State Central Committee, virtually withdrew from the contest for the Post-office. BAKER had made a ferocious onslaught on him for personal reasons, and RABE yesterday notified the Executive that if the rejection of his universally-conceded claims to the Post-office was necessary to the rejection of improper men, pressed for other places from influential quarters, he was ready to be sacrificed. Accordingly, RABE was overslaughed, and PARKER appointed, instead of BAKER's man, M. S. WHITING. RABE's unselfish conduct in this fight has won general respect and admiration. It is also understood that ROBT. DENIO is settled upon for Melter and Refiner in the Mint. It is further believed that Capt. RICHARD CHENERY has been agreed upon for Navy Agent at San Francisco.

DISTRICT-ATTORNEY OF NEW-YORK.

E. DELAFIELD SMITH was to-day appointed District-Attorney of New-York.

NAVY AGENT FOR NEW-YORK.

It is rumored, to-night, that DUTCHER is beaten by D. D. T. MARSHALL, for Navy Agent at New-York, but no appointment is yet announced.

THE BOSTON APPOINTMENTS.

Several of the Massachusetts delegation in Congress, are expected back here to-morrow to fix up the remaining appointments. They will recommend RICHARD H. DANA for District-Attorney, JOHN S. KEYES for Marshal, Dr. PHELPS for Surveyor, and EZRA LINCOLN for Sub-Treasurer. Probably they will all be appointed.

MOVEMENTS OF THE FOREIGN ENVOYS.

The Department of State is very busily engaged making out instructions to newly-appointed Envoys and agents of the Government. Messrs. CLAY, CORWIN, ADAMS, BURLINGAME, MARSH and DAYTON can leave as soon as they arrange their private affairs. It is understood, in consequence of our present peculiar position with the Spanish Government, that CARL SCHURZ must proceed to his post at once.

SECRETARY OF LEGATION TO LONDON.

I am authorized to state that the report, some time since, that Mr. ADAMS, Minister to England, had protested against the appointment of WILSON, as his Secretary of Legation, is wholly untrue. He is perfectly satisfied with the appointment, although it makes very little difference, except socially, as the Secretary acts entirely free from and independent of the Minister. They are both awaiting instructions and preparing for their departure together.

MR. CAMERON AND THE WAR DEPARTMENT.

Secretary CAMERON has now fairly settled himself into the business of the War Department, and is giving it close attention. I understand it is his purpose to study carefully the entire condition of the Army, with a view to the development of whatever reforms may be needed to secure greater efficiency and economy in its operations. It is quite eight years now since the counsels of the veteran SCOTT have been allowed to have any weight in the arrangements made for the conduct of this branch of the public service. During Mr. PIERCE's Administration, JEFF. DAVIS, of course, could not tolerate the advice of one under whom he had served once as a subordinate: and during the last four years it did not suit Secretary FLOYD's purposes to have the War Department administered upon strictly military principles, because that necessarily interfered with speculative and swindling schemes. The change of Administration has brought with it a new condition of affairs, and we may hope that the country will be allowed the benefit of Gen. SCOTT's wisdom and experience, applied in every proper way to the military establishment.

THE TIMES INDORSED.

The leader in yesterday's TIMES has created great sensation in political circles, and finds a ready echo in the breast of every thinking man who wishes the Administration well.

THE TRIALS OF SECRETARY CHASE.

No sooner does Mr. CHASE find himself somewhat relieved of office-seekers, than he is assailed by a horde of claimants upon the Treasury, demanding money. He takes it very patiently, but from his excessive labors seems much worn and exhausted.

THE DEATH OF JUDGE MCLEAN.

The death of Judge MCLEAN, announced in this city to-day, created very general sorrow. A tribute of respect will be paid by the members of the Bar in this city at an early opportunity. Some have begun to speculate, already, upon his successor. TRUMBULL's name is mentioned, and some say this vacancy insures the appointment of CRITTENDEN. SAMUEL F. VINTON and THOMAS EWING, both of Ohio, will probably be pressed.

THE LATE AMERICAN MINISTER TO PERU.

I am assured that RANDOLPH CLAY's connection with the Government, as Minister to Peru, was not terminated, as stated, because the President disapproves the course of the late Administration on the Peruvian claims. Mr. CLAY has simply achieved the fate of many other diplomats whose places are wanted for Republican incumbents. The new Administration has not yet in any way indicated its policy on the claims in question.

A CARD FROM CAPT. REYNOLDS.

Capt. A. W. REYNOLDS, U. S. A., publishes a card here, denying the statement of the TIMES, that he was partly responsible for TWIGGS' surrender in Texas.

Com. PAULDING succeeds STRINGHAM in the Bureau of Detail.

The report that Capt. WYNDER, son-in-law of Gov. GOODWIN, of New-Hampshire, had resigned his commission on account of secession, is not true. He is in California on service, having recently been ordered there; and, although a Southern man, says he will stand by our flag while a star remains. The gentleman who resigned is a son of Gen. WYNDER, of Maryland.

Capt. VAN BRUNT and Purser PETIT are ordered to the *Minnesota*.

By order of the President all further appointments of Consuls are postponed for several weeks.

Senator HALE, of New-Hampshire, left for home to-day.

DISPATCH TO THE ASSOCIATED PRESS.

WASHINGTON, Thursday, April 4.

Capt. BARRY's Company of Artillery left here to-day for New-York. From twenty-five to thirty carpenters, engaged by the Government, went in the same train, but for what purpose is not publicly known.

The Gulf Squadron is to be commanded by Capt. STRINGHAM. The reasons for the increase of the naval force in that quarter are conjectural. The extreme caution which characterizes the Administration on this as well as other military subjects, occasions many warlike rumors. The Government seems to have come to the determination, in the language of a Cabinet officer, "to be known only by its acts."

The steamer *Pawnee*, now lying off the Washington Navy-Yard, will probably leave for parts unknown on Saturday.

The following officers have been ordered to the steamer *Minnesota*, destined for the Gulf: Capt. Van Brunt, Com. Chase, Lieutenants Werden, Wainwright, Badger, Johnson, Foster and Mitchell, and Watson Smith, Master, and Franklin Jackson, Chief Engineer.

Extreme solicitude is everywhere manifested relative to the movements concerning Forts Pickens and Sumpter. The fear is expressed that a collision may be precipitated.

Information has been received here, stating that Lieut TALBOT left Charleston to-day with important dispatches for Washington.

A reliable private dispatch from Charleston says that it is supposed Major ANDERSON's supplies were cut off to-day, causing considerable commotion and anxiety as to the final result.

Capt. GORGAS, who recently resigned in the Army, has tendered his services to the Confederate States. He is a native of Pennsylvania, and was formerly in command of the Charleston Arsenal.

In addition to the other Maine appointments, heretofore stated, are JAMES WEEKS, Postmaster at Bangor.

DWIGHT B. BARNARD, Postmaster at Calais.

WM. B. SMITH, Collector at Machias.

TRUMAN HARMEN, Collector at Belfast.

The following appointments have also been made:

JAMES F. BABCOCK, Collector at New-Haven.

LAPANDER R. WEBB, Surveyor at Peoria, Ill.

JOHN YOUNGS, Collector at Sandusky, Ohio.

DAVID MORGAN, Postmaster, Minneapolis, Min.

EDWIN COWLES, Postmaster, Cleveland, Ohio.

SAMUEL ANDREWS, Postmaster, Camden, N. J.

SAMUEL WOOD, Collector, Paso del Norte, New-Mexico.

The President to-day made the following San Francisco appointments: IRA H. RANKIN, Collector; BENJ. W. MUDGE, Appraiser-General: SAMUEL H. PARKER, Postmaster; R. J. STEVENS, (Senator BAKER's son-in-law,) Superintendent of the Mint.

OUR WASHINGTON CORRESPONDENCE.

DESPERATE EFFORTS OF THE VIRGINIA SECESSIONISTS—THE STATE WILL REMAIN IN THE UNION—THE GREAT STRUGGLE TO COME—THE EXPORT DUTY ON COTTON, ETC.

WASHINGTON, Wednesday, April 3, 1861.

The Secessionists in the Richmond Convention are making desperate efforts to create the impression that their cause is gaining strength among the people; but all accounts from the interior, except their own, concur in stating that the pestilent fever is abating, and that the public mind is becoming calm and indifferent to their appeals. Secession has, from the beginning, been an affair of the politicians, and has never had any hold upon the popular heart. It is a fruit of disappointed ambition, the offspring of hatred and resentment in the oligarchy which has lost the control of the Federal Government. The cause touches not the honor nor the interests of the people, and is merely an affair of hair-splitting platform-builders. The "Democratic" demagogues have for thirty years ridden the negro hobby, and have been determined to keep it as their own peculiar property. The Whigs, or Opposition, have been compelled to abandon the field of politics, or keep up neck and neck with the "Democracy," in exactions upon the Federal Government, and the result of this disgraceful competition is, that each, and especially the Democracy, finds itself committed to platforms and *ultimatums* which can only be consistently maintained by voting themselves out of the Union.

This was the case at the late election, and everybody supposed that the Secessionists would sweep the State. But the result proved that the people of Virginia have far more self-reliance than they had credit for; and instead of yielding to the clamor of the demagogues, they overwhelmed them with disgrace, by electing five Union men to one Secessionist. If the question of holding a Convention had been submitted, they would have voted it down by thousands, and there the matter would have ended. But this was not allowed. The delegates were assembled, and immediately the Secessionists began to insist that their opponents should come up to their platforms and pledges, and demand "guarantees" and "compromises" of the Federal Government and the effect is to keep the people in a state of feverish agitation.

But I predict that they will not dare to pass a Secession Ordinance and submit it to the popular vote. They are conscious of their weakness, and hence the perpetual discussions, and delays, and preparations, which it is hoped will keep up the excitement until some fortunate collision between the Federal and Confederate forces shall take place. The States which have been voted out of the Union are doubtless really anxious to avoid collision; but the attorney for Bardell, in the famous case of Bardell *vs.* Pickwick, was not more anxious to be *kicked*, than are the Secessionists in the Border Slave States to witness an attempt at *coercion* against their Southern neighbors

It is said that the Secessionists at Richmond have purchased out the *Whig*, heretofore a Union paper, and that it will shortly open its batteries upon the Stars and Stripes. The editor of the *Whig*, Mr. RIDGWAY, who is a vigorous writer, will, I hear, commence a new enterprise in journalism, in the cause of the Union.

A majority of the people of Richmond and the adjacent country are probably for secession—or at least the dominant oligarchy has managed to establish a reign of terror at that great negro mart; but the great heart of the State, the valley, with the entire West, and probably half of the district east of the mountains, is sounder to-day than they were three months ago.

I have no fears for the result of the struggle now going on in Virginia. I believe that it will be kept up until 1864, when the great fight is to take place between the East and West—between the slaveholding and non-slaveholding interests—on the basis of taxation. Slavery has been, and is yet, the pet interest of Virginian society. It is taxed to the extent of only about one-third of land or other property, while the enormous State debt of forty-one or two millions has been incurred in building railroads and canals in the slave region. The non-slaveholders of the West have at length become aroused on this vital subject, and the irrepressible conflict has begun. By the terms of the Constitution, it cannot be changed until 1865; but the questions then to be decided are already mooted, and the non-slaveholders are daily becoming bolder and more imperative in their demands of even-handed justice. I have not yet seen the result of the recent census, as it regards the relative strength of Eastern and Western Virginia; but the white population of the latter can be little less than double that of the former.

One of the most stupid things yet done by the Confederate States is the export duty they have laid upon cotton. When the whole manufacturing and commercial world is on the look-out for new supplies of cotton, in order to provide against a possible deficiency consequent upon the failure of the Cotton States to meet the demand, their Government steps in to aid the movement, and puts in a bounty upon the production of the article in foreign countries by taxing that of their constituents. It may be hoped that this folly will not be persisted in. It could only proceed from ignorance and conceit; and while it will stimulate rivalry, and thus tend to break down the curse of the cotton monopoly, it will at the same time give the cotton-growers of North Carolina, Tennessee and Arkansas ample protection in the American market.

The treasonable spirit which rules the councils of the Virginia Legislature is manifested in the fact, that while it has authorized the seizure of the guns manufactured at the Bellona Foundry for the United States, not the slightest opposition has been made to the sale of arms by a Richmond manufacturer to the Southern traitors. The folly of this piece of meanness is illustrated in the fact that the Bellona guns are small, the whole thirty costing only thirteen or fourteen thousand dollars. They are in no way necessary to the defence of Fortress Monroe, which is amply provided with the materials of defence. The secession fright has been entirely without adequate foundation, but the occasion serves to illustrate the treasonable spirit which prevails about Richmond.

It is said that MACKLIN, the army officer who surrendered the public property at one of the forts in Texas, not content with turning over the stores on hand, sent off to a considerable distance for a supply of specie, intended for the payment of the troops, in order that it might fall into the hands of the traitors.

OBSERVER.

IMPORTANT FROM CHARLESTON.

A SCHOONER FIRED INTO FROM MORRIS ISLAND.

WASHINGTON, Thursday, April 4.

A dispatch just received here states that the mortar batteries on Morris Island, last evening, fired into an unknown schooner which attempted to enter the harbor without displaying her colors. Three shots were fired.

Major ANDERSON immediately dispatched a messenger to Gov. PICKENS to demand an explanation.

A violent gale was blowing at the time, and the vessel put to sea again.

A FLAG OF TRUCE FROM FORT SUMPTER.

WASHINGTON, Thursday, April 4.

Another dispatch from Charleston has been received, which states that two officers had landed from Fort Sumpter with a white flag, and had gone to head-quarters with Col. HATCH.

LATER.—The officers are Lieut. SNYDER and Lieut. TALBOT. Lieut. SNYDER subsequently returned to Fort Sumpter, and Lieut. TALBOT left for Washington this evening.

It was a New-Jersey schooner which was fired into, loaded with ice. One shot went through her.

SUPPLIES FOR FORT SUMPTER CUT OFF.

WASHINGTON, Thursday, April 4.

Still another dispatch has reached here from Charleston, which reports that JEFF. DAVIS has directed Gen. BEAUREGARD to cut of Major ANDERSON's supplies of food and mails.

All officers of the Confederate Army on leave of absence are ordered to their respective commands.

The crisis is rapidly approaching. Thirty laborers at Fort Sumpter, whose time is out, want to leave, but are not permtited.

DISPATCHES FROM CHARLESTON.

CHARLESTON, Thursday, April 4.

Charleston has to-day been in a state of excitement unequaled since the first secession movement. A crisis is at hand. The appearance of a schooner off the harbor last evening, and her attempt to pass the batteries, her being fired into, and her subsequent mysterious disappearance, have aroused apprehensions of the most serious character. The military leaders have been unusually active all day, and members of the Convention now in session, belonging to the several fortifications, have been ordered to their stations.

A thousand rumors are in circulation, the principal of which indicates that Fort Sumpter will be attacked in the course of two days, and that the attack will be from the forts.

Lieut. TALBOT, of Fort Sumpter, lately promoted, went to Washington this forenoon, as bearer of dispatches to the Government.

The Charlestonians generally say there shall be no more boys' play. Evacuate or fight is the prevailing sentiment.

Major ANDERSON will soon have to surrender in self-defence, though it is believed that an attempt will be seriously made at reinforcement.

WELCOME B. SAYLES, Special Agent of the Post-Office Department of the Southern Confederacy, left to-night direct for Washington. After a thorough examination into the postal arrangements in the Southern section, he has had interviews with Postmaster-General REAGAN and nearly all the postmasters.

The old mail arrangements will probably be continued until the Confederate States are ready to conclude their own, which will be shortly.

Two companies left the arsenal to-night for Savannah.

CHARLESTON, Wednesday, April 4.

Later advices are understood to have been received from Montgomery, ordering further supplies to Major ANDERSON to be cut off.

No further communication will be allowed between the Fort and Federal authorities.

The danger is imminent, and members of the Convention wait here, expecting a conflict before Saturday.

REPORTED LETTER FROM FORT SUMPTER.

BUFFALO, Thursday, April 4.

The *Commercial Advertiser* publishes a letter this afternoon signed "Johnson McNeill," a private in the Army who enlisted at Buffalo a year ago, and who is now with Major ANDERSON in Fort Sumpter. There is not a doubt as to the genuineness of the letter, which, on account of the soldier's inability to write well, was written by a sergeant and brought by a passenger to New-York on the last steamer. He says:

"We have enough to eat and drink, and sufficient to keep us for *four months*. Our fuel is scarce, but that is nothing. The rebels think we have been idle, but they nor any one else will ever know how many men we have in this garrison. We have got sufficient to hold the fort against the whole South in a body. Major ANDERSON is a true soldier and so are the other officers, and the men would die for him. I only wish we had a chance to give the rascals hell, and we will do it too. If we ever go out of this fort it will not be with the wish of our officers. As to sending us men and supplies it is all nonsense to talk about it. It cannot be done. We are all right if old LINCOLN will only have the back-bone to stand by us."

OUR CHARLESTON CORRESPONDENCE.

SOUTH CAROLINA A SUBLIME MYSTERY—THE MERCURY PLAYING AN APRIL FOOL!—A FICTITIOUS ACCOUNT OF THE MORRIS ISLAND BATTERIES—A VERY ANCIENT NEGRO CUPID—THE PEOPLE PRAY FOR SOMETHING TO TURN UP—THE CONVENTION HAVE A GRAND JUNKETING.

CHARLESTON, C. S. A., Monday, April 1, 1861.

The more I see of the men of Charleston, the more convinced I am that very many of them act, talk, and behave like perfect children. They started the secession ball, not because they had "niggers stolen from them, but because they wanted absolute free trade, and some of them a free-and-easy *slave* trade. They are now about to ratify the Provisional Constitution, which puts in force, with slight modifications, the old United States Tariff of 1857, which they kicked overboard so unceremoniously on the 20th of December, 1860. They hate and detest the Stars and Stripes of the old Union, yet they unanimously indorse a close imitation of that flag. They denounce ANDERSON in the bitterest terms "for his act of war in removing from Fort Moultrie to Fort Sumpter;" yet they, with spasmodic intervals, supply him with all the luxuries of the market, and allow him and his men to "live like fighting-cocks." They denounce the North theoretically, and practically endeavor to live on the best terms with her people. They even assail your correspondent as being the representative of, what they are pleased to call, "a vile Black Republican sheet;" they threaten him with the surveillance of the dreadful Vigilance Committee, and insinuate that he will shortly have notice to quit; yet the same people will go out of their way to give him exclusive information, and socially open to him their hearts, their homes, and even their purses. In fact, South Carolina in general and Charleston in particular is a sublime mystery, and cannot be estimated or measured by any of the commen-sense rules that govern one in their intercourse with ordinary people. It is to be hoped that one of these days some acute physiologist will give us a proper analysis of them, so that when another crisis comes, we shall be better prepared to meet it than we have this late revolutionary one.

What do you think of a sheet like the *Mercury*, that arrogates for itself absolute perfection in journalism, publishing the following leading editorial on this 1st of April, under the caption, "Floating Battery?"

"The flag of the Confederate States will be flung to the breeze from the Floating Battery at 10 o'clock this morning. The proportions of the flag are 20 by 12 feet, and it will be raised at a height of sixty feet. An oration suitable to the occasion will be delivered. Refreshments have been generously provided."

Over one thousand persons hastened to the Custom-house which Uncle Sam commenced to build a long time ago. They waited in vain for the flag—in vain for Col. DURYEA, the Governor's Aid, the orator, and in vain for the $15 brandy, champagne, &c., that were to be poured out lavishly on the occasion. They finally went home, a crowd of men, crinoline and soldiers, feeling that they were the silly victims of an April-fool trick the leading paper in Charleston (next to the *Courier*) had perpetrated. This is another proof of childishness.

I observe that the *Herald* has at last discovered that Charleston correspondence is somewhat necessary, and has sent down some one to examine the fortifications in the harbor. If the gentleman had ever seen big guns before he would not have made so many gross errors. He mixed up columbiads and howitzers in the most heterogeneous manner, and has *magnified largely* the real strength of the Morris Island works. When he comes across a short range shooting-iron, a *howitzer*, which will send perhaps a half mile, and calls it a *columbiad*, which will send from two to three miles, the supposition is that he was out of his reckoning altogether, as the sailors say. A copy of the letter was sent to Gen. BEAUREGARD by an officer I am well acquainted with. The General carefully read it, and remarked very quietly "That it would do to send North, but he was not aware before that they had so many guns."

I visited, yesterday afternoon, an ancient negro, who has reached the ripe period of *one hundred and twenty-five years*. His history is a very curious one, and he is indirectly connected with that horrible catastrophe, the burning of the *Pulaski*, the *Echo* negroes, who were in Fort Sumpter in 1858, and with ALBERT SUMNER, of Boston, who had an interest in him once. The old fellow now looks more like an ape than a human being: he is bent with the weight of years, and is enabled to totter along with the aid of a stick that reaches above his head; his language is a perfect gibberish, but his eyes have a remarkable animal brightness. He lives and thrives in a place where white men cannot stay over night with impunity after the first of June. Mr. MISSROON, his owner, allows him to do as he pleases, clothes and feeds him, and gives him a comfortable cottage to live in. CUPID, as he is called, may have sprung from a black Venus in his native Africa, but he is a perfect parody on the name now. CUPID and NED, a youth of ninety, belonged to the late Mr. BALL who was burnt up in the *Pulaski*. Mrs. BALL was a Miss PELL, of Boston. For years the suit of PELL *vs.* BALL, agitated all South Carolina. The most eminent counsel could not determine whether the husband or wife was burnt up first, and this very important point brought down Mr. SUMNER, from Boston, who was nearly related to

[*Continued on Eighth Page.*]

The New-York Times.

VOL. X....NO. 2977. | NEW-YORK, SATURDAY, APRIL 6, 1861. | PRICE TWO CENTS.

THE IMPENDING CRISIS.

[illegible] to Bombard Sumpter in Forty-eight Hours.

[illegible] and Military Preparations of the Government.

The Steamships Atlantic and Illinois Chartered as Transports.

The Powhatan to Sail Immediately.

Activity at the Navy-Yards and Military Posts.

Views of the Southern Commissioners.

Action of the Virginia Convention Against Secession.

OUR WASHINGTON DISPATCHES.

WASHINGTON, Friday, April 5.

MATTERS AT CHARLESTON.

A dispatch received in this city, from a reliable person in Charleston, states that Gen. Beauregard, before sunrise this morning, left for Morris Island, for what specific purpose, however, was only known to himself and, perhaps, Gov. Pickens. The General is reported to have stated that Maj. Anderson had now but two alternatives—to evacuate Fort Sumpter within forty-eight hours, or suffer a bombardment.

SOUTHERN COMMISSIONERS' VIEWS.

Lieut. Talbot is expected here to-morrow night with dispatches from Major Anderson.

In conversation last night, Crawford, one of the Commissioners from the Southern Confederacy, said he anticipated only peace, and declared that he spoke advisedly in saying that the Confederate States desired nothing else. But, if Lincoln did not desire peace, they were prepared to accept whatever was in store for them. That they would wage civil war rather than submit to coercive execution of any law of this Government, and should maintain their independence at all hazards. He claims that the Confederate States' Government is growing daily in strength, and can afford to wait peaceably for the development of Lincoln's policy. To-day he again declared his conviction that there was nothing in the rumors of warlike movements by the Administration.

TREASURY NOTES TO BE ISSUED.

The Secretary of the Treasury has definitely concluded to issue Treasury notes, redeemable in two years, for the balance of the eight millions recently advertised. He will issue them after a few days' opportunity to enable all who desire to offer for them. No formal bids are to be asked, however. One offer has already been received for two millions at one-eighth per cent. premium.

SECRETARY CHASE'S CAPABILITY—QUICK WORK.

When the new Administration came in, Secretary Chase found five millions of dollars of certificates of deposit awaiting the issue of the Loan stock last previously bid for. The balance of this was issued last week—*per contra* the acceptances of bids for the new loan were received in New-York on Wednesday last, and one million sixteen hundred thousand dollars of the stock has been already issued by the Department—the certificates of deposit being received in the morning and the stock issued to the bidders for full amount the same day. This promptness will continue to characterize each day's transactions. There has never been anything approaching this celerity in the history of the Government. It is the more marked in view of the pressure of appointments and other business.

AN APPOINTMENT IN VIRGINIA.

Dr. Fisher, of Fauquier County, Virginia, was appointed to-day Marshal of Eastern Virginia. He is a decided Union man.

THE NEW-YORK APPOINTMENTS.

It is now said the New-York appointments will not be made until the last of next week. Charles A. Stetson is here, looking to be appointed Marshal, in the event of the name of Capt. Schultz being withdrawn.

CALIFORNIA APPOINTMENTS.

The appointment of D. W. Cheeseman as Sub-Treasurer of San Francisco was issued to-day, and is highly creditable to the Administration. He accepts the office at the earnest pressure of his friends. The reported appointment of Stevens, for Superintendent of the San Francisco Mint, seems to have been premature, as no commission is yet issued. The names of the Surveyor of the Port of San Francisco, Naval Officer, Navy Agent, Surveyor-General, and some other minor California appointments are still unannounced.

MISCELLANEOUS APPOINTMENTS.

Edward Prentice, has been appointed Collector at New-London, Conn.

Mr. Babcock, Editor of the *Palladium*, has been appointed Collector at New-Haven, Conn.

Major George T. Whittington, is strongly pressed by leading Republicans and Union men for Collector at Alexandria, Virginia.

Hon. Green Adams, of Kentucky, is in town, but has received no commission yet for the Sixth Auditorship, to which he was reported appointed. It is, however, probable he will get it.

Elisha Whittlesey, the new First Comptroller, is expected to assume office on Monday.

Dr. Chamberlain, of Keene, N. H., is to be Chief Clerk of the Sixth Auditor's Office. This is an important position, having under its control a hundred and sixteen clerks.

DIDN'T GO SOUTH.

The statement published in New-York that a Clerk in the Treasury Department had gone to Mobile on financial business for the Department is erroneous. He received leave of absence at a time when his services were much needed, only because the death of his brother there made his presence for a short time indispensable.

INQUIRERS FROM CANADA.

A company of gentlemen are in town from Canada, for the purpose of prospecting and gaining a more correct idea of our national affairs than they can do at home. They express great surprise at the death-like quietude in Washington and the apparent indifference of the people with whom they come in contact. They are gentlemen of wealth, and seem much interested in our troubles. They will call upon the President, whom they have a great curiosity to see, before leaving, and thence go South to Charleston and New-Orleans.

DISPATCH TO THE ASSOCIATED PRESS.

WASHINGTON, Friday, April 5.

It is understood that the Secretary of the Treasury will receive offers for Treasury Notes, redeemable in two years, for the balance of the Loan not taken under the last notice. An offer has been made for two millions, at an eighth per centum premium.

D. W. Cheesman has been appointed Assistant-Treasurer at San Francisco; Jas. G. Zalen, Postmaster at Hudson; Chas. H. Prinison, Postmaster at Corning, N. Y., and Nehemiah D. Sperry, Postmaster at New-Haven; Ed. Prentiss, Collector at New-London; Thos. H. Turner, Marshal for the Eastern District of Virginia; Chas. S. Loring, a Chief-Engineer in the Navy.

The Interior Department has under consideration the subject of the organization of the Land Offices in the new Territories of Dacotah, Colorado and Nevada.

It is not true that the Southern Commissioners have taken a house in Washington. It is well understood that the length of their sojourn here will be dependent on circumstances.

Much alarm exists here on account of the military preparations of the Government, which preserves entire silence.

OUR WASHINGTON CORRESPONDENCE.

SENTIMENT IN NORTH ALABAMA—THE APPOINTMENT OF A UNITED STATES JUDGE—WHAT THE CONFEDERATE STATES MUST COME TO—ENORMOUS TAXATION—NORTHERN OFFICERS WITH SOUTHERN WIVES, ETC.

WASHINGTON, Thursday, April 4, 1861.

The appointment of a District Judge for North Alabama, is said to have been made at the instance of Alabamians themselves, who don't mean to recognize the Government of Jeff. Davis. I know not how extensive and out-spoken the Union sentiment is in that region, but it cannot be forgotten that the Palmetto flag was torn down some two months ago, at Athens, the place at which the Court is to be held, and that the Stars and Stripes were run up in its stead, amid the rejoicings of the people. I know nothing of Mr. McLane, who has been appointed to the Judgeship, but it is not to be supposed that he would accept the position, much less seek it, if he was not confident that his authority will be sustained by the people.

It was in this very region that resistance was made in the early part of the Winter to the payment of taxes, which were levied to pay some expense connected with the secession movement, and it is apprehended that similar resistance, on a more formidable scale, will take place whenever the Government of the Confederate States shall resort to direct taxation as a means of meeting its obligations.

That this odious and unpopular resort to direct taxes must be made at no distant day, in order to keep life in the Montgomery Government, there can be no sort of doubt, and whenever it occurs, we may look out for a general and wide-spread disaffection, rebellion and anarchy. The receipts from Customs in the Confederate Republic, in spite of their supposed advantages over the Government of the Union as it regards revenue laws, will be insignificant. If the independence of that Republic were acknowledged, and peace restored, its revenue from this source would be inconsiderable, and in the actual state of things, it will bear no proportion to the expenditure which will become necessary. The recent Congress held at Montgomery has already authorized the raising of an army of ten thousand men, which at a moderate estimate will cost three millions of dollars. They must also have some sort of a navy, and with the civil service, the public expenditure cannot fall below eight or ten millions per annum, in a time of proposed peace. The purchase of vessels and their equipments for the naval service is an extraordinary expenditure, which will have to be incurred in the very outset. No respectable force of this kind could be procured and got ready for sea without an expenditure of millions, in addition to the ordinary annual outlay.

It is obvious that the Government of the Confederate States will be unable to raise these great sums, either by taxing the people or straining their credit. They may raise their army of ten thousand men because there is no great difficulty in enlisting recruits in times of pecuniary distress, but their payment will be more difficult. Not six months will elapse from the time this force is called into service, before embarrassments of the most threatening nature will overtake the Cabinet of Mr. Davis. It will be rather more difficult to procure vessels for their navy; but they will probably be able, by one means or another, to fit out as many small craft as they will be able to maintain. It is to be hoped that they will succeed in their efforts in this way. They will never be able to build a navy capable of hurting anybody but themselves. Its expense will be more formidable to the people who pay the taxes which will be necessary to support it, than to the enemies of the Republic.

It is said that Capt. J. Gorgas, whose resignation was alluded to a day or two ago, has tendered his services to the Cotton Confederacy. He is from Michigan, but married a Mobile lady. His abandonment of the flag of his country, furnishes another instance of the subordination of Northern epaulettes to Southern petticoat rule, of which the rebellion of the oligarchy has furnished several. Adjutant-General Cooper, Farren, and two or three others, if I mistake not, were drawn into treason by such gentle persuasives. A story is told of an honest Hibernian, who, when in the act of marrying a wealthy Southern lady, responded to the usual interrogatory of the parson—"Patrick, wilt thou take this woman to be thy wedded wife?"—by declaring with emphasis, "Yes, be jabers, and the *nagers* too." It seems that the Northern chivalry who have allied themselves to the South by the matrimonial tie, are not a whit behind Patrick in the thoroughness of their attachment.

The Times article, on "a policy" for the Administration, has created quite a sensation in political circles. The feeling seems to be general, without distinction of party, that the time for action has arrived. There are those who still think that it is practicable to reinforce Fort Sumpter; but the prevalent belief is, that necessity, as well as policy, calls for its speedy evacuation. For my own part, I have believed for several weeks that the most effectual way to kill the Secessionists off, and cause a powerful reaction against them, is to withdraw the force from Forts Sumpter and Pickens. There is entire unanimity for secession in these portions of the seceded States, and the only effect of holding the forts is to irritate and inflame the populace. The case is quite different with regard to the troops on the western borders of Texas. There the Union sentiment is predominant, and the presence of the troops is necessary to protect the people from Indian and Mexican marauders. Wherever the Union sentiment is strong, it should be recognized and encouraged; but in districts which are thoroughly alienated in feeling, the better plan would evidently be to leave the people to themselves. It will not be twelve months before a reaction will take place even in these, if they are left to the consequences of their folly; while any attempt at coercion will only strengthen the disaffection in the Border States.

The withdrawal of the forces from Forts Sumpter and Pickens would give a death-blow to secession in Virginia and North Carolina, where it still has a strong foot-hold. The friends of union are contending bravely, and they still have the people with them; but it is not probable that they could maintain their ground if actual hostilities were to commence.

All Union men of the South concur in the opinion that the sure method of destroying secession is to withdraw the troops from Sumpter and Pickens. I have not seen or heard of a dissentient from this. It is here that the shoe pinches; and whoever looks into the Southern newspapers will see that the Secessionists predict coercion, and the Unionists repel the charge, and maintain that a pacific policy will be pursued. OBSERVER.

IMPORTANT NEWS FROM CHARLESTON.

CHARLESTON, Friday, April 5.

A terrible moment is evidently at hand. The news from Washington and New-York to-night corroborates the general impression that within twenty-four hours war will be upon us.

Every man has been ordered on duty, and the utmost activity prevails. The State is prepared for any emergency.

The highest officials say the present state of things cannot last but a short time longer.

The excitement throughout is intense, and everything wears a warlike aspect.

OUR CHARLESTON CORRESPONDENCE.

NEW-YORK ENLIGHTENING THE CHARLESTONIANS ABOUT THEIR OWN FORTIFICATIONS—GOV. PICKENS AND GEN. BEAUREGARD HOLD A COUNCIL OF WAR—A NEW BATTERY AT MORRIS ISLAND—A FUNNY STORY OF A FREE LOAN — WIGFALL SPREADING HIMSELF IN CHARLESTON—COAL $10 A TON.

CHARLESTON, C. S. A., Tuesday, April 2, 1861.

The sensation sheet of Charleston is fearfully excited, this morning, because your correspondent has sent to New-York a full account of the batteries at Morris Island. He pitches into the Times as "that virulent Abolition sheet," pitches into "Jasper," and is splenetic generally. He, however, is obliged to acknowledge frankly "*that our people, apparently, have to go to New-York papers to learn facts about our own affairs!*" and, to prove it, republishing the whole letter. When he lives a few more years, he will learn that when New-York journalists want to find out anything, they generally discover a way, even if they have to storm columbiads, mortars and howitzers to do it.

Gov. Pickens was excited last night—in fact he was tremendously aroused—and sent for Gen. Beauregard. The General came immediately and with his usual calm and self-possessed manner, quietly asked what was the matter. "Look at that, Sir," said the consort of the divine Cleopatra, handing him a dispatch fresh from Maj. Heiss, of the telegraph. The General read, looked blue, and looked angry, but said nothing, but a *Council of War* kept the lights burning at the Executive Head-quarters much later than I am in the habit of seeing them. Those lights are a sort of political barometer, and they breathe peace and quietness according, as they are put out early or the reverse. I stationed a special to watch them, and he reported at 3 A. M. that they were still burning. It is rather disagreeable to be kept awake by what may turn out a lying telegram, but in the emergencies of nations, one's sleep is not of the slightest consequence. The dispatch from Washington stated very positively that "the pressure from the extreme wing of the Republican Party was so strong that Lincoln hesitated about Col. Lamon's return with the order for the evacuation," which was fully decided on, as the Colonel himself said in this city, and as I telegraphed last week, "that reinforcements were looked upon as feasible," etc. There has been considerable activity this morning in all the military departments, and evidently something is intended of a serious nature. It is extensively credited that Gen. Beauregard and Gov. Pickens wish to relieve Major Anderson from his distressing predicament. They know he will not evacuate without full military orders, and they have his assurance that "he believes that he cannot be reinforced without a fearful loss of life." They propose, therefore, since his own Government procrastinate so strangely about him to come to his relief by starving him out. It is a novel method of showing your friendship for any one by withholding his daily food, but they really admire and worship his bravery and his soundness, and they think they will help him, since his own Government won't. This is the actual programme, as given to me by a high official this morning.

There is a point on Morris Island called Oyster Point. It is very important, militarily speaking, and has been strengthened within forty-eight hours by a new battery of four twenty-four pounders. It will now be called Oyster Point Battery.

This point is near the Morris Island inlet; the distance across the neck of land is only about fifty yards, so that the guns, being *en barbette*, they can attack any force that may attempt to enter in boats through the inlet, where the water is over six fathoms deep, while previous to any such attempt the columbiads, a little further up the channel, can rake the vessels at a distance. Nature, art, and first-class military genius are rapidly making this harbor a perfect Gibraltar of strength.

Edward Frost, Secretary of the Treasury of South Carolina, has recently submitted his report to the Convention through Gov. Pickens. He states that after the act of secession, the exigencies of the State demanded a loan of $400,000; $150,000 for the Ordnance Bureau, and $250,000 for general military defence. This amount was taken up at par by the banks, and has all been spent, I believe. He congratulates the people on the fact that very soon the Confederate Government will refund the expenses that has been so cheerfully incurred, and "the people will be relieved from the pressure." This will be welcome news to a great many. He adds that $22,275 have been voluntarily contributed. With the exception of Mr. Benjamin Mordecai's $10,000, these free-will offerings have been made with the understanding that the names of the givers should not be published. In connection with these free loans, I wish to mention a curious little circumstance. About the time that wise people saw that South Carolina was determined to precipitate a revolution, a certain Hebrew gentleman of this city, who ought to live in Wall-street, went on to New-York and became a "*Bear*," on the strength of what he knew here, as a broker, of the real political complexion of affairs. He speculated freely in Rock Island, Pacific Mail and Erie, and quietly bagged $50,000 in less than a month. One day he astonished his brother Hebrews by returning to this city and cutting an immense dash. When the free gifts to the State became fashionable, the little broker was coerced by his friends, who wished to play on his love of the dust, by telling him that he must help the State in her hour of need. It was a bitter pill for him, but as he was very timid, they made him swallow it, and he gave $500. It is said that he has been sick ever since.

The immortal Wigfall, Hon. Louis T. Wigfall, of seceded Texas, is here, the lion of the Mills House. I saw him last night, in a cloud of smoke, cutting his usual pranks, and telling his broad stories, which may be or may not be mentioned to ears polite. He is a son of the Palmetto, and has a brother, a divine, in one of the up-country districts.

The Convention are constantly sitting in secret session. No one knows what they are about. Their wives and daughters are delighting the disconsolate tradesmen, who find the times decidedly dull. Any one who wishes to speculate in coal had better do so at once. It brings $10 a ton here. JASPER.

THE NOTE OF PREPARATION.

IMPORTANT MOVEMENTS IN THE ARMY AND NAVY.

The conflicting character of the reports and rumors touching the movements of the Army, and of naval vessels, many of which have turned out to be incorrect, have naturally made the public distrustful of any intelligence on that subject which is not a record of facts actually accomplished. Avoiding all mere speculations on so important a subject, it will be our object, as far as possible, to report only such movements of the Government forces as can be relied upon as correct, or which have actually occurred.

The exciting topic of conversation throughout the City yesterday was the reported activity of the War Department; the concentration of Government troops at this point, and the rumored expeditions about being dispatched from this port. To ascertain the facts of the case, diligent inquiry was made in the proper quarters, and in the absence of any positive statements of the officers who are connected with the expeditions on foot, our reporters were left to judge mainly from actual observation as to what is going on.

The steamship *Atlantic*, of the North Atlantic Company, has undoubtedly been chartered by the Government as a transport for troops, and will sail to-day. She is lying at the old Collins dock, foot of Canal-street, having on Thursday evening been hauled from the north side of the dock, where she lay outside of the *Baltic*, to the berth at the south side. On the pier, and on board the ship great activity prevailed throughout Thursday night, and all day yesterday. A large gang of men were employed in coaling the vessel, putting on board large quantities of salt provisions and army-bread; in packing the ice-houses with fresh meats, and cabin stores, such as poultry, game, and beef. Carpenters were busy below in making such alterations in the lower hold and in the berth-deck as would be necessary for the sleeping accommodations of six hundred men. The steward's force was actively employed in overhauling the saloons and state-rooms, putting in mattresses and bedding, and dusting out the place generally. The cook was heating up his coppers, and cleaning and scouring up things in the galley and making preparations to feed a large company of passengers, while the engineer and his assistants were cleaning up the engine, and evidently getting ready for a sudden start. On the dock, in close conversation with the agents of the steamer, were observed several army officers, who were evidently urgent that matters generally should be hurried up, and the ship got ready for sea instanter. Mr. Clark, the shipping agent, who furnishes the crew and hunts out the stow-aways, was busy about the ship, while John Maquin, now known as the steamboat pilot *par excellence*, walked in dignity and leisure up and down the dock as if waiting the word of command to take the ship out.

Shortly after 2 o'clock Capt. A. G. Gray, late in command of the *Baltic*, appeared at the Custom-house and cleared the ship coastwise. In answer to questions as to her particular destination, he replied that he had been directed to get the ship ready for sea, but he knew nothing whatever as to where she was going. Cols. Keese and Brown appeared to have the sole direction of the expedition, judging from their frequent interviews with the owners, and by their presence at the Quarter-Master's office in State-street, where they were directing affairs generally. At the latter place several Army officers reported themselves during the day, each with his baggage, or with his valise in hand. Everything indicated unusual activity and a movement in some direction.

The steamer *Illinois*, of Vanderbilt's Southampton and Havre line, which had been got ready to sail on Saturday, has also been chartered by the Government for the purpose of transporting troops. Accordingly, arrangements have been made with the steamer *City of Baltimore* to take out the *Illinois'* mails, passengers, and specie. Being already coaled, provisioned, and manned, there will be very little delay in dispatching her. She is capable of accommodating five hundred troops. She has recently had attached Densmore's patent paddle-wheels, which greatly increases her speed and comfort as a sea-going steamer. It is probable that the *Powhatan* will convoy both the *Atlantic* and *Illinois* to their destination.

The United States revenue-cutter *Harriet Lane* yesterday returned from sea, and came up to the City.

Yesterday morning it was decided, in obedience to instructions from Washington, to put the *Powhatan* steam frigate in commission, and send her off, at all hazards, before nightfall. Capt. Foote, Lieut. Almy, and Mr. Brady have not slept for nights, owing to the press of business in equipping this vessel. All day yesterday extra hands were working on her. Capt. Brevoort, of the marine barracks, sent down the marines, consisting of a full frigates' guard, at 1 o'clock; at 1½ the crew were sent over in boats from the receiving ship *North Carolina*, and cheered their old vessel heartily on reaching her; and at 2 o'clock the ensign was hoisted, and the *Powhatan* was turned over by Capt. Foote to Capt. Mercer, and his officers. All hands then were mustered on the quarter deck, and the ship duly declared in commission for a special cruise. As the armament is likely to be used somewhat briskly, new and strong planks have been substituted for the old ones under the guns. The boilers have not been touched, but the caulkers and carpenters made an excellent job of her hull, in the brief time allotted to them.

The following are the officers ordered to the *Powhatan*:

Captain—Samuel Mercer, of Maryland.
Lieutenants—Egbert Thompson, New-York; Harris, Queen, Geo. W. Brown, Downes, Gamble, McDermot, Smith, Phelps, Brysen.
Purser—Gulick.
Surgeon—Wilson.
Chief Engineer—Newell.
Assistant Surgeon—Laws.
First Assistant Engineers—W. Lamdin, Lt. Broome, Jas. F. Samdin.
Second Assistant Engineers—Jackson McEbwell, John Purdy.
Third Assistant Engineers—E. Laws, H. McIlvain, Frank Fletcher.
Carpenter—Connelly.
Sailmaker—Stevens.
Gunner—Duycker.
Boatswain—McCloud.
Captain's Clerk—J. H. Bulkley.
Purser's Clerk—Wm. Beale.

The *Powhatan* is a first-class side-wheel steamer, of 2,415 tons burthen, and was built at Gosport in 1850. She carries 11 guns and about 300 officers and men. Her service list includes two general cruises and one special cruise. She returned from China last Summer, and was about to be put in ordinary when she was ordered suddenly to the Gulf of Mexico. She was to have been stripped on Monday, when the instructions to get her ready for sea came from Washington. She is the only steam frigate ever converted from the "lying-up" condition into the commission state, *in the space of three days*. She will probably convoy the *Atlantic*.

There are no special orders to fit out any other man-of-war here at present. The corvette *Savannah* will probably be put in hands to-day, or early next week, but it will be done in compliance with directions to have her placed in a state of readiness, which the Commandant received weeks ago. The work on the *Roanoke* and *Wabash* is going ahead uninterruptedly. There is a rumor that the former will be taken out of dock to let some other ships in. The revenue and surveying fleet remain in the stream in *statu quo*. A large concourse of visitors assembled at the Navy Yard yesterday.

The Companies H and R, spoken of above as having arrived from Washington, belong to the Second Artillery. They were sent to the National Capital immediately before Mr. Lincoln's election.

New-York was last night enlivened by detachments of Uncle Sam's soldiers, with plethoric purses, from Fort Hamilton, who came over to spend one jolly evening before "the fray." They are all "mad for fighting."

The steamer *Water Witch*, of the Home fleet, was to have gone into commission yesterday at Philadelphia.

AFFAIRS AT GOVERNOR'S ISLAND.

Our reporter visited Governor's Island, yesterday, and found men actively engaged in loading a lighter with mortar-shells. Major Thornton, of the Ordnance Corps, who has charge of the munitions of war on the island, was superintending their labors. When asked whether he was at liberty to say anything concerning the destination of the *materiel*, or of any contemplated military movements, he replied politely, but firmly, that he could not, but that his visitor might freely visit any part of the island and see for himself all that was to be seen. The lighter arrived at Governor's Island yesterday morning, laden with provisions. These were speedily removed, and while the soldiers, clad in dark blue flannel working shirts, were engaged in rolling the shells, one by one, on to the vessel, Major Thornton occasionally reminded them that they must work expeditiously. On the dock, besides a large quantity of these mortar shells, were piles of the smaller but more destructive balls, with which columbiad guns are loaded. Two of these guns, weighing 15,000 pounds each, were on an adjacent wharf, at which lay a schooner, the *John N. Genin*, which arrived there yesterday, and which, it is conjectured, is to be laden with munitions of war. Within a month past two other schooners have been thus laden at the same pier, and have departed for parts unknown. In the vicinity of the wharves are collected 37,000 shells, a large number of gun carriages, and other war-like contrivances, on each of which are painted the words "Capt. Vogdel, U. S. A., Fort Pickens, Fla." Whether they are designed to be sent to the fortress mentioned in the superscription, is a question that is open to debate. Major Thornton would not say, but he observed that what was written might be intended to mislead unofficial inquirers. It is a fact, which may have some significance, that this same Major Thornton, of Albany, was stationed on the same island during the Mexican War, and superintended the embarkation thence of 47,000 shells, which were sent to Vera Cruz to be used in the reduction of that place. What they effected there our readers know. Major Holmes, who is a native of North Carolina, and graduated at West Point in 1829, is in command of all the troops stationed there, except those connected with the Ordnance Department under Major Thornton. Recruits are arriving daily at the island from the recruiting-offices in New-York, Boston, Rochester, Carlisle, Penn., and elsewhere. The Major examined 36 of these, just arrived yesterday, and more were expected the same day from Carlisle. The Commandant has orders to fill up the companies under his command to the war complement—84 men—as speedily as possible.

We asked an officer of rank what the feeling was among the men with regard to the possibly impending war. He replied that they did not care. If ordered to fight they would fight; and he added that there were no better soldiers in the world. The same officer said that two officers of the detachment now at this post had refused to go South to fight; he declined to name them. We could, of course, obtain no definite information with regard to the meaning of the military movements now in progress. Col. Keese and Col. Brown, and a few staff officers, we were told, are the only ones in New-York who know the orders of the War Department. Major Holmes, who has been for some years Commandant at Governor's Island, is to be relieved in June by Col. Smith.

A detachment of United States recruits arrived yesterday from Buffalo, and were immediately sent over to Governor's Island to be detailed for regimental service.

Capt. Barry's Company of Artillery, and Companies H and K Second Infantry, accompanied by some mechanics, reached town early yesterday morning, and joined the Sappers and Miners at Fort Lafayette. A company or two from Fort Columbus were also to have gone up last night. These troops are all under orders to depart soon for some destination, the latitude of which no one can find out. There are now 491 men at Fort Hamilton.

A Board of Army Officers have been in session for three days at the Quartermaster's Office, in this City, for the purpose of distributing the available troops stationed in the Harbor of New-York. They have not yet made any official report. Col. Harvey Brown, Second Artillery, presides on the Board.

REPORTS FROM NEW-ORLEANS.

NEW-ORLEANS, Thursday, April 4.

A second company of Zouaves, numbering 100 men, left this city this evening to join the battalion of Zouaves before Fort Pickens.

It is reported here that the United States steam sloop-of-war *Brooklyn* arrived off Pensacola harbor on the 31st ult., from Key West.

Advices from Indianola state that the United States steamer *Mohawk*, together with the steamers *Star of the West* and *Empire City*, were lying outside of Pass Cavallo bar, waiting the arrival of the Federal troops from Brazos, to transport them to New-York. The steamer *Fashion* has been chartered by the Federal Government to transport the troops from Indianola to Pass Cavallo bar. Ten companies are expected to arrive shortly from San Antonio.

THE SOUTH CAROLINA CONVENTION AND THE NEW CONSTITUTION.

CHARLESTON, Friday, April 5.

The final vote took place in the Convention to-day on the adoption of the permanent Constitution of the Southern Confederacy. The whole number of members of the Convention is 172, of whom 146 voted for and 16 against the Constitution. Ten were absent.

There is nothing new as to Fort Sumpter or other matters.

CUTTING OFF THE SUPPLIES.

From the Charleston Mercury, April 3.

We understand the liberal supplies heretofore permitted to Major Anderson will shortly be cut off. Yesterday, a dispatch was received from the Commissioners to Washington, advising a change of policy. In their opinion, no more roast beef—no more barrels of potatoes—in short, no more supplies of any description, should be suffered to reach Fort Sumpter. A decision has been reached here. Fort Sumpter must shortly provision itself. To-morrow the garrison must fall back upon its own stores. Its licensed intercourse with the city must cease. But there is something more to be mentioned. A dispatch has been sent to President Davis, in which immediate action is not indirectly hinted at. No reply has yet been received, but a telegraphic reply is hardly to be looked for. The mail will undoubtedly bring an answer. Our citizens, we are aware, are excited in regard to these matters. Patience with them, however, has become a cardinal virtue. Let them exercise it.

THE VIRGINIA STATE CONVENTION.

RICHMOND, Friday, April 5.

In the Convention to-day the sixth resolution was up in the Committee of the Whole.

It was amended on motion of Mr. Critcher, by inserting the words, "dissolve their connection with," in lieu of the words, "cast off obedience to."

Mr. Moore moved to strike out the word "wrongs" and insert "causes," the idea being that "wrongs did not impel States to secede," which was rejected by a large majority. Some other amendments were defeated.

Mr. Bouldin moved to amend by inserting "earnestly desire" in lieu of the words "indulge the hope." Agreed to.

Mr. Wise moved to strike out the whole, and insert the substitute contemplating resistance to wrongs, indulging in the desire for an adjustment, and that Virginia should not offer or adopt any terms of adjustment which might not be acceptable to the seceded States, and restore them to the Union.

The Committee refused to strike out—ayes, 55; noes, 83.

Mr. Wise moved to amend by adding the last clause of the foregoing substitute, which was rejected, 64 to 74.

The resolution was adopted as follows:

Resolved, Deeply deploring the present distracted condition of the country, lamenting the wrongs that have impelled some of the States to dissolve their connection with the Federal Government, but sensible of the blessings of the Union, impressed with its importance to the peace, prosperity and progress of the people, we earnestly desire that an adjustment be reached by which the Union may be reëstablished in its integrity, and peace, prosperity and fraternal feelings be restored throughout the land.

The seventh resolution was then taken up, and amended on motion of Mr. Wise by striking out all from the words "Governments" to the last sentence. Yeas, 68; Nays, 67.

Mr. Leake moved to amend by adding a declaration that the North must abstain from interference with Slavery in the States and common Territory, and abandon all hostile political organizations. Rejected—40 to 93.

The seventh resolution, as amended, was adopted.

The eighth resolution was passed by for the present.

The ninth was taken up.

Mr. Conrad moved to strike out the first line of words, "exercise of this right," and insert, "withdrawal from the Federal Government." Agreed to.

Other amendments were offered, pending which the Convention adjourned.

THE RICHMOND WHIG.

RICHMOND, Friday, April 5.

There is good authority for stating that the Richmond *Whig* will not advocate secession, but will stand by the policy of presenting an ultimatum to the North.

THE WOES AND TRIBULATIONS OF SOUTHERN CORRESPONDENTS.

From the Charleston Courier.

CHARLESTON, Tuesday, April 2, 1861.

EDITORS OF THE COURIER: I notice in a morning's paper a left-handed compliment paid to the "Special Correspondent" of the New-York Times in Charleston. It seems that I am selected as a rest for them to throw a little harmless fire at the Government of South Carolina. Although I admire the frankness which acknowledges that some have to consult that "virulent Abolition sheet," the New-York Times, for general information concerning the fortifications on Morris' Island, yet I must be permitted to question the violation of all press etiquette, as shown in publicly announcing my name in connection with the letter alluded to. The paper referred to seems disturbed at my facts; but I believe the citizens of Charleston prefer facts to fiction. Because I have stated things as they really are in the city, I have been denounced by extremists at the North as "*a rank Secessionist.*" In this connection, I beg to call attention to the inclosed paragraph from the New-York Times. JASPER.

ANOTHER CORRESPONDENT.

From the Mercury.

THE HARBOR BATTERIES.—The *Herald's* correspondent must have worn magnifying glasses when he visited the harbor. He found and described more batteries than the engineers, as yet, have reported to head-quarters.

A CARD FROM AN ANXIOUS IRISHMAN.

To the Editor of the Charleston Mercury:

Under existing circumstances, as far as my own affairs are concerned, it is most painful to me to be obliged to rush into print. But, in times like the present, delicacy must be waived; and every man, strangers particularly, in a community so *serenely* agitated by the grand movement of Southern Independence and nationality, should appear before a watchful, and, perhaps, rather suspicious public, in his true colors. I hope, therefore, you will permit me, through the columns of your widely-circulated, spirited and uncompromising paper, to *explain myself* briefly to the good and chivalrous people of Charleston.

Having had the pleasure of making the acquaintance of two gentlemen since my arrival here, and having seen a good deal in their company, one of whom was a fellow-passenger on the steamer *James Adger*, from New-York, and who has since turned out to be no less a person than the correspondent of the New-York Times. The other is an Englishman, of agreeable manners, and much intelligence, but unfortunately strongly suspected of being the correspondent of the New-York *Tribune*. Of either circumstance I was not aware till within the last few days. The latter gentleman has, however, pledged his honor to me that he is not the "Simon Pure," and is simply here on commercial business, which I have reason to believe is true. I feel it, however, incumbent upon me to declare that, directly or indirectly, *I am in no way connected with either of the gentlemen, or I have any political communication with the North.*

As regards my own coming here, I am not afraid to admit, though I may return to the North, that I came down here to try my chance on the battle-field, being fully impressed with the belief, before I left Baltimore, that fight was inevitable, and would be immediate. My sympathies have ever been with the chivalrous and sunny South, and I gave public utterance to my secession sentiments at Barnum's Hotel; and the day I left New-York I avowed my Southern proclivies on the door of the Merchants' Exchange in Wall-street. Soon after my arrival here I did myself the honor of tendering my services as a soldier to His Excellency, Gov. Pickens. But my letter, in which were inclosed a printed statement of my antecedents, and testimonials from such mercantile houses as Messrs. Howland & Aspinwall, of New-York, was suppressed, nay pocketed, by a false friend, who undertook to hand it to the Governor.

Suspecting foul play, I sought an interview with His Excellency, which he kindly condescended to grant me, and in the presence of his most amiable family, I had the distinguished honor of explaining the nature of my visit. His Excellency was pleased to applaud my motives, and good-naturedly held out a prospect of giving me a position. Although I have not had the good fortune to succeed in getting it, *and that His Excellency's wishes have been frustrated*, I am nevertheless grateful to him for the manner in which he received me. I shall never forget his courtesy, urbanity and generous frankness. *He strikingly reminded me, both in person and manner, of the great O'Connell, whose personal friendship and confidence I had the honor of enjoying.*

Though disappointed in the object I had in visiting Charleston, I rejoice that the Southern Confederacy is not only established, but will be recognized by the Northern Government, as well as by foreign Governments, without the shedding of blood. It will prove to the world that the American people, North and South of "Dixie's" line, are possessed of coolness, forbearance and wonderful common sense.

Apologizing for thus trespassing upon your invaluable space, I have the honor to remain, Sir, your obedient servant, PATRICK H. O'CONNOR.

LETTER FROM FORT SUMPTER.

From a reliable correspondent at Fort Sumpter, the Philadelphia *North American* gathers the following particulars:

"No order for the evacuation of the fort had reached there up to the 31st inst. On the previous Saturday, the Convention, on the invitation of Gen. Beauregard, had visited the defences in Charleston harbor. Rapid firing of shot and shell took place from the batteries on Cummings' Point. Thirty of the laborers employed at Fort Sumpter were to leave on Monday, the 1st inst. The provisions in the fort were nearly exhausted, and but four days' bread remained.

An amusing incident occurred a few days ago, upon the arrival of the steamboat with the private effects of one of the officers, which had been left at Sullivan's Island. Supposing that Fort Sumpter was at last to be evacuated, the troops at the different batteries around mounted upon the breastworks and sand-hills to watch the departure. Just before the arrival of the boat Major Anderson had given orders for the repair of the large flag, which had become torn. While the steamer was lying at the wharf the flag was lowered, when the troops around set up a loud shout, which, however, was suddenly checked by seeing a storm-flag running up to the mast-head, that soon floated out as defiantly as ever.

The fuel in the Fort was scarce, but the troops were using drift-wood which has been caught. None of the gun carriages had been burned, as has been reported.

The New-York Times.

VOL. X....NO. 2979. NEW-YORK, TUESDAY, APRIL 9, 1861. PRICE TWO CENTS.

THE WAR CLOUD.

Preparations for Attacking Fort Sumpter.

Intention of the Administration to Send in Provisions.

Continuation of Naval and Military Preparations.

SAILING OF THE BALTIC AND ILLINOIS

The Captain of the Powhatan Superseded.

Interesting from Pensacola and Fort Pickens.

IMPORTANT NEWS FROM CHARLESTON.

CHARLESTON, Monday, April 8.

Everything is now prepared for action. All vessels have been ordered to keep out of the range of fire between Fort Sumpter and Sullivan's Island.

The famous Floating Battery is expected to sail at 7 o'clock P. M., for a point somewhere near Fort Sumpter.

A house has just been blown up near the five-gun battery.

Business is entirely suspended, and the most intense excitement prevails. JASPER.

PREPARATIONS FOR THE COMING STRUGGLE.

CHARLESTON, Sunday, April 7.

Gen. BEAUREGARD, this morning issued an order, and sent a special messenger to Major ANDERSON, giving him an official notification that all intercourse between Fort Sumpter and the city would be prohibited from that date.

All the posts have been strengthened, and two additional regiments are hourly expected from the interior.

MILITARY MOVEMENTS.

CHARLESTON, Monday, April 8.

Gen. BEAUREGARD has ordered out 5,000 more troops. Companies of volunteers are constantly arriving and being put in position in the harbor. New batteries are also being constructed.

MAJOR ANDERSON'S MAIL FACILITIES.

CHARLESTON, Monday, April 8.

Major ANDERSON'S mail facilities have not been cut off as reported; only his supplies.

IMPORTANT FROM MONTGOMERY.

MONTGOMERY, Monday, April 8.

The Cabinet has been in session all day, and something serious is anticipated to be on the *tapis*. Important news is expected here from the Confederate States Commissioners at Washington.

OUR WASHINGTON DISPATCHES.

WASHINGTON, Monday, April 8.

FALSE REPORTS—THE CABINET A UNIT.

The day has been one of exciting rumors, most of which were, upon investigation, found devoid of foundation or sense.

It was currently reported that there had been a row in the Cabinet, and that Mr. SEWARD and Mr. CHASE were to retire, the latter to take the place upon the Supreme Bench, to fill the vacancy caused by the death of JUDGE McLEAN; the former because the President had overruled him in his policy. Another rumor assigned the Treasury to Mr. CAMERON. Of course this is all stuff. I am authorized to announce that the assurance given in the TIMES, of entire unity in the Cabinet, is absolutely correct. Not the slightest difference exists between Mr. SEWARD and the President on any point.

There is a strong pressure to put CHASE on the Supreme Bench, than whom no better judge or lawyer could be selected. But he is now thoroughly conversant with the policy of the Administration respecting national matters, and has commenced the establishment of a system of reform in the Treasury Department which would require at least a month for his successor to understand, and follow out. Besides, Mr. LINCOLN would regard any change in the Cabinet, so soon, for any reason, as an indication of weakness. Notwithstanding, Mr. CHASE would, it is understood, have the appointment, if no other duties called him elsewhere. He does not desire his own advancement at the expense of the interests of the Government. He could have gone to the Supreme Bench, instead of the Cabinet, weeks ago if he had chosen.

CANDIDATES FOR THE SUPREME BENCH.

Among those mentioned to succeed McLEAN are SWAYNE, and Judge GHOLSON, of the Supreme Bench of Ohio. The latter will be backed by the entire Bar of Ohio, and by Senators TRUMBULL, FESSENDEN, and CRITTENDEN. Judge LOGAN, of Illinois, a member of the Peace Convention, is also backed by the Bar of his State.

GOVERNMENT INTENTIONS TOWARDS FORT SUMPTER.

Lieut. TALBOT, who returned to Fort Sumpter with instructions to Major ANDERSON, is expected to arrive there to-morrow morning. There certainly is no present purpose to reinforce Sumpter. Nevertheless, an attempt will be made to send in supplies or provisions, via an unarmed vessel. If the Secessionists choose to fire upon her, they will have themselves initiated whatever disasters or trouble shall follow.

While the President sees no necessity for reinforcing Fort Sumpter while Charleston is not threatened with foreign invasion, he is determined to fulfil his constitutional duty, as laid down in his Inaugural. He cannot, therefore, abandon Sumpter, or any other public property, so long as the Government has power to hold it.

In this view of the case he must feel the small force now holding it, and will do so, unless the rebels are strong enough to drive them out. Thus, as you will see, the question of peace or war is entirely in the hands of JEFFERSON DAVIS, who, it is well known, has control of the Charleston troops, whom he has hitherto restrained, notwithstanding Gov. PICKENS' disposition to yield to the pressure for an immediate bombardment of Sumpter.

The *Herald's* story of stipulations having been agreed upon for the evacuation of Sumpter is unfounded, as you probably supposed.

THE GOVERNMENT LOAN.

Notwithstanding the exciting rumors of the last few days, the indications are that the four millions Treasury notes will be taken at a handsome price, fully vindicating the sagacity of Secretary CHASE in rejecting speculative bids for the late loan.

I understand Secretary CHASE has addressed a letter to Ex-Secretary DIX, expressing his appreciation of the high public spirit displayed by the latter, and by the Banks of Commerce and America in their efforts to sustain the public credit, instead of depressing it in the late loan biddings.

MOVEMENTS OF TOM CORWIN.

TOM CORWIN left to-day for New-York, and will leave by the first conveyance for Mexico, to assume the duties of his position. He has received his instructions; they are of the most explicit character, covering the entire ground of our policy towards the new Mexican administration, and giving assurances of the friendly relations and intentions of this Government towards that. The position of the rebellious American States is also fully discussed, and the Mexican Government is called upon to sustain its present relations of non-recognition of the so-called Confederate States. Of the same character will be the instructions to the European Ministers.

CASSIUS M. CLAY is expected to arrive every day. His papers are all prepared, and ready for him.

CALIFORNIA APPOINTMENTS.

WILLIAM SCHMOLTZ is appointed Coiner at the San Francisco Mint. The choice could not be bettered. The remaining California appointments will probably be announced to-morrow. It is understood that SAMUEL J. RIDGE will be Appraiser-General, and B. W. MUDGE, Assistant Appraiser. The announcement of the appointment of Capt. SCHULTZ, as Marshal of New-York, is premature.

The trial of GODARD BAILEY was not called up to-day. It is now expected to come up Wednesday.

Capt. BRITON and Col. SUMNER have been ordered to the Pacific coast.

DISPATCH TO THE ASSOCIATED PRESS.

WASHINGTON, Monday, April 8.

The State Department replied to-day to the note of the Confederate State Commissioners, declining to receive them in their official capacity, but expressing deference for them as gentlemen. The Secretary expressed a peaceful policy on the part of the Government, declaring a purpose to defend only when assailed. The reply is of such a character as to require a continuation of the correspondence. It is not known when the Commissioners will leave Washington; not, however, for some days.

However much the reports of Southern designs on Washington may be discredited, it is certain that officers high in authority are taking precautionary measures for the safety of the Capital. The anxiety to hear from Fort Sumpter and other Southern points where conflicts are apprehended, is intense.

ALEXANDER DUVALL has been appointed Collector of Richmond, Va.

The following appointments were made to-day:

WM. L. ADAMS, Collector at Astoria, Oregon.

HARRISON B. BRAND, of Missouri, Superintendent of Indian Affairs, Central Superintendency, St. Louis.

GEORGE M. OSGOOD, Postmaster at Cambridge, Mass.

OUR WASHINGTON CORRESPONDENCE.

THE POLICY OF THE ADMINISTRATION—CONDITION OF BUSINESS—AMALGAMATION IN THE SOUTH—A MIXED RACE, ETC.

WASHINGTON, Sunday, April 7, 1861.

Rumors are rife in the city in regard to the policy of the Administration; and if we are to believe the *quid nuncs*, war is immediately at hand between the North and South. Everyone asks the question, shall we have war? Men of business are peculiarly sensitive on this point, and manifest the utmost solicitude. The effect of the unsettled and uncertain state of public affairs has been to prostrate all enterprise, and cause a general stagnation in business. Notwithstanding the crowds of office-hunting strangers here, most of whom are still able to pay their weekly bills, the times were never harder, and a profound state of apprehension exists that things will grow worse.

The same dearth of business prevails in Baltimore, and it is gratifying to see that the public misfortunes have brought the Secessionists to see the sad consequences of their folly. The Baltimore *Sun*, which, for seven or eight months, has ridden the secession hobby under whip and spur, at length sounds a signal for retreat, and calls aloud for peace. It at length sees that the mad career it has pursued has prostrated every industrial enterprise in Baltimore, instead of bringing to it the trade of the whole South, as was fondly anticipated. "Our interest," says the *Sun*, "is *peace*, nay, *our very necessity* is peace." This is now the *sine qua non* and the *ultimatum* of that journal. "The Border Slave States," it says, "ought to declare *peace* to be their *ultimatum*." This is certainly a great improvement in the tone of a journal which, up to a very recent period, has insisted that the Border Slave States should demand the adoption of the Crittenden resolutions, or other similar concessions from the North, as indispensable conditions of reunion. The *Sun's* policy now is to recognize the Confederate States, or, at least, not to attempt an enforcement of the laws in them, and seems quite reconciled to the idea of remaining in the old Union on condition of being at peace with the new one. It seems to abandon altogether the idea of joining the Confederate States. This return to moderation in the tone of the most widely circulated journal published south of Mason and Dixon's line, I regard as a hopeful sign of returning reason. The *Sun*, by pursuing a moderate course, can accomplish a great deal in the cause of restoring the spirit of Union and harmony.

I have reason to believe that the confident statements of the dispatches from this city in regard to the policy of the Administration should be taken with a grain of allowance. A few days will determine, but I shall be surprised if the warlike predictions are verified by the event.

I notice in the TIMES of the 4th a statement signed "A Virginian," the object of which is to correct an error, which he attributes to you, in regard to the legal *status* of persons having negro blood. The writer has, doubtless, misunderstood your position when he attributes to you the idea that "all persons in the South having any proportion, however small, of African blood in their veins, are held to servitude." This implies that you never heard of the free negroes in that section, which is absurd. But what I wish to call attention to is an error into which the writer has himself fallen. He says, that "in Virginia, where there is only one-eighth of African blood, and seven-eighths of white blood, the law declares such a person to be a free white—and the white column is every year augmented by such persons passing into it." The natural inference from this statement is, that when a *slave* ceases to have more than one-eighth of African blood, he becomes free; but this is by no means the case. The law referred to, defines who are mulattos or free colored persons; and while it confers all the privileges of a white citizen upon a free person having only one-eighth of negro blood, the immunity has no application to slaves. The consequence is, that there are slaves in Virginia as white, and often whiter than their masters. But there are no white "free negroes," if I may be allowed the solecism, for the reason, as stated by "A Virginian," that when they pass the third degree in descent from the African *properitus*, they cease to be regarded in law, or in fact as free negroes, and take rank with the whites—for the most part doubtless with the "poor whites," but occasionally also with the "first families."

I called attention to this law in a letter to the TIMES last Summer, and warned the Southern people of the fatal corruption of blood which is rapidly going on in this way, in spite of their strong prejudices against negro equality. The present generation of Southerners is still full of the pride of ancestry, and no people could be more tenacious of their Anglo Saxon origin, than those who are ready to go to war for the right of extending and perpetuating Slavery. But in spite of pride, prejudice, religion, morality and legal restraints, the process of amalgamation is rapidly going on and will in the course of time overthrow the barriers of cast; and the Southern people will be recognized by themselves and by the world as a mixed race—half European and half African. I have long seen that the true cause of the apparently slow increase of the free negroes, in the North and South, is to be found in the fact adverted to by "A Virginian," viz.: That they become white, and take rank with the whites.

This evil is inconsiderable in the Free States, owing to the small per cent. of negro population; but in the South, and especially in the Confederate States, the two races are nearly equal in numbers, and the tendency is to an increase in the proportion of the African element. True, the negroes are held in Slavery, and the fact of their bleaching out produces no change in their condition in the eye of the law. But this cannot always be the case. A turn of the wheel of fortune, which Mr. JEFFERSON declares to be a thing by no means impossible, may put all classes on terms of political equality. Indeed, he asserts, and all history and experience sustain him in the assertion, that the revolution must, at some day, come. But even without any sudden disruption of society, the slow but certain effect of amalgamation is to reduce all classes to a common color and common social condition. The Northern Slave States, by sending their bondmen South, and substituting free white labor, will escape this degradation; but fate seems to have fixed upon the Cotton Confederacy as the abode for all time of a mulatto race similar in complexion to that of the Moors and other semi-African people.

I learn that Fort Sumpter will be evacuated in a few days. This point is now no longer doubtful. The President is decided in favor of the measure as an inevitable necessity. The ground will be taken that the Fort could not be reinforced without a bloody conflict, which would serve to alienate the Border States, and destroy all hope of Union between the North and South. The abandonment of the position will not be a recognition of secession, either in purpose or in fact. The possession of Fort Pickens will probably be retained, simply because it is practicable without raising additional military force, and with no great risk of a collision. It is the great superiority of position which the rebels have at Charleston that makes the danger of collision so imminent. But at Fort Pickens no such advantage emboldens them to attack the Government forces. For these reasons, it is probable that the latter post will be reinforced, and the former abandoned. OBSERVER.

OUR CHARLESTON CORRESPONDENCE.

TWO EXTRAORDINARY SENSATIONS—A WHITE FLAG FROM SUMPTER WITH TWO OFFICERS—LIEUT. TALBOT AND LIEUT. SNYDER—GREAT STIR IN MILITARY CIRCLES—THE FLOATING BATTERY UNDER ORDERS.

CHARLESTON, C. S. A., Friday, April 5, 1861.

We had two very extraordinary sensations Wednesday evening—a firing into a schooner sensation, and a Wigfall sensation. It would be difficult to say which bore off the palm. Let me describe both correctly. The city was startled late in the afternoon by firing from Morris Island. It was supposed at first to be mere practice shots; but those who had the best glasses could see that a schooner was the object, and what that schooner meant and where she came from, and what she wanted in this harbor, remained a sublime mystery until late yesterday afternoon. I enlisted a Charleston pilot in my service, and finally he brought me the following. It seems that about 4 P. M. a schooner was seen beating up the channel. She had no pilot aboard, as was evident from the fact that she failed to give the usual signal to the guard boat. As she still kept on her way, apparently shaping her course for Fort Sumpter, she was fired into by the Fort Morris Battery, they sending a shot across her bows. Still she kept on, but throwing to the breeze the Stars and Stripes. When she came abreast of the Mortar Battery, they sent some very heavy shot, but not pointed at her hull, but which nevertheless hit her. As she still persisted, they sent a shell which burst close to her rudder. My informant said in his rough, sailor parlance, that he was quite near at the time and called out to the captain, "Why in h—ll don't you heave to?" The captain of the schooner was evidently bewildered, and didn't know what to do. When the shell was fired he hove to in desperate haste. Major ANDERSON, who had been carefully scanning the whole thing with his glass, immediately sent the Fort boat, and detailed Capt. SEYMOUR and Lieut. TALBOT to row over at once to Morris Island to ask an explanation of the firing, and to obtain permission to visit the schooner. This was granted, and they immediately went on board. After tarrying awhile, they returned to the Fort and the schooner put at once to sea. It has been blowing a gale for several days, and on Wednesday evening, the entire bay was white with foam. To this may be ascribed the fact that although a coast steamer was sent in pursuit of the unknown vessel, she returned at midnight stating that she was unable to find her. The fact of the visit of the officers from Fort Sumpter has led all Charleston to believe that the schooner had provisions and men for the Fort, and that she was the *avant courier* of a fleet on the way, and that the raising of the United States flag was well understood by Major ANDERSON. As I know that she had a cargo of ice on board, I look upon this surmise as amounting to nothing, but the Charlestonians persist in thinking that there was something immense intended, which they happily upset. The Captain of the *Shannon* evidently thought that ice was in demand here, notwithstanding the $2 duty per ton. He certainly did his best to come in, but I fancy he will not care to repeat the experiment. So much for that sensation. Now for WIGFALL.

It is certainly unfortunate that DU CHAILLU did not carefully anatomize the great Ex-Texan Senator ere he carried to Europe his new treasures of Mammalia. I am confident Belgrave-square and the Faubourg St. Germain would have looked at it as a rare specimen. It was duly announced that the Ex-Senator would speak at 10 P. M., precisely, from the balcony of the fashionable Mills House. At that hour a crowd, that would have done justice to St. Tammany in her palmy days, assembled and densely packed the street. Ten, 10½, and 11 rolled on, but still he came not. The band went it strong on "Dixie" and the "Southern Marseillaise," and then went it strong over again. They played a new tune, too, which relates to "Fort Sumpter has caved in" which certainly was rather premature. At last the immortal appeared in the parlor. He said he had been to see some ladies, and had forgot all about the sovereign people. Intended to smoke first anyhow, and take a pretty stiff glass of *eau de vie*. At last he appeared. What an extraordinary hodge podge; quotations from Don Juan, interspersed thickly with bar-room slang; SHAKESPEARE, sandwiched with low vulgarisms; and SCOTT, interweaved with the choice twang of the stable. I sent a report of the speech, but reading WIGFALL and seeing him are two very different things. Quietly and deliberately did that heavily-bearded man with the jolly phiz and the somewhat sensual countenance, tell his absorbed listeners that "next Spring he hoped to be in the saddle, and invade Washington with an army of about 500,000 men." Fresh, too, from Senatorial pap in that very city, and well lined with those agreeable things that Washingtonians understand so well how to appropriate. Ungrateful WIGFALL! posterity will stamp you as the last seceder, who gave the last stab at the exposed vitals of a dismembered Union.

A heavy sea was running yesterday, but about 11 A. M. a boat had left Fort Sumpter, as I supposed would be the case, from the previous day's firing. Slowly they rode over the rough waves and approached the city, two officers in their heavy boat cloaks and five oarsmen, also two trunks. As they approached the *Adger's* wharf, at 12½ o'clock, I saw Lieut. TALBOT bearing a *white flag*, to enable him to enter safely the hostile port of Charleston. Strange, suggestive, melancholy spectacle, which ABRAHAM LINCOLN and all his Cabinet ought to have witnessed. A guard was stationed over the little boat, the *Moultrie*, and Lieutenants TALBOT and SNYDER, accompanied by the Quartermaster-General, HATCH, hastened on foot to Governor PICKENS' Head-quarters. The interview lasted one hour and a half, then a carriage drove down with one of the Governor's Aids, two other Palmettoans and Lieut. SNYDER, a stern, determined looking man, with a bronzed face and a somewhat Germanic cast of countenance. While the officers were absent, the apparently half-starved and *bleached* looking men who manned the *Moultrie*, had indulged in sundry private arrangements of tobacco and the ardent, which they had carefully stowed away in divers private places. Ere the boat left the pier, the policeman of the C. S. A. ruthlessly turned up everything, and carried all the little arrangements ashore. The poor fellows, who told me they were laborers, looked absolutely wild with disappointment, but they could not help themselves. Discipline is discipline, but it certainly was very small potatoes in the C. S. A. official to deprive those unfortunate fellows of their anticipated comforts. There are thirty of them now there, whom Major ANDERSON has no use for, and would gladly discharge, but as they have mouths, and probably pretty big ones, it is the policy now of the South Carolina Government to let them eat up the fortress—in other words, the more men the quicker they will be starved out.

There is a great stir in military circles. I saw none of the careless lounging last night at the Mills House and Charleston Hotel that one ordinarily witnesses among the officers on leave. Many of them were summoned to their posts ere the sun set, and it is generally understood that if nothing is done in Washington, within a very short time, that they will take the initiative here. Lieut. TALBOT did not leave immediately, as some telegrams may state, but had to wait until last evening. Capt. HAMILTON, of the Floating Battery, has orders to get her in readiness immediately. No more mail facilities and no more supplies for Major ANDERSON. JASPER.

MILITARY AND NAVAL MOVEMENTS.

CONTINUED ACTIVITY AT THE NAVY-YARD AND MILITARY POSTS.

THE STEAMSHIPS BALTIC AND ILLINOIS READY FOR SEA—THE HARRIET LANE TRANSFERRED TO THE NAVY AND ORDERED AWAY—RUMORED RESIGNATION OF CAPT. MERCER, OF THE POWHATAN FRIGATE.

Public attention continued to be mainly engrossed, yesterday, with the great activity in the military and naval departments of the Government. Without any positive knowledge of the destination of the ships, speculation ran high as to where they were bound, and, in some cases, bets were freely offered that they were destined for this or that point of the South, according to the favorite theory of each person.

As soon as the *Atlantic* left her dock, the steamship *Illinois* took her berth to receive cargo. The provisions and ordnance stores, howitzer-carriages and ammunition were hastily put on board, and, with her coal, loaded the steamer heavily by the stern. There was, however, a large space still left in the forward hold, which would be filled, when the steamer would draw about twenty feet.

This vessel carries an immense cargo. Her accommodations for troops are also very good, and, it is believed, with her improved feathering paddle-boats, she will make excellent time, notwithstanding she is so deep.

The military chest, in the shape of two of HERRING'S safes, with some $50,000 in gold and silver, was brought down by Adams' Express wagon and lowered into the specie room—a safe compartment in the extreme after part of the ship. The *Illinois* had her whole crew on board, and will be ready to receive her troops and depart some time to-day. A canal-boat load of wood was among the articles put on board.

On board of the *Baltic* nothing could exceed the industry which everywhere prevailed. Steam was got up on Sunday night, and the engines tested and found all right. All through Sunday, and late into the night, the work of loading her continued, and from an early hour yesterday morning every possible variety of articles intended for the use of the troops continued to arrive at the pier, by teams and in lighters. Immense quantities of bacon, packed for transportation on mules, flour in sacks, soap, and all kinds of preserved meats and vegetables, packed in boxes, vinegar and molasses in portable kegs, stove-coal, sewed in strong small canvas bags; coal by the hundred ton in gunny sacks—probably for steamers' use, and every other article that can be reckoned among Quartermasters' stores. There were also many cases, evidently containing United States muskets, and fixed ammunition by the ton, packed in snug boxes, most of it marked as shrapnel for heavy twelve-pounder boat howitzers.

At the upper deck were some eight or ten boats, including those built expressly for use in the surf, with the requisite quantity of oars and other appliances for their use. About one hundred bales of hay were piled on the after deck, and an equal quantity lay upon the dock ready to go on board.

Outside of the gate were gathered a motley crowd watching the arrival of each particular consignment, and amusing themselves with queries as to what each package contained.

At noon fires were lighted under the boilers of the *Baltic*, and at 4 o'clock the steam was up, and, so far as that was concerned, she was ready to start. It is probable that she will leave at the noon tide to-day. Mr. GRAHAM, former First Assistant Engineer of the *Adriatic*, is Chief Engineer.

THE HARRIET LANE TRANSFERRED TO THE NAVY.

The steamer *Harriet Lane* on Sunday hauled down the Revenue flag and hoisted the Stars and Stripes, indicating that she has been transferred to the Navy Department. This was anticipated some weeks since, when her armament was increased. Her commander, Capt. JOHN FAUNCE, has frequently declared that he would fight under the American flag as long as it continued to fly over one city or town of the United States. She sailed from her anchorage off the Battery at 10 o'clock yesterday morning, destined, it is said, for the South. Who knows?

The surveying steamer *Vixen* has returned to the yard.

RUMORED RESIGNATION OF THE POWHATAN'S COMMANDER—DEPARTURE OF TROOPS, &C.

Yesterday was a busy one at the Army quarters in this neighborhood, but quiet and uneventful in Naval circles. The ordinary work at the Navy-yard went on as usual, but at Governor's Island, Fort Hamilton, and Bedloe's Island, unusual excitement prevailed. There seems to be a growing impression among well-informed persons that both the reinforcement of Fort Pickens, and the recovery of the Texas forts, are contemplated by the Government.

The Navy-yard folks were astonished yesterday to see Capt. SAMUEL MERCER, the commander of the *Powhatan*, walking among them, in citizen's clothes. The papers all said he had gone to the ocean in his vessel, but *they* were "at sea" instead of him. His resignation was currently reported during the day; but *he has not sent it in*. His detachment, moreover, is a Government measure, the meaning of which is only known to the Cabinet. Capt. MERCER is a native of Maryland, from which State he was appointed in 1815. He has done over 26 years service, of which 19 were spent at sea. He never was popular with sailors, his manner being austere and distant, characteristics which Jack especially dislikes.

THE NAVY-YARD.

No orders have been received to fit out the *Savannah* or *Perry* for immediate sea service, as stated. The former was yesterday hauled into the wharf to have her three heavy guns taken out, as they interfered with the workmen, who are preparing her for "the ready state." Besides, their removal facilitated the labor of putting her in the dry-dock, into which she was floated at 11 A. M., the steam frigate *Roanoke* having been previously taken out. The water tanks of the *Wabash* were commenced on, for the first time, yesterday. Their appearance on the wharf would make an unsophisticated person suppose it impossible to place them all in one vessel. The *Roanoke's* removal from the dry-dock has been partly occasioned by the necessity for examining the *Savannah's* bottom, and partly by the fact that whatever work remains to be done on her, can be, by good management, prosecuted at the wharf. The brig *Perry* was hauled alongside the Hudson-avenue dock, to be operated on at the leisure of the authorities. Her movements have not been actuated in any way by "the crisis."

THE NORTH CAROLINA.

A 3,000-ton line-of-battle ship, looks very lonesome with only 120 men on board. This is exactly the case with "the North." She has 60 recruits, 44 marines, and about 20 permanent men, who might be left out, as they have done all the duty Providence gave them power to perform. The short-watches of the *Powhatan* were made up on board the receiving-ship, and many of the actors who were to open the "Nautical Theatre" on the 1st of April have gone to play more important parts than those on the programme at the "Scuttle Butt." The condition of the *North Carolina* is not satisfactory. It is even doubted whether she could be removed two rods with safety. She was built at Philadelphia forty-one years ago, and has been so long at the Navy-yard that even green reporters know her from "the last arrival."

DEFENCELESS CONDITION OF THE NAVY-YARDS.

The attention of the Government has been called to the utterly defenceless condition of the different Navy-yards. Millions of dollars' worth of public property and vast quantities of war munitions are left to the protection of a couple of hundred men. What good are cannon without men to work them? A well-disciplined force of [illegible] men could take any Navy-yard in the Union to-morrow with its present garrison. The marines are supposed to be the "navy's military arm," on which the Administration chiefly relies for the guardianship of the yards. Here, then, is the force available for this purpose:

	Marines.
Brooklyn Yard	60
Norfolk Yard	75
Boston (Charlestown) Yard	55
Portsmouth, N. H., Yard	25
Total	211

These figures are over the mark. In reply to those who argue that sailors are always on hand, it may be useful to state that there are not, as a general thing, twenty available and efficient persons at any of the places named, except New-York, which could be reinforced from Governor's Island. Why not put some of the soldiers crowded out of military barracks in the Navy yards.

THE DEPARTURE OF TROOPS FROM GOVERNOR'S ISLAND.

Yesterday morning active doings progressed at Governor's Island. As early as 8 o'clock orders from the Head-quarters of the army were received, directing the equipment of *three* Companies of recruits. Then the bustle commenced. The detail was hung up in the different rooms; men crowded round it, climbed on each other's shoulders, on benches, boxes, and piles of clothing to see whether their names were on the list. Those who were mentioned on it no sooner learned the fact than they began the final preparations. As nearly everybody's knapsack had been packed for weeks, and everybody's cartouche-box filled with the war allowance, and everybody's everything in readiness for the road, a concentration of the different accoutrements and "conveniences" was only necessary. The ambulance was next put in order for departure; the baggage-masters took charge of the wagon-loads of articles confided to them, and placed the indispensable sentinels over it, with the customary orders that their live bodies must never cease to protect it, implying, naturally enough, that their dead bodies could do very little to attain that end. At 2 o'clock there were no unbelted men to be seen. Muskets standing by the wall; soldiers swaggering up and down the parade-walks, pulling on their gloves, wiping out "the nipple," or tightening the chin-strap, conversed freely on the weather, the price of vegetables, the scarcity of grass in Texas, and the quality of the soup. But no one seemed to talk of, or care about, his destination. One, indeed, went so far as to wish he knew whether there were any pretty girls where they were going, "wherever that was." At 3, the following troops left the Island:

	Men.		Men.
Company C	68	Company B., (left since Saturday)	15
Company C	67		
Company E	47	Company F	100
Company D	100		
Total			397

These soldiers, except the 15 men of Company B., are recruits, nominally lettered to facilitate transportation. The regiments to which they will be assigned are not known.

FORT HAMILTON.

Yesterday the commanding officers of Companies H and K received instructions to have their men ready for embarkation at 2 o'clock on board the steamer *Illinois*. Accordingly, all hands were mustered under arms, the baggage put upon the wharf, and the final preparations for departure completed. All day did the poor fellows wait, lounging about, expecting the arrival of the transport, but she did not come. At last, about 4 P. M., the steam-tug *Catalina* came alongside the wharf, her captain handed an envelope to Commanding-officer BROWN, the result of which was the embarkation of the soldiers on board, and their subsequent transfer to the *Illinois* and *Baltic*.

LATEST—DEPARTURE OF THE STEAMERS ILLINOIS AND BALTIC.

These steamers have at last put off, where, we are still unable to tell. The mystery which has enveloped the whole business was kept up to the last moment.

On Sunday morning the *Baltic* seemed to be safe at her wharf for two or three more days, while steam was going in the *Illinois*, and she was thought to be ready for a start at any moment. Yet the *Baltic* was off first, starting at 5½ o'clock last evening, while the *Illinois* did not go away till long after night had set in. About 100 soldiers went by the *Baltic*, and in cargo she took 8,000 bags of oats and an immense quantity of general forage, which seemed intended for the horses in Texas; but there were also a great number of wheelbarrows, picks, spades and similar implements suited for throwing up of earth-works, &c.

The *Illinois* has been roughly refitted for the accommodation of troops, besides being absolutely crammed with miscellaneous material in bulk and packages. She will go over the bar with a draft of more than 20 feet. Some of the soldiers under orders to sail in her were grumbling last night at the idea of being cribbed and cabined in the spare room between decks. She could handsomely accommodate four hundred, and take near a thousand tons of freight as well. She carries a formidable assortment of rockets, bengola lights, and similar pyrotechnic signals.

THE CHARTERED FLEET.

The services of three additional steamers have been engaged by the Government, making the chartered fleet at present as follows:

	Men.	Tons.
Coatzacoalcos	40	1,000
Fashion	22	1,000
Atlantic	60	2,000
Baltic	60	2,000
Illinois	[illegible]	[illegible]
Ocean Queen	40	[illegible]
Yankee	14	[illegible]
Thomas Freeborn	14	[illegible]
Total	300	[illegible]

The tonnage and number of men are not exactly correct, but will give an idea of the extra force employed. The *Coatzacoalcos* and *Fashion* are expected here every day; the *Ocean Queen* and steamships *Yankee* and *Freeborn* were chartered yesterday. The *Baltic*, *Atlantic* and *Illinois* have sailed, as already stated.

IMPORTANT FROM THE GULF FLEET.

THE SHIPS PROVISIONED—PROGRESS OF SECESSION—WAR PREPARATIONS—WATER TANKS MADE INTO BATTERIES—THE BROOKLYN'S TROOPS NOT LANDED—THE WYANDOTTE'S PRIVILEGES—COMMODORE CUNNINGHAM'S PLOTS—THE MARINES LOYAL ALL ROUND—THE STAR SPANGLED BANNER IN KEY WEST—THE MORALE OF THE FLEET.

ON BOARD THE UNITED STATES STEAM-CORVETTE BROOKLYN, OFF PENSACOLA, Monday, April 1, 1861.

The Home Fleet is provisioned at last. I am in a hurry to have this important news conveyed to the hundreds of people who have friends on board the different vessels. The *Brooklyn* got the necessaries at Key West, where her officers had quite an adventure.

On the 26th day of March, 1861—I am particular about the date, you see—the grand flag of the Confederate States of America met a sad catastrophe. It was most unceremoniously hauled down from over one hundred houses in Key West, by command of the *Commander* of Fort Taylor. He politely informed the citizens that they should not carry their Southern enthusiasm to extremes, and that two nations should not rule Key West at the same time, for the present, at all events. Having taken in plenty of stores and provisions at the "Key," this good ship steamed out of harbor, gracefully dipped the Star Spangled Banner as she passed the forts, and arrived here. Of course, distributing the welcome and needed necessaries among the Squadron, was the first thing they did.

If you imagine that the Southern tacticians are idle, you are mistaken. Our telescopes show them to us day and night. Bees are not busier than they. What do you think has been their last move? They have actually hit upon the really splendid idea of converting water-tanks into formidable batteries. Any unsophisticated reader, that may be induced to smile at this step, should be compelled to attempt their destruction with shot and shell. Sand is packed firmly, tightly and "danced on" in them, and they literally line the road from Fort McRae to the Warrington Navy-yard. They have evidently been arranged by a practiced engineer. Fort Barrancas is now in genuine fighting trim. I do not exaggerate the fact when I say that 120 guns are as admirably arranged there, and an efficient manual force—I don't know the number—as well detailed, as it is possible to make them. Every crevice in the fort, which is not needed for shot or shell, is fairly crammed with all the requirements needed in a fortress.

The troops that came out here in the steam-corvette *Brooklyn*, 200 in number or thereabouts, were yesterday transferred to the United States frigate *Sabine*, bag, baggage and belts. Why this has been done I cannot say. Perhaps the *Sabine's* launches are better adapted for conveying soldiers over to Pickens in a quiet way, than ours. To send these big boats "secretly" alongside the steamer might create suspicion; to transfer them in open day to the frigate excites none, and leaves them at *the very hatchway where said boats are secured*. I quote the word "secretly" because it is blotted out of all our dictionaries. The American forces here can do nothing without its enemies knowing the ins and outs of it. What matter if we could say the same of our opponents, but we cannot. Anything our spy-glasses do not see is a mystery to us. How does the difference arise? Capt. ADAMS, of the *Sabine*, thinks that it is our fault. There are several persons who agree with Capt. ADAMS.

By the way, note the fact that the transfer of the troops to the *Brooklyn* on the 31st of March, must make all the news "bogus" that told of their being sent to Pickens on the 28th of February, and subsequent and previous days. We all differ with you all about reinforcing this fort. It could be done by this fleet in eight hours. There is no insurmountable difficulty about it—*but one*. I allude to the indisposition of Mr. CAMERON to strengthen Lieut. SLEMMER, until he is surrounded like Major ANDERSON. Perhaps I should say "until his great advantages over the enemy" are counterbalanced, but maybe there is not much difference in the terms.

We owe one favor—no small one, I can tell you—to the Secessionists. They permit the steam gun-boat *Wyandotte* to run in and out to Pensacola, and all around, without molestation. It is a piece of kindness that we would sincerely appreciate, even lessened as it is, in importance, by the prohibition her officers are under to buy provisions, were it not that there is a bit of poison in it, which makes it treacherous. We have *sailors* here, who are not at all as pure as men should be. No man in America knows this better than Commodore CUNNINGHAM, whom the United States Government made an officer of. He would now instill insidious venom into these sailors, by circulating private "explanations of the case" among them. Let me here state one grand thing, successfully accomplished by the traitors. They have got Union men to be considered "Abolitionists," in the strongest sense. On ship and shore this fallacy has been cleverly circulated. I dare not calculate its influence, in the aggregate, upon future events. Persons who know nothing about the material of which our army and navy are composed, cannot form an idea of it.

The Marine Guard of the *Wyandotte* gunboat has been sent on shore (on Rosas Island), to do picket guard for the tired-out garrison there. Let me here name one bright spot in the Navy. It is the Marine corps. Extra loyalty in trying times seems to be a characteristic—I had nearly said a peculiarity—of Marines everywhere. WILLIAM, the Conqueror, put "Royal" to their title, that his appreciation of their devotion might be shown. America should call them "National," because when every other branch of their country's service has black spots in it, the Marines loom out in moral grandeur—true, unapproachable and brave. I am delighted to see by the papers, and to learn from private letter, that the corps at home is just as its representatives are here. Oh, that we had ten thousand Marines!

I have just received a queer item from Key West. That it is not put in the proper place in my letter, is the messenger's fault—not mine. There is a company of Southern soldiers there, called the Island Guards. They were lately on parade. They had a grand Palmetto (or C. S. A.) flag, which was brought down to the drill-ground by the Captain. But even in the ranks of Secessionists, there are men whose Union memories are not dead. The greater portion of the Company *would not go through their exercises under* the banner. "Why not?" asked their officer. "Well, we don't wish to," said the majority. "But you are citizens of the C. S. A. *now*," said the Captain. "Then why didn't they keep the flag we're used to?" answered the men. Enraged, the Captain dismissed the volunteers. But like all good stories, this has its bitter part. The Captain resigned.

The *morale* of this ship's company is generally good. It is not because I am a "Brooklyn man" that I claim for this ship the character of the best in the Squadron. As a proof, she is called "The floating Abolition h—ll," by our enemies. Even in the nickname there's a mine of meaning. It goes from shore to ship-board, and stirs bad thoughts in many people. You know, I suppose, that "city chaps," as they are called, abound in our man-of-war. Now, a New-York, or Baltimore, or Philadelphia "city chap" has many weaknesses; but I doubt whether he has a greater one than that which springs from his hatred of "Abolitionists." Don't you see, therefore, that "the floating Abolition h—ll" has diplomacy underneath? The *St. Louis* is not very sound, *morally*—the *Sabine* derives all her Unionism from an indefatigable, patriotic commander—the steamers' *personnel* are about on a par with their timbers. There's nothing to boast of in either. But when United States Judges send convicted thieves and man-slaughterers into the service, what great virtue can one expect to find in it?

We are without a commander and without orders. Where are the supply and our dispatches? I am

[Continued on Eighth Page.]

The New-York Times.

VOL. X.....NO. 2981. NEW-YORK, THURSDAY, APRIL 11, 1861. PRICE TWO CENTS.

THE IMPENDING WAR.

EXCITEMENT AT THE NATIONAL CAPITAL.

Anticipated Raid of the Secessionists.

THE DISTRICT MILITIA ORDERED OUT.

Intentions of the Administration Regarding Fort Sumpter.

Object and Result of Lieutenant Talbot's Mission.

What is Thought of the Refusal to Allow him to Return to the Fort.

SOUTH CAROLINA TO BE HELD RESPONSIBLE.

OUR WASHINGTON DISPATCHES.

WASHINGTON, Wednesday, April 10.

RUMORED PLOT TO SEIZE THE CAPITAL.

The officers of the District Militia were yesterday ordered to have a meeting at 10 o'clock this morning, in consequence of information relative to a contemplated movement for the seizure of this city by the Secessionists under McCULLOUGH. Near midnight, however, orders were issued for the assembling of the militia at their armories this morning, and officers have been engaged summoning the men ever since 5 A. M.

The armories are now all full of men. The understanding is that they are to be drafted for service at the different public buildings; but this is not yet definitely known.

There is much excitement and anxiety here, although it is not very apparent on the streets.

Among the troops ordered out is SCHAFFER's National Rifles, which are believed to be Secessionists. The call for actual service will of course compel all the traitors to retire from the corps.

MORE ABOUT THE DEFENCE OF WASHINGTON.

Seven Militia Companies reported to Gen SCOTT this morning, and between six and eight hundred of them volunteered for any service in which the President might desire them to act. Very many however, refused to act. Out of seventy men among the National Rifles sixteen resigned. A large number will be drafted to make up the quota. Subsequently they repaired to the Commissary's Department and received their equipments and rations for the night. They will be stationed about the several public buildings at night, and most of them will be relieved from duty during the day.

The city resounded throughout the day with martial music; and the tramp of soldiers about the streets, and movments of companies, added much to the excitement and made the day very lively. Among these troops are many of the ablest citizens of Washington. To-day's work has proven that the Militia of the District is generally sound for the Union.

A WEAK INVENTION.

A dispatch was received here this morning by one of the city editors from one MARTIN, dated at Charleston, stating that the United States vessels had arrived off the Bar, and were moving up towards Fort Sumpter, when the Charlestonians opened fire upon them, and were responded to by Major ANDERSON and Fort Moultrie; that the fight was raging fiercely, and that Major ANDERSON's defeat was probable.

This was enlarged upon as the story passed from mouth to mouth.

The dispatch was taken to President LINCOLN, who simply said he doubted it, but immediately summoned the Cabinet together and excluded all visitors.

The whole town was thrown into a fever of intense excitement, and people, even to-night, can hardly be made to discredit the dispatch, although it was very soon discovered to be a stupid hoax. Every one here nearly is on the *qui vive*, expecting to hear war news from the South.

THE TREACHEROUS TREATMENT OF LIEUT. TALBOT.

The Cabinet considered the refusal of the Charleston authorities to allow Lieut. TALBOT to return to Fort Sumpter. It is not known what they will do, but it is understood, on good authority, that the Government and Major ANDERSON also, will demand an explanation from Gov. PICKENS. If this action was by his authority or consent, the Administration will then decide what course to pursue. Gov. PICKENS and South Carolina will be held responsible, as it is not the intention of President LINCOLN to treat with JEFF. DAVIS or the Confederacy officially. All the Southern Union men denounce this violation of the rules of war with indignation, and speak of it openly as the meanest of treachery. Should Major ANDERSON, in this contingency, act upon his own discretion and attack the town, the Government will sustain him fully.

THE SOUTHERN COMMISSIONERS DISGUSTED.

The Southern Commissioners are still here, but leave for the South to-morrow morning in disgust, protesting that they have been humbugged and deceived.

THE POLICY OF THE GOVERNMENT.

While many Naval Officers express the belief that the attempt to provision Fort Sumpter will be successful, others of excellent judgment usually think otherwise; but the decision of the Administration in the matter was made independent of the question of probable success. The President considers it his duty to make the effort at all events. If successful resistance is made by the Charleston forces, then will arise the grave question whether the Government shall exert its whole power to reinforce and resupply the fort irrespective of cost.

There need be no doubt that the Government has the power, for the law gives the President full authority to summon the militia of all the States, if necessary, to suppress rebellion against the Federal Government. It has been contended that this power could only be exerted in support of judicial process. But that is clearly an error, as will be seen on examination. At all events, the Administration is satisfied of its power under that law and will not hesitate to exercise it if it is considered necessary.

THE SOUTHERN MAILS.

Mr. BLAIR will cut off the South Carolina mails this week, and stop all postal communications, if Major ANDERSON is not allowed free and uninterrupted communication with the authorities at Washington. The first authoritative report to him of any assumption over, or interruption of the mails in the South, will put an end to their mail facilities.

MATTERS IN MARYLAND.

Great excitement was caused in Baltimore today by a scorching Union article in the Baltimore *Clipper*, denouncing the Southern Confederacy and its acts. The article has provoked threats of an assault on the author.

Gov. HICKS and many prominent Marylanders assure the President that Maryland will be loyal if he does not provoke or commence the war, which he certainly will not do.

THE D. C. DISTRICT-ATTORNEYSHIP.

Mr. E. C. CARRINGTON, of this city, is assured by Messrs. BATES and LINCOLN that he shall be appointed Attorney for this District. He is a nephew of Mr. FLOYD, and will have to conduct that case in the Indian Bond fraud, prosecution if it ever comes up. So far as I can learn, the appointment will not give general satisfaction, and is not the President's first choice, but is pressed by Mr. BATES.

A PROSPEROUS TREASURY.

Mr. CHASE has now all the money he needs for present contingencies, and is paying all current obligations which are necessary. He calculates upon a slightly increased revenue the present month. He has had no occasion yet to touch the funds received on the last loan. All the stock for the New Loan has been issued for which bids were received.

DISPATCH TO THE ASSOCIATED PRESS.

WASHINGTON, Wednesday, April 10.

Ten companies, or about one-fourth of the volunteer militia of the District of Columbia, are mustering to-day for inspection, the order having been issued from the Government head quarters last night. Several days ago the company officers were directed to immediately report the number of effective men. This unexpected movement has given rise to many surmises, especially as reports prevail, believed to be correct, that these ten companies are to be drafted into immediate service.

Much excitement everywhere exists, heightened in a great degree by bogus dispatches, professedly from Charleston, of a stirring battle in the vicinity of Fort Sumpter.

There is no doubt that the military movements here in progress are connected with precautionary measures for the defence of the Capital from an apprehended attack from the South.

The Federal forces in Washington are to be strengthened this week by at least one additional artillery company.

WASHINGTON, Wednesday, April 10—P. M.

During this afternoon various volunteer companies proceeded to the War Department, and were inspected by Assistant Adjutant General MCDOWELL. Several hundred men were mustered into service.

Two or three broken companies were rejected, the number of each being below forty-two members.

An attempt is making to-night to bring them up to this minimum, in order to their acceptance.

Of the National Rifles, over sixty members, only one half consented to be mustered in. The reason for this, as in other similar cases, was that some of the men were apprehensive they would be ordered to some point beyond the limits of the District of Columbia, while others were unwilling to take the oath, which they conceive, in the event of the secession of Maryland and Virginia, would compel them to fight against those States. It is said they were informed that the oath must be taken unconditionally, and the infraction of which would expose them to punishment under the rules and articles of war.

At a late hour of the afternoon two companies appeared at the War Department, some of the members without uniforms, but the Adjutant-General had retired for the day.

Capt. CARRINGTON's Company, about 80, were mustered in to a man. The accepted companies have already been placed on duty, guarding their respective armories.

Immense crowds gathered in front of the War Department to witness the proceedings attendant on the inspection and mustering into service.

A new Military Department, formed of Maryland and the District of Columbia, is to be established, with Col. C. F. SMITH as Commandant, and Capt. TALBOT, Adjutant.

SHERMAN's Artillery, from Fort Ridgely, Minnesota, which was ordered to Newport, but countermanded, and two companies of cavalry, are expected here to-morrow. The latter will come without horses, which will be purchased in this market.

The President has appointed S. P. BROWN, of Maine, Navy Agent; GEORGE N. BEALE, of Maryland, Navy Storekeeper at Washington, and ELISHA WHITTLESEY to his former position as First Comptroller of the Treasury.

TITIAN J. COFFEY, of Pittsburgh, has entered upon his duties as Assistant Attorney-General. ARCHIBALD ROANE, till recently Chief Clerk of that Department, has gone to Montgomery, and the place thus vacated is filled by RICHARD BATES, the son of the Attorney-General.

There is reliable information to show that the late publication that Gen. AMPUDIA was marching on Brownsville is false. On the contrary, he has retired from the army, gone into the interior, and has no means, even if he had the disposition, to enter upon such an enterprise; beside the Constitutional Government is opposed to any such movements.

OUR WASHINGTON CORRESPONDENCE.

THE ADMINISTRATION DISPOSED TO KEEP STATE SECRETS—THE MOVEMENTS OF TROOPS—WHAT IS TO BE DONE IN TEXAS—TWIGGS'S TREASON.

WASHINGTON, Monday, April 8.

Every good citizen must rejoice that the new Administration manifests a disposition to guard more faithfully its State secrets than did its predecessors. The promulgation of the purposes of the Government while these are yet not entirely formed, or when disclosure would tend to defeat or embarrass them, is quite as weak as it is undignified. But this reticence may be carried too far, and lead to more mischief than it is designed to prevent. A wise discrimination should be observed by the Administration, not only in keeping secret that which ought to be confidential, but also in giving to the public through the Press whatever can be told with propriety. By this course a great deal of unnecessary and vexatious anxiety will be spared the public mind, and business will be less seriously affected than if the imaginations of men are permitted to run entirely wild upon all questions of Government affecting the people. For a week past the public mind has been in a fever of agitation relative to the sudden movements of troops, and the evident preparations for their embarkation. If these troops are designed to be landed where they will invite attack or precipitate new disturbances, it is well, doubtless, to let nothing be officially known upon the subject to the public. But, on the other hand, if the [illegible] of the Administration, that they are designed for peaceful purposes are true, why not let the public know at once the fact, that the public mind may be quieted, and business tranquilized.

In looking over the movements of troops arranged for in New-York during the last few days, one is led to the conviction that the Government is making provision for two distinct and opposite necessities of the public service—that it has been preparing to bring troops home from Texas, and at about the same time, to *send* reinforcements not only to the Gulf forts, but to Texas also. Steamers for transports have been fitted up in your port, with stalls for horses on deck, and the hold full of provisions. This fact would seem to indicate very clearly that they are going to Texas to bring north the cavalry and artillery, of which the army of the Southwest had an over-proportion. Fort Clarke, Texas, on the Mexican frontier, was at one time garrisoned by four companies of flying artillery, in pursuance of an order of Secretary FLOYD, making it a school for artillery practice. The Second Cavalry have also been garrisoned for a long time in Texas, and the treasonable agreement between TWIGGS and the Texas Secession Commissioners anticipated and prevented the fulfillment of the wishes of the Federal Government to send troops into the Territory of New-Mexico, because it stipulated for the embarkation of the entire force "by sea from Brazos or Indianola." Hence the Second Cavalry, which could so much easier and better have marched direct to Arizona, are compelled to proceed to New-York by sea, and thence, by the way of Independence, to make a land journey of several thousand miles in order to reach the same destination, which, under ordinary circumstances, could have been attained by a journey of a few hundred miles.

The case of the Second Cavalry is cited to illustrate the workings of TWIGGS' traitorous compact, because that corps is certain—unless actual war intervenes—to be sent at once to some of the Western Territories. The Texas Secession Commissioners foresaw that,—and also that the cavalry would naturally proceed to Arizona, whence they could any day take up their line of march to reënter Texas; hence the stipulation that the troops should go out "by sea" It is naturally asked "Why has Col. WAITE, who succeeded Gen. TWIGGS in command of the Military Department, proceeded to carry out the treasonable agreement of his predecessor, which can have no basis of legality?" The answer, doubtless, is found in the fact that TWIGGS' treason had so demoralized the troops under his command, that they cannot be depended upon. Per consequence they are to come out of Texas, and to the North, where, whoever among their officers is wavering in fidelity to the Union, may be weeded out by transfer or resignation. This done they will be ready to take up the march again over the Plains, soon as the Spring grass is high enough to make the journey practicable. It is a duty which Government owes to the faithful officers in the Army of the Southwest, to promote their riddance of all who sympathize with secession, lest infidelity in the hour of necessity should cast discredit and suspicion upon the true men and traitors alike.

But there are other transports which have left New-York *with troops*. If DUNCAN's battery, so recently stationed in this city, has been sent to sea, with horses, &c., it is evident they have gone somewhere else than to the forts on the Gulf. If this be so, where else can they have gone except to Texas? Certainly not to Forts Pickens, Taylor or the Tortugas—for there is no room at these posts for the employment of flying artillery. Reinforcements for the Gulf forts would consist only of artillerists, familiar with the management of heavy sea-coast guns; and the flying artillery, doubtless, have gone to Texas, to replace in part the demoralized troops withdrawn thence. Nowhere else within the Union are such troops needed at present—and on the western frontier of Texas their absence is almost daily sacrificing the lives of the settlers to the remorseless savage. Add to the theories thus developed, the suggestion that a portion of the warlike preparations of the last week look to the reinforcement and resupply of the Gulf ports—particularly of Pickens—and we have a satisfactory solution of those preparations, and a much less exciting one than that which has so alarmed the public mind, and so seriously affected the value of property of various descriptions.

The treachery of TWIGGS, and its effect upon the army of the Southwest, present a striking illustration of the influence which false political teachings, pursued through a course of years, may have upon the mind of its pupils. To Northern officers TWIGGS' conduct could have but one aspect—that of damning treason, and treachery as mean and degrading to the perpetrator as it was injurious to the public weal. But the minds of many Southern officers had been prepared for it by the insidious inculcation of the Calhoun doctrine, that an officer's duty to his State is paramount to that owed to the Federal Government under his oath. Few Southern officers have gone the entire length anticipated by their unscrupulous political teachers, who in putting forth their dogmas intended that their teachings should culminate in the delivery of the entire army over to the seceding South, whenever they, as Southern politicians, desired its services. The military education of the officers has defeated their plan in part; but while it has spared the army the disgrace of wholesale treason,—Calhounism has so sapped the loyalty of many a Southern soldier, as to make him look at least with lenient eye on such an act as was the disgraceful surrender of TWIGGS. The future historian, while stamping with the seal of ineffable disgrace those who like TWIGGS have shamelessly repudiated their oaths and obligations to support the flag, will also point to the teachings of CALHOUN as the moral virus which poisoned the hearts and judgments of many a gallant man, and led him to abandon the service of his country, from false ideas of duty, just when fidelity and firmness were needed most. S.

TROOPS DESTINED FOR TEXAS—DUTY OF THE GOVERNMENT—BEN M'CULLOCH AND HIS DESIGNS, ETC

WASHINGTON, Tuesday, April 9, 1861.

It is highly probable that the troops recently embarked at New-York are destined for Texas. This is the general impression in Washington, and is fully borne out by the circumstances of the case, the nature of the equipment, as well as by the policy which has been thus far developed on the part of the Administration. It seems to be highly probable also, that this transmission of troops to Texas has been invited by Gov. HOUSTON, who, as a friend of the Union, has been placed in extraordinary circumstances. Of the seven Governors of the rebellious States, he is the only one who has opposed the movement, and refused to recognize the pretended act of secession. He has given way before the physical force of the rebels, but has refused to recognize the rightful authority of the Government *de facto* which they have established, and issues a powerful appeal to the sober second thought of the people in the form of a proclamation. The fact is well known also, that a large portion of the Texan population, if not a majority, is loyal to the Union; and that it has been overpowered by the organized band of outlaws, known under the title of the Knights of the Golden Circle.

The fact seems to be lost sight of, that the Federal Government is authorized and bound to "repel invasion" of the States even when not called upon by the local Legislatures or the Governors. Texas has been invaded by Indian tribes, and is threatened by lawless bands of Mexicans. Here, then, is legitimate ground for interference, in addition to the ordinary right of the Executive to send troops to any part of the Union.

The right of the Executive to protect the States against "domestic violence" is to be exercised at the call of the Legislature, if in session, or at that of the Governor. It is probable that Gov. HOUSTON has exercised this right of calling upon the President for aid, for the double purpose of repelling invasion and quelling violence.

But it is, of course, legitimate for the Federal Government to enforce the laws of the Union, and the President is bound by his official oath to enforce them, wherever it is practicable, without regard to the call of the State authorities, and for these reasons combined, there can be little doubt that the chief part of the forces which have been sent South are destined for Texas. I have heretofore called attention to the high moral obligation which rests upon the Government to protect the Union-loving population of Western Texas against the Indian and Mexican marauders; and the same duty of protection is equally strong as against the robber-bands which have assumed the fanciful title of Knights of the Golden Circle. The opportunity is a favorable one for giving the friends of Union a rallying-point, and a guaranty of protection in their efforts to overthrow the usurpation of the "Democratic" oligarchy. Wherever the friends of Union have a foot-hold, they should be sustained by Federal forces; and, if need be, the Union militia should be called out and paid by the Government. If the traitors are permitted to arm and organize, the friends of Union should be encouraged to do likewise.

The announcement in one of our cotemporaries, that secret agents sent out by Mr. LINCOLN, immediately on his accession to power, returned some days ago from Europe, with assurances from the Governments of France and England that the Confederate States would not be encouraged or countenanced in their efforts to gain independence, bears the marks of absurdity upon its face. In the first place, sufficient time had not elapsed, between the inauguration of the new Government and the announcement, for the agents to go and return, supposing them to spend a sufficient time abroad to obtain such important information. And in the second place, the idea of sending secret agents post-haste to England and France, to ascertain whether the Governments of those countries would sustain Mr. LINCOLN'S Administration in the enforcement of the laws—in other words, whether this Government would be permitted to exist any longer, is too preposterous for belief. It is simply incredible that a proceeding so undignified, and so unworthy of a great people, could be authorized by any Administration.

It is possible that private gentlemen may have undertaken such a mission, on their own motion, and that they may have drawn some such inference from the declarations of English and French ministerial officers; but it is utterly improbable that the supposed agents had any official sanction.

The announcement that BEN MCCULLOCH, the Texan Ranger, was seen emerging from a house in the First Ward, one morning last week, is said to be true, and it is stated, with confidence, that the house referred to is occupied by an Ex-United States Senator, who pretended to represent a Free State, up to the 4th of March. MCCULLOCH, it is reported, woke very early that morning, and was seen in the Ex-Senator's house, and afterwards passed over the Long Bridge into Virginia at a sweeping pace. He is reputed to be a man of desperate courage, but it is silly to suppose it possible that he would attack the Capital at the head of his Knights of the Golden Circle, backed by the corn-stalk militia of Virginia. No formidable military organization could be made within five hundred miles of Washington, for its seizure, without sounding the notes of preparation for weeks or months before getting ready to march. The friends of Union in this city are far more numerous and well organized, and far more ready to defend the city, than any band of outlaws to attack it; and in addition to this security, we have several hundreds of United States troops, armed to the teeth, the very sight of which here, last Winter, struck terror into the hearts of the traitors, and caused them to deny and ridicule the idea of an attack on Washington.

Capt. WITHERS, who has resigned his position in the army, is said to be a good Union man, but has been constrained to the course he has adopted out of deference to his father-in-law, a Texan gentleman, who threatened to disinherit his family if he continued longer in the service. The resignation of Major HOLMES takes his acquaintance by surprise. He is of North Carolina, if I mistake not, instead of Virginia, as announced. It is believed that the Secessionists are making great efforts to induce Southern Army and Naval officers to resign, as a means of weakening the confidence of the people in the Government. But it is a good thing to get rid of such officers, however meritorious in other respects, as acknowledge a doubtful allegiance to the Government. So both sides will be pleased at these resignations.

The statement that Mr. CLAY, of Kentucky, who has been appointed Minister to Russia, has advertised his estate for sale, is a mistake. His real property amounting to about twenty-two hundred acres of splendid farming land, in Madison County, Kentucky, is entailed, and he could not sell it if he would. The truth is, that he has advertised his furniture and farming utensils, and fine stock of cattle, for sale, with the view of renting out the estate during his absence in Europe.

OBSERVER.

THE VIRGINIA STATE CONVENTION.

RICHMOND, Wednesday, April 10.

The twelfth resolution came up.

Mr. CARLISLE moved to strike out a portion making an indispensable condition that no attempt be made to reinforce or recapture the forts, &c. Rejected—17 to 104.

Mr. WISE moved to add a clause declaring that all the forts in the limits of the seceded States ought to be evacuated for purposes of pacification. Lost—5 to 67.

The resolution, as amended, was adopted.

The following is the resolution:

The people of Virginia will await any reasonable time to obtain answers from the other States to these propositions of amendment. We are aware of the embarrassments that may produce delay, but we will expect, as an indispensable condition, a pacific policy will be adopted towards the seceded States, and no attempt be made to subject them to Federal authority; nor to reinforce any of the forts situated on the main land, or within the harbors of any of the seceded States, nor to recapture the forts, arsenals or other property of the United States within their limits, nor exact payment of imposts on their commerce, nor any measure calculated to provoke hostilities or collision. The forts, arsenals, magazines, and other places ceded to the United States, and situated on the mainland, or for the protection of the harbors of the seceded States, ought, for the purposes of pacification, be evacuated by the authorities of the Federal Government.

The thirteenth resolution was then taken up.

The Convention then took a recess.

Much excitement was occasioned by the reports that an attempt will be made to reinforce Fort Sumpter to-day or to-morrow. The extreme Unionists in the Convention say they are not to be moved by telegraph dispatches, and indicate that they will stand by the Government if the steamers are attacked. The conservatives entertain different sentiments.

After recess the Convention amended the thirteenth resolution, and passed it. It is as follows:

Resolved, That in the opinion of this Convention, the people of Virginia would regard any action of the Federal Government, or of the Confederate States, tending to produce a collision of forces, pending the efforts to effect an adjustment of existing difficulties, as unwise and injurious to the interests of both, and they would regard any such action on the part of either as leaving them free to determine their own future policy.

Pending the consideration of the 14th resolution the Convention adjourned.

LATEST FROM CHARLESTON.

THE FLOATING BATTERY PLACED IN POSITION.

CHARLESTON, Tuesday, April 9.

Everything is quiet to-night as regards excitement. People are becoming accustomed to suspense.

The floating battery has been towed into position between Sullivan's Island and Fort Sumpter.

Senator WIGFALL, of Texas, and EDMUND RUFFIN, of Virginia, (nearly 70 years of age,) shouldered muskets and joined the army as privates. Numbers of old men have done the same. Even cripples are anxious to fight, and may be seen riding with the cavalry.

The fleet is not yet in sight, but is expected off Stono to-night.

Troops continue to arrive in the city from the interior.

CHARLESTON, Wednesday, April 10.

The floating battery, finished, mounted and manned, was taken out of the dock last evening and anchored in the cove near Sullivan's Island.

Our people are not excited, but there is a fixed determination to meet the issue.

An additional regiment of 1,000 men is hourly expected from the interior.

The Convention has just adjourned, subject to the call of the President. Before adjourning, it passed resolutions approving the conduct of Gen. TWIGGS, in resigning his commission and turning over the public property under his control to the authorities.

Gov. PICKENS was in secret session with the Convention to-day.

About 1,000 troops were sent to the fortifications to-day; 1,600 more go down to-morrow.

Messrs. Wigfall, Chestnut, Means, Manning, McGowan and Boyleston have received appointments in Gen. BEAUREGARD's Staff.

A large number of the members of the Convention, after adjournment, volunteered as privates.

About 7,000 troops are now at the fortifications.

WASHINGTON, Wednesday, April 10.

The Charleston *Courier* of yesterday morning reports the arrival of Lieut. TALBOT there on Monday. He had a conference with Gov. PICKENS and Gen. BEAUREGARD, but was not allowed to communicate with Major ANDERSON at Fort Sumpter. Lieut. TALBOT started back for Washington last night. It is understood that the nature of his conference with Gov. PICKENS and Gen. BEAUREGARD was to obtain permission for an unarmed store-ship to victual the garrison at Fort Sumpter. Permission was refused. It is generally believed that the unarmed store-ship will be accompanied with moral force. Every preparation is made to prevent any relief being sent into Fort Sumpter.

THE WAR EXCITEMENT.

STATE OF FEELING AMONG THE PEOPLE.

THE NAVAL AND MILITARY EXPEDITIONS—MOVEMENTS AT THE NAVY-YARD AND MILITARY POSTS.

Little else was talked of, yesterday, but the war news. On emerging from their homes, men eagerly sought the morning papers, in expectation of the startling intelligence which has so long been threatened from the South, and many expressed their disappointment that affairs in the secession line were so long in coming to a focus. On the cars, in the ferry and steamboats, in the hotels and bar-rooms, knots of citizens gathered, and warmly discussed the movements of the Government, and particularly the probable character of the late expeditions, their destination, and the chances of success in provisioning or reinforcing Fort Sumpter. While there was here and there one who questioned the wisdom of the step, the mass of people expressed the most earnest wish for the success of the attempt, and nine out of ten men who said anything went in strongly for sustaining the Government of the country against all traitors, North or South.

The newspaper bulletins were the centre of attraction to eager crowds, and a few glaring capitals at any corner were sufficient to draw a large crowd, who anxiously peered over each other's shoulders to catch a glimpse of the latest telegraphic dispatch from Charleston or Washington.

The mistaken announcement that the *Baltic* and her consorts were due off Charleston yesterday, with the prophecy of stirring events from that quarter, created additional excitement. The fact is, the *Baltic* and *Illinois* did not go to sea, as announced, on Monday night. Both of them lay at anchor until Tuesday morning, the *Illinois* at Quarantine, and the *Baltic* at the S. W. Spit. Both steamers crossed the Bar nearly together about 7 o'clock on Tuesday morning, and at 7:30 they discharged their pilots and continued on their voyage southward. Being very deep, the *Baltic*, although a fast sailer, can hardly be expected to make more than ordinary speed. The *Illinois* was loaded to a draft of 20½ feet aft, but with her improved feathering paddles, although they were submerged 10 feet, she is reported to have gone off with unusual celerity, her wheels making 14¼ turns per minute with only 16 pounds of steam. Allowing 60 hours for them to reach Charleston—providing Charleston is their destination—these steamers will not arrive off the Bar until 7 o'clock this (Thursday) evening. Making the necessary allowance for night time, during which little could be done towards the arrangements for entering the harbor, it will be noon of to-morrow (Friday) before any movement can be made.

The steamer *Uncle Ben*, which was compelled to return, after proceeding as far as Barnegat on account of a damaged pump, started again on Tuesday evening, being only some twelve hours behind the other steamers.

The *Atlantic*, which went to sea in company with the *Powhatan* on Sunday night, if bound to Charleston, probably arrived thither yesterday morning, and must have been magnified by the excited optics of the Carolinians into the "six steamers" reported as being off the bar.

The *Harriet Lane* probably convoyed the *Baltic* and *Illinois*.

THE CHARTERED FLEET.

We gave on Tuesday a hastily got-up table of the chartered fleet. The following is correct as regards the tonnage, and nearly so as regards the men in the vessels. Of course all hands usually on board are included, merely to show the number of extra persons whose services have been engaged by the Government.

Vessels.	Tons.	Men.
Coatzacoalcos	1,500	75
Fashion	500	40
Atlantic	2,845	80
Baltic	2,885	71
Illinois	2,123	60
Ocean Queen	2,802	75
Yankee	400	14
Uncle Ben	300	14
Empire City	1,650	50
Star of the West	1,500	54
Total	16,505	536

A CLUE TO THE DESTINATION OF ONE OF THE SHIPS.

At the Troy arsenal unusual bustle has been observable within the past week. Lieut. BALCH, stationed at that place, was, on Friday last, ordered to repair at once to Fort Pickens, and report himself for duty there. Singularly enough, he arrived in the city the evening before the departure of the *Baltic*, and left next day. How, and where he went immediately from here are mysterious. Major MORDECAI, of the North Carolina Ordinance Department, who is now nominally commander at Troy, being really absent in his native State, Lieut. STRONG fills his place. There is only one other commissioned officer, Lieut. PORTER. The works at the arsenal are prosecuted with the utmost vigor, even on Sunday. The preparation of cartridges chiefly occupies the employes at present.

Several small sailing vessels are also reported to have been chartered by the Government, probably for the same purpose as those which have already been dispatched.

THE NAVY-YARD.

There is no doubt that orders for the immediate fitting-out of the United States ships *Wabash*, *Perry* and *Savannah*, have been received at the Brooklyn Navy-yard.

The housing of the *Wabash* was removed, yesterday, extra hands put to work on her, and preparations were made to put coal on board, which shows that the authorities are in a hurry to have her completed for commission. From the appearance of things, her machinery will be finished by Mr. KING very soon and steam will probably be applied on Saturday. The rigging, carpenter's work and ordnance, were taken in hands, to be hurriedly got ready. The *Wabash* is in fine condition, rates 40 guns, but does not carry more than 25, is 3,200 tons burthen, and was built at Philadelphia in 1856. Having been constructed of timber, fresh and green from the woods, and subsequently sent to a warm climate, she was, at one time, deemed unsound, but is now all right. She will be fit for commission in three weeks.

The brig *Perry*, whose state of readiness is to be turned into condition for active service, will be rigged to-day. Some riggers are to be taken on to expedite the job. Six days will suffice to put her in duty trim. The *Perry* is 280 tons burden, carries 6 guns, and was built at Gosport in 1843. She has cruised on nearly every squadron, and was last attached to the Paraguay expedition. She can be made ready for sea in three weeks.

The corvette *Savannah*, now in the dry dock, is to be prepared also, we should judge. She can be put in the commissioned state in five weeks. The *Savannah* is a sailing corvette, 1,726 tons burden, is rated for 24 guns and 300 men, and was built at Brooklyn in 1842. She was a 50-gun frigate until 1859. Her last duty was performed as Flag-ship of the Home Squadron, the *Cumberland*, now to be replaced by the *Minnesota*, relieving her.

Commodore STRINGHAM, the newly-appointed Commander-in-Chief of the Home Squadron, was to leave this City last night to join his ship at Boston. He could sail in less than ten days for Pensacola.

The marine garrison of the Brooklyn Navy-yard was to have been paid off yesterday, Major RUSSELL, the Disbursing Officer of the Marine Corps, having been ordered from Head-quarters at Washington for that purpose.

GOVERNOR'S ISLAND.

Everything was quiet and dull on Governor's Island yesterday, but it is evident that another *exodus* of troops is imminent. The quarters are being cleared out for the reception of fresh soldiers.

Major J. P. HEINTZMAN, First Infantry, will take command of the Island, *vice* Major HOLMES, who left on Tuesday evening, until 30th of June, when Col. SMITH, previously detailed for the post, will report for duty. Major HOLMES is a native of Pennsylvania, and was appointed from that State in 1826 to a Brevet Lieutenancy in the Third Infantry. He was breveted in 1847 for distinguished service in the Mexican war.

THE RECRUITING BUSINESS.

Since the commencement of the month applications for enlistment have been unusually numerous, recruits presenting themselves by threes and fours, but in the absence of any special orders on the subject, none but really good men are taken.

At the principal recruiting rendezvous in Chatham-street, 317 men were enlisted during the six months ending March 31, and 1 296 rejected in the same period, showing a monthly average of 62 enlisted and 216 rejected.

Of the rejected candidates many would be eligible in case of war; such, for example, as those foreigners who were refused in consequence of not speaking much English. The Chatham-street book shows that out of every twelve men enlisted ten are foreigners, Irishmen and Germans predominating.

THE COMING TROOPS.

We have already stated that the steamers *Coatzacoalcos* and *Star of the West* are expected here daily, with the remainder of the garrison of Texas. The first of these troops embarked on board the steamer *Fashion* at Indianola, on the afternoon of the 30th ult., to be subsequently transferred to the *Coatzacoalcos*, which they were. They mustered as follows:

	Men.
1. Company D, Second Cavalry	79
2. Company B, Second Cavalry	84
3. Company B, Second Cavalry	64
4. Company I, Second Cavalry	63
5. Company G, Second Cavalry	67
6. Company F, Second Cavalry	80
7. Company H, First Infantry	64
8. Company A, First Infantry	60
9. Company I, First Infantry	58
Total	570

Nos. 1 and 2 come from Camp Cooper; No. 3 from Camp Colorado; No. 4 from Camp Verde; Nos. 5 and 6 from the City of Brownsville; No. 7 from Camp Cooper; No. 8 from Camp Verde; No. 9 from the City of San Antonio, in which the Texas Rangers assembled to accept the surrender of Gen. TWIGGS' command.

The following officers accompany the soldiers: Infantry—Capts. King, Caldwell and Carpenter. Cavalry—Capts. Palmer, Stoneman, Brackett and Jenifer; officers Oakes and Whiting, Company K. Companies G and E had been brought up from Brazos Santiago to Indianola in the steamer *Arizona*, there not being convenient room for them on board the steamship *Daniel Webster*, which brought the artillery companies here some time since.

The following statement gives as nearly as possible the number of troops that have recently left this port within the past three or four days. Of course, the rumors about 2,000 having left in the steamers are without foundation:

Steamers.	Men.
Atlantic	358
Illinois	100
Baltic	400
Total	858

THE STATE MILITIA.

The militia of the State have evidently received some orders recently, judging from their increased attention to drilling and other signs of activity.

THE CHARLESTON NAVY-YARD.

The *Minnesota* received her masts on Monday, and the lists of stokers and firemen had already been filled up. There were applicants enough to man half a dozen frigates.

Orders have been forwarded from Washington to have the *Mississippi* fitted out as soon as possible. SAMUEL H. BROWN has been appointed Master Laborer at the Yard, in place of JOHN ROWNSAVILLE, removed.

THE PHILADELPHIA NAVY-YARD.

At the Philadelphia Navy-yard the steamer *Water Witch* has just been put in complete sea trim. She will probably sail the present week, with an unusually large crew of sailors and marines. The other vessels at the Yard are the *Jamestown*, 22 guns, which could be prepared for sea in ten days; and frigate *St. Lawrence*, 50 guns; in case of emergency she could be ready for sea in three weeks. There are 75 men on the receiving ship, and 100 marines in the barracks.

MORE WAR VESSELS WANTED.

PHILADELPHIA, Wednesday, April 10.

Dispatches from Washington state that the sloop-of-war *Jamestown* and the frigate *St. Lawrence*, now at the Navy-yard here, are to be fitted out for sea forthwith.

CAPT. MERCER AND THE POWHATAN.

PHILADELPHIA, Wednesday, April 10.

The *Bulletin*, of this evening, authoritatively denies the statements relative to Capt. MERCER, of the *Powhatan*, and says they do him great injustice. The facts are as follows: He left the ship at Staten Island by instructions from Washington. These instructions directed the command of the ship to be given to Commodore PORTER.

SAILING OF THE PAWNEE.

NORFOLK, Va., Wednesday, April 10.

The *Pawnee* sailed at 6 o'clock P. M. yesterday, with sealed orders for the South.

Arrivals in the City.

Commodore Armstrong, of the U. S. Navy; Hons. W. M. Converse and family, of Norwich, and W. T. Wilkinson, of Wisconsin; Gen Jas. W. Nye, of New-York, and J. P. Hamlin and W. A. Tuttle, of Boston, are at the Astor House.

C. H. Doolittle, of Utica; W. Dorlen, of Troy; Col. Nixon, of Cincinnati; A. G. Gilbert, of Albany; S. B. Dyer, of Paris; T. R. Rigson, E. B. Huntingdon and Dr. Hayward, of Boston; F. Moore, of Detroit, are at the Fifth-avenue Hotel.

Hon. H. S. McCombs, of Delaware; L. C. Jones, of Hartford; W. G. Nolan, of Texas; Dr. Eldridge, of Elmira; J. A. Millard, of Troy; G. N. Wanen, C. Rice and S. H. Perkins, of Boston; B. R. Nickerson, of California; J. E. Yeatman, of St. Louis; Dr. Saunders, of Kentucky; D. T. Vail, of Troy; S. S. Crocker, of Taunton, Mass; and N. B. Fletcher, of Providence, are at the St. Nicholas Hotel.

Capt. W. Wright, of Texas; Lieut. Fitzree and N. Owens, of the U. S. A.; A. Rubrey, of England; J. S. Rarey, the horse tamer, of Ohio; J. D. Fry, of California; J. W. Thomson, of Tennessee; D. C. Buchlin, of California; and W. S. Renney, of Arkansas, are at the Metropolitan Hotel.

Abraham Lincoln

Jefferson Davis

Bombardment of Fort Sumter by the batteries of the Confederate States, April 13, 1861

The New-York Times.

VOL. X.....NO. 2983. NEW-YORK, SATURDAY, APRIL 13, 1861. PRICE TWO CENTS.

THE WAR COMMENCED.

The First Gun Fired by Fort Moultrie Against Fort Sumpter.

THE BOMBARDMENT CONTINUED ALL DAY.

Spirited Return from Major Anderson's Guns.

The Firing from Fort Sumpter Ceased for the Night.

Hostilities to Commence Again at Daylight.

The Correspondence which Preceded the Bombardment.

The Demand for a Surrender and Major Anderson's Refusal.

THE RELIEF FLEET OFF THE HARBOR.

How the News is Received in Washington.

OUR CHARLESTON DISPATCHES.

CHARLESTON, Friday, April 12.

The ball has opened. War is inaugurated.

The batteries of Sullivan's Island, Morris Island, and other points, were opened on Fort Sumpter at 4 o'clock this morning.

Fort Sumpter has returned the fire, and a brisk cannonading has been kept up. No information has been received from the seaboard yet.

The military are under arms, and the whole of our population are on the streets. Every available space facing the harbor is filled with anxious spectators.

CHARLESTON, Friday, April 12.

The firing has continued all day without intermission.

Two of Fort Sumpter's guns have been silenced, and it is reported that a breach has been made in the southeast wall.

The answer to Gen. BEAUREGARD'S demand by Major ANDERSON was that he would surrender when his supplies were exhausted, that is, if he was not reinforced.

Not a casualty has yet happened to any of the forces.

Of the nineteen batteries in position only seven have opened fire on Fort Sumpter, the remainder are held in reserve for the expected fleet.

Two thousand men reached this city this morning and embarked for Morris Island and the neighborhood.

CHARLESTON, Friday, April 12.

The bombardment of Fort Sumpter continues.

The Floating Battery and Stephens Battery are operating freely, and Fort Sumpter is returning the fire.

It is reported that three war vessels are outside the bar.

CHARLESTON, Friday, April 12.

The firing has ceased for the night, but will be renewed at daylight in the morning, unless an attempt is made to reinforce, which ample arrangements have been made to repel.

The *Pawnee*, *Harriet Lane*, and a third steamer are reported off the bar.

Troops are arriving by every train.

LATER DISPATCHES—HOSTILITIES STILL PROGRESSING.

CHARLESTON, Friday, April 12.

The bombardment is still going on every twenty minutes from our mortars. It is supposed that Major ANDERSON is resting his men for the night.

Three vessels-of-war are reported outside. They cannot get in. The sea is rough.

Nobody is hurt. The floating battery works well. Troops arrive hourly. Every inlet is guarded. There are lively times here.

CHARLESTON, Friday, April 12.

The firing on Fort Sumpter continues.

There are reviving times on the "Palmetto coast."

CHARLESTON, Friday, April 12—3 A. M.

It is utterly impossible to reinforce Fort Shumpter, to-night, as a storm is now raging.

The mortar batteries will be playing on Fort Sumpter all night.

FROM ANOTHER CORRESPONDENT.

CHARLESTON, Friday, April 12.

Civil war has at last begun. A terrible fight is at this moment going on between Fort Sumpter and the fortifications by which it is surrounded.

The issue was submitted to Major ANDERSON of surrendering as soon as his supplies were exhausted, or of having a fire opened on him within a certain time.

This he refused to do, and accordingly, at twenty-seven minutes past four o'clock this morning Fort Moultrie began the bombardment by firing two guns. To these Major ANDERSON replied with three of his barbette guns, after which the batteries on Mount Pleasant, Cummings' Point, and the Floating Battery opened a brisk fire of shot and shell.

Major ANDERSON did not reply except at long intervals, until between 7 and 8 o'clock, when he brought into action the two tier of guns looking towards Fort Moultrie and Stevens iron battery.

Up to this hour—3 o'clock—they have failed to produce any serious effect.

Major ANDERSON has the greater part of the day been directing his fire principally against Fort Moultrie, the Stevens and Floating Battery, these and Fort Johnson being the only five operating against him. The remainder of the batteries are held in reserve.

Major ANDERSON is at present using his lower tier of casemate ordnance.

The fight is going on with intense earnestness, and will continue all night.

The excitement in the community is indescribable. With the very first boom of the guns thousands rushed from their beds to the harbor front, and all day every available place has been thronged by ladies and gentlemen, viewing the spectacle through their glasses.

The brilliant and patriotic conduct of Major ANDERSON speaks for itself.

Business is entirely suspended. Only those stores open necessary to supply articles required by the Army.

Gov. PICKENS has all day been in the residence of a gentleman which commands a view of the whole scene—a most interested observer. Gen. BEAUREGARD commands in person the entire operations.

It is reported that the *Harriet Lane* has received a shot through her wheelhouse. She is in the offing. No other Government ships in sight up to the present moment, but should they appear the entire range of batteries will open upon them.

Troops are pouring into the town by hundreds, but are held in reserve for the present, the force already on the island being ample. People are also arriving every moment on horseback, and by every other conveyance.

CHARLESTON, Friday, April 12—5 P. M.

Capt. R. S. PARKER brings dispatches from the floating battery, stating that up to this time only two have been wounded on Sullivan's Island. He had to row through Major ANDERSON'S warmest fire in a small boat.

Senator WIGFALL in same manner bore dispatches to Morris Island, through the fire from Fort Sumpter.

Senator CHESNUT, another member of the staff of Gen. BEAUREGARD, fired a gun, by way of amusement, from Mount Pleasant, which made a large hole in the parapet.

Quite a number have been struck by spent pieces of shell and knocked down, but none hurt seriously. Many fragments of these missiles are already circulating in the city.

The range is more perfect than in the morning and every shot from the land tells.

Three ships are visible in the offing, and it is believed an attempt will be made to-night, to throw reinforcements into Fort Sumpter in small boats.

It is also thought, from the regular and frequent firing of Major ANDERSON, that he has a much larger force of men than was supposed. At any rate, he is fighting bravely.

There have been two rain storms during the day, but without effect upon the battle.

Everybody is in a ferment. Some of those fighting are stripped to the waist.

IMPORTANT CORRESPONDENCE PRECEDING THE BOMBARDMENT.

CHARLESTON, Friday, April 12.

The following is the telegraphic correspondence between the War Department at Montgomery and Gen. BEAUREGARD immediately preceding the hostilities.

The correspondence grew out of the formal notification by the Washington Government, which is disclosed in Gen. BEAUREGARD'S first dispatches.

[No. 1.]

CHARLESTON, April 8.

L. P. WALKER, Secretary of War:

An authorized messenger from President LINCOLN, just informed Gov. PICKENS and myself that provisions will be sent to Fort Sumpter peaceably, or otherwise by force.

(Signed.) G. F. BEAUREGARD.

[No. 2.]

MONTGOMERY, 10th.

Gen. G. T. BEAUREGARD, Charleston:

If you have no doubt of the authorized character of the agent who communicated to you the intention of the Washington Government to supply Fort Sumpter by force, you will at once demand its evacuation, and if this is refused, proceed in such manner as you may determine, to reduce it. Answer.

Signed, L. P. WALKER, Sec. of War.

[No. 3.]

CHARLESTON, April 10.

L. P. WALKER, Secretary of War:

The demand will be made to-morrow at 12 o'clock.

Signed, G. F. BEAUREGARD.

[No. 4.]

MONTGOMERY, April 10.

Gen. BEAUREGARD, Charleston:

Unless there are especial reasons connected with your own condition, it is considered proper that you should make the demand at an early hour.

(Signed) L. P. WALKER, Secretary of War.

[No. 5.]

CHARLESTON, April 10.

L. P. WALKER, Secretary of War, Montgomery:

The reasons are special for 12 o'clock.

(Signed) G. F. BEAUREGARD.

[No. 6.]

CHARLESTON, April 11.

L. P. WALKER, Secretary of War:

Demand sent at 12 o'clock. Allowed till 6 o'clock to answer.

(Signed) G. F. BEAUREGARD.

[No. 7.]

MONTGOMERY, April 11.

Gen. BEAUREGARD—Charleston:

Telegraph the reply of Maj. ANDERSON.

(Signed,) L. P. WALKER, Secretary of War.

[No. 8.]

CHARLESTON, April 11.

To L. P. WALKER, Secretary of War:

Maj. ANDERSON replies:

"I HAVE THE HONOR TO ACKNOWLEDGE THE RECEIPT OF YOUR COMMUNICATION DEMANDING THE EVACUATION OF THIS FORT, AND TO SAY IN REPLY THERETO, THAT IT IS A DEMAND WITH WHICH I REGRET THAT MY SENSE OF HONOR AND MY OBLIGATIONS TO MY GOVERNMENT WILL PREVENT MY COMPLIANCE." He adds: "Probably I will await the first shot, and if you do not batter us to pieces, we will be starved out in a few days."

Answer. G. F. BEAUREGARD.

[No. 9.]

MONTGOMERY, April 11.

Gen. BEAUREGARD—Charleston:

We do not desire needlessly to bombard Fort Sumpter, if Major ANDERSON will state the time at which, as indicated by him, he will evacuate, and agree that, in the meantime, he will not use his guns against us unless ours should be employed against Fort Sumpter. You are thus to avoid the effusion of blood. If this or its equivalent be refused, reduce the fort as your judgment decides to be the most practicable.

(Signed) L. P. WALKER, Secretary of War.

[No. 10.]

CHARLESTON, April 12.

L. P. WALKER, Secretary of War:

HE WOULD NOT CONSENT. I write to-day.

G. F. BEAUREGARD.

MR. FOX'S VISIT TO FORT SUMPTER.

CHARLESTON, Friday, April 11.

Intercepted dispatches disclose the fact that Mr. FOX, who had been allowed to visit Major ANDERSON on the pledge that his purpose was pacific, employed his opportunity to devise a plan for supplying the fort by force, and that this plan had been adopted by the Washington Government, and was in progress of execution.

THE KENTUCKY VOLUNTEER REGIMENT.

LOUISVILLE, Friday, April 12.

Dispatches have come here to hold the Kentucky Volunteer Regiment in readiness to move at a moment's notice from the War Department at Montgomery.

EXCITEMENT IN MOBILE.

MOBILE, Friday, April 12.

There is intense excitement and rejoicing here. Fifteen guns have been fired in honor of the attack on Fort Sumpter

THE CONFEDERATE STATES CONGRESS.

MONTGOMERY, Friday, April 12.

An extra session of the Confederate States Congress has been called for April 29.

THE NEWS IN WASHINGTON.

WASHINGTON, Friday, April 12.

The town was thrown into intense excitement to-night by the report of the commencement of hostilities at Charleston this morning at 4 o'clock. The more so because of the previous news of peace and landing of provisions at Fort Sumpter. The news came to-night from the Associated Press agent at Charleston, giving all the particulars of the correspondence between BEAUREGARD and Major ANDERSON, the commencement of the attack by the Secessionists, and ANDERSON'S response from his batteries.

The news was posted at once in all the hotels, and the wildest scene of excitement ensued. Among the Union men here there was general rejoicing that an issue was made at last, while no advocates of Southern rights were to be found.

Major ANDERSON'S fame is on every one's tongue about the hotels and streets. The news was at once taken to the White House. All visitors will be excluded, and the Cabinet summoned to await further information and act upon it. One thing I am certain of, from positive knowledge—that if this last information proves true, the Administration will support ANDERSON and his course with the whole power and means of the Government, at all hazards.

A crowd assembled at the telegraph office to await further news.

Everyone had been waiting anxiously all day for the report of an attack upon the Government supply vessels, which it was ascertained last evening would probably approach Charleston harbor some time during the night or this morning. The surprise occasioned by the report from repeated dispatches that they had entered the harbor without molestation, and were landing the supplies without any difficulty, present or apprehensive, created nearly as great an excitement as the later reports of battle. The President was informed by dispatches to three different parties, announcing the safe landing, until he finally concluded that they must be correct, and that better counsels were prevailing among the Southern men.

CABINET COUNCILS.

Mr. LINCOLN summoned the Cabinet together the second time to consult. They had met once at 10 A. M., and now convened again at 1 o'clock P. M. There was general rejoicing at the prospects of peace and final adjustment of our national difficulties, dampened somewhat, however, by fear that it would prove false. LINCOLN said to a friend that if these advices were correct, the crisis had been passed, and the whole question settled without firing a gun. He added that he did not consider the Government at war with the South, and did not intend it should by his act. It was in this view that the provisioning of the fort was ordered to be attempted, unaccompanied by armed demonstration. The President further said, while assuming that the supplies had been landed, that he did not consider maintaining supremacy of the Federal Government any victory over the South, but simply a vindication of the faith he had always reposed in the ultimate good sense, and sense of justice among the American people. The War Department did not place any reliance to-day on the peace dispatches. Secretary CAMERON declared that he saw no escape from conflict at both Forts Sumpter and Pickens.

LATER.—Notwithstanding a violent rain-storm, people are still thronging the streets, anxious to get the details of the fight at Charleston, but very little has leaked out except the leading statement that the fight has begun. The last rumor on the streets is that a breach has been effected in the walls of Fort Sumpter. Military men here say if this statement is part of the Associated Press news, it throws discredit on the whole story, as Fort Sumpter is too strong to be thus speedily reduced by any battery in the possession of the enemy. The motive of the statement that a breach has been effected, is supposed to be to discourage the President from sending additional forces there on the idea that the whole affair would be ended before reinforcements could arrive. This surmise is strengthened by the failure to get news of the arrival of the transports at Charleston, as there can be no doubt that some of them reached there before this. The President is anxious but calm at this trying hour of responsibility, confident in the rectitude of his course, and its approval by the people.

FOREIGN ASPECT OF SECESSION.

Mr. SEWARD and the President have consulted frequently with the foreign diplomats here concerning the present condition of our national affairs and the course of their respective Governments. On the part of the representatives of England and France, it is well understood that there is no sympathy whatever for the South. Lord LYONS says that he sees no benefit to be derived by the English Government, or any foreign Power, from the subremacy of its people; that there is, of course no prospect of foreign supremacy on this continent in any event; while England and the United States have become so strongly united in mutual interests, that misfortune to one is disaster to the other in all points of material interests. The Southern Commissioners had reason to discover these facts while in Washington, and have probably given DAVIS and his compatriots some new ideas not at all flattering to their vanity and visions of ultimate success.

VIRGINIA TRAITORS.

The report that R. A. PRYOR, of Virginia, has joined the staff of BEAUREGARD, gives color to the rumor that several companies had left Richmond for Charleston, to join the rebel forces. Under the circumstances, the Virginia Committee who arrived to-day, will get only cold comfort from Mr. LINCOLN, although they will be treated courteously, as the Administration cannot disclose its purposes while a rebellious army is opposing its power.

THE TRAITORS' MAILS TO BE STOPPED.

Should the news of to-night be confirmed, the Postmaster-General will suspend at once all mail communications with the rebel States.

THE DEFENCE OF WASHINGTON.

Two companies of the Second Cavalry are ordered to this city, to be selected by the officer in charge of the corps. Although Washington is not under martial law, all possible precautions are taken to guard against surprise. Mounted videttes are stationed at all the approaches to the city, at a distance of several miles, to give notice of any coming hostile force.

FROM ANOTHER CORRESPONDENT.

ANOTHER ACCOUNT OF THE NEWS AT WASHINGTON.

The first dispatches from the seat of war were received in this city about 7 o'clock this evening. The excitement caused by the meagre intelligence was most intense. Bulletins were posted at the principal hotels, where immense crowds gathered to discuss the probable results. It is almost needless to say that while there was but one opinion as to the end, there was an infinite variety of conjectures as to the *modus operandi*. The public sentiment is very decided that in the war inaugurated to-day the Government will prove to be the victor.

NEVER THOUGHT OF EVACUATION.

There is no foundation for the long stories told of the original purpose of the Government to evacuate Fort Sumpter. Mr. LINCOLN has not entertained any such purpose. He has entertained no purpose but to maintain possession of the Government property and enforce the laws. All statements that negotiations were entered upon for the departure of Major ANDERSON'S command were mere *canards* got up for the purpose of covering political defeats. The policy of the Administration never depended upon the contingency of evacuation. It was fixed within ten days after Mr. LINCOLN'S inauguration. If evidence were wanting of this, it would be found in the fact that the Government was prepared to dispatch such quantities of men and material as left the port of New-York within four days.

FORETHOUGHT OF THE ADMINISTRATION—ITS EFFECT.

The rapid shipment of supplies, men and munitions was the result of forethought and previous preparation—the end of means long before matured. The Government continues to receive assurances of the popularity of the measures it has inaugurated. These come from all quarters, and from men of all parties. I was talking with a gentleman from Maryland this evening, who assured me that the steps taken to maintain the supremacy of the General Government had done more to stifle secession in his State than all the compromise propositions. He was at home yesterday when a dispatch was received that a conflict had taken place in the harbor of Charleston. About forty persons were present, including Republicans and "very few" Douglas Democrats and Bell-Everett men. There was a universal expression of hope that the Government would succeed. This feeling pervades the Border States to an extent that surprises all. The stern realities of an actual conflict appear to have sobered the people and brought them to realize the duties of the Government and their own responsibility as citizens.

DEMOCRATIC INDORSEMENT OF MR. LINCOLN'S POLICY.

I met a Democrat to-day, whom I have known all through the excitement of the last election as an out-and-out friend of the Southern Secessionists. He is a New-Yorker, and widely connected with its business, he himself being one of the heaviest dealers in sugars in your City. I was astonished to hear him proclaim unguardedly his approval of the policy of the Administration, his hope that the vigor displayed in the beginning would continue to the end, and his willingness to make all the sacrifices which war imposes upon commercial enterprise. He says that the prominent Democrat of the State of New-York who shall venture to give his aid and comfort to the Southern Confederacy is doomed to political oblivion. I could multiply a dozen such instances in my experience of to-day.

NO EXTRA SESSION OF CONGRESS.

There is little probability of an extra session of Congress. As was telegraphed you yesterday, there is no necessity for such a session. The Government has all the power which Congress could confer, except the money.

MONEY PLENTY.

Until the limit of Treasury Notes is reached, the Government has as much means at its disposal as its wants are likely to exhaust before the regular period for the assembling of the National Legislature. Were it to be called together now, it could do nothing more to maintain the national honor than Mr. LINCOLN is now doing, while it might seriously jeopardize the early success of the Government forces by needless but exciting debates. In the hands of a prudent, just and decided President, and an intelligent and harmonious Cabinet, the national honor and the national integrity is much safer than experience has proved it would be in the keeping of Congress.

LEO.

GENERAL WASHINGTON NEWS.

THE MORRILL TARIFF NOT SO BAD.

The alleged imperfections and imprudences of the Morrill Tariff, upon which an extra session has been defended, are found to be largely exaggerated, if not entirely unfounded. Mr. BARNEY assures me that he will find no difficulty in executing the law with his present force, and that its provisions are quite as explicit as such laws are usually made, and that the changes from the previous system are not so violent and general as is supposed. A gentleman from Maryland told me today that the new tariff was doing much to keep that State loyal. He represents the iron and coal interests of the State, and he thinks the same beneficial influences will be felt in Virginia and North Carolina, in both of which States the mining interests are fast becoming paramount.

FINANCES OF THE CONFEDERATE STATES.

The financial embarrassments of the "Confederate States" are betraying themselves at every turn. Yesterday's TIMES exposed some of the evidences of the pecuniary troubles of secession by calling public attention to the fact that the $5,000,000 of the $15,000,000 loan of the Confederate States are being "apportioned among" (that is, *forced* upon) the Banks of New-Orleans, Mobile, &c. Have you noticed, also, that the very first of the $1,000,000 Treasury Notes, issued by the Provisional Government of the seceded States, were taken "by the Secretaries of War and the Treasury in payment of their quarter's salaries." The significance of this fact is apparent when it is remembered that the test of financial soundness in any Government consists of its ability to pay all Government dues in gold.

An old Clerk of the Treasury Department, who was South last week on private business, met there Ex-Secretary HOWELL COBB, with whom he had some conversation relative to the financial condition of the Government of the United States. Mr. COBB'S experience in the Southern Confederacy does not seem to have improved his judgment at all in the matter of financial estimates, for he continues to come as wide of the mark as ever. In the conversation referred to, he expressed the opinion that the revenues of the Treasury would be only about $1,000,000 per month; that, under this state of facts, the funds would be speedily exhausted, and that, as there is authority to borrow only $27,000,000, which, with the $1,000,000 per month for the ensuing year, would foot up only $39,000,000, while the expenses of the Government must be about $65,000,000, the Treasury must be bankrupted inevitably.

The figures in the Department show, in fact, an increase of revenue over last year, and the revenue is coming in at the rate of $3,000,000 per month, instead of $1,000,000, which Mr. COBB graciously allows. During the two weeks ending April 9, 1860, the receipts in the Treasury were $1,471,241 48. The receipts during the corresponding fortnight of 1861 were $1,500,667 34; increase in 1861 $29,425 81.

It should be remembered, too, that these results are attained at a time when the new Tariff is operating unfavorably towards the Treasury, because goods are withdrawing from bond for consumption in cases where the duty is less under the old Tariff than under the new, while merchandise which can be taken out of bond at *reduced* duties under the new Tariff are allowed to remain. Unless a war shall occur, Government is likely to have abundant means during the coming year.

SUMPTER AND PICKENS CANNOT STAND BOMBARDMENT.

Gentlemen skilled as engineers, and whose judgment is usually sound, express the opinion that neither Pickens nor Sumpter can withstand bombardment, if their assailants are not operated against by land forces. The forts in question were not constructed to sustain a siege, but to defend harbors against hostile fleets. For the latter purpose they are admirably adapted; no "wooden walls" could withstand the fire from their batteries, or do themselves harm; but a well-sustained fire from different points on the adjacent shores, it is maintained, will reduce them both in time,—unless they have men enough and guns enough to promptly demolish the assailing forts.

SWAGGERING NAVAL OFFICERS.

An agent of the Navy Department might be profitably employed in an occasional stroll through the hotel lobbies at Washington, to notice the language and deportment of some who wear the naval buttons, and yet constantly and publicly swagger about the folly of the Government undertaking to bring the "Southern Confederacy" to terms. It is not often that a naval officer thus dishonors the button,—but when he does, if he has not the manliness to resign, it would be advisable to ship him to sea somewhere where he could do no harm if he should take the notion to turn traitor.

A. B. DICKINSON, on Thursday, formally accepted the mission to Nicaragua.

GUARD DUTY BY THE CLERKS.

It is suggested that the Secretaries of the various departments call upon the clerks to perform guard duty at each Department where they are stationed. In this way all the loyal employes will be very easily discovered, and the shakey ones detected. I have the assurance that the experiment is to be tried in connection with the present military movements in the city.

AFFAIRS IN NEW-GRANADA.

The Government of New-Granada has no force with which to render effective its recent decree blockade of the forts of Rio Hacha, Santa Martha, Carthagena and Zapote, in the Atlantic, these forts being in the complete possession of the revolutionists. So far as the Pacific is concerned, the forts of Buenaventura, Tumaco, etc., have been partially blockaded for the past six months or more, by small vessels fitted out at Panama—but I believe this does not directly much concern American interests, although it does so indirectly, as the business of the Panama Railroad is somewhat lessened by any disturbances affecting the trade of the Pacific.

UNABATED RUSH FOR OFFICE.

There was a great rush at the White House again to-day of office-seekers. Most of them failed to gain admittance on account of the exciting news. The entire remainder of the Boston appointments were made, to-day, as follows:

Surveyor, CHARLES A. PHELPS.

Navy Agent, EUGENE L. NORTON.

United States District-Attorney, RICHARD H. DANA.

Marshal, JOHN S. KEYES.

A strong, but unsuccessful effort to defeat this slate was made.

The crowd of New-York office-seekers is increasing. CHARLES A. STETSON denies that he is a candidate for Marshal, or any other office.

CALIFORNIA APPOINTMENTS.

The following additional appointments have been made for California:

Appraiser, JOHN P. ZANE.

Collector at Monterey, JOHN T. PORTER.

Collector at Stockton, S. W. SPERRY.

Collector at Benicia, S. M. SWAIN.

Collector at San Diego, JOSHUA SLOANE.

Collector at San Pedro, OSCAR MACY.

WM. BELL has been appointed Postmaster at Great Salt Lake City, Utah Territory.

DISPATCH TO THE ASSOCIATED PRESS.

WASHINGTON, Friday, April 12.

The Virginia Commissioners arrived in this City, this morning, and during the afternoon they visited the President, not in their official capacity, and were received by him directly after the Cabinet meeting adjourned.

The President has made the following Massachusetts appointments:

CHAS. A. PHELPS, Surveyor of the Port of Boston in place of FLETCHER WEBSTER, who was removed at the earnest request of the Massachusetts Congressional delegation; EUGENE L. NORTON, Navy-Agent at Boston; RICHARD H. DANA, District-Attorney; JOHN S. KEYS, Marshal; JOHN A. GOODWIN, Postmaster at Lowell.

C. C. P. BALDWIN, Marshal, and GEORGE HOWE, Attorney for Vermont.

JAMES C. AIKEN, Marshal, and ED. G. BRADFORD, Attorney for Delaware.

LANSING G. VANCE, Postmaster at Morristown, Pennsylvania.

HARMON BENNETT, Postmaster at Norwich, New-York.

THE NEWS IN NEW-YORK.

Yesterday was a day of excitements. Rumors apparently well grounded concerning the progress of affairs at Charleston flitted through Wall-street, pervaded the thoroughfares and produced sensations of surprise, indignation and rejoicings, according to the nature of the mind to which they were brought. Dispatches were received stating that President DAVIS had, after consultation with his Cabinet, directed Gen. BEAUREGARD to allow unmolested passage of the Federal transports with their loads of supplies for Fort Sumpter, thereby obviating immediate hostilities; others that Maj. ANDERSON and Gen. BEAUREGARD were consulting together, and the probabilities were that the Fort would be surrendered so soon as its supplies were exhausted; and still others announcing that the war had actually begun. The first-mentioned dispatch was generally credited, and the feeling was almost universal that a great moral victory had been achieved by the United States Government.

At 5 o'clock in the afternoon, however, all uncertainty was set at rest. The telegraphic wire brought the long looked-for intelligence that WAR HAS BEGUN, and that the forces of the Confederated Traitors have struck the first blow. Expected as was the news, it produced a most remarkable and wide-spread sensation. Many had hoped the contest might yet be avoided; others thought the Federal Government would back down rather than shed blood; and others were certain that a Divine Providence would interfere to prevent so fratricidal a strife. The bulletin boards were surrounded; the streets near them were blockaded, and the fast-gathering multitude were only satisfied when the self-appointed reader had read himself hoarse in the frequent repetition of the brief announcement of the facts. Hundreds of anxious inquirers besieged the telegraph and publication offices, confident that there might yet be some item of information which was withheld from the masses, and they were only appeased when told that they were in possession of all, and that until this morning's papers were out they could have no more.

"Good, good," exclaimed many a one, as he read the statement, or as it was repeated to him by a friend, "at last we have reached a crisis: something *must* be done." The feeling of rejoicing was everywhere to be met, that Major ANDERSON had not lowered his flag, and that President LINCOLN had determined to sustain, even at so fearful a cost, the honor of the country. Of the very many with whom we conversed, and from whom we heard the freeest expression of opinions, we did not find a single individual who did not respond heartily to the sentiment, "Thank Heaven we have a Government." Speculations and wagers of all kinds were the order of the night, as to the probable effect of this or that battery, of the arrival and probable action of the fleet, and of the result of this first contest; and very long odds were offered and taken that Sumpter would silence Moultrie, and that the fleet, on arrival, would find but little to do. However that may be, the war has begun—the aggressors were the Confederated forces, the Federal post has returned vigorously the fire, and the entire moral support of the North stands about the President in this trying moment, as will the entire physical force stand at his side if a more trying hour should come.

THE PENNSYLVANIA WAR BILL.

HARRISBURGH, Friday, April 12.

The War bill passed both Houses to night, without amendment. Gov. CURTIN waited at the Executive office to sign it. It is signed.

The Charleston dispatches about hostilities were announced in both Houses, and produced a profound sensation.

Mr. SMITH, a *Democratic* member of the House, after the Charleston dispatches were received, changed his vote to aye on the War bill. All the Democrats of both Houses voted against it. The bill appropriates $500,000 for the purpose of arming and equipping the militia; authorizes a temporary loan; provides for the appointment of an Adjutant-General, Commissary-General, and Quartermaster-General, who, with the Governor, are to have power to carry the act into effect.

EFFECTS OF THE WAR IN BALTIMORE.

BALTIMORE, Friday, April 12.

The Charleston news was not generally promulgated here until after midnight. It produced a profound sensation, and general expressions of regret at

[*Continued on Eighth Page.*]

The Charleston Mercury.

SPONTE SUA SINE LEGE FIDES RECTUMQUE COLENTUR. VINDICE NULLO

VOLUME LVI. CHARLESTON, S. C., SATURDAY, APRIL 13, 1861. NUMBER 11,1[illegible]5

THE MERCURY.

SATURDAY, APRIL 13, 1861.

April Twelfth, 1861.

We stated yesterday that on Thursday, at three o'clock, p. m., General BEAUREGARD had made a demand upon Major ANDERSON for the evacuation of Fort Sumter through his Aids, Colonel CHESNUT, Captain LEE, and Colonel CHISHOLM, and that Major ANDERSON had regretfully declined, under the circumstances of his position. It was, however, understood that unless reinforced he would necessarily yield the post in a few days—say by the fifteenth. An effort was, therefore, made to avoid an engagement, without incurring greater risk of reinforcement. At one and a half, A. M., Colonel CHESNUT and Captain LEE reached Fort Sumter from General BEAUREGARD, and, we gather, were prepared to enter into any arrangement for non action as to Fort Sumter, if no assistance were given to the efforts of reinforcement; but postponement merely to mature hostile plans was impossible. No satisfactory agreement being proposed, and time being important, at three and a half o'clock a. m., Major ANDERSON was notified that, at the expiration of an hour, the batteries would open their fire upon him. The Aids then passed thence in a boat to Fort Johnson, and Col. CHESNUT ordered the fire to begin. Precisely at four and a half o'clock a shell was fired from the signal battery on James' Island, which, making a beautiful curve, burst immediately above Fort Sumter. Within fifteen minutes all the Carolina batteries were in full play. The inhabitants of Charleston forthwith thronged to the East Bay Battery and other points of observation, and excitement prevailed through the day amid various and stirring rumors put afloat from time to time. Major ANDERSON, having no oil to light up his casemates, and the morning being slightly murky and drizzly, did not respond until broad day. At a quarter before six he opened his fire by a shot at the Iron Battery on Cumming's point; then at Fort Moultrie; the Floating Battery, located at the west end of Sullivan's Island; the Dahlgren Battery; the Enfilade Battery, Major TRAPIER's Battery, and Fort Johnson, interspersing his attentions by paying respects to the numerous mortar batteries, by which he, encased in brick, is surrounded. Hour after hour has the fire on both sides been kept up, deliberate and unflagging. The steady, frequent shock of the cannon's boom, accompanied by the hiss of balls, and the horrid, hurtling sound of the flying shell, are now perfectly familiar to the people of Charleston. While the early sun was veiled in mist, we saw shell bursting within and illuminating Fort Sumter, or exploding in the air above, leaving a small thick cloud of white smoke to mark the place. We saw solid shot striking the dark walls, and in each instance followed by a fume of dust from the battered surface. One man was visibly stricken prostrate on the wharf, and carried in the fort; and several guns were dismounted. The walls, too, in several spots, were damaged. And while Sumter has certainly and manifestly been injured, no loss is yet sustained on our part. Fort Moultrie is intact, and the Iron Battery is ready for continued work, after a full and fair trial of its powers of resistance; also the Floating Battery. The practice of our soldiers, as marksmen, has been excellent and highly satisfactory to officers of science and experience; and, great gratification, at the last accounts, six o'clock, p. m., not one man of our army has suffered injury.

The *Pawnee* and *Harriet Lane* are lying off North Channel bar, with another ship, supposed to be the *Baltic*; at ship bar a war ship, judged to be the *Illinois*. Whether they will attempt to reinforce Fort Sumter in barges to-night, or land troops on Morris Island for an engagement, or will try to run the gauntlet of our channel batteries and Fort Moultrie, remains to be seen, and we will see.

Secession in Virginia.

If Virginia succeeds in withdrawing from the Union, it is believed that Maryland will follow; and the National Capitol will then be within the limits of the new Confederacy. That the spirit of secession is gaining ground in Virginia day by day is manifest. It has gained members of its Legislature and the Convention. Cities and towns that originally voted for remaining in the Union have recently, by their votes, declared in favor of secession. Southern Confederacy and disunion flags that were lately torn down and trampled in the dust as soon as raised, are now not only permitted to float on the breeze, but are flying in various parts of the State. Meetings are held and resolutions adopted in favor of secession. President Lincoln's appointed mail agents are forbidden to discharge their duties under penalty of tar and feathers. At the election in Richmond the Union candidate was defeated by 1000 majority. The Legislature have passed a resolution, forbidding the removal and delivery of guns at Fortress Monroe by the United States Government. The Richmond *Whig* and Lexington *Valley Star*, which have hitherto earnestly opposed secession, have been purchased by the Disunionists, and will hereafter advocate secession. It is proposed, also, to buy over every purchasable paper in the State that has favored the Union cause. It is intimated that the prominent politicians of the State propose holding a Convention, at which, without a vote of the people, Virginia will be declared out of the Union.

It is not our purpose here to account for this change in the popular sentiment, but the hesitating policy of the Administration has doubtless operated to bring it about. From the Washington correspondence of the Philadelphia *Press*, written by "Occasional," who is known to be Col. J. W. Forney, we make the following extract, bearing upon this subject:

"Although the Union sentiment pervades Virginia and Maryland, no sane man can doubt to-day that the active spirits in both these States are the Secessionists, and that the friends of the country there, as elsewhere, relying upon the justice of their cause, and upon the idea that nothing can permanently interfere with the integrity and strength of the Union, are idle and indifferent. And yet it would be vain to deny that the chief Federal authorities have literally become alarmed at the indications in the two Commonwealths which originally ceded the ten miles square in which the capital of the country is located. Virginia and Maryland, as I write, are in the hands of the Disunionists. Mr. Lincoln cannot appoint a friend of the Union in either without arousing against him a local excitement, and if he dared to select a Republican for a post-office, mail agency, or collector of the port, such appointee would be expelled in utter disgrace.

"The Convention now in session at Richmond presents an uncommon spectacle to the country. Elected by an overwhelming majority pledged to the Union as it is, man after man has been subtracted from the Union column, until the friends of the nation are now glad to boast that they control it by a small and uncertain majority. Even James Barbour, chosen a delegate over an avowed Secessionist, in the Culpeper district, by announcing himself in the canvass as an unalterable friend of the Union, has, within a few days, taken ground in favor of the Southern Confederacy; and it is stated, with some emphasis, that Sherard Clemens, John T. Harris, and other well known Union men, are leaning to the same side. Should the ordinance in favor of secession pass the Convention, the most serious fears may well be entertained as to the safety of this capital. The President, worried by office hunters, has passed many sleepless nights in thinking over our national troubles. If he demands a force bill, the Border States will retire from both branches almost in a body. They have, from Virginia to Missouri, through their conventions, legislatures, and newspapers, declared that the Cotton States should not be coerced. If he suggests a peace policy, his own party will be divided and decimated. The National Legislature, in that event, will be a scene of terrible excitement. What, then, is the Executive to do, to remove the obstacles to a lasting peace? I confess that I am at fault to suggest a remedy. When the wisest statesmen pause before this unusual problem, no intelligent or patriotic American can be blamed for hesitation and doubt. It is this state of public feeling which strengthens the idea of a recognition of a Southern Confederacy. A peaceful separation—the only method through which we can restore trade to its accustomed channels, and open the way for a renewal of that confidence and security which have enabled us to sustain and maintain our commercial relations with other countries."

THE CONFEDERATE STATES VS. NEW ENGLAND.—The census returns demonstrate that while the New England States have increased but about 18 per cent. in the ten years, the seceded States have increased 23 per cent., and those boasted States, New York and Pennsylvania, 25 per cent.

BOMBARDMENT OF FORT SUMTER!

Splendid Pyrotechnic Exhibition.

FORT MOULTRIE IMPREGNABLE.

THE FLOATING BATTERY AND Stevens' Battery a Success.

"Nobody Hurt" on Our Side.

ETC., ETC., ETC.

As may have been anticipated from our notice of the military movements in our city yesterday, the bombardment of Fort Sumter, so long and anxiously expected, has at length become a fact a[illegible]lished. The restless activity of the night b[illegible] was gradually worn down, the citizens who had thronged the battery through the night, anxious and weary, had sought their homes, the Mounted Guard which had kept watch and ward over the city, with the first grey streak of morning were preparing to retire, when two guns in quick succession from Fort Johnson announced the opening of the drama.

Upon that signal, the circle of batteries with which the grim fortress of Fort Sumter is beleaguered opened fire. The outline of this great volcanic crater was illuminated with a line of twinkling lights; the clustering shells illuminated the sky above it; the balls clattered thick as hail upon its sides; our citizens, aroused to a forgetfulness of their fatigue through many weary hours, rushed again to the points of observation; and so, at the break of day, amidst the bursting of bombs, and the roaring of ordnance, and before thousands of spectators, whose homes, and liberties, and lives were at stake, was enacted this first great scene in the opening drama of what, it is presumed, will be a most momentous military act. It may be a drama of but a single act. The madness which inspires it may depart with this single paroxysm. It is certain that the people of the North have rankling at their hearts no sense of wrong to be avenged; and exhibiting to those who expect power to reconstruct the shattered Union, its utter inadequacy to accomplish a single step in that direction, the Administration of the old Government may abandon at once and forever its vain and visionary hope of forcible control over the Confederate States. But it may not be so; they may persist still longer in assertions of their power, and if so, they will arouse an independent spirit in the South, which will exact a merciless and fearful retribution.

But to return to our report. The act which we have undertaken to record was so unique as might be supposed there were few incidents to mark it. Below we have presented the reports as they successively arrived from the different batteries, and which when placed on our bulletin board, were received with the most eager interest by the mass of anxious friends who at every instant of the day came crowding to our office.

There were several circumstances, however, developed by the day's experience which it is important to notice.

It affords us infinite pleasure to record that Fort Moultrie has fully sustained the prestige of its glorious name. It fired very nearly gun for gun with Fort Sumter. We counted the guns from eleven to twelve o'clock, and found them to be 42 to 46, while the advantage was unquestionably upon the side of Fort Moultrie. In that fort not a gun was dismounted, not a wound received, not the slightest permanent injury sustained by any of its defences, while every ball from Fort Moultrie left its mark upon Fort Sumter. Many of its shells were dropped into that fort, and Lieut. JOHN MITCHEL, the worthy son of that patriot sire, who has so nobly vindicated the cause of the South, has the honor of dismounting two of its parapet guns by a single shot from one of the Columbiads, which at the time he had the office of directing.

The famous iron batteries—the one at Cumings' Point—named for Mr. C. H. STEVENS, the inventar, and the celebrated Floating Battery, constructed under the direction of Capt. HAMILTON, have fully vindicated the correctness of their conception. Shot after shot fell upon them and glanced harmless away, while from their favorable position their shots fell with effect upon Fort Sumter, and the south-east pancopee, under the fire of the STEVENS' battery, at nightfall, if not actually breached, was badly damaged. At this battery the honor of firing the first gun was accorded to the venerable EDMUND RUFFIN, of Virginia, who marched to the rendezvous at the sound of the alarm on Monday night, and who, when asked by some person who did not know him, to what company he belonged, replied, "to that in which there is a vacancy."

It were vain to attempt an exhibition of the enthusiasm and fearless intrepidity of our citizens in every department of this eventful day. Boats passed from post to post without the slightest hesitation under the guns of Fort Sumter, and with high and low, old and young, rich and poor, in uniform or without, the common wish and constant effort was to reach the posts of action; and amid a bombardment resisted with the most consummate skill and perseverance, and with the most efficient appliances of military art and science, it is a most remarkable circumstance, and one which exhibits the infinite goodgoodness of an overruling Providence, that, so far as we have been able to learn from the most careful inquiry, not the slightest injury has been sustained by the defenders of their country.

It may be added, as an incident that contributed no little interest to the action of the day, that from early in the forenoon three vessels-of-war, two of them supposed to be the *Harriet Lane* and *Pawnee*, lay just beyond the bar, inactive spectators of the contest. Whether they will attempt to enter during the night and encounter the batteries on either side that line the shore, is yet to be determined; if so we will present the records of a bloody issue in our next.

Fort Sumter did not return the fire of our batteries for over two hours, and ceased firing at seven o'clock, p. m., though our men continued to the hour of our going to press.

Annexed are the reports above referred to, which appeared on our Bulletin.

FLOATING BATTERY, April 12—9, a. m.—1861.

Captain R. S. PARKER reports from Sullivan's Island to Mt. Pleasant that everything is in good order at Fort Moultrie. "Nobody hurt." The embrasures have stood well. The Floating Battery has been struck eleven times, but the balls failed to penetrate. Major ANDERSON is concentrating his fire on the Floating Battery and the Dahlgren Battery, under command of Lieut. J. R. HAMILTON. No houses on fire, as has been rumored. A number of shells from Fort Moultrie have dropped into Fort Sumter, and one of the barbette guns has been dismantled. A steamer, supposed to be the *Nashville*, hove in sight about 8 o'clock, but, upon hearing the firing, put back to sea.

FLOATING BATTERY, 10½ o'clock.

All right here; not a man wounded, though ANDERSON has concentrated [illegible] heavy fire on us. The battery stands well. [illegible]LOGAN, M. D.

FLOATING BATTERY, 11 o'clock.

Nobody hurt up to this hour. [illegible] working. [illegible] the roof, and [illegible] strikes the battery, the shock is not perceptible.

CAMP BOMAR, SULLIVAN'S ISLAND, 1 P. M.

No fleet in sight yet. Sumter badly damaged in parapet guns and buildings. Lieutenants RHETT and MITCHEL are at Moultrie in command of the battery bearing on Sumter. Captain HAMILTON has a DAHLGREN gun at the Cove, doing great mischief, and gets, *with the Floating Battery*, commanded by Lieutenants YATES and HARLESTON, nearly all ANDERSON's attention. *No one killed* yet on our side or injured.

RIPLEY *is in his shirt sleeves*, working his guns himself. The work is progressing finely.

LETTER FROM AN OFFICER IN COMMAND OF THE SUMTER GUNS ON FORT MOULTRIE.

FORT MOULTRIE, 1 o'clock.

We are all unhurt, and if the war steamers now off the bar do not give us trouble to-night, I have great expectation of success.

RIPLEY is every inch a soldier. Indeed, I cannot speak in too high terms of our officers and men.

Our gun practice has been fine. It has been satisfactory to Col. RIPLEY. Every now and then whilst I write seated between two of my Columbiads a shot from ANDERSON hisses spitefully over my head.

To Lieut. MITCHEL, under my command, belongs the honor of having *first* dismounted two guns for ANDERSON at one shot.

In haste, yours.

FORT MOULTRIE, 4½ p. m.

We commenced firing this morning at 4½ a. m., and have continued a steady fire until the present, and are still firing. The balls from Fort Sumter are doing little or no damage, not a person having been injured. The Morris Island batteries appear to be doing a great deal of injury to their side of Sumter.

Major ANDERSON has one gun bearing on Fort Johnson, one on each of the lower batteries on this Island, and five on Fort Moultrie. At present there are three United States war-vessels off the harbor. All the guns bearing on them are loaded and manned, ready for action.

MORRIS ISLAND, 8 a. m.

The batteries are doing great execution, and have received no injury.

STEVENS' BATTERY, MORRIS ISLAND, 10 a. m.

Everything going on well. The battery has been struck ten times without being injured. Everybody in good spirits, and no one hurt.

MORRIS ISLAND, 12 m.

Two of the guns on the iron battery have been partially disabled, but no one injured.

MORRIS ISLAND, 3½ p. m.

We have repaired the injury done to iron battery, and have commenced firing with the same success. No one injured.

FORT JOHNSON, 2 o'clock.

ANDERSON has fired two shots, but without effect.

The official reports made to Headquarters last night from the several forts and batteries, state that no person was injured; and that four out of every six shells fired, fell inside Fort Sumter.

The schooner *Petrel*, J. L. JONES, commanding, while lying off the mouth of Hog Island Channel, was fired into from Fort Sumter, about half-past 8 o'clock. One shot took effect in the bow of the schooner, and several passed over her. Captain JONES reports that the fire of Sumter is principally directed against the Floating Battery, the Four Gun Battery, and the DAHLGREN Battery on Sullivan's Island, with little apparent effect. Most of the shell, from the Mortar Battery on Morris Island, are falling in Sumter, while the shot from STEVENS' Battery are breaching the Fort rapidly.

Letter from "Occasional."

[*Correspondence of the Philadelphia Press.*]

WASHINGTON, March 22, 1861.—Shall the Southern Confederacy be recognized by the Administration of Mr. Lincoln? This is the question that begins to excite the attention of the country, North and South. Like that which preceded the proposition to evacuate Fort Sumter, which may now be regarded as almost finally decided upon, this discussion will awaken intense resentment in many quarters, particularly among those who have taken the ground from the beginning that the revenues ought to be collected, even if bloodshed should ensue. But may not the Administration in this, as in the Fort Sumter matter, be driven by circumstances to recognize the Confederacy? Many Republicans take the ground that it is better to pursue this course than to embark in the fruitless undertaking of collecting the revenue at the risk of precipitating a conflict with the seceded States. The paralysis that has settled upon business, the growing demands upon the Treasury of the United States, the daily resignations in the army and the navy, not to speak of other indications, all establish the fact that we are in the midst of extraordinary exigencies, and that no past example of administrative skill or party craft can be imitated to deliver us from the novel and threatening occurrences of which we are the creatures. One politician regrets that General Jackson is not on the stage to take the place of Mr. Lincoln; but he ought to reflect that the hard realities and new difficulties the latter has to deal with, would have perplexed any man, and could not have been immediately baffled and disposed of, even by the iron will and prompt courage of the Hero of New Orleans. *General Jackson ought to have lived when Disunion reared its horrid front in the Buchanan Administration*, and then, doubtless, his foresight would have crushed rebellion by anticipating its designs, and by arming the government at all points to meet the monster, when he finally exposed his purpose. Another politician, while denouncing the evacuation of Fort Sumter, and railing at the Cotton States, declares it were far better to get rid of the latter forever than to be making ineffectual efforts to bring them back into the Union. Others—and this class is rapidly increasing—assert that the only way to produce anything like system out of disorder is to recognize the Southern Confederacy, and to leave its authors and engineers to their own fate—in other words, to their own people, who, it is predicted, will soon become sick of the experiment, and at last, convinced that the Republicans have not intended to do them wrong, and that the loyal States of the old Government can prosper without them, will depose their leaders, and demand readmission into the Union. It ought to be borne in mind that throughout the Border Slave States, whose adhesion to the Union is of the first and last importance, there is a unanimous sentiment against coercion. Now, this sentiment is alike against collecting the revenues if such a step is to be taken amid warlike preparations. Meanwhile, it is not to be denied that the free States themselves are greatly disturbed and divided in regard to these issues. The great anti-slavery party is by conscience and conviction, by record and by nature, a peace party, and the Democratic party, with some exceptions, stands upon the idea that nothing can be done to enforce the laws upon the revolutionary States of the South until every honorable means has been tried to convince them that their rights are safe in the Union, and that the Administration of Mr. Lincoln intends no assault upon their institutions. These are undeniable, notorious, abounding signs of the times.

The alternative of an extra session, in order to take some steps in regard to the new tariff, is demanded by a number of leading Republican journals, and may be set down as another proof of the eagerness of the people in regard to the future. And what does this future promise to us? If we may judge from intelligence from all quarters of the Union, nothing but bankruptcy, poverty and despair. Spring approaches with no indications of revival in trade in the great cities; our shipping interest is at a stand-still; there being no market for manufactures, our forges and furnaces will be suspended, or entirely stopped; and, although money may be said to be plenty, capitalists clutch it tightly in their hands, because they see no safety in investments when the Government itself seems to be rocking to its ruin, or, like a rotten ship in a stagnant sea, slowly falling to pieces. Something must be done, and that soon! A National Convention can only be called after the lapse of a certain time, during which interval our complications and distresses will be multiplied. Is there no remedy immediately at hand by which temporary relief may be obtained, and the public mind so tranquilized as to give the Administration a chance to look around?

View from Charleston housetops during the bombardment of Fort Sumter

The Charleston Mercury.

DAILY PAPER, Ten Dollars per annum, payable half yearly in advance.

VINDICE NULLO
SPONTE SUA SINE LEGE FIDES RECTUMQUE COLENTUR.

COUNTRY PAPER—Three a Week—Five Dollars per annum in advance.

VOLUME LVI. | CHARLESTON, S. C., MONDAY, APRIL 15, 1861. | NUMBER 11,126

THE BOMBARDMENT OF FORT SUMTER.

Surrender of Major Anderson.

Full Particulars.

We closed the report of the grand military diorama in progress on our Bay amid the clouds and gloom and threatening perils of Friday night. The firing, abated in the early evening, as though for the concentration of its special energies, commenced again at ten o'clock, and amid gusts of rain, and clouds that swept the heavens, the red hot shot and lighted shells, again streamed from the girt of batteries around, and concentrated in fearful import over Fort Sumter. Of the effects little was visible, of course, and anxious citizens, who from battery, spire and housetop, had bided the peltings of the storm, mute spectators of the splendid scene, could only wait the opening of the coming day for confirmation of the hopes and fears with which the changes in the scene successively inspired them.

As dawn approached, the firing again abated, and when the rising sun threw its flood of light over the sparkling waters from a cloudless sky, it was but by random shots from outlying batteries, with scarce an answer from Fort Sumter, that spectators were assured the contest still continued, and that human feeling was not in harmony with the grace and glory of the scene. It was but a little while, however, before the energy of action was restored, and as the work of destruction still went on, it was feared that still another day of expectation and uncertainty was before us. But at 8 o'clock the cry arose from the wharves, and rolled in one continuous wave over the city, "FORT SUMTER IS ON FIRE!" The watchers of the night before, who had retired for a few moments, were aroused, occupations were instantly suspended, and old and young, either mounted to their points of observation, or rolled in crowds upon the Battery, to look upon the last and most imposing act in this great drama.

The barracks to the south had been three times set on fire during the bombardment of the day before, but each time the flames were immediately extinguished. Subsequently, however, a red-hot shot from Fort Moultrie, or a shell from elsewhere, found a lodgment, when the fact was not apparent, and the fire, smouldering for a time, at length broke forth, and flames and smoke rose in volumes from the crater of Fort Sumter. The wind was blowing from the west, driving the smoke across the fort and into the embrasures, where the gunners were at work, and pouring its volumes through the port holes; the firing of Fort Sumter appeared to be renewed with vigor. The fire of the Fort, long, fierce and rapid, however, was gradually abated, and although at distant intervals a gun was fired, the necessity of preserving their magazines and of avoiding the flames, left the tenants little leisure for resistance. But the firing from without was continued with redoubled vigor. Every battery poured in its ceaseless round of shot and shell.—The enthusiasm of success inspired their courage and gave precision to their action; and thus, as in the opening, so in the closing scene, under the beaming sunlight, in view of thousands crowded upon the wharves and house tops, and amid the booming of ordnance, and in view of the five immense ships sent by the enemy with reinforcements, lying idly just out of gun shot on the Bar, this first fortress of despotic power fell prostrate to the cause of Southern Independence.

At about 9 o'clock the flames appeared to be abating, and it was apprehended that no irreparable injury had been sustained; but near 10 o'clock a column of white smoke rose high above the battlements, followed by an explosion which was felt upon the wharves, and gave the assurance that if the magazines were not exploded, at least their temporary ammunition were exposed to the element still raging. Soon after the barracks to the east and west were in flames, the smoke rose in redoubled volume from the whole circle of the fort, and rolling from the embrasures, it seemed scarcely possible that life could be sustained. Soon after another column of smoke arose as fearful as the first. The guns had long been completely silenced, and the only option left to the tenants of the fortress seemed to be whether they would perish or surrender.

At a quarter to one o'clock, the staff, from which the flag still waved, was shot away, and it was long in doubt whether, if there were the purpose, there was the ability to re-erect it. But at the expiration of about twenty minutes, it again appeared upon the eastern rampart, and announced that resistance was not ended. In the meantime, however, a small boat started from the city wharf, bearing Colonels LEE, PRYOR and MILES, Aids to Gen. BEAUREGARD, with offers of assistance, if perchance the garrison should be unable to escape the flames. As they approached the fort the flag appeared, and, as the firing from our batteries was unabated, they started to return, and had progressed, perhaps, the larger portion of the way when a shout arose from the whole circle of spectators on the islands and the main land, announced that the white flag of truce was waving from the ramparts. A small boat had already been seen to shoot out from Cumming's Point in the direction of the fort, in which stood an officer with a white flag upon the point of his sword. This officer proved to be Col. WIGFALL, Aid to the Commanding General, who, entering through a port hole, demanded the surrender. Major ANDERSON replied, that "they were still firing on him." "Then take your flag down," said Col. WIGFALL; "they will continue to fire upon you so long as that is up." And further intercourse, resulting in a surrender of the fort, upon terms definitely arranged by Major JONES, the Chief of Gen. BEAUREGARD's staff, was held, which will be more distinctly set forth in other portions of the paper. The boat, with other Aids from Charleston, had returned, and, receiving Col. WIGFALL, they all came over to the city; and thus was inaugurated the closing act in the military drama.

In the afternoon Major JONES, Cols. CHESNUT and MANNING, with other officers and the Chief of the Fire Department and the Palmetto Fire Company, went down to Fort Sumter, and the details were concluded. We have not now the time to make a detailed description of the fort. It is enough to state at present that the walls are uninjured. Upon one of the faces (to the west), exposed to the water battery, it had received eighty shots; the other, equally exposed to this battery and to Fort Moultrie, had received more. Many of the doors to the embrasures had been driven in, but the permanent injury was slight; the balls penetrated but about 8 or 10 inches, removing about a half bushel of material. The cornice of the parapet in many places was knocked off, but all the parapet guns dismounted had been restored to their positions, and their carriages seemed then but little injured by the flames. The wall was most disfigured by the balling from Cummings' Point, but then there was little progress to a breach. Some of the casement guns were dismounted, and the devastation within the fort was great; the gunners were covered with fragments of shells. The barracks were swept entirely away, and there was nothing left but a loose mass of brick and mortar. A more detailed account of the effect of the bombardment upon the fort will be found in another column.

The Fight as Seen from Cummings' Point.

[FROM A SPECIAL CORRESPONDENT ON MORRIS ISLAND.]

On Thursday morning, when I came to Morris Island, it was evident that the term of preparation and practice was soon to close. The men all expected the order to open fire that night. And, indeed, there were reasons enough to justify the belief that it would be given. It was generally known that a fruitless demand for the surrender of Fort Sumter had been made that afternoon. And, from what was known of Gen. BEAUREGARD, nobody imagined that he would delay action many hours after such a refusal. Besides, the unusual proceedings at the batteries bearing on Fort Sumter showed plainly that we were upon the eve of battle. The sandbags, which screened from ANDERSON's view the 42 pounders at the Point Battery, were hastily removed as soon as it was dark; the works in the neighborhood of the Point were all lit up with lanterns; the guns were loaded, shotted and sighted, and the men were kept at their posts long after their usual time for retiring. Thus matters stood until a few minutes after 8 o'clock, when, to the great chagrin of the impatient young gunners, their officers gave the order to return to their quarters. The companies accordingly filed off, as usual, to their camps, the tattoo resounded over the dark sand hills, the tents were soon tenanted, and the men forgot their disappointment in sleep.

THE BOMBARDMENT OPENED.

A light rain commenced falling soon after midnight and continued, with intermissions, for several hours. At half past four o'clock in the morning of Friday the more wakeful of our men were aroused by the distant boom of a shell. We afterwards learned from the sentinels that it came from the Fort Johnson mortar battery. In a moment the camps were all astir. The long roll summoned a few drowsy ones to the ranks, and the eager squads, convinced that the time for action had at last arrived, trotted off at a quick pace towards their respective posts. Everything being in readiness, the three batteries of Morris' Island bearing upon Fort Sumter, opened immediately. It was not yet daybreak, and the scene, which at that moment was novel, was picturesque as well. The course of the shells on their fiery way could be easily traced until they exploded in a white cloud of smoke, followed by a dull detonation, over the parapets of Fort Sumter. The effect of the solid shot was also perceptible with the naked eye. At each discharge of the guns, either the water adjacent to the fort would be dashed up in great sheets of spray, or the dense brown cloud of crumbling brick and mortar would mark the spot upon the ramparts hit by the balls. Meanwhile we could see that the batteries at other points in the harbor were as actively employed as our own. Ever and anon the shells flew out from the mortar batteries at Fort Johnson, Sullivan's Island, and Mount Pleasant. The Floating Battery, stationed in the Cove, was quite hidden from our view by the smoke from its own guns, but it was not difficult to see the effective execution of its 42 pounders upon the north parapet of Fort Sumter. Quite a large portion of the Sullivan's Island shore was also wrapped in the white smoke, but the incessant flashing from the merlons of Fort Moultrie assured us that RIPLEY was hammering away with characteristic vigor. At first the Morris Island batteries alternated regularly with the others, but later this arrangement was found embarrassing, and our batteries fired at the discretion of the officers commanding them.

HOW THE GUNS WERE MANNED.

Here, perhaps, I ought to give some account of the men who worked the guns in this portion of the harbor. The batteries which bore upon Fort Sumter from Morris Island are three in number, mounting in all six guns and six mortars. The outermost of these is the now famous TRAPIER Battery, in itself a monument of engineering science and energy. It is composed of massive beams and sandbags, and contains at this time three eight-inch mortars. When the work was first built, it also mounted some heavy guns; but these have been removed, their carriages and closed embrasures remaining to show the position which they occupied. The TRAPIER Battery was manned by the Marion Artillery, Captain KING, assisted, towards the close of the bombardment, by the Sumter Guards, Captain RUSSELL. The former company labored incessantly at their pieces, from the opening of the bombardment until Saturday morning. Their fire was skillful, and but very few of their shells failed to explode either in or over the fort.

The next work, and nearer to the city than the TRAPIER battery, is the STEVENS, or Iron Battery—a novelty in military engineering—planned by and constructed under the supervision of an estimable son of this State. The efficiency of this unique fortification was a matter of no little concern to many previous to the action; but all doubts were immediately dispelled by Major ANDERSON's tests, as I shall presently relate. The Iron Battery contains three heavy Columbiads. It is flanked by immense slopes of sand bags, and these are burrowed very curiously, but securely, with places to retreat, which the soldiers call "rat-holes," but which are in reality very dry, capacious and comfortable chambers, except, perhaps, that the ceiling might be a trifle higher. And here I may as well say that all the fortifications have one or more of these rat-holes, to be used as a magazine, a hospital or as quarters for the relief according to circumstances.

Passing from the Iron Battery, we come to the Point Battery, a large work containing three ten-inch mortars, two 42 pounders, and the newly arrived rifle cannon, presented to the State by CHARLES K. PRIOLEAU, Esq., now in Liverpool, and junior partner in the firm of JOHN FRASER & Co. It will, doubtless, be a great satisfaction to that gentleman to know that his timely gift was so serviceable to our troops. The gun has patent sights attached, by means of which the greatest accuracy of range was obtained, and each of its conical balls crashed through its mark with telling effect.

Both these last named important posts, the Iron and Point Batteries, were held by the Palmetto Guards, Capt. CUTHBERT—a gallant corps, which, for numbers, alertness, efficiency and unexampled coolness in action, won the respect and admiration of all who saw them during the fight. I think that their officers must be proud of such men and I know that those officers are not unworthy of their command. The two batteries manned by the Guards were commanded by Major STEVENS, of the Citadel Academy. Capt. CUTHBERT devoted himself especially to the direction of the Iron Battery. The rifled cannon was worked by a squad of the Palmetto Guards, under the superintendence of Capt. THOMAS, of the Citadel Academy.

I should not omit to mention the fine looking companies in charge of the long line of batteries pointing to the Ship Channel and extending along the whole extent of the Morris Island beach. Although they were not called into action, we cannot forget that it is to their sleepless vigilance we must attribute the indisposition of the fleet to reinforce ANDERSON's garrison. Perhaps through the foolhardiness of our enemies, they may yet have an opportunity of vindicating their valor in the fight as well as their vigilance on the watch.

ANDERSON OPENS HIS BATTERIES.

At half-past six o'clock a dull unpleasant drizzle began to fall, and the leaden sky betokened a dreary day. Our guns kept pounding indiscriminately at the walls, parapet and quarters of Fort Sumter, but for nearly two hours no reply came. The Fort seemed as if all within were asleep; not a casemate was opened, and there was no movement noticeable in any portion of the post, excepting the flapping of the United States flag, floating defiantly from a very lofty staff. Thus things continued until a few minutes after 7 o'clock, when a shout from the hundreds peeping over the sandbags announced that ANDERSON had opened fire. He began with his heavy casemate guns bearing upon Cumming's Point. His first efforts were directed to batter down the Iron Battery. For a time his shots were watched with intense interest, but after fifteen minutes' firing it became apparent that he could make no serious impression upon the iron-cased roof. Ball after ball rebounded from the close layers of railroad iron, and splashed their way harmlessly through the marsh beyond. Most of his shots were aimed too high, and whizzed above the battery without striking it. These went ricochetting over the surface of the water, tearing up vast masses of the sea-weed, and giving a terrible fright to hundreds of the sea-fowl, which rose in every direction from the marsh. The effect of the shots which hit the iron battery was not perceptible to those within, except by the noise of the concussion, and even this was not so loud as we had expected.

At half-past 7 o'clock the flash from the parapet of Fort Sumter announced that ANDERSON had begun to work his barbette guns. This, however, did not continue very long, for the continual explosion of our shells in every direction, on and around the parapets, soon admonished him of the risk of exposing his men in that position.

At twenty minutes before 8 o'clock an alarm from our guard boats cruising about the Bar announced a steamer in the offing. Looking out from the crest of the sand hills with my glass I could descry, in the far distance, a large steamer very similar in appearance to those which ply between Charleston and New York. It was afterwards ascertained to be the *Nashville*. Later in the day three other vessels were seen—two of them evidently men-of-war. They made no attempt, however, to come in, but lay together in the offing throughout the day.

About half-past 10 o'clock a shot from ANDERSON struck the middle port of the Iron Battery, crushing in the iron plates that protected the guns, making an indenture of several inches. The ball did not penetrate, but glanced off like the others over the marsh. The force with which it struck the door, however, unfortunately so disarranged the lever by which the port was opened and closed, that it was found impossible, during the remainder of the day, to work that gun. The other two kept up a brisk fire throughout the whole of the bombardment.

The firing from all the batteries on both sides of the harbor was maintained steadily until nightfall. Major ANDERSON, during the afternoon, appeared to have become convinced that his efforts to riddle the Iron Battery were ineffectual, for the steady fire which he had kept up against Cummings' Point was transferred to Fort Moultrie, the Dahlgren and the Floating batteries on the other side of the Bay. He took care, however, at irregular intervals of fifteen or twenty minutes, to send a shot whizzing over our heads, and this kept our men upon the *qui vive*. At one time I noticed that the direction of his shots against Morris Island was changed from the Point batteries to those farther out. Perhaps he meant to rake the camps, the sight of which was plainly enough indicated by our flags. If such was his design, his aim was very creditable, for the balls—some said grape—whistled a few feet above the heads of the Sumter Guards, who had been detached from the 17th Regiment, and posted as a reserve at the head of the line of tents to act as a relief to the Marion Artillery at the TRAPIER Battery. Whenever a flash from the southeastern casemate announced that a shot was coming, it was somewhat ludicrous to notice the sudden dodge of hundreds of heads behind the sand hills, and the abject prostration of such of the darkeys as had not already betaken themselves to the other extremity of the Island.

A few minutes before 7 o'clock, the fire from Fort Sumter ceased. Shortly afterwards our guns also stopped firing. At half-past 7 the rain, which had been lowering all day, began to fall in torrents, and most of our men sought such shelter as was to be had. The storm was a trying one. The wind howled drearily over the sand hills, and the rain descended with a force and volume, against which the slight tents and leaky sheds—the only available cover—were a poor protection. The storm continued, with an occasional lull, until near morning. Meantime our gallant young gunners at the Mortar Batteries, nothing daunted by the disagreeable rain, had kept up their firing of shells during the entire night, though at somewhat longer intervals than before. The Sumter Guards deserve special mention for the alacrity with which they performed the laborious and unpleasant duty of strengthening the foot of the Iron Battery with sandbags. For many hours of the night during the worst of the storm they worked steadily, lifting the wet and heavy bags into position, and when day broke the face of the work was even stronger than on Friday.

SECOND DAY OF THE BOMBARDMENT.

Saturday morning, the 13th of April, a day long to be remembered in our annals as marked by the close of the most extraordinary bombardment on record, came in bright and glorious. The clouds had cleared away, but the rain had left the ground moist, and the air pleasantly cool. About sunrise a vigorous fire was re-opened from our guns. The effects of the first day's bombardment could now be easily seen without the aid of a glass. The south and east facades of Fort Sumter were completely pitted by balls, and from what we had seen of the fire from Sullivan's Island and the Cove, we knew that the north facade could not be in much better condition. The edge of the parapet was in many places cut off, a number of the guns were dismounted, and the embrasures of the casemates were so battered, that the regularity of their outline could hardly be distinguished. The chimneys and roof of the barracks were also perforated in many places by our balls. The guns of Fort Sumter did not re-open fire until seven o'clock, when the shots began to pour in quick succession from the casemates pointing towards Fort Moultrie. RIPLEY's men returned shot for shot, and at each discharge from Sullivan's Island, we could see great fragments of the parapet of Sumter toppling over into the water.

FORT SUMTER ON FIRE.

At ten minutes after 8, a. m., a thick black smoke was seen issuing from the southern portion of Fort Sumter, and a moment later a wild shout of triumph rang along the sand hills, and was heartily echoed across the water from Sullivan's Island and Fort Johnson, as we saw the red flames piercing the top of the barracks and borne eastward by the high wind, wrapping the entire parapet in dense clouds of smoke. The sight infused new confidence into our men, and the bombardment immediately became far more rapid and fierce than at any previous time. The singular coolness with which our gunners had, until then, performed their duty, seemed for a moment to have given way to the excitement of the novel scene. The bombs flew so thick and fast that we could see them exploding in groups over the flaming fortress, while only a few seconds intervened between the hammering fire of the heavy ordnance.

The fire blazed furiously, until the whole line of the barracks on the south side of Fort Sumter was swept away, leaving only some of the crumbled, blackened and tottering chimneys towering over the ramparts. Then the fire burned lower, the flames sank behind the parapet, and we were left in ignorance as to their further progress. In the course of the forenoon we noticed several violent explosions, apparently doing serious damage to the fort, but whether these were caused by the fire communicating to hand grenades and like combustibles, or to the magazines, we could only conjecture. During the progress of the conflagration, for a long time Maj. ANDERSON maintained a steady and terrible firing against Fort Moultrie, but very few guns were fired towards Morris Island.

THE FLAGSTAFF SHOT AWAY.

At a quarter before 1 o'clock another tremendous cheer from the watchers upon our batteries called me to my point of observation, just in time to see the flagstaff of Fort Sumter bearing the flag of the United States falling heavily inside the Fort. From this auspicious moment the impression became general among our men that the fortress would be ours before night fall.

For fifteen or twenty minutes I could see no ensign over the fort, but, at the end of that time, I descried a large United States flag elevated amid the smoke close on the north wall of the fort. Meantime a small boat had shot out from the beach of Cumming's Point towards the wharf of Fort Sumter. I afterwards learned that it contained Col. LOUIS T. WIGFALL, Aid to Gen. BEAUREGARD, and Private GOURDIN YOUNG, of the Palmetto Guards. Col. WIGFALL bore a flag of truce upon his sword. A white flag also waved upon Fort Sumter, and in a short time the conclusion of the negotiations was announced to us by the disappearance of the United States flag from the fort.

THE SURRENDER ANNOUNCED.

The rest is briefly told. Col. WIGFALL returned and notified the Captains of the several companies to inform their respective commands that the fort was unconditionally surrendered.

The scene that followed was altogether indescribable. The troops upon the hills cheered and cheered again. A horseman galloped at full speed along the beach, waving his cap to the troops near the Lighthouse. These soon caught up the cry, and the whole shore rang with the glad shouts of thousands.

The first burst of exultation over, all eyes were turned to the fleet in the offing, and the guards resumed their wonted rounds upon the batteries which have so nobly vindicated the independence of the State.

INCIDENTS OF THE BATTLE.

Although during the thirty-four consecutive hours through which the bombardment lasted, not a man was in any way injured upon our side, it cannot be said that our men altogether escaped Major ANDERSON's balls. As Captain JONES was standing in the Point Battery a spent ball, which had struck the sand bags above, rolled over striking him upon the back of the neck, but not with sufficient force to hurt him. The ball—a 32 pounder—was preserved as a memento of the occasion.

The first gun fired from the Iron Battery at Cumming's Point was discharged by the venerable EDMUND RUFFIN. He subsequently shot all the guns and mortars used during the action.

The bright-quartered flag of the Marion Artillery floated proudly over the TRAPIER Battery during the whole of the bombardment. On Saturday morning, when the men at these mortars were relieved by the Sumter Guards, the splendidly broidered blue banner, presented by some ladies a short time ago to the latter Company, was placed side by side with the ensign of the Marion's, and the rest of the action was fought with both flags waving overhead. It was noticed as a singular coincidence that at the very moment when the emblems of the Game Cock and the Swamp Fox were first fluttering together from the crest of the battery, the fire was discovered issuing from the parapet of Fort Sumter.

During the drenching rain Friday night, an alarm was given owing to a boat having attempted to pass the beach batteries on Morris Island. It was finally overhauled, and found to contain two sailors on a drunken frolic, who were dismissed with a reprimand for their rashness.

The New-York Times.

VOL. X....NO. 2984. NEW-YORK, MONDAY, APRIL 15, 1861. PRICE TWO CENTS.

Editorials

The Fall of Sumpter.

It is by no means impossible, after all, that what seemed at first to be a national calamity, and which rendered yesterday a memorably dark day in the experience of every patriot, was after all a substantial and crowning advantage, anticipated and provided for in the plans of the Administration. Its policy has been uniform and consistent—to protect the property of the Government, and enforce its laws. It will yield nothing belonging to it unless dispossessed by superior force, but it will not weaken the reputation of its military arm, by a reckless waste of men or means in the maintenance or attempted recapture of any comparatively valueless position. This arm is wielded by that illustrious Chief and Patriot, whose forty years of active service have never known dishonor or defeat, who, in the disappearance of our great leaders, is providentially left to us, and under whose guidance, though we may not for the time be advised of his plans, we are always sure of being led to substantial success.

It is altogether probable that Fort Sumpter could not, at any reasonable cost, have been relieved, after Mr. LINCOLN assumed the reins of Government, till he had collected the Army and Navy, dispersed by Mr. FLOYD, in order to render Washington and the forts and magazines at the South an easy prey, and could assume something like vigorous offensive action. It was important that Fort Sumpter should be retained as a point upon which to concentrate the military strength of the rebels, securing to him precious hours in which to concentrate his forces upon more important and menaced points. To abandon, it would instantly relieve a large force to operate against Washington and Fort Pickens. To hold this force inactive till they could be re-inforced in a manner to defy attack, was a master-stroke of policy, and does credit even to Gen. SCOTT's military reputation.

This advantage being gained, the Administration was then prepared to test the question whether the Confederated States would allow the sending of supplies to a handful of famished soldiers, cooped up in Fort Sumpter. To relieve their wants was an act of mercy as well as peace. To prevent it, would be an act of war. This war the rebels have inaugurated. Major ANDERSON's orders were to act as he did at Fort Moultrie—to consult the emergency; to yield, if necessary, to superior force. The fleet did not render assistance, as it could not without the risk of being disabled, and, perhaps, destroyed. Government was too weak in its naval arm to encounter any such risks. It would interfere with its proper command of the sea, and with its plans, to commence an immediate enforcement of the revenue laws at the ports of the rebel States. Fort Sumpter, as a strategetic point, is of no sort of consequence. It was constructed solely for defence against foreign invasion, which is not contemplated by the Government.

The port of Charleston, we learn by way of Montgomery, is *blockaded*. Every vessel entering or leaving it is to pass the *surveillance* of a ship-of-war. No wonder that "the Charlestonians regarded with execration the fleet that refused to come to the rescue of the gallant ANDERSON." It was not the plan of the Administration that they should go to his rescue at too great a peril. It was from the start destined to an entirely different field and mode of action. Neither the retention or surrender of Fort Sumpter could have any bearing on the policy the Government had marked out for itself. This was an isolated case, that stood solely on its own merits. Government could not allow its Flag to be disgraced by retreat. *It is strengthened in every part by the surrender of the Fort.* It may not attempt, at present, its recapture, but will notify the Confederated States that, till it is restored, *the commerce of Charleston must pass over the deck of a ship-of-war.*

The first act in the drama which has terminated in the surrender of Fort Sumpter, instead of being a defeat, is, when we come to look at its effects, a most brilliant success. It has thrown upon the Confederated States the entire responsibility of commencing the war. It has given us time to arm for offensive operations, and *to collect and to place before every Southern port a fleet sufficient to enforce the revenue laws, and to protect our commerce from Southern pirates.* We still hold every point of value in the Gulf—Fort Pickens, Key West and Tortugas. We turn the Confederated States upon themselves. We hold the command of the sea, upon which they cannot even float Alderman BOOLE's scows. Their armies, which they have collected and armed with such cost, they may turn against each other, to help to stifle the little freedom of thought or expression that may yet exist. They are harmless against us. The little commerce that may still seek their ports must submit to our revenue laws.

All this the Confederates at Montgomery may, in their impotent rage, contemplate with the same execration that the people of Charleston did the fleet that refused to expose itself to fire. Water is not their element. We command the avenue upon which their existence depends. They have commenced the war. We now propose to give them a taste of our power without exposing ourselves to their attacks. Mr. JEFFERSON DAVIS had good cause for being sick in bed at the reception of the news. The magnitude of the advantage gained at Washington, and the utter inability of the Confederate forces to cope with us in the arena we have chosen in which to carry on the contest, accounts for the lowered tone adopted at Montgomery and the feeble salvo of *seven* guns at their triumph. We are now prepared for a contest in a field in which we hold their lives in our hands, and on which they cannot harm us to the extent of a hair. We are prepared to follow up such a contest till they are entirely satisfied.

The People and the Issue.

The reverberations from Charleston harbor have brought about what months of logic would have been impotent to effect—the rapid condensation of public sentiment in the Free States. The North is now a unit. Party lines have shriveled, as landmarks disappear before the outpouring of volcanic lava. The crucial test of this is New-York City—the spot most tainted by the Southern poison. Not the thick insulation which the commercial spirit puts between the conscience and duty—not the obliquity engendered by long years of the most perverse political education—have been able to withstand the electric fire of loyal indignation evoked by the assassin-stroke aimed at the heart of the Republic. There are now no such ardent supporters of the Government as those who have been life-long Democrats. It is a fact full of omen, and one which persons imperfectly acquainted with the impulses that lie at the bottom of the popular heart could never have anticipated, that the very roughs of the City are aroused, and bring their passionate devotion to the cause of their country. One intense, inspiring sentiment of patriotism has fused all other passions in its fiery heat. Let the Administration now know that twenty millions of loyal freemen approve its act, and imperiously demand the vindication of the integrity and majesty of the Republic.

Viewed in the light of these events, the lull that for so many weeks reigned in the public spirit becomes very intelligible. A suspense—a long, dumb, unconscious waiting, very pathetic in its character—held the people's mind. Treason so vile paralyzed thought and will. The way was not clear what to do. It could not at first be believed that the country really held men so insane, so suicidal, as to attempt to transform such threats as theirs into deeds. The sheer demonism which marked the programme of social construction put forth by the Slave Power, caused it rather to assume the aspect of a terrific species of irony. And then, when the designs of the rebels became only too apparent, and it was evident that naught but the exercise of sovereign Might could avail to check those frenzied men, there was honest hesitancy in resorting to the force of arms. Civil war runs counter to the theory of the Republic. The framers of our Government made such provisions as would forever render rebellion unnecessary. All experience has shown how easily this Government can be induced to change its rulers, if any good reason for doing so was presented, and earnestly and persistently forced upon public opinion. Besides this, there was a doubt in many minds as to the degree to which the theory of Democracy allowed of opposition to the avowed and deliberate will of sovereign States. On the whole, it presented itself as a painful, perplexing problem. That problem has at length been solved by the public conscience, and the solution sweeps away forever the sophistries as to State Rights and coercion which entangled the subject. The lull is over—and an equinoctial storm of popular indignation has ensued.

In entering upon this struggle, the great community of Free States does so, prepared to bring to bear on the vindication of its national honor inexhaustible material resources. Her census shows returns which, under other circumstances, would have been the wonder of the world. It has, indeed, been industriously declared by timid croakers that "war is national ruin." There is no more absurd chimera. The Free States are richer and more populous than England was under PITT, when she fought the long fight with NAPOLEON, and vastly stronger than France when she battled triumphantly against all the Continental powers.

As to moral force, it panoplies the Republic as with a wall of fire. She enters the contest with that triple arming which justice gives to a cause. The moral conscience of the world is on her side. It is true that the rebels, lured by the support of that European element whose sympathies are contingent with the rate of duties levied on imported goods by the United States, have hoped for the recognition of the European Powers. That delusion is doomed to be rudely dispelled. The rulers of England and France do not dare to recognize that League. The unmaking of Ministries would hang on the decision, and they know it.

The Administration is not brought face to face with a *Revolution*. This is not the attitude. It has to deal with a plot, a conspiracy. There will be no "fraternal blood" shed, unless it be the blood of men who are willfully and persistently in the position of traitors. The right of revolution is not denied:—changes, prompted by causes material or moral, and effected through legal and constitutional means, are contemplated with calmness. But that Treason should be claimed as a right—that anarchy should rule—it is this which thrills with indignant amazement. How profound has been the humiliation, how hot the indignation, are shown in the tumultuous surgings of passion that are now baptising with one common sentiment of constitutional unity and patriotic devotion every loyal American heart.

The New-York Times.

VOL. X....NO. 2984. NEW-YORK, MONDAY, APRIL 15, 1861. PRICE TWO CENTS.

FORT SUMPTER FALLEN.

PARTICULARS OF THE BOMBARDMENT.

The Fort on Fire and the Garrison Exhausted.

NO ATTEMPT AT REINFORCEMENT.

The Cessation of Firing and the Capitulation.

NO LIVES LOST ON EITHER SIDE.

Major Anderson and his Men Coming to New-York.

How the News was Received in Washington.

Call for Seventy-Five Thousand Militia.

AN EXTRA SESSION OF CONGRESS

War Feeling Throughout the Northern and Western States.

FORT PICKENS REINFORCED.

CHARLESTON, Saturday, April 13—Evening.

Major ANDERSON has surrendered, after hard fighting, commencing at 4½ o'clock yesterday morning, and continuing until five minutes to 1 to-day.

The American flag has given place to the Palmetto of South Carolina.

You have received my previous dispatches concerning the fire and the shooting away of the flag-staff. The latter event is due to Fort Moultrie, as well as the burning of the fort, which resulted from one of the hot shots fired in the morning.

During the conflagration, Gen BEAUREGARD sent a boat to Major ANDERSON, with offers of assistance, the bearers being Colonels W. P. MILES, and ROGER PRYOR, of Virginia, and LEE. But before it reached him, a flag of truce had been raised. Another boat then put off, containing Ex-Gov. MANNING, Major D. R. JONES and Col. CHARLES ALLSTON, to arrange the terms of surrender, which were the same as those offered on the 11th inst. These were official. They stated that all proper facilities would be afforded for the removal of Major ANDERSON and his command, together with the company arms and property, and all private property, to any post in the United States he might elect. The terms were not, therefore, unconditional.

Major ANDERSON stated that he surrendered his sword to Gen. BEAUREGARD as the representative of the Confederate Government. Gen. BEAUREGARD said he would not receive it from so brave a man. He says Major ANDERSON made a staunch fight, and elevated himself in the estimation of every true Carolinian.

During the fire, when Major ANDERSON's flag-staff was shot away, a boat put off from Morris Island, carrying another American flag for him to fight under—a noteworthy instance of the honor and chivalry of South Carolina Seceders, and their admiration for a brave man.

The scene in the city after the raising of the flag of truce and the surrender is indescribable; the people were perfectly wild. Men on horseback rode through the streets proclaiming the news, amid the greatest enthusiasm.

On the arrival of the officers from the fort they were marched through the streets, followed by an immense crowd, hurrahing, shouting, and yelling with excitement.

Several fire companies were immediately sent down to Fort Sumpter to put out the fire, and any amount of assistance was offered.

A regiment of eight hundred men has just arrived from the interior, and has been ordered to Morris Island, in view of an attack from the fleet which may be expected to-night.

Six vessels are reported off the bar, but the utmost indignation is expressed against them for not coming to the assistance of Major ANDERSON when he made signals of distress.

The soldiers on Morris Island jumped on the guns every shot they received from Fort Sumpter while thus disabled, and gave three cheers for Major ANDERSON and groans for the fleet.

Col. LUCAS, of the Governor's Staff, has just returned from Fort Sumpter, and says Major ANDERSON told him he had pleasanter recollections of Fort Moultrie than Fort Sumpter. Only five men were wounded, one seriously.

The flames have destroyed everything. Both officers and soldiers were obliged to lay on their faces in the casemates, to prevent suffocation.

The explosions heard in the city were from small piles of shell, which ignited from the heat.

The effect of the shot upon the fort was tremendous. The walls were battered in hundreds of places, but no breach was made.

Major ANDERSON expresses himself much pleased that no lives had been sacrificed, and says that to Providence alone is to be attributed the bloodless victory. He compliments the firing of the Carolinians, and the large number of exploded shells lying around attests their effectiveness.

The number of soldiers in the fort was about seventy, besides twenty-five workmen, who assisted at the guns. His stock of provisions was almost exhausted, however. He would have been starved out in two more days.

The entrance to the fort is mined, and the officers were told to be careful, even after the surrender, on account of the heat, lest it should explode.

A boat from the squadron, with a flag of truce, has arrived at Morris Island, bearing a request to be allowed to come and take Major Anderson and his forces. An answer will be given to-morrow at 9 o'clock.

The public feeling against the fleet is very strong, it being regarded as cowardly to make not even an attempt to aid a fellow officer.

Had the surrender not taken place Fort Sumpter would have been stormed to-night. The men are crazy for a fight.

The bells have been chiming all day, gun firing, ladies waving handkerchiefs, people cheering, and citizens making themselves generally demonstrative. It is regarded as the greatest day in the history of South Carolina.

FORT SUMPTER EVACUATED.

CHARLESTON, via AUGUSTA, Saturday, April 13.

FORT SUMPTER HAS SURRENDERED.

The Confederate flag floats over its walls.

None of the garrison or Confederate troops are hurt.

Another correspondent says:

The bombarding has closed

Major Anderson has drawn down the stripes and stars, and displays a white flag, which has been answered from the city, and a boat is on the way to Sumpter.

CHARLESTON, Saturday, April 13—P. M.

The Federal flag was again hoisted over Fort Sumpter, when PORCHER MILES, with a flag of truce, went to the Fort.

In a few minutes the Federal flag was again hauled down by Major ANDERSON, and a white one unfurled.

CHARLESTON, Saturday, April 13.

Gen. BEAUREGARD, with two Aids, have left for Fort Sumpter.

Three fire companies from Charleston are now on their way to Sumpter to quell the fire before it reaches the magazine.

Fort Sumpter has unconditionally surrendered.

Ex-Senator CHESNUT, Ex-Governor MANNING and W. P. MILES have just landed and marched to Gov. PICKENS' residence, followed by a dense crowd wild with joy.

It is reported that the Federal flag was shot away by the Palmetto Guards at Morris Island.

In all two thousand shots have been fired. No Carolinians killed.

Major ANDERSON and his men, under guard, were conveyed to Morris Island.

The bells are ringing out a merry peal, and our people are engaged in every demonstration of joy.

It is estimated that there are nine thousand men under arms on the islands and in the neighborhood.

THE LATEST DISPATCHES.

CHARLESTON, Saturday, April 13.

I have seen W. PORCHER MILES, who has just returned from a visit to Fort Sumpter. He assured me that no one was killed at Fort Sumpter. This is reliable, and puts at rest all previous reports about Sumpter.

Maj. ANDERSON has reached the city, and is the guest of Gen. BEAUREGARD.

Our people sympathize with Maj. ANDERSON, but abhor those who were in the steamers off our bar and in sight of our people, and did not even attempt to reinforce him

The Fairfield regiment, one thousand strong, has just passed the *Courier* office, on their way to Morris Island.

There are now ten thousand men under arms in the harbor and on the coast.

Judge MAGRATH, who has just returned, reports that the wood-work and officers' quarters at Fort Sumpter are all burnt.

None of the officers were wounded.

The Fort will be taken possession of to night by the Confederate troops.

A boat from one of the vessels outside the harbor communicated with Gen. SIMONS, in command of the forces on Morris Island, and made a request that one of the steamers be allowed to enter the port for the purpose of taking away Major ANDERSON and his command. An arrangement was agreed upon by the parties to stay all proceedings until 9 o'clock to-morrow.

CHARLESTON, Saturday, April 13.

Hostilities have for the present ceased, and the victory belongs to South Carolina. With the display of the flag of truce on the ramparts of Sumpter at 1½ o'clock, the firing ceased, and an unconditional surrender was made.

The Carolinians had no idea that the fight was at an end so soon.

After the flag-staff of ANDERSON was shot away, Col. WIGFALL, Aid to Gen. BEAUREGARD, at his Commander's request, went to Sumpter with a white flag, to offer assistance in extinguishing the flames. He approached the burning fortress from Morris Island, and while the firing was raging on all sides, effected a landing at Sumpter. He approached a port-hole, and was met by Maj. ANDERSON. The Commandant of Fort Sumpter said he had just displayed a white flag, but the firing from the Carolina batteries was kept up nevertheless.

Col. WIGFALL replied that Major ANDERSON must haul down the American flag; that no parley would be granted; surrender or fight was the word. Major ANDERSON then hauled down his flag, and displayed only that of truce.

All firing instantly ceased, and two other of Gen. BEAUREGARD's staff—Ex Senator CHESTNUT and Ex-Governor MANNING—came over in a boat and stipulated with the Major that his surrender should be unconditional for the present, subject to the terms of Gen. BEAUREGARD.

Major ANDERSON was allowed to remain with his men in actual possession of the fort, while Messrs. CHESTNUT and MANNING came over to the city, accompanied with a member of the Palmetto Guards, bearing the colors of his Company. These were met at the pier by hundreds of citizens, and as they marched up the street to the General's quarters, the crowd was swelled to thousands. Shouts rent the air and the wildest joy was manifested on account of the welcome tidings.

After the surrender, a boat with an officer and ten men was sent from one of the four ships in the offing to Gen. SIMONS, commanding on Morris Island, with a request that a merchant ship or one of the vessels of the United States be allowed to enter and take off the commander and garrison of Fort Sumpter.

Gen SIMONS replied that if no hostilities were attempted during the night, and no effort was made to reinforce or retake Fort Sumpter, he would give an answer at 9 o'clock on Sunday morning.

The officer signified that he was satisfied with this, and returned. This correspondent accompanied the officers of Gen. BEAUREGARD's staff on a visit to Fort Sumpter. None but the officers were allowed to land, however. They went down in a steamer and carried three fire engines for the purpose of putting out the flames. The fire, however, had been previously extinguished by the exertions of Major ANDERSON and his men.

FORT PICKENS AND THE HARBOR OF PENSACOLA.

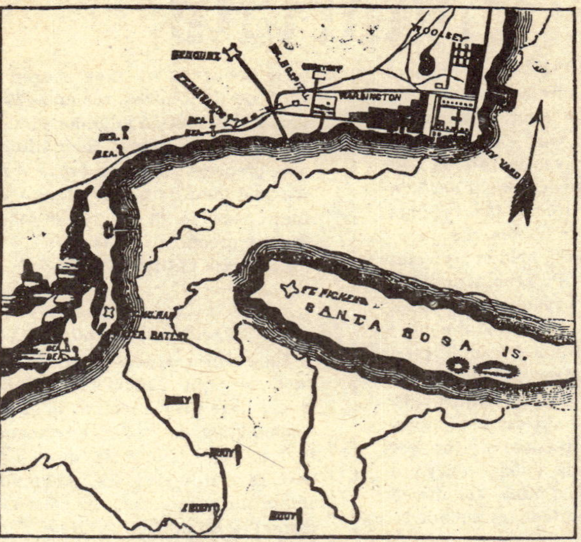

The visitors reported that Major ANDERSON surrendered because his quarters and barracks were destroyed and he had no hope of reinforcements. The fleet lay idly by during the thirty hours of the bombardment and either could not or would not help him; besides, his men were prostrate from over-exertion.

There were but five of them hurt, four badly and one, it is thought, mortally, but the rest were worn out.

The explosions that were heard and seen from the city in the morning, were caused by the bursting of loaded shells. These were ignited by the fire, and could not be removed quick enough. The fire in the barracks was caused by the quantities of hot shot poured in from Fort Moultrie. Within Fort Sumpter everything but the casemates is in utter ruin. The whole thing looks like a blackened mass of ruins. Many of the guns are dismounted. The side opposite the iron battery of Cummings' Point is the hardest dealt with. The rifled cannon from this place made great havoc with Fort Sumpter. The wall looks like a honey-comb. Near the top is a breach as big as a cart. The side opposite Fort Moultrie is honey-combed extensively, as is that opposite the floating battery.

Fort Moultrie is badly damaged. The officers quarters and barracks are torn to pieces. The frame houses on the islands are riddled with shot in many instances, and whole sides of houses are torn out.

The fire in Fort Sumpter was put out, and recaught three times during the day.

Dr. CRAWFORD, Major ANDERSON's surgeon, is slightly wounded in the face. None of the Carolinians are injured.

Major ANDERSON and all his officers and men are yet in Fort Sumpter. I approached near enough to the wall to see him bid adieu. In addition to this, conversations were had, which have been repeated to me.

A boat was sent from the Fort to night to officially notify the fleet at the bar that Major ANDERSON had surrendered. It is not known when the Carolinians will occupy Fort Sumpter, or what is to be done with the vanquished.

Everyone is satisfied with the victory, and happy that no blood was shed.

In the city, after the surrender, bells were rung and cannon fired.

CHARLESTON, Sunday, April 14.

Negotiations were completed last night. Major ANDERSON, with his command, will evacuate Fort Sumpter this morning, and will embark on board of the war vessels off our bar.

When Fort Sumpter was in flames, and ANDERSON could only fire his guns at long intervals, the men at our batteries cheered at every fire which the gallant Major made in his last struggles, but looked defiance at the vessels of war, whose men, like cowards, stood outside without firing a gun or attempting to divert the fire of a single battery from Sumpter.

Five of ANDERSON's men are slightly wounded.

CHARLESTON, Sunday, April 14.

The steamer *Isabel* is now steaming up, and will take Gen. BEAUREGARD to Sumpter, which will be turned over by Major ANDERSON to the Confederate States. ANDERSON and his command, it is reported, will proceed to New York in the *Isabel*.

CHARLESTON, Sunday, April 14.

Maj. ANDERSON and his men leave to-night in the steamer *Isabel* at 11 o'clock for New-York.

The fleet is still outside.

It was a thrilling scene when Maj. ANDERSON and his men took their formal leave of Fort Sumpter.

THE TIMES CORRESPONDENT IMPRISONED.

WILMINGTON, N. C., Sunday, April 14.

I saw the first gun fired at Fort Sumpter at 4 o'clock, A. M., April 12. I witnessed the battle for six hours. At noon I was arrested by order of Gen. BEAUREGARD as a Federal spy, and was imprisoned for twenty-four hours, and then sent out of the city by Gov. PICKENS, destitute of funds. In Wilmington I was aided by Mr. PRICE, of the *Daily Journal*, and will be with you in thirty-six hours.

There are conflicting reports as to the number killed. It is generally believed that nobody is hurt. JASPER.

PROCLAMATION BY THE PRESIDENT.

SEVENTY-FIVE THOUSAND VOLUNTEERS AND AN EXTRA SESSION OF CONGRESS.

BY THE PRESIDENT OF THE UNITED STATES.

A PROCLAMATION.

Whereas, The laws of the United States have been for some time past, and now are opposed, and the execution thereof obstructed in the States of South Carolina, Georgia, Alabama Florida, Mississippi, Louisiana and Texas, by combinations too powerful to be suppressed by the ordinary course of Judicial proceedings, or by the powers vested in the Marshals by law,—now, therefore, I, ABRAHAM LINCOLN, President of the United States, in virtue of the power in me vested by the Constitution and the laws, have thought fit to call forth, and hereby do call forth, the militia of the several States of the Union to the aggregate number of seventy-five thousand, in order to suppress said combinations, and to cause the laws to be duly executed.

The details for this object will be immediately communicated to the State authorities through the War Department. I appeal to all loyal citizens to favor, facilitate and aid this effort to maintain the honor, the integrity and the existence of our national Union and the perpetuity of popular government, and to redress wrongs already long enough endured.

I deem it proper to say that the first service assigned to the forces hereby called forth will probably be to repossess the forts, places and property which have been seized from the Union, and in every event the utmost care will be observed, consistently with the objects aforesaid, to avoid any devastation, any destruction of, or interference with property or any disturbance of peaceful citizens in any part of the country, and I hereby command the persons composing the combinations aforesaid to disperse and retire peaceably to their respective abodes, within twenty days from this date.

Deeming that the present condition of public affairs presents an extraordinary occasion, I do hereby, in virtue of the power in me vested by the Constitution, convene both Houses of Congress. The Senators and Representatives are therefore summoned to assemble at their respective Chambers, at 12 o'clock noon, on Thursday, the fourth day of July next, then and there to consider and determine such measures as in their wisdom the public safety and interest may seem to demand.

In witness whereof, I have hereunto set my hand, and caused the seal of the United States to be affixed.

Done at the City of Washington, this fifteenth day of April, in the year of our Lord one thousand eight hundred and sixty-one, and of the Independence of the United States, the eighty-fifth.

By the President, ABRAHAM LINCOLN.

WILLIAM H. SEWARD, Secretary of State.

AID FOR THE GOVERNMENT.

Advices from Albany state that Gov. MORGAN will to-morrow issue a call for twenty-five thousand men, for the assistance of the Federal Government.

A private letter from Gov. CURTIN, of Pennsylvania, to a prominent citizen of New York, states that he can have one hundred thousand Pennsylvanians in Washington within forty eight hours, if required.

THE AVAILABLE MILITIA.

Should the Government require it, a military gentleman states that the following number of men can be forthcoming at short notice, and probably in a out the following contingents:

Maine	5,000	Michigan	10,000
New-Hampshire	5,000	Illinois	15,000
Vermont	5,000	Wisconsin	5,000
Massachusetts	15,000	Iowa	5,000
Rhode Island	2,500	Minnesota	5,000
Connecticut	5,000	Kansas	2,500
New-York	25,000	Indiana	5,000
New-Jersey	2,000		
Pennsylvania	30,000	Total	154,500
Ohio	12,500		

The estimate would give to an army of three divisions: 62,500 for the Eastern, 51,500 for the Central, and 37,500 for the Western Divisions. This would do to make a beginning.

THE NEWS IN WASHINGTON.

WASHINGTON, Sunday, April 14.

THE EXCITEMENT AT THE CAPITAL.

The excitement here throughout the day has been intense. People gather in groups on the streets and in the hotels, discussing affairs at Charleston and the probabilities of the future.

There is great diversity of opinion relative to the reliability of the news that Major ANDERSON has surrendered. The dispatches to the Associated Press are evidently full of blunders, which cast suspicion on the whole.

DISPATCHES TO THE PRESIDENT.

The President, nevertheless, has intelligence which satisfies him that the news is too true. Private dispatches from Charleston, signed by trusty men, also confirm it; but as the telegraph is known to have been constantly tampered with by the secession authorities, it is feared that even private dispatches may have been mutilated for the purpose of cutting the Government off from all possible means of correct information.

THE CREDIBILITY OF THE TELEGRAMS.

The statement that the fleet had asked a cessation of hostilities until morning especially puzzles everybody, for if the Fort had surrendered the fleet could only have asked a cessation for its own sake, and we have thus far no information that it had been engaged. The vessels had only to steam out of range.

Still the opinion of men of high military authority here is that the news of the surrender is too true. They say no battery for the defence of the harbor could long withstand a skillful bombardment by heavy metal, where the garrison assailed is too weak to reply effectively and distract or annoy the assailants.

Besides, it is well-known here, and I have it from an authentic official source, Major ANDERSON's provisions were all exhausted yesterday, leaving him without an ounce to refresh his men after their hard day's work. There is apparently good reason here to believe the report that Major ANDERSON has embarked seaward.

Still many wagers were taken here to-day that the whole story of the surrender is false. The Union men absolutely refuse credence.

STREET FIGHTS IN WASHINGTON.

To-day's excitement has betrayed many secessionists who held public office, and who could not conceal their joy at the reduction of Fort Sumpter. Several fights occurred, and decided knock-downs. Gen. NYE, among others, has knocked down a couple of secessionists within the last day or two. The fact is, Northern men have got tired of having treason crammed offensively down their throats, and are learning to resent it by force, the only argument the chivalry seem to appreciate.

JOHN M. BOTTS ON SECESSION.

Hon. JOHN M. BOTTS, who is here, is violent in his denunciations of secession. He has been all day the stoutest disbeliever in the story of Major ANDERSON'S surrender. He insists that the whole story is manufactured for the purpose of precipitating Virginia into the secession movement. He predicts that it will utterly fail.

THE COURSE OF VIRGINIA.

Everybody here sees that now war has commenced, the question which the Virginia Convention has to decide is simply whether Virginia will declare war against the United States or stand by the Government; whether she will invite the battle upon her soil, to her utter ruin, or aid in bringing the fratricidal strife to a speedy termination by sustaining the Government and Union.

THE NORTH A UNIT.

The news from the North of the unanimity of public sentiment in favor of the Government and the strongest policy for the suppression of rebellion gladdens every heart. It is fully believed that all partisan considerations henceforth will be suspended, and that every effort will be directed to saving the country.

THE PRESIDENT'S PROCLAMATION.

You have the President's proclamation, making a requisition for seventy-five thousand volunteers, called from all the adhering States except California and Oregon. That news will thrill like an electric shock throughout the land, and establish the fact that we have a Government at last.

UNANIMITY OF THE CABINET.

The Cabinet is a unit on these measures, and no man among them was more decided and active in their support than Mr. SEWARD, who urged conciliation and forbearance until the Disunionists were put clearly and thoroughly in the wrong.

THE QUOTA OF TROOPS FROM EACH STATE.

The War Department is engaged to-night in calculating the number of troops which each State is entitled to furnish. New York will be entitled probably to ten regiments. Pennsylvania and Massachusetts to a few less. The estimates are based upon the Federal representation of the States.

This proclamation is the fruit of a prolonged Cabinet meeting held last night.

THE BLOCKADE OF SOUTHERN PORTS.

No policy relative to closing the ports of the Seceding States is yet understood to be settled upon in detail. It is probable, however, that arrangements will be speedily made to cut off all communication with them by sea. There need be no doubt about the power of the Government to do this under its authority to prevent smuggling.

But, independent of that, the occasion justifies the Executive in assuming responsibility. He may well emulate Gen. JACKSON, who, when Bon LETCHER asked him under what law he could bring the Nullifier leaders of South Carolina to Washington for trial and execution, replied that if the Attorney-General could not find a law for it, he would get another Attorney-General who could. Self-preservation is the Government's first duty, and its masters, the people, will justify it in every wise measure addressed to that end.

ACTIVITY OF GEN. SCOTT.

Gen. SCOTT has been at work all day, with all the energy of the soldier in the prime of life, making calculations for the disposition of the forces to be raised.

PROBABLE ATTEMPT TO SEIZE WASHINGTON.

The Administration has satisfactory information that the Confederate States have proposed, immediately after reducing Fort Sumpter, to march on Washington with their army of twenty thousand men, for which they will have nothing else to do. Until recently, JEFFERSON DAVIS was disposed to postpone that step until the secession of Virginia and Maryland was effected, but as he despairs of that now, he believes that at the approach of his army those States will immediately unite their forces with his. Men who know those States well say he is in error.

PREPARATIONS FOR ITS DEFENCE.

There is one regiment of volunteers now in Baltimore ready to obey the call of the Government immediately, and they will be mustered into service. Virginia also is ready to furnish her quota. The Government designs to bring a force of volunteers to this city not only strong enough to defend it against all comers, but to render an attack on it improbable. Several additional companies of regulars are also ordered here. It is not improbable that this point will be made a grand rendezvous from which troops can readily be sent wherever required.

THE SINEWS OF WAR.

Congress is called in extra session on the 4th of July,—a glorious day for a glorious work! This is essential in order to get the money that will be needed to enable the Government to sustain itself, and to pay as it goes. War is a costly experiment, as the Disunionists will find. It is no longer child's play, and will impoverish them utterly in a few months, if they persist in it, for they must themselves be the aggressors, and transport their troops and supplies long distances. The hopelessness of their unrighteous struggle must speedily force itself upon their minds when they learn how vigorous is the Government in its present hands, and how unanimous the people are in sustaining it.

MARTIAL LAW AT THE CAPITAL.

The President had not at nine o'clock to-night determined upon putting Washington under martial law. But there is little doubt that it will be done within a day or two. If so, it is hoped that possession will be taken of the telegraph office to prevent its employment by Disunionists for treasonable purposes.

CUTTING OFF THE MAILS.

The rumor that it has been decided to cut off all the mails from the seceded States is premature, to say the least. The Government does not recognize secession, and does not wish to punish the true men of the South together with the traitors. Wherever the mails are interfered with, they will be cut off, but probably not elsewhere. At least no determination otherwise has yet been arrived at by the President, notwithstanding his reference to the subject in the following letter to the Committee of the Virginia Convention, delivered by the President yesterday:

To Hon. Messrs. Preston, Stuart and Randolph:

GENTLEMEN: As a Committee of the Virginia Convention, now in session, you present me a preamble and resolution in these words:

Whereas, In the opinion of this Convention, the uncertainty which prevails in the public mind as to the policy which the Federal Executive intends to pursue towards the seceded States, is extremely injurious to the industrial and commercial interests of the country, tends to keep up an excitement which is unfavorable to the adjustment of the pending difficulties and threatens a disturbance of the public peace; therefore,

Resolved, That a committee of three delegates be appointed to wait on the President of the United States, present to him this preamble, and respectfully ask him to communicate to this Convention the policy which the Federal Executive intends to pursue in regard to the Confederate States.

In answer, I have to say that having, at the beginning of my official term, expressed my intended policy as plainly as I was able, it is with deep regret and mortification I now learn there is great and injurious uncertainty in the public mind as to what that policy is, and what course I intend to pursue. Not having as yet seen occasion to change, it is now my purpose to pursue the course marked out in the inaugural address. I commend a careful consideration of the whole document as the best expression I can give to my purposes. As I then and therein said, I now repeat, "The power confided in me will be used to hold, occupy and possess property and places belonging to the Government, and to collect the duties and imports; but beyond what is necessary for these objects, there will be no invasion, no using of force against or among the people anywhere." By the words "property and places belonging to the Government," I chiefly allude to the military posts and property which were in possession of the Government when it came into my hands. But if, as now appears to be true, in pursuit of a purpose to drive the United States authority from these places, an unprovoked assault has been made upon Fort Sumpter, I shall hold myself at liberty to repossess it, if I can, like places which had been seized before the Government was devolved upon me; and in any event I shall, to the best of my ability, repel force by force. In case it proves true that Fort Sumpter has been assaulted, as is reported, I shall, perhaps, cause the United States mails to be withdrawn from all the States which claim to have seceded, believing that the commencement of actual war against the Government justifies and possibly demands it. I scarcely need to say that I consider the military posts and property situated within the States which claim to have seceded, as yet belonging to the Government of the United States as much as they did before the supposed secession. Whatever else I may do for the purpose I shall not attempt to collect the duties and imposts by any armed invasion of any part of the country; not meaning by this, however, that I may not land a force deemed necessary to relieve a fort upon the border of the country. From the fact that I have quoted a part of the Inaugural Address, it must not be inferred that I repudiate any other part, the whole of which I reaffirm, except so far as what I now say of the mails may be regarded as a modification.

Postmaster-General BLAIR sent special agent BRYANT to Pensacola last week to reëstablish the Post-office there. BRYANT stopped at Montgomery on his way, where Confederate States Postmaster REAGAN forbade him to fulfill his mission, but failed to give any reason therefor.

RECRUITS FOR THE SECESSION ARMY.

Recruiting for the regular army of the Southern Confederacy has been going on sometime at Baltimore. The men are sent South via Norfolk as rapidly as they are obtained. Recruiting was also going on for the same service in this city yesterday. No objection is made to it, as it is deemed desirable to be rid of such men. A reliable Union man as Collector at Baltimore now, would do much good in watching these enlistments and detecting anticipated efforts to obtain a navy for the Confederated States at that port.

FORT PICKENS.

The Government has no advices from Fort Pickens, but you may rely upon it that relief has been sent to it. Dispatches hence to Pensacola have positively announced the fact to Gen BRAGG, and it is very probable that fighting has begun there also by this time. No apprehension is entertained on its behalf, as it has abundant men and supplies, and, if needed, additional forces can be sent it from Fort Taylor and Tortugas.

While the Executive does not indicate his purpose in that respect, it is generally understood to-night that the contest will be waged at Charleston vigorously for the vindication of the flag at that point and the recovery of the public property there.

MISCELLANEOUS MILITARY MATTERS.

Five additional companies of the District militia were mustered into service to-day, making 1,500 men here now under arms.

The National Rifles, a Disunion corps, held a meeting last night to rejoice over the reduction of Fort Sumpter and reorganize their corps. Martial law would suppress this nest of traitors.

One POWELL, a clerk in the Sixth Auditor's office, and an officer in the District militia who last week took the oath to support the Government, stated publicly on the street to-day, that if Maryland should secede he would go with her. He will probably lose both his office and commission to-morrow. No mercy henceforth will be shown to Disunionists in the public employ.

Twenty men from the Second Cavalry were stationed all last night as a guard at the White House. Mounted troops are stationed to-night outside the city, with rations for their horses. They are guarding every approach to the city. They are stationed four at each point, and relieved every four hours. Signals have been arranged for more speedy communication. One hundred and fifty men are stationed in the Post-office Department; three hundred at the Treasury; two hundred at the Capitol, and two hundred near the White House. Gov. CURTIN, of Pennsylvania, who is in town, received dispatches to-day, assuring him that Pennsylvania volunteers to any

[Continued on Eighth Page.]

The New-York Times.

VOL. X....NO. 2986. NEW-YORK, WEDNESDAY, APRIL 17, 1861. PRICE TWO CENTS.

Editorials

The Contest and the Relative Strength of Parties to It.

From the progress of the inventive arts, the chances of war among nations possessing an equal amount of courage and endurance are almost exactly measured by the amount of *money* a belligerent can command. Money is equivalent to numerical superiority in men, in ships, in means of locomotion and subsistence, and in the perfection and completeness of instruments of destruction. Success is no longer an attribute of a particular nationality, or the fortune of a particular General, or a matter of accident, but depends upon *mass*, and the skill with which this is wielded. The combatant excelling in these two conditions must in the end win, no matter what reverses it may at first suffer from want of preparation, or training, or habitude.

This premise, which is universally conceded, should relieve us of any concern as to the result of the contest in which we are now engaging, no matter how wide may be its range, or the extent to which it may be pushed. We may concede personal courage to our opponents, fully equal to our own, and still leave them in hopeless inferiority as to their ability to maintain anything like an equal fight. The Confederate States contain a white population of 2,500,000, or about one-eighth of the population of the Northern States. The latter can, if necessary, bring a force *eight times greater* into the field. All the Slave States together have a white population of only 8,000,000, against 19,000,000 in the North. Measured by numbers, the North is twice and a half as powerful, assuming all the Southern States to be a unit in sentiment and purpose. But this is impossible. Missouri in no contingency will join the Gulf Confederacy, neither will Delaware, nor Maryland, nor Western Virginia, nor Eastern Kentucky, nor Tennessee. In case of hostilities, the proper *surveillance* over the negro would compel at least one-half of the white males to remain at home as a local police, increasing the disparity to such a degree as to render it the height of fool-hardiness for the South to venture upon the contest.

How is it with regard to munitions of war? In heavy ordnance and the like the South may be pretty well supplied, from the forts they have seized and plundered. But in the seceding States there is neither a powder-mill nor a foundry for the casting of cannon, nor an establishment for the manufacture of arms. Did any such establishment exist they could never turn out material or arms that could match those manufactured at the North. The seceding States to day are being supplied from ourselves with everything they use. But for this source they could not put a regiment in the field. Disarm them, and they must remain so until they can again supply themselves by purchase. The Southern States are a people without artisans. Labor is held in disgrace. The greater portion of the white population are ignorant. To say that such a people can supply the very first conditions upon which success depends, a proper armament, and compete with the trained skill of the North, is an absurdity that carries its own refutation. Take away the arms the Federal Government have distributed through the South, or that have been stolen, and they would be impotent for any military exploit whatever.

They are equally weak in their commissariat. The seceding States cannot manufacture a yard of clothing fit for soldier's wear, nor raise the food for his rations. These must be supplied from the North, if at all. They are still weaker in the grand *sine qua non*—Cash. This the seceding States are literally without, and with the exception of one or two points, never had any. It is the law there, that the crop is realized and spent, long before it is gathered. Charleston was looked upon as the richest city South, in proportion to its population. Yet Charleston is almost completely exhausted. The State is so pressed that it cannot carry on the work necessary to complete its Capitol. All its banks are broken, with hardly a dollar of coin in their vaults. Its contributions to secession are forced loans. There is no other city South that had any money except New-Orleans, and this can be had only by forced loans from the banks. This resource will soon be exhausted, and then there must be an end both of borrowing and of forced loans. With all the bluster displayed, the $15,000,000 loan cannot be sold to voluntary purchasers. Nor can a second loan be put off, should this one be wrung from unwilling victims. The moment a State secedes its credit is ruined. The conviction is universal that secession will end in *repudiation*. A people that so readily trample under foot the most sacred obligations, will not be long in throwing off a debt the moment it is regarded as a burden. Nominally, Virginia is still a loyal State; but the fear that she will secede, has caused her bonds to fall to 57—the same bonds that a few years ago were sought after at 115, and but for secession would to-day be selling at a handsome premium!

Seceding States, individually, cannot borrow, because they deny all legal responsibilities. The Confederate States cannot, because they allow any one to secede from them at will, and because they embrace two *black sheep* among them, Mississippi and Florida. No one will trust a firm where these two are leading members, neither at home nor abroad, nor among themselves. In whatever direction the Confederate States may look, they can get no money, except by spoliation, which soon exhausts what it feeds on. Their people have none, and they can show their face in no foreign market.

The South lies entirely at the mercy of the North in their innumerable points vulnerable to attack. They want 200,000 men as a defence against 10,000 on board a well-appointed fleet. One day this force could threaten Norfolk; the next Wilmington; the next Charleston; the next Savannah; then Florida, Mobile, New-Orleans and Galveston. No one could tell where the blow was to be struck, and consequently every menaced point would have to be well guarded. Such a fleet and force could in six months put the whole South in a perfect frenzy, by constantly hovering upon their coast with hostile demonstrations. They could not touch it, and could only regard it from their shores with impotent rage.

What is the contrast the North presents to this picture? Vast wealth proffered to Government with a generous hand—hundreds of millions, if necessary, and with it a half a million of men, supplied by a homogeneous, united and enthusiastic people. Each State can place and maintain a respectable force in the field, and several of them, armies. Every one of them can raise any required amount of money at the legal, and many of them at much lower rates of interest. The credit of all is without stain. The value of their securities is unaffected by the civil war. Contrast the bonds of the State of New-York with those of Virginia, the former selling at *double* the price of the latter. The new war loan of New-York will be eagerly sought for; while, if Virginia secedes, she cannot borrow a dollar. Suppose these two States to be pitted against each other, does any one doubt the issue?

On the land, the Northern States alone constitute a first-class military power, in their wealth and the number of men they can arm and maintain in the field. The skill of their artisans is the admiration of the world. In food they can supply a continent. To say that such a people cannot overmatch one rude to the last degree in all its industries, capable of producing neither their food, nor clothing, nor arms, nor means of locomotion—a people, the greater portion of whom are unskillful and untrained, and impatient of all discipline or restraint—is to affirm that ignorance is stronger than intelligence, poverty than wealth, and wild insubordination than training and culture.

The North have an immeasurable advantage in its command of the sea. All the Southern produce must float upon it to market. We consequently hold in our hand the very elements of their existence. We could reduce them to beggary without moving or equipping a soldier. A few ships stationed off their forts would do all this. With the mercantile marine in our harbor, which could be got ready for sea at a week's notice, we could almost instantly throw 100,000 men upon any point to be attacked. We might threaten a dozen points at the same moment, and so divide and distract the enemy, that resistance at the point where the blow was to be struck would be impossible. With the command of the sea in our hands, the South, with ten times their present means, could not defend themselves. They have more than 5,000 miles of frontier line to protect, requiring thrice the number of men they could bring into the field. With such a frontier to guard, how supremely silly are all threats of invading the *North*.

In this contest the Government has only steadily, but firmly, to pursue the course it has marked out, and ultimate success must follow with as much certainty as matter obeys its laws.

Major Anderson.

The *Courier and Enquirer* makes a most disingenuous attempt to shuffle out of the responsibility of its gross attack upon the honor and loyalty of Major Anderson, for by quoting part of a paragraph from a telegraphic dispatch from Washington in the Times of Monday. Our correspondent stated that *suspicions* of Major Anderson's fidelity were excited in Washington by the news of his surrender; but he adds the following, which the *Courier and Enquirer* omits in its quotation:

"I think the facts, when known, will, however, show that Major Anderson *deserves the commendation of the country, for a most brave and vigorous defence of his command, and that he did not surrender until it became an inevitable necessity.* He will probably show, by his official communication to the Government, that his men had not tasted bread for the five hours previous to the surrender; that they were utterly exhausted with the labor of firing the heavy guns; that a shell from the Cummings Point Battery fell among the shells of the Fort, causing an explosion and setting fire to the wood-work of the Fort, and that the smoke of the burning structures was so dense as to render it impossible to continue the combat, and that his force was unable to put out the flames, or even to save their own private property. *It was under these circumstances that he was at last compelled to hoist a flag of truce, and eventually to stipulate for a surrender.*

The *Courier and Enquirer* has no right to quote the Times in support of its assault, and it certainly has no right to garble the paragraph by which it seeks to shield itself.

The *Courier and Enquirer* publishes the following extracts of letters written by Capt. Doubleday, from Fort Sumter:

Fort Sumter, Tuesday, Jan. 8, 1861.

I notice in the papers that the *Star of the West* has been sent here with 250 troops, but this is so improbable, we do not believe it. It requires a war-vessel to enter the harbor now. * * * So far they have staved off actual hostilities; *but if they fire upon any vessel which runs up the American flag, we will give them a taste of our columbiads.*

Jan. 9.—Early this morning I saw the *Star of the West*, with two American flags hoisted, approach the battery opposite to us on Morris Island. It was a beautiful sight, and my heart beat to see it. The battery is sheltered from our direct fire by some high sand hills. I saw a shot fired from it at the steamer, and immediately notified Major Anderson, and caused the long-roll to be beat. The men were rapidly formed at their guns. The enemy continued to fire upon the American flag; and as the steamer kept on her way, Fort Moultrie opened its fire in addition. I told the Major that guns were pointed and ready to fire; *but he would not permit us to do so. I felt deeply mortified to stand still and look on, without doing anything to assist the vessel. Though we did not see the steamer's name, yet we had no doubt it was the Star of the West, with troops on board.*

*Jan.*14.—Major Anderson's orders from the Government, while in Fort Moultrie, were, to act strictly on the defensive.

Feb. 6.—Major Anderson is a Southern man by birth and feeling, and sympathises with the South in its demands, but *considers secession as an unjustifiable means of securing them.* His situation here is a cruel one, and I feel deeply for him. He says if Kentucky secedes he will resign and go to Europe, for he will never fight against her nor the Stars and Stripes. I consider him as an honorable and brave man, placed in an exceedingly difficult situation. Much as we differ as to the propriety of some of his acts, and in political belief, I have a high respect for him as a man and an officer.

The *Courier and Enquirer* has quoted Capt. Doubleday as authority for its denunciations of Major Anderson. These extracts give an unqualified denial to the imputation. Instead of furnishing the slightest support for its censure, they afford the strongest possible evidence of its injustice.

Major Robert Anderson

The New-York Times.

VOL. X....NO. 2986. | NEW-YORK, WEDNESDAY, APRIL 17, 1861. | PRICE TWO CENTS.

THE COMING STRUGGLE.

Patriotic Responses to the Government Appeal.

MEN AND MEANS IN ABUNDANCE.

How the Call for Volunteers is Received in the Border States.

THE EXPECTED ATTACK ON FORT PICKENS.

Call on the Confederate States for 32,000 More Troops.

The Departure of Major Anderson and his Men from Charleston.

The Virginia Convention in Secret Session.

OUR WASHINGTON DISPATCHES.

WASHINGTON, Tuesday, April 16.

RUMORED BOMBARDMENT OF FORT PICKENS.

A rumor is circulating in town that the Government has received a dispatch from Pensacola announcing the commencement of the bombardment of Fort Pickens. This is erroneous, and if an attack has been made the Government has no advices of the fact.

MARYLAND RESPONDS LOYALLY.

Maryland has responded, through her constituted authorities, announcing that *she will promptly furnish her quota of men for the maintenance of the Government.*

Baltimore is reported as strong for the Union. There is to be a large meeting there of Minute Men to-night, and it is understood that two regiments will be raised on the spot to-night. The editor of the *Clipper* is among the leaders of the Union men. There are threats of destruction of the *Clipper* office, but it will not be permitted by the people, although some of the leading officials and military men in that City are rank Secessionists.

DELAWARE FOR THE UNION.

No official advices yet from Delaware. But there is good reason to believe that she will not fail in her duty in the present crisis.

KENTUCKY REFUSES HER QUOTA OF TROOPS.

The Secretary of War has received dispatches to-day from Gov. MAGOFFIN, of Kentucky, that he should not respond to the call for forces, and that no soldiers would, with his consent, leave the State to coerce any of the Southern sisters of Kentucky. A private dispatch is also received by a gentleman connected with a strong Union paper in Kentucky, stating that the State authorities would allow no troops to join the Federal forces, nor any Federal force to pass through the State. There was great excitement throughout the State upon the reception of the proclamation. A dispatch from Louisville says there is great danger of a mob attacking the *Journal* office, which, under the gallant PRENTICE, still stands out boldly for the Union.

GOVERNMENT RECRUITING IN KENTUCKY.

Major WOOD, of the Second Cavalry, has been ordered to Kentucky on recruiting duty.

NORTH CAROLINA, MISSOURI AND VIRGINIA TROOPS NOT FORTHCOMING.

Gov. ELLIS, of North Carolina, also telegraphed the President that he could not respond, as he had doubts of his authority and right to do so. His dispatch is regarded by the Administration as courteous and gentlemanly, which can hardly be said of Gov. MAGOFFIN's communication.

The Governor of Missouri also refuses to respond. Gov. LETCHER, of Virginia, also has unofficially refused.

INDEPENDENT CORPS COLLECTING.

The Secretary of War will accept an independent corps of Volunteers from any of the States where the Governors of such States refuse to call out the militia. Two regiments from Kentucky, two from Tennessee, and two from Missouri. "Independent" it is expected will be tendered and accepted to-morrow. The War Department mustered in a large number of Volunteers to-day. The National Rifles of this city, of which so many members refused to take the oath, is now fully filled up by volunteers, all of whom took the oath and are each day performing guard duty. They were complimented by Adjt.-Gen. THOMAS, and cheered by the ladies from windows and the crowds in the streets as they passed.

KANSAS COMPLAINS OF NEGLECT.

The citizens of Kansas now here complain bitterly that their State was not called upon, and say they will tender a regiment anyhow.

THE MASSACHUSETTS QUOTA DOUBLED.

The quota of Massachusetts was doubled to day, giving her one brigade of four thousand men. Gen. B. F. BUTLER, late the Democratic candidate for Governor of that State and member of the Charleston Breckinridge Democratic National Convention, will command the Brigade. Three companies will report at Washington and one at Fort Monroe.

GOV. SPRAGUE PROFFERS PERSONAL AID.

The voluntary offer of Gov. SPRAGUE of Rhode Island, to bring on his own forces and head them, has changed the mind of very many men, and excited a strong Union feeling in Maryland and elsewhere. The defection in the North was expected. This puts an end to it, and has an excellent moral effect.

THE SECESSIONISTS ENROLLING.

Dr. C. BOYLE, the Commander of the National Volunteers of this city, "secession corps," says that one hundred and twenty men joined the corps last evening. One advantage of martial law here would be that such men could be summarily disposed of at once.

CABINET COUNCILS.

The Cabinet has been engaged all day on military and naval affairs, and civil appointments have the go-by for the present. The sudden emergency which has arisen demanding instant preparation on a large scale for war, necessarily demands constant and severe labor on the part of the Executive Government, in considering and deciding upon the plans of operation presented by the military authorities.

The TIMES' articles of to-day upon the crisis have attracted marked attention here in official circles. I know at least one member of the Cabinet who expressed to-night decided admiration of their vigor and accurate measurement of the necessities of the hour.

WHAT WILL VIRGINIA DO?

Opinions here continue divided relative to the probable course of Virginia. Some of her citizens sojourning here are positive she cannot be dragged out of the Union, except by revolution, which would give her a civil war of her own. A greater number think her Convention will pass the Ordinance of Secession, but that her people will reject it. If Virginia secedes, it is a distinct declaration of war against the General Government, and the first thing she will have to do is to possess herself of Fortress Monroe, Harper's Ferry, and other public property, which will at once precipitate an hundred thousand men upon her in support of the Government, devastating her territory, and concentrating on her head all the plagues which the seven "Confederate States" have raised, and should share alone. Instead of preserving her domestic institutions by this, her own citizens are assuring her that war will make her a Free State within ninety days; while, if she continues to stand, she may yet stem the tide of disunion, and save blood and the dreadful arbitrament of the sword.

RUMORED IMMINENT ATTACK ON WASHINGTON.

There is a report here to-night that the Virginia Secessionists are approaching Washington. It created a sensation, but it is not true.

Capt. JUNIUS PALMER's company of Indiana cavalry, which arrived here only Saturday last, is already fully mounted and ready for efficient service.

THE APPOINTMENTS.

BEN. HARDIN HELM, of Kentucky, is appointed Paymaster of the Army, to fill the vacancy occasioned by resignation to-day.

No New-York appointments are announced yet, but the impression prevails that the President has definitely settled upon WAKEMAN for Surveyor, DENNISON for Naval Officer, and BLATCHFORD for Assistant Treasurer. The hitch is still relative to the Marshalship.

The Massachusetts delegation, having completed their appointments, have all gone home. All of them have signified their desire to join in the defence of the Union.

The city is unusually quiet to-night, but all the usual points are guarded strongly.

BRADFORD R. WOOD, our new Minister to Denmark, leaves here to-morrow, and sails in the *Fulton* on her next trip.

Rev. E. N. KIRK and others, of Boston, have arrived here from Richmond, where they debarked from steamer *South Carolina*, from Boston for Charleston, but which failed to go to the latter port, in consequence of the recent exciting events.

DISPATCH TO THE ASSOCIATED PRESS.

WASHINGTON, Tuesday, April 16.

It is said that the orders for the Rhode Island and Massachusetts regiments, under the recent levy, to proceed immediately to this City, have been countermanded, for the reason that arrangements are not yet made for their accommodation.

Col. ELLSWORTH has had strong inducements offered him to proceed to New-York City and organize a regiment of Zouaves. He probably left this morning, to be joined there by a number of the members of his old corps, who will take an active part in the organization and instruction of the regiment. If he does not go thither he will repair to Illinois for a similar purpose. He last night declined the commission in the army which has been at his disposal for some weeks.

Twenty tons of shell and grapeshot were removed from the Washington Navy-yard to Georgetown to-day, in view of a possible attack on Washington from that direction.

Several additional companies of volunteers were mustered into service to-day.

The Government has directed that no more copies of the Coast Survey Report be sent to the Seceded States.

The following are the telegraphic responses made by the Democratic Governors of North Carolina and Kentucky to the War Department, in reply to the requisitions for troops.

Prominent gentlemen of the Union Party in these States, now here, aver that these Governors misrepresent the people, and have been assured by Secretary CAMERON that the services of independent companies volunteering directly to the Federal Government will be accepted:

RALEIGH, April 15, 1861.

Hon. SIMON CAMERON, Secretary of War: Your dispatch is received, and if genuine, which its extraordinary character leads me to doubt, I have to say in reply that I regard the levy of troops made by the Administration for the purpose of subjugating the States of the South as in violation of the Constitution and a usurpation of power. I can be no party to this wicked violation of the laws of the country, and to this war upon the liberties of a free people. You can get no troops from North Carolina. I will reply more in detail when your call is received by mail.

JOHN W. ELLIS,
Governor of North Carolina.

FRANKFORT, Ky., Tuesday, April 16.

Hon. SIMON CAMERON, Secretary of War:

Your dispatch is received. In answer, I say emphatically that Kentucky will furnish no troops for the wicked purpose of subduing her Sister Southern States.

B. MAGOFFIN, Governor of Kentucky.

It appears by a telegraphic dispatch, published in the North Carolina *Rough Notes* newspaper of Monday, that Governor ELLIS sent the following dispatch:

To Capt. CRATON:

Can you take Fort Macon with your Company?

OUR WASHINGTON CORRESPONDENCE.

MILITARY APPEARANCE OF THE METROPOLIS—IMPORTANCE OF PRECAUTIONARY MEASURES—THE CAPTURE OF FORT SUMTER—EFFECT UPON THE BORDER STATES, ETC.

WASHINGTON, Monday, April 15, 1861.

The regular force concentrated at this point, with the volunteers and militia, which are being enlisted and drilled for active service, give to the Federal Metropolis quite a military appearance, and remind one of the accounts we read of the European Capitals, in which almost every third man to be met in the streets is a soldier. The revolt of our Southern aristocracy against the people is thus producing effects not dissimilar in outward aspect from those which result from the arbitrary Governments of the Old World, in which the people have no control, and against which they are prone to revolt. The importance of preserving the Seat of Government and the public archives fully warrants and even demands these precautionary measures; but to my mind they give ample assurance of safety. It would be simply impossible for the rebels to surprise the Government, and seize the Capital, before thousands of reinforcements could be brought here from the Free States. There may be in the rowdyism of Baltimore elements of danger to the peace of Washington, but on the side of Virginia I see no reason to apprehend dangers which cannot be intercepted by forces now here. The gentlemen of Virginia have the qualities which fit them for command, but they have around them none of the materials which are necessary to constitute the rank and file of an army. Every gentleman expects to be an officer, while the inferior classes are either too indolent or too proud to serve in the ranks, or too degraded to make efficient soldiers. The Western Virginians are a hardy race, but luckily they are friends of the Union, and may be safely relied upon to repel an invasion of the Capital by the rebels from the Confederate States.

The great majority of the people of Washington, being friends of the Union, are deeply mortified at the capture of Fort Sumter. All day yesterday there was a prevalent indisposition to believe the reports from Charleston; but this morning, when no loop remains to hang a doubt upon, consolation is found in the Proclamation of the President, which gives assurance that the Government will be maintained and the rebels punished for their temerity.

It remains to be seen what will be the effect of the recent events upon the Border States. If the Union men remain firm—if they show a spirit of true attachment and loyalty to the Government bequeathed to them by their fathers, the Administration should apportion at least ten thousand of the militia or volunteers called for to them, and commit the protection of the public property within the limits of these States to their hands. By this policy confidence will be inspired, the cause of Union will be strengthened, and the irritation natural to be expected from the introduction of Northern, or even regular soldiers, would be avoided. Intelligent men in the military service, as well as civilians, concur in the opinion that this will be the true policy of the Government. There is great danger that the collision at Charleston, and the call for troops, will strengthen the Secession feeling in the Border States, but they will, at the same time, have the good effect of drawing the line unmistakably between the genuine friends of the Union and those so-called Unionists who are perpetually insisting upon "additional guarantees."

I conversed this morning with an intelligent Virginian from Norfolk, who informs me that the workmen employed in the Navy-yard at that place are firm friends of the Union, and may be relied upon to resist an attempt on the part of the Secessionists to seize the Yard. They comprehend the nature of Southern society well enough to see that a Southern Confederacy would have but little use for a navy, and little use for their labor. They say that the South is an agricultural country, without manufactures or commerce, and that such a country could ill afford the expense of a naval establishment; and, in fact, would have little use for one. This spirit among a large and useful body of men, located at the right point, should be fostered.

The recapture of the Charleston forts is regarded by military men as a task of herculean proportions. With Forts Moultrie, Sumter and Pinckney, and the batteries on the shore, with a bar at the mouth of the harbor, and with the malaria of tropical marshes, an attacking force will have to encounter obstacles which might challenge the most formidable military Power. It is evident from the tone of the Proclamation, that the President will refrain from taking advantage of the peculiar social organization which exists in South Carolina. A foreign enemy would not hesitate to assail the Confederate States in this, their weakest point, and there cannot be a shadow of doubt as to the result of such tactics; but the humane and paternal spirit which actuates the Government in its efforts to chastise the rebellion of misguided citizens, forbids the adoption of a course which would be fatal to a whole section of the country, and equally disastrous to the law-abiding and to the rebellious.

It is probable that under these circumstances the Government will adopt, as it regards Fort Sumter, the policy of blockading the entrance to the harbor, in place of besieging the fortresses. The effect of a blockade would be to destroy the commerce of Charleston, and at the same time protect the public revenue. The Secessionists would have no remedy against this policy. They have no naval fleets or sailors, and no means of resistance. The consequence would be the transfer of the trade of the State to Wilmington, in North Carolina.

The same policy of blockade should be extended to Savannah, Mobile, New-Orleans, Galveston, and other points where it is practicable to import foreign goods; and its effect must be the speedy reduction of the Seceded States. The whole external commerce of the Confederate States, under such a system would be destroyed, and they would be indebted to the adjacent ports of the loyal States, or to the navigation of the Upper Mississippi and Ohio for whatever they have hitherto received, either from Europe direct, or from the North by coasting vessels. In the meantime, the large military force which has been called for will be amply sufficient to retake and reinforce the forts and arsenals which are in any way essential to the control of the outlets to the sea, and to protect and defend the friends of the Union in the disaffected States whenever they may call for assistance.

OBSERVER.

IMPORTANT FROM CHARLESTON.

A Reliable Account of the Commencement of Hostilities.

Experience of the Times Correspondent as a Prisoner of War.

From Our Special Correspondent.

WASHINGTON, Tuesday, April 16, 1861.

At last safe at the Federal Capital, which will not remain so long, if the North does not arouse itself from its inertia. I will take up the thread of my narrative, which was so rudely broken off by the infamous arrest, alluded to by telegram.

A witness of the cannonading of Fort Sumter for six hours, and having had a full description of it by gentlemen who witnessed it up to Saturday at 2 P. M., I can perhaps give a far more accurate account of it than the absurd ones sent North by the telegraph. After mailing my letter of April 11, I investigated all the points of interest in the city, found the Battery crowded with ladies, who remained there all night; the city, constantly patrolled by mounted volunteers and infantry in large numbers; while at Gen. PICKENS' and Gen. BEAUREGARD's head-quarters there was evidence of intense activity. At 1 A. M. I repaired to the long Adger Pier, and there, mounted on a cotton bale, I quietly awaited the opening gun, armed only with an opera glass. My sole companion was a fair young girl, a bride of only three months, who, with her little brother, awaited the opening of the war. Her husband had left her to join the Palmetto Guards, and she shed bitter tears as the day slowly dawned. At 10 minutes past 6 o'clock precisely, the first shot was fired from the Five-mortar Battery on James' Island, followed in quick succession by the Iron Battery at Cumming's Point, the Floating Battery, Fort Moultrie, and the one at Mount Pleasant. At 6 A. M., Dr. ROBERTSON, an intimate, personal and professional friend, hurriedly approached me and inquired if Fort Sumter had opened fire. At 6½ o'clock precisely, the first gun was fired from Fort Sumter, directed at Stevens' Point, and soon the conflict became general on either side. The sun rose on as beautiful a morning as the world has ever seen, but soon the clouds gathered thick and fast, and nature poured forth her torrents as though frowning on the infamous spectacle. At times, the fort was completely hidden from view, yet the iron hail sped on its murderous work, and the distinctive sounds of shot and shell could be clearly marked out as they cut the thin air with fearful rapidity.

Whenever the haze lifted, I could discover the sacred flag of our country proudly spreading itself to the breeze. Although the shot fell around it thick and fast, yet it seemed to possess an absolute power of intangibility, and nothing could disturb it. The scene was solemn in the extreme. Even the crowd that now lined the wharf forbore, hushed the rude jest, and seemed at last to comprehend that war was at last inaugurated, and that, too, by South Carolina.

Dropping for a time the account of my arrest as a "Federal Spy," let me assure your readers that Sumter was not "enveloped in flames" at any time; that the men were not sent out on a raft to collect water to extinguish the fire, simply because there was plenty of the article inside; that the fort was not breached at all, and that it was not a blackened mass of ruins when the curtain dropped on the last act of the tragedy. No boat left Morris Island with a United States flag for Major ANDERSON when his own was shot away, simply because the Morris Island boys had no such flag to offer. They so hate the Stars and Stripes that they would have sooner been bitten by the moccasins of their own swamps than touch an emblem of the country they have cast off. It was a pretty telegraphic fiction, but very false. Major ANDERSON surrendered simply because *he found that the fort could not continue the siege for any length of time.* He found that the United States vessels were not coming in, and he wished to prevent a useless shedding of blood. The paper warriors may accuse him of cowardice, but a purer, truer, more honest man does not walk this world. Now for the arrest.

I left the Adger Pier at half-past ten, and proceeded to my rooms in King street to obtain a little refreshment before returning to my labors. While thus employed, I heard the hurried tread of armed men on the stairs, and then a hasty knock; when I opened the door I saw a crowd of ten rough customers armed with revolvers which protruded from their coats. On asking what this meant, and by what authority they acted, they pointed to their six shooters as a sufficient warrant for their proceedings. They had evidently fortified their courage with copious glasses of whisky, and expected a terrific combat with that peaceable gentleman, the TIMES' correspondent. To gain time for thought I invited them all in, and requested them to partake of the hospitalities of my private locker. Abashed at my quiet manner, they seemed inclined to back out, and all but one went down stairs. He informed me that I was arrested by order of the Government of South Carolina, being suspected of furnishing information to the Federal Government at Washington, and that I must go to the Guard-house. He would not permit me to call on friends who could have effectually disposed of this false charge, but hurried me off. Arriving at the office, I was ordered to take off every article of value, watch, purse, pocket-book, etc. Even private letters from dear friends were consigned to his black list, and then I was thoroughly thumped and percussed, to see if I had any secret pockets, with cyphers, etc. I was thrust into a foul dungeon reeking with bad rum and worse tobacco, and my only couch a couple of blankets black with filth and alive with vermin. By standing on extreme tiptoe on the end of the lounge, I could just look out on the yard, where I could hear the policemen talking about the spy they had just got hold of. One of them said that I would probably be hung the next morning at sunrise in the prison yard, and the frequent sound of the hammer during the night gave extreme plausibility to this supposition. This was probably deliberately intended to torture me. Another said that the Cadets of the Citadel would have a drum-head court-martial on me as soon as Sumter was surrendered, and that I would be shot by a platoon at their encampment, adding that I was particularly obnoxious to them because I spoke in one of my letters of their *impertinence* in firing into the *Star of the West.* Another, a brutal wretch, whom I afterwards recognized as that of an Ex-Municipal Policeman under Mayor WOOD, said that he had heard that the Government meant to make an example of me and shoot me, *à la Sepoy* from the mouth of a sixty-four pounder. With these remarks close under my window, with the infernal cannonading of Fort Sumter brought close to my ears by the fresh inland breeze, and surrounded by rats, mice, bedbugs, and other vermin, I passed the night.

I found from the conversation of those men that I had been under their constant surveillance for the past three months, and that they had orders to bring the TIMES daily to the leading officials of Charleston. Pacing my cell, unable to sleep, worn out with constant duty for the last fifty-two hours, at last the morning dawned. At 9 o'clock I was waited upon by a somewhat cheery-faced official, who facetiously asked me if I felt hungry. I told him that he must be aware that I had not tasted food for *twenty four hours*, and that I had come to the conclusion that the chivalrous people of Charleston meant to reduce me by a slow process of starvation. He seemed ashamed of the acts of his superiors, and said I should not suffer for food. He cooked a nice breakfast, and brought it himself, leading me to infer that he was not a brute, if his masters were. At 10 the under keeper came, and I told him that it was an infamous disgrace to the people of Charleston to thrust a gentleman into a reeking cell, intended only for drunken Irish and negroes, and promised him that if he would work for me he would not lose anything by it. At 12 he brought a man who said he had orders from Gov. PICKENS to send me away from the city *at once.* I urged him to let me call on my banker's, and get some funds, but he peremptorily declined, and said that if the soldiers saw me in the streets, they would certainly tear me in pieces. At the office they returned my property, minus that famous editorial "Wanted a Policy," a piece of petty larceny which I did not think South Carolina would be guilty of. I found that they had examined everything. Among the articles were several clippings from the *bogus* Charleston correspondence of the *Tribune*, wherein I was charged with being a Secessionist. These must have nonplussed them exceedingly. Forcing me to thrust my things in my trunks in the most hurried manner, I was conveyed to the Northeastern Railroad Station, with only $15 to take me to New-York. I expected that I would be spotted on the road by the self-appointed bloodhounds, and took measures accordingly. I felt sure that South Carolina knew that if an open and avowed correspondent of the leading daily sheet of the North was murdered openly in the streets of Charleston, that the act would damn her in the eyes of the whole civilized world; but she had not the slightest compunctions about telegraphing to every leading station North, South, East and West in the C. S. A. to "catch, mob, seize, hold and possess, at any hazard, the body of *Jasper.*" I determined, therefore, to openly state to all interrogatories that I was from Charleston, and bound to New-York. I surmised that this would throw them off their guard, as they would naturally suppose that the man they were in search of would not dare to avow this. It answered admirably. Ten miles from the city a well-dressed man, with a very suspicious air, approached and asked as follows:

STRANGER—Are you the TIMES correspondent?

JASPER—No, Sir. My impression is that he is still in jail, in fact Gov. PICKENS told me so just before I left the city.

S.—Ah, you know Gov. PICKENS?

J.—Oh yes, very well.

S.—I beg your pardon, Sir. I evidently have made a great mistake. But don't you think he is abroad?

J.—I do not. (*Exit Mr. Nonplussed.*)

Just beyond, four old men were seated whom I recognized as members of the Convention that had just adjourned, and also ex-Members of Congress, who had fed freely from the Federal pap. They were slightly winy, and at every station ran out and shouted to the crazy crowd, "Fort Sumter is taken, the d—d DOUBLEDAY is killed." As they were talking very loudly, I resolved, as my life was in imminent danger, to listen closely. The most bloated one of the crowd told his companions that he was sure I was the man—he would swear to it. "It would not do for us old fellows to be engaged in it, but let us pass him on, and if the Vigilants catch him at the next station by God they'll hang him to the first tree." At Florence, where we stopped for supper, I found that every one was rudely staring at me, and therefore thought it expedient not to expose myself. I had just obtained a seat, when several ruffians approached, and the spokesman said, "Will you give me your name, Sir, your business, where you come from, and where you are going? It is necessary that you should do so, and see to it that you speak the truth; if you don't you will swing for it. Answer every question." I then went through another set of questions; they made me stand up, and examined my points as they would a slave at the "Mart." They could elicit nothing. I have not been in Charleston three months for nothing, and parried every question. The whistle sounded, and they hurried off, swearing "that there was something wrong about me, but they'd be d——d if I hadn't bluffed them somehow." Intolerably disgusted with this last exhibition of Palmetto chivalry, I determined to put on a "secession cap," give my moustache a Southern twist, and rant about secession with every one that came along. At every station, until I reached the United States of North Carolina, the spies came in, but I had foiled them fully by this last arrangement, and reached Wilmington, N. C., in safety. I wish here to thank, in the warmest manner, Mr. FANNING, of the telegraph office, and Mr. PRICE, of the *Daily Journal*, for their courtesies, material and otherwise. Mr. F. said that telegrams had been sent to all points of the compass, and he evidently thought that I had had a narrow escape.

It was painful to witness the secession mania cropping out so strong along the entire length of the Railroad in North Carolina and Virginia. At every station the question was "Is Sumter taken?" and when the response was "yes," they danced with joy.

I have called on Mr. LINCOLN; also on Gov. SEWARD and Gen. SCOTT. Mr. LINCOLN still exhausts himself in appointments, and the old hero of Mexico works night and day. In conversation with a member of his Staff, who superintended the plans for the construction of Fort Sumter, he assured me that no breach could have been made in the walls in so short a time. He evidently approved of the course of Major ANDERSON, and led me to infer that Gen. SCOTT fully indorsed his movements. Let the infamous maligners of the hero of Sumter take a note of this.

In glancing at the first real stab to the Republic has received in the inauguration of civil war, as openly invited by South Carolina, I would observe that the boasted victory of ten thousand men arrayed against 65 artillerists, 15 musicians, 9 officers and 30 laborers, divested of all gasconade and flummery, is simply a very paltry and contemptible conquest, after all.

I went to Charleston with the kindest feelings towards the South and her people. I have buffeted for them the wave of Northern fanatics. I have stated facts that frequently put them in a much higher light at the North. I was helping earnestly in the good work of recementing peaceful feelings between the two sections. They received me cordially, and promised me the most ample protection. In my hour of need, when madmen were trying to kill me, they stood aloof and lifted not a finger in my defence. Was this brave, was it manly, was it chivalric? Was it not rather low, contemptible and infamous? In the Crimea and in the Italian war the person of a correspondent was as sacred as that of the priest ministering to the dying on the battle-field. It has been left for the State that prides herself on her chivalry to inaugurate a system that would disgrace His Sable Majesty the Cannibal of Dahomey, who kills six men every morning, by way of a slight appetizer.

Has the so called Gamecock State any apology to make for this low-bred and vile outrage?

JASPER.

LATEST DISPATCHES FROM CHARLESTON.

CHARLESTON, Tuesday, April 16.

The Federal fleet stopped three vessels coming in last evening, one with the Spanish flag, one with the British, and the other with the American. They were detained a short time and then allowed to proceed. The fleet determined to interfere no more until orders were received from Washington.

Troops continue to pour in from all parts of the States. Half-disciplined as many of them are, they undergo rigid drills. It is estimated that there are 10,000 in and about the city. Three regiments are encamped near the Race Course, and two at Rikersville, three miles beyond.

Gen. BEAUREGARD is very active—strengthening every position. He has offers of regiments from Alabama and Georgia, but the Carolinians are so eager to serve that he declines any other aid. He says he can get 50,000 men from this State. At Columbia every man, from 16 to 60, is under arms. Ten companies from the State Capital are now here.

It is thought by good authority that there is no doubt but the British Government will recognize Southern Independence at a very early day. The same is true of France.

The *Isabel* has just come into port from the outside. She brings the information that the Federal fleet has weighed anchor and sailed, in company with the *Baltic*, for New-York.

The *Baltic* has Major ANDERSON and command aboard.

THE WAR EXCITEMENT.

NEW-YORK.

TROY, N. Y., Tuesday, April 16.

At the immense demonstration in this city last evening in favor of the Stars and Stripes, a motion was made to adjourn in a body to the residence of Gen. WOOL, where, on behalf of the citizens, an address was made by MARTIN J. TOWNSEND, to which Gen. WOOL responded that his heart was rejoiced at this glorious demonstration of patriotism. Never, by any former compliment bestowed upon him, had he been thrilled by such a measure of joy. It is true that he had fought under the old flag, but he had done no more than his duty towards the best Government that ever existed. He had fought under the Stars and Stripes that were carried in triumph by WASHINGTON and under which JACKSON closed the second war for independence at New-Orleans in a halo of glory. Will you permit that flag to be desecrated and trampled in the dust by traitors now? Will you permit our noble Government to be destroyed by rebels in order that they may advance their schemes of political ambition and extend the area of Slavery? No, indeed, it cannot be done. The spirit of the age forbids it. Humanity and manhood forbid it, and the sentiments of the civilized world forbid it. My friend, that flag must be lifted up from the dust into which it has been trampled, placed in its proper position and again set floating in triumph to the breeze. I pledge you my heart, my hand, all my energies to the cause. The Union shall be maintained. I am prepared to devote my life to the work and to lead you in the struggle. [Deafening applause, cheers for the Union and Gen. WOOL.]

ALBANY, Tuesday, April 16.

The excitement about war continues to-day, although a heavy rain-storm prevails.

Last night, Senators SPINOLA, CONNOLLY and others, were serenaded by Democrats and Republicans for their votes on the war bill.

To-day a dispatch addressed to THOMAS C. FIELDS was read in both Houses, stating that a crowd had been at the New-York *Herald* office and compelled them to hoist the American flag, and that the *Herald* was out for the Union. The reading of the dispatch was received with loud applause.

POUGHKEEPSIE, N. Y., Tuesday, April 16.

A meeting of the military of this city will be held this evening.

AUBURN, N. Y., Tuesday, April 16.

An artillery company is rapidly filling up in this city. The Forty-ninth Regiment, under Col. RICHARDSON, will be immediately filled up to its full complement of ten companies of 100 men each. The war spirit is fully aroused in this city. The stars and stripes are flying in all directions, and all parties are in favor of sustaining the Government.

PENNSYLVANIA.

PHILADELPHIA, Tuesday, April 16.

This afternoon a mob of a couple of hundred boys visited the residence of JOSIAH RANDALL, he bringing out the American flag. They then formed in procession to march to the residence of WM. B. REED.

Mayor HENRY started in pursuit, and met them on the route. The Chief of Police arrested the ringleader. The Mayor then addressed the crowd, and ordered them to disperse, stating that this reckless spirit had gone too far, and that he would permit no further indulgence of it. He cautioned them that if it was necessary to take life to accomplish the preservation of peace that extremity would be resorted to.

The crowd scattered, and it is not probable that their demonstrations will be renewed.

P. G. WATMOUGH and L. P. ASHMEAD, formerly Lieutenants in the United States Navy, who resigned years ago on account of entering into other avocations, though now wealthy, have tendered their services to the Secretary of the Navy, prompted by love for the Union.

Mayor HENRY has issued a proclamation declaring that treason against the Union will not be permitted, nor will violence to persons or property of inhabitants be tolerated. He requires all good citizens to make known every person aiding the enemy by enlisting men or furnishing munitions of war or provisions. The laws of the State and Federal Government must be obeyed, and the peace and credit of the city shall be preserved. May God save the Union.

The State Legislature has enacted a law making any connivance with the enemy's Government punishable with $5,000 fine and ten years' imprisonment.

The Second Regiment of the Second Brigade, Col. CONROY commanding, tendered their services to the Government this evening. They are one thousand strong. This Regiment comprises the Irish companies of the city, and its prompt response to the call shows the injustice of the suspicions created against its commander. These suspicions against prominent officers of the State Militia have been shown to be unfounded, as well as many other instances, since the President's Proclamation, all seeming to cheerfully respond in the hour of danger.

TRENTON, Tuesday, April 16.

Our city continues to be quite excited. Gov. OLDEN has ordered Company A, of the City Battalion, to the State Arsenal, under apprehensions that the arms would be taken away. Some think the apprehensions are generally groundless. A crowd with a drum and fife are marching through the streets to-night. An attack on the *True American* office is apprehended, because the American flag is not displayed.

WESTCHESTER, Penn., Tuesday, April 16.

A large meeting was held here last night, in response to a call for military. The meeting was addressed by JOHN HICKMAN and other prominent men. Major WYCK offered to raise a company. Rolls for enlistment received numerous signatures, and money was collected for their equipment.

POTTSVILLE, Pa., Tuesday, April 16.

Several Companies have responded to the President's proclamation. A Company of Light Infantry and the Washington Artillery leave to-morrow for Harrisburgh and Washington.

The citizens are preparing to raise funds to aid the families of volunteers.

CARLISLE, Tuesday, April 16.

Adjutant HULBERT, by order of Capt. BENROSE, has issued a call for volunteers of Cumberland County.

READING, Pa., Tuesday, April 16.

The Ringgold Flying Artillery of Reading, Capt. JAMES MCKNIGHT, 120 men, with four field pieces, received a requisition from the Governor this morning, to set out this evening, at 6 o'clock, for Harrisburgh, to place a rendezvous for the first Pennsylvanians in the field.

There was a large and enthusiastic Government meeting at Tyrone, Blair Co., to-night. Speeches were enthusiastically received. Ex-Senator BIGLER arrived after the adjournment, and expressed himself unequivocally for the Government and he was determined to sustain it to the last. Two military companies from Tyrone, two from Altoona, and two from Hollidaysburgh, will leave to-morrow for Harrisburgh.

ERIE, Penn., Tuesday, April 16.

A large meeting of citizens, irrespective of party, was held here last evening. Resolutions were adopted pledging the hearts and hands of Erie City and County to maintain the integrity of the Government and honor of the Flag.

The Wayne Guards of Erie and other companies will offer their services to the Governor.

MASSACHUSETTS.

BOSTON, Tuesday, April 16—P. M.

In accordance with the call of the Commander-in-Chief of the companies comprising the four Regiments ordered to report for service in this City, they commenced arriving before 9 A. M. this morning, the companies first arriving not having received their orders until last night. Already about 30 companies have arrived, numbering over 1,700 men in uniform, and with these are several hundred who are importunate to be allowed to join the ranks.

Notwithstanding the cold, a northeast rain has been falling all day. The streets are crowded, and the appearance of a Company on its march from the dépôt to Faneuil Hall, is the signal for the most enthusiastic cheers. The various Companies are quartered in Fanuel Hall and other large buildings, and their wants are amply provided for by the Adjutant and Quartermaster-General, as well as by the Governor's Aid. The outfits of the troops have commenced arriving from the Arsenal, and to-morrow each man will be provided with the necessary articles for active service.

The troops are a fine-looking body of men, and are in the best of spirits, all eager to hasten to where their services may be needed.

The bark *Manhattan*, which arrived here this forenoon from Savannah, had a secession flag hoisted. A crowd proceeded to the wharf, and compelled Capt. DAVIS to take it down, and hoist the Stars and Stripes.

The Board of Aldermen have tendered Faneuil Hall for the quarters of the Massachusetts Volunteers until their departure for service. The Stars and Stripes are now floating from the old Cradle of Liberty.

LAWRENCE, Tuesday, April 16.

Our City Government this morning appropriated $5,000 for the benefit of the families of those who have volunteered to defend the country's flag.

CONNECTICUT.

NEW-HAVEN, Tuesday, April 16.

The Mechanics' Bank, of this City, this morning tendered to Gov. BUCKINGHAM $25,000 for the use of the State in supporting the National Government.

The Elm City Bank has just tendered to the Governor of the State $50,000 towards meeting the present National emergency, with liberty to draw at sight.

NEW-HAVEN, Tuesday, April 16.

The Directors of the Mechanics' Bank of this city this morning unanimously voted to offer $25,000 to the Governor of the State to aid him in equipping and moving any forces he may be called upon to furnish in defence of the Government.

The Elm City Bank has this day telegraphed to Gov. BUCKINGHAM to draw at sight on them for $50,000 for the same purpose.

The Fairfield County Bank has offered $20,000, and a private gentleman $50,000.

NORWICH, Conn., Tuesday, April 16.

Gov. BUCKINGHAM has issued a proclamation calling for volunteers, to rendezvous at Hartford. The Thames Bank, of this city, have just voted to tender $100,000 to Gov. BUCKINGHAM, to assist in equipping the troops in support of the Government.

NORWALK, Monday, April 16.

The Fairfield County Bank has offered $50,000 to Gov. BUCKINGHAM.

NEW-HAMPSHIRE.

CONCORD, N. H., Tuesday, April 16.

New-Hampshire responds to the President's proclamation, and will furnish the troops required. The Concord Union Bank has tendered a loan of $20,000 to the Governor, and all the Directors, with the Cashier, agree to contribute $100 each to the support of such families of the volunteers of this city as may fall in defending the flag of the country.

NEW-JERSEY.

The people of Hudson County are becoming thoroughly aroused in regard to national difficulties, and they stand united in their determination to support the Federal Government, and in Hudson County alone nearly or quite the *quota* of men required from the State can be raised.

Brigadier-Gen. HATFIELD, not having the authority to offer the services of the Brigade to the General Government uninstructed, has called a meeting of the representatives of the several companies on Friday evening next, to consult and determine what duty and honor require of them under the circumstances. The meeting will be held at the Hudson House, Jersey City.

E. C. HOPPER, Captain of Company B, Second Regiment, has called a meeting of his Company at the Hudson House, on Thursday evening next, to take action in reference to offering their services to the Government.

On Monday afternoon, a coasting schooner was discovered lying in the bay, with a Palmetto flag flying at its masthead. A party of "glass-house boys" procured a boat, and proceeding to the vessel, ordered the Captain to lower the flag and substitute in its place the Stars and Stripes. The Captain refused, when they threatened to pitch him overboard and sink the vessel. The American flag was soon spread out to the breeze, when it was heartily cheered and the Palmetto was stowed away below.

A Union meeting was held last night at the Hudson House, in Jersey City, for the purpose of taking action to raise volunteers, whose services are to be tendered to the Federal Government. J. W. SCUDDER, Esq., was chosen President; two Vice-Presidents from each Ward were also chosen, and C. H. DUMARS acted as Secretary. At the head of the hall was displayed a large American flag, together with the portraits of Gen. GEORGE WASHINGTON, Gen. SCOTT and HENRY CLAY. The following-named gentlemen were appointed a Committee to prepare resolutions to be presented at a future meeting: Thomas R. Potter, John H. Low, Hon. Samuel A. French, David Smith, Chas. A. Woolsey and J. O. Rouse.

A motion was adopted authorizing the above Committee to confer with the Minute Men, who have called a meeting with a view of concert in action.

Col. GREGORY, of the Second Regiment, said that the quota of men for New-Jersey was four regiments of 780 men each, and that about one half of these were to be raised in Hudson and Essex Counties. It was the intention of the Hudson Brigade to volunteer *en masse.*

A motion, by Mr. POTTER, to open a roll for signatures, was received with applause, and adopted.

Stirring speeches were made by Dr. H. D. HOLT, Hon. N. C. SLAIGHT, BENJAMIN VAN RIPER and JOHN H. LOW.

During the speaking cheers were given for the Stars and Stripes, the Federal Government, Major ANDERSON, &c.

BENJAMIN VAN RIPER advocated the striking down of every Northern man who advocated secession, and all traitorous newspapers.

Mr. JOHN LOW proposed that at some future period they call upon the proprietors of the *American Standard*, in Jersey City, the editors of which had so much maligned the Government, and make them hoist the American flag, or make them leave the town." This proposition was received with tremendous cheering, and cries of "Let's do it to-night." The roll was then opened, and thirty names were signed. In a few minutes. Three groans were given for "JEFF. DAVIS," after which cries were made to go to the *Standard* office. After the adjournment a crowd of about 200 persons went around in front of the *Standard* office, where they hooted and yelled, and demanded that a flag be hung out, and threats to sack the office were freely made. Nothing further than yelling and groaning was done, and the party promised to come again if the flag was not displayed to-day (Wednesday.) The mob also went around to the house of one of the proprietors, and there made a noisy demonstration.

The Hudson Guards met last night in Cooper Hall, Jersey City, for preliminary action, with a view of offering their services to the country.

The Directors of the Bank of Jersey City had a

[Continued on Eighth Page.]

The Charleston Mercury.

VINDICE NULLO
SPONTE SUA SINE LEGE FIDES RECTUMQUE COLENTUR.

VOLUME LVI. | CHARLESTON, S. C., WEDNESDAY, APRIL 17, 1861. | NUMBER 11,128

THE MERCURY.

WEDNESDAY, APRIL 17, 1861.

Must We Have War?

The Past makes the Present—the Present, our Future. What is to be the future of the present events which press upon us with their stern and stirring realities?

Our readers know that we have repeatedly declared that we did not believe that a war between the North and the South would be the result of a dissolution of the Union by the secession of the Southern States. With the sound of our cannon still ringing in our ears, we are of the same opinion still.

That the brutal fanatics who sit in the high places at Washington are ready to plunge the whole country into contest and blood, we have never doubted. It was a thorough conviction of their treacherous and desperate hatred of the South that compelled us to urge, as the only course of safety for the South, a prompt and eternal separation from their power.

Events have shown that our estimation of this brutal and bloody faction was correct. Large portions of the people of the seceding States did not believe it. The Frontier Slave States have not believed it. They have still believed that there were feelings of respect, feelings of fraternity towards the people of the South, from the great body of the people of the North. Hence they have lingered in the foul embraces of a Union, mastered by Abolitionism, whose one great policy was the subjection of the South to the dominion of the North—whose one great passion was to destroy the South. Slowly but surely time has lifted the veil from the hideous and loathsome features of Abolitionism enthroned in Washington. Its inauguration by cannon and bayonets, manifested at once its *principle* and its *reliance* for success—*despotism* and *force*. OLIVER CROMWELL praying whilst CHARLES the I.'s head was being cut off, was the example of its bloody hypocrisy.

With LINCOLN's Proclamation, and his requisition for troops to march upon the South, the standard for the conquest of the South is at last unfurled. Thirty years' agitation and hate at last breaks forth in its eager cries for blood. It is most natural. Thank God, the consummation is in our day, whilst we have yet the power to resist—the capacity to save ourselves from its meditated devastation, insurrection and horrors.

But will Northern hate and fanaticism fail in its prey? Will it not at least carry through the South one long track of blood, which will tell to future ages its fierce invasion and stern efforts for conquest? We answer no!

Fortunately for the world, it is never all mad. The first great result of the meditated invasion of the South, will be to unite the South together. United together, the South is invincible. The North knows this as well as the South. On this account, we rejoice at the late demonstrations in Charleston Bay, and the war policy declared at Washington. Virginia will soon be with us; and the other Frontier States will follow her lead. They are forced to take sides, by the Abolition Government at Washington. They must help to conquer us, or aid us in our defence. We cannot doubt the result. The miserable fanatics and charletans at Washington are pursuing the very course of policy we most earnestly desire them to pursue, and will defeat and destroy their power for evil in the effort to exercise it. We deprecate war; but we frankly confess, that if war is necessary to consolidate the South, it is far preferable to the Slaveholding States being divided. It is very far preferable to a mixed Confederacy of Slave and Free States. The demonstration of war upon the South will, however, prevent war, by raising up such a power to meet it, through a united South, as will ensure its defeat. War between the North and the South can only exist by the Frontier Slave States joining the North against the South; and this we deem an impossibility.

But will not Fort Pickens be held like Fort Sumter? and will we not be compelled to shell them out? Yes! But this will not be war. Will not our coast be blockaded? Very probably. But this will be war on sea, where we cannot reach them. But a campaign war—a war of invasion for conquest, by the North against the South, we do not expect to see. It will be most fatal to the interest of the North, whilst it may be most beneficial to the South in uniting them together in one *exclusive* destiny; but, in our judgment, it will never take place. War or no war, the Confederate States are equal to the great enterprise they have assumed, of protecting their rights, liberties and institutions.

Abolition Anticipations.

We publish to-day the editorial of the New York *Tribune* on the "approaching conflict" in the Bay of Charleston, to reinforce Fort Sumter. By this time the *Tribune* will have learned that its vaticinations may sometimes prove incorrect. The first great requisite in successful war, is to appreciate your enemy as he deserves. Neither the Government at Washington, nor the wretched fanatics who support its policy, seem to understand the people of the South. Their contempt, from our long submission to their insulting aggressions, blinds them to a true estimate of our characteristics. Hence they bully and boast, and receive the fate of pretensious fools and bullies. The discreet commanders of the 2500 soldiers in the fleet off our bar understand the difficulties of their position; and to the infinite chagrin and mortification of our infantry on Morris Island, have declined to land their troops, or make any attempt to reinforce Fort Sumter. They would have been, in all probability, utterly destroyed. What a pity the Editor of the *Tribune* had not been in command, to carry out his well conceived military operations! or that "eminent soldier who planned the expedition!"—what a pity!

Our Washington Correspondence.

WASHINGTON, April 14.

Abolition Astonishment—The Accounts of the Bombardment—Growth of the Secession Feeling in Washington—Discomfiture at Willard's Hotel—Anderson Stock Low—The Snubbing of the Virginia Commissioners, etc., etc.

Yesterday morning all Washington was startled by the report of the first day's operations in the reduction of Fort Sumter. The Black Republicans were quite taken aback. For a week past their swollen pride and insolence here has been intolerable. Many of them were fully of the opinion that at the first appearance of the Federal armada South Carolina would back down, and the whole difficulty be settled by an absolute submission to the Federal power. Hence, a report, *via* New York, that President DAVIS had given orders "not to fire upon the storeship for Sumter," found a ready credence. But whether resistance was made or not, all the Republicans looked forward to an easy and assured triumph. Even Southern men felt somewhat uneasy and apprehensive as to the result. The great strength of Sumter and the skill of ANDERSON's officers and men, the difficulties of a combined attack by a fleet, and a body of 2500 to 3000 regular troops—taking the Confederate troops in separate divisions—were difficulties calculated to make the most sanguine of our friends here wish the fight were over and the victory won. Such, to speak frankly, were my own feelings. The accounts of the first day's bombardment dispelled most of these apprehensions, and showed plainly enough our friends had the enemy at a disadvantage.

During yesterday Southern men began to be hopeful—Republicans doubtful; and when, in the evening, the news got out that the flag of the Confederate States was waving over Sumter, the whole town was in a ferment. Secessionists who have been "under the weather" all through the winter and spring, became all of a sudden as "plenty as blackberries." *Silent sympathisers* for long months with the South began to enquire how they could become members of the "National Volunteers," a military organization which has stood alone in the city with the secession flag unfurled. At the date of this writing the secession party here is growing so fast that I question much whether, in a few days, THE MERCURY will be ultra enough to suit them.

The Black Republicans are shaken up amazingly. Last night they refused to believe the news. It was not true. LINCOLN had got despatches from Charleston (of all places in the world!) that the United States flag was waving over Sumter. Army and navy men did not understand how so strong a fortress could fall in thirty-six hours. It was absurd and impossible. So the Black Republicans retired, uneasy and incredulous, to their "virtuous couches." LINCOLN and his confidential advisers held a stew over it up to one o'clock at night; when, unable to fix up things to his satisfaction, he retired to his royal couch.

"Uneasy lies the head that wears a crown."

But sometimes the tongue *lies* easy enough, *vide* the "pacific" mission of Capt. FOX and Col. LAMOND to Major ANDERSON.

Sunday morn comes and brings them all no better news. Strolling into "WILLARD's," the Black Republican Headquarters, it was pleasant to note the subdued look of the whole crowd. There was a perceptible want of dash, of hope, of that quality which the French call *elan*. They were evidently meditating profoundly upon the mutability of human affairs. Sumter had *not* "knocked Moultrie into a cocked hat." The batteries at Cummings' Point had *not* been demolished. Five hundred men at Moultrie had *not* been killed. The pleasant rumor of the day before, that Gen. BEAUREGARD had "sent a flag of truce to ask time to bury his dead," had exploded before the lights of telegraphic history. In fact, "nobody was hurt." What a pity! If ANDERSON had only been killed, how it would have excited the Northern feeling! Sumter lost, and the "sympathy dodge" lost, too, at the same time. "Truly Fortune has a spite at us to-day"!

At the door of WILLARD's a group was gathered of Black Republican military *savans*. They had not seen much of actual war, except perhaps a fist-fight between boys, but they had *heard* of battles, and had had dreams of Sumter "shelling Charleston." The latter they had read about in the *Tribune*. War upon women and children to demonstrate that we "have a Government." But albeit, unused to the camp, these gallant men who came here to storm the Secretary's anti-chamber for offices, gave to the listening public *their* views about the Sumter business. As to ANDERSON having done his duty in the premises, that was all humbug. He had been merely pretending to fight. It was all arranged before hand between him and the Charlestonians that they were not to hurt one another. No! ANDERSON was a traitor like all the rest of them. The idea of bombarding each other two days and not killing anybody, was absurd, preposterous and impossible. In point of fact, ANDERSON stock is so low this morning among the Republicans, that I should hesitate to give you the quotations. *Per contra*, the Secessionists have no doubt that he has done all that a brave man could do under the circumstances, and they are now delighted that he is now in a position to get fresh provisions, lamb and greens and green peas, *ad libitum*. Charleston hospitality is no bad article, as I know personally.

You will see, of course, the President has given the Virginia Commissioners a curt and insolent reply to their request to be informed of his intentions. Poor Virginia! Her honor unluckily placed in the hands of men like JOHN LETCHER, STUART and SUMMERS, who each day delight in exposing her to some fresh shame and insult. Her people are a patient, forgiving, long suffering race, or they would take these traitors and hang them to the nearest lamp-post or gallows.

It is hardly possible to tell, yet, what will be the effect of yesterday's proceedings upon the Northern mind. If a battle shall be fought to-day, it will have a great effect in shaping results. My belief is, however, the President will call Congress together and ask for means to push on the war. In the meantime, he will most likely carry on the war so lamely begun.

The President and Cabinet were in session all this morning instead of going to Church. A Coercion Parson, this morning, in the usual prayer for them, put in an extra amount of unction. All right enough. They need it badly. But, he should get ready the prayer for persons undertaking a journey—for old Virginia will soon make LINCOLN's "Scotch Plaid" necessary for his comfort.

SOUTH.

Our New York Correspondence.

NEW YORK, April 13.

The Fort Sumter News in Gotham—Lincoln's Extravagance—The Effect of the Surrender of Sumter—Lincoln's Perfidy—The Mails, etc., etc.

The city, ever since the fire was opened on Fort Sumter, up to the final announcement of its surrender, which occurred at a late hour this afternoon, has been in the greatest state of excitement. Nothing else, scarcely, has been talked about. Tremendous efforts are being made by Black Republican leaders and papers to excite and unite the North against the South, even in this city, whose interest is to be sacrificed to the demoniacal madness of Abolitionism; and, during the present excitement, they may succeed to some extent. But there yet remains among the masses large bodes of people who do not sympathise with Lincoln's government, and who denounce his usurpation of the 'war-making power. A paper is in circulation in favor of calling a meeting to condemn LINCOLN's unconstitutional course. Still the North talks loudly in favor of crushing out the South. You will see that several free States propose offering volunteers to LINCOLN; but this military boasting, after all, appears larger on paper than in reality.

LINCOLN's Government is spending money at a rapid rate. The steamers *Illinois*, *Baltic* and *Atlantic* were chartered at the rates of $2000 per day, and to be found in fuel.

The three steam tug boats, having been heavily loaded with coal, had to encounter the recent gale, which, Captain BERRY states, was the most severe he has witnesed on our coast for two years. They only effected insurance on them at the rate of 4 per cent. per month.

The steamship *Kangaroo* has been detained till Sunday morning, at 6, a. m., for the purpose of carrying the latest news from Charleston to Europe.

No event could have possibly happened, and could have so utterly disappointed and galled the Black Republicans, as the *surrender of Fort Sumter*. The moral effect of your glorious and victorious attack, will be very great, both in this country and in Europe. The next news we hope to hear is the surrender of Fort Pickens to the Confederate troops.

There are several facts showing the treachery and false pretences of LINCOLN's Government, besides that connected with the visit of Mr. FOX to Major ANDERSON. I have received the statement from the highest and most reliable authority, that the Peace article which some time back appeared in the *National Intelligencer* was examined by LINCOLN, and approved by SEWARD and other members of his Cabinet, and fully endorsed by him and his advisers before it appeared in the *Intelligencer*. How completely have they belied all the positions taken by that article!

SIDNEY.

P. S.—It is said that LINCOLN will forthwith stop the Southern mails. Then, the only course for intercourse with this city is that previously suggested to you, which ought to be carried out by the Confederate Government.

The Cabinet of the Confederate States — Attorney-General Benjamin, Secretary Mallory, Secretary Memminger, Vice-President Stephens, Secretary Walker, President Davis, Postmaster Regan, Secretary Toombs

The Charleston Mercury.

VINDICE NULLO SPONTE SUA SINE LEGE FIDES RECTUMQUE COLENTUR.

VOLUME LVI. CHARLESTON, S. C., FRIDAY, APRIL 19, 1861. NUMBER 11,130

THE MERCURY.

FRIDAY, APRIL 19, 1861.

For What Are We Contending?

For more than thirty years the people of South Carolina have been contending against the consolidation of the Government of the United States. Created a Confederation of Republics whose central power, authority and jurisdiction, were carefully limited by the compact of the Constitution, and made conformable to, and within its proper limits, co-ordinate with the original and reserved powers, authority and jurisdiction of the several States of which it was composed, the United States Government has steadily usurped powers not granted—progressively trenched upon State Rights. Not a bald, irresponsible, unchecked, vulgar democracy of mere numbers, was organized by the instrument of Federation between the States; but a well adjusted, duplicate system, harmonious and complementary—the central common Government performing its allotted functions within its prescribed sphere, and each State Government performing all other functions of Government not expressly yielded to the other. If that Government became practically omnipotent, it was clear that it must be a most fearful despotism—a despotism of one section of the Union over the other—a despotism of Manufacing over Agricultural States—of Free States over Slaveholding States. Earnestly and faithfully have our public men at Washington contended against this fatal consummation. It was not for free trade only in 1853—it was not against anti-slavery fanaticism only in 1852—it is not now against our preclusion from our Territories, or the vulgar crew who fill the high places at Washington, that we have set up for ourselves a separate destiny. These are all effects of one great cause—the consolidation of the Federal Government. As *facts*, we have been obliged to meet them—but the facts themselves were comparatively insignificant. They were like the ship money which HAMPDEN refused to pay—like the three pence a pound on tea, which our fathers resisted. They proved to us that we were the slaves of a consolidated despotism—that self government, and the security which self government alone can impart—and liberty, and the princeless self-esteem and proud repose, which liberty only can inspire—were no longer our inheritance or possession. It was in vain that South Carolina endeavored to prove that this despotism existed. We had the forms of a free representative government. There was a party in the Northern States *professing* those principles of limitation and restriction, which might yet be restored to ascendency in the government, and make it again a free government. There was a deep reverence and attachment to the Union, which blinded the understandings of some of the brightest intelligences of the South. These all conspired to carry the South on in the chains of a sectional despotism, which looked, in its final consummation, to nothing short of our absolute subjection and ruin. South Carolina, by her secession, forced the test of the nature of the government under which we lived. It has proved itself. As one scale of hypocrisy after another fell off of its poisonous surface, it stood forth a pure, fierce monster of despotism. The *National Intelligencer*, of Washington, for forty years the central organ of Consolidation, identifies its policy with the New York *Tribune*. BLAIR, the mouth-piece of JACKSON Democracy in 1833, and JOHNSON, of Tennessee, its modern prototype, and DOUGLAS and BUCHANAN, now join with LINCOLN and CHASE and SEWARD in the grand effort to establish, *by the sword*, what has long existed as a policy—*the despotism of a consolidated government under the Constitution of the United States*. The matter is now plain. State after State in the South sees the deadly development, and are moving to take their part in the grand effort to redeem their liberties. It is not a contest for righteous taxation. It is not a contest for the security of slave property. It is a contest for freedom and free government, in which everything dear to man is involved. Shall we submit to the sectional and remorseless despotism of a majority of the Northern States, with no restraints on their lawless will, no checks on their omnivorous rapacity? That is the question. Every man, every boy in the South answers No! And they will fight the foul usurpers and tyrants, if they dare the issue of war, as long as the streams run and the sun shines on our vallies.

Washington City.

We sincerely hope that no effort will be made by citizens of the South to take possession of the city of Washington, and to expel the officials of the Government of the United States from their abodes or offices. If any such effort is made before Virginia and Maryland shall have seceded from the Union of the United States, it will be very disastrous to the cause of secession. It will raise the State pride of the citizens of these proud Commonwealths, who will not be able to see, with indifference, their territories lawlessly invaded and used for an unlawful purpose. And when these States have seceded, it will be for *them* to settle their relations towards Washington. The course of JAMES the Second, we think, will be followed. That Scotch cap and military cloak will again be called into service; and the Black Republican horde, who now defile the high places at Washington, will fly like rats out of a burning barn. Let them go. Do not pollute the soil of Virginia or Maryland with their mean blood. Let them go. To keep them in Washington, after Virginia and Maryland have seceded, you will have to put them in a three-story jail. Do not dignify them by chasing them—much less killing them.

FORT SUMTER.

Official Correspondence Between General Beauregard and Major Anderson, Previous to the Bombardment.

[Copy.]

HEADQUARTERS PROVISIONAL ARMY, C. S. A.,
Charleston, S. C., April 11, 1861—2, p. m.

SIR: The Government of the Confederate States has hitherto forborne from any hostile demonstration against Fort Sumter, in the hope that the Government of the United States, with a view to the amicable adjustment of all questions between the two Governments, and to avert the calamities of war, would voluntarily evacuate it. There was reason at one time to believe that such would be the course pursued by the Government of the United States, and under that impression my Government has refrained from making any demand for the surrender of the fort.

But the Confederate States can no longer delay assuming actual possession of a fortification commanding the entrance of one of their harbors, and necessary to its defence and security.

I am ordered by the Government of the Confederate States to demand the evacuation of Fort Sumter. My Aids, Colonel CHESNUT and Captain LEE, are authorized to make such demand of you. All proper facilities will be afforded for the removal of yourself and command, together with company arms and property, and all private property, to any post in the United States which you may elect. The flag which you have upheld so long and with so much fortitude under the most trying circumstances, may be saluted by you on taking it down.

Colonel CHESNUT and Coptain LEE will, for a reasonable time, await your answer.

I am, sir, very respectfully,
Your obedient servant,
(Signed) G. T. BEAUREGARD,
Brigadier General Commanding.

Major ROBERT ANDERSON, Commanding at Fort Sumter, Charleston Harbor, S. C.

[Copy.]

HEADQUARTERS, FORT SUMTER, S. C.,
April 11th, 1861.

GENERAL: I have the honor to acknowledge the receipt of your communication demanding the evacuation of this fort; and to say in reply thereto that it is a demand with which I regret that my sense of honor and of my obligations to my Government prevent my compliance.

Thanking you for the fair, manly and courteous terms proposed, and for the high compliment paid me,

I am, General, very respectfully,
Your obedient servant,
(Signed) ROBERT ANDERSON,
Major U. S. Army Commanding.

To Brigadier General G. T. BEAUREGARD, commanding Provisional Army C. S. A.

[Copy.]

HEADQUARTERS PROVISIONAL ARMY, C. S. A.,
Charleston, April 11, 1861—11 p. m.

MAJOR: In consequence of the verbal observations made by you to my Aids, Messrs. CHESNUT and LEE, in relation to the condition of your supplies, and that you would in a few days be starved out if our guns did not batter you to pieces—or words to that effect;—and desiring no useless effusion of blood, I communicated both the verbal observation and your written answer to my communication to my Government.

If you will state the time at which you will evacuate Fort Sumter, and agree that in the mean-time you will not use your guns against us, unless ours shall be employed against Fort Sumter, we will abstain from opening fire upon you. Colonel CHESNUT and Captain LEE are authorized by me to enter into such an agreement with you. You are therefore requested to communicate to them an open answer.

I remain, Major, very respectfully,
Your obedient servant,
(Signed) G. T. BEAUREGARD,
Brigadier-General Commanding.

Major ROBERT ANDERSON, Commanding at Fort Sumter, Charleston Harbor, S. C.

[Copy.]

HEADQUARTERS, FORT SUMTER, S. C.,
2.30, a. m., April 12, 1861.

GENERAL: I have the honor to acknowledge the receipt of your second communication of the 11th inst., by Col. CHESNUT, and to state, in reply, that cordially uniting with you in the desire to avoid the useless effusion of blood, I will, if provided with the proper and necessary means of transportation, evacuate Fort Sumter by noon on the 15th instant, should I not receive, prior to that time, controlling instructions from my Government, or additional supplies; and that I will not, in the mean time, open my fire upon your forces, unless compelled to do so by some hostile act against this fort or the flag of my Government by the forces under your command, or by some portion of them, or by the perpetration of some act showing a hostile intention on your part against this fort or the flag it bears.

I have the honor to be, General,
Very respectfully,
Your obedient servant.
(Signed) ROBERT ANDERSON,
Major U. S. A. Commanding.

To Brigadier General G. T. BEAUREGARD, Commanding Provisional Army C. S. A.

[Copy.]

FORT SUMTER, S. C., April 12, 1861,
3.20 a. m.

SIR: By authority of Brigadier General BEAUREGARD, commanding the Provisional Forces of the Confederate States, we have the honor to notify you that he will open the fire of his batteries on Fort Sumter in one hour from this time.

We have the honor to be, very respectfully,
Your obedient servants,
(Signed) JAMES CHESNUT, jr,
Aid-de-Camp.
STEPHEN D. LEE,
Captain S. C. Army and Aid-de-Camp.

Major ROBERT ANDERSON, United States Army, Commanding Fort Sumter.

FOR THE MERCURY.

Has the President of the Confederate States a Right to Issue Letters of Marque and Reprisal?

"Inter arma silent leges."

Your paper of this morning contains President DAVIS' Proclamation, "inviting all those who may desire service in private armed vessels on the high seas, to make application for commissions or letters of marque and reprisal to be issued under the Seal of these Confederate States." The question I propose for your consideration, is this: Has the *President* of the Confederate States the power to issue "letters of marque and reprisal under the Seal of these Confederate States?"

There cannot be two opinions upon the subject. He has no such power. The Provisional Constitution of the Confederate States, under which he is acting, has distinctly and unequivocally vested this power in "the Congress" alone, and has no where given a particle of power over this subject to the President.

In the sixth section of the First Article of the Constitution, granting powers to *Congress*, are the following words: "To declare war, *grant letters of marque and reprisal*, and make rules concerning captures on land and water." Here, the power to grant letters of marque and reprisal is vested in Congress alone, and follows the power "to declare war." President DAVIS has just as much power "to declare war" against the United States as to grant letters of marque and reprisal. He has power to do neither. Both are exclusively within the authority of the Congress of the Confederate States.

If you will turn to the second section of the Second Article of the Constitution, ordaining the powers vested in the President, you will find that his whole military power consists in the following clause: "The President shall be Commander-in-Chief of the Army and Navy of the Confederacy, and of the militia of the several States when called into actual service of the Confederacy."

I suppose it requires no argument to show that where a power is not granted in the Constitution to the President, he cannot have it; and that where it is *expressly granted to Congress*, that of itself is an absolute negation of it to any other department of the Government.

A CAROLINIAN.

Interesting from Pensacola.

Our Warrington Correspondence.

HEADQUARTERS PROVISIONAL ARMY,
Warrington, Fla., April 13, 1861.

The Feeling Among the Southern Troops Around Fort Pickens—The Mercury's Correspondence—How the Confederate Posts are Garrisoned—Topography of Pensacola and its Surroundings—A Night Alarm—Fort Pickens and its Surroundings—Condition of the Sand Batteries—Likelihood of a Breach—The old Palmetto Regiment Represented, etc., etc., etc.

The long agony of doubt and suspense which has, for months, paralyzed the energies of our people, is at length over. We breath freer now that we know the worst, and can prepare to meet it. This place is now to become the grand theatre of the struggle, and the focal point of national interest. It will be the pleasing duty and earnest endeavor of your correspondent daily to inform the public mind, and relieve the public anxiety, by communicating through the columns of THE MERCURY an authentic report of all military operations at this point. When he ceases to do so, you may take it for granted that he has gone down beneath the tide of battle, and sleeps with the dead, among the victims of war.

Just a month ago, the work of reinforcing this point began. At that time the garrison here consisted of five companies of Alabama twelve months volunteers. In addition to this battalion, there was a remnant of a militia company, under Capt. O'HARA, from Mobile, a company of Florida militia, and another squad of twenty Florida militia. This entire force, which constituted the garrison at this place on the 13th of March, barely numbered 500 men. The first reinforcement was the company of "Red Eagles" from Mobile, Alabama, under command of Capt. BEN LANE POSEY. They arrived on the 15th of March, and were placed immediately in command of the Barrancas Redoubt. Captain O'HARA's militia and the Florida militia were then disbanded.

Reinforcements then began to pour in from all points. They have been arriving almost every day since the 20th ult. The result is now an aggregate of 5000 men. They consist of the following elements:

A brigade of Mississippians	1,700 men.
3 battalions of Alabamians	1,400 "
9 companies of Floridians	600 "
3 battalions of Georgians (not all here)	1,100 "
2 companies of Louisianans (Zouaves)	200 "
	5000

It may be necessary to explain the topography of this locality, for the better understanding of our position here. Warrington Navy Yard is about eight miles from Pensacola. It is about two miles from Fort Pickens, which is on the southern point of Santa Rosa Island. This Island, which is about forty miles long, and an average of a mile wide, divides the waters of the Gulf from those of Pensacola Bay. The entrance from the Gulf to the Bay is about one mile wide. It lies between the south end of Santa Rosa Island, on which stands Fort Pickens, and a land-spit of the main land just opposite, on which stands Fort McRae. Fort Pickens is 500 yards from the end of the Island, and Fort McRae is so near the water that its base is washed by every wave that breaks upon the beach. Pickens and McRae are 2000 yards apart. The main land opposite Fort Pickens is semi-circular in form, the Navy Yard forming the northern point, and Fort McRae the southern point. The space between is occupied by the village of Warrington, which extends parallel to the beach for a mile. Next comes the Marine Hospital; next Barrancas Barracks; next Fort San Carlos de Barrancas; next the Lighthouse; and last, Fort McRae. The further point of any part of this semi-circle, is not exceeding two miles from Fort Pickens. One thousand yards in the rear of Fort Barrancas stands Barrancas Redoubt. These are all the points in the field of operations which have "a local designation and a name." I have given this minute topographical description of the field of operations for future reference by your readers, whom I advise to preserve it for that purpose; it will greatly assist them in understanding the letters written from this place.

I will next give you a statement of the positions occupied by the several corps of the army. The navy yard is occupied only by Capt. LEE's company of Georgians from Atlanta. It has 110 men. Sixty-eight of them being machinists, it has been converted into a corps of sappers and miners. The south end of Warrington—the Barrancas barracks, Fort Barrancas and Barrancas Redoubt—are occupied by the Alabamians. Barrancas Redoubt, the most important of all these positions, is occupied by the "Red Eagles," under Captain BEN. LANE POSEY, who is commandant of the redoubt. The space between the redoubt and Barrancas barracks is occupied by the Georgians. The Mississippi brigade is posted between Fort Barrancas and Fort McRae, immediately in rear of the light house. Fort McRae was occupied yesterday by an Alabama company under Capt. DRAPER.

Last night, about 7 o'clock, I was startled by the firing of cannon at the fleet. I was about to start to call on some friends in the Mississippi brigade. I heard five guns fire at intervals of about three minutes each. I went down to the Light House, and found that two companies of Mississippians had just left to reinforce Fort McRae, where an attack was anticipated. The light of the Light House was extinguished. The officer of the day came galloping past, with orders to call out all the troops under arms. Many of the troops slept on their arms all night, and some never slept at all.

The firing was to announce the arrival of the storeship *Relief* with provisions for the garrison and fleet. Reinforcements were probably thrown into Fort Pickens last night. The elements were favorable for it, and the time was doubtless improved. A collision is probable now at any moment. All the batteries were supplied with ammunition to-day. The *Wyandotte*, which has been plying about the bay at pleasure, was notified yesterday evening to leave, and if she comes in again she will be fired on. We are looking for a steamer to arrive to-night from Mobile, with a large cargo of Quartermaster's stores. Her entrance may be interfered with, and that will, if it happens, produce a collision.

Our main reliance for offensive operations is upon the small batteries along the beach. There are three of these in the navy-yard, mounting about four 32's each. There is another battery—an admirable one—in the south end of Warrington. It is just opposite the main gate of Fort Pickens, which is distinctly visible from it. This battery will knock down the gate. The best battery of all is one of three ten-inch Columbiads, between Fort Barrancas and the Light House. It will be finished to-morrow. The next best is a battery of four eight-inch Columbiads, just below the Light House. This has been finished for some time. These bear on the south side of Fort Pickens, which is a mere brick wall only four feet thick. This part of the fort was never finished. Columbiads will soon demolish it. That will be very well; but then comes "the tug of war." It will be an "imminent deadly breach" indeed to rush into, and hecatombs of men will perish in it.

The fleet lies usually about six miles from Fort McRae. It has lately taken a nearer position in line of battle to rake with its broadsides the island approaches to Fort McRae.

Such are, in detail, the items of fact, and I hope of interest, in regard to our military condition. I will send you by telegraph and mail the earliest and most authentic information of all military operations at this theatre of war.

There are among the troops here three of the few survivors of the Palmetto Regiment. LARY O'BANNON, of Barnwell, who was in Company D, is here as Quartermaster, with the rank of Captain. OCTAVIUS T. GIBBS, who was in Company B, is Captain of a company from Mississippi. BEN LANE POSEY, who was in Company E, is Captain of the "Red Eagles" from Mobile. Col. GLADDEN, the only surviving field officer of the Palmetto Regiment, will be here in a few days in command of a regiment from Louisiana. PETER LAKEY, of Orangeburg, who was conspicuous in the Kansas raid, is here, a Major of a Georgia Battalion. These are the South Carolinians whom I have met here in a few days past. All of them occupy high and honorable positions, and in "the hour which tries men's souls," they will not shame their nativity or their past history.

LA PALMA.

CHARLESTON MERCURY

EXTRA:

Passed unanimously at 1.15 o'clock, P. M., December 20th, 1860.

AN ORDINANCE

To dissolve the Union between the State of South Carolina and other States united with her under the compact entitled "The Constitution of the United States of America."

We, the People of the State of South Carolina, in Convention assembled, do declare and ordain, and it is hereby declared and ordained,

That the Ordinance adopted by us in Convention, on the twenty-third day of May, in the year of our Lord one thousand seven hundred and eighty-eight, whereby the Constitution of the United States of America was ratified, and also, all Acts and parts of Acts of the General Assembly of this State, ratifying amendments of the said Constitution, are hereby repealed; and that the union now subsisting between South Carolina and other States, under the name of "The United States of America," is hereby dissolved.

THE UNION IS DISSOLVED!

The New-York Times.

VOL. X....NO. 2989. NEW-YORK, SATURDAY, APRIL 20, 1861. PRICE TWO CENTS.

HIGHLY EXCITING NEWS.

SOUTHERN PORTS TO BE BLOCKADED.

A Day of Riot and Blood in Baltimore.

Pennsylvania and Massachusetts Volunteers Attacked.

Two Massachusetts Men Killed and Several Wounded.

They Return the Fire and Kill Seven of the Rioters.

The Secessionists Nonplussed at Harper's Ferry.

The Arms Destroyed and the Building Burnt.

Departure of the Seventh Regiment of New-York.

The Most Impressive Scene Ever Witnessed in Broadway.

THE WAR SPIRIT THROUGHOUT THE NORTH.

PROCLAMATION FROM PRESIDENT LINCOLN.

WASHINGTON, Friday, April 19.

The President has issued a proclamation, stating that an insurrection against the Government of the United States has broken out in the States of South Carolina, Georgia, Alabama, Florida, Mississippi, Louisiana and Texas, and the laws of the United States, for the collection of the revenue, cannot be effectually executed therein, conformably to that provision of the Constitution, which requires duties to be uniform throughout the United States, and further a combination of persons engaged in such insurrection have threatened to grant pretended letters-of-marque, to authorize the bearers thereof to commit assaults on the lives, vessels and property of good citizens of the country, carefully engaged in commerce on the high seas, and in the waters of the United States.

And whereas the President says an Executive proclamation has already been issued, requiring the persons engaged in these disorderly proceedings to desist, therefore calling out a militia force for the purpose of repressing the same, and convening Congress in extraordinary session, to deliberate and determine thereon. The President, with a view to the same purposes before mentioned, and to the protection of the public peace, and the lives and property of its orderly citizens, pursuing their lawful occupations, until Congress shall have assembled and deliberated on the said unlawful proceedings, or until the same shall have ceased, has further deemed it advisable to set on foot a BLOCKADE OF THE PORTS within the States aforesaid, in pursuance of the laws of the United States and the laws of nations, in such cases provided.

For this purpose a competent force will be posted so as to prevent the entrance and exit of vessels from the ports aforesaid.

If, therefore, with a view to violate such blockade, a vessel shall attempt to leave any of the said ports, she will be duly warned by the commander of one of the said blockading vessels, who will indorse on her register the fact and date of such warning; and if the same vessel shall again attempt to enter or leave the blockaded port, she will be captured, and sent to the nearest convenient port for such proceedings against her and her cargo as may be deemed advisable.

ABRAHAM LINCOLN,
President of the United States.

WM. H. SEWARD, Secretary of State.

OUR WASHINGTON DISPATCHES.

WASHINGTON, Friday, April 19.

The President's proclamation will be issued to-morrow, announcing the blockade of the Southern ports.

THE MASSACHUSETTS TROOPS ATTACKED.

The Massachusetts men were attacked on their passage to Baltimore. The Sixth Regiment turned and fired on the mob, killing several.

Our New-York troops must be prepared to fight their way through.

VIRGINIA MONEY DEPRECIATED.

Virginia money has been quoted here for several days at 12½ and 15 per cent. discount, and a President of one of the prominent Banks says that probably it will go down to 25 per cent. discount. In consequence of this great and prospectively greatest depreciation of Virginia currency, some shrewd speculators have hit upon a novel method for avoiding the loss by discount. One party went yesterday to Alexandria, where Virginia notes are received at par, and purchased $1,000 worth of flour. It is understood that others have gone there with large amounts of the same currency, to purchase bacon. These speculations are prompted by the expectation of a large consumption of these articles in the city. Government is already bringing in large quantities of provisions for troops, and storing them in the vaults of the public buildings.

CASSIUS M. CLAY'S COMPANY.

The following are the names of a portion of those who have volunteered for the defence of the Capitol, under the command of CASSIUS M. CLAY:

James W. Wye..........New-York City.
Hiram Smith..........Rochester.
A. H. Ryington..........Norwalk, Conn.
Ray W. Potter..........Brooklyn, N. Y.
James W. Lomers..........Champlain County, N. Y.
Samuel P. Dinsmore..........New-York City.
C. H. Foster..........Hartford County, N. Y.
John S. Clark..........Auburn, N. Y.
David Wilmot..........Pennsylvania.
George R. Smith..........Omahaha, N. T.
John O. Donnell..........New-York.
Charles H. Bailey..........Omaha, N. T.
William Porter..........New-York City.
S. C. Greene..........Buffalo.
William E. Lansing..........Madison County, N. Y.
B. F. Mudgett..........Brooklyn, N. Y.
J. H. Hobart Ward..........New-York City.
D. D. Connover..........New-York City.
John N. Gennin..........New-York City.
Charles A. Perkins..........Oswego, New-York.
James Millward..........New-York City.
S. H. Lathrop..........New-Mexico.
A. G. Lawrence..........Cleveland.
Alonzo Welch..........Saratoga, N. Y.
Nehemiah Lathrop..........New-York City.
Geo. R. Sherman..........Rockland County, N. Y.
John Woodruff..........New Haven, Conn.
George B. Van Brunt..........New-York City.
Charles A. Clark..........New-York City.
Thomas Dyer..........Chicago, Ill.
Silas B. Dutcher..........New-York City.
Willis Patten..........New-York City.
C. S. Bushnell..........New-Haven, Conn.
Francis W. Rice..........Panama, New-Granada.
O. S. Ferry..........Norwalk, Conn.
Joseph Hawes..........Panama, New-Granada.
W. B. Chase..........Washington, D. C.
James S. Chalker..........Hartford, Conn.
H. D. Webster..........Omaha Nebraska.
David Butterfield..........New-York City.
John G. Camp..........New-York City.
Geo. S. Gregory..........New-York City.
James G. Slaight..........Brooklyn, N. Y.
R. R. Sloan..........Ohio.
Cyrus Newlin..........Philadelphia.
Calvin Hueson..........Rochester, N. Y.
James P. Craig..........Randolph, Ill.
Hugh Tyer..........New-York City.
William L. Lockwood..........New-York City.

THE SAFETY OF WASHINGTON.

Many people ask, "Will it be safe for women and children in Washington, in view of the threatened war?" and residents here are receiving numerous appeals from distant friends to leave the city for some more Northern refuge. All such indications of fear are idle. There *has* been danger of an outbreak here and in the neighborhood of the little squad of traitors who are scattered among the great mass of Unionists who comprise the population of the District; but there are not enough of them to get up a respectable riot, and they will not attempt it. As to the seizure of the Capital by a Southern army—that will never be effected if a million men can hold the Stars and Stripes over it,—for above all other points, this is the one which the Government will retain in its possession until it has been proven that the Secessionists can subjugate the rest of the American people,—and that time we apprehend here is not immediately at hand.

THE BENEFITS OF A FIGHT.

If there are still in the North any who hesitate about the propriety of effective measures to support the Government, and who fear and tremble lest a collision of arms is to render a perpetuation of the Union between the North and South impossible, it would do them good to hear the sentiments expressed by Southern gentlemen in this neighborhood—men who know the South, and who have independence enough to express their views freely and without stint. I remember that during the late session of Congress, an outspoken and honest Southern member, conversing with a member from New-England with respect to the disturbances between the sections, remarked, "We are going to have a fight with you, and somebody's going to get hurt; but after that we shall like each other better than we ever have since the foundation of the Government."

I confess that at the time it did seem as though the mode suggested was rather a rough sort of introduction to good fellowship; but in conversing to-day with another Southron, he expressed the same idea, in a form of argument which carried with it great force. "The masses of our people," he said, "don't understand the people of the North. You don't fight duels, nor do various other things which Southern education holds to be indispensable to a reputation for courage. They have consequently settled down into the conviction that 'Yankees' are 'cowards'—and while they despise them for that, they hate them also because they don't give them opportunity for more violent demonstrations upon their persons. They don't *respect* the people of the North—and so they don't believe Northern men when they disclaim any purpose of oppressing the South, and of interfering with Slavery in the States. Cowardice they look upon as the quintessence of meanness—and lying they consider its natural companion. Hence it is that they refuse to give the North credit for an honest motive in its Anti-Slavery sentiments, and hence they believe the demogogues, who profess to see nothing in your hostility to Slavery extension except an offensive purpose to humiliate the South, and force her to inequality in the Union. Now we are about to have a conflict; they will learn that Northern people are not cowards, but as brave and determined as themselves. The knowledge of that fact will inspire them with respect for you, give them confidence in your truth, and make us all better friends than the two sections ever can be until they have each learned, by a stern experience, that the other is worthy of respect and confidence."

There certainly is wisdom and sound logic in the argument,—and if the dread trial by the sword must come, there is some consolation in the anticipation that good will ultimately flow from the evil.

DISPATCH TO THE ASSOCIATED PRESS.

WASHINGTON, Friday, April 19.

It is reliably stated by parties direct from Richmond that the ordinance of secession was publicly proclaimed yesterday. The vote on its passage is kept secret.

On inquiry at the Post-office Department it is ascertained that no measures are in progress for discontinuing any of the Southern mails. On the contrary, the contractors from that section recently here have arranged for facilitating the transportation. The Postmaster-General has discretion to suspend them only in cases of obstruction.

Capt. PAULDING, Commander EMMONS, and Lieut. WOODHULL constitute the Board of Detail, through whom all the naval preparations are made.

The Chief Clerk's room is the only one in the Navy Department accessible at times to the public.

The city is comparatively quiet this morning.

Those who feared an attack on Washington during last night were not even alarmed by any extraordinary notes of warning or precaution.

Rumors have been circulating for a week that the Philadelphia appointments have been made. As soon as the President actually makes them they will be seen.

Major A. M. HANCOCK, of Kentucky, has been appointed Consul to Malaga.

HARPER'S FERRY BURNT.

The Post Deserted and Fifteen Thousand Stand of Arms Destroyed.

BALTIMORE, Friday, April 19—11 A. M.

Harper's Ferry was burnt last night, and abandoned by the United States troops.

CARLISLE, Penn., Friday, April 19.

Lieut. JONES, late in command at Harper's Ferry, arrived here with his command of 43 men at 3 P. M., to-day.

Lieut. JONES, having been advised that a force of 2,500 troops had been ordered by Gov. LETCHER to take possession of Harper's Ferry, and finding his position untenable, under directions of the War Department, destroyed all the munitions of war, Armory, Arsenal and all the buildings. He withdrew his command under the cover of night, and almost in the presence of 2,500 troops. He lost three men.

Fifteen thousand stand of arms were destroyed.

The command made a forced march of thirty miles, last night, from Harper's Ferry to Hagerstown, Md. Lieut. JONES and command look much worn and fatigued. They were most enthusiastically received by our entire population.

THE CUMBERLAND AT HAMPTON ROADS.

BALTIMORE, Friday, April 19.

The United States corvette *Cumberland* is at Hampton Roads, and not inside Norfolk harbor. She is caulked anew. It is said she got up anchor last night.

The *Illinois*, from Charleston, is due at Norfolk, with troops for Fort Monroe. Attempts may be made to prevent her from landing them, which the *Cumberland* can effectually oppose. Her presence is most opportune. Everything is quiet at Norfolk to day.

STARTLING FROM BALTIMORE.

The Northern Troops Mobbed and Fired upon—The Troops Return the Fire—Four Massachusetts Volunteers Killed and Several Wounded—Several of the Rioters Killed.

BALTIMORE, Friday, April 19.

There was a horrible scene on Pratt-street, to-day. The railroad track was taken up, and the troops attempted to march through. They were attacked by a mob with bricks and stones, and were fired upon. The fire was returned. Two of the Seventh Regiment of Pennsylvania were killed and several wounded.

It is impossible to say what portion of the troops have been attacked. They bore a white flag as they marched up Pratt-street and were greeted with showers of paving-stones. The Mayor of the city went ahead of them with the police. An immense crowd blocked up the streets. The soldiers finally turned and fired on the mob. Several of the wounded have just gone up the street in carts.

At the Washington dépôt, an immense crowd assembled. The rioters attacked the soldiers, who fired into the mob. Several were wounded, and some fatally. It is said that four of the military and four rioters are killed. The city is in great excitement. Martial law has been proclaimed. The military are rushing to the armories.

Civil war has commenced. The railroad track is said to be torn up outside of the city. Parties threaten to destroy the Pratt-street bridge.

As the troops passed along Pratt-street a perfect shower of paving stones rained on their heads.

The cars have left for Washington, and were stoned as they left.

It was the Seventh Regiment of Massachusetts which broke through the mob. Three of the mob are known to be dead and three soldiers. Many were wounded. Stores are closing, and the military rapidly forming. The Minute Men are turning out.

BALTIMORE, Friday, April 19—2:30 P. M.

Affairs are getting serious. Before all the cars got through, great crowds assembled at various points and commenced obstructing the road.

Reports are now arriving that the mob are tearing up the track.

It is understood the principal portion of the troops have got through.

BALTIMORE, Friday, April 19—4 P. M.

A town meeting has been called for 4 o'clock.

It is said there have been 12 lives lost.

Several are mortally wounded.

Parties of men half frantic are roaming the streets armed with guns, pistols and muskets.

The stores are closed.

Business is suspended.

A general state of dread prevails.

Parties a short time ago rushed into the telegraph office, armed with hatchets, and cut the wires. Not much damage was done.

BALTIMORE, April 19—5 P. M.

R. W. DAVIS, of the firm of PEGRAM, PAYNTER & DAVIS, was shot dead during the riot, near Camden Station.

It is reported that the Philadelphians are now at the outer dépôt.

The President of the Road has ordered the train back, at the urgent request of the Mayor and Governor. They are already off.

The citizens who were mortally wounded are, JOHN MCCAN, P. GRIFFIN and G. NEEDHAM.

Four of the Massachusetts troops were killed and several wounded, but it is impossible to learn their names.

As far as ascertained, only two of the Massachusetts soldiers were killed, belonging to Company C. Their bodies are now at the Police Station.

At the same Station are the following wounded:

Sergeant AMES, of the Lowell City Guard, wounded in the head, slightly.

Private COLUM, of the same place, shot in the head, not serious.

Private MICHAEL GREEN, of Lawrence, Mass., wounded in the head, by stones.

H. W. DANFORTH, Company C, Sixth Regiment, of Massachusetts, slightly wounded.

So far as known at present, seven citizens were killed, including Mr. DAVIS, before mentioned, and JAMES CLARK.

Half a dozen or so are seriously wounded, though it is believed not fatally.

Comparative quiet now prevails. The military are under arms, and the police are out in full force.

There is a large mass meeting here to-night, addressed by the Mayor. The Governor was present.

PHILADELPHIA VOLUNTEERS SENT BACK.

PHILADELPHIA, Friday, April 19.

The Philadelphia Volunteers have been turned back, because without arms or equipments.

THE MASSACHUSETTS TROOPS IN WASHINGTON.

PHILADELPHIA, Friday, April 19.

A special dispatch from Washington says that the Massachusetts Regiment, except 120 men, arrived there at 5 o'clock. They report that three of their members were killed.

OUR BALTIMORE CORRESPONDENCE.

WARLIKE NEWS FROM THE SOUTH—VIRGINIA SECEDED—ATTACK ON HARPER'S FERRY—GOV. HICKS—EXCITEMENT IN BALTIMORE—RESIGNATION OF COL. HUGER, U. S. A., &C.

Correspondence of the New-York Times:

BALTIMORE, Thursday, April 18, 1861.

The news from the South is of the most warlike character. Every effort at preparation is being made for the anticipated conflict; and private dispatches, from unprejudiced sources, represent the feeling of resistance as unanimously extreme.

I have reason to believe, on reliable authority, that the Virginia Convention have, in secret session, by a large majority, repealed the ordinance by which she became a member of the Confederation; that it has not been made public, because of the desire first to mature some plan of prompt and general action; that some fifteen hundred or two thousand troops are now *en route* for Harper's Ferry, and that ere this reaches you that post will be in their possession.

Serious fears are entertained by the Baltimore and Ohio Railroad Company, in consequence of information imparted from different sources, that their bridge over the Potomac will be destroyed. The President, Mr. GARRETT, has this moment, by special engine, sent an influential agent there with a view to the protection of the Company's property.

The Norfolk boat of this morning also brings intelligence that the Navy-yard there had been seized, and that vessels had been sunk in the channel, to prevent the men-of-war, lying under the guns of Fortress Monroe, from leaving.

Gov. HICKS has not yet responded, either affirmatively or negatively, to the requirements of the Secretary of War, in regard to the quota of troops from Maryland. The statement in the papers of yesterday that he had done so, are not true.

There is great excitement in this city. A serious disposition is manifested in certain quarters to obstruct the passage of Northern troops through the State. Public opinion is, as yet, too equally divided to permit any open demonstration, and the Mayor and Board of Police are determined on preserving order. The Police force is a well disciplined and efficient one, but has no general authority beyond the Municipal limits.

Col. B. F. HUGER, commandant at the Pikesville Arsenal, near this City, on Monday, resigned his commission in the United States service.

The clouds deepen, and all who seriously regard the political atmosphere, are trembling at the impending crash. CECIL.

THE CITY MILITARY EXCITEMENT.

The Seventh Regiment off for Washington.

The Seventy-first, Twelfth and Sixth Regiments Ordered to Leave To-morrow.

The Metropolis Alive with Military Excitement—The People Bid the Seventh God Speed—The Union and its Flag to be Upheld—The Rhode Island Troops En Route.

Yesterday was a sad, and yet triumphant day for New-York. It was sad that a thousand of our noblest citizens should be so suddenly called away from their homes—perhaps to death—to defend the Constitution and the laws. It was a triumphant vindication of the loyalty of our citizens thus promptly volunteering to the hardships of a soldier's life. Never before were the people roused to such a pitch of patriotic enthusiasm. There have been gala days, and funeral pageants, and military shows, and complimentary receptions, and triumphal processions that filled the streets with crowds of curious, wondering, sympathetic people, but never has there been developed such a universal, heart-felt, deep-rooted, genuine enthusiasm. The American colors were prominent everywhere—on housetops, on flag-staffs, on horses attached to all kinds of vehicles, on ropes stretched across the streets, on the masts of shipping in the harbor, on breastpins, on the lappets of coats, on the fronts of men's hats—on all sides the glorious old red, white and blue waved in the joyous breeze and dazzled the eye with their bright colors. The awful solemnity of civil war came pressing home to our people who had sons and brothers and fathers just departing, perhaps never to return. The news of the difficulties in Baltimore, the struggle of the troops with the rabble, the reported death of many, the rumors of an attack on the Capital, the tearing up of railroad tracks, and all the attendant horrors of internecine warfare, struck terror into many a stout heart, while the tears of kind-hearted women flowed copiously as a rain-storm. The excitement was heightened to a great degree by the announcement of the fact that the Sixth, Twelfth and Seventy-first Regiments had likewise been ordered to leave for the seat of war this afternoon. Appended are the details of the various movements:

DEPARTURE OF THE SEVENTH REGIMENT.

IMMENSE ENTHUSIASM—EXCITING AND IMPRESSIVE SCENES AND INCIDENTS.

The intelligence that the Seventh Regiment, the "crack" Regiment, the almost adored military body, of this City, would leave for Washington yesterday afternoon, created an excitement scarcely surpassed by anything that has transpired since the first news of the attack on Fort Sumter. Although it was announced that 3 P. M. was the time for the assembling of the Regiment at their Armory, over Tompkins Market, Broadway was the scene of gathering for hundreds of people long before noon. The march of the second installment of Massachusetts troops, early in the forenoon, was but an incentive to their patriotism. If they had to wait many hours, as indeed they had, they were prepared to stand on the tip-toe of expectation till their favorite Regiment passed, even if nightfall came. The aspect of Broadway was very gay indeed. Minus the firing of pistols and the explosion of Chinese crackers, it was many Fourth of Julys rolled into one. The Stars and Stripes were everywhere, from the costliest silk, twenty, thirty, forty feet in length, to the homelier bunting, down to the few inches of painted calico that a baby's hand might wave. It would be invidious to say from what buildings the National flag was displayed, because it would be almost impossible to tell from what buildings it did not wave, and never, if flags can be supposed to be animated with any of the feelings of their owners, with a purer devotion to the Union. Evidently, all political partisanship was cast aside. But the gayest, and in this respect, the most remarkable thoroughfare, was Cortlandt-street. Lafayette-place, where the Regiment was to form previous to marching, was very attractively dressed—a huge flag being displayed from the Astor Library, among numerous others from private buildings. But Cortlandt-street showed a gathering of flags, a perfect army of them. They were not, in that comparatively brief space from Broadway to the Jersey City Ferry, to be numbered by dozens or by scores, every building seemed like "Captains of Fifties." It was flag, flag, from every window from the first floor to the roof, from every doorway,—in short, it was flag, flag,—and of quite large sizes, too, till the wearied eye refused the task of counting them. Such was the display along the route of the "Seventh." Such is and will be the route for all noble troops entering our City from the New-England States.

Around the Armory of the Seventh Regiment crowds gathered at an early period of the day, and moved on, only to be replaced by other crowds. So the excitement was kept up, till towards three o'clock the throng became stationary. It was, by no means, an ordinary crowd. Well-dressed ladies, men whose checks can be honored at the best Banks for as many dollars as would build a church of excellent architecture, were among them. They were about to witness the departure of the Seventh Regiment, too probably, to the battle-field. Though the flags waved gaily over them, their faces wore a grave look—not sad exactly, but it was no time for mirth.

From all quarters the members of the Regiment, in full fatigue dress, with their knapsacks and blankets, kept pouring into the Armory. Guards at the doors kept the crowd, who had no business inside, from entering, but the building was filled to its utmost, notwithstanding, by the members, their relatives and friends. There were many touching scenes of farewell-taking, but these were merely episodes. Mothers, wives, sisters, will weep on such occasions, but there was no faltering among the men. A heartier shake of the hand than usual, to a friend,—a warmer kiss—let it be reverentially said—to a wife or mother, and the manhood of the soldier grew the greater, and he trussed his knapsack the tighter to his back as he gave the last adieu.

They formed in Lafayette-place about 4 P. M., in the presence of an immense crowd, each window of each building being filled with such fair applauders as might cheer the heart of the forlornest bachelor, if there was any such among these noble soldiers. Once in line, they proceeded through Fourth-street to Broadway, down that great thoroughfare to Cortlandt-street, and across the ferry, in boats provided for the purpose, to Jersey City. The line of march was a perfect ovation. Thousands upon thousands lined the sidewalks. It will be remembered as long as any of those who witnessed it live to talk of it, and beyond that, it will pass into the recorded history of this fearful struggle. The Regiment was escorted by a band of Zouaves, who volunteered for the occasion. Their gay uniform and peculiar step revived the excitement that had begun somewhat to droop among the crowd that had waited for hours, the regiment not reaching the Park till 5½ o'clock. After the Zouaves came, a strong body of police, and after the police, THE REGIMENT. Not as, on festival days, not as on the reception of the Prince of Wales, but, nobly and sternly, as men who were going to the war. Hurried was their step, not so regular as on less important occasions. We saw women, we saw men shed tears as they passed. Amidst the deafening cheers that rose, we heard cries of "God bless them." And so along Broadway, and through Cortlandt-street, under its almost countless flags, the gallant Seventh Regiment left the City.

The excitement in Jersey City, long before they had crossed the ferry, was scarcely less intense, and when they landed there, they found they were by no means in a foreign State. It seemed that all the people of the sister city had turned out. It was a reënaction of what their fellow-townsmen and townswomen had done for them. White handkerchiefs, waved by the ladies' hands, were as numerous as the dog-wood blossoms in Spring, and it was proved that a Jerseyman can raise as hearty a cheer as the best New-Yorker. And so it was till all were fairly disposed of in the cars, and the cars moved off.

We regret to have to record an accident in this connection. One of the Medical Staff accompanying them, a German gentleman, was crushed in Jersey City between an express wagon and a car. He was so injured that he was unable to give his name. He was duly taken care of.

Two or three incidents connected with the occasion of this departure of the Seventh may be properly taken notice of. While at the Armory, before starting, news was brought of the attack at Baltimore on the Pennsylvania troops, and the subsequent bloodshed. It was at first disbelieved, but afterwards became credited. Of course there was not the first indication on the part of any member of backing down. On the contrary, it seemed to inspirit them the more. One old gentleman, a veteran of the Regiment, earnestly begged, on hearing it, that he might be supplied with a regimental suit, knapsack and appurtenances, and as he could not be accommodated, he left for home, vowing that he would supply himself, and follow on to-day. By the way, we learn that about 100 more members of the Regiment intend to leave here on Monday. The Twelfth, Ninth and Seventy-first Regiments leave to-day.

Another incident was, that previous to the departure of the Regiment a splendid American flag was presented to them by E. H. SIMON, Esq., of Company A, Seventy-first Regiment. An appropriate expression of sentiment accompanied the presentation, which was feelingly responded to by Col. LEFFERTS.

One of the members of the Regiment was to have been married on Monday, and the cards of invitation had been issued. But he went yesterday, all the same, to serve his country. The ardent wishes, not only of his friends, but of thousands who never saw his face, will be that he may return at no distant period, unhurt, and with his due share of honor, to fulfill the happy contract.

A false report was spread, and gained credence by its being published in some of the evening papers, and announced on their bulletins, that, owing to the exciting news from Baltimore, the track having been torn up and a fight progressing, the Seventh would march down Canal-street and embark on board the *Baltic* for Washington. This, of course, was not true.

While the Regiment was passing down Broadway, opposite the store of Messrs. BALL, BLACK & Co., Major ANDERSON appeared on the front balcony, and was immediately greeted with prolonged shouts of applause. Each company of the Regiment, with their officers, Col. LEFFERTS and Col. SHUMWAY, stopped, took off their caps, and cheered with the heartiest will. The crowd of spectators, learning the occasion, shouted with all their power, till the gallant Major, after bowing several times, had to retire. He had afterwards to leave the building by a side door, to escape the enthusiastic attentions which the people were prepared to bestow upon him.

On the Corn Exchange, as on the Merchants' Exchange, at the Stock Exchange, and in commercial circles generally, the utmost enthusiasm prevailed. As the gallant Seventh Regiment was under marching orders for the National Capital, several young merchants, serving in its ranks, bade adieu to their associates at the Corn Exchange. No words of regret were heard, but many an earnest "Good-bye," and "God bless you, my brave fellow." Offers of money to defray expenses were freely made. Assurances to those who were leaving young families behind that these should not be neglected were generously given. The sentiments interchanged were truly inspiriting. The Government should be supported, rebellion should be suppressed, the public property defended and the laws enforced. The Corn Exchange is thoroughly satisfied that its representatives—the MALLONS, the HERRICKS, and others—in the ranks of the glorious "Seventh" will do their duty, faithfully and well.

On the railroads between this and Washington, it is intended that the Seventh Regiment shall be preceded by a Pilot Engine, to insure safety. The Engineer Corps have howitzers loaded with grape and canister. Probably the troubles at Baltimore will interfere with the Pilot Engine.

The great meeting to be held to-morrow was also a leading topic at the Merchants' Exchange. All the members and subscribers not absent on military duty, decided to attend,—adopting the following resolution unanimously, and amidst vociferous cheering:

Resolved, That the members of the New-York Corn Exchange close their places of business to morrow, Saturday, April 20, at 2 P. M., and attend the meeting to be convened at Union Square at 3 P. M., in support of the General Government of the United States of America.

We are requested by Quartermaster WINCHESTER, of the National Guards to say that packages, or letters, in stamped envelopes, for members of the Seventh Regiment, while on duty in Washington, will be received by Mr. HOEY, Superintendent of Adams Express Company, and forwarded *free of charge*. They should be addressed, care of Quartermaster WINCHESTER, and delivered at the office of Adams Express Company previous to 4½ P. M.

THE SEVENTH REGIMENT AT NEW-BRUNSWICK.

NEW BRUNSWICK, N. J., Friday, April 19.

The Seventh Regiment of New-York, numbering nine hundred and ninety-one men by actual count, reached New-Brunswick at 8¾ P. M. The route thus far has been one continued ovation, and at every station on their route they have been greeted with the booming of cannon and the shouts of thousands of the patriotic citizens of New-Jersey, who have almost lined the road, and houses at a distance of half a mile from the road were seen to be illuminated.

PHILADELPHIA, Friday, April 19—11 P. M.

The Seventh Regiment has not arrived yet, though expected more than an hour since. It is reported they will go on board the *Keystone State*, and be taken to Washington *via* the Potomac. The streets are thronged to witness them march. They were at New-Brunswick at 9 o'clock, but it will be 12 ere they reach here.

THE VOLUNTEERING EXCITEMENT.

THE SEVENTY-FIRST REGIMENT.

At the Head-quarters of this Regiment, in Centre Market, there was a great rush of members, volunteers and friends, on the announcement of the arrival of orders to leave for Washington. In Company E alone there are 250 recruits, although only that number was required for the whole corps. It is supposed that at least 500 men will be ready to obey the summons. There was much chagrin, however, that the order had not come earlier, and many complaints were made that the Seventh Regiment had more notice, better equipments and a subscription fund to help them pay expenses, while the other regiments ordered out had short notice, imperfect equipments and no pecuniary aid. In view of these facts, a Committee was deputized to wait upon the other regiments and together apply to Gen. SANDFORD for an extension of time, if only for twenty-four hours. Many of the members are dependent upon daily labor for the support of their families, and require time to make the necessary domestic arrangements. The recruiting, however, proceeded rapidly. Much gratification was expressed at the fact of Col. VOSBURG being the senior Colonel, and therefore commander of the battalion ordered to go to-day.

We are requested to state that volunteers for the Seventy-first Regiment, to leave for Washington on Sunday morning, will be received at the Armory, Centre Market, all day Saturday.

TWELFTH REGIMENT.

The arrival of Col. BUTTERFIELD from Washington, with the orders for the Sixth, Twelfth and Seventy-first to depart for Washington to-day, set the City in a fever of excitement. At the various drill-rooms of the Twelfth Regiment, the crowds that poured in continually kept the rooms filled to overflowing. There were no less than 600 recruits enrolled during the day. At least 400 men of the regular Regiment, ready uniformed and equipped, will be ready to leave to-day. The Old Guard, exempt and honorary members of the Regiment, met promptly, and took measures to help those going, and keep up the organization here, and be prepared to go on in a few days if necessary. The Regiment joined in the request for an extension of the time—having every confidence in being better able to be properly equipped at longer notice. The volunteers will not go until they can be better equipped and partially drilled. A semi-Zouave uniform is to be furnished by the Government for the entire corps. Col. BUTTERFIELD is using every effort to have the Regiment do credit to the City and the State.

The members of the Old Guard, also the exempt members of the Twelfth Regiment, are requested to meet, in citizens dress, at No. 594 Broadway, this Saturday afternoon, at 2½ o'clock, for the purpose of acting as a guard of escort to the Twelfth Regiment on their departure from this City.

THE SIXTH REGIMENT.

The head-quarters of this Regiment presented a lively scene last evening, on the occasion of the preparations for leaving for Washington to-day. Col. PINCKNEY was surrounded by his wondering officers, who bothered him with endless questions as to the minutiæ of the trip. The utmost chagrin was evinced that no longer notice could be given, and many officers avowed that their commands could not turn out at so slight warning. The armorers' room, the company quarters and the crowded drill room resounded with the busy note of preparation, the buzz of conversation among the visitors and the continued administering of the oath of allegiance to volunteers.

SACRAFICES OF THE VOLUNTEERS.

Some of the most remarkable instances of patriotic sacrifice of self-interests ever known were developed among the instances of volunteers. In the Seventh Regiment many men of fortune and high social and political positions turned out in the ranks. In the Sixth, Seventy-first and Twelfth the same scenes were presented. In all, lovers left their sweethearts, sons their parents, fathers their families; and many a pillow was wet last night with the tears of those who sorrowed in all the sadness of bereavement. But the women of New-York came bravely to the work. They put courage into the hearts of the young soldiers, and even with fair hands helped to arrange uniforms, and to stow cartridges. We might give numberless instances of the most noble self-denial ever known under similar circumstances.

THE SCENE AT BARNUM'S MUSEUM.

The Astor House, Barnum's Museum, and all the buildings in the vicinity, were crowded to excess to witness the passage of the military. A respectable mass meeting gathered in front of the Astor House, and listened to speeches which were extemporized by various gentlemen. Loud cheers continually rent the air in response to every patriotic sentiment.

A SCRAMBLE FOR FLAGS.

At the corner of Broadway and Duane streets, an amusing scene occurred, on the occasion of some one from the top of a building throwing a quantity of flags into the air, which were borne by the breeze for some distance, and excited a *furore* of patriotic enthusiasm from a vast crowd.

THE TWELFTH, SEVENTY-FIRST AND SIXTH REGIMENTS TO LEAVE ON SUNDAY.

The efforts of the Colonels and other officers of the above regiments to procure an extension of time were successful, and Gen. SANDFORD extended the time to Sunday. The battalion, under command of Col. VOSBURGH, who is the senior Colonel, will assemble at 7 A. M., and proceed to the National Capital.

THE RHODE ISLAND ARTILLERY.

The Providence Marine Artillery arrived in the steamer *Empire State* yesterday, at 6 A. M., and anchored off the Battery, to await orders. These were duly received and the troop proceeded to Jersey City and were transferred to the steamer *Kill von Kull*. They left at noon for Elizabethport, intending to proceed thence *via* rail by Easton, Penn. The following is the list of officers: Capt. C. H. Tompkins; Lieuts. W. H. Reynolds, B. F. Remington, J. Henry, C. Barstow, Augustus M. Power. The steamer brought 150 men, and a full battery of six pieces, four six-pounders, and two howitzers, which are to be replaced very soon by a full battery of James' rifled cannon.

There were thirty men sent back this afternoon by the *Empire State* to Providence, these being in advance of the number required to man a battery. They were greatly disappointed, and will probably unite with another battery of artillery now in course of formation in Providence. Sergeant HARKNESS was compelled to return on account of sickness.

Gen. CYRUS E. DYER, Commissary and Quartermaster of the Rhode Island Regiment, is stopping at the Astor House.

Col. ARNOLD and Gov. SPRAGUE's staff passed through the City yesterday, *en route* for Washington. The Infantry belonging to the Rhode Island Regiment, will probably arrive off the Battery this evening, in the steamer *Empire State*, accompanied by Gov. SPRAGUE, and the aids and officers of the regiment.

COL. ELLSWORTH'S VOLUNTEER REGIMENT OF FIREMEN.

The preliminary arrangements for the organization of a Regiment of Zuaves from the ranks of the New-York firemen having been completed on Thursday, yesterday was actively spent in recruiting, and by nightfall the roll at each rendezvous was well filled. Indeed, the firemen are so enthusiastic in the matter, appreciating so highly the complement which the Administration has paid them in inviting their aid, that Col. ELLSWORTH would find no difficulty in obtaining a corps 2,000 strong instead of 860, which is the limit. To-night the companies will meet at their respective head-quarters, and afterwards assemble either at the Arsenal or Palace Garden, as may be designated, and their perfect their organization into companies. They will be formed into squads of four each, who will act as comrades during the campaign, marching, drilling, tenting and messing together. The rolls of the different companies will then be open for the reception of signatures at the General Head-quarters, where the election for officers of the regiment will take place.

The financial affairs of the organization promise to be placed in a flourishing condition, as several wealthy gentlemen of the City, who feel deeply interested in the success of the movement, have volunteered their services and material aid, to put the Regimental exchequer in good condition. It is also proposed to raise sufficient funds in this way to uniform the Regiment before it shall leave the State, and thus relieve the Federal Government of the expense.

It was decided yesterday that the uniform should consist of a grey felt hat, skull fatigue cap, red shirt, (firemen's,) grey jacket, grey flowing pants, (Zouave,) gaiters and blue overcoat. A firm of merchant tailors have contracted to have the requisite number of these uniforms ready by Wednesday night next, and the Regiment will be ready to muster 12 o'clock to-night. We understand that a very fine stand of colors is to be presented to the corps by the Fire Department before it departs from the City. Col. ELLSWORTH has received several letters from prominent merchants, and also from two or three of the City Banks, offering material aid to assist him in the enterprise, and the fact nobly attests their patriotism.

THE NEW REGIMENT.

A recruiting-station, for the Ninth and Fifteenth Wards, has been opened by Acting Major J. MANSFIELD DAVIS, on the southwest corner of Tenth-street and Sixth-avenue, for the new Regiment about being organized, under the command of Ex-Col. DURYEA, late of the Seventh Regiment, National Guard. Maj. DAVIS is just the man for the work, and the young men of those Wards who desire to render their country a service cannot find a better place to enroll their names.

MORE TROOPS FROM MASSACHUSETTS.

Yesterday morning the military spirit of the City was cheered by the arrival of the Eighth Regiment of the Massachusetts Militia, following close upon the heels of the Sixth Regiment, which passed through our streets on Thursday. They numbered nine hundred men, filling eighteen cars, which left Boston on Thursday night at 6 P. M. Their list of officers is as follows: Colonel, Timothy Moore; Lieutenant-Colonel, E. W. Hincks; Major, Andrew Ellwell; Adjutant, G. W. Cresey; Paymaster, R. G. Asher; Quartermaster, A. A. Ingalls; Surgeons, B. Breed and W. W. Tapley. The companies are from Salem, Marblehead, Lynn, Newburyport and Pittsfield. Alighting at the dépôt at Twenty-Seventh-street, they proceeded to the Fifth-avenue Hotel where four companies took breakfast. Three companies breakfasted at the Lafarge House, and three at the Astor. As the entire Regiment passed the Brevoort House on Fifth-avenue, Major ANDERSON was loudly cheered. They left, at noon, yesterday, for Washington.

The Third and Fourth Massachusetts Regiments left Boston *via* Fall River, on Wednesday, where they embarked on the *State of Maine* for Fort Monroe.

An Irish Regiment is in course of formation at Boston.

The Fifth Regiment of Massachusetts will march immediately.

THE OLD CITIZENS AROUSED.

A meeting of the old citizens upwards of fifty years will be held at Palace Garden, Fourteenth-street, between Sixth and Seventh avenues, on Monday, the 22d day of April, at 7½ P. M., for the purpose of organizing a volunteer regiment for the defence of our City, in the absence of our sons and young men, who may be called away for the defence of the General Government in perpetuating our beloved nation, founded by our immortal WASHINGTON and his associates under the Providence of God.

LIFE INSURANCE AND VOLUNTEERING.

At a meeting of delegates from sixteen Life Companies doing business in this City and elsewhere, held this day, April 19, 1861, the following resolution was passed for the consideration and final decision of the Boards of Directors of the several Companies:

Resolved, That it is the opinion of this Committee that the several Life Insurance Companies should give their consent to those assured by them to enter into the Military and Naval service of the United States for such a period and upon such terms as may be agreed. It is understood that an advanced rate will be charged.

COL. WILSON IS WILLING TO GO TO BALTIMORE.

To the Editor of the New-York Times:

I understand that the people of this City think that if 2,000 men would volunteer to go to Baltimore, they could keep a passage for the troops now on their way to the seat of war. I have 2,000 men who will volunteer to march to Baltimore on Monday afternoon, at 5 P. M., and hold and protect all Union troops passing through. We will want rifles and swords, bayonets, plenty of ammunition, COLT's pistols, knives, gray shirts, felt hats, stout shoes and pants. Respectfully, yours,

WILLIAM WILSON, Colonel,

WILSON'S VOLUNTEERS.

The head-quarters of this Regiment is at No. 618 Broadway. Col. WILSON has already raised 1,500 men, and can raise 2,000 active, muscular young men, good and true, providing that a musket with a sword bayonet, ammunition, a flannel shirt, a felt hat and a good pair of shoes is furnished to each man. He guarantees to start for Baltimore, or anywhere else the Government chooses to send them, by 5 o'clock Monday.

COL. DURYEA'S VOLUNTEER REGIMENT.

At a meeting held last evening at the head-quarters of the Fifth Ward Volunteers now forming, to be enrolled into the "Advance Guard" of Volunteer Militia, to be commanded by Ex-Col. DURYEA, of the famous Seventh Regiment. Mr. CHAS. W. LEWIS was elected Chairman, and Dr. F. G. PETIT JEAN, formerly Surgeon in the French service, was elected Secretary. The purpose of the meeting was stated by the Chairman,—to elect a Captain of the Company,—and nominated JAMES L. WAUGH, formerly Captain of Fifth Company National Guards,—an officer of undoubted experience, and one who would stand by the National flag at all hazards. The members present entered into an election, which resulted in the unanimous

Continued on Eighth Page.]

Demonstration in Union Square, New York, to support the government, April 20, 1861

The New-York Times.

VOL. X....NO. 2990. NEW-YORK, SUNDAY, APRIL 21, 1861. PRICE TWO CENTS.

THE UNION FOREVER!

Immense Demonstration in this City.

THE ENTIRE POPULATION IN THE STREETS.

Over One Hundred Thousand People at Union-square.

The Metropolis Streaming with Banners and Streamers.

Processions, Speeches and Resolutions.

LETTER FROM ARCHBISHOP HUGHES.

Addresses by John A. Dix, Daniel S. Dickinson, Wm. M. Evarts, Senator Baker, Henry J. Raymond, Moses H. Grinnell Wm. F. Havemeyer, Fernando Wood, Wm. Curtis Noyes, Rich'd O'Gorman, D. D. Field, Hiram Ketchum, John Cochrane, and Others.

The Empire City, yesterday, spoke in tones of thunder for the Union, the Constitution and the enforcement of the laws. The largest meeting, without exception, that was ever held on this continent, and the most enthusiastic, was that which came together at Union-square and in the vicinity yesterday—for the hundred thousand and unnumbered thousands more who responded to the call were too numerous to find standing room within the limits of the Square itself. Into the adjoining thoroughfares the crowds overflowed, and Broadway from Fourteenth-street almost to the Battery was a surging mass of human beings all the afternoon. The stores were closed, and everywhere, on house-tops and mastheads, and on men's hats and next their hearts, and even in ladies' bonnets were the Stars and Stripes,—the emblem of a Union which the people have declared "must and shall be preserved." They who of late, and not without some show of reason, have upbraided Americans for the seeming apathy with which they first heard how that flag had been dishonored, should have seen the demonstration of yesterday. Union-square was a red, white and blue wonder. Countless little flags were hung from windows or waved by ladies and children who looked forth from them. Not only the adjacent hotels,—the Clarendon, the Everett, the Union Place, the Monument House,—displayed national colors in profusion, but from nearly every private house, from Spingler Institute and from the Church of the Puritans, the flag of our Union waved proudly.

STAND NO. 1.

The happy possessors of green tickets, to the number of several hundreds, were admitted to the main stand of the meeting, fronting on the statue of WASHINGTON—on the site of the memorable spot where the dedication ceremonies of the statue took place. Among those present were some of the most distinguished of New-York's merchants, jurists and literati. The stand was crowded to excess with the wealth and talent of the City. DODWORTH'S band furnished music, a stout corps of police quelled all approaches from unwarranted intruders, flags waved from all points, and the glorious colors of Old Sumter itself floated from a friendly tree, where they were placed by the identical HART, who nailed it to the flagstaff of Major ANDERSON'S fortress, after it was shot away from the enemy. As HART ascended the tree to adjust the flag, Superintendent KENNEDY shouted to the people his name, and as it was echoed from mouth to mouth through the vast concourse, cheer upon cheer rent the air, and finally HART was obliged to come forward and speak.

SPEECH OF POLICEMAN HART, OF FORT SUMTER.

Mr. HART, who, it will be recollected, is the Metropolitan policeman who went to Fort Sumter as escort to Mrs. ANDERSON, advanced to the front platform, and spoke as follows:

I see many patriotic hearts around me, which we would have rejoiced to have had with us at Fort Sumter. This (pointing to the flag) is the flag that we nailed to the flagstaff of Fort Sumter, and nobly we defended it until the last. I want you of New-York to volunteer to nail that flag again to Fort Sumter. [Thunders of applause.]

The time previous to the arrival of the speakers was occupied in the diversions of the surging crowd, the raising of a time-honored American flag on the statue of WASHINGTON, and the display of a huge American Eagle. Soon the swaying of the outskirts of the mass announced

THE APPROACH OF MAJOR ANDERSON,

who seemed to be borne almost upon the shoulders of the people through the dense mass. In vain did the well meaning policemen endeavor to keep back the tide—their task was as fruitless as that of Mrs. Partington; for the eager populace pressed closer and closer to view the hero of the first battle in the pending war. The enthusiasm ran to the highest pitch, as the object of it all rose to view on the stand, and was placed in sight of the multitude. Nervous and agitated as he never was in the face of the enemy, he acknowledged the homage, and renewed greetings were given from the assembled thousands as far as the eye could reach—from Fourteenth-street and Broadway round to the corner of Fifteenth-street and Fourth-avenue. In like manner were Surgeon CRAWFORD, Capt. DOUBLEDAY and Capt. FOSTER greeted, and it was long before the tumult of their welcome could be subdued.

At last, R. H. MCCURDY, Esq., mounted a prominent point, and amid the din announced that Dr. SPRING, the venerable pastor of the Brick Church, would invoke the Divine blessing. The sight of Dr. SPRING'S white hairs streaming in the breeze tended greatly to allay the storm, but it was in vain that he endeavored to make himself heard twenty feet from the stand. In feeble and trembling tones he spoke as follows:

SPEECH OF DR. SPRING.

Mr. PRESIDENT: I feel myself very happy, as a native born American and a son of one of the Revolutionary officers, and as a member of Christ's Church, and one of his ambassadors, to be permitted to bear my testimony in favor of this noble cause. My past views on the agitated questions of the country are well known to those of you who are familiar with the Press. I have seen no occasion to alter them. I adhere to them as now. But the question now is, not between Slavery and Anti-Slavery—not between Republicanism and Democracy, but between law and anarchy, between Government and no Government. And permit me to say that all the other questions are evanescent, they are mere phantoms; they shrink into nothingness compared with the grand question of Government and no Government in this country. It is with high pleasure that I lift my voice on behalf of that Church which I represent, and I cheerfully accept the invitation to open this meeting with prayer.

Dr. SPRING then uttered an impressive prayer appropriate to the occasion.

RECEPTION OF HON. JOHN A. DIX.

Mr. MCCURDY then said: I have now the honor of presenting to you, as Chairman of this meeting, Hon. JOHN A. DIX. All who are in favor of that will say "Aye." An universal shout greeted Mr. DIX as he advanced to the front of the stand, and put the question on the adoption of the following list of officers, likewise proposed by Mr. MCCURDY. The list was adopted, and the meeting stood organized as follows:

President—JOHN A. DIX.

VICE-PRESIDENTS.

Peter Cooper,	Greene C Bronson,	W. B. Astor,
W. M. Evarts,	W. C. Bryant,	Pelatiah Perit,
George Bancroft,	John A. King,	James Boorman,
Stewart Brown,	John J. Phelps,	R. B. Minturn,
Berry Grinnell,	Moses Taylor,	O. D. F. Grant,
W. E. Dodge,	Watts Sherman,	Edwin Croswell,
L. G. B. Cannon,	Jno. D. Wolfe,	Seth B. Hunt,
Freder'k Bronson,	F. A. Conkling,	A. J. Williamson,
D. H. Arnold,	Edwin Dobbs,	Joseph Stuart,
R. H. McCurdy,	Joseph W. Alsop,	E. E. Morgan,
Willis Blackstone,	Nath. Hayden,	John Lloyd,
Chas H. Russell,	Robt Kay,	Benj. L. Swan,
Jno. C. Jones,	David Hoadley,	Robt J. Taylor,
Jas. N. Phelps,	James Low,	John Ewen,
Jos. A. Briggs,	John D. Jones,	Wm. C. Bryce,
Henry F. Vail,	A. B. Baylis,	Elnathan Thorne,
W. B. Maclay,	Fred. Kapp,	Alex. Duncan,
George Folsom,	Andrew Carrigan,	A. C. Kingsland,
Isaac Ferris,	J. Auchincloss,	M. Franklin,
D. R. Martin,	Wm. Chauncey,	H. B. Chaflin,
William Bryce,	A. S. Hewitt,	S. B. Althause,
Peter Lorillard,	Erastus Brooks,	Joseph Seligman,
S. Livingston,	W. H. Osborn,	A. A. Vanderpoel,
W. W. De Forest,	Anson Herrick,	Theodore Fowler,
Daniel Leroy,	S. L. Mitchill,	Augustus Schell,
Chas. Christmas,	J. B. Varnum,	William Hall,
Charles A. Secor,	John T. Hoffman,	Hamilton Fish,
Luther Bradish,	Fernando Wood,	A. T. Stewart,
Morris Ketchum,	Jonathan Sturges,	J. J. Astor,
John Cochrane.		

SECRETARIES.

J. Smith Homans,	J. T. Johnston,	D. D. Lord,
George A. Vogel,	Chas. B. Norton,	John Bigelow,
Shepard Gandy,	C. H. Marshall, Jr.,	Fletcher Westray,
Jas. G. De Forest.		

SPEECH OF HON JOHN A DIX.

Mr. DIX on taking the Chair, said:

FELLOW-CITIZENS: We have come together to express our determination to uphold the authority of the Government, and to maintain inviolate the honor of the country. The circumstances under which we are assembled are calculated to fill any patriotic heart with the deepest concern. For the first time in our day civil strife has broken out in the bosom of our prosperous and happy country, and has been pushed by unscrupulous men to the extremity of war and bloodshed. With no provocation whatever, from the Federal Government, they have turned their arms in fraternal hatred against it, even when it was administered by those who were actuated by the most friendly dispositions towards them. But I do not doubt, when the present excitement shall have passed away, when those who have thus arrayed themselves against the Government of the country, shall have learned from a disastrous experience that their true interest lies in peace, all will concede, on a review of the past, in a spirit of fairness and moderation, that there was no just ground for alienation. [Applause.] But, fellow-citizens, I feel that all such considerations are inappropriate to the hour. The time for action has come. Practical issues are upon us, to be dealt with under a just sense of the responsibilities they have brought with them. The Constitution of the United States has been spurned and repudiated. The authority of the Government has been resisted by military force. The flag of the Union has been insulted, in more than one instance torn down and even trampled under foot. Most of us were born, and all of us have lived, in prosperity and peace under the protection of the Constitution; we have regarded our allegiance to the Union as second only to our religion in the sanctity of its obligations: and we have venerated the national standard, under which WASHINGTON and JACKSON, and the host of gallant men who were their compatriots in arms, or who followed in their footsteps, achieved undying honors for themselves and their country. [Enthusiastic applause.] We should be less than men if we could look with indifference on these outrages on all we hold most dear. There is no justification for the course of the Confederate States in overturning within their limits the authority of the Federal Government. They have no excuse for it. This is no time for elaborate argument. Let me say in a word, that no respectable defence of the right of secession has ever fallen under my notice. No man contends that there is any warrant for it in the Constitution. There is but one way for a State to go out of the Union—the way in which all came in—by the concurrence of the common authority. In no other manner can the terms of separation be agreed on. [We don't want to separate.] Whatever preliminary action there may be, it must come to this conclusion at last. It is an omitted case in our political compact. The framers of the Constitution did not contemplate the dissolution of the Union. They framed the Government for themselves and their posterity. The repudiation of its authority by one of its members was not foreseen or provided for. It is a case which cannot be reached by the powers vested in Congress or in the Executive; and the States are necessarily remitted to the exercise of their united sovereignty for the solution of a problem which concerns the existence of all. It was for this reason that a Committee of which I was Chairman, in an address to our Southern brethren, adopted at a meeting in Pine street, in December last, recommended that the States should meet together for consultation, and if they could not settle their difficulties amicably and preserve the Union, that they should arrange the terms of separation and save the country from the horrors of civil war. We implored them to pause, in order to give us time for an effort to restore harmony and fraternal feeling. We appealed to them in language of entreaty, which would have been humiliating if it had not been addressed to brethren of the same political family. To this appeal, enforced by the concurrence of eminent citizens of this State, who had always been the most strenuous advocates of Southern rights, the States, to which it was addressed, responded by setting the authority of the Union at defiance, by seizing the public forts and arsenals, by seducing Federal officers from their allegiance, and, in one instance, by confiscating the treasure of the Government. For months these outrages were submitted to with no effort on the part of the Government to resent or punish them, in the hope that under the guidance of better counsels, those who committed them would return to their allegiance. This forbearance, unexampled in the history of nations, and falsely interpreted into a pusillanimous surrender of its authority by the Federal Government, had only the effect of invigorating the spirit of resistance, until at last the slender force in Fort Sumter was attacked—some 6,000 or 7,000 men against 100—and compelled, after a heroic resistance, to evacuate it. [Cheers for Fort Sumter.] The gallant commander of that handful of loyal men who sustained this unequal contest, is now before you. [Tremendous applause for Major ANDERSON.] There hangs the flag under which they upheld the honor of their country; and its tattered condition shows the desperate defence they made. [Enthusiastic cheering.]

It is under these circumstances that the General Government has appealed to the country to come to its support. [We will, we will.] It would have been treacherous to its trust if it had not determined to uphold the authorities confided to it.

And, here, fellow-citizens, it is important that we should clearly understand the position of the late Administration on this question. It is due to this Administration, as well as the last, that we should all understand it. I shall be very brief, but I must ask your close attention for the few moments that will be needed.

On the 3d of December last, in his annual Message to Congress, the late President made a strong and unanswerable argument against the right of Secession. He also indicated his purpose to collect the revenue and defend the forts in South Carolina. In a special message to Congress on the 8th of January he declared (I use the language of the Message,) "the right and the duty to use military force defensively against those who resist the Federal officers in the execution of their legal functions and against those who assail the property of the Federal Government is clear and undeniable." [Cries of "Good for him!" and loud cheering.] The authorities of South Carolina were repeatedly warned that if they assailed Fort Sumter it would be the commencement of a civil war, and they would be responsible for the consequences. [Cheers.] The last and most emphatic of these warnings is contained in the admirable answer of Mr. HOLT, Secretary of War, to Mr. HAYNE, the Commissioner from South Carolina, on the 6th of February. It is in these words: "If, with all the multiplied proofs which exist of the President's anxiety for peace and of the earnestness with which he has pursued it, the authorities of that State shall assault Fort Sumter and peril the lives of the handful of brave and loyal men shut up within its walls, and thus plunge our common country into the horrors of civil war, then upon them and those they represent must rest the responsibility." [Enthusiastic applause and waving of hats.] I believe the letter from which I read this extract has never been published, for I, as a member of the Administration at the time it was written, have a right to say that it had the cordial approval of the late President and all his constitutional advisers. [Cheers for Gen. DIX.] And this brings me to the point I wish to make. I violate no confidence in making it. It is this: If South Carolina had tendered war to the late Administration as she has to this—I mean by a hostile and deadly assault—it would have been unanimously accepted. [Prolonged cheering.] I repeat, then, that this Administration has done no more than its duty. Nay, I believe, that self preservation rendered necessary what it has done. I have no doubt that the Confederate leaders at Montgomery have entertained, and still enter[tain] the design of marching upon Washington to overthrow the Government, taking its place and pretending itself to the nations of the world as the true representative of the people of the United States. [Cries of "Never; never; they can't do it."] Against this usurpation and fraud, if it shall be attempted, I trust we shall contend with all the strength God has given us. [Cries of "We will."] I am for supporting the Government. I do not ask who administers it. It is the Government of my country, and as such I shall give it in this extremity all the support in my power. I regard the pending contest with the Secessionists as a death-struggle for Constitutional Liberty and law—a contest, which, if successful on their part, could only end in the establishment of a despotic Government, and blot out, wherever they were in the ascendant, every vestige of National Freedom. You know, fellow-citizens, that I have always been in favor of adjusting controversies between the States by conciliation, by compromise, by mutual concession—in a word, in the spirit in which the Constitution was formed. Whenever the times shall be propitious for calm consultation, they will find me so still. But, until then, let us remember that nothing could be so disastrous, so humiliating, and so disreputable to us all as to see the common Government overthrown or its legitimate authority successfully resisted. Let us, then, rally, with one heart, to its support. I believe it will act with all the moderation and forbearance consistent with the preservation of the great interests confided to it. There is no choice left out to acquiesce in its surrender to revolutionary leaders, or to give it the means it needs for defence, for self-preservation, and for the assertion of its authority, holding it responsible for their legitimate use. Fellow-citizens, we stand before the statue of the Father of his Country. The Flag of the Union, which floats over it, hung above him when he presided over the Convention by which the Constitution was framed. The great work of his life has been rejected, and the banner by which his labors were consecrated has been trampled in the dust. If the inanimate bronze in which the sculptor has shaped his image could be changed to the living form which led the armies of the Revolution to victory, he would command us in the name of the hosts of patriots and political martyrs who have gone before, to strike for the defence of the Union and the Constitution.

Mr. MCCURDY read the resolutions, as follows:

Whereas, The Union of the States, under the guidance of Divine Providence, has been the fruitful source of prosperity and domestic peace to the country for nearly three-quarters of a century; and,

Whereas, The Constitution, framed by our Revolutionary fathers, contains within itself all needful provisions for the exigencies of the Government, and, in the progress of events, for such amendments as are necessary to meet new emergencies; and,

Whereas, An armed combination has been formed to break up the Union by throwing off the obligations of the Constitution and has, in several of the States, carried on its criminal purpose by seizing forts, arsenals, revenue vessels, and public treasure, and, finally, by assaulting Fort Sumter, a fortress of the United States occupied by a slender but heroic garrison, and capturing it by an overwhelming force after a gallant defence, thus setting the authority of the Government at defiance, and insulting the National Flag; and,

Whereas, The Government of the United States, with an earnest desire to avert the evils of civil war, has silently submitted to these aggressions and insults with a patient forbearance unparalleled in the annals of history, but has at last deemed it due to the public honor and safety to appeal to the people of the Union for the means of maintaining its authority, of enforcing the execution of the laws, and of saving our country from dismemberment, and our political institutions from destruction; therefore,

Resolved, That the Declaration of Independence, the War of the Revolution, and the Constitution of the United States, have given origin to this Government, the most equal and beneficent hitherto known among men; that under its protection the wide expansion of our territory, the vast development of our wealth, our population, and our power have built up a nation able to maintain and defend before the world the principles of liberty and justice, upon which it was founded; that by every sentiment of interest, of honor, of affection, and of duty we are engaged to preserve unbroken for our generation, and to transmit to our posterity, the great heritage we have received from heroic ancestors, that to the maintenance of this sacred trust we devote whatever we possess, and whatever we can do, and in support of that Government under which we are happy and proud to live, we are prepared to shed our blood, and to lay down our lives.

Resolved, That the founders of the Government of the United States have provided, by the institution of the Supreme Court, a tribunal for the peaceful settlement of all questions arising under the Constitution and laws; that it is the duty of the States to appeal to it for relief from measures which they believe unauthorized; and that attempts to throw off the obligations of the Constitution and to obtain redress by an appeal to arms, can be considered in no other light than as levying war against the United States.

Resolved, That the Constitution of the United States, the basis and the safeguard of the Federal Union, having been framed and ratified by the original States, and accepted by those which subsequently became parties to it, is binding upon all; and that any assumption by any one of them of the rights delegated to the Federal Government, without first seeking a release from its obligations through the concurrence of the common sovereignty, is unauthorized, unjust to all others, and destructive of all social and political order.

Resolved, That when the authority of the Federal Government shall have been reestablished and peaceful obedience to the Constitution and laws prevails, we shall be ready to confer and cooperate with all loyal citizens throughout the Union, in Congress or in Convention, for the consideration of all supposed grievances, the redress of all wrongs, and the protection of every right, yielding ourselves, and exacting from others to yield, to the will of the whole people, as constitutionally and lawfully expressed.

Resolved, That it is the duty of all good citizens, overlooking past differences of opinion to contribute by all the means in their power, to maintain the Union of the States, to defend the Constitution, to preserve the National Flag from insult, and to uphold the authority of the Government against acts of lawless violence, which, if longer unresisted would inevitably end in breaking down all the barriers erected by our fathers for the protection of life, liberty and property and involve the country in universal anarchy and confusion.

Resolved, That a Committee of twenty-five be nominated by the President, or appointed by this meeting, to represent the citizens in the collection of funds and the transaction of such other business in aid of the movements of the Government, as the public interests may require.

Hon. DANIEL S. DICKINSON was next introduced, and was received with a storm of applause.

SPEECH OF HON. DANIEL S. DICKINSON.

Mr. DICKINSON said: I am invited, Mr. President, and my fellow citizens, to attend and address this meeting in the language of its call, "without regard to previous political opinions or associations, to meet to express their sentiments in the present crisis in our national affairs, and their determination to uphold the Government of their country, and maintain the authority of the Constitution and its laws." I embrace the opportunity with alacrity, and have traveled 200 miles and upwards this morning that I might do so, for I look with extreme apprehension and alarm upon the danger which threatens us as a whole, recently a united people. I would know no section in this great material heritage of Freedom, which stretches from ocean to ocean, from the far frozen North to where it is fanned by the gentle breezes of the tropics; no division or strife among or between children of a common father and brothers of the same household; but the demon of discord has inaugurated his fearful court in our midst, and the crisis is to be met like every other vicissitude. A somewhat extended service in the National councils, at a period of unusual interest, gave me an opportunity for much and mature reflection, upon the relations between the North and the South; upon the duties each section owed to itself and the other, and to the cause of Free Government, under a hallowed compact upon the constitutional guaranties secured, and upon that fraternal regard which, by every consideration that could influence civilized and Christian men, each section and its people should at all times cultivate toward the other. I have looked upon all these of the same common faith, and though scattered over an area so vast, divided into sections, subdivided into numerous States, and the two sections committed to different systems of industry, as mutually conducive to one great interest, as essential to each other to promote the common enjoyment, and as bound together to the same immortal destiny. None of these views of what should and ought to, and might have been, have been changed, but recent untoward events have served to confirm them beyond the shadow of a doubt, and to increase regrets that those so strong so little, and of such incalculable value, could not have been put forth before it was too late! But now, in common with every lover of his country, I am called to meet that we should be aroused from these dreams of a people's security, happiness and glory, by a conflict of blood. Until recently I had hoped that time, and a returning sense of patriotism and reference to the scenes and trials of the Revolution, a thought of the great names, and greater memories of those who wrought out the noble lot we should enjoy, and above all, a sense of duty we owed to ourselves, to each other, to our country and its Constitution, to our descendants, to the cause of liberty throughout the earth, would bear this great question far above and beyond the field of vitiated and demoralized politics, and save the Union; not in mere form, but the Union of our fathers, in the spirit of the Constitution, the Union purchased by the blood poured out at Lexington, and Bunker Hill, and Saratoga and Yorktown; the Union of the great spirits of '76, the Union of the stars and stripes, which though torn and disfigured, is dearer than ever; the Union over, which every patriot in every section can exclaim, in the language of the British Poet, "With all thy faults, I love thee still!"—the Union which can never be destroyed in the affections of the American people. Yes,

> "You may break, you may shatter the vase if you will,
> But the scent of the roses will hang round it still."

But these anticipations have not been, and are not to be realized. Six months since we were enjoying unexampled success—now ruin runs riot over this fair land, and all for madness. Numerous States have passed ordinances of secession from the Union, and have seized the Federal property within their reach; they repudiate and disown its authority, assault its flag, and defy its power; have deliberately, and with an overpowering force, attacked and reduced a partially garrisoned and unoffending fortification, because they assumed to regard the gallant Major ANDERSON, with his loyal men, who reposed in peace, a kind of Minister Plenipotentiary of the United States, near, and rather too near, the Government of South Carolina; and now they have threatened, as is asserted upon what seems to be good authority, to march against the Federal Capital. Troops marching to its defence have been murdered. War is, therefore upon us, with all its terrible realities—a civil, intestine war, against and between brethren! It were profitless to inquire for original or remote causes; it is no time for indecision or insult to; it is no time for crimination or recrimination, or for reviving partisan issues; it is no time to inquire whose hand governs the helm, nor who placed him there, if as prescribed by the Constitution, nor by what name he is known in the political jargon of the day. But, the only inquiry should be, does he propose to steer the good Ship of State according to the chart of the Constitution, between the Scylla and Charybdis which threaten her pathway, and will he uphold the Constitution and administer the laws with the firmness, justice, and forbearance, with a wisdom, mercy, and discretion, becoming the Chief Magistrate of such a people, in such an exigency; and if he does that, and that only, he should be, and will be, triumphantly sustained; not by political parties extant or obsolete, nor those serving partisans, but by the patriotic pulsations of the great popular heart. Our reverses are chargeable as well to a demoralized sentiment as to sectional disturbance. The country is cursed with the "canker of a calm world and a long peace—rank with mean ambition—swarming with office hunters and plethoric with treasury-mongers. Like the plagues of Egypt, they have filled the beds, and boards, and kneading troughs of the Republic, and poisoned the very fountains of political morality." My desires and efforts, and anxieties and prayers, have been for peace, that everything might be yielded that could be consistent with a nation's dignity and honor, and our great Republic could yield much to a portion of its erring people, rather than provoke or even permit a conflict of hostile forces; and even yet I invoke the benign spirit of conciliation! The Government must arm, and that in a manner commensurate with its vast resources, and becoming the priceless interests confided to its keeping,—becoming a great, generous, and forbearing people, and becoming the lamentable occasion; but it should put on its armor for preservation, not for destruction; not for aggressive war, but for defensive peace; not for subjugation or coercion, but to arrest tumult, lawlessness and disorder; not to despoil others, but to keep its own; to maintain the supremacy of the Constitution, and to vindicate the laws, to put down insurrection, and to repel invasion; to maintain the power and dignity of the nation, and preserve its flag inviolate; to save, if saved can be, the Union, already dissevered, from the final overthrow and destruction with which it is menaced. The contemplation of even the most brilliant success upon the field of blood, brings me in this controversy only heart sickness and sorrow, for I cannot forget that it is a war between those who should have loved, and cheered, and consoled each other, along the bleak and desolate pathway of life's perilous pilgrimage, and that we may say of him who falls in the wicked and unnatural strife:

> "Another sword has laid him low,
> Another and another's,
> And every hand that dealt the blow,
> Ah me! it was a brother's."

But I would assert the power of the Government over those who owe it allegiance and attempt its overthrow, as Brutus put his signet to the death warrant of his son, that I might exclaim with him, "Justice is satisfied and Rome is free." I would defend our Government, and its territory, and its citadel, that we may not weep like women over that we fail to defend like men. In this fraternal strife, let us by no means forget the numerous patriotic hearts at the South, that beat responsive to the Union sentiment; how long and how faithfully they have endured, how much of assault and contumely they have withstood, what interests, political, social and material, they have sacrificed, how long and how safely they have buffeted the angry waves which have beat around them!

They have loved and cherished the Union, and have clung with a death-like tenacity to the pillars of the Constitution—to uphold and sustain it—and may God bless them. Let us remember them in this the evil day of our common country, and do nothing to cast impediments in the way of their patriotic progress and endurance.

The action of our own noble State may be potential in this gloomy crisis. She has power, and must interpose it—wealth, and must proffer it—men, and must rally them to duty; and should employ her mighty energies to silence this accursed din of arms, and tumult and murder, at an early moment, in the name of the Constitution and the Union, of justice, forbearance, humanity and peace.

> "'Tis not the whole of life to live,
> Nor all of death to die."

And this commercial Emporium of the Western hemisphere, the offspring of Free Government and unrestricted enterprise, under a glorious Union, where they concentre and are diffused. Great in natural advantages and material wealth, great in architectural magnificence and commercial renown, great in an active and enterprising population, in the arts and sciences in her institutions of religion, charity and learning; but greater in her mighty moral energies for good, when the waves of madness heave, mountain high, and threaten universal destruction. She can, in the plenitude of her power, speaking with united voice do much to silence the war whoops which Christian civilization has borrowed in this day of light from savage barbarism. She can do much to roll back and calm the angry agitation of the waters with the stern commands of peace. Then let her stretch forth her strong arm in support of the Constitution and the Union. Let her sustain the Government in its lawful authority, in upholding inviolate our glorious flag—emblem of a more glorious Union, in defending its territory, in preserving that Union, if possible, from further disruption and destruction, and proclaim how by the measures of justice and wisdom, every disaffected State to the Union it once loved, and cherished and adorned. And if when all efforts at conciliation have failed, the surges of internal passion shall run more madly still, an armed force must meet for destruction upon the field of battle, when it is covered with the dead and dying, and the shrieks of the wounded are ascending to heaven, let us be able to exclaim with Cæsar when he saw the field of Pharsalia strewn with his fallen countrymen—"They would have it so!" The States of the South alleged common grievances against the Free States, and suggested the necessity of further guarantees. There was a large and powerful party in the Free States, in sympathy with them in this demand, and if all the Southern States had moved with solemn deliberation and in concert, it is obvious that satisfactory guarantees would have been provided, or that if not, a peaceful separation could have been secured, and civilization and Christianity and freedom have been spared the disgrace which must disfigure the page of history, so long as ink shall stand a faithful sentinel on paper, and darken the dreamy shadows of tradition, when history shall have faded away. But some rushed hastily to pass ordinances of secession without waiting for the concert of aggrieved sisters, or even the sanction of their own people—some seized the Federal property within their reach, and armed for avowed conflict, and menaced the Federal Government, and thus reduced all chances for conciliation, either for restoration or final peaceful separation. One initiation has produced another, one false and impetuous movement has initiated another, until all national hope of peace has left us, I fear, forever, and we must drink, drink to the dregs, the cup prepared for us. There was nothing in the relations of the two sections, importunate as they were, which ever rendered a resort to arms either justifiable or necessary, and the inauguration of war, over questions capable of pacific adjustment, will be condemned and execrated wherever civilization finds a resting-place, and the widow's wail, and the orphan's tears haunt the last moments of its existence. For myself, in our Federal relations, I know but one Union section, one flag, one Government. That section embraces every State; that Union is the Union, sealed with the blood and consecrated by the tears of the Revolutionary struggle; that flag is the flag known and honored in every sea under heaven, which has borne off glorious victory from many a bloody battle-field, and yet stirs with warmer and quicker pulsations the heart's blood of every true American, when he looks upon its Stars and Stripes wherever it waves. That Government is the Government of WASHINGTON, and ADAMS, and JEFFERSON, and JACKSON—a Government which has shielded and protected not only us, but God's oppressed children who have gathered under its wings from every portion of the globe—a Government which, from humble beginnings, has borne us forward with fabulous celerity, and from humble beginnings made us one of the great and prosperous Powers of earth. The Union of the States was a bright vision of my early years—the pride of my manhood, the ambition of my public service. I have sacrificed upon its altar the best energies and choicest hopes of a life chequered by vicissitude and trial. I had believed the contemplation of its beauties would be the companion of approaching age, and in after times the beguiler of vacant and solitary hours. And now, that its integrity is menaced, its fair proportions disfigured, it is still dear to my heart, as a great fountain of wisdom from which incalculable blessings have flowed. I have rejoiced with it in its heyday of success and triumph, and will by the grace of God, stand by it in its hour of darkness and peril, and by those who uphold it in the spirit of the Constitution, when the timid falter and the faithless fly, and when the skies lower and the winds howl, and the storm descends and the tempest beats—when the lightnings flash, and the thunders roar, and the rains dash, and the proud ship Union creaks and groans with the expiring throes of dissolution, I will cling to her still as the last refuge of hope from the fury of the storm; and if she goes down, I will go down with her, rather than survive to tell the story of her ignoble end. I will sustain that flag of stars and stripes, recently rendered more glorious by ANDERSON, his officers and men, wherever it flutters, over the sea or over the land; and when it shall be despoiled and disfigured, I will rally around it still as the Star Spangled Banner of my fathers and my country, and so long as a single stripe can be discovered, or a single star shall glimmer from the surrounding darkness, I shall cheer it as the emblem of a nation's glory and a nation's hope. And, could I see again my beloved and bleeding and distracted country all peacefully reposing beneath it, as in days gone by, I would almost swear with the devoted Jephtha, that infatuated leader of the hosts of Israel, that I would sacrifice to the Lord the first living thing that I should meet on my return from victory. [Tremendous applause.]

SPEECH OF SENATOR BAKER.

Senator EDWARD D. BAKER, of Oregon, was then introduced. He mounted a table and was received with great applause. He said:

The people in their majesty to-day meet to sustain the majesty of the Constitution, [cheers,] and I come a wanderer from the far Pacific to record my oath anew with you of the great Empire State to-day. The hour for conciliation is passed. [Applause.] The gathering for battle is at hand, [cheers,] and the country requires that every man should do his duty. [Cheers.] Fellow-citizens, what is that country? ["Freedom."] Is it the soil on which we tread? Is it the gathering of familiar faces? Is it mere lecturing and talk? Nay, more than these, is it power, and might, and majesty alone? No! Our country is more, far more than all these. The country which demands our solace, our love, our devotion, our hearts' blood, is more than all the e. [Applause.] Our country is the history of our fathers; our country is the tradition of our mothers; our country is past reunion; our country is present power and pride; our country is future hope and destiny; our country is greatness, glory, truth, constitutional liberty, and, above all, Freedom forever. [Great applause.] These are watchwords under which we fight, and we will shout them out till the stars hear in the sky in the stormiest shock. [Loud applause.] I have said that the hour for reconciliation is past. It may return, but not to-morrow, nor next week. It will return when that tattered flag (pointing to the flag of Sumter over his head) is avenged. [Long and continued applause.] It will return when rebellious traitors are taught obedience and submission; it will return when a rebellious Confederacy are taught that the North, though forbearing, is not fearful; it will return when again the ensign of the Republic streams over every rebellious fort, and every rebellious State; then, as of old, the ensign of the power and dignity, and majesty and the peace of the Republic. [Cheers.] Young men of New-York; No Young men of the United States, you are told that this is not to be a war of aggression. In one sense true; in another, not. We have committed aggression upon no man in all the broad land. In their rebellious nest, in their traitorous camp, no man, no truthful man, can say that he has been ever disturbed, though it be for a single moment, either in life, liberty or estate. The day that began this unnatural, wicked, rebellious warfare their rights were more secure, their property more guarded by us—not by themselves—guarded more securely than any people ever did have property guarded from the beginning of the world. [Cheers.] We have committed no aggression; we have violated no compact; we have exercised no unholy power; we have been loyal, constitutional and just. A majority of the Union, we will govern our own Union in our own way. We are all Democrats, we are all Republicans. We acknowledge the sovereignty of the people. Under the Constitution and beneath that flag, let traitors beware.

In this sense, then, young men of New-York, we are not for a war of aggression; but in another sense—speaking for myself as a man of honor, who has been a soldier, and as a Senator—I say in another sense, I am for a war of aggression. I propose to-day, now, as we did before in Mexico—to conquer peace. [Cheers.] I propose to go to Washington, and beyond. [Cheers.] I do not desire to remain entirely supine, inactive, fearful; till the war is brought to our midst. [Cheers.] I will meet them on the threshold of their gathering—[cheers]—there in the very seat of their power, and dictate the rebellious terms of peace. [Cheers.] It may take $30,000,000—it may take $300,000,000—what then? We have it. [Cheers.] Loyally, nobly, grandly, do the merchant princes of New-York respond to the ardent appeal of the United States Government. It may cost us 75,000 lives; it may be 75,000 lives; it may be 750,000 lives; what then? We have them. [Great cheering.] The blood of every loyal citizen of this Government is dear to me; my sons and theirs—young men grown up beneath my eye and care are here—they are all dear to me; but if the organization, the destiny, the renown, the glory, the freedom of a Constitutional Government, the only hope of a free people demand it, let them all go. [Tremendous cheering.] I am not now speaking timorous words of peace. I speak to kindle a spirit of manly, determined war. [Cheers.] I speak in the midst of the Empire State, amid scenes of past suffering and past glory; with the defences of the Hudson above me, the scenes of the struggle on Long Island before me, [cheers,] the statue of WASHINGTON in my very face, [cheers,] the tattered, unconquered flag of Sumter [great cheering] waving in the hand which I can almost now imagine trembles with excitement of battle. [Cheers.] and where I speak I say my mission here to-day is to kindle the heart of New-York for war. [Great cheering.] War, sudden, bold, determined forward war this day. [Renewed cheering.] The Seventh Regiment has gone. [Three times three deafening cheers.] Let seventy and seven more follow. [Cheers and cries of "Bravo."] "Of old," said the great historian, "beneath the banner of the Cross, Europe precipitated itself upon Asia"—beneath the banner of the Constitution let the men of the Union precipitate upon the disloyal Confederate States. [Immense cheering.] A few more words and I have done. [Cheers and cries of "Good."] Let no man underrate the dangers of this controversy. Civil war for the best of reasons—upon the one side the worst, upon the other always dangerous to liberty—is always fearful, bloody. Yet, fellow-citizens, there are worse things than fear, doubt, dread, danger or blood. Dishonor is worse. [Great cheering.] Perpetual anarchy is worse. [Cheers.] States commingling and forever severing is worse. And Traitorous secession everywhere is worse, and to be demeaned and belittled in the eyes of the Old World—perhaps star after star blotted out—[cries of "Never"] stripe after stripe obscured or dimmed.—to have men blush for shame throughout generations to come—these are worse than blood. [Enthusiastic and long continued cheering.] People of New-York, on the eve of battle, allow me to speak as a soldier. Few of you know of me, my career has been obscure [cries of "No"] and distant, but I can say that I have seen you tried. It was once my fortune to lead the gallant New-York regiment in the shock of battle. I was then leader upon the bloody heights of Cerro Gordo, [cheers,] and know well what New York can do when her blood is up. [Prolonged cheering.] Again and once more we will march, but not for revenge. We have nothing to avenge. It is not much that that tattered flag was lowered [pointing to the Sumter flag over the statue of WASHINGTON] when guarded by 70 against 10,000; it is not much that starvation effected what the enemy could not compel. [Cheers.] We have something to punish—as yet little or nothing to revenge. The President, himself a hero without knowing it, [cheers,] says there are wrongs to be redressed, enough endured to march to battle and to victory, because we don't choose to endure these wrongs any longer. They are wrongs not merely against us; they are not wrongs against us in one sense, but against our Union, [cheers,] against the Constitution, against human hope and human freedom. [Enthusiastic cheers.] This. If it be revenge, is dictated by these tattered stripes, and we will revenge them. [Enthusiastic cheers.] New-York, already while I speak, following in the wake of a man so eloquent, and, what is better, so conservative and well known—even while I speak the object of the meeting is accomplished; on the wings of lightning goes forth that the heart of this great mart of commerce, New-York, by one hundred thousand of her people speaks to the country, and declares that she will loyally sustain the Government. [Cheers.]

ANOTHER HERO FROM FORT SUMTER.

When Senator BAKER had concluded, Lieut. HALL, who formed one of the garrison of Fort Sumter, was introduced, and was received with overwhelming demonstrations of applause.

Hon. ROBERT J. WALKER was next introduced, and amid great confusion spoke as follows:

SPEECH OF HON. ROBERT J. WALKER.

FELLOW-CITIZENS: It is well that more than a hundred thousand of the freemen of the great State of New-York should be assembled on this occasion in the view of the flag of our country held by the image of its immortal founder—the great and glorious WASHINGTON. [Loud cheers.] Never, my countrymen was a more important epoch in the history of the world. From the dawn of civilization down to the present period so vast a question, so important in its results, so permanent in its influence for good or evil, was never before submitted to the consideration of any people. That portion, fellow-citizens, is this: Shall this Union be maintained and perpetuated, [yes, yes,] or shall it be broken and dissolved? [No, no.] Shall the flag which floated over the army of Washington, bearing on it the kindred emblems of our country's glory—shall that flag under which our fathers fought the war of the Revolution, and the war of 1812, shall it be stricken down? [No, no.] Yet there are certain States which claim to have seceded from the American Union. That claim is not founded on the Constitution. The Constitution of our country recognizes naught of Secession. The articles of confederation which precedes the Constitution declared that it was to be perpetual, and each one of the States of this Union pledged itself to its sister States that this Union would be perpetual, and she cannot now violate her faith without the destruction of the Constitution. Fellow-citizens, our country has been successful in every war. [Applause.] Against open enemies we have nothing to fear. But if this doctrine of secession is to be permitted and recognized by the American people, our Union is destroyed forever. If such a principle is to be maintained we have no Government, and our flag is a vain symbol. Secession is political suicide—[applause and cheers]—the self-destruction of a glorious nation—a nation spilling its own life-blood. If we do not now stop at the threshold, now and forever, this Government cannot be maintained, but we shall fall into universal anarchy, and become the scorn and scoff of the civilized world. And now to this question. What is your response? Will you sustain the Government? [Loud cries of "Yes!" "Yes!"] Will you maintain the Union, and support the laws? ["Yes!" "Yes!"] Gentlemen, your patriotic response is echoed from the Atlantic to the Pacific coast. Everywhere the voice of the American people declares in thunder-tones that the flag shall be maintained—that the Government shall be supported and that the Union shall be perpetual. [Loud and vociferous cheers.] Now, gentlemen, I will detain you but a little longer, because there is important intelligence from Washington to be communicated to you. Bear in mind that your flag has been assailed over Fort Sumter. Bear in mind, too, that we have a capital which bears the name of the Father of our Country, and where now is—however I may have opposed his election—the President of my country. [Loud cheers.] That capital is endangered. I shall never ask who commands the Ship of State when he sails under the flag of our Union, and guides it by the chart of the Constitution. [Cheers.] I regret most deeply this war. But we must fight it out until our glorious flag floats over every fort, and every vessel, and every acre of soil recognized as its national symbol. [Prolonged cheering.]

The President then made the following announcement:

The steamer *Baltic* is now at the foot of Canal street. Men are wanted to go in her, to proceed to Washington to-morrow. Other steamers will be ready, and if the men of New-York go there to-morrow morning they will be received on board and armed. [Tremendous cheers.]

And, fellow-citizens, I have another announcement to make; Mr. BAKER, of Oregon, who has just addressed you, proposes to raise a Brigade of New-Yorkers if the State will equip the men. [Prolonged cheers.]

LETTER OF ARCHBISHOP HUGHES.

The President then read the following letter from Archbishop HUGHES:

NEW-YORK, April 20, 1861.

DEAR SIR: Unable to attend the meeting at Union-square, in consequence of indisposition, I beg leave to state my sentiments on the subject of your coming together, in the following words:

Ministers of religion and ministers of peace, according to the instructions of their Divine Master, have not ceased to hope and pray that peace and union may be preserved in this great and free country. At present, however, that question has been taken out of the hands of the peacemakers, and it is referred to the arbitrament of a sanguinary contest. I am not authorized to speak in the name of any of my fellow-citizens. I think, so far as I can judge, there is the right principle all among them whom I know. It is now thirty years since, a foreigner by birth, I took the oath of allegiance to this country, under its title of the United States of America. [Loud cheers.] As regards conscience, patriotism, or judgment, I have no misgiving. Still desirous of peace, when the Providence of God shall have brought it. I may say that since the period of my naturalization, I have none but one country.

In reference to my duties as a citizen no change has come over my mind since then. The Government of the United States was then, as it is now, symbolized by a National Flag, popularly called "The Stars and Stripes." [Loud applause.] This has been my flag, and shall be to the end. [Cheers.] I trust it is still destined to display in the gales that sweep every ocean, and amid the gentle breezes of many a distant shore, as I have seen it in foreign lands, its own peculiar waving lines of beauty. May it live and continue to display these same waving lines of beauty, whether at home or abroad, for a thousand years, and afterwards as long as Heaven permits, without limit of duration.

JOHN HUGHES, Archbishop of New-York.

Loud calls were now made for Mayor WOOD, who responded as follows, being greeted with favorable demonstrations:

SPEECH OF HON. FERNANDO WOOD.

Mayor WOOD was then introduced. He was received with loud applause and a few hisses. He said: The Chairman has announced that Col. BAKER, the gentleman who has so eloquently addressed you to-day, proposes to raise a brigade of New-Yorkers if New-York will bear the expense. I here, as Mayor of this City, so far as I have the power to speak, pledge for the Corporation that same. [Loud applause.] When I assumed the duties of the office I have now the honor to hold, my official oath was that I should support the Constitution of the United States and the Constitution of the State of New-York, [cheers,] and infer from that that it is my duty, as it is consistent with my principles and my sense of right, to support not only the Constitution but the Union, the Government, the laws, and the flag, and in the discharge of that duty I care not what past political associations may be severed. [Great applause.] I am willing to give up all sympathies, and, if you please, all errors of judgment upon all national questions. [Applause.] In this great contest, representing, as I do, if not the whole, at least a portion of the community, I am willing to say here that I throw myself entirely into this contest with all my power and with all my might. [Loud applause.] My friends, the greatest man, next to WASHINGTON that this country has ever produced, has said that the Union must and shall be preserved. [Loud cheers.] and in that connection he said—and it is directly pertinent to the present contest—peaceably if we can, but forcibly if we must. [Cheers.] Why, gentlemen, what is the nature of that Government? The Government of the United States is founded upon the representative principle. It is the popular voice which the representatives speaks in making the laws. The laws are simply, therefore, the expression of the popular will; and the administration of the law, your Chief Magistrate, in so far as he acts within the law, represents the popular will; that will must be sustained at all hazards and under all circumstances. [Cheers.] My friends, it has been said here to-day that your flag has been insulted; aye, not only has your flag been insulted, but a Secretary of war, assuming to represent the Confederate States, has said that the Confederate flag would fly over Faneuil Hall, at Boston. My friends, if that banner can ever be carried to Faneuil Hall, in Boston, it must be over the dead body of every citizen of New-York. [Great applause.] And in behalf of New-York, I am prepared to say to you here, and through the Press to our friends of the South, that if that flag shall ever float over the National Capitol, every man, woman and child, will enlist in the war. I am with you in this contest. We know no party now. We are for maintaining the integrity of the National Union intact. I call upon every man, whatever may have been his sympathies, to make one great phalanx in this controversy, that we may, in the eloquent language of the Senator who has preceded me, proceed to conquer a peace. [Long-continued applause.] It has already been announced by your Chairman that the *Baltic* and other vessels are ready to take 5,000 men to-morrow to the Capital at Washington. I urge every man to respond to the call. [Loud cheering.]

Ex-Gov. HUNT was then introduced, and made a very eloquent and admirable address. The controversies of the past, he said, must be forgotten. We must all rally for the salvation of the country. The Capital was in danger, and he trusted our preparations would be ample for its defence. He hoped the time would come when all our sectional differences might be settled by a national Convention. But at present our duty is to defend the Capital and rally to drive back rebellion. Gov. HUNT was greeted with loud applause.

WM. M. EVARTS, Esq., was then introduced. He spoke as follows:

MR. CHAIRMAN AND GENTLEMEN: I shall not detain this immense crowd more than three minutes with what I have to say. I regard this as a business meeting, commencing the greatest transaction this generation of man has ever seen. [Applause.] We stand here but in the second generation from the men who declared our independence, fought the battles of the Revolution, and framed the Constitution under which we live—and the question for us to decide is whether we are worthy children of such men, and whether our descendants shall curse as we bless our fathers. [Cheers and exclamations of assent.] I can tell you that you have something more to do than you have done hitherto, which has been simply to read the glorious history which you have delighted in reading. You have to write a history which your children will glory in and bless you for. [Applause.] I tell you that when Providence puts together the 19th day of April, 1775, on which day was spilt the first blood at Lexington, and the 19th day of April, 1861, when was shed the first blood at Baltimore, it means something. [Tumultuous cheering.] I tell you that when the Statue of WASHINGTON sustains in its firm hand the splintered flag-staff of Fort Sumter, it means something also. [Renewed cheering and cries of "Three cheers for the flag," which were given.] And there is but one question left, and that is, whether you mean something also. If you mean something, do you mean enough, enough ENOUGH?—of time, of labor, of men, of blood, to seal and sanction the glories of the future of America. [A tremendous affirmation was the response.]

I tell you, gentlemen, that your ancestors fought for the sacred independence, liberty and equal rights which we enjoy, and every enemy of that liberty, independence and equal rights has told you that those ideas are inconsistent with Government. It is for you to show that the Government of the people means that the people must obey the Government, [applause]; and having shown what the world never saw till the Declaration of our Independence, what a people that governs itself can do in peace, you are to show what a people that governs itself must accomplish when it—the people—wages war against rebels and traitors. [Loud cheering.] I tell you that each man here is fighting his own quarrel and protecting the future of his children, and with this sentiment you need no argument and no suggestion to carry you through the conflict, but this, that you should remember your fathers and care for your children. [Applause.] Now, allow me to say that I have a most eloquent and patriotic, and earnest letter from my friend JAMES T. BRADY, who is detained in a distant State. I would read it, but you will read it to-morrow in the newspapers. [Calls for the reading of the letter were then made, but Mr. EVARTS left the stand without reading it.]

Mr. DIX then came forward, and said that the meeting had passed a resolution to appoint a Committee of twenty-five persons, to receive funds in support of the public authorities, and authorizing him to name them.

Mr. DIX followed the announcement of the Committee with the statement that the *Tribune* Association had subscribed $1,000 for the object in view, and the announcement was received with applause.

Mr. EVARTS then moved that the name of Gen. DIX be added to the Committee, and the question was put and carried.

The following resolution was then passed amid the utmost enthusiasm, and with three times three huzzas:

Resolved, That New-York adopts the wives and children of our citizens who may fall in the defence of the Union.

Hon. R. C. SCHENCK, of Ohio, then came forward and made a stirring speech—declaring that party lines and State lines were all abolished, and that now we were a nation of freemen fighting for our liberties and for the Constitution of our country. He had just come from Massachusetts, and spoke eloquently of the preparations made in that noble State to save the Capital and the Union.

Mr. DIX—I have just received a telegraphic dispatch from Gov. MORGAN.

ALBANY—6:35 P. M.

I have been enabled to respond, without delay, to the requisitions of the War Department, and am prepared to meet future demands from the present organized military force, at least until the volunteers be got ready.

I am in communication with the Secretary of War,

[Continued on Eighth Page.]

The Charleston Mercury.

VINDICE NULLO
SPONTE SUA SINE LEGE FIDES RECTUMQUE COLENTUR.

VOLUME LVI. CHARLESTON, S. C., MONDAY, APRIL 22, 1861. NUMBER 11,132

THE MERCURY.

MONDAY, APRIL 22, 1861.

President Lincoln a Usurper.

It would be absurd, we suppose, to expect the Abolitionists, in possession of the Government at Washington, to observe or respect the Constitution. Mr. SEWARD openly declared in the Senate that they were governed by "a higher law" than the Constitution. They must, by their own professions, be as profligate in their administration of the Constitution as they are tyrannical in their policy. Still, in the great matter of war, given exclusively by the Constitution to Congress to inaugurate, it might be supposed that the most brutal fanaticism might pause in its usurpations. But President LINCOLN does not pause. He boldly calls for seventy-five thousand men of the militia of the Northern States, to conquer and subdue seven sovereign States who have left the late Union of the United States. The justification of this act is put, by his adherents, on the Act of 1795. That act contemplates the case of an obstruction of the laws of the United States, "by combinations in a State too powerful to be suppressed by the ordinary course of judicial proceedings, or by the powers vested in the Marshals." It supposes the existence of Courts of the United States—the existence of Marshals,—and to aid the Courts and the Marshals in enforcing the laws against unlawful combinations, "The President of the United States to call forth the militia of such or of any other State or States, as may be necessary to suppress such *combinations*."

Now, is the secession of a whole State, *unanimously* (as was the case in South Carolina), with the instant abolition of the Courts of the United States and its Marshal, "*a combination in a State*," such as the Act of 1795 contemplates? What authority in the State is this militia to support? And, when six other States stand in the same position, how absurd is the pretension that this Act of 1795 contemplated such a state of things and now authorizes the President of the United States to call for seventy five thousand men, of the militia of the other States, to conquer them, and force them back into a union with the conquering States. And, when we remember that the power to coerce a State to a submission to the authority of the laws of the United States was distinctly made in the Convention which framed the Constitution of the United States and rejected, it is plain that the Act of 1795 has no bearing upon the present state of things. President LINCOLN's call on the States to furnish troops to subdue the seceding States is, therefore, a flagrant usurpation.

But what does the usurpation mean? Will the militia troops, called out by President LINCOLN, really enter upon the enterprise of subduing the seceding States to the authority of the United States? The term of their service will answer that question. The South is unconquerable. But if the South is to be conquered, it clearly must be by a regular army, duly equipped, and with well trained officers to command it. It must be a work of time—perhaps the work of years, with many a hard battle to fight, with a people used to arms, fighting for their institutions and homes. Now, the seventy-five thousand men President LINCOLN calls into the field will have their term of service ended in three months, with no power, as the laws now exist, to continue their service. The Act of 1795 prescribes that "the use of the militia so called out may be continued, if necessary, until the expiration of thirty days after the commencement of the next session of Congress." The next session of Congress takes place on the 4th day of July. Of course, the service of these troops expires on the 4th day of August next—a little over three months from this time. Will troops, whose term of service so soon expires, enter upon the enterprise of conquering the South? Not a man of them will cross the Potomac or the Ohio, or will be seen on our coasts. They are to protect the cowardly incendiaries in Washington, who are at the head of the United States Government, and to keep up the fortunes of Black Republicanism by war demonstrations and agitations for the benefit of that party.

The fact, too, that the Act of '95 limits the period of the services of the troops it authorizes the President to call forth, to thirty days after the next Congress meets, shows the nature of the authority it confers. It is *temporary*, and only to meet a *sudden emergency*, which Congress, not being in session, cannot meet. But has the secession of the seven States constituting the Confederate States, been an affair which Congress could not meet? It took place when the Congress of the United States was in its regular session—three months before it adjourned. Congress knew of it—considered it—legislation to meet it was proposed and rejected—and now this foul usurper and malignant fanatic digs up the Act of '95, and affects to use its sanction, in defiance of the refusal of the late Congress to act—to call forth seventy-five thousand men to make war upon the South. He will, probably, before the grand drama of blood he has endeavored to open, is closed, see cause to deplore the "higher-law" depravity which has governed his counsels. Seeking the sword, in spite of all moral or constitutional restraints and obligations, he may perish by the sword. He sleeps already with soldiers at his gate, and the grand reception room of the White-House converted into quarters for troops from Kansas—border ruffians of Abolitiondom.

Reorganization.

The Montgomery *Mail* speaks of Virginia and the future of the Confederate States as follows. The news from Ohio, Illinois and Indiana, arming enthusiastically to conquer or desolate the South, at the bidding of LINCOLN, does not seem, however, to favor its policy of reorganization:

Before this week passes away she will be with us, both her people and her government. Before this week passes away her breast will be bared as our shield, and her arm as our defence. Nay more, she will put her seal upon the future. The rest of the Border States will follow her "as bone of her bone and flesh of her flesh," and forthwith the *Mississippi river and its tributaries will become established as an* uncorrosive chain, binding together in indissoluble bonds of friendship and confederated alliance, the entire South, *Northwest and Pacific, uniting and linking each and every part heart to heart*, while the vista of Republican liberty and Patriarchal institutions, shall yet again open out upon immeasurable fields fanned by the breezes of the Caribbean Sea, assuring the grandest realm of freedom on which the sun ever shone, towering above the lofty altitude of Rome even in the days when that proud mistress of Dominion culminated over the Nations and Provinces of earth.

The Sixth Massachusetts regiment fighting their way through Baltimore, April 19, 1861

The New-York Times.

VOL. X.....NO. 2993. | NEW-YORK, WEDNESDAY, APRIL 24, 1861. | PRICE TWO CENTS.

THE WAR NEWS.

Virginia Troops Threatening Washington.

THE CAPITAL CONSIDERED SAFE.

MARTIAL LAW DECLARED IN BALTIMORE.

The Business of the City Entirely Ruined.

THE BURNING OF GOSPORT NAVY-YARD.

Immense Amount of Government Property Destroyed.

Departure of Over Three Thousand Troops from New-York.

ADVICES BY GOVERNMENT MESSENGERS.

GEN. SCOTT ORDERS A DEMONSTRATION UPON BALTIMORE—ARMSTRONG GUNS COMING FROM ENGLAND.

By the arrival of two Government messengers, who left Washington late on Saturday night, we have intelligence from the National Capital. At that time they report that no fears were felt for the safety of the city, but the authorities were anxious regarding Fort Monroe, of the reinforcement of which they had not heard. The messengers came on to Baltimore as rapidly as possible, reaching there early Sunday morning; but deeming it imprudent to put themselves within reach of the mob which now reigns there, they did not enter the city. The Railroad authorities took them in charge, however, and dispatched them by carriage to Cockeysville, a point 13 miles from Baltimore, as has already been stated. While waiting here they heard the whistle of a locomotive engine, and asked the landlord of the hotel where they were stopping if a train had lately reached that point from the North. He replied that it had, and that there were 3,500 men just over the hill. Apprehensive that this might be a force of Secessionists, the messengers were about changing their course, when they learned that the troops were from Pennsylvania. As the messengers were entrusted with instructions *from Gen. Scott to Gov. Curtin ordering a demonstration upon Baltimore, in view of the disturbances there,* they authorized the officer in command of this force to push ahead, and taking an engine hastened forward to Chambersburgh, where they found 3,500 more Pennsylvanians making their way to Philadelphia. These troops were ordered to join the detachment at Cockeysville, and in all probability by the present time the force which was thus augmented has been further increased to 10,000 or 12,000, for these messengers report that the Pennsylvania border was thoroughly alive with enthusiasm, and a determination to revenge those who had been stricken down by the mob in the streets of Baltimore. Almost every male in the smaller towns had enlisted, and all were determined to march directly on Baltimore. These facts and the positive orders of Gen. Scott to Gov. Curtin to make a demonstration in force upon Baltimore render the telegram received this morning to the effect that the troops at Cockeysville had been ordered back to Harrisburg, exceedingly improbable.

We also learn through the same channel by which we receive this information, that *orders have been dispatched to England by the Government for twenty Armstrong guns,* which may be expected to arrive here at an early day.

FROM WASHINGTON AND BALTIMORE.

LACK OF PROVISIONS AT THE CAPITAL—THE CONDITION OF BALTIMORE—CAPTURE OF 24,000 STAND OF ARMS BY FOURTEEN BOYS FROM WASHINGTON.

A gentleman who left Washington at 3 o'clock on Sunday last has just given us important information regarding the state of affairs at the Capital. At the time he left the number of military, including volunteers, was not more than 5,000 or 6,000. The Massachusetts and Pennsylvania Regiments, to the number of 1,500, which arrived in Washington on Friday and Saturday, were quartered in the Capitol—the former being situated in the Old Hall of Representatives and the Senate Chamber, and the latter in the New House of Representatives. Troops had been quartered in the different Departments, and business generally was suspended. On Sunday it was rumored that martial law was to be proclaimed on the succeeding day, and, as confirmation of the statement, it may be stated that the clerks in the different departments had all been armed, and notified to be ready for service at a moment's notice.

The Georgetown Heights were held by troops of the regular army. Great anxiety was felt with regard to a want of provisions. All supplies were cut off by the Secessionists, and a drove of cattle had been intercepted at the Long Bridge across the Potomac. Our informant arrived at Annapolis junction, fifteen miles from Annapolis, where he learned that the Seventh Regiment from New-York, with a detachment of 100 Massachusetts soldiers, and a portion of unarmed troops from Pennsylvania had reached Annapolis on a ferry-boat from Ferryville, opposite Havre de Grace. The railroad from Annapolis junction to Washington was open, but he could not say whether it was open from Annapolis to the junction. There were rumors that the track had been torn up. He arrived at Baltimore at 5½ P. M. Sunday. He found the city in possession of the mob and military, who acted in concert. Armed men were moving in every direction, and yelling like enraged devils. Carts, carrying munitions of war, were in motion constantly. Gov. Hicks was acting with the military, whether from choice or on compulsion he could not say. The men in arms appeared to be mostly Americans, and were all young men from 15 to 20, scarcely any being over 30 years of age. The mob seized arms wherever they could find them, and had broken open many stores where arms were to be had. On Monday it was reported that the Pennsylvania troops who had been sent to Cockeysville, Md., had been ordered back to Harrisburgh. This caused the excitement to abate, as there was a design to send down 3,000 men from Baltimore to intercept them. There was a general talk in the streets of attacking Fort McHenry, but no demonstrations had been made in that direction when he left. He left Baltimore at 11 A. M. Monday, in a covered butcher's wagon for Havre de Grace. The wagon contained five passengers, one of whom was a Northern member of Congress. They took the old turnpike road, and were closely watched, but not otherwise molested. They found the telegraph poles cut down for ten miles this side of Baltimore. They arrived at Havre de Grace, and were conveyed across the Susquehannah in ferry boats in time to take the evening train for Philadelphia. Twelve hundred Pennsylvania troops were waiting at Ferryville, opposite Havre de Grace, to be taken in a boat to Annapolis. A strong police force is stationed on the line from Ferryville to the Delaware State line, to keep the route open. An attempt had been made to blow up a stone bridge on this line, but it was frustrated. They passed a Government train going to Ferryville with more Pennsylvania troops.

On Friday night last, fourteen boys from Washington, went down to Alexandria and boarded a steamboat lying at the dock; awoke the captain, told him that he was superceded in command, ordered the firemen to fire up, and before they knew what was the meaning of the surprise, the steamboat was on its way to Washington. On arriving at Washington, it was found that 24,000 stand of arms were stowed away in the boat, intended for the Secessionist Army.

Lieut. Maury, of the National Observatory at Washington, disappeared on Friday last, and has left for parts unknown. Capt. Scott has been placed in command of the Observatory. Many families were leaving Washington in anticipation of an attack upon the City.

From the gentleman who gives us this information, we learn that Mr. Winans, the Baltimore millionaire, has advanced $500,000 to the Confederate authorities, $500,000 to the State of Maryland, and that he has his whole force of workmen at present, engaged in the manufacture of pikes, which may be designed for service in the streets of Baltimore.

VIRGINIA TROOPS THREATENING WASHINGTON.

HARRISBURGH, Tuesday, April 23.

Caleb Cushing arrived here yesterday and left for Washington on Sunday. He says that Gen. Lee with 5,000 Virginia troops was covering Arlington Heights.

The camp at Cockeysville had broken up, and the troops were returning here to go South *via* the Susquehanna River.

Lieut. Jenifer, reported as having deserted the Carlisle Barracks, had a full knowledge of the plans of the Government. Dispatches for his arrest have been sent in every direction.

Caleb Cushing narrowly escaped injury from the people of Carlisle and Chambersburg. He stated that he was on his way to Massachusetts to join a regiment for the defence of the Union.

He left last evening.

LATER FROM BALTIMORE AND WASHINGTON.

PHILADELPHIA, Tuesday, April 23.

Cornelius Wendell, with his family of five children, has just come in from Washington. He left on Monday morning, at 10 o'clock. There was great excitement in the city.

When the Secessionists found they were bluffed at Harper's Ferry, they started for Alexandria, where four thousand men are encamped. The number of Secessionists near Washington is estimated at six thousand, of whom four thousand are at Long Bridge, and two thousand near Arlington Heights.

Heavy cannonading was heard on Saturday night, and crowds were at the Washington Navy-yard without ascertaining anything definite before Mr. Wendell left.

Ladies and children are being sent away rapidly from Washington. The Secessionists declare their intention of seeing the Capital this week, and Mr. Wendell says that they seem determined to try it. He went by railroad to Baltimore, and found that city in the hands of a mob. No churches have been burned or property injured, but tremendous excitement prevailed, and no man was safe who did not agree with the mob. He paid $300 to get from Baltimore to New-York, with five children, all under 13 years old.

The appearance along the road was funereal. Long lines of carriages and other vehicles, filled with people, were flying from Baltimore, and so great was the crowd that quick travel was impossible.

Washington is well guarded by 8,000 troops, and Lieut. Gen. Scott feels confident that no force can be brought to bear sufficient to capture it.

HARRISBURGH, Tuesday, April 23.

A merchant of Baltimore has arrived here, *via* Frederick and Hagerstown. He left Baltimore yesterday afternoon. There were no Union flags flying, and but few secession flags. No attack had been made on Fort McHenry. He thinks there were no more than 200 Federal troops there. He believes the Federal troops can now pass through the city unassailed.

Military drilling, and marching to the sound of music, were alone to be seen. Business was entirely suspended, and there will not be a solvent house in Baltimore within a week. Virginia money was at 30 per cent. discount yesterday.

The same gentleman was at Washington on Sunday evening. There were no Virginia troops on Arlington Heights. This is one day later than Caleb Cushing's report.

He says the Baltimoreans will not attack Washington.

He reports the Eighth Massachusetts and Seventh New York Regiments at Annapolis. Some fighting had occurred, but he is unable to give any particulars, save that they are able to protect themselves.

Maryland money was refused entirely by the Banks of Harrisburgh, yesterday, at any price. The brokers buy it at a heavy discount.

STILL LATER FROM BALTIMORE.

HAVRE DE GRACE, Tuesday, April 23.

The Baltimore papers of this morning received here say that the excitement of Sunday had been succeeded by comparative quiet and good order, and that the people were tired of startling rumors.

In every direction scouts had been sent to guard the approach of any bodies of men.

Nearly all the bar-rooms in the city were closed on Monday.

During the morning (Monday) several messengers from the Cockeysville camp brought information of the movements of the Northern troops. It is reported that a number of from 2,000 to 3,000 troops were there, and short of provisions. They permitted no citizen of Maryland to pass over any bridges without a strict examination.

By order of Marshal Kane, several wagon loads of bread and meat were sent to the camp of the Pennsylvanian troops, a number being sick and suffering. Three of them died, and were buried within the encampment.

The troops had abandoned their encampment and were supposed to be waiting for the cars to return to Harrisburgh or within the borders of Pennsylvania.

Only about one-half of them were armed.

The Governor of Maryland has issued a proclamation, convoking the Legislature to meet on the 26th.

A special election will be held in Baltimore to-morrow for delegates to fill vacancies.

On Monday afternoon the excitement in the city had abated somewhat.

A mail had been dispatched North by a wagon to the Susquehannah River, and thence by railroad.

The Baltimoreans complain greatly for the want of mail and telegraph facilities.

The steamer *Locust Point*, from Boston, for Little Rock, Ark., has been seized, also a large quantity of saltpetre and brimstone, from Pittsburgh for Cincinnati, at Canton station.

No provisions of any kind are allowed to be transferred from Baltimore.

Violence has been offered to Henry W. Hoffman, the newly appointed Collector of Baltimore, at Harper's Ferry, as he was about coming to the city to take possession of the office.

Several Northerners have been arrested as suspected spies, but discharged.

The city is now well supplied with arms. The City Volunteers are largely increasing. Fresh arrivals are constantly coming in from the country. Between three and four hundred colored residents have offered their services.

The Southern Rights Convention have nominated the following candidates for delegates: John C. Brune, Ross Winans, Henry M. Warfield, Dr. J. Hanson, Thos. F. Parkin, Scott H. M. Morfitt, S. Teagle Wallis, C. R. Pitts, W. G. Harrison, Lawrence Sangston.

ARRIVAL OF THE BALTIMORE AND WASHINGTON MAILS IN PHILADELPHIA.

PHILADELPHIA, Tuesday, April 23.

The letter mail from Baltimore and Washington arrived here this afternoon, having left Baltimore yesterday afternoon.

Our advices from Washington on Sunday night say that Capt. Elzey, of the United States Army, had resigned. He is a Marylander, and was in command of the Augusta Arsenal when it was surrendered, since which he was ordered to Fortress Monroe.

It was rumored also that Col. May, of Maryland, had also resigned.

Alexandria, Va., was in great commotion, and secession flags were flying in every direction. The people were preparing for war, and recruiting was progressing quite rapidly. Three Union men were required to leave.

The Government had been strengthening the positions of the public buildings in Washington.

The Capitol is surrounded with hastily thrown up defences, and barricades were erected around the Treasury Department. Precautionary movements were made in every direction.

A number of Secession Washingtonians had left for Virginia.

The local trade at Alexandria and down the river was entirely suspended. Provisions and flour have advanced in price.

An express from Baltimore is to be started at 3 o'clock A. M.

THE VERY LATEST FROM BALTIMORE.

PHILADELPHIA, Tuesday, April 23.

It is reported by arrivals from Baltimore at 6 o'clock this morning, that martial law was proclaimed, and all the citizens ordered in their houses.

All the places of amusement, &c., have been closed.

A gentleman who arrived from Baltimore this evening, leaving there at 9 o'clock this morning, states that when he left, the report was current in the hotels that news had reached there, *via* Annapolis, that Fort Pickens was captured with serious loss of life. It is only given as a rumor. He also says that Baltimore had been put under regular militia law when he left. Although strong guards were on duty, the city is quiet.

From Annapolis the very latest private dispatches received in this city last night, at 8 o'clock, state that the Northern troops, from the steamers *Maryland* and *Boston*, had landed at Annapolis without obstruction, and intended to march immediately to Annapolis junction. The citizens of the town and neighborhood were preparing to give them a Guerilla fight in their march.

The Northern troops had taken horses for the purpose of transporting artillery and baggage.

TROOPS TO PASS THROUGH BALTIMORE.

BOSTON, Tuesday, April 23.

A private dispatch to Messrs. Sprague & Co., from Philadelphia, states that the Government has released the steamer *P. Sprague* from her charter to convey troops from Philadelphia, in consequence of Maryland having guaranteed the safe transit of 5,000 troops through Baltimore daily.

A letter from a member of the Fourth Massachusetts Regiment, dated on board the steamer *State of Maine*, confirms the attempt to poison the Regiment when off New-York, by prussic acid mixed with brandy.

A member of the Easton company had died.

THE GOVERNMENT CANNOT PURCHASE PROVISIONS IN BALTIMORE.

A gentleman, who left Baltimore last Friday afternoon, says that he had an interview with the Collector of Baltimore just before starting, who informed him that he had received instructions from the Government to purchase and forward provisions, and although there was plenty in the city, no one would sell to the Government for fear of the mob.

GEN. BEAUREGARD ADVISES LADIER TO LEAVE WASHINGTON.

A lady here received a letter yesterday from her sister in Washington who is an intimate acquaintance of the sister of Gen. Beauregard, who is now visiting Washington. Gen. Beauregard's sister has urged this lady in Washington to leave with all her effects at once, but why or on what account is not stated.

NEWS FROM THE SOUTH.

MOVEMENT OF GOVERNMENT VESSELS WITH TROOPS.

The schooner *S. B. Wheeler*, of Wilmington, Del., from Galveston in 14 days passage, arrived this morning, reports that on the 22d inst., 20 miles south of Absecomb, saw three steamers with troops on board; on the same day, off Barnegat, saw two others—all bound South.

Nothing unusual was going on in Galveston when the *Wheeler* left.

FROM SAVANNAH.

ARRIVAL OF LARGE NUMBERS FROM THE SOUTH—WHAT THEY ARE DOING DOWN THERE.

The steamer *Florida*, which arrived from Savannah this forenoon, brought a large number of passengers, among them many business men and families, who were but too glad to escape from the place. All business is said to be at an end both there and in Charleston. They were throwing up sand batteries at Tybee, evidently expecting an attack from the sea. Troops in large numbers continued to occupy Charleston, and there was a general belief that a fleet would soon appear off the port to attack the place. The steamer *Isabel* has been taken and fitted up as a man-of-war. The old tugboat *Huntress* had been converted into an armed revenue cutter; they also have a small steamer called the *Everglade* running about the harbor. The *Nashville* had been detained at Charleston, and the *Florida* only escaped by adopting a *ruse*.

The news of the attack on the Massachusetts troops in Baltimore, and the reported killing of 130 of them, set the town wild with excitement and rejoicing. Gov. Letcher, of Virginia, had made a requisition on Beauregard for two Regiments. The vessels going in past forts Pulaski and Johnson are always fired at, and compelled to dip the Stars and Stripes to the Confederate flag.

FROM CHARLESTON.

A gentleman from Charleston who left last Thursday, says that the Southern troops were in most excellent condition and discipline. It was the intention of the Southern Confederacy to march North an army of from 50,000 to 60,000 men, and they expect an addition of at least 50,000 men in going through Virginia.

Mr. Russell, of the London *Times*, was in Charleston when our informant left.

FROM FORT TAYLOR AND KEY WEST.

By the arrival of the *Cahawba* at New-Orleans from Havana on the 18th, we learn that the *Mohawk* had arrived at the latter port. The *Cahawba* left the *Empire City* from Texas at Havana with 600 troops for Key West on the 15th.

The *Atlantic* from New-York with troops, was anchored near Triangle Shoals; on the 13th communicated with Fort Taylor. She left the 14th for Sand Key.

The *Powhatan* appeared off the harbor of Key West on the 14th and exchanged signals with the *Crusader*.

The garrison at the Fort Taylor and Key West barracks are engaged drilling at the guns.

The *Atlantic* brought commissions for some of the Federal appointees.

The commanding officer of Fort Taylor was appointed Postmaster of Key West.

MOVEMENTS IN NEW-ORLEANS.

NEW-ORLEANS, Monday, April 22.

The free colored population, at a meeting, have resolved to tender their services to the Government for the defence of the State.

A meeting was called to-night to adopt measures to clear the city of Abolitionists. Several have been arrested already.

FAMILIES LEAVING VIRGINIA.

Capt. Collins, of the schooner *O. H. Lee*, from York River, arrived this morning, bringing as passengers Mr. E. W. Evans, lady and family, G. F. Southwell and lady, James Cross and family, and several others, who were compelled to leave Williamsburgh for expressing themselves favorable to the Union. They were given but few hours to get ready to leave, the feeling was so bitter against them. The schooner was boarded by Lieut. Cosnahan and Sergeant Taliaferro, with a boat's crew of six men, for the purpose of seizing her, but finding her papers all right, and the Captain being a favorite man, she was given a passport and allowed to proceed.

BURNING OF GOSPORT NAVY-YARD.

Eleven Vessels Scuttled and Burned—The Steam Tug Yankee Tows the Cumberland to Sea—Norfolk Not on Fire.

We have already noticed the fact that the steamtug *Yankee*, which went to Charleston with the fleet of relief, was obliged to put into Norfolk in distress on the 14th, her smoke-stack having been carried away in a severe storm. She has just arrived at this port, and a gentleman who returns in her gives us particulars of her further experience.

The *Yankee* lay at the Navy-yard until Friday, the 18th, when the Virginia Custom-house officers came over in a tug and demanded the surrender of the *Yankee*. Commodore McAuley, who was in command of the Navy-yard, refused to comply with this demand, saying that if they attempted to take her from the yard he would sink them where they lay. The *Cumberland* immediately beat to quarters, and brought her 11-inch pivot gun which was charged with shell to bear upon their tug, and they deemed it advisable to leave forthwith.

On Saturday evening, at 9 o'clock, the *Pawnee*, arrived from Washington, with 200 volunteers and 100 marines, besides her own crew, and at once the officers and crew of the *Pawnee* and *Cumberland* went to the Navy-yard and spiked and disabled the guns, and threw the shot and small arms into the river. At 10 o'clock, the marines, who had been quartered in the barracks, fired them, and came on board the *Pawnee*. This movement was premature, for it was the intention to fire all the buildings simultaneously. A party of officers, meantime, were going through the different buildings and ships, distributing waste and turpentine, and laying a train so as to blow up the Dry Dock. The were engaged in this work until 2 o'clock, when the train was fired. At 3 o'clock, the *Yankee*, to the Captain of which, Charles Germain, much credit is due, came along and took the *Cumberland* in tow, the *Pawnee* taking the lead. All the vessels beat to quarters, the guns were manned, and everything was in readiness to carry out the threat of Commodore McAuley, that if a gun was fired from either shore he would level both Portsmouth and Norfolk. At this time the scene was indescribably magnificent, all the buildings being in a blaze, and explosions here and there scattering the cinders in all directions.

The Government vessels had been scuttled in the afternoon before the *Pawnee* arrived, to prevent their being seized by the Secessionists, who had been in arms in both Norfolk and Portsmouth, under the command of Gen. Taliaferro. Their number is estimated at some 1,400 men. The scuttling was done between 12 and 2 o'clock on Saturday. Lest this mode of destruction should not be complete, however, trains were laid on them and the vessels were fired with the buildings.

The following are the names of the vessels which were destroyed: *Pennsylvania*, 74 gun-ship; steam-frigate *Merrimac*, 44 guns; sloop-of-war *Germantown*, 22 guns; sloop *Plymouth*, 22 guns; frigate *Raritan*, 45 guns; frigate *Columbia*, 44 guns; *Delaware*, 74 gun ship; *Columbus*, 74 gun ship; *United States*, in ordinary; brig *Dolphin*, 8 guns; and the powder-boat.

Of these the *Merrimac*, *Plymouth* and *Germantown* were ready for sea, but the *Pawnee* made her appearance at the yard too late to save them. The *Merrimac*, in fact, had had steam on only a few hours previously.

The *Yankee*, as we have already said, left the yard with the *Cumberland* in tow about 3 o'clock. The fleet proceeded down the river until 9 o'clock, when it came to anchor within a mile of the point where wrecks were known to have been sunk for the purpose of obstructing the navigation. Boats were sent out to take soundings in order to ascertain whether some other passage than the regular channel could not be found. All efforts proved unsuccessful, so the fleet raised anchor and forced their way directly through the wrecks. The *Cumberland* caught one of the sunken vessels and carried it along with her, and apprehensions were at first entertained that she might be carried on to Sewell's Point, where it was supposed that the rebels had erected batteries. Meantime the *Keystone State* came up from Washington with marines, and by her help and that of the *Yankee*, the *Cumberland* was towed into deep water and the wreck was disentangled. She then went up under protection of the guns of Fort Monroe and came to anchor. While the vessels lay there, four men, who had been employed in the Navy-yard, succeeded in making their way down the river, and reported that they left everything in flames, and the smoke and flames could easily be seen from the *Cumberland*. The rebels, too, they reported were fearful of attempting to arrest the flames, because they apprehended that a train was laid to blow up the buildings.

The *Yankee* left on Tuesday morning for New-York. She reports that the *Pawnee* and *Keystone State* had got the crew of the *Pennsylvania*, and the Marines who occupied the barracks, on board, to carry them to Washington. Both left for the Capital at 9 o'clock, where they probably arrived early this morning.

Our informant states that the value of the property destroyed was estimated at $50,000,000.

Yesterday morning the *Yankee* spoke the *Baltic* and *Coatzocalcos*, both bound for Washington, with troops, who cheered most lustily as they passed. They probably reached their destination at noon to-day.

FROM ANOTHER SOURCE.

The steamtug *Yankee*, Capt Germain, from Charleston Bar on the 15th, *via* Norfolk 21st, P. M., arrived here this morning, bringing three passengers from the Navy-yard at Gosport. She has had very heavy weather, both on the outer and home passage, having lost her smoke-stack, and received considerable other damage. On arriving at Charleston bar, and finding the fleet had gone, she put back for Norfolk, where she arrived on 17th, at 4 P. M., and finding a movement on foot to seize the boat, proceeded to the Navy-yard, and placed the steamer under the guns of the vessels there. On the 18th, the Custom-house officers came to seize her, when the Commodore of the yard refused to give her up, saying if they attempted to take her by force, he would blow her out of water before they could reach Norfolk. This quieted the mob who had congregated.

The *Yankee* took the *Cumberland* in tow to Fortress Monroe. On the way she grounded on Orris Island, and it took two hours to get her off.

The Secessionists observing the escape of the *Cumberland*, commenced obstructing the channel below her.

After towing the frigate down, the *Yankee* proceeded to New-York.

The *Pawnee* left Washington last Friday night, with an extra detachment of officers, men and marines, with Flag-officer Paulding on board, and proceeded to Fortress Monroe, where she received the Third Massachusetts Regiment, just arrived hence for the Navy-yard at Gosport. At this place it was found that the officers in charge had commenced destroying the public property, finding it would fall into the hands of the enemy. They had scuttled all the ships, (the *Cumberland*, being the only ship in commission,) cut down the shears, and rendered most of the other property useless. The object of the rioters having been partly frustrated by the scuttling of the ships, it was determined that the Federal forces should leave, and preparations were made to complete the demolition of the property. The *Pawnee*, with the *Cumberland* in tow, assisted by the *Yankee*, started out, and after passing the Navy-yard sent up a rocket—a preconcerted signal to apply the match—and in an instant, ships, ship-houses and store-houses were in flames, and so rapid were they that Commodore Rogers, of the Navy, and Capt. Wright, of the Engineers, were unable to reach the point of rendezvous, where the boat was in waiting, and were necessarily left behind. Among the most valuable property destroyed were the line-of-battle ship *New-York*, on the stocks; *Merrimac*, first-class screw; *Germantown*, sloop-of-war just ready for sea; *Plymouth* and *Dolphin*, brigs; also the *Pennsylvania*, *Columbia* and *Potomac*, frigates; *Columbus* and *Delaware*, liners; all of the last named being hulks and nearly worthless. Large quantities of provisions, cordage and machinery were also destroyed—besides buildings of great value—but it is not positively known that the dock was blown up.

The burning of the Navy-yard at Norfolk was done by the Union men, who are in a majority, but comparatively unarmed.

The *Cumberland* was 60 short of her complement. When the *Pawnee* came up to the Navy-yard, both the *Cumberland* and *Merrimac* lay broadside to her, with guns loaded, thinking she was in the hands of the Secessionists. On board the *Pawnee* an opinion prevailed that a similar state of affairs existed on board those ships, and was ready accordingly. When the *Cumberland* hailed, "What steamer is that?" the answer was, "The *United States* steamer *Pawnee*." The cheering on board the vessels and on shore told how satisfactory this reply was.

The Union men employed in the Navy-yard cut down the flag-staff, so that it could not be used by the enemy.

The guns in the Navy-yard and at St. Helena were spiked.

The *Yankee* has gone to the Navy-yard at Brooklyn.

GLIMPSES OF WAR.

OUR WASHINGTON CORRESPONDENCE.

WASHINGTON, Saturday, April 20, 1861.

The telegraph has told you of the leading incidents that are weaving themselves through the warp of time, and shaping the figures of History. But the magnetic chord vibrates only to the harsh strokes of great events, and, like History, records but master movements. Shall I trace, in a few of the details of the hour—the trifles of the moment—the waifs that float by almost unnoticed on the rushing tide of revolution?

It is a warm, sunny day, this 20th day of April. The air is redolent of bursting buds, and the Capital Park is jubilant with the gushing songs of the birds and the humming of the honey-bees. The Northern air that has "aggressed" upon us for a week past has been driven back by the rebellious South wind, that comes, fresh from the fair faces it has carressed, and the waving tresses through which it has wantoned, to enchant the soul with its balmy breath, and entrance the mind with its dreamy sweetness. Shall we not go where its fullness shall be drank in—where we shall be intoxicated with its soft and lingering embrace? In the pleasure grounds of the Capitol—as nowhere else—can we realize the luxury of this warm sunshine and this flower-perfumed air.

But it is the Capitol no more—for the Capitol signifies order. It should be the temple of legislation—the abode of the oracle that gives us just and wise law—the soil in which peace, and commerce and enterprise and civilization should have their chief and sure foundations. But the Capitol is not now the symbol of advancement. It has become the temple of Mars—it has been re-dedicated to the God of War—it is crowded with armed men.

It needs password and countersign now to cross its porch, and to gain admittance. I must have safe passage from an "officer of the day," and give proper token of my loyalty to a sentinel marching to and fro, with a bronzed face that betokens service and the resolution which grows out of service—backed by a fixed bayonet on a musket that looks as though, if occasion required, it could throw bullets with a penetrating force that might leave an unsightly orifice, through which the breath of life would be diverted to the great detriment of the human system. Thanking fortune that I have successfully run the gauntlet of the gentleman with the unsightly combination of steel, powder and lead, let me jot down some of the strange scenes by which I found myself surrounded.

In the House wing of the Capitol I found the quarters of the Pennsylvania Regiments—the first command to reach Washington in response to the call of the Government. The troops were billetted through the various retiring rooms and offices of the House—the Representative Hall being reserved for the Seventh Regiment. Armed men and the rude implements of carnage massed in these marble corridors and gorgeous rooms, awakens me to a deep sense of the power and the *abandon* of military rule. I realize the desolation now which war brings in its train. On the luxurious damask and brocatel covered sofas lay stretched men who probably never before reposed in such magnificence. Over the tapestrial carpet of the floor are strewn in profusion and disorder, the suddenly accumulated stores of the Commissary's Department—here a slab of bacon, there a quarter of beef, or a saddle of mutton, or a Virginia ham—a sea biscuit, tin drinking cups, papers of pepper, bags of salt and cans of vinegar filling up the insterlices, and rounding up the pyramid. Upon the rich and costly bronze ornaments—upon the gas chandeliers, and upon the gilt brackets that held back the silk and lace curtains, were festooned knapsack and belt, cartridge-box and bayonet-scabbard—the smaller implements and surroundings of a soldier.

In the halls and corridors the men were being drilled and taught the expertness of carnage. In broad contrast to the dark and polished Tennessee marble wainscoting, are the blue uniforms and rough bearing of the men. Upon the rich encaustic tiling falls with a dull, heavy sound the iron-shod butts of musket and rifle. The arched and frescoed ceiling echoes and reëchoes the ringing clatter of the ramrod, as the recruits perfect themselves in the manual of loading their pieces.

In the Senate Chamber are quartered the Massachusetts regiments—the cool and brave men who endured insults and threats from the mob at Baltimore, yesterday, until they could endure no longer, and then resolutely fought their way through the rebel city, and continued their journey to the Capital. Upon the cushioned sofas of the galleries of the Senate Chamber, the men found excellent couches. When I visited them this morning, they had concluded breakfast, and the guard for the day being detailed, the remainder of the command were at their ease. In the Vice-President's chair, sat Col. Jones, the commandant of the force—a frank, free-hearted, soldierly-looking man. The Clerk's desk was occupied by the Adjutant and his assistants, engaged in making up the muster-roll, returns and requisitions incident to active service. The privates were engaged at the Senators' desks, writing letters. I had a woman's curiosity, almost, to know what were the varying shades in which these new heroes were painting, with pen and ink, the pictures of their first battle. You will recollect that the passage through Baltimore was on the Anniversary of the battle of Lexington—and that yesterday, as on that memorable occasion, the first shock of the conflict fell upon the stout hearts of New-England men. Were they thinking, as they wrote this morning, of the concurrence of these events? were they repeating, as did their grandsires after the triumph of Concord, the oath that consecrated their lives and their property to avenging the blood of the martyrs who fell on the opening battle field of the Revolution.

It was a novelty to see how suddenly these men had adapted themselves to the position in which they are placed. They occupied the Senate Chamber with as much repose of manner as they could have exhibited in the workshops and fields from which they were enlisted. It was a kind of poetic justice that filled Wigfall's abandoned seat with a stalwart man fresh from his forge, while Mason and Hunter were succeeded by operatives from the factories of Lowell. The stationery in use was the residuum of the last Session, having the usual engraved headings of the Senate and House of Representatives.

Some of these Massachusetts men have the tokens—the scars and casualties of yesterday's combat. One showed me a bruise on the forehead, where a paving stone had grazed him. An inch more to the right, and he would have been instantly killed, as was his companion, young Stevens. Another one showed me a battered button—the upper one of his great coat—upon which a ball had struck, and left a deep indenture. Narrow chances, those, were they not?

All the statuary in the halls of the Capitol, and in the old Rotunda, has been boxed, to preserve it from injury through carelessness. The pictures in the panels have also been faced over with heavy planking, which secures them from harm. I almost regret that some of them have been the object of such precaution. A brief campaign might be atoned for, if a few of the exaggerations in marble, some of the burlesques on canvas, and a goodly portion of the Capitol extension could be subjected to the rude shock of the contending armies.

The porticos of the Capitol building are barricaded to the height of about eight feet. The iron plates for the new dome are used for the breastworks between the marble columns. Behind these are placed barrels of cement, piles of stone and timber, forming an impenetrable barrier, in the rear of which the troops could take shelter in case of an attack. It seemed a strange contradiction to see the workmen, engaged in the construction of the portico, going on with their labor of laying the foundations amid thousands of armed men; the click of the chisel, the stroke of the hammer and the ring of the trowel blending with the word of command, the challenge of the guard and the tramp of the battalions drilling in the corridors. So reluctant is civilization to recede before the advancing desolation of war, that the artizan lingers to enrich with his skill the parapet and dome that the morrow may see leveled to their foundations. Within musket range of the outposts of the troops are even now a score of men chiseling in marble the flowers and clusters of grape and ivy wreaths, with which the finished portions of the Capitol are so profusely decorated.

The cooking for the troops is done in the basement of the building, which is said to afford ample accommodations for the culinary department. A most accessible portion has been reserved for the Seventh Regiment. I did not penetrate below the first floor—but I could judge by the vast quantities of supplies that were being transported "down below," that the Commissary's department might laugh a siege to scorn.

Have I given the readers of the Times a glimpse of the realities through which we are passing at the Capital of the nation? Between the outlines, let them fill in a few bruised and battered men—let them see the ghastly forms of the dead that were slaughtered at Baltimore, yesterday, and they will have a sketch that bears to the imagination the semblance of war. Let them look through the history of the past, and realize the fiendish purposes that have prompted the desolation that seems to be impending, and let them swear, that be that desolation what it may, the sun of peace shall never rise again upon the living cause of all our present tribulations. LEO.

OUR BALTIMORE CORRESPONDENCE.

BALTIMORE, Sunday, April 21, 1861.

I came over from Washington last night to watch the progress of events, and see the condition of the city and the drift of the popular sentiment.

At every dépôt the train from the Capital was besieged by crowds anxious to hear particulars of the combat in Baltimore, and the prospect at Washington. At three stations, we found military companies mustered—the officers of which came with us to Baltimore, to offer the aid of their commands to the City authorities. They all seemed to concur in the opinion that we were in the midst of great events, to which they were destined to give shape, and that there be no excessive disasters, except to the unfortunate mortals and munitions of war (whisky and Jamaica) with which they might come in contact.

We reached the Baltimore dépôt without any interruption to the train, and the hotel unmolested. In the office there was a little talk, but not as much as is usual when an important election is pending. I noticed as very apparent, a general disposition to refrain from expressing opinions. All were anxious for *news*—and my budget of Washington gossip was readily accepted—but nobody knew what was going on about them here in Baltimore—nobody was willing to utter sentiments.

In the streets of the lower part of the city, however, there were immense crowds, warm discussions, and the high pitch of excitement which discussion engenders. The mob—for Baltimore-street was one vast mob—was surging to and fro, uncertain in what direction to move, and apparently without any special purpose. Many had small secession cards pinned on their coat collars, and not a few were armed with guns, pistols and knives, of which they made the most display.

I found the greatest crowd surging around the telegraph office, waiting anxiously, of course, for news. The most inquiry was as to the whereabouts of the New-York troops—the most frequent topic, the probable results of an attempt on the part of the Seventh Regiment to force a passage through Baltimore. All agreed that the force could never go through—all agreed that it would make the attempt if ordered to do so, and none seemed to entertain a doubt that it would leave a winrow of the dead bodies of those who assailed it in the streets through which it might attempt to pass.

As the wires of the telegraph leading to New York had been cut, there was no news to be had for the crowd from that direction. Of course, too, I could not telegraph any information for your Sunday issue.

I found the police force entirely in sympathy with the Secessionists and indisposed to act against the mob. Marshal Kane and the Commissioners do not make any concealment of their proclivities for the Southern Confederacy. Mayor Brown, upon whom

Continued on Eighth Page.]

The New-York Times.

VOL. X....NO. 3013. NEW-YORK, SATURDAY, MAY 18, 1861. PRICE TWO CENTS.

THE SECESSION REBELLION.

The Latest News from the Federal Capital.

Probable Intentions of the Secessionists.

Important Letter of Secretary Seward.

Why it is Treason to Sell Steamships to Seceders.

A MILITARY EXPEDITION FROM ANNAPOLIS.

Ross Winans Conditionally Discharged.

BLOCKADE OF CHARLESTON HARBOR.

BRITISH SHIPS NOT ALLOWED TO ENTER.

Overwhelming Vote for the Union in Kentucky.

Capt. Montgomery Menacing the Texas Secessionists.

Another Capture of Rebels in Missouri.

SPECIAL DISPATCH FROM WASHINGTON.

WASHINGTON, Friday, May 17.

It is ascertained beyond cavil that the report of the desecration of the Tomb of WASHINGTON, and the removal of the remains, is wholly untrue. The Government has this from a reliable messenger, who visited Mount Vernon and returned to-day. He found everything unmolested, and Mount Vernon in its usual quiet condition. There was no indication about the Tomb of its having been molested, and the messenger was not interfered with nor questioned—seeing only the keeper of the place and the servants who usually wander about the grounds. A letter from Col. LEE to a gentleman in this city, which has been shown to a member of the Cabinet, says that the whole statement of the removal, or any such intention, is without the slightest foundation.

TROOPS INSULTED IN BALTIMORE.

The statement made by some of the Baltimore papers, that all the troops recently passing through Baltimore have not been molested nor insulted, is incorrect. Ringgold's Artillery was grossly insulted nearly all the way through the streets, but no offensive attack was made upon them. The commanding officer restrained his men from inflicting deserved chastisement upon the insulting fellows who thronged the sidewalks.

The Government is changing as rapidly as possible the old muskets of the troops when they arrive, and supplying with Minié and Sharp's rifles. They intend to have these old arms inspected, and such as are of sufficient value are to be rifled and supplied with the best modern improvements for breech-loading and cap-locks. This can be done at a slight expense to the Government, and make efficient and valuable arms.

The Michigan Regiment, which arrived last night, paraded to-day, and made a splendid personal appearance. They were highly spoken of by Gen. MANSFIELD, Secretary CAMERON and Gen. SCOTT, whom they called upon and saluted. They went at sundown to the Washington Monument Grounds, and discharged their arms as a salute to the monument.

THE NEWS FROM THE SOUTH.

The dispatches from the South that the rebels are nearly completing an arrangement for an attack on Washington, is not believed. The Government has, however, received such information from secret agents in the South, but it is presumed that they have been made to believe these things by the leaders to deceive their own people at home, and to draw the attention of the Government here from points in Virginia to Washington. Gen. SCOTT will, however, protect Washington, without abandoning his plans of operation at other points. Three companies have been stationed at the Long Bridge the past two nights—one on the Virginia side, one near the draw, and one on the Washington side.

SECRET SERVICE.

Four men were picked from each company in the District to-day and ordered to report at a certain point for immediate service. It is not known what they are to do, but it is presumed they are for scouting service. They are the best men and most trustworthy that could be selected.

The Rhode Island troops are now in camp, having completed the removal of their baggage and equipments to-day. They have a fine location. The men are much better satisfied with camp life than their location at the Patent Office.

The Zouaves moved their camp this afternoon. They will be in their new position ready for drill to-morrow.

ARREST OF A SPY.

A spy named WOOD was arrested to-day, and placed in close confinement. He is from Newark, N. J. Last evening he called upon Gen. SCOTT, and professed to tell him what was going on among the rebels of Virginia. He then applied to the General for money to pay his expenses while on a scouting expedition in Virginia. Gen. SCOTT gave him thirty dollars, and he left, ostensibly to obtain information. This morning he visited the New-Jersey regiments, and was reported as endeavoring to tamper with the troops, endeavoring to persuade them to leave the service of the Government. He was thereupon arrested, and stands a fair chance of being hung as a spy and a traitor.

THOS BENBOW died at the hospital this morning, from congestion of brain. He was a private in Company F, Twelfth New-York Regiment. His remains were taken this afternoon to New-York, by an escort of a Sergeant and a few members of the Company. Company K, Twelfth Regiment, will receive them at New-York, and the remains will be interred with military honors. This is the first death from disease among the military.

LEO.

DISPATCH TO THE ASSOCIATED PRESS.

WASHINGTON, Friday, May 17.

Col. MCDOWELL, Assistant Adjutant-General, has been promoted to the position of a Brigadier-General. Col. THOMAS, the Adjutant-General, was, a short time ago, elected to a similar rank.

The Virginia newspapers received to-day, note continued arrivals of Confederate troops, and their departure for points not designated.

The following important letter was yesterday written by the Secretary of State:

DEPARTMENT OF STATE, WASHINGTON, May 16, 1861.

SIR: I have received your letter of yesterday's date asking me to give you in writing my reasons for considering an acceptance on your part of Gov. LETCHER'S proposition to purchase the steamships *Yorktown* and *Jamestown*, recently seized by his orders and now in his possession, an act of treason. With this request I readily comply. An insurrection has broken out in several of the States of this Union, including Virginia, designed to overthrow the Government of the United States. The Executive authorities of the State are parties to that insurrection, and so are public enemies. Their action in seizing or buying vessels to be employed in executing that design is not merely without authority of law, but is treason. It is treason for any person to give aid and comfort to public enemies. To sell vessels to them which it is their purpose to use as ships-of-war, is to give them aid and comfort. To receive money from them in payment for vessels which they have seized for these purposes would be to convert the unlawful seizure into a sale, and would subject the party so offending to the pains and penalties of treason, and the Government would not hesitate to bring the offender to punishment.

I am, Sir, your obedient servant,

WM. H. SEWARD.

To G. HEINEKEN, Esq., Agent New-York and Virginia Steamship Company, Washington.

Citizens of the seceded States, in order to receive patents for inventions, must take the oath prescribed by law, acknowledging their allegiance to the United States.

The statement that ROSS WINANS, of Baltimore, was unconditionally released, is unfounded. There is authority for stating that he was only released, by order of the Government, on his giving a parole of honor that he would do no act, openly or covertly, hostile to the Government of the United States.

A general army order has been issued, stating that there will be added to the General Staff of the Army four Quartermasters and eight Assistants, to be promoted and selected according to existing laws and regulations. There will be added to the Medical Department ten Surgeons and twenty Assistants. The Surgeons will be promoted from the senior Assistant Surgeons, and the Assistants appointed from civil life, after having passed the usual examination by the Board from the Medical Department of the Army. Due public notice of the appointment and time and place of meeting of the Board will be given.

Mr. HERBERT, Superintendent of Mount Vernon, says there is no foundation for the report that the remains of WASHINGTON have been removed from their resting place. This is in accordance with a statement heretofore emanating from this correspondence.

Brig.-Gen. MANSFIELD to-day issued an order as follows:

I advised by telegraph the agent of Adams Express Company at New-York, Philadelphia and Baltimore, that in the future no Express matter, inclusive of letters, will be permitted to go south of this City into Virginia. Last evening Col STONE seized, by my order, the Express matter, and stopped all contraband goods, and allowed the rest to go forward.

Ex-Gov. A. H. REEDER, of Pennsylvania, well known in connection with the early history of Kansas, was to-day appointed Brigadier-General by the President.

The opening of the line of travel from Baltimore North and Northwest, has been the signal for a rush of travel to Washington. Yesterday and to-day's trains brought hundreds of passengers.

The Irish Brigade, over 1,000 strong, tendered by Major MULLIGAN, was to-day accepted by Secretary CAMERON for service during the war. Its probable destination is Washington.

The Departments daily receive bushels of letters from applicants for places, military and civil, most of which ask for replies. It is proper therefore to state that it is the inflexible rule that letters relating to such subjects, though read and filed, are not and cannot be answered.

OUR WASHINGTON CORRESPONDENCE.

WASHINGTON, Thursday, May 16, 1861.

The occupation of Baltimore by the National troops is significant of the purpose of the Administration to advance upon Harper's Ferry in a very few days, and the precaution is by no means unnecessary, if we consider the character and numbers of the Secessionists in that largest of the Southern cities. Nothing seems to be more probable than that an attack upon the rebels at the Ferry, while Baltimore was left free to fester and foment treason, would be to invite "a fire in the rear." It is not surprising, therefore, that Gen. SCOTT has put a rope around the necks of the traitors in that city before proceeding to disperse those south of the Potomac.

The probability of an immediate attack on the enemy is rendered stronger, if we consider that there would seem to be no other way of explaining necessity of occupying Baltimore. The smoldering embers of secession were known to exist there, but with strong forces all around the city there was no danger of an outbreak, without an immediate and powerfully exciting cause; and but for the suggested movement, good policy would have dictated the wisdom of leaving the city to itself. We may, for these reasons, look for stirring events at no distant day—probably a bloody battle, or a general rout of the ill-organized bands collected about Harper's Ferry.

The telegraphic reports from Harrisburgh, that Col. ANDERSON had informed Gov. CURTIN that Ex-Vice-President BRECKINRIDGE would take a command under him in support of the Union, is thought to be too good to be true. If true, it is highly important and significant, since it would indicate that Kentucky, in the estimation of that over-cautious statesman, is for the Union. It will be admitted, also, that the name of Mr. BRECKINRIDGE would give immense strength to the cause of Union in all the States which have yet to vote upon the question of Union or disunion.

This is in some respects the strangest war that ever was waged. Who before ever heard of a Government extending its mail facilities to whole provinces in open rebellion, while the rebel Postmasters make their regular quarterly returns to the Government against which they have waged war, and call for supplies of stamps as often as they have occasion? Yet this is now actually the case. I am assured that within a week the Post-office Department sent $4,500 worth of stamps to New-Orleans, and $1,500 worth to Charleston! This is a fair illustration of the "independence" of the Confederate States. They steal all they can lay their hands upon, and then turn mendicant to get more.

The rumored robbing of Mount Vernon, of the bones of WASHINGTON, is not credited. The crime seems to be so unnatural and so abhorrent to the minds of men, that even the companions of FLOYD are thought to be superior to it. The Romans believed parricide to be impossible, and, therefore, made no law for its punishment; and the Americans cannot suspect even traitors and rebels of violating the tomb of the Father of his Country. If, however, the improbable rumor shall turn out to be true, it will more than verify the imputations heretofore cast upon the character of Col. WASHINGTON, the proprietor of Mount Vernon—that he grew rich by speculating in the bones of his illustrious kinsman—for, not content with selling them to the ladies of America, he is represented as stealing them back again, probably with a view of selling out again to the Confederate States. He has already dishonored the name he bears, to an extent which is humiliating to every true American; but it may be hoped, for the honor of human nature, that he has spared them this disgrace.

The refusal of the Government to receive a black regiment of Canadian fugitives into the public service, cannot fail to impress the people of the South favorably. Thus far the course of events tends to demonstrate that the South should look to the Federal Government for protection against the negro population, instead of the "Confederate States." While the former has repeatedly refused to receive aid from slaves or to harbor runaways, the latter has been employing negroes, slave and free, in building fortifications, and in some instances negroes have been armed and officered as soldiers.

The "Confederate States" having no other reserve for revenue than direct taxes, will be glad enough to sell their cotton to the hated Yankees in order to enable their people to pay the taxes. Their Congress, in the exuberance of pride and vain-glory, when they were still laboring under the hallucination of supposing that cotton was king, laid a tax on the exportation of that article. But when they find themselves at the mercy of their enemies, they will be glad enough to suspend the collection of this duty, and to send the cotton North, over the interior routes of communication.

The difficulty of getting cotton to market, and the necessity of having an unwonted supply of breadstuffs, provisions, and food for horses in these war-like times, will very probably cause unusual attention to be given to the latter articles, to the neglect of the former; and it will not be surprising if the cotton crop shall fall to one-half that produced last year. This event has been anticipated by the cotton consumers of Europe, and hence the herculean efforts which have been made to stimulate the production of other regions of the world. It will be a miracle if the cotton planters are not ruined by their rebellion. Every event seems to conspire for their destruction. There is imminent danger of the immediate and violent overthrow of Slavery; and at any rate, there is a strong probability that the institution will be materially modified before the termination of the war. These are the direct consequences likely to flow from the rebellion, and to them will be added, in all human probability, the destruction of the value of slaves by the destruction of the monopoly now enjoyed in the production of cotton. The opinion gains ground daily, that whatever else may happen, Slavery will be destroyed or fatally wounded in the conflict of arms; and from present appearances it encounters the greatest risks at the hands of its friends.

Mr. SMITH, familiarly known as "Extra Billy," of Virginia, is in the city. He is a Secessionist, but is allowed to walk the streets with impunity. No Northern ex-member would be permitted to promenade the streets of Richmond, and even a Northern Democrat, unless he were believed to be an enemy of the Federal Government, would be permitted to go at large. This simple fact illustrates the difference between freedom and Slavery. He was seen on the avenue to-day in company with and in familiar conversation with Gen ASHLEY, of Ohio, one of the most sterling and thorough-going Republicans in the country. No doubt the Ex-Governor of Virginia felt all the more comfortable for the companionship of a "Black Republican" for once.

The Government has no reason to exclude Secessionists from Washington, or from any other portion of the country north of the Potomac. If they come here or go further North, for the purpose of spying out the weakness of the Federal forces, or the lukewarmness of the people in the cause of Union, they will go back with a flea in their ears. So long as they refrain from efforts to smuggle contraband articles, or to foment sedition in this City and Maryland, they should be permitted to travel unmolested. They will carry home anything but encouraging news.

OBSERVER.

IMPORTANT FROM MARYLAND.

AN EXPEDITION INTO SECESSION.

ANNAPOLIS, Friday, May 17.

One hundred men, Capt. THOMAS' company, (Thirteenth New-York Regiment,) with two pieces of artillery and three days rations, went down the Bay yesterday on the propeller *Wm. Woodward*, to retake the Smith Point light-ship, towed a few miles up the Great Wycomico. The Secessionists have two more in their possession.

It was not determined in Washington to-day where Major BUTLER would be sent.

A train ran off the track, last night, between Washington and Annapolis Junction, injuring one man and destroying seven cars.

Col. PRATT has made excursions into the country of several miles from the Junction.

WILLIAM H. ANTHON has left for Washington to assume the duties of Judge Advocate-General for New-York.

Parties direct from Harper's Ferry say there are only about 4,000 troops there. There were many Unionists among them, who were induced to enlist by the false report of another John Brown raid at Harper's Ferry.

One object of scattering so many troops in so many counties of Virginia, is to make sure of a secession majority by their votes.

THE DISCHARGE OF ROSS WINANS.

BALTIMORE, Friday, May 17.

ROSS WINANS has been honorably discharged, according to orders from Washington.

All is quiet in this city this morning.

The Philadelphia Camp is visited by thousands. It presents a splendid appearance.

Many of the men and officers are visiting people in the city.

More troops are expected *via* Perryville.

Following is the *Sun's* account of the release of Ross Winans:

"Ross WINANS, Esq., arrested on Tuesday night, at the Relay House, by order of the Administration, was released yesterday, without even an examination. It appears that the charge against him was treason, in having furnished material aid to Virginia. The charge was founded upon mere rumor, in which there was no truth. It appears that within an hour after his arrest he was taken to Annapolis by special train, and there provided with a comfortable room.

On Wednesday a steam-tug was sent for him, and he was brought up to Fort McHenry, where he was comfortably provided for, and where he was treated with great courtesy by the officers. His release was obtained through the influence of some personal friends, upon whose statements Mr. LINCOLN ordered his release, through Gen. SCOTT. The order for arrest him had been issued to any commissioned officer."

LATEST REPORTS FROM BALTIMORE.

BALTIMORE, Friday, May 17.

The city is very quiet to-day.

One company of artillery regulars passed through to Washington.

The Eighth New-York Regiment have been ordered back to Washington. They seem loath to leave the pleasant camp at the Relay House. The men there are in good health. Very few are on the sick list in either of the three regiments.

THE BALTIMORE AND OHIO RAILROAD.

CAMDEN STATION, Friday, May 17.

To C. W. Peevel, Esq.

The reports in the Eastern papers this morning, about the destruction of the bridges on our road, are untrue. The only ground for them is the attempted destruction of the small culverts near Point of Rocks, by which, however, no injury was done. The statements are of the same as the report in a New-York morning paper, "That I asked General SCOTT to take possession of us as a military road." W. P. SMITH.

A TIMES CORRESPONDENT ARRESTED AS A SPY.

HARPER'S FERRY, Friday, May 17.

E. F. UNDERHILL was arrested here to-day by the Secessionists on a charge of being a spy. He had been to Wheeling to attend the Convention as Reporter for the NEW-YORK TIMES, and was on his way back to Baltimore.

UNION TRIUMPH IN KENTUCKY.

LOUISVILLE, Friday, May 17.

The official vote in eighty-nine counties for the Union Delegates to the Border State Convention is 96,561. Eighteen counties are yet to be heard from. The aggregate Presidential vote in November was 146,216.

FRANKFORT, Ky., Friday, May 17.

The House yesterday concurred in the Senate bill legalizing the suspension of specie payments by the Kentucky Banks.

The House also passed resolutions that Kentucky should maintain a strict neutrality during the present contest, and approving of Gov. MAGOFFIN'S refusal, under existing circumstances, to furnish troops to the Federal Government.

IMPORTANT FROM ST. LOUIS.

ANOTHER CAPTURE OF SECESSIONISTS.

ST. LOUIS, Friday, May 17.

Several Union men having been driven from Potosi, on the Iron Mountain Railroad, a detachment of volunteers, under command of Capt. COLE, was sent on Tuesday night to protect the loyal citizens in that section.

Capt. COLE reached Potosi at 3 o'clock this morning, and surrounded the town with a chain of sentinels, and shortly after daylight a hundred and fifty citizens were taken prisoners and formed in line.

The Union men were recognized and released. About fifty secessionists were liberated on parole, and nine of the leaders were brought to the City prisoners of war.

A lead manufactory belonging to JOHN DEAN was taken possession of and some four hundred pigs of lead seized.

On the return trip the troops dispersed a company of cavalry at De Soto, and captured thirty horses they left behind in their flight. The Stars and Stripes were then hoisted on a pole just ready to receive a secession flag. Another prominent Secessionist was arrested here, and another at Victoria, make twelve in all, who are now in the arsenal.

Thirteen American families arrived here last night, having all been driven from different towns on the Pacific Railroad for supporting the Union.

Gen. PRICE has issued orders instructing the Brigadier-Generals to immediately organize the militia of their respective Districts and hold them in readiness for active service. The officers and soldiers are strictly enjoined to afford all the protection in their power to the persons and property of the citizens of the State, without reference to political principles, the organization being simply to protect the people in their rights under the Constitution of the State, and the United States troops are warned to avoid collision with any armed bodies, unless absolutely required to protect the lives, liberty, and property of the people. The flag of the State of Missouri is the only one to be used by the militia.

Nearly 900 Irishmen have been enrolled in the United States service here, and will probably be organized into a separate regiment.

LETTER FROM GENERAL HARNEY.

MILITARY DEPARTMENT OF THE WEST, ST. LOUIS, May 13, 1861.

My attention has been called to publications in several of the city papers to the effect that the volunteers under my command at this post were disorderly, and that they were acting to some extent in defiance of the discipline of the army.

I deem it my duty, and it affords me great pleasure to say, that these publications are wholly unfounded, and do great injustice to the volunteers. These troops have submitted cheerfully and with alacrity to the discipline of the service, and nothing has come under my observation, or been reported to me, that should subject them to the injurious publications to which I have alluded. I beg to express my entire disapproval of such unfounded publications, as they are only calculated to injure the public service, and create disquiet and ill feeling in the community.

W. S. HARNEY,

Brigadier-General U. S. Army, Commanding.

IMPORTANT FROM ALBANY.

PROCEEDING OF THE MILITARY BOARD.

ALBANY, Friday, May 17.

Nothing of special interest was done by the State Board to night.

The Companies of W. R. MCDONALD, of New-York, and Capt. HENRY BALDWIN, of Steuben, were accepted.

The three Companies discharged from service to-day, by the State Board, were from New-York. They desired their release from the State Board in order to join a regiment accepted directly by the Federal Government and proceed at once to active duty, without the harassing delay to which volunteers are subjected under the Board. The resolutions for their discharge were introduced by Secretary of State JONES, and opposed by Attorney-General MYERS. The companies are indebted to the exertions of Major FARNHAM for the accomplishment of their wishes.

MOVEMENTS IN NEW-YORK.

ALBANY, Friday, May 17.

Little business of interest was transacted by the Military Board this morning.

The companies of Capt. MAHER, Capt. ISAAC L. TAYLOR and Capt. JOSEPH KELLER were released and discharged further service on their own application.

The Board organized another Utica Regiment, composed of the following companies:

Capt. Jennings, 77 men; Capt Capleman, 77 men; Capt Arrowsmith 77 men; Capt Wetmore 77 men; Capt. Brencle, 77 men; Capt. D. Smith, Jr., 77 men.

The election of the following officers for the Cayuga Regiment was confirmed; Col. JOHN S. CLARK, Lieut.-Col. CLARENCE A. SEWARD, and Major JAMES H. LEDLIE.

The following companies have been accepted: FRANCIS J. MCHUGH, of New-York, 79 men; DOMINICK O'CONNER, of New-York, 79 men; MICHAEL MURPHY, of New-York, 78 men.

PORT JERVIS, Orange Co., N. Y., May 16.

A company of volunteers, numbering 88 men, under command of THOMAS HOLT, left here on Tuesday morning last for New-York, to join the Sickles Brigade. They were accompanied by the entire Fire Department of the village, and a large concourse of citizens, with the Delaware Artillery corps, under Lieuts. ST. JOHN and BRODHEAD, as escort in their march through the streets to the dépôt, where the Captain was presented with a handsome sword by a few of his fellow townsmen. The cars moved from the dépôt amid the roar of cannon, waving of flags handkerchiefs and cheers.

CANANDAIGUA, Friday, May 17.

The third company of volunteers from Canandaigua, left here for Albany, this evening, amid the cheers of the people. Other companies are forming here, and great enthusiasm still prevails.

THE MILITARY CAMP AT ELMIRA.

ELMIRA, N. Y., Friday, May 17.

Five companies have arrived here since yesterday, from Angelica, Peterboro, Palmyra, Mt. Morris, and Candor.

Capt. WHITLOCK'S company, from Ithaca, now here, has been ordered to join Col BAKER'S Regiment, in New-York. They leave this evening.

MOVEMENTS IN NEW-JERSEY.

TRENTON, N. J., Thursday, May 16.

Capt. HATFIELD'S company, of Elizabethtown, have enlisted for three years. They arrived here at 1:45 P. M., and were escorted to their quarters at the State Arsenal by Capt MURPHY'S company. They numbered eighty men, besides the officers, and their uniform excited admiration.

CAPTURE OF A SUBMARINE BOAT.

PHILADELPHIA, Friday, May 17.

Quite an excitement was created in the upper part of the city this morning by the seizure of a submarine boat, the invention of DE VILLEROI, a Frenchman. It was going down the river and struck on an island. Four men were found aboard. VILLEROI says he was about taking it to the Navy-yard to test, but the officers of the yard disclaim any knowledge of him. The boat was constructed some time since for raising wrecks and other submarine work, but was never put in active use. It is cigar-shaped and made of iron; 30 feet long. It supplies its own air and will be useful in running under a fleet.

REPORTS FROM CINCINNATI.

CINCINNATI, Friday, May 17.

The report about BRECKINRIDGE is entirely unfounded.

The First Regiment, Guthrie Grays, Col BASLIE, 1,000 strong, passed through the city to-day for Camp Dennison, sixteen miles above, looking towards Western Virginia.

Gen. MCCLELLAN, Commander of the Western District, has sent five thousand guns for use of the Kentucky Union men. Their particular destination is unrevealed.

Col. ANDERSON is still in Cincinnati. He is likely to receive a grand ovation in Louisville. Cincinnati performed prodigies in his honor yesterday.

CINCINNATI, May 17, 1861.

DAN RICE'S circus flotilla was menaced by the mob last midnight. They demanded that RICE should hoist the Union flag instead of his own. He brought a howitzer, charged with slugs, to bear on the mob, and defied them; put on steam and stood for the Kentucky shore, where he is now safely moored.

The Bank of the Ohio Valley was thrown out to-day by the Cincinnati Clearing House. Other banks sound.

THE BLOCKADE OF NORFOLK.

THE YANKEE WITH THREE PRIZE STEAMERS IN TOW.

PHILADELPHIA, Friday, May 17.

The steamer *City of Richmond* has arrived from Washington, *via* Fortress Monroe. She left at Washington the steamer *Boston*, to sail yesterday for Annapolis. She reports, last evening, 30 miles south of Cape Henlopen, saw steamer *Yankee*, with three prize steamers in tow, bound north.

Orders for building one of the seven sloops-of-war were received at the Philadelphia Navy yard. The ship is to be pushed rapidly forward.

FROM THE CHESAPEAKE.

A VESSEL WITH A LARGE CARGO OF TOBACCO CAPTURED BY THE BLOCKADING SQUADRON.

The United States transport *Cahawba*, J. B. BAKER commanding, arrived yesterday from Washington, D. C., making the passage in 46 hours, where she landed the Second Connecticut Regiment. Capt. BAKER wishes to express publicly his thanks to Mr. GEO. F. MOORE, pilot of the gun-boat *Quaker City*, for volunteering to pilot the *Cahawba* from Hampton Roads to Washington City and back to the entrance of Chesapeake Bay. The pilot who was on board being confined to his room by sickness, and had it not been for the kindness of Mr. MOORE, the *Cahawba* would probably have been detained a day at Hampton Roads, as pilots are very scarce and not reliable in those waters. The following gun boats are on the blockading squadron and doing effective service: *Harriet Lane*, off the mouth of James and Elizabeth River; *Monticello*, off York River; *Quaker City*, at mouth of Chesapeake Bay. The *Dawn* and *Yankee* were at anchor off Fort Monroe, waiting orders. The steam-frigate *Minnesota*, Flag officer STRINGHAM, arrived off Old Point Comfort on the morning of the 13th inst. All well.

On the night of the 14th inst. gun boat *Quaker City* towed to sea the ship *Argo*, of Bath, (Me.,) with cargo of tobacco, from Richmond, Va., valued at $150,000. There was a prize-crew placed on board by Flag-officer STRINGHAM, of the squadron, her destination being New-York.

THE CHARLESTON BLOCKADE.

BRITISH SHIPS TURNED AWAY.

The movements of the steamship *Niagara*, the first vessel of the blockading fleet which has arrived off Charleston harbor, are thus noticed in the Charleston *Courier* of the 13th and 14th inst:

"This steam frigate, which it was reported some days since was coming off this port to blockade the harbor, was first noticed off here at an early hour on Saturday, by Pilot-boat No. 4, then outside the bar, and also from the steeple of the Custom-house.

The pilot-boat had observed in the offing on Friday evening what appeared to be a merchant ship bound in, and which, not being in sight on Saturday, was no doubt ordered off. Towards midday the *Niagara* disappeared, but returned off the port in the afternoon.

On Saturday Capt. ROBERT LOCKWOOD, pilot in Boat No. 2, (the *W. Y. Leitch*) took to sea the schooner *Minnehaha* for Baltimore; soon after leaving which vessel outside, he made a square rigger standing in for the bar. Being anxious to board, but not liking the *Niagara*, then in sight, he concluded to send his large boat into port, and take to his skiff with a trusty hand.

He reached the vessel about 7 P. M., and found her to be the British bark *Hilja*, from Liverpool, consigned to Messrs. R. MURE & Co. The tide being too late to get her into port, he remained on board during Saturday night, his skiff being taken on deck and carefully placed away. On Sunday morning, it being calm, he was unable to get her under way, and about 8½ A. M. she was boarded by a boat from the *Niagara*, commanded by Lieut. R. L. MAY, who informed the captain of the *Hilja* that the port was blockaded—the rebels inside having fired on Fort Sumter with a garrison of less than 100 men; gave him a Yankee paper containing the latest news, and mentioned that an army of 100,000 men had landed in Louisiana. The Captain of the *Hilja* informed the boarding officer that he was short of water, and requested a supply from the *Niagara*, but he was informed that the frigate had less of that article than was necessary for her. The following is a copy of the indorsement of Lieut. R. L. MAY on the papers of the *Hilja*:

"Boarded May 12th, and ordered off the whole Southern coast of the United States of America it being blockaded. (Signed) R. L. MAY, Lieut. U. S. Steamship *Niagara*."

The officer remained by the *Hilja* for about twenty minutes, when he left. The boat's crew had a revolver each in a belt attached to the waist. Mr. LOCKWOOD left the *Hilja* about 10 A. M., and reached the city in his skiff, accompanied by a valuable boat hand, who remained faithful, although appearances indicated that the boy had only to open his mouth when he might have had a passage to some other place than "Dixie's Land."

The *Hilja* went off during the day, and will proceed to the British Provinces. The British ship *Monmouth*, from Liverpool, and the ship *Gen. Parkhill*, from the same place, were seen off the bar yesterday, and were ordered off; and we understand that the *Niagara* had previously sent off three other square-rigged vessels. During Sunday the *Niagara* went well off shore, accompanied by two of the above vessels, and while she was absent the British ship *A. & A.*, Capt. HUTCHINSON, from Belfast, stood in from the eastward, when the *Niagara* made after her; but the ship, having much the start, was run into shoal water, where the frigate could not well approach her, when the *Niagara* put about and stood South. If the boats of the *Niagara* fail to board her before this morning, she may get into port, with the aid of steam, in the morning. The race was anxiously watched from the wharves, and also by a party of gentlemen who were out in the pilot-boat *Rover*, Capt. EVANS. They went alongside and spoke the ship.

From the Courier of the 14th.

The British ship *A. & A.*, from Belfast, which was reported in our last issue as having anchored near the outer buoy of North Channel, after having been chased by the *Niagara*, escaped being boarded by the man-of-war on Sunday night, and was successfully towed into port by the steamer *Gordon*, yesterday morning. The officers of the *Niagara* supposed the *A. & A.* to have been ashore when she anchored. She was so close in, but in this supposition they were mistaken, and the ship has got into a port where she will make a most superior freight, say about 1⅛d. for Upland, and 1¾d for Sea Island Cotton.

The British ship *Susan G. Owens* went to sea yesterday for Liverpool, and it was rumored that she was boarded by a boat from the *Niagara*, and her papers strictly examined; but the pilot who took her to sea informs us that he watched her closely after she got outside until she had almost disappeared, and that no such event took place. She was, when last seen, going off finely, with all her canvass set. So far as we can ascertain, no outward bound vessel has yet been stopped.

The *Niagara* was about ten miles Southeast from the Ship Bar yesterday, and was there visited during the afternoon by ROBT. BUNCH, Esq., Her Britannic Majesty's Consul at this port, who left the city about 2 P. M. in the steamer *Charleston*, and proceeded on board the *Niagara*, where he was received with the usual salute, and had every courtesy extended to him, and every matter in regard to the blockade satisfactorily explained. All neutral vessels now in this port would be allowed a reasonable time to depart, but nothing further would be allowed to come in. The *A. & A.*, which got in yesterday, and whose manner of getting into port rather disturbed the nerves of some cotton shippers, will be allowed to go unmolested. All open letters for masters of foreign vessels expected here will be received on board the *Niagara* and given to the parties when they come off the Bar but no sealed communications will be received. A fleet of eight or ten sail, with Commodore STRINGHAM, is expected off here shortly when the blockade will be rigidly enforced all along the coast. They expressed a willingness to have supplied the *Hilja* with water, but the Captain sailed off in such haste that it could not be done.

The commander of the *Niagara* was pained at the position he had to occupy in reference to the seceded States, but he intended to carry out his orders. Mr. BUNCH says the *Niagara* is a formidable looking ship, has a noble crew of about six hundred men, is loaded down with provisions and war materials, decks piled up with shot and gun of the most formidable size. The only Charleston ships ordered off have been those reported; say, the *Monmouth*, *Gen. Parkhill* and *Hilja*, all from Liverpool. The *Eliza Bonsall*, *Sir Allan McNabb*, &c., have not yet been seen. Several other British vessels have been ordered off, two of which it is said were bound to Savannah, but their names we did not learn. No vessels appeared off this harbor on Monday, so far as we could see or learn, and the *Niagara* had a quiet day, but she keeps steam on all the time and moves rapidly when under way.

MOVEMENTS OF CONNECTICUT TROOPS.

HARTFORD, Friday, May 17.

The Third Regiment of Connecticut Volunteers leave on Monday for Washington, completely armed and equipped.

GEN. PRENTISS TO GOV. MAGOFFIN.

CAIRO, Ill., Friday, May 17.

Gov. MAGOFFIN, of Kentucky, has sent a messenger to Gen PRENTISS, commanding the United States forces here, demanding an explanation of the arrest of a traitor and spy, a resident of Columbus, Ky. Gen. PRENTISS declined making a written communication in reply, and said that he denied the right of Gov. MAGOFFIN or any other man, excepting the proper United States authorities, to interrogate him.

It is said that Gov. MAGOFFIN has ordered all secession flags flying in Kentucky to be lowered.

A message was received here, to day, from Paducah, asking support for the Union men.

IMPORTANT FROM THE SOUTHWEST

THE REBELS TAKEN IN THE REAR.

The New-Orleans papers of Saturday and Sunday bring highly important intelligence regarding a movement upon the Texas frontier. The *Picayune* of the 12th says:

"We learn by the steamer *J. M. Sharp*, which arrived this morning from Jefferson, Texas, that news reached that place on Tuesday last, by express, in a letter to J. M. & J. C. MURPHY, that MONTGOMERY, of Kansas notoriety, at the head of 3,000 men, had taken Fort Washita. Messengers had been sent to Marshall and other places, for men, money, guns, powder and lead. Capt. BILL YOUNG, with about 600 men, was on the march trying to oppose MONTGOMERY. This news was corroborated last Wednesday at Shreveport. The greatest excitement prevailed throughout the country. The bells were ringing when the *Sharp* left Jefferson, for the purpose of calling a town meeting. Already a large meeting had been held at Shreveport.

A correspondent of the *Picayune* writes:

In connection with the reported taking of Fort Washita by the notorious MONTGOMERY of Kansas Abolition fame, it may be as well to state that three weeks ago I learned in Galveston, on undoubted authority from St. Louis, *via* New Orleans, and published it in the Galveston *News*, that Mr. LINCOLN'S Secretary of War had, about a week before, sent a dispatch to Major MONTGOMERY, U. S. A., at St. Louis, to instruct Major EMORY (who has something to do with the Overland Mail route) to concentrate all the force he could at Forts Washita, Cobb and Arbuckle, which posts are just outside of the Northern frontier of Texas, and parallel with it.

Major EMORY was to use his own discretion as to when and how to carry out the order. This news has doubtless ere this reached the Texas frontier.

Major MONTGOMERY, you will remember, was taken prisoner the other day by the Arkansas State troops, at or near Fort Smith, on the western frontier of that State, and the point of departure of the overland stage.

Fort Washita is on the Comanche Reserve to the northwest of Texas, and will afford MONTGOMERY an excellent opportunity, backed by those Indians, who all hate the Texans, to depredate in our own State. Col. BAYLOR and some thousands of experienced Texas Rangers are on that frontier, and now that the C. S. Government gives these brave men and indomitable Indian fighters the authority and means to protect themselves, MONTGOMERY and his band will stand but little chance of holding the fort.

The *Delta* of Saturday evening has this documentary evidence of the reality of this raid:

Governor MOORE this morning received the following letter, signed, it will be seen, by a number of prominent citizens of Northwest Louisiana:

SHREVEPORT, Louisiana, May 8, 1861.

GOVERNOR THOS. O. MOORE—*Dear Sir*: Inclosed we forward you a handbill just received from Marshall, Texas. The names of many of these gentlemen are known to us, and we have no doubt they at least believe the contents of the handbill. Send us arms by all means—arms for mounted companies. Telegraph the Montgomery Government, if necessary. Send all sorts of arms and ammunition immediately. In haste.

J. M. LANDRUM, THOS. H. MORRIS,
A. FLOURNOY, SR., J. S. FLOURNOY,
T. P. HOTCHKISS, J. N. HOWELL,
H. J. G. BATTLE, F. P. AUSTIN,
THOS. J. ALLEN.

An express has just reached this place, stating that MONTGOMERY, of Kansas, at the head of 2,000 or 3,000 men, had taken possession of Forts Washita and Cobb, on our northern frontier, and threaten invasion of our State and the devastation of our County. Col. W. C. YOUNG, at the head of 600 men, was holding them in check, and dispatched runners, calling upon the people for help.

LET OLD HARRISON RESPOND TO THE CALL.

We have the men ready to go, but we need horses and money. Let every man having a horse or any money answer this appeal from the northern part of our State by offering both to such as are ready to march and drive the invader from our soil.

Our County Court has this day issued the bonds of the county, bearing ten per cent interest, in obedience to the action of the public meeting held last Saturday, the 4th inst. These bonds are now ready for sale. Let every man that can raise $50 come forward and buy at least one of these bonds. The money thus raised will be invested for the purpose of purchasing arms and ammunition for the defence of our country, and the cause appeals to every patriot to do what he can.

A public meeting will be held in Marshall on Thursday next, at 11 o'clock, to take action in the matter; at which time let every citizen be present and report what amount of money he will invest in the bonds of the County, and what number of horses he can furnish. We must have money, or ruin and desolation stare us in the face.

A. POPE, GILL McKAY,
J. M. MORPHIS, A. E. LEMMONS,
WM. BRADFIELD, G. B. LIPSCOMB,
F. S. BASS, W. P. LANE,
J. N. COLEMAN, G. B. ADKINS,
J. F. WOMACK, W. H. DIAL,
G. G. GREGG, J. A. HARRIS.

MARSHALL, Tuesday Evening, May 7, 1861.

LATER REPORTS FROM TEXAS.

NEW-ORLEANS, Friday, May 17.

Texan advices say that Col. VAN DORN had succeeded in causing the surrender of the remaining Federal troops in Texas.

Texans in large numbers were doubtless on the upper frontier taking necessary steps to defend the State against incursions, from unfounded rumors at Montgomery that the Abolitionists were marching to capture the forts on the upper border.

THE PENNSYLVANIA TROOPS.

PHILADELPHIA, Friday, May 17.

The Adjutant-General has issued orders designating the Pennsylvania Regiments mustered into service by numbers in order. Col. PATTERSON'S Regiment, at Washington, is the Seventeenth; LEWIS', LYLE'S and MOREHEAD'S, at Baltimore, are the Eighteenth, Nineteenth and Twenty-second respectively; Col. DARE'S, on the line of the railroad, is the Twenty-third; Col OWEN'S Irish Brigade (still here) is the Twenty-fourth; Col GRAY'S Scott Legion (also here) is the Twentieth. The latter regiment is composed largely of officers and soldiers of the Mexican War. They have been uniformed in the regular United States Army dress, and expect to start soon.

HARRISBURG, Friday, May 17.

Two regiments are being formed to-day, out of men now encamped at Camp Curtin, by consolidating companies. The Philadelphia Regiment, for three years, has been finally accepted. It was composed jointly of five companies Col. SMALL'S Regiment, and five of ROBERT G. MARCH'S companies. The officers here have agreed to elect RUSH VAN DYKE chief-surgeon of the consolidated regiment.

REPORTS FROM HARRISBURGH.

HARRISBURGH Friday, May 17.

Nearly all the members of the Legislature have gone home. Few are still lingering to get companies accepted. The Governor is overwhelmed with applications to receive companies, but will positively receive no more until the General Government issues another requisition. Great indignation is felt among the military that fourteen additional regiments are to be taken from New-York.

The Governor goes to Chambersburgh to morrow, to review the troops. Several high State dignitaries will accompany him.

Fifteen regiments, under the new military bill, are to be distributed according to the number of troops already in the field from each County, also its population, except a discrimination against the rural districts, in order that sufficient producers will be left at home for harvest purposes—the State to pay no expense until marching orders be received by the companies.

MOVEMENTS OF IOWA TROOPS.

BURLINGTON, Iowa, Friday, May 17.

Companies C, E and I, Fourth Artillery, from Fort Randall, Capt. GETTY commanding arrived here to-day. They leave to-night for Chicago.

REPORTS FROM BOSTON.

BOSTON, Friday, May 17.

The United States brig *Bainbridge* is now under sailing orders, and was hauled into the stream to-day. Repairs on the steam frigate *Mississippi* are completed, and she is expected to sail Tuesday. Commodore MERVINE, Flag-officer of the Gulf Squadron, will sail in her.

A proposition is before the Legislature for aid in erecting a monument over the remains of WHITNEY and LADD, the two soldiers killed at Baltimore.

The Governor, accompanied by both branches of the Legislature, visited the Forts to day.

[*For Additional Rebellion News, see Eighth Page.*]

The New-York Times.

VOL. X....NO. 3019. NEW-YORK, SATURDAY, MAY 25, 1861. PRICE TWO CENTS.

HIGHLY IMPORTANT NEWS.

The War for the Union Commenced in Earnest.

Advance of Thirteen Thousand Government Troops into Virginia.

Alexandria, Arlington Heights and Other Points Occupied.

Occupation of Alexandria by the Fire Zouaves.

Col. Ellsworth Assassinated by a Rebel.

HIS MURDERER INSTANTLY PUT TO DEATH

FULL DETAILS OF THE OCCURRENCE.

Vigorous Preparations for Holding the Positions Secured.

Rebel Troops Threatening the Cumberland Valley.

SPECIAL DISPATCH FROM WASHINGTON.

WASHINGTON, Friday, May 24.

As I telegraphed last night, the Zouaves were ordered to enter Alexandria this morning. In accordance with this order, the command was embarked on the steamers *Baltimore* and *Mount Vernon*. About 5 o'clock they reached Alexandria. Just before reaching the wharf the commander of the *Pawnee* sent a flag of truce to the rebel forces giving them one hour in which to withdraw from the town. The *Baltimore* and *Mount Vernon* then made fast to the wharf. As the steamers approached the rebel sentinels fired their guns in the air and retreated back upon the main body, said to have been about five hundred strong. Simultaneously with the landing of the Zouaves the first Michigan Regiment entered Alexandria by the road leading from Long Bridge, and proceeded direct to the railroad dépôt, of which they took possession, capturing a troop of rebel cavalry numbering one hundred, with their horses and equipments.

The Zouaves landed in good order in double quick time, each company forming in company order on the street facing the river. Company E, Capt. LEVERIDGE, was the first to disembark. Capt. LEVERIDGE'S Company was at once detailed to destroy the Railroad track leading to Richmond, which service they promptly performed. After detailing Company E, Col. ELLSWORTH directed the Adjutant to form the Regiment, and then with his Aid, Lieut. WINSER, and a file of men, started for the Telegraph office for the purpose of cutting the wires.

Col. ELLSWORTH and his detachment proceeded in double quick time up the street. They had proceeded three blocks, when the attention of Colonel ELLSWORTH was attracted by a large secession flag flying from the Marshall House, kept by J. W. JACKSON. Col. ELLSWORTH entered the hotel, and meeting a man in the hall asked, "Who put that flag up?" The man answered, "I don't know; I am a boarder here." Col. ELLSWORTH, Lieut. WINSER, the chaplain of the regiment, Mr. HOUSE, a volunteer aid, and the four privates, went up to the roof and Col. ELLSWORTH cut down the flag.

The party were returning down the stairs, preceded by private FRANCIS E. BROWNELL, of Company A. As they left the attic, the man who had said he was a boarder, but who proved to be the landlord, JACKSON, was met in the hall, having a double-barrel gun, which he leveled at BROWNELL. BROWNELL struck up the gun with his musket, when JACKSON pulled both triggers of the gun. The contents lodged in the body of Col. ELLSWORTH, entering between the third and fifth ribs. Col. ELLSWORTH was at the time rolling up the flag. He fell forward on the floor of the hall and expired instantly, only exclaiming "My God."

Private BROWNELL, with the quickness of lightning, leveled his musket at JACKSON, and fired. The ball struck JACKSON on the bridge of the nose, and crashed through his skull, killing him instantly. As he fell BROWNELL followed his shot by a thrust of his bayonet which went through JACKSON'S body.

The companions of Col. ELLSWORTH, seven in number, immediately posted themselves so as to command the halls of the hotel, and threatened to shoot the first man who showed his head outside of a door. In this way they stood for ten minutes. Their protracted absence alarmed Adjutant LEOSER, who ordered Company A, Capt. COYLE, to search for him. The Company found their commander dead, and their comrades in possession of the hotel. A surgeon was then sent for, but Col. ELLSWORTH was dead long before his arrival.

The Company made a litter of muskets, and placing the body of the Colonel on it, returned to the boat, leaving, however, a detachment to guard the hotel, and make prisoners of all its occupants. The body was brought to the Navy-yard, and there remains, awaiting the action of the War Department. After fitting ceremonies here, his remains will be taken to Mechanicsville, New-York, for interment. His family reside at Mechanicsville. There were no other demonstrations of opposition to the occupation of the city.

TROOPS ON ARLINGTON HEIGHTS.

Sixty of the Metropolitan Rifles went to Arlington Heights last night to do guard duty and scout. They returned this morning early. The sixteen hundred men, mostly New-Jersey troops, ordered there, had not then arrived. Their advance, however, is throwing up entrenchments to-day.

The Michigan Regiment will be there to-day, making three thousand in all, with a battery.

Ten thousand Federal troops are on the Virginia side at noon to-day.

There is a battery at each end of the Long and Chain Bridges, and one at Alexandria with the Zouaves. By peremptory orders from Gen. SCOTT no civilians are permitted to pass either way to-day.

WASHINGTON, Friday, May 24—P. M.

The movement of troops last night was much larger than was at first supposed. We have now about 11,000 men in Virginia. They occupy all the uplands commanding Washington, and extend down below Alexandria. The men in the field are the New-York Eighth, Fifth, Seventh Twelfth, Twenty-fifth, Twenty-eighth and, Sixty-ninth, and the "Pet-Lambs;" also three New-Jersey regiments. The Rhode Islanders and one Michigan regiment, together with a portion of the Seventy-first New-York, are on river duty.

The men on the Heights are throwing up earthworks, and preparing for batteries. No fighting has taken place, the rebels as yet having no forces in front of our lines.

The Sixty-ninth crossed the river below Georgetown, and took position on the Orange and Manassas Gap Railroad, which runs out of Alexandria.

They took up some of the rails, and awaited in ambush the arrival of the train, which they supposed would leave Alexandria with the fugitives. When it came it was surrounded, and the train captured. About seven hundred persons were on board, including 300 men. The entire party were held as prisoners of war, and will be kept as hostages for the fair treatment of any loyal citizens that may fall into the hands of the rebels.

Among the prisoners captured by the troops this morning, are several persons who have been ringleaders in the rebellion movements in Virginia. Dr. BOYLE is one. He will stand a good chance of treading air. The excitement among the troops in Washington is most intense. All are anxious to join their comrades in the field, and every regiment hopes to be favored. The commanding officers are besieged with importunities for the privilege of being ordered out. Notwithstanding the departure of eleven thousand men last night, the force remaining in Washington is quite as large as it was a week since, and almost every train brings a regiment.

One hundred cavalry were taken prisoners near Alexandria.

Senator CHANDLER and friend, who were permitted to go over as special aids, have just returned.

The New-York troops have gone in the direction of the Manassas Gap Junction, beyond Alexandria.

The District troops are now in possession of Arlington Heights.

PROBABLE MOVEMENT ON HARPER'S FERRY.

It is probable that the Ohio troops moved down from the West upon Harper's Ferry last night, and that they were supported by a column from Pennsylvania. It is also probable that a simultaneous movement was made against the rebels at Norfolk. Our communications do not extend to those points. So that I cannot say positively that these movements were executed, but it is likely that Virginia was invaded on all sides at the same time. LEO.

FULL DETAILS OF THE MOVEMENTS.

WASHINGTON, Friday, May 24.

The New-York Sixty-ninth and Twenty-eighth Regiments, with Lieut. DRUMMOND'S Cavalry and a battery, passed the Chain Bridge about midnight last night. They first took possession of the Loudon and Hampshire Railroad, seized the train, arrested the passengers, took the cars and engine, and took one secession soldier, who was on board the train, prisoner. They held the position to-day on the road.

The Regiments who went over were the New-York Twelfth, Sixty-ninth, Seventh, Twenty-fifth, Twenty-eighth and Fifth; the New-Jersey Fourth, Third Michigan, First Rhode Island, three Companies of the Seventy-first New-York, Second New-York, two Companies; and the Rhode Island Batteries; ELLSWORTH'S Zouaves; three Companies Cavalry, Regular Army; three Companies of the Ohio Regiments; one Company of the Massachusetts Fifth, and twenty-five hundred District troops. Col. RICKET'S Battery went over to-day. Several Detached companies were also sent over—in all thirteen thousand men. The quota ordered were fourteen thousand, but the order for one New-Jersey Regiment was countermanded.

The Zouaves are to-night anchored on a steamer in the river, to prevent them from avenging the death of ELLSWORTH. Lieut.-Col. FARNHAM has had all he could do to keep them from burning the town. They swear the most terrible revenge.

Col. WILCOX, of the Michigan Regiment, is in command to-night of the army on the Virginia side.

Sherman's Battery returned to-night to this city.

At seven o'clock Alexandria was comparatively quiet. The citizens are in great fear.

The New-York Seventh are stationed about an eighteenth of a mile from the Long Bridge, at Jackson City, or Columbia Springs.

The camp-fires are easily discernable from this city at various points. Two guns of Sherman's Battery command the Long Bridge to-night.

THE VIRGINIA PRISONERS.

The thirty-six Virginia Cavalry, prisoners, were brought up to the Navy-yard this afternoon. They are very glum and ill-natured. Their conversation and answers to inquiries are very comical and amusing.

A large body of men are at Arlington Heights, but it is not known exactly who they are, except one New-Jersey regiment and some District Volunteers.

Most of the District Volunteers returned to-day.

Several hundred men are vigorously at work digging trenches and erecting fortifications.

The District Volunteers led the van in the march last night.

Twenty prisoners were in irons at 2 o'clock to-day at Alexandria. All the prisoners taken this morning were confined for a time in the slave pen at Alexandria. It was the only good purpose that I ever kew a slave pen to serve.

The Government very properly prohibited the passage of citizens into Virginia to-day, but immense quantities of provisions and tools for throwing up entrenchments, were sent to the troops stationed on the heights.

STRENGTHENING POSITIONS.

The troops are actively engaged in constructing fortifications, and preparing for the permanent occupation of the country covered by the movement made last night. This movement was planned by Gen. MANSFIELD, and executed under his personal supervision. He knew the exact point of ground that each Regiment should occupy, and at daylight each Regiment was in its place. So quietly was all this done, that only the newspaper people were aware of the sudden exit of thirteen thousand men.

It is creditable that the Sixty-ninth was given the post of danger, and that the duty assigned it was faithfully and fearlessly executed.

COL. ELLSWORTH'S REMAINS.

The body of Col. ELLSWORTH will leave Washington by the afternoon train to-morrow. They will be carried from the Navy-yard, and followed to the dépôt by the President and Cabinet, and a large body of troops.

The last thing Col. ELLSWORTH did last evening before leaving Washington, was to write a letter to his father, E. D. ELLSWORTH, of Mechanicsville, N. Y., and another to Miss CARRIE SPAFFORD, at Rockford, Ill., to whom he was engaged to be married. His last act, as he left the tent to embark on the steamer, was to look at her portrait, and to place it in his bosom.

Col. ELLSWORTH'S body was placed in the engine-house at the Navy Yard this morning. The house was heavily draped with American flags, crape and boquets of flowers. It was guarded by the Zouaves, a company of the Seventy-first New-York, and some regulars. Thousands of people assembled there to see the remains during the day, the President's family among the number.

The body of JACKSON still lies on the floor of his house, where he was shot.

Lieut. STRIKER, Company B; Seargeant ALCOCK, of the Staff, Company A; BROWNELL, Company A, who shot JACKSON; Corporal ESLING, Company A, and some others, compose the military escort of ELLSWORTH'S remains to New-York.

The Zouaves have the flags and Jackson's gun, which was taken. Gen. SCOTT will give it to them to keep.

AFFAIRS AT ALEXANDRIA.

At 8 o'clock, when Sergeant ALCOCK left Alexandria, everything was quiet.

Hundreds of women and children have come over to-day from Virginia. Alexandria will be nearly deserted within a day or two.

Col. ELLSWORTH'S body will be interred at Mechanicsville, near Troy.

NO DISPATCHES BY THE PERSIA.

There were no dispatchhes received at the State Department by the *Persia*. This is accounted for by the fact that neither Mr. DAYTON nor Mr. ADAMS had arrived at their Embassies when the *Persia* sailed. The private letters received show unmistakably that the British Ministry was in sympathy with the Southern Rebels. The letter from France induce the belief that the French Government will be more friendly to the United States Government than the British. All the letters received indicate a prevalent belief through Europe that the dissolution of the American Union is a fixed fact, and that European Governments are acting upon such a theory.

Since the news brought by the *Persia*, Lord LYONS has maintained a studied silence, declining to speak upon te political questions in dispute. It is evident that he does not himself know what will be the policy of his Government, and that he is surprised at the position assigned to Great Britain in accordance with the last advices. If the British Government should determine to recognize the Southern Confederacy, Lord LYON'S will probably resign. His opinions that a different policy would prevail, have been so freely expressed, that he cannot in honor represent a different course of action. Indeed, as for that matter, if England is against the United States, the dismissal of Lord LYON'S will be promptly made out.

GUN-BOATS, ARMS, &C., IN ENGLAND.

I am permitted to present the following extract from a letter dated London, May 11, written by a well-known shipping merchant of your city to a prominent member of the Union Defence Committee. The specifications to which he alludes are now before the Navy Department, and there is every likelihood ef prompt action being taken upon his suggestions:

LONDON, Saturday, May 11.

* * * * Amongst other things the want of gun-boats has been pressed upon me by reading some article in the NEW-YORK TIMES and *Evening Post*, and accordingly I made application to one of the best builders in the country, who has built a great many for this Government, always to their entire satisfaction, and he has furnished me with the inclosed statistics for gun boats built of teak or oak, fastened throughout with copper bolted through and through. The great difficulty is the time it will take to build them. They can be built of iron in about half the time, and I think would in every way be equal, and in many respects superior to wood. Mr. LAIRD has built for Continental Governments, and is building for France now.

I also send a note concerning three fine iron ships that can be ready for sea at a week's notice. They can be had for £35,000 each, and cost when new £65,000, though now as good as when first built. There is no difficulty in strengthening them for carrying heavy guns forward and aft. There are other ships to be had, but generally at extravagant prices; but these three I have examined carefully, and feel confident of their being in perfect order.

I write to you that you may communicate with the proper authorities through such channels as may be best. I notice that Mr. ASPINWALL has been asked by Government to charter or secure some ships, and, at first, was inclined to write to him; but, on reflection, thought it best to send through you. My time is at my country's service without fee or reward, save the consciousness and pleasure of doing my mite in repelling the unholy attacks upon its honor and its flag.

Our enemies are here working their treasonable schemes. I met them at Brussels, buying arms and ammunition. They *have purchased nearly one hundred rifled cannon* in this country, which are soon to be shipped, probably from Liverpool. I hope to be able to send word by *what vessels*, in time to have them seized. I hear of them at Manchester and Birmingham, in search of rifles, &c. Their head-quarters is at the new hotel, Westminster, and I learn that our Consul-General, CAMPBELL, a Southern man, meets, counsels and advises them. Our new Consul has just arrived, and I am happy to say is active in thwarting their plans.

I feel it a pleasure to mention the active efforts o Mr. FORSTER, member of Parliament, to head off all attempts for recognition of the Southern Confederacy, and to have it proclaimed that no vessel will be permitted to fit out from this country as a privateer, nor any subject of Great Britain to enlist as against a nation with which she is at peace. I am sure that the sympathies of this whole nation are with the North, keenly as they feel the probable effects upon the manufacturing interests.

Our friend, Col. FREMONT, is so excited about the condition of things at home, that I doubt if he remains here. He is quite prepared to abandon his work here for *self*, and tender his services, if needed, to his country. He would make a splendid General, so cool, clear and prompt in his plans, and with executive ability as a soldier unsurpassed. I do not know a man who could rally so many *young men* to follow him as he. Should he go home, I hope he will be called at once to fill one of the highest positions in the army. He is very much courted here, and his views are sought after with much avidity.

MAILS IN THE SOUTH.

On the first of June it is probable a proclamation will be issued, suspending all mail operations in the rebel States. As fast as they are conquered, and return to their allegiance, the mail facilities will be restored.

It has been ascertained definitely that until to-day the rebels have had constant advices of Government operations. The information was collected by their spies, who went to Alexandria, and transmitted it thence by telegraph. That game was blocked last night.

GEN. SCOTT'S INTENTIONS.

There is not likely to be another forward movement for some days. Gen. SCOTT has perfect faith in his superiority of numbers, and will move onward only so fast as he can maintain an advance. The campaign may be slow, but it will be sure. It crawls now, but it will run when the time comes for haste. Let the friends of the Union have *faith* and patience. Gen. SCOTT has never failed the country, and his military skill and ability are as clear and vigorous as ever. With him there is no such word as *fail*. He will certainly crush this rebellion.

THE ZOUAVES' REVENGE.

I hear, at 12 o'clock, from a gentleman just arrived from Alexandria, that the Zouaves have commenced executing their threats of vengeance, and have already shot three violent secessionists. The people at Alexandria who were sympathisers with JACKSON have been compelled to flee for the safety of their lives. The most intense excitement exists.

Mr. WOODS, the correspondent of the London *Times*, who was on the Prince of Wales tour, arrived here this evening, in company with J. W. FORNEY, of the Philadelphia *Press*.

The *post-mortem* examination of the body of Col. ELLSWORTH, by Dr. EUGENE REGUENT, Dr. HOLMES and Dr. SHELDON, disclosed these facts: that the contents of the gun entered the chest a little to the left of the breast-bone, between the second and third ribs, causing a lacerated wound about an inch and three-quarters in diameter, fracturing the third rib; then passed through the left lung, lacerating the arch of the aorta and its branches. The heart and the pericardium were not injured. The slugs, three in number, lodged in the spinal column, fracturing the third and fourth vertebrae, and the third rib. She medical examination was made by order of President LINCOLN, under care of Col. H. D. STOVER, of New-York.

THE MASSACHUSETTS STAFF OF GEN. BUTLER.

Gen. BUTLER has formally resigned his commission as Brigadier-General of the Massachusetts Volunteers. This discharges his present Staff, as the Army regulations compel him to appoint his Staff from the regulars or the three years' volunteers.

His Staff in Maryland has consisted of Major CLEMENCE, Lieutenant-Colonel PARKER and Capt. HAGGERTY.

Capt. HAGGERTY will, probably enlist for the full term of three years, and he, accordingly, remains with the General.

Capt. R. S. FAY is appointed Military Secretary, the only staff appointment left entirely discretionary to the General.

Major CLEMENCE and Col. PARKER may, therefore, be expected Northward shortly. LEO.

DISPATCH TO THE ASSOCIATED PRESS.

WASHINGTON, Friday, May 24.

Within a few hours past there have been stirring and important military movements. It was suspected yesterday that orders had been given for an advance of troops into Virginia, but these being necessarily of a secret character, the exact truth could not therefore, at that time, be reliably ascertained.

The New-York Second, Twelfth, Seventh and Seventy-first Regiments, the New-Jersey and Michigan Brigades, and ELLSWORTH'S Zouaves were, so far as is at present ascertained, constituted the forces which advanced upon Virginia. The Washington City National Rifles, Capt. SMEAD, at about 10 o'clock last night passed over the Long Bridge, which is about a mile in length and unites Washington with the Virginia shore, and remained at the latter terminus, until between 1 and 2 this morning, acting as an Advance Guard. These were followed by other district volunteer companies, acting in a similar capacity; subsequently the New-York Second and Twelfth Regiments, and the Michigan and New Jersey Brigades crossed the bridge. The Virginia pickets having been previously driven in by the Advance Guard, one of the regiments took the road leading to Fairfax Court-house, about twenty miles from Washington, while another one —the Jersey—stopped at the forks, a mile from the long bridge, to await orders.

An advance into Virginia was also made from another point—namely: at the mouth of the Potomac Aqueduct, at Georgetown.

The Seventh New-York Regiment were among the troops, and after several hours' march, occupied a point between the Bridge and Columbia Spring, on the line of the Washington and Alexander Railroad.

It is understood that orders were issued yesterday for two regiments to proceed to and occupy Alexandria, and it is stated at this time that Col. ELLSWORTH'S Zouaves crossed over in boats, while it is equally certain that preparations were made to seize Arlington Heights, which plainly overlooks Washington, and there is but little, if any, doubt, that all these orders have been executed. It was at least 2 o'clock this morning before all the troops reached their places of designation. The troops which did not repair to Alexandria and Arlington Heights were required to guard important intermediate points between Washington and Alexandria. The *District of Columbia* did not return to Washington until 6½ o'clock this morning.

From 6.000 to 10,000 troops were sent over into Virginia this morning.

Firing was heard occasionally by the driving in the Virginia pickets.

Washington is all excitement this morning, owing to these proceedings, and further events are looked for with intense solicitude.

NINE O'CLOCK.

The New-York Zouaves, Fourteenth, and Sixty-ninth, and Jersey regiments hold Alexandria, while Arlington Heights are occupied by several other regiments.

The entrance into Alexandria was attended by an event which has cast the deepest gloom over this community. Col. ELLSWORTH, who had hauled down the secession flag from the Marshall House, was soon after shot by a concealed foe. His dead body has been brought to the Washington Navy-yard.

Accounts from Alexandria are somewhat confused, but there is no doubt of the fact that a man named JACKSON, who shot Col. ELLSWORTH, was instantly put to death—some say by both bullet and bayonet.

When the Federal troops reached Alexandria, the Virginia soldiers fired at them and fled.

Visitors to that city say that the scenes were intensely exciting.

Federal vessels were in the meantime before Alexandria.

It seems to be true, that a body of Federal troops has advanced to Fairfax Court-house, to take possession of the Junction of the Orange and Alexandria and Manassas Gap Railroad, with a view of intercepting the advance of Virginia troops towards Alexandria, from Richmond and other points.

Nearly 3,000 troops arrived here yesterday, comprising some from New-York and the two Ohio regiments. A third Connecticut regiment came in this morning.

WASHINGTON, Friday, May 24—11 o'clock A. M.

It is reported that as the Virginia troops retired from Alexandria one of them was killed by a return shot from the Federal forces. There is a prospect of capturing the fugitives. Among the forces sent over to Virginia were two batteries and two companies of artillery. Numerous wagons, with spades, picks and other entrenching tools, also passed into that State. The proceedings attending the movements of the troops were conducted with the best possible order.

The new of the death of Col. ELLSWORTH was not generally known throughout Washington until towards 10 o'clock to-day. The excitement was intense, especially among the military, who express the greatest impatience and desire to be sent over to Virginia.

From a spyglass view of Alexandria, the Stars and Stripes are prominently flying from various quarters.

Several captures having been made in Hampton Roads before the expiration of the fifteen days from the notice of the blockade, restitution in such cases has been ordered.

WASHINGTON, Friday, May 24—1 P. M.

Numerous wagons, with camp equipage, are passing through the streets, to-day, to the Federal troops in Virginia. Nothing of peculiar note has been received up to this hour.

Postmaster-General BLAIR prepared an order to-day discontinuing the transmission of the United States mails in Virginia and other seceding States, and annulling all contracts for the same. Tennessee is excepted from the operation of the order, for the reason that that State has not yet formally seceded. This course of the Postmaster-General is under the act in relation to the subject, passed at the last session of Congress. Contractors will be immediately notified of this decision. The mails for the South, from Washington, were stopped at the crossing-place by the Federal troops, and were returned to the Post-office here.

Judge AMY, bearer of dispatches, had an interview with the President and Secretary of War to-day, and tendered to them three regiments from Kansas, to co-operate with the Iowa regiments in camp at Keokuk, and the Illinois regiments in camp at Quincy, to protect the Union men of Northwestern Missouri and to secure a safe transit of stores and provisions over the Hannibal and St. Joseph Railroad to the West.

Orders have been issued by the War Department to Capt. RENO, of Fort Leavenworth, to supply the Kansas regiments with arms and military equipments, and also horse equipments for a regiment of cavalry. The arrangement will furnish at once over 10,000 men, who will remain in camps in their respective States, ready to take possession of the Hannibal and St. Joseph Railroad, between those points, as soon as any further demonstrations are made by JEFF. THOMPSON, of St. Joseph, and his secession followers, to interrupt transportation through Missouri.

Mr. AMY reports good rains in Kansas, and says the crops in that State never looked more prosperous.

The State militia are being organized into eleven regiments, and the State authorities have determined to equip them as well as possible for home defence, having decided to discountenance any invasion of the State of Missouri, unless Missouri shall secede, or invade Kansas, or the safe transit across the State be interrupted. With these arrangements, and the prompt and decisive steps adopted by Gen. HARNEY, and the coöperation of Gen. PRICE, the President expects peace to be maintained in Missouri and Kansas.

Judge AMY reports a great want of suitable clothing for the military in Kansas, and has applied to the Government for a supply, which will be granted.

The cavalry of Secessionists captured at Alexandria to day, have been brought to the Washington Navy-Yard.

Passengers from that city, to-day, say that the Fire Zouaves have been amusing themselves riding about on the horses.

The other prisoners are in custody.

The Federal troops are quartered at the Mansion House.

At two o'clock this afternoon, the body of JACKSON still lay where he was killed.

The troops between here and Alexandria have made good progress in throwing up entrenchments.

Col. WILCOX, of the Michigan Regiment, is in command of Alexandria.

The ferry-boats between Washington and that city will resume their trips next week.

The flags all over the city are half mast to-day, and the bells are tolling in respect for Col. ELLSWORTH. It is probable his remains will be brought to the President's House and conveyed thence to the cars. To-morrow afternoon they will be transported to New-York, of which State was a native. He was aged about 27 years.

There are about twelve Secessionists under charges in the common jail,

Many of the troops here are in readiness to march at a moment's warning.

The President has appointed JOHN G. STEPHENSON, of Indiana, Librarian of Congress, and the following-named gentlemen Postmasters: JOHN CHAPMAN, at Salem, Mass.: EDWARD A. CHASE, Lynn, Mass.; WM. H. HASKELL, Gloucester, Mass.

COL. ELLSWORTH'S REMAINS.

WASHINGTON, Friday, May 24, 1861.

Chas. A. Stetson, Astor House:

Col. ELLSWORTH'S remains will leave at 2½ o'clock to-morrow (Saturday) P. M. They will go to the Astor with a guard of six men and a lieutenant. Make such preparations as you see fit. I should say No. 41. You know what to do and will do it. We are heart-broken, and Virginia has contracted a debt that centuries of groveling cannot wipe out. We occupy Alexandria. ALEX STETSON,

Quartermaster First Regiment N. Y. Zouaves.

[We understand that the body will be laid in state in the Governor's Room, City Hall, as the Astor House does not afford sufficient accommodations for the occasion. The body will probably reach this City Sunday morning.—ED. TIMES.]

COL. ELLSWORTH'S FUNERAL.

The Ellsworth Fire Zouave Fund Committee will meet this (Saturday) afternoon at 5 o'clock, at the Astor House, Room No. 51, to make final arrangements for the funeral obsequies of the late Col. E. E. ELLSWORTH. By order

A. J. DELATOUR, Chairman, *pro tem.*

GEO. F. NESBITT, Secretary.

ACTION OF THE FIRE DEPARTMENT.

A meeting of the Fund Committee, recently appointed by the Fire Department to superintend the equipment and departure of the First Regiment Firemen Zouaves, Col. ELLSWORTH, was held at the Astor House yesterday afternoon, A. F. OCKERSHAUSEN acting as chairman. The following preamble and resolutions were unanimously adopted:

Whereas, This Committee (who have so recently aided in organizing the above regiment, to go forth in defence of our Constitution, our Union, and our Flag) having learned with deep sorrow of the death of Col. ELLSWORTH, while in the discharge of his duty, and while hauling down the flag of traitors, do most deeply sympathize with his afflicted family and friends, and the regiment he so ably commanded in this lamentable disaster. A gallant, brave and energetic officer has fallen in his country's cause, and his State and the nation mourns his loss. Therefore,

Resolved, That this Committee will attend the funeral obsequies of the late Col. ELLSWORTH, and they invite the Trustees, the President, and officers and ex-officers, and the Fire Department generally, to join in paying their respects to the soldier who chose to command a regiment of the New-York firemen, and has proved himself worthy of the confidence reposed in him.

Resolved, That a Committee of Six from this body be appointed to proceed to Washington to take charge of the honored remains and escort them to this City, or such place as the family and friends of the deceased may designate.

Resolved, That a Committee of Five be appointed with power to make such arrangements as they may deem necessary, upon the reception of the remains in this City.

The Committee appointed to take charge of the body on its arrival in this City, organized by the appointment of A. DELATOUR, No. 25½ Wall-street, as Chairman, and JAMES KELLY, Receiver of Taxes, Secretary.

The following gentlemen comprise the Committee of Arrangements: John Decker, Chief of the Fire Department; Henry B. Venn, Henry A. Burr, Zophar Mills, James G. Watkins, and George F. Nesbitt.

The Committee appointed to proceed to Washington departed immediately by the cars last evening. The parents of the deceased were notified by telegraph of their bereavement. They reside at Malta, Saratoga County, in this State Nothing definite can be known in regard to the funeral ceremonies until their arrival.

THE SEVENTY-FIRST REGIMENT.

RESERVE BATTALION SEVENTY FIRST REGIMENT AMERICAN GUARD.

The members of this battalion and ex-members of the regiment are requested to attend a meeting to be held at the Armory, Centre Market, this evening, at 8 o'clock, to take suitable action upon the decease of Col. ELLSWORTH, of the New York Zouaves, and the reception of his remains in this City. By order of

CHAS. H. PIERSON,

Commanding Reserve Battalion.

THE NEWS OF COL. ELLSWORTH'S DEATH.

MECHANICSVILLE, N. Y., Friday, May 24.

The assassination of Col. ELLSWORTH has caused in this, his native town, the utmost sorrow and indignation. The father of Col. ELLSWORTH happened to be in the telegraph office when the melancholy intelligence was received, and the first intimation he had of it was seeing the operator weeping. Mr. ELLSWORTH'S grief was indescribable on learning the sad news. He left, in company with his wife, for New York this evening, on the *Francis Skiddy*. All the flags in town are at half-mast. The sympathy expressed for his parents is universal. The Colonel was their only living son. About a year since his younger brother, a young man of much ability, died in Chicago.

A great excitement was created by one WALLMAN, a Dutch peddler, who thought his death was all right, and expressed sentiments favorable to the traitors. He was allowed by the citizens twenty minutes to leave town, and left with the band playing the Rogue's March, with orders to return no more.

POUGHKEEPSIE, Friday, May 24.

Upon the report of the death of Col. ELLSWORTH, the flags were lowered half mast, and the fire bells tolled.

PITTSBURGH, Pa., Friday, May 24.

Col. ELLSWORTH'S death was received here with profound sorrow. All the flags in the city were at half-mast.

REBELS ON THE POTOMAC.

THE CUMBERLAND VALLEY THREATENED.

CHAMBERSBURGH, Penn., Friday, May 24.

Beyond all doubt 9,500 Confederate troops are now posted between the Point of Rocks and Williamsport, on the Potomac. 7,000 are Virginians, and the rest Alabamians, Mississippians, Carolinians and Georgians. There are also 300 Cherokees, armed with tomahawks, scalping knives and rifles. They are from North Carolina and Georgia. The Virginians are well armed, but short of provisions.

Between the Point of Rocks, 8 miles below, and Williamsport, 23 miles above Harper's Ferry, there are thirty-five pieces of cannon at various points. Twenty of these are brass field-pieces

Great apprehension prevails in the Cumberland Valley of invasion from Virginia. 10,000 head of cattle, and 5,000 horses could be seized by a sudden eruption of an expeditionary corps, holding the Valley five days, even if finally driven back into Virginia.

A forward movement of Virginia may be expected at any moment. CAMPBELL'S Flying Artillery, six pieces, has been ordered to this place, but two additional regiments of infantry, and a battalion of Cavalry, are absolutely needed here to prevent a devastation of the whole Valley. There should also be three batteries of six twelve-pounders.

REPORTS FROM BALTIMORE.

BALTIMORE, Friday, May 24.

The news from Washington has produced a profound sensation here. The Old Point boat, this morning, reports that General BUTLER threw out a guard of three hundred men at the United States Hotel, principally to guard a splendid well of water, belonging to Col. SEGAR, which was wanted for the use of the garrison.

Nothing is known relative to Sewall's Point. A movement had not taken place when the steamer left.

A steamer arrived at Fort McHenry this morning with a large supply of gun carriages and other military stores. Col. Morehead's regiment came across the river this morning, marched up Broadway and proceeded to Patterson Park. They made a fine display.

REPORTS FROM ST. LOUIS.

ST. LOUIS, Friday, May 24.

The State troops at Jefferson City, numbering about 4,000 men, were ordered to disband, yesterday, by Gen. PRICE. At first they refused to obey, but it is believed that they will quietly disperse and return to their homes.

A ten-inch howitzer, an eight and a-half inch mortar, and three hundred rounds of cartridges, ball, shell and cannister were shipped from the Arsenal, yesterday, destined for Cairo.

MOVEMENTS OF THE SEVENTH.

ALEXANDRIA BRIDGE, Friday, May 24.

The Seventh Regiment left Camp Cameron at 1:20 this morning, each man having sixty rounds of ball cartridge. They touched the "sacred soil of Virginia" at 4 A. M., landing at the Alexandria Bridge, near which they are encamped.

They will throw up earthworks to-morrow morning, fortify men being detailed from each company. I just left them, all well and full of enthusiasm. JASPER.

THE STEAMER PEERLESS.

TORONTO, Friday, May 24.

Steamer *Peerless*, recently sold to agents of the American Government, left here for New-York to-day.

THE COAST GUARD SERVICE.

SAG HARBOR, Friday, May 24.

The revenue cutter *Crawford*, Capt. CARSON, arrived in our bay to-day. She comes after her crew, who enlisted at this place.

BLOCKADE OF THE MISSISSIPPI.

The following note appears in the New Orleans *Picayune:*

BRITISH CONSULATE, NEW-ORLEANS, May 17, 1861.

EDS PICAYUNE: Although I have not received any official notice regarding the time when the blockade of the Mississippi River will be established, it may be important to those interested to give such information as I have received from Washington:

"Neutral vessels will be allowed fifteen days to leave port after the actual commencement of the blockade, whether such vessels are with or without cargoes, and whether the cargoes were shipped before or after the commencement of the blockade."

I may add that it is rumored that the blockade will be effectually established on or about the 26th inst.

I am, Sirs, your obedient servant,

WM. MURE, H. B. M. Consul.

[*For Additional Rebellion News, see Eighth Page.*]

The New-York Times.

VOL. X....NO. 3019. NEW-YORK, SUNDAY, MAY 26, 1861. PRICE THREE CENTS.

THE SECESSION REBELLION.

False Reports of Fighting at Alexandria.

All the Troops in Washington Ordered Under Arms.

Large Bodies of Them Thrown into Virginia.

Astonishing Celerity of their Movements

ONLY A SKIRMISH BETWEEN PICKETS.

The Obsequies of Col. Ellsworth.

Highly Important from Fortress Monroe.

Reported Capture of the Sewell's Point Battery.

GEN. BUTLER RECONNOITERING.

SPECIAL DISPATCH FROM WASHINGTON

WASHINGTON, Saturday, May 25.

The false alarm of a fight in the neighborhood of Alexandria, which was raised about one o'clock to-day, had one great advantage—it tested the disposition of our troops, and made manifest their efficiency. As the signal went from camp to camp that the rebels were attacking the wing, there was a prompt and decisive response of "ready," and they were ready. I never realized until to-day the celerity of movement which drill and discipline insures.

SHERMAN'S battery of six-pounders made the distance from their quarters to Long Bridge at the rate of nine miles an hour. The Massachusetts Fifth were under arms, in line, and off to the Bridge before there appeared to be time for the orders to be ready.

N. P. BANKS is in town. It is understood to be settled that he will be made a Major-General.

The Massachusetts Fifth were ordered to be ready' with all their equipments, at 5 o'clock, but up to this time have not left the Treasury building. All the other Regiments ordered over the river to-day, when the false alarm was given, have gone back to their camps.

I have just seen a member of the New-York Seventh, who says he is from there this evening. He says everything is quiet. The work at Arlington Heights was going on lively. He says there was great excitement when the alarm was given on the other side; that a large body of men were advancing, some miles distant, upon their post.

The troops who went over the river confidently expected a fight' but not a man flinching when the order was given, that I can learn.

Gen. MANSFIELD regrets the false alarm, but is much gratified at the spirit manifested by the troops.

Col. COOPER was at the Relay House to-day, with several companies reinforcements.

ANOTHER ZOUAVE SHOT.

JOHN BUTTERWORTH, of the Zouaves Sargant of the Guard, Company I., was shot about 3 o'clock this A. M., by the sentry. He was challenged three times, but failed to reply, thinking the sentry knew him. He died in five minutes. The sentry was justified, of course. It is a good lesson.

Lieut. Col. FARNHAM will succeed ELLSWORTH in command by unanimous election.

JACKSON'S body is in possession of his friends.

Lieut.-Col. NOBELSDORFF and Major KUNE, of Chicago, are here to urge the acceptance of a German Regiment, commanded by FRED. HECKER, Commander of Revolutionary forces in Baden in 1848. NOBELSDORFF was a distinguished officer in the Prussian army. KUNE was a member of Gen. BEM'S staff in the Hungarian Revolution. Every member of the regiment has seen service. The Chicago Irish Regiment is accepted, which makes the Germans jealous.

If Col. MIX'S Mounted Rifles are accepted, Col. PARKER, recently of BUTLER'S staff, will probably join in the command.

ARLINGTON HEIGHTS.

The Sixty-ninth have been under arms all day, and are much exhausted, but full of spirit.

A body of the Seventy-first went across the river on the steamer *James Gay* to-night.

Dr. BOYLE is not among the prisoners taken by the Federal troops. He barely escaped.

The Zouaves have the horses and arms of the captured cavalry. They have seized a case of Colt's revolving rifles, and one of double barrelled shot-guns.

The camps and equippage of the troops on the other side go over to-morrow.

I learn from Baltimore that JOHN MERRIMAN, one of the leading Secessionists, is now in confinement at Fort McHenry. He has been one of the most active and dangerous of the Maryland traitors, according to my informant. He is charged with being the leading spirit in the burning of the bridges.

The Secessionists are very active, holding secret meetings there every night. They are certainly plotting some new scheme of mischief. But the agents of the Government and Union men of Baltimore are on their tracks, and are sure to discover the movement.

They are becoming very restless under the lax order of the military rule now administered there. Scarcely a Union flag is to be seen in the streets while hundreds were to be seen when Gen. BUTLER was in command. Secession doctrines and abuse of the Administration are freely indulged in.

These facts have been brought to the attention of the President and Gen. SCOTT.

SEWELL'S POINT BATTERY.

There are many doubts expressed by officers of the Government and military men of the truth of the report received last night at the War Department of the capture of Sewell's Point Battery by Gen. BUTLER. It is deemed impossible that in one day he could so dispose his forces as to assist the water force in such an undertaking. He reached the Fort late Wednesday night, and it takes one day to get the news from there, so that he had necessarily but one day to do all this. I am positively assured by the chief clerk and operator at the War Department that they have no such positive news, but expect it will be done.

Last night Col. BUTLER, the General's brother, received from him a dispatch stating, "I shall take Sewell's Point as soon as possible." We expect, therefore, to hear of an attack there soon.

COL. ELLSWORTH'S FUNERAL.

The funeral of Col. ELLSWORTH to-day was an imposing spectacle. The ceremonies were held at the White House. The sermon, preached by Rev. Dr. PINE, was exceedingly appropriate to the occasion, the preacher giving a national character to the discourse by denouncing the killing of ELLSWORTH as murder. He stigmatized those engaged in this rebellion against the Government as assassassins.

The purpose of the Government was to give to the funeral of Col. E. the solemnity and dignity of a notional event. The President and the highest civil and military officers followed the body, and the military escort represented every branch of the service. The pall-bearers were J. G. NICOLAY, the private Secretary of President LINCOLN; AUGUSTUS HAIGHT, and ROBERT H. MORRIS, of the State Department, Col. STOVER, of New-York, and Hon. J. N. ARNOLD, M. C, from Illinois. Messrs. HAIGHT and STOVER accompanied the remains to New-York; and in addition, Messrs. L. D. BOOMER, E. C. LEARNER and STEPHEN GALE, of Chicago, Ill., accompanied the body by request, and as the representatives of the President.

The citizens of Illinois at present in Washington raised a sum of money for the purpose of purchasing a flag, to be presented to the Zouaves. The regiment has already eleven flags, and so express a desire that the money shall be given to the parents of Col. ELLSWORTH.

SUBSCRIPTION FOR COL. ELLSWORTH'S FAMILY.

A meeting was held this evening of non-residents, for the purpose of recommending a general subscription throughout the country, the subscriptions to be limited to one dollar each person. Gov. BANKS presided, and ABRAM WAKEMAN was Secretary. Messrs. JOHN COCHRANE, WALDO HUTCHINS and SIMON H. MIX presented appropriate resolutions, and speeches were made by Gov. BANKS, CALEB LYON, ISAAC N. ARNOLD, M. C., of Chicago, and JOHN COCHRANE.

Mrs. JOHN J. ASTOR was appointed General Treasurer, and REUBEN H. WALWORTH. EDWARD C. DELAVAN and JAMES M. COOK, of Sarotoga, were appointed an advisory Committee.

MOVEMENT OF TROOPS.

LATER.—The Massachusetts Fifth will march to-night to reinforce the troops in Virginia. They will be accompanied by two companies of Flying Artillery.

Speaking of Virginia, I looked to-day down ten feet into her sacred soil, the troops having penetrated to that depth in throwing up entrenchments They are making frightful scars upon the Old Dominion.

The Highland Regiment reached Washington to-night.

Col. WESTBROOK has tendered to the War Department a regiment of thoroughly drilled troops, and they will probably be accepted. LEO.

FROM ANOTHER CORRESPONDENT.

FORT SEWARD, ARLINGTON HEIGHTS, VA., Saturday, May 25.

The troops along Arlington Heights have been under arms all day expecting an attack. Large bodies of U. S. troops crossed Alexandria bridge in consequence of firing in that direction.

The Sixty-ninth are rapidly completing formidable earthworks, and will work all night, an attack in force from Culpepper Court-house being expected to-morrow or the day after at furthest. As an acknowledgment to Gov. SEWARD for his kindness, since they have been here, their fort is called by his name.

The wildest reports have been in circulation all day, and the secession feeling showed itself strongly in Washington when it was believed that the Union forces had suffered a reverse. The men of the Fifth, Twenty-eighth and Sixty-ninth are well, and in high spirits. H.

DISPATCH TO THE ASSOCIATED PRESS.

WASHINGTON, Saturday, May 25.

Western Virginia is an exception to the order of the Postmaster-General for the stoppage of the mails in the seceded States. Every facility will be afforded for postal accommodations in that section.

There is a great deal of coal on the way from Cumberland, Maryland, to tide-water, the principal or only difficulty in the way of which is the refusal of the rebel troops at Harper's Ferry to allow the boats to pass that point. From present indications, this obstruction will not probably long continue.

It cannot be ascertained that anything of especial moment took place at Alexandria last night. There is no doubt, however, the Government has sent on advance parties to take such measures regarding the railroads, bridges, etc., as to impede the advance of the Confederate troops.

The remains of Col. ELLSWORTH were this morning conveyed to the East room of the President's house, where, for several hours, they lay in state. The coffin was draped with the American flag and adorned with choice flowers. The face was exposed to the public. Many persons, principally soldiers, visited the White House to take a farewell look at him.

WASHINGTON, Saturday, May 25—P. M.

Owing to the immense throng of anxious gazers on the remains of the deceased, the funeral *cortége* delayed moving from the Executive Mansion till near 1 o'clock. All along the line of Pennsylvania-avenue flags were displayed at half-mast and draped in mourning. Every available point, including the windows, balconies and house-tops were thronged with anxious and sorrowful gazers. Various testimonials of respect were paid. All the bells of the City were tolled, and the heads of the soldiers and troops uncovered. Several companies of the City Corps, followed by the New-York Seventy-first Regiment, Marines, and the local Cavalry Corps, formed the military escort, with their arms reversed and colors shrouded.

The hearse was followed by a detachment of Zouaves, one of whom, the avenger of Col. ELLSWORTH, carried the identical secession flag, torn down by the deceased.

Then followed the President, accompanied by Secretaries SEWARD and SMITH, and the rest of the procession was composed of carriages, containing the captains of the Zouave Regiment.

The head of the procession reached the dépôt at about 1:40, and the train, with the remains, will soon start.

THE FALSE ALARM.

WASHINGTON, Saturday, May 25—3 P. M.

At 2 o'clock, this afternoon, the Massachusetts and other troops were hurrying to their quarters for a hasty advance towards Alexandria, where a fight is reported in progress, the extent of which is not known. Three guns have been fired, which is the signal for all the troops here to get under arms. Great excitement prevails throughout the city. Soldiers and private citizens in crowds are hurrying in every direction. A full light battery, at a few moments' notice, thundered over the Long Bridge. Gen. MANSFIELD and Staff led the advancing troops from Washington.

Intense anxiety prevails throughout the city.

WASHINGTON, Saturday, May 25—4 P. M.

The report of an engagement is incorrect, although believed at head-quarters and acted upon by signal guns.

There is no fight in progress.

WASHINGTON, Saturday, May 25—4½ P. M..

An account, just received from Virginia, which seems to be truthful, says the cause of alarm was that the Federal picket guard at Little Falls Church, near Arlington, were driven in by Secessionists. The latter were soon put to flight. The Sixty-ninth New-York Regiment left their work at the entrenchments and are now drawn up in line on the brow of the hill. The troops which hastily left the city this afternoon, are halting within a mile's [illegible]ce. The artillery and cavalry passed on in the direction of Alexandria.

WASHINGTON, Saturday, May 25—5 P. M.

Some of the troops who so hastily crossed the river this afternoon, have returned to this City, disappointed in their expectations of meeting the enemy. The proceedings, however, demonstrate the facility and expedition with which forces can be thrown into Virginia.

The President, while in the procession to-day, accompanying the remains of Col. ELLSWORTH to the cars, was informed by a courier of stirring hostilities on the Virginia side. Gen. MANSFIELD was similarly advised, and this was the foundation of the military movements here to-day. A dense smoke was meanwhile seen on the line of Arlington Heights, and cannonading heard. The latter, however, were funeral minute guns, and the former probably from camp fires. The troops now here have been ordered to hold themselves in readiness to march at a moment's notice. The utmost watchfulness on the part of the military authorities to guard against the approach of the secession troops is everywhere manifest.

OUR WAR CORRESPONDENCE.

The March into Virginia—The Fifth, Twenty-eighth and Sixty-ninth New-York State Militia—First Night's Campaigning.

IN CAMP, ARLINGTON HEIGHTS, VA., Friday, May 24, 1861.

Last night that event so threateningly denounced by Gov. LETCHER took place. The "sacred soil" of Virginia received the imprint of thirteen thousand feet on march to the vindication of the Union.

Visiting the Sixty-ninth Regiment in their quarters in the Catholic College, on Georgetown Heights, last evening, the scene was strange and impressive in the highest degree. The men had no idea they were about to start for Virginia, but knew that a move in some direction was contemplated, though few of them thought the line of march would be given until the beginning of next week.

Nevertheless, the main halls and corridors of the college presented a bustling and busy scene, the Commissary, Quartermaster and Adjutant superintending the distribution of vast quantities of clothing—red flannel shirts, woolen socks, heavy marching shoes, blankets and general equipments.

Moving through the companies of men led up by their officers to receive these supplies, the dark robed figures of the Holy Fathers of the College presented a striking contrast. Calm, pale, clad in long black robes reaching to the ground, and wearing the peculiar black cap of their order, the ministers of religion formed a stern back-ground to the brilliancy of uniforms, the glitter of arms and the glare of light which made up the scene on entering.

Passing out into the moonlight, we could see, from the brow of the hill on which the college is built, the leafy Heights of Arlington, across the river; the long aqueduct, which also serves as a bridge, and is guarded at either end by Uncle Sam's artillerymen; the City of Alexandria in the distance, across the water; and the beautiful tree-crowned islands lying between this point and that city. Before us, the calm of Nature seemed unbroken; not a breath of wind stirring, and the shadow of the smallest branch being reflected in the water.

Turning round, however, the two vast piles of red brick buildings which form the main portion of the College, were all alight with excitement—save in that wing of one of them still occupied by the fifty or sixty students, who remain, out of the three hundred lately gathered at this seat of learning. More than forty of the older students, hailing from the South, are now, it is said, lieutenants in the Confederate Army. The peace of the Academy has given place to the clang of arms; and the Holy Fathers have only to fear that the regiment which succeeds the Sixty-ninth may not be so amenable to the mild discipline of religion and persuasion.

Let me say, at this point, that nothing can be kinder, more considerate or thoughtful than the Brotherhood of this institution have shown themselves. Father EARLY, in particular, might sit for the portrait of a model priest of the olden time—courtly, bland acquiescent, polished, handsome and insinuating: a middle-aged, calm, resolute man, as much at home in the drawing-rooms of Washington or Paris as in his cloister, and yet never losing sight of "the Church" wherever he may be, or whatever his occupation. But to return:

By two o'clock last night everything was in readiness for the road, the men still believing that they were not to start until to-day, and expecting every moment to be dismissed and sent to their quarters. At half past two, however, the orders were given to take up the line of march; and by three o'clock this morning the head of the Sixty-Ninth could be seen winding over the narrow pathway on one side of the aqueduct, while the rear guard were still defiling through the main gate of their quarters, and stretching in tortuous curves through all the intervening streets.

On this march were engaged the Fifth New-York Regiment, Col. CHRISTIAN SCHWARZWAELDER, almost entirely German; the Twenty-eighth, of Brooklyn, and a squadron of skirmishing cavalry known as the President's Body Guard. On the Georgetown side, the bridge is defended by a battery of flying artillery, completely enfilading its entire length; while on the Virginia side, two or three companies of District Militia have heretofore been stationed to prevent any attempt on the part of the Secessionists towards blowing up or otherwise destroying the aqueduct. As Washington so completely depends on this work—we might say for its very existence—this guard-duty is one of the safest positions that could be assigned to the local soldiery of the Federal Capital.

Over the aqueduct marched the troops—their shadows, forty feet below, on the calm surface of the Potomac, advancing steadily along the water in fantastic procession. Suddenly, at the end of the bridge, the line wheeled upon the road for Alexandria—not a bugle sounding, not a drum beating; the deep silence of the trees on each side and overhead being utterly unbroken; every eye straining through the little patches of moonlight shimmering down through the leaves, to catch sight of any lurking foe; and every ear alert for the sharp ring that was to announce another officer picked off by some assassin marksman.

Then out into the broad moonlight, and over long patches of meadow land and grassy uplands—again plunging into the woods and again reappearing in open country. Here and there were beautiful mansions embosomed in trees, their white walls and green verandahs wearing none the less an air of comfort for the heavy dews that were falling; the weariness of the men under the novel weight of their full accoutrements and ammunition; the undulating character of the country, and the very doubtful prospect looming up in the immediate future of a nap for two hours on the wet grass, and then to work at entrenchments with the first daylight. Let the owners of those mansions sleep peacefully in their beds while they may! It is not forever that such acts as the murder of Col. ELLSWORTH, of which we have only this moment heard, can fail to draw down a frightful retribution alike on the just and the unjust.

Arriving at a distance of about four miles from Georgetown, the Fifth and Twenty eighth were posted for camp duty, first breaking down the bridges in advance of them, to prevent a sudden attack by the Secessionists. These two regiments mustered in the march about 700 men each—the Twenty-eighth, perhaps, 800; but this latter body still need a good deal of drill and experience, being for the most part composed of men wholly new to military duties. The Fifth did very fairly and appeared in excellent spirits, the moonlight march, the silence, and the mystery of our destination having doubtless some attractions for the German mind.

As for the Sixty-ninth, they turned out more than twelve hundred muskets, leaving yet another hundred—the newly arrived Zouaves—in their late head-quarters at the College. This Regiment has grown into great favor in Washington—not a single one of its members ever having become amenable to the police authorities in any way; and its discipline and efficiency having frequently been made the subject of complimentary notice by Gens SCOTT and MANSFIELD. For very much of the good order and moral restraint existing in the ranks, it is doubtless indebted to the ceaseless and zealous exertions of Father THOMAS MOONEY, an admirable specimen-priest of the true Irish type, who, if he were not chaplain, would certainly be a candidate for Colonel—fate and a sanguine temper giving him equal adaptation to the sword of the spirit and the "regulation sword"—a veritable son of the church-militant. But this again is a digression.

The Fifth and Twenty-eighth being posted in a position which, to describe, must be seen by daylight, the Sixty-ninth then wheeled back, four of its companies being stationed on a hill about half way between the aqueduct and the advance, to keep open communication, three companies being detailed under orders of an engineer officer of the United States, to throw up fortifications and entrenchments for a camp, to be occupied by the regiment; and the balance having their post of duty assigned on a narrow strip of land, sloping down from the Aqueduct canal to the shore of that arm of the Potomac which runs up past Georgetown, where they are to keep open and protect a military ferry that has been established between the District of Columbia and Virginia—this ferry having its Virginian terminus exactly at the foot of the road to Alexandria. It is not difficult to conjecture what this means, and the less so as rafts laden with horses and boats carrying field pieces, are already passing over.

But your correspondent is very weary, as doubtless his readers may also be. In the first experience of campaigning, everything is so novel that one is apt to attach personal value to trifles which may prove of no general interest. This is a fault, however, of which time promises a speedy cure. Reluctant to complain of anything under the sudden and fearful pressure which has brought so many thousands into the field, he would only express a hope on behalf of the Regiment, that tents, artillery, a few waggons and a regular commissariat may be supplied as soon as possible by the War Department. Commissary RICHARD DOWDING has really been of invaluable service, and has the thanks of all the men. Quartermaster TULLY also labors energetically, and while the Regiment was in the College it had every reason to be satisfied. But there is reason to fear that the health of the men cannot long hold out, if kept working in the trenches all day under a broiling sun, and allowed to sleep at night without any other covering than their blankets and the sky for a counterpane.

Of Col CORCORAN, let me add that I have never seen a man so lavish of himself while so scrupulously careful of others. His health is very far from being robust, and yet he works without cessation, while paying the most minute attention to any symptoms of sickness or even weakness in the men under his command. Lieut.-Col. NUGENT is also an efficient and painstaking officer. I must now close, as this letter has to go by Engineer-Capt. JAMES B. KIRKER, who is sent back to New-York on business connected with the regiment. He is accompanied by Major TAYLOR, Inspector of the Fourth Brigade.

In a few days, if there be no immediate advance, I will endeavor to visit the other regiments, and report their movements and condition. Of the shooting of Col. ELLSWORTH we know but little here, beyond the bare fact of its occurrence, and that the Fire Zouaves did *not* hang all the men in the house from which the shot proceeded. The indignation, however, is unspeakable; but these are matters not to be written about—not to be talked about. They are felt, remembered, and will bear their fruits. Lieut. GILES, who, with Lieut. MURPHY, *captured* DE GRANVALL, the spy, at Annapolis Junction, has been a little under the weather, but is now fully recovered. All the men of the regiment in good health. No signs of epidemic disease; nor will there be likely, as Arlington Heights are cool and pleasant, if they only give us tents and camp equipage. Capt. MEAGHER of the Zouaves, who came on with Major BAGLEY'S command, is ill, and confined to bed in Washington. H.

IMPORTANT FROM FORT MONROE.

REPORTED CAPTURE OF SEWALL'S POINT BATTERY.

WASHINGTON, Saturday, May 25.

The *Yankee* arrived here to-day, from Fortress Monroe, and brings the report that General BUTLER yesterday captured Sewall's Point, with a loss of 84 killed and wounded; that the enemy lost between three and four hundred killed and wounded; that many prisoners were taken—perhaps 600, and that on Thursday evening the enemy's pickets near the Fort were surprised, and 300 prisoners brought to the Fort. The War Department has information to the same effect.

LANDING OF GEN. BUTLER AT HAMPTON.

BALTIMORE, Saturday, May 25.

The steamer *Adelaide* arrived from Fortress Monroe, early this morning. The correspondent of the Associated Press there sends the following:

FORTRESS MONROE, Friday, May 24.

Gen. BUTLER suddenly made his appearance yesterday in Hampton, at the head of the Vermont Regiment, on a reconnoissance. The rebels attempted to burn the Long Bridge, but were frustrated by the activity of the Advance Guard.

To-day (Friday,) he extends a reconnoissance several miles up the peninsula between James and York Rivers

The Troy and Vermont Regiments have encamped near Hampton, this being the occupation of Virginia soil by Federal troops.

The *James Adger*, after landing the Troy Regiment, sailed for New-York.

The *Harriet Lane* has gone to Charleston.

The blockading squadron off Fort Monroe consists of the *Minnesota*, *Cumberland*, *Yankee*, *Star*, (formerly *Monticello*,) *Quaker City*, and other small craft. The officers of the squadron, this morning, called on Gen. BUTLER.

There are several prizes in the harbor.

The arrival of the frigate *Mississippi* is expected, that active operations will be undertaken against Sewell's Point.

In the action of last Sunday, particulars of which you have, three of the four guns of the rebels were dismounted, and it is well understood here that at least half a dozen men were killed. The battery was to contain thirteen guns.

The Michigan Regiment is expected soon from Washington, also several regiments from New-York and Boston.

FURTHER FROM FORTRESS MONROE.

BALTIMORE, Saturday, May 25.

The morning steamer from Norfolk is in. Gen. BUTLER only took nine hundred men, and did not go as far as Lyndhaven, but to a point nearer Fortress Monroe, where he is encamped. He will wait there until reinforcements arrive from New-York, when he will resume his march for Norfolk. He has expressed his determination to take the Navy Yard, or perish in the attempt.

The Virginians are busily engaged in strengthening their positions. A floating battery has been placed on the flats near Craney Island, and five new batteries are now completed between Lyndhaven and Loudon Bridge. There are ten thousand men at Norfolk with outposts thrown out towards Loudon Bridge, which is twelve miles east. There are five thousand men at Portsmouth and five thousand at Gosport. A gentleman from Richmond says that a millions of dollars have been expended in fortifying York River to defend Richmond, and that there are fifteen thousand troops there. He says the people of Richmond fully expect to be attacked, but are confident of their ability to defend the city. The Petersburgh cavalry company is still there.

Later advices from Norfolk state that Gen. BUTLER has gone on a reconnoissance up the peninsula between James and York rivers.

The New-York and Vermont regiments are encamped near Hampton.

The officers of the steamers *Minnesota*, *Cumberland*, *Monticello*, *Quaker City* and *Yankee*, now blockading Chesapeake Bay, held a consultation this morning with Gen. BUTLER, when further details of the attack were agreed on.

Reinforcements of troops from New-York were hourly expected, when the attack on Sewell's Point would be made.

TRIP OF THE JAMES ADGER TO AND FROM FORTRESS MONROE.

The *James Adger* left the dock at New-York on Wednesday afternoon at 5 P. M., and anchored off the Battery until Thursday at 12:30 A. M.. at which time she got under weigh and proceeded to sea. We had on board the Second Regiment, New-York State Volunteers, of Troy, numbering 800 men.

During the voyage the men were in fine spirits, and with the exception of the indispensable accompaniment to the unaccustomed voyager, sea sickness, they enjoyed the best possible health.

On Friday, May 24, at 3 A. M., we arrived at the wharf at Fortress Monroe, and at 9 A. M. all the troops were landed. Upon their arrival at the Fortress, they received orders from Gen. BUTLER, who is now in command of the Federal troops at that For-

[*Continued on Eighth Page.*]

MAP OF THE SEAT OF WAR.

SCALE OF MILES

G. WOOLWORTH COLTON N.Y.

The New-York Times.

VOL. X....NO. 3028 — NEW-YORK, WEDNESDAY, JUNE 5, 1861. — PRICE TWO CENTS.

THE SECESSION REBELLION.

IMPORTANT FROM THE FEDERAL CAPITAL.

Official Account of the Battle at Philippi.

Complete Rout of Two Thousand Rebels.

COL. KELLY NOT KILLED.

An Advance of the Federal Troops To-day Towards Manassas Gap.

Night Alarms Along the Entrenchments.

IMPORTANT FROM FORTRESS MONROE.

The Yankee Gone to Norfolk with a Flag of Truce.

Gen. Butler Preparing for an Advance.

FATE OF THE NAVAL BRIGADE.

Rumored Withdrawal of the Insurgents from Harper's Ferry.

SPECIAL DISPATCH FROM WASHINGTON.

WASHINGTON, Tuesday, June 4.

Señor HURTIDO, the New Granadian Commissioner for the settlement of the Panama claims, was presented to the President to day. By agreement, a delay of eighty days is to occur, before the Commissioners enter upon the discharge of their duties. The condition of the Government of New-Granada, threatened to be overthrown by a revolution, is the reason assigned by the Minister for asking the delay, and our excuse for granting it. By the way, it is probable that Gen. HERRAN will again be sent as Minister to this country, in the event of the success of Gen MOSQUERA.

THE NAVAL BRIGADE.

Col. BARTLETT, who arrived in Washington to-day, denies that his brigade has been ordered back to New-York. Indeed, he represents it as standing high in the estimation of Gen. BUTLER.

Parson BEECHER left for New-York this P. M., having succeeded in securing the acceptance of the Brooklyn Phalanx.

Preparations for repelling an attack, were made at Fort Corcoran, last night. Information of the probable attack of a rebel column, had been officially communicated to Col. CORCORAN, with instructions to hold his force in readiness to repel it. In accordance with orders from the War Department, the Fifth New-York fell back to a position abreast of the Sixty-ninth, and the Twenty-eighth, New-York, was placed as a reserve in position from the *tête-de-pont* of the Sixty-ninth to the Aqueduct Bridge. The Thirteenth New-York, crossed the river, and was divided into two battalions, one of which was held in reserve at the foot of Corcoran Hill, with orders to support the right of the Sixty-ninth in case of a general attack. The other battalion of the Thirteenth took position in the rear of the Fifth, to support that regiment and to skirmish from the foot of Corcoran Hill to the *tête-de-pont*.

In the afternoon the Sixty-ninth had constructed an abattis extending three quarters of a mile, from the foot of the bastion to a ravine through which the rebels would have to advance to make an attack. The men slept behind this work on their blankets, each in the place he was to occupy in case of an attack.

REPORTED ADVANCE OF REBELS.

About 3 o'clock, this morning, the outposts of the Second Company of United States Dragoons galloped in with a report that the rebels in force, with cavalry, infantry and artillery, were advancing, and not more than three miles distant, with the evident purpose of attacking.

Col. CORCORAN ordered large bonfires to be lighted three hundred yards in front of his lines, for the double purpose of deceiving the enemy and enabling his men to see the rebels as they advanced. Two companies of United States Dragoons, under Lieut. TOMPKINS, made a short excursion from the outposts, and reported having heard firing. One scout represented that he had seen a column of infantry drawing field-pieces or carts. Another scout represented having seen cavalry in force on Cross Road.

Notwithstanding these statements, however, nothing more was heard of the rebels, nor were any to be seen at daylight within range of the field-glasses. With the mist of the morning, infantry and cavalry and artillery had melted away, like the baseless fabric of a dream, and the Sixty-ninth, stacking their muskets, with pickaxes and spades resumed work in the trenches.

The Seventy-ninth have gone into quarters at Georgetown College, lately occupied by the Sixty-ninth.

A company of recruits for the Twelfth were sworn in to-day.

JOSEPH A. NUNEZ, of California, declines the appointment of Commission to La Paz. He will be appointed a Paymaster in the Army.

I am reliably informed that Mr. LITTLEJOHN has written a letter declining the appointment of Consul to Liverpool, and asking the appointment of Mr. WRIGHT, of Oswego, as his successor. It is doubtful if Mr. LITTLEJOHN'S declination will be accepted.

BIDS FOR THE FIFTH QUARTERS.

The bids for the purchase of the hides, tallow, horns and hoofs of the cattle killed by the United States within the military district of Washington were opened to-day. The highest bid was that of JOHN CRAIG & Co. at $10 52 per head. The lowest bid was JACOB SHARP at $3. The price heretofore paid was $5 63. It is doubtful if the highest bidder will give the security required, as his price is higher than the same articles would command in New-York.

THE FIGHT AT PHILLIPPA.

A special Cabinet meeting was called to-day.

Important dispatches have just reached Gen. SCOTT, giving details of the fight at Phillippa, last night, twenty miles from Grafton. The enemy was some 2,000 strong, and was surprised in camp. Fifteen to twenty were killed in the conflict, several prisoners were taken, and a large quantity of arms and ammunition, tents, &c., fell into the hands of the Federal forces, commanded by Cols. KELLEY and CRITTENDEN. Col. KELLEY, of the First Virginia Union Volunteers, is reported killed. The enemy was completely routed, and retreated into the interior of Virginia.

The Department Buildings are being draped in mourning to-day, on account of the death of Judge DOUGLAS, whose remains are expected here on Thursday or Friday for interment in the Congressional Burial Ground.

THE WASHINGTON CITY ELECTION.

The City election for Collector, Surveyor, Register, Aldermen and Council occurred here yesterday. The vote was small, and little interest was manifested in it. The unconditional Union ticket is believed to have prevailed by slight majorities, though the vote is close.

The Scotch Highlanders, Seventy-ninth Regiment, arrived at 3 o'clock this morning. They make a fine show, and are greatly admired. The novelty of their costume is striking, and the Highlanders are just now the lions of the hour.

I learn that the Second Brigade in New-Jersey, under the original levy of the President, has been mustered into service, and numbers about 3,000 men. They are encamped near Trenton, and now await orders. The Brigade is made up of three regiments of stalwart men, who have enlisted for the war.

MOVEMENTS IN VIRGINIA.

Within the past twenty-four hours no movements have been made among the troops at Alexandria of material consequence. I passed a few hours in camp over the river to-day, and found about five or six hundred of the men busily engaged in squads at the trenches. The weather continues intensely hot, but no serious illness prevails.

The number of secession troops, in and around Fairfax, and between that point and Manassas Gap, is now set down at not exceeding four thousand six hundred in all.

A forward movement of a portion of our forces is ordered to-day, and an advance of some three or four miles will be made by the van in the next twelve hours.

AFFAIRS IN NEW MEXICO.

Major MYERS, United States Army, arrived in Washington to-day from New-Mexico, over the Plains. The Major was stopped by secession troops *en route* hither at Osage River Bridge, 100 miles from St. Louis. The rebels examined him cautiously, and demanded his arms, but afterwards suffered him to proceed. He thinks that serious trouble may be anticipated in New-Mexico from the State of affairs eastward, and fears are entertained that some recent political movements, in behalf of the Territory, may not prove so advantageous to the people there as was at first hoped for by those most deeply concerned in the welfare of that region of country.

MAJ.-GEN. BANKS.

Maj.-Gen. BANKS remains at Willard's yet. I am able to state that, although up to yesterday hopes were entertained by certain prominent members of the Government that Gen. BANKS would accept the Quartermaster General's Department, it has now been definitely decided that he goes into the field, though no location has as yet been fixed on for his assignment. I learn that he will await instructions here, and that he will lose no time by returning even to Chicago, where his family still remain, but will go to duty immediately upon receiving orders.

D. T. MOORE, British Despatch Agent, so well known from New-York to Washington, has been in the service forty-five years, having been appointed to this post May, 1816, during the reign of George III. Yesterday he filed with the British Minister the necessary evidence and documents, and asks to be placed upon the Civil Pension list.

AFFAIRS AT FORTRESS MONROE.

A messenger arrived from Fortress Monroe this morning. The troops there continue to enjoy good health. Some half dozen members of the Troy (N. Y.) Regiment were on trial for the alleged robbery of a man and woman at Hampton. The Judge-Advocate on this occasion is N. ST. JOHN GREEN, a prominent Boston lawyer, and brother to DURELL GREEN, lately appointed Colonel in the United States Army. The citizens of Hampton and the residents in the immediate neighborhood of the Fortress, have conceived some alarm at the heavy augmentation of troops there, and appeared more especially concerned at the presence of Col. DURYEA'S Zouave Regiment, whom they stand in fear of. Most of the inhabitants are getting away from the vicinity and from Hampton as fast as it is practicable.

The value of negroes there is now rendered but nominal, and Cuffee is moving off also with an alacrity which is surpassed only by the locomotion of Massa, though in a different direction. Fugitives still flee to the fort. Gen. BUTLER has now about 115 negroes, not 350 as reported, employed in and about the fortress. Many families have departed in the direction of York. One man, a Mr. JONES, had twenty slaves, all but one of whom left him, and sought refuge in the fort. This last chattel was devoted affectionately to ole massa, and declared he loved him. "I'll nebber leab yer, massa—nebber!" swore this chattel, a very promising sable, "I'll stick to my ole massa 'long's I lib!" and master and man left together for the interior. Next morning, when massa rose to proceed on his journey, his devoted property had decamped for the North, taking with him massa's horse, and neither Cuffee nor horse have since been heard from.

Judge THOS. RUSSELL, Hon W. T. DAVIES and Hon J. MORRISSEY, a Commission from Gov. ANDREW, of Massachusetts, to look after her troops, arrived at Fortress Monroe on Monday, in the steamer *Cambridge*, from Boston. As the steamer entered the mouth of the Bay in the night, a false light decoyed her, and she ran ashore on the sand beach, whence she got off after considerable trouble. Brig.-Gen. PEIRCE, of Massachusetts, was on board, with some fifty sappers and miners, and the cargo comprised provisions, tents and munitions for the Third and Fourth Massachusetts Regiments at the fort.

There are between eight and nine thousand troops now there, and accessions are constantly arriving. Gen BUTLER'S plans are not known, of course, but it is understood that he is preparing for a decisive and important movement.

The Massachusetts quota of the regular Army appointments was decided upon to-day. The old Bay State gets one Lieutenant Colonel, six Captains, twelve First Lieutenants, and six Second Lieutenants, as her portion of the officers in the new levy. The names of the fortunate appointees have not as yet been made public.

Sixty members of the Seventy-first Regiment came in this morning with the Scotch Regiment, and about thirty recruits for the Ninth New-York Regiment also accompanied them.

HEAVY ORDNANCE.

A large number of guns of heavy calibre have lately been taken down to the wharf here, in readiness for shipment away.

The *Freeborn* steamer is repairing damages at the Navy-yard.

The Rhode Island steamer *Sea Gull* left for Providence to-day, after discharging stores for the troops now here from that State.

A party of marines arrived to-day from the ship *Allegheny*, at Annapolis, to be placed on Board the boats running up and down the river here.

The New-York Fifth returned to this side the river to-day.

All the troops in Washington to-night are ordered to sleep on their arms.

Gen. WEBB is in Washington. He will to-morrow morning formally signify his acceptance of the Brazil mission.

The President had to-day a diplomatic dinner, at which all the heads of the Departments were present.

ACCIDENT TO SENATOR HARRIS.

A serious accident occurred to Senator HARRIS to-day. He was crossing a street near the Treasury Department, and attempted to avoid a passing carriage. In doing so he ruptured the muscles of the lower part of the leg. He was in great pain for some time, but is suffering less this evening. He will be confined to his room for some days.

An attempt was made to-day to close up the New-York appointments, but the attempt failed. The stick appears to be on the Surveyor. Negotiations are going on to-night, but without much chance of agreement.

Paymaster PANGBORN has been ordered to report for duty on board the *Vincennes*, at Boston.

LEO.

DISPATCH TO THE ASSOCIATED PRESS.

WASHINGTON, Tuesday, June 4.

Lieutenant WEST, formerly in command of the steamer *Philadelphia*, has been ordered to join the *St. Lawrence* at Philadelphia.

The *Keystone State* left here last night, probably for New-York.

The vessels at the Washington Navy-yard, for immediate service, are the *Baltimore*, *Philadelphia*, *Anacosta* and *Freeborn*. They are well supplied with ammunition and stores, and are awaiting orders.

The secession prisoners about forty in number, are still on board the *Powhatan*. They are exceedingly well treated.

Several of the regiments here have for some nights past been ordered to hold themselves in readiness for duty at a minute's warning. There is much anxiety on their part for forward movements.

The New-York Highlanders did not arrive until 2 o'clock this morning. They are quartered for the present at Georgetown College.

OUR WAR CORRESPONDENCE.

The Service in Virginia—A Night Alarm Along the Intrenchments—Promptness of our Troops—Threatenings of the Rebels—Want of Artillery, &c.

HEAD-QUARTERS FIRST BRIGADE,
DEPARTMENT EASTERN VIRGINIA,
Monday, June 3, 1861.

Last night, about 12 o'clock, the advanced pickets of the rebel army fired on the outposts of the Twenty-eighth New-York Regiment, who returned the compliment, and forthwith a general alarm was sounded. The Fifth New-York had fallen back early during the day to a position abreast of the Sixty-ninth, on the left-hand side of the road leading to Fairfax Court-house; and immense progress had also been made in constructing a *tête-de-pont* to protect the Aqueduct Bridge, in the rear of, and below Fort Corcoran, the main work of defence at this end of the line.

In an instant after the firing, the bugles of the Fifth, Twenty-eighth, and Sixty-ninth sounded the officers' call and the drums beat to arms. Being in Fort Corcoran, and confining my correspondence to things personally seen or heard, I must speak mainly of the conduct of the Sixty-ninth, though I learn that all the regiments along the line from here to Alexandria did their duty equally well—one continuous roll of drums and ringing of bugle calls running down the whole range of hills from this point.

In three minutes from the call to arms, the Sixty-ninth were mustered in full equipments along the ramparts—Col. CORCORAN commanding, under the orders of Acting Brig.-Gen. HUNTER, who has command of the three New-York regiments forming the Brigade at this point. Silence was ordered, and the strictest silence preserved, with only occasional whispered jokes amongst the men, and the sound of falling tents outside the lines, as they were struck in order to leave clear fronts of fire from the parapets. There was none, or but very little, "skulking" that I could see—even the new recruits, some of whom are still unprovided with firearms, picking up shovels and spades and falling into line on the banquette along with their more lucky brethren carrying muskets.

On the ramparts, too, stood Judge DALY and RICHARD O'GORMAN, armed with revolvers, and eager to discharge any duty that might be assigned to them. Also JOHN SAVAGE, who volunteered into the ranks and carried a musket. JOHN O'MAHONY, also a visitor to the Camp, volunteered as Col. CORCORAN's aid, and was in the saddle for action. Father MOONEY too, had his place, and did much to encourage the men. But the alarm was not followed by a general attack, as expected—two Orderly Dragoons attached to Col. HUNTER, soon returning from the camp of the Twenty-eighth with intelligence that all was quiet—the men who had fired on the Twenty-eighth's pickets having immediately disappeared into the trees out of which they had emerged. On this, by orders of Col. HUNTER, the men were dismissed to sleep on their arms, with the exception of about 100 stationed in the bastions and half a company, under Capt. HAGGERTY, sent forward to reconnoitre towards the Twenty-eighth, on the road to Fairfax Court house. Early in the evening, I should have commenced by stating, scouting parties had been sent forward from the Sixty-ninth about three miles in advance of the Twenty-eighth, as there had been whispered information from high sources that the attack (now positively set down for to-night) was to have been made last night.

Scarcely had the men lain down after the first alarm, the staff officers being still assembled in the Colonel's tent, before another roll of musketry, with a spattering fire, came from the same direction, and again the bugles sounded and the drums rolled amongst the woody hills from Fort Corcoran to Alexandria. It was a pitch black night; no moon, and not a single star to be seen; the very night of all others favorable to an attack, and this second alarm (about 2 o'clock this morning) made us sure that the first skirmishers were now being followed up by the main force.

Again the ramparts were manned as before, unbroken silence prevailing that we might hear what was being done in advance of us. But all was still. At length Col. HUNTER, Col. CORCORAN and staff, accompanied by Quartermaster TULLY as a volunteer, rode down the road to ascertain what was this second alarm, but returned in less than an hour with the news that it was only a repetition of the former bush-fighting, and that, as the Twenty-eighth and Company B of the Second Dragoons were now thoroughly on the alert,—the latter under command of Lieut. TOMPKINS,—we might again retire to sleep, if sleep we could, until aroused by another alarm.

And we did sleep, all of us; for we were thoroughly tired, both officers and men. A dress parade had been held during the day, and the Sixty-ninth reviewed by Col. HUNTER. In the afternoon, the men had been hard at work in the trenches, and finally, these two alarms had kept them awake and on foot in the pitch-black, sultry, suffocating air—the only lively sights to be seen, being enormous lightning-bugs, flitting over the surrounding woods and hills, and strangely taking the appearance of rockets or pyrotechnic signals of some kind, thrown up by the rebel army.

But this morning we have gained intelligence from high sources, which leaves no doubt, apparently, that the "smoke" of last night had real "fire" behind it. On high authority it is rumored that an attack in force is to take place to-night—the main weight of it falling, probably, on this end of the line, as the position commanding (to a certain extent) all the others in succession. In consequence of this, the Thirteenth New-York has been sent to reinforce us; and our men have already constructed—since the news came, about four hours—an *abattis* or breastwork of felled trees, from the reëntering angle of the bastion on the extreme right, away past the hospital, and so on down to the river. Intense activity also prevails in the earthworks, the men having received double rations, and working as cheerfully and incessantly as so many beavers.

The Fifth New-York, I regret to say, has not been treated well, and have not behaved well, to use the mildest phrase. The men are suffering from sickness, and some of its officers appear to be at loggerheads. For this reason it received orders to report at Washington this afternoon, leaving its place here to be filled by the Thirteenth New-York, whose bugles I hear cries up the hill (4½ P. M.) as I write. The Sixty-ninth are cheering and hurrahing for their arrival; but the Fifth who have been ordered peremptorily to remain on the field until to-morrow morning, observe for the most part an unfortunate silence. The Thirteenth look well, appear in high condition, and will be put to work immediately to assist in carrying out the *abattis* in the line from the left bastion down to the woods which lie between this hill and Arlington House, where the Eighth New-York is stationed.

Will you believe it that we are still without artillery, although two bastions are completed, with banquette and sodded parapet,—the whole work being in an advanced condition, and capable, with guns, of a powerful defence. Of course, they can send us if they have them to spare, a couple of guns from Sherman's Battery; and the Eighth New-York have five or six pieces, well served, they say, and ready for service. The Eighth, however, are stationed in a thick wood, where artillery could be of no possible service; while we front an open plain, varied with undulations of greater and less depth, but with full a clear mile in front of us to be raked by artillery. On the other hand, the Eighth are in a central position, where Gen. McDOWELL has his Head-quarters, and I doubt not that it is all right as it is and that my speculations and all other non-professional criticisms on military movements are utter bosh and tomfoolery.

Gen. McDOWELL, I may say, has the look of a soldier every inch. He is tall, burly, bluff, in the very prime of life, with features indicating remarkable animal and physical strength. He is constantly in the saddle, and has the full confidence and respect of the men, especially the Irish element, on whom physical stature and strength never fail to make an impression. Col. HUNTER, commanding the Brigade at this position, is an officer of middle age, with remarkable gentleness of manner, courtesy and firmness. His deliberate and calm course of action acts as a sedative of the most powerful kind on those apt to be excited, while his vigilance is all the more effective from the fact that he never allows his cool judgment to be moved for an instant from its balance. He served with distinction through the Mexican War, and has since held various positions of importance. He is now Colonel of the Third Cavalry, a regiment in process of being raised.

I know not whether I can have this letter posted this evening or not. The bridges are guarded, with orders to let none pass either way, except with orders from head-quarters to general head-quarters; but possibly Col. HUNTER may be sending in dispatches to the War Department by one of his dragoon orderlies,—of whom he has now four in constant attendance. There are about 60 dragoons of Company B, Second Cavalry, now in advance of us, with the Twenty-eighth, their orders being to fall back slowly on our position if the enemy appears in force to-night. A more busy or intensely exciting scene than the camp now presents I have never seen. All the Sixty-ninth are at work in the trenches, and to-night each man will lie down in his blanket on the banquette, on the very spot he is to fight upon, should the attack be made.

It is curious for one who has often speculated on what must be a soldier's feeling on entering battle for the first time, to note the calmness and absolute carelessness with which the boys are making their preparations,—examining the caps of their guns, wadding, counting their cartridges, burnishing up their arms, oiling the stock of their bayonets, so that they may come off and again be put on easily, and going through all the other routine necessary to be done. Then they leap into the trenches with a shout, having stacked their arms above them on the banquette, seize pick and shovel, and dig and pick, and throw up earth and trundle their wheelbarrows, as if they were preparing for some immense merry-making to come off to-night. Of course, the attack may be postponed until to-morrow night; but it is not probable, from the positiveness of the information. At any rate, it has to come soon, if ever; and I find it a relief from thought to write during the interval of two hours allotted for dinner and rest.

Will you beg the Defence Committee to send on to us light suits of flannel and straw hats for the men? The Havelocks sent by Mrs. Judge DALY, and the many patriotic ladies who assisted her, have been of great—infinite—service; but we want straw hats, for the regulation caps under the Havelocks are too heavy. The weather is intensely hot and bright, a light shower to-day having only laid the dust, without cooling it. In haste I must now conclude, being requested to give the thanks of the Regiment to the many friends who have forwarded articles for their comfort. Very obediently yours, H.

RUMORED EVACUATION OF HARPER'S FERRY.

CHAMBERSBURGH, Tuesday, June 4.

A person from Sharpsburgh, Md., states that the rebels have sent over five hundred sick back to Winchester. The prevailing diseases are small pox and diarrhoea.

There are about 200 men at Sheppardstown on the Virginia side.

It is the general belief that Harper's Ferry has been evacuated by the secession troops, the evidence being the burning of cars.

COL. KELLY NOT DEAD.

HOPES ENTERTAINED FOR HIS RECOVERY.

CINCINNATI, Tuesday, June 4.

Col. KELLY, wounded at the Philippi action, is not dead, as reported last night. He was seriously wounded in the breast. The ball has been extracted, and hopes are entertained for his recovery.

FROM FORTRESS MONROE.

FORTRESS MONROE, Monday, June 3,
via BALTIMORE, Tuesday, June 4.

Only some fifty of the men belonging to the Naval Brigade will return to New-York in the steamer *Coatzacoalcos* to-day. The others will remain for one week, as citizens, laboring for their rations, and not as a military organization.

Col. BARTLETT is much better, and goes to Washington to-night with several of his officers. This is the best Gen. BUTLER can do for them.

It is believed that the Brigade was ordered back to New-York, partially on account of a misunderstanding between the President and Secretary of War. Mr. LINCOLN having accepted the Brigade without consulting Mr. CAMERON.

The steam tug *Yankee* left for Norfolk this morning with a flag of truce. Heavy firing from Sewall's Point was heard as she passed.

The *Cambridge* arrived this morning from Boston.

THE MARYLAND BRIDGE-BURNERS.

PHILADELPHIA, Tuesday, June 4.

The *habeas corpus* case of the bridge-burners, who were taken to York, Penn., came up before Judge CADWALLADER this morning.

Mr. WILLIAMS, of Baltimore, was counsel in the case, but he did not appear, but Mr. WHARTON, who is associated with him, announced that the prisoners had been discharged by order of the War Department.

Mr. WHARTON stated that Mr. WILLIAMS had left the city for fear of violence, but his fears were evidently unfounded. The people took no interest in the matter, as fifty persons were not at the hearing.

THE BORDER STATE CONVENTION.

FRANKFORT, Ky., Tuesday, June 4.

The Border State Convention adjourned yesterday *sine die*, after adopting the National and State address.

UNEMPLOYED NEGROES IN RICHMOND, VA.

LOUISVILLE, Ky., Tuesday, June 4.

The Richmond *Whig* says there are 5,000 unemployed negroes there. Manual labor is stagnant.

IMPORTANT FROM LOUISVILLE.

LOUISVILLE, Ky., Tuesday, June 4.

Union flags are constantly raising amid great enthusiasm. They are flying at half mast to day, in consequence of the decease of Senator DOUGLAS.

Hon. JOHN J. CRITTENDEN consents to run for Congress in the Lexington District.

Mr. MALLORY was renominated for the Seventh District by acclamation, at Lagrange, yesterday.

Immense quantities of provisions day and night are going by way of Sheperdsville, 18 miles south of Louisville, on the Louisville and Nashville Railroad, thence to be sent by rail South, if the transmission thereto shall not be interdicted.

The *Journal* is informed that there are 2,000 soldiers at Camp Irondale, near Richmond, two miles from the Kentucky line; the same number at Camp Cheatham, near Springfield, Tenn.; that the measles was very prevalent among them; also, that well-attended Union meetings had been held privately at Nashville Saturday, notwithstanding the suppression of the Union sentiment there by the Secessionists.

The *Journal* editorially says that Col. ANDERSON will take no military command here, but goes to the mountains of Pennsylvania on account of his failing health.

AFFAIRS IN MISSOURI.

THE SUPERSEDING OF GEN. HARNEY.

Correspondence of the New-York Times.

ST. LOUIS, Saturday, June 1, 1861.

The news that Gen. HARNEY had been recalled, so anxiously expected since the duplicity of his conduct became fully apparent, when he went down on his knees before STERLING PRICE, produced a feeling of sincerest joy throughout the city yesterday morning. Spreading like wildfire from one end of the city to the other, you could read it in the smiling and cheerful faces of all true Union men; hope dawned once more, and a new energy seemed to have pervaded the whole community. The down-crushing feeling of distrust at once gave way to hopeful views of the future, and the people of St. Louis felt sure again, that with HARNEY out of harm's way, and Col. BLAIR and the brave Capt. LYON as their leaders, they would be a match for the whole gang of Secessionists throughout the State.

For some time past rumors have been current here that Gen. HARNEY would soon be recalled and superseded by Gen FREMONT. Little faith, however, was put in this statement, as such a step would necessarily involve a complete change in the ruinous policy the Administration has heretofore pursued towards the Border States.

It was, on the contrary, feared that Missouri and Kentucky would be sacrificed as Virginia has been sacrificed, for there can be little doubt now that Virginia might have been saved to the Union by the same means employed towards Maryland. Gen. HARNEY did all he could to make such a sacrifice possible. During the short time of his command here, he has done more to strengthen secession and crush the Union cause in the State, than the most sanguine of CLAIB. FOX JACKSON'S party could have anticipated. In fact his recall did not come a day too soon, and coming as it did, it has in all human probability saved Missouri from the horrors of a civil war, and a foretaste of the pleasures of JEFF. DAVIS' Southern Elysium. For I am fully convinced that there is a deep-laid plot, as I have repeatedly informed your readers, to tear Missouri and Kentucky out of the Union at any sacrifice, and that in this scheme of the rebel chief at Montgomery, his main coadjutors are CLAIB. FOX JACKSON, Gov. of Missouri, and Gov. MAGOFFIN, of Kentucky. The plan by which Missouri would have been carried for the cause of the Southern rebellion can easily be traced out. Gen. HARNEY had withdrawn all the troops from the surroundings of St. Louis. One of the regiments had been sent away to Bird's Point. It was hoped that Col. BLAIR'S would leave next; in fact, the telegrapher stated it; but the moment we heard this piece of news confirmed by the telegraph, we at once knew it must be a lie. Col. BLAIR having gone, representations would have been sent to Washington that Missouri was quiet and out of all danger, and that Capt. LYON might be very conveniently spared. Then we should have had but a few companies left, and the Home Guards would undoubtedly have been immediately disbanded. Perhaps the State of Missouri, being now considered loyal, beyond a doubt, might even have been generously supplied with some of the arms now in possession of the Home Guards. For who can tell now far a generosity might have gone, which did not blush to place the United States in the position of a criminal in order to spare the feelings of a traitor like Gov. JACKSON? And then! could a few companies of United States Volunteers have protected St. Louis against a sudden attack of several thousand well-armed secession troops, thirsting to take revenge for the disgrace inflicted upon their party by the taking of Camp Jackson? Well, Gen. HARNEY has been recalled! *Te deum laudamus!* We breathe freer. But, we also should like an investigation. The people of Missouri would be glad to know what policy the Administration really does intend to pursue in regard to their particular case. Shall the Union men in the interior be protected? Will the Government at Washington furnish the Union men of our State with arms, to form themselves into Home Guards, as was done in the case of our city? The people of Missouri would like to know why it took a paper, containing Gen. HARNEY'S dismissal, two weeks to reach St. Louis, on its way from Washington—just time enough to allow him to do so much more mischief to the Union cause? In fact, why was it made out at so early a date? Did the War Department keep it in readiness, *expecting* to make an early use of it? And, did the Government send a man here, as Chief Commander, whose dismissal it was thought proper to have handy for any emergency? The whole affair is enveloped in mystery, and needs some explanation.

The *Missouri Republican* of this morning contains Gen. HARNEY'S answer to the writ of *habeas corpus*, in the case of McDONALD, wherein Gen. HARNEY has given the first official notification of his withdrawal from the Western command. Perhaps you have heard of this McDONALD. He is another of those Merrymen, of whom Gen. CADWALADER, in Baltimore, has caught a specimen, by the name of JOHN, and who are more trouble than they are worth, and who ought all to be hung, after which ceremony the officers could have no objection to the serving of ever so many writs of *habeas corpus*. This McDONALD gains very cheap notoriety and excellent grub and lodgings over in Illinois by refusing to swear allegiance to the Government; and his ambition and appetite being thus gratified at public expense, he leads a very comfortable life, as in duty he is bound to. The case is just the counterpart of the Baltimore MERRYMAN'S, so why inflict your readers with a recital of it? Major URIEL WRIGHT, one of our political orators, half fish and half fool, who regards everything from a legal point of view—and would have made a capital lawyer in the trial about the shadow of an ass, which excited the ancient city of Abdera to such an unusual degree some few centuries ago—finds the case a splendid opportunity to deliver himself of his opinions on all political questions that disturb the country, and of the large drops of perspiration that break out all over his body, and tremble aghast at the orator's terrible power of speech. And so, he being happy, and his client being happy, and the jury pocketing their fees, and the Judge listening dreamingly to the Major's soporific ebullitions; why should then a fuss be made about the matter? Gen. HARNEY, however, in his answer, seems terribly excited about the supremacy of the law, which should be upheld; having evidently forgotten all that he once said about the "military" law. He concludes, however, with the gratifying assurance that he has no power over the body of the said McDONALD, as he has just received an order for his recall from the Western command, dated Washington, May 16.

Gen. LYON is, of course, his immediate successor, and will probably remain so until Gen. FREMONT arrives, to take charge of the Western Department. In Gen. LYON the people of St. Louis have unlimited confidence; in fact, he is the idol of their hearts. No man is more beloved than he, among the troops as well as the citizens. There is no doubt that he will shortly repair all the injuries Gen HARNEY has done to our cause. He has the power, and I am sure he has the will, to do so. Immediate action is necessary. In every district of the State, Gov. JACKSON causes his subordinates to enroll men under the infamous military bill, in some places secretly, in others openly. The Secessionists are hard at work in every corner of the State, and it is apparent that they are collecting their troops at some unknown point in the the Southern parts of Missouri for some bold stroke against an exposed point of the United States forces. Large quantities of lead are purchased with army scrip and transported over the border to the rebels in Arkansas. It is absolutely necessary that something be done immediately to stop these proceedings. For the purpose of protecting the interior, we can spare a large number of troops. Let them immediately take possession of the most important places in the State, organize the Union men of these places as Home Guards, and keep a strict watch on all suspicious movements of the enemy. All boats entering or leaving this port ought to be strictly searched, and no railroad train be allowed to leave without inspection. Capt. LYON yesterday made an arrangement with the North Missouri Railroad, to have all the trains searched by an inspector, appointed for that purpose by the United States, and paid by the Company. This is a very judicious movement, and it is to be hoped that a similar arrangement will be entered into with the other railroads. It would also be advisable to notify the Banks that they must not advance any money to the Government for the purpose of buying arms, which ought to go towards paying the interest on the State bonds, due July 1, on penalty of an indictment for treason.

A few words in conclusion, in regard to the conduct of the Press in this city. Not one of the journals published here has had the courage, openly, to condemn Gen. HARNEY'S conduct, which every loyal citizen regarded with suspicion. Even the German papers kept a sullen silence. THE NEW-YORK TIMES has been, I believe, the first journal in which his treaty with PRICE, was boldly criticised, and his conduct put in a true light. Now, that he has been recalled, we can, of course, feel safe again; but if he had remained, to do more mischief, a great responsibility would have rested upon the journals that saw the impending danger, and did not dare to utter a voice of warning.

MORE SEIZURES IN ST. LOUIS.

The Missouri *Democrat*, of June 1, says:

"Having received information that a large quantity of munitions of war was expected to arrive by rail Thursday night or early Friday morning, Gen. LYON authorized Gen. SWEENEY, of the reserve corps brigade, to dispatch troops to each of the depôts in the city. Two companies attended the arrival of each of the trains, but nothing contraband was found. The troops were kept at the North Missouri depôt during most of the forenoon. An arrangement was at last made by which the Government is to select, and the Railroad Company to pay an Inspector, whose business shall be to see that no goods contraband of war pass over the lines without the approbation of the Government, and that such goods attempting to pass be seized. A similar arrangement will doubtless be made with each of the Railroad Companies.

From the above incident rumor projected the absurd story that the United States troops had taken possession of the various lines of railroad leading out of St. Louis.

On the previous day, seizure was made of five kegs of powder and a quantity of bar lead, shipped on the North Missouri Road, by order of Messrs. D. A. JANUARY, THOS. E. TUTT & Co. and R. P. OBER & Co., to parties in the townships of Allen and Mexico. The shipper was Mr. LAFLIN, powder merchant, to whom Gen. LYON ordered the goods to be restored—this gentleman pledging himself to ship no more contraband articles without the consent of the United States military authority here, obtained in each instance.

MILITARY AND NAVAL MOVEMMNTS.

The attention of general officers of the army belonging to the staff and regiments, has been called to the order of the War Department, permitting them to appear on horseback during service in the field, comparisoned as their comrades of the regular mounted troops. They may wear over the saddle, housing of dark blue cloth, with the usual adornments of gold-lace, a blue web surcingle, black leather bridle, yellow collar, black leather holsters, with gilt mountings, yellow metal or gilt stirrups. Officers of the Corps of Engineers and Topographical Engineers, have the same privilege.

The following horse regiments, for mounted soldiers, are published for the information of officers raising dragoon and cavalry regiments. Although put down for the regular army, volunteers are to be provided with them. The things needed are, one bridle, one watering bridle, one halter, one saddle, one pair of saddlebags, one saddle-blanket, one surcingle, one pair spurs, one curry comb, one horse-brush, one picket pin, one link, one lariat, one nose-bag. The "uniform bridle" must have a double rein. The amount of provender mentioned in the regulation list, will be made known to the men when they join their respective companies. In buying steeds for the service, stallions should get first preference, geldings next. Mares, heavy or light in foal, should not be taken to the field.

A detachment of United States Marines left Washington on Saturday for Portsmouth, N. H., where they are to constitute a guard for the United States sailing frigate *Santee*, which is to go in commission next week. This vessel was 37 years on the stocks, being launched in 1855. She about to commence her first cruise, on which she will carry 500 sailors, 50 marines and 60 guns. Like all our frigates, she is 1,726 tons burthen. The liner *Alabama*, which was put on the stocks at the same time, has not yet been launched. The Naval Board recommended her for conversion to a steamer. The old *Dale* and the *Marion*, late of the African Squadron, are also fitting out. There are 1,100 men working in the Yard. Officers in the United States service at Portsmouth were all sworn in anew last week. Commodore PEARSON, of New-Hampshire commands the Yard; Lieut. COLVOCORESSES, a native of Greece, being executive officer.

New-York, which has turned out the real successful steamers in the Navy, is to construct only one of the new vessels, while Portsmouth, Boston and Philadelphia are to build two each. The *Brooklyn* and *Iroquois* are, without exception, the best ships of their respective classes in the service. They never broke down, unlike all the others lately built, except the *Mohican* and *Hartford*. It now appears that New-York is to do all the "jobbing" and the other cities the building, for the service. The keel of the *Adirondack* is now on the blocks in the Western Ship-house, and Mr. DELANO feels confident that she shall be a second *Iroquois*.

One year ago Lieut. TOMPKINS, of the Second United States Cavalry, was a private in the regiment of which Capt. EWELL was First Lieutenant. At the skirmish near Fairfax a few days ago, they met as enemies—the former as a Lieutenant leading his old comrades, the latter still only a Captain—but of the Secessionists. One, by his patriotism, won a commission and a victory; the other, by resigning, lost both.

The usual routine movements only went on yesterday at Fort Hamilton, Governor's and Bedloe's Islands. The troops from Texas have made their camp at the fortified village as comfortable as possible, under the circumstances. Detachments of recruits from various offices were sent over to Fort Columbus last evening.

The United States frigate *Potomac* was taken in hands at the Navy-yard, to be hauled alongside, but being fast in the mud she could not be moved. Some "digging" will be tried at her bed to-day. This morning the chartered steamer *Daylight* will go in commission. The *Savannah's* entire armament is now on board. The *Vandalia* is still in the stream.

The orders for the *Roanoke* and *Colorado* are being made out at the Navy Department. Those for the latter will be sent to Boston to-morrow.

THE WRECKING STEAMER DIRIGO.

This remarkable and highly useful invention now lies off the Battery, for the inspection of the board of Underwriters and others interested. It has recently arrived from Bangor, where she was built some three years ago, and has been employed until last Spring on the St. Lawrence River, when she was dispatched to the wreck of the steamship *Hungarian*, lost in February, 1860, off Cape Sable, U. S. She was of the greatest service in saving cargo, the machinery of the steamer and her boilers, carrying them while in the slings to Yarmouth, N. S., a distance of 60 miles.

She has two purchases and is capable of lifting 100 tons weight and steaming off with it.

She is square-rigged forward, and has ten separate engines four of which constitute her propelling power, of 50 horse. Two are attached to the purchases, and the remaining four work her pumps, of which she has two—one capable of discharging 100 tons of water per minute, and the other 50 tons.

It is the intention of her owner, Capt. S. B. PRATT, to offer the use of the steamer to the Government for raising and pumping out any vessels sunk in channels or otherwise obstructing navigation.

SAILING OF THE SCOTT LIFE GUARD.

The United States steam transport *Alabama*, with the First Regiment Scott Life Guard, sailed yesterday (4 h) for Fortress Monroe.

ARRIVAL OF THE SUSQUEHANNA.

SANDY HOOK, Tuesday, June 4.

The United States ship *Susquehanna*, fifteen days from Cadiz has arrived here, she mounts ten guns, with a complement of 315 officers and men. The following is a list of her officers:

Captain, George N. Hollins; Lieutenants J. N. Barney, H. R. Davenport, J. Young, Wm. Given, A. W. Weaver, J. H. Gilles, J. G. Walker; Master, C. Merchant; Surgeon, Jos. Beale; Assistant Surgeon, Chas. Martin; Paymaster, F. Senae; Lieutenant of Marines, J. H. Joner; Chief Engineer, George Sewell; Midshipmen, J. L. Hoole, T. L. Dorwin, F. L. Hoge; First-Assistant Engineers, S. D. Hibbart, L. A. Williams; Second Assistant Engineers, W. P. Dessiano, B. C. Bampton; Third-Assistant-Engineers, J. De Kauffi, J. D. Renshaw; Third-Assistant Engineer, A. S. Green; Boatswain, C. H. Hacker; Gunner, A. Lovett; Sailmaker, W. M. Mahoney; Carpenter, J. M. Baer.

SAILING OF THE SUSQUEHANNA.

SANDY HOOK, Tuesday, June 4.

The United States frigate *Susquehanna* is off the Hook, anchored. She is bound to Boston.

[For other Rebellion News see Eighth Page.]

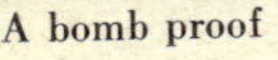

A bomb proof

Battle of Philippi, June 3, 1861

Charge of Duryee's Zouaves at the Battle of Bethel

The New-York Times.

VOL. X....NO. 3034. | NEW-YORK, WEDNESDAY, JUNE 12, 1861. | PRICE TWO CENTS.

THE GREAT INSURRECTION.

Startling Intelligence from Fort Monroe.

A Conflict with the Rebel Forces at Great Bethel.

The Rebels Intrenched in Force, with Batteries of Rifled Cannon.

Gallant Charge of the Federal Troops.

Their Ammunition Gives Out and They Retire with Loss.

INCAPACITY OF BRIGADIER-GEN. PIERCE.

The Loyal Forces Firing on One Another.

Thirty of the Federal Troops Killed and One Hundred Wounded.

The Batteries Reported to Have Been Subsequently Carried.

Rumored Evacuation of Harper's Ferry.

Withdrawal of the Rebels from Point of Rocks.

THE SKIRMISH AT WILLIAMSPORT.

FORTRESS MONROE, Va., Monday, June 10.

Last night about 2 o'clock quite a large force left camp, under command of Brig.-Gen. PIERCE, with the design of breaking up marauding expeditions on the part of the enemy, for the purpose of running off the negroes and white men to work on their batteries. The forces were transported safely over Hampton Creek in barges manned by the Naval Brigade, under supervision of Lieut. CROSBY, of the frigate *Cumberland*. The force had proceeded about three miles beyond the creek when they were fired upon by the New-York Seventh Regiment, who had marched down from Newport News, for the purpose of joining in the expedition.

The Seventh was established in a copse of wood at an angle of a road, and their fire was quite destructive. Sergeant CAREY, of Company A, Col. TOWNSEND's Regiment, was killed. Lieut. STONE, of the same Regiment, a sergeant and nine privates, were wounded, some seriously. The fire was returned, and the Seventh fired one charge of grape from a howitzer, which passed over the heads of the troops of the Third, doing no harm.

The precise state of matters was then mutually ascertained, and the forces uniting proceeded towards Little Bethel church, five miles from Hampton. There they came upon the advanced guard of the enemy, defeated them and drove them back taking thirty prisoners, including one lieutenant.

Advancing towards Big Bethel, in York county, they came upon the enemy in force, and a sharp engagement ensued, in which the artillery played an important part on both sides.

No details have reached us of the action, and I must await them before I can give further accounts.

Gen. BUTLER was busy keeping open communication with the post.

The conduct of the men has been most admirable under the hottest fire. The Naval Brigade received the highest compliment for their efficient conduct. In working the boats they were of the greatest service throughout the night and day.

LATER.

The contest at Great Bethel was more severe than was at first apprehended. The enemy were so strongly intrenched in and protected by batteries, that after more than two hours and a half severe fighting, our ammunition giving out, we were obliged to fall back, which we did in perfect order.

The details, as near as can be, in the confusion, ascertained, are as follows:

Brig-Gen. PIERCE, with the First, Second and Third New-York, from this post, joined with detachments from Newport News from the Fourth Massachusetts, First Vermont, and Seventh and Ninth New-York, with two light field-pieces, under Lieut. GREBLE, and a squad of regulars, drove into the enemy, numbering four thousand men, and soon came upon their position, protected by the fire of six heavy batteries, mounted with six and twelve pound howitzers and heavy rifled cannon. The engagement immediately became warm, the guns under Lieut. GREBLE returning the intensely hot fire from the enemy's batteries.

After some time Gen. PIERCE gave the order to charge on the battery, and Col. DURYEE'S Zouaves gallantly marched in quick time under a scorching fire up to near the ramparts of the battery, where a broad ditch intervened, which could not be passed, when the gallant lads fell back.

Col. TOWNSEND'S Regiment also went near to the battery, but meeting the same obstruction were also compelled to retire.

After over two hours' hot contest the ammunition for the field pieces and the muskets gave out, and the order was given to retire, which was effected in perfect order.

Want of time prevents any details. We lament the loss of Lieut GREBLE, of the United States artillery, one of the most brave, gallant and chivalrous officers in the service, who died bravely at his gun from a cannon shot, which struck him in the forehead, killing him instantly.

Our loss in killed and wounded is about seventy-five, among the latter I mention:

Capt. KILPATRICK, of the Zouaves, was shot in the leg.

Lieut. DUMONT, Company B, of the same regiment, had a bayonet wound in the leg, not serious, and others slightly wounded.

I shall forward a list at the earliest possible moment. The enemy's loss was heavy. Every one on our side behaved most bravely and did their duty.

OTHER ACCOUNTS.

FORTRESS MONROE, Monday, June 10, *viâ* BALTIMORE, Tuesday, June 11.

This has been an exciting and sorrowful day at Old Point Comfort. Gen. BUTLER having learned that the rebels were forming an intrenched camp with strong batteries at Great Bethel, nine miles from Hampton, on the Yorktown Road, he deemed it necessary to dislodge them; accordingly movements were made last night from Fortress Monroe and Newport News.

About midnight, Col. DURYEE'S Zouaves and Col. TOWNSEND'S Albany Regiment crossed the river at Hampton, by means of six large batteaux, manned by the Naval Brigade, and took up the line of march, the former some two miles in advance of the latter. At the same time, Col. BENDIX'S regiment, and detachments of the Vermont and Massachusetts regulars at Newport moved forward to form a junction with the regulars from Fortress Monroe, at Little Bethel, about half way between Hampton and Great Bethel. The Zouaves passed Little Bethel about 4 A. M. Col. BENDIX'S Regiment arrived next, and took a position at the intersection of the roads. Not understanding the signal, the German Regiment, in the darkness of the morning, fired upon Col. TOWNSEND'S column, marching in close order, and led by Lieut. BUTLER'S son, and aid of Gen. BUTLER, with two pieces of artillery. Other accounts say that Col. TOWNSEND'S regiment fired first. At all events, the fire of the Albany regiment was harmless, while that of the Germans was fatal, killing one man and seriously wounding two others, with several other slight casualties. The Albany regiment, being back of the Germans, discovered from the accoutrements left on the field, that the supposed enemy was a friend. They had in the meantime fired nine rounds with small arms and a field-piece. The Zouaves, hearing the firing, turned and also fired upon the Albany boys. At daybreak, Col. ALLEN'S and Col. CARR'S Regiments moved from the rear of the Fortress to support the main body; the mistake at Little Bethel having been ascertained, the buildings were burned and a Major with two prominent secessionists, named LIVERY and WHITING, made prisoners. The troops then advanced upon Great Bethel in the following order, namely: the Zouaves, Col. BENDIX, Lieut.-Col. WASHBURNE, Col. ALLEN, and Col. CARR. At that point our regiments formed and successively endeavored to take a masked secession battery. The effort was futile, our three small pieces of artillery not being able to cope with the heavy rifled cannon of the enemy, according to some accounts thirty in number. The rebel battery was completely masked, so that no men could be seen, but only the flashes of the guns. There were probably less than a thousand men behind the batteries of the rebels. A well-concerted movement might have secured the position, but Brig.-Gen. PIERCE, who commanded the expedition, appears to lost his presence of mind. The Troy Regiment stood for an hour exposed to a galling fire, when an order to retreat was at last given, but at that moment Lieut. GREBBLE, of the United States Army, and in command of the artillery, was struck by a cannon ball and instantly killed. He had spiked his gun, and was gallantly endeavoring to withdraw his command.

Capt. GEO. W. WILSON, of the Troy Regiment, after the order to retreat was given, took possession of the gun, and with Quartermaster MCARTHUR brought it off the field, with the corps of the beloved Lieutenant. Both were brought to Fortress Monroe this evening.

There are probably twenty-five killed, and one hundred of the Federal troops wounded.

Lieut. BUTLER deserves the greatest credit for bringing off the killed and wounded. Several of the latter are now in the Hospital here.

I should have stated that Col. MCCHESNEY'S Regiment formed a reserve.

Col. HAWKINS' Regiment moved from Newport News during the day, and an armed vessel went up to Newport News, expecting the *Cumberland*.

All the regiments are now probably up at their former quarters.

Great indignation is manifested against Brig.-Gen. PIERCE.

Gen. BUTLER has been ubiquitous, doing all in his power to save our men and the honor of our cause.

BALTIMORE, Tuesday, June 11.

The special correspondent of the *American* returned from Fortress Monroe this morning, with a full report of the battle at Great Bethel. For several days past Gen. BUTLER has been advised of movements of a considerable body of Confederate troops in the vicinity of the village called Great Bethel, which is about 12 miles from the Fortress, and near the road conducting to Yorktown. Believing from reliable reports that they had thrown up intrenchments, and generally extending their outer line of pickets, he determined, after consultation with other officers, to whip them away, and accordingly gave orders to several regiments to hold themselves in readiness to march at a moment's warning. At the same time, the Chief of the Ordnance Department received orders to send a battery of howitzers, which was soon under line of march, comprising four 12 pounders and a detachment of U. S. Artillery, under Lieut. GREBBLE and other officers. A party of the Naval Brigade was also quickly mustered, for the purpose of conveying troops across Hampton Creek, which was done by means of fishing boats sent down, on Saturday, from the Susquehanna River.

The detailed force of the Volunteers consisted of three regiments, the Albany Regiment, Col. TOWNSEND; the New-York Zouaves, Col. DURYEE, and the Seventh Regiment, Col. BENDIX, with companies from other regiments, comprising a force of nearly 3,000 men.

The command moved at 12½ o'clock on Sunday night with the Zouaves nearly one hour ahead, and owing to a most unfortunate mistake in relation to signals, two of the regiments got into a collision when the regiment of Col. BENDIX, mistaking that of Col. TOWNSEND for that of the enemy, fired into them, and did not discover their mistake until the dawn of day, when their supposed enemy left them masters of the field. It is not known exactly how many were killed or wounded, but the number will not be considerable.

After an explanation and a mutual understanding between the two Regiments, it was then agreed to move on to Great Bethel, and the entire force took up the line of march, which is three miles from the place where the error was committed.

As soon as the right of the column got near the place they were apprised of the presence of the foe, who were very strongly intrenched, and who opened fire upon them with a battery of rifled cannon. The Federal troops promptly responded, but the volleys of the infantry and the small park of howitzers were unavailing against such a formidable battery, and in the course of half an hour a retreat was sounded, and executed in good order.

The Regiment moved well and the men, it is acknowledged on all sides, acted with a spirit of determination. The most melancholy feature of the battle was the killing of Lieut. GREBBLE.

It was almost impossible to tell the number of killed and wounded on the side of the Federal troops, but I was told by Gen. BUTLER that his estimate was about 30 killed and 100 wounded.

It was feared that Major WINTHROP, Aid to Gen. BUTLER, had been killed, as he could not be found.

When the news of the action reached the Fortress the utmost sadness prevailed, and there was a mournful aspect visible throughout. The first wounded man that reached the Fortress was private JAS. GARBETT. He came in in an ambulance, which was very carefully driven.

As soon as Gen. BUTLER heard of the affair, which was about 7 o'clock, he mounted his horse and rode at the top of its speed to Newport News Point, for the purpose of ascertaining all the facts in the case.

Col. DIMICK also rode around the ramparts, and, inspecting the side near the land approach, ordered the howitzers and mortars to be gotten ready.

About 9 o'clock P. M. the steamer *Catalina* reached the wharf, with some of the dead and wounded. In the meantime, nearly all the armed fleet proceeded up the James River, to Newport News Point.

The hospital for the regular force and the regiments of volunteers who are stationed in the Fortress, is in first-rate order, and under the directorship of Dr. CUYLER will continue so.

It is officially announced that the health of the garrison is excellent and but few are on the sick-list.

I have endeavored to get a full list of the killed and wounded in the affair at Great Bethel, but succeeded only partially, as but few of them had reached the place up to the time of the departure of the boat, which usually leaves at 4 o'clock, but was detained for your correspondent until 9 P. M.

The following are the names of some of the wounded, all of Col. TOWNSEND'S Regiment:

JOHN CONNELLY, Company A, in the knee; in no danger.

FREDERICK BACON, Company A, severely.

JOSEPH RICHARDS, Company C, bayonet in the thigh; slight.

PHILIP SWEENEY, thigh-bone fractured; bad.

W. C. CODY, Company F, shot in the abdomen; mortal.

JAMES GABBETT, Company G, fractured thigh-bone by shot; not mortal.

Lieut. E. W. STONE, Company H, beyonet wound in the knee; slight.

The following are among the wounded at the Big Bethel battle:

S. F. SOUTHEM, Company H, Fourth Massachusetts Regiment; seriously, in the lung.

JOHN DANN, Company H, DURYEE'S Regiment, shot in the arm.

JOHN CONWAY, Company H. DURYEE'S Regiment, shot in the leg; not bad.

C. GHENT, Company K, Col. BENDIX, shot in the left chest; seriously.

FRANK A. BAKER, of Company —, shot in the calf of leg; only a flesh wound.

Of these, such as are contusions are singularly cheerful.

Amongst the killed was Lieut. GREBBLE, of the U. S. Artillery. He was struck upon the right side of the forehead by a rifled cannon, the ball of which tore away the upper part of the head.

He was an efficient officer, and greatly beloved by his brother officers, who, as may be expected, are keenly grieved by the sad bereavement. His funeral will take place on Wednesday, and his remains will be deposited in a metallic coffin, specially ordered from Baltimore.

Orderly Sergeant GOODFELLOW, of Company D. of the First New-York Regiment, was struck by a cannon ball and dropped dead. Three members of the same company were badly wounded.

It appears that the Albany Regiment, under Colonel TOWNSEND, were in reserve.

It was thought that Lieut. Col. GRINNELL had been killed, as he was missing.

Capt. JUDSON KILLPATRICK, of Company H of the Zouaves, was wounded in the fleshy part of the thigh by the bursting of a shell, but gallantly led his company across the field to the attack.

SPECIAL DISPATCH FROM WASHINGTON.

WASHINGTON, Tuesday, June 11.

The unfortunate affair at Great Bethel, near Newport News, and its disastrous consequences, are the theme of conversation in every circle. The rashness of Gen. PIERCE is universally condemned, and his unfitness to command is as universally conceded. Such blunders as marching men into an enemy's country without food and without ammunition, are denounced as inexcusable crimes, and such as call for punishment.

Lieut GREBLE, among the killed, was one of our first officers,—probably one of the best artillerymen that we have. He leaves a young wife and two children, resident in Philadelphia. His father left Washington this morning, to visit his son, expecting to find him in command of the batteries at Newport News, and, of course, alive and well. It will be a terrible blow for him to find only the mangled corpse of his brave boy.

THE ENEMY'S WORKS CARRIED.

I am told that Postmaster-General BLAIR says that Gen. BUTLER last night assaulted the enemy's works at Bethel, where PIERCE was repulsed, and carried them by storm. I hope it is true.

THE QUARTERMASTER'S DEPARTMENT.

It has been finally determined to detail Capt. MEIGS to the Quartermaster's Department. It is stated that he has never done a day's duty in the field, and has no practical knowledge of the details of the office. If so, of course he has no errors to unlearn. He is honest, but is understood to be one of the most extravagant of all public men.

GEN BUTLER'S CONTRABAND.

"Contrabands" are beginning to be plenty through all our camps over in Virginia. At a moderate estimate, there are five to ten chattels attached to each regiment, and "more a-coming." They are held subject to the claims of their owners, but not likely soon to be called for, as their owners just now appear to prefer straight necks to moveable goods.

TROOPS AT THE CAPITAL.

Within the limits of the capital there are now encamped or quartered seventeen regiments of volunteer troops, numbering in the aggregate fully eighteen thousand picked men, thoroughly armed, equipped and provisioned. These troops are under the supervision of Gen MANSFIELD. In addition to these there are stationed upon the heights surrounding the city at Alexandria and beyond the bridges, twenty other full regiments, amounting to over twenty-two thousand soldiers, including regulars, under command of Gen. MCDOWELL. Here are forty thousand men, besides those sent forward yesterday, and those stationed at the Relay House near by and at Annapolis—an army competent for any present emergency in this quarter, ready, willing and anxious for "business."

The Garibaldi Guard is encamped on East Capitol-street, three miles from town. This regiment reports nine hundred and seventy-four men, in good condition, ready to move at the sound of the bugle.

The Second New-York Regiment are a little to the rear of the Garibaldians, and are getting very proficient in drill. They, too, are ready to move.

A private named SHANE, of the Sixty-ninth New-York Regiment, was accidentally shot in the shoulder, in camp, this morning. The wound is not dangerous.

The newly-arrived Michigan Second went into camp this forenoon, near the Aqueduct Works, above Georgetown.

The Ohio regiments and the splendid Scotch Highlanders, many of the latter in tartan plaid and buskins, paraded this afternoon, and attracted marked attention.

Hon. JOHN COCHRANE, of New-York, is authorized by Gen. CAMERON to raise a regiment, to be commanded by himself, it is said, which will be accepted when ready. He will leave for home to-morrow.

FRANKS FOR SOLDIERS.

Hon. CHAS. H. VAN WYCK, of the Tenth New-York District, arrived to day. He has been busy at the camps, and has been very kind to the soldiers everywhere. He has franked thousands of letters. Mr. VAN WYCK called on the City Postmaster this evening, and informed him that he should distribute amongst the troops fifty thousand franked envelopes for their use to-morrow. He will remain in town till Congress comes together, when he proposes to offer a bill for the benefit of volunteers, which shall contain provisions authorizing the Colonels of regiments to frank all letters sent to their families, and also making return letters from such friends free when addressed distinctly to any named regiment hereafter actually in the service of the United States. This is a good move in the right direction, and the originator of the proposal not only deserves the thanks of the troops, but the credit of the plan.

TWO SCHOONERS BURNT.

The propeller *Resolute* arrived at the Navy-yard last night. Capt. BUDD, during his absence, seized two schooners down the river, which had been engaged in carrying provisions to the enemy. They were old vessels, and he fired and burned them both to the water's edge. The *Resolute* leaves again to-night.

The steamer *Reliance* went down yesterday towards the mouth of the Potomac, to aid in guarding the river.

The Washington Insurance Company has ordered its outstanding policies canceled and to be returned, in consequence of the threatening state of the times.

The *Monticello* has left this port for a cruise on the river to-day.

JUDSON MILLER is appointed Collector, and HENRY THOMAS Deputy at Georgetown, D. C.

JOHN L. HAYES is appointed Chief Clerk of the Patent Office, *vice* SHUGERT removed.

Sixty United States soldiers from Governor's Island arrived here to-day

Mayor BERRET has vetoed the bill to reduce the city officials' salaries here.

MORE CONTRABAND.

Three slaves were taken into one of the camps yesterday. A Mr. WEBB, of Virginia, claimed to be their owner, and demanded them. The Colonel refused, deeming them contraband. They were sent over to Gen. SANDFORD'S quarters, upon his order, where WEBB again presented himself, and Gen. SANDFORD sent for a wagon at his own expense, into which the three negroes were placed and sent back to Virginia, to the entire satisfaction of their secession master. This act on Gen. SANDFORD'S part has given rise to much comment to day, and he gets very little credit in any quarter save among the rebel slave owners over the river.

ANOTHER BRIGADIER GENERAL.

Ex-Gov. STANTON, of Kansas, has been commissioned as a Brigadier-General in the United States Army, and has been detailed for duty at New-Mexico, where he is to raise two regiments. One of these regiments is to be commanded by ST. VRAIN, and is to be enlisted from the native New-Mexicans; the other regiment is to be composed of Americans, and commanded by KIT CARSON.

The Mounted Rifles and the detachment of the First Cavalry, now on duty at Mexico, are to come home. They are to be replaced by the recruits sent out under Capt. GRANGER. Gen. STANTON'S head quarters will be at Sahta Fé.

THE NEW YORK TROOPS.

Gov. MORGAN and Attorney-General MYERS reached Washington this afternoon. They come to make some arrangements about the troops now enlisted. It seems to be the misfortune of our State that it is always sending officials here to see about troops, but are never sending any troops. If they would send fewer high cocklelorums and more high privates, the State would appear to better advantage on the field of battle.

Speaking of sending troops, I am authorized to say that the Government wants troops, and will receive any regiments that may come to Washington. If regiments come on their own responsibility they will be received, whether they have State authority or not for their coming.

As an evidence that the Government wants troops which it cannot get, I state the fact that the Government ordered two regiments from the Elmira dépôt, one of which was to be Col. CLARK'S Cayuga Regiment. Only Col. CLARK'S Regiment came through, no other being in readiness. Six regiments ready to come were ordered from Wisconsin, because they were ready, and more would have been taken if they had offered.

The Presidennt, Secretary SEWARD, and Senator BAKER, visited the Navy-yard this afternoon, and were received with the customary salute. They witnessed some splendid practice with the large Dahlgrens and James' rifled cannons, and then a practice drill of the Seventy-first.

THE POSITION OF BELGIUM.

The Government has despatches from Belgium, giving the strongest assurances that the Government of that country will not openly or covertly favor the rebel confederacy. Of course there will be no more arms sold to the rebels from that quarter. Private letters also assure the Government that the statements about the sale of arms to the rebels by the factories of Belgium are gross exaggerations.

THE CASE OF CAPT. BALL.

I am informed by a gentleman who knows Capt. BALL intimately, that the stories afloat of his return to the rebel army are all wrong. He is represented as a Christian, who will fully abide by his oath of allegiance. Previous to taking the oath, and having it administered to his men, he made a speech to his troop, explaining to them the nature of the obligation they were about to incur, and assuring them that he should himself religiously adhere to the promise he was about to make.

BALLOON SERVICE.

Prof. LOWE, the balloon man, is in Washington, and has proposed to the Government a system of reconnoitering which promises to be effective. It will be tested to morrow, if the necessary arrangements can be completed. The balloon will be sent up from the President's grounds, and will contain the Professor and an experienced telegrah operator. It will be held to the proper height by a cord. It will also be connected to the earth by insulated wires, which will be attached to the recording machine in the War Department. The operator in the balloon will thus communicate directly with the War Department. Of course, the same experiment would be practicable in the field, the operator in the balloon, above the smoke of the contest, giving information of all that was transpiring in the enemy's camp.

ANOTHER MOVEMENT OF TROOPS.

There is another movement of troops to take place in the morning. Five regiments are under orders to leave, and will do so at once. They are doubtless to cross the river and go up on the Leesburgh line. LEO.

FROM ANOTHER CORRESPONDENT.

WASHINGTON, Tuesday, June 11.

FINAL ACCEPTANCE OF THE BROOKLYN PHALANX.

Rev. HENRY WARD BEECHER has again been in Washington seeing about the acceptance of the Brooklyn Phalanx, which he has maintained for the last ten days at his private expense. He has just informed me of the unconditional acceptance of the regiment. He says this time there is no mistake about it. It may be worth while to correct a malicious statement, that a son of Mr. BEECHER holds a prominent command in the Phalanx. His position is that of Lieutenant.

COMMUNICATIONS WITH MEXICO.

The active and efficient Mexican *Chargé*, Señor ROMERO, is stirring the matter of postal communication with Mexico. Consequent upon the representations of Señor ROMERO, it is said the Administration is about to place an armed dispatch steamer between New-York and Vera Cruz, or between Havana and Vera Cruz, which shall make semi-monthly trips, carrying Government dispatches and a regular mail.

At present it appears as though our Minister to Mexico, Mr. CORWIN, was entirely abandoned by his Government. The importance of having speedy and frequent communication with that Ambassador, at this time, can scarcely be overestimated.

DISPATCH TO THE ASSOCIATED PRESS.

WASHINGTON, Tuesday, June 11.

From the best available sources it is believed that the entire secession force of Virginia does not exceed 50,000 or 60 000.

Gen. BEAUREGARD has issued a proclamation from Manassas Junction, extravagantly picturing the deplorable consequences of the expected invasion of Federal troops.

Hon. Mr. BUFFINGTON, of Massachusetts, has visited the Fifth Regiment of that State at Alexandria, and will proceed to the Relay House to-night to visit the Eighth, next to Fortress Monroe, his business being connected with the interests of Massachusetts troops at these points.

The President, to-day, called on Gov. MORTEN, of Indiana, for six additional regiments.

Cols. S. MEREDITH, W. L. BROWN, and MCMILLEN, are each to command a regiment.

The remaining three regiments are to organize as formerly.

Great credit is due to Senator H. S. LANE, for his untiring efforts in behalf of his State.

Cols. MCMILLEN and BROWN served in the Mexican War, the former with Col. BAKER'S Regiment, of Illinois, and the latter with Senator LANE'S Ioniana Regiment. They are known as gentlemen of fine military skill, and the friends of Col. BROWN, who are now here, predict that from his good character and indomitable energy, the country will be effectually served.

Captains of companies wishing to join his regiment, will report to him at Logansport, Indiana.

The most satisfactory assurances are received from Belgium that there will be no recognition of the Southern Confederacy in any form by that Government. An entirely friendly feeling toward the United States Government is manifested.

The statements which the Confederates put forth in regard to supplies of arms imported by them from that country, are ascertained, on undoubted authority, to have been greatly exaggerated.

The reception recently of a *Chargé d'Affaires* from Chili by this Government was marked by an interchange of the kindliest sentiment, and there is no doubt the American Minister accredited to that country will be welcomed in a like amicable spirit.

The appointment of CHARLES ROBINSON as Minister to Peru, renews the diplomatic intercourse with that country, and, as a consequence, Mr. ZAGANA, who was dismissed by President BUCHANAN, simultaneously with the return of Minister CLAY to this country, will in all probability again come hither to represent Peru. It will be recollected that the latter was instructed to ask for his passports in the event of a non-compliance with the positive and unchangable demands of the late Administration, which precluded the consideration of the modified mode as proposed by Peru of settling the controversy between the two Governments. Thus friendly relations with these two South American Republics have been restored.

Capt. DRAKE DEKOY, aid to Gen. MANSFIELD by his courtesy and assiduous devotion to duty and efficient dispatch of the business connected with his position, is reported so to have won upon his official superiors, that his promotion to a Colonelcy is rumored as a mark of the high appreciation of his character.

The forces which left here yesterday under Col. STONE, have concentrated at Tennellytown, about four miles from Washington. The Advance Guard Owens' Cavalry, proceeded to Rockville, ten miles further. The main column will march in that direction to-night.

The New-York Twelfth, Syracuse First, and Second Ohio Regiments, and the New-York Seventy-ninth, paraded to-day, and were reviewed by the President, Lieut.-Gen. SCOTT and Gen. SANDFORD. The first-named is expected to go to Virginia very soon.

The regiment of mounted riflemen, and four companies of dragoons in New-Mexico, are ordered hence probably in this direction.

ED. N. STEBBINS, of Pennsylvania, has been appointed Paymaster and Storekeeper at the Washington Arsenal, in place of Mr. BENSON, who resigned.

WM. PAMER and ED. JUDD, of New-York, have both been appointed Paymasters in the Army.

The Confederate troops for the past two days, it is reliably ascertained, have been moving from Harper's Ferry to Winchester, and thence towards Manassas Junction, as fast as wagons can be procured to convey their baggage.

AFFAIRS AT HARPER'S FERRY.

TROOPS WITHDRAWN FROM POINT OF ROCKS.

FREDERICK, Tuesday, June 11.

From a gentleman well conversant with the localities in and around Harper's Ferry, who left Hagerstown early this morning, I learn that 10,000 United States troops are between the town of Greencastle, nine miles from the former place, and Chambersburgh, from whence they are marching.

Yesterday, the Virginians destroyed about twenty-five canal-boats in the vicinity of Harper's Ferry, with the intention, it is supposed, of preventing their being used to transport Federal troops across the Potomac.

The troops recently at Point of Rocks have certainly been withdrawn, and are now with the main body at Harper's Ferry.

Much disaffection is reported to exist among the Kentuckians on Maryland Hights, and a rumor is current here that in a few days they intend displaying the Stars and Stripes, and probably deserting in a body.

THE FIGHT AT WILLIAMSPORT.

BALTIMORE, Tuesday, June 11.

The Williamsport correspondent of the *American* says:

"The fight at Clear Spring continued all day yesterday between the Home Guard, of Clear Spring and Williamsport, and the Virginians, who were endeavoring to destroy Dam No. 5, on the Chesapeake and Ohio Canal.

No one on the Maryland side was hurt, but two horses and one man were killed on the Virginia side.

The Virginians had destroyed all the canal boats on the Maryland side, between Williamsport and the Ferry.

THE ADVANCE FROM CHAMBERSBURGH.

THE FORCE UNDER GEN. PATTERSON—THE BRIGADES ORGANIZING—WHEN AND HOW THE ADVANCE IS TO BE MADE—STRENGTH OF THE REBELS.

Correspondence of the New-York Times.

CHAMBERSBURGH, Penn., Sunday, June 9, 1861.

The army corps at this point, under command of Major-Gen. PATTERSON, is being rapidly organized and placed on an efficient footing, and only awaits artillery, which will arrive probably in a few days, to commence active operations. It comprises among its forces one and a half regiments U. S. regulars, about half a regiment of which are cavalry. Two of the divisions will be commanded by United States officers, which will inspire confidence and give steadiness to the corps. All the regiments of Pennsylvania Volunteers that are to be engaged on this line are now here, with the exception of Col. JARRETT'S, which is to be here to-morrow. Col. CAMPBELL, of the Twelfth, is stationed on the North Central Road, near Melville, and may easily be brought here to coöperate, if necessary. Col. ZEIGH'S Sixteenth Regiment, arrived here from York yesterday, and went into camp about two miles and a half south of this place, on the road to Greencastle; they, together with a company of the U. S. Second Infantry, which also arrived yesterday, with the band, and Col. DIXON H. MILES, U. S. A., form the nucleus of a Fifth Brigade, now organizing. Five companies, B, D, G, H and K, under command of Capt. O. S. SHIPPARD, reached here to-day from Carlisle Barracks, where they arrived from Washington yesterday. They also joined Col. MILES'S Brigade. A Michigan regiment is expected to arrive to-morrow and will be joined to Col. MILES'S command. One company of U. S. Artillery, with battery, &c., now at Carlisle from Washington, will be here to morrow or Tuesday, and join the same Brigade.

The Eleventh Regiment of Pennsylvania Volunteers, Col. JARRETT, is expected here to morrow from Havre de Grace, and will, probably, form the nucleus for a Sixth Brigade, with a regiment of Rhode Island Volunteers, Col. BURNSIDE, with light battery, &c., which is to arrive at Harrisburgh on Monday night, from Washington, and will be immediately sent on here. Two Ohio regiments are expected here shortly, which will complete the force intended for this point.

A regiment of Indiana Volunteers, Col. LEWIS WALLACE, now at Cumberland, has been placed under command of Gen. PATTERSON.

The aggregate force under Gen. PATTERSON then may be placed at about 20,000 men, and will be supplied, about Tuesday or Wednesday, with about six field batteries (six guns each) and perhaps one or two howitzers.

I think no advance to Hagerstown, or beyond Greencastle, will be made before the arrival of the artillery—that is to say, before Wednesday or Thursday.

As soon as the other brigades are in a condition to support them, Col. THOMAS and Gen. WILLIAMS, with the First and Second Brigades, will probably be ordered to proceed to Hagerstown, and, leaving a sufficient force there, push guards beyond, and advance to Williamsport, and, as the other regiments come up, proceed to Martinsburgh. It is not probable that the enemy will make any decisive stand between this and Martinsburgh, but it is not to be presumed from this that there is to be no resistance. The position of the rebels in and around Harper's Ferry is a very strong one, and operating upon interior lines, they have a great advantage. Two courses are open to them. They may simply draw in their outposts and concentrations at Harper's Ferry and await the attack; or, if strong enough, they may (and this appears the more probable course) watch a favorable opportunity to attack any portion of the line of the invading army, destroy their communications, and attempt to beat them in detail. A glance at any map, and bearing in mind the points in occupation of the enemy, at Harper's Ferry, Point of Rocks, Shepherdstown, Martinsburgh and opposite Williamsport, all in a circuit of about thirty miles, and varying not more than from eight to fifteen miles apart, will show the strength of their position in a strategical point of view. Too much caution cannot be used; the consequences of a defeat now, not merely in a material but in a political point of view, cannot be over-estimated. Gen. PATTERSON, himself an officer of experience, and with an able and experienced staff, is fully equal to the position, and, although he may displease the rash and inexperienced, will doubtless, by his conduct of this campaign, vindicate the judgment of the General-in-Chief in assigning him to this important command, and realize the expectation of the public at large.

The present constitution, division and location of the army is as follows:

First Brigade, Col. George H. Thomas, U. S. A., Commanding, at Greencastle, 12 miles in advance of the place, towards Hagerstown.

Two Companies U. S. Artillery / One Company U. S. Infantry	Capt. Doubleday.
One Company Independent Rangers	Capt. McMullen.
Four Companies U. S. Cavalry	Col. Thomas.
One Company Penn. Cavalry	Capt. James.
Sixth Regiment, Pennsylvania	Col. J. Nagle.
Twenty-first Regiment, Penn	Col. J. F. Ballier.
Twenty third Regiment, Penn	Col. C. P. Dare.

Second Brigade, Gen. E. C. Williams, immediately in rear of First Division, near Greencastle.

Seventh Regiment, Pennsylvania	Col. W. H. Irwin.
Eighth Regiment, Pennsylvania	Col. A. H. Emby.
Tenth Regiment, Pennsylvania	Col S. A. Merideth.
Twentieth Regiment, Penn	Col. A. H. Grey.

Third Brigade, Brigadier-General Geo. C. Wyncoop, Camp Chambers, 3½ miles in advance of Chambersburgh.

First Regiment, Pennsylvania	Col. Sam. Yoke.
Second Regiment, Pennsylvania	Col. Stambaugh.
Third Regiment, Pennsylvania	Col. J. P. Minier.
Twenty-fourth Regiment, Penn	Col. J. T. Owen.

Fourth Brigade, Brigadier-General James S. Negley, Camp Paterson, three miles in advance of Chambersburgh.

Ninth Regiment, Pennsylvania	Col. Longnecker.
Thirteenth Regiment, Penn	Col. Rowley.
Fourteenth Regiment Penn	Col. Johnston.
Fifteenth Regiment, Penn	Col. R. S. Oakford.

Fifth Brigade, Col. Dixon H. Miles, U. S. A., Commanding, Camp Brady, 2½ miles in advance of Chambersburgh.

Sixteenth Regiment Pennsylvania Volunteers, Col. Zeigle.

One Company United States Second Infantry, Lieut. Spencer. Other Companies expected.

Five Companies United States Third Infantry, (Battalion) under command Major O. S. Sheppard.

One Company United States Artillery, with battery, &c., expected on Tuesday.

One Regiment Michigan Volunteers, Col. ——, expected to-morrow, from Harrisburgh.

One Regiment Rhode Island Volunteers, Col. Burnside, with light battery, expected from Washington, *viâ* Harrisburgh, on Tuesday.

There will probably be some change in the constitution of the last three Brigades, and a Sixth will be formed, particularly if the two Ohio Regiments arrive.

AFFAIRS IN WESTERN VIRGINIA.

RAPID MOVEMENTS OF FEDERAL TROOPS.

CINCINNATI, Tuesday, June 11.

A special dispatch to the *Gazette*, from Grafton, says that the Indiana Zouaves experienced no trouble in reaching Cumberland. No Secessionists were seen on the way. The people of Cumberland were friendly.

One hundred army wagons, with a full supply of horses, are at Parkersburgh, *en route* for Grafton.

Companies of Virginia Volunteers are rapidly organizing under Gen. MORRIS' proclamation.

Arms were issued to-day to two fully organized companies from Fairmount, and others are reporting themselves from the South and East.

The railroad is clear to Cumberland, and trains are running again. Travel is reviving.

Many delegates passed through Cumberland to-day, *en route* to the Wheeling Convention.

A special dispatch from Wheeling to the *Commercial* says that delegates to the Convention are fast arriving here. Over five counties east of the Alleghanies will be represented. The feeling predominant is for a Provisional Government.

A collision occurred at Glencoe, thirteen miles from Wheeling, on the Central Ohio Railroad to-day, killing four of the employes on the road, smashing an engine and shattering one or two cars.

SOUTHERN NEWS THROUGH LOUISVILLE.

LOUISVILLE, Tuesday, June 11.

The Surveyor of the Customs at Evansville, Indiana, has notified steamers that the transportation of provisions to Smithland and Paducah, Kentucky, is in violation of the instructions of the Government, and will be prohibited.

The New-Orleans and Mobile mail-boats were stopped on the 8th inst.

The British ship *Independence* and the Bremen ship *Gabain*, went to sea from New-Orleans on the 6th inst. The ships *Mamaroneck* and *Parsons*, for Liverpool, were abandoned inside the bar at Pass a l'Outre at the same time.

Two small vessels of war appeared on the 6th inst. at the mouth of Bienvenue Bay, ten miles from New-Orleans, where the British landed in 1813. Gen. TWIGGS has occupied the Martello Tower at that point.

The Charleston *Mercury* of the 6th inst. reports that a privateer captured off Georgetown a Portland brig valued at $40,000.

Savannah papers of the 7th inst, state that the ship *Sebasticook*, of Bath, Maine, had been seized by the Collector of the port, in consequence of remaining there longer than allowed by law.

A special dispatch from Charleston to the New-Orleans *Picayune*, dated the 8th inst., says that Gov. PICKENS has published a notification against sending funds to the North, such being in conflict with the law on the subject.

OPERATIONS AT CAIRO.

CAIRO, Monday, June 10.

Gen. PRENTISS yesterday sent two companies, under the command of Capt. JOSLYN, to Mound City, to guard that place, as it had been threatened by a band of Kentucky rebels.

Col. SHUTTNER, in command at Bird's Point, to-day broke up a camp of Secessionists near Norfolk, Mo., and succeeded in capturing 18 rebels, who are being examined before Gen. PRENTISS. A number of others made their escape.

THE SIXTY-NINTH REGIMENT.

ARLINGTON HEIGHTS, Tuesday, June 11.

Two companies of the Sixty-ninth Regiment, of New-York, advanced towards Fairfax Court-house last night. Private CORNELIUS SHEEHAN was shot, while bathing, by an accidental spent ball from some muskets which had been loaded, and discharged for the purpose of cleansing them. The ball passed into his right shoulder. The wound is not considered dangerous.

THE ONONDAGA VOLUNTEERS.

ALBANY, Tuesday, June 11.

Postmaster SEDGWICK, of Syracuse, is here on his way to Washington to pay the Twelfth Regiment of Onondaga Volunteers the sum of $7,000, which he has secured for them from the State Military Board.

[*For other Rebellion News see Eighth Page.*]

The Charleston Mercury.

SPONTE SUA SINE LEGE FIDES RECTUMQUE COLENTUR. —VINDICE NULLO

VOLUME LVI. CHARLESTON, S. C., WEDNESDAY, JUNE 12, 1861. NUMBER 11.17[illegible]

THE MERCURY.

WEDNESDAY, JUNE 12, 1861.

Debts due an Alien Enemy.

When a war breaks out between two nations which have had commercial intercourse with each other, their citizens will own property in these nations respectively. Can the citizens of one nation, owning property in the other nation, sell this property to citizens of the other nation, and thus escape loss or confiscation? We suppose that all over the Confederate States there are transferences of stocks and bonds due in the Confederate States by citizens of the United States. In some cases, powers of attorney to sell are sent on to Southern agents to sell and transfer property.

In our opinion, all such sales and transfers are fraudulent and void. By the laws of nations *every species of private contract made with subjects during war is unlawful.* The drawing and negotiation of Bills of Exchange between subjects of the powers at war, and the remission of funds in money or bills to the enemy's country, are equally unlawful. Buying from an enemy, or selling to an enemy, is a contract, and unlawful. Any trading whatever, whether in goods, or stocks, or bonds, or notes, between the citizens of belligerents, is forbidden by the laws of nations. The universal sense of nations have acknowledged the demoralizing effects which would result from the admission of individual intercourse between the states at war. The whole nation is embarked in one common bottom, perhaps struggling for its existence, and must be reconciled to one common fate. Every individual of the one nation must acknowledge every individual of the other nation as his *own enemy*, because he is the *enemy of his country.* This being the duty of the citizen, a hostile or disloyal character is attached to trade or contracts with the enemy of his country. So, also, the presumption is, that every thing which issues from a hostile country is, *prima facie*, the property of the enemy. As such, it must stay to be amenable to confiscation or appropriation, as the exigencies of the war may require; and to attempt to change its character as enemy's property, and thus to avoid the legitimate consequences of war in its effect on the enemies of a country, is fraudulent and illegal. It will, we suppose, be difficult for the people of the Confederate and of the United States to realise at once that they are no longer citizens of the same government; and still more difficult, that they are enemies. But war has its duties as well as peace, and we should endeavor to understand and practice them.

Retaliation.

THE CONDITIONS UNDER WHICH WE ARE TO FIGHT THIS WAR.

The judicial murder of the citizen, LATIMER, if he had a trial at all, inaugurates the most horrid necessity of civil war—retaliation. When, in the war of the Revolution, Col. HAYNE was executed by the British, under the sentence of an incompetent military tribunal, the officers of the Southern American army unanimously called, in writing, upon Gen. GREENE to retaliate upon the British officers who were captive. GREENE notified the British General that he would retaliate, not upon militia, but upon British regular officers; and he at once clapt up several of them in close confinement with a view to their execution. This cured the mischief. Unless our Government adopts this plan, not simply for the protection of our soldiery, but our citizens, we shall hear of the most brutal outrages and murders every day. And no army, officers or men, will be willing to fight, unless the conditions of the war are equal and reciprocal on both sides. Further, the murder of JACKSON, defending his own house against the marauder—the execution of LATIMER, for the simple discharge of the same duty—the horrid excesses which have been perpetrated at Alexandria and elsewhere upon life, honor, and all that is precious to civilization, puts the aggressor totally out of the pale and protection of war, law and humanity. The Zouaves deserve no better fate than to be shot down unsparingly in their tracks—no quarter allowed them—and if taken, hung outright—not as soldiers, but as outlaws, murderers and plunderers. The wild justice of retributive vengeance, in all such cases, must supersede ordinary forms, and technical pleadings and common jurisdiction; and every prisoner now in our hands should be held in close duresse, as a life bondsman, pledged to doom and execution, at the tidings of one Southern soldier or citizen hung or butchered by the remorseless enemy. Nothing less than this will bring these land pirates to their senses. This justice, promptly administered, unsparingly and sharply as the offence, will cure the evil, and check the sanguinary thirst of these marauding demons for the blood of our people. Let it be done, and quickly.

NOTES OF THE WAR.

From our Special Correspondent.

CAMP GREGG, FAIRFAX COUNTY, VA., June 7, 1861.

A Scouting Party and What it Accomplished—Caution of the Enemy—The Richland Rifles—On the Alert—Capture of the Horse Company at Alexandria, and what came of it—A Nice Question—Good Health in Camp—The Encampment at the Junction, &c., &c.

The same tantalising condition of expectation and uncertainty continues. We are very well assured that there will be a battle, and that the battle ground is now before us; but when the ball will open is the question we have no present means of solving, and so still sleep upon our arms.

In the meantime, however, we have some little to enliven us. Three evenings ago our scouts were driven in by a party whose precise character we were unable to discover, and to be advised upon the subject the next night, Capt. DAVIS, Fairfield Volunteers, with Lieut. BOAG, Richardson Guards, Lieut. CLYBURN, DeKalb Volunteers, Mr. ROBUSKI, 1st Orderly to the Colonel, Private BOAG, of Richardson Guards, and Lieut. JOHNSTON, of Capt. POWELL's Cavalry, and Quartermaster DOUGLASS, of the Virginia Flying Artillery, started on a scout. They scoured the tract of country intervening between this place and Fairfax, and finding nothing to reward their enterprise, had their passes renewed by Colonel EWELL, commanding at Fairfax, and plunged into the enemy's country beyond. They drove in the enemy's pickets to within a mile or two of Fell's Church, at which point they learned he was in some considerable force, and turning to the left, in the hope of intercepting some of his scouts, they started one and drove him into Vienna, which place they took by storm. Like the man who won the elephant in the raffle, however, they were quite at a loss what to do with it. The inhabitants were unanimously disaffected, but they were too many to be brought off. The party was too small to hold the place, if they had had orders to do so; and hence, therefore, after a very decided assertion of authority, they started back and arrived in camp the afternoon of yesterday, with no other damage than the fatigue of a hard ride, and no advantage but that which consisted in assuring the enemy that we are on the alert and are not afraid to meet them.

The attack upon our own scouts was again repeated, however, and, as it appeared that there were no detachments of the enemy in the field, it become evident that the disturbance was occasioned by disaffected persons in our neighborhood. To provide for these a suitable entertainment, Capt. MILLER was sent out last night with a detachment of his Richland Rifles, to lie in wait for them. And arrangements were so made as to render it reasonably certain that if they appeared again they would be taken. But there is often something to defeat "the best laid schemes of mice and men," and so it happened here. Capt. POWELL, two of whose troop of horse were to act as decoys, to be certain that in the event of a skirmish, there should be no mistake as to whether his men were friends or enemies, gave them the rallying cry, intending that they should use it only, of course, when reassembling; but he little recked of their excessive zeal. The enemy appeared as usual, but in greater force, and was ready to give them a chase, when, without firing a pistol, they dashed off, shouting the cry at the top of their voices, and thus assuring him that there were others at hand to aid them, he prudently withdrew. After this, nothing could be done, of course. Our party continued, and had reason to know that the enemy also lingered about, and had, in fact, sent a detachment round to intercept the scouts, but finding he was counter moved, he did not expose himself; and daylight coming on, our party returned. The character and location of this enemy, however, has thus been pretty well determined, and it will go hard with us if it shall not yet be my fortune to give an account of them.

Before they fired upon our scouts; last night they did not; and it is to be supposed, therefore, that it was their intention to take them alive, and extort the information necessary to a full knowledge of our position.

Our two regiments are some little distance apart, but both strongly posted, and the stand can be made to advantage, whether the one or the other point may be attacked. We have reason to know that the plan of movement is now being considered by the enemy, but are assured also that it is not yet determined on.

When Alexandria was taken, the enemy, for the purpose, it is supposed, of throwing our forces off their guard, gave them notice that they must evacuate or surrender by nine o'clock, and entered the town a little after six. Most of the troops had moved off, or were in the act of moving, so as not to be intercepted; but Captain BALL, commanding a troop of horse, and relying on the faith of the enemy that they would not enter before nine o'clock, was taking his breakfast when the enemy entered, and his whole troup was captured. They have since been held as prisoners until yesterday, when they were released upon taking an oath not to serve against the United States. It may, perhaps, present a nice question in morals whether an oath so extorted can bind them, or whether, when their homes are sacked and burned, they cannot raise their arms to defend them. Some declare their purpose to regard their oaths; some to take the consequences of a violation. The enemy will, doubtless, claim to hang them if he takes them again in arms, and it is probable that we may have here re-enacted one of the most painful scenes of our Revolution.

It is strange how soon a people become indifferent to danger. The tract of country between this position and the enemy must soon become a battle ground, but few have left it—few have put their things in readiness to leave. All are engaged about their customary avocations. Women, as well as men, await the issue. The gentleman, the proprietor of Chantilly, where I spent the night of the attack on Fairfax, has been absent for the last three days at Richmond, while his family remain at home. And yesterday morning Capt. DAVIS and his scouting party were sumptuously breakfasted by a family within four miles of the enemy's outposts.

The health of our forces is good. There are still some cases of measles, but they are generally mild and manageable; and though our troops have been much exposed—our pickets have been extensive, and guard duty has been very onerous, all are exposed in all sorts of weather, during some portions of the day or night—they bear it bravely, and seem only in better spirits the more they have to do.

Camp Pickens—the name of the encampment at the Junction—is constantly assuming a more military and formidable aspect. The number has been increased, the lines extended, and for some time, at least, it would seem to be intended to be the headquarters of the forces in this department. Our authorities seem now to be impressed with the importance of protecting the communications in the rear of Harper's Ferry, and some 1200 men were sent into that field yesterday. Others will doubtless follow; and as, by Proclamation of the Governor, the militia of Virginia have at last been called out, it is beyond question that we will soon have enough in numbers, at least for every point now threatened.

The militia were ordered to be in readines to assemble, and the places of rendezvous were indicated more than a month ago; but they only now have been actually ordered out. For regular warfare, they will, of course, not be reliable; but for the irregular action, necessary to impede and cripple an invading army, they will soon be efficient—as efficient, perhaps, as any irregular soldiers ever were.

L. W. S.

—o—

CAMP GREGG, June 8, 1861.

The Lines Closing—The Projected Movement Against Harper's Ferry—Old Point—The Fight at Acquia Creek—Camp Incident—Our Officers, &c., &c.

Still no battle, but the lines are closing. The enemy has taken post at the White House, on the south side of the Potomac, within about three miles of Mount Vernon, and within about twelve miles of Fairfax Station, on the Orange and Alexandria Railroad. This position is about fifteen miles from Fairfax Court House, and about twenty from Manassas Junction, where the mass of our forces is still situated. Some three thousand troops were landed there Thursday, and they are taking measures to defend the place. Whether they propose a simultaneous movement from that and other points on Manassas, or intend to move thence by land on the batteries at Acquia Creek, which they have been unable to take by water, or merely intend to hold it as a strong position, for whatever uses it may be put to, does not appear.

The four brigades, comprising eighteen regiments, and about 15,000 men, assembled at Chambersburg, Pa., under General PATTERSON, is about moving down to Hagerstown, in Maryland, and in the direction of Harper's Ferry. Whether it is their purpose to march directly on Harper's Ferry, or cross to Martinsburg, in Virginia, some twenty-five miles from Hagerstown, and move thence, with MCCLELLAN's forces from the West, on Winchester, in the rear of Harper's Ferry, or merely to hold Hagerstown as a strong position, is also uncertain; but I am inclined to think they will not open the campaign by battering their brains out against the heights of Harper's Ferry, and that if they move at all at present, it will be to invade Virginia, and take that position in reverse. The report that they had already crossed the Potomac, of which I spoke yesterday, though as well authenticated as a report could be, was, as I supposed it was, untrue.

With respect to movements at Old Point Comfort, my means of information are not better than your own; but it would appear that there are there not more than 10,000 men, and, with that force, they will not attempt a march through the centre of the State. It would also appear that that gimblet-eyed man, BUTLER, as he is called, will not have whatever of a field is open there to himself. The redoubtable BANKS, of Massachusetts, has been put in charge of field operations, such as there may be, and thus the hero of no battle, BUTLER, has, to an extent at least, been superseded. His genius, however, seems to be in entertaining fugitive slaves, and that he can indulge as well within the walls of the fortress.

Such is the condition of the three great military departments in this State. LANE, of Kansas infamy, has invaded Arkansas, and possessed himself of Pocahontas, against which the forces of that State are being concentrated. But in reference to matters in that quarter, I cannot undertake to speak with any confidence. He is reported to have a force of 8000, but I cannot think it is near so great: while against even that force, Arkansas can have little difficulty in making head.

With respect to movements in this particular department, I have little to say in addition to what I said yesterday. The affair at Acquia Creek was more important even than we thought it was. The *Pawnee* was not sunk, but only for the reason that she was run upon the Maryland flats opposite, where she now lies. While I have it upon evidence, I cannot question that there were seventy dead bodies carried up to Washington by the steamers *Freeborn* and *Anacosta.* They were able to leave the scene of action. Of this mortality and of the sinking of the *Pawnee* the official reports are silent; and as with respect to this and the engagement at Fairfax, the enemy have shown themselves such unmitigated liars, it is fair to presume also, that they have lied with respect to all others, and that the engagements at Pigg's Point, near Norfolk, and at Phillipi, in the west, have been equally disastrous to them.

Of the first it was reported that Wednesday last the cutter *Harriet Lane*, cruising about Pigg's Point, was opened upon by a masked battery, and that firing fifty-eight shots she retired from the action with only five wounded; but it is confessed that our gunners shot with astonishing precision, and that the cutter was struck some eight times, from which we are compelled to record some mortality at least.

Of the engagement at Phillippi also it was reported that Col. KELLY was despatched, with about 3000 men from Grafton, where the forces of Gen. MCCLELLAN were assembled, to Phillippi, where there some 15,000 secessionists; that he surprised them, routed them, and took 5000 stand of arms, their ammunition and baggage, without the loss of a man, and with only KELLY himself mortally wounded. But I hear it upon the authority of a gentleman, who professes to know, that there were some few of the assailants killed.

Men who fight for money and show can never stand against men who fight for their homes and wives and children. And with that prudence which I am sure our officers will practice, I contemplate the results of every meeting with the most perfect confidence.

The incidents of our camp life differ little from the incidents of camp life everywhere. Liquor shops expelled from the village reappear upon the outskirts, and there is the usual vigilance and activity between officers on the one side, and liquor dealers on the other, to take each other at a disadvantage, while the soldiers look upon the game with the greatest possible complacency, or from a spirit of mischief lend a hand to both sides. Captain GIBBES, then the officer of the day, led a gallant charge a few days since upon an establishment then three mile off, and took a barrel or two; while this morning Captain DAVIS made a seizure almost within the lines, and opening it in the road before the tents. The mischievous compound now runs trickling down the declivity, while quite a number of the men stand around affecting to lament the waste of the material.

Our gallant Colonel of the First exhibits sleepless vigilance. He would rather not retire; and that he may not be compelled to do so, is availing himself of every natural advantage of his position, and our pickets are not only vigilant, but industrious in measures of defence. Col. KERSHAW, with whom is now Gen. BONHAM and Staff, has also a fine position, which he is instant to defend. Both do what can be done, both inspire the utmost confidence and devotion in their men, and both will be sustained to the last in any position they may take.

L. W. S.

Our Richmond Correspondence.

RICHMOND, VA., JUNE 4, 1861.

Picturesque Scenes on the Cars—Defences of Norfolk—Gen. Huger—Appearance of our Troops—Louisiana takes the Palm for Discipline—Politics, &c., &c.

The line of railroad from Florence to this city is a sort of military panorama, presenting an endless variety in costume and physique. In one car you find the Georgia or Carolina volunteer, with the monotonous grey suit, and, in some instances, with the addition of a grey flannel shirt; in the next, the Louisiana Zouave, in blue pea-jacket, blue peg-top trowsers, white gaiters, and the inimitable and neatly fitting New Orleans shirt, of such color and material as pleases the fancy of the wearer. Then, again, the eye rests on one or more groups of the simon pure Zouave. The blue jacket, the yellow sash in heavy folds around the waist; the crimson trowsers—of the fullest conceivable pattern—the black and white leggins and gaiters, the black belt and knife, and the small red fez and yellow tassel fitting jauntily on the back of the head. The flannel shirt, which is made to fit low on the shoulders, exposes the entire neck and face, and you would readily think yourself among the heros of the Malakoff, particularly if you had seen their antics in, on top, and around the railroad cars when in motion. Some ladies in an adjoining car nearly fainted at the apparent recklessness of these military curiosities, who, in the open country, I would mention, take great pleasure in slipping out of the car windows, and domiciling themselves for a convenient season on the roof of the cars, as they say, with a French accent, "for to enjoy the fine prospect." Our uninitiated "lads in grey" look very complacently, and seem to enjoy the "style" very much.

Owing to the number of troops and the necessary accumulation of camp equipage, and "*materiel de guerre*," travel is much suspended along this great seaboard thoroughfare. The Railroad Companies seem to have placed their trains entirely at the disposal of the Quartermaster-General, and hence it is that an ordinary traveller cannot count too certainly on making the regular connections at the different stations. Much time is lost on the road, and if, as was the case with a number of passengers last week, the station should be as uninviting as Weldon, the twelve hours detention is onerous in the extreme. Weldon is to our "Zouave friends" what Gallipoli was to their Eastern namesakes on their way to the Crimea, a sort of "wretched place," where fluids were abundant but abominable to the taste, and where the groceries were very low in quality and quantity of stores, and very high in price. Most of these novel characters, however, were provided with crackers and cheese, and the provision tariff at Weldon was not largely encouraged.

When I left Charleston some interest was felt in regard to the military district embracing Norfolk, Portsmouth and the Gosport Navy Yard, in view of the large concentration of Northern State troops at Fortress Monroe, under Gen. BUTLER. The peculiar position of this stronghold, and its partial isolation from the main line, has enabled LINCOLN's troops to spread over a portion of the adjoining county towards and even beyond Hampton; but "the offending hath this extent no more." They will find it difficult to do more than hold their ground, as the extensive works now being erected under Gen. HUGER's direction will, in a day or so, and even now may be said to offer insurmountable obstacles to their proposed aggressive movements.

In military matters it is not wise to speak in detail. Suffice it to say, that increased confidence is felt by the people in that section; and if working eighteen hours out of the twenty-four will ensure success, General HUGER and his efficient and talented staff of officers will be rewarded for their untiring exertions.

Looking around Richmond, one is struck with the manly, and, generally, the substantial appearance of the troops. It is nothing more than proper to say, however, that so far as good equipment and excellence in the drill is regarded, Louisiana is much in advance of all other States. The several commands here are certainly the best prepared for immediate service. The Battalion of Light Artillery particularly is a splendid offering from the opulent Crescent City to the Confederate States.

The Alabama, Georgia and South Carolina regiments are all in much the same relative condition—fine, able-bodied men, enthusiastic for the cause, and delighted at the near approach of hostilities; but they were not ready for the field when they left home; and it is a fact that should be mentioned for our guidance in the future, that the present system of militia service is a broken reed, upon which no Southern State should hereafter depend. It is not enough that men should only know to which "beat" or "patrol" they are attached—it is not right for politicians in commission to tell their companies, regiments, brigades and divisions, about their courage and bravery, and all that. It would be better if a system should be founded which would make the commissioned officers instructors in the all-important primary duties of the soldier; not only learn men how to *muster*, but how to shoulder arms and carry arms; the wheelings and flankings; the loadings and firings; their duties in camp and on guard; have it understood that musters are not for fun and amusement, but for *work*; and then when the State wants ten regiments, men will slip out to the front who are, to some extent, informed of their high duties.

Of course, in our present emergency the troops from the South are equal, and in almost all cases superior, to the Northern State troops, and as sure as the sun rises they will drive back the foe; but experience is useful only as we profit by it, and as our next war may be with disciplined soldiers—and it may come suddenly—we should look to our own wants *now*, when mistakes can be corrected and wise precautions taken.

Politically, people talk of the treachery of Gov. HICKS and JOHNSON, of Tennessee; of the election in the latter State where the Union sentiment still lingers; of the probable future of Maryland, Kentucky and Missouri, and of the chances of a battle, which all true Southern men hope for, as a necessity in our present, apparently, star-gazing condition. The frequent *surprises* have had the effect of bringing down the press on the officers in command; but the true policy in all such cases is to have these words written on the back of the delinquent parties commission—"discharged from the service of the Confederate States." President DAVIS' health is much improved.

The New-York Times.

VOL. X....NO. 3037. NEW-YORK, SATURDAY, JUNE 15, 1861. PRICE TWO CENTS.

HIGHLY IMPORTANT NEWS.

Harper's Ferry Evacuated by the Rebels.

The Bridge Blown Up and the Government Buildings Destroyed.

Retreat of the Rebels Towards Winchester.

THEIR DESTINATION MANASSAS JUNCTION.

Probable Retirement of the Combined Forces to Richmond.

IMPORTANT MOVEMENTS IN MISSOURI.

Open Treason of Gov. Jackson and the Other State Officers.

A Collision Expected Between the State and Federal Troops.

Latest Intelligence from Fortress Monroe.

A Flag of Truce Sent to Yorktown.

FORMIDABLE FORTIFICATIONS ALONG THE ROAD.

SPECIAL DISPATCH FROM WASHINGTON.

WASHINGTON, Friday, June 14.

The news of the evacuation of Harper's Ferry by the rebels was received at the War Department to-day about 12 o'clock. They went away with baggage down the road to Winchester, destroying all they could not carry, and, like a steam-plow, taking up the railroad track and burning the bridges as they run.

This result I telegraphed you three weeks ago must take place. They could not stay at the Ferry, and had to run. Where they have gone is the question now. Down to Winchester by rail, thence by a march of twelve miles to Strasburg or Front Royal, and then by railroad again to Manassas Junction; and doubtless to-night they are there or thereabouts, unless the Leesburgh column has taken the liberty of burning bridges and destroying a portion of the track from the Gap to the Junction.

How long will they stay at Manassas? There is a wide difference of opinion about this point. Some see in this evacuation of Harper's Ferry, and the retreat upon Manassas, an immediate attack upon Washington. Among some of the transient visitors and the oldest inhabitants, the danger of an attack on the city is very imminent—but, depend upon it, the rebels at Manassas will not move towards Washington. Their next movement will be another retreat—a retreat in the direction of Richmond. They will stay at Manassas until, like locusts, they have eaten up the country, and then they will,

"Fold their tents, like the Arabs, and as quietly steal away."

There is no help for them. They must go. They have not provisions, nor transportation, nor field artillery in such quantity as will justify a forward movement, and least of all a movement that brings them face to face with the forty-five thousand men and two or three hundred field and siege guns. Depend upon it, the wind that next fills the sails of the rebel ship must blow from, not towards, the North.

MR. BURLINGAME APPOINTED TO CHINA.

The State Department has dispatches announcing the withdrawal of Mr. BURLINGAME, our Minister to Austria. Mr. BURLINGAME did not present his credentials, the Austrian Court having, in a most delicate manner, notified Mr. BURLINGAME that it would be under the necessity of declining to receive him. There is to be no ill-feeling to grow out of this affair, the Austrian Government having given the most satisfactory assurances of its good feeling, by being the first to proffer its aid to support the Government in crushing this rebellion.

It is probable that Hon. HENRY WINTER DAVIS will be appointed to succeed Mr. BURLINGAME, and that the appointment will be made at an early day.

Mr. BURLINGAME has been appointed Minister to China, a higher and more lucrative position than he now occupies.

P. C. KANE, of New-York, has been appointed a Captain in the Army. He is a brother, I believe, to the late Dr. KANE.

The Capt. POPE, who was to-day appointed a Brigadier-General, is the same gentleman whom President BUCHANAN court-martialed for accompanying President LINCOLN to Washington.

Commissioner WOODS has appointed Major WM. B. CHASE, of Washington, Chief Clerk in his office. He is fortunate in securing the services of a gentleman, and one so well qualified to fill the position. It is probable that SAMUEL STRONG will be appointed Superintendent under Mr. WOODS.

THE BALTIMORE ELECTION.

The peace and quiet of the election in Baltimore, is said to be due to the energy of Gen. BANKS. Previous to the election he addressed a note to Mayor, stating that he had detailed a force to sustain the civil authorities in maintaining public order, and that he had instructed them to be vigilant and prompt, and to make his orders effective, "he had given each man forty rounds of ball catridge." The Mayor and Marshal KANE appeared to understand "that last remark."

The experiments with the balloon that were to be made to-day did not come off, the Gas Company failing to supply the motive power. It will certainly go up to-morrow.

The War Department to-day received a large quantity of insulated wire for field purposas, and also a number of recording instruments.

I see about Washington several gentlemen connected with the Police Department of New-York. If they told the truth, they would say they were here to arrest several members of "the ring" who were indicted by the last Grand Jury of New-York.

We have a number of distinguished arrivals to-day, among them Major THACKER and Senator HARCOURT, of Albany. I thought, too, I heard the laugh of Capt. SCHULTZ, somewhere in the halls of Willard's.

A MOVEMENT OF THE SIXTY-NINTH.

At 1 A. M., this morning, two hundred and fifty of the Sixty-ninth, under Lieut.-Col. NUGENT, accompanied by fifty of Company B, Second United States Cavalry, under Lieut. MASON, were hurriedly advanced to the two new bridges erected on the Loudon and Hampton Railroad, between BALL'S Cross Roads and Alexandria, Gen. McDOWELL having received positive information that an attempt in force to destroy the road would be made. The information was correct enough, but the strong force on the ground prevented any attack by the rebels, whose scouts were seen falling back as the cavalry advanced.

Two of the twenty-four-pounder columbiades were mounted yesterday on Fort Corcoran, the first being christened "Hunter," in honor of the officer commanding one brigade. The officiating Chaplain remarked that it was a promising and patriotic infant, being able to speak in thunder tones for the Union at the moment of its birth.

Great desire is felt by the men on Arlington Heights to have the Senty-ninth sent over to join their brigade, the Highlanders now having no other employment than to kill the mosquitoes, which fasten on their bare legs just across the river, and within sight of the camp. The presence of the Seventy-ninth, abreast of the Sixty-ninth, would bring a generous emulation between Irishmen and Scotchmen, that could not fail to be of service. As Secretary CAMERON'S brother is Colonel of the Seventy-ninth, will the Secretary of War be pleased to make a not of this request?

SECRETARY SEWARD IN VIRGINIA.

Secretary SEWARD to-day visited Virginia, and the intrenched camp of the Sixty-ninth. He was honored with a hearty welcome and a *reveille*, which he repaid with a characteristic speech.

Col. MEIGS has entered upon his duties as Quartermaster-General. He retains Major SIBLEY in the Department, but the Major is promoted to be a Colonel.

UNIONISTS IN VIRGINIA.

A scouting party who visited Falls Church recently, nine miles from this city, were handsomely received by the residents there, who expressed the hope unreservedly that the Federal forces would shortly occupy that place.

At Fairfax Court-house about 700 Confederate troops are reported to be encamped at latest advices.

Several excellent field pieces have just been forwarded to Alexandria, for the use of the Zouaves there. They are to be mounted on the extensive entrenchments built by that regiment at Alexandria.

A BRUSH WITH THE REBELS.

At Annapolis, Major MORGAN, of the Thirteenth Brooklyn Regiment has just returned from Queenstown, where he had a brush with his forces with the enemy. He brought one prisoner and five hundred stand of arms. He was assaulted from the bushes, but drove the rebels out and secured their arms.

Several friends of the late Senator DOUGLAS met at the National, last evening, Hon. JOHN B. HASKINS in the chair. It was voted to procure a suitable monument in his honor, and arrangements were discussed for pronouncing an eulogy upon Judge DOUGLAS' character on the 4th of July next. Another meeting will be held next week at the City Hall on this subject.

MILITARY MOVEMENTS.

From Rockville it is reported that the regiments which left here Monday, together with a portion of MAGRUDER'S Battery, left that town on Wednesday evening, advancing Northwestward.

Several of the subordinate officers at Fortress Monroe have resigned their positions since the Bethel fight, on account of their dissatisfaction with Brig.-Gen. PIERCE, and others threaten to do so.

The British Minister here has been applied to by certain wives of Irish soldiers now in the rebel army, who have never been naturalized, to take action for their relief. The British Consul has been directed by Lord LYONS to take testimony in this matter, and then release will be demanded.

The Nineteenth New-York Regiment, now at Kalorama, will be paid off at once. Paymaster WOODRUFF is here with the money.

The First and Second Ohio and the Connecticut Regiments left Washington this evening. They went across Long Bridge, down in "Ole Virginny," towards Dixie.

We have the thermometer at 97° in the shade to-day. Good, calm weather, but a little bit over-hot for fighting, except at long range. LEO.

DISPATCH TO THE ASSOCIATED PRESS.

WASHINGTON, Friday, June 14.

The Government finds itself seriously embarrassed in the management of the present military campaign, by the premature publication of sufficient information to disclose its purposes to the public, South, as well as North. Portions of its plans for the movements of the troops have thus been made known, and has enabled the rebels to frustrate the successful execution of them. This it is no longer disposed to allow to be done, and yet it is unwilling to exclude the Press from the advantages afforded by the telegraph, and therefore is reluctant absolutely to prohibit the transmission of dispatches for publication.

In view of this state of things, it is suggested that editors of the leading journals in Philadelphia, New-York, Boston and other cities, immediately meet at Washington and come to some satisfactory understanding, which will relieve the Government from further embarrassment, and, yet, afford the Press all the facilities it can reasonably desire, under the circumstances.

FRANCIS W. RICE, a correspondent of the newspaper Press, has been appointed Consul at Aspinwall.

Postmaster-General BLAIR has dispatched to the Postmaster at Louisville the following:

"The order requiring mail matter coming from disloyal States to be held for postage, was not intended to prevent its delivery upon the payment of the postage."

As an explanation of the above, it will be recollected that the late order of the Postmaster-General required letters from the seceded States to be immediately forwarded to the Dead Letter Office, but this is not intended to cover cases where the letter has arrived at its place of delivery and the person to whom it is addressed offers to pay to the United States for the postage due thereon. In such cases it may be delivered upon the payment of the postage.

The most extravagant and improbable rumors are from day to day circulated, which, though unentitled to belief, occasion much painful apprehension and inquiry. Trifling events are often magnified into importance, and imaginations represented as realities.

The appointment of Hon. ANSON BURLINGGAME as Minister to Austria was to-day changed to that of Minister to China.

STEPHEN A. HURLBURT and Captain JOHN POPE, the latter of the Army, both of Illinois, were to-day appointed Brigadier Generals of the forces of that State.

PHILLIP PENDLETON, now engaged receiving Virginia troops at Williamsport, under the proclamation of Col. LAMON of this city, was to-day appointed additional Paymaster in the Army.

The Committee appointed, yesterday, in regard to the erection of a Douglas monument, etc., met this evening, and unanimously selected Col. FORNEY to deliver the eulogy on the 3d of July. THOS. C. FIELDS was made Corresponding Secretary; GEO. W. McLEAN, Monument Secretary, and J. J. McELHONE, Chairman.

On the recommendation of the Colonel of Ordnance, the use of percussion caps by the troops is prohibited, except when firing with cartridges. In drilling at the manual of arms either a burnt cap will be used to protect the cone, or the man will be instructed not to pull the trigger with sufficient force to bring the hammer down.

The New-York Seventy-first, to-day, arrested a spy at the Navy-yard. The letter on his cap indicated that he is a member of the Piscataway (Maryland) Rifles. There have been no arrivals or departures at the Navy-yard to-day. There are six steamers at the wharf, and there is great activity in the shops, preparing guns and ammunition.

The volunteer battalion near Chain Bridge, two miles above Georgetown, are making fine progress with their intrenchments, and preparing to mount guns so as to command the whole Virginia shore and sweep the bridge, if necessary.

From what is known of the movements of Col. STONE'S force they are to protect the line of the Potomac.

The First and Second Ohio Regiments broke camp to-night and passed into Virginia.

REPORTS FROM ALEXANDRIA.

ALEXANDRIA, Friday, June 14.

A slave belonging in Maryland, and who fled here and took abode with the Zouaves, was delivered up to his owner this afternoon, on producing the proper authority.

The military railroads are being pushed forward with great rapidity.

Active military movements here are predicted, on the news from Harper's Ferry, in order to prevent the enemy from concentrating their troops.

HARPER'S FERRY EVACUATED.

RETREAT OF THE REBELS AND DESTRUCTION OF THE BRIDGE.

FREDERICK, Md., Friday June 14.

It is here reported, upon the authority of a messenger who arrived here this morning from within one mile of Harper's Ferry, that the bridge across the Potomac at that point was blown up and entirely destroyed, between 4 and 5 o'clock this morning. The explosion was distinctly heard, and the smoke of the burning structure seen by parties here.

The messenger further reports that all the troops have been withdrawn from the Maryland shore, and that the town of Harper's Ferry has been evacuated by the great body of the troops recently there. A small force is still there, probably the rear guard of the retreating army.

It is reported that eight car loads of provisions were destroyed to prevent them falling into the hands of the Federalists, who are supposed to be concentrating upon Harper's Ferry, from the directions of Greencastle and Cumberland.

The wife and family of Gen. HUGER were at the Ferry last night, and had engaged a private conveyance from the city to take them to a point further southward, but were compelled to accompany the column by its sudden flight.

The destruction of the bridge may be regarded as certain. Confirmatory intelligence of the fact has been received here within a few minutes. A gentleman of this city, who was at Harper's Ferry last night, saw the preparations being made for the blowing up of the structure.

The bridge at Shepardstown was also burnt last night.

LATEST FROM HARPER'S FERRY.

FREDERICK, Md., Friday, June 14.

A resident of this city, who has just returned from Harper's Ferry, states that the bridge has been entirely destroyed, with the exception of the piers, which are left standing. The tressle-work of the railroad within the town was also destroyed. The Government buildings were being severally burnt when he left there at 11 o'clock this morning. The armory was first fired and destroyed. The rifle works, it is supposed, will follow next. All the machinery had been transported into the interior several days ago. He estimates that there are some 4 000 troops yet in the town. The main body, it is said, has been pushed on to Charlestown and to a point near Leesburgh.

THE REBELS MOVING TO WINCHESTER.

BALTIMORE, Friday, June 14.

A letter received at the office of the *American* from Berlin, on the Baltimore and Ohio Railroad, confirms the burning of the Harper's Ferry Bridge. The correspondent heard the explosion, and went up to see the conflagration.

All the troops are gone from the Maryland side, and they were hurrying out of Harper's Ferry as rapidly as possible.

The letter states that the town will be troopless by 12 o'clock to night.

They are moving towards Winchester in great haste.

A correspondent at Williamsport writes that at 7 o'clock Thursday evening a messenger arrived at the secession post, opposite to that town, at the top of his speed, and called in all the pickets and they all left with equal speed.

From a correspondent at Sharpsburgh it is ascertained that two Virginians were shot at Dam No. 5 and that an attack was being made on a warehouse at Mercersville, which the people were preparing to resist, the purpose being to rob it.

REPORTS FROM SHARPSBURGH.

SHARPSBURGH, via HAGERSTOWN, Friday, June 14.

Reliable escaped Virginians report that the Confederate troops left Harper's Ferry, to-day, one part retreating to Winchester and another into Loudon County. This would seem to indicate that a retreat to Manassas Junction is intended.

The railroad bridge at the Ferry was blown up one hour after sunrise this morning. The remaining Government buildings were all burnt.

The railroad bridge at Martinsburgh was burnt to-day. Also the bridge at Shepardstown.

A dark smoke is still ascending from the burning buildings at the Ferry.

REPORTS FROM WILLIAMSPORT.

WILLIAMSPORT, Friday, June 14.

The Shepardstown Bridge was burnt last night by the rebels, the smoke and flames being distinctly seen here.

The Confederate pickets have been withdrawn from all points 20 miles above and 10 miles below here.

A rumor reached here this morning that the enemy are throwing up earthworks at Shepperd's Ford, between Dam No 4 and Shepherdstown Bridge.

A gentleman arrived here this morning, who visited Stewart's Camp at Hainesville, four miles this side of Martinsburgh. Last evening the camp was broken up and the troops moved to Martinsburgh.

THE MARYLAND CONGRESSIONAL ELECTION.

BALTIMORE, Friday, June 14.

Complete returns from the Third District elect LEARY, Union candidate, by 375 majority. This District gave BRECKINRIDGE a majority last Fall.

In the Sixth District as far as heard from, the returns favor the election of CALVERT, Union candidate. The result is uncertain.

We have nothing from the First District yet.

CALVERT, Union, is 1,500 ahead in the Sixth District, with Charles, St. Mary's and Calvert to hear from.

The general impression is that the whole Union delegation, except H. WINTER DAVIS, is elected.

BALTIMORE, Friday, June 14—P. M.

Mr. CRISFIELD, (Union) is elected in the First District. He has 124 majority in Queen Anne; 490 in Caroline; 4 0 in Dorchester, and Henry, (Secessionist) has 20 in Talbot.

It is now believed that H. WINTER DAVIS is the only Union candidate defeated, and he is beaten by Hon. HENRY MAY, who claims to be an uncompromising enemy of secession and an independent Union man. He was undoubtedly supported by a large majority of Union men in his District.

THOMAS' majority in Washington County is 4,000.

The Baltimore *American* notices the Fourth District election as follows:

"In the Fourth District, Mr. MAY is elected over Mr. DAVIS by over two thousand majority. This result has not surprised and still less disappointed us. When Mr. DAVIS was nominated we declared that he was not the choice of the Union men of the District, and that he could not be elected. Mr. DAVIS and his friends, however, persisted in burthening the Union cause with the dead weight of his personal and political unpopularity, and the result has proved the truth of the declaration we then made. The whole contest has been unfortunate in its manifold cross purposes, but it is some consolation to know that Mr. MAY, the successful candidate, although not so decided in his expression of Union sentiments as could be wished, is yet one upon whom the secessionists cannot depend for any 'precipitation' movements."

IMPORTANT FROM MISSOURI.

OPEN TREASON OF THE STATE OFFICERS.

HERMANN, Mo., Friday, June 14.

A gentleman from Jefferson City, says the steamer *White Cloud* was loading at that place yesterday, with cannon and military stores. It was said that Gov. JACKSON and all the State Officers were to embark in her for Arrow Rock, a strong point about sixty miles above, on the Missouri River.

Capt. KELLY'S Guard, of one hundred men, were the only troops at the Osage Bridge, or Dodd's Island.

ST. AMHERST, (9 miles from Jefferson City), FRIDAY, June 14—8 P. M.

A special agent, who was sent down from Jefferson City with the mail, has just returned here, having left here this P. M. He says the Governor and all the State Officers left there yesterday, and that the last of the soldiers left to-day at 2 P. M., taking with them all the locomotives (of which I understand there were five,) and cars, and burning the bridge at Grey's Creek, three miles west of Jefferson City, also one above there, after they had passed over them.

It is supposed the Governor has ordered his forces to concentrate either at Boonsville or Arrow Rock, probably the latter.

It is thought that Gen. LYON will push on after him, and should he meet with no detention, he will not be more than twenty four hours behind him.

The Moreau bridge, forty-one miles this side of Jefferson City is unharmed, but the western span of the Osage bridge, nine miles this side, is burned.

MOVEMENTS OF TROOPS IN MISSOURI.

ST. LOUIS, Thursday, June 13.

The steamer *Iatan*, with the Second Battalion of the First Regiment Missouri Volunteers, under command of Lieut. Col. ANDREWS, one section of Totten's Light Artillery, and two companies of regulars, under Capt. LATHROP, and the steamer *J. C. Swan*, with the First Battalion of the First Regiment, under Col. BLAIR, and another section of Totten's Battery, and a detachment of Pioneers, and Gen. LYON and Staff, numbering 1,500 all told, left here this afternoon for some point up the Missouri River, supposed to be Jefferson City. Horses, wagons, and all necessary camp equipage, ammunition and provisions for a long march, accompanied the expedition.

In the case of O. A. BURBITT, arrested for treason before Judge TREAT, United States District Court, to-day, an examination was waived, and the prisoner was released in $10,000 bond for trial before the United States Circuit Court, July 8.

In the cases of Col PARSTON, EDWARD BLENNERHASSETT and EDWARD O. PIONEERS, examination was postponed till to-morrow on the two former, and the latter was dismissed.

ST. LOUIS, Friday, June 14.

Seven more companies of troops and a battery of six guns went out on the Pacific Railroad last night. The steamer *D. A. January* was bought yesterday by the Government.

LATEST REPORTS FROM ST. LOUIS.

ST. LOUIS, Friday, June 14.

The steamers *January* and *Swan*, of the Missouri River expedition, passed Herman, about eighty miles above here at 4 o'clock, and the steamer *Louisiana*, also belonging to the expedition, passed Washington, thirty miles this side, about the same time.

The Second Regiment, under Col. BORNSTEIN, went out on the Pacific Railroad this afternoon, fully provided with camp equipage and munitions of war.

It is conjectured that this regiment will embark on the steamer *Louisiana*, at Herman, and follow the expedition under Gen. LYON.

Under guarantee of protection from the Federal Government, the Pacific Railroad Company is taking energetic measures to immediately repair the bridges on that road.

The *Evening News* learns that two regiments of Iowa volunteers are encamped at Keokuk.

Four hundred Illinois troops, from Quincy, have been concentrated at Hannibal, Mo., by order of Gen. LYON, for the purpose of holding North Missouri and checking Gov. JACKSON'S movements in that region.

It is said that a portion of this force will be sent to Lexington and St. Joseph's.

The *Evening News* also, says that there are a considerable number of Confederate troops assembled in Arkansas, and the Indian Territory, and Northern Texas, for an advance into Kansas and Missouri, to seize the Newbown lead mines and march to the assistance of Gov. JACKSON'S movement. He invites them.

INTERVIEW BETWEEN GEN. LYON AND GOV. JACKSON.

FAILURE OF NEGOTIATIONS.

From the St. Louis Democrat, June 12.

Gov. JACKSON and Gen STERLING PRICE, having, through T. T. GANTT and Judge WM. A. HALL, solicited an interview with Gen. LYON, and agreeing to come to St Louis for such purpose, Gen. LYON, at the request of Mr. GANTT, signed the following paper, guaranteeing them from arrest on their journey to and from the city, and during their sojourn here up to the 12th:

HEAD QUARTERS DEPARTMENT OF THE WEST, ST. LOUIS, MO., June 8, 1861.

It having been suggested that Gov. CLAIBORNE F. JACKSON and Ex-Gov. STERLING PRICE are desirous of an interview with Gen. LYON, Commanding this Department, for the purpose of effecting, if possible, a pacific solution of the domestic troubles of Missouri, it is hereby stipulated on the part of Brig. Gen. N. LYON, U S A, Commanding this Military Department that should Gov JACKSON and Ex.-Gov PRICE, or either of them, at any time prior to, or on the 12th day of June 1861, visit St. Louis for the purpose of such interview, they and each of them shall be free from molestation or arrest on account of any charge pending against them or either of them, on the part of the United States, during their journey to St. Louis, their stay at St. Louis and their return from St. Louis to Jefferson City. Given under the hand of the General Commanding, the day and year above written.

N. LYON, Brig.-Gen. Com.

This being sent, or presented to the parties to whom the passport was given, they left Jefferson City by special train, and arrived as is already known. Yesterday morning Gen. LYON sent them an invitation to visit the Arsenal, which they felt unwilling to accept, notwithstanding Gen. LYON offered them an escort. They, however, sent word by THOMAS L. PRICE, Esq., that they thought as they had come all the way from Jefferson City to see Gen. LYON, he should meet them at the Planters. This the General did not hesitate to do, as he desired to treat them courteously, and meet them in a spirit of peace if they so desired it, and only invited them to the Arsenal because it was his head quarters, and being so occupied with necessary calls upon him, felt loth to leave his important post for so long a time. He, however, as soon as was made known to him the wish of Gov. JACKSON, at once ordered his horse, and invited Col. F. B. BLAIR, Jr., and Major CONANT to accompany him.

They went at once to the Planters' House, and were soon in company with Gov. JACKSON, Ex Gov. PRICE, and THOS L. SNEAD, the latter private Secretary to the Governor.

The conference was of some four hours' duration, and the views of the parties were very freely given. Gov. JACKSON opened the conversation by making professions of peace, but soon put Gen. PRICE forward as his mouth-piece, only now and then repeating his desire, "Not to have any troops on either side. The United States troops must leave the State, and not enter it, and he would disband his own troops, and then we should certainly have peace."

Gen. PRICE went on at some length, to justify his course as in *perfect* harmony with his understanding with Gen. HARNEY, and that he had not violated its one iota.

When asked by Gen. LYON how his course was in concert with Gen. HARNEY'S second proclamation, in which Gen. H. denounced the military bill as treasonable and unconstitutional, and when Gen. LYON said Gen. HARNEY must have sadly changed on the agreement not being lived up to, Gen. PRICE made further remark that he had made no further agreement whatever with Gen. HARNEY about the enforcement or carrying out of the military bill.

At this moment a kind friend sent to Gen. LYON a copy of the following memorandum, which was sent from Gen. H. as the only basis upon which he would treat:

MEM. FOR GEN. PRICE.

MAY 21, 1861.

Gen. HARNEY is here as a citizen of Missouri, with all his interests at stake in the preservation of the peace of the State.

He earnestly wishes to do nothing to complicate matters, and will do everything in his power consistently with his instructions, to preserve peace and order.

He is, however, compelled to recognize the existence of a rebellion in a portion of the United States, and in view of it he stands upon the proclamation of the President, itself based upon the laws and the Constitution of the United States.

The Proclamation commands the dispersion of all armed bodies hostile to the supreme law of the land.

Gen. HARNEY sees in the Missouri Military bill features which compel him to look upon such armed bodies as may be organized under its provisions, as antagonistic to the United States within the meaning of the Proclamation, and calculated to precipitate a conflict between the State and the United States troops.

He laments this tendency of things, and most cordially and earnestly invites the coöperation of Gen. Price to avert it.

For this purpose, Gen. HARNEY respectfully asks Gen. PRICE to review the features of the bill in the spirit of law, warmed and elevated by that of humanity, and seek to discover some means by which its action may be suspended until some competent tribunal shall decide upon its character.

The most material features of the bill calculated to bring about a conflict are, first, the oath required to be taken by the militia and "State Guards"—(an oath of allegiance to the State of Missouri, without recognizing the existence of the Government of the United States;) and secondly, the express requirement, by which troops within the State, not organized under the provisions of the military bill, are to be disarmed by the *State Guards.*

Gen. HARNEY cannot be expected to wait a summons to surrender his arms by the State troops.

From this statement of the case, the true question becomes immediately visible, and cannot be shut out of view.

Gen. PRICE is earnestly requested to consider this, and Gen. HARNEY will be happy to confer with him on the subject whenever it may suit his convenience.

N. B.—Read to Gen. PRICE in the presence of Major H. S. TURNER on the evening of the 21st of May.

The confusion and mortification into which Gen. PRICE was thrown by this paper, made him an object of pity, and after a few moments of hesitation he said he did not remember hearing the paper read. He said Gen. HITCHCOCK and H. S. TURNER were to see him, but he did not see or hear of such a paper.

The conversation then became somewhat animated, Gov. JACKSON still saying little, and Gen. PRICE insisting that no armed bodies of United States troops should pass through or be stationed in the State, as such would occasion civil war—that Missouri must be neutral, and neither side should arm—Gov. JACKSON to give protection to Union men, and to disband his State troops.

On the other hand, Gen. LYON laid down his views as a servant of the Government, somewhat to this effect: That if the Government withdrew its forces entirely, secret and subtle measures would be resorted to, to provide arms and effect organizations which, upon any pretext, could put forth a formidable opposition to the General Government, and even without arming, combinations would doubtless form in certain localities to oppress and drive out loyal citizens, to whom the Government was bound to give protection, but which it would be helpless to do, as also to repress such combinations, if its forces could not be sent into the State. A large aggressive force might be formed and advanced from the exterior into the State to assist it in carrying out the secession programme, and the Government could not, under the limitation proposed, take posts on these borders to meet and repel such force. The Government could not shrink from its duties nor abdicate its corresponding rights; and, in addition to the above, it was the duty of its civil officers to execute civil process, and, in case of resistance to receive the support of military force. The proposition of the Governor would at once overturn the Government privileges and prerogatives which he (Gen. LYON) had neither the wish nor authority to do. In his opinion, if the Governor and the State authorities would earnestly set about to maintain the peace of the State, and declare their purposes to resist outrages upon loyal citizens of the Government, and repress insurrections against it, and in case of violent combinations needing the coöperation of the United States troops, they should call upon or accept such assistance, and in case of threatened invasion, the Government troops took suitable posts to meet it, the purposes of the Government would be subserved, and no infringement of the State rights or dignity committed. He would take good care in such faithful coöperation of the State authorities to this end, that no individual should be injured in person or property, and that the utmost delicacy should be observed towards all peaceable persons concerned in these relations.

Upon this basis in Gen. LYON'S opinion, could the rights of both the General and State Governments be secured, and peace maintained. It was proposed by Gov. JACKSON that they should go into a correspondence, which Gen. LYON disapproved, as their views were widely apart, and such a course would not make matters any better; but he was willing that each one should briefly put down their views, and let them be published. To such a statement Gov. JACKSON was not disposed to agree.

Gov. JACKSON and Gen. PRICE returned to Jefferson City last night, at 6 o'clock, by special train.

IMPORTANT FROM VIRGINIA.

LATEST ADVICES FROM FORTRESS MONROE.

FORTRESS MONROE, Thursday, June 13, via BALTIMORE, Friday, June 14.

There have been no military movements of importance to-day.

The statement in my yesterday's dispatch that the rebels had retired from Great Bethel is true, so far as their main body is concerned, but the place is still held by them and can be occupied by a large body at short notice.

Capt. H. E. DAVIS, son of Judge DAVIS, Lieut. CHARLES H. SEAMAN and Dr. MARTIN, of Col. DURYEE'S Regiment, yesterday entered the enemy's lines with a flag of truce, and went to within half a mile of Yorktown. They saw a formidable battery at Great Bethel, but were not allowed to examine the works, and from there to Yorktown were conducted by bridle paths. They were escorted by a Sergeant and four troopers, who met them at Newmarket Bridge, three miles from Hampton, to which point the secession pickets now extend. They were courteously treated by Col. J. B. MAGRUDER, who commanded at Great Bethel. There was a large encampment of cavalry at Yorktown, and the place was being strongly fortified. There are also batteries between Great Bethel and Yorktown.

The Secessionists report one killed and five wounded at the engagement at Great Bethel, and express a wish that Gen. PIERCE may be retained in command.

Major WINTHROP was shot by a Louisiana rifleman while heading a vigorous charge. He was buried by the rebels, and his heroism greatly praised. I have just brought his hat and spurs from the Zouave camp.

Two Zouaves died prisoners, viz.: BENJAMIN F. HOPPER and JOSEPH L. TAYLOR, nephew of MOSES TAYLOR.

The rebels represented that they had other prisoners, whom they were willing to exchange. Capt. PHILIPS has to-day visited the Fortress with a flag of truce in reference to the same.

There was an alarm last night, and the whole garrison turned out.

Gen. BUTLER and Quartermaster TALLMADGE have this afternoon gone to Newport News.

The mercury yesterday stood at 92° in the shade.

Reconnoissances have been made both from Fortress Monroe and Newport News.

It is reported that JEFFERSON DAVIS was at Richmond last week.

DIRECT FROM OLD POINT COMFORT.

The United States steamer *Quaker City*, Commander O. CARR, United States Navy, commanding, arrived yesterday morning in 21 hours from Old Point Comfort and Hampton Roads.

She was relieved on the blockade off the Capes of Virginia, by the United States gun-boat *Star.*

The *Quaker City* has been constantly under steam for 48 days, (having been among the first of the blockade fleet,) and during this time has rendered active and efficient service.

The *Quaker City* comes home by order of the Government, and will return to her station in four or five days. She brings to New-York the valuable lenses of the Cape Henry light-house, captured by the *Quaker City*, which the Secessionists had taken down, and were attempting to remove.

List of officers.—Commander, Overton Carr, U. S. N; Master, Thos. W. Wilson; Acting-Master, S. W. Mather; Surgeon, Dr. E. B. Dalton; Purser, H. J. Bulley; Chief Engineer, Solon Farrer; First Assistant Engineer, Wm. D. Pendleton; Second Assistant Engineer George Farrer; Third Assistant Engineer, William E. Moore.

PROCEEDINGS OF THE WHEELING CONVENTION.

WHEELING, Va., Friday, June 14.

In the Convention, to-day, Mr. CARLILE, from the Committee on Business, reported an ordinance vacating the seats of all the State officers now in rebellion against the United States; providing for a Provisional Government and for the election of officers; also providing that the State, county and municipal officers immediately take the oath of allegiance to the United States. The ordinance was made the special order for Wednesday next.

In the afternoon a spirited debate ensued on the declaration reported yesterday. Mr. DORSEY, of Monongalia, took strong ground for an immediate division of the State.

Mr. CARLILE took the ground that Congress, at the coming session, would not be likely to recognize the division, which recognition is necessary, until the rebellion in the Southern States is put down, the object of Congress being to restore every original State to the Union. This done, Congress would recognize the Provisional Legislature, and with the consent of the Legislature and Congress, separation could be effected at an early day.

Five hundred stand of arms, and a loan from Massachusetts, arrived here to-day, for distribution to the Home Guards in this and the adjoining counties. More are expected to-morrow.

INTERESTING FROM NORFOLK.

PHILADELPHIA, Friday, June 14.

A refugee from Norfolk brings a copy of the *Transcript* of the 25th, containing the names of the men who voted for the Union ticket, notwithstanding the threats of assassination.

He says the *Merrimac* was just afloat when he left, and he ridicules the idea of her being used for offensive purposes. No other vessel was raised.

IMPORTANT FROM CAIRO.

THE OPERATIONS OF GEN. PRENTISS.

Correspondence of the New-York Times.

CAMP DEFIANCE, CAIRO, Sunday, June 9, 1861.

"NEUTRALITY" IN KENTUCKY.

Last evening, Gen. PRENTISS was honored by a communication from another of those patriotic sons of Kentucky, who are so eager to protect her "sacred soil" from pollution by the presence of the lawful troops of the Government to which her citizens owe paramount allegiance, while they tolerate so amiably the invasion and occupancy of armed traitors, avowedly nursing disloyal sentiments and inaugurating enterprises whose fit punishment is the gallows. In this case, however, the fool so palpably predominates over the hypocrite, that the latter gravitates into the realm of the ridiculous. A doctor in Paducah, to whom Gov. MAGOFFIN once wrote a letter concerning a Mass meeting to be held in his neighborhood, has succeeded, through a miraculous elasticity of logic, in so extending his "little brief authority," as to furnish him a warrant for controlling the movements of the army of the United States.

The letter, with Gen. PRENTISS' reply, so well illustrates the folly of those instruments employed by rebellion, and the practical good sense with which their impertinences are met, that I subjoin both.

PADUCAH, Ky., Saturday, June 8, 1861.

To Gen. Prentiss, commanding forces at Cairo, Illinois:

SIR: Inclosed please find a copy of my instructions from His Excellency, the Governor of Kentucky, which, among other things, required that I shall restrain any infraction of the attitude of self-defence assumed by the State. Especially you will restrain all movements looking to a disregard of the authority of the State in her sovereign relations.

The immediate occasion of this note is this: I have received positive information that a large body of the troops under your command, with arms in their hands, and under command of United States officers, crossed over from Cairo on Thursday last to disperse a body of unarmed militia, which had assembled for military instruction, in the county of Ballard, agreeably to the laws of this State; that they place guards around the houses and over the persons of our citizens on the march, to prevent intelligence of their approach from being communicated and other steps, all wearing the appearance of hostile intentions.

The Governor and people of Kentucky had hoped that after the declaration of their neutrality they would have been left free from menace or threat, to solve for themselves the momentous questions which so imminently threaten the peace of the State, and which in other States has resulted in the overthrow of the civil and the substitution of the military authority, and carrying in their train of evils bloodshed and anarchy.

I shall hope to hear from you by the return of Lieut. GERARD, the bearer hereof.

I have the honor to be, &c., &c.,

JNO. M. JOHNSON.

The following is a copy of the instructions of Gov. MAGOFFIN to Dr. JOHNSON, to which he refers in the above letter.

[COPY]

COMMONWEALTH OF KENTUCKY, EXECUTIVE DEPARTMENT, May 2, 1861.

DEAR SIR: Rumors have reached me to the effect that a mass meeting of the Southern portion of the State will be held at Mayfield on Monday next, the 27th inst., and apprehending that measures may be taken detrimental to the domestic peace of this State, you are requested to attend its session, and lay before the citizens assembled there my proclamation of the 20th May, and enjoin upon them a true and sincere observance of its recommendations. You will please exert your utmost influence to induce, upon the part of those citizens and others in that region of the State, a respect for the position held by Kentucky, as set out in that proclamation, and to restrain from any infraction of the attitude of self defence as assumed by the State. Especially you will restrain all movements looking to a disregard of the authority of the State in her sovereign relations. Report to me what you do in the premises. Respectfully yours,

(Signed) B. MAGOFFIN.

To Dr. JNO. M. JOHNSON.

To these State Sovereignty documents, Gen. PRENTISS returned the following pointed reply:

HEADQUARTERS FIRST BRIGADE ILL. VOLUNTEERS, CAMP DEFIANCE, CAIRO, June 8, 1861.

To Dr. J. M. Johnson:

SIR: I received your letter of this date, and have read it carefully. Permit me to say that *I hold myself responsible to my Government for my official acts.*

Trusting you will assure Union citizens of Kentucky that I am ready to render aid to them at all times when solicited, and believing that my Government will approve of my course in this, I remain,

Yours respectfully, B. M. PRENTISS, Brig.-Gen. First Brig. Ill. Volunteers.

OCCUPATION OF MOUND CITY.

Last evening a deputation of citizens of Mound City, a few miles above Cairo, on the Ohio, visited Gen. PRENTISS, and stated that a plan had been revealed, by which the rebels intended to make a night raid on the town, destroying the Marine Railway there, and a foundry capable of being used, if needed, for Government purposes. To guard against any such contingency ten companies from Col. COOK'S Regiment were sent up to-day, under command of Capt. JOSLYN, to occupy the point.

There was a dispatch received to-day, from St. Louis, to the effect that JEFF. THOMPSON would arrive here on the *Meteor* steamer. An examination was instituted, on the arrival of the *Meteor*, but the disunion ex-Mayor of St. Joseph proved to be *non est.*

Since the stoppage of the mails South, we get news from that quarter with more difficulty. Appearances indicate that all eyes are turned on Virginia, except so far as defence is undertaken against a threatened attack from Cairo. ZOUAVE.

CAMP DEFIANCE, CAIRO, Tuesday, June 11, 1861.

CAPTURE OF SECESSIONISTS.

Gen. PRENTISS receives from citizens of Missouri and Kentucky, almost daily, applications for protection from the persecution of Disunionists. On one of these applications from Missouri, he has recently acted. It became apparent to him, from testimony, that companies of men, in neighborhoods not remote from this place, were perfecting military organizations for traitorous purposes, and were driving out such loyal citizens as were opposed to their proceedings. The precise settlement implicated, is one located near the Missouri River, about ten miles below Cairo, and rejoices in the euphonious appellation of Rush Ridge.

Accordingly, about 12 o'clock night before last, a hundred and fifty men from Col. SHUTTNER'S German Regiment, at Bird's Point, were detailed under command of Capt. HASSFURTHER, to proceed to the suspicious locality, under guidance of one of its citizens, and make certain arrests. This duty they discharged efficiently, and returned, yesterday, about 2 o'clock P. M., having in custody eighteen *suspects*, whom they delivered over to the General for examination. The men were the ordinary class of Missouri farmers and white laborers, with the exception of one man, a Scotch schoolmaster, whom the evidence subsequently given, proved to have acted as a sort of leader in the whole disloyal business.

The men did not appear at all pleased with the attentions of the "d——d Dutch," and were evidently glad to be brought over to Gen. PRENTISS' quarters, where they arrived about sunset, and after eating supper, which was supplied them at the St. Charles, were placed upon an examination with a view of determining their immediate destiny.

This examination proved to be more interesting than I had expected. It was conducted with mingled kindness and severity by Gen. PRENTISS, and served to expose the secret working of the secession mind in border neighborhoods. It seems that a self defensive military company had been organized some time since; but upon the news of the capture of Camp

[Continued on Eighth Page.]

Battle of Boonville

Harper's Ferry

The New-York Times.

VOL. X....NO. 3041. NEW-YORK, THURSDAY, JUNE 20, 1861. PRICE TWO CENTS.

HIGHLY IMPORTANT NEWS.

The Particulars of the Battle of Booneville, Mo.

Brilliant Ruse de Guerre of General Lyon.

UTTER ROUT OF THE REBEL FORCES

IGNOMINIOUS FLIGHT OF GOV. JACKSON.

IMPORTANT FROM WESTERN VIRGINIA.

Another Fight at Phillippa Expected.

Threatening Demonstrations on the Line of the Baltimore and Ohio Railroad.

A New Governor Nominated by the Wheeling Convention.

Position of the Federal Column Under Col. Stone.

Unsuccessful Attempt of the Rebels to Cross the Potomac.

The Result of the Reconnoissance from Fortress Monroe,

SPECIAL DISPATCH FROM WASHINGTON.

WASHINGTON, Wednesday, June 19.

Lieut. WOOLLEY, of the Twenty-fifth New-York, died at the encampment of that regiment this afternoon at 4 o'clock. He was a Supervisor of Albany City. His body will be sent home for interment.

The reported return of a regiment of the rebels to Harper's Ferry on Monday was true. They came back for some mechanics proficient in rifle making. Having impressed as many of these mechanics as they could find, the regiment retreated with them under a guard.

SUPPLIES FOR THE REBELS.

It is ascertained that the rebels have lines of communication across the Potomac from Budd's Ferry down. Small boats are used in the night, which are concealed in the bushes by day, and thus avoid the observation of our cruisers. Only letters and newspapers are conveyed thus, the supplies of provisions going in through Kentucky and Tennessee, instead of *via* Baltimore and Frederick, as heretofore.

A broker in Baltimore lately took $10,000 in Virginia money to Richmond, and obtained a draft on New York for the amount at seven and one-half per cent. Why was this done? Can your brokers explain?

The Fourth Pennsylvania Regiment have crossed the river with wagons, &c., to take position on the Virginia side toward Vienna.

JOHN H. SMITH, who refused to take the oath at the Treasury Department, was yesterday removed.

Col. STONE's command is still occupied in guarding the Maryland bank of the Potomac, the ferries opposite Leesburgh, and ten miles further up the river.

THE REBELS IN WESTERN VIRGINIA.

From Romney Col. WALLACE reports that the rebels retreated summarily to Winchester, and that he secured and brought their tents to Cumberland Camp. The rout of the Disunionists at Romney was total. Several funerals took place in the town next day. One of the rebel Captains was killed, and one Major was taken prisoner, and a member of the Virginia Legislature.

At Alexandria, business is entirely at a stand-still, and the town, ordinarily sufficiently dull, is now positively stupid in its appearance. The police arrangements have been transferred to a detachment from the Massachusetts Fifth, and general good order prevails among the inhabitants, most of whom are sulky and uncommunicative. However, there is one shop there, a saddlery and leather establishment, the only one in the town where such articles can be had at all, the proprietor of which has repeatedly refused to furnish a belt or strap, or to do any repairs for the Federal troops.

The rebel forces are to-day reported to have left Fairfax.

The First and Second Ohio Regiments have fallen back to a point along the railroad near Ball's Cross-roads. Two of the Connecticut regiments are stationed further up on the road towards Fairfax, and pickets are thrown out on both sides. Our troops now line the way from Alexandria and for several miles southwest.

The Twenty-first Regiment, from Elmira, N. Y., came in this afternoon at 3 o'clock.

ANOTHER BRIGADIER-GENERAL.

Senator LANE, of Kansas, has been appointed Brigadier-General in the regular army. He leaves for Kansas at once to organize his brigade, two regiments of which will remain in Kansas—three others to be stationed in Northwestern Missouri, to look after the Secessionists in that region.

A MERITED PROMOTION.

Capt. CHARLES G. HALPINE, of the *Leader*, has been promoted to the rank of Assistant Adjutant-General of Col. HUNTER's Brigade.

ADVANCE OF THE FEDERAL LINES.

Gen. McDOWELL's line has advanced about four miles towards Fairfax, occupying strong positions. At latest accounts, the eleven hundred troops who made the assault at Vienna had fallen back upon Centreville. It is stated that no rebel troops are to be seen in or around Fairfax Court-house. They have all fallen back to join BEAUREGARD's forces, evidently at Manassas junction.

THE HARPERS FERRY REBELS.

The rumors that Gen. JOHNSTON's forces, which retreated from Harper's Ferry, had turned with a view to attack a wing of our army, are false. He is reported at Martinsburgh, *en route* to Winchester, with his entire force, still retreating. His retrograde movement, if it were originally intended as strategic, has proved a failure. LEO.

DISPATCH TO THE ASSOCIATED PRESS.

WASHINGTON, Wednesday, June 19.

Some time ago application was made to the Secretary of War to obtain the admission, duty free, of drillings imported for the use of the Cadets of the United States Military Academy, and was refused by him, on the ground that the policy of the Government should at all times be to prefer domestic manufactures in all instances of purchases for the public service, and to resort to foreign markets for such articles only as cannot be obtained in this country. By the following, it will be seen that the Secretary of War has pursued a similar course in reference to a recommendation of the Engineer Department for the admission free of duty of 250 tons of gas-coking coal and 23 tons of cannel coal, imported for the use of the Military Academy. The Secretary of War cannot countenance this importation of coal by approving of this recommendation. A better article of coal, of all kinds, can be secured in this country than can be brought from Europe, and it is deemed due the great industrial interests of the country that the Government should foster and encourage its own resources instead of those of foreign countries.

Among other rumors which have found their way into the Press is that the Ohioans took the enemy's masked battery at Vienna.

Equally untrue is the report that the Federal troops have taken quiet possession of Fairfax Court-house.

There is official authority for both these denials.

The two Pennsylvania regiments which arrived yesterday were, this morning, reviewed by the President and Secretary of War.

The Rhode Island regiment have returned to their camp near Washington.

The *Star* says: "There is reason to believe that the lines of the disunion troops extend from the neighborhood of Occoquan, as far as Centreville, and that they are intrenching with heavy guns in the neighborhood of Fairfax Station, 3½ miles from Fairfax Court house and 14 miles from Alexandria. It is supposed they may purpose an extension of their forces up along the line of the Orange and Alexandria Railroad, now rebuilding, with the view of attacking the Zouaves who are guarding the repaired bridges this side. All the indications go to show that the disunion troops are being pushed forward from Manassas Junction, by daily installments, to points nearer the Federal lines."

Speaker ALLEN and Hon. ALBERT G. PORTER have succeeded in procuring a requisition for four additional three-years' regiments from Indiana, to be raised in the southern part of that State. It is said that companies almost enough to complete them are already raised. Thus Indiana will have 25 regiments. This will entitle them to a Major-General, in which case Brig.-Gen. MORRIS, now serving so gallantly with the three-months' volunteers, will probably be appointed to that position.

The War Department has also accepted, or authorized to be raised, four additional regiments from Wisconsin, and the same number from Iowa, one of those from the latter State to be cavalry; all the others infantry.

The two companies of the New-York Seventy-first Regiment, who went to Port Tobacco, Md., several days ago, have returned to Washington. Although they were unsuccessful in their search for concealed arms, &c., they obtained much valuable information for the Government.

The opinion is that the military company who had been drilling weekly in that neighborhood, have gone to the relief of the Secessionists at Aquia Creek. It seems that Port Tobacco has been a head-quarters for such recruits.

The *Mount Vernon* received orders to-day to get immediately under weigh for some point down the river, and amply manned and munitioned, departed.

It is evident that the Secessionists intend to interfere with the navigation of the Potomac by erecting batteries on its banks.

The announcement is officially made to-day that the President, in consequence of the pressure of public business, is obliged to decline receiving any visitors from this time until the opening of the session of Congress.

JOHN BRADSHAW, of Indianapolis, has been appointed a Brigade Quartermaster.

The Douglas Monument Committee met to-day, Hon. JOHN B. HASKIN in the Chair.

Present, JOHN F. ENNIS, J. J. McELHONE, GEO. W. McLEAN, THOS. C. FIELDS, and ANDREW M SADLADE.

They reported that Col. JOHN W. FORNEY would deliver an eulogy, and Prof. HENRY, of the Smithsonian Institution had kindly proffered the use of the lecture-room of the Institution, of which Judge DOUGLAS was one of the Regents, for the delivery of the eulogy on the 3d of July. Prof. HENRY was selected to preside. The Committee had under consideration the use to which the Douglass fund should be appropriated, but owing to a large number of communications upon that subject being laid before them, it came to no final conclusion.

The following resolutions, proposed by THOMAS C. FIELDS, of New-York, were adopted:

1. *Resolved*, That an address to the citizens of the United States be prepared and published, setting forth the objects of this Committee.

2. *Resolved*, That the President appoint an Auxiliary Committee for each State, to consist of not more than eleven, nor less than three members; such Committees to report to this Committee.

3. *Resolved*, It is recommended that the friends of the late Senator DOUGLAS, without distinction of party, assemble in their respective towns, cities and villages, on the evening of the 3d of July next, for the purpose of forming Relief and Monument Associations for their several localities, when donations and subscriptions will be received and forwarded to the Treasurer hereafter to be appointed.

The friendly aid of the ladies of the United States is requested. The Auxiliary Committees will be announced Friday evening next, to which time the Committee adjourned.

Two hundred recruits for the First German Rifle Regiment of New-York arrived to-day, thus filling the regiment, which will be supplied with new Enfield rifles, recently imported.

The Twenty-first Regiment (Buffalo, N. Y.) arrived this afternoon.

The Twenty-fourth and Twenty-sixth Pennsylvania and the First Massachusetts Regiments, which reached here yesterday, went into camp this afternoon, the last to guard the approaches to Chain Bridge, above Georgetown.

The Federal forces in Virginia, under Gen. McDOWELL, have advanced their position four miles to-day in the direction of Fairfax Court-house. The pickets on each side are almost within hailing distance.

THE VIRGINIA SIDE OF THE POTOMAC.

MOVEMENTS OF THE SIXTY-NINTH REGIMENT—THE RAILROAD TO VIENNA—BOGUS UNIONISTS—GRAND PARADE ON THE RACE COURSE—IMPORTANT ARRESTS—THE UNFORTUNATE AFFAIR AT VIENNA, ETC.

Correspondence of the New-York Times.

CAMP LINCOLN, ARLINGTON HEIGHTS, VIRGINIA, Tuesday, June 18, 1861.

Last Sunday, while on dress parade, the Sixty-ninth New-York Regiment was stampeded to some purpose. Orders came about 2 o'clock P. M. for the whole regiment to prepare for instant action, and take up its line of march to this point, where the railroad track is crossed by the turnpike road to Fairfax Court-house. Forty rounds of ammunition per man and two days' rations were to accompany us, the orders being to support the Connecticut regiment under Gen. TYLER, which had been fired upon while going up the railroad towards Vienna.

Five minutes after receiving the telegraphic message from Gen. McDOWELL, Col. HUNTER and Staff were in motion towards the scene of supposed danger,—the famous Company B, Second U. S. Cavalry, under Lieut. TOMPKINS, clattering hard behind us,—each soldier with his carbine in his right hand, to shoot down any skirmishers who might try to pick us off from the thick woods on either hand; and each officer with his revolvers lying loose in the holsters before him.

But all was quiet on our arrival, except a stray shot to the left just as we neared the railroad track; and from inquiries made in the neighborhood, it soon became clear that the Connecticut regiment, which we had been sent forward to support, had already returned safely along the line and over the newly-reconstructed bridges, (supposed to have been reburned,) about half an hour before our arrival.

As an illustration of how little the people of this region can be believed, I may mention that, while making a brief excursion in company with Lieut. SAMUEL W. STOCKTON, of the First Cavalry, we called at the house of a man named FERAS, about half or three-quarters of a mile up the Fairfax Road, in advance of where our cavalry were stationed. He received us with great cordiality, inviting us to enter, offering the hospitalities of his house, and sending out his children to play with us. He talked "Union" somewhat too strong for both our stomachs, assuring us that "all the men round there were unconditional Unionists," and so forth—the fact being well known that his wife, who had retired at our approach up the lawn, is one of the bitterest Secessionists in the country. On leaving, we mutually remarked that he "Talked twice two sweet to be honest," and to-day he is a prisoner in the guard-house of Fort Corcoran, on incontestible evidence proving him to be a First Lieutenant in the secession cavalry. Let me add that Lieut. S. W. STOCKTON is nephew and newly-appointed Aid to Col. HUNTER, commanding this brigade, the Aid previously appointed having been promoted to be Assistant Adjutant General of the brigade, with the rank of Captain.

Finding all quiet at the railroad crossing, and sending details of ten men each to see that the track was clear up and down the line, and the bridges in good order, Col. HUNTER awaited the arrival of the Sixty-ninth, nor had he long to wait. In less than half an hour after our arrival, we heard sweeping over the hills behind us, a mighty chorus of about 1,300 voices chanting the "Star-Spangled Banner," and this, although the men had been advancing nearly four miles, with full accoutrements, blankets, and forty rounds of ammunition per man. It was a sublime spectacle as the heads of the column debouched through the deep-cut road leading over the brow of the hill; and never shall I forget the excited faces and flashing eyes of the men as Col. HUNTER rode up to halt them where they were, and advance two companies down the road to support the cavalry if necessary. Nine cheers and a "tiger" were given for the Colonel as he rode up, the unearthly clamor startling our horses and backing them down the hill almost on their haunches. But such blank faces as came, when the Colonel announced to Col. CORCORAN that all was quiet and no present chance of any engagement! It was really a curious and amazing spectacle,—the men dropping their jaws, their faces losing the flush, their eyes resuming a natural expression, and the fatigue, which they had not previously felt, instantly beginning to tell on them. But there was no help for it; and so, leaving the Engineer Company under Capt. QUINLAN and the "Faugh a Ballaghs," under Capt. PATRICK KELLY, to support the dragoons, the balance of the regiment and Col. HUNTER returned to Fort Corcoran for the night,—Lieut. STOCKTON remaining as a volunteer with Lieut. TOMPKINS and the cavalry.

Yesterday a grand parade was ordered at the Race Course near the Long Bridge, the Thirteenth and Sixty-ninth New York form this Brigade, and the Connecticut and New-Jersey Regiments forming in review before Secretary of War CAMERON and Gen. RUNYON, of New-Jersey. On the ground I noticed THURLOW WEED and Senator ABEL, of New-York, several members of the Cabinet, and many of the foreign Ministers,—Lord LYONS not included, perhaps because he knows himself to occupy a suspected and doubtful position. There were about six thousand men under arms; and Gen. McDOWELL used the significant phrase when the review was over: "Thank Heaven! this ends the show part of our duties. We must buckle down to business now." Fort Corcoran is to be much more heavily armed than was at first supposed, our battery consisting of sixteen sixty-four-pounder Columbiads and four twenty-four-pounder howitzers. Four of the latter are in place and seven of the former—the old hills round this neighborhood shaking yesterday when the first sixty-four-pounder gave out its deep voice for the Union.

But while the parade was in progress some important steps were made at the railroad crossing. The Engineers arrested one prisoner, and fired at an armed man, who escaped by plunging into the woods; while the other company arrested a Captain and four troopers of the secession army, Lieut. FERAS amongst the number; also obtaining the full muster-roll of the troop, and seizing a whole pile of valuable secession papers. The prisoners are now in Fort Corcoran, and the papers in the War Department—Lieut. TOMPKINS and his men having the muster-roll, and scouring the country now, while I write, to seize every man whose name appears thereon.

All during the day, however, rumors had been afloat that the Ohio troops, under Col. McCOOKS, had been heavily attacked while proceeding to Vienna; and about 12 o'clock last night orders came from Gen. McDOWELL to send four companies of the Sixty-ninth, supported by "Company B," Second Dragoons, to extricate the Ohio men out of their difficulty. Just as these companies were forming outside the fort, on the Fairfax road—Col CORCORAN in command, and carrying with him one of the 24-pound howitzers—three cavalry men dashed up with news that the "Cleveland Greys," a company of the Ohio Regiment, had been torn to pieces by a discharge of grape-shot, while passing in the railroad car, and that 1,500 rebel soldiers were between McCOOKS and a return to the main body of our Division. On this, Col. CORCORAN added another company to his command, and started at once for the scene of action—where everything was profoundly quiet in our immediate neighborhood, but where the wounded men, being carried back, showed us that this, at least, was not a false alarm.

At daybreak this morning, Gen. McDOWELL sent orders to have the balance of the Sixty-ninth advance to support their Colonel,—though all is quiet on the railroad at last advices,—Fort Corcoran meanwhile being garrisoned by one company of the Sixty-ninth, one company of artillery (regular service) and two companies of the Thirteenth New-York. Col. HUNTER has also received orders to hold himself in readiness to advance with the Thirteenth at any moment,—the Twenty-eighth New-York, forming the third regiment of this Brigade, seeming to be considered more an ornament than for use and taking no part in any of the demonstrations. We expect hot work and plenty of it before nightfall; but again the cowards who fired on a railroad train with grapeshot and then fled may keep at a safe distance. Father MOONEY, who has just come in, tells me that the wounded of the Ohio men this morning presented a fearful spectacle, while the amputations and other operations necessary were being performed. No men of the Sixty-ninth are yet reported hurt, but I will try and send you a postscript from their camp this afternoon, the chances seeming to be, in the judgment of those who should know, that the rebels will now fall back on Fairfax Court-house, and make a stand there in force. If so, they can hardly hold the place long, as our men are eager for the attack, in strong force, and the place was not fortified with any strength at last reports. It is hard to collect one's thoughts in such a whirl of business and excitement—this letter having been twice interrupted since its commencement to examine prisoners in two cases and administer the oath of allegiance, with due caution as to the "instant halter" penalty in case of any violation.

But is it not something like madness to send troops by railroad through an enemy's country? If the rebels want to stop them in force, it can be done by felling a single tree, or rolling a stone across the track; while with the men packed in open cars, and unable to defend themselves, they can be fired at securely from the woods on either hand, and the shooters make their escape easily before the train can be stopped, and a company of skirmishers put in motion. The better opinion seems to be that we are in for a guerilla warfare, in which case all the regiments forming the main body of the army should march on foot, with flank companies thrown out to skirmish in advance, and to right and left. Col. McCOOKS, of the Ohio Regiment is said to be a brave but impulsive officer, who acted wholly on his own discretion in going on so far as Vienna, his orders having simply been to guard the railroad bridges within two or three miles of that city. I have heard this moment, from Lieut.-Col NUGENT, who has just returned, that all is quiet around the Sixty-ninth, and that the battery which fired into the Ohio Regiment, yesterday, has been withdrawn and cannot anywhere be found by our troops, who are scouring the whole neighborhood. Col. NUGENT says that there were two charges of grape fired into the Ohio men while on the cars, killing four and wounding seven; and that another discharge took place while the Ohioans were picking up their wounded. McCOOKS had with him when fired upon, only two hundred and fifty of his men, the rest being scattered along the line at the various bridges. There are now four thousand three hundred of the Union soldiers on the road, with Company B, Second Cavalry, and we all expect orders to march forward this afternoon towards Vienna, whither the fifteen hundred rebels are said to have retreated. The force consists of the First and Second Ohio, First Connecticut and Sixty-ninth New-York. Col. HUNTER, with the Thirteenth, starts in half an hour to join the advance. Last accounts report the enemy fortifying Vienna, and making full preparations to give us a warm reception. My correspondence after this may become irregular, if our mail facilities are not kept up; but I will write whenever possible. H.

IMPORTANT FROM MISSOURI.

THE SLAUGHTER OF REBELS AT BOONEVILLE.

ST. LOUIS, Tuesday, June 18.

The *Democrat* has just received the following dispatch from Jefferson City. Mr. GORDON, of St. Louis, and other gentlemen from above give the following account of the battle of Booneville:

Gen. LYON landed four miles below Booneville, and opened a heavy cannonade against the rebels, who retreated and dispersed into the adjacent wood, whence, hidden by brushes and trees, they opened a brisk fire on our troops. Gen. LYON then ordered a hasty retreat to the boats, and the rebels, encouraged by this movement, rallied and followed the troops into a wheat field. Gen. LYON halted, faced his troops about, and bringing the whole force of his artillery to bear, opened a murderous fire on the rebels, *three hundred* of whom were killed, and the balance fled in all directions, leaving their arms on the field. Gen. LYON then moved forward and took possession of Booneville.

Gen. PRICE was taken with violent diarrhœa at the beginning of the battle, and was taken on a steamer and carried to his home in Charaton.

Gov. JACKSON viewed the battle from a distant hill, and fled for parts unknown after the defeat of his forces.

There is great rejoicing among the Union men here, and the Stars and Stripes are hoisted on the Capitol, guns are fired and the Star-Spangled banner was played by regimental bands.

Scouting parties will be sent out in all directions to-morrow, to cut off the retreat of the rebels.

The steamer *J. C. Swan* has arrived with two cannon, ammunition and artillery men, which have been planted at Col. BORNSTEIN's head-quarters.

JOHN FITZPATRICK, one of the most violent Secessionists of the State, took the oath of allegiance to the United States Government in the presence of all the officers here to day.

REPORTS FROM JEFFERSON CITY.

JEFFERSON CITY, Wednesday, June 19.

People living near Syracuse have arrived to-day, saying that 600 State troops retreating from Booneville, with 6 cannon, reached Syracuse yesterday. They said they were going to draft men from the neighborhood and would take at least every one who could furnish a horse. Various reports as to the number of killed were in vogue. The probabilities are that about 150 were killed. There is no possible doubt that a battle was fought, and the State forces completely routed, but the telegraph being out of order between here and Booneville, we cannot get entirely authentic accounts of the affair.

BRIG.-GEN. LYON.

Brig.-Gen. NATHANIEL LYON, whose brilliant exploit at Booneville is now the theme of every tongue, is a native of Connecticut, having been born near the birthplace of Hon. GIDEON WELLES, Secretary of the Navy. He graduated with honors at the West Point Academy, and entered the regular army as a Second-Lieutenant in the Second Infantry, his first commission bearing date on the 1st July, 1841. He was promoted to a Brevet First-Lieutenancy shortly afterward, subsequently to a Captaincy. He has occupied the latter rank practically since the 11th of June, 1851, and was booked for advancement to a higher position at the first opportunity, he being entitled to that title by brevet, before his recent appointments to a Lieutenant-Colonelcy and a Brigadier Generalship.

AFFAIRS IN WESTERN VIRGINIA.

OPERATIONS OF THE REBEL FORCES.

GRAFTON, Wednesday, June 19.

Information thought to be reliable says that 1,500 Confederate troops are in the neighborhood of Beverly and Phillippa, and that an attack will be made on the latter place; there is no doubt but the rebels in Western Virginia have been largely reinforced, and soon a grand movement is contemplated.

The Federal troops will be equal to the emergency. Large reinforcements will probably reach here in a few days.

A force sufficient to guard the Cheat River Bridge has been sent forward from here.

The rebel forces from Romney burned the railroad bridge over New-Creek, twenty miles west of Cumberland, early this morning, and marched on to Piedmont, which place they now hold.

The telegraph wires east of Piedmont were cut by them.

Their number is variously estimated at from 2,000 to 4,000.

Notice was given of their approach to the town, and the citizens were preparing to leave when our informant left.

All the engines belonging to the Baltimore and Ohio Railroad, were fired up and sent West, to Grafton, and the greatest excitement prevailed.

A company of citizen-soldiers, who were guarding the bridge, are reported to have retreated on the approach of the rebels.

The Piedmont telegraph operator closed the office and fled, and we have no means of ascertaining what damage is being done. Communication by railroad, between Cumberland and this place, is now cut off.

PROCEEDINGS OF THE WHEELING CONVENTION.

WHEELING, Va., Wednesday, June 19.

The time of the Convention was occupied to-day with a debate on the ordinance for reorganizing the State Government.

Mr. WEST, of Wetzel, offered an amendment, that no one who voted for secession be allowed to hold office in the State during the war.

This was supported by Mr. WEST and his colleague, Mr. MARTIN, who, among other statements, said that the Secessionists in his County were in the habit of taking the oath of allegiance and afterwards repudiating it. There was no confidence in the oath of men, who had to learn to disregard an oath to be good Secessionists.

The amendment was lost—Ayes, 10; Nays, 66.

The ordinance was finally passed—73 to 3.

The ordinance provides for the entire reorganization of the State Government; every officer to be obliged to swear allegiance anew to the United States, and repudiate the Richmond Convention.

The Convention will now proceed to choose a Governor and Council. A new State seal and other emblems of authority had been ordered.

WHEELING, Va., Wednesday, June 19—P. M.

FRANK PIERPONT, of Marion County, was unanimously nominated for Governor by the Convention in caucus to day.

WHEREABOUTS OF COL. STONE.

WASHINGTON, Wednesday, June 19.

Accounts of an entirely reliable character this morning, received from Poolsville, dated 9 o'clock last night, say that Col. STONE is still there, and not at Leesburgh, as has heretofore been frequently reported.

Yesterday afternoon, the enemy attempted to make a crossing at Goose Creek, having arrived opposite Edwards' Ferry in force, estimated by officers in command of the guard there at from eight to nine hundred men. They made use of a ferry-boat which they had withdrawn from the Potomac River. Col. STONE had given orders, as he himself communicates, that if any attempt was made to move the boat a fire should be opened on it.

In compliance with these orders, Lieutenant HASBRUCK fired from his 12-pounder field howitzer a spherical case shot, which burst directly in range, and covered the boat with a shower of bullets and fragments. The effect was excellent. The horse of a mounted officer leaped overboard, and the boat was rapidly drawn back to shore. The enemy then formed in line along the crest of the bank, and commenced firing, but a few well-directed spherical case shots dispersed them, and sent them flying towards Leesburgh.

IMPORTANT FROM FORT MONROE.

RECONNOISSANCES TOWARDS GREAT BETHEL.

FORTRESS MONROE, Tuesday, June 18, *via* BALTIMORE, Wednesday, June 19.

During the last two nights important reconnoissances have been made from Fortress Monroe and Newport's News, in the direction of Great Bethel. Last night a strong detachment was at New-Market bridge. The region about the mouth of Back River has also been examined by scouts.

Lieut. BUTLER and Mr. WINTHROP yesterday visited Great Bethel with a flag of truce, for the body of the lamented Major WINTHROP. The mission was entirely successful. The party were kept waiting at a distance from the fortification until the body could be procured. They were most courteously treated by the Confederate Officers, and Gen. MAGRUDER sent his compliments to Gen. BUTLER.

No information was obtained relative to the force at Great Bethel.

According to the latest accounts there were five Regiments at Yorktown.

Major WINTHROP's body is now being conveyed to the Baltimore boat, and will be taken to Boston.

S. G. GILLIES, of Col. McCHESNEY's Regiment, was buried to-day. He was accidentally shot while on guard by the sentinel nearest to him.

Col. McCHESNEY has resigned his command on account of illness, and returned to New-York.

Gen. BUTLER is on the Rip Raps to-day, experimenting with a rifled gun.

FROM ANOTHER CORRESPONDENT.

FORTRESS MONROE, Tuesday, June 18.

The expedition yesterday to enable Capt. SMITH, of the Topographical Engineers, to make a reconnoissance, returned late in te evening, having traveled twenty-five miles. It went to Newmarket Bridge and to Newport's News, then five miles up James River, passed over to the east branch of Buck River, and returned by Newmarket Bridge.

Beside a critical survey of this district, much valuable information was obtained concerning the position, strength and purposes of the enemy, who, in considerable force, occupy the district between Hampton and Buck River, with the evident intention of drawing nearer to Old Point. They are making a survey of the routes and bridges, and it is the opinion of Capt SMITH that their plan is to throw forward bodies of men so as to occupy the district between Hampton and Yorktown.

To-day Capt. SMITH is engaged in reconnoitering between Newmarket Bridge and the east branch of Buck River, with reference to works to check these purposes.

Other reconnoissances will follow, and a complete survey will be obtained of what has become a district of much strategic importance, lying between Hampton and Yorktown.

Nothing is known of the reported concentration of troops above Newport's News. The rumor is doubted. The steamers seen on James River are probably carrying guns to be transported to Yorktown.

Yesterday Lieut. GEORGE H. BUTLER with others proceeded to Big Bethel to bring away the remains of Major WINTHROP. At Little Bethel a picket took their message to Col. MAGRUDER, who sent Capt. KILSEN, of Louisiana, to receive them. Two hours after Col. MAGRUDER came, and they were handsomely received. With Col. MAGRUDER were Col. DE RUSEY, brother of the Chief of the Engineers at Fortress Monroe, Col. HILL, of North Carolina, and other late officers of the army.

None of Lieut. BUTLER's party were permitted to go near the batteries. The body of Major WINTHROP was taken up by Col. MAGRUDER's men, and escorted to the wagon by a force of 300, who fired a volley. Most of them had shot-guns. An escort was offered to Hampton, but Lieut. BUTLER declined it.

Col. MAGRUDER and others spoke in the highest terms of Major WINTHROP's bravery. He was distinctly seen for some time leading a body of men to the charge, and had mounted a log, and was waving his sword and shouting to his men to "Come on!" when a North Carolina drummer-boy borrowed a gun, leaped on the battery, and shot him deliberately in the breast. He fell nearer to the enemy's works than any other man went during the fight.

He wore the sword of Col. WARDROP, of the Massachusetts Third, and it was supposed that it was Col. W. who fell. The sword has been sent to North Carolina as a trophy. It has on it the name of Col. W.

From what he saw and heard, Lieut. BUTLER is convinced that the rebels had not less than ten killed and a large number wounded. Their battery was constructed and served by Maj. RANDOLPH and the battle was fought principally by North Carolina troops.

The Virginia cavalry is spoken as fit only for scouts; two regiments that had been sent for reached Big Bethel from Yorktown just as our forces retreated, having marched fifteen miles in two hours and a half. They were completely exhausted.

The remains of Maj. WINTHROP will leave to-night for New York with an escort.

A second experiment with the Sawyer projectile, from the Rip Raps, was tried to-day. Ten shots were fired, eight of which fell either inside of or a short distance from the rebel battery on Sewall's Point. The firing was witnessed by Gen. BUTLER, Col. DIMMICK, and a large party of gentlemen and ladies, and was regarded as extraordinary, especially as the battery could not be seen at the Rip Raps. The men in the rebel camp were seen from the tug to scatter in all directions.

The *Minnesota*, with the crew of the privateer *Savannah* on board, came into the Roads this morning.

BALTIMORE, Wednesday, June 19.

The Norfolk boat came up with colors at half-mast this morning, in honor of the remains of Major WINTHROP, which were on board.

An officer from Fort Monroe says the trial of rifled cannon at the Rip Raps was highly satisfactory. Many balls went clear over Sewall's Point, and fell into the water between that and Crany Island.

One ball burst over the enemy's works, and produced a sensation. Men could be seen mounting horses and hastening off.

ADVENTURES OF A FLAG OF TRUCE.

PRIVATE LETTER FROM AN OFFICER IN THE FIFTH NEW-YORK ZOUAVES.

CAMP HAMILTON, FORTRESS MONROE, Va., Friday, June 14, 1861.

When you see Mr. and Mrs., and Miss ——, give them, through me, the respects of Col. MAGRUDER, who begged to be particularly remembered to them. The Colonel is commander of the secession forces at Yorktown, and had command of the battery that *slaughtered* our men the other day, and is altogether a big gun among the enemy; so yesterday I drove up to Yorktown and called on him. I was also introduced to several officers and privates of the rebel army, took dinner in the camp near Yorktown, and had a grand time generally. To explain: On Monday, when the awful news came to our camp, I prepared the hospital for the wounded and got everything ready, and when they came, we were all prepared to give them prompt and kind attention; and then I heard the sickening news that, owing to inexcusable negligence, no rear-guard had been appointed to bring away the wounded, and that everybody had been left to shift for himself, and that consequently our wounded men had been left on the field. This so disturbed me that I went to the Colonel, and volunteered to go after them. He consented. I received a detail of men to accompany me, and pull the hand carts, and started about 7 in the evening. At Hampton Creek we had a rough time. Boats were bringing over men as fast as possible, and it was very dark before we got over.

On the other side, much confusion prevailed; men were getting horses and guns over, while cannon was planted so as to command all the streets, to prevent the attack of cavalry, which was momentarily expected. We were told that all the wounded found were brought in, that the enemy were furious, and would slaughter us if they found us. But I knew that two or three of our wounded were left, and started out with a flag of truce. It was, I assure you, very dreary and lonely, as we passed through the deserted streets of Hampton, and out into the quiet country, looking ahead for the first sight of an enemy. At last I heard the tread of a horse, and rode ahead, and gave command to prepare for them. When the [illegible] near enough, I ordered "halt," and asked who was there and where they were going. No answer. I could make out through the gloom of the evening that there was a wagon, containing three or four men in uniform, who sat looking at me, and I at them; and thus we sat for nearly five minutes. It was [illegible] liar," but as I heard no click of a trigger, I remained safe and quiet until my question was answered, and then I discovered it was our chaplain and one or two other chaplains and surgeons, who had been separated from their regiments. They had been bringing the wounded until our men fell back, and the cavalry came out from the battery and pursued them into the wagons containing the wounded and fired at the same time the flag of truce—and they had to run for their lives; they hid in the woods, and after dark managed to escape. They told us the wounded were prisoners and could not be got, and that the bridge over the next creek, a little further on, was torn up, so that we could not cross except by swimming.

I would still have gone, but we could not get the wagons across, and could not certainly have got the wounded, so I turned back with the chaplains, and got home after infinite trouble in crossing the creek.

It was fortunate we were stopped, for the enemy was wild and exasperated, and would have murdered every one of us, without respecting the flag of truce or my mission as surgeon.

But I could not give it up with that; so, yesterday, having obtained permission from Gen. BUTLER, I started with Capt. DAVIES and a private, named SEAMAN, for the wounded, one of whom belonged to Capt. DAVIES' company. We were all on horseback, with a white flag, carried by Capt. DAVIES.

Everybody the night before, and who saw us in the morning, said good-bye to us, for no one expected to see us again. And, as for ourselves, at least myself, I was fully convinced that we would be shot, or if we were only imprisoned we would be lucky. We rode mile after mile without seeing any one, until turning a corner we came plump on a body of cavalry, fifteen or twenty in number; and a brutal-looking set they were. Instantly every revolver was drawn—by them of course—for going with a flag we had no weapons whatever. Capt. DAVIES advanced with the flag, and SEAMAN and I were ordered to halt. Capt. DAVIES gave the leader the order of Gen. BUTLER, who slowly read it, and, when done, he turned his head and spoke a few words to his men, who cocked their revolvers, and two or three with guns cocked them, and held them up at us, ready for action. We were ordered to advance and I assure you it was an intensely interesting moment as we sat there looking into each others eyes—they with hate, we with distrust and suspicion; expecting every moment to hear the command "fire."

My sensations were peculiar, I acknowledge, and not to be envied; for though we had been expecting to be shot by the pickets in the woods at any moment, that would have been sudden, and instantly done with; but now to be bulleted in cold blood was not a cheerful prospect. However, after debating among themselves, we were surrounded by an escort and ordered to advance. At first they were gloomy and silent, but gradually they thawed out, and we were on talking like friends. We now learnt from them that we must go to Yorktown, by order of Col. MAGRUDER that all men *taken* were to be brought to him. We, of course, had to submit, and then began the longest ride on horseback, and the most tiresome of any kind, I ever underwent. In the hot sun on the dusty road, it was bad enough, and we longed to get into the shade; but when we were gratified, we found it was worse than the road. They took us a long detour through the woods, to prevent our seeing batteries and fortifications with which they have *blockaded the road*. There was a path through the woods, but it was rendered impassable by trees felled *across it, ditches dug, &c., &c.*, and we were compelled to plunge through the underbrush and thickets, scratching and tearing ourselves, and nearly ruining our horses. At length we reached the road again, and had ten miles' travel to complete the journey.

We met a good many secession troops, principally cavalry, all desperate looking characters, who looked very black at us, but nothing occurred. We had a particularly narrow escape from being shot, which occurred at a village called Cockleton. When we came near the village we saw a crowd of the inhabitants around the school-house door, talking with the members of a company of infantry, dressed in a remarkably shabby uniform. As soon as our white flag and pantaloons became visible, every man of the company rushed into the school-house for his gun, or crawled around the corner of the house, the others cocked their pieces, and would undoubtedly have fired, if, by so doing, they had not been liable to shoot also their own men. The officer leading us rushed ahead and spoke a few quick words to the Captain of the company, waving at the same time the white flag. The Captain ordered every man to fall into line; no one obeyed; they glared at us, with muskets on their shoulders, waiting for us to come abreast, to fire. The Captain drew his sword, threatened with it each man, and got them into line. "Shoulder arms;" but this they would not do; the butts of the muskets instinctively sought their shoulders; with a gigantic curse, the Captain [illegible] them, and fear brought the muskets into position. After more swearing and howling, he compelled them to order arms, and then our guide gave the word "forward!" and we *rushed* through. We should undoubtedly have been shot by the soldiers or citizens in a dozen places on the road, had it not been for the energetic conduct of the officers who guided us.

About 1 o'clock we arrived within less than a mile of Yorktown, and saw, near by, where CORNWALLIS surrendered, and which is now fortified and defended by the worthy descendants of the Tories of the Revolution.

We were taken into the rebel camp, and then to Col. MAGRUDER. We were introduced to many Colonels, Majors, Captains and privates (the latter wealthy gentlemen of Virginia, owning plantations on the James River.) We were treated very kindly, had a grand dinner and a nap after it, and bottles of wine opened for us.

They kept us, however, till 5 o'clock, probably to prevent our seeing the movements of military, for as we came through those horrible woods again, we caught sight of a huge howitzer, drawn by four horses, just disappearing through the woods. We had a long, fatiguing ride home, where we arrived about [illegible] in the morning. We had to leave our horses at Hampton, we being too weak and they too tired to be got across. You can imagine how tired I was when I tell you that the others, having crossed in a small boat to our side of the creek, which boat they were going to send back to me, I, having charge of the horses, tied them up and fell fast asleep on the grass, though, having no longer the flag of truce, I was liable to be attacked and cut up into hash at any moment. But don't be horrified; I knew there was no chance of any attack, and so slept comfortably and soundly.

The next morning we were great heroes, having done more than any others, been further and got more information.

We had rode sixty miles on horseback, and about ten on foot, from Hampton here, (having lost the way down to camp.)

We found they had buried our dead, and that our wounded had all died and been buried.

So we returned from a hazardous excursion, but one which none of you will say was rash on my part, since it was only my duty—or at least one which the ordinary feelings of humanity would prompt me to perform.

You ask me what position WINTHROP held? He was an Aid to Gen. BUTLER, but was murdered at Bethel on Monday. One of the rebel captains told me how he was shot while gallantly leading his company. A young Louisianian in the battery saw him and said he would shoot him in the breast, pointing at the same time to a place on his own breast where he meant to hit him. He fired and hit within one-eighth of an inch of the spot he said he would. When the villain told me this I had to shut my eyes and turn one side, that he might not see the expression of rage on my face and in my eyes. But WINTHROP will be avenged.

THE BUFFALO REGIMENT.

BALTIMORE, Wednesday, June 19.

The regiment from Buffalo, *via* the Northern Central, passed through for Washington at 10 A. M.

[*For Additional Rebellion News, see Fifth and Eighth Pages.*]

The New-York Times.

VOL. X....NO. 3067. NEW-YORK, MONDAY, JULY 22, 1861. PRICE TWO CENTS.

CRUSHING REBELLION.

The Greatest Battle Ever Fought on this Continent.

The Whole Rebel Army of Manassas Engaged.

FEARFUL CARNAGE ON BOTH SIDES.

Advance of the National Army in Three Columns.

The Enemy's Position Attacked by Flank.

Incessant Roar of Artillery and Rattle of Small Arms.

The Rebels Routed and Driven Behind the Manassas Lines.

The Battle to be Renewed To-Day.

THE PRIVATEERS COMING TO GRIEF

Another Vessel Recaptured and Brought to This Port.

The Commander and His Mates Killed by the Colored Steward.

[illegible] of the Rebel Congress at Richmond.

JEFF. DAVIS' MESSAGE.

TREMENDOUS BATTLE AT BULL'S RUN.

BULL'S [illegible], Sunday, July 21—2 P. M.

The great battle occurred to-day, and the result is not certain at the moment I write. Both sides have fought with terrible tenacity. The battle has been hot and steady for three hours, and the loss must be very heavy—certainly not under one thousand on each side.

The Union Army advanced from Centreville in three columns at 3 o'clock this morning. Col. RICHARDSON commanded the column by the road to Bull's Run, where the action of Thursday took place, and Col. MILES lay on the rear end at Centreville to support him.

Gen. TYLER commanded the centre division, which took the Warrenton Road—Gens. SCHENCK and Col. SHERMAN being in advance. He had the three Connecticut Regiments, two from Michigan, two from Wisconsin, and the Sixty-ninth and Seventy-ninth, from New-York. Gen. McDOWELL, with Col. HUNTER and a very powerful division, went out on this road, which leads directly forward to Manassas, crossing Bull's Run by a stone bridge, which had been mined.

The attack by these two points was intended mainly as a feint. The real attack was by HUNTER, who took a narrow road two miles out leading to the right, having HUNT'S and the Rhode Island batteries, and leaving Col. KEYES on the [illegible] at the crossing of the roads as a reserve. [illegible] were to proceed high up the stream, cut himself a path through the woods, cross over, and turn the position of the rebels on the north.

I went out with the centre column. At ten minutes before six we halted about a mile this side of the position of the rebels. The Sixty-ninth and Seventy-ninth Regiments of New-York were thrown the to right, in the woods, and the First and Second Ohio and the Second New-York to the left in advance.

The thirty-pound Parrott gun was planted in the middle of the road, and at ten minutes past six it threw two shells into the battery of the enemy, but without eliciting any response. Ten minutes after, we heard firing on our left from RICHARDSON'S column, which was continued at intervals for two hours, but without eliciting any reply.

Our column remained silent, firing now and then a gun, and at twenty minutes to eight, AYRES' Battery, formerly SHERMAN'S, fired five or six rounds into the enemy, but without response. At a quarter before nine shots were rapidly exchanged between the opposing skirmishers, and GARDNER, of Lacrosse, belonging to the Rhode Island Regiment, was reported killed.

At about ten o'clock heavy clouds of dust showed that reinforcements were coming up to the rebels from Manassas, and was continued through the next three or four hours.

At 11 o'clock AYRES' Battery went to the front; the Sixty-ninth, New-York, was ordered to deploy into the field in front, and firing was heard from HUNTER'S Division, on the extreme right, far in advance.

The Ohio regiments were pushed forward with the Second New-York, and ran upon a masked battery of four guns, which killed and wounded quite a number of both. Of the latter, MICHAEL McCARTY, Sergeant of Company H, was wounded, and afterwards was reported dead. Lieut. DEMSEY received a slight wound. Some twenty or thirty of the Ohio regiment broke and run, but the rest stood firm, as did the Second New-York.

CARLISLE'S Battery was brought to the front on the right, and soon drove the rebels out of the masked battery.

It was now 11½ o'clock, when HUNTER'S column appeared across the Run, advancing on the flank of the rebels, and the engagement soon became very active in his position. He kept steadily advancing, pouring in a steady fire of artillery and musketry.

The whole Brigade under TYLER was ordered forward to his support. The Sixty-ninth and Seventy-ninth New-York, the First, Second, and Third Connecticut, and the Second Wisconsin were sent in. A constant roll of musketry marked HUNTER'S advance, and the artillery from our column played incessantly on the flank of the rebels. So far as I could see, the latter were pushed backward a considerable distance to the road directly in front of where I stood, across which they charged twice with the bayonet upon our troops, but were repulsed each time. Our men crossed the road and poured in upon them a terrible fire of artillery and musketry.

I write this at 2½ o'clock, and am compelled to close in order to avail myself of a special messenger to Washington. The fight is still going on with great energy. The rebel batteries have again commenced firing upon us, and their balls and shells fall thick upon the road and in the field which I had selected as my observatory.

Gen. SCHENCK and two batteries are ordered up to repulse an attempt of cavalry to outflank us. I shall try to send the result in a later dispatch.

H. J. R.

SPECIAL DISPATCHES FROM WASHINGTON.

WASHINGTON, Sunday, July 21—2 P. M.

Fronting Bull's Run is the main battery of the rebels, flanked on each side by slanting batteries, which protect the entire crossing of the creek. The right battery can be flanked, but the left cannot.

Our troops moved onward last night at 6 o'clock, numbering about forty-five thousand. Gen. PATTERSON'S column is reported moving down the Winchester Road with about fifteen thousand men, and is expected to join to-day. Eleven thousand troops left Alexandria this morning, so that by night we shall have a superior force there, although this morning we stood forty-five thousand against sixty thousand rebels.

What was done last night we do not know positively, but I am just in receipt of a report that a battle was commenced last night, and has continued all day.

The frequent discharge of heavy guns can be heard distinctly at Long Bridge, and this has continued since 6 this morning.

WASHINGTON, Sunday, July 21—5½ P. M.

This morning a general engagement took place along the entire line. After a terrific fight, with great slaughter on both sides, each and every battery was taken.

The fight progressed most fiercely, and the firing only ceased when the rebels were forced within their Manassas lines.

The principal fight took place three and a half miles this side of Manassas. Couriers have been dispatched for further intelligence, and may be expected in very soon.

This news is corroborated by dispatches now before President LINCOLN, Gen. SCOTT and Gen. MANSFIELD. Gen. MANSFIELD says the enemy's guns and equipments are in the hands of our forces.

Now, on to Richmond!

WASHINGTON, Sunday, July 21—8 P. M.

That this city has been in the greatest possible excitement you can well imagine. Bulletins have been received hourly by the President, and at the War Department. Several of them have been made public, being read at the corner of Willard's Hotel to vast crowds, who cheered vehemently, and seemed fairly intoxicated with joy.

Dr. PULLISTON, who has just returned, says that our artillery was played beautifully, and with terrific effect. Very many prominent men were on the field, and others were stationed at a distance of three-quarters of a mile. Senator BIGLER was one of the former.

It seems idle to add anything to the detailed account of Mr. RAYMOND, with the exception of what I learn from official sources. Gen. SCOTT received the following from an official courier:

FAIRFAX C. H., 5½ P. M.

The enemy accepted battle in full force. A great battle was fought and a victory won. The rout of the enemy was complete.

The Fourth Regiment, Pennsylvanians, are on their way from Centreville, their time being up. They had legal a right to leave, but there can be but one opinion as to their courage. Dr. PULLISTON met them on their way hither, and accosting the Major of the Regiment, said. "where are you going?" "Home," replied he—"our time is up." "But didn't they want you to stay?" "Oh, yes, they would have been glad of us, but we have done much hard work, and didn't care to stay." Whereupon the Doctor gave him a good blowing up, and went on.

An eye-witness informs me that members of a regiment on the right made a stampede, bnt were brought up by Col. BLENKER'S regiment, which supported them, and brought them again to order.

The Zouaves, of New-York, were very badly cut up, but behaved with great gallantry, and are spoken of by all as being worthy of the highest praise.

I hope to send later confirmatory news.

WASHINGTON, Sunday, July 21—11½ P. M.

Quartermaster SAMPSON, of the New-York Thirty-first, has just come in. He left Mr. RAYMOND at Fairfax Court-house. Mr. SAMPSON agrees with Dr. RAY, of the Chicago *Tribune*, in the belief that the battle will be renewed to-morrow. Col. HUNTER, who was shot through his cheek, has arrived, and though seriously, is not mortally wounded.

From all accounts it is evident that this has been the greatest battle ever fought on this continent. It has resulted in serious mortality on both sides.

Col. HUNTER'S column did most of the fighting, and suffered very severely. Col. SLOCUM, of the Second Rhode Island, is reported dead.

It would be gratifying to know of the safety of several Senators and hosts of Representatives who were spectators, and who have not been heard from.

HOWARD.

FROM ANOTHER CORRESPONDENT.

WASHINGTON, Sunday, July 21.

An arrival from the battle-field, as late as 5½ o'clock, says that the conflict was being carried on with vigor and success beyond Bull's Run, and three miles in advance of the battle-field of last Thursday. Reports of cannonding were heard here so late as 10 o'clock this evening, and it is supposed that our troops were still engaging the enemy at or near Manassas Junction.

From the thousand and one rumors around the city, it is impossible to send anything reliable. Each man tells a different story, and all profess to have been eye-witnesses to the events they narrate. It is certain, however, that there has been a desperate and destructive fight, and that the contest has been equally stubborn on both sides. The supremacy of the cavalry of the rebels gave them great advantage. They charged repeatedly upon our infantry, and caused great harm. The Fire Zouaves sustained several of these charges, and were finally broken.

It is now 12 o'clock. Mr. RAYMOND has not yet reached Washington.

LEO.

BULLETINS OF THE BATTLE.

WASHINGTON, Sunday, July 21.

The following bulletins were received in official quarters, during the progress of the battle, from the telegraph station about four miles from Bull's Run:

FAIRFAX COURT-HOUSE, Sunday, July 21—11 A. M.

There is rapid firing from heavy guns and frequent discharges of musketry.

11:40.—The fighting is very heavy, and apparently more on our left wing.

11:50.—There is evidently a battle toward our left in the direction of Bull's Run, and a little north. The firing is very rapid and heavy.

1:45.—Heavy guns are heard again, and apparently nearer. The musketry is heavy and nearer.

2 P. M.—The musketry is very heavy and drawing much nearer. There is evidently a movement more to our left.

2:45 P. M.—The firing is a little farther off, and apparently in the direction of the Junction. Less heavy guns and more light artillery, as near as I can judge.

3 P. M.—The firing has ceased ten minutes since.

3:35 P. M.—The firing has almost entirely ceased, and can only be heard with difficulty. I shall telegraph no more unless there should be a renewal of the battle, which has been so gloriously fought for the old Stars and Stripes, and from all indications here our troops have at least stood their ground.

FAIRFAX COURT-HOUSE, Sunday, July 21—3:50 P. M.

Our courier has not yet returned. Quartermaster BARTON, of the Second Regiment of Michigan, has just passed, and says that the officers, men, and citizens at Centreville say a general engagement of the whole line had taken place, three and a half miles this side of Manassas, and that our troops had driven and forced the Secessionist lines back to Manassas. We expect a courier now every moment.

CENTREVILLE, Sunday, July 21—4 P. M.

Gen. McDOWELL has ordered the reserves now here under Col. MILES to advance to the Bridge over Bull's Run, on the Warrenton road, having driven the enemy before him. Col. MILES is now three or four miles from here, directing operations near Blackburn's ford.

FAIRFAX COURT-HOUSE—4:45 P. M.

Two of our couriers have returned, but are unable to communicate in person with Gen. McDOWELL. One of the couriers was on the field of battle. He says our troops have taken three masked batteries, and forced the enemy to fall back and retire. He says the battle was general on Bull's Run for some distance. One of the batteries taken was in a wheat field, and the other some distance from it, and the third still further on.

5.20 P. M.—Another dispatch says that the Nationals have won the day. The loss on both sides is heavy, but the rout of the rebels is complete. The batteries at Bull's Run are silenced, and two or three others taken.

5.45 P. M.—The firing has ceased. We shall send another courier there in a few minutes. The Colonel went at 4 o'clock and will be back soon.

A still later report, not official, but from apparently reliable source, says that the column under Col. HEINTZELMAN has followed the rebels to Manassas Junction, and has opened fire on their entrenched camp, and was then shelling them.

The cannonading can occasionally be heard in Washington from Georgetown Heights.

The head-quarters of the Army is inaccessible to-night, the President and Cabinet being privately with Gen. SCOTT and Staff, and other distinguished gentlemen.

PREPARATIONS FOR THE BATTLE.

CENTREVILLE, Sunday, July 21,
via Fairfax Court House, Sunday, July 21.

We have successfully outflanked the enemy. At 2½ o'clock this morning the various regiments about Centreville were formed for march, and at 3 o'clock they were in motion in the direction of Perryville, leaving Bull's Run to the left. At 6 o'clock the first gun was fired by a thirty-pound rifled cannon, sent ahead to batter the masked batteries that might be encountered on the road. There was no reply from the enemy, and the advance moved on.

At Gen. McDOWELL'S head-quarters, three miles beyond Centreville, the greater part of the army moved to the right, to avoid a bridge some distance beyond, said to have been undermined. They will pass over upon pontoons prepared by Capt. ALEXANDER, of the Engineer Corps, and who has inspected the country minutely in a previous reconnoisance, and to whom, in a great measure, the plan of the campaign is due.

A general battle is expected to-day or to-morrow, and which will probably decide the fate of the whole campaign.

If Gen. JOHNSON has not yet formed a junction with Gen. BEAUREGARD, he will be entirely cut off by this manœuvre. Thrown back upon the mountains, his army will become utterly demoralized, and probably fall into the hands of Gen. McCLELLAN, who is advancing beyond the Blue Ridge. And if he has formed a junction with Gen. BEAUREGARD, it opens our communication with Gen. PATTERSON'S column; and thus reinforced, the National army can crush out opposition.

If we are driven back the army can retreat upon Centreville, and keep open the communication with Washington. If Gen. BEAUREGARD remains where he is, his communications in the rear are endangered, and Manassas Junction being situated in the apex of a triangle formed by railroads, a movement in his rear would destroy his communications with Richmond.

The only danger the National troops run by this flank march would be by a sudden advance of Gen. BEAUREGARD upon Centreville, interrupting communications and cutting off our supplies. But this manœuvre would be desperate, as cutting himself off from supplies, and placing himself in an exhausted country, and between the National troops and the Potomac.

The Sixty-ninth New-York Regiment was assigned the post of honor in advance. The members of this regiment have agreed unanimously to serve, although their time is now out.

All the New-York regiments will follow this example.

For five hours one steady column of troops passed through Centreville.

The *morale* of the soldiers is excellent. All are anxious for a battle, and when informed of the purpose to advance, the enthusiasm was beyond all description.

It is supposed that Gen. BEAUREGARD'S forces are larger than ours.

A battle is imminent at any moment, but it may not take place till to-morrow night.

Telegraphic wires are rapidly following the Army, and offices were opened this morning at Fairfax Court-house, with Messrs. BUELL and BENTON as Army operators.

EFFECTS OF THE BATTLE IN WASHINGTON.

WASHINGTON, Sunday, July, 21.

The most intense excitement is everywhere existing to hear further from the field of battle. Every returning spectator of the event is immediately surrounded to relate his observations.

The demand for intelligence is insatiable, and unauthenticated rumors prevails, which serve to confuse the truth.

The smoke from the battle could be seen from the eminences in Washington.

A number of members of Congress, and even ladies, went to the neighborhood of Bull's Run, to witness the battle. One of them reports Col. HUNTER, of the Third Cavalry, acting as Major-General, was seriously, if not mortally, wounded.

It is stated with confidence in all qurrters that Col. CAMERON, of the Seventy-ninth Regiment, and brother of the Secretary of War, and Col. SLOCUM, of the Second Rhode Island Regiment, were killed.

DISPATCH TO THE ASSOCIATED PRESS.

WASHINGTON, Sunday, July 21.

The orders to move yesterday evening, at 6 o'clock, were countermanded till early this morning; our troops meantime cutting a road through the woods, in order to flank the enemy's batteries.

The Secretary of War has received a dispatch that the fighting was renewed at Bull's Run this morning. Our troops engaged the enemy with a large force, silenced their batteries, and drove the Secessionists to the Junction.

The city is wild with joy.

Firing was heard in this city to-day from the direction of Bull's Run, from 11 till about 3. There was a cessation till nearly 5, and at 7 this evening the reverberation of cannon was again audible.

A gentleman who arrived to-night says at 3 o'clock this afternoon the Second and Third New-Jersey Regiments were ordered to march forward from Vienna, the First sending their baggage back to Camp Trenton. Other troops were hurrying forward to the scene of hostilities, and there is much military excitement and bustle in the direction of all the camps.

It is not doubted in military quarters that Gen. JOHNSTON was enabled to effect a junction with the Confederates some time during yesterday.

Official dispatches were sent to Gen. McDOWELL at 2 o'clock this morning.

The New-York Thirty-seventh Regiment passed over into Virginia this morning, the band playing "Dixie," amid the cheers of the soldiers and citizens.

Gen. McDOWELL has caused the following order to be issued:

"Capt. VARIAN'S Battery of Light Artillery, attached to the Eighth Regiment of New-York Volunteers, State Militia, having completed the period of its enlistment, is honorably discharged from the service of the United States, and will march to Alexandria and report to Gen. RUNYON, to be mustered out of the service of the United States.

The material of the Battery will be turned over to the Ordnance officer of this command."

This battery, it will be recollected, started from New-York within 24 hours' notice. It has at all times rendered prompt, willing and efficient service, and gained the approbation of high military gentlemen.

The body of private BLACK, of the Fourteenth New-York Regiment, State Militia, who was accidentally shot two months ago, went forward to-day, under an escort, to his relatives in Brooklyn.

FROM FORT PICKENS.

The steam transport *City of New-York*, which arrived last night from Fort Pickens, brought on four passengers, viz: Lieut. McCRAY, of the United States Army, who was discharged by Col. BROWN, commander at Fort Pickens, owing to his secession principles, (he was born in Virginia,) Mr. SIMMONS, First-Lieutenant of the United States steam gun-boat *Huntsville*, who fell down the hold of the vessel and injured his spine; also a fireman of the steam-frigate *Mississippi*, who returns sick, and a volunteer belonging to Col. WILSON'S Regiment.

THE REBEL GOVERNMENT.

JEFF. DAVIS' MESSAGE TO THE SOUTHERN "CONGRESS."

RICHMOND, VA., via NEW-ORLEANS,
Saturday, July 20.

The Message commences as follows:

In my Inaugural I called attention to the causes which formed the Confederacy. It is now only necessary to call attention to such facts which have occurred during the recess, and to matters connected with the public defence.

He then congratulates Congress on the accession to the Confederacy of three equal sovereign States. (Mentioning the several States.) It was deemed advisable to remove the several departments and archives to Richmond, to which place Congress already removed the seat of Government. After the adjournment of Congress, the aggressive movements of the enemy induced prompt and energetic action. The accumulation of the enemy's forces on the Potomac, sufficiently demonstrated that his efforts were directed against Virginia, and from no point could necessary measures for her defence and protection be so efficiently directed as from our own capital.

The rapid progress of the last few months, stripped the veil behind which the true policy and purposes of the Lincoln Government were concealed, and they are now fully revealed. The Message of their President and the action of their Congress at the present session confess the intention for the subjugation of the seceding States by a war of folly which is equaled only by its wickedness. It is a war by which it is impossible to attain the proposed result. Whilst the dire calamities cannot be avoided by us, it will fall with double severity on themselves. Commencing in March last with an affectation of ignorance of the secession of the seven States, which organized the Confederate Government, persisting in April in the absurd assumption of the existence of a riot, which was dispersed by a *posse comitatus*, and continuing in the successive months the false representations that these States intended an offensive war, in spite of conclusive evidence to the contrary, furnished as well by official action as by the basis of the Constitution, the President of the United States succeeded in deluding the people of those States into the belief that it was the purpose of this Government, not peace at home, but conquest abroad; not the defence of our liberties, but the subjugation of the people of the United States. The series of manœuvres by which the impression was created, the act by which they were devised, and the perfidy by which they were executed, are already known. Could it be supposed they would make openly their success a subject of boast and self-laudation in the Executive message?

Fortunately for the truth of history, LINCOLN'S Message minutely details the attempt to reinforce Fort Sumter, in violation of an armistice, of which he confesses to have been informed only by rumors too vague and uncertain to create any attention. The hostile expedition dispatched to supply Fort Sumter, is admitted to have been undertaken with a knowledge that its success was impossible. The sending of a notice to the Governor of South Carolina, of an intended ruse for the accomplishment of the object, and, quoting from the Inaugural, there could be no conflict unless these States were the agressors, he proceeds to declare his conduct as in the past for the future, was the performance of this promise, which could not be misunderstood. In defiance of our statement that he gave notice of the approach of the hostile fleet, he charges these States with being the assailants of the Union of the States. The world cannot misunderstand this unfounded pretence. LINCOLN expresses concern that some foreign nations have so shaped their actions, as if they supposed the early destruction of the Union probable. He abandons the further disguise, and proposes to make the contest short and decisive, and confesses even an increased force might be demanded. These enormous preparations, a distinct avowal that the United States are engaged in a conflict with a great and powerful nation, compelled to abandon the pretence of dispersing rioters and suppressing insurrection, and driven to the acknowledgment that the Union is dissolved, they recognize the separate existence of the Confederate States by indirection. By the embargo and blockade, by which all commerce between the two is cut off, they repudiated the foolish idea that the inhabitants of the Confederacy are still citizens of the United States, for they are now waging an indiscriminate war upon them, with a savage ferocity unknown to modern civilization.

He compares the present invasion to that of Great Britain of 1781, (?) which was conducted in a more civilized manner. Mankind will shudder at the outrages committed on defenceless females by those pretending to be our fellow-citizens, and will depict the horror which they regard the deliberate malignity which, under the pretext of suppressing insurrection, make a special war on the sick, women and children, by carefully devised measures to prevent their obtaining medicines necessary for their cure.

The sacred claims of humanity, respected by all nations, even in the fury of the battle, by a careful deviation of an attack from hospitals, are now outraged by the Government, which pretends to desire to continue fraternal connections. Such outrages admit of no retaliations unless the actual perpetrators are requited.

Col. TAYLOR'S mission to Washington was to propose an exchange of the prisoners taken on board the privateer *Savannah*, and to inform Mr. LINCOLN of our determined purpose to check all barbarities on prisoners of war by such retaliation as would effectually put an end to such practices. Mr. LINCOLN'S promised reply has not yet been received.

Reference is made to the peculiar relations existing between this Government and the States usually termed the "Border Slave States," which cannot properly be withheld from notice. Our people are animated by sentiments towards the inhabitants of these States, which expression in your enactment refusing to consider them enemies, or authorize hostilities against them. A large portion of the people of those States regard us as brethren, and if they were unrestrained by the actual presence of large armies, the subversion of civil authority and a declaration of martial law, some of them at least, would joyfully unite with us. But they are, with almost entire unanimity, opposed to the prosecution of the war waged against us. These are facts of which the daily recurring events warrant the assertion that the President of the United States, in refusing to recognize in those, our late sister States, the right of refraining from an attack on us, justifies his refusal by the assertion that the States have no other power than that reserved to them in the Union by the Constitution.

The new Constitutional relation between the States and General Government is a fitting introduction to another assertion of the Mefsage, that the Executive possesses the power of suspending the *habeas corpus*, delegating that power to military commanders at discretion; and both these propositions claim respect equal to that which is felt for the additional statement of opinion of the same paper, that it is proper in order to execute the laws, that the same single law made to meet the extreme tendencies of the citizens for liberty; that practically it relieves more of the guilty than the innocent, should to a very limited extent be violated. We may well rejoice that we have forever severed the connection with a Government that thus tramples on all principles of constitutional liberty, with a people in whose presence such avowals could be paraded.

Our operations on the field will be greatly extended by reason of the policy which heretofore secretly entertained, is now avowed and acted on by the United States. The forces hitherto raised have proved ample for the defence of the seven States which originally organized the Confederacy. With the exception of those fortified islands whose defences is effectually aided by the preponderation of naval force, the enemy has been driven completely out of those States, and now at the expirration of five months from the formation of the Govenment, not a single hostile foot presses their soil. The forces, howeaer, must necessarily prove inadequate. On account of the invasion by half a million of men now proposed by the enemy, a corresponding increase of our forces becomes necessary.

The message refers to the abundant crops with which we have been cheered, the most abundant known in our history. Many believe the supply adequate to two years' consumption. The citizens manifest laudable pride in upholding their independence, unaided by any resources other than their own, and the subscription to the loan proposed by the Government, cannot fall short of fifty millions of dollars, and will probably exceed that sum.

[Owing to some unexplained cause, the remainder of the "message" has failed to come to hand.]

JEFF. DAVIS' PRIVATEERS.

Arrival of Another Recaptured Prize Vessel—The Commanding Officer and Two of His Mates Killed and Thrown Overboard.

The schooner *S. J. Waring*, of Brook Haven, SMITH, master, hence for Montevideo, July 4, with an assorted cargo, came up to the City yesterday P. M., and we gather the following intelligence from those on board:

On the third day out from port, the 7th inst., when 150 miles from Sandy Hook, in lat. 36°, long. 69°, was brought to by the privateer brig *Jeff. Davis*, which sent a boat full of men alongside, and ordered the Captain of the schooner to haul down the United States flag, and declared her a prize to the C. S. A. They ransacked the vessel, and took from her what they wanted—such as charts, quadrant, provisions, crockery, &c., and after returning to the schooner a second time, they put a prize-crew of five men on board without arms, and took away Capt. FRANCIS SMITH, the two mates and two seamen, leaving the steward, two seamen and Mr. BRYCE MACKINNON, a passenger, on board. The prize-crew were MONTAGUE O'NEIL, a Charleston pilot, in command; one named STEVENS, as mate, and MALCOLM LIDDY as second mate, and two men.

At 3 P. M. the schooner was headed South—probably for Charleston or near by. The remaining crew and the passenger were in hopes of a recapture by some United States vessel, and made themselves agreeable and sociable to the privateersmen, and in consequence they suspected nothing until the night of the 16th of July, when 50 miles to the southward of Charleston.

Seeing no prospect of their hopes being realized, and the prize captain and first mate being asleep in their berths, and the second mate at the wheel, the others dozing or asleep, the preconcerted plan was carried into effect by the steward, WILLIAM TILLMAN, (colored,) killing the three with a hatchet, and throwing the bodies overboard. It was all finished in five minutes. One of the remaining men was tied up that night, and both were released in the morning, on promise to help work the vessel, and were treated accordingly.

After retaking the vessel the charge of her devolved on the steward. Neither he or the rest understood navigation, but having once got hold of the land he brought her safely up to pilot ground, when Mr. CHARLES E. WARNER, of the pilot-boat *Jane*, took charge of her.

One of the schooner's men, DONALD McLEOD, refused to assist in her recapture, the whole duty falling on the steward. She has anchored off the Battery.

The names of the schooner's men are as follows:

WM. TILLMAN, steward.

WM. STEDDING, seaman who assisted.

DONALD McLEOD, seaman who refused.

The prisoners on board are named JAMES MILNOR, of South Carolina, and JAMES DAWSETT, of New-Jersey, who appears to be an innocent sort of person.

Officers NESBITT, SULLIVAN and GURSKER, of the Harbor Police, arrested the prisoners and also brought ashore the steward.

There was no insurance on the vessel. She was built in Port Jefferson, L. I., in 1853, and is owned by JONAS SMITH & Co. of this City.

STATEMENT OF JAMES E. DORSETT, ONE OF THE PRIVATEER'S CREW.

JAMES E. DORSETT and JAMES MILNOR, the two privateersmen, are confined in the cells of the Detective office. DORSETT is an intelligent young man, [illegible] prepossessing in manner. He cheerfully answered [illegible] questions which were put to him last evening by [illegible] reporter. He said:

I was born in New-Jersey, and on the 4th of March last shipped at Jersey City on the schooner *Stagg*, for a voyage to Key West. Our cargo was taken in at Pier No. 36 East River, and we reached Key West and Bay Port, Fla., early in May. It was determined that our return cargo should be cedar, and about the 10th of May we went to Cedar Keys for a load, but our vessel was detained there by the merchants, as security for a debt alleged to be due them by [illegible] ASHBAR, her owner.

A man named [illegible], acting as agent for the cedar dealers, was dispatched to New-York in relation to the seizure, and a day or two after his departure, some people from Bay Port came on board the schooner and unbent the foresail and main [illegible], which they carried ashore. A few days after [illegible] Capt. TUCKER, of Fernandina, came over to Bay Port and took possession of all the Northern vessels at the latter place as prizes to the Southern Confederacy. Three vessels were seized in all. The *Stagg*, *Annie Smith* and *Daniel Townsend*. The officers and crews of these prizes, by direction of Capt. TUCKER, were all put on board a small schooner, (excepting [illegible] TOWNSEND, brother of the captain of the *Daniel Townsend*, and myself, who were forcibly retained,) and told to make the best of their way North. They were sent off with a small stock of provisions, barely sufficient for a few days' subsistence on short allowance.

After the departure of our companions, TOWNSEND and myself were carried to Fernandina, where we received urgent offers to enlist in the secession Army. These we firmly declined, and remained on board the vessel. After a few days, Capt. TAYLOR raised a company of 40 men, and conveyed them to Bay Port to protect the seized vessels, as it was believed that the United States steamer *Crusader* would attempt to retake them. All this time I had been serving my captors in the capacity of cook. We did not long remain as a guard for the prizes, but were soon relieved by another company from Fernandina, to which place Capt. TUCKER returned us. We had been thus far treated kindly during our involuntary captivity, and Capt. TUCKER seemed so well pleased with us that he promised to pay us for our services and send us home. This promise he subsequently refused to fulfil, and renewed his offers of enlisting in the Secession Army. I told him that I would not become a soldier, and TOWNSEND also objected. The Captain then told TOWNSEND that he should appoint him a ship-keeper, and detail him to watch his brother's vessel. He also informed me that I could have that night to think over his offer of enlisting, and that he would see me next day. Accordingly, the following morning, he sent for me, and finding me persistent in my desire to go home, placed a paper in my hand which proved to be a notice that I had been drafted as a soldier.

That very day, the steamer *Cecil* came into port from Savannah, Geo., and I determined, if possible, to escape by her. I, therefore, at the first opportunity, stole away, and concealed myself on board of that vessel, remaining in my hiding-place until she left. After getting fairly at sea, I emerged from confinement, and paid for a deck-passage to Savannah, where I arrived the latter part of May.

At Savannah I put up at a sailor's boarding-house, kept by a man named RAY, where I remained until my means were entirely exhausted, being unable to find conveyance North. RAY discovering that I was penniless, said I had better join the Southern Navy, and conducted me to a shipping-master's office. I expressed my disinclination to enter the service, but RAY said I must ship, as I owed him money which he could not afford to lose these hard times. The proposition was then made me to join the privateer, *Jeff. Davis*, which I was informed was fitting out in Charleston Harbor. Three or four Northern men were there also, in the same predicament as myself, and after consultation we decided to sign the shipping articles. In taking this step, we believed that the privateer would soon fall into the hands of a United States

[Continued on Eighth Page.]

The Charleston Mercury.

VOLUME LXXIX. CHARLESTON, S. C., MONDAY, JULY 22, 1861. NUMBER 11,208

THE MERCURY.

MONDAY, JULY 22, 1861.

The Great Battle Yesterday.

Sunday, the Day of Battles, has added another great conflict to its bloody calendar.

A battle, such as the New World had never yet beheld, has been fought at Manassas.

The hireling hosts of our ruthless foes, after a desperate fight of ten hours, have been routed, at the point of the bayonet, by the Southern troops.

But the victory, we fear, has been dearly won. We glance at the first accounts which have been flashed to us over the wires, ere the smoke of the combat has cleared away from the gory field—and, as we catch the names of the illustrious fallen, which have already reached us, with no heart for triumph or exultation over the glorious issue, we await, with anxious hearts, the fearful details of the fray.

The President's Message.

In our *Extra*, of yesterday, we laid before our readers the Message of President DAVIS to the Confederate Congress, assembled at Richmond on the 20th inst. We republish it this morning for the convenience of our country readers.

The President, after congratulating the country upon the accession of North Carolina and Tennessee, addresses himself to a brief refutation of the falsehoods of President LINCOLN'S Message, and an exposure of the malice and follies of the United States Government towards us. The truth, in reference to the past and present relations and conduct of the two Governments will, doubtless, be understood by Europe.

His action in reference to the prisoners he holds in retaliation for the outrages committed upon citizens of the Confederate States, now prisoners of the United States Government, will be approved by the country. We think the policy should be strictly adhered to—an eye for an eye, and a tooth for a tooth—ignominy for ignominy, and chains for chains. Nothing else will be satisfactory or effective.

We are gratified at his remark that we may well rejoice that we have forever severed our connection with a Government that thus tramples upon all principles of constitutional liberty, and with a people in whose presence such avowals could be hazarded.

As regards the necessary increase of our army to meet the emergency presented by the late action of the United States Congress, he refers the Congress to the report of the Secretary of War.

The Secretary will report concerning the financial projects of the Government.

The Morning Press—The Mails.

The Press of Charleston has always been under serious disadvantages on account of this fact: that in making up schedules on the great mail routes, the circumstance of this being an important commercial city has, seemingly, been lost sight of, and the arrivals and departures of railroad trains and steamers have been so fixed (whether intentionally or otherwise we cannot, of course, say) that our people and the press have to be much inconvenienced.

As an instance of this indifference to our wants, we would mention the very great difficulty experienced at the completion of the Northeastern Railroad, to have the time saved by the building of that road made available to the public. So great was the complaint that the President of the Chamber of Commerce was sent to Washington to have the matter satisfactorily adjusted, and he was successful in securing to the community a connection twice a day with the Wilmington and Manchester Road. The time of making up the mails, however, was not what we had a right to expect.

We have already spoken of the endless delay in the transmission of letters and papers to Richmond. This delinquency is yet to be corrected, for during the last week the delays have been as frequent as ever. We now call attention to our connection with the Southwest, by the Charleston and Savannah Railroad. A letter or newspaper for Macon, Ga., or any point on this route beyond Savannah, leaves Charleston by the Charleston and Savannah Railroad at 9½ a. m., and arrives in our sister city at 2½ p. m., *one hour and a quarter* after the train has left for Macon and beyond. These letters and newspapers are quietly laid over in the post office until 11 o'clock p. m., *a delay of more than eight hours*, or three hours longer than the running time between the two cities. It is urged that to alter the schedule of the Georgia Central Road would involve great changes, which the President of the road does not feel called upon to make. The Charleston and Savannah Railroad is running on faster time than most of our Southern roads, and the hour and a quarter cannot be made up on this road; hence it follows that some of the *same time* on the route from Richmond south to Florence, should be made available to the public in order to bring the connection with the North, by the Northeastern Railroad to Charleston, an hour and a half to two hours earlier than the present time.

A careful examination of the time table will show that a great deal more than two hours can be saved. For instance, the running time from Richmond to Weldon, *eighty-six miles*, is *six hours*, or fourteen and one third miles an hour; on the Charleston and Savannah Railroad the running time is about twenty miles an hour. If, then, the roads from Richmond to Weldon would increase their speed to twenty miles an hour, which is the rate of travel on the Weldon and Wilmington Road, the time needed would be gained; the Northeastern Railroad train would reach Charleston at 6 a. m. instead of 8 a. m.; the Charleston and Savannah Road would start at 7½ a. m. instead of 9½ a. m., and would reach Savannah at 12.45 p. m., three quarters of an hour before the day train to Macon leaves, giving passengers ample time for dinner in Savannah. This would give Charleston a rapid communication with Savannah, Milledgeville, Macon, Columbus, Montgomery, and other important points, and would not interfere with the connection at Savannah with the Gulf Road and the Florida steamers. More than this, it puts the seaports of Norfolk, Wilmington, Charleston, Savannah, Pensacola, Mobile and New Orleans on the great line of travel and the mails.

At another time we will speak of our mail facilities with the upper part of our own State.

Inexcusable Ignorance—The States Sovereign.

To the Editor of the Charleston Mercury:

In the President's Message, lately issued from the Cabinet of Messrs. LINCOLN, SEWARD & Co., it is declared that the word "sovereignty of the States," it is BELIEVED, is not in any of the State Constitutions. Now, in the State Constitution of te most fanatical and furious of the States who have coerced the Cabinet into its war policy, Massachusetts, Part 1, Art. 4, it is declared that "the people of this Commonwealth have the sole and exclusive right of governing themselves, as a free, sovereign, and independent State: and do, and forever hereafter shall, exercise and enjoy every power, jurisdiction and right, which is not, or may not hereafter be by them expressly delegated to the United States of America, in Congress assembled."

In regard to the Declaration of Independence, the "Colonies" are not only declared to be severally "free and independent States," three times, but they claim to be exactly what Mr. LINCOLN denies a sovereign State to be—that is, "political communities without a political superior"—"absolved from all allegiance to the British Crown and ALL political connection TOTALLY dissolved." They also claimed, and at once exercised that most sovereign of all rights—which President LINCOLN cannot constitutionally do—that is, "full power to levy war, and to do all other acts and things which independent States—*not dependent, not having any superior.*"

In their Confederation of 1778, as "*The United States of America*," Article 2, declares that "EACH STATE RETAINS ITS SOVEREIGNTY," &c., of course asserting that it was as sovereign States they now confederated as "the United States of America.'

When the nine States who formed the Constitution of the United States in 1787, seceded without leave, asked or given, from that "PERPETUAL UNION," they did so each one severally as "sovereigns," and having undisputed right to do so.

The articles of ratification of this new Constitution by New York, Virginia and Rhode Island expressly declare that "the powers of government may be reassumed by THE STATES whensoever it shall become necessary to the happiness of their people."

The people, who, it is asserted by this declaration, may re-assume the powers of government, are the people of these States alone and separate. The Conventions represented, spoke for and acted for the people of these States only. They were not charged with caring for the rights of any but the people of these States. They were not acting in this matter with the people of other States, nor the people of other States with them. Each State was left to ratify the Constitution or not, as it thought fit. This declaration being made part of the ratification of their constitutions, when they spoke of the "powers of Government" which may be re-assumed, they referred especially to those powers which were then being conferred on the new Government of the United States; otherwise it was out of place. The people of these States, acting for themselves only, and not for others—acting as a separate people, and not jointly with others—were then, of themselves and by themselves, conferring certain powers on the new Government; and these powers thus and then conferred, they reserved the right to re-assume to themselves, the people of these States, by the act of the people of these States, whenever the people of these States should find that so to do was necessary to their happiness. Whether this was to be done under the Constitution or in spite of it, is no matter. The declaration made on such an occasion, meant this, or it meant nothing.

It is not true that the Constitution of 1787, as the Constitution of the United States, of 1776, the United States declares itself to be a PERPETUAL form of government; nor, if it did, does the common sentiment of mankind recognise any form of government as entitled to be perpetual and unchangable. It is certain that the people of these States did not accept it as perpetual, but, on the contrary, openly protested, from the start, against its being considered perpetual. You cannot turn up the evidence that the Constitution of the United States is the law in these States, without turning up on the same record, proof that the people of these States claim the right of withdrawing,

New York State Militia charging a Confederate battery at the Battle of Bull Run

by their own separate acts, as they conferred them, the powers given by them by that Constitution, to the General Government, and merely of abrogating the Constitution so far as these States are concerned. That record must stand so until we ratify the Constitution anew, in another form of words, in another sense.

Now, this right (whether under or over the Constitution, they were not careful to define), *which these States, by their records, claim and assert the seceded States have exercised, and* THEY HAVE DONE NOTHING MORE.

We have thus proved—1. That in the Articles of Confederation each State retained its SOVEREIGNTY, freedom and independenc, &c.; that it was in virtue of this State sovereignty alone, the Deputies of the twelve States represented in the Federal Convention adopted the seventh Article of the Constitution, viz: "The ratifications of the Conventions of nine States shall be sufficient for the establishment of this Constitution BETWEEN THE STATES so ratifying the same," in direct violation of the thirteenth Article of the Confederation, viz: "*The Articles of this Confederation shall be inviolably observed* by EVERY *State*, and the Union *shall be perpetual; nor shall any alteration at any time hereafter be made in* ANY *of them, unless such alteration shall be agreed to in a Congress of the United States, and be afterwards confirmed by the Legislatures of* EVERY *State.*"

2. The exercise of this sovereignty in the ratification by eleven States was an act of secession by them, from Rhode Island and North Carolina, each being bound to the others, by solemn compact, not to alter or amend.

3. That this principle was the basis of the resolutions (drawn by Mr. MADISON and Mr. JEFFERSON,) of Virginia and Kentucky in 1795, and of "MADISON'S Report" thereon.

We might show, also, that this principle was proclaimed by Mr. QUINCY, of Massachusetts, in the House of Representatives, in 1811, when Louisiana applied for admission as a State. That it was maintained by Massachusetts, Connecticut and Rhode Island, in their respective Legislatures in 1814, and by their deputies in the Hartford Convention (which assembled in a time of war) in that year. *The principle* was unqualifiedly maintained, but not acted out, *merely* from considerations of expediency, for the moment; and an early peace removed the principal cause of New England's complaint, and that this fundamental principle and nothing more has been acted upon by the secession of South Carolina, Mississippi, Florida, Alabama, Georgia, Louisiana, Texas, North Carolina, Tennessee, Arkansas and Virginia.

Thus every one of the original States (*North Carolina* perhaps excepted) stands committed, theoretically and practically, to the principle of secession *as an inherent and legal right of State sovereignty, in virtue of their powers reserved.*

If, then, secession be treason, all the original States which were parties to the Constitution at its formation and ratification, except perhaps North Carolina, and not the present seceded States alone, are guilty of it. But how a sovereign State, in the exercise of its united and embodied powers, can commit treason, or be punished for it, may be difficult to comprehend by any other than an arbitrary military despotism.

Finally, we have shown that the LINCOLN despotism is based upon the most inexcusable ignorance of the most fundamental and undeniable facts.

BATTLE OF BULL'S RUN.

[*From the Richmond Examiner.*]

For more than a week the commanding general of the Confederate forces at Manassas has been anticipating an advance of the enemy, and has so arranged his troops as to be prepared at all points. At Fairfax Court House, Gen. BONHAM was stationed, with six regiments of infantry, composed of four from South Carolina (KERSHAW, CASH, WILLIAMS and BACON) and two from Virginia (PRESTON and WITHERS), with two batteries of light artillery (SHIELD'S Howitzers and KEMPER'S Company), and about five hundred cavalry, under command of Col. RADFORD, of Virginia.

At Fairfax Station, about four miles distant from the Court House, and on a line with it, Gen. EWELL, of Virginia, was posted with three regiments of infantry, two Alabama (SIEBLES' and RHODES), and one from Louisiana (SEYMOUR'S). These regiments were stationed at intervals of a mile from each other, RHODES' 5th Alabama Regiment guarding the Braddock road approach from Alexandria, which intersects the country road between the Court House and the Station. At both places, infantry works had been thrown up for the protection of the troops, and at the Court-House, particularly, extended lines of defence, including two or three masked batteries, had been constructed.

At Centreville, a commanding eminence on the turnpike road, between Fairfax Court House and Bull Run, Col. Cocke was stationed with his Regiment and Latham's Light Battery. The object of these preparations was to resist the incursion of anything short of a large army into the interior, and in the event of the approach of a force under twenty thousand men, to give battle and drive them back. At the same time, orders had been issued, in case of an overwhelming demonstration of the enemy, to fall back on Bull Run, the selected battle ground. To provide for this contingency, the troops for more than a week past have been trimmed of all superfluous baggage, and been under orders to keep on hand constantly three days' provisions in advance. Quartermaster and Commissary supplies have been kept in limited amounts, and the wagons held in constant readiness to move off with camp equipage, &c.

We are particular in stating these minute details to give the reader an idea of what was antipated by the commanding general, and of his arrangements to meet the contemplated contingency.

On Thursday, the enemy felt his way cautiously up from Alexandria and Washington, in three separate columns, of probably fifteen thousand each—one down the railroad, another the Braddock road, and the third from the direction of Falls Church. Our pickets were driven in about two o'clock, and our troops, after firing several hundred rounds, withdrew in order before the advancing foe, and fell back on the banks of "Bull Run," a stream about four miles from Manassas and eight from the Court House.

The "Run" is about sixty feet wide and easily fordable for infantry at this season of the year, but its points of defence against an adversary attempting to cross, are inviting to the military eye. Here the retiring forces were met by Gen. Longstreet's Brigade, consisting of the 11th, 17th and 1st Virginia Regiments, under the command respectively of Colonels Garland, Corse and Moore, together with artillery from New Orleans. Our troops bivouacked for the night in expectation of the fight opening at daybreak. But the enemy approached cautiously, beating the roads and woods in advance of them with skirmishers, until about four o'clock in the afternoon, when their main body arrived within a half mile of the Run, and made three several attempts to advance on it, and each time were repulsed with great slaughter.

The reports of the loss of the enemy are conflicting, varying it from five to fifteen hundred. Certain it is, their retreat had every appearance of a signal rout, leaving, as they did, their dead behind them, and losing six pieces of their artillery. Two of the Virginia Regiments pursued them for some distance, and captured quite a number of prisoners. The Confederate loss is estimated at about one hundred killed, wounded and missing. It is said the enemy, in their several advances, behaved at first with much spirit, quickly rallying and closing up their mowed columns, but finally broke, and gave way under the murderous execution of our musketry and artillery.

On Wednesday afternoon despatches were sent to Gen. Johnston to repair with a portion of his command to reinforce Gen. Beauregard at Manassas. Johnston has his entrenchments at Winchester strongly fortified and defended with heavy artillery, as to be able to spare at least half his command without any risk. The propriety of these instructions is vindicated by the despatch in another column announcing that Patterson has left Martinsburg, and is on his way across the Potomac. Johnston, by this time, is at Manassas, prepared to take part in the fight to-day, should it occur.

The enemy, as they advanced, displayed their accustomed Vandalism, burning and destroying as they went. The villages at Fairfax Court House, Germantown and Centreville were reduced to ashes, and men and women were fleeing in every direction. Such are the well authenticated accounts of passengers by the Central train of yesterday.

FURTHER PARTICULARS.

Information derived from gentlemen who left Manassas Junction at 8 o'clock yesterday morning causing us to lay before our readers the important particulars of the great victory achieved by our troops on Thursday.

At dawn on that day, the enemy recommenced their advance upon our lines. The Washington Artillery went out to meet them, and a skirmishing fight between the opposing forces of flying artillery immediately began and lasted until 11 a. m. At this hour their whole front, infantry and artillery continuing still to advance, our infantry also pushed forward and the fight became general.

The battle continued with unabated fury for three hours, when, about two o'clock, p. m., the enemy's centre giving way before the combined fire of our artillery and the charge of our infantry, their whole force fell back precipitately and in disorder.

But, after an interval of an hour, during which there was some unimportant skirmishing, at three o'clock, p. m., the enemy again returned to the charge with redoubled impetuosity, and again, after severe fighting, were they driven back at the point of the bayonet.

A third time they were rallied and brought up, but only to be repulsed quickly and with great slaughter.

It was now five o'clock, p. m., and the enemy made no attempt to renew the fight, but retreated hastily, leaving the field, strewn with the bodies of their dead and wounded, in possession of the Confederates.

The battle had extended along the creek, "Bull's Run," a distance of over a mile, and within this space the enemy had left 986 of their men dead or mortally wounded. Our loss, as counted that night, was 137 killed, wounded and missing, but by the next morning this number was reduced to less than sixty by the return of stragglers, who had been scattered and lost in the woods during the night. The enemy threw chain-shot and fired upon our hospital while the yellow flag, which secures immunity in civilized nations, was flying. General Beauregard had a narrow escape, a ball having passed through the kitchen of a house where he was partaking of dinner. The General has displayed qualities of the highest order as a military commander, with, perhaps, the exception of indifference to his own life, now so valuable to the Confederacy. He exhibited great coolness during the engagement, and was in all parts of the field.

The Alexandria Riflemen are said to have particularly distinguished themselves, having crossed the ford in the face of a terrific fire from the enemy's artillery, and fought hand to hand with the Yankee hirelings.

The famous Sherman battery, upon which the enemy evidently based so much hope of success, was almost utterly annihilated. Some say there is scarcely a corporal's guard of them left. Our First Regiment of Virginia Volunteers, under Colonel P. T. Moore, is said to have fought desperately. Three separate charges were made by it with the bayonet, and in each instance the enemy fled like sheep. Among the enemy's dead were many officers, whose uniforms indicated high rank, though their names were unknown. Before the departure of the train for Richmond yesterday morning, the enemy had sent in a flag of truce to General Beauregard, asking permission to bury their dead, which was, of course, granted.

The number of the enemy actually engaged in this battle is variously estimated at between five and ten thousand, whilst our force little exceeded 3500.

Only eight of our men are certainly known to have been killed, which, with those who are so severely wounded as to leave little or no hope for their recovery, will, perhaps, bring our actual loss up to twenty. Few of our men who were struck are dangerously hurt. About twenty of them came down last evening by the Central cars, the most severely wounded of whom was a Captain of the Washington Artillery, who was wounded in the leg by the explosion of a shell. Col. P. T. Moore, who was struck early in the fight, arrived by the same train. His wound had not been dressed, and, from the loss of blood and the jolting of the cars, he was very much exhausted when he reached home, but he is considered in no danger. The ball took effect on the inner side of his arm, and glancing from the bone—which is not thought to be broken—came in contact with one of his ribs, producing a very painful but not dangerous wound. Lieut. Wirt Harrison, wounded in the instep by a buck-shot, and Mr. Knauff having received a musket ball through the hand, also reached home yesterday evening. Major Carter Harrison and Captain James K. Lee were so severely wounded as to render their removal to Richmond dangerous. We could not ascertain the character of Major Harrison's injuries, but Capt. Lee is said to have been struck in the back, near the spinal column, by a bullet, which passed entirely through his body. He is thought to have been accidentally shot by one of his own men. The remains of Lieut. Humphrey Miles, of Company G, First Regiment of Virginia Volunteers, were brought down and delivered to his friends.

One of the Washington Artillery was killed, and seven wounded. The most of these latter were struck during the explosion of a shell, which was thrown by the enemy after the battle was over, and whilst they were in retreat.

It was reported that seven guns of the Sherman Battery had been captured by our troops, but others who seem to have had good opportunities of information deny the truth of this statement. But all agree that we secured many hundred rifles and muskets, besides a vast quantity of sidearms.

The New-York Times.

OL. X....NO. 3068. NEW-YORK, TUESDAY, JULY 23, 1861. PRICE TWO CENTS.

DISASTER TO THE NATIONAL ARMY

Retreat of Gen. McDowell's Command from Manassas.

Full Details of the Engagement.

But 20,000 of the National Forces in Action.

90,000 REBELS IN THE FIELD.

The Retreat of Our Forces on the Eve of Victory.

A Panic Among the Teamsters and Civilians.

Exaggerated Statements of Our Losses.

Measures of the Government to Retrieve the Disaster.

GENERAL M'CLELLAN IN COMMAND.

Offensive Operations to be Resumed Immediately.

GEN. PATTERSON AT HARPER'S FERRY.

Latest intelligence from Western Virginia and Missouri.

Editorial Correspondence of the N. Y. Times.

WASHINGTON, Monday Morning, July 22, 1861.

I came in from Centreville last evening for the express purpose of sending you the latest intelligence of the great battle of yesterday. I left Centreville at half-past 5 and reached here at midnight. I sent a dispatch to the office, but, as it is to be subjected to the censorship of the Government, which gives no hint of what it refuses permission to pass, I have no means of knowing whether its contents reached you or not. I must therefore repeat its contents.

The battle yesterday was one of the most severe and sanguinary ever fought on this Continent, and it ended in the failure of the Union troops to hold all the positions which they sought to carry, and which they actually did carry, and in their retreat to Centreville, where they have made a stand and where Gen. McDOWELL believes that they are able to maintain themselves.

As I telegraphed you yesterday, the attack was made in three columns, two of which, however, were mainly feints, intended to amuse and occupy the enemy, while the substantial work was done by the third. It has been known for a long time that the range of hills which border the small, swampy stream known as Bull's Run, had been very thoroughly and extensively fortified by the rebels,—that batteries had been planted at every available point, usually concealed in the woods and bushes which abound in that vicinity, and covering every way of approach to the region beyond. These are the advanced defences of Manassas Junction, which is some three miles further off. Until these were carried, no approach could be made to that place; and after they should be carried others of a similar character would have to be overcome at every point where they could be erected. The utmost that military skill and ingenuity could accomplish for the defence of this point was done. Gen. McDOWELL was unwilling to make an attack directly in face of these batteries, as they would be of doubtful issue, and must inevitably result in a very serious loss of life. After an attack had been resolved upon, therefore, he endeavored to find some way of *turning* the position. His first intention was to do this on the Southern side,—to throw a strong column into the place from that direction, while a feigned attack should be made in front. On Thursday, when the troops were advanced to Centreville, it was found that the roads on the south side of these positions were almost impracticable,—that they were narrow, crooked and stony, and that it would be almost impossible to bring up enough artillery to be effective in the time required. This original plan was, therefore, abandoned; and Friday was devoted to an examination by the topographical engineers of the Northern side of the position. Maj. BARNARD and Capt. [illegible] reconnoitred the place for miles around, and reported that the position could be entered by a path coming from the north,—though it was [illegible] long and circuitous. This was selected, therefore, as the mode and point of attack.

On Saturday the troops were all brought closely up to Centreville,—and all needful preparations were made for the attack which was intended for the next day. Yesterday morning, therefore, the Army marched—by two roads—Col. RICHARDSON with his command taking the Southern, which leads to Bull's Run, and Gen. TYLER the Northern—running parallel to it at a distance of about a mile and a half. The movement commenced at about 3 o'clock. I got up at a little before 4, and found the long line of troops extended far out on either road. I took the road by which Colonel HUNTER with his command, and Gen. McDOWELL and staff, had gone, and pushed on directly for the front. After going out about two miles Colonel HUNTER turned to the right—marching obliquely towards the Run, which he was to cross some four miles higher up and then come down upon the intrenched positions of the enemy on the other side. Col. MILES was left at Centerville and on the road, with reserves which he was to bring up whenever they might be needed. Gen. TYLER went directly forward, to engage the enemy in front, and send reinforcements to Col. HUNTER whenever it should be seen that he was engaged. Perhaps the following very rough diagram may render the relative position of these several localities somewhat more intelligible:

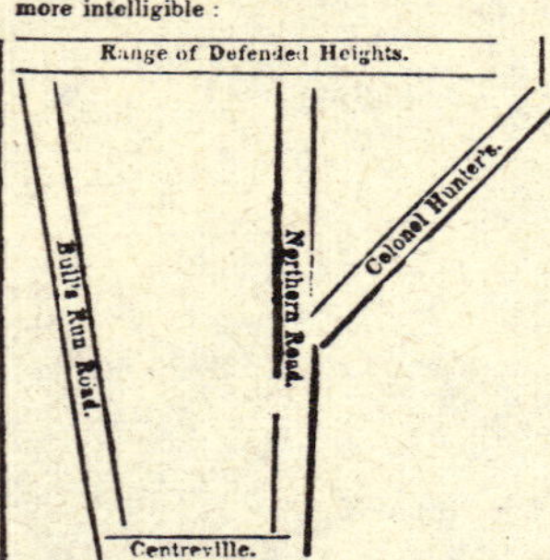

I went out, as I have already stated, upon what is marked as the northern road. It is hilly, like all the surface of this section. After going out about three miles, you come to a point down which the road, leading through a forest, descends;—then it proceeds by a succession of rising and falling knolls for a quarter of a mile,—when it crosses a stone bridge and then ascends by a steady slope to the heights beyond. At the top of that slope, the rebels had planted heavy batteries, and the woods below were filled with their troops and with concealed cannon. We proceeded down the road to the first of the small knolls mentioned, when the whole column halted. The 30-pounder Parrott gun, which has a longer range than any other in the army, was planted directly in the road. Capt. AYRES' battery was stationed in the woods a little to the right. The First Ohio and Second New-York Regiments were thrown into the woods in advance on the left. The Sixty-ninth, New-York, the First, Second and Third Connecticut regiments, were ranged behind them, and the Second Wisconsin was thrown into the woods on the right. At about half past six o'clock the 30-pounder threw two shells directly into the battery at the summit of the slope, on the opposite height, one of which, as I learned afterwards, struck and exploded directly in the midst of the battery, and occasioned the utmost havoc and confusion. After about half an hour Capt. AYRES threw ten or fifteen shot and shell from his battery into the same place. But both failed to elicit any reply. Men could be seen moving about the opposite slope, but the batteries were silent. An hour or so afterwards we heard three or four heavy guns from Col. RICHARDSON'S column at Bull's Run, and these were continued at intervals for two or three hours, but they were not answered, even by a single gun. It was very clear that the enemy intended to take his own time for paying his respects to us, and that he meant, moreover, to do it in his own way. Meantime we could hear in the distance the sound of Col. HUNTER'S axemen, clearing his way, and awaited with some impatience the sound of his cannon on the opposite heights. Time wore along with occasional shots from our guns, as well as those of Col. RICHARDSON'S column, but without, in a single instance, receiving any reply.

At a little before 11 o'clock, the First Ohio and Second New-York, which were lying in the wood on the left, were ordered to advance. They did so,—passing out of the road and climbing a fence into a wood opposite, which they had barely approached, however, when they were met by a tremendous discharge of a four-gun battery, planted at the left in the woods, mainly for the purpose of sweeping the road perpendicularly and the open field on its right by which alone troops could pass forward to the opposite bank. They were staggered for a moment, and received orders to retire. Capt. AYRES' Battery (formerly SHERMAN'S) was advanced a little, so as to command this Battery, and by twenty minutes of vigorous play upon it, silenced it completely.

At half-past 11 we heard HUNTER'S guns on the opposite height, over a mile to the right. He was answered by batteries there, and then followed the sharp, rattling volleys of musketry, as their infantry became engaged. The firing was now incessant. HUNTER had come upon them suddenly, and formed his line of battle in an open field, at the right of the road. The enemy drew up to oppose him, but he speedily drove them to retreat and followed them up with the greatest vigor and rapidity. Meantime, for some three hours previous, we had seen long lines of dense dust rising from the roads leading from Manassas, and, with the glass, we could very clearly perceive that they were raised by the constant and steady stream of reinforcements, which continued to pour in nearly the whole day. The Sixty-Ninth, Seventy-ninth, Second and Eighth, New-York—the First, Second and Third Connecticut, and the Second Wisconsin, were brought forward in advance of the wood and marched across the field to the right, to go to Col. HUNTER'S support. They crossed the intervening stream and drew up in a small open field, separated from Col. HUNTER'S column by a dense wood, which was filled with batteries and infantry. Our guns continued to play upon the woods which thus concealed the enemy, and aided materially in clearing them for the advance. Going down to the extreme front of the column, I could watch the progress of Col. HUNTER, marked by the constant roar of artillery and the roll of musketry, as he pushed the rebels back from point to point. At 1 o'clock he had driven them out of the woods and across the road which was the prolongation of that on which we stood. Here, by the side of their batteries, the rebels made a stand. They planted their flag directly in the road, and twice charged across it upon our men, but without moving them an inch. They were met by a destructive fire, and were compelled to fall still further back. Gradually the point of fire passed further away, until the dense clouds of smoke which marked the progress of the combat were at least half a mile to the left of what had been the central position of the rebels.

It was now 2½ o'clock. I was at the advanced point of the front of our column, some hundred rods beyond the woods, in which the few troops then there were drawn up, when I decided to drive back to the town, for the purpose of sending you my dispatch. As I passed up the road the balls and shell from the enemy began to fall with more than usual rapidity. I did not see the point from which they came; but meeting Capt. AYRES, he said he was about to bring up his battery, supported by the Ohio Brigade, under Gen. SCHENCK, to repel a rumored attempt of cavalry to outflank this column. As I went forward he passed down. Gen. SCHENCK'S Brigade was at once drawn up across the road, and Capt. AYRES' guns were planted in a knoll at the left, when a powerful body of rebels, with a heavy battery, came down from the direction of Bull's Run, and engaged this force with tremendous effect. I went to Centreville, sent off my dispatch, and started with all speed to return,—intending to go with our troops upon what had been the hotly contested field, never doubting for a moment that it would remain in their hands. I had gone but a quarter of a mile when we met a great number of fugitives, and our carriage soon became entangled in a mass of baggage-wagons, the officer in charge of which told me it was useless to go in that direction, as our troops were retreating. Not crediting the story, which was utterly inconsistent with what I had seen but a little while before, I continued to push on. I soon met Quartermaster STETSON, of the Fire Zouaves, who told me, bursting into tears, that his Regiment had been utterly cut to pieces, that the Colonel and Lieutenant-Colonel were both killed, and that our troops had actually been repulsed. I still tried to proceed, but the advancing columns rendered it impossible, and I turned about. Leaving my carriage, I went to a high point of ground and saw, by the dense cloud of dust which rose over each of the three roads by which the three columns of the Army had advanced, that they were all on the retreat. Sharp discharges of cannon in their rear indicated that they were being pursued. I waited half an hour or so, to observe the troops and batteries as they arrived, and then started for Washington, to send my dispatch and write this letter. As I came past the hill on which the Secessionists had their intrenchments less than a week ago, I saw our forces taking up positions for a defence if they should be assailed.

Such is a very rapid and general history of yesterday's engagement. I am unable to be precise or profuse in matters of detail, and must leave these to a future letter.

I hear nothing, on every side, but the warmest and heartiest commendation of our troops. They fought like veterans. The rebels did not, in a single instance, stand before them in a charge, and were shaken by every volley of their musketry. I do not mean to praise any one at the expense of another. The Sixty-ninth fought with splendid and tenacious courage. They charged batteries two or three times, and would have taken and held them but for the reinforcements which were constantly and steadily poured in. *Indeed it was to this fact alone* that the comparative success of the rebels is due. We had not over 20,000 men in action, the rest being held behind as reserves at Centreville; while the enemy must have numbered at least 60,000.

The Fire Zouaves before they had fairly got into action, were terribly cut up by a battery and by musketry, which opened on their flank. They lost a great many of their officers and men.

Col. HUNTER, who led the main column of attack, received a severe wound in his throat; he was brought to this city, but I understand that he cannot recover, if indeed he is not already dead. I have heard the names of many others reported killed or wounded, but deem it best not to mention them now, as the rumors may prove to be unfounded.

About a mile this side of Centreville a stampede took place among the teamsters and others, which threw everything into the utmost confusion, and inflicted some very serious injuries. Mr. EATON, of Michigan, in trying to arrest the flight of some of these men, was shot by one of them,—the ball taking effect in his hand. Quite a number of Senators and members of the House were present at the battle.

I shall be able to ascertain to-morrow the cause of the retreat of Col. HUNTER'S column after the splendid success it achieved. I would gladly, though in the face of evidence unable, believe what is rumored here, that this column did indeed hold its ground, and that the retreat was confined to the other columns. I fear this will not prove to be the fact.

H. J. R.

SPECIAL DISPATCHES TO THE N. Y. TIMES.

WASHINGTON, Monday, July 22.

Stragglers from the Army create great but needless excitement, by stories that the rebels are coming to Washington. There is not the slightest cause for any such apprehension. The Army is falling back upon Arlington, and new regiments are constantly arriving from the North.

It is not easy to account for the panic which occasioned the first movement of retreat, but the most probable account is, that it was caused by a charge of cavalry, which was repulsed by the regiment upon which it was made, but which threw another, upon which in turn, it fell into confusion.

The Army, in its retreat from Centreville, was protected in rear by Col. MILES' Reserve.

Some fifty or one hundred of the Fire Zouaves have just arrived here. The rumor is circulated that this is all that is left of the regiment, but this is not so. These are only those who have come on singly in advance.

Exaggerated statements about the losses of individual regiments increase the excitement and cause heedless grief. The official list will be published as speedily as possible. All access to the Army across the Potomac is impossible.

DISPATCH TO THE ASSOCIATED PRESS.

WASHINGTON, Monday, July 22.

After the latest information was received from Centreville at 7½ o'clock last night, a series of events took place in the intensest degree disastrous.

Many confused statements are prevalent, but enough is known to warrant the statement that we have suffered in a degree which has cast a gloom over the remnants of the Army, and excited the deepest melancholy throughout Washington.

The carnage is tremendously heavy on both side, and on ours it is represented as frightful. We were advancing and taking the masked batteries gradually but surely, and driving the enemy towards Manassas Junction, when the enemy seemed to have been reinforced by Gen. JOHNSTON, who, it is understood, took command, and immediately commenced driving us back, when a panic among our troops suddenly occurred, and a regular stampede took place.

It is thought that Gen. McDOWELL undertook to make a stand at or about Centreville, but the panic was so fearful that the whole Army became demoralized, and it was impossible to check them either at Centreville or Fairfax Court-house.

Gen. McDOWELL intended to make another stand at Fairfax Court-house, but, our forces being in full retreat, he could not accomplish the object.

Beyond Fairfax Court-house the retreat was kept up until the men reached their regular encampments, a portion of whom returned to them, but a still larger portion coming inside the intrenchments.

A large number of troops fell on the wayside from exhaustion, and scattered along the route all the way from Fairfax Court house.

The road from Bull's Run was strewed with knapsacks, arms, &c. Some of our troops deliberately threw away their guns and appurtenances, the better to facilitate their travel.

Gen. McDOWELL was in the rear of the retreat, exerting himself to rally his men, but only with partial effect.

The latter part of the Army, it is said, made their retreat in order. He was completely exhausted, having slept but little for three nights. His orders on the field did not at all times reach those for whom they were intended.

It is supposed that the force sent out against our troops consisted, according to a prisoner's statement, of about 30,000 men, including a large number of cavalry. He further says, that owing to reinforcements from Richmond, Strausburgh, and other points, the enemy's effective force was 90,000 men.

According to the statement of two Fire Zouaves, they only have about 200 left from the slaughter, while the Sixty-ninth and Seventy-ninth Regiments frightfully suffered in killed and wounded. The number cannot now be known.

SHERMAN'S, CARLISLE'S, GRIFFIN'S, and the West Point Batteries, were taken by the enemy, and the eight siege and 32 rifle cannon, the latter being too cumbrous to remove. They were two miles the other side of Centreville. Such of the wounded as were brought to the Centreville Hospital were left there, after having their wounds properly dressed by Surgeon FRANK H. HAMILTON.

The panic was so great that the attempt to rally them to a stand at Centreville was entirely in vain. If a firm stand had been made there our troops could have been reinforced and much disaster prevented. Gen. McDOWELL was thus foiled in his well-arranged plans.

It is supposed all the provision trains belonging to the United States Government were saved. Some regimental wagons were overturned by accident, or the wheels came off, and had, therefore, to be abandoned. Large droves of cattle were saved by being driven back in advance of the retreat.

It is supposed here, to-day, that Gen. MANSFIELD will take command of the fortifications on the other side of the river, which are able, it is said, by military engineers, to hold out against any force the enemy may bring against them. Large rifled cannon and mortars are being rapidly sent over and mounted.

An officer just from Virginia, (10:30,) reports that the road from Centreville to the Potomac is strewed with stragglers. The troops are resuming the occupations of the fortifications and intrenchments on the line of the Potomac.

Col. MARSTON'S New-Hampshire Regiment reached here this morning. He was wounded. Col. HEINTZELMAN was also wounded in the wrist. In addition to those reported yesterday, it is said that Col. WILCOX, the gallant commander of a brigade, was killed. Also Capt. McCOOK, a brother of Col. COOK, of Ohio.

The city this morning is in the most intense excitement. Groups are everywhere gathered inquiring the latest news.

Wagons are continually arriving, bringing in the dead and wounded. Soldiers are relating to greedy listeners the deplorable events of last night and early this morning. The feeling is awfully distressing. Both telegraph communication and steamboat communication with Alexandria is suspended to-day to the public. The greatest alarm exists throughout the city, especially among the female portion of the population.

ANOTHER ACCOUNT OF THE ORIGIN OF THE PANIC.

WASHINGTON, Monday, July 22.

The following is an account of the inauguration of the panic which has resulted so disastrously to our troops. It receives additional interest from the subsequent events:

All our military operations went swimmingly on, and Col. ALEXANDER was about erecting a pontoon across Bull's Run. The enemy was seemingly in retreat, and their batteries being unmasked, one after another, when a terrific consternation broke out among the teamsters, who had incautiously advanced immediately after the body of the Army, and lined the Warrenton road. Their consternation was shared in by numerous civilians, who were on the ground, and for a time it seemed as if our whole army was in retreat. Many baggage wagons were emptied and their horses galloped across the open fields, all the fences of which were torn down to allow them a more rapid retreat. For a time a perfect panic prevailed, which communicated itself to the vicinity of Centreville, and every available conveyance was seized upon by agitated civilians. Wounded soldiers cried on the roadside for assistance, but the alarm was so great that numbers were passed by.

Several similar alarms occurred on previous occasions, when a change of batteries rendered the retirement of the artillery necessary on our part, and it is most probable that the alarm was owing to the same fact.

The reserve force at Centreville was immediately brought up, and marched in double quick step in the following order:

Col. EINSTEIN'S Twenty-seventh Pennsylvania Regiment, with two guns; the Garibaldi Guards and Col. BLENKER'S First Rifle Regiment, with its batteries, followed at several miles distance by the DeKalb Regiment.

When our courier left, at 4½ o'clock, it was in the midst of this excitement. Two new masked batteries had been opened by the rebels on the left flank, and that portion of the division had its lines broken and demanded immediate reinforcements. The right was in good order. The battery erected on the hillside directly opposite the main battery of the enemy was doing good execution and additional guns were being mounted. On his arrival at Fairfax Court-house, he was overtaken by a Government messenger, who reported that our Army was in full retreat toward Centreville. They were followed by less agitated parties, who stated that the report of the retreat was owing to the fact that the alarm among the teamsters had communicated itself to the volunteers, and even, in some instances, to the regulars, and the lines were broken, and that a retirement of our forces across Bull's Run was rendered necessary.

Col. HUNTER passed, at the same time, in a vehicle, wounded.

Ayres' Battery was also reported as lost.

Crowds of carriages and baggage wagons came rushing down the road.

The telegraph office was closed against all private business, and in an hour the alarm had been communicated all along the road to Washington.

DISASTERS OF THE BATTLE.

WASHINGTON, Monday, July 22.

The Rhode Island Battery was taken by the rebels at the bridge across Bull's Run, where their retreat was cut off. Their horses were all killed. It is reported that the Black Horse Cavalry made an attack on the rear of the retreating Army, when the latter turned and fired, killing all but six of the assaulting party.

The Seventy-first, New-York, lost about half their men.

The following regiments were engaged in the fight:

The First, Second and Third Connecticut Regiments.

The First Regiment of Regulars, composed of the second, third and eighth companies.

Two hundred and fifty Marines.

The Eighth and Fourteenth New-York militia.

The First and Second Rhode Island.

The Seventy-first New-York.

The Second New-Hampshire.

The Fifth Massachusetts.

The First Minnesota.

The First Michigan.

The Eleventh and Thirty-eighth New-York.

The Second, Fourth and Fifth Maine, and the Second Vermont Regiments, besides the several batteries.

Add to killed, Lieut.-Colonel FOWLER, of New-York Fourteenth. Add to wounded, Col. LAWRENCE, of Fifth Massachusetts Regiment; Capt. ELLIS, of Seventy-first New-York, (badly)

Col. FARNHAM and Major LOZIER, of the Zouaves, are not killed, but badly wounded.

The following is a partial list of the officers killed and wounded:

KILLED.—Capt. McCOOK, the Major and Lieutenant-Colonel of the Zouaves; Capt. GORDON, Company H, Eleventh Massachusetts; Capt. FAY, Company H, Second Rhode Island; Col. SLOCUM, of the Second Rhode Island; Col. SLOCUM, of the Twenty-second New-York; Col. WILCOX, of the First Michigan.

WOUNDED.—Col. TOMPKINS, of the New-York Second; Col. FARNHAM, of the Fire Zouaves; Col. HUNTER, United States Army; Col. CORCORAN, Sixty-ninth New-York Regiment, and Col. CLARK, Eleventh Massachusetts.

Capt. RICKETTS, of the Artillery, and two New-York Regiments, have gone over to Virginia.

It is vaguely reported that Gen. PATTERSON'S division arrived in the vicinity of Manassas this morning and commenced an attack on the rebel forces. He was within twenty-five miles of the battle-ground yesterday, but the exhausted condition of his men prevented him from coming to the aid of McDOWELL.

It is also reported that 4,000 of our troops have been sent back towards Fairfax, from the other side of the river.

It was the remnant of the Zouaves that were attacked by the Black Horse Cavalry and repulsed them, leaving but six to return. The gallant regiment now numbers but a couple of hundred.

It is probable that the number of killed and wounded is magnified by large numbers who are missing, probably wandering through the woods.

The lowest estimate may be placed at 4,000 to 5,000.

It is represented in many quarters that the Ohio regiments showed the greatest consternation, probably from want of confidence in their commanding officers. It is known that on the day previous to the battle a large number of them publicly protested against being led by Gen. SCHENCK, and it was only through the importunities of Col. McCOOK, in whom they placed all confidence, and other officers, that they were prevented from making a more formidable rebellion.

The Pennsylvania Fourth was not in the action, having left for home on the morning of the battle, their term of service having expired.

It was known to our troops at the time of the battle, yesterday, that Gen. JOHNSTON had formed a connection with BEAUREGARD on the night of the first action at Bull's Run.

Our men could distinctly hear the cars coming into Manassas Junction, and the cheers with which the Confederates hailed their newly arriving comrades. They knew that the enemy was our superior in numbers and in their own position.

These facts were further confirmed by prisoners taken, deserters and spies, but they were not probably known at Washington, and the officers in leading our men into action only obeyed orders.

Gen. SCHENCK, as well as the older field officers, acted admirably. He collected his forces and covered the retreat, and up to the last moment was personally engaged in the endeavor to rally his men to make a stand at Centreville.

It was the arrival of fresh reinforcements to the enemy in superior numbers that turned the scale of battle.

The enemy before now might, perhaps, have more to boast of if they had followed up their advantage last night.

THE NATIONAL AND REBEL LOSSES AT BULL'S RUN.

WASHINGTON, Monday, July 22,
Via BALTIMORE, Monday, July 22.

I have spent eight hours in carefully questioning the returned soldiers in various parts of the city. Our losses are far less severe than was at first reported by scared civilians and running soldiers. There are probably not 300 killed, and perhaps not 200. For example, the Second Connecticut Regiment, returned, which was reported in the morning as badly cut up, lost but a dozen.

The New-Haven Grays have all returned unharmed, yet this regiment was exposed to frequent volleys of cannon and musketry.

Again, 200 of Ellsworth's Fire Zouaves were reported to have been surrounded in the road and annihilated by the Black Horse Cavalry. On the contrary, they cut down and destroyed the Cavalry, and suffered little loss themselves.

In this encounter, the New-York Seventy-first, also reported as used up, suffered but little; and so of others. Few of the vast number of balls fired by the rebels took effect. On the contrary, all the instances detailed by our men, show that the enemy suffered severely.

Three New-York Fire Zouaves, who were scouting in the advance, hunted the rebels on the sly, like squirrels, among the bushes, and chalked down 26 as positively killed by them.

The New-York Seventy-first came upon a rifled gun. It lost eight men, but in return killed the whole of the 18 rebels secreted.

BETTER NEWS FROM THE SEAT OF WAR.

WASHINGTON, Monday, July 22.

The number of killed and wounded is gradually decreasing. Six hundred Zouaves have returned.

Rest satisfied that we will furnish information as soon as possible regarding names, &c., but there is too much liability to mistake for haste.

It is now understood that Col. WILCOX, reported killed, is living, though badly wounded.

The Government entertains no apprehension for the safety of the Capital. Preparations not only for the defensive, but for the renewal of offensive operations are going on vigorously.

Gen. McDOWELL has returned to his head-quarters at Arlington Heights. The regiments comprising his Army will resume their position. Most of them have already done so.

GEN. McCLELLAN ASSIGNED TO THE COMMAND OF THE POTOMAC.

WASHINGTON, Monday, July 22.

Gen. McCLELLAN has been summoned by the Government from Western Virginia to repair to Washington to take command of the Army of the Potomac.

Gen. ROSENCRANZ takes his place in command of the Army of Western Virginia.

The *Corps d'Armee* at Washington is to be instantly reorganized and increased. The orders have already been given. Offers of regiments already raised and being made, will be accepted with such rapidity as to insure that this will be accomplished in a few days. Large reinforcements from various districts are already on the way hither, orders having been telegraphed for them yesterday, while the battle was in progress.

DISPATCH FROM SECRETARY CAMERON.

OUR REGIMENTS NOT SO BADLY CUT UP.

Mr. C. A. STETSON, of the Astor House, has received the following dispatch from Mr. Secretary CAMERON:

C. A. Stetson, Astor House:

In reply to your dispatch, I am happy to be able to say that our loss is much less than was at first represented, and the troops have reached the forts in much better condition than was expected. The Department is making vigorous exertions to concentrate at this point an overwhelming force, and the response from all quarters has been truly patriotic. A number of regiments have arrived since last evening. There is no danger of the Capital or the Republic.

SIMON CAMERON.

SECESSION ACCOUNT OF THE BATTLE.

RICHMOND, Va., Sunday, July 21,
via NEW-ORLEANS, Monday, July 22.

A fight commenced near Manassas, at 4 o'clock this morning, and became general about 12. It continued till about 7, when the Nationalists retired, leaving us in possession of the field. SHERMAN'S Battery and Light Artillery was taken. It was a terrible battle, with great slaughter on both sides. It is impossible to give details to-night.

REBEL ACCOUNT OF THE FIRST FIGHT.

LOUISVILLE, Monday, July 22.

A special dispatch to the Nashville *Union* from Manassas, 18th, says that at the fight at Bull's Run Gen. BEAUREGARD commanded in person. The enemy was repulsed three times in great confusion and loss. The Washington Artillery of New-Orleans, with seven guns, engaged SHERMAN'S fifteen guns, and, after making the latter change position fifteen times, silenced and forced them to retire. Large quantities of arms were taken. Our loss was trifling. Maj. HARRISON and two privates were killed. Capts. DULANY, CHITTMAN and three privates were wounded. A National officer of high rank was killed, and $700 in gold taken from his body.

THE EFFECT OF THE NEWS IN THIS CITY.

The news of our national disaster fell upon the public with overwhelming force. It came at a time when the full torrent of exultation at a supposed victory was spreading itself through the City, and cheering hearts that might be rendered desolate by the first details of the fight. No one was prepared for a check so abrupt. When the first dirty newsboy whirled through the streets, shrieking at the top of his ominous voice, "Defeat of the Union Army," no one felt the slightest disposition to buy an extra. It was regarded as a smart commercial fraud, which ought to be put a stop to by the police. But bad tidings travel apace, and in a short time it was known that a reverse had really been encountered. The newsboys—who, if they wrong as a rule, are sometimes wronged as an exception—were then in demand. Their stock of papers was rapidly exhausted, and the supply not being able to keep pace with the demand, the fortunate possessor of an extra became a sort of animated bulletin. Circles that constantly increased gathered around him, and heard with consternation the unhappy tidings. From 11 A. M. until midnight business, as an absorbing and distinct pursuit, was virtually suspended. Those who made a show of attending to it were so disheartened and preoccupied that they will probably regret having done so. In Wall-street, where the death of one's grandmother has a commercial value, the reverse was considered disadvantageous to our cause to the extent of 4 per cent. Securities declined to that extent.

No event of the present war, not even excepting the capture of Fort Sumter, has caused so intense an excitement, or stimulated our population to a greater expression of patriotism. The usual mid-day resorts were crowded. It is months since they have presented so animated an appearance. The various dispatches to the Press were compared with a closeness which, if practiced daily, would be fatal to penny-a-liners. The slightest discrepancies were commented upon, and a general complaint prevailed that there was a lack of details. When, later in the day, Mr. RAYMOND'S letter was received, and it became apparent that portions of his former dispatches had been eliminated in Washington, there was a strong and decided expression of disapprobation. If we were defeated, they said, why was the news suppressed until after Wall-street had had an opportunity of operating on the basis of a victory? We repeat simply what we heard.

The surprise and consternation excited by the intelligence had somewhat subsided when a different feeling took possession of the masses. The blow had been felt—how severely no one can describe—but when the stupor it had caused passed off the eye was clear, the muscle braced and the purpose strong. It could be avenged. Northern men, they said, are all the better for being beaten once or twice. We know our foe now, and woe to him. For each man that has fallen, a dozen will spring to fill his place. So genuine was the impulse of renewed patriotism, that the various recruiting offices in the City secured more men yesterday than they have done on any previous day of the past month. It is cold water that hardens steel, and disaster that proves the metal of a nation. A rumor prevailed during the day, that the Seventh

[*Continued on Eighth Page.*]

The New-York Times.

OL. X....NO. 3069. NEW-YORK, WEDNESDAY, JULY 24, 1861. PRICE TWO CENTS.

THE GREAT REBELLION.

The Victory of Sunday, and How it was Lost.

Exaggerations of the First Reports Corrected.

THE NATIONAL ARMY NOT ROUTED.

A Body of Troops Still at Centreville.

Our Loss in Killed and Wounded not Over Six Hundred.

The Rebel Loss Estimated at Three Thousand.

THEIR TROOPS IN NO CONDITION TO PURSUE.

Shocking Barbarities Perpetrated by the Rebels.

They Make Targets of the Wounded Soldiers, Mutilate them with Knives, and Fire at the Hospital.

Brilliant and Dashing Bravery of the Fire Zouaves.

They Annihilate the Black Horse Cavalry.

Lists of Our Killed and Wounded.

SPECIAL DISPATCHES FROM WASHINGTON.

WASHINGTON, Tuesday, July 23.

The feeling is much better here to-day. The enormous exaggerations of the runaway soldiers have ceased to have the effect which attended them yesterday. Our loss in killed and wounded will not much exceed six hundred, though the missing may be three times that number.

It is understood that the Government has already taken the necessary steps to bring one hundred thousand men into the field here, and this renews the confidence and determination of the people.

Col. Ramsay's regiment has been accepted, and ordered to report at Washington within twenty days, and muster in by hundreds.

The losses of the New-York and other regiments have been greatly overstated. The Seventy-first has not lost over thirty in killed and wounded. The Fire Zouaves suffered more severely, as did also the Sixty-ninth. Capt. T. F. Meagher had a horse shot under him, but is untouched. All our losses were in advancing—none in falling back. There was no panic in front. This was confined mainly to the wagon drivers, straggling soldiers and fugitive officers, at the rear of the columns.

Our greatest deficiency was in cool and competent officers. The men fought nobly, and were ready for anything which experienced commanders would order them to do.

Gen. McDowell behaved admirably. He was active, cool, and attended to everything in person, so far as possible; but he had not a sufficient staff, and was not properly supported by his subordinates. Major Wadsworth, of New-York, one of his aids, showed the utmost gallantry and devotion. He exerted himself to rally the forces when they first fell back, and towards the close, after having his horse shot under him, seized the colors of the wavering New-York Fourteenth, and called on the boys to rally once more to the glorious old flag. Private Tyler took hold of the colors with him, and the regiment rallied to another charge, but without success. Major Wadsworth, as the Army retreated, remained at Fairfax Court-house, and devoted himself to purchasing everything needful for the wounded, of whom about a hundred and fifty were at that place.

Gov. Sprague behaved with conspicuous gallantry, and insisted on making a stand for another fight at Centreville, but the men were too much demoralized by the panic which sprung up in the rear.

Col. Burnside displayed great activity and courage at every stage of the fight, and is eager to renew it. Cols. Hunter and Heintzelman have sent word that, in spite of their wounds, they will take the field again in two days, if desired. When the Fourteenth New-York entered the field, they passed a wounded major of the rebel army, who begged for water. A private gave it to him, and he offered his gold watch in return. The private declined to take it, but the Major insisted, as he said some one else would get it if he did not. The testimony is universal to the barbarity and ferocity with which our wounded were treated by the rebels. Gen. Scott is in good spirits, and hard at work. Russell got a report of the fight off in time for the Boston steamer.

FROM ANOTHER CORRESPONDENT.

WASHINGTON, Tuesday, July 23.

I have gathered the following lists of killed and wounded in the Fire Zouaves.

John Gleason, Company I, wounded.

James Hurley, Company I, killed by a pistol-shot in his own hands.

Michael Kane, Company F, wounded.

Barber, Company C, killed.

Murray, Company C, killed.

David Small, Company I, killed.

James McNamee, Company I, wounded and left.

James Norton, Company I, wounded.

John O'Brien, Company I, wounded.

Thos. Goodwin, Sergeant-Major, Company I, wounded in the foot.

Patrick Cook, Company I, wounded and left.

Chas. Lynch, Company I, wounded in the hand.

Jas. McGuire, Company I, killed.

Robert Brown, Sergeant, Company B, killed.

Gorman, Company B, killed.

James Williams, Company H, wounded

Bragdon, Company H, wounded.

Coon, Company I, killed.

Wm. Heap, Company H, wounded.

Terrance Ryan, Company A, wounded.

Wm. Waters, Company K, wounded.

Hasler, Company K, killed.

Carroll, Company K, wounded.

David Fleming, Company K, wounded.

John Drout, Company K, wounded.

John Finn, Company K, wounded.

Capt. Coulter and Capt. Bryant, of the Seventy-ninth, are killed.

The following are wounded in the Seventy-first:

Capt. Dunham, Company G.

Capt. Hart, Company E.

Capt. Ellis, Company F.

John Morrissey, Company H, wounded.

John Cobb, Company H, wounded.

H. W. Linderbeck, Company H, wounded.

Lieut. Embley, Company H, wounded.

The Seventy-first are gathering at the Navy-yard in their former encampment. They estimate their loss in killed, wounded and missing, at eighty to one hundred. The survivors are in the best condition, and in good spirits.

The surgeon who was in charge of the one hospital at Centreville, states that when he left there yesterday morning at 9 o'clock, the rebel pickets were within one hundred rods of the village. There were in the hospital 120 when he retired. Of course, they fell into the hands of the rebels. He estimated our wounded at not exceeding 400 to 500.

Col. Corcoran is still missing at 9 o'clock this morning, but hopes are entertained that he is safe.

During the fight, the rebels carried American flags to deceive our men, when small squads that had got separated from their regiments, approached these flags, they were fired upon and slaughtered. The rebels also fired upon the wounded, standing them up for targets, and then firing at them. One of the Connecticut men saw this done.

A number of the Second New-York saw the rebel Sharp-shooters fire upon and kill two vivandieres who were giving wine and water to the wounded.

The rebels also shot at ambulances, bringing off the wounded. They also fired point blank at the buildings used as hospitals, and it is said by some that they fired the buildings.

Capt. Haggerty, of the Sixty-ninth, was killed in a charge. When his body was found, his throat was cut from ear to ear, and his ears and nose were cut off. Many of the wounded were found thus disfigured.

It is charged very positively that Capt. Alexander, of the regular army, who was in command of a battery, showed cowardice, and was the first to run away.

Arnold Harris, a former officer in the Army, a former proprietor of the *Union* and *States* newspapers, and a strong Secessionist, has been sent to recover the body of Col. Cameron.

When the colors of the Sixty-ninth were captured by the Virginians, two of them seized the flags and were going off with them, when Lieut. Matthews, of Company K, Fire Zouaves, fired and killed both the Virginians, and recovered the flags.

Capt. Wildey, of Company I, Zouaves, killed two out of four Mississippians who were dragging a gun. All our men agree in representing that the rebel infantry will not stand a fair fight, even with three to our one. They gave way whenever attacked, when not supported by artillery.

WASHINGTON, Tuesday, July 23—2 P. M.

Capt. Todd, of Brattleboro, Vt., and the Major of the Second Vermont, are among the wounded.

The stragglers are gradually gathering together, but very slowly. Most of them are ambitious of telling their own stories, and as they have crowds of listeners, they do not like to go again into camp.

The Government has taken possession of the rolling stock and tracks between this city and Baltimore, and will hold all for the use of Government.

Two hundred volunteer surgeons came from Philadelphia this morning.

The body of Col. Kennedy, of the Tammany Regiment, will be sent to New-York by the train this afternoon.

The first installment of Col. Van. Allen's regiment of cavalry, from New-York, reached Washington last night. It consisted of Capt. Fitzsimmons' company from Rochester, eighty-five men and horses.

The remnants of the regiments composing Gen. McDowell's Army occupy the lines they left before their advance upon Manassas.

Many of the citizens of Washington are again leaving the city, fearful of an attack from the rebels under Beauregard. The Secessionists of Washington make no concealment of their exultation. The prisoners taken from the rebels and in confinement in Washington are liberally supplied with cakes, pies, wines and clothing by women who commend them as the greatest patriots in the country.

Among the dispatches received at the Washington office to-day, was the following, addressed to a member of one of the regiments quartered at Arlington Heights, of course of the Sixty-ninth:

NEW-YORK, July 23, 1861.

Your wife wishes to know if you are dead, alive or wounded. If dead, please send the body on.

A spectator of the scene tells me that the Zouaves literally decimated the Black Horse Cavalry, the celebrated rebel troop. About the middle of the battle the Zouaves fired by platoons upon the rebel infantry stationed in the woods. After they had fired they discovered a troop of horse coming down on their rear. They carried the American flag, which deceived Col. Heintzelman, and made him believe they were United States Cavalry, and he so told the Zouaves. As they came nearer, their true character was discovered, but too late for all the Zouaves to reload. The regiment faced and received the cavalry as they came down, with leveled bayonets, which threw them into confusion. Then away went muskets, and the Zouaves went in with their knives and pistols. They seized horses and stabbed their riders. In this hand-to-hand conflict the Black Horse Troop were handled in their own professed way of fighting. The sequel showed the Zouaves to be the most expert handlers of the knife.

When the fight was over, there were not twenty of the four hundred cavalry left alive. Men and horses had been cut to pieces by the infuriated red-shirts. This troop of cavalry had boasted they would picket their horses in the grounds of the White House.

The telegraph office here is besieged by a crowd sending messages to friends. The capacity of the office is not equal to the extraordinary demand upon it, which will account for any delay in the receipt of answers to inquiries. LEO.

WASHINGTON, Tuesday, July 23—6 P. M.

The following are the wounded in the Twenty-seventh Regiment, N. Y. V., Col Slocum, as fully as they could be ascertained, at the Head-quarters of the regiment, up to 4 o'clock this afternoon:

Thomas Betts, Company B. thumb shot off.

Charles Miller, Company D, shot in the hand.

W. N. Bawker, Company C. flesh wound in left breast.

J. W. Butler, Company C, rib broken.

H. O. Wheeler, Company C, shot through the foot.

Martin Green, Company C, shot through the leg.

Sergeant G. Williamson, Company C, fractured ribs.

Wm. Gerret, Company C, Wound in the ankle.

J. Williams, Company C, slightly wounded.

Daniel Meanish, Company A, wounded in the head and back.

Daniel Favington, Company A, wounded in the groin.

Wm. D. Giles, Second Corporal, Company A, wounded in the shoulder.

Levi Daniels, Company A, wounded in the leg.

Andrew Biesinger, Company A, wounded in the hand.

Nathaniel Wright, Company A, wounded in the leg.

Chas. H. Dick, Company A, wounded in right arm.

S. J. Steele, Company G, wounded in the abdomen.

W. J. Runnell, Company D, bayonet wound in thigh.

Thomas G. Wier, teamster, dislocation of elbow.

Samuel Sedgwick, Company H, wounded in ankle joint.

Lieut. Phillips, Company G, contused wound.

Col. H. W. Slocum, wounded in the thigh.

Lieut.-Col. J. J. Chambers, contused wound in the leg.

Surgeon N. S. Barnes, contused wound in the knee:

The following are additional to the names heretofore sent of the Fire Zouaves:

Wm. B. Smith, Company K, shot through the leg.

W. Dwyer, Company D, wounded in the foot.

Henry Shields, Company B, wounded in the leg.

Thos. Thompson, Company A, wounded in the hand.

W. H. Underhill, Company A, wounded in the leg.

Robert Duffield, Company F, shot through the thigh.

Robert Dyer, Company F, finger shot off.

Michael Connell, Company F, shot through the arm.

Edward Sweeny, Company F, shot across the breast.

The following are additional to the list of the Seventy-first:

Wm. Broome, Company F, shot in the leg.

—— Merrill, Company F, shot in the throat.

Thos. Deavy, Company G. shot in the leg.

Abby, Company F, wounded in the breast.

Fred. Gilbert, Company G, shot in the leg.

Beverly Clark, Company F, shot in the arm.

John Eagleston, Company F, lost a finger.

Wm. Behan, Company F, shot in both legs.

C. Broome, Company F, shot in the arm.

F. Porter, Company H, Fourteenth Massachusetts, is wounded.

Lieut. G. Martin, Company G, Fifth Maine, wounded.

Lieut. Graham, Company D, Eleventh Massachusetts, is wounded in the hand.

Col. Lawrence, Fifth Massachusetts, was struck by a spent ball, not seriously.

Daniel W. Whittemore, Company A, of the Second New-Hampshire, is wounded in the leg

Isaac Derby, same Company, had his left arm shot off.

Arthur T. Pickett, Second Sergeant, Company I, Thirty-eighth, New-York, is wounded in the hands and legs by the bursting of a shell.

Lieut. Brady, Company D, same Regiment, has his wrist bone broken by a ball.

The body of Col. Kennedy, of the Tammany Regiment, was sent to New-York by the train to-day, in charge of his brother, John A. Kennedy, Superintendent of Police. Funeral ceremonies were had in the rooms of Geo. W. McLean, at Willard's, and the pall-bearers were officers of a corresponding rank to the deceased.

Ex-Vice-President Breckinridge visits the rebel prisoners taken at Fairfax and at Centreville, and does not, in his interviews with them, conceal his sympathy with them and their cause.

Henry Winn, of Mass., has been appointed clerk to the Senate Committee on Foreign Relations, in place of Ben: Perley Poore, who is to be Colonel of a Rifle Regiment, now being raised in Massachusetts.

The removal of Gen. Patterson was in response to strong remonstrances from Philadelphia, from men who questioned his loyalty. It will be recollected that after the surrender of Sumter, the people of Philadelphia demanded that certain persons should display the American flag, and that the first house visited by the excited populace was that of Gen. Patterson. The unerring instincts of the mob pointed him out then, as a sympathiser with the rebels, and later events go far to prove they were correct.

The colors of the Fifth Massachusetts Regiment were lost in the last fight, but rescued by one of the reporters, Mr. Stedman, of the *World.*

It is well authenticated that in several instances our men fired upon each other. Company I, of the Thirty-eighth Regiment New-York Volunteers, suffered severely from such a mischance.

The Government is making extensive arrangements for the arrival and care of troops. The Commissioner of Public Buildings, Mr. Woods, is engaged in fitting up barracks where arriving regiments can be properly cared for until prepared to go into camps. There is to be no more red-tapeism in that direction.

For the past twenty-four hours there is manifest for the first time real efficiency in several of the Departments, and a knowledge that the country expects now every man to do his duty.

Our loss of field pieces is not so great as I have heretofore estimated it. Every gun of Capt. Ayres' battery, formerly Sherman's, was brought off safe—only some caissons being lost. The loss of baggage wagons will not exceed fifty. In small arms, our loss is at least three thousand.

The colonels of our regiments appear to have been in the thickest of the fight, if we may judge by the casualties. The returns show four killed and seven wounded. There were thirty-six in the engagement, which gives a ratio of one in three killed or wounded.

DISPATCHES TO THE ASSOCIATED PRESS.

WASHINGTON, Tuesday, July 23.

The weather is bright and beautiful after the heavy rain of yesterday. This morning Pennsylvania-avenue and the streets present a lively appearance. The soldiers, in various garbs, are either wending their way to their respective places of rendezvous, or entertaining still anxious and curious persons with additional incidents of the battle and the subsequent stampede. Various groups are brightening up their muskets, or repairing the damages to their small arms and wardrobe.

The scene among the military in some quarters resemble those attending a dismissal after a grand holiday display. Whilst some of the soldiers are almost sinking under their pedestrian fatigue, those who were more fortunate in flying to Washington either on horses cut from the baggage-wagons or in vehicles, make a comparatively neat appearance.

Amid the hasty gathering of so many odds and ends of regiments, under such distressing circumstances, it is no wonder that the charities of our citizens are solicited. They are generously dispensed.

The morning is being occupied in putting affairs in order on the Virginia side, within the original National lines. From the indications around us, the business of repairing the commissariat and ordnance damage is in lively progress. The boats are again running to Alexandria.

The Fire Zouaves will rendezvous at the head-quarters of the Twelfth Regiment to-day, when some accurate knowledge of their losses will be ascertained in killed and wounded.

The last seen of the gallant Col. Wilcox, of the First Michigan Regiment, was lying wounded on the battle field. He is either dead, or a prisoner.

In the First Michigan Regiment the following are known to be killed:

Capt. Withington, Company B.

Capt. Butterworth, Company C.

Lieut. Casey, Company G.

Lieut. Monck, Company F.

Orderly Sergeant Lewis Hartmeyer, Company H.

Orderly Sergeant Hartmeyer, Company A.

Privates—Richard Jones, Company A; James Kelly, Company F, and both the color-bearers.

Privates Cunningham, of Company A, and John Stafford, of Company G, are among the wounded.

Major Bidwell took the place of Col. Wilcox, and managed to bring the regiment out of the field in the best possible order.

A Zouave drummer-boy, who was taken prisoner but escaped, reports that the Secessionists have an immense number of prisoners in their hands. It is supposed they were principally picked up on the way.

Fifteen members only of the First Ohio Regiment are missing. The officers are all safe.

WASHINGTON, Tuesday, July 23—6 P. M.

Our losses have been greatly exaggerated. It is now well ascertained that the killed will fall short of a thousand. The rebels did not follow our retreating forces after they passed Bull Run.

Col. Einstein, of the Pennsylvania Twenty-sixth Regiment, returned to the battle-field about 11 o'clock on Sunday night, and brought off six pieces of artillery, which he delivered to the commanding officer on the Potomac yesterday evening. The Colonel reports that the field was clear and not an enemy in sight.

The President and Secretary of War are vigorously at work reorganizing a powerful Army.

Within the last twenty-four hours over 60,000 fresh men, with a number of batteries of artillery, have been accepted. A number of regiments have arrived, and every day will bring immense reinforcements to the National Capital. Ten new regiments will be in Baltimore by this evening.

The response from every quarter has been most gratifying and truly patriotic.

LATEST DISPATCHES FROM WASHINGTON.

WASHINGTON, Tuesday, July 23—10 P. M.

The following letter was received this morning from Capt. Tyler, which seems to indicate that some of the troops must have stood ground at Centreville, and the rebels not have advanced immediately, if at all:

HEADQUARTERS, NEAR CENTREVILLE, Monday, July 22.

To Capt. Tyler, Assistant Commissary-General, Alexandria:

For God's sake send me some forage. I have 325 horses and nothing for them to eat.

(Signed) CAPT. GIBSON, Of the Franklin Brigade.

The state of affairs at Alexandria does not seem to indicate that we hold a position more advanced than that before the march commenced. No persons are allowed to pass beyond the lines, which seem to be within four or five miles. So stringent is this regulation, that a lady in the perils of childbirth was refused a pass this afternoon, to go to her home in Fairfax County, where she had left her children.

The utmost excitement continues to prevail in Alexandria. The citizens generally seem to anticipate the advance of the rebels within 48 hours. It is known, however, that the Manassas Railroad is not obstructed as far as Springfield, and the Loudon road as far as Camp Upton.

But fifty men of Company E, Capt. Leveridge, Fire Zouaves, have returned out of ninety-seven. They were immediately returned to their old post, the arduous duty of guarding the Government warehouses at Alexandria. This composed the extreme right of the Zouaves and formed three times under a hot fire. All four Sergeants were wounded. The following are among their casualties:

Killed—Thomas W. Chambers, Sanderson.

Gilbert Brower and Sergeant Leary were both left on the field dangerously wounded. Sergeant Meeks lost an arm. Private Post Peter Delmotte, Private Inness, shot both legs. Bates Franklin Holliday and Waterhouse.

The following wounded have been brought into the hospital at Georgetown:

James Canwell, Fourth Maine.

John McCreeran, Sergeant R. C. Kelley, John Hayes, John O'Keefe; Corporals Henry Rice, Mathew Dailey, John Keilahan, Pat. Riley, Richard A. Kelly, James Hyland, Wm. Chosey, Peter Gillery, Joseph Gallagher, Thomas Kernan, Corporal Thomas Egan, John Gallagher, Thomas Sheehan, David Thyuu, all of the New-York Sixty-ninth.

A. S. Mainard, H. Ginley, C. A. Garvin, R. J. Simpson, Wm. Fuller, L. M. Preston, J. W. Marden, G. Maynard, J. D. Bahaw, W. S. Lynch, D. M. Bond, Harvey McDaniels, Cornelius Letrevin, of the Wisconsin Second; Joseph Dayton, Third Connecticut.

G. T. Newton, do.

James Card, Second Maine.

Christopher Cummings, New-York Sixty-ninth.

John Falken, New-York Thirty-third.

Thomas J. Whiton, Connecticut Third.

Charles C. Mills, Connecticut First.

J. B. Gilmore, Minnesota First.

Charles McElroy, Connecticut First.

J. D. Wilson, Second New-York Volunteers.

Florence Dingman, Michigan Second.

C. Baker, New-York Thirteenth.

Fred'k Scherfenberg, Minnesota.

James A. Galt, New-York Thirteenth.

James Duffy, do.

Pat. Gusmigan and Thos. Welsh, New-York Seventy-ninth.

D. M. Mason, John Falrose and George Craig Third Maine.

J. Mitchell, New-York Seventy-ninth.

C. Fluntford, New-York Thirteenth.

J. Frazier, Corporal, New-York Seventy-ninth.

John Carpenter' Third United States Infantry.

George W. Kennedy, Corporal, New-York Seventy-ninth.

Henry R. McCullum, Second Wisconsin.

J. Flamery, Second Wisconsin.

A. Bugbee, Second Wisconsin.

O. D. Glading, Second Infantry.

W. Jenkins, Third Maine Volunteers.

G. W. Smith, Eleventh New-York.

Asher A. Walker, Eleventh New-York.

J. S. Reet, Second New-York.

E. B. Blockiston, Fourth Maine.

D. J. Riley, Second New-York.

Carl Erbach, Second United States Artillery.

Mishael Maher, Eleventh New-York Volunteers.

W. H. Gordon, Fourth Maine.

J. B. St. Clare. Lieutenant New-York Seventy-ninth

Gudhelp Woonsor, Second Wisconsin.

Roderick Black, New-York Seventy-ninth.

Jacob Schaff, Third Connecticut.

M. Malcolm, New-York Seventy-ninth.

Burnam Dunbar, Vermont Second.

H. Ames, New-York Fourteenth.

C. C. Busbee, Wisconsin Second.

W. Rouse, do.

C. C. Dowe and Lieut. A. A. Meridan, do.

J. Sullivan, New-York Sixty-ninth.

A. McKean, New-York Thirteenth.

J. W. Burgess, Connecticut First.

Barney Mulligan, New-York Thirty-eighth.

W. Dutcher, Wisconsin Second.

C. A. Keyes, do.

Col. Maistow, New-Hampshire Second; musket ball, arm broken and wounded in the breast; doing well.

Capt. Hiram Rollins, New-Hampshire Second; shot in shoulder; severe wound; he will recover.

Capt. Todd, Brattleboro, Vermont Second, shot in throat; ball passed completely through, within one inch of jugular vein; will recover.

Major Gidmore, Vermont Second, of Montpelier; wrist shattered by Minié rifle ball, not dangerous.

Private Henning, Montpelier, Vermont Second; wounded in thigh by rifle ball.

Col. Lawrence, Massachusetts Fifth; shot in the shoulder, and also wounded in the abdomen by splinters of wood. In no danger.

Capt. Gordon, Massachusetts Eleventh, died from his wounds.

Andrew Hill and F. Nelson, privates in Vermont Second, wounded in legs with rifle balls; not very serious.

Lieut. Wall or Hall, New-York Eighth, wounded by fragment of shell, seriously.

Lieut. Lorraine, of Sherman's battery, painfully wounded in the foot by ball.

[Priestly Oldham Craig, Second Regiment artillery, dead.

Dr. B. Buckstone, of Fifth Maine; Dr. A. Allen, of Third, and Dr. A. A. C. Williams, of First, (whose regiment was not in the action, but volunteered to go with the Fire Zouaves,) were taken prisoners—the two first at the hospital and the latter on the battle-field, after being wounded.

The number killed, wounded and missing in the Vermont Second, is less than 50. This number will probably be lessened by detachments yet to report themselves. The regiment is in camp at their old quarters outside of Alexandria.

Capt. Todd, of Brattleboro, wounded in the throat, and Sergeant-Major Guman in the wrist. All doing well.

Lieut. Cobart Hitchcock, of the Marine Corps, while gallantly engaged with a battery, was instantly killed by a shot from a rifled cannon.

The number of killed in the regiment is small. The wounded are doing well.

LATER.

No official returns of the dead and wounded have yet been made out.

It may be safely stated that no National troops, in a body, are either at or South of Fairfax Court-house.

Gen. McDowell is at Arlington.

THE KILLED AND WOUNDED OF THE FOURTEENTH REGIMENT.

LIEUT.-COL. FOWLER ALIVE.

Hon. J. S. T. Stranahan and A. J. Benson, Esq., returned from Washington last evening, bringing with them the following list of killed and wounded of the Fourteenth (Brooklyn) Regiment, Col. A. M. Wood. These gentlemen also bring the gratifying intelligence that Lieut.-Col. Fowler, of the Fourteenth, before reported dead, was at Arlington Heights, alive and well. The rumor of his being killed is supposed to have been founded upon the fact that when Col. Wood was wounded, he took him from the field, and his disappearance led to the supposition that he had fallen. The safety of Col. Fowler was at once communicated to his wife, who, for the twenty-four hours previous, had mourned him as dead.

The following list embraces all the killed as far known:

1. John Davenport.
2. Wade, formerly in the employ of David W. Wetmore.
3. Schell.
4. Fagan, Company F.
5. Brown.
6. Francis F. Head, formerly of Company D, and Ensign of the Regiment. A brother is Sergeant-Major of the Regiment. Deceased was single, 22 years of age, and has a father, Mr. Henry Head, residing at No. 89 Fulton-avenue.
7. Kelly.
8. Sullivan.
9. Minott.
10. Van Horn.
11. McManus.
12. J. Snyder, Company C, 35 years old, single. Resided at No. 72 Adelphi-street.
13. P. M. Dagnall, Company C, 21 years old, single. Resided at No. 186 Fulton-street.
14. Mansfield.
15. Dietz.
16. Smith.
17. Prescott.
18. Adams.
19. Scott.
20. Van Horn.
21. Baldwin. (There are three of this name in the regiment.
22. McCarty.
23. Morrill.
24. Clay

It is supposed that this is not a full list of the killed. The following-named persons are reported to be seriously wounded:

1. Middleton.
2. Jones.
3. Spear.
4. Conrad A. Ten Eyck, of Company C, 21 years old, single, and resided at No. 82 Cranberry-street.
5. De Witt.

Several others are slightly wounded.

OUR TROOPS IN POSSESSION OF CENTREVILLE.

WASHINGTON, Tuesday, July 23.

I have just returned from Alexandria. I could not get out of the pickets in the vicinity.

Capt. Tyler received a letter this morning from Capt. Gibson, of the Franklin Brigade, dated Centreville, asking for horse fodder, from which it appears that our troops are still there.

INCIDENTS OF THE BATTLE.

Correction of Exaggerations—The Enemy in No Condition for Pursuit—Another Solferino Stampede—Straggling Soldiers—Treatment of the Wounded by the Rebels.

Editorial Correspondence of the New-York Times.

WASHINGTON, Monday Evening.

Public feeling grows somewhat more settled and resolute in regard to the defeat of Sunday. The first reports brought by the stragglers and fugitives from the Army, and marked by all the exaggerations of men in a panic, created a feeling of consternation and intense alarm. Men were looking for the instant appearance of the rebel army against Washington,—for an immediate uprising of the Secessionists of Baltimore, and for the immediate overthrow of the Government. Reflection and more accurate intelligence has modified this feeling very essentially;—and the Washington public begin to realize that the American Government is not so near its end as they were inclined at first to suppose, and perhaps to hope. The earliest reports represented the defeat as an entire and disgraceful rout, which had completely broken up the Union Army.

It was asserted that the entire baggage train of the force, with all their horses, wagons and equipage of every kind collected at such an enormous cost, had fallen into the hands of the enemy, and that the rear of the Army was left without protection of any kind. It now appears that our Army retreated in very good order as far as Centreville, where it was protected from pursuit by the reserves, under Col. Miles; that no attempt was made to capture the baggage wagons which had nearly all been left between Centreville and Fairfax, and went back with the Army to the latter place, and that the only material which fell into the hands of the rebels was such as had been hastily, and not very creditably, abandoned on the road between Bull's Run and Centreville.

It is pretty evident that the enemy was in no condition for pursuit. A powerful force of cavalry might have done great execution upon the rear of our retreating columns; and they did make an attempt of this sort upon the Warrenton Road, but a volley from Col. Blenker's regiment, which was sent out from Centreville to cover the retreat, soon put them to flight. The pursuit extended but a short distance, and was attended by no important results.

It will delight the heart of my excellent old friend of the *Herald*, to learn that I became involved in another stampede, not quite so extensive or disastrous as that of Solferino, but one sufficiently disgraceful to answer his purpose. As soon as it was understood in the crowd of teamsters, fugitive soldiers and miscellaneous hangers-on of the army at Centreville, that our columns were retreating, they became very considerably excited,—and this feeling rose to panic when they heard the sound of cannon in the rear, as they supposed it to indicate that the enemy was pursuing in force. After I had driven something over a mile from the village on my way to Washington, the crowd in the rear became absolutely frenzied with fear, and an immense mass of wagons, horses, men on foot, and flying soldiers, came dashing down the hill at a rate which threatened destruction, instant and complete, to everything in their way. The panic spread as they proceeded, and gathering strength by its progress, the movement became absolutely terrific. The horses caught the frenzy of the moment, and became as wild as their masters. My driver attempting to check the speed of our carriage, found it suddenly crushed under the weight of an enormous Pennsylvania Army wagon which crushed it like an egg-shell. The opportune arrival of another carriage containing a couple of Congressmen, relieved me from the dilemma, and took me to Washington. Previous to my mishap I was overtaken and passed by a solitary horseman, who proved to be Mr. Russell, of the London *Times*, who was profoundly disgusted with this movement, and was making all possible haste to get out of it.

The most discreditable feature of this stampede was the very large number of soldiers who had straggled away from their regiments during the battle, and who now threw away their muskets, blankets and knapsacks, and ran as if their lives depended on their speed. For a long time no attempt was made to stop them. But near Fairfax, a New-Jersey regiment had drawn up across the road, and compelled every soldier upon whom they could lay hands to go back to his regiment. They were dragged out of carriages and from the backs of horses, and turned backward with the greatest rigor. Many of them managed, however, to pass the guard, and the road all the way to Washington was crowded with these timid and fugacious warriors. How they were suffered to pass Long Bridge, having neither pass nor countersign, is among the mysteries which I have no thought of fathoming. But they made their appearance on the street corners and in the barrooms of the city with the early dawn,—and each speedily became the central point of a steadily swelling crowd, who learned the bloody history of this awful battle from the lips of these heroes, every one of whom had staid in the very thickest of the fight until his regiment was all cut to pieces, and he was left the sole survivor. It was these men who gave to the masses in Washington their knowledge of the terrible defeat the Union forces had sustained. Why Gen. Mansfield has suffered them thus to roam the streets all day, filling the public ear with their prodigious lies, and creating an intense and dangerous fever of the public mind, I cannot imagine. They ought either to be forced into the strict discipline of military

[*Continued on Eighth Page.*]

The Charleston Mercury.

VINDICE NULLO — SPONTE SUA SINE LEGE FIDES RECTUMQUE COLENTUR.

VOLUME LXXIX. CHARLESTON, S. C., THURSDAY, JULY 25, 1861. NUMBER 11,211

NOTES OF THE WAR.

From Our Own Correspondents.

THE REVERSE IN WESTERN VIRGINIA.

ARMY OF THE POTOMAC, CAMP PICKENS, July 19.

The First Whiff of the Coming Tempest—Movements in the West—The Disasters to Gen. Garnett's Command—Outline of the Retreat, etc., etc.

I sent you, yesterday, a brief and somewhat rambling account of the engagement Wednesday. I had just returned from a trip to Central Virginia, in the hope of more perfect information as to the movements of Gen. GARNETT. I was out of the fight, therefore, but as our own troops were not in it, to any serious extent, I do not so much regret it as I would have done. That, however, we regard as only the first whiff of the coming tempest, and still have the ship trimmed and bow on. Last night was one of anxious suspense. It was reported that the enemy was advancing, in force, upon all the crossings of Bull Run. Our men were in position and on their arms. Each person had his post, watchwords were out, and whether there would be a strike or not, at any instant, was a question perpetually present to every watcher of the immense mass of men within the lines of the Army of the Potomac. Each slept, if he slept at all, in instant readiness for the opening note of the grand orchestra.

It did not come, however; night faded into morning, and men rose to a day of uncertainty and expectation. Reports were about that the enemy had gone off, but they were contradicted; scouts with the utmost hardihood pushed their investigations almost into the very lines of the enemy. Their reports were constantly brought to headquarters, and, as the result, the whole army has taken up the line of march, so much of it, at least, as has been held in reserve, and now, at ten o'clock, they are filing on by every practicable pass to what are expected to be the scenes of action.

The positions are the same as those mentioned yesterday, strengthened, however, by Gen. JOHNSTON's forces from Winchester, and Gen. HOLMES' from Fredericksburg. Other regiments also have arrived from Richmond, and I listen now to the first sounds of the opening combat at some point upon the line of defences, as strong as human hearts and human arms can well make them. So far I have reserved the ability to go to whatever point may be attacked.

Pending this condition of suspense, I will give you the results of my inquiries in the West. Your readers are generally aware that the enemy under Gen. McCLELLAN had assembled in force at Phillipi, and that our troops, under Gen. GARNETT, had been assembled at Beverly. The positions of these places will be seen upon the map, to which, for the better understanding of affairs there, I would advise your readers to refer. It will be seen that Gen. GARNETT's position was in the Tygart Valley, between the Cheat and Rich Mountains, which are the first of the Alleghanies met with in marching West. The force of Gen. GARNETT amounted to only 6000, that of McCLELLAN to near, if not quite 20,000. Ours were undrilled and unequipped; theirs were the best they have in service. To enter this valley and meet Gen. GARNETT, Gen. McCLELLAN advanced with two columns—one by Buchanan and the other by Leesburg. To meet him, Gen. GARNETT himself advanced to Laurel Hill, in the direction of Leesburg, about ten miles, and sent a detachment of about 2000 troops under Col. PEGRAM to the top of Cheat Mountain, in the direction of Buchanan. The enemy advanced until he met these two forces at both points, and then came to a pause, the object and result of which were uncertain. He came to contest about the 5th or 6th instants, and what would be his further movement did not appear until the morning of the 11th, when a large part of his Buchanan column appeared in the rear of Col. PEGRAM's forces, having crossed the mountain on his flank. That this was his object, might have been anticipated; for I have myself seen a young man in the action who says he heard their axes as they were cutting their road round them. The enemy appearing in his rear, Col. PEGRAM, at the loss of his camp equipage and two guns, drew off his men to a position of tolerable security. Then he became concerned excessively about his loss, and, declaring his unalterable purpose to recover his guns, called for a volunteer force of three hundred men to go and take them. The call was responded to, and they advanced to within sight of the enemy's encampment, apparently unseen, and were in ambush, where another company of their own were coming up, and being mistaken for the enemy, were about to be fired on. The effort to prevent this attracted the attention of the enemy, who at once moved to surround them. This defeated the enterprise, and Col. PEGRAM giving the order to his troops to make their way across to Laurel Hill as well as possible, went back to the main body of his forces. These he led by a circuitous route back to Beverly, which place he reached next morning; but soon after the enemy entered and captured a considerable portion of his force, and was himself taken prisoner. Gen. GARNETT, upon learning the first defeat of Col. PEGRAM, ordered a large force to fell the trees across the road from Rich Mountain to Beverly, to impede the enemy while he himself prepared to retreat to Beverly. This he accomplished in good order to within four miles, when he discovered that his orders had been mistaken, and that instead of cutting the trees on the Rich Mountain road, his men had cut them on the Laurel Hill road. Instead of impeding the enemy, therefore, they impeded him, and thinking then that it would be imprudent to urge further his return to Beverly, which place, however, had not then been occupied by the enemy, he started off to the east over Cheat Mountain. His labors and privations must have been fearful, but seemed to promise success. When returning to the rear of his army attacked by the enemy, to restore order, he was shot. After this some were killed and some were taken prisoners, but much the larger portion of his force arrived safely at Petersburg, in the valley east of Cheat Mountain, and Sunday evening were in comparative safety.

The remnant of Colonel PEGRAM's command fell in with Colonel SCOTT, commanding the Forty-fourth Regiment Virginia Volunteers, and arrived about the same time safely at Monterey on the same side of Cheat Mountain, lower down than Petersburg. Colonel SCOTT had been ordered to join Colonel PEGRAM, and was on his way from Beverly when the attack was made. He could have fallen on the enemy's rear while engaged with Colonel PEGRAM, but did not do so, and retreating continued on to Monterey, without giving that assistance to our routed forces or that impediment to the enemy which might have been expected.

This is a brief outline of the fearful experience under Gen. GARNETT's command. What are to be the further movements of Gen. McCLELLAN does not appear. He may go east to join Gen. PATTERSON, or west to meet Gen. WISE; but while it would have been more probable that he would join Gen. PATTERSON, since Gen. PATTERSON has himself withdrawn from the Harper's Ferry District, if this be true, he will have no longer a motive to do so. It might be desirable, perhaps, to have him at Washington; but there will be an unwillingness to expose Western Virginia to our forces, under Generals FLOYD and WISE, and the chances are that he will be continued in that department, and more especially will this be the case if it be true, as has been stated, that Gen. Lee has himself gone to the West to take the command of Gen. GARNETT's forces.

L. W. S.

THE DAY BEFORE THE BATTLE.

ARMY OF THE POTOMAC, CAMP PICKENS, July 20.

Preparations for the Great Battle—Incidents of the First Fight at Bull Run—The Artillery Duel—The Field after the Battle—Unburied Dead—Firing at our Hospital—The South Carolinians "up a Tree"—Trophies—The Final Arrangements for Defence, &c., &c.

The condition of suspense noticed in my letter of this morning, has remained unbroken. The enemy's pickets have been often seen on the other side of Bull's Run, and there have been indications of their being in force and ready to advance, but they have not advanced. A few minutes ago three guns were fired at a point to the east of the place where the railroad crosses, but the purport of it has not transpired. In the meantime, our forces have been arranged and compacted to the utmost possible efficiency, and provisioned and supplied, have crossed the stream and are advancing on the enemy at Centreville. All things indicate that aggressive action will be taken. Very vast accessions have been made to the army at this point, in the several forces under General HOLMES, at Frederick, General JOHNSTON, at Winchester, and General EVANS, at Leesburg; and the artillery and cavalry have all been thrown forward.

The many incidents of the engagement, Thursday, are still the subject of attention. The two batteries of artillery stationed on the rising ground on either side of the creek, more than a mile apart, had a regular duel. They had the field to themselves. The infantry intervening, was below on the banks of the creek. Both batteries had reputations to sustain; both had the ability with which to sustain it, and it is claimed by our side unanimously, and established by the fact that the Washington Artillery were completely triumphant. They lost but one man killed, and few wounded, while the guns of SHERMAN's Battery were often forced to change position, and at last was completely silenced.

I said that the only regiments engaged were the First, Eleventh and Seventeenth Virginia, but under Gen. LONGSTREET's command were also the Sixth Louisiana Regiment, Col. HARRY HAYES, which did effective service, and lost one man, while some twelve were wounded.

The losses in Col. GARLAND's Regiment were one killed, Maj. CARTER HARRISON, a most gallant and lamented officer, and five wounded.

The scene of conflict is painful. I mentioned yesterday, that, under a flag of truce, the enemy undertook to bury their dead, but did not bury all. I now learn that they did not even ask to bury their dead, or make any effort to do so, and a gentleman on the ground, and at pains to count them, states that more than sixty men were found rotting in the field. Some were, doubtless, carried off, but it argues a singular want of humanity that they should permit those to be unburied. Many of them were buried by our men, but the task was so offensive that the party was forced to desist.

Another evidence of a spirit unusual in Christian warfare was in their firing on our hospital. This was a large barn on a hill, quite conspicuous, and visible to the enemy, over which the yellow flag floated; but it was not only shot at, but the firing was so constant and so close that the Surgeons had to remove the wounded to the cover of a hill, and one of the ambulances, when in the act of transporting them, was struck by a ball.

THE GREAT BATTLE.

BULL RUN, SUNDAY MORNING, July 21, 10 o'clock.

On the Field of Battle—A Sublime Scene—The Dark Columns of the Enemy Advancing—His Batteries Open Fire—Our Men at First Lie Perdu—Our Flank Movement—Terrible Firing—The Enemy Driven Back—Scene of the Conflict Changed to Stone Bridge—Gallantry of Gen. Evans' Small Force—Our Losses—President Davis on the Field—How he Was Received, etc., etc.

It seemed to be conceded that this was to be the day of trial for which we have been working for many months past, and, in common with the immense mass of men assembled here, I have taken my position upon Bull Run to share the fortunes of the contest.

The scene, a moment since, and yet, is unutterably sublime. Upon the hill, just one and a third miles off, the enemy are placing their artillery. We see them plunging down the Centreville road to the apex of the eminence above Mitchell's Ford, and deploying to the right and left. Dark masses are drifting on with the power of fate in the road. We see the columns moving, and, as they deploy through the forests, we see the cloud of dust floating over them, to mark their course. When the dust ceases, we are sure that they have taken their position. The firing now commences from two batteries to the right and left of the road. It is constant, and another has been opened about a mile lower down. That, however, has been firing for an hour past. The guns are served with great rapidity and precision, and, as we are within range, and uncertain, therefore, when they will favor us, there is quite an interest in the position. Our own troops are in the dense forest that lies below us on Bull's Run. They are still; not a gun has yet been fired, and there would seem to be nothing to indicate their presence. Of their presence and their readiness the enemy is advised, however, and is making all the headway he can. Of the precise position, however, they are still unadvised: and in every clump of trees, and all along the line, they are plunging shots. So far, however, none have told. Our own batteries are in reserve, ready for a spring to any point that may come to be available. The hospital is again the object for their fire; and the battery, I mentioned as a mile below the ford, having heavier guns than mere field pieces, and one at least rifled, is now playing upon it.

The object, however, of most intense interest is a line of dust that begins to rise above the mass of forest lying for miles away to the right of the enemy. That it is a moving column is evident, but whether of our own or the enemy is the principal question. If ours, we are taking the enemy in flank. If theirs, they out-flank us. It moves towards the enemy, and a courier that joins us reports that it is the brigade of Gen. COCKE. On it goes. There is no corresponding column of the enemy. The movement promises success. The enemy may have stationed a force in anticipation, but if not, we fall upon their flank.

HALF-PAST TEN O'CLOCK A. M.—There is firing on our flanking column. The enemy has opened their battery upon it half way. The column responds. The firing becomes rapid—musketry! rapid. Generals BEAUREGARD, JOHNSTON and BONHAM, have just come to the hill where I have been standing. The whole scene is before us—a grand moving diorama. The enemy have sent a ball from their rifled cannon at us. Another. They pass over us with a sound that makes our flesh crawl. All have left the spot but Generals BEAUREGARD, BONHAM and JOHNSTON, and their aids. The firing has ceased at the head of our flanking column. It is renewed again, nearer, I think, to the enemy. Another ball exactly over our heads. A very sustaining force follows our flanking column. The enemy, firing at our Generals, has dropped a shot among the wagons in the edge of the woods below, and they dash off. Another shot follows them as they fly, and plunges in the ground but a few feet behind one of them.

ELEVEN O'CLOCK.—The firing has been awful. The heads of the flanking and resisting columns are distinctly visible from the smoke that rises above them; and they stand stationary for a long time, but at last the enemy's column goes back—a column of dust rises in their rear—a shout rises that roars loud as the artillery from our men—the enemy's fire slackens—our reserves advance—the dust rises on to the position lately occupied by the enemy—we triumph, we triumph, thank God! The dust still rises in the rear of the enemy, as though they were retreating rapidly.

QUARTER BEFORE TWELVE O'CLOCK.—The enemy make another stand. Again, there is the roar of musketry, long like the roar of distant and protracted thunder. Again, the roar, but always at the head of the enemy's column. A column of dust rises to the left of our forces and passes to the enemy's right. It must be intended to flank them. It is fearful to think how many heart-strings are wrung by the work that now goes on—how many brave men must be mangled and in anguish.

Again, the enemy has fallen back to another point half a mile in the rear; and the spirals of the smoke curl up the side of the mountain in the background. The whole scene is in the Piedmont valley, which I have often noticed to have slept so sweetly to the west of Centreville, and sweeping on down to the south. It is nearly level, or seems so, and the Blue Ridge rises to form the dark background of a most magnificent picture.

TWELVE O'CLOCK, NOON.—The batteries first opening have been silent for half an hour, and the whole extended valley is now the thick of the fight. Where the enemy last took his stand retreating, the fight is fearful—the dust is denser than the smoke. It is awful. They have been repulsed three times—so it is reported by a courier—and now they have taken their bloodiest and final stand.

HALF-PAST TWELVE O'CLOCK.—The firing now is at its height. Never until now have I dreamed of such a spectacle; for one long mile the whole valley is a boiling crater of dust and smoke.

QUARTER BEFORE ONE O'CLOCK.—The fray ceases; Gens. BEAUREGARD and JOHNSTON dash on to the scene of action, and as we cannot doubt that the enemy has again fallen back, it looks as though they were on their way to Washington.

ONE O'CLOCK.—Column after column is thrown in from all along the line of Bull's Run to fall upon the left flank of the enemy, and the firing is again renewed as though nothing had been done. An effort would seem to have been made to outflank us, and it has brought on another engagement further off, but on a line with the first. The cannon established on the hill was a feint at the Mitchell's Ford, while of both armies the effort was to outflank. These guns now but play at the columns of dust as they rise from the infantry and cavalry as they tramp past; and as those columns near the point where I stand, they have brought a dozen balls at least within 100 yards.

FIFTEEN MINUTES PAST ONE O'CLOCK.—The firing has almost entirely ceased, but still our reserves are pouring in. The enemy seems to be making an attempt to cross at Mitchell's Ford. All at Mitchell's Ford is a feint, and it is now certain that the grand battle ground for empire is now to the west, beyond the Stone Bridge, on Bull's Run, and I go there.

EVENING.—At two o'clock I arrived on the ground; but of the further scenes of this eventful battle, I have nothing more to say, save this only, that at five o'clock the enemy was at last driven from the field, leaving most of the guns of SHERMAN's Battery behind them, with an awful list of dead and wounded.

It will be evident to any one who becomes familiar with the events of the day, that I misapprehended many of the occurrences. The attack was made at a point above the Stone Bridge on Bull's Run by the whole disposable force of the enemy, led by General McDOWELL. The importance of the movement was not at first estimated, and it was met by Gen. EVANS, with only the Fourth South Carolina Regiment, Colonel SLOAN, the Independent Louisiana Battalion, Major WHEAT, and two guns of the Washington Artillery. The charge of the enemy was met with an intrepidity that was beyond all praise, and the whole column of the enemy was held at bay until reinforcements came. These were led on by Colonel JACKSON, Colonel BARTOW, General BEE, General JONES. The conflict went on in a fierce and terrible struggle of the Confederate troops against great odds, and amidst terrible slaughter.

At the crisis of the engagement two regiments of South Carolinians, KERSHAW's and COCKE's, were ordered to advance. KEMPER's battery was attached to KERSHAW's. As these troops advanced, they were joined by PRESTON's regiment, of COCKE's brigade. A tremendous charge was made, which decided the fate of the day. After acts of incredible valor, the enemy were driven off far to the north. As they retreated on the Braddock Road to Centreville, a charge was made upon them by a portion of our cavalry, and I think of the Radford Rangers. They dashed upon them about a mile away, and the dust above them for ten minutes rose up as from the crater of a volcano. The punishment was severe and rapid.

Colonel HAMPTON's Legion suffered greatly. It came last night and marched directly into battle. When I went upon the ground I heard that Colonels HAMPTON and JOHNSON were both killed, but afterwards I met Colonel HAMPTON riding from the field, wounded badly, but exhilarated at the thought that his men had exhibited surpassing intrepidity, and that General BEAUREGARD himself had relieved him and led his Legion into battle.

Colonel SLOAN's Fourth Regiment South Carolina Volunteers suffered as much. They stood decimated at every fire until reinforcements came, and they exhibit a sad remnant of the noble body of men that entered into battle.

The Second Regiment, Colonel KERSHAW, did fearful execution at the crisis of the contest, but suffered less.

The Fourth Alabama Regiment, Colonel JONES, and the Eighth Georgia Regiment, Colonel GARDNER, suffered greatly.

Wearied and worn and sick at heart, I retired from the field whose glory is scarcely equal to its gloom, and I have not the time or strength to write more. I send my field notes as they are.

President DAVIS came upon the ground just as the battle ended, and the wildest cheering greeted him. He rode along the lines of war worn men who had been drawn off from action, and he seemed proud of them and of his right to command such noble men, but it was tempered with a feeling of regret that their right to his respect had been vindicated at so dreadful a sacrifice. Many wounded still stood in the ranks, and exhibited the unalterable purpose to stand there while they had strength to do so.

How many of the enemy were killed we have no means of knowing, but it must have been much greater than our own. Our men shot with the utmost possible coolness and precision, and they must have claimed this compliment.

We took SHERMAN's Battery, sixteen guns, and three guns from those batteries that opened upon us first above Mitchell's Ford.

These are facts reported to me on the ground at sundown, but they are not necessarily correct. I have hesitated to state any thing, but upon the whole have thought it best. I will send a corrected list of our casualties to-morrow.

There was an engagement at the batteries above Mitchell's Ford, in which the Fifth, Seventh and Eighth South Carolina Regiments were engaged, but the facts have not transpired beyond the taking of the guns.

L. W. S.

From a Special Correspondent.

BULL RUN, July 19.

The First Fight at Bull Run—Where the South Carolinians were Posted—The Brooks Guards—Fair Carolina Photographs not in the Hands of the Enemy—The Retreat to Bull Run—The Repulse—Our Loss and the Enemy's—Kemper's Battery, &c., &c.

I send you a few notes of my observations of the battle of Bull Run, fought on the 18th, between the army of the Potomac, under General BEAUREGARD, and the "grand army" of the North, under General McDOWELL.

The expectation of an attack, which had almost died out, was revived by well grounded reports and suspicious appearances on Monday and Tuesday; and on Wednesday morning expectation was changed into certainty by the booming of cannon, followed by the rattling of small arms and the rapid head of hastening couriers. The Yankees were advancing on Fairfax C. H., where BONHAM's Brigade of South Carolinians held the advance post of the Confederate Army. They were firing upon one of our pickets. Captain HAILE, with the whole of his company and half of the Brooks Guards, was on picket from two to four miles from camp, and the enemy was advancing across their line of retreat at about one mile. From Col. KERSHAW's camp (the most advanced) the glitter of the enemy's guns in the morning sun illumined hill after hill. But there was no time for observation. The "long roll" beat, and each company fell promptly into line. Col. KERSHAW gallops in, and to the interrogatory "How is the picket?" replies "All right." Capt. RHETT was ordered to take the other half of his company and hold a house, at the intersection of the two roads, until the picket reached that point. "The Brooks," elated at the prospect of a fight, and anxious for the fate of their exposed comrades, set off at a brisk rate, and soon reaching their place of destination, were preparing to keep the Yankees at bay until the safe passage of their friends, when the picket arrived at a double quick. The Brooks Guards greeted their captain with three hearty cheers, who recalled those that had been deployed, and the whole column (two companies) set off to join the regiment. The Yankees were then about a quarter of a mile on the right. They reached the camp just in time to join the regiment without having a moment to pause, and, therefore, lost most of their baggage. Yesterday the lamentation at the loss was great, but to-day it is said that our deserted baggage was burned, and the deprivation is spoken of much more cheerfully. For it now leaks out that the chief cause of grief was, not the loss of all their worldly goods, but the fear of the Yankee camp being brightened by the counterfeit presentments of many Carolina girls (the company having been largely supplied with amiable photographs)!

The retreat of the leading division of the army from Fairfax C. H. to Bull Run was a masterpiece of tactics. It was made in the very face of a vastly superior enemy, for twelve miles, without loss. KERSHAW's Regiment, with KEMPER's Light Battery, brought up the rear, every now and then halting, and showing so threatening a front, that the enemy preferred to follow at a safe distance, and thus threw away an admirable opportunity.

Yesterday they assailed our forces in entrenchments here at Bull Run, and, after being twice driven back with great slaughter, were compelled to retreat. They left in our hands two cannon, one 24 lb rifled cannon and one 6-pounder, and near three hundred muskets, besides small arms, pistols, &c. Our loss was seven killed and fifty wounded. Theirs, nine hundred killed; wounded unknown. I will send you, by the first opportunity, a shell which fell and buried itself inside the Brooks Guards' entrenchment. None of KERSHAW's Regiment were wounded. The credit of this fight is due chiefly to the Washington Artillery of New Orleans, the 1st and 17th Virginia Regiments and the Louisiana 7th, assisted by KEMPER's Light Battery, which was protected by the 2d South Carolina Regiment (KERSHAW's). The 17th Virginia Regiment highly distinguished itself. At one time one of its batteries drove a whole regiment of the enemy before it at the point of the bayonet to the top of a hill, where it was obliged to fall back to the Run, the enemy's discomfited regiment having been reinforced by four others. Being joined at the "Run" by the other battalion, this gallant regiment awaited the near approach of the five opposing, delivered a telling fire, and charged on them with the bayonet, chasing the whole, five to one, across the field at full speed. General BEAUREGARD checked the pursuit. KEMPER, covered by one battalion of the Second Palmetto Regiment, under KERSHAW, sallied out from the entrenchments just at this juncture, threw two shells into the flying infantry of the enemy as they attempted to rally, and scattered them anew. Captain KEMPER is a gallant and accomplished young officer, and has been attached to KERSHAW's Regiment.

To-day we have constantly expected a renewal of the attack. But the Yankees appear to require more breathing space after yesterday's bout. We hope to give them a thorough drubbing to-morrow.

All the South Carolinians are well, except Col. KERSHAW, who was kicked on the ankle by a horse. No bones are broken, but it is painful. Private BROWN, of the Palmetto Guard, died of a sun-stroke during the retreat from Fairfax Court House, on Wednesday.

Battle of Bull Run, July 21, 1861

War balloon at General McDowell's headquarters preparing for a reconnaissance

The New-York Times.

VOL. X—NO. 3072. NEW-YORK, SUNDAY, JULY 28, 1861. PRICE THREE CENTS.

Editorials

Our Defeat to Inaugurate a Plan for the War.

The reverse at Bull's Run is undoubtedly the first step of our Government toward the adoption of a competent plan of military operations, if not of a well defined policy as to the war; the absence of such policy is the only explanation for our defeat. Unless a person has some definite object, he wastes his strength in extravagant, futile, and often contradictory efforts, in precisely the same manner that our own has been wasted in the campaign in the Eastern States. In Missouri, Gen. Lyon was instructed to clear the State of rebels, which he did in a most summary manner. There were really no difficulties in the way of a skillful commander, because he had a definite object and abundant means for its execution. Common sense was the only other element wanting to insure success; and this Gen. Lyon appears to possess in an eminent degree. There was no sufficient motive to thwart him while he was too far from Washington to have his plan of operations interfered with. To Gen. McClellan was confided the task of driving the enemy out of Northwestern Virginia—a duty which he promptly accomplished, because a straightforward one, to which he could direct his undivided energies and skill. In a short month his campaign was brought to a glorious termination, allowing him to be called to duty elsewhere.

The campaigns in Missouri and Western Virginia have shed lustre upon our arms; but when we come to the Eastern States, this agreeable picture is wholly reversed. We call out vast bodies of troops, keep them in positions and cantonments where they are almost entirely unemployed till the period of the enlistment expires; the monotony of their camp life being broken only by a few ill-considered and ineffectual attacks upon the positions of the enemy, in which our soldiers make a prodigal display of personal daring to be stung to the quick by defeats. Our movements seem to be the result of a momentary impulse, not of any definite or great plan. Why was the enemy allowed to collect 90,000 men at Manassas Junction, to receive the attack of some 20,000 of our own troops, while nearly twice that number, charged with the duty of preventing a junction of the forces under Johnston with those under Beauregard, were idling their time away in camp at Harper's Ferry? It does not help the matter to say that the period of enlistment of one-half of Patterson's command had nearly expired, paralyzing his movements to such a degree that he could not act offensively. If Patterson could not move safely against Johnston, then the attack on Manasses Junction was sheer madness. But the force directed against this position was in the same condition that Patterson alleges his to have been. The time of a number of regiments in McDowell's command was to expire within four days from the first real battle of the campaign. Suppose we had held the advance gained only by the united exertions of the whole Army, what was to become of those left behind, when deserted by one-half of their comrades? Who ever heard of a campaign being inaugurated with an Army so composed? A regiment has no sufficient motive to fight to-day whose time is out to-morrow. It encounters all the dangers without reaping any advantage of the contest; the day after the battle the men composing it go into private life. Nothing can be more demoralizing to those left behind than to see, perhaps in the midst of battle, regiment after regiment leaving for home to be disbanded. It is no wonder that our men were repulsed, but that they fought as well as they did.

We know that Gen. Scott is not responsible for such follies. But who is? The President does not claim to be a military man, or to direct the movements of our forces. Where does this power, so potent for mischief, and never for good, reside? Is it not the same influence to which are to be referred the blunders and mismanagement in the organization of the Army, and the entire indifference and neglect shown to meritorious officers seeking to have accepted their services and those of their men, and dancing attendance in Washington week after week, often with the strongest recommendations from the President and Gen. Scott, to come home at last utterly wearied and disgusted with the treatment received? To get anything like satisfactory answers to proffers of service has frequently been impossible, unless made through particular channels through which alone the official ear could only be reached and influenced.

Upon this power, busied with its own schemes the disaster at Bull's Run has fallen like a clap of thunder. Since the battle-sixty thousand men have, without shuffling or equivocation, been accepted for the war. Henceforward the necessities of the crisis, not schemes of petty personal ambition, are to guide and direct affairs. A definite plan of the campaign must now be entered upon. The real magnitude of the contest has just burst upon us. We shall be compensated for our defeat by the lesson it has taught. Its causes will be so thoroughly sifted, that their recurrence will be effectually guarded against. The machinery of the War Department will be thoroughly overhauled and ventilated. Hereafter troops will be collected in large bodies with some definite object; and more than all, capable officers will take the place of those incapable. The reverse, for the first time, will set us in the Eastern States, methodically at work. The instant a right beginning is made a successful issue of the contest is not far distant.

The Hard-hearted Confederates.

Some months ago the plan of the Confederates for quieting the revolution they were about inaugurating in this country was, to frame a new Constitution for the seceding States, and then let into their league such of the Middle and Western States as, on due contrition for past hostility to Pro-Slavery rule, and good promise of dutiful behavior in the future, should be found worthy of Southern association. But New-England it was thought best to exclude entirely, as sinners too hardened for salvation in the Black Republic.

Mr. JEFFERSON DAVIS modified the plan slightly in his message to the Montgomery Congress, wherein he prayed to be "let alone," and expressed the extreme pleasure with which he would drop the sword, and make friendly and favorable treaties with the free-soil, semi-barbarians of the United States. But the hardness of the Union heart to these tenders of the rebel olive-branch, has quite disgusted the organs of Mr. DAVIS, and they now are taking new and higher ground. Whenever the United States are fairly whipped, ruined and starved (as they unquestionably will be, by rebel accounts, in a few weeks,) and shall ask Mr. DAVIS to call off his war-dogs, and grant them a peace, the Richmond (Va.) *Examiner* suggests a clause to be put into the treaty, the nature of which will be gathered from the following extract from its columns:

"There is a greater danger to be apprehended from a hasty and incautious peace than any we have as yet suggested, and which we have, therefore, reserved for separate consideration. It is bad enough to deal with Northerners—to have them visit us, and to be forced to visit them—but it would be ruinous to have them come down upon us in shoals as numerous as the mackerel and cod about their coasts, to seize the ballot-box and control the helm of State. Unless the terms of peace exclude them this they will certainly do. The Yankees are not farmers, and few will remove to the Northwest. We have been their customers—have bought most of their manufactures—and, if we refuse to go to them, they will certainly (unless prevented) come to us. Lowell and Salem, Boston and Hartford, and every other town and village in New-England, will empty their scoundrel bosses, their filthy factory hands and starving laborers upon us. They will change the whole tone and character of our society, and soon, uniting with the Submissionists, abolitionize one-half of the South.

No treaty of peace will be worth a fig that does not effectually exclude Yankee notions and Yankee people. Our tariff should discriminate against their goods, and our naturalization laws against themselves."

That is, indeed, the unkindest cut of all. Dixie's land has proved to be so good a place for "permanent investments" of Northern capital; so delightful a place for Northern born men to sojourn in; so difficult a country for them to "tear themselves away from," when the heat of war made migration to the northward politic, that it will be a heart-breaking matter to find that not only are they expelled from the comforts of Southern hospitality, but that the door is to be irrevocably closed, bolted and barred against them. How will they survive it?

The Regimental Officers.

Our columns are read by large numbers of the officers at present in service in the volunteer regiments of the United States. We desire, on the part of the public, to address them some sober words under the present crisis. In every great disaster the popular mind always seeks some scapegoat on which to lay the blame. The people are fast tending to the point of fastening it on the officers of our regiments, since the late defeat. The facts thus far are certainly supporting—though not fully proving—this judgment. The men, in large numbers of regiments, testify that they knew and saw nothing of their officers during the battle; they fought, as they expressed it, "on their own hook"—in one instance a Quartermaster leading the regiment. The Army officers—who, it is true, are not so disinterested witnesses—all agree that the majority of the volunteer officers were utterly incompetent to their place. But the great and damning fact is, that twenty thousand men, in the moment of victory, were seized with an unaccountable panic, and that no officer had moral control enough over them to hold them back. A single word from some brave officer, in whom they had learned to have confidence, might have turned the whole rout, and saved this nation the greatest disgrace which has ever fallen on its arms. But in the majority of the regiments, the regimental officers either were panic-stricken themselves, or found, in the moment of extreme trial, that they had not the slightest influence over their men.

Our American pride droops in the dust, to think that there was no gallant corps of officers to throw themselves before the frightened mass, and say, "Fly! but over our dead bodies!" or that but two brigades were all that were left to defend our rear and collect the ruins of the flight, when no enemy pursued! The conduct of the officers since, during the disorganization of the regiments in Washington, bears out the accusations of the men. We hear of frightened Colonels in attics, and of officers deserting their men for days, while frequenting the hotels and bar-rooms. Of course, to all this, there are noble exceptions. The heroic dead in the ravines near Manassas need no commendation. They were officers who preferred death to dishonor, and who understood their high responsibilities.

Many, too, who survived, in various regiments which need not be particularized, did their duty bravely, through all that long day's battle, and the shameful retreat. Their regiments honor them, and future battle-fields will show the confidence they have in them. We mean another class of men—men who know more of book-keeping than battles; whose sole qualifications for their place as officers, are, having been the principal clerk or young politician of their village; who have no military experience or moral power. These men have taken the lives and happiness of tens of thousands of people on their shoulders, without ever thinking of or caring for the responsibility. We are rejoiced to hear that Congress recommends an "Examining-Board" for our volunteer officers, so that we may at least be sure of some military education.

But this is not the most vital defect. Many of our volunteer officers have military education enough for their positions. West Point does not necessarily make a good leader. The want is deeper and more radical. It can be corrected by every civilian who is now in command, if he will only set himself to the work. Let him remember that WASHINGTON, in his first campaign, was a militia officer, while BRADDOCK was a regular. The first thing to be considered is, that the men under command are like children, and must be carefully cared for, and their confidence be acquired. It is a mistake to suppose that this can be done best by affected joviality or familiar manners. A leader should always withhold himself from too great familiarity. Men whose lives are to be in the hands of their commander, do not care that he should be a joker or "a good fellow." They merely want to prove perfect confidence in his head and his nerve. He must first establish their respect by the most undoubted, even reckless, valor. Then in the long marches, the camp, the bivouac and the barracks, it must be seen that their colonel, or major, or captain, is always working first after the comfort of his men, and then after his own. Here our officers are shamefully deficient. A little care of the men in peace, would give them a vast control in war. A leading officer should feel that for the campaign, power over his soldiers is what he is to aim at—not comfort, or "having a good time." With power, comes hereafter honor, success, and, perhaps, the salvation of his country. His glory should be that he has his regiment or company in thorough control. His discipline should be the severest, while his kindness should know no bounds.

Let him be in the habit of requiring unyielding obedience. Men in danger will always yield to the strong will and unshaken courage. His soldiers are his children, and he must command. All observers of our Army agree that the officers do not exercise enough *moral* control over their men. A good leader ought to be constantly using his tact to stir up the spirits of the troops. If a band will not play at the end of a long march, they should be whipped into it. The soldiers should be personally encouraged. A good speech will inspirit men before a battle, and a good joke can break up a panic.

There is as yet little of the *esprit du corps* among our soldiers, which keeps men firm in danger, and exposes them fearlessly to the greatest perils. The commanders should cultivate it. The place of Colonel, or Major, or Captain, must now be considered a high one, and the nation should demand that the best and bravest men fill it. Reorganize our officers, and we shall easily beat the enemy. Continue the present system, and we might as well give up to the Southern Confederacy.

The New-York Times.

VOL. X....NO. 3079. NEW-YORK, SATURDAY, JULY 27, 1861. PRICE TWO CENTS.

THE GREAT REBELLION.

Highly Important News from Washington.

ANOTHER CRY OF DANGER TO THE CAPITAL

Plans and Intentions of the Rebel Leaders.

A Corps d'Armee to Cross the Potomac and Make an Attack in the Rear.

Simultaneous Movements to be Made Against McClellan, Butler, Banks and Rosencranz.

Troops Still Pouring into Washington.

An Important Expedition from Fortress Monroe.

Capture of Ten Rebel Schooners and Sloops.

RETURN OF WAR-WORN HEROES.

Enthusiastic Reception of the Eighth and Seventy-first.

SPECIAL DISPATCH FROM WASHINGTON.

WASHINGTON, Friday, July 26.

The Postmaster-General and the Mexican Minister have concluded an arrangement for a mail between some point in the United States and Vera Cruz. The terms of a contract for transportation have also been arranged, and the whole matter virtually concluded.

CASUALTIES IN THE THIRTY-EIGHTH.

The following is an official list of the killed, wounded and missing of the Thirty-eighth New-York Volunteers, Col. WARD. By the way, this Regiment and the Twenty-seventh, Col. SLOCUM, were quite as much in the fight as any other two regiments, the Zouaves, Sixty-ninth and Seventy-ninth not excepted:

KILLED.

Wm. E. Straight, Orderly Sergeant, Company I.
Samuel Ashworth, Third Sergeant, Company B.
John McBride, Fourth Corporal, Company I.
Wm. Wier, James H. Hart, Chas. Paulson, G. Robinson and Louis Williams, privates of Company B.
John Osman, of Company H.
James Flynn, of Company F.

WOUNDED.

Capts. Hugh McQuade, Company F, severely and a prisoner; Robt. F. Allason, Company C, slightly.
John Brady, Jr., Second Lieutenant Company D, badly wounded in the wrist.
Thomas S. Hamblin, First Lieutenant Company F, badly, and a prisoner.
Arthur T. Pickett, Second Sergeant Company I, and N. Schermerhorn, Second Sergeant Company H, slightly.
B. S. Stevens, First Corporal Company H, slightly.
Marvin P. Lord, private Company B, slightly; Walter Kniffin, slightly; A. Klaila, Company C, dangerously; J. Maier, Company C, dangerously; A. Scharf, Company C, mortally; J. Schmelfening, Company C, mortally; William Chambers, Company D, slightly; Martin Donahoe, ditto; John O'Brine, Company E, ditto; Anthony Walton, Company E, ditto. Privates Company F—John McIntyre, slightly; Patrick McCann, twice slightly; Martin O'Neill, ditto; Thomas Murphy, do.; Wm. Fielding, ditto; Edward Sweeney, G, ditto; Benj. Taylor, Company G, ditto; Hugh F. Dunnigan, Company H, severely; Barney Mulligan, Company H, ditto; Hugh McLaughlin, Company H, ditto; Sylvanus Greer, Company I, slightly; Edwin Close, Company I, ditto; Theo. B. Hamilton, Company I, ditto, Orlando B. Hurley, Company I, ditto.

MISSING.

Charles J. Murphy, Quartermaster.
Stephen Griswold, a prisoner.
Major James D. Potter.
Company A—Privates Michael Ahern, Gevert Jersen, Alexander Kar, John McNamaara, John McMahon No. 1, Jacob Schindler.
Company B—Privates John Green, Edward H. Kellogg, Louis Lesnard, Michael McGrain, Ferdinand Kelly, Laurence Dill, Thomas Fay, Corporal Alfred C. Bowers.
Company C—Privates R. Gabitch, T. Hoefer, J. Wirt, A. Mirt, A. Keller, S. Shaublein, A. Ahr.
Company D—Privates Jas. B. Clority, Geo. Cisco, Mathew Dollard, Lewis Walsrode, John Gallagher, Calvin T. C. Gould. Geo. A. Kennaston, Philo E. Lewis, Jonathan Coward, Edw. Donnelly, George Hart, Geo. Hanna, and Corporal Chas. Stothoff.
Company E—Sergeant Watson Mallory; Privates Henry Brown. Philip Donahue, Thos. Hollahan, John Hendry, Saml. Hart, John Kelsey. David Lyon, Edw. Marsh, John McEornon, Jas. Shine, Jas. Wilson.
Company F—Sergeants Moss and Donahue; Corporal Maloney; Privates Jas. Nelson, Timothy Sullivan, Mich'l. Dowling, Mich'l. Kennedy, Jas. Shepherd, Wm. Fielding, Pat. Coyle, Mich'l. Reims, Henry Hilliard, Laurence Mooney, John Holland, Wm. Mackay.
Company G—Privates Thos. H. Karr, Pat. McGinn, Wm. H. Millett, Chas. J. Ridiker, Geo. Wright.
Company H—Privates Wm. Lane, John Lanphier, Wm. Ross, Luther L. Mills, James Underhill.
Company I—Privates Wm. Breese, Chas. Sear, Irving C. Smith, John Jackson, Isaac Canan, Wm. Bolan, Byron Swazee, Edward Chevalier, John Gumbleton.
Company K—Privates James McCormick, James A. Coburn, Wm. Todd, Wesley Sumner, Jos. Trombley, Corporal Boutwell.

AN ALABAMA MUSTER ROLL.

I saw to-day the muster roll of Company B, Sixth Alabama, dated July 8, which was picked up at Fairfax Station. At that date there were fifty-six reported for duty, and thirty-seven sick. One death and one desertion are reported.

ASSEMBLAGE AT A FIRE.

There was a fire in H-street to-day, which brought out in one strong picture the different classes of men now in Washington. The controlling spirits were the Zouaves, but on the brakes of one engine I noticed members of regiments from eight different States.

TROOPS AND INTRENCHMENTS.

The War Department has accepted the regiment tendered by Col. NORTHEDGE, of New-York, and ordered it to rendezvous at Bedloe's Island. The regiment is one thousand strong.

An immense amount of labor is being done upon the fortifications around this city. They are being mounted with heavy siege guns and supplied with vast quantities of munitions and projectiles. Seamen have been brought from the naval station at Annapolis to teach the soldiers how to work the guns.

The immense dépôt for the reception of troops, which Mr. WOODS is fitting up, is rapidly approaching completion. It will have accommodation for 3,000 men, with rooms for officers, pools for bathing, hospital for the sick and broken down, &c. Attached will be a storehouse, kitchen and oven. These things should have been done in the beginning. The indifference heretofore manifested by the authorities for the care and comfort of troops arriving in Washington, begat much dissatisfaction, and was the cause of demoralization which has never been entirely cured.

The troops continue to arrive in great numbers the arrivals averaging three to four thousand a day.

IN FOR THE WAR.

The Twenty-sixth Regiment, New-York Volunteers, Col. CHRISTIAN, whose term of service has expired, have enlisted for the war, and been accepted by the President. The regiment is now the extreme outpost of the Army on the Potomac. The State of New-York owes them a suit of clothes, and they need them badly. At parade some appear minus coats and some minus pants. The State should do its duty.

The War Department has also accepted the Fifty-fifth Regiment New-York Militia, Col. DE TROBIAND, which has enlisted for the war.

The Nineteenth Regiment New-York Militia, Col. WOOD, from Orange County, has also been accepted for the war, with permission to be mustered in by companies.

EXTENDING THE OUTPOSTS.

Our outposts are gradually being extended again in the direction of the victorious rebels.

LONG CABINET MEETING.

The Cabinet had a protracted session to-day, being held together for more than four hours. Of course, Washington is filled with rumors as to the character of the business which required so long a sitting. I presume the extraordinary condition of the Government, and the means of extricating it from the embarrassment resulting from the battle of Bull's Run, was all that occupied the Heads of Departments.

ADJOURNMENT.

It is not probable now that Congress will adjourn earlier than the last of next week. The direct tax bill drags, but it will pass. The details appear to be crude, and the opponents of the bill are industrious in proposing amendments calculated more to damage than perfect the measure. One thing is certain, that Congress will do all in its power to give efficiency to the Army and Navy, and to give value and security to the public debt.

DISPATCH TO THE ASSOCIATED PRESS.

WASHINGTON, Friday, July 26.

Cols. DUMONT, MILROY and WALLACE, of Indiana, who have distinguished themselves in Western Virginia, have been, or will be, appointed Brigadier-Generals, in addition to J. J. REYNOLDS, of that State. Brig.-Gen. MORRIS will be honorably discharged from the service to-morrow.

Major-Gen. SANDFORD, of New York, Brig.-Gen. RUNYON, of New Jersey, and Brig.-Gen.'s COX, SCHLEICH, and BATES, of Ohio, will also respectively be honorably discharged; the first named, August 15th, the last named, 27th, and the others on the 30th inst.

According to general orders No. 45, in the future no volunteer will be mustered into the service, who is unable to speak the English language.

Capt. VAN VLIET has been appointed Quartermaster of the Army of the Potomac, and has entered upon his duties.

G. S. TALLIAFERRO, late a clerk in the Treasury Department, who was arrested a week or two since at Port Tobacco, on a charge of carrying correspondence between the Secessionists of this city and Virginia, was released to-day on taking the oath of allegiance.

Col. FRED. W. LANDER, one of Gen. MCCLELLAN's aids, who so greatly distinguished himself in the battles of Western Virginia, is in Washington. He refuses to-night the compliment of a serenade from his friends.

Gen. MCCLELLAN himself arrived here to-night, and privately proceeded to his hotel.

Among the incidents worthy of special note, connected with the battle Sunday, was the visit of the Secretary of War, accompanied by a few friends, for the purpose of witnessing the engagement. After spending several hours at Gen. MCDOWELL's Head-quarters, on Saturday, and hearing the evidence in relation to the possibility of Gen. JOHNSTON having joined forces with Gen. BEAUREGARD, he ordered his team and started for Washington to forward reinforcements. On his arrival at Washington, he drove directly to the President's and Gen. SCOTT's Head-quarters to inform them of his views. Four regiments which were under marching orders for Harper's Ferry to join Gen PATTERSON's column, were started South, and five others ordered to be ready Sunday morning. Three of the regiments thus ordered, had reached Fairfax before the retreat commenced.

Judge MCKEON, Gen. BULLARD and Prof. MCCOY, all of New-York, had an interview with the President to-day, to request the calling into the field of Major-Gen. WOOL. The deputation were kindly received. They responded that New-York, which has furnished 50,000 volunteers, has confidence in that veteran, and wondered why he was retained in Troy. The President stated that there was no decision to keep him out of active service, and that their representations would be duly considered.

Ten thousand volunteers have arrived at Washington within the last 48 hours.

The following is a list of the killed, wounded and missing in the Second Ohio Regiment:

KILLED.

Surgeon ALFRED POWELL.
Lieut. J. W. DEMPSEY.
Lieut. SAMUEL IRWIN.
Sergeant A. DONETT.

Privates.

— Stroud,	Thomas J. Lanagan,
Patrick Bush,	John Cregan,
John McFarland,	— Carrier,
Wm. Maxwell,	Michael McCarty,
Wm. B. Aird,	Andrew Morrow,
Robert Tape,	Patrick McCormick,
James Murphy.	

WOUNDED.

Joseph Morrison, slightly;	Patrick Larkin,
James McNamara,	John H. Morris,
Geo. Taylor, Color Serg't;	Sergeant J. D. Wilson,
Corporal W. A. Tucker, slightly;	J. McTiernan, badly;
	P. Mollen,

A. Fitzpatrick,	John Bush,
P. H. Dennin, dangerously;	Adolph Wabucks,
I. G. Fernson, slightly;	Daniel Morrow.

TAKEN PRISONERS.

Assistant-Surgeon J. S. FARGUSON, Assistant-Surgeon W. A. CONNOLLY, Hospital Teamster HOWARD, Surgeon's Boy, JOSEPH.

MISSING.

Second Lieut. Henry Simpson, Company B.
Sergeant-Major Wm. J. Thomas, Company B.
And one hundred and forty others.

DESERTER.

Second Lieut. Frank R. Mott, Company I.

Major BIDWELL, acting commander of the Michigan First, in his official report of the engagement on Sunday, says his loss, which was heavy, occurred mostly in front of the enemy's batteries. The loss of officers is large, proportionately to men. No troops could have maintained their formation any length of time under such a fire. They were hurried into action after a march of 12 miles over an exceedingly dusty road, with little or no time for rest or refreshments. But the fatigue the men evinced, and their courage, coolness, and endurance, entitle them to the highest praise. Col. RICHARDSON, in his report, gives great credit to the Michigan Second and Third for covering his retreat.

The following is the loss of the Michigan First: Went into the field with 475 men and 25 officers; lost 9 officers and 108 men, as follows:

Col. WILCOX, wounded and prisoner.

KILLED—David Jones, Charles Kauffman, George Rhodes, Wm. Maetzke, (color bearer,) Nathan Steinbregh and James Kelly.

Captains WHITTINGTON and BUTTERWORTH are supposed to be killed.

The following are missing from the Regiment, and probably many were killed, as they went into the woods when the Regiment charged and did not come out:

J. N. Barker, Albert W. Russell, Jacob N. Trask, John Archer, John Stritz, Wm. E. Thornton, Edward A. Cross, S. Clinton, Charles H. Palmer. Additional missing: Lewis Hartmeyer, Hubbard Smith, Franklin Balls, W. A. Cunningham, Hubert Eagan, Nelson M. Farrar, Henry Hutchinson, Joseph Ingersoll, Charles Ingles, John Arndt, Charles Chipman, Frank De Pease, J. Bailey, Daniel J. Briggs, George Rhodes, Charles B. Whitcomb, George D. Drury, D. Marcy Holmes, Charles C. Harvey, John D. Swails, Charles V. Brinkhorhoff, Ralston Walker, Henry A. Brower, Asaria Dubois, John Gregg, Michael Hoag, William Johnson, Melauchter Martin, Noah Porter, Walker Wait, Wm. Cornelius, John B. Newell, John Rauser, John Lang, Barnard Mauch, (probably dead,) J. J. Bame, Peter Baier, Henry Brink, Henry Brunner, Charles Ewers, Gustavus Goldsmith, Joseph Hubbell, Smith Sheppard, James Kelley, J. M. Cozey, (dead or prisoner,) Andrew Craig, Lieut. M. A. Parks, Murray Baker, George Phillip, Charles B. Moore, Frederick Lanmar, Wm. Smith, Wm. V. Marks, Clement Longsberry, Charles Kent, Albert M. Edwards, Horace Blanchard, Christian Bloom, P. E. Pomeroy, George Barker, John Reich, Wm. C. Moore.

The following are wounded:

Captains Charles M. Lum and Wm. A. Graves. Privates N. Johnson, W. Kidd, Thomas Martiamery, J. Witherspoon, J. H. Starkweather, Charles Derwan, Curtis Fowler, J. P. Vandermaker, John A. Shoeter, Wm. Sugle, Jacob Zeet, Emil Schub, Gottleib Maude, Fred. Salter, Wm. Wolfe, O. J. Person, John Sheffer, Josiah Flomerfelt, Joshua Frolverton, Henry Field, Hiram S. Brownell, Thos. O'Neill, Hiram Lane, Wm. A. Graves, Darius C. Bradish, James H. Fowler, Wm. H. Fleming and Richard A. Watt.

The following wounded were brought to the Washington Infirmary to-day:

Capt. A. D. Bean, Maine 4th; Winfield Fuller, Jas. Hunter and George Miller, Fire Zouaves; N. C. Mathews, Maine 4th; A. Ackerman, New-York 12th Volunteers.

Private M. WORDEN, Michigan 1st, brought to this Infirmary yesterday, died this afternoon.

REPORTS FROM ALEXANDRIA.

ALEXANDRIA, Friday, July 26.

The conduct of the soldiers in Alexandria to-day, has been very excessive, drunkenness being predominant, and the guard-houses, slave-pens and jail are nearly all full.

The Provost Marshal's Guard visited three drinking-houses, to-day, which had been selling liquor after having been notified, and destroyed all remaining on hand.

Gen. RUNYON has issued an order to arrest, after to-day, all soldiers found in the streets after 5 o'clock, excepting those having passes.

JOHN HUGHES, of Company A of Mozart Regiment of New-York, broke and run from the guards about dusk this evening, while they were endeavoring to handcuff him, and being called on to halt he refused, when he was shot down dead by a member of his own company.

——— CHAMBERLAIN, of Company A Second Maine Regiment, died at the hospital to-day.

It is stated on military authority that the secession pickets extend to within three miles of Fort Corcoran, in the vicinity of the former Camp Upton.

Union men were seized early this morning near the Chain Bridge, two miles above Georgetown, by secession scouts.

It is ascertained as a fact that the rebels were kept well informed of all our movements. Their gradual withdrawal from Fairfax Court-house and advanced posts, was a portion of their plan in drawing our troops into the ambuscades which led to ruin and death. Hence the imperfect condition of their earthworks at Fairfax and other points, which excited ridicule among military men.

REBEL ACCOUNTS OF THE BATTLE OF BULL'S RUN.

LOUISVILLE, Friday, July 26.

A special dispatch to the Charleston *Mercury*, dated July 23, says: As soon as it became evident that the enemy meant to give battle, President DAVIS hastened to the scene of action, arriving in time to take part in the battle. He immediately assumed command of the centre. Gen. BEAUREGARD was commander of the right wing, and Gen. JOHNSTON of the left. It was against Gen. JOHNSTON's command the enemy concentrated their best troops, who fought most obstinately. At one time the left was pressed so severely that the issue of the conflict in that direction seemed doubtful. It was here that Col. BARTON's Georgia Regiment was posted, which was so terribly cut up that a large body of our troops from the centre was sent out at a critical moment to the left's assistance and turned the tide of the battle. The enemy broke and fled before the impetuous charges of the Southerners, and the battle soon became a route.

LOUISVILLE, Friday, July 26.

A dispatch from Richmond, July 22d, says:

Soon after prayer in the Confederate Congress, the following dispatch was read to that body:

MANASSAS JUNCTION, Sunday Night.

Night has closed upon a hard fought field. Our forces were victorious. The enemy was routed and fled precipitately, abandoning a large amount of arms, ammunition, knapsacks and baggage.

The ground was strewed for miles with those killed, and the farm houses and the ground around were filled with wounded. Pursuit was continued along several routes towards Leesburgh and Centreville until darkness covered the fugitives. We have captured several field batteries, stands of arms and Union and State flags. Many prisoners have been taken.

Too high praise cannot be bestowed whether for the skill of the principal officers or for the gallantry of all our troops. The battle was mainly fought on our left. Our force was 15,000, and that of the enemy estimated at 35,000.

(Signed) JEFFERSON DAVIS.

Another dispatch says the entire Confederate force was about 40,000, and the entire forces of the United States near 80,000.

No particulars are received of the dead and wounded.

L. M. BRUSH has been arrested at Manassas as a spy, with Federal passes on his body.

THE NEW PENNSYLVANIA TROOPS.

HARRISBURGH, Friday, July 26.

On Sunday night last, Gov. CURTIN was urgently requested to push on troops to the Capital, and within the ensuing four days ten infantry regiments, nearly 11,000 picked men, thoroughly uniformed and equiped, and most of them regularly drilled in camps of instruction for two months, were thrown forward, and an additional regiment will be sent on before the close of the week. Great pains had been bestowed by the State authorities upon this Army, which was organized under the supervision of Brig.-Gen. GEO. A. MCCALL, long an officer in the regular Army, through all grades of which he has passed with distinction.

The State has also an artillery regiment, and a regiment of 1,200 cavalry nearly ready for service, which has been accepted by the Secretary of war.

To the foresight and energy of Gov. CURTIN is chiefly owing the ability of the State to contribute so promptly and efficiently to the National safety in the present emergency.

THE CAPITAL IN DANGER.

Project of the Rebels for Capturing Washington—Lee to Arouse Baltimore—Beauregard to Engage McClellan and Henningsen to Dislodge Rosencranz.

From Our Own Correspondent.

WASHINGTON, Thursday, July 25, 1861.

In these exciting times, when so many rumors, having only an imaginary foundation, are gaining currency, it is bad policy to add to their number, but I will be pardoned for communicating a project which a military officer of high rank has just assured me is now entertained by the rebels for gaining possession of the Capital. The recent success of the Confederate forces at Manassas has determined their leaders to adopt another plan of campaign,—to give up the offensive and take up the defensive. They think it is useless now to defend Richmond, but they deem it necessary to occupy this city and Baltimore, and to accomplish that end they have not only agreed upon the following plan of operations, but they have begun to put it into practice.

According to my authority, Gen. LEE, who has now, as you know, set his *corps d'armée* in motion, under the pretext of attacking our army in Western Virginia, really intends to direct his force upon the upper Potomac, which he will cross at a distance of about forty miles from Washington. Once there, he will be joined by the Secessionists, who are secretly organizing all over Maryland, and will then attack Washington on its unfortified and defenceless side. At the same time, BEAUREGARD will make a movement against MCCLELLAN, whom he will keep busy within his own lines, thus preventing his taking part in the defence of the city. JOHNSTON will be left to watch and counteract PATTERSON's movements; a strong column will be sent against BUTLER from Richmond, and PRYOR, the chevalier of the bowie-knife, and HENNINGSEN, the companion of WALKER, the fillibuster, will dislodge ROSENCRANZ from the position he occupies in Western Virginia. Such, according to the information I have received, is the plan the rebels have adopted.

I know the Administration expressed the opinion, the other day, that Washington cannot be taken. I know such is not their opinion to-day; and that they are expecting momentarily to hear of the approach of Gen. LEE. I know also that a great many persons, mainly the politicians, will lull the people into mistaken confidence. What will be the consequence? The nation suddenly aroused by the catastrophe at Bull's Run, will, under these soothing assertions, go to sleep again, until awakened by a new disaster. Shall we suffer this to take place, or shall we prepare ourselves against all contingencies of the kind? Shall we maintain our Army on the same footing, allowing lack of discipline to rule supreme, soldiers to leave their camps for the indulgences of cities, regiments to remain disorganized, the city unfortified, soldiers commanded by lawyers and merchants, officers in peace, civilians in war? Shall we continue to have no camps in which our soldiers may be inured to the fatigue of a long march, no schools to instruct them in the tactics of war, and in the evolutions indispensable to the success of a campaign? to evolutions by battalions, regiments and divisions?

If the state of things in which we have lived hitherto, is going to last, permit a man who knows what armies are, and what they must be, what the defences of a country must consist of, what are the requirements and eventualities of war, to tell you that there is no use for you to send any more men to Washington. The best thing we can do is to make peace with the South, and as honorable a peace as we can. You know well, from what I have already said in the TIMES, that I have some right to advise, and you may testify to the truth of that on which I have repeatedly insisted, that our army was not properly organized, and, consequently, not ready to march; that our fortifications were insufficient; that our soldiers ought not to be sent under fire before being prepared, by three months, at least, of severe and thorough drilling; and that it was useless to undertake a campaign unless there was homogeneity, compactness and unity, between the different branches of the Army. Though I have the greatest repugnance against reminding you of these facts, the fear I have of seeing a renewal of the same mistakes urge me to speak as I do. I cannot sit quietly, and contemplate with a cold indifference, the destruction of our Army, the ruin of our country, and the dishonor of our flag. I accuse nobody of responsibility for what has happened, because I believe it is everybody's fault; but I think it is the duty of every good citizen to oppose with all his might the repetition of the errors, mistakes and follies, which have been committed since the opening of this campaign, and that is why I sincerely and openly express my doubts, anxieties and fears.

A bearer of dispatches has arrived at Washington from Gen. LYON's Camp in Missouri. He states that JACKSON is now in the extreme Southwestern part of the State, where he has been joined by MCCULLOCH, and that both intend to make an inroad in Kansas. The Cherokee Indians have joined the rebels, notwithstanding the strenuous opposition made by JOHN ROSS, their President.

POLITICS IN OHIO.

CLEVELAND, Friday, July 26.

The Republican State Central Committee met at Columbus yesterday. All parts of the State were represented.

Resolutions were passed, declaring it not now expedient to call a Convention of the Republican Party for the nomination of officers to be chosen at the coming State election.

Resolved, That the Democratic Central Committee be requested to unite with this Committee in a call for a joint convention, for the purpose of nominating a suitable State ticket.

The call is to be addressed to all who are in favor of an unconditional preservation and a union of the States, the maintenance of the integrity of the National Government, and a vigorous and continuous prosecution of the war.

In case of a refusal by the Democratic Central Committee to accept these propositions for a union by the 9th of August, the Executive Committee are directed to issue to the people of Ohio a call for a Convention.

Delegates to the nominating Convention are to be chosen without reference to party, on the simple basis of the maintenance of the Government and the suppression of the rebellion against it.

ANOTHER REBEL REVERSE IN WESTERN VIRGINIA.

CINCINNATI, Friday, July 26.

Gen. COX occupied Charleston on the Kanawha yesterday, the rebels retreating and burning the bridges. A rebel steamer was abandoned and burnt. It is supposed the rebels will be met by Col. ROSENCRANZ's column, sent out some days ago to intercept their retreat.

GEN. BANKS' DIVISION.

MOVEMENTS OF THE COLUMN—GEN. PATTERSON'S EXCUSES—SIZE OF GEN. JOHNSTON'S FORCE.

Correspondence of the New-York Times.

HARPER'S FERRY, VA., Wednesday, July 21, 1861.

I wrote you on the 19th from Charlestown. Since then, on Sunday last, as you are aware, we came to this place, and JOHNSTON, being relieved from all anxiety as to this force, hastened to join the Confederate army at Manassas, where, according to the reports received here, he rendered efficient service. Gen. PATTERSON left Bunker Hill on Wednesday, the 17th, and on the following day JOHNSTON started with the main body of his forces for Manassas. On Saturday the rear-guard, left to watch our movements, proceeded to join him, leaving no troops behind but a few of local militia.

Since our arrival the General has turned his attention to finding out excuses for his extraordinary conduct. He never intended to attack or follow up JOHNSTON. Although JOHNSTON was plainly sent or left in the vicinity of Winchester, to watch this column and prevent its operating on the right of the enemy in the attack on Manassas, and although the business of Gen. PATTERSON was as plainly to rout JOHNSTON's force or to keep them where they were, or to follow them, yet the egotism of Gen. P. seemed to have induced him to imagine that JOHNSTON had some special spite against him, and was bent upon following and attacking him. Hence a host of exaggerated reports constantly sent on to Washington in regard to the movements and designs of the enemy. JOHNSTON plainly did not care what became of this column, so long as it did not go where it could aid our troops in the main attack on the Manassas line, and hence the moment he found, by our march to and delay at Charlestown, that we had no design of taking part in that movement, he made all speed to arrive there with his forces in time to take part in the action, in which, I regret to say, he appears to have been successful. The Washington Battery of New-Orleans, with 8 heavy guns, which is said to have done such execution on our troops on Sunday, was reported to have been with JOHNSTON at Winchester.

The reported strength of the enemy while we were at Bunker Hill did not go beyond 25,000. They were said to be strongly intrenched, and to have felled trees and fences and barricaded the road. The reasons first assigned for not attacking him (although I repeat, it was never intended to attack him when we left Martinsburgh,) was, first, the unwillingness of our troops to advance further on the eve of the expiration of their term of service; and, second, the superior strength and position of the enemy.

The slander upon our troops I have already disposed of, in my letter of the 19th. In regard to the second reason, it is to be observed that, although, if true, a sufficient reason for not attacking the enemy in their lines, it was no reason whatever for moving away from him and leaving him free to join the forces at Manassas. An army of 20,000 men might well detain, or at least delay, for a long time, the movements of a force even of 40,000 men, particularly if they were embarrassed by a train of heavy guns. The reason given is inconsistent with itself. The fact that JOHNSTON remained in the neighborhood of Winchester as long as this force was in that vicinity, and intrenched himself there, proves that he was not so strong as has been subsequently reported, and also proves that he would not have ventured to move with this army hanging upon his rear, and certainly could not have moved with such rapidity with his heavy guns as to have arrived in time for the action at Manassas.

Since arriving here this force has been rapidly dwindling away; no serious effort has been made to retain them. Ten regiments of Pennsylvania three months' men have already been sent on their way home, and some even that volunteer to stay longer if needed.

Gen. SCOTT is justly incensed at the impotent conclusion to which this column has been brought, and has by no means been satisfied with the excuses that have been showered upon him. He, doubtless, sees through them.

The last report hailed here with joy is, the enemy's forces at Winchester were over 40,000, including 1,000 cavalry and sixty guns—many very heavy, some even Columbiads. This absurd report is seized upon here as though it was true, and if true an excuse, forgetting that if true it was the more important to keep it here. But it is plainly untrue. How is it that if true it never reached us until we left the neighborhood of Winchester? Is it likely that after the experience of the rebels of the great caution—I might say timidity—of Gen. PATTERSON, they would, on the eve of the decisive struggle at Manassas, have detailed so large a force to keep in check 22,000 men? I think clearly not. I saw this morning a man from the neighborhood of Winchester, who says that the force under JOHNSTON did not exceed 20,000, that even with the citizens of the place and a considerable portion of unarmed militia, who express willingness to fight, and which it is the habit of Virginia to estimate as soldiers, it would be impossible to make up 40,000.

But I leave this painful subject—the case is too plain for argument. In any other country, Gen. PATTERSON would be shot. Adjutant RYNO was shot for not doing enough, although he gained a victory. He ought, certainly, to be court-martialed. At all events, he is a disgraced man, and, as a soldier and public character, entirely ruined. He never was eminent for bravery, or for anything else, that I know of. He is a man of wealth, and has managed to keep himself at the head of the military organization in Philadelphia. But in the Mexican war his courage was impugned. He was always either sick or buying sugar when any fighting was to be done. Moreover, his heart is not with the North in this contest. He has, from the first, done nothing but create and magnify difficulties. I have always thought and have said that his design, from the first, was to dally and putter away the time until the terms of the three months' men expired. I am surprised that Gen. SCOTT tolerated him so long.

The instincts of the people in these cases are seldom at fault. They never had confidence in Gen. PATTERSON, and, during the first excitement upon the news from Sumter, the mob threatened his house and compelled him to show his colors.

THE TWELFTH NEW-YORK STATE MILITIA.

CAMP MCDOWELL, HARPER'S FERRY, Tuesday, July 23, 1861.

To the Editor of the New-York Times:

In the late unfortunate battle which took place at Bull's Run, the statement is made that the Twelfth New-York Regiment fled before the enemy, and otherwise conducted themselves in a most disgraceful manner. Too many, I fear, do not understand the distinction between the Twelfth New-York S. M., and the volunteers. The former, Col. BUTTERFIELD's regiment, was not in MCDOWELL's column, but in that of Gen. PATTERSON. Should we be called into action, you may rely upon our regiment proving itself an honor to the City and State.

By giving this communication a place in your paper you will greatly oblige myself as well as the regiment generally.

Yours, very truly,
CHAS. A. CARLETON,
Engineer Corps N. Y. S. M.

IMPORTANT FROM FORT MONROE.

SUCCESSFUL EXPEDITION TO BACK RIVER.

Correspondence of the New-York Times.

FORTRESS MONROE, Wednesday, July 24, 1861.

Gen. BUTLER has again given proof of his determination to perform his duty to the Union in the direction of movements against the enemy, when properly supported, by sending an expedition, with artillery, to attack a battery on Back River. This battery is supposed to be one that the Disunionists planted soon after their retreat from Bethel, in anticipation of another attack from the Union troops. The expedition left quietly, this afternoon, as if for occasional practice, and consists of both land and sea forces. Portions of the California regiment, under Col. BAKER, United States Senator from Oregon; of the Tenth New-York, under acting Col. ELDER; the Naval Brigade, under Major WHITTEMORE, and others not here named, constitute the command. The infantry marched from their encampments over the tongue of land that separates the battery of the enemy from the Fortress, while the Naval Brigade and their compatriots were towed by steam tugs in boats around by water. The attack will probably be made simultaneously from both quarters at the appointed time. Suitable guides are provided and everything is arranged in the best possible manner, considering the comparatively limited period that has been allowed Gen. BUTLER for the training of his artillery horses. One of the pieces is Sawyer's rifled cannon.

But little, if anything, is known of the expedition outside of the fortress. Surgeons SMITH and DE LITTLE accompany it in their professional capacity, thoroughly provided for action. I am much mistaken in the genius of the man who designed, and the mettle of those personally engaged, if this does not prove as gallant an affair as any of MCCLELLAN's or either one of BUTLER's at Annapolis, Baltimore or the Relay.

Our ships-of-war continue every moment on the alert. The *Minnesota* and *Roanoke* are both wide awake. Steam is kept up every moment. Should the *Jamestown* and *Yorktown* come to *this town* they will find us all *in* town.

NEPTUNE.

FORTRESS MONROE, Thursday, July 25.

Lieut. CROSBY, yesterday, took charge of an expedition to Back River, consisting of 300 men and seven field pieces, upon the propeller *Fanny* and two launches, belonging to the ships of war in the harbor and to the Naval Brigade. Back River is properly an arm of the sea, about midway between Old Point and York River.

The expedition was entirely successful. Lieut. CROSBY surprised and burned nine sloops and schooners belonging to Confederates, and brought off one valuable prize, a schooner laden with bacon, corn and furniture; the last article belonging to parties about to take refuge up the York or Rappahannock River.

LA MOUNTAIN will, this evening, make an ascension from Hampton to reconnoitre the position of the Confederates in the vicinity.

Mr. DUNNING, of the Sanitary Commission, leaves for Washington to-night. He reports a gratifying improvement in sanitary affairs about the fortress and the camps during the past few days.

JEFF. DAVIS' PIRATES.

EXAMINATION OF THE SUMTER PRIVATEERSMEN.

UNITED STATES COMMISSIONER'S COURT.

Four of the crew of the privateer *Sumter*, who were placed in charge of the bark *Cuba*, Capt. SPROUL, after her capture, and who were subsequently recaptured by the crew of the *Cuba*, and arrived at this port on Sunday last, was brought up for preliminary examination yesterday, before United States Commissioner OSBORN. ALGERNON S. SULLIVAN, Esq., who has been retained by JEFF. DAVIS' oligarchy, appeared for the prisoners; and G. P. ANDREWS, Esq., conducted the examination for the Government. The pirates names are HUDGINS, a Virginian, who acted as Captain; SPENCE, an Englishman; DAVIDSON, a Scotchman; O'BRIEN, an Irishman; and DONNELLY, an American.

Capt. J. D. SPROUL, of the *Cuba*, was the only witness examined, and his story did not differ from the account already published. He said they were brought to by a shot from the *Sumter*, while off the southern coast of Cuba, on the 4th of July, the *Sumter* at the time displaying the American flag. They were boarded by a party from the *Sumter*, who said she was a United States vessel. Capt. SPROUL and officers were taken on board the *Sumter*, when they were informed that their vessel was a prize to the C. S. A. They were afterwards transferred to their own vessel, and taken in tow by the *Sumter*, which also had another prize, the brig *Machias*, in tow. The *Machias* broke loose from the *Sumter* on the 5th, and the privateer went in chase of her, and failing to connect again with the *Cuba*, the latter vessel was left to make her way into port. On the 12th of July, the crew of the *Cuba* retook their vessel from the pirates, and sailed for New-York. The pirates did not willingly surrender the vessel, as some of them stated on their arrival here, but offered all the resistance in their power.

The cross-examination of Capt. SPROUT failed to elicit anything of importance for the defence of the pirates, and on his testimony the Commissioner ordered them committed to await the action of the Grand Jury.

GEN. FREMONT'S STAFF.

ST. LOUIS, Friday, July 26.

The following officers are officially announced as composing the Staff of Gen. FREMONT:

Capt. J. C. KELTIN, Assistant Adjutant-General and Acting Commissary; Brevet-Major JOHN MCKINSTRY, Assistant Quartermaster; Surgeon S. G. J. DECAMP, Medical Director; Lieut.-Col. T. P. ANDREWS, Assistant Paymaster.

COL. CORCORAN AND CONGRESSMAN ELY PRISONERS.

PHILADELPHIA, Friday, July 26.

The *Bulletin* has a special dispatch from Washington which states, on the authority of a letter from Leesburgh, Va., that Col. CORCORAN and Congressman ELY are prisoners at Manassas.

The dispatch also states that Col. WADE HAMPTON was killed, and that the rebels are taking care of our wounded and burying our dead.

The scouting parties of the rebels came within three miles of Washington last night.

COL. PINCKNEY'S REGIMENT COMING HOME.

BALTIMORE, Friday, July 26.

The Sixth Regiment, Col. PINCKNEY, have been honorably relieved from duty, their term of service having expired on the 19th of July, and the regiment will leave for New-York on Saturday noon, and probably arrive on Sunday.

THE BLOCKADE OF GALVESTON.

BOSTON, Friday, July 26.

The United States steamer *South Carolina*, Commander ALDEN, was off Galveston on the 7th of July. She had captured eleven vessels since establishing the blockade, on the 3d inst. One of the prizes had arrived at Pensacola, under command of Capt. RODNEY BAXTER, with dispatches for Commodore MERWINE.

RESPONSE OF VERMONT.

MONTPELIER, Friday, July 26.

Vermont will furnish one company of Sharpshooters in response to the call in loyal States.

[*For other Rebellion News see Second, Fifth and Eighth Pages.*]

Battle of Wilson's Creek, August 10, 1861

General Stone's Division at Edward's Ferry, October 20, 1861

The New-York Times.

VOL. X....NO. 3090. NEW-YORK, SUNDAY, AUGUST 18, 1861. PRICE THREE CENTS.

THE GREAT REBELLION.

Important News from the National Capital.

The First Seizure Under the President's Proclamation.

Large Amount of Goods Intercepted at Annapolis Junction.

Communication Between Baltimore and the Rebels Cut Off.

The Departments of Northeastern Virginia and Washington Joined.

GEN. McCLELLAN IN COMMAND.

Withdrawal of the Rebel Forces to Fairfax Court-house.

A Fight Expected in Western Virginia.

Important Seizure of Money by Gen. Fremont.

The Rebels Threatening Fortress Monroe.

Philadelphia Vessels Captured by Pirates.

SPECIAL DISPATCH FROM WASHINGTON

WASHINGTON, Saturday, Aug. 17.

A heavy seizure of goods destined for the rebels was made near Annapolis Junction to-day. The goods were bought by parties in Baltimore for Richmond dealers. A draft for $4,975 was sent to pay for them. With the goods were also seized the teams and wagons by which they were being conveyed, and a number of letters to officers in the rebel Army. Besides the value of the goods, this seizure is important, as the man in charge of the goods furnishes also much information of the manner in which communications are kept up between Baltimore and the rebel States.

SHELLING THE WOODS AT MATHIAS POINT.

Since the affair at Mathias Point, the steamer *Freeborn* went down and shelled the woods from whence the rebels fired, clearing them up and rendering them untenable, for the time being at least.

THE SEVENTY-NINTH MUTINEERS.

The court-martial will take up the case of the mutineers of the Seventy-ninth on Monday.

PASSES.

Gen. PORTER, the Provost-Marshal, commenced issuing passes to-day. Lieut. BACHE has charge of that department, but all passes are signed by Gen. PORTER. The greatest caution is observed in granting them, and a record is kept of all issued.

BRIGADIERS.

EGBERT L. VIELE, of New-York, has been appointed a Brigadier-General of the volunteers. [illegible], of California, has also been appointed a Brigadier. Both are graduates of West Point, and served with distinction in the Mexican War.

ENGLAND AND THE BLOCKADE.

Notwithstanding the rumors about the dissatisfaction of England and France at the alleged ineffectiveness of our blockade, there has been no intimation from any Government with which we have commercial intercourse, of any intention or desire to violate it. Indeed, all nations have thus far practically respected it.

CONSULAR APPOINTMENTS.

The list of consular appointments has been completed for the present. No more changes will be made, except an exigency arises, similar to that at Curaçoa.

CHANGE IN DEPARTMENTS.

A general order was issued by Gen. SCOTT to-day, uniting the military departments of Washington and Northeastern Virginia into one department, to be called the Department of the Potomac, under Maj.-Gen. McCLELLAN, who is ordered to proceed to organize the troops under him into divisions and independent brigades. By this change, Gen. MANSFIELD is left without a command, and no intimation has been given him as yet as to what duty he will be assigned. His staff will remain as heretofore. The new department includes Northeastern Virginia, the District of Columbia, and Maryland, as far as Bladensburgh.

EXPERIMENT WITH A NEW GUN.

The President for three mornings has been visiting the Navy-yard, experimenting with a newly-invented mechanical gun, which is worked by a crank in the hands of the gunner, and throws seventy balls per minute. The implement is said to be the invention of a poor mechanic of New-York, and is not yet patented. The President feels a lively interest in the experiments of new fire-arms.

RECRUITING BRISK.

Intelligence from the different recruiting stations states that the plan of mustering men into the service singly is rapidly filling up the ranks of regiments now forming.

SUPERINTENDENT OF PUBLIC BUILDINGS.

The reappointment of Mr. WOOD, as Superintendent of Public Buildings, gives general satisfaction. He has resumed the duties of his position, and it is generally believed that he will be confirmed by the Senate at the coming session.

ECONOMIZING EXPENSES.

In the Land Bureau of the Interior Department, Judge EDMONDS, the Commissioner, has reduced the force of clerks over fifteen per cent. Whilst economizing as far as possible in the Bureau, he is exacting the strictest attention to the duties of the office from subordinates.

AN ELOPEMENT.

To the great scandal of all good and virtuous people in Washington, a beautiful woman, the wife of a highly respectable citizen and the mother of three children, has seceded from her husband, a strong Union man. She eloped with a Washington merchant, a Secessionist, and the couple are now in Dixie, whither the husband will probably not care to pursue his erring wife. The children are here with the father. The absconding lover leaves assets to the amount of two thousand dollars to pay debts amounting to thirty thousand.

JAPANESE VOUCHERS.

The Consul at Hakodadi, Japan, has forwarded to the State Department the original Japanese vouchers, with the translations, for the expenditures made on behalf of the Consulate. They are very voluminous, considering the small amount of matter contained in them. One is a bill presented by Mr. GOO-SO-GO-YO-YAH-KAS-KE—whoever he may be—of Chig-gah-si-ma, Hakodadi, for sixty-two bundles of charcoal and two hundred and twenty sticks of fire-wood, furnished to sailors. The aggregate cost thereof in Japanese currency reaches the portentous figure of 48,550. Reduced to United States currency, the amount is $12 14. The bill with signature and seal fills three pages of Japanese paper.

DISPATCH TO THE ASSOCIATED PRESS.

WASHINGTON, Saturday, Aug. 17.

The Confederate forces have nearly all fallen back to Fairfax Court-house, thus widening the distance separating the hostile forces. The pickets of both Armies, however, occupy nearly the same advanced positions as heretofore.

Ex-Minister FAULKNER is not, as has been stated, merely detained as a hostage for the return of Messrs. HARRIS and MAGRAW, who went to the Confederate camp for the purpose of recovering the body of the late Col. CAMERON, but for good and satisfactory reasons to the Government, apart from any such considerations.

The reporter of the Associated Press at Washington learns that a statement is published in Philadelphia, and perhaps in other papers this morning, as coming from him, that Secretary CAMERON is to be removed. Nothing whatever of this kind was transmitted by the reporter, who by this publication desires to relieve himself from even a suspicion of giving currency to a statement utterly destitute of any foundation in fact.

MUTINY OF THE SEVENTY-NINTH.

Correspondence of the New-York Times.

WASHINGTON CITY, Wednesday, Aug. 14.

The usual quiet of the city has been somewhat disturbed to-day by the mutinous conduct of the Seventy-ninth Regiment. It appears that an order was sent to them last night to strike their tents early this morning, and march to some other locality—to join SICKLES' Brigade, as was generally understood. When the morning came the men refused to obey the order, as they had previously agreed among themselves—not a man would move—not an order would they obey, and the officers were compelled to strike the tents without assistance. This only increased the excitement, which continued until 9 or 10 o'clock, when a number of cake and beer venders, with plenty of whisky, made their appearance, and the men began to drink and to become intoxicated, when the mutiny increased and the whole regiment was in a state of terrible excitement; all order was at an end; the officers were grossly insulted, and at last the more violent began to fight among themselves.

Early in the day Col. STEVENS, the newly-appointed Colonel of the regiment, calmly endeavored to bring them back to duty. He called them together and addressed them, and then went among them and personally appealed to them to obey the orders of their superiors, but all his gentle remonstrances and patriotic appeals were treated with contempt. Then he read the Riot Act, but this they laughed to scorn. At last he sent to the War Department a statement of the case, whereupon a regiment of infantry, two companies of cavalry, and several pieces of ordnance, were sent to subdue these turbulent spirits, and after a deal of trouble the regiment finally formed and left the field, arriving in the city about dark, escorted by the cavalry, while the infantry brought up the rear.

The cause of the difficulty appeared to be a general belief that the Government had acted in bad faith toward them, in not fulfilling its promises. It appears that after the Bull Run fight, in which they suffered severely, and lost their Colonel, (CAMERON,) that they desired to return to New-York, reorganize and return; to this end, they entreated their Lieut.-Col. ELLIOTT to make such an arrangement with the Secretary of War; and, finally, Col. ELLIOTT informed them that the Secretary had complied with their wishes. A number of the men claim that this order was read to them on parade, but Col. ELLIOTT informed me that it was not read, although it was generally understood that they were to go home, recruit and reorganize, although no day was set for their departure. Some assert that they were to go immediately after they elected a Colonel; but instead of this, the Secretary of War appointed Col. STEVENS, who was an officer of the regular Army, and to cap the climax, the order for their return to New-York was countermanded, upon which, they determined to resist. The idea appeared to prevail that the Zouaves were sent home to reorganize, because they refused to do duty, and they supposed they could accomplish the same thing by a regular and stubborn mutiny.

Late in the afternoon I went to the encampment, which was situated at the head of Seventh-street, on a beautiful hill, overlooking the city. A thousand people, in carriages, on horseback and on foot, stood at a respectful distance from the scene of the confusion, as a fight was seriously apprehended. On the way I met a few straggling soldiers, but they were all intoxicated, and more impertinent than intelligent. When I reached the encampment, the cavalry occupied the summit of the hill, in the rear, the infantry on either side, and the batteries in the road in front. The camping ground was covered with knapsacks, canteens, haversacks, blankets, guns, every variety of camp equipage, mixed up with prostrate soldiers, who could no longer stand or keep awake. Guards of armed men held some as prisoners, who resolutely refused to obey orders, and who were ready and anxious to fight anything or anybody—some were tied, and one man insisted upon insulting and abusing the officers, and could only be silenced by the application of a gag, but the moment it was taken from his mouth he began again, more furious than ever; at last, exhausted, he stretched himself upon the ground, and went to sleep.

As the regiment marched off the field, a large majority of them appeared to be intoxicated; they were noisy and riotous on the march; some refused to march, and were compelled to go into the ranks by force. One man, more stubborn than the rest, declared he would not go. The Captain and a private seized him and forced him along. He was about to resist with great violence, when an officer of the regular Army approached and told the Captain that he would be justified in killing him; whereupon the soldier staggered into the ranks and moved off as well as his drunken legs could carry him.

The whole scene was disgraceful in the extreme, and nothing but the large and superior force brought to bear upon them prevented the disbanding and desertion of the entire regiment. Let it be understood that the officers of the Seventy-ninth did not sympathize in this mutiny, but did all in their power to prevent it and to quell it.

A company of Zouaves was raised, a few days ago, in Philadelphia, composed entirely of French and Italians who served in the Crimean and Italian wars. Many of them have the original Zouaze dress as worn in the Crimea. They are called the Zouaves d'Afrique, of Philadelphia. They are commanded by Capt. CHAS. H. T. COLLIS, an American, who was here yesterday, and arranged for their immediate employment. They were ordered to Harper's Ferry.

RICHMOND.

From the Philadelphia Press.

The mutineers were encamped on the side of a hill, which was rather sparsely wooded. The cavalry first came on the ground, and one of the companies formed on the hilltop. The infantry marched past, and were drawn up on the side of the hill, the line extending to the base, and at an angle with the horsemen. The command was then given by Col. STEVENS to the Seventy-ninth to fall in, and was obeyed with some reluctance. The line was formed on the road at the bottom of the hill, and the regiment marched up towards Fourteenth-street, with colors flying and band playing. A few were so intoxicated that they could not obey the orders, and they were left on the the field to be arrested by the patrol. The regiment marched up the road in tolerably good order, although the soldiers manifested a defiant and disagreeable spirit. Some were shouting and cheering, especially as the cavalry passed, while others who did not have arms, were carrying sticks on their shoulders. The cavalry and infantry followed them until they arrived on Fourteenth-street, where the order was given to halt.

They halted on a part of the street sparsely inhabited, and about the distance of a furlong from their encampment. On each side of the road were large meadows, soft, marshy, low, and in some parts rendered impassable by the recent rains. After the Seventy-ninth had halted, the cavalry rode over into the meadow about fifty paces from the road, and formed in a line parallel with the road. The infantry then came up, and formed in line at right angles with the cavalry and extending across the road into the meadow on each side. The mutinous regiment was directed to form in line on the side of the road, parallel with the cavalry. The regular battalion was then marched up the road and formed on the other side of the street, immediately opposite and facing the Seventy-ninth, while the cavalry retired to a more distant part of the meadow.

The lines having been formed, Gen. PORTER and his staff, accompanied by Col. STEVENS and Major SYKES, rode up to the centre. After a moment or two of delay, an aid of Gen. PORTER read the orders of Gen. McCLELLAN in a remarkably clear and distinct tone of voice. The orders have not yet been published, and what I write of them is merely from recollection. He stated that he had heard with pain and sorrow of the disaffection which existed among the members of the Seventy-ninth Regiment; that he had listened attentively to their alleged grievances, and, after examining them with care, was compelled to say that they were of the most frivolous character. At a time like this, when the country needed the services of her children, the exhibition of such a spirit as that manifested by the Seventy-ninth could only come from the basest motives which could actuate the soldier, and would lead to the belief that their conduct was prompted by cowardice. As a punishment he ordered that the regiment should be deprived of its colors, until, by future good behavior and honorable service on the field of battle, its soldiers showed themselves worthy to bear them. The ringleaders of the mutiny were to be placed in arrest, and the regiment was to be ordered to fall in by company and march to the quarters assigned them in Virginia, and, if they refused to obey this order, *they were to be fired upon.*

The scene during the reading was exceedingly impressive. The sun was just going down, and in the hazy, uncertain twilight, the features and forms of officers and men could scarcely be distinguished. Immediately behind his aid was Gen. PORTER, firm and self-possessed. Col. STEVENS was in front of his own regiment, endeavoring to quiet his rather nervous horse. In the rear of the regulars, and a little distance apart, Gen. SICKLES sat carelessly on horseback, coolly smoking a cigar and conversing with some friends. At one time during the reading a murmur passed through the line of the mutineers, and when that portion of the order directing the regiment to surrender its colors was read, a private in one of the rear cried out in broad Scotch tones—"Let's keep the colors, boys!" No response was made by the remainder of the regiment. Major SYKES at once rode up the line to where the voice was heard. It would have been more than that soldier's life was worth, had he been discovered at the moment, in pistol range, by any of the officers. When the reading was concluded, a voice cried out "fire," and a number of spectators in the rear of the Infantry, supposing the work of death about to commence, ran a little distance to escape the balls.

After the orders had been read, Gen. PORTER said to Col. STEVENS, "Point out the leaders." A squad of men were detailed from the battalion to accompany the Colonel, who went from company to company and designated the obnoxious members. They were marched to the rear to the number of forty or fifty, and placed under arrest. This operation took some time, and it was dark before the arrest was completed. The final order was then given to wheel by company into column, and march to the quarters in Virginia. This was the order which they had disobeyed in the morning, and which, if again disobeyed, would have been followed by a fire from the regular infantry. There seemed to be a moment's delay, but the mutinous volunteers, evidently seeing that resistance was useless, reluctantly obeyed, and took up the line of march to their quarters. The arrested leaders were taken to the guard-house, while the remainder of the regiment was escorted by the cavalry and the battery.

ORDER READ TO THE SEVENTY-NINTH.

The following is the order read to the Seventy-ninth Regiment on Wednesday:

"The General Commanding has heard with the deepest pain of the acts of insubordination on the part of the Seventy-ninth Regiment. Without attempting to enter into a discussion of the causes, it is sufficient to say that they are frivolous and groundless.

That these acts have thrown disgrace upon the regiment and the service, and taking place at this time, they give rise to the strongest suspicions of the most abject cowardice. The regiment has forced upon the Commanding General an issue which he is prepared to meet.

The men are ordered to lay down their arms and return to duty. All those refusing to do so will be fired upon immediately. If they comply with the order, the ringleaders only will be punished.

The colors of the regiment are taken from them, and will be returned only when their conduct in camp shall have proven that they understand the first duty of a soldier—obedience; and when, on the field of battle, they shall have proved their bravery. The names of the leaders in this revolt will be sent to the Governor of New-York, to be placed in the archives of the State. A court martial will be held forthwith."

THE MASSACHUSETTS BANKS.

BOSTON, Saturday, Aug. 17.

The Boston Banks agree to take ten millions, and the country banks five millions, as the first installment of the Government loan.

Col. F. W. LANDER is on a visit to his father in Lynn, who lies at the point of death.

THE "MEAGHER BRIGADE."

From the Boston Herald.

We have been requested to publish the subjoined letter from Capt. THOMAS F. MEAGHER, of the Sixty-ninth New-York Regiment, written in reply to a note addressed to him by a gentleman in this city inquiring whether he (MEAGHER) had authorized any person to enlist men in this city for a New-York Brigade "to be commanded by him." It will be seen that Mr. MEAGHER's letter effectually disposes of the matter:

WASHINGTON, Aug. 14, 1861.

MY DEAR ——: I did not receive your letter informing me of the fact that certain parties in Boston were organizing an Irish Brigade for the war, and doing so in my name, and apparently with my authority, until this late moment. Previously I had heard rumors of such being the case, but they were so very vague that I took no notice of them. Now, however, that I learn something positive about the matter, I write, fully authorizing you to state—and to to state so in the most public and emphatic terms—that I have not authorized, in any way whatever, directly or indirectly, the organization of the brigade in question, and that, moreover, I hold the parties who have had the impudence and dishonesty to use my name for the purpose, as nothing less than brazen swindlers and impostors, and accordingly denounce them and their scheme to the public, and warn the public of Boston—the Irish portion of it especially—to beware of and spurn them.

Be so good as to let this statement and these sentiments of mine be known and published, wherever, and as extensively, as the fraudulent mischief done by these parties has spread. And believe me, with sincere regard, very truly your friend,

THOS. FRANCIS MEAGHER.

TROOPS FROM CALIFORNIA.

The St. Louis *Democrat* of Aug. 15 makes this improbable statement:

"We learned last evening, from reliable sources, that the State of California has offered the Government 50,000 troops, and that the War Department has accepted them.

The first order from the War Department went out last night by the Pony Express. It directs four regiments of infantry and one of cavalry to proceed to Western Texas. It is stated in official quarters that the 50,000 men will reach the Mississippi Valley within forty days."

THE WAR IN MISSOURI.

SEIZURE OF $50,000 BY U. S. TROOPS.

ST. LOUIS, Saturday, Aug. 17.

A detachment of U. S. troops from Cape Girardeau seized fifty-eight thousand dollars belonging to the bank at St. Genevieve yesterday, by order of Gen. FREMONT, and brought it to this city to-day. It is understood this money was being used or would be used for the benefit of the secession cause in that section.

The statement in the late news from California, that J. C. PALMER had left that State for the purpose of taking charge of the Commissary Department under Gen. FREMONT is untrue. Mr. PALMER has no connection whatever with Gen. FREMONT.

ST. LOUIS, Saturday, Aug. 17—P. M.

It appears now that the fifty-eight thousand dollars, seized at St. Genevieve yesterday, was at the request of the Directors of the Parent Bank here, to whom it was transferred to-day by Gen. FREMONT.

Dispatches reached here, to-day, that a train conveying troops over the Hannibal and St. Joseph Railroad was fired into by the Secessionists near Palmyra, and one soldier killed and several wounded. Gen. POPE immediately sent orders to Gen. HURLBUT to take such force as he deemed necessary to Marion County, quarter them on the people, and levy contributions of horses, mules, provisions and such other things as are useful to soldiers, amounting to $10,000 on the inhabitants of the County, and $5,000 more on the citizens of Palmyra, as the penalty for this outrage.

GOV. JACKSON'S FORCE, ETC.

KANSAS CITY, Mo., Saturday, Aug. 17.

We learn from reliable sources that six hundred State troops, well drilled and equipped, leave Fayette, Harvard County, to-day, with the intention of joining Gov. JACKSON's forces in the Southern part of the State. Four hundred of them are said to be mounted.

OUR ST. LOUIS CORRESPONDENCE.

DANGER TO CAIRO FROM THE REAR—DESIGNS OF THOMPSON AND HARDEE—THE MISSOURI HOME GUARDS—SECESSION OUTRAGES, ETC.

ST. LOUIS, Tuesday, Aug. 13, 1861.

Those who have attentively watched the progress of events in the West will not be surprised to hear that the flame of secession has spread to Southern Illinois, and that one of the greatest dangers to which Cairo is at present exposed is that of invasion from the rear. Should the rebels under JEFF. THOMPSON succeed in taking Cape Girardeau, they would be in possession of two good steam ferries across the Mississippi, and, once over the river, the counties of Alexander, Union, Jackson, Johnson, Williamson, Hamilton, Jefferson and Washington would be in a blaze. There would be no difficulty in forming a connection with bands of Secessionists from Paducah, Ky., the Illinois Central would be rendered impassable, and Cairo left at the mercy of its foes.

Loyal men in that portion of Illinois are feeling very uneasy at this state of things. But a very few weeks ago the Secessionists were secret in all their movements, held their meetings at night and were extremely careful not to be found out. But now, confident either of strength or approaching success, they are bold, defiant and threatening. I am reliably informed that anonymous letters are daily received by gentlemen high in office, from persons who profess to be afraid to sign their names, giving a most alarming account of the state of things in that region.

But thus far the mysterious designs of THOMPSON and HARDEE have been frustrated by the skillful manœuvres of Gen. FREMONT, with his small and neglected force. His name is a tower of strength to loyal men and a terror to his foes. No sooner did he appear at Cairo, than the rebels evacuated Charleston in hot haste, fled to New-Madrid, and yesterday it was reported that the entire right wing had recrossed the Mississippi at that place.

The fortification of Cape Girardeau has effectually prevented any movement in that direction. Pilot Knob is so strong that all advance upon Jefferson City is checked by that route. So that for the present, at least in this part of the State, the rebels will have to confine themselves to their favorite mode of warfare—robbery and murder.

The Home Guards of Missouri, to whom the State and the nation owe so much, are to be reorganized and sworn in for three years or the war. St. Louis is to have five regiments of infantry, besides cavalry and artillery. This organization will do more towards putting down the infamous guerilla system inaugurated by the rebels than all the volunteer regiments which can be raised.

Capt. CHARLES ZAGONYI, a Hungarian, late of your City, has been directed to raise a company of picked mounted men, to serve as a body guard for Major-Gen. FREMONT. They will be constantly on guard near the General's head-quarters, and will relieve the minds of many friends of his who know the state of feeling here.

The hatred of the Union in this city is almost as amusing as it is painful. As elsewhere at the South, those who give freest expression to it are the women and children. A man with a military cap or buttons runs in a short walk as trying a gauntlet of scornful looks and insulting words, as usually would fall to his lot in a long life. But the hardest thing to bear is a way the prettiest Secessionists have of covering up their faces with a shawl or fan when they meet you; letting one eye out, which says, as plainly as eyes can speak, "See what you lose by being a vile Hessian."

Accounts of outrages continue to come in from all quarters of the State. The latest is from Potosi, on the Iron Mountain Railroad, where a body of mounted rebels dashed in on Saturday evening just at dusk, shooting an old man who was quietly sitting on his doorstep. The Home Guards were taken by surprise, but rallied and drove the assaulting party off, with a loss of one killed and five wounded—two of them fatally.

Potosi is, I understand, to be immediately occupied by our troops. The rich lead mines there are a tempting bait for the enemy, who are sadly in want of that necessary article.

St. Louis is to be at once and thoroughly fortified and secured against any attack from within or without, the plan having been already decided upon by Gen. FREMONT.

The superintendence of the work will be intrusted to Col. HASSENDEUBEL, one of the heroes of Carthage, and the whole will be under the direction of Brig.-Gen. ASBOTH, whose rare abilities as a military engineer have won the highest encomiums from scientific men ever since his career in Hungary, and are a sufficient guarantee that the work will be well and thoroughly done.

Major GEO. E. WARING, late of the Garibaldi Guard, arrived here on Saturday, and is already actively engaged in the organization of his new cavalry regiment, the "Fremont Hussars," which is encamped on the race-course, about three miles out of the city. The officers of this regiment have all, without exception, seen active service.

The city is full of rumors this afternoon in regard to the recent battle at Springfield. One account giving us another brilliant retreat, with the death of McCULLOCH, and the other asserting that we have been entirely cut up, Gen. LYONS killed, and that a victorious army is marching upon St. Louis. You will learn the truth as soon probably as we do.

J. W. S.

OUTRAGES AT CYNTHIANA, OHIO.

From the Cincinnati Press, Aug. 15.

Reliable information is received in our city that the Secessionists in the vicinity of Cynthiana have begun their nefarious work at that point. For some days past they have been sorely troubled by the shipment of arms, ammunition and military clothing from this city for the use of the Union men, who, it is well known, are forming themselves into companies throughout the State for the protection of the interests of the Union. This fact, it seems, has become fully known to the people near Cythiana, and as they are of strong Disunion character, they determined to put a stop to it so far as railway facilities are concerned. Last night, in pursuance of their intentions, they set fire to and completely destroyed about fifteen hundred feet of the trestle work on the road beyond Cynthiana, thereby preventing the shipment of all goods, stores, &c., beyond that point. As a consequence, supplies cannot be sent any further in that direction for the present, but we may congratulate ourselves that previous to the outrage a large amount of arms and ammunition had gone forward, and we hope safely reached its destination.

THE WAR IN WESTERN VIRGINIA.

A LARGE REBEL FORCE NEAR ROMNEY.

BALTIMORE, Saturday, Aug. 17.

A letter from Westernport, Md., opposite Piedmont, dated the 13th inst., says that the National scouts, last Sunday night, succeeded in capturing three notorious secession bridge-burners, at New Creek.

A force of a eleven hundred Secessionists is reported near Romney. The National troops are at New Creek Bridge, and expected to be attacked by them. The Nationals have been reinforced.

A large number of fugitives from Virginia, men, women and children, in great distress, are daily passing through Westernport, seeking refuge.

MOVEMENTS OF GEN. ROSECRANS.

Correspondence of the Cincinnati Times.

CLARKSBURGH, Va., Aug. 11, 1861.

It is said that one is compelled to go from home to hear the news, but the Cincinnati morning dailies bring it to our doors. The intelligence in one of the journals of Friday morning was rich and rare. Gen. ROSECRANS was highly delighted with it. He had "killed fifteen hundred rebels," which was some source of gratification, but was deeply pained at the loss of "five hundred National troops." His grief, however, was somewhat softened by learning the fact that he had in quiet possession as prisoners of war, Gov. WISE and all his rebel companions, who escaped the sanguinary battle-field alive!

Of course he felt gratified that he had *personally* accomplished all this, while at least a hundred miles from the scene of the reported action. He is obliged to the Cincinnati Press for the "metropolitan" way in which they captured WISE and thrust him into his arms. The General intended to take him in a brief period if he continued to lay around loose in the Kanawha region. The trap was about ready, when the job was taken off his hands by the newspapers, and WISE was bagged! Of Course, the General, who is a business man, can now turn his attention to some other quarter, and, from certain indications, that other quarter may be an important one.

A FLAG OF TRUCE FROM A REBEL GENERAL.

For some days back, rumors have been afloat that the rebel General LEE was advancing upon Western Virginia, with a strong force, to coöperate with WISE, or to assume command of the forces, and endeavor to drive the National troops from the State. There were no foot-prints, however, which specially indicated his presence anywhere in Western Virginia, until two or three days ago, when a flag of truce was sent to Gen. REYNOLDS, of the First Brigade, who is in command of the forces at Cheat River Gap. The proposition, as I understand it, was an exchange of prisoners. The real object, however, was, undoubtedly, to get within our lines for the purpose of taking observations in regard to numbers and preparations for an attack.

The design failed, however, as the bearer of the flag was compelled to halt at least two miles from where our men were in camp. Where the bearer of the flag came from, or what distance, was unknown. But the proposition came from Gen. LEE, or purported to—and if from him, of course rumor must for once be correct in Western Virginia. If he is here he is undoubtedly advancing by Cheat River pass, with the expectation of falling upon our forces this side of the mountains, and whip them before they are fairly aware of his presence. We have, however, some four thousand men in the immediate locality, and a larger number within a march of forty-eight hours.

If Gen. LEE is in Virginia, it is not probable that he would go over the same ground that WISE has so recently laid waste, but would hope to catch our men sleeping upon their victories won at a more remote period, and where they have been resting in fancied security. He may, perhaps, catch Gen. ROSECRANS asleep, but *when* he does, Gen. LEE will find no difficulty in spreading himself miscellaneously through Western Virginia. No doubt, if he should come in strong force he would be enabled to make good progress until our Army could be concentrated, as, from very necessity, they are now scattered over a line of nearly three hundred miles. But the position of affairs is changed from what they were previous to the rout at Rich Mountain, Laurel Hill and Corrack's Ford. *We* are now on the defensive, occupy the strongholds, and guard the passes. The advance must be made by the rebels, and not by the Union forces, if they propose to regain the positions which they have lost in the contest thus far.

A CHANGE OF HEAD-QUARTERS.

The report of the advance of an enemy has not yet assumed sufficient definiteness as to warrant its being given as a positive fact, with details of localities, strength, &c., but as an indication that "something is in the wind," I can state potitively that Gen. ROSECRANS will remove his headquarters from Clarksburgh within the next 48 hours, unless circumstances should require further delay. What particular section he is bound for, is not known beyond his "military family," but my own opinion is, that he will make his head-quarters for the present at Buckhannon or Beverly, the former 28 miles from Clarksburgh, and the latter some 15 or 20 miles from Cheat Mountain Pass. If he is going in that direction, put this and that together, viz: the reported advance of the rebel forces, the flag of truce, and the movement of Gen. ROSECRANS. It all looks as though there might yet be a little sharp work in this section of Western Virginia. Besides the indications to which I have alluded, the forces which have been on the move, have had their "forward march" in the direction of Buuckhannon and Beverly.

POSITION OF THE OPPOSING FORCES.

CLARKSBURGH, Monday, August 12.

There still remain twenty-two counties of what is known as Western Virginia—the extreme southwestern portion—that are supposed to be yet a hot bed of Secessionists. Of no importance in themselves, these counties only deserve attention as they command the road to Cumberland Gap, and the entrance to loyal East Tennessee. Neither the Government nor rebel troops have yet entered this section in force, but the rebels are known to have now a body of some strength stationed at the Gap itself.

The situation at present is briefly this: The Cheat Mountain Gaps, the key to this whole country, are held by a strong force—a portion of Gen. REYNOLDS' Brigade—the remainder of which is stationed at Beverly, Huttonville and in that vicinity. Other portions of Gen. ROSECRANS' command are scattered over almost the whole of the northwestern part of Virginia, guarding the Railroad lines from Wheeling and Parkersburgh down to Grafton, and thence eastward through the Cheat River country, Oakland, Altamont and almost to Cumberland; occupying the Kanawha Valley by Gen. COX's Brigade, and holding towns like Weston, Buckhannon, Summersville, Phillippi and Bealington. Thus much of our position may, perhaps, be safely made public.

The enemy, on the other hand, are concentrated at two important points—Covington, near the entrance to the Kanawha Valley, and Monterey, opposite the Cheat Mountain Gaps. Rumor has it that Gen. LEE is himself at the latter point, organizing a force to attack the Gaps, and attempt another eruption into Northwestern Virginia. It is even said that some of his troops are now in the mountains. On how reliable evidence this rests, I can scarcely say as yet; though I confess that, on some accounts, the idea of the rebels attempting to reconquer Western Virginia seems anything but probable.

Still, it is known that they have a strong force at Staunton, and there are pretty well authenticated accounts of additional regiments having been ordered to that point from the extreme South. They may be there for the purpose of eventually attempting to wipe out the disgrace of Philippa, and Laurel Hill, and Cheat River, and Rich Mountain; or it may be that their intention is to keep up the feint of an inroad on Western Virginia, so as to maintain the diversion of National troops from the East, while they, on the other hand, are on the line of a railroad, and can be run to Manassas or Richmond in a couple of days if needed. The latter certainly seems the more probable hypothesis, and would be in harmony with their plans as hitherto developed.

But, should the rebel leaders really intend another attack on Western Virginia, a glance at the map will show that they must make it in one of two ways—reinforce WISE and force their way back from Covington into the Kanawha Valley again, or reinforce the troops at Monterey, and either attack our position at the Cheat Mountain Gaps, or attempt to find some other pass through the mountains, so as to approach Beverly and Laurel Hill once more. WISE's position at Covington being connected with Staunton by rail, it is very easy either to throw forces down to him, or to move his command up to strengthen the body threatening the Gaps. Of the two, the latter would now seem the more probable attempt. But LEE, or whoever really commands the rebels at Monterey, will hardly try a direct passage through the Gaps. A much more probable thing would be an attempt to find or cut a new road across the mountains, so as to come down at an unexpected point, and take ROSECRANS in the flank.

In any event, the Cheat Mountain Gaps are the important point. It was through these that PORTERFIELD's first motley crew entered Western Virginia and approached Grafton. Through these they retreated, when scared away from Philippa; through these McCLELLAN, supinely enough, permitted GARNETT to enter again, with his Laurel Hill and Rich Mountain army. That door is now shut. We will be well enough to hold it so, and Gen. ROSECRANS seems fully awake to the fact.

Hence, there is now going on a gradual concentration of our forces towards the Gaps, and Gen. ROSECRANS himself is to move his head-quarters in that direction—to Buckhannon, at least—in a few days. Gen. COX, too, it is expected, will be brought up from the Kanawha, and the strength of the brigade be added to the force already here, while some of the new troops from Ohio and Indiana take his place.

IMPORTANT FROM FORT MONROE.

THE REBELS PREPARING FOR AN ATTACK.

FORTRESS MONROE, Friday, August 16.
via BALTIMORE, August 17.

Gen. BUTLER yesterday assumed the responsibility of paying the New-York regiments. About $20,000 had been deposited for some time at Old Point, for the want of a paymaster.

The ship *Fair Wind*, of Boston, with a cargo of guano, was this morning towed up the Roads by the *S. R. Spaulding*, in a disabled condition. She was ashore on Hog Island.

The British brig-of-war *Gladiator* was yesterday cruising off the Capes.

A flag of truce yesterday conveyed Mr. WHEELER, formerly United States Minister to Nicaragua, to the Confederate pickets beyond New-Market Bridge.

A flag of truce is just in from Norfolk with Corporal HURLBUT, of the Connecticut Regiment, released by the Confederates for his attention to Col. GARDNER after the battle of Bull Run. He states that a considerable number of released prisoners, including several chaplains, will reach Old Point to-morrow.

In his opinion the Confederates are actively preparing for an attack on Fortress Monroe. That measure is now popular in the Confederate camps, and appropriate material is being collected in large quantities at Norfolk. The attack upon Fortress Monroe will be made within one week, he thinks.

BALTIMORE, Saturday, Aug. 17.

The report about an intended attack on Fortress Monroe is considered here as a perfect absurdity.

REPORTS FROM LOUISVILLE.

STATEMENT OF A YOUNG MAN FROM RICHMOND—PEACE MEETING, ETC.

LOUISVILLE, Ky., Saturday, Aug. 17.

A young man from Richmond, of secession proclivities, apparently well informed of the designs of the Confederate Army, says that they intend an immediate advance. He predicts fighting at the Relay House on the 18th inst., and says that the Southern Army is well provided with blankets, &c., for a Winter campaign, and that they are in a high state of discipline. He says that there is also a universal desire to attack Washington.

A peace meeting called by prominent Secessionists for this evening, was held at the Court-House. As the crowd entered the hall many were singing the Star-Spangled Banner.

JAMES SPEED, Unionist, was called to the Chair, and JAMES TRABUE, Secessionist, was also nominated by the persons calling the meeting. A division of the house took place, when SPEED was declared elected. The Secessionists, numbering a hundred, then withdrew, shouting for the Southern Confederacy.

Speeches were made by Messrs. SPEED, [illegible], HARLAN and others, and the resolutions were adopted with but one dissenting voice.

The preamble and resolutions are as follows:

The preamble sets forth that there is no mistaking the position of Kentucky in the present civil war, as she is unalterably for peace.

Resolved, That while this State desires to be true to the Union, she also desires to have peace with the States.

Resolved, That we earnestly desire the restoration of peace to every part of our beloved country, and as the speediest and surest mode of effecting that result, we appeal for a cessation of the war now being made on the Union.

Resolved, That we behold in a dissolution of the Union a remedy for no evils, but an aggravation of all.

Resolved, That we do not see how peace, enduring and substantial, to be attained by the establishment of two independent Governments within the present Union.

Resolved, That we deprecate the attempt being made to produce by force a disruption of the Union.

Resolved, That for the purpose of restoring peace all patriotic men abandon the sectional parties at the North and at the South, and that the rights of the Government should not be abandoned while it dictates to armed rebellion.

Resolved, That the neutrality of Kentucky but foreshadowed her love for peace, and that all negotiations looking to the constitutional settlement of all sectional differences, and to the preservation of the Union, shall have her hearty coöperation.

Resolved, That we are unwilling that any foreign Power shall own the mouth of the Mississippi River or any ports of the Union, and therefore are unalterably opposed to the dissolution of the Union; that we are for our country, now and forever, whether assailed by foreign or domestic enemies.

The resolutions were unanimously passed by the crowd, who filled the hall to overflowing.

SOUTHERN ITEMS THROUGH LOUISVILLE.

LOUISVILLE, Saturday, Aug. 17.

It is denied along the Nashville Railroad, that the Confederate authorities take money from those passing northward, but it is known that they take the gold *in transitu*, in some cases giving the owners currency therefor, which is at a discount of at least 8 per cent.

A dispatch from the Nashville *Union and American* to the Louisville *Courier*, says that President DAVIS has issued a proclamation ordering all residents of the Confederate States, who do not recognize the Confederacy to depart within forty days under pain of being condemned as aliens and enemies.

The same dispatch corrects yesterday's dispatch by saying that a battle took place at Lovettsville, Va., instead of Leesburgh, wherein two hundred and fifty Nationals and fifty Confederates were killed, and eleven hundred and fifty Nationals made prisoners, the latter not being able to recross the river, it having meanwhile swollen.

The Richmond *Examiner* says that official sources indicate that two hundred and ten thousand Confederates were in the field at the time of the passage of the bill authorizing the President to call out four hundred thousand volunteers.

The Richmond *Dispatch* is advocating Norfolk as the great Atlantic port of America.

The Confederate Congress has resolved to adjourn on the 19th inst., to meet in November next.

SUPPRESSION OF THE ST. LOUIS HERALD.

CARD FROM THE EDITOR TO THE PUBLIC.

I received the following notice last evening:

[illegible] No. 12.

OFFICE PROVOST MARSHAL,
ST. LOUIS, August 14, 1861.

To Col. JOHN MCNEIL, *Commanding Home Guards:*

You are hereby ordered to suppress the newspaper called the *Morning Herald*. I will not allow the publication of the same from the date of this order.

(Signed) J. MCKINSTRY,
Major United States Army, Provost Marshal.

I have been a law abiding citizen of this city from my infancy, and am so still; I therefore bow submissively, trusting that justice will yet be done by a discriminating public. I can only assure the patrons of the *Morning Herald* that I will endeavor to resume publication as soon as I can possibly do so, without violating law or orders issued by those in power.

JAMES L. FAUCETT.

[For other Rebellion News see Second and Eighth Pages.]

The Charleston Mercury.

VOLUME LXXIX. CHARLESTON, S. C., THURSDAY, AUGUST 29, 1861. NUMBER 11,241

THE MERCURY.

THURSDAY, AUGUST 29, 1861.

The Enemy on the Coast.

There was considerable talk upon the streets yesterday, in consequence of despatches having been received in the morning stating that a large fleet of U. S. war vessels had suddenly left Hampton Roads and sailed South. Later in the day despatches from Wilmington (published elsewhere in our columns), conveyed the intelligence that the fleet had passed Cape Hatteras on Monday afternoon. Still later the news came in from the harbor entrances that the hostile vessels were in the offing. Their number was variously stated, but all agreed that the fleet was a large one. We are inclined to credit the estimate of our Wilmington correspondent, who says that the vessels were ten in number.

Whether it shall prove to be part of the enemy's plan of campaign to attack our coast or not, we may be certain that there is no lack of the vindictive spirit which would prompt such an attempt. The article in another column, copied from the New York *Times*, shows clearly enough what we have to expect, unless we are ready and watchful at all points. How far we *are* ready the enemy may learn from the iron throats of many a "masked" battery, of the location of which, as yet, he little dreams.

Fort Hatteras as seen from Fort Clark

Admiral Silas Stringham, commander of the Federal fleet at Hatteras Inlet

Matthew F. Maury, inventor of the Confederate water mines

NOTES OF THE WAR.

From Our Own Correspondent.

CHARLOTTESVILLE, VA., August 24.

"Dixie in the Mountains"—The Old Dominion Aroused—A Sunset Walk—The Grave of Thomas Jefferson—Monticello and its present Owner—A Charming Landscape, etc., etc.

I am sitting by one of the south windows of the Farish House, a better kept and better provided hotel than any I have found since I left home, ruminating on my experiences of the past week and wondering what I shall have to say to THE MERCURY this afternoon. Shreds and patches of intelligence, some of them span new and sparkling, some dull, faded and worn, all about as curious and worthless as the jumble of a pedlar's pack, come out piece-meal from my scrap bag; but I can never stitch them them into any useful or even pleasing pattern, and contented with my poverty of invention, I throw aside the paltry ruff, and go on gazing listlessly out of my casement at the lovely prospect beyond.

The cool western breeze which is rippling the tasselled corn into endless waves, comes laden with the hum of war from the distant Alleghanies. The dull rumble of the ambulances, bringing in the sick and wounded from the front, echoes up the hill-side. A company of stalwart lads, hardy mountain boys, flushed with vigor and excitement, and burning with desire, are passing the window *en route* for the unknown perils of the battle field and camp hospitals; and a little girl of only seven summers dances along the pavement by their side, watching the glorified drummer with eager eyes and keeping time with her tiny hands to the martial strain of "Dixie."

Go where you will over this broad land, the air is instinct with strife. War, horrid war, is shaking it to its very centre—flaming out from the deathful-grinning fortresses by the mouth of the Chesapeake, and drowning with its sonorous clangor the pastoral songs of harvest-home on the teeming upland. For an injured people have roused with a battle cry from their long dream of Northern faith and justice and brotherhood, and risen at last

> To the higher aims
> Of a land that has lost for a little her lust of gold,
> And love of a peace that was full of wrongs and shames,
> Horrible, hateful, monstrous, not to be told:
> And God's just doom shall be wreaked on a giant liar."

And yet the fields are clothed with as fresh a green as if the land were lapped in universal calm. The mists of the mountain slopes are as soft, the broken shafts of sunlight lie as quietly athwart the lawns, and the wavering shadows chase each other as merrily over the meadows, as if the tear-threaded cobwebs were still trembling in the cannon's throat and all men's good had become each man's rule. On that bare crag yonder, standing out sharply against the orange sky, the Sage of Monticello sleeps as undisturbed as if the fierce democracy were not shaking into ten thousand fragments the great government whose foundations he laid, and the dust of that other and noble Virginian does not stir in its bed by the Potomac, though the capital he founded and which bears his name, heaves with the convulsions of a people to whom he bequeathed the freeest government on earth, destined soon to be supplanted by the lawless terrors of anarchy or an iron despotism.

This is a strange parenthesis, you will say, for one whose theme should be of charging squadrons and iron-hearted warriors; but I cannot get my morning's trip out of my head, and I think a little walk in the mountains will not do any harm to you, who have been breathing fire and smoke all the week. It will cool your head and clear your brain for the coming work, to take a dip into the clear stream which washes the feet of Monticello, THOMAS JEFFERSON's residence and fitting burial place.

I would advise you, in the first place, to take a horse, instead of a hack, as I imprudently did this morning; so, if you will mount the office Pegasus, and come with me, I will carry you across as pretty a range of hills, and up as magnificent a gorge, as ever that hard-ridden steed has climbed in Switzerland. First, you will pass, for a couple of miles, over a billowy sweep of corn and wheat land, whose rise and dip is so regular and wave-like, that one fancies a heaving ocean of land to have been rocking here once, and suddenly petrified into eternal rest by the angry genius of the mountain. Plunging into a deep but narrow stream, where your horse's girth will be wet, and your feet, too, if you don't take the precaution to sling them up on his withers, you may stop—a moment only, for the sun is setting fast—and look back over your shoulder at the village, encircled by the ripe harvests which the busy mowers are reaping. The soft "swath" of the scythe, the sharp clack of the mill where the circling horses are thrashing out the grain, the brawl of the streamlet, the glow on the distant fields, the dark, dank foliage of the frowning mountain in front, form so sweet a picture, that one is unwilling to leave it for the hard ascent that promises a wider but certainly not a lovelier prospect above.

General Benjamin Butler, commander of the Federal troops

Bombardment of Forts Hatteras and Clark by the Federal fleet

Through devious and uncertain ways, now winding along a tobacco patch, now by corn rows so steep that the golden tassels of one row shake off their pollen at the roots of another, stumbling up over loose stones that go clattering down behind and splattered all over with the inevitable mud, you gain the first ledge and come right out of the dense chesnuts upon a picturesque cottage and fine glade, where you are almost tempted to turn round for another look, but desist for fear of losing the charm of the *curonable*(?) which the mountain top promises. Straight up alongside of a deep gorge, down which a biscuit, dropped from your saddle, would fall two hundred feet, and sometimes turning a sharp angle where the water has cut an almost perpendicular chasm, you climb, and climb, and climb, with a densely wooded wall of rock on one hand and the dark precipice threatening you on the other, until you unexpectedly emerge in a small clearing around which a somewhat dilapidated, square, brick wall runs. The iron gate is open, and as your enter, the eye, glancing over a dozen or more marble slabs and head-stones, rests on a grey granite pyramid, supported by a block of the same material, rudely hewn and blackened with age, which you know at once to be JEFFERSON's tomb. There is no name on the monument, only the dates of a birth and death. The conceit is a childish one, and in wretched taste, and yet I cannot help thinking that the dusty incumbent who holds the stone in *mort main* is rather flattered by the surprise of his visitors, if the "dull cold ear of death," contrary to GRAY's philosophy, ever catches any mortal accounts. Around the great statesman, and philosopher and man of letters, lie his children and their offspring. And from his lofty resting place he can keep watch and ward over the State he loved, and served and honored.

From the cemetery a narrow path through the field or the longer carriage road leads up to the front of the old mansion which crowns the brow of Mount Monticello. It was planned by JEFFERSON himself, and is built of good, durable brick, which has stood the ravages of the weather remarkably. To the front and rear a colonnade projects from the central hall, which traverses the entire building, and on either side of this project spacious wings of an irregular pentagonal shape. A covered wing connects these with the servant's halls and rooms which run at right angles with and at some distance from the main building, and the smooth shaven and well wooded lawn encircles the entire group.

To the ceiling of the portico in front a large compass is attached, and fronting the guest as he enters the door, and immediately over it, stands the dial of the old family clock, whose gilded hands refuse to mark time for the more recent owner of the venerable mansion. The property is now in the possession of a Captain LEVY, United States Navy; and as the United States has confiscated the Pennsylvania estates of Senator MASON, Virginia might well retaliate by handing over this ancestral property to the nearest lineal descendant of its illustrious founder.

From the brow of the plateau to the north of the house, the panorama unfolded is transcendently beautiful. The coy village, embowered(?) in waving crops, and sweeping in a gentle curve through the slope of the rolling valley, lies nestled in the protecting arms of the gray old mountains, like some blooming Vivien in the embrace of a sage and doating Merlin. The pencil might delineate, but no words can describe, the exquisite charm of this soft cabinet picture. The ever varying lights and shades of that delicious prospect only the educated eye can appreciate, and the whole is fused into a bit of landscape poetry, which he who has once made it his own, will recall as a possession and a joy forever. J. D. B.

Our Fairfield Correspondence.

FAIRFIELD DISTRICT, August 27.

Diet for Our Army—Corn vs. Wheat—Advantages of Using the Unbolted Wheat Meal—Bountiful Crops—What the Ladies of the Back Country are Doing—The Noble Spirit in which They are Working for Our Troops, etc., etc.

We see, in a late number of your paper, a complaint about flour alone being furnished our army in Virginia. As you suggest, corn bread is the proper diet, being that which our Southern people are mostly in the habit of using. If, however, this cannot be easily obtained, we would suggest the unbolted wheat meal. This we have been using for several months, in feeding our blacks, as well as at our own table. Even if the soldier cannot sift it, the bran is so much softer than that of corn, that it makes excellent bread without this operation, so necessary with the other. Mixed with a little lard, or grease from fried bacon, it is excellent; but without either of these, a little milk or buttermilk causes it at once to rise, and become very light. The truth is, with simple water and salt only kneaded in, it is fine. So much do some of our neighbors like it, that they declare, after this year's experience, that they intend hereafter to have a portion of their wheat so ground and kept every year. It is certainly the most easily digested bread that is, or can, be used. Urge its importance upon our authorities, and the health of our dear friends in the army everywhere will soon improve.

SCOTT's threat to starve us out is not likely, under God's blessing, to succeed this year; for never, in my experience of near thirty years as a planter, have I seen such an abundance as is now in the fields. Corn, that upon fields that would usually yield not more than ten or twenty bushels per acre, are now counted good for double that amount, while at the same time, at least one-fifth more has been planted. And what is still better, it is safe from all disaster, save only freshets in the rivers. Cotton, too, is extraordinary in its promise; while of wheat, oats and rye there is the greatest abundance. Sweet potatos and turnips, too, were never more promising. It does indeed seem that the Great Giver of all good has smiled upon us in our harvests, as well as upon our cause in the field of battle.

I am happy to inform you that our ladies are doing everything in their power to aid and relieve our soldiers. Associations are being everywhere formed for this purpose, and are now working with a will in the good cause. Almost every day boxes of medicines, and such dainties as will meet the demands of the sick and suffering, are being sent off to Virginia and elsewhere that they may be needed. Nor will this cease till this unrighteous war that is now being waged upon us by those who once insultingly claimed to be our brethren is over, and every sick and wounded soldier dismissed from the hospital. More than this, looms and cards, long idle, are now busy weaving up strong, warm wool cloth, for winter use, all of which will be made into coats and pants, and sent on when needed. We know of a blind lady, unable to do anything else, whose delicate fingers are now busy knitting socks for the soldiers, an example worthy of imitation, but no exception to the general rule, among the wives and daughters of us backwoodsmen, in this day of common suffering and common effort. If your low-country ladies beat us in their sacrifices and offerings upon the altar of country, they will have to bestir themselves, I assure you. So high is the spirit of our women, that I do not believe there is a single one that would not be ready to play the part of Mrs. MOTTE, of the Revolution, and string the bow that was to fire her own dwelling, sooner than that a Yankee footstep should disgrace its threshold.

The New-York Times.

VOL. X....NO. 3102. NEW-YORK, SUNDAY, SEPTEMBER 1, 1861. PRICE THREE CENTS.

THE GREAT REBELLION.

News from Gen. Butler's Expedition.

The Rebel Batteries at Hatteras Captured and Destroyed.

Movements of the Rebel Forces Near Washington.

A SECESSION FLAG ON MUNSON'S HILL.

A Large Body of Cavalry Manœuvering in the Vicinity.

HIGHLY IMPORTANT FROM MISSOURI

Martial Law Proclaimed Throughout the State.

The Confiscation Law to be Enforced.

Encouraging News from Gen. Rosecrans.

The Remains of General Lyon in New-York.

SPECIAL DISPATCH FROM WASHINGTON.

WASHINGTON, Saturday, Aug. 31.

The Government has information to-night that Gen. BUTLER's naval expedition proceeded as far as Cape Hatteras, where the forces were landed and the rebel batteries taken, and destroyed. No particulars have been received, but it is anticipated that the rebels could not have made much resistance, as they were not likely to have had a heavy body of men in that vicinity.

SECRETARY SEWARD RETURNED.

Secretary SEWARD returned to Washington this evening, bringing with him all the members of his family.

OTHER ARRIVALS.

Hon. CHRISTOPHER ROBINSON, our Minister to Peru, is now here awaiting instructions.

Hon. GEO. OPDYKE arrived here this morning.

GEN ROSECRANS SAFE.

Advices received by the Department from Gen ROSECRANS assure us of his confidence in his ability to maintain his position against any force the rebels will be likely to concentrate in his vicinity.

REBEL FLAG ON MUNSON'S HILL.

A large secession flag has been raised by the rebels on Munson's Hill. It was visible with a glass, this afternoon, from the top of the ship-house at the Navy-yard. A considerable cavalry force was also seen going through their evolutions.

VISIT TO THE NAVY-YARD.

The President and Secretary WELLES visited the Navy-yard last evening.

ANOTHER SEIZURE OF SMALL BOATS.

Another expedition from the Navy-yard left yesterday afternoon, to secure any additional small boats not seized between the city and Fort Washington. Thirteen were taken and brought to the Navy-yard.

ANOTHER DENIZEN OF FORT LAFAYETTE.

Lieut. W. H. WARD, late of the *Macedonian*, resigned his position several weeks since. He reached New-York on the store-ship *Relief* yesterday, and by order of the War Department, has been arrested and conveyed to Fort Lafayette. He is a native of Virginia, but was appointed to the Navy from Ohio, of which State he is still a citizen.

APPOINTMENT.

THOS. GALES FOSTER, of Philadelphia, an old reporter, and a nephew of the late JOS. GALES, has been appointed to a second-class clerkship in the War Department.

GEN. SHERMAN TRANSFERRED TO KENTUCKY.

Brig.-Gen. FITZ-JOHN PORTER has taken command of the brigade lately commanded by Gen. SHERMAN, who has been assigned to the Department of Kentucky, under Gen. ANDERSON.

THE REBEL PICKETS.

None of the rebel pickets were seen nor heard of from Ball's Cross Roads during last night or this morning.

DISCHARGED FROM ARREST.

Mr. SEYBOLD, a roving correspondent of the *Tribune*, arrested a few days since as a spy, has been discharged. There was no proof against him.

ARREST OF MARYLAND REBELS.

The arrest of Senator MCKAIG, of Maryland, and other Secessionists at Cumberland, has given great satisfaction to the friends of the Union here. It indicates a purpose on the part of the Government to hold in check the nest of treasonable legislators which has so earnestly endeavored to turn Maryland over to the rebels.

COLONEL OF THE SIXTY-NINTH.

Capt. THOS. F. MEAGHER has been appointed Colonel of the New-York Sixty-ninth. The Sixty-ninth, the Third New-York Irish Regiment, two from New-England, and one from Philadelphia, are to be organized as an Irish Brigade, under Gen. SHIELDS as commander.

SUPERSEDED.

Col. BRADLEY, who was appointed by Gov. MORGAN to supersede Maj. PATRICK in looking after the interests of the New-York troops, has arrived. Maj. PATRICK feels indignant at his removal, of which he had received no notification, and which, as far as he is aware, was without just cause.

DISPATCH TO THE ASSOCIATED PRESS.

WASHINGTON, Saturday, Aug. 31.

It seems certain that the Administration at present has no intention whatever to avail itself of the permissive sanction given by Congress to the collection of duties on shipboard, or to the entire closing of ports, which on the land side are in the possession of the insurrectionary authorities. Our Government will rely on the existence and efficiency of its blockade, for a sufficient answer to any reclamation which may be made by foreign Governments in regard to their maritime rights. The *Intelligencer* of to-day contains an article to the above effect, and this Telegraphic Agency has such authentic information as warrants the expression of the correctness of the statement.

Lieut. W. H. WARD, late of the *Macedonian*, who lately resigned and arrived in New-York in the *Release* on Friday, has been ordered to spend the watering season at Fort Lafayette.

The Navy Department had the Potomac River examined last night, between this city and Fort Washington, for boats which might be used in transporting contraband articles across. The catch brought up to the Navy-yard numbered thirteen.

Letters to Western Kentucky to the continued Post-offices should be addressed *via* Louisville.

Gen. MARTINDALE, of New-York, has been assigned to the command of a brigade in the Department of the Potomac. He is now on the other side of the Potomac.

NEWS FROM FORTRESS MONROE.

CANNONADING HEARD AT HATTERAS INLET.

FORTRESS MONROE, Friday, Aug. 30, }
Via BALTIMORE, Saturday, Aug. 31. }

The gun-boat *Iroquois*, from the blockade off Savannah, arrived last evening. She reports having heard heavy cannonading when off Hatteras Inlet, and also spoke a brig which had met the National fleet. We have no other intelligence of the expedition.

One of the Confederate prisoners, retained for some days at Old Point, expressed the opinion that the National vessels would be blown up by submarine batteries which Lieut. MAURY had placed in Hatteras Inlet and other assailable points on the Carolina coast.

Since the quarrel between the Alabama and Virginia troops at Yorktown, which resulted in the killing of eight men, the Virginia Regiments have been transferred to Norfolk. The Alabamians accused the latter of cowardice.

This morning a small secession tug-boat, mounted with rifled brass cannon, ran out from Norfolk to within two and a half miles of Newport's News. She fired twenty-three shots at the United States frigate *Savannah*. No person was injured. The tug was in range of but two of the *Savannah's* guns, and SAWYER's rifled cannon on shore. When they were brought to bear upon her, she ran down towards Old Point and fired two shells, one of which exploded near the *Seminole* and the other close to the Rip Raps. The fire was returned, whereupon she retreated behind Sewall's Point.

IMPORTANT FROM LOUISVILLE.

SUCCESS OF GEN. BUTLER'S EXPEDITION.

LOUISVILLE, Ky., Saturday, Aug. 31.

A special to the *Courier*, of this city, from the *Union and American*, of Nashville, dated to-day, says that dispatches from Richmond state that Gen. BUTLER, commanding a fleet of one hundred guns and four thousand men, arrived at Fort Hatteras on Tuesday, and opened fire on the Fort, which was vigorously returned by the garrison of three hundred men, under the command of Capt. BARROW, formerly of the U. S. Navy. After twenty rounds had been fired, the ammunition of the Fort was exhausted, and the entire garrison surrendered. The fort was built a few months since.

The same dispatch says that it is believed in Richmond that the blockade has been effectually broken by the arrival of the British ship *Alliance* at Beaufort, N. C.

President DAVIS is reported as convalescent.

An engagement took place at Cross Lanes, Virginia, on the 26th inst., between 3,000 Confederate soldiers and 900 National troops, resulting in our favor.

Commercial intercourse with the North, under a limitation, is to be enforced by penalties during the war. Letter correspondence is also prohibited.

Advices from Matamoras to the 25th inst. state that a British schooner from the blockade of Newbern, and has arrived at that port, (Matamoras.) She has sailed again for Charleston. A sloop from Charleston also ran the blockade.

Two regiments of the Brigade of the Home Guards of Louisville, under command of Gen. JOUATT, paraded through the streets this evening. They made a fine appearance, and were well armed and uniformed. Several companies of the Brigade, uniformed and unarmed, not having participated in the parade to-day, are on parade in the streets to-night.

The shock of an earthquake was distinctly felt here to-day, persons being aroused by its violence from sleep. The shock lasted several minutes.

The statement from Washington, that Mr. GUTHRIE had sent advices to this city of an apprehended outbreak of hostilities in Kentucky, is untrue.

TREASON NOT TOLERATED IN CONNECTICUT.

Correspondence of the New-York Times.

BRIDGEPORT, Friday, Aug. 30, 1861.

Treason in this portion of the State is about crushed out. The sympathizers with the Southern rebellion are disheartened, terrified. Their organ being destroyed, they have no means of promulgating their principles over the signature of "Senex," "Truth," &c., and they dare not talk openly concerning their real sentiments. Many who before were active in getting up "peace meetings," now avow themselves in favor of conquering a peace; but they will have to sit some time longer upon the stool of repentance before they will be received in full communion. The [illegible] that of the fellow who [illegible] received as that [illegible] church upon probation. About [illegible] he was found in a state of intoxication, and upon being questioned concerning his condition, replied: "Why, you see, they took me up on probation for six months, but I behaved so well they let me off at three." When the converts show "fruits meet for repentance," they will be received and the right hand of fellowship extended to them.

An impromptu Union meeting was held in this City on Monday evening last, which has done much to strengthen the hands of the loyal citizens and quiet disloyalists. It was a gathering without regard to former political opinions, but Republicans and Democrats united in expressing their attachment to the Union under which we have prospered, the Constitution upon which that Union is based, and the flag of that Union which has never yet been trailed in the dust before a foreign foe, and never trampled under foot save by those who have enjoyed its protection, and have now set at defiance its authority. Among those in attendance was [illegible], who was invited to a seat upon the platform, and cheer upon cheer was given as the venerable representative of "Old Hickory's" Administration accepted the invitation. He has been passing the Summer in this city with his family, and has employed his time in writing the life of ANDREW JACKSON, which with him is a "labor of love."

A few days since, a regular secession flag was pulled down a few miles from this City, by some of our returned volunteers, and another brought in by Deputy Sheriff BARNUM.

E. B. SCHNABLE, of Pennsylvania, who was arrested at Morris, Litchfield County, on Wednesday night, was one of the most eloquent and popular speakers that ever visited this State, and for that reason was a more dangerous ally of the enemy. His receptions in this city have always been perfect ovations, and immense crowds would stand and listen to him for hours. His race, however, is run here, and his future receptions will be of another character.

The city is doing nobly in raising volunteers for the war. One company of over one hundred, under command of Capt. FITZGIBBONS, a brave and deservedly popular officer, has already gone to the rendezvous at New-Haven.

Capt. FREDERICK FRYE, who wears by descent the badge of the order of Cincinnati, is raising another company. At the battle of Bull Run, he showed himself not unworthy of the order of merit which he possesses.

Four other companies are forming, so that, when full, our city will have over five hundred of its "bone and sinew" fighting the battles of the Union. Pretty good, is it not, for a city of 13,000 inhabitants, and with strong secession influences at work.

P. T. BARNUM, the great showman, as he calls himself, is *exhibiting* wonderful and commendable energy in the cause.

UNION.

IMPORTANT FROM MISSOURI.

PROCLAMATION OF GEN. FREMONT.

ST. LOUIS, Saturday, Aug. 31.

The following proclamation was issued this morning:

HEAD-QUARTERS OF THE WESTERN DEPARTMENT, }
ST. LOUIS, Aug. 31. }

Circumstances, in my judgment, of sufficient urgency, render it necessary that the Commanding General of this Department should assume the administrative powers of the State. Its disorganized condition, the helplessness of the civil authority, the total insecurity of life, and the devastation of property by bands of murderers and marauders, who infest nearly every county in the State, and avail themselves of the public misfortunes and the vicinity of a hostile force to gratify private and neighborhood vengeance, and who find an enemy wherever they find plunder, finally demand the severest measures to repress the daily increasing crimes and outrages which are driving off the inhabitants and ruining the State.

In this condition the public safety and the success of our arms require unity of purpose, without let or hindrance, to the prompt administration of affairs.

In order, therefore, to suppress disorders, to maintain, as far as now practicable, the public peace, and to give security and protection to the persons and property of loyal citizens, I do hereby extend and declare established martial law throughout the State of Missouri. The lines of the Army of occupation in this State are for the present declared to extend from Leavenworth, by way of the posts of Jefferson City, Rolla, and Ironton, to Cape Girardeau, on the Mississippi River. All persons who shall be taken with arms in their hands, within these lines, shall be tried by Court Martial, and, if found guilty, will be shot. The property, real and personal, of all persons in the State of Missouri, who shall take up arms against the United States, or who shall be directly proven to have taken active part with their enemies in the field, is declared to be confiscated to the public use, and their slaves, if any they have, are hereby declared free men.

All persons who shall be proven to have destroyed, after the publication of this order, railroad tracks, bridges or telegraphs, shall suffer the extreme penalty of the law.

All persons engaged in treasonable correspondence, in giving or procuring aid to the enemies of the United States, in disturbing the public tranquillity by creating and circulating false reports or incendiary documents, are in their own interest warned that they are exposing themselves.

All persons who have been led away from their allegiance are required to return to their homes forthwith; any such absence without sufficient cause will be held to be presumptive evidence against them.

The object of this declaration is to place in the hands of the military authorities the power to give instantaneous effect to existing laws, and to supply such deficiencies as the conditions of war demand. But it is not intended to suspend the ordinary tribunals of the country, where the law will be administered by the civil officers in the usual manner and with their customary authority, while the same can be peaceably exercised.

The Commanding-General will labor vigilantly for the public welfare, and in his efforts for their safety hopes to obtain not only the acquiescence, but the active support of the people of the country.

(Signed) J. C. FREMONT,
Major-General Commanding.

MOVEMENTS OF THE REBELS.

ROLLA, Mo., Friday, Aug. 30.

The correspondent of the St. Louis *Democrat* furnishes the following items:

Parties from Springfield report that a skirmish had taken place in Vernon County, east of Fort Scott, between Col. MONTGOMERY, of the Kansas forces, and the rebel troops under Gen. RAINS. Reinforcements had been sent to RAINS from Springfield.

Six thousand rebels were encamped at Pond Spring. Another encampment of over five thousand men was at a spring south of the Fayetteville Road.

Gen. MCBRIDE, with one thousand men, passed through Dade County, last week, in a northwest direction, and one thousand men were at Dry Leads, in Dade County, devastating the country of every vestige of property belonging to Union men.

REPORTED REPULSE OF THE REBELS AT LEXINGTON, ETC.

ST. LOUIS, Saturday, Aug. 31.

The *Republican* has a dispatch saying that the Secessionists, 4,500 strong, attacked the 430 Home Guards and National troops in the intrenchments at Lexington on Thursday, and were repulsed with the loss of 60 killed. None of the National force was killed. This needs confirmation.

CHARLES MCLAREN, BASIL W. DUKE and JAMES H. CARLISLE, secession Police Commissioners, have been removed by Gov. GAMBLE.

The report that Palmyra was occupied by the Secessionists, under MARTIN GREEN, a few days ago, is untrue.

The money belonging to the Fayette Bank, seized by Secessionists on Wednesday, has been returned.

NO INFORMATION FOR THE ENEMY.

ST. LOUIS, Saturday, Aug. 31.

Provost-Marshal MCKINSTRY has issued orders peremptorily forbidding any person passing beyond the limits of this county, without a special permit from his office, and railroad, steamboat, ferry and other agents, are prohibited from selling tickets to any one not holding a pass from the Provost-Marshal. This order is aimed specially to reach parties leaving the city for the purpose of communicating information to the enemy.

SEIZURE OF TOBACCO.

BOSTON, Saturday, Aug. 31.

The United States Marshal to-day seized 50,000 pounds of tobacco, the alleged property of JAMES THOMAS, Jr., of Richmond. The tobacco reached here *via* Nashville and Louisville.

STATE POLITICS.

ELECTION OF DELEGATES TO THE DEMOCRATIC STATE CONVENTION.

ALBANY, Saturday, Aug. 31.

Hon. ERASTUS CORNING and PETER CAGGER were elected Delegates to-day to the Democratic State Convention.

SYRACUSE, Saturday, Aug. 31.

The Convention of the Second Assembly District of Onondaga County, was held at the City Hall at 2 o'clock to-day, for the purpose of electing two delegates to the Democratic State Convention, which assembles in Syracuse on the 4th of September. A full delegation was present, and the Convention in every respect was harmonious.

A series of resolutions, reflecting the sentiments of the Democratic Party in the present struggle, were unanimously adopted.

These resolutions argued a return to the Democratic line of liberal policy towards every State in the Union, in which event a large hope was entertained by the Convention for a speedy adjustment of the present difficulties.

The delegates elected are Hon. DENNIS MCCARTHY and JOHN A. GREEN, Jr.

ALBANY, Saturday, Aug. 31.

JOSEPH C. YATES, of Schnectady, comes out in a card, repudiating the action of the Democratic State Committee, and indorsing the policy of union with the Republicans.

SENECA FALLS, N. Y., Saturday, Aug. 31.

The Democratic County Convention held at Bearytown to-day was largely attended, and the utmost unanimity and enthusiasm prevailed. Hon. A. WOODWARD, of Lodi, and JAMES MCLEAN, of Waterloo, were elected to the State Convention.

BATAVIA, Saturday, Aug. 31.

DEAN RICHMOND, Esq., and Hon. H. J. REDFIELD were to-day elected Delegates from Genesee County to the Democratic State Convention.

BUFFALO, Saturday, Aug. 31.

The First and Second Assembly Districts in Convention to-day elected the following Delegates to the Democratic State Convention: First District—RICHARD FLACK and C. K. LOOMIS. Second District—WILLIAM P. SUTTON and A. P. LANSING.

SARATOGA, N. Y., Saturday, Aug. 31.

AMASA KEITH, of Saratoga Springs, and EDGAR L. FURSMAN, of Schuylersville, are elected delegates from the Second Assembly District of this county to the Democratic State Convention, to be held at Syracuse on the 4th inst.

MEETING OF DELEGATES TO THE DEMOCRATIC STATE CONVENTION.

At a meeting of the delegates to the Democratic State Convention, held at Mozart Hall on Saturday at 3 P. M., Judge DALY was called to the Chair and L. F. COZENS appointed Secretary.

The following gentlemen answered to their names:

I.—S. B. Williams, Ben. Ray.
II.—James Wadsworth, P. Garrick.
III.—Harris Bogart, M. L. Harris.
IV.—B. Maloney, J. McMahon.
V.—Robert L. Linn, J. Flynn.
VI.—Thomas Cassin, James S. Durning.
VII.—P. W. Engs, J. M. Harrington.
VIII.—P. McKnight, John Galvan.
IX.—Peter Fullmer, J. W. Nash.
X.—George C. Genet, George Kuster.
XI.—P. G. Moloney, N. Hill Fowler.
XII.—J. Belleisheim, P. Daly.
XIII.—J. A. McMaster, B. F. Fairchild.
XIV.—J. B. Borst, T. B. Voorhees.
XV.—Gilbert Dean, S. Boardman.
XVI.—Roger Dolan, F. J. McDonough.
XVII.—Dunham J. Crain, John Conway.

After several addresses and the transaction of general business, the delegates adjourned to meet at the Voorhees House, Syracuse, on Tuesday, Sept. 3, at 6 P. M.

DEMOCRATIC PRIMARY ELECTIONS.

The primary meetings of the Tammany section of the Democratic Party were held last evening, to elect delegates to the Democratic State Convention. The successful candidates are understood to be in favor of a vigorous prosecution of the war, this being at present the principle issue between the Tammany and Mozart divisions of the party.

ARRIVAL OF THE REMAINS OF GEN. LYON

Yesterday afternoon the body of Gen. NATHANIEL LYON arrived in this City, *en route* to Connecticut, of which State the late General was a native and where his remains will be interred. The escort in charge of the body, which is composed of officers and civilians, is as follows:

Major H. A. Conant, Quartermaster of Gen. LYON's Division; Capt. Edgan, of Gen. Fremont's Staff; Dr. Lyon, cousin of Gen. Lyon, and of Gen. Fremont's Staff; Capt. Plummer, of U. S. A., who is a personal friend of Gen. Lyon, and wounded in the battle of Springfield; Lieut. Clark, of the Missouri Home Reserve, and eight privates: Mr. Brantfort Knowlton, Mr. J. B. Hossler, Webster Man, (a brother-in-law of Gen. Lyon,) M. P. McJuillen, Cincinnati *Gazette*, and Junius H. Brome, Cincinnati *Evening Times*.

On the arrival at the foot of Cortlandt-street the body was placed in the waiting-room of the Ferry-house, in consequence of the Seventh Regiment not having arrived. Finally, the corpse was put into a hearse drawn by four white horses, and was taken to the City Hall, preceded by the Third Company of the Seventh Regiment. Arriving at the Park, the coffin was taken up by eight privates who had accompanied it from St. Louis, and carried to the Governor's room. It will be guarded by a detachment of the Seventh Regiment until its departure on Monday. The body is only partially embalmed, on account of its having become partly decomposed before found. In such a case it will be impossible for the features of the deceased to be exposed. To-morrow from 9 A. M., till 1 P. M., the public will be admitted into the room, where Gen LYON lies in state. The body is placed in a metallic burial case, which is inclosed in a mahogany coffin. At half-past three o'clock the funeral procession will start from the City Hall and proceed to the New-Haven dépôt where the body will be taken in charge by Gov. BUCKINGHAM. The line of march will be up Broadway to Twenty-seventh-street, and from thence to the dépôt.

THE REMAINS OF GEN. LYON.

PHILADELPHIA, Saturday, Aug. 31.

The remains of Gen. LYON passed through this city at 8 o'clock this morning, escorted by the military to the Trenton Railroad Dépôt. The flags of the city are at half-mast. Numbers crowded the streets through which the procession passed.

TRENTON, N. J., Saturday, Aug. 31.

The remains of Gen. LYON passed through this place at 11 o'clock this morning. During the passage through the city minute guns were fired, the bells tolled, and flags displayed at half-mast.

HONORS TO THE LATE GEN. LYON.

RECEPTION OF HIS REMAINS IN ST. LOUIS.

From the St. Louis Democrat, Aug. 28.

From 12 to 1 o'clock yesterday some thousands of citizens—men, women and children—thronged the streets in the neighborhood of Gen. FREMONT's Head-quarters, corner of Eighth and Chouteau-avenue, to witness the public tribute of respect and honor to the deceased Gen. LYON, and the solemn military procession which was to follow his remains through the city to the place of their departure for the East. On the evening previous the body was conveyed from the undertaker's, on Fifth-street, to the residence of Col. BRANT, Gen. FREMONT's Head quarters.

At 12½ o'clock, Capt. EDGAR, formerly of the New-York Seventh Regiment—who accompanied the relatives of Gen. LYON from New-York on their errand to Springfield, to take charge of the remains, and who was the bearer of the white flag to the enemy—master of ceremonies, aided by Major CONANT, of Gen. LYON's staff, who had been at the side of the deceased hero from the battle of Booneville to the battle of Springfield, began making dispositions of the infantry and cavalry according to the order and arrangement previously published.

Two fine companies of cavalry, Capt. TILMAN's, a Chicago company, Capt. ZAGONYI's, of the Fremont Body Guard, for some time stationed on the north side of the street, facing South, moved down below Seventh-street, and a section of Capt. CARLIN's Battery of Ohio Light Artillery, consisting of twenty-four horses, about forty men and two pieces of cannon fell in behind them. This section of the Artillery company was followed by a section of the Third Regiment United States Reserve Corps, under Col. MCNEIL, occupying the whole width of the street. After the forward portion of the procession had been arranged, there was a few moments of pause and silent waiting for the pall-bearers. The moment they appeared bearing the coffin down the steps, which was decked with fresh flowers, the American flag thrown across the lid, a thousand hats were lifted from the heads of the multitude.

The coffin was borne by the following officers: Col. F. P. Blair, Col. Andrews, Col. Salomon, Col. Osterhaus, Majors Conant, Sturgis, Scofield, and Capt. Gates.

Attached to the hearse were four dark bay horses driven by Mr. ARNOT.

Immediately after the coffin was placed in the hearse, the relatives of the deceased, Mr. KNOWLTON, a cousin, and Mr. HESLER, a brother-in-law, accompanied by Lieut. CLARK, entered a carriage following the hearse.

Following these were Gen. Fremont and staff, Capt. J. C. Kelton, Major J. McKinstry, Col. Andrews, Gen. Asboth, Col. Woods, Major Eaton and Capt. Harris, all mounted. Also Capt. Able, United States Navy, in a carriage.

A carriage, occupied by the Mayor of the city, and one or two members of the City Council, came next in the procession.

The rear was closed by the remaining half of the Conant Light Artillery Company and a division of Col. MCNEIL's Regiment, led by Major MARSH.

The procession, being thus formed, moved, shortly after 1 o'clock, down Chouteau-avenue to Fifth-street, up Fifth to Washington-avenue, down Washington to the levee, and up the levee to the ferry landing. A multitude of thousands was gathered on the levee, to witness in silent reverence the procession to the ferry-boat. Many public and private houses through the city, especially the residences on Fifth-street, were hung with mourning. Many of those who once were the political enemies of the deceased, were constrained to join in the common public manifestation of sorrow. The whole city seemed to be solemnized by the presence of that cold body from which a noble and heroic spirit had so lately departed.

The horse that walked, saddled and bridled, without any rider, immediately in the rear of the hearse, was the horse rode by Gen. LYON when he was killed. His favorite, a dappled gray stallion, was killed under him at Wilson's Creek.

The position of Gen. SIEGEL, commanding the procession, was immediately in front. He sat in the splendid saddle lately presented to him on behalf of his friends in St. Louis.

On arriving at the ferry-landing, Gen. FREMONT and Staff dismounted and proceeded in solemn procession, with the pall-bearers in the rear of the hearse as it passed on to the boat. This solemn ceremony was witnessed by tens of thousands of eager and saddened spectators. The General and Staff returned rapidly to their horses, and with a quick march the long procession began its return, half proceeding northward up the levee, and half escorting Gen. FREMONT down the levee and up through the city to his head-quarters. The ferry-boat crossed the river rapidly, and the body was immediately placed upon the train in waiting.

The railroad car provided by the Adams Express, and in which the coffin was deposited, was heavily hung, within and without, with mourning. The centre seats having been removed, the coffin was placed in a box covered and lined with silk velvet, on a stand in the centre of the car. Alongside lay the sword and pistol which were on him when he fell.

As an act of courtesy to him, members of Company K, of the Third Regiment Missouri Reserve Corps, who volunteered their services as guard over the body of Gen. LYON while it lay in the city, were appointed escort of the remains to the East, along with the friends in charge.

The following are the officers and privates mentioned who went as an escort: Major H. A. Conant, Capt. Edgar, Capt. Plummer, Lieut. Clark, and privates Joseph P. P. Taylor, E. P. Freeman, Chas. H. Howland, Edmund S. Bidden, E. P. Rice, Wm. Zukoski, Fred. H. Hersum and Wm. K. Patrick.

Capt. EDGAR was not certain where the body would be taken, to Webster, Massachusetts, or to Connecticut. This will be determined by friends in the East. The route is to be through Cincinnati, Pittsburgh, Philadelphia and New-York, and the funeral party will probably be detained at each of these points a few hours.

FROM BALTIMORE.

ARREST OF A FEMALE TRAITOR—THE MILITARY HOSPITAL—MOVEMENTS OF TROOPS, &C.

BALTIMORE, Thursday, Aug. 29, 1861.

The Weems steamers, three in number—the *Martha Washington*, *Planter* and *George Weems*—yesterday resumed running from this city up the Patuxent River, on the Chesapeake Bay shore. They were suspended by orders from the War Department at Washington two weeks ago, on account of a contraband trade having been imposed upon them without, it is believed, the knowledge of the owners—a quantity of pistols having on one occasion been found upon one of the steamers. They are allowed to resume their trips only upon coming under the control of the Custom-house officers, and no passengers are to be conveyed except such as can produce passes from the Provost Marshal.

MRS. THOMAS J. WARRINGTON, wife of one of the most able lawyers in this city, was arrested about 6 o'clock yesterday morning, upon the charge of having in her possession communications of a treasonable character. At the time of her arrest she was getting into a carriage intending to proceed to the Light-street wharf to take passage in a steamer for the Eastern Shore. She has a son in the rebel Army, and circumstances have led the military authorities to suppose treasonable correspondence has been held between them, and that this journey was to see him, either in the Southern portion of the State, or to cross the Potomac for that purpose. A valise, which she carried, contained no proof beyond the finding of a gentleman's fine shirt. She was taken to Fort McHenry and there searched by females, but nothing objectionable being found upon her, she was released by order of Gen. DIX, and provided with an escort to her home. When arrested by Lieut. MORRIS, her indignation knew no bounds, and she threatened to shoot the officer should he presume to lay hands upon her.

An extensive military hospital is being inaugurated in this city by Government. The Adams House and the National Hotel have been taken for that purpose, and will be supplied with one thousand bed and other conveniences for the sick and wounded. The medical stores now at Frederick are being removed, and the National is being prepared for immediate use, and to which the patients now in that place will soon be brought.

On Tuesday evening a detachment of 240 men arrived in this city by the Northern Central Railroad, *en route* for Washington, to join the infantry regiment of Col. HAY, which will bring it up to the regulation standard. A train, consisting of sixteen large cars, filled with cavalry horses, arrived at the same time, over the Philadelphia road, intended for the companies of cavalry which have already passed through. Three large cars, loaded with brass field-pieces and carriages, also arrived, and will proceed to Washington without delay.

On the same evening, between six and seven hundred men belonging to the Philadelphia infantry, under command of Col. MCNULTY, arrived over the Northern Central Road, from Harrisburgh, and proceeded immediately to the Capital. They were all recruits, unarmed and without uniforms, all of which will be supplied them on their arrival at Washington, where they will go immediately into a camp of instruction and be thoroughly drilled. The required standard of 1,046 men will soon be attained and sent forward.

A detachment of 263 United States Cavalry also arrived by the same route, under command of Col. EMERY, and passed on to Bladensburgh, where they will await further orders. The men were all fully uniformed and equipped, and have experienced considerable Army service.

About 3 o'clock, yesterday afternoon, the First Regiment United States Chasseurs, from New-York, under command of Hon. JOHN COCHRANE, Colonel, reached this city in a special train, and marched through our streets to the Washington station, where another special train conveyed them to the latter city.

The Eighteenth Massachusetts Regiment, Col. BARNES, numbering 782 men, reached here last night at a late hour, by the Northern Central Railroad, and proceeded immediately to Washington. Recruits will soon join the regiment, bringing its numbers up to the requisite standard.

The intrenchments on Federal Hill are rapidly progressing, while the old buildings which have stood so long upon the grounds will be speedily demolished.

ARGUS.

PRIMARY PEACE MEETINGS—STATEMENT OF A VIRGINIA REFUGEE—SHOOTING CASE, ETC.

BALTIMORE, Friday, Aug. 30, 1861.

Primary Peace meetings were held in the various Wards of the city yesterday, to choose delegates to constitute a Convention which will select eleven delegates to represent the City of Baltimore in the State Convention, to assemble in this city on the 10th of September next. The following are the peaceful Ward delegates chosen:

Second Ward—Wm. Stevens, Wm. S. Gorton, Emanuel Weinman, Hugh Auld, Cyrus Nagly. One bitter Secessionist, the remainder Southern sympathizers.

Third Ward—Capt. Francis W. Wilson, Ezra Whitman, Dr. John F. Monmonier, Andrew J. George and Hugh Gifford. All Southern sympathizers.

Fourth Ward—George W. Herring, Wm. H. Vickery, Dr. J. W. Houck, Robert Y. Banks, Leonard Pasano. Two violent Secessionists, the balance Southern sympathizers.

Fifth Ward—Wm. H. Cowan, James L. Mills, Wm. C. Cunningham, Joseph Beard, and Dr. M. M. Taylor. Notorious Secessionists.

Sixth Ward—J. S. George, W. H. Johnson, Thomas W. Morse, Thomas S. Austin and James R. Leane. Three rank Disunionists and two Southern sympathizers.

Seventh Ward—James P. Thomas, James Webb, W. A. Glanville, Wm. J. O'Brien and Thomas Wilkinson. Southern sympathizers.

Ninth Ward—Col. M. J. Cohen, Wm. Hawrand, A. D. Miller, John F. Poe, Dr. James A. Steward. All Secessionists.

Tenth Ward—Lewis W. Wolf, Ambrose M. Emery, Henry James, Robert W. Wall, Augustus Albert. Strong Secessionists.

Eleventh Ward—John Stuart, Thomas J. Hutchins, Israel Cohen, John Williams and Theodore Parsons. Secessionists and Southern sympathizers.

Twelfth Ward—James S. Forbes, Charles C. Gibson, George H. Brice, Charles G. Kerr and William Krebs. Disunionists and Southern sympathizers.

Thirteenth Ward—W. H. Rasin, Chas. Miller, John S. Gosnell, Chas. T. Tyson and J. C. Smith. Strong Southern sympathizers.

Fourteenth Ward—Ross Winans, Livingstone King, Wesley Starr, George U. Porter, Hugh Hamilton. Uncompromising Secessionists and Southern sympathizers.

Sixteenth Ward—Dr. C. C. Richardson, F. C. Bowers, Dr. Wm. C. Kloman, Dr. Bautz, John W. High. All Secessionists.

Eighteenth Ward—Samuel Hollingshead, Wm. M. Wilson, Felix McCurley, Dr. George Tolson and Wm. A. Schaeffer. All Secessionists.

Twentieth Ward—Dr. Thomas Sappington, Benjamin Horn, H. Crout, William Ortwine, Wendall Bollman. Secessionists and Southern sympathizers.

These are the gentlemen selected by the *Peace Party* of this city to nominate delegates to the State Peace Convention, and are composed of ultra Disunionists, thin-skinned Unionists, and Southern sympathizers.

Strong efforts are being made to obtain Executive mercy in the case of ALEXANDER GALE, condemned to execution on Friday of next week, for the murder of a negro named JOHN EVANS. GALE, who is a slave of Col. GEORGE R. HOWARD, has been confined in jail nearly two years. He was first tried by the Circuit Court of Baltimore, and, the jury disagreeing, the case was transferred to Towsontown, and a verdict of murder obtained.

The evidence showed that the prisoner was employed as a deck-hand on the sloop *Ellen*, Capt. WOODS, and while lying in the basin became involved in a quarrel with the deceased. Both had been drinking, and during the absence of the Captain were encouraged to fight by a white man. The deceased made several attempts to kill the prisoner, who gave him one fatal wound with a small penknife in self-defence. From the respectable character of the petition for Executive clemency, it is thought that a commutation of his sentence, if not an unconditional pardon, will be obtained.

Last evening about 6 o'clock the *Ben. Deford*, steamer, Capt. WM. A. HALLETT, which had been employed by Government for the transportation of about 350 sailors from Boston to Washington, came up the harbor to take in a cargo of assorted merchandise for her return trip.

Capt. HALLETT states that while running up the Potomac a schooner was discovered displaying a signal of distress. He immediately stopped the boat, and a Virginia refugee on board the schooner desired to be taken to Washington. He was taken on board the *Deford* by order of a United States Naval officer, and landed at the Navy-yard in Washington. He gave a very intelligent description of the appearance of the country bordering upon the Potomac through which he had passed. Farms of the most extensive area and improved cultivation have been completely ruined and desolated. The fields have been ravaged, the houses pillaged, the young men impressed into the rebel service, and the women and children in a state of constant alarm, while himself had abandoned a fine estate to escape personal outrage.

A probable fatal case of shooting occurred last evening in the camp of the Sixteenth Massachusetts Regiment, stationed at Prospect Hill, near Greenwood Cemetery in this city. The name of the unfortunate man is ANDREW J. SPROWL, of Boston, and belonged in Company I. He had been placed on guard in the immediate vicinity of a member of the same company named STEPHEN SCOTT. Rumor says that the two had been engaged in a quarrel on the previous day, and that a revival of it had occurred on the morning of yesterday. [illegible] The report of the musket created an alarm in the camp, and it being supposed that the man had been shot from a house in the neighborhood, a squad of men was detailed to discover the fact. The ball, which was of the Minié pattern, entered the back near the left shoulder-blade, and passing entirely through the body, escaped between the third and fourth ribs at the breast. He was immediately attended by the surgeon of the regiment, who, last evening, entertained but slight hopes of his recovery. SCOTT was pointed out by several, who stated that they saw the [illegible] fired and the man fall. He was immediately placed under arrest and will be subjected to a court-martial. He admitted the shooting, but alleged that it was purely accidental—that he leveled his musket without thought at his comrade, and without intending to discharge it. SCOTT, it is believed, bears a good character, although at times unguarded in his ways. SPROWL is about [illegible] years of age, of exemplary character, and has a wife and two children residing in Boston.

The Twenty-first Massachusetts Regiment, which [illegible] at Patterson's Park in this city since Sunday last, received yesterday morning orders to repair immediately to Annapolis Junction, to relieve the [illegible] Regiment, hitherto detailed there, and which had been ordered to Washington.

ARGUS.

THE ILLINOIS VOLUNTEERS.

Brig.-Gen. HURLBUT, of the U. S. A., detailed as Major-General of the Illinois Volunteers, arrived at this City last Friday evening *en route* for Chicago, at which point his head-quarters will be fixed for some brief time. He has been staying at the Metropolitan, but leaves for the West to-morrow. [illegible]

THE SKIRMISH NEAR BALL'S CROSS ROADS.

The following, from Col. H. C. HOFFMAN, Colonel of the Twenty-third New-York Regiment, gives a correct version of the skirmish [illegible]

[*Continued on Eighth Page.*]

The New-York Times.

VOL. X....NO. 3113. NEW-YORK, FRIDAY, SEPTEMBER 13, 1861. PRICE TWO CENTS.

STIRRING INTELLIGENCE

Another Victory in Western Virginia.

TOTAL ROUT OF THE THIEVING FLOYD.

Brilliant Success of the Ohio Troops Under General Rosecrans.

The Rebels Driven Out of a Strongly Intrenched Position.

Capture of all their Camp Equipage, Baggage, Wagons, Horses, etc.

IMPORTANT FROM MISSOURI.

The Rebel Forces Under Martin Green Scattered.

Another Force of Five Hundred Routed.

Reported Capture of Six Hundred More.

Gen. McClellan's Report of the Skirmish at Lewinsville.

The Privateer Sumter Said to be Wrecked.

GREAT VICTORY IN WESTERN VIRGINIA.

CLARKSBURGH, Va., Thursday, Sept. 12.

A battle took place about 3 o'clock Tuesday afternoon, near Summerville. Gen. ROSECRANS after making a reconnoissance, found FLOYD'S army, 5,000 strong, with 16 field pieces, intrenched in a powerful position, on the top of a mountain at Cannix Ferry, on the west side of Gauley River. The rear and extreme of both flanks were inaccessible. The front was masked with heavy forests and a close jungle.

Col. LYTLE'S Ohio Tenth Regiment, of Gen. BENHAM'S Brigade, was in advance, and drove a strong detachment of the enemy out of camp this side of the position, the site of which was unknown. Shortly afterwards his scouts, consisting of four companies, suddenly discovered themselves in the face of a parapet battery, and a long line of palisades for riflemen, when the battle opened fiercely. The remainder of the Tenth, and the Thirteenth Ohio, were brought into action successively by Gen. BENHAM, and the Twelfth afterwards by Capt. HARTSUFF, whose object was an armed reconnoissance. The enemy played upon our forces terrifically, with musketry, rifles, canister and shell, causing some casualties. Col. LYTLE led several companies of Irish to charge the battery, when he was brought down by a shot in the leg.

Col. SMITH'S Thirteenth Ohio engaged the enemy on the left, and Col. LOWE'S Twelfth Ohio directly in front. LOWE fell dead at the head of his regiment early in the hottest fire by a ball in the forehead.

MCMULLEN'S howitzer battery and SNYDER'S two field pieces meantime were got into the best position possible under the circumstances, and soon silenced two of the rebel guns.

The fire slackened at intervals, but grew more furious as night approached, when the German Brigade was led gallantly into the action by Col. MCCOOK, under the direction of Adj.-Gen. HARTSUFF, but after a furious fight of three hours ordered the recall of the troops, and the men laid on their arms within a short distance of the enemy, each ready to resume the contest the next morning.

The thief, FLOYD, fled during the night, and sunk the boats in the river, and destroyed the temporary bridge which he made when he first occupied the position. The turbulence and depth of the river, and the exhaustion of the troops, made it impossible to follow him. He left his camp equipage, wagons, horses, large quantities of ammunition, and fifty head of cattle.

Our loss is fifteen killed and about seventy wounded—generally flesh wounds. The rebel loss is not ascertained. They carried their dead and wounded with them. Their loss was certainly serious. Capt. MCGROUTY, of Cincinnati; Capt. MCMULLEN and Lieut. SNYDER, of Ohio, are among the wounded, but not dangerously.

Twenty-five of Col. TYLER'S men, who were taken by FLOYD at Cross Lane, were recaptured, and FLOYD'S personal baggage and that of his officers, was taken by Gen. BENHAM'S Brigade, which suffered most. It was commanded by him in person, and Col. MCCOOK led his brigade.

Gens. Rosecrans and Benham, Col. McCook, Col. Lytle, Col. Lowe, Capt. Hartsuff, Capt. Snyder' Capt. McCullen Burke of the Ohio Tenth, and the other officers, displayed conspicuous personal gallantry. The troops were exclusively from Ohio, and showed great bravery.

OFFICIAL REPORT OF THE BATTLE.

WASHINGTON, Thursday, Sept. 12.

Lieut.-Gen. SCOTT to-night received a dispatch from Gen. ROSECRANS, giving a few of the particulars of his action with FLOYD, stating that the enemy was driven from his intrenchments across the Gauley River. He says FLOYD was punished severely, a number of his troops being killed, and a quantity of camp equipage taken, while the loss on our side was small.

The following is Gen. ROSECRANS' official report, in full:

HEAD-QUARTERS, ARMY OF VIRGINIA, CAMP SCOTT, Wednesday, Sept. 11, 1861—P. M.

To Col. E. D. Townsend:

We yesterday marched seventeen and a half miles, reached the enemy's entrenched position in front of Connifix Ferry, driving his advance outposts and pickets before us. We found him occupying a strongly entrenched position, covered by a forest too dense to admit its being seen at a distance of three hundred yards. His force was five regiments, besides the one driven in. He had probably sixteen pieces of artillery.

At 3 o'clock we began a strong reconnoissance, which proceeded to such length that we were about to assault the position on the flank and front, when night coming on, and our troops being completely exhausted, I drew them out of the woods, and posted them in the order of battle behind ridges immediately in front of the enemy's position, where they rested on their arms till morning. Shortly after daylight a runaway contraband came in, and reported that the enemy had crossed the Gauley during the night by means of the ferry and a bridge which they had completed.

Col. EWING was ordered to take possession of the camp, which he did at about 7 o'clock, capturing a few prisoners, two stand of colors, a considerable quantity of arms, with Quartermaster's stores, messing and camp equipage. The enemy have destroyed the bridge across the Gauley, which here rushes through a deep gorge, and our troops being still much fatigued, and having no material for immediately replacing the bridge, it was thought prudent to encamp the troops.

We occupied the ferry and captured the camp, sending a few rifle cannon shots after the enemy to produce a moral effect. Our loss will probably amount to 20 killed and 100 wounded. The enemy's loss had not been ascertained, but from report it must have been considerable.

(Signed) H. S. ROSECRANZ.

SPECIAL DISPATCH FROM WASHINGTON.

WASHINGTON, Thursday, Sept. 12.

There is much feeling here among leading men, caused by the action of Gen. MCCLELLAN in ordering the return of fugitive slaves, or, rather, their arrest in camps and imprisonment in jail to await the claim of their masters. This is in contravention of the spirit of the letter addressed by the Secretary of War to Gen. BUTLER, for it constitutes our troops but an army of negro catchers. It is directly in contradiction to the letter of FREMONT'S proclamation, which has been unanimously accepted by the people of the loyal States as the true interpretation of our relation to the slaveholders in rebellion against the Government.

CONSUL AT AUX CAYES.

H. H. SANDFORD, of Kentucky, has been appointed Consul to Aux Cayes.

THE BALTIMORE EXCHANGE.

The Government having prohibited the transportation of the Baltimore *Exchange* through the mails, that paper comes out, this morning, with a tirade of abuse of the Government, and a threat that it will continue to aid the rebels.

It is probable that the papers indicted by the Grand Jury of Westchester County will be prohibited from passing through the mails.

RECONNOITERING.

The Secretary of State reconnoitered the rebel intrenchments at Munson's Hill in person, to-day. After taking a distant view of the big guns, he reviewed Gen. BLENKER'S Brigade, and was escorted back to Washington by a detachment of cavalry detailed by Gen. BLENKER. It is a little remarkable that the rebels did not salute the Secretary.

NO MORE CONSULS.

The list of consular appointments is now full, and the State Department has published the names, stations, etc., in a pamphlet, for the use of the public. Those who did not get appointed, can have the satisfaction of learning who did, by sending for a copy.

COTTON IN ENGLAND.

The Government is in receipt of valuable information by the last steamer, relating to the present stock of cotton in the English warehouses, and the prospect of a supply from other sources than the rebel States. This information leaves no room to doubt that the Manchester mills will be able to run on full time for an entire year, even without touching one pound of the new crop. The information obtained from the Spinners' Association has greatly and agreeably suprised the manufacturers, and led them to soften down very much in their demand for a speedy termination of the war. The fact that our Eastern mills have shipped raw material to England has astonished the European spinners, who had supposed our factories to be closed for the want of supplies.

INTERCEPTED CORRESPONDENCE.

The assortment and reading of intercepted correspondence has become a heavy tax upon the Department charged with that branch of the service—so great, indeed, as to make it necessary to detail extra clerical force for that duty. Were I permitted to detail results, the country would have no cause to complain of the zeal and energy of the Department in respect to ferreting out rebels.

THE NATIONAL ZEITUNG.

Based upon trustworthy information received by the Government of the disloyal sentiments uttered by the *National Zeitung*, of New-York, the Postmaster-General has directed that that journal be denied the facilities of the United States mail.

A NEW HOSPITAL.

A portion of the north wing of the Patent Office has been converted into a hospital for the uses of the Indiana troops.

THE SINKING OF THE TIGRESS.

I have learned the particulars of the sinking of the *Tigress*. She was steaming up the river, the *State of Maine* being bound down. Each vessel tried to avoid the other, but by some awkwardness they did not clear, and the *State of Maine* struck the *Tigress* amidships, sinking her almost immediately. There were fifteen persons on the *Tigress*, all of whom were saved.

SERREL'S POST-NOTES.

SERREL has failed thus far to obtain possession of his forty thousand pounds in post-notes. They are held by Gen. SPINNER, United States Treasurer, who declines to give them up, except upon order of Secretary CHASE.

GEN. HEINTZELMAN TO HAVE A DIVISION.

Gen. HEINTZELMAN is to have command of a Division in our Army.

THE VIRGINIA BRIGADE.

Col. WARD LAMON has already raised for his Virginia Brigade about twenty-five hundred men. As recruiting has ceased in Northern Virginia, consequent upon the retreat of our troops to Maryland, he will proceed at once to Illinois under the authority of the War Department, to obtain troops to complete the Brigade. He is authorized to muster in and draw subsistence for the men as fast as they enlist.

GEN. LANDER.

Gen. LANDER has been assigned to command a Brigade in the Army of the Potomac. He leaves for his command to-morrow.

MORE CONTRABANDS.

Four contrabands arrived at the Navy-yard today from the flotilla. Three were slaves of a man named FIELDING LEWIS, residing near the Rappahannock, and the fourth an intelligent house-servant, named JAMES LAWSON, who was owned by Col. TAYLOR, of the rebel Army, whose residence is situated but a short distance from the Potomac, in King George County. LAWSON states that between Aquia Creek and Mathias Point there are about two thousand troops of the rebel Army, besides some seven hundred militia. One North Carolina Regiment is included in the two thousand. At Hasspatanss Hill a body of troops are stationed. The force along the shore was being increased, in view of an expected attack from our flotilla. At Potomac Creek they had a battery of five guns, one of which was not mounted. Two were rifled cannon. He saw the battery on Saturday week. The troops are supplied with food and provisions by the farmers and planters, who furnish them without any apparent reluctance. The militia are miserably equipped, and are in poor discipline. The slaves have been hopeful that the war would result in good to them, but statements have been constantly made to them that those who have run away have been sold by the Northern men into worse Slavery, or sent to Africa. This has caused many who otherwise would have attempted to escape to hesitate. LAWSON was at Manassas with his master before and after Bull Run. He reports that since the battle the rebels have extended their intrenchments from a few miles back of Alexandria to near Culpeper Court-house, beyond Manassas. Coin was very scarce, the only money in circulation being shinplasters. LAWSON thinks a large force would not be required to capture the whole shore from Aquia Creek to Mathias Point.

NEWS FROM BELOW.

The *Ceres* arrived this evening from the Potomac flotilla. She reports all quiet below.

NAVAL PENSIONS GRANTED.

Naval pensions were granted to-day as follows: JOHN B. MILLER, of the *Mississippi*, $6; JOHN H. LAWRENCE, $4, and BENJ. F. FULLER, of the *Brooklyn*, $9 per month.

JOS. BAYARD, of Lockport, a private in the New-York Twenty-eighth Regiment, who suffered the loss of a foot, was allowed a pension of $6 per month.

GEN. M'CLELLAN'S MOVEMENTS.

Gen. MCCLELLAN was across the Potomac today. He did not return until late.

THE REBELS AT MUNSON'S HILL.

The rebel flag was not hoisted to-day on Munson's Hill, nor were the sentries posted on the works as heretofore. Their pickets, however, were not drawn in. The cause of this change is a matter of conjecture. Some suppose that it is a feint, designed to invite an attack; others, that the main body of their force were moved up the river toward Lewinsville, fearing in consequence of yesterday's reconnoissance, that a movement would be made against them by our forces.

SERENADE TO MR. HOLT.

To-night Hon. JOSEPH HOLT was serenaded at his residence. He appeared on the balcony and responded to the compliment in a brief, hopeful and eloquent speech.

DISPATCH TO THE ASSOCIATED PRESS.

WASHINGTON, Thursday, Sept. 12.

Gen. MCCLELLAN'S dispatch to the Secretary of War is very brief. He merely says that Gen. SMITH made a reconnoissance with 2,000 men to Lewinsville, remained there several hours and completed their examination of the ground. When the work was completed and the command had started back, the enemy opened fire with shell by which two men were killed and three wounded.

GRIFFIN'S Battery, he says, silenced that of the enemy, and our men came back in perfect order and excellent spirits. The men behaved most admirably under the fire. He concludes by remarking, "We shall have no more Bull Run affairs."

The firing in the direction of the Chain Bridge, this morning, was from artillery practice.

Two dead bodies were recovered from the Lewinsville field by a detachment of the Nineteenth Indiana Regiment, to-day. No further tidings have been heard of Lieut. HANCOCK, who is reported killed, the body not having been found. The presumption is that he was taken prisoner.

A man supposed to be a spy was arrested to-day in the neighborhood of Chain Bridge, and was taken to the head-quarters of Gen. SMITH heavily ironed.

Everything has been remarkably quiet in the neighborhood of Bailey's and Bull's Cross Roads to-day. The residence of Mr. BALL, to the right of Ball's Cross Roads, is alternately occupied by our pickets and those of the Confederates—ours during the day and theirs at night.

Hon. MOSES F. O'DELL arrived here to-day. He comes specially to look after the troops hereabout from the Southern part of New-York, particularly those from Kings County, who are sick or otherwise needing attention.

THE SUMTER REPORTED LOST.

WRECKED ON THE ISLAND OF TRINIDAD.

Capt. ATKINSON, of the bark *Venus*, from Curacoa, arrived yesterday, reports that the Venezuelan Consul at Curacoa had received advices from Carracas, Venezuela, to Aug. 22, which stated that the privateer *Sumter* had gone ashore on the Island of Trinidad, Port of Spain, about the 20th August, and had become a total wreck.

[The latest previous intelligence from the *Sumter* left her at Surinam on Aug. 20, whither she had gone for a supply of coal, which had been refused her. It is possible that her captain may have been compelled to beach the *Sumter* in consequence of this failure; but the present shape the intelligence given above cannot be considered perfectly reliable.—ED. TIMES.]

PREVIOUS REPORTS OF THE SUMTER.

The following is a copy of a letter received by ELWOOD WALTER, Esq., Secretary of the Board of Underwriters of the Port of New-York:

CURACOA, Thursday Aug. 22.

The privateer steamer *Sumter* was seen off Porto Cabello, 14th inst., with a new prize, supposed the bark *Teresa*, that had left Maracaibo for New-York, with a cargo of coffee. On the 15th, a steamer, flying the American flag, passed before the harbor, that reported herself as the *Keystone State*. Commander SCOTT, in search of the *Sumter*. The pilot that went out to her, could not learn where she was bound to, but by last accounts from St. Thomas, we learn the *Keystone State* was bound to Cienfuegos. The pilot reports her as quite a new steamer,—the *Keystone State* being five years old. It is supposed the steamer that passed only assumed the flag and name to gain information for her own purpose.

IMPORTANT FROM MISSOURI.

REPORTED CAPTURE OF SIX HUNDRED REBELS.

JEFFERSON CITY, Wednesday, Sept. 11.

A gentleman from Georgetown, Pettis County, reports that the army of Gen. PRICE was encamped, on Saturday night last, on the Warrensburgh Road, near Clinton, in Henry County, destined, it was thought, for Lexington.

Another messenger from Sidalia brings information that Dr. JAMISON, the Kansas jay-hawker, with a small force from that State, had fallen upon a party of five hundred rebels, under the notorious Dr. STAPLES, and completely routed them, and killed their leader. If this be true, the most difficult part of restoring peace in Pettis County and the adjoining counties, has been accomplished. This man, STAPLES, and the Capt. MAGOFFIN captured some days since, have been the principal instigators of secessionism in these counties.

The same messenger states that Col. MARSHALL'S Illinois Cavalry had surrounded 600 rebels under Capt. SHELBY, a short distance below Lexington, and taken the whole force prisoners. SHELBY had two cannon. This latter report needs confirmation. It has been known, however, for several days, that SHELBY'S band had taken a position at the place indicated after abandoning the siege of Lexington.

THE REBELS UNDER GREEN SCATTERED.

HENNEWELL, Mo., Tuesday, Sept. 10.

Gen. POPE'S command marched for the rebels under GREEN on Sunday night, and at daylight Monday reached their camp, but GREEN, having received notice of the approach of our troops, had fled, and his forces scattered in every direction, leaving much of their baggage, provisions and forage, and the public property they had captured at Shelbina. GREEN'S force numbered about 3,000, and Gen. POPE'S troops, having made a forced march of 23 miles, they were unable to pursue him. At the latest accounts it was understood that the bulk of GREEN'S horde had crossed the Northern Missouri Railroad, and were making for the woods in Chariton County. Gen. POPE followed in pursuit with the Sixteenth Illinois and Third Iowa Regiments, after giving them a few hours rest, but, as GREEN'S forces are mounted, there is but little prospect of overtaking him.

OFFICIAL ACCOUNTS FROM GEN. POPE.

WASHINGTON, Thursday, Sept. 12.

The following dispatch was received to-night at the head-quarters of the Army:

ST. LOUIS, Sept. 12, 1861.

Col. E. D. Townsend, Assistant Adjutant-General:

The report of Gen. POPE to-day from Hunneville says he made night marches on GREEN last Sunday, who, however, got notice of his approach, but was successful in continuing the dispersion of 3,000 rebel forces, leaving behind them much baggage, provisions and forage; also the public property seized by GREEN at Shelbourne. Gen. POPE'S infantry was too much fatigued to pursue. The horsemen, however, followed in pursuit ten or fifteen miles, until the enemy scattered.

The railroad east of Brookfall is open, and no more secession camps will be made within 20 miles.

Gen. GRANT telegraphs that the first gun is in position at Fort Holt, Kentucky.

(Signed) J. C. FREMONT, Major-General Commanding.

ANOTHER ATTEMPT UPON A RAILROAD BRIDGE.

MEXICO, Mo., Monday, Sept. 9.

Another fiendish attempt to destroy the lives of our soldiers was made a day or two since, on the North Missouri Railroad. The timbers of a bridge were partially burned, in expectation that a train with troops would be precipitated into the creek below; but the design of the villains being known the train stopped here, and the troops are now encamped at this place, where they will remain until the bridge is repaired.

NATIONAL WOUNDED AT SPRINGFIELD.

ST. LOUIS, Wednesday, Sept. 11.

Dr. FRANKLIN, senior Surgeon of Gen. LYON'S Brigade, has arrived from Springfield, and reports that all the National wounded, remaining in the place, have been retained by order of the rebel commander, and held as hostages for the safety of the Secessionists now in the hands of the National authorities. Dr. FRANKLIN was told that for every rebel shot or hung under FREMONT'S recent proclamation, our wounded, the National soldiers, would be shot.

Capt. KIDD, of the rebel Army, arrived last night with a flag of truce. It is conjectured that he brings a proposition for an exchange of our wounded soldiers now at Springfield for all the secession prisoners now in the hands of the Federal authorities throughout the State.

Mrs. WILLOW and a free colored woman, named HANNAH COURTNAY, were arrested yesterday, for selling poisoned pies to the soldiers at Camp Benton.

Acting Quartermaster-General MCKINSTRY has issued orders forbidding all officers, agents, or other employes in the Quartermaster's Department, and all contractors with said department, from dealing in any way with persons not known to be loyal to the United States Government, and all officers, agents, employes, and contractors are directed to use the utmost vigilance to prevent the disbursement of any moneys of the United States for the benefit of its enemies.

Gov. GAMBLE has returned here, arriving last night. The *Republican* learns that his mission was to get money and arms to enable him to get out the State troops under his proclamation, in which he was entirely successful. The money will be placed to his credit in the Sub-Treasury, and the arms will be forwarded as fast as possible. Gov. GAMBLE had no other object in view in visiting Washington than to procure means to secure the peace of the State by arming her own citizens, and all reports of his interference in others matters are untrue.

With a view of promoting the health and comfort of the troops in and near St. Louis, Gen. FREMONT has appointed a Sanitary Committee of five gentlemen, who shall serve voluntarily and be removable at pleasure. The general object of this commission shall be to carry out such sanitary regulations and reforms as the well-being of the soldiers shall demand; it shall have authority, under the direction of the Military Directors, to select, fit up, and furnish suitable buildings for Army and brigade hospitals, in such places and in such manner as circumstances may require; attend to the selection of women nurses under authority of Miss DIX, and coöperate with the surgeons of the various hospitals in providing male nurses; and consult with the commanding and regimental officers with regard to the sanitary and general condition of the troops, and aid them in providing proper means for the preservation of health and preventing sickness, by wholesome, well-cooked food, and obtain from the community at large such additional means of increasing the comfort, promoting the moral and social welfare of the men in camp and hospital as may be needed, and cannot be furnished by Government regulations. This Committee is not intended to interfere with the Medical Staff or other officers of the Army, but to coöperate with them, and aid them in the discharge of their present arduous duties.

COMPLETION OF A RAILWAY, ETC.

ST. LOUIS, Thursday, Sept. 12.

The connection between the Pacific and Iron Mountain Railroad was completed to-day. This junction of roads was made by order of Gen. FREMONT, and will enable the Government to transport troops and any stores from one section of the State to another without reshipment. Troops can also be transferred from the river without the delay of marching through the city.

It is reported that Capt. BOYD, commanding the Secession forces in Buchanan County, marched into St. Joseph, on Saturday last, and plundered the stores of some $40,000 worth of goods.

The latest advices from Paducah state that the impression prevails that the enemy would not attack that place.

The circulation of the Dubuque *Herald* has been interdicted in this County by order of the Provost-Marshal.

Capt. HAZARD, of the United States Navy, has arrived from Boston.

FROM GEN. BANKS' ARMY.

RAILROAD OPERATIONS OF THE REBELS.

POINT OF ROCKS, Wednesday, Sept. 11.

Union men from Martinsburgh on Saturday, report that the rebels have taken up the entire track on the Baltimore and Ohio Railroad from that town to North Mountain, a distance of 9 miles, and transported the rails, etc., to Manchester, for the extension of the Alexandria, Loudon and Hampshire Railroad, from Strausburgh to that point. The track torn up was lately relaid by the company.

At Duffield's station, on the Baltimore and Ohio Railroad, the rebels were busily engaged in taking down seven or eight new and first-class locomotives for transportation on to Winchester. These locomotives had but recently been put upon the route; some of them are of the heaviest kind, and were probably spared by the rebels in the recent conflagrations on account of their adaptibility to transporting troop-trains in Virginia.

Hon. DAVID C. STROTHER is still held prisoner by the rebels, probably in Richmond. His son, "Porte Crayon," is a guest or *attaché* of the Engineer Corps of Gen. BANKS' column.

The new system of Army signaling is becoming a fixed institution. The appointees are compelled to pass a thorough examination in mathematics, engineering, astronomy, &c, and many changes are made in the corps for want of proficiency.

SECESSION MEETING AT ROCKVILLE.

ROCKVILLE, Tuesday, Sept. 10.

On Saturday last a primary meeting was held here by the Secessionists to elect delegates to the Baltimore Convention to nominate State officers. About six delegates from Montgomery County were present. Their meeting was a secret one.

The most prominent of those present were Thomas Lausdale, of the Tridelphia Mills, near Baltimore President; Alex. Kilgow, W. V. Bowie, D. H. Bowie, Henry W. Viers, J. W. Campbell, Nich. D. Offutt, John W. Jones, M. Green, M. Fields, (Editor), Lewis Shatts, Geo. Peters, Thos. Nolan, S. M. Lyddana, John Brewer, A. Garrett, M. Dettrick, (Jailor and Bailiff), Geo. Peterson, W. T. Reed, Thos. Hunter, Lem. Mike Letton, John Spates, (Register), Samuel Riggs, E. C. Bell, J. S. Carman, (School Teacher), Ben. Cooley, (Mail Contractor), J. A. T. Kilgow, E. S. Wooten, R. A. Sheckels, Isaac Young, and others.

A Committee, consisting of Isaac Young, W. V. Bowie, J. A. T. Kilgour and Ben. Cooley, was appointed to draft a series of resolutions, which they reported, and were adopted. These resolutions were lengthy, and of a strong secession character. Among them were the following, in effect:

Resolved, That we, delegates from Montgomery County, while respecting the Federal Government and its laws, still love our State, and will oppose the Federal Government in bringing Northern Abolitionists upon our soil

Resolved, That we will oppose the Northern Abolitionists in endeavoring to arrest citizens loyal to the State of Maryland.

Delegates were appointed to the Baltimore Convention, but their names could not be ascertained.

JOHN W. JONES, one of the members of the meeting, is said to be a rampant Secessionist, and an owner or lessee of the building in which the telegraph office is located.

THOS. NOLAN, lately arrested on a charge of having shot a picket, was another. ED. C. BELT is represented as being a fanatical Secessionist, as is also R. A. SHECKELS.

During the day outside Secessionists thronged the town, and boldly proclaimed their sentiments. Many of them, as well as the delegates, were armed with revolvers and knives, striking terror to the hearts of the quiet Union men. Deep threats were made of what would be done to the Abolition hordes.

It is stated that the Secessionists of this town are well provided with ammunition and weapons, and that a resident citizen has been teaching the sword exercise.

SOUTHERN NEWS THROUGH LOUISVILLE.

LOUISVILLE, Thursday, Sept. 12.

A special dispatch to the *Journal*, from Washington, dated the 11th, says that Gen. MCCLELLAN has carried Hall's Hill, with a loss of 15 killed, and that Gen. BANKS' command was within a short distance. A general battle, the dispatch states, is expected tomorrow.

The Evansville *Journal* says the steamer *Sue Evaz*, under the command of the gun squad from that place, had captured a boat with 1,000 barrels of salt, destined for the Confederate States.

The Southern papers say that Capt. W. F. LYNCH, late of the United States Navy, has been appointed Chief of the Bureau of Detail and Equipment in the Confederate Army.

Col. JONES, of the Fourth Alabama Regiment, died at the Orange Court-House, Va., on the 26th, from wounds received at the battle of Bull Run.

W. BOYD, late Clerk in the National War Department, had arrived at Richmond with full information respecting matters at Washington.

LOUISVILLE, Thursday, Sept. 12.

A special dispatch from Washington to the *Journal*, of the 12th, says cannon are roaring in the distance, and a battle is going on.

Several guns recently in possession of the State Guard were taken from this city yesterday, and nearly a hundred more were found under a hay-stack in the suburbs of the city.

The steamer *Treadwater*, BELL, old and of little use, was seized by the National authorities at Smithfield to-day. She had been conveying provisions up the Tennessee River.

The Nashville *Union and American* congratulates the Confederates States upon the election of Gen. ALBERT SIDNEY JOHNSTON, to the command of the Western Division of the Confederate Army.

The Richmond *Examiner*, of the 9th, says that since the battle at Cross Lanes, Western Virginia, Gen. FLOYD has been waiting for supplies. On Saturday there were brought down fifteen prisoners who were taken straggling through the woods since the dispersion of Col. TYLER'S command.

Gen. FLOYD was at last accounts about one mile and a half beyond Gauley Bridge. The enemy was in full force at Gauley Bridge, and were strongly posted in the vicinity of Gauley Road, occupying Hawk's Nest above the Kanawha. The enemy had been outflanked by Gen. CHAPMAN, who held his position with 2,000 militia. The same paper says before many hours, the Potomac will be effectually closed by batteries. The Chief of the Ordnance in Virginia, in responding to the call for all the field artillery, says that ten batteries are now ready for immediate duty, and eight or ten more could be ready soon.

Among the above 15 prisoners which have arrived in Richmond, were W. H. RAYNOR, of Rhode Island and Lieut. C. J. MURPHY.

The *Examiner* also says that JEFF. DAVIS has so far recovered from his recent severe illness as to take an airing on Saturday in a carriage.

IMPORTANT FROM FORT MONROE.

INCREASE OF THE NATIONAL FORCES.

FORTRESS MONROE, Wednesday, Sept. 11, Via BALTIMORE, Sept. 12.

In view of the increasing importance of Fortress Monroe as a basis of offensive operations against the Confederates, there is to be a large increase in the military and naval forces.

There was heavy firing this morning on Sewall's Point. The Confederates were trying the range of their guns.

A deserter states that the Confederate force there numbers only about 2,000 men.

Quartermaster TALLMADGE is making arrangements to quarter contraband slaves at Old Point in comfortable wooden barracks outside the fortress.

AFFAIRS AT FORTRESS MONROE.

PREPARATIONS FOR THE FALL CAMPAIGN—THE IMPORTANCE OF THE RECENT BLOW—THE UNION SENTIMENT IN NORTH CAROLINA—AFFAIRS AT THE FORTRESS.

Correspondence of the New-York Times.

FORTRESS MONROE, Sunday, Sept. 8, 1861.

The Government is preparing to follow up the late victory of Hatteras with vigorous measures. Brig.-Gen. JOHN F. REYNOLDS having been designated, will soon repair to that post and assume command, under Major-Gen. WOOL. This is a judicious selection, and relieves those who had apprehensions that the cause now prospering so finely on the coast might receive a check from injudicious hands. It is understood that a fleet of gun-boats will, within a few days, be placed in Pamlico Sound, and that there will be a land force in the neighborhood to meet emergencies. The country should not, however, expect too much for the present. The season, in fact, is not far enough advanced to commence land operations in the South. Nevertheless, had Gen. WOOL at his command a sufficient force, it would not be ten days before the country would rejoice over the most satisfactory results. I understand that the General has in his eye the precise spot where he is anxious to plant a blow that will make rebellion quake. The plan is matured in his own mind, and he only asks the support of the Government. The old veteran is fully in the work, and was never more vigorous or active. Commodore STRINGHAM, too, to whom too large a share of the credit of the Hatteras victory cannot be given, is aroused, and chafes under delay. He wants to keep his squadron of matchless frigates and gun-boats at work, and does not doubt that, in conjunction with Gen. WOOL, another victory might be achieved before the echoes of the rejoicings over the capture of Hatteras have died away. With the field before us which the late expedition and victory opened, Fortress Monroe becomes the point of first magnitude. The flank movement, so auspiciously began, can be carried on from no other point. We have information that the greatest concern prevails among the rebels at Norfolk and vicinity, lest they will be taken in the rear—a contingency which they have wholly omitted to prepare for. Great as the traffic carried on by the rebels through Hatteras Inlet is now known to have been, it is small compared with their expectations as to the future. Indeed, they relied on this avenue as the chief one of supply of many things of greatest need. Pamlico and Albemarle Sounds had already become a very pirate's cave, the entrance to which they were right in saying, could not be successfully blockaded. The storms and tempests which are said to be the delight of the pirate, and which prevail nowhere with such fury as on the Hatteras coast, gave them almost perfect security; what was wanting their guns would supply—while Charleston, Savannah, and the other leading ports on the coast, were closed by a blockade which, in spite of all that England may pretend, is as perfect as one can well be—the rebels counted surely on keeping Hatteras Inlet open, which was equivalent to keeping free more than two hundred miles of coast. This key point taken, we can easily imagine how they may be filled with consternation, while the smothered Union feeling in the old North State takes hope in the prospect of deliverance. It was not five hours after the fall of Hatteras became known at Richmond, when regiments on their way from the Cotton States to the Potomac were turned back, while the demand for ten thousand troops went forward from Newbern to Richmond. Thus the blow fell as crushingly on the flank of the rebel Army on the Potomac as on the State troops who were left behind to guard the coast defences of North Carolina. You cannot make a movement on the Southern coast; you cannot mount a gun at Hatteras or embark a soldier from Fortress Monroe, without producing an effect like a hundred shells bursting on the flank of BEAUREGARD. No fleet ever braved the ocean with such terror to the foe as will the fleet of gunboats on Pamlico Sound, if the Government only places the necessary force at the command of Gen. WOOL. It will be folly to expect results from mere pretences. The blows must be real, inflicting punishment on the head of foes, and giving protection to friends.

We have the most positive information of the existence of a lively Union feeling in the Old North State, which only awaits the manifestation of National authority to join the Armies of the Union against rebellion. The ordinance of secession never was sanctioned by the people. The State was rushed out of the Union in defiance of the popular judgment, and not an hour since has opposition to the JEFF. DAVIS treason failed to grow stronger and deeper. My information is direct and reliable that the great mass of the people are "all right for the Union." While most of the politicians have taken sides for the rebellion, Vigilance Committees armed and threatening, though comparatively few in numbers, have been able to overawe thousands of unarmed, unambitious Union men, right at heart, though without leaders. The country awaits in the expectation, though with a feeling bordering on impatience, the following up of the victory of Hatteras with a vigorous policy, commencing with the reinforcement of Gen. WOOL.

In the more immediate neighborhood of the fortress there is nothing of stirring interest. The papers bring us the news of much that never happened, and we are amused at speculations—"hopes, doubts and fears"—the foundation for which no man can perceive. Of the growing improvement of Gen. WOOL'S forces, under the substitution of discipline and drill for a disregard of both, we are abundantly assured. The rebels appear to have given up all intention, at least for the present, of attacking Newport's News, though they stand in constant dread at Norfolk of the bombardment. Defences which before the bombardment of Hatteras were deemed impregnable they are engaged in strengthening, and strong as their batteries are at Sewell's Point and Craney Island, we have evidence that the confidence of the rebels in them is not near as great as it was.

There were taken at Hatteras a number of trophies, such as flags, some of them very beautiful, presented by ladies, with defiant inscriptions, swords and other such sort of things. These, Gen. BUTLER—whose principal share of the battle was to receive them—omitted to take due care of, but permitted to be scattered. Some he took himself, some he gave to friends, and others he permitted to be retained by individuals who thought they were most entitled to them. Pretty much everybody got something, except the Navy, which got nothing except the sword of Commander BARRON, which he gave to Commodore STRINGHAM. These scattered trophies, especially the flags, the Commodore has for the last few days been engaged in looking after, with the view of depositing them in the proper places, and in the name of the Navy, no doubt, at Washington. I am glad to say that tolerable success has attended his efforts, he having come into possession of four or five flags and some swords. As we go on gaining victories, we will learn how things should be conducted, and what to do with the trophies. In this case it was but natural that the Commodore, under whose direction upwards of two thousand shells were thrown, which won the victory with scarcely a single shot from any other quarter, should look around for something to show for it.

For other Rebellion News see Second and Eighth Pages.]

The New-York Times.

VOL. XI....NO. 3132. NEW-YORK, SATURDAY, OCTOBER 5, 1861. PRICE TWO CENTS.

THE GREAT REBELLION.

FIGHTING IN WESTERN VIRGINIA.

Everything Quiet Around Washington.

Arrival of Gen. Wool on his Way to the West.

Gen. Fremont Not Superseded nor Ordered to Washington, nor to be Court-martialed.

IMPORTANT NEWS FROM MISSOURI.

The Reported Evacuation of Lexington.

Price Said to be Moving Towards Independence.

The Strength and Position of the National Forces.

Interesting Facts and Rumors From the South.

Gustavus W. Smith a Major-General in the Rebel Army.

SPECIAL DISPATCH FROM WASHINGTON.

WASHINGTON, Friday, Oct. 4.

I rode along our advanced outposts to-day, and found all quiet. The rebel pickets appeared this P. M. near Falls Church, but made no demonstrations. They were mostly laying on the grass, their horses being tied to the trees.

FORTIFYING MUNSON'S HILL.

The New-York Thirty-seventh Regiment are busily engaged in throwing up the fortifications on Munson's Hill. They are now very formidable. It will be utterly impossible for the rebels to approach with artillery of long range enough to assail the works.

THE NAVAL EXPEDITIONS.

I understand that Gen. MCCLELLAN has, or will send a request, through the correspondent of the Associated Press, that all papers will abstain wholly from mentioning the Naval preparations of the Government for any expedition against the South.

ANOTHER PICKET SHOT.

This morning a soldier attached to the Garibaldi Regiment, while on picket-duty, was fired at by the rebel pickets, seven balls entering his body. He is still alive, although his recovery is doubtful.

REBEL ARTILLERY PRACTICE.

The rebels have been engaged during the day in artillery practice at Burke's Station, on the Orange Railroad.

GEN. WOOL AND GEN. FREMONT.

Gen. WOOL arrived in this city to-day, and I am now entirely satisfied that my statement in this morning's TIMES was correct. Gen. FREMONT has neither been superseded nor ordered to this city under arrest.

THE CHARGES AGAINST GEN. FREMONT.

The following is the result of inquiries to-day, in official quarters: The charges preferred by Col. FRANK P. BLAIR against Major-Gen. FREMONT, on the 26th of September, have not yet reached Washington. According to the revised Army Regulations, charges are required to be transmitted through the superior officer, which in this case is Gen. FREMONT himself. A copy of the charges, however, has been received to be filed, in the event that Gen. FREMONT himself shall neglect or decline to transmit the original document to the War Department.

Gen. WOOL, it is thought by those well-informed in military circles, will proceed to the West under specific instructions.

WESTERN DEPARTMENT QUARTERMASTER.

In response to a request of Gen. FREMONT for a Quartermaster for the Western Department, as Brig.-Gen. MCKINSTRY has taken the field, Major ROBERT ALLEN has been appointed to that position. He has the reputation of being one of the best officers of that kind in the employment of the Government.

GEN. SHERMAN TO HAVE COMMAND IN KENTUCKY.

It is further ascertained that Brig.-Gen. SHERMAN will be promoted to a Major Generalship, and will take command of the Department of Kentucky, the delicate state of Gen. ANDERSON'S health alone rendering this arrangement necessary.

TRAITORS IN MAINE.

Secretary SEWARD to-day addressed to the Governor of Maine the following letter:

DEPARTMENT OF STATE, WASHINGTON, Oct. 4, 1861.

GOVERNOR: Application has been made to the President for the release of ROBERT ELLIOTT, a political prisoner held in custody at Fort Lafayette.

The evidence taken in his case shows that he had not only conceived the purpose of treasonable coöperation in the State of Maine with the insurrectionary citizens arrayed in arms in other States for the overthrow of the Government and the Union, but that he had even gone to the extreme length of getting up an unlawful force to operate, in Maine, against the lawful action of the State and of the Federal Government. His associates in that treasonable enterprise since his arrest have taken an oath of allegiance to the United States.

The proceeding is very proper in itself, but the representations they make, that they and he were loyal to the Union at the time when they were combining in arms against it, cannot be accepted, at least, in his behalf. It appears that he is too intelligent to misunderstand the legitimate tendency of his criminal acts. He cannot be released. On the contrary, your vigilance in ferreting out the conspiracy, and in arresting it by denouncing it to the Government and the country, is deemed worthy of especial commendation.

If any of the other offenders are still persisting in their treasonable course, you will, I am sure, not fail to give information to this Department. I have the honor to be, very respectfully, your obedient,

(Signed) WM. H. SEWARD.

To His Excellency, ISRAEL WASHBURNE, Augusta, Me.

NO FEES FOR PASSPORTS.

It having been reported to the State Department that agents who are employed by individuals to procure passports are in the habit of exacting a fee from those for whom the passports are requested, alleging as a reason therefor that a fee is charged by the Department, notice is given that no fee has ever been charged by the Department for a passport; that such a charge is expressly forbidden by the act of Congress of the 18th of July, 1856, in regard to all passports, except those issued by the agents of the United States in a foreign country, and in the latter case the fee is limited to the sum of one dollar.

ACCOUNTS OF DECEASED SOLDIERS.

The Second Auditor of the Treasury has been instructed, in settling the accounts of deceased soldiers, to credit them with the one hundred dollars' bounty granted by Congress.

A DISHONEST QUARTERMASTER.

One of the leading Regular Army officers in the Quartermaster's Department has been found to be dishonest, and will be removed. This will make some stir among some contractors.

A large contract was given out for oats to-day at 48 cents per bushel.

NEWS FROM THE UPPER POTOMAC.

Information from Gen. BANKS' command has been received to-day, to the effect that the enemy in the vicinity of the Potomac seems to be continuing their retreat.

MORE SHOOTING AT DARNESTOWN.

A letter from Darnestown, Md., says about six o'clock last evening, just after parade, private SAML. D. MARTIN, of the Forty-sixth Pennsylvania Regiment, shot Col. SAML. D. KNIPE and his son, CHAS. D. D. KNIPE, with a revolver. Col. KNIPE was shot badly through the shoulder and right arm, and his son through the right hand. MARTIN is a half-brother to LANAHAN, the murderer of Maj. LEWIS, of the same regiment, and has exhibited bad blood to Col. KNIPE for some time.

MARTIN was immediately placed under arrest.

ALL QUIET ON THE LOWER POTOMAC.

An arrival from the Lower Potomac reports all quiet. During the fog on Wednesday morning the *Resolute* ran close under the batteries at Aquia Creek, and was fired upon with shells. No one was injured. The sound of drum and fife was heard continually on shore throughout Wednesday night, but the cause of it was not known.

NO MORE DEPREDATIONS.

All depredations by our troops on the other side of the Potomac have ceased, and both public and private property is respected.

DEPREDATIONS TO BE PUNISHED.

An army order has just been issued announcing that all depredations upon private property will be severely punished, that no remission of the death penalty for such outrages will be exercised, &c., and that the commanders of guards over such property will be held responsible as the principals.

STRICKEN FROM THE ROLLS.

The name of Capt. ALEXANDER W. REYNOLDS, Assistant Quartermaster in the regular Army, has been stricken from the rolls, for absenting himself from duty, and failing to report his name for duty.

MORE SHARP-SHOOTERS.

H. W. STOUGHTON, of Randolph, Vt., has been commissioned to raise an additional company of sharp-shooters, to be attached to BERDAN'S Regiment.

A BALLOON ASTRAY.

A mysterious balloon, with two men in it, passed over this city about 5 o'clock this afternoon, from west to east, at a great heighth. The sensationists have it that it was in the service of the traitors, and that it had C. S. A. conspicuously painted on its sides; others say, which is more probable, that it was one of Prof. LOWE'S, which had parted its fastenings and started off on its own hook.

NEW-JERSEY TROOPS REVIEWED.

The New-Jersey troops were reviewed this afternoon at their camp by Gen. MCCLELLAN and his Staff. Their appearance was very fine.

EXPENDITURES LESSENING.

Expenditures of the Government for military purposes are no longer increasing, but are greatly lessening.

MISCELLANEOUS NEWS.

The balloon used for observatory purposes broke its fastenings this afternoon, and took an easterly direction. Its loss will at once be replaced by another.

ALBERT L. MCGILTON, Lieutenant-Colonel of the Second Pennsylvania Regiment, was to-day elected Colonel of the Fourth Pennsylvania Reserve.

Major MORLEY, Superintendent of Military Railroads, has caused to be constructed a sidelong, or turn-off to the Loudon and Hampshire Railroad, near Falls Church, by which the transportation of supplies to the troops in that vicinity is greatly facilitated.

E. R. PENNINGTON, son of Gen. PENNINGTON, has been appointed Captain of the Twelfth Infantry.

J. H. GROVE, of Pennsylvania, and WM. CHAMBERS, of Illinois, have been appointed Brigade Surgeons.

Gen. MCCLELLAN has officially named the twenty-nine forts and three batteries in the vicinity of Washington.

Postmaster Gen. BLAIR left Washington this afternoon for Portsmouth, N. H., to bring home his family.

GREAT UNION MEETING AT WESTCHESTER, PENN.

LETTER OF EX-PRESIDENT BUCHANAN.

WESTCHESTER, PENN., Friday, Oct. 4.

At the great Union Meeting at Hayesville, Chester Co., on the 1st inst., the following letter from Ex-President BUCHANAN was read:

WHEATLAND, near Lancaster, Penn., Sept. 28, 1861.

DEAR SIR: I have been honored by your kind invitation as Chairman of the appropriate Committee to attend and address a Union Meeting of the citizens of Chester and Lancaster Counties, to be held at Hayesville on the 1st of October. This I should gladly accept, proceeding, as it does, from a much valued portion of my old Congressional district, but advancing years and the present state of my health render it impossible. You correctly estimate the deep interest I feel, in common with the citizens who will there be assembled, in the present condition of our country. This is, indeed, serious; but our recent military reverses so far from producing despondency in the minds of a loyal and powerful people, will only animate them to more mighty exertions in sustaining a war which has become inevitable by the assault of the Confederate States upon Port Sumter. For this reason, were it possible, waiving all other topics, I should confine myself to a solemn and earnest appeal to my countrymen, and especially those without families, to volunteer for the war, and join the many thousands of brave and patriotic volunteers who are already in the field. This is the moment for action—for prompt, energetic and united action—and not for the discussion of peace propositions. These we must know would be rejected by the States that have seceded, unless we should offer to recognize their independence, which is entirely out of the question.

Better counsels may hereafter prevail, when these people shall be convinced that the war is conducted, not for their conquest or subjugation, but solely for the purpose of bringing them back to their original position in the Union, without impairing in the slightest degree any of their constitutional rights.

Whilst, therefore, we shall cordially hail their return under our common glorious flag, and welcome them as brothers, yet, until that happy day shall arrive it will be our duty to support the President with all the men and means at the command of the country, in a vigorous and successful prosecution of the war. Yours, very respectfully,

(Signed,) JAMES BUCHANAN.

THE SITUATION IN MISSOURI.

Gen. Fremont's Position---His Action Contrasted with that of Gen. Lyon---Number of the National Forces---Movements of the Rebels, etc.

From Our Own Correspondent.

JEFFERSON CITY, Tuesday, Oct. 1, 1861.

Notwithstanding the very small attention with which Western operations are regarded, (unless a defeat occur,) this place is just now one possessing military elements of the greatest interest. Not only is it a point at which Gen. FREMONT is to demonstrate to an anxious public his fitness or unfitness for the tremendous responsibilities he has assumed, but it is also one at which are being created events and circumstances which ere long will decide the long-disputed question as to the fate of Missouri. Here are concentrating all the talent, the material, the energies, of the Department of the West—here are the actors rehearsing their parts preparatory to another drama, such as was shown at Springfield, Carthage, Booneville, Lexington.

One Thursday of some months ago, JACKSON issued his treasonable proclamation from this very place. Friday Gen. LYON drove him a fugitive from his Capital, and the next Monday dislodged him from Booneville and hunted him from the State. People who remember this are disposed to grumble as they reflect that two weeks have elapsed since the fall of Lexington—for two weeks has secession held high carnival over the spot rendered sacred by the gallant defence of MULLIGAN—for two weeks has it been permitted to rejoice, to fortify, to recover its breath—and as yet nothing more has been done than to transport an army to this point, which, in point of time and difficulty of travel, is not half way to Lexington. If two weeks are required to get a sufficient force to this point, how long will it take to get that same force over the balance of the route?

I believe that Gen. FREMONT is a hard worker; he labors incessantly to promote the cause in which he is engaged; he leaves nothing undone that can be done by personal effort, or advanced by personal sacrifice; yet, in spite of all this, things seem to advance with supernatural slowness. Never seemed there motions before, which looked so exactly like rest; but possibly, in view of the gigantic task before the National troops, it is well that nothing should be done hastily—that nothing should be adventured prematurely.

When one reviews the course of Gen. LYON—sees him routing secession from two distant and important points in less than a week—the rapidity of his march in the hottest months of Summer from Booneville to Springfield—the wind-like velocity with which he swooped upon Forsyth, Dug Springs and Curran—his omnipresence, his untiring vigilance, the facility with which he clapped an extinguisher upon every blaze of treason that broke out in or near the scene of his operations; when one remembers all this, he cannot but at least contrast the light, effectual movements of then, with the ponderous slowness of those of to-day. May it not be that Gen. FREMONT is too much embarrassed with the etiquette of war—with a cumbrous, unwieldly staff—with the panoply and externals of conflict? There may be use of private secretaries *of* private secretaries *of* private secretaries—of certain ceremonies, head-quarters approachable through a pathway lined by glittering swords, bands making the air sick in languishing with the stirring music of silver instruments, red tape formalities, and a thousand other similar things and operations; but yet their effect, although brilliant to friend and observer, is of doubtful utility upon the ragged Secessionists who hide themselves and their shot guns behind every bush in Northern Missouri.

If our foe was a polite one, his appreciation might be moved, his loyalty excited, by witnessing the gallant efforts made on his account, were he to see the magnificent trappings and caparisons, hear the beautiful music, watch the admirable evolutions. But, unfortunately, our Secession friend is an unkempt blackguard—wrapped in the contemplation of "treasons, stratagems and spoils." His soul has no appreciation for the beautiful music of Hungarian airs, poured upon the resonant and delighted air from costly silver instruments. Clad in a shirt innocent of soap and water, he appreciates not at all the gilded trappings of our gallant array; sneaking in the recesses of the dim woods, and coolly priming his old flint-lock rifle, he cares absolutely nothing for the gleam of beautiful muskets, the clank of heavy sabres, or the intricate deadliness of improved revolvers.

To him, LYON, with his old white hat, his stern countenance, his common every-day soldiers, was a dreaded reality—they feared him in life and respected him in death. One long roll from his battered old drums carried a more wholesome terror into the hearts of secession than will a thousand airs from Norma, born under the breath and manipulations of skillful Teutonic *artistes*. They knew he was never fettered by formalities, and only found courage to attack him when confident in the strength of an overwhelming force.

But it is to be hoped that ere long Gen. FREMONT will demonstrate that, in spite of all these apparent drawbacks, he is competent to the position he has undertaken to fill—and thus at once satisfy the earnest hopes of the country, and make good his own assertion to that effect.

The arrival of troops at this point is about the only event of importance. There are now here some ten thousand men, while probably from fifteen to twenty thousand more have gone forward, and are now located at Booneville, Glasgow, Georgetown, Lamine Bridge and Sedalia. This force is in all respects the flower of Western troops. It includes some 2,500 cavalry, a formidable force of rifled and other artillery, and infantry armed in many cases with COLT'S revolving rifles, sword bayonets, and other modern improvements. In addition to this, the material—the baggage, clothing, tents, &c.—is of a first-class character; rendering the present force in all respects one of the most efficient ever organized in the East or West. Whether the results to be accomplished will be important in proportion to this, is, of course, a question of time—one that will probably meet with solution some time within the next two or three weeks.

I have many doubts as to the efficiency of the organization now being constructed to war with secession. The troops of the enemy are all mounted—they move from point to point with incredible celerity. At the appearance of an equal or superior force, they scatter in a few hours in every direction, and in an equally short space of time concentrate at points miles away. Their agents extend to every point of the State—they know all our plans, and are able, at any moment, to hurl immense forces upon a point not sufficiently protected, but whose apparent remoteness from danger has been thought its security. Fighting under no rule, taking the ambuscade and shot-gun in preference to the open plain and the bayonet or cannon; Indians in attack, cavalry in retreat; present always when least expected, yet never found when hunted for, they are a peculiar, a subtle, dangerous foe, and one which requires different treatment from that of any other in the civilized world. Hence I permit myself to doubt the propriety of warring with them as we would with England or France. Columns of infantry and the heavy *impedimenta* of our troops cannot catch them unless they wish it; and they never wish it, unless satisfied that an immense superiority of numbers will give them an easy victory. To meet such men we want light cavalry, we want men that can travel as fast as they can, and who, when the moment for action comes, are equally ready to use their sabres as dragoons, or, dismounted, take to the trees and operate as infantry. We want light artillery, four and six pounders, and only such baggage as may readily be moved from point to point. When we have more of this force, we can reasonably begin to hope upon one that will be able to hunt out and cope successfully with these secession guerillas, that now mock our efforts to bring them to a fair battle.

A gunboat built at St. Louis and designed to proceed up the river and clear out the masked batteries supposed to be located this side of Lexington, has not arrived as far as here yet; and probably, owing to her immense weight and great draught, will be unable to ascend at all. The plan of making a ball-proof boat, and loading her with heavy artillery to clear the Missouri of batteries, was a capital one,—its only drawback is, that it can't be made practicable. She is yet in St. Louis, I believe, a model of immense strength and terrible destructive power; but at present is of no further use than to afford her friends the dubious satisfaction of thinking that she might do fearful execution if only able to get in the right position. However, if St. Louis be attacked, the *New Era* would be found to be of immense utility.

Yesterday all the commissioned officers who were captured at Lexington, with the exception of Col. MULLIGAN, reached this point under escort of Capt. CHAMPION, of the Confederate service. They left there the day after I did, and bring no later intelligence from that point than that contained in my last letter. Some of them state that Gen. PRICE unearthed from the fortifications several hundred bombs, which had been buried there by his predecessors in treason, of whose existence the National troops were ignorant.

Major TANNER died to-day of his wounds, and as I write, a military *cortège*, with reversed arms and step in accord with the movements of a solemn dirge, is passing my window to do honor to his remains.

A forward movement on the part of FREMONT, in the direction of Lexington, is talked of for to-morrow. The whereabouts of MCCULLOCH are still as mysterious as ever. I honestly believe him dead from the effects of a wound received at Springfield.

GALWAY.

LEXINGTON EVACUATED BY THE REBELS.

JEFFERSON CITY, Thursday, Oct. 3.

Gentlemen who have arrived this evening from Sedalia confirm the report of the evacuation of Lexington by the rebels, and also bring intelligence of the probable occupation of that place by Gen. STURGIS.

Major BAKER, of the Home Guards, who was among the prisoners taken at Lexington, and who refused to give his parole, escaped from the rebels on Monday night and arrived at Sedalia this morning. He says that all the Confederates left Lexington on Monday afternoon, and that their rear-guard, as it left, were fired upon with shell, by Gen. STURGIS, who just then appeared on the opposite side of the river. Several were wounded by the shells. When they first left Lexington, Major BAKER thinks it was the intention of Gen. PRICE to march direct on Georgetown, but information having been brought to him that Gen. SIEGEL was advancing with 40,000 men, he moved Westward towards Independence. Whether the main body of the rebels pursued this route any distance, Major BAKER is unaware, as during the confusion among the rebels upon the reception of the news of the large force of SIEGEL and the reported pursuit by STURGIS in the rear, he (BAKER) escaped.

Major BAKER thinks Gen. PRICE'S effective force will number about 25,000 men, in addition to which he has some 15,000 irregular troops, whose principal occupation is foraging; but this portion of the Army had pretty much left the main body before Major BAKER escaped.

Gen. SIEGEL, who is in command of our advance guard, had all his preparations made for an attack last night, and had the enemy made his appearance he would have met with a warm reception.

Our forces are mostly stationed at Otteville, Sedalia and Georgetown. The distance from Otteville to Sedalia is twelve miles, and from Sedalia to Georgetown four miles. We have also something of a force under Gen. POPE at Booneville, only twenty-five miles northeast of Sedalia.

THE REPORTED REMOVAL OF FREMONT.

ST. LOUIS, Thursday, Oct. 3.

The following dispatch, received here, to-day, will set the matter of Major-General FREMONT'S removal at rest:

WASHINGTON, Thursday, Oct. 3.

Gen. FREMONT is not ordered to Washington, nor from the field, nor is any court-martial ordered concerning him. (Signed,) WM. H. SEWARD.

ST. LOUIS, Thursday, Oct. 3.

The report in the afternoon dispatches of the removal of Major-Gen. FREMONT has created intense indignation among the mass of Unionists, and great rejoicing among the Secessionists.

The recruiting rendezvous for an Irish regiment was closed on the receipt of the news, and a meeting in the Second Ward this evening, for the formation of a Home Guard, adjourned without action.

A gentleman who visited Benton Barracks this afternoon, reports that the greatest excitement exists there among the troops, amounting almost to mutiny.

A mass meeting is called for Saturday, for an expression of opinion relative to the removal of Gen. FREMONT.

Gen. MCKINSTRY has been ordered to the Department of Cumberland, Kentucky.

A gentleman from Sarcoxie says that Judge CHENAULT had hung nine men for loyalty to the Union.

BAD STATE OF AFFAIRS IN MISSOURI.

NUMBERS OF THE REBELS—DANGER THAT THE NEXT BATTLE WILL BE LOST BY GEN. FREMONT.

Correspondence of the New-York Times.

CHICAGO, Tuesday, Oct. 1.

Rev. S. H. OLMSTEAD arrived here this morning from Platte City, Mo., which place he left about a week ago. He has been pastor of the Bapitst Churches at Booneville and Platte City, for five or six years past. He gives a very deplorable account of affairs in that section of the State. Since the surrender of Lexington, the Secessionists have become more bold and defiant, and many who have hitherto maintained a position of neutrality, have thrown off their disguise and gone to join PRICE and MCCULLOCH. All is anarchy and confusion and lawlessness, and everybody in that region has given up the idea of saving any property that is convertible or destructible. He looks upon the Union cause as lost for the present in Missouri, and anticipates that, should a battle occur, Gen. FREMONT will be beaten by the overwhelming force of the rebels. When he left, MCCULLOCH was understood to be within two days' march of Leavenworth, on his way to join his forces with those of PRICE.

Mr. OLMSTEAD is a Union man, and says that his life has not been safe for the past six months, on account of his having made Union speeches. But he made out to remain until after the surrender of MULLIGAN, when he was compelled to leave, almost destitute. He represents that the conduct of some of the officers of the National forces has tended to exasperate the people. He referred to Col. SMITH, of the Illinois volunteers, as having plundered the inhabitants in St. Joseph and the surrounding country to a shameful extent. About two weeks ago a band of Jayhawkers, in one of their marauding expeditions, met the scouts of Col. SMITH'S Regiment, and after a short fight, fled. The regiment pursued, and, on arriving opposite Platte City, planted its cannon, commenced firing upon the city with shell and round shot, without giving any notice. There was terrible consternation among the women and children, who fled from the town as rapidly as possible. Mr. OLMSTEAD placed his family in a carriage and drove seven miles into the country. On his return, the next day, he found his dwelling completely riddled with balls, his books strewn about, and everything of any value

[Continued on Eighth Page.]

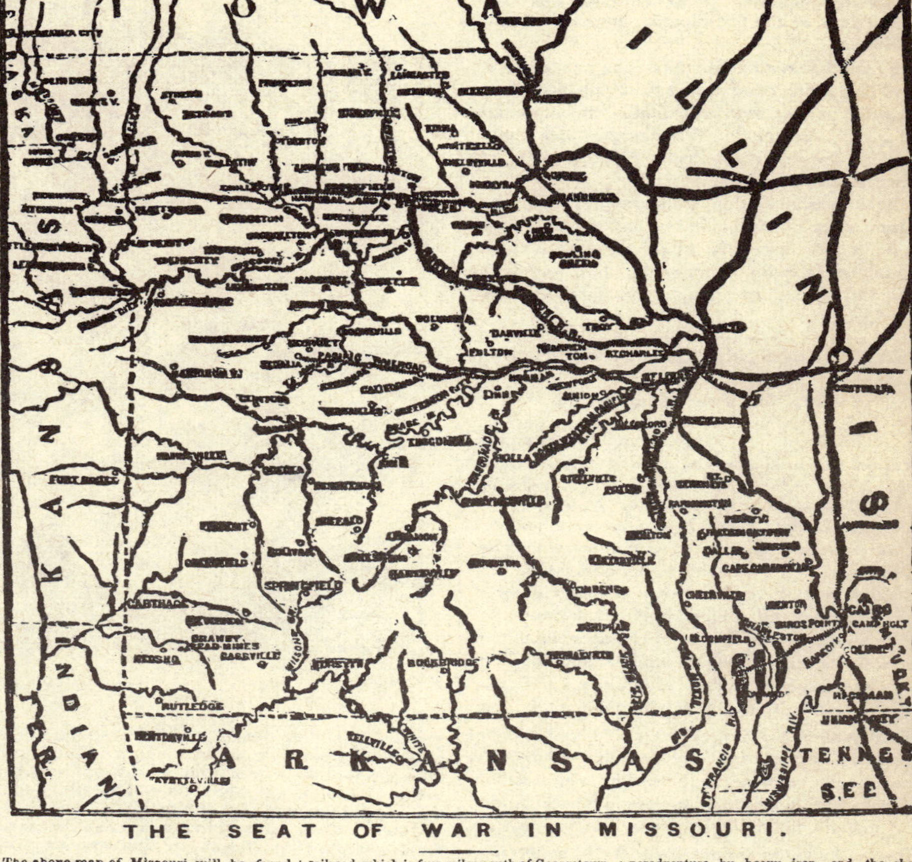

THE SEAT OF WAR IN MISSOURI.

The above map of Missouri will be found full of interest at the present moment, when all eyes are turned toward that State, in view of the extraordinary events occurring there. If a line be drawn from a point just back of Bird's Point, bearing northward and verging towards Cape Girardeau, then deflecting westward, passing a little south of Ironton, and continuing on in the same general direction between Rolla and Waynesville to Versailles; thence, circling around to the west of Sedalia and Georgetown, and turning sharply eastward to Arrow Rock; and thence taking both banks of the Missouri, westward to Kansas City, the northern limit of insurrectionary domination in Missouri will be very accurately described. All south and west of the line thus drawn is under subjection to the rebels, and it is nearly one-half of the territory of the State.

The head-quarters of Major-Gen. FREMONT are now removed to Jefferson City. He has concentrated nearly his whole force there, and is pushing his columns freely up the railroad to Syracuse, to the Lamine Bridge, to Otterville, a few miles beyond the Lamine, and to Sedalia, the terminus of the railroad, which is four miles south of Georgetown. He is supposed to have 15,000 men at these points. Gens. SIEGEL and DAVIS are in command at Sedalia of these advancing forces. There were a few Union troops stationed at Booneville, and at a point some distance above on the opposite side of the river, but we believe they have been withdrawn to join the columns advancing from Jefferson City towards Georgetown. There were about 5,000 troops at Rolla, where there is an immense amount of valuable stores. Three regiments of these men have been ordered to march overland towards Georgetown, a distance of full sixty miles, leaving Rolla quite weak—two regiments being a very small force to defend so much property.

Certain steamboats have gone up the Missouri River from Jefferson City with troops, destination not known. In addition to this, it should be known that the new gun-boat *New Era*, just completed at St. Louis, has gone up the Missouri, to aid the Army in its present advance. This vessel is shot and shell-proof. The engines, boilers and wheels are all protected beyond any peradventure by heavy iron, and the sharp-shooters (300 in number) and gunners aboard are in no danger from bullets from shore. She has several Dahlgren guns—84-pounders—in place, under bomb-proof decks, directed by experienced gunners, and it is expected that they will destroy with the greatest ease any obstacle within a distance of three miles. It is added that she can't be sunk, perforated, burned, nor blown up. If this boat shall reach Lexington, and break up PRICE'S control of the river, his situation will be much worse than it now seems. Gen. STURGIS was last reported on his return from Kansas City toward Jefferson. His whereabouts and Gen. LANE'S, we are not certain of.

Our Missouri letter, to-day, says that the troops now in the field, under FREMONT, are splendidly equipped, accompanied by unsurpassed artillery, and at least 2,500 cavalry.

Of Gen. PRICE'S position and purposes, we can know but little. He is believed to command fully 40,000 men—all at Lexington recently, and all his best generals around him. What will be his policy now, we can only conjecture. If he has evacuated Lexington and gone West, then he is safe again, and will elude capture.

The Charleston Mercury.

. . . Five Dollars per annum, payable . . . in advance.

—VINDICE NULLO
SPONTE SUA SINE LEGE FIDES RECTUMQUE COLENTUR.

COUNTRY PAPER—Thrice a Week—Five Dollars per annum, in advance.

VOLUME LXXIX. CHARLESTON, S. C., MONDAY, OCTOBER 21, 1861. NUMBER 11,285

When the Election for the President and Vice-President of the Confederate States shall take Place.

By the first section of "the Act to put in operation the Government under the Permanent Constitution of the Confederate States," the States are to appoint Electors for President and Vice-President, on the *first Wednesday in November*, eighteen hundred and sixty one.

By the second section, it is provided, that "the Electors for President and Vice-President shall meet in their respective States on the *first Wednesday in December*, eighteen hundred and sixty one, and proceed to vote for President and Vice-President.

THE SOUTHERN COMMERCIAL CONVENTION.

From Our Own Correspondent.

MACON, Ga., October 18.

What the Convention has Done—Direct Trade Resolutions Laid on the Table—Strange Position Taken by Gen. Duff Green—Discriminating Enactments too Dangerous to the North—Development of a New Political Element—A Renewal of Intercourse with the Yankees to be the Inducement for Peace, &c., &c.

The action of the Convention in regard to deciding against the propriety of an advance by Government to the planters; the opening of our ports free to the world's commerce, and allowing the exportation of Cotton in return for importations, has already reached you. But there was one important matter passed over, which requires the early, and earnest attention of the country. I mean the resolutions, proposing the needful preparatory Legislation to prevent our trade and finance falling again under the control of New York. These resolutions, I think, expressed the sentiment of the country, as they certainly did aim a deadly blow at the North, as appeared upon the debate. They were:—

1st. To place a discriminating duty of twenty per cent on all Foreign Goods imported into the Confederate States through or for account of Northern parties for a period of ten years.

2nd. To place a direct income tax upon all Northern Exchange or Bills payable there, for a similar period.

3rd. Recommending our Banks and Merchants, to make all our Cotton produce Bills, accepted payable in Europe, at least to the extent of our Foreign importations.

These resolutions were known as the "Direct Trade Resolutions," the friends of direct trade taking the position, that because of the artificial means employed in the late Union to direct our trade North, it became absolutely necessary for the South to aid Southern trade, by Legislative enactment, to break away from the restraint upon our commerce so long and so unjustly imposed by the United States Government. These resolutions were postponed in the Business Committee, and passed over from time to time until it was too late to debate them. They were however called for by the Convention in the last hours of its session, and would have passed but for the argument put forward by Gen. Duff Green as Chairman of the Business Committee, followed by a Parliamentary movement which cut off debate and laid them on the table.

The position taken by Gen. Green, was, that these resolutions were so fatal to Northern Commerce with the South, so destructive of all hope of New York ever again participating through the importation of our goods in our wealth, through the discount of our Cotton Bills and the control of our Exchanges, that to pass them would be to prolong the war. That the direct trade resolutions in fact would make any adjustment with the North impossible—and prevent any RECONSTRUCTION of the commercial and financial connections between the North and South. These views suddenly put forward, had great weight with the Convention. All debate being cut off by the nature of the motion with which Gen. Green closed the argument, the direct trade resolutions were tabled. The greatest excitement followed this unexpected debate. The direct trade men were only the more convinced of the importance of their measures from the fact, that their opponents considered them *too dangerous to the North*. They believed that the free trade resolution unless practicalized by direct trade, would not give to the South the full measure of commercial benefit desired. It was also contended for, and I think with great force, that one of the objects, if not the *paramount object* of the Convention was to indicate the necessary preparatory means, to prevent the North from ever again having any control over our trade. For one, I am free to confess, that the objections urged by Gen. Green were to my mind the very reason why the direct trade resolutions should have passed. The fact that they were so dangerous to the North, is the best evidence of their necessity to the South.

In order to allow the utmost harmony to prevail it was afterwards infomally agreed to suppress the exciting debate which flowed from this unexpected position of Gen. Green. But I understand that the direct trade resolutions will be taken up soon in another form and pressed upon the consideration of Government.

Outside of the interest to the mercantile community which these resolutions possess, a significant and important political element is developed by their defeat as above stated. There is no doubt, that the result was brought about by a powerful Georgia influence, and that parties in high position in the Government from this State, are opposed to disrupting by Legislation those commercial and financial ties which are only suspended, and which are to be preserved as an *inducement for peace* to the North, as well as a basis of adjustment of the terms of that peace. What the ultimate social and political result of such commercial and financial RECONSTRUCTION will be, is a matter of grave concern to the Southern people. As your correspondent give the simple facts. They are certainly significant and pregnant with great events hereafter.

Retreat of Federal troops after the fight at Ball's Bluff

Our Richmond Correspondence.

RICHMOND, October 17.

Squally Aspect of Things—We Continue to Fall Back—Results of the Defensive Policy—McClellan's and Lee—Postage Stamps at Last—Flags for Manassas—A Traitor in the War Office—Neglect of the Sick—Second Torriani Concert, etc., etc.

Things look squally enough this mild, hazy autumn morning. I find in them a sufficient cause for the sad aspect which the community and some of the Cabinet have presented for some time past. This, then, is the pass to which we have been brought by the purely defensive policy. Is Gen. LEE's West Point dogma, that "volunteers are worth nothing until all enthusiasm has been crushed out of them," substantiated? Is it also President Davis', and is he now satisfied? Whether Lee really asserted this, I know not; he is so accused; but one thing is very certain—if we go on as we are now going, there will soon be no enthusiasm either in the volunteers or in the people. There must be precious little of that noxious element remaining in troops who, for three months, have been doing nothing but dig dirt and fall back.

We do not apprehend a general engagement at Manassas. McClellan's idea is to drive us slowly and surely before him, and possibly (?) attack (?) us again at Bull Run on our front and upon both flanks. Hence the movement in the direction of Winchester, if, indeed, such a movement has been made, and the late reconnoissance by ships at Evansport. I shall not be at all surprised to hear, ere long, that our army has fallen back to Rappahannock Station, some twenty or thirty miles in rear of Manassas, and already fortified for our reception. So much for the defensive policy.

Joy! for Postage Stamps have come at last.—They are ornamented with the head of President Davis, printed in green ink.

An order from Manassas, for the making of twenty-five regimental flags of a peculiar description, has been received here, and our young ladies have gone hard to work at them. This circumstance excites considerable speculation. Before the battle of Manassas an enormous quantity of flannel was used in the making of wing-badges, which were thrown away after the battle of the 16th, because similar badges were seen on the shoulders of the enemy. Now we need flannel for underclothing. We wager that the pattern of these new flags has already reached New York; for the recent publication, in the *Herald*, of the names of the officers in the Confederate Army, shows conclusively that there is a traitor in the War Office.

The sick sent down from Manassas are oftentimes shamefully neglected. I heard, last night, of a young South Carolina invalid who was found in the act of going to bed on the grass in the Capitol Square. He was taken to a gentleman's house and kindly cared for. There seems to be no understanding between the authorities at Manassas and those in charge of the hospitals here. Southern people are kind and hospitable to a fault, but here there is a lack of forethought and system. The Executive will not remove incompetents.

The second Torriani Concert, given last night, was thinly attended. HERMES.

The Surprise of the Mississippi Blockaders.

The following graphic account of the late naval exploit of Com. HOLLINS at the Passes of the Mississippi, is taken from the New Orleans *Bee:*

Quietly and unsuspectingly the Lincoln ships were riding at anchor, and all on board of them, except the watch on deck, were in their bunks asleep, and perhaps dreaming of a victorious ascent to the Crescent City, and the booty and beauty they would find in its thoroughfares. It was fifteen minutes before four o'clock, the moon had set, and all was silence and darkness, when suddenly a cry of alarm went up from the deck of one ship, and it was answered from one to another, for they had discovered a long, low, black object skimming down the current that, from its very indistinctness, and shape unseen before, almost palsied them with fear.

THE MANASSAS.

It made straight for the broadside of one of the sloops of war, (reported by Com. Hollins to be the Preble) and ran into it with a tremendous concussion. One long, fearful shriek arose from the men on board, who had been only the preceding instant aroused from their sleep by the cries of the watch, and then the stricken vessel became the scene of terrible confusion, and her men ran up on deck, expecting to go to the bottom of the river every moment. Hardly had the officers of the other vessels had time to comprehend the nature of our attack when they perceived the gunboats steaming down the river toward them. The shock of the collision had been so great as to throw the engines of the Manassas off their centre and render her perfectly helpless. The solid live oak sides of the Preble had been cut into, but not torn to pieces, and the Manassas was thrown back by the rebound.

When she was some distance from the enemy her commander, Capt. Charles Austin, told the engineer to give her all the power she was capable of, and so much steam was crowded on, the gauge could not record it.

The vessels were lying up stream, and the one best seen from the Manassas was the Preble, so Capt. Austin steered her diagonally across the river, right for that ship's bow, striking her between the cat-head and the bowsprit, and cutting her right open.

The force of the concussion and the noise of the crash were tremendous, as the Manassas had been going at thirteen knots. Every one on board of her was knocked flat down. As soon as the engineer could regain his feet he backed the engines, and she drew off easily, but with whole sheets of the Preble's coppering and pieces of her wood sticking to the prow.

The consternation on board the Preble was extraordinary. Her officers and men seemed to be rushing about in every direction, shrieking and screaming. They were crying: "Fire! Murder! Oh! my God! The ship's afire! It's going to blow us up! We're lost!" and similar wild ejaculations. Some of them actually jumped overboard in their fright.

The Manassas recovered herself and Captain Austin saw that he was beside the Richmond with a fine chance to run into her amidships, and he again told the engineer to crowd on the steam. It was just then that the accident to her machinery was discovered, and one engine would not work at all.

At this moment the Richmond gave her a broadside, and immediately after the Vincennes gave her another. Most of the balls went over her, but some six or seven struck her, making slight indentations in her iron sheathing. Her flagstaff and chimney were shot away, and Capt. Austin and the engineer went up on top and cut away the wreck of the chimney.

She then made the best of her way from them, crippled as she was, and they fired several more broadsides at her without doing any more damage. She will be repaired and ready for service again by to-morrow morning, and Capt. Austin, who is delighted with her success, says he will guarantee to sink every vessel, from the Niagara to the Water Witch, that dares to enter the river again.

AFFRIGHT OF THE ENEMY.

The Richmond and Water Witch, having steam up, cut their cables and threw out hawsers to the Vincennes and Preble with all the haste that their fears pushed them to, while at the same time they fired their broadsides at the cause of their fright. But in their hurry, confusion and terror they fired wild, and only a few balls struck the Manassas, these doing her no harm. Our gunboats now came within range, and at once opened fire upon the vessels, and kept up an iron rain upon them all the time they were getting under way. It did not take the Lincolnites long to get off, however, and they started down the Southwest Pass with all the speed they were capable of. The McRae, Ivy and Tuscarora were close after them for awhile, and the firing was kept up uninterruptedly until half-past four o'clock.

Still the terror-stricken blockaders kept up their flight, and so great was their wild haste to reach the open gulf that they ran hard aground on the bar. The Preble, which had been settling steadily, despite the incessant working of all her pumps, now sank and creened over on her beam ends. Her men were taken off upon the other vessels. She is a total loss, although the enemy may succeed in saving her rigging and some other articles of value by wrecking her. Never more, however, can she float upon the water, or menace our coast.

THE FINAL CANNONADE.

At nine o'clock the McRae, Ivy and Tuscarora came up within range of the stranded vessels and opened fire upon them, hulling them several times, and doing some damage to their rigging.—But the enemy, although fast aground, had complete use of their guns, and in the broad light of day they could now see with what insignificant boats they had to contend against. They recovered from their panic when they found they could not run away, and replied to the peppering of our little craft with whole broadsides. For one hour this cannonading continued, and then Commodore Hollins withdrew his boats and quietly returned the way he came. His twelve or fourteen guns were no match for their forty, nor were his frail craft able to withstand shot as well as their staunch bulwarks. To have approached them too close would probably have cost him the boats that had cleared the river once, and might be needed to clear it again.

The New-York Times.

VOL. XI....NO. 3149. NEW-YORK, FRIDAY, OCTOBER 25, 1861. PRICE TWO CENTS.

THE GREAT REBELLION.

Highly Important News from Various Points.

Quiet Along the National Lines Across the Potomac.

Full Particulars of the Battle of Monday.

Approximate Estimate of the National Loss.

THE OBSEQUIES OF COL. BAKER.

The Rebel Steamer George Page Cruising on the Lower Potomac.

From the Mouth of the Mississippi and Fort Pickens.

EXPOSURE OF REBEL MENDACITY.

Hollins' Story of the Defeat of the National Fleet a Humbug.

The Rebels Terribly Whipped at Santa Rosa.

SPECIAL DISPATCH FROM WASHINGTON.

WASHINGTON, Thursday, Oct. 24.

THE NATIONAL LOSS ON MONDAY.

The official number of the killed, wounded and missing at the Leesburgh fight have been received. We had 79 killed and drowned, 141 wounded, and there are 193 missing. The missing may be prisoners or straggling.

THE RECENT REBEL MOVEMENT.

An evidence that the falling back of the Confederates at Fairfax Court-house, three weeks ago, was a sudden and unexpected movement, is furnished in the fact that they set up telegraph poles, and stretched the wires upon them, from Fairfax to Falls Church, and had only completed the work on the Thursday previous to the Sunday when our troops advanced. They removed the wire as they fell back, but had not time to remove the poles, which are still standing, ready for Government wires, when our troops shall make an advance.

NO CHANGE IN THE SITUATION.

Scouts who have penetrated from the centre of our lines to near Fairfax, report the same situation of the respective lines as yesterday.

A RECONNOISSANCE BEYOND VIENNA.

A reconnoissance in force, was made to-day from Gen. SMITH's Division, consisting of two companies of Col. FRIEDMAN's Cavalry, five companies of Infantry and two pieces of artillery. The result was the capture of eight rebels, fully uniformed, beyond Vienna, and further information obtained of the position and forces of the rebels in the neighborhood of Fairfax Court-house.

A VENTURESOME RECONNOISSANCE.

Major PALMER, of the Coast Survey, made a successful reconnoissance beyond Falls Church to-day, obtaining valuable information of the roads and topography of the country. Major PALMER had an escort of six cavalry. He was shot at four times, and what is remarkable, each of these four shots struck the same man and horse in the escort. One ball struck the horse, a second the saddle, a third the man, and a fourth the horse. None of them inflicted any serious wounds, the range being too long.

ABSURD AND FRIGHTFUL RUMORS.

The city has been filled to-day with the most absurd and frightful rumors. I was told to-day at WILLARD's by gentlemen who really believed what they said, that Gen. STONE had been drowned, Gen. BANKS taken prisoner, and that Gen. McCLELLAN had only escaped a similar fate by the most desperate riding. Then I was told that ten thousand men had crossed the Potomac at Mathias Point, and were marching up to take Baltimore. Of course there was no foundation for either of these stories, but yet they were generally believed. If some of them get in the papers I shall not be surprised.

THE FUNERAL OF COL. BAKER.

The funeral of Col. BAKER, to-day, was very largely attended, and was in all respects an imposing display. The body of the deceased lay in state in the main parlors of Col. WEBB's mansion. His uniform, as he wore it when he was killed, was examined by many curious spectators. The bullets had cut through the hat and coat, one ball going through his head just over the ear, and another going through the body from hip to hip. The body was escorted by the Pennsylvania Zouaves, and followed by the Thirty-sixth Pennsylvania and the Fourth Rhode Island, a detachment of his own regiment, his relatives, the President and his Cabinet, and a large number of distinguished citizens. Mrs. LINCOLN also united with her husband in paying this last tribute of respect to an old and valued friend.

The hearse was proceded by a detachment of twelve men from the California Regiment, selected from those who rescued the body of BAKER on the field from the enemy. They had previously carried the coffin from the house to the hearse, and at the Cemetery deposited it in the vault.

After the process of embalming has been completed, the body will be sent to California, and buried on Lone Mountain, near the grave of Senator BRODERICK. The Committee of citizens from the Pacific coast, now here, intrusted with the arrangements, consists of Senators LATHAM and McDOUGALL, Gen. DENVER, GEORGE N. WRIGHT, M. E. FLANAGAN, SAMUEL B. SMITH, of California, and GEORGE K. SHELL, E. M. BARNUM and CHARLES S. DREW, of Oregon, and WILLIAM H. WALLACE, of Washington Territory.

At the request of those charged with the arrangements for the funeral of Col. BAKER, Secretary SEWARD invited the Diplomatic Corps to be present. All except two accepted the invitation. Baron GEROLT, being indisposed, sent his regrets. Lord LYONS did not receive the notice in time to be present, but sent to the Secretary a note in which he pays a high tribute to the talent and courage of the deceased.

THE REBEL FIASCO AT NEW-ORLEANS.

The Navy Department has at last official advices from the fleet off the mouth of the Mississippi. Commander HOLLINS proves to have run away almost before he saw our ships, and to have put back with all speed to New-Orleans. We lost no vessel, nor did the rebels do any damage to any of them, or kill or wound a man. The rebel battering ram fouled with the *Richmond*, and the two were drifting down towards one of our vessels, which got out of the way. As soon as the ram and the *Richmond* could be separated, each turned tail and made a straight wake for a safe port. HOLLINS hardly saw one of our vessels.

THE REBEL STEAMER PAGE ON THE POTOMAC.

The *Star* of this evening has rumors that the rebel steamer *Page* has been seen crowded with men in the vicinity of Shipping Point, Evansport and Budd's Ferry, and that small boats have been crossing the river at those points, and that the *Page* ran near the Maryland shore, and fired shots at our troops stationed there.

Several oyster boats that have arrived to-day were fired at, but not injured, by the rebel batteries. They report that the rebels are unloading the *Fairfax*, and have possession of the schooners *Mary Virginia* and *Blossom*.

It is reported at Alexandria that the *Page* ran within two miles of the *Harriet Lane*.

EFFECTS OF CLOSING THE POTOMAC.

Since the closing of the Potomac by the rebels, the Baltimore and Ohio Railroad is necessarily making extensive arrangements for the largely increased business which it must do if the army of the Potomac remains much longer in its present position. Long sidlings have been put in at frequent intervals, in such a manner as to substantially answer the purpose of a double track. Switches have been laid in every direction from the dépôt, and storehouses built for the reception of freight. It became imperatively necessary that these arrangements should be made, and it will probably in a short time be a military necessity that the War Department shall resume possession of the line between this city and Baltimore and Annapolis, and so be able to control the running of trains and the transportation of supplies and munitions of war.

MERCHANTS ENTITLED TO THEIR PAY.

Provost Judge FREESE persists in his decision that New-York merchants are entitled to a *quid pro quo* for their goods. Messrs. CHAPMAN, LYON and NOYES, and J. T. MOORE, I believe, of the firm of C. W. & J. T. MOORE, Broadway, have secured goods in satisfaction of their claims. It seems that according to Judge FREESE's idea, it is only necessary for the claimant to show that he sold the goods, and that the purchaser is in Secesh and won't pay. One of the Alexandria merchants complained to the President of the decision, but was informed that the authority of the Provost Judge's Court was fully recognized.

NO MORE CONFLICT OF AUTHORITY.

The President has instructed the Deputy United States Marshal for this District to refuse to serve any writ of *habeas corpus* upon a military commander, and to inform the Judges of the District Court that in all matters pertaining to military affairs he has suspended the operation of the writ.

ANOTHER REGIMENT OF CAVALRY.

Col. FRIEDMAN was to-day authorized by the War Department to raise another regiment of cavalry, and a letter from the Assistant-Secretary of War was sent to Gov. CURTIN in furtherance of that object.

ARTILLERY TARGET PRACTICE.

This A. M., CARLISLE's United States, WEEDAN's Rhode Island, and FOLLETT's Massachusetts Batteries, were employed in target practice at short range from Minor's Hill. The firing was admirable, and that of the Volunteer Companies was highly creditable, notwithstanding the limited period of time since their organization.

A REVIEW TO TAKE PLACE.

There is to be a grand review of the troops in Gen. FITZ JOHN PORTER's division to-morrow afternoon.

VIRGINIA GETTING TIRED OF IT.

The Government has advices from Louisville that accounts received there from Virginia represent that the citizens of that State are becoming very tired of the presence of the rebel troops, and anxious that they should leave the State, even though it brings Virginia under the rule of the Union. The occupation has already impoverished the State of everything to be eaten or worn, or used in any shape. Between the masters who have sent their slaves South, and the slaves who have taken themselves North, there is no prospect were the South to succeed, that Virginia would have slaves enough within her borders to make it politic or profitable for her to maintain the institution. She is struggling literally for a shadow, and exhausting her strength in the effort to grasp what is constantly receding.

NOT ALLOWED TO PROCEED.

A few days since Mrs. KERRIGAN, wife of Col. JAMES E. KERRIGAN, of the New-York Twenty-fifth, now under arrest, went with another lady beyond our outposts into Secessia. The avowed purpose was to visit the house of the lady, but they were compelled to turn back without reaching there.

ARRESTED AS SPIES.

The Provost-Marshal of Alexandria has in his custody two mysterious gentlemen, arrested while prowling near Gen. HEINTZELMAN's outposts, under circumstances that led to a belief that they were spies. Failing to give a satisfactory account of themselves, and their physiognomies being decidedly against them, they were locked up.

ANOTHER ARREST.

PRESLEY HAYCOCK, a Virginian, residing north of Fall's Church, was taken into custody, to-day, on a charge of disloyalty. He has a brother in the rebel army, and another who is a prisoner in Washington. He refused to take the oath of allegiance, and is still held as a prisoner.

LIQUOR SELLERS FINED.

Two river skippers, who sold liquor to citizens of Alexandria, in evasion of the license laws, were arrested by Provost Marshal GRIFFITH's orders, and fined $5 each.

THE REBEL MAILS FROM RICHMOND.

It is alleged that even now there are letters and papers received regularly in Alexandria from Richmond and other points South. Doubtless the arrests of spies recently will make these mails less regular.

CONGRESSIONAL ELECTION IN ALEXANDRIA.

The election in Alexandria, to-day, for a member of Congress to represent the Seventh District, took place on the theory that there was no election on the 23d of May. Nearly all the votes were given for S. F. BEACH, who will be declared elected. Congress will, of course, decide upon the validity of the election.

THE UNION MOVEMENT IN ALEXANDRIA.

The Union movement in Alexandria is progressing. A Union flag-staff will be raised on Saturday.

RECRUITS FOR THE NINETEENTH NEW-YORK.

Major LEDLIE, of the New-York Nineteenth, returned to Washington this morning. He has been at home for some time recruiting three additional companies for the regiment. The regiment is also to have a battery attached, and when reorganized is expected to be one of the finest in the service. Major LEDLIE will probably be promoted in a few days to the rank of Colonel.

SANDERSON A BRIGADE COMMISSARY.

JAMES M. SANDERSON, the Caterer, has been appointed Commissary of Gen. WADSWORTH's Brigade.

ISAAC BELL, of your City, I notice this evening among the guests at Willard's.

THE BATTLE AT EDWARDS' FERRY.

FULL DESCRIPTION OF THE ENGAGEMENT.

Repulse of the Union Forces—Heavy Loss—Gallant Conduct of the Men.

LIST OF THE KILLED AND WOUNDED.

From Our Special Correspondent.

EDWARDS' FERRY, UPPER POTOMAC, Sunday—6 P. M.

The Union troops have commenced shelling the rebels on the Virginia shore across the river, whether merely to drive them out or as preliminary to an advance, we shall probably know in the morning. As I intend to make my letter, as far as possible, a journal from hour to hour of what actually takes place under my own observation, I shall not attempt to anticipate movements, but only record what I see and hear. The firing commenced at 4:35 this afternoon, from VAN ALLEN's Battery of two Parrott guns,—12-pounders,—the shells going well over to the Virginia side, to the north of Goose Creek. Their explosion is very distinctly heard. Seven shells have been thrown within ten minutes, without eliciting any response from our friends across the water. Gen. STONE is directing the movement. The tenth and eleventh shells fired were long range, the explosion not being heard for ten seconds. The next two exploded in five. The direction given to the shells is varied so as if possible to find out the location of the rebels, who are supposed to be concealed in a thick wood to the southwest, on the hill, and apparently a mile from the mouth of Goose Creek. The fourteenth sounded like a solid shot, and the three following shells, which made a loud explosion, brought no answering shot from the rebels.

At five minutes to 5 P. M. the battery in charge of Lieut. FRINK, situated in a field to the southeast and some quarter of a mile from the Ferry, also opened with shell, the two batteries keeping up the fire with rapidity, each missile exploding beautifully. Just as the sun is going down, the First Minnesota and Second New-York came down over the hill, and take the road to the Ferry. The sun sets gloriously, reflecting his rays from the thousands of bayonets which line the road. The firing is renewed again from both VAN ALLEN's and FRINK's Batteries. The troops are marching to the river with the intention either of crossing or of working a feint to do so, with a view of trying what effect the movement may have upon the enemy.

The air is perfectly still, and the close of this pleasant Sabbath is impressively calm and beautiful. The view of the Virginia hills from where I stand, near the battery, is almost enchanting. The echo of each report of our guns is heard from the opposite hills as distinctly as the report itself, and the explosion of each shell makes the third distinct report caused by each discharge. Something which resembles the sound of a drum-corps is distinctly heard from the Virginia side. The troops are drawn up along the bank in open order, and the order is now again passed along the lines to "Fall in." There goes a boat-load of troops across the river, which looks like a real movement.

The two companies, after landing, were recalled, but at 12 o'clock three regiments crossed over, encamping on the Virginia side. This was evidently designed as the opening of the campaign in Upper Virginia, and to-morrow, no doubt, the whole force encamped near here will be thrown over. There is every prospect of lively, I hope not of disastrous, times. The rebels will not do anything we wish them to. I now proceed to the camp near the Monocacy, to observe movements.

MONDAY MORNING.

The engagement has been renewed this morning. At daylight, portions of the Massachusetts Twentieth, Col. LEE, and the Massachusetts Fifteenth, Col. DEVENS, not over 300 in all, crossed over three-quarters of a mile below Conrad's Ferry. They crossed the island, which at this point is about 150 yards wide, and three miles in its extreme length. These two companies—viz., I and D, commanded respectively by Captains BARTLETT and CROWNINGSHIELD—met with no opposition on landing, and pushed on until they had reached the open space. This company (H, of the Fifteenth Regiment) went ahead as skirmishers, and were met in an open field by a company of 70 rebels, who fired the first volley, wounding ten and taking two prisoners. The company charged on them, and drove them back, but were in return driven back by a large cavalry force, besides a Mississippi rifle company.

This ended the contest for the morning; but a straggling fire was kept up on both sides until 1:30 P. M., when the rebels renewed the engagement with great fury. They attacked in front and on the right flank. At this time Gen. BAKER's Brigade was arriving. They consisted chiefly of the Philadelphia Zouaves, under command of Col. BAXTER.

Col. VAUGHAN, of the Rhode Island, had also arrived, and, with the greatest difficulty, succeeded in getting one of his six-pounder guns up the ascent, being obliged first to dismount the gun. This piece, with the two mountain howitzers belonging to the Twentieth Massachusetts, were all the heavy guns on the field. The fire was kept up from the right flank and front with great activity, the rebels raining a perfect storm of balls upon the Union forces. The Twentieth, although mostly raw recruits, stood the enemy's fire like veterans. They ran up to the brow of the hill, delivered their fire, and only fell back to reload and repeat. This continued until 5½ P. M., the Union forces maintaining their position steadily against the deadly, raking cross-fire from the front and left of the woods.

At this juncture Gen. BAKER, who had dismounted from his horse, and was advancing at the head of his command, coolly, but resolutely encouraging his men, received a ball through his head, killing him instantly. The General's blood bespattered Capt. CROWNINGSHIELD, who stood beside him at the moment. He never spoke. His body was immediately taken to the rear by his men, who freely wept at their loss. He was placed in a scow, and transported to the island, and thence to the Maryland shore. His remains were sent to Edwards' Ferry, and thence to Poolesville. His horse, which had been left standing, was afterwards shot. A small canvas satchell, containing his papers, I saw in the hands of a young man to whom they were delivered shortly before he fell.

This was the turning point of the battle. The rebels were five to one of the Union force, and the latter were finally ordered to leave the field. The retreat was made after the Bull Run pattern, with slight improvements, the men rolling, sliding, and almost turning summersaults down hill, to escape the galling fire which now assailed them from all points. The rebels were constantly reinforced, screaming like furies at each onset. Before retreating they threw the six-pounder down the hill into the river. The howitzers were left on the field, and fell into the enemy's hands.

The Fifteenth and Twentieth Massachusetts Regiments suffered very severely, losing a large part of their numbers in killed and wounded.

The Tammany Regiment covered itself with glory. Capt. O'MEARA often rallied his command, throwing defiance into the very teeth of the enemy, and showing the rebels that he could *scream* equal to the worst of them. Capt. O'MEARA took charge of the landing, and refused to let any but wounded men enter the boat, ordering the sound troops to go back and pepper the rebels. His conduct was very gallant throughout, evincing a true and lofty courage. Lieut. MESSER took command of the scow, and continued to ferry over the wounded, who poured down the hill. Several times the rebels fired upon him as he was crossing with the wounded men. The fourth boat-load was capsized, by the men rushing into it in too great numbers, and the whole party, about fifty in number, well and wounded, were precipitated into the stream. Ten of the party, at least, were drowned. A great many tried to swim the river, and sank from exhaustion. One half of those who are missing were drowned in this manner. It is not yet known how many of our men have fallen into their hands. *The destruction of life has been far greater, in proportion to the numbers engaged, than at Bull Run.*

The officers of Company A, Massachusetts Twentieth, are reported safe. Officers of Company C—Capt. DREHER wounded in the face. Lieut. WESSELHOEFT swam the river, but has not been seen.

Capt. CROWNINGSHIELD, of Company D, was slightly wounded in the arm, and has not reported. Lieut. PERRY has not reported. Neither has the Captain. Lieut. MESSER, same company, was exposed to great danger, the balls whistling all around him, but he escaped unhurt.

Of Company E three officers were wounded. Among the wounded of Company A is Lieut. HOLMES, who was shot in the breast. He is the son of OLIVER WENDELL HOLMES.

Capt. BADO, of Company G, swam the river with young WESSELHOEFT, but has not been seen.

Capt. PUTNAM, of Company H, lost his right arm, which was amputated at the old farm house on the island. He is doing pretty well.

Lieut. HALLOWELL, Company H, swam the river, and constructed a raft on which to transport the wounded from the Virginia shore.

Lieut. STURGIS is unhurt. Company I—officers all safe.

WILSON SIBLEY, Company G, Fifteenth Massachusetts, swam the stream, by advice of an officer who plunged in and went ahead. When they got half way across and in the strongest of the current, some twelve rebels fired at him. He saw their movement and dived at the flash, thus escaping their bullets. The officer was shot through the head, gave one loud outcry and sank to the bottom.

A young man who, a moment before, appealed to the Captain to help him, on seeing his friend shot, sank exhausted.

CHARLES HEAD, of Co. D, Fifteenth Massachusetts, says that when he was swimming across, he saw at least one hundred persons also making the same effort to escape from the tender mercies of the rebels. Among them he observed Col. BEVINS. There were many crying for "help," but he thinks not more than two-thirds reached the island in safety. He himself gave out when several rods from the shore, and sank to the bottom, but contrived to walk ashore.

I arrived at the ferry, and crossed over shortly after 3 o'clock P. M. Only three scows were in use, carrying say fifty men each, and occupying at least thirty minutes in getting each load over! I met wounded men returning in their comrades' arms, and bleeding from feet, legs, chest, head, arms, and every other description of wounds. I assisted in conveying them to a comfortable place in a large shed near the river, and proceeded toward the scene of action. Soon I reached an old farm-house, which was being used as an hospital. Groups of soldiers and persons not in uniform were crouching behind a corn-crib, built of logs, to shelter themselves from the bullets, which were now singing fearful music over our heads. The aim appeared to be at the house containing our wounded. In the yard, and covering its whole space, lay the wounded, dead and dying, in every stage of mutilation. The house contained two rooms, which were also full to repletion. Not a square foot of space remained unoccupied by the bleeding, wounded congregation. I took off my coat, and for half an hour rendered such assistance as an amateur surgeon could render. There was, as usual, a plentiful lack of surgical assistance, twenty poor fellows calling for aid, where only one or two could be attended to.

It was dark before the conflict closed, and I then recrossed the river and worked until this hour, (7 A. M. Tuesday morning,) in transporting the wounded in boats and litters to places of safety. I took my horse and rode to Edwards' Ferry, where I obtained a canal boat, in which a large quantity of hay was placed for the comfort of the wounded. I reached the Ferry, and by 2 o'clock this morning we had about forty poor wounded soldiers on board, and quietly proceeding to the Ferry. Some fifty wounded were taken to a barn half a mile from the line of the canal. A large number who could not be removed remained at the farm-house on the island, and multitudes were left dead and dying on the bank of the Old Dominion, their groans waking mournful echoes from the hills and woods. The officers have suffered severely. There is no way of ascertaining the actual number of casualties.

STATEMENT OF LIEUT. MESSER.

Lieut. MESSER, of Company D, Twentieth Massachusetts Regiment, who was among the first to gain a position on the Virginia side, about 4 o'clock A. M., gives me the following description of the localities. The landing, which was made in a batteau carrying only 28 men at a time, was upon a steep, clayey bank, ten feet high, very slippery. Having gained the top of this muddy bank, they struck a path which they followed to the left for about one hundred yards, when they filed right, went up over the hill, at an angle of 45 degrees, the top of which was some 100 feet above the river level. Here they came to an open space 150 yards wide and 200 long, which was surrounded on the right, left and front with a dense forest, in which the enemy were strongly posted, but entirely protected from view. In the rear was the steep hill which they had ascended. On the centre of the opening was a gully, and at the left a cow path; thus, with the river behind them, the troops fought desperately. To think of retreat was equivalent to death by bullet, by drowning, or of torture and imprisonment among the rebels. The fact that Gen. STONE was known to have crossed at Edwards' Ferry, with a strong force, (it was between three and four thousand men,) with the intention of attacking the rebels in the rear, gave them great courage. How dreadful must have been the suspense waiting—waiting with such fearful odds against them—fighting in momentary expectation that they should hear the roar of friendly cannon in the enemy's rear. The reason why the reinforcements did not arrive in time to coöperate is not yet explained. A story prevails here (at Edwards' Ferry, where I am now writing,) that our force yesterday lost four out of six pieces of artillery after crossing into Virginia. It is not generally credited here.

Gen. STONE sent an order late last evening to hold the island at any cost. The artillery and Harris Cavalry, in consequence, remained on the Canal line. It was generally believed that the rebels would shell us out of the island in the morning, if possible.

As I write, (7.30 A. M., Tuesday,) the rebels are firing from their side of the river. Possibly an engagement is now going on. The Sixteenth Indiana and Sixth Pennsylvania have just passed to cross the river. The firing increases, and affairs look like a general engagement to-day. We are where the rebels could reach us easily with shells. There is another camp of the Twentieth Massachusetts just arrived—Capt. JOHN SAUNDERS, of Salem. The space surrounding the ferry is now compact with men and horses.

PARTIAL LIST OF KILLED AND WOUNDED.

Brig.-Gen. E. D. Baker, killed.

Capt. Sloan, Fifteenth Massachusetts, wounded in foot.

Charles G. Snow, Company G, Fifteenth Massachusetts.

L. E. Ball, Company G, Fifteenh Massachusetts.

Sergt. John N. Davies, slightly.

Wm. Coles, California Regiment.

James Cranberger, killed—fell in his brother's arms.

Lieut.-Col. Ward, lost a leg; remaining on the Island.

Washington Carpenter Haskins, Rhode Island Third Battery, slightly.

Frank Graich, Company H, Fifteenth Massachusetts, arm.

John Pierce, arm.

Samuel T. Smith, Company C, Fifteenth Massachusetts, of West Boylton, hip.

Wm. A. Edson, Company A, Second Massachusetts, kidneys.

Thos. Dwyer, Company A, South Boston, thigh.

John Handy, Company H, Baker's Brigade.

Capt. Watson, Oxford, Mass., Company E, Twenty-fifth Massachusetts, shot while swimming the river.

Capt. Getchell, Blackstone, also shot in the river.

R. K. Cooper, Company C, Fifteenth Massachusetts, killed.

George Cutler, Lancaster, Mass., killed.

Wm. Lawrence, Litchfield, Mass., killed.

Sergeant John Merchant, Company A, Twentieth Massachusetts Regiment, killed.

Willis A. Cook, Company C, Fifteenth Massachusetts, killed.

A. L. Fuller, Company C, Clinton, Mass., killed.

Col. Lee, of the Massachusetts Twentieth, a prisoner.

A. H. Rice, Fifteenth Massachusetts, Company G; ball through hip, abdomen and arms.

Frank Elles, Company A, BAKER's California Regiment; wounded through arm—has the bullet in his pocket.

Wm. J. Holland, Company G; shot through hip.

Thomas A. Southwick, Company H, Fifteenth Massachusetts; wounded in knee and thigh.

Geo. W. Hobert, Company A, First California; ball through his back.

F. H. Marble, Company G, Fifteenth; two balls in shoulder and one in back. Laid eight hours in mud and rain before being discovered.

Henry H. Allen, Company A, California Regiment; shot in the thigh—flesh wound.

Wm. J. Cole, Company H, Fifteenth Massachusetts; left hip.

Lieut. Holmes, son of Oliver Wendell Holmes, wounded in breast.

Samuel Sibley, Company H, Fifteenth Massachusetts, bullet through each thigh and one in knee.

Henry A. Callar, Company H, Fifteenth Massachusetts, through lower part of the body.

Albert Stackpole, Company F, Twentieth Massachusetts, through shoulder.

The wounded were mostly sent down to Edwards' Ferry by canal boats, and were carried thence in ambulances to Poolesville.

A heavy northeast rain-storm has been prevailing for 18 hours, and the Potomac is rapidly rising. The difficulty of crossing will soon be greatly increased.

Half of the Fifteenth Massachusetts are reported to be killed, wounded, or missing. The Twentieth is nearly as badly broken up. I saw a member of the Twentieth Massachusetts to-day who had been over to the Virginia shore to look after our comrades. He was fired on, and compelled to leave. The condition of the wounded who came down to Edwards' Ferry this morning by a leaky canal-boat—the rain having wet many of them to the skin—was pitiable indeed. They are by this time safely in hospital.

The following are reported safe in the Massachusetts Fifteenth: Capt. G. C. Joslin, Lieut. Bartlett, Lieut. Corbin, Company I; Col. Deven, Major Keenboll. Lieut.-Col. Ward lost one leg—amputated at the house on the island.

I have no time for further details. E. S.

FURTHER REPORTS OF KILLED AND WOUNDED.

PHILADELPHIA, Thursday, Oct. 24.

Adjutant NEWLIN, of the California Regiment, is reported badly wounded.

Capt. HICKS, of Company P, California Regiment, is killed.

Capt. BERREL, of New-York, of Company G, California Regiment, is wounded.

LATEST REPORTS FROM UP THE RIVER.

APPROXIMATE ESTIMATE OF THE KILLED, WOUNDED, PRISONERS AND MISSING.

WASHINGTON, Thursday, Oct. 24.

Gen. McCLELLAN is now at his headquarters.

From the best data obtained from Harrison's Island up to late this evening, it is believed that the number of killed was 79; wounded in our possession and in possession of the enemy, 141; missing, now prisoners in the hands of the enemy, and wandering in the woods on both shores of the river, not exceeding 400; total loss in killed, wounded and missing, 620. This will be reduced by men returning to camp, as they are constantly coming in.

The officers and men behaved with the most extraordinary courage. They were pressed by an overpowering force, but stood firm until their whole supply of ammunition was exhausted, and then retreated to the river, and threw their guns and swords into the river, to prevent the enemy from getting possession of them. Col. RAYMOND LEE and Staff were furnished with a skiff to make their escape. The Colonel gallantly refused, and gave orders to use it for conveying the wounded across the river. It was filled with wounded, who reached the Maryland shore in safety, and the humane and gallant officer was taken prisoner. All credit is due to him.

Col. COGSWELL took command when Col. BAKER fell, and behaved with the greatest coolness and gallantry. He also is a prisoner.

Gen. McCLELLAN returns with renewed confidence in the action a efficiency of his soldiers. The conduct of Col. BAKER, in his effort to rescue the Massachusetts and other men under fire, was heroic beyond description.

WASHINGTON, Thursday, Oct. 24—10 P. M.

Col. OWENS, of the Second California Regiment, arrived here to-night, direct from Edwards' Ferry, and has related the following additional particulars in regard to the recent engagement:

The force was 1,730 on our side, and of the number killed, wounded and missing, 207 belonged to Col. BAKER's Regiment.

Capt. VAUGHN, who was sent over to bury the dead, reports that a large number of the rebels who were slain were carried away, while others were interred on the battle-field.

The impression is that their killed, so far, exceeded ours, owing to the efficiency of our artillery.

Lieut.-Col. WISTAR, who was wounded in the shoulder, arm and jaw, is considered out of danger.

Capt. MARKOE was wounded in the arm and taken prisoner.

Lieut. WILLIAMS, of Capt. PUTNAM's Company, was killed.

Col. OWENS further states that, immediately previous to the fall of Col. BAKER, the rebels made a flank movement to turn the latter's line.

Col. BAKER perceiving this, immediately wrote an order to be conveyed to the Tammany companies which had just arrived, and while the right was facing his command to meet the flank movement, and about giving orders to charge, he was killed, falling ten feet in advance of his column.

The field on which the battle was fought is circumscribed within an area of six acres.

Lieut. BRAMHALL, who was taken prisoner, reports that Col. HILTON, of the rebel army, was killed at the commencement of the engagement.

ANOTHER SKIRMISH ON TUESDAY.

The National Forces Withdrawn from the Virginia Side.

EDWARDS' FERRY, Wednesday, Oct. 23.

Yesterday Capt. VAUGHN, of the Rhode Island Battery, went over the river with a flag of truce, to recover some of the dead, and ascertain the fate of others. He was detained by the enemy, and had not returned at nightfall.

About 5 P. M., to-day, a rebel brigade was seen proceeding in the direction of Conrad's Ferry, and disappeared behind a wood, where it is stated there is an earthwork, mounting seven guns. The point is between the river and Leesburgh, two miles from the latter place, and about three miles from Edwards' Ferry.

It is supposed they are the same troops which attacked our pickets yesterday. About the same hour Gen. ABERCROMBIE sent word to headquarters that the enemy's force was advancing towards his position on the Virginia side from above and below, and asking for reinforcements. His command was seen drawn up in line of battle near the shore, and orders were issued to push over a strong force to his relief. Up to the present hour (10 P. M.) no attack has been made.

Five persons were arrested at Poolesville to-day, on a charge of being secession spies. They were examined and remanded to safe keeping.

The skirmish of yesterday was fought on our side exclusiuely by the independent corps of Andrew's Massachusetts Sharpshooters and Company K of the Nineteenth Massachusetts Regiment. The enemy's force consisted of one regiment each from Louisiana, Mississippi and Virginia. They attempted to flank our little force, but the terrible fire from the Sharpshooters—a rebel falling at each shot—and the firmness of Company K prevented the execution of their plan. The loss of the enemy was great, while only one of our men was killed. The skirmishers were aided by seveaal shots from our batteries on the Virginia shore.

EDWARDS' FERRY, Thursday, Oct. 24.

Yesterday on learning that a large force of the enemy were approaching and had arrived at two points, above and below, and in the immediate vicinity of the Ferry, it was judged advisable to withdraw the portion of our troops from the Virginia shore, both at Edwards' Ferry and Harrison's Island. This was rendered the more necessary from the high state of the water and the gale which made it a matter of impossibility to throw once a sufficient force to make our positions there perfectly secure against a general attack. The forces at Harrison's Island were removed first in the face of, and unmolested by a large body of, the enemy, who wisely, perhaps, forbore to make any demonstration. Gen. STONE commanded the Division opposite Edwards' Ferry, and removed them during the tempestuous storm in the night safely, and without any accident, he being among the last to leave the shore.

The numbers of the enemy are not known to outsiders, but it is inferred that they had between 13,000 and 30,000. Their positions were in dangerous proximity to the Ferry, and a night attack would have been disastrous to our small numbers there. This morning none of their encampments or troops are visible, except, perhaps, one occasionally passing along the road through the openings of the forest.

IMPORTANT FROM MISSOURI.

Ben McCulloch's Force Reported to be Cut to Pieces.

Defeat of the Rebels at Big Hurricane Creek.

ST. LOUIS, Thursday, Oct. 24.

Col. MORGAN, with 220 men of the Eighteenth Missouri, and two pieces of artillery, had a fight with some 400 rebels at Big Hurricane Creek, Carroll County, last Saturday, killing 14, taking eight prisoners, and putting the balance to flight.

Col. MORGAN had 14 wounded and two mortally.

It is believed at LaClede that the notorious MARTIN GREEN had deserted Gen. PRICE, and is trying to raise another band of outlaws in North Missouri.

The following is a special dispatch to the *Democrat* from Jefferson City:

Col. MAGRUDER arrived from Tipton to-night, and reports it is rumored and believed there that LANE and MONTGOMERY had intercepted BEN McCULLOCH, or some one assuming that name, in his attempt to join Gen. PRICE, and cut his whole army to pieces.

This report is also believed here.

We are reliably informed that about 500 rebels are congregated in and around Fulton, Calloway County, whose design is to seize some passing steamer or ferry for thmselves, and burn the Osage bridge, on the Pacific railroad. A formidable and vigilant guard will be maintained at the bridge.

Gen. FREMONT is said to have discovered 160,000 bushels of Corn buried at Warsaw, and delivered it over to the United States Paymaster.

IMPORTANT FROM KENTUCKY.

THE REBEL STRENGTH IN COLUMBUS.

CAIRO, Thursday, Oct. 24.

Col. BUFFORD and Capt. DREWER, of Gen. McCLERNAND's staff, accompanied by several other gentlemen, went to Columbus yesterday on the propeler *Sampson* for the purpose of exchanging prisoners. The party were cordially received by Gens. POLK and PILLOW, and 16 prisoners were released. The town is well fortified. A battery of eight 24-pounders is placed at the upper end of the town.

Two forts are being built about 1½ miles from the town, but no guns are mounted.

The number of rebels in Columbus is not over 10,000.

THE ELECTION IN WESTERN VIRGINIA.

WHEELING, Va., Thursday, Oct. 4.

The election for a division of the State, as ordered by the ordinance passed at the last Convention, came off throughout Western Virginia to-day. The vote in this city was not full, but overwhelmingly for "Division."

The reports from the interior, so far as received, show still greater unanimity for it. Thirty-nine Counties are included in the new State.

Messrs. LAMB, PAXTON and BATTELLE are elected delegates from this County to the Convention, which meets on the 26th of November to frame a Constitution.

[*Further Rebellion News see Second and Eighth Pages.*]

The New-York Times.

VOL. XI.....NO. 3154. NEW-YORK, THURSDAY, OCTOBER 31, 1861. PRICE TWO CENTS.

THE GREAT REBELLION.

Departure of the Naval Expedition from Fortress Monroe

Affairs Unchanged Along the Lines of the Potomac.

The Rebel Batteries Down the River Shelling the Maryland Shore.

PROGRESS OF THE WAR IN THE WEST.

FIGHTING IN NEW-MEXICO.

Four Hundred Rebels Dispersed in Missouri.

IMPORTANT FROM HAVANA.

The Rebel Commissioners Slidell and Mason Received with Distinction.

The Steamer Theodora Gone to Charleston Again.

SPECIAL DISPATCH FROM WASHINGTON.

WASHINGTON, Wednesday, Oct. 30.

NOT GOING INTO WINTER QUARTERS.

I think I have sufficient authority for explicitly denying the statement that the army of the Potomac would go into Winter quarters within the lines of the present encampment or intrenchments. No such purpose is entertained by the Government, and no such suggestion has been made by Gen. McClellan. Indeed, within the past forfnight the activity of preparation has been greater than within the same time for the last two months. Of course, an army is to remain in and around Washing to defend the Capitol, and doubtless we shall have a large camp of instruction. For the men and horses constituting this force, Winter barracks will be provided, and timely preparations are making for this; but beyond this there is nothing being done that looks like inaction during the Winter months.

NO NEW MOVEMENTS.

Since the rebels have ran away from Gen. McCall's division, there is nothing of interest to report, the movements and position of our own forces being contraband. Our scouts range the country round for ten to fifteen miles, but find nothing except the desolated tracks of the rebel hordes.

There is a report in circulation here that the rebels were firing on Banks' camp to-day, but there is no truth in it. All is quiet in his camp.

AFFAIRS ON THE LOWER POTOMAC.

The rebel batteries on the Potomac have been ineffectually playing upon our forces engaged in erecting counter batteries on the Maryland shore. The rebel steamer *Page* appears to be aground in Quantico Creek. She cannot escape without risking a few shots from our guns.

Two prisoners arrived at the Navy-Yard to-day, having been captured by our river force on suspicion of being spies. One was taken at Port Tobacco.

THE CONFLICT OF JURISDICTION.

Deputy-Marshal Phillips represented to the Circuit Court, to-day, that he did not serve the rule issued by that body on the 22d inst., to be served on Gen. Porter, Provost-Marshal for the District of Columbia, because he was ordered by the President of the United States not to serve the same, and to report to the Court that the privilege of the writ of *habeas corpus* has been suspended for the present, by order of the President, in regard to the soldiers of the army of the United States within this District. The Deputy-Marshal respectfully disclaims all intention to disobey or treat with disrespect the orders of the Court.

Chief-Justice Dunlop delivered an opinion to the Court, as follows:

Rule to show cause against Gen. Andrew Porter, Provost Marshal of the District of Columbia, why an attachment of contempt of court, issued against him for obstructing the process of this Court, and the administration of justice under it.

The return made by Deputy-Marshal Phillips, the 26th of October, we will order to be filed, though we do not doubt our power to regard it as insufficient in law, and to proceed against the officer who has made it. The existing condition of the country makes it plain that that officer is powerless against the vast military force of the Executive, subject to his will and order, as Commander-in-Chief of the army and navy of the United States.

Assuming the verity of the return, which has been made on oath, the case presented is without parallel in the judicial history of the United States, and involves the free action and efficiency of the Judges of this country. The President, charged by the Constitution to take care that the laws be executed, has seen fit to arrest the process of this Court, and to forbid the Deputy Marshal to execute it. It does not involve merely the question of the power of the Executive in civil war to suspend the great writ of freedom, the *habeas corpus*.

When this rule was ordered to give efficiency to that writ, no notice had been given by the President to the Courts or the country of such suspension here, now first announced to us, and it will hardly be maintained that the suspension could be retrospective. The rule in this case, therefore, whatever may be the President's power over the writ of *habeas corpus*, was lawfully ordered, as well as the writ on which it was founded. The facts on which the rule was ordered by the Court are assumed to be true, as respects the President, because the President had them before him, and has not denied them, but forbade the Deputy Marshal to serve the rule on Gen. Andrew Porter. The President, we think assumes the responsibilities of the acts of Gen. Porter, set forth in the rule, and sanctions them by his order to Deputy Marshal Phillips, not to serve the process on the Provost Marshal.

The issue ought to be and it is with the President, and we have no physical power to enforce the lawful process of this Court on his military subordinates. Against the President's prohibition we have exhausted every practicable remedy to uphold the lawful authority of this Court. It is, therefore, ordered this 30th day of October, that this opinion of the Court be filed by the Clerk and made part of the record, as explaining the grounds on which we now decide not to order any further proceedings in this case.

Associate Judge Marshall said: As a member of this Court and on its behalf I wish it understood that notwithstanding the blow leveled at this Court, I do distinctly assert the following principles:

First—That the law in this country knows no superior.

Second—That the supremacy of the civil authority over the military cannot be denied; that it has been established by the ablest jurists, and I believe recognized and respected by the great Father of the country during the Revolutionary war.

Third—That the Court ought to be respected by every one as the guardian of the personal liberty of the citizen in giving ready and effectual aid by that most valuable means, the writ of *habeas corpus*.

Fourth—I therefore respectfully protest against the right claimed to interrupt the proceedings in this case.

So the Judges of the Circuit Court here have decided that their edicts ought to be obeyed, and that if they had the power they would enforce them, but, "as the Court knows herself" that it cannot be done, the Judges content themselves with entering a protest against the military authorities, and Gen. Andrew Porter in particular, and directs that all further proceedings in the case be stopped. The Court is discreet, certainly, and it is probable that the sentinels will now be withdrawn from pacing up and down before the doors of the Judges.

THE GREAT EXPEDITION.

It is certain that no one outside of the naval expedition knows where the first blow will be struck. It is probable, however, that the earliest news concerning its operations will come through Southern channels.

THE STORY ABOUT CAPT. DUPONT'S CLERK.

The *Tribune's* story of the running away of Capt. Dupont's clerk grew out of what the boys call "a sell." Some wag innocently remarked that "the clerk had gone to parts unknown," with all the papers, orders, etc. Without stopping to think that he himself was ignorant of the destination of the fleet, the vigilant "special" at once informed the *Tribune* that the clerk had gone to secesh.

AFFAIRS IN ALEXANDRIA.

Gen. Montgomery, Military Governor of Alexandria, has issued an order forbidding the sale of liquor to soldiers in his District.

Provost-Marshal Griffith has been authorized by the Provost Court to seize a number of secession songs and pamplets, offered for sale by a bookseller of Alexander. Judge Freese says he will not permit the sale of any such documents, neither will he allow the utterance of secession sentiments in any shape.

I send you by mail a copy of the decision of Provost Judge Freese, of Alexandria, in the case of Bowen, Holmes & Co., of New-York, and Hallowell & Co., of Philadelphia, against Witmer & Co., of Alexandria. It is on this decision that an appeal is to be made to the President, and the opinion of Judge Freese is intended as a precedent to cover all civil cases of a similar nature. If the decision is sustained, it will equal in importance the *coup d'etat* of Gen. Butler as to the contrabands.

VALUE OF PROPERTY IN WASHINGTON.

I have before alluded to the enhanced rates of rents in Washington since the Army of Occupation came here. The effect has also been to raise the value of real estate. A gentleman showed me a piece of property to-day that last June would not have sold for twenty thousand dollars, that is now rated at fifty thousadd. Indeed, the owner will not not part with it at that price.

THE MILITARY EXAMINING BOARDS.

There are, at this time, in Heintzelman's and Franklin's divisions, two examining boards in full blast, and judging from the character and military reputation of their members, those gentlemen who have entered the service for pastime will discover, when too late, that they have mistaken their calling, or find their "occupation gone." The very names of the officers composing these Boards strike terror to aspiring military novices. In Heintzelman's Division they are Col. Pratt, Thirty-first New-York Volunteer Regiment; Col. Simpson, Second New-Jersey Regiment, U. S. A.; Col. Hawman, Thirty-seventh New-York Regiment, U. S. A. In Franklin's Division, Col. Ward, Thirty-eighth New-York Regiment; Col. Herbert, New-Jersey First Regiment; Col. Poe, Second Michigan Regiment, U. S. A. We sympathise with the victims who may come within their clutches.

A RARE PROMOTION.

Chas. A. Austin, of Massachusetts, has been promoted from an ordinary seaman to be master's mate. This is a most rare, if not the first occurrence of the kind, and will assure Jack that good conduct is sometimes rewarded with promotion.

A DEFAULTING OFFICER.

A Lieutenant-Colonel of a Massachusetts regiment has resigned his commission, and the resignatinn is accepted, when, unfortunately, he has borrowed several hundred dollars from the regimental fund.

UNIFORMS FOR THE ARMY CHAPLAINS.

The army Chaplains held a meeting this morning, at Trinity Church, in this city. The principal object appeared to be the concentration of their efforts so as to procure the passage of a law more clearly defining their position and rank, their relations to other officers, and the uniform they should wear. The law now prescribes that they shall have the pay of Captains of Cavalry, but does not designate their uniform. It was finally determined to present this matter to the President and the proper military authorities, through a Committee, and to agree upon what action it is necessary Congress shall take in order to remedy the evils complained of.

THE NUMBER OF THE SICK.

The weekly reports from the hospitals, show the following as the number of inmate for the week ending Oct. 25: On E-street, 80; Seminary, 120; Union, 163; Columbian, 231; Circle, 42; Alexandria, 134. Total, 820. This is a decrease since last week.

COL. EINSTEIN.

Col. Einstein has been mustered out of the service, and, indeed, mustered from Washington to Philadelphia.

NOTABILITIES.

Among the notabilities at Willard's to-day, I notice Gen. Butler, Wm. B. Thomas, Collector of Philadelphia, Hon. O. B. Matteson and Count Corwin.

SECRETARY SEWARD IN THE CAMPS.

Secretary Seward, and Assistant Secretary Seward, to-day visited the camps on the Virginia side.

SENATOR WILSON'S NEW POSITION.

Senator Wilson to-day entered the service, as a member of Gen. McClellan's Staff.

LEUTZE'S PICTURE IN THE ROTUNDA.

Leutze, the artist, has commenced painting the large picture for the vacant panel of the great rotunda. The subject is allegorical, typifying the advance of population Westward. The design was described last Spring, when it was first exhibited here. The sketch is very graphic and spirited.

SOLDIERS TO BE SHOT.

It is understood that Gen. McClellan has issued an order for the shooting of four soldiers found guilty of sleeping at their picket posts.

MISCELLANEOUS NEWS.

Some members of the Thirty-third New-York Regiment, owing to gross misconduct, to-day got into difficulty with citizens in the neighborhood of Lewinsville. Two of the former were severely injured. Gen. Hancock sent out a detachment and promptly placed the soldiers under arrest.

Col. Henry L. Scott, one of the Inspectors-General and son-in-law of Lieut.-Gen. Scott, has been retired by the Army Board, owing to his physical disability.

The Navy Department will take no notice of applications for places of masters or master's mates where the ages of the applicants are not stated, and references to the last employers given.

Capt. Henry B. Davidson, of the Tennessee First Cavalry, having left his regiment July 1st, on thirty days' leave, and having failed to report for duty, has been dropped from the rolls.

IMPORTANT FROM HAVANA.

Arrival There of the Rebel Commissioners to Europe.

THEIR ENTHUSIASTIC RECEPTION.

Return of the Theodora to Charleston.

The steamship *Columbia*, Capt. Adams, from Havana at 5 P. M. on the 25th inst., arrived here yesterday morning.

The *Columbia* encountered strong northerly gales, with a heavy head sea, during most of her passage.

The *Columbia* brings intelligence that the Confederate steamer *Theodore*, formerly the *Gordon*, a vessel of 518 tons burden, Capt. Lockwood, left Havana on Wednesday afternoon, the 23d inst., for Charleston, having been in port a week. She sailed from Charleston for Cardenas, where she landed Messrs. Slidell and Mason, Confederate States Commissioners for Europe, and afterwards proceeded to Havana—Messrs. Slidel and Mason taking the land route to Havana. The Commissioners were received with the highest consideration, from the Captain-General down.

The *Theodora* is supposed to have taken with her a large quantity of arms and provisions, such as coffee, &c. She was prescuted while there with a silk flag by Southern ladies. She took out with her about twenty passengers, including Mr. Meade, late United States Minister to Brazil.

Consul-Gen. Shufeldt telegraphed to the Commander of the steam-frigate *San Jacinto*, at Trinidad, on the 24th, to proceed at once to Havana.

The British Consul called on the Confederate Commissioners, in full uniform, and presented them to the Captain-General.

From the *Diario de la Marina* we learn that the *Theodora* arrived at Cardenas on the morning of the 17th October, with a view to ascertain if the two Envoys were in time to take the Spanish mail steamer to Cadiz. The steamer in question had, however, left on the 16th.

The *Theodora* cleared at Havana for Nassau, N. P., the British Consul giving the necessary papers.

The blockade seems to interfere very slightly with intercourse between Havana and the rebel ports. The British schooner *R. Burrows* reached Havana from Mobile on the 16th inst., with full files of Southern paper. The *Burrows* had of course run the blockade. A few days later the British brig *Maj. Barbour* performed the same feat at New-Orleans, reaching Havana in safety, bringing details of the Hollins victory.

The capture of the steamer *Salvor* by the *Keystone State* had caused much sensation at Havana.

Capt. Coxetter, late of the privateer *Jeff. Davis*, is in Havana. He came in the *Theodora*, and was left there for no good.

Things look quite warlike in Havana, a large vessel was in the harbor fitting out for Mexico.

From the Diario de la Marina, Oct. 18.

Yesterday, in the afternoon, the Confederate steamer *Teodora*, or *Theodore*, arrived at the port of Cardenas, having on board two distinguished persons from the South, sent by President Davis in the character of Ministers Plenipotentiary to the Governments of England and France.

The steamer in question sailed from the port of Charleston; but we are not aware why she has put into Cardenas. Certainly the mere fact that she brings two Ministers Plenipotentiary, *en route* to Europe, appears to indicate that some event has occurred of great importance in favor of the South. This is only conjecture on our part, but we do not believe it to be without foundation, and we would add that, in our opinion, these plenipotentiaries go to ask the recognition of the Confederation of the Southern States from the principal Powers of Europe. We expect shortly further advices in regard to this matter.

After the foregoing was written, we received the following dispatch from our Cardenas correspondent:

CARDENAS, Thursday, Oct. 17, 1861.

The steamer *Theodora*, from Charleston, brings the Envoys of the Confederate States near the Governments of England and France. The Envoys are Mr. Slidell, of New-Orleans, and Mr. Mason, of Virginia. They have touched at this port to learn if they can overtake the mail steamer for Cadiz.

From the Diario de la Marina, Oct. 19.

This morning, at 7 o'clock, the Confederate steamer *Theodora*, which arrived day before yesterday at Cardenas, entered our port. Mr. Slidell and Mr. Mason, the Commissioners from the South, have not arrived in her, but we understand will come by rail to this capital the day after to-morrow.

THE GREAT NAVAL EXPEDITION.

Its Departure on Tuesday Morning at Daylight.

THE FLEET SPOKEN OFF CAPE HENRY.

FORTRESS MONROE, Tuesday, Oct. 29, }
Via BALTIMORE, Wednesday, Oct. 30. }

The great fleet sailed this morning—the *Wabash* taking the lead at daylight, when the gun was fired as a signal, and the *Cahawba* bringing up the rear. The vessels, about fifty in number, formed in line a few miles down the Roads, and went out between the Capes in splendid style. The *Baltic* had the *Ocean Express* in tow, the *Vanderbilt* the *Great Republic*, and the *Illinois* the *Golden Eagle*. The morning was the most beautiful of the season, and the scene the finest ever witnessed on this continent.

There is no news from Old Point.

REPORT BY THE TRANSPORT THOMAS SWANN.

The United States steam transport *Thomas Swann*, Capt. Hamilton, from Baltimore forty-eight hours, and Fortress Monroe twenty-four hours, arrived yesterday morning. The sailing vessels of the United States fleet were under way Monday, at 5 P. M., and the steamers were getting under way when the *Thomas Swann* left.

On Monday, the 28th, at midnight, off Hog Island, she passed four steamers bound south.

PROGRESS OF THE FLEET.

Capt. Hamilton, of the United States steam transport *Thomas Swann*, reports on the 29th inst., off Cape Henry, passed twenty vessels belonging to the Naval Expedition, all under convoys. Spoke them, and they all reported that they were bound South.

THAT STARTLING REPORT.

The following card appears in the Philadelphia *North American*:

TO THE PUBLIC.

My brother-in-law, Alexander McKinley, a native and citizen of Philadelphia, and a member of its bar, is the private and confidential secretary of Flag-Officer Dupont. To this post of honor and confidence he was invited by Capt. Dupont, and he is now discharging his responsible duty on board the flag-ship *Wabash*. Private letters have been received from him to-day dated Oct. 27. The New-York *Tribune* of to-day, under its editorial head, has circulated a report which has been copied into the *Evening Bulletin* of this city, under the caption of "Startling Report," that "the private secretary of Commodore Dupont had absconded, carrying with him the maps and charts, and even the sealed orders of the Commodore." The natural effect of this rumor is that Mr. McKinley's name has been most unkindly referred to. I pronounce the whole story to be a vile calumny, and have, by the advice of counsel, taken measures to trace it to its source, meaning to hold strictly responsible all who contribute to the defamation of an innocent and absent man. J. W. FAIRES,
No. 245 South Thirteenth-street.
PHILADELPHIA, Oct. 29, 1861.

DIAGRAM OF THE BATTLE OF BALL'S BLUFF.

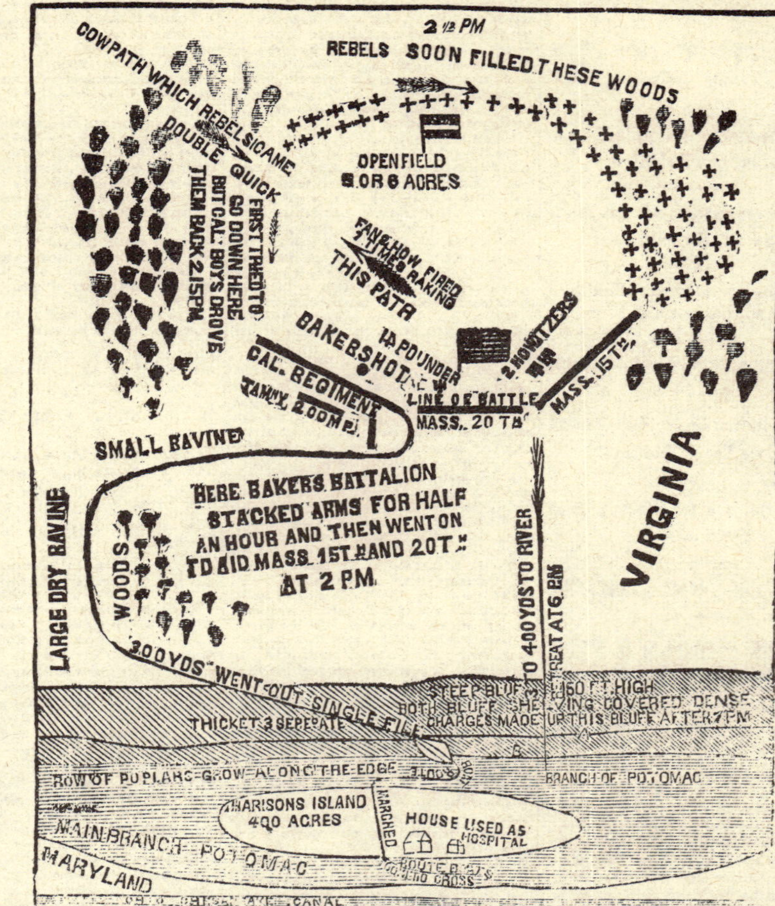

IMPORTANT FROM MISSOURI.

FOUR HUNDRED REBELS DISPERSED.

JEFFERSON CITY, Tuesday, Oct. 29.

A special dispatch to the St. Louis *Republican* says:

Gen. Prentiss, who left St. Louis on Monday last with a force of infantry to surprise and capture the rebels at Fulton, in Calloway County, has returned, and reports that before he reached Fulton, Gen. John R. Henderson, of the State Militia, had made a compromise with the rebels at Dyer's mills, near Concord, by which he agreed that the United States would not make any arrests if the rebels would lay down their arms and return to their homes.

Gen. Prentiss acquiesced in the compromise, but on the first violation of it will visit severe vengeance upon the offenders.

The rebels were 400 strong, and Gen. Henderson's force numbered 1,500. The proposition for compromise came from the rebels.

THE CONGRESSIONAL INVESTIGATING COMMITTEE.

ST. LOUIS, Wednesday, Oct. 30.

The Congressional Committee closed their labors last night. It is understood that they made a searching investigation into the alleged frauds and irregularities of the Government officers of this Military Department. The result of their examination will be made public in a few days.

IMPORTANT FROM MEXICO.

DEFEAT AND ROUT OF PARTIES OF REBELS.

KANSAS CITY, Tuesday, Oct. 19.

The Santa Fé mail furnishes the following interesting items:

"About the 4th inst. a party of New-Mexico volunteers, under Capt. Mink, was surprised at Alimosa, thirty-five miles bely Fort Craig, by 110 Texan rebels, and their horse stampeded. Capt. Mink proposed to surrender his company, but his men dissented, secured their horses and retreated to Fort Craig. Subsequently about one hundred United States troops, from Fort Craig, pursued the rebels, overtook them, killed their Captain and ten men, wounded about thirty, and killed thirty horses. The balance of the Texans escaped to Messella.

Another band of rebels who had been encamped on the Arkansas River were being pursued by a company of Confederate States dragoons, from Fort Wise, and a company of New-Mexicans.

THE TRIAL OF PIRATES AT PHILADELPHIA.

PHILADELPHIA, Wednesday, Oct. 30.

Eben Lane, the last of the *Jeff. Davis* pirates was acquitted on the ground that, being the navigator of the *Enchantress* after her capture, he must have delayed her progress, preventing her arrival at a rebel port; because, in sixteen days the vessel only made 250 miles. Lane alleges that he sailed the vessel North during the night and South during the day.

Thomas Quigley, David Mullens and Edward Rockford, were convicted of piracy last evening.

The schooner *Specie*, captured off Savannah, bound for Havana, has arrived at the Navy-yard.

DEPARTURE OF REBEL PRISONERS FOR BOSTON.

Yesterday evening, the rebel prisoners—numbering 900—who have been confined in Fort Lafayette, Fort Wood, and on Governor's Island, left on the steamer *State of Maine* for Boston, at which place they will be incarcerated in Fort Warren. A guard of 100 men, commanded by Capt. Updegraff, accompanied them, so as to make sure that none lose themselves on the way.

AFFAIRS ON THE UPPER POTOMAC.

THE LATE DISASTER.

A Full History of the Movement Across the Potomac, and the Disaster which Followed it—Where the Responsibility Belongs.

From Our Special Correspondent.

POOLESVILLE, Tuesday, Oct. 29, 1861.

It is now a week since the battle took place between the opposing forces which met this side of Leesburgh. During that time many versions of the affair have been given, all more or less incorrect, and the country has been balancing between the blame which certain correspondents insist should fall upon Gen. Stone and the unbounded praise which the same parties lavish upon the late Col. Baker. I have prepared, from official documents—the same from which Gen. Stone has made up his report—the following statement, which embraces every movement, every order and every result up to the time when Gen. Banks assumed the command and the general retreat was ordered. Before giving that statement, I will remark that the order said to have been found upon the person of Col. Baker, signed Stone, and ordering him to go on to Leesburgh, is a forgery. Gen. Stone is not Napoleon and does not sign his dispatches Stone, nor does he address Colonels as Generals, nor does he write ungrammatical orders. I have his word for it, that the document is a forgery.

It seems that on the 20th instant, Gen. Stone, having been advised of the movement of Gen. McCall to Darnestown, determined to make a demonstration to draw out the intentions of the enemy at Leesburgh. Consequently he proceeded, at 1 P. M., to Edwards' Ferry, from this point, with Gorman's Brigade, the Seventh Michigan Volunteers, two troops of the Van Alen Cavalry and the Putnam Rangers, sending at the same time to Harrison's Island and vicinity four companies of the Fifteenth Massachusetts Volunteers, under Col. Devens, (who had already one company on the island,) and Col. Lee, with a battalion of the Twentieth Massachusetts. And to Conrad's Ferry, a section of Vaughn's Rhode Island Battery and the Tammany Regiment, under Col. Coggswell. A section of Bunting's Y. Y. S. M. Battery, under Lieut. Bramhall, was at the time on duty at Conrad's Ferry, and Rickett's Battery, already posted at Edwards' Ferry, under Col. Woodruff.

The movement of Gen. McCall, on the day previous, seems to have attracted the attention of the enemy, as just previous to the arrival of Gen. Stone at Edwards' Ferry, a regiment of infantry had appeared from the direction of Leesburgh, and taken shelter behind a wooded hill near Goose Creek, 1¼ miles from the position of the Union troops at the ferry. Gen. Stone ordered Gen. Gorman to display his forces in view of the enemy, which was done, without inducing any movement on their part, and then ordered three flat boats to be passed from the canal into the river, at the same time throwing shell and spherical shot into and beyond the wood where the enemy were concealed, and into all cover from which fire could be opened on boats crossing the river, to produce an impression that a crossing was to be made. Orders were also sent to Col. Devens, at Harrison's Island, some four miles up the river to detach Capt. Philbrick and twenty men to cross from the island and explore by a path through woods little used, in the direction of Leesburgh, to see if he could find anything concerning the enemy's position in that direction; but to retire and report on discovering any of the enemy. The launching of the boats and shelling at Edwards' Ferry caused a rapid retiring of the force which had been seen there, and Gen. Stone caused the embarkation of three boat-loads of thirty-five men each, from the First Minnesota, who, under cover of the shelling, crossed and recrossed the river, the boats consuming in crossing from three to seven minutes. The spirit displayed by officers and men at the thought of crossing the river was most cheering, and satisfied the General that they could be depended on for most gallant service, whenever more than demonstration might be required of them.

As darkness came on Gen. Stone ordered Gorman's Brigade and the Seventh Michigan to fall back to their respective camps, but retained the Tammany Regiment, the companies of the Fifteenth Massachusetts and artillery near Conrad's Ferry, in their position, waiting the result of Capt. Philbrick's scout, he (Stone) remaining with his Staff at Edwards' Ferry. About 4 P. M., Lieut. Howe, Quartermaster of the Fifteenth Massachusetts, reported to Gen. Stone that Capt. Philbrick had returned to the island after proceeding unmolested to within a mile and a half of Leesburgh, and that he had there discovered, in the edge of a wood, an encampment of about thirty tents which he approached to within twenty-five rods without being challenged, the camp having no pickets out any distance in the direction of the river. Gen. Stone at once sent orders to Col. Devens to cross four companies of his regiment to the Virginia shore, and march silently, under the cover of night, to the position of the camp referred to, to attack and destroy it at daybreak, pursue the enemy lodged there as far as would be prudent with the small force, and return rapidly to the island, his return to be covered by a company of the Massachusetts Twentieth, which was directed to be posted on a bluff directly over the landing place. Col. Devens was ordered to use this opportunity to observe the approaches to Leesburgh and the position and force of the enemy in the vicinity, and in case he found no enemy, or found him only weak and in a position where he could observe well and be secure until his party could be strengthened sufficiently to make a valuable reconnoissance, which should safely ascertain the position and force of the enemy, to hold on and report. Orders were dispatched to Col. Baker to send the First California Regiment to Conrad's Ferry, to arrive there at sunrise, and to have the remainder of his brigade in a state of readiness to move after an early breakfast. Also to Lieut.-Col. Ward, of the Fifteenth Massachusetts, to move with a battalion of a regiment to the river bank opposite Harrison's Island, to arrive there by daybreak. Col. Devens, in pursuance of his orders, crossed the river and proceeded to a point indicated by a scouting party, Col. Lee remaining on the bluff with 100 men to cover his return.

In order to distract attention from Col. Devens' movement, and at the same time to effect reconnoissance in the direction of Leesburgh from Edwards' Ferry, Gen. Stone ordered Gen. Gorman to throw across the river, at that point, two companies of First Minnesota, under cover of fire from Rickett's Battery, and sent a party of thirty-one Van Alen Cavalry, under command of Maj. Mix, accompanied by Capt. Chas. Stewart, Assistant Adjutant-General; Capt. Murphy, Lieuts. Pierce and Gouraud, with orders to advance along Leesburgh road until they should come to the vicinity of the battery, which was known to be on that road, and then turn to the left and examine the heights between that and Goose Creek, see if any of the enemy were posted in that vicinity, ascertain as nearly as possible their number and disposition, examine the country with reference to the passage of troops to the Leesburgh and Georgetown turnpike, and return rapidly to cover behind the skirmishers of the First Minnesota.

This reconnoissance was most gallantly made by all in the party, which proceeded along the Leesburgh road nearly three miles from the ferry, and when near the position of a hidden battery came suddenly on a Mississippi regiment about thirty-five yards distant, received its fire and returned it with their pistols. The fire of the enemy killed one horse, but Lieut. Gouraud, the gallant Adjutant of the Cavalry Battalion, seized the dismounted man, and drawing him on his horse behind him carried him safely from the field. One private of the Fourth Virginia Cavalry was brought off by the party, and as he was well mounted and armed his mount replaced the one lost by the fire of the enemy. Meantime Col. Devens on the right, having in pursuance of his orders arrived at the position indicated by the scouts as the site of the enemy's camp, found that the scouts had been deceived by the uncertain light, and had mistaken the openings in the trees for a row of tents. He found, however, wood in which he concealed his force from view and proceeded to examine the space between that and Leesburgh, sending back word to Gen. Stone that thus far he could see no enemy. Immediately on receipt of this intelligence, which was carried by Lieut. Howe, Quartermaster of the Fifteenth Massachusetts, Gen. Stone ordered a non-commissioned officer and ten cavalry to join Col. Devens, for the purpose of scouring the country near him while he continued his reconnoissance, and to give him due notice of the approach of any enemy, and that Lieut.-Col. Ward, with his battalion of the Fifteenth Massachusetts, should move on to Smart's Mill, half a mile to the right of the crossing-place of Cols. Devens and Lee, where, in strong position, he could watch and protect the flank of Col. Devens on his return, and secure a second crossing-place more favorable than the first, and connected by a good road with Leesburgh. Capt. Candy, Assistant Adjutant-General in Gen. Lander's Staff, served on Gen. Stone's Staff during the day, and accompanied the cavalry.

For some reason never explained at headquarters, neither of those orders were carried out. The caval-

[Continued on Eighth Page.]

The New-York Times.

VOL. XI....NO. 3150. NEW-YORK, SUNDAY, OCTOBER 27, 1861. PRICE THREE CENTS.

THE GREAT REBELLION.

Affairs in the Vicinity of Washington.

Grand Review of Gen. Fitz John Porter's Division.

Heintzelman's Pickets Advancing Down the Potomac.

The Excelsior Brigade Occupying the Opposite Side.

Critical Situation of the Rebel Steamer Page.

Her Retreat to Aquia Creek Cut Off.

Further Particulars of the Battle Near Leesburgh.

Official Report of the Santa Rosa Fight.

Demoralization of the Rebel Forces in Missouri.

SPECIAL DISPATCH FROM WASHINGTON.

WASHINGTON, Saturday, Oct. 26.

The grand review of Gen. FITZ JOHN PORTER'S Division took place to-day near Hall's Hill, and for a meteorological wonder, it did not rain. Many distinguished citizens and ladies from different parts of the country were present to witness the spectacle. Besides Generals MCCLELLAN and FITZ JOHN PORTER, and their respective Staffs, Generals McDowell, Morrell, Martindale, Butterfield, Barry, Stoneman, Keys and Burns, and Colonels Pickel and Averill, with their respective Staffs, and other well known military commandants, were present and participated in the review. The Prince DE JOINVILLE and Dr. RUSSELL, of the London *Times*, were in prominent positions near Gen. MCCLELLAN.

At 10½ o'clock the brigades were formed in lines. At 11 o'clock the firing of the artillery announced the arrival of Gen. MCCLELLAN and Staff upon the field, accompanied by Gen. PORTER. They rode in front of the lines, from right to left. This being concluded, the troops—infantry, artillery and cavalry—passed in marching review before Gen. MCCLELLAN, the bands, in turn, performing the national and other inspiring airs. The marching was repeated in double-quick time, and this feature added much to the spirit of the occasion. The brigades then formed columns of grand divisions in close order, then deployed into lines, changed fronts, and afterwards fired by files, companies and battalions.

The review was the finest that has yet taken place. The troops were in admirable condition and drill, and as the division has prided itself on its being the most perfect, each regiment, in a spirit of emulation, tried to excel the others. The marching was admirable, and in the evolutions in line the troops exhibited a wonderful promptness and mobility. The firing, too, was such as to secure the commendation of all present. Besides the perfection of the troops, it may be appropriately stated that Gen. FITZ JOHN PORTER, in addition to his qualities as General, is the best-looking man in the service.

AFFAIRS ALONG THE LINES.

Everything has been quiet to-day along the centre of our lines. There is nothing of interest on our right wing, towards Prospect Hill. The military telegraph reports that the rebels make no demonstration near Conrad's or Edwards' Ferries.

All the troops of the right wing will have a grand review, near Maj.-Gen. MCCALL'S headquarters, on Tuesday morning, at which the President and Cabinet, Gen. MCCLELLAN and Staff, and others, will be present.

SCOUTING AT FLINT HILL.

A scout sent out by Gen. WADSWORTH, early this morning, reached Flint Hill. from which point he had an excellent view of the situation about Fairfax Court-house. No rebel troops were visible, though considerable smoke was rising from a piece of woods back of Fairfax and between it and Germantown. Later, he saw a dozen rebel cavalry approaching, and after coming within a half mile of Flint Hill they wheeled to the left and ascended to a hill half a mile northwest, where he discovered a body of infantry, numbering about sixty, which he had not previously noticed. He then returned to our lines.

THE LOWER POTOMAC—PRECARIOUS POSITION OF THE PAGE.

The steamer *Reliance* came up from the flotilla last night, bringing up Capt. Fox, Assistant Secretary of the Navy, and at 1 o'clock she left the Navy-yard to rejoin the flotilla.

It is reported that the ice boat, which has a fine battery of four guns, and another steamer run up past the Matthias Point battery in the night, and that they are now between the rebel steamer *Page* and Aquia Creek, with the *Yankee* and *Resolute* lying at Stump Neck, opposite Cockpit Point, and the other steamers below Evansport. The *Page* is in rather a critical situation. She was lying near the captured schooner *Fairfax* yesterday evening, and was supposed to be aground.

On board the flotilla at Indian Head heavy firing was heard yesterday afternoon in a southeasterly direction.

Two schooners, bound up with stores, ran the blockade the night before last without receiving a shot.

The Assistant Secretary of the Navy, Mr. FOX, returned from the Lower Potomac to-day, and denies that there are any permanent batteries at Mathias Point. The Reliance, which brought Mr. Fox up, has returned to the flotilla.

A vessel arrived at Alexandria to-day, having been boarded by the rebel steamer *Page*, and allowed to pass up on the assumption that Alexandria is in the Confederate States.

ADVANCING DOWN THE POTOMAC.

Gen. HEINTZELMAN is quietly advancing his pickets along the southern side of the Potomac, while SICKLES goes down on the northern side.

ORDER RELATING TO THE SUBSISTENCE, ETC., OF VOLUNTEERS.

The following order was issued to-day from the Adjutant-General's Office:

First—United States and Disbursing officers will supply subsistence to and subsequent to muster for all volunteer organizations raised under proper authority' whether originally granted by the Governors of the loyal States or directly by the War Department Subsistence prior to muster will be paid from the appropriation for collecting, drilling and organizing volunteers, and subsequent thereto from the appropriation for the subsistence of the army.

Requisitions for funds for the former expenditures will be made upon the Adjutant-General, and for the latter upon the Commissary General of Subsistence.

Accounts for expenditures under the first head will be rendered to the Adjutant-General, and under the second, to the Commissary General of Subsistence.

Second—The attention of officers supplying subsistence to volunteers in process of organization into companies and regiments, both prior to and subsequent to muster, is called to the exorbitant prices demanded and paid.

Rations in kind will hereafter be issued wherever cooking facilities can be furnished to the troops, whether in squads or larger bodies.

If the rations cannot be contracted for at a reasonable rate, subsistence will be procured in bulk and issued to the volunteers.

In no case should the cost of the rations uncooked exceed nineteen cents, and at most of the points in the Western States it should not exceed fourteen cents.

When cooking facilities cannot be furnished, contracts for the rations cooked may be made at reasonable rates, and the necessity for the same must be clearly stated in the accounts.

When board and lodging are necessary, the price for each soldier should be stated, and the aggregate cost of both must not exceed forty cents per day.

Third—No bands for volunteer regiments will in future be mustered into the service, and vacancies that may hereafter occur will not be filled. All members of the bands now in service, not musicians, will be discharged upon the receipt of this order, by their respective regimental commanders.

THE CONFLICT OF AUTHORITY.

In the Circuit Court this morning the Judges asked the Clerk if there had been any return to the writ issued against Gen. PORTER, the Provost Marshal.

The Clerk answered: "There was none."

District Attorney CARRINGTON, in behalf of Deputy Marshal PHILLIPS, presented a paper with an affidavit of Mr. PHILLIPS, stating that the writ had not been served, because he had been ordered by the President not to serve it, and because the privilege of the writ of *habeas corpus* had been suspended for the present, by the order of the President, in regard to soldiers in the army of the United States, within the District of Columbia.

Mr. CARRINGTON offered to submit an argument to the Court in behalf of Marshal PHILLIPS, but the Court announced that it did not propose to take any steps against him.

As the return presented a rare question, the Court desired to hold it under advisement, and an adjournment was made until Wednesday morning next.

THE DIPLOMATS AND COL. BAKER'S FUNERAL.

While Lord LYONS was prevented by an accidental circumstance from receiving the invitation to attend the funeral of Col. BAKER in time to avail himself of it, the French Minister similarly excused himself to the Secretary of State, and the Envoy from Prussia says his absence on that occasion was caused by indisposition, for which he expresses his regret.

TO HAVE A BRIGADE.

It is understood that Col. LANSING, of the New-York Seventeenth Volunteers, is to be assigned the command of a brigade. It is a good selection.

APPOINTED A CAPTAIN.

JOSEPH RUPERT PAXTON, of Philadelphia, has been appointed a Captain in the Fifteenth Regular Infantry. Mr. PAXTON recently received, also, the appointment of Consul to Bahia, Brazil, but in view of the greater honor now offered him, he will, it is presumed, decline that office.

BRIGADE MARCHING.

Gen. WADSWORTH'S Brigade is daily being marched from six to eight miles, with musket, knapsack, blanket, overcoat, haversack and canteen, to accustom the men to the fatigues of moving in heavy marching order. Yesterday they marched from TAYLOR'S, up the Leesburgh Pike, to a point three miles distant, and then countermarched to their quarters. The men bear the exercise well, and are daily becoming more able to endure the fatigue of a heavy march.

REBEL REMINISCENCES.

The houses occupied by the rebel troops, when they were posted nearest our lines, are found to be defaced by all sorts of rude inscriptions. They are, in the main, the names of the regiments and companies quartered there, imprecations not very chaste against the Yankees and the "Lincoln Government," rude figures, &c., &c. The walls of UPTON'S and FEBRY'S houses, which are the headquarters respectively of Gens. WADSWORTH and KEYES' Brigades, are thus defaced, and from it the visitor learns that companies from the Second Louisiana, the Second Georgia, Seventh Virginia and First Maryland Regiments had been present near there on picket. A rude picture of a man hanging on a gallows, has written under it "Abraham the First." A rebel flag is represented, on which is a scroll containing the words "Death before Dishonor—Death before Defeat." The full muster-roll of the Independent Grays, First Maryland Regiment, is written in pencil on the wall. Ninety-one names are recorded, beginning with Capt JAMES M. HERBERT, and followed by the Lieutenants, GEORGE R. BOOTH, WM. K. HOWARD, and NICHOLAS SNOWDEN. Among the privates are the names of JAMES E. HOWARD and CHARLES HOWARD, following each other, and included in a brace, opposite which is written, "Sons of CHARLES HOWARD, Police Commissioner in Fort Lafayette." There is also inscribed after the name of the company, the following: "Sept. 10th, arrived here. It is now the 17th. Fighting every day at long range between our sentinels and the Yankees; killed one day before yesterday." Some rhyming rebel has given vent to his feelings in the following sensible statement and self-evident proposition:

"I will eat when I'm hungry,
I will drink when I'm dry;
If the Yankees don't kill me
I will live till I die."

THE MISSES SCOTT REDIVIVUS.

The residence of the Misses SCOTT, about three-quarters of a mile west of Falls Church, is again within our lines. The young ladies profess to be loyal, and they strenuously deny the charge of being a party to the capture of Capt. KELLOGG of the Connecticut Regiment. They say that his arrest was effected without their contrivance or design, and that the Captain's over-gallantry in insisting upon accompanying them home against their caution and wish, placed him within the power of the rebel pickets, who saw his approach, and hence he was caught. The household consists of Mrs. SCOTT, her two daughters, and some negroes.

LIEUT. ROSS, OF THE ANDERSON ZOUAVES, KILLED.

As the train from Baltimore to this city, due here at 5:30 Friday evening, was nearing this city, a person was seen on the track by the engineer but not in sufficient time to enable him to stop the engine before the unfortunate man was struck by the cow-catcher, thrown from the track and severely injured. The train was stopped as soon as possible, and the man was picked up in a state of insensibility, and placed in as comfortable a position on the train as circumstances would allow. Dr. JONES, Assistant Surgeon of the navy, happened to be on the train, and rendered such assistance as could be rendered in the case. On the arrival of the train in Washington, the injured man was transferred to the Army Infirmary, near the City Hall, and, on examination, showed he had received a serious fracture of the pelvis and other injuries, from which he died in the course of two hours. The papers found upon his person indicated him to be W. R. ROSS, First Lieutenant in the Anderson Zouaves. How he came to be walking on the track at the time is not known.

VISIT TO THE CAMPS.

Yesterday Judge HARRIS and Secretary CAMERON visited several camps in Virginia—among them that of the Ira Harris Cavalry.

FORT ELLSWORTH COMPLETED.

President LINCOLN was to have viewed Fort Ellsworth as completed to-day, but was detained in Washington on business. Commander WAINWRIGHT is in command, with four hundred seamen, to man the guns. The battery in the vicinity is under the command of Lieut. ALLEN and eighty seamen. Both positions are considered impregnable.

SECESSIONIST MARYLANDERS CAUGHT.

A good story is told of a stratagem invented by a detachment of one of Gen. SICKLES' regiments, to decoy some Marylanders, who were suspected of being secession spies. Inducements were held out to the suspected persons to proceed at a given time to the Virginia shore, to join the rebel forces At the appointed time, instead of finding means of transportation, the rebels found a squad of Union troops, who quietly caged them.

BEEF WANTED.

The Commissary's Department advertises for 12,000 head of beef cattle, to be delivered as follows: 4,000 at Washington, on or before the 20th of November; 4,000 at Harrisburgh, by the 30th of November; 4,000 at York, Chambersburgh, or Harrisburgh, on or before the 30th day of January. Proposals are to be presented on or before the 15th day of November at 12 o'clock.

A SOLDIER'S FUNERAL.

The funeral of Private ABRAHAM RUSSELL, of Company F, Third Maine Regiment, took place in Alexandria to-day.

Corporal PHILIP CASEY, of the Thirtieth (Troy) Regiment, died yesterday in camp.

AN ALEXANDRIAN WOMAN ARRESTED.

One of the so-called ladies of Alexandria was to-day taken to the Provost Marshal's office, and publicly reprimanded for insulting a Union officer.

IMPORTANT FROM MISSOURI.

DEMORALIZATION OF JEFF. THOMPSON'S REBEL COMMAND.

PILOT KNOB, Mo., Saturday, Oct. 26.

Col. PLUMMER has returned with his command to Cape Girardeau. Col. CARLIN now occupies Fredericktown, with a regiment of infantry, a squadron of cavalry, and two pieces of artillery. THOMPSON and his rebel band were pursued twenty-two miles beyond Fredericktown, on the Greenville road, when the chase was abandoned. The rebels are probably now at Greenville. but they are completely demoralized, and will doubtless continue their retreat. The detachment sent out to bury the dead after the battle, reported near two hundred of the rebels killed and left on the field. Our loss was six killed and about forty wounded, one mortally.

FROM FORTRESS MONROE.

FORTRESS MONROE, Friday, Oct. 25, via BALTIMORE, Saturday, Oct. 26.

Nothing new has occurred in the vicinity of Old Point.

The *Cambridge* is in from the blockade off Beaufort, and reports that the *Albatross* lost two men, drowned, in a fruitless attempt to land men south of Beaufort.

AFFAIRS IN BALTIMORE.

THE BALTIMORE AND OHIO RAILROAD—MILITARY MOVEMENTS—DURYEE'S ZOUAVES UNDER MARCHING ORDERS, ETC.

BALTIMORE, Friday, Oct. 25, 1861.

A short time since the Baltimore and Ohio Railroad Company, were notified by Government, that in case an effectual closing of navigation in the Potomac river should occur, a necessarily increased demand would be made upon the Washington Branch Road, for the transportation of army supplies. That event has taken place; but the Railroad Company having exercised the utmost diligence in accumulating freight cars at this terminus of the road, Government is not likely to be embarrassed much from the insufficiency of supplies, which was to be apprehended by such an event.

The Company have a good road, with single track, running from Locust Point to a junction with their main road in this city, and the transports, steamers, and other vessels, loading with stores and supplies at New-York and other places, have been ordered to this port to discharge at Locust Point, and the freight transported from thence to Washington by railroad. The transports began to arrive to-day, and the Company feel confident they can now supply any demand likely to be made upon them for freights.

Quite an important movement has been made in the troops hitherto quartered in this city—two or three regiments having departed for Washington. The Duryee Zouaves, who have so long occupied Federal Hill, are under marching orders, and will probably leave in a day or two—leaving behind them an enduring monument of their skill and industry, in the large and efficient fort which now incloses the brow of the hill.

The Seventh Maine Regiment, who have also for some weeks past been engaged in fortifying Potter's Hill, in the eastern part of the city, took their departure this afternoon for Washington, lamenting the death of the Colonel, THOMAS H. MARSHAL, which occurred this morning at a private residence in this city. His death was occasioned by a severe attack of typhoid fever. His wife was with him during his sickness, and was present at his death. An escort of the regiment remained to convey his remains back to his home in Maine. The command is now under Lieut.-Col. SELDEN CONNOR. The death of their commander, who was universally beloved, spread a heavy gloom over the regiment. The Third New-York Regiment came up from Fort McHenry this afternoon, and proceeded at once to Washington. The city is all astir to-day with moving regiments.

Yesterday pilots were put on board the fleet comprising the great naval expedition at Fortress Monroe. It is conjectured that the fleet is not destined to a very distant point, as the provisions placed on board are not sufficient for a lengthy expedition.

ARGUS.

IMPORTANT FROM THE UPPER POTOMAC

Full Particulars of the Disaster of Monday.

Additional Lists of the Killed and Wounded.

The Fearful Odds Against the National Forces.

How Col. Baker was Killed, and Who Killed Him.

SCENES AND INCIDENTS OF THE BATTLE.

From Our Special Correspondent.

POOLESVILLE, Thursday, Oct. 24, 1861.

I have already sent you a hurried account of the battle of Monday, and some of its incidents. From the statement of those engaged with the enemy, and from personal observation, I am enabled now to furnish you additional particulars of the highest interest.

Company G, California Regiment, Capt. LOUIS BIERAL, crossed at Conrad's Ferry about 2 P. M., taking the route by Conrad's Ferry. They left camp at daylight, but were obstructed in the march along the canal. The only transports were two scows, capable of carrying forty men each. It took two loads of all these boats, occupying about an hour to get over. The shore where the landing was made was a heavy clay' and the rise of the hill very rocky. There was no regular path.

Capt. BIERAL led his Company into action at 2½ P. M. His position was in the centre of the opening. The enemy were strongly posted in the woods, which in front were very dense. He posted his color guard ten paces in front of the line, and opened upon the enemy in the thicket.

A perfect shower of balls rained from the invisible enemy, whose position could only be known by the smoke of their guns. Their aim was low, striking our boys in their feet and legs. The men made good use of GRIFFIN'S six and twelve-pounder howitzers, which were placed on the right, and kept up the fire briskly. The original party in charge of the guns was shot away, and Company G, with the assistance of Col. WISTAR and Col. COGSWELL, placed the heaviest gun in position. This was 4 o'clock P. M.

After the fight had progressed some time, Gen. BAKER became evidently convinced that it was a hopeless contest, and addressing Quartermaster YOUNG' who was acting as his Aid, asked him if there was any means to recross the river, beside the boats on which they had come over. Mr. YOUNG replied, "There is nothing." The General answered, "Then let us do all we can, and die bravely." Addressing the men he said, "I will not ask you to go where I do not lead." Three cheers greeted the General's remark. He stood with his right hand in the breast of his coat, and was continually in front of his command. He said, "Fire low, boys, and fire steady, keep cool, and don't get excited."

A large force of the enemy were discovered advancing upon a double-quick through an open lane at the left of the ground, when the gun was wheeled in that direction, and fired. As the smoke of the gun blew away, a wide opening was observed in the enemy's ranks. They then made a charge from the front, and the enemy were again driven into their covert, after they had advanced to within five feet of our colors.

The firing from the right had now nearly ceased—only an occasional stray shot from persons posted in the trees to pick off the officers. At this juncture, a person, wearing a gray jacket and blue pants, appeared, riding a dark brown horse, and beckoned with his hand to the Union forces, saying, "We are friends; come this way, boys." Firing instantly ceased for two minutes, Gen. BAKER and the Assistant Adjutant-General saying, "Cease firing; you are shooting your own men." The next moment Gen. BAKER said, "Soldiers, there is JOHNSTON on the left; give them a volley."

By this time the enemy had flanked us on the left. The Adjutant-General inquired "Who are you," addressing his inquiry to the flanking party. He was answered, "We are Confederates, you Yankee sons of b——s." This confusion arose from the fact that Gen. BAKER had posted Company A as a skirmishing party on the left. The order was then given to charge, and the Unionists pressed into the woods on the left, but they met an overpowering force and fell back.

A very tall man now stepped from behind a tree, and, with a revolver, fired at Gen. BAKER, within five feet of his person. Six discharges were made, and nearly all the balls entered the General's body. He fell on his back, partly against a tree, and died instantly. The rebel who had shot the General then sprang forward, and was in the act of taking his body or stripping off his sword, when Capt. BIERAL ran forward, placed his revolver at his ear and shot him dead.

A heavy volley of musketry followed, which drove the boys back. Acting-Adjutant HARVEY said, "Soldiers, who will volunteer to rescue the General's body?" Capt. BIERAL answered the summons, and was followed by Sergt. JAMES CLARK, Lieut. JOHN MURRAY, private STEEHAN and a half dozen others. They raised him up, and bore him from the field. Three or four of the rescuing party were shot in the act and fell, but succeeded in taking the General's body safely across the river.

Capt. BIERAL resumed command of his company, and the fight went on half an hour, when the firing ceased. Capt. BIERAL spoke an encouraging word to the color-bearer, and as Company D had lost their officers, and had no one to lead them, he offered to take command. They followed into the edge of the woods, charging with the bayonet. A strong reinforcement of the enemy, however, arrived at this moment, and drove them back, and they retreated in good order down the hill. Every wounded man was removed from the field, and the commanders were the last to leave.

The retreating soldiers met a boat-load of about 40 men coming over the river, but seeing that the day was lost, they hesitated to land, although they had nearly reached the shore. Some of the party waded in and jumped on board the already heavily-loaded scow, which was capsized about twenty feet from the shore.

A shower of bullets was coming down the hill, and their muskets had already been thrown overboard. Those who could swim struck out for the island shore whilst the more timid endeavored to swim back. The larger proportion of the boat's company, however, are believed to have sank at once. Those who remained on the shore were taken prisoners immediately. Among them were Adj.-Gen. HARVEY and, as is supposed, Col. COGSWELL, of the Tammany Regiment.

Capt. BIERAL was now concealed some 200 yards to the left, and witnessed the firing of the rebels upon his retreating men—many of whom were shot while swimming, and sank to the bottom. He remained there nearly half an hour, in company with the Color-bearer, and Corporal JAMES BLACK, of Company G. They then swam across. Just as they landed, Capt. BIERAL received some slight wounds in his arm and side.

The firing on the island was just as severe as on the field. The rebels certainly fired at the hospital—at the wounded—at persons in the river—into the thicket, where the Union men were supposed to be concealed—and kept up their firing until about 9 o'clock P. M.

No braver men ever confronted an enemy on the field. The rebel officers themselves declared they thought we had a much superior force, and asked at one time, "Where are all your men?" On being answered that they were all engaged, he said, "Why, if we had known that, we could have eaten you all up."

The presence of the two pieces of artillery caused the rebels to think that we had a large reserve. This no doubt protracted the fight. At a time when our men were fairly used up, Capt. BIERAL took off his cap and called for cheers, crying out that reinforcements were at hand. This fearless conduct kept the rebels in constant check, and looking to the rear.

Col. COGSWELL, who is supposed to be a prisoner, fought with great courage and gallantry. The command devolved on him after Gen. BAKER fell, and well did he sustain his position.

Col. WISTAR was wounded in the left cheek, but stood his ground, cheering on his men, until his right elbow was shattered. His sword fell to the ground, but he coolly picked it up with his left hand, and was assisted to the rear.

A Captain of the Fifteenth Massachusetts was seen to come down to the river, and offer his gold watch to any one who would assist him to swim across, declaring that he would rather die than be taken prisoner. No one was able to accept his offer and he jumped in, and, after a brief struggle, sank to the bottom.

Private PETER FARNEY, of Company G, thinks he was the last man who swam from the river bank opposite the field of battle. He states that as near as he could judge, from eighty to a hundred soldiers lay wounded and helpless on the bank.

STATEMENT OF CORPORAL PIPER.

Corporal FREDK. PIPER of Company P, First California Regiment, was wounded in the right hand, and when he reached the river he plunged in with his clothes on. Five or six men sank beside him; their outcries were terrible. "My God!" "Oh, oh!" "Help!" were heard from all parts of the river. He swam with one hand for fifty yards, and struggled on, he hardly knew how, until he reached the opposite bank.

To go back: Mr. PIPER remained concealed behind a rock, a clump of bushes protecting him from view, until 12 midnight. During this time he saw the enemy's pickets, and heard them challenging our men who struggled, one after another, into their lines. In response to the question "Who goes there?" he often hears the answer, "a friend in distress." These, he supposes, were our men who went in to deliver themselves up. At midnight the enemy rallied some two or three hundred men, and discharged a deadly volley among the bushes where our men were concealed. Eighteen or twenty men fell killed or wounded. A few moments of quiet followed, and the demand from fifty voices was heard, "Surrender." They answered, "Don't fire, we surrender." "Fetch that regiment here," was then demanded by a rebel officer, at the same time he commanded our men to "lay down their arms and come out." At this a large number rushed to the river bank and plunged in. "Come back, come back, you Yankee sons of b—s," was the next exclamation, followed by another volley and straggling shots at the men in the water. A large number were heard to give one outcry of distress and sink. The dead and wounded, in large numbers, lay scattered along the shore, and remained there through the night.

Reinforcements to the enemy were arriving at the place all night, shouting and singing as they came. Mr. PIPER says that Gen. BAKER stood beside his regiment, coolly encouraging them. The men lay flat on the ground for half an hour, the fire of the enemy going over them, but a great many rebel pickets or sharpshooters were stationed in the trees, and shot the men on the ground and picked off the officers. To clear the woods they charged with the bayonet. The first battalion yielded slightly, but were soon met by another regiment coming up behind, who delivered their fire over the shoulders of the first, while the bayonets were interlocked. They were not over ten yards distant, and out of the hundred and fifty of our men forty were shot down. The remainder of them fell back and lay down on their faces, receiving the volley of the whole regiment.

Gen. BAKER at this time saw an officer, whom he supposed to be JOHNSTON, riding a white horse, and asked for a pistol. As a private was in the act of handing him one, he received his death wound and fell. The enemy rushed forward to obtain his body but they were met by a dash of our men, in obedience to an officer's command, and a momentary struggle followed to obtain possession of the brave man's body. As a rebel officer stooped to clutch it, he fell, pierced by a bullet, and a bayonet pinned him to the ground. The Adjutant-General, who had run forward, exclaimed, "Handle him tenderly, men, I have lost the best friend I had in the world."

The sun was now quite low, the woods to the west casting their dark shadow over the bloody scene. Overwhelming reinforcements continued to strengthen the rebel army, who were well sheltered by the woods and rifle pits. Our men were shot down faster than they could be sent across by the scows. The Commander had fallen in sight of the whole lines, casting a gloom over the struggling ranks; the day was evidently lost. Fighting had been going on in an irregular way for two or three hours, while the enemy poured well-directed volleys from full ranks upon our scattered and demoralized forces. The cannon were spiked and thrown down the hill. The wounded, who lay scattered over the encouraged the men in every possible way to continue the fight, but it was useless to do so, and the officers all being shot, wounded or made prisoners, the Unionists retired down to the edge of the river, which was only some fifty yards distant. Here, exhausted and hopeless, they awaited some opportunity to cross, looking at their friends who stood in large numbers on the opposite shore, who could render no assistance.

AFFAIRS ON HARRISON ISLAND.

First Lieut. MAT. SMITH, of California Regiment, Company P, left the island on Tuesday, at 2 P. M. There were then holding the place about 2,000 men, consisting of the Nineteenth Massachusetts, a portion of the Tammany Regiment, 600 strong, the Rhode Island and Ninth Regiment Batteries, and a regiment of New-York Rifles. The wounded had all been removed during the night. Capt. RITMAN, of Company D, California Regiment, Col. DEVEREUX, Lieut. SMITH, Col. BAXTER, of the Philadelphia Zouaves, aided in removing them. Two died in the hospital, and were buried near by. Their names I could not learn. The rebels invited our men across to carry away the wounded. A number were brought across and sent to Edwards' Ferry, and thence to Poolesville.

A notice was sent from the rebel lines, under a flag of truce, for our forces to evacuate the island in six hours. It must be confessed that they have a good position from which to enforce the mandate, being situated on a bluff more than fifty feet above the river level. We shall hold the place, however, until driven out. The Forty-sixth Pennsylvania and a portion of the Ninth New-York State Militia Battery occupy the tow-path opposite the island.

The following is the report, as it now stands, of the first battalion of BAKER'S California Regiment. It may be modified for the better hereafter:

	Men
Total engaged, eight companies, say	780
Killed (so far as known)	8
Wounded	34
Missing	272
Commissioned officers dead, Lieut. H. S. D. WILLIAMS, of Company A, who fell on the field at the head of his men, with musket in hand	1
Commissioned officers missing	8

All who escaped swam the river. Many arrived at the camp having on nothing but a pair of drawers.

Four hundred arms and accoutrements were delivered to this command, and were either broken up or thrown into the Potomac to prevent them from falling into the hands of the enemy. Color-Sergeant VANSANT, of Company P, acted with great gallantry. He was always in front of the lines, proudly bearing aloft his standard, which was riddled with balls. The staff was cut in two, but he gathered up the pieces and carried them off the field, burying them where he hopes hereafter to recover them.

Color-Sergeant WOOD and Corporal HARTLEY acted with great presence of mind, and won the admiration of their commanders.

Corporal RANDALL, of Company D, is reported dead. He had three balls in his body.

Capt. RITMAN had a narrow escape. While going from the hospital to the river, a volley of at least 100 bullets was fired at him, but he went on, if possible to render assistance to the men in the river. He saw the heads of men above the surface of the water for a half mile. A great many were calling for help, but there was none at hand. The only boat on that side was a small one, capable of holding fifteen persons—the scow having been sunk.

Col. ISAAC J. WISTAR, of the California Regiment, was slightly wounded in the face, and severely in the arm. They expect to save his arm.

Sergeant-Major BASTIAN was wounded severely in the breast and arm. Expect to save his arm.

Lieut. WADE, Company D, was severely wounded, but he will recover.

Capt. HICKS was shot through the shoulder.

JOS. D. WILLIAMS, First Lieutenant of Company A, died of his wounds, and his body has been forwarded to his friends in Philadelphia.

THE WOUNDED AT THE BATTLE OF CONRAD'S FERRY.

The following is a list of the wounded, in the hospital at Camp Observation, of the First California Regiment:

John Stanley, Co. G, shot through the shoulder; ball taken out of his back; will recover.

Edward Wisner, Co. A, ball through one shoulder, and extracted from the other; will probably recover.

Edward Mann, Co. G, flesh-wound in the thigh; doing well.

Lieut. Robert Templeton, Co. K, shot in right shoulder; ball not yet extracted.

William Hartley, Co. D, shot through right forearm; expect to save his arm.

Stephen W. Mackay, Co. G, shot through the wrist; doing well.

Frank J. Lambert, Co. H, shot in the right arm; flesh-wound.

Corporal Frederick Piper, wounded in the back of the hand; doing well.

In Hospital at Poolesville:

Joshua Steinbeck, Sergeant Co. G, through thigh.
Wm. McDonald, Co. G, several wounds, but doing well.
Henry H. Kohler, Co. G, leg.
William Smith, Co. G, hip.
Louis Rand, Co. G, thigh.
Charles C. Ferguson, Co. P, killed. His body was riddled with balls.
James Patterson, Co. D, thigh.
Corporal Snow, Co. C, wounded in shoulder.
Henry Rikee, Co. D, leg.
Thomas Pilling, Co. A, leg.
Wm. Brunt, Co. G, slight wound in his eye.
Geo. Seusenderferg, Co. C, wounded.
John Stanley, Co. G, shoulder.
Lieut. William Cole, Co. G, shot in foot.
William Fisher, Co. A, finger shot off.
James Calligan, Co. N, slightly in finger.
Joseph Conell, Co. H, shot in chin.
R. S. Goslin, Co. H, thigh.
Charles Reynolds, Co. G, slight in thigh.
Samuel G. Murphy, Co. G. leg.
James R. Little, Co. L, wounded through both legs.

MOVEMENTS AT EDWARDS' FERRY.

EDWARDS' FERRY, Thursday, Oct. 24—P. M.

Having completed the list of the wounded, in the hospitals at Camp Observation and Poolesville, I hastened down here to see what was going on. The frequent firing from this direction indicated that a battle was progressing on the Virginia side opposite to this place. To bring up the narrative of events here, I must go back to Sunday, the day before the action near Conrad's Ferry. During Sunday night. the Second New-York State Militia crossed over the river at this point, for the purpose, as was supposed, of holding the Ferry on the opposite bank of the Potomac. They soon commenced scouting, but met with only a few of the rebels. They captured one Secessionist who is detained in the guard-house, on the opposite side of the street where I am writing He is a fine-looking man, and no doubt classes himself among the first families.

The First Minnesota followed—seven companies getting over before daybreak. The Telescope sharp shooters, from Massachusetts, who crossed with them, attracted much attention. Three companies of cavalry were the next to cross, taking up an advanced position, where they met the enemys' pickets, and had a brief skirmish. Several of the rebels were killed, and the prisoner before mentioned was captured. No general engagement took place, the enemy falling back to their favorite covert, the woods where they kept at a safe distance from our sharp shooters. Several of them were reached at a distance of half and three-quarters of a mile.

Reinforcements continued to cross in small detachments, and the belief was that it was the intention to outflank the rebels at Conrad's, where our men had engaged the enemy early in the morning. For some unaccountable cause, however, but probably on account of the known strength of the rebel forces and batteries between Edwards' and Conrad's Ferries, the passage of troops was stopped, and our men were kept within retreating distance of Edwards' Ferry, leaving Gen. BAKER, with his small and tardy reinforcements, to sustain the whole brunt of the battle going on above.

In the evening the troops were ordered back, and when parts of two regiments had landed on the Maryland shore, orders came to stop the withdrawal of the troops, as Gen. BANKS' Division had arrived to sustain us. The same two regiments were accordingly retransported to the Virginia shore during that night. On Tuesday several other regiments went over. From that time there was a great *show* of transporting troops across, but, with the exception of a small scow-load, none actually crossed over. There was not at any one time over two pieces of artillery on the Virginia side, viz., two 12-pounders, of Col. REYNOLDS' Rhode Island Battery. On Monday three small scow-loads, each carrying say fifty men, were sent across.

About noon a canal-boat was got through a sluice-way into the Potomac, and orders were sent to stop all canal-boats passing either way, and appropriate to use such as were fit for service. This looked like action again. All tow-lines that could be got hold of were seized, greatly to the grief of the Captains, who were left boatless, tow-lineless and disconsolate. Seven other boats were got into the Potomac on Wednesday, affording preparations for crossing one regiment after another in rapid succession. But the river was now swollen by the heavy rains that were falling. thus increasing the current to such a volume that boats could not be poled over. As yet not all the lines that could be found would span the river, and, at last, when the last rotten tow-line had been bent on, and the two shores were connected, the line parted with the first strain, and the boat had to return.

Men were now set to cutting poles, and mules were brought into requisition to have the boats up the stream along shore, in order to get a good "offing." At noon, however, obstruction in another form arose. A stiff breeze sprung up from the northwest, and rendered all further attempts to cross by these means utterly futile. not to say dangerous.

Meantime some sharp skirmishing was had with an advanced body of the enemy's pickets, the firing for a few minutes being very sharp on both sides. In this engagement Gen. LANDER was wounded in the leg. Gens. ABERCROMBIE, BANKS, GORMAN, COOPER and others were on the field.

This (Thursday) morning, Gen MCCLELLAN arrived about 9 o'clock, and assumed command of operations, or, at least, actively coöperated with the other Generals.

Meantime the four thousand and odd troops were left alone on the enemy's shore, there being no possibility of reinforcing them. The banks of the Potomac were lined with troops bivouacing on the wet grass, many of whom were actually suffering for food Some of them had eaten nothing for twenty-four hours.

The object of all these movements having been accomplished, on the plans of the Generals being changed, a final order was issued to have all the troops brought back again. Rumors prevailed that JOHNSTON was advancing from Manassas with fifty thousand or some other fabulous number of men and that it was deemed prudent to quit the sacred soil for the present. But now they were again confronted with the northwest gale and rapid current.

[*Continued on Eighth Page.*]

The New-York Times.

VOL. XI....NO. 3161. NEW-YORK, FRIDAY, NOVEMBER 8, 1861. PRICE TWO CENTS.

THE GREAT REBELLION.

Continuance of the Fighting in Western Virginia.

A Decisive Movement About to be Made by the National Forces.

Gen. Rosecrans Reinforced with Artillery.

HIGHLY IMPORTANT FROM KENTUCKY.

An Expedition from Cairo Against Columbus.

A Warm Action Going on at Last Accounts.

IMPORTANT NEWS FROM MISSOURI.

A Better Feeling in the National Army.

The Chances for a Great Battle More Remote.

Rebel Report of the Capture of the Privateer Sumter.

SPECIAL DISPATCH FROM WASHINGTON.

WASHINGTON, Thursday, Nov. 7.

CHEERING NEWS FROM EUROPE.

The news from Europe at the State Department is understood to be eminently satisfactory. Official dispatches corroborate the impressions given by the telegraphic reports already published in the newspapers. Unofficial communications from loyal citizens of the United States, residing in Paris and London, say that in France Prince NAPOLEON has cast off all reserve, and declared that the insurrection cannot prevail; and other letters say that secession is dead in France, or, at least, that it gives no signs of life.

THE REBELS ON THE UPPER POTOMAC.

A letter received to-night from Darnestown says the latest reliable information from the Virginia side of the Upper Potomac induces the belief that the rebels are strongly reinforcing their posts and fortifications at and around Winchester, as well as on their river frontier, fearing a simultaneous advance of Gen. KELLY from the direction of Romney, and of Col. GEARY from Sandy Hook. Some persons estimate the number of rebels at Winchester as high as 15,000, while it is known that their forces at the river posts are being increased daily. Recently they have resumed firing on our pickets, but this mode of warfare has not yet proved very sanguinary nor successful to the assailants. The letter further says during yesterday the Potomac River rose so high as to compel our pickets to forsake the towpath of the canal, so at present there is no danger of either of the contending armies crossing in force.

AFFAIRS DOWN THE POTOMAC.

Gen. SICKLES left town this evening, for his headquarters on the Lower Potomac.

There is no news of importance from the Potomac flotilla to day. The *Yankee* came up for repairs, and her commander, Capt. EASTMAN, has been ordered to another vessel. The name of the *Moun Vernon* has been changed to the *Mount Washington*, and that of the *Powhatan* to the *King Philip*, there being already a *Mount Vernon* and a *Powhatan* among the National steamers off the Southern coast.

THE BATTERIES ON THE POTOMAC.

Gen. SICKLES has been in the city for two days awaiting the arrival of his batteries. He expresses the opinion that the rebel batteries on the Potomac are not of the formidable character supposed. They have been erected at six different points, namely: Freestone Point, Shipping Point, Evansport, above and below Aquia Creek, and Mathias Point. At one time there were five guns —field pieces—at Freestone Point, but there is good reason to believe that the battery has since been abandoned. No shell were ever fired from them to the Maryland shore. At Shipping Point, the work has embrasures for seven guns, and they have there one gun from which 10-inch shell have been thrown to the Maryland shore. It is believed that this gun was originally intended to be conveyed to Mathias Point. It required from 30 to 40 yoke of oxen to move it. The remainder of the guns at Shipping Point are field pieces. At Evansport the battery of field pieces is concealed, but no firing has ever been done from it which could not be easily done with four guns. The battery above Aquia Creek is concealed, and as it has not been fired from for some time, it is not known what is its strength. That below the creek is also concealed, but it is regarded as a strong battery, as the point is an important one to hold to protect the dépôt of the Fredericksburgh Railroad. The battery at Mathias Point was concealed by a small undergrowth, but it is believed that there are no guns there at the present time, though it is stated that a large wood-pile on the Point conceals a number. The situation of Mathias point makes it a dangerous one to hold, as it can be assailed from the river, and as a large marsh is in its rear, a retreat could be easily cut off. From Freestone to Mathias Point is three miles, and Gen. SICKLES does not believe that the rebels have more than 25 guns on the whole distance. These are distributed at the points located where the channel of the river runs close to the Virginia shore. There is no indication of the rebels being present in any force except at Evansport. Our scouts have crossed the river about the mouth of Occoquan and have discovered no troops or pickets.

ANXIETY IN REFERENCE TO THE FLEET.

No further intelligence has been received from the fleet, and the anxiety to hear the result of the expedition is intensified with each day's delay.

QUIET ALONG THE LINES.

Nothing has transpired for several days to disturb the quiet along our lines. Foraging parties accompanied by strong escorts, daily go beyond our outposts, and they return successful, without so much as getting a sight of the rebels.

NO INFORMATION FROM GEN. ROSENCRANS.

The Government has no information from Gen. ROSENCRANS' army of particular interest.

THE EUROPEAN INTERVENTION IN MEXICO.

Two of the chief instruments in bringing about the proposed European intervention in Mexico are GABRIAC and MIRAMON. Mr. BARRON, one of the great English capitalists in Mexico, and whose fortune is at stake, has been in England for some months, and, doubtless, has done his share of this business.

The three parties above mentioned constitute a curious and extraordinary combination for the present age. It is doubtful whether a more Jesuitical trio can be found in either hemisphere, and under influences wielded by this trio, three of the principal Powers of Europe have been induced to combine and reestablish the Powers of Darkness in Mexico.

The influence the old despotic, bigoted anti-progressive Church Party in Mexico has exerted in the matter may be estimated when it is known that MIRAMON has been appointed Lieutenant-General—second in command—of the Spanish forces destined to invade his native country.

THE BLOCKADE AT CHARLESTON.

A highly intelligent and trustworthy gentleman, who has been on duty in connection with the blockading squadron off Charleston, assures me that since five weeks ago, Capt. MARSTON took command of the station, it is absolutely certain that no vessel has put to sea directly from that harbor. Through the narrow channels leading among the Sea Islands to Savannah, and even to points on the coast of Florida, small craft, such as schooners of light draught and sloops, may have made their way, but the watch of these passages is not carried on by the orders of the the squadron, and would in fact, be beyond its powers. My informant has reason to believe the surveillance was much less perfect while Capt. MERCER had charge of the station. When Capt. MARSTON arrived to supersede that officer, his flag-ship, which had put to sea several days before on account of a storm, had not returned, and was actually absent a week, while the *Vandalia*, without the aid of steam, held her own close to the port, but of course without the means of watching every outlet, or of pursuing a steam vessel of the enemy.

THE ESCAPE OF THE SUMTER.

Intelligence has been received that the *Sumter*, when chased by the *Brooklyn*, as she was running the blockade at Charleston, fearing capture, had already thrown overboard one of her heaviest guns, and as it became more and more probable that she must fall into our hands, the Captain had about determined to surrender, when the *Brooklyn* hauled off and abandoned the chase. As it has been thought worth while to institute a Court of Inquiry in the case of GUSTAVUS H. SCOTT for abandoning the search for the *Sumter* when it was not in sight or its whereabouts known, it is a little singular that the conduct of the officers of the *Brooklyn*, in abandoning a chase ror the same vessel when it was in full sight, should not be thought worthy of an investigation.

THE CIVIL CASES IN ALEXANDRIA.

Attorney-General BATES is of the opinion that no matter what circumstances may exist at Alexandria the military authority has no right to interfere in civil matters. The affairs of Judge FREZE's Provost-Court remains *in statu quo*, or as far as civil proceedings are concerned—the property of the rebel debtors being still held by the Court until some positive and final action by the President on the specific question submitted to him in the test case of BARLEY & TRIPLETT. It is still asserted that the President is desirous of securing to Northern merchants, by means of Provost-Courts, the millions of dollars due them from rebels in arms against the Government.

CIVIL OFFICERS TO BE DEPOSED.

An order will shortly be issued deposing all the civil authorities of Alexandria who refuse to take the oath of allegiance. Judge FREESE has decided that they are already deposed by the action of the Wheeling Convention

JOHN A. WASHINGTON'S ESTATE.

The estate of JOHN A. WASHINGTON has been placed in charge of Commander LEE, of the United States Navy.

ACCOUNTS OF THE LIVERPOOL CONSULATE.

The quarterly accounts from the Liverpool Consulate, just received by the State Department, disclose the extent of the embezzlements and thefts of BEVERLY TUCKER, Mr. BUCHANAN's Consul at that port, of all the moneys received and in possession of the Consulate when he left, including the many thousands for the support of sick and disabled seamen. Not a dollar was left, and the Government was compelled to send over funds to pay the liabilities of the Consulate, to prevent the personal property belonging to it from being seized by the bailiff. From private sources I learn that TUCKER's style of living was luxurious and so extravagant that he left private debts unpaid in Liverpool amounting to $200,000. A half dozen such men in office abroad from the rebel Confederacy would haste the termination of the war.

THE NEW MINISTER FROM SWEDEN.

Count PIPER, the new Minister Resident from Sweden and Norway, had his first audience of the Secretary of State to-day at the Department. It is officially communicated to the Government that the selection of this distinguished statesman, a lineal descendant of Count PIPER, identified with the glorious history of his country in the period of CHARLES the Twelfth, of Sweden, is designed as a special mark of respect and good will on the part of Sweden toward the United States. It is not unlikely that the Government of the United States will make some suitable recognition of this action on the part of Sweden.

THE RETIREMENT OF GEN. SCOTT.

An order has been prepared, officially informing the army of the retiracy of Lieut.-Gen. SCOTT, and embodying the letter in which he states his reasons for this voluntary act.

GEN. MITCHELL IN WASHINGTON.

Gen. MITCHELL, who recently tendered his resignation, has arrived in Washington.

SEPARATION OF FAMILIES.

Many cases of the separation of families by reason of the rebellion, and of a very distressing character, are coming to the knowledge of the State Department. Sickness, or other unavoidable causes, have kept members of families—many of them ladies—in the South, until intercourse between the States became extremely difficult or their means became exhausted; and hence they have been compelled to remain away from their friends, —often suffering extreme poverty in addition to the anxiety of mind proceeding from their being unable to communicate by letter. In such cases, letters designed for their friends in the South, can be forwarded from Fortress Monroe whenever a flag of truce is sent down. They are first examined by one of Gen. WOOL's Staff, to ascertain that they relate to instances of distress, and contain no information that will be of service to the enemy. Hence, such letters should be brief, legibly written and unsealed, and should contain money to pay the postage in the Southern mails. Those written in cypher or illegibly written, are very apt to be set aside as treasonable.

MINISTER TO JAPAN.

Hon. ROBT. H. PRUYN, Minister to Japan, is now in the city to receive his instructions from the Government in reference to the affairs of his mission. He will return to Albany to-morrow, to remain a few days preparatory to taking his departure for Jeddo.

AN APPOINTMENT.

Lieut. CHARLES H. POWERS, of Rochester, one of the most efficient executive officers in the service, has been appointed an Assistant Adjutant-General, and has been assigned to the Staff of Gen. MARTINDALE.

RETURN OF SECRETARY SEWARD.

Secretary SEWARD returned to the city last night.

THE SANITARY COMMISSION.

Dr. BELLOWS, President of the Sanitary Commission, has forwarded to the State Department a detailed account of a visit to the rebel State and war prisoners in Castle William. He says that when first brought there, when no preparation had been made to receive them, ill-clothed and sick from the voyage, there was, no doubt, more or less inconvenience suffered. Their wants had been supplied with alacrity, and the prisoners were better supplied and fed than many of our own soldiers in the field. In conclusion, Dr. BELLOWS states that it would be a great consolation to believe that our own prisoners were treated half as well.

CAPTURE OF A REBEL DOCTOR.

A reconnoitering party from Gen. SMITH's division, yesterday, when near Vienna, arrested Dr. HUNTER, a surgeon in the rebel army. He will be brought to Washington.

RAILROAD ARRANGEMENTS.

The Government Railroad Department has been in negotiation for some time with the several Railroad Companies between Washington, New-York, Boston and Buffalo, for a more expeditious arrangement of trains, by which communication with different parts of the North will be more frequent. The arrangements are nearly completed, awaiting only the final action of a Convention to be held in Philadelphia on Monday next.

The Post-office Department will be represented by Assistant Postmaster-General McCLELLAN, and the War Department by THOS. H. CANFIELD, Assistant General Manager of Railroads for the Government.

Capt. MORLEY, the General Manager, has been compelled, on account of ill-health, to ask leave of absence for a few days, during which time Mr. CANFIELD will discharge the duties of that office.

CONSUL TO BAYONNE APPOINTED.

WM. MORAN, of Philadelphia, has been appointed Consul to Bayonne, France.

REVIEW OF BUELL'S DIVISION.

A grand review of Gen. BUELL's Division is to take place to-morrow.

MAJOR VOGDES.

Major ISRAEL VOGDES, who was taken prisoner by the rebels on the occasion of the attack on Col. BILLY WILSON's Regiment at Santa Rosa island, is a grand nephew of Mad ANTHONY WAYNE, of the Revolution. Col. HAYMAN, of the New-York Thirty-seventh, a cousin of Major VOGDES, is also a grand nephew of the Revolutionary General.

CAPT. SEMMES OF THE PRIVATEER SUMTER.

HIS DEPARTURE FOR EUROPE.

It has already been announced that Capt. SEMMES, commander of the privateer *Sumter*, had arrived in Europe, though considerable doubt is thrown over the statement. The following extract of a letter from a gentleman who went out in the steamer *Edinburgh*, may throw some light upon it:

"OFF QUEENSTOWN HARBOR, Monday, Oct. 21, 1861.

* * * We have several Consuls aboard. Mr. BAKER for Greece, Mr. ECCLESTON for Cadiz, and MURPHY for Frankfort. There is also a bearer of dispatches, Capt. LANMAN, United States Army, of Philadelphia. Among the lady passengers are several Southern ladies, going to Europe to stay during the war. They are very bitter Secessionists, talking much about it and making great boastings. One of them claimed she had sold Confederate bonds in New-York.

An accident occurred which created quite a stir yesterday in our ship. A Mrs. SOUVAN, of Baltimore, a young, handsome widow, appeared at the dinner-table with a secession flag wrapped around her, and made herself very conspicuous. Several passengers complained of it, but, as Capt. ROSKILL was not present, the matter passed by till tea-time when she again appeared with it. This widow claims to be a relative of the CARROLL who signed the Declaration of Independence, as we are informed. She is young and good-looking, and had before had quite a flare with a Mr. S——B, of New-York, who had addressed a letter to her rather familiarly on the boat, and whom she took to task at the dinner-table one day, greatly to his mortification At the tea-table quite a discussion took place about the flag and the Union, the Consular gentlemen taking part in it. Suddenly a champion appeared for the flag in the person of a man who had all along in the trip pretended to be a British Post Captain, by the name of BURNSIDE, but whom most of the passengers thought greatly acted like a Southern man. He was evidently acquainted with the seafaring life. *This Capt. B. now avowed himself as Capt. Semmes, of the Sumter; said he had got a letter from the British Consul at Laguayra to Lord Lyons, and had been introduced by the latter as a British subject to Gov. Seward and other officials at Washington*; and he said he had visited our army on the Potomac, &c. None of the Northerners knew his identity, though Capt. LANMAN thinks he does. The Southern ladies claim they were informed in New-York that Capt. SEMMES was aboard of the steamer when she left New-York. He made his disclosure when under the influence of liquor, as was thought at the time. He avows his trip to Europe to be for the purpose of buying war-vessels, and expects to meet DUDLEY MANN, YANCEY, &c., in London. He will be watched now pretty sharply in London, while he stays there. He had quite a quarrel with Mr. S——, of New-York, calling the latter a blackguard, and pretending that Mr. S—— had followed him as a spy, which the latter disclaims. Of course there was quite a row being got up in the saloon, and the Captain was sent for, who quieted it, and Capt. SEMMES retired to bed.

About 140 Irish disembarked here; going to stay in Ireland till the war is over, as business was dull in America. Yours, &c., W.

FROM FORTRESS MONROE.

BALTIMORE, Thursday, Nov. 7—1 P. M.

The boat from Old Point has just arrived. She experienced a heavy gale in the Bay; had some of her upper works damaged, and lost a large anchor.

She brings no tidings of the great fleet. There had been no arrivals from the southward.

The *S. R. Spaulding* has not yet returned to Hatteras Inlet.

ANOTHER ARREST.

CLEVELAND, Ohio, Thursday, Nov. 7.

MATTHEW F. MAURY, of New-Orleans, was arrested here to-day by the United States Marshal. A large number of letters to parties in the rebel States were found in his trunk.

The Southern Coast and its Railroad Communication with the Interior.

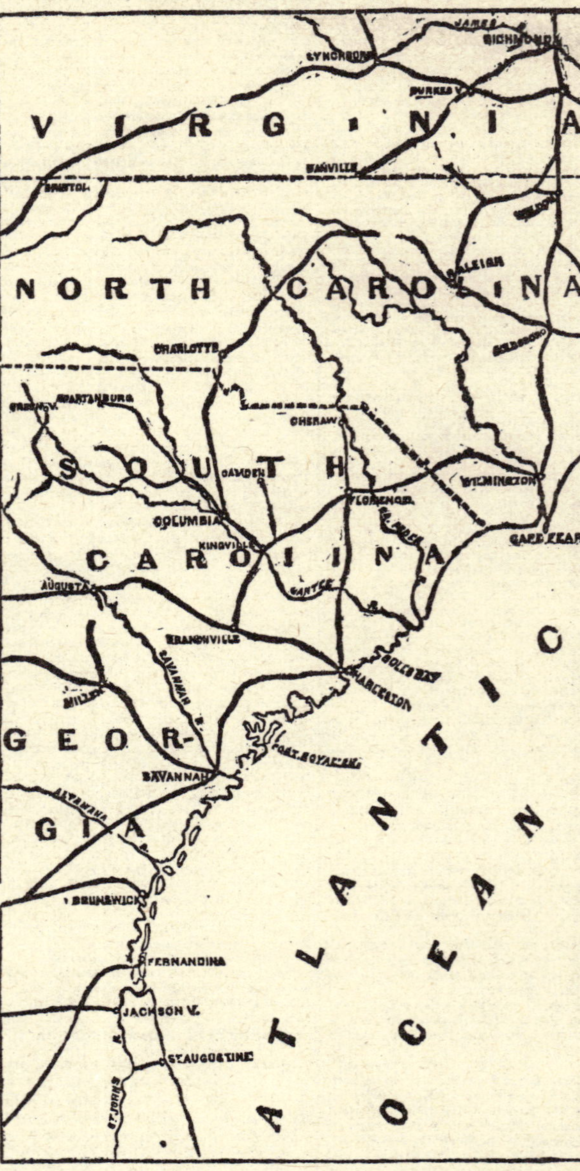

Bull Bay and the Coast to Charleston.

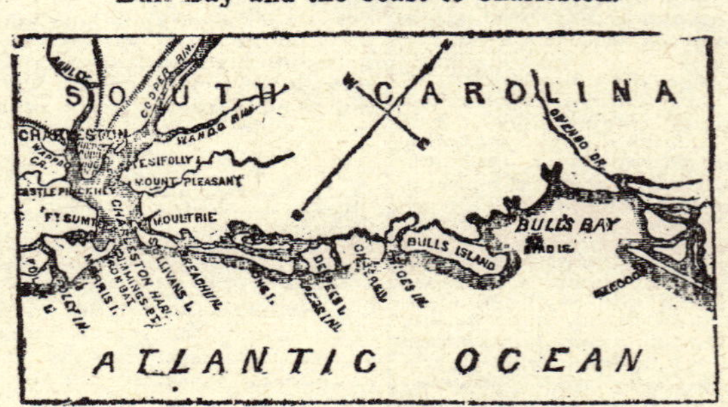

Charleston, Port Royal Entrance and Beaufort.

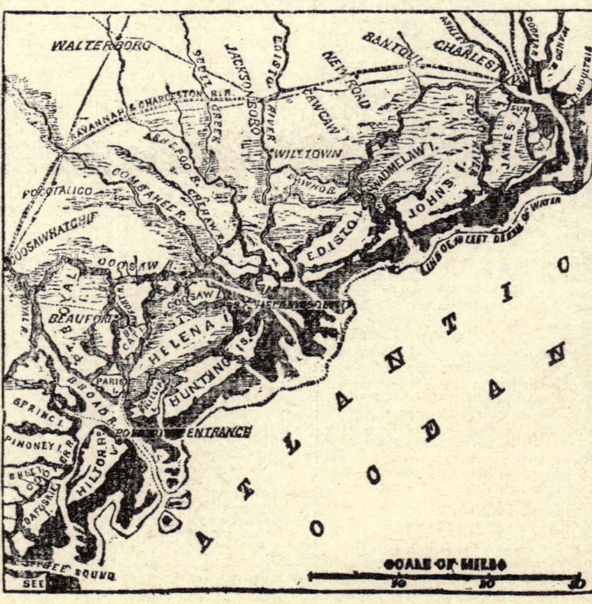

THE NAVAL INVASION.

PORT ROYAL AND BEAUFORT.

Topographic and Hydrographic Sketch of the Region of the Expediton.

ITS STRATEGIC FEATURES.

History and Romance of the Locality.

It seems quite certain that the Naval Expedition from which the whole country awaits intelligence with so much anxiety, is intended to operate upon the coasts of South Carolina and Georgia,—with a view primarily of establishing dépôts for receiving stores and reinforcements, and also of moving upon Charleston or Savannah and opening a port for the exit of cotton. It is more than probable that PORT ROYAL is one of the points selected for landing:—whether the other is Bull's Bay, north of Charleston, or Brunswick, south of Savannah, is as yet unknown:—and will depend on which of the two cities is to be first assailed.

The Maps which we publish this morning, give a clear and complete view of the whole locality. The first sketches the sea coast and the railroad lines connecting Charleston and Savannah with the interior. A force entering Port Royal, by marching a few miles into the interior, and destroying the railroad, can destroy communications between Savannah and Charleston,—and by dividing to the right and left, can cut off both cities from Augusta and the West. On the other hand, a force landing in Bull's Bay, and marching to the rear of Charleston, can cut off that city from its connection with Columbia and the North —so as to delay, very considerably, troops proceeding to its relief.

Unquestionably the central point of interest, in connection with this expedition, is

PORT ROYAL AND BEAUFORT.

Port Royal Entrance is an inlet from the Atlantic, in latitude 32° 8′ N., fifty miles southwest of Charleston, and fifteen miles northeast of Tybee Inlet the entrance of Savannah River. The opening from the Atlantic is between Edding Island and Hilton Head Island, and at that point is about three miles wide. The prolongation inward of Port Royal Entrance is called Broad River and Port Royal River. Running up this for about twenty-five miles, bending off eastward through the Coosaw River, and coming out to the Atlantic again through St. Helena Sound, you have an irregular area of about twenty-five miles by fifteen. This amphibious region is cut up by numerous rivers, creeks and inlets into a great many islands (Sea Islands) of various sizes, the chief of which are "Port Royal," "St. Helena," "Paris," "Ladies," "Coosaw," "Morgan," "Dathaw," "Edding," "Chaplin," "Prentis" and "Hunting."

Along the coast of South Carolina as in North Carolina and Georgia, stretches a low and narrow sand bar—a kind of defensive outwork of the land, seldom inhabited except by lost Indians and runaway negroes, who subsist by hunting and fishing. At distant intervals there are shallow breaches through which the quiet tide steals in twice a day, swelling the natural lagoons and damming the outlet of the fresh water stream till the current is destroyed and turned back, and their flood dispersed far and wide over the debatable land of the Cypress Swamp. Then, when the heavy rains in the interior have swollen the rivers, their eddying currents deposit all along the edges of the sandy islands and capes the rich freight they have brought from the calcareous or granitic mountains in which they rise, with the organic waste of the great forests through which they flow. This is the soil of the rice and cotton plantations, which are always found in such parts of the tidal swamps adjoining the mainland or the sandy islands as are left nearly dry at the ebb of the water.

The entrance to Port Royal is the best channel for ships through the bars in the whole range of ports below Norfolk. BLUNT's *Coast Pilot* gives the following directions for entering:

"Steering for Port Royal harbor, the course, after taking bearings, is due west for St. Michael's Head, within fifteen leagues of which will be found from twenty to twenty-five fathoms water. Land is made in clear weather at a distance of six leagues, in twelve fathoms water. Port Royal Entrance is known by a small grove of trees, which stand on the west side of it, and tower above all the other trees like a high-crowned hat; hence this grove is called the Hat of Port Royal. The entrance to Port Royal is between two immense breakers—one on the north called Cole's Care, the other to the southward, called Martin's Industry; between these two breakers lies the entrance of the channel into Port Royal Harbor, which is about a mile wide. Continue to steer as aforesaid, between the two breakers, until you bring Phillip's Point to bear N. N. W., then steer directly for it, and you will have, as you proceed, 9, 8 and 7 fathoms water. When you are abreast of Phillip's Point, give it a small birth, and steer up N. and W., ½ W., in 6 and 5 fathoms; in the latter depth you may anchor—very safe harbor."

Ships which draw 14 or 15 feet water, may go in at Tybee and proceed through land to Beaufort in Port Royal Islands; and from Beaufort, vessels of 8 or 9 feet water may go through land to Charleston. From Charleston vessels drawing 7 or 8 feet water may go through land to the river Medway, in Georgia, which lies thirty miles south of Savannah. On this coast it is observed that Northeast, Easterly and Southeast winds cause higher tides than other winds, and also somewhat alter their course. At Port Royal entrance the tide flows, on the change and full days of the moon, at 7½ o'clock. About six leagues from the land, in twelve fathoms water, the flood sets strongly to the southward, and the ebb to the northward; farther off from the shore there is no tide at all. Near to the entrance of the harbor there is a strong indraught during the flood-tide, and an outset with an ebb-tide.

Within Port Royal entrance, even over the bars there are three and a half fathoms water or twenty-one feet, and probably twenty-seven feet at high tide. We append, as interesting in this connection, the respective draught of the various transports:

Steamers.	Tons.	Draft, ft.
Ariel	1,296	14
Atlantic	2,845	20½
Alabama	1,261	13½
Baltic	2,723	21
Belvidere	1,600	—
Ben Deford	1,060	—
Champion	—	—
Cahawba	1,643	11
Coatzacoalcos	1,500	8
Daniel Webster	1,035	11
De Soto	1,675	15
Empire City	1,751	14
Ericsson	1,902	16
Florida	1,261	15
Illinois	2,123	19
Locust Point	462	16
Marion	800	13
Matanzas	875	—
Mercedia	1,070	10
Ocean Queen	2,802	16
Oriental	1,000	—
Parkersburg	715	10
Philadelphia	1,238	11
Potomac	448	—
Roanoke	1,071	10
Santiago de Cuba	1,850	15
Spalding	—	—
Star of the South	960	—
Vanderbilt	3,360	20
Winfield Scott	—	—

"Vessels that enter Port Royal Sound," says the *Coast Survey Report*, 1859, "will find in the Colleton River, at the neck and at its confluence with the Checkessee, a capacious, completely protected and acceptable anchorage in from four to seven fathom waters. Colleton Neck is only eleven miles from the Charleston

[*Continued on Eighth Page.*]

The Charleston Mercury.

DAILY PAPER—TEN DOLLARS PER ANNUM, PAYABLE HALF YEARLY IN ADVANCE. | VINDICE NULLO SPONTE SUA SINE LEGE FIDES RECTUMQUE COLENTUR. | COUNTRY PAPER—THRICE A WEEK—FIVE DOLLARS PER ANNUM, IN ADVANCE.

VOLUME LXXIX. | CHARLESTON, S. C., MONDAY, NOVEMBER 11, 1861. | NUMBER 11,303

THE MERCURY

MONDAY, NOVEMBER 11, 1861.

The Battle of Port Royal.

The Battle of Port Royal will be remembered as one of the best fought, and best conducted battles, which have signalized the war in which we are engaged.

If Gen. Ripley had been appointed a General in command two months sooner, every thing would have been in a better state of preparation. But these two previous months were wasted in doing nothing for our defence. Within the time left to him, Gen. Ripley did all that untiring energy and skill could accomplish, to put our coast in the state of partial preparation our enemies will encounter. The two islands of Hilton Head and Bay Point, with their extreme limits constitute the two points which guard the entrance to Port Royal Sound, about three miles in width. On these two points, two Forts were erected—Fort Walker on Hilton Head—and Fort Beauregard on Bay Point. The time we possessed, enabled us to make them only earthworks, without any protection from shells or bombs.

The Island of Hilton Head was commanded by Gen. Drayton. The officers immediately superintending the artillery and conducting the fire of Fort Walker, were Col. Wagener, Major Arthur Huger and Capt. Yates, of the regular service, especially detailed by Gen. Ripley to aid in directing the artillery. Col. Dunovant commanded at Fort Beauregard, but he generously allowed Capt. Elliott, of the Beaufort Artillery, to direct and conduct the batteries of the Fort.

The day was beautiful—calm and clear, with scarcely a cloud in the heavens—just such a day as our invaders would have ordained, if they could, to carry on their operations.

In such a sketch of the battle as, amid the excitement and thousands of baseless rumors, we are enabled to present to our readers, a brief review of the earlier events of this memorable week will not be uninteresting.

PRELIMINARY OPERATIONS OF THE ENEMY.

The great fleet of the enemy passed our Bar on Sunday, the 3d inst., and on the following day was anchored off Port Royal entrance. About 4 o'clock on Monday afternoon, Com. Tatnall, with his "mosquito fleet" ran out from the harbor and made the first hostile demonstration. The immense armada of the invaders, numbering, at that time, thirty-six vessels, was drawn up in line of battle; and as our little flotilla steamed briskly up to within a mile of them, and opened its fire, the scene was an inspiriting one, but almost ludicrous, in the disparity of the size of the opposing fleets The enemy replied to our fire almost immediately. After an exchange of some twenty shots, Commodore Tatnall retired, and was not pursued.

About seven o'clock on Tuesday morning, several of the largest Yankee war steamers having come within range, the batteries of Forts Walker and Beauregard were opened, and the steamers threw a number of shells in and over our works, inflicting no damage upon Fort Walker, and but slightly wounding two of the garrison of Fort Beauregard. This engagement lasted, with short intervals, for nearly two hours, when the enemy drew off. The steamers made a similar, but shorter reconnoisance, on Wednesday evening, but without any important results. On the next day (Wednesday), the weather was rough, and the fleet lay at anchor five or six miles from shore. During the day, several straggling transports came up, swelling the number of vessels to forty one. All Tuesday night, and all day Wednesday, and Wednesday night, our men stood to their guns, momentarily expecting an attack, and obtaining only such scanty rest and refreshment as chance afforded.

THE DAY OF THE BATTLE.

Thursday dawned gloriously upon our wearied but undaunted gunners, and all felt that the day of trial had at last arrived. Scarcely had breakfast been despatched, when the hostile fleet was observed in commotion. The great war steamers formed rapidly in single file, and within supporting distance of each other, the frigate *Minnesota*, the flag ship of Com. Dupont, in the van. As the long line of formidable looking vessels, thirteen in number, most of them powerful propellers, with a few sailing men-of-war in tow, swept rapidly and majestically in, with ports open and bristling with guns of the heaviest calibre, the sight was grand and imposing. This was at half past eight o'clock. Until the *Minnesota* came within the range of and directly opposite to our batteries on Hilton Head, all was still. Suddenly, the fifteen heavy guns of Fort Walker, which had been aimed directly at the huge frigate, belched forth their simultaneous fire, and the action was begun. Almost immediately afterwards, the batteries of Fort Beauregard, on the other side of the entrance, also opened their fire. The enemy at first did not reply. But, as the second steamer came opposite to Fort Walker, the hulls of the first three were suddenly wrapped in smoke, and the shot and shell of three tremendous broadsides, making, in all, seventy five guns, came crashing against our works. From this moment, the bombardment was terrific and incessant. One by one the propellers bore down upon our Forts, delivered their fire as they passed, until nine had gained the interior of the harbor, beyond the range of our guns. The *Minnesota*, still followed by the others, then turned round and steamed slowly out, giving a broadside to Fort Beauregard, as she repassed. Thus the battle was continued, the enemy's vessels sailing in an eliptical curve, pouring one broadside into Bay Point, and then sweeping around to deliver the other against Hilton Head. This furious fire from some four hundred guns, many of them of the 11-inch Dahlgren pattern and some even of 13-inch bore (for a sabot of that diameter was found in Fort Beauregard), was maintained incessantly, and the roar of the cannonade seemed most continuous. Meanwhile, our garrisons were making a gallant defence. They kept up a vigorous and well directed fire against their assailants, and notwitstanding that their best gun was dismounted at the beginning of the action, they succeeded in setting fire to several of the ships. Whenever this happened, however, the enemy would haul off and soon extinguish the flames. The effect of our guns was, in many instances, plainly visible from the Forts. Although the sides of the *Minnesota* are of massive strength, several of her ports were knocked into one. Nor was she the only vessel upon which this evidence of the power of our fire could be seen. Many of the other steamers were likewise badly hulled.

After some time spent in sailing round and delivering their broadsides in rotation, in the manner we have described, the enemy's steamers adopted another and more successful plan of attack. One of them took a position inside the harbor so as to enfilade the batteries of Fort Walker, while several opened a simultaneous enfilading fire from the outside. Besides this terrific cross fire, two of the largest steamers maintained the fire in front of the Fort. Thus three furious converging streams of shot and shell were rained amongst the brave little garrison for hours. The vessels came up within a half mile of the shore, but nearly all our guns had, by this time, become dismounted, and we were no longer able to reply with serious effect.

Soon after 11 o'clock, the batteries of Bay Point were silenced. The fire of Fort Walker, as far as the guns that remained were concerned, was not a whit slackened, until one o'clock. By that time the dreadful condition of the fort became too apparent to be longer disregarded. The guns lay in every direction, dismantled and useless; the defenses were terribly shattered, the dead and dying were to be seen on every side, and still the iron hail poured pitilessly in.

FORT WALKER ABANDONED.

In this strait, it was determined to abandon the fort. A long waste, about a mile in extent and commanded by the enemy's guns, intervened between the garrison and the woods. Across this they were ordered to run for their lives, each man for himself; the object being to scatter them as much as possible, so as not to afford a target for the rifled guns of the fleet. The preparations for running this perilous gauntlet were soon made. Knapsacks were abandoned, but the men retained their muskets. Each of the wounded was placed in a blanket and carried off by four men. The safety of the living precluded the idea of removing the dead. And thus, the gallant little band quitted the scene of their glory, and scampered off, each one as best he could, towards the woods. The retreat was covered by a small detachment who remained in the Fort for an hour after their comrades had left. Among those who remained were Capt. Harms, with six men, Lieut. Melchers with four men and Lieut. Bischoff, with four men. These worked three guns until about two o'clock, when they also quitted the post.

The abandonment of Fort Beauregard was equally a necessity. The garrison were exhausted and in momentary danger of being cut off. When Col. Dunovant ordered a retreat, tears of mortification and indignation filled the eyes of Captain Elliott at the sad necessity. The retreat was admirably conducted, and rendered entirely successful by the prudent energy of Capt. Hanckel, one of General Ripley's Aids, who had got together some twelve flats at Station Creek, by which the troops passed safely over to St. Helena Island. From there, they passed to Beaufort Island, and reached the train at Pocotaligo without the loss or injury of a man. In this Fort none were killed, and but five were wounded, and two of these were wounded by negligence in loading a cannon, by which hot shot was driven on the powder, without the wet wad preceding it.

EVACUATION OF BAY POINT.

The rest of the story is briefly told. Late Thursday night the garrison of Fort Walker had collected at the landing, in the hope of being able to reach Bluffton by water. Luckily, several small Confederate steamers were within hail.—But here a ludicrous mistake occurred. The retreating troops imagined the little steamers to be Yankee gun-boats; while the crews of the steamers were convinced that the troops were a body of disembarked Yankees. Acting upon this double delusion, a deal of mutual reconnoitering was made, and it was only after a vast variety of strategic approaches, that they reached the conclusion that it was "all right." A quick trip to Bluffton followed.—Thence the troops marched to Hardeeville, 17 miles distant. The road along which they dragged their exhausted frames was filled with a heterogeneous throng of fugitives of all conditions, carriages, carts and conveyances of every description that could, by any possibility, be pressed into service. The spectacle was a sad one.

Thus ended the defence of Port Royal. The mortification of the disaster is lessened by the consciousness that our troops deserved success.

What injury we did to the enemy, we do not know. Our firing was, of course, less efficient than theirs. Our troops were volunteers—theirs were picked artillerists. Yet, it is very remarkable how few were killed or wounded, amongst our troops. This battle, in this respect, was very much like the battle of Fort Sumter. How so many cannon could have been dismantled and rendered useless, and yet so few of those who worked them injured, seems very marvellous. Our troops did their duty faithfully and bravely, and fought until to fight longer would have been sheer folly. Though encountering immense odds, no signs of cowardice marked their conduct. Officers and soldiers exemplified the ancient character of the State, and deserve our profound gratitude and admiration.

Our Policy.

Our enemies have invaded South Carolina for two purposes—1, to gratify their hate and revenge—and 2, to gratify their avarice. The first we have to meet with fighting; but the last must be defeated by *policy*, where fighting fails. To defeat their avarice, our policy should be to destroy the objects their avarice proposes to feed on. General plunder is undoubtedly designed; but the special objects of their appropriations will undoubtedly be our slaves, and cotton. What shall we do with them? Shall we leave them on our plantations to be appropriated by our invaders? It appears to us, our true policy is, to take off of our plantations, our slaves, horses and cattle—and to burn up our cotton. To leave our horses to arm them, our cattle to feed them, our slaves to strengthen them, and our cotton to enrich them, or to run their factories, appears to us to be the worst policy possible.

Captain S. F. Dupont

Bombardment of Fort Walker, Hilton Head, Port Royal Harbor by the United States fleet, November 7, 1861

The New-York Times.

VOL. XI....NO. 3164. NEW-YORK, TUESDAY, NOVEMBER 12, 1861. PRICE TWO CENTS.

THE GREAT REBELLION.

Glorious News from South Carolina.

Confirmatory Intelligence Through Two Distinct Channels.

Beaufort in Possession of the National Forces.

Three Forts Captured After Two Days' Fighting.

The Rebel Losses Acknowledged to be Heavy.

Seizure of the Railroad Between Charleston and Savannah.

A Stampede of Southern Troops in Virginia.

Particulars of the Loss of the Transport Union.

FRENCH WAR VESSELS WRECKED.

News from Western Virginia, Kentucky, and Missouri.

THE GREAT EXPEDITION.

NEWS FROM MEMPHIS BY WAY OF CAIRO.

CAIRO, Monday, Nov. 11.

Memphis papers received to-day contain dispatches from Savannah fully confirming the landing of the naval expedition at Beaufort, and capture of three forts at Port Royal, Hilton Head and Bay Point. The Federal forces had possession of the town of Beaufort. The rebels acknowledge their loss very heavy.

New-Orleans papers also received to-day speak of an immense fleet off Ship Island.

OUR DISPATCHES FROM FORT MONROE.

FORTRESS MONROE, Sunday, Nov. 10.

The steamship *R. Spaulding* arrived from Hatteras Inlet this morning with the Twentieth Indiana Regiment.

A deserter, who reached the Inlet in a small boat, stated that news had been received on the main land of the taking of two Rebel forts at Port Royal, and the landing of a large National force.

Beaufort had also been taken by our troops.

No particulars have arrived, but the main fact corresponds with the news received a few hours since from Norfolk by a flag of truce. Great excitement prevailed on the arrival of the news at Norfolk.

From the same source we have a rumor that the railroad above Beaufort has fallen into the possession of our troops, with an immense quantity of stores.

Five deserters who reached Newport's News this morning, state that the rebels up James River are in consternation, and also bring the improbable rumor, that our troops had advanced up the Railroad, as far as Charleston.

The captain of the United States gunboat *Albatross* reports that he discovered the *Union* ashore on the 6th inst., about eight miles to the eastward of Bogue Inlet, but, in consequence of the heavy weather had no communication with the shore until the following day, when he landed with a flag of truce, and learned from the captain of a rebel company the following particulars:

The *Union* went ashore, or rather was ran ashore in a sinking condition on the 1st inst., and soon after broke in two in front of the smoke-stack. The crew, seventy-three in number, and fifteen horses were saved. The men are prisoners at Fort Macon and Raleigh, N. C. Large quantities of stores were seen piled up on the beach.

At the time of the disaster, the steamer *Winfield Scott* was in company with the *Union*, and the Captain of the latter expressed the opinion, that his consort was lost, she having suddenly disappeared.

Nothing is known concerning the rumored loss of the *Ocean Express*.

There are rumors of three Federal vessels having gone ashore.

The French frigate *Calabria* was burned to the water's edge, on Friday night, off Hatteras. All hands were saved.

FROM ANOTHER CORRESPONDENT.

FORTRESS MONROE, Sunday, Nov. 10, }
Via BALTIMORE, Monday, Nov. 11. }

The gunboat *Albatross*, from the blockade on the North Carolina coast, which arrived last evening, reports that on Wednesday, the 6th, she sighted a wreck about eight miles north of Bogue Inlet, N. C., but the sea was so high she could not make her out, though a flag of truce was hoisted on shore.

Next day she stood in again, when another flag was hoisted. On communicating, she learned that the wreck was the United States steam-transport *Union*, belonging to the fleet, loaded with horses and provisions, and that she went ashore on the night of Friday, the 1st inst. All hands were saved. When she struck she was badly stove, with four feet of water in her hold. She was run square on shore, and broke in two abaft the smoke-stack. Capt. GARVIN and eighty others were divided in two parties, and sent to Fort Macon and Raleigh.

The beach was strewn with the cargo and dead horses. She had 67, all but 15 of which were killed before going ashore.

The rebel officers informed the officers of the *Albatross* that Capt. GARVIN had said he feared the *Winfield Scott*, with two regiments, had foundered and gone down, because she was in company shortly before the *Union* struck, and suddenly disappeared. It was at night, and this conclusion is much doubted.

The rebels reported also that two vessels of the fleet were ashore near Charleston, and others below Hatteras. Nothing was heard of the *Ocean Express* or the names of any of the others alleged to be lost.

The *Spaulding* has also arrived from Hatteras. Lieut. LOWRY reports that on Wednesday [illegible] last heavy firing was heard south of that place, and news was received that the French war steamer *Prona* was on Ocracoke Beach. Lieut. LOWRY, with the gunboat *Underwriter*, was dispatched to her.

The sea was very high, and we could not get nearer than three miles. Lay there all night, making signals. In the morning, finding the *Underwriter* in a damaged condition, returned to Hatteras. At 11 o'clock the same day, the French steamer was seen to blow up, with a loud explosion and dense smoke. It was supposed she had been abandoned and blown up. This and another French war steamer have been in the neighborhood some time, but have repelled all intercourse with our ships.

Before the *Spaulding* left, Gen. WILLIAMS received intelligence from the main shore that the expedition had entered Port Royal and captured the batteries and Beaufort. It was reported through the same source that the *Mayflower* and another ship belonging to the fleet were wrecked.

Nothing has been heard from the fleet except the above. Nothing whatever has been received here concerning the fighting at Port Royal, except the first report through Norfolk, that one gunboat was disabled by the rebel guns, and another aground in a critical situation. Excepting the wrecks, the belief is that the expedition is successful.

REPORTS RECEIVED IN BALTIMORE.

BALTIMORE, Monday, Nov. 11.

An officer of the Twentieth Indiana Regiment, who came from Hatteras Inlet, arrived here in the Old Point boat. He says that he had a long conversation with the party who brought the news to Hatteras Inlet. This party was not a deserter, but a private citizen—a man of considerable intelligence, who had crossed the Sound at the risk of his life, to bring news to the National troops.

The officer reports that his conversation corresponds precisely with what has already been transmitted over the wires.

Outside of this statement there is a report that, in taking Beaufort, a large part of the town was burnt.

FURTHER REPORTS FROM BALTIMORE.

BALTIMORE, Monday, Nov. 11.

Capt. DOWELL, of the Twentieth Indiana Regiment, which returned to Fortress Monroe from Hatteras, says that he found it almost impossible to remain longer on that narrow neck of land on account of the loss of camp equipage and stores. Although the men have suffered severe privations, the number on the sick-list is very small. All are now comfortably quartered near Fortress Monroe.

Col. HAWKINS' New-York Regiment will return by the next trip of the steamer. These men have suffered more severely in health than the Indiana Regiment. Over 100 are on the sick list.

Capt. DOWELL gives the following statement in reference to the reception of the news from the fleet at Hatteras Inlet:

Capt. DOWELL states that the day previous to the departure of the steamer *S. R. Spaulding*, a man was observed paddling across in a small canoe from the main land to the peninsula, and as soon as he reached shore he proceeded to the quarters of the Twentieth Indiana Regiment, and stated that the people of North Carolina had received tidings of the great naval expedition; that it had succeeded in effecting landings at the ports of Port Royal and Beaufort. At the first named place that they had experienced no difficulty in landing, as there was but a small settlement on the coast; but at Beaufort a considerable fight took place, which lasted for near two days.

The man stated that he was not a deserter from the rebels, for he would not join them, being a Union man in heart and principle. He seemed to be very intelligent, and his only object in making the visit was to communicate to the National troops the success of the naval expedition.

He remained on the place until the *Spaulding* made her departure.

Capt. DOWELL brings intelligence of the loss of the French man-of-war *Cantilabria*, near Beaufort. She was of about 2,500 tons, and after vainly endeavoring to ride the gale got aground upon a shifting sand bar. Notwithstanding the incessant exertions of her officers and crew she had to be abandoned, and all hands, including the officers, soldiers and seamen, were compelled to find shelter on shore as best they could. The vessel was afterwards boarded by a detachment by order of the commanding officer and blown up. The reason of this proceeding was not known. It was impossible for the wreckers to reach the vessel.

RUMORED RETURN OF THE VANDERBILT.

BALTIMORE, Monday, Nov. 11.

It is reported by the boat from Old Point that a steamer came in the Capes last evening and continued up the Bay without stopping. She was thought to be the *Vanderbilt*, with dispatches from the Great Fleet. Nothing has been heard of her arrival yet at Annapolis Roads.

There is nothing but outside report to warrant the statement that "at last accounts our troops had advanced to within twelve miles of Charleston."

REPORTED STAMPEDE OF REBEL TROOPS.

PHILADELPHIA, Monday, Nov. 11.

A special dispatch to the *Inquirer*, dated Fortress Monroe, says that two fishing-smacks took refuge under the guns of the *Cumberland*. The Captains were Baltimoreans. They reported they had been fishing in James River, supplying the rebel troops. When they left the report was current that Charleston had been attacked, and state that on Friday last several regiments were sent South from the James and York Rivers. The embarkation took place in great haste. The shores of the James River were almost deserted.

THE NEWS AT WASHINGTON.

WASHINGTON, Monday, Nov. 11.

There is most intense excitement here to hear further particulars in regard to the great expedition.

Utterly groundless rumors are circulating,—among others, that Charleston has been bombarded.

No intelligence whatever concerning the great expedition had been received in any quarter up to noon to-day, additional to what has already been telegraphed North to the general Press.

THE GREAT EXPEDITION.

ITS DESTINATION KNOWN IN THE SOUTH—HOW WAS IT DIVULGED?

Correspondence of the Philadelphia Inquirer.

WASHINGTON, Nov. 9, 1861.

It is astonishing how the Confederates obtain a perfect knowledge of all our movements. It appears from information received here that *the positive destination of our fleet was known even in New-Orleans on the 17th ult.—weeks before it was known in the North!*—and extra troops were dispatched from points south of Charleston to defend the approaches of that coast. Port Royal in particular, from its known advantages, received the special attention of the Confederates, and their best man (TATNALL) was placed in command of that location.

I need not say that the Government is sorely perplexed in consequence of this continued leakage of its plans, but it seems to be just now wholly powerless in the matter.

The report in this instance that the destination of the fleet was divulged by means of a mail thoughtlessly put on board a vessel shamming distress, and taken to Charleston, receives but little credence, as, even if this occurrence was true, the blockading vessel from which the mail was sent had no knowledge of the actual destination of the fleet, (which had not then even sailed,) and could not therefore state where it was bound.

Besides, the plans were solely in the confidence of the President, his Cabinet, Gen. SCOTT, Capt. DUPONT, and perhaps one or two others, and how they were known through the entire South as early as the 18th of October, is a question that may well puzzle even a Philadelphia lawyer.

It proves one thing, however, that, despite the careful precautions of the Government, *there must still be spies in the shape of professed friends, enjoying both its confidence and its secrets.* It has been thought by some that much valuable information might have been purloined or obtained from the telegraph [illegible] here, but I have reason to know that such a proceeding would be absolutely impossible. All that remains is for the Government to use, if possible, even greater exertions than hitherto, to ferret out those guilty of promulgating its secrets, as otherwise the Government wheels must be more or less blocked continually.

Additional details of the engagement before Beaufort are awaited with an anxiety never before excelled. The number of men and weapons brought to bear against our fleet and the brave troops on board, makes it almost certain that the slaughter there has been most bloody on both sides, and the whole country will await news of the final issue with the deepest feelings of solicitude. The contest has, of course, ere this been decided, and official intelligence of the same should reach us by Monday at the latest. It is expected that, in the event of a successful landing at Beaufort, which is here believed probable, railroad communication will be suspended by our troops, and the telegraph office seized. These will be two most important steps, as speedy information of the existing condition of affairs will thus be cut off from other parts of the State and the South. The Navy Department have full confidence in the success of our forces, and information respecting the same is probably now in Norfolk, but withheld by order of the Confederate authorities.

THE DISASTER TO THE GOVERNOR.

Correspondence of the New-York Times.

U. S. STEAM BARK YOUNG ROVER, NORTHERN ATLANTIC BLOCKADING SQUADRON, 40 MILES N. E. CHARLESTON, S. C., Saturday, Nov. 2, 1861. }

This morning, about 8 o'clock, saw from the mast-head the "Star Spangled Banner," Union down, floating at half-mast upon a vessel about eight miles distant, "dead to the windward," and, hastening to her relief, found it was the United States steamer *Governor*, having on board 400 troops, bound down with the fleet, which had been passing some time before. She had been separated from the fleet during the heavy gale of the previous night. She was entirely disabled, her rudder gone, her machinery broken, and she was leaking badly. They wished to be taken off, as the vessel must go the bottom in a short time. Not being able to take them all on board, we went for assistance, crowded on all canvas, and finally came within signaling distance of the United States frigate *Sabine*, which immediately made sail and followed us back to the steamer. The frigate being amply supplied with men and boats, and having plenty of room, declined our proffered assistance; and we went on our way, rejoicing that we had been the humble means of saving 400 lives, although it was not done without risk to our own ship, as the sea was running very high.

This ship goes in for repairs now, to Hampton Roads. It is commanded by JOHN HUMPHREY, Volunteer Lieutenant Commanding. The following is a list of her officers, also: J. B. Studley, J. H. Eldridge, Geo. Williams, Masters; E. D. G. Smith, Acting Surgeon; Geo. W. Stone, Acting Paymaster; James Patterson, Acting Assistant Engineer.

OUR DISPATCHES FROM WASHINGTON

WASHINGTON, Monday, Nov. 11.

GRAND TORCHLIGHT PROCESSION—SPEECHES, ETC.

A grand torchlight procession, in honor of the accession of Gen. McCLELLAN to the post of Commander-in-Chief of Army of the United States, took place to-night. The demonstration was planned and executed by Gen. BLENKER'S Division, and was carried out with the taste and success which characterize such efforts on the part of foreign citizens. The division marched over Long Bridge, and after forming in Fourteenth-street, lighted their torches and marched past Willard's, Pennsylvania-avenue, to the President's House, where Mr. LINCOLN appeared and witnessed the spectacle as the procession passed. Rockets and Roman candles followed each other in quick succession.

The procession then marched around Lafayette-square, and halted in front of Gen. McCLELLAN'S residence, where Gen. BLENKER and staff were cordially received by the Commander-in-Chief, Secretaries SEWARD and CAMERON, and Gens. MARCY, FRANKLIN, SMITH, ANDREWS, PORTER, VAN VLIET, and others, including many ladies.

A protracted serenade followed, during which there was a splendid exhibition of fireworks, which closed with an allegorical piece representing Justice, with the sword and scales, standing under the "Stars and Stripes," and a spread eagle.

Loud calls were made for Gen. McCLELLAN, which being ineffectual, the call was made for Secretary CAMERON, who appeared on the balcony and said:

SECRETARY CAMERON'S SPEECH.

SOLDIERS: I am very glad to see you here to-night, and especially since you have come to do honor to your gallant and brave young General. [Cheers.] It is an evidence to my mind that every one of you is determined to do his duty. [Cheers.] The greater portion of your number I believe are Germans. Coming as I do from the State of Pennsylvania, whose population is composed for the most part of Germans or their descendants, it makes me still more happy to meet you, for the Germans of Pennsylvania have fought in every battle-field that has given glory to our country. [Cheers.] I know that when the brunt of battle comes, you will do as nobly as did the Germans in the battles they fought for our common liberties. [Loud cheers.]

The calls for Gen. McCLELLAN were then renewed, in response to which he appeared upon the balcony with Gen. BLENKER. There was an evident desire to make Gen. McCLELLAN deliver a speech, but he, as usual, blushingly retired.

Secretary SEWARD was then loudly called for. He appeared on the balcony and said:

SECRETARY SEWAARD'S SPEECH.

FELLOW CITIZENS AND SOLDIERS: I see before me the one part of our army gathered for the defence of the Union—[cheers]—an army as large as any Monarch on the face of the earth has ever, in the tide of time, brought into the field,—as brave as any;—and yet it is an army that contains not a single conscript. [Cheers.] Every soldier is a volunteer, and nearly every volunteer is a citizen. It may be well so, for you have come here to defend an experiment—the first in the history of the world which has existed for eighty years and has never demanded of any citizen or subject the sacrifice of his liberty or his life against his consent. [Cheers.] I knew, when this struggle began, that we should find soldiers and seamen; that we should find all we wanted except in one particular, and your gathering to-night shows me that that want is now supplied. What is that want? It is a General.—and you have him here to-night. And, fellow-citizens, whoever is the sovereign of this continent of America, ought to be, and must be, the sovereign of the world. [Cheers.] Who is sovereign in America? Is it the Queen of Liberty, as she walks abroad over this vast continent, wrapt in her flaming robe; or is it Cotton? [Laughter.] Whoever is here who is in favor of Cotton, let him shout to the top of your voice. What? not a voice for King Cotton? What, then, say you for the Queen of Liberty? [Loud cheers.]

Amid loud calls for Gen. BLENKER, he appeared and addressed the assemblage in a brief but telling speech, spoken with a marked German accent. He said:

GEN. BLENKER'S SPEECH.

CITIZENS AND SOLDIERS: I will say but a few words, and those few words are these. I swear to you that, if we are before the enemy, I will fight with the thousands of volunteers I see before me, and better than I speak your noble language. [Loud cheers.]

After bidding farewell to Gen. McCLELLAN, Gen. BLENKER gave the order to march, and the procession moved through the city and across the river.

GOOD ADVICES FROM KENTUCKY.

Private advices from Kentucky continue to give a very encouraging account of the progress of the campaign against the rebels in that State.

A RECONNOISSANCE TO PEACOCK'S HILL.

Yesterday Gen. HANCOCK sent out five companies of the New-York Forty-ninth and three of cavalry to Peacock's Hill, five miles beyond Lewinsville. They discovered no signs of the recent presence of rebel pickets, except a few extinguished camp fires. The cavalry went three miles beyond, and was informed that the place had but recently been occupied by rebel troops. They brought in a prisoner.

MOUNT VERNON WITHIN OUR LINES.

In front of the left wing of our army below Alexandria our picket lines extend from the mouth of the Accotink up the Accotink Ridge ten miles in front of Fort Lyon and four in front of Mount Vernon, which estate is now within our lines. The rebel pickets appear about two or three miles beyond our lines, and about the same distance this side of the Occoquan.

FIELD WORKS AT FAIRFAX STATION.

Scouts in the direction of Fairfax Station state that the rebels have thrown up two field works at that point, and that Gen. EWELL is there with five regiments.

A Virginian residing near the mouth of Pohick Creek has reported to Gen. RICHARDSON that the rebels are throwing up a work at or near that point. As he is extremely anxious to sell forage to the Government, his statements are looked upon with suspicion, as being intended to prevent our commanders from sending out foraging expeditions in that direction. The general belief is that they have no force near Occoquan.

FROM THE LOWER POTOMAC.

The *Resolute* arrived to-night from the flotilla. She reports a new six-gun rebel battery, five miles above Mathias Point. It opened upon the *Freeborn* this morning, but none of the shots hit. Oyster pungies continue to run the blockade nightly, and to-day four passed up in broad daylight.

THE PENSACOLA.

This war-steamer is still lying in the Potomac, opposite Alexandria, and though commenced nearly four years since, is still uncompleted. Its keel was laid about the same time as the *Brooklyn*, which latter, built by contract, was quickly finished, and has since made a three years' cruise. The cause of the delay is the costly experiment which is being tried in her engines, in which Mr. SICKELS is endeavoring to avoid the difficulties which caused the failure of the *Lancaster's* machinery, which was constructed nearly on the same principle. The *Pensacola's* machinery is of the most complicated character, and has cost thus far about $300,000, while that of the *Brooklyn* and other vessels of the same class only cost about one-third of that sum. If no unforeseen accident occurs, the engines will probably be completed this week and a trial of them given.

AT THEIR POSTS AGAIN.

Secretary CAMERON, Adjt.-Gen. THOMAS, and Quartermaster-Gen. MEIGS, arrived in this city to-day, and were at their posts in the War Department.

THE BALTIMORE AND OHIO RAILROAD.

Owing to the inconvenience which would be occasioned the Government by the interruption of transportation on the railroad between Baltimore and this city, should any malignant rebel tear up the track or destroy the bridges, Gen. McCLELLAN has established a strong guard over the road, extending the entire distance between the cities. The sentinels are all within hailing distance of one another.

RAILROAD TIME-TABLES.

Information has been received here that the Railroad Convention which met in Princeton to-day adopted the following time-table, to take effect on the 18th inst.: Leave Washington at 6 and 11 A. M. and 5 P. M., arriving in New-York at 6 and 10 P. M. and 4 A. M.; leave New-York 7 A. M. and 6 and 11 P. M., arriving in Washington at 6 P. M. and 6 and 9:30 A. M. Trains leaving Washington at 5 P. M. go through direct to New-York every day.

A SCOUT.

One of Gen. FRANKLIN'S scouts, named THOMAS P. EDWARDS, Corporal of Company D, Third New-Jersey Regiment, in company with a private of the same regiment, named NEWBERN, penetrated the rebel lines recently to within three miles of Fairfax Court-house. At the house of DAVID FITZHUGH they encountered three rebel scouts, one of whom shot EDWARDS, the ball passing through the fleshy part of the arm, and entering his side, and lodging near his spine. NEWBERN shot two of the rebels, and then with EDWARDS, who walked about thirteen miles in spite of his wound, escaped. EDWARDS is now in the Seminary Hospital, at Alexandria, and likely to recover.

A REVIEW OF GEN. FRANKLIN'S DIVISION.

Gen FRANKLIN'S Division will be reviewed by Gen. McCLELLAN on Thursday.

THE FUTURE VICEROY OF MEXICO.

Reliable advices received here state that the Spanish Government, in placing MIRAMON second in command of the Spanish forces about to invade Mexico, promised to make him Viceroy of that country in case the invasion should prove successful. This is but the repetition of the St. Domingo programme. SANTANA, who sold his country to the Spaniards, has been made Captain-General of that part of the island of St. Domingo now in possession of Spain.

SUFFERING ABOUT WINCHESTER.

If it be true that fifteen thousand [illegible] are quartered near Winchester, it must intensify the sufferings of all the people there. A lady who recently escaped from there and crossed the Potomac, says that the stock of coal there is entirely exhausted, and that though there is an abundance of wood in the vicinity, there are no horses and wagons with which to transport it to the villages, they having been all seized by the rebels and carried off. The gas works of Winchester were stopped a month ago, owing to the stock of coal being exhausted, and the candles then on hand were used up weeks since. Of cotton and woolen goods, and boots and shoes, there is scarcely any left. Poor families, many of whose husbands and sons are in the rebel army, having gone there voluntarily, or been pressed into the service, have but little food, and less clothing and fuel, and are consequently suffering greatly. A case recently occurred, showing that no better state of things exists about Richmond. A merchant from that city came a few weeks since, and bought the whole of the remaining stock of general merchandise of a Winchester merchant and transported it to Richmond to sell.

GEN. GRANT.

Gen. GRANT, the hero of the battle of Belmont, is a resident of Galena, Ill., and was appointed on the recommendation of Hon. ELIHU B. WASHBURNE. He graduated at West Point in 1837, and was breveted First Lieutenant for gallant and meritorious conduct at Molina del Rey, and breveted Captain for similar conduct at Chepultepec. He resigned his commission in 1855, and was in many battles in Mexico.

LIGHT-HOUSES ON THE SOUTHERN COAST.

No efforts have yet been made to reëstablish the light on Fort Hatteras. The rebels removed the first-class fresnal lenses from the lighthouse months since, and as they have no difficulty in crossing the Sound from the main land, it would be impossible to keep the light there at present, except a force was stationed there to protect it. Chandeleur Island, near the mouth of the Mississippi, being now in possession of our forces, the light will be reëstablished there soon.

SALT AND SHOES FOR THE REBELS.

The license of the Government to Northern shippers to trade in salt and shoes, etc., with loyal citizens of the Southern States, spoken of by a morning paper, is likely to test the honesty of the parties so engaged. Suppose, when the vessels get into Southern waters, a rebel citizen offers a better price for the cargo than the loyalist, what will happen? This query will probably dispose of the whole question whether such licenses are to be issued or not.

TRESPASSES UPON PRIVATEP PROERTY.

In view of the military occupation of Alexandria and Fairfax Counties, and the practical abrogation of the Civil Courts, an immunity has

[*Continued on Eighth Page.*]

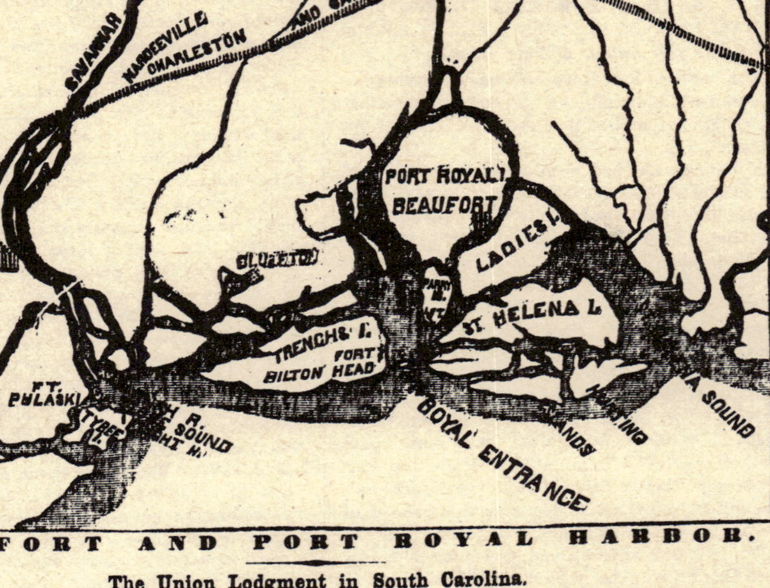

BEAUFORT AND PORT ROYAL HARBOR.

The Union Lodgment in South Carolina.

The certainty that Port Royal and Beaufort are the regions at which the Naval Expedition has struck its first blow, and the brilliant success that has attended operations there, lend those localities increased interest. To satisfy this we republish a clear and complete map of

PORT ROYAL AND BEAUFORT.

Port Royal Entrance is an inlet from the Atlantic, in latitude 32° 8' N., fifty miles southwest of Charleston, and fifteen miles northeast of Tybee Inlet, the entrance of Savannah River. The opening from the Atlantic is between Edding Island and Hilton Head Island, and at that point is about three miles wide. The prolongation inward of Port Royal Entrance is called Broad River and Port Royal River. Running up this for about twenty-five miles, bending off eastward through the Coosaw River, and coming out to the Atlantic again through St. Helena Sound, you have an irregular area of about twenty-five miles by fifteen. This amphibious region is cut up by numerous rivers, creeks and inlets into a great many islands (Sea Islands) of various sizes, the chief of which are "Port Royal," "St. Helena," "Paris," "Ladies," "Coosaw," "Morgan," "Dathaw," "Edding," "Chaplin," "Prentis" and "Hunting."

Along the coast of South Carolina as in North Carolina and Georgia, stretches a low and narrow sand bar—a kind of defensive outwork of the land, seldom inhabited except by lost Indians and runaway negroes, who subsist by hunting and fishing. At distant intervals there are shallow breaches through which the quiet tide steals in twice a day, swelling the natural lagoons and damming the outlet of the fresh water stream till the current is destroyed and turned back, and their flood dispersed far and wide over the debatable land of the Cypress Swamp. Then, when the heavy rains in the interior have swollen the rivers, their eddying currents deposit all along the edges of the sandy islands and capes the rich freight they have brought from the calcareous or granitic mountains in which they rise, with the organic waste of the great forests through which they flow. This is the soil of the rice and cotton plantations, which are always found in such parts of the tidal swamps adjoining the mainland or the sandy islands as are left nearly dry at the ebb of the water.

The entrance to Port Royal is the best channel for ships through the bars in the whole range of ports below Norfolk. Within the Roads, even over the bar, there are three and a half fathoms water, or twenty-one feet, and probably twenty-seven feet at high tide. The command of waters, too, which the possession of Port Royal entrance gives, is immense. Ships which draw 14 or 15 feet water, may go in at Tybee and proceed through land to Beaufort in Port Royal Islands; and from Beaufort, vessels of 8 or 9 feet water may go through land to Charleston. From Charleston, vessels drawing 7 or 8 feet water may go through land to the river Medway, in Georgia, which lies thirty miles south of Savannah. The entrance of the harbor, as is shown on the map, *was* protected by batteries on Hilton Head and Parry's Island. Masses of smoking ruins now only show where they *were*.

Port Royal Island, the chief of the group above mentioned, is surrounded by the Broad, Port Royal, Coosaw and Beaufort Rivers, and is about twelve miles long and six wide. On the east side of the island, and about mid-way, stands the town of Beaufort, on Beaufort River, the approach of which does not admit vessels of over eleven feet draft. Beaufort is about ten miles from the sea, and sixteen miles from the Charleston and Savannah Railroad, and this important line is itself directly approachable by water through Broad River and St. Helena Sound and Combahee River. A force moving up the river from Beaufort, *via* Beaufort and Coosaw and Port Royal rivers, would strike the Charleston and Savannah Railroad at about midway between Charleston and Savannah, and about 50 miles from either city—a fact which renders obvious the immense strategic importance of that line. Beaufort is the Newport of South Carolina, and has a white population of about one thousand. It is thus described by Sir CHARLES LYELL, in his *Travels in the United States*:

"Beaufort, a picturesque town composed of an assemblage of villas, the summer residences of numerous planters, who retire here during the hot season, when the interior of South Carolina is unhealthy for the whites. Each villa is shaded by a verandah, surrounded by live oaks and orange trees."

The possession of the fine harbor of Beaufort or Port Royal thus gives command of one of the most important, and, for the designs the army of the Union has in view in making a lodgment on the Southern coast, most advantageous bases of operation in entire rebeldom. Beaufort District has an area of 1,540 square miles. The surface is low and level, and the soil sandy and alluvial, producing cotton, rice, etc., in great abundance. Our troops will thus find themselves lodged in the richest district (South Carolina term of county) in the State—yielding some fifty million pounds of rice annually, and thirteen thousand bales for the finest quality of cotton, the famous long-staple sea-island, the very kind Europe most wants. Here are over six millions of dollars' worth of crops, subject at once to confiscation, if their proprietors persist in their disloyalty. It is also one of the most thickly settled districts of the State, the population in 1850 being 38,805. Of these no less than 32,279 are negro slaves—a property representing *twenty millions* of dollars! It is on this spot that the shaded maps of negro distribution show the nightliest shade. *We shall thus literally carry the war into Africa!* The place is admirably suited for a vast camp of instruction, and with proper defences it will not be found difficult to hold this whole district against any force the rebels can bring against us. What a splendid nucleus of loyalty in the very heart of the birthplace of secession.

The New-York Times.

VOL. XI....NO. 3166. | NEW-YORK, THURSDAY, NOVEMBER 14, 1861. | PRICE TWO CENTS.

THE GREAT EXPEDITION.

Arrival of the Bienville with Official Dispatches and Correspondence.

The Accounts of Capt. Dupont and Gen. Sherman.

A Full Narrative of Events by Our Own Correspondent.

COMPLETE SUCCESS OF THE EXPEDITION

How Forts Beauregard and Walker were Taken.

Terrific Bombardment of Between Four and Five Hours.

Gallant Conduct of the National Vessels.

The Defeat and Utter Rout of the Enemy

Forty-three Pieces of Cannon Captured.

Beaufort Abandoned by All but the Negroes and One Drunken White Man.

Fifteen Thousand National Troops Landed.

Proclamation of Gen. Sherman to the South Carolinians.

The U. S. gunboat *Bienville*, Commander Chas. Steedman, and A. E. R. Benham, Executive Officer, arrived at this port at 6½ o'clock last evening, from the Great Naval Expedition, via Fortress Monroe, where she left dispatches for Commodore Goldsborough, and whence Capt. Steedman proceeded to Washington with dispatches for the Army and Navy Departments. These dispatches, from Capt. Dupont, who commanded the naval portion of the Expedition and from Gen. Sherman, who commanded the military branch, will be found below, together with a detailed narrative of the operations of the Expedition since it left Hampton Roads.

The fleet arrived at Port Royal on Monday, the 4th inst.

On Tuesday the smaller gunboats rounded into the channel under a fire from the forts, which did no damage.

On Wednesday the weather prevented active operations, but on Thursday morning, 7th inst., the men-of-war and the gunboats advanced to the attack.

The action commenced at 10 A. M., and was hotly carried on on both sides, and lasted about four hours, at the end of which time the rebels were compelled by the shower of shells to abandon their works and beat a hasty retreat.

The day after the fight the *Seneca*, and two other gunboats, under the command of Lieut. Ammen, proceeded up to Beaufort, and found but one white man in the town, and he was drunk.

After the capture of the forts the whole army, about 15,000 men, were safely landed and established on shore.

THE GOVERNMENT ACCOUNTS.

Washington, Wednesday, Nov. 13.

Capt. Steedman arrived here at noon to-day bringing official dispatches from the great naval Expedition. He is also the bearer of two rebel Confederate flags, one Palmetto flag, and the American flag first hoisted in South Carolina over Fort Walker. Capt. Steedman reports that the captured forts are magnificent, with covered ways, and bomb-proof. All that our troops had to do was to occupy them. They can be held against any opposing force.

Among the most efficient vessels were found to be the new gunboats, and of which the Navy Department had twenty-three constructed expressly for such purpose, and their success both in the gale and under fire was perfect.

Commander Drayton, who commanded the *Pocahontas*, is the brother of Gen. Drayton, who commanded the rebel forts.

Capt. Steedman, who brings the dispatches, is the son of a former Mayor of Charleston.

On the reception of the official dispatches, the following order was issued:

General Order.—The Department announces to the navy and to the country its high gratification at the brilliant success of the combined navy and army forces, respectively commanded by Flag-Officer S. F. Dupont and Brig.-Gen. J. W. Sherman, in the capture of Forts Walker and Beauregard, commanding the entrance to Port Royal harbor, South Carolina. To commemorate this signal victory, it is ordered that a national salute be fired from each Navy-yard at meridian on the day after the reception of this order.

(Signed) GIDEON WELLES.

PRIVATE LETTER FROM CAPT. DUPONT.

The following is a portion of a private letter from Flag-officer Dupont, to the Assistant Secretary of the Navy:

Wabash, Port Royal, Nov. 8, 1861.

My Dear Mr. Fox: During the disheartening events of our passage my faith never gave way, but at some moments it seemed appalling. On the other hand, I permit no elation at our success, yet I cannot refrain from telling you that it has been more complete and brilliant than I ever could have believed. I have been too fatigued to send a detailed official account of the battle. My report is full up to the eve of it, and I think will interest you; but I had to content myself with a succinct account, which I think will be liked as well as a more detailed narrative. This I will however, forward in time for the Secretary's report. I kept under way and made three turns, though I passed five times between the forts. I had a flanking division of five ships to watch, and old Tatnall, too, who had eight small and swift steamers ready to pounce upon any of ours, should they be disabled. I could get none of my big frigates up. I thought the *Sabine* would have gotten clear up to the *St. Lawrence*. I sent no word, however, and the *Savannah* was blown off. I do not regret it now, except on their account. I believe my plan was clever. I stood against the tide, and had the management the better in consequence. Their confidence was extreme that they could drive us away. They fought bravely, and their rifle guns never missed. An 80-pounder rifle ball went through our mainmast in the very centre, making an awful hole. They aimed at our bridge where they knew they could make a hole if they were lucky. A shot in the centre let water into the after-magazine, but I saved a hundred lives by keeping under way and bearing in close. We found their sights graduated at six hundred yards. When they once broke the stampede was intense, and not a gun was spiked. In truth I never conceived of such a fire as that of this ship on her second turn, and I am told that its effect upon the spectators outside of her was intense. I learn that when they saw our flag flying on shore the troops were powerless to cheer but wept. Gen. Sherman was deeply affected, and the soldiers are loud and unstinting in their expressions of admiration and gratitude. The works are most scientifically constructed, and there is nothing like Fort Walker on the Potomac. I did not allow the victory to check our ardor, but dispatched some vessels, under Capt. Gillis, over the other side. To-day I have sent an expedition to Beaufort to save the light vessels, but they were fired instantly after the surrender.

Beaufort is deserted. The negroes are wild with joy and revenge. They have been shot down, they say, like dogs, because they would not go off with their masters. I have already a boat at Skull Creek, and the communication between Savannah and Charleston is cut off."

PRIVATE LETTER FROM ANOTHER OFFICER.

The following is an extract from a private letter from one of the officers engaged in the bombardment:

"I am sure our success will rejoice your hearts; it has been complete, and terror runs over the whole country. The negroes are wild, and plundering their masters' houses. The whites have been driving the negroes away by force, and shooting them down, but they still come to the gunboats. The moment Gen. Drayton took to his horse in the panic of the 7th, his two hundred servants went directly to the *Wabash*. This is worthy of notice, as putting down the nonsense that the slaves were ready to fight for their masters. They surrounded Capt. Ammen in crowds at Beaufort, one of them, calling out, in the joy of his heart, 'I didn't think you could do it, massa.'"

CAPT. DUPONT'S OFFICIAL REPORTS.

The following are the official dispatches to the Navy Department:

FIRST DISPATCH.

Flag-Ship Wabash, off Hilton Head,
Port Royal Harbor, Nov. 6, 1861.

Sir: The Government having determined to seize and occupy one or more important points upon our Southern coast, where our squadrons might find shelter, possess a dépôt, and afford protection to loyal citizens, committed to my discretion the selection from among those places which it thought available and desirable for these purposes. After mature deliberation aided by the professional knowledge and great intelligence of the Assistant Secretary, Mr. Fox, and upon taking into consideration the magnitude to which the joint naval and military expedition had been extended, to which you have called my attention, I came to the conclusion that the original intentions of the Department, if carried out, would fall short of the expectations of the country, and of the capabilities of the expedition, while Port Royal, I thought, would meet both in a high degree.

I therefore submitted to Brig.-Gen. Sherman, commanding the military part of the expedition, this modification of our earliest matured plans, and had the satisfaction to receive his full concurrence, though he and the commanders of the brigades very justly laid great stress on the necessity, if possible, of getting this frigate into the harbor of Port Royal.

On Tuesday, the 29th of October, the fleet under my command left Hampton Roads, and with the army transports, numbered 50 vessels. On the day previous I had dispatched the coal vessels, twenty-five in number, under convoy of the *Vandalia*, Commander Haggerty, to rendezvous off Savannah, not wishing to give the true point of the fleet. The weather had been unsettled in Hampton Roads, though it promised well when we sailed. But off Hatteras it blew hard, some ships got into the breakers, and two struck, but without injury, on Friday, the 1st of November. The rough weather soon increased into a gale, and we had to encounter one of great violence from the Southeast, a portion of which approached to a hurricane. The fleet was utterly dispersed, and on Saturday morning one sail only was in sight from the deck of the *Wabash*. On the following day the weather moderated, and the steamers and ships began to reappear. The orders were opened, except those in case of separation. These last were furnished to all the men-of-war by myself and to the transports by Brig.-Gen. Sherman. As the vessels rejoined reports came in of disasters. I expected to hear of many, but when the severity of the gale and the character of the vessels are considered, we have only cause for great thankfulness.

In reference to the men-of-war, the *Isaac Smith*, a most efficient and well-armed vessel for the class purchased, but not intended to encounter such sea and wind, had to throw her formidable battery overboard to keep from foundering; but thus relieved, Lieutenant-Commanding Nicholson was enabled to go to the assistance of the chartered steamer *Governor*, then in a very dangerous condition, and on board of which was our fine battalion of marines, under Maj. Reynolds. They were finally rescued by Capt. Ringgold, in the *Sabine*, under difficult circumstances, soon after which the *Governor* went down. I believe that seven of the marines were drowned by their own imprudence. Lieut.-Com'd'g Nicholson's conduct in the *Isaac Smith* has met my warm commendation. The *Peerless*, transport, in a sinking condition, was met by the *Mohican*, Commander Gordon, and all the people on board, twenty-six in number, were saved under very peculiar circumstances, in which service Lieut. J. W. Miller was very favorably noticed by his commander.

On passing Charleston, I sent in the *Seneca*, Lieut. Commanding Ammen, to direct Capt. Lardner to join me with the steamer *Susquehannah*, off Port Royal, without delay.

On Monday, at 8 o'clock in the morning, I anchored off the bar with some twenty-five vessels in company, with many more heaving in sight.

The Department is aware that all the aids to navigation had been removed, and the bar lies ten miles seaward with no features on the shore line with sufficient prominence to make any bearings reliable. But to the skill of Commander Davis, the fleet Captain and Mr. Boutelle, the able Assistant of the Coast Survey, in charge of the steamer *Vixen*, the channel was immediately found, sounded out and buoyed. By 3 o'clock, I received assurances from Capt. Davis that I could send forward the lighter transports, those under eighteen feet, with all the gunboats, which was immediately done, and

PORT ROYAL HARBOR AND BEAUFORT.

The Scene of the Engagement.

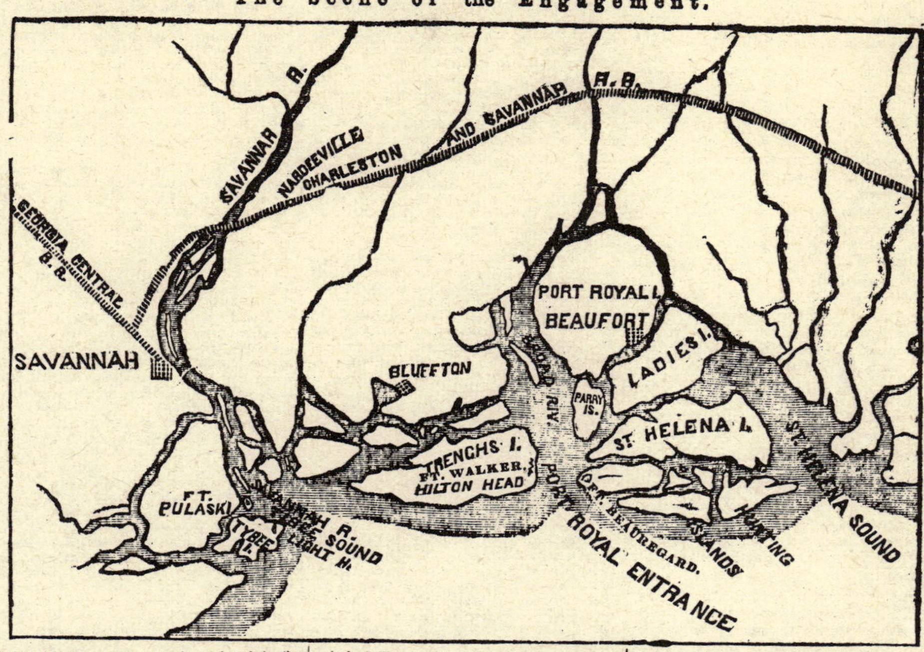

before dark they were securely anchored in the roadstead of Port Royal, South Carolina. The gunboats almost immediately opened their batteries upon two or three rebel steamers under Commodore Tatnall, instantly chasing him under the shelter of the batteries. In the morning Commander John Rodgers, of the U. S. steamer *Flag*, temporarily on board this ship, and acting on my staff, accompanied Brig.-Gen. Wright in the gunboat *Ottawa*, Lieut. Commanding Stevens, and supported by the *Seneca*, Lieut. Commanding Ammen, made a reconnoissance in force, and drew the fire of the batteries on Hilton Head and Bay Point sufficiently to show that the fortifications were works of strength and scientifically constructed.

In the evening of Monday Capt. Davis and Mr. Boutelle reported water enough for the *Wabash* to venture in.

The responsibility of hazarding so noble a frigate was not a light one, over a prolonged bar of over two miles. There was but a foot or two of water to spare, and the fall and rise of the tide is such that if she had grounded, she would have sustained most serious injury from straining, if not totally lost. Too much, however, was at stake to hesitate, and the result was entirely successful.

On the morning of Tuesday the *Wabash* crossed the bar, followed closely by the frigate *Susquehannah*, the *Atlantic*, *Vanderbilt*, and other transports of deep draft, running through that portion of the fleet already in. The safe passage of this great ship over the bar, was hailed with gratifying cheers from the crowded vessels. We anchored, and immediately commenced preparing the ship for action. But the delay of planting the buoys, particularly on the Fishing Rip, a dangerous shoal we had to avoid, rendered the hour late before it was possible to leave with the attacking squadron.

In our anxiety to get the outline of the forts before dark, we stood in too near these shoals, and the ship grounded. By the time she was gotten off, it was too late, in my judgment, to proceed, and I made signals for the squadron to anchor out of gunshot, from the enemy. To-day the wind blows a gale from the southward and westward, and the attack is unavoidably postponed. I have the honor to be, Sir,

Respectfully your obedient servant,

S. F. DUPONT, Flag Officer.

Commanding South Atlantic Blockading Squadron.

SECOND DISPATCH.

Flag-ship Wabash, off Hilton Head,
Port Royal Harbor, Nov. 8, 1861.

Hon. Gideon Welles, Secretary of the Navy, Washington:

Sir: I have the honor to inform you that yesterday I attacked the batteries of the enemy on Bay Point and Hilton Head, and Forts Walker and Beauregard, and succeeded in silencing them after an engagement of four hours' duration, and driving away the squadron of rebel steamers under Commander Tatnall.

The reconnoissance of yesterday made us satisfied with the superiority of Fort Walker, and to that I directed my especial efforts, engaging it at a distance of eight hundred, and afterwards at six hundred yards. But the plan of attack brought the squadron sufficiently near Fort Beauregard to receive its fire, and the ships were frequently fighting the batteries on both sides at the same time. The action was begun on my part at 26 minutes after 9, and at half-past 2 the American ensign was hoisted on the flag-staff of Fort Walker, and this morning at sunrise on that of Fort Beauregard. The defeat of the enemy terminated in utter rout and confusion. Their quarters and encampments were abandoned without an attempt to carry away either public or private property. The ground over which they fled was strewn with the arms of private soldiers, and the officers retired in too much haste to submit to the incumbrance of their swords. Landing my marines and a company of seamen, I took possession of the deserted ground, and held the forts on Hilton Head till the arrival of Gen. Sherman, to whom I had the honor to transfer their command.

We have captured forty-three pieces of cannon, most of them of the heaviest calibre, and of the most improved design. The bearer of these dispatches will have the honor to carry with him the captured flags, and two small brass field-pieces, lately belonging to the State of South Carolina, which are sent home as suitable trophies of the success of the day.

I inclose herewith a copy of the general order which is to be read in the fleet to-morrow morning at muster.

A detailed account of this battle will be submitted hereafter. I have the honor to be, very respectfully, your obedient servant, S. F. DUPONT,

Flag-Officer, Commanding South Atlantic Blockading Squadron.

P. S.—The bearer of dispatches will also carry with him the first American ensign raised upon the soil of South Carolina since the rebellion broke out.

S. F. D.

GENERAL ORDER TO THE FLEET.

Flag-ship Wabash, Hilton Head,
Port Royal Bay, Nov. 8, 1861.

General Order No. 2.—It is the grateful duty of the Commander-in-Chief to make a public acknowledgment of his entire commendation of the coolness, discipline, skill and gallantry displayed by the officers and men under his command, in the capture of the batteries at Hilton Head and Bay Point, after an action of four hours' duration.

The Flag-officer fully sympathises with the officers and men of his squadron in the satisfaction they must feel at seeing the ensign of the United States flying once more in the State of South Carolina, which has been the chief promoter of the wicked and unprovoked rebellion they have been called upon to suppress.

S. F. DUPONT,

Flag-officer Commanding South Atlantic Blockading Squadron.

CASUALTIES IN THE ACTION.

Flag-ship Wabash, off Hilton Head,
Port Royal, Nov. 8, 1861.

Hon. Gideon Welles—Sir: I have the honor to report the following casualties in the action of yesterday in the capture of the batteries at Hilton Head and Bay Point:

Wabash—Killed, one—Thomas Jackson, coxswain, captain of a gun. Slightly wounded, two—Alfred Hernsey, seaman, and Wm. Wall, seaman.

Susquehannah—Killed, two; John P. Clark, Orderly Sergeant, and Wm. Price, second coal heaver. Wounded severely, one; Samuel F. Smart, first-class boy. Wounded slightly, two; Patrick Dwyer and Samuel Holbrook, second grade.

Pawnee—Killed, two; John Kelly, Orderly Sergeant, and Wm. H. Fitzhugh, first-class boy. Wounded slightly, three; Alfred Washburn, Master's Mate; Jacob House, ordinary seaman, and Patrick Quinn, ordinary seaman.

Mohican—Killed, one—John A. Whittemore, Third Assistant Engineer. Wounded seriously, three—W. Thompson, Isaac Seyburn, Acting Master, and Sherman Bascom, ordinary seaman. Wounded slightly, four—Mayland Cuthbert, Third Assistant Engineer; John O. Pittman, Master's Mate; John W. Townsend, ordinary seaman, and Charles Browne, ordinary seaman.

Bienville—Killed, two—Patrick McGuigan and Alexander Chambers. Wounded slightly, three—Peter Murphy, Alexander Ferey and Wm. Gilchrist.

Seminole—A few slightly wounded; the number not reported.

Total—Killed, 8; wounded severely, 6; wounded slightly, 17. Killed and wounded, 31.

I have the honor to be,

Respectfully, your obedient servant,

S. F. DUPONT,

Flag-officer Commanding United States Atlantic Blockading Squadron.

SUPPLEMENTAL DISPATCH.

Flag-Ship Wabash, Off Hilton Head,
Port Royal, Nov. 9, 1861.

Hon. Gideon Welles:

Sir—Since writing my official dispatches, I have sent gunboats to take possession of Beaufort, and to protect the inhabitants, but I regret to say they have fled, and the town is abandoned to the negroes, who are reported to me as in a lawless condition. The light vessels, which I hoped to have made use of, were destroyed on the desertion of the forts by the rebels. The post-office was visited, and a number of documents, letters, &c., obtained. I have covered Scull Creek, the mouth of Broad River, and have cut off this communication between Charleston and Savannah. Respectfully, your obedient servant,

S. F. DUPONT, Flag-Officer,

Commanding U. S. Atlantic Blockading Squadron.

OFFICIAL REPORT OF GEN. SHERMAN.

Headquarters Expedition Corps,
Port Royal, S. C., Nov. 8, 1861.

Adjutant-General United States Army, Washington, D. C.:

Sir: I have the honor to report that the force under my command embarked at Annapolis, Maryland, on the 21st of October, and arrived at Hampton Roads, Virginia, on the 22d.

In consequence of the delay in the arrival of some of our transports, and the unfavorable state of the weather, the fleet was unable to set out for the Southern coast until the 29th, when, under the convoy of a naval squadron in command of Commodore Dupont, and after the most mature consideration of the object of the expedition by that flag-officer and myself, it was agreed to first reduce any works that might be found at Port Royal, S. C., and thus open the finest harbor on the coast that exists south of Hatteras.

It was calculated to reach Port Royal in five days at most, but in consequence of adverse winds and a perilous storm on the day and night of the 1st of November, the fleet arrived at Port Royal bar not until the 4th, and then but in part, for it had been almost entirely dispersed by the gale, and the vessels have been straggling in up to this date.

The transport steamers *Union*, *Belvidere*, *Oceola* and *Peerless* have not arrived. Two of them are known to be lost, and it is probable all are.

It is gratifying, however, to say that none of the troop transports connected with the land forces were lost, though the *Winfield Scott* had to sacrifice her whole cargo, and the *Roanoke* a portion of her cargo, to save the lives of the regiments on board. The former will again be unable to put to sea. The vessels connected with the naval portion of the fleet have also suffered much, and some have been lost.

After a careful reconnoissance of Port Royal Bay it was ascertained that the rebels had three field-works of remarkable strength, strongly garrisoned, and covered by a fleet of three gunboats, under Capt. Tatnall, late of the United States Navy, besides strong land forces, which the rebels were concentrating from Charleston and Savannah. The troops of the rebels were afterwards ascertained to have been commanded by Gen. Drayton.

One of the forts, and probably the strongest, was situated on Hilton Head, and the other two on Philip's Island. It was deemed proper to first reduce the fort on Hilton Head, though to do this a greater or less fire might have to be met from the batteries on Bay Point. At the same time our original plan of co-operation of the land forces in this attack had to be set aside in consequence of the loss during the voyage of a greater portion of our means of disembarkment, together with the fact that the only point where the troops should have landed was from 5 to 6 miles (measuring around the intervening shoal,) from the anchoring place of our transports; altogether too great a distance for successful debarkation with our limited means. It was therefore agreed that the place should be reduced by the naval force alone. In consequence of the shattered condition of the fleet, and the delay in the arrival of vessels that were indispensable for the attack, it had to be postponed until the 7th inst.

I was a mere spectator of the combat, and it is not my province to render any report of this action. I deem it an imperative duty to say that the firing and maneuvering of our fleet against that of the rebels and their formidable land batteries, was a masterpiece of activity and professional skill, that must have elicited the applause of the rebels themselves, as a tactical operation. I think that too much praise cannot be awarded to the science and skill exhibited by the flag-officer of the Naval Squadron, and the officers connected with his ships. I deem the performance a masterly one, and ought to have been seen to be fully appreciated.

After the works were reduced I took possession of them with the land forces. The beautifully constructed work on Hilton Head was severely crippled, and many of the guns dismounted. Much slaughter had evidently been made there, many bodies having been buried in the fort, and some twenty or thirty were found some half a mile distant. The island, for many miles, was found strewed with army accoutrements and baggage of the rebels, which they threw away in their hasty retreat. We have also come into possession of about forty pieces of ordnance, most of which is of the heaviest calibre and of the most approved modes, and a large quantity of ammunition and camp equipage.

It is my duty to report the valuable services of Mr. Boutelle, assistant in the Coast Survey, assisting with his accurate and extensive knowledge of this country. His services are invaluable to the army as well as to the navy, and I earnestly recommend that important notice be taken of this very able and scientific officer by the War Department.

I am, very respectfully, your ob't servant,

T. W. SHERMAN,

Brigadier-General Commanding.

GEN. SHERMAN'S PROCLAMATION TO THE PEOPLE OF SOUTH CAROLINA.

After landing and taking possession of the forts, Gen. Sherman issued the following proclamation:

To the People of South Carolina:

In obedience to the orders of the President of these United States of America, I have landed on your shores with a small force of National troops. The dictates of a duty, which, under the Constitution, I owe to a great sovereign State, and to a proud and hospitable people, among whom I have passed some of the pleasantest days of my life, prompt me to proclaim that we have come amongst you with no feelings of personal animosity; no desire to harm your citizens, destroy your property, or interfere with any of your lawful laws, rights, or your social and local institutions, beyond what the causes herein briefly alluded to may render unavoidable.

Citizens of South Carolina: The civilized world stands appalled at the course you are pursuing! Appalled at the crime you are committing against your own mother, the best, the most enlightened, and heretofore the most prosperous of nations. You are in a state of active rebellion against the laws of your country. You have lawlessly seized upon the forts, arsenals and other property belonging to our common country, and within your borders with this property you are in arms, and waging a ruthless war against your Constitutional Government, and thus threatening the existence of a Government which you are bound by the terms of the solemn compact to live under and faithfully support. In doing this you are not only undermining and preparing the way for totally ignoring your own political and social existence, but you are threatening the civilized world with the odious sentiment that self-government is impossible with civilized man.

Fellow-Citizens: I implore you to pause and reflect upon the tenor and consequences of your acts. If the awful sacrifices made by the devastation of our property, the shedding of fraternal blood in battle, mourning and wailing of widows and orphans throughout our land, are insufficient to deter you from further pursuing this unholy war, then ponder, I beseech you, upon the ultimate, but not less certain result which its further progress must necessarily and naturally entail upon your once happy and prosperous State. Indeed, can you pursue this fratricidal war, and continue to imbrue your hands in the loyal blood of your countrymen, your friends, your kinsmen, for no other object than to unlawfully disrupt the Confederacy of a great people—a Confederacy established by your own hands, in order to set up were it possible, an independent Government, under which you can never live in peace, prosperity or quietness.

Carolinians: We have come among you as loyal men, fully impressed with our constitutional obligations to the citizens of your State. Those obligations shall be performed as far as is in our power, but, be not deceived; the obligation of suppressing armed combinations against the constitutional authorities is paramount to all others.

If, in the performance of this duty, other minor but important obligations should be in any way neglected, it must be attributed to the necessities of the case; because rights dependent on the laws of the State must be necessarily subordinate to military exigencies, created by insurrection and rebellion.

W. SHERMAN, Brig.-Gen. Commanding.

Headquarters, S. C., Port Royal, S. C., Nov. 8, 1861.

DETAILS OF THE EXPEDITION.

Narrative of Events from the Sailing of the Fleet to the Occupation of Port Royal.

The Departure from Hampton Roads—The Voyage Down the Coast—The Great Storm—Damage to the Vessels—Losses, &c.

The Arrival on the South Carolina Coast—Description of the Entrance to Port Royal.

The Bombardment of Forts Beauregard and Walker.

Daring Manœuvres of the Fleet—A Tremendous Rain of Shot and Shell.

Helter-Skelter Rout of the Rebels and Occupation of their Works.

Special Correspondence of the New-York Times.

Steamship Atlantic, Hampton Roads,
Monday, Oct. 28, 1861.

The unsettled condition of the weather still deters the departure of the Expedition. As there is little wind and the sea is smooth, our inactive state is an inexplicable mystery to thousands in the fleet, and occasions much grumbling. But we must exercise charity and excuse the dissatisfied. Ignorant landlubbers! none of them ever heard of a barometer, and don't know how surely it indicates the temper of the elements.

How tediously the time passes. Few of the many now "cabined, cribbed, confined" on shipboard, are provided with reading matter, or other means of pastime, and even the fortunate in this respect do not generally avail themselves of their privileges. A deep-rooted feeling of *unrest* seems to possess every one in his waking moments. Little occurs to break the monotony of our condition, which is an unvarying round of eating and sleeping—especially eating. One might suppose, from the appearance of things, that the chief end of life was to gormandize. The soldiers seem to devote their time exclusively to consuming rations; and in the cabin, the celerity with which the meals follow each other conveys the notion to my mind that the purveying department contemplates changing us all into cormorants. I can scarcely find opportunity to write on the dining-room tables—the only convenient place—for almost as soon as one cloth is removed another is spread. If adipose tissue is not developed by such treatment, then must the lean kine of Pharaoh's dream have representatives on board.

Capt. Eldridge has just received sailing orders from the flag-ship, and the entire fleet will get under way to-morrow morning. This announcement is hailed with great joy by all, and as it forms the topic of remark, countenances are lighted with smiles, which for days have been grimly clouded. I shall adopt the maritime custom of keeping "a log," and jot down each evening the occurrences of the day that you may be fully informed of all that happens connected with the "Great Expedition."

Tuesday, Oct. 29

Before sunrise, this morning, the Union-jack at the foremast-head of every transport in the fleet, announced that the vessels were getting up steam. Presently, the majestic *Wabash*, leader of the fleet, moved slowly from her anchorage toward the mouth of the bay. Very soon afterwards gunboats, transports, and other craft followed in the same direction, each hastening to the position assigned it in the order of sailing. The sun rose above the horizon, midway between Capes Charles and Henry, and his great red disk reflected itself upon the glistening sides of the passing vessels, enveloping them in a murky haze, through which they faded into perspective like spectral forms. Gradually the roadstead, which for days had presented a magnificent and novel appearance, became deserted, vacant, and unpleasantly strange to the vision. The *Atlantic* was last to leave, in order that Capt. Saxton, Chief Quartermaster of the Expedition, whose quarters are on board, might have ocular proof of the departure of all the fleet. The *Golden Eagle*, one of the sailing vessels, caused some detention by grounding near the Rip Raps; but two or three tugs went to her assistance, and after an hour's puffing, fussing and pulling, hauled her off. The *Illinois* then took her in tow, and carried her seaward. It was now near 12 o'clock, and the *Atlantic* steamed toward the fleet, whose hulls, like black hummocks, loomed indistinctly against the horizon, far off to the eastward. There can be no doubt that the watchful enemy at Sewell's Point has communicated the news of our departure to Norfolk, thence to be telegraphed to every Southern city.

The fleet moved slowly, and the *Atlantic* soon overtook them. The vessels were arranged in parallel lines, apparently occupying an area of about four miles in length, and three in width. I can best convey an idea of their positions by the following table:

LEFT COLUMN.	CENTRE COLUMN.	RIGHT COLUMN.
Baltic.	Wabash.	Empire City.
Ocean Express.	Atlantic.	Oriental.
Illinois.	Vanderbilt.	Florida.
Golden Eagle.	Great Republic.	Philadelphia.
Locust Point.	Ocean Queen.	Roanoke.
Star of the South.	Zenas Coffin.	Matanzas.
Parkersburgh.	Potomac.	Ben Deford.
Belvidere.	Winfield Scott.	Ferry-boat.
Coatzacoalcos.	Union.	Governor.
Marion.	Ericsson.	Peerless.
Mohican.	Cahawba.	Daniel Webster.
	O. M. Pettit.	Augusta.
	Seminole.	Ariel.
		Mercury.

A line of gunboats extended along the whole front of the fleet, of which the *Curlew*, *Isaac Smith*, *Pawnee* and *Ottawa* were to the left of the *Wabash*, and the *Unadilla*, *Seneca*, *Pembina*, *R. B. Forbes*, and *Penguin* to the right. The gunboats *Pocahontas* and *Alabama* protected the left flank.

The vessels were stationed with an interval of four cables' length between the columns, and at one and a half cables' distance in line ahead, and moved with their relative positions well maintained. The wind blew gently from the west, and there was but little sea. After passing Cape Henry an east by south course was steered, and the "sacred" sand-spit of Virginia had disappeared from view by 5 o'clock. The *Wabash*, with all her sails set, careened gracefully in acknowledgment of the evening breeze; the *Atlantic*, her engines running at quarter speed, following demurely in her wake, and the other vessels came slowly and haughtily forward in their columns. Unconsciously the novel scene led me to think of the immense wealth and power of a Government which could put so mighty a fleet afloat; and I fervently prayed for its preservation and success to that Mightier One who could destroy it with a breath.

The sun sank gorgeously. As his great red disk slowly descended, a bank of orange-colored clouds reflected his fading beams upon the ships, which soon

The New-York Times.

VOL. XI....NO. 3168. NEW-YORK, SUNDAY, NOVEMBER 17, 1861. PRICE THREE CENTS.

THE GREAT REBELLION.

Highly Important and Gratifying Intelligence.

Capture of the Rebel Commissioners, Slidell and Mason.

The Frigate San Jacinto Takes Them from the English Mail Steamship Trent.

Particulars of the Capture—Protest of the Rebels.

Sketch of the Commissioners, and of Capt. Wilkes, Commanding the San Jacinto.

HOW THE NEWS WAS RECEIVED IN WASHINGTON

Highly Important News from Kentucky.

A Rebel Army of Forty Thousand Threatening Cincinnati, Louisville and Lexington.

Floyd's Forces Driven Back in Western Virginia.

The Armies of McCulloch and Price Gone to Arkansas.

The Late Movement of National Troops into Eastern Virginia.

Terrible Panic in the South Following the Battle of Port Royal.

THE CAPTURE OF MASON AND SLIDELL.

DISPATCHES FROM FORTRESS MONROE.

Fortress Monroe, Friday, Nov. 15.

The United States steam-frigate *San Jacinto*, Capt. Wilkes, arrived in the Roadstead at 12½ P. M., having on board the rebel Commissioners, Slidell and Mason.

They were taken from the English mail steamer on the 8th instant off Bermuda.

Lieut. Fairfax and thirty-five armed men went from the *San Jacinto* with five officers, who boarded the steamer and picked out the Commissioners.

Messrs. Slidell and Mason made feeble resistance, but were induced to leave with Lieut. Fairfax.

The captain of the steamer raved and swore, called the United States officers "piratical Yankees," and other abusive names.

One of the secretaries of the rebel Commissioners, named Eustace or Hurstace, also showed resistance; but himself and colleague accompanied their employers to confinement.

Mr. Slidell had his wife and four children on board, who were allowed to proceed to Europe.

Commodore Wilkes came ashore and had a lengthy conversation with Gen. Wool.

He expressed his opinion that he had done right, and said that, right or wrong, these men had to be secured, and if he had done wrong, he could do no more than be cashiered for it.

When it became known that these two worthies were in Hampton Roads, the excitement was immense.

Some reported that quarters would be provided them on the Rip Raps, but either the frigate will proceed to New-York, or some other vessel will be sent there with the prisoners on board, and deliver them at Fort Lafayette.

FROM ANOTHER CORRESPONDENT.

Fortress Monroe, Friday, Nov. 15.

The U. S. steamer *San Jacinto* has just arrived from the Coast of Africa, *via* the West Indies, where she has been cruising for some six weeks.

Old Point was electrified by the tidings that the *San Jacinto* had on board Messrs. Slidell and Mason, who were going abroad as Ministers of the Southern Confederacy to France and England.

Capt. Wilkes reported the news at headquarters in person, and will forward his dispatches to Washington to-night.

They had embarked on board an English mail steamer. Hearing of the fact, Capt. Wilkes determined to take them, and coming up with the steamer in the Bermuda Channel, he sent aboard and demanded the surrender of the arch rebels. The reply was, that there was not force enough to take them.

Capt. Wilkes thereupon sent an additional force and at the same time put the *San Jacinto* into a convenient position.

Messrs. Slidell and Mason were then surrendered.

The English steamer took them on board, knowing who they were, their destination and business.

Capt. Wilkes is understood to have acted on his own responsibility.

Messrs. Slidell and Mason asked permission of Gen. Wool to send letters to their friends, which was granted. The letters were open, of course.

The *San Jacinto* will leave for New-York direct this evening.

FURTHER PARTICULARS FROM BALTIMORE.

Baltimore, Saturday, Nov. 16.

An officer of the *San Jacinto* has arrived here on the steamer from Old Point, with dispatches for the Government. He hurried off to the railroad dépôt immediately upon his arrival and took a special train to Washington. We shall, doubtless, soon hear something official in regard to the arrest of Messrs. Slidell and Mason.

The name of the British vessel from which Messrs. Mason and Slidell were taken has not as yet been ascertained.

All the documents and papers of Messrs. Slidell and Mason were seized. Their families were allowed to proceed.

The captain of the British vessel delivered up Messrs. Slidell and Mason under a protest.

This is the substance of the reports by the passengers by the Old Point boat.

FROM ANOTHER CORRESPONDENT.

Baltimore, Saturday, Nov. 16.

I have been enabled to gather a few facts concerning the arrest of Mason, Slidell, McFarland and Eustis. After Capt. Wilkes had brought the English steamer to, he sent his First Lieutenant and other officers to board her. The Lieutenant informed the Captain that his object was to arrest the four gentlemen, who, with the other passengers, had gathered on deck to see what was going on. Mason asked if he would take them by force, to which he replied, he was ordered to bring them along with him, and he always obeyed orders. The families of the traitors felt terribly aggrieved, and after consultation it was decided to offer them free passage to New-York with their husbands. This they declined, and continued their journey to St. Thomas.

Capt. Wilkes stood at the side of his vessel when the prisoners came up. Mason and Slidell, both of whom knew him perfectly well, passed over the side quietly, but without recognition. Eustis followed, and was swaggering offensively by, when Capt. Wilkes said, "I am Captain of this ship, Sir;" whereupon Eustis, touching his hat, said, "I beg your pardon, Sir," and passed on.

Capt. Taylor, a passenger home from the Coast of Afcica, and who was bearer of dispatches to the Government, gave up his room to Mason. They did not leave the vessel at Fort Monroe, but coals having been obtained, they were put at once *en route* for fort Lafayette.

SEMI-OFFICIAL ACCOUNT OF THE ARREST.

Washington, Saturday, Nov. 16.

Capt. Taylor, who has arrived here with dispatches, reports that when the *San Jacinto* stopped at Cienfuegos, the escape of Slidell and Mason was ascertained. Proceeding thence to Havana, it was understood they had taken passage on the 7th inst. on the British mail steamship *Trent*, plying between Vera Cruz, by way of Havana, and St. Thomas and Southampton.

While the *San Jacinto* was in the narrowest part of the Bahama Channel, about twenty-four miles to the westward, she met the packet, and, as usual in such cases, fired a shot across her bows and brought her to. Two boats were sent to her, under the command of Lieut. Fairfax, who, boarding the packet, arrested Mason and Slidell, who were personally known to him.

They at first objected to being removed without the employment of force for that purpose. However, they were soon after removed without further trouble, and conveyed to the *San Jacinto*. Their respective Secretaries, Eustis and McFarland, were also brought on board, and are now on their way to New-York.

The packet had no other save her own flag.

The remainder of the passengers, including the ladies connected with the Slidell and Mason party, were not molested, and were therefore left free to pursue their journey.

The official dispatches are voluminous, and include several accounts of the capture, together with the protest of Mason and Slidell against being taken from a British ship.

SKETCH OF THE REBEL COMMISSIONERS.

JAMES M. MASON.

James Murray Mason is a native of Virginia, and springs from one of the very first of its families. He was born in 1797, in what was at that time a part of Fairfax County, on Anadostan Island, which is encircled by the Potomac River, just above the present metropolis of the Union. His first ancestor in Virginia was George Mason, who was a member of the English Parliament in the reign of Charles I. He was a strong upholder of the King, and resisted the measures adopted against him by the Parliament. Subsequently he became an officer in the army of Charles II., and commanded a regiment of cavalry in the campaign against the "Roundhead" troops of Oliver Cromwell. After the defeat of the royal forces at Worcester, in 1651, he made his escape disguised as a peasant, and, embarking for America, landed at Norfolk. Soon afterward he established a plantation in Westmoreland County, on the Potomac, on which river he and his lineal descendants have lived for more than two hundred years.

Our present subject began his education at the primary schools in Virginia and in Georgetown, D. C.; and graduated in 1818, at the University of Pennsylvania, in Philadelphia. He commenced the study of law at the College of William and Mary, Williamsburgh, Va., afterward entered as a student the office of the late Benjamin Watkins Leigh, at Richmond, and obtained a license to practice in 1820. In the same year he removed to Winchester, where he entered upon the practice of his profession. In 1826 he was elected to the Virginia House of Delegates, and was twice reelected. He also served as a member of the Convention called in 1829 to revise the Constitution of that State.

In 1837 he was elected to Congress, where he served but one term. In 1847, he was elected to the Senate, to fill the seat of Joel Pennybacker who died during the session. He was reëlected in 1849, for the term commencing on the 4th of March, 1851, (the session of the Legislature being biennial,) and he was again elected to the Senate in December, 1855, for the term commencing on the 4th of March, 1857, and to expire on the 4th of March, 1863. He was thus a member of the Senate for fourteen years. His position as Chairman of the Senate Committee on Foreign Relations which he held for several sessions, may be said to have given him a *quasi* superintendence of the proceedings of the State Department, and brought him into intimate contact with Buchanan and other dignitaries and conspirators at home and abroad. During his long Congressional career he has never distinguished himself by bringing forward or carrying out any of those great and beneficent acts of legislation which alone can make a prominent position illustrious. He was violently, pro-Slavery, and took a memorable part in the debates on the Fugitive Slave law, on the Kansas-Nebraska bill, and on all questions which involved in any way the everlasting negro. He will be remembered as the principal concocter of the Fugitive Slave bill.

Mason is a man of narrow and feeble intellect, of virulent temper and of insolent manners; and why Jeff. Davis ever sent him as a plenipotentiary to England, is one of those Confederate mysteries which it is not given to ordinary mortals to comprehend. His position in the Senate made him somewhat acquainted with foreign affairs, and it is most likely on this plea that he has got himself appointed. The probability, however, is that, morally and intellectually blind though he be, he had eyesight enough to foresee the disaster that was about to fall upon the cause on which he had staked his neck, and, being an arrant coward, obtained the appointment as a means of escape from the ruin which he saw would soon overtake him. Even this miserable subterfuge, however, has failed him, and he is now in the iron clutch of the Government over whose utter destruction he has lately been reveling.

Mason is not only a knave, but a hypocrite. He found it convenient through life to class himself as a Democrat, though a man with less democracy in his composition or manners never existed. He wrote disunion letters to South Carolina, and Union letters to Massachusetts, and in the debatable ground of Washington, when it suited his schemes, or his plans of personal advancement, he was everything to all men—except being honest and truthful. As far back as September, 1855, he wrote to a public affair in South Carolina: "But one course remains for the South—*immediate, absolute and eternal separation*. Better, far better, to stand toward the Northern States as we stand to the rest of the world—enemies in war, in peace friends—than to remain halting under a common Government, enemies in the guise of peace, or friends at war." And yet, only two years later, he said, in a speech delivered to an audience assembled on Bunker Hill: "I shall tell it in old Virginia, when I return to her hallowed land, that I found the spirit of Massachusetts as buoyant, as patriotic, as completely filled with the emotions that should govern patriotism, when I visited Bunker Hill, as it was when that battle was fought."

During the secession excitement in the last regular session of Congress, when one State after another was rushing out of the Union, Mason was equally double-faced. As long ago as March last, he said in the Senate that "he recognized no allegiance to this Government; he recognized and acknowledged no allegiance to this government; none whatever." And yet, for a considerable time after this, he retained his seat in the United States Senate. He will now, it is to be hoped, have an opportunity to straighten up and rectify his mischievous political career.

JOHN SLIDELL.

This arch-conspirator is a native of the State of New-York, to which he now returns loaded with eternal infamy. He was born in the year 1793, and as soon as he reached manhood, he went to New-Orleans, to seek his fortune. He arrived there "poor, friendless and alone;" but, as he had received a good education in his native State, he shortly undertook the practice of law in that city. His skill and adroitness soon won for him a high place at the New-Orleans bar. His success as a lawyer was unparalleled even in that city of sudden successes; and he was retained on one side or the other, in almost every important lawsuit which arose. After fifteen or twenty years' toil at the bar of New-Orleans, he accumulated a princely fortune and a wide reputation. His first public service appears to have been as United States District Attorney at New-Orleans, to which office he was appointed by Gen. Jackson. He was frequently sent to the State Legislature of Louisiana, and was afterwards chosen one of the Louisiana delegation to Congress. In the House he was remarked for his tact and skill as a manager, and his shrewdness and coolness in debate. At times, under provocation, he would become excited, and the words would flow from his lips in a torrent; but this rarely happened. His temper was generally thoroughly under command.

While a member of Congress, Slidell was selected by the President to act as Minister-Plenipotentiary and Envoy-Extraordinary to Mexico. The circumstances imparted unusual importance to the mission. War was actually on the point of breaking out. Taylor was on the Rio Grande, and the American squadron lay off Vera Cruz. Previous to firing the first gun, however, President Polk, professing still to be anxious to preserve peace, and Mexico having intimated that a new Envoy from the United States would be received, Slidell was accredited. The mission did not achieve any useful purpose. After many and futile discussions, the Mexican Government refused to receive Slidell, and he finally demanded his passports and returned home.

After his return, he began to develop his ideas of the necessity of conquering Mexico, and subjugating the Spanish, Indian, and other races, not excepting the negroes, which added greatly to his popularity in the South.

When Mr. Soule vacated his seat in the Senate to fill the post of Minister to Madrid, Slidell was appointed to succeed him for the unexpired term; and, at the close of this term, he was reëlected for six years. In the caucuses of the extreme Southern Party with which he acted, no member's advice carried more weight than Slidell's. He spoke little, but kept a close eye on affairs and on the wires.

During Buchanan's reign, he was the controlling spirit of that miserable old man; and all the atrocious acts of the late Administration, particularly for the last year of its existence, are traceable to him. He taught Cobb how to swindle, and Floyd how to steal, and twisted old Buck's nose and conscience as if they were wax. He has been mentioned for many important diplomatic missions, but, excepting the unsuccessful one to Mexico, obtained none. He was, when caught, on his way as Jeff. Davis' Plenipotentiary to France; but in this, too, he has wretchedly failed. In person, Slidell is striking; of middle height, stout figure and with a bold mein. He is utterly unprincipled, and his political career in Louisiana a record of villainies that it would be heard to parallel. In 1844, by the celebrated Plaquemine frauds, he defrauded the Whigs of the vote of Louisiana, and thereby defeated Henry Clay and made Polk President. For his infamous work at this time he acquired the *soubriquet* of Baron Plaquemine. Again, at a later day, in the matter of the Houmas Land Grants, in Louisiana, he was guilty of frauds so palpable and outrageous that even New-Orleans, with its easy virtue, almost spewed him out. By this he acquired the *nom de plume* of Old Houmas. But his crowning fraud on the people of Louisiana and on his country was when he swindled his adopted State out of the Union.

In catching him we have undoubtedly caught the most accomplished scoundrel, and the ablest engineer of conspiracy in all the South—Jeff Davis himself not excepted.

CAPTAIN CHARLES WILKES.

The name of Capt. Charles Wilkes, who so neatly nabbed Slidell and Mason, is a name known both in navigation and in science. He was born in this State in 1805, and originally entered the naval service of his country in 1818, at the early age of 13 years. In 1838, having previously distinguished himself by his scientific ability, he received from the American Government the command of a naval expedition intended to explore the countries bordering on the Pacific and Southern Oceans. His command consisted of two sloops-of-war, a brig and two tenders, and he himself had the grade of Captain. Leaving here shortly after his appointment, he doubled Cape Horn, crossed over to Polynesia, Van Dieman's Land and Australia, advancing as high as the 61st degree of south latitude; he then visited the Feejee Islands and Borneo, and returned to New-York in 1842, after having visited Singapore and the Cape of Good Hope. This memorable expedition of four years was fertile in useful observations, which Capt. Wilkes recounted in a very able work in five octavo volumes, entitled *A Narrative of the United States Exploring Expedition*. In 1848 the Geographical Society of London presented him with a gold medal, as a token of their appreciation of his labors. He has also, since then, published a work entitled *Western America*, which contains valuable statistical details and geographical facts and maps relating to California and Oregon. Commodore Wilkes received his present commission in 1855. He has been in the service altogether forty-three years. Ten of these years he has been on sea service; twenty-six engaged on shore or other duty, and seven years unemployed. For some years, latterly, he has been assigned to special duty near Washington. He is now returning from the Coast of Africa with the United States steamer *San Jacinto*. On his way home he found orders to cruise around the coast of the West Indies to look out for privateers or vessels attempting to run the blockade, which duty he has been performing for the past six weeks. While engaged in this business he fell in with the vessel containing the two rebel Plenipos. The whole country now rings with applause of his bold action.

THE NEWS OF THE CAPTURE IN WASHINGTON.

Washington, Saturday, Nov. 16.

The city was made joyful to-day by a rumor which gained currency about noon, to the effect that ex-Senators Mason and Slidell, the Envoys of Jeff. Davis to England and France, respectively, had been taken at sea, and were now prisoners on board a United States vessel of war. An hour later, Capt. Alfred Taylor, of the navy, arrived by a special train from Baltimore, bearing dispatches to the Government, from Commodore Wilkes. These official documents, numbering near a dozen, give full particulars of the capture, and are at present in the hands of the Government, to be fully examined before publication. The general facts connected with the arrest are as follows:

Commodore Wilkes, while returning from the Coast of Africa, in the *San Jacinto*, stopped at Havana to take in coal, and while *there*, learned that Messrs. Mason and Slidell were to leave on the 7th, on the British Mail steamer *Trent*, for England. Capt. Wilkes heard, about the same time, that the *Sumter* was off Laguayra, and he determined to capture her if possible.

While steaming through the Bahama Channel he encountered the *Trent*, and brought her to by firing two shots across her bow. Lieut. Fairfax, of the *San Jacinto*, was immediately sent on board with a boat's crew and marines, and asked of the master of the *Trent* to see his passenger list. This was denied, and Lieut. Fairfax then stated that his purpose was to take into custody Messrs. Slidell and Mason, whom he knew to be on board, and those who accompanied them. The rebel envoys were soon recognized, and they refused Lieut. Fairfax's demand that they should proceed aboard the *San Jacinto*, and immediately went below to their state-rooms. They were followed, and Lieut. Fairfax told them that if they refused to go peaceably, he should be compelled to use force. They still refused, when the marines, stepping forward and taking them by the shoulder, they made no further opposition.

Messrs. Eustis and McFarland, the Secretaries of the rebel Envoys, were also arrested. Slidell and Eustis had their families on board the *Trent*, and the prospect of a separation occasioned an affecting scene. Commodore Wilkes subsequently offered to allow their families to accompany them, but the ladies refused, preferring the voyage to England and a protracted separation from their husbands, rather than the risk of an imprisonment in the North. Slidell's family consisted of his wife, four children and two servants; Eustis' of his wife, two children and a servant. The baggage of the prisoners was transferred to the *San Jacinto*, and it is said that it contains important documents, and among them their instructions from Jeff. Davis' Government. Any mail matter which had been intrusted to them had probably been transferred to the English mail.

No opposition was offered by the officers of the *Trent* to the arrest, other than a verbal protest though one man who has charge of the mails on board indulged in some gasconade about the outrage committed, and was loud in his assertions that the blockade would be raised within a month after the news reached England.

After their transfer to the *San Jacinto*, the prisoners united in drawing up a statement of the facts connected with their arrest, which they addressed to Commodore Wilkes, and accompanied it by a request that it be forwarded to the United States Government. It does not materially differ from the narration I have given above. The signature attached to the document were evidently written while under a feeling of trepidation, and they approximate to the irregularity of that of Stephen Hopkins, of 1776.

Slidell and Mason are well known. Eustis was formerly a Member of Congress from Louisiana. He married a daughter of Mr. Corcoran, the Washington banker, who, it is said, has betrayed much uneasiness to-day in reference to the arrest. McFarland is a son or nephew of William H. McFarland, a bank President in Richmond, a strong Union man, and one of the last to succumb to the pressure of the rebellion. He is a bachelor.

On the *San Jacinto* the prisoners were treated with marked kindness by Commodore Wilkes and his officers. They conversed freely upon various subjects, but politics were not alluded to. When they arrive in New-York they will be transferred to Fort Warren.

On reaching Hampton Roads, Capt. Taylor, of the United States sloop-of-war *Saratoga*, was landed at Fortress Monroe, to convey dispatches to the Government.

Of course everybody is rejoiced that the arch rebels are in custody, but the circumstances connected with their arrest have created some apprehensions of consequences. The right of search has always been asserted by Great Britain, and has been denied by the United States. England and France have not recognized the rebel States as a nation, but have recognized them as belligerents, and the point is now presented of an insurgent claiming to be a diplomatic envoy from a State not yet recognized, arrested while traveling, on a vessel of the nation to whom he is accredited, and taken from it by a vessel of the nation against which he is in rebellion, and which still claims him as its subject. It seems to be conceded that Commodore Wilkes acted in the matter without instructions, and whatever instructions may have been given to the Atlantic fleet to effect their capture in the *Theodora*, it was hardly contemplated that they should be taken in a British vessel. In view of the intricate question of international law likely to be raised, there is a casting about for precedents, and in the streets even Grotius, Puffendorf, Vattel and Wheaton are learnedly appealed to for justification. I am informed that the Secessionists of Baltimore called upon the British Consul to-day and asked what Great Britain would do in the matter, and that he expressed the opinion that the act did not interfere with any law of nations; and that, in view of all the facts, probably no notice would be taken of it. Members of the Cabinet think that the case presents an opportunity to test the point whether the British Government will accept its own doctrines when the American Bull goads the British Ox and the general feeling seems to be that the most that will be required will be, that the United States Government apologize for the act, which it will do and hold on to the prisoners.

IMPORTANT FROM KENTUCKY.

The Rebel General, Johnston, Reported to be Advancing with a Large Force.

National Troops Concentrating to Check Him.

Cincinnati, Saturday, Nov. 16.

On Wednesday afternoon Brig.-Gen. Thomas ordered Gen. Sheoff to fall back by forced marches from Camp Calvert, near London, Ky., to Danville, where the National forces will concentrate to oppose Gen. Sidney A. Johnston, who is reported to be advancing and threatening Cincinnati, Louisville, or Lexington, with 40,000 men.

The Fourteenth, Seventeenth and Thirty-eighth Ohio and Thirty-third Indiana Regiments immediately took up the march, but a majority of the Tennessee Brigade refused to turn their faces backward, and it was deemed expedient to order them, with the Third Kentucky Regiment, to return to their old camp.

Zollicoffer has united his forces with those of Johnston, leaving only a few hundred men at Cumberland Gap. The ford is entirely deserted.

Our troops were at Crab Orchard Springs on Saturday morning.

IMPORTANT FROM THE KANAWHA.

Floyd Driven Back from all His Positions.

He Steals Another March on the National Troops.

Cincinnati, Saturday, Nov. 16.

Advices from Gen. Rosecrans' headquarters state that on the 10th Gen. Cox's Brigade crossed the Kanawha and New Rivers, and drove the rebels back three miles from all their positions. Gen. Schenck's column intended attacking them in the rear, but was prevented crossing the River from high water.

Gen. Benham's Brigade moved up and began to feel their front, when a sharp skirmish took place, lasting from 4 P. M. till dark, when Gen. Benham's force lay on their arms waiting for morning. The rebels began their retreat, and were well on their way to Raleigh before the movement was discovered.

Gen. Benham pursued them 25 miles amidst a drenching rain, but seeing little chance of overtaking them turned back.

In the skirmish with the rear guard, Co.. Crogran of the rebel cavalry and a few others were killed. The loss on our side was two.

A PARTY OF MEN DROWNED.

Point Pleasant, Va., Saturday, Nov. 16.

A sad accident occurred at Camp Piatt, twelve miles above Charleston this morning. Capt. Bell, of Company K, Fourty-fourth Ohio Regiment, and eleven of his men, while crossing the Kanawha in a skiff ran under the steamer *Commodore Perry*. The Captain and seven of his men were drowned, and the remainder saved.

[*For other Rebellion News, see Eighth Page.*]

IMPORTANT FROM THE SOUTH.

The Great Fleet Understood to have Gone to Pensacola.

Excitement Produced by the Capture of Port Royal.

THE PANIC AT SAVANNAH.

Reported Arrival of the Steamship Fingal.

The Black Flag in South Carolina.

NEWS BY WAY OF FORTRESS MONROE.

Fortress Monroe, Friday, Nov. 15, }
Via Baltimore, Saturday, Nov. 16. }

The fleet is understood to have gone to Pensacola.

News of another exploit may be expected soon.

A dispatch from Savannah, the 14th, states that the fleet had passed Fernandina, standing southward.

Private advices represent that the capture of Port Royal has produced the greatest excitement throughout the South, and especially along the seaboard, from the cities and villages of which the people are fleeing in the greatest precipitation.

A dispatch from Charleston to the Richmond *Enquirer*, the 14th, states that Gen. Sherman had taken possession of Pickney Islands, seized all the able-bodied negro men and sent them to the fleet.

No attempt has been made to land on the main-land.

A flag of truce to-day brought about one hundred supporters of the Union, including about twenty-five women. They relate a sad tale of suffering and oppression. A number of persons have recently been thrown into prison for not supporting the rebellion, including Mr. Pendon, Baptist minister.

The victory at Port Royal greatly depressed the rebels and encouraged the Union men, of whom there are large numbers.

The *Merrimac* is still in the dock, and it is the opinion of intelligent men that she will never float. She is being encased with three layers of inch boiler-iron.

The Georgia Planters' Convention recommend that in case the war continues, and the present cotton crop remains unsold, no crop should be planted next year.

A resident of Norfolk thinks there are nearly twenty thousand rebel troops in and near that city.

NEWS BY WAY OF BALTIMORE.

Baltimore, Saturday, Nov. 16.

We have Petersburgh, Va., papers of the 14th inst. They appear to be very much in the dark as regards the operations of the fleet.

Lynchburgh, Va., Wednesday, Nov. 13.

It is reported, but not confirmed, that the Union men of Tennessee have taken possession of Bristol.

The panic at Savannah, in consequence of the victory of the fleet, was so great that even men were running away. Small-ware merchants, who were packing up their goods to leave, had been notified by the authorities that they would not be permitted to carry off their goods.

The Savannah *Republican* is indignant at this cowardly desertion in time of danger, and urges Gen. Lawton to issue an order preventing any able-bodied man, under sixty years of age, from leaving.

The Norfolk *Day Book* of yesterday contains the following:

Macon, Ga., Thursday, Nov. 14.

The Planters' Convention have adopted a resolution indorsing the defensive measures of the Government, and recommending a discriminating duty of twenty per cent. on the productions of the United States.

It was also resolved that if the war should continue and the present crop remain undisposed of, the planters should not plant next Spring beyond the wants of home consumption.

Savannah, Thursday, Nov. 14.

The Federal fleet is reported to have passed Fernandina yesterday, bound South. Great activity prevails in strengthening the defences of the city, and a general feeling of security prevails.

The same paper says that the steamer *Fingal* has arrived at Savannah with a cargo of war munitions, &c.

The Richmond *Dispatch* says:

"We have information that the authorities of South Carolina have communicated with the Government upon the subject of hoisting the black flag, to which allusion has been made since the attack upon the coast of that State. It is believed that Gen. Lee has received orders from the War Department urging that 'those captured must be regarded as prisoners of war.' It is said that this will be disregarded by the authorities of South Carolina; that the same course will be pursued, which Gov. Wise adopted at the time of the John Brown raid, and that when South Carolina is done with the invaders the Confederate Government can have them."

THE BOMBARDMEFT OF PORT ROYAL.

The Philadelphia *Press* publishes some interesting extracts from private letters by an officer of the *Wabash*. He writes:

"After our first attack, we hauled off to repair damage, and in about two hours renewed the assault.

After the resumption of our fire, the rebel batteries ceased to reply. Our guns carry two miles with effect, and were then within seven hundred yards of them.

Commodore Dupont declared that '*they might sink his ship, but he would not move from his position until the forts had surrendered.*'" * * * *

In the fort I found a gray suit, the uniform of a Captain or Lieutenant of the Savannah Guards, which belonged to a son of the famous Gen. Huger—pronounced 'Hugee.' I am led to believe this from the fact that in the breast-pocket I found a fine linen handkerchief, marked 'Joseph Huger,' in indelible ink. In the right side-pocket were three Minié rifle-balls, a number of musket-wads, and a five and three cent piece.

On the front of the cap is a palmetto tree, and as neat a specimen of such work as I ever saw. Yesterday, when on shore, I was in charge of a boat's crew, and had no time for trophy-hunting. To-day, however, I may take a trip through the camp, and endeavor to find the materials for an interesting letter. I am told that we have captured more property than the expedition has cost; and you know that is no small sum.

Here are bales of cotton piled up ready for shipment, and but for our opportune arrival it might ere this have been *en route* for an English port. There is a plantation which mustered two hundred negroes. They are coming off to us at every opportunity, and I expect every one will be aboard our vessel before we leave.

When the rebels retreated, they never spiked a gun. They might have destroyed their entire camp, but their flight was so precipitate that they left everything in excellent order. Their magazines were found to be filled with shot, shell and powder sufficient to withstand a ten-days' bombardment.

One of the contrabands, in answer to a question as to how many of the rebels were killed, replied that the General who owned him *had threatened him with death if he ever divulged the secret*. He says that two full regiments were killed, probably meaning two *companies*.

We found some of the corpses lying at a mile's distance from the fort, thus showing that they must have commenced retreating before our fire had been discontinued. *I expect we will have another battle in a few days, probably at the fort up the Bay.* We do not want it badly, however, for we now have sole control of Port Royal harbor.

NEWS BY WAY OF NORFOLK.

From late numbers of the Norfolk *Day Book* and Charleston *Courier*, we extract the following important items:

"On Monday, placards were posted in Norfolk that on Wednesday a flag of truce would visit Old Point, and all persons having passes from headquarters, by registering their names at the Mayor's Office, would be permitted to leave the city. In a half an hour after the announcement was made public, a

The New-York Times.

VOL. XI....NO. 3169. NEW-YORK, MONDAY, NOVEMBER 18, 1861. PRICE TWO CENTS.

THE GREAT REBELLION.

Further Particulars of the Capture of Slidell and Mason.

How the Capture was Effected, and How They Behaved.

Their Papers in Possession of the Government.

How the Affair is Regarded in Washington.

No Difficulty with Great Britain Apprehended

AN UNFORTUNATE FORAGING PARTY.

A Number of the New-York Thirtieth Captured.

THE NEW OCCUPATION OF VIRGINIA.

Movements of National Troops into Accomac and Northampton Counties.

PROCLAMATION OF GEN. DIX.

THE CAPTURE OF MASON AND SLIDELL.

We announced in the TIMES of yesterday morning the capture of the two rebel Commissioners, Messrs. MASON and SLIDELL. The following dispatches, from our Washington correspondent, give the particulars of the capture, with various interesting incidents attending it:

WASHINGTON, Saturday, Nov. 16.

The city was made joyful to-day by a rumor which gained currency about noon, to the effect that ex-Senators MASON and SLIDELL, the Envoys of JEFF. DAVIS to England and France, respectively, had been taken at sea, and were now prisoners on board a United States vessel of war. An hour later, Capt. ALFRED TAYLOR, of the navy, arrived by a special train from Baltimore, bearing dispatches to the Government, from Commodore WILKES. These official documents, numbering near a dozen, give full particulars of the capture, and are at present in the hands of the Government, to be fully examined before publication. The general facts connected with the arrest are as follows:

Commodore WILKES, while returning from the Coast of Africa, in the *San Jacinto*, stopped at Havana to take in coal, and while *there*, learned that Messrs. MASON and SLIDELL were to leave on the 7th, on the British Mail steamer *Trent*, for England. Capt. WILKES heard, about the same time, that the *Sumter* was off Laguayra, and he determined to capture her if possible.

While steaming through the Bahama Channel he encountered the *Trent*, and brought her to by firing two shots across her bow. Lieut. FAIRFAX, of the *San Jacinto*, was immediately sent on board with a boat's crew and marines, and asked of the master of the *Trent* to see his passenger list. This was denied, and Lieut. FAIRFAX then stated that his purpose was to take into custody Messrs. SLIDELL and MASON, whom he knew to be on board, and those who accompanied them. The rebel envoys were soon recognized, and they refused Lieut. FAIRFAX's demand that they should proceed aboard the *San Jacinto*, and immediately went below to their state-rooms. They were followed, and Lieut. FAIRFAX told them that if they refused to go peaceably, he should be compelled to use force. They still refused, when the marines, stepping forward and taking them by the shoulder, they made no further opposition.

Messrs. EUSTIS and MCFARLAND, the Secretaries of the rebel Envoys, were also arrested. SLIDELL and EUSTIS had their families on board the *Trent*, and the prospect of a separation occasioned an affecting scene. Commodore WILKES subsequently offered to allow their families to accompany them, but the ladies refused, preferring the voyage to England and a protracted separation from their husbands, rather than the risk of an imprisonment in the North. SLIDELL's family consisted of his wife, four children and two servants; EUSTIS' of his wife, two children and a servant. The baggage of the prisoners was transferred to the *San Jacinto*, and it is said that it contains important documents, and among them their instructions from JEFF. DAVIS' Government. Any mail matter which had been intrusted to them had probably been transferred to the English mail.

No opposition was offered by the officers of the *Trent* to the arrest, other than a verbal protest, though one man who has charge of the mails on board indulged in some gasconade about the outrage committed, and was loud in his assertions that the blockade would be raised within a month after the news reached England.

After their transfer to the *San Jacinto*, the prisoners united in drawing up a statement of the facts connected with their arrest, which they addressed to Commodore WILKES, and accompanied by a request that it be forwarded to the United States Government. It does not materially differ from the narration I have given above. The signatures attached to the document were evidently written while under a feeling of trepidation, and they approximate to the irregularity of that of STEPHEN HOPKINS, of 1776.

SLIDELL and MASON are well known. EUSTIS was formerly a Member of Congress from Louisiana. He married a daughter of Mr. CORCORAN, the Washington banker, who, it is said, has betrayed much uneasiness to-day in reference to the arrest. MCFARLAND is a son or nephew of WILLIAM H. MCFARLAND, a bank President in Richmond, a strong Union man, and one of the last to succumb to the pressure of the rebellion. He is a bachelor.

On the *San Jacinto* the prisoners were treated with marked kindness by Commodore WILKES and his officers. They conversed freely upon various subjects, but politics were not alluded to. When they arrive in New-York they will be transferred to Fort Warren.

On reaching Hampton Roads, Capt. TAYLOR, of the United States sloop-of-war *Saratoga*, was landed at Fortress Monroe, to convey dispatches to the Government.

FURTHER PARTICULARS.

WASHINGTON, Sunday, Nov. 17.

The papers found in the possession of SLIDELL and MASON have been received, and are now in possession of the State Department.

When Lieut. FAIRFAX, of the *San Jacinto*, reached the deck of the *Trent*, he met the Captain and inquired if he had MASON and SLIDELL on board. He hesitated in answering, when Mr. FAIRFAX discovered MASON at a distance seated. Observing this, the Captain stated that they were on board, and Mr. FAIRFAX approached the rebel Envoy, and inquired if he was not Mr. MASON. MASON arose and stated that he was, when Mr. FAIRFAX announced that he had orders for his arrest. MASON turned to the Captain and asked if he intended to allow this outrage to be committed upon his flag. The Captain made some response, which was inaudible to my informant. Mr. SLIDELL at that moment came up from the cabin, and he also was informed by Mr. FAIRFAX that he had orders for his arrest.

The ladies of the suite coming up at the moment, a conversation in an under tone was commenced, which was followed by a very effecting scene, as it became apparent that they were to be separated. They expressed themselves confidently that they would never see Mr. SLIDELL or Mr. MASON again, and when the offer was made to his family to accompany him, Mr. SLIDELL objected, and asked that they continue the voyage.

In a private conversation, it is supposed that they gave to EUSTIS and MCFARLAND instructions what to do when they reached Europe, and were much astonished to learn that they were also to be transferred. Their baggage was brought up and examined, and various papers which were supposed to be of service to the Government were taken possession of. A considerable amount of money was found. Their wearing apparel was transferred to the boats, and soon the prisoners were on board the *San Jacinto*. MASON was very haughty in his manner for a time after reaching the vessel, but SLIDELL was pleasant and easy in his manner.

Lieut. FAIRFAX is by birth a Virginian, and is one of the family of that name in the Eastern part of the State. Gen. FAIRFAX, a rebel Virginian, who played a prominent part in the effort to bring Northwestern Virginia into the rebellion, is a member of the same family. The Lieutenant entered the naval service from North Carolina, and it is said that he is a distant relation of MASON, whose arrest he made. Those who know him speak in high terms of his loyalty and integrity.

The apprehensions which were felt yesterday of difficulties that might arise with England in consequence of the act of Capt. WILKES, have been much lessened to-day, in view of the cordial approval which it has received at the hands of the Government, and the further fact that English authorities are abundant sustaining the legality of the proceeding.

Great confidence is expressed by those high in authority, that Great Britain will not take issue with our Government in the matter, but coinciding with the doctrine that the conveyance of ambassadors, agents or dispatches from a belligerent is a violation of neutrality, will, when placed in possession of the whole truth in the case, leave it where it now is.

GENERAL NEWS FROM WASHINGTON.

WASHINGTON, Sunday, Nov. 17.

SECRETARY CHASE RETURNED.

Secretary CHASE returned to the city to-day.

A PLEASANT PARTY.

This morning a party, consisting of Secretaries SEWARD, CAMERON and SMITH, Assistant Secretaries SEWARD, SCOTT and SMITH, Gov. ANDREW, Col. RITCHIE, Gen. VAN VLEIT, Col. FORNEY, Mr. THAYER and other distinguished citizens, with several ladies, left on a special train for Annapolis. Gov. HICKS and daughter and Gen. BURNSIDE met the party on their arrival, and a salute was fired in honor of the event by the Twenty-third Massachusetts, at the Naval School. Subsequently a dinner was partaken of at the City Hotel, after which two brigades, under command of Gen. BURNSIDE, were reviewed. The troops presented a splendid appearance, and their proficiency in drill elicited the applause of the visitors.

AN UNFORTUNATE FORAGING PARTY.

At 8 o'clock yesterday morning a foraging party, consisting of six wagons and teamsters, twenty corn pickers, and fifty-seven of the New-York Thirtieth Volunteers, under command of Capt. LANDON, proceeded to DULIN's house, four miles west of Falls Church, on the Fairfax road. The party halted in DULIN's corn-field, and sentinels were stationed on the edge of the field to give alarm in case of an approach of the enemy, and about twenty were stationed about the wagons. It was arranged that in case of an alarm the men were to rally about the wagons. At 2 o'clock the supplies had been obtained, and the party was about to set out on their return, when a sentinel on the northwest part of the field fired a shot and ran to the wagons. Some of the men at the time were eating dinner in DULIN's house. Capt. LANDON and Lieut. ANDREWS attempted to rally the men, in the midst of which about eighty of the rebel cavalry dashed through the field and captured them and a few of the privates, who had remained by the wagons. The others fired upon the rebels, and then in a panic ran to the timber, about a hundred yards east, where for a few moments they kept up an irregular firing upon the cavalry as they approached, during which two were seen to fall from their horses. The rebel cavalry had by this time become scattered, and they commenced scouring the timber in search of our men, who began a retreat, each man for himself. About 3½ o'clock the first one arrived at headquarters, near Upton's Hill, and told the story. Within a half hour fifteen more had come in, and by this morning two-thirds of the party made their appearance.

At four o'clock, Major TARBELL, of the New-York Twenty-fourth, took two hundred and fifty men and marched out to DULIN'S and scoured the vicinity in search of our men or the enemy, but were unable to find anybody except a few stragglers, who were making their way to our lines. DULIN, though a professed Union man, and whose property has been devastated by the rebels when they formerly occupied it, and BRUSH, a neighbor, were suspected of having conveyed information to the rebels on the arrival of the foraging party. Both were taken into custody, and are now held in our camps. Capt. LANDON was in the Mexican war. The conduct of our troops in the affair was disgraceful in the extreme. Their force was ample to have resisted the attack and beaten back the cavalry, had they rallied, as was prearranged, and stood their ground. Not one of our men, so far as is known, was wounded. To-day a scouting party went out to DULIN'S, and passing some distance beyond found our wagons, loaded, deserted, the rebels being unable to carry them off owing to the bad state of the road. The horses, however, had been taken. Teams were sent forward and the wagons and forage brought in.

The names of the missing men are as follows: Capt. W. W. Landon, Lieut. Jas. W. Andrews, Corpls. P. Coony, G. H. Vanderzee, and M. White; Privates P. Frazier, Geo. McWharton, L. Hartigen, Sen.; Harris Stafford, John Sleight, D. B. Morris, A. Holtzein, N. H. Rowland, Cole Stanton, C. Elms, Wm. Peck, N. W. Porter, Thos. Porter, Walter Minick, Douis Marto, H. C. Smith, Robt. Wayland, Wm. McDCormick, D. Stickles, Freeman Clapper and Jas. Morrison.

DEATH OF LIEUT. SNYDER.

Lieut. GEO. W. SNYDER, of the Engineer Corps, U. S. A., died at 7 o'clock this morning, in this city, of typhoid fever. Lieut. SNYDER was a native of Schoharie County, New-York. He entered West Point, and graduated in 1856. He was one of the garrison at Fort Sumter, from its occupation by Major ANDERSON until its evacuation, and during the bombardment commanded a portion of the men. His gallant conduct elicited in the published accounts at the time the highest praise. Fort Ellsworth and six other fortifications opposite Washington were constructed under his direction. His health has not been good since the privations he suffered at Sumter, and three weeks since he was seized with the malady which caused his death. He was but twenty-eight years of age, but was one of the most talented members of the engineer corps.

BURNING OF THE NORFOLK NAVY-YARD.

The Senate Committee is still investigating the facts connected with the abandonment and destruction of Norfolk Navy-Yard. Already sufficient proofs have been elicited to show the culpability of the naval authorities at that point in pursuing the course they did.

NAVIGATION OF THE POTOMAC.

Five schooners passed down the Potomac yesterday, unmolested by the rebel batteries.

THE CALIFORNIA PRISONERS.

An order was sent to-day from the Government to have Dr. GWIN, CALHOUN BENHAM and Mr. BRENT confined in Fort Lafayette.

DECISIONS UNDER THE TARIFF LAW.

The Secretary of the Treasury has made the following decisions under the tariff act of March last: Lithographic handbills or show-bills are liable to entry to duty at a rate of 15 per cent., as printed matter. Woolen jackets not made on frames, but hand-knit, open in front, with buttons and sewed button-holes and pockets, were properly charged a duty at the rate of 12 cents per pound, and in addition 25 per cent. The decision of the collector of Boston, assessing a duty of 40 cents per pound, in addition to the 10 per cent. *ad valorem* on cigars costing $8 per thousand, is affirmed by the Secretary of the Treasury.

INTERESTING AUCTION SALES.

The household furniture and horses of Dr. GWINN are advertised to be sold at auction on Tuesday next, at his late residence, corner of Nineteenth and I-streets.

The personal property of the late Senator DOUGLAS will also be sold at auction to-morrow. The bidding is expected to be brisk in the desire to obtain mementoes of the departed statesman.

GOV. RANDALL IN TOWN.

Gov. RANDALL, of Wisconsin, arrived yesterday, and to-day paid a visit to the regiments from that State. He was received with great enthusiasm.

ACCIDENTALLY KILLED.

Private KLUM, of the New-York Thirtieth, was killed to-day by the accidental discharge of a gun.

GEN. DENVER GOING TO KANSAS.

Gen. DENVER, of California, left to-day, for Fort Leavenworth, where he will report to Gen. HUNTER.

A DEARTH OF NEWS.

The newsboys are no longer permitted to cross into Virginia, and the soldiers are annoyed at the dearth of newspapers.

GEN. SUMNER.

Gen. SUMNER yesterday had an interview with with the President and Gen. MCCLELLAN.

IMPORTANT FROM FORT MONROE.

Sailing of the San Jacinto for New-York.

AN ATTACK UPON NEWPORT'S NEWS EXPECTED.

FORTRESS MONROE, Saturday, Nov. 16.

The *San Jacinto* sailed for New-York to-day.

A flag of truce went to Norfolk to-day, but brings no newspapers nor intelligence of any kind.

The gunboats *Cambridge*, *Mount Vernon* and *Lockwood* have gone up to Newport's News to-night.

The rebels have assembled in considerable force at Great Bethel. An attack upon Newport's News is by no means improbable.

The gunboat *Young Rover* has been sent to the York River.

The *Cambridge*, just from the Rappahannock, brings no news.

The recent fire at Norfolk consumed a large quantity of valuable stores, including nearly their entire supply of oil.

The *S. R. Spaulding* leaves for Hatteras Inlet to-night, having in tow two schooners, loaded with frame houses for the troops, and stores.

The *Belvidere* will also leave for Port Royal to-night.

THE EXPEDITION TO THE RAPPAHANNOCK RIVER.

OFFICIAL REPORT OF COMMANDER PARKER.

U. S. STEAMER CAMBRIDGE, RAPPAHANNOCK RIVER, Nov. 9, 1861.

SIR: I have the honor to report that on the 6th instant I ordered a detachment of thirty men from this vessel, under the command of Lieut. GIVEN, assisted by Acting Masters ELDRIDGE and STRONG, and Midshipman CUSHING, to proceed in the United States steamer *Rescue* to the Cunitomen Creek and capture a schooner reported to me to be loaded with firewood; and in the event of not succeeding in this, to burn her.

The schooner was found to be hard and fast ashore, and, as it was impossible to move her, she was burned in obedience to my orders to this effect, together with a large quantity of firewood piled upon shore. No resistance was met with till the *Rescue* began to return, when a body of rebel troops, armed with rifles, on both sides of the creek—supposed to be about 130 in number—with a rifled cannon in a masked battery, attacked her, but without effecting much damage to our party. The rebels were concealed by thick underbrush and a house, from which they fired.

Acting Master STRONG was struck with a spent rifle ball, but not seriously hurt, and no other person was wounded.

The expedition was perfectly successful, and the duty performed in a spirited and brilliant manner.

The detachment returned to this vessel about 5 P. M., having been absent on this duty a little more than four hours.

I herewith forward Lieutenant GIVEN's report of the affair:

I have also to report that, having been informed by a contraband, that there were three companies of rebel troops encamped at the town of Urbana, near a large magazine of powder, I proceeded, on the 8th inst., to that place, and endeavored to dislodge them and blow up the magazine with our battery, assisted by the *Rescue*. After bombarding the encampment for an hour and a-half, the magazine was perforated several times with our shot and shell, but we were unable to destroy it, the depth of water not allowing us to approach the enemy nearer than one mile and a-half. The rebels did not reply, except by musketry, when a boat from the *Rescue* attempted to approach the shore. There were no casualities in this action on our side.

Since our arrival in this river, this vessel has been actively engaged in maintaining the blockade.

Respectfully, your obedient servant,

WM. A. PARKER, Commander.

Flag Officer L. M. GOLDSBOROUGH, Commanding U. S. A. B. Squadron, Hampton Roads.

AN IMPORTANT MOVEMENT.

A Large Body of National Troops Thrown into Accomac and Northampton Counties, Va.

Proclamation of Gen. Dix to the Inhabitants.

One of the most significant movements of the United States troops, is that planned by Major-Gen. DIX, and directed toward the occupation of Accomac and Northampton Counties, Va. Particulars of which were given exclusively given in yesterday's TIMES. These counties form what is known as the Eastern Shore of Virginia, and are in what was formerly WISE's Congressional District. The inhabitants, as a mass, have refrained from active participation in the rebellion, though very many young men have entered the Confederate army. Accomac is understood to be prepared to array herself for the Union, but Northampton is hostile.

Gen. DIX, with the approbation of the Government, has been maturing the plan of operations which is now being successfully executed. He has sent thither, by way of Pomake Sound and River, the following forces, under direction of Gen. LOCKWOOD, of Delaware, viz.:

Seventeenth Massachusetts—Col. AMORY.
Fifth New-York—Col. WARREN.
Twenty-first Indiana—Col. MCMILLEN.
Sixth Michigan—Maj. BACON.
Fourth Wisconsin—Col. PAYNE.
"Mann's" Massachusetts Battery.
Troop of Cavalry—Col. RICHARDS.
CORNELL'S Legion, from Maryland.
Second Delaware—Col. WHEATON.
The Home Guards—Col. WALLACE.

In all about five thousand well disciplined and effective men, which entered Virginia yesterday.

On Thursday last, Gen. DIX sent the following proclamation to Gen. LOCKWOOD, for distribution among the people of the counties:

PROCLAMATION TO THE PEOPLE OF ACCOMAC AND NORTHAMPTON COUNTIES, VA.

The military forces of the United States are about to enter your counties as a part of the Union. They will go among you as friends, and with the earnest hope that they may not by your own acts be compelled to become your enemies. They will invade no right of person or property. On the contrary, your laws, your institutions, your usages, will be scrupulously respected. There need be no fear that the quietude of any firesides will be disturbed, unless the disturbance is caused by yourselves. Special directions have been given not to interfere with the condition of any person held to domestic servitude, and in order that there may be no ground for mistake or pretext for misrepresentation, commanders of regiments or corps have been instructed not to permit such persons to come within their lines.

The command of the expedition is intrusted to Brig.-Gen. HENRY H. LOCKWOOD, of Delaware—a State identical in some of the distinctive features of its social organization with your own. Portions of his force come from counties in Maryland bordering on one of yours. From him and from them you may be assured of the sympathy of near neighbors, as well as friends, if you do not repel it by hostile resistance or attack.

This mission is to assert the authority of the United States, to reopen your intercourse with the loyal States, and especially with Maryland, which has just proclaimed her devotion to the Union by the most triumphant vote in her political annals; to restore to commerce its accustomed guides, by reestablishing the lights on your coast; to afford you a free export for the produce of your labor, of a free ingress for the necessaries and comforts of life which you require in exchange, and in a word to put an end to the embarrassments and restrictions brought upon you by a causeless and unjustifiable rebellion.

If the calamities of intestine war which are desolating other districts of Virginia, and have already crimsoned her lands with fraternal blood, fall also upon you, it will not be the fault of the Government. It asks only that its authority may be recognized. It sends among you a force too strong to be successfully opposed,—a force which cannot be resisted in any other spirit than that of wantonness and malignity. If there are any among you who, rejecting all overtures of friendship, thus provoke retaliation and draw down upon themselves consequences which the Government is most anxious to avert, to their account must be laid the blood which may be shed, and the desolation which may be brought upon peaceful homes. On all who are thus reckless of the obligations of humanity and duty, and all who are found in arms, the severest punishment warranted by the laws of war will be visited.

To those who remain in the quiet pursuit of their domestic occupations the public authorities assure all they can give peace, freedom from annoyance, protection from foreign and internal enemies, a guaranty of all Constitutional and legal rights, and the blessings of a just and parental Government.

(Signed,) JOHN A. DIX,
Major-General Commanding.

HEADQUARTERS, BALTIMORE, Nov. 13, 1861.

What effect this will produce is as yet matter for conjecture, but it is believed that its reception will be favorable.

THE TRAITORS FROM CALIFORNIA REARRESTED.

On Saturday afternoon, Superintendent KENNEDY, in accordance with instructions received from the Secretary of State, rearrested Ex-Senator GWIN, J. CALHOUN BENHAM and J. L. BRENT, the trio who had been arrested by Gen. SUMNER. Dr. GWIN's arrest was effected at the New-York Hotel during the afternoon, and that of the other two in the evening. They were all taken to Fort Lafayette, to await the arrival of traitors MASON and SLIDELL by the *San Jacinto*, when the whole party will be conveyed to Fort Warren, Boston Bay.

BENHAM's baggage contained, among other papers, two slips cut from the *Tribune* of the 11th of May, 1860, and the TIMES of May 11, 1860, being articles descriptive of himself at the time of his appointment as United States District Attorney by Ex-President BUCHANAN.

The baggage of all the prisoners contained revolvers, pistols, dirks and bowie-knives.

Dr. GWIN appeared to be profoundly displeased at having fallen into the hands of the authorities.

INTERESTING FROM BALTIMORE.

THE SEIZURE OF THE SCHOONER MARYLAND BY THE REBELS AND HER RECAPTURE—PROBABLE STRENGTH OF THE REBEL BATTERIES ON THE POTOMAC, ETC.

Correspondence of the New-York Times.

BALTIMORE, Friday, Nov. 15, 1861.

From Lieut. C. H. COLBURN, of the Eleventh Massachusetts Regiment, Company H, attached to Gen. HOOKER's Brigade, on the Maryland shore of the Potomac, and who arrived in this city this evening, I have the following interesting particulars of a rebel attack upon the schooner *Maryland*. The schooner was loaded with wood, and yesterday, while passing the rebel battery off Pig Point, and directly off the encampment of the Massachusetts Eleventh, became becalmed. The crew, immediately on perceiving preparations making by the rebels to attack their vessel from the Virginia shore, dropped their anchor and, taking to their boats, rowed away to the United States flotilla, which was anchored about four miles up the river.

Lieut. W. L. CHANDLER, of the Eleventh, in command, and accompanied by Lieut. COLBURN and two or three others, immediately leaped into a small boat and put off for the schooner. When they reached her they discovered that the rebels were approaching from the opposite shore in superior force. The guns of the rebel battery now opened a brisk fire upon the vessel, which, together with the near approach of the rebel crew in the boat, compelled them to abandon her, having made the discovery that no one was left on board.

Soon after the rebels reached the schooner, dark volumes of smoke were seen bursting up the cabin hatchway, while the rebel demons danced about the deck, cheering and yelling like wild men, and continuing their loud cries until they had entered their boat and gained the Virginia shore.

A gentle breeze now began to sweep up the river, and no sooner had the rebels deserted the burning vessel than the men of the Eleventh again rowed back to her, and amid a rapid fire from the rebels, hoisted her anchor and extinguished the flames—which they found confined to the cabin—set the sails, and slowly and steadily swept up the river, amid the cheers of the National forces, who had now gathered upon the bank, and carried the schooner safely beyond the range of the enemy's fire.

The *Maryland* was lying close in to the Maryland shore. Another schooner, which was lying becalmed about quarter of a mile below the *Maryland*, also followed, and passed by the battery without damage. Over one hundred shots were fired upon the schooner *Maryland*, only two of which took effect, and those above-deck, doing little or no damage.

The steamer *Yankee*, as soon as the schooners had cleard the rebel fire, steamed down and took them in tow, carrying them up to the Government flotilla, where the *Maryland* was again handed over to her crew.

The impression is prevalent among the officers of both HOOKER's and SICKLES' Brigades, that the batteries on the Virginia shore of the Potomac, are not so formidable and potent in their character as has been apprehended. It is believed that most of the batteries consist of field-pieces, which are changed from point to point on the river, giving rise to the supposition that their batteries are more numerous than is actually the case.

Upon preparations being made by Gen. HOOKER to fire upon the rebels with his battery, upon the above occasion, the rumbling wheels of the enemy's pieces were distinctly heard receding from the shore. They have but one gun at this point which ranges across the river, and that is a thirty-two pounder, the balls of which are often thrown nearly into the camp of the Eleventh Massachusetts Regiment.

The secession element of this city are appalled at the suicidal threat of the South in reference to hanging the Northern prisoners who are selected to retaliate against the execution of the crew of the *Savannah*. "Why!" exclaimed one, "the North would send down her armed legions thick as the locusts of Egypt, to avenge their deaths!" The report is not credited here.

The following is from the Charleston *Mercury*, of the 10th, which was received by the steamer *Georgeana*, from Fortress Monroe this morning:

"LIST OF VESSELS IN CHARLESTON.—Steamships, 2; ships, 2; barks, 2; brigs, 4. The steamers were the *Isabel*, Capt. ROLLINS; and the *Cahawba*, Capt. BLACKHAM. There were no schooners in port over one hundred tons. The following schooners reached Charleston on the 9th: Schooners *James H. Ladson*, with 2,550 bushels of rough rice; *George Chisholm*, 190 barrels of rice; *Gen. C. C. Pinckney*, 14 bales superior cotton; *Guide*, 2,350 bushels rough rice; *H. Lowndes*, 2,500 bushels rice; *Coquette*, 2,600 bushels rice; *Elyria*, 2,323 bushels rice; *Edisto*, 1,600 ditto." ARGUS.

THE ENGAGEMENT AT PIKETON, KY.

LOUISVILLE, Sunday, Nov. 17.

A slight snow, the first of the season, occurred here this morning.

The Mount Sterling *Whig* has a report from THOMAS TURNER, one of Gen. NELSON's Aids, relative to the late Piketon engagement. He says that at Prestinburgh, the National army divided into two colums, one under Col. SILL, *via* John's Creek, and the other met the enemy by another route.

At Ivy Creek the latter had a sharp engagement for one hour and twenty minutes, routing the rebels—killing six and wounding 24. The rebels reported to the Unionists that they lost from 200 to 300, of whom 40 were killed, and about 60 wounded.

Another account says the National loss was six killed and 17 wouned.

The previous account from Cincinnati appears to have been greatly exaggerated.

CONSOLIDATION OF REGIMENTS.

GENERAL HEADQUARTERS STATE OF NEW-YORK, ADJUTANT-GENERAL'S OFFICE, ALBANY, Nov. 8, 1861.

SPECIAL ORDERS, No. 483.—Special order No. 452 is hereby rescinded. In accordance with general orders No. 78 from this department, and with general orders No. 71 from the War Department, the organizations heretofore known as the "Clinton Guard" and the "Astor Regiment" are hereby consolidated into a regiment, to be designated as the Sixty-first (61st) Regiment of New-York State Volunteers.

The following persons are appointed Field, Staff and Company Officers of the Sixty-first Regiment thus organized, and will be commissioned when the field, staff and company muster-rolls, certified to by the mustering officers, shall have been filed in the office of the Adjutant-General of the State.

Col. SPENCER W. CONE, Lieut.-Col. Francis C. Barlow, Major William C. Massett.

Staff Officers.—Adjt. David E. Gregory, Quartermaster Robert H. Ellis, Surgeon Asa B. Snow, Assistant Surgeon Andrew Merrill, Chaplain John Ross Baumes.

Company Officers.—Co. A—Capt. Edward Z. Lawrence, First Lieut. Wm. E. Butterfield, Second Lieut. Walter H. Maze. Co. B—Capt. Jas. I. Trenor, First Lieut. Dennis A. Moore, Second Lieut. Thomas G. Morrison. Co. C—Capt. Kent O. Brady, First Lieut. Wm. McIntyne, Second Lieut. Wm. H. Coltis. Co. D—Capt. Joseph M. Carville, First Lieut. David Henriques, Second Lieut. George W. Scott. Co. E—Capt. David Jackson, First Lieut. Wm. H. Roome, Second Lieut. Edgar Belcher. Co. F—Capt. Theodore Russell, First Lieut. Geo. D. H. Watts, Second Lieut. Albert L. Blowers. Co. G—Capt. Arthur L. Brooks, First Lieut. Wm. Keech, Second Lieut. Henry A. Gates. Co. H—Capt. Edward P. Mount, First Lieut. Manton C. Angell, Second Lieut. Dexter C. Leland. Co. I—Capt. Eugene M. Deming, First Lieut. Jerome J. Woodruff, Second Lieut. Lucien Cadwell. Co. K—Capt. Charles T. Ripley, First Lieut. Cornelius P. Bergen, Second Lieut. Walter F. Jones.

Brig.-Gen. YATES is charged with the execution of the details of this order.

By order of the Commander-in-Chief.

THOS. HILLHOUSE, Adjutant-General.

THE NEWS FROM EUROPE.

ADDITIONAL BY THE NIAGARA.

OUR PARIS AND LONDON CORRESPONDENCE.

Mr. Slidell Expected in Paris---What He was to Do.

FRANCE, ENGLAND AND THE BLOCKADE.

The Possibilities of an Anglo-American War.

The Protest of the President Against the Mexican Expedition.

Further Light upon the Cotton Question.

The mails from Europe by the steamship *Niagara*, which left Liverpool on the 2d inst., calling at Queenstown on the 3d, were received here on Saturday evening.

We are thus placed in possession of important letters from our correspondents at Paris and at London.

We are also enabled to lay before our readers interesting extracts from European exchanges.

A portion of the latter appeared in our Sunday edition.

THE REBEL COMMISSIONERS TO EUROPE.

The Arrival of Mr. Slidell looked for with Especial Interest—Object of his Mission—Effect of the Financial Success of Mr. Chase upon the Secessionists—Pamphlets—The Constitutionnel upon Mr. Everett, &c.

From Our Own Correspondent.

PARIS, Friday, Nov. 1, 1861.

The Southern Commissioners, who are now at Paris, look forward to the arrival of Mr. SLIDELL with a great deal of pleasure. They have immense confidence in his abilities, and anticipate, upon his arrival, being able to offer to the European Governments new inducements for taking their Government under their protection. Since the word protection has slipped from my pen, I may say that I have heard it mentioned that one of the new inducements Mr. SLIDELL is authorized to offer to the French Government as the price of a recognition, is that of giving to France, what is called in diplomacy, *a protectorate* over the new Confederacy, with such commercial advantages as must be irresistible. Of course I have no means of guaranteeing the truth of this rumor. One thing, however, is certain—great hopes are built upon the diplomacy which Mr. SLIDELL will inaugurate upon his arrival.

Mr. YANCEY, who is making himself very popular at Paris, gave a grand dinner the other day to his friends at the Restaurant Philippe.

We have heard from a gentleman who has ramifications in secession society, that the ready taking of the second and third National Loan has struck the secession gentlemen with more dismay than any event that has occurred in the history of the war. They still counted, it seems, upon divisions in the North, and perhaps a little upon its cupidity. But since it is now not a question of "who will take the loan?" so much as "who shall we let have it?" the tables are quite turned, and we can understand their disappointment. The first and ablest, and most efficient General in the nation, is evidently SALMON P. CHASE.

For some time we had enjoyed an intermittence in the paroxysms of *brochures* on the American question, but the enemy is again at work in this line, and now we have *The Policy of France and of Humanity in the American Conflict*, by M. BARRILLON, a Lyons official and silk manufacturer. M. BARRILLON writes 40 octavo "long-primer" pages to prove that disunion was the inevitable destiny of the great Republic, that the habits of the people and their opposite commercial interests required it, and that Slavery is an enormity which ought to be eradicated, if by no other means than by the force of arms, and finally that France is the country which has the arms to do it. Like the author of a preceding pamphlet, he thinks that, since European bayonets will be required to destroy Slavery in America, it is easier to fight against eleven States than against thirty-four. He therefore goes for disunion!

The *Constitutionnel* has published entire, and with a commendatory prefcae, Mr. EVERETT's beautiful address to the Prince NAPOLEON at Boston. We have reason to believe that this publication was made by a request coming from high place.

An article from the *Siècle*, which you published in the TIMES a month ago, regrets that so little attention is paid to the American question in France. We beg leave to suggest that this indifference exists only in the *Siècle* office, just where it ought not to exist, for of all the leading journals of Paris it is the one which contains the least on the question. And yet the *Siècle* is the leading republican paper of France, and avows the most sympathy for the United States, its people and institutions. MALAKOFF.

FRANCE, ENGLAND AND THE BLOCKADE.

Rumored Intention of the European Powers to Turn the Mexican Expedition Against the United States.

From Our Own Correspondent.

PARIS, Friday, Nov. 1, 1861.

A French paper developes at length the theory that the heavy and useless armaments which the French and English are sending out to Mexico are not destined for the coercion of that Power, but for the liberation of cotton in the Southern States. He gives the following as the composition of the fleet: On the part of France, six vessels—the *Imperial*, the frigates *La Guerre* and *L'Active*, another of the same rank, a corvette and a cutter. The *Imperial* will be the flag-boat

The New-York Times.

VOL. XI....NO. 3170. | NEW-YORK, TUESDAY, NOVEMBER 19, 1861. | PRICE TWO CENTS.

THE GREAT REBELLION.

IMPORTANT NEWS FROM WASHINGTON.

Attempt of the Rebels to Capture the Brooklyn Fourteenth.

They are Repulsed, with Considerable Loss.

The Expedition to the Eastern Shore of Virginia.

Landing of the Troops in Accomac.

Favorable Reception of General Dix's Proclamation.

IMPORTANT FROM SANTA ROSA ISLAND.

Another Attempt of the Rebels to Surprise Billy Wilson's Zouaves.

Lamentable Failure—They are Shelled Off by the Fleet.

Preparations for the Rebels at Newport's News.

SPECIAL DISPATCH FROM WASHINGTON.

WASHINGTON, Monday, Nov. 18.

THE BATTLE OF PIKETON NOT A HOAX.

A dispatch from Cincinnati states that the reported battle at Piketon was a hoax. If a hoax, it was one which resulted in the capture of twenty-seven hundred prisoners. The misapprehension arose from the fact of two battles having been fought. On the first day, the main battle was fought, in which four hundred were killed and twenty-seven hundred taken prisoner. The following day, however, the rebels rallied, and in the skirmish that ensued they lost between thirty and forty men. That we have not earlier received full intelligence from Gen. NELSON is attributed to the fact that Piketon is nearly 150 miles from railroad communication, and the intervening space is over a mountainous district, and at this season of the year over bad roads.

CAPT. WILKES AND THE REBEL COMMISSIONERS.

Capt. WILKES was sent to the coast of Africa especially to bring home the *San Jacinto*, and it was only when he arrived in the West Indies that he heard of the escape of Messrs. MASON and SLIDELL. Therefore, his arrest of them could not have been pursuant to orders. Capt. WILKES acted in accordance with the principle of international law. He tendered to the ladies accompanying the Mason and Slidell party a passage on his ship, and the use of the cabin, with all the delicacies and attentions they might require, but they declined his gallant and considerate invitation.

THE ARREST NO VIOLATION OF LAW.

The *Intelligencer* of this morning has an able article, reviewing the act of Capt. WILKES in the light of international law. Its purpose is to show the entire justification of the arrest, and I learn upon good authority, that in the estimation of diplomats the positions therein assumed are well founded, and are sustained both by precedent and the teachings of standard writers.

CAPT. WILKES SUSTAINED.

There is an increasing confidence in the entire correctness of Capt. WILKES' act in taking SLIDELL and MASON, and I am informed that Secretary CHASE has expressed his regret that he did not also seize the vessel. Count DE GUROWSKI is certain that Great Britain will not take exception to the act, in view of the fact that English writers on International Law class powder, ball, Ambassadors and hemp, even, as belligerent—thus disagreeably sandwiching MASON and SLIDELL as contraband of war.

A FALSE ALARM.

This afternoon, while a review of a portion of Gen. McDOWELL's Division was taking place, a courier arrived, stating that the New-York Fourteenth Militia, of Brooklyn, had been captured beyond Fall's Church, on the Fairfax road. Gen. WADSWORTH's Brigade was immediately ordered out, and they proceeded from Bailey's Cross Roads west by the Columbia turnpike, if possible to surround the attacking party. At the same time, the cavalry and artillery left by the Fairfax road, only to learn that the report was a gross exaggeration. The facts, as near as I can learn, are these: The Brooklyn Fourteenth proceeded out on a foraging expedition to near BRUSH's house, at 10 o'clock this morning, and while they were engaged in getting on a supply of corn, a body of rebel cavalry drove in our pickets, and wounded one man. They were successfully driven back, it is stated, with a loss of seven.

MISSING MEN OF THE THIRTIETH NEW-YORK.

There are still some twenty-eight missing in connection with the capture by the rebels on Saturday of a detachment of the foraging party.

AGENCIES FOR ARMS TO BE WITHDRAWN.

The War Department will soon issue a circular addressed to the Governors of the loyal States, requesting the withdrawal of their agents for the purchase of arms, both at home and abroad, as the Government has received advices to the effect that a sufficiency of arms will be secured through its own agency to meet the demands which may from time to time arise. This arrangement will very much facilitate the speedy delivery of arms, and remove the temptations to speculators to withhold for better contract prices, at the expense of the Government.

THE CALIFORNIA TRAITORS.

The protest by the authorities at Panama against Gen. SUMNER's arrest of GWIN, BENHAM and BRENT turns out to be without authority of the New-Granadian Republic.

AFFAIRS ON THE LOWER POTOMAC.

The steamer *E. B. Hale* arrived at the Navy-yard on Saturday night. For a week or two past, she has been stationed at Stump Neck to watch the rebel steamer *George Page*, but the opening of the new rebel battery at Cockpit Point, forced her to move from that exposed position, and she now lies at Deep Point, when on the lookout. Her officers have no objections to an encounter with the *Page*, as they have a staunch little steamer and a fine battery aboard.

The *Dawn* ran the blockade of the Potomac River on Saturday night week, the *Hetzler* on last Tuesday night, and six schooners on Thursday night last—all bound down. Since then none but small vessels have passed either way.

All the vessels which have left Washington or Georgetown, have passed through safely, and none are now at Indian Head.

The rebels are busy at Freestone Point, and it is supposed they are building a strong work for a battery there.

VISITORS EXCLUDED.

The heads of Departments have been so much annoyed by visitors that they have not been able to commence their annual reports. They have, therefore, been compelled to resolve to exclude all visitors until after the meeting of Congress, and in view of this determination, parties who contemplate visiting Washington for the purpose of having interviews with the heads of Departments, are advised to defer their journey hither until after the assembling of Congress.

CONTRACTS FOR BEEF CATTLE.

The contracts for supplying the Government with three lots, each of four thousand head of cattle on the hoof, deliverable at Washington, Harrisburgh, York or Chambersburgh, as the Government may determine, were awarded today, as follows: The first to EDWARD McQUADE and WM. T. HILDRUP, of Pennsylvania, at $3 98, the contract to continue four months from Nov. 30; the second to JAMES LOWTHER and ISRAEL PAINTER, of Pennsylvania, at $3 57½, the contract to continue four months from Dec. 31; the third to RUFF, SANGER & Co., at $3 55. The bidders below these figures withdrew their bids, or failed to respond. The contract stipulates that the cattle shall have an average weight of 1,300 pounds, and that no animal shall be received weighing less than 1,000 pounds.

NO MORE VOLUNTEERS TO BE CALLED FOR.

The statement that the President intends to issue a proclamation, calling upon the States for two hundred thousand more volunteers, is without foundation. When the half million volunteers called for by act of Congress have been recruited, none will be received except in the regular service.

MILITARY APPOINTMENTS.

The following military appointments were made to-day, viz; Assistant Adjutant-Generals of Volunteers—Capt. Leonard Scott, for Gen. Paine's Brigade; Capt. George A. Hicks, for Gen. Burns' Brigade; Capt. John Pound, for Gen. Price's Brigade; Capt. Andrew C. Kemper, for Gen. Wade's Brigade; Capt. Wm. Van Dohn, for Gen. DURYEE's Brigade. Capt. Charles A. Reynolds, to be an Assistant Quartermaster in the regular service. Wm. Sheffler to be an Aid-de-Camp to Major-Gen. Banks.

GEORGE D. KELLOGG, of Chicago, has been appointed Assistant Adjutant-General of Volunteers, with the rank of Captain, and assigned to Gen. STANLEY's Staff.

MILITARY STOREKEEPER.

EPHRAIM D. ELLSWORTH, father of the late Col. ELLSWORTH, has been appointed Military Storekeeper by the President, but is not yet assigned to duty.

THE FLEET IN THE WESTERN DEPARTMENT.

The President has appointed Capt. A. H. FOOTE Flag-officer of the fleet in the Western Military Department. He thus ranks with the Major-General. This arrangement obviates any possible conflict of authority between the commanders respectively of the land and water forces.

FOR THE WESTERN GUNBOATS.

Yesterday, four hundred seamen, who have been stationed at Fort Ellsworth, and two hundred marines, left for Cairo, to man the gunboats there.

A SHARP TRANSACTION.

To day an *exposé* of a sharp transaction, to say the least, came to light. A Brigade Commissary made a requisition upon the Commissary Department for 150 barrels of flour. The requisition was filled, and the Commissary, it is said, sold the flour to a dealer in sutlers' stores, receiving therefor over $1,000. Subsequently the dealer sold the flour to another party, and received the money for it. He in his turn offered it for sale to Maj. BECKWITH, the Commissary of Subsistence, who identified it and made a seizure. The facts were explained, and the last dealer called upon the first for his money, who returned it this afternoon. It is said that this is one of a series of similar transactions that have taken place between the same parties, and by which the Government has been swindled.

PRISONERS TO FORT MACKINAW.

It is proposed to send a portion of our prisoners of war to Fort Mackinaw.

COL. FRISBIE IN COMMAND OF A BRIGADE.

Col. FRISBIE, of the New-York Thirtieth Regiment, is now in command of the brigade formerly under Gen. KEYES.

GEN. SUMNER'S FAMILY.

Gen. SUMNER's daughters are married to Virginians. One, EUGENE E. McLEAN, is now an invalid in Richmond. He was a Quartermaster in the regular service at Baltimore, where he resigned at the beginning of the present difficulties. The other, ARMISTEAD LONG, was a Lieutenant in the regular service, and was an aid to Gen. SUMNER when he resigned and went South. Gen. SUMNER's two sons are Lieutenants in the regular cavalry, one in the First and the other in the Fifth Regiment.

COL. GRAHAM.

Col. GRAHAM, of the Fifth Regiment, Excelsior Brigade, is in the city under arrest. It is rumored that the reason of his arrest is the burning of some buildings on Matthias Point by his command, on the occasion of the recent reconnoissance there.

PROPERTY OF GEN. WALBRIDGE CONFISCATED.

Intelligence has been received of the confiscation of some landed property belonging to Gen. HIRAM WALBRIDGE in South Carolina.

THE REBELS OF ALEXANDRIA KEEPING FAST.

The 15th inst. being the day appointed by JEFF. DAVIS for a day of fasting and prayer throughout the rebellious States, the secessionists of Alexandria, as dutiful rebels, past the day with empty stomachs.

MITTENS WANTED.

Our troops are suffering for the want of mittens and gloves. No provision is made by the Government for the supply of these needed articles, and donations will be gratefully received by the men. A half million pairs are now wanted.

YANCEY'S SON.

The superscription on the letter written by YANCEY to his son, is as follows: "B. C. YANCEY, Captain Artillery, C. S. A., Fort Morgan, Mobile." It was inclosed in an envelope, directed to Messrs. HOBART & FORSTER, New-Orleans.

PAYMENT OF MISSOURI TROOPS.

Col. HARDING, of Missouri, has made an arrangement by which the three months Home Guards of that State, mustered into service under the authority of the late Gen. LYON, will be paid.

A FULL REGIMENT IN NEW-JERSEY.

A requisition for guns for the Ninth New-Jersey Regiment was made to-day upon the Ordnance Department. The regiment numbers 1,200 men.

CONTRABAND WHEAT.

The fourteen thousand bushels of wheat captured by our troops at Harper's Ferry are now at Georgetown being ground into flour. The flour has been turned over to the Commissary's Department.

CONSULS APPOINTED.

The following-named Consuls have been appointed: GEORGE KENT, of Maine, at Paso del Norte, Mexico; MAX EINSTEIN, of Pennsylvania, at Nuremburg; WM. IRWIN, of Pennsylvania, at Bahia, Brazil; ALLEN FRANCIS, of Springfield, Ill., at Victoria, Vancouver's Island.

THE AMERICAN CLAIMS AGAINST NEW-GRANADA.

The Commissioners to settle American claims against New-Granada met today, and the calendar was called and three cases were taken up.

THE CONSUL TO BUENOS AYRES.

HINTON ROWAN HELPER, our Consul to Buenos Ayres, left for New-York to-day, and will proceed to South America on the 7th proximo.

A GRAND REVIEW TO TAKE PLACE.

A grand review of several Divisions is to take place in Virginia on Wednesday, on which occasion the world at large will be permitted to be present without the trouble of obtaining passports.

PRENTICE IN TOWN.

GEO. D. PRENTICE, of the Louisville *Journal*, is in the city, and has been cordially welcomed by his numerous friends.

FROM A PRISONER IN RICHMOND.

The following private letter has been handed in for publication:

PRISON HOSPITAL, RICHMOND, Va., Nov. 13, 1861.

FRIEND GILES: I have received a note from Sergeant O'DONOHUE, of Company K, inquiring about LUKE DOYLE, of Company B—your company. His leg was amputated and he died in the General Hospital on the 17th of September last. I have written you a letter once, but got no answer, and was glad to hear through my wife of your getting home safe. DENNIS SHORTER is here, well from his wound. He told me the last he saw of you, you were taking a man's musket out of his hand and using it yourself on the battle-field of Bull Run, July 21. I am in good health, and I am helping to take care of the wounded men in this hospital. Tell Sergeant O'DONOHUE that SHAUGHNESSEY, whom he inquired for, is here, getting on quite well now. He had quite recovered at one time, but gangrene set in, and he had to come to hospital again. HUGHES, whom he inquired for, has been sent to Columbia, S. C., with others.

They say that Col. CORCORAN is one of those whose lot it is to be hung in retaliation in case the privateersmen in New-York and Philadelphia are hung. I read an article to that effect in one of the papers here on Monday last.

I would write you a long letter if I thought it would go. Give my respects to all my friends, and accept the same from, yours sincerely, P. R. DUNNE,
Engineer Corps Sixty-ninth Regiment, N. Y. S. M.
To Capt. WILLIAM M. GILES, Company B, Sixty-ninth Regiment.

THE EASTERN SHORE OF VIRGINIA.

Our Map of Accomac and Northampton Counties, the Destination of Gen. Lockwood's Expedition.

We present above a minute and faithful map of the eastern shore of Virginia, the destination of an expedition which Major-Gen. DIX has dispatched from his command at Baltimore. The counties of Accomac and Northampton occupy the lower extremity of the peninsula, of which Delaware is the base, the Atlantic and Chesapeake Bay washing the two sides. The seaboard exhibits the common characteristics of the Atlantic coast, in its numerous islands of sand, with inlets and interior sounds; the principal of these being Chincotague Island, inlet, and sound, famous for oysters, the favorites of epicures. It is from the Atlantic side of Accomac and Northampton that the Northern supplies of the bivalves are chiefly drawn. The Chesapeake shore is closely indented with bays and inlets, often the estuaries of small inland streams. From Cape Charles, the Southern extremity, to Cape Henry, the opposite gate-post of the Chesapeake waters, the distance is about fifteen miles. To Old Point Comfort it is nearly thirty.

Accomac County is only known to fame as long time the home of Ex-Gov. WISE, whose seat "Only, near Onancook," was the place at which his not infrequent letters, public and private, were for many years dated. The county covers some 480 square miles, principally of a sandy alluvium, naturally fertile, but sadly abused by slave cultivation. The population, which is represented to be mainly loyal to the Union, numbered in the census of last year 10,687 whites, and 4,507 slaves. Northampton County, at the southward of Accomac, with one-fourth less area than the latter county, has less than one-half the population. It numbers 2,004 whites, 3,872 slaves; the preponderance being dangerously in favor of the latter; and we discover, what is always noted where such disproportion exists, a community almost unanimously given over to treason. It is not the practice of the insurgent Government to leave such dispositions without encouragement. Troops have therefore been sent across the bay; the inhabitants have joined them in large numbers; and, pushing into Accomac, they have found sympathy at a village, euphoniously named Pungoteague, which they have intrenched and surrounded with batteries more or less formidable.

It is to repress this this demonstration, and to afford support to the alarmed Unionists, that Gen. DIX has sent a force of about 4,000 men to occupy the peninsula. These entering the Pocomoke Sound and River, had, at the latest advices, landed at Newtown, a point just above the Maryland line, whence they will be able to advance without difficulty in pursuit of the rebels. From this point also the judicious proclamation of Gen. DIX has been promulgated, and, as we learn, with satisfactory effect.

THE REBEL COMMISSIONERS.

Arrival of the San Jacinto off this Port—She is Ordered to Boston.

The *San Jacinto*, with Messrs. MASON and SLIDELL on board, was telegraphed at 3 P. M., yesterday, when off Squan. Mr. ROBERT MURRAY, United States Marshal, embarked on board the steam-tug *Achilles*, and intercepted her, and in pursuance of orders received from Washington, she was ordered to Boston; no communication from the shore to be allowed with her, until after the delivery of her prisoners at Fort Warren.

Marshal MURRAY will proceed to Boston in the *San Jacinto*, to deliver in person the prisoners to Col. DIMMOCK, at Fort Warren.

IMPORTANT FROM HAVANA.

The Embarkation of Slidell and Mason on board the Trent—Southern Captains and the Blockade—The Mexican Expedition.

The Mail steamer *Cosmopolitan*, A. C. CROCKER, Esq., Commander, from Havana, Nov. 12, arrived here yesterday morning.

Messrs. SLIDELL and MASON, the Confederate Commissioners, with their families and suite, sailed from Havana on the 7th inst. by English steamer *Trent* for Southampton *via* St. Thomas, having received marked attention from parties in Cuba, which followed them to their embarkation.

Secession merchant captains, of which there are a large number at Havana, pronounce the blockade only inconvenient, and hand you almost daily for perusal papers of late date from the ports they last sailed from.

C. G. HELM, now residing in Havana, has no official relation with the Confederates, so far as known in that city.

The Spanish fleet bound to Mexico, are all ready to sail, and only await the arrival of vessels from Spain now past due. The expedition goes down strong, and will bring about terms which can be accepted, or will levy on property and adjudicate.

THE CALIFORNIA PRISONERS OF STATE.

Ex-Senator GWIN, J. CALHOUN BENHAM and S. L. BRENT, who were confined in the First Ward Station-house since Saturday evening, were yesterday morning removed, under charge of Capt. SILVEY, to Fort Lafayette.

THE EXPEDITION TO ACCOMAC.

Four Thousand Troops Preparing to Land—Favorable Reception of Gen. Dix's Proclamation, &c.

BALTIMORE, MONDAY, Nov. 18.

The steamers *Georgia* and *Georgiana* arrived this morning from Newtown, Worcester County, Maryland. Four thousand Federal troops were preparing to go into Virginia. On the way up the Potomac River a boat was sent ashore with Gen. DIX's proclamation, which was read to a large number of Virginians in a farm house, who declared it entirely satisfactory, and claimed the protection of the Government against the Secessionists, who were forcing them into the rebel ranks against their will. The gunboat *Resolute* had been giving them protection through the day, but at night they would have to seek shelter in the woods.

IMPORTANT FROM SANTA ROSA.

Another Attempt by the Rebels to Capture Billy Wilson's Zouaves—A Lamentable Failure.

Mr. SAVAGE, U. S. Vice-Consul at Havana, who had been to Key West on business, and who returned to Havana on the 10th inst., reports that 1,500 rebel troops had been discovered by the Union patrol, some twenty miles from the fort, on Santa Rosa Island. The patrol immediately informed the commander of the fleet, who sent a force and shelled them off the island with great loss. It is supposed the object was to get together some 5,000 or more rebels, and by a forced march to Col. WILSON's camp make another night attack upon them. The greatest vigilance is exercised by the commander of the Zouaves.

MILITARY AND NAVAL INTELLIGENCE.

Several officers recently appointed from civil life have reported to Col. LOOMIS, on Governor's Island, making the total number of officers on the rolls upwards of forty. There is not sufficient accommodations for so many officers in Fort Columbus, and six of them have, therefore, been transferred to Fort Wood, Bedloe's Island.

Some of the Cape Hatteras prisoners still remain on Governor's Island, sick in hospital.

The following regular regiments, or portions of them, stationed at California, are under orders for the States, and may shortly be expected here: Fourth, Sixth and Ninth Infantry, and the First Cavalry, numbering, with the detachment which passed through the City on Friday, about 3,000 men.

The United States bark *Fernandina* was put into commission on Saturday afternoon at the Brooklyn Navy-yard with the customary formalities. The following is a list of her officers:

Acting Volunteer Lieutenant in Command, GEORGE W. BROWN; Acting Master and Executive Officer, J. R. Dickenson; Acting Masters, M. S. Harris and S. P. Clark; Acting Assistant Surgeon, E. Pray; Acting Assistant Paymaster, William D. Hempstead; Masters' Mates, H. Heath, J. C. Robinson and R. Rhodes.

The *Fernandina* carries an armament of six 32-pounders, and a crew of about ninety men, and is in every respect a useful-looking craft. She left the yard yesterday and anchored off the Battery, where she will receive her powder.

The steamer *Henry Andrews* will be put into commission to-day. Her officers and crew are ordered to be on board this morning.

The steamer *De Soto*, which has been off the battery during the past few days taking in powder, sailed yesterday.

The steamer *Bienville* has been repaired and supplied with stores, and is ready for sea again. She will sail to-day.

The storeship *Relief*, having been thoroughly cleansed out, is now ready to receive her stores. The chartered steam transport *Coatzacoalcos* went up the East River yesterday for repairs.

The work of paying off the employes at the Yard has commenced, and will take two or three days.

Preparations are being made for mounting, permanently, six guns, captured during the Mexican war and sent to the Yard a few months ago. They are the only trophies of the kind in the Yard.

SEIZURE OF THE W. R. KIBBY FOR RUNNING THE BLOCKADE.

The bark *W. R. Kibby*, which has heretofore figured somewhat conspicuously as a slaver, has now turned up in a new light. It will be recollected that the *Kibby* was condemned as a slaver, and sold by the United States Marshal of this District. She was purchased by a firm in South-street, and fitted out for a trading-voyage to St. Thomas, whither she sailed with a cargo. She there took out papers from the British Consul and went to Key West, whence she proceeded to Texas, successfully running the blockade. At Brazos and Matamoras she took in a cargo of hides and $20,000 in specie, with which she started for Halifax. Falling short of provisions on the way, she put into this port on Sunday to get a fresh supply. She was immediately seized by the United States Marshal, the Captain arrested and sent to Fort Lafayette, and the vessel detained as a prize.

FROM CAMP MUDDY BRANCH, MD.

CAMP MUDDY BRANCH, Saturday, Nov. 16.

The northeaster of yesterday gave way to a freezing gale from the northwest. Ice formed last night, and the ground continues to freeze to-day. The contrast of the present temperature with that of the week previous cannot but prove very detrimental to the health of the army and horses, unprotected as all are from the inclemencies of the weather. It is to be hoped, for the sake of the men who have left comfortable homes for the defence of the Union, that the military authorities will not delay a moment beyond the actual necessities of the case to provide comfortable quarters for those whose duty it is to guard our frontiers or meet the enemy in combat during the coming Winter.

Private FLANDERS PERKINS, of Company F, New-York Eighth Regiment, died of typhoid fever on Thursday. He was a native of Elba, Genessee County.

P. M. ENGLE, Esq., long the efficient Assistant-Quartermaster of Gen. BANKS' Division, has been rewarded with a commission as Captain in the regular army, and appointed Brigade-Quartermaster. He is a gentleman of fine accomplishments, a native of Germany, and received a European military education. Officers and men of this division indulge the hope that he will be detailed for this division.

The New-York Nineteenth, Col. LEDLIE, were quite elated yesterday by the appearance of Major LAWYER, Paymaster for that regiment. They have recently received a complete outfit of clothing, including warm and substantial overcoats. Their new tents are expected in a few days.

JOHN CHANDLER, of Cumberland, Md., but formerly a resident of Darnestown, was arrested there yesterday by the Provost Guard. It is reported that he is charged with being a spy, while others say he was clandestinely selling articles contraband of military rule.

Gen. ABERCROMBIE, who has been on a visit to a sick daughter in Philadelphia, has returned, and resumed the duties of his position. Col. FLETCHER WEBSTER, of the Twelfth Massachusetts, was acting Brigadier-General in his absence.

AFFAIRS AT FORTRESS MONROE.

A Spanish Bark Captured off Charleston—Preparations for a Fight at Newport's News, &c.

FORTRESS MONROE, Sunday, Nov. 17,
via BALTIMORE, Monday, Nov. 18.

There has been no flag of truce to-day, and there is no intelligence whatever from the South.

A Spanish bark, taken off Charleston by the *Alabama*, has arrived, in charge of a prize crew, and will sail to-night for New-York. The [illegible] on board, and will probably be released.

Our naval force at Newport's News has been increased in order to check the rebel expedition fitting out in James River, of which three formidable fire-boats are said to form a part.

Gen. PHELPS' command are building comfortable huts for Winter quarters, and Newport's News will, in a few days, present the appearance of a large frontier village.

AID FOR LOYAL NORTH CAROLINIANS.

We are handed the following letter by the Secretary of the "North Carolina Committee of Relief," appointed at the meeting held at Cooper Institute on the 7th inst.

The importance of prompt and liberal donations to so worthy and true a charity will be seen at once:

FORTRESS MONROE, Va.

W. E. Dodge, Jr., Esq., Secretary North Carolina Committee of Relief:

DEAR SIR: Rev. Mr. TAYLOR and myself arrived here yesterday morning, and have received from the officers of the steamer *S. R. Spaulding*, and of the Twentieth Indiana Regiment, just returned to Hatteras, the most deplorable accounts of the destitution of the people on the Banks. If your Committee propose to do anything for their relief, for God's sake *let it be done quickly*. Capt. HOWES, of the *Spaulding*, says they need *immediately* 500 barrels of flour. Most of them can pay, but the trouble is they cannot buy. I beg you to use your best efforts to hurry forward the arrangements of the Committee, even if you do not accomplish so much as you originally proposed.

Yours, respectfully and truly,
CHARLES HENRY FOSTER.

I earnestly second Mr. FOSTER's request [illegible].
M. A. TAYLOR.

Any contributions may be sent to J. [illegible], Treasurer Manhattan Bank, or to any member of the Committee, who will cause the same to be acknowledged through the public prints.

Donations of supplies may be sent to W. E. DODGE, Jr., Secretary, No. 21 Cliff-street, New-York, freight on same to New-York being paid, and due notice given by mail.

THE STEAMSHIP CONSTITUTION.

PREPARATIONS FOR EMBARKING GEN. BUTLER'S DIVISION.

BOSTON, Monday, Nov. 18.

The steamship *Constitution* came up to Long Wharf at 9 o'clock this morning. Her running time from New-York was 29 hours, a heavy gale blowing throughout the passage. The working of the ship and her engines was eminently satisfactory. She was visited by at least 5,000 people this afternoon.

After embarking the troops at Boston, she will proceed to Portland, Wednesday afternoon, where the Maine Twelfth Regiment, Col. SHEPLEY, will be taken on board. The regiments embarking will include the Massachusetts Seventy-sixth, Col. JONES, (late of the Massachusetts Sixth, which marched through Baltimore, April 19.)

FOR THE NAVAL EXPEDITION.

The steamship *Admiral*, with the Fifty-third Regiment, D'EPINEUIL Zouaves, sailed from Quarantine for Annapolis, Sunday, 6.30 P. M.

IMPORTANT FROM MISSOURI.

Gen. Halleck in St. Louis—Positions of the Different Divisions of the National Army.

ST. LOUIS, Monday, Nov. 18.

Gens. HALLECK and HAMILTON arrived here this morning.

Gens. STURGIS and WYMAN arrived here last night.

The Divisions of Gens. HUNTER, STURGIS and POPE have reached different points on the Pacific Railroad, where they will await orders from Gen. HALLECK.

Gen WYMAN's Brigade reached Rolla on Saturday, and the Divisions of Gens. SIGEL and ASBOTH will arrive here to-day or to-morrow.

Gen. WYMAN brought a number of rebel prisoners, among them Col. PRICE and several other officers.

RETURN OF THE ARMY FROM SPRINGFIELD.

From the St. Louis Evening News.

Intelligence from Springfield apprises us of the breaking up of the Federal camp at that place, and the commencement of the return march of the army. The divisions of Gens. STURGIS and SIGEL are on their way to Rolla, and the remainder of the army, consisting of the divisions of POPE, McKINSTRY and ASBOTH, are marching towards Sedalia through Warsaw.

As we have already intimated, the plan for future operations in Missouri probably contemplates the establishment of garrisons at the most important posts in the Southwest and on the Missouri River, and the release of the main body of the Southwest army for active service in another quarter—most probably Southeast Missouri or Southwestern Kentucky.

By a late order, the Department of the West is divided into two Departments—that of Missouri, including the States of Missouri, Arkansas, Illinois, Iowa, Minnesota, Wisconsin, and that portion of Kentucky lying west of the Cumberland River; and that of Kansas, including Kansas, the Indian Territory, Nebraska, Dacotah, and Colorado. The Department of Missouri is to be under command of Gen. HALLECK, with his headquarters at St. Louis; and the Department of Kansas under command of Gen. HUNTER, with his headquarters at Fort Leavenworth.

The arrangement of the parts of these new Departments foreshadows, to some extent, the plan of future operations. The field of Gen. HALLECK's most important service will be in Southeast Missouri and Southwestern Kentucky; and in that region he will no doubt find his battle-fields. Gen. HUNTER will operate in Southern Kansas, and find his battle-fields there and in the Indian Country.

WHO FIRST SUGGESTED AN ATTACK ON BEAUFORT?

To the Editor of the New-York Times:

You will be doing an act of simple justice by stating, that to Mr. ROBERT FREEMAN, of your City, is due the credit of first suggesting to the Government the expedition to Beaufort. Mr. FREEMAN laid this scheme before Gen. WOOL last April, and after his retirement to Troy, before Gens. DIX and BANKS. Gen. DIX, at Mr. FREEMAN's request, made the suggestion to Gen. SCOTT, who approved it, but insisted on postponing its execution till Fall, from over-caution in regard to the health of the troops, although assured of the perfect healthfulness of the locality.

Probably after this war, our military authorities will be somewhat better informed as to the special characteristics of different localities in our country.

CORNING, N. Y., Nov. 15, 1861. F. H. R.

THE PRISONERS AT RICHMOND, VA.

PHILADELPHIA, Monday, Nov. 18.

The *Bulletin* has letters from prisoners at Richmond, Va., giving the names of many Philadelphians, members of Col. BAKER's regiment.

DEATH OF AN ARMY NURSE.

WESTCHESTER, Pa., Monday, Nov. 18.

Miss DEBBY HUGHES, the Washington nurse, so badly injured by the recent railroad accident, died at noon to-day of tetanus.

[For other Rebellion News see Second and Eighth Pages.]

The New-York Times.

VOL. XI....NO. 3171. NEW-YORK, WEDNESDAY, NOVEMBER 20, 1861. PRICE TWO CENTS.

THE GREAT REBELLION.

IMPORTANT NEWS FROM WASHINGTON.

Particulars of the Attack Upon the Brooklyn Fourteenth.

Another Speech by Secretary Cameron.

His Faith in the Ability of the Government to Crush the Rebellion.

LATE INTELLIGENCE FROM PORT ROYAL.

Beaufort Not Yet Occupied by the National Troops.

Interesting Details of the Condition of Affairs There.

THE FLEET NOT YET GONE SOUTH.

Success of the Expedition to the Eastern Shore of Virginia.

Gen. Butler's Division Embarking at Boston.

SPECIAL DISPATCH FROM WASHINGTON.

WASHINGTON, Tuesday, Nov. 19.

A RECEPTION TO PRENTICE.

This evening, a reception was given by Col. JOHN W. FORNEY, at his residence, to GEORGE D. PRENTICE, of the Louisville *Journal*. A numerous assemblage of distinguished citizens was present, among whom were Secretaries Cameron and Smith, Assistant Postmaster-General Kasson, Assistant Attorney-General Coffey, Senators Wilkinson, McDougal, Trumbull and Pomeroy; Adjt.-Gen. Thomas; Gens. Porter and Sykes; Hon. Robert J. Walker, Prof. Bache, Hon. Thos. H. Clay and many others. An hour passed in agreeable conversation, during which Mr. PRENTICE was introduced to the company. A fine supper was then partaken of, at the close of which Secretary CAMERON made a few remarks

SECRETARY CAMERON'S REMARKS.

He said that we were in the midst of a great war—much greater than anybody believed when it commenced. The most important portion of the country, in its relations to the war, was Kentucky, and he was gratified to announce that we had present a gentleman who had done more than any other man towards the preservation of the Union. [Applause.] He only regretted that he had not the power of language to say to that gentleman what he felt was due to the services he had conferred upon the country. He referred to Mr. PRENTICE, of the Louisville *Journal*. For himself, he (Mr. CAMERON) had never had a doubt as to the result of the war. He had faith in the Anglo-Saxon race, which covered this continent. He had still greater faith in the virtue, intelligence, courage and enterprise of the great white laboring population scattered over the Northern States, in achieving our final success. He had always loved and respected the people of the South, but he had felt that the great North was in the end to carry liberty over the world by virtue of its force, its courage and its constancy. In looking into our National troubles, he had felt doubtful of but two or three of the States. He had felt that if Kentucky was but true to herself and the Union, Tennessee would be found ready to second her; and while he saw commercial interests, personal feelings, pride of family and other adverse influences at work, he felt no further doubt when he saw that that great paper opened its columns in favor of the Union. He then felt that the Union was safe. [Applause.] In conclusion, he gave the "health, long life and prosperity of Mr. PRENTICE, of the Louisville *Journal*. [Renewed applause.]

MR. PRENTICE'S REMARKS.

Mr. PRENTICE made a few remarks. He said that he merely wished to say, in response, that he agreed with his distinguished friend in his estimate of the magnitude of this war, and he could only add that he thought the Secretary of War was equal to it.

RELATIVE TO SEIZURES OF VESSELS.

Secretary CHASE has issued the following regulations to be observed in regard to seizures of vessels, made in pursuance of the sixth section of the act of July 13th, last.

First—All such seizures must be made by the Collectors of Customs or other proper revenue officer, except in case of his absence or disability, or where immediate action is necessary, and no such officer is at hand to make the seizures.

Second—In all cases of seizures the Collector, or other officer acting in his stead, shall notify the proper District-Attorney, who will at once institute proceedings for the condemnation of the vessel. After the commencement of such proceedings, if it shall appear to the satisfaction of the District-Attorney instituting them, that the vessel is owned in part by persons not citizens of any State, or part of State, in insurrection against the United States and not residing therein, and that she will not be employed in aiding the existing rebellion, or in violating any law of the United States, such vessel may be discharged on bail being given according to the course of admiralty proceedings for the share or shares owned by any person or persons residing in any such insurgent State or part of State, in which case the proceedings so instituted will be prosecuted without delay, to the condemnation and sale of such insurgent interest, and as to the remainder of the vessel, the forfeiture thereof will be remitted.

Third—Should there be any unusual delay in the commencement of such proceedings, or should there be any other circumstances rendering it proper, in the judgment of the Collector, or other officer acting in his stead, that the vessel should be released from custody, before the commencement of proceedings, the same may be done, provided the Collector, or other officer acting in his stead, shall be satisfied that no such improper use as before mentioned is to be made of the said vessel, and one or more of the loyal owners, residing in the loyal States, shall give a bond, with sufficient sureties, to the United States, in double the value of the share or shares thereof owned in any such insurgent State, or part of State, with the condition that the vessel shall be safely, and in good order, returned to the Collector, or other officer, in whose custody she may be, within such time as he shall direct, and without any change in the ownership of said share or shares, and with the further condition that the vessel shall, at all times, be subject to any order or decree of the Court in which any proceedings for her condemnation may be instituted, or of any appellate Court to which the same may be removed, and with the further condition that any costs, or other moneys, which shall be awarded by either of said Courts in said proceedings, shall be paid, together with such other conditions as the Collector or other officer shall deem just and expedient in order to secure the objects contemplated by the act aforesaid. The execution of such bond, and the discharge of the vessel shall not delay the institution or prosecution of proceedings for the condemnation of the insurgent interest, but the same shall be commenced and prosecuted in all all respects, so far as practicable, in the same manner as if the vessel still remained in the custody of the officer. The District-Attorney will notify the Collector, or other officer making the seizure in his stead, of the commencement of the suit, of the result of the trial and of the time of sale, if a sale be ordered, and the result thereof.

THE SKIRMISH OF THE BROOKLYN FOURTEENTH.

Mention was made in a previous dispatch of a skirmish yesterday afternoon, two miles and a half southwest of Falls Church, since which time additional particulars have been ascertained The charge upon our pickets near BRUSH's house, was made by three hundred or more rebel cavalry, and this occasioned the stampede. There was heavy firing on both sides, our men gallantly standing their ground, but were compelled to retreat to the reserve in consequence only of the superior force and cavalry advantage of the enemy, who, as it was yesterday stated, fell back on the advance of our reinforcements. The charge of the rebel cavalry was made on the pickets of Company H, Fourteenth Brooklyn Regiment. The following are the names of the killed: Privates Seymour and Walter Taylor; Mortally wounded, Private William Stryker; Missing, Lieut. Gunman, Sergt. McNeill, Privates W. A. Judden, Daniel McCauley, George Kohler, E. Rich, J. F. Rich, William Campbell, Clinton Pettit and Nathaniel Lyon. This morning a strong force was sent out by order of Gen. McDOWELL to the neighborhood where the skirmish took place. The dead bodies of SEYMOUR and TAYLOR were found stripped of their clothing, and the skulls mashed in as if done by the butt of a carbine. No other wounds were visible. It is, therefore, supposed that the men were beaten to death. A woman living in the vicinity stated that the rebels carried away three of their own dead, together with six wounded. From her description of the uniform, two of the latter belonged to the Brooklyn Regiment.

THE OATH NOT TO BEAR ARMS.

By direction of the Government the oath not to bear arms against it has been administered to 29 rebel prisoners at the old Capitol. Another has signified his desire to take the oath of allegiance. These proceedings are preliminary to their release, for an equal number who have been or may be relieved by the rebel authorities.

REBEL PRISONERS RELEASED.

The following is a correct list of the rebel prisoners recently released from the Old Capitol Prison and sent South:

Sixth Alabama—J. L. Coffey, William Lailin, P. G. Alvord, T. J. Bates, A. J. Smith.

Fifth Alabama—D. D. Figuet.

Fourth Alabama—Thos. Hudson.

Governor's Guards, Va.—S. S. Green.

Radford, Va., Regiment—Daniel Porter, G. A. Thomas and J. A. Leadbeater.

Eighth Georgia—Samuel Gavitt, S. Reich, J. Calvin, Wm. N. Barron, S. L. Eastmead, J. R. Payns, G. H. Gramburg, F. Ward.

Fourth South Carolina—Roger Pinckney, W. J. N. Barton, H. Comanier, R. H. Lewis.

Second South Carolina—Wm. James.

Ninth Virginia—W. A. Wilson, C. Lang.

Nineteenth Virginia—J. A. Winfield.

Hampton Legion, South Carolina—H. H. Fornell.

Second Mississippi—R. Walker, Col. R. R. Boone, W. M. F. Thompson.

First Battalion, Texas—Wm. Johnson.

Sixth North Carolina—W. Burrows.

Citizen—Geo. Minor, who resides near Falls Church.

All of the above prisoners were committed by Gen. MANSFIELD, except the last named.

LORD LYONS AND THE LATE CAPTURE.

I am informed that Lord LYONS has stated in private circles that SLIDELL and MASON would be given up to Great Britain.

A LETTER FROM COL. LEE.

A letter has been received by Capt. CHARLES CANAY, Assistant Adjutant-General to Gen. LANDER's Brigade, from Col. LEE, of the Twentieth Massachusetts Regiment, now a prisoner at Richmond. Col. LEE states that he and the other imprisoned officers have been very kindly treated, and makes inquiries as to the disposition of the enemy captured at Ball's Bluff. The rebels say that fewer of the Massachusetts officers would have been killed had they not been too proud to surrender.

A MOVEMENT OF THE REBELS.

It was rumored last night in Gen. PORTER's Division that the rebels had moved down towards our lines, two miles this side of Vienna, and that the purpose of their movement was to seize all the forage beyond our lines in the vicinity.

THE GRAND REVIEW.

The grand review which takes place to-morrow will be the most brilliant military spectacle that has ever transpired on the continent, and many thousan citizens are preparing to cross the river in the morning to be present. Several Governors and many members of Congress will join in the review.

THE CASE OF MR. DULIN.

Mr. DULIN, whose arrest I mentioned, for supposed complicity with the rebel cavalry in attacking one of our foraging parties at his place on Saturday, is still in custody. He has been examined, but proofs indicate his innocence of the charge. He has always been regarded as loyal among the Union men of Fairfax County.

MEN OF THE THIRTIETH NEW-YORK CAPTURED.

Beside the twenty-six members of the New-York Thirtieth mentioned as taken prisoners near DULIN's House, I have to add the following: Sergt. W. H. WEBSTER, Company A: Privates A. M. SIMMONS, Company I., and DANIEL CONNOR and FREDERICK RILEY, Company K.

COMMANDER OF THE MISSISSIPPI FLEET.

Capt. A. H. FOOTE has been appointed flag-officer of the fleet in the Mississippi River.

CHIEF ENGINEER OF STAFF.

Gen. CULLOM has been appointed by Gen. HALLECK Chief Engineer of his Department, and Chief of Staff.

THE CASE OF COMMANDER POORE.

The Court-martial in the case of Commander POORE, of the *Brooklyn*, assembled yesterday. The Court consists of Commanders BREEZE, LEVY and JARVIS, and Capts. LATTIMER and CHAUNCEY. Several witnesses have already been examined.

COMMISSARY APPOINTED.

W. W. LELAND, the great stock raiser of Western Texas, has been commissioned by the Secretary of War as Commissary of Subsistence, and assigned to the staff of Brig.-Gen. MEAGHER, of the Irish Brigade, with the rank of Major.

APPOINTED A LIEUTENANT.

JOHN R. MYRICK has been appointed Second Lieutenant Third Artillery.

THE FRAUDS OF A COMMISSARY.

The frauds which I alluded to yesterday, as having been committed by a Brigade Commissary, have been continued for some time, and efforts have been heretofore made by Major BECKWITH to prevent them. The Commissary is a Capt SCHUTTE, of BLENKER's Division, and the plan of operations has been to take the wheat flour furnished by the Commissary, trade it off for rye flour, and receive from the dealer the difference in cash—from $2 to $3 a barrel. Charges will probably be preferred against Capt. SCHUTTE.

COL. WARD H. LAMON.

I am credibly informed that Col. WARD H. LAMON sent in his resignation as United States Marshal for the District of Columbia, that he might assume command of his Brigade, and that the President refused to accept the resignation, stating that he could not spare him from his position as Marshal, at least for the present.

SLIDELL A LAND-OWNER IN MINNESOTA.

During the months of August and September, 1857, JNO. SLIDELL and ELISHA RIGGS, the Banker, bought in joint account, with land warrants and cash, ten thousand acres of land in the Menosha and district, Minnesota.

BUILDING A BRIDGE.

A train of cars, with timber and bridge builders, went out to-day beyond Springfield. They found no rebels, and they met with no obstruction. They passed five miles beyond our lines.

SALE OF SENATOR DOUGLAS' FURNITURE.

The furniture of the late Senator DOUGLAS was yesterday sold at auction, bringing fair prices, or about two-thirds of its cost. A gallery containing about fifty pictures, with busts of himself, Gen. JACKSON and the Empress JOSEPHINE, has been reserved.

A POST-OFFICE DECISION.

The Postmaster-General, this afternoon, decided that the Act of 1825, relative to post-offices and post-roads, empowers him to declare the streets of cities post routes. He has accordingly issued an order declaring the streets of the different cities post routes, and has ordered private postal service to be at once discontinued.

TROOPS STILL OFFERED.

Tenders of troops continue to be made to the War Department, and it is probable that before the meeting of Congress the half a million authorized to be accepted will be supplied. Offers of additional regiments of cavalry are declined, owing to a sufficiency of that branch of the army.

JUDGE MERRICK.

The guards have been withdrawn from the residence of Judge MERRICK, who has resumed his seat on the Circuit Court Bench.

PENNY POSTS IN PHILADELPHIA.

The Postmaster-General has issued an order to have the private penny-posts in Philadelphia discontinued at once, or be subject to prosecution.

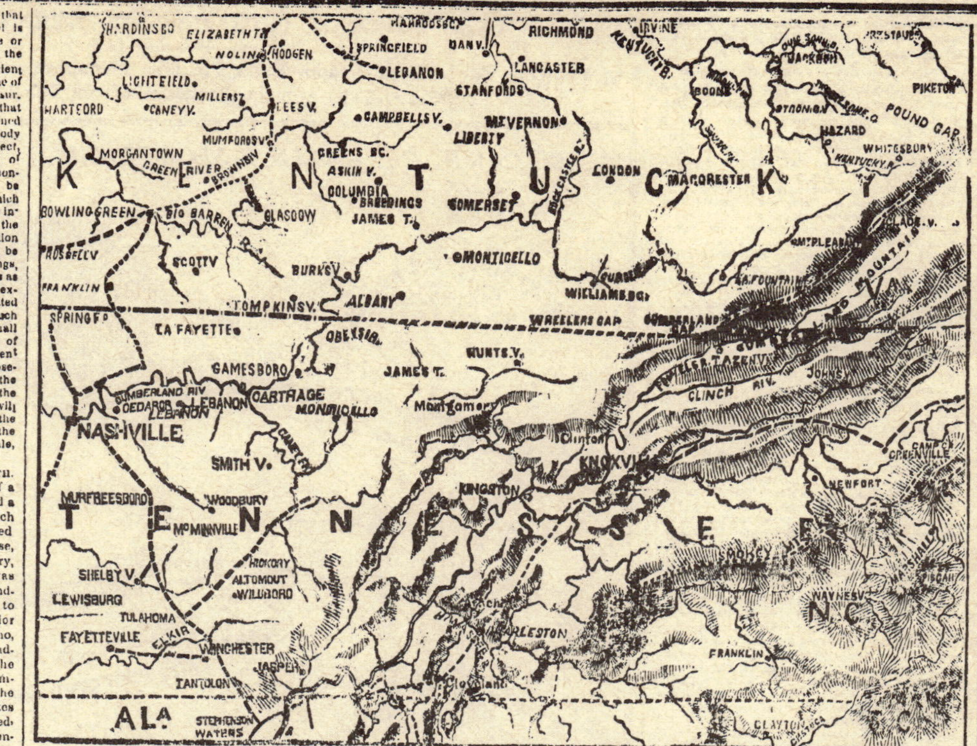

EASTERN KENTUCKY AND TENNESSEE.

Map Exhibiting the Actual and Prospective Seat of War in that Section; with the Railroads and Railroad Bridges.

The map we lay before the readers of the TIMES, this morning, is especially intended to represent those portions of Tennessee and Kentucky where military operations are active, and where the population in sympathy with the cause of the Union are promoting it, by destroying important railroad bridges upon the rebel lines of communication. The latest intelligence from Kentucky, leaves Gen. NELSON, after winning the splendid engagement at Piketon, pausing at that point, without affording any indication whether he proposed to proceed southward through Pound Gap or Cumberland Gap, or to remain, in order to keep the Secessionists of Eastern Kentucky in check, while Gen. THOMAS, now in strong force at London, advances toward Cumberland Gap, and attacks LEE, who is said to hold that pass at the head of 25,000 rebels. Our Ohio correspondent suggests that the mountains of that district afford other entrances into Tennessee beside those held by the enemy, naming especially Wheeler's Gap, some thirty-five miles westward of the Cumberland Gap. It is not impossible that Gen. THOMAS contemplates turning the flank of LEE, by availing himself of these undefended passes. In the meantime, Gen. BUCKNER, at the head of 30,000 rebels, holds Bowling Green, throwing forward his advance guard as far as Green River, the bridge over which has been destroyed by his orders. The headquarters of the Union army, which at present contents itself with barring BUCKNER's march northward, remains at Elizabethtown, with the advance at Nolin.

The Unionists of Tennessee, deprived of arms, and yet in eager sympathy with the movement for the emancipation of the State, are playing a most important part in burning the bridges upon the several railroads in the Eastern counties, over which the rebel armies and supplies must be transported. The superb viaduct over the Cumberland, above Nashville, is one of these fated bridges, the destruction of which places BUCKNER in a situation of serious danger should a retreat become necessary. The bridges over the Hiawassee River, at Charleston, over Lick Creek, in the same county, and over the Holston River, in Jefferson County,—points below and above Knoxville—cut off travel upon the line of the East Tennessee and Georgia, and Tennessee and Virginia Roads at three vital points. The Georgia State Road is severed by the demolition of a bridge fifteen miles east of Chattanooga, thus suspending approach from the direction of Georgia and the Carolinas. The loss of the five bridges we have named, the location of which will be seen by reference to the map, must not only cause the rebels most serious embarrassment in the conduct of their operations, must deplete their forces by the numbers of troops necessary to protect the remaining bridges, and must fill them with profound alarm at the undercurrent of hatred these daring acts of incendiarism so clearly reveal.

THE OCCUPATION OF ACCOMAC.

The Rebels Laying Down Their Arms and Claiming Protection—The National Flag Flying, &c.

SALISBURY, Md., Tuesday, Nov. 19.

All the troops, except the Purnell Legion and the Second Delaware Regiment, left Newton yesterday for Dixie.

A messenger with a flag of truce had arrived in Newton and communicated to Gen. LOCKWOOD that those in arms in Accomac had laid down their arms and claimed his protection. Capt. RICHARDS' Cavalry, with Capt. MERRILL as guide, had advanced as far as Drummondstown to learn their determination.

A messenger just from Newton as the boat left Salisbury, informs our correspondent that Capt. MERRILL had returned, and that the cavalry did not go below Drummondstown, but that the Stars and Stripes are floating over the place.

OUR BALTIMORE CORRESPONDENCE.

BENEFICIAL EFFECT OF THE MOVEMENT INTO ACCOMAC AND NORTHAMPTON—THE FIRST LANDING MADE—READING GEN. DIX'S PROCLAMATION—A REBEL FORCE DISBANDED, ETC.

BALTIMORE, Tuesday, Nov. 19th.

The appearance of the strong force sent by Gen. DIX to the eastern shore of Virginia, together with his proclamation to the people of Accomac and Northampton counties, (previously published in the TIMES), has had a very beneficial effect among the residents of that vicinity.

The steamer *Georgiana*, with a portion of Gen. LOCKWOOD's command, in endeavoring to make a landing got aground off Sax Island on Virginia shore and lay there the greater part of Saturday and Sunday, by which time the crew had run short of provisions, and it was determined to send a boat ashore to procure some. In the boat was Mr. WALTEMEYER, Sutler of Purnell Legion, and an officer, who had no sooner landed than they were invited to a large farm-house where about twenty-five Union men were assembled who seemed much interested in the party, having seen the steamer loaded with men, and desired to know the object of their visit. Gen. DIX' Proclamation was then read to them by the officer, and gave general satisfaction. They hoped the Secretary of War would send a force there to protect them from the rebels, who were determined to resist the advance of any National troops, and alleging that they feared being impressed into the rebel service, many having already been forced in the ranks. They were protected during the day by the gunboats *Ajax* and *Reliance* stationed near the shore, but at night had been forced to flee into the woods, to escape impressment, and were satisfied, were it not for those gunboats, they would had no protection, but all would have been impressed. An additional gunboat was sent to their aid by Commodore GOLDSBOROUGH, Naval Commander at Fortress Monroe.

The Union men reported the feeling of resistance stronger in Northampton than in Accomac. Some rather substantial earthworks had been erected and cannon mounted, and they need not be surprised to meet a masked battery as they advanced. Enough was gained by the interview to show there was a strong determination to resist the advance of Government troops. At first they refused to sell any provisions to the boat's crew, on the ground that it was the Sabbath, but finally consented to supply them gratuitously. This ended the interview, and the boat soon pulled for the steamer.

On the advance of our forces into the interior, they were met at intervals by farmers and residents, who acknowledged themselves to have recently belonged to a regiment of Virginia cavalry, but reported the whole force, numbering about *thirty-five hundred men, disbanded and returning to their homes*. Gen. LOCKWOOD and command would remain in that region, to preserve order and restore confidence to loyal men, but it is not thought any resistance would be offered him.

Through a secession source I learn that it is rumored at Old Point that the Government had been informed that no flag of truce would be allowed to pass till a period of thirty days had expired. Since then it is stated, on better authority, that the time was limited to twenty days. Something of importance is evidently going on at Norfolk and contiguous points which the Confederates are anxious to conceal. I cannot vouch for the truth of this rumor, but give it for what it is worth.

Another good haul of contraband was made to-day in this city by Deputy Provost-Marshal McPHAIL. The goods comprising United States muskets, shot-guns, pistol and musket cartridges, cannister and grape-shot, beds and bedding, a few of WINANS' famous pikes, and twenty-four scaling-ladders, intended to be used in taking Fort McHenry, in all six good wagon-loads were taken from a warehouse—where they had been concealed since the 19th of April—and removed to the armory.

I will send further particulars to-morrow in relation to the expedition to Accomac—at which time I hope to give official information.

AFFAIRS ON THE UPPER POTOMAC.

FROM GEN. BANKS' DIVISION.

DARNESTOWN, Monday, Nov. 18.

The division teamsters and wagon-masters received two months' pay on Saturday.

A preliminary meeting, by many of the commissioned officers, was held on Saturday night, to form a Masonic lodge for this division. Many distinguished men were present.

Everything in the shape of locomotives, machinery, &c., belonging to the Baltimore and Ohio Railroad, have been removed by the rebels and taken in the direction of Winchester. Even the double track for 20 miles has been torn up.

Last week Major STONE, chief of the Provost Guard, with a company of cavalry, paid a visit to the neighborhood of Sandy Spring, Montgomery County, Maryland. He made the arrest of Rev. SAMUEL LEECH, a clergyman of the Methodist persuasion, whom he sent to Fort McHenry. Other cases where parties were charged with disaffection, were investigated and dismissed. Much to the regret of his subordinates of the Guard, and the pleasure of his regimental command, Major STONE has rejoined his regiment, having been promoted from a Captaincy to a Majority during his absence on detached service.

The First Brigade, and probably others, have been ordered to report their full strength, equipments, &c., to Washington, immediately. A rumor has been circulated in camp that Gen. BANKS, with his command, will be ordered to some more active duty this week.

JOHN CANDLER, of Cumberland, and JOHN ROWZEE, of this district, have been discharged from arrest by Gen. BANKS.

The Massachusetts regiments are making preliminary arrangements to celebrate Thanksgiving in camp. Turkies, chickens and pumpkins are being procured.

THE TRANSPORT SERVICE.

The United States steam transport *Whilldin* sailed last evening for Locust Point. She carries a full cargo of provisions and ammunition, also Wiard's Battery, consisting of two 12-pounders and four 6-pounders, rifled.

The United States steam transport *Eastern State* has been sold to the Government.

[*For other Rebellion News, see Eighth Page.*]

NEWS FROM SOUTH CAROLINA.

Arrival of the Atlantic from Port Royal.

Beaufort Not Yet Occupied by the National Forces.

THE TOWN STILL DESERTED.

The Great Fleet at Anchor in Port Royal Harbor.

OPERATIONS OF GEN. SHERMAN'S ARMY.

Full Details of Events from the Correspondents of the Times.

The United States steam transport *Atlantic*, Capt. ELDRIDGE, arrived at this port at about 11 o'clock yesterday morning from Port Royal, S. C., which place she left on the 16th at 3 P. M. She brings no news of interest, nothing of importance having transpired since our last advices. She has on board a number of passengers, and invalids from the army and navy, also six prisoners.

Everything remained quiet. The troops had been all stationed, and were well. Several visits had been made to Beaufort by a regiment or so, but they retired again, leaving the place deserted.

There had been no communication from the opposite side of the Island confirming the rumor that the Union pickets had been attacked.

The stores and ordnance had nearly all been landed, and several of the transports will soon be ready to leave.

The dispatch relative to a fleet being seen at Fernandina, Florida, bound south, was undoubtedly an error, as the Federal fleet still remained in Port Royal Harbor on the 16th.

The *Atlantic* brings a number of secession trophies and one bale of cotton.

We are indebted to Purser J. B. FORDHAM for the following list of passengers and memoranda of her passage and list of vessels now lying in Port Royal harbor, South Carolina:

The *Atlantic* left her anchorage at 3 P. M., Nov. 16, crossed the bar at 4:50 P. M., with passengers and mail to Col. D. D. TOMPKINS, Quartermaster, U. S. A., New-York.

The ship was piloted over the bar by Lieut. ROBERT PLATT, U. S. N., and found not less than 25 feet of water in the channel, thus demonstrating the fact that the largest vessels may enter that grand harbor with perfect safety. There is 22 feet at low water

The following is the passenger list of steamship *Atlantic*, from Port Royal:

Capt. Ladue, Quartermaster United States Army; Col. Henry Moore, Forty-seventh Regiment New-York Volunteers; W. T. Crane, special artist *Frank Leslie's Newspaper*; O. G. Sawyer; Lieut. Harbaugh, U. S. A.; Mr. Allen, Forty Eighth New-York Volunteers; Capt. Boyd, U. S. Marine Corps; Capt. Hull, U. S. A.; Maj. Pangborn, U. S. Paymaster; Dr. Bloodgood, U. S. N.; Capt. Blethen; Mr. Newcomb, First Officer of the steamer *Peerless*; Capt. Litchfield, and A. R. Calden, Chief Engineer steamer *Governor*; Messrs. Johnson, Rogers, Duryea; Lieut. F. A. Sawyer, Forty-seventh New-York Volunteers; John A. May, Chief Engineer, and Samuel C. Wise, First Assistant Engineer, steamer *Peerless*; T. C. Entwistle, Engineer U. S. steamer *Vixen*; Capt. McNutt, Ordnance Corps, U. S. A.; five wounded men from U. S. squadron; eight teamsters; seven sailors crew of the prize brig *Providentia*; twelve men from steamer *Peerless*; three shepherds from U. S. Quartermaster's Department.—Total, 57.

The *Atlantic* left in Port Royal Harbor, S. C., the following vessels:

United States frigate *Wabash*, gunboats *Pawnee*, *Mohican*, *Seminole*, *Flag*, *Unadilla*, *Seneca*, *Pembina*, *Curlew*, *R. B. Forbes*, *Ottawa*, *Isaac Smith*, *Mercury*, *O. M. Pettit*, ferryboat; sloop-of-war *Pocahontas*; gunboats *Penguin* and *Augusta*; transports, (steamers,) *Baltic*, *Vanderbilt*, *Ocean Queen*, *Ariel*, *Philadelphia*, *Empire City*, *Cahawba*, *Roanoke*, *Marion*, *Oriental*, *Matanzas*, *Star of the South*, *Parkersburgh*, *Locust Point*, *Potomac*, *Winfield Scott*, (condemned,) *McClellan*, *Daniel Webster*, *Illinois*, *Ben De Ford*; ships *Great Republic*, *Ocean Express*, *Golden Eagle*, *Zenas Coffin*—1 bark, 2 brigs, a large number of coal schooners and six traders.

Sailed—*Susquehannah*, (frigate,) *Bienville*, *Coatzacoalcos*, *Connecticut*, *Rhode Island*, *Vandalia*, sloop-of-war. The *Savannah* and *Sabine*, frigates, are off Tybee and Port Royal.

OUR PORT ROYAL CORRESPONDENCE.

The Change Produced After the Landing of the National Troops—Capabilities of the Harbor—A Regular Line of Steamers to Run to New-York—Stores of Cotton—The Influx of Contrabands—Effects of the Blow upon South Carolina, &c.

PORT ROYAL, S. C., Sunday, Nov. 10, 1861.

This place has now been in the hands of the Federal forces for three days, and although only the troops are landed, the change produced is remarkable. In the first hurry and confusion, amid which I wrote an account of the events of Thursday, I had no opportunity to do more than note the more salient of those events and the merest outside of circumstances. Some of the significance of the circumstances and the account of the effects as well as of the events themselves, I shall attempt now to set before you. And first, of the importance of Port Royal: doubtless, an endeavor will be made to depreciate the consequence of this place, and to lessen in the eyes of the world the results of our victory; but the attempt must eventually prove futile. Port Royal is the finest harbor on the South-eastern coast, the only excellent one between Norfolk and Key West; its natural advantages infinitely transcend those of either Charleston or Savannah; it is large enough for twenty armadas like that now riding securely within its inclosure. There are twenty-three feet of water on its bar at low tide; indeed, the presence inside of such vessels as the *Great Republic*, the *Wabash*, and the *Atlantic*, whose superiors in size and draught do not exist in the world, sufficiently attests the capacities of the bay. The land is comparatively high, the climate salubrious—none of the malaria so common in this region infest the neighborhood; on the contrary the South Carolinians have been wont to resort to this spot in the Summer for its coolness and health-provoking airs. Since our arrival the weather has been as delicious as at the North in the balmiest days of June or September.

The position of Port Royal is equally admirable, whether considered in a military, naval or political light. It is between Savannah and Charleston, and doubtless within a few days the communication between those important towns will be easily cut off. The network of inland waters that extends in either direction will enable us, if we choose, to transport troops on gunboats, either to Savannah or Charleston, without going within range of the guns of Fort Pulaski, at the former place, or Sumter or Moultrie at the latter. We can thus attack the two largest towns in South Carolina and Georgia at their weakest point, besides being able to run up into their country and annoy and frighten them wherever they make a military demonstration. The Island of Hilton, on whose northern point stands one of the forts just captured, extends to Ty-

The New-York Times.

VOL. XI....NO. 3180. | NEW-YORK, SATURDAY, NOVEMBER 30, 1861. | PRICE TWO CENTS.

THE GREAT REBELLION.

Further Reports About the Engagement at Fort Pickens.

The Navy-Yard Destroyed, and Bragg Calling for Reinforcements.

Official Announcement of the Capture of Tybee.

The Island Within Easy Mortar Distance of Fort Pulaski.

The National Flag now Flying in all the Rebel States but Two.

Important Results Accomplished by the Eastern Virginia Expedition.

CONDITION OF AFFAIRS AT WASHINGTON.

Another Reconnoissance to Fairfax Court-house.

SKIRMISHING ON THE UPPER POTOMAC.

SPECIAL DISPATCH FROM WASHINGTON.

WASHINGTON, Friday, Nov. 29.

OFFICIAL ANNOUNCEMENT OF THE CAPTURE OF PORT ROYAL.

Dispatches have been received at the Navy Department from Flag-officer DUPONT, dated Port Royal, 25th inst., giving the gratifying intelligence that the flag of the United States is flying over the territory of the State of Georgia. Tybee Island, which he says is within easy mortar distance of Fort Pulaski, has been taken possession of, and the approaches to Savannah completely cut off. On the Island is a strong martello tower, with a battery at its base.

ONLY TWO STATES LEFT.

The National flag now floats over the soil of every seceded State except Alabama and Arkansas. In Virginia it floats over one-third of the State; in North Carolina, at Hatteras Inlet; in South Carolina, at Port Royal and a half-dozen neighboring Islands; in Georgia, on Tybee Island; in Florida, at Key West, Santa Rosa Island and other points; in Mississippi, at Ship Island; in Louisiana, at Chandeleur Island; in Texas, at El Paso; and in Tennessee, at Bristol' Elizabethtown, and other points in the eastern part of the State.

ARRIVAL OF RELEASED OFFICERS.

Lieuts. JOHN L. WORDEN and ROBT. SILDEN, of the navy, and Mr. WILLIAM A. ABBOTT, also of the navy, arrived in this City to-day—the first from New-York, and the others direct from Richmond *via* Norfolk and Fortress Monroe. All three were recently released, having been exchanged for rebel officers. They met with a hearty welcome at the Navy dépôt.

THE CASE OF LIEUT. WORDEN.

Lieut. WORDEN had been seven months a prisoner in the Montgomery Old Jail, he having been arrested by order of Gen. BRAGG, on his way North, after he had conveyed the order to the fleet off Pensacola to reinforce Lieut. SLEMMER, at Fort Pickens. Believing that the dispatches that he bore from the Government to Capt. ADAMS, of the fleet, would be opened by the rebels, he opened them himself, committed their contents to memory, and destroyed them. On applying to Gen. BRAGG to be permitted to go to the fleet, he was asked if he carried dispatches. As he stated that he had only a verbal order, he was permitted to go out. Having delivered his order he returned, and he subsequently learned that it had been determined by BRAGG that night to attack the fort—he not being aware that the order conveyed by Mr. WORDEN was to reinforce. The reinforcement foiled him in his plans, and the attack which would otherwise been successful, was not made. To shield himself from the censure that he deserved, in permitting Mr. WORDEN to go to the fleet, BRAGG ordered his arrest, stating that WORDEN had represented that his verbal order was of a pacific nature. It was because of this misrepresentation that Mr. WORDEN was held so long in custody. The feeling of the rebel Secretary of War, L. P. WALKER, was most bitter against him, and had he remained in office it is probable that Mr. WORDEN would not have been exchanged. He was kindly treated at Montgomery. Many of his old associates in the navy, now in the rebel service, visited him, and did all they could to effect his release. Among them was Mr. ALLISON, formerly Paymaster in the Navy, and a son-in-law of Chief-Justice TANEY, and now Paymaster of rebel marines. He also saw Commander INGRAHAM and Lieut. ISAAC N. BROWN.

LIEUT. SELDEN'S ACCOUNT OF AFFAIRS IN RICHMOND.

Lieut. SELDEN states that in Richmond the feeling of anger, indignation and chagrin, at the arrest of SLIDELL and MASON was beyond all description. They had previously been exulting in the success of the rebel envoys in reaching Cuba, and they were certain that they would reach Europe without difficulty. He states that it is the severest blow which the rebel Government has yet received. Mr. SELDEN says that, up to the time of his leaving Richmond, two days since' he had heard nothing of the proposed removal of the rebel Capital to Nashville. Being a Virginian himself, he was treated with additional indignity and severity on account of his loyalty, and by none more than his own relatives, who live in Richmond and vicinity.

A SKIRMISH ON THE UPPER POTOMAC.

From a gentleman who left Hancock, Md., yesterday morning, I learn that on Wednesday last, a company of loyal Virginians, attached to LAMON'S Brigade, were fired upon from across the Potomac by a regiment of rebels. The loyalists sheltered themselves behind the back of the Chesapeake and Ohio Canal, and returned the fire with spirit. Five of the rebels were seen to be carried off. A messenger was sent to the commandant of the Thirteenth Massachusetts Regiment, at Williamsport, for reinforcements, and four companies and two batteries of artillery were sent to their relief, they arriving at daylight yesterday morning, before my informant left, at which time the fight had been resumed.

A RECONNOISSANCE TO FAIRFAX COURT-HOUSE.

A reconnoissance was made yesterday by a squadron of the Lincoln Cavalry, under command of Capt. W. H. BOYD. They proceeded to within about a mile of Fairfax Court-house, when they observed rebel infantry partially concealed in rifle pits, which extended across the turnpike. A few rebel cavalry were also in the rear and within rifle range. Shots were exchanged, the Lincoln Cavalry using carbines, and using every precaution to prevent a surprise by deploying on foot to the right or left. The squadron returned in good order, having accomplished the object of the reconnoissance. One of our troops had his arm slightly gazed by a ball, and a rebel was killed. The cavalry and infantry of the enemy were seen to change their positions by falling back into the town.

A rumor, generally circulated and believed here to-day, that our troops occupied and held Fairfax, is without the slightest foundation in fact. The position still remains the same as it has been for the last month.

THE CAPTURE OF THE BRITISH SCHOONER MABEL.

In giving an account of the capture of the British schooner *Mabel*, by Commander YARD, of the sloop-of-war *Dale*, Capt. DUPONT says that she has been brought into Port Royal harbor. She purported to be from Havana, and bound to New-York, but at the time of her capture she was heading for St. Catharine's Sound. Her cargo consisted of 7 bales of blankets, 4 cases of cloth, 3 boxes of starch, 25 boxes of tin, 120 bags of coffee, 20 bbls. of potatoes, 350 pigs of lead, 30 bags of shot, 1 box of shoes, 6 bags of arrow-root, 1 case of pistols, (revolvers,) 2 cases of cavalry swords, and 2 cases of stores. The *Mabel* was formerly named the *John W. Anderson*, of Baltimore, and there is strong presumption of her intention to run the blockade. She will be sent to Philadelphia for adjudication.

THE SLAVES ON GOVERNOR'S ISLAND.

When the prisoners from Hatteras Inlet reached Fort Columbus, two slaves belonging to an officer, and brought with the others, were placed on the Island and no further notice taken of them. When the prisoners were removed the contrabands still remained, but insular life not being pleasant, and supposing themselves to be held as prisoners under a supposition of disloyalty, they forwarded a request to Washington, stating they were willing to take the oath of allegiance. The Government having no prejudice against color, sent an order to the military authorities on Governor's Island, to-day, to administer the oath of allegiance and release them.

LOYAL SENTIMENTS IN VIRGINIA.

From two trustworthy sources intelligence has been received of the increasing strength of the loyal sentiment in Frederick, Jefferson and Bulkley Counties, in Virginia. On Tuesday a lady arrived at Hancock, from Martinsburgh, with her children. Her husband, a loyalist, had fled to Maryland four months ago, and it was with the greatest difficulty that she was able to get permission to pass the rebel lines to Maryland. She states that in Berkley County the greatest suffering exists among the families of Union men who are now fugitives. During the past fortnight she states that the expression of Union sentiments had been growing stronger, and that on the occasion of the approach of Capt. SUMZ, with a scouting party of a 150 cavalry, to within five miles of Martinsburgh, the joy of the loyal families was unbounded, on the supposition that it was the beginning of an advance by our troops; but that when the party returned they were in despair. As a sample of the prices of provisions, she states that salt was selling in Martinsburgh at $6 a peck.

AFFAIRS AT WINCHESTER.

A gentleman who left Winchester on Sunday last, also brings encouraging news. He has been for three years a resident of Frederick County, and is well acquainted with the people and the locality. He says that the fortifications there are of no strength, and would be of but little service against a well-arranged attack; that JACKSON, the rebel General, has only a brigade of troops and an indefinite number of badly armed, poorly disciplined and lukewarm militia; that he has sent to Centreville for reinforcements, but has been refused them, with a statement that he must defend the vicinity with his present force. Since the success of Gen. KELLY at Remoney, an alarm has been apparent among the rebels in Frederick and Hampshire Counties, and all are notified that no resistance, at present available to them, can prevent the successful taking of Winchester by our troops, because of their inefficiency and cowardice. A. McDONALD, who was defeated by Gen. KELLY and Gen. CARSON, of the militia, had been compelled to resign. WM. L. CLARK, a Western man by birth, but an active rebel, and President of the Winchester and Potomac Railroad, immediately after the occupation of Romney, had packed up his personal property and left for Richmond. The Loyalists were growing bolder. The practice of compelling men whose loyalty was suspected, to take the oath of allegiance, had been stopped, as it was feared, that in the event of an advance of our forces, the loyal men, then in the ascendancy, would retaliate upon them with great severity. The rebels themselves say that a majority of the people are submissionists, and no better than Yankees. A fact, which is significant in estimating the division of public sentiment is, that there has never been an instance in Frederick County in which the property of a known loyal man has been confiscated, though this has been done in the adjoining county, Shenandoah. The family of GEORGE RYE, a leading Union man, now a fugitive, have been turned out of their home at Woodstock, the county seat, and are now living on the charity of friends.

FRENCH NAVAL OFFICERS IN WASHINGTON.

Admiral REYNAUD and Capt. C. MARQUIS DE MONTAIGNAC, of the French fleet now on our coast, arrived in Washington yesterday, and to-day were presented to the President by Secretary SEWARD. During the forenoon they visited the Navy-yard in company with Secretary WELLES, where they were received by Commander DAHLGREN and other officers, in ful dress. A salute was fired, and the Stars and Stripes hoisted with the French Tri-color. In the evening they were present at a dinner given at Secretary SEWARD'S. Secretary WELLES, Assistant-Secretary FOX, Commodore GOLDSBOROUGH and Commander DAHLGREN were also among the invied guests.

SIR JAMES FERGUSON.

Sir JAMES FERGUSON having been accused of acting as a spy when visiting this country, it is only an act of justice to him to say that he was charged by many persons in the South with letters to be delivered or distributed through the post-office in the North, and that on arriving at Washington and being advised that such a conveyance of correspondence was prohibited by the Government, he at once repaired to the State Department and surrendered all the letters to the Government.

A REPEATING BREECH-LOADING RIFLE.

SPENCER'S new repeating breech-loading rifle was tried by a board of army officers, by order af Gen. McCLELLAN, on Friday. They made a satisfactory report and recommended its introduction into the service. An order for a supply had previously been issued by the Navy Department.

COL. BERDAN'S SHARPSHOOTERS.

Col. BERDAN will grant no more commissions to raise companies of sharpshooters for his brigade, as enough have already been granted to more than well fill it. Those wishing to join the corps must enlist under captains holding commissions prior to the present date.

ARMY APPOINTMENTS.

The following army appointments have just been made:

Second Lieut. Richard R. Crawford and Samuel Breck, Jr., to be Assistant Adjutant Generals, with the rank of Captain.

Capt. Joseph C. Andenreid, Capt. Wm. P. Sanders and Joseph C. McKibbin, to be Aids-de-Camp to Gen. Halleck, with the rank of Colonel.

John Haskins, to be Aid-de-Camp to Gen. Halleck, with the rank of Colonel.

Charles Weston, to be Military Storekeeper in the Ordnance Department.

James Fuller, to be Commissary of Subsistence of Volunteers, with the rank of Captain.

Hiram B. Wetzell, to be Assistant Quartermaster of Volunteers, with the rank of Captain.

R. Morris Copeland, to be Assistant Adjutant-General of Volunteers, to report to Gen. Banks, with the rank of Major.

GEN. BANKS' MOVEMENTS.

Gen. BANKS returns to Darnstown to-morrow.

MOVEMENTS OF COM. GOLDSBOROUGH.

Com. GOLDSBOROUGH leaves to-morrow for his fleet

COM. CRAVEN ASSIGNED TO BLOCKADING SERVICE.

Commodore CRAVEN has been detached from the Potomac flotilla, to be assigned to a command in the blockading fleet.

THE ACCOUNTS AGAINST THE SICKLES BRIGADE.

Maj. BAIRD, of the Inspector General's Department, is to proceed to New-York to investigate the accounts against the Sickles Brigade.

THE COURSE OF LECTURES.

Letters have been received from WENDELL PHILLIPS, HENRY WARD BEECHER, HORACE GREELEY and GEO. W. CURTIS, signifying their acceptance of the invitations sent them to each deliver a lecture in a course to be given this Winter in Washington.

DEATH OF SURGEON ALEXANDER.

Dr. W. T. ALEXANDER, Assistant Surgeon to Col. BAYARD'S First Pennsylvania Cavalry Regiment, who was wounded in the skirmish at Drainesville, died to-day. It was thought yesterday he would recover.

DEATH OF LIEUT. CONKLIN.

Lieut. CONKLIN, of Thirtieth New-York, died yesterday, and to-day his body was escorted to the cars with military honors.

A MEMBER OF THE BROOKLYN FOURTEENTH DEAD.

Private HENRY LEE, Company A, New-York Fourteenth Volunteers, died this morning and was buried at Fall's Church with military honors.

RETURNED TO CAMP.

WM. MOODY, missing from Third Pennsylvania Cavalry since the skirmish last Tuesday, returned to camp yesterday. No dead bodies have since been found on the spot, as asserted.

A THANKSGIVING VISIT.

The Secretary of War visited Gen. JOHN FITZ PORTER'S headquarters on Thanksgiving day.

A THANKSGIVING SUPPER.

A supper was given in camp on Thanksgiving Day by the officers of the Fourteenth New-York to Gens. PORTER and MORRELL, with their staffs, and the Colonels of MORRELL'S Brigade. Speeches were made by the two Generals, by Capt. LOCKE, Assistant Adjutant-General, and by Cols. McQUADE, WOODBURY, CASS and BLACK.

IMPORTANT POST OFFICE ORDER.

WASHINGTON, Thursday, Nov. 29.

POST OFFICE DEPARTMENT, Nov. 29, 1861.

It has been reported to this Department that some Postmasters have declined to receive United States Treasury notes, payable on demand, when presented to them in payment for postage stamps and stamped envelopes.

Postmasters are, therefore, informed that these notes are to be received and disbursed by them, as equivalent, in all respects, to coin.

By order of the Postmaster-General.

(Signed) H. N. SEEVLY,
Third Assistant Postmaster-General.

LETTERS FROM PORT ROYAL.

Eighteen hundred letters were sent from Port Royal in the last mail.

PROVISIONS FOR OUR FORCES NEAR SAVANNAH.

Mr. TOMPKINS, of New-York, has been instructed to send three steamers, loaded with provisions, to our forces near Savannah.

PATENTS ISSUED.

Between Jan. 1 and Sept. 30 2,581 patents were issued and 15 extended; 3,514 applications were received.

AFFAIRS ON THE UPPER POTOMAC.

A SKIRMISH AT SANDY HOOK.

SANDY HOOK, Friday, Nov. 29.

A little excitement was occasioned here, this afternoon, by the Confederates throwing about thirty shells at the quarters of some companies of the Twenty-eighth Pennsylvania Regiment, under command of Major HECTOR TYNDALL, at Harper's Ferry. The Major tried long range Enfields at them, but the distance, being 2,000 yards, was too great. Although some of the firing from the rebels was fair, nobody was hurt! The men are being well deployed, and ready for closer range, which the rebels would not give.

CAPTURE OF FEDERAL OFFICERS IN MISSOURI.

ST. JOSEPH, Mo., Thursday, Nov. 28.

A band of rebels, under the notorious ST. GORDON, captured Capt. ROBB, Capt. WHITE and Lieut. MOONLIGHT, three United States officers, from the railroad train at Weston to-day.

The rebel STEIN, with 50 of his followers, is reported to be near Weston.

THE SCENE OF OPERATIONS IN WESTERN FLORIDA.

Map Showing Santa Rosa Island, Forts Pickens, Barrancas and McRae; Warrington, the Navy-Yard, and the Positions of the Rebel Batteries.

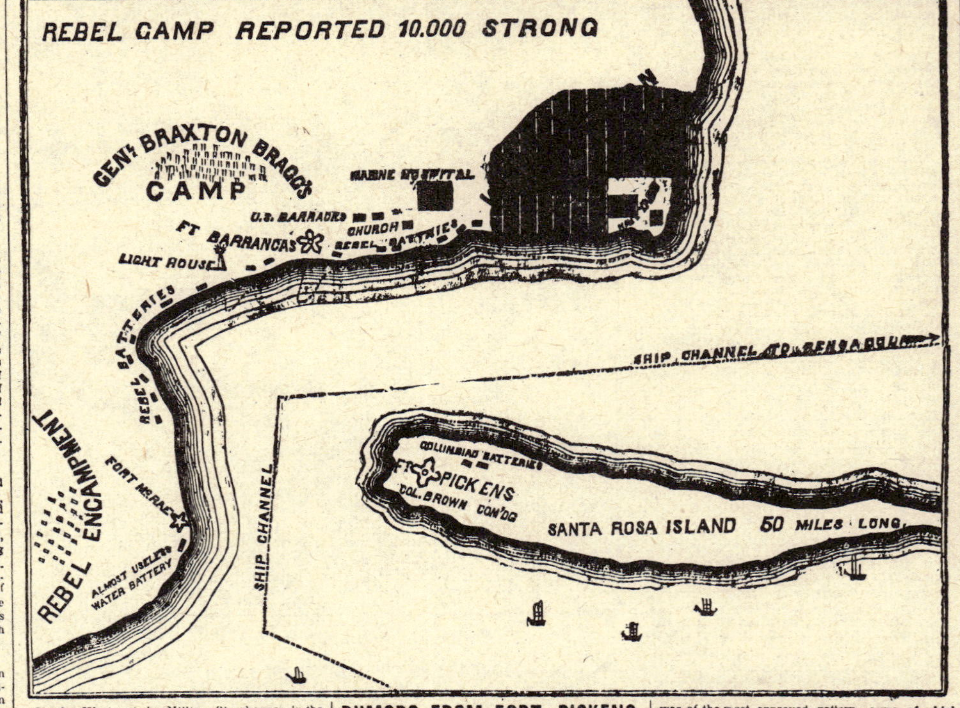

RUMORS FROM FORT PICKENS.

Further Rebel Accounts of the Engagement.

No Breach Made in the Walls of the Fort.

The Navy-Yard and a Considerable Quantity of Army and Ordnance Stores Destroyed.

Pensacola Evacuated by Order of Gen. Bragg.

A LOUD CALL FOR REBEL REINFORCEMENTS

The Reported Damage to the National Vessels.

REBEL ACCOUNTS VIA NORFOLK.

Correspondence of the Philadelphia Inquirer.

FORTRESS MONROE, Wednesday, Nov. 27, P. M.

Passengers by a flag of truce from Norfolk, this morning, furnish some further particulars in regard to the fight at Fort Pickens. These particulars, it must be remembered, come through rebel sources. Gen. BRAGG had not made a breach in the fort, as was before reported.

Great excitement was prevalent throughout the South respecting the battle, but it was thought that BRAGG would be able to force Col. BROWN to surrender.

A messenger arrived from Pensacola on Sunday last, with a peremptory order for reinforcements.

Gen. BRAGG was at that time hopeful of early success, and was replying at intervals upon the fortress with great effect. His regular salvos are described as being really terrible.

The General was perfectly cool and confident. No breach had yet been made, but on Monday one would be manifest, when BRAGG expected reinforcements, and would storm with fresh troops and ordnance.

Col. BROWN had concentrated a perfect storm of hot shot and shell upon the Navy-yard, and it had been burned down, together with all of the out-buildings, and a considerable quantity of army and ordnance stores.

Pensacola had been evacuated by order of Gen. BRAGG.

Col. BROWN had called to his assistance five vessels of war, all of which had been driven off by the batteries. The steam-frigate *Niagara* was almost riddled with bullets, and the *Colorado* was thoroughly disabled.

Gen. BRAGG had declared to his troops that he would never surrender, and the greatest enthusiasm prevailed among the men.

On Tuesday, Gen. BRAGG would engage Col. BROWN in front, and land a large force on the island so as to take him in the rear.

The United States steam gunboat *Cœur de Lion*, Capt. ALEX. HAMILTON, arrived at Fortress Monroe on Wednesday, from Washington, which place she left on Sunday last, having successfully run the Potomac blockade. She had forty-two shots aimed at her, of which she received but one, doing very little harm. The *Cœur de Lion* had on board Prof. LOWE, the Government aerial navigator, and Prof. STARKWEATHER, of Boston, his assistant. Prof STARKWEATHER goes to Port Royal, with apparatus complete, to aid Gen. SHERMAN in making reconnoissances.

On Tuesday evening a rebel flag of truce was brought to by a blank shot from the gun-boat *Gen. J. E. Wool*, and upon boarding her she was found to have on board a few letters from our poor fellows who are prisoners of war, and one gentleman with a foreign air, a consumptive cough, and a trunk full of generalities.

This gentleman said he had very urgent business in Baltimore, and would like to go up on the *Louisiana*; but Capt. DAVIS, the Provost Marshal, detained him, and then started for the headquarters of Major-General WOOL for instructions.

After Captain DAVIS had explained matters, Gen. WOOL determined to detain the man and await orders from Washington.

The "poor refugee" entered his name on the register of the hotel as "BRIAN O'HARRA, Puerto Rico, W. I."

He says the new iron British steamer *Fingal* arrived off Tybee about two weeks since from Southampton, *via* Puerto Cabello, where she had seen the rebel steamer *Sumter* often.

The *Fingal* was loaded with arms and munitions of war of the most approved pattern, some of which were being used against Fort Pickens. She ran into Beaufort in a storm, and is now at Charleston, about to be fitted for a man-of-war, and will carry a powerful battery of Whitworth rifled cannon.

The gentleman spoke in a manner to lead us to believe that he must have been either an officer or a special agent on board of the *Fingal*.

He says the Southerners have raised a great deal more grain than usual this season, and that they are not suffering for the want of anything but luxuries, which they are willing to forego for the sake of their so-called independence.

When we asked this man how he got South, he said he left New-York and went through Kentucky and when we asked how he got to Puerto Cabello he seemed confused and refused to explain.

Upon examining his trunk some valuable papers were found, the contents of which it would not be proper to publish. Some were sealed and stamped by "ROBERT BUNCH, Her Majesty's Consul at Charleston, S. C." These were directed to "His Excellency, Lord LYONS, H. B. M., Minister Plenipotentiary at Washington," &c., &c., and were carefully consigned to the care of a special agent, who will take them to Mr. SEWARD for inspection.

A LATER DISPATCH—NO NEWS.

BALTIMORE, Friday, Nov. 29.

The boat from Old Point has arrived. A flag of truce had brought down two or three ladies from Norfolk, but no news. The rebels are evidently endeavoring to keep back Southern news.

THE FORT PICKENS AFFAIR.

The news from Western Florida is still very meagre, and, being from rebel sources, is still very dubious. The rebels, however, talk a good deal less loudly of their own doings, while they are singularly reticent about ours. They had not breached the walls of Fort Pickens nor captured the Fort, but they *were* greatly excited, were calling for reinforcements, and swearing they would never *surrender* alive, while Col. BROWN had burned down the Navy-yard and the town of Warrington, and the rebels had evacuated Pensacola. This is certainly a considerable "come down" from the news of two days ago. But still it is so unsatisfactory that the public will not be contented till reliable advices arrive, and these must now be very close at hand.

We give to-day a map, more concise and definite than any that has yet been published, of the immediate scene of the action, and of the different forts, batteries and camps, both of the National forces and the rebels. The entrance of the bay, between Santa Rosa Island on the east, and the mainland on the west, is about a mile wide, but within it expands into a capacious harbor, from 4 to 10 miles in width, and entirely landlocked. Fort Pickens is on the extreme point of the long, narrow Santa Rosa, and various batteries and other works, described by us three days ago, have been erected here.

On the mainland to the west are the rebel works and rebel encampments, which have been so often described. Opposite the lower part of the island is Fort McRae, and about a half a mile to the north, and immediately in front of the entrance, (the west shore making an abrupt turn to the east,) stands Fort San Carlos de Barrancas. In rear of this fort is situated Gen. BRAXTON BRAGG's main camp. Near the fort are the lighthouse, extensive barracks and the naval hospital. About a mile above the hospital is the navy-yard, situated on Tartar Point, where the shore bends again to the north. The village of Warrenton lies immediately adjacent to the wall of the Navy-yard.

The town of Pensacola, reported as evacuated, is eight miles in a northeasterly direction from the Navy-yard, and why Gen. BRAXTON BRAGG should have ordered its evacuation, if he had positively determined to breach Fort Pickens "on Monday," it is hard to see. It appears much more likely that BRAGG anticipated the destruction of his forts and batteries by the very troops he was on the point of "forcing to surrender," and an immediate assault on Pensacola by the vessels of war which he had just "riddled with bullets." It will be seen, by the line of the ship channel to Pensacola, in our map, how close to rebel forts, and their line of shore batteries, our vessels had to run when playing on the enemy, or when making their way to the city. (The ship-channel line running westward in the map, does not of course indicate the direction in which lies Pensacola; just about the point at the tip of the arrow, the channel turns sharply up the bay to the city.)

It is hardly likely that Col. BROWN could have seized and held Pensacola or Warrington, or either of the rebel forts. His force is too small to permit him to spare a detachment for any such work as that. If he shelled out the rebels in front, kept them at bay in the rear, (from which they had been for some time preparing to attack him,) burned their army and ordnance stores, their barracks and towns, and maintained his own position, it will be a triumph sufficiently great, and will, moreover, have prepared the way for the occupation of the mainland at our convenience. The whole number of National troops at Pickens, as we stated the other day, was but eleven hundred regulars and Wilson's Zouaves, while the rebels claimed to have something like ten thousand men. As to the "five vessels" which Col. BROWN called to his assistance, it is impossible to conjecture what ships they were; but it is quite likely that the frigate *Colorado*, which had just returned from a run down to the vicinity of the Balize about the time the ball opened, brought along with her some of the blockading vessels, which had been released from duty by the completion of the fortifications on Ship Island.

The whole account we take to be eminently favorable to the National arms; and if BRAGG had not bragged that he would never surrender alive, we should soon expect to see him and his men along here, to keep company with his fellow-North Carolinian and fellow-traitor, Commodore BARRON.

PENSACOLA BAY AND CITY.

Pensacola harbor is the best harbor on the Gulf of Mexico. It is completely landlocked, and has twenty-two feet of water on the bar at low tide. East Bay admits frigates of the largest class, and is entirely sheltered from all winds. The town of Pensacola, which is the principal seaport of West Florida, had, a year ago, a population of about 4,000; but a great part of these fled from the ruin and terror that had overtaken the city. The houses are generally old-fashioned Spanish structures. The Alabama and Florida Railroad, which connects the town with Montgomery, (Ala.,) was completed shortly after secession. That part of the road then unbuilt was finished with great haste by DAVIS' orders, so that troops and munitions might be hurried forward for the capture of Fort Pickens. Although that is nine months ago, however, Pickens is as yet uncaptured—nor, we judge by the latest news, is it likely soon to be captured. The climate is exceedingly healthful, except for occasional and rare visitations of yellow fever. The creole element predominates in the resident population. In 1814, Gen. JACKSON drove out the British, who had established themselves there by permission of the Spaniards, and assaulted and took the city and adjacent forts. Again in 1818, Gen. JACKSON, in consequence of Indian incursions on United States territory, took possession of Pensacola, and obliged Fort Barrancas, to which the Spanish Governor had retired, to capitulate. In 1821, the whole territory was ceded to the United States. We hope it will turn out that Col. BROWN is no unworthy successor of Gen. JACKSON.

DOINGS ON THE REBEL COAST.

OUR HILTON HEAD CORRESPONDENCE.

OCCUPATION OF TYBEE ISLAND—THE PRELIMINARY RECONNOISSANCE—SHALL BEAUFORT BE OCCUPIED?

HILTON HEAD, S. C., Monday, Nov. 25, 1861.

Two or three days ago Com. ROGERS was sent in the *Flag* to make a reconnoissance of Tybee Roads and to place buoys in the channel. On Friday night he returned and reported his belief that Tybee was abandoned. He was ordered to return with his own steamer, the *Flag*, supported by the gunboat *Seneca* and steamer *Pocahontas*, to make a reconnoissance in force. Last night he sent back the *Seneca* to report that he had taken possession of the Island, after firing several shells on shore without eliciting a response. The *Flag*, *Pocahontas* and *Augusta* anchored in the Roads last night and were about landing to take possession when we left. Yesterday, our boats put out and saw the enemy at Fort Pulaski; this, as you know, is a casemated fort. Our vessels now have all moved up and secured good Winter quarters without the necessity of putting to sea in case of violent blows. The anchorage where there is 20 feet water at low tide is from 2 to 2½ miles distant from the Fort, which has not, as yet, tried its range on the vessels.

The *Pawnee*, *Unadilla*, *Pembina* and *Vixen* have gone to St. Helena Sound to reconnoitre. They carry peaceful messages to the people, all of whom seem to have fled in terror, so alarmed were they by the capture of their strong positions at Hilton Head.

Gen. SHERMAN is strongly urged by some of his advisers to occupy Beaufort with two-thirds of this division, and to let the coming fleets from the North go further down the coast for whatever supplies may be necessary.

The weather is growing cold now, and warm clothing is much needed. Several thousand blankets are in the storehouses for use at a future time.

One hundred thousand feet of lumber was secured in Beaufort a day or two ago by Quartermaster SAXTON, and brought down. Hardly any of the inhabitants remain there. We buy everything offered for sale when anyone is present to sell; but commerce is mostly carried on by the negroes.

WANDERER.

THE ARMY AND NAVY.

Thursday being Thanksgiving Day, there were no movements at the Brooklyn Navy-yard, which was closed. All the recruiting offices, with the exception of No. 98 Chatham-street, were also closed, and there was no necessity for this one being open, as the Medical Examiner's office in Grand-street was closed, and if any recruits had presented themsemselves for enlistment they could not have been passed.

To provide for the examination of such non-commissioned officers as may be recommended by their commanding officers for promotion to the rank of Second Lieutenant in the regular army, a Board, consisting of the Professors of Mathematics and Ethics, and the Commandant of the Cadets, will convene at the Military Academy, West Point, on the first Monday of September in every year. Hitherto, a Board of army officers has convened in Washington for this purpose, in accordance with General Order No. 17, Oct. 4, 1854.

The report that Senator WILSON intends to bring in a bill during the ensuing session of Congress, to abolish the office of sutler, in the army, has caused great commotion among army sutlers and their friends. Even at a small post like Governor's Island, the sutler makes a very nice thing of it. Lager beer is allowed to be sold there, but nothing stronger. On the frontiers sutlers have been permitted, and indeed expected, to keep liquors, the sale of which was, however, restricted.

The business done at the Brooklyn Navy-yard yesterday was merely of a routine character.

ARRIVAL AND DEPARTURE OF THE SEVENTY-SEVENTH REGIMENT.

This regiment, Col. McKEAN, which has been quartered for some time past at Saratoga Springs, arrived in this City yesterday on its way to the seat of war. On landing the men were marched to the Park Barracks, where a substantial meal was provided for them. The men during their stay at Saratoga were fully uniformed and equipped, but were not armed. When at the Park Barracks they were furnished with Enfield rifles. After obtaining refreshments the men were drawn up into line in front of the City Hall, and were presented with a regimental flag and guide colors by HIRAM KETCHUM, Esq., who made a brief and appropriate speech. Col. McKEAN, on receiving the flags, said that he felt justly proud in handing the flag just presented, to Color-Sergeant BEMIS, a descendant of the BEMIS in whose fields one of the fifteen battles of the Revolution had been fought. The regiment then marched down to Pier No. 1, North River, and took the boat for Amboy. Subjoined is a list of the officers:

Colonel—J. B. McLean; Lieutenant-Colonel—J. C. Henderson; Major—Seldon Hetzel. Co. A—Capt. A. W. Arnold; Co. B—Capt. B. J. Judson; Co. C—Capt. C. C. Hill; Co. D—Capt. John Carr; Co. E—Capt. Lewis Wood; Co. F—Capt. J. B. Andrews; Co. G—Capt. Calvin Rice; Co. H—Capt. A. F. Beach; Co. I—Capt. Franklin Norton; Co. K—Capt. N. S. Babcoek.

THE RELEASED FORT WARREN PRISONERS.

BOSTON, Friday, Nov. 29.

The eleven Kentuckians recently released from Fort Warren, being destitute of means, were to-day sent to their homes at the expense of the City of Boston.

The New-York Times.

VOL. XI....NO. 3186. | NEW-YORK, SATURDAY, DECEMBER 7, 1861. | PRICE TWO CENTS.

IMPORTANT FROM PORT ROYAL.

ARRIVAL OF THE TRANSPORT VANDERBILT.

Gen. Viele's Expedition not yet Started.

BEAUFORT STILL UNOCCUPIED.

Important Reconnoissances of the Adjoining Country.

The Whole Tract from Tybee to Charleston Deserted by the Whites.

Immense Quantities of Cotton to be Secured.

Destruction of Storehouses by Rebel Incendiaries.

GENERAL GOOD BEHAVIOR OF THE BLACKS.

The United States steam transport *Vanderbilt*, Capt. LE FEVRE, from Port Royal, S. C., Dec. 3, with mails and passengers to Col. D. D. TOMPKINS, U. S. Quartermaster, arrived at this port yesterday morning.

Nothing of importance had trranspired since the sailing of the *Rhode Island*. Gen. VIELE's expedition was fitting out with all possible haste, and would leave on its mission as soon as more troops arrived, which would be very soon, as they were expected at any moment.

The harbor at Port Royal has been buoyed off, so that a vessel drawing twenty-five feet of water can enter with perfect safety.

The health of the troops continues good.

Beaufort still remains unoccupied by the National troops. Visits are daily made by officers of the army and navy to that place.

The schooner *Western Star* was to sail for New-York in a day or two, with a cargo of cotton.

The work of digging intrenchments on Tybee Island was progressing rapidly, the laborers being protected by two National gunboats.

Two National gunboats were also lying off Beaufort for the purpose of repelling any advance which might be made by the rebels to occupy the island.

Our intrenchments at Hilton Head have been strengthened. Two piers are in course of construction, and several storehouses have been erected.

Transports were busily discharging. The following vessels were at Port Royal when the *Vanderbilt* left:

British frigate Immortalite.
United States frigate Wabash.*
United States gunboats Mohican, Pembina, Ottawa, Curlew, R. B. Forbes, Isaac Smith, Mercury, O. M. Pettit, Penguin, Augusta, Florida, Bienville.
Transports—Steamers Ariel, Daniel Webster, Philadelphia, Matanzas, Oriental, Empire City, Cahawba, Roanoke, Star of the South, Parkersburgh, Locust Point, Winfield Scott, (condemned,) Potomac, Ben Deford, Atlantic. Ships Great Republic, Ocean Express, Golden Eagle, Zenas Coffin, and a number of brigs and schooners coal-laden.

Capt. R. SAXTON, Chief Quartermaster at Port Royal, has ordered the immediate return of the *Vanderbilt* with a cargo of supplies required by the Quartermaster at that point. It will be recollected that the *Vanderbilt*, in the recent Naval Expedition, was freighted with a large assorted cargo of ordnance, commissary and quartermaster's stores, together with two regiments of soldiers, including all their camp equipage, rations, baggage, &c., &c.; also, Gen. SHERMAN's entire brigade staff officers. Besides, she towed the *Great Republic*.

The following are the passengers by the *Vanderbilt*:

Major J. L. Hewett, paymaster U. S. A.; Saml. F. Barr, sutler of Sherman's E. C.; Capt. C. H. Farrell, of Gen. Vele's Staff; Chas. A. Weed, Gov. Supercargo, Capt. John A. Falconer, New-York Seventy-ninth Regiment; E. W. Wallam, paymaster's clerk; Lieut. Horatio Belcher, Eighth Michigan Regiment; W. McClellan, master carpenter; Wm. H. Beard, of Brooklyn; Capt. Foster Willis, steamer *Mayflower*; John J. Ross, Ninth Maine Regiment; W. J. Skinner, U. S. Engineers. Also, 13 discharged teamsters and carpenters, and 35 invalid seamen and soldiers.

Among the passengers of the *Vanderbilt*, is Capt. L. CHRISTIE, and five of his crew of schooner *Albion*, who were taken prisoners whilst trying to run the blockade at Charleston.

It will be remembered that the *Albion* reached this port about a week ago in charge of a prize crew.

Capt. CHRISTY states that after his vessel was captured by the *Penguin* he was put on board a Spanish vessel and taken into Port Royal.

He says several vessels run the blockade off Savannah while he was at that place. Capt. CHRISTY resides at Savannah, where a portion of his family now are. He is a native of New-York City.

He also brings home one secession spy taken at Port Royal. He is a German, and gave his name as CONRAD MARTIN. He says he came to this country about four years ago, and has lived most of the time at Beaufort, where he has worked at shoemaking. When our troops captured Fort Walker, the wealthy planters, residing in Beaufort, took a hasty departure for the interior, and he followed them, taking the precaution, however, before he went, to bury his trunk a distance of several feet in the earth. The crafty negroes were not long in discovering the spot, as MARTIN, on his subsequent return to repossess himself of his worldly treasures, found out. His next move was to search for his trunk. He traveled over several plantations, but could not find it. He then jumped into a boat, and engaged four negroes to row him across a stream, and on reaching land was surprised to find himself surrounded by a company of Highlanders, and a prisoner in their hands. What action the Government will take in his case is not yet known.

OUR PORT ROYAL CORRESPONDENCE.

Important Events of a Few Days—The Reconnoissances on the Mainland—The Country Deserted by the Whites, from Tybee to Charleston—Quntities of Clothes Discovered—Fortifications Deserted—The Negroes Welcoming the Union Soldiers, &c.

HILTON HEAD, PORT ROYAL, S. C., Sunday, Dec. 1, 1861.

The events of the past few days have not been salient ones; the building of stables for eleven hundred horses, the erection of ordnance storehouses, and the appointment of cemeteries, are scarcely themes that strike the public attention, vastly important as they are to the comfort and safety of the new population landed upon this shore. The throwing up of entrenchments and the mounting of guns are more purely military in their aspect, and a complete description of the changes wrought here by the officers of the engineer and ordnance corps would undoubtedly interest the country, but prudence forbids any such detail. There are left only the reconnoissances, which have been important and extended, and a statement of the results developed by them.

The reconnoissances since my last letter have been a renewed one, under Capt. GILMORE, Chief of Engineers, to Tybee Island, and one westward, half way to Charleston, under Lieut. P. H. O'RORKE, also of the Engineer Corps. The former completed the investigation begun by Gen. SHERMAN, in person, a few days earlier. He went on the steamer *Ben De Ford*, with three companies of volunteers as an escort, and spent a day or two exploring the condition of the island. No other defences were discovered than those I have described in a previous letter, and these, as then stated, were completely abandoned. Some other results of the reconnoissance were of a nature not proper for publication.

Lieut. O'RORKE made his reconnoissance under an escort of three companies of the New-York Seventy-ninth and three gunboats, the *Pawnee*, (flag-ship,) Capt. DRAYTON; the *Pembina*, Capt. BANKHEAD, and the *Curlew*. Capt. BOUTELLE, of the Coast Survey, whose intimate knowledge of this coast renders his presence almost indispensable on such occasions, also accompanied the expedition in his vessel, the *Vixen*. Lieut. O'RORKE first traveled the length of St. Helena Island to St. Helena Sound, where he was met by the gunboats; thereafter, his progress was partly by land and partly by water. On Otter Point, the northern extremity of St. Helena Sound, he found a small field work, which had been mounted with four or five guns, but was entirely abandoned. From here the party sailed up several of the rivers that penetrate the interior. On the Ashepoo they found a fort, and on the Coosaw another, both in the condition of that on Otter Point. The greatest distance traveled inwards from the sea was twelve or fifteen miles, but at one time the party was only thirty-two miles from Charleston. Everywhere the whites had deserted their residences, leaving the negroes behind; in several instances they set fire to the cotton-houses at the approach of the Union forces, but with these exceptions, their property remained undisturbed. No pillaging had taken place. National troops were sometimes quartered in gentlemen's houses, where the furniture of the drawing-rooms was scrupulously guarded from use, and the silver plate that, in their haste, was left on the sideboards, was subjected to no damage. The blacks told the same story here as everywhere else; their masters had fled with the greatest trepidation after the fall of Port Royal; had endeavored to persuade the slaves to accompany them, and had even shot some who refused. But, as elsewhere, the blacks had remained behind, and welcomed the new-comers. For seven miles further inward than it was thought advisable to advance, the whites were said to have abandoned the country.

It is thus definitely ascertained, that from Tybee Island, within a mile and a quarter of Fort Pulaski, up to Otter Point, not much more than thirty miles from Savannah, the entire seaboard of South Carolina is in our hands; her white population fled; her planters' houses abandoned, and often pillaged by the blacks; the cotton houses frequently burned by the rebels themselves, (sometimes the cotton has been buried,) and the slave population left to take care of itself. The efforts to carry off the slaves have been in nearly every case abortive. No love for masters, no fear of their cruelty, no apprehension of the Yankees has been sufficient to alarm the blacks. They all look upon us as friends; and where they do not come within our lines, say that all that restrains them is the dislike of leaving their families and the "tings"—their little property. They have a cat-like clinging to their old quarters, and do not generally manifest any desire to quit them. When they have fled in large numbers, it has been always towards our lines, but so far as I can learn it has been because of the efforts of their masters to take them off. This they resist, but they manifest no peculiarly vindictive spirit. They complain of bad treatment, but I cannot learn that they display any desire to revenge themselves. They chuckle indeed with infinite glee over Southern disasters; they tell of the lies they told their former owners, of their pretences to love them, of their forced obedience; they believe in the power of the Unionists to overthrow the Southern rule; they are willing to act as guides or scouts, (occasionally;) to work; to give all information; and the more intelligent they are the readier to aid us. But unless provoked by the foolish attempts of the rebels to carry them off, I doubt whether they will attempt any injury to the persons of the whites. The plundering indeed presages evil, but if the rebels set the example by firing their own cotton-houses, they need not be surprised to find it imitated. If they persist in their attempts at forcibly restraining the slaves and in firing at them, the worst consequences are likely to follow.

The health of the command is not so good as might be desired; congestive and typhoid fevers are prevalent, but by no means epidemic. There is, however, a great lack of hospital stores, and I am authoritatively informed that the patriotism and benevolence of those at home could hardly be better employed than in providing additions to these stores. The need for such luxuries as the sick require is pressing, and even bedding, sheets, and other of the more obvious necessities of the hospital have not been furnished. Requisitions have been made for them, but months may elapse before in the official routine the command will be supplied. The women of New-York who feel inclined to devote a portion of their means or their energies to the cause, in behalf of which these men sicken and die, have here a fitting opportunity. The cause of this strange state of affairs is no neglect on the part of the present Medical Director of the command; Dr. GEO. COOPER, who was appointed to his position only a day or two before the expedition sailed from Annapolis.

VAGABOND.

THE RECONNOISSANCE UP THE ASHPOO RIVER.

VESSELS ENGAGED IN THE SERVICE.

Our correspondent with the great Naval Expedition, states that the *Pawnee*, *Pembina* and *Curlew* were the vessels engaged in the reconnoissance up the Ashpoo River in South Carolina. We append a brief description of these gunboats.

The *Curlew* was in New-York about ten days ago, having her machinery arranged. She is about 380 tons burden. Her armament consists of six 32-pounders and a rifled 20-pounder Parrott on the forecastle deck. Her principal officers are:

Lieutenant Commanding—WATMOUGH.
First Lieutenant—George H. Haywood.
Masters—Robert Spavin, Horatio Parish, Caleb A. Curtis.
Assistant Paymaster—W. A. Aiken.
Assistant Surgeon—Celso. Prerucci.
First Assistant Engineer—George R. Ewer.
Third Assistant Engineers—John Lloyd, True Swasey, Arch. D. McConnell.

The *Pembina* is one of the new twenty-three gunboats, with whose shape and appearance every New-Yorker, at least, is now familiar. She was engaged in the action at Port Royal entrance, and had her steam-chest perforated by a round shot. Her principal officers are:

Lieutenant Commanding—P. CROSBY.
Lieutenant and Executive Officer—C. H. Cashman.
Acting Masters—Rodgers, Mills, Powers.
Acting Paymaster—E. Stewart.
Acting Assistant Surgeon—A. W. H. Hawkins.
First Assistant Engineer—J. Young.
Third Assistants—Van Horenburg, N. B. Clark, J. S. Smith.

The *Pawnee* carries twelve 9-inch guns, and is a vessel of 1,289 tons. She has performed rigid blockade duty during the Summer. At one time she had a very smart engagement with the rebel batteries at Aquia Creek. She fought at Port Royal, with the rest of the squadron, and was struck nine times in her hull. One of the balls entered the ward-room, knocked down bulkheads, and finally lodged in an iron safe. The *Pawnee's* principal officers are:

Lieutenant Commanding—R. H. WYMAN.
Lieutenants—Maxwell, McCrea, Eastman, Blue.
Midshipmen—Snell, Daniels.
Surgeon—Gunnell.
Paymaster—Abbott.
Chief-Engineer—W. H. Rutherford.
Third Assistant Engineers—Hardee, Trilley, Champion, Adamson, Sellman.

OPERATIONS IN SOUTH CAROLINA.

Scene of the Recent Reconnoissances Made by our Forces.

* Fort Beauregard. ** Fort Walker. Rough shading on interior of Map indicates Swamps.

THE COTTON AT PORT ROYAL, WASTED AND DESTROYED.

Extract of a Letter Dated

HILTON HEAD, Dec. 1, 1861.

Gen. SHERMAN will not allow a pound of cotton to go, unless there is a *white* owner to buy it from. Cotton is used freely for 15,000 soldiers' beds, and *is wasted and scattered round in every direction.* Cotton houses are *full* of the finest sea island cotton, and the negroes burn it up nightly by orders of their masters. Capt. SAXTON, the chief Quartermaster of the expedition, wants to *take the cotton and load every return ship with it, but Gen. Sherman will not give his consent.* Certain parties have hired the negroes about here to pick and gin the cotton, paying them five cents a pound for their labor. Gen. SHERMAN is in ill health, being badly afflicted with the dispepsia.

MAP OF EASTERN TENNESSEE.

Morristown, the Scene of Parson Brownlow's Exploit, and the Surrounding Region.

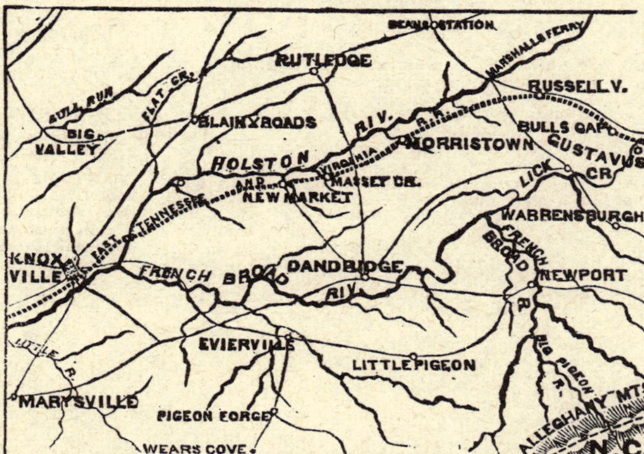

THE NEWS FROM EAST TENNESSEE.

The important news which we published yesterday of the exploit of the gallant Parson BROWNLOW in East Tennessee, is again directing universal attention to that quarter of the scene of operations. The patriots of that region have become wearied out waiting on the dilatory and wavering movements of the National forces in Eastern Kentucky, and have been driven to desperation by the outrageous persecutions of the rebel authorities, State and Confederate; and now, after having destroyed the bridges on the various railroads over which the rebel hordes might be precipitated upon them, they have taken the field, drawn the sword, and won the first battle that has been fought in that State.

It is a striking and significant fact that the mountainers dwelling along that part of the great Appalachian range which sweeps through the middle Slave States have been, and still are, warmly devoted to the National Union. In Western Maryland, Western Virginia, Western North Carolina, Eastern Tennessee, Northern Georgia, and Northern Alabama, the people were strongly opposed to secession, and bitter against all the schemes of the conspirators; and when, finally, by fraud and villainy, the latter succeeded in achieving their ends, these men not only refused for months to succumb to the secession traitors, but, at different points, began organizing in various ways, both peaceful and belligerent, so as to reverse their doings, and to regain a position in the old Union and under the old flag. (The fact that the slaves are comparatively few, and thinly scattered along this mountain range, may account for the predominance of Union feeling and conviction. There is settled all through here a free, independent yeomanry, with all the traditions and conditions of liberty, and with but little interest in African Slavery.)

Western Virginia may now be said to be redeemed; for, though the rebel bushwackers may keep up a petty warfare for an indefinite period, the National forces are fortified in strong mountain positions from which no rebel force can ever expel them, while the newly organized State Government will see to it that peace is maintained, and that the marauders are driven from every foot of the soil over which its boundaries may be extended.

The scene now opens further westward in the adjoining State of *Tennessee*, and the campaign begins with a success under BROWNLOW precisely as did the campaign in Western Virginia under KELLY. Operations at the present point, however, are of far greater importance to the war, in its general aspect, than those that have taken place in any other part of the Southwest. We have urged over and over again, in this journal, the fundamental importance to the Union cause of our obtaining possession of the East Tennessee and Virginia Railroad. It requires but a glance at any correct Railroad map to establish this proposition. The road may be said to begin at Memphis, on the Mississippi River, and proceed by way of the Memphis and Charleston Railroad to Chattanooga, in the southeast corner of Tennessee, and thence through Knoxville, by way of the Virginia and Tennessee Railroad, to *Richmond*. This is the sole route used by the rebel States of the Southwest in this war, in reaching the army of rebellion in Virginia. Along this long fertile line are found the men of war and the provisions for war. And by this route alone is it possible to draw supplies to Virginia in sufficient abundance and with necessary dispatch, to support the army that JEFF. DAVIS has in the field. For a distance of 240 miles, that is to say, from Chattanooga, Tenn., to the State line near Abingdon, Va., this road lies wholly in *East Tennessee*, and in the midst of as loyal and warlike a population as can be found in the Union.

Morristown is not far from the centre of this district, and on this line of road. Geographically, it is situated in Granger County, East Tennessee, about thirty miles south of Cumberland Gap, and 226 miles east of Nashville. Militarily, it is a strategic point of vast and vital importance.

If Gen. BROWNLOW has really gained the reported victory, and if the loyal mountaineers of East Tennessee—of whom there are at least forty thousand—flock to his standard in sufficient force to enable him to maintain himself, he will not only have outflanked and cut off ZOLLICOFFER and LEE, and raised the National banner well down in the centre of the rebel territory, but he will also command the great rebel railroad of the Southwest.

We publish this morning, however, three items of news which cannot be agreeable to Parson BROWNLOW. One is, that the National troops at Camp Hoskins, Pulaski County, Ky., which, since the disgraceful retreat of Gen. SCHOEPF, are the nearest reinforcements to the East Tennesseeans, are about to retire northward before the rebels, thus isolating BROWNLOW even more than he has been. The second is, that Gen. ROSECRANS, a part of whose forces were reported some time ago to be preparing for a diversion into Kentucky or East Tennessee, has gone northward as high as Wheeling, Va., for the Winter. And third, instead of *his* going to East Tennessee, his adversary, the rebel thief FLOYD, and his command, had been ordered there, and on the 3d inst. were within thirty miles of the East Tennessee and Virginia Railroad. And yesterday morning it was announced that the rebel, Gen. CRITTENDEN, had arrived at Knoxville, in BROWNLOW's rear, to take the field with his forces.

These things look bad enough, undoubtedly; but Gen. Parson BROWNLOW is a man of resources, and if FLOYD, ZOLLICOFFER or CRITTENDEN come up on him with an overwhelming force, he can at all events destroy the railroad, disband and retire his forces to the mountains, and there wait for the bright morning, which we hope is not far off, when, from the gray Cumberland Mountain peaks the persecuted loyalists can descry the flag of the Union advancing from fold Kentucky.

IMPORTANT FROM SAVANNAH.

An Immediate Attack on Fort Pulaski Expected.

BALTIMORE, Friday, Dec. 6.

A dispatch from Savannah in the Richmond papers of yesterday, dated the 4th inst., says:

"Sixteen of the ships of the enemy are now inside the bar, and an attack on Fort Pulaski is hourly expected."

REBEL NEWS FROM TYBEE.

The Savannah *Republican* publishes a letter from Fort Pulaski direct, dated Nov. 25, from which we make the following extract:

"The enemy appeared around Tybee Point about 7 o'clock A. M., yesterday. The sentinel reported them, and the assembly was beat. We were ordered to the guns—there we awaited them. The enemy, composed of a frigate and one gunboat, rounded the point, and commenced throwing shot and shell on Tybee. Not having received a reply, they dispatched the gunboat for more vessels. About 4 o'clock the gunboat came back with two more very large vessels; soon after a long train of small boats were seen to leave the vessels and head for the shore. About 6 o'clock the Federal flag was seen flying on Tybee Island. About 7 o'clock at night, Capt. READ, of the Irish Volunteers, took a squad of his men and went over to the island, and got in sight of the Yankees—he could see them all around the fire—but, finding that he could not effect his object, which was to burn the large hospital, there being too many men around the house, he returned, and burnt all the houses on his way, including Capt. KING's large house; also, the platform where the boat lands. They also brought off an old negro, the property of Mr. KING, whom the picket had left. He is now at the fort.

This morning the Federal flag could be seen flying on the lighthouse. There are three large vessels off the point now, and another gunboat has just arrived.

The island is naturally protected by large sand-hills, which could have protected our men from the shells of the enemy.

I think a thousand men would whip them off the island in two hours. The enemy have a foothold on all the Southern States bordering on the Atlantic, but I think they have gained very little by taking Tybee Island. I do not think they can get enough rice and cotton on Tybee to pay the cost of the expedition, as they say they did at Port Royal.

Capt. S. has gone out to burn some fishermen's huts on the island.

We have plenty of ammunition and men, and we defy them to come in range of our guns—we will show them the difference between taking Port Royal and Fort Pulaski.

LATEST FROM TYBEE.

From the Savannah *News* of the 28th we extract the following:

"The steamer *Ida* arrived from Fort Pulaski at 4 o'clock, yesterday afternoon, having left at 2 o'clock. Capt. CIRCOPELY reports six Federal vessels still inside the bar. Five more vessels, supposed to be transports, arrived yesterday noon, and can be seen outside the bar, making eleven vessels in all now in sight of Fort Pulaski. From their movements it was thought the vessels outside would come in over the bar last evening. The vessels inside lie at anchor about four miles from the fort, and out of the reach of our guns. One, a large frigate, can be seen from the Exchange and the balconies of the stores on the bluff.

Between 10 and 11 o'clock yesterday morning, a party of Yankee troops, armed with muskets, were observed from the fort advancing along the beach towards King's landing. Two or three round shot and shell were fired at them from the fort. When the first shell was fired, the Yankees prostrated themselves on the ground; after the second shell burst over them, they arose and fled to the cover of the woods. They afterwards appeared on the beach, out of the range of the guns of the fort. It is not known whether any of them were hit by our shot and shell, but those who saw the bursting of the shell, which made the sand fly in their immediate vicinity, are under the impression that they were not entirely harmless.

NEWS FROM THE SOUTH.

Movements of the Thieving Floyd—A Flag of Truce from Norfolk—A Message from Gov Letcher, &c.

BALTIMORE, Friday, Dec. 6.

The Richmond *Dispatch*, of yesterday, says that it is currently reported, that Gen. FLOYD's command has been ordered to another important post for duty.

A telegram, dated Nashville, 3d inst., says that Gen. FLOYD has fallen back to within thirty miles of the Virginia and East Tennessee Railroad.

FORTRESS MONROE, Thursday, Dec. 5, via BALTIMORE, Friday, Dec. 6.

A flag of truce came down from Norfolk bringing several Charleston passengers, but no news of any kind.

Gen. WOOL also dispatched a flag of truce to Norfolk with a number of letters and considerable clothing for the Union prisoners at Richmond.

The *Illinois* will leave here for Port Royal with troops for Gen. SHERMAN this evening.

The Norfolk *Day Book* of to-day contains a message from Gov. LETCHER, the main points of which is his regret that Fortress Monroe is not in possession of the Confederate States.

The Rebel Congress, at its session of the 3d inst., passed a resolution of thanks to Gen. STERLING PRICE, for his active services in Missouri during the campaign.

Gov. LETCHER urges a forward movement. He says the banks of the Potomac is not the place to fight, but the banks of the Susquehanna.

FROM NEW-ORLEANS.

LOUISVILLE, Ky., Friday, Dec. 6.

The New-Orleans *Crescent*, of the 25th of November, contains the weekly bank statement to the 22d of November, as follows:

Circulation	$6,958,000
Deposits	18,403,000
Specie	13,771,000

There had been no sales of Cotton or Tobacco. Sugar was selling at 3c.@3⅞c. ℔ lb. Molasses, 14c. @21c. ℔ gallon. Flour, $11 50@$12 ℔ bbl. Corn, $1 ℔ bushel. Whisky, rectified, $1 10 ℔ gallon, and Rye, $2 25. Lard, 29c.@30c. ℔ lb. Beef—Mess, $33. Pork—Mess, $45. Bacon, 22c.@25c. ℔ lb.

Nov. 26—Texas cattle sell at $20@45 per head; hogs, $10@$13 per 100 lbs.; sheep, second quality, $3 @$5 per head; veals, $8@$13 per head.

The New-Orleans *Crescent* also says that the decrease in the Exchange of $274,000 on the week is attributed to a desire to place funds in England to invest in merchandise, sterling having been freely taken at 125 to 126. We are not aware of any prospective improvement in commerce to warrant these figures, which are much higher than in the bankruptcy of 1837 and 1840.

It is bruited about that some parties are placing all their funds in Europe for fear, perhaps, the highway robbers of the world may penetrate our good city.

DURYEE'S ZOUAVES AGAIN IN BALTIMORE.

BALTIMORE, Friday, Dec. 6.

The Fifth New-York Regiment returned from the eastern shore of Virginia yesterday. This morning, they made a grand parade here, marching from Federal Hill through the city to the headquarters of Gen. DIX. They bore with them a large secession flag, which they captured in the land of Dixie. The flag was carried union down. On depositing it at headquarters, the battalion gave three tremendous cheers for Gen. Dix and the American Union.

NAVIES OF THE WORLD.

The Naval Strength of America, England and France.

Growth, Prospects and Present Condition of Each.

The condition of political affairs both in Europe and America, gives increased interest to the relative strength of the leading Powers, especially on the sea. The combined expedition against Mexico, shows that the Western Powers do not intend to remain idle spectators of events on this side the Atlantic, and our own internal commotions create an opportunity which cannot fail to be tempting to powerful and ambitious nations. In view of these circumstances, we have compiled the following condensed statement of the condition and strength of the three leading navies of the world.

THE AMERICAN NAVY.

The American navy may be said to have been reconstructed since the fall of Sumter. Every one knows that through the infernal treachery and ingenuity of traitors in the Buchanan Administration, the American navy had been so scattered and disabled that at the outbreak of the rebellion it was practically useless. Though the register showed 89 men-of-war, mounting 2,302 guns, the National Government could not assemble half a dozen vessels to meet a sudden emergency. To make the case still worse, four ships of the line, four frigates, two sloops-of-war and a brig were destroyed at the burning of the Gosport Navy-yard. This reduced our nominal number of guns to about 1,800. But these figures fell very far short of the actual number at the command of the Navy Department. As late as July last only twenty vessels of the regular navy, mounting barely 400 guns, had been collected for service in the blockade. Twenty-two ships, mounting 336 guns, were still on foreign stations, and the remainder, numbering about 1,000 guns, were in different Northern Navy-yards, fitting out for service, or used as receiving ships. Indeed, of this last class, so many were useless for the urgent need of the Government that their names and the number of their guns merely served to swell the register, and to mislead people into supposing that our navy was much stronger than it really was. Thus the *Ohio*, (84,) receiving-ship at Boston; the *North Carolina*, (84,) receiving-ship at New-York; the *Vermont*, (84,) in ordinary at Boston; the *New-Orleans*, (84,) on the stocks at Sacketts' Harbor; the *Alabama*, (84,) on the stocks at Kittery; the *Virginia*, (84,) on the stocks at Boston; the *Constitution*, (50,) school-ship at Newport; the *Brandywine*, (50,) in ordinary at New-York; and the *Franklin*, (50,) in ordinary at Portsmouth, are all included in the list, and their total guns (664) must be subtracted from the efficient regular naval force under the control of the Government. In July last the *regular* naval force, either fitting out or in commission on the Southern coasts did not exceed forty vessels nor amount to over 750 guns. Day by day, however, the blockading fleet continued to receive additions from vessels ordered home from foreign stations. Of a fleet of eighteen ships-of-war that carried the American flag in foreign waters, thirteen have returned home. Six gunboats and sloops, carrying 88 guns, have been left on the Pacific coast—one, the *Saratoga*, (18,) on the coast of Africa, and one, the *Pulaski*, (1,) on the coast of Brazil. Thus the efficient force of the navy of the United States—efficient, that is to say, for the blockade and the purposes of the rebellion—is equal (omitting receiving ships and ships of the line that have been on the stocks for fifty years) to about seventy vessels of all rates, carrying between 1,200 and 1,300 guns. When we reflect upon the condition of this same navy only six months ago, we can well afford to congratulate the Department on its efforts.

It is not only in gathering together our scattered squadrons, or in refitting our ships, that the Government has evinced a remarkable and determined energy. Besides this great labor, an altogether new navy has sprung into life, and has already distinguished itself in the war. Eight new steam sloops were ordered by Congress, and their construction was immediately commenced. They have been all launched except two, and these are in a very forward state. The sloops are about 1,000 tons burden, and carry each [illegible] guns. The construction of twenty-three new gunboats for the regular navy was also ordered by the Government. We believe that all of them have been launched—many have been for weeks in commission, and some were engaged in the capture of the Port Royal forts. Their commanders declare them to be very serviceable for blockading purposes—much more serviceable than such huge [illegible] vessels as the *Niagara*. These gunboats are about 500 tons each. They are pierced for [illegible] guns, but only carry four each. Besides these, six additional screw sloops, twelve side-wheel steamers and three iron-clad steamers have been built or in an advanced stage of construction.

While the attention of Government was thus turned to the construction of new war vessels, it did not neglect the obvious policy of purchasing and chartering such steamers and sailing vessels as it could turn to profitable account. More than two hundred and fifty vessels, of all classes, have been purchased or chartered by Government for the purposes of the war; and for those purchased out-and-out for the navy, over $5,000,000 have been paid. From the Secretary of the Navy's report we learn that seventy-nine steamers (side-wheels and propellers) have been purchased by Government and have been converted into efficient gunboats. In following the rebels up creeks and inlets, and in capturing small craft striving to run the blockade, many of the smaller gunboats have done invaluable service. These seventy-five purchased vessels, carry 341 guns. At the present time the *effective* navy of the United States may thus be classified:

SUMMARY OF EFFECTIVE VESSELS IN THE UNITED STATES NAVY.

	Sailing. Ships.	Sailing. Guns.	Steam. Ships.	Steam. Guns.
Frigates	6	300	[illegible]	[illegible]
Sloops (old and new)	17	342	[illegible]	[illegible]
Brigs	2	12	[illegible]	[illegible]
Small side-wheel steamers	—	—	[illegible]	[illegible]
Iron-clad steamers	—	—	[illegible]	[illegible]
Gunboats (new)	—	—	[illegible]	[illegible]
Steamers purchased and converted into gunboats	—	—	[illegible]	[illegible]
Ships purchased	13	52	[illegible]	[illegible]
Barks purchased	18	78	[illegible]	[illegible]
Brigs purchased	2	4	[illegible]	[illegible]
Schooners purchased	24	49	[illegible]	[illegible]
Totals	82	837	[illegible]	[illegible]
Total effective vessels				[illegible]
Total guns				[illegible]

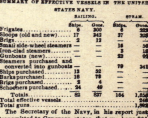

The Secretary of the Navy, in his report just transmitted to Congress, states that we have [illegible] vessels, 2,557 guns, and 22,000 seamen, but he includes, in his list, receiving-ships and ships of the line that have been on the stocks since 1818. [illegible]

The New-York Times.

VOL. XI....NO. 3188. | NEW-YORK, TUESDAY, DECEMBER 10, 1861. | PRICE TWO CENTS.

NEWS FROM WASHINGTON.

The Condition of Affairs in Western Tennessee.

Union Men Awaiting the Arrival of the National Army.

IMPORTANT PROCEEDINGS IN CONGRESS

The Disasters to the National Arms to be Inquired Into.

Proposed Investigation of the Conduct of the War.

An Exchange of Prisoners Recommended.

The Question of Slavery in the District of Columbia.

A Delegation of Western Indians on a Visit to Washington.

PROCEEDINGS OF THE REPUBLICAN CAUCUS

OUR SPECIAL WASHINGTON DISPATCHES.

WASHINGTON, Monday, Dec. 9.

THE REPUBLICAN CAUCUS.

The caucus of the Republicans to-night was attended by about forty members. A large number have deliberately determined not to compromise themselves by engaging in a mere party movement in regard to the policy of the war. Of course the most ultra men of the party were present. All newspaper men and outsiders were carefully excluded, and I am consequently enabled to give to the public only a sketch of the proceedings. My informant in some cases declining to furnish me with the names of speakers, though giving me the substance of the debate.

Mr. POMEROY, of Kansas, was chosen Speaker, and Mr. MCPHERSON, of Pennsylvania, Clerk. Hon. THADDEUS STEVENS opened the ball, saying that the design of the meeting was to ascertain the opinions of the Republicans in Congress on the policy of the war, with a view to shaping legislation and controlling the result. He felt that there was imperative necessity for such action. The war lingers. He was free to say that the South could never be subdued as long as they were allowed to keep four millions of slaves to clothe and subsist them, while they put every able-bodied white man into the field. Mr. STEVENS was in favor of compensating loyal masters in the South, but emancipation should be declared and made universal. The speaker was severe on the military authorities. He declared that Gen. MCCLELLAN was trying to control the Legislative and Executive powers of the nation; that he had threatened to resign unless the President should cause Mr. CAMERON's report to be amended before received or reported to Congress. Mr. STEVENS closed with some earnest and energetic declarations of his relentless purpose to overthrow the slave system, and sat down with applause from his side of the caucus.

Mr. DIVEN, of New-York, replied to Mr. STEVENS. He said he did not understand the object of the caucus when he came to it, nor had Mr. STEVENS much enlightened him. If the object was to secure the perpetuation of the Republican Party, the call was legitimate; but if it was to provide a policy for the war, the caucus was very improper. All poltical parties were supporting the Government. There were hundreds of thousands of men, besides the Republicans, interested in the conduct of the war, and its result. They were entitled to be heard, and they would be heard. All were united in one general opinion, that the war must be prosecuted with vigor, and by the swift bullet, the gleaming sabre, and the bursting shell. That was the way to end the war—not by resolutions or acts of Congress, but by fighting. Suppose we pass an act declaring that the slaves of all rebels shall be free. That will not make them free; on the contrary, their rebel masters will continue to use them and rally for a more desperate defence, knowing the nature of the ruin threatened. How was the rebel army obtained? By the cunning lies of the rebel leaders. The people of the South had been made to believe that the Republicans were unconstitutional and revolutionary, and meant to destroy all that they call their rights. Shall we verify the predictions of our enemies? In reply to an interruption by Mr. STEVENS, the speaker said he would be ready to strike down Slavery by a blow, and let loyalists and rebels suffer alike, if that were the only alternative of saving the Union; but he thought we were very far from being reduced to that extremity. The speaker complimented the President for his firmness, not doubting his devotion to free principles, but believing his conservative policy to be true wisdom. He said if gentlemen wished to attack the President, and deprive him of his prerogatives as the Chief Magistrate, they would find it much harder work getting him out of the Presidency than they had putting him in. In conclusion, the Speaker presented these resolutions as expressing the sentiments of patriotic Republican on the present occasion.

Resolved, That the Philadelphia Platform of 1856, and the Chicago Platform of 1860, embody the political faith of the Republican Party, and that this meeting recognize no right of a Congressional Convention to add or take from that statement of principles.

Resolved, That we are rejoiced to know that all political parties are giving a loyal support to the war, and that nothing should be done by the Republicans to create dissensions or revive party distinctions in the prosecution of the same.

Ten minute speeches were afterwards made by Messrs. POTTER, DIVEN, BINGHAM, KELLY, EDWARDS, LANE, CAMPBELL, ASHLEY and DAVIS. The discussion is represented as having been very spirited. The feeling seemed to be in favor of confiscating the slaves, and all other property of the rebels, and their aiders and abetters, but not to interfere with those of the Unionists.

The attendance of Representatives and Senators was not as large as was desired, hence no vote was taken, and the caucus adjourned till Wednesday night.

MR. STEVENS' RESOLUTIONS.

Mr. STEVENS, of Pennsylvania, has modified his resolutions in several important particulars, namely, declaring there can be no solid and permanent Union so long as Slavery exists, and that all slaves be proclaimed free, compensation to be made to loyal masters, who have been and continue to be supporters of the Union.

THE DECEASED MEMBERS OF CONGRESS.

As to-morrow and Wednesday will be devoted to proceedings consequent on the death of Senators BAKER and BINGHAM, the House has postponed the consideration of the various Slavery propositions until Thursday.

FUGITIVES FROM TENNESSEE.

Hon. EMERSON ETHERIDGE to-day received information from Paducah that large numbers of Tennesseeans, [illegible] Weakley, Carroll and Henderson Counties in West Tennessee, are arriving there. They have fled from their homes, escaping with the utmost difficulty, in order to avoid being drafted into the rebel service, and desire to take up arms for the Government. Gen. PAYNE has asked for authority to muster them into service. They represent that in Weakley, Henderson, Carroll, Hardin and McNarry Counties the Union feeling is very strong, and the Unionists in the [illegible] and impatient for the arrival of the National troops, on whose approach a general uprising of the people would take place. The immediate aid of Government is necessary, and will redeem Tennessee from the rebel yoke. Mr. ETHERIDGE goes to Paducah immediately, and we trust will carry with him from Headquarters assurances of speedy and effectual assistance.

EMANCIPATION IN KENTUCKY.

We understand that the President has been assured that the Legislature of Kentucky will soon emancipate all slaves in that State, reimbursing loyal men for losses sustained thereby.

CARRYING THE NATIONAL FLAG TO NEW-ORLEANS.

Prominent men from the West believe that the army from the Western States can, before Spring, carry the Stars and Stripes in triumph to New-Orleans.

A VISIT OF INDIAN DELEGATES.

To-day eight Indian delegates from the Seminoles, Cherokees and Creeks, were presented to the Secretary of the Interior. They were sent hither by the loyal men of their Nations, to examine into the condition of the Government and its power to overthrow the rebels. On their introduction to the Secretary they, through an interpreter, gave us the reason for the partial disaffection of their tribes, their apparent abandonment by Government, the absence from them of its troops and agents, and the inducements and threats of the rebel emissaries, who represented that the Government was overthrown and unable longer to protect and aid them, while the Confederacy was ready to enter into treaties with and assist them, if they would join it, and if not, would destroy them. Their [illegible] and surprise at the strength and stability presented through the West and at Washington. Secretary SMITH replied, explaining to them their duties and their relations to the Government.

SENATOR WILSON'S BILL RELATING TO COURTS-MARTIAL.

Senator WILSON's bill relative to courts-martial in the army, provides that in the time of war, the commander of a Division or separate Brigades may appoint general courts-martial, and may confirm, execute, pardon and mitigate their sentences, provided that the sentences of such courts, extending to loss of life, or the commission of a commissioned officer, shall require the confirmation of the General commanding the army in the field to which the Division or Brigade belongs; and provided further, that when a Division or Brigade commander shall be the accuser or prosecutor of an officer under his command, the court shall be appointed by the next higher commander.

THE ALLOTMENT BILL.

The Allotment bill of the same Senator provides that the Paymaster-General shall assign one or more Paymasters, now in service, to each State from which volunteeers have been or may be accepted, whose duty it shall be to receive and distribute to the families of the volunteers such portion of their pay as they may allot. Section 2d provides for the appointment by the President of three persons in each of such States, whose duty it shall be to visit the several Departments in said State, and procure the allotment tickets from volunteers. Sec. 3d provides that these persons shall receive no pay or emoluments from the Treasury of the United States.

PARSON BROWNLOW.

Private letters have been received in this city fully confirming the statement that Parson BROWNLOW is in the field at the head of a force of some 3,000 men. The card from him published in a Richmond paper, denying the report that he had taken up arms, was issued a month ago. The reported conflict at Morristown is fully credited here, and great anxiety is felt to have aid sent as rapidly as possible into Tennessee and Kentucky.

A TELEGRAPH DOWN THE COAST.

Mr. CYRUS W. FIELD has been in the city for several days, consulting with the Government in reference to establishing a line of telegraphic communicatioa from Washington, to extend along the lines of the coast. He proposes that the wires be extended to Fortress Monroe and Newport News from our present lines, and thence by submarine cable across to Cape Charles, and along the coast to Hatteras Inlet, Bull Bay and Port Royal. Then as soon as Fernandina shall be taken, that it be extended to that port and crossing the peninsula of Florida to Cedar Keys, and thence to Fort Pickens, Ship Island, Chandeleur Island, and around the mouths of the Mississippi to Galveston, when that port shall fall into our hands. A branch line is proposed to extend from Cedar Keys to Key West and the Tortugas. The length of the main wire will be about fifteen hundred miles, and the branch for Cedar Keys to Key West and Tortugas and Tortugas about four hundred miles.

THE NEW EXCHANGE OF PRISONERS.

About two hundred prisoners of war in Washington and the Northern cities have been released by order of the Government, and will be forwarded from Fortress Monroe under a flag of truce. Each prisoner gave his parole not to take up arms against the United States Government until exchanged, and it is understood that each is to procure an exchange from among our prisoners now in the South. Since the Port Royal victory the rebels have been more anxious than our own Government to effect an exchange. The following is a list of the prisoners released from the old Capitol prison:

Jas. Silks, J. H. Howard, W. A. Prince, J. O. Perkins, T. T. Buck, J. T. Pool, J. W. Davis, J. T. Mays, W. Mallow, E. M. Hancock, A. C. Landstreet, R. Paulding, J. S. Walker, Thos. Hays, L. B. Buckley, R. Gray, M. T. O. Keefe, T. A. Hammond, W. C. Humphries, A. T. Holmes, Jas. Kershaw, T. W. Branch, Geo. Howard, A. Porter Rose, J. B. Driskell, A. J. Sigler, C. H. Knott, S. E. Vaden, Wm. Davis, Dr. J. M. Fleming.

THE APPROACHES TO SAVANNAH.

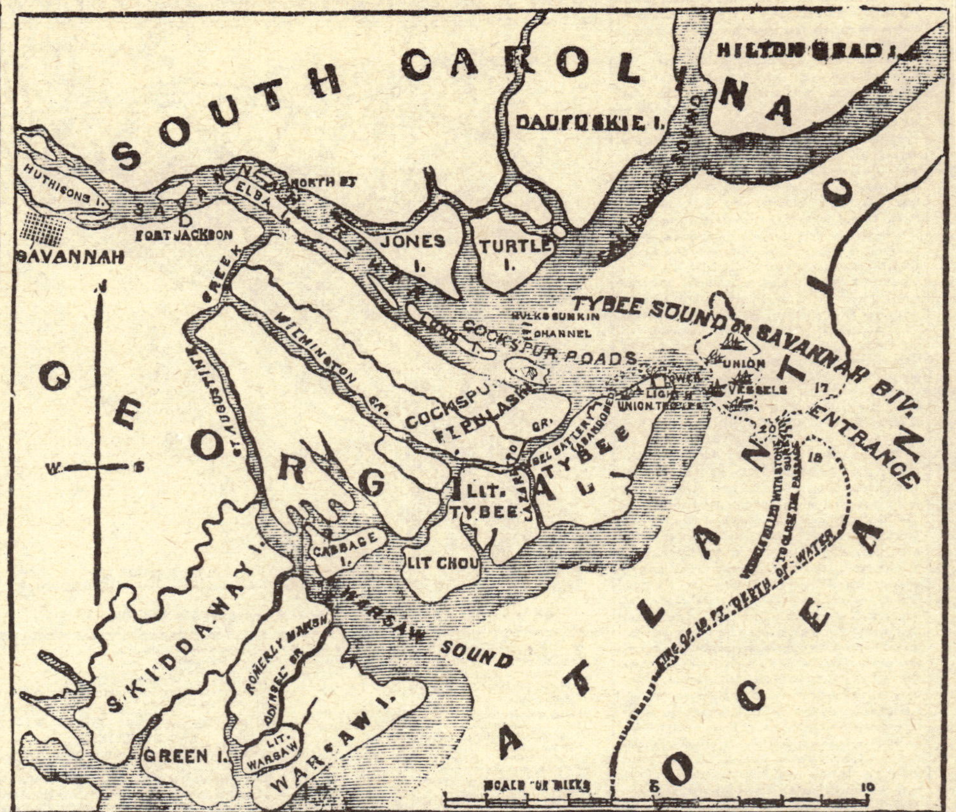

BALLOON RECONNOISSANCE ON THE LOWER POTOMAC.

Yesterday, a protracted balloon reconnoissance was made from the river opposite Gen. HOOKER's headquarters. While the balloon was up, the rebel batteries fired at it with shell, many of which burst directly under it, though none within less than 200 feet. As the shells exploded the occupant of the car defiantly waved the American flag.

CONDITION OF THE REBEL FORCES.

A deserter from the rebel forces on the Lower Potomac crossed to Gen. HOOKER's Division yesterday. He represents that the rebel army between the river batteries and Manassas Junction numbers twenty-five or thirty thousand, is well armed, and clothed and supplied with provisions, and have abundant artillery. The soldiers have not been paid since the beginning of the war, and on this account are dissatisfied. A great desire to desert is manifested, many of the men being Unionists impressed into service.

IMPORTANT GENERAL ORDER.

General Orders No. 104 invites the attention of officers to the following, in addition to the orders of the Secretary of War, embraced in the regulations for the recruiting service:

First—The large number of enlisted men discharged on "certificates of disability" has attracted the notice of the General-in-Chief, and as it is an especial duty to render the rank and file of the army as efficient as possible, the attention of Superintendents and other officers concerned either with the enlistment of men, or their discharge on account of disability, is directed to the judicious discharge of their respective duties. Evidence is abundant, as attested by the records of the Adjutant-General's Office, that many men have been enlisted who were "unfit for service," prior to or at the date of their enlistment. It should be borne in mind that the law provides for the enlistment of "effective and able-bodied men," and if any officer shall enlist any person contrary to the true intent and meaning of the law, it is further provided, for every offence, "he shall forfeit and pay the amount of the bounty and clothing which the person so recruited may have received from the public, to be deducted out of the pay and emoluments of such officer." With this object in view paragraphs 980 and 981 of the Revised Regulations must be strictly complied with. A sense of duty will cause an enforcement of the laws and regulations governing the service, and these must be the guidance of the officers obtaining recruits. Officers cannot be too circumspect in the discharge of their duties, and they are called upon to comply strictly with all regulations applicable to the subject.

Second—As to minors every precaution should be taken to prevent their enlistment, except as provided by the regulations. A true record of the age is of great value. In a majority of cases the recruiting officer may be justified in recording the age as stated by the person offering to enlist, yet many cases occur in which he should rely more upon his own judgment and less on the recruit's affirmation, in ascertaining his probable, if not his actual age, in every doubtful case. Therefore, as to the minority or over age of the man, it become the duty of the officer to judge for himself to a certain extent, and not, in any case, to accept a recruit who under anxiety to enlist manifestly misstates his age.

Third—It will be observed the regulations at this time contain no direct prohibition to enlist married men in the regimental service. This must be governed by the want of laundresses for companies, and in the general service by the Superintendents.

Fourth—It is enjoined upon all Superintendents and other officers, commissioned and non-commissioned, to conduct the service with diligence, unceasing personal attention and economy.

[Official] By command of Major-Gen. McCLELLAN.

L. THOMAS, Adjutant-General.
THOS. M. VINCENT, Assistant Adjutant-General.

BEN. WOOD IN THE HOUSE.

Hon. BEN. WOOD took his seat in the House to-day.

THE COURT-MARTIAL OF KERRIGAN.

The Court-martial in the case of Col. KERRIGAN met to-day, on the corner of Pennsylvania-avenue and Seventeenth-street. Gen. CASEY presides, and Col. MCCORL is Judge-Advocate. EDMUND L. HEARNE, of New-York, appeared in behalf of the prisoner. The charges are five in number, and they and the specifications, when formal verbiage is taken from them, are as follows:

FIRST CHARGE—Reputed neglect of duty. *Specification*—That from June 28 to Oct. 18, in New-York and Virginia, he failed and neglected to give to his officers and men practical or theoretical instructions in the tactics and in the school of the battalion and company.

SECOND CHARGE.—Conduct to the prejudice of good order and military discipline. *First Specification*—That at Hall's Hill, in Virginia, on the 14th and 15th of October, he suffereed and permitted privates and non-commissioned officers of his regiment to engage in

ENTRANCE TO CHARLESTON HARBOR.

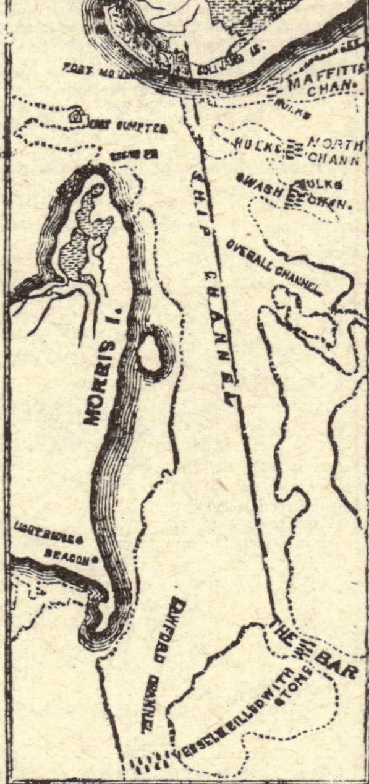

disorderly language, and to make noisy disturbances without any attempt to suppress the same. *Second Specification*—That on the 15th of October, in camp at Hall's Hill, upon inspection and review, he permitted many privates to appear on parade in a state of unseemly disarray and filth, their pantaloons unbuttoned and their underclothes and persons exposed.—*Third Specification*—Thot he restored to duty without trial, on the 4th of September, one PATRICK GAFFNEY, a deserter from Company I. *Fourth Specification*—That he allowed GAFFNEY, a deserter from the 25th of July, who remained absent till the 4th of September, and when restored to duty without trial, to be paid for the intervening period.

THIRD CHARGE—Violation of the forty-fourth article of war. *Specification*—That being commanded by Brig.-Gen. MARTINDALE, his superior officer, to assemble with the commissioned officers of his regiment, for the purpose of examination and instruction by Gen. MARTINDALE, did, after being present at the rendezvous on the 16th of October, absent himself, without permission, and without being dismissed or relieved.

FOURTH CHARGE—Disobedience of orders in violating the ninth article of war. *Specification*—That being commanded by Gen. MARTINDALE, his superior officer, in the execution of his office, to return to his (KERRIGAN's) quarters for instruction and examination, from which he had absented himself as previously stated, did wilfully refuse to obey.

FIFTH CHARGE.—Lying out of camp without leave of his superior officer. *Specification*—That on the night of Oct. 14, he did absent himself and lie out of camp at Hall's Hill, without the knowledge of his commanding officer.

SIXTH CHARGE—Drunkenness on duty. *Specification*—That he was drunk on duty on the 27th of September, while his regiment was moving from the camp on Morton's farm to Hall's Hill.

To all of these Col. KERRIGAN entered a plea of Not Guilty, except as to that which charges him with lying out of camp at night, to which he pleads guilty. The examination of witnesses will commence to-morrow morning at 10 o'clock.

THE CASE OF GEN. PATTERSON.

Gen. PATTERSON called for a Court of Inquiry nearly a month ago, but owing to the absence of the Secretary of War, at the time, no action was taken. Recently he has renewed his demand, and the subject is now under consideration. As an inquiry would affect Gen. SCOTT, as well as PATTERSON, the propriety of granting it, during the absence of the former, may well be doubted.

A GREAT NUMBER OF VESSELS WANTED.

During the coming few weeks the Navy will require a large number of vessels, now fitting out, and it is earnestly hoped that fishermen and others, returning from summer cruises, will enlist in this branch of the Government service. Several thousand will be needed.

COL. MULLIGAN ARRIVED.

Col. MULLIGAN arrived here to-day. His business is supposed to be connected with the disaster at Lexington.

CHARLESTON AND SAVANNAH.

The Points of Operation of the Stone Fleet.

The Secretary of the Navy, in his report published in this journal on Wednesday last, says that the southward bound stone fleet is intended to obstruct the channels of *Charleston* Harbor and the *Savannah* River; and this, says he, "if effectually done, will prove the most satisfactory and economical method of interdicting commerce at these places." We give herewith a view of the points referred to, and their water approaches, from which a clear idea of the "rat-holes" to be stopped up can be obtained. One detachment of the fleet, consisting of twenty-five stone-laden old whalers, sailed four weeks ago, and it is supposed, has by this time operated on the Savannah River. The next detachment, consisting of twenty vessels of the same kind, is now leaving from different points, and is understood to be intended for the approaches to Charleston. The names and tonnage of the vessels, which have been purchased by the Navy Department for the present expedition, are as follows:

Names.	Where Purchased.	Tons.
Ship Montezuma	New-London, Conn.	424
Ship America	New-London, Conn	418
Bark Edward	New-Bedford, Mass.	340
Bark Mechanic	Newport, Mass.	335
Bark Messenger	Salem	216
Ship India	New-Bedford	366
Ship Newburyport	Gloucester	341
Ship Wm. Lee	Newport	311
Ship Emerald	Sag Harbor, N. Y.	518
Ship New-England	New-London, Conn	375
Bark Dove	Lew-London, Conn	151
Ship Valparaiso	New-Bedford	402
Bark Noble	Sag Harbor	274
Ship Majestic	New-Bedford	297
Brig Stephen Young	Boston	199
Ship Bogota	New-York	300
Bark Peri	Portland, Me	265
Bark Jubilee	Portland, Me	233
Ship Margaret Scott	New-Bedford	330
Bark Marcia	Portland	343
Total, 20 vessels, of		6,438

These vessels are laden with upwards of six thousand tons of stone. The vessels themselves, and the mode of sinking them, have been already described; so that anything in regard to these at present is unnecessary.

Seven of these craft sailed from New Bedford yesterday. Six will sail from Boston to-day, and five from New London to-morrow. Two will leave New-York in time to rendezvous and report to the officer commanding the blockading squadron off Port Royal entrance.

At *Savannah*, as will be seen by the map, the stone ships will be sunk nearly opposite Tybee Island, at a point where the channel converges from two directions of approach. This will not, of course, interfere with the movements of our light draft gunboats. Opposite Cockspur Island the rebels themselves have sunk some old hulks in the channel, to prevent the approach of our men-of-war to Savannah; but if they imagine these alone would keep us from the city, should we desire to enter it, they cannot be very well acquainted with the various expedients in navigation which we may adopt. The ship channel at that point where our hulks are to be sunk varies from eighteen to twenty feet in depth; and it is believed that a perfectly effective blockade can be here established. It is only 250 yards across, and can be completely barred by half a dozen vessels. Some of the hulks will be sunk at other points north and south of that indicated in our map.

Vessels requiring fourteen feet of water can ordinarily go up to the wharves of Savannah, and larger vessels go to Five Fathom Hole, four miles below; but with our batteries on the different islands in the vicinity of Tybee Sound, and with the stone fleet in the channel, it will be hard work for even a rebel cock-boat to make its way up to the doomed city of Savannah without our permit.

In *Charleston* harbor the vessels will be sunk [see map] near the bar, a short distance below Morris Island, on the upper end of which, it will be remembered, the batteries were placed that first opened fire upon Fort Sumter. The outer harbor of Charleston, lying within the bar, extends from Sullivan's Island to the South Channel, below the lighthouse, a distance of six miles. This bar consists of successive ranges of sand banks, which stretch away before the entrance for several leagues; and, as these ranges consist in part of quicksand, they are liable, from storms and undercurrents, to occasional change of locality. Between these successive ranges of sand are formed several channels of varying depths of water; and it is these channels that the great stone fleet will block up.

Until recently the channels in use were but three—the Ship channel, with 16 feet water at ebb; the Overall channel, with 14; and Lawford's, or the South channel, with but 10 feet. Since the blockading fleet appeared off the harbor, several other safer channels, skirting along near Sullivan's Island, have been used by the rebels—Swash channel, Maffit's channel, etc. Of these, the principal one is Maffit's channel, which was discovered about two years ago, and named after its discoverer, an officer of the Coast Survey. By this channel, vessels pass out and in close to the shores of Sullivan's Island; it is more free from shoals, is of bolder cut, and more direct passage than any of the others. Before secession times, great efforts were being made to increase the depth and facility of this channel; and a dredge steamer of great power, worked by suction, was constantly employed removing sand and mud from its bed. They might as well have saved their dredging, for henceforth Maffit's channel, as well as the others, will be rendered impassable.

The best of these channels may, at high water, give a depth of 18 or 20 feet. The average rise of the tide upon the coast is about 7 feet. The approach to the coast is easy enough, and the shoaling gradual. The Ship channel is about 11½ miles from the city of Charleston, while that of Maffit is only about 7. It was by Maffit's channel that the several vessels which have lately violated the blockade, effected their ingress and egress.

It is the duty of the stone fleet to block up each and every one of these "rat-holes" leading into that breeding-nest of treason, Charleston. When once the hulks are sunk, the shifting sands of the vicinity will probably wash in and settle in around them, until there is formed an impassable and almost irremovable barrier to the commercial greatness of which the Charlestonians have so often had visions.

This stone fleet will save JEFF. DAVIS a good deal of very painful work. It will be remembered that in his late message he said that he was hard at work collecting statistics of all the vessels which succeeded in running the blockade, to transmit to those foreign Powers that were willing to give him a hearing. When the stone-fleet gets to its destination, at the bottom of these harbors, there will be two ports—and those two as important as any in his dominions—from which JEFF. will be saved the tedious labor of collecting the statistics of the violation of the blockade. Now that he will have leisure, and considering the gloomy aspect of his affairs, it would be well for him to employ this spare time in the recitation of his *paternosters*.

FIGHTING ON THE UPPER POTOMAC

Attack of the Rebels on the National Pickets at Dam No. 5.

SUCCESSFUL RESISTANCE OF OUR TROOPS

THE REBELS FORCED TO ABANDON A BATTERY

Their Loss Fifteen or Twenty Killed, and Many Wounded.

FREDERICK, Md., Monday, Dec. 9.

Col. LEONARD, of the Thirteenth Massachusetts Regiment, arrived here this morning from Williamsport, with important advices from the Upper Potomac.

On Saturday afternoon, a rebel force, consisting of a battery of six pieces, and about 400 infantry and 200 cavalry, made their appearance at Dam No. 5, on the Virginia side, and commenced throwing shells and shot at the Dam and houses on the Maryland shore, burning a barn and riddling all the houses within range, continuing the fire until dusk.

The only Union forces there to oppose the enemy were a company of the Massachusetts Thirteenth, on picket duty, and an unarmed Illinois regiment. As the Massachusetts company was armed with smooth-bore muskets, their fire was not effective at that distance.

Early on Sunday morning, they resumed the fire with artillery and small arms, and, emboldened by the slight resistance met with on Saturday, came down to the very brink of the river, and exposed themselves without fear.

During the night Col. LEONARD dispatched a canal boat from Williamsport, and another company of his regiment, armed with Enfield rifles, who were concealed as skirmishers along the Maryland shore. On the renewal of the attack the riflemen opened fire from their concealment, and in a short time the rebel artillerists were compelled to abandon their battery in hot haste, their infantry and cavalry leaving the ground about the same time.

The rebel loss is believed to be about 15 or 20 killed, and many wounded.

For the want of a sufficient infantry force, and a battery to protect our movements, Col. LEONARD was compelled to let the rebel guns remain in position, and, after nightfall, the rebels returned and took them off. The rebel battery consisted of three Parrott 10-pounders, one 12-pounder, carrying the Sawyer shell, and two smooth-bore 6-pounders. Some of their infantry were armed with improved long-range rifles.

This force came from Bath. The cavalry and infantry came by country roads, but the battery came by railroad from Martinsburg. They are probably *en route* to Winchester or Harper's Ferry, and stopped at that point to destroy and thus impede canal transportation.

This morning the rebels were in considerable force, and kept up a scattering fire with rifles upon our men whenever visible. One Union soldier was struck twice and severely wounded, but this is the only casualty on our side during the whole affair.

At 1 o'clock last night a portion of the First Brigade here was put in readiness to start to Williamsport, but at a later hour the order was countermanded.

This noon a battery of Parrott guns was forwarded to Harper's Ferry by train, to be in readiness should the rebels again wish to test their skill in projectiles.

ANOTHER ORDER BY GEN. HALLECK.

ST. LOUIS, Monday, Dec. 9.

Gen. HALLECK has issued orders, stating that the Mayor of the City will require all municipal officers immediately to subscribe to the oath of allegiance prescribed by the State Convention in October last, and directs the Provost-Marshal to arrest all State officers who have failed to subscribe to such oath within the time fixed by the Convention, and attempt to exercise civil authority in violation of the ordinance.

LOCAL MILITARY MOVEMENTS.

INSPECTION OF THE FOURTH AND FIFTH REGIMENTS, IRISH BRIGADE.

Yesterday, at Fort Schuyler, the Fourth and Fifth Regiments of the Irish Brigade were inspected by Maj. ALLCOCK, aid-de-camp to Gen. YATES. The different companies were well represented. Great credit is due to Acting Brig.-Gen. MEAGHER for his untiring exertions in bringing the brigade to its present effective strength. Maj. ALLCOCK complimented the officers on the healthy and soldierly appearance of the men, and requested the officers to get their lady friends to supply their men with needle-cases, as those articles were the most useful *souvenirs* they could have. On Thursday a steamer will convey the men to Amboy on their way to Springfield, nine miles below Alexandria, where the other regiments of the brigade are stationed. All members of the brigade are requested to report themselves at Fort Schuyler to-morrow morning; if they do not they will be left behind.

THE WARREN RIFLES.

This regiment was inspected on Saturday last at the Red House, Harlem, by Major ALLCOCK. At present the Warren Rifles number five hundred and sixty-one men, the majority of whom were present. The men presented a very creditable appearance, especially when it is taken into consideration that it is not yet quite seven weeks since the first man was mustered into the service of the United States. It is stated that the regiment will be attached to Gen. BURNSIDE's Division.

The New-York Times.

NEW-YORK, WEDNESDAY, DECEMBER 11, 1861.

NEWS FROM WASHINGTON.

Important Dispatches Received from Our Ministers in Europe.

General Sympathy for the National Government.

Gradual Approach of the Enemy Toward our Lines.

Their Strength Estimated at only One Hundred Thousand.

IMPORTANT NEWS FROM NORTH CAROLINA.

The Unionists of that State Acting in Concert with those of Eastern Tennessee.

Charges of Treason Preferred Against Col. Kerrigan.

THE PROCEEDINGS OF CONGRESS.

A Proposition to Divide the Session.

OUR SPECIAL WASHINGTON DISPATCHES.

WASHINGTON, Tuesday, Dec. 10.

IMPORTANT DISPATCHES FROM EUROPE.

Mr. GOODRICH, special bearer of important dispatches from our Ministers in Europe, arrived here this morning, and laid the documents before the Secretary of State. Mr. GOODRICH has been trave'ling for some time in Europe, and has had frequent interviews with the leading men throughout that country. The sympathy is almost universal with the Federal Government, and against the rebels.

THE NATIONAL LOAN.

Messrs. JOHN A. STEVENS, HENRY VAIL and JAS. GALLATIN, a Committee from the bankers of New-York, are here looking after the interests of the capitalists in connection with the National Loan.

JOINT INTERVENTION IN MEXICO DECLINED.

Our Government has replied to the invitation of England, France and Spain to take part in the expedition against Mexico, declining to have anything to do with it.

THE SUPPOSED STRENGTH OF THE REBELS.

It is believed, from all that can be gathered, that the rebel force in front of our lines numbers at least one hundred thousand men.

THE UNIONISTS OF NORTH CAROLINA.

A letter from a citizen in the western part of North Carolina to a friend in Washington has passed the rebel lines, and was to-night placed in the hands of Gen. McCLELLAN. It brings the clearest confirmation yet received that there is a large and determined organization of Unionists in that State. They are in constant communication with the Unionists in East Tennessee, and await only the dawn of hope for a general rising. They expect a reinforcement of BROWNLOW by the National forces, and will accept that movement as the signal for their own action.

A MEETING OF COMMITTEE CHAIRMEN.

There was a meeting of the Chairmen of the Business Committees of the House this evening, the principle object of which appears to have been to consider the expediency of having a long or a short term at the present session. As the questions that are to come before the present Congress are more momentous than any that ever yet came up before a deliberative body, the majority of those present were not disposed to favor limiting any debate that did not overstretch reasonable bounds, or to adopting any line of policy calculated to shut out a ray of light upon any subject of importance under consideration.

A PAMPHLET ON THE WAR.

A pamphlet was laid on the desks of several Senators and members to-day, written by CHARLES ELLET, Civil Engineer, in which the author discusses at some length the management of the present war, and animadverts pretty severely upon Gen. McCLELLAN'S policy of conducting affairs so far. Its appearance has caused much comment in political circles.

REPORTER OF THE SUPREME COURT.

Among the candidates for the office of Reporter to the Supreme Court are J. M. CARLISLE, EDWARD M. STANTON, R. H. GILLETT and PHILIP R. FENDALL, all residents of Washington.

THE BUTLER AND LEHMAN CONTESTED ELECTION

The House Committee on Elections will report on the contested case of JOHN M. BUTLER and Mr. LEHMAN on Thursday next, the evidence and arguments having all been submitted.

SLAVERY IN THE DISTRICT OF COLUMBIA.

The bill introduced by Mr. HUTCHINS, of Ohio, yesterday, proposes unconditionally to abolish Slavery in the District of Columbia.

THE PRIVATEERS.

It is currently stated that the Military Committee of the House favor the treatment of the privateers captured by our vessels as prisoners of war.

SENATOR POLK, OF MISSOURI.

Hon. TRUSTEN POLK, of Missouri, is expected daily in Washington, to resume his seat in the United States Senate. He will be confronted by the following letter, written by him to one P. S. WILKES, just before the battle of Wilson's Creek. WILKES was editing a secession paper in Southwest Missouri. Nothing else will be needed to secure POLK'S expulsion as a traitor:

DEAR SIR: Above I send my check to you for the *Equal Rights Gazette*. It is all I can do, and I could not do even that much until now. You have heard of the difficulty that the *Bulletin* has fallen into. I hope to have it "ante up" there at the rate of $200. I hope the friends there have made arrangements which will insure the permanence of the paper. It has been and is doing good service. I have made a speech (yesterday) on the state of affairs, Southern rights, and the position of Missouri, present and future, which I will send you as soon as published, in pamphlet for distribution. In the meantime, I will send it to [illegible], and if the *Gazette* can stand the draft on its columns, and you approve of it, and think it will do good in forming correct puolic sentiments in Southwest Missouri, please have it published. Dissolution is now a fact; not only a fact accomplished, but thrice repeated. Everything there looks like inevitable and final dissolution. Will Missouri hesitate a moment to go with her Southern sisters? I hope not. Please let me hear from you. I would be glad to keep posted as to the condition of things in Southwest Missouri. I like Gov. JACKSON'S position. It looks like adherence to the "Jackson Resolutions." I am truly your friend,

TRUSTEN POLK.

P. S. WILKES, Esq., Springfield, Mo.

THE REBELS ADVANCING.

A dispatch was received at headquarters late last evening, stating that two regiments of infantry and one of cavalry, of rebels, had made their appearance in front of Gen. BLENKER'S Division. It was reported, also that a pretty large rebel force had taken possession of Springfield—a place which had been abandoned by them some time ago. The rebels have been advancing quietly in the direction of our lines for some days, in several directions, evidently with a view of ascertaining our position.

SHELLING REBELS ON THE LOWER POTOMAC.

The Secretary of the Navy to-day received the following letter from R. H. WYMAN, Lieutenant, commanding the Potomac flotilla, dated

UNITED STATES STEAMER HARRIET LANE, }
OFF MATAMORA CREEK, Monday, Dec. 9, 1861. }

SIR: I have the honor to report to you that this morning, at about 9½ o'clock, seeing the enemy's pickets, three camp wagons and a mounted officer coming down the road to the southward of Freestone Point, and halting at some buildings near the beach, directed the steamers *Jacob Bell* and *Anacosta* to shell the buildings. I stood in with this vessel as far as the draft of water would admit to protect them in the event of the enemy's bringing a field battery to Freestone Point.

After shelling the buildings and hill, and driving back the pickets, Lieut.-Commanding McRAE landed with a few men, and fired four houses, which have since burned to the ground. They contained sutlers stores, flour, &c. As eighteen hours elapsed before the fire subsided, I judge that the quantity of stores must have been considerable. The enemy fired but a few musket-shot.

REBEL ARTILLERY PRACTICE.

The rebels fired yesterday from their battery opposite Budd's Ferry an eighty-four-pound shell, which passed over "Posey's House," where some of the Massachusetts officers are quartered, and buried itself in the field beyond.

All the small sloops and schooners that were below the blockade have succeeded in running up safely.

Our reporter, out near Falls Church, to-day, could hear distinctly the echo of the rebel artillery all day, practicing at Centreville.

Near Alexandria there could be heard, all the afternoon, heavy and steady firing down the Potomac, supposed to be near Freestone Point.

REVIEW AT BAILEY'S CROSS ROADS.

Eight regiments of Gen. McDOWELL'S Division were out on review to-day at Bailey's Cross Roads. They were practiced in division evolutions and firing.

THE TRIAL OF COL. KERRIGAN.

The trial of Col. KERRIGAN was proceeded with to-day. The detail for the Court is as follows: Brig.-Gen. SILAS CASEY, President; Brig.-Gen. L. P. GRAHAM, Brig.-Gen. I. A. PALMER, Brig.-Gen. JOHN G. PARKE, all of volunteer service; Col. FRANK WHEATON, Second Rhode Island Volunteers; Col. T. W. STOCKTON, Michigan Volunteers; Col. E. P. CHARMAN Eighth Pennsylvania Cavalry; Col. W. W. H. DAVIS. Hundred-and-Fourth Pennsylvania Volunteers; Col. J. W. ALLEN, Ninth New-Jersey Volunteers; Col. JOHN BEARDSLEY, Ninth New-York Cavalry; Col. J. B. HOWELL, Eighty-fifth Pennsylvania Volunteers. First Lieut. J. A. McCOOL, Third Infantry, Judge Advocate.

General Order No. 174 was received from Gen. McCLELLAN, directing the Court to sit without regard to hours.

Judge HEARNE, of New-York, appeared as counsel for Col. KERRIGAN, and leave was granted by the Court for accused to have the assistance of Hon. REVERDY JOHNSON.

Three new charges and specifications were served on Col. KERRIGAN at the City Prison last night, to the following effect:

Charge Seventh and Specification.—Charges that said JAS. E. KERRIGAN, Colonel of the Twenty-Fifth New-York Volunteers, did on the 27th day of August, 1861, shamefully abandon his post, which he had been commanded to defend and hold at Munson's Hill, Fairfax Co., Va.

Charge Eighth and Specification—Charges accused with withdrawing the pickets of his regiment without orders from their position on the outposts of the camp at Munson's Hill, when the enemy was advancing there on the 27th of August.

Charge Ninth and Specification—Charges accused with leaving his camp, and visiting and communicating with the enemy on the 25th of July, and on divers other days and times between the 25th of July and the 1st of October.

On the reading of these additional charges, the accused asked for a week's delay to prepare his defense. The Court refused to grant any time at all, at present, but concluded to proceed with the trial on the original charges, promising to grant all necessary time when the new charges were taken up.

Witnesses Major H. L. SAVAGE, Capt. A. H. FERGUSON, THOMAS P. ABBOTT and Gen. JOHN H. MARTINDALE were examined, and all testified to gross neglect of his duties by Col. KERRIGAN.

TRIAL OF SURGEON-GEN. FINLAY.

A General Court-martial met this morning, for the trial of Surgeon-Gen. FINLAY, on charges preferred by Dr. TRIPLER. The charges were not read to-day, and the Court adjourned until Thursday. The charges originated, it is alleged, as follows: On being ordered to Philadelphia, instead of reporting to his superior, Dr. FINLAY, Dr. TRIPLER reported to the Sanitary Commission, thereby showing great discourtesy to his superior officer. When taxed with this impropriety he replied offensively, whereupon Dr. FINLAY requested him to leave his office, and for this charges have been preferred against him for conduct unbecoming an officer.

THE SURRENDERED REGULARS.

The regular troops surrendered to the rebels in New-Mexico by Maj. LYNDE, and released on parole, consisting of one company of the Third Cavalry and five companies of the Seventh Infantry, are to be stationed on the Northern frontier, and will probably garrison the posts of Detroit, Fort Niagara, Fort Ontario, Sackett's Harbor and Rouse's Point. The duties required of them are such as they can perform without violating their paroles.

The posts mentioned have not been occupied by troops for several years past, and are much out of repair. Col. C. A. WAITE, of the First Infantry, is assigned to the command of a district embracing the above named posts.

A FUGITIVE.

Yesterday, Mrs. ANDERSON, of Maryland, a daughter of Mr. MINOR, who was taken prisoner at his residence, near Falls Church, and was released a few weeks ago and sent to Norfolk, applied at the jail for a slave belonging to her father, and who has been confined since last August, he having been arrested after his escape from Virginia. She pretended that the slave belonged in Maryland, but the facts having been ascertained, her request was refused.

EXCHANGES.

Among other proposals for an exchange of prisoners, the rebel authorities offer to exchange Capt. RICKETTS, of the Regular Artillery, who was captured at Bull Run, for a Mr. DELISLE.

Messrs. O'GORMAN, DALY and SAVAGE had interview to-day with the President, the Attorney-General and Gen. McCLELLAN on the subject of arranging the exchange of prisoners. They all acquiesce in the necessity of the adoption of some plan which should bring about this object.

PROMOTED.

Capt. FRANCIS G. YOUNG, of New-York, late Brigade Quartermaster of Col. BAKER'S Brigade, has been appointed an Assistant Quartermaster in the United States Army. Capt. YOUNG'S claims were pressed by the most influential citizens of New-York and New-England, and the appointment is regarded as most judicious.

GEORGE H. LITTS has been promoted to First Lieutenant of Company B, Major BARKER'S McClellan Dragoons, and P. PURLEY PAGE elected Second Lieutenant of the same company.

CAPT. BOYD MADE PROVOST-MARSHAL.

Capt. BOYD, of the Lincoln Cavalry, who made the successful reconnoissance to Fairfax Court House, a few days ago, and for which he was complimented by Gen. McCLELLAN, has been detached from his regiment and now performs the duty of Provost-Marshal for the Division under Gen. FRANKLIN. His company performs patrol duty.

APPOINTMENTS.

A number of appointments, made during the recess of Congress, have been sent to the Senate for confirmation.

PENSIONS.

The following pensions were granted on Saturday: JOHN IRWIN, private, Co. E, First Regiment United States Artillery, who was burned and maimed by the bursting of a gun at Fort Sumter, during the bombardment; total disability; $8 per month.

B. WASHBURN, private, Co. E, Second Regiment Maine Volunteers, injured at Bull Run; total disability; $8 per month.

WASHINGTON ELLIS, Corporal, Co. E, Fifth Regiment Maine Volunteers, injured at Bull Run; half disability; $4 per month.

JAMES BEAVER, private in Captain BLACKMORE'S Company, First Regiment Tennessee Militia, War of 1812; total disability; $6 per month.

SUSAN DEAN, (widow of WILLIAM J. DEAN, private, Co. A, Second Regiment Maine Volunteers, killed at Bull Run,) $5 50 per month.

A MEETING OF SUTLERS.

There was a meeting of sutlers here this evening, for the purpose of organizing an opposition to Senator WILSON'S bill for the abolition of sutlers. There were about forty persons present. Nothing was done beyond making arrangements to procure signatures to a remonstrance against the passage of such a law.

PLATES FOR VESSELS OF WAR.

The Navy Department invites proposals for furnishing, fitting, and securing to vessels of war iron plates of 33 inches thickness, and 15½ feet in length, to have planed edges and countersunk holes, to be bent to the shape of the vessel from stem to stern, and fastened to the timbers with conical-headed bolts of 1½ inches in diameter. It is understood that the Department designs to thus clothe vessels of war with the least possible delay.

THE CAMPAIGN IN MARYLAND.

On Saturday Mr. SEWARD dined with Gen. DIX in Baltimore. He had a protracted consultation with him in reference to the campaign about Baltimore.

THE LATE MINISTER TO NEW-GRANADA.

Hon. GEORGE W. JONES, late Minister to New-Granada, has arrived in the city. He states that both parties in that Republic sympathize with the North in the present struggle.

THE CLAIMS AGAINST NEW-GRANADA.

Judge UPHAM, the umpire under the Claims Convention with New-Granada, has arrived here, under a call from the Commissioners, and is considering the point submitted to him by them in regard to the liability of New-Granada to make provision for the settlement of claims contemplated by that treaty.

RETIRED UPON FURLOUGH PAY.

Commanders E. R. THOMPSON and OVERTON H. CARR, and Lieut. JAMES A. DOYLE, United States Navy, have, upon recommendation of the Board, now in session in New-York, been retired upon furlough pay.

DISMISSAL FROM THE NAVY.

Commander F. A. NEVILLE, a native of Virginia, late of the receiving ship *Ohio*, has been dismissed from the navy.

SECRETARY CHASE'S SYSTEM OF FINANCE.

A well-known gentleman of financial ability has prepared and will publish, this week, a pamphlet explanatory of the Secretary's proposed system of national finance.

THE WAY TO SEND LETTERS.

The following is an extract from a recently-intercepted Southern letter:

"I suggest that you send your letters through Hon. JAMES M. MASON, at London. In this way they will be sure to reach their destination."

URGED FOR A BRIGADIERSHIP.

Hon. C. B. CALVERT, of Maryland, and Hon. R. H. DUELL, of New-York, waited upon the President yesterday, urging the appointment of Col. JOHN C. ROBINSON as a Brigadier-General. The latter commanded at Fort McHenry, on the 19th of April, and now commands a Brigade at Annapolis Junction.

FOUR DAYS OF BEAUTIFUL WEATHER.

We have had four days consecutively of the most charming and Spring-like weather, most suitable for operations in the field.

HAD HIS POCKET PICKED.

A. A. JOHNSEN, of Pittsburgh, had his pocket picked this afternoon, at the railroad dépôt, of about eight thousand dollars, in drafts and money. The drafts were upon J. J. CISCO, New-York, signed by Capt. H. JONES BROOKS, Quartermaster,—one for five thousand dollars, and one for nineteen hundred, and eight hundred dollars in Pittsburgh notes. It was taken from him just as he was leaving for New-York on the 5 o'clock train to-night.

FAILING TO MAKE CONNECTIONS.

The express train from New-York to Washington, in many instances, fail to make connections, owing to the trains being overloaded with recruits. To obviate future difficulty, Mr. CALFIELD, manager of the Government Railroads, has made arrangements for a through train from New-York every twenty-four hours for recruits, who will not be permitted to occupy the express train.

THE NEW MORGAN TENT

JOHN McCLANE, of New-York, has succeeded in introducing to the Government the new Morgan tent and orders have been given for manufacturing them.

MECHANICS AT THE WASHINGTON NAVY-YARD.

Eighteen hundred mechanics are employed at the Navy-yard, their monthly wages amounting to one hundred thousand dollars.

THE SANITARY COMMISSION ADJOURNED.

The Sanitary Commission adjourned on Saturday night until next January, unless sooner called together by the Executive Committee.

RECOGNIZED.

The President has recognized PEDRO PABLO [illegible] as Vice-Consul of the Republic of Chili for the port of New-York.

IMPORTANT NEWS FROM SONORA.

Some months since, the Church Party in the City of Mexico, anticipating the intervention of the European Powers to establish a monarchy in the country, took measures to establish the nucleus of a party in the distant States. In the State of Sonora, some five hundred Reactionists made a stand for the purpose of revolutionizing the State. A telegraphic dispatch dated San Francisco, Dec. 9, has been received in this city by a Mexican gentleman, stating that the Reactionary Party in Sonora had been thoroughly beaten and dispersed by the Liberal forces, and that order under the Constitutional Government is completely restored.

SENATORS ELECTED TO THE REBEL CONGRESS, ETC.

A copy of the New-Orleans *Delta*, of Nov. 24, which reached here to day, announces that WM. L. YANCEY and CLEMENT C. CLAY were elected Senators from Alabama to JEFF. DAVIS' Senate on the 21st ult.

The Houston *Telegraph* of the 16th announced that WIGFALL had been elected Senator from Texas, and that OLDHAM, WALL and HEMPHILL were candidates to fill the other vacancy.

In a letter from Austin, dated Nov. 14, the writer states that Gen. HEBERT is making formidable preparations for defending the Texas coast.

JAS. L. BEAL, a member of one of the Red River regiments in the rebel army, had been hung as a spy.

The *Delta* announces that the messenger of the South Western Express Company would leave New-Orleans on the 27th of November, and that the proprietor has advantages which must make the South independent of the mail blockade.

THE PROCEEDINGS OF CONGRESS.

SENATE.

WASHINGTON, Tuesday, Dec. 10.

Messrs. FESSENDEN, of Maine, (Rep.,) and SUMNER, of Massachusetts, (Rep.,) presented petitions for the emancipation of slaves under the war power.

Mr. SUMNER presented a petition from FRANCIS A. TREADWAY, setting forth that he had some time ago presented a complaint to the Supreme Court against JEFF. DAVIS and others, but was told they were improper papers, after he had presented the complaint to the Magistrates' Court, but with no effect. Referred to the Committee on Judiciary.

Mr. FOOTE, of Vermont, (Rep.,) offered a resolution that WALDO P. JOHNSON, of Missouri, by sympathizing with and participating in rebellion against the United States, has been guilty of conduct incompatible with his duty as Senator of the United States, and that he be therefore expelled from the Senate of the United States, which was laid over.

Mr. WILSON, of Massachusetts, (Rep.,) introduced a joint resolution to provide for the payment of the Commissioners who were appointed to investigate the claims of the Western Military Department. Referred to the Committee on Finance.

Mr. HARLAN, of Iowa, (Rep.,) introduced a bill to authorize the President to acquire territory for the settlement of free persons of African descent. Referred to the Committee on Public Lands.

Mr. WILSON, of Massachusetts, (Rep.,) introduced a bill for the reorganization of the Medical Department of the Army, which was referred to the Committee on Military Affairs.

Mr. HALE, of New-Hampshire, (Rep.,) called up the resolution offered yesterday that the Committee on Judiciary be instructed to inquire into the expediency of abolishing the present judicial system of the United States, and establishing another in pursuance of the Constitution, and it was agreed to.

Mr. NESMITH, of Oregon, (Dem.,) introduced a bill to provide for the protection of overland emigrants to California and Oregon. Referred to the Committee on Territories.

Mr. HARRIS, of New-York, (Rep.,) introduced a bill relative to the sale of spirituous liquors in the District of Columbia. The bill is designed to render more operative the bill passed last Summer, and provides for trial by any Justice of the Peace. It was referred to the Committee on Judiciary.

Mr. CHANDLER, of Michigan, (Rep.,) announced the death of Hon. KINSLEY S. BINGHAM, late Senator from Michigan, and gave a brief sketch of the life of the late Senator. He went to Michigan in the early his tory of the State from New-York, and soon became a favorite of the people, being elected Governor of Michigan in 1854, again in 1856, and soon after to the Senate of the United States. In the Senate, the deceased was well known for the purity of his life, sound judgment and fidelity to the country.

Mr. CHANDLER offered the customary resolution, that the Senate go into mourning thirty days, and do now adjourn.

Mr. KING said he rose to pay a tribute to a wise and good statesman, and a true man. He was a genuine specimen of the citizens of free government, and was always devoted to his country with his whole heart.

Mr. CLARK spoke of the dead Senator as a true and conscientious man, whose true merit was known only to his friends, and was always true to his country, and firm and unwavering in the discharge of his duty.

Mr. SUMNER paid a tribute of worth and excellence to the deceased, saying that the Senator was always firm for right, and against oppression and wrong. He was one of those beautiful natures where God joined the mildest manners to the bravest mind. He was always opposed to Slavery, and any compromise with evil. Such a Senator is ill spared at such an hour as the present, though he still lives by example. Those who knew him here, and in the State that loved him, will cherish his memory with affectionate pride.

The resolution was agreed to, and the Senate adjourned.

HOUSE OF REPRESENTATIVES.

WASHINGTON, Tuesday, Dec. 10.

Mr. ROSCOE CONKLING, of New-York, (Rep.,) offered a resolution, which was adopted, requesting the Attorney-General to report his views as to the means of obtaining a retrocession of that part of Virginia formerly belonging to the District of Columbia.

Mr. POTTER, of Wisconsin, (Rep.,) from the Committee on Public Lands, reported a bill providing homesteads to actual settlers, and providing a bounty for soldiers in lieu of grants of public lands. He explained that the homestead feature of this bill was heretofore passed, but there is an addition that all soldiers, marines and seamen shall be entitled to it by the provisions of this act.

It also contains a section giving a bounty of $30 to the three months volunteers.

The further consideration of the bill was postponed till Wednesday week.

The House concurred in the resolution from the Senate for a Joint Committee to inquire into the conduct of the present war, with power to send for persons and papers.

Mr. PENDLETON, of Ohio, (Dem.,) moved that the memorial of Messrs. HOWARD, GATCHELL and DAVIS be referred back to the Committee on Judiciary, with instructions declaring that Congress alone has the power, under the Constitution, to suspend the privilege of the writ of *habeas corpus*; that the exercise of that power by another Department of the Government is a usurpation, and dangerous to public liberty; that the persons above named be delivered to the Marshal to the end that they may be indicted, with the right of a speedy trial, if there be probable cause for such proceeding.

Mr. PENDLETON said:

Mr. SPEAKER: These memorialists are members of the Board of Police of the City of Baltimore. On the 1st day of July last, at the dead hour of night, they were arrested and conveyed to Fort McHenry, by a detachment of United States soldiers under Gen. BANKS. They were in the performance of the duty assigned to [illegible] of their State. The peace of the city was then unbroken. The [illegible] Courts were in full operation within her limits. Judges, Marshal and the District-Attorney were in the exercise of their accustomed functions. The process of the Courts, if I am correctly informed, had not been interfered with, except in one memorable instance, and then by the authority of the President of the United States himself. These gentlemen were arrested without a warrant. They have been detained without an indictment. They are deprived of their liberty without process of law. They have not been confronted with their accusers. They are not informed of the nature of the accusation against them. They have been denied the right to a speedy and public trial by an impartial jury. The President of the United States, in his Message to this House, in response to a resolution of it, has declined to furnish the grounds for their arrest. On the very same day when he did so, while their petition for redress of a great grievance was pending before the House, the President had them conveyed out of the district and State in which they had been arrested and where, if at all, they had committed the crime, first to Fort Lafayette and then to Fort Warren. They are arbitrarily held by military power. They are entirely helpless. They have presented their memorial to Congress, asking that Congress may examine their case or that it may be remitted to the judicial tribunal, to be legally heard and determined, and my colleagues on the Judiciary Committee can find no more fitting response to a reasonable request like this than that this respectful petition shall lie unanswered on this table. The writ of *habeas corpus* was invented for the purpose of meeting the exigencies of just such a case as this. It commands that the body of a prisoner shall be produced, that the cause of his commitment may be inquired into, and that he may be discharged if he is illegally held, or remanded if he is held by competent authority on a charge of crime. These gentlemen would have been glad to avail themselves of this writ, which the President commanded his General to suspend, and to hold them at his own sole will and pleasure. The President, in his message at the extra session of Congress, gave us his reason for his action in the matter. He says: "I have authorized that the writ of *habeas corpus* be suspended," and before he did so he talked considerably of his right and the propriety of doing so. The privilege conferred by the *habeas corpus* is to institute and command an inquiry as to whether a person is held by competent authority under a charge of crime. If a person is so held he is remanded, and if he is not he is discharged. That provision of the *habeas corpus* act has never been invaded by the executive power till now. Sir, the object of this suspension and the effect also of it is to prevent inquiries into the legitimateness of the imprisonment under military power. The object of this evasion of the great charter of liberty is to enable military officers, or others who have like power, to arrest and imprison men though they have committed no crime against the laws of the land; and to punish them, not as the law prescribes, but in whatever way those who have the power may ordain. If I rightly construe the Message of the President, he claims authority to seize, to hold and detain all persons not engaged in the land and naval forces—not men engaged in enterprises against the Government, but all persons whom he may suspect, and to imprison them without regard to the provisions or process of law. The President further claims the authority of the Constitution of which it is a complete violation, to arrest whoever in his judgment he may think proper. The President says his authority is derived by implication, and because, I suppose, he deems it inconvenient to have the right to suspend the writ of *habeas corpus* vested in Congress alone. Now, the only clause which refers to the subject is one which provides that the writ of *habeas corpus* shall never be suspended except in case of rebellion or invasion, or under circumstances when the public safety demands it. This is undoubtedly the only implication that can be derived authorizing the suspension of the writ of *habeas corpus*. Who shall suspend it? That is the question. It is not vested in the Executive exclusively, nor in Congress exclusively, but in all the departments of the Government. I grant that under the arbitrary rule of ELIZABETH, of England, and during the early part of the reign of CHARLES the First, it was exercised by these monarchs, but CHARLES was compelled as the price of his throne to assent to the Bill of Rights, by which he bound himself never to imprison a man without due process of law. CHARLES did not stand by his interpretation of the ancient constitution, and after ten years of struggle with his people, he lost his throne and his life as the penalty of his infraction of it. His successor tried all means and every kind of scheme to retain this arbitrary power, which was at last swept away forever by the great charter. We are told by the eminent historian, MACAULAY, that CHARLES II. sought to repeal the *habeas corpus* act, for that he hated it as only tyrants can hate whatever stands between them and their own despotic wills. And this *habeas corpus* act was the most stringent curb ever imposed by a Legislature on tyranny. When WILLIAM and MARY came to the throne they declared that the Crown did not possess the power of suspending the writ of *habeas corpus*, and from that hour to this, one hundred years before the adoption of the Constitution of the United States, England had no monarch during all her foreign wars and intestine troubles, wayward and wicked enough though some of them were, who dared to suspend the writ of *habeas corpus*, or who ever claimed that they had the power to imprison a citizen without the process of law. All history to which I have had access confirms this view of the case. HUME and MACAULAY claim this right as the principal in the great structure of the English Constitution. But here, according to this novel theory of government, the President may suspend the Constitution and the laws of the United States made under it. He may, as it is claimed, do all this, supersede them all, disregarding the limitation enjoined for the exercise of his prerogatives. He may abolish all the laws of the land, and substitute in their place his own will. He may abolish the whole system of Government built up and bequeathed to us by our Revolutionary fathers, and he may build up for himself a new and entirely different system. All this he may do, it is claimed, rightfully, legitimately, and without interference. I hold this assumed position is untenable and indefensible; that there is no warrant for it in the Constitution, or in the principles which underlie the theory of our Government, nor in the genius of the American people, nor in the spirit of liberty which is the boast of our institutions. Such a proposition will destroy the law, as it is utterly inconsistent with the law. It will reduce this nation, if deliberately adopted as the theory of government, to the condition of Slavery; and I say that any nation that will willingly adopt it is lost to all sense of manly independence, is lost to the appreciation of its own dignity and national rights, and for them the yoke of the slave is the only fitting emblem. We are told, in defence of this theory, that it would not exist only in cases of rebellion against the Government. We are also told that it was not intended that the Constitution of the United States should be inoperative in times of civil war. Our fathers hoped that civil war might never befall us, but they knew human nature too well to expect that we should forever enjoy profound repose. They had freed themselves from the yoke of oppression, they had successfully conquered enemies without and Tories within, and then they formed a Constitutional Government, recognizing in it that honesty and good sense which marks the patriot. Is it to be supposed that they would adopt a Constitutional Government to be operative only in time of peace, and that that Constitution should be superseded whenever discord or war would present an opportunity to set it aside and substitute for it the will of military power? The Constitution gives to the several departments of the Government all the power ever intended to be used for any purpose. If the laws of the United States are too lenient, they may be made more stringent. If Judges are imbecile, let them be impeached. Let the whole machinery of Government be revised and improved, if you will; but whoever goes beyond that to support the Government, would destroy the Constitution under the pretence of preserving them. The Government has no right to break down the constitution to uphold itself. It never was intended for a moment that the Constitution under any circumstances should be superseded. The President holds office under the Constitution, you sit there under it, the Judges sit and pass judgment in virtue of the provisions of that instrument alone, and if you supercede it, neither you nor the Judges, nor the President himself, possesses any more power than the humblest man in the land. Supersede the Constitution! You might as well try to repeal all laws for the guidance of society, and let the nation go adrift to ruin at once. The only way to preserve the Government is to preserve the Constitution, to observe its limitation, and to obey its prohibitions. When the Constitution falls, then indeed the Government falls. This is not the way to preserve governments. Ambition makes its own opportunity, and under this system of superseding the Constitution in times of public calamity, the public mind will become degraded, the people on every fresh occasion for the exercise of this power will yield still a little more to those encroachments, till the public will be destroyed, the public intellect warped, the national character tarnished and the national life of liberty and independence overthrown. They will become the plaything of every tyrant, and each successive invasion of their rights will be tamely submitted to until all apppreciation of independence and rights and freedom is forever lost. It is vain to say that this is an idle dream—the realization of the fact is before us. Six months ago, when the *habeas corpus* act was first suspended in the case of MERRIMAN, who was held on a charge of treason, the public mind was intensely excited. Now what is the fact? Citizens are committed and imprisoned because in the public newspapers they dare criticise the acts of the Government. Newspapers have been suspended, and the whole power of the Government despotically exercised without a public murmur. We are told also that when this public danger shall have passed away the Constitution will be restored to its pristine vigor, and the people will be allowed to resume their accustomed liberty. When was this ever so? When were the invaded and restricted rights of a people ever restored to their exact position except by the sword? When was liberty once surrendered ever restored except by blood? For the willful surrender of their rights no nation ever resumed them only through the agonies of a revolution, and you cannot make a nation sensible of rights that in time of danger possesses no rights. You cannot increase and strengthen virtue, and courage, and patience in a people, by teaching them that in times of great public calamity and danger to the State, they must rely for their safety, not on their own virtue, and courage and constancy, but on the power and good will of their rulers. No free nation ought ever listen for a moment to the arguments of State necessity. The history of those people who have been so deceived is written in the wreck of free institutions. It is marked with wrongs, with high hopes destroyed, and noble aspirations violated and trampled upon. If we look over the pathway of desolation thus exposed to view, we may easily imagine that we see the spirit of American independence and American freedom hovering over this day, tearfully praying it too may not be added to the long list of victims immolated on the altar of State necessity. This argument of State necessity always proceeds from the Executive power. It is the voice which issues from the throne itself, and unless speedily answered, unless answered now, ere long comes the mandate to surrender to military power. An imperial throne rises on the ruins of an overthrown republic; oaths are violated, liberties swept away, rights trampled on, and a nation is prostrated in the dust. This is but the familiar picture which presents the dire effect of a people submitting to the plea of State necessity. We are further told that in times of great public danger the people ought to sustain the hands of their rulers by confiding in their integrity of motives and disinterestedness of action. Yes, sir, I would sustain them with the public confidence while they adhered to the provisions and principles of the Constitution; but I would paralyze them, sir, with distrust, whenever they commenced the work of usurpation. It was DEMOSTHENES, in his divine phillippic, who told the Athenians that the surest defence of a free people against tyranny was distrust. The Athenians did not heed his warning, and from that hour to this Grecian independence and Grecian liberty have been but a name. WILLIAM, Prince of Orange, wisely taught the same lesson to the Dutch when PHILIP of Spain asked their confidence in his Administration, and they wisely heeded the lesson, and the immortal glories which clustered for two hundred years around the Dutch Republic testifies to the truthfulness of the axiom. I, Sir, speak not in behalf of the memorialists—upright and honest men as they are, and unjustly deprived of their liberty, as I know them to be—I speak in behalf of the Constitution, I speak in behalf of the liberties of the nation, I speak in behalf of my constituents, I speak in behalf of myself, and in behalf of you, my colleagues on this floor. And I say here that the proposition that the President has the power to suspend the writ of the *habeas corpus*, arbitrarily and without reason, without regard to the principles and provisions and process of law, to detain the citizen of any portion of this country, is utterly and entirely indefensible. And I further say, that it becomes every member of this House, in virtue of his oath, taken here before the tribune of the people, to support and preserve the Constitution, and in virtue of the position we hold here to support the framework of the Government, and as representatives of the people, solemnly in the face of Heaven and of our responsibilities to protest against it.

Mr. BINGHAM, of Ohio, (Rep.,) replied, that all his colleague had just said, or could say, had been fully and satisfactorily answered by the argument of the Attorney-General heretofore submitted. Notwithstanding the ability of his colleague, he (PENDLETON) had not been able to disguise the fact that the time has come when contemplated by the words of the Constitution for suspending the writ of *habeas corpus*. It was imputed that some power should do so. This conceded, then his colleague's argument destroyed itself. It implied a censure on this House in not discharging the duty long ago required by the oath which they had all taken to support the Constitution. His colleague's position was that Congress alone can suspend the writ, while conceding the time has come for its suspension. When rebellion lifted up its head over a large portion of this Republic, and essayed to shake down the pillars of the Constitution and drench the land in fraternal blood, it was no time to be splitting hairs as to whether Congress or the President should first exercise the power. Did his colleague contemplate a general jail delivery, or wish to confine his sympathies to the rebels and conspirators of the City of Baltimore? Had he no sympathy for those confined in the old Capitol? Why should they not also be discharged? Assuming his colleague's position to be right, the conclusion results, his colleague was derelict in duty in not moving a suspension of the writ in accordance with the oath he had taken to maintain, protect and defend the Constitution. The laws are to be executed, and not only executed by force, but by the sword against the powers of rebellion. It did not lie in the mouths of the memorialists to claim the benefit of the Constitution, every provision of which they had trampled under foot.

On motion of Mr. BINGHAM the whole subject was tabled—108 against 26.

A message was received from the Senate, announcing the death of Senator BINGHAM, of Michigan.

Eulogies were delivered by Messrs. BEAMAN, TROWBRIDGE and GRANGER, of Michigan, Mr. SEDGWICK, of New-York, and Mr. ASHLEY, of Ohio.

The usual resolutions of respect were passed, after which the House adjourned.

IMPORTANT FROM KENTUCKY.

Zollicoffer not Advanced North of the Cumberland.

LOUISVILLE, Tuesday, Dec. 10.

Gen. ZOLLICOFFER has not advanced North of the Cumberland River, as reported. Gen. SCHOEPF has withdrawn to Somerset, and there awaits reinforcements.

GARRETT DAVIS ELECTED U. S. SENATOR.

FRANKFORT, Ky., Tuesday, Dec. 10.

Hon. GARRETT DAVIS has been nominated for Senator in place of the traitor BRECKINRIDGE, by one majority over Hon. JAMES GUTHRIE.

FRANKFORT, Ky., Tuesday, Dec. 10—P. M.

GARRETT DAVIS was elected United States Senator for the remainder of JOHN C. BRECKINRIDGE'S term to-day, by a vote of 84 to 12.

THE NEW SENATOR FROM KENTUCKY.

GARRETT DAVIS, who has just been elected by the Legislature of Kentucky to fill the place in the United States Senate lately occupied by the expelled traitor BRECKINRIDGE, is one of the ablest public men in Kentucky. He is a native of that State, 58 years old, is a lawyer by profession and has acquired great distinction at the bar, and a very lucrative practice. He was a Representative in Congress from the Bourbon District in Kentucky for eight years, from 1839 to 1847. His residence is Paris, the county seat of Bourbon, one of the wealthiest "blue grass" counties in the State. When he left the public service, so high had he risen as a forensic debater and a skillful parliamentary tactician, that he was justly regarded as one of the very foremost of the Whig leaders. His health forced him out of congressional life. But ever since his retirement he has had a leading part in shaping the State policy, and no important movement has been made without consulting him.

He has taken a very active part in his own State against secession. When the secession troubles broke out, he went to Washington and procured from the President arms for the Home Guards, a military organization raised chiefly upon his suggestion, to counteract BUCKNER'S army of the secession militia. By this movement, he and the other Union patriots foiled BUCKNER completely in his efforts to "precipitate" Kentucky.

As a public speaker, DAVIS is cogent and forcible. He is a master of sarcasm when aroused against a foe; he is relentless and unsparing. His elocution is by no means graceful, nor is his voice agreeable, yet he possesses great power over the masses. They have faith in his honesty, and loved the bold, determined character of the man. He is very energetic in his manner, and has great breadth and strength of brain. The rebels hate him more bitterly and curse him more deeply than any other man in the region in which he lives—which is the best evidence of his devotion to the Union. Mr. DAVIS is short in stature, quick and active in motion, and his presence is not imposing. His want of physical is in marked contrast to his mental vigor.

There is no doubt that he will prove a worthy representative of the bold, unflinching Union sentiment of Kentucky. He was nominated for the Senate by but one majority over Hon. JAMES GUTHRIE, Secretary of the Treasury under PIERCE.

The New-York Times.

VOL. XI—NO. 3192. NEW-YORK, SATURDAY, DECEMBER 14, 1861. PRICE TWO CENTS.

IMPORTANT FROM THE WEST.

Preparations for a Great Battle in Kentucky.

Expected Collision Between Schoepf and Zollicoffer.

Gen. Buell's Army Moving Forward to Green River.

Sixty Thousand National Troops on the Line between Louisville and Nashville.

TROOPS STILL POURING INTO KENTUCKY.

A Simultaneous Movement at all Important Points Expected.

POSITION OF THE OPPOSING FORCES.

REPORTS FROM CINCINNATI.

CINCINNATI, Friday, Dec. 13.

The Frankfort (Ky.) *Gazette* has a dispatch, which says that when the stage left Somerset, at 11 o'clock, on Wednesday, there had been no fighting.

The Postmaster wrote as follows:

"We are expecting to fight hourly. The enemy are close upon us, with a force estimated at from 8,000 to 15,000 men. Our force is about 5,000 effective men. Both citizens and soldiers complain of Gen. THOMAS for not having sent reinforcements to Gen. SCHOEPF."

As it cannot interfere with the plans laid down, it is not improper to state that the plans of Gen. BUELL was that Gen. THOMAS should get in the rear of Gen. ZOLLICOFFER.

Letters to-night express apprehensions about the result, should Gen. ZOLLICOFFER force Gen. SCHOEPF to an engagement before Gen. THOMAS arrives.

An officer arrived from London this evening says that the rumor there was that after some picket fighting Gen. ZOLLICOFFER began to retreat again. If this should prove true Gen. THOMAS will not be in time to intercept him.

Troops continue pouring into Louisville. Four regiments passed through yesterday.

The *Commercial* of this city has a dispatch which says: "The Paymaster from London reports that Gen. CRITTENDEN is at Cumberland Gap with fifteen hundred men and a large force in the vicinity."

A letter to the Representative from Wayne County says that Major HELVETI, and three others captured with him by the rebels, were killed after their capture.

All the leading men have been driven from Owensville, Bath County, and the town is in possession of 400 rebels, who are committing the greatest excesses.

The Louisville *Journal* of yesterday, says that all Indiana regiments which have a minimum number of men, have been ordered into Kentucky. This order will throw from nine to ten thousand troops into Kentucky during this and the coming week.

Gen. ROSECRANS arrived at Cincinnati the day before yesterday. A public reception was given him at the hall of the Catholic Institute last night.

CINCINNATI, Friday, Dec. 13—P. M.

The *Commercial's* Frankfort dispatch says that no fight had taken place up to 8 o'clock to-day at Somerset.

ZOLLICOFFER was advancing, and is near that town with 9,000 men, and reinforcements are probably coming to his assistance.

The Thirty-first Ohio Regiment left Stamford this morning at daylight, at the double-quick, to assist Gen. SCHOEPF.

The dispatch says, without doubt, there is a rebel force at Orningsville.

HUMPHREY MARSHALL is invading Eastern Kentucky with a formidable force.

The Mount Sterling *Whig* issues a call to the Unionists to resist their certain danger.

REPORTS FROM LOUISVILLE.

LOUISVILLE, Ky., Friday, Dec. 13.

A letter from Somerset, dated the 7th inst., confirms the capture by the rebels of Major HELVETI and Capt. PRINCE.

J. R. RICHARDSON, Postmaster at Somerset, writes on the 10th inst. as follows:

"Gen. ZOLLICOFFER has crossed the Cumberland River twenty miles below Waitsborough, on a bridge of coal-barges, with from 9,000 to 15,000 troops. We expect to fight to-morrow. The National forces under Gen. SCHOEPF are six regiments, with two batteries."

The *Democrat* discredits the above, failing to get confirmation from its correspondent.

The Bowling Green *Courier* deprecates the discouraging effect of the burning of Whippoorwill Bridge on the Memphis branch railroad by the Nationals. Its correspondent says nothing to indicate a forward movement of either army this Winter.

Tennessee money that fifteen to twenty days ago was fifteen to twenty per cent. discount, is now thirty five per cent discount.

The *Courier* says that fifteen thousand Kentuckians are in the rebel army.

THE SKIRMISH AT JACKSONVILLE.

BAGDAD, Ky., Friday, Dec. 13.

A party of rebels have been endeavoring to make the Union men take the oath of allegiance to the Southern Confederacy in this section, and Col. WHITAKER, on learning of it, sent a squad of soldiers to arrest them, when the rebels fired upon Col. WHITAKER's men. The odds were too great, and Col. WHITAKER dispatched to Capt. LEE, at Louisville, for assistance, who arrived this afternoon, immediately proceeding with the troops to Jacksonville, where the skirmish last evening took place.

FORWARD MOVEMENT OF THE NATIONAL FORCES.

From the Cincinnati Commercial, Dec. 11.

A dispatch from Louisville last night informs us that Gen. BUELL's army (which, on the direct Louisville and Nashville line, is not less than sixty thousand strong) is moving forward to Green River. The remarkable quietude of this army for so long a period renders this movement more significant. That a general advance is in progress is further indicated by the marching from Louisville, on Monday, of the Second, Thirty-first, Twenty-fourth, Sixth, Ninth, Tenth, Twenty-first and Thirty-third Ohio regiments. Gen. MCCLELLAN's plan is well understood to be that *a simultaneous advance shall take place—on the Mississippi, against Columbus, Ky.; in Central Kentucky, upon Bowling Green; from Romney, upon Winchester; from the Potomac, into Eastern Virginia; from Fortress Monroe, upon Yorktown or Norfolk; and that Butler's, Burnside's and Sherman's coast expeditions shall make demonstrations at the same time.* If this be the case—and we do not profess to have either official or semi-official information—movements at all important points may be expected when one takes place; and the forward movement in Kentucky is the signal of a general advance.

SITUATION OF THE OPPOSING FORCES.

From the Chicago Tribune, Dec. 11.

The position of affairs in Northeastern Kentucky, on the line to Cumberland Gap, is as follows: The two East Tennessee regiments remain at Camp Calvert, near London, just where they halted when the pursuit of ZOLLICOFFER was abandoned. ZOLLICOFFER has come back into the State, but by another road, taking the turnpike through Whitely and Wayne counties to the north bank of Cumberland River, below Somerset. This place, the present headquarters of Gen. SCHOEPF's command, is about thirty miles east of London. ZOLLICOFFER has all the way from 9,000 to 12,000 troops. He was evidently heading for Bowling Green when the advance of our troops threatened his rear. Gen. SCHOEPF has now, at Somerset, (or had at last accounts,) the following troops, with more, probably, to come:

2d Ohio Regiment	Col. Len. A. Harris.
17th Ohio Regiment	Col. John M. Connell.
38th Ohio Regiment	Col. Ed. D. Bradley.
50th Ohio Regiment	Col. James P. Fyffe.
Kentucky Infantry	Col. Wm. A. Hoskins.
Kentucky Infantry	Col. Thos. J. Bramlette.
Kentucky Infantry	Col. Henry Grider.
1st Ky. Cavalry (portion)	Col. Frank Wolford.
Capt. Standart's Ohio Battery	
And another battery.	

Gen. SCHOEPF commands the troops, assisted by Gen. JESSE T. BOYLE. They number some 7,000 men, and when joined by the force at Camp Calvert, there will be 10,000 at least. Unless Gen. THOMAS again interferes, SCHOEPF will make quick work of the rebel gang and of the "masterly" intrenchments that are said to hold Cumberland Gap, and will be promptly on hand to the relief of the gallant BROWNLOW. So near the line, we hope he will not be prevented this time in the great undertaking. Our last information from Somerset was to the effect that the rebels had chosen strong positions on the other side of the river, and would have to be shelled out. The two camps were almost within shot distance of each other, and hair-breadth escapes of skirmishing parties were of daily occurrence.

Gen. GEO. B. CRITTENDEN, the new rebel Commanding-General of East Tennessee and East Kentucky, is at Cumberland Gap, in force, with thirty days' rations, and it is feared that he may advance into Kentucky. The Union troops at London and Wild Cat, on the Lexington and Cumberland road, are reported to have been withdrawn to Somerset, and CRITTENDEN would find no serious obstacles to an advance other than the condition of the roads, which on that route are said to be bad. We should have some big news from that quarter before many days, despite the rumor that SCHOEPF is under orders not to fight unless attacked.

FROM GEN. SCHOEPF'S BRIGADE.

Correspondence of the Cincinnati Times.

GEN. SCHOEPF'S BRIGADE,
TWO MILES NORTH OF SOMERSET, Ky.,
Friday, Dec. 6, 1861.

I yesterday wrote you that it was then supposed that the enemy would attempt to cross the Cumberland River a short distance below the point at which we were then stationed. In anticipation of this movement on the part of the rebels, Gen. SCHOEPF ordered one company of Col. WOLFORD's First Kentucky Regiment of Cavalry, under the command of Capt. DILLION, to proceed without delay to Mill's Springs (that being the point where the enemy were expected to cross) as a reconnoitering party.

The Seventeenth Ohio, Col. CONNELL, and Capt. STANDART's battery of artillery, were also ordered to follow up the advance of the cavalry. Capt. DILLION, with the cavalry, after having proceeded about seven miles, which was about one half the distance to Mills' Springs, halted and encamped for the night. The Seventeenth Ohio and STANDART's Battery, coming up with the cavalry, and finding them encamped, also halted and encamped. After taking up the line of march in the morning to proceed to the point designated, and before reaching it they were informed that the enemy had been engaged in crossing the river during the entire night. And that a force of over four thousand had succeeded in gaining a landing upon this side of the river, and were still crossing in large numbers.

The enemy had also a battery of eight guns planted upon the heights on the opposite of the river, which commanded the shore on this side. While the Federal forces continued to advance they suddenly came upon the reconnoitering forces of the enemy. The enemy being in greatly superior numbers the small force of Federalists were soon surrounded, when Maj. HELVETI, of the cavalry, and eighteen of his men, were taken prisoners by the enemy. Capt. PRINCE, of the Engineering Corps, were also at the same time taken prisoners.

The Federal forces then fell back to Fishing Creek, where they intrenched, awaiting the approach of the enemy. At midnight Gen. SCHOEPF received intelligence that the enemy, twelve thousand strong, had crossed the river, and were then advancing upon the forces at Fishing Creek. Col. HOSKINS, with the Kentucky regiment, had left Camp Goggin at dark, on the road to Fishing Creek. The Thirty-eighth Ohio remained at Camp Goggin. Gen. SCHOEPF having received correct intelligence of the advance of the enemy in large force, and not deeming his small force sufficient to meet them, his position such as could be easily turned, and his retreat cut off, ordered a retreat of all the forces six miles east of the position formerly occupied by the Seventeenth Ohio, and beyond the town of Somerset.

At 11 P. M. the Thirty-eighth Ohio received the order to fall back, together with the remaining portion of the Kentucky regiment. Everything was moved with order and quietude. On arriving at Somerset, at 3 A. M., we found the Seventeenth Ohio, and Col. HOSKINS' Kentucky regiment, which had arrived one hour previous. In passing through the town we found the inhabitants in the highest excitement. Almost every thing was being removed from the place. Bedding, furniture, stores of all kinds, men, women and children, were being promiscuously stowed into carriages, carts, wagons and coaches. Every available beast of burden was brought into requisition—the donkey, the horse, the mule and the ox—to bear away all of worth and value, beyond the grasp of the Vandal foe, whose approach to their now deserted hamlets was momentarily expected.

THE MISSISSIPPI EXPEDITION.

Correspondence of the St. Louis Democrat.

CAIRO, Ill., Sunday, Dec. 8, 1861.

The naval force, which is to take so important a part in the great military drama which is so soon to be enacted in the Mississippi Valley, begins to make something of a show here. We have at this point now four of the new St. Louis gunboats, one of the new tugs, besides the old boats—as the *Tylor, Lexington* and *Conestoga* are termed—together with the receiving ship *Maria Denning*. These make already quite a fleet; and with the great quantities of ammunition and naval supplies lying about, and the liberal sprinkling of naval uniforms, and sturdy sailors, Cairo just at present, presents quite as much the appearance of a marine town, as it does of a military post. As I write, the *Benton* and *Essex* are momentarily expected, and before this reaches you, they, too, will have been joined to the fleet here; and ere the end of the week, quite likely, we shall have pretty much the entire flotilla from St. Louis. The gunboats from Mound City will not be finished for a fortnight or three weeks yet. The gunboats which are here are being rapidly completed and prepared for active service. The carpenters and engineers are busy from morning to night, and the interior arrangements already begin to assume a very "ship shape" appearance. The machinery has been adjusted, guns lashed, ammunition taken aboard, so that some of them are already in fair fighting condition. Commodore FOOTE has been here for some days, and gives to these arrangements the most constant personal supervision.

A correspondent of the Cincinnati *Commercial* writes, under date of Cairo, Dec. 8:

"Six rebel gunboats arrived at Columbus yesterday, some of the names of which I obtained. They are each reported to be pierced for fourteen guns. They are not iron-plated, as thought, but are generally boats of immense power and speed. One of their most powerful gunboats, the *Tuscarora*, took fire, accidentally, near Helena, Ark. Having a large amount of powder and shell on board, her crew had to leave her with the greatest haste. Some lives are said to have been lost by drowning.

The famous *Manassas*, Commodore HOLLINS, broke her battering-ram below Memphis, and is now at that city repairing damages. She draws ten feet of water.

Of the other six gunboats at Columbus, I have obtained the following names, viz: the *J. B. Howard* and the *Marquis de la Habana*, a vessel cut out under the guns of Vera Cruz a year or two ago. These two last rank as frigates.

The Confederates at Columbus now claim to have sixty thousand men in force, and daily receiving fresh reinforcements.

The *Benton* and *Carondolet*, gunboats, from St. Louis, are now here and rapidly arming—the others are under the way, in convoy of the *W. H. B.*

The naval men here are anxiously awaiting orders to go down and engage the rebel fleet, and are eager for the fray. They express their hearty wishes to get a fair chance at them, and will not fail to maintain the honor of the flag of the Union, and perch victory again on its top, if the rebel flotilla will fight and not run away. They may beat us in showing their heels, but cannot in a fair stand-up battle.

At Columbus, the land batteries are being rapidly depressed, in order to get the range of our boats when they come down.

Col. DICKENS, from the cavalry regiment of Illinois, arrived yesterday, per cars. Five hundred of them were, soon after their arrival, sent down the river per steamers *Aleck Scott* and *Montgomery*—destination unknown. They will doubtless soon be heard from, and are on active service.

Yesterday morning a number of shells were fired from Fort Cairo, in order to test them. They burst correctly and beautifully, and the practice was highly satisfactory to the officers.

Commodore FOOTE, of the Flotilla of the West, is here, and pushing forward naval preparations with great energy and vigor.

The *Conestoga* gunboat, after a long cruise up and down the Ohio, Tennessee and Cumberland rivers, arrived here yesterday for supplies, and left in the afternoon for Paducah.

KENTUCKY ADMITTED INTO THE SOUTHERN CONFEDERACY, ETC.

RICHMOND, Tuesday, Dec. 10.

The *Examiner* of this morning says that Congress, while in session, passed a bill admitting Kentucky into the Southern Confederacy. The admission is complete, as Commissioners were appointed at Russellville, and empowered to act in behalf of Kentucky.

A bill has been introduced in the Confederate Congress prohibiting the importation of negroes from Africa.

The Alabama House of Representatives has passed a bill legalizing the suspension of specie payment by the chartered banks of that State.

The report of superseding Gen. PRICE by Gen. HEATH is denied.

The Governor of Mississippi has made a call upon the inhabitants for arms.

REPORTED WRECK OF THE UNITED STATES STEAMER ANNIE TAYLOR.

A LIEUTENANT AND NINE MEN CAPTURED BY THE REBELS.

CAIRO, Friday, Dec. 13.

The following is from the Memphis *Appeal* of the 11th:

"NEW-ORLEANS, Dec. 10.

Lieut. SHEPARD, of the Confederate steamer *Mobile* has arrived at Rashear City, with a Lieutenant and nine other Federal prisoners, taken from the United States steamer *Annie Taylor*, which was wrecked near Sabine Pass.

THE MICHIGAN LEGISLATURE.

DETROIT, Thursday, Dec. 12.

Gov. BLAIR has issued a proclamation for an extra session of the Legislature, to assemble on the 2d proximo.

THE MISSISSIPPI, FROM CAIRO TO MEMPHIS.

E. Wells, N.Y.

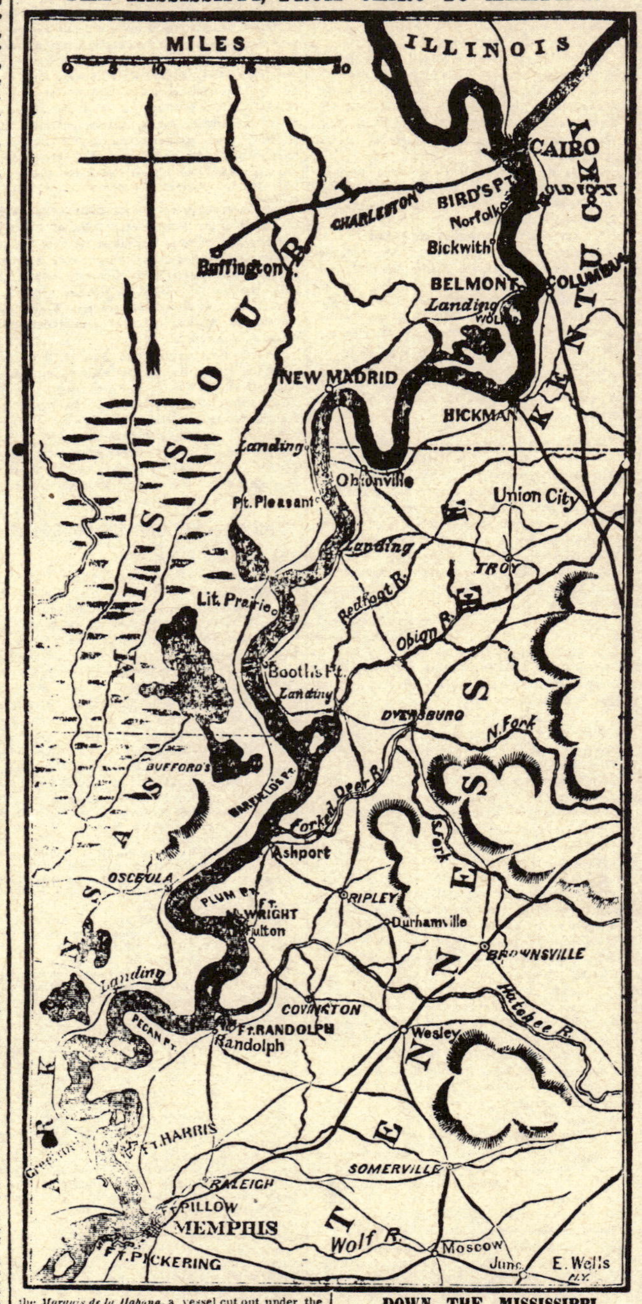

DOWN THE MISSISSIPPI.

FROM CAIRO TO MEMPHIS.

One of the boats of the great naval river expedition, now nearly ready at Cairo, has a flag-staff erected on its upper deck, from the top of which floats the American flag, while on the bottom is nailed a sign, "For Memphis and New-Orleans." The impression generally prevails in our Western Army, as well as among the river rebels, that the grand flotilla will shortly cut its moorings at Cairo, and start on this perilous voyage down the Mississippi among the innumerable river batteries and river rebels—flanked on the land sides by fifty or a hundred thousand Union soldiers. Whether the belief is correct that it will certainly go down the Mississippi, in preference to any of the other streams in the vicinity, a short time now will tell. But the fact that we have a choice of navigable rivers near by, which penetrate into the very heart of the South, may well keep the rebels in a terrible state of perturbation as to where the blow *will* be struck. For fear it *should* start down the Mississippi one of these fine Winter mornings, however, we give a map of the course and windings of that river, from Cairo to Memphis, indicating also the towns, forts, and other natural and artificial points of defence between these two places.

THE NAVAL FORCE.

Cairo at present presents as much the appearance of a marine town as it does of a military post. Naval uniforms, jolly jack tars, jaunty young officers, naval supplies, iron-clad gunboats, and all the paraphernalia of "life on the river wave," now give a novel appearance and furnish a new phase of life to that marshy, muddy and unhealthy, but all-important military and naval strategical point. At the latest advices, the last gunboat for the fleet, building at St. Louis, had left for Cairo, and the mortar-floats, &c., building at other points, were leaving for the point of rendezvous daily. The dispatch with which these boats have been built and equipped exceeds anything in our naval history. Some of them are already in fighting condition—the guns lashed, ammunition taken aboard, machinery adjusted, and men and officers all aboard; and it looks as if it could not be long before the whole thing was under way—for somewhere.

The expedition will consist of a fleet of eleven gunboats, 38 floating batteries, and 28 river steamers. There are now over two hundred pieces of cannon of the heaviest calibre, at Cairo, ready to be mounted on them.

DESCRIPTION OF ONE OF THE GUNBOATS.

The dimensions are to be: Length over all, 175 feet; breadth of beam, 51½ feet; depth of hold, 6 feet. The sides are sloped at an angle of about 45 degrees, and nothing but a plunging shot from a high bluff could strike the surface at right angles. They are sheathed with wrought iron plates 2½ inches in thickness, securely bolted to each other and through the heavy three-feet oak timber beneath. Each plate has been severely tested by shots from rifled cannon at different distances, and is now calculated to resist any missile known to modern warfare. The bow is pierced with four port-holes, through which protrude the muzzles of four 32-pound Parrott guns; the stern has three pieces of the same sort, and the sides have each six formidable 10-inch columbiads. When ready for service, little will be presented above the water-line save the muzzles of the guns and the top of the smoke-stacks. The boilers and the machinery are all under water; and this part is so divided with water-tight compartments that, in case a ball should enter one, it can do no material damage. In strength and effectiveness these gunboats are equal to any frigate in the navy, and seems as though able to cope with HOLLINS' famous ram itself. This brief outline of the flag-ship *Benton* will serve as a specimen for nearly all the balance. Take them altogether, they are about as formidable looking instruments of destruction as ever navigated American waters.

The mortar-floats, or floating batteries, are built of pine logs three-ply thick. They will carry one 64-pound columbiad each, and will be used only for throwing shells among the rebels on shore.

THE FLEET AND ITS OFFICERS.

A few days more will put the entire fleet in working order. Too much praise cannot be bestowed upon the naval officers for the great work they have accomplished in an unprecedentedly short time, without the convenience and appliances of a navy-yard. Generals GRANT and MCCLERNAND, also at Cairo, have been vigorously at work night and day, and straining every nerve in forwarding the business of preparation. The great work of demolishing the rebel batteries and opening the Mississippi, has, no doubt, got mainly to be done by these gunboats and their aids. The work is difficult and extremely perilous, but our gallant navy, in action, has always been equal to the demands of the country upon it.

The military part of the expedition will, it is believed, be under the general command of Maj.-Gen. HALLECK, who has now his grand army organized at St. Louis and other points, and this will be joined by the columns of Gen. GRANT at Cairo, and that of Gen. SMITH at Paducah. There will probably be between 50,000 and 75,000 men in the expedition.

The naval part of the expedition will be under the command of Commodore FOOTE, who has superintended the construction and armament of the gunboats. Commodore FOOTE is an open-hearted, affable sailor and gentleman, and is known in the navy as one of its most efficient officers. He distinguished himself in China by the bombarding and breaching of a Chinese fort, the fort being, in all respects, a superior work of masonry. The feat called forth the praise of all foreign naval officers on that coast.

The following is a list of the naval officers now at Cairo, intended for command in the "Flotilla of the Western Waters:"

Flag-officer, A. H. Foote.	Capt. Steimbel,
Capt. W. D. Porter,	Lieut. Phelps,
Capt. A. H. Kelty,	Lieut. Shirk,
Capt. Dove,	Lieut. Wilson,
Capt. Mack,	Lieut. Paulding,
Capt. Pennock,	Lieut. Bishop,
Capt. Winslow,	Midshipman Lord.
Capt. Roger Perry,	Master's Mate Butler.

We know nothing as to the time when the expedition will start, nor as to its destination, nor would we state such things if we knew. But the above facts are all known and published at Cairo, and of these no concealment is even there attempted to be made.

REBEL PREPARATIONS FOR THE FLEET.

For the reception of this fleet the rebels have made immense preparations along the Mississippi from Columbus, a few miles below Cairo, to Memphis. These preparations are of four kinds. First, to prevent our fire in the rear, they have a large land force, which they claim amounts to sixty thousand men at Columbus alone. Secondly, they have river batteries heavily mounted, and forts (see map) at all the main strategic points on the river. Third, they have a fleet of six gunboats at Columbus to meet ours, and further below they now have HOLLINS' ram, which, we learn, has again got its nose broke some way or other. And fourth, it is believed they have sunk, or are ready to sink, old hulks at different points in the channel of the river, near Columbus, so as to prevent the passage downward of our flotilla. Columbus itself is now fortified as strongly as it can be—probably as strongly as Manassas. Indeed, the rebels call it the "Manassas of the West." A little northward of the town, upon a ledge of chalk bluffs, they have extensive earthworks and fortifications, and below the town also they have earthworks immediately on the bank of the river. The high banks of the Mississippi here offer great natural advantages of defence against attack by the river. Columbus is the northernmost point on the Mississippi possessed by the rebels; and was the first place they seized on Kentucky soil when she declared her neutrality. It will be remembered how neatly FREMONT checkmated their hopes of making it a point of aggression by seizing Paducah as soon as they had seized Columbus.

The rebels have also batteries thrown up at New-Madrid, at the great bend of the river; and they claim that these alone can destroy or drive back any flotilla the Yankees may attempt to send down. Some fifty miles above Memphis again is Fort Wright, situated on what are known as the Chickasaw Bluffs. It is said to have ten guns mounted. Fort Randolph, further down, is an immense series of earthworks and fortifications; and it is here that the celebrated Gen. PILLOW was said to have stretched a chain across the river to prevent the descent of our gunboats. Fort Harris, ten miles above Memphis, has a parapet eight feet in height, and is said to mount eight 32-pounders. Immediately to the north of the city of Memphis, is Fort Pillow, which mounts six cannon and two mortars. The cotton bale barricades erected by PILLOW in the streets of Memphis, of whose great strength we heard so much half a year ago, have now been removed; and the city itself, in its own immediate vicinity, is not very strongly defended. Fort Pickens, below the city, is of no strength.

One can form some idea from these details, and by looking at the map, what an amount of work has to be done before our Western boys can reach Memphis by the Mississippi. But yet our Western Generals and soldiers, who know all these things thoroughly, say that they expect to spend their New-Year's day in Memphis. And if we may judge of the plan of attack from certain recent movements in Kentucky, we should not wonder if they did.

THE ESCAPE OF THE SUMTER.

Serious Charge Against the Commander of the Gunboat Iroquois.

The brig *Thomas W. Rowland*, Capt. ROWLAND, from Rio Janeiro *via* St. Thomas, Nov. 27, arrived at this port on Thursday night.

Capt. ROWLAND states that the Captain of the United States gunboat *Iroquois* is entirely and alone to blame for the escape of the *Sumter* from Port Royal, Martinique. The captain of the gunboat sent a man on shore at Port Royal with signal lights, and gave him instructions to signalise to him the movements of the *Sumter*, and on the night of the 23d of November, signals were made by the man on shore that she was leaving the harbor, but no notice was taken of it by the Captain of the *Iroquois*. His first Lieutenant tried to persuade him to give chase, which they could easily have done, as the *Sumter* drew one foot more water than the *Iroquois* did, but he would not comply, saying it would be very unpleasant for him to capture her, as he and Capt. SEMMES had been schoolmates, and had sailed together, and Capt. SEMMES had been his superior officer; and another reason was that he did not want to break the neutrality laws. The movements of the *Sumter* were seen from the deck of the *Iroquois*, she (the *Sumter*) taking a southerly course, when the captain of the *Iroquois* gave orders to proceed to St. Thomas, not making the least effort to capture the privateer, although he had been lying off the port several days for that purpose. On these facts becoming known at St. Thomas, the greatest indignation prevailed among the Americans in port, and all others friendly to the United States.

RUMORS ABOUT THE REBEL COMMISSIONERS.

HALIFAX, Friday, Dec. 13.

It has been strongly reported here to-day that Messrs. BRECKINRIDGE and HUNTER applied for passage by the *Canada*, but were refused, in consequence of a telegram from Secretary CAMERON, warning the agents of the Cunard line against conveying rebels. Mr. CUNARD emphatically contradicts the report.

IMPORTANT FROM REBELDOM.

A Renewal of the Fight at Fort Pickens Anticipated.

AN EXPECTED ATTACK ON NORFOLK.

Arrest of Slaves on their Way North.

The Late Destruction of Property Near Port Royal.

Excitement Relative to Drafting in Tennessee.

Gov. Harris Driven from Nashville to Memphis.

THE CONDITION OF LOUISIANA

COMMERCIAL AND FINANCIAL INDICATIONS.

NEWS BY WAY OF FORTRESS MONROE.

FORTRESS MONROE, Thursday, Dec. 12, via BALTIMORE, Friday, Dec. 13.

A flag of truce left here this morning for Norfolk, in charge of Capt. MILWARD, with a large quantity of letters and express matter for the South. The boat returned with passengers from Richmond, who are British subjects, and two from Norfolk.

The Norfolk *Day Book* has dates from Pensacola to Dec. 8. There had been no further fighting, but Gen. BRAGG hourly anticipated a renewal of the attack from Fort Pickens. The National vessels were flitting in and out of the harbor in the most bewildering manner to the rebels. Sometimes there would be a dozen in the evening, and all but two disappear before morning.

The Montgomery *Mail*, of the 6th inst., congratulates its readers on the report that old HARVEY BROWN has died of a wound received in the late fight at Fort Pickens. Passengers up from that city this morning, say that the report is firmly believed, but not positively known to be true.

The *Day Book* of Thursday was considerably excited in relation to a rumor that Norfolk is to be attacked. It suggests that additional obstructions be placed at the entrance of the harbor, and if no done by the military authorities, urges that the City Councils take it in hand.

The Norfolk *Day Book* speaks of an important arrest there of a number of slaves in the act of making their escape to the North. They had with them fifteen hundred dollars in stolen money. An examination of their case was had before the Mayor, but for prudential reasons the report of it is withheld.

The Richmond *Dispatch*, of Wednesday, contains the following mail items:

The Charleston *Courier*, of the 9th, says that on Wednesday a detachment of the Beaufort Artillery, 22 men, passed over to the island and visited Beaufort, where the utter desolation and abandonment were relieved only by the presence of one light and a barking dog.

There were no signs of the enemy, either on land or water. Our men then proceeded to the work of destruction. The chief object was to destroy the crops of cotton and provisions on Paris Island, which being near the enemy, was crowded with negroes who had flocked there to escape from the control of their owners. Owing to the want of boats, this object was but partially effected. Seven hundred bales of cotton, and seven hundred bushels of corn, were burnt on Dr. THOMAS FULLER's plantation. Returning to Battery Plantation, the work of destruction was resumed. The torch was successively applied to the cotton of twelve other plantations, and the contents of five barns were emptied and consumed. Seventeen crops, amounting to nearly four thousand bales, were thus effectively removed from the fangs of the destroyer.

The *Courier* says that the English steam ship-of-war *Racer* arrived off Charleston harbor on Friday, and brought dispatches to the British Consul. The *Racer* left next day for Port Royal.

The *Courier*, of the 9th, says: "On Friday last, there were in sight near this harbor the steamship *Susquehanna*, two side-wheel gunboats, a store ship, a large schooner, supposed to be laden with coal, and the Sweedish bark *Winona*. We hear that this last vessel was bound to this port, supposing there was no blockade, which want of information will be unfortunate for her owners, as she will no doubt be seized."

The Richmond *Dispatch* has among its telegrams the following:

SEIZURE OF A SCHOONER—BOLDNESS OF THE HESSIANS.

AUGUSTA, Ga., Tuesday, Dec. 10.

The Charleston *Courier* of this morning says that the Lincoln fleet seized a schooner on Saturday, and that a steamer was seen passing on Monday with a floating battery or dock in tow.

The Charleston *Mercury* of to-day says: "The Yankee invaders are getting bolder. A small body of them were seen near Port Royal on Sunday.

At Richmond, Wednesday, the war excitement was high. The storm of war was expected to burst momentarily somewhere.

A dispatch dated Memphis, Dec. 10, says, New-Madrid is now fortified. Two regiments were sent there yesterday.

The rumored contemplated attack on Cairo has been abandoned.

The Savannah *Republican* urges President DAVIS to send WM. C. RIVES and JOHN J. WARD as Commissioners to France and England.

The iron ram *Manassas* arrived at Columbus Sunday.

IMPORTANT STATEMENTS OF REFUGEES.

CINCINNATI, Friday, Dec. 13.

The *Commercial* says: "We had, yesterday, a very interesting interview with two Union refugees from Louisiana, who succeeded in making their way from New-Orleans to Nashville, through the rebel lines, to the Ohio River. They confirm the report of the utter stagnation of business in New-Orleans, and constant apprehensions of attack, and scarcity of all the necessaries of life. All men between the ages of eighteen and forty five were being impressed into service.

Memphis is strongly fortified on the river side. There were two gunboats at the landing. A regiment of infantry and a few companies of artillery comprised all the troops at that point.

The two Union refugees arrived at Nashville on the 6th inst. The city was in a high state of excitement on that day and the following, owing to an attempt being made to draft citizens into the army. The in-

1862

The New-York Times.

VOL. XI—NO. 3223. NEW-YORK, TUESDAY, JANUARY 21, 1862. PRICE TWO CENTS.

GLORIOUS NEWS.

A Great National Victory in Kentucky.

Zollicoffer's Army Twice Defeated and Routed.

DEATH OF ZOLLICOFFER.

Attack on Gen. Schoepf at Somerset.

A Battle Lasting from Daylight until 3 o'clock P. M.

The Rebels Utterly Routed and Driven Back to Their Intrenchments.

Combined Attack upon Them by Generals Schoepf and Thomas.

THE ROUT RENDERED COMPLETE.

Capture of All the Rebel Cannon. Quartermaster's Stores, Tents, &c.

The National Flag Flying Over "Zollicoffer's Den."

HEAVY LOSS OF LIFE ON BOTH SIDES.

THE BATTLE AT SOMERSET.

CINCINNATI, Monday, Jan. 20.

A battle took place at Somerset, Ky., on Saturday, between Gen. SCHOEPF's and Gen. ZOLLICOFFER's forces.

The battle lasted from early in the morning till dark.

Gen. ZOLLICOFFER was killed and his army entirely defeated.

The loss is very heavy on both sides.

A CONFIRMATION FROM LOUISVILLE.

LOUISVILLE, Ky., Monday, Jan. 20.

Gen. THOMAS telegraphs to headquarters that on Friday night, Gen. ZOLLICOFFER came up to his encampment, and attacked him at 6 o'clock on Saturday morning, near Webb's Roads, in the vicinity of Somerset.

At 3 o'clock on Saturday afternoon Gen. ZOLLICOFFER and BAILIE PEYTON had been killed, and the rebels were in full retreat to their intrenchments at Mill Springs, with the National troops in hot pursuit.

No further particulars have been received in regard to the losses on either side.

THE SECOND BATTLE, ON SUNDAY.

LOUISVILLE, Monday, Jan. 20.

Gen. THOMAS, on Sunday afternoon, followed up the rebels to their intrenchments, 16 miles from his own camp, and when about to attack them, this morning, he found their intrenchments deserted, the rebels having left all their cannon, quartermaster's stores, tents, horses and wagons, which fell into our hands. The rebels, dispersing, had crossed the Cumberland in a steamboat and nine barges at White Oak Creek, opposite their encampment at Mill Springs. Two hundred and seventy-five rebels were killed and wounded, including Gen. ZOLLICOFFER and BAILIE PEYTON dead, who were found on the field. The Tenth Indiana lost seventy-five killed and wounded. Nothing further of the National loss has yet reached here.

THE STARS AND STRIPES FLOATING OVER THE REBEL FORTIFICATIONS.

THE DEATH OF GEN. ZOLLICOFFER CONFIRMED.

CINCINNATI, Monday, Jan. 20.

A combined attack was made, to-day, (Sunday,) on Gen. ZOLLICOFFER's intrenchments at Mill Springs, Wayne County, Ky., resulting in a complete victory. The Stars and Stripes now float over the fortifications. We captured all their camp property and a large number of prisoners. Our loss is heavy. Gen. ZOLLICOFFER's dead body is in the hands of the Nationals.

DETAILS OF RESULTS ACHIEVED.

CINCINNATI, Monday, Jan. 20.

A Lexington correspondent of the *Commercial* gives the following account of Saturday's battle:

Gen. ZOLLICOFFER, learning that the National force had appeared in his rear, marched out of his intrenchments at 3 o'clock Saturday morning, and attacked Gen. SCHOEPF in camp. The pickets were driven in at an early hour, and the attack was made before daylight. The battle is reported to have raged with great fury until 3 in the afternoon, when Gen. ZOLLICOFFER, having been killed, the whole force of rebels fled in confusion to their camp. The loss is not stated, but is thought to be heavy. The BAILIE PEYTON killed is a son of the ex-member of Congress from Tennessee of that name. Our victory has been very decisive, and will result in a rout of the whole force defending the right flank of Bowling Green.

THE NEWS IN WASHINGTON.

WASHINGTON, Monday, Jan. 20.

The news from Kentucky causes intense delight. It is everywhere credited. No official confirmation, however, has been received up to 9 o'clock to-night.

One o'clock, A. M., 21st.—The Government, this morning, received official intelligence of the victory in Kentucky similar to that previously received by the Press.

THE SCENE OF THE GREAT VICTORY IN KENTUCKY.

Map Showing Somerset and the Cumberland River, with its Relations to Cumberland Gap, the Tennessee and Virginia Railroad, Knoxville, Nashville, Bowling Green and Columbus.

THE LOCATION OF THE BATTLE.

We have more good news this morning from Eastern Kentucky. Our last advices from that quarter, a week ago, announced the rout of HUMPHREY MARSHALL; to-day we chronicle an action and a victory of far greater importance. The situation preceding the battle, and the facts in the case, are as follows:

Gen. SCHOEPF, as everybody knows, has been stationed, for the last three months, at the little town of Somerset, [see Map,] Southeastern Kentucky, about six miles north of the Cumberland River, with a force of some 8,000 men under his command—the object being to prevent the advance of the rebels any further North until such time as we were prepared to move on Tennessee, through Cumberland Gap. On the Cumberland River itself, and on both of its banks, [see Map,] near directly south of SCHOEPF's position, the rebel ZOLLICOFFER has for some time had his stronghold, with a force of about the same strength as his adversary. About ten days ago, however, ZOLLICOFFER, dreading an assault, was reinforced by the division under the rebel CRITTENDEN, (eldest son of Senator CRITTENDEN,) who has lately been stationed at Knoxville, Tenn., and still later at Cumberland Gap. CRITTENDEN, being a Major-General, outranked ZOLLICOFFER, who was only a Brigadier, and consequently took command of the whole rebel force on the Cumberland, numbering probably some 15,000 men. Previous to this junction, however, Gen. BUELL had detached from his main body a division under Gen. THOMAS, to do the very thing which ZOLLICOFFER dreaded—attack him "in the rear." At the latest advices from that quarter, our forces under THOMAS had reached the town of Burkesville, [see map] on the Cumberland River, about thirty miles southwest of what is known as "Zollicoffer's" Den." It was then expected that THOMAS would at once move up the river on the rebels and assault their works. Putting together the dispatches that have reached us concerning the affair from Louisville and Cincinnati, and it appears that the rebels were assailed by the combined forces of our two Generals, driven from their fortification and completely routed. It would seem that ZOLLICOFFER first imprudently came up on last Saturday and assaulted our position in the vicinity of Somerset, but that his army was repelled by Gen. SCHOEPF and he himself slain. His forces were pursued and a combined attack by THOMAS and SCHOEPF was next day made upon his works on the Cumberland River, which resulted in a complete and overwhelming victory for the Union banner. At latest accounts the Stars and Stripes were floating over the rebel fortifications.

This position of ZOLLICOFFER on the Cumberland was one of the three great rebel strongholds in Kentucky—the first being at Columbus, in the extreme west, soon to be assailed by the great flotilla; the second at Bowling Green, in Central Kentucky, now imminently menaced by Gen. BUELL, and the third and most important of all, in the east, being the one which has just succumbed before our gallant troops. Naturally the latter position was the strongest of the three and indeed it was for defence one of the very strongest points possible. Selecting the mountainous region on both sides of the Cumberland River at a point where its course runs from due south to due west, and where the hills, although immediately upon the banks, rise to an altitude of 300, 350 and 400 feet above the level of the river, ZOLLICOFFER occupied and fortified these hills, commanding all approaches by the river from both directions, as well as through the valleys of the creeks on the north and on the south. Behind these immense natural and artificial defences the rebels were posted, capable apparently of bidding defiance to the assaults of any force. His forces on the north side of the river, prior to his reinforcement by CRITTENDEN's troops, consisted of six regiments, stationed on a height 400 feet above the river, commanding the approach from both directions, and on the south side of four regiments, commanding the valley of Meadon Creek, and a depression though the hills from the south, about a mile to the west. The geographical position of this intrenchment is as follows: From Somerset, about fifteen miles southwest; from Columbia, forty miles southeast, and about six miles below the head of steamboat navigation. The position commands all the coal mines, and many of the salt wells south of the Cumberland. Unluckily for the rebels, their main body moved out of this strong post to assail our forces, and as Gen. THOMAS came up opportunely as they began to fall back, he pursued them, and the glorious victory above chronicled is the result.

The column of Gen. THOMAS, when he left Columbia to move forward, consisted of 15,000 well-appointed men. They were nearly all Western troops—mostly from Ohio, Indiana and Kentucky. In Gen. SCHOEPF's Brigade were the two famous regiments of East Tennessee, who have been burning for a fight with their enemies and persecutors for nearly half a year.

This victory opens the way for our gallant army of the West to penetrate into East Tennessee, through Cumberland Gap; [See map;] and if promptly followed up to the capture of the Virginia and East Tennessee Railroad, will *compel the rebels to evacuate Bowling Green, and will compel Beauregard to retire from Manassas.* The position of the different points mentioned, and their relation to Cumberland Gap and the Tennessee and Virginia Railroad, to Knoxville, Nashville, Bowling Green and Columbus, and to our main body at Munfordsville, will all be found on our map. The rebels propose to make the Ohio River the boundary line of their bloody despotism, but they are rapidly retreating from that line.

Brig.-Gen. SCHOEPF, to whom this glorious Union victory is in great measure due, is a Hungarian officer of great distinction. Compelled to leave his own country on the fall of its liberties, he took refuge in this City. From here he went to Washington, and his great abilities and genius were discovered by Hon. JOSEPH HOLT, who procured him a situation in one of the Departments, and was afterward the means of procuring him a command in the army. Absurd stories have been extensively circulated by the Press about his being at one time a porter in one of the hotels in this city; but in truth he never held any such position. He was appointed five months ago to Eastern Kentucky as Brigadier-General, and was there first brought into notice by the disastrous engagement and retreat at Wildcat. Gen. SCHOEPF, however, was in no way to blame for that melancholy affair. His present victory will elevate his fame high in public estimation, and confirm the opinion of those who know that he is one of our most scientific and bravest soldiers.

SOMERSET.

Somerset, says a Western correspondent, is a small one-horse town of about fifteen hundred inhabitants. Is not remarkable for beauty or business, but like almost all other interior Kentucky towns, is a dull and dreary-looking place. The buildings are nearly all wooden structures, and the business parts, especially, are rather ricketty-looking affairs. There are but two brick buildings in the place, one of which is the Court-house, and is a most magnificent structure, being about on a par with an ordinary smoke-house.

IMPORTANT FROM CAIRO.

The Late Movement Down the River Explained—A Reconnoissance in Force—Evacuation of Camp Beauregard by the Rebels, &c.

CHICAGO, Monday, Jan. 20.

A special from Cairo to the *Journal* says that Gen. GRANT and Staff arrived in town yesterday morning. Gen. PAINE's Brigade reached Fort Jefferson on Saturday night. Gen. MCCLERNAND's Brigade will arrive to-morrow. The object of the expedition was a reconnoissance in force of all that part of Kentucky upon which portion operations against Columbus will necessarily be performed, and a demonstration to aid Gen. BUELL's right wing, our forces have been eminently successful—the Engineer Corps, under Gen. WEBSTER, having a full and accurate knowledge of the country.

It is understood that Gen. SMITH has taken the camp equipage and whatever was left in Camp Beauregard, and the rebels fled to Columbus. Gen. MCCLERNAND's Brigade went to within seven miles of Columbus, and encamped Thursday night in sight of the rebel watch-fires. They afterwards visited the towns of Milburne, Lovelaceville, Blandville, surveying all the roads as they went. Part of Gen. SMITH's command will return to Paducah to-day.

CAIRO, Monday, Jan. 20.

A gentleman from New-Orleans, who arrived here last night, reports that when he left there the citizens were daily expecting that Fort Pike, commanding the entrance to Lake Pontchaitrain, would be attacked and captured by the Nationals from Ship Island.

There were not over 5,000 troops in the city, and not exceeding 2,000 more could be raised in case of emergency. There are no batteries on the river above or below the city.

The only defences against attack from the gulf are two forts on the opposite side of the river, towards the mouth. He thinks the city could be easily captured by a small force.

Gen. MCCLERNAND's Brigade has returned from its expedition and taken their old quarters.

The Twentieth Illinois Regiment, which has been encamped at the mouth of the Mayfield Creek since the expedition started, will be up to-night.

COL. GARFIELD'S VICTORY.

THE LATE FIGHT AT PRESTONBURGH.

From the Cleveland Herald, Jan. 16.

Capt WILLARD, of Company F, Forty-second Regiment, arrived here last night on his way home to Ravenna. He was not in the Prestonburgh fight, being detained by sickness a few miles back of Paintville, but obtained many incidents of the battle from those who were in it.

Prestonburgh is about twelve miles beyond Paintville. After the cavalry skirmish at the latter place, Col. GARFIELD pushed on with the advance of his Brigade for Prestonburgh. Before reaching that place he found the enemy posted on and behind a range of hills. The Federal force forming the advance was less than 700, but Col. GARFIELD at once prepared to make an attack.

A body of the enemy was posted on a commanding hill, and it became necessary to dislodge them. The Fourteenth Kentucky volunteered for the service, as they knew the nature of the ground. Said Col. GARFIELD: "Go in, boys; give them—*Hail Columbia!*"

The hill was cleared, and soon the reserve of the Brigade came in at the double quick. As soon as he saw them Col. GARFIELD pulled off his coat and flung it up in the air, where it lodged in a tree, out of reach. The men threw up their caps with a wild shout, and rushed at the enemy; Col. GARFIELD, *in his shirt-sleeves*, leading the way.

As the Federal troops reached the top of the hill, a rebel officer shouted in surprise, "Why, how many of you are there?" "Twenty-five thousand men, d—n you!" yelled a Kentucky Union officer, rushing at the rebel. In an instant the rebels broke and ran in utter confusion.

Several instances of personal daring and coolness are related. A member of Capt. BUSHNELL's company in the Forty-second was about to bite a cartridge when a musket ball struck the cartridge from his fingers. Coolly facing the direction from which the shot came, he took out another cartridge and exclaimed, "You can't do that again, old fellow."

Capt. WILLARD says that the two men killed on our side were Kentuckians. The loss of the enemy is not known. In addition to the twenty-seven bodies found on the field, a number of human bones were found in several of the houses burned by the rebels in their retreat from Prestonburgh. A rebel officer reported at a house where he called at during his flight, that they had killed 500 Federals, and lost 250 of their own men. It is not unlikely that the killed, wounded and deserted will amount to that number, as numerous desertions took place previous to the battle.

The rebels burned most of their camp equipage and baggage. Some arms fell into the possession of our forces, and a large number of knapsacks and overcoats. The property found was wretchedly poor, the coats being made almost entirely of cotton.

Acting Adj.-Gen. CLAPP writes to the same paper from Prestonburgh, Jan. 11, giving the following list of wounded. The two Union soldiers killed belonged to the Fourteenth Kentucky.

David Hall Co. A, Forty-second Regiment, severe in shoulder.

Sherman Leach, Co. A, Forty-second Regiment, slightly in the leg.

Wm. Gardner, Co. G, Forty-second Regiment, dangerously in the neck.

Jacob James, Co. G, Forty-second Regiment, dangerously in abdomen.

Fred. Coffin, Co. F, Forty-second Regiment, dangerously in the thigh.

Charles Carlton, Co. F, Forty-second Regiment, very dangerously, leg amputated.

Jacob Griffith, Co. H, Forty-second Regiment, slightly in the elbow.

Henry Forney, Co. C, Forty-second Regiment, very slightly.

Frank Miller, Co. A, Fortieth Regiment, in the foot, slightly.

Second Lieut. Thos. Lilley, Co. A, Fortieth Regiment, severely in the arm.

James W. Rose, Co. B, Fourteenth Kentucky Regiment, in thigh, badly.

W. Chapman, Co. E, Twenty-second Kentucky, slightly in the neck.

Alexander Bell, Twenty-second Kentucky, severely in arm.

The enemy is in full retreat toward Abington, Va. Our men are too much exhausted to follow. The Big Sandy Valley is effectually cleared of rebels.

DISTURBANCES AMONG THE NEGROES.

From the Frankfort (Ky.) Yeoman, Jan. 17.

We have just learned of a reliable gentleman of New Castle, the circumstances of a very unusual occurrence in that place just before Christmas, which we deem it proper should be placed before the people of Kentucky. Some forty or sixty negros, all slaves, had been engaged in killing hogs for one of the citizens of New Castle, at night. About that time, and after the work was over, *they paraded the streets of the town in a body, between the hours of ten and twelve, uttering all sorts of disorderly sounds, singing political songs and shouting for Lincoln.* They seemed to take special pains to make their unusual and disorderly demonstrations in front of the residences of one or two prominent Southern Rights citizens. They continued their tumultuous proceedings for an hour or o without interruption from either officers or citizens, and finally dispersed of their own account.

We deem it due to the peace and security of the Commonwealth to give this information to the public, in order that other communities may be put on their guard, and be prepared to suppress in their incipiency all such dangerous movements on the part of the slave population.

We also learn from the same gentleman, that about the same time, or shortly after, a party of slaves in Henry County, belonging partly to Union and partly to Southern Rights men, made off from the county, taking with them a wagon and horses, with a full supply of provisions belonging to their owners, and made their escape into Indiana. They were immediately pursued by their owners into Indiana and overtaken; but the owners were notified by the population that they should not arrest the slaves, and, in fact, were themselves notified to leave the State without delay. A second visit of the same and other parties, with proper certificates, as the gentleman who gives us the facts is informed, was made with the same result.

We are also informed that numerous houses and barns, belonging to residents of Henry County, *have recently been fired and burned to the ground by the negroes, and that in consequence a general feeling of insecurity prevails throughout the entire community.*

GEN. BUTLER AND GOV. ANDREW.

BOSTON, Monday, Jan. 20.

In the Legislature, to-day, a voluminous correspondence was presented, relating to the difficulties between Gov. ANDREW and Gen. BUTLER. Some of it is said to be of a very spicy character, particularly that which has reference to the appointment of officers under Gen. BUTLER. The Governor charges unfitness of character against some of the officers under BUTLER, to which the latter replies, charging the appointment of a man guilty of adultery, alluding to an officer who was alleged to have run away with Mrs. BRANNAN, whose disappearance from Staten Island caused so much excitement a few years ago. The correspondence was ordered to be printed.

REPORTS OF A DESERTER FROM THE REBELS.

PHILADELPHIA, Monday, Jan. 20.

JOHN JOHNSON, a Jerseyman, impressed into the rebel service in New-Orleans in April last, escaped from Manassas ten days since, and has arrived here on his way home. He estimates the force at Manassas at 40,000, at Leesburgh 30,000, and at Occoquan at 15,000. He did not hear of the Port Royal victory until he got within the National lines. The defeat of the rebels at Dranesville had a depressing effect on the rebel army. The loss was conceded at 800 killed, wounded and missing. He says the Louisiana Regiment, to which he was attached, contains a large number of steamboatmen, anxious to escape to the National lines.

NAVAL AFFAIRS IN BOSTON.

BOSTON, Monday, Jan. 20.

There are now eleven vessels of war at the Navy-yard, finishing, repairing, undergoing operations, or awaiting stores or orders, and three on the stocks. Among these are the ship-of-the-line *Vermont*, frigate *Macedonian*, and steam sloop-of-war *San Jacinto*. The *Ino* yet lays in the stream. The sloop-of-war that is building will be one of the most powerful and beautiful of her class in the Navy. There are two months' pay due the workmen in the yard.

NEWS FROM FORTRESS MONROE.

A Flag of Truce to Craney Island—Ex-President Tyler Seriously Ill—New Rebel Brigadiers, &c.

FORTRESS MONROE, Sunday, Jan. 19, *via* BALTIMORE, Monday, Jan. 20.

A flag of truce went to Craney Island to-day, with two persons who came down from Baltimore last night to go South.

The following is all the news we can gather from Southern papers received.

Ex-President JOHN TYLER is very ill at Richmond.

A dispatch dated Macon, Ga., says that the accounts from the wheat region are very favorable, and that the crops never appeared more promising thus early.

The following Brigadier-Generals have been confirmed by the Congress at Richmond:

HENRY HEATH, of Virginia; JOHNSON R. DUNCAN, of Louisiana, and S. WOODS, of Alabama.

Dates from Havana to the 9th inst. have been received at New-Orleans. Business was extremely dull on the island.

The Norfolk *Day Book* gives a rumor, that the Federal Secretary of the Navy and Secretary of the Interior have resigned, and that Messrs. COLFAX, of Indiana, and HOLT, of Kentucky, will succeed them.

The U. S. steamer *Sumter* arrived yesterday afternoon.

The troops on board the *Constitution* will come ashore to-morrow for exercise.

GEN. LANE'S STAFF.

Correspondence of the Philadelphia Press.

WASHINGTON, Sunday, Jan. 19.

The following is the list of Gen. LANE's staff. They are appointed as staff-officers to Gen. MCCLELLAN, and detailed to Maj.-Gen. HUNTER, to be by him detailed to Gen. LANE—this arrangement being rendered necessary in the case of a Brigadier-General who has a Major-General's command:

1. Wm. H. Merritt, Iowa, Colonel. Behaved with great gallantry as commander of Iowa regiment at Springfield.

2. Judson Kilpatrick, New-York, Lieutenant-Colonel. Graduate of West Point, and distinguised for gallant conduct at Great Bethel; since detached from the army to serve as Lieutenant-Colonel of the Harris Cavalry.

3. John Ritchey, Kansas, Major. Commanded regiment in Kansas Brigade at Morristown and Drywood—known as the man who shot Arms, United States Marshal of Kansas.

4. V. Antwerp, Iowa, Major. A graduate of West Point.

5. F. J. Weed, Kansas, Major. Served in Kansas Brigade.

6. C. Vaughan, Kansas, Major. Behaved with great gallantry under Gen. Lane.

7. J. R. McClure, Kansas, Captain. Commanded and lost a foot at Springfield.

8. Wm. Kyle, Illinois, Captain.

9. Wm. A. Phillips, Kansas, Captain. Well known as the Kansas *Tribune* correspondent.

10. A. P. Russell, Kansas, Captain. Had a command at Springfield.

11. Wm. O. Donnell, Kansas, Captain. Connected with Lane through all the Kansas troubles.

12. James M. Rice, Illinois, First Lieutenant.

13. Wm. R. Dole, District of Columbia, First Lieutenant. Son of Commissioner of Indian Affairs.

14. James Christian, Kansas, First Lieutenant. A leading Douglas Democrat.

15. J. M. Winchell, Kansas, First Lieutenant. A prominent candidate for the United States Senate when Lane and Pomeroy were elected, and correspondent of the NEW-YORK TIMES.

16. A. J. MEAD, Kansas, First Lieutenant. A member of the first Free State Council of Kansas.

17. J. B. Carter, Pennsylvania, First Lieutenant. In the Kansas Brigade.

18. A. L. Reed, Kansas, First Lieutenant. A man of mark in the Kansas troubles.

19. Fred. A. Brown, New-York, Second Lieutenant. In service in Kansas Brigade.

20. Volney Hickok, Illinois, Second Lieutenant. Known as the author of several poetical effusions of merit.

21. W. W. Roberts, Kansas, Second Lieutenant. Formerly of Oberlin, Ohio.

Gen. LANE left this (Sunday) afternoon for Chicago, preparatory to taking the field. He is accompanied, as will be seen by the above, by staff officers remarkable for their high standing and distinguished military skill. All arms of the service are represented, and all will, doubtless, acquit themselves in their new positions in a manner honorable to the cause and themselves.

Before Gen. LANE left, he, in conjunction with his colleague, Senator POMEROY, induced the Government to mount and equip, as cavalry, the remainder of the gallant Kansas regiment which fought with such unparalleled bravery at Springfield, as a mark of appreciation of its valor. The request was warmly seconded by Gen. MCCLELLAN. It will be remembered that this regiment lost, in killed and wounded, 270 out of 650 men—the remainder marching off the field under orders, after clearing it of the enemy, to the sound of martial music.

THE MISSOURI UNITED STATES SENATORSHIP.

ST. LOUIS, Monday, Jan. 20.

JOHN B. HENDERSON, a Douglas Democrat, a member of the State Convention, an uncompromising Union man, and Brigadier-General in the State service, has been appointed by Lieut.-Gov. HALL to fill TRUSTEN POLK's seat in the United States Senate.

A passage was made through the ice opposite the city yesterday, and the ferry-boats are now running. Two days more of mild weather will probably break the gorge below, and entirely clear the harbor of ice.

THE STEAM-FRIGATE HARTFORD.

PHILADELPHIA, Monday, Jan. 20.

The steam-frigate *Hartford* dropped down to Fort Mifflin yesterday afternoon, and will sail as soon as her powder can be taken on board.

THE EIGHTY-FIRST NEW-YORK REGIMENT.

OSWEGO, Monday, Jan. 20.

The Eighty-first New-York Regiment, Col. Ed[illegible] Rose, left Fort Ontario this morning for Albany, *en route* to the seat of war.

THE UNITED STATES SHIP ST. LOUIS.

The United States ship *St. Louis* is now at the Philadelphia Navy-yard, awaiting the arrival of her crew. She mounts twenty guns, and will probably go into commission Tuesday or Wednesday next. Her Commander, M. C. MARIN, is a native of Florida, and is a loyal Union man. The following is a correct list of the officers of the *St. Louis*:

Commander—Matthias C. Marin.
Lieutenant—James A. Greer.
Surgeon—Albert L. Gihon.
Assistant Surgeon—Fk. B. A. Lewis.
Assistant Paymaster—Judson P. Post.
Marine Officer—Wm. J. Squires.
Master—Wm. F. Stewart.
Acting Masters—John E. Johnson, George Cables, Joshua Rowe.
Master's Mates—Allen Hixie, Hazard Marsh, Peter Fagan, M. V. Furman.
Boatswain—Francis M. Loud.
Gunner—Geo. P. Cushman.
Carpenter—David Jones.
Sailmaker—J. E. Crowell.
Surgeon's Steward—John L. Connelly.

THE TRANSPORT SERVICE.

The United States steam-transport *Planet* sailed Sunday evening for Locust Point, with a full cargo of subsistence stores and gun-carriages.

The United States steam-transport *New-York*, lying at Pier No. 9 North River, is also loading for the above port. She will carry 1,500 barrels of potatoes, and other stores.

The schooner *Anna R. Hayes*, which arrived on the 18th from Philadelphia, has a cargo for Government, consisting of rifled cannon, ammunition and anchors.

GEN. SHERMAN'S FORCE TO BE AUGMENTED.

The steamer *Oriental*, recently arrived at this port from Port Royal, will probably sail to-day for Annapolis, where she will take on board the Forty-seventh Pennsylvania Regiment, numbering nearly one thousand men, and then proceed to Hilton Head. The *Oriental* has been expressly fitted up for the conveyance of troops, and on this trip will take out a large supply of water.

THE NEWS FROM EUROPE

OUR CORRESPONDENCE BY THE ARABIA.

The Question of Acknowledging the Rebel Confederacy.

Menacing Attitude of the British Government.

Effect of the Pacific News from America.

Disappointment of the War Journals.

POPULAR PEACE MOVEMENT IN ENGLAND.

MORE PARLIAMENTARY ORATORY.

TONE OF THE FRENCH PRESS.

Mr. Thurlow Weed in Answer to Capt. Maury.

Miscellaneous and General Intelligence.

The Royal Mail steamship *Arabia*, from Liverpool on the 4th, and Queenstown on the 5th, arrived here early yesterday morning.

A telegraphic summary of her news was given in the TIMES of Thursday last, and a few extracts indicating the state of opinion in England touching the *Trent* affair, appeared in a small portion of our morning issue of yesterday.

We now add important correspondence from London, with ample extracts from our British and Continental exchanges.

The *Moniteur de la Flotte*, in alluding to the application made to the French Government to supply men-of-war to convey goods from Havre and other ports to the United States, observes:

"The journals which mention the matter might have added that the Government could not possibly accede to the wish expressed by the Chambers of Commerce, the ships-of-war having peculiar internal arrangements and a heavy war material, which does not allow them to carry merchandise. To convert them into transports it would be necessary to take out a great part of their guns, and they would thus be exposed to dangers which might arise from a mere misunderstanding. What war vessels can do, and what they will do, is to convoy merchant vessels and protect French trade in all the seas which it frequents."

A Frankfort letter states that Mr. MURPHY, the American Consul in that city, recently received a letter, apparently from the two burgomasters, informing him that his passport was ready, as the Germanic Confederation had recognized the Confederation of the Southern States. Mr. MURPHY, suspecting some trick, sent the document to the burgomasters, who at once declared that their signatures had been rather cleverly imitated.

Mr. GEORGE FRANCIS TRAIN, the American railroad contractor, having occasion to speak at Darlington on the 2d, thus referred to the American Secretary of State:

"Mr. SEWARD had been represented as hostile to this country; but I deny it. He is my friend, and I had the pleasure of his acquaintance when he was over in this country. I presented him to LAMARTINE in Paris, and heard his views about England. I can tell you Mr. SEWARD now bears to this country the kindest of feelings. You will get back from America, I know, a most courteous dispatch. There may be a little delay, but no war."

THE AFFAIR OF THE TRENT.

A Better Feeling with the Opening of the New Year—Confidence in Peace—Stocks and Cotton Up—The Position of France—The Question of the Blockade—Good Effect of Mr. Seward's Correspondence, &c.

From Our Own Correspondent.

LONDON, Saturday, Jan. 4, 1862.

The new year, unlike its predecessor, has begun with a general improvement in feeling and temper. The news which was received on the morning of the 1st, has restored general confidence, and it is easy to see that the war-party is now laboring again at up-hill work. They cannot now doubt that MASON and SLIDELL will be surrendered, or growl at the cowardice of the American Government in allowing itself to be bullied. The friends of peace and the loyal American [illegible] since made up their minds on the subject. They say that we, in holding those men, are doing either right or wrong. If we are doing wrong, we should give them up. If we are doing right, we should still be fools to fight England about them just now. We have all eternity to settle our account with England; why force a contest now when we are in the worst possible state for it? Feeling confident that the good sense of the American people will see the matter in its true light, the peace party here has got on its legs again and is striking out with fresh vigor. The *Times* has changed its tone, and has returned to its old tactics of quiet irritation, in which it is always successful. The stock market made a prodigious jump, and the advance has been well maintained. Cotton, too, has advanced a half-penny per pound, which is perhaps the best sign of all, as it indicates that the blockade is considered secure. It is not impossible that if the men are given up without extra irritation, that our friends here will be able to take a stand in Parliament that will put a stop to any blockade-breaking projects; always supposing that no untoward accidents happen.

It is of the more importance that such an attitude should be successfully taken, as the attitude of France becomes more and more equivocal. Some persons explain her late haste to indorse the demand of England as caused by a sincere wish to preserve peace; others, as a quiet device to England, to engage her in a war which would leave the Continent free; others, as a further development of that universal policy by which NAPOLEON is endeavoring to make himself the umpire of all mankind; but, whatever may be the cause, and I do not undertake to guess which of these is nearest the truth, it is worth while to remember the fact that already, several months ago, the Government of France urged England to recognize the South, and that then England returned a flat refusal to the proposition. [illegible] have all along been very generally known, but now the fact is stated in the public journals, and is undoubted. France is hostile to our [illegible]

Battle of Mill Springs (Logan's Crossroads), January 19, 1862

Embarkation of General McClernand's brigade at Cairo, January 10, 1862

The New-York Times.

VOL. XI----NO. 3228. NEW-YORK, MONDAY, JANUARY 27, 1862. PRICE TWO CENTS.

THREE DAYS LATER FROM EUROPE.

ARRIVAL OF THE EUROPA AT HALIFAX.

How the Rendition of Mason and Slidell was Received.

Mr. Seward's Dispatch Perfectly Satisfactory.

Insulting Tone of the British Press Toward the Rebel Commissioners.

The British Government would Have Done as Much for Two Negroes.

Further Denunciation of the Stone Blockade.

The Nashville Still Watched by the Tuscarora.

THE SUMTER EXPECTED AT SOUTHAMPTON

Commercial and Money Affairs.

HALIFAX, Sunday, Jan. 26.

The R. M. steamship *Europa*, Capt. ANDERSON, from Liverpool at 3 P. M. of the 11th, and Queenstown on the 12th, arrived here at 10½ o'clock last night. The wind was then and is still blowing a hurricane, with a heavy sea.

The *Europa* has neither troops nor stores, the Government having discontinued shipments by the Cunarders.

The *Europa* has 18 passengers for Boston, £6,500 for Boston and £64,000 for Halifax.

THE TRENT AFFAIR.

It was said that notwithstanding the pacific solution of the American question, warlike preparations at Woolwich have not been relaxed. The steamers *Spartan* and *Ajax* continued to take in heavy stores for Halifax and Jamaica.

No official notice had yet been given at Portsmouth respecting any discharge of hired mechanics or laborers, but it was understood that the reduction takes place in April.

A Cabinet council, summoned for the 14th, had been countermanded, Mr. SEWARD's dispatch having been considered in a council held on the 9th.

The *Times* understands that an answer will be returned, expressing gratification at the disavowal of Commodore WILKES' act, accepting the satisfaction rendered, and assuming that the precedent in the *Trent* case will rule the case of the schooner *Eugenia Smith*. As to the general discussion of the law of neutrals, the Government will decline any answer until they have had an opportunity of submitting the whole note to their law officers. There are propositions in this note which are not at all admissible, and after the delivery of the prisoners these points may be properly raised and discussed.

The *Morning Post* announces that a thorough understanding had been arrived at with the American Government. Not only had they given the required reparation, but in doing so Mr. SEWARD will have succeeded in impressing on the English Government the notion that they have not only present indemnity, but also no small pledge of future security.

The *Times* says rumor fixes England's expenses, owing to the late difficulty, at £2,000,000; but the *Times* expects that when all the bills are in, it will be double that sum, and that the money has not been thrown away.

The *Daily News* is eulogistic of the course pursued by the Washington Government, and bitterly denounces the policy of the *Times* and *Post*.

The *Times* has a strong editorial on the reception due to MASON and SLIDELL; says they are *about the most worthless booty it would be possible to extract from the jaws of the American lion*—having long been known as blind and habitual haters and revilers of England.

The *Times* sincerely hopes that Englishmen will not give these fellows anything in the shape of an ovation. The civility due to a foe in distress is all they can claim. England has returned them good for evil; and even now, if they can, they will only entangle her in a war with the North. *England would have done just as much to rescue two negroes*. Let MASON and SLIDELL, therefore, pass quietly on their way, and have their say with anybody who may have to listen to them.

The other journals advise a similar course, and allude to MASON's strong advocacy of the Fugitive Slave law, to prejudice the public against him.

THE STONE BLOCKADE.

The *Times* reiterates its denunciation of the stone blockade of Charleston harbor, and says among the crimes which have disgraced the history of mankind it is difficult to find one more atrocious than this. Even the fierce tribes of the desert will not destroy the well which gives life to the enemy.

The *Times* protests in the strongest terms against such proceedings, and asserts that no belligerent has the right to resort to such a warfare.

THE TUSCARORA AND NASHVILLE.

Great interest had been excited relative to the movements of the *Tuscarora* and *Nashville*. At the latest dates they continued at Southampton, watching each other. The *Tuscarora* remained at her anchorage, about a mile from the dock mouth, with her fires banked up and ready to slip her anchor and start at a moment's notice. She only required coals, water and provisions, which were being supplied her. On her arrival Capt. CRAVEN communicated with the captain of the frigate *Dauntless*, expressing regret at Prince ALBERT's death, and asking if he might fire, as a tribute of respect, twenty-one minute guns. He was notified that the Queen had requested that no guns be fired in the vicinity of Osborne. The compliment, therefore, although fully appreciated, could not be accepted.

The *Nashville* continued in dock. The Government had observed the strictest neutrality towards her, and nothing whatever had been permitted to be done to her but what was absolutely necessary to make her seaworthy. Neither powder, guns, nor munitions of war had been put on board. During the night of the 9th, three armed men from the *Tuscarora* were discovered reconnoitering the *Nashville*, and were ordered off by the dock superintendent. Fires were lighted on the *Nashville* on the 10th, and there was an impression she was about to sail, but she made no movements. The *Tuscarora* was on the alert with steam up.

The *Sumter* was reported to have left Cadiz for Southampton.

It was also reported that another National vessel was cruising in the channel, and might be expected at Southampton.

The *Morning Herald* is surprised that the Government has not given orders to the authorities at Southampton to warn the *Tuscarora* that she must either quit port at once, or wait until twenty-four hours have elapsed after the departure of the *Nashville*. We should not, says the *Herald*, have allowed the *Nashville* to lie in wait within the mouth of the Mersey for American packets and merchantmen. Therefore, we cannot, without a gross violation of our duty as neutrals, allow the *Tuscarora* a license we should have refused her enemy. The *Herald* holds out the course of the French authorities at Martinique between the *Iroquois* and *Sumter* as an example to follow.

GENERAL ENGLISH NEWS.

Dr. RUSSELL, in his correspondence to the *Times*, predicts the fate of the American Government will be sealed if January passes without some great victory.

MCLARIN, mate of the American ship *Ganges*, had been committed for trial in London, for murdering one of the crew at sea.

The London Money market on the 10th opened firm, but toward the close showed some slight reaction, Consols closing at ⅛ decline, attributed solely to realizations after the advance.

The market on the 11th was dull but steady.

Since the reduction of the Bank *minimum* of Thursday, to 2½ per cent., money has been pretty plentiful in the open market, at 2¼ per cent. for the best bills and was offered on the Stock Exchange at 1 per cent.

There had been a considerable advance in Saltpetre, under the idea that the export prohibition would soon be removed.

FRANCE.

The Bourse was firm and advancing; Rentes, 68f. 65c.

The monthly returns of the Bank of France showed a decrease in cash of over 18,000,000 of francs.

The increase in bills discounted was nearly 61,000,000 francs.

The Paris correspondent of the *Morning Post* asserts that the French official circles felt much satisfaction at the pacific termination of the *Trent* affair, while the effect on the Bourse was an immediate rise of 1 per cent.

The *Moniteur* of the 11th says a feeling of profound regret and indignation has been aroused in England as well as France by the vindictive act of destroying the port of Charleston.

SPAIN.

A Cadiz telegram of the 10th says the American Consul had received orders to protest against the admission of the *Sumter* into that port. It was said Spain would protect the prisoners brought by the *Sumter*.

The suspension of SHEA's Bank, at Madrid, is attributed to heavy defalcations in the junior partner. The liabilities were estimated at £250,000, and upward.

ITALY.

The majority of the Chamber of Deputies had unanimously resolved to continue to support RICASOLI's Government.

GERMANY.

A violent shock of earthquake was felt at Dresden on the 9th. It extended as far as Leipsic. No damage is reported.

HOLLAND.

The Ministers had tendered their resignations.

RUSSIA.

It was reported that Russia had sent an embarrassing ultimatum to Rome to the effect that if the Pope does not condemn the conduct of the Polish clergy, Russia will recognize the Kingdom of Italy.

TURKEY.

The Turks at Tripoli have maltreated several Christian inhabitants. The French Consul demanded indemnity, and a French frigate had arrived off the port.

INDIA AND CHINA.

Additional telegrams had been received in anticipation of the arrival of these mails.

At Calcutta, Dec. 15, the produce markets were active. Rice freights to England, 72s. 6d.

After the *coup d'état* at Peking, a new regency was established, under the two Empresses.

The state of affairs was encouraging.

The rebels were in the vicinity of Shanghai, and the foreigners were prepared for an attack.

Ningpo was also in a state of alarm from the same cause.

At New-Zealand affairs looked peaceful. Sir GEO. GREY had accepted the invitation of the natives for a conference.

THE LATEST VIA QUEENSTOWN.

QUEENSTOWN, Sunday, Jan. 12.

The *Journal* of St. Petersburg publishes an article congratulating Mr. SEWARD on the uprightness and intelligence of his policy, and demanding that the *Trent* incident may become the starting-point of negotiations for the recognition by the Powers of common principles upon the question of the neutral flag. It also expects England to give the world solemn guarantees for the future by signing a convention, which, by insuring universal respect for the rights of neutral Powers, would contribute to the maintenance of peace, and mark the progress of civilization.

TURIN, Thursday, Jan. 12.

In reply to a motion made by Signor CRISPI in the Chamber of Deputies, for explanations relative to the late events at the Castle Moro, Baron RICASOLI stated that according to dispatches received by the Government, almost all the leaders of the movement had been arrested, and order restored.

PARIS, Wednesday, Jan. 11—Evening.

Rentes firm at 68f. 60c.

PARIS, Sunday, Jan. 12.

A decree by the Emperor appoints Marshal MAGNAN Grand Master of the Freemasons in France. The Grand Master has hitherto been elected by the Freemasons themselves.

Another decree regulates the taxation of foreign bonds and shares.

ROME, Sunday, Jan. 12.

The Bourbon Committee has deprived CHIANONE of the command of the brigands for having disobeyed his instructions by shooting prisoners.

WAS IT THE SUMTER?

The Montreal *Advertiser*, which is in the interest of the rebels, and has manifested an accurate knowledge of their affairs, makes the following statement concerning the rebel privateer at Cadiz:

"The Confederate privateer, or rather public armed ship, which has been playing the mischief with American ships off Cadiz, is not the *Sumter*, which is yet on her old beat; but one of the new vessels for which the *Nashville* took officers to Europe. Her name and that of her consorts will be known soon enough; in the meantime there will be weeping and wailing among the underwriters of Federal war risks."

ARRIVAL OF A PRIZE BARK.

The prize bark *Jarger Leorentzen*, (Danish,) in charge of prize-master Lieut. GERAUD, from Rio Janeiro to Havanna in 56 days, to which port she was going for orders, has arrived at this port. She has a cargo of 4,800 bags of coffee, and was captured Dec. 26, in lat. 7° N., and long. 38° 30', W., by United States ship *Morning Star*, in consequence of informality in her papers, from which it was supposed she was destined for New-Orleans. On the 16th inst. while off Bermuda, spoke brig *John Butler*, bound to Antigua. The *Butler* had lost her deck load, and had sustained some damage. The *Leorentzen* experienced heavy easterly winds on her way from Bermuda.

The Storm at Boston.

BOSTON, Sunday, Jan. 26.

The storm cleared up about midnight. It is fine and breezy to-day. The night mail train from New-York, which was delayed by a freight train off the track, arrived at 2 P. M. to-day.

IMPORTANT FROM FORTRESS MONROE.

Not a Word of News from the Burnside Expedition.

The Vessels Disappeared from Pamlico Sound.

WRECK OF THE TRANSPORT LOUISIANA.

Acknowledgment by the Rebels of their Defeat at Mill Spring.

HOW THEY ACCOUNT FOR IT.

THE CAPTURE OF CEDAR KEYS, FLORIDA.

FORTRESS MONROE, Saturday, Jan. 25.

The storm has cleared away, and the sun is now shining.

In consequence of the rough weather the *George Washington* has not made the trip to Cherrystone since Tuesday.

The *Adelaide* did not arrive from Baltimore until about 1 o'clock this afternoon.

The *Georgiana* was detained last night. She left this afternoon for Baltimore.

A flag of truce this afternoon took to Craney Island several rebel officers, who arrived yesterday morning from Baltimore. The boat also brought back several passengers to go North.

The U. S. transport *Louisiana*, of Gen. BURNSIDE's Expedition, formerly of the line between Old Point and Baltimore, has been beached to prevent her falling into the hands of the rebels. She was burnt. All hands were saved.

The light-boat on the Middle Shoal, placed there to supply the absence of the Cape Henry Light-house, went ashore last night on Pleasure-house Beach. The crew were taken to Norfolk.

The Norfolk *Day-Book*, of Saturday, contains not a word of Gen. BURNSIDE's Expedition, excepting a paragraph on the weather, saying that it is under the impression that the Burnside Expedition is the cause of it all. Somebody relieved themselves yesterday by wishing that said fleet would either go to the bottom or go home, as they were tired of such bad weather, and never expected to see better while they are menacing the South.

An extract is given from the Newbern *Progress*, of Thursday last, which says, in reference to the reported presence of the fleet in Pamlico Sound:

"Up to this writing, (Wednesday) we are not sure that there is now, or ever has been, a Yankee gunboat over the swash at Hatteras or not. The latest news we have is from Capt. HILL, who arrived here, yesterday, from Matamuskeet, Hyde County, through the Sound, and says he saw nothing in the Sound in the shape of a gunboat. We shall probably hear more before going to press, as Col. G. B. SINGLETARY sought and obtained permission from the Commanding General to go on a reconnoitering expedition down the river. He left Tuesday evening."

A postscript added to the above article says:

"Col. SINGLETARY had not arrived when we went to press, and we are still in doubt."

A dispatch, dated Wilmington, 24th, says there was a heavy wind from the east-northeast all night, and to-day, up to 9 o'clock this morning, there is nothing new from the coast, except an apparent wreck drifting shoreward this morning, fifteen miles east of New Inlet.

The rebels at last admit their defeat in Kentucky. The *Day Book* says, under the head of "Further particulars from the Somerset disaster—Not so so bad as first reported by our side—Six thousand Confederates attack fourteen thousand Federals:"

"The Petersburgh *Express* sends us the following: Gen. CRITTENDEN began the attack at 7 o'clock Sunday morning. The enemy was supposed to be 1,500, but afterward found out to be 14,000 strong. Gen. ZOLLICOFFER was killed early in the action. Gen. CRITTENDEN was wounded, Col. CARROLL took command of the forces, and recrossed the Cumberland River. Our loss was three hundred. The enemy lost four or five hundred. RUTLEDGE's and MCCLURG's batteries were left on the field. We marched 7 miles. The enemy were repulsed three times and fell back to their fortifications. They then outflanked us. We retreated to our breastworks, were surrounded and crossed the Cumberland River under fire, eight o'clock Sunday night. We lost all our horses, tents, equipments, eleven guns, spiked, or thrown into the river. Cols. POWELL, BATTLE, STOKES and CUMMINGS were wounded. Maj. FAGG was wounded in the hip. Gen. ZOLLICOFFER's body has not been recovered. Our forces were 6,000. We are still falling back."

A second dispatch dated Petersburgh, 24th, says:

"A despatch from a friend at Knoxville has just been received, saying that Gen. CRITTENDEN rallied at Monticello, and will make a stand there. The disaster to our forces was very much exaggerated by the fugitives.

The paragraph relative to the loss of the *Louisiana* is founded on a prevailing report at Norfolk.

The Norfolk *Day Book* has an article from the Charleston *Mercury* headed "Important from Florida," giving the particulars of the capture of Cedar Keys. There were three schooners and five fishing smacks loading there at the time the "Yankees" took the place. The schooners were loaded with lumber and turpentine. The *Mercury's* informant thinks they were destroyed by the owners on Thursday night, 16th, as soon as it was ascertained that the Yankees intended to attack the town. The President of the Railroad went down with two companies of infantry to protect the property, and a message was sent to Gen. WAPIER for assistance. During Thursday firing was heard in the direction of Cedar Keys, and our fleet no doubt, has taken the place.

THE MARYLAND LEGISLATURE.

PEARCE AND KENNEDY REQUESTED TO RESIGN.

BALTIMORE, Sunday, Jan. 26.

Resolutions were introduced into the Maryland Senate on Saturday, to request Senators PEARCE and KENNEDY to resign, on the ground that their sentiments are in direct conflict with the settled view of the people of the State, and that it is right and proper that the State should, at this critical juncture, be represented by Senators whose hearts beat responsive to the throb of devotion to the integrity of the Union, felt by the great popular heart of the State.

AN ESCAPE INTO DIXIE.

BALTIMORE, Friday, Jan. 24.

The British schooner *Edwin*, Capt. GORDON, which cleared hence 14th inst. for Barbados, has been run ashore near Back River, in the bay, the cargo landed and the vessel burnt. The Captain and certain passengers, who went from here concealed in the vessel, escaped into Virginia. It now turns out that the Captain and owners are citizens of North Carolina, and she was put under the British flag to enable them to carry our their designs.

THE ARMY AND NAVY.

The naval recruiting returns for last week show that three hundred and twenty-five men were shipped in this City, one hundred and eighty of whom were for Capt. PORTER's mortar fleet, and the rest for general service. This is a larger number than has been shipped in any week during the last six months. The number of disposable seamen on board the *North Carolina* is eight hundred.

Lieut. WORDEN, who has been in charge of the South-street naval rendezvous since November, is appointed to the steamer *Ericsson*.

Recruiting for the regular army presents no new feature. The business done here last week was of the slightest possible character. The general service offices did not enlist a single recruit, and the regimental offices were not much more fortunate. A small detachment of recruits, enlisted during the last ten days for the Fifth Artillery, were sent on Saturday to Harrisburgh, Penn., where the regiment is being organized. The official headquarters of the regiment are at Fort Pickens, Pensacola. The Eleventh Infantry, headquarters at Fort Independence, Boston harbor, has two recruiting offices here, which have not yet met with much success.

The battalion of the Twelfth Infantry, at Fort Hamilton, has not received any addition to its strength lately. Between seventy and eighty men are still required to bring up this battalion to the authorized standard of eighty men. Some of the recruiting offices in the country are said to have as many men as would complete the battalion, but are holding them back for the second battalion, which will be organized as soon as the first is full.

A report is current in military circles, that, in consequence of the new infantry regiment filling up so very slowly, they will be consolidated and sent off to the war. Should this be the case, it is very probable that some three hundred of the newly appointed officers will be mustered out of the service. The date of the organization of these new regiments is 14th May, 1861—nearly eight months and a half ago.

The very stormy weather, on Saturday, put a stop to all outside work at the Brooklyn Navy-yard. The only changes since Friday are the floating of the gunboat *Forbes* into the dry dock, and the hauling of the sloop-of-war *John Adams* into the berth vacated by the *Owasco*, near the storehouse, to facilitate the discharging of her stores.

The following is a complete list of all vessels at present in the Navy-yard, and shows what they are doing:

Name.	Guns.	What Doing.
North Carolina	84	Receiving ship.
Sabine	50	In commission, receiving stores.
John Adams	22	Out of commission, discharging stores
Richmond	22	In commission, receiving stores, &c.
Oneida (new)	9	Fitting out, nearly completed.
Octorara (new)	7	Fitting out, nearly completed.
Kanawha (new)	4	In commission, ready for sea.
Owasco (new)	4	In commission, ready for sea.
Dacotah	9	Repairing boilers, &c.
Forbes	6	In Dry Dock for repairs.
Verona	10	Altered at private ship-yard, and now being armed and got ready for commission.
Jackson	8	
Sachem	5	
Uncas	5	
Currituck	5	
Corwin	4	Revenue cutter.
Adirondack, (sloop-of-war,) on the stocks.		
Lackawanna, (frigate,) on the stocks.		

In addition to the above there are sixteen vessels belonging to Capt. PORTER's fleet, which are receiving their armament and stores. We printed a correct list of them on Saturday.

There are about 3,610 men at the military and naval stations around New-York. They are distributed as follows:

	Men.		Men.
Governors Island	570	North Carolina	800
Fort Hamilton	800	Marine Barracks	210
Fort Lafayette	65	Vessels in harbor, ab't	900
Bedloe's Island	65	West Point, about	200
Total			3,610

THE EIGHTH NEW-HAMPSHIRE REGIMENT.

BOSTON, Saturday, Jan. 25.

The Eighth New-Hampshire Regiment, Col. FEARING, arrived from Worcester this afternoon, and is temporarily quartered in Faneuil Hall.

The storm prevented the transportation of the regiment to Fort Independence.

THE SEVENTY-EIGHTH REGIMENT (CAMERON RIFLE HIGHLANDERS.)

This regiment, Col. S. M. ELLIOTT commanding, has now nearly its full complement of men. Gov. MORGAN has given orders that all requirements for the complete organization of the regiment should be furnished. Companies or skeleton companies attaching themselves to the Seventy-eighth will retain their company organization, with their own officers. The headquarters of the regiment are at No. 246 Fourth-street.

OUR CAIRO CORRESPONDENCE.

CAPT. PORTER ON A WHALING EXPEDITION.

UNITED STATES GUNBOAT FLEET,
FORT JEFFERSON, Saturday, Jan. 18, 1862.

In order that your readers may form a correct estimate of the authors of the subjoined correspondence, respectively, a brief explanatory statement seems to be necessary. MARSH MILLER, the commander of the rebel gunboat *Grampus*, is one of the most desperate and at the same time cowardly men in Secesh. We have driven him before us at least a dozen times, and now he sends us this absurd challenge. The *Grampus* is well known to be a species of spouting-fish, and this particular one frequently runs up the Mississippi to blow, and then runs down again. We are going down the river to-morrow to see if his courage is up to the standing point; but we are afraid he will draw a bee line to Columbus, as he has heretofore always done.

The public well know that Capt. PORTER is not one of the rose-water heroes, and he will not be expected to waste compliments on men whose treasonable and cowardly conduct he holds in supreme contempt. The following is a verbatim copy of his first dispatch to the Commander of the *Grampus*, written after he had repeatedly driven the craven rebel down under the shelter of the land batteries at Columbus:

PORTER TO MILLER.

Come out here, you cowardly rebels, and show your gunboats. PORTER.

MILLER'S REPLY.

MARINE HEADQUARTERS,
COLUMBUS, Ky., Jan. 13, 1862.

Commander Porter, on United States Gunboat Essex:

SIR: The iron clad steamer *Grampus* will meet the *Essex*, at any point and time your Honor may appoint, and show you that the power is in our hands. An early reply will be agreeable to

Your obedient servant, MARSH J. MILLER,
Capt. Commanding C. S. I. C. Steamer *Grampus*.

CAPT. PORTER'S REJOINDER.

UNITED STATES GUNBOAT *Essex*,
WM. D. PORTER, Commanding,
FORT JEFFERSON, Saturday, Jan. 18, 1862.

To the traitor Marsh Miller, commanding a Rebel Gunboat called the Grampus:

Commander PORTER has already thrashed your Gunboat Fleet; shelled and silenced your Rebel Batteries at the Iron Banks; *chased your miserable and cowardly self down behind Columbus*; but if you desire to meet the *Essex*, show yourself any morning in Prentys' Bend, and you shall then meet with a traitor's fate—if you have the courage to stand.

God and our Country; "Rebels offend both."
(Signed.) PORTER.

Our flag-ship, the *Benton*, has been condemned Her machinery does not work satisfactorily, but Capt. PORTER thinks she is fast enough for our purpose. He says we don't contemplate *running*, and for this reason he would rather have them all slow, so that if they get into a tight place they will be obliged to fight their way out. Capt. P. only believes in running when the enemy lead the way. SIGNAL.

FATAL ACCIDENT—THE RESULT OF INTEMPERANCE.—Yesterday, Coroner WILDEY held an inquest, at No. 94 Baxter-street, on the body of JOSEPH MCCABE, a native of Ireland, thirty-four years of age, who, while intoxicated, on Saturday night, attempting to ascend a stair, fell over a banister a distance of twelve feet, and was killed immediately. The jury rendered a verdict of death by accident, resulting from intemperance.

THE WAR IN KENTUCKY.

Details of the Battle of Mill Creek.

FULL ACCOUNT OF THE ACTION.

Desperate Fighting on Both Sides.

DEATH OF ZOLLICOFFER.

Total Rout and Demoralization of the Enemy.

Gen. Crittenden Probably Hiding in the Woods.

Special Correspondence of the Cincinnati Gazette.

CAMP NEAR SOMERSET, Tuesday, Jan. 21.

The enemy, under the immediate command of Maj.-Gen. CRITTENDEN, marched, eight regiments strong, from their camp, last Saturday night. Their mounted grand guards were skirmishing through the greater part of the night with ours. Col. WOLFORD's cavalry were doing outpost duty that night, and by their behavior then, and in the battle afterward, completely cleared away the reproach which some unworthy officers have brought upon them. They will always fight well when WOLFORD is with them. The Tenth Indiana occupied a wooded hill on the right of the road. On the left was a field, stretching down the hill for several hundred yards. In front of the woods was another field of about twenty acres.

The enemy formed in these two fields, attacking the Indiana troops both in front and upon their left flank. A section of Capt. STANDART's Battery had been brought up, and was stationed in the road. The attack here was made about 7 o'clock in the morning. Col. MANSON coming up to the position just after the attack began, and seeing that his men must be overpowered before the other regiments could come up, ordered his men to fall back, which they did in good order, fighting as they went. Capt. STANDART reluctantly gave up the privilege of "giving the enemy one good blizzard" from that point, and retired, too.

Immediately to the rear of the woods where the Tenth were stationed is another field, with a steep descent to a ravine, and then comes another dense forest. On the left of the road the clearings continue to the ravine, the sides of which at that point are covered with a growth of scrub oaks and other timber.

After crossing the river another field lies on the left of the road. The Tenth retired through the field on the right of a road, and through the woods for about a hundred and fifty yards to the rear of the ravine. At this point, Col. FRY's Fourth Kentucky came up and formed along the fence which separates the road from the field on the left. There is no fence on the right of the road at that point. The two regiments here formed in the shape of a "V," its point toward the enemy advancing from the ravine, behind which they had reformed after their temporary success in the first attack. For nearly an hour they tried to break that "V," but failed.

What rebel regiments came through the woods to attack the Tenth at this place, I have not learned. Those which attacked Col. FRY were BATTLE's Tennessee and the Fifteenth Mississippi, the "Wigfall Rifles," and the "Mississippi Tigers," as they loved to call themselves. These were the crack regiments of the enemy, and they sustained their reputation. Again and again they charged across the field, but were always met by the terrible fire of the Kentucky Fourth, and driven back.

At the point of the "V" died Gen. ZOLLICOFFER. He fell nearer our camp than any other man of his army. He was with BATTLE's Regiment, his own home friends, born and brought up around him at Nashville. A short distance from him, to his right, a party of his men had been broken from their comrades and were herding together like frightened deer. Col. FRY's men were just about to fire on them. Col. FRY himself was at the right of his regiment at the point of greatest danger. Gen. ZOLLICOFFER was on foot and within a few feet of the Colonel. A gum coat concealed his uniform. Seeing the condition of his men, as the Colonel rode up, Gen. ZOLLICOFFER said to Col. FRY, "Colonel, you would not fire upon your friends, would you?" Col. FRY supposed, from the General's manner and remark, that he was one of our own officers, and at once replied, "Certainly not, Sir; I have no such intention." He turned and rode a few steps, when one of the General's aids fired at him, wounding his horse. Believing that he was tricked, Col. FRY at once wheeled and fired at the General. The latter raised his hand to his breast and fell dead. Another ball struck him at the same moment, I believe, in the arm.

Here, too, fell young BAILIE PEYTON, son of a venerable man, well known to the nation. Young PEYTON, like his father, struggled long against disunion. He was hissed and insulted last May for telling his love for the old Union.

It was near this point that my only personal friend, so far as I know, in the Southern army, was wounded. You remember ALLAN BATTLE. There is no one of the Oxford boys of four years ago who does not remember and love him, and who did not mourn when we heard that he had joined the rebel army. Married into one of our best known and most respected Ohio families, educated in a Northern college, (Miami University,) and with so many ties of friendship binding him to the North, it was no thoughtless spirit or bitter hatred which made him take up arms against us. Last June he took his young wife to her father's and then returned to Nashville to close up his father's unsettled affairs, intending then to go North again, and await the issue of what must be, to him, a sad contest. But the tide in Nashville was too strong for him. His father and brothers were in the army. All the young men of the South were rushing into it. To carry out his first intention would be to separate himself forever from his own family and from his birthplace, for to the men of the South their independence seemed at that time *un fait accompli*, and one who deserted them then would always be a marked and proscribed man.

And so he went into the army. I talked about him with a wounded prisoner, the color-bearer of BATTLE's regiment. He spoke of him with an affection which you and many others of our acquaintance will echo. He said that ALLAN had often told him of his hatred of this war and his unwillingness to fight; "the best friends he had in the world outside of his own family." ALLAN was the adjutant of his father's regiment. The color-bearer, marching beside him, had his leg broken by a ball, and fell. Young BATTLE caught up the flag, advanced a step, waving it, when he too was shot in the shoulder. He fell, and, rising again, was struck by a bullet on the cheek. He was able to walk from the field, and made his escape. This prisoner did not think that either of the wounds was dangerous, though another told me that he was badly wounded. He related the incident in the same way.

The death of their General does not seem to have greatly disheartened the enemy. They continued their attacks with as much vehemence as ever. The Second Minnesota Regiment came up and formed along the fence, on the left of the Fourth Kentucky. The rebels still extended their line to flank us on that side. The Fifteenth Mississippi charged up to the fence, and the men in the two regiments fought hand to hand, catching hold of each other's guns, and trying to drag them through and over the fence, but it was all in vain.

MCCOOK's gallant Dutchmen came up to support the Tenth, forming on their right, and with them, driving the enemy out of the woods, over the ravine, up the hill, across the field to the right of the road. The Fourteenth Ohio, which, with the Ninth, had marched all night to get to the battle, together with the two East Tennessee and the Twelfth Kentucky regiments, were coming up. The enemy themselves were in danger of being outflanked and cut off from their retreat. STANDART's Battery was in full play, with deadly effect, on their centre. KINNEY's and WHITMORE's were advancing. There was no help for it, the day was lost to the rebels, and they must retreat. They were pushed back, flying as they went across the fields. Our deadly Minié balls told fearfully on their ranks; yet the loss was not all theirs. Many of our brave fellows dropped. Col. WOLFORD's horse was shot under him, as he charged upon their centre. BOB MCCOOK was wounded, and his horse shot under him. But a bullet through the heart would hardly stop *him*.

On they went. The enemy is driven through the woods, where, an hour and a half before, they nearly surrounded the Tenth, the heroes of Rich Mountain. Many regiments are completely broken, and run for the forests on the left. WOOD's Alabama regiment breaks for a swamp, and scatter there. It has a home look to them, and is a safer place than the road or the fields. Some regiments act together, and form in a field a mile to the rear of their first position. But STANDART's shells, thrown from the hill where the section was so nearly taken, begin to fall among them. They fly again, pursued by our victorious troops. For the third and last time they form, only to be scattered as before.

After this the rout is complete. Panic-stricken, they fly in all directions. The pursuit is pressed up to the very intrenchments of the enemy. Two of their pieces have been taken. The third, which they took with them, is only saved to be left behind in their flight across the river. Our cannon open on their camp, our shells falling into their most effective battery, killing four of the men at their guns and driving the rest away. The darkness of nightfall only prevents a general assault, and our troops lie down, hoping in the morning to complete the good work of that Sabbath, a work they had not sought, for they were resting that day, preparatory to the attack which Gen. THOMAS had intended to make on Monday.

I rode over the battle-field in the evening. Our men were burying the dead, but many still lay ghastly where they fell. The wounded had been all taken up. The same kind treatment was extended to the enemy's wounded which was given to our own. The universal remark which they made to me as I passed through the hospital was: "We never expected to be treated so. We have been misled. We expected to be served like dogs should we fall into your hands. You are kinder to us than we would have been to you." The only difference was in the burial of the dead. Those of the enemy were laid together in common pits. Our own were buried in separate graves, and on many of them I saw young cedars already planted by their comrades.

Beside one of the graves prepared for the enemy's killed, I noticed several lying ready to be interred. One poor boy lay in the exact position, as I was told, in which he was found. He rested on his side, his head lying on his right arm, while his left hand was loosely closed on his right elbow. His eyes were closed, and he looked as though he had just fallen asleep.

I need not tell you how we marched that night, through the horrible mud, nor how our boys have been dropping in all day, worn out with fatigue, disappointed because they had all the labor with none of the glory of victory, and only consoled by the promise that a few days more will see us on our way to Tennessee. There is nothing to oppose us now. CRITTENDEN's army is no longer, and never again will be, an army. Totally demoralized, scattered to the winds, they will go home or be captured piecemeal. We wait only for our provision train and the means of crossing the river.

And now my long and imperfect story of the battle is ended. I fear that I have not given in all things a correct account of it, but I have done my best to do so. If I have given the credit of this, the most decisive victory of the war, to some regiments which properly belongs to others, or have made mistakes in my description of what they all did, I can only say to them that if they will but let me know when they next have a fight in time for me to be there, I will tell exactly what they do, and give them all full justice.

It will be a matter of surprise to the whole nation that the rebels should leave their fortified camp on the river to attack us in the open field. The fact is they knew that they either had to fight or retreat. Gen. BOYLE's Brigade had cut off their river communication with Nashville and threatened their rear. They knew that Gen. THOMAS was advancing on the Columbia Road, and that his regiments had necessarily become scattered by reason of the bad roads and high water. They had found out that we had taken possession of Hudson's Ford. They believed that Fishing Creek was so high, that Gen. SCHOEPF's forces could not cross, and were totally unaware of the arrival of the two Tennessee regiments, and the Twelfth Kentucky at Gen. THOMAS' camp. In danger of being surrounded completely and starved out, they had either to retreat or do what they did—try to cut us up piecemeal. They thought that they were attacking but three regiments. They made the attempt, and were bitterly foiled. They left on the field of battle one hundred and fifty dead and as many wounded, besides the many whom they succeeded in sending away before the pursuit became too hot for them. Our loss was 38 killed and 134 wounded.

One mystery still remains unraveled. Where is Major-Gen. GEORGE B. CRITTENDEN? Nothing was seen of him after the battle turned against him. It appears that he did not get back to his camp, for the order of retreat was signed by "Col. CUMMINGS, Acting Brigadier-General, in command of the troops." Did he put on a "hat, a kerchief and a muffler, and so escape?" I think that any woman's gown might fit him since this battle of Cliff Creek, without hunting for that of "my aunt, the fat woman of Brentford."

There is a strange rumor floating through the country and in our camps that he was cut off from the main body of his army, and with two regiments is still hiding somewhere in the woods this side of the river. Nobody can tell the exact spot, but the forests are wide and wild, abounding in squirrels and woodchucks, and there are still some chickens left on the scattered farms. I don't believe anyone will ever be able to find the mythical rebels, but I have no doubt that the children in the western part of Pulaski County will, for a long time be afraid to go out alone at night, or into the woods in daytime, and that they will grow up with the fixed idea, which they will in turn transmit to their descendants, that somewhere upon the hills, on the Cumberland or among the wild cliffs of Fishing Creek, wanders a lost Major-General with a sword ten feet long and eyes like balls of fire, and with him two thousand gigantic Tennesseeans who live on babies and applejack, drink JEFF. DAVIS' health from gourds full of blood, and sing "Dixie" in the tree tops all night long in the full of the moon.

THE NARRATIVE OF ANOTHER WITNESS.

Correspondence of the Cincinnati Commercial.

ZOLLICOFFER'S (LATE) ENCAMPMENT, Jan. 20, 1862.

Here I sit in a cedar log cabin, inside the intrenchments of the wonderful position of old "Zolly," to write you a letter, on contraband paper, with a contraband pen and contraband ink. Where shall I begin—what shall I write first? There are incidents enough, if all recounted, to fill a volume; things that took place in this, the most complete victory, and most overwhelming, total overthrow, the secession army has yet met with in this rebellion. To begin at the beginning, and tell the story straight:

Just at daybreak on Sunday morning, the 19th of January, sharp firing commenced with the pickets [illegible] the same spot where the firing was last Friday n[illegible]; the long roll beat in the Indiana Tenth, a[illegible] they formed instantly and marched to the suppo[illegible] of their pickets. The Tenth and KINNEY's batter[illegible] were close together, and half a mile in advance of everything. The battery got ready for action [illegible] on the instant, and awaited orders. By the way [illegible] STANNARD's battery and WETMORE's four gun batte[illegible] were both in park, one on each side of KINNE[illegible] battery. The First Tennessee was about a quarter of a mile in the rear of these batteries, in the woods. The Fourth Kentucky, Col. FRY, was the next regiment on the road, half a mile in the rear of the ba[illegible]; it was forming as I ran past, getting to my own regiment, (for I slept in KIN[illegible] battery;) the Second Tennessee, another quarter of [illegible] mile in [illegible] rear of the Fourth Kentucky. By this time [illegible] cavalry were running their horses all over the [illegible] country, in every direction except toward the [illegible]ing, which still continued at intervals. The Second was just getting breakfast, and supposing it to be only a picket fight, kept on cooking and eating, though very few had eaten anything when the column of our force appeared, coming on in our rear. Lieut.-Col. TREWHIT promptly got us into line, and double-quicked us into the road ahead of the advancing column; the Fourth Kentucky had gone when we reached their encampment. The firing still continued, and very briskly; we kept on at double-quick, all hoping and believing that we would have a chance to smell burnt powder. But when opposite the encampment of the Tenth Indiana, up rode the Colonel and halted us for further orders; we all thought, if we didn't say it, d—n further orders.

The Tenth Indiana went into the woods about a quarter of a mile in advance of their tents, to the support of their pickets; and bravely did they support them, too, for over half an hour, against the whole force led against them; and never retreated a step, nor gave an inch of ground, until nearly surrounded by overwhelming numbers; then, to save themselves from being entirely surrounded, they unwillingly gave way. Here was a crisis; and yell on yell went up from the lantern-jawed Secessionists; they thought the day was all their own. But, happily, any disastrous consequence was prevented by the arrival of the Fourth Kentucky and Ninth Ohio, to the support of the gallant Tenth. Again our men made a stand; now there was fighting in good earnest; and the Second Minnesota joined in with the Tenth, and the Fourth, and the Ninth Ohio. Volley after volley rattled in quick succession, and sometimes it seemed as though there was only one continuous volley, interrupted now and then by the growling of the "yellow pups," which had been brought to bear on the enemy; and when they once commenced they distributed their favors freely in all directions, in the shape of shot and shell; and, gentlemen, excuse me from being the recipient of any such favors. There were only two or three shots from cannon fired by the enemy, and they were either badly aimed, or the pieces were out of range, for the shot did not disturb anybody. Once they threw a shell into the air, which burst when some four or five hundred feet high. No damage was done by it, and their artillery seemed to be of no use to them whatever; while, on the contrary, ours seemed to be of immense use to us, and it was most ably and effectively handled. After a little more than two hours of hard fighting, a most tremendous volley of musketry, followed by a ringing shout from our side, seemed to have decided the battle in our favor, for, from that time, although firing was kept up at intervals, the Secessionists, whipped and cowed, began their retreat, which, in about twenty minutes more, became a total rout; and from the indications along the road, which we afterward passed over, the flight appeared to have been a regular race from that point back to their intrenchments, to see who could get there first, and the devil take the hindmost.

All the credit and honor of this battle is due to the

[Continued on Eighth Page.]

The Charleston Mercury.

DAILY PAPER—Ten Dollars per annum, payable half-yearly in advance.

VINDICEX NULLO
SPONTE SUA SINE LEGE FIDES RECTUMQUE COLENTUR.

COUNTRY PAPER—Three a Week—Five Dollars per annum, in advance.

VOLUME LXXX. CHARLESTON, S. C., WEDNESDAY, FEBRUARY 5, 1862. NUMBER 11,366

THE MERCURY

WEDNESDAY, FEBRUARY 5, 1862.

The Exportation of Cotton.

Our readers will remember how earnestly we have urged the policy of allowing no cotton or tobacco to be exported from the Confederate States. If left to fighting, we knew, that peace could be obtained only after a long and bloody struggle; but God had placed in our hands an instrumentality by which the interests of other nations were so powerfully controlled, that their intervention has been certain to compel the raising of the blockade, and a consequent peace at no distant day. That day was the working up of all the cotton of the last year's crop in Europe. It was as certain to come as the seasons. We had only to hold on to our cotton, and prevent its exportation from the Confederate States, and the result was inevitable. The inefficient blockade of our ports is no more consistent with the laws of nations than the seizure of Messrs. MASON and SLIDELL. National honor compelled the Ministers of Great Britain to interpose in the latter case; but *national necessity* must compel them to interpose in the former. In the main, the good sense and patriotism of the people have sustained the policy of preventing the exportation of cotton. The Legislature of Louisiana has passed a law to that effect; but still the love of gain in individuals has, in some instances, violated it. We will not now discuss the sophistries by which a course, so plainly prolonging the war and assisting our enemies, by taking away the inducement of foreign nations to break the blockade, are usually supported. If we want arms, the best way (probably the only sure way, now, to obtain them) is to compel foreign nations to break the blockade. If we want supplies of munitions of war, and clothing for our armies, force the breaking of the blockade. If we want peace—success to our cause—hold on to every bag of our cotton, until the millions in Europe, to whom it is bread and life, shall, by their sufferings and cries, compel their governments to break the blockade, and bring them cotton. This policy is now on the eve of victory. A very few more weeks, if supplies are not sent from this country, must force the alternative on foreign nations, of running or raising the blockade. Let us stand together in enforcing this policy, stronger than rifles and cannon, to defeat our foes and bring us peace. It is our only—our last instrumentality for a short war.

James Mason

John Slidell

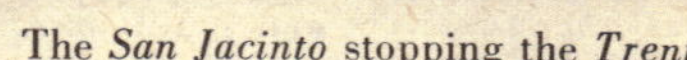

The *San Jacinto* stopping the *Trent*

Captain Charles Wilkes,
commander of the *San Jacinto*

The outrage over the *Trent* — Lord Lyons communicating Earl Russell's dispatch to Secretary Seward

The Charleston Mercury.

DAILY PAPER—Ten Dollars per annum, payable half-yearly in advance.

VINDICE NULLO
SPONTE SUA SINE LEGE FIDES RECTUMQUE COLENTUR.

COUNTRY PAPER—Three a Week—Five Dollars per annum, in advance.

VOLUME LXXX. CHARLESTON, S. C., MONDAY, FEBRUARY 3, 1862 NUMBER 11,364

THE BURNSIDE EXPEDITION.

THE VESSELS IN THE GALE.

GREAT LOSS AND SUFFERING.

The latest papers received from the North, by the way of Norfolk, are those of the 29th ult.—We get from them some important news of the Burnside Expedition. As great interest exists in the public mind concerning the disaster sustained by the fleet, we devote all our available space to the following summary, which we make up from our different sources of intelligence.

OFFICIAL DESPATCHES FROM GENERAL BURNSIDE.

A special messenger, with official despatches from General Burnside, reached Washington on the 28th ult. They are dated "Headquarters, Department North Carolina, Hatteras Inlet, January 26, 1862." The messenger left Hatteras on Sunday. General Burnside states:

We left our anchorage at Annapolis on Thursday, the 7th, and after a protracted passage, owing to dense fogs, arrived at Fortress Monroe on Friday night, at 12 o'clock. Leaving Fortress Monroe on Saturday, at 10 o'clock in the morning, we proceeded at once to sea, but owing to fogs on Sunday and Sunday night, our progress was very slow.

On Monday, the 13th, the weather cleared, with a heavy wind and rough sea, which caused our vessels to labor very heavily, and some were obliged to cut loose from the vessels they were towing. Most of them, however, passed over the bar and anchored inside the harbor, about 12 o'clock noon, on the 16th, just in time to escape the severe storm on Monday night and Tuesday.

The propeller City of New York ran on the bar, at the entrance of the harbor, and, owing to the severe weather and want of small boats, we could render her no assistance. She was laden with stores, and was lost.

The General also says he had been led to suppose that he would find experienced pilots at Hatteras, but he had great difficulty in accomplishing his wish for want of proper accommodations. He adds that he would commence that day to build a wharf for the landing of supplies. The men were cheerful and patient, and he would proceed with confidence.

After the arrival of the expedition at Hatteras, the enemy made their appearance in one or two vessels on a reconnoitering expedition. Our boats gave chase and drove them back. The transports and other vessels grounded will be got off by the aid of a tug-boat. Only one was lost (the City of New York), and no lives, with the exception of the three above referred to.

THE YANKEE NEWSPAPER ACCOUNT.

By the arrival of the steamer Eastern State, at Fortress Monroe, we have direct and official intelligence of the arrival of the Burnside expedition at its destination. The recent storms were unusually severe at Hatteras, and consequently delayed and crippled the expedition; but when the Eastern State left everything looked favorable.

The expedition sailed from Hampton Roads on the 11th and 12th instants, and consists of one hundred and twenty five vessels, of all classes. They arrived at Hatteras between the 12th and 17th, having been greatly retarded by severe storms and adverse winds, which prevailed about that time. After their arrival they experienced a series of storms of such unparalled severity that for two days in succession, it was impossible to hold communication between any two vessels of the fleet.

After the first storm, it was discovered that, instead of vessels drawing eight and a half feet being able to go over the swash, or bars, as General Burnside had been informed, no vessel drawing over seven and a quarter feet could pass into Pamlico sound. No vessel either could pass the outside bar drawing over thirteen feet, unless skilfully piloted; consequently the steamer City of New York struck on the bar, loaded with a cargo valued at $200,000, and consisting of powder, rifles and bombs, and proved a total loss. The captain and crew, after bravely remaining in the rigging for forty hours, were saved.

The gunboat Zouave dragged her anchors, stove a hole in her bottom, and sunk, proving a total loss. Her crew were saved.

The steamer Pocahontas went ashore near the lighthouse, and became a total wreck. Ninety valuable horses, belonging to the Rhode Island battery, were on board, and were all drowned, including several valued at five hundred dollars each.

The Grapeshot parted her hawser, by which she was towed, and went down at sea. Her crew were saved.

An unknown schooner, laden with oats; and another schooner, also unknown, were all lost on the beach. Six of the crew of the latter perished.

The steamer Louisiana struck on the bar, where she still remains. The report of her having been burned is entirely incorrect. She may be got off.

The Eastern Queen, and also the Voltigeur, are ashore. The latter will probably be got off.

The steamer New Brunswick, of Portland, Maine, is reported among the lost. She had the Ninth Maine Regiment aboard, about 700 in number.

The water vessels had not reached their destination when the Eastern State left, and had it not been for the condensers on board of some of the vessels and on shore, terrible sufferings would have occurred. As it was, the water casks were old whisky, camphene and kerosene oil casks. It is thought that the Union pilots of Hatteras have proved themselves traitors, having intentionally run several vessels ashore.

One of the storms can only be described as terrific. The waters in every direction were covered with foam, the waves dashing with a clear sweep across the Hatteras shore, and completely cutting off the post from all outside communication. The current was rushing at the rate of five miles per hour, and the chop seas prevented Gen. Burnside from answering any of the signals of distress or communicating with his generals. At one time flags would appear Union down on a number of vessels, indicating a want of water, coal or provisions.

Col. J. W. Allen, Ninth Jersey regiment, and Surgeon F. S. Weller, with a boat's crew, and the second mate of the Ann E Thompson, when they found that the troops needed water, manned the lifeboat in order to reach the General. Unfortunately the boat was swamped, and the colonel, surgeon and mate were drowned. The boat's crew were saved.

Despite all these adverse circumstances, Gen. Burnside has succeeded in getting over the bar one half of his vessels, all the gunboats, and seven thousand troops. Everything appeared in a satisfactory condition when the Eastern State left.

The large transports with the troops remained outside of the bar, until the arrival of the S. R. Spalding, from Port Royal, on the 23d, when Captain Howes volunteered to bring them all inside. This was accomplished yesterday afternoon, the Eastern State passing the last as she left. A portion of the gunboats chartered by Gen. Burnside for the expedition refused to proceed further than Fortress Monroe.

Fall weather has now set in, and the schooners are making their appearance with water and coal, and everything looks promising. The General is confident of ultimate success, and has the respect of every man under his command.

General Burnside left Fortress Monroe on the Picket, but subsequently took possession of the Spaulding, which he will occupy as his flag ship. She will be used for taking the remaining troops over the bar. The only troops that have been landed are the Twenty-Fourth Massachusetts regiment, and the Rhode Island battery. Col. Hawkins' regiment goes with Gen. Burnside's expedition, and their places will be supplied by the Sixth New Hampshire. There has been no loss of life except what is above mentioned. Eleven deaths have occurred since the fleet sailed.

Different statements are received at Hatteras from the surrounding population in relation to the disposition and intentions of the enemy.—Some who come in say that they are completely frightened and will not make a stand. Another report is, that large masses of troops will be concentrated in the vicinity, and still another story, confirmed by many, is, that their exertions will be directed chiefly to placing obstructions in our progress to Norfolk. The rebels keep a good lookout for our movements with their gunboats. Two of them made their appearance immediately after the storm, but disappeared when chased.

ADDITIONAL PARTICULARS—CONDITION OF THE FLEET.

From the Baltimore *American*, of the 29th ult., we get the following additional information in reference to the position of affairs at Hatteras Inlet when the steamer *Eastern State* left there:

STEAMER POCAHONTAS.

The Pocahontas went ashore on Saturday night week, ten miles north of Hatteras. Before she went ashore her wheel chain broke and her boilers were rolled off their legs. The engineer managed to keep steam up until she was beached, about twenty yards from shore. The crew landed, carrying a large hawser ashore, which they made fast to the beach.

The crew and soldiers on board in charge of the horses numbered eighty men. Those left on board escaped to the shore by the hawser. Some of the horses had been previously thrown overboard to lighten the boat. In three quarters of an hour afterwards the boat broke into three pieces and floated ashore. In the after cabin, when it came ashore, one of the horses was found quietly eating hay. Of the ninety horses on board only twelve came ashore alive. The men built large fires on the beach, and the light from them was probably taken by the rebels for the burning of a steamer. The crew afterwards made their way to the village at Big Kinnekeeth, where they were succored by the inhabitants, and afterwards came down the sound to Hatteras. The soldiers marched down the beach. The officers and crew were quartered on board the Louisiana. The officers are—Henry North, captain; Mr. Cator, first mate; Josiah Linthicum, second mate; Tone Hamilton, engineer, and others. They will come up by the next arrival.

THE LOUISIANA.

The Louisiana went ashore on Tuesday night, the 14th, on the inner bar, at Hatteras Inlet. On Thursday, the 23d, the steamer got afloat, but during a gale on the 24th again went ashore, the steamer New Brunswick having run over and carried away her anchor. The vessels also collided, and considerable damage was done to the upper works of each. The New Brunswick floated off, but the Louisiana still remained ashore. She remained tight, and would be got off at the first high tide. Her position was not considered dangerous. Capt. William H. Phelps was exerting himself to get her afloat, and, from the able manner in which he handled her during the storm, it was believed he would succeed.

THE VOLTIGEUR.

The bark Voltigeur was ashore inside the inlet. All her cargo was safe, but the vessel would not probably be got off.

THE GUNBOAT ZOUAVE.

This gunboat, a purchased vessel, bilged on the 15th, inside the inlet, and sunk on the bar. All her guns and stores were taken off.

THE CITY OF NEW YORK.

This vessel struck on a bar outside the inlet on the 13th. She broke in two and went to pieces on the next day. Nothing was saved from her.—Parts of her cargo floated into the inlet. The officers and crew were all saved.

General Pierre G. T. Beauregard, C.S.A.

COAL SCHOONER LOST.

A schooner, loaded with coal, struck on the inner bar on the 15th. Her crew were saved. A barge, name unknown, was lost outside.

STEAMSHIP SUWANEE.

This steamship was ashore inside the bar, but would be got off.

When the Eastern State left, the last ship outside, the Aracon, was going in, towed by the S. R. Spaulding. Several of the troop ships, drawing too much water, were lying inside the inlet, but could not pass over the inner bar. The troops on board these vessels were landed and transferred to boats inside the bar. There were about one hundred vessels in the sound and the remainder in the inlet.

REBEL RECONNOISSANCE.

On the 21st two rebel gunboats came down the sound reconnoitering. Several of our gunboats started after them, and shots were exchanged, but the thick fog prevented any long pursuit.

THE VESSELS LOST AND DISABLED.

THE LOUISIANA.

The Louisiana, disabled, is the largest steamer of the fleet, being one of the only two vessels which could carry an entire regiment. She is said to be the largest, finest and fastest steamer ever built at Baltimore, and was only chartered the day before the sailing of the fleet from Annapolis. Her hull is nearly 300 feet in length, of corresponding breadth of beam, with splendid state-rooms, and originally cost, including furniture, tackle, outfit, etc, about $105 000. She was built in 1852, by Mr. Hugh A. Cooper, the machinery made by Charles Reeder, and has made over twenty miles per hour. For more than three weeks the steamer has been attached to the Burnside expedition. Her principal officers are as follows: Captain, Philips; First Mate, Jacob Kirwan; Engineers, George W. Akers and Vance Wilson; Clerk, James Aspril. The Sixth New Hampshire regiment, Colonel Nelson Converse, were on board.

THE GRAPESHOT.

The Grapeshot, reported to have parted the hawser by which she was towed, and to have gone down at sea, was one of the floating batteries sent with the expedition. She was formerly a canal boat, was almost solid from deck to keel, and was divided into five compartments. She had but one deck. She was under the command of Master's Mate N. B. McKean, and carried two guns.

THE ZOUAVE.

The Zouave, also sunk, was a propeller gunboat, carrying four guns—one thirty-pounder Parrott rifled gun, two twelve-pounder Wiard rifled guns, and one twelve-pounder boat howitzer. She was commanded by Captain William Hunt.

Companies A, B, C, F, G and K, of the Twenty-fifth New York Regiment, were on board the Zouave. This regiment was attached to General Foster's command. His staff were also on board.

THE EASTERN QUEEN AND THE VOLTIGEUR.

Both of these vessels are reported ashore. The Eastern Queen is a side wheel steamer, under the command of Captain Collins. The Fourth Rhode Island, Colonel J. D. Rodman, attached to General Parke's brigade, were on board. The Voltigeur is a purchased sailing troop bark, under command of Captain William Bay. She had on board a portion of the Eleventh Connecticut, Colonel T. H. C. Kingsbury.

THE CITY OF NEW YORK.

The City of New York was an African vessel, 573 tons, fifteen feet draught, and with two decks. She was built of white oak, copper and iron fastened, and was launched at Hoboken in 1852. She has a vertical engine of three hundred horse power. She was one hundred and seventy feet long, with twenty-six feet beam, and formerly ran on the line between Boston and Philadelphia.

THE POCAHONTAS.

The Pocahontas was an old steamboat, built some twenty years ago, and used to run on the Chesapeake Bay. For some years she has been laid up in ordinary, and was only chartered a few days before the sailing of the expedition.

LATEST REPORTS FROM NEWBERN.

The Newbern N. C. *Progress*, of Saturday, gives us the following:

The latest news we have from Burnside and his expedition was received here early yesterday morning by the arrival of the Albemarle from Portsmouth. The news has nothing new, but is a confirmation merely of the news heretofore received, to wit: That a very large fleet is there.—The number of vessels in the Sound, however, has been increased from twenty to thirty-six.

The statement published the other day that three hundred men had been lost by the wrecking of a bark on the bar, which came to the Ocracoke people through a Yankee who professed to have deserted and was seeking conveyance to this place, has been contradicted by five other Yankees who visited Ocracoke subsequently, who say that only three persons were lost. Heavy firing has been going on occasionally at Hatteras for a few days, the object of which is not fully defined, supposed, however, to be target practice.

Since, through the indomitable energy of Col. Singletary, we have got a boat placed upon our river and a regular line of communication established, we are comparatively easy here, being in a condition to watch the movements of the enemy. Whenever an advance movement is made we will be as likely to know it here as the people at any other point, and shall continue to give whatever information we can that we know to come from "reliable gentlemen," regardless of the taunts of country newspapers; and predict that people abroad will soon learn, if they have not already, that all the "reliable" information they receive from the fleet comes through this place, unimportant as many ignorant persons suppose it to be.

The Charleston Mercury.

DAILY PAPER—Ten Dollars per annum, payable half-yearly in advance.

VINDICE NULLO SPONTE SUA SINE LEGE FIDES RECTUMQUE COLENTUR.

COUNTRY PAPER—Thrice a Week—Five Dollars per annum, in advance.

VOLUME LXXX. CHARLESTON, S. C., TUESDAY, FEBRUARY 4, 1862. NUMBER 11,365

THE MERCURY.

TUESDAY, FEBRUARY 4, 1862.

The Success of Our Cause.

We have never doubted the success of our cause; and events, although they have enlarged the sphere of contest, and promise to render it more bloody, does not, in the least, render doubtful the result. But we frankly confess that we did not anticipate these events. We did not anticipate the temporising and hesitation which produced the war. We did not anticipate the course of our Government in carrying on the war by a stand-still, defensive policy. We did not anticipate the course of foreign nations, in tolerating an insufficient and illegal blockade of our ports. These things no man could have anticipated. But, nevertheless, there is not a sign in the Southern heavens which betokens submission to Yankee domination. On the contrary, every day's experience, bringing with it the most untoward circumstances, but deepens and strengthens the determination of the Southern heart to win liberty and independence in this great contest. Has the possession of Port Royal won over to the enemy a single man in South Carolina? Is the spirit of South Carolina in the least broken by the occupancy of our hated enemies of a portion of our soil? Has the raid on Hatteras, or the expedition in Pamlico Sound, now preparing to harass her people and burn her towns, subdued, in the least, the people of North Carolina? Will the battle of Mill Creek, and the fall of Zollicoffer, unnerve the spirit of the people of Tennessee? In fact, does not every success (as they call it) of our enemies, tend more certainly to defeat their object of subduing us to their dominion, by uniting the Southern people in a more intense hatred and determination to resist it? Our danger has been compromise and a false peace. The war has developed the characteristics of our Yankee foes. The Southern people generally were totally ignorant of them; but every day which continues the war, develops their hateful characteristics. Their very successes develope them. The grand attempt of their stone-fleet to destroy Charleston harbor—their Confiscation Acts—their murders—their burnings in the Frontier States—their wanton destruction of property—their conduct towards our slaves—all tend to defeat their object. They are making sure that separation, which they produced by their folly, and which now they endeavor to defeat by their wickedness. They are the best friends of the Disunionists of the South. They establish, by the most undisputable proofs, the soundness of the disunion policy, and show to the world that, like a nest of rattlesnakes, they are only fit to live by themselves. Nor can we fail to see, that we of the South are to make the last stand on record for free representative government in the world. It is gone forever in the North. Their contest now with us, is a contest between despotism and conservative liberty to the Southern white race. It is more—it is a contest for abolition and the ruin of the country; for no man can doubt the doom of slavery under their despotic dominion. The redemption and independence of the Confederate States are more certain, if that is possible, than they have ever been.

THE WAR ON THE COAST.

YANKEE NEWS FROM PORT ROYAL.

THE BLOCKADE OF CHARLESTON.

We have received Northern papers of very recent dates, which contain some interesting letters from Port Royal and the blockading squadron off this coast. We make up a full summary of the news contained in these accounts:

THE YANKEE COLONY IN SOUTH CAROLINA—A NEWSPAPER TO BE PUBLISHED—APPEARANCE OF "THE CITY" OF HILTON HEAD.

HILTON HEAD, January 30.

Though we have settled down in our places here, and have fortified ourselves so that we may remain here till doomsday for all the forces Secession may bring against us; yet our aggressive tendencies are not at all deadened, and our commanders, unless I am greatly mistaken, are not yet satisfied with the work they have done in carrying the Stars and Stripes into the Southern territory. Yankee energy and ingenuity among the soldiers, are, however, at work in the meantime, to make this place a model of a Northern growing prosperous city on Southern soil. We have a postoffice established here, and I understand that the postmaster, Mr. Joseph Sears, is also on the point of establishing a weekly newspaper here, to be called the New South. Many of the officers have had their wives or families brought here, or have sent home for them, and women and children, and people in civilians' dress, are numerous about the town. It is looking here more like a city and less like a camp.—Yankee vessels within the waters hereabout, and merchant vessels from the North, are quite frequent here. A long wharf of four or five hundred feet extends into the harbor, giving every facility for loading and discharging vessels. A battalion of the First Massachusetts Cavalry, Col. Williams, arrived here last week.

A FLAG OF TRUCE AND A "PLEASANT INTERVIEW."

Since the affair on the first, one entire brigade of Tennessee troops have arrived at Port Royal Ferry and reinforced Gen. Donelson, who is now in command there. The rebels have received other reinforcements, and are now very strong at that point.

A flag of truce was sent to Port Royal Ferry, in charge of Dr. Kimball, Brigade Surgeon. The object was to exchange the body of a Confederate soldier for that of one of our men, who was taken prisoner while wounded, and who subsequently died in the enemy's hands. Dr. Kimball was met by some Confederate officers, who promised to carry his communication to the commanding officer, and return an answer on the following day, at 12 o'clock. On Thursday, Dr. Kimball again crossed the ferry in a small boat, with a flag of truce, and was again met by a number of officers of the South Carolina regiments.—They gave him a note from Gen. Donelson to Gen. Stevens, covering a surgeon's certificate of the death of the private in their hands, and that the body was too much decomposed to exhume and exchange. Upon this reply being made known, the body of the rebel soldier was returned to Beaufort, and decently buried. The South Carolinians inquired whether there were any Massachusetts regiments on the Island, and if so, they expressed a great anxiety to have them placed in front, where they could cut them to pieces. They were assured that they would have occasion to meet the New Englanders some of these days, and that they would not find them at all backward for a fight. The interview was very pleasant.

THE "GALLANTRY" OF THE YANKEES IN THE FIGHT ON NEW YEAR'S DAY.

I append the following General Order from the Commander-in-Chief, complimenting Gen. Stevens and the men under him for their bravery and gallantry in the affair of the 1st:

GENERAL ORDER NO. 1.

HEADQUARTERS, E C.,
HILTON HEAD, S. C., Jan. 7, 1862.

The General Commanding desires to express his gratification at the good conduct exhibited by the troops under command of Brigadier General Stevens, when engaged on the 1st instant, in capturing and destroying the enemy's batteries on the Coosaw river.

The conduct of this affair confirms him in the conviction that our troops, when ordered to march ahead, will know no obstacle, and will promptly and in good order penetrate wherever ordered.

The thanks of the Commanding-General are specially due to Brig. Gen. Stevens for the energy and good judgment evinced in the preparation and prosecution of this affair.

To Flag Officer Dupont, commanding blockading squadron, and to Commander R C. P. Rodgers, commanding the naval portion of this expedition, and the officers and men under his command, the thanks of the country and army are likewise due. The energy, alacrity and efficiency which supported the land forces on this occasion, though nothing more than what could have been expected from that distinguished branch of the service, will ever be gratefully remembered.

By order of Brigadier-General T. W. SHERMAN.
LOUIS H. PELOUZE, Capt. Fifteenth
Infantry, Acting Assistant Adjutant General.

NEWS FROM NORTH EDISTO.

From North Edisto we have further intelligence of operations in that quarter, and the state of affairs at the Negro Colony of Botany Bay Island. The latter has increased greatly of late, and the prospect of a still larger increase are very fair. Over one thousand contrabands—men, women and children—are now there, and Captain Ammen, of the Seneca, has taken measures to supply them abundantly with corn and other articles of food, so there is no danger of their suffering from want in that respect. On the 2d and 3d the Penguin, Commander Budd, went to Bear Bluff, and collected a large quantity of maize, and destroying the balance remaining, and also a house occupied by rebel soldiers, who had fired upon them. Captain Ammen encourages the collection of corn by the negros, and feels no apprehension of immediate want.

Commodore Dupont and General Sherman are anxious to hold possession of North Edisto in force as a base of operations; but their force is exhausted, and they are reluctantly compelled to wait until the much desired reinforcements arrive. The sooner they are sent the sooner something will be accomplished in this quarter. Both the military and naval arm must be reinforced before operations are commenced which shall materially advance our interests in this department.

INCIDENTS AT STONO INLET.

Stono Inlet, one of the most important, if not the most important, channel of communication to Charleston, has been closely blockaded for a long time past by some of Flag Officer Dupont's squadron. More recently the sloop-of-war Pocahontas, Commander G. B. Balch, has been engaged in blockading duty off that point, and she has lately drawn the fire of the strong batteries

The Union ironclad fleet, commanded by Admiral Dupont, firing upon Fort Sumter

at that point, and ascertained their strength. She had quite an exciting little interview with the Confederates on Cole's Island, on the 28th of December. On the afternoon of that day a Confederate steamer came down through one of the inland channels and passed in front of Stono Inlet. Commander Balch directed a ten-inch shell to be thrown at her, but it fell short, and after a second had been fired, the steamer had crossed the inlet and entered a channel on the other side, escaping injury from our shells. The steamer doubtless brought down a reconnoitering party, but the fire of the Pocahontas must have prevented the party from obtaining the desired end.

Soon after this little affair two batteries on Cole's Island opened fire on the Pocahontas with rifled guns, but all the shots dropped short. The enemy could not be reached by the guns of the Pocahontas, and she withdrew, after obtaining the desired information. While attempting to get within range she touched ground, but no injury was sustained by her. Commander Balch had the last fire, and stood out into deeper water, and came to anchor.

WHAT THE DESERTERS SAID.

Nothing of importance occurred off Stono until yesterday, when some deserters came on board in a sail boat, from the rebel army. They represented themselves as Northern men in the rebel army, and asked protection. They were welcomed aboard by Commander Balch, who assured them of his protection. They belonged to the Lucas Artillery, commanded by Major Lucas, whose headquarters were on Cole's Island. They had obtained a pass from the Captain of Company A, of the battery, countersigned by Major Lucas, to go outside the bar to dredge for oysters, and to return by two o'clock, p. m. After they had got outside they made rapid way for the Pocahontas. They gave a great deal of important information in regard to the state of affairs at Stono and throughout the State.

The Confederates at Stono have been sleeping on their arms for weeks, expecting the arrival of Burnside's expedition. They are in want of provisions, such as beef, salt and coffee.

The enemy have greatly strengthened their force on the coast; but we have no cause to take them where they are in strength. Col. Heyward is in command of Cole's Island which is defended by four batteries of fifteen guns of heavy calibre. Major Lucas commands the artillery force on the Island, and is abundantly supplied with ammunition and munitions of war. There are about eight hundred and fifty troops on the Island. But they will not trouble us, as that is not the road to Charleston.

THE BLOCKADE.—HOW THE ELLA WARLEY ESCAPED.

We get the following paragraphs from the letters of a correspondent of the New York *Tribune* on board one of the blockading vessels:

Our naval operations furnish no items of news. Our vessels, however, maintain a strict blockade upon the coast from Cedar Keys to Charleston, and it is a most fortunate vessel that succeeds in running the blockade. Indeed, but one has run it for several months, and that one was the Isabel, which took advantage of a thick fog, when objects could not be discerned half a ship's length, and ran into Charleston through the Maffit channel. She happened there at the time when there were unfortunately only one steamer, the Mohican, and a sailing bark, the Gemsbock, off the bar, the other two steamers being unavoidably absent in coaling and repairing for a couple of days. As it was, the Isabel suffered considerable damage from the shot and shells of the Mohican, her stern being nearly carried away by a well directed shot from the sloop-of-war.

THE STONE BLOCKADE OF MAFFIT'S CHANNEL.

Maffit's channel, one of the rat holes to Charleston, and a more important one than we were led to suppose, is to suffer the same fate that befell the main ship channel. It is to be filled up with the old stone fleet, which is now here awaiting its doom. Maffit's channel has deepened since the coast survey was made, and now we have good reason to believe twelve to fifteen feet of water can be carried in it. It is now by far the best channel in the harbor, and Commodore Dupont has determined to sink fifteen or sixteen old ships in it, at a point where it will be impossible to run a ship in the night or in a fog, when they are once scuttled. This will relieve us of a troublesome channel to guard. The work of sinking the fleet will commence this week; but Flag Officer Dupont will keep a sufficient number of steamers off the bar to blockade it, whether the stone fleet experiment be successful or not.

ANOTHER ACCOUNT OF WHAT THE DESERTERS SAID.

Stono Inlet, which we are now blockading, is the key to Charleston, among the Sea Islands in this vicinity. It is well fortified, as we learn from four deserters who came on board of us to-day in an old boat, being pursued by a boat filled with men who were unable to overhaul them. Had they been taken, they say, they would have been shot to morrow morning. The fortifications extend from east to west. Fort Marion has two 32's and one eight inch Columbiad; Fort Ripley, three 42 pounders and one ten inch; Fort Palmetto, four 32 pounders, two of them rifled, and one ten inch in rear of bastion, which mounts two 18 pounders. One and one-half miles back of this, on Stono River, stands Fort Pickens, mounting nine 24 pounders.

My informant says the privates get no coffee, no whisky, no salt, in fact nothing but salt meat and bread and water; says he has heard much about their corn, but he has seen none in the four months he has been quartered here; that they have recently received troops from North Carolina; that some of the Bull Run men are here; that Lieutenant Barnwell was accidentally shot dead a few days since; that the men are all anxious for a fight, and a settlement one way or the other.

I think vessels drawing five or six feet of water, of good speed, might easily drive them from their batteries, and open the way to Charleston, as Fort Pickens can be shelled from Stono batteries.

THE YANKEES AT TYBEE—WHAT THEY THINK OF FORT PULASKI.

From Fort Pulaski we have reports down to twelve o'clock yesterday. Some two companies of infantry were landed at their pier, brought down by rebel steamers a few days past. They have been exercising the men at the guns, with considerable precision in firing since that time, and yesterday succeeded in throwing a fuse shell within three hundred yards of the Pawnee.

We have discovered upon one of the salients of Fort Pulaski a rifled gun of heavy calibre, evidently one of the hundred pound Armstrong guns brought over by the Fingal. It possesses a great range, but the projectiles employed do not burst with any degree of certainty. The fire, however, is very accurate, and it may prove a bad customer for us when we have occasion to get within range. The Confederates have several rifled guns of the most approved pattern, of English and Confederate make.

A contraband who was picked up by the Connecticut Seventh, and who had left Savannah, reported a considerable number of the rebel forces in and around that city, and stated that the river was defended by fire-rafts, to some extent.

A VISIT TO DAUFUSKIE ISLAND.

Yesterday, in company with several officers of the ship, I went on shore for a visit to Melrose, the plantation of Mr. Stoddard, of Savannah, situated on Daufuskie Island, about five miles from the anchorage. The Island is in the custody of a Provost Marshal, and a detachment of sappers and miners are doing picket duty and keeping up a general surveillance, communicating with the companies on Hilton Island.

The mansion house is built in the Southern style, with capacious galleries, extending around the entire area of the building, with a large hall, commodious rooms, and every possible appliance conducing to comfort and luxury. The outhouses are numerous, including a carpenter's, wheelwright's and blacksmith's shop, extensive stabling, coach and wagon houses, mills, dairies, bake-houses and paint room. The negro quarters are deserted, with the exception of a few antique specimens, including a veritable "Uncle Tom" and "Old Mamma," useless from age and infirmity. The rest of the slaves have been disposed of, and, from what we could gather, at nominal prices.

A LIGHTSHIP FOR THE YANKEES.

The steamer McClellan, Captain Gray, arrived yesterday from New York, with a fine lightship in tow, which is to be moored off Martin's Industry shoals in a day or two. It is singular that the Lighthouse Board should have allowed so much time to elapse before placing a light at that important point. It will be the only light from the Capes of Virginia to Cedar Keys on the Atlantic coast, and will be of immense value to mariners who are blown upon the coast.

The New-York Times.

VOL. XI----NO. 3239. NEW-YORK, SATURDAY, FEBRUARY 8, 1862. PRICE TWO CENTS.

ANOTHER GREAT VICTORY.

The Capture of Fort Henry on the Tennessee River.

THE WAR CARRIED INTO TENNESSEE.

Official Dispatches from Gen. Halleck and Commodore Foote.

The Battle Fought Entirely by the Gunboats.

Desperate Resistance of the Rebels under Command of Gen. Tilghman.

The Rebel Commander and a Large Number of Officers and Men Captured.

Panic and Flight of Four Thousand Rebel Infantry.

EVERYTHING LEFT BEHIND THEM.

The Gunboat Essex Disabled by a Shot Through Her Boiler.

Immense Strategic Importance of the Victory.

DISPATCH FROM MAJ.-GEN. HALLECK.

ST. LOUIS, Friday, Feb. 7.

The following is announced from Headquarters: Fort Henry is ours! The flag of the Union is re-established on the soil of Tennessee. It will never be removed.

By command of Maj.-Gen. HALLECK.

W. W. SMITH,
Captain and Aide-de-Camp.

DISPATCH FROM FLAG OFFICER FOOTE.

WASHINGTON, Friday, Feb. 7.

Secretary WELLES has received the following dispatch:

U. S. FLAG SHIP CINCINNATI, OFF FORT HENRY, TENNESSEE RIVER, Feb. 6, 1862.

The gunboats under my command, the *Essex*, commander PORTER; the *Carondelet*, Commander WALKE; the *Cincinnati*, Commander STEMBEL; the *St. Louis*, Lieut.-Commanding PAULDING; the *Conestoga*, Lieut.-Commanding PHELPS; the *Taylor*, Lieut.-Commanding GWINN, and the *Lexington*, Lieut.-Commanding SHIRK, after a severe and rapid fire of one hour and a quarter, have captured Fort Henry, and have taken Gen. LLOYD TILGHMAN and his Staff, with sixty men, as prisoners.

The surrender to the gunboats was unconditional, as we kept an open fire upon the enemy until their flag was struck.

In half an hour after the surrender, I handed the fort and prisoners over to Gen. GRANT, commanding the army, on his arrival at the fort in force.

The *Essex* had a shot in her boilers, after fighting most effectually for two-thirds of the action, and was obliged to drop down the river. I hear that several of her men were scalded to death, including the two pilots.

She, with the other gunboats, officers and men fought with the greatest gallantry.

The *Cincinnati* received thirty-one shots, and had one killed and eight wounded, two seriously.

The fort, with twenty guns and seventeen mortars, was defended by Gen. TILGHMAN with the most determined gallantry.

I will write as soon as possible.

I have sent Lieut.-Commanding PHILLIPS and three gunboats after the rebel gunboats.

(Signed,) A. H. FOOTE, Flag-Officer.

DETAILS FROM CAIRO.

CAIRO, Ill., Friday, Feb. 7.

Fort Henry, on the Tennessee River, surrendered yesterday at 2 o'clock in the afternoon, after a most determined resistance.

The fight, which lasted one hour and twenty minutes, was conducted by the gunboats *Cincinnati*, *Essex* and *St. Louis*.

The *Cincinnati* fired 125 rounds, and received 34 shots from the rebel guns, but only one man was killed.

The *St. Louis* fired 110 rounds, but received no damage.

The *Essex* was disabled after firing ten rounds, by a ball striking her boiler. Thirty-two persons on board of her were scalded to death. Capt. PORTER, her commander, was badly scalded, but not dangerously so.

Two rebel Generals, one Colonel, two Captains, and one hundred privates, were taken prisoners.

The fort mounted seventeen guns.

The land forces did not reach the scene of the action until two hours after the surrender of the fort.

The Memphis and Ohio Railroad bridge, fifteen miles above the fort, has been taken possession of by our troops.

DETAILS FROM CINCINNATI.

CINCINNATI, Friday, Feb. 7.

The *Gazette* and *Commercial's* Cairo correspondence give the following account of the bombardment and capture of Fort Henry:

Yesterday at 12½ P. M., the gunboats *Cincinnati*, *St. Louis*, *Carondelet*, and *Essex*, the *Tyler*, *Conestoga*, and *Lexington*, bringing up the rear, advanced boldly against the rebel works, going to the right of Painter Creek Island, [see TIMES' diagram,] immediately above where, on the east shore of the river stands the fortifications, and keeping out of range till at the head of the island, and within a mile of the enemy, passing the island in full view of the rebel guns. We steadily advanced, every man at quarters, every ear strained to catch the Flag-Officer's signal-gun for the commencement of the action. Our line of battle was on the left, the *St. Louis* next, the *Carondelet* next, the *Cincinnati* (for the time being the Flag-ship, having on board Flag-Officer FOOTE,) and the next the *Essex*. We advanced in line, the *Cincinnati* a boat's length ahead, when at 11:30, the *Cincinnati* opened the ball, and immediately the three accompanying boats followed suit. The enemy was not backward, and gave an admirable response, and the fight raged furiously for half an hour. We steadily advanced, receiving and returning the storm of shot and shell, when getting within three hundred yards of the enemy's works we came to a stand, and poured into him right and left. In the meantime the *Essex* had been disabled, and drifted away from the scene of action, leaving the *Cincinnati*, *Carondelet* and *St. Louis* alone engaged.

At precisely forty minutes past one, the enemy struck his colors—and such cheering, such wild excitement, as seized the throats, arms, or caps, of the four or five hundred sailors of the gunboats can be imagined. After the surrender, which was made to Flag-officer FOOTE by Gen. LLOYD TILGHMAN, who defended the fort in a most determined manner, we found that the rebel infantry encamped outside the fort, numbering four or five thousand, had cut and run, leaving the rebel artillery company in command of the fort.

The fort mounted seventeen guns, most of them 32-pounders, one being a magnificent 10-inch columbiad. Our shots dismounted two of their guns, driving the enemy into the embrasures. One of their rifled 32-pounders burst during the engagement, wounding some of their gunners. The rebels claimed to have but eleven effective guns worked by fifty-four men—the number all told of our prisoners. They lost five killed and ten badly wounded. The infantry left everything in their flight. A vast deal of plunder has fallen into our hands, including a large and valuable quantity of ordnance stores.

Gen. TILGHMAN is disheartened. He thinks it one of the most damaging blows of the war. In surrendering to Flag-Officer FOOTE the rebel General remarked, "I am glad to surrender to so gallant an officer." Flag-Officer FOOTE replied, "You do perfectly right, Sir, in surrendering, but you should have blown my boat out of the water before I would have surrendered to you."

In the engagement the *Cincinnati* was in the lead, and flying the Flag-officer's pennant, was the chief mark. Flag-Officer FOOTE and Capt. STEMBEL crowded her defiantly into the teeth of the enemy's guns. She got thirty-one shots, some of them going completely through her.

The *Essex* was badly crippled when about half through the fight, and crowding steadily against the enemy. A ball went into her side-forward port, through the heavy bulkhead and squarely through one of her boilers, the escaping steam scalding and killing several of the crew.

Capt. PORTER, his Aid, L. P. BRITTON, Jr., and Paymaster LEWIS, were standing in a direct line of the balls passing, Mr. BRITTON being in the centre of the group. A shot struck Mr. BRITTON in the top of his head, scattering his brains in every direction. The escaping steam went into the pilot-house, instantly killing Messrs. FORD and BRIDE, pilots. Many of the soldiers, at the rush of steam, jumped overboard and were drowned.

The *Cincinnati* had one killed and six wounded. The *Essex* had six seamen and two officers killed, seventeen men wounded, and five missing. There were no casualties on the *St. Louis* or *Carondelet*, though the shot and shell fell upon them like rain.

The *St. Louis* was commanded by LEONARD PAULDING, who stood upon the gunboat and wrought the guns to the last. Not a man flinched, and with cheer upon cheer sent the shot and shell among the enemy.

PURSUING THE FLYING REBELS.

PADUCAH, Ky., Friday, Jan. 7.

Gen. SMITH, on the west, and Gen. GRANT on the east side of the Tennessee River, are pursuing the retreating rebels. It is reported and credited by some of our officers that the rebel troops at Fort Henry was not true to the rebel cause, and took advantage of the opportunity offered by an attack to run away from a fight that was distasteful to them.

REPORTS FROM LOUISVILLE.

LOUISVILLE, Friday, Feb. 7.

Three large steamers—*Benjamin J. Adams*, *E. H. Fairchild* and *Battic*—left here for the Cumberland and Tennessee Rivers this evening.

All quiet along the line of the Louisville and Nashville Railroad.

A dispatch from Gen. HALLECK to Gen. BUELL, this evening, says: "We have taken Fort Henry. The enemy has retreated on Paris, leaving part of his guns. Our cavalry are in pursuit.

Gen. GRANT will attack Fort Donelson to-morrow.

THE NEWS IN WASHINGTON.

WASHINGTON, Friday, Feb. 7.

The news from Fort Henry has diffused general joy, and stimulated the openly expressed desire for additional victories.

Mr. SEDGWICK caused the dispatch from Flag-Officer FOOTE to Secretary WELLES, to be read to the House, and it was received with great demonstrations of applause.

CONFIDENCE OF THE REBELS.

The following dispatch, received by way of Fortress Monroe, shows that the rebels were confident of being able to repulse an attack upon the fort:

MEMPHIS, Thursday, Feb. 6.

Three Federal gunboats appeared on the Tennessee River yesterday, and opened fire on Fort Henry. The latter responded. There was no damage done to the Fort. The Federals are landing troops two miles from the fort. An attack is expected. The Confederates are in full force on the Tennessee River. No damage from the Federals is apprehended.

OUR FIRST VICTORY IN TENNESSEE.

We have cheering news this morning from Tennessee. The United States soldiers and sailors have at last attained a foothold in that State, after a brilliant naval engagement—a foothold at a point, too, most important for operations, which will now very soon be begun, against Nashville, Memphis, and the whole of the rebel region of the Southwest. As Gen. HALLECK says in his brief bulletin of victory: "The flag of the Union is reëstablished on the soil of Tennessee. It will never be removed." It must henceforth be borne steadily southward to the Gulf of Mexico.

Our late military operations in the West have been remarkable for one thing; they have uniformly achieved the purpose for which they have been undertaken. We have had several considerable actions in, and on the line of Kentucky, and *we have not there yet suffered one defeat.* This augurs well for our success in the two decisive engagements which must yet be fought there ere the rebel hordes are finally expelled from the soil of that proud and loyal State. The battle and the victory at Fort Henry, on the Tennessee River, which this morning we record, and the subsequent seizure of an important strategic point on the line of the Memphis and Ohio Railroad, are, in their bearings on the pending general advance of our troops from Kentucky, by far the most important events that have taken place in that section since the war began. Not on account of the greatness of the rebel force defeated—for it was not very great—nor on account of the deeds of valor wrought by our brave troops—though we doubt not they have earned laurels as gay as ever decked a soldier's brow; but because the points gained give us the control of the direct line of railroad which connects the great rebel force at Columbus with that at Bowling Green—and because, also, it clears away another, and perhaps the last, of the obstacles which have heretofore prevented the southward advance of the grand Western army under Gen. DON CARLOS BUELL. There is another and stronger rebel fort on the Cumberland, a few miles eastward of the scene of our present victory but considering the fact that our troops are now in the rear of that fort, and learning, as we do, from the West, the movement that is on the *tapis* to bring it down as suddenly as Fort Henry has been brought down, we look upon the victory we have gained as being full and complete, as regards the object in view. Look at the map at that part of Tennessee where Fort Henry is located, and at that point of the Memphis and Ohio Railroad which our troops now hold, and see how far we have penetrated in the rear of Bowling Green—see how far in the rear of Columbus—how convenient we are for sweeping down on the railroad to Memphis—see how near we now are to Nashville—and how Nashville is related to the whole State of Tennessee, and that again to the whole of the rebel States of the Southwest, and some idea will be had of the value of the present advance and victory.

THE SCENE OF OUR NAVAL VICTORY IN NORTHERN TENNESSEE.

Diagram Showing the Location of Fort Henry and its Guns, together with its Relations to Fort Donelson, the Nashville and Memphis Railroad, and Other Important Points.

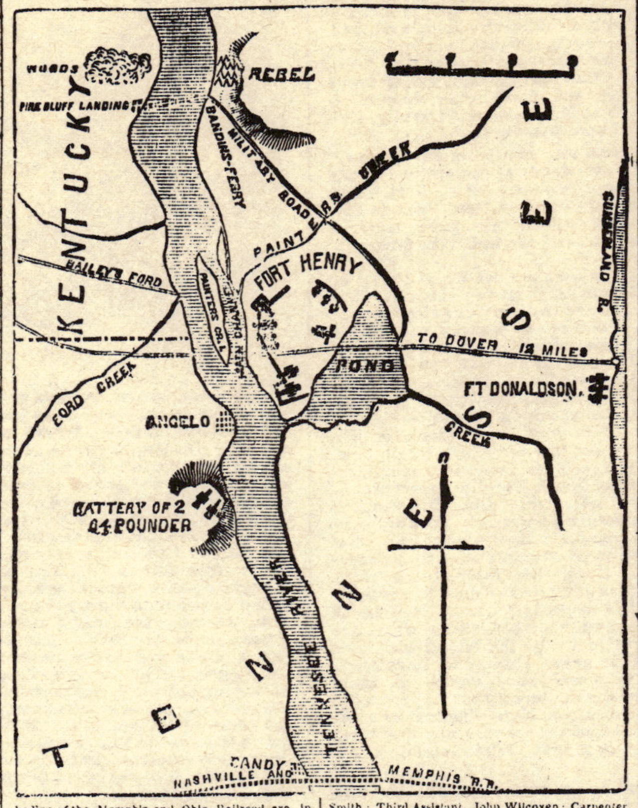

THE BATTLE, AND THE FORCES ENGAGED.

From our telegrams, and the official dispatch of Commodore FOOTE, it appears that *this victory was entirely a naval one*—the troops of the expedition not having come up to the scene of action until the rebels had surrendered. The gunboats engaged are a part of those strong iron-clad river boats, or turtles, which were built, within the last few months, at St. Louis, Carondelet, and other points, and which were originally destined for the expedition down the Mississippi. Commodore FOOTE mentions nine of these vessels as having been in the engagement, and we herewith give a complete and correct list of the officers of the fleet and of all these boats, with their armament, and other details of interest.

THE GUNBOATS AND THEIR OFFICERS.

The following are the officers in command of the fleet, which was brought into action, and of each boat:

OFFICERS OF THE FLEET.

Flag-officer—ANDREW H. FOOTE, U. S. N.
Fleet-Captain—Commander A. M. Pennock, U.S.N.
Ordnance Officer—Lieut. J. P. Sanford, U. S. N.
Ordnance-Lieutenant—Byron Wilson.
Flag-Lieutenant—James N. Prickett.
Flag-officer's Secretary and Acting Paymaster-in-Chief—S. Henriques.

GUNBOAT ESSEX.

Commander, H. D. PORTER, U. S. N.; First Master, Robert K. Riley; Second Master, James Lanning; Third Master, Theodore P. Ferry; Fourth Master, George W. Walker; Assistant Surgeon, Thomas Rice; Acting Paymaster, J. H. Lewis; Pilots, J. McBride, Marshall H. Ford; Masters' Mates, James B. Gray, Samuel B. Brittan; Chief Engineer, Charles Blissell; First Assistant Engineer, R. J. Stearns; Second Assistant Engineer, George D. Simon; Third Assistant Engineer, J. Weitzel; Gunner, M. B. Snyder; Armorer, —— Fletcher; Carpenter, Thomas Steel.

GUNBOAT CARONDELET.

Commander, HENRY WALKE, U. S. N.; First Master, Richard K. Wade; Second Master, John Dorety; Third Master, Charles C. Gray; Fourth Master, H. A. Walke; Pilots, William Henton, Daniel Weaver; Surgeon, James S. McNeely; Paymaster, George J. W. Nexsen; Master's Mates, Theodore L. Gillman, Edward E. Brennard; Chief Engineer, W. H. Faulkner; First Assistant Engineer, Charles H. Caven; Second Assistant Engineer, Samuel S. Brooks; Third Assistant Engineer, Augustus F. Crowell; Carpenter, O. Donaldson; Gunner, Richard Adams; Armorer, H. H. Rhodes.

GUNBOAT CINCINNATI.

Commander, R. N. STEMBEL, U. S. N.; First Master, vacant; Second Master, —— Pratt; Third Master, Charles G. Perkins; Fourth Master, John Pearce; Surgeon, Jacob Kinsey; Paymaster, Baron Proctor; Pilots, Isaac D. Gaugh, H. Attenborough; Masters' Mates, Jas. McB. Stembel, Philip Shell; Gunner, —— Morton; Carpenter, Thomas B. Gregory; Chief Engineer, W. McGarland; First Assistant, Samuel Lovejoy; Second Assistant, J. Armstrong; Third Assistant, W. J. Sherman; Armorer, Benj. Marshall.

GUNBOAT ST. LOUIS.

Lieutenant Commanding, LEONARD PAULDING, U. S. N.; First Master, Samuel Black; Second Master, James Y. Clemson; Third Master, Charles S. Kendrick; Fourth Master, Alexander Fraser; Acting Paymaster, Lewellyn Curry; Surgeon, —— McDill; Master's Mates, S. H. McAdams, James P. Paulding; Pilots, Frank Riley, Robert G. Baldwin; Gunner, —— Hall; Chief-Engineer, W. Carswell; First Assistant, T. F. Ackeman; Second Assistant, James L. Smith; Third Assistant, John Wilcoxen; Carpenter, Robert H. Medill.

GUNBOAT CONESTOGA.

Lieutenant Commanding, PHELPS, U. S. N.; First Master, John A. Duble; Second Master, Charles P. Noble; Third Master, Benjamin Sebastian; Assistant Surgeon, William H. Wilson; Acting Paymaster, Alfred Phelps; Chief-Engineer, Thomas Cook; First Assistant Engineer, Alex. Magee; Third Assistant Engineer, Michael Norton; Master's Mates, James Kearney, Richard H. Cottee; Gunner, Henry Hamilton; Carpenter, Andrew Woodlock; Armorer, James O'Niel.

GUNBOAT TAYLOR.

Lieutenant Commanding, W. GWIN, U. S. N.; First Master, Edward Shaw; Second Master, Jason Goudy; Third Master, James Martin; Pilots, John Sebastian and David Hiner; Chief Engineer, Samuel Goble; First Assistant Engineer, D. Edward Weaver; Second Assistant Engineer, Edward W. Goble; Third Assistant Engineer, Oscar S. Davis; Armorer, Elihu Stevens; Acting Paymaster, W. B. Coleman; Assistant Surgeon, T. H. Kearney; Carpenter, Thomas Russell; Gunner, Herman Peters, U. S. N.; Master's Mates, Ferdinand T. Coleman and Edward D. Brainard.

GUNBOAT LEXINGTON.

Lieut. Commanding, J. W. Shirk, U. S. N.; First Master, Jacob S. Hurd; Second Master, Martin Dunn; Third Master, James Fitzpatrick; Fourth Master, Sylvester Poole; Pilots, Joseph McCammant, Wm. Ford; Chief-Engineer, Joseph Huber; First Assistant-Engineer, Wm. H. Meredith; Second Assistant-Engineer, Wm. Bishop; Acting Paymaster, A. J. Taylor; Assistant-Surgeon, G. W. Garver; Master's Mates, vacant; Armorer, Reuben Strong; Carpenter, Richard Carroll.

ARMAMENT OF THE GUNBOATS.

	Guns.		Guns.
Essex	9	Conestoga	9
Carondelet	13	Taylor	9
Cincinnati	13	Lexington	9
St. Louis	13		

These guns are all in battery, and none are less than 32-pounders—some are 42-pounders, some 64-pounders, and one (on the *Essex*,) throws a shell weighing *one hundred and twenty-eight pounds*. In addition to these, each boat carries a Dahlgren rifled 12-pounder boat howitzer on the upper deck. Several of the larger guns on each boat are rifled.

DESCRIPTION OF THE GUNBOATS.

The gunboats used in the expedition are part of those which were built for Gen. FREMONT's grand Mississippi flotilla. They have already been fully described in the TIMES by our correspondent at Cairo, but we will again give a brief general description of them.

The boats are built very wide, in proportion to their length, giving them almost the same steadiness in action that a stationary land battery would possess. They are constructed upon the same principle as the famous iron battery at Charleston, the sides sloping both upward and downward from the water line, at an angle of 45 degrees. The bow battery on each boat consists of solid oak timber 26 inches in thickness, plated on the exterior surface with iron 2½ inches thick. The side and stern batteries are somewhat thinner, but have the same thickness of iron over that portion covering the machinery. The boats are not plated on the roof, which consists of a 2½ plank. Of course a shot falling upon this deck, even at an acute angle, would go through, and a heavy shell so entering would blow up the boat; but the chances of this occurring are not as one in a thousand.

The boats are intended, in action, to be kept "bow on;" hence the superior strength of the bow battery. Broadsides can be delivered with terrible effect while shifting position. To facilitate movements in action, the engines and machinery are of the most powerful kind. The boilers are five in number, constructed to work in connection with or independently of each other. In case of damage done to any one or more of them, a valve closes the connection between the damaged and undamaged boilers, and the latter operate as if nothing had happened.

The most dreadfully savage contrivance upon these boats is that to prevent boarding. Each boat is supplied with a number of large hose-pipes for throwing *hot water* from the boilers, with a force of 200 pounds pressure to the square inch. Any human being who shall encounter this terrible stream of hot water will be boiled in an instant.

The three last-mentioned boats in our list (the *Conestoga*, *Taylor* and *Lexington*,) are not of the same model or character as the others, being simply Mississippi River steamboats rebuilt with perpendicular bulwarks and pierced for guns.

THE REBEL FORT HENRY.

Fort Henry, situated in Tennessee, upon the Tennessee River, and a short distance from the northern boundary of the State, was constructed last Summer by the rebels. It is an earthwork, and stands in the river bottom, about the high water mark, just below a bend in the river, and at the head of a straight stretch of about two miles. It, therefore, commands the river for that distance down stream, and very little else. The land around it is a little higher than the fort, and a portion of it is covered with heavy timber. On the opposite side of the river are three hills commanding the fort completely. The armament of the fort, according to Commodore FOOTE's report, was twenty guns and seventeen mortars. It consisted, we understand, of two 64-pounders, eight 32-pounders, four 12-pounders, and the rest 6-pounders, most of them smooth-bore. It was also supported by a battery of two guns planted on the commanding hills on the opposite side of the river, but of whose capture we have no record. A small creek setting into the Tennessee just at the south of the fort admits back water into the low lands behind the fort, forming a pond of marsh. Across this a bridge or causeway has been constructed, giving communication by means of a military road (see diagram) recently cut directly back to Fort Donelson, at Dover, on the Cumberland River. From a point on this road back of the pond another road has been cut, leading around under the bluffs back of the bottom land to the Pine Bluff landing, six miles below the fort. The chart of the fort, which we give, will furnish an idea of the position of the guns of the battery on the west side of the Tennessee, and of the relation of Fort Henry to Fort Donelson, which at latest accounts, was still unreduced.

Until lately, the garrison of the place was but one regiment, the Tenth Tennessee, 900 strong, and composed mostly of Irishmen; but since the fort was menaced, reinforcements of two Mississippi and one Louisiana regiments, have been sent, and likely also some additional Tennessee troops. The Memphis *Appeal* of the 12th of January said that the rebel authorities had taken into consideration the critical condition of Fort Henry, and that vigorous and energetic preparations had been made, by land and river, to meet our advance. The whole force was placed under command of Gen. LLOYD TILGHMAN, of Kentucky, a graduate of West Point, and reported an able commander. He is now a prisoner in our hands, and this most important and strategical position is in possession of United States troops.

COMMODORE FOOTE.

Commodore ANDREW H. FOOTE, who so gallantly led the gunboats in the action at Fort Henry, is a native of Connecticut, and entered the service from that State in 1822. Since that time he has been continually in service, making the whole time of his naval career extend over forty years. He is still, however, full of the fire and vim of youth, and is one of the best specimens of the old sea dogs in America. Over twenty years of his time he has been on ocean service, cruising in almost every sea; ten years he has been on shore duty, and twenty years of his time has been what is dessignated as unemployed. He received his commission as commander in 1852, and was last at sea in 1858. Since that time he has been on service in the Brooklyn Navy-yard; but about eight months ago was assigned to the duty of superintending the putting up of the great Mississippi flotilla. Commodore FOOTE is known in the navy as one of its most efficient officers, and distinguished himself greatly in China by the bombardment and breaching of a Chinese fort, the fort, in all respect, a superior work of masonry. The last called forth the praise of all foreign naval officers on that coast. Commodore FOOTE is an affable gentleman, and, as will be seen by his reply to the rebel TILGHMAN, *never surrenders*.

CAPT. PORTER.

Capt. PORTER, of the gunboat *Essex*, who is reported as badly scalded by the bursting of his boat's boiler, is a native of Louisiana, but entered the navy from Massachusetts in 1823. He is a son of the renowned Commodore PORTER, who figured so prominently in the war of 1812. He has been thirty-eight years in the service, and has seen twelve years sea duty, five years shore duty, and the rest of the time unemployed. He was last at sea in 1850, and was then and has been since until recently in command of the sloop *St. Marys*. His commission as naval commander dates only since 1855. When the Mississippi flotilla was projected, he was detailed to the command of a gunboat. The Captain christened his boat the *Essex*, after his father's renowned vessel, and judging from precedent, Capt. PORTER is the "bull-dog," or fighting man of this expedition. He has Dahlgren guns for his armament, and delights in "shelling." He worked prodigiously getting his boat ready, and since then he has been cruising round, stirring up the rebels wherever he could find them.

It was the boast of Commodore PERRY that he built some of his vessels on Lake Erie in twenty-six days. Capt. PORTER took the ferry-boat *New Era*, completely stripped her of everything but the framework of her hull, and entirely remodeled, rebuilt, and planked her, strengthened her with additional timbers and knees, caulked her, put in bulkheads, built strong and ample gun-decks, cased her hull with iron plates, in fact, constructed a new vessel, carrying nine heavy guns, and floated her out of her dock in *fourteen days*. The mechanics tell with considerable zest how, on the fourteenth day, Capt. PORTER, who had been crowding the work night and day, without giving notice, opened the gates of the floating dock, let on the water, and, to the astonishment of the industrious artisans aboard, the craft was in her element.

It is earnestly to be hoped that the gallant Captain will speedily recover, and be ready once more for active duty on his loved element.

GEN. TILGHMAN.

The rebel commander of Fort Henry, who was so gallantly captured by our navy boys, is a native of Maryland; entered West Point as a cadet in 1831; was made brevet Second Lieutenant in the First Dragoons in 1836, but shortly after resigned, and became division engineer on the Baltimore and Susquehanna Railroad, and afterward on the Baltimore and Ohio Railroad. In the Mexican war he reëntered the service as volunteer Aid-de-Camp to Col. TWIGGS, and was present at the battles of Palo Alto and Risaca de la Palma. He commanded a Volunteer till October, 1846, and in January, 1847, was made Superintendent of the defences of Matamoras; finally he acted as Captain of Volunteer Artillery in HUGHES' regiment from August, 1847, till July, 1848. At the close of the war he again entered civil life, and was chosen principal Assistant Engineer in the Panama Isthmus Railroad. On the breaking out of the war he was acting as railroad engineer, but joined the rebels, and was appointed to command at Fort Henry, where he has been ingloriously captured.

THE GREAT MORTAR FLEET.

The Vessels Nearly All Ready—Their Number and Appointments—Operations to Commence Immediately.

A number of the vessels attached to Commodore PORTER's mortar fleet have sailed South to the point of rendezvous, and others will soon follow. The expedition has been forming here for some months, and many experiments have been made to test the strength of the mortars.

The heavy mortars were cast at Pittsburgh, and have an average weight of about 17,000 pounds. The diameter of the bore is 13 inches, and the depth 35 inches, with a thickness of metal around it of 15 inches. The diameter of the trunnions is 15 inches, and the complete length of the mortar is 50 inches. They may be used alike upon sea or land, and are elevated or depressed by means of projections on the breech. It is stated that accurate firing may be made at a distance of 2¾ miles.

The circular platform which sustains the mortar carriage is constructed of heavy timber 1 foot in depth and 12 feet in diameter, and is made to revolve so that the mortar may be aimed in any direction.

The mortar carriage is made mostly of wrought iron, having a length of about 9 feet and a height of 4 feet. It weights about two tons, and is capable of resisting a pressure of about 150 tons.

The bombshells to be used weigh, unfilled, 200 pounds each, and when filled an additional weight of 12 pounds is given. About 8,000 of these missiles have been manufactured for the fleet.

Each vessel has been provided with two 32-pounders, weighing 3,700 pounds. They are smooth-bore and throw solid shot and shell.

Instructions to be observed in time of attack have been transmitted by Government to the officers of the fleet, and a convenient code of signals has been adopted. The vessels, which are mostly schooners, of two and three hundred tons burden, number twenty-one in all. The side-wheel steam gunboat *Octorara* is to be the flag-ship of the flotilla.

LATER FROM PORT ROYAL

Arrival of the United States Sloop-of-War Savannah.

SAILING OF THE EXPEDITION FOR THE SOUTH.

The United States sloop-of-war *Savannah*, Commander JOHN S. MISSROON, arrived at this port last night from Port Royal, S. C., making the passage in eight days. The *Savannah* went into commission in June last, and since has been engaged in arduous blockade; her crew are suffering from its effects, on which account she has been ordered home. The holding of Tybee Island by the seamen of the *Savannah* and gunboats in the Savannah River, until relieved by the New-York Volunteers, was a signal service. She brings no news of importance from Port Royal, except the sailing of the Expedition for the South on the 26th, including all the light-draft steamers, several gunboats and several thousand troops. Everything remained quiet at Port Royal. The following is a list of officers of the *Savannah*:

Commander, JOHN S. MISSROON; Lieutenant, A. W. Johnson; Surgeon, Henry C. Mayo; Paymaster, A. W. Russell; Assistant Surgeon, Job Corbin; Acting Masters, Samuel C. Gray, Wm. F. Shankland and Charles W. Zimmerman; Lieutenant Marines, W. B. McKean; Captain's Clerk, J. W. McLellan; Paymaster's Clerk, Wm. J. Littlejohn; Boatswain, Wm. Winchester; Gunner, N. B. Willets; Carpenter, Amos Chick; Sailmaker, R. L. Tatern.

AFFAIRS ON THE UPPER POTOMAC.

An Outrage of the Rebels under a Flag of Truce—Houses at Harper's Ferry Shelled and Destroyed by the National Forces, &c.

SANDY HOOK, Friday, Feb. 7.

This forenoon, Capt. BAYLOR and three of his men, concealed behind a stone wall, just above Harper's Ferry bridge, one either black or painted, by displaying a flag of truce, induced a loyal Virginian over; when nearly across, Capt. BAYLOR and two others fired and killed the ferryman.

Our batteries on the heights then shelled the buildings. Subsequently the men crossed and set fire to the twelve houses, including the Wager and another hotel, railroad buildings, etc. The whole lower part of the town was reduced to ashes. A necessity existed for burning the buildings, as they had been hiding places for the rebel riflemen, who had been annoying our troops for weeks past.

The number of rebels was not known, but many were seen to mount their horses and leave the outskirts of the town by the Charlestown road.

This afternoon the rebel flag of truce, in the hands of three of BAYLOR's men, came to the ferry, but were warned off by Col. GEARY. Large numbers of rebel pickets, mounted, were stationed all the afternoon near Bolivar.

THE ARMY AND NAVY.

The United States gunboat *Dawn* arrived yesterday at the Brooklyn Navy-yard for repairs. She left Fortress Monroe on the morning of the 6th. She brings no news of importance. The following is a list of her officers:

Lieut.-Commanding, A. G. CLARY; Lieut. and Executive officer, E. Drayton; Asst.-Paymaster, F. Parker; Asst.-Surgeon, J. W. Sherry; First Asst.-Engineer, M. B. Cates; Third Assistants, D. Tomlinson and T. P. Gee; Master's Mates, J. G. Underhill, J. Barrett and Charles M. Cooley.

The chartered schooner *Annie Glover* left the Yard yesterday for Ship Island. She takes several mechanics and a cargo of castings for machinery, and other stores.

The brig *Caroline* sailed for Panama with ordnance stores, &c.

The mortar schooner *Para* left the Yard yesterday. There are now only three sailing vessels belonging to Capt. PORTER's mortar fleet remaining at the Yard. It is said that all these vessels will rendezvous at Hampton Roads, and wait there until the steamers detailed for the fleet are ready. These steamers are the *Octorara*, *Westfield* and *Clifton*, and possibly others.

The carpenters have nearly completed their work on the frigate *Sabine*, now lying in the stream, and it is expected that she will sail immediately.

The sloop-of-war *Richmond* is having the remainder of her armament placed on board, and will, it is reported, sail on Monday. The statement which we made a few days ago, relative to the preparations which were being made on board the *Richmond* for the reception of Gen. SCOTT, who was expected to go to Key West, was quite correct. The naval authorities were positive that the General was going to Key West, as stated.

It was reported a few days ago, that the steamship *Fulton* had been chartered by the Government and was coaling at the foot of Beach-street, North River; but it now appears that the *Fulton* has had her coal bunkers full for some weeks, and there is some doubt whether she has been chartered or not.

The Twenty-Eighth Massachusetts Volunteers remain on Governor's Island, but are ready to start at a few minutes' notice. They expect to go to Hilton Head in the clipper ship *S. R. Mallory*, which, with the clipper *Tycoon*, has been chartered by the United States Quartermaster for the conveyance of this regiment and the Seventh New-Hampshire. The latter regiment will go to Fort Jefferson, Tortugas.

REPORTED EVACUATION OF ROMNEY.

PITTSBURGH, Penn., Friday, Feb. 7.

The Wheeling *Intelligencer* of yesterday learns that the rebels evacuated Romney last night.

WASHINGTON, Friday, Feb. 7.

The War Department has received a dispatch that Gen. LANDER now occupies Romney, the rebels having retreated.

A LETTER FROM GEN. SIGEL.

The following brief communication from Gen. SIGEL, to a friend in Detroit, sets at rest the oft-disputed question as to whether he did or did not, lately, resign his command in Missouri. It has been authoritatively published in the German papers:

ST. LOUIS, Sunday, Jan. 26, 1862.

ESTEEMED SIR: In relation to the contents of your letter of the 16th inst., received by me yesterday, in St. Louis, I can, unfortunately, only say that a variety of circumstances of a personal nature, but, more especially, the regard and consideration I owe to the troops under my command, have compelled me to send in my resignation. You will, however, not take it amiss in me that I have no desire to leave my command at the moment when the last blow is to be struck against the army of the enemy in Missouri. For the latter reason I have not insisted upon immediate dismissal, but hope that it will be accorded so soon as the Government shall have been fully acquainted with the cause of dispute.

Thanking the Germans of Detroit who have so warmly interested themselves in my behalf—and thereby, too, in their own—I send you cordial greeting, and am yours, most sincerely,

FRANZ SIGEL.

To C. MARXHAUSEN, Esq., Editor of the *Michigan Journal*, Detroit.

THE MAINE LEGISLATURE.

AUGUSTA, Me., Friday, Jan. 7.

Mr. SMART's resolves, slightly amended, in favor of confiscating, liberating and also arming the slaves of rebels, if it be a military necessity, have passed the Senate to-day by a vote of 24 against 4.

The New-York Times.

VOL. XI—NO. 3240. NEW-YORK, MONDAY, FEBRUARY 10, 1862. PRICE TWO CENTS.

THE BURNSIDE EXPEDITION

The Attack upon Roanoke Island Commenced.

REPORTS RECEIVED FROM THE REBELS.

The National Forces Said to Have Been Twice Repulsed.

THE REBELS CONTRADICTING THEMSELVES

Late Advices from Our Special Correspondent.

FORTRESS MONROE, Saturday, Feb. 8.

A flag of truce from Craney Island, to-day, brought over several ladies, to go North.

A lady passenger by the flag of truce reports that Gen. HUGER to-day informed her that he had received a dispatch from Roanoke Island, to the effect that the National forces had advanced to Roanoke Island and had been twice repulsed. The attack commenced at 7 o'clock, yesterday morning, and the fight was still going on when the latest news was received.

NORFOLK, Saturday, Feb. 8.

A messenger, arrived to-day from Roanoke Island, reports that four Federal steamers were off the Island last night, and a large number of vessels were twelve miles below the Island. An attack was expected at this point.

Gen. WISE is in better health.

OUR EXPEDITIONARY CORRESPONDENCE.

The Fleet at Anchor in Pamlico Sound—Sabbath Observances—Drills—Music—Chaplains—Loss of the Steamer E. H. Herbert.

MONDAY, Feb. 3—4 o'clock A. M.

The days of our tribulation are not yet accomplished; the spell is still upon us—the spell of weather, I mean; and the great invading fleet of Uncle Sam still rides majestically at anchor in the breezy Sound of Pamlico, where, to all appearances, it might ride until July, if it is to wait for "settled weather." The wind has been blowing "stiff" from the Northeast for twenty-four hours, and yesterday no boats, except they were strongly manned, dared to venture away from the ship's side. Consequently there was no visiting, no orders—except a call on the regiments of the first brigade for a morning report—and no mail.

The troops, pent up on board of their ships, improved the last Sabbath before the attack according to their individual tastes. It was rumored that the day would be observed with more than the usual solemnity, the chaplains being requested to return thanks to the Almighty for our progress thus far, and invoking His benediction upon our arms. But no such order came from "Headquarters." We have outgrown those old-fashioned notions. The prevalent idea in the management of this *windy* campaign seems to be fully embodied in that terse remark attributed to CROMWELL, "Pray to God, but keep your powder dry," with particular emphasis on the powder. I trust it will not all end in smoke.

The New-England troops excel in the musical faculty, and in every regiment from Massachusetts, Connecticut or New-Hampshire music-teachers or good singers abound, and many an otherwise tedious evening has thus been beguiled by the elevating influence of music. In this respect no regiment, perhaps, is more favored than the Massachusetts Twenty-third, composed chiefly of Salem, Marblehead, Danvers and Boston men. Many of the officers were members of the best musical societies, and leaders or pillars in their church choirs at home. Could their friends have looked in upon us on board of the *Highlander*, during many of the boisterous nights we have been anchored in this Sound, while the storm howled without, they might have heard:

—"Perhaps Dundee's wild, wrarbling measures rise,
Or plaintive martyrs, worthy of the name,
Or noble Elgin beat the heavenward flame."

On board of the *Huzzar*, which carries the left wing of the Twenty-third, they have their full share of sweet singers, and a very excellent band of music, under the lead of HENRY C. BROWN, of Boston. In the centre of the fleet, which covers an area of some two miles of the bay, is anchored the *S. R. Spaulding*, the present flag-ship of Gen. BURNSIDE. From her high decks he can easily survey the entire fleet, and observe all that is going on. On the deck of one or two vessels near us are gathered quiet groups of soldiers, and the sublime strains of "Old Hundred" which float across the waters, human voices mingling with the bands, testify that they are engaged in religious worship. To many of these brave and earnest men it will be, perhaps, their last Sabbath on earth. On the hurricane deck of the *Admiral* the officers of the Twenty-fourth Massachusetts, with a portion of their troops, whose bright bayonets gleam like polished silver in the morning sunlight, are practising their skirmish calls. Their movements are watched from neighboring vessels with much interest, and with something of amusement, while the officers and men wheel right and left by turns, fall down, rise up, practice the double-quick, deploy by fours, &c., all at the sound of the bugle.

The following are the skirmish calls for the First Brigade:

Forward	Dixie.
Quick time	Ellen Bayne.
Double-quick	Yankee Doodle.
Display as skirmishers	Girl I Left Behind Me.
Retreat	Pop Goes the Weasel.
Halt	Same as in U. S. Tactics.
March by the right flank	Hail Columbia.
March by the left flank	Red, White and Blue.
Commence firing	Half Officers' Call.
Cease firing	Same as in U. S. Tactics.
Lie down	Same as in U. S. Tactics.
Rise up	Same as in U. S. Tactics.
Rally by fours	Same as in U. S. Tactics.
Rally by platoons	Same as in U. S. Tactics.
Rally on the reserve	Old Dan Tucker.
Rally on the battalion	Wait for the Wagon.

Copies of the above have been furnished to the troops, and the regimental bands are practicing the calls.

The strong northeaster which prevails renders these efforts at drill on the contracted space of the steamer's dock somewhat difficult, and not a little unpleasant. The thermometer stands at 43°, a temperature which keeps many of the men below decks, and makes fire comfortable.

It is understood that orders will be issued to start in the morning. We are undoubtedly to make our first landing at Roanoke Island, carrying with us three days' provisions. As this will not reach you until long after this event has passed, there is no longer any necessity of withholding thus much from the public. This point taken and fortified, the army and naval force will move rapidly to another place. As circumstances must in a great measure govern our movements, it would be premature to say anything further. It is even doubtful whether it is yet determined which way the army will move.

To-day the sky is still overcast, the wind blows with its accustomed strength, and, as yet, there are no signs of a movement. I have risen at an early hour to scratch a few last notes, expecting that the steamer *Suwanee* will leave with dispatches this morning. Appearances indicate, however, that she will be detained until the fleet moves northward.

LOSS OF STEAM-TUG E. H. HERBERT—CREW SAVED.

In my account of the narrow escape from shipwreck experienced in my last trip from Fort Monroe reference was made to a steamer which sailed in company with us, but turned back after getting as far as Hatteras Shoals. This was the *E. H. Herbert*, of Baltimore, Capt. WM. MATHER. She was abandoned in a sinking condition the following day, Friday last, her captain and crew being rescued by Capt. SETH C. AVERY, of the schooner *Wm. H. Mailler*.

When she reached the entrance of the sine, off Hatteras, her engine became disabled, so that the little steamer could not make half her usual speed, compelling her to put back, which she did, with the hope of reaching Cape Henry. They reached the vicinity of New-Inlet late on Friday afternoon, when just as night was about closing around them, and the vessel was going down, Capt. AREY discovered the vessel heading toward him with her colors set Union down. It was a most providential deliverance. There was only time for the Captain of the tug to clear away his boat, and with his hitherto despairing crew, to step out of his sinking craft. A heavy squall from the northeast struck the vessels at this moment, which rendered abortive all efforts to save anything on board, and in which she soon disappeared from view and went down. The Captain and crew were brought to Hatteras Inlet, arriving safely on Saturday evening. The Captain's name is WILLIAM MATHER; Engineer, H. C. HANCOCK, Pilot, GABRIEL MACOMBER. The other names I have not learned.

NEGLECT TO PROVIDE PILOTS.

The individual who has in charge the business of seeing to the piloting in of the strange vessels continually arriving here, is much complained of for neglecting to send out pilots when they are wanted by vessels in the offing. The *Mailler* lay off the bar over four hours with colors flying for a pilot, and no attention whatever was paid to the signal. As night was coming on, and as he had already experienced two gales of wind in the gulf, Capt. AREY determined to put her in. He was unacquainted, but succeeded in finding his way through the breakers and reached his anchorage in safety. The schooner *R. C. Stannard*, of Baltimore, was in company with the *Mailler*, and did not get in until Monday. He was off the bar with all his signals set for forty-eight hours.

FINAL ARRANGEMENTS.

Gen. BURNSIDE has been quite busy, during the last two days and nights, in completing final arrangements for his departure. These have embraced the necessary distribution of water and provisions to the fleet—some six days' supply; the apportionment and command of the troops; programme of landing; the distribution of Lieut. FRICKER's signal corps, on which great reliance must be placed, for the transmission of information from one point to another, day and night, and the inspection of the fleet generally.

The small fleet of steam-tugs, which arrived on Thursday from Fortress Monroe—the terriers of the navy—will be chiefly relied upon to tow the sailing transports to places of convenient landing.

As I am writing this on the deck of the *Spaulding*, the scene presented is of the liveliest description. The wind has died to a calm, and glimmers of sunshine give hope of a bright afternoon and a pleasant morrow.

On all sides, steamers, sailing transports, gunboats and naval vessels are grouped together, their decks alive with expectant troops, who are as jubilant as children just released from school at the prospect of moving away from this place, so long the theatre of their confinement, perplexity, and hopes deferred. The regimental Bands are sounding the strains of "Dixie," "Red, White and Blue," and other patriotic airs across the still waters of the sound. Among them, ringing out with clarion notes, is the shrill bugle of "JOE GREEN," of the Rhode Island Fourth Regiment. All ears pause to listen, and breathless silence reigns while his magic fingers are on the keys of that silver bugle. The scene is well calculated to raise the long-depressed feelings of the poor fellows who have so heroically endured their protracted imprisonment on shipboard, in this most stormy and disagreeable part of the coast. They will fight hard for a footing upon any portion of *terra firma* whenever the opportunity may present itself.

TIME FIXED FOR DEPARTURE.

MONDAY, 3 P. M.

General BURNSIDE has just announced to his officers his intention to start to-morrow, Tuesday morning. Each vessel has a ten-days' supply of water and provisions; and as everything is nearly ready as it can well be, there is no longer any known reason for delay. The sky is at present clouded over, and the wind is canting to the southeast, from which there is a light air prevailing.

As the mail will be sent on board the *Suwanee* at once, and as I have nothing further to refer to, until we reach that long-looked-for island called Roanoke, I close my letter under the inspiring strains of "Sweet Home," from Gilmore's Band, of the Twenty-fourth Massachusetts, and hoping to send you cheering news from the old North State by the next mail.

I ought not to omit mention of the valuable services which have been rendered to the entire command by Mr. WILLIAM D. HALE, of New-York, for his efforts in the distribution of the soldiers' large mail, which has arrived here during the week. Mr. HALE is a worthy son of Mr. JAMES W. HALE, late of the *Journal of Commerce*.

E. S.

IMPORTANT FROM MISSOURI.

The National Army About to Move Against Price—Preparations of the Rebels for Battle.

ROLLA, Saturday, Feb. 8.

The news from the West indicates that the preparations for a decided blow against the enemy are nearly completed. The forces for this movement are nearly all concentrated at the point whence it is intended to move against the adversary, and in a few days the whole command will be on the march westward.

Gens. SIGEL's and ASBOTH's divisions have reached Lebanon, and Major WRIGHT's battalion of cavalry has moved thirteen miles west of that point.

Gen. DAVIS' Brigade was reported to be crossing the Osage River on Wednesday, and a portion of it was expected to arrive at Lebanon on Thursday.

Two of Major WRIGHT's scouts report that PRICE has made a speech to his troops, telling them they were surrounded, that they must fight or surrender, and that they all decided to fight. PRICE is said to have been heavily reinforced from Arkansas, and to have collected large supplies of provisions on the road leading from Springfield to Fayetteville.

Capt. WOOD had arrived at Waynesville with 72 rebel prisoners, including five captains, taken between Lebanon and Springfield.

NEWS FROM FORTRESS MONROE.

Movement of Troops—Reported Destruction of the Rebel Steamer Calhoun—More Prisoners for Exchange.

FORTRESS MONROE, Saturday, Feb. 8,
Via Baltimore, Sunday, Feb. 9.

An order was issued from headquarters yesterday for the Tenth New-York Regiment, now attached to the garrison of the fortress, to remove to Camp Hamilton, as soon as the weather will permit, in order to make room for the companies of artillery recently arrived.

The following is from Southern papers:

The New-Orleans correspondent of the Charleston *Courier* reports the burning of the rebel steamer *Calhoun*.

NEW-ORLEANS, Friday, Feb. 7.

Four hundred and ninety-two prisoners left yesterday for North Carolina, to be exchanged.

MILL SPRING PRISONERS.

LOUISVILLE, Saturday, Feb. 8.

Forty-six prisoners, captured at the Mill Spring fight, were brought here to-night. Among them are Lieut.-Col. M. B. CARTER, of the Twentieth Tennessee, and three Lieutenants of other rebel regiments.

THE VICTORY AT FORT HENRY.

Acknowledgment of Defeat by the Rebels.

Reported Destruction of the Bridge on the Memphis Railroad.

Additional Particulars of the Engagement.

GREAT VALUE OF THE PROPERTY CAPTURED.

Brief rebel reports of the recent affair at Fort Henry, Tennessee, are received by way of Fortress Monroe.

A dispatch from Clarksville says that Fort Henry has fallen into the hands of the enemy, our force retreating to Fort Donelson. Federal gunboats are at Danville, Tennessee, and the bridge at that place has been destroyed by the Yankees. 20,000 Federals formed the attacking column.

MEMPHIS, Friday, Feb. 7.

Fort Henry was captured by the Federals yesterday, after two hours' fighting.

FURTHER PARTICULARS OF THE FIGHT.

CINCINNATI, Sunday, Feb. 9.

Special dispatches to the *Gazette* and *Commercial*, dated Fort Henry, 8th, give the following intelligence:

Directly after the capture of Fort Henry, the gunboats *Lexington*, *Tyler* and *Conestoga*, started up the river with instructions to proceed as far as they saw fit. Yesterday the *Carandelet*, in charge of Cols. WEBSTER, RIGGINS, and *McPherson*, of Gen. GRANT's staff, made a reconnoisance as far as the bridge of the Memphis and Clarkesville Railroad, at Danville. They found quarters had been built at the bridge, and occupied by some troops, and there was also found a large quantity of army supplies, commissary stores, wagons, &c. The inhabitants were deserting their dwellings for miles around, and fleeing in every direction. The bridge at Danville was partially disabled by the first gunboats which went up the river. Another of the piers was crippled so as to completely prevent the passage of trains.

There were but eight guns captured by DICKEY's Cavalry and Col. LOGAN, instead of fourteen. Nearly all the guns were spiked with telegraph-wire, which was easily removed. They are brass 6-pounders, and in fine order. All the prisoners taken (about 100) were sent to Cairo yesterday. The amount of property captured will exceed $1,000,000.

Reconnoissances have been made by Col. LOGAN and others, to within a mile of Fort Donalson. Gen. GRANT and Staff will make a reconnoissance this afternoon beyond Danville.

Dispatch to the Chicago Evening Journal.

CAIRO, Friday, Feb. 7, 1862.

I arrived from Fort Henry on the gunboat *St. Louis* this morning. We left the fort at 9 o'clock last evening.

Our gunboats took one 128-pounder, one 24, rifled two 42-pounders, ten 32-pounders, one 24 siege-gun, two 12-pounders, one 6-pounder cais-on in the fort.

A rifled shell was fired directly into the muzzle of the 128-pounder. Seven guns were disabled. Thirty-one shots struck the *Cincinnati*, seven struck the *St. Louis*, and fourteen struck the *Essex*.

The *Cincinnati*, *Carondelet* and *St. Louis* were within 300 yards of the rebel batteries when the flag was hauled down on the Fort.

No one was injured. The *St. Louis* is as good as new. She fired 126 shots during the engagement; 53 five-second rifle 7 inch shells, weighing eighty pounds; 15 ten-second ditto; 2 fifteen-second ditto; 17 five-second and 6 ten-second 8-inch shells.

The *Cincinnati* fired 136 shots. The *Essex* fired 35 shells.

The *Essex* was disabled by a round shot that entered a forward port, passing through a heavy bulwark into her boiler. She reports 26 killed, wounded and missing. Her pilots, MARSH FORD, of Pittsburgh, and JAS. MCBRIDE, of Cincinnati, were scalded, and died.

Capt. PORTER's clerk, S. B. BRITTON, was killed, a round shot taking off his head. Two were killed on the *Cincinnati*. The second master, HEWITT, lost a leg, but will probably recover.

Our prisoners are Brigadier-Gen. Floyd Tilghman; Capt. H. L. Jones, of Kentucky, Acting-Quartermaster; Capt. J. H. Hayden, Chief of Engineers; Capt. John McLaughlin, Quartermaster; Major W. L. McComico, Assistant Adjutant-General; Capt. Jesse Taylor, commanding garrison; Lieuts. J. Ormsley, Watts and Fred. J. Weller, and Capt. G. R. G. Jones, and sixty privates.

In the evening, three 6-pounders and five rifled field-pieces were recovered that had been taken into the woods.

The *Lexington* and *Conestoga* went up the river, it was supposed to destroy the bridge of the Clarksville and Memphis Railroad, last night.

Gen. SMITH, on the west side of the river, had captured the whole camp equipage of two regiments, and it was believed a number of prisoners.

At least six hundred shots were fired during the engagement. It was a most terrific cannonade.

The guns were well served.

I saw six dead rebels. Their loss could not be ascertained, the dead having been taken away.

The scene inside of the rebel intrenchments was terrible. In three rows of their log barracks not one escaped, shot and shell having torn everything to splinters.

On the *Cincinnati* one was killed, P. CASSIDY, of St. Catherines; eight wounded, one of whom, WM. LAKEMAN, will die. Capt. PRATT may save his leg.

Our land force on the east side of the river encamped at Fort Henry last night.

AN HOUR BEFORE THE BATTLE.

Dispatches to St. Louis Papers.

STEWART CO., TENN., CAMP HALLECK,
Four miles north Fort Henry,
Wednesday, 11 A. M., Feb. 5.

The night passed perfectly quiet, the enemy making no demonstration upon us whatever.

It seems to-day palpable that they have no idea of leaving their intrenchments.

Our cavalry's scouts were busy yesterday afternoon driving in the pickets several times, but meeting no parties of the enemy. They keep close in their holes.

Steamers were plying on the river above, during the whole night, evidently carrying reinforcements to the fort.

Some of the enemy's steamers could be plainly seen this morning.

When the *Iatan* arrived with her troops she saw a rebel gunboat, supposed to be the *Dunbar*, above the head of the Island.

The *Lexington* and *Conestoga* went after her on each side of the Island, and the rebel boat retreated.

One of our gunboats pulled up two torpedoes in the chute of the Island below the fort. They were made of boiler iron and pointed in the shape of a cone, with a fuse and match at the lower end, with a bag of powder weighing 80 pounds.

Two Confederate mail-carriers were taken by our troops near Fort Henry. They reported 15,000 men at Fort Henry. Reports have been received here of balloons and rockets being sent up from the fort.

A salute was fired at the fort about 10 or 11 o'clock last night.

The weather this morning is quite foggy, but the sun now appears to be gradually making its appearance.

The troops enjoyed a good night's rest, and are now in a fine condition to meet the enemy.

The rebels sent up a large signal balloon last night, which rose well in the air, and floated away to the north of us.

REPORTS FROM ST. LOUIS.

ST. LOUIS, Mo., Sunday, Feb. 8.

A correspondent of the *Republican* says that the property captured at Fort Henry, is valued at upwards of $200,000.

Nine hundred prisoners were transferred from here to Alton to-day, where quarters have been prepared in the old Penitentiary.

Fifteen hundred cavalry and a battery of light artillery left yesterday for Fort Henry. A regiment of cavalry also left for Rolla.

OUR PADUCAH CORRESPONDENCE.

A MOVEMENT IN EARNEST—DESCRIPTION OF THE WORKS TO BE ATTACKED—FORT HENRY—THE FORCE PROBABLY THERE—FACILITY OF ITS REINFORCEMENT—EFFECT OF THE LATE RECONNOISSANCE IN FORCE—RECONNOISSANCE YESTERDAY BY THE GUNBOAT ESSEX.

PADUCAH, Wednesday, Feb. 5, 1862.

A genuine movement is now going on up the Tennessee River, intended for the reduction of Fort Henry. Four of the new gunboats and the three old ones constitute the naval force, while the land forces consist of about fifteen thousand infantry, one thousand cavalry, and seven batteries of field artillery. The expedition goes under the command of Brig.-Gen. U. S. GRANT, Brig.-Gens. C. F. SMITH, JOHN A. MCCLERNAND and LEW. WALLACE, commanding brigades. The force as above stated may be further augmented by troops now at Cairo and arriving there daily. The force is drawn from Cairo, Bird's Point, Fort Holt, this place and Smithland, including perhaps one or two regiments direct from St. Louis. I have not been able to obtain a list of the regiments comprising the land forces. All from this post are taken, but two regiments. On Monday the first troops passed here on the transports, and preceded by the gunboats, proceeded up the Tennessee to a point five miles below the Fort, and were landed on the eastern side of the river. They have been followed by fleet after fleet of transports—the boats rapidly coming and going—until now nearly the whole force must have reached the point of debarkation.

In December last I gave you a description of Fort Henry and its surroundings. All that has since been ascertained, by reconnoissance and otherwise, confirms me in the opinion of the correctness of that report. But, as stated at that time, a large number of hands were employed throwing up additional intrenchments. This work has been prosecuted with energy from the middle of December until the latest accounts. Let me briefly recapitulate the main points of my former account, that the reader may better understand the situation of the coming engagement, the result of which (for weal or woe) will probably be heralded to you by the telegraph before this letter shall reach your hands. Fort Henry is situated on the east bank of Tennessee River, upon its brink, about high water-mark. It is simply a large bastioned earthwork, not casemated, and, so far as is known, without bomb-proofs. To properly understand its position, let the reader take a common school or other map of Tennessee, and he will observe that the line of the northern boundary of the State strikes the Tennessee River on its east bank some miles further north than that at which it leaves the river again westward, so that a fort could be built that much further north on the east than on the west bank of the river, without trespassing upon the territory of Kentucky. The fort was first laid out, and at least partially constructed during the neutrality dispensation in Kentucky; and the rebel military authorities and engineers, wishing to get as far north as possible with their fortification, lest the soil of Tennessee should be polluted by the tread of the Lincolnite invader, placed it upon the point which will be readily seen upon the map where the northern line of the State strikes the river on its eastern shore. The fort thus built upon the sand is commanded on the opposite side of the river by a hill, the occupation of which by an enemy would render the position in the main work wholly untenable.

When I referred to this subject in December, preparation was being made to fortify this hill. I now learn that the contemplated fortifications have been made, but that they consist simply of two turrets on the hillside, one above the other, and mounted with a few heavy guns. It is said that these new works only look toward the river, and are unprotected in the rear; but I am disposed to think that it will be found otherwise. Even the foolish men who built their political fort in the river bottom, so low that recently by their own account the water was within four feet of their magazine, and within six feet of their guns—even these disciples of GID. PILLOW could hardly have erected earthworks commanding their main work upon the opposite hill, and left them wholly unprotected in the rear. I judge that it will be found that there are intrenchments and rifle pits on the western declivity of this hill, to protect the works from assault by infantry.

The ground to the rear of Fort Henry, on the east side, is also higher than the fort, but is supposed to be occupied by bodies of infantry and light artillery, with which the post has been recently reinforced. At the time of the late reconnoissance toward that place, which Gen. SMITH was ordered to make in force, it is reported in Southern papers that BUCKNER, with four regiments, was sent from Bowling Green to reinforce Fort Henry, and it is understood that the place has been considerably reinforced since that time.

It is supposed by some that the garrison is, or soon may be, augmented to some twelve or fifteen thousand. Such may be the force which our army may to-morrow or next day be called upon to confront. The Memphis, Clarkesville and Louisville Railroad passes within an easy day's march of Fort Henry, crossing the Tennessee River eighteen miles above it, communicating with Bowling Green, Clarkesville and Dover, on the east, and Columbus on the west. As the rebel chiefs have impressed all the rolling stock of the railroads into their service, it will be easy to precipitate reinforcements upon the fortifications of the Tennessee and Cumberland with great rapidity.

Had the present expedition been dispatched in its full force, without the forewarning which has been given, success would have been certain. As it is, I have strong hopes of a good result, but not altogether without misgivings of possible failure or even disaster. May the result gloriously dispel my foolish fears. The rebels have lately been giving out extravagant reports of their numerical strength at Fort Henry—an old trick to delay the attack, for which they are not yet fully ready. I have heard estimates even as high as forty thousand of the troops at that place, but have no idea that there is to-day so many as twelve thousand there.

On yesterday the gunboat *Essex* approached within about two miles of the main work at Fort Henry, and threw over two hundred shells into or at the fortifications. She was replied to vigorously by the guns in the Fort. One shell struck the *Essex* on the iron plating of her bow, and glanced off. Another went through her cabin, where she is not plated, passing within a few feet of the Captain. No considerable damage done, and nobody hurt, on our side. Up to the latest accounts we have to-day, the bombardment had not been renewed. Such are the reports brought down by officers who have returned, and no doubt substantially correct. So soon as the forces are ready the new gunboats will proceed nearer, within easy range, and persuade the rebels that the work of yesterday was a mere reconnoissance, as it was.

TENNESSEAN.

HIGHLY IMPORTANT MOVEMENT.

East Tennessee to be Invaded by Three Armies—Knoxville and the Railroad to be taken Possession of.

CINCINNATI, Saturday, Feb. 8.

An Indianapolis dispatch to the *Commercial* says that Gen. THOMAS' division is said to have made a forward movement, and will invade East Tennessee at three different points simultaneously. Gen. CARTER goes through Cumberland Gap, Gen. SCHOEPF by the Central route, and Gen. THOMAS, with MANSON and MCCOOK's brigades, will cross at Mill Spring. They will advance immediately on Knoxville, where they will take possession of the railroad, cutting off supplies and communication with the rebel Government.

THE ARMY AND NAVY.

The Naval recruiting returns for last week, give a total of 280 men shipped here, 130 of whom were booked for Capt. PORTER's mortar fleet, and the remainder for general service.

Recruiting for the army continues very slow. Two men and several boys were sent to Governor's Island from this City last week. Strong, intelligent boys, between the ages of 14 and 18 years, are much wanted for the company of field musicians, several having lately been sent to regiments. In referring last week to the length of service of the Sergeant in charge of the boys, Sergeant CHARLES HENKE, we made a slight mistake. He has been in the army nearly forty years, and has, therefore, very few seniors in the service.

Eleven men enlisted in the country for the Eighth Infantry arrived at the headquarters, Fort Hamilton, on Friday evening. The Eighth has now on the rolls about ninety men, all told. Capt. THOMAS G. PITCHER, of Company I, is in command. Another recruiting office for this regiment has been opened at No. 147 Eighth-avenue.

At the Brooklyn Navy-yard, on Saturday, the steamer *Varuna* hauled into the stream, and her berth was taken by the sloop-of-war *Dacotah*. The latter has commenced to test her engines, and for this purpose will have steam up seventy-two hours.

The barkentine *Horace Beals* has left the yard, and the schooner *Norfolk Packet* is in the stream. There is now only one sailing vessel, the bark *A. Houghton*, belonging to the mortar fleet left at the Yard. The following steamers will form part of the fleet: *Octorara*, *Westfield*, *Clifton*, *John P. Jackson* and *Forbes*. The *Octorara* has been floated out of the dry dock, and the *Cayuga* and *Forbes* floated in. The latter will be overhauled again, as she was found to leak very fast.

The sloop-of-war *Savannah*, from Port Royal, arrived at the Yard for a new mainmast, stores, &c. She saluted Commodore PAULDING, and the salute was returned by the *North Carolina*.

The following vessels are at the Navy-yard:

Name.	Guns.	What doing.
North Carolina	84	Receiving ship.
Sabine	50	Ready for sea.
Richmond	22	Nearly ready for sea.
Savannah	22	Arrived for repairs.
Oneida (new)	9	Fitting out.
Dacotah	9	Fitting out.
Cayuga (new)	9	In dry dock.
John Adams	22	In ordinary.
Dawn	4	Fitting out.
Sachem	5	Fitting out.
Uncas	5	Fitting out.
Currituck	5	Fitting out.
Octorara (new)	9	Fitting out.
J. P. Jackson	—	Fitting out.
Westfield	—	Fitting out.
Clifton	—	Fitting out.
Forbes	4	In dry dock.
Corwin	4	Revenue cutter.
A. Haughton	3	Mortar vessel, fitting out.
Norfolk Packet	3	Mortar vessel in the stream.
Lackawanna (frigate)	—	On the stocks.
Adirondack (sloop)	—	On the stocks, nearly comp'e.
St. Lawrence	50	Off the Battery.

The following shows the forces in the harbor at the present time:

	Men.		Men.
Governor's Island	1,500	North Carolina	700
Fort Hamilton	900	Marine Barracks	150
Fort Lafayette	65	Vessels in harbor	1,400
Fort Richmond	7		
Bedloe's Island	60	Total	4,782

Since guns have been mounted in Fort Richmond, Staten Island, a small guard has been placed there.

DEPARTURE OF THE ST. LOUIS FROM PHILADELPHIA—BAD WORK AT THE NAVY-YARD—THE OFFICERS, ETC.

Correspondence of the New-York Times.

UNITED STATES SHIP ST. LOUIS,
OFF NEWCASTLE, Del., Friday, Feb. 7, 1862.

Among the multitude of your readers there are doubtless some whose "pulses throb responsive to our own," and to whom an occasional stray waif from our goodly ship will be a pleasure, and if you should consider your correspondent's effort worthy an insertion, others will in time follow which may be more interesting.

The *St. Louis* was put into commission on the 31st January, and a crew of one hundred and forty men and twenty-seven marines were placed on board, after which we dropped down to Fort Mifflin, where we took on board our powder and shell. Sunday, Feb. 2, we were towed to our present location to avoid the ice and refit. To refit? you will naturally exclaim—yes, to refit. No vessel, I venture to say, left the Philadelphia Navy-yard in as wretched condition as this. The idea of a ship going to sea without a "pump" in working order, independent of many minor deficiencies, is simply preposterous. There is evidently much negligence, if not culpability, in the discharge of duty by the heads of some of the departments of the yard, which should be rigidly investigated, and when traced, those implicated should be promptly and summarily dealt with. But for a succession of snow-storms since we left, our comforts would have been complete, and we could desire little more.

I am happy to say that a better set of officers and men than ours never trod the decks of any of Uncle Sam's cruisers; everything, in spite of the inclemency of the weather and the uncomfortable *et ceteras* of a vessel lately put in commission, goes as merry as a marriage bell. The commander, M. C. MARIN, is a model gentleman, and thoroughly conversant with his profession, and if his future deportment is foreshadowed by the present, our cruise cannot fail to be a pleasant one. Our executive officer, Lieut. JAMES A. GREER, is everything that we could desire of a gentleman in his position. Invariably courteous and affable in manner, as well as discriminating and just in the execution of his official duties, he has already won golden opinions. Our ship, under his efficient supervision, has already attained that look which plainly indicates man-of-war. Out of chaos he has brought regularity and *discipline*, which is the essential of a vessel of war. Most of the officers are gentlemen selected from our merchant marine, for their proficiency in their profession, and are a most estimable set of fellows. The crew also begin to put off the longshore-man, and assume the jaunty look of the jolly "jack tar." She may not have the honor to participate in the suppression of the rebellion, our destination being the Mediterranean, but if the occasion presents, our services will be effectively rendered, and should, perchance, good fortune lead us into the company of JEFF. DAVIS' pets, rest assured they will meet a warm reception.

We leave to-morrow, and will receive our first mail in Cadiz, Spain, touching at the Western Islands. All incidents, and everything that will be interesting to your readers, will be forwarded on all available occasions.

The following is the list of the officers: Commander, M. C. MARIN; Lieutenant, James A. Greer; Surgeon, Albert L. Gihon; Assistant Surgeon, F. B. A. Lewis; Assistant Paymaster, Judson S. Post; Second Lieutenant Marines, Wm. S. Squires; Sailing Master, Wm. F. Stewart; Acting Masters, Geo. Cables, Joshua Rowe, John E. Johnson; Masters' Mates, Peter W. Fagan, Allen Hoxie, Hazerd Marsh, Henry Lane; Boatswain, Francis McLoud; Acting Gunner, Geo. P. Cushman; Carpenter, Daniel Jones; Acting Sailmaker, I. E. Crowell; Captain's Clerk, ——— ; Paymaster's Clerk, James L. Neller.

The armament of the *St. Louis* is as follows: 4 8-inch shell guns of 55 cwt.; 13 32-pounders of 33 cwt.; 2 Parrott rifled guns, 20-pounders; 1 light 12-pound boat howitzer.

P. W. F.

THE GREAT MORTAR-BOAT FLOTILLA.

The Organization of Capt. Porter's Fleet.

Formidable Character of the Expedition.

Mortars, their Origin and Uses—Concerning Shells and Fuses—Service of Mortars—Range and Elevation—Dimensions and Weight of Heavy Mortars—Monster Mortars of Former Times—The Three Great Mortar Fights of the Century.

The powerful flotilla of Mortar-Boats which has been, for some weeks past, fitting out at the Brooklyn Navy-yard, under the superintendence of Commodore PORTER, is now nearly ready for sea, and may be expected to start for somewhere during the coming week. Concerning what particular rebel stronghold they are intended to beleaguer and bombard, official reticence, as yet, has made no sign. Whether, indeed, Captain PORTER himself is precisely aware of the point where his expedition is to make itself offensively felt, is exceedingly doubtful. One thing, however, is certain; if he does know, he keeps his information hermetically bottled up from all access to inquisitive outsiders. It is, of course, prudent and judicious to conceal the details of our military and naval preparations as completely as possible; for disclosures made here, to satisfy the curiosity of a loyal public, soon find their way far South, and, forewarning, teach the rebels to forearm themselves. To fit out expedition after expedition—as our resources enable us to do—ready to strike blows at any vital part of rebeldom that we may find exposed, and at the same time to keep the rebels in anxious suspense as to the exact spot where the blow shall fall, is one of the most important advantages pertaining to the National cause in the prosecution of this war. This same mortar fleet keeps half-a-dozen rebel towns and fortresses upon the very tenter-hooks of disquietude and terror, simply because its special mission is involved in mystery. Did Norfolk, or Savannah, or New Orleans, or Mobile—any *one* of them—know definitely that *it* was Capt. PORTER's destined victim, then might it make defensive preparations—concentrate troops, intrench itself, mount guns, work itself up to the requisite pitch of patriotic desperation, make up its mind heroically to perish to the last man on its desecrated threshold e'er it would inhale an atmosphere polluted by the breath of the ruthless invader—and, in point of fact, all that sort of thing. But, whilst it is in suspense, it cannot do this. It doesn't care to assemble soldiers, to waste time in digging trenches, to gather cannon, when the first authentic intelligence it receives may be to the effect that these things are not wanted there, but a hundred or five hundred miles away. For this, and divers other cogent reasons, the less Capt. PORTER's mortar fleet—its composition, armament, method of dispatch, and eventual destination—is advertised, the better. It is a case in which the rebels should be allowed to obtain the earliest reliable information; and, though we may feel a little envious of them on this account at first, we shall, in the long run, be inclined to come to the conclusion that, late news as we shall get it, is more welcome than such exclusively early information as is made through the medium of 13-inch shells.

ORGANIZATION OF THE FLEET.

That Capt. PORTER's flotilla will be a most thoroughly equipped and formidable naval attacking force, there is every reason to expect. Capt. PORTER has made the mortar branch of the ordnance service his peculiar study, and, in that specific department, is looked upon by the profession generally as an officer of uncommon expertness and ability. An assault upon a place with bombs projected from mortars is, in many respects, very different from an assault with shot and shell projected from cannon, carronades or howitzers. Big, ponderous ships-of-war are not needed where the firing can be made at long ranges, often from behind sheltering bluffs, or at such an angle, "in shore," as prevents the guns of the fort assailed being brought to bear with any appreciable effect. Such vessels as the *Niagara* and *Wabash* can do immense execution with a succession of broadsides; but, to range up in broadside order at all, a ship's timbers must be of prodigious strength, and the ship itself must have the resistive power which size and weight alone can give. Mortars cannot be fired broadside on, as the direction they give to projectiles is, technically speaking, vertical, and broadside firing is nearly horizontal. Moreover, it is only when the attacking force has command of the sea and of the position which it chooses to occupy, that mortar boats are brought into requisition. The boats themselves, are thus not required for actual fighting purposes, though, of course, they may get occasionally peppered, during a sharp engagement; but the danger of this is not so great as to make it matter of primary consideration. Small vessels, therefore, of moderate staunchness and limited cost are quite as good for the mortar service as the most expensive craft that could be built. Though small, a vessel can bear the lateral recoil of successive discharges of the heaviest mortars, without perceptibly careening, and, if reasonably staunch, she can coast with safety down to the place to be assaulted. She must be braced and bolted a good deal about the deck, though, for there is tremendous wear and tear of platforms, and of all woodwork thereunder fastened, consequent on the mortars recoiling angularly downward, instead of running back like ordinary guns. To bear the strain thus created, Capt. PORTER has had the decks of all his vessels underlaid with massive timber beams, interlaced and riveted, and extending (where the main pressure of recoil occurs) almost through to the kelson. The mortars themselves rest upon circular revolving platforms, of novel and ingenious construction. By means of a very simple arrangement of machinery these platforms can, when the mortars are fired, be lifted from their rollers, and planted firmly on the solid beds beneath; and when a change of aim is desirable, they can be as easily elevated, and turned in any direction the gunners please. These platforms are a great improvement on those adopted in the British Navy.

The vessels collected by Capt. PORTER are mostly brigs and schooners, of sufficient stoutness, which have all been interiorily remodeled under his personal superintendence. The flagship will be the steam gunboat *Octorara*, and the "sail of the line" are to be divided into three divisions as follows: First Division (Lieut. WATSON SMITH commanding), schooners *Norfolk Packet*, *Oliver Lee*, *William Bacon*, *Arletta*, *O. P. Williams*, *Para*; Second Division (Lieut. W. W. QUEEN commanding), schooners *T. A. Ward*, *George Mangum*, *Adolphus Hugel*, *Matthew Vassar, Jr.*, *Sidney C. Jones*, *Maria J. Carlton*, *Orvetta*; Third Division (Lieut. R. RANDOLPH BREESE commanding), schooners *J. Griffith*, *Racer*, *Sarah Bruen*, *Henry Jones*, *Dan Smith* and the brig *Sea Foam*. Most probably, after meeting at some appointed rendezvous, other steamers will be employed to tug the sailing craft to their anchorage upon the field (if one may use the word) of action.

MORTARS, THEIR ORIGIN AND USES.

So little have mortars, and the effective service to which they can be put, been heard of in recent warfare, that few people know very accurately what they are, what are their uses, why they are so named, and wherefore they should be substituted for this and that wondrous cannon that there is so much talk about. To satisfy the last conjecture first: First, Because the cutting down of expenditures in a comparatively small way, seems to be the hobby of the hour. It does not take so much powder to fire a shell from a mortar as from a columbiad, and extensive bombardments can consequently be indulged in with the former for

The New-York Times.

VOL. XI—NO. 3243. NEW-YORK, THURSDAY, FEBRUARY 13, 1862. PRICE TWO CENTS

THE BATTLE OF ROANOKE

Overwhelming Success of the Burnside Expedition.

Roanoke Island and Elizabeth City Captured.

The National Forces Pushing on to Edenton.

Total Destruction of the Rebel Flotilla.

Three Hundred Rebels Killed and Twenty-five Hundred Taken Prisoners.

REPORTS OF THE NATIONAL LOSSES.

FORTRESS MONROE, Tuesday, Feb. 11, via BALTIMORE, Wednesday, Feb. 12.

By a flag of truce to-day we learn the complete success of the Burnside Expedition at Roanoke Island.

The Island was taken possession of, and Commodore LYNCH's fleet completely destroyed.

Elizabeth City was attached on Sunday, and evacuated by the inhabitants. The city was previously burned, but whether by our shells or the inhabitants is not certain.

The first news of the defeat arrived at Norfolk on Sunday afternoon, and caused great excitement. The previous news was very satisfactory, stating that Yankees had been allowed to advance for the purpose of drawing them into a trap.

The rebel force on the island is supposed to have been only a little over three thousand efficient fighting men.

General WISE was ill at Nag's Head, and was not present during the engagement.

When the situation became dangerous, he was removed to Norfolk.

All the gunboats but one were taken, and that escaped up a creek, and was probably also destroyed.

One report says that only seventy, and another that only twenty-five of the Confederates escaped from the Island.

General HUGER telegraphed to Richmond that only fifty on the island escaped.

There appears to be no bright side of the story for the rebels.

The Richmond *Examiner*, this morning, in a leading editorial says:

"The loss of our entire army on Roanoke Island is certainly the most painful event of the war. The intelligence of yesterday by telegraph is fully confirmed. Twenty-five hundred brave troops on an island in the sea were exposed to all the force of the Burnside fleet. They resisted with the most determined courage, but when fifteen thousand Federal troops were landed against them, retreat being cut off by the surrounding element, they were forced to surrender. This is a repetition of the Hatteras affair on a large scale."

The following dispatches on the subject are taken from the Richmond papers of this morning:

NORFOLK, Monday, Feb. 10.

The latest news states that Capt. O. JENNINGS WISE, son of Gov. WISE, was shot through the hip and disabled, though his wound was not mortal. Maj. LAWSON and Lieut. MILLER were mortally wounded. About 300 Confederates were killed. Our wounded numbers over 1,000. The number of Yankees wounded is about the same. Midshipman CAMM had his arm shot off. The other casualties are as yet unreported.

A late arrival this morning says that Elizabeth City had been shelled and burned by the Yankees, and that the enemy was pushing on to Edenton.

SECOND DISPATCH.

NORFOLK, Monday, Feb. 10.

A rumor has prevailed that Commodore LYNCH's fleet of gunboats had been captured. It is not regarded as true, but it is believed that all were burned by the Confederates to prevent their capture, with the exception of one, which was endeavoring to make its escape. The fleet went to Elizabeth City from Roanoke Island, and was probably burnt at the former point.

THIRD DISPATCH.

NORFOLK, Monday, Feb. 10.

A dispatch was received at Richmond, at midnight, stating as follows:

"A courier arrived here this afternoon at 4 o'clock and brought the intelligence that Elizabeth City was burned this morning by its inhabitants. During the conflagration the Federals landed a large force. All our gunboats excepting one were captured by the enemy.

Gen. WISE has not yet arrived at Norfolk."

The following "very latest" we copy from to-day's *Norfolk Day Book*:

"A courier arrived here yesterday afternoon about 3 o'clock, from whom we gather the following information:

The enemy advanced in full force upon Elizabeth City yesterday, about 7 o'clock, and began an attack upon that place. The citizens, finding resistance vain evacuated the place, but, before doing so, set fire to the town, and when our informant left, it was still in flames. We have also to record the capture, by the enemy, of all our little fleet, except the *Fanny*, or *Forrest*, our informant is not certain which. This eluded the enemy, and made up Pasquotank River. She was pursued, however, and fears are entertained that she was captured. It is said that before our boats surrendered they were abandoned, and that their crews succeeded in making their escape. If so, we are at a loss to conjecture why the boats were not fired before they were abandoned. The disaster to our little fleet is attributed to the fact that having exhausted their supply of coal and ammunition, they proceeded to Elizabeth City for the purpose of obtaining a supply. Every effort was made to obtain coal, but without success, and the boats could not, therefore, return to the island and lend any assistance whatever to our forces.

All the details as published with reference to the capture of Roanoke Island are confirmed by the courier, who represents our loss at three hundred killed and wounded, and that of the enemy not less than one thousand killed.

Great havoc was made among the enemy while coming up the road leading to the fort. Our forces brought to bear upon them two 32-pounders, and at every fire their ranks were terribly thinned. The places of the fallen, however, were quickly filled.

The Park Point battery was manned by the Richmond Blues and most nobly did they defend it. During the conflict they were attacked by a whole regiment of Zouaves, and though completely overpowered they stood their ground. They did not yield a foot, until all but seven of them had fallen bleeding to the ground.

There is good reason to believe that had Col. HENNINGSEN, with his artillery, been on the Island, it would not have been forced to surrender.

The lack of field-pieces was sadly felt, and had they been at hand, perhaps the enemy never would have been able to have landed their forces.

Col. HENNINGSEN had orders, we understand, to report to Roanoke Island, but by some misunderstanding, he mistook Elizabeth City for his place of destination.

Capt. TAYLOR, of this city, is represented as having greatly distinguished himself."

In addition to the above, there are many rumors we might give, but as they are nothing more than rumors, we prefer withholding them. Among them, however, is one worthy of notice, that Gen. WISE had been shot while on his way in an ambulance. The statement, so far as we have been able to learn, is untrue. We can only account for it by supposing that the name of the General was confounded with that of his son, who was reported among the killed.

It is reported that one regiment from Massachusetts was badly cut up, but is impossible to ascertain which of the five it was that were attached to the Expedition.

All the Southern papers received to-day are unanimous in admitting a complete victory to our troops, and in saying that the loss of the island is a very serious one.

The news received to-day occasions great excitement at Old Point. A steamer with official dispatches from Gen. BURNSIDE is hourly expected.

The prisoners captured, numbering at least 2,000, will be here in a few days.

MAILS FOR THE BURNSIDE EXPEDITION.

Letters left in the care of FRANK E. HOWE, No. 283 Broadway, or at the Astor House, will be forwarded to the Burnside Expedition to-morrow, the departure of the steamer having been postponed one day.

AFFAIRS AT FORTRESS MONROE.

Arrival of the Released Prisoners—News from the South—The Position at Savannah—The Rebel Authorities Stopping the Manufacture of Whisky.

FORTRESS MONROE, Tuesday, Feb. 11, via BALTIMORE, Wednesday, Feb. 12.

A flag of truce was sent to Craney Island early this morning, to inform Gen. HUGER that the prisoners of war from Fort Warren arrived in the bark *Trinity* last night.

The bark was accordingly towed up opposite Sewall's Point by the steamer *Rancocas* and the tug *Adriatic*, and at about 1 o'clock the rebel steamer *West Point* came out from Norfolk, and the prisoners were transferred. They numbered four Captains, three First Lieutenants, six Second Lieutenants, two Third Lieutenants, and 384 others, rank and file and colored servants. They were taken at Hatteras and Santa Rosa, and are the last of the prisoners of war at Fort Warren, except Commodore BARRON.

The passage here from Boston has been quite unpleasant on account of the crowded condition of the vessel. But the prisoners are all enjoying as good health as could be expected.

It was generally supposed here that the small-pox was on board the vessel, but on the authority of Lieut. BUELL, who comes in charge from Fort Warren, the statement is positively denied.

The prisoners having been transferred to the *West Point*, the *Trinity* was towed back to her anchorage in the Roads.

Several passengers were brought back from Norfolk, including Capt. J. S. MOORE, of the transport *Osceola*.

The *Osceola* was a part of Gen. SHERMAN's expedition, and was wrecked on the coast of Georgia Nov. 2, and the Captain and the whole crew taken prisoners.

The latest intelligence from Savannah is that the National gunboats were at Wall's Cut, an opening which communicates with Savannah without passing Fort Pulaski.

There has been some skirmishing between the Nationals and rebels at Port Royal Ferry.

The city of Savannah was being strongly fortified.

We find the following additional news from various parts of the South, in the papers received to-day:

Ex-Gov. W. CAMPBELL declines the tender of the appointment of a Brigadier-General, and assigns as a reason his physical incapability to perform the duties of the office. He was to have filled the place vacated by the death of Gen. ZOLLICOFFER.

The bill to raise troops to meet the requisition on Virginia by the President of the Confederate States, passed both branches of the Virginia General Assembly on Monday in secret session.

The bill provides that all companies now in the field shall be filled up, to the number of one hundred men; that the Governor shall call for volunteers for this purpose, and that if the requisite number be not thus enlisted, the deficiency is to be made up by draft from the enrolled militia.

The injunction of secrecy has been removed from a bill passed by Congress, appropriating two millions of dollars for the benefit of the State of Kentucky.

JAMES LYONS is probably elected to Congress, to supply the vacancy caused by the death of JOHN TYLER.

The War Department has issued an order for the seizure of all corn in the hands of distillers or others, to be used for the purposes of distillation. This step is taken, not only on account of the pernicious effects of the unlimited manufacture of whisky, but also because of the exorbitant prices the Government is obliged to pay for an article indispensable to the subsistence of the army.

IMPORTANT FROM CENTRAL KENTUCKY.

National Troops in Motion Towards Bowling Green.

CINCINNATI, Wednesday, Feb. 12.

The weather is improving and the roads drying.

The *Commercial* says that our army in Central Kentucky is in motion. Gen. NELSON's Division is marching along the Glasgow turnpike. Gen. MITCHELL's Division had crossed Green River on Monday morning, taking the advance of the Union column to Bowling Green.

GEN. HUNTER'S EXPEDITION.

Preparations for the Advance—Concentration of Troops and Supplies in Southern Kansas.

LEAVENWORTH, Tuesday, Feb. 11.

The greatest activity prevails at Fort Leavenworth in preparations for the expedition to start from here under Gen. HUNTER. Troops and supplies are being concentrated in the Southern portions of the State, and the indications appear favorable for an early advance. The General himself is working earnestly and unceasingly in the perfection of the details of the expedition, and every department is pushed to its utmost capacity. Seven regiments of cavalry, four regiments of infantry and three full batteries of artillery, with Parrott and Weird guns, are now *en route* from the East, and are daily expected to join the expedition, which will be one of the most formidable yet organized during the war.

DIAGRAM SHOWING THE POSITION OF ROANOKE ISLAND.

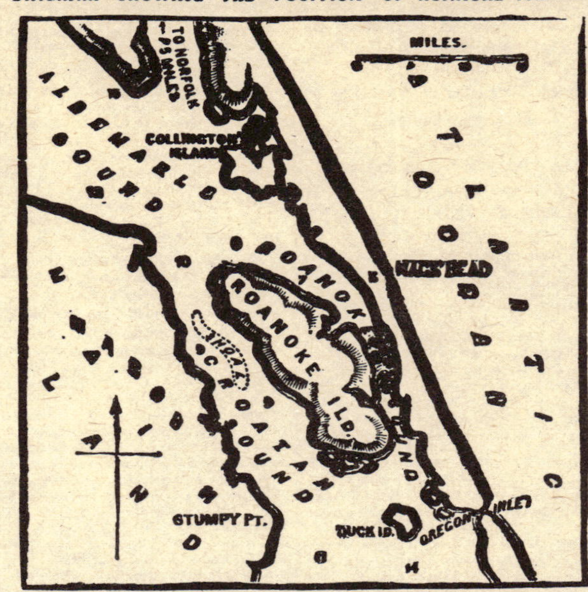

The above diagram will show more clearly than the large map we gave yesterday the position and some of the relations of Roanoke Island, of whose capture we have now definite intelligence. We have already described the island, and need not now recapitulate. It may be said, however, that it is seven miles long and three broad, and has good natural means of defence, which had been well improved by the rebels. The rebel earthworks, which were strong, were thrown up about the centre of the island, and our troops had to debark on its southern end, and march up a distance of between two and three miles, to the rebel position. On the mainland opposite, there were also defences; and on the narrow strip of beach to the east, at the point marked as Nag's Head, there was lately a rebel force stationed; but as we have no account of fighting there, it may have been that the whole of the rebel forces were concentrated on the island. The waters between the island and the outer beach, designated Roanoke Sound, are not navigable by large vessels; so that the movements of our gunboats were mainly in Croatan Sound. It will be seen how perfectly Roanoke Island here forms the key of the inland navigation at this point.

OPERATIONS IN TENNESSEE

Flag-Officer Foote's Report of the Battle of Fort Henry.

The Advance of the National Gunboats into Alabama.

Six Rebel Steamers Burned and Three Captured.

QUANTITIES OF MILITARY STORES SEIZED

The National Forces Everywhere Received with Joy.

Enthusiastic Exhibition of Loyalty to the Government.

THE EXPEDITION UP THE TENNESSEE.

OFFICIAL REPORT TO FLAG-OFFICER FOOTE. ETC.

WASHINGTON, Wednesday, Feb. 12.

The following is Lieut.-Commanding PHILLIPS' report to Flag-Officer FOOTE, received to-day at the Headquarters of the Army, by telegraph from Cairo:

GUNBOAT CONESTOGA, RAILROAD CROSSING OF THE TENNESSEE RIVER, Feb. 10, 1862.

SIR: We have returned to this point from an entirely successful expedition to Florence, at the foot of Muscle Shoals, Alabama. The rebels were forced to burn six of their steamers, and we captured two others, beside the half-complete gunboat *Eastport*. The steamers burned were freighted with rebel military stores. The *Eastport* has about 250,000 feet of lumber on board. We have captured 200 stand of arms and a quantity of clothing and stores, and have destroyed the encampment of Col. CREWS. At Savanna, Tenn., we found the Union sentiment strong.

(Signed) PHILLIPS, Lieut.-Com'g.

REPORTS FROM CINCINNATI.

CINCINNATI, Wednesday, Feb. 12.

Special dispatches to the *Gazette and Commercial*, dated Fort Henry, the 10th inst., give the following account of the gunboat Expedition up the Tennessee River.

After the capture of Fort Henry, the *Lexington*, *Conestoga* and *Tyler* gave chase to the rebel steamer *Dunbar*, and on reaching the Memphis and Louisville Railroad Bridge, set fire to a portion of it and captured some stores, &c. They then passed on in chase of the *Dunbar*, but did not overtake her. It is supposed that she escaped by running up some creek.

During the night the gunboats went to Florence, Alabama, the head of navigation, and two hundred and fifty miles from Paducah. Everywhere along the river they were received with astonishing welcome by numerous Union families in Southern Tennessee and Northern Alabama, and at the towns along the river the old flag was looked upon as a redeemer, and hailed with shouts of joy.

Capt. GWYNN, of the *Tyler*, has recruited thirty men for service on the gunboats, and says he can get enough for the whole fleet.

The people of Florence are so delighted at finding the Stars and Stripes once more giving protection to them that they were prepared to give a grand ball to the officers of the gunboats, but they could not remain to accept of their courtesies.

Wherever our boats landed, and the people became assured that we did not come to destroy, but to save they seemed to have no means too extravagant to express their delight and joy.

Our gunboats captured four steamers, including an unfinished gunboat, and burned seven others.

They captured a large quantity of stores and one hundred and eighty stand of arms.

One boat goes up the river this morning.

REPORTS FROM ST. LOUIS.

ST. LOUIS, Wednesday, Feb. 12.

A special dispatch to the *Republican*, dated Fort Henry, 11th inst., states that the gunboats *Conestoga*, *Tyler* and *Lexington* returned from Upper Tennessee last night.

The boats went as far as Florence, Ala., and were received with the wildest joy along the river.

Old men cried like children at the sight of the "Stars and Stripes," and invited the officers and men of the gunboats to their houses, and told them all they had was at their disposal. Large numbers were anxious to enlist under the "Old Flag," and the *Tyler* brought down 250 men to fill up the gunboats' crews.

Our officers were assured that if they would wait a few days whole regiments could be raised, and if the Government would give them arms to defend themselves, they could bring Tennessee back into the Union in a few months.

They said that when the secession ordinance was passed, armed men stood at the polls and everything went as certain politicians said.

At Savanna, Eastport and Florence the officers and men of our gunboats went ashore without arms and mingled freely with the people.

The Union men along the river comprise the wealthy and best portion of the inhabitants, large numbers of whom have American flags.

Not a gun was fired either going or coming.

The rebel gunboats *Eastport*, *Sallie Ward* and *Muscle*, only partially finished, were captured and are here. The *Eastport* had 250,000 feet of lumber on board, and the *Ward* had a quantity of iron plating.

The steamers *Sam. Kirkman*, *Linn Boyd*, *Julia Smith*, *Sam. Orr*, *Appleton* and *Belle* had been burned by the rebels to prevent them from falling into our hands.

The railroad bridge at Florence was not destroyed.

A quantity of papers were captured on the *Eastport*, belonging to Lieut. BROWN, late of the Federal Navy. Among them were letters from Lieut. MAURY, stating that submarine batteries could not be used successfully in the rapid streams of the West.

One hundred and fifty hogsheads of tobacco, and a quantity of other freights, will be brought down from the mouth of Sandy River to-morrow.

A daily line of packets has been established between Fort Henry and Cairo.

Nothing during the war has been so prostrating to the rebels as the late victory of the gunboat expedition mentioned above.

THE REPORT OF FLAG-OFFICER FOOTE.

WASHINGTON, Wednesday, Feb. 12.

The following is an official copy of the report of Flag-Officer FOOTE to the Navy Department relative to the capture of Fort Henry:

CAIRO, Ill., Feb. 7, 1862.

SIR: I have the honor to report that on the 6th inst., at 12½ o'clock P. M., I made an attack on Fort Henry on the Tennessee River, with the iron-clad gunboats *Cincinnati*, Commander STEMBEL, the flag ship; the *Essex*, Commander PORTER; the *Carondelet*, Commander WALKER, and the *St. Louis*, Lieutenant-Commanding PAULDING; also taking with me the three old gunboats *Conestoga*, Lieutenant-Commanding PHELPS; the *Tyler*, Lieutenant-Commanding GWYNN, and the *Lexington*, Lieutenant-Commanding SHIRK, as a second division, in charge of Lieutenant-Commanding PHELPS, which took a position astern and in shore of the armed boats, doing good execution there in the action, while the armed boats were placed in the first order of steaming, approaching the fort in a parallel line.

The fire was opened at 1,700 yards distance, from the flag-ship, which was followed by the other gunboats, and responded to by the fort. As we approached the fort, slow steaming till we reached within 600 hundred yards of the rebel batteries, the fire both from the gunboats and the fort increased in rapidity and accuracy of range.

At twenty minutes before the flag was struck, the *Essex* unfortunately received a shot in her boiler, which resulted in the wounding and scalding of twenty-nine officers and men, including Commander PORTER, as will be seen in the inclosed list of casualties.

The *Essex* then necessarily dropped out of line astern, entirely disabled, and unable to continue the fight, in which she had so gallantly participated until the sad catastrophe.

The firing continued with unabated rapidity and effect upon the three gunboats as they continued still to approach the fort with their destructive fire, until the rebel flag was hauled down, after a very severe and closely-contested action of one hour and fifteen minutes.

A boat containing the Adjutant-General and Captain of Engineers came alongside after the flag was lowered, and reported that Gen. LLOYD TILGHMAN, the commander of the fort, wished to communicate with the Flag-officer, when I dispatched Commander STEMBEL and Lieutenant-Commanding PHELPS, with orders to hoist the American flag where the secession ensign had been flying, and to inform Gen. TILGHMAN that I would see him on board the flag-ship. He came on board soon after the Union had been substituted for the rebel flag on the fort, and possession taken of it.

I received the General and his Staff, and some sixty or seventy men, as prisoners, and a hospital ship, containing sixty invalids, together with the fort and its effects, mounting 20 guns, mostly of heavy calibre, with barracks and tents capable of accommodating 15,000 men, and sundry articles, which, as I turned the fort and its effects over to Gen. GRANT, commanding the army on his arrival in one hour after we had made the capture, he will be enabled to give the Government a more correct statement of than I am enabled to communicate from the short time I had possession of the fort.

The plan of the attack, as far as the army reaching the rear of the fort to make a demonstration simultaneously with the navy, was frustrated by the excessively muddy roads, and the high stage of water preventing the arrival of our troops until some time after I had taken possession of the fort.

On securing the prisoners, and making the necessary preliminary arrangements, I dispatched Lieut.-Commanding PHELPS with his division up the Tennessee River, as I had previously directed, and as will be seen in the inclosed orders to him, to remove the rails, and so far render the bridge of the railroad for transportation and communication between Bowling Green and Columbus useless, and afterwards to pursue the rebel gunboats, and secure their capture if possible.

This being accomplished, and the army in possession of the fort, and my services being indispensable at Cairo, I left Fort Henry in the evening of the same day with the *Cincinnati*, *Essex* and *St. Louis*, and arrived here this morning.

The armed gunboats resisted effectually the shot of the enemy, when striking the casemate.

The *Cincinnati*, the flag-ship, received thirty-one shots, the *Essex* fifteen, the *St. Louis* seven, and the *Carondelet* six—killing one and wounding nine in the *Cincinnati*, and killing one in the *Essex*, while the casualties in the latter from steam amounted to twenty-eight in number. The *Carondelet* and *St. Louis* met with no casualties.

The steamers were admirably handled by the Commanders and officers, presenting only their bow guns to the enemy, to avoid the exposure of the vulnerable parts of their vessels.

Lieut.-Commanding PHELPS, with his division, also executed my orders very effectually, and promptly proceeded up the river in their further execution after the capture of the Fort. In fact all the officers and men gallantly performed their duty, and considering the little experience they have had under fire, far more than realized my expectations.

Fort Henry was defended with the most determined gallantry by Gen. TILGHMAN, worthy of a better cause, who, from his own account, went into action with eleven guns of heavy calibre bearing upon our boats, which he fought until seven of the number were dismantled or otherwise rendered useless.

I have the honor to be, very respectfully, your obedient servant, H. H. FOOTE, Flag Officer.

Hon. GIDEON WELLES, Secretary of the Navy, Washington, D. C.

LIST OF CASUALTIES.

U. S. FLAG STEAMER CINCINNATI, Feb. 6, 1862.

SIR: I have the honor to report that the casualties on board this vessel during the bombardment of Fort Henry, from the effects of the enemy's fire, were: Killed, 1; wounded, 9. Total, 10. Respectfully,

R. N. STEMBEL, Com., U. S. N.

To H. H. FOOTE, Commanding naval forces, Western waters.

FLAG-OFFICER H. H. FOOTE—*Sir*: As Capt. PORTER is unable to write, he has directed me to send you a list of killed, wounded and missing on this vessel:

W. D. Porter, Commander, scalded.
J. H. Lewis, Paymaster, scalded.
T. P. Perry, third master, scalded badly.
S. B. Brettan, master's mate, killed by a cannon shot.
James McBride, pilot, killed by scalding.
Wm. H. Ford, pilot, killed by scalding.
John Matthews, Quartermaster, scalded badly.
A. D. Waterman, Captain of forecastle, missing.
Henry Gemper, fireman, missing.
Samuel Bayer, fireman, scalded badly.
John Lautz, fireman, missing.
James Coffey, seaman, killed by scalding.
N. McCarty, seaman, scalded.
H. Hagan, seaman, scalded.
Dana Wilson, seaman, killed by scalding.
Ben. Harrington, seaman, scalded badly.
Wm. O'Brine, seaman, scalded badly.
Thomas Mullen, seaman, scalded slightly.
W. H. Maxey, seaman, scalded badly.
T. Sullivan, seaman, scalded badly.
James Bedard, seaman, missing.
J. P. Beers, seaman, killed by scalding.
John O. Hara, seaman, scalded.
John Castello, seaman, scalded.
J. J. Phillips, seaman, scalded.
B. Lula, seaman, scalded.
H. Reynolds, seaman, missing.
James Argus, seaman, scalded.
Thomas Millett, seaman, scalded badly.

In addition to the above, we had nineteen soldiers scalded, of whom several have since died.

Very respectfully, your obedient servant,
ROBERT K. RILEY,
Ex Officer United States gunboat *Essex*.

SPECIAL ORDER NO. 3.

UNITED STATES GUNBOAT TAYLOR, PADUCAH, Feb. 2, 1862.

Lieutenant-Commanding PHELPS will, as soon as the fort shall have surrendered, upon a signal from the Flag-ship, proceed with the *Conestoga*, *Taylor* and *Lexington* up the river to where the railroad bridge crosses, and if the army shall not already have got possession, he will destroy so much of the track as will entirely prevent its use by the rebels.

He will then proceed as far up the river as the stage of water will admit, and capture the enemy's gunboats and other vessels which might prove available to the enemy.

A. H. FOOTE,
Flag-Officer commanding naval forces in Western Waters.

THANKS TO COMMODORE FOOTE.

WASHINGTON, Wednesday, Feb. 12.

The following was sent to Commodore FOOTE last Sunday:

NAVY DEPARTMENT, Feb. 9, 1862.

Flag Officer A. H. Foote, U. S. N., Commanding U. S. Naval Forces, Cairo, Illinois:

Your dispatch, announcing the capture of Fort Henry, by the squadron which you commanded, has given the highest gratification to the President, to Congress, and the country. It was received and read in both Houses of Congress in open session. The country appreciates your gallant deeds, and this Department desires to convey to you and your brave associates its profound thanks for the service you have rendered.

GIDEON WELLES,
Secretary of the Navy.

MOVEMENTS OF NATIONAL TROOPS.

ST. LOUIS, Wednesday, Feb. 12.

A Cairo special dispatch to the *Democrat* says that passengers by the Evansville packet report passing at Paducah, this morning, eleven transports laden with troops.

The Forty-sixth, Thirty-first, and Fourth Illinois regiments, a battalion of the Twenty-ninth Illinois, and a company of the Eighth Wisconsin, left here this afternoon.

Signal fire balloons, apparently sent up from Mayfield by the rebels, have been seen here the past few nights.

Advices from Fort Henry say that much reliance was placed on the 20-pound Parrott guns of the First Missouri Artillery, three batteries of which are there under Major CAVENDER.

Four more regiments marched from there last night on reconnoitering parties, and went within one mile of Fort Donelson. A squadron of our cavalry barely escaped capture by 900 rebel cavalry, supported by infantry.

GEN. HITCHCOCK A MAJOR-GENERAL.

ST. LOUIS, Wednesday, Feb. 12.

The *Republican* learns that Gen. HITCHCOCK has accepted the appointment of Major-General of Volunteers. Should Gen. HALLECK take the field in command of the Southern Expedition, which is considered probable, Gen. HITCHCOCK will remain at the head of the Department here.

FROM PORT ROYAL.

The bark *Charles Kean*, Capt. SWAN, arrived at this port yesterday, from Port Royal, S. C., in eight days. Matters remain as at last accounts. Vessels were arriving daily from Northern ports, with stores, ammunition, &c. The health of the troops was good. The *Charles Kean* lies at anchor near the South Ferry, Brooklyn.

A DAY LATER FROM EUROPE

THE TEUTONIA OFF CAPE RACE.

The U. S. Steamer Tuscarora Ordered out of Southampton Waters.

THE NASHVILLE PERMITTED TO REMAIN.

THE CRUISE OF THE SUMTER.

Our London and Paris Correspondence.

Prospects of Intervention in America.

MR. SEWARD'S LATE DISPATCHES.

Napoleon III. on the American Question.

TONE OF THE FRENCH PRESS.

The Journals of Madrid on the War.

The steamship *Teutonia*, which left Southampton on the morning of the 1st inst., passed Cape Race at 6 o'clock yesterday morning, and was intercepted by the news-yacht of the Associated Press.

The steamship *Australasian*, from New-York, arrived at Liverpool on the 1st.

The steamship *Asia* took the mails of the steamship *Etna*.

The United States gunboat *Tuscarora* has been ordered off the dock off Southampton by the British Government, and has taken up a position near the Needles.

The pirate *Nashville* was still in Southampton dock.

The reported naval engagement in the Mediterranean is not confirmed.

The WINDHAM lunacy case ended on the thirty-fourth day, and a verdict was rendered in favor of young WINDHAM.

The *Times'* City Article of Jan. 31 says Consols continued dull at 92⅜ a 92½ for money, and 92⅞@93 for March 6. Numerous transactions took place in the Discount market at 2 ₽ cent. On the Stock Exchange the rate of advances was 1½ a 2 ₽ cent. French Rentes declined; quoted at 71f. 10c.

American securities were dull.

The statement of Secretary SEWARD, implying that the American Government held themselves bound after subjugating the rebels, to restore the destroyed harbors, or open better ones, added considerable to the disquiet of Federal bondholders, since it makes a further indefinite addition to the prospects of the ultimate amount of debt. It is believed that even if the war were wound up immediately, the debt of America would, at the rate of interest that must be paid, involve an annual charge on the revenue equal to more than half the total required for the national debt of England.

A new Ministry has been formed in Holland.

The Russians have been defeated in Circassia.

Many wrecks are reported in the Black Sea.

French troops are being rapidly dispatched to Mexico.

The Herzegovian insurgents have reëntered the places from which DERVISH PACHA had driven them, without resistance. The Turks had concentrated at Pigsissa, and advanced on the 29th to Gbriska, the inhabitants withdrawing to Austrian territory.

The *Teutonia* reports passing through great quantities of ice. On the 7th, in lat. 49° 40′, lon. 32° 30′, passed steamship *Parana*.

No later markets came by the *Teutonia* than those received by the *Jura*.

By the *America* and the *Jura* we receive highly interesting letters from our Correspondents in Paris and London: and also full files, from which we derive important additions to the extracts contained in our issue of yesterday.

THE AMERICAN QUESTION.

THE ATTITUDE OF FRANCE.

Prospects of Intervention—Adroit Game of the English Press—Sufferings of the Working Classes—The French Campaign in Mexico—The Ball at the Tuileries.

From Our Own Correspondent.

PARIS, Friday, Jan. 24, 1862.

The uneasiness in American circles about a foreign intervention in our affairs increases rather than diminishes. *In French circles the opinion is almost universal that France and England will interfere before a month.* This opinion I have heard expressed by journalists so sober and so prudent in general, that my faith in the justice and the good dispositions of the French Government have been somewhat shaken. While willing to admit that all the superficial indications point to an interference, I am yet unwilling, however, to believe that the French Government has arrived at that point. The Ministers, the Government people, the Government Press, appear to be ready for an intervention; but the Emperor and the Prince NAPOLEON will hesitate before plunging into a policy so fatal to French interests. Not many days ago, the Emperor is reported to have said to the English Ambassador that he thought it right and fair to allow the American Government further trial of force against the insurrection; and notwithstanding the noise that has been raised for the last few days on the subject, I have seen nothing to indicate that the Emperor holds any other view than that expressed above.

The French Government has probably protested against the closing of the Southern ports with stones, but if it has, it is done in more becoming language than that employed by the English Foreign Office for the same purpose. The French Government will not take upon itself to judge the motives of the American Government in the accomplishment of such an act.

In London they continue to write to Paris that the French Government is taking the lead in the matter of a recognition of the Confederacy, and the declaration of a nullity of the blockade, while in Paris they write to London that it is the English Government which is taking the lead. Are we not permitted to draw from this fact the conclusion that neither party desires to be the first to engage in the dirty business? The statement so often repeated that in July last the

The Charleston Mercury.

DAILY PAPER—TEN DOLLARS PER ANNUM, PAYABLE HALF-YEARLY IN ADVANCE.

SPONTE SUA SINE LEGE FIDES RECTUMQUE COLENTUR. —VINDICE NULLO

COUNTRY PAPER—THRICE A WEEK—FIVE DOLLARS PER ANNUM, IN ADVANCE.

VOLUME LXXX. CHARLESTON, S. C., THURSDAY, FEBRUARY 13, 1862. NUMBER 11,373

NOTES OF THE WAR.

INTERESTING NEWS FROM THE NORTH.

THE BOMBARDMENT OF FORT HENRY.

The New York *Herald*, of the 8th, puts us in possession of the very last Northern accounts of the attack and capture of Fort Henry, and other interesting intelligence, a summary of which we give below:

BOMBARDMENT AND SURRENDER OF FORT HENRY—THE MEMPHIS AND OHIO RAILROAD IN THE HANDS OF THE NORTHERN TROOPS.

A Northern despatch, dated Cairo, February 7, says:

We have taken Fort Henry. It was surrendered to Commodore Foote yesterday, at two o'clock in the afternoon, after a most determined resistance. The fight, which lasted an hour and twenty minutes, was conducted by the gunboats Cincinnati, Essex, and St. Louis. The Cincinnati fired one hundred and twenty-five rounds, and received thirty-four shots from the rebel guns; but only one man was killed. The St. Louis fired one hundred and ten rounds, but received no damage. The Essex was disabled after firing ten rounds, by a ball striking her boiler. Thirty-two persons on board of her were killed, being scalded to death. Captain Porter, who commanded her, was badly scalded, but not dangerously so. One rebel General, one Colonel, two Captains, and one hundred privates, were taken prisoners. The fort mounted twenty guns and seventeen mortars.

The land forces did not reach the scene of the action until half an hour after the surrender of the fort. The Memphis and Ohio Railroad bridge, fifteen miles above the fort, has been taken possession of by our troops.

DETAILS OF THE BATTLE.

The following details of the fight, are from the correspondence of the Cincinnati *Commercial*:

Yesterday, at half-past 12 p. m., the gunboats Cincinnati, St. Louis, Carondelet and Essex, the Tyler, Conestoga and Lexington bringing up the rear, advanced boldly against the rebel works, going to the right of Panther Creek Island, immediately above, where, on the east shore of the river, stands the fortifications, and keeping out of range till at the head of the island and within a mile of the enemy, passing the island in full view of the rebel guns. We steadily advanced, every man at quarters, every ear strained to catch the flag officer's signal gun for the commencement of the action. Our line of battle was on the left of the St. Louis, next the Carondelet, next the Cincinnati (for the time being the flag-ship, having on board Flag-Officer Foote), and the next the Essex.

We advanced in line, the Cincinnati a boat's length ahead, when, at half-past eleven, the Cincinnati opened the ball, and immediately the three accompanying boats followed suit. The enemy was not backward, and gave an admirable response, and the fight raged furiously for half an hour. We steadily advanced, receiving and returning the storm of shot and shell, when, getting within three hundred yards of the enemy's works, we came to a stand and poured into him right and left. In the meantime the Essex had been disabled, and drifted away from the scene of action, leaving the Cincinnati, Carondelet, and St. Louis alone engaged.

CONFEDERATE COLORS STRUCK.

At precisely forty minutes past one o'clock the enemy struck his colors, and such cheering, such wild excitement as seized the throats, arms or caps of the four or five hundred sailors of the gunboats, can be imagined.

After the surrender, which was made to Flag-Officer Foote by General Lloyd Tilghman, who defended his fort in a most determined manner, we found that the rebel infantry, encamped outside the fort, had cut and run, leaving the rebel artillery company in command of the fort.

THE FORT.

The fort mounted seventeen guns, most of them thirty-two and thirty-four pounders, one being a magnificent ten-inch columbiad. Our shots dismounted two of their guns, driving the enemy into the embrasures. One of their rifled thirty-two pounders burst during the engagement, wounding some of their gunners. The rebels claimed to have but eleven effective guns, worked by fifty four men—the number all told of our prisoners. They lost five killed and ten badly wounded.

GASCONADE.

The infantry left everything in the fight. A vast deal of plunder has fallen into our hands, including a large and valuable quantity of ordnance stores.

Gen. Tilghman is disheartened. He thinks it one of the most damaging blows of the war. In surrendering to Flag-Officer Foote, the rebel General remarked, "I am glad to surrender to so gallant an officer." Flag-Officer Foote replied, "You do perfectly right, sir, in surrendering; but you should have blown my boats out of the water before I would have surrendered to you."

CASUALTIES.

In the engagement the Cincinnati was in the lead, and, flying the Flag-Officer's pennant, was the chief mark. Flag-Officer Foote and Captain Stembel crowded her defiantly into the teeth of the enemy's guns. She got thirty-one shots, some of them going completely through her. The Essex was badly crippled when about half through the fight, and crowding steadily against the enemy. A ball went into her side forward port, through her heavy bulkhead, and squarely through one of her boilers, the escaping steam scalding and killing many of the crew. Captain Porter, his aid, C. P. Britton, jr., and Paymaster Lewis, were standing in a direct line of the balls passing, Mr. Britton being in the centre of the group. A shot struck Mr. Britton on the top of his head, scattering his brains in every direction. The escaping steam went into the pilot house, instantly killing Messrs. Ford and Bride, pilots. Many of the soldiers, at the rush of steam, jumped overboard and were drowned.

The Cincinnati had one killed and six wounded. The Essex had six seamen and two officers killed, seventeen men wounded and five missing. There were no casualties on the St. Louis or Carondelet, though the shot and shell fell upon them like rain. The St. Louis was commanded by Leonard Paulding, who stood upon the gunboat and worked the guns to the last.

Not a man flinched, and with cheer upon cheer sent the shot and shell among the enemy.

DESCRIPTION OF THE GUNBOATS.

The St. Louis and Cincinnati are pierced for thirteen guns each, the Essex for nine guns. The bow guns are heavy 84 pound rifled cannon; the others are 8 inch columbiads. The sides of the boats, both above and below the knee, incline at an angle of forty-five degrees, and nothing but a plunging shot from a high bluff could strike the surface at right angles. The iron plating has been severely tested by shots from rifled cannon at different distances, and has shown itself to be utterly impervious to any shots that have been sent against it, even at a range of three hundred yards.

The boats, it will be perceived, are built very wide, in proportion to their length, giving them almost the same steadiness in action that a stationary land battery would possess. They are constructed on the same principle as the famous iron battery at Charleston, the sides sloping upward and downward from the water line at an angle of forty-five degrees. The boats are built so that in action they could be kept "bow on;" hence the superior strength of the bow battery. Broadsides were so arranged as to be delivered with terrible effect while shifting position. To facilitate movements in action, the engines and machinery are of the most powerful kind. The boilers are five in number, constructed to work in connection with, or independent of, each other. In case of damage done to any one, or more of them, a valve was arranged to close the connection between the damaged and undamaged boilers, and the latter operate as if nothing had happened.

IMPORTANCE OF THE SEIZURE OF THE RAILROAD.

The capture of the Memphis and Ohio Railroad bridge, as mentioned in the above despatch, secures an important strategical position, to which others must, in the course of military events, be auxiliary. It in effect turns the enemy's left flank, cuts off the communication between Memphis and Bowling Green, from which the latter is dependent for its supplies, and isolates Columbus from Bowling Green; so that for all military purposes communication is cut off between the rebels at these points. No doubt the Federal force will push on until they reach the Nashville and Memphis Railroad, near Camden, Tenn. This point, once in our possession, will cut off Hickman and Memphis from Nashville. This accomplished, then good-bye to Gens. Johnson, Beauregard, Buckner, and the rebel host. There will be no necessity then to attack Columbus or Bowling Green. Starvation will do the work. The New Orleans Delta, in a late edition, says: "The safety of the whole South depends on the result of the battle at Columbus. This place once taken, there can be no effectual resistance at other points." In military philosophy a position turned and besieged is equal to a place captured.—Hence, according to the New Orleans Delta, the safety of the whole South is in jeopardy.

OFFICIAL REPORT OF COMMODORE FOOTE.

U. S. FLAG SHIP CINCINNATI,
OFF FORT HENRY,
TENNESSEE RIVER, February 6, 1862.

The gunboats under my command—the Essex, Commander Porter; the Carondelet, Commander Walker; the Cincinnati, Commander Stembel; the St. Louis, Lieutenant commanding Paulding; the Conestoga, Lieutenant commanding Phelps; the Taylor, Lieutenant commanding Gwinn, and the Lexington, Lieutenant commanding Shirk—after a severe and rapid fire of one hour and a quarter, have captured Fort Henry, and have taken Gen. Lloyd Tilghman and his staff, with sixty men, as prisoners.

The surrender to the gunboats was unconditional, as we kept an open fire upon the enemy until their flag was struck. In half an hour after the surrender, I handed the fort and prisoners over to Gen. Grant, commanding the army, on his arrival at the fort in force.

The Essex had a shot in her boilers, after fighting most effectually for two thirds of the action, and was obliged to drop down the river. I hear that several of her men were scalded to death, including the two pilots. She, with the other gunboats, officers, and men, fought with the greatest gallantry. The Cincinnati received thirty-one shots, and had one man killed and eight wounded, two seriously. The fort, with twenty guns and seventeen mortars, was defended by Gen. Tilghman with the most determined gallantry. I have sent Lieutenant commanding Phillips and three gunboats after the rebel gunboats.

A. H. FOOTE, Flag Officer.

Commodore Andrew H. Foote, U.S.N.

General Joseph E. Johnston, C.S.A.

GENERAL JOHNSTON'S ADDRESS TO THE ARMY OF THE POTOMAC.

We publish below a soul-stirring address from General JOHNSTON to the Army of the Potomac, in regard to the re enlistment question, the all-absorbing topic of conversation in the camps and elsewhere. We have reliable authority for saying that the troops in the Army of the Potomac are rapidly re-enlisting, and we cannot doubt that this address will serve to arouse the volunteers in other portions of the country:

GEN. JOHNSTON'S ADDRESS.

HEADQ'RS DEP'T OF NORTHERN VA.,
February 4, 1862.

Soldiers: Your country again calls you to the defence of the noblest of human causes. To the indomitable courage already exhibited on the battle field, you have added the rarer virtues of high endurance, cheerful obedience, and self sacrifice. Accustomed to the comforts and luxuries of home, you have met and borne the privations of camp life, the exactions of military discipline, and the rigors of a winter campaign. The rich results of your courage, patriotism, and unfaltering virtue, are before you. Entrusted with the defence of this important frontier, you have driven back the immense army which the enemy had sent to invade our country and to establish his dominion over our people, by the wide-spread havoc of a war inaugurated without a shadow of constitutional right, and prosecuted in a spirit of ruthless vengeance. By your valor and firmness you have kept him in check, until the nations of the earth have been forced to see us in our true character—not dismembered and rebellious communities, but an empire of confederate States, with a Constitution safe in the affections of the people, institutions and laws in full and unobstructed operation, a population enjoying all the comforts of life, and a citizen soldiery who laugh to scorn the threat of subjugation.

Your country now summons you to a nobler and a greater deed. The enemy has gathered up all his energies for a final conflict. His enormous masses threaten us on the West; his naval expeditions are assailing us upon our whole Southern coast; and upon the Potomac, within a few hours' march, he has a gigantic army, inflamed by lust and maddened by fanaticism. But the plains of Manassas are not forgotten, and he shrinks from meeting the disciplined heros who hurled across the Potomac his grand army, routed and disgraced. He does not propose to attack this army so long as it holds its present position with undiminished numbers and unimpaired discipline; but, protected by his fortifications, he awaits the expiration of your term of service. He recollects that his own ignoble soldiery, when their term of service expired, "marched away from the scene of conflict to the sound of the enemy's cannon," and he hopes that at that critical moment Southern men will consent to share with them this infamy. Expecting a large portion of our army to be soon disbanded, he hopes that his immense numbers will easily overpower your gallant comrades who will be left here, and thus remove the chief obstacle to his cherished scheme of Southern subjugation.

The Commanding General calls upon the twelve-months' men to stand by their brave comrades who have volunteered for the war, to re-volunteer at once, and thus show to the world that the patriots engaged in this struggle for independence will not swerve from the bloodiest path they may be called to tread. The enemies of your country, as well as her friends, are watching your action with deep, intense, tremulous interest. Such is your position that you can act no obscure part. Your decision, be it for honor or dishonor, will be written down in history. You cannot, will not draw back at this solemn crisis of our struggle, when all that is heroic in the land is engaged, and all that is precious hangs trembling in the balance.

Deck of a gun-boat engaged in the attack on Fort Henry

The Charleston Mercury.

DAILY PAPER—Ten Dollars per annum, payable half-yearly in advance.

SPONTE SUA SINE LEGE FIDES RECTUMQUE COLENTUR.—VINDICE NULLO

COUNTRY PAPER—Three a Week—Five Dollars per annum, in advance.

VOLUME LXXX. CHARLESTON, S. C., FRIDAY, FEBRUARY 14, 1862. NUMBER 11,374

A Free Press.

A Republic is a Representative Government, under the control of the people, for whom it exercises its delegated powers, and to whom it is responsible. It is an organization based upon the principle that the people are capable of discriminating between truth and error, folly and wisdom, and right and wrong; and are competent to carry out, in the conduct of the Government—both by men and measures—the discriminations they make. To be in a position to exercise judgment, and by that means to shape the course of their Government, facts and opinions must be elicited and put before the people for canvass. There is no means for informing the people, and for evoking their proper judgment, so competent as the press. To muzzle the press, is to suppress facts and opinions which may be necessary to the correct judgment of the people. Whatever militates against the freedom of the press, wars upon the people's means of obtaining light for the control of their Government—strikes at the root of republican freedom itself. Its practical effect is to put the people, their Government and their measures in the hands of those who, having gained their confidence, would keep them in the dark, and direct affairs without responsibility.

A free press is absolutely necessary for the preservation of liberty in any country. It may become, and to a certain extent always is, licentious. What power is free from abuse; and where can perfection be found in the world? But even a licentious press is far less evil than a press that is enslaved, because both sides may be heard in the former case, but not in the latter. A licentious press *may* be an evil; but fair play is allowed. The evil is open to remedy. An enslaved press *must* be so: for an enslaved press suppresses truth, and may cause error to be more current than truth, folly than wisdom, and wrong more powerful than right, without the benefit of correction. False statements, foolish counsels and unjust actions are given currency and applause, without comment or contradiction. A licentious press cannot effect these things; for if it gives poison, it gives also the antidote, which an enslaved press withholds. An enslaved press is doubly fatal. It not only takes away the true light, for in that case we might stand still, but it sets up a factitious one, that may drag us to our destruction.

The Richmond *Examiner* published in its columns, a short time since, a bill which it said had been reported by a Committee to Congress, in which heavy penalties were provided against any one who should publish in the papers anything with respect to our armies. Such a bill is the SEDITION ACT over again, passed during the administration of JOHN ADAMS in '98—with this difference only: that the former applies to our *Armies*, and the latter applied to the *Government*. The Sedition Act overthrew the Federal party of that day; and we have no idea that any Act destroying the liberty of the press, will pass Congress.

THE INVASION OF NORTH CAROLINA.

MOVEMENTS IN ALBEMARLE SOUND.

FURTHER PARTICULARS OF THE ROANOKE ISLAND DISASTER.

OPINIONS OF THE PRESS.

From our exchanges we get some further news of the operations of the BURNSIDE expedition on the North Carolina coast. The following is from the Wilmington *Journal*, of Wednesday evening:

PROBABLE DESIGNS OF THE INVADERS—MOVEMENTS OF THE YANKEE GUNBOATS.

The Yankee gunboats are said to have passed up to Winton, the county seat of Hertford county, on the Chowan River. The Chowan is formed by the confluence of the Meherrin and Nottaway rivers. The main branch of the Nottaway is the Blackwater, which is crossed by the Seaboard & Roanoke Railroad, about half way between Weldon and Portsmouth, though rather nearer to the latter place. The Blackwater is navigable up to the railroad, as a steamer has been running regularly in connection with the railroad trains, although necessarily a small one, owing to the narrowness and crookedness of the stream. The movements of the Lincoln gunboats would seem to indicate a desire to force their way up as far as the Portsmouth Road, so as either to obtain possession of it, or at least cut off communication by that line.

Although capable of doing much harm to the people resident on the shores of the sounds and the rivers emptying into them, it is evident that there would be no strategetic end to be served that would repay the vast outlay of men and money that the Burnside expedition has occasioned, unless either Norfolk is attacked or possession obtained of some leading line of Railroad; and therefore it is, we take it, that the attention of our authorities will be, or at least ought to be, directed to the protection of the lines of communication, especially of water communication leading from the navigable waters of Albemarle and Pamlico sounds, in the direction of any of our public works. The Blackwater, although deep, is so narrow and crooked that it might be stopped by trees felled across it.

It is not believed that the enemy can or will attempt to force his way to a railroad by way of the Roanoke. The idea is that he will try to push up the Chowan and Nottaway to the junction of the latter with the Blackwater, and then try to march to Carrsville, about 16 miles from Suffolk.

THE ENEMY'S GUNBOATS PURSUE THE CONFEDERATE STEAMERS.

We get the following interesting paragraphs from the Norfolk *Day Book* of Wednesday:

The fleet, after falling back from Roanoke Island, ran up the Pasquotank river for the purpose of receiving ammunition, which was expected from Norfolk. On Sunday, the enemy's vessels crossed the Sound, and early on Monday morning advanced up the Pasquotank river. Our vessels had then gained the battery on the river, and were drawn up for the purpose of co-operating with it, if occasion should require it. Captain Parker, of the Beaufort, was detailed by Commodore Lynch to the command of this battery.

Owing to the dense fog which prevailed on Monday, the Federal fleet came within to or three hundred yards of our fleet and battery before being discovered. Our fleet was therefore compelled to retire again, and the battery was abandoned. Before it was left, however, all the guns were spiked. The fleet proceeded towards Elizabeth City, closely pursued by the enemy. After proceeding some distance, two of the vessels were overtaken and captured, one, which would have been captured, was burned, and three—the Beaufort, Empire and Raleigh—succeeded in making their escape.

THE BURNING OF ELIZABETH CITY.

The report of the burning of Elizabeth City and its capture by the Federalists is fully confirmed. The town was attacked on Monday morning about 8 o'clock, and was set on fire and evacuated after a fight of about a couple of hours duration. The torch was applied by the patriotic citizens themselves, and although the destruction was only partial, yet a sufficient display of self-sacrifice has been made by these gallant Carolinians to satisfy the enemy that they are fighting a people they never can subdue.

The Confederate steamer Forrest, attached to Commodore Lynch's fleet, and which was undergoing repairs at Elizabeth City, we are glad to say, was not left to the enemy, as at first reported, but was burned by the citizens before they left the town.

THE ENEMY AT EDENTON.

A special train of the Seaboard and Roanoke Railroad arrived in Portsmouth, yesterday, about one o'clock. Information was brought that the enemy had entered Edenton, and taken possession. This news was communicated through Dr. Warren, of Edenton, to the people of Suffolk, and forwarded by them to us. We have received no confirmation as yet of the statement, and it may be that the intelligence is premature. The enemy was represented as being on the way to Blackwater, and the non-arrival of the boat due from there yesterday seemed to corroborate the statement.

FURTHER PARTICULARS OF THE BATTLE OF ROANOKE ISLAND.

The Richmond Blues and McCullough's Infantry are represented as having conducted themselves nobly during the battle. Not a man among them but displayed the utmost coolness and intrepidity, and the greatest havoc was made by them among the foe. They kept at one time two regiments at bay, and finally at the point of the bayonet drove them up to their arm-pits into the Sound. Before surrendering, each man coolly broke his gun against the trees, determined that, though they fall into the hands of the enemy, they should be useless.

THE CASUALTIES.

Our loss was not over one hundred killed and wounded, while that of the enemy is estimated at at least one thousand killed. Indeed we have information that at Old Point the number is estimated at fifteen hundred killed. The beach is represented as being strewn with their dead bodies, and the probability is that when the truth comes out it will be found that this victory has been purchased by the Yankees with a fearful outlay of life.

The excitement of the battle, in which he was physically unable to participate, has had a very favorable effect upon the health of Gen. Wise. We regret to add that Capt. O. Jennings Wise was among the killed, and not wounded only, as at first reported. He was in command of the Richmond Blues, and received a wound shortly after the engagement began, which disabled him. While his comrades were bearing him from the ground, a shot from the enemy penetrated his body, inflicting a mortal wound. He died almost immediately. It is related that after he had fallen on the field one of his men approached him and enquired if he was badly hurt. His reply was: "Never mind me! Fight on, men! fight on! and keep cool!" Capt. Wm. Selden, of Norfolk, attached to the Engineer Department, was also among the killed.

TREACHERY THE CAUSE OF THE DISASTER.

We learn that a man named Doe, who lived on Roanoke Island, and who knew of a landing place on the marsh that others were ignorant of, deserted, went over to the enemy and piloted them into the landing, after giving them all the information about our forces and fortifications. It appears that Colonel Shaw got wind of his intended desertion, and told him that if he attempted to desert he would blow him out of the water; but Doe afterwards got a chance and made his escape, and in consequence of that escape we have this terrible disaster.

WHO IS TO BE BLAMED FOR THE DISASTER?

The Newbern *Progress*, of Wednesday, says:

Roanoke Island might have been held, but the Government at Richmond seems oblivious to the existence of North Carolina, save when men are wanted. 8,000 or 10,000 men would have held the island, but it is not likely that 20,000 can retake it. It was well known to the government that Burnside was at Hatteras, with a powerful fleet and a heavy force, weeks ago, with every reasonable indication that Roanoke Island was to be the point of attack; and, in view of these facts, not only our State, but the country, has a right to know why some of the movable troops about Norfolk, Petersburg, and Richmond, were not sent to the relief of the brave 2,500 who have fell into Yankee hands.

We write without any further particulars than those given yesterday morning, but with our knowledge of the country we know that Elizabeth City, Edenton, Plymouth, Winton, Murfreesboro' and Gatesville are entirely at the mercy of the enemy; and at the latter place the enemy are only 30 miles from Suffolk and less than 50 from Norfolk. A few thousand men and a few heavy guns could have checked the enemy at Roanoke Island, but probably a hundred thousand could not now prevent their depredations.

The people are beginning to complain a good deal about the way in which things are managed at Richmond, and certainly they have some cause.

The Norfolk *Day Book*, of Wednesday, has the following strong editorial article on the subject of the disaster:

The fact cannot longer be concealed that criminal negligence is chargeable somewhere for the disastrous overthrow of our brave and gallant men at Roanoke Island.

The fact cannot longer be concealed, because it is upon the tongue of every reflecting man. As a public journal, devoted to the public cause—a cause in which all possess and realize the deepest interest—this paper is averse to the suppression of a grievance of such magnitude from any sicklied or sentimental fear that injury is to accrue to the true interests of the people by a free comment and exposure. Thus to wield the engine of the press, we regard as the true glory and noble aim of the press of a free people. When it ceases thus to speak, the benefits of its mission are lost or unattained, and it becomes but the panderer to power. This is the position which it now occupies under the heel of the Northern despotism.

If the public press is to be muzzled or to muzzle itself from fear of bringing down upon the heads of those in authority the merited condemnation which mal-administration justly demands—if it is to maintain silence from fear of exposing even to our enemies the patent fact that some of our men in authority are derelict in duty and lack the qualifications which their positions demand—then, the printers' type may be as well sent back to the foundery, abuse of power in high places go unexposed, the perpetrators continue their mal-administration, the public interests be suffered to languish, be disregarded and criminally imperilled. The brave men who fought the enemy at Roanoke Island, and many of whom poured out their blood like water in the futile attempt to maintain their stand against an overwhelming force, were sacrificed to a criminal neglect to reinforce them. This is the fact which has impressed itself upon the public mind, and to which we hesitate not to give utterance and an objective form.

Notwithstanding the knowledge possessed by every man in our midst, and within the bounds of the Confederacy, of the fitting out of the Burnside expedition—notwithstanding its reported presence hovering off the Carolina coast—notwithstanding its proclaimed arrival off Roanoke Island, disclosing the manifest intention of the enemy to attack that devoted Island, and to possess it as another stragetic base for future and more important operations—notwithstanding the fact, known to our men in power, that this important post was not sufficiently manned; that the force there was inadequate to defend it against the attack by which it had been menaced for weeks—notwithstanding this, and more which might be stated, yet that handful of brave and devoted men were suffered to remain there insufficiently reinforced, and to await the moment when, apparently uncared for, they were to be "butchered to make" a Northern "holiday," and to furnish the demoralized press of the savage and soulless North a fit theme for their truculent boastings and fiendish huzzas. Such is the culpable neglect which demands ventilation and calls for remedial interposition of the Executive arm of the Government at Richmond. If the vulnerable points on our extended coast are to be defended at all, let them be defended effectively, or at least with some reasonable regard to the overpowering forces which have hitherto been concentrated against them. To garrison them with a force so inadequate as that which fough to the death at Roanoke, is to convert them into slaughter pens, and criminally sacrifice the lives of our brave and devoted men. Such, it is melancholy to reflect, was the lamentable fate of O. Jennings Wise and his Spartan band, seven of whom escaped to bring the tidings of their untimely doom.

But more. We ought to have had in the Sound twenty gunboats or more—such even as could have carried, each, one effective rifled gun.

Ten months have elapsed since the Navy Yard here came providentially into our possession by desertion—and fifty such gunboats might have been easily constructed there, armed, manned, and placed at the mouths of the numerous and small streams in the sound and elsewhere. But there has not one single one such been here constructed. This is a startling fact, and evinces what the public regard as culpable negligence.—Although within a few hours ride of this great and inestimable depot to the Confederacy, Mr. Secretary Mallory has not once visited the Navy Yard since he warmed his official seat, nor has he manifested that administrative energy in the matter of these gunboats which the time demands from him and from all who have been placed in positions of importance such as he and others occupy in these perilous times. The disaster at Roanoke Island by no means consists alone in its mere capture, nor in the loss of the band of braves there sacrificed.

Its most important and designed results are yet in the womb of futurity, and unless they are at once thwarted by diligence, foresight and energy, manifested in the proper quarters, the intentions and hopes of the Burnside expedition may yet be fully effected and realized. Let it never be lost sight of for a moment at a time, that this point—this Navy Yard—is one of incalculable importance to the Southern Confederacy.

The Flag of the South.

The Richmond *Examiner*, in alluding to the subject of the new flag to be selected for the Confederate States, thus offers an original design:

Before we get our national emblem, we must get rid of stars and stripes in all their variations. So, too, of all arrangements of red, white, and blue. Nothing can be gotten from either but plagiarisms—poor imitations—feeble fancies. Our coat of arms must be not only in accord with the higher law of heraldry, but, above all, original,—our own, and not another's.

Not one of the thousand writers on this topic has yet presented an original or appropriate idea. Yet there is a thought which starts to the mind's eye:

The national emblem of the equestrian South is the horse. Its colors are black and white. Its shield is the sable horse of Manassas on a silver field; its flag is the white flag with the black horse. Both colors are already united to make the grey of the Confederate uniform; and emblem and colors are alike suggestive of the country and its history; and neither belong to any other nation of christians.

Charge of Hawkins' Zouaves upon the Confederate batteries on Roanoke Island

The Charleston Mercury.

DAILY PAPER—TEN DOLLARS PER ANNUM, PAYABLE HALF-YEARLY IN ADVANCE. | VINDICE NULLO—SPONTE SUA SINE LEGE FIDES RECTUMQUE COLENTUR. | COUNTRY PAPER—THREE A WEEK—FIVE DOLLARS PER ANNUM, IN ADVANCE.

VOLUME LXXX. CHARLESTON, S. C., WEDNESDAY, FEBRUARY 19, 1862. NUMBER 11,37[illegible]

THE MERCURY.

WEDNESDAY, FEBRUARY 19, 1862.

The capture of Nashville is the heaviest blow that has, thus far, been dealt us by our Northern enemies. With the exception of our beleaguered stronghold at Columbus, the whole of Kentucky is now at the mercy of the invader, and the seat of war has suddenly been transferred to Central Tennessee. The wily McCLELLAN understands the difference between the hardy troops of BUELL and the doughty New Englanders of his own "Grand Army." Assured of the safety of Washington, he is too sagacious to risk his Yankee soldiers beyond their entrenchments; but, in the meantime, he is affording to his columns in Tennessee every advantage which the immense preponderance of the North in the material resources of war can give. We may look for the campaign in Tennessee to be marked by all the vigor of which the enemy is capable, and we must prepare to meet the invasion with all the strength that we can bring against it, and with the obstinate valor of men who feel that they are fighting for existence itself.

In the meantime, the war on our seacoast promises to assume new activity. But two months more remain, before the diseases of the climate will begin to do their work with SHERMAN's marauders. Those two months are likely to be memorable in the annals of Savannah and of Charleston. Our telegrams to-day mention that pontoon and engineer regiments have already been despatched to Port Royal. The opening of the ball in our neighborhood cannot be delayed much longer. The Georgians, who keep watch and ward at the threatened gates of our sister city, will never unbeseem the fame of those who have so nobly upheld the banner of the Empire State in the bloodiest struggles of the war. Let us, of South Carolina, emulate their resolve to conquer or to die—animated by the thought that we are contending for all that is dear to the human heart, and nerved by the assurance that, if we fail, there will be nothing left to us to live for.

The Defensive Policy.

[*From the Richmond Dispatch.*]

If the South is pleased with the defensive policy, there is certainly one point of agreement at any rate between the belligerents—the North approve it heartily. That section has the rare and agreeable excitement of being at war and at peace at the same moment. It has not heard in all its borders from the beginning of this conflict one hostile gun; it has never known an evil of war save its financial embarrassments. Its fields are safe from the tramp of hostile squadrons; its firesides are never quenched in blood; its dwellings and towns do not light the sky with fearful conflagrations, its women and children are not in fear of being shelled out of their houses or of suffering barbarities worse than death. They enjoy the luxury of reading, in their comfortable parlors, accounts of the inflictions of these calamities upon the people of the Southern Confederacy, with no such uncomfortable drawback as the faintest dream of retaliations upon themselves. They are, therefore, in the vein to cheer on the war hounds with the most enthusiastic alacrity, and enjoy the gaieties of life with even more than ordinary gusto. We are not, therefore, surprised to see brilliant accounts of the splendor of Presidential levees in Washington, and the roystering fun and frolic of the New York Park. There is a charming exhilaration in the sport of throwing stones at the frogs in a pond, who, unhappy creatures, have not the ability to reciprocate the compliment. The more pusillanimous a race, the more delightful is a combat in which there are blows to give and none whatever to take.

We may fancy in our ignorance and blindness that war to be effective must be aggressive as well as defensive, and that the best way to overcome an antagonist is not merely to parry his blows. In all encounters between man and man, and in all other wars that we have ever heard of, such a thing as striking back is considered not only honorable, but expedient. Whether such a process will excite an enemy to fresh indignation, does not usually enter into the calculation of fighting men, and, if it did, it is a question which must depend upon the character of the adversary. Without derogating from the martial capabilities of the Northern people, we incline to the opinion that an aggressive warfare against them would stir up quite as much apprehension as rage, and that they infinitely prefer a kind of warfare in which they read of battles in newspapers, and have nothing to do with them personally.—They boast that they have now in the field an army of seven hundred thousand men, raised almost entirely since the period when it became evident that this war was to be on the part of the South strictly defensive. Whether that number has been raised or not, it is certain that they have placed in the field all who are willing to go, and have exhausted their exchequer in efforts to carry on the war. Their spirit and their energies have risen in proportion to the immunity of their own soils and homes from danger. Their newspapers have been more belligerent, and their politicians more truculent, as they have discovered that the hostile foot of the South is not to be planted on their own territory. If they had the means, they would carry on the war at least as long as Great Britain carried on the war against the American Colonies; for Great Britain herself was not more secure from an American invasion in the Revolution than the North is from the South in the present contest.

We trust that with the opening of the spring campaign the enemy will be made to feel that there are blows to take in this contest as well as blows to give. We have given the defensive plan a fair trial, and have seen its results. A larger number of our gallant soldiers have perished by disease in camp and hospital than we could have lost by a march from the battle field of Manassas to the city of Philadelphia. Henceforth, we must make up our minds that this is war, and that for every drop of Southern blood which has been shed, and for every hour our soil has been polluted by the footsteps of invasion, we will have compound interest in laying waste every accessible foot of Northern territory with fire and sword.

DAILY PAPER—TEN DOLLARS PER ANNUM, PAYABLE HALF-YEARLY IN ADVANCE. | VINDICE NULLO—SPONTE SUA SINE LEGE FIDES RECTUMQUE COLENTUR. | COUNTRY PAPER—THREE A WEEK—FIVE DOLLARS PER ANNUM, IN ADVANCE.

VOLUME LXXX. CHARLESTON, S. C., MONDAY, FEBRUARY 24, 1862. NUMBER 11,381

THE MERCURY.

MONDAY, FEBRUARY 24, 1862.

Our Revolution.

Despondency is ever the result of weakness. When dangers are distant, to descry them, with weak men, is an offence; to warn of their coming is to excite distrust or dislike; and when dangers do come, to cower before them is the usual refuge of such. It is the part of the truly brave seldom to make an undue estimate of the dangers or difficulties before them, but to see things as they are, because passions are not permitted to pervert judgment. Their hopes and expectations are not beyond the warrant of events, and fears neither hide nor magnify the truth. Hence, when disasters come, the truly brave are neither surprised nor alarmed, and their will is ready to meet the disasters present. Indeed, their spirit and resolution rises higher, because a mightier task is before them, and the wrong inflicted by disaster inspires a deeper anger, indignation and resentment. These strong passions kindled by opposition, rouse and sustain them in resistance. All truly brave men, therefore, have been greatest when most pressed. Constancy is a virtue only known in trial and peril. The indomitable spirit of the Roman people was only seen when, after the loss of three pitched battles their Senate rose up and thanked their defeated General "that he had not despaired of the Republic."

We, of the Confederate States, it seems, must soon prove that we are worthy of independence and liberty. We would have preferred to have won them more easily. Whether we would have kept them, if thus won, may be questionable. A vast portion of our people, neither realized the characteristics of the Northern people, nor the dangers which long, like a gathering cloud, have impended over their existence and institutions. It has required red-handed war to teach us our true relations towards these people, and to force us into that antagonism necessary for a permanent separation. Some of our rulers have clung with pertinacity to the hope of compromise and a re-union with them; and this vain, and (if realized) fatal hope, has spread a spirit of inactivity and weakness over our arms. That delusion, we trust, is fast passing away; and the stern alternative of utter subjugation or independence is forced upon us. In this state of things, let the people of the Confededrate States make up their minds to meet their destiny. That destiny is either to be an enslaved and undone People forever, or to be free and self-existant. They have the choice, and fighting manfully is the only way to independence. The Northern people cannot give to conquered subjects rights which they have not themselves. They have set up a military despotism over themselves, and they have nothing else to offer us. The only difference between us and themselves would be this: their despotism is *for their benefit*—to conquer and to overrun us; for us, it would be a despotism *without benefit*. It is a despotism of a mob—ferocious, avaricious and fanatical—armed with hatred for us and our institutions. Submission to such a despotism must be destruction. Safety—liberty—existence itself, depends on our successful resistance to their domination. We can do it; and, with God's help, we will do it. "A strenuous *will* must stimulate our determinations, and excite our utmost efforts to give them a practical result." It is the time for a display of systematic energy.

A Lesson of History for Generals Commanding Armies.

At Baylen, in Spain, on July 19, 1808, DUPONT, and twenty-one thousand French troops, laid down their arms to double their number of Spaniards, who had surrounded them in the mountains. NAPOLEON, when he heard of it, gave vent to the following observations: "That an army should be beaten, is nothing—it is the daily fate of war, and is daily repaired; but, that an army should submit to a dishonorable capitulation, is a stain on the glory of our arms never to be effaced. Wounds inflicted on honor are incurable. The moral effect of this catastrophe will be terrible. They say General DUPONT had no other way to prevent the destruction of the army—to save the lives of the soldiers! Better, far better, to have perished with arms in their hands—that not one should have escaped. Their death would have been glorious; we would have avenged them. You can always supply the place of soldiers. Honor alone, when once lost, can never be regained."

None of the Generals connected with this surrender, were ever employed again. On May 1st, 1812, an Imperial decree forbade, *on pain of death*, any capitulation in the field which should amount to a laying down of arms.

Hoc caverat mens provida Reguli,
Dissentientis conditionibus
Fœdis, et exemplo trahenti,
Perniciem veniens in œvum.
Si non periret immiserabilis
Captiva pubes.

To the Editor of the Charleston Mercury:

I send you an article from the Richmond *Whig*, which you will oblige me by inserting in your columns. You have been ahead of others in denouncing the war policy which the Government of the Confederate States has pursued; and predicted too wisely the fatal consequences which would ensue. You have been denounced in turn. Time, and the events thickening around us, now tells the truth. Your admonitions have been in vain; but all men, it appears to me, will honor you for your sagacity, independence and patriotism.

A SUBSCIBER.

—

I would like to know whether a plain citizen may presume to express any opinion at all on the war, through a public journal, without incurring contempt as a "croaker," an "ignoramus," a "silly alarmist," &c., even if the editor should forbear to throw his production under the table. Is all the wisdom of the country concentrated in "officials?" and are the people at large without common sense, and a parcel of cackling geese, because they venture to have an opinion in any wise acquired, except by second-hand process, from "the heads of Department?" It is candidly confessed, that men having the best opportunities for information are, as they ought to be, the best informed; but does this fact exhaust the sum of information, or prove the wisest use has been made of superior knowledge of existing and surrounding circumstances? And suppose the clearest dictates of wisdom have been slighted, shall no one venture to insinuate that this may be the state of the case, lest he should be called a "croaker!" Is everything to be approved as proper and wise, lest we should call in question the infallibility of "the powers that be?"

This has heretofore been the state of public sentiment, and one would think of the *Press*; for I will venture to say that there are not one hundred men, and women, and *children*, and *negros*, all told, either North or South, who could make up an expectation at all on the subject, who have not been woefully disappointed in every calculation and expectation since the date of the battle of Manassas. Swear every one on a bible, and he will tell you that no arguments or reasonings *could have brought him to believe*, for one moment, that our armies would have been kept in inaction, inertness and stagnation from the 21st of July till the close of the year, except in skirmishes and accidental engagements. I defy mortal man to point out in history, since its earliest dawn, a like instance of a victorious army remaining inactive, or acting only on the defensive, for so long a time; especially when it was known that a powerful enemy was exerting every energy to recover strength from a crippled and demoralized condition, to renew his attempt to subjugate its people; and when such inaction, beyond all things, most favored the designs of the enemy. If McClellan had had the privilege of securing *one wish*, and *only one*, as to the preparation of means, *that wish* would most naturally have been, that all things should remain quiet till he had mustered into service, and thoroughly drilled, an overwhelming army, and prepared a powerful navy and all the munitions of war.

We have done exactly what he would have had us do. When *our* forces would make a demonstration at Manassas, *he* would make one on the Peninsula to draw off action from the Upper Potomac, so as to have time to mature his plans; and thus has he manœuvred for six months—first making demonstrations on one point, and then on another, for no other purpose under Heaven, except to get time to mature his plans. A general engagement was what, of all things, he most deprecated. We have been *most gloriously* acting out the fable of the "*terrapin* and *the hare*."

From this state of inaction and false security has resulted the loss of Hatteras, of Port Royal, of Beaufort, of Fort Henry, of Roanoke, and of Donelson. The enemy were regarded with such contempt that any kind of a ditch was thought to be sufficient to keep them off. Now, let me ask a few questions. If the forts were insufficient, was it because they could not have been made vastly stronger in the same time given, and with the same means effected? Were they as strong as they could have been made? And if not, why were they not? Could a stronger force have held them? And if so, why was such a force not placed in them? Was the force under Gen. Wise the largest which could have been placed on Roanoke Island? And if so, why were the defences not made stronger? How does it happen that *none*, or *few* of our forts are *bomb proof*—why is it? Was there not time, and was there not means? And if a large force could have been spared for Roanoke, why was it not sent there? Would it not have been a most wise and judicious disposition of even twenty thousand troops, if necessary, to hold so vital and important a post as that? How can such neglect as is manifest, even to an idiot, be excused or palliated by the country? A powerful fleet, numbering more than a hundred vessels, is about to attack an important point on our coast; and a grand army of two thousand five hundred men is sent to oppose these ships, and fifteen thousand or twenty thousand troops besides! Has the country no right to ask how this is, nor to know? And if no more men could be spared, why sacrifice this little Spartan band in a defenceless position? Would it not have been better to evacuate the Island, and fortify Elizabeth City, or some other defenceless point, and thereby save the men and the arms?

I shall, no doubt, be told that I am an "*ignoramus*," "*a croaker*," and a *very presumptuous intermeddler*, but it is evident to the merest *fool* among the *silliest*, that there is something wrong somewhere, and that somebody is either *traitorous* or *utterly incompetent*; or that we are an exceedingly *weak* and *defenceless* people.

The New-York Times.

VOL. XI----NO. 3247. | NEW-YORK, TUESDAY, FEBRUARY 18, 1862. | PRICE TWO CENTS.

GLORIOUS VICTORY.

THE FALL OF FORT DONELSON.

Johnston and Buckner, the Rebel Generals, Captured.

FIFTEEN THOUSAND OTHER PRISONERS.

Escape of Floyd and Pillow with Five Thousand Men.

Floyd Denounced by the Rebels as a Black Hearted Traitor and Coward.

Heavy Losses in Killed and Wounded on Both Sides.

Immense Amount of War Material Captured.

THE OFFICIAL DISPATCHES.

Flag-officer Foote Gone to Attack Clarksville.

AUTHENTIC PLAN OF FORT DONELSON.

REPORTS FROM ST. LOUIS.

ST. LOUIS, Monday, Feb. 17.

Fort Donelson surrendered at 9 o'clock yesterday morning to the land forces. The gunboats were present at the time. *An immense amount of war material are among the trophies of the victory.*

Gen. FLOYD skulked away the night before the surrender.

The gunboat *Carondelet* has arrived at Cairo with a large number of our wounded. Many have also been taken to the Paducah hospital.

This city is wild with excitement and joy. The news was read at the Union Merchants' Exchange, creating the most intense enthusiasm. "The Star Spangled Banner" and the "Red, White and Blue" were sung by all present, after which they adjourned and marched to head-quarters, twelve or fifteen hundred strong, where three rousing cheers were given for HALLECK and FOOTE. Gen. HALLECK appeared at the window, thanked the people for the hearty demonstration, and said:

"*I promised when I came here, with your aid, to drive the enemies of the flag from your State. This has been done, and they are now virtually out of Kentucky, and soon will be out of Tennessee.*"

The "Star Spangled Banner" was repeated, and with louder cheers for the Union the crowd dispersed.

Judge HOLT wept for joy when he heard the news. Many of the stores were closed, the city decorated with flags, and evidence of the greatest joy everywhere manifest.

Gov. YATES, Secretary HATCH and Auditor DUBOIS of Illinois, left for Fort Donelson this morning to look after the wounded Illinois troops.

A requisition has been made for all the steamboats in this vicinity to be held in readiness for transportation of troops or Government stores.

REPORTS FROM CHICAGO.

CHICAGO, Monday, Feb. 17.

A special to the *Times*, dated Fort Donelson, 16th, says:

"Fort Donelson surrendered at daylight this morning unconditionally. We have Gens. BUCKNER, JOHNSTON, BUSHROD and 15,000 prisoners, and 3,000 horses. Gens. PILLOW and FLOYD, with their brigade ran away on steamers without letting BUCKNER know their intentions.

Gen. SMITH led the charge on the lower end of the works, and was the first inside the fortifications. The Fort Henry runaways were bagged here.

The prisoners are loading on the steamers for Cairo.

Our loss is heavy—probably 400 killed and 800 wounded. We lose a large per centage of officers: Among them are Lieutenant-Colonels IRWIN of the Illinois Twentieth, WHITE of the Thirty-first, and SMITH of the Forty-eighth; Colonels JOHN A. LOGAN, SAWYER and RANSOM are wounded. Maj. POST, of the Eighth Illinois, with 200 privates, are prisoners, and have gone to Nashville, having been taken the night before the surrender. The enemy's loss is heavy, but not so large as ours, as they fought behind entrenchments.

We should have taken them by storming Saturday, if our ammunition had not given out in the night.

Gen. MCCLERNAND'S Division, composed of Gens. OGLESBY'S, WALLACE'S and MCARTHUR'S Brigades, suffered terribly. They were composed of the Eighth, Ninth, Eleventh, Eighteenth, Twentieth, Twenty-ninth, Thirtieth, Thirty-first, Forty-fifth, Forty-eighth and forty-ninth Illinois Regiments.

Gen. LEWIS WALLACE, with the Eleventh Indiana, Eighth Missouri, and some Ohio regiments, participated.

TAYLOR'S, WILLIARD'S, MCALLISTER'S, SCHWARTZ'S and DRESSER'S Batteries were in the fight, from the commencement.

The enemy turned our right for half an hour, but our lost ground was more than regained.

Gen. LANMAN'S Brigade of Gen. SMITH'S Division was the first in the lower end of the enemy's works, which was done by a charge of bayonets.

As nine-tenths of the rebels were pitted against our right, our forces on the right were ready all night to recommence the attack.

On Sunday morning they were met on their approach by a white flag, Gen. BUCKNER having sent early in the morning a dispatch to Gen. GRANT surrendering.

The works of the fort extend some five miles on the outside.

The rebels lose forty-eight field-pieces, seventeen heavy guns, twenty thousand stand of arms, beside a large quantity of commissary stores.

The rebel troops are completely demoralized, and have no confidence in their leaders, as they charge PILLOW and FLOYD with deserting them.

Our troops from the moment of the investment of the fort, on Wednesday, lay on their arms night and day, half the time without provisions, all the time without tents, and a portion in a heavy storm of rain and snow.

CHICAGO, Monday, Feb. 17.

A special from Fort Donelson says: The forces were about equal in numbers, but the rebels had all the advantage of position, being well fortified on two immense hills, with their fort near the river, on a lower piece of ground. From the foot of their intrenchments, rifle-pits and abattis extended up the river, behind the town of Dover. Their fortifications on the land side, back from the river, were at least four miles in length. Their water battery, in the centre of the fortifications, where it came down to the river, mounted nine heavy guns.

The rebels were sure of success. In any other cause and against less brave troops, they could easily have held the position against a hundred thousand men.

The business of getting the different brigades in position for attaching the new arrivals to the different divisions, took up the greater portion of Friday night.

At daylight Saturday, the enemy opened on the Eighteenth Illinois, when Col. OGLESBY'S Brigade was soon engaged, and was soon followed by WALLACE'S and MCARTHUR'S Brigades, the latter acting under Gen. MCCLERNAND, as the position of the troops had been changed during the night, and Gen. GRANT had been called away during the night to the gunboats.

The movements of all the troops, except those attached to MCCLERNAND'S Division, were made without anything except general orders.

At a suggestion from Gen. MCCLERNAND, Gen. WALLACE sent up four regiments to support his division, who were nearly out of ammunition.

From the commencement till near 10 o'clock the fighting was terrific. The troops on the right were disposed as follows: MCARTHUR'S Brigade, composed of the Ninth, Twelfth, Forty-first, Seventeenth, and Nineteenth Illinois Regiments; next Gen. OGLESBY'S Brigade, consisting of the Eighth, Thirteenth, Twenty-ninth, Thirtieth, and Thirty-first Illinois Regiments, SCHWARTZ'S and DRESSER'S batteries; next was Gen. WALLACE'S Brigade, of the Eleventh, Twentieth, Forty-fifth, and Forty-eighth Illinois Regiments. These three brigades composed Gen. MCCLELLAND'S Division, and bore the brunt of the battle.

It was found that the enemy was concentrating his main force to turn our right, which was done by our men getting out of ammunition, and in the confusion of getting up reinforcements, retreating about half a mile. As soon as the division, which had stood its ground manfully for three hours, retired, the enemy occupied the field, when Gen. GRANT ordered Gen. SMITH to move forward his division and storm the enemy's works on our left. This order was obeyed with great alacrity, and soon the cheers of our daring soldiery were heard, and the old flag displayed from within the enemy's entrenchments.

Gen. GRANT then sent word to Gen. MCCLERNAND that Gen. SMITH was within the enemy's intrenchments and ordering their forces to move forward and renew the attack on the right. One of Gen. WALLACE'S Brigades—the Eleventh Indiana, Eighth Missouri and some Ohio Regiments—was rapidly thrown into position and Company A, of the Chicago Light Artillery, was planted in the road, and as the rebels, supposing we were in retreat, came, yelling, out of their works into the road, the Chicago boys poured a hailstorm of grape and canister into their ranks, slaughtering dozens of them.

Simultaneously with this the infantry commenced firing at will, and the rebels went pell-mell back into their works, our men advancing and taking possession of the ground lost, and a hill besides. Fresh troops who had not been in the action were then thrown forward, and as the shades of night drew on were in a strong position to participate in a simultaneous attack to be made on Sunday morning.

Gens. OGLESBY, WALLACE and MCARTHUR'S brigades did the hardest fighting, and have suffered terribly. They would undoubtedly have held their first position but for the failure of their ammunition. The ammunition wagons were some distance off the hills preventing their being moved.

Some of our best officers and men have gone to their long homes.

Hardly a man that went over the field after the battle, but discovered some comrade who had fallen.

We lost three Lieutenant-Colonels, and at least one-quarter of all the other officers were wounded or killed.

During Saturday night a contraction of all our lines was made for a simultaneous assault from every point, and orders were given by Gen. GRANT to take the enemy at the point of the bayonet. Every man was at his post. The Fifty-seventh Illinois was on the extreme right.

At daylight the advance was made, and when the full light of day broke forth, white flags were hung in many places on the enemy's works.

An officer at a convenient point was informed that they had stacked their arms and surrendered early in the morning, the following correspondence having passed between the commanders:

GEN. BUCKNER TO GEN. GRANT.

HEAD-QUARTERS, FORT DONELSON, Feb. 16.

SIR: In consideration of all the circumstances governing the present situation of affairs at this station, I propose to the commanding officer of the Federal forces the appointment of Commissioners to agree upon terms of capitulation of the forces at this post under my command. In that view I suggest an armistice until 12 o'clock to-day.

I am, very respectfully, your obedient servant,

L. B. BUCKNER, Brig.-Gen., C. S. A.

To Brig.-Gen. U. S. GRANT, commanding United States forces near Fort Donelson.

GEN. GRANT TO GEN. BUCKNER.

HEADQUARTERS ON THE FIELD, FORT DONELSON, Feb. 16.

To GEN. S. B. BUCKNER—*Sir:* Yours, of this date proposing an armistice and the appointment of Commissioners to settle the terms of capitulation is just received. No terms except unconditional and immediate surrender can be accepted.

I propose to move immediately on your works.

I am, very respectfully, your obedient servant,

U. S. GRANT, Brig.-Gen. Com'd'g.

GEN. BUCKNER TO GEN. GRANT.

HEADQUARTERS, DOVER, Tenn., Sunday, Feb. 16.

Brig.-Gen. U. S. Grant, U. S. A.:

SIR—The distribution of the forces under my command incident to an unexpected change of Commanders, and the overwhelming force under your command compels me, notwithstanding the brilliant success of the Confederate arms, to accept the ungenerous and unchivalrous terms which you propose.

I am, Sir, your servant,

S. B. BUCKNER, *Brig.-Gen., C. S. A.*

Our force was soon in the enemy's works, when the rebel officers gave up their swords.

The bulk of the rebels are chagrined as they knew of the surrender long before our men were apprised of it. PILLOW and FLOYD had planned and executed their escape during the night, taking with them FLOYD'S Brigade and a few favorites, occupying what few small steamers they had. The prisoners are loud in their denunciations of the runaways.

Many of them acknowledged the hopelessness of their case, and intimated a willingness to take an oath of allegiance, and return to their homes. To the question put to an officer, as to how many prisoners we had, he replied, "*You have all out of twenty-five thousand who were not killed, or did not escape.*"

It is impossible to get a list of the killed and wounded, as all the killed have not yet been brought in, and are mixed with the rebel killed. As far as ascertained the following is a list of the killed and wounded:

EIGHTH ILLINOIS.

Killed—Capt. Wilson, Lieut. Shuts and Lieut. Marsh. Wounded—Capt. Hannah.

NINTH ILLINOIS.

Killed—Capt. Shaw, Lieut's Boyce, Churchill, Kenyon, Vohr, Duncan, and Orderly-Sergeant Billard. Wounded—Capt. Robinson, Capt. Becker, Lieut. Fulton, Lieut. Leber.

ELEVENTH ILLINOIS.

Killed—G. Park, Richard Woodman, Milton Boggs, James McCatlin, Simeon Sloane, Caleb Griffiths, E. Morris, all of Company G. Wounded—Andrew McKer, Lieuts. Dean, Wilcox, Murray, Blackstone; Capt. Carter (slightly).

EIGHTEENTH ILLINOIS.

Killed—Lieut. Manzur, Captain Craig, Sergeant Pethill. Wounded—Col. Lawler, (in the arm,) Capt. Wilson, Lieut. Toole.

TWENTIETH ILLINOIS.

Killed—Lieut.-Col. Erwin. Wounded—Capt. Kearard, Lieuts. Archdeacon and King.

THIRTIETH ILLINOIS.

Killed—Adjutant Kirkpatrick.

THIRTY-FIRST ILLINOIS.

Killed—Lieut.-Col. White, Capt. Williamson. Wounded—Col. Logan, (ball through the shoulder.) Adj. Capeheart, Capts McCook, Summerfield, Dr. McCook.

FORTY-EIGHTH ILLINOIS.

Killed—Lieut.-Col. Smith.

FORTY-FIRST ILLINOIS.

Killed—Capt. True.

The composition of the rebel forces was as follows:

Regiments			
Tennessee	11	Virginia	4
Mississippi	8	*Cavalry Battalions.*	
Texas	1	Alabama	1
Kentucky	2	Tennessee	1
Arkansas	1	Mississippi	1

THE KILLED AND WOUNDED.

CHICAGO, Monday, Feb. 17.

A private message this evening to the Sanitary Commission from Cairo, says that there are 300 killed, 600 wounded, and 109 missing, at Fort Donelson.

ST. LOUIS, Monday, Feb. 17.

All the wounded on both sides at Fort Donelson will be brought here and placed in the hospitals. A dozen or more surgeons, with a corps of hospital nurses, left this afternoon for the battle-field to assist in their transportation.

CINCINNATI, Monday, Feb. 17.

The steamer *Allen Collier* leaves to-night, with twelve surgeons and over 100 boxes of supplies for Fort Donelson. Three thousand dollars were subscribed in a short time for the relief of the wounded. The United States Sanitary Commission telegraphed to Gen. HALLECK to send to Cincinnati as many wounded soldiers as he saw proper, saying that the citizens of Cincinnati would most gladly provide for them.

INDIANAPOLIS, Ind., Monday, Feb 17.

A special train left at 7 P. M., for Fort Donelson with physicians, 25 volunteer nurses, and a large quantity of hospital stores. A citizens' meeting has been called, to make arrangements for taking care of the wounded that will be sent here.

Gov. MORTON leaves for Fort Donelson to-night.

PLAN OF FORT DONELSON.

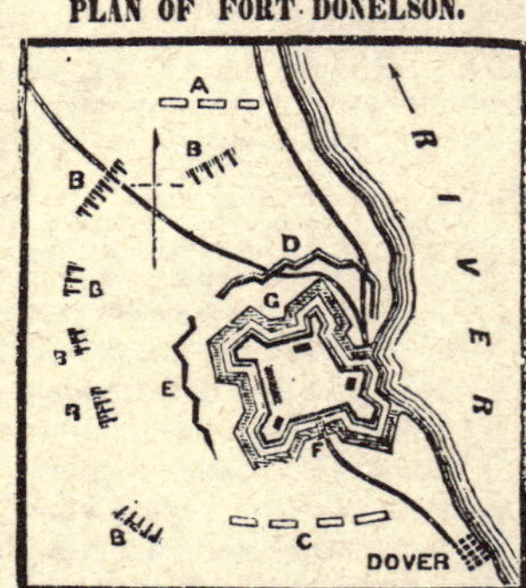

REFERENCES TO THE PLAN.

A.—Gen. SMITH.
B.—Union Field Batteries.
C.—Gen. MCCLERNAND.
D.—Rebel Redoubts.
E.—Rebel Rifle Pits.
F.—Draw Bridge.
G.—Ditch around the Fort.

OFFICIAL BULLETINS OF THE VICTORY.

REPORT OF FLAG-OFFICER FOOTE.

CAIRO, Monday, Feb. 17, 1862.

Hon. Gideon Welles, Secretary of the Navy:

The *Carondelet* has just arrived from Fort Donelson, and brings information of the capture of that Fort by the land forces, yesterday morning, with fifteen thousand prisoners.

JOHNSTON and BUCKNER were taken prisoners.

The loss is heavy on both sides.

FLOYD escaped with 5,000 men during the night.

I go up with the gunboats, and as soon as possible will proceed up to Clarksville.

Eight mortar boats are on their way, *with which I hope to attack Clarksville.*

My foot is painful, but the wound is not dangerous.

The army has behaved gloriously.

I shall be able to take but two iron-clad gunboats with me, as the others are disabled.

The trophies are immense.

The particulars will soon be given.

A. H. FOOTE, Flag-Officer.

REPORT OF BRIG.-GEN. CULLUM.

CAIRO, Feb. 17, 1862.

To Major-Gen. McClellan:

The Union flag floats over Fort Donelson. The *Carondelet*, Capt. WALKER, brings the glorious intelligence.

The fort surrendered at 9 o'clock yesterday (Sunday) morning. Gens. JOHNSTON (A. SIDNEY) and BUCKNER, and fifteen thousand prisoners, and a large amount of material of war are the trophies of the victory. Loss heavy on both sides.

FLOYD, the thief, stole away during the night previous, with five thousand men, and is denounced by the rebels as a traitor. I am happy to inform you that Flag-Officer FOOTE, though suffering with his foot, with the noble characteristic of our navy, notwithstanding his disability, will take up immediately two gunboats, and with the eight mortar boats which he will overtake, will make an immediate attack on Clarksville, if the state of the weather will permit. We are now firing a National salute from Fort Cairo, Gen. GRANT'S late post, in honor of the glorious achievement.

(Signed,) GEO. W. CULLUM,
Brig.-Gen. Vols. and U. S. A., and
Chief of Staff and Engineers.

THE REBEL GENERALS CAPTURED.

GEN. ALBERT SIDNEY JOHNSTON.

Gen. JOHNSTON, who was captured at the fall of Fort Donelson, and is now in our hands as a prisoner of war, is one of the five "Generals" of the rebel army. The other four being BEAUREGARD, LEE, COOPER and J. G. JOHNSTON. He was in chief command of the rebel Department of Kentucky, to which he was appointed as the successor of BUCKNER, four months ago. He is considered by military men the ablest General in the rebel service.

He is a native of Mason County, Ky., was born in 1802, and is now consequently 60 years of age. His father was a native of Connecticut. He was a student at Transylvania University, and subsequently graduated at West Point in 1826. During eight years succeeding he served in the army as a Lieutenant and Adjutant of the Sixth Infantry, and engaged in the campaign against BLACK HAWK, in which he acted as Adjutant-General of the Illinois troops, with the rank of Colonel. He subsequently resigned his commission in the army, and in 1836 removed to Texas. He entered the Texan army as a private soldier, but Gen. RUSK soon discovered his strategic abilities and made him Adjutant-General of his command. He soon rose to be senior Brigadier-General of the Texan army, was promoted to succeed Gen. FELIX HOUSTON, which led to a duel between them, wherein JOHNSTON was wounded. In 1837 he took the command-in-chief in Texas, and in 1839 he acted as Secretary of War of the new Republic, under President LAMAR. He participated also in the Indian fight on the River Neuces, in which the Cherokees, 700 strong, were defeated. In 1840 he retired from office and settled on his plantation near Galveston. He labored hard for the annexation of Texas. In 1846, at the request of Gen. TAYLOR he went to Mexico, and arrived there shortly after the battles of Resaca de la Palma and Palo Alto. He was elected Colonel of the First Texas Regiment, and served in that capacity for six months. He then served as Aid to Gen. BUTLER in the battle of Monterey; and for his conduct on that day he was recommended by Gen. TAYLOR for the appointment of Brigadier-General, but the position was bestowed upon Caleb Cushing. After this battle he retired to a plantation in Brazoria County, Texas, where he remained, until appointed by Gen. TAYLOR, in 1849, as Paymaster in the army. When the enrollment of four new regiments was proposed by the Pierce Administration, the Texas Legislature asked that he be appointed one of the Colonels; and he was accordingly appointed by JEFF. DAVIS, then Secretary of War, Colonel of the Second Cavalry, with his headquarters at San Antonio, Texas. There he remained till 1857, the greater part of the time in command of the Department of Texas. In the latter part of 1857 he received the command of the United States forces sent to coerce the Utah Mormons into obedience, and conducted the remarkable expedition across the Plains to Salt Lake City, in the Spring of the succeeding year. He was put in command of the Military District of Utah, and received the brevet rank of Brigadier-General. On the close of the Mormon troubles he was sent to California, and on the death of Gen. CLARKE assumed the command of the Department of the Pacific. Shortly after the rebellion got under way, his loyalty was suspected, and Gen. SUMNER was sent out to supersede him. Before Gen. SUMNER reached California, JOHNSTON had left his command to join the rebels. For fear of being caught, he took the overland route, with three or four companions, on mules, and passed through Arizona and Texas, and thence to Richmond. At first he was appointed to a rebel command on the Potomac; but, upon the great importance of the Western Department being seen by JEFF. DAVIS, he was appointed to take chief command at Bowling Green. He then did everything possible to strengthen that position, and bring as large a force as could be got for its defence. Only a month ago, he issued an earnest appeal to Kentucky and Tennessee to furnish him with fifty thousand more men. But Gens. BUELL and HALLECK were "too much" for him. A week ago his position was outflanked, and the National army was in his rear; and last Monday, he and the greater part of his command left for Fort Donelson, to make a desperate stand against our advancing columns. He had just time to get his army in position for battle, when the fort was assaulted, and he and all his command there stationed taken prisoners. Gen. JOHNSTON stands a little over six feet high, is of a large, bony, sinewy frame, with a grave, gaunt and thoughtful face; possesses quiet, unassuming manners—forming, in all, a soldier of very imposing appearance.

SIMON BOLIVAR BUCKNER.

Gen. BUCKNER, the second prisoner in rank captured at Fort Donelson, is a Brigadier-General in the rebel army, and for some months was in chief command in the rebel Western Department. He is a native of Kentucky, a graduate of West Point, and is now 38 years of age. In 1844, he was appointed, by brevet, Second Lieutenant in the Second Infantry, and next year he was Acting Assistant Professor of Ethics at West Point. In 1846, he was transferred to the Sixth Infantry, in which he went to Mexico, and was breveted First Lieutenant for gallant conduct at Contreras and Cherubusco, at which latter battle he was wounded. He was subsequently breveted Captain for gallant conduct at Molino del Rey. In 1847 he was Regimental Quartermaster, subsequently Assistant Instructor in Infantry Tactics, and in 1852, Commissary of Subsistence, with the rank of captain. When the secession movement began, he took an active but secret part with them, and as commander of the Kentucky State Guard, he exercised a powerful influence on the fighting element of his native State. Last Summer he visited Washington, represented himself there as loyal, ingratiated himself into Gen. SCOTT'S confidence, obtained permission to inspect all the fortifications in that vicinity, made Hon. ROBERT MALLORY and others believe that he wished to take active service in the army of the United States, returned to Louisville, and remained for a brief period, without giving public indication that he contemplated any disloyal movement, but all this time was holding conference with JEFF. DAVIS and the conspirators. Subsequently he managed to seduce a large part of the State Guard into the rebel service, and for this was appointed to command at Bowling Green. He is an adroit, skillful, bad man. The days of his active treason, however, are now ended.

GEN. BUSHROD.

Gen. BUSHROD, we believe, is a Kentucky Militia General. He is not a graduate of West Point and is unknown to fame either in military or civil life.

HOW THE NEWS WAS RECEIVED.

Rejoicings in the City—Gen. Scott on Broadway.

Many were the anxious hearts carried to business yesterday. Over the matutinal muffin was read the fact that the right wing of the intrenchments at Fort Donelson had been carried, and that the Stars and Stripes waved over those works. In ferry-boats, omnibuses and cars men earnestly discussed the position of our troops, and confidently asserted that it was only a question of time with regard to the beleaguered fort. Yet, notwithstanding this confidence in the success of our troops, anxiety was depicted on many faces, and further news was looked for with the deepest interest.

Before noon the news arrived of the defeat of the rebels, and their surrender to the Union General. Every bulletin was soon surrounded with an eager crowd, who, with greedy eyes devoured the news. Newsboys were flying about with "Extras," and in an almost incredible short space of time the glorious news was all over town. Then came hand-shakings and congratulations that are impossible to describe, but which were fervent, honest and loyal.

At the City Hall, Custom-house, and other public buildings, the National flag was flung to the breeze. On the hotels and principal buildings on Broadway the National Standard was also raised, making the City present as gay an appearance with regard to colors, as it did at the commencement of the war.

When the excitement was at its height Gen. SCOTT was seen in a carriage on Broadway. As soon as he was recognized cheer after cheer went up, and he was followed to a store where he was about to make some purchases. The crowd was so great, such an interest being taken in the General, that the Police were obliged to clear a passage through the people, in order to allow him to make his exit from the store.

From there the General drove to the Leather Manufacturers' Bank, on Wall-street, where he was immediately surrounded by brokers, merchants and others, who cheered him lustily. On the veteran General leaving the bank further enthusiasm was manifested, and continued until the General had entered his carriage, and was driven rapidly away.

In the evening BARNUM'S Museum was brilliantly illuminated, every pane of glass in the building having a light behind it. The effect was most pretty, and it made that portion of Broadway almost as light as day.

The news of the capture occasioned great excitement in business circles, and gave unbounded satisfaction to all parties. At the Produce Exchange, the news was received with most enthusiastic cheering. Very few seemed surprised, though many were evidently pained to hear that FLOYD had stolen 5,000 men from the rebel ranks and fled to parts unknown.

THE UNION DEFENCE COMMITTEE.

The following communication has been sent in for publication:

OFFICE, No. 30 PINE-STREET,
NEW-YORK, Monday, Feb. 17, 1862.

At a special meeting of the Committee, held this day, Mr. DRAPER, Vice-Chairman, presiding, the following resolutions, submitted by the Chair, were unanimously adopted:

Resolved, That in further acknowledgment of the loyal and gallant conduct of the Union forces, now engaged in suppressing rebellion, this Committee desire to express their admiration of the strategic skill of the commanding Generals, the determined ardor and dashing bravery of the officers, soldiers and seamen engaged in the investment, assault and capture of Fort Donelson, on the Cumberland River, in Tennessee.

Resolved, That the public heart of the country overflows with gratitude to the heroic men who have added a new glory to our national annals.

Resolved, That the memory of the patriots who have maintained the national honor at the sacrifice of their lives, becomes a sacred trust of a grateful country; and that the wounded and suffering defenders of the Union are entitled to the sympathy of all who appreciate principles of loyal duty and devoted patriotism.

Resolved, With the view to give public expression of the grateful sense entertained by the people in regard to the recent successes of the National arms, this Committee recommend that the citizens of New-York, Brooklyn and vicinity, be invited to assemble in mass meeting on the day made illustrious by the birth of WASHINGTON—the 22d of February, inst.

Resolved, That a Select Committee be appointed to make the necessary arrangements for the meeting, and to give public notice of the time and place; and that His Honor the Mayor be requested to preside.

REJOICING THROUGHOUT THE COUNTRY.

BOSTON, Monday, Feb. 17.

Mayor WIGHTMAN has issued a congratulatory proclamation on the capture of Fort Donelson, and directing a salute of 100 guns at noon to-morrow, also that the church bells be rung and the national flags be displayed from the public buildings.

The patriotic citizens will fire 500 guns on the Common to-morrow.

Resolutions were unanimously passed in both branches of the Legislature, to-day, presenting the thanks of the people of the State to the gallant officers and soldiers of the army, and the sailors of the navy of the United States, on the occasion of the series of brilliant victories recently won by their courage and skill in the States of South Carolina, Georgia, Missouri, North Carolina, Virginia, Kentucky and Tennessee, and the Governor was requested to order a salute in honor of these great successes of the arms of the Union.

Dispatches from Maine, New-Hampshire and Vermont, announce the general manifestation of enthusiasm and thanksgiving for the glorious result.

PHILADELPHIA, Monday, Feb. 17.

The news of the greatest victory of the war operates like sunshine, of which we are entirely destitute to-day. Crowds are gathering, under umbrellas, in the vicinity of Third and Chestnut streets, and "extras" find a ready demand.

The arrangements for the grand celebration of our victories, appointed for the 22d of February, will be made on a much more extensive scale, in view of this almost overwhelming disaster to the rebel cause.

Flags are being profusely thrown out in every direction.

The occasion is one of great public rejoicing.

In the midst of the joy over the news at the Commercial Rooms in the Merchants' Exchange, a proposition was started to raise a fund of $100,000 to educate and provide for the orphans of the slain on our side, and $5,000 was raised in a few minutes. The rest will be easily obtained. Besides this beneficence, the Cooper Shop Refreshment Committee have had under consideration the establishment of a home for the benefit of all wounded, maimed and sick soldiers after the rebellion is crushed. A charter for a "Soldier's Home" has been obtained, and the erection of a suitable building will shortly be commenced. It is stated that one gentleman has signified his intention of subscribing $40,000 for this purpose.

ALBANY, Monday, Feb. 17.

Rejoicings in honor of the glorious victory of the Federal arms, and the capture of rebel Generals, has kept the city in a blaze of excitement till a late hour to-night. The Capitol, State House, City Hall, Governor's residence, Van Vechten Hall, and other buildings, were brilliantly illuminated, huge bonfires blazed in State and Washington streets, and the whole city is a scene of rejoicing.

ROCHESTER, Monday, Feb. 17.

The news of the taking of Fort Donelson was received here with the wildest enthusiasm. Flags waved from the principal buildings, and there seemed to be a spontaneous burst of patriotic feeling. The bells were rung, cannon fired, bonfires lighted, dwellings illuminated, fireworks exhibited, &c. Speeches were made by the Mayor and others at the City Hall. Bands of music were out, and the streets were filled with people till a late hour. It was a general jubilee.

TROY, Monday, Feb. 17.

The war news caused great rejoicing in this city, and there was a large display of bunting. This evening 100 guns were fired, and the bells of the churches rung. A salute was fired at the Watervliet Arsenal.

POUGHKEEPSIE, Monday, Feb. 17.

One hundred guns were fired here, and all of our bells rung this afternoon, in honor of the capture of Fort Donelson.

CHICAGO, Ill., Monday, Feb. 17.

The news of the surrender of Fort Donelson, received this morning, created the wildest enthusiasm. Business of all kinds was temporarily suspended. The Boards of Trade adjourned at an early hour. The people claim the honor of the victory for Illinois the troops there being twenty-five regiments of infantry of Illinois, six of Iowa, and four of Indiana. There were also four regiments of Illinois cavalry, and six companies of artillery from Wisconsin.

AUBURN, Monday, Feb. 17.

One hundred guns were fired in this City, over the Fort Donelson victory.

GENEVA, Monday, Feb. 17.

The citizens of Geneva are all rejoicing. Bells are ringing, cannon are firing, and bonfires burning, over the great victory at Fort Donelson.

NEWS FROM FORTRESS MONROE.

Telegraphic Communication with Washington and New-York—Anticipated Visit of the Secretary of War.

FORTRESS MONROE, Sunday, Feb. 16,
via BALTIMORE, Monday, Feb. 17.

The propeller *Planet* arrived this afternoon from Baltimore, having on board the sub-marine cable to be laid across the Bay from this point to Cape Charles.

The line has already been completed from Wilmington, Del., to Cape Charles, and also from the headquarters of Gen. WOOL, about a mile and a half up the beach, to the place selected for the crossing. The line will be sunk in a few days, and as soon as the necessary arrangement can be made, this Department will be connected directly by telegraph with Washington and New-York, and the Government and the public will become informed of the important news transmitted hence from 12 to 24 hours earlier than at present.

The line will be under the management of Mr. W. H. HEISS, of the United States Military Telegraph, and will be of the greatest value to the Government.

The *Fernandina* sailed this afternoon. Wind northeast. Weather clear.

In anticipation of a visit from the Secretary of War, the Tenth New-York Regiment was ordered to parade at 7 o'clock this morning, and the Secretary was to be received with a salute and other honors.

IMPORTANT FROM KENTUCKY.

The Evacuation of Bowling Green.

PART OF THE TOWN BURNED.

Movements of the National Forces.

Eighty Thousand Men Concentrating on the Cumberland.

CINCINNATI, Monday, Feb. 17.

This morning's *Commercial* has the following special dispatch:

"On learning that the rebels were evacuating Bowling Green, Gen. BUELL ordered a forced march by Gen. MITCHELL to save if possible the railroad and turnpike bridges on Big Barron River. They, however, had all been destroyed when Gen. MITCHELL reached the banks of the river.

The brigades of Gen. BRECKINRIDGE and Gen. HINDMAN were, until Thursday evening, at Woodland Station.

The rebels left nothing at Bowling Green except a few old wagons.

A part of the town, it is reported, is being burnt.

It is believed now that no rebel forces exist in Kentucky east of the direct road from Bowling Green *via* Franklin to Nashville.

Gen. CRITTENDEN is trying to organize another army at Carthage, on the south bank of the Cumberland. This is the only rebel force on the line from Bowling Green to Nashville.

Gens. BRECKINRIDGE and HINDMAN'S Brigades have fallen back on Russellville, where Gens. BUCKNER'S and FLOYD'S Brigades have been stationed for some time. Gens. JOHNSTON and HARDEE were also believed to be at that point on Friday.

It is believed that, with the exception of the above brigades, the whole rebel army has been moved to Fort Donelson and Clarksville.

What movements may have been made by the rebel forces can only be conjectured, but the probabilities are that they have concentrated their whole force on the Cumberland.

If, however, they have not done so, the divisions of Generals NELSON and MITCHELL will be ample to cope with all they may have between Bowling Green and Nashville.

It is believed that the divisions of Gens. MCCOOK and THOMAS embarked at the mouth of Salt River, on steamers for Cumberland, on Saturday night, and that the troops who have been in camps of instruction at Bardstown, were at Louisville yesterday embarking for the Cumberland.

Three Indiana regiments, and a battery of artillery, leave New-Albany to-day.

The aggregate of these reinforcements is perhaps 40,000.

Gen. BUELL, we understand, goes with Gen. MCCOOK'S Division, to take command in person on the Cumberland, where our forces will be, by to-morrow night, 80,000. While he presses the enemy on the Cumberland with his tremendous force, their flank and rear are pressed by the heavy divisions under Gens. NELSON and MITCHELL.

Since writing the above we learn that ten regiments now in Ohio camps are ordered at once to the Cumberland.

RUMORED CAPTURE OF SAVANNAH.

FORTRESS MONROE, Sunday, Feb. 16,
Via BALTIMORE, Monday, Feb. 17.

By a flag of truce from Norfolk, we learn that fighting has been going on near Savannah, and that city has probably been captured.

IMPORTANT FROM MISSOURI.

The Pursuit of Price by Curtis and Sigel.

Capture of a Portion of the Rebel Supplies.

SPRINGFIELD, Sunday, Feb. 16.

The following is a special to the St. Louis *Democrat*:

"According to the latest advices the Federal army is in vigorous pursuit of the rebels. Gen. PRICE'S army was on Crane Creek, twenty-nine miles from here, on Friday evening, and our forces five miles in the rear, preparing to make an early start in pursuit the next morning. Gen. PRICE had placed his train in advance.

About 100 wagons, containing supplies for him were brought into this place from Forsyth, only a few hours before his retreat. The rebel sympathizers here claim that Gen. PRICE will be reinforced by twelve or fifteen regiments from Bentonville, Ark., under Gen. VAN DORN, but Gen. SIGEL, who was advancing on the rebel columns by a different route than that pursued by Gen. CURTIS, may strike a blow on their flank, and upset Gen. PRICE'S calculations.

Four rebel officers and thirteen prisoners fell into our hands on Friday, and are now here. The officers are the notorious Col. FREEMAN, Major BARRY, Aid de Camp to Gen. MCBRIDE; Capt. DICKINSON, Chief Engineer; and Capt. DONELL, Quartermaster.

A pony express has been established by Capt. BALDWIN between Rolla and this point.

Obituary.

Hon. WM. PENNINGTON, of New Jersey, died at his residence, in Newark, on Saturday evening last. Mr. PENNINGTON was in the 66th year of his age. In 1837 he was elected Governor of New-Jersey, and for seven successive terms of one year each he was re-elected. President TAYLOR appointed him Governor of Minnesota, and the Senate confirmed him, but Mr. PENNINGTON declined the position, and subsequently was appointed by President FILLMORE one of the Judges to settle claims under the Mexican treaty. A union of the Republicans and Conservatives elected him to Congress in 1858, from a District which had previously been largely Democratic, and on Feb. 1, 1860, he was chosen Speaker of the House, after one of the bitterest contests on record. In 1861, Mr. PENNINGTON was renominated for Congress, but local causes contributed to his defeat, after a very close canvas, in which he ran largely ahead of his ticket.

There are painful rumors in circulation in Newark, to the effect that Gov. PENNINGTON'S illness was brought to its lamentable conclusion by the mistake of a druggist, who carelessly put up morphine, when the prescription called for quinine. The fatal blunder was not discovered until the medicine had been administered. The matter will undoubtedly undergo an investigation.

General Ulysses S. Grant,
the hero of Fort Donelson

General John B. Floyd

General Simon Buchner,
who surrendered Fort Donelson

General Gideon J. Pillow

Surrender of Fort Donelson, February 16, 1862

The New-York Times.

VOL. XI---NO. 3251. | NEW-YORK, SATURDAY, FEBRUARY 22, 1862. | PRICE TWO CENTS.

THE SIEGE OF FORT DONELSON.

Full Details from Our Special Correspondents.

INVESTMENT OF THE POSITION.

THE ATTACK BY THE GUNBOATS.

Desperate Attempts of the Rebels to Raise the Siege.

Irresistible Bravery of the National Forces.

THE SURRENDER.

Large Number of Field Batteries Captured

The Confederate Soldiers Attempt to Shoot Floyd.

Partial List of the Killed and Wounded.

THE REGIMENTS TAKEN PRISONERS.

IN CAMP NEAR FORT DONELSON, SATURDAY, Feb. 15, 1862.

It was determined by Gen. GRANT to make the attack upon Fort Donelson from two directions—by land from the direction of Fort Henry, and by water up the Cumberland, assisted by an adequate column of troops on the banks. Tuesday night, the Fifty-seventh Illinois, Col. BALDWIN, arrived at Fort Henry, on the steamer *Minnehaha*.

Gen. GRANT directed Col. BALDWIN to return immediately down the river, stop all transports with troops, proceed down the Tennessee and up the Cumberland, keeping in the rear of gunboats, which would be found ready to start at Paducah on his arrival. The order also added that he should reach the vicinity of Fort Donelson Wednesday afternoon, disembark his troops, and be ready, in conjunction with the column from Fort Henry and the gunboats, to make an attack upon Fort Donelson Thursday morning. The plan seemed easy of accomplishment, so far as keeping "on time" is concerned, but in this respect quite a failure ensued.

Cooks were immediately set at work to provide the three days' rations ordered, and this took until midnight to accomplish. The *Minnehaha* then started out and reached Paducah about daylight, stopping and turning back on the way some eight or ten transports, loaded with troops.

Upon reaching Paducah we found that only a portion of the gunboat fleet had arrived, and this necessitated another delay. Toward night, however, the stragglers came slowly creeping up the river, and soon after the whole fleet started, and by 10 o'clock we had reached Smithland, at the mouth of the Cumberland River. The scene here was magnificent beyond description—the night was as warm as an evening in August in our more northern latitudes, a full moon looked down from an unclouded sky, and glanced off from bayonets, plumes and sword-hilts without number. At intervals long jets of fleecy smoke burst out along the parapets of the two forts on the height overlooking the town, and the boom of the welcome went reverberating over the hills, till from the long distances in Kentucky, it came back like a whisper. In turn the bands on the boats charmed the ear with most eloquent music, which, added to the effect of scores of gaily dressed ladies promenading the upper decks, gave the scene more the character of some vast drawing-room gathering—so much like was it, that no one would have been surprised had the whole crowd suddenly resolved into eddies of whirling waltzes or the swift changeful currents of quadrille or gallopade.

It was midnight before the fleet again got under way, and from that time our progress against the rapid sweep of the Cumberland was of the slowest possible description. On the morning of Thursday, by about 9 o'clock we made Eddyville—a small town on the east bank of the river, and distant only about forty-five miles from Smithland. If one may judge from the demonstrations of those who stood on the shore watching our passage, a more loyal town than Eddyville exists nowhere beneath the sun. The women waved handkerchiefs of all colors, or in lieu of that an apron or bonnet; the men swung their hats and vociferated alternately "Hurrah for the Union!" and "Hurrah for LINCOLN!" until hoarse beyond utterance; even the dogs of Eddyville were loyal, and barked and wagged their tails in patriotic joy at the National inundation. There was only one case, however, that bore the marks of sincerity. An old man whose head was as white as a snow-drift, stood on the shore leaning heavily on his cane and watching with seeming apathy the passage of the boats, whose full appearance his faded eyes probably failed to catch. Just as the *Minnehaha* passed opposite him the magnificent band of the Fifty-seventh struck up "Yankee Doodle." Its strains seemed to awaken stirring memories in the old man's mind—off went his hat, and with a vim that sent his hair flying around his head like a snow-bank lifted by the wind, he gave three hearty cheers for the Union—the Union in which himself, his children and his grandchildren had been born, reared and protected.

Eddyville is a nice little town, and probably is quite as good as that ancient scriptural city which numbered at least one righteous man among its inhabitants. It is probably some time since the high bluffs which environ it have had their echoes busy translating the patriotic airs of "Hail Columbia," "Star Spangled Banner" and "Yankee Doodle," and much good, I hope, may the exercise do those for whose benefit it was intended.

It was close upon midnight when the fleet reached the point below the Fort, where the disembarking was to take place; and then a savage wind was driving hail, sleet and snow directly in our teeth, as the work of landing the troops was commenced. A more disagreeable job never was undertaken and finished; however, by daylight the troops were all ashore, and the storm had cleared off, leaving the ground frozen hard and covered to the depth of an inch with snow.

The column which thus reached here, by way of the Cumberland, numbered not far from 10,000 men, who were conveyed in fourteen transport steamers; the column which came from Fort Henry, across the country, under Gen. GRANT in person, was composed, in round numbers, of 20,000 men, and included infantry, some fifteen or seventeen batteries of artillery, and from twelve to fifteen hundred horsemen. Before proceeding further in the history of affairs, I will write of the movements of this force.

The land forces left Fort Henry at 10 o'clock Wednesday morning. The route lay along the Dover road, and as there had been no rain for the last few days, and the weather was mild and cheerful, the progress was comparatively rapid. In some four hours after starting the head of the column had entered the ravines to the rear, and taken up a position within about two miles of Fort Donelson. This position was not taken till after frequent and short delays, the surroundings were carefully examined, and their entire freedom from masked batteries and other favorite secession man-traps fully ascertained.

The rest of the day was spent in bringing the remaining part of the forces into position, which was done by extending both up and down a line parallel with the river, and then bending in the extreme right and left, thus inclosing the fort in a semicircular line and completely surrounding it. This was not done without much trouble. The enemy's pickets and sharpshooters seemed endless in number, and had to be driven from every ravine and hill-top, at an expense of much blood-letting. No very serious damage resulted, however, to our forces, and by night they had driven the rebels completely within the line of their fortifications, and had sharpened their appetites for a more serious brush on the day following.

Thursday morning dawned beautifully, and seemed to smile upon the efforts of the National troops. The men cheerfully accepted the omen, and determined to make the most of the weather and their rifles during the day—a determination which was fully carried out ere night, and which gave many a poor fellow a leaden passport for ferriage over the Dark River.

Among the operations projected was one to force a reconnoissance close up to the fort, and thus early settle the character of the neighboring ground with a view to the more important operations of the future. The ground around the fort is a rolling upland, covered with heavy timber and dense undergrowth, and broken for miles around into ravines, bordered by precipitous bluffs, whose sides, steep and rocky, almost forbid the passage of even a goat. The fort itself is situated upon a high bluff, which slants with an easy descent to a point at the water's edge on the north, and is probably not less than one hundred feet above the level of the water. To the rear the bluff has been to some extent leveled for the distance of a mile. On this artificial table land stands the fort, whose lines of fortifications and rifle pits cover the entire leveled space. Bordering this fortified portion is a ravine of no great depth, across which, and forming its outer boundary, is a timbered ridge, or rather a series of ridges, for it is divided at intervals by ravines which flow in all directions like streams emptying into a river.

Moving toward this ridge about 10 A. M. Thursday, was a body of National troops, composed in all of about five regiments of infantry and some three or four batteries of artillery. The National troops were met, at a distance of a thousand yards or so, by a heavy force of the enemy, and a sharp engagement ensued, which, however, was confined mainly to artillery practice and "bushwhacking" on both sides. The enemy gradually gave ground, and in an hour had taken refuge within their works, and our troops were in possession of the series of hills which lies adjacent to the ravine next to the outer line of fortifications. The distance from these ridges to the nearest defences of the rebels was not more than three hundred yards, and being covered with timber, while they are slightly higher than the works, they afforded a capital position for our sharpshooters, of which they were not slow to avail themselves.

Among the rest who disposed themselves along these ridges were BIRGE's celebrated regiment of riflemen, and from that time forward, a secession head above the parapet, for ever so brief a period, was sure to go down with a hole bored through it about the size of one that might be made with a three-quarter auger. This regiment did most effectual service. Each member is dressed in gray, with a gray felt cap, whose top is rigged "fore-and-aft" with squirrel tails dyed black. Their weapon is a heavy rifle, carrying conical ball, with an effective range of about 1,000 yards. On this occasion, as indeed upon every other since, they fought pretty much in the places and after the manner that happened best to suit individual fancies. Lying flat behind a stump, one would watch with finger on trigger for rebel game with all the excitement of a hunter waylaying deer at a "salt-lick." Woe to rebel caput that was lifted ever so quickly above the parapet for a glance at Yankee operations fifty eyes instantly sighted it, and fifty fingers drew trigger on it, and thereafter it was seen no more. Writhing over on his back, the sharpshooter would reload and then twist back in all the operation, not exposing so much as the tip of his elbow to the enemy.

About 11 o'clock three regiments—the Fourth Illinois on the left, the Forty-ninth on the right, and the Eighteenth in the centre—under command of Col. MORRISON, started on double-quick down the declivity with a view of storming the outer breastwork. As they reached the bottom of the bluff Col. MORRISON received a ball in his hip, and fell from his horse. Seeing their leader fall, and nobody appearing to take his place, the regiments wavered, and finally fell back, gaining the top of the hill in good order, but with considerable loss.

Again in the course of the day the Twenty-fifth Indiana make a break for a breastwork in front of them, but were met by a force of the enemy triple their own, and were, after fighting desperately for nearly an hour, forced to retire.

These were the main efforts of the land forces during the day, aside from the bushwhacking—this was kept up as long as the light would permit a man to sight a barrel. Once during the night the enemy sallied out in force, and made a determined attempt to capture TAYLOR's Chicago Battery, but were driven back with a heavy loss as their only recompense. The whole day was of the busiest and most exciting description. There was not a single instant from 10 o'clock until night that the woods were not filled with the sharp crack of small arms, the heavy roar of artillery, and the swift, whistling rush of the rebel grape-shot as it scoured incessantly through the timber—a perfect tempest of iron hail.

Our total loss through the day was believed at the time to reach about 30 killed and 170 wounded. This large number of casualties resulted, to a great extent, from the imprudence of the men themselves.

THE FORT DONELSON FORTIFICATIONS.

Diagram Showing the Main and Upper Fort, the Rifle Pits, and the Water and Field Batteries; and the Manner in which the Position was Invested by the National Forces.

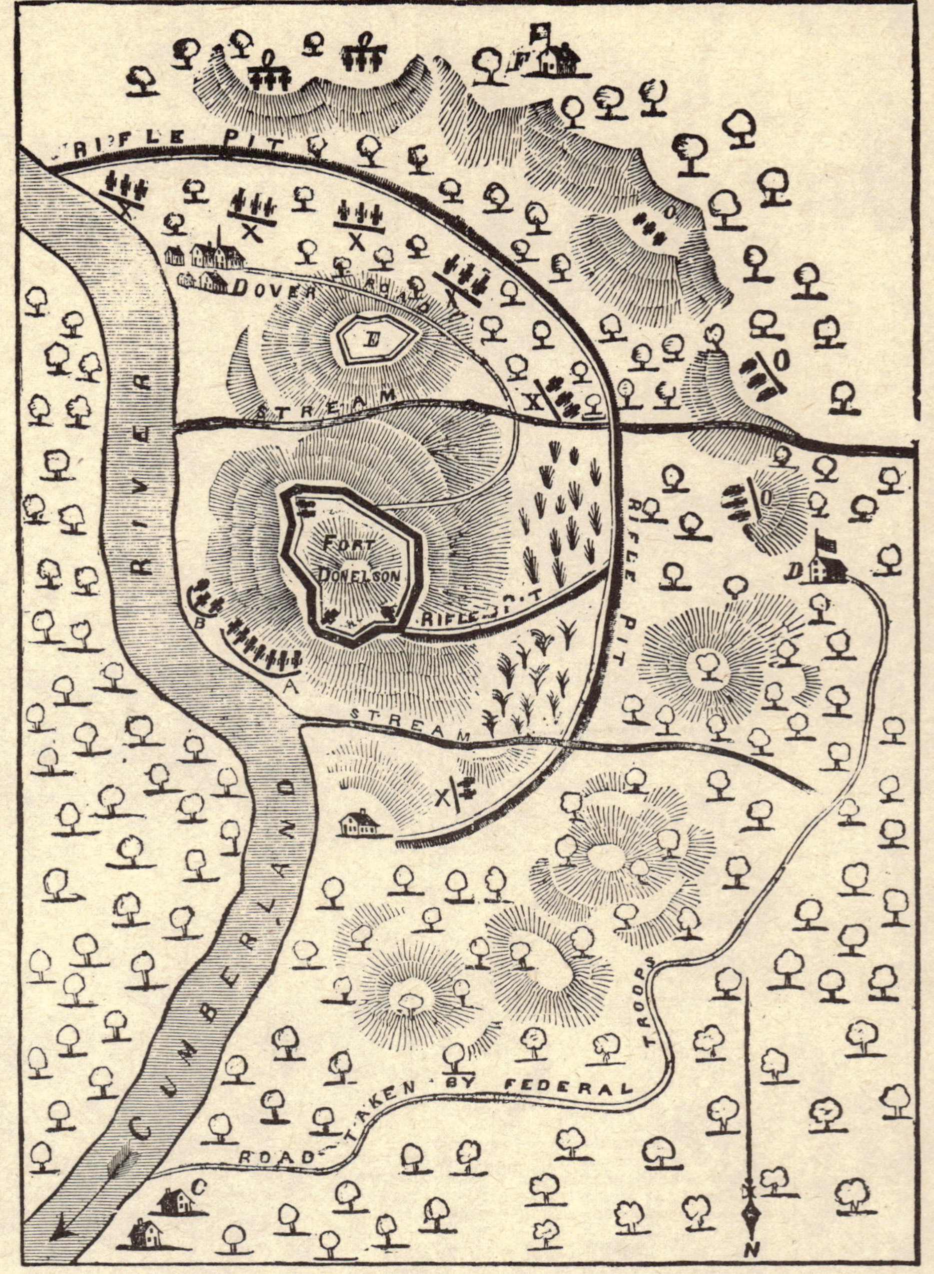

A—Water Battery, 9 guns.
B—Water Battery, 3 guns.
C—Landing National troops.
D—Gen. GRANT's Headquarters.
E—Breastwork.
F—Gen. MCCLERNAND.
O—National Batteries.
X—Confederate Batteries.
To the right of the Fort are Abattis.

They were so anxious to fight that they hesitated at no exposure to obtain a shot at the enemy. A large number of the wounds were caused by falling limbs, which were wrenched off by the fiery showers of grape sent from the rebel batteries.

During the time that the land forces were engaged, the iron-clad gunboat *Carondelet*, went up and singly engaged the rebel batteries. She fired 102 shots, and received no great damage in all the tremendous fire to which she was exposed, save in the case of a single shot. This, a monster mass of iron, weighing at least 128 pounds, entered one of her forward ports and wounding eight men in its passage, dashed with terrific force against the breastwork of coal-bags in front of the boilers, and there was stopped. Soon after this she retired from the unequal contest, having covered herself with glory for having so long singly withstood the enormous force of the rebel's entire water batteries.

Thus ended the operations of Thursday. The results, although accompanied by a comparatively heavy loss on our side, were in the main satisfactory. The courage and eagerness of our troops were tested, the range and bearing of the enemy's guns obtained, and a thorough examination made of all the grounds adjacent to the fort.

Friday, the work of disembarking the troops and stores brought by the transports was commenced. By noon the forces had all landed, and were on their way to join the main body.

The only event of importance that occurred during the day was a heavy engagement between the gunboats and the fort. About 2 P. M. the fort threw a few shells at the transports, but, however, failed in reaching them by about half a mile. Soon after the whole fleet of seven gunboats moved up—the four iron boats in advance and ahead, the three wooden boats at a discreet distance in the rear. At about a mile the iron boats opened from their bow guns, and were replied to promptly by the fort.

I secured a position about half-way between the boats and fort, a little out of the line of fire, and there for two hours had the pleasure of listening to a concert of the most gigantic order. At first the roar from fort and boats was unbroken for a single instant, so rapid was the firing, while the air high overhead seemed filled with a million of hissings, as the heavy storm of shells tore furiously ahead on their mission of destruction. In about half an hour, the fire from the fort began to slacken, and shortly after was continued from only three guns—the rest apparently having been silenced by our fire. At this time the boats were within some four hundred yards, and were on the point of using grape-shot, when a shot disabled the steering apparatus of the *Louisville*, by carrying off the top of the wheelhouse, and knocking the wheel itself into fragments. There was a tiller aft, and this was instantly taken possession of by the pilot—but he had scarcely reached it, ere the rudder was carried away by a shot from the *Taylor*. Of course the boat became instantly unmanageable, and swung around, receiving a shot in the wood-work towards the stern, which, I believe, wounded several seamen. Under these circumstances, it was thought best to retire, and accordingly the whole fleet fell back to the position it had occupied in the morning. The most serious damage sustained during the action was from one of those monster 128-pound shots, which passed through a bow-port of the *Louisville* and dismounted the second gun on the starboard quarter, killing three men and wounding six others. A captain of one of the guns was cut completely in two, and spattered his brains over Capt. DOVE, who stood by him, and otherwise so mangled him that scarcely a resemblance to humanity remained. The same boat also received a shot near the water-line, which, while it did not penetrate the hull, started the timbers so as to set her leaking badly. During the night, however, all damage was repaired, and this morning she is as ready for active service as ever. The total loss on the *Louisville* was six killed and eight or ten wounded. One of the other gunboats had some of her woodwork shot away, but was not materially damaged.

The iron boats in action were:

Louisville, Capt. B. M. DOVE.
St. Louis, Lieut.-Com. PAULDING.
Carondelet, Lieut.-Com. KELTZ.
Mound City, Lieut.-Com. ———.

The other three boats were the wooden ones—*Taylor*, *Lexington* and *Conestoga*.

There is a boat about to leave for Cairo, and I have concluded to mail this without awaiting the result of the final assault. Affairs look encouraging—the fort is completely invested, and will probably be stormed either this afternoon or to-morrow morning.

The rebels have a flag flying from the fort which is thought to be a black one.

FORT DONELSON, Tenn., Monday, Feb. 17, 1862.

My last letter closed with the doings of our troops up to Friday night, and at that point in the progress of the siege I will resume the history of events.

Friday night was one of the severest description. The men being without tents, and in many cases without fire, suffered intensely. Hundreds were frost-bitten, and from facts related to me since the surrender by some of the rebels, I have no doubt but that many of our wounded men, who fell in the fight of Friday, and were unable to walk in, were actually frozen to death. This circumstance is a terrible one, and inexpressibly shocking, but there was no help for it. During the various conflicts of Friday, the scene was constantly changed from point to point and were not again visited by our troops. Men would fall at these places, and being unable to get away, were obliged to stay where they fell. In some cases, a few of our wounded were cared for by the rebels, although they were without fire, and could give them but little valuable assistance.

Saturday morning opened cold and lowering, as if in sympathy with the bloody drama which its first grey beams inaugurated. All the day the tide of battle raged along the ground which had hitherto divided the hostile forces, and swallowed in its bloody depths more brave lives than were lost in all the days before.

On the extreme right of the National line was Gen. MCCLERNAND's Division, composed of three Brigades as follows:

FIRST BRIGADE—COL. OGLESBY COMMANDING

Eighth Illinois, Lieut.-Col. Rhoades.
Eighteenth Illinois, Col. Lawler.
Twenty-ninth Illinois, Col. Reardon.
Thirtieth Illinois, Lieut.-Col. Dennis.
Thirty-first Illinois, Col. John A. Logan.
Swartz and Dresser's Batteries.
Stewart's, Dollin's, O'Harnett's and Carmichael's Cavalry.

SECOND BRIGADE—COL. W. H. L. WALLACE.

Eleventh Illinois, Lieut.-Col. Hart.
Twentieth Illinois, Col. Marsh.
Forty-fifth Illinois, Col. Smith.
Forty-eighth Illinois, Col. Harney.
Twenty-fifth Kentucky, Col. SHACKLEFORD.
Taylor's and McAllister's Batteries.
Seventh Illinois Cavalry, Capt. Kellog.
Fourth Illinois Cavalry, Col. Dickey.

THE THIRD BRIGADE,

as made up, is commanded by Gen. PAYNE, who, however, was not present. It has only two regiments:

Eighth Wisconsin, Col. MURPHY.
Forty-ninth Illinois, Col. W. R. MORRISON.

These three Brigades occupied the entire ground from the centre of the National line to its extreme right. The balance of the line from the centre to the extreme left, was held by the Second Division under Gen. C. F. SMITH.

Early on the morning of Friday—almost before it was fairly light—the enemy poured forth in a mass of not less than 3,000 men, and hurled themselves with tremendous force against the Forty-fifth and Twelfth Illinois Regiments, that were nearly on the extreme right. Accompanying them were twelve batteries of Artillery. The Forty-fifth and Twelfth sustained the shock manfully for a short time, and then withdrew. The Eighteenth and Ninth Illinois soon after came to their support, and for a short time held the enemy in check. Soon after, the Thirtieth, Thirty-first, and Eleventh Illinois Regiments, the Eighth Missouri, Fifty-eighth Ohio, and Twenty-fifth Kentucky, and WILLARD's Battery were added to the National force, and the fight became of terrific proportions. MCALLISTER's Battery took position on an eminence, and for four hours their heavy twenty-four-pounders were not silent for a single instant. During all this time they were exposed to a heavy fire from the Rebels, who had erected batteries so as to command MCALLISTER's position from three points—two directly in front, and one on his right. TAYLOR's Battery stood a little to the rear of the other, and somewhat to the left—the other National batteries were distributed at various points along the line, as the nature of the ground would permit—all kept the air incessantly filled with their music, and with showers of grape and shell.

This is but an outline of the position of the National forces, for there can be strictly no correct sketch given, as at no time during the fight were the regiments stationary. Now they pushed forward, again fell back, withdrew, and were replaced by others. The fight itself was prolonged and desperate. Now it rolled over a hill, anon poured along a ravine, always in the woods, and always marking its track in characters of blood. The conflict was not conducted according to any particular military plan—men stationed themselves behind trees, logs, rocks, anything that would afford shelter, and blazed away whenever a hostile head appeared.

The Twenty-fifth Kentucky Regiment was on the extreme right, and was attacked by a swarm of the enemy with such vigor that they broke and fled in disorder. At another part of the National line the attack was conducted by such overwhelming numbers that the line was broken through, and the battle seemed well-nigh likely to become a total rout on the part of the National forces. It was at this last gap broken through the National line that MCALLISTER's Battery was stationed, and where for a time it fell in the hands of the rebels. The battery had only 150 rounds of ammunition, and at about 10 o'clock these were all fired away—not a single shot was left. Capt. MCALLISTER in vain endeavored to obtain a supply from the rear; a shot from the enemy passed through three of his horses; another tore off the trail from one of the guns; a third smashed the wheel of a second gun. Just at this time, a heavy force of the enemy obtained a cover near him, and opened fire at about two hundred yards with musketry. Hitching six horses to the only undamaged gun, he endeavored to haul it off, but the weight was so great, and the road in such a muddy condition, that it was found impossible to get along with it, and after dragging it a half mile, it became mired, and he was reluctantly obliged to leave it. The horses were driven off, dragging the limbers and empty caissons, and the guns were left to their fate. In the course of the day a tremendous charge on the part of our troops reoccupied the lost ground, closed up the gap and recovered the pieces. They were found where they were left, their great weight—being 24-pound siege guns—probably preventing the enemy from taking them away.

The fight raged from daylight until nearly noon without a moment's cessation, and resulted in the enemy's being driven back to his intrenchments. The battle-ground extended over a space some two miles in length, every inch of which was the witness of a savage conflict. *The rebels fought with the most determined bravery*, and seemed bent upon breaking through the right wing at any cost. They poured against our lines a perfect flood, and it was only by a bravery that equaled their own, and a resolute determination to conquer that outlasted their efforts, that our gallant soldiers were at length enabled to stay the fierce tide, and finally to hurl it back to its former boundaries. Our men determined that they *would* win, and win they did, with a gallantry that entitles every man to the name of hero.

The whole of the fight was of the most terrific character. Without a single moment's cessation the rebels poured into our forces perfect torrents of canister, shell and round shot, while their thousands of riflemen hurled in a destructive fire from every bush, tree, log or obstruction of any kind that afforded shelter. The roar of the battle was like that of a heavy tornado, as it sweeps through some forest on its mission of destruction. Small arms kept up an incessant cracking, mingling with which came up occasionally the roar of company or division firing, while over all came every moment or two the resonant thunders of the batteries.

Never fought men better than did ours on this bloody day. They clung to a position till driven from it by the direst necessity, and in many individual cases, men refused to retreat, but stuck to their tree or bush till the enemy's force rolled about them, and swallowed them up. Many in this way were taken prisoners, while others found a speedier, bloodier end to their daring. The victory was a costly one. Some of the regiments were cut completely to pieces, others were reduced to a size that scarcely left them a respectable company, while all suffered more or less severely. Lieut.-Col. QUINN, of the Twentieth Illinois, while gallantly urging on his men in the hottest of the fight, was struck by a grapeshot that cut his heart completely out. *The mortality among officers was terrible.* Major Post, of the Eighth Illinois, Capt. Rigby, Acting Major of the Thirty-first Illinois, Lieut.-Col. White, of the same regiment, Lieut.-Col. Smith, of the Forty-eighth; Capt. Craig, Company A, and Lieut. Skeats, Company F, all of the Eighteenth; Capt. Wilson, Company F, Eighth, Capt. Swartout, Company H, Eighth Missouri; Capt. Shaw, Company B, Lieut. Vore, Company E, and Lieut. Boyce, all of the Eleventh Illinois; Adjutant Kirkpatrick, of the Thirtieth, Capt. Mendel, of the Seventh, Capt. Brokeck, of the Forty-ninth Illinois; Lieut. Mausker, of the Eighteenth Illinois; Adjutant Chipman and Capt. Slaymaker, of the Second Iowa, were among those who met their death on this bloody battle-field.

Our entire loss is not yet known, but will reach a figure not much short of six hundred, killed and wounded. The number of men wounded is beyond all precedent, but in an unusually large number of cases, they are not of a serious nature. The enemy used, generally, the "buck and ball" cartridge; that is, a cartridge with one ball and three buckshot. Almost everybody got a scratch from one of the latter; one could scarcely go anywhere where the air was not filled with them.

Affairs had scarcely quieted down, on the right wing ere the ball was opened in Gen. SMITH's Division, on the left. The Second, Seventh and Fourteenth

[Continued on Eighth Page.]

The Charleston Mercury.

DAILY PAPER—TEN DOLLARS PER ANNUM, PAYABLE HALF-YEARLY IN ADVANCE.

VINDICES SULLÆ [illegible]
SPORTS SUA SINE LEGE FIDES RECTUMQUE COLENTUR.

COUNTRY PAPER—THREE A WEEK—FIVE DOLLARS PER ANNUM, IN ADVANCE.

VOLUME LXXX. CHARLESTON, S. C., TUESDAY, FEBRUARY 25, 1862. NUMBER 11,392

THE MERCURY.

TUESDAY, FEBRUARY 25, 1862.

Retrospective.

We commend to the perusal and reflections of our readers, as appropriate, the following editorials taken from our columns last year. They will see what were then our views, and what the suggestions we offered; how far they have been justified by events; and how far they have proved erroneous.

WHAT SORT OF FIGHTING?

[*From the Mercury, May 30, 1861.*]

A correspondent cautions our people not to suppose the men whom the defenders of the South are about to meet in battle, will be defeated without hard fighting. The caution is timely, for we do not doubt the contest will be bloody beyond anything known in the annals of this country. The Southern people are accustomed to the use of fire-arms and of horses. They are naturally a warlike people, and by education and training are better fitted for command. Our soldiers have more individuality, and more character, as soldiers, than those of the North. Our officers are likely to prove abler, we think. But those who entertain the idea that Northern troops will not fight in such a cause as this—one they think worth fighting for—their means of money-making—are mistaken. Although they are brought up to think courage a special virtue when found in a man, and not a matter of course, as is regarded at the South, still there are a large number of men there as brave as any in the world. With the ferocious hate against us which they manifest, and the bitter fear they feel of losing their all in the way of profits and consequence by successful disunion, it would be folly, after they have gone such lengths already, to expect anything short of a desperate attempt to subdue and subjugate us by ball and bayonet. Gen. Scott is a man of capacity in planning, and is thorough in his preparation. He has had time to drill the volunteers mustered in, and has a pretty good number of regulars. He will, undoubtedly, put his best foot foremost, and meet us with the best forces in the service, taking every advantage that he is able to conceive and execute. He must, of course, fail in the effort to conquer the South. But the result of the first one or two battles is *important*, and will turn *on the relative number of Southern troops in the field and on the completeness of preparations.* We have officers of great ability, and troops that on equal terms are invincible. What odds they may be required to vanquish, and what disadvantages they will be able to surmount, experience must prove as occasion shall call. Southern troops will rally after repulse; we are inclined to think Northern volunteers will not. Nor will the latter stand heavy charges of cavalry. Ours will. A few effective victories on our part would ensure the immediate recognition of our independence abroad, show the North the folly of their undertaking, and speedily re-establish *peace.* Defeat would have the contrary effect of *prolonging the war.* We should look matters squarely in the face. The North will open the ball with hard fighting.

THE TACTICS OF THE NORTH.

[*From the Mercury, May 31, 1861.*]

Night and day, for the last two months, has the Northern Government been making herculean efforts in its department of war. Preparation on the most gigantic scale has gone on steadily and unflagging under the intelligent and able superintendence and direction of General Scott. An immense body of volunteers have been thrown into camp, and are drilling eight hours a day under competent officers of West Point training.—The arms at hand have been distributed, and all who are to engage soon in the battle have been thoroughly equipped with the best weapons.—Factories, for the manufacture of cannon, rifles, sabres, bayonets and ammunition of every description, are in full operation at the North during the whole twenty-four hours of each day. Agents have long since been sent abroad to Europe to procure and forward, as fast as possible, cargos of improved arms, and already they have begun to arrive. Great efforts have also been made for the health, comfort and supplies of Northern troops. Energy and promptitude have characterized their movements both in Maryland and St. Louis, and their success along the Border has, so far, been complete. They have, in the West, obtained and secured the great repository of arms for that section, equipped our enemies of St. Louis, Illinois, Indiana and Ohio, leaving the resistance men of Missouri poorly provided, Kentucky unarmed and overawed, and Tennessee also with a meagre provision for fighting, dependent on the Cotton States for weapons of defence. Maryland has been cowed and overpowered, Washington rendered as secure as may be, while Virginia is invaded and Richmond threatened with capture.

In all this, the military proceedings of the North, since the fall of Sumter, have been eminently wise. For the purpose of overpowering, disheartening and gaining the first advantages, which, both at home and abroad, are of immense importance, the concentration of all the forces available as promptly as possible, has been clearly the course of generalship and true economy. The first blow is said to be often half the battle. The war policy of Scott and the Northern Government has all the effect of the first blow. The final result we cannot, in the slightest degree, doubt. The effort to conquer the South must fail. The immediate success will depend, in a great measure, *upon the number of troops now got ready, and the efficiency of the preparation made for them by the Confederate Government during the same period Scott has been at work.* Let us not commit the mistake of underrating our enemy, or of supposing that, in modern warfare, it is only the courage of a people and the relative military talent of their field officers that decide the issues of war. Ability in combinations and bravery in executing them, may fail of success where the *material is wanting or deficient.* An hour's delay of a corps of reserve lost the battle of Waterloo; and Napoleon fought the battle with the best troops in the world. They were cut to pieces.

THE NAVY OF THE CONFEDERATE STATES.

[*From the Mercury, August 10, 1861.*]

When the history of the present contest comes to be written by the historian who will tell the story of the struggle for our liberty to the grandchildren of the men of 1861, nothing, probably, will surprise them more than that, for months after the formation of a Government, the keel of not a single war steamer was laid by the Confederate States. With the spring and summer before us, and the certainty that, after the equinoctial gales' the enemy will be upon us, and that the blockading fleet will shake off its inaction, and cast about for opportunities of telling aggression, we seem to have sat down in a kind of torpor, waiting for some foreign Hercules to pull us out of the mire. Without an effort, the conclusion seems to have been arrived at, that it is either useless or impossible to build up or buy up a navy with the resources furnished by the Southern States, and console ourselves for this want of energy with the hope, that because England and France want cotton, "they will wipe out the blockaders." Perhaps, since the resources of the Confederacy are questioned in naval matters, we may ask further evidences of the diplomatic astuteness of our agents in their efforts to embroil England and France in our quarrel, and with their aid to destroy the fleet that is destined to annoy and threaten us so long as this war lasts. Let us rely on ourselves, asking no favors of any nation; and, unto the very last, let us fight our battles under our own flag alone. The only peace we will ever get from the Northern despotism is the one we shall conquer; and to rely on the possible interference of a foreign nation—one, too, who has done as much as any other to fan the flames of fanaticism against us—seems only the result of weakness and imbecile despondency. Our forests of timber, our mountains of coal and iron, our fields of hemp and cotton, upbraid us for this idleness—this enervation. God has given us these things, yet we seem unmindful of their uses. To-day there is not a vessel in the United States navy but what sails on a Southern keel, and spreads Southern canvas to the breeze.

If in anything the enemy has displayed energy, it has been in the *reorganization of its navy.*

What, then, has our Government done? The demon of doubt may have paralyzed for awhile the energies of the Navy Department; but surely the first shot that hurtled across the waters of our harbor against "Sumter," should have exorcised that demon.

A few merchant steamers and river boats have been purchased, we are informed, and are in a course of preparation for active service upon our inland waters, where the enemy will send their iron-clad gunboats and floating batteries.—*We have yet to learn of the probable construction of any such vessels on our part, and what has been done in Europe, is in the way of purchase.* Is not five months' time long enough to have procured some naval defence?

There may be reasons for the present inactivity, but, until the future reveals them, we are bound to believe and express the conviction forced upon us, that the Navy Department at Richmond has not displayed the energy and concentration which the circumstance that surround and menace us demand. To the people of this State we can only say again and again to prepare, and to rely on themselves alone in warding off the dangers of the coming winter.

NOTES OF THE WAR.

THE DOINGS OF THE BURNSIDE EXPEDITION—PARTICULARS OF THE CAPTURE OF THE CONFEDERATE GUNBOATS IN THE PASQUOTANK RIVER—DESTRUCTION OF ELIZABETH CITY, ETC.

The correspondent of the New York *Tribune* gives the following account of the expedition of Commander ROWAN to Elizabeth City, and the destruction of the Confederate gunboats:

After the great victory of Roanoke Island, and as soon as suitable preparations could be made, a portion of the fleet proceeded to Elizabeth City, for the purpose of capturing the rebel navy, which, it was said, had made a stand at that point, with the intention of resisting our force to the last. Orders were also given to burn what steamers the rebels were building at that place, but not to destroy or molest any other property belonging to the citizens.

The expedition, in command of Captain S. C. Rowan, left Roanoke Island on Sunday, at 3 o'clock p. m. It was composed of the following steamers: Delaware, Lieutenant Commanding Quackenbush, the flag ship; Underwriter, Lieut. Commanding W. N. Jeffers, Louisiana, Lieutenant Commanding Murray; Lockwood, Acting Master Graves; Seymour, Lieutenant Commanding Wells; Hetzell, Lieutenant Commanding Davenport, Shawsheen, Acting Master Woodruff; Valley City, Lieut. Commanding Chaplin; General Putnam, Acting Master Hotchkins; Commodore Perry, Lieutenant Commanding Flusser; Ceres, Acting Master Hayes; Whitehead, Acting Master French; Blinker, Acting Master Giddings, making fourteen in all.

The distance to Elizabeth City from Roanoke Island is some thirty-five or forty miles. About an hour after the squadron left the island we discovered two rebel steamers some five miles off, making for Elizabeth City, with all possible speed, and were doubtless carrying the news of our approach.

This was about an hour before sundown, and under full head of steam all hands gave chase, in hope we might capture the two steamers before dark; but after a hard run of over an hour, we were satisfied that the job could not be accomplished, and on arrival at the mouth of Pasquotank river, on which Elizabeth City is situated, it was decided to anchor for the night, and proceed to give the enemy battle early in the morning.—We were then some twelve or fifteen miles from Elizabeth City.

The squadron anchored across the river, so that nothing could pass in the night, and all hands were ordered to have their side arms by them, so as to be ready for the enemy, should he attack us before morning. It was a beautiful moonlight night, but no enemy came in sight until morning, when just at the break of day a loaded schooner was discovered coming down the river, and of course was an easy prize. She was taken by the steamer Shawsheen, which also gave chase, fired a gun across the schooner's bow, which brought her to; but the Seymour having started first, reached the schooner just in time to nab her, and carry off the honors, which of course she was entitled to. At this writing I have not learned with what the schooner is loaded; doubtless with supplies for the enemy. The Seymour took her prize in tow, and was soon in company with the squadron.

We came in sight of Elizabeth City about 8 o'clock, and as we approached we discovered the enemy's steamers, seven in number, in line of battle in front of the city ready to receive us. A fort was also discovered on a point which projected out some considerable distance—one-fourth of a mile, perhaps—in front of the rebel line of steamers; and directly opposite of this fort was a schooner anchored, on which were two heavy rifle guns; the distance between the fort and this schooner being about half a mile. Four large guns were mounted on the fort, and it was thought by the rebels that no fleet of ours could pass this narrow channel; consequently they considered themselves safe, with the assistance of their navy, drawn up between the city and fort.

At the sight of the enemy everything was in readiness for battle. To describe the wild delight of our brave blue jackets when they first discovered the enemy is more than the pen can describe.

The charge was short and desperate, and without any exception is one of the most brilliant ever made by the American navy. All eyes were on the Commander, Rowan, to see what the first order would be, as we were rapidly approaching the foe.

In due time he ran up the signal to engage the enemy in close action, hand to hand. We were then about two miles from the enemy. This was a signal for a test of speed, as well as the signal for a deadly encounter with a desperate foe, whose all was staked upon this final engagement. For a distance of two miles it was a race between our steamers in their eagerness to outstrip each other, and to be first to meet the enemy of the Republic.

The river began to narrow as we approached the city. The point where the fort was situated necessarily brought our steamers nearer together, making them sure marks for the enemy's guns; indeed, it would be a miracle if a shot from one of the enemy's guns did not strike some one of our steamers. Under the circumstances, most any other commander would have thought it advisable to first attack the fort and silence the guns on both sides of that narrow point, and then attack the rebel steamers; but not so with the brave and intrepid Rowan, whose motto is to charge bayonets on the enemy whenever and wherever he may be found. In action, the position of the commander's ship is in the centre of the squadron. The Delaware, Capt. Rowan's flag ship, was at the head of the advancing column, and led the van. No attention was paid to the fort or armed schooner, as they dashed by them through a perfect torrent of shells and grape, boarded the rebel steamers, and engaged them at the point of the bayonet, as the panic stricken rebels leaped into the water in every direction. Many were killed by the bayonet and revolver in this hand to hand fight, and sank below the water. Their real loss will, doubtless, never be known to us; the slaughter, however, was fearful, and the struggle short and desperate—not more than fifteen minutes in duration.

The fort and armed schooner were deserted quite as soon as were the rebel steamers, for it was made quite as hot work for those behind the guns as it was for their confederates on the gunboats. Our loss is two killed and about a dozen wounded—all seamen. The death struggle was brief. In less time than it would take to write a telegraphic despatch the victory was ours.

The Commodore Perry was in the advance, and made for the rebel steamer Sea Bird, the flag ship of the rebel navy, on which were Commodore Lynch, and run her down, cutting her through. The Ceres run straight into the rebel steamer Ellis, and run her down in like manner, boarding her at the same time. The Underwriter took the Forrest in the same style, while the Delaware took the Fanny in fine shape, she having received ten shots from our squadron, which made daylight through her in as many places.—The Morse, Shawsheen, Lockwood, Hetzell, Valley City, Putnam, Whitehead, Blinker and Seymour also covered themselves with glory. Every officer and man in our entire squadron behaved like a hero, one as brave as the other, all through this desperate charge. The terrified rebels, as they forsook their gunboats, fired them, and thus all but the Ellis were burned, including a new one on the stocks. Four were burned, one captured, and two made their escape—the Raleigh and Beaufort. They are in the canal which leads to Norfolk, but are not able to go through, on accounts of the locks having been destroyed; consequently they will be captured before this reaches you, as they can go only some few miles towards Norfolk.

The log books of the steamers, together with the signal book of the rebel navy, and all their naval signal colors, fell into our hands, with many other records and papers, which places us in possession of much that is valuable.

This great naval victory gives us full possession of all the inland waters of North Carolina. We have learned where the rest of the rebel steamers, now few in number, can be found, and rest assured that they are all destined to fall into our hands in short order, perhaps before this reaches you.

The following are the names of the seven steamers which we encountered to-day, with their commanders: Ellis, Capt. C. W. Cooke; Raleigh, Capt. Alexander; Fanny, Capt. Taylor; Beaufort, Capt. Parker; Accomac, Capt. Sands; Forrest, Capt. Hoover; Seabird (the rebel flag ship), Commodore Lynch.

All these commanders were educated in the United States Naval Academy. Capt. Cooke is taken prisoner by our forces. As I have already said, the Raleigh and Beaufort escaped.

When it became evident that nothing but disaster awaited them, the rebels, after firing their gunboats, fled to the village, and commenced firing the principal buildings. It is said that Colonel Martin, of Hatteras memory, fired considerable of his own property before fleeing. An officer of the Wise Legion was caught mounted riding through the village, pointing out the buildings to be burnt. The village had been deserted by most of the population. Those who remained were in great fright, and under the delusion that the object of our visitation was to burn the town, and that they would be cruelly treated. Captain Rowan availed himself of the first moment to disabuse them of this idea, and assured them that he came to give them protection, and besought them to cease inflicting injury on themselves by setting fire to their beautiful village. A prominent physician came to the dock and sought a conversation with Captain Rowan, who repeated these assurances, which had the effect to stay the further application of the torch. But several of the best buildings were already in flames, among them them the Court House.

"TREASON IN WASHINGTON."

A committee of the Yankee Congress recently appointed to "smell out" treason among the employees of the LINCOLN Government, has reported the following list of persons as "disloyal to the Government of the United States, and in sympathy with the attempt of the rebels to overthrow the present Government." The evidences in these cases, we are assured, "was deemed conclusive by the committee":

Henry Clay Pruess, clerk, War Department.
James M. Wright, clerk, War Department.
James Grosler, clerk, War Department.
Wm. D. Bell, clerk, War Department.
L. M. Morton, clerk, War Department.
T. W. Durnell, clerk, War Department.
Henry Robinson, clerk, War Department.
Patrick Jordan, messenger, War Department.
John S. Conrad, assistant surgeon, Georgetown.
Zephaniah Jones, contractor for the Army.
W. W. Lamee, clerk, War Department.
Jno. Tyler Powell, captain, Volunteers.
Wm. M. Ferguson, captain, National Guards.
Robert P. Dodge, Paymaster, U. S. Army.
John McCobb, clerk to do., U. S. Army.
Lloyd Harrison, Lieutenant, U. S. Army.
—— Throckmorton, Lieutenant, U. S. Army.
John Hollohan, Quartermaster's Dept.
John Thompson, Quartermaster's Dept.
W. W. Jacobs, clerk, War Dept.
Edmund H. Brooke, Paymaster Gen's Bureau.
M. B. Goodwin, Paymaster Gen's Bureau.
Walter Cadmen, Paymaster Gen's Bureau.
John Gould, clerk, War Dept.
Marvin Sheckles, clerk, Quartermaster's Branch.
John O. C. Clark, Quartermaster's Branch.
Harvey Tilden, captain, regular army.
W. O. Williams, lieutenant, regular army.
Richard W. Barnaclo, lieutenant, D. Volunteers.
Daniel Burcher, quartermaster, Maryland brigade.
Ferris T. Hyatt, quartermaster's department.
Thomas A. Delano, quartermaster's department.
Samuel McPherson, wagonmaster, U. S. Army.
C. J. Hamilton, sup. of ambulances.
——— Springman, army teamster.
George Wright, foreman, U. S. Arsenal.
Daniel O'Connell, workman, U. S. Arsenal.
James Goodwin, workman, U. S. Arsenal.
Charles Keller, workman, Arsenal.
Lewis Julian, workman, Arsenal.
Pasco Keller, workman, Arsenal.
Andrew Coyle, firm of Coyle & Brothers, contractors for lumber.
Joseph Troxwell, firm of Morrison & Co., contractors for flour.
John Laird, watchman, Capitol Extension.
Wm. Ashdown, foreman U. S. Arsenal.
——— Nolan, laborer, War Department.
Joseph Ward, watchman, Capitol Extension.

Employed at U. S. Arsenal, Washington, D. C.

Libren Anderson	Alfred Deegle,
Stephen Dudley,	Isaac Miller,
Daniel Moran,	Peter McGuinise,
Henry Dudley,	Lewis Locke,
Benj. Harrison,	Rodney Brooks,
Frederick White, cl'k,	Thomas Simmons.

The New-York Times.

VOL. XI----NO. 3253. NEW-YORK, TUESDAY, FEBRUARY 25, 1862. PRICE TWO CENTS

THE CAMPAIGN IN TENNESSEE.

MORE GOOD NEWS.

Nashville Occupied by General Buell's Forces.

The Tennessee Troops Called in by Gov. Harris.

A Strong Reaction in Favor of the Union.

Flag-Officer Foote's Proclamation to the People of Clarksville.

IMPORTANT ORDER FROM GEN. HALLECK.

ST. LOUIS, Monday, Feb. 24.

A special dispatch from Cairo to the *Democrat* says the latest intelligence from the Cumberland is that Gen. BUELL's forces occupy Nashville; that Gov. HARRIS has called in all the Tennessee troops, and that a strong reaction has occurred among the people.

THE SURRENDER CONFIRMED.

LOUISVILLE, Monday, Feb. 24.

Reliable private information received to-night assures us that Nashville is virtually in possession of the National forces.

THE CITY OF NASHVILLE.

By the capture of Nashville, we obtain possession of the largest city in the rebel States which has yet been occupied by our troops. Nashville, the capital of the State of Tennessee, is a city of 30,000 inhabitants. It is situated on the Cumberland River, 200 miles (following the windings of the stream) above its junction with the Ohio. The city is built chiefly on the south side of the river, on the slopes, and at the foot of a hill rising from it. It stands upon a solid rock, elevated to the height of from 50 to 175 feet above the level of the stream. It is a place of great trade, and is an important railroad centre. There are five railroads radiating from the city, namely: the Tennessee and Alabama, the Louisville and Nashville, the Edgefield and Kentucky, the Nashville and Chattanooga, and the Nashville and Northwestern. Steamboats and *gunboats* ascend from the mouth of the Cumberland to Nashville, and the river is navigable by boats of 1,500 tons for 50 miles above the city, and by smaller boats to the Falls, 500 miles.

Nashville is generally well built, and there are numerous imposing public edifices. One of the finest of the former is the new capitol, situated on an eminence 175 feet above the river, and constructed of a beautiful variety of fossiliferous limestone. It is built in the Grecian style of architecture, cost over a million of dollars, and is considered the handsomest State Capitol in the Union. There are many other fine public buildings. There were at secession time, five daily newspapers, eight weeklies, and eight monthlies.

The commerce of Nashville was very large, and was carried on by river, rail and turnpike. The average annual shipments are 30,000 bales of cotton, beside tobacco, wheat, corn, bacon and hogs. The neighborhood is a famous stock-raising country, and has a high reputation for blood-horses and other stock. The value of taxable property is about $15,000,000.

Twelve miles east from the city is the Hermitage, the famous residence of ANDREW JACKSON, over which will once again be raised the glorious flag which the stern old hero loved. Among the residents of the city is the late JOHN BELL; and there are known, also, to be a strong and more enduring Union element than he was made of.

By the possession of Nashville, taken in connection with our late occupation of Cumberland Gap, and Forts Henry and Donelson, we gain military possession of nearly the entire State of Tennessee. The rebels of the Southwest are now all crowded into Columbus and Memphis. These strongholds, too, must now soon fall.

FROM FORT DONELSON.

COMMODORE FOOTE'S PROCLAMATION TO THE CITIZENS OF CLARKSVILLE, ETC.

CAIRO, Saturday, Feb. 22.

Everything is quiet at Fort Donelson.

The rebels, before evacuating Clarksville, fired a railroad bridge crossing the Cumberland at that point.

Commodore FOOTE issued the following proclamation:

Inhabitants of Clarksville at the suggestion of Hon. CAVE JOHNSON, Judge WISDOM and the Mayor of the city, who called upon me yesterday after our hoisting the Union flag on the forts, to ascertain my views and intentions towards the citizens and private property. I hereby announce to all peaceably disposed persons that neither in their persons nor property shall they suffer molestation by me or by the naval forces under my command, and they may safely resume their business avocations with assurances of my protection. At the same time I require all military stores and army equipments shall be surrendered, no part of them being withheld or destroyed; and further, that no secession flag or manifestation of secession feeling shall be exhibited. And for the faithful observance of these conditions I shall hold the authorities of the city responsible.

(Signed,) ANDREW H. FOOTE.

The Nashville papers advise the undermining of some of the bluffs on the Cumberland River, on the approach of our gunboats, either to destroy them or obstruct the channel.

IMPORTANT ORDER FROM GEN. HALLECK.

ST. LOUIS, Sunday, Feb. 23.

HEADQUARTERS DEPARTMENT OF MISSOURI, Feb. 23.

The Major-General commanding this department desires to impress upon all officers the importance of preserving good order and discipline among their troops. As the armies of the West advance into Tennessee and the Southern States, let us show to our fellow-citizens of these States that we come merely to crush out rebellion and restore to them the peace and benefits of the Constitution and the Union, of which they have been deprived by selfish and unprincipled leaders. They have been told that we come to oppress and plunder. By our acts, we will undeceive. We will prove to them that we come to restore, not to violate the Constitution and the laws. In restoring to them the glorious flag of the Union, we will assure them that they shall enjoy under its folds the same protection of life and property as in former days. Soldiers, let no excess on your part tarnish the glory of our arms.

The orders heretofore issued from this Department in regard to pillaging, marauding and the destruction of private property, and stealing and the concealment of slaves, must be strictly enforced. It does not belong to the military to decide upon the relation of master and slave. Such questions must be settled by the civil Courts. No fugitive slave will be admitted within our lines or camps except when specially ordered by the General commanding.

Women and children, merchants, farmers, mechanics and all persons not in arms are regarded as noncombatants, and are not to be molested, either in their persons or property. If, however, they assist and aid the enemy, they become belligerents, and will be treated as such. As they violate the laws of war, they will be made to suffer the penalties of such violation.

Military stores and public property of the enemy must be surrendered, and any attempt to conceal such property by fraudulent transfer or otherwise, will be punished, but no private property will be touched unless by order of the General commanding.

Whenever it becomes necessary forced contributions for supplies and subsistence for our troops will be made. Such levies will be made as light as possible, and be so distributed as to produce no distress among the people. All property so taken must be receipted fully and accounted for as heretofore directed.

These orders will be read at the head of every regiment, and all officers are commanded to strictly enforce them.

By command of Maj.-Gen. HALLECK.

W. H. McLEAN, A. G.

THE WESTERN VICTORIES.

The Strategy of the Union Army on the Cumberland—Buell's Part in it—McClellan, Buell, Halleck and Grant, Joint Heirs of Fame.

From Our Own Correspondent.

WASHINGTON, Tuesday, Feb. 18, 1862.

In the general joy that diffuses itself through the nation over the brilliant triumph of the Union armies, no jealousies have, so far, been permitted to intrude; but the full measure of honor and praise is freely given to every one of our skillful and heroic Generals who has led his columns to victory. And surely there is glory and fame enough for all. Let each have his full share, for each one feels that he receives a double portion in the generous heartiness with which his brother officers concede his dues.

Your correspondent has already attempted to point out, in a conspicuous manner, the masterly combinations of Gen. McCLELLAN, which have been brought to bear with such crushing effect upon the great rebellion. Gen. McCLELLAN's relation to the war was national, not local and limited; and hence have arisen all the misconceptions of his conduct in the popular mind that have so much wronged him. He had to treat the rebellion as a unit—to comprehend all its vast proportions—to hedge it in, even in its continental area—and to crush it, not only in one State, but everywhere. Hence, while a captious critic was vehement about the army of the Potomac, as if nothing was going amiss except in front of Manassas, Gen. McCLELLAN had to consider every rebel fort, fortress and line of defence, in all the fourteen States engaged in the assault upon the Government, and to prepare his measures, not to beat the enemy in one point only, when they could so easily retreat to another, but to beat them at all points, and by annihilation render their cause irreparable. The pen of history may do justice to Gen. McCLELLAN's strategy, but it can never do justice to the moral heroism with which he has endured the terrific storm of slander and unappeasable abuse that for six weeks has fallen on his devoted head while he was patiently waiting for the readiness of all his preparations and the consummation of his designs.

Gen. GRANT has received a quick and well-deserved acknowledgment of his valiant services at Fort Donelson, in the promotion which the President and Senate have just conferred upon him. Certainly a more gallant and determined officer never led an invincible soldiery to victory, and his *prestige* is second now to that of no General in our army. It is true, he fought with large odds in his favor, but he fought skillfully, persistently, humanely and successfully.

But a third General has a share in the proud fame that has been won on the Cumberland—and so large a share, too, that it is due to him and to the full truth of history, that it should be distinctly known and acknowledged. It neither detracts from the magnitude of McCLELLAN's merits, nor from the renown of GRANT's splendid battle, nor from HALLECK's earnest and sympathetic contribution to victory. The great rebellion is overthrown by the skillful dispositions of the campaign on the Tennessee and Cumberland Rivers; and for the plan of the campaign, as wrought out to such triumphant success, Gen. BUELL, more than any one else, is entitled to the credit. Your correspondent speaks of what he personally knows, and will proceed to relate.

When Gen. BUELL was assigned to the command of the Department of the Ohio, last Fall, he possessed, as he now possesses, the fullest confidence of Gen. McCLELLAN in his military genius and calm bravery. His appointment was McCLELLAN's own work, and shows the latter's prudence and sagacity in the choice of men to execute great trusts. Gen. BUELL was ordered to go to Kentucky—then invaded by the rebels and fortified for their battle line in the West—make himself acquainted with his field of operations, devise such plan of campaign against the enemy as he should find necessary, and report to Gen. McCLELLAN, who promised to support him to the full extent of his demands. Up to this time, the public mind had been directing the campaign in Kentucky solely to an advance through Cumberland Gap into East Tennessee, to seize the Virginia and Tennessee Railroad. Secretary CAMERON, when he visited Gen. SHERMAN at Louisville, the 16th of October, gave Gen. SHERMAN, then commanding in Kentucky, the following directions, as set forth in Adjutant-Gen. THOMAS' rather celebrated report: "He [the Secretary of War] was tired of defensive war. * * He desired that Cumberland Ford and Gap should be seized, and the East Tennessee and Virginia Railroad taken possession of." Gen. MITCHELL, of Cincinnati, was eager to take the head of the column in Kentucky and move in that direction; and because he was not permitted by Gen. SHERMAN to do so, he came to Washington and tendered his resignation to the President of the command of the Ohio Department. A few days subsequently the Western Military Departments were reconstructed, and Gen. BUELL placed in command at Louisville, with such full powers from Gen. McCLELLAN as have been recited. Two evenings before he started to his post, he requested the presence of your Washington correspondent at his house, with a map of the States of Tennessee and Kentucky, of which States the latter had extensive topographical knowledge. Gen. BUELL then proceeded to inquire minutely into all the possible routes of invading Tennessee, and how the enemy's forces were then distributed—which facts, from social reasons, I had kept better than he. Gen. BUELL's first and most careful inquiries were directed to the Cumberland Gap topography, and the feasibility of the scheme recommended by Secretary CAMERON, and urged vehemently by the Press everywhere, through the lively sympathy then felt for the East Tennessee patriots. The mountainous character of the country through which the Gap had to be reached, the roughness of the roads to that place and beyond, rendering the conveyance of artillery so difficult and slow, and subjecting an army, at every mile, to formidable resistance, were dwelt upon, and that direction of advance discouraged. On the other hand, the movement of troops from Cairo up the Cumberland River, by transports and gunboats, against Nashville, so as to get in the rear of BUCKNER's army, was urged as the only mode of successfully breaking the rebel line and compelling their evacuation of Kentucky. The success of this movement might, moreover, insure the loss of their army at Bowling Green. A gentleman of Gen. McCLELLAN's Staff (Col. T. T. GANTT) was present at this interview, and gave a ready indorsement to the merit of the suggestions. The only doubt raised at the time was whether the gunboats then building to descend the Mississippi would not be of too heavy draft to be used on the Cumberland, and whether or not Gen. HALLECK, a Major-General, would be willing to detail so large a part of his army (40,000 was the number indicated as necessary) to help execute a leading part in the campaign of Gen. BUELL, who was only a Brigadier.

There the interview closed, and Gen. BUELL in two days left for the West, taking with him *the map on which the movements had been traced.* Not long afterwards your correspondent wrote to Gen. BUELL, reviving this subject and suggesting to him—to save any offence to Gen. HALLECK, to refer the proposed plan to headquarters, and let the order be issued from Washington for the "coöperation of the two Departments in executing it. Gen. BUELL replied to this letter (the *date* should be noted) as follows:

LOUISVILLE, Dec. 3, 1861.

MY DEAR SIR: * * * To any one who has occasion to study the matter in hand as I have, your views cannot fail to have force. *Coöperation is the important thing,* and THAT I AM TRYING TO EFFECT. Secrecy is hardly less important, and so I hope that no plan of operations in Kentucky will be discussed, lest it should suggest as much to the enemy as to ourselves. *I wish the public to forget awhile that we are here.* Truly yours, D. C. BUELL.

In conformity with this suggestion of quietness and secrecy, qualities that so remarkably distinguish Gen. BUELL, the fact of his labors in this direction has never before been mentioned publicly. But that he did seize upon this plan of a campaign, and that he matured and presented it to headquarters; that it was thoroughly approved by Gen. McCLELLAN, and every facility given to combine and effect it, is a truth that their correspondence on the subject fully attests. A few days before Gen. McCLELLAN was taken sick, (about the first of the year,) the member of his Staff who was present at the first interview on this subject with Gen. BUELL, indicated to your correspondent that Gen. McCLELLAN wished some further data in regard to the probable rise of water in the Cumberland River, and suggested that I should call to see him. But his illness became so severe that the meeting did not take place, and the bank-full condition of the Cumberland soon solved all remaining doubts. The brilliant realization of all that Gen. BUELL hoped for from the "coöperation" he was "trying to effect," and *did* effect, is before the world. The plan was simple—irresistible. It was the hurling of the entire force of two of the most powerful military departments in the country upon the weak point of the enemy's lines. *The plan was Buell's*; it was a part of Gen. McCLELLAN's circle of assault; the hearty coöperation was HALLECK's, and the imperishable, blood-bought glory of battle is GRANT's. There is honor and fame enough in this great achievement to satisfy the utmost ambition of all the Generals dividing it. Long may their laurels be green, and long may they live to enjoy the plaudits of a grateful country! YORK.

The Expedition up the Tennessee and Cumberland—The Great Strategic Plan of the Campaign—Justice to Brig.-Gen. D. C. Buell.

From Another Correspondent.

WASHINGTON, Saturday, Feb. 22, 1862.

Justice to one of the most valuable officers in the American army, seems to render it proper for me to say what follows. The expedition up the Tennessee and Cumberland rivers has, beyond doubt, been the great master-stroke of military strategy in the war. It has broken the back of the rebellion, and that rebellion, however it may linger in pain for a time, must die. Flag-Officer FOOTE has won laurels, and Gen. GRANT a Major-Generalship, in the execution of this great plan. Gen. HALLECK has won honors, and Gen. HUNTER has been publicly thanked. All this is well. I would not detract from the honors of any.

But to what military man is due the credit of the great plan itself? To Brig.-Gen. D. C. BUELL, commanding the Department of the Ohio. For two months has that officer been urging this plan upon those without whose coöperation it could not be carried out. Not more than a fortnight after Gen. BUELL's arrival at his headquarters in Louisville, *his mind was made up that an expedition should be sent up the Tennessee and Cumberland, in the main features of the plan the same as has been adopted.* Circumstances outside of his plan, and for which he was not responsible, prevented his forces from being as near Bowling Green at the time of its evacuation, as he might have desired; but the strategy which forced the evacuation of a position almost impregnable at the season needs no apology.

The plan of Gen. BUELL could not, however, be carried out without the coöperation of the gunboat flotilla, which did not belong to Gen. B.'s command. And another masterly feature of this great plan was the concentration of the forces of Gens. HALLECK and BUELL upon the rebel centre. To obtain this combination of forces, and to secure the coöperation of the fleet, it was necessary to await the readiness of Gen. HALLECK's command. The gunboats had to be got ready; and, as I wrote you from Paducah some time ago, the whole great Western movement was delayed for the completion of these boats and their readiness for action.

In the meantime, Gen. BUELL repeatedly suggested his plan, and asked for the desired coöperation. At length he obtained what he desired, and the plan was carried out substantially as he had proposed. I speak what I know, and could go much *deeper* into the matter if I saw proper. While, therefore, Gen. GRANT and Flag-Officer FOOTE are entitled to their honors, and other officers to theirs, let Gen. BUELL receive the credit which is due a great master of strategy for the plan of the campaign.

Under the circumstances, I regret to see an item like the following, in a late number of the *Tribune*:

"A telegram from Louisville in our last apprised us that Maj.-Gen. BUELL and his staff were on Monday evening regaled with a sumptuous feast at the Galt House in honor of the capture of Fort Donelson. Had Gen. B. been one of those Generals who know what this war is about, we think he would not have been in Louisville on Monday evening, but with the advance divisions of his army, somewhere across Green River. Unless the rebels are utterly 'gone in,' there is likely to be fighting down there about these days."

The dispatch only spoke of a supper *tendered*. Gen. BUELL is one of the most laborious workers in the army. Scarce a night finds him in bed before 2 or 3 o'clock in the morning. Anybody can tender Gen. BUELL a supper; but did he eat it? From my knowledge of that officer, I should say he was very certain not to neglect his duties five minutes for any occasion of carousal whatever. When he came to Kentucky, he found not more than 20,000 effective drilled troops under his command. The reinforcements sent him were almost universally raw recruits; and while he waited for the coöperation above spoken of, and for transportation, he has organized them into an efficient army.

It so happened, by some means, that though the Tennessee River expedition was sent at Gen. BUELL's instance, he was not notified of any immediate intention to send it until it was already on its way up the river. The rapid rebel concentration on the Cumberland rendered it necessary for Gen. B. to send large reinforcements in that direction; and he remained some days in Louisville superintending that movement. TENNESSEEAN.

COLUMBUS NOT EVACUATED.

ST. LOUIS, Monday, Feb. 24.

The *Republican's* Cairo dispatch says that the reports about the evacuation of Columbus are entirely false. The rebels are still there in strong force. None of the garrison has been withdrawn, and they evidently intend making a desperate stand there.

IMPORTANT FROM FORT MONROE

Release of Cols. Lee, Wood and Cogswell, and Other Union Prisoners.

A Gloomy Time at Jeff. Davis' Inauguration.

THE FALL OF NASHVILLE REPORTED.

A Victory Claimed for Price at Sugar Creek.

Telegraphic Communication with Fort Monroe.

BALTIMORE, Monday, Feb. 24.

The Old Point boat has arrived here, having left Fortress Monroe yesterday.

She brings fourteen released officers, including Col. WOOD, of the Fourteenth (Brooklyn) New-York Regiment, who was wounded and captured at the battle of Bull Run; Col. LEE, of the Twentieth Massachusetts Regiment, captured at Ball's Bluff; Col. COGSWELL, of the Tammany Regiment; and Capt. KEFFER, of BAKER's California Regiment.

Col. WOOD was paroled, and had the liberty of moving about the City of Richmond previous to leaving. He was present at the inauguration of JEFF. DAVIS, and states that *no enthusiasm was manifested on the occasion, hardly a cheer being raised.*

Col. LEE, of the Massachusetts Twentieth, says that just before leaving Richmond, on Saturday evening, he was taken aside by a distinguished officer of the rebel Government, who privately assured him that *an official dispatch had just been received of the fall of Nashville.*

FORTRESS MONROE, Sunday, Feb. 23, via Baltimore, Monday, Feb. 24.

The steamship *Adelaide*, from Baltimore, did not arrive until 10 o'clock last night.

The *Georgianna* came in at her usual time this morning.

Both will return to Baltimore to-night.

The *Adelaide* brought down the rest of the Sixth Wisconsin Regiment, and conveyed them to Newport's News this morning.

Gen. JOHN E. WOOL, with Col. CANNON and Major JONES, of his Staff, went with the steamer *Rancocas*, this morning, under a flag of truce, to meet by appointment Gen. HOWELL COBB, off Craney Island, for the purpose of opening negotiations for a general exchange of prisoners.

The *Rancocas* became disabled, however, after proceeding some distance, and having put back to Fortress Monroe, the steamer *Adelaide* was taken for a substitute.

The *Adelaide* was met by the *William Selden*, and Gen. WOOL having stepped on board the latter a consultation of about an hour in length took place between the two Generals.

The result of the interview is not known.

The *Hoboken*, with the submarine cable to be laid across the Bay, did not leave until about 2½ o'clock this afternoon.

A connection having been made between the cable and the land-wire at its terminus on Beach Grove, above the fort, constant communication is had between the *Hoboken* and Gen. WOOL's headquarters.

Everything was progressing satisfactorily up to 4 o'clock this afternoon, when Mr. HEISS telegraphed that he had proceeded about five miles out.

There is no doubt about the line being successfully laid, and if the weather is favorable, the line will be open to-morrow forenoon.

The *George Washington* left at half past 9 o'clock this morning for the James River, to receive about 390 released Union prisoners.

She has now (5 o'clock) returned. The released prisoners go to Baltimore to-night. Among them are Cols. COGSWELL, LEE and WOOD, Lieut. HARRIS, and about a dozen other officers; also the crews of the schooner *Ocilla*, captured in the Gulf of Mexico on the 1st of November, and the brig *Elsinore*.

The largest number of the prisoners returned belong to the Tammany and First California Regiments.

A large proportion of the prisoners were captured at Ball's Bluff.

There are now no Union prisoners remaining at Richmond.

The released prisoners left Richmond last night, but the boat got aground and did not reach the rendezvous until about 3 o'clock this afternoon.

The whole number of released prisoners is about three hundred and ninety.

A few copies of Richmond papers are received, from which the following news is obtained:

A dispatch dated Fort Smith, via Clarksville, Ark., and Chattanooga, Tenn., says that Gens. PRICE and HERBERT are fighting the enemy, to-day, at Sugar Creek, in Benton County, Ark. The result is not known. Our troops are confident of success.

LATER.—The enemy lost 700 men, and our loss is 100. We have gained another great victory.

(Signed) ALBERT PIKE.

The Richmond *Dispatch* is lauding Gen. PRICE for his great victory as announced in ALBERT PIKE's dispatch.

The Richmond *Whig*, of Friday, has a bitter article on the Davis Administration. It says:

"Judging by results so far, *it is the most lamentable failure in history*, and suggests to the reflecting mind, that the most signal service which that Government can now render to the country is *the surrender of the helm to abler and better hands*. In view of the past, the present and probable future, *the pageant of to-morrow is a bitter mockery, and a miserable compensation for the ruin of a free people*. A child with a bauble—an old man with a young wife, are partial illustrations of the deplorable folly."

The *Dispatch* contains the programme for the inauguration ceremonies; also a proclamation of JEFF. DAVIS announcing Friday, the 28th inst., as a day of fasting, humiliation and prayer.

The surrender of Savannah was rumored at Richmond.

FURTHER FROM FORTRESS MONROE.

BALTIMORE, Tuesday, Feb. 24.

The released prisoners say that the Captain of the steamer that brought them stated that he expected another party of prisoners to be waiting for him on his return to City Point. They were from Salisbury, North Carolina, and Alabama. The next lot to come after these will be those from Charleston and Columbia, South Carolina, including Col. CORCORAN, who might be expected on Thursday or Friday. The party who came to-day includes all who were in Richmond except three, who were too sick to be removed. The following are the officers:

Col. M. Coggswell, Forty second New-York; Wm. R. Lee, Twentieth Massachusetts; Col. A. M. Wood, Fourteenth New-York; Maj. Paul Revere, Twentieth Massachusetts; Surgeon E. H. Revere, Twentieth Massachusetts; Capt. Henry Bowman, Fifteenth Massachusetts; Capt. F. J. Keller, First California; Capt. G. W. Rockwood, Fifteenth Massachusetts; Capt. R. Williams, Twelfth Indiana; Lieut. J. C. Freeman, First Virginia; Lieut. J. E. Guerre, Fifteenth Massachusetts; Lieut. Wm. Harris, First California; Lieut. B. F. Hancock, Nineteenth Indiana; Lieut. E. B. Hull, First Virginia; W. E. Merrill, Engineer Corps, U. S. A.; W. B. Vassells, Fifteenth Massachusetts, and Lieut. George H. Wallace, Forty-second New-York.

The whole party went to Washington this afternoon, after spending a merry day with the Union men of Baltimore. Col. LEE says information was given him about the surrender of Nashville, by a prominent citizen of Richmond, not by an officer of the rebel Government, and that a dispatch was received by JEFF. DAVIS whilst reading his inaugural.

The prisoners all speak of a strong Union Party in Richmond, who are in high glee at the Union victories. They were compelled, for their own safety, to keep quiet, but took frequent occasion to make their sentiments known to the prisoners, extending to them various acts of kindness, which had to be stealthily performed.

There was a large attendance to witness the inauguration, but the enthusiasm was very subdued. Those who were on parole could not get near enough to hear the address, and it was not printed before they left.

The Savannah *Republican*, of Wednesday last, says:

"Notwithstanding the hostile demonstrations of the enemy and the show of formidable preparations for an attack on this point, no material change in the attitude of affairs has taken place during the past few days. Some twenty vessels are still at anchor off our Skidaway batteries, about the same number as formerly are to be seen in the vicinity of Wallscut and Mud River. One or two of the latter have advanced a little higher up, or nearer the main channel. Small boats prowl about in the river between Fort Jackson and Fort Pulaski, but keep at a respectful distance from the guns of either fort. Our telegraphic communication is effectually cut off from the latter fort, and water communication has to be maintained under the fire of their gunboats and a floating raft battery which the enemy have established near Venus Point, and which effectually commands the river. Gunboat skirmishes are of almost hourly occurrence.

THE BURNSIDE EXPEDITION.

Operations Renewed by the National Forces.

Occupation of Winton on the Chowan River.

A REBEL BATTERY SHELLED OUT.

The Richmond *Dispatch*, of Saturday, has the following:

"SUFFOLK, Va.- Friday, Feb. 21.

Capt. NICHOLS, of the Petersburgh Artillery, arrived here this afternoon from Winton, where he had been stationed with a battery. On yesterday he was shelled out by the Yankees. They had seven steamers, all of which had passed up the river. Capt. NICHOLS had a horse shot from under him. Two of his men were wounded. The town of Winton is in ashes. Our troops retreat to Murfreesborough."

Another dispatch, dated Norfolk, 21st inst., says:

"The Federal forces again ascended the Chowan River yesterday to Winton, with several gunboats and a large number of troops. The Confederates opened a heavy fire upon them. The Yankees landed and burnt the town. The Southerners retired. Our loss is said to be two men. The humbug Congressman, C. H. FOSTER, was among the killed Yankees."

PRISONERS AT LOUISVILLE.

LOUISVILLE, Monday, Feb. 24.

The steamer *Argonaut*, from Cairo, arrived from Jeffersonville this afternoon, with 194 of the Fort Donelson prisoners, including Gen. BUCKNER and Staff. They were in charge of a detachment of National soldiers, under command of Capt. WALKER, and were sent to Indianapolis by special train this afternoon.

THE GUNBOAT ESSEX.

ST. LOUIS, Monday, Feb. 24.

The gunboat *Essex* arrived from Cairo to-day. She will immediately be put on the ways, 50 feet added to her length, her machinery lowered into the hold, and repaired throughout in the most thorough manner.

Capt. PORTER, who came on the *Essex*, is improving rapidly. His face and hands are pretty severely scalded, but he inhaled no steam, and will be ready for duty soon again.

RELEASE OF FORT WARREN PRISONERS.

BOSTON, Monday, Feb. 24.

Many of the Fort Warren prisoners were released on Saturday, on their taking the oath of allegiance, agreeable to a late order from Washington.

The following, however, declined their liberty, except on unconditional terms: Wm. G. Harrison, Wm. H. Winder, Henry M. Warfield, and W. H. Getchell. It is thought the fort will hold out as long as they do.

M. W. BARR was among the released.

THE PROBABILITIES.

The correspondent of the Philadelphia *Ledger* telegraphs from Washington:

"It is rumored on fair authority, that a movement is on foot to induce the Government to consent to an armistice, with a view to the assembling of a Convention of the States, in hope that some satisfactory conclusion of the war might be reached and the Union once more restored to its original beauty and integrity. From all that I can learn, however, I do not think that such a movement will be successful, though it is by no means improbable but what the South, in its present dilemma, would quickly agree to the proposition.

Quite a large number of the prisoners recently liberated by the rebels, arrived here this morning for the purpose of receiving their back pay.

The intelligence of the spread of the Union feeling at Nashville, and the probable peaceful surrender of the city, has induced several families from thence, but lately residing here, to make preparations for their return, which they will do on the first appearance of actual safety to their persons and property.

Per contra, advices have been received here to the effect that the rebels, headed by BEAUREGARD and JOHNSON, will certainly make a stand at that point, and defend the city wherever assailed. The rebels claim to have 70,000 troops in Nashville, while its approaches, they say, are fortified so strongly as to defy assault.

COL. ANNISANSEL.

An order issued by Secretary STANTON relative to Col. ANNISANSEL whom Gen. LANDER accused of cowardice in the recent brilliant affair at Blooming Gap, has already been published. The Wheeling *Intelligencer* gives the following sequel to the affair:

Gen. LANDER has concluded to suspend the death penalty, and that he will simply disgrace the recreant Colonel by depriving him of his sword and commission, and ordering him forthwith out of his military jurisdiction.

Col. ANNISANSEL is what is known as a Franco-Swiss-man by birth—that is, he was born in the French part of Switzerland. He has been in this country several years, and was until recently a teacher of music at Cannonsburg and Pleasant Hill Female Seminaries in Washington County, Pennsylvania. He was indefatigable in getting up the First Virginia cavalry, and everybody supposed that he meant "business" in so doing. But it would seem that he intended simply, like a good many others, to feather his cap and his nest.

Destructive Fire in Boston.

BOSTON, Monday, Feb. 24.

A destructive fire broke out at 9½ o'clock this evening, in MATTHEW's Block, a large five-story granite structure, between Commercial and North streets, and Clark and Fleet streets. The block was totally destroyed. Owing to the high wind the flames extended across Commercial-street to SARGEANT's Wharf, sweeping every building from the wharf. The fire is still burning. Loss estimated at $500,000.

IMPORTANT FROM THE SOUTH.

How the Fall of Fort Donelson is Received.

Shrieks of Wrath from the Rebel Press.

Lessons to be Learned from Northern Perseverance.

The Rebels Whistling to Keep their Courage Up.

A Warning Against the Foreign Residents of Richmond.

THE FALL OF FORT DONELSON.

AN OUTBURST FROM THE REBEL PRESS—"THE BLOODY BARBARIANS."

From the Richmond Dispatch, Feb. 19.

After three days of the most desperate fighting ever witnessed on this continent, (so declares a veteran regular officer,) the most desperate fighting against the most tremendous odds, in which day after day the multitudinous host of invaders were driven back past their own camps, our glorious Spartan band, from sheer exhaustion, has been borne down by a new avalanche of reinforcements piled upon the already enormous weight against which they have hitherto struggled with complete success, and has suffered one of those misfortunes which are common to war, but which entail no dishonor on our cause, and which will only animate to the most stern and undying resistance every true Southern heart.

If these bloody barbarians, whose hands are now soaked to the elbows in the life-blood of men defending their own homes and firesides, dream that they are now one inch nearer the subjugation of the South than when they started on their infernal mission, they prove themselves to be fools and madmen, as well as savages and murderers. They have taught us a lesson, we admit; they have admonished us to be more wary and circumspect, to husband with greater care our limited resources, and not to underrate our enemy.

But they have also placed between them and us a gulf that can never be crossed by their arts or arms, and a universal determination to die, if die we must, for our country, but never permit her to be subjugated by the most malignant, the most murderous, the meanest of mankind, whose name is at this very moment such a by-word of scorn and reproach throughout Europe, for their combined cruelty and cowardice, that their own ambassadors cannot stand the scorn of the world's contempt, and are all anxious to fly back to the United States.

Their success at Fort Donelson, gained only by vast superiority of numbers, will only have the effect of converting the whole population of the South—men, women and children—into an immense army, who will resist them at every step, and everywhere "welcome them with bloody hands to hospitable graves." The glorious valor of our troops at Fort Donelson is not dimmed in the slightest degree by their inability to hold their ground against overwhelming odds: but, on the contrary, shines through the black clouds of disaster with a radiance which will kindle the whole South into a blaze, and surround their own names with a halo of imperishable venom.

THE CRISIS.

From the Richmond Dispatch.

The crisis of the war is upon us, and reverse upon reverse comes in quick succession. We have scarcely recovered from the depression consequent upon our defeat at Fort Henry and Roanoke, ere we are called upon to meet a still heavier calamity in the fall of Fort Donelson, and the surrender of our brave troops holding that important post. It is true the facts concerning this last disaster have not yet reached us from sources entitled to belief; but enough is known to convince us that we have sustained another staggering blow.

We have not been of those who entertained the belief that our arms would always be successful, or that it was within the bounds of possibility our small army could meet and drive back the overwhelming hordes of the enemy at every point at which they could penetrate, and are not, therefore, taken by surprise, nor greatly discouraged, by the untoward events which have taken place in the West and on the Atlantic coast. We have not known our own strength, although we have been greatly too confident of the weakness and cowardice of our foe. If these disasters shall turn our thoughts in upon ourselves, and shall arouse us to the full comprehension of our perilous situation, and to the energy and activity requisite for the occasion, they will not have overtaken us in vain.

We do not believe the defeat at Fort Donelson is of the proportion our telegraphic columns would give us to understand. It must be remembered, the intelligence they furnish comes from the enemy, who are not apt to depreciate the victories they gain. And we see much to encourage us even in this dark hour. Our permanent Government is launched upon the stormy sea, it is true, but we think her timbers are stout enough to bear the strain, and that the noble structure will be none the worse for the rough usage to which it has thus early been subjected.

The War Department received, on Monday evening, from Gen. A. S. JOHNSTON, a telegram, announcing the fall of Fort Donelson, but couched in so ambiguous a style that it becomes necessary to request more intelligible information. No answer has as yet been received from that officer, probably on account of the interruption of telegraphic communication, occasioned by the severity of the weather.

A BLAST FROM THE ENQUIRER.

From the Richmond Enquirer, Feb. 19.

The fortitude of our people is again to be tried, and the metal of which their courage is made once more to be tested, by the last news from Fort Donelson. We have met with heavy disaster there. The wretches who are invading our country were enabled, by the facilities of river transportation, to bring up reinforcements to their previously whipped troops, and have overwhelmed us with numbers. We are without the necessary facts and explanations to justify comment upon the tragedy of last Sunday. We have had experience enough already to show the folly of premature criticisms. We must have *patience*. Such reports as have reached us are chiefly from the North, and are given in the telegraphic column.

But this thing we must do. By the mangled body of every man who fell at the hands of the scoundrel murderers who have invaded the country of those who never did them any harm—by the homes which we have established by our industry—by the beautiful land which we have inherited from our fathers—by the families that we love—by all that is noble and patriotic and brave, and in the fear and fervently invoking the favor of God—we must all resolve, in our inmost souls, and vow with an irrevocable vow, that we will resist the enemy to the last extremity, and that we will die if we cannot live freemen!

And this vow we must set about making good. Let cowards tremble, if they will! Let vile niggards count their treasures in agony. But what brave or generous citizen would wish to survive the ruin of his country? Who would desire to live when odious and vulgar despots have foot upon our necks? No, fellow-citizens, let us, as did our fathers, pledge our honor to each other and to the world, that our lives and our fortunes shall be devoted to the vindication of our liberties; and that, if these are lost, not shall survive the wreck, for nothing would be worth saving!

Courage, then, people of the Confederate States! You have now one of those "opportunities" which, if improved, make nations famous, and make brave men renowned! History awaits our action to make up the record of glory or infamy. Any man can be brave when there is no danger. Any soldier can be enthusiastic when cheered by a round of successes. It is *adversity* that *tries men's souls*, and distinguishes between the true man and the false—the genuine and the counterfeit! Let us as individuals and let us a people, seize this opportunity for true glory. Let us stimulate each other's courage, and emulate each other's zeal! If one man falls let two step forward to take his place! This fight must be redeemed. We *will* have the victory!

What if we have reverses? 'Tis the fate of war; a war without disasters is a winter without storms. But we will bear them like patriots and brave men, and, both in our fortitude and our daring, we will show ourselves worthy to be free. If we do not, we do not *deserve* to be free.

Of the extent of the disaster which we have suffered at Donelson, we are very uncertain. We must believe that the Federal account is greatly exaggerated.

The wires were not working yesterday to Nashville, after the morning. The War Department received no news, save a dispatch from Gen. A. S. JOHNSTON in the morning. He was at Nashville. *Gen. Floyd was there also, with a portion of the Fort Donelson command. The dispatch said "he had saved a thousand."* The number captured by the enemy can

The New-York Times.

VOL. XI—NO. 3262. NEW-YORK, FRIDAY, MARCH 7, 1862. PRICE TWO CENTS

IMPORTANT FROM WASHINGTON.

A Message from President Lincoln.

Proposition to Aid the Border States in the Gradual Abolishment of Slavery.

Government Opposition to the Designs of the Allies in Mexico.

Another Finance Measure from the House Committee of Ways and Means.

The Publication of the Fremont Documents.

ALEXANDER CUMMINGS' DEFENCE.

Army and Navy Promotions and Confirmations.

MESSAGE FROM PRESIDENT LINCOLN.

WASHINGTON, Thursday, March 6.

The President to-day submitted to Congress the following Message:

Fellow-citizens of the Senate and House of Representatives:

I recommend the adoption of a joint resolution by your honorable bodies, which shall be substantially as follows:

Resolved, That the United States ought to coöperate with any State which may adopt a gradual abolishment of Slavery, *giving to such State pecuniary aid*, to be used by such State in its discretion, to compensate for the inconveniences, public and private, produced by such change of system.

If the proposition contained in the resolution does not meet the approval of Congress and the country, there is the end; but if it does command such approval, I deem it of importance that the States and people immediately interested *should be at once distinctly notified of the fact, so that they may begin to consider whether to accept or reject it.*

The Federal Government would find its highest interest in such a measure, as one of the most efficient means of self-preservation. The leaders of the existing insurrection entertain the hope that the Government will ultimately be forced to acknowledge the independence of some part of the disaffected region, and that all the Slave States north of such parts will then say, "The Union, for which we have struggled, being already gone, we now choose to go with the Southern section." *To deprive them of this hope substantially ends the rebellion*, and the initiation of emancipation completely deprives them of it, as to all the States initiating it. The point is not that all the States tolerating Slavery would very soon, if at all, initiate emancipation, but that while the offer is equally made to all, the more Northern shall, by such initiation, make it certain to the more Southern that *in no event will the former ever join the latter in their proposed Confederacy.* I say "initiation," because, in my judgment, gradual and not sudden emancipation is better for all.

In the mere financial or pecuniary view any member of Congress, with the census tables and the Treasury reports before him, can readily see for himself, how soon the current expenditures of this war, would purchase, at a fair valuation, all the slaves in any named State.

Such a proposition on the part of the General Government, *sets up no claim of a right by Federal authority to interfere with Slavery* within State limits, referring, as it does, the absolute control of the subject in each case, to the State and its people immediately interested. It is proposed as a matter of *perfectly free choice* with them.

In the annual Message last December I thought fit to say: "The Union must be preserved, and hence all indispensable means must be employed." I said this not hastily, but deliberately. War has been, and continues to be, an indispensable means to this end. A practical reacknowledgment of the National authority would render the war unnecessary, and it would at once cease. *If, however, resistance continues, the war must also continue*, and it is impossible to foresee all the incidents which may attend and all the ruin which may follow it. Such as may seem indispensable or may obviously promise great efficiency toward ending the struggle, must and will come.

The proposition now made, though an offer only, I hope it may be esteemed no offence to ask whether the pecuniary consideration tendered would not be of more value to the States and private persons concerned than are the institution and property in it, in the present aspect of affairs.

While it is true that the adoption of the proposed resolution would be merely initiatory, and not within itself a practical measure, it is recommended in the hope that it would soon lead to important results. In full view of my great responsibility to my God and to my Country, I earnestly beg the attention of Congress and the people to the subject.

(Signed,) ABRAHAM LINCOLN.

OUR SPECIAL WASHINGTON DISPATCHES.

WASHINGTON, Thursday, March 6.

HOW THE PRESIDENT'S MESSAGE WAS RECEIVED.

The President's Message to Congress to-day creates profound interest. The friends of the Union's reconstruction are delighted and strengthened, while the radicals are proportionately distressed. But the latter have been obviously downhearted for several days. Nothing remains for them but to give up their principles and to keep their share of the offices, or to assail the Administration and lose their comfortable places. It is a dilemma that will be differently met by different moral organizations.

It was evident that a document of such an important character was not generally anticipated. The reading was called for by Mr. STEVENS, of Pennsylvania, and, on his motion, referred to the Committee of the Whole on the State of the Union, in which it will be discussed. Some of the members apparently not fully understanding it, as pronounced from the desk, perused the manuscript at their seats. The subject therein discussed forms to-night a theme of earnest conversations. The message of a similar character transmitted to the Senate was not read.

THE SECRETARY OF STATE ON MEXICAN AFFAIRS.

The Secretary of State is preparing a dispatch on the subject of Mexican affairs, in which the determination of the United States to resist the designs of European Powers to establish monarchial institutions on this continent will be energetically set forth. It will be laid before the Committee on Foreign Affairs of both Houses, with the other papers that are soon to be submitted.

THE DEFENCE OF GEN. FREMONT.

Every witness who testified before the Committee on the Conduct of the War was put upon his honor not to reveal his evidence before them. The publication, therefore, of Gen. FREMONT's evidence in the *Tribune*, when the Committee only last Saturday unanimously resolved that it should not be done, creates the greatest amazement. The papers of the Committee have not been violated, for they were examined to-day, and found sealed as they were first filed. As Gen. FREMONT's friends here freely censure the breach of privilege and honor, the *Tribune* will be compelled to relieve Gen. FREMONT of any responsibility in the premises, if the facts will allow it.

THE CAVALRY FORCE.

The statement that by the reduction and reorganization of the cavalry force a large increase of the expense of this corps would result, is untrue. I am authorized to state by the Senate Military Committee, the reduction in the expenses in the cavalry corps, by reducing the regiments to forty, will be about three millions dollars per annum. The entire expense of mounting, equipping and supporting a cavalry regiment for one year is $680,000.

THE PURCHASE OF COIN.

The bill reported from the Committee of Ways and Means to-day authorizing the purchase of coin and for other purposes, provides that the Secretary of the Treasury may dispose of any bonds or notes bearing interest authorized by law, for coin, at such rates and upon such terms as he may deem most advantageous to the public interest, and may issue under such rules and regulations as he may prescribe certificates of indebtedness such as were authorized by the act "to authorize the Secretary of the Treasury to issue certificates of indebtedness to public creditors," approved March 1, 1862, to such creditors as may desire to receive the same in the discharge of checks drawn by disbursing officers upon sums placed to their credit on the books of the Treasurer, upon requisitions of the proper Department, as well as in the discharge of audited and settled accounts, as provided by said act. It is further provided that the Demand Notes authorized by the act of July 17, 1861, and by the act of Feb. 12, 1862, shall be receivable and shall be lawful money and legal tender in like manner, and for the same purposes, and to the same extent, as the notes authorized by the act to authorize the issue of United States Notes, and for the redemption or funding thereof, and for funding the floating debt of the United States, approved on the 25th of last month.

FUNERAL OF GEN. LANDER.

The military display attendant on the funeral of Brig.-Gen. LANDER this afternoon was large and impressive. A number of the most distinguished gentlemen connected with the army, navy and civil positions were present. Flags everywhere are at half-mast.

PROMOTIONS FOR GALLANT CONDUCT.

The President, in addition to other officers promoted for gallant conduct, has nominated Brig.-Gen. THOMAS to be a Major-General, as a recognition of his late eminent services in Kentucky. Also Col. HARVEY BROWN to be a Brigadier-General by brevet; Major ARNOLD to be Lieutenant-Colonel by brevet; Capt. HILDT to be Major by brevet; Major TOWER to be Lieutenant-Colonel by brevet; Capts. Allen, Chalfin, Closson, Robertson, Blunt, Duryea and Langdon to be Majors by brevet; and First Lieuts. McFarland, Shipley, Jackson, Pennington, Seely, Frank E. Taylor and Todd to be Captains by brevet.

APPOINTMENTS IN THE NAVY CONFIRMED.

Capts. BELL, MCKEAN, DUPONT, GOLDSBOROUGH and FARRAGUT were to-day confirmed by the Senate as Flag-Officers of the Navy, and J. J. WITZIG, E. M. SHIELD and THOMAS B. STILLMAN as Inspectors of Steamboats.

POSTMASTERS CONFIRMED.

The following were confirmed as Postmasters: B. L. Cult, Hannibal, Mo.; T. Good, Allentown, Penn.; L. Smith, Watertown, N. Y.; P. H. Agan, Syracuse, N. Y.; D. R. Bacon, Leroy, N. Y.; C. O. Eastman, Claremont, N. H.; T. K. Ware, Fitchburgh, Mass.

CONSULS CONFIRMED.

The following named Consuls were confirmed: J. R. Fairlamb, at Zurich; H. Young, Santa Cruz; Alexander Henderson, Londonderry; Charles H. Edwards, Alicante; Abraham Hanson, Bissao; Elias Wample, Laguayra; Thomas Spencer, Hilo; Wm. H. Evans, Cyprus.

COLLECTORS CONFIRMED.

The following were confirmed as Collectors of the Customs: Wm. H. Mills, at Pass del Norte; L. Haven, Chicago; J. E. Stalker, Annapolis, Md.; Wm. L. Ashmore, Burlington, N. J.; Charles A. Perkins, Oswego, N. Y.; Charles T. Swift, Barnstable, Mass.; Nathaniel T. Sargeant, Kennebec, Me. And the following as Surveyors of the Customs: Geo. Howland, Tiverton; W. W. Gorton, Patuxet, R. I.; W. Thornberry, Paducah, Ky.; J. R. Meeker, Nosqually, Washington Territory.

OTHER CONFIRMATIONS.

The following were also confirmed: C. W. Chatterson, Indian Agent, Cherokee Agency; C. H. Hale, Superintendent of Indian Affairs, Washington Territory; Thomas S. Nelson, Recorder of Land Titles in Missouri; S. R. Juneson, Receiver of Public Moneys for Nebraska; H. Stout, Attorney, and J. L. Gibbs, Marshal, of Utah; E. D. Shuttuck, Attorney for Oregon; W. Wasson, Marshal for Nevada.

In addition to the above, a large number of army nominations were confirmed, but none of field officers.

MR. FOSTER OF NORTH CAROLINA.

CHARLES HENRY FOSTER has returned to Washington, and again presented his petition for a seat as member from the Second Congressional District of North Carolina. The case is before the Committee on Elections.

POSTAL MATTERS.

Postal communication is entirely reopened to Accomac and Northampton Counties, Virginia.

The Post-office Department is ready to establish, as soon as Congress shall give the authority, free delivery in cities with uniform rates of postage for local and general letters.

[*See Eighth Page for Proceedings of Congress.*]

EUROPE AND MEXICO.

INTERESTING STATEMENTS AND DEVELOPMENTS FROM MR. EDWARD E. DUNBAR.

Correspondence of the New-York Times.

WASHINGTON, Wednesday, March 5, 1862.

Last evening there was quite a large social gathering of Senators, Representatives and other gentlemen who take a special interest in our foreign relations, at the residence of Mr. EDWARD E. DUNBAR, of New-York, now temporarily sojourning in Washington.

Mr. DUNBAR entertained his company with a most interesting account of the European coalition against Mexico. In his remarks, Mr. DUNBAR stated that while Spain was preparing to conquer Mexico on her own account, erect a monarchy and place a Spanish Prince on the throne, England proposed a tripartite coalition against Mexico to NAPOLEON, who at first declined, but finally yielded, believing, in common with other European statesmen, that the American Union was irretrievably broken; and England having conceded to him his plan of establishing an Austrian Duke on the Mexican throne, in consideration of which, Austria was to cede Venetia to Italy and the latter country to cede the island of Sardinia to France, Spain was obliged to enter into the tripartite alliance, but she knew nothing of the programme agreed upon by England and France, and which she will, doubtless, strenuously oppose, but be obliged to yield at last to the dictum of England and France.

Mr. DUNBAR regarded the expedition to Mexico as the initiative of a new European policy—or rather an old policy revived—on the American Continent, retrogressive in its character, and fraught with the greatest damage to Republican institutions. The European Allies were now thoroughly committed to this policy, and it was to be feared that their pride, and what they considered their material interests, bound up in a political necessity, would not permit them to withdraw. When, therefore, news of the Union victories, and the manifestation of Union sentiment in States and sections supposed to be irredeemably committed to secession, reached Europe, there was reason to believe that the Allies would hasten their movements in Mexico, afford aid directly or indirectly to the South, and find cause of quarrel with the North.

M. DUNBAR's address was full of great thoughts and strong National sentiment. The following are the closing remarks:

"CHATAUBRIAND says: 'God rises behind men. The Providential event comes after the human event.' How true this is proving in our distracted country. The human event with us was based on an insane struggle for political power. That issue is rapidly disappearing and behind it rises the Providential event with appalling distinctness. It is no longer a question of negro Slavery in these United States—the North against the South or the South against the North. The great question now before the whole American people, both North and South is, whether they will consent to be divided into two or more nationalities, and exist as inferior Powers subject to the dictation of European policy and diplomacy, as the Spanish American Republics have existed, or whether they will stand up UNITED and invincible, the conscious representatives of freedom and progress, and assert and maintain that independence and proud preëminence they so recently held, against each and every foe."

There was a strong desire expressed that Mr. DUNBAR should repeat his address at the Smithsonian Institution. C. B.

NEWS FROM THE UPPER POTOMAC.

The Rebels Reported to be in Full Force at Winchester.

Occupation of Bunker Hill by Our Troops.

Rapid Progress on the Baltimore and Ohio Railroad.

CHARLESTOWN, Va., Thursday, March 6.

Reliable intelligence states that the rebels are in full force at Winchester. They have completed formidable earthworks on this side, mounted with sixty guns, including field batteries.

Bunker Hill was occupied by our forces yesterday, as the extreme outpost on the West.

There is some movement of troops to-day.

A scouting party of cavalry reports that Ashby's rebel cavalry, last night attempted to cut them off when near Berryville, but were foiled in the attempt.

Four regiments, with a four-gun battery, attempted, on the 3d inst., to flank Col. GEARY, near Lovettsville, but were driven off without a battle.

Yesterday, several deserters were brought into town by the cavalry. Among them was Lieut. ARTHUR MARKELL, of the Fifth Virginia Volunteers.

A squad of the Van Alen's Cavalry, to-day, captured a rebel picket, five in number, near Bunker Hill. They belonged to the Second Virginia Infantry. The prisoners were carried before the Division Provost Marshal, Lieut.-Col. ANDREWS, of the Massachusetts Second, for examination.

The work on the Baltimore and Ohio Railroad progresses rapidly, and every point is strongly protected from the Cumberland to Harper's Ferry, and every facility is being afforded to the Company. A large force is employed on the bridge and iron trestle-work at the Ferry. The work has been found in better condition than was at first supposed by the Engineer, and ten days is fixed as the time at which through connection can be made.

All the commands of this division are in the best condition and anxious for an attack by the enemy.

CHARLESTOWN, Thursday, March 6—8 P. M.

Smithfield, seven miles northwest of this place, was occupied to-day by a strong force.

Gen. BANKS has issued a general order, forbidding all kinds of depredations or marauding upon the property of citizens. He says no officer or soldier shall disturb in any manner the ordinary business of the country. He has appointed Major S. H. D. CRANE, of the Wisconsin Third, as the officer in charge of all seizures of property for the use of the army.

Country supplies, which, on our arrival, were cut off, are now coming in more freely.

Public sentiment in regard to our presence is gradually undergoing a favorable change, and faces which scowled upon the Union soldiers, now smile in pleasant intercourse with the officers and men.

The army storehouses here are fast filling up with confiscated articles of produce and manufactures, and such as are required are being issued to the army. The seizures to-day include five hundred barrels of flour and two hundred bushels of wheat, the latter in bags marked "Confederate States."

REBEL REPORTS FROM WINCHESTER.

A correspondent of the Richmond *Dispatch*, writing from Camp Mason, near Winchester, says the troops in that direction are improving in health, and but little sickness exists. A portion have received marching orders, but to what point is not known. "It seems to be pretty well known that the enemy are threatening Winchester from Romney and Williamsport. 'Stone-Wall' JACKSON, of course, will be prepared to meet them."

The same correspondent, writing on the 28th, says:

"The enemy have succeeded in crossing the Potomac and taking possession of Charlestown, in Jefferson County. The cars that left here this morning for that place, returned a short time after, not deeming it prudent to advance near the town. The Yankees are reported to be in large force, and will, no doubt, advance toward Winchester in a day or two."

The *Dispatch* also contains the following:

"Private letters from Winchester furnish information that Gen. JACKSON had caused the removal of the Quartermaster and Commissary stores from that point, in anticipation of an early attack from the enemy. The same letters also state that a report prevails that the enemy have crossed, or were crossing, in large force, at Williamsport. The distance from Williamsport to Winchester, by the Martinsburgh and Winchester turnpike, is 34 miles, and the roads are represented to be almost impassable. Whether the enemy will risk an attack at this time, or in a very short time, is extremely doubtful, unless his facilities for transportation are much more extensive and efficient than we have reason to believe them to be. At any rate, we feel well satisfied that Gen. JACKSON will make a gallant stand before yielding the place, which he will only do when overpowering numbers render it prudent and necessary."

The Richmond *Examiner* of the 3d inst. says:

"A report was brought down by passengers on the cars yesterday, that seventeen Yankee regiments were at Leesburgh; that Gen. JACKSON had been compelled to fall back upon Winchester, and that Gen. JOHNSTON was moving reinforcements to him at that place. Nothing confirmatory of this report had been received at the War Department; but as it comes by a gentleman who is well known in the city, and was circulated yesterday very generally among some of our public men, we mention it as not an improbable story."

IMPORTANT FROM TENNESSEE.

How Nashville Suffered from a Rebel Mob.

The Contrast Presented by the Union Forces.

Gen. Grant's Declaration of Martial Law.

OUR CLARKSVILLE CORRESPONDENCE.

THE CONDITION OF NASHVILLE—WANTON DESTRUCTION BY THE REBELS—THE RIVER NAVIGABLE FOR THE LARGEST STEAMERS—THE WOUNDED REBELS—GEN. GRANT'S PROCLAMATION OF MARTIAL LAW.

CLARKSVILLE, Tenn., Tuesday, Feb. 25, 1862.

Our accounts from Nashville present the sad picture of a city under the rule of a mob, and that, too, of the most desperate character. Had the Unionists been able to reach that city a week sooner, much wanton destruction of private and public property would have been prevented. As it is, however, all the bridges, both railroad, turnpike and highway, including the magnificent iron suspension bridge, have been either burnt or otherwise totally destroyed. The stores and shops of citizens have been entered and pillaged—no distinction having been made by the rebel outlaws between the advocates of secession and the lovers of Union. All suffered alike at the hands of this band of marauders, who carried away everything they could possibly use, and destroyed what they could not take away.

The leaders of this gang of thieves were cavalry men of Col. FORREST's Texan Rangers, who claim to have cut their way through our army at Fort Donelson, but who really ran away in the night with PILLOW and FLOYD, and quartered themselves in this fashion upon the inhabitants of what they chose to make their city of refuge. The gunboat *Cairo* was dispatched from here to Nashville last Sunday afternoon, and as the sight of such vessels has heretofore put to flight all such rascals, it is hoped that whatever is left of the city will enjoy a degree of quiet to which it has latterly been a stranger. The *Cairo* was sent in accordance with a suggestion of Gen. BUELL, by Gen. C. F. SMITH, commanding this division, a messenger from Gen. BUELL having reached him Sunday noon, with the intelligence that the former officer was within nine miles of Nashville, was still advancing, and expected to meet with some resistance. It is understood now that Gen. BUELL has left a sufficient garrison there, and is pushing on to Murfreesboro, the forces of Gen. NELSON having had sufficient time to effect a junction with him. The high stage of water in the Cumberland is most favorable to the operations and movements of the National army. The river is higher now than it has been during the last eight years, and the largest Ohio and Mississippi steamers can navigate it as easily as they can navigate their own waters.

The rebels, when they began to turn their attention to the importance of strengthening Fort Donelson, established an extensive hospital at this place. During the three days of the contest for the possession of that fortification, a large number of their wounded were brought up from Dover and placed in it, but when, on Sunday morning, the valorous and self-sacrificing surgeons heard of the fall of the fort, they imitated the example of their Generals, and sought safety in flight. Two only remained.

As a natural consequence, the mortality among the wounded has been enormous, and but for the assistance rendered by the surgeons of the gunboats which had arrived here, not many who entered that hospital would have left it alive. Four days after the hegira of these medical officers, eleven more came down from Nashville under a flag of truce, for the purpose of removing these wounded prisoners to that city, but left behind all of our wounded, who had been previously sent there. Their request was, of course, denied, but they were permitted to remain, if they chose, and attend to the wounded here. This they had the manliness to do, and matters at the hospital are now improving a little. We captured all the rebel surgeons at Fort Donelson, but immediately released them, with the simple understanding that, should any of ours be taken prisoners hereafter, and not given up, they should immediately report themselves for an exchange. The terms were accepted, and the Medical Staff of both armies worked side by side there, attending to National and Confederate wounded men alike.

The conduct of the soldiers left at this point thus far has been much to the delight and surprise of the citizens. Many of them, who left their homes when they learned that the "Lincolnites" were coming among them, have returned, and every day increases the population of this half-deserted burgh. I have not yet learned of the return of any of the negroes who were sent by their owners to Arkansas for safety. A negro insurrection was greatly dreaded last week, when no one except the civic authorities held possession of the town, and even now the heads of some holders of this species of property rest uneasily on their pillows.

The city has been placed under martial law. Col. JOHN COOK, of the Seventh Illinois, acting as commander of the post, and Capt. ESTABROOK, of the same regiment, as Provost-Marshal. Their labors are not likely to be very severe, inasmuch as nearly all the public property of the enemy has been taken care of, and there is little or no business going on in town. The stores are mostly closed, the few that are still kept open have no stocks of any account on their shelves, and there is little incentive for any one to engage in commercial pursuits until Tennessee is placed in a position very different from that she occupies at present. The Postmaster absconded ten days ago, being in debt to both Governments,—showing the deluded Southrons that those who steal at Washington will be very apt to continue the practice at Richmond,—leaving his friends and two sets of bondsmen to lament the loss of their mails and money. Our own mail system has not yet been extended to this point.

The money in circulation here is mostly home-made, passing in exchange for a good article of about half price; it consists of South Carolina, Georgia and Tennessee bank notes, which are issued *ad libitum*, and Confederate notes, which I suppose are manufactured quite as freely. The State currency, for the lack of something better, will buy what few articles are for sale in this region, but the secession notes are simply worthless. What they will do for money after the restoration of peace nobody knows.

Below Clarksville, on the eastern bank of the Cumberland, the rebels have erected three earthworks which they dignify with the title of forts. They had already mounted five guns in them, and had them nearly completed, when the loss of their fortifications at Dover caused them to suspend their labors, and give up the design altogether. There was no sort of use for them, but the citizens thought their own town must be walled about, forgetting that if Donelson fell there was no hope left for them. They have given to the whole thing now the name of Fort Humbug, and have put into our hands five more guns than we should have taken had they stopped to think a moment before they undertook to fortify themselves so strongly. The weather is warm and mild, the roads are good except where covered with back water from the river, and everything looks favorable for army movements.

The appended proclamations have just been received:

HEADQUARTERS DISTRICT WEST TENNESSEE, FORT DONELSON, Tenn., Feb. 22, 1862.

GENERAL ORDERS No. 7.—Tennessee, by her rebellion, having ignored all laws of the United States, no Courts will be allowed to act under State authority, but all cases coming within the reach of the military arm, will be adjudicated by the authorities the Government has established within the State.

Martial-law is therefore declared to extend over West Tennessee. Whenever a *sufficient* number of citizens return to their allegiance to maintain law and order over the territory, the military restriction here indicated will be removed.

By order of Major-Gen. U. S. GRANT.
JOHN A. RAWLINS, Ass't. Adj.-General.

HEADQUARTERS SECOND DIVISION DIST. WEST TENN., CLARKSVILLE, Tenn., Feb. 24, 1862.

GENERAL ORDER No. 11.—The sale of any spirituous or intoxicating liquor, in any quantity, is prohibited; should any one violate this order, he will be placed under guard, for trial by Court-martial, and his liquor seized and held for hospital purposes.

By order of Brig.-Gen. C. F. SMITH.
THOS. J. NEWSHAM, Ass't. Adj.-General.

IMPORTANT FROM COLUMBUS.

A Skirmish with Rebel Cavalry—Heavy Cannonading Heard at New-Madrid—The Rebels in Strong Force There—Items from the Rebel Papers.

CHICAGO, Thursday, March 6.

A special to the Chicago *Tribune* from Cairo, says:

The National pickets at Columbus were driven in yesterday by the rebel cavalry. The woods in the vicinity of the town were shelled by the gunboats. The rebels fled.

It is reported that heavy cannonading was heard at Columbus at 4 o'clock this morning, in the direction of New-Madrid. The rebel army at that point numbers 40,000 men, having been largely reinforced from Columbus and Memphis. They also have eight wooden gunboats.

From late rebel papers we glean the following:

The steamer *Cambridge* was sunk on the 23d ult. near Grand Glaise. Forty-two lives were lost.

The machinery from the various workshops in Nashville was removed prior to the evacuation of that place to Chattanooga.

The people of the South are warmly urging and demanding JEFF. DAVIS to take the field.

A bitter contest is going on at Memphis as to whether the town had better be burned on the approach of the Federal gunboats.

REGULATION OF TRADE.

ST. LOUIS, Mo., Thursday, March 6.

A general order issued this evening states that Surveyors and other Custom-house officers and agents in this Department, as well as those on the Cumberland and Tennessee Rivers, are expected to respect the permits issued by the Surveyor of either of the posts of the Ohio River, and bearing his official signature and seal. Military officers in command of posts where there are no Custom-house officers, or acting in concert with such officers, will in like manner respect these permits. Sealed baggage, while the seals remain unbroken, will also be respected by officers. Goods, wares or merchandise in transit thus covered by permits, and baggage thus sealed, will be allowed to go forward to their places of destination, unless there is good and satisfactory reason for their detention, or information received from reliable sources. Until further orders, the transportation of this Department is not open to munitions of war, except unless special regulations with military authorities. Whisky for the time being is prohibited in the resumed commerce of the Cumberland and the Tennessee. By order of Major-Gen. HALLECK.

IMPORTANT FROM SHIP ISLAND.

Capture of the Rebel Steamer Magnolia, with Four Hundred Bales of Cotton—A Dozen Oyster Boats Seized, &c.

BOSTON, Thursday, March 6.

The gunboat *Saxon*, from Ship Island Feb. 22, arrived here this morning. Capt. SNOW reports seeing a vessel, supposed to be the gunboat *Kensington*, which towed out the ship-of-the-line *Vermont*, on Sunday last, at 3 o'clock, off Cape Hatteras.

He also reports that the steamer *South Carolina* had captured the rebel steamer *Magnolia*, while attempting to run out of Mobile. She had 400 bales of cotton on board. The Engineer attempted to blow her up, but the escape of steam only killed himself. The *Magnolia* is a large side-wheel steamer.

The health of the regiments at Ship Island was good.

The weather was very hot, the thermometer standing in 95 degrees in the shade.

The supply of oysters for New-Orleans had been cut off by the capture of a dozen oyster boats, with thirty-six prisoners.

The sloop-of-war *Hartford*, with the paymaster on board, had arrived.

WASHINGTON's birthday was celebrated in good style by the troops. Gen. PHELPS issued an order of the day of a highly patriotic character.

FROM FORTRESS MONROE.

FORTRESS MONROE, Wednesday, March 5, *via* BALTIMORE, Thursday, March 6.

The gunboat *Mt. Vernon* has arrived from the blockade off Wilmington.

A flag of truce was sent to Craney Island to-day, but has not yet returned.

The wind to-day is northwest.

THE FORT DONELSON PRISONERS.

BOSTON, Thursday, March 6.

Forty-nine rebel officers from Fort Donelson reached this city this morning, in charge of a detachment of the Ohio Twentieth. They are principally from Kentucky, Tennessee, Alabama and Mississippi, and comprise all the Colonels, Lieutenant-Colonels and Majors captured. They were sent to Fort Warren.

COL. LEE AT HOME.

BOSTON, Thursday, March 6.

The public reception of Col. LEE and other officers of the Massachusetts Twentieth, at Roxbury last night, was a very cordial affair. Gov. ANDREW, the Mayors of Boston and Roxbury, and other gentlemen made speeches. Col. LEE responded briefly, in words of glowing patriotism and devotion to our country and its flag. A large number of ladies were present.

SONS OF VERMONT.—The Sons of Vermont held a large and enthusiastic meeting at the Fifth-avenue Hotel last evening, there being about 200 of the Sons and descendants of the Green Mountain Boys present. After a lengthy and happy interchange of sentiment, the Committee on Reception and Arrangements made a report that all arrangements had been completed for the reception of Vermont soldiers, and presented a badge with the Vermont coat of arms and the motto, "Welcome Sons of Vermont." The Committee also presented a beautiful banner, which was received with cheers, and the report adopted. It was voted to hold a reception at the Metropolitan Hotel this evening at 8 o'clock, and the "Sons" and their wives and daughters of all descendants of Vermoners are invited to be present. Tickets may be had at the Metropolitan Hotel.

IMPORTANT FROM THE SOUTH

Great Excitement in the Rebel Capital.

Full Particulars of the Arrest of John Minor Botts and Other Prominent Citizens.

Significant Demonstrations of the Union Men.

PROCEEDINGS OF THE REBEL CONGRESS

The Proposition to Burn the Cotton and Tobacco Crops.

Notes of Alarm from the Mississippi Valley.

Attack of the New-Orleans Press on Gen. A. S. Johnston.

A CARD FROM C. J. FAULKNER.

THE ARREST OF UNION MEN.

From the Richmond Examiner, March 3.

On Saturday night, Capt. GOODWIN, by order of the Government, proceeded with a party of select men to the farm of JOHN MINOR BOTTS, and took him, and all of his papers and private correspondence, in custody. Leaving an officer in charge of the papers and house of BOTTS, Capt. GOODWIN brought him prisoner to this city, and lodged him in MCDANIEL's negro jail, situated in Blankinship's alley, some fifty yards north of Franklin-street.

Capt. GOODWIN then went to the farms of VALENTINE HECKLER and FRANKLIN STEARNS, and took both of these well-known Union men, and all of their papers and letters, and brought them to this city.

BOTTS' and HECKLER's letters and papers [illegible] yet been examined. STEARNS' have undergone only a cursory examination, and so far, nothing of interest has been found among them, except several letters from his friend BOTTS, begging for money.

We are under the impression that, as yet, the Government is in possession of no positive information that would convict Botts of treason. But he is known to be the recognized leader of all the disaffected—all the low Germans of the Red Republican, Carl Schurz school, and of the vile remnant of the Union Party.

Against Stearns' and Heckler's loyalty the Government has been for a month in the possession of the most conclusive evidence; and it feels confident of its ability to prove that both of these men have been loud in their denunciations of what they have been pleased to term the "Rebellion," and have, over and again, expressed their willingness to sacrifice their entire property to restore the dominion in the South of the United States Government.

The man WARDWELL, another party arrested, has, since the beginning of the war, been known to every citizen as a blatant and defiant Union man.

MILLER, who has also been lodged in jail, is the chief or high priest of the secret Black or Red German Republican Societies of Richmond, some of whose members, it can be proved, have, since the reverse of our army at Fort Donelson, *boasted that they had thousands of arms and abundance of ammunition concealed in the city, and that the men were enrolled who would use them on the first approach of the Yankee army.*

An Irishman, named JOHN M. HIGGINS, has also been arrested and put in the same prison. HIGGINS is a connection of Col. CORCORAN, of the Yankee army. Two of HIGGINS' aunts married two of CORCORAN's uncles. A letter from CORCORAN to HIGGINS, advising the latter to send his wife and family North, and containing assurances that he (CORCORAN) would have them safely conveyed under flag of truce, has recently been intercepted by our Government. Whether our Government has any evidence of HIGGINS' intention to follow CORCORAN's counsel, has not transpired.

It is said that STEARNS, the whisky man, on approaching the prison, surveyed it with a most contemptuous expression, and remarked, "*If you are going to imprison all the Union men you will have to provide a much larger jail than this.*" Mr. STEARNS will, we think, be not a little mistaken in his calculations. If the Government use its power wisely and firmly, this great Union party, on which STEARNS, and others like him, have based such great expectations, will, in a day, dwindle into ridiculously small proportions. By neglect, idle, ignorant and vicious persons have been allowed with impunity to boast their treason in our streets.

The rumor that the above-mentioned parties had been arrested was on every tongue yesterday morning, but no one could, with certainty, say whence the rumor originated, or whether it was authentic. And not until a late hour in the evening was it known to be a fact that the parties were confined in MCDANIEL's jail. Very soon after the information became generally diffused, a crowd collected in the vicinity, and the matter was freely discussed. Not a man was there but expressed himself in unmeasured terms of approbation of the course of the Government. The only apprehension that seemed to be felt was, that the Government would not be thorough and summary enough in its treatment of traitors. *The universal Yankee sympathizers dangling from as many lamp-posts would have a most wholesome and salutary effect.*

While standing in the crowd, near the jail, our attention was attracted to a great quantity of burning paper flying out of one of the chimneys. It was immediately suggested that the prisoners, not having been properly searched, were destroying private and perhaps treasonable documents which they had about them.

We have reason to believe that many other arrests will be effected within the next twenty-four hours. We forego to mention names, lest we might throw some impediment in the way of the authorities.

Now that the Government appears really in earnest in the suppression of treason, it becomes every citizen who knows a man or set of men inimical to our country and cause to point them out.

It will be recollected that, on Thursday last, JOHN GOLD and ELIAS PAULDING were arraigned for having made use of treasonable language, and that it appeared on investigation that GOLD had proclaimed himself a Union man, *and announced that the Stars and Stripes would soon wave from the top of our capitol, and that Elias Paulding amended Gold's announcement with an emphatic "That's so."* We stated in our last paper that the Mayor had turned both parties over to the Confederate authorities. In this we were mistaken. The Mayor had merely committed them for further examination, and they were accordingly brought into Court on Saturday and again committed till this morning.

UNION MEN IN THE POLICE COURT.

From the Richmond Examiner, Feb. 28.

JOHN GOLD and ELIAS PAULDING were arraigned in the Mayor's Court yesterday for avowing themselves subjects of the Lincoln Government, and expressing sentiments disloyal to the Southern Confederacy. JOHN GOLD is an Irishman; ELIAS PAULDING, the other prisoner, is a man about 50 years of age, and apparently an American. WILLIAM HAMMOND, a McCulloch Ranger, and another member of the same company, were sworn as witnesses.

HAMMOND deposed: I was taking supper last night at Ford's, and the conversation at the table turned on the late affair at Roanoke Island, and the subsequent treatment of our men by the Yankees. I said we had been treated about as well as prisoners of war could expect. GOLD spoke up, and asked if any one ever had been maltreated under the Stars and Stripes. He said he himself was a soldier, and a member of the Polish Brigade. *That he had been dragged to the recruiting-office in New Orleans with a halter about his neck, and forced to enlist. He said he was a citizen of Philadelphia—that the Star Spangled Banner had once waved over this city, and would soon do it again.* This man PAULDING, at this, spoke up and said: "That's so." I then left the table and went into the front room, and when GOLD and PAULDING came out I arrested GOLD, and told my comrade to arrest PAULDING, and we carried them to the watch-house. At the watch-house GOLD repeated that he was a citizen of Philadelphia, and had a wife and four children there, *and said he claimed the protection of the United States, and that he did not recognize the Confederate Government.* He showed a medical discharge from the Polish

The New-York Times.

VOL. XI—NO. 3263. | NEW-YORK, SATURDAY, MARCH 8, 1862. | PRICE TWO CENTS.

NEWS FROM WASHINGTON.

How the President's Message is Received.

MAILS TO THE SOUTH PACIFIC.

Probable Passage of a Law to Compel Vessels to Carry the Mails when Required.

The Bill for the Occupation and Cultivation of Cotton Lands Passed in the Senate.

The Case of Gen. Fremont Considered in the House.

Speeches of Messrs. Blair of Missouri, and Colfax of Indiana.

OUR SPECIAL WASHINGTON DISPATCHES.

WASHINGTON, Friday, March 7.

THE PRESIDENT'S MESSAGE.

The more the President's Message is discussed the more difficult is it to define the position of parties in regard to it. One great point, however, is gained—the subject is universally discussed with more calmness than has ever before characterized a question about Slavery.

DEPARTURE OF GOV. JOHNSON FOR TENNESSEE.

Gov. ANDREW JOHNSON, accompanied by his son, Col. ROBERT JOHNSON, WILLIAM A. BROWNING, Secretary, &c., Hon. HORACE MAYNARD, and Hon. EMERSON ETHERIDGE, Clerk of the House, left Washington this afternoon for Nashville, via Harrisburgh, Pittsburgh, Cincinnati and Louisville.

THE MAILS TO THE SOUTH PACIFIC, VIA PANAMA.

The Senate Committee on Post-offices, at their meeting to-day, authorized Mr. COLLAMER to report Mr. SUMNER's bill to provide for the carrying the mails from the United States to foreign ports, with a recommendation that immediate action be had, so as to provide for carrying the mails to the South Pacific before the 21st inst., after which date Commodore VANDERBILT has notified the Postmaster-General he will refuse to take the mails. The bill, as reported, provides that any vessels clearing from a foreign port shall take and receive any mail matter placed on board said vessel by the United States Consul or by the port officers of such foreign port or place, for the United States, and shall deliver the same to the Post-office of the place aforesaid in the United States.

ALLOTMENTS OF THE NEW-YORK SOLDIERS.

The Allotment Commissioners from New-York to-day closed up the objects of their mission, having visited upwards of 70 regiments, and handed over to the Paymaster-General all the certificates, so that that officer can complete what remains to be done. They have been eminently successful.

THE NEW GUNBOATS.

The Senate Finance Committee having rejected the appropriation of $15,000,000 in the Naval Appropriation bill for the construction of gunboats, the Secretary of the Navy has addressed letters to the Naval Committee of both Houses, stating that unless some provision is made at once for these boats, the Department would be compelled to suspend operations, which had already been commenced.

TRANSPORTATION OF ARMY SUPPLIES.

The contracts for transportation of army supplies for the next two years from Fort Leavenworth and Kansas City to posts west of these points, including all in Kansas, Nebraska, Utah, Colorado and New-Mexico, were to-day awarded by Gen. MEIGS to IRWIN, JACKMAN & Co., the former contractors.

NO MILITARY MOVEMENTS.

Intelligence from every part of the military line of the Potomac, to-day, reports nothing of material interest.

CONFIRMATIONS BY THE SENATE.

The Senate to-day confirmed the following as Brigadier-Generals of Volunteers: Major Lawrence Graham, of the Second Cavalry; Eleazar Paine, of Illinois; Wm. A. Richardson, of Illinois; Daniel Butterfield, of New-York; W. T. Ward, of Kentucky; Major George Sykes, of the Thirteenth Infantry; Capt. David S. Stanley, of the Tenth Cavalry; Thomas A. Davies, of New-York; Col. Philip St. George Cooke, of the Second Cavalry; and Capt. Joseph B. Plummer, of the First Regiment of Infantry, for gallant conduct at Springfield and Fredericktown, Mo.

The Senate also confirmed HENRY VAN RENSSELAER to be Inspector-General, with the rank of Colonel, and THOMAS HILLHOUSE, of New-York, to be an Assistant Adjutant-General of Volunteers, with the rank of Major.

THE PROCEEDINGS OF CONGRESS.

SENATE.

WASHINGTON, Friday, March 7.

The message of President LINCOLN, suggesting the passage of a joint resolution providing for cooperation with any State for the abolition of Slavery, with pecuniary compensation, was read and referred to the Judiciary Committee.

Mr. SUMNER, of Massachusetts, (Rep.,) presented a memorial, signed by many prominent merchants of New-York, asking that immediate action be provided for the transportation of the mails from New-York to Panama.

Mr. ANTHONY, of Rhode Island, (Rep.,) presented a memorial from the officers and seamen on board the steamship *Governor*, asking for compensation for losses from wrecking that vessel.

Mr. FOSTER, of Connecticut, (Rep.,) presented a memorial from merchants of New-York, calling attention to the cotton lands on the Southern coast.

Mr. WADE, of Ohio, (Rep.,) moved to take up the bill to provide for the occupation and cultivation of the cotton lands.

The motion was agreed to by Yeas 25, Nays 11.

Mr. DAVIS, of Kentucky, (Union,) said, some time since the Legislature of Kentucky passed a resolution requesting his predecessor and colleague to resign. His colleague had not resigned, and fifteen days since the Senator from Minnesota offered a resolution for the expulsion of his colleague. The Kentucky Legislature are now in session, and they want to know when that question is to be acted upon. If he is to be expelled, the Legislature do not want to adjourn and allow a disloyal, traitorous Governor to appoint any one to take the place of his colleague.

Mr. TRUMBULL, of Illinois, (Rep.,) said the Committee were doing the best they could, and would make a report soon.

Mr. POWELL, of Kentucky, (Opp.) said that he was a little surprised at the zeal of his colleague, but would only say that he (POWELL) was anxious for an investigation to be had. The action of the Kentucky Legislature was a matter between himself and that Legislature. He (POWELL) could make it plain to the Senate, and would do so, that his action in the Senate at the last session was entirely in accordance with the will of the people, as expressed by the resolutions, to wit:—to preserve a strict neutrality in Kentucky. He (POWELL) was perfectly willing to abide by the decision of the people of Kentucky at any time. He only intended to ask the attention of the Senate to a brief statement to vindicate himself, after the Committee had reported, and all the Senators had spoken.

Mr. CARLILE, of Virginia, (Union,) said that he was sorry to see that Senators were determined to press the bill. He did not believe that the Government held supreme control over all the lands of the country. The bill proposes to substitute the Government in place of the present masters of slaves, and to make the Government one great, lordly slaveholder, with a great brood of petty agents. The provisions of the bill make humane treatment of the slaves impossible. There are also appeals coming here to us from thousands of the white race, who have been turned out of their homes, and these appeals have more force for him (CARLILE) than any that could come from the negro race. This bill will take from the treasury immense sums of money, which could be better used in the proposed scheme of colonization.

Here the morning hour expired.

The Chair called up the special order.

Mr. WADE, of Ohio, (Rep.,) moved to postpone the special order, and proceed to the further consideration of the bill.

Motion agreed to, by Yeas, 23; Nays, 16.

Mr. PEARCE, of Maryland, (Opp.,) thought the bill impracticable, and a most extraordinary and political blunder. The money that it would cost the Government to provide for these indigent persons would make the Treasury more indigent than themselves even.

The bill was then passed, by Yeas, 28; Nays, 14.

NAYS—Messrs. Browning, Carlile, Cowan, Davis, Henderson, Kennedy, McDougall, Pearce, Powell, Rice, Saulsbury, Thomson, Wilson of Missouri, and Wright—14.

The Senate went into Executive session, and then adjourned till Monday.

HOUSE OF REPRESENTATIVES.

WASHINGTON, Friday, March 7.

On motion of Mr. COX, of Ohio, (Dem.,) it was resolved that the Secretary of War communicate to this House the number, age, and condition of the Africans who have been under the supervision of Major-General JOHN E. WOOL, commanding at Fortress Monroe, Va., since he has had control of that Department, together with the amount of work or service performed by them, the pay, if any, which they have received, and the cost to the Government for their maintenance and support.

Mr. GURLEY, of Ohio, (Rep.,) introduced a bill to secure to pilots, engineers, sailors, and crews upon the gunboats and war vessels their bounty and pensions.

The House then proceeded to the consideration of the bill to authorize the Secretary of the Treasury to purchase coin, and for other purposes.

Mr. PENDLETON, of Ohio, (Dem.,) inquired of Mr. STEVENS whether in his (STEVENS') opinion it was necessary to authorize the sale of the five hundred millions of bonds recently authorized, in order to realize sufficient coin for the payment of the interest, which could not be more by next July than forty millions on the six hundred and fifty millions of indebtedness.

Mr. STEVENS, of Pennsylvania, (Rep.,) did not think it necessary, but it was found by the Secretary of the Treasury that these bonds cannot be sold except at a great sacrifice, which he did not choose to make. Hence, he suggested the passage of the bill, so that the specie section of the recently enacted United States note law may not be repudiated. Mr. STEVENS added in reply that the new five hundred million bonds have not yet been issued.

Mr. PENDLETON expressed himself satisfied with the explanation, and would vote for it. He, however, offered an amendment, which was agreed to, reasserting that the demand notes shall be receivable for duties on imports.

With this exception, the bill was then passed as originally introduced.

Mr. HARDING, of Kentucky, (Union,) rising to an explanation, said that he had noticed in the newspapers that the Chairman of the Committee on Territories had reported a bill providing for Territorial Governments in the seceding States, and for their subsequent admission into the Union. This subject had been discussed in the public prints. He (HARDING) was at a loss to ascertain how this information was obtained.

Mr. ASHLEY, of Ohio, (Rep.,) the Chairman of the Committee, informed his colleague thereon, that the Committee authorized him to report the bill, and under instructions he (ASHLEY) had moved its printing and recommitment to the Committee.

Mr. HARDING remarked that the newspapers also said that the Senate's Committee on Territories had concurred in the provisions of this bill.

Mr. ASHLEY replied that he was not aware that that Committee, with the Chairman of whom he had been in consultation, had come to any conclusion on the subject. If the newspapers had made a misstatement, the Chairmen of neither of these Committees was responsible for it.

Mr. HARDING said that only four out of the nine members of the Committee had agreed on this bill, and yet it was sent out as the report of the majority of the Committee.

Mr. ASHLEY further explained that he gave printed copies to those who asked for them.

The conversation here terminated.

The bill to render valid and to authorize the extension of the patent granted JOHN S. MINE, for an improvement in the manufacture of lampblack, was passed by a vote of 73 against 39.

The House then went into Committee of the Whole on the State of the Union, the bill regulating the franking privilege being nominally under consideration.

Mr. BLAIR, of Missouri, (Rep.,) proceeded to speak of the Military Department of the West under Gen. JOHN C. FREMONT. Mr. BLAIR said a very great pressure had been brought to bear through the newspapers to force Gen. FREMONT back into a command, and to force the Administration against its judgment, expressed after deliberation, to employ him in some one of the military departments. He (BLAIR) had seen it stated in telegrams that Gen. FREMONT had again and again demanded a trial. This is not true.

Mr. RIDDLE, of Ohio, (Rep.,) asked on what authority the gentleman made the last statement?

Mr. BLAIR, resuming, said: No demand for a trial has been made, unless it has been done within the last two or three days. Gen. FREMONT had not made the demand at all, for he (BLAIR) had taken pains to satisfy himself of the fact by inquiry at the office of the Adjutant-General and at that of the Judge-Advocate of the army. It was most extraordinary that an officer of the army, charged with crime, mutiny and misconduct of the war, and deposed from his command in consequence of these charges, should not ask a trial. He ventured the assertion that if Gen. FREMONT will demand a trial, the Administration will grant it. It had also been heralded that the Committee on the Conduct of the War had demanded his (FREMONT's) restoration. He (BLAIR) undertook to say that such was not the fact. It was simply a publication of some of FREMONT's partisans, and it was also said through the Press that FREMONT was to be restored to a command. He (BLAIR) did not know whether this was so or not, but inasmuch as this information came in somewhat the shape of other publications, he believed it was of the same character. There were preliminary symptoms which foreshadowed and announced the simultaneous appearance of the statement made by Gen. FREMONT in his defence before the Committee, and the speech of his aid-de-camp (SHANKS) in this House. The statement and the speech inaugurate a new campaign and a new field, and the battle is to be fought with weapons far different than the rude instruments of war—with proclamations, which, up to this time, in Gen. FREMONT's hands have had no serious effect. He (BLAIR) commended Gen. FREMONT's choice of weapons. Certain it was that his proclamations did not help the enemy as much as his exposed and isolated posts at Lexington and elsewhere. His proclamations did not injure the Administration as much as a single purchase of worthless arms and the erection of useless earthworks. He (BLAIR) did not believe that Gen. FREMONT was authorized to publish his statement, which was extraordinary in its character.

Mr. GOOCH, of Massachusetts, (Rep.,) member of the Committee on the Conduct of the War, said that Gen. FREMONT having presented a large number of documents, was requested by the Committee to prepare a concise statement as to the administration of affairs in his Department, which he (FREMONT) did at a subsequent period. Gen. FREMONT again appeared before the Committee and was questioned. When he was about to leave the room he was requested not to give information to anybody outside, of what he had stated to the Committee. He (GOOCH) understood Gen. FREMONT to acquiesce in the request, as he had in all others made by the Committee. He (GOOCH) only wished to add that the publication was made without the knowledge and against the consent of the Committee.

Mr. BLAIR—Was it all published?

Mr. GOOCH—His (FREMONT's) statement and documents, and not the portion in response to the inquiries of the Committee.

Mr. BLAIR said FREMONT's statement was as extraordinary as the manner in which it found its way into print. It was an apology for disaster and defeat, and ingenious in the suppression of important facts and suggestions of others which never existed. In this he shows he is a better apologist for defeat than a General to achieve victories. Mr. BLAIR proceeded to speak of his early friendship for FREMONT. He now had no private griefs. And it was only for the reason that FREMONT was found to be incompetent for his position that he recommended his removal. He had acted from considerations of public duty. He then spoke at length of the disasters at Springfield and Lexington, to show that these were attributable to FREMONT's incompetency. Those by whom he surrounded himself had settled themselves down upon us like obscene birds of prey. No men have as bad characters as those who are FREMONT's familiars. Of course there are honorable exceptions. No greater slander was uttered by any man than that, at the time FREMONT went to St. Louis, it was a rebellious city. The declaration of martial law was, therefore, superinduced by his apprehension of imaginary danger. Mr. BLAIR also examined FREMONT's contracts and other transactions. He spoke for about two hours, the time having, by unanimous consent, been extended.

Mr. COLFAX, of Indiana, (Rep.,)—I did not intend to reply at this time, and am, therefore, ill-prepared to answer the elaborate charges made against Gen. FREMONT by the gentleman from Missouri. While I differ from him in regard to the supercedure of FREMONT in the command of the Department of the Northwest, I wish to be distinctly understood to say that, no matter who is in command, I sustain that General, with all my heart and soul, and strength and mind, who acts most effectually and efficiently against the enemy. I believe it my duty to do so, for this, under God, is our only hope of putting down this gigantic and Satanic rebellion. But I must say that I deeply regret that the gentleman should have indulged in the remarks he did, in debating a grave question like this; that on such an occasion he should have mingled personalities and charges which would be better indulged in on some more fitting arena. I will not touch upon the opening of the remarks of the gentleman, with regard to his and his family's previous relations with Gen. FREMONT, for I am here to speak in vindication of history, of the fair record of the present day, and to prove that my friend's feelings and judgment are perverted by prejudices. The gentleman opposite had been the friend of Gen. FREMONT up to the latter end of August. Up to that time he (Mr. BLAIR) was the warm and devoted friend, the champion and admirer of Gen. FREMONT. Up to that time no charges had been made by him. From the time the war broke out, I tried, in my humble sphere, to sustain confidence in our Generals. I endeavored to preach forbearance and unity. I implored men to cease deprecating Generals in the field. I felt that when they went forth the cause of the country rested on them; that they had the lives of our brave soldiers on their hands, and that they should be supported. Whenever the Administration superseded them, well and good. Let them go. With regard to the charges to-day reiterated on this floor against Gen. FREMONT, I will first say that I do not claim for Gen. FREMONT the character of a perfect man. As all men are fallible, so he had his faults. He was an impulsive and impetuous man. But I regret that he published the statement of defence he did. But Gen. FREMONT must have concluded that he had already abided his time long enough. After six months, under the whip and spur and lash of howling enemies, he held, and, with an abandonment of self and a reticence which has commanded the admiration of friends and the approval of the civilized world, waited patiently his vindication since the day he was deposed from his command to the present. Now, without disparaging others, I say that he is the only Major-General in the United States Army who has gone with his troops away from headquarters in pursuit of the enemy, performing long marches, fording rivers, and never halting till he had brought the foe to bay. Others, no doubt, were willing to do all in their power to the same end—but this is the only instance at the time of this determination and courage of Gen. FREMONT. And now I say that no man can believe the aspersion ventured upon by the gentleman from Missouri, that Gen. FREMONT is a timid man. Every schoolboy in the country knows the history of the man, and that history disposes of that aspersion. Whether, as a General, he was fitted for the command of the Western Department or not, he is a brave and fearless man, a man who has met death in various forms, and encountered perils in every shape; a man who has written his name on the page of history as a great discoverer—adventurer, if you will; one who has raised the Stars and Stripes on distant soil, through privation and toil and suffering, to the improvement of science and the glory of his country. Last of all, even while he knew the sword of Damocles was suspended over his head by a single hair, he went with his army in pursuit of the enemies of his country, leading the advance in person, not bringing up the rear, as is customary with Generals in command. No, Sir, Gen. FREMONT is no coward, but a brave and fearless man. With regard to the charges about the contracts, desiring to be frank, I say that I do not approve of the contracts made by Gen. FREMONT with regard to the fortifications for Missouri; but in making these contracts, it must be supposed that he was guided by the opinion of the head engineer of the department with regard to the price. But if his outlay in this respect was improvident and extravagant, I have only to express the hope that the expenditures of the public money in other departments have been managed with scrupulous economy. We all know the charge brought against him by Adjutant-Gen. THOMAS, that the horses purchased by him were ring-boned and spavined, &c. Now, when I came to Washington I found that there were fourteen hundred horses, purchased for the army of the Potomac, condemned, and not a paper in the country had a word to say about it, but because a few horses were condemned in FREMONT's command, all sorts of charges are brought against him. The gentleman from Missouri had been very eulogistic of St. Louis, its patriotism, &c. Now, I wish I could believe all he said in its favor. I, indeed, believe with him, that the great bulk of the people are loyal, but I as firmly believe that the wealth and capital, and social influence of St. Louis, were strongly on the side of secession, even since Gen. HALLECK took command of that Department. They held an election in that city for a Chamber of Commerce, and what was called the "secession ticket" was elected by a large majority, in the face even of the Major-General of the United States commanding. In speaking of the sentiments which actuated a portion of the people of that city, I speak of its wealth and capital as being strongly on the side of secession; and so strongly was this feeling manifested, that General HALLECK compelled the Chamber of Commerce to take the oath of allegiance. I know St. Louis is loyal, and one of the strongest proofs of that is found in the fact that, when their deposed General came back, after he came back degraded and deposed from his command, without power or place, they gathered around him in tens of thousands to welcome him. I take that as a strong proof of their loyalty. The gentleman (Mr. BLAIR) says that up to the time of the death of LYON he had been a warm friend of FREMONT. Now, the fact is that LYON's death occurred on the 10th of August, and it is seen that the gentleman's friendship continued for FREMONT till even after this—continued for him whom he has since arraigned as a guilty criminal, as one whose skirts are stained with the blood of that brave officer—arraigns him now of a crime, which, if guilty, he must be guilty of murder, if he (Gen. FREMONT) had the power to relieve him and did not. But though LYON died early in August, it is not till September that the gentleman from Missouri considers FREMONT guilty, because for twenty days after he did not accuse him of the crime. Mr. COLFAX quoted several dispatches from Gen. SCOFIELD HARDING, and Gen. LYON himself, to show the impossibility of reinforcing LYON, even before the withdrawal of the large drafts of troops from the Southwest for the protection of Washington, and continued. It was under, therefore, the most adverse circumstances that Gen. FREMONT took command at St. Louis; and it was for raising an army to protect the Union, and to put down rebellion, that he has been condemned from one end of the country to the other. The gentleman opposite declared here that Cairo did not need reinforcements, but I say it did. FREMONT had at this time a few regiments, three of three-months' men—men who had not yet received any pay, and who would not reenlist, but were, in consequence of neglect, determined to abandon the service. Now, I submit to this House, and to the country, the consideration of the two points to be reinforced. One was at the end of a common wagon road, from whence LYON could have retreated if he could not maintain himself; the other was at the mouth of the Ohio, which commanded the Mississippi and the Missouri Rivers at Cairo, the furthest point south we then had in our possession. It was then in great danger of being wrested from us, and rebel Governors and leaders had sent down troops to seize it for the Secessionists. Now, Gen. FREMONT could only reinforce one of these two points, and he chose the most important, and went to Cairo. Mr. COLFAX read letters and dispatches from Gen. PRENTISS, to show the imminency which demanded the strengthening of Cairo, and continued: Cairo was at that time threatened by the enemy, thirty thousand strong. He had with him only eight regiments, and only two of these he had a right to hold. He did the best he could. He got together all the force he could muster, and went down on steamboats to Cairo. And for this, too, he was condemned all over the country, because, indeed, he should have traveled by steamboats and thus make a parade. But it was actually necessary to do so, in order that he might impress the rebels with the conviction that he commanded a larger force than he really did. There were also great complaints made because Gen. FREMONT went in a carriage to the boat. I inquired into this matter, and the fact is that his friends brought the carriage to his house for the purpose of conveying him to the wharf. When he saw the carriage he refused to enter it, saying, "No, I will not go in this state." His friends insisted, because they feared he would be assassinated on the way if he went on foot, while at the same time it was necessary, as Major-General, to show himself from an open carriage to loyal people. A good deal was also said about the six thousand dollar house he rented in St. Louis. I also inquired into this charge, and found that all his immediate officers were quartered in the same house, which was also used for the officers of the Department, as there was no time for traveling from office to office. A great public saving was effected in this way, and yet for this also has Gen. FREMONT been denounced. Another of the charges brought against him was with regard to the purchase of five hundred tons of ice, with which it was sneeringly said there should be glorious times making sherry cobblers for the Staff. From inquiry I ascertained that this ice was ordered on the requisition of the Surgeon-General. At the time the requisition was made for the ice, half the troops were sick from using the muddy waters of the streams in the vicinity of the camps, and when the sick men were sent to the hospitals they remained sick, for even there they had none but this impure water, which first prostrated them. Of one regiment—the Twenty-second Illinois—the majority were in hospital from malaria and the use of bad water. The ice was procured, not to follow the army, but to be used in the hospitals by the sick and wounded soldiers—for the use of the men who had shed their blood for the country. For this Gen. FREMONT had been denounced all over the country, and to these charges and accusations he has been silent and forebore to answer up to this time. The gentleman (Mr. BLAIR) said that the hundred days of FREMONT were the saddest days that had ever befallen the loyal men of the Northwest. I differ with him there, also. Oh, no; there were sadder days than those. It was after Gen. FREMONT was deposed, when the gallant army, with which he had driven off the enemy, was ordered to fall back. Then it was that the loyal men, who had so long suffered from the presence of the rebels, and who hailed the glorious Stars and Stripes with acclamations as the promise of safety and security, and with clasped hands and joyful faces cheered once more for the Union—it was when these people forsook their homes to follow in sad procession the retreating army, to avoid the halter and the gibbet, hopeless and fondless, the days following that which saw Gen. FREMONT deposed. These were the saddest days for the people of the Northwest. The gentleman from Missouri characterized the proclamation issued by Gen. FREMONT as bombastic. I have this to say about that proclamation: I never quarreled with the President because he saw fit to say that that proclamation should be modified. I regret that he did so, but I know Mr. LINCOLN is as honest a man as lives on this continent, and he acted, no doubt, from convictions of duty, and while I differ with him in respect to that proclamation, I would be the last to asperse an act of his. The President said it should be modified. But Gen. FREMONT said the President must then modify it himself; he would bow to the order as a subordinate should to the rebuke of his chief. The gentleman (Mr. BLAIR) might have refrained from his remarks with reference to what he called the "mutiny" at Springfield. Now, he had it from distinguished authority, that a spirit of insubordination was manifested all over the camps when it was known that their General was superseded in his command. It was then that he delivered his farewell to the army, and the whole country was seized with admiration when they saw how a brave and noble man was stricken down can fall without a word of complaint and without a murmur. Gen. FREMONT's conduct on the occasion should have shielded him from at least one charge of the gentleman opposite. Even those New-York papers, which had most persistently denounced him, expressed in eulogistic language their admiration of his conduct in that trying moment. It is true he could not escape an ovation in St. Louis on his return; but in Cincinnati, when he learned, as he was passing through it, that the citizens were determined to give him an ovation, he avoided it by keeping on his way, even declining to accept of its hospitalities. Has there ever been a man stricken down from high position under a presence of untoward circumstances, who has borne himself so meekly? I speak as an independent member of this House, not having had one fact communicated to me by Gen. FREMONT. Now, with regard to the proclamation. What difference was there between it and the declaration of that distinguished man, ANDREW JOHNSON, one of the most loyal men living? JOHNSON declared that no rebel had a right to own anything. That was all that FREMONT said, clothed in the language of a proclamation. He said, "The real and personal property of rebels shall be confiscated, and the slaves of any shall be free men." JOHNSON says: "No rebel has a right to own anything." I don't see any difference, and yet no person has attempted to condemn JOHNSON. I come now to the fall of Lexington. I happened to be in St. Louis on the 14th of September, and found the whole city excited with the news which had just reached there, that PRICE was marching upon the gallant defender of the town of Lexington, and when my friend speaks about the Home Guard, it appears to me that Col. MULLIGAN didn't bear very high testimony to their gallantry then. But I saw Lieut.-Gov. HALL, and he told me that PRICE was marching toward Lexington with 15,000 men, and that FREMONT ought to send out a column to interrupt him. I asked him how many men FREMONT had, and he said he thought he had 20,000. I thought if he had that number he certainly could snap out some; and I went to Gen. FREMONT, full of zeal for the reinforcement of MULLIGAN, and told him what Lieut.-Gov. HALL had said, and that if he had twenty thousand men some ought to be sent out. He said: "I will tell you, confidentially, what I would not have known in the streets of St. Louis for my life. They have got the opinion that I have twenty thousand men here. I will show you what I really have got." He rang the bell, and his Secretary came and brought the muster-roll for that day, and by that muster-roll he had in St. Louis, and within seven miles round about, less than eight thousand men, and only two of them full regiments. It was a beggarly array of an army, and it was all needed to defend that city at that time. But I asked him if he could not spare some of these? Sir, the tears stood in his eyes as he handed me two telegraphic dispatches he had that day received from Washington. I will read them, that you may see how little was at his command to reinforce MULLIGAN. Mr. COLFAX then read the dispatches ordering him to send 5,000 armed infantry to Washington, and continued, I have shown you that he had men, but no guns; and when he bought guns, the necessity for which was imperious, he was denounced from one end of this country to the other because they were not Springfield rifles of the best quality. Yet he must send five thousand well-armed infantry to Washington at once, and this draft on him was to be replaced by troops from Kansas, or wherever he could best gather them. I asked him, "What can you do (and my heart sank within me as I asked the question) here with an inferior force, and your best forces sent away to Washington?" Said he, "Washington must be in danger, and they must have my troops, though Missouri fall, and I fall myself." After I had heard that, I would have been a traitor to my convictions if I did not stand up to defend this man, who was willing to sacrifice himself to defend the imperiled Capital of the country.

Mr. BLAIR said Gen. FREMONT made a return to Secretary CAMERON about the same time, which showed that he had 55,000 men in his department.

Mr. COLFAX—I am coming to that very point. He telegraphed to Washington that he was preparing to obey the order received, and I doubt not it made his heart bleed, knowing the strait MULLIGAN was in. Then he telegraphed to Gov. MORTON and Gov. DENNISON for more troops, and the answer he received was, that they had received orders to send all their troops East. So there his reliance failed. My friend says that it cannot be shown that he moved any of his men until after Lexington had fallen. Lexington fell on Friday, the 22d of September. I well remember the day. Here are dispatches to Gen. POPE, on the 16th of September, and dispatches from Gen. STURGIS to Col. DAVIS, hurrying the men. The wires were hot with orders hurrying the men to reinforce MULLIGAN. POPE telegraphed, on the 17th of September, that his troops would be there day after to-morrow, which would have been two days before Lexington surrendered, and STURGIS thought he should be there on Thursday. Col. MULLIGAN told me himself, that if STURGIS had appeared on the opposite side of the river, he thought PRICE would have retired. Thus, from three sources, FREMONT sent on troops to reinforce MULLIGAN, but he failed to do it because the elements seemed to be against him, and not because he did not seek to do so in every possible way that he could to send succor to him. At this very time there were all the different posts in Missouri to be held; his three months' men were rapidly retiring, and his best men sent to Washington; PRICE, with 15,000 men, marching to Lexington; MCCULLOCH threatening Rolla, HARDEE threatening Ironton, and POLK and PILLOW at Columbus; and all over the State were organized bands of rebels—about 80,000 men—threatening him, and he with an inadequate force to meet them. And while thus struggling, from every side were launched against him the poisoned arrows of hate and partisan enmity, and while FREMONT was out hunting the enemies of his country somebody was in St. Louis hunting up witnesses against him, and giving *ex parte* testimony taken there; and while he was facing the foe, endeavoring to secure victory, a synopsis of the testimony was sent upon the wires all over the country, so that the public mind should be poisoned against him and his overthrow might be the easier. I think, in the name of humanity—if there is no such word as justice—they should at least have sent him this evidence after he came back to his post, but to this very hour the Committee have not sent him this testimony at all. My friend says FREMONT has not demanded a trial. If the charges were made against him to the War Department, and if they think them substantial enough to reserve any attention, it is their business to put him on trial.

Mr. WADSWORTH, of Kentucky, (Union,) was understood to make some inquiry about the contracts for the fortifications of St. Louis, and the contracts for clothing and supplies.

Mr. COLFAX—I have said, that I did not defend the fortification contracts; but even then there may be injustice done him by *exparte* testimony. If Gen. FREMONT could prove that he had acted on the advice of competent men, and that work of this kind, day and night, hurrying all the while, was worth something like what he paid, it would at least be sure palliation for it. But I do not know what his defence is. He directed Gen. MCKINSTRY to make the best bargain he could, and then he approved it, whatever the decision was; and yet Gen. FREMONT is held responsible for all that Gen. MCKINSTRY had done. But Gen. MCKINSTRY was not appointed by him, but was sent there by the Government before Gen. FREMONT got there. When FREMONT was superseded, this was the condition of things in Missouri, and it is the proudest and noblest vindication that he can have that the whole State was more tranquil than was Western Virginia or Kentucky. I don't care whether you say anybody else did it or FREMONT, but such was the fact. In the second place his army was headed and was further South than any other army in the Union at that day. In the third place, it was headed in the right direction. In the fourth place, the men under his command, who, if he had been this imbecile, foolish and timid man that my friend has talked about, would have scorned and despised him for leading them into the jaws of death. These men were filled with loyalty and enthusiasm for him, and the brave Life Guard, with ZAGONYI at their head, who performed the most brilliant achievement of the war—though my friend says they did nothing at Springfield, they charged on an enemy ten times their force, with the war cry of, "Fremont and the Union"—and when they came back to St. Louis they were dismissed from the service for words spoken at Springfield, refused rations and forage for their horses, and treated with scorn and contempt. Those brave men, who dared to charge on an enemy ten times their force, with the war cry of their chieftain, whom they loved and for whom they would have given their blood, should at least be spoken kindly of in the halls of Congress. In the fifth place, he had marched his army, although the Adjutant-General had said it could not be done for the want of transportation, yet he had marched his army after the enemy, and in the right direction, until the moment when he was suppressed and he fell. In the sixth place, when he left Missouri every mile of its railroad was running to full capacity, and left behind him in the City of St. Louis an evidence of good sense, if not genius—he connected all the railroads around the levee so that you can use the whole amount of transportation upon one road, and then he left. Adjourned till Monday.

IMPORTANT FROM KENTUCKY.

Great Extent of the Earthworks at Columbus.

Additional Interesting Particulars of the Evacuation and Occupation.

The Rebel Force There Only Eighteen Thousand.

CAIRO, Thursday, March 6.

A second visit to Columbus has revealed many facts of interest. Col. BUFORD, who has made a complete examination of the earthworks, says they are six miles long.

THE OCCUPATION BY OUR FORCES.

CAIRO, Wednesday, March 4.

Commodore FOOTE, Gen. CULLOM and Gen. SHERMAN, with six gunboats and four mortarboats, the Twenty-seventh, Forty-second and Forty-fourth Illinois, and Seventy-first Ohio, left here this morning at daylight, for Columbus, which place they reached at 9 o'clock, and found it occupied by 250 of the Second Illinois Cavalry, under command of Lieut.-Col. HAAS.

This officer left Paducah on Sunday night, and took possession of Columbus last evening at 5 o'clock, about two hours after the last of the enemy had left.

From citizens of the place I learned the following particulars:

The evacuation began last Wednesday night, and continued until yesterday. The force there was 18,000 strong, a part of which went by land in the direction of Union City, while the other part, with their stores, were taken down the Mississippi by twenty transports, which had been sent up from below for this purpose.

Most of their stores and cannon were removed, and their barracks, extending over an area of a mile, were burned.

Some private property was fired, but not purposely.

The ten cannon which mounted their water battery were thrown into the river.

The 128-pounder, which bursted and wounded Gen. POLK last Fall, was left.

The mammoth chain which Gen. PILLOW had stretched across the river to obstruct its navigation, can be seen hanging from the bluffs into the water.

The business houses were closed, and all but six families had fled.

The printing material of the *Confederate News* had been thrown into the river.

A large quantity of bacon was poisoned, and left for our troops.

The railroad leading to Union City was torn up, the dépôt at Columbus burned, and a bridge over Alton Creek destroyed.

The fortifications had been mounted by two hundred cannon.

A great quantity of shot, from 64 down to 12-pounders, and a lot of torpedoes were left behind.

The bluff upon which they were fortified is 100 feet high, and a temporary railroad had been constructed to haul their cannon up to their works.

The citizens said the enemy at New-Madrid were to be reinforced by the rebels who went down the river, and those who went into the interior would make a stand at Union City.

The Twenty-seventh, Forty-second and Fifty-fourth Illinois had marched from the transports up to the fortifications when I left.

Commodore FOOTE, with the flag-ship *Cincinnati*, has just returned. The other gunboats are on their way up.

EXECUTION OF A SOLDIER.

BALTIMORE, Friday, March 7.

Private JOSEPH H. KUHNS, of the Second Maryland Regiment, will be hung, at Fort McHenry, to-day, between the hours of 12 and 3 o'clock, in the presence of the whole division of Gen. DIX, for the murder of Lieut. J. DAVIS WHITSON. The military are now assembling and marching to the fort.

THE GUNBOAT TUSCARORA.

BOSTON, Friday March 7.

The national gunboat *Tuscarora* remained near Gibraltar, February 15. She had changed her anchorage from Algesiras to Orange Grove, bringing her within three miles of the steamer *Sumter*, but still in Spanish waters.

TRADE WITH NASHVILLE, TENN.

LOUISVILLE, Ky., Friday, March 7.

The military restrictions on trade between Northern ports and Nashville, Tenn., have been removed.

UP THE TENNESSEE RIVER.

The Late Engagement at Pittsburgh Landing.

Probable Loss of the Enemy Twenty Killed and Two Hundred Wounded.

The Union Strength in Southern Tennessee.

ST. LOUIS, Friday March 7.

A special dispatch to the St. Louis *Democrat*, dated Cairo, 6th inst., says that Lieut. GWIN, of the gunboat *Tyler*, reached here last night from the Tennessee River.

The enemy had not renewed their attempt to fortify Pittsburgh landing.

Lieut. GWIN landed under a flag of truce, and was permitted to go 8 mile from the river before being stopped by the pickets of the enemy.

The object of Lieut. GWIN was to obtain an exchange of prisoners, which had been taken last Saturday.

On the morning after the engagement nine dead bodies and one hundred wounded were found in the encampment of the enemy, which had been removed three miles from the river.

Lieut. GWIN thinks the loss of the rebels in the engagement was twenty killed and two hundred wounded. Their force engaged was 1,000 infantry, 300 cavalry and six pieces of artillery.

At Corinth, Miss., eighteen miles from the Tennessee River, the rebels have 1,500 or 2,000 troops.

At Henderson Station, a mile from the Tennessee River, were from 1,000 to 2,000 rebels.

At Bear Creek, seven miles back of Eastport, Miss., there were from 800 to 1,000 of the enemy.

It was reported that the rebels were fortifying Chicahawa.

The result of the recent election in Hardin and McNary Counties shows the strength of the Union sentiment in Southern Tennessee. The former gave 500 out of 1,000 votes for the Union candidate, and the latter 200 majority out of 1,800 votes.

Lieut. GWIN says that the cry of the people is to send us arms and sufficient force to protect us in organizing ourselves, and we will drive the rebels out of Tennessee ourselves.

DISPATCHES FROM FLAG-OFFICER FOOTE.

WASHINGTON, Friday, March 7.

The Navy Department has received full dispatches from Commodore FOOTE, concerning the recent expedition to Pittsburgh, near the Mississippi line, a synopsis of which has already been published. It appears that, during the action, the gunboats *Lexington* and *Taylor* expended 45 eight-inch shells, 25 six-inch shells and 16 stand of grape. Several of the rebels were seen to fall, but the full extent of the damage to them could not be ascertained.

THE GUNBOAT FIGHT IN TENNESSEE.

Correspondence of the Chicago Post.

CAIRO, Monday, March 3.

The discovery of a new rebel battery on the Tennessee River, mentioned by telegraph, was made in this wise. Hearing that the rebels were planting a new battery somewhere near Savannah, the wooden gunboats *Taylor* and *Lexington* were ordered to make a reconnoissance up the river and shell them out. The boats left Fort Henry Friday morning, and proceeded slowly, examining the shores carefully as they went along. They were accompanied by the transport *Izetta*, with two companies of the Thirty-second Illinois Regiment. They passed Savannah about 10 o'clock Saturday morning, having as yet discovered no signs of the expected battery. But now the transport was ordered to keep well in the river, as at any moment a shell or round shot might announce the unpleasant proximity of the object they were in quest of.

Eight miles above Savannah we came to a little town called Pittsburgh, a miserable looking little hamlet, as they nearly all are in this region. There is an island here in the river, called Diamond Island, and just as we came out of the channel at its head, *bang!* went a rebel cannon, and a 24-pound shot came plunging toward us from the rebel battery situated less than half a mile in our advance. It was followed by two other shots from smaller guns, before our big guns responded. We steamed right on toward them, and opened at about six hundred yards, with shell. Their battery consisted of one 24-pounder rifled gun, and three 12-pounder howitzers. The 24-pounder fired only six shots, when it was silenced, either by our fire or from some other cause. The three smaller guns blazed away for about twenty minutes, when they also ceased firing, not a single one of their shots from the beginning having touched either of our boats. Our gunboats kept up their fire for half an hour longer, shelling the woods in all directions.

When the firing commenced, a small body of rebel infantry was also discovered, who undertook to put in practice the plan which some Memphis newspaper editors proposed, viz.: To conceal themselves on the bank and pick off the pilots of our gunboats. They soon found they might as well attempt to swallow an oyster without opening the shell. A few discharges of grape sent them helter skelter over the brow of the hill.

After the woods had been shelled pretty thoroughly, and nothing more been seen or heard of the enemy, about forty soldiers and marines, under command of a lieutenant, were sent ashore to reconnoitre the neighborhood. They proceeded up the long slope of the hill to the distance of a thousand yards or more from the landing, when they suddenly found themselves face to face with two or three regiments of rebel infantry, who immediately shot at them. Our men returned the compliment, and immediately retired to the shelter of a log house, some five hundred yards from the shore, where they made a stand, and peppered away at the rebels as vigorously as if they expected to drive back the rebel ten or fifteen hundred.

The gunboats hesitated to reopen on the rebels lest they should kill some of our own men, but waited in the momentary expectation that they would return to the boats. They did not do so, however, until the Lieutenant commanding (whose name I cannot learn) discovered that the rebels were flanking him on both sides, for the purpose of making prisoners of his little command. He then ordered a retreat, and the gallant forty made the best time they could to the boats, which they reached with the loss of three men killed and seven or eight wounded. The rebels pursued hotly, and getting behind trees fired both at our men in the boats and at the gunboats, perforating the latter with a good many musket balls, but injuring no one except the officer in command of the boat howitzer on the upper deck, one of whose legs was shattered by a Minié ball, rendering amputation necessary.

The gunboats reopened their batteries with grape, which caused the rebels to retreat with most undignified rapidity over the hill again. Seeing and hearing no more of them, the gunboats moved down the stream a short distance and lay at anchor. Having none but fifteen-second fuse shells, the gunboats were unable to do the execution at short range which they could have done with shorter fire. Accordingly, the *Lexington* was dispatched to Cairo for a supply of the desired ammunition, while the *Taylor* remained to look after the new rebel battery. The place where it was found is a sort of natural fortification, the hill furnishing a hollow just over the first ridge, in which the rebel infantry took shelter from our fire. In this particular it resembles Fort Donelson.

Trouble with the Indians in Colorado.

CHICAGO, Friday, March 7.

The Denver *News*, of the 24th, says that a delegation from Conegos and Gaudaloupe Counties arrive in that city, to lay before the Government information respecting the threatened difficulties with the Utah Indians. They represent war as imminent. A number of fights recently occurred between the Utahs and Arapahoes. It is said that an alliance between the latter tribe and four other tribes, has been made for the purpose of warring on the Utahs the coming season. Settlers in the counties named fear one party or the other may encroach on the white settlements.

The New-York Times.

VOL. XI—NO. 3264. NEW-YORK, MONDAY, MARCH 10, 1862. PRICE TWO CENTS.

HIGHLY IMPORTANT NEWS.

Desperate Naval Engagements in Hampton Roads.

Attack Upon our Blockading Vessels by the Rebel Steamers Merrimac, Jamestown and Yorktown.

The Frigate Cumberland Run Into by the Merrimac and Sunk.

Part of Her Crew Reported to be Drowned.

SURRENDER OF THE FRIGATE CONGRESS.

Engagement of the Rebel Steamers with the Newport's News Batteries.

The Minnesota and Other Vessels Aground.

CESSATION OF FIRING AT NIGHT.

Opportune Arrival of the Iron-Clad Ericsson Battery Monitor.

A Five Hours' Engagement Between Her and the Merrimac.

The Rebel Vessel Forced to Haul Off.

THE MONITOR UNINJURED.

FORTRESS MONROE, Saturday, March 8.

The dullness of Old Point was startled to-day by the announcement that a supicious looking vessel, supposed to be the *Merrimac*, looking like a submerged house, with the roof only above water, was moving down from Norfolk by the channel in front of the Sewell's Point batteries. Signal guns were also fired by the *Cumberland* and *Congress*, to notify the *Minnesota*, *St. Lawrence* and *Roanoke* of the approaching danger, and all was excitement in and about Fortress Monroe.

There was nothing protruding above the water but a flagstaff flying the rebel flag, and a short smoke-stack. She moved along slowly, and turned into the channel leading to Newport's News, and steamed direct for the frigates *Cumberland* and *Congress*, which were lying at the mouth of James River.

As soon as she came within range of the *Cumberland*, the latter opened on her with her heavy guns, but the balls struck and glanced off, having no more effect than peas from a pop-gun. Her ports were all closed, and she moved on in silence, but with a full head of steam.

In the meantime, as the *Merrimac* was approaching the two frigates on one side, the rebel iron-clad steamers *Yorktown* and *Jamestown* came down James River, and engaged our frigates on the other side. The batteries at Newport's News also opened on the *Yorktown* and *Jamestown*, and did all in their power to assist the *Cumberland* and *Congress*, which, being sailing vessels, were at the mercy of the approaching steamers.

The *Merrimac*, in the meantime, kept steadily on her course, and slowly approached the *Cumberland*, when she and the *Congress*, at a distance of one hundred yards, rained full broadsides on the iron-clad monster, that took no effect, the balls glancing upwards, and flying off, having only the effect of checking her progress for a moment.

After receiving the first broadside of the two frigates, she ran on to the *Cumberland*, striking her about midships, and literally laying open her sides. She then drew off, and fired a broadside into the disabled ship, and again dashed against her with her iron-clad prow, and, knocking in her side, left her to sink, while she engaged the *Congress*, which laid about a quarter of a mile distant.

The *Congress* had, in the meantime, kept up a short engagement with the *Yorktown* and *Jamestown*, and having no regular crew on board of her, and seeing the hopelessness of resisting the iron-clad steamer, at once struck her colors. Her crew had been discharged several days since, and three companies of the Naval Brigade had been put on board temporarily, until she could be relieved by the *St. Lawrence*, which was to have gone up on Monday to take her position as one of the blockading vessels of the James River.

On the *Congress* striking her colors, the *Jamestown* approached and took from on board of her, all her officers as prisoners, but allowed the crew to escape in boats. The vessel being thus cleared, was fired by the rebels, when the *Merrimac* and her two iron-clad companions opened with shell and shot on the Newport's News batteries. The firing was briskly returned. Various reports have been received, principally from frightened sutler's clerks. Some of them represent that the garrison had been compelled to retreat from the batteries to the woods. Another was that the two smaller rebel steamers had been compelled to retreat from their guns.

In the meantime the steam-frigate *Minnesota*, having partly got up steam, was being towed up to the relief of the two frigates, but did not get up until it was too late to assist them. She was also followed up by the frigate *St. Lawrence*, which was taken in tow by several of the small harbor steamers. It is rumored, however, that neither of these vessels had pilots on board them, and after a short engagement, both of them seemed to be, in the opinion of the pilots on the Point, aground. The *Minnesota* either intentionally or from necessity, engaged the three steamers at about a mile distance, with only her two bow guns. The *St. Lawrence* also poured in shot from all the guns she could bring to bear, and it was the impression of the most experienced naval officers on the point that both had been considerably damaged. These statements, it must be borne in mind, are all based on what could be seen by a glass at a distance of nearly eight miles, and from a few panic-stricken non-combatants, who fled at almost the first gun from Newport's News.

In the meantime darkness approached, though the moon shone out brightly, and nothing but the occasional flashing of guns could be seen. The *Merrimac* was also believed to be aground, as she remained stationary, at a distance of a mile from the *Minnesota*, making no attempt to attack or molest her.

Previous to the departure of the steamer for Baltimore, no guns had been fired for half an hour, the last one being fired from the *Minnesota*. Some persons declared that immediately after this last gun was fired, a dense volume of vapor was seen to rise from the *Merrimac*, indicating the explosion of her boiler. Whether this is so or not, cannot be known, but it was the universal opinion that the rebel monster was hard aground.

Fears were of course entertained for the safety of the *Minnesota* and *St. Lawrence* in such an unequal contest; but if the *Merrimac* was really ashore, she could do no more damage. It was the intention of the *Minnesota*, with her picked and gallant crew, to run into close quarters with the *Merrimac*, avoid her iron prow, and board her. This the *Merrimac* seemed not inclined to give her an opportunity to do.

At 8 o'clock, when the Baltimore boat left, a fleet of steam-tugs were being sent up to the relief of the *Minnesota* and the *St. Lawrence*, and an endeavor was to be made to draw them off the bar on which they had grounded. In the meantime the firing had suspended, whether from mutual consent or necessity, could not be ascertained.

The rebel battery at Pig Point was also enabled to join in the combined attack on the *Minnesota*, and several guns were fired at her from Sewall's Point as she went up. None of them struck her, but one or two of them passed over her.

The Baltimore boat left Old Point at 8 o'clock last night. In about half-an-hour after she left the wharf, the iron-clad Ericsson steamer *Monitor* passed her, going in, towed by a large steamer. The *Monitor* undoubtedly reached Fortress Monroe by 9 o'clock, and may have immediately gone into service; if not, she would be ready to take a hand early on Sunday morning.

The foregoing are all the facts as far as can be at present ascertained, and are, probably, the worst possible version of the affair.

THE LINE OF THE POTOMAC FROM HARPER'S FERRY TO CHETANK POINT.

Map Showing the Cockpit Point Batteries, Yesterday Evacuated by the Rebels, and Taken Possession of by Our Troops; Leesburgh, from Which the Rebels were Driven on Saturday Morning by Col. Geary, and All Other Important Points.

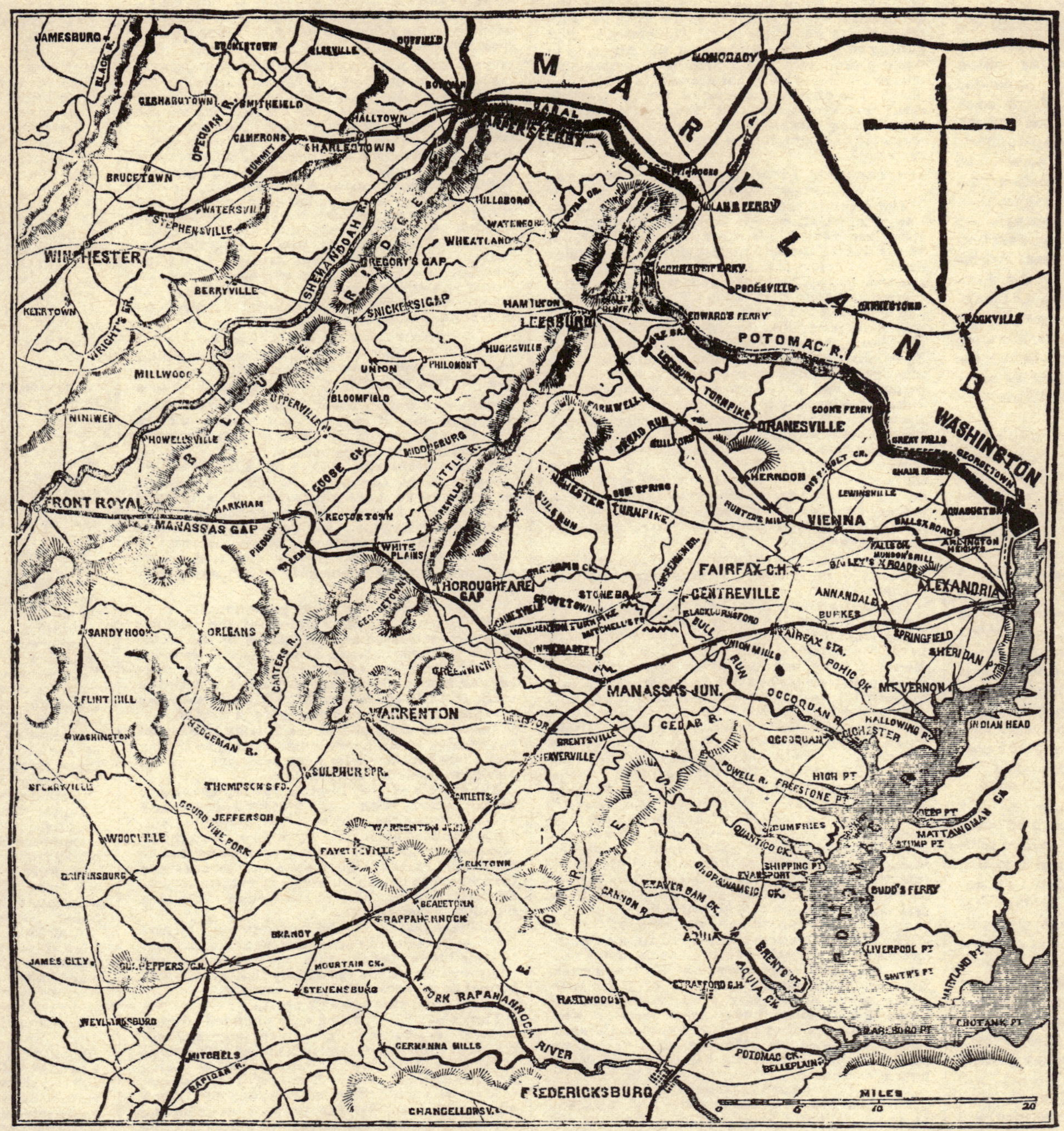

LATER AND BETTER NEWS.

A Five Hours' Engagement Between the Ericsson Battery and the three Rebel Steamers

The Rebel Vessels Driven Off—The Merrimac in a Sinking Condition.

WASHINGTON, Sunday, March 9—6:45 P. M.

The telegraph line to Fortress Monroe is just completed, and a message from there states that after the arrival of the *Monitor*, last night, she was attacked by the *Merrimac*, *Jamestown*, and *Yorktown*. *After a five hours' fight they were driven off, and the Merrimac put back to Norfolk in a sinking condition.*

OFFICIAL.

[BY TELEGRAPH FROM FORTRESS MONROE.]

WASHINGTON, Sunday, March 9—7 P. M.

The *Monitor* arrived at Fortress Monroe last night.

Early this morning she was attacked by the three vessels—the *Merrimac*, the *Jamestown* and the *Yorktown*.

After five hours' contest they were driven off—the *Merrimac* in a sinking condition.

The above is official.

DISPATCH AUTHORIZED BY GEN. WOOL

FORTRESS MONROE, Sunday, March 9.

The *Monitor* arrived at 10 P. M., last night, and went immediately to the protection of the *Minnesota*, lying aground just below Newport's News. At 7 A. M. to-day the *Merrimac*, accompanied by two wooden steamers, the *Yorktown* and *Jamestown*, and several tugs, stood out toward the *Minnesota*, and opened fire. The *Monitor* met them at once, and opened fire, when the enemy's vessels retired, excepting the *Merrimac*. *The two iron-clad vessels fought, part of the time touching each other, from 8 A. M. till noon, when the Merrimac retreated.* Whether she is injured, or not, it is impossible to say.

Lieut. J. L. WORDEN, who commanded the *Monitor*, handled her with great skill, assisted by Chief-Engineer STIMERS.

The *Minnesota* kept up a continuous fire, and is herself somewhat injured. She was moved considerably to-day, and will probably be off to-night.

The *Monitor* is uninjured, and ready at any moment to repel another attack.

[Sent by order of Gen. WOOL.]

WASHINGTON, Sunday, March 9.

The following was received to-night by Major-Gen. MCCLELLAN from Gen. WOOL, dated Fortress Monroe, at 6 o'clock this evening:

"Two hours after my telegraphic dispatch to the Secretary of War last evening, the *Monitor* arrived. She immediately went to the assistance of the *Minnesota*, which was aground, and continued so until a few moments since. Early this morning she was attacked by the *Merrimac*, *Jamestown* and *Yorktown*. After a five hours' contest they were driven off, the *Merrimac* in a sinking condition. She was towed by the *Jamestown*, *Yorktown* and several smaller boats toward Norfolk, no doubt, if possible, to get her in the dry-dock for repairs. The *Minnesota* is afloat and being towed toward Fortress Monroe."

THE VESSELS ENGAGED.

THE ERICSSON BATTERY MONITOR.

The new Ericsson battery, or, as she is now called, the *Monitor*, which left this port for Southern waters last Wednesday, has already had her first engagement with the enemy, and has come out victor. It appears that she arrived in Hampton Roads last Saturday night, just after the rebel battery *Merrimac* had been playing havoc with our blockaders. She came to the rescue precisely at the right moment. Yesterday morning she was set upon by the *Merrimac*, the *Jamestown* and the *Yorktown*. After a five hours' fight she drove them all off, the *Merrimac* putting back to Norfolk in a sinking condition. As the public will now be anxious to know something of the style and power of this iron-clad vessel, which has thus routed the famous rebel iron-clad floating battery, we append a full account of her, furnished by our correspondent, who accompanied her on a recent trial trip from this harbor.

DESCRIPTION OF THE VESSEL.

The designer and builder of the *Monitor* was Capt. ERICSSON, famous in connection with the invention of a mode of propelling vessels and working engines by the motor-power of caloric, or heated air. Capt. ERICSSON is a Swede by birth, but his remarkable and persevering scientific efforts have been carried on principally in this City for the last ten years.

By an act of Congress passed last Summer, the Secretary of the Navy was authorized to advertise for proposals to build one or more iron-clad vessels, all proposers to furnish their own plans. An appropriation of $1,500,000 was made to build such vessels, providing that the plans met with the approval of three commanding officers of the navy. The Board appointed consisted of Commodores JOSEPH SMITH, HIRAM PAULDING, and Capt. CHAS. H. DAVIS. Capt. ERICSSON sent in a plan which was accepted, with the understanding that the vessel was to be finished in one hundred days. The contract bears date the 4th of October, 1861.

The keel of this vessel was laid on the 25th of October, and so rapidly was the work performed, that the engines were put into the vessel and operated on the 31st of December last. The construction of the vessel was under the superintendence of Engineer ALBAN C. STEINERS, and Assistant Engineer ISAAC NEWTON, who were detailed from the frigate *Roanoke*, by Government, for that purpose. Annexed are the dimensions of the *Monitor*:

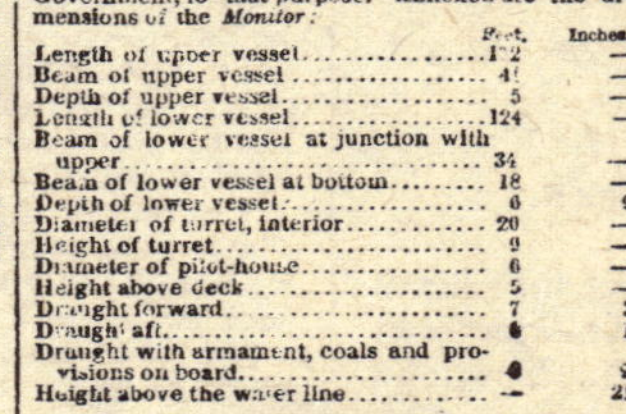

	Feet.	Inches.
Length of upper vessel	172	—
Beam of upper vessel	41	—
Depth of upper vessel	5	—
Length of lower vessel	124	—
Beam of lower vessel at junction with upper	34	—
Beam of lower vessel at bottom	18	—
Depth of lower vessel	6	9
Diameter of turret, interior	20	—
Height of turret	9	—
Diameter of pilot-house	6	—
Height above deck	5	—
Draught forward	7	3
Draught aft	[illegible]	1
Draught with armament, coals and provisions on board	[illegible]	9
Height above the water line	—	21

THE ARMAMENT.

The armament consists of two 11-inch Dahlgren guns, which are the heaviest now used by the navy. The lower part of the gun-carriages upon which the upper part slides when the gun is run in or out, consists of solid, wrought iron beams, extending the whole diameter of the turret, with their ends secured to it in such a manner that they essentially form a part of it. These beams are planned perfectly true, are seven inches deep by four inches wide, and are placed perfectly parallel in the turret, both guns pointing in the same direction. This permits the officer working the guns to take his aim by sights fixed with the turret instead of with the guns, in the usual way, which requires personal exposure when taking the aim. The ports through the side of the turret are only sufficiently wide to permit of the passage through them of the muzzle of the guns, and with just enough addition, vertically, for the elevation required. Inside of these swing iron pendulums, which close them against the enemy as soon as the gun recoils. The whole is made to revolve by a pair of steam engines placed beneath the deck, the handle which governs them passing up into the turret convenient to the hand of the officer who aims the gun.

HER AMMUNITION.

At the Novelty Iron Works a quantity of solid wrought iron shot was forged for the *Monitor*; each one weighing 187 pounds. These were intended for perforating and sinking iron clad vessels of the enemy whose sides are the ordinary height above the water line. Besides these she carries a quantity of cast iron shots, weighing 175 pounds each, and one hundred round of shells, in weight 155 pounds each.

THE MACHINERY.

Mr. C. H. DELAMATER fitted this vessel with machinery. It consists of two horizontal tubular boilers, containing 3,000 square feet of fire surface, and two horizontal condensing engines, of forty inches diameter of cylinders, by twenty-two inches stroke of pistons. The propeller is nine feet diameter, sixteen feet pitch, and has four blades. Her speed is about six and a half knots an hour. All her machinery is below water-line.

THE MONITOR'S OFFICERS.

The following were the officers of the *Monitor* when she left this port, six days ago:

Lieutenant Commanding—JOHN S. WORDEN.
Lieutenant and Executive Officer—S. D. Green.
Acting Masters—L. N. Stodder and J. W. Webber.
Acting Assistant Paymaster—Wm. F. Keeler.
Acting Assistant Surgeon—D. C. Logue.
Chief Engineer—A. C. Steiners.
Engineers—First Assistant, Isaac Newton; Second Assistant, Albert B. Campbell; Third Assistants, R. W. Sands and M. T. Sunstron.
Acting Master's Mate—George Frederickson.

THE SCIENTIFIC PLAN OF THE MONITOR.

Capt. ERICSSON's idea in building the *Monitor* was to give the greatest buoyancy to the vessel, and as small a target as possible to the enemy, so as to enable him to completely protect every part, all its attachments and every person on board, when under the fire of an enemy. He conceived that to do this was to build a broad flat-bottomed vessel with vertical sides and pointed ends, so that it requires but a shallow depth to displace water sufficient to buoy itself up, though loaded with an impregnable armor upon its sides, and a bomb-proof deck upon which is placed a shot-proof revolving turret containing two of the heaviest Dahlgren guns. To insure such a vessel the power of locomotion, it was only necessary to suspend beneath it a vessel of ordinary strength, sufficiently narrow and sloping at the sides, that if, as actual experiment has proven possible, the enemy's missile should pass below the shot-proof upper vessel, these sides can only be hit at such an acute angle that little harm is likely to ensue, and in its length approaching the bow only so nearly that its raking stem may receive the shot fired from directly ahead in the same way, and at the stern giving sufficient space to permit the dipping shot coming from directly aft to pass under the shot-proof end, directly on its course, without hitting the rudder, which is placed abaft the propeller.

The sides of the upper vessel are first formed of plate-iron, half an inch thick, outside of which is attached solid white oak, twenty-six inches thick, which again receives the rolled iron armor of five inches thickness. The bomb-proof deck is supported by well-stanchioned and diagonally braced oak beams, ten inches square, placed with their faces twenty-six inches apart, upon which is laid planking seven inches thick, covered with rolled plate-iron one inch thick. As the bottoms of these beams are on a level with the water-line, the armor above water is supported by a backing of forty-one feet in depth. The lower vessel is of iron, one-half inch thick, made in the usual manner, and contains, in its after part, the steam machinery and coal, and in the forward part—the poop being divided by a wrought iron bulkhead—the quarters for the officers and crew, and the ammunition and stores. In describing the upper and lower vessel, it must not be imagined that they are constructed separately; they form, together, one vessel; it is only as respects form that they can be regarded as two.

The Pilot-House and Anchor.

The pilot is protected by a shot-proof pilot-house which alone weighs 22,000 pounds. The house stands five feet above the level of the deck. The anchor is suspended from a circular well, open at the bottom, situated in the extreme bow of the upper vessel, and connected with the capstan in the bow of the lower one. An arrangement is also provided for taking soundings below the water line.

The Turret.

The turret spoken of above is for the protection of the men while working the guns; in fact, no one is exposed or seen by the enemy. The turret revolves, and consists, first, of a rolled plate iron skeleton, one inch thick, to which is riveted two thicknesses, of one inch each, of rolled iron plates. Outside of these riveted plates are six thicknesses, of one inch each, of rolled iron plates. Outside of these riveted plates are six thickness, of one inch each, of rolled plates bolted firmly to the first two thicknesses with screw bolts, having deep countersunk heads on the outside and nuts within, so that if in action the enemy's shot should loosen any of the plates they can easily be refastened. The seams are vertical, and these break joints with each other, consequently no shot can strike the seam of more than one thickness. The top is covered with a bomb-proof roof, placed six inches down within the turret, and perforated with holes. In addition to the above the gunners are protected by a shield, within the turret, of one and a half inch thickness.

FOR WHAT THE MONITOR WAS INTENDED.

The Ericsson Battery was not intended for an ordinary cruiser, but for the defence of our harbors and coast, and for operations such as those in which she has just achieved such a signal success. She is enabled to carry eight days' fuel, and thus can proceed easily from port to port along our seaboard. Provisions for three months can be stowed away in her, and a condensing apparatus for supplying fresh water to the officers and crew is fitted up on board.

THE LAST TRIAL TRIP OF THE MONITOR AND ITS RESULTS.

Last Monday the *Monitor* went on a trial trip down the Bay, about five miles beyond Fort Lafayette. Her steering qualities were found to be all that could be desired.

The guns were fired to test the question which had been mooted, of whether the concussion within the turret would not be so great as to injure seriously the ears of the men. First, a blank cartridge was fired, with the hatches in the roof open. Then a charge of canister, weighing 135 pounds, with 15 pounds of powder, with the hatches still open, and finally the same charge with the hatches closed, as they will be under the fire of the enemy. It was found that in every case the concussion in every part of the interior of the turret was considerably less than when standing near such a gun fired in the open air. The sailors stationed at the guns, and who expected to handle them shortly against the enemy, all expressed themselves delighted at the success of the trial. The speed of the vessel by the chip log was 6¾ knots, the engines making 65 revolutions.

The last heard of the *Monitor* previous to this news of her success, was by a bark which arrived here yesterday morning. The bark reported that, on the 7th inst., at 10 P. M., off Barnegat, she passed the *Monitor* in tow, bound for Fortress Monroe.

This magnificent success in her first trial, will settle all questions as to her efficiency.

LIEUT. WERDEN.

Lieut. J. R. WERDEN, it will be recollected, at the commencement of the rebellion was captured by the rebels, after having conveyed dispatches from the Government to the National fleet off Pensacola, and imprisoned several months at Montgomery. He was exchanged a short time ago, and was immediately assigned to the *Monitor*, in which, as will be seen from the dispatches, he has done most efficient service.

THE MERRIMAC.

The *Merrimac*, the iron-plated rebel steamer which attacked the Ericsson Battery, was formerly the United States screw-frigate of the same name. She was built at the Navy-Yard at Charlestown, Mass., in 1855; and her last active service was in the Pacific Squadron. At the time of the rebel attack on the Norfolk Navy-Yard, she was lying there in ordinary, as a store and receiving ship. She was a ship of 3,200 tons burden, and was pierced for forty guns. When the Navy-yard was assailed, she was set fire to, scuttled and sunk, by the National officers, in preference to letting her fall into the hands of the rebels. A recent official report on the subject, made to the rebel authorities, stated that she was sunk and burned to her copper line and down through to her berth-deck, which, with her spacious gun-deck, were also burned. After the rebels had got possession of the Yard, they proceeded to raise the hull of the *Merrimac*, and to convert her into a vessel of war for their own purpose. Her hull was cut down to within three feet of her water-work, and a bomb-proof house built on her gun-deck. She was then iron-plated, and her bow and stern steel clad, with a projecting angle of iron for the purpose of piercing a vessel. She had no masts, and there was nothing to be seen over her gun-deck, with the exception of the pilot-house and smoke-stack. The bomb-proof was three inches thick, and made of wrought iron. Altogether she looked like a most formidable war-ship. But when her iron sheathing was half on, it was tested by columbiads and found inefficient. She was then additionally strengthened, until she was so heavy that she bade fair to become unmanageable, and even to sink by her own weight. In a description published some two or three months ago, her armament was stated as consisting of four 11-inch navy guns on each side and two 100-pounder Armstrong guns at the bow and stern. But no doubt great changes have been made in her armament before this time. The Norfolk *Day Book* of the 6th ult. had an article describing the attempt to convert the *Merrimac* into an impregnable iron plated man-of-war as a failure. It began thus:

"We have scarcely patience enough left to condemn in temperate language the reckless impropriety of two of our cotemporaries, who have seen fit, in their thirst for notoriety, to thrust before the public the fact that the *Merrimac* has proved an abortion."

It was further said, that

"The calculation in displacement was erroneous. An error amounting to more than two hundred tons was discovered when the ship was floated off. The chief subject of regret is, that when she was shored up again the ship caught upon the blocks and received a considerable strain; consequently, some parts of the machinery have been taken up, and a quantity of dead-wood will have to be introduced to correct the

[Continued on Eighth Page.]

The Charleston Mercury.

VINDICE NULLO — SPONTE SUA SINE LEGE FIDES RECTUMQUE COLENTUR.

VOLUME LXXX. CHARLESTON, S. C., WEDNESDAY, MARCH 12, 1862. NUMBER 11,394

THE MERCURY.

WEDNESDAY, MARCH 12, 1862.

Our Shipments of Cotton.

We published yesterday a paragraph from the Columbia *Carolinian*, intimating some grave suspicions as to the real destination of the cotton shipments made from the various blockaded ports of the Confederate States. From such information as we can gather, we feel assured that, though there has probably been some illicit trade between the Yankees and persons in Southern ports, it has never reached the extent which the *Carolinian* seems to fear. We are glad to be able to say that, although the money profits to be reaped by selling Southern cotton to the Yankees at Nassau and Havana would be very great, the owners of all the more important vessels employed in running the blockade have steadfastly refused to entertain the tempting offers of those buying on Northern account. Neither the steamer hinted at by the *Carolinian*, nor any other steamer, as far as we can learn, has carried out cotton for other than the European markets.

We are assured, however, that many of the small sailing vessels which have run the blockade at Charleston, Mobile, Georgetown and Savannah, have sold their cargos of cotton, rice and naval stores at Nassau and Havana to parties avowedly purchasing for the Northern market. There is every reason to believe that the cargos were thus sold to the Yankees with the full knowledge and previous consent of the shippers. The unlawful character of these transactions is in no wise palliated by the fact that, owing to the small size of the vessels, the cargos were inconsiderable in amount. But it is certainly mere justice that, in denouncing this traffic with the enemies of our country, we should carefully discriminate between those shippers who have yielded to, and those who have spurned, the considerations of gain which such a traffic offers.

Conscription.

The Governor and Executive Council of South Carolina have, we learn, decided to make a radical and important change in the mode of raising troops in this State, whenever they may be needed hereafter, as long as the war shall last. On and after the 20th of the present month, all requisitions upon the State for troops will at once be filled *by conscription*, which very many persons, well informed on the subject, regard as the most effective and equitable plan. The conscripts will be mustered in *for the war*. *No volunteers*, for any arm of the service, will be received after the 20th inst. All field and line officers, from the grade of Colonel down to that of Third Lieutenant, will be appointed by the Governor and Council. The non-commissioned officers of each company will be appointed by the Captain, with the approval of the commanding officer of the Battalion or Regiment. These, we believe, are the main features of the new military regulations, which will probably be published in a few days.

THE GREAT NAVAL BATTLE IN HAMPTON ROADS.

FULL DETAILS OF THE ACTION.

The latest intelligence concerning the signal victory recently achieved by the naval forces of the Confederate States in Hampton Roads, will be found in our summary of telegraphic news. The following detailed accounts of the engagement, taken from the Norfolk *Day Book* of Monday, will be found interesting:

THE ENGAGEMENT OPENED—SPEEDY SINKING OF THE FRIGATE CUMBERLAND.

At a quarter past eleven o'clock on Saturday, the iron-clad steamer Virginia cast loose from her moorings at the Navy Yard, and made her way down to Hampton Roads towards the blockading fleet lying off Newport News. She reached their neighborhood after some detention at the obstructions below at two o'clock. Here she found the two first class sailing frigates Cumberland and Congress. The enemy seemed entirely unaware of our intention to attack them, and it is said, were so completely lulled into security that the Virginia had got down to Sewell's Point before they took the alarm. With a determination to pay her respects to the Cumberland first, the Virginia bore down for that vessel, and while passing the Congress she gave her a broadside by way of a salute. Her operations on the Cumberland were performed in the short space of fifteen minutes' time, at the end of which the Cumberland sank just where she had been lying. The Virginia, on approaching her, and getting within point blank range, fired her bow gun several times, and ran into her, striking her fairly with her ram, which made her reel to and fro, and sent her speedily to the bottom, but while going down, we understand, the aft gun of the Cumberland was discharged at the Virginia, with what injury we know not. The object in first getting rid of the Cumberland was probably to destroy the very heavy armament which that frigate carried, it being the heaviest in the Yankee navy. The officers and crew of the Cumberland made their escape as best they could, many of them being captured by our gunboats. The wounded on board, it is believed, went down with the vessel.

THE CONGRESS ATTACKED.—AFTER A STUBBORN RESISTANCE SHE SURRENDERS.

The Virginia next turned her attention to the Congress, which vessel, it is said, gallantly resisted her inevitable fate for nearly an hour, but finally finding the ship rapidly sinking, she hauled down her colors and made for the beach, where she was run as high aground as possible. Her officers and crew were taken off by our gunboats, and while she had her flag of truce hoisted, and was being relieved of her killed and wounded by our boats, the Yankees on shore at Newport News, disregarding the flag of truce, with Minie muskets fired into her and killed several of their own men, and slightly wounded in the arm Mr. John Hopkins, one of our pilots, attached to the Beaufort. While the Virginia was engaged with the Congress with her bow gun she poured broadside after broadside into the shore batteries of the enemy at Newport News. One discharge from the bow gun of the Virginia, says one of the prisoners, capsized two of the guns of the Congress, killing sixteen of her crew, and taking off the head of a Lieutenant Smith, and literally tore the ship to pieces.

THE STEAM FRIGATE MINNESOTA AND THE ST. LAWRENCE JOIN IN THE "FREE FIGHT" AND GET AGROUND.

While the engagement was going on between the two frigates and the Virginia, the enemy's steam frigate Minnesota put out from Old Point to their assistance. She laid well over towards Newport News, but not entirely out of the range of our batteries on Sewell's Point, which opened on her with what effect we are unable to say, but she replied to them without any damage whatever. The Minnesota got aground when within a mile or two of Newport News Point. There she stuck, unable to get off, while the Confederate steamers Patrick Henry and Jamestown peppered her with their batteries, while the Virginia was attending to the shore batteries at Newport News. The frigate St. Lawrence then came up to the assistance of the Minnesota, and she also got aground, and a steam frigate, supposed to be the Roanoke, put off from Old Point with the same intention, it is supposed, but seeing the sad havoc which the Virginia was playing with the Federal vessels, she put back to Old Point.

BURNING OF THE CONGRESS.

The frigate Congress was set fire to, on Saturday night, by a boat's crew from some of our vessels. She illuminated the whole Roads and river, and about midnight her magazine exploded with a tremendous noise. Her conflagration afforded a rare sight to many thousands of spectators who lined the shores of our harbor to witness the spectacle of a ship on fire. Many articles of value, we learn, were removed from her by our gunboats before being fired.

OTHER INCIDENTS.

The James River steamers arrived at the scene of action, it is said, about one hour after the engagement commenced. They easily passed the Newport News' batteries, and, after joining in the fight, rendered very efficient aid.

Several small prizes were said to have been taken by our gunboats from the Yankees, one of which, the schooner Reindeer, was brought up to the Navy Yard on Saturday night. Two others were said to have been carried over to Pig Point on Saturday.

Tugs and steamers were sent to the assistance of the Minnesota and St. Lawrence from Old Point, after they grounded, but their efforts to haul them off were unavailing.

The report that the Congress was fired by the Federals to prevent her falling into our hands, is without a shadow of truth. She was fired by hot shot from the Virginia, for firing into our boats while she had a flag of truce at the time flying, after she had struck her colors and surrendered to us.

Among the prisoners taken off the Congress was the slave Sam, the property of ——— Drummond, Esq., of this city, who escaped to the enemy some time in October last. He is now safe, having reached his home sooner, and under different circumstances, than he anticipated.

The first gun fired in the engagement is said to have been fired by the Confederate gunboat Beaufort, at the frigate Congress. All of our steamers and gunboats are said to have been managed with the utmost skill and dexterity, rendering great assistance to the Virginia in this magnificent and successful engagement.

By this daring exploit we have raised the James River blockade, without foreign assistance, and are likely, with the assistance of the Virginia, to keep open the communication.

THE FIGHT ON SUNDAY BEGUN.

The engagement was renewed again on Sunday morning, about 8½ o'clock, by the Jamestown, and several of our gunboats, firing into the Minnesota and St. Lawrance. Some detention occurred on board the Virginia on Sunday morning, we learn, or she would have commenced the engagement much earlier than 8½ o'clock; at which time she, together with the Patrick Henry, Jamestown and our other gunboats, opened fire on the Minnesota, which still lies hard and fast aground. The tide being at ebb, the Virginia did not take the channel, where the Minnesota lay, probably for fear of grounding, but getting within a good range of her, she opened fire with terrible effect, completely riddling her, and rendering constant exertion at the pump necessary to prevent her from filling.

THE ERICSSON BATTERY MAKES HER APPEARANCE.

Early in the morning, the Ericsson Battery, now called the Monitor, was discovered off Newport News Point, she having gone up there during the night. A sharp encounter soon took place between her and the Virginia, during which time they were frequently not more than 30 or 40 yards apart. Unfortunately, the Virginia ran aground, and the Ericsson, using her advantage, poured shot after shot into her, but without doing any serious damage. In a short while, however, the Virginia succeeded in getting off, and putting on full head of steam, ran her bow into the Ericsson, doing, as it is thought, great damage. Notwithstanding the firing were much heavier than on Saturday, there was no casualties on either of our vessels—not a man being in the least injured by shot from the enemy or otherwise.

DESTRUCTION OF THE GUNBOATS.

Several of the enemy's gunboats being within range, they were tapered with a shell or two from the Virginia, with telling effect, and in every case disabling or sinking them. One of these laying alongside the Minnesota, had a shell thrown aboard of her, which, on bursting, tore her asunder, and sent her to the bottom.

Having completely riddled the Minnesota, and disabled the St. Lawrence and Monitor, besides, as stated above, destroying several of the enemy's gunboats—in a word, having accomplished all that they designed, and having no more material to work upon, our noble vessels left the scene of their triumphs and returned to the yard, where they await another opportunity of displaying their prowess.

RETURN OF OUR FLEET TO NORFOLK.

On the arrival of the Virginia at the Yard her men were mustered and addressed by the commanding officer in terms of praise for their noble bearing during the engagement. They responded with hearty cheers, and expressed a desire to again re-enact the scenes through which they had just passed whenever opportunity presented.

The injury sustained by the Patrick Henry was not as great as at first supposed—being so trifling that a few hour's repairs were sufficient to place her in readiness for action.

The officers of the Virginia are represented as having acted with the utmost courage and bravery during the contest. It is related of Capt. Buchanan that during the thickest of the fight he remained on the deck of the Virginia, and that he discharged musket after musket at the enemy as they were handed up to him. It was while thus exposed that he received the wound of which mention is made above.

It is said that all of the batteries on Newport News were silenced except one, and that our shot and shell were thrown with such unerring aim and precision among the enemy that great numbers of them were killed and wounded.

THE ENEMY'S LOSSES.

The enemy's loss, killed and wounded, during the two day's battle, is exceedingly large, and estimated as from six to twelve hundred. The scene around the Congress is represented as being heart-sickening. The officers of the Beaufort, who ran alongside of her on Saturday night, and who boarded her for the purpose of removing the wounded aboard of her, and who were brutally fired upon by the enemy, while engaged in this work of mercy, represented the deck of the vessel as being literally covered with the dead and dying. One of them assures us that as he went from fore to aft, his shoes were well nigh buried in blood and brains. Arms, legs, and heads were found scattered in every direction, while here and there, in the agonies of death, would be found poor deluded wretches, with their breasts torn completely out.

Of the crew of the Cumberland, but few survived to tell the tale. As she went down her crew went with her, excepting some few who were taken as prisoners by us, and a few others who escaped to the shore. Out of the five hundred aboard of her, it is estimated that not over a hundred, at most, escaped, the remainder either being killed by our shot or drowned as the vessel went down.

Twenty-three prisoners were brought up to this city on Saturday night. These were all taken off the frigate Congress by the gunboat Beaufort, whilst our other gunboats took off others. One of these prisoners died while on his way to the city. He and another one wounded, were shot by their own forces, while being saved from the sinking frigate Congress. The wounded prisoners were carried to the hospital.

Of course, the greater part of those on board the gunboats were also drowned, as there was not sufficient time for them to have made their escape. Added to this very many in the camps of the enemy at Newport News were killed by the shells which the Virginia threw among them.

OUR LOSSES.

On our side the loss was indeed small, and when we consider the storm of shell, to which at times they were subjected, we can but wonder while we rejoice that so few of them suffered injury.

On the Virginia there were two killed and eight wounded. Among the wounded, we regret to mention, Capt. Buchanan and Lieutenant Minor. These wounds, however, we are happy to state, are but slight.

A shot entered the port hole and struck the gun on the muzzle, knocking off a piece nine inches long. This disabled the gun, which was immediately replaced by another of the same calibre.

On the Raleigh, Midshipman Hutter was killed, and Captains Tayloe and Alexander wounded—the first mentioned quite severely.

On the Beaufort, Gunner W. Robinson and two seamen were wounded. This was all the damage sustained by this vessel among her men. Two Yankee prisoners aboard of her were struck by the balls of their friends, one of them killed and the other severely wounded. The former was standing in the door of the wardroom at the time the Beaufort was alongside the Congress, and one of the shower of balls sent by the enemy on shore, from their Minie muskets, struck him on the forehead, penetrating his brain and killing him almost instantly.

On the Teaser, one man was wounded very slightly.

On board the Patrick Henry a shot entered one of her ports, we understand, and passed through one of her boilers, disabling it. She was compelled to haul off temporarily for repairs. There were four men killed and three wounded on board of her. Other damage not material.

Andrew J. Dalton, a printer, who left our office a few days since to join the Virginia, and who was at the bombardment of Sumter and participated in several other engagements during the war, we learn was one of the wounded on board that vessel on Saturday.

While the loss of the enemy is counted by hundreds, ours, as will be seen from the above, amounts to only seven killed and seventeen wounded. This loss on our part, as small as it is, was not the work of the enemy's shots from their vessels, but the result, for the most part, of the fire of muskets from ashore.

During the contest, the mainmast of the Raleigh was carried away. The flag staffs of the Virginia were also cut down.

FREEMEN!

AVOID CONSCRIPTION!

The undersigned desires to raise a Company for the Confederate States service, and for that purpose I call upon the people of the Counties of Jefferson and Hawkins, Tenn., to meet promptly at Russellville, on SATURDAY, JULY 19th, 1862, and organize a Company.

By so doing you will avoid being taken as Conscripts, for that Act will now be enforced by order of the War Department. Rally, then, my Countrymen, to your Country's call.

S. M. DENNISON,
Of the Confederate States Army.

CHARLESTON, Tenn., JUNE 30, 1862.

Captain Franklin Buchanan, commander of the *Merrimac*

John Ericsson, inventor of the *Monitor*

Lieutenant John Worden, commander of the *Monitor*

Battle of the *Merrimac* and the *Monitor* in Hampton Roads, Virginia, March 9, 1862

The New-York Times.

VOL. XI—NO. 3265. NEW-YORK, TUESDAY, MARCH 11, 1862. PRICE TWO CENTS.

Editorials

An Advance on the Potomac.

We hear of renewed clamors at Washington for an immediate advance of the army of the Potomac. Our successes at the West have fairly intoxicated the minds of some of our civic warriors at Washington, and they demand a movement in front of the Capital without delay, and without the slightest regard to the circumstances of the case. This unreasonable temper will, of course, be greatly encouraged by the news of this morning, that the rebels are actually in retreat.

We trust that these clamors will not be allowed to have one whit more effect than they have had hitherto. Gen. McClellan has shown by the best of all tests, *success*, that his plans of the campaign have been judicious, and admirably adapted to secure the triumph of the Union cause. And he is fairly entitled to the continued confidence of the whole country and to the undisturbed prosecution of his unfulfilled designs. Nothing is more certain than that he has formed a plan for the expulsion of the rebels from Centreville and Manassas, and for their capture. It is not enough that they be driven away, or forced to abandon those points. *They must not be suffered to escape.* And Gen. McClellan must be allowed to complete his plans for cutting off their retreat before he is forced to disturb them in their present position.

No one who watches the military movements of the day on the Potomac, can fail to see that a most comprehensive plan is in process of execution for the defeat, destruction and capture of the rebel forces in Virginia. Upon the two wings the movement has already commenced. What is to be done in the rear is as yet matter of conjecture. But when all things in all quarters are ready, no one can doubt that the grand concentric movement will be made. To compel the Commanding General *to make it before*, would be only to sacrifice success to the demands of a temporary and a doubtful sentiment.

In spite of all the detraction of which he has been the object, Gen. McClellan has thus far proved himself abundantly competent to his high responsibility, and adequate to the duties of his high command. He has shown himself a superb strategist—competent to the largest combinations and the most extended operations in the field. His plans are now upon the very eve of consummation. But a few days can elapse at the farthest, before they will be put to the test. He is a rash and an unwise man who would, from any feeling of impatience, force them to execution before they are fully ripe. We do not anticipate from either the President or the Secretary of War any such unsafe and disastrous counsels.

Iron-clad Vessels.

The affair of the *Merrimac* has proved incontestibly the absolute necessity of iron-clad vessels in naval warfare. All the experiments and speculations in the world become of little importance in presence of the decisive test which she encountered. All our best and most formidable wooden vessels proved to be utterly ineffective against her mail-clad sides; and nothing but the most fortunate circumstance that we had just completed *one* war vessel of the same sort, enabled us to resist her raid upon our naval defences. But for the opportune presence of the *Monitor*, we do not see what could have prevented the *Merrimac* from destroying every one of our vessels in Hampton Roads, and then proceeding by a similar process to clear the Southern coast of our blockading squadron.

We trust this incident, disastrous as it has been to us, will convince Congress of the absolute necessity of at once ordering the construction of enough iron-clad gunboats to meet every probable emergency. Not long since, they rejected a proposition to appropriate $15,000,000 to this purpose. Recent events have shown that there is no possible way in which that sum of money can be put to better uses. We shall always need vessels of precisely this class. Even if the rebellion should end at once, and all danger of foreign war should for the time pass away, we need them as part of the permanent defences of the country; and there is no better time than this for entering upon the work of their construction.

There is another point, in this connection, which needs explanation. During the last eight or ten years, the Government has invested over half a million of dollars in Stevens' Battery—an iron-clad vessel, resting upon substantially the same principles as those just tested, and certain to be, if successful, the most formidable engine of the kind ever constructed. The inventor has invested a very large private fortune in the work, and a few hundred thousand dollars more would insure its completion. Every dictate of interest and of honor—every motive of economy and of public safety—requires that this tremendous weapon should be made effective at the earliest possible moment.

Just at this point a Congressional Committee steps in, and, without assigning a single valid reason, arrests its progress and forbids its completion. They admit that, upon the testimony of professional men in every department, it promises to fulfill all the conditions that can be required of it. They acknowledge its power, its speed, its invulnerability, its easy management, and everything essential to its success. But—as will be seen by reference to an article in another column—without witnessing a single experiment, although the inventor had prepared them at his own cost,—without assigning a single valid objection, or alleging anything beyond a vague conjecture in disparagement of its claims, the Committee has pronounced judgment against it, and Congress refuses to authorize its completion.

The *Monitor* (foreground) vs. the *Merrimac*

Why is this? Why, at such a moment, when the country needs everything it can secure in the way of effective preparation for defence, does the Committee refuse to sanction the completion of such a work? Is it because the contract is already made—because there is no room for further speculation, no chance to make money out of it as a Government job? We trust Congress will give renewed attention to this subject, and take pains to procure such information as will enable it either to satisfy the country that the Battery is a failure, or else take early steps for its completion. Those who are best acquainted with its capabilities assert that it could sink the *Merrimac* in half an hour. If this is so, the country cannot afford to dispense with its services.

Coast and Harbor Defence.

We give in another column an abstract of an elaborate memorial to Congress, recapitulating the great features of the Stevens Battery, as approved by the whole Board of Government Examiners, completely refuting the objections of the majority, and setting forth in detail, the fighting qualities and the results of experiments relative to that vessel.

Nothing could be more erroneous than the impression which generally obtains, that the report of this Board, taken as a whole, and with reference to the several professions of its distinguished members, is unfavorable to the completion of this great work. On the contrary, the Board *unanimously approved* all its great features. They admit that all the parts of the vessel above water, and intended to be shot-proof, are "efficiently protected against the heaviest ordnance now afloat in any part of the world;" that the speed, even at one-half the boiler pressure proposed, will be seventeen knots, or nearly twenty statute miles an hour; that the vessel's facilities of manoeuvring are remarkable and unprecedented; and that the weight and efficiency of broadside are 50 per cent greater than those of our heaviest steam frigates.

The majority of the Board then make certain objections, which, according to the standard authorities in such matters, are wholly of an engineering character. Now, the only engineering experts on the Board—Prof. Henry (who made an entirely favorable minority report) and Mr. Stimers—were equally divided in opinion on these objections; therefore, there is *no majority report of experts against any feature of this vessel.*

Hence it was eminently proper for Mr. Stevens to put to the highest possible test those points which were left in dispute by the experts of the Board. As the only material objection of the majority, according to Prof. Henry, was that the Battery was not strong enough to go to sea, Mr. Stevens therefore invited the very men who *have built* above two-thirds of the iron ships that the country has produced—and they will be admitted by Congress to be the highest possible authority—to decide the matter finally; and their unanimous report was that the Battery would be strong enough to stand any weather at sea.

The following objections of the majority—the demolition of the decks by firing over them; the inability of the sides to support their load; and the choking of the pumps by coal and the *débris* of the bilge, are refuted by the results of *actual trial*, as witnessed and verified by experts. The objection that the boilers can safely carry but twenty-five pounds of steam, is answered by the certificate of the United States Supervising Inspector of boilers, who, having tested them, states that they can carry fifty pounds according to law. The other objections are just as fully and satisfactorily answered, in the memorial referred to.

If it is possible to make a clearer case than this, we cannot divine the process by which it would be done. In fact, the costly and elaborate experiments made by Mr. Stevens, and these certificates of the highest professional authorities, not only relieve Congress of the responsibility it must ordinarily feel in acting upon such novel questions, but they convert the report of this Board into an indorsement of his plans, by settling in his favor the points left unsettled by them.

In addition to all this, the facts that the Government already has an interest of half a million dollars in the vessel; that its total cost will be about half that of the European iron-clad vessels of the same size, but of inferior speed, protection and broadside, as admitted by the Board; and that the smaller iron-clad vessels now ordered, cannot possibly cope with such fast and heavy vessels as the *Warrior*, for instance—these facts must, and will, we think, speedily settle the question of completing this great work. We cannot see any pretext, much less a reason, why Congress should longer refuse to grant the necessary appropriation.

The New-York Times.

VOL. XI—-NO. 3265. NEW-YORK, TUESDAY, MARCH 11, 1862. PRICE TWO CENTS

ANOTHER GREAT BATTLE.

A Most Glorious Victory in Arkansas.

The Combined Rebel Army Under Price, McCulloch, Van Dorn, and McIntosh, Defeated.

A Desperate Battle, Lasting Three Days.

FINAL ROUT OF THE ENEMY.

OUR CAVALRY IN FULL PURSUIT.

Capture of Guns, Flags, Provisions, &c., in Large Quantities.

Our Loss in Killed and Wounded One Thousand.

THAT OF THE ENEMY STILL LARGER.

ST. LOUIS, Monday, March 10.

The following is an official dispatch to Maj.-Gen. MCCLELLAN:

The army of the Southwest, under Gen. Curtis, after three days' hard fighting, has gained a most glorious victory over the combined forces of Van Dorn, McCulloch, Price and McIntosh. Our loss in killed and wounded is estimated at *one thousand!* That of the enemy was still larger. Guns, flags, provisions, &c., were captured in large quantities. Our cavalry are in pursuit of the flying enemy. (Signed)

H. W. HALLECK, Major-General.

THE SOUTHWESTERN ARMY AND ITS MOVEMENTS.

ST. LOUIS, Monday, March 10.

Correspondence of the Missouri Democrat.

CROSS HOLLOWS, Ark., Saturday, March 1.

Vigorous reconnoissances are kept up to watch the enemy's movements, and foraging parties are active in obtaining supplies. Pork and beef are purchased in the vicinity in abundance, and about half the quantity of flour required is obtained in the same manner, and all our forage.

PRICE, whose retreat is acknowledged on all hands to have been ably conducted, has found refuge in Boston Mountains. From two deserters who came into camp yesterday, it is ascertained that he is encamped on Cove Creek road, while MCCULLOCH is posted one and a half miles distant. The latter had burnt the village near the Indian frontier, known as Caul Hill. The supplies of the rebel army are obtained from Van Buren.

It is stated on good authority that PRICE and MCCULLOCH had a violent quarrel before leaving Cross Hollows.

At Fayetteville we found all the telegraphic dispatches up to the time of the evacuation by the rebels. A dispatch from MCINTOSH to HEBERT, in command at Cross Hollows, urges him to press forward and reinforce PRICE at Springfield at all hazards, as that point is important to be held by the Confederates.

Ex-Senator JOHNSON, of Missouri, who opened a recruiting office at Springfield for the rebels previous to PRICE's departure, was the first to reach Fayetteville where he stopped several days.

The clemency of Gen. CURTIS, and judicious policy inaugurated in relation to the treatment of the citizens of Benton County, is bringing its reward in the general confidence already showing indications of being restored among fugitives who fled at our approach. Confederate bills, which were 25 cents discount on our arrival in Benton County, have suddenly become valueless, and the inhabitants refuse to take them.

Maj. WRIGHT learns that the citizens of Keetsville knew of the intended attack on that place, and communicated the intelligence to the rebels, but kept all intimation of it from Capt. MONTGOMERY. On the afternoon before the fight, the ladies of the village left, one by one, and during the attack all were out. Maj. WRIGHT learns that there are 5,500 rebels in Cedar County and in Dade County, Mo. These parties are committing depredations, and swearing vengeance against Union men.

The health of the troops has been good, particularly on the march.

THE CHASE AFTER PRICE.

SKIRMISHING WITH THE REAR GUARD—A REPULSE—M'CULLOCH'S WINTER QUARTERS—RELICS—BURNING OF BENTONVILLE AND FAYETTEVILLE.

Correspondence of the New-York Times.

CAMP HALLECK, ARKANSAS, Sunday, Feb. 23, 1862.

We are at the head waters of the Osage Creek, and about 20 miles from the Cherokee nation, having marched about 250 miles into the heart of Secessia Skirmishing between our advance guard and the rear of Gen. PRICE, began about five miles north of Springfield, and has continued up to this time. Our column is under the command of Acting Major-Gen. CURTIS, assisted by Gens. SIGEL, RAINS and ASBOTH. We have about 20.000 men and 70 pieces of artillery. We have captured in all about 70 prisoners, but no part of PRICE's train or ammunition.

The results of the skirmishing thus far have been unimportant. In the sharpest attack, a cavalry charge, we lost nine killed and about twelve wounded. The enemy's battery was so well served and securely planted that our men were compelled to retire.

The reports have been that PRICE was to make a stand at the old battle-ground of Wilson's Creek. This is a very strong point. Many evidences of the conflict of Aug. 10 are traceable.

It now reported that PRICE and MCCULLOCH have made up their differences and have joined hands and forces, and are to make a stand at Boston Mountain or on the Arkansas River. This is probably not reliable. Gen. VAN DORN is said to have taken the command with a body of 2,000 cavalry.

In Cross Hollows, four miles from this point, MCCULLOCH's army had their Winter quarters; $35,000 were expended alone for the lumber used in the construction of barracks and stables, which were of the most comfortable kind, extending in a straight line more than half a mile. A beautiful parade-ground, a fine stream of pure water, and a grist-mill, were near by. The barracks, with their contents, and large quantities of commissary stores and camp furniture, were burned a few days since, when the rebels heard the booming of Yankee cannon through these mountainous regions. The stables are still standing, and the mill is grinding secession wheat and corn for Union troops. About 100 blooded game cocks, with silver gaffs, are all that is left to show that this has been made classic ground.

PRICE and his army have industriously reported through this whole country the wrongs which would be inflicted upon the unprotected persons who remained at home, and the consequence has been that men, women and children are fleeing from us as though the angel of destruction were our attendant. A few days ago, when our troops entered the town of Bentonville, the women shrieked and fainted with terror, and would not believe that they would not all be butchered at once. We are now waiting for our commissary trains and some reinforcements, when we shall move on; but all hopes of bagging the man who *never retreats* are abandoned. By the march of the two armies the country is left in ruin and desolation.

Bentonville and most of Fayetteville have been laid in ashes—the first by our men, because one of their comrades, who had been taken prisoner, was found in a sink with his brains dashed out. The latter the enemy have burned, with large quantities of powder and ammunition.

To-day the weather is like the middle of April in New-York, although it has been quite cold. The roads are very muddy, and rapid movements will be impossible without some improvement. No New-Yorker can imagine how we live here. Our bills of fare would astonish, if not disgust some of our epicures. Facilities for writing are limited. A report is in circulation that one of our commissary trains has been cut off. One of our messengers, with mail and dispatches, has never been heard from.

ST. LOUIS.

THE REBELS FALLING BACK

Their Lines Along the Potomac Being Withdrawn.

Evacuation of Centreville, Winchester, and Other Important Points.

Their Batteries on the Lower Potomac Deserted.

EVIDENCES OF A GREAT PANIC.

Splendid Pieces of Artillery Left in Position.

SPECIAL DISPATCH FROM WASHINGTON.

WASHINGTON, Monday, March 10.

My dispatch last night stated that the appearance of rebel scouts near Vienna was a feint, to cover their retreat. The latter part of the message failed to reach you—why, I know not, as it would have informed you of the great event that to-day convulses Washington—the general abandonment by the rebels of their Potomac line of defences.

From Winchester on the west, to the Cockpit batteries on the east, covering a front of [illegible] miles, the rebels have precipitately withdrawn. Their retreat bears many evidences of a panic. Splendid guns were left in position in the Potomac batteries—some of them spiked, some not harmed. Valuable ammunition and stores were left at some places, that came into quiet possession of our troops. It can hardly be doubted that their wary leaders, as usual, obtained full information from traitors among us of the impending advance of our great army, and that they fled to get out of danger.

There seems to be uncertainty to-night whether the rebels have evacuated Manassas, but they are certainly gone from Centreville—at all events, after a diligent search in the extensive trenches there, late this afternoon, none were found.

Civilization and improvement follow the enemy's retreat from the Potomac. Seven miles of telegraph were built and put in operation to-day, southward in Dixie.

The contrabands and fugitives who have escaped the rebel lines and report their retreat, say they are retreating to Gordonsville, but it is doubted whether they can attempt a stand there. They will hardly stop short of Richmond, and they will not be allowed to tarry long there.

There are many theories of the rebel retreat. Some suppose that their purpose is to throw their whole army on BURNSIDE and annihilate him; but to surrender all Virginia to gain a partial victory is not sensible warfare. The probability is that the army is so reduced by the refusal of men to reënlist, that DAVIS finds it folly to attempt to hold Virginia.

Our Government takes no step backward, and Virginia will soon be as free from rebel armies as Tennessee, and a Provisional State Government will be peacefully erected, with, perhaps, JOHN MINOR BOTTS for Governor.

The radicals are sorry to gain so much without losing many thousand soldiers at Manassas, but the soldiers' families will be satisfied.

To-day was the most animated and exciting that Washington has seen since last July. The streets were early crowded with cavalcades, and horses at all the livery stables rose rapidly to nearly double their former price. Newspaper reporters swarmed thickly forth, and expressed an ardent desire and intention which they had long held in check, to visit the memorable plains of Bull Run. Numbers of them, doubtless, will sleep to-night near that field of battle.

Persons visiting Washington on business with the head of the Government need not apprehend that they will find "Old ABE" absent and playing soldier in front of Richmond, as the *Tribune* repeatedly intimates. The President's signature being necessary to give efficacy to the acts of Congress for the support and prosecution of the war, it is believed he will continue his duties here—at least till Congress adjourns.

It rained slightly in the early part of to-day, but the day closed beautifully. The earth is greatly dried within ten days, and the roads in Virginia are said to be rapidly hardening.

FROM ANOTHER CORRESPONDENT.

WASHINGTON, Monday, March 10.

It is rumored and believed here that the rebel army is retreating from Centreville and Manassas.

Lieut. WISE, commanding the Potomac flotilla, in his official report to the Navy Department, confirms the rumors of the abandonment of the rebel batteries at Cockpit, Shipping and other points along the Potomac, and also the burning of the steamer *Page* and other rebel craft.

COMMODORE DUPONT'S OPERATIONS IN GEORGIA AND FLORIDA.

Diagram Showing Brunswick, Ga., its Harbor and Channel, and its Relation to the Adjoining Islands and Coast.

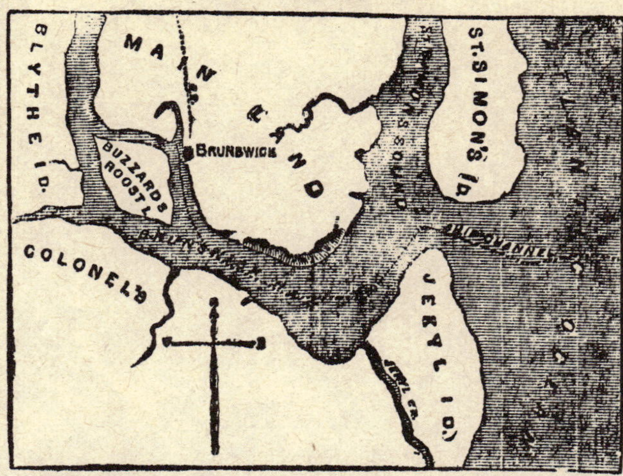

Diagram Showing Fernandina, Fla., the Location of Fort Clinch, and the Character of the Adjoining Coast.

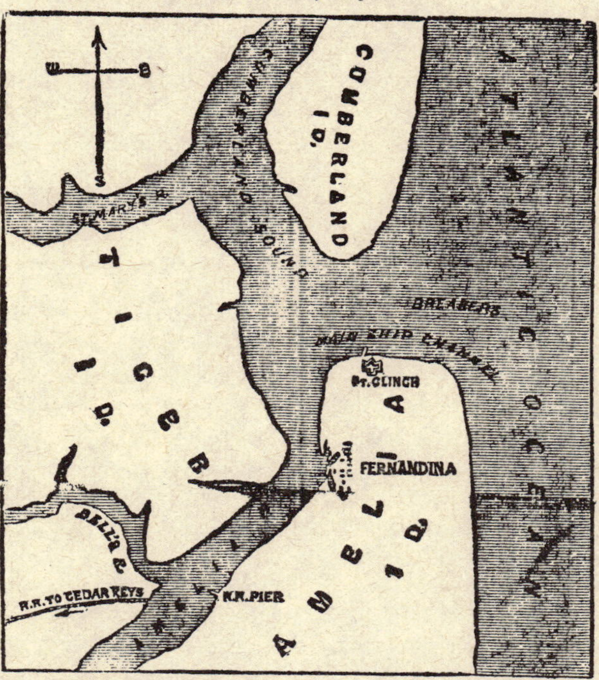

Outline Map Showing the Relations of Brunswick, Ga., and Fernandina, Fla., to Each Other, and to the Contiguous Regions.

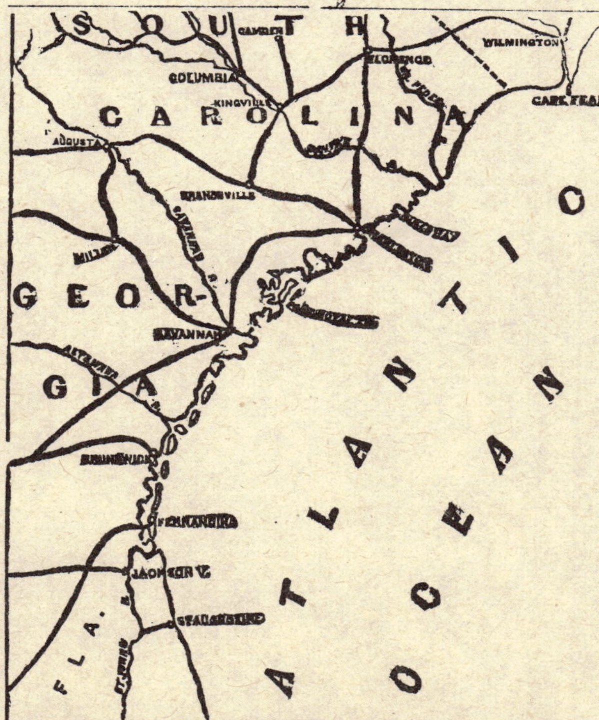

RUMORED EVACUATION OF WINCHESTER.

CHARLESTOWN, Va., Monday, March 10.

It is currently rumored and believed that Winchester was fully evacuated yesterday.

A reconnoissance is out this morning to ascertain the facts.

The intelligence from other quarters greatly encourages all friends of the Union, as indicating a speedy termination of hostilities.

CHARLESTOWN, Va., Mo[illegible]ch 10.

It is now ascertained beyond a d[illegible]at Winchester has been evacuated by the rebels. The prominent places between here and Winchester are occupied by our troops.

THE EVACUATION OF CENTREVILLE AND WINCHESTER CONFIRMED.

WASHINGTON, Monday, March 10.

There is no longer any doubt that the rebels have evacuated Centreville, Winchester and other important points, indicating a general falling back of their forces.

OPERATIONS ON THE COAST

Brilliant Successes of the Fleet Under Commodore Dupont.

Capture of Brunswick, Ga., and Fernandina, Fla.

Inglorious Flight of the Rebels from Both Places.

Cannon and Munitions of War Captured.

Old Fort Clinch "Retaken, Held and Possessed."

An Exciting Race Between a Gunboat and a Railroad Train.

BALTIMORE, Monday, March 10.

The United States steam gunboat *Alabama*, Capt. LANIER, arrived here this morning, direct from Fernandina, Fla., bringing Capt. DAVIS, late Flag-Officer of the South Atlantic Squadron, as bearer of dispatches from Commodore DUPONT to the Navy Department, announcing the capture of Fernandina and Brunswick by the fleet under his command.

We are indebted to Capt. DAVIS for an outline of the operations of the fleet since it left Port Royal about the 1st of March, on what was announced as an important expedition, the place of destination having been held back at the request of the Government.

The first point of the coast approached by the fleet was the town of Brunswick, Ga., the enemy abandoning their works and precipitately flying at the approach of the gunboats. It was taken possession of, and gunboats left in charge. This gives the Government the control of the whole coast of Georgia from South Carolina to Florida.

Brunswick being disposed of, the fleet moved twenty miles further to Cumberland Sound, the entrance to the harbor of Fernandina, Fla. The fleet entered Cumberland Sound in the following order:

The *Mohican*, Flagship of Com. DUPONT,

The *Ottawa*.	The *James Adger*.
The *Seminole*.	The *Florida*.
The *Pawnee*.	The *Seneca*.
The *Flag*.	The *Huron*.
The *Bienville*.	The *Pembina*.
The *Alabama*.	

They were followed by the small armed steamers *Isaac Smith*, *Potomska*, *Penguin* and *Ellen*. Next came the armed revenue cutter *Henrietta*, and armed transports *Empire City*, *Boston*, *Belvidere*, *Star of the South*, *George's Creek*, and the brig *Gen. Wright*.

When the expedition came in sight of Fort Clinch the rebels were discerned making hasty flight, but they fired two or three shots from the barbette guns of the fort. The shells of the fleet, however, caused a hasty evacuation, and Fort Clinch was immediately taken possession of, and the flag of the Union raised on an old staff which has been so long disgraced by traitor colors.

This is the first of the old Southern forts of the Union that has been recovered since the proclamation of President LINCOLN, declaring they must all be restored to the Union.

As the fleet approached the fort a train of cars was observed leaving Fernandina, and, as the track runs some three miles along the shore of the Sound, Commodore DUPONT sent one of the gunboats in pursuit of her. An exciting race took place, the steamer throwing shells at the flying train, some of them falling in such close proximity that some of the fleeing rebels jumped from it, and took to the bush. Among the latter is said to have been late Senator YULEE, of Florida, accompanied by his servant. The train of course outrun the gunboat, and thus escaped.

The old casemated Fort Clinch having been taken possession of, the Union flag was speedily raised. From the eight rebel earthworks abandoned by the enemy twelve large guns fell into our possession, including one immense rifled gun, of 120 pounds calibre. Five of them were found in Fort Clinch, and the others were in the earthworks. The rebels had hastily removed a portion of their guns, which were said to be at St. Johns further up the Sound. An expedition was preparing to go up and capture them, when the *Alabama* sailed. Considerable ammunition was also captured, and the same evening the rebel steamer *Darlington*, loaded with wagons, ammunition and camp equipage, was also captured while endeavoring to escape.

The expedition accomplished its mission on the 4th of March, the anniversary of the inauguration of President LINCOLN.

The troops of Gen. WRIGHT were landed, and Commodore DUPONT handed over to his possession the forts and earthworks, which were quickly garrisoned.

Most of the male inhabitants of Fernandina had fled, and the city was also taken possession of. This has been one of the most useful ports to the rebels, a large number of vessels having run the blockade from here.

OFFICIAL ANNOUNCEMENT OF THE SUCCESSES.

WASHINGTON, Monday, March 10.

The Navy Department has received the following:

BALTIMORE, March 10.

To Hon. Gideon Welles, Secretary of Navy:

I arrived this morning, and will come on in the next (four o'clock) train. The enemy has abandoned his heavy fortifications at St. Simons and Brunswick Georgia. Fort Clinch and Fernandina, and St. Marys, Florida, are ours.

(Signed,) C. H. DAVIS, Captain U. S. N.

Senator GRIMES to-day read a dispatch announcing the capture of St. Marys and Fernandina, Fla., and St. Simons and Brunswick, Ga.

Fort Clinch and Fernandina, and St. Marys, Florida, are ours.

REPORT OF FLAG-OFFICER DUPONT.

Capt. DAVIS, late Fleet-Captain of the North Atlantic Squadron, arrived here to-night, bringing an official dispatch from Commodore DUPONT, of which the following is a copy:

FLAG-SHIP MOHICAN, HARBOR OF FERNANDINA, Fla., March 4, 1862.

SIR: I had the honor to inform you in my last dispatch that the expedition for Fernandina was equipped, and waiting only for suitable weather to sail from Port Royal. I have now the pleasure to inform you that I am in full possession of Cumberland Island and the Sound of Fernandina, and Amelia Island, and the river and Town of St. Mary's.

I sailed from Port Royal on the last day of February, in the *Wabash*, and on the 2d inst., entered Cumberland Sound by St. Andrew's Inlet, in the *Mohican*, Commander S. W. GORDON, on board of which ship I have hoisted my flag. The fleet comprised the following vessels, sailing in the order in which they are named: *Ottowa*, *Mohican*, accompanied by the *Ellen*, *Seminole*, *Pawnee*, *Pocahontas*, *Flag*, *Florida*, *James Adger*, *Bienville*, *Alabama*, *Keystone State*, *Seneca*, *Huron*, *Pembina*, *Isaac Smith*, *Penguin*, *Potomska*, the armed cutter *Henrietta*, the armed transport *McClellan*, the latter having on board the battalion of marines, under the command of Major REYNOLDS, and the transports *Empire City*, *Marion*, *Star of the South*, *Belvidere*, *Boston*, and *George's Creek*, containing a brigade under the command of Brig.-Gen. WRIGHT.

We came to anchor in Cumberland Sound, at 10½ on the morning of the 2d, to make an examination of the channel, and wait for the tide. Here I learned from a contraband, who had been picked up at sea by Commander LANIER, and from the neighboring residents on Cumberland Island, that the rebels had abandoned in haste the whole of the defences of Fernandina, and were even at that moment retreating from Amelia Island, carrying with them such of their munitions as their precipitate flight would allow.

The object of carrying the whole fleet through Cumberland Sound was to burn the heavy works on the south end of the Cumberland, and the north end of Amelia Island. But on receiving this intelligence, I detached the gunboats and armed steamers, of light draft from the main line, and placing them under the command of Commander P. DRAYTON, of the steam-sloop *Pawnee*, I ordered them to push through the Sound at the utmost speed to save public and private property from threatened destruction; to prevent poisoning wells, and to put a stop to all those outrages, by the perpetration of which, the leaders of this nefarious war, hope to drive and exasperate the Southern people.

In the meantime I went out of the Sound and came by the sea to the main entrance of this harbor. In consequence of bad weather, I was unable to cross the bar till this morning. Commander DRAYTON, accompanied by H. R. P. RODGERS, with the armed launches and cutters, and the small armed companies from the *Wabash*, had arrived several hours before me. Immediately on his entering the harbor, Commander DRAYTON sent Lieut. WHITE, of the *Ottawa*, to hoist the flag on Fort Clinch, the first of the National forts, on which the ensign of the Union has resumed its proper place since the first proclamation of the President of the United States was issued. A few scattering musket shots were fired from the town by the flying enemy, when it was discovered that a railroad train was about to start. Commodore DRAYTON, on board the *Ottawa*, and Lieut.-Commanding STEVENS, chased this train for two miles, and fired several shells at it, aiming at the locomotive, some of which took effect. It was reported that the Hon. DAVID YULEE, late a Senator of the United States from the State of Florida, escaped from this train and took to the bush.

Commander C. R. P. RODGERS pushing ahead with the launches, captured the Rebel steamer *Darlington*, containing military stores, army wagons, mules, forage, &c., and fortunately secured the drawbridge, which was held during the night by the second launch of the *Wabash*. There were passengers, women and children, in the *Darlington*, and the brutal Captain suffered her to be fired upon, and refused to hoist a white flag, notwithstanding the entreaties of the women. No one was injured. I send the Captain of the steamer home a prisoner. His name is JACOB BROCK. He is a native of Vermont, but he has been a resident of Florida for twenty-three years.

The same night Commander C. R. P. RODGERS ascended the St. Mary's with the *Ottawa*, and took possession of the town, driving out a picket of the enemy's cavalry. Early in the morning the town of Fernandina was also occupied by a party of seamen and marines from Commander DRAYTON's command. In both places the inhabitants had fled, by order, it is said, of the rebel authorities. A company of seamen and marines, under Lieut. MILLER, was sent from the *Mohican* to hold Fort Clinch. It is reported to me by Lieutenant Commanding DOWNES, of the *Huron*, that the whole structure of the railroad on the Fernandina side, including the swinging drawbridge, is quite uninjured.

The rebels have done some damage by fire to the tressle work on the other side of the river, but I am not yet informed of its extent. Several locomotives, baggage cars, tenders, freight cars, and some other property besides that found in the steamer *Darlington*, have been recovered.

The whole number of guns discovered up to this time is thirteen, embracing heavy 32-pounders, 8-inch guns, and one 80 and one 120-pounder rifled guns The towns of St. Mary's and Fernandina are uninjured. I visited the town, Fort Clinch, and the earthworks on the sea face of the island. It is impossible to look at these preparations for a vigorous defence without being surprised that they should have been voluntarily deserted. The batteries on the north and northeast shores are as complete as art can make them. Six are well concealed and protected by ranges of sand-hills in front, contain a perfect shelter for the men, and are so small and thoroughly covered by the natural growth and by the varied contours of the land, that to strike them from the water would be the mere result of chance. A battery of six guns, though larger, and affording, therefore, a better mark, is equally well sheltered and masked. The batteries and the heavy guns mounted on Fort Clinch command all the turnings of the main ship channel, and rake an approaching enemy. Beside them, there was another battery of four guns on the south end of Cumberland Island, the fire of which would cross the channel inside the bar. The difficulties arising from the indirectness of the channel and from the shoalness of the bar would have added to the defences by keeping the approaching vessels a long time exposed to fire, under great disadvantages, and when the ships of an enemy had passed all these defences, they would have to encounter a well constructed and naturally masked battery at the town, which commands the access to the the inner anchorage.

We are told that Gen. LEE pronounced the place perfectly defensible. We are not surprised at this, if true. We captured Port Royal, but Fernandina and Fort Clinch have been given to us.

We had, in the expedition, Mr. W. H. DENNIS, an assistant in the Coast Survey, who possessed accurate local knowledge of a part of the ground we passed over, of which indeed he had made the topographical map under the direction of the superintendent. He was zealous and active, and it gives me pleasure to mention him. The *Empire City*, on board of which was Gen. WRIGHT, grounded on the bar. As soon as he arrived, in another steamer, immediate steps were taken to transfer to him the forts and all authority and possession on the land.

I desire to speak here of the harmonious counsels and candid coöperation, which have marked throughout my intercourse with the able officer. Our plans of action have been matured by mutual consultations and have been carried into execution by mutual help.

I take great pleasure in reminding the Department that one principal and ultimate object of the Naval Expedition, which I have the honor to command, was in the first conception to take and keep under control the whole line of sea coast of Georgia, knowing, to use the language of the original paper "that the naval power that controls the seacoast of Georgia, controls the State of Georgia."

The report that the fortifications at St. Simons armed with heavy columbiads, had been abandoned, which first reached me at Port Royal, is confirmed. This being the case, the entire seacoast of Georgia is now either actually in my possession or under my

[Continued on Eighth Page.]

Battle of Pea Ridge, March 8, 1862

The New-York Times.

VOL. XI—NO. 3266. NEW-YORK, WEDNESDAY, MARCH 12, 1862. PRICE TWO CENTS.

MANASSAS EVACUATED.

The Rebel Stronghold Occupied by the Union Forces.

Evidences of the Precipitate Flight of the Rebels.

Jackson's Force Deserted at Winchester.

Hospital and Commissary Stores and War Materiel Left Behind.

The Works and Quarters Left Uninjured.

Accommodations for One Hundred and Fifty Thousand Men.

Supposed Stand of the Rebels at Gordonsville.

SPECIAL DISPATCH FROM WASHINGTON.

WASHINGTON, Tuesday, March 11.

The rebels have evacuated Manassas. We occupied it this morning.

Dispatches received at headquarters this forenoon stated positively that the rebels had not evacuated Winchester. If this is so,—and those best authorized to know report it,—Gen. JACKSON's rebel army is assuredly cut off and will be captured.

This abandonment of a splendid army corps at Winchester could not have been designed, and is further proof of the haste and confusion of the flight from Centreville and Manassas.

The officer commanding the Union forces at Manassas sent in a messenger to-night. I had the fortune to meet him, and get many particulars concerning the condition of things at Manassas. That famed rebel post was occupied this morning about 10 o'clock, and the Union flag was unfurled over the works.

Everything at Manassas was found in great confusion, the flight of the rebels having been precipitate in the extreme. Persons in the vicinity allege that the abandonment of the place was quite recently resolved on, and the guns were begun to be removed about a week ago. Intense alarm seized the rebel forces, and thenceforward a wild haste characterized all their movements.

The last rebel troops left the place last Friday. Their works were left entire and unharmed, and finer, it is said, are not to be found in the country. The log-huts are remarkably comfortable, and the accommodations ample for one hundred and fifty thousand men. Our army have come into possession of commissary and hospital stores in large quantities, besides wagons, tents, caissons and hundreds of other valuables. It is proper to add, however, that statements quite contradictory of these are received, and it is hard to decide which are true.

The statements of all persons in the vicinity concur that the rebel forces have retired to Gordonsville. This would place them behind the Rappahannock River, the crossing of which by the Union army could be strongly resisted, as the bridge is 1,200 feet long, and that the rebels will doubtless destroy. The country about Gordonsville is rolling, and susceptible of good defences, though the Rappahannock bottom is wide, and only about two feet higher than the water in its usual Winter stage. But though the rebel officers may have designed to stop at Gordonsville, it is by no means certain they have done so, as they retreated in a most excited and disorderly manner.

At Gordonsville the rebels would have the advantage of a narrower front than at Manassas, and less easily flanked. The reason of their sudden retreat from Manasses was the belief they had of an intention on the part of Gen. MCCLELLAN to turn their right flank by a march through Fredericksburgh.

If the rebels are pursued from Manassas to Gordonsville ever so vigorously, it is not likely they could be caught up with under a week, if they destroy the railroad as they go. Those persons who are so exasperated because the rebels were not advanced upon two months ago, forget that they could have run away as easily then as now, and the pursuit of them been far more difficult and dangerous.

Dispatches from Gen. HEINTZELMAN, to-day, confirm in every particular the report of the panic retreat of the rebels from the Potomac batteries. Confusion reigned everywhere. For miles in the interior, men were burning their houses, their fodder, and other farm wealth, and fleeing in dismay to the South.

The *Stepping Stones*, late yesterday evening, towed from Quantico to Budd's Ferry a barge containing the picket guards of 500, and, returning, towed to the Maryland shore the barge containing the stores mentioned.

The rebel steamer *Page* is lying in Quantico Creek, burned to the water's edge.

A reconnoissance was made this forenoon across the Occoquan, scouring the country for five miles west of that stream. All the late rebel camps in that vicinity were found deserted and destroyed.

The Lincoln Cavalry, while scouting in the vicinity of Burke's Station, on the Orange and Alexandria Railroad, fourteen miles out, yesterday captured thirteen secession prisoners. Eleven of these prisoners passed through Pennsylvania-avenue this morning, in charge of a guard.

TELEGRAMS FROM THE ADVANCE.

FAIRFAX COURT-HOUSE, Va., Monday Noon, March 10.

On Sunday morning, a squad of cavalry, numbering ten or twelve, passed through here, going toward our lines, but returned in an hour or two and went toward Centreville. In the evening the Union troops occupied Fairfax. Your correspondent, finding no enemies around, encamped at Fairfax for the night. A few rude trenches are all the military defences about this place. The roads are found to be good, and, so far, unimpeded. All the Union troops ordered have come up. No accident has occurred.

Everybody has run away from about Fairfax who could. The houses are mostly empty, fences are gone, and desolation prevails. The Court-house and Church are in good condition.

TUESDAY MORNING.

Last night was cold, but the soldiers are all fresh and fine this morning. The movement to this place has been a great success. As much order reigns as though the troops were still at Arlington Heights. No stragglers are loitering along the road,—and the army of to-day is in striking contrast with the army of July. No facts could more conclusively show the wisdom of long and patient training of men in camp before attempting to handle them in the field. This army is invincible, and can go "On to Richmond!"

CENTREVILLE, Tuesday, March 11.

Yesterday morning our forces, amounting to upward of two thousand, proceeded to Centreville, and occupied the village about 4 o'clock in the afternoon. It was altogether deserted.

The entire command thence proceeded to Manassas, arriving there in the evening.

The rebels had destroyed as much of their property as they could not carry away, by fire and otherwise. The bridges, railroad track and dépôt in that vicinity were extensively damaged, and nothing but wreck and desolation was apparent.

LATER.

Upon close examination it was discovered that the rebels before evacuating their much boasted stronghold, had set fire to such of their commissary stores as they could not conveniently carry off. The place presented a scene of the utmost desolation, a mass of charred and blackened ruins. The rebels also blew up the bridges along the line of the Orange and Alexandria Railroad for some miles below Manassas. Such of the locomotives which were out of repair were also destroyed, it is supposed by being blown up, and the vicinity of the dépôt is covered by fragments of machinery belonging to the destroyed locomotives.

It is said the rebels left Centreville on Sunday morning. Large numbers of contrabands have reached our lines (which now extend beyond Manassas Junction,) and are still coming in by droves. On our way from Centreville yesterday morning, we passed at least one hundred, who were making their way to Washington. Some of the fugitives claim to have come twenty miles west of Manassas. They all agree in saying that the rebels left the latter place in great precipitation, and that the destruction of their commissary stores was commenced at an early hour on Sunday. The contrabands state that a portion of the force which left Manassas passed northwardly, but this is considered improbable. But if they did, it was for the purpose of reinforcing JACKSON, at Winchester.

They also state that all the bridges along the route which they came, had been blown up by the rebels in their retreat, and that the greater portion of the track is also torn up.

The earthworks at Centreville had been greatly misrepresented. They were not of the formidable character supposed. The enemy before evaccating had somewhat injured them by breaking the embrasures and casemates; so at Manassas, which, however, has not been fully examined. On our troops arriving at Fairfax Court-house, they found not more than a dozen families. The soldiers rushed into the Court-house and brought away some of the records; but this being discovered, the officers directed their return.

When our troops learned that Manassas had been evacuated their spirits suddenly became depressed, as they had anticipated a spirited conflict with the enemy.

About a mile and a half before reaching Centreville, a number of graves was discovered, principally of Alabama troops. The graves were marked with head and foot boards, with the names of the deceased thereon. A guard was placed near them, as if to shield them from mutilation, although it was not supposed such an act could be committed.

Most of the contrabands above alluded to were happy in their liberty, and remarkably communicative, to the extent of their limited knowledge.

THE EVACUATION OF OCCOQUAN.

WASHINGTON, Tuesday, March 11.

Official information, to-day, reports that the enemy formerly encamped back of and below Occoquan have retreated, destroying everything they could not carry on their backs. They left on Saturday. Our troops took possession this morning, and were welcomed by a part of the inhabitants with great joy. Every boat in the vicinity, and anything that would float, had been destroyed. The rebels told the villagers they were going to fall back to the Rappahannock.

A call from the Governor of Virginia on the militia of the State, for 10,000 men, was proclaimed in the streets of Occoquan on the 9th inst., by an officia who immediately departed. Nearly all the able bodied men of the village left with the rebel army. A few refused to go.

The rebel force which has thus retreated was composed of three Texan, one Georgia and one Mississippi regiment, and the Hampton Legion.

THE LINE OF THE POTOMAC FROM WASHINGTON TO ITS MOUTH.

Showing Manassas, Fredericksburgh, and the Line of the Rappahannock, and their Relations to Richmond.

WINCHESTER NOT EVACUATED.

JACKSON'S FORCES STILL THERE.

An Armed Reconnoissance to Within Five Miles of the Place.

BUNKER HILL, Tuesday, March 11.

The intelligence of the evacuation of Winchester, yesterday, was premature. It was Berryville that the reconnoissance reported evacuated. The latest intelligence from Winchester is to the effect that the town is occupied by at least one brigade of infantry. Other troops are also there. There is a strong suspicion that a portion of the forces which evacuated Centreville have been ordered to reinforce Winchester.

The pickets were undisturbed last night. An active scouting was continually kept up.

STEPHENSON'S DEPOT, 5 miles from Winchester, Tuesday, March 11—P. M.

The forces under Gens. HAMILTON and WILLIAMS, constituting an armed reconnoissance, have reached this point without any serious opposition.

FROM THE UPPER POTOMAC.

A RECONNOISSANCE BY COL. GEARY.

The Bones of Union Soldiers Bleaching on Ball's Bluff.

LEESBURGH, VA., Tuesday, March 11.

Col. GEARY, Acting Brigadier-General of troops here, made a personal reconnoissance yesterday as far as CARTER's Mills. The trail of the retreating enemy was blackened with the ruins of granaries, ashes of hay and grain stacks, fences, etc. He found the bridge over Goose Creek had been burned after our occupation here on Saturday. The enemy have completely fallen back. The command continues to make captures from rank Secessionists.

The loyal feeling is growing, and many persons come forward to take the oath of allegiance daily.

LEESBURGH, VA., Tuesday, March 11.

Col. GEARY, with some of his officers and a detachment of the First Michigan Cavalry, rode to Ball's Bluff to-day, and buried the whitened bones of the brave Union soldiers who fell upon that field in October last. Impressive remarks preceded this humane act, and a monument of gross rebel neglect was hidden from human sight.

SPECIAL DISPATCH FROM HARPER'S FERRY.

HARPER'S FERRY, Tuesday, March 11.

About thirty State prisoners are now in prison here—the prison, the engine-house rendered famous by JOHN BROWN. Among them are Lieut.-Col. WHITE, of the Fifty-sixth Virginia, captured yesterday at Leesburgh, by Col. GEARY; and RITCHIE, also captured by GEARY, a farmer near Leesburgh, who stamped to death, at Ball's Bluff, a wounded soldier, while the latter was asking aid.

Contrabands are pouring in, and are set to work by Government. Thirty, yesterday, arrived. They report the rebels as evacuating Manassas, and falling back on Richmond. Slaves are impressed to transport stores and cannon from Manassas.

No guns were found at Leesburgh but wooden Quaker guns. The rebels left the night before GEARY arrived—said to be four thousand in all.

A large thirty-two-pounder was found disabled, being burst, on Tuesday, on the third discharge, killing sixteen rebels and wounding eight.

HENDERSON's Virginia Cavalry, on Saturday night, came near Shenandoah Furnace, seven miles from here, and abused the family of a Virginia soldier in GEARY's regiment.

There was a cavalry skirmish near Winchester last night, and one National soldier was killed. The rebel loss is unknown.

RECEPTION OF THE NEWS.

IN NEW-YORK.

ALBANY, Tuesday, March 11—1½ P. M.

One hundred guns are now firing at the Capitol Park in honor of the National victory at Manassas. The roar of the guns mingle with the patriotic cheers of the legislators and people.

ALBANY, Tuesday, March 11.

This city has been the scene of rejoicing all day over the capture of Manassas. Every street is decorated with flags—voluntary processions have been formed, and many patriotic demonstrations made.

IN NEW-ENGLAND.

BOSTON, Tuesday, March 11.

The occupation of Manassas by our forces, and the series of victories now being reported, causes a highly jubilant state of feeling all over New-England.

IN OHIO.

CINCINNATI, Tuesday, March 11.

The news of the retreat of the rebels from Manassas absorbed the attention of the business community to-day. Not much was done in any department of trade.

FROM KEY WEST AND PORT ROYAL.

Arrival of the Oriental—Confirmation of the Capture of Brunswick and Fernandina—Vessels Lying at Key West and Port Royal.

The United States transport *Oriental*, Captain TUSO, arrived at this port at 10½ o'clock last night, from Key West and Port Royal. She left the former port on the 4th inst., at 4 P. M., and arrived off Port Royal at 4 P. M. of the 6th; was detained outside 20 hours for want of a pilot. She left Port Royal at 5 P. M. of the 8th, and experienced fine weather the entire passage.

She brings no news, except that the United States gunboat *Verona* had just arrived from Fernandina, (Fla.,) bringing intelligence of the success of Commodore DUPONT's expedition, and confirming the news of the capture of Fernandina and Brunswick, all of which we have had in detail by the *Alabama* at Baltimore. Everything remained quiet, both at Key West and Port Royal. The troops were in good health and spirits.

The following vessels were at Key West: U. S. steamship *St. Jago de Cuba*, U. S. steamship *R. R. Cuyler*, U. S. gunboats *Pinola* and *Owasa*, U. S. brig *Bainbridge*, Spanish prize bark *Teresita*, brigs *Samuel Welsh*, of Philadelphia; *Rebecca Sheppard*, of Philadelphia; *Almore*, of Waldoboro; schooner *Louisa Frazer*, of New-Jersey, and several others. Commodore PORTER's bomb fleet, consisting of 21 vessels, were to sail next day for Ship Island.

The following vessels were at Port Royal: Steamers *Atlantic*, discharging; *Mississippi* and *Matanzas*, for Ship Island, with Gen. BUTLER and Staff and 1,400 men; *Cahawba*, *Ben. de Ford*, *Cosmopolite*, *Delaware*. Ship *Charter Oak*. Barks *Magnolia*, *Fanny Elsser* and others. Also, U. S. frigate *Susquehanna*. The gunboat *Verona* had just arrived from Fernandina. The U. S. gunboat *Kensington*, Commander CROCKER, just arrived from Boston, after a long and boisterous passage, short of coal and disabled. The *Oriental* brings the following passengers:

Capt. Yeaton, Col. Edward W. Serrell, Capt. Reaney, Capt. Alexander Annan, Capt. A. C. Eady, Maj. B. H. Hill, U. S. A.; Capt. Calfin, Mrs. Col. Van Zandt, Lieut. Rocher, Lieut. R. Ruges, G. W. Harcourt, James Breckinridge, P. Springstein, H. Elkin, J. C. Saxton, Lieut. John Stark, 10 soldiers, and 15 in steerage.

We are indebted to Purser ANTONIO LABENS, of steamer *Oriental*, for favors.

BATTLE OF PEA RIDGE.

Official Report of Gen. Curtis to Gen. Halleck.

BEN McCULLOCH KILLED.

Brilliant Manœuvres by the Union Army.

DESPERATE FIGHTING ON BOTH SIDES.

FINAL ROUT OF THE REBELS.

ST. LOUIS, Tuesday, March 11.

The following is the official report of Gen. CURTIS to Gen. HALLECK:

HEADQUARTERS ARMY OF THE SOUTHWEST, PEA RIDGE, Ark., March 9.

GENERAL: On Thursday, the 6th inst., the enemy commenced an attack on my right wing, assailing and following the rear guard of a detachment under Gen. SIGEL to my main lines on Sugar Creek Hollow, but ceased firing when he met my reinforcements, about 4 P. M.

During the night I became convinced that he had moved on so as to attack my right or rear. Therefore, early on the 7th I ordered a change of front to the right—my right, which then became my left, still resting on Sugar Creek Hollow.

This brought my line across Pea Ridge, with my new right resting on Head Cross Timber Hollow, which is the head of Big Sugar Creek. I also ordered an immediate advance of the cavalry and light artillery, under Col. OSTERHAUS, with orders to attack and break what I supposed would be the reinforced line of the enemy. This movement was in progress, when the enemy, at 11 A. M., commenced an attack on my right. The fight continued mainly at these points during the day, the enemy having gained the point held by the command of Col. CARR, at Cross Timber Hollow, but was entirely repulsed with the fall of the Commander, McCULLOCH, in the centre, by the forces under Col. DAVIS. The plan of attack on the centre was gallantly carried forward by Col. OSTERHAUS' who was immediately sustained and supported by Col. DAVIS' entire division, supported also by Gen. SIGEL's command, which had remained till near the close of the day on the left. Col. CARR's division held the right, under a galling, continuous fire, all day. In the evening, firing having entirely ceased in the centre, and the right being now on the left, I reinforced the right by a portion of the Second Division, under Gen. ASBOTH. Before the day closed I was convinced that the enemy had concentrated his main force on the right. I commenced another change of front, forward, so as to face the enemy where he had deployed on my right flank in a strong position. The change had only been partially effected, but was in full progress, when, at sunrise on the 8th, my right and centre renewed the firing, which was immediately answered by the enemy with renewed energy along the whole extent of his line. My left, under Gen. SIGEL moved close to the hills occupied by the enemy, driving him from the heights, and advancing steadily toward the head of the Hollows. I immediately ordered the centre and right wing forward, the right turning the left of the enemy, and cross-firing on his centre. This final position of the enemy was in the arc of a circle. A charge of infantry, extending throughout the whole line, completely routed the whole rebel force, which retired in great confusion, but rather safely, through the deep, impassable defiles of Cross Timber. Our loss is heavy. The enemy's can never be ascertained, for their dead are scattered over a large field. Their wounded, too, may many of them be lost and perish. The force is scattered in all directions, but I think his main force has returned to Boston Mountains.

Gen. SIGEL follows him toward Keittsville, while my cavalry is pursuing him toward the mountains, scouring the country, bringing in prisoners and trying to find the rebel Major-Gen. VAN DORN, who had command of the entire force at this, the battle of Pea Ridge.

I have not as yet statements of the dead and wounded, so as to justify a report, but I will refer you to a dispatch which I will forward very soon.

Officers and soldiers have displayed such unusual gallantry that I hardly dare to make distinction. I must, however, name the Commanders of Divisions: Gen. SIGEL gallantly commanded the right, and drove back the left wing of the enemy; Gen. ASBOTH, who is wounded in the arm, in his gallant effort to reinforce the right; Col. and Acting-Brig.-Gen. DAVIS who commanded the centre, where McCULLOCH fell on the 7th, and pressed forward the centre on the 8th; Col. and Acting-Brig.-Gen. CARR is also wounded in the arm, and was under the continuous fire of the enemy during the two hardest days of the struggle.

Illinois, Indiana, Iowa, Ohio and Missouri may proudly share the honor of victory, which their gallant heroes won over the combined forces of VAN DORN, PRICE and McCULLOCH at Pea Ridge, in the mountains of Arkansas.

I have the honor to be, General,
Your obedient servant,
SAMUEL R. CURTIS, Brigadier-General.

LATEST REPORTS FROM SPRINGFIELD.

Special to the Missouri Republican.

SPRINGFIELD, Mo., Monday, March 10.

A messenger who arrived this morning at 8 o'clock reports that the battle lasted from Thursday morning till Saturday evening, and that our loss was about 450 killed and wounded. The rebel loss was about 1,000 killed and wounded, and 1,000 taken prisoners, among them Col. McRAE, of an Arkansas Regiment.

The attack was made from the North and West, our army being completely surrounded. Gens. VAN DORN, PRICE, McCULLOCH and McINTOSH were present with about 25,060 men. Gens. McCULLOCH and McINTOSH are reported mortally wounded.

The attack from the rear was made by Gen. McCULLOCH, and was met by Gen. SIGEL, who routed him completely. His corps scattered in wild confusion. We have also captured a large amount of stores, cannon, teams and ammunition.

THE LOCATION OF THE BATTLE.

The location of the battle can be seen from any ordinary map of Arkansas, or of the United States. It was in the extreme northwestern part of the State, and in the northwesternmost county (Benton.) A range of hills (of the Ozark range) will be seen sweep-

[Continued on Eighth Page.]

The New-York Times.

VOL. XI—NO. 3267. NEW-YORK, THURSDAY, MARCH 13, 1862. PRICE TWO CENTS.

NEWS FROM MANASSAS

Reports of Our Correspondent with the Advance of the Army.

The Rebel Evacuation Commenced on Friday Last.

THE PANIC AMONG THE REAR GUARD.

The Rebels at Winchester Now Said to Have Escaped.

Great Strength of the Rebel Fortifications.

Concentration of the Rebel Army at Gordonsville.

SPECIAL DISPATCHES FROM WASHINGTON.

WASHINGTON, Wednesday, March 12.

A courier from the Union troops in the direction of Brentsville, Va., brings reports to 5 P. M. yesterday. Up to that time they had sustained their difficult march with much fortitude, and but few lagged behind. All are much disappointed at the flight of the rebels. The smoke of burning property near Manassas can be plainly seen from camp.

The roads in many places are very bad.

Contrabands coming into our lines report that officers commanding the twelve months "Confederate" troops advised their men to disband and repair to their homes.

Great columns of smoke seen in the direction of Brentsville, indicated the abandonment and destruction of the enemy's works.

A correspondent of the TIMES, who accompanied the advance upon Centreville and Manassas has just come in. He was in every fort at Centreville, and went with the first column that crossed the Bull Run battle-field and entered the famous stronghold, Manassas. He corrects many previous statements we have had of the evacuation of those places by the enemy.

It was only last Friday that the retreat of the rebels from Centreville commenced. Gen. JOHNSTON left on Friday morning; Gen. SMITH left on Saturday afternoon, and Col. STUART last Monday, the day our army left camp on the Potomac.

The retreat was conducted very orderly at first. Everything was carefully cleaned up at Centreville—nothing left that could be useful to us. The forts were well planned and very formidable. They command the roads, and the fire of not less than a hundred guns could be converged upon any approach to the defences; but the guns were never brought from Manassas to mount the Centreville forts. A railroad track extended from Manassas to Centreville, and a telegraph line. The rebel Generals had their headquarters at Centreville all together, and a more convenient and complete military establishment could not be found in Washington than they had.

Through Manassas the enemy continued their retreat as quietly as it began. They carried off all their heavy guns from Manassas—forty to sixty in number—part of their army marching by turnpike to Warrenton, and part to Gordonsville, where it was said they would make a stand.

It was on Monday evening that the first sign of panic was noticed at Manassas. A part of STUART'S rear-column was preparing a train to move Southward by railroad, when they learned some excited rebels had set fire to the bridges ahead of them. They immediately began to burn, destroy, and run away in general confusion. Five hundred barrels of flour, piled up in ranks, had their heads stove in. Barrels of molasses suffered the same way, with more loss to the commodity; and a hundred and sixty barrels or kegs of powder were left which they did not well know how to destroy in safety to themselves.

It seems to be confirmed that the enemy had, two weeks since, between fifty and sixty thousand troops at Centreville and Manassas, and that they only began their retreat last Friday. Why they went is a mystery; as that number of men, in the fortifications they had prepared, would have been equal to three times their force assailing them from without. They must have feared to trust their men whose enlistments were expiring, or their powder, which many accounts agree is of very inferior quality.

But the strangest news brought by the TIMES correspondent is that Gen. JACKSON and one-half his army, whom Gen. BANKS yesterday supposed he was closely watching in Winchester, went down the railroad to Manassas one week ago, and quietly marched off southward. The other half are said to be moving southward in the valley of the Shenandoah.

Reconnoissances beyond Manassas show that all the damage possible to be done in a brief time has been done to the railroad that took the rebels off. The last of the rebels left Manassas on Monday evening. On Monday night our scouts approached the place. On Tuesday, about 1 o'clock, P. M., the correspondent of the TIMES, attended by a detachment of Union troops, entered the works.

MANASSAS STATION, ORANGE AND ALEXANDRIA RAILROAD, WEDNESDAY NIGHT.

Many contrabands from beyond Manassas came in to-night, reporting great demoralization in the rebel army. Gen. SUMNER gave employment to as many as wished to stay, and passes to the rest to go to Washington. He stated his determination to use his command in no case to return them. The troops to-day, in their eagerness to keep up with the main column, divested themselves of everything not deemed indispensable, throwing away knapsacks and extra clothing, and carrying only their blankets.

The following persons deserted from the rebels and came to our camp here, on Saturday and Sunday last:

James Thornton, 27th Virginia.
John Chasty, 20th Georgia.
John Kehoe, 20th Georgia.
Dennis Collins, 20th Georgia.
Joseph Burgess, Hampton Legion.
James Martin, formerly attached to Company G, 17th Virginia; connected now with no company, but in the employ of the Confederate Government.

On Tuesday a number of rebel pickets were captured by the Union advance in Virginia, and turned over to the Chaplain of a regiment to catechise. The Chaplain reported:

A Second Lieutenant, two Corporals and eleven privates, all of the First Maryland Regiment. The Lieutenant was JOS. K. STEWART, a West Pointer, smart and reticent.

Corporal SHEANS, wounded badly in the left thigh, bullet through right hand, sabre cut in wrist.

Private JAS. W. SWANN, from Baltimore, enlisted at Harper's Ferry.

THOMAS B. ANGEL, from Washington; has a brother-in-law, WM. RIPLEY, in Washington, doing Government work; has a family in Washington; was forced into the rebel service in Winchester.

JOHN H. DURST, Maryland; ERNEST GLOSSNER, and WM. WENSELL, Germans.

JIMMY MCMANUS, Irishman, joined the rebels voluntarily; would fight the Yankees like h—ll, if he had a chance.

THOMAS GAVEN.

ED. ENGELHARDT—was forced into the rebel service; glad to get away.

JOHN GOLDEN.

LATER.—Five more rebels have come in and surrendered themselves.

FROM ANOTHER CORRESPONDENT.

WASHINGTON, Wednesday, March 12.

Information received from a gentleman direct from Manassas, who left there at 10 o'clock this morning, represents the condition of the army as about the same as it was yesterday afternoon. The report prevalent that the rebels were again concentrating in that vicinity is without foundation; on the contrary, there is little if any doubt that the rebels have retired toward Gordonsville, and that they rest, with their advance at the Rapidan River, their camps extending back to Gordonsville, twelve miles.

WASHINGTON, Wednesday, March 12—P. M.

Accounts received from Manassas to-night state that nothing of much value to our army was found at that place. The wagons, about thirty in number, were old and worn out, and had evidently been impressed into the service. The "contrabands" from the surrounding country came in and helped themselves to whatever clothing they could find, and also to the commissary stores, such as flour, bread, meat and cooking utensils, which the enemy had left behind them.

It was ascertained from the prisoners captured yesterday, namely, Capt. WOODS and four privates of the Louisiana Tigers, at the first station on the Orange and Alexandria Railroad, beyond Manassas, that a company of that corps had just retired as our forces advanced into Manassas.

The works deserted by the enemy are not occupied by our troops.

A large number of rebels in leaving Bull Run took the Warrenton Turnpike leading towards Richmond.

The rebel rear guard, on passing through Gainesville, six miles from Bull Run, fired and destroyed the village.

MOORE'S extensive flouring mills, at the foot of Bull Run Mountain, and six miles from the Stone Bridge, were also burned.

The railway stations and bridges, for the distance of about fifteen miles, were also destroyed yesterday morning.

It is supposed from what could be gathered, making a fair average for the number the huts could contain, that the rebel troops at Manassas did not at any time exceed 60,000 men, and not more than 30,000 have occupied that section within the last two months.

Information to-night, received from Winchester, is that our forces to-day took possession of that town.

THE PLAN OF THE CAMPAIGN.

The following private letter, written by a gentleman of extended military experience, has been handed us for publication:

NEW-YORK, Saturday, March 8, 1862.

DEAR SIR: Your kind note is just received, and in reply I would say that I am sure you do no more than express the patriotic anxiety of many others in reference to the apparent inactivity of our army on the Potomac, and I therefore will gladly express my opinion regarding it, in vindication of those whose capacities as military leaders are mainly concerned.

I must, however, confine myself to abstract principles of strategy, the correctness of which, of course, you or any other unprofessional man must take for granted, but the refutation or contradiction of which from any professional source, I may safely challenge. It will, moreover, be necessary for me, for the moment, to pass by the general plan of the campaign, and to present elementary explanations of principles which I may have to cite, simply because I wish this little treatise to be clear to the most unmilitary mind.

To begin with, I must tell you that all military operations, no matter of what magnitude, are reducible to the simplest principles of tactics which govern the single soldier. For as all evolutions or manœuvres of companies, battalions, regiments, etc., are no more than the aggregations of the simple movements of the single soldier, so are the bases of whole campaigns, the developments of them and the subsequent evolutions therefore, as I have said, are reducible to the simplest principles of tactics governing the individual soldier.

What, then, is the permanent factor in the planning of any military operation? It is the true conception of its simplest tactical nature, or, as it is called in military parlance, the determination of its "tactical aspects." This is in strategy what the diagnosis is in medicine, and you will at once not only perceive its importance, but also how it is possible that anything contrary to the laws of strategy should be evident to a thorough military mind and eye, from its superficial operation, and without it being necessary for the critic to be in camp or on the Staff of any Commanding General.

Now, if a skillful physician determines the diagnosis of any disease, a layman may refer to a *Materia Medica* and look up the remedy. But if you treat a patient afflicted with inflammation of the lungs for typhoid fever, nothing but a miracle, or his strong constitution, or an accident, but surely not your treatment, can cure him, for that positively tends to killing him, and any man attending the patient during such treatment can certainly not claim the doctor's degree for what he did.

Let us apply this same logic to our campaign, and see how our military doctors acted, and whether they determined on the right diagnosis, and what it was. Let us suppose that we want to drill a single soldier; what have we, first of all, to do? Can we lay him down, or sit him upon a chair? Certainly not. We must put him on his feet. What do his feet represent? Surely they are his base.

Next, what does the direction mean in which his face is turned? Surely it is the direction in which the enemy is supposed to be; for it is he whom he has to face, and in facing your man to the right, left, or about—these movements mean no more nor less than the change of position of your assailant, or your own intention to flank him; while your march forward means the occupation of the ground you traverse, or the marching backward, the yielding of the ground you gave up to the enemy.

If, then, we had to go through a campaign, what would be the first thing to do? Certainly a base would have to be taken. Next, we turn our face to ward the enemy.

Now, common sense, without any knowledge of natural philosophy, tells us that a rod, if held upright in the air, will be more liable to break in proportion to its length. If, therefore, we want to strengthen it, we must place props under it. It follows, then, that in multiplying our single soldier, or prolonging his base thousands of times by aggregation, we will need props, or supports. These, then, are in operation on a large scale, and, in military phraseology, called strategic points, and, more specifically, they are termed keys to our whole position, or to any specific part of it.

Now, do you think that the plan of a campaign, or its strategic points, can arrange themselves, without any one to attend to it? Certainly not. Every one knows that a squad of soldiers want their non-commissioned officers, a Company their commissioned officers and Captains, the Regiment its Staff, the Brigade its General, and so on until the whole army must be divided into corps of special denominations, and each of these must have their commanders, until the whole has its Commander-in-Chief, from whom all orders in conformity with the general plan of the campaign, and for its systematic and harmonious working can, and ought only to emanate. System, then, and organization are required, and are in military matters more, perhaps, than in any others, the very soul and substance.

We will now proceed to the consideration of our position, or to use the same figure of speech we employed above, we will examine the nature of the disease of our military organism, and form our diagnosis.

For this purpose we will have to ask ourselves the following questions, viz:

1. Where are we?

We are on a line running from the mouth of the Potomac along that river to the Ohio, and thence to the Mississippi on the one hand; and again on the Atlantic Coast from Chesapeake Bay to the Gulf of Mexico.

2. Where is the enemy?

The enemy is within the periphery thus described.

3. What do we want to do?

We mean to occupy, conquer, or hold all the area of territory inclosed by the above periphery.

4. How are we to do this?

By marching over it, for when that is done the military object which we have in view is attained.

5. What is the position of the enemy?

His position is evidently a "central" one.

6. What is our own position?

Ours is, in consequence of what we have already said, a "peripheric" one.

7. What have we, therefore, to do, in accordance with the laws of strategy, in the case before us?

The law in the case is as follows: Whenever the reciprocal position of two contending armies is such that the one finds itself in a "peripheric," the other in a "central" position, the only salvation for the former lies in its closing the periphery, or, in other words, completing the circle upon the enemy.

8. What has the enemy to do, in accordance with those very same laws?

The law applicable to the defence of a central position is as follows: To unite the mass of the forces against whichever army of the enemy first approaches, remaining on the defensive on all other points, and keeping all the lines of communication with the centre open and unimpaired.

Knowing this, we also know where our basis lies, viz.: It is from the Potomac, along the Ohio, up to the Mississippi; and as it is the multiplied basis of 500,000 single soldiers, it is long, long, indeed, and liable to break unless we support it, which we consequently do by fortifying as many strategic points as are necessary for this purpose. But what is to be done with our territory beyond our base line? We will consider this point in its proper place. Now, from what I said in the beginning of this little treatise, it appears that the greatest military operations should be reducible down to the simplest principles of tactics for the individual soldier, and we have thus far done this.

We now want to move over the ground we intend to occupy or hold. How shall we do this? Well let us descend to the simple evolutions of a single file, squad, or company, under similar circumstances, and see what they would have to do.

We see clearly that our file, squad, company or regiment would have to perform a left-wheel movement while marching with a movable pivot. But which of the two wings of our squad or of any larger force will have to make the longest steps in a left-wheel movement? Surely, the right wing. Our whole grand campaign, then, is in its tactical aspect simply a left wheel movement *en march*, and as it is so, our right or Western wing or army has to make the longest strides, because it is on the sweeping wing, and its advance, our left wing, or army of the Potomac, has to follow slowly, or *aligné*. Whenever this simple movement or evolution is performed, then indeed our campaign is at an end, for we will have traversed the whole area inclosed by the Potomac, Ohio, Mississippi and the Gulf, and that area is ours: and more than this we did not desire to accomplish. You see now clearly that it is not this General, or that one, or this opinion or that one, which suggests that the right or left of our army should move; for chance or opinion has no applicability to the principles of strategy, or even of tactics, for they are as unalterable as the first principles of mathematics or of the laws of nature itself. The point to be fixed was, to reduce the campaign to its simple, "tactical aspect," and all the subsequent evolutions naturally proceed from that.

Will you now wonder that our left wing, or the army of the Potomac, did not move, or does not even now rush on headlong? Could it or can it do so, I ask you? Certainly not; for it is on the pivot side of our left wheel movement, and has consequently to slowly follow over the diagonal to—a place I have no desire to name. For it to do otherwise would be as wise as for a single soldier, when assailed on his right, to make a left face, or turn his back to his assailant. Hence, you may see how utterly erroneous the former move upon Manassas was, not because you were not prepared, or poorly so, but because you did just the contrary to that which was necessary; for even if you had confined yourself to the occupation of Virginia alone, which was not and could not be your sole object, you still had to perform a "left wheel," and a central position to assail, and you were therefore wrong, in view of both the objects before you. You will also see how completely ruinous was the neglect of your Western army, which had almost not a man, while you accumulated thousands on your left. Finally, you may see that the "backbone" of this rebellion, as it is popularly called, is not East, but out West, or in the Appalachees, on the sweeping wing of our whole army.

The question will now suggest itself to you, what do we mean by our naval expeditions, and how with regard to the territory on the right of the Mississippi, and with regard to Texas? You must still bear in mind that we are in a "peripheric position," and that we have therefore to "complete the circle" upon the enemy, which we do by investing the whole Atlantic coast, and by an army in Kansas and another in Texas. But our uninterrupted base line ends with the Mississippi; beyond that we have only "partisans," as they are called in military parlance, or Generals who with their *corps d'armée* keep our right as safe and protected as our fleet on the Atlantic does our left, thus helping to complete the circle upon the enemy.

And now I suppose one more doubt and question may arise in your mind, as there will in those of many others, viz.: How are you to understand the simple movement of a "left wheel" as the illustration of a campaign of such magnitude, with so many *corps d'armée*, each moving on its own base, and having to overcome its own obstacles? Well, the explanation is plain enough.

Suppose you want to perform a left wheel with a regiment over broken ground, (say trees, bogs, underbrush, or a solitary rock being the obstacle,) what will you do? You will order those obstacles to be removed, and the Companies in whose track they are will have to do so. So will the Commander-in-Chief give the general order and plan of any campaign, while the execution of the details will have to be left to the various commanders of the *corps d'armée*, and if they find obstacles in their way, they must find means to remove them, "*but without disturbing the harmony of the whole;*" and no corps must any more get ahead, or remain behind the *alignement* of all the extended operations, than a single soldier must do the same as one of a squad. Rest assured that there is no "chance" in military matters, for if you are elated by a chance success to-day, you may as well be prepared to meet with similar "chance" discomfiture to-morrow.

And now you may put one more question to me, viz.: What is the use of any advance on our part along the Atlantic coast upon the main, if a simple left wheel movement of our land forces will perform and complete the task?

Because the enemy is in a central position, and as he is likely to defend it in accordance with the laws already laid down, we have, after completing the circle upon him, to defeat the operation of his law—first, by interrupting his line of communication with his centre, and next by forcing him to take the offensive, simultaneously upon a primary and several secondary lines, by which course his forces are necessarily divided, and his destruction becomes a question of mere physical force. You may, therefore, rest assured that, thus far, whether you attribute it to chance, inspiration, or thorough knowledge, the right course has been pursued, of late, in every respect, and we may reasonably entertain hopes for the future.

But let me tell you, before I close this, that military operations, like the web of Penelope, bear the seeds of their own destruction within themselves, unless systematically and vigorously carried out. To allow any outside opinion or pressure to interfere in any way with the systematic operations of the campaign, or to divert any of its various arms to the execution of any strategic scheme, however advantageous they may be, if untimely, is likely to create confusion in the operations of the campaign, the plan for which can only emanate from the Commander-in-Chief and his *Etat-Major*, unless we choose to hand over the whole matter to *farceurs*, who may then arrange a general war cotillion, according to the fancies of all the honorable political Generals, wherever they may be.

Very respectfully,
Your obedient servant, D.I.M.

THE GREAT PLAN OF THE CAMPAIGN.

Diagram Exhibiting the Grand Lines of Military Movement of the Union Armies, as Planned by Lieut. Gen. Scott, and now being Carried Out.

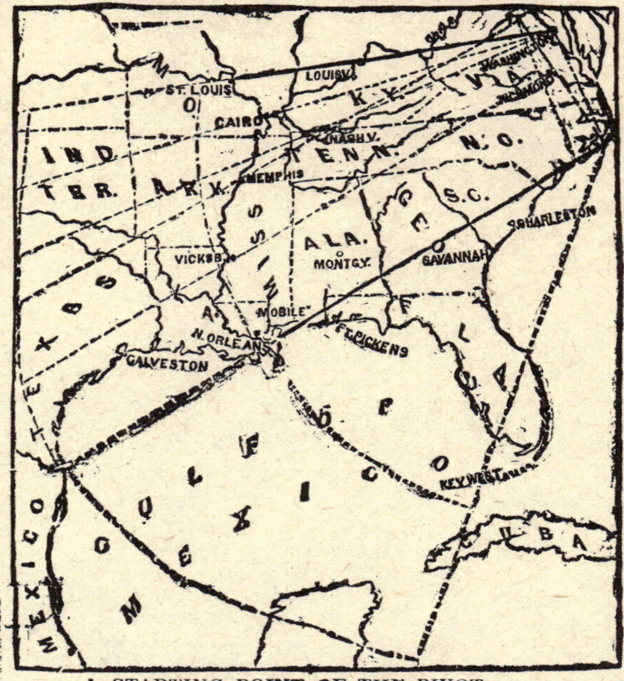

1. STARTING POINT OF THE PIVOT.
2. DIAGONAL TERMINUS OF THE PIVOT.

Great Wool Sale at Providence.

PROVIDENCE, Wednesday, March 12.

At the great Wool sale here to-day, the attendance of dealers from New-York, Philadelphia, Boston and Hartford, and manufacturers, was large. The prices realized were 2½@5 ℔ cent. lower than the average of sales in the market, viz.:

Ohio XX....50c.	@51¼c.	Ohio No. 4..44¼c.	@ —
Ohio X......48½c.	@50c.	N. Y. S. ex..45c.	@45½c.
Ohio No. 1..49c.	@49½c.	N. Y. S., 1...44c.	@44½c.
Ohio No. 2..48c.	@48½c.	N. Y. S., 2...43c.	@ —
Ohio No. 3..40c.	@ —	N. Y. S., c'n.40c.	@ —

IMPORTANT FROM WASHINGTON.

War Bulletins Issued by the President.

THE ORDER FOR A FORWARD MOVEMENT

Gen. McClellan Relieved of the Command-in-Chief.

He Takes the Field at the Head of the Army of the Potomac.

A NEW DIVISION OF DEPARTMENTS.

Gen. Fremont Assigned to a Command in Western Virginia and Eastern Tennessee.

Gen. Halleck in Command of the Department of the Mississippi.

Enthusiastic Reception of Gen. McClellan by the Army.

IMPORTANT PROCEEDINGS OF CONGRESS.

[OFFICIAL.]

WAR BULLETINS.

EXECUTIVE MANSION, WASHINGTON, Jan. 27, 1862.

THE PRESIDENT'S GENERAL WAR ORDER, NO. 1.

Ordered, That the 22d day of February, 1862, be the day for a general movement of the land and naval forces of the United States against the insurgent forces.

That especially,
The army at and about Fortress Monroe,
The army of the Potomac,
The army of Western Virginia,
The army near Munfordsville, Ky.,
The army and flotilla at Cairo,
And a naval force in the Gulf of Mexico,
be ready for a movement on that day.

That all other forces, both land and naval, with their respective commanders, obey existing orders for the time, and be ready to obey additional orders when duly given.

That the Heads of Departments, and especially the Secretaries of War and of the Navy, with all their subordinates, and the General-in-Chief, with all other commanders and subordinates of the land and naval forces, will severally be held to their strict and full responsibilities for the prompt execution of this order.

ABRAHAM LINCOLN.

EXECUTIVE MANSION, WASHINGTON, March 8, 1862.

THE PRESIDENT'S GENERAL WAR ORDER, NO. 2.

Ordered, First, that the Major-General commanding the army of the Potomac proceed forthwith to organize that part of said army destined to enter upon active operations, including the reserve, but excluding the troops to be left in the fortifications about Washington, into four army corps, to be commanded according to seniority of rank, as follows:

First corps to consist of four divisions, and to be commanded by Maj.-Gen. I. MCDOWELL.

Second corps to consist of three divisions, and to be commanded by Brig.-Gen. E. V. SUMNER.

Third corps to consist of three divisions, and to be commanded by Brig.-Gen. S. P. HEINTZELMAN.

Fourth corps to consist of three divisions, and to be commanded by Brig.-Gen. E. L. KEYES.

2. That the divisions now commanded by the officers above assigned to the commands of corps shall be embraced in, and form part of their respective corps.

3. The forces left for the defence of Washington will be placed in command of Brig.-Gen. JAMES WADSWORTH, who shall also be military Governor of the District of Columbia.

4. That this order be executed with such promptness and dispatch as not to delay the commencement of the operations, already directed to be undertaken by the army of the Potomac.

5. A fifth army corps to be commanded by Maj.-Gen. N. P. BANKS, will be formed from his own and Gen. SHIELDS' (late Gen. LANDER'S) Division.

ABRAHAM LINCOLN.

EXECUTIVE MANSION, WASHINGTON, March 11, 1862.

THE PRESIDENT'S GENERAL WAR ORDER, NO. 3.

Major-Gen. MCCLELLAN having personally taken the field at the head of the army of the Potomac, until otherwise ordered, he is relieved from the command of the other Military Departments, he retaining command of the Department of the Potomac.

Ordered, further, That the two Departments now under the respective commands of Generals HALLECK and HUNTER, together with so much of that under Gen. BUELL as lies west of a north and south line, indefinitely drawn through Knoxville, Tenn., be consolidated and designated the Department of the Mississippi, and that until otherwise ordered Maj.-Gen. HALLECK have command of said Department.

Ordered, also, That the country west of the Department of the Potomac and east of the Department of the Mississippi be a Military Department, to be called the Mountain Department, and that the same be commanded by Major-General FREMONT; that all the Commanders of Departments, after the receipt of this order by them respectively, report severally and directly to the Secretary of War, and that prompt, full and frequent reports will be expected of all and each of them.

ABRAHAM LINCOLN.

THE NEW MILITARY DEPARTMENTS.

GEN. MCCLELLAN'S DEPARTMENT.

The Department of the Potomac, to which Gen. MCCLELLAN is now confined by the President's War Order, No. 3, has the following geographical boundaries:

The States of Delaware and Maryland, the District of Columbia, and that portion of Virginia east of the Alleghany Mountains and North of James River, excepting Fortress Monroe and sixty miles around the same.

GEN. HALLECK'S DEPARTMENT.

The Department of the Mississippi, as newly constructed, embraces the late Departments of HALLECK and HUNTER, and the greater part of that under BUELL. It will extend over the following region:

Dacotah, Nebraska, Colorado, the Indian Territory west of Arkansas, and Kansas—being HUNTER'S late Department; Missouri, Arkansas, Iowa, Minnesota, Wisconsin, Illinois, Indiana, and the States of Kentucky and Tennessee as far west as the town of Knoxville, and to a line from thence run north and south indefinitely—being all of HALLECK'S and nearly all of BUELL'S late Departments. This Department is by far the largest, geographically, of the three newly-constructed Departments, and comprises more than one-half of the entire territory of the United States.

GEN. FREMONT'S DEPARTMENT.

The new Mountain Department will include the following sections:

That part of Virginia west of the Alleghany Mountains, lately commanded by Gen. ROSECRANS; that part of Tennessee west of Knoxville, that part of Kentucky west of a line drawn north from the same town, and the States of Ohio and Michigan.

OUR SPECIAL WASHINGTON DISPATCHES.

WASHINGTON, Wednesday, March 12.

GEN. M'CLELLAN AND THE ARMY OF THE POTOMAC.

The Department having formally announced that Gen. MCCLELLAN has taken the field in person, it is not improper to say that he left Washington last Monday, and is leading his great Potomac army upon the flying rebels of Virginia. His reception among the troops, as he passed to their head, was one of the grandest ever witnessed in the country. The largest body of men ever put in motion at once since the battle of Solferino moved from the banks of the Potomac on that day. For many miles, on divers roads, the embattled ranks pressed forward, and the cheers that hailed the General at one point of the lines was taken up by regiment after regiment, and division after division, until the whole vast army rent the heavens with shouts of welcome.

Gen. MCCLELLAN rode through the ranks in motion his cap ever in his hand, returning the salutes of the enthusiastic soldiers. It is only hoped by his friends that the country will patiently give him half the time that was accorded to the Western General who pursued his foe from Lexington, Missouri, to Arkansas.

GEN. M'CLELLAN'S POSITION.

The relief of Gen. MCCLELLAN from the command of the Western Department, is only just to him. It would be wrong to keep him responsible for campaigns which, while he is in the field, he cannot personally supervise. While his enemies see in this change his humiliation, his friends see his justification and safety.

GEN. FREMONT'S RESTORATION TO COMMAND.

The restoration of Maj.-Gen. FREMONT to a command, was, under the circumstances, a proper deference to the opinions of a very large, intelligent and respectable body of men in Congress, whose good will it is desirable for the President to retain. The President's action would have been more gratifying if FREMONT'S new command had been more important. It includes only ROSECRANS' and GARFIELD'S troops and there are no rebels in arms in the Department for even this small force to operate against.

NO COUNCIL OF WAR HELD.

The statement published that last week a council of war in Washington decided, eight to four, that the army of the Potomac could not be moved against the enemy at present, is entirely untrue. The Generals were unanimous that an advance was possible and proper. The only difference was as to the plan of the proposed attack.

NO TAX ON FLOUR.

Hon. ALFRED ELY having received about fifty letters from millers residing in New-York, appeared before the Committee on Ways and Means, recently, in opposition to the proposed tax of ten cents on every barrel of flour. The result was this tax was stricken from the bill.

THE CLAIMS COMMISSION AT ST. LOUIS.

JOSEPH HOLT arrived here to-day from St. Louis. The Commission for the settlement of the claims in the Department of Missouri, under FREMONT'S administration, have completed their labors. They will make their report in a few days. The aggregate amount of claims presented amounted to $10,000,000. The sum awarded is considerably below that figure.

THE SECRETARY OF WAR AND HARBOR DEFENCES.

The Secretary of War was before the Military Committee of the Senate to-day for two hours. The Secretary has under consideration the important subject of harbor defences in the Northern cities.

VOTES OF THANKS.

The speedy action taken by Congress, in passing resolutions of thanks to our gallant Naval Commanders, will have a good effect in the service. The Naval Committee of the Senate have reported two to-day—one to Commander FOOTE and Capt. WORDEN.

COST OF THE MONITOR.

The *Monitor* cost less than $250,000, and was contracted to be finished in ninety days.

THE STEVENS BATTERY.

Mr. STEVENS is here with a model of his battery. It has been visited and examined with deep interest to-day, by Naval Committees of Congress, and receives universal applause. Can New-York do nothing to promote its completion? By working day and night it could be finished in sixty days.

THE AQUIA CREEK BATTERIES.

By an arrival at the Navy-yard to-day it was ascertained that the rebel batteries were evacuated at Aquia Creek yesterday morning. Whether permanently or not, there are no means of ascertaining.

GEN. FREMONT.

Gen. FREMONT will return to Washington either this evening or to-morrow morning.

THE RAILROAD TO MANASSAS.

Repairs have already been commenced on the bridges injured by the rebels at Bull Run, and the probability is the railroad to Manassas will be in running order this week.

SENATOR SHERMAN'S CONFISCATION BILL.

The bill introduced in the Senate, to-day, by Mr. SHERMAN, of Ohio, is as follows:

SEC. 1 Authorizes the President to take possession of all property and persons, as follows: 1. Of persons hereafter acting as officers in the army and navy of the rebels. 2. Of persons hereafter acting as President, Vice-President and members of Congress of the so-called Confederate States. 3. Of the Governors of the States, members of the Legislatures and Judges of the States in rebellion, who hereafter take the oath to support the rebel Constitution. 4. Of persons holding offices of honor in the United States, who hereafter may hold offices in the said Confederate States; and, 5. Of persons owning property in the loyal States who may hereafter assist or give aid to the rebellion.

SEC. 2 provides that to recover possession of such property in the loyal States proceedings be instituted in the name of the United States, in the District where the property is found, and if the property is sold the proceeds be deposited in the Treasury of the United States.

SEC. 3 provides that property seized where judicial proceedings are obstructed shall be held till judicial proceedings are restored, when a suit shall be instituted.

Articles of a perishable nature are to be sold or used as the service requires, and no person described in the first section of the bill shall hold any person to

[*Continued on Eighth Page.*]

The Charleston Mercury.

VINDICE NULLO
SPONTE SUA SINE LEGE FIDES RECTUMQUE COLENTUR.

VOLUME LXXX. CHARLESTON, S. C., TUESDAY, APRIL 8, 1862. NUMBER 11,417

THE MERCURY

TUESDAY, APRIL 8, 1862.

The Victory of Shiloh.

The ides of March have come and gone. The crisis of our fate has been met. The grand catastrophe of the war has been enacted. Once more the people of the South, released from the shackles with which their energies have been bound, and following the true instincts of every Southern heart, have risen up, in the majesty of their power and the splendor of their courage, and have trampled down and crushed before them, in the burning wrath of outraged honor and wounded pride, this mongrel herd of Northern rabblement which has been thrown upon us. Standing upon no; paltry principle of defence, but boldly advancing upon them in their position, in serried columns, fairly we met them, sword to sword, and bayonet to bayonet, and hand to hand, and eye to eye—and nobly our gallant troops swept the foe before them, like chaff before the angry gale. They have but done now what their brave hearts have ever been prepared to achieve. Let pæans, long and loud, be sung, and let the fierce huzza of triumph, ring from the lips of a gladdened people, in honor of the brave who live—in honor of the brave who fell. No holiday pastime—no laggard diplomacy—no push-pin warfare, this upon the plains of Shiloh. But the Genius of *War*, himself, was there, and once more, as at Manassas, at Ball's Bluff, and at Donelson, he has kindled the Southern heart, and blazed in his eye, and nerved his hand with his fiery passion and desperate resolve to grapple with death, and to conquer victory. And may his spirit still be abroad amongst us—let still the thunders of his javelin go forth—cry havoc, and forward, to our brave boys. Smite, and slay, and capture, and still forward, forward, brave boys—forward from the banks of the Tennessee across the waters of the Ohio. Hands off! says Europe. And hands off! say we. And as there is a living God, we will drive this insolent, bartering marauder—this tribe of hucksters—back to the farthest hills of his barren pasture. Let but Executive power stand aside, and let our people fight, and let our great Generals lead them on, and from this time forth, our lost opportunities will be redeemed, as from field to field, victory will soar above and perch upon our advancing arms.

But in the midst of the proud triumph, we cannot but pause a moment in saddest grief over the inevitable fate of war. Ten thousand stricken hearts must yield their tribute to patriotism, in a life-long lamentation over the heroic dead. A thousand strong hearts, that but yesterday beat high with the instincts of life, are stilled forever. But it is the fate of life, and it is written, that "men must work, and women must weep"—weep those tears, which are the saddest and the sorest things for us to witness and to bear.

A great General, too, has fallen. ALBERT SIDNEY JOHNSTON, the veteran of many a field, has fought his last battle. Goaded on by our late disasters, his high spirit could not brook imputations, and, rushing onward at the head of his troops, he fell a victim to misfortunes, which were brought upon us by no fault of his. He is gone, but his spirit will live—live and move along the blazing line of many a field to come—live amidst the roar of artillery and the clash of arms—live in the cry for vengeance, and live in the shout of victory—and it will live on the pages of a great history yet to be written—live in monumental marble, and live in the hearts of a grateful people.

Battle of Shiloh, April 6, 7, 1862

RICHMOND NEWS AND GOSSIP.

(FROM OUR OWN CORRESPONDENT.)

RICHMOND, Friday, April 4.

From Washington—McClellan's Big Army Demoralized—Old Scott Despised—Mr. Simms' Losses—King Cotton Upheld—Want of Brains—Capt. Morgan—Attorney General Watts, etc., etc.

A traveller (ex-Senator GWIN) just from Washington, via the Underground Railroad, gives some interesting news. He says MCCLELLAN has an army of 180,000 men, fine looking, well drilled and equipped, and 400 pieces of artillery. But both the young Napoleon and his men have been disconcerted and almost demoralized by Johnston's evacuation of Manassas. McClellan knew of the evacuation, but after it had taken place the force of public opinion compelled him to advance. The consequence was, that his men got to Manassas ahead of the provision trains, and, owing to the state of the roads, it was impossible to feed them. They became mutinous, and finally McClellan was forced to tell each man to take care of himself and make his way back to the Potomac as best he could. A stampede equal almost to that of Bull Run ensued. The people in Washington thought the army had been whipped again. McClellan at once fell in the public estimation and lost ground with his men. Thus the high-blown reputation of Napoleon No. II collapsed, and the morale of a splendid army, eager for fight and confident of victory, was seriously impaired.

Our traveller thinks that the grand "on to Richmond," by way of Manassas, has been abandoned, and that the attack in tremendous force will take place on the Peninsula, combined with a naval assault on the James and York rivers. The Yankees are determined to have Richmond at any cost. Nobody at Washington seems to entertain doubt of the speedy subjugation of the South. The expenses of the Lincoln concern amount now to four millions a day, but the Treasury notes sell at par. A signal victory will bring them down "by the run," as sailors say. Old Scott is in New York city, neglected by the Yankees themselves. This is a *resume* of the traveller's news; no doubt he imparted still more valuable information to the authorities. Hence, probably, the protracted consultation between the President and Gens. Lee, Loring and Johnston.

The recent losses of W. Gilmore Simms, Esq., as detailed in THE MERCURY, have excited the warmest sympathy among his friends and admirers in this city. Surely the hand of misfortune is laid heavily upon him. The suggestions of THE MERCURY should at once be carried out. South Carolina would be recreant to herself did she not sustain a son who has done so much to honor her.

The Examiner devotes a vigorous article, this morning, to King Cotton. The editor says, "If King Cotton has lost his sceptre for a time, it has been from the incapacity of his ministers." He then shows how we have been undone by the want of brains in the Administration; but closes his article cheerfully by saying, that "It were only necessary from the first for King Cotton to assert his sovereignty for all the world to acknowledge it." This opinion is based on the assumption that common sense and energy are to rule hereafter.

The spies that were to have been hung to-day have been respited by the President. I hear that they have made important confessions, which have led to the arrest of two other conspirators. Captain Jno. Morgan, the famous Partisan, reached the city last night, and the town is all agog to see him. Attorney General Watts has not yet arrived, nor has he been heard from, so far as known. Hot weather brings the people out in swarms—especially young officers on horseback.

HERMES.

THE NEWS OF THE WAR.

ANTICIPATIONS OF THE GREAT BATTLE NEAR CORINTH.

A correspondent of the New Orleans *Delta*, writing on the 31st ult., in regard to the great battle expected for some weeks past, in the neighborhood of Corinth, Miss., and which has at last actually taken place, said:

The forces, it is believed, will be about equal. In that event, it is not difficult to guess the result, as our Generals command the best troops in the world.

The correspondent of the Savannah *Republican*, writing on the 3d inst., says:

From all I can learn, the enemy is straining every nerve to render his next blow as effective and crushing as possible. The largest army ever seen on this continent is being concentrated in Tennessee, preparatory to the great movement upon the Memphis and Charleston Railroad, at or near Corinth. Troops are being drawn from the Potomac, from the line of the Ohio, from Missouri, and from all other points where they can be spared. The control which the enemy has of the northwestern rivers, and the early reconstruction of the Baltimore and Ohio Railroad, will give him great facilities in the rapid movement and concentration of his forces.

THE YANKEES IN JACKSONVILLE, FLORIDA.

The Gainesville, Fla., *Cotton States* says:

We learn that the commanding officer of the Yankee forces at Jacksonville has issued a circular to the citizens of that place, and to those living in the counties bordering on the St. John's. Gov. Milton has received a copy of the circular, but we have not learned its contents. The enemy are taking preliminary steps for the formation of a Provisional Government. A convention is to be held for the purpose of selecting delegates to represent them in the Federal Congress, and for other officers. We also learn that the traitor, Titus (Col. Hopkins' son-in-law), has given in his adhesion to the tyrant Lincoln, as also several others who have heretofore been prominent lawyers of Jacksonville, and are now using their influence to promote the cause of the vandals.

OUR PRISONERS TAKEN AT FORT DONELSON—HOW THEY ARE TREATED—STATEMENT OF AN ESCAPED PRISONER.

Lieutenant WILSON, of GRAVES' battery, captured at Fort Donelson, reached Corinth, Tennessee, on the twenty-ninth ultimo, having effected his escape from Camp Chase, Columbus, Ohio. He made his way uninterruptedly through Indianapolis, Terre Haute, Evansville, and Henderson, to the Tennessee line. Lieut. WILSON made his exit from the military prison by a novel mode, which it would be impolitic to state, but through which many more of our men may yet be enabled to escape. He makes the following report of the prisoners confined at Columbus, Ohio:

Reaching Columbus, the prisoners were divided into two parties, and placed within a half acre enclosure, surrounded by a fence twenty feet high, with a platform on top, for the use of the sentinels. Thirty or forty were placed in rooms heated by barrel staves, where they remained twenty-four hours without anything to eat. Owing to the filthy condition of the prison quarters, a great deal of sickness prevails, and a number of deaths have already occurred.

If compelled to remain in their present situation through the summer weather, a large amount of disease and suffering must ensue. The prisoners are allowed the same quality of food as the Federal soldiers, with the exception that, instead of coffee, parched beans are furnished. The fare supplied is of such an inferior character that it is not eaten, $50,000 having been sent from Kentucky to the prisoners, with which purchases of whatever is desired are procured.

Large quantities of clothing have also been sent from Kentucky, and our soldiery are made as comfortable as the circumstances of their condition will admit of. Captain Ross, formerly of the United States service, who commanded a battery of heavy guns at Donelson, has been released on his parole, and reports himself every five days at headquarters. No proposals for the release of prisoners have yet been made, although several, through the intercession of Northern acquaintances, have been set at liberty.

Horace Maynard was in Columbus shortly after the arrival of the prisoners, and was instrumental in the release of three Tennesseeans, who took the oath and were discharged. All the field officers captured at Fort Donelson have been sent to Fort Warren, the remaining commissioned officers being at Camp Chase, Columbus, Ohio.

Lieut. Wilson represents a unanimity of feeling in the North with reference to the rebellion, which they affect to believe is nearly at an end; there are, however, many sympathizers with us in Southern Indiana, some of whom afforded Lieutenant Wilson facilities for reaching Kentucky. While at Indianapolis, a number of negros belonging to Lieutenant Wilson and others, were taken from them and set at liberty.

The New-York Times.

VOL. XI—NO. 3291. NEW-YORK, THURSDAY, APRIL 10, 1862. PRICE TWO CENTS.

THE BATTLE OF PITTSBURGH.

Important Particulars of the Terrible Struggle.

The Fight Continued Through Two Days.

Partial Success of the Enemy on Sunday.

Opportune Arrival of Gen. Buell's Forces.

Final Defeat and Flight of the Rebels.

Gen. Albert Sidney Johnston's Body Left on the Field.

Other Prominent Rebel Officers Killed.

Our Probable Loss in Killed, Wounded and Missing Five Thousand.

Gen. Wallace Killed and Gen. Prentiss taken Prisoner.

Occupation of Corinth by Our Forces.

CAIRO, Wednesday, April 9.

Further advices from Pittsburgh Landing give the following about the battle:

The enemy attacked at 4 o'clock Sunday morning, the brigades of Gen. SHERMAN and PRENTISS being first engaged. The attack was successful, and our entire force was driven back to the river, when the advance of the enemy was checked by the fire of the gunboats.

Our force was then increased by the arrival of Gen. GRANT, with the troops from Savannah, and inspirited by reports of the arrival of two divisions of Gen. BUELL's army.

Our loss that day was heavy, and, besides the killed and wounded, embraced our camp equipage and 36 field guns.

The next morning our forces, now amounting to 80,000, assumed the offensive, and by 2 o'clock P. M. had retaken our camp and batteries, together with some 40 of the enemy's guns and a number of prisoners, and the enemy were in full retreat, pursued by our victorious forces.

Our casualties were numerous, and include Gen. GRANT, wounded in the ankle, slightly.

Gen. W. H. WALLACE, killed.

Gen. SMITH, severely wounded.

Col. HALL, Sixteenth Illinois, killed.

Col. LOGAN, Thirty-second Illinois, wounded severely.

Col. DAVIS, Forty-sixth Illinois, wounded, severely.

Major HUNTER, Thirty-second Illinois, killed.

Col. PEABODY, Twenty-fifth Illinois, severely wounded.

Our killed, wounded and missing are not less than 5,000.

CHICAGO, Wednesday, April 9.

The *Times'* account of the battle at Pittsburgh Landing on Sunday and Monday, says that the enemy surprised Gen. PRENTISS' Brigade, which was in the advance, five miles beyond Pittsburgh, at 5 o'clock on Sunday morning, taking two regiments prisoners and capturing the General. The fight continued during the entire day, the enemy driving our forces back to Pittsburgh with fearful loss.

Gen. BUELL, with Gen. NELSON's Division, arrived at 4 o'clock, and turned the tide of battle.

The enemy was commanded by Gens. POLK and BEAUREGARD, who suspended the attack about 4 o'clock.

On the morning of Monday, the troops having rested on the field, and being reinforced by Gen. NELSON's Division, supported by the gunboats, drove the enemy back and occupied their former position, completely routing the rebels, who were immediately followed by several thousand cavalry, who at last accounts were some miles beyond Corinth.

The *Tribune* places our loss at from 600 to 1,000 killed and 3,000 to 4,000 wounded. The rebel loss is twice that number. *Six of our batteries were taken and retaken six times.*

The *Times* says that Gen. BEAUREGARD had given orders not to destroy any of the camp equipage taken on Sunday, as he *expected a complete victory the next day.*

CHICAGO, Wednesday, April 9.

The *Tribune's* special from Cairo, 9th, gives the following summary of reports gathered from persons who witnessed the battle at Pittsburgh Landing.

The National army was posted between two streams, about four miles apart, that run into the Tennessee nearly at right angles, within about two miles from Pittsburg. The left front was commanded by Gen. PRENTISS, who had several raw regiments. In his rear was Gen. SHERMAN, with his division, completely cutting it off from the main army.

Gen. MCCLERNAND put himself at the head of his troops and cut his way through the rebels, and rejoined the army.

The fight had now become desperate, and on Gen. GRANT's assuming command, the enemy were driven back, and the National forces occupied at night nearly the same position they did in the morning. The fight lasted 15 hours.

During the night, Maj.-Gen. LEW. WALLACE came up from Crump's Landing, with 19,000 troops, and in the morning the battle was renewed with great fury.

THE FIELD OF CONFLICT IN THE SOUTHWEST.

Showing Number Ten, and the Rebel Defences on the River to Memphis; also, Pittsburg Landing, Corinth and the Line of the Tennessee River.

neither party seeming disposed to yield. Between 11 and 12 o'clock the fight was terrific.

Soon after noon, Gen. BUELL had crossed the Tennessee, and attacked the enemy in flank with 40,000 men. The rebels were soon routed, Gen. BUELL pursuing them with 12,000 men, mostly cavalry, and the *latest rumors were that he had taken Corinth.*

Eight hundred wounded are reported to be on one steamer, on the way down. Gen. HALLECK is expected here in the morning *en route* for Tennessee. Several barges of ice are ordered to go up the Tennessee to-night for the use of the wounded.

THE FIRST DETAILED REPORTS.

The following dispatch reached us yesterday morning too late to be inserted in our regular morning edition, but was issued at an early hour in an "Extra:"

PITTSBURGH, *via* FORT HENRY, Wednesday, April 9—3:20 A. M.

The greatest battle of the war has just closed, resulting in the complete rout of the enemy, who attacked us at daybreak Sunday morning. The battle lasted without intermission during the entire day, and was again renewed on Monday morning, and continued undecided until 4 o'clock in the afternoon, when the enemy commenced their retreat, and are still flying toward Corinth, pursued by a large force of our cavalry. The slaughter on both sides is immense.

The fight was brought on by a body of three hundred of the Twenty-fifth Missouri Regiment, of Gen. PRENTISS' Division, attacking the advance guard of the rebels, which were supposed to be the pickets of the enemy in front of our camps. The rebels immediately advanced on Gen. PRENTISS' division on the left wing, pouring volley after volley of musketry, and riddling our camps with grape, cannister and shell. Our forces soon formed into line and returned their fire vigorously, and by the time we were prepared to receive them, had turned their heaviest fire on the left centre of SHERMAN's Division and drove our men back from their camps, and bringing up a fresh force, opened fire on our left wing, under Gen. MCCLERNAND. This fire was returned with terrible effect and determined spirit by both infantry and artillery, along the whole line for a distance of over four miles.

Gen. HURLBURT's Division was thrown forward to support the centre, when a desperate conflict ensued. The rebels were driven back with terrible slaughter, but soon rallied and drove back our men in turn. From about 9 o'clock, until night closed on the bloody scene, there was no determination of the result of the struggle. The enemy exhibited remarkably good generalship. At times engaging the left with apparently their whole strength, they would suddenly open a terrible and destructive fire on the right or centre. Even our heaviest and most destructive fire upon the enemy did not appear to discourage their solid columns. The fire of Maj. TAYLOR's Chicago Artillery raked them down in scores, but the smoke would no sooner be dispersed than the breach would again be filled.

The most desperate fighting took place late in the afternoon. The rebels knew that if they did not succeed in whipping us then, that their chances for success would be extremely doubtful, as a portion of Gen. BUELL's forces had by this time arrived on the opposite side of the river, and another portion was coming up the river from Savannah. They became aware that we were being reinforced, as they could see Gen. BUELL's troops from the river bank, a short distance above us on the left, to which point they had forced their way.

At five o'clock the rebels had forced our left wing back so as to occupy fully two-thirds of our camp, and were fighting their way forward with a desperate degree of confidence in their efforts to drive us into the river, and at the same time heavily engaged our right.

Up to this time we had received no reinforcements. Gen. LEW. WALLACE failing to come to our support until the day was over, having taken the wrong road from Crump's Landing, and being without other transports than those used for Quartermaster's and Commissary stores, which were too heavily laden to ferry any considerable number of Gen. BUELL's forces across the river, those that were here having been sent to bring up the troops from Savanna. We were, therefore, contesting against fearful odds, our forces not exceeding thirty-eight thousand men, while that of the enemy was upwards of sixty thousand.

Our condition at this moment was extremely critical. Large numbers of men, had straggled toward the river, and could not be rallied. Gen. GRANT and staff, who had been recklessly riding along the lines during the entire day, amid the unceasing storm of bullets, grape and shell, now rode from right to left, inciting the men to stand firm until our reinforcements could cross the river.

Col. WEBSTER, Chief of Staff, immediately got into position the heaviest pieces of artillery, pointing on the enemy's right, while a large number of the batteries were planted along the entire line, from the river bank northwest to our extreme right, some two and a half miles distant. About an hour before dusk a general cannonading was opened upon the enemy, from along our whole line, with a perpetual crack of musketry. For a short time the rebels replied with vigor and effect, but their return shots grew less frequent and destructive, while ours grew more rapid. The gunboats *Lexington* and *Tyler*, which lay a short distance off, kept raining shell on the rebel hordes. This last effort was too much for the enemy, and ere dusk had set in the firing had nearly ceased, when, night coming on, all the combatants rested from their awful work of blood.

Our men rested on their arms in the position they had at the close of the night, until the forces under Major-General WALLACE arrived and took position on the right, and General BUELL's forces from the opposite side and Savanna were now being conveyed to the battle-ground. The entire right of Gen. NELSON's Division was ordered to form on the right, and the forces under Gen. CRITTENDEN were ordered to his support early in the morning.

THE SECOND DAY'S BATTLE.

Gen. BUELL having arrived on Sunday evening, in the morning the ball was opened at daylight, simultaneously by Gen. NELSON's Division on the left, and Major-Gen. WALLACE's Division on the right. Gen. NELSON's force opened up a most galling fire on the rebels, and advanced rapidly as they fell back. The fire soon became general along the whole line, and began to tell with terrible effect on the enemy. Generals MCCLERNAND, SHERMAN and HURLBURT's men, though terribly jaded from the previous day's fighting still maintained their honors won at Donelson, but the resistance of the rebels at all points of the attack was worthy a better cause.

But they were not enough for our undaunted bravery, and the dreadful desolation produced by our artillery, which was sweeping them away like chaff before the wind. But knowing that a defeat here would be the death blow to their hopes, and that their all depended upon this great struggle, their Generals still urged them on in the face of destruction, hoping by flanking us on the right to turn the tide of battle. Their success was again for a time cheering, as they began to gain ground on us, appearing to have been reinforced; but our left, under Gen. NELSON, was driving them, and with wonderful rapidity, and by eleven o'clock Gen. BUELL's forces had succeeded in flanking them, and capturing their batteries of artillery.

They however again rallied on the left, and recrossed, and the right forced themselves forward in another desperate effort. But reinforcements from General WOOD and Gen. Thomas were coming in, regiment after regiment, which were sent to Gen. BUELL, who had again commenced to drive the enemy.

About three o'clock in the afternoon Gen. GRANT rode to the left, where the fresh regiments had been ordered, and finding the rebels wavering, sent a portion of his body-guard to the head of each of five regiments, and then ordered a charge across the field, himself leading, as he brandished his sword and waved them on to the crowning victory, while cannon balls were falling like hail around him.

The men followed with a shout that sounded above the roar and din of the artillery, and the rebels fled in dismay, as from a destroying avalanche, and never made another stand.

Gen. BUELL followed the retreating rebels, driving them in splendid style, and by 5½ o'clock the whole rebel army was in full retreat to Corinth, with our cavalry in hot pursuit, with what further result is not known, they not having returned up to this hour.

We have taken a large amount of their artillery and also a number of prisoners. We lost a number of our forces prisoners yesterday, among whom is Gen. PRENTISS. The number of our force taken has not been ascertained yet. It is reported at several hundred. Gen. PRENTISS was also reported as being wounded. Among the killed on the rebel side was their General-in-Chief, A. Sydney JOHNSTON, who was struck by a cannon ball on the afternoon of Sunday. It is further reported that Gen. BEAUREGARD had his arm shot off.

This afternoon Gens. BRAGG, BRECKINRIDGE and JACKSON were commanding the rebel forces.

Our loss in officers is very heavy. It is impossible at present to obtain their names. The following were among the number:

Brig. Gen. W. H. WALLACE, killed.

Col. PEGRAM, Acting-Brigadier-General, killed.

Col. ELLIS, Tenth Illinois, killed.

Maj. GODDARD, Fifteenth Illinois, killed.

Lieut. CANFIELD, Seventy-second Ohio, mortally wounded, since dead.

Lieut.-Col. KYLE, Forty-first Indiana, mortally wounded.

Col. DAVIS, Forty-sixth Illinois, mortally wounded.

Gen. W. T. SHERMAN, wounded in the hand by a cannon ball.

Col. SWEENY, Fifty-second Illinois, Acting Brigadier-General, wounded. Received two shots in his only remaining arm, having lost one in Mexico; also a shot in one of his legs. Col. SWEENY kept the field until the close of the fight, exciting the admiration of the whole army.

Col. DAVE STUART, Fifty-fifth Illinois, Acting Brigadier-General, shot through the breast on Sunday, returned to the field on Monday.

Col. CHAS. CRAFTS, Thirty-first Illinois, Acting Brigadier-General, shot through the right shoulder, not dangerously.

Col. HAYNE, of the Forty-eighth Illinois, wounded slightly.

Col. C. MCKAY, of the Seventeenth Kentucky, wounded slightly.

Lieut.-Col. STOUT, of the Eighteenth Kentucky, wounded slightly.

Lieut.-Col. MORGAN, of the Twenty-fifth Indiana, wounded badly in the head.

Col. MASON, of the Seventy-first Ohio, wounded slightly.

Maj. EATON, of the Eighteenth Illinois, (Acting Colonel,) wounded fatally.

Maj. [illegible], of the Eleventh Illinois, wounded slightly.

Capt. IRVING W. CARSON, Gen. GRANT's scout, head shot off by a cannon ball.

Capt. PRESTON MORTON, wounded mortally—since dead.

Capt. DILLON, of the Eighteenth Illinois, killed.

Capt. MACE, of the Fifth Illinois, killed.

Capt. CARTER, of the Eleventh Illinois, killed.

Maj. PAGE, Fifty-seventh Illinois, killed.

Gen. GRANT and staff were in the field, riding along the lines in the thickest of the enemy's fire during the entire two days of the battle, and all slept on the ground Sunday night, during a heavy rain. On several occasions Gen. GRANT got within range of the enemy's guns, and was discovered and fired upon.

Lieut.-Col. MCPHERSON had his horse shot from under him when alongside of Gen. GRANT.

Capt. CARSON was between Gen. GRANT and your correspondent, when a cannon ball took off his head and killed and wounded several others.

Gen. SHERMAN had two horses killed under him, and Gen. MCCLERNAND shared like dangers. Also Gen. HURLBURT, each of whom received bullet-holes through their clothes.

Gen. BUELL remained with his troops during the entire day, and with Gen. CRITTENDEN and Gen. NELSON, rode continually along the lines, encouraging their men.

OUR FORCES OCCUPY CORINTH.

CAIRO, Wednesday, April 9.

An officer who left Pittsburgh Landing on Monday evening reports that *our forces occupy Corinth, and that Gen. Johnson's body had been found on the field.*

He also confirms the report that BEAUREGARD had his arm shot off.

There have been no arrivals from the Tennessee River since early this morning. A boat is expected to-night.

THE BODY OF GEN. JOHNSTON.

WASHINGTON, Wednesday, April 9.

The following was received at the War Department this evening:

"Gen. A. SIDNEY JOHNSTON's body was left on the battle-field, and is in our possession, as well as the bodies of a large number of other prominent officers."

BEAUREGARD AND HELL.

ST. LOUIS, Wednesday, April, 9.

The *Democrat's* special from Cairo says that the rebels were pursued by about 8,000 of our cavalry.

Rebel prisoners say that BEAUREGARD made a speech to his troops before entering the fight, saying he "*would water his horse in the Tennessee River or in hell—and that the fight before them was hell unless successful.*"

THE HEROES OF THE BATTLE.

Sketches of Some of the Commanders at the Battle at Pittsburgh Landing, and of Some of the Killed and Wounded Officers.

The hasty dispatches that were received yesterday of killed and wounded officers are probably both incomplete and incorrect in many particulars. Indeed, some of those reported dead have already turned up, and others will doubtless do so. Under these circumstances it might be both injudicious and painful to give sketches of the officers reported fallen until the facts are definitely ascertained. We will briefly notice some of those honorably engaged in the battle, and some of the fallen, regarding whom the statements seem to be authentic. The officers in chief command were Major-Gen. GRANT, who acted so gallantly on Sunday, and Major-Gen. BUELL, who was in joint command on Monday.

MAJ.-GEN. ULYSSES S. GRANT.

Gen. GRANT is just forty years of age, is a native of Ohio, a graduate of West Point, and served honorably in the Mexican War, having been attached eleven years to the Fourth Regiment United States Infantry, serving as Second and First Lieutenant, as Quartermaster and as Captain. After his resignation he settled in Missouri, and moved from there to Illinois, in 1850. Upon the breaking out of the present war, he offered his services to Gov. YATES, and was appointed Colonel of the Twenty-first Illinois Volunteers, and served until promoted as a Brigadier-General, with commission and rank from the 17th of May, 1861. He was engaged as Colonel and Acting-Brigadier-General in several of the contests in Southeastern Missouri; and his course as Commander of the Southern District of Missouri has been thoroughly scrutinized, and among his most praiseworthy acts was the occupation of Paducah and stoppage of communication and supplies to the rebels *via* the Tennessee and Cumberland Rivers. He was the planner of the battle of Belmont, and had chief command of the troops at the capture of Fort Donelson. After the latter event, a new district was created, under the denomination of the District of West Tennessee, and he was created a Major-General, and assigned to the command of it. But it was reported that he was under a cloud with the superior military authorities, and the most absurd stories were circulated as to the cause thereof. The simple fact was that there was some dissatisfaction with his "strategy" at Fort Donelson. When the expedition went up the Tennessee, he was not at first put on duty; but was very soon after assigned to the command of that heavy column. His personal bravery and dash is undoubted. He is a man of plain exterior, light hair, blue eyes, five feet nine in height, plain and retiring in his manners, firm and decisive in character, esteemed by his soldiers, never wastes a word with any one, but pays strict attention to his military duties. He is one of the hard-fighting school of Generals.

GEN. BUELL.

Gen. DON CARLOS BUELL is 42 years old, was born in Ohio, reared in Indiana, graduated at West Point, has been twenty years in the army, and his service has been almost continuous. He served with great distinction in the Mexican war, as Lieutenant, Captain and Adjutant, until at Churubusco he received a severe wound from a bullet, which passed through the upper part of his chest. At the time the present war broke out, he was a Lieutenant-Colonel in the Regular army, in California, but he was appointed a Brigadier-General by Congress, and was ordered to take command of a division of the army of the Potomac. On the resignation by Gen. ROBERT ANDERSON of the command of the Department of the Ohio, he was assigned to that important position, and it was under his eye that the magnificent army which lately marched from Bowling Green to Nashville, was raised and drilled. The various battles of Gen. GARFIELD against HUMPHREY MARSHALL, the battle of Mill Springs, where ZOLLICOFFER was killed, and various other important actions in Kentucky, were the emanations of his skill, and his military management in Kentucky was of the highest order. On the recent reconstruction of Departments in the Southwest, he was subordinated to Gen. HALLECK, but was at the same time created a Major-General. He left Nashville with his fine army a fortnight ago, and arrived at Pittsburgh Landing, at a most opportune moment to achieve a triumph for the previously wavering National arms. Gen. BUELL is remarkable for industry and energy, his coolness and self-possession are such that it is believed he could think as calmly, and form his plans as deliberately in a tempest of grape as in the quiet of his tent; and in the regular army he is esteemed as emphatically a fighting man. He is of compact frame, very deep chest, indicating great vital power, possesses almost herculean strength in his arms, and can lift prodigious weights at arm's length; has light hair and full beard; blue eyes, which are steady and unmoved in danger; carriage erect, step measured; and, in short, is such a type of man as is produced by long service in the American army.

GEN. W. H. WALLACE.

Brig.-Gen. W. H. WALLACE, who was the only General officer killed at Pittsburgh Landing, was a native of Illinois, a graduate of West Point, and, previous to the present war, had seen service on the Pacific frontier, as a Captain of the Washington Territory Mounted Volunteers, in which position he took part in the Indian War of 1855. At the opening of this war, he raised and obtained the Colonelcy of the Eleventh Illinois Regiment of Volunteers. With his regiment he was at Fort Henry, and from there went to Fort Donelson, at which battle he was Acting Brigadier-General, and immediately afterward was confirmed as Brigadier-General by Congress. He was a very skillful and gallant officer, and his loss will be deeply mourned by the brave soldiers of the West.

GEN. C. F. SMITH.

Major-Gen. SMITH, who was severely wounded at the battle, is already well known to the country for his immense personal bravery at Fort Donelson. He is a Pennsylvanian, graduated at West Point in 1825, and held successively several responsible positions in the Academy until 1843. He went to Mexico as Captain, but, for various gallant acts, was soon breveted Colonel. In 1854 he received regular promotion as Major of the First Artillery, and in 1855 was made Lieutenant-Colonel of the Tenth Infantry, which rank he held up to the opening of the war. He then received a commission as Brigadier-General, and was appointed to the command of the forces at Paducah, Kentucky. Various preposterous charges of disloyalty were here brought against him by personal enemies, but all these he has since disproved in a most splendid manner.

COL. T. W. SWEENEY.

Col. SWEENEY, whose conspicuous gallantry is mentioned in the dispatches, is THOMAS W. SWEENEY, Captain of Co. D, Second United States Infantry. He is a native of Ireland, but has been long resident in this country, and when war was declared between the United States and Mexico he was one of the first to volunteer his services. He served with great distinction in various engagements, as Second Lieutenant in a New-York volunteer regiment, and was seriously wounded, losing his right arm. As a reward for his services, he had the option of receiving either a pension or a commission in the regular army, and immediately chose the latter, and was, accordingly, appointed Second Lieutenant in the Second Infantry, March 3, 18[illegible], and ordered to report for duty on Governor's Island, where he remained some months. Since then he has served with his regiment in various parts of the frontiers, and has the reputation, among the regulars, of being a good soldier, but a strict disciplinarian. He was on recruiting service in this city from June, 1858, to June, 1860, when he was relieved. At the close of the year he set off to join his regiment in Nebraska. He has been in active service ever since the commencement of the rebellion, and has previously distinguished himself under the lamented Gen. LYON, in Missouri, where he acted as Brigadier-General.

THE REBEL GENERAL KILLED.

GEN. ALBERT SIDNEY JOHNSTON.

Gen. JOHNSTON, the bogus report of whose capture at Fort Donelson gave him a biographical fame two months ago, is now certainly disposed of at last, as his dead body is in our hands. He was one of the five rebel "Generals," the other four being BEAUREGARD, LEE, COOPER and JOE JOHNSTON. He was for half a year commander of the rebel Department of Kentucky, with his headquarters at Bowling Green, which famous stronghold he evacuated six weeks ago. He is 60 years of age, a native of Kentucky, and graduated at West Point in 1826. He was engaged in the Black Hawk war, in the Texan war of independence, in the Mexican war, and in the war against the Mormons. He was Brigade-General in command of the Military District of Utah, and at the opening of this rebellion, was in command of the Department of the Pacific. Shortly after the rebellion got under way, his loyalty was suspected, and Gen. SUMNER was sent out to supersede him. Before Gen. SUMNER reached California, JOHNSTON had left to join the rebels. For fear of being caught, he took the overland route, with three or four companions, on mules, and passed through Arizona and Texas, and thence to Richmond. At first he was appointed to a rebel command on the Potomac; but upon the great importance of the Western Department being seen by JEFF. DAVIS, he was appointed to take chief command at Bowling Green. He did everything to strengthen that position, and bring as large a force as could be got for its defence. But, on being outflanked by our advance up the Cumberland, he incontinently deserted his stronghold, fled to Nashville, from thence to Decatur, and from thence to Corinth, and now has fallen—a traitor to his native State and to his country. JOHNSTON was a little over six feet high, of a large, bony, sinewy frame, with a grave, gaunt and thoughtful face; of quiet, unassuming manners—forming, in all, a soldier of very imposing appearance. He was considered by military men the ablest General, for command, in the rebel service, and his loss will be a severe blow to the tottering rebellion.

RELEASE OF STATE PRISONERS.

BOSTON, Wednesday, April 9.

The Commissioners have ordered the release of the following Members of the late Maryland Legislature from Fort Warren: Hon. E. G. Kilbourne, of Ann Arundel County, Speaker of the House of Delegates; Josiah H. Gordon, of Alleghany County; Dr. Charles McGill, of Washington County; Clark J. Durant, of St. Mary's County; Dr. Mills, of Carroll County; and Messrs. Claggett, of Frederick, and Jones, of Talbot County.

OPERATIONS ON THE MISSISSIPPI.

Commodore Foote's Official Report of what he Found at Island Ten.

Seventeen Officers and Three Hundred and Sixty-eight Privates Captured.

Four Rebel Steamers, Seventy Heavy Cannon, and Immense Quantities of Provisions and Ammunition Taken.

Two Steamers and the Gunboat Grampus Sunk by the Rebels.

The Great Floating Battery Found Ashore.

DETAILS OF PRELIMINARY OPERATIONS.

WASHINGTON, Wednesday, April 9.

The following was received at the Navy Department this morning:

FLAGSHIP BENTON, ISLAND NO. 10, April 8, (*via* CAIRO.)

Hon. Gideon Welles, Secretary of the Navy:

I have to inform the Department that since I sent the telegram last night, announcing the surrender to me of Island No. 10, possession has been taken of both the Island and the works upon the Tennessee shore, by the gunboats, and the troops under command of Gen. BUFORD. Seventeen officers and three hundred and sixty-eight privates, besides one hundred of their sick, and one hundred men employed on board the transports, are in our hands unconditionally prisoners of war. I have caused hasty examination to be made of the forts, batteries, and munitions of war captured. There are eleven earthworks, with seventy heavy cannon, varying in calibre from 32 to 100-pounders rifled. The magazines are well supplied with powder, and there are large quantities of shot and shell, and other munitions of war, and also great quantities of provisions. Four steamers afloat have fallen into our hands, and two others, with the rebel gunboat *Grampus*, are sunk, but will be easily raised. The floating battery of sixteen heavy guns, turned adrift by the rebels, is said to be lying on the Missouri shore, below New-Madrid. The enemy upon the mainland appear to have fled with great precipitation after dark last night, leaving in many cases half prepared meals in their quarters, and there seems to have been no concert of action between the rebels upon the Island and those occupying the shore, but the latter fled, leaving the former to their fate. These works, erected with the highest engineering skill, are of great strength, and with their natural advantages would have been impregnable if defended by men fighting in a better cause. A combined attack of the naval and land forces would have taken place this afternoon or to-morrow morning had not the rebels so hastily abandoned their stronghold; to mature the plans of attack having absolutely required twenty-three days of preparation. Gen. POPE is momentarily expected to arrive with his army at this point, he having successfully crossed the river yesterday under a heavy fire, which, no doubt led to to the hasty abandonment of the works last night. I am unofficially informed that the two gunboats which so gallantly ran the fire of the rebel batteries a few nights since, yesterday attacked and reduced a fort of the enemy opposite, dismounting eight heavy guns.

The following is a copy of the order of Gen. MCCALL on assuming command of the rebel forces on the 5th inst.:

SOLDIERS: We are strangers, commander and commanded, each to the other; let me tell you who I am. I am a General made by BEAUREGARD, a General selected by BEAUREGARD and BRAGG for this command when they knew it was in peril; they have known me for twenty years; together we have stood on the fields of Mexico; give them your confidence now; give it to me when I have earned it. Soldiers, the Mississippi Valley is intrusted to your courage, to your discipline, to your patience. Exhibit the vigilance and coolness of last night and hold it.

(Signed) W. D. MCCALL,
Brigadier-General Commanding.

I regret that the painful condition of my feet still requiring me to use crutches, prevented me from making a personal examination of the works; I was, therefore, compelled to delegate Lieut.-Com. S. PHELPS, of the Flag-ship *Benton*.

A. H. FOOTE, Flag-Officer,
Commanding Naval Forces.

COMMODORE FOOTE CONGRATULATED BY SECRETARY WELLES.

WASHINGTON, Wednesday, April 9.

The following congratulatory letter was sent to-day to Flag-officer FOOTE by telegraph:

NAVY DEPARTMENT, Wednesday, April 9.

Flag-officer A. H. Foote, Commanding Gunboats on Western Waters:

SIR: A nation's thanks are due you and the brave officers and men of the flotilla on the Mississippi, whose labors and gallantry at Island No. 10, which surrendered to you yesterday, have for weeks been watched with intense interest. Your triumph is not the less appreciated because it was protracted, and finally bloodless.

To that Being who has protected you through so many perils, and carried you onward to successive victories, be the praises for his continued goodness to our country, and especially for this last great success of our arms.

Let the congratulations to yourself and your command, be also extended to the officers and soldiers who coöperated with you.

GIDEON WELLES, Secretary of the Navy.

OUR ISLAND TEN CORRESPONDENCE.

EVENTS PRECEDING THE CAPTURE OF THE ISLAND —HOW COL. BISSELL GOT THE TRANSPORTS TO GEN. POPE—THE CARONDELET RUNNING THE GAUNTLET OF THE REBEL BATTERIES, ETC.

ABOVE ISLAND NO. 10, Saturday, April 5, 1862.

My last letter gave you the particulars of a gallant affair on the part of our troops, in spiking the most formidable rebel battery at this place—an operation whose daring has scarcely ever, until yesterday, been equaled, and which stamps the impress of hero upon every man who was engaged in it. Gallant as was this, it has been equaled, if not excelled, in the enterprise by which the *Carondelet* was, last evening, run by the rebel guns, and moored in com-

[*Continued on Eighth Page.*]

The Charleston Mercury.

DAILY PAPER—Ten Dollars per annum, payable half-yearly in advance. | SPONTE SUA SINE LEGE FIDES RECTUMQUE COLETUR.—VINDICE NULLO | COUNTRY PAPER—Three a Week—Five Dollars per annum, in advance.

VOLUME LXXX. | CHARLESTON, S. C., THURSDAY, APRIL 10, 1862. | NUMBER 11,419

The Currency.

We see it deliberately proposed that the whole currency of the Confederate States should be Treasury Notes of the Government of the Confederate States; and that the notes of all the Banks in the Confederate States should be superseded and withdrawn. This, we have no doubt, is the policy of the Government at Richmond.

The whole circulating medium for currency in the Confederate States is estimated, by the Secretary of the Treasury, at ninety millions of dollars.

When the Banks met in Convention, and agreed to receive the Treasury Notes of the Government of the Confederate States on deposit or in payment of their dues, it was a fair proposition to divide with the Confederate Government the currency of the country. As it was then, it consisted almost exclusively of their notes. They assented to the limitation and withdrawal of a portion of their notes and to the substitution therefor, of the Treasury Notes of the Confederacy. Could they have been expected to do more than this? If they had proposed and consented to yield the whole field of the currency to the Confederate Government, what would have been the consequence? Without the issue of their notes, when specie payments were suspended, they could make no discounts—they could do no business—they would have to close their doors; to make dividends, they would have to collect their debts from their debtors, if this was possible. But this is impossible; for, from one end of the Confederacy to the other, stay laws, preventing the collection of debts, have been passed. The only other alternative would be, to do nothing—nothing in making loans—nothing in collecting debts—in a word, utter ruin. Without issues, the Banks could not use their credit. Their stocks would pay no dividends, and would soon be valueless. Did the Banks mean this when they consented to receive as currency the Treasury Notes of the Confederate Government, and to give them a circulation instead of their own notes? We are sure they could have meant no such folly. They meant to divide the currency with the Confederate Government. Of the ninety millions of currency required for circulation, the Confederate Government would take fifty or sixty, and they the rest. This was fair. It was more than fair—it was patriotic. But now the policy is deliberately entertained of absorbing the whole currency of the Confederate States by the Treasury Notes of the Confederate Government, and practically annihilating the Banks of the States.

Is this wise, and is it practicable, if it is wise? If the Banks were, to-morrow, to protect themselves, by refusing to receive the Treasury Notes of the Confederate Government on deposit or in payment of their dues, what would be the effect? A sudden and most disastrous depreciation of Treasury Notes. A blow would be struck at the credit of the Confederate Government it would never recover. What wise statesman would force the Banks to such a policy, which they may be compelled to adopt to preserve their existence? The existence of the Banks is not merely the preservation of so much capital. Destruction of the Banks is ruin incalculable to the whole property and industry of the country. Annihilate Bank credit, and all other credit perishes. A wise government would foster, instead of breaking down, the main-springs of credit in a country. Its credit is only the result of the general credit of the country.

And when it is obvious to the best financial knowledge and experience, that the destruction of the credit of the Banks is totally unnecessary, it is astonishing that it should find countenance in any quarter. If the Confederate Government should absorb the whole currency, it would amount to a very small relief. Admit that the Banks are left forty or fifty millions of the currency, and what is this to a Government spending three millions a week? If it is dependent on the circulation of its Treasury Notes *as currency*, it is clear that it must soon—nay, it is already at the end of its credit. Its resources are exhausted. But the Confederate Government does not depend on the circulation of its Treasury Notes, *as currency*, to maintain its credit. Its credit rests on the confidence of capitalists in its ability to pay. That clause in the Treasury Note Act which provides that Treasury Notes may at any time be vested in Eight Per Cent. Bonds, enables the capitalist, at any time, to realize by them a profitable investment, whilst it prevents the Notes from depreciating. Just in proportion as these notes depreciate, in the same proportion will they occasion loans to the Government by its Bonds. Thus, the whole available property of the country is brought into requisition to support the Government, whilst the credit of the country is sustained by the support of a sound currency. But there must be a limit to the issues of Treasury Notes. In good faith, it ought not to have issued more Treasury Notes, bearing no interest, than the proportion of the currency it agreed with the Banks it should absorb—say *sixty millions of dollars*. Beyond this amount, it ought to have issued Treasury Notes, *bearing an interest*, which would tend to withdraw them from circulation. By this wise policy, the Banks, the great sources of credit, would be enabled, by doing business, to keep alive the commercial interest of the country, and the evils of a redundant currency would be avoided. But if the Confederate Government shall attempt to supply the whole currency of the country, by a wild and reckless issue of Treasury Notes, *bearing no interest*, inevitable disasters must follow. These notes must be depreciated. They must also depreciate Bank notes, as the Banks put them upon a par with their notes by receiving them at their counters. Hence every thing will have an artificial and increased value. The Confederate Government, in six months, will have to pay more for its Government and army supplies, than the whole amount of the superfluous and vicious currency it may put forth will produce. And then the derangement, injustice, confusion and ruin which a falsely inflated currency will occasion, will be beyond calculation. We regret to say that we fear the Confederate Treasury policy is very far from conforming to the principles we have very briefly endeavored to expose. The matter is one of vital importance. False steps now taken will be remediless. Let the voice of the business men, financiers and brokers of the country be heard ere it be too late. We earnestly warn the country of the consequences of a short-sighted, selfish financial policy on the part of the Government. Its end will be ruin. It must be prevented.

THE NEWS OF THE WAR.

We gather from our exchanges some additional and interesting information bearing upon the recent battle at Shiloh. Previous to the conflict, the heroic and lamented ALBERT SYDNEY JOHNSTON issued the following stirring address to the Southern forces:

HEADQUARTERS ARMY OF THE MISSISSIPPI,
CORINTH, MISS., April 3, 1862.

Soldiers of the Army of the Mississippi! I have put you in motion to offer battle to the invaders of your country. With resolution and disciplined valor, becoming men fighting as you are for all that is worth living or dying for, you can but march to decisive victory over the agrarian mercenaries who have been sent to despoil you of your liberties, your property and your honor.

Remember the precious stake that is involved in this contest; remember the dependence of your mothers, your wives, your sisters, and your children, is upon the result.

Remember the fair, broad, abounding land, the happy homes and the ties that would be dissolved and desolated by your defeat.

The eyes and hopes of eight millions of people rest upon you. You are expected to show yourselves worthy of your race and your lineage: worthy of the women of the South, whose noble devotion in this war have never been exceeded, at any time.

With such incentives to brave deeds, and in the trust that God is with us, your Generals will lead you confidently to the combat, fully assured of ultimate and glorious success. (Signed)

A. S. JOHNSTON, Gen. Comd'g.

[Official]
JOHN M. OTEY, JR., A. A. A. General.

The Richmond *Examiner*, in summing up its news of the battle, first gives Gen. BEAUREGARD'S despatch, and adds:

A despatch was also received by Gen. Cooper from the telegraph operator at Corinth. The date of this despatch is in advance of that of Gen. Beauregard, and states that we were then pursuing the retreating enemy beyond his encampments; that we had possession of his camp, and had taken all his camp equipage, military stores, and a vast amount of arms and ammunition. The despatch states that the news continues to be more favorable every moment. We may state that Gen. Beauregard has a reputation with the Government for remarkable moderation of tone and expression in his despatches; and that the impression obtained in official circles that the "complete" victory he announces has been the most important and decisive action of the war. The news was instantly telegraphed by the Government to Gen. Magruder, and was announced to our command on the Peninsula.

In addition to the despatch copied above, two despatches were received in other quarters of the War Department confirming in all respects the intelligence of our victory, and stating that we had taken six thousand prisoners and one hundred guns. It is thought in official quarters that the number of prisoners taken is even larger than this.

General Beauregard is understood to be in a position to give him *the entire control of the Tennessee river, cutting off the enemy's transports and intercepting his retreat in that direction*. The enemy is thus confined in a hostile country, broken with mountains and streams, from which the second "grand army" of the North can certainly not extricate itself with the ease and celerity of the famous retreat from the plains of Manassas.

The Tennessee river has been an avenue by which the enemy has massed a heavy army near the junction of the Memphis and Charleston and the Mobile and Ohio Railroads. Our force is estimated to have been 90,000 men.

The Atlanta *Confederacy* publishes the following despatch, dated Chattanooga, April 7:

The fight near Corinth was terrific. Our victory was complete, but the loss very heavy. Sydney Johnston, Gen. Claiborne of Arkansas, and Col. Bate of Tennessee, were killed. We have taken 80 pieces of cannon. The entire force of the enemy, it is thought, will be captured.

The *Confederacy* has the following speculations on the subject of the battle:

One of the despatches in our paper yesterday morning, says that a part of Buell's army were at Duck River. Another says Buell himself did not come up in time to take part in the fight. By these, we understand that he was making an effort to concentrate his army with Gen. Grant's to attack our forces at Corinth; that only a part of his army had reached its destination, and that our forces had fallen upon them and precipitated the fight just in the nick of time—just before the enemy were ready for it. One of our despatches indicates that our forces were fighting Buell's army on Monday. We have no doubt that another battle will be fought with Buell's forces very soon, if it was not on Monday.

Several very powerful iron-clad gunboats have been building at New Orleans during the fall and winter. The press has been silent about them till of late. The Yankees have found it out, and consequently there is no longer any reason for us keeping silent.

It is believed these boats left New Orleans last Saturday, and that by this time they are having a conflict with the Lincoln gunboats above Island No. 10. Of course they will sink them or run them far up the Mississippi or Ohio at once. The main object, it is believed, is to go to the mouths of the Tennessee and Cumberland, near Cairo, and bag all the gunboats and transports, with the whole retreating Lincoln army, as they go out of Tennessee from the face of our victorious legions, as they march on Nashville and on into Kentucky. This is a magnificent programme, if it works out as well as it is laid down.

THE GREAT BATTLE OF SHILOH—YANKEE SPECULATIONS IN REGARD TO THE RESULT—THE STRENGTH AND EQUIPMENTS OF THE CONTENDING ARMIES.

Our great victory at Shiloh will rather put the Yankees to blush after their boastful and confident predictions of the result. Our latest Northern papers show that they counted, with almost perfect confidence, on whipping us, and that "it was the general belief of all the prominent officers of General GRANT'S command that the rebels would retreat on their approach." To show what bright anticipations the Yankees had of the battle, when hourly impending, we make some extracts from a letter in the New York *Herald* of the 1st:

The hosts are being marshalled on both sides for a grand battle. From all the indications the impending battle will be the most *important of any that has yet been fought in this war*. All our scouts concur in the statement that the rebels are concentrating the main body of their forces at Corinth, Mississippi. Troops arrive there daily from Georgia, Louisiana, Alabama, Mississippi and Tennessee. Scouts estimate them now at seventy-five thousand, but forty-thousand is, doubtless, nearer correct. Beauregard is in command.

The rebels have forces at Iuka and other points on the Memphis and Charleston Railroad. A courier started from our headquarters two days ago across the country to Buell's advance. We still await the return of transports from Paducah. Rebel gunboats are in this neighborhood. Deserters continue to come in from rebel posts. They say half the soldiers would desert if they could. One deserter says, out of ninety-five in his company in one of the Purdy regiments, thirty-four had deserted, and twenty more were eager to do the same. Our troops, for a week past, have been under orders to march at an hour's notice, with ten days' rations. Our forces at Pittsburg *are being rapidly augmented, steamer after steamer arriving continually, laden with fresh troops.*

The latest advices from the rebel camp at Corinth give the strength of the force there at 70,000 strong. Recent indications relative to the persistent efforts of the rebels to fortify the town of Corinth would seem to demonstrate an intention to make a vigorous resistance there. It is, however, *the general belief of all the prominent officers of General Grant's command that the rebels will retreat on our approach*; but should a battle occur at Corinth, it will doubtless be one of the hardest fought and bloodiest affairs of the present war.

We take the following from the correspondence of the Chicago *Times*:

The rebel troops are pouring into Corinth, both as the nearest point to the body of our army and as a convenient rendezvous for the railroad line. In two days last week our scouts saw fifteen trains, loaded with soldiers, enter the town. Many of their troops are supposed to be the raw militia, half armed and unorganized, that have been gathered by the recent levies; but the numbers are becoming formidable. Sixty thousand is the lowest figure to which the official information will reduce them; and, after making all the necessary discounts and deductions, I cannot see now we can work them down to an actual number of less than thirty-five or forty thousand. With Beauregard at their head, it will be seen that this force will not let our expedition remain without anything to do.

A correspondent of the St. Louis *Republican*, writing to that paper under date of the 27th ult., gives the following particulars in regard to the Yankee army at Corinth:

Few rivers (Tennessee) have ever had as imposing sight on their banks. Sixty thousand men and miles of horses, wagons, cannon, and so forth, are there; although everything is bustle and preparation, there is no confusion. The law of order was never better illustrated. It is a vast military machinery, where men are the springs and wheels all moving regularly, surely on in the great work of preparation. Wagons are loaded before they seem hardly to have reached the goods, and tents are moved in a fraction of the usual time. There is no lounging or anxiety to shirk, but universal cheerfulness and confidence. The tone of the Western army is completely changed. It is no longer "if we capture such a place," but "when we capture it." The soldiers there think of nothing but victory. They have confidence in themselves, and the haunting terror of apprehension has fled. They believe now that as they march forward it is to conquer. This peculiarity, so different from the gloom produced by reverses and inactivity, at once strikes the stranger.

A happier, healthier, more efficient army than that now at Savannah and Pittsburg never, probably, went to war. Each regiment is burning to win laurels to wear with their companions who got fame and scars at Fort Donelson. Opposed to this noble army is a rebel force of forty-five thousand, lying in wait behind their works, eighteen miles distant. Corinth is a position naturally strong, and formidable defences have been erected there. Rifle pits, redoubts, abattis, and other means of strength, from behind which to hurl destruction upon an assailing force, have been constructed. The very best rebel military talent—embracing Beauregard, Bragg, and others—is concentrated there, and at Corinth will be fought the great decisive battle of the Western campaign. Forty heavy guns, and a great number of field pieces, are possessed by the enemy, and immense stores of provisions are gathered in. The flower of the South are congregated there to offer battle, and they cannot retreat except by sacrificing everything.

The road between the Union camps and Corinth is a long and excellent turnpike, and the distance can be easily traversed in a day. Gen. Grant has his headquarters at Savannah, while the bulk of the army lays at Pittsburg. Parade grounds and spots for comfortable quarters are being cleared, and everything gives token of a week's longer stay there. During that time Gen. Buell is expected to reach a point from which he can carry out successfully the part assigned him.

SCENE IN MEMPHIS, TENN.

EATING-HOUSE KEEPER. "Corned Beef — Beans — Glass of Whiskey — Four Dollars Ninety-Five. What's this? (*looks at Confederate Note.*) Guess you'd better keep this; I'd rather take your Word!"

The New-York Times.

VOL. XI—NO. 3292. NEW-YORK, FRIDAY, APRIL 11, 1862. PRICE TWO CENTS

THE BATTLE OF PITTSBURGH.

A Clear and Graphic Account of the Two Days Action.

Splendid Generalship Displayed on Both Sides.

Indomitable Bravery of Our Troops Against Great Odds.

Opportune Service of the Gunboats Tyler and Lexington.

The Movement of the Union Army which Caused the Rebel Retreat.

Seventy Thousand Men Engaged on Each Side.

The Rebels Reinforced by Price and Van Dorn.

Reported Capture of John C. Breckinridge.

CINCINNATI, Thursday, April 10.

A correspondent of the *Times* writes the following account of the Pittsburgh battle:

Our forces were stationed in the form of a semicircle, the right resting on a point north of Crump's Landing, our centre being in front of the main road to Corinth, and our left extending to the river in the direction of Hamburgh, four miles north of Pittsburgh Landing.

At 2 o'clock, on the morning of the 6th, 400 men of Gen. PRENTISS' Division were attacked by the enemy, half a mile in advance of our lines. Our men fell back on the Twenty-fifth Missouri, swiftly pursued by the enemy. The advance of the rebels reached Col. PEABODY'S Brigade just as the long roll was sounded, and the men were falling into line. Resistance was but short, and they retreated under a galling fire, until they reached the lines of the Second Division.

At 6 o'clock the attack had become general along our whole front. The enemy, in large numbers, drove in the pickets of Gen. SHERMAN'S Division, and fell on the Forty-eighth, Fiftieth and Seventy-second Ohio Regiments. Those troops were never before in action, and, being so unexpectedly attacked, made as able a resistance as possible, but were, in common with the forces of Gen. PRENTISS, forced to seek the support of the troops immediately in their rear.

At 10 o'clock the entire line on both sides was fully engaged—the roar of cannon and musketry was without intermission from the main centre to a point extending half way down the left wing. The rebels made a desperate charge on the Fourteenth Ohio battery, which, not being sufficiently supported by infantry, fell into their hands. Another severe fight occurred for possession of the Fifth Ohio battery, and three of its guns were taken by the enemy.

By 11 o'clock, a number of commanders of regiments had fallen, and in some cases not a single field officer remained; yet the fighting continued with an earnestness which showed that the contest on both sides was for death or victory. Foot by foot the ground was contested, and finding it impossible to drive back our centre, the enemy slackened their fire, and made vigorous efforts on our left wing, endeavoring to outflank and driving it to the river bank. This wing was under Gen. HURLBURT, and was composed of the Fourteenth, Thirty-second, Forty-fourth and Fifty-seventh Indiana; Eighth, Eighteenth and Twenty-first Illinois. Fronting its line, however, was the Fourteenth, Fifty-seventh and Seventy-seventh Ohio, and Fifth Ohio Cavalry of Gen. SHERMAN'S Division. For nearly two hours a sheet of fire blazed from both columns, the rebels fighting with a vigor that was only equaled by those contending with them.

While the contest raged the hottest, the gunboat *Tyler* passed up the river to a point opposite the enemy, and poured in broadsides from her immense guns, greatly aiding in forcing the enemy back.

Up to 3 o'clock the battle raged with a fury that defies description. The rebels had found every attempt to break our lines unavailing. They had striven to drive in our main column, and finding that impossible, had turned all their strength upon our left. Foiled in that quarter, they now made another attempt at our centre, and made every effort to rout our forces before the reinforcements which had been sent for should come up.

At 4 o'clock there was a short cessation in the fire of the enemy, their lines falling back for nearly half a mile, when they suddenly wheeled, and again threw their entire forces upon our left wing, determined to make a final struggle in that quarter, but the gunboats *Tyler* and *Lexington* poured in their shot thick and fast, with terrible effect.

Meanwhile Gen. WALLACE, who had taken a circuitous route from Crump's Landing, appeared suddenly on the enemy's right wing. In the face of this combination of circumstances, the rebels felt that their enterprise for the day was a failure, and as night was approaching, fell back until they reached an advantageous position somewhat in the rear, yet occupying the main road to Corinth. The gunboats continued to throw shells at them until out of range.

After a wearied watching of several hours of intense anxiety, the advance regiments of Gen. BUELL appeared on the opposite bank of the river. The work of passing the river began, the Thirty-sixth Indiana and Sixty-eighth Ohio being the first to cross, followed by the main portions of Gens. NELSON and BRUCE'S Divisions. Cheer after cheer greeted their arrival, and they were immediately sent to the advance, where they rested on their arms for the night. All night long steamers were engaged ferrying Gen. BUELL'S force across, and *when daylight broke, it was evident the rebels, too, had been strongly reinforced.*

The battle was opened by the rebels at 7 o'clock, from the Corinth road, and in half an hour extended along the whole line. At 9 o'clock the sound of artillery and musketry fully equalled that of the previous day. The enemy was met by our reinforcements and the still unwearied soldiers of yesterday, with an energy they certainly could not have expected.

It became evident they were avoiding the extreme of our left wing, and endeavoring, with perseverance and determination, to find some weak point by which to turn our force. *They left one point but to return to it immediately, and then as suddenly would, by some masterly stroke of Generalship, direct a most vigorous attack upon some division where they fancied they would not be expected; but the fire of our lines was as steady as clock-work, and it soon became evident that the enemy considered the task they had undertaken a hopeless one.*

Further reinforcements now began to arrive, and took position on the right of the main centre, under Gen. WALLACE. Gens. GRANT, BUELL, NELSON, SHERMAN and CRITTENDEN were everywhere present, directing movements for a new stroke on the enemy. *Suddenly both wings of our army were turned upon the enemy, with the intention of driving them into an extensive ravine. At the same time a powerful battery, stationed in the open field, poured volley after volley of canister into the rebel ranks.*

At 11½ o'clock the roar of the battle shook the earth. The Union guns were fired with all the energy that the prospect of the enemy's defeat inspired, while the rebels' fire was not so vigorous, and *they evinced a desire to withdraw.* They finally fell slowly back, keeping up a fire from their artillery and musketry along their whole column as they retreated. They went in excellent order, battling at every advantageous point, and delivering their fire with considerable effect; but from all the divisions of our lines they were closely pursued, a galling fire being kept upon their rear.

The enemy had now been driven beyond our former lines, and were in full retreat for Corinth, pursued by our cavalry.

The forces engaged on both sides in this day's battle are estimated at about 70,000 each.

ACCOUNTS RECEIVED IN CAIRO.

CAIRO, Thursday, April 10.

An arrival from Pittsburgh Landing says that the rebels, in making the attack on Sunday morning, carried the Stars and Stripes, and wore the Federal uniform.

Gen. Bragg is reported to have been killed. Provisional Governor JOHNSON, of Kentucky, is wounded, and was taken prisoner.

It is stated that Gen. PRENTISS escaped in the confusion of the rebels' retreat on the second day's fight.

Our total loss is about 7,000. This is the estimate of the military commanders who were in the engagement. Of this number about 2,000 were taken prisoners, the balance are killed and wounded, in the usual proportions.

Gen. WALLACE, of Illinois, was reported dead, as it was thought impossible that he could live; he was, however, living on Wednesday, and improving. He was shot in the back of the ear, the bullet coming out of his nose.

Gen. HALLECK passed Cairo to-day, *en route* for Pittsburgh Landing.

Five thousand prisoners are expected to arrive here to-night from Island No. 10.

Every preparation is being made here for the reception of our wounded from Pittsburgh.

ACCOUNTS RECEIVED IN CHICAGO.

CHICAGO, Thursday, April 10.

A special to the Chicago *Tribune*, from Cairo, says:

We are just beginning to get reliable details from the great battle at Pittsburgh. From several gentlemen who were on the field after the fight, the following is gathered:

Gen. PRENTISS' Brigade, consisting of the Sixty-first Illinois, Seventeenth Wisconsin, Twenty-fourth Indiana and Seventy-first Ohio, were attacked while eating their breakfast, by what seemed to be the entire rebel force. Gen. PRENTISS had no artillery, and his brigade was cut to pieces and forced to retire. PRENTISS and many of his men were taken prisoners.

At 12 o'clock, the entire line was engaged, but in full retreat. At 4 o'clock the enemy had taken SCHWARTZ'S Battery of six guns, DRESDEN'S Battery of four guns, and WATERHOUSE'S Battery, also, two Ohio batteries, names not known. Thousands of our soldiers who had taken refuge under the bank of the river utterly refused to fight, and in fact, they could not, as officers and men were mixed in inextricable confusion.

The army at this time seemed to be utterly defeated. At this juncture the gunboats *Lexington* and *Tyler* opened a tremendous fire of shot and shell upon the enemy, and kept it up every half hour during the night. Some of the shells set the woods on fire, and many dead rebels were burned.

At 7 in the evening the firing had generally ceased. About midnight the rebels attempted to plant a battery within 300 yards of our siege guns, but were driven away by the gunboats and siege guns, supported by three regiments of Gen. MITCHELL'S Division, which had arrived and crossed the river about 6 in the evening.

Our informants persist in estimating our loss on Sunday at 3,000 killed and 5,000 wounded as being a low figure.

During the night the rebels were reinforced by Gens Van Dorn and Price, from Arkansas, with a very large force.

Gen. LEW. WALLACE came up with the Eleventh and Twenty-third Indiana, Forty-fourth Illinois, and Eighth Missouri, and WILLARD'S Battery, and in the morning fiercely attacked the enemy's left wing. They went into the fight at the double-quick, with tremendous shouts, and did terrible execution. By 10 o'clock they had driven the rebels back two miles.

At about 10 o'clock the rebels were reinforced, and for a few minutes our men were forced to yield.

The other divisions of Gen. BUELL'S army now appeared, and at once became fully engaged. For two hours all the destructive elements of the earth seemed to be striving for the mastery on this fatal field; but at last the Southern chivalry broke and fled in all directions.

Gen. BUELL followed the flying foe with 12,000 troops, mostly cavalry, smiting without mercy, those who would not surrender. *He was reported to have taken Corinth with all its immense stores of arms and ammunition.*

The rebel troops were mostly from Texas, Mississippi and Louisiana, with many from Georgia and Alabama.

Our informants say that they could ride through the battle-field where our forces were posted, *but the dead was so thick in the enemy's lines that they could not do it there.* They assure us that the rebels occupied our camps on Sunday night, and took care of our sick and wounded, destroying nothing, *expecting confidently to have our entire army the next day. They thought the battle already fought and won.*

On Monday, Gen. McCLERNAND cut his way through the enemy that had surrounded him. Most of his troops behaved with great gallantry, but the Fifty-third Ohio was ordered to the rear in disgrace for refusing to fight.

Our informants state that John C. Breckinridge is taken prisoner. They say they saw him pass to the general headquarters.

THE REPORTED OCCUPATION OF CORINTH.

WASHINGTON, Thursday, April 10.

Up to 4 o'clock, this afternoon, the Government had received no official dispatch confirmatory of the occupation of Corinth by our troops.

THE WOUNDED IN THE GREAT BATTLE.

The Western Sanitary Commission has an overwhelming task before it, in providing for the wounded soldiers on the battle-ground of Pittsburgh. It therefore appealed to the East for assistance, in the subjoined telegram:

WESTERN SANITARY COMMISSION,
ST. LOUIS, April 9, 1862.

James A. Roosevelt, No. 94 Maiden-lane, New-York:
Send us shirts, drawers and sheets, all you can. Great battle. Sending four hospital steamers to Gen. GRANT.
J. E. YEATMAN, President.

We are authorized to say that contributions for the above object, either in money or goods, will be taken charge of, and properly forwarded, by J. A. ROOSEVELT, No. 94 Maiden-lane, or may be sent direct by Adams' Express to JAS. E. YEATMAN, President Western Sanitary Commission, St. Louis.

AID FOR THE WOUNDED.

ST. LOUIS, Thursday, April 10.

Two steamers fitted up as floating hospitals left here yesterday for Tennessee River, and large contributions of all kinds of supplies are being made to-day to furnish two more, which will leave this evening. The Western Sanitary Commission is moving earnestly and with energy in this matter, and every effort will be made for the speedy relief of our wounded soldiers at Pittsburgh Landing.

Col. KELTON, Assistant Adjutant-General, and Gen. KETCHUM, are in charge here, while Gen. HALLECK is in the field.

CHICAGO, Wednesday, April 9.

The Board of Trade to-day unanimously voted $2,000 for the benefit of the wounded in the battle of Sunday and Monday. Subscriptions of nearly half as much more were raised.

LOUISVILLE, Wednesday, April 9.

A large meeting of the citizens, the Mayor presiding, was held here this evening, to make arrangements for taking care of the wounded from Corinth. $2,500 were contributed, and any further amount desired offered.

The steamer *Commercial* left for the Tennessee River to-night, with medical and other supplies. The steamer *Diligent* will leave to-morrow, with nurses and supplies. Any amount of hospital accommodations in the city were offered.

MILWAUKEE, Wednesday, April 9.

The Chamber of Commerce, on the Governor's recommendation, held a meeting to-day for the relief of the wounded at Pittsburgh Landing. After subscribing liberally, the doors were thrown open for the reception of hospital stores. To-night the room is well filled, and an agent of the Governor, accompanied by the surgeons, will leave to-morrow to render all the aid possible for the comfort of the wounded.

LOUISVILLE, Thursday, April 10.

Telegraphic communication was opened between Savanna, Tenn., and this city this afternoon.

Forty physicians and nurses arrived from Frankfort this evening, and will immediately leave on the steamer *Autocrat* for Fort Donelson and Pittsburgh Landing. Several other boats, with similar aid, are passing down the river from this city and elsewhere.

CINCINNATI, Wednesday, April 9.

A boat has been commissioned to take physicians, nurses and stores to the scene of the Tennessee battle. A meeting of the Chamber of Commerce was held to-day, and a committee of five appointed to solicit subscriptions to purchase necessaries for the wounded, and a large amount was raised in a short time. The Committee appointed will go to Columbus to-night to urge the Legislature to make appropriations, charter other boats, and secure necessary supplies. It is probable three or four boats will leave here this week for Tennessee. A large number of nurses have tendered their services.

REJOICINGS IN MASSACHUSETTS.

BOSTON, Thursday, April 10.

Gov. ANDREW has ordered a salute of one hundred guns to-morrow, at noon, in honor of the recent victories.

Resolutions were unanimously adopted in both branches of the Legislature to-day, in furtherance of the suggestions of the Secretary of War inviting the citizens of the Commonwealth to join, on Sunday next, in a general *Te Deum* in honor of our recent victories, and congratulating the Western States upon the valiant deeds of their soldiers in the Valley of the Mississippi.

The Board of Brokers voted to-day $500 in aid of the wounded at Pittsburgh Landing.

REJOICING IN RHODE ISLAND.

PROVIDENCE, Thursday, April 10.

By order of Lieut.-Gov. ARNOLD, a National salute was fired here this afternoon, in honor of the great victory in Tennessee.

IMPORTANT FROM NEW-MEXICO.

The Texans Ordered to Evacuate the Territory.

WASHINGTON, Thursday, April 10.

The following was received to-day by the Secretary of War:

KANSAS CITY, Thursday, April 10.

The Santa Fé mail has arrived. The Texans, 1,300 strong, had evacuated Santa Fé, and were marching up the river. It was reported that Col. CANBY had intercepted an express with orders to the commander of the Texan forces to evacuate the Territory and return to Texas. Col. HOUGH had left for Fort Union with 1,400 men, to make a junction with Col. CANBY. The Texans were exacting contributions and forced loans from the inhabitants. Clothing was being taken from the merchants without regard to politics or circumstances.

Correspondence of the Missouri Republican.

FORT UNION, Sunday, March 23, 1862.

Our column, under command of Col. HOUGH, is breaking up camp for a forward movement South toward the rebel forces. The Texan army occupies a strong position in the vicinity of Albuquerque, seventeen miles south of the dépôt, about midway between this and Fort Craig, where Col. CANBY was at last accounts. The Texans have taken up this as a strategical point, doubtless intending to march upon either column as they leave their stronghold of Fort Union or Craig, and by their superior force, which is estimated at 2,400, and 21 pieces of artillery, whip one, and face about and assault the other column before they can form a junction.

It would seem that Col. HOUGH and Col. CANBY, the Department Commander, are not acting in concert, and sound men fear that this movement—one of the most difficult of military combinations—may not prove successful, and render our dépôt at Fort Union which is the only supply dépôt left us, comparatively defenceless. I can scarcely believe, however, that Col. HOUGH will march beyond supporting distance of this dépôt. The Texans are occupying Santa Fé, 100 miles south of here, with from 100 to 200 troops.

OPERATIONS IN VIRGINIA.

Great Strength of the Rebels at Yorktown.

Their Force Reported to be Sixty Thousand Strong.

General Joe Johnston in Command.

The Merrimac Still Detained by Bad Weather.

NEAR YORKTOWN, Wednesday, April 9—1:20 P.M.

The weather still continues unfavorable for military operations. It has been raining for nearly two days. The creeks are very much swollen, and the low grounds covered with water, making the roads almost impassable, even for empty wagons.

Information received shows that *the rebels have a force of sixty thousand*, which is rapidly being added to by troops from the neighborhood of Richmond, which is one day from Yorktown by railroad and river, they having four steamers and sixteen transports in use, and by the time the roads are in condition for the Union army to move *the rebels may be able to meet them with one hundred thousand men.*

The flower of their army, with the best arms, are in a strongly-intrenched position. Previous to our troops occupying the present position, the military authorities had no means of ascertaining the extent of the rebel works. Information obtained through deserting contrabands and other sources, shows that the enemy have *nearly five hundred guns*, some of them of the largest calibre.

The rebel General, JOHNSTON, with some of his forces, has arrived, and taken command in person, showing that they intend making *a desperate resistance to the advance of our troops at every point.* Their intrenchments extend entirely across the Peninsula, from the James to the York River.

The cheering news from the Western Department arrived here to-day, and our troops are wild with enthusiasm over the result, and are anxious to be led to action and similar deeds of valor.

REPORTS RECEIVED THROUGH BALTIMORE.

BALTIMORE, Thursday, April 10.

The Old Point boat has arrived.

The news of the capture of Island No. 10 caused great rejoicing and enthusiasm.

The storm still continued, but had somewhat abated toward evening.

Reports from the Army represent our brave forces facing exposure undauntedly, and meeting it with characteristic ingenuity in the way of improvised shelter. The enthusiasm and anxiety to meet the enemy was unabated, and confidence in Gen. McCLELLAN was unbounded. Though the storm at this time is unfortunate, the time has not been lost, and the retreat of MAGRUDER and his forces, or their defeat, is about as certain as any possible future event.

The prospect of clearing up is looked for with anxiety at Old Point, in the belief that sunshine and the *Merrimac* will come together. All seem confident that she will be captured or sunk if she comes out.

REPORTS RECEIVED IN WASHINGTON.

WASHINGTON, Thursday, April 10.

The latest news received from Cherrystone reports everything quiet in the vicinity of Fortress Monroe. A strong wind was blowing, and the sea running very high.

OUR ARMY AT YORKTOWN.

POQUOSIN BAY AND AFFAIRS AT SHIPPING POINT—GEN. WOOL'S CORPS—SIGNIFICANT MOVEMENTS.

From Our Own Correspondent.

POQUOSIN BAY, Va., Monday, April 7, 1862.

Poquosin Bay is perhaps not laid down in the geographies immediately accessible to most of the readers of the TIMES. It is a small bay, a few miles below the mouth of York River, jutting into the peninsula far enough to make a very safe harbor for at least a hundred vessels, of the size and draft usually found in these waters. The rebels appear to have thought it of sufficient importance to defend it very formidably, for on the western shore of the bay, and just south of a little creek called Cheeseman's Creek, that runs into it from the direction of Yorktown, they built four water batteries, and erected a continuous breastwork a quarter of a mile long. The woods adjacent are full of "elegant" wood huts, and a long, well-built shed for horses, showing that a large body of cavalry had lain here.

There were no guns in the batteries, however. They had been removed, and the place evacuated by the rebels, for what reason I cannot guess, unless under a panic fear of capture. They left everything uninjured, and I assure you the buildings afford capital quarters for a lot of Union soldiers that I saw enjoying them.

Poquosin Bay is reached by a channel of eighteen feet depth, and I saw one of our best Potomac gunboats, that perform police duty around "Old Virginia's shore," glide in as easily as she could into New-York harbor.

The fortified place on this bay is called "Shipping Point," by the natives. There is a place further up the Potomac, of the same name, that has become rather famous in our Winter's history of the blockaded Potomac. But the folks here are innocent or careless of the fact, or claim their place as the old "original" Shipping Point. Notwithstanding the danger of confusion, it must continue to be thus known. This lower Shipping Point is only about ten miles southeast of Yorktown. A portion of the Union army on the peninsula have their headquarters about six miles from this landing, which would put them within four miles of Yorktown. It is supposed that the rebels have discovered this fact, judging by the frequent firing they have indulged in, and I hope, therefore, I shall not be considered guilty of furnishing "valuable information" to the enemy. Poquosin Bay has no well-built wharfs, and I saw two "Yankee" regiments a few moments since wading ashore from their transports. Doubtless before these beavers leave here they will greatly improve the commercial facilities of Shipping Point. They will do, within a week, more to advance the usefulness of this admirable little haven than the Virginians have done in a hundred years. Perhaps, after all, it will turn out that this war has not been a bad speculation for the Old Dominion. I have met many enterprising Northern soldiers with a keen appreciation of Southern soil, Southern skies and Southern harbors, longing for the return of peace and the sale of confiscated rebel lands at low rates. The "Chinese Wall" has been broken down by the "invasion" of the Vandals, and it will be said of Virginia, as was said of ancient Greece, that though "taken," she has in turn taken the hearts of her conquerors, and will even polish their civilization.

I shall make an overland trip from Poquosin Bay to the Union headquarters, and being just now of an archæological turn of mind, I will try to visit "Yorktown," the scene of the close of the American revolution. The roads are very bad at present, but the soil is sandy, and only a day or two will be needed to render them passable.

The official reports from Fortress Monroe inform you that "cannonading has been heard in the direction of Yorktown." I saw a young Lieutenant at Poquosin Bay, who had had communication with the Union forces. He reports no material mischief done on either side. But it is thought there will be "somebody hurt," if the enemy does not discreetly move his position.

Fortress Monroe is not so busy a scene as it was ten days ago. Many transports have left Hampton Roads. About sixty left the day I reached the Fortress. Whither they have gone, or whether they will return, it is unnecessary to state. Gen. WOOL has a model army in his Department; not so large as some other *corps*, but yet large enough to do far more than he has been allowed to attempt. They are the very *élite* of the grand army of the United States. Gen. WOOL has always been distinguished for the superiority of his discipline. He makes of the rawest volunteers soldiers equal to veterans in an incredibly short time. When he took command of volunteers in the Mexican war, no officer was so odious to them. He converted them into soldiers, and after one or two successful battles, many of his men came to him, with tears in their eyes, and apologized for their former conduct toward him, and thanked him for *making* them to do their duty in the beginning of their campaign.

The *Merrimac* has so long been talked about and looked for at Fortress Monroe that many are beginning really to think she will never come out again. They say, (and with apparent good reason,) that if she had not been afraid or unable to come out, she would certainly have come when there was so vast a number of well-laden transports here. Her destruction or her capture of property, supposing her to have been successful, would have been incalculable.

Col. LEE, of the Massachusetts Twentieth, is at Fortress Monroe, waiting for an exchange to go forward, when he will take the head of his regiment again.

YORK.

THE MOUNTAIN DEPARTMENT.

Occupation of Monterey by Gen. Milroy—The Enemy's Scouts in Sight—The Enemy Reported to be Fortifying, &c.

WHEELING, Thursday, April 10.

The following is from a telegram just received here from Gen. MILROY, who is working vigorously to carry out Gen. FREMONT'S orders and plan of active operations in his district. Tremendous rain and snow-storms have raged throughout the mountain region for several days, rendering movements of troops almost impossible.

There is no sign yet of the much needed and promised reinforcements.

MONTEREY, Wednesday, April 9.

Arrived here yesterday at 2 o'clock. Weather terrible. Rain and snow continually for two days. Fear that I will be out of provisions, as I learn that Greenbrier River, in our rear, is impassable. Rear guard of the enemy at McDowell. Their mounted scouts in sight to-day—driven in by our scouting party. Enemy reported fortifying east side of Shenandoah Mountains.

DISPATCH FROM GEN. FREMONT.

WHEELING, Thursday, April 10.

E. M. Stanton, Secretary of War:

Gen. MILROY is in possession of Monterey and Crabbelton. The enemy's mounted scouts are still in sight of Monterey. Their rear guard was driven back by our troops. They are reported fortifying themselves east of the Shenandoah Mountains.

(Signed,) J. C. FREMONT,
Major-General Commanding.

DEPARTMENT OF THE SHENANDOAH

EDENBURG, Va., Thursday, April 10.

All is quiet. The enemy's pickets have not been seen during the severe storm of the past two days.

The Baltimore and Ohio Railroad.

BALTIMORE, Thursday, April 10.

The Directors of the Baltimore and Ohio Railroad have passed the following:

Whereas, Publications have been made in some journals of the Northern and Western States, alleging disloyalty on the part of the officers and employés of this Company, and assigning this as a reason why the Government of the United States have not at an earlier period assisted the Company in opening the road to its terminus; and

Whereas, The officers of this Company have the entire confidence of the Government, as is well known to this Board, and that the delay of the Government in furnishing the necessary assistance to enable the Company to open the road, has not been owing to the causes alleged; and

Whereas, This Board, in accordance with our views, are opposed to the employment of any persons by the Company who are known as disloyalists; therefore,

Resolved, That the employment, in any capacity whatever, of any person known to be disloyal to the Government will meet with the unqualified disapprobation of the Board, and if any persons now in the employ of the Company shall be discovered to be disloyal to the Government, the removal of such person is imperatively demanded.

Resolved, That no person shall be appointed to any position or employed in any capacity by the officers of this Company, except loyal citizens of the United States.

Wool Sale in Boston.

BOSTON, Thursday, April 10.

The auction sales to-day, of six hundred thousand pounds of wool, was well attended, and higher prices realized than expected by purchasers. Before the sale there was a disposition to bear prices, but towards the middle the auctioneer rallied upon bidders, and the sale closed at firm prices, ranging from 43c. to 48c., average 45c. for Ohio and Pennsylvania fleece and extra Washington County fleece. The principal purchasers out of this market were Messrs. BULLOCK & SONS, of Philadelphia; ROBINSON & Co., of Philadelphia; C. LULING, J. RIPLEY, VAN BLARCOMB & Co., of New-York. The lots were all taken without reserve, to *bona fide* bidders. The wool was purchased in Pennsylvania and Ohio, by G. W. BOND & Co., who acted as agents for several capitalists, without regard to price. The sale was satisfactory to both holders and purchasers.

THE COMMISSIONERS OF CHARITIES AND CORRECTIONS.—Yesterday afternoon the above Board held its semi-monthly meeting. The regular weekly statement shows that on March 29, 1862, there were remaining in the various Institutions 7,711, and since admitted 1,943, making a total of 9,564. A communication was received from Dr. ALEXANDER B. MOTT, inquiring of the President if wounded soldiers, who had no homes, could be furnished with accommodations at Bellevue Hospital. The answer was in the affirmative, provided they paid $3 per week. The use of the Tombs court-yard was granted by the Board for the execution of WM. HAWKINS, who is now under sentence of death. CHARLES M. JEFFERDS, who is now under sentence of death, also sent a communication to the Board, requesting permission to take exercise at the City Prison, or else be transferred to the Hospital. The request was referred to the Warden of City Prisons, with instructions that while he (JEFFERDS) should be treated with all liberality, he must not be permitted to go beyond the rule, in all cases to be adhered to, of safe keeping. The Board then adjourned.

OPERATIONS ON THE MISSISSIPPI.

The Prisoners and Spoils [illegible] at [illegible] Ten.

Nearly the Entire Rebel Force Prisoners

One Major-General and Three Brigadiers.

Seventy Rebels Killed and Wounded on the Island.

ST. LOUIS, Thursday, April 10.

A special to the *Republican*, from Island No. 10, says that two hundred hogsheads of sugar, and several hundred barrels molasses, eighty cannon, four hundred wagons, one hundred and twenty-[illegible] horses, sixty mules, five thousand stand of arms, thirty pieces of light artillery, and great quantities of blankets, clothing, &c., have fallen into our hands.

The total number of prisoners captured is five thousand. One Major-General, (MAKALL,) and three Brigadier-Generals, (GAULT, WALKER and [illegible].) The prisoners are being embarked as rapidly as possible for Illinois.

We also took about 16,000 solid shot, and immense quantities of ammunition.

CAIRO, Thursday, April 10.

With a few exceptions the whole rebel force around Island No. 10 are now prisoners. An attempt was made by them to cross Lake Reelfoot on rafts, but they were surrounded and compelled to surrender. Thirteen guns were taken, instead of the number previously reported.

The prisoners say that seventy men were killed on the island by our mortars.

GREAT ACHIEVEMENT BY THE ENGINEERS.

The following extracts from a private letter, written by a member of Col. BISSELL'S Engineer Regiment to a friend in Rochester, give a description of the obstacles surmounted in order to furnish the necessary means of transportation to Gen. POPE'S forces. The achievement was certainly the most remarkable engineering exploit of the war thus far. The writer says:

"After the surrender of the forts at New-Madrid, we (Col. BISSELL'S Engineer Regiment) were engaged for four days unspiking guns, changing batteries, establishing new works, and other engineering matters. Then we were sent over by Gen. POPE to ascertain whether it was not practicable to establish batteries opposite Island No. 10, so as to enfilade their works on the Kentucky shore. We spent three days in the swamps in canoes, with darkies as guides, but found the project impracticable. Col. BISSELL, however, stated that he could, by hand labor, get steamboats and flatboats through the woods and bayous, and by that means land our forces nearly opposite New-Madrid, and take all the enemy's works in the rear. Gen. POPE at once gave him *a carte blanche*, and he sent to Cairo for four steamboats, six flats, and such guns as could be spared. They sent the steamers *W. B. Terry, John Trio, Gilmore* and *Emma*, with the barges, a quantity of lumber, &c., and one eight-inch columbiad and three 32-pounders. Tools we did not need, for the regiment carries everything from the heaviest ropes and screws down to fine steel drills for unspiking guns. Our route is about twelve miles long, of which two miles were through timber, and the remaining ten through narrow, crooked bayous grown up full of brush and small trees. We have cut our way right through, the track being fifty feet wide, in which thirty are required for the hulls of the boats. The timber is cut four feet below the surface of the water. In one short stretch we cut seventy-five trees thus deep, not one less than two feet through. The machines were rigged from rafts and our lowest flats, and worked each by about twenty men. In the first place, three large launches went ahead to cut out and push out of the track the underbrush and driftwood; then three rafts followed, on which were the men who cut down and cut off the trees; then the scows, then two large barges, then one of the steamboats. Very large lines were provided to run from the capstan of the steamboats, and haul out by snatch-blocks what the men could not handle. Then followed the rest of the fleet, men being engaged all the time converting the flatboats into floating batteries. From the river to the levee the distance is about 500 feet; here the water was shallow and the route full of stumps; it took one whole day to pass this—then the cut in the levee. Here the fall was over two feet and the rush of water was tremendous. The largest boat was dropped through with five lines out ahead. Then a cornfield, overflowed from a cut in the levee. Here was something of a channel cut by the swift water, and we got along nearly a quarter of a mile to the woods; here was the labor—two straight and long miles to the nearest point in the bayou. Then it took eight days to get through. Then Wilson's Bayou, then East Bayou, then St. John's Bayou, which empties into the Mississippi at New-Madrid. If you have never seen a Southern swamp, you have no idea how thick it is; a New-York elm swamp does not begin. It sometimes took twenty men a whole day to get out a half sunken tree across the bayou. Such a place as that kept us all back, and none of the rafts or flats could get by, and all had to wait. The water after we got into the woods was about six feet deep, with a gentle current setting across the peninsula. In the East Bayou the current was tremendous, and the boats had to be checked down with heavy head-lines. Here we found some obstructions caused by drift-heaps, but cutting off one or two logs would start all down the current.

This is the hardest job I have ever seen undertaken, but Col. BISSELL is so far down now as to call it successful, for we are in sight of the fences on the ''tother side of Jordan.'"

An engraving of the saw used in cutting off the stumps is then given, and the writer adds by way of description:

"At each end of the saw a rope 30 feet in length is fastened and carried to boats upon which men are stationed. Ten men man and work each rope. When the saw runs right we have cut off a stump two feet in diameter in fourteen minutes. Often it pinched and run crooked; then a gang would be two or three hours on one of the same size. If there happened to be any brush under the water it added much to the labor; it all had to be fished up and got out of the way."

COTTON COMING.

From the Louisville Democrat, of the 8th.

The *Glendale* arrived here, yesterday, from Pittsburgh Landing, Tennessee River, with some two hundred bales of cotton, shipped by the planters to their brokers, in this city. One of our houses received 108 bales, another 74, and a third a smaller number, making about two hundred bales. *This cotton was shipped by the planters for their own benefit, and is not confiscated cotton.* Some of the planters of that region, now here, represent that large quantities of cotton have been burned, but not by the planters. It is done by the rebels, at the command of the military authorities. It is only a few days since [illegible] planters from the interior applied to Gen. [illegible] for assistance in saving their cotton from [illegible] the hands of the rebels, and he sent [illegible] hundred men, with a large transport[illegible] brought no small amount within our [illegible] was safe. Talk about the planters burning their cotton! All such tales are nothing else than [illegible]

FORT LAFAYETTE PRISONERS.—[illegible], who arrived here in the Schooner *Edwards* from Tampico on the 7th ult., and was arrested on suspicion of being a rebel agent, was yesterday released on parole by the Commissioners appointed to [illegible] into the cases of prisoners confined at Fort [illegible]. WM. T. SMITHSON, a Washington baker, declined to take the oath of allegiance and was [illegible] the Fort. The following persons were [illegible] ed by the Commissioners and recommended [illegible] ers of war: Thos. E. Sanders, [illegible] Baker, Thos. C. Fitzpatrick, Joseph [illegible] Hughes, John Greenough, Jeremiah [illegible] Redman. Geo. Hale—all of them [illegible]

The New-York Times.

VOL. XI—NO. 3290. NEW-YORK, WEDNESDAY, APRIL 9, 1862. PRICE TWO CENTS.

THE SEAT OF WAR IN THE SOUTHERN, EASTERN, AND MOUNTAIN PARTS OF VIRGINIA.

Indicating the positions now held by the Rebels, and some of the positions held by the Union Army; and showing, also, the Railroad Lines of Retreat for the Rebels.

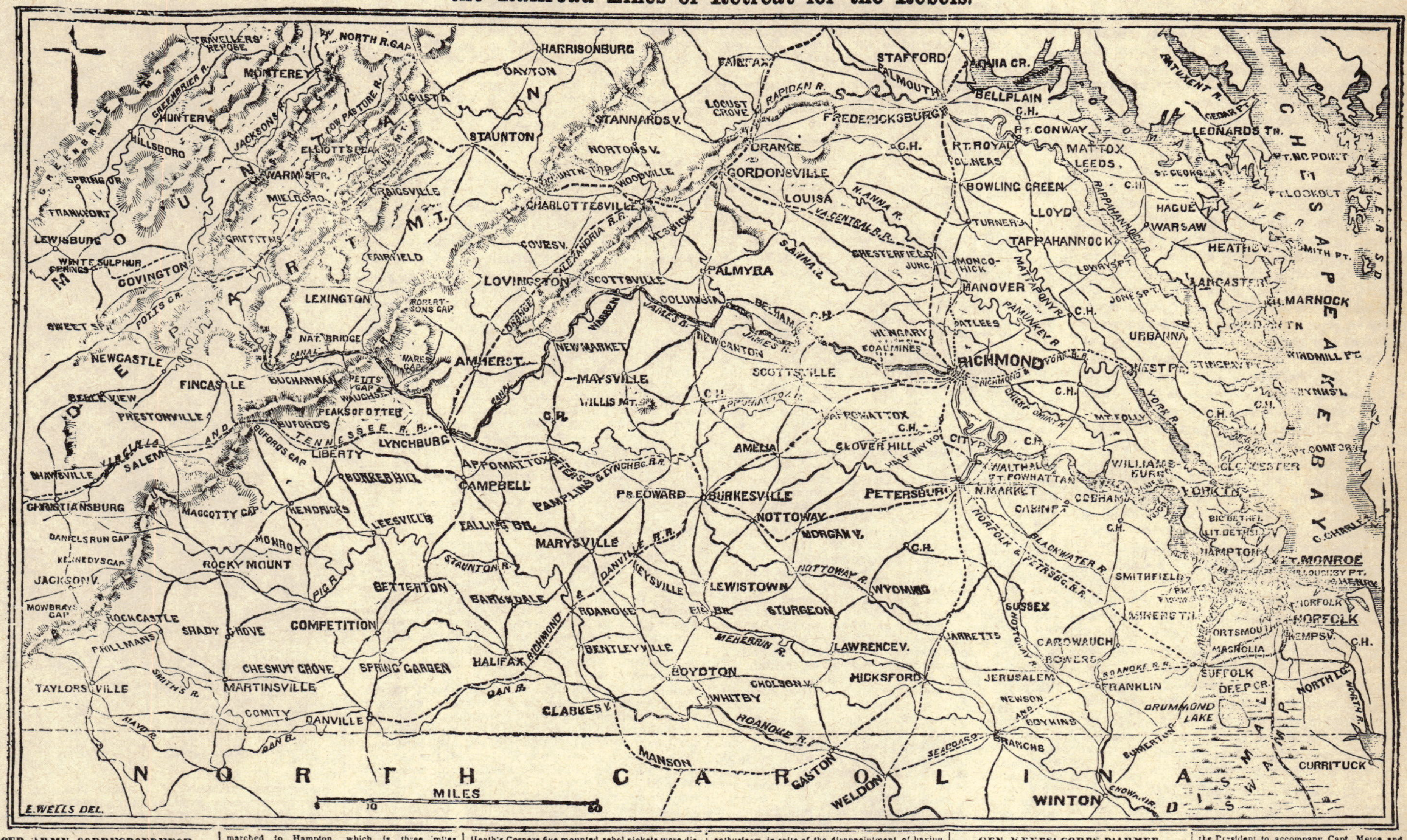

OUR ARMY CORRESPONDENCE.

GEN. PORTER'S DIVISION.

Departure from Alexandria—The Voyage down the Potomac—Arrival at Fortress Monroe—One Night Amid the Ruins of Hampton—Encampment Near New County Bridge—A Reconnoissance at Big Bethel.

From Our Special Correspondent.

NEAR NEW COUNTY BRIDGE, Va., Friday, March 28, 1862.

On the 21st of March, the Division under command of Gen. PORTER left its temporary quarters at Cloud's Mills, Va., and proceeded to Alexandria, where it embarked on a fleet of thirty-six steam and sailing vessels, and at 11 o'clock the following morning, commenced moving down the Potomac. The embarkation was conducted with the utmost order and precision, and without accident of any kind. A fall of rain the night previous made the roads somewhat yielding, but did not tend to dampen the ardor of the troops, who expressed their willingness to march a greater distance, along roads in worse condition, so delighted were they at the prospect of soon being brought face to face with the enemy.

The flight of the rockets from the *Daniel Webster*, Gen. PORTER's flagship, was the signal for the fleet to get under weigh, and shortly after the vessels with crowded decks and streaming pennants, amid the hearty shouts of the troops, glided slowly from their anchorage and piers on their way southward. The *Daniel Webster*, having on board the Fourth Michigan Regiment, took the lead, closely followed by the *Elm City*, *State of Maine* and *Knickerbocker*, bearing respectively Gens. MARTINDALE, MORELL and BUTTERFIELD, with their Staffs. The other vessels of the fleet came in regular order. Your correspondent secured a passage on the flagship, thereby having facilities for becoming acquainted with any important event which might happen on board any of the vessels. Nothing of moment, however, occurred. Some uneasiness was caused on the afternoon of the 21st by a report to the effect that the *Knickerbocker* had sprung a leak, and the pilot deemed it unsafe to enter the Bay that night; but an investigation proved that the leak was not of a serious character.

A signal corps attached to the expedition rendered valuable service by their system of rapidly communicating from one vessel to another.

The soldiers, occupying every part of the boat, enjoyed themselves amazingly, and frequently engaged each other's attention by pointing out places and objects of interest on the banks of the river. Our point of destination was unknown to but few, consequently much speculation was had in reference to it, which continued to be indulged until the fleet had fairly arrived under the protecting guns of Fortress Monroe. At about 9 o'clock in the evening, it being considered imprudent to advance in the darkness, without the guide of light-houses, the vessels came to anchor within ten miles of the mouth of the river, where they remained until 6 o'clock the next morning. They then proceeded on their course and arrived in good order at Fortress Monroe at about 4 o'clock in the afternoon. Some of the regiments disembarked that night and were marched to Hampton, which is three miles west of the fortress, where they were joined on the following day by the remaining troops of the division. HAMILTON's Division, which had sailed from Alexandria a few days in advance of PORTER's, was already encamped at Hampton. In referring to Hampton, it would be more proper to say the ruins of that place, for scarcely any thing remains of that once favorite rural district but lonely chimnies, heaps of mortar and brick, scathed trees, and despoiled gardens. The flaming torches of seven hundred rebel fiends, in a single night last Summer, was the cause, as is familiarly known, of this wholesale and wicked desolation. They did not even hesitate to wreak their insatiate vengeance on the sacred memories of the dead, as the defaced, dislocated, and shattered tombstones, plainly testify. Lest any desecration should be caused on the part of our troops, to the graveyard surrounding the ruins of a church, which was built over two centuries ago, a guard was stationed over it night and day. This precaution, however, was unnecessary, for not a Union soldier had the inclination to even speak but softly as he moved with cautious tread over that ancient and hallowed ground.

Gen. PORTER's Division left Hampton on Tuesday, the 25th, and proceeded up the peninsula to within about a mile and a half of New-County Bridge, and about two and a half miles from Hampton. At 3 o'clock on Thursday morning an order was issued to the Second and Third Brigades to prepare for a

RECONNOISSANCE AT BIG BETHEL.

At a few minutes past 7 the Third Brigade, Gen. BUTTERFIELD, accompanied by GRIFFIN's Battery, formed in line and led the way to Big Bethel, taking the direct road thither, and after proceeding some distance, met, unexpectedly, Gen. MORELL's Brigade, who intended to go by a different route. The two Brigades met upon the same ground where, on the 10th of June last, the unfortunate collision occurred between two Union regiments, but on this occasion every precaution had been taken to prevent a similar disaster. Here the brigades parted, the Second taking the road leading to the right, and the Third pushing forward as originally planned, preceded by a line of skirmishers, composed of a portion of Col. BERDAN's Sharpshooters, who were followed by Company H, Seventeenth Regiment, Capt. GROWER, supported by a line of skirmishers from the same regiment. Then came the other companies of that regiment, GRIFFIN's Battery, the Forty-fourth, Eighty-third, Twelfth and STOCKTON's Michigan Regiments. The Brigade moved in the order indicated, and when arrived within a mile of Big Bethel, encountered an obstruction, consisting of a number of large trees felled across the road, which were soon thrown aside by the pioneers. Everything was then got in readiness for an attack in case the enemy should be found in position at the works of Big Bethel. A careful disposition was made of the force, and if the enemy had showed fight at that place he would bitterly have repented his rashness. A few rebels who were stationed behind the works fled precipitately at the approach of our skirmishers, and shortly after the American flag was planted thereon by Lieut. S. HOWLAND ROBBINS, one of Gen. BUTTERFIELD's aids. Gen. BUTTERFIELD, at the head of three regiments, then took a road leading to the left, and proceeded a distance of three miles, for the purpose of reconnoitering the country, and driving out the enemy, should he show himself at other works which were visible beyond. Upon arriving at these works, they were ascertained to be about a quarter of a mile beyond Heath's Corners, and to the right in front of a house owned by Mr. CARROL PRESBEY. At Heath's Corners five mounted rebel pickets were discovered, who sped away with the greatest possible dispatch. They were pursued by our skirmishers until the latter had come up to the works.

It was ascertained that these earthworks extended from Big Bethel to James River—a distance of ten miles—and were evidently designed to prevent a flank movement by our troops. This extensive range was the only formidable feature they presented. All the works were abandoned. In the rear of the works, at Heath's Corners, lives a man named CALLONY, who reported that a company of the Second Louisiana Regiment, Capt. CURTIS, had been there the preceding morning, also that the Tenth Louisiana Regiment was there about a fortnight ago, and staid one day. He further stated that the nearest works from that point were three miles distant, at WALL's farm, and were strongly built. On the right of the road leading to Heath's Corners, and across a morass, was another work, near the house of widow HEATH, which was unapproachable on account of the deep mire. On the return of the force they were followed by the rebels to Heath's Corners, near to the position where they were first seen.

The Second Brigade, under command of Gen. MORELL, with MARTIN's Massachusetts Battery and the Eighth Pennsylvania Cavalry, arrived at Big Bethel, and pursued a road leading to Rosetown, a distance of two miles. No earthworks or fortifications were observed on the route. They learned, however, from an inhabitant that two companies of rebel cavalry had left Rosetown fifteen minutes before their arrival. In one house an Irishman was discovered secreted under a bed. He had blackened his face, hoping by this means to pass himself off as a negro, but the imposture was detected, and the Irishman taken to headquarters.

A party of skirmishers advanced two miles beyond Rosetown to Smithville. A strong fortification was observed here, behind which were about 700 rebels. Our troops did not attack the fort, their purpose being only to reconnoitre. When turning a sharp corner three rebel cavalry officers were seen by the signal corps, who immediately gave chase. One of the rebels was shot, and his sword and belt were picked up.

The result of the reconnoissance was eminently satisfactory, and the whole force returned the same evening, in good order, to their quarters behind New-County Bridge. WHIT.

GEN. SUMNER'S CORPS D'ARMEE.

The Advance Upon Manassas—Camp Life—A Letter from the Chaplain of the New-York Sixty-sixth.

HEADQUARTERS SIXTY-SIXTH REGIMENT, N. Y. S. V., (Col. PINCKNEY,) SANGSTER'S STATION, Va., Tuesday, March 11, 1862. Nine miles from Manassas.

I write on the ground by a camp-fire, under the strangest and most romantic circumstances. Nothing could surpass the grandeur of this extempore encampment, and words will fail, I am afraid, to give you much idea of it as it strikes the senses of those who are in the midst of it. Our exhilaration at leaving the dull monotony of the tented camp, where we have endured all manner of dull, wintry hardship, within sight of the Capital, and at last making the advance, of course adds zest to our feelings; and yet here is something truly grand. After two days' severe march, through deep woods, we at last emerged upon a wide expanse of open, hilly country, and Gen. SUMNER's Division now rests from its toils, full of the highest enthusiasm, in spite of the disappointment of having the enemy escape the anaconda, and give us yet a chase, perhaps to the Gulf.

Some twelve thousand troops are here resting on their arms for the night. A part rests on an immense open hill, a part in heavy woods on the left, on a steep hill, with woods intervening, while others occupy a hill in front.

I have just strolled through the whole command. Gen. SUMNER bivouacks on the right, on a little rise of land, and from this point the whole may be taken in at a glance.

Thousands of camp-fires glowing in every direction, showing a most variegated scene,—horses picketed by thousands,—artillery drawn up in grim array.

On the left of Gen. FRENCH's Brigade, the Sixty-sixth Regiment of New-York occupy the most prominent position. Bivouacking in a heavy piece of woods on a steep hill-side, their fires by hundreds light up the whole with wondrous splendor, the flames rising high among the lofty trees, and the smoke lit up with lurid light above, casting the forest in relief, as though the trees were interspersed with auroral columns. Here you may recall all that you ever read of romance in wild wood life, and multiply its multitudes and extent, and you can imagine something of what is not to us imagination or fiction, but *reality*.

The men are scattered around in booths, or under shelter-tents, made of india-rubber blankets, or by hundreds rolled up in blankets on the bare ground, like so many mummies. Others are discussing chickens, (rebels',) or even larger animals, making merry over their campaign cooking—so rich, compared with the ordinary camp rations. They have bid adieu to their tents with the utmost alacrity. Meanwhile the bands lend their inspiring strains, answering one another from hill to valley, and echoing through the woods with peculiar sweetness. Over the whole, serene, the same as from the beginning of creation, shine unclouded stars and moon.

The headquarters of the chiefs are, of course, object of peculiar interest. The veteran hero of Mexico, and Kansas, and Utah—a splendid man—Gen. SUMNER, now commanding a *corps d'armée* with as much composure as though it were a regiment, surrounded by a brilliant staff, and surveying the whole scene, with couriers coming and going; and not far away, the model of a Brigadier-General, pacing back and forth, with hands behind him, before his fire, every now and then stopping to receive a messenger or dictate an order—the heroic FRENCH—every inch a man of war, who defied Gen. TWIGGS in Texas, and brought off the only battery in the State, defying the rebels to take a gun, through a wild march of five hundred miles, from beneath his flag.

Or you may visit Col. PINCKNEY, of our Sixty-sixth, seated on a log before his booth, like a chieftain of the olden time, receiving his Captains and regulating the wild enthusiasm of his command.

I have tried to give you a picture most difficult to draw. But think of the money that it has cost to get up this little entertainment, the intelligence, science and experience here concentrated, and you may fill the details for yourself, drawing very deeply on imagination before you can come near what is real.

To-morrow we move on Manassas, but not through fire and blood, as we thought this morning. The anaconda, winding through so many woodland roads, with slow but determined advance from the Potomac toward the rebel strongholds, have frightened the foe, and he has slipped away from his hole, and we must have a long chase yet. * * * *

My desk has been the ground and the light precarious, so you must excuse all mistakes.

JAMES H. DWIGHT.

GEN. KEYES' CORPS D'ARMEE.

Sketch of the Commander—His Military Services.

HEADQUARTERS GEN. KEYES' CORPS D'ARMEE, WASHINGTON, Friday, March 21, 1862.

The Press, echoing the impulses of the great popular heart, developes the military spirit as fast as the people can follow it. At the outset of the rebellion we had a correspondent to each regiment; soon they became so numerous that a "Press Brigade" was formed, and now we make another leap and divide our brigades and divisions into *corps d'armées*. Your correspondent having been assigned to the above command, finds that he will have to describe, amplify and glorify the valorous deeds of some 400 Captains, 800 Lieutenants, some 40 Colonels, Adjutants, Majors, and Chaplains, and any quantity of Sergeants, Corporals and privates, making a grand total of over 40,000 men, selected from the volunteers of New-York, Pennsylvania, Maine, Massachusetts, Rhode Island, Vermont and Wisconsin—a tremendous responsibility for one pen, which, however, having shed considerable ink before, buckles to the good fight again, with a determination to lay before the public the truth.

Gen. ERASMUS D. KEYES, the commandant of the fourth *corps d'armée*, was born in Massachusetts. He was appointed a cadet at West Point in 1828, from Maine, graduating sixth in his class; in 1832 he was ordered to report to the Third Artillery as Brevet Second Lieutenant. Under Col. CUMMINGS, of the Second Infantry, he took an active part in the Black Hawk war. During the first whisperings of secession in South Carolina, in 1832, he was stationed at Charleston. Gen. SCOTT appreciating his services at that time, invited him to become one of his military family, and on his staff he remained nine years, being with him during the Patriot difficulties in Canada, the removal of the Cherokees, etc. In 1841 he was made Captain of the Third Artillery, and served in Florida. While passing through New-Orleans with a number of Seminoles, an insurrection broke out among the blacks, which was quelled by his promptness. In 1842 he was appointed head of the Department of Artillery and Cavalry at West Point; remained there four years, devoting himself to the study of military tactics. In February, 1849, he was ordered to the Pacific coast, and was stationed there eleven years. During this time he greatly distinguished himself in the Indian campaigns by his intrepidity, nerve and self-possession. Not forgetting the claims of civil life, he was assiduous in improving the tone of society, was a leading man in all matters appertaining to the improvement of San Francisco, and personally superintended the Harbor improvements. In 1858, as a tribute to his daring courage in the Indian wars on the Pacific coast, as well as his civil services, he was made Major of the First Artillery, and in 1859 returned to New-York. Gen. SCOTT again recalled him to his Staff, making him Military Secretary, with the rank of Lieutenant-Colonel. Stationed at Washington during the stormy Winter of '60–'61, while YULEE and his traitor band were plotting treason in their Senatorial seats, Col. KEYES carefully watched the pulse of the tide which was so rapidly drifting the country into war, and, had his repeated warnings been heeded, measures would have been taken which might have rendered impossible the consummation of the designs of the arch conspirators.

In April, 1861, Col. KEYES received an order from the President to accompany Capt. MEIGS and Col. BROWN to New-York, and there superintend the expedition for the relief of Fort Pickens. When Washington was in such imminent danger, during the week subsequent to the bombardment of Fort Sumter, Col. KEYES took charge of the 5,000 volunteers that flocked to the National Capital.

At Bull Run Col. KEYES served under Gen. TYLER. After the rout commenced, instead of falling back on Washington, he retired to Fall's Church, where he remained two days, and saved and sent to Washington over two hundred wagon-loads of stores, ordnance, &c., which otherwise would have fallen into the hands of the enemy. He also recovered all the tents which were deserted by the panic-stricken soldiery. For this Col. KEYES received the thanks of the entire country, and the President was not slow in placing him at the pinnacle of his profession. After commanding a brigade for three months, under Gen. McDOWELL, he was ordered to the command of a division to relieve Gen. D. C. BUELL, and within a few days has been assigned to the Fourth Corps d'Armée. Can the country doubt that such a man will fail to lead his 40,000 to victory and imperishable renown?

JASPER.

GEN. HUNTER'S DEPARTMENT

The Voyage From Hampton Roads—Arrival at Port Royal—Skirmish at Edisto—Loss of the Steamer Empire.

From Our Own Correspondent.

STEAMER ATLANTIC, PORT ROYAL HARBOR, Sunday, March 30, 1862.

The good steamer *Atlantic*, bearing Gens. HUNTER and BENHAM, with their Staffs, left Fortress Monroe on Friday afternoon at 4 o'clock, and reached this place this morning. The voyage was entirely devoid of incident.

The coast about Port Royal disappointed me. It is low and sandy; Hilton Head is but little above high tide. But the harbor is truly royal in extent, and the channel, though intricate, equal in depth to that of New-York. Government has replaced the buoys, and a light-ship lies each night near the bar. Over the site of the rebel Fort Walker, on the south-side, the Stars and Stripes floated proudly in the evening breeze; and where was only an old plantation house a few months ago, now appeared a little village of barracks and government offices. A fine new wharf, T-shaped, has also been built out into the bay, on piles. Riding at anchor, in different parts of the harbor, were about fifty vessels of all sorts and sizes—mostly large. All the coasts in sight are covered with forests—mainly the emblematical palmetto; I could almost fancy that I saw the rattlesnake coiled around its stem. It was a satisfaction to see headless trunks of some which our shot have decapitated.

Of course, we had plenty of visitors, both from the shore and the ships in port. The mails have been sent in by the pilotboat; but numbers had old acquaintances to see or inquire after, and all were anxious for news by word of mouth. Fortunately, the passengers had no occasion to go ashore till they pleased, and so the evening was undisturbed by the bustle and care of departure.

My voyage ended. It is only proper that I pay my honest tribute to the admirable condition of the *Atlantic*, under the experienced charge of Capt. ELDRIDGE, and Purser FORDHAM. Everything makes for comfort

The Charleston Mercury.

DAILY PAPER—Ten Dollars per annum, payable half-yearly in advance.

VINDICE NULLO SPONTE SUA SINE LEGE FIDES RECTUMQUE COLENTUR.

COUNTRY PAPER—Thrice a Week—Five Dollars per annum, in advance.

VOLUME LXXX. CHARLESTON, S. C., SATURDAY, APRIL 26, 1862. NUMBER 11.432

THE MERCURY.

SATURDAY, APRIL 26, 1862.

Styles of Fighting.

McCLELLAN, last July, after the lesson of Manassas, declared that henceforth the war of the North upon the South should be one of artillery. The remark was sagacious—the policy was wise. It has been carried out in the operations of the United States from that time to this, and those operations have been marked with much success. The Southern troops are superior in their fighting qualities, from their education and their opportunities, if from nothing else. With the rifle and bayonet—the horse and sabre, they are better fighters than their Northern foes. In equal numbers they can generally defeat them. But the North has superior facilities for procuring and making ordnance. With powerful earthworks mounting numbers of guns, or with fleets of distant gunboats, long taw is a comparatively safe and formidable kind of warfare. It was this which defended Washington; it is this which has reduced so many of our works; it is this which saved GRANT's army at Shiloh. We believe it is to be the basis of McCLELLAN's operations on the Peninsula, and HALLECK's on the Tennessee River. Time is the friend of this warfare of Northern engineer and artillerists. Activity on our part is their apprehension; celerity and dash are fatal to it. Inferior in ordnance, with few gunboats, we must be inferior in that kind of war. It is clearly our policy, then, to fight infantry fights and cavalry fights, as much as possible, in the open field, to take the foe before their heavy works and heavy guns are put into fighting condition, and to give them systematically as little time as possible for preparations. We do not want works. Advancing armies have no need of them. We should not permit them to have works either, if capable of preventing it. Our present difficulty is arms. Activity and success can procure these from the foe. Rapidity of movement and Southern impetuosity can anticipate and overmatch these ordnance preparations, this heavy artillery war. Let us have no more Manassas dilly-dally. Philadelphia and Cincinnati are the goals, and nothing but the double-quick will take us there.

THE NEWS OF THE WAR.

THE ENEMY'S OPERATIONS AT THE MOUTH OF THE MISSISSIPPI—STRENGTH OF THE YANKEE FLEET ETC.

The following from Fortress Monroe, published in the Baltimore *American*, exposes the plan of the Federal attack on the forts below New Orleans:

THE EXPECTED ATTACK ON NEW ORLEANS.

The mammoth steamer Constitution arrived here last night from Ship Island, bringing dates up to Sunday, March 16th. Commodore David D. Porter's mortar fleet, with the Harriet Lane as the flagship, left Ship Island on the 14th inst., and was to be followed in a few days by Commodore Farragut's fleet of sloops-of-war and gunboats. Their destination was understood to be the Southwest Pass, from which they were to open fire on Forts Jackson and Philip, which guard the passage to New Orleans. The departure of this immense fleet is reported to have been a grand sight, stretching in line for many miles along the ocean, as far as the eye could reach, in the following order:

First Division—Schooners Norfolk Packet, Olive A. Lee, Pera, C. V. Williams, Arietta, William Baron, Sophronia.

Second Division—Schooners Z. A. Ward, Sidney C. Jones, Matthew Vassar, Maria J. Carlton, Orvitta, Adolph Hugel, George Mangham.

Third Division—Bark Horace Beals, schooners John Griffiths, Sarah Brinn, Racer, brig Sea Foam, schooners Henry James, Dan Smith.

Reserve Steamers—Steamers Octorara, Harriet Lane, Owaska, Westfield, Clifton, Miami, Jackson, R. B. Forbes.

Commodore Farragut's fleet consists of the sloop-of-war Hartford, his flagship, the Pensacola, the Brooklyn, and the gunboats Pinola, Sciota, Itaska, and most of the other ten new gunboats, recently built, with other small class war steamers, said to number twenty-three in all.

It is presumed by the officers on board the Constitution that the work of reducing Forts Jackson and Philip was commenced some days since. It was supposed that some of the mortar boats would take position in an inlet in the rear of Fort Jackson, while the others would advance up the Southwest Pass within shelling distance, and endeavor to drive the forces out of the forts. In the meantime the gunboats would silence a battery erected about a mile below the forts for the protection of a barricade in the river, intended to prevent the passage of Commodore Farragut's fleet up in front of the forts. This barricade was said to be composed of logs chained together, and fastened to the shores by heavy chains. It was fixed so as to be opened to allow the passage of rebel vessels at pleasure.

When this barricade shall be removed and the channel of the river opened to the entire fleet, a sharp and decisive contest may be anticipated. If the forts should continue impervious to the bombs of the mortar fleet, those who are acquainted with the character and energy of Commodore Farragut, anticipate that he will lead his whole fleet directly under their guns, and, by repeated broadsides of grape and shrapnel, endeavor to drive the gunners from their posts. We may, therefore, expect exciting news from New Orleans in a few days.

The troops still remain at Ship Island, and were in good health and spirits. They were being perfected in drill, and becoming most efficient troops. Gen. Butler had not arrived when the Constitution left, but they passed him going in with reinforcements.

THE ABOLITION MISSIONARIES AT BEAUFORT, SOUTH CAROLINA.

The following racy letter, by the New York *Herald's* Hilton Head correspondent, will repay perusal. It is dated Hilton Head, South Carolina, March 15, and appears in the *Herald* of the 22d ult:

The military, civil, political, philanthropic and abolition circles hereabouts were deeply agitated last week by the announcement of the arrival of forty or fifty missionaries from as far east as Boston, and from the wicked city of New York. The excitement became more general, and if possible, more intense, when it was given out by those who pretended to be well informed on the subject, that a portion of this band of missionaries was composed of the gentler sex, and that the whole troupe was then upon the steamship Atlantic, at anchor in the harbor, and about to precipitate themselves upon the abodes of the wicked in and about the Department of South Carolina. The truth of some of the rumors was soon established by the testimony of various witnesses, who had fortunately boarded the Atlantic at an early hour, and had seen and conversed with the novel importation from the North. If any doubted them, their doubts were soon removed by the appearance on shore of several light-haired, long-whiskered, spectacled individuals, with umbrellas in one hand and a mysteriously covered package, suggestive of tracts, in the other, followed by several ladies prim and antiquated, and of a general Bostonian style, such as are observed in William Lloyd Garrison's soirees or at Wendell Phillip's re-unions. These began to perambulate the island, and attracted very general attention.

The fact of the arrival of the missionaries being conclusively settled, conjecture was at once rife as to what they were to do here. Some asserted that they had come to hold a woman's rights convention on Hilton Head, where they could express their opinions freely and with perfect safety, and to labor in a field where their doctrines would be received and accepted by the lords of creation, who, being away from their better halves, could investigate the subject uninfluenced by fears or favors. Others, and, as it was soon apparent, the better informed, suggested that they were missionaries to the contrabands in this quarter—a large, and, as it seems, influential class of people, whose demoralized and barbarous state had lately become known to the philanthropists of Boston and New York, and whose welfare was near to their hearts. It soon became generally known that there were sixty of these missionaries on the Atlantic, twelve or fifteen of whom were ladies, and the remainder gentlemen of large expectations and liberal ideas. Among them are men of all trades and professions, and well calculated for anything except a successful pursuit of agriculture and contrabands. The ladies are from Boston and New York, and propose to conduct an industrial school, and teach the young contrabands' ideas how to shoot, and their fingers the art of plain sewing. The entire institution was gotten up by, and is under the direction of Mr. Edward L. Pierce, the Government Agent.—This much of their plans.

The day after the Atlantic's arrival, the missionaries, with that fine appreciation of the comforts of this life, which has always characterised them, transferred themselves, bag and baggage, to the village of Beaufort—known to them by reputation as the Newport of the South—and then, with a rare forethought, selected the finest mansions in the village, and straightway settled down to their task.

The landing of the Pilgrims at Plymouth Rock could not occasion more surprise and astonishment to the innocent natives of that region than did the advent of our missionary friends to the soldiers and contrabands in Beaufort. Several affecting scenes occurred, but I can describe but one. Mrs. French, a leading lady, whose regard and veneration for the contrabands had been greatly intensified by the speeches of the Reverend Mr. French and Mr. Pierce at *post prandial* meetings on the Atlantic coming out, and by the resolutions passed at the same, in which it was resolved that the negros should be addressed as brothers and sisters, and considered in that light. Mrs. French becoming thoroughly imbued with the abolition and loving ideas which were advanced always after a hearty dinner, was fully prepared to meet the contrabands in a sisterly spirit by the time the missionaries were ready to land.

Arriving at Beaufort, the party stepped ashore, and soon came across the peculiar institution in full feather. Mrs. French rushed on and embraced a colored female, who was startled not a little by the peculiar style of the salute, and in the words of the resolutions, exclaimed: "You are my sister! (Closer embrace). You are my equal and you are my sister!" Thus, with other sweet converse, did she her time beguile, and after a charming interview of this friendly character with the negro woman, whose eyes protruded from mingled fear and pleasure, Mrs. French moved on with the missionaries to green fields and pastures new. That was one of the incidents that marked the arrival of the missionaries in the field of their labors. There are others equally disgusting and novel, if I would but write them. The above will suffice, however, as it shows the drift of the missionary movement. The truth of the matter is, that nearly all of the missionaries are rabid abolitionists of the Garrison school, and the leaders, Mr. Pierce and the Rev. Mr. French, are a trifle ahead of their fellows in their fanaticism.

GENERAL M'CLELLAN AND HIS POLICY—WHAT THEY SAY ABOUT HIM IN WASHINGTON.

The editor of the Springfield (Massachusetts) *Republican*, who has been on a visit to Washington, writes to his paper—which, by the way, has heretofore been a McCLELLAN paper—as follows.

A Boston Bostonian—of that kind whose reverence for men in authority outlived even Gardner Know Nothingism—drew me into a vacant corner at Willard's Hotel, and, with an air of mingled horror and sadness, said, in a whisper, "Isn't this rather a free-talking town?" I was obliged to confess that, next to discomfort, scandal was a Washington weakness. My friend was shocked as well puzzled, by the way that Congressmen, Cabinet Ministers, men in authority and men out, have been swashing McClellan with the rough sides of their tongues for the last ten days.

Nor men alone—women—the wives of civilians and army officers—daughters of the Cabinet—the belles of public and private drawing rooms, join the eager fray, with tongues sharpened by original serpentine association, and fired with the love and jealousy that are the monster passions to the crinoline mind. Is McClellan a greater man than Napoleon, or a monster humbug? Is he plotting for a compromise and the Presidency, or has he a scheme of rebellion extermination so deep and great that no other mind can imagine or comprehend it? The visitor at Washington can take his choice, and find plenty of conclusive arguments for either judgment. But you must believe him either a fool or a demi-god. The war of friends and enemies has reached the point where no compromise is permitted. Those of us who don't believe him either must hide our diminished heads and wait till the storm is over.

Indeed, it is very difficult for an earnest, candid seeker of the truth to reach a correct judgment as to General McClellan's management of the campaign; and his relations to its successes and failures. There is no doubt of a great abatement of confidence in him on the part of the Cabinet and Congress. The President, too, measures what he gave him before without stint. It is not easy to see why, with nearly a quarter of a million of the oldest and best troops of the Union at his command, General McClellan permitted the rebels to press their lines in upon him at all points, and to hold the Potomac, both above and below Washington, all winter—why he refused to seize fine opportunities to cut off large detachments of their armies—why he denied the Navy Department the co-operations it has for months asked to take Norfolk and seize the Merrimac before she could execute the mischief that has since startled the country; or why he could not join the naval forces in clearing the Potomac of the rebel batteries, for which they were long ago ready—why, in the only "stirring up" that he gave the enemy, the preparations for an advance and retreat was so feeble as to result in the Ball's Bluff tragedy—why he kept General Halleck in check for weeks after that officer was ready to move onward—why he opposed General Butler's Southern expedition until overruled by the War Department—why he kept promising to move onward, and never did until the President had repeated twice or thrice positive orders to do so—and why, when he did so, he permitted himself to repeat the farce of the King of France, in marching up the hill and then marching down again?

That all these and many more similar things are true of his course as commander-in-chief I have the most abundant reason to believe. That he has almost sinned away by postponement and inaction his day of grace with President and Cabinet, those most cognizant of the opinions of the latter sufficiently know. The new Secretary of War, Mr. Stanton, has been growing in impatience with, and estrangement from, him ever since he assumed that office, and, but for the President's cautious policy, it is quite likely Gen. McClellan would have been dethroned from the leadership of the Army of the Potomac.

There was a tremendous pressure from the Senate and a portion of the Cabinet for a change; but the President was firm and said that, though he relieved him from the general command, in part because he was not satisfied with his course, he had confidence that, now he had taken the field at the head of his especial division of the army, he would push forward the campaign as rapidly as possible, and prove worthy of the position.

He has certainly so far trifled with his own opportunities as to put his reputation and position at the hazard of an accident. He cannot stand up under a failure, be that failure even the result of no fault of his own. And herein is his severest self-criticism, for no man, public or private, has the right to place himself, or let himself be placed, where he cannot stand up before the public

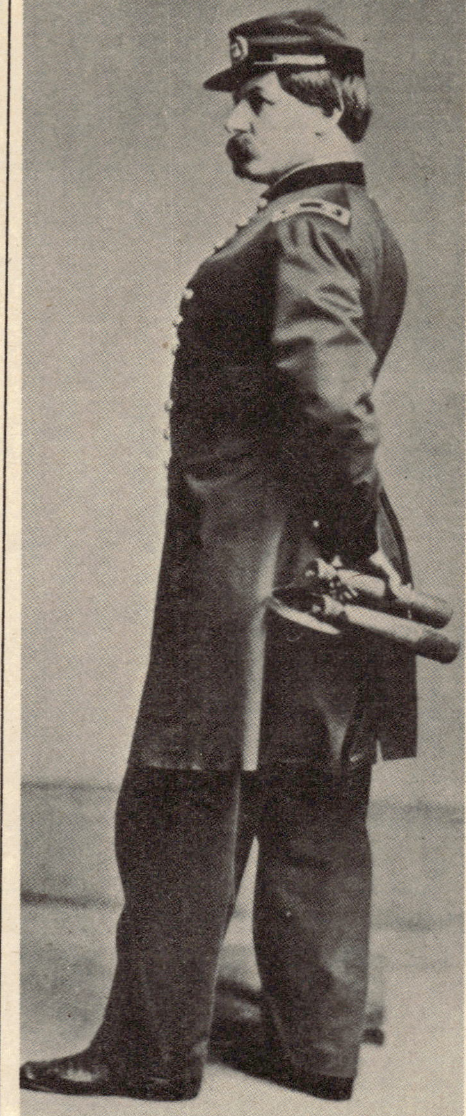

General George B. McClellan

against the accident of a single occasion. No man in America ever had such opportunities as Gen. McClellan. To no man was ever given, so generously or so fully, such public faith.

MORALS IN THE YANKEE METROPOLIS.

The picture often presented by Southern journals of the nauseating stench of corruption which pervades every class in Washington, from the occupants of the White House down through the departments of Congress, to the most servile lick-spittles who fawn at the feet of power, has been considered by many overdrawn; but the half has not been told. The following, the most humiliating confession we have yet seen, is from the pen of Horace White, of the Chicago Tribune, in his Washington letter to that journal. Referring to the morals of Washington, it says:

"The tone of morality here is considerably lower than it has ever been before. This is admitted on all hands, and can be proved, or rather needs no proof, for the air is heavy with public and private guilt. A few years ago a high Austrian official, whose peculations were discovered, applied the lancet to his own veins, and another similarly situated hanged himself. There is no such sense of shame here. Any coroner's jury in Washington would find a verdict of insanity for such conduct, and the verdict would be accepted in good faith."

The Southerners, as a class, had a very nice sense of honor, so far as the public treasury was concerned. When they held the power here there was comparatively little thieving, and when any was discovered it was promptly exposed and denounced. There has been a change—*a dreadful change—for the worse.* The frauds and attempted frauds on the treasury, in one channel and another, come so fast, and from such unexpected quarters, that one is bewildered in contemplating them. Yet nobody has been brought to justice, and nobody seems to think it possible that anybody should be brought to justice.

"O! those rascally contractors!" says some honest man in the rural districts. For every dollar wrongfully taken by a contractor, five have been taken by public servants. And in this matter Republicans are just as bad as Democrats, and Democrats just as bad as Republicans. Congress has its due proportion of vagabond politicians, who think they will never have another chance, and who are bound to have "their share" of the golden, or rather paper, stream. The honest men are in a lean minority, powerless to stay the tide of corruption, but not, we trust, wholly powerless to expose it.

The Charleston Mercury.

DAILY PAPER—TEN DOLLARS PER ANNUM, PAYABLE HALF-YEARLY IN ADVANCE.

VINDICE NULLO
SPONTE SUA SINE LEGE FIDES RECTUMQUE COLENTUR.

COUNTRY PAPER—THREE A WEEK—FIVE DOLLARS PER ANNUM, IN ADVANCE.

VOLUME LXXX. | CHARLESTON, S. C., MONDAY, APRIL 14, 1862. | NUMBER 11,422

THE MERCURY.

MONDAY, APRIL 14, 1862.

The accounts of the great battle of Shiloh come straggling in at last, but in a form so confused and contradictory that the real condition of our affairs in the West is still, in many important respects, a mystery. Enough is known, however, to render it certain that the battle of Sunday, the 6th instant, although a mere preliminary engagement, was not a whit less bloody than the contest which has made memorable forevermore the Plains of Manassas. The victory was ours, and our soldiers slept upon the field which they had so dearly won. But the morrow brought another and a still more desperate conflict. The odds against us were appalling. All day long the picked armies of the North and of the South wrestled obstinately upon the banks of the Tennessee. Finally the enemy was driven from his positions, and soon afterwards our own victorious troops were recalled to resume their former lines at Corinth. Of the results of the two day's fighting we have, as yet, no satisfactory intelligence. It would seem that BUELL, as well as SYDNEY JOHNSTON, was killed; that the carnage on both sides was awful, and that we captured at least seven thousand prisoners. This last item will be an excellent offset to our heavy loss at Fort Donelson. But the battle of Shiloh was in no respect decisive. It simply taught the invader something of the men whom he would have to face, and it has induced both sides to redouble their energies in preparation for the tug of war which it yet to come. Heavy reinforcements for the enemy are being hurried down those great highways of invasion, the Tennessee and Cumberland rivers, and the entire militia of Louisiana and Mississippi has been called out to strengthen our own reserves. When the hostile hosts are once more ready, we shall hear of a fray, the like of which this Continent has never yet beheld.

THE NEWS OF THE WAR.

Stirring war news pours in upon us, thick and fast, from every quarter of the Confederacy.—From the following summary, which we gather and condense from various sources, our readers will be enabled to obtain a bird's-eye view of the vast and complicated military operations in the invaded regions of the South :

THE FALL OF FORT PULASKI.

The Savannah *Republican* of Saturday says :

The firing of the enemy was kept up the whole of Thursday night at intervals of about a half hour, so ue two or three shells only being fired at a time.

Yesterday morning the most terrible bombardment of the siege commenced soon after daylight. The guns were louder and more rapid than at any time previous, and the windows of the city shook as if rocked by an earthquake; indeed the very earth trembled with the fierce cannonade. Such was the fire that even the confident began to feel uneasy for the fort. The bombardment of Sumter was no approach to it, either in the number of guns or the size and weight of the shot. At 2 p. m., the firing ceased altogether.

Later.—We learn that Fort Pulaski, after a most gallant defence, against guns vastly superior to its own, surrendered to the enemy at 2 o'clock, p. m., yesterday. Corporal Law, of the Phœnix Riflemen, stationed at Thunderbolt, brings the information direct. He reached the Fort at 5 o'clock, a. m., yesterday, and started on his return trip immediately after the flag was struck. The surrender was unconditional. Seven large breaches were made in the south wall of the Fort by the battery of eight Parrott guns at King's Landing ; all the barbette guns were dismounted, and three casemate guns, leaving but one gun bearing on that point. Three balls had entered the magazine and a clear breach had been made in it. The balls were conical and steel pointed, and propelled with such force as to pass entirely through the wall at nearly every fire. The garrison, it is said, fought with the greatest bravery and determination, until it became folly to contend with such fearful odds. No lives were lost during the terrible bombardment of the fort. Four men only were wounded—three have lost a leg and one an arm, each—all privates :—one of the Wise Guards, one of the Montgomery Guards, and two of the Oglethorpe Light Infantry. No names are given. The Oglethorpes occupied the most exposed portion of the Fort. Lieut. Hussey was stunned, but not seriously hurt. Col. Olmstead sent no official despatch, but a verbal message that the garrison had done all that men could do. He attempted to signalize to Causton's Bluff yesterday morning, but such was the fire that no human being could stand on the ramparts for even a moment. Nearly a thousand shell, of the largest size, were thrown into the Fort from the Federal batteries. It will be gratifying to know that, though much exhausted, all the garrison are well except the four wounded men. This account may be relied on as correct. It is corroborated by another witness, a signal man, who went down and returned in company with Corporal Law.

In addition to the above, we learn that the enemy brought two of their large vessels into the river yesterday, anchoring one abreast of the Fort, and the other opposite their battery at Oakley Point.

An official despatch received by us from Savannah, on Saturday morning, announces that the above account is "fully credited in official quarters." From the account of the surrender, which appears in the Savannah *News*, we take the following :

A courier arrived in the city last night, from whom we learn that the Fort was breached in several places by the heavy rifled Parrott guns, twelve of which were in the King's Point battery, distant about a mile and a quarter from the Fort. Early in the day all the guns in the barbette except two were dismounted or otherwise disabled by the fire of the enemy's batteries, and seven of the casemated guns bearing on the batteries disabled. The shot and shell of the enemy's batteries having made extensive breaches in the walls of the Fort, their fire was directed towards the magazine, the location of which they had doubtlessly learned from deserters, and which was in imminent danger of being exploded, having been breached in three places.

The fort having become untenable under the terrific fire of the heavy guns of the enemy, nearly all our guns that could be brought to bear against their batteries having been disabled, and the magazine being in imminent danger, a longer resistance was deemed hopeless, and the fort was surrendered about two o'clock in the afternoon. Our informant states that the effect of the enemy's batteries on the walls of the fort was utterly demolishing, and that the strong masonry heretofore deemed almost impregnable, offered but a feeble resistance to the steel-pointed shot of the immense Parrott guns.

THE BATTLE OF SHILOH.

The accounts of the battles which took place in the West on the 6th and 7th instants, are somewhat confused. We give them, however, such as they are. The Atlanta *Commonwealth* says :

We have seen and conversed with a gentleman who left Corinth on Wednesday night, in company with four thousand of the prisoners, bound for Tuscaloosa, Ala. There was severe and sanguinary fighting on Sunday and Monday, but had been none since, at least up to the time of the departure of our informant. The loss of the Confederates in killed and wounded, up to that time, was between four and five thousand, and that of the Federals was estimated at about twenty thousand. As graphically expressed by our informant, "There was a perfect sea of dead Yankees on the field." [The entire loss of the enemy, in killed, drowned, wounded, and prisoners, we learn from another source, is estimated at Corinth to be thirty thousand.] Up to Monday night our men were too busy attending to our own wounded to give any attention to those of the enemy.

Up to the time our informant left, seven thousand prisoners had been brought in, and large numbers were continually arriving. The division under General Polk drove five thousand of the enemy into the river, and it is estimated that not less than two hundred found a watery grave. Among the enemy's killed is Gen. Wallace, and among the captured by our forces are General Prentiss and several Colonels who were acting Brigadiers. The former of whom is reported being quite insolent in his deportment. Before leaving Corinth on the cars, he remarked to the crowd assembled that if he had time he would make them a speech, and make them good Unionists in ten minutes.

In reference to the death of Gen. Buell, it is stated by five Confederate soldiers who had been taken prisoners and escaped, that the colors of the Federal army were draped in mourning for his loss, and that he was killed early in the action on Monday. This is confirmed by the admission of six hundred prisoners who came in on Wednesday, and by a despatch received here by private parties from Mobile. In consequence of these disasters the Federal army is reported to be in disorder.

The death wound of General Johnston was inflicted on the calf of his right leg, and was considered by him as only a flesh wound. Soon after receiving it, he gave an order to Gov. Harris, who was acting as a volunteer aid to him, who, on his return to Gen. Johnston, in a different part of the field, found him exhausted from loss of blood, and reeling in his saddle. Riding up to him, Gov. Harris asked : "Are you hurt ?" to which the now dying hero answered : "Yes, and I fear mortally," and then, stretching out both arms towards his companion, fell from his horse, and soon after expired. No other wounds were discovered upon his person.

We get the following additional despatches from various sources :

A despatch from Corinth to the Mobile Tribune says that an armistice of three days has been asked for by the Federals for the purpose of burying their dead. Twelve thousand are reported to be killed, many thousands wounded and many more thousands made prisoners. Buell certainly killed.

A private despatch, dated Corinth, April 8th, says, that in the late battle Major General W. J. Hardee, of Savannah, was slightly wounded; First Lieutenant William A. Reid, of Savannah, now attached to the First Louisiana Regiment, and Major John Bowen, formerly of Savannah, now a citizen of Missouri, were also slightly wounded. Killed: Colonel Patterson and Colonel Patton, Arks. ; Colonel Deas, Ala. ; Colonel Kit Williams, Tenn. ; Major Mimms, Tenn., and Colonel Duke. First Louisiana Regiment badly cut up; also 16th 21st and 22d Alabama Regiments. Colonel Bates' Regiment badly cut up. Enemy's baggage and ammunition, with 88 guns, fell into our hands.

All concur in our victory being complete.—Drove them to their gunboats both days. They commenced shelling—we retreated. Their loss, lowest estimate, 18,000 in killed on the field : Generall Buell among them. Many of their and our wounded were burnt by the woods taking fire. We destroyed much of their ammunition, these being too much for us to haul off. The whole militia of Louisiana and Mississippi have been called out, and coming up.

It is reported, by a despatch to a gentleman in Atlanta, that the Federal cavalry have taken possession of Huntsville, Alabama. If so, then the Memphis and Charleston Railroad is in possession of the enemy.

GRAND VICTORY—SIX THOUSAND EIGHT HUNDRED PRISONERS CAPTURED—TWENTY-FIVE MILLIONS WORTH OF PROPERTY SECURED, INCLUDING ARIZONA AND NEW MEXICO.

The Richmond papers obtain from Mr. W. H. MACWILLIE, Delegate elect from the Territory of Arizona, a copy of the following important and interesting letter :

MESILLA, March 2.

We have just received, by express from Fort Craig, important news. A battle was fought between the forces of Gen. Sibley and Gen. Canby, on the 21st February, which resulted in the complete defeat of the latter with great loss.

The particulars as given by the courier disclose the fact that this has been the most closely contested battle of the war, and perhaps the bloodiest for the numbers engaged. General Sibley, with his command, numbering, rank and file, two thousand three hundred men, left Fort Thorn, eighty miles below Fort Craig, about the twelfth of February, with the intention of taking the latter place. On arriving in the vicinity of Craig, he learned from some prisoners, captured near the post, that General Canby was in command of the Federal forces in the Fort, that he had twelve hundred regular troops, two hundred American volunteers and five thousand Mexicans—entire force near six thousand four hundred men. Notwithstanding this superior force, he boldly advanced, and, on the 19th, crossed the river near Fort Craig, and, making a detour of some miles, arrived on the morning of the twenty-first in sight of the river, three miles above the Fort, where a large body of the enemy were stationed to receive him. It seems that all the enemy's forces, with the exception of their artillery and reserve, were upon the same side of the river to which our troops were advancing. A portion of Col. Baylor's regiment, under command of Maj. Pyon, numbering 250 men, were the first to engage the enemy. Alone and unsupported for one hour, they held their positions amid a hail of grape, canister and round shot. At that time they were reinforced and the battle became general. The enemy then made an attack upon our right wing, and were repulsed. A general movement was then made upon our line with more success, a portion of our left wing being compelled to fall back and take a new position. This was about two o'clock.—The enemy now supposed they had gained the day, and ordered their battery across the river, which was done, and the battery was planted upon the bank. As soon as the battery opened Gen. Sibley knew it had crossed, and immediately ordered a general charge, which was performed as Texans only can do it. Starting at a distance of eight hundred yards, with their Camanche war-whoop, they reserved their fire until within thirty yards of the battery, when they poured a deadly fire, with double barrelled shot-guns and pistols, immediately into the horror-stricken ranks of their foes. They sprang into the river, and, in crossing, numbers were killed. Capt. Teel's battery now coming up, closed this sanguinary contest, with shell and grape, as they fled down the opposite side of the river to the fort. The battle lasted nine hours. Our loss is thirty-eight killed and one hundred and twenty wounded ; that of the enemy, as given by themselves, is three hundred killed, four or five hundred wounded and two thousand missing.

The result of this battle is conceived of more importance to the Southern Confederacy than any that has been fought during the war. It will give us the Territories of Arizona and New Mexico, about twenty-five million dollars worth of property, and will greatly add to the prestige of our arms.

We are now expecting to hear of the capture of Fort Craig, with all the troops and military stores in the Territory.

The above letter is from Judge S. Hare, Confederate Judge, resident of Mesilla.

Mr. Macwillie has subsequently received a letter informing him, without further particulars, of the capture of Fort Craig with 6,800 prisoners, and all the munitions and military stores.

The cannon captured embraced the greater portion of those belonging to Fort Union, which is the only Federal military post remaining in New Mexico.

Bombardment and capture of Fort Pulaski, April 11, 1862

The New-York Times.

VOL. XI—NO. 3296. NEW-YORK, WEDNESDAY, APRIL 16, 1862. PRICE TWO CENTS.

THE WAR IN THE SOUTHWEST.

An Important Movement Against the Rebels.

Their Communications Below Corinth Cut off by Our Forces.

[illegible]e Bridges on the Mobile and Ohio Railroad Destroyed.

A FLAG OF TRUCE FROM BEAUREGARD.

Gen. Grant's Official Report on the Way to Washington.

ANOTHER GREAT BATTLE IMMINENT

PITTSBURGH LANDING, Tenn., Monday, April 14.

A force of four thousand men, on five transports, left this landing on Saturday night, accompanied by the gunboats *Tyler* and *Lexington*, and proceeded up the Tennessee River to a point near Eastport, Miss., where they landed, and proceeded inland to Bear Creek Bridge, and *destroyed the two bridges on the Mobile and Ohio Railroad*, one measuring 121 feet, and the other 210 feet in length.

A cavalry force of 150 men was found there, who, after having four killed, "skedaddled" in the most approved Southern style. The expedition returned Sunday night, without having lost a man.

This was one of the most successful operations of its kind during the war, *completely cutting off communication of the main rebel body at Corinth with Alabama and the rest of the Confederacy, except New-Orleans.*

A flag of truce arrived at the outposts yesterday, with the son of Gov. Johnson, of Kentucky, asking for his father.

ST. LOUIS, Tuesday, April 15.

Several gentlemen connected with the Army at Pittsburgh, arrived here yesterday. Among them is Capt. Lagow, of Gen. Grant's Staff, who is the bearer of Gen. Grant's official report of the battle of Pittsburgh. They left the army on Friday night.

Gen. Halleck arrived in Pittsburgh on Friday, and immediately assumed command of the army.

Gen. Grant, in his official report, estimates our loss 1,500 killed and 3,500 wounded. The loss of the enemy in killed and left on the field is greater than ours. In wounded an estimate cannot be made, as many must have been sent to Corinth and other places. The loss of artillery was great, many pieces being disabled by the enemy's shot; some losing all their horses and many men. Not less than 200 horses were killed.

The rebel army has its headquarters at the foot of [illegible] Ridge, extending two miles from Corinth. The advance of the National troops is eight miles from Pittsburgh Landing, *leaving a space of only two miles between the opposing armies. A battle may be fought at any moment. We have the strongest assurance that our army is ready for the encounter.*

CINCINNATI, Tuesday, April 15.

The *Commercial* has information from a reliable man, who left the battle-ground on Thursday evening. He estimated our loss in killed at from 1,200 to 1,500; wounded, 3,500 to 4,000, and missing, 2,500. The rebels lost more in killed than we did, but not so many wounded. About 1,000 unwounded rebel prisoners were taken, and about 1,200 wounded. Up to the time he left 2,200 rebels had been buried.

Our troops retook on Monday all the batteries lost on Sunday, and captured twelve pieces from the enemy. The rebels were so confident of their ability to hold our camps which they took on Sunday, that with a single exception they did not destroy them.

On Tuesday Gen. Beauregard sent a flag of truce, requesting permission to bury his dead, and saying:

"Owing to the heavy reinforcements you received Sunday night and Monday, and the fatigue of my men, *I deemed it prudent to retire and not renew the battle.*"

The permission was not granted.

The bearer of the flag admitted that Gen. Beauregard received a slight wound in the left arm.

DEATH OF GEN. WALLACE.

CAIRO, Sunday, April 13.

The body of Gen. Wm. H. L. Wallace, killed in the battle of Pittsburgh Landing, has arrived here; also, nearly 300 prisoners. The twice-repeated report of the escape of Gen. Prentiss from the enemy is now contradicted; it is no doubt untrue.

PARTIAL LIST OF THE WOUNDED.

Dispatch to the Cincinnati Gazette.

ABOARD STEAMER COMMODORE PERRY, EVANSVILLE, April 11.

We send you a list of wounded taken from the field at Pittsburgh Landing, and conveyed aboard steamer *Commodore Perry* on the 8th inst., the day after the fight at that place. We arrived there on Tuesday, at 4 P. M., with 500 troops from Nashville, expecting to be in time for the fight, but were a little too late, so I immediately organized those under my command and sent them into the field to gather up the wounded and bring them aboard. We left there Wednesday, at 3 P. M., under the advice and assistance of Dr. Murray, Medical Director of Gen. Buell's forces, one of the most kind and efficient surgeons in the field. Every attention was shown us at Paducah by Drs. Austin and Haines, contributing largely to the comfort of the wounded. The officers and men of the 48th Indiana, quartered at that place, seemed to vie with each other in their attentions to the wounded. Under the kind and attentive assistance of Capt. M. A. Hawes, of the 30th Indiana, Lieut. Posey, of the 29th Indiana, and Drs. King and Meeker, of the 29th and 9th Indiana, the wounded were amply provided for. Capt. Andrews, in command of the boat, has left nothing undone that could contribute to the comfort of the men. The following is a list of the wounded under our care:

COMMISSIONED OFFICERS.

Second Lieut. J. Raft, 32d Indiana, slightly; Capt. M. S. Stuart, 30th Indiana, slightly; Capt. Wm. Dauson, 30th Indiana, slightly; Capt. J. B. White, 30th Indiana, slightly; 2d Lieut. L. S. Brown, 26th Kentucky, slightly; 2d Lieut. S. A. Saxton, 54th Ohio, slightly; 2d Lieut. A. B. Stanley, 26th Kentucky, slightly; 2d Lieut. S. C. Scott, 31st Indiana, slightly; Capt. Peter Emery, 6th Kentucky, slightly; Capt. Edward Johns, 32d Indiana, slightly; Capt. S. L. Allen, 29th Indiana, slightly; Capt. Casey, 29th Indiana, slightly; 2d Lieut. G. Woodmause, 39th Indiana, died of wound April 9; Maj. Fred. Arn, 31st Indiana, killed.

NON-COMMISSIONED OFFICERS AND MEN.

—— Pierce, 9th Indiana, slightly; William Mitchell, 9th Indiana, slightly; M. H. Horne, 9th Indiana, do.; George Blackman, 9th Ind., do.; C. H. Morriss, 9th Ind., do.; C. E. Peaples, 9th Ind., do.; O. Brakeman, 9th Ind., do.; C. H. Gould, 9th Ind., do.; David Miller, 9th Ind., do.; James Marsh, 9th Ind., do.; Joseph Brooks, do.; John Marsh, do.; J. H. Weir, do.; Isaac Peterson, do.; Hiram Peterson, do.; Wm. Ryder, do.; Hanson Beck, do.; Wm. B. Gillman, do.; Peter Stenbury, do.; Thomas Brown, do.; W. H. Stewart, do.; A. B. Winfield, do.; J. W. Morehouse, do.; Chas. Morris, do.; T. W. Graham, do.; J. Abbett, do.; J. Morrow, do.; J. Reprogle, do.; Jonas Bartlett, do.; A. W. Porter, do.; Amos Daghoff, do.; Silas Rees, do.; Luther Johnson, do.; John Grant, do.; Murrey McConner, seriously; Solomon Hanna, do.; Henry Burgiss, do.; C. S. Wise, do.; Lewis Kesler, do.; Peter Caneral, do.; Jno. Deardorff, slightly; Chas. Kellsey, do.; Jessee Seigett and Adam Shaller, do.; D. W. Haydor, slightly; Lewis Roberts, seriously; A. L. Pierce, slightly; S. H. Tabor, slightly; J. N. Becker, slightly; A. F. Morris, seriously; Nathan Rector, slightly; Israel Finch, slightly—all of the 29th Indiana. J. A. Chester, slightly; Benj. Evans, seriously; Peter Kingsugall, do.; H. B. Mabendey, slightly; C. Coe, seriously; Elane Rice, do.; Jacob Miller, do.; William H. Cole, do.; Milton Mitchell, do.; J. S. Eneard, slightly; J. W. Green, do.; H. C. Hawnall, slightly; George Myers, do.; John H. Geller, seriously; Orderly Cogley, slightly; D. Kohler, do.; J. Engert, do.; E. Chase, do.; A. Whitney, do.; J. Kynor, do.; J. Mood, do.; W. H. Coffin, seriously; J. McGowan, slightly; Jas. Woodworth, do.; Geo. Nagens, do.; Abner Beck, do.; Geo. Magers, do.; Wm. Jenkins, do.; Elam Rice, do.; George Maners, do.; Paris Henderson, do.; Daniel T. Welch, do.; F. Douglas, seriously; Wm. Enwert, slightly; C. W. Price, do.; E. S. West, do.; Fred. Flager, do.; Daniel Roger, do.; Joseph Buffet, do.; John H. Gillen, do.; R. H. Craig, do.; Dev. Kalahan, do.; John Olt, do.; T. S. Conly, do.; B. E. Mondervelt, do.; J. H. Bennett, do.; Wm. Foine, do.; D. F. Beach, do.; Henry C. Green, seriously; S. Bishop, slightly—all of the Thirtieth Indiana. Wm. McConnell, slightly; M. Cramer, seriously; Geo. Hasse, slightly; J. Ford, seriously; P. Romain, do.; W. D. Carder, do.; S. B. Irens, do.; R. E. Hurburt, do.; S. Erly, do.; A. Finly, do.; A. Wright, do.; J. S. Welch, slightly; J. G. Morris, do.; Wm. Archer, do.; John Lawrence, do.; J. Schultz, do.; Jacob Crowder, do.; W. H. Phelps, do.; A. Brown, seriously; C. Beuford, [illegible]; A. Harper, do.; J. H. Cless[illegible], do.; Capt. M. L. Stuart, do.; Capt. J. B. White, do.; Capt. Dawson, do.; Martin Whitmore, do.; J. Worman, do.; R. McCash, do.; W. H. Allen, do.; J. Davis, seriously; J. Elliott, slightly; J. Michael, seriously; S. Gairton, slightly; T. M. Lane, slightly; J. Fidler, slightly; J. S. Hall, do.; C. A. Bennett, do.; W. Baker, do.; C. H. Castler, do.; J. Utley, seriously; J. Huffman, slightly; A. Carson, do.; H. McCulloch, do.; H. Bush, do.; C. Mozert, do.; B. F. Eatsell, do.; J. McGraw, do.; W. Neff, do.; A. Horriss, do.; D. Pollock, do.; D. S. Irish, do.—all of the Thirty-first Indiana. N. T. Ryman, slightly; G. H. Mahon, do.; J. Stevens, do.; T. Jacoby, do.—all of the Thirty-second Indiana. F. Jacoby, slightly; G. Creaver, do.; C. Clendar, seriously; J. Elman, do.; J. Brant, do.; J. G. Weachler, do.; J. Wack, slightly; L. Knit, do.; J. Wantz, do.; J. Theobald, do.; J. Roeker, do.; P. Ketch, seriously; C. Miller, slightly—all of the Twenty-fourth Ohio.

Dr. Norriss P. Wiltney, Fifteenth Regulars; John Bush, N. Shuttler, W. Landis, Nineteenth Regulars.

J. Shelby, slightly; George Hauzer, do.; John Lester, do.; J. Bunn, do.—all of the 11th Indiana.

F. Eush, slightly; A. Berryman, do.; G. W. Durham, do., of 30th Indiana. R. Anderson, slightly; C. Barthoa, do.; F. Murray, do., 6th Indiana. W. J. Crossby, slightly, 39th Indiana. J. J. Williams, slightly; W. C. Elliott, seriously; J. Bailey, do.; H. Harrick, do.; J. Jackson, slightly, 21st Iowa.

D. B. Glenn, slightly, 54th Ohio; S. Ingle, slightly; J. H. Kirchberger, do.; Simon Coll, do.; P. Ullmer, do.; J. C. Schrenker, do.; W. Miller, of the 40th Ill.; R. Wiley, do., 11th Ky.; R. Harney, slightly; W. B. Rhodes, seriously, 45th Ill.; P. Maloy, slightly, 15th Regulars; C. A. Ahman, slightly; S. McDonald, do.; H. Weldiner, do.; W. G. Hasbing, do.; R. Hunt, do.; J. Bridges, seriously; N. Webster, slightly; N. Weeks, do.; J. W. Evans, seriously; Z. Weir, do.; J. Kelley, slightly; L. D. Jones, do.; J. S. Low, do.; D. Clark, do.; W. C. Davis, do.—all of 77th Ohio.

L. Gross, slightly; A. Burroughs, do., 8th Wisconsin; B. W. Sarver, slightly, 15th Michigan.

C. Simonds, slightly, 23d Indiana; F. Shuber, slightly, 54th Ohio; J. L. Doline, slightly, 34th Illinois; D. C. Young, slightly; W. F. Corple, do.; S. R. Wertz, do.; J. J. Brown, do.; J. Gillett, do.; J. H. Riggard, do.; M. Buhan, do.; J. Everett, do.; J. Bornhizer, do.; Otho Lizer, do.; G. Tondine, do.; W. Carr, do.; D. Hinman, do.; J. M. Baird, do.; Thomas Butler, do.; J. A. Noel, do.; J. Barnlizer, do.; J. Watson, do.—all of the 7th Illinois.

C. P. Long, slightly; J. Walker, F. McKinness, do.; J. E. Larkin, do.; M. Haupton, do.—15th Michigan.

C. F. Trar, seriously, 16th Regulars; E. Picket, seriously, [illegible], seriously, 6th Kentucky; A. Lane, slightly, 24th Ohio; T. J. Moody, slightly, 25th Indiana; L. B. Jones, slightly, J. Shook, slightly, 6th Kentucky; J. D. Mileson, slightly, 19th Ohio.

A. Green, slightly, 23d Indiana; J. Davis, slightly, 25th Indiana.

J. S. Parker, slightly, 49th Illinois.

P. Reice, seriously, 23d Wisconsin; D. Grover, seriously, 19th Regulars; J. McDonald, seriously, 16th Iowa; J. M. Brower, slightly, 6th Ohio; J. Fairchild, slightly, 14th Wisconsin; E. Austin, seriously, 25th Indiana; John Webber, slightly, Charles Hainer, seriously, 24th Iowa; L. C. Peck, seriously, 16th Regulars; D. D. Patterson, seriously, 15th Regulars; J. Williams, seriously, 6th Iowa; B. F. Hutchinson, seriously, 18th Wisconsin; A. N. Coon, seriously, 16th Wisconsin; D. Nornpool, slightly, 49th Illinois.

D. McClain, seriously; S. J. C. Bryant, seriously, 7th Ill.; J. Donahao, seriously, 11th Ind.; J. E. Chatfield, seriously, 15th Ill.; Wm. S. Lathrop, slightly, 2d Ky.; A. B. Mankin, slightly, 11th Ill.

D. Sullivan, seriously; 32d Ind., Hendleam, seriously; Wm. Sabler, slightly; 15th Mich., C. Weldon, slightly.

Rebel prisoners—Maj. Samuel T. Love, 27th Tenn., mortally wounded; David Smith, Jackson Artillery, mortally wounded.

B. J. BLOWNEY, Major Commanding, Aboard *Commodore Perry.*

AID FOR THE WOUNDED.

ST. LOUIS, Tuesday, April 15.

Hon. Edwin M. Stanton, Secretary of War:

We sent a boat laden with supplies and attended by doctors and nurses, to the seat of war. Will you pay the expenses of the boat alone, and enable us to use the money raised for the wounded? We have a number already here, and more on the way. Answer immediately. (Signed,) J. M. DELPH.

DOWN THE MISSISSIPPI.

Com. Foote and Gen. Pope en Route for Memphis.

CAIRO, Saturday, April 12.

The Flag-officer (Commodore Foote) left New-Madrid to-day with the flotilla and mortarboats, *en route* for Fort Pillow, accompanied by a large body of troops.

FROM THE FLORIDA COAST.

Interesting Dispatches from Commodore Dupont—A Colony of Contrabands Established.

WASHINGTON, Tuesday, April 15.

The Navy Department has received dispatches from Commodore Dupont, inclosing a communication from Commander Godon, dated United States steamer *Mohican*, March 30, from which it appears that on the 17th ult., with the launches and another armed boat, he entered Jekyl Creek, and proceeded to Dubignon's place, where he discovered a deserted battery of three guns commanding that stream, and the remains of a camp of some 200 men. A considerable number of cattle remained on the island, but were very wild upon our men approaching them. On the 22d the *Bibb* made her appearance, and Capt. Boutelle at once commenced placing the buoys for the bar and channels. Commander Godon says: Contrabands continued to come to us. I sent a number by the *Potomska* to Fernandina, and also several by the *Connecticut*. We landed our field-pieces and a strong force on Colonel's Island, and obtained what we needed; and that night, after again firing a shell or two at Fancy Bluff, proceeded to St. Simons. There I landed all the contrabands, with their corn and provisions, tools, &c., and, having housed them, set them to work. Already they have planted potatoes. To-morrow they will begin to prepare the land for corn.

They have set up their mill, and I have told them they are to plant cotton, and thus to become of use to themselves. They seem contented, but, without a vessel at the other end of the island they are in danger of being interfered with by soldiers landing in that direction and approaching them at night. St. Simon's is a fine, rich island, about ten miles long; on the north end is a village, Frederica. It is said to be healthy, and a thousand blacks could be usefully employed here and made self-supporting. Such a colony, properly managed, would do much good. Those now here, some forty in number, live on T. Butler King's place, under cover of our guns.

THE FALL OF FORT PULASKI.

An Unconditional Surrender on Friday Afternoon Last.

Terrible Bombardment by the National Batteries.

Seven Large Breaches Made in the South Wall.

Over a Thousand Shells Exploded within the Fort.

NO LOSS OF LIFE REPORTED.

FORTRESS MONROE, Monday, April 14.

A flag of truce went up to Craney Island this afternoon, and brought back two Norfolk papers. They were taken to headquarters, and, although containing the important information of the unconditional surrender of Fort Pulaski, an effort was made, in accordance with the policy that prevails here, to keep even good news from the representatives of the Press. I am, however, able to give you the substance of the glorious news, as published in the Savannah *Republican*.

The *Republican* says, substantially, that it learns with deep regret, that after a gallant defence, against guns mostly superior, Fort Pulaski surrendered at 2 P. M., yesterday, the 11th. Corporal Law, of the Pulaski Guards, who did not leave Fort Thunderbolt until after the flag was hauled down, brings the intelligence of the event. The surrender was unconditional. *Seven large breaches were made in the south wall by the National battery of eight Parrott guns*, at King's Landing. All the barbette guns on that side were dismounted, and also three of the casemate guns, leaving but one gun bearing on that point. *Three balls entered the magazine, and a clean breach was made in it.*

The balls used were conical, and were propelled with such force that they *went clear through the walls at nearly every fire.*

Col. Olmstead, who was in command, telegraphed the previous evening that *no human being could stand upon the ramparts for even a single moment*, and that over 1,000 large shells had exploded within the fort.

The *Republican* publishes the above as a postscript to a part of its edition, and makes no comments, nor gives any particulars as to the number of men and officers in the fort at the time of the surrender. It says, however, that none of its defenders were killed, and but four wounded.

FROM ANOTHER CORRESPONDENT.

The steamer *Rancocas* went out this afternoon with a flag of truce, and was met by a rebel boat having on board Lieut. Preston, of S. C.

A copy of the Norfolk *Day Book* was brought back containing highly important information. It states that the Union forces captured Fort Pulaski on Friday night after a fight of a few hours. It is also stated that every one of the steel-pointed shot from our guns went through the walls of the Fort as if there had been no impediment.

We lost none in killed. The rebel loss was none killed, and only four wounded. The surrender was unconditional.

NEWS RECEIVED IN BALTIMORE.

BALTIMORE, Tuesday, April 15.

The Savannah *Republican*, of the 12th, announces the unconditional surrender of Fort Pulaski on the previous day.

Seven large breaches were made in the walls by our batteries of Parrott guns at King's Landing, and all the barbette guns on that side, and three casemate guns, were dismounted.

Three balls entered the magazine.

Col. Olmstead, the rebel commander, signaled, the day previous to the surrender, that our fire was so terrible that no human being could stand upon the parapet for even a moment.

FORT PULASKI.

The best description of Fort Pulaski is that given by Mr. Russell, of the London *Times*, who visited it less than a year ago, shortly after its seizure by the rebels. The same description will answer for the present day, as it has undergone few alterations except to mount a few guns:

SAVANNAH, Ga., May 1, 1861.

It is said that fools build houses for wise men to live in. Be that true or not, it is certain that "Uncle Sam" has built strong places for his enemies to occupy. To-day I visited Fort Pulaski, which defends the mouth of the Savannah River and the approaches to the city. It was left to take care of itself, and the Georgians quietly stepped into it, and have been busied in completing its defences, so that it is now capable of stopping a fleet very effectually. The river at Savannah is as broad as the Thames at Gravesend, and resembles that stream very much in the color of its waters, and the level nature of its shores. Rice fields bound it on either side, as far down as the influence of the fresh water extends, and the eye wanders over a flat expanse of mud and water, and green osiers and rushes, till its search is arrested on the horizon by the unfailing line of forest. In the fields, here and there, are the whitewashed square wooden huts, in which the slaves dwell. At one point a small fort, covering a creek by which gunboats could get up behind Savannah, displayed its "garrison on the walls, and lowered its flag to salute the small blue ensign at the fore, which proclaimed the presence of the Commodore of the Naval force of Georgia on board our steamer. The guns on the parapet were mostly field-pieces, mounted on frame-works of wood, instead of regular carriages.

After steaming down the river about twelve miles the sea opened out to the sight, and on a long, marshy, narrow island near the bar, which was marked by the yellowish surf, Fort Pulaski threw out the Confederate flag to the air of the Georgian 1st of May. The water was too shallow to permit the steamer to go up to the jetty, and the party landed at the wharf in boats. A guard was on duty at the landing—tall, stout young fellows, in various uniforms, or in rude mufti, in which the Garibaldian red shirt and felt slouched hats predominated. They were armed with smooth-bore muskets, (date 1851,) quite new, and their bayonets, barrels and locks were quite bright and clean. A few minutes' walk led us to the fort, which is an irregular pentagon, with the base line or curtain face inland, and the other faces casemated and bearing on the approaches. The curtain, which is simply crenellated, is covered by a redan surrounded by a deep ditch, inside the parapet of which are granite platforms, ready for the reception of guns. The parapet is thick, and the counterscarp are faced with solid masonry. A draw bridge affords access to the interior of the redan, whence the gate of the fort is approached across a deep and broad moat, which is crossed by another drawbridge. As the Commodore entered the redan the guns of the fort broke out into a long salute, and the band at the gate struck up almost as noisy a welcome. Inside, the parade presented a scene of life and animation very unlike the silence of the city we had left.

The garrison of the fort is 650 men, and fully that number were in and about the work, their tents being pitched inside the redan or on the terreplein of the parapets. The walls are exceedingly solid and well built of hard gray brick, strong as iron, upwards of six feet in thickness, the casemates and bombproofs being lofty, airy, and capacious as any I have ever seen, though there is not quite depth enough between the walls at the salient and the gun-carriages. The work is intended for 128 guns, of which about one-fourth are mounted on the casemates. They are long 32s with a few 42s and columbiads. The armament will be exceedingly heavy when all the guns are mounted, and they are fast getting the 10-inch columbiads into position *en barbette*. Everything which could be required, except mortars, was in abundance—the platforms, and gun-carriages are solid and well made, the embrasures of the casemates are admirably constructed, and the ventilation of the bombproof carefully provided for. There are three furnaces for heating red-hot shot.

It will take some hard blows before Georgia is driven to let go her grip of Fort Pulaski. The channel is very narrow, and passes close to the guns of the fort. The means of completing its armament have been furnished by the stores of Norfolk Navy-yard, where between 700 and 800 guns have fallen into the hands of the Confederates; and, if there are no columbiads among them, the *Merrimac* and other ships, which have been raised, as we hear, with guns uninjured, will yield up their Dahlgrens to turn their muzzles against their old masters.

THE ARMY AND NAVY.

An order for the better regulation of Military Hospitals, and for facilitating the discharge of soldiers unfit for service, has been issued from the War Department.

All General Hospitals are placed under the direction of the Surgeon-General. The chief medical officer, to whom the charge of all the general hospitals in a city may be intrusted, will make out certificates of disability for such men as, in his judgment, should be discharged. The certificates must give such medical description of the cases, with the degree of disability, as may enable the pension-officer to decide on any claims to pension which may be based upon them. These certificates are to be forwarded to the Military Commander, who is authorized to give discharges, and furnish final statements of pay and clothing due to the soldier.

The Military Commander is instructed to collect stragglers and send them to their proper stations, or discharge them on certificates of disability, as above, if unfit for service. He will also send such patients as are reported fit for duty to their regiments, under proper escort. Convalescent, wounded, or feeble men, capable of acting as cooks, nurses and attendants, are to be employed as such, instead of being discharged. All officers and enlisted men of volunteers, who are on parole not to serve against the rebels, will be considered on leave of absence until notified of their exchange or discharge. They will immediately report their address to the Governors of their States, who will be duly informed from the Adjutant-General's office, as to their exchange or discharge. The duties of Military Commanders will devolve upon the following officers:

District of Columbia	On the Military Governor.
City of Baltimore	On the Commander of the Middle Department.
City of Philadelphia	On Lieut.-Col. H. Brooks, Second Artillery.
City of New-York and Military Posts in vicinity	On Brevet Brig.-Gen. Harvey Brown.

The iron-clad sloop-of-war *Galena* arrived at the Navy-yard yesterday at 11 A. M., and immediately hauled under the shears to receive her armament. She will carry four 9-inch Dahlgren guns, and two 100-pound Parrott guns. Her rig is what is known in naval circles as that of an hermaphrodite brig, viz.: brig rigged forward and schooner rigged aft. As might be expected there was a good deal of bustle and excitement at the yard when the *Galena* came in, and a crowd of people thronged the wharf anxious to inspect her, but no one was permitted to go on board unless passed by a Naval officer. Among the crowd on the wharf we observed several would-be critics passing judgment on the untried vessel, and deciding to their own satisfaction how far she was shot-proof, and what were the defects of her armature. When the *Monitor* was at the yard there were very few outsiders who thought they should like to be aboard of her either at sea or during action.

The supply steamer *Massachusetts* will be put into commission to-day, under the command of Lieut. Cooper, who, we may mention, is to be presented with a handsome and valuable gold watch, by the Navy-yard employes, as a token of their appreciation of his gentlemanly and obliging disposition while Executive officer of the yard.

The General Order relative to the recruiting service, referred to about ten days ago, was not correctly given. As we stated at the time, it applied to the Volunteer force only. The following is a correct copy of the order:

"The recruiting service for Volunteers will be discontinued in every State from this date (April 3d.) The officers detached on Volunteer recruiting service will join their regiments without delay, taking with them the parties and recruits at their respective stations. The Superintendents of Volunteer recruiting service will disband their parties and close their offices, after having taken the necessary steps to carry out these orders. The public property belonging to the Volunteer recruiting service will be sold to the best advantage possible, and the proceeds credited to the fund for collecting, drilling, and organizing volunteers."

Capt. Donald C. Stith, who has been dismissed from the service, belonged to the Fifth United States Infantry, not the Maryland Fifth Infantry, as published yesterday.

A detachment of one hundred blue jackets left the *North Carolina* Monday, for Cairo, Ill., accompanied by a guard of marines. Mr. John Byrnes, carpenter of the *North Carolina*, went in charge of them.

Capt. Gansevoort, Chief of the Ordnance Department at the Yard, will take command of the sloop-of-war *Adirondack*, now fitting out. Capt. Gansevoort is a native of this State, and has been in the service since March 4, 1823. His last sea service was in 1856, since when he has been on duty on shore. Lieut. William G. Temple will succeed Capt. Gansevoort in the Ordnance Department, and another officer will be detailed, *vice* Temple.

The destination of the store-ship *Release* is the Mediterranean squadron, not the blockading squadron, as printed.

Arrival of the United States Frigate Sabine.

The United States frigate *Sabine*, Capt. Cadwallader Ringgold, from a cruise in search of the United States ship *Vermont*, arrived at this port last evening. The *Sabine* left Hampton Roads March 12, and on the 29th of March, off Bermuda, fell in with the *Vermont*, lying unmanageable in the trough of the sea; kept in company with her for two days, during which time supplied her with sails, rigging, &c. April 1, during a heavy squall, parted company, and saw nothing of her since; left her in a good condition, and she would make for Port Royal.

The *Sabine*, since leaving Hampton Roads, has had a succession of heavy gales from all quarters of the compass, and during which she behaved nobly.

The following is a correct list of the officers of the *Sabine*:

Captain—Cadwallader Ringgold.
Lieutenant and Ex.-Officer—H. C. Blake.
Paymaster—J. George Harris.
Surgeon—J. J. Abernethy.
Master—C. A. Walker.
Acting Masters—J. Ewer, J. K. Beatie, W. R. Hathaway, E. B. Hennessey, D. E. Taylor.
Assistant-Surgeon—D. M. Skinner.
Lieutenant Marines—W. R. Remey.
Captain's Clerk—E. Brown, Jr.
Paymaster's Clerk—C. D. Boss, Jr.
Acting-Master's Mates—L. H. White, E. M. Noe, B. W. McKeever, Jas. Courtney.
Carpenter—G. E. Beucham.
Sailmaker—T. E. Chavalier.
Acting-Gunner—C. Seymour.
Acting-Boatswain—R. Robinson.

The *Sabine* was towed up to the Navy-yard.

Rebel Prisoners En Route to Fort Warren.

ALBANY, Tuesday, April 15.

The rebel officers Major-Gen. Makall, Gens. Brown and Gaunt, and Majors Davidson and McCall, and Capt. Sellner arrived here this morning, under charge of Capt. Selfridge, United States Army. They breakfasted at the Delevan House, and proceeded on to Fort Warren.

OLD POINT AND YORKTOWN

Nothing Seen of the Merrimac on Monday or Yesterday.

Fears of the Rebels for the Safety of Richmond.

One of the Rebel Papers Shows How the Monitor, the Naugatuck and the Galena Might Take the City.

PROGRESS OF THE SIEGE OF YORKTOWN.

Rebel Batteries on the York River Shelled by Our Gunboats.

SPECIAL DISPATCH FROM WASHINGTON.

WASHINGTON, Tuesday, April 15.

I have just received the following under date of Fortress Monroe, April 14:

Although the weather has been unusually fine to-day, the *Merrimac* has not made her appearance. The opinion prevails with many, that she will remain as a protection to Norfolk, while the rebel troops that have been stationed there will be removed to Yorktown, to take part in the impending battle. The apparent desertion of some of their batteries around the Point, would seem to confirm this opinion.

The Norfolk *Day-Book*, received by flag of truce, claims the battle at Pittsburgh Landing as a great rebel victory. They state that Van Dorn and Price joined forces with Beauregard, and gave battle again on Wednesday with great success.

The Captain of the Rebel boat that met the *Rancocas* admitted the defeat of the Rebel Army at Pittsburgh Landing on Monday.

Up to this hour, 5 P. M., we have no important news from our army before Yorktown.

DISPATCH FROM FORTRESS MONROE.

FORTRESS MONROE, Monday, April 14.

A Richmond paper contains an editorial, exhibiting considerable fear for the safety of that City. It intimates that the *Monitor*, *Naugatuck* and *Galena*, all armored vessels, might easily come up James River, and by their invulnerability and powerful guns take and keep possession of the city. To prevent such a result, it proposes that the channel of James River shall be obstructed by stone, which it says is abundant for the purpose, and should be used at once.

The *Merrimac* has not come out, and nothing has been seen of her to-day. The tide has been low, and this may have kept her in. Early in the morning a rebel tug ran out from behind Sewall's Point, but soon returned. Later in the day there was a large fire in the woods on the Point, apparently from the burning of brush, which engaged the attention of the curious, and gave rise to some speculations that the rebels were building a new battery there.

WASHINGTON, Tuesday, April 15.

Dispatches received from Old Point up to 9 o'clock this morning, report all quiet there. Various rumors were current about the *Merrimac*, but nothing reliable was known. She had not made her appearance up to the hour above referred to.

THE LATEST NEWS FROM YORKTOWN.

BEFORE YORKTOWN, Tuesday, April 15.

Yesterday morning about two o'clock, a section of artillery was posted within half-a-mile of the rebel works near the river, supported by sufficient infantry to prevent their being captured. Fifteen shots were fired into the rebel earthworks before they were able to bring their guns to bear, when our men withdrew without damage.

A fine view was yesterday obtained of the position of the rebels both at Yorktown and Gloucester, from Fairchild's house, at the mouth of Wormlith's Creek. Twenty-four guns were seen in the water-battery at Yorktown, and nine at Gloucester. At the latter place a large number of workmen were engaged in erecting new works.

At Yorktown the old works used during the siege of 1780 were still visible and readily distinguished from those of recent construction. Heavy guns were mounted on their walls, and the rebel flag was flying from its battlements. The principal wharf was covered with commissary stores, while the river was dotted with sails. Every one appeared to be busy, as though the coming struggle depended upon his individual exertions.

Late in the afternoon, a schooner anchored a short distance above the wharf, was burnt.

The flotilla was yesterday afternoon engaged in shelling out a body of rebels, who were engaged in constructing a shore battery, about four miles below Gloucester. The result of the firing was not known.

On Saturday, Corporal Walter H. Bean, Company E, Berdan's Sharpshooters, was shot through the neck and back while on picket.

Last night things were remarkably quiet. A slight shower occurred this morning, but the sun soon made its appearance.

DISPATCH FROM GEN. WOOL.

FORTRESS MONROE, April 15—4 P. M.

Hon. E. M. Stanton:

Nothing has occurred since my dispatch of this morning to disturb the quiet then represented. The fine weather is very favorable to the operations at Yorktown, and it is probable that Gen. McClellan will soon be able to open his batteries at the fortifications of the enemy.

The French Minister honored me with a visit this morning. He has gone to Norfolk and will go to Richmond. On entering the fort I gave him a salute of thirteen guns.

(Signed) JOHN E. WOOL, Major-General.

OPERATIONS ON THE YORK RIVER.

WASHINGTON, Tuesday, April 15.

The steamer *Yankee*, Capt. Eastman, arrived at the Navy-yard to-day, having left York river at 6 o'clock yesterday morning.

The *Yankee* went about eight miles up the York river on Sunday night, and anchored off Gloucester Point, where the steamers *Penobscot*, *Marblehead*, and *Wachusett* were already lying.

The rebel batteries at the Point, which are said to be very extensive, mounting mostly 100-pound rifle guns, tried the range of their guns on the steamers about 2 o'clock yesterday afternoon, the shot falling very little short of the *Marblehead*. The vessel then dropped down the river, and, about three miles below the Point, discovered a party of rebels building a battery on the North bank, on whom the *Yankee* opened fire at the distance of three-fourths of a mile. The rebels seemed loth to abandon their works, and although the shells of the *Yankee* fell in their midst, they did not leave the vicinity, but took refuge in the woods and behind some neighboring log houses. The *Yankee*, after firing some 60 or 70 shot and shell during an hour and a half, left the scene, the other boats having come up to do their share.

As the *Yankee* was leaving, the boats of the *Marblehead* were on the way to the shore to burn the houses behind which the rebels had taken refuge.

During the engagement a battery up the river fired some eight or ten shots, but they fell far short of them. The guns in the batteries at Gloucester Point are said to be only in a position to [illegible] vessels below them in the middle of the river, and light-draught vessels can approach within a short distance of the point with safety by hugging the shore.

LETTER FROM OUR CORRESPONDENT.

AFFAIRS IN FRONT OF YORKTOWN.

CONGRESSMEN AND GOVERNMENT OFFICERS ON A LEE SHORE—ROADS ON THE PENINSULA—LIFE IN CAMP.

IN FRONT OF YORKTOWN, Friday Morning, April 11, 1862.

Yesterday morning I left the comfortable quarters I had found in farmer Huder's house near Ship Point, intending to reach the front of the army, somehow, during the day. I waded through the mud to the landing, to find some opportunity of sending a letter to the Times. The steamers were all anchored out in the bay, and there was no transportation to them except such as persons in my situation might invent. I soon found two others seeking the same object, and we three borrowed a leaky skiff, wherein we set sail; not much wiser, in some respects, than the three "wise men of Gotham" that once "went to sea in a bowl." Your correspondent, being the best seaman of the three, had to do the rowing. The wind was still high, the three days' storm not having abated, and the bay very rough. The mile and a half of pulling at the oars then and there performed by me cost an hour's time and the sorest pair of hands I have had for some years. But I was rewarded by success and the commendation of my comrades, and that is what a "soldier" chiefly values.

On board the boat, the *King Philip*, I found Senator Grimes, Mr. Sedgwick, of the House, Col. Lee, of the Massachusetts Twentieth, and one or two others who had come up with us the day before, and had spent the dreary day and night on board, rocked by the waters and housed by the rain, with nothing to amuse them but a score or more of transports around, loaded with horses, hay, commissary stores, heavy guns, mortars, shot and shell, which rocked as ceaselessly as they, with no prospect apparently of ever reaching a landing. Occasionally our imprisoned and desperate legislators did what other men do in such trying circumstances—they took something to drink; and wondered when the war would end, if it progressed at this rate.

The successful voyage of your correspondent to the weather-bound ship, inspired the distressed parties with the thought of themselves reaching land; which they were soon enabled to do through the courtesy of the *King Philip's* Captain, who sent them off in a long-boat. Not long after, I found them wandering in the rebel village of camp-huts, much surprised at their neat construction and comfort. We all met at length at the head-quarters of Gen. Thos. Francis Meagher, and while there, a messenger arrived from the headquarters of the army. It was Hon. E. B. Washburne, who had "piled" into a forage wagon the evening before, determined to see what he could of the famed Peninsula and the vicinity of Yorktown. Capt. Fox, of the navy, had followed behind the wagon, mounted on that abhorrence of a sailor, a horse. It was a perilous movement for a seaman to leave his official element; and when, in the morning, Mr. Washburne returned alone, hardly recognizable through the several coatings of mud that encased him, we were fearful the right arm of the navy had been lost. But in a short time the Captain, too, returned. Both had a tale of horrors to outpour, regarding the state of the country they had traversed. They had ridden to camp through a pitiless rain—the whole surface of the earth a sea of mud, the roads patched just badly enough to compel a man to shun them wherever he could turn off, only to find the roadside worse, enforcing his immediate return. It was nightfall when they reached Gen. McClellan's headquarters. These were in a dreary open field, the floor of the tents being mud, and mud ankle deep everywhere outside of the tents. And the General's quarters were a specimen of the quarters of the great army—rain, mud and darkness threw a pall over everything.

Capt. Fox and Mr. Washburne, having rejoined their friends at Ship Point, they all proceeded on board the *King Philip*, and your correspondent was duly commissioned to take the Captain's horse back to the army; which public service he, being on foot, most willingly and gallantly performed.

I shall never be able to make any human being realize what a desperate road it is that leads from Ship Point to the place where Gen. McClellan's headquarters were pitched. I recalled all that I had ever read of the road from Balaklava to the front of Sebastopol, over which the French and English armies first drew their stores and siege guns. That was universally conceded to be the worst road ever seen, and the English language, and probably the French, was exhausted in describing it. But this road must have been worse than that. This road crossed frequent sloughs, over which poles had been thrown cross-ways, to make a corduroy road. But the immense rains had so saturated the soil, that everything was soft, three feet deep by the plummet, and the poles floated in the mud as they would in water. They would turn under the horses' feet, trip and throw them down, catch in the wagon-wheels, and torment where they were designed to help. Here and there a cleared place on the road-side would be seen, an old field or heather, which would tempt the thoughtless teamster or horseman aside. But sorrow for all such. The smooth surface covered a treacherous quicksand. The wagons would plunge in to their hubs, from which no horse or mule power could extricate them; and the mounted horse would struggle with such desperate contortions as nearly to dislocate his limbs and unseat his rider. Six miles had we of this road. It was a sea of mud, boundless and fathomless. We might have added endless, if we had been required to go beyond the six miles. Wagons were stuck fast along the whole line of march. Mules were seen sitting down on their haunches in the mud, buried up to their bellies in the mud, lying down on their sides in the mud, falling exhausted in their traces. Teamsters thrashed, slashed and swore—and swore, slashed and thrashed. It was of no avail; for nothing short of omnipotence could draw an army's retinue through that Stygian bog. The dry wind and the sun, that seemed to have bidden the earth farewell, were the only source of hope for feeding the grand army of the Potomac.

I did not reach Gen. McClellan's camp till 2 P. M. It was somewhat improved from Mr. Washburne's description, but yet only a vast muddy bull pen in appearance. Gen. McClellan was absent reconnoitering near Yorktown, and selecting a site for a new camp. I was, however, kindly received by Gens. Marcy and Williams, and Cols. Kingsbury and Astor, and other members of his staff. Col. Astor kindly proffered to pilot me nearer to Yorktown, and after an hour's rest I started toward that famed spot, about four miles distant. Having approached near Gen. Heintzelman's camp, Col. Astor showed me the road and left me to pursue my course. I rode along some distance and asked for Gen. Butterfield's camp, Gen. B. being in Heintzelman's corps. I was pointed still ahead, and rode on till I saw a frowning fortification

[Continued on Eighth Page.]

The New-York Times.

VOL. XI—NO. 3306. NEW-YORK, MONDAY, APRIL 28, 1862. PRICE TWO CENTS.

NEW-ORLEANS OURS!

Acknowledgment of its Capture by the Rebels.

Dispatches from Gen. Wool and Gen. McDowell.

Fort Jackson Passed by Our Forces on Thursday Morning.

GREAT EXCITEMENT IN THE CITY.

Strict Martial Law at once Proclaimed.

Cotton and Steamboats Reported to be Burnt.

The National Forces Before the City on Friday at Noon.

Last Gasp of the Rebel Telegraph Operator.

DISPATCH FROM GEN. WOOL.

FORTRESS MONROE, Sunday, April 27.

Hon. E. M. Stanton, Secretary of War:

A fugitive black, just arrived from Portsmouth, brings the Petersburgh *Express* of yesterday, which contains the following dispatch:

NORFOLK, Friday, April 25.

The enemy passed Fort Jackson at 4 o'clock yesterday morning.

When the news reached New-Orleans, the excitement was boundless.

Martial law was put in full force, and business was completely suspended.

All the cotton and steamboats, excepting such as were necessary to transport coin, ammunition, &c., were destroyed.

At 1 o'clock to-day the operator bade us good by, saying that *the enemy had appeared before the city.*

This is the last we know regarding the fall. Will send particulars as soon as they can be had.

The negro bringing the above, reports that the rebels have two iron-clad steamers nearly completed, and that it is believed that the *Merrimac* will be out to-morrow. JOHN E. WOOL.

DISPATCH FROM GEN. McDOWELL.

HEADQUARTERS OF THE DEPARTMENT OF THE RAPPAHANNOCK, April 27, 1862.

Hon. E. M. Stanton, Secretary of War:

I have just returned from the camp opposite Fredericksburgh. I was told the Richmond *Examiner* of the 25th had been received in town, announcing as follows:

"New-Orleans taken." "Great destruction of property, cotton and steamboats." "Steamboats enough saved to take away the ammunition." "Great consternation of the inhabitants."

IRWIN McDOWELL, Major-General.

THE CAPTURE OF NEW-ORLEANS.

The news of the capture of New-Orleans, which we received from the South at a late hour last night, clears up gloriously the mystery which for some time has hung around the movements of our navy and army upon the Lower Mississippi. We had already had intelligence that our bombketches had opened fire upon Fort Jackson, 60 miles below the city, and yesterday morning we published news derived from the rebels that one of our gunboats had run past that work. But the defenders of the fort, it was said, had sent word to their friends that they were confident of their strength, and were able to endure the shelling as long as our fleet was able to keep it up. That news was up to Tuesday last. It appears certain that, notwithstanding the rebel bombast, Fort Jackson, and probably, also, Fort St. Philip, on the opposite side of the river, were reduced that very day; for by the gray dawn of Wednesday morning, our armada had steamed past the fortifications, and by noon it appeared, with power and terror, before the Crescent City. At this point the telegram stops short, and leaves us completely in the dark as to what has been done during the past four days. Whether Gen. BUTLER, as is probable, sent in a demand for the capitulation of the city, and what may have followed—a compliance with, or refusal of the terms of the demand—we do not yet know. But it is altogether unlikely that any serious attempt was made to defend the city itself. Indeed, New-Orleans was utterly incapable of defence, when once our fleet got in front of it. With a hundred gun and mortar-boats riding high above the city, ready to pour down upon it a torrent of fire and iron, it would be madness for the rebels to dream of any other terms than unconditional surrender. It has been thought that the land force accompanying the expedition was too small to repossess a city, which must still count somewhat like a hundred and fifty thousand inhabitants. And so it would be if the military contingent had to act alone. But the fact is, that the naval arm when once raised over the city, was of itself sufficient to hold it in complete subjection. And the only work for the troops would be to seize and garrison some few important positions in the city, raise the Stars and Stripes over the United States property and other public places, and act as a repressive police force. The rebels will be disarmed; the Union element, which is known to be strong in New-Orleans, will be organized; and Gen. BUTLER, from his headquarters in the St. Charles Hotel, will put in force whatever other measures are necessary for the securing of public order.

The seizure of this, the greatest city of the Jeff. Davis Confederacy, will be a terrible disheartenment for the rebels, and is in itself almost equivalent to a defeat of BEAUREGARD'S army at Corinth, if that army has not yet been destroyed by the forces of Gen. HALLECK. At all events, it will compel the rebels of the Southwest to fight their last battle on their present line of operation. BEAUREGARD is pressed, if not already assailed, by HALLECK in front; Gen. MITCHEL will prevent his retreat toward Mobile; BUTLER forbids his approach to New-Orleans; and our gunboats can *pass up the Mississippi and attack Memphis in front*—acting in conjunction with Commodore FOOTE above. The way is also opened for the gunboats to pass up the Red River and across the entire State of Louisiana to Shreveport; to pass up the Arkansas River and through the entire State of Arkansas to Fort Smith; and to pass up the Yazoo River and through a great part of the State of Mississippi. In fact, it opens up a passage through more than a half of the remnant of a Confederacy still nominally held by the rebel rulers. Thus, by this splendid stroke of our river navy, we see not only the fall of the Southern Metropolis, but also a moral and territorial gain for the National cause, which far overshadows in importance even this. If the news be allowed to reach the rebel army at Corinth—and it certainly cannot be kept from it for more than a day or two—it must complete its demoralization; for it will demonstrate beyond a peradventure that the cause in which it fights is hopeless. There can be no prospect to the rebels of recapturing the city; for the railroad leading to it will be destroyed, and a descent by the river is impossible. The whole of Southern Louisiana is a vast plain, and in no event can the rebels make a stand anywhere near the city.

New-Orleans is the great commercial and financial emporium of the South. It is to the Gulf coast what New-York is to the Atlantic coast. Its fall will be to the South a worse blow even than the capture of New-York by an enemy would be to the North. Through it more than half of the cotton crop of the entire South passes to the world, while its exports of sugar, molasses, tobacco and corn exceed those of any other Southern city. There is probably not much cotton there now, but the fact that we also virtually possess a great part of the cotton-growing territory, will secure its speedy export with or without the will of the planters.

It is nearly half a century since an enemy appeared before New-Orleans. That enemy was repulsed with a slaughter which renders memorable the plains of Chalmette. But this time an army captures the City almost without loss of blood—though it has doubled its population many times since then. Such are the advances made by science; and such are the irresistible powers which the Nation now brings into the field against its enemies.

The Mississippi is now virtually opened throughout its entire length. That was the work which the men of the Northwest laid out for themselves a year ago. The West has done a good share of the work; but it has been left to the men of the East to complete it.

THE CITY OF NEW-ORLEANS.

The population of New-Orleans, by the last census, was 168,472. This has, undoubtedly, been largely decreased since the rebellion. The commerce of the city, which was its main support, has been totally ruined, and thousands of the people have fled to the country, or anywhere that they could find a scanty subsistence, while other thousands have been drafted into the rebel army. The city is the emporium of the Mississippi Valley, and is situated on the left bank of the river, about a hundred miles from its mouth. The older portion of the city is built on the convex side of a bend of the river, which here sweeps around in a northeast, east, and southeast course. From this location it derives its familiar soubriquet of the "Crescent City." In the progress of its growth up stream, the city has now so extended itself as to fill the hollow of a curve in the opposite direction, so that the river front presents an outline somewhat resembling the letter S. It stretches or straggles along the bank of the river some six or seven miles, with an average depth of one mile, it only being possible to build on the narrow strip of land lying immediately on the edge of the river, the highest point being in front, and then rapidly *sinking in the rear until lost in interminable swamps.* In the rear of New-Orleans, a half a mile, perhaps, beyond the suburbs, is the Metairie ridge, a narrow strip of high land two or three feet above high water mark, of an average of a half mile in width; then you come again to the swamp, which continues to the shores of the lake beyond, almost as dense as any in the surrounding valley, gloomy and peculiar and uninhabited, except by alligators and buttemes. The front of New-Orleans is of course on the river, and from the peculiarity of the country, and the levée which serves to protect the city from being overflowed by the Spring rise, our fleet, when it reached the city, *must have been above the ground on which the city is built, and commanded it as from an eminence.* This circumstance, with the fact that the breaking of the levée by a cannon-shot, or a few minutes' work with the spade, *would submerge the whole place*, makes New-Orleans, with its defenceless rear, the weakest and least protected place of any commercial importance in the world. The defences of the city were so fully and, as the event has proved, accurately described in the TIMES of Monday last, that it is not necessary now to rehearse the facts. What has become of the rebel gunboats and rams, of which we have heard so much, it is hard to conjecture.

The most important railroads terminating at New-Orleans, are the New-Orleans, Jackson and Great Northern, which, until lately, united it with the great railroad systems of the Eastern and Northern States, and the New-Orleans, Opelousas and Great Western, extending westwardly a short distance into Texas. The great avenue, however, of the trade and commerce of the city, is the Mississippi River. Along the river front of the city the levée, or artificial embankment to keep the city from inundation, is extended by a continuous series of wooden wharfs. A sort of esplanade is thus formed, several miles in extent, which, during the busy season, presents a scene of wonderful variety and animation. Cotton bales, sugar hogsheads, negroes and mule-drays are in great abundance. Among the notable buildings are the branch mint of the United States—which the rebels seized a year ago and stole a part of the coin—the Custom-house, one of the most massive structures in America, but not yet completed, the cathedral of St. Louis, and sixty other churches, the St. Charles Hotel, which cost $590,000; the hospital, banks and benevolent institutions. On Jackson-square is a bronze equestrian statute of Gen. JACKSON, by CLARK MILLS. The New-Orleanians will now remember Gen. JACKSON as the man who said, "The Union must and shall be preserved."

The population of New-Orleans has long been remarkable for the diversity of its elements. About one-half of the whites are of foreign birth, and among these the French and Spanish are predominant. There is also a large number of Northerners. Those who know the city best believed that it would surrender when the forts defending it should fall. The mass of the permanent population is composed of intelligent men, and the commercial interests have always had a more clear idea of the folly of this rebellion than the people in the interior. At all events, after the forts alluded to fall, and the gunboats, which are not really formidable, are taken, New-Orleans is helpless—more helpless indeed than any other city can be.

THE NEWS IN WASHINGTON.

WASHINGTON, Sunday, April 27.

The city is wild with rejoicing to-night over the news of the advance of our gunboats upon New-Orleans, in spite of the resistance of Forts Jackson and Philip, and the probable surrender of that city from the vile clutches of rebeldom, and its return to loyalty and trade with all the world. New-Orleans is probably in possession of Gen. BUTLER at present writing. The President is in high glee over the news.

FROM ANOTHER CORRESPONDENT.

WASHINGTON, Sunday, April 27.

The news from New-Orleans, which has come through several rebel sources, is deemed here to be of the utmost importance.

What Old England failed to do with all her power, has been handsomely accomplished by New-England. The manner in which the success at Forts Jackson and St. Philip was followed up is highly commended. In thirty hours our brave men consummated their victory, and appeared before the great city of the southwest to receive its submission.

This is but a foretaste of southwestern operations.

No mention is made by the rebels of their iron-clad "turtles" and "rams" that were to annihilate the Yankee fleet; which leads to a suspicion that the common estimate of the rebel motive power from their own misrepresentations, has been a mistake. It is pretty clear that on this occasion they could not stop to conceal the truth.

THE CAPTURE OF NEW-ORLEANS BY THE BUTLER EXPEDITION.

Map Showing the Topography of New-Orleans and the Surrounding Country, with the Line of the Mississippi River from its Debouchure to the City.

IMPORTANT FROM SHIP ISLAND.

Activity in Military and Naval Movements—The Expected Attack on New-Orleans—Gen. Butler's Forces to go Through the Lakes, &c.

From the Boston Journal of Saturday Evening.

The ship *Black Prince*, Capt. HOWES, arrived here this morning, from Ship Island 6th inst., *via* Havana 15th, where she touched to convey Government dispatches to the United States Consul at that port. She also brings a large mail to this port.

Several transports had recently arrived at Ship Island. The ship *Parliament*, from Boston, reached there on the 4th inst., and landed all her horses in good order. The ship *Western Empire*, from Boston, was also as fortunate in carrying her freight of horses. The ships *Great Republic*, from Portland, and the *Eliza* and *Ella*, and bark *Wild Gazelle*, from Boston, had arrived out with stores, forage, &c. A large number of transports were left in port when the *Black Prince* sailed, and among them the steamer *Mississippi.*

Letters received by this arrival state that the health of the troops at the Island was very good. Capt. JOHN A. NELSON, of the Thirtieth Massachusetts Regiment, has been appointed Provost-Marshal by Gen. BUTLER.

At the time the *Black Prince* sailed, preparations were making for the attack on New-Orleans, and it was then expected that the attack would be made about the 14th inst. Nearly all the troops at Ship Island would participate. The steamers *Mississippi* and *Matanzas* were at the island, and might join in the expedition. The expedition to Pass Christian, which has been mentioned in the Southern papers, was undertaken by the Ninth Connecticut Regiment, Col. CAHILL. A small battery was captured and a Mississippi regiment driven out. A few of our men were wounded, but none killed. Nothing was known of the rebel loss.

A letter from Ship Island of the 3d of April mentions that the brigade of Gen. WILLIAMS had sailed for New-Orleans, and that the other brigades were expected to follow immediately. The rumor which we had several days ago of the capture of Fort Pike, between Lakes Borgne and Ponchartrain, is probably well founded. It was by this route that Gen. BUTLER expected to penetrate to New-Orleans, while the fleet reduced the forts on the river.

There was a great deal of dissatisfaction in the Twenty-sixth Regiment M. V. at the position assigned to it in the brigade. As one of the oldest regiments in the service, being recruited from the old Sixth, which was attacked in Baltimore, it was felt that a higher position was due to it than that of the fifth company. It was maintained, too, that Col. JONES was entitled to the appointment of Brigadier, and there were rumors that he would resign. But he effectually disposed of these reports and all disaffection by a speech at the end of a regimental review, in which he said that the Twenty-sixth and its officers had come out to fight the enemies of their country, and although their position might not be such as they desired, yet it was their duty to show in a humbler position that they were entitled to the advancement which they now thought was their due.

NEWS FROM FORTRESS MONROE.

The Galena Put in Fighting Trim—All Her Yards and Masts Taken Out—A Flag of Truce, &c.

FORTRESS MONROE, Saturday, April 26.

All the yards and lower masts of the *Galena* have been taken out, and nothing can be seen above deck but the smoke-stack.

A flag of truce to Craney Island to-day took up a number of letters for prisoners and others at the South, and also the Secretary of the Spanish Legation at Washington.

The weather is disagreeable. Wind northeast.

Harper's Weekly, on its arrival here this morning, was seized by Major JONES, on account of objectionable editorials and a map of the vicinity of Yorktown.

WOUNDED FROM PITTSBURGH LANDING.

PITTSBURGH, Penn., Sunday, April 27.

The steamers *Marengo* and *Hailman*, sent from this city to Pittsburgh Landing, returned to-day, with seventy wounded, who were placed in the Marine Hospital. The boats started with nearly 500, all of whom were left at points on the river near their homes. Among the wounded are two rebel prisoners.

THE SIEGE OF YORKTOWN.

Gallant Dash of a Company of Massachusetts Men.

Capture of one of the Rebel Works.

Fourteen Rebels Captured and the Work Destroyed.

Our Loss Four Killed and Twelve Wounded.

HEADQUARTERS OF THE ARMY OF THE POTOMAC, CAMP WINFIELD SCOTT, Saturday, April 26, 1862—11 A. M.

Hon. E. M. Stanton, Secretary of War:

Early this morning an advanced lunette of the rebels on this side of the Warwick, near its head, was carried by assault by Company H, First Massachusetts Regiment. The work had a ditch six feet deep, with a strong parapet, and was manned by two companies of infantry, no artillery.

Our men moved over open, soft ground, some six hundred yards, *received the fire of the rebels at fifty yards, did not return it, but rushed over the ditch and parapet in the most gallant manner.*

The rebels broke and ran as soon as they saw that our men intended to cross the parapet.

Our loss was three killed, and one mortally and twelve otherwise wounded. We took fourteen prisoners, destroyed the work sufficiently to render it useless, and retired.

The operation was conducted by Gen. C. GROVER, who managed the affair most handsomely. Nothing could have been better than the conduct of all the men under fire.

The supports, who were also under artillery fire of other works, were companies of the First and Eleventh Massachusetts.

In spite of the rain, our work progresses well.

(Signed) G. B. McCLELLAN, Maj.-Gen.

FROM THE CORRESPONDENT OF THE ASSOCIATED PRESS.

CAMP WINFIELD SCOTT, DEPARTMENT OF THE POTOMAC, Sunday, April 27.

During Friday the enemy constructed a rifle-pit in front of the lines of Gen. HAMILTON, with a view of picking off the men working our field-pieces, which had been posted in a position to prevent them from strengthening their works. At daylight, yesterday morning, three companies of the First Massachusetts Regiment, and two of the Eleventh, were sent out to endeavor to capture those who might occupy it by getting between them and their reserve. The result was in every way successful, with the loss of three killed and thirteen wounded. The number of the killed and wounded on the part of the rebels must have been equal, if not more, than ours. Fourteen of the enemy were taken prisoners, and brought to headquarters, and were, to-day, taken on board the prison boat *John R. Thompson.*

The following is the official list of killed and wounded, all belonging to Company H, First Massachusetts Regiment:

KILLED.—George P. Noyes, Wm. D. Smith and Walter B. Andrews.

WOUNDED.—Allen A. Kingsbury, mortally, Company H; George L. Stoddart, George H. Campbell, Wm. H. Montague, Thomas Crittick, Horace A. Simms, George H. Stone, Wm. H. Lane, O. C. Cooper, Wm. T. Wright, James W. Spooner, Wm. P. Hallocue, Thomas Archer.

The boat from Old Point, last night, brought up about twenty paymasters. Their arrival will be hailed with much joy by the troops.

Paymaster CAMERON was attacked with congestion of the brain yesterday on the way up from Fort Monroe. He is better to-day.

About 10 o'clock to-day the enemy opened a brisk fire on our men near York River, without doing any damage.

One of the gunboats shelled the rebel works near Yorktown this afternoon for about an hour.

The enemy responded, but without doing any harm.

The rain has ceased, and everything indicates pleasant weather once more.

HEADQUARTERS, NEAR YORKTOWN, Saturday, April 26, VIA BALTIMORE, April 27.

It is still raining, making the roads next to impassable.

The rebels opened their battery at Yorktown, this morning, on three canalboats, while passing into Wormley's Creek. The nineteenth shot exploded in one of the boats, without injuring any one, when, apparently satisfied, they ceased.

Col. CROCKER and Maj. CASSADY, of the Ninety-third New-York Regiment, on Thursday afternoon passed through our outer pickets. Letters have been received from them to the effect that they are safe and well, and seemed to be much pleased with the cordial reception they received. The sentry told them he was the outer guard. The affair will undergo an investigation.

Everything is remarkably quiet.

OUR ARMY BEFORE YORKTOWN.

ACTIVITY OF THE REBELS—PREPARATIONS FOR THE SIEGE—INEFFECTUAL FIRING—A DRENCHING RAIN.

CAMP WINFIELD SCOTT, Near Yorktown, Va., Thursday, April 24, 1862.

Day and night the rebels continue to work on their intrenchments with the utmost vigor, and without suffering any serious molestation from our guns. Their miserable flag, which flaunted in proud defiance over a parapet on the day of our arrival, is less conspicuous to-day. The infantry and cavalry that our fire forced to precipitately retreat to the extreme rear of their works, are now assembled with additional numbers in the position which they previously occupied. Above the earthworks prancing steeds and active men, which two weeks ago cautiously avoided the least exposed situations, indicate a boldness engendered solely by our own philanthropic forbearance. Numerous rifle-pits, of sufficient depth to conceal from view the marksmen within, have been recently formed by the enemy, who have taken special care to remove the excavated earth, so that the ground at a safe distance may not have the appearance of an unbroken surface. The sound of the tattoo at night, and of the reveille at morn, is wafted to us from the rebel camps, and occasionally throughout the day lusty shouts and cheers emanating from the same quarter can be distinctly heard. The progress our own army has made in its preparations to annihilate the stronghold before it, including the intrenchments, rifle-pits and other barriers that have lately sprung up to increase the strength of that stronghold—to bring to a plebeian level the lofty arrogance that marks the bearing of rebellion leaders—to change the seeming exultant spirit of rebellion followers that vents itself in loud huzzas, to a real sentiment of feeling that cries, equally loud for clemency, your correspondent at present is denied the privilege of transmitting. The exigency of the occasion requires that the strictest silence should be observed upon all subjects connected with the movements of the army. It is not unreasonable to suppose that these movements are important; consequently the impatience of the public to be informed of their nature and extent may become doubly enhanced, but it is to be hoped that every patriot will admit that the injunction placed upon correspondence by Government is wise and opportune. As a fair exchange, the journalists here respectfully submit that their letters be allowed to pass through the mails without detention. If this course is adopted, a letter, when published, will be its own monitor, and the public will be served with the latest unprohibited news.

In referring to the movements of the army it may not be a breach of confidence to state that under the careful guidance of its able leader, all the preparations essential to meet and conquer a large opposing force have been made. When the siege is once commenced, it is presumed that facilities will be extended to furnish the public with particulars and events as they occur.

Within the past three days an exchange of two or three shots at intervals has become quite a common affair. At night we are not unfrequently awakened by the whiz and explosion of a rebel shell, which, passing over or through a wood, increases the reverberation, and gives one the impression that it was rather familiar, especially for the lateness of the hour. These outbursts of the enemy, however, are now getting to be generally regarded as a common nuisance, instead of a common danger, and the boys are often heard calling upon the Corporal of the guard to put under arrest the missile that falls within a few yards of their feet. Last week a daring, but reckless act was successfully accomplished by a private in the Seventeenth New-York Regiment, who, upon observing a shell strike quite near him, sprang forward with a pail of water and extinguished the ignited fuse. A sensation, if not a complete surprise, was given to a party of bathers the other day, by the descent of a 32-pounder in their very midst. After a brief consultation it was decided not to leave the pool until their ablutions had been performed. In the morning it is the usual practice of a regiment returning from picket duty to bring to their camp as trophies two or three shot or unexploded shells, which the enemy had volunteered to distribute among them the preceding night. A large variety of these projectiles have found their way to many of the brigade or division headquarters, where they attract considerable attention. It is a singular fact, not lightly to be commented upon, that so few casualties have occurred among our men during all the irregular and promiscuous firing of the enemy. It is true that dozens of their shells do not explode, but even in that case they are liable to have the same effect as a round shot; and bursting and falling as they do, above, among, and on every side of our regimental picket guard, it is almost inconceivable how they escape injury.

Another drenching rain has made the roads so fearfully deep with mire that passage across them is next to an impossibility.

Various absurd rumors, such as "the enemy evacuating Yorktown," "the fall of Richmond," the capture of rebel Generals," and other rumors of similar import, have been current to-day, but will probably be superseded before sundown by some startling fiction of tremendous magnitude. WHIT.

Another Letter from John Bright.

JOHN BRIGHT, M. P., has written to Mr. JAMES FORSYTH, of Troy, the following answer to a note from that gentleman under date of Feb. 24:

ROCHDALE, Thursday, April 10, 1862.

DEAR SIR: I write you a short note to thank you for your letter of the 24th of February last. It is a great gratification to me to know from many letters from the States, that my speech, to which you so kindly refer, has given so much satisfaction amongst your countrymen. It was spoken to your people as much as to ours, and I believe it has done good in both countries.

At this moment there is here the utmost tranquility in regard to American questions, and it is rare to find a man who professes sympathy for the South. My own clear opinion is, that an overwhelming majority of the English people would rejoice greatly at the complete success of your Government and the restoration of your Union. I hope this may soon be realized, and that you will not fail to fix an incurable wound in the grand evil which has been the one cause of your trouble.

We are interested in the proposition of the President to compensate the States which are willing to give up their slaves, and hope it may produce a good effect, though it is very difficult for men who have exercised an absolute authority over all about them to consent to give up their power. We are looking for tidings from Virginia, and from your great river, where events of the greatest moment are now taking place.

With many thanks for your very kind letter, believe me always with great respect, yours,

JOHN BRIGHT.

JAMES FORSYTH, Troy, U. S. A.

THE WAR IN THE SOUTHWEST.

Important from Gen. Halleck's Army.

Reported Engagement Between the Advance Guards.

OUR FORCES PUSHING FORWARD.

Beauregard Said to be Moving Troops to Memphis.

Indications of the Desperation of the Rebels.

ST. LOUIS, Saturday, April 26.

A special dispatch to the Missouri *Democrat*, dated Cairo to-day, says:

"*Passengers who reached here this morning on the steamer N. W. Thomas, which left Pittsburgh Landing Thursday night, bring the highly important intelligence that an engagement took place on Thursday, between the advance guards of the National and rebel armies; that the rebels were driven back towards Corinth, and that Gen. Halleck was pushing his whole army vigorously forward.*"

CHICAGO, Saturday, April 26.

A special dispatch from Cairo, to the *Journal*, says that a reconnoissance was made toward Corinth on Thursday, and when nine miles out they surprised a rebel camp, and advanced to Pea Ridge, within six miles of Corinth. They remained from 11 o'clock in the morning until 3 o'clock in the afternoon, but no signs of the enemy were seen.

Mr. STEVENSON, of Danville, Ill., who accompanied the reconnoissance, *heard the constant rattle of cars and sounding of steam whistles towards Memphis, and thus got the impression that the rebels were evacuating Corinth for Memphis.*

CHICAGO, Sunday, April 27.

A special from Cairo to the *Times* says:

"Passengers from Pittsburgh report that, on Thursday, over thirty deserters from the rebel army entered our camps, and begged to be enrolled among our troops. *They all corroborated the statement received the day before relating to the evacuation by the rebels of their present position, and asserted that Beauregard had withdrawn a considerable portion of his force for the defence of Memphis.*"

LATEST FROM PITTSBURGH LANDING.

CAIRO, Sunday, April 27.

The river is still rising, and in some places gradually making its way over the levée.

The steamer *McClellan*, from Pittsburgh Landing at 4 o'clock on Saturday, has arrived.

The rebels are inaugurating a system of guerilla warfare along the Tennessee River. Boats were fired on yesterday a short distance above Fort Henry.

Our army is steadily advancing toward Corinth. Gen. POPE'S Division is on the extreme left, four miles above Pittsburgh Landing.

A reconnoisance in force, on Thursday, encountered a large force of rebel infantry and cavalry eight miles from the Landing. The rebels formed in line of battle, and after firing one volley retreated in great disorder, with considerable loss. Fifty-nine prisoners were taken. The roads have been improving, but the rains on Friday rendered them again unpassable.

The *McClellan* brought down the body of Gen. C. F. SMITH.

The Memphis *Avalanche* of the 23d says that a raft, upon which was a large field piece, and a 13-inch mortar, and sixteen of our men, was captured by the rebels, near Fort Wright, and taken down the river. It still insists that the Battle of Shiloh was a rebel victory.

Gens. BUELL and BEAUREGARD had effected arrangements for an exchange of wounded prisoners.

Passengers by the *McClellan bring further accounts of Corinth being evacuated by the rebels, who will make their next stand at Columbus, Miss.*

Col. TURCHIN'S Brigade had moved back from Tuscumbia to Huntsville, where Gen. MITCHEL is encamped.

DEATH OF MAJ.-GEN. SMITH.

PITTSBURGH LANDING, Friday, April 25, *via* LOUISVILLE, Saturday, April 26.

Maj.-Gen. C. F. SMITH died at Savanna, Tenn., at 4 o'clock this afternoon, of dysentery. He was taken sick shortly after the occupation of Savanna by the forces under him, and has been suffering and sinking slowly for some weeks, though his condition was not thought to be dangerous until the past week. His family have been notified of his death, and are on their way to Savanna.

REPORT OF GEN. HALLECK.

PITTSBURGH LANDING, April 27.

Hon. E. M. Stanton, Secretary of War:

Major-Gen. C. F. SMITH died at 4 o'clock, P. M., on the 25th. His remains have been sent to St. Louis, where they will be buried with military honors. He is a great loss to this army. I have not directed military honors to be paid to his memory here, but wait your order.

The enemy has been strongly reinforced since the last battle. H. W. HALLECK, Major-General.

OFFICIAL WAR BULLETIN.

WAR DEPARTMENT, April 27.

Order directing military honors to be paid to the memory of Major-Gen. C. F. SMITH.

This Department has learned, with deep regret, that the gallant Major-Gen. C. F. SMITH, whose patriotic valor and military skill were signally exhibited at the capture of Fort Donelson, died at Savanna, in Tennessee, at the hour of 4 o'clock P. M., on the 25th of this month, and it is ordered that the customary honors be paid to his memory.

EDWIN M. STANTON.

IMPORTANT REPORTS FROM MEMPHIS.

CHICAGO, Sunday, April 27.

The Memphis *Avalanche* of the 24d says, that on the 11th eighty Federal cavalry *took possession of Pocahontas, Ark.*

"There are 10,000 Federal troops at Doniphan, Mo."

[*Continued on Eighth Page.*]

The Charleston Mercury.

DAILY PAPER—TEN DOLLARS PER ANNUM, PAYABLE HALF-YEARLY IN ADVANCE. | VINDICE BELLO — SPONTE SUA SINE LEGE FIDES RECTUMQUE COLENTUR. | COUNTRY PAPER—THREE A WEEK—FIVE DOLLARS PER ANNUM, IN ADVANCE.

VOLUME LXXX. | CHARLESTON, S. C., WEDNESDAY, APRIL 30, 1862. | NUMBER 11,435

THE MERCURY.

WEDNESDAY, APRIL 30, 1862.

Is Charleston to be Saved?

Charleston is not difficult of defence against land attacks. So long as we have the rivers and harbor, a respectable force can hold it against heavy odds, and concentration is easy. General LEE is said to have expressed the opinion that the field-works thrown up for its defence were strong to an extent almost ridiculous. But of what avail are field fortifications while the city is exposed to the ingress of iron-clad gunboats by the water approach. So long as the entrance to our roadstead is unobstructed, the labors on land, however well directed, are labors thrown away, or expended for the benefit of the enemy. Charleston can be saved but in one way, and that is by keeping the Yankee fleet out of our water approach. We believe that the harbor can be efficiently obstructed, and that within a short time—time enough to save it from water attack. JOHNSTON and BEAUREGARD may employ their land forces, and the malaria of our summer will co-operate in preventing an attack by land, for some time, at least.

But to save Charleston from the gunboats, energy is necessary on the part of our State authorities and our citizens. The task is one of great magnitude, requiring a large force of hands, and great courage and zeal in the expenditure of labor. Gen. RIPLEY has performed an immense amount of efficient work within his military district. He has contended with great difficulties in the obtainment of sufficient force. He has stretched his authority to the utmost in helping himself, when others should have supplied him. He has been employed on labors not so vital as the harbor defences; and, unless he receives at once the force needed, and is put in the way of obstructing the harbor, Charleston will, in all probability, fall. He has done all that a man could do to get at this work long since. He has not had the opportunity. It is now late, but we trust not yet too late.

Our people and the State authorities must make up their minds either to throw the ordnance of our Forts into the sea, and blow them up, evacuating Charleston to the enemy, or they must see that our harbor is obstructed and Fort Sumter secured from Parrott guns on Morris Island. The time has fully come to face this alternative, and the sooner we get to a conclusion the better. Croakers are a useless class. We repeat that, in our opinion, Charleston can probably be saved by prompt and untiring energy.

THE NEWS OF THE WAR.

THE FALL OF NEW ORLEANS.

The Richmond papers of Monday throw but little light on the capture of New Orleans. The *Examiner* surmises as to the direction General LOVELL will take. On the supposition that he will join General BEAUREGARD at Corinth, it is calculated that an immediate action will occur there, or that an attempt will be made there at once to move the forces under BEAUREGARD eastward. The situation is said to admit of no other alternative.

The loss of the great cattle country of Texas is accounted as not the least disastrous result of the ill-timed fall of New Orleans; and some appreciation of this loss may be made when it is known that droves of cattle to the amount of more than two hundred thousand head were being driven through to New Orleans at the time of its unexpected capture by the Yankees.

It is understood that the subsistence of its armies in the field is likely to be a question of immediate concern to the government. Much of the cattle country in Virginia is already in the hands of the enemy, and the *Examiner* thinks that a sudden concentration of our forces in Virginia or to the eastward is among the measures contemplated by the Government.

The Richmond *Enquirer*, (government organ,) in commenting upon the event, says:

We need not say that this is an unexpected and heavy blow. The Confederacy had been plied with emphatic and continued assurances from New Orleans, that the defences of that city were complete and impregnable. They had had a long time for preparation, and we were assured that the time was diligently improved. Forts and shore batteries, we were told, lined the river bank, rendering it impossible for the enemy to ascend. And if these were not sufficient, iron-clad steamers of giant proportions and impenetrable mail, floated in the channel, ready to demolish every opponent. A large and well-appointed army was there to resist a land attack. In short, those who had most at stake and who should have been hardest to please,—we mean the citizens of New Orleans and the officers entrusted with its defence,—united in confidence and daily assurance that New Orleans was perfectly secure. And yet New Orleans has fallen!

It remains to be told why it was that all these preparations and assurances proved fallacious.—It remains for the government to hold stern inquest into all the circumstances of this deplorably calamity. The occasion demands it, and demands that negligence and incapacity, wherever they may attach, shall be summarily punished or prescribed. They have brought upon us a heavy misfortune, and sternly must they answer it.

This disaster must not dishearten us, and must not enfeeble our efforts. On the contrary, we must redouble our exertions and we must redeem the fortunes of the war! What we have lost at New Orleans, must be regained elsewhere. We must strike with renewed zeal, for we have increased necessity. We must and will win the fight. There is no alternative but utter ruin and eternal infamy. Deliberately and under solemn conviction we say it, far better would it be for every man, woman and child that stands on Southern soil, to go beneath the sod, than under the yoke of the rapacious and brutal North. We most carry on this war, therefore, if with diminished advantages, at least with renewed energy! The Mississippi and its banks, may temporarily pass out of our control. Our States, East and West, may thereby have to wage separate fight; but yet it will be the same fight. A blow struck in Missouri will be felt in Virginia. A blow in Carolina or Virginia, or Kentucky, will be felt in Missouri. Then let every brave man, whether East or West, nerve his arm for new exertions; and may the soul of every citizen thrill with the courage which makes the hero, and prepares for glorious deeds.

We have but small room to profit, so far as naval operations are concerned, by the disaster at New Orleans; for we have but little water left us in possession. The ports of a few cities, on the Atlantic coast, are all that we now have to defend. But surely we shall hereafter be better able to judge of the strength of our defences, and of what is required, than we have just proven ourselves. Men who have been considered as conjoining eminent professional skill with great practical sense, have deceived themselves and the country at New Orleans. No such confidence can be felt again, as to other points. And it is well,—for the distrust will cause a careful examination of our remaining water defences. Norfolk will, doubtless, be the next aim of the enemy's naval operations. If that be lost we shall have to close our Navy Department, until, on land, we shall have won back our waters.

One effect of the fall of New Orleans will be to liberate, for more active operations, the large army which has been stationed there for its defence. Thirty thousand men have been compelled to stand by and see a great city taken by comparative hundreds, because they could not reach them. But if joined to Beauregard, they shall enable him to overpower Buell and redeem Tennessee and Kentucky, who shall say that we have not gained more than we have lost?

The past shows that however unpropitious fortune has proved to us on water, we can triumph on land. Let us increase our exertions there.—Let our generals and government realize, as they must and will, the necessity that is upon us for a daring, brilliant, energectic, skillful campaign that shall cause us to forget our past misfortunes in our future rejoicings. Let us have *diligence* among our officers, in the place of foolish boastings; and a healthy distrust of the completeness of our defences which shall inspire constant vigilance, in the place of that insane self confidence, in itself disgraceful, and which has been the source of so many humiliations. And no man must stand for a day in the way of the cause, We trust that the President will always, and without a moments' hesitation, and in disregard of interested clamor, dismiss or supersede any man who shows himself indolent or incapable, and will fill his place with a man of better promise. The country is in an exigency and needs her best men to lead her bravest men!

REPORTS FROM MEMPHIS.

The correspondent of the Savannah *Republican*, writing from Memphis, on the 17th instant, says:

The military authorities have allowed but little to transpire respecting affairs at Fort Pillow, lest it should reach the enemy below New Orleans, and influence his movements. For the same reason, we hear but little here of what is transpiring at New Orleans. According to our latest accounts, the Federals were still trying to gain the rear of Fort Pillow by way of Forked Deer River, but they had not met with much success, owing to the shallowness of the stream and the immense amount of drift wood a few miles above the mouth. The bombardment of the fort was still kept up.

It is probable that the estimates of our killed and wounded during the battle of Shiloh have been too small. The returns come in slowly; but such as have been received would indicate that our total loss cannot be much, if any, less than 4,000. This includes many whose wounds were very slight, and who have not gone to the rear on account of their injuries. Of the entire number wounded, it would be no exaggeration to say, that at least 1,500 of them have been on their feet all the time. The timber afforded very great protection, and our troops were sharp enough to take advantage of it: otherwise, our casualties would have been much greater, and the wounds more fatal.

It is currently reported that Gen. Crittenden has resigned his position in the army. He and Gen. Carroll, of this city, were suspended from their commands just before the late battle, at the instance of Major General Hardee, in consequence of their intemperance; and it is supposed that Gen. Crittenden sent in his resignation in consequence of this proceeding. Gen. Carroll was attached to Gen. C.'s command. The whole country will approve of the course pursued by Gen. Hardee, while no sober man will regret that Crittenden has left the army. He is one of the cleverest men in the world, and no one questions his courage or loyalty, but his habits are such as to render him wholly unfit to command.

King Jeff the First. "Let them Burn! Let the Women and Children Suffer! I'm Bound to keep Warm!" (*Harper's Weekly*)

YANKEE OPERATIONS IN NORTH ALABAMA.

We get the following from the Mobile *Advertiser*:

We learn from gentlemen from the vicinity of Huntsville that the five thousand Yankees occupying that beautiful little city are carrying things with a high hand—and carrying off things with both hands. They plunder and destroy at will, and will probably get rich by thievery. One of their first performances was to go out to Gov. Chapman's place, in the neighborhood of the city, where they stole thirty mules, and, among other things, the carriage and horses of General L. P. Walker, in which they drove back to town in glee. A large number of persons have fled from the city, leaving their all at the mercy of the enemy, and what that mercy is they are showing. The notorious Judge George W. Lane—he whom Lincoln appointed Judge of the Northern District of Alabama about a year ago—is stated to be on most fraternal terms with the invaders, and to employ himself in pointing out to them persons who are unmitigated rebels.

The enemy are securing considerable cotton by means of threats to the planters should they burn it. Quite a number had burned their cotton, and some of these had been captured.

The Yankee forces are spreading through the country in the neighborhood of Tuscumbia, which is in their possession; but they are closely observed by Colonel Helm's Kentucky cavalry. A skirmish occurred a few days since between a party of these and some Yankees within the limits of the town. There were twenty-one of our men, only four of whom showed themselves. The enemy, after five of their number were killed, fell back, with the intention of drawing our men into an ambush, but they were too shrewd for them. We understand that the bridge at Florence was burned by our men.

General Kirby Smith, at last accounts, was in Knoxville, superintending certain shipments, and is now at Bridgeport, Ala., where he is concentrating a large force for early action. General Humphrey Marshall is in a position to aid General Smith in his endeavors to prevent the junction of Fremont's forces with those of Buell.

A correspondent of a Northern paper writes:

Our readers have been considerably exercised concerning the whereabouts of the division of the army under Gen. Mitchell. He has been heard from at Inka, Miss. It will be recollected that he left Nashville and proceeded southward, by way of Murfreesboro', at the same time that Buell started across the country from Nashville to Columbia and Pittsburg. Nothing was heard from him for several weeks, outside of military at least. Yesterday intelligence was brought that he had arrived at Decatur, at the head of Muscle Shoals, forty-four miles by railroad above Tuscumbia, where there is a bridge across the Tennessee river, used by the Memphis and Charleston Railroad. Crossing this bridge to the western side of the river with his division, he burned the bridge, and thus destroyed the communication with Virginia, whence the rebels have for weeks past brought immense supplies and large numbers of troops. The bridge across Bear Creek had been previously destroyed by the gunboats Lexington and Tyler and a detachment of troops from this post; but the breaking off of the communication was necessarily but temporary, as the stream was comparitively an insignificant one, and could be easily spanned by a temporary structure, or, if necessary, forded.

The destruction of the Decatur bridge must be exceedingly annoying to the rebels, necessitating the employment of steamers and flat boats to ferry over their troops. A gentleman familiar with the region informs me that there are three steamers above the shoals, and any quantity of barges, so that the mere destruction of the bridge does not absolutely destroy communication.—Gen. Mitchell, to make his work altogether effectual, has torn up the railroad track as far as Iuka, which is 20 miles east of Corinth, near the Alabama line. From Decatur he proceeded to Florence, and destroyed the railroad bridge there. The wreck has been floating down the Tennessee for 24 hours, furnishing incontestible evidence of the thoroughness of its destruction.

Gen. Smith (Paducah Smith) is in command of the post at Savannah. He has been on the sick list for some time, and until quite recently has been considered convalescent. I understand to-day that his disease has taken an unfavorable turn, and that fears are entertained for his recovery.

The wounded are dying at Savannah at the rate of eight or ten a day.

A SPY HUNG.

RICHMOND, April 29.—TIMOTHY WEBSTER, the spy, convicted by Court Martial, was hung to-day at Camp Lee, near this city.

Sixteen Yankee soldiers, captured by some of Stonewall JACKSON'S men, and eight Unionists, arrived here this evening from the Valley.

FROM THE WEST.

MEMPHIS, April 28.—(*Despatch to Savannah Republican.*)—I give you below the condition of affairs at New Orleans, as obtained here from what is considered reliable sources:

The Federal gunboats passed up to New Orleans without reducing Forts Jackson and St. Philip. General LOVELL retired with the military and able-bodied men, after which the Mayor surrendered the city on a pledge that persons and property would be protected. The specie in the banks and the public property were all removed from the city. All the cotton in the city was burnt. General LOVELL is at Pass Manchoe, on Lake Ponchartrain. The ram *Louisiana*, and one gunboat, are at Fort Jackson; the rest are destroyed. The enemy lost several of their boats. General BEAUREGARD has issued orders for the destruction of all cotton within the enemy's reach.

The armies near Corinth are very active, and a battle is considered imminent at that point. The weather is good, and favorable to military operations. The bombardment of Fort Pillow continues, but with what result, has not transpired.

The New-York Times.

VOL. XI—NO. 3307. NEW-YORK, TUESDAY, APRIL 29, 1862. PRICE TWO CENTS.

THE CAPTURE OF NEW-ORLEANS.

The City Occupied by Our Forces.

Additional Particulars from Rebel Sources.

A PANIC THROUGHOUT THE SOUTH.

Preliminary Operations of Our Squadron in the Gulf.

The Entrance of Our Flotilla into the Mississippi Passes.

GREAT OBSTACLES OVERCOME.

Reconnoissance Toward the Rebel Forts.

FULL DETAILS OF THE EXPEDITION.

OUR DISPATCH FROM FORTRESS MONROE.

FORTRESS MONROE, Sunday, April 27, *Via* BALTIMORE, Monday, April 28.

Five contrabands left Portsmouth, opposite Norfolk, at 1 o'clock last night, and arrived here this morning. They bring several late papers and much valuable information. They are intelligent men, and give interesting accounts of affairs in the vicinity of Norfolk. They confirm the reported capture of New-Orleans by our forces, and state that much excitement prevails in the South regarding it.

I send extracts from the Richmond *Enquirer* of the 26th, in which the appearance of the National gunboats before New-Orleans is announced.

[The following telegram announcing the fall of New-Orleans was embodied in Gen. WOOL's dispatch published yesterday, but we reproduce it for the sake of completeness.—ED. TIMES.]

THE FALL OF NEW-ORLEANS.

From the Richmond Enquirer, April 26.

The following telegram from Mobile, dated April 25, was received in Richmond at 11 o'clock P. M.:

"The enemy passed Fort Jackson at 4 o'clock yesterday morning.

When the news reached New-Orleans the excitement was boundless. Martial law was put in full force, and business was completely suspended.

All the cotton and steamboats, excepting such as were necessary to transport coin, ammunition, etc., were destroyed. At 1 o'clock to-day, the operators bade us good-bye, saying that the enemy had appeared before the city, and this is the last we heard from the Crescent City.

This is all we know regarding the fall. Will send particulars as soon as they can be had."

EDITORIAL COMMENTS.

From the Richmond Enquirer, April 26.

Affairs are critical at New-Orleans. On Thursday, according to intelligence received here, two of the enemy's gunboats passed Fort Jackson, and commenced to make cautious observations in the river above. The same information stated that the *Louisiana*, the iron-clad battery, was in position to resist them.

On yesterday, there were reports that an additional number of the enemy's vessels had run by the forts. Telegraphic intercourse with the city of New-Orleans was very difficult, on account, it was stated, of the excitement prevailing there, which had caused a general interruption of business.

THE NEWS FULLY CONFIRMED.

The City of New-Orleans Occupied by the National Forces.

FORTRESS MONROE, April 28, 1862.

To Hon. E. M. Stanton:

News of the occupation of New-Orleans by our forces is confirmed to-day.

No further news. (Signed,)

JOHN E. WOOL, Major-General Com'g.

To the Associated Press:

A flag of truce to-day took dispatches and letters to prisoners. No papers were received.

The telegraph operators having left New-Orleans, there is no news from there. The operators attempted to return, but *found the city occupied by the National forces.*

There is no other news.

WASHINGTON, Monday, April 28.

The President has received a special dispatch, to-night, from a source altogether different from that through which the information came yesterday, of the fall of New-Orleans, confirming the same. The President thinks it is a mistake, however, in announcing the city as fallen. He says it fell when it went down with rebeldom, and that now it has risen.

IMPORTANT FROM THE GULF

Preparations for the Expedition Against New-Orleans.

Full Details of the Movements of the National Forces.

The United States steamer *Connecticut*, Commander WOODHULL, from the blockading squadron, arrived at this port yesterday, bringing the mails and about two hundred sick and wounded seamen, from the various ships of the blockading squadron. She has also several refugees from Texas, who were taken from Matamoras by the United States gunboat *Montgomery*.

The *Connecticut* left the Southwest Pass April 12. The ships of the expedition to New-Orleans were all inside the Passes, and were making preparations to move. They had their decks sanded, and were all ready for action. The crews of the ships along the coast are all in very good health.

The following are the passengers by the *Connecticut*:

Welsh, and about 100 sick and wounded seamen and soldiers.

The following are the names of the refugees.

Dr. E. Larned, Thos. McBride, Hy. Corning, Wm. Robertson, Martin Sharp, Timothy Cronin, Leon Tallmann.

LETTERS FROM OUR SPECIAL CORRESPONDENT.

OFF PILOT TOWN, Southwest Pass of the Mississippi, Saturday, March 29, 1862.

The destination of Commodore PORTER's mortar flotilla is no longer a secret. It is bound to the Crescent City. The bomb-schooners are now anchored within the Mississippi Passes, and the large naval fleet of Commodore FARRAGUT, which is to operate conjointly with them, is also here, or hovering along the coast not far away, in readiness for entering the river at the shortest notice.

I last wrote from Ship Island, just after the arrival there of the flotilla from Key West, when none but the leaders of the expedition knew how long we should tarry, nor whither our departure would take us. But there was no undue curiosity manifested. Seafaring men seem to be contented creatures, and Captains and crews settled themselves down to routine life, as though unceasing drills with mortar, cannon and small arms were the height of happiness. Without warning, however, on Saturday morning, the 15th inst., after the flotilla had been at Ship Island four days, a signal was made by the flag ship to get under weigh, and the signs of prompt obedience were immediately to be seen. Sails were unloosed, the windlasses were manned, and in twenty minutes the twenty-one vessels were bowling along with a fair wind for Pass à l'Outre. As they swept from the roadstead, in a single line, equidistant, the beauty of the scene must have partially recompensed the soldiers on the sand island for their disappointment at the sudden departure. They had confidently hoped, poor fellows, that the advent of the flotilla augured a move for themselves from their dreary post, and their grief must have been poignant when the vessels, like spectres, disappeared from their sight.

The next morning the fleet was close to the uninviting mud-banks which mark the entrance to the Mississippi. But there was no wind, and the larger number of the vessels could not make headway against the current, which set them seaward again, and Tuesday morning dawned before they had reassembled. It has been evident from the beginning that Commodore PORTER does not wish to spend time in idleness. While awaiting the concentration of the fleet at Pass à l'Outre, he kept his flagship, the graceful *Harriet Lane*, which had preceded the flotilla from Ship Island, flitting about continually. Now, she generously caught hold of a helpless schooner and dragged her into line; and again, relaxing her man-of-war dignity, she would seize three of the little vixens and dash off with them up the river, as easily as a regular tugboat. After three days' labor, which was often interrupted by the densest of fogs, all the schooners were anchored within the Pass. This result was hastened by the arrival of the steamers *Clifton* and *Westfield*, both of which are gunboats attached to the expedition.

Meanwhile, the schooners had been making their warlike toilettes, and it was interesting to observe the rapidity with which the change was effected in their dress. The flotilla is divided into three divisions of seven vessels in each, and each division prepared itself for action at a given signal. Then you looked upon the little craft and saw the graceful rig and trim looks of pleasure yachts, and in a few moments more they would present the saucy mien of vessels of war. There is a spirit of friendly emulation, a healthy rivalry, existing in the flotilla with reference to rapidity in executing orders, and this manœuvre of metamorphosing the hound into the bulldog, afforded one of the best opportunities it has had for exhibition. The men were put to their trumps. In less than ten minutes after each division had been signalized to "house topmasts," the sails were stripped from the masts, the rigging cast loose, running gear unrove, and the spars upon the decks of every vessel. Some of the crews were three or four minutes ahead of the others, but all did more than well.

But with the "housing" of the topmasts, the work of preparation was not entirely done. The heavy standing rigging of the foremasts was brought in to the masts and "frapped" around them, the forebooms and gaffs were unshipped and secured with the topmasts on the outside of the vessels, in a manner which is likely to prevent accidents from splinters in case a shot should strike them, and the main decks were cleared of everything which could impede the rapid handling of the guns. These precautionary measures having been adopted, the fleet is now in fighting trim, fierce and formidable.

The stay at Pass à l'Outre was short. The hindmost vessels had scarcely taken position within the entrance, when another order was given to get under way. An opinion prevailed, naturally enough, that the flotilla was to pass up the river until it encountered rebel obstructions; but such was not the plan of procedure. Some of the vessels (as many as the steamers could manage) were taken in tow, and the rest, with a favorable wind, followed under sail. After reaching the head of the Passes, where the frigates *Hartford* and *Brooklyn*, with five or six gunboats, have stationed themselves as grim sentinels, the flotilla was directed down stream again, and is now anchored about four miles from the entrance of the Southwest Pass, opposite Pilottown.

This Pilottown is a hamlet of about a dozen houses, which, as the name signifies, was formerly the abiding place of the Mississippi pilots. Months since the rebel rulers in Louisiana made these people desert their homes, and the sole occupants of the place, until within a week or two, have been a family of Germans, who live by oystering and fishing, and who refused to obey the mandate which called upon them to relinquish their possessions. The town is located upon a mud bank, and consists of one street, which runs perhaps half a mile, along the margin of a bayou. The houses, one of which is of considerable size, and had been used as a hotel, are generally well constructed, and superior in every respect to what one might look for in such a locality. Each of them contains some of the heavier kind of household furniture, which could not be conveniently removed in the hurry of the proprietors' departure. But it is a very odd village. It is not founded upon a rock nor upon the sand, but upon the water. The buildings are supported upon piles, driven into the mud, and the Mississippi flows beneath them. There is but one promenade, a plank walk, a few feet wide, which also rests upon piles, and extends the length of the village. Some water is fenced in in front of each house, and some water is fenced in in the rear of each house, but for what purpose it is difficult to imagine, except that the inhabitants wished to delude passers-by into the belief that they owned flower and kitchen gardens. I can only think of one class of persons whom living here would please, and that is sportsmen of indolent propensities. They could sit at the upper-story windows, and pop away at canvas-back, widgeon, teal, and other waterfowl, which, at early morning, seek minnows and shrimp in these watery inclosures. During my visit to this aquatic region, I tried to find points of resemblance to the description of the deserted "Sweet Auburn," but was not successful in a solitary instance.

The town is now garrisoned by a squad of marines, under Lieut. HEISLER of the flag-ship *Hartford*, and the Stars and Stripes float once more from the staff on the pilot's look-out, where, before [illegible] times, the brave flag always floated. Commodore FARRAGUT has made the place a spar-yard, and the sheds and jetties at the easterly end are piled with spare booms, topmasts and other material, belonging to vessels-of-war, which would be in the way during a battle. In a fight, there is always more danger on ship-board from splinters than from all other causes, and it is fortunate that a convenient place has been found for storing the hamper from which they are produced.

The flotilla has now been here nearly two weeks, and there are no means of telling how much longer it may be delayed. Two causes, I am informed, hinder our advance. The first is, that all the gunboats have not arrived, and without their aid the dismantled schooners could not stem the current and get into line of battle; and the second, that all the steam vessels must replenish their coal-bunkers before they are ready for action. Tugs and colliers are hourly expected. Until they come, we must cultivate patience.

This detention, however, will not be without advantages. On the mortar vessels the crews in a great degree are novices in the use of guns of any description, and drilling is necessary. For the past few days the exercises of this kind have been almost incessant, and the men work with commendable zeal. Much of my time is passed on board the schooner *Para*, Capt. HOOD, (to whom I am indebted for many courtesies,) and in witnessing the drills the hours are relieved of much of the tediousness which would otherwise mark them. Capt. HOOD and his officers do much by their example in the way of instructing the men. A very animating scene is often presented when drilling is in progress simultaneously upon all the vessels, and the air is resonant again and again with sturdy cheering, which tells of victory over the imaginary foe.

But the drilling of the crew is not all that entertains me. There are a hundred little things in the daily routine of life on board a war-vessel which make time pass quickly to an interested observer. Listening to the strange and comical calling and piping of the boatswains is a perennial pleasure. They whistle shrilly through a silver pipe upon the slightest pretence, and follow usually with an order uttered in the hoarsest and harshest tones which vocal organs may make. The Captain of the *Para* wants his gig, and SIMPSON, the boatswain, gives a series of chirps and twitters, and then comes in measured cadence from the cavernous depths of his lungs a sound, which is interpreted "away, there, gigsmen, away!" He pipes for everything. There is piping to shorten sail, and piping to make sail; piping to wash clothes and to hang them up to dry; to quarters, and to dismiss from quarters; when a boat comes alongside, and when a boat leaves. But SIMPSON's most elaborate pipes are for dinner and liquor. Upon these occasions he fairly exhausts himself with his whistle, and it is with difficulty that he manages to jerk out the one word, "grub," or "grog," which follows. The "grog" call is made twice a day—at 8 A. M., and 12 M. It is thought so musical, that if we had an Ixion on board I am sure his wheel would stop, or a Sisyphus, his stone would cease rolling. At its sound all work is suspended, and the crew march up to the Master-at-Arms. This functionary has previously stationed himself upon deck with a few half-gill measures and a tub of whisky. As each man files along he receives a measure full of the liquor, which he drinks upon the spot. But these calls and growls of the boatswain are useful in spite of their comicality. His pipes can be heard far above the roaring of the sea and the howling of the wind, when lungs alone would be unable to make orders understood.

I had very nearly forgotten to mention that the gunboat *Owasco*, on her trip from Ship Island to the Passes, a few nights since, captured two rebel schooners, laden with cotton, which had run the blockade from New-Orleans. They were concealed under Chandeleur Island, Mississippi Sound, when discovered, and sought to elude detection by lowering their sails. Their names, I believe, are the *President* and *Eugenia*. Prize crews were sent on board, with orders to go to Key West. The sailors and officers of the prizes were distributed among the flotilla. I have conversed with some of them respecting matters at New-Orleans, but I do not place sufficient reliance in the statements to warrant me in repeating them.

Two sad accidents have occurred since the flotilla anchored here. EDWARD BARRY, of Boston, a hand on board the *Norfolk Packet*, while washing off the side of the vessel, fell into the water and was drowned; and a boat belonging to the *Maria J. Carlton*, attempting to go alongside the *T. A. Ward*, which was under way, was swamped, resulting in the loss of FRANCIS BIRD, the coxswain. Capt. JACK was in the boat when the casualty occurred, and he, as well as the five oarsmen, had a narrow escape from drowning.

The following is a list of the vessels comprising the mortar fleet, with their commanders:

FIRST DIVISION—LIEUT. WATSON SMITH, COMMANDING.

No. 1. Schooner *Norfolk Packet*, Watson Smith, Lieutenant Commanding.
No. 2. Schooner *Arletta*, Acting Master Thomas E. Smith.
No. 3. Schooner *Sophronia*, Acting Master John A. Darling.
No. 4. Schooner *Para*, Acting Master Geo. N. Hood.
No. 5. Schooner *C. P. Williams*, Acting Master Amos R. Langthorn.
No. 6. Schooner *William Bacon*, Acting Master Wm. P. Rogers.
No. 7. Schooner *Oliver H. Lee*, Acting Master Washington Godfrey.

SECOND DIVISION—LIEUT. WALTER W. QUEEN, COMMANDING.

No. 8. Schooner *S. A. Ward*, Walter W. Queen, Lieutenant Commanding.
No. 9. Schooner *Adolph Hugel*, Acting Master Hollis B. Jenks.
No. 10. Schooner *Mathew Vasser*, Acting Master Hugh H. Savage.
No. 11. Schooner *George Mangham*, Acting Master John Collins.
No. 12. Schooner *Maria J. Carlton*, Acting Master Chas. E. Jack.
No. 13. Schooner *Sydney C. Jones*, Acting Master Robert Adams.
No. 14. Schooner *Orvetta*, Acting Master Francis E. Blanchard.

THIRD DIVISION—R. R. BREEZE, LIEUTENANT COMMANDING.

No. 15. Barkentine *Horace Beales*, R. R. Breeze, Lieutenant Commanding.
No. 16. Schooner *John Griffith*, Acting Master Henry Brown.
No. 17. Schooner *Racer*, Acting Master Alvin Phinney.
No. 18. Schooner *Sarah Bruin*, Acting Master Abraham Christian.
No. 19. Schooner *Henry James*, Acting Master Lewis Pennington.
No. 20. Schooner *Dan. Smith*, Acting Master Geo. W. Brown.
No. 21. Brig *Sea Foam*, Acting Master Henry E. Williams.

OFF PILOTTOWN, S. W. PASS OF THE MISSISSIPPI RIVER, Wednesday, April 2, 1862.

Only those who have spent three weeks as we have, in strict isolation from the world, can understand how profound was the feeling of joy which yesterday afternoon pulsated through every heart in the Western Gulf Squadron, at the announcement that the steamer *Connecticut*, with mails from home, was off the bar. She had been expected several days earlier, and the anxiety to receive her news had been greater than usual, in consequence of our latest advices, papers of the 5th of March, having left affairs in that interesting state which augured the quick approach of important movements. We are now in a measure relieved of this tantalizing suspense. For, although the mails have not yet been distributed, the substance of the news has passed from mouth to mouth until all have heard it, and await with keener zest the delivery of the newspapers containing the particular accounts. I have not yet been able to ascertain what are the latest dates brought down, but I shall long remember the eagerness with which I glanced through a well-worn copy of the TIMES of the 10th ultimo, giving the news of the disastrous attack upon our vessels in Hampton Roads by the *Merrimac*, and the gallant fighting of the *Monitor*. I was not able to retain the paper long enough to inform myself respecting the evacuation of Manassas, and the proposal before Congress of gradual emancipation of the slaves, but had to be satisfied with the bare fact that such was the news. To-day, if the mail shall have been distributed, I will know all.

This matter of distributing mails in the navy causes much complaint. There seems to be no system about it, and often letters or newspapers remain for weeks within a stone's throw of their destination before being delivered. The most flagrant instance of carelessness of this kind was made known a day or two since. The gunboat *Owasco*, on leaving New-York early in February, brought with her a mail for the fleet. Most of it should have been distributed at Key West six weeks ago, but those to whom the bags were intrusted stowed them away in the vessel's sail-room, where they remained forgotten until last week. Even then they were found by accident. But a truce to grumbling, if I would send the news.

Five weeks since, when I attached myself to the mortar flotilla, its destination was a secret which I made no effort to learn. I determined to follow wherever it went, leaving time to make its developments. In a previous letter I have said that we are bound to New-Orleans. Now, I have to furnish information respecting the forces which are to operate with us. The glory of the achievement is not to rest entirely upon us. It has to be shared with a large and powerful squadron of war vessels under Commodore FARRAGUT, to whose general control the conduct of operations is confided. But the mortar fleet still holds its position as the main stay and prominent feature of the expedition.

During the three weeks that I have been at the Passes, the time has been exclusively devoted to preparing for the attack upon the rebel strongholds, with whose reduction rebellion will have been annihilated. Forts St. Philip and Jackson are nearly opposite each other, about thirty miles from the entrance of the river, and seventeen from the Head of the Passes, where our advanced vessels are anchored. Both these works were unfinished when the rebellion commenced, but the rebels have since had ample time to strengthen them, and they have not failed to render them as nearly impregnable as possible. Fort Jackson only has a tier of casemated guns. All the others are mounted *en barbette*. As the river between the two forts is not more than 700 yards wide, an idea may be formed of the proximity at which the fighting will be done when the vessels attempt to pass up. Recent reconnoissances have determined that the rebels have probably 175 guns bearing upon the channel. Some of these are of heavy calibre, but nothing can long resist the force which will be brought to oppose them. There is always one advantage on the side of ships against forts. The former can concentrate their fire upon one object, and at the same time be so diffused themselves as to disconcert the garrison.

The names of the war-vessels here, exclusive of the mortar-flotilla, are as follows:

Hartford, flagship of Commodore FARRAGUT, steam-sloop, 22 guns, Commander RICHARD WAINWRIGHT.

Brooklyn, steam-sloop, 22 guns, Commander T. T. CRAVEN.

Richmond, steam-sloop, 22 guns, Commander ALDEN.

Pensacola, steam-sloop, 22 guns, Commander C. M. MORRIS.

Mississippi, side-wheel steamer, 16 guns, Commander SMITH.

Of gunboats, we have the *Iroquois*, Lieut.-Commanding DE CAMP; *Varuna*, BOGGS; *Oneida*, LEE; *Katahdin*, PREBLE; *Kennebec*, RUSSELL; *Kineo*, RANSOM; *Winona*, NICHOLS; *Wissahicon*, SMITH; *Pinola*, CROSBY; *Sciota*, DONALDSON; *Montgomery*, (side-wheel,) HUNTER.

In addition to these, we have attached to the mortar-flotilla, the *Harriet Lane*, (flag-ship of Commodore D. D. PORTER,) Lieut.-Commanding WAINWRIGHT; *Westfield*, Commander W. B. RENSHAW; *Clifton*, Lieut.-Commanding BALDWIN; *Owasco*, GUEST; *Miami*, HARRELL.

There are now expected daily the *Aroostook*, Lieut.-Commanding BEAUMONT; *Penobscot*, CLITZ; *Marblehead*, NICHOLSON; *Maratanzo*, side-wheel, ——; *Wachusett*, [illegible]; *Chocura*, PATTERSON, and *Dacotah*, Commander MCKINSTRY.

The *Iroquois*, *Wissahickon*, *Varuna* and *Oneida*, are first-class gunboats, very heavily armed. The others are vessels of the second class, each carrying one 11-inch pivot gun, two 24-pounder howitzers, and a 20-pounder rifled Parrot gun.

This is a terrible force to be arrayed against the recusant people of Louisiana; almost double the number of guns and vessels which Commodore DUPONT used so gloriously at Port Royal. But that was a pigmy affair in comparison with the gigantic character of the obstacles to be overcome here. Imagine the storm of destruction which these guns alone can raise, and then think of the fury which can be added to it when 21 mortars simultaneously hurl their missiles. Each mortar shell weighs 200 pounds, (the weight of a barrel of flour,) and five of these shells can be thrown from the entire fleet each minute. Their flight may be guaged with the utmost accuracy. Is it not right to believe that this weight of metal will prove irresistible? When the attack will be made cannot even be conjectured. Commodore FARRAGUT is determined not to move until all his vessels are here. The *Pensacola* and *Mississippi*, two of the largest, are aground on the bar, where they will remain until a heavy southwest gale comes to deepen the water.

The *Hartford* and *Brooklyn*, with from three to four gunboats, form the vanguard of the squadron. They are anchored at the Head of the Passes, in the very place where HOLLINS' ram last Summer bore down upon the *Richmond*, *Preble* and *Vincennes*. Four days since I went up as a guest of the officers of the gunboat *Kineo*, to visit this place. There is not so much to interest there as down at Pilottown. For a week or two a pleasant excitement was furnished by expecting a second call from HOLLINS, for whom a reception had been prepared. He, however, has not chosen to come, and our vessels, though unrelaxing in their vigilance, have almost given up the idea of his coming. Every day a little tug leaves the forts and comes within sight of our ships, but she is so fleet that our boats have no chance of getting her within range of their guns.

While I was at the Head of the Passes a reconnoissance was made in the gunboats *Kennebec* and *Wissahicon*, under the direction of Fleet Captain BELL. The vessels approached within two miles of the forts, and remained exposed to their fire for some minutes. The rebels have cut down the trees on the river banks, which obstructed the view. As soon as our vessels appeared Fort St. Philip opened fire upon them with two rifled guns, which are supposed to be each of 100-pound calibre. Twenty-five or thirty shots were fired, and a shell exploded within twenty yards of the *Kennebec*. She changed her position and another shell burst directly in her wake, showing that the rebels have practiced sufficiently to have the exact range of the channel. Below Fort St. Philip, and opposite a line of eight schooners, which are moored across the stream, is a small earthwork, probably protecting one end of a chain cable, which the schooners support. This obstruction will not prove formidable, however. We have ways of overcoming it. It is supposed that the vessels may be prepared as fire-ships, but preparations have been made to meet that contingency. There is a rumor that the enemy has secured quantities of heavy drift-wood, which is to be let loose upon our vessels with the force of an avalanche when they arrive opposite the forts. The only thing that gives color to the statement is the fact that very little drift-wood is seen floating down the stream. It is scarcely among the possibilities to hold drifting trees and heavy logs sufficiently long against the force of the current for such a purpose. If the plan were tried it would prove only a temporary obstruction, and none of our vessels except the two or three paddle-wheel steamers would suffer injury.

I observe that each of the large steam vessels belonging to the squadron has taken a very prudent course for protecting their machinery. Heavy chain cables have been securely bolted upon their sides, forming a perfect armor for that part of the ship in which the engine is located. Of course other measures have been taken for putting the vessels in fighting trim. Everything which is unserviceable during a fight has been removed and placed ashore at Pilottown. Thus denuded of their topmasts and other light hamper, they have an air of strength and massiveness, which is simply terrible.

I mentioned that the *Mississippi* and *Pensacola* were aground on the bar. They have been there more than a week attempting its passage. The armament of both has been removed, but neither has been lightened sufficiently to cross until the water becomes higher. Fogs down at the bar seem to be perennial, and impede operations greatly. The steamers *Clifton* and *Westfield* have both been at work upon the helpless vessels; but having exhausted coal, they have had to suspend operations.

The health of the entire squadron is excellent. The mortar captains, a jolly set of fellows, may become ill, however, if something is not done soon. They begin to fret at the lack of opportunity for ridding themselves of the large amount of superfluous energy with which they are imbued. H. J. W.

DISPATCHES TO THE GOVERNMENT.

Active Operations of the Fleet in the Gulf—The Affair at Pass Christian, &c.

WASHINGTON, Monday, April 28.

By the arrival of the steamship *Connecticut* at Hampton Roads on Saturday, the Navy Department has received dates from the Mississippi River to April 12, including dispatches from Flag-Officer FARRAGUT and Capt. PORTER of the bomb flotilla. At that time the steamships *Mississippi* and *Pensacola* were over the bar, and the flotilla moving to be in readiness to take their positions. It appears from these documents that while sailing from Ship Island to Pass a l'Outre, with the mortar flotilla, Lieut.-Commanding GUEST, in the *Owasco*, leading, the schooners at night chased and captured the two Confederate schooners *Eugenia* and *President*, loaded with cotton, and bound for Havana, they having escaped through Britain Island Passage.

The captain of the *Eugenia* was a noted blockade breaker. He was the commander of the *Miramon*, when she was captured. He gave his word of honor to Commodore MCKEAN to come out of Mobile after getting provisions, and leave our waters forever. He broke his word, and in the *Eugenia* has made several successful voyages.

According to information obtained from one of the prisoners, the soldiers would fight a little at Fort Jackson, but when that fell, "people in New-Orleans think the rich and big men would all clear out and leave the rest." Times are hard. There is no work excepting for carpenters, who get four dollars per day working on the gunboats. They are paid in Confederate notes, and in many stores these will not pass. There are five gunboats on the Lake, beside the two new ones not yet equipped, and a good many in the river. Some went up the river a short time ago, with the steam-ram and ten thousand men.

Capt. MORRIS reports the death of FREDERICK BETH, captain of the after guard, and NICHOLAS T. CONNOR, coxswain; also, the injuring of JAMES PAU, seaman, and Acting-Master JOHN D. ROBERTSON. The former sustained a contusion in the head; the latter a fracture of both bones of the left leg. The accident happened on board the *Pensacola* by the parting of a hawser.

Flag-officer FARRAGUT incloses a report from Acting-Master THOMAS PICKERING, to Lieut.-Commanding HUNTER, commanding steamer *Montgomery*, of the capture of the schooner *Columbia*, of Galveston, loaded with cotton, and bound to Jamaica. The expedition was attended with much danger. Those engaged in it not only encountered a heavy sea at night, but was fired upon from the fort at St. Louis Pass, Texas, a shot passing through the side of the launch. Owing to a strong flood tide and head wind, and the rebel's long roll having been beaten, the party from the *Montgomery* not being able to bring out the schooner with safety, destroyed her by fire.

The steamship *Hatteras* having captured the steamer *Wallis* off Ship Island, sold her to Gen. BUTLER for a transport vessel.

An expedition from the United States bark *Pursuit*, captured the rebel steamer *Florida*, which was lying about twenty miles above St. Andrew's Town. They succeeded in cutting her out, and on their way up the bay, also captured the sloop *Lafayette*, with fifteen bales of cotton on board. On the way down the expedition was induced, by a flag of truce, to send a boat ashore, when within gunshot distance there rose from the bushes a party of about thirty or forty men, and fired on the boat, killing one of the seamen and wounding several others.

Flag-officer FARRAGUT, under date of April 10, communicates reports made to him by Lieut.-Comdg. READ, of the steamer *New-London*, dated March 26 and April 5, of two engagements between his vessel and others and some rebel steamers. He says: "On the afternoon of the 2d instant, we left Ship Island in company with the United States steamer *J. P. Jackson* and the transport steamer *Henry Lewis*, with the Connecticut Ninth Volunteer Regiment on board, to coöperate with the army for the purpose of effecting a landing at Biloxi. The landing was made the evening of the same day, the *New-London* and *J. P. Jackson* anchoring off the town. The next day about 4½ P. M., the troops embarked, when all got under way, and embarked for Pass Christian, intending the following day to effect a landing at Pass Christian. At 10 P. M., having taken a favorable position for the night, we came to anchor. On the 4th of April at 4:40 A. M., three rebel steamers were discovered standing down to make an attack. The action was immediately begun by the *New-London*, *Jackson* and *Lewis* with the rebel steamers *Oregon*, *Pamlico* and *Carondelet*, and after its continuation about thirty minutes, the *Lewis* was withdrawn on account of the crowded stated of her decks, and the *New-London* and *Jackson* continued the fight for one hour and forty-five minutes, when the enemy withdrew, apparently much injured. About 9 A. M., the United States steamer *Hatteras* joined us, and being senior officer, took command, while the landing was being effected at Pass Christian. A rebel merchant steamer appeared to the eastward, and was immediately pursued by the *New-London* and *Jackson*. After a chase of one hour she was captured. She proved to be the rebel steamer *P. C. Wallis*, loaded with turpentine, resin and lime.

NEWS FROM FORTRESS MONROE.

Fears at Norfolk of an Attack by Burnside—Concentration of Rebel Troops at South Mills—The Rebel Steamer Merrimac Expected, &c.

FORTRESS MONROE, Sunday, April 27.

Contrabands inform me that the most intense excitement exists around Norfolk, and great fear is felt of an attack by BURNSIDE. Nearly all of the troops have been sent from Norfolk, Portsmouth and Suffolk, to South Mills, to repel any advance that BURNSIDE might make.

The current rumor around Norfolk was that the *Merrimac* would come out to-morrow and try to pass up York River, to destroy our shipping now there. They state that steel wedges have been prepared, with a view of boarding the *Monitor*, and tightening her turret so that it cannot revolve, and for cutting loose her sheathing. The *Merrimac's* prow, or cutter, is now twelve feet long, made of wrought iron, and steel-pointed.

The citizens are evidently becoming very uneasy, and many are leaving for more secure localities. It seemed to be generally conceded by every one, they say, that New-Orleans had fallen.

THE WAR IN THE SOUTHWEST.

Important from Gen. Halleck's Army.

The National and Rebel Pickets only Half a Mile Apart.

CAIRO, Monday, April 28.

The steamer *Estella*, from Pittsburgh Landing has arrived.

The army is still gradually advancing, but everything was quiet.

A reconnoissance on Friday discovered that the enemy were strongly posted at Pea Ridge, three miles beyond our line of pickets, but we did not advance to attack them.

There is news from Fort Pillow. The mortars still fire occasionally.

Refugees from Memphis report a strong Union feeling existing there, and that *the majority of the people are anxiously awaiting the arrival of our forces to take possession.* It was not believed that the city would be burned, but all the cotton, sugar and molasses will be destroyed.

VAN DORN, PRICE and JEFF. THOMPSON, were at Memphis with about 6,000 miserably clad troops. They remain there to drive the people into submission to the conscription act, which is being enforced.

Hundreds of the inhabitants are leaving daily to avoid impressment. Most of the twelve-months' men, whose term of service is about to expire *refuse to reënlist under any circumstances*, and are deserting in large numbers.

CHICAGO, Monday, April 28.

A special to the *Times* from Cairo to-day, says Pittsburgh advices of Sunday night say that the roads are improving, and preparations for the coming battle progressing speedily. *The pickets of the two armies are now only half a mile apart.*

There is much sickness among our troops, the result of fatigue and exposure and unhealthy climate.

Refugees report that Gen. VILLIPIGUE is still in command at Fort Wright, and has a force of six or eight thousand men. The guns from Fort Randolph have been taken there. A large number of negroes are constantly at work strengthening the fortifications.

There is a report, which is deemed reliable, that the gunboat fleet is coming up the river to attack our flotilla, and then will make a bold stroke for the possession of the Mississippi. On the reception of this report, a steamer was immediately dispatched to Island Number Ten, having on board gunners sufficient to man the batteries there.

Refugees report that a despotic censorship is enforced in all parts of the Southwest, and public prints dared to utter nothing derogatory to the Rebellion. They say that the Union men there are as *firm and loyal as ever, and rejoicing at the near approach of the Federal army.*

Union clubs meet nightly at Memphis, and are holding correspondence with similar clubs in nearly every large city of the South.

Gen. PRENTISS, and the other Federal prisoners, who had been at Memphis, *received marked attention from Union people.* He was taken to Tuscaloosa. Fort Harris, just above Memphis, has been overflowed by a crevasse, and much damage caused to the surrounding country.

The *Tribune's* Cairo dispatch says that rebel cavalry had appeared in considerable force on the river, twenty miles below Savanna, and a gunboat had been sent down the river to watch their movements. All the Tennessee River boats now carry brass pieces in their bows, and each side is also armed with a guard on the hurricane deck, to return any fire from guerrilla bands.

DEPARTMENT OF THE RAPPAHANNOCK.

Fredericksburgh Not Yet Occupied by our Forces—Large Rebel Force in the Vicinity—A Number of Prisoners Captured—Possibility of a Battle.

WASHINGTON, Monday, April 28.

I have just come in from Falmouth. Everything is as yet in *statu quo*. Fredericksburgh is not yet occupied by our troops. Yesterday the rebel pickets could be plainly seen on the hills a mile and a half back of the town. In company with another correspondent I spent the most of the day there, but the pickets didn't think us worth capturing. The sound of the church-going bell was not heard there, as two of the bells have been shipped to Richmond to be cast into cannon, and the other one is cracked.

The rebel cavalry descend into the town every night, and are rapidly forcing away the few Union men remaining. On Friday night they captured five of our soldiers who straggled over there. Gen. MCDOWELL, on his arrival at Falmouth on Monday, issued orders forbidding any visits to be interchanged between the shores, on any pretence whatever.

We have every reason to believe that the rebels are in force, not more than twelve miles from Fredericksburgh, and under command of Gen. SMITH. All accounts agree in estimating the number at between 10,000 and 15,000. No young men are to be seen at Fredericksburgh, all having gone with the Southern army.

Sixteen Confederate soldiers were brought in this evening from Fredericksburgh, members of different companies of the Ninth Virginia Cavalry. Five of them were surprised in their beds night before last by a squad of the First New-Jersey Cavalry, six miles beyond Fredericksburgh. Our cavalry were informed of their whereabouts by a negro, who swam the Rappahannock to give the information, and led our soldiers to the house by a mountain path, enabling them to avoid the rebel pickets. The prisoners are all young, intelligent and educated, claiming to be gentlemen as well as rebels, and they state that the whole regiment is composed of similar material. Five of the prisoners were taken in a store in Falmouth, where they had gone for shelter from the rain. The others are deserters, who state that they were part of the force that fought behind the barricades at Falmouth on Friday night. They belonged to a cavalry regiment, which was to be reorganized into artillery, for which reason they deserted. The prisoners taken against their will are sullen and uncommunicative, and refuse to state where the enemy is or in what force, but the others give all the information they can, freely. It seems pretty certain that the rebels have a considerable force not far from Fredericksburgh, and hoped to induce us to occupy the town with a regiment or two, that they might swoop down and capture it. The exploit which gave us the rebel prisoners was well planned on the part of the New-Jersey Cavalry, and boldly executed.

It is quite possible that a battle may soon occur near the Rappahannock, but it is equally possible and probable that everything will remain quiet for a month. C. H. W.

The Charleston Mercury.

DAILY PAPER—Ten Dollars per annum, payable half-yearly in advance. | VINDICO NULLO SPONTE SUA SINE LEGE FIDES RECTUMQUE COLENTUR. | COUNTRY PAPER—Three a Week—Five Dollars per annum, in advance.

VOLUME LXXX. CHARLESTON, S. C., MONDAY, MAY 5, 1862. NUMBER 11,439

THE MERCURY.

MONDAY, MAY 5, 1862.

The Capture of New Orleans.

We have been favored by an interview with an intelligent gentleman of character, who has just come from New Orleans, where he was at the time of its fall. From him we obtain the following particulars of the capture of the city:

The Yankee fleet consisted of seventy boats of various descriptions—gunboats, mortar boats, steam frigates, &c. The defence of New Orleans rested upon two forts, Jackson and St. Philip, a few inferior batteries above the forts, and a fleet of twenty boats, the strongest of which were the *McRae* (carrying seven 32-pounders and one 9 inch gun), and the *Manassas Ram*. The *Louisiana* (carrying eight large guns) was a complete failure. She had to be towed down the river and used as a floating battery, for the two large wheels working in the middle of the boat interfered with one another and rendered her unman-[illegible] [illegible] an old hulk roofed with iron. [illegible] fire was concentrated chiefly on [illegible] work was only a battered shell. [illegible] garrison were said to have [illegible] and fortitude. Three of the [illegible] said to have passed by without the knowledge of the forts. The river is about a mile wide, and covered with heavy fog at night. The naval engagement extended for some miles up the river. Exchanges of broadsides and collisions were continuous, until but one of the Confederate boats—a steam hulk with one gun—returned to the city, and was burned and turned adrift. A Galveston steamer sunk one of the best of the Yankee gunboats after running into her three times. She was soon sunk herself. The *McRae* was seen gallantly exchanging broadside for broadside with two double-bank frigates. She was commanded by Capt. TOM HUGER, of Charleston, and was sunk. Her commander is said to be in New Orleans, wounded, having saved his life in one of the small boats, it is supposed. The *Manassas*, commanded by Lieut. WARLEY, of South Carolina, disappeared, but it was not known whether she betook herself to one of the bayous, was captured or sunk. The conduct of the Confederate Navy was desperate in the gallantry and devotion displayed. But their fight was hopeless from the beginning. The great *Mississippi* steam ram had just been launched a few days, and would not have been ready to operate for forty days more. She was a propeller, with three screws and sixteen engines, to carry twenty guns of the largest calibre. Her projection, or ram, was twenty feet of solid timber, to be shod with an additional steel point. She was three times as large and powerful as the *Virginia*, floated beautifully, and was sea-going. All the naval officers who saw her say that she was the finest ship in the world, and it is confidently asserted by officers of high rank, that without a gun she could have destroyed the whole Yankee fleet. She was to have been ready by the 1st of February. The contractor was a M. TIFT, a brother-in-law of Mr. MALLORY. The woodwork was finished long ago, and there has been great anxiety and impatience about the dilatory manner of completing the iron work and machinery. The people of New Orleans and the surrounding country offered the Government and its agents all their mechanical resources and workmen. They were declined, until three days before the attack. Up to that time night work had not been put upon the boat. $100,000 bounty was, some time since, offered to the contractor to get it ready in time. Rewards were offered to others. LOVELL said, to the remonstrances of citizens, that his hands were tied, and that he could do no more than he was doing. Governor MOORE said that matters were going on well, and that the city was safe. He could do nothing. The citizens offered money and labor to fortify the levee between the city and the forts, but their offers were declined as unnecessary. Three days before the appearance of the Yankee ships at New Orleans, Governor MOORE quietly departed with his chief counsellors by way of the Carrollton Railroad, about dark, having a steamboat and picket of soldiers at that point. Anonymous letters probably caused it. Two days before the surrender of the city an excited crowd, prepared with a rope, appeared at

General Mansfield Lovell, who commanded New Orleans

the ship-yard in search of the contractor of the *Mississippi*. He was gone. The *Mississippi* was burned and sunk by the authorities.

Our informant states that there is a feeling of profound exasperation against the Administration and its agents. The people feel that they have been systematically trifled with and sacrificed. When the Yankee officers landed, five Sicilians, who cheered them, were shot down by the crowd. All who showed any signs of favor were knocked down as traitors. The feeling was intense. All the cotton was burned, and all the tobacco, except that claimed by the French Government. The sugar and molasses remains in the city, as private property, in immense quantities. Much, however, is on the plantations still; the crop being very large. Gen. LOVELL carried off, by railroad, the machinery of the workshops and iron mills, and all the rolling stock of the railroad. The machinery is important, and entitles him to credit. In preparation for the defence of the city he has either been permitted to do little, or has done little of his own accord. His forces are at a camp of instruction at Jackson, Mississippi, protecting the railroad where it crosses Pearl River. He is not expected to reinforce BEAUREGARD, except as a reserve corps. His forces are said to be about twenty thousand. Twelve thousand foreign denizens in New Orleans had organized to fight in defence of New Orleans, but declined going off to fight in the Confederate cause.

Recruits have been pouring in to General BEAUREGARD, who fully possesses the hearts and the confidence of the Western people. To the extent of his capacity of arming them, it is supposed he will have men. It is believed in New Orleans that his army numbers one hundred and twenty thousand, but many are sick from limestone water. There is a feeling of perfect certainty of defeating BUELL and HALLECK in a signal manner. Corinth is far enough from the gunboats to give opportunity for capturing or destroying them. Hence it has been selected as the battle field. General and troops are alike confident.

THE FALL OF NEW ORLEANS—FULL AND INTERESTING PARTICULARS.

We have some further accounts of the capture of New Orleans. The gunboats of the enemy suffered terribly in their attempt to pass Forts Jackson and St. Philip. The Confederate gunboat *Gen. Quitman* ran into one of them, and both sunk in a very few minutes, with all on board. The *McRae* also went down, firing her last broadside just as she was sinking beneath the waters. The Yankee boats which succeeded in getting up to the city bore honorable testimony of the spirit of our men and the accuracy of their aim. Some of them were completely riddled by our shot, and all were more or less damaged. They were not iron-clad, or did not appear to be. As the boats were coming up the river a crowd was collected on the levee, among whom was a small knot of traitors, who hurrahed for the Union. An immediate response to this demonstration was given by revolvers in the hands of the citizens, who fired into them, killing three and wounding six. The statement by Commodore FARRAGUT, that women and children were shot and killed, is a base fabrication. When the officer bearing the demand for the surrender of the city landed on the levee, he was greeted with a welcome and shake of the hand from a solitary individual. The officer passed on, but his friend soon after paid the penalty of his treason with his life. We transfer to our columns the full account of the fall of the city, as given in the *Delta*:

At the moment it was announced that the ships had passed the forts, it became evident to all reflecting persons that the city was defenceless.—Steps were then taken to render it a barren conquest. By order of the Governor and military authorities, all the Government munitions and stores were sent away. Such material of war as could not removed was destroyed. Orders were also issued to destroy all the cotton in this city. This was done. The troops under the command of Gen. Lovell were marched to the interior lines of the city—a few miles below, these lines would have been formidable against an army advancing by land; but the batteries near the river were quite weak and ineffective against the ships—especially in the present stage of the river—the high surface of the water enabling them completely to command the surrounding country. In the condition of affairs it was quite obvious that the enemy's fleet would meet with no serious obstacle in passing up the river. Accordingly it was announced at an early hour that they were coming. Their vessels came up slowly, as if feeling their way—the Hartford, the flag-ship of Com. Farragut, leading. Then followed the Brooklyn, the Richmond, and nine other ships, big and little. As these ships approached the batteries, about six or seven miles below the city, our artillerists opened upon them from both sides of the river, but as the guns were only 24's, they produced but little effect. The ships replied with several broadsides, which showed that they completely commanded our batteries. The batteries, though manned by unpracticed gunners, kept up the fire for some time, but with no effect, and under such discouraging circumstances as to render it an obvious policy to withdraw the gunners and the troops. The batteries were accordingly abandoned, and the troops were marched to the Jackson Railroad. In the meantime the hostile squadron steamed up the river. A terrible and melancholy spectacle was presented to the victorious ships. The whole levee, for miles, was wrapped in smoke, from the burning cotton and gun carriages, which the authorities had ordered to be consumed. In the river were many hulls of burning ships, the *debris* of our fleet and of the merchant vessels and steamers which contained cotton.

The squadron proceded up the river, the great multitude clustered on the levee looking on in disgust and horror at the dismal spectacle. As they passed a few shots were fired by some of our soldiers, but without orders. The ships did not reply, but proceeded slowly along our levee. A feeble cheer was raised on board of one of the ships, which was responded to by something like a cheer from a few persons in the crowd. The [illegible] such or not, drew upon the [illegible] were suspected of giving them, [illegible] or so of pistol shots, by which several persons were wounded. The squadron being advanced, the foremost ship as far as the Fourth District, came to an anchor—the ships to the number of thirteen taking up positions in front of the city so as to command the several streets. After remaining in this position for a half hour, a boat came ashore with two officers; one containing Captain Bayleis, second in command of the squadron, Capt. Farragut being flag officer, and a Lieutenant. These officers were greeted on touching the shore with the most uproarious huzzas for "Jeff. Davis and the South," and with the most threatening demonstrations. They had neglected to bring a flag of truce, and it was a proof of the good sense of even an infuriated multitude that they were allowed to land. They, however, proceeded under the protection of some gentlemen, who undertook to conduct them to the Mayor's office, in a drenching rain, followed by a furious and excited mob. Though no violence was offered to the officers, certain persons, who were suspected of favoring their flag and cause, were set upon with great fury and very roughly handled. On arriving at the City Hall, it required the intervention of several citizens to prevent violence being offered to the rash ambassador of an execrated dynasty and Government.

The Mayor received the Federal officers in his office, with proper dignity. Capt. Bayleis stated the purport of his mission. He had been sent by Capt. Farragut to demand the surrender of the city, and the elevation of the flag of the United State over the Custom House, the Postoffice, the Mint and the City Hall. The Mayor replied that he was not the military commander of the city, that he had no authority to surrender it, and would not do so, but that there was a military commander now in the city, and he would send for him, to receive and reply to the demand.

A messenger was dispatched to Gen. Lovell. In the interval a number of citizens who were present, got into conversation with the U. S. naval officers. The Lieutenant seemed to be a courteous, well behaved gentleman, who bore testimony with apparent earnestness to the vigor and valor of the defence of our forts, and was quite communicative. The senior officer was more reserved, but still more large in his professions of peaceful intents. It was difficult, however, for him to conceal the bitter sectional hate of a Massachusetts man against a true Southern community. In the course of the conversation, however, this officer remarked that Capt. Farragut deeply regretted to see the spirit of incendiarism

Admiral David G. Farragut, who commanded the New Orleans assault fleet

which prevailed in the city in the destruction of cotton and other things. The Mayor remarked that he differed with him; that the destruction was of our own property, and did not concern outsiders. Capt. Bayleis replied that it looked like biting off one's nose to spite his face. The Mayor replied that we had judged differently.

After a while Gen. Lovell arrived in front of the City Hall, and was greeted with loud cheers by the crowd outside. On entering the Mayor's office, Capt. Bayleis introduced himself as second in command of the United States squadron in front of the city. Gen. Lovell replied: "I am Gen. Lovell, of the Army of the Confederate States, commanding this Department." The officers then shook hands, and Capt. Bayleis stated his mission to demand the surrender of the city, and the elevation of the United States flag over the Custom House, Mint and Postoffice—adding that he was instructed by Capt. Farragut to state that he came to protect private property and personal rights, and especially not to interfere with the negro property.

Gen. Lovell replied that he would not surrender the city, nor allow it to be surrendered; that he was overpowered on the water by their superior squadron, but that he intended to fight them on land as long as he could muster a soldier; that he had marched all his armed men out of the city; that he had evacuated it; and if they desired to shell the town, destroying women and children, they could do so. That it was to avoid this he had marched his troops beyond the city limits, but that a large number even of the women of the city had begged him to remain, and defend the city even against shelling. He did not think he would be justified in doing so. He would, therefore, retire and leave the city authorities to pursue what course they should think proper.—Capt. Bayleis said that no such purpose was entertained by Capt. Farragut, reiterating the expression of his regret at the destruction of cotton. Gen. Lovell interrupted him by saying that it was done by his authority. Captain Bayleis said that he had no doubt that General Lovell had done his duty, and they were doing theirs. It was then concluded that Captain Bayleis and the other officers would return to their ships, that the Mayor would call the Council, and lay before it the demand of Captain Farragut. The officers requested to be protected in their return to their ships, and General Lovell directed Colonel Lovell and Major James to accompany them. The officers accordingly proceeded to the rear of the City Hall, where they took a cab and proceeded to the wharf.—During the interview an immense and excited crowd of people had congregated about the City Hall, who alternately hurrahed for Jeff. Davis, for General Lovell, and most vigorously grouned for "Lincoln and his squadron."

To calm this multitude, Pierre Soule addressed them in a few eloquent and effective words, counseling moderation, self-possession, fortitude and confidence in their cause, declaring that the honor of the Government and city was in safe hands, and that Gen. Lovell's answer to the demand to surrender was worthy of the commander of a brave people.

Gen. Lovell, on appearing on the steps, was also loudly cheered. He addressed the multitude in a short speech, declaring his purpose not to surrender the city, but to retire with his army and fight the Lincolnites, whom they could always whip on land. He briefly sketched his course in the preparation of the defence of the city. Had done all he could do with the means at his disposal. That he came here six months too late, and it was beyond his resources to contend successfully against the enemy's power on water.

He advised the citizens to bear themselves manfully, never to stoop or submit to the Lincoln domination, and to wait with patient fortitude for the deliverance from bondage which must soon come to them. The General then mounted his horse, and accompanied by his staff, rode to the Jackson Railroad, where he took the last car, having already sent his army ahead of him.

The New-York Times.

VOL. XI—NO. 3309. NEW-YORK, THURSDAY, MAY 1, 1862. PRICE TWO CENTS.

Editorials

The News from New-Orleans.

The news we receive from the rebels concerning New-Orleans is a remarkable medley, and the only fact that appears in it clear and certain is that the city is really in our possession. The fleet passed Fort Jackson just a week ago this morning, and by noon of next day it appeared before the Crescent City. A demand for the surrender of the city was immediately made by the commander of the naval squadron, which the rebel General refused to comply with; but immediately after his refusal, he and his forces evacuated the city, and fled northward by railroad, nearly a hundred miles. Commodore Farragut, instead of opening fire upon the rebellious city, then entered into a correspondence with the civil authorities, the result of which is not told; but the terms of the dispatch we give this morning, dated Mobile, Sunday, indicate that the city functionaries were trying to induce our naval commander to ask *them* to surrender the city; and the only thing they seemed to fear was that he would not renew his demand. It is said that "*he promised* the Mayor's Secretary, who visited the fleet by flag of truce, *that he would make a renewed demand* for the surrender of the city; but," alas! "he has not done so up to this hour, 5 o'clock" (Sunday.) That certainly looks exceedingly like a parallel to the authentic tale of Capt. Scott's coon, whose anxiety to avoid the bullets of the huntsman led him to invite himself down from the tree—a historical narrative, well known and much admired by all Orleanians. But if Commodore Farragut had not repeated his demand for a capitulation by 5 o'clock, it is probably he did so by 5½ o'clock; or, more likely still, the Mayor, waiving all needless ceremony in the matter, chivalrously took the initiative, and offered to give up what he knew he could not keep. For the Richmond papers, of Monday morning, definitely proclaimed to the startled rebels of the capital, and in the ears of Jeff. Davis himself, that "New-Orleans was in the possession of the enemy." The latest of our dispatches concerning the city is from Mobile, Monday, and that announces the evacuation of all the fortifications erected for the defence of New-Orleans on the lake in its rear—so that, from the battered forts, sixty miles below the city, to the point to which Lovell retreated, eighty miles above it, there was nowhere an enemy who offered any resistance. No mention is made in any of the dispatches of Gen. Ben. Butler, who was in chief command of the whole expedition, military and naval; and it is evident that he was not with the fleet when it appeared before the city, as, if he had been, the negotiations for capitulation would have been carried on by and with him, instead of Commodore Farragut. It is very likely that Farragut was waiting for his appearance from Friday, when the first demand for surrender was made, until Sunday night at five o'clock, when the second demand had not yet been sent to the anxious Mayor. It was understood, however, that Gen. Butler was to approach New-Orleans, with the Army of Occupation, by way of the Lakes, reduce the fortifications on their shores, and march to the possession of the City *via* the famous Shell Road; and this view is confirmed by our special dispatch from Washington this morning. If he reached his point of debarkation by Sunday or Monday of this week, however, as he must have done, he would find no hostile batteries or forts lining the shore, as the rebels themselves had destroyed them all; and the way would be clear for a triumphal march into the greatest city of rebeldom. By this route (*i. e.* by Lakes Borgne and Pontchartrain) our vessels could keep up free communication with the city; and if the forts on the Lower Mississippi were not reduced, they will now be cut off from supplies, and a speedy surrender is inevitable. They were only of value as defences to the city; and that being in our hands, it is better not to waste powder on their destruction, but to preserve as much of them as possible for our own uses. But we shall have authentic details concerning the whole affair before many days, as a steamer was doubtless dispatched North as soon as the work was completed. In the meantime, the rebel dispatches we already have, leave no doubt of the fact that our forces are in actual possession of the city.

The rebels, it would seem, propose making another stand—probably a "desperate stand"—for the defence of the capital of the State. Baton Rouge is 120 miles above New-Orleans, on the eastern bank of the river; and the rebel steamboats, at the lastest advices, were running with the rebel troops, stores and ordnance to Manchac, fifteen miles below that place, while the forces of Gen. Lovell were said to have fled to Tangapaho, which is within supporting distance of the capital, to its northeast. The rebel papers mentioned last Summer that Baton Rouge and Manchac had been strongly fortified, as an extra safeguard in case the fall of New-Orleans, that impossible event, should possibly happen. They hope here not only to defend the State Capital, but also to prevent the advance of our steamers into the rich cotton valley of the Red River. But, if all their gunboats that were not captured by us were burned by themselves, they must have a poor hope now of preserving the capital, or any part of the State, or of the Mississippi Valley. Gov. Moore, of Louisiana, will doubtless soon be added to the list of fugitive rebel Governors.

Prisoners of war as depicted by *Harper's Weekly*

The Legislative Address.

In other columns we give place to the manifesto addressed by the representatives of all parties in the State Legislature to their constituents. It recites a clear and comprehensive narrative of the events which have carried the country into the vortex of revolution, with the comment necessary to give a true interpretation to a history so pregnant with results, and so directly bearing upon the reorganization of party, and the future political condition of the country. The authors of this paper place the responsibility of the war, not directly upon the slaveholders, but upon the political leaders of the South, reluctant to part with the control of the National Administration. The election of Mr. Lincoln was the signal of rebellion, not because it endangered the interests of Slavery, but because it placed the Government in Northern hands, with the patronage needful to perpetuate the possession. Against the political leaders of the South, the address would have all the penalties of treason directed; it calls for a moderate scheme of confiscation applicable to the slaveholder, as a too willing accessory to rebellion, but has no punishment to urge against the ignorant and deluded rag-tag and bob-tail of Southern society, who have composed the heroic armies of the revolt. The Administration of Mr. Lincoln, both in its conduct of domestic and foreign affairs, meets with the entire approval of the signers. They find it their duty to support the President's plan of emancipation, the policy of abolishing Slavery in the District of Columbia, and in general to lend their cordial concurrence to the conservative line of conduct which Mr. Lincoln and his leading advisers have marked out for themselves. The restoration of the Union, the enforcement of the Constitution and laws, are the objects of the war. The President, in the view of these gentlemen, is laboring wisely and bravely to promote those objects, and the people of New-York are engaged to be his loyal and steadfast auxiliaries.

The value of the present movement can only be judged by reference to the antecedents of the persons who share in it. Twenty-one names are of Republicans, elected by a strictly partisan vote; forty-five are Republicans and twenty-two Democrats, elected on Union tickets; and one a Democrat chosen as such. Of twenty-nine Senators and Assemblymen, whose names are not affixed to the address, about one-third are said to have been absent from Albany at the time the declaration was determined upon and signed. A majority of the remainder were Republicans; the names of only nine Democrats, whether absent or dissenting, failing to appear at the foot of the document. This extraordinary concord amounts practically to unanimity. The obligations of party are thrown aside by the Legislature, in order that those of patriotism may be more perfectly assumed; and what is more to the purpose, and what must afford the President the heartiest satisfaction, is, that this able paper obviously represents the sentiments of nine-tenths of the population of New-York. In fact, no act of the Legislature more thoroughly expresses the will of its constituency than this timely, noble, and patriotic manifesto.

Rebel Treatment of our Fallen Soldiers.—The report of the Committee on the Conduct of the War, in reference to the atrocities perpetrated by the rebels upon the bodies of our soldiers who have fallen in battle shows, in its true colors, the character of the parties to the contest we are waging. By the rules of modern warfare the moment a man has fallen he is entitled to all the care that an enemy is able to bestow upon its soldiers similarly situated; and if death ensues, to all the rites of Christian sepulture. The rule is based upon the fact that modern wars are waged, not to wreak personal hate or vengeance, but to vindicate a principle or alleged necessity of State. The moment a soldier, from any cause, ceases to be a combatant, his person is respected, according to well-established and humane laws. It is only savages that burn at the stake; tear out and devour the heart of a victim, as the highest manifestation of infernal prowess and hate; display in ferocious triumph mutilated remains; convert skulls into goblets, human jaws into spurs for cavalry riders; or strip the flesh from the bones, to carve on the latter ghastly devices and mementoes of the fight. But many of these, and still greater outrages, are asserted by the present Committee to have been committed upon those of our soldiers who fell at Bull Run, and careful examination, it is stated, shows that in every important engagement gross outrages against humanity have been committed.

It should be remarked, however, that the report of the Committee confines itself to a general statement of results; and presents none of the evidence that led to the revolting conclusions arrived at. While, therefore, in the absence of actual testimony, we are willing to hold in abeyance all extreme opinions on this matter, it must still be confessed that there are many elements of Southern society and education that are calculated to give this barbarous *bent* to the Southern character. Slavery has begotten in the minds of the ruling caste a thorough contempt for the persons of the inferior one, and the same feeling of contempt is naturally transferred to whoever stands in hostile relations to it. Slavery surely tends to brutalize the mind, trampling as it does upon every sentiment of pity, humanity, or justice. We must remember, too, that the civilization of the South is a composite one, made up of Caucasian and African elements, and that it displays the very worst features in the natures of each—arrogance, imperiousness and brutality on one side, resulting from strength; and timidity, cunning, treachery and desire for revenge on the other, from a sense of weakness. Where two races come together, and in the most intimate of all relations, as the mixture of color shows, the higher falls much more than the inferior ascends. Southern character is composite like Southern society—infinitely boastful, vainglorious; full of dash, without endurance; treacherous, cunning, timid and revengeful. We must expect to see this civilization display its true character on every occasion. We stand aghast, but we can, at present do no more. The spectacle will not be forgotten and will sink deepinto the hearts of our people. It will be to the North an irresistible argument for the superiority of its own institutions, and of their value as the bases of our Government. It will not render us less humane, but will add infinitely to the value of our cause.

The New-York Times.

VOL. XI—NO. 3317. NEW-YORK, SATURDAY, MAY 10, 1862. PRICE TWO CENTS.

NEWS FROM FORTRESS MONROE.

Highly Important Movements in Progress.

Sewall's Point Shelled by our Vessels of War.

The Susquehannah, San Jacinto, Seminole, Dacotah, Monitor and Naugatuck Engaged.

Feeble Response of the Rebel Batteries.

APPEARANCE OF THE MERRIMAC.

Unsuccessful Attempts to Draw her into an Engagement.

GREAT PANIC AT NORFOLK.

Gen. Burnside Reported to be at Weldon, N. C.

PROBABLE SPEEDY FALL OF THE CITY.

DISPATCHES FROM FORTRESS MONROE.

FORTRESS MONROE, Thursday, May 8, via BALTIMORE, Friday, May 9.

Shortly before noon to-day, the *Monitor*, *Naugatuck*, *Seminole*, *Susquehannah*, *Dacotah* and *San Jacinto*, in the order in which they are named, steamed up towards Sewall's Point, Capt. LARDNER, of the *Susquehannah*, in command of the expedition. As soon as within range, fire was opened with shot and shell against Sewall's Point. Most of the shots were good ones. It was nearly half an hour before a reply was made from the Point. The Rip Raps next opened fire, and then the *Naugatuck* for the first time. Several shots were fired from the single gun on the extremity of the Point, when one from the *Monitor* struck in the vicinity, doubtless disabling the gun, as it has not fired since. The position of the *Monitor* was far in advance of the rest of the fleet and she continued in motion until within a mile or two of the Point, when considerable execution must have been done by her accurate firing. The *Naugatuck* kept in the back-ground, the range of her Parrot gun enabling her to do so. Sewall's Point battery replied briskly. The Rip Raps fired occasionally, and a continued fire was kept up from the gunboats. The affair was comparatively uninteresting from this point of view on account of the distance, so details cannot be given. At about 1 o'clock a black smoke was seen to arise, supposed to have been occasioned by combustible shells being thrown into the woods. It soon died away, however, and disappeared. Nothing more occurred until a little before 2 o'clock, when the firing was very feeble from the Point. The *Monitor* about this time returned from her advanced position and joined the fleet. In the distance nothing of her could be seen but a small square dot in the water. At 2¼ o'clock a very dense black smoke arose rapidly from the Point, caused, probably, by the burning of the rebel barracks or other buildings. At about 2½ o'clock the *Merrimac* made her appearance, when the fleet returned, with the exception of the *Monitor*. The *Merrimac* is still (5 o'clock) off the Point. The *Monitor* is ready to attack her. The *Seminole* has returned to the Lower Roads. There is no prospect of a fight at present—5½ o'clock. The *Monitor* has returned—the *Merrimac* is in the same position.

The crew of the steam tug which deserted from the enemy, report there is great excitement in Norfolk this morning; that *Gen. Burnside, with a large force, is within a few miles of Weldon*, and that the rebel troops are evacuating the city with all possible speed.

Sewall's and Pig Points, they say, are already abandoned, and preparations were making to destroy the Navy-yard and other public property.

A MORE DETAILED ACCOUNT.

BALTIMORE, Friday, May 9.

The special correspondent of the *American* sends the following, relative to affairs in Hampton Roads and the Peninsula;

FORTRESS MONROE, Thursday, May 8.

This has been a most stirring and exciting day at Old Point, and all are anticipating the early fall of Norfolk.

At 11 o'clock, the steamer *Naugatuck* was observed raising steam, and about 12 o'clock she moved out by the side of the *Monitor*, which vessel had also cleared her deck for action, taken down her awning and pipes and stood forth in full fighting trim.

11¾ *o'clock.*—The gunboat *Dacotah* has just moved up in line of battle, with two little batteries, followed by the sloop-of-war *Seminole* and the *San Jacinto*. The flag-ship *Minnesota* is also under steam.

12 *o'clock.*—The *Naugatuck* has moved up toward Elizabeth River, followed by the *Monitor* and *Dacotah* in line of battle. The *San Jacinto* follows slowly. Heavy firing can still be heard from the direction of James River, where, as you have already been informed by telegraph, the *Galena* and other gunboats have gone. The sidewheel steamer *Susquehannah* has just moved up, passing the *Seminole* and *San Jacinto*. In the meantime the *Dacotah*, *Monitor* and *Naugatuck* had reached the channel and taken a position off Sewall's Point, and the *Dacotah* fired a shot toward Craney Island. A second shot from the *Dacotah* struck the beach at Sewall's Point.

12:30 *o'clock.*—The *Susquehannah* moves up, and takes the lead of the *San Jacinto* and *Seminole*. No answer from either of the rebel forts, and the *Dacotah* and *Monitor* are steaming up Elizabeth River. The *Naugatuck* is lying off toward the mouth of the James River. Presently, the *Dacotah* and *Monitor* approach Craney Island and Sewall's Point. The *Dacotah* fires every few minutes alternately at Sewall's Point and Craney Island, the enemy making no reply, although all the balls reach their intended destination. The *Monitor* is now taking the lead, but has not fired. In the meantime the *Seminole* and *Susquehannah* open on Sewall's Point, and two shots are fired from the Point, the latter falling short of the *Monitor*, which is now a mile above the other vessels.

12:40 *o'clock.*—The rebels are firing rapidly from Sewall's Point, principally at the *Monitor*, while a continual succession of shells are being poured on the enemy from the *Susquehannah*, *Dacotah*, *Seminole* and *San Jacinto*, broadside after broadside. The Rip Raps also throw occasional shells into Sewall's Point.

12:50 *o'clock.*—The *Susquehannah*, *Dacotah*, *San Jacinto* and *Seminole* are pouring shells, and the *Monitor* threw her first two shells from a point full a mile and a half ahead of the other vessels. The guns from Sewall's Point fall short of the regular fleet, and many of them explode high in the air at half distance. The *Monitor* is still moving forward, firing an occasional shot; whilst the Rip Raps and a float, lying in line of battle, are still firing steady.

1 *o'clock P. M.*—The *Monitor* is now within a mile of Sewall's Point, moving slowly forward and firing. The enemy are also firing briskly from Sewall's Point at the *Monitor*, and shells are falling thickly around her. Craney Island is also joining in the fight, and has just thrown several shells at the *Monitor*, one of which exploded directly over her. The *Monitor* moved steadily forward, occasionally firing and receiving shells and shot from the rebel batteries with perfect indifference.

2 *o'clock, P. M.*—During the past hour there has been but little if any change in the progress of the bombardment. The *Monitor* has fallen back and lays alongside of the *Susquehannah*, probably for the purpose of communicating with her. The *Naugatuck* in the meantime, has been throwing shells into Pig Point, and the fleet have also thrown a number of shells in the same direction.

2¼ *P. M.*—The *Monitor* and *Dacotah* are moving along again slowly up the mouth of the Elizabeth River. A dense black smoke has commenced to rise from Sewall's Point, indicating that our incendiary shells thrown there have fired the barracks. The *Dacotah* continues to throw her shells directly into the Point, the explosions of which can be distinctly seen. The shells from the Point mostly fall short and splash along in the water or explode in the air, the constant changing in position of our vessels destroying the range of the rebel gunners. They are, however, making quite a determined fight from their works, giving our fleet almost shell for shell and shot for shot. Sewall's Point is almost enveloped in smoke from the constant explosion of shells and the smoke from its own guns, and the fire raging in the vicinity must make it a hot place for suffering humanity.

2:30 *P. M.*—The *Monitor* has laid out of action for nearly an hour. She is probably cooling her guns. Four larger vessels throw occasional shots, all of which appear to enter the works of the enemy, or explode within the woods beyond. The Rip Raps has also kept up a constant cross-fire, throwing a large number of shells in the rear of the Point batteries. The Rip Raps battery has the range of Sewall's Point perfectly.

2:45 *o'clock P. M.*—The rebel monster *Merrimac* now makes her appearance on the scene. She has just passed from behind Sewall's Point, and is running down slowly toward the National fleet. Her black hull can be seen moving slowly along shore, in front of Craney Island batteries. Simultaneously with the appearance of the *Merrimac*, the *Monitor* started up from behind the wooden vessels, and moved up to meet the enemy. Dense volumes of smoke ascend from the pipes of the *Merrimac*. The *Monitor*, with only a puff of white steam escaping, looks in the distance like an atom on the surface of water. The larger vessels have drawn aside and left. The *Monitor* and the *Naugatuck* are now in the approaching path of the *Merrimac*. The contestants are yet two miles apart.

3 *P. M.*—The *Minnesota* fires her signal gun, and the long roll is being beaten in the fort. The *Minnesota* is starting to come up from her anchorage below the fort. The vessels of the fleet had been lying quietly at anchor for the last half hour, when the signal from the flagship ordered them all to return. The *Susquehannah* led the way, followed by the *San Jacinto*, *Seminole*, *Dacotah*, and the *Monitor* bringing up the rear, all apparently using the greatest speed toward the fort.

To spectators this seemed rather mortifying, but as they moved down in line the *Monitor* was observed to halt and the *San Jacinto* and *Dacotah* also followed her example, leaving the *Susquehannah* and *Seminole* moving ahead. The four steamers and the *Monitor* having taken their positions, the *Merrimac* also halted, and the five vessels thus stood not more than a mile and a half apart, the *Merrimac* apparently not willing to come further down, and the *Monitor* unwilling to go further up. The *Minnesota* also steamed up in front of the fortress wharf, followed slowly by the *Vanderbilt*, when both stopped. After laying in this position the *Minnesota* turned round and steamed back, and the *Vanderbilt*, without turning, backed water slowly down the river. Whilst all this manœuvering was going on, firing had entirely ceased from all points.

3:40 *P. M.*—The *Merrimac* now turns round and steams back toward Norfolk, with her rebel flag flying impudently. The Baltimore steamer *Georgiana* has laid out in the stream with steam up all the afternoon, ready to escape from danger at the earliest moment. The *Minnesota* and *Vanderbilt* have gone back to their anchorage. The *Dacotah* again proceeded up toward the *Merrimac*, and the monster starts toward the mouth of Elizabeth River. The *Dacotah* is now within easy range of Sewall's Point, but the batteries there do not open on her. She and the *Monitor* have both stopped, and the *Merrimac* is lying stationary about a mile in advance of the Craney Island batteries. (Here commenced an important movement, which cannot be made public just yet.)

The *Vanderbilt* and *Arago* have now steamed up in front of the wharf, and have again halted.

The *Merrimac* has run back under the guns of Craney Island, and the *Monitor* is steaming off toward her, at full speed.

The *Minnesota* is also coming up again at full speed, the effort being to draw the rebels out again.

4:45 *P. M.*—For the past hour the fleet has been moving back and forward, but the *Merrimac* still lies under the guns of Craney Island.

The *Monitor* is lying about a mile and a half from the *Merrimac*, and the *Dacotah*, *Susquehannah* and *Seminole* are still in the rear. The *Naugatuck* is also moving up toward the *Monitor*.

The *Minnesota*, *Arago* and *Vanderbilt* have gone back to their anchorage, and there is no prospect of a fight to-night.

The troops are going on board the transports, and the war vessels, including the *Monitor*, have all returned to their anchorage.

The President viewed the action from a tugboat lying about a mile in the rear of the fleet. He has just returned, and, as he passed up the wharf, was vociferously cheered by the troops.

LATEST.—Our fleet having retired, the *Merrimac* is again steaming out. The *Monitor*, *Dacotah* and *Naugatuck* are still, however, in position off Sewall's Point.

An officer of the *Seminole* states that the rebel flag-staff on Sewall's Point was twice shot away during the bombardment. The first time it fell it was picked up, and a rebel in a red shirt jumped on the ramparts with a stump of the staff and the flag, and waved it, when another shell struck him, killing him, and, it is supposed, others near him.

Of the many shots fired at the fleet by the rebels, not one struck any of our vessels. Some went over their masts, but most fell short. The rebels could be distinctly seen from the vessels carrying off their dead and wounded.

THE NAVAL OPERATIONS BETWEEN FORTRESS MONROE AND NORFOLK.

Diagram Exhibiting the Water-Passage to Norfolk and Portsmouth, the Evacuated Rebel Batteries at Sewall's Point, and all the Locations of Interest in the Vicinity of Hampton Roads.

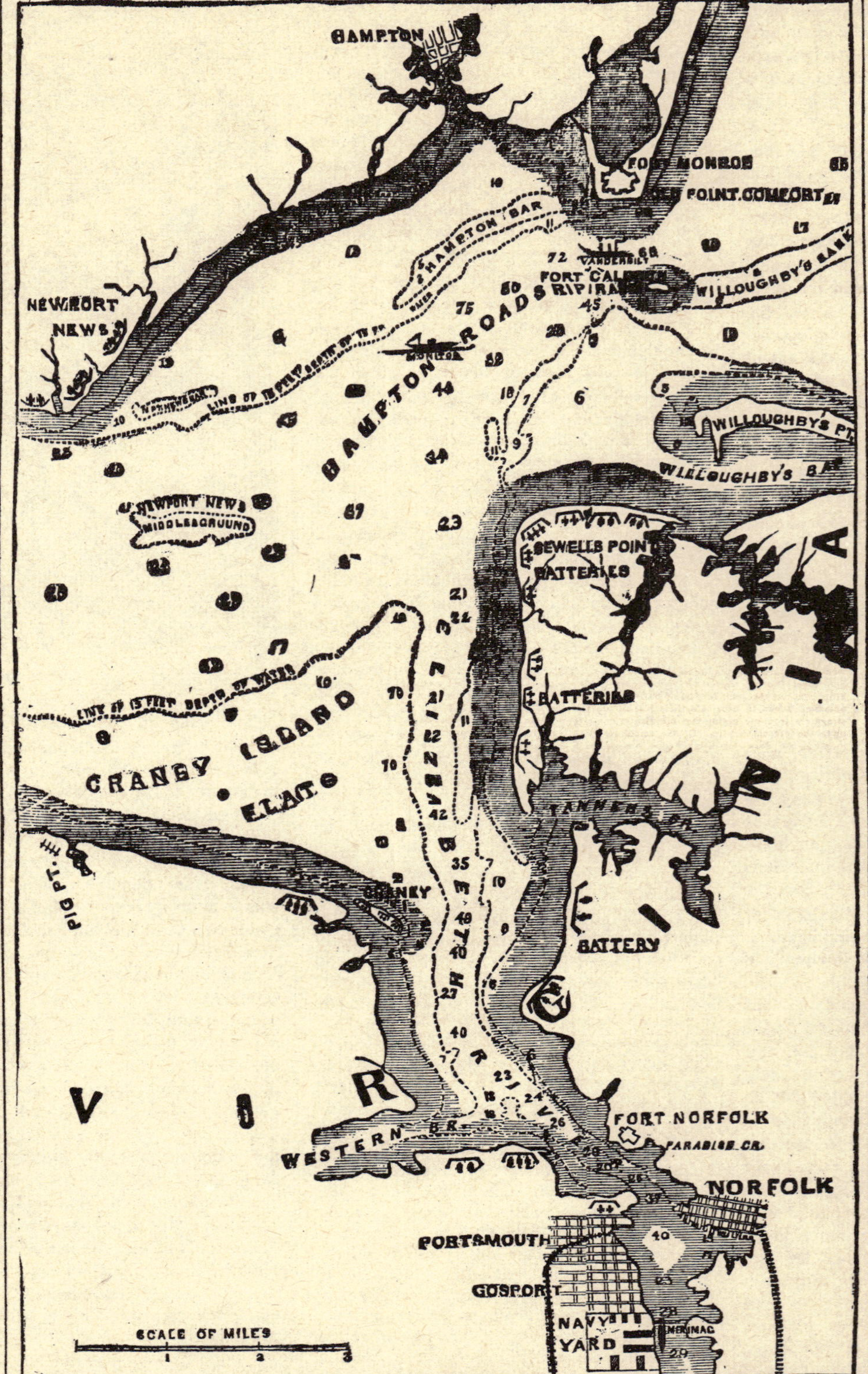

OUR FORTRESS MONROE CORRESPONDENCE.

FORTRESS MONROE, Thursday, May 8, 1862.

Old Point was astir at an early hour this morning, with rumors of anticipated events of an important nature. The visit of the President and two members of his Cabinet indicated that something unusual was on foot, and this was fully realized by the events of the morning.

A BOAT FROM THE ENEMY.

Early this morning, the steam-tug *J. B. White* arrived at Newport's News, and voluntarily surrendered to Gen. MANSFIELD. She had on board three citizens beside the crew. They state that the boat was sent to bring a large gun from Sewall's Point to Norfolk. When past the picket-boats of the enemy, they shut off steam, and drifted with the tide past the rebel batteries to Newport's News. The *J. B. White* was owned by COURTRIGHT, BARTON & Co., of Erie, Penn., and was brought around, before the commencement of the rebellion, to the Chesapeake and Albemarle Canal, to be used in towing vessels.

Important news was brought by those on board. The rebels commenced evacuating Norfolk yesterday. Orders had been given to blow up the public buildings, but on petition of the citizens action was suspended. The greatest consternation was prevalent—many fleeing in every direction. Many were secretly praying for the arrival of our troops. BURNSIDE was reported as being within a few miles of Norfolk. The troops around Norfolk would be used to protect the railroad. It was thought that the *Merrimac* would have her guns taken off and be scuttled. We will know the truth of this report before many hours.

The *Galena*, *Aroostook* and *Port Royal* gunboats left the Roads at 6 o'clock, this morning, and went up James River. *It is said that this movement is made by direct order of the President.* The rebel boats *Yorktown* and *Jamestown* are now up the river, and must be captured or destroyed.

Our boats passed Pig Point battery without being fired upon, but at present writing, (10½ o'clock A. M.,) heavy firing is heard from Day Point.

11 *o'clock.*—The boat from Newport's News reports the safe passage of our gunboats past the Day Point batteries. They were still pushing up the river.

BOMBARDMENT OF REBEL BATTERIES.

At 11 o'clock the *Dacotah*, *Monitor* and *Naugatuck* were observed moving up the channel. The rigging of vessels and the tops of houses were soon covered with spectators, eager to witness the expected engagement. At 12¼ o'clock the *Dacotah* opened the first fire on Sewall's Point battery, and was soon seconded by shots from the *San Jacinto*, *Seminole* and *Susquehannah*. Our fleet had taken position in the channel leading up Elizabeth River, from which they could shell the batteries on both sides of them. They were not long in waiting for a reply, for the rebel batteries gave a speedy acknowledgment of the attention paid them. The bombardment was now fairly open.

The day was beautiful, the harbor smooth and the atmosphere very clear. In quick succession the fleet poured forth its iron storm on the rebel batteries, and the curling smoke from over or in the strongholds of the enemy told that it was not without some damage to them. Soon the water-spouts rapidly arose in close proximity to the *Monitor*, informing her that the enemy's shot and hatred was mainly intended for her. The balance of the fleet had stopped, but the *Monitor* still pursued her course up the channel, a mere speck on the water, unmoved by the shot that fell on every side of her, and only at long intervals returning the fire, to remind them she was not the harmless craft she seemed to be. When a mile or more beyond the rest of the fleet, and within range of the Craney Island battery, she opened fire upon them, but with what damage to the enemy I could not tell at the long distance from which I beheld it.

Commodore GOLDSBOROUGH anchored with his flagship, in the rear of the fleet, and directed operations.

At 2½ o'clock, a smoke was seen to arise from behind Sewall's Point, which from first appearance was mistaken for the *Merrimac*; but as it increased in density, it revealed the fact that the woods on the point of the enemy's barracks were on fire. The *Monitor*, after shelling Craney Island for about an hour, returned alongside the other vessels.

The heavy firing was still kept up with spirit, the heavy reports making the vessel on which I write this communication fairly tremble at each discharge. To add to the general chorus, the sullen, yet heavy sounds of firing up James River, informed us that the *Galena* and her consorts were having hot work. The Sawyer guns on the Rip Raps also joined in the bombardment, and sent many well-directed shots into the works of the foe.

"Where is the *Merrimac?*" was asked by every one. It was now high tide, the most favorable time for her appearance, and from her past actions we did not think she would long be absent when she once knew that our fleet had changed from their old positions, and had even ventured to shell their batteries. Every one expressed an ardent hope that she would add to the interest of the day by coming out and exhibiting her prowess with the *Monitor*. Still she was not visible, and our only amusement was to see our fleet throw its storm of shell into the point.

The President, Secretary of War, Secretary CHASE, and Assistant-Secretary of War TUCKER, were among the spectators of the fight, looking on with evident satisfaction at the punishment of the enemy's batteries.

3 *o'clock.*—"Here comes the *Merrimac*," shouts some man from the rigging, and all eyes are turned to a little column of black smoke that made its appearance around the Point. Telescopes are brought into requisition, and his assertion is verified. The firing from the fleet ceased, the *Monitor* again took her place in the van; the ramparts of the fort, and every available lofty pinnacle is black with anxious spectators. The *Merrimac* slowly approached, and as she neared our fleet, the *Susquehanna* and *Dacotah* began slowly to retire.

Everything was silent. The fleet, or part of it, moved noiselessly about, and the thousands of spectators gazed in silent hope or fear at the approaching contest.

Every eye was fixed on the *Monitor*, who was to be the David for this rebel Goliah. Only her turret and flagstaff, floating the glorious old Stars and Stripes, could be seen above water; but on that little speck hung the hopes of the fleet. The *Minnesota*, at this juncture, headed up the harbor, to play her part in the programme. She has an old score to settle with the rebel monster, and welcomes the opportunity. The *Merrimac* still nearer approaches, and, with humiliation, we see all of our fleet retire, with the exception of the *Monitor*, to a point nearly in front of the fort. The *Merrimac* moves in front of the line of vessels with her old saucy air, taking care, however, to keep aloof from the *Monitor*, who retains her place with an air as independent as her distinguished rival. It is evidently the desire of Commodore GOLDSBOROUGH to entice the *Merrimac* further into the harbor.

4 *o'clock.*—After looking on for a half hour, with an impudence truly refreshing, the *Merrimac* has turned and headed for Craney Island. The fleet is taking its former position at the entrance of the Norfolk channel, while a few excellent shots from the Rip Raps are paying parting respects to the *Merrimac*. I have no time for comments, as the Baltimore boat is about starting, and will merely add that the expectations of the day have hardly been realized, as we had confidently hoped that this would be the last day for the *Merrimac*. Why our vessels did not move on her, Commodore GOLDSBOROUGH alone knows and can tell.

W. W. C.

FROM GEN. M'CLELLAN'S ARMY.

Still Crowding the Rear of the Retreating Foe.

A GREAT BATTLE AT WEST POINT.

Thirty Thousand Rebels under Lee Defeated by Gens. Franklin and Sedgwick.

Lee Flanked and Driven Back to the Chickahominy.

A Junction Between Gens. McClellan and Franklin.

The Galena nearly Opposite Williamsburgh

DISPATCH FROM FORTRESS MONROE.

FORTRESS MONROE, Thursday, May 8.

I learn by steamer from Yorktown, that Gen. MCCLELLAN had advanced twelve miles beyond Williamsburgh, and has had several skirmishes with the enemy, routing them with heavy loss.

The embarkation of troops for West Point was progressing with great rapidity, and a heavy battle had taken place on Wednesday afternoon between the troops under Gens. FRANKLIN and SEDGWICK, and the rebels under LEE, who were endeavoring to make their way to Richmond. It is said to have been the severest battle on the Peninsula, and *the rebels were totally defeated and flanked, being driven back toward the forces under Gen. Johnston on the Chickahominy.*

The whole number of Federals killed and wounded was 300.

The enemy were driven back by our gunboats with great slaughter.

They had not less than 30,000 men, while our whole force was not over 20,000 landed. Had it not been for the gunboats, they would, perhaps, have been defeated.

DISPATCH FROM GEN. McCLELLAN.

WILLIAMSBURGH, Va., May 9—12 M.

To the War Department:

I heard a few minutes ago that the *Galena* was aground off Hog Island—I judge not badly, for the reason that Capt. ROGERS does not throw over his coal. I have sent him all the assistance he asks.

My troops are in motion, and in magnificent spirits. They have all the air and feelings of veterans. It would do your heart good to see them.

I have effected a junction with Gen. Franklin.

Instructions have been given so that the navy will receive prompt support, whenever and wherever required.

GEO. B. McCLELLAN,
Major-General Commanding.

FROM WILLIAMSBURGH ON THURSDAY.

WILLIAMSBURGH, Thursday, May 8, Via WASHINGTON, Friday, May 9.

The details of the engagement of Monday are so voluminous and incorrect that it will be necessary to await the report of Gen. MCCLELLAN, which is now being prepared.

Deserters from the enemy are hourly coming in.

Gen. JAMISON has been appointed Military Governor and Provost Marshal of the town of Williamsburgh.

The official report of the killed and wounded being too lengthy to send over the military telegraph, it has been forwarded by mail.

The expedition up York River has been most successful, and we now occupy West Point. Heavy firing has been heard in that direction, but the particulars are not known. Yesterday the advance guard of our cavalry had a skirmish with the rear guard of the enemy, about seven miles from here. *The main body of the enemy have retreated across the James River.*

The general impression with military men is that the rebels have made their last stand in Virginia.

For a distance of some ten miles beyond Williamsburgh the road is lined with broken army wagons in the retreat of the enemy.

Brig.-Gen. JAMES H. VAN ALEN has been appointed Military Governor and Commandant of Yorktown and Gloucester, with Capt. CYRUS HALDEMAN for Adjutant-General.

Gen. VAN ALEN has appointed Capt. REVERE, of the Forty-fourth New-York Regiment, to be Provost Marshal.

NEWS RECEIVED IN WASHINGTON.

WASHINGTON, Friday, May 9.

MCCLELLAN'S dispatch, saying he has effected a junction with Gen. FRANKLIN'S Division, is supposed to mean that the wings of the two forces touch each other, forming a perfect military line from the mouth of the Chickahominy to New-Kent, and enveloping the rebel army in a fold that will rapidly close upon and crush them.

H. J. R., of the TIMES, writes from the front of the army on Wednesday, as follows:

"I hear this morning reports which indicate a more thorough demoralization of the enemy than I had assumed. It is said that a heavy force of cavalry, sent in pursuit, has taken some twenty pieces of their artillery, and found a very large quantity of arms thrown away."

The total killed and wounded of the Union army in the Williamsburgh battle, at the latest accounts from camp received to-night, is reported thus:

Killed—Two hundred and thirty.

Wounded—Seven hundred and sixty-four.

Missing—Sixty-nine.

THE BATTLE OF WILLIAMSBURGH.

ADDITIONAL LISTS OF KILLED AND WOUNDED.

LIST OF KILLED, WOUNDED AND MISSING OF THE ELEVENTH REGIMENT MASSACHUSETTS VOLUNTEERS.

Richard Moylan, private, Company A—killed.
Jas. J. Pierce, private, Company A—killed.
Wm. H. McMahon, private, Company A—killed.
Henry C. Granger, private, Company B—killed.

[Continued on Eighth Page.]

The New-York Times.

VOL. XI—NO. 3317. NEW-YORK, SUNDAY, MAY 11, 1862. PRICE THREE CENTS.

OPERATIONS IN VIRGINIA.

Another Cannonade of Sewall's Point.

The Object of the Demonstration on Thursday.

Official Report of Commodore Goldsborough.

The Measures Taken to Dispose of the Merrimac.

The Work of Gen. McClellan's Army.

Detailed Reports of the Battle of Williamsburgh.

OFFICIAL LISTS OF KILLED AND WOUNDED.

FORTRESS MONROE, Friday May 9. }
via BALTIMORE, Saturday, May 10. }

The *Merrimac* remained off the point all night.

The *Monitor* went up this forenoon and fired a few shots into Sewall's Point.

The Rip Raps battery also opened briskly, a large number of the shots striking in the wood.

Many comparisons are drawn between the enterprise of the naval fleets here and at New-Orleans.

REPORT OF COMMODORE GOLDSBOROUGH.

U. S. FLAGSHIP MINNESOTA, }
HAMPTON ROADS, Va., May 9, 1862. }

His Excellency the President of the United States:

SIR: Agreeably to a communication just received from Hon. EDWIN M. STANTON, I have the honor to report that the instructions I gave yesterday to the officers commanding the several vessels detailed to open fire on Sewall's Point, were—that the object of the move was to ascertain the practicability of landing a body of troops thereabouts, and to reduce the works if it could be done; that the wooden vessels should attack the principal works in enfilade, and that the *Monitor*, to be accompanied by the *Stevens*, should go up as far as the works, and there operate in front. On the *Merrimac's* appearance outside of the works, the *Monitor* had orders to fall back into fair channel-way, and only to engage her seriously in such a position that this ship, together with the merchant vessels intended for the purpose, could run her down. If an opportunity presented itself, the other vessels were not to hesitate to run her down, and the *Baltimore*, an unarmed steamer of light draught, light speed, and with a curved bow, was kept in the direction of the *Monitor*, expresely to throw herself across the *Merrimac*, either forward or aft of her plated house, but the *Merrimac* did not engage the *Monitor*, nor did she place herself where she could have been assailed by our ram-vessels to any advantage, or where there was any prospect whatever of getting at her. My instructions were necessarily verbal, and, in giving them, I supposed that I was carrying out your wishes in substance, if not to the letter. The demonstration resulted in establishing the fact that the number of guns at the principal works on Sewall's Point has been essentially reduced, and is not greater than about seventeen, and that the number of men now stationed there is comparatively quite limited. The quarters connected with this work were set on fire by our shells, and no doubt seriously injured.

I am, very respectfully, your obedient servant,
(Signed,) L. M. GOLDSBOROUGH,
Commanding Naval Blockading Squadron.

THE BATTLE OF WILLIAMSBURGH.

Connected Account of the Engagement—Strength of the Rebel Position—Fort Magruder—The Forces Engaged on Each Side—Seventeen Pieces of Artillery Captured from the Rebels.

From Our Own Correspondent.

WILLIAMSBURGH, Va., Wednesday, May 7, 1862.

Now that the smoke of the battle has somewhat cleared away, I am able to give you a more connected account of the engagement, on Monday, between our advance guard and a large force of rebels who opposed our entrance into this town. The position from which the rebels assailed our forces was an exceedingly strong one, being along the line of defences established by them just below Williamsburgh, last Spring, previous to their fortification of Yorktown and Warwick Creek. Near the centre of a broad plain, at the upper side of which stands Williamsburgh, and right across the turnpike road leading to the city, they erected a substantial bastion, large enough to accommodate six or seven thousand men, and commanding the place in every direction, so that a force approaching it from any point must be exposed to a raking fire for three-quarters of a mile or more. Well supplied with artillery, and defended with determination by a force of 5,000 men, this bastion would give a world of trouble to an army of five times that number. It was supported by five smaller flanking works of the same pattern, on the right, and two on the left, each of them having platforms for two guns, the large work being fitted for five guns.

The approach to the plain thus defended from the direction of Yorktown was by two roads; the one on the left, taken by HOOKER's Division and its supports, being a straight path through the woods. That on the right, along which HANCOCK advanced, led over a brook or creek, which had been dammed at this point, where the road crossed it through a defile in such a way as to convert the defile into a deep pond, passed at the lower side by a narrow causeway, commanded by an earthwork looking down upon it at a height of fifty feet, and from a bold bluff on the further side. Over this causeway troops would be compelled to march four abreast for a distance of more than one-eighth of a mile, exposed to the fire of a fort above the reach of their artillery. For some reason, however, this position has never been occupied. Probably it was intended to mount artillery there, as the occasion demanded. The fact that this work, and the flanking works about Fort Magruder, were none of them occupied on Monday, shows plainly that the rebels had not proposed to make any decided stand against us here. Indeed, the command of the York River, secured to us by the evacuation of Yorktown, made their position at this point of the Peninsula untenable, as we could easily throw a force above them to take them in the rear.

The rebels had, in fact, pushed on several miles beyond Williamsburgh with their main body, before our advance approached on Sunday night, retaining a small force only at the forts in their rear. But, leaving everything behind them, our troops pushed on so rapidly after the rebels, struggling through the mud with their heavy wagons, that they found it absolutely necessary to hold us in check long enough to secure their retreat. Accordingly, on Monday morning, troops were hurried back to the support of their rear guard, occupying Fort Magruder. They continued to come in all through the day, supplying fresh troops to oppose our men. Commencing with a small force, each party continued to swell its numbers with reinforcements, until the rebels had finally fifteen or twenty thousand men on the ground, and we about the same number. The rebels had the advantage of hurrying their troops along more rapidly, so that some of our men were compelled to stand their ground for hours against a much superior force opposing them.

The contest was for the possession of the woods surrounding the plain in which stand the forts. Through these our troops advanced to the attack; Gen. HANCOCK's Brigade, of Gen. SMITH's Division, KEYES' Corps, on the right, and a portion of Gen. HOOKER's Division on the left. Here was the heaviest fighting. Gen. HOOKER's Division suffered more severely than any other. They were in the advance of the army on the left, approaching on Sunday night to within four or five miles of Williamsburgh. By 4 o'clock on Monday morning, Gen. GROVER, who led the advance, had his brigade in motion, and marched them into the woods on the left of the plain before Williamsburgh, whose fortifications I have described. Here two or three companies of the First Massachusetts, and two companies of the Second New-Hampshire, were sent forward as skirmishers; the remainder of the First Massachusetts being posted in the edge of the wood on the left, and eight companies of the Second New-Hampshire in a similar position on the right. The Eleventh Massachusetts and the Twenty-Sixth Pennsylvania was then sent along the edge of the woods to the right, and at once briskly engaged the enemy, whom they drove to the protection of Fort Magruder.

An artillery fight then commenced, our troops occupying the enemy's rifle-pits, picking off their gunners and silencing their guns. The rebels then opened fire from the woods, at a considerable distance on the left, where they were hidden from sight, using their artillery to support an attempt to turn our left flank. The New-Jersey Brigade was sent to oppose this flanking force, and were soon furiously engaged. At this point was the main contest, the rebels making a desperate effort to turn our position. In the midst of the conflict the troops engaged fell short of ammunition, and reinforcements were sent for. The First Regiment of the Excelsior Brigade, Seventieth New-York Volunteers, Col. DWIGHT, was sent forward with a portion of the Second New-Hampshire, to sustain the attack, now at its height, the enemy throwing a heavy column forward and pressing furiously on our men, and forcing them back for a time by weight of numbers.

Col. DWIGHT's regiment suffered more severely than any other, he being himself badly wounded in the head, and taken prisoner. Lieut.-Col. FARNUM was also wounded in both knees, but not seriously. Six out of the ten captains in the regiment were killed, and the regiment very badly cut up. It is impossible, indeed, to ascertain their loss at present, stragglers from the regiment continuing to come in up to the present writing. Of the remaining regiments of the Excelsior Brigade, one was posted in front and the others held in reserve, all being more or less engaged before the close of the day.

Meanwhile Gen. PECK's brigade, the advance of Gen. COUCH's division, arrived on the ground at 1 o'clock, having marched up from Lee's Mills, ten or twelve miles back, that morning, in the midst of a pouring rain, and through mud ankle deep. But Gen. HOOKER being sore pressed, they were marched at once into the fight, taking a position on the right of Gen. HOOKER, in the center of our position, where they were at once exposed to the full force of the enemy's fire. For two hours they held their position against great odds. Twice they were driven back, and twice they rallied again, and recovered their ground.

When the brigade first reached the ground the One Hundred and Second Pennsylvania advanced to the front and delivered their fire and fell back, giving place to the Ninety-eighth Pennsylvania, which held their ground until the One Hundred and Second rallied, and the two maintained the position. The Fifty-fifth New-York, DE TROBRIAN's Zouaves, came up on the left and then retired, while the Sixty-second New-York held the rebels in check, and the One Hundred and Second and Ninety-eighth Pennsylvania delivered a cross-fire. The Fifty-fifth then formed a new line of battle and advanced to the support of the Sixty-second, and the Ninety-third Pennsylvania came up and opened fire on a battery commanding the road, until the rebels were finally driven back at all points.

Toward the close of the afternoon the Seventh Massachusetts and the Second Rhode Island came in and were held in reserve, but were not called into action, though coming under fire. The Second Rhode Island fully sustained its reputation even at Manassas, and both regiments would have done good service had the opportunity occurred. The Seventh Massachusetts marched coolly through a raking fire of grape and canister to reach their position, but fortunately lost none of their number.

BURNEY's Brigade and others of KEARNEY's forces reached the ground just at night. I have not learned what share they bore in the engagement. Gen. PALMER, of Gen. CASEY's Division, with his brigade and two regiments of Gen. KEIN's Brigade, arrived on the ground somewhat later, and assisted in holding it during the night.

These particulars relate entirely to what transpired on the left of our advance. A brisk fight was, at the time, going on at the right where HANCOCK's Brigade was especially engaged. The contest was much less fierce here—the rebels devoting their main strength to a contest for the woods held by Gen. HOOKER, which, I since learn, they swore to take if it cost 20,000 men. But Gen. HOOKER was of different mind, and determinedly maintained his ground against a superior force until reinforcements arrived to enable him to make good his position. He was everywhere active, having two horses shot under him during the day. His Adjutant, Capt. DICKSON, was wounded, but not seriously.

The desperation of the fight is shown by the fact that the woods in which the troops fought was lost and won four times. One of HOOKER's batteries was carried by the rebels with a bold dash, but a cross-fire from PECK's troops compelled them to retire before they could drag it away with them, and they sought shelter in their rifle-pits.

The troops opposed to us were the Fourth, Fifth, Sixth, Ninth South Carolina regiments, Gen. ANDERSON's Brigade; the Second, Third, Seventh and Eighth, KERSHAW's Brigade; the First, Seventh, Eleventh and Seventeenth Virginia, HILL's Brigade; the Fourteenth Louisiana, the Fourteenth Alabama, and probably the whole of WILCOX's Brigade; the Fourth, Sixth, Eighth, Ninth, Tenth, Eleventh and Twelfth Alabama; the Twenty-fourth Virginia; the Second Florida; the Fourteenth and Seventeenth Louisiana, and the Nineteenth Mississippi. The last three regiments were badly cut up. The Nineteenth Mississippi is said to have been 1,500 strong. A portion of these forces formed the division of Gen. LONGSTREET. Gen. EARLEY and Gen. RAINES were also in command, and, it is said, JOHNSTON himself. A portion of LATHAM's Battery, celebrated at Manassas, was also in the engagement.

I enumerate above twenty-six regiments, whom I learn were in the fight, from the statements of the rebel prisoners in our hands. It is not probable that this covers their entire force, which was very heavy, for a rear guard, and certainly well handled. Some of the most reliable of the Southern troops were engaged, and the large proportion from South Carolina and Alabama will be noted, fifteen out of the twenty-six regiments being from these two States.

The rebels lost heavily; Gen. RAINES being reported killed, though this is uncertain, and Gen EARLEY wounded. Colonels WARD, of the Second Florida, and MOTT, of the Nineteenth Mississippi, were killed, and Col. WOODARD, of the Tenth Alabama, is missing. Among the regiments suffering the most severely was the Twenty-fourth Virginia, nearly every officer of which was either killed or wounded.

During the night of Monday the rebels beat a retreat, and with the dawn of Tuesday morning the rear of their line was discovered passing over the plain into Williamsburgh beyond, and so continuing their retreat toward Richmond, leaving the town for our occupation. Gen. JAMESON was at once appointed Military Governor of the place by Gen. MCCLELLAN, and proceeded to occupy it with his brigade, who were marched up the high street of the ancient village to the good old tune of "Yankee Doodle." As they entered the town at one end the rear guard of the rebel cavalry were disappearing at the other. A squadron of the Fifth Pennsylvania Cavalry, a brigade of infantry and company of artillery, were at once sent in pursuit. The latter did not get far beyond the town, on account of the impassable nature of the roads. The cavalry continued in pursuit for some four or five miles, picking up twenty or thirty prisoners, and securing four pieces of artillery—two 32-pounders, one 12-pounder, and one carronade, besides a number of other pieces of artillery, amounting to seventeen in all. They were but half an hour behind the last of the rebel cavalry, but being in small force, were unable to push on.

All along the way were the usual evidences of a hasty retreat; blankets, knapsacks and muskets strewing the wayside, and in one place two poor fellows who had been wounded, were left in a wagon to care for themselves. They piteously entreated that they be sent for, which was promised.

In Williamsburgh, the churches, the University buildings, and other public buildings, as well as many private dwellings, were found filled with wounded, left behind the rebels in their hasty exodus. In fact, there was scarcely a house in town that did not have at least one. Here and there among them was one of our wounded men, who had fallen into the rebels' hands and been left behind with the rest. I found two left in this way in the open plain below Williamsburgh, where they had been exposed to a chilling rain through the night, with no covering but a blanket. With this exception they had been treated with kindness, their wants being supplied so far as possible while they continued in the enemy's hands. In addition to the wounded found in Williamsburgh, a large number were found scattered in different places outside the village. The whole number coming into our hands cannot be less than one thousand, Gen. PECK stating to me that six hundred were found in one spot.

The rebels have the grace to send in some of their surgeons, with a flag of truce, so that our doctors were relieved of a portion of the labor of caring for them. The ladies of the town were also present with their attentions, and the rector of the Episcopal Church, Rev. Mr. AMBLER, did credit to his cloth by remaining at his post, visiting those who were wounded and in prison.

The rebels did not undertake to bury any of their dead, and the battle-field presented a ghastly spectacle on the following morning, as the sun rose on these scores of dead faces upturned to Heaven, as if pleading for a Christian interment. No prayers could be said over them, and they were hastily gathered together, in trenches, and covered with the sod. When I visited the scene of the encounter, early this (Tuesday) morning, our men were busy at this work, and the traces of the fight of the day previous were still fresh before me. Here was one poor fellow with a minié ball through his breast, and there another horribly torn with a flying bit of shell; now singly, and then in groups, I came upon them as they lay upon the wet sod of the wheat-field about Fort Magruder. There was almost a fascination in the ghastly sight, as the sense grew blunted to it, and the bruised and torn frames of flesh ceased to remind you too closely of the men that once dwelt there.

Here and there was a dead horse, too, and the plain was strewn in all directions with overcoats and knapsacks, blankets and bed-quilts, caps and shoes, left behind in the eagerness to press forward. In one of the redoubts I found two wounded rebels, who had been left by their comrades, and attended to where they lay by our surgeons, until they could be removed. They seemed cheerful, and lay quietly reading a couple of New-York newspapers, which had been handed to them, doubtless with the kindly purpose of cheering them with reports of Southern victories.

The scene in the woods, where the severest struggle occurred, was even more horrible, the dead and wounded on both sides lying together in heaps, marking the localities of the fiercest contests. It will be days before the bodies of all the slain can be searched out and buried. Our own have been gathered to-day as rapidly as possible, and the rebels will be taken care of speedily. A message was sent by flag of truce, offering them an opportunity to return and take care of their slain, but the brutal answer came back, that if we wanted them buried more than they did, we might do it ourselves. It was such an answer as might have been expected from the men who placed torpedoes in our road; and the barbarism exhibited in this, appears also in the indifference with which the Confederate Generals have turned their backs upon those who could no longer be of service to them.

Beside the wounded rebels left upon our hands, we have secured a large number of prisoners, approaching one thousand in number, as near as can be estimated. Some of them were found concealing themselves in closets and corners in Williamsburgh, and our troops have been unearthing them at intervals during the day. A number have also came voluntary forward and given themselves up, glad to get so easily out of what they begin to consider a bad scrape. Among these is an Irishman, who, after pocketing $600, paid for serving as a substitute, thus cancels his bargain. But with these and other evidences of faint-heartedness, there is still many as determined as one rebel soldier, who declared that the South would never submit until there was a bayonet at every door and a guard in every house.

The rebels are clearly determined to dispute our passage to Richmond, and all accounts agree that the river Chickahominy is to be their line of defence. They have no works of consequence this side of that, and, in fact, no line which will enable them to present a front to an advance from West Point, as well as to our approach up the Peninsula. They declare that Richmond shall never be taken so long as there is an old woman left to fight in its defence; but so it was at New-Orleans, at Port Royal, and in North Carolina, and other points now quietly held by our forces.

FROM ANOTHER CORRESPONDENT.

WILLIAMSBURGH, Va., Wednesday, May 8, 1862.

The battle of the 6th inst. is proven to have been upon a much larger scale than was at first supposed, and the number of the killed and wounded on both sides exceeds considerably the figures given at the close of the engagement. The most severe fighting occurred on our left, at which point we sustained our heaviest losses.

The battle was opened at 7 o'clock A. M., by the First Massachusetts and Second New-Hampshire Regiments, under command of Gen. HOOKER, who took a position behind a field strewn with fallen timber, at the right of a road leading from Warwick and joining the main road at a point within a mile of Williamsburgh. At the junction of these two roads was situated the principal rebel fort, called Fort Magruder, in the rear of which were located several barracks. Two batteries—WEBER's United States and BRAMHALL's New-York—formed in position in front of the regiments. With this small force on our side the battle was commenced. The batteries directed their fire at first upon Fort Magruder, and as the engagement progressed, were obliged to respond to a fire received from a breastwork at the left of the main fort. At 8 o'clock the Eleventh Massachusetts and Twenty-sixth Pennsylvania regiments came up, and were ordered by Gen. HOOKER to deploy through the woods, in the rear of the other regiments, in order to open communication with Gen. SUMNER, who was stationed on the main road. At the same time the Fifth, Sixth, Seventh and Eighth New-Jersey regiments were sent to the left of the road, and formed in position on a line with the troops on the other side. Our batteries opened a rapid fire on the fort, which was responded to promptly by the rebels. The rebels also threw shell and grape-shot into the woods, where our forces were drawn up in line, making the position an exceedingly difficult one to hold.

At 10 A. M. the Seventieth, Seventy-second, Seventy-third and Seventy-fourth New-York, also under command of Gen. HOOKER, came up and passed over to the left of the New-Jersey Brigade. Meantime, three regiments of the rebels came out of the fort and made a charge on the batteries, but this movement was counteracted by a similar one made by the First Massachusetts and Second New-Hampshire, and the rebels were compelled to retire to their fort. They soon reappeared, however, with increased numbers, and made a charge upon our whole front, but our troops advanced and met the charge with great courage, and for a while seemed to have gained the advantage. The rebels observing the critical position of their advanced force, sent out reinforcements from the fort who, coöperating with the troops already there, succeeded in forcing our men back to the woods. Our men rallied again, however, and poured a tremendous volley into the rebel ranks, causing their men to fall by dozens. The enemy returned the fire with vigor, but could not withstand the impetuosity of our bayonet charge, and fell back again to his lines. A third time the rebels came up to contest the ground, and a third time our men advanced to repel them. Our men, by this time, had become quite fatigued, and not a little disheartened by not receiving reinforcements. Gen. HOOKER had sent to Gen. SUMNER for more men, but they did not make their appearance until afternoon. The fight was now in the balance, and the two forces were alternately driven back. At last the rebels, by sending out fresh troops, were enabled to hold the ground, and our men retired with a heavy loss. The enemy emboldened by this apparent victory, attempted to make a flank movement on the left. They now held possession, and occupied rifle pits which we found deserted in the morning, and from which they kept up a destructive fire on our men. 6,000 rebels were seen to leave the forts and pass along the woods to our left. At this time all the force we had to oppose them was the regiment above named. In this critical juncture Capt. SMITH, of the Fourth New-York Artillery, came up with his pieces and formed in battery in the middle of the road, and immediately commenced a raking fire upon the enemy's front, causing him to falter, and giving our own men time to recover somewhat from the confusion which the enemy's fire had occasioned. WEBER's and BRAMHALL's batteries had been abandoned on account of the utter impossibility to get them off the field. The horses were shot, and the wheels were sunk in a deep mire. The rebels found it equally difficult to get them over to their side, and did not succeed in taking but four pieces to their lines. While tugging to get the others away, SMITH's Battery gave them a charge of canister, causing them to retreat in a hasty manner. Soon after Gen. KEYES, who had been making strenuous efforts all the morning to get his troops formed, sent Gen. PECK, with his brigade, to the assistance of Gen. HOOKER, Gen. PECK taking a position on the right of the road. Gen. KEARNEY also arrived, with BERRY's Brigade, and took a position at the extreme left in order to prevent flanking by the enemy. Before arriving on the ground Gen. BERRY ordered his men to lay aside their knapsacks and all other cumbersome articles, that their progress to the field might not be in the least impeded. The Third Michigan was ordered to the left as a support, while Gen. BERRY moved forward with the remaining regiments, arriving on the ground at about 2½ P. M. The Fifth Michigan, Col. TERRY, proceeded to the left of the road in front of fallen timber and the rifle pits, while the Thirty-seventh New-York, Col. HAYMAN, went still further to the left. The Second Michigan occupied a position on the right of the road. As soon as these arrangements were completed, an order was given for the troops under Gen BERRY to advance and charge upon the enemy, which they did in a splendid manner, driving the enemy entirely out of the timber. At this charge the enemy lost 63 men killed. The enemy being posted in the rifle-pits caused our troops much annoyance. The Fifth Michigan, however, soon compelled them to retreat, although in so doing it lost a great many of its men.

Of course, the enemy had the advantage of being protected, while our men were obliged to expose themselves in bold relief. Our bullets could not penetrate the earth-works around the rifle-pits, and the only way to drive the enemy out, was to make a bayonet charge. This charge was made in a splendid manner by the Fifth Michigan in front, and the Thirty-seventh New-York at the left, the men pushing up to the pits near enough to bayonet the riflemen behind them. By this charge considerable loss was occasioned on both sides.

The enemy made frequent attempts to turn our left, and were as often repulsed. Col. TERRY was slightly wounded by a stray shot in the early part of the engagement, but this did not deter him from leading his regiment forward.

Gen. PECK, who occupied a central position, that is a position between our right and left wings, deserves great credit for his coolness and courage. At one time his men had the fire of three different forts directed upon them, but they stood up unflinchingly and maintained their position, and finally compelled a body of infantry, which came out to meet them, to precipitately retire.

The Fifth Wisconsin, Forty-ninth Pennsylvania, Thirty-third New-York and Sixth and Seventh Maine, under command of Gen. HANCOCK, formed our force on the right wing, until about 5 P. M., when it was increased by the arrival of Gen. CASEY's Brigade. The brilliant charge made by Gen. HANCOCK's command, whereby the rebels lost 100 killed and 200 wounded, besides about 150 taken as prisoners, has been fully recorded in your columns.

It is estimated that the enemy lost, during the engagement, 500 killed, 1,500 wounded, and 500 taken prisoners. Among the killed are two Brigadier-Generals, besides several line officers.

Our loss is severe, and may possibly equal that of the enemy. A large number of our line officers were killed and wounded, and 200 of the Excelsior Brigade were taken prisoners.

During yesterday and to-day our ambulances have been constantly employed in bringing the wounded from the woods and fields to the hospitals in the village. The wounded thus conveyed are mostly of the enemy. The rebels did not stop to bury their dead or care for their wounded, and during the whole of Monday night the battle-field was covered with their dead, dying and suffering. This state of things was rendered doubly severe in consequence of the rain which had been falling in torrents since morning, and which continued to fall during the night. The soil was soft and clayey, and in many instances the men lay half buried from view.

Although during the day the rebels from one of their forts hoisted a flag of truce and fired a volley into our men who were approaching it, we forgot the dastard and cowardly act when attending to the wants of their wounded.

The William and Mary College, the Episcopal Church, Court-house, and several other buildings are used for the wounded soldiers. When the rebels fled the town they left their wounded in barns and along the streets. The men were subsequently taken into the buildings where they now lie by our own soldiers. Seventeen Surgeons come in yesterday under a flag of truce.

This morning a troop of cavalry and two batteries advanced six miles from here. Gen. KINNES' Brigade went out at about 11 o'clock. The position of the enemy was discovered, but no battle ensued. At about dark another body of cavalry and another battery went out to the same place to support the force already there. Nothing of importance transpired during the night. WHIT.

FROM ANOTHER CORRESPONDENT.

ESTIMATES OF THE LOSS—THE COMMISSARY DEPARTMENT.

CAMP BEYOND WILLIAMSBURGH, Va., }
Thursday, May 8, 1862. }

A battle has been fought with the enemy's rear guard just outside of Williamsburgh, where light earthworks had been erected, beside other intrenchments. The Commanding General sets down the loss on either side to be about two thousand killed, wounded and missing—*one-third killed* outright. Yesterday and day before, we have been busily engaged in burying the dead and hunting up the wounded. Gen. HOOKER's Division has suffered the most—having held certain ground for five hours in front of a heavy abbatis—when Gen. PECK's Brigade came to his support, and Gen. HANCOCK charged the enemy, putting him to flight. Bayonet wounds are plenty—the rebels having stood firm until a charge was made, when they fled in the utmost confusion. Our cavalry and horse artillery are still in pursuit, but the roads are terrible, which impedes their progress much.

Gen. FRANKLIN's Division has arrived at West Point, and is reported to be engaged with the enemy. We may yet cut off his retreat.

I should judge there were about twenty thousand of our men engaged in the battle on the 5th, and about the same number of rebels.

Yesterday five hundred head of beef cattle were distributed to the different brigades on the battle-field, having been driven from Fortress Monroe. Col. CLARKE, Chief Commissary, and Capt. BUCHANAN, Assistant Commissary, both of Gen. MCCLELLAN's Staff, are indefatigable in their exertions to keep the army well supplied with fresh beef. Our stores are now ascending the river, under charge of Capts. BELL and PORTER. No doubt the dépot will be at West Point.

Headquarters move to-day. The Commanding General is in the best of spirits, and everything goes on well.

No more accidents than those already related have happened from the bursting of torpedoes, although there are many yet to be seen in places.

SIONARA.

ADDITIONAL LIST OF KILLED AND WOUNDED.

BALTIMORE, Saturday, May 10.

The steamer *Commodore*, from Yorktown, is now in the harbor, with between 600 and 700 sick and wounded soldiers, who will go into the hospitals here.

The following is a list of the killed and wounded at the Williamsburgh battle:

FIFTH EXCELSIOR REGIMENT—COL. CURTIS COMMANDING.

Sergt. John Dutton, killed,
W. Spritt, killed,
John S. Veiner, wounded,
S. McFarland, wounded,
Lewis Elmuck, wounded,
Sergt. B. Jordan, killed,
W. Pollock, killed,
Henry Phillipins, killed,
Charles Emery, killed.
James Dougherty, killed.
2d Lt. Purdy, wounded.
1st Sergt. F. M. Brown, wounded.
Corp. J. Towers, wounded.
Thos. Trainer, wounded.
Corporal James Hockliff, killed.
James Bruce, killed.
Jacob Suynam, killed.
Isaac E. Milligan, killed.
Fras. T. Stevens, killed.
Sergt. H. Du Bois, killed.
Matt. Ferns, wounded.
A. E. Inoyn, wounded.
A. W. Smith, wounded.
F. Cameron, killed.
Jas. G. Smith, wounded.
J. W. Baker, wounded.
J. V. Littlefield, wounded.
W. Laughlin, wounded.
S. Melville, killed.
Thos. McRady, killed.
Jas. P. Smith, killed.
Thos. Crooker, killed.
Albert Reed, killed.
Martin Nix, killed.
Capt. Geo. H. Quarterman, slightly wounded.
Thos. Ferris, wounded.
Peter Sullivan, wounded.
John Alligar, wounded.
Caleb March, killed.
T. W. Ryan, killed.
Chas. Rhinefeldt, killed.
John Shoemaker, killed.
Abner Space, killed.
Sergt. P. A. Ryder, killed.
Corpl. J. R. Burns, killed.
George Dwyer, killed.
Corp. C. Linn, wounded,
Fred. Schroeder, wounded,
Charles Chrundies, killed,
Corp. Liuriff, wounded,
Wm. Schmidt, wounded,
James Ronsell, wounded,
Pat. Kennedy, killed,
John Dyer, killed,
P. H. McGulley, killed,
Morris Hagan, wounded.
John G. Keech, wounded.
Albert Bird, wounded.
2d Lt. De Sonche, wounded.
Sergt. J. Harman, killed.
F. J. McDonald, killed.
Wm. H. Hart, killed.
Corp. I. Bell, wounded.
H. Rusking, killed.
Sergt. J. Richardson, killed.
Isaac C. Bailey, killed.
Oliv. D. Sudden, wounded.
W. H. Fleming, wounded.
Wm. Bostwick, wounded.
Jas. Gormley, wounded.
Thos. Rooney, wounded.
Wm. Baker, wounded.
E. McLevy, wounded.
D. Williams, wounded.
E. Lewis, wounded.
Geo. Cadmus, wounded.
Sam. Cady, wounded.
B. De Groot, wounded.
W. F. Young, wounded.
O. Hiscock, wounded.
W. G. Vilas, wounded.
E. R. Pierson, wounded.
J. H. Hodges, Jr., killed.
Sgt. J. V. Smith, killed.
J. S. Daugler, killed.
W. McGlom, killed.
Robt. Youmans, killed.
Joseph Jefferson, killed.
Daniel Zindle, killed.
Edward Maginnis, killed.
D. McGovern, killed.
John Odell, killed.
Wm. Shaw, killed.
Henry Leinard, killed.

FIRST REGIMENT EXCELSIOR BRIGADE.

Col. Dwight, severely wounded.
Lieut.-Col. Farnum, severely wounded.

Killed.

Second Lieut. Wm. H. Kilburn.
Sergeant John E. N. Houten.
Sergeant Robert Harvey.
Corporal Joseph Winters.
Corporal Charles Gankle.
Corporal Chas. Ryerson.
John Whitford,
Fred. Cain,
Victor Gastner,
Thomas Hallowell,
J. Bergen,
David Hallowell,
T. Bruen,
Jacob Nees,
Sergeant Aug. Cook,
Henry Beekman,
Joseph Frith,
Henry Ulleweiller,
Michael McPaigue,
James McGee,
Michael Kirk,
Aulon Springler,
John Tracy,
Wm. Howard,
Orwin C. Knapp,
John Davy,
Matthew McCann,
W. A. Wicker,
John Riley,
Simon M. Renoe,
Capt. John Mitchell,
Sergeant Edward Burley,
Jona Hilton,
Henry Kissick,
Michael Ryan,
Michael O'Connell,
Lieut. Frank H. Nelson,
E. S. Belknap,
James Bragg,
J. C. Wright,
Ed. Kennedy,
Charles H. Fuller,
W. C. Strickles,
Capt. Jacob Bruner,
Lieut. W. Miller,
Sergeant W. P. Finley,
Corporal D. C. W. Young,
J. C. Earl,
Fred. Ball,
John E. Dearing,
Jesse Geipenger,
Capt. H. R. D. Reilley,
Corporal W. R. Mills,
Corporal John Beck,
Alpheus Lambert,
James Dunning,
M. F. Knapp,
S. Leonard,
Henry Smith,
Capt. W. H. Bugbee,
Second Lieut. Hearick Haynor,
Sergeant J. W. Wooster,
Sergeant John O'Leary,
Corporal Alfred O. Parkes,
Patrick Murphy,
Thomas Harrington,
Charles Durgen,
Francis Tone.
Peter Donohue,
John McMullen,
Joseph Walker,
Corporal Henry Braio,
Corporal E. F. Moore,
Wm. Cooke.
Alfred Barnum,
James McMann,
Byron Walworth.

Wounded.

First Lieut. B. W. Hoxie,
Ord'y Sergt. A. Belcher,
Corporal J. Hervey,
P. L. Afforvitel,
J. Rowan,
A. Dolan,
J. Davenport,
D. Clarke,
R. Howard,
J. C. Teffeny,
J. Westervelt.
Capt. Daniel Mahen,
Capt. Comerford,
Thomas Mifard,
John Clarke,
James Fountain,
Peter Shelton,
Christian Right,
August Frost,
First Lieut. Philip Miles.
Corporal D. B. Price.
Act. Lieut. S. W. Howe,
James Sullivan,
Wm. McFarland,
Joseph Meis,
P. C. Flick,
Dennis Falvey,
George W. Meade,
John Belden,
Philip Callahan,
James Calfield,
Joseph Johnson.
Wm. Wakefield.
Corporal J. Conkley,
J. H. Garrahard,
J. Kitchell,
J. M. Pouse,
Capt. J. McCarnby,
Sergeant John Sheridan,
John Bouelph,
C. L. Hilliard,
S. M. Lewis,
Thos. Murphy,
John Quinn.
J. G. Rosenoratz,
Geo. Warren,
James Haley,
Tim. Riendon,
Jere. E. Cochran,
John Loftus,
Daniel Mullane,
Corporal Jno. Franklin,
James Hyland,
George Hebard,
Alex. White,
Martin Rigby,
A. C. Strickler,
Wm. Law,
Charles Ebling,
John McCarty,
Lieut. Jas. F. Dennerton,
Corporal S. Craft,
T. Scanless,
James Cathcart.
John Campbell.
Thomas Dardis,
J. Montgomery,
D. M. Russell,
Jacob Kinzie,
Wm. Webber,
Wm. Russell,
Rudolph Frank,
Lieut. G. P. Stevens,
Sergeant Jos. W. Craw,
Sergeant H. B. Myers,
Corporal Alex. Harrison,
Chas. S. Cockell,
Corpl. Wilson L. Derarne,
Wm. H. Price,
Wm. Constable,
Samuel Garven,
Robt. McKinzbry,
Hiram Saxton,
Elias Branch,
Ira Putnam,
Mark Worthington,
Dexter D. Patrick,
Averill J. Rounay,
John M. Smith,
Anthony Emerling,
Moses Mabee,
Fred. Hatfield,
Lieut. Geo. Robinson,
Sergeant J. Stevenson,
Corpl. W. H. Wilkinson,
Thomas Allen,
Chas. Glassier,
John Hammett,
David Hitchcock,
Wm. Lasler,
John Pangborn,
J. Clegg,
Peter Irvine,
J. Markham,
J. Lesler,
1st Lieut. C. E. Dodge,
Corporal James Lowe,
N. E. Fountain,
Thos. Larkin,
Robt. Marines,
D. H. Mead,
Thos. Ross,
Wm Sergeant,
Sergeant John Currie,
A. F. McHaney,
Thos. Haloran,
Wm. McKean,
Patrick Murray,
Sergeant Alex. Theis,
James Sweeney,
F. Rainbow.
John Buck.
Morgan Sutton,
James Spahr.
Robt. McClelland,
F. H. Smith,
Thomas Evans,
James Felter,
Lieut. Henry Ellesson,
Sergeant Saml. Kelly,
Tim. Sullivan,
George Smith.
Eugene McCarthy,
Aug. Walker,
Benj. Turner,
Chas. Burgess.

[*Continued on Eighth Page.*]

FROM NEW-ORLEANS.

Further Particulars From Our Correspondents.

Interesting Scenes and Incidents.

Additional Reports to the Navy Department.

Comments of the New-Orleans Press on the Capture.

A MESSAGE FROM MAYOR MONROE.

The Business Prospects of the City.

QUARANTINE STATION, BELOW NEW-ORLEANS, }
Sunday, April 27, 1862. }

Our ships have been pretty well riddled, and we have had both killed and wounded on board all of them, but, thank God, much fewer than we had reason to anticipate.

The following order was observed in the attack, the squadron being divided into two divisions:

The Second Division, commanded by Capt. T. BAILEY, advanced first, viz:

Gunboat *Cayuga*, Lieut. Commanding HARRISON.
United States steamship *Pensacola*, Capt. H. W. MORRIS.
United States steamship *Mississippi*, Commander M. SMITH.
United States steamship *Oneida*, Commander S. P. LEE.
United States steamer *Varuna*, Commander C. S. BOGGS.

At 2½ o'clock they got under weigh, and by 3½ o'clock they were within the range of Fort Jackson. After firing in several broadsides, they continued onward, to engage Fort St. Philip, at short range, on the right bank of the river, while the First Division, consisting of the following ships, came up in gallant style, to continue the engagement with Fort Jackson:

Flagship *Hartford*, Flag-Officer FARRAGUT.
U. S. steamer *Brooklyn*, Capt. CRAVEN.
U. S. steamer *Richmond*, Commander ALDEN.
U. S. steamer *Iroquois*, Commander DECAMP.
Gunboat *Scioto*, Lieut.-Commanding DONALDSON.
Gunboat *Wissahicon*, Lieut.-Commanding A. SMITH.
Gunboat *Kineo*, Lieut.-Commanding RANSOM.
Gunboat *Katahdin*, Lieut.-Commanding PREBLE.
Gunboat *Kennebeck*,* Lieut.-Commanding RUSSELL.
Gunboat *Winona*, Lieut.-Commanding CROSBY.
Gunboat *Itasca*,* Lieut.-Commanding COLWELL.
*These did not succeed in passing the forts.

As soon as the squadron passed the forts, we fell in with the enemy's fleet, which we engaged, and soon destroyed nearly all their vessels, which were either sunk or set fire to and abandoned. The U. S. steamer *Mississippi* had the honor of capturing the celebrated ram *Manassas*, which gave such a fright to our squadron in August last. She had already given the *Mississippi* a poke in the ribs, and had injured several of our ships, when Capt. SMITH signalized the flagship for permission to give chase, which being granted he approached her in gallant style, and ran her ashore, where she was captured and destroyed.

Proceeding on our way up the river we arrived at the Quarantine Station, where we captured a body of 500 men, who laid down their arms; a regiment of rebel troops also surrendered to Capt. BAILEY on the opposite side of the river.

In an hour we were under way again, steaming along with the Stars and Stripes floating from our mast-heads. Many of the houses displayed white flags as we passed, and some of the inhabitants waved their handkerchiefs at us.

At sundown we came to anchor a few miles below the celebrated "English Turn," and remained all night to bury our dead. At 5 A. M. on the 25th we got under weigh, again ascending the river in line. The appearance of the country had been gradually changing its character as we proceeded on our way. On each side of the river there were fine sugar plantations, with gangs of negroes peacefully working in the fields, and beautiful mansions, surrounded with trees and orange groves, in full bloom. Everything looked so calm and peaceful that we almost imagined there would be no more resistance, but as we approached the city round Slaughter-House Point, the boom of the cannon put an end to these fancies.

A brisk fire was opened on us from each side of the river, but our march was onward, and engaging each battery in turn, at short range, we silenced them all in less than thirty minutes, and came to anchor at noon in front of the city. Before our arrival the Vigilance Committee had fired all the steamers and cotton-ships lying along the levee, and the clouds of black smoke that enveloped the fleet and the city gave a grand but fearful aspect to the scene. More than fifty fine ships and steamers were destroyed, and the loss of property must have amounted to several millions of dollars. A kind Providence appeared to lead us throughout the whole contest, and even at this last moment the windows of Heaven were opened, sending down a copious rain, which tended greatly to limit the extent of the conflagration.

MONDAY, April 28.

Fort Jackson and Fort St. Philip surrendered to Commander D. PORTER at 12 o'clock M. The conditions were: Arms and all public property to be surrendered, and officers and men to be placed on parole not to take up arms again during the war, unless regularly exchanged. I have just returned from a visit to the forts, and the rebel troops are evacuating.

Gen. DUNCAN, commanding the coast defences; Col. HIGGINS, commanding Fort Jackson; Commodore MITCHELL, and many other officers, were taked prisoners.

Commander MCINTOSH was killed, and Capt. HUGER was seriously wounded.

All the above officers formerly belonged to our navy. What a blow this will give to rebeldom, for read what the *Daily Delta* of the 19th inst. says:

"The name of New-Orleans has never once been coupled with defeat or surrender. She has been crowned with the prestige of victory. Shall she be uncrowned, and loaded with the humiliation of conquest by the most hated and loathsome of foes?"

MORE OFFICIAL DOCUMENTS.

REPORT OF CAPT. BAILEY.

U. S. GUNBOAT CAYUGA, AT SEA, May 7, 1862.

Hon. Gideon Welles, Secretary of the Navy.

SIR:—Having found it impossible to get the Colorado over the bars of the Mississippi, I sent up a large portion of her guns and crew, filling up deficiency of both in the different vessels, and with my aid, Acting Midshipman Higginson, steward and boat's crew, followed up myself, hoisting by authority of the Flag-Officer my red distinguishing flag as second in command, first on the Oneida, Commander Lee, and afterwards on the Cayuga.

The brave, resolute, and indefatigable officer, Commander D. D. PORTER, was at work with his mortar fleet, throwing shell at and into Fort Jackson, while Gen. BUTLER, with a division of his army in transports, was waiting a favorable moment to land. After the mortar fleet had been playing upon them for six days and nights without perceptibly diminishing their fire, and one or two changes of programme, Flag Officer FARRAGUT formed the ships into two columns, "Line ahead," the column of the Red under my orders being formed on the right, and consisted of the *Cayuga*, Lieut.-Commanding HARRISON, bearing my flag and leading the *Pensacola*, Capt. MORRIS; the *Mississippi*, Commander SMITH; *Oneida*, Commander J. P. LEE; *Varuna*, Commander C. L. BOGGS; *Katahdin*, Lieut.-Commanding PREBLE; *Kineo* Commander RANSOM, and the *Wissahickon*, Lieut.-Commanding A. A. SMITH.

The column of the Blue was formed on the left and

The New-York Times.

VOL. XI—NO. 3319. | NEW-YORK, TUESDAY, MAY 13, 1862. | PRICE TWO CENTS.

THE CAPTURE OF NORFOLK.

Editorial Correspondence of the New-York Times.

Interesting Particulars of the Advance Upon and Occupation of the City.

The Destruction of the Navy-Yard by the Rebels.

Proclamations Issued by Gens. Wool and Viele.

THE LAST OF THE MERRIMAC.

Character of the Rebel Fortifications on Craney Island.

Gen. Wool's Report to the War Department.

About Two Hundred Cannon Captured.

OCEAN VIEW, OPPOSITE FORTRESS MONROE, Saturday evening, 8 o'clock.

NORFOLK and Gosport Navy-yard again belong to the United States! Our troops under Gen. WOOL entered and took possession of the town at 5 o'clock this afternoon, receiving its surrender at the hands of the Mayor and Common Council. All the troops who had been holding it under Gen. HUGER were withdrawn yesterday,—the public buildings and public property in the Navy-yard were all destroyed,—the people remained in the city, and our forces entered into peaceable possession, being encamped two miles out of the town, in what is called the Intrenched camp, which was very strongly fortified, and in which 30 pieces of cannon fell into our possession. Brig.-Gen. EGBERT L. VIELE has been appointed Military Governor of the place, and the strongest assurances were given by Gen. WOOL and by Secretary CHASE, who accompanied him throughout the march, that the persons and property of all the inhabitants should be treated with the utmost respect.

This is the general summary of the intelligence as I have just received it at this point from Gen. WOOL and Secretary CHASE, who have this moment returned from Norfolk in the carriage heretofore used by Gen. HUGER. The details of the expedition as well as its origin, are worthy of more specific mention. For some time past Gen. WOOL has been of the opinion that Norfolk might be taken without great cost: but nothing definite had been done in regard to it, partly because the coöperation of the Navy Department could not be secured, and partly because such a movement was not consistent with the general plan of the campaign which had been decided upon. After the fall of Yorktown and the withdrawal of the great body of the rebel army, it was believed that the abandonment of Norfolk would speedily follow as a necessary consequence. When Gen. McCLELLAN, therefore, on Monday after the fall of Yorktown, telegraphed to Gen. WOOL asking for more troops in order to make an effective pursuit of the rebels up the York River, Gen. WOOL declined to send any on the ground that it might become necessary for him to take and hold Norfolk.

On Thursday the little steamtug *J. B. White* came in from Norfolk, having deserted from the rebel service. She had been sent to bring in a couple of schooners from the mouth of Tanner's Creek; the officers in charge of her being Northern men, and having been long desirous of escaping from the rebel *régime*, considered this a favorable opportunity for effecting their object. They slipped past Craney Island without attracting any hostile observation, and then steered directly for Newport's News. On arriving they reported to Gen. WOOL that *the rebel troops were evacuating Norfolk*—that very many had already gone, and that not over two or three thousand remained, and even these, it was confidently believed, would very speedily be withdrawn. They were men of intelligence and of evident sincerity, and their statements commanded full confidence.

Under these circumstances Gen. WOOL decided to make a military demonstration upon Norfolk. A large body of troops was embarked upon the transports lying in the Roads, and all preparations were made with a view to *a landing on Sewall's Point during Thursday night.* Several of our vessels were sent to shell the Point during the preceding day, and as you have already heard, they did it with a good deal of effect. But they received very vigorous replies from the batteries there, and were finally put to flight by the appearance of the *Merrimac*, which came up to take part in the conflict. This vigorous demonstration on the part of the rebels satisfied the military authorities that the attack could not safely be made at that time, or at that point. The troops were accordingly disembarked on Friday morning, and the expedition was for the time abandoned.

On Friday Secretary CHASE, who had been spending several days here, as had also President LINCOLN and Secretary STANTON, learned from a pilot familiar with the coast, that there was a place where a landing could be effected a mile or so beyond Willoughby Point,—and that a very good road led directly from that shore to Norfolk. In company with Gen. WOOL and Col. T. J. CRAM, of the Topographical Engineers, Secretary CHASE on Friday crossed over in the steam revenue-cutter *Miami*, and sent a boat to sound the depth of water and examine the shore, with a view to a landing for troops. While doing so, they perceived signs of a mounted picket guard on the shore above, and not deeming it safe to venture too far, they pulled back for the *Miami*. On their way, however, a woman was seen in a house on shore waving a white flag. The boat's crew at once returned, and were told by the woman that her husband had fled to the woods to avoid being forced into the rebel service by the mounted scouts who came every day to find him, and that on his last departure he had instructed her to wave a white flag on the approach of any boats from the Union side. She gave the party a good deal of valuable information concerning the roads and the condition of the country between there and Norfolk. Secretary CHASE and Col. CRAM went ashore and satisfied themselves that a landing was perfectly feasible. On returning to Fortress Monroe they found that President LINCOLN and Secretary STANTON, on examining the maps, had been led to make a similar exploration and had come to a similar conclusion, though the points at which the two parties had struck the shore proved to have been a mile or two apart.

The result of all this was that Gen. WOOL decided upon an immediate march upon Norfolk *from that point*, and orders were at once issued to carry it into effect. The steamer *Adelaide*, which was filled with freight and passengers for Baltimore, was stopped half an hour before her time of sailing, and with half a dozen others, was at once occupied by the infantry and artillery destined for the expedition. They began to embark at about 4 o'clock, on Friday afternoon, and by midnight several of them had started for the opposite shore. A vigorous bombardment was open from the Rip Raps upon Sewall's Point, and kept up for two hours, to induce the belief that this was the intended point of debarkation. The steamers crossed over, and at daylight preparations were made for landing. The shore is a smooth sandy beach,—the sand being very deep as you leave the water, and suddenly rising into long mounds ten or fifteen feet high, thrown up by the heavy winds blowing in upon the shore, and forming a complete breastwork around the fields which they invade. The water, shallow at the shore line, deepens very gradually, and only at some fifty feet out becomes deep enough for vessels drawing five or six feet of water. Three or four canal-boats were towed over, and placed side by side lengthwise of the coast,—an inclined platform was constructed to the land, and this served for a temporary wharf across which the troops, cannon, and other indispensables of the expedition were landed. The infantry regiments were landed first, and started at once upon their march. The negroes, who alone remained behind, said that a mounted picket had been there the day before, but had left, saying that the Union men were coming over in a day or two. The troops were landed, and started forward in the following order:

Twentieth New-York, Col. MAX WEBER.
Sixteenth Massachusetts, Col. P. T. WYMAN.
Ninety-ninth New-York, Col. WARDROP.
First Delaware, Col. J. W. ANDREWS.
Fifty-eighth Pennsylvania.
Tenth New-York, Col. BENDIX.
One hundred Mounted Riflemen.
FOLLETT'S Battery, Light Artillery, six pieces.
HOWARD'S Battery, four pieces.

One leading object of pushing forward the infantry rapidly was to secure, if possible, the bridge across Tanner's Creek, by which the route to Norfolk would be shortened several miles. The route lay through pine woods and over roads in only tolerable condition. At about 1 o'clock the leading regiment, under MAX WEBER, came to the bridge and found it burning, having just been set on fire by a body of men who had planted a couple of small guns on the opposite bank, which they opened upon our advance. Gen. MANSFIELD, who had come over from Newports News, at Gen. WOOL'S request, to join the expedition, thought this indicated an intention to resist the further progress of our troops, and that nothing could be done without artillery and a larger force. He accordingly started back to hurry up the batteries and to provide for bringing over a portion of his command as a reinforcement. Gen. WOOL, however, meantime decided to push forward. The column marched back about two miles and a half to a point where a diverging road led around the head of Tanner's Creek, and took that route to Norfolk. Nothing further was heard from the party that had fired upon our column, and it was evident that the demonstration was merely intended to protect them in the destruction of the bridge. They fired about a dozen shots, none of which took effect.

Our troops pushed rapidly forward in spite of the heat of the day, and at 5 o'clock reached the intrenched camp, some two miles this side of Norfolk, which had been very strongly fortified with earthworks on which were mounted twenty-nine pieces of artillery. No troops were in the place, and our forces passed through it on their way to the town. Just before reaching it they were met by a flag of truce, to which an officer was at once sent forward to inquire its object. Receiving the information that it was to treat for the surrender of the city, the officer returned, and Gen. WOOL and Staff, with Secretary CHASE, advanced to meet the Mayor of the city, who had come out under the flag. Both parties dismounted and entered a cottage by the roadside, when the Mayor informed the General of the evacuation of the city and of the object of his visit.

It seems that a meeting was held at Norfolk some days since, not long, probably, after the evacuation of Yorktown was resolved upon, of the rebel Secretary of War, Gen. HUGER, Gen. LONGSTREET, and some others of the leading military authorities, at which it was determined not to attempt to hold the City against any demonstration of the National forces to effect its capture. This decision was followed by the withdrawal of the main body of the troops; and this (Saturday) morning, after it was understood that our troops had landed at Ocean View, and were advancing upon the City, Gen. HUGER addressed the following letter to the Mayor:

HEADQUARTERS OF THE ARMY, NORFOLK, May 10, 1862.

Hon. W. W. Lamb, Mayor:

SIR: The troops which formerly defended this neighborhood having been removed elsewhere by order of the Government, I have not the means to defend the city, and have ordered the forces off, and turn over the charge of the city to yourself and its civil officers.

I have the honor to be, very respectfully, your obedient servant, BENJ. HUGER, Major-General.

Upon receiving this note, the Mayor immediately convened the Select and Common Councils of the city, and the following action was taken:

At a joint meeting of the Select Council and the Common Council of the City of Norfolk, held on the 10th of May, 1860, the following preamble and resolutions were adopted:

Whereas, An official communication has been received by the Mayor of the city from Maj. Gen. HUGER, announcing that the troops which formerly defended this neighborhood having been withdrawn, he has no longer the power to defend the City, and that he turns over the charge of it to the Mayor and civil officers;

Therefore, *Resolved*, That Capt. JAMES CORNICK and C. H. ROWLAND, Esqs., President and Vice-President of the Special Council, and J. B. WHITEHEAD and G. W. CAMP, Esqs., President and Vice-President of the Common Council, be, and they are hereby appointed a Committee to coöperate with the Mayor in conferring with the Federal Military Commander, and assuring him that no resistance can or will be made to the occupation of the city by the United States forces, but that the citizens expect and claim protection to persons and property during such occupation.

Resolved, That the Committee proceed to meet the Commanding-General of the United States forces, and communicate this action to him.

(Signed) F. G. BROUGHTON, Jr., Clerk.

These proceedings were taken this morning, and the Committee designated in these resolutions proceeded, in company with the Mayor, to meet Gen. WOOL.

The Mayor, after presenting these resolutions, said he had come in conformity with the instructions they contained to surrender the city into the hands of the United States, and to ask protection for the persons and property of the citizens.

Gen. WOOL replied that *his request was granted in advance*,—that the Government of the United States had not the slightest wish or thought of interfering with the rights of any peaceable citizen, and that all should have full protection against violence of every kind. The first thing he had done on setting out in the morning had been to issue an order, prohibiting under the severest penalties any interference whatever with the private property or rights of any citizen, and this prohibition should be enforced with the utmost rigor. He begged the Mayor to rest assured that everything he had asked should be granted.

A general conversation then took place between the officials on each side, in which their sentiments and opinions were freely interchanged. Special stress was laid by the city representatives on the fact that they had discountenanced, in every way possible, all the propositions that had been made for the destruction of private property, and the burning of the bridge across Tanner's Creek was characterized as an utterly useless and unauthorized act. Capt. CORNICK said that if the Government had ordered the city to be burned, he should of course have submitted; but he had given public notice that if any member of any Vigilance Committee, or anybody else, without full authority from the Government, should attempt to set his house on fire, he would shoot him on the spot. The Mayor concurred in these sentiments, and expressed the strongest determination to do everything in his power for the preservation of the public peace and of social order.

The party then broke up to go the City Hall for the formal inauguration of the new military authorities. The Mayor invited Gen. WOOL and Secretary CHASE to ride with him in his carriage, and they proceeded together, followed by the General's bodyguard and the troops. After entering the City Hall the Commanding General issued the following

GENERAL ORDER, NO. 1.

HEADQUARTERS DEPARTMENT OF VIRGINIA, NORFOLK, May 10, 1862.

The city of Norfolk having been surrendered to the Government of the United States, military possession of the same is taken in behalf of the National Government by Maj.-Gen. JOHN E. WOOL.

Brig.-Gen. VIELE is appointed Military Governor for the time being. He will see that all citizens are carefully protected in all their rights and civil privileges, taking the utmost care to preserve order and to see that no soldier be permitted to enter the city except by his order, or by the written permission of the commanding officer of his brigade or regiment, and he will punish summarily any American soldier who shall trespass upon the rights of any of the inhabitants.

(Signed.) JOHN E. WOOL, Major-General Commanding.

Immediately after issuing this order Gen. WOOL with his Staff and Secretary CHASE withdrew, and rode back in the carriage used only this morning by Gen. HUGER, across the country to Ocean View, the place of debarkation, which they reached at a little after 8 o'clock. The only report of the surrender of the city which preceded them was brought by a negro, who arrived about twenty minutes in advance, and said that he left Norfolk at 5½ o'clock, and that he then saw a body of our horsemen and one regiment of infantry inside the works. He had walked all the way, and his report was speedily confirmed by the appearance of the General in person, who at once went on board the steamboat *Pioneer* and returned to Fortress Monroe—stopping on the way to announce the result to the Flag-officer of the fleet on board the *Susquehanna*.

Gen. VIELE at once entered upon the discharge of his duties. His first act was to issue the following, which was freely posted and circulated throughout the town:

PROCLAMATION.

NORFOLK, Va., May 10, 1862.

The occupancy of the cities of Norfolk and Portsmouth is for the protection of the public property, and the maintenance of the public laws of the United States. Private associations and domestic quiet will not be disturbed, *but violations of order and disrespect to the Government will be followed by the immediate arrest of the offenders.* Those who have left their homes, under the anticipation of any acts of vandalism, may be assured that the Government allows no man the honor of serving in its armies who forgets the duties of a citizen in discharging those of a soldier, and that no individual rights will be interfered with. The sale of liquor is prohibited. The office of the Military Governor and of the Provost-Marshal are at the Custom-house.

(Signed) EGBERT L. VIELE, Brigadier-General United States Army, and Military Governor.

Immediately after Gen. WOOL left the City Hall, a large concourse of citizens assembled around the City Hall and called loudly for a speech from the Mayor.

Mayor LAMB came forward and addressed them briefly, confining himself mainly to a recital of the incidents of the day. He said that he had had nothing to do with deciding the result; that had been done by the superior authorities. The citizens of Norfolk had been deserted by their friends, and all the city authorities could do was to obtain the best terms possible for themselves and their property. He was happy to assure them that in this he had been successful. The Commanding General of the United States troops had conceded everything they had asked, and had guaranteed the preservation of order. He enjoined upon the citizens the maintenance of peace and quiet, and exhorted them to abstain from all acts of violence and disorder. If the decision had rested with him he would have defended the city to the last man; but their Government had decided differently, and they must yield to its authority. The Mayor's remarks were cheered by the crowd, who also gave three cheers for President DAVIS with a great deal of enthusiasm, and also responded with less heartiness to a demand for three groans for LINCOLN.

Gen. HUGER left Norfolk only two hours before the entry of our troops. Before the army withdrew, the following letter was addressed to the Mayor:

NORFOLK, May 10.

DEAR SIR: I am directed by Major-Gen. HUGER to hand over to you all the provisions in my possession for distribution to the poor and needy of our community, discriminating in favor of the families of the volunteers who are absent on service.

In the press and hurry of the moment I cannot furnish an inventory of the stock on hand. But there are several hundred barrels of flour at the tobacco warehouse and at the store of ODOM & CLEMENTS. At the store of W. D. REYNDERS & Co. there is also a large amount of bacon, and in the building occupied by me there are many articles for the needy.

W. H. SMITH.

Thus ends this day's work. It has been vigorous and effectual. The embarkation of the expedition began last night at 4 o'clock. It was landed upon a slightly-known shore, without a wharf, early next day. Gen. WOOL slept in Fortress Monroe last night,—marched with his troops some twenty miles, captured Norfolk, and was in bed again in his own quarters before midnight. The President and Secretary of War were awakened to hear the news, and received it *en deshabille*, and with great exultation. They all slept the better for it.

One of the neatest little exploits of the campaign was performed by Capt. DRAKE DE KAY, of Gen. MANSFIELD'S Staff, while awaiting the General's arrival at a house called *Moore's Ranche*, a kind of Summer hotel kept by a man named MOORE, at Ocean View, the place of debarkation. All the white men, and most of the women of this vicinity had fled—it was said by those they had left behind, to the woods, to prevent being forced into the rebel service. Capt. DE KAY, while supper was being prepared, mounted his horse and determined to explore the country, followed only by his negro servant. As he was passing a swamp toward evening, he came suddenly upon *seven* of the secession troops, who were lurking by the roadside, and were armed with double-barreled guns. The Captain turned and shouted to his (imaginary) company to prepare to charge—and then riding forward rapidly, revolver in hand, told the men they were his prisoners, as his cavalry would soon be upon them, ordered them to discharge their pieces and deliver them to him, which they did without delay. He then informed them that his only "company" was his negro servant, and directed them to follow him into camp. An hour later, just after Gen. WOOL had returned from Norfolk, the Captain rode to the beach and informed Col. CRAM, as Chief of the General's Staff, that the seven prisoners, whom he had marched to the beach, were at his disposal. Their arms were taken away, and on *promising* to take the oath of allegiance, the men were at once dismissed. One of them proved to be MOORE himself, who came over to his house, where he found half-a-dozen of us in full possession, and just preparing to discuss a very comfortable supper which his colored cook had got ready for us. Like nearly all the rebel soldiers in this section, he said that he had been *forced* into the service, and was only awaiting a chance to run away; but his statements on this point did not obtain, to say the least, any *more* credit than they deserved. The guns of this little squad, who were probably one of the rebel pickets scattered through the woods, were all handsome and effective double-barreled fowling-pieces.

Later—Destruction of the Merrimac.

FORTRESS MONROE—Sunday Morning.

The first news that greeted us this morning was that the *Merrimac* had been blown up by her officers, and was no longer to dominate our fleet in Hampton Roads. The news at first seemed too good to be true. Careful observers, however, and among them Capt. GADSDEN, of the *Arago*, reported that they had seen and heard the explosion at about 4½ o'clock this morning, and that they thought they could not be mistaken. Early in the morning, on hearing the report, Commodore GOLDSBOROUGH ordered the two tugs *Zouave* and *Dragon* to go down to Craney Island on a reconnoissance. They did so, and very soon returned, reporting that the *Merrimac* was no longer to be seen, that pieces of timber and other indications of a burned and wrecked vessel were floating in the neighborhood where she had lain the night before, and that the report of her explosion was doubtless true. Previous to their return they were followed by the *Monitor* and *Naugatuck*, and the *San Jacinto*, the *Susquehanna*, the *Mount Vernon*, the *Seminole* and the *Dacotah* steamed in the same direction. These vessels ran down below Craney Island, and lay off the city. On Craney Island were two or three negroes, who said that the *Merrimac* had been brought back the night before about a mile from where she had been lying,—and that early this morning she was blown up, her officers and crew having gone ashore in small boats, and having started at about 8 o'clock across the country for Suffolk. They said they were about 200 in number.

Large fragments of the wreck were also found floating around, which rendered this story almost certain to be true.

I understand that the officers of the *Monitor* and *Naugatuck* discovered, early this morning, two dead bodies floating in the water, which they had no doubt were those of two sailors belonging to the *Merrimac*. They were not examined, however, nor were any means taken to identify them.

Last night a man in gray naval uniform, accosted Gen. VIELE, at the Atlantic hotel, and wished to know if he would be arrested. The General told him certainly, if he wore that uniform. This morning he made his appearance in the same uniform again, and was arrested. He proved to be the sailing master of the *Merrimac*. He knew nothing of her having been destroyed, but said that her latest orders from the Government were *to go up the James River* for protection against the Federal gunboats. TATNALL had tendered his resignation rather than take her up the York River, but had withdrawn it on receiving notice of this change in her destination. The prisoner was taken on board the *Monitor*, and had a long conversation with Lieut. JEFFERS about the contest between the two vessels. He said no shots from the *Monitor* had penetrated the *Merrimac*, or injured her in any way except by starting her timbers; and that the only shot which entered her was one from the *Cumberland*, which struck her port-hole, split the gun, killed two men and wounded seventeen, including Capt. BUCHANAN. This man did not concede that the *Merrimac* was afraid to fight the *Monitor*, but he intimated very plainly that there had been great dissatisfaction among the crew, and great difficulty in bringing them to obey orders. He thought they would not blow her up so long as there was any chance of making her useful in the James River or elsewhere; but that if this project had been given up, they would be very likely to dispose of her in that way.

I have no doubt whatever of the destruction of the vessel. It became, in fact, a necessity after the surrender of Norfolk. She could only go twelve miles up the James River, as the water was not deep enough for her,—and our gunboats are already far beyond that point. If it was certain that the rebels were determined to make another stand in front of Richmond, I should think it strange that they should consent to forego all aid from this formidable vessel, which might at least prevent other gunboats from going to the assistance of the attacking army. But the destruction of the *Merrimac* confirms the impression I have received from the recent military movements of the rebels, and which I have more than once expressed, that *Virginia has been substantially abandoned by the rebel Government.*

VISIT OF PRESIDENT LINCOLN AND SECRETARIES STANTON AND CHASE TO NORFOLK.

President LINCOLN, who has been staying here, as have also the Secretaries of War and the Treasury, for several days, and whose presence and personal participation in the movements of the last week, have been of the utmost importance to the country, decided to start for Washington this morning in the steamer *Baltimore*. On hearing the reported destruction of the *Merrimac* confirmed he concluded first to take a look at this latest of the ships which has been recovered for the Union. Taking Gen. WOOL on board the steamer accordingly, under charge of Commodore GOLDSBOROUGH, they went down to Norfolk, where the Commodore left for his flagship, and Gen. WOOL remained to transact business connected with the affairs of this new Department. The President did not go ashore, but after taking a look at the city started immediately for Washington. His visit here has been of the most unostentatious, but certainly of the most useful sort. He has given his personal attention and care to every department of operations here, and has brought a very excellent and safe judgment to bear upon matters which required something more than mere professional knowledge and skill for their solution. And I do no injustice to others in saying that much of the vigor and success of the recent operations here is due to the stimulus of his presence.

Latest from Norfolk.

NORFOLK, Sunday, May 11—2 P. M.

I seized the first opportunity, to-day, to take a look at the fortifications by which Norfolk has been so long defended against our fleet. It is easy to see that their strength has not been exaggerated. The works on Sewall's Point are quite extensive, intended for forty guns, only twenty-three of which, however, have ever been mounted, and of these only seven now remain. Craney Island—long, low and level—stands just at the entrance of the channel, and has upon it a very formidable series of skilfully constructed earthworks, intended for fifty guns, of which thirty-nine had been mounted,—mostly nine and ten inch Dahlgrens, though there were also rifled and Parrot guns among them. There were also nine finished casemates on the north bastion, and five unfinished. The works are all admirably constructed. Next beyond Craney Island, on the right, is a most beautiful semi-circular water battery, with eleven casemates, and finished in as fine style as any works of a similar kind I have ever seen. Still further on, upon the same side, is still another battery, while on the opposite shore stands Fort Norfolk. All these works together constitute a gauntlet which it certainly would not be prudent in any but the most powerful vessel of war to attempt to run. Then, too, just below these batteries, directly across the channel, has been driven a line of piles, an opening being left in the middle for the passage of vessels, intended, however, to be closed in an emergency by sinking the immense hulk of the old *United States*, which lies close by for preparation. Upon these piles, the *San Jacinto*, as she was going in to-day, stuck fast for a couple of hours, but finally extricated herself without injury.

The rebels succeeded in almost completely destroying the Navy-yard last night. Hundreds of them were busy in setting fire to all the buildings and all the vessels, and this morning little remained but smoking ruins and a dismal desolation. The great Eastern and Western ship-houses, the marine barracks, officers' quarters, smiths' shops, engine houses, &c., were all consumed. The rebels had built and launched two iron vessels, mounting four guns each and built in water-tight compartments, so as to be raised or sunk at pleasure. These were not intended to be propelled, but to be used as stationary batteries for harbor defence, or else to be towed out to operate against our wooden vessels. They were burned, but not so seriously injured as to be entirely useless. A number of small vessels and schooners were also burned. Great efforts were made to destroy the dry dock, but they were unsuccessful.

The magnificent Naval Hospital remains untouched. Even the vandalism which has marked so many of the acts of the rebels during this war, shrank from the sacrilege of firing this splendid structure.

A good deal has been said in conversation here of the feeling of the citizens of Norfolk. All the public indications of sentiment in the city thus far have certainly been on the side of secession. Scarcely half a-dozen men have ventured to come out boldly as Union men. The general tone of conversation, where you succeed in getting any, is dull, discontented and sour. I do not regard this, however, as an infallible indication of settled political sentiment. The people unquestionably feel that they have been abandoned by their friends and *conquered* by the North. This is never a pleasant feeling, and men must be pardoned for not being able to conquer it on the instant. I saw nothing, during my stay in the city, which was it is true very short, to indicate that spiteful hatred of the Union and its friends which has been manifested in other quarters.

The negroes were out in full force,—and were all in their most smiling holiday attire. Whether it was the military show, always so fascinating to the negro mind, or the equally strong passion for something new, or a sanguine perception that all this conquest is for their behoof, I do not pretend to say; but they certainly seemed to be the parties most deeply interested in the pageant of to-day. Quite a number of Irishmen were in the streets, and they were mainly quite free to proclaim their satisfaction at the changed aspect of affairs. I had quite a political talk with a dozen or so of plain, respectable people collected on the wharf. They deplored the existing state of things, but thought the Abolitionists mainly to blame for it, and said they were glad no more blood had been shed, because it would only exasperate the feelings of the people, and it seemed after all that we should be *obliged* to live together again as friends by-and-bye.

From what they could learn they thought the state of things very critical at Richmond. The understanding, when Gen. HUGER withdrew the troops from Norfolk was, that they were to go direct by railroad to Petersburgh, and thence to Richmond, with a view to a general concentration of all the Southern troops for the defence of that city. But they expressed a good deal of apprehension lest McCLELLAN should reach Richmond in advance of such a concentration and therefore either frustrate it at once, or form a junction with BANKS and McDOWELL from the other side. They had advices from Richmond to Friday morning, but they

[*Continued on Eighth Page.*]

THE CITY OF RICHMOND AND ITS DEFENCES.

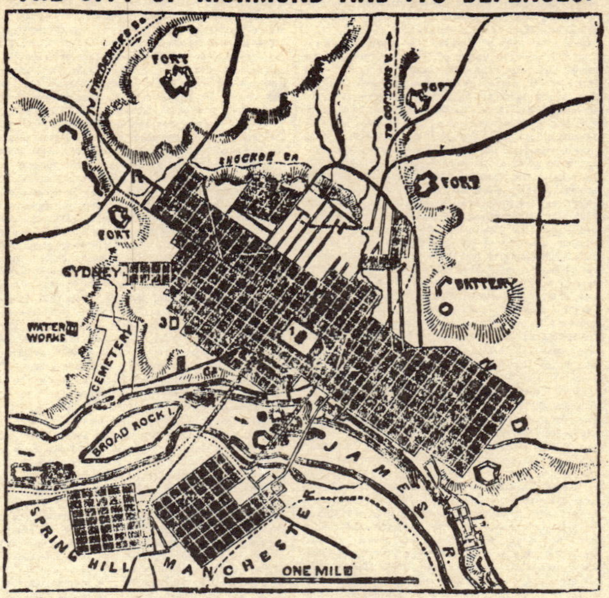

1.—Capital.
2, 2, 2.—Railroad Dépôts.
3.—Penitentiary.
4.—Poorhouse.
5.—City Hall.
7.—State Arsenal.

THE CITY OF RICHMOND.

We give herewith a diagram, showing the minute topography of the famous rebel Capital, upon which Gen. McCLELLAN, is now advancing with such rapid strides. The city, by last census, had a population of thirty-eight thousand souls; but the great influx of civil and military official and refugees from other parts of the State, has probably raised it, of late, to a much higher figure. It is situated at the head of tide-water, at the lower falls of James River, about one hundred and fifty miles from its mouth. The city occupies a most picturesque situation, being built on Richmond and Shockoe hills, which are separated by Shockoe Creek and surrounded by beautiful scenery. It is regularly laid out and well built, the streets, which are lighted with gas, crossing each other at right angles. On Shockoe Hill are the State Capitol and other public buildings. The Capitol is an imposing edifice, and contains in its central hall HOUDON'S celebrated statue of WASHINGTON. On the east of the square is the Governor's mansion, now occupied by the drunkard and traitor LETCHER. JEFF. DAVIS resides in a private mansion, which was purchased for him by the rebel Government. The city has many fine public buildings, six banks, thirteen newspapers and twenty-three churches. In one of the three Presbyterian churches JEFF. DAVIS worships.

The falls of James River afford immense water-power, and there are very extensive factories, including four cotton and about fifty tobacco factories, flour mills, rolling mills, forges, furnaces, machine-shops, &c., the latter of which, and particularly the Tredegar Iron Works, have been of immense service to the rebels in turning out ordnance and material of war. The annual exports of Richmond before the rebellion reached to near $7,000,000, and its imports three quarters of a million; but since it had the honor of being the rebel capital, its foreign commerce has been extinguished. Vessels or gunboats drawing ten feet can ascend to within a mile of the city, at a place called Rockets, from which the rebel capital could be conveniently shelled. Vessels of fifteen feet draught ascend to Warwick, three miles below. A canal has been built around the falls, and above them there is navigation for over 200 miles. The James River and Kanawha Canal, intended to extend to Covington, is completed for 200 miles.

Richmond has very extensive railroad communications, being the terminus of five roads, running to Fredericksburgh and the Potomac, (now in our hands,) to West Point and the York River, (in our hands,) to Petersburgh and Norfolk, (partly in our hands,) to Danville, Va., to Jackson's River, by the Central Railroad, and from these the connections lead all through the Southern States. Opposite the city are the two towns of Spring Hill and Manchester.

Richmond was founded in 1742, became the Capital of the State of Virginia in 1779, and in June, 1861, it was made the seat of government for the "Confederate States of America, whose Congress assembled there on July 20. Its history since then is only too familiar to the country. Around the city are various hills extending a great distance, on the most important of which fortifications were erected last Summer, in the days of the On to Richmond cry. Some of these will be found indicated in our diagram. What fate may now awaits the city depends upon JEFF. DAVIS and his army.

The Charleston Mercury.

VINDICE NULLO — SPONTE SUA SINE LEGE FIDES RECTUMQUE COLENTUR.

VOLUME LXXX. CHARLESTON, S. C., THURSDAY, MAY 15, 1862. NUMBER 11,448

THE MERCURY.

THURSDAY, MAY 15, 1862.

The fate of the Capital, though still a mystery to us, is probably fixed before these words can meet the eyes of our readers. The telegraph, yesterday, brought no tidings from Richmond, and we have nothing later than the brief despatch, dated Tuesday night, announcing that the enemy's gunboats had ascended the James River as far as City Point. The subsequent silence may have been accidental, but it looks ominous. We fear that we shall have the story of New Orleans over again, and that we have lost, through imbecility, sloth and delay, what the Grand Army of McCLELLAN could never have won. But we will hope for the best.

City Point, the head of deep water navigation on the James River, is nearly thirty miles below Richmond. For the past fortnight, the work of obstructing the channel, at a point some miles higher up, has been vigorously going on. Upon the efficacy of the obstructions rests the safety of the city; and before this, we presume, that efficacy has been put to the test.

The fall of Richmond would, indeed, be a heavy blow. It is difficult to estimate the vast quantities of stores and public works which must be destroyed or abandoned in the event of such a disaster. The capture of the seat of Government would sadly shake the confidence of Europe in our ability to achieve our independence. We see it stated that the unofficial advice given in a friendly spirit to gentlemen of high position by Count MERCIER, during his late visit, was never to surrender the Capital.

But happily, the wealth and the strength of this Confederacy do not reside in its cities. We have ceased to hope for encouragement or aid from the Powers of Europe; and the rebels of to-day, relying only upon themselves, will yet show to the world that their spirit cannot be broken by reverses, and that they are no degenerate sons of their fathers—the rebels of our first Revolution.

RICHMOND NEWS AND GOSSIP.

(FROM OUR OWN CORRESPONDENT.)

RICHMOND, Monday, May 12.

Big Battle To-Day—Doubtful—Johnston's Position—Jackson and Heth—Miniature Bombs, &c., &c.

On the street you are told that the great fight which is to decide the fate of Richmond, will certainly come off to-day, and some go so far as to declare that they can hear the cannonading now (11 a. m.) going on. It may be so, if JOHNSTON has made the attack. McCLELLAN is cautious, and now that Norfolk is given up, his plan would be to advance in the direction of Petersburg before giving battle on the Peninsula, so as to divide our forces. Two of Johnston's divisions had crossed the Chickahominy Swamp and the others were crossing, when McClellan pressed his rear so hard that he was compelled to recall the two that had crossed, and make a stand with the swamp in his rear, with only two narrow bridges to facilitate his passage. I learn that he protested against going to the Peninsula, but Davis forced him to it. Instead of attacking McClellan at once, as the whole army desired, he began to dig dirt, and now we see the end of it. The retreat from Yorktown would have added fresh laurels to his reputation, if he had succeeded in crossing the swamp. But Johnston is brave and prudent, even in the estimation of those who do not love him; his own skill and the pluck of his men may extricate him from the difficulty. There are some advantages in having the swamp in his rear. The men will fight desperately, and the facilities for running to Richmond on every pretext will be cut short, for the bridges are easily guarded, and it is a perilous job to wade the swamp.

The Enquirer notifies the Confederacy that the attack on Grant at Shiloh was made *under the instructions* (Enquirer's italics) of the President. This proves Davis' unapproachable wisdom, according to the Enquirer. The idea of fighting one army in preference to two, of course would not have occurred to anybody else. Soldiers from Beauregard's army complain that his hands are tied; and it is in everybody's mouth that Jackson's last despatch to the War Department was, "Send me more men and no more orders." Administration organs may grind out flattery as much as they please; but the day will come when military men will have an opportunity to vindicate themselves, and the truth.

I have nothing in regard to the victories of Jackson and Heth which will not reach you in the papers. You may be sure that "the whole of Milroy's army" is not and will not be "captured," for the simple reason that most Yankees have as many legs as a centipede. Among the missiles used by the enemy at Williamsburg were miniature bombs, about the size of a man's thumb, and filled with shot. They explode on striking an object, are intended to blow up caissons, and are shot from a peculiar rifled gun. We had an invention of this sort at Manassas, but it failed.—A captain came up yesterday, and declared that in the fight on Friday evening we captured 300 prisoners. Nobody else ever heard of the fight.—Whole trains of stragglers have been sent back to Johnston, but still the hotels, streets and the streets leading to the city, are filled with them.—The resident population of Richmond is estimated at 75,000 or 80,000, and provisions are so dear and high that we have to send away on parole all the Yankee prisoners, to keep from feeding them. Two soldiers were murdered last week by Baltimore Plugs. It is said the President has gone down to the big fight. Hope it is true.

HERMES.

IS NOT CHARLESTON TO BE DEFENDED?

To the Editor of the Charleston Mercury:

I appeal to you, as the representative of Carolina chivalry, to have the above question answered.

It was with a feeling of humiliation I never before experienced, I heard, a little while ago, from a gentleman just returned from Charleston, that Charleston possibly *would not be defended*—that dear old Charleston may be surrendered to LINCOLN's abolition vandals when his gunboats sail into the harbor.

Can these things be? Is this inference correct? Shall history record the fact that the very seat and centre of the most glorious revolution the world has ever seen, was given up without a struggle?—that Charleston fell like Roanoke; and that, though her citizens had the intelligence to understand her rights, they lacked the spirit to maintain them? Shades of Rutledge, Moultrie, and Jasper forbid it! But if, indeed, this decree is already written in the Book of Fate, then let us know it at once, that patriots may have the chance to die before so terrible a doom shall overtake them.

Is it really true that no lingering spark yet remains of the spirit of 28th June, 1776, among the sons of Carolina? If so, how dared they begin the strife of 1861, that they have not the courage to carry on to its legitimate result? Is every man there a Bob Acres, whose courage has oozed out at his fingers' ends. No: it cannot be. At least I, for one, will not believe it, until the deed is done.

That there may be, and are, craven-hearted men in your midst, I do not doubt; and with these there are, doubtless, timid property-holders, who shed the tears of a coward and a miser whenever they contemplate the destruction of their shingles and tiles, their brick and mortar, by hostile shells; but, by the glorious memories of the Past, I will yet believe that there are tens of thousands ready not only to sacrifice property, but life itself, in defence of Carolina honor.

For the benefit of those whose recreant hearts cannot be incited to the performance of their duty, please publish the following poem, which loses nothing by having been written forty years ago. I leave them to make the application and draw the parallel, when the banner of Yankeedom floats from your Custom House. MARION.

Georgia, May 10, 1862.

THE NEWS OF THE WAR.

THE EVACUATION OF NORFOLK AND THE BURNING OF THE MERRIMAC.

The Virginia papers teem with the particulars of and comments upon the evacuation of Norfolk and the loss of the *Merrimac-Virginia*. With regard to the latter event, the Petersburg *Express* says:

There are but two rivers in the Confederate States which can accommodate a vessel drawing as much water as did the Merrimac. When she last left the Navy Yard, her draft was 22 feet.—Upon going down Thursday, and driving off the bombarding fleet from Sewell's Point, she lay to under the guns of Craney Island, that she might protect the evacuation of both the Island and the Point. Early Friday morning, the iron-clad vessels Monitor and Galena moved up in the direction of Newport's News, and lay off at a distance of two miles in shoal water. The guns of the Merrimac were very powerful, but of short range, and it was out of the question to think of engaging the Federal vessels unless they would come into deep water. All day Friday those vessels maintained their position, and Saturday morning the Roads was filled with naval vessels of various descriptions. The guns at Craney Island and Sewell's Point had been dismounted, and the Merrimac was compelled to hover close by, to protect the retreat of our troops from those points. Saturday afternoon the troops all got off from Craney Island, those at Sewell's Point having left in the morning.

A council was now held among the officers, and it was determined to try and get into James River, but upon consultation with the pilots, the commander was assured that the vessel could not be run in James River, unless her draft was reduced to 18 feet. This fact was announced to the crew, who received the information with loud cheers, and went to work with great industry, throwing out coal, ballast, etc., to lighten the vessel. By midnight she was lightened to the required draft, but [illegible] new difficulties interposed. She had come up so high as to expose her hull, thus rendering her as vulnerable as any wooden vessel, and the pilots came to the conclusion, that even with only 18 feet, at the present low stage of the water in James River, caused by the strong westerly winds, they could not carry her any distance beyond Newport's News.

General Thomas J. (Stonewall) Jackson

To think of giving battle in the now exposed condition was out of the question, and to remain in her then position rendered her capture only a matter of time. It was then determined to destroy her, and steps were immediately taken to consummate the deed. Her roof, already covered with tallow and other fatty matter, was saturated with oil, and her decks also received a copious supply of the same material. Her crew, numbering 350, were then safely disembarked in small boats, and ten men detailed to apply the torch. This was accomplished by laying small trains of powder from each port to various parts of the ship, which, upon being ignited, speedily enveloped the noble vessel in a sheet of flame. The waters were brilliantly illuminated for miles, but not a boat's crew from any of the Federal vessels dared approach the burning mass to extinguish the fire and secure the prize. She continued to burn until 4 o'clock, when the fire reached her magazine and caused an explosion which shook the earth at Suffolk, 32 miles distant, and sent her enormous guns and nine hundred tons of iron plating flying in the air to a height of three or four hundred feet.

The plates, heated to a cherry red, we are told, presented an awful but magnificent sight. A moment or two more, the flying fragments fell into the water, and all that remained of the most formidable war vessel ever constructed, was her charred and burning hull. We can well imagine the fiendish delight with which our enemies chuckled over this annihilation of what had been to them a "rod of terror" since the 6th of March last, and how soundly Gen. Wool must have slept for the first time since the terrible havoc of that memorable day.

Commodore Tattnall, who it now appears, retained the command of the Virginia at the solicitations of the government, arrived in Richmond on Monday night. The crew of the Virginia have been sent down to the batteries on the James river.

STONEWALL JACKSON'S MOVEMENTS.

The *Dispatch* says:

The news from "Stonewall" Jackson, if it be correct, is glorious. It was rumored in Staunton yesterday morning, and generally credited, that he had completely and effectually dispersed the army of Milroy, and that they were scattered, panic stricken, in every direction. Portions of them had taken the route through Pendleton county, and these were being hotly pursued, and numbers captured; others were breaking their guns and divesting themselves of every article calculated to impede their progress. Ashby is said to be in possession of the enemy's stronghold on Cheat Mountain.

THE FIRING OF THE GOSPORT NAVY YARD.

The Richmond *Dispatch* says:

The Navy Yard was successfully fired and destroyed by a party of eight or ten Marylanders, under command of Lieutenant Spotswood. The dock was blown up by pyrotechnics, under direction of Mr. Thomson, also a Marylander; its gates and ends being effectually blown out, so that the damage may be considered irreparable. Every building and shed in the yard was totally consumed, except the moulding department, which unavoidably was left uninjured, owing to the want of proper combustibles. Having laid waste everything, and applied the torch wherever practicable, the firing party proceeded to St. Helena, opposite, destroyed or burnt all the quarters there, and, arriving at Portsmouth, fired every pound of cotton and tobacco, etc., leaving naught but ashes in their wake. Such was the success of the party under Lieut. Spotswood, that scarcely anything of value was left untouched or intact—all was complete wreck and destruction. All steamers and vessels in both ports were burned and consumed to ashes, and the old "United States" being filled with rock and sunk in the harbor. After leaving the latter place, a party of Marylanders, under Lieut. A. P. Butt, burned all the quarters and government buildings below Portsmouth and Suffolk. Thus the enemy, in occupation of those places, will find nothing but ruins and ashes to reward their labors.

The New-York Times.

VOL. XI—NO. 3323. NEW-YORK, SATURDAY, MAY 17, 1862. PRICE TWO CENTS.

NEWS FROM WASHINGTON.

Thanks to Gen. Wool for the Capture of Norfolk.

What is Thought of Gen. Hunter's Proclamation.

THE FIRST MAILS FOR NEW-ORLEANS.

Probable Appointment of a Military Governor for Kentucky.

NEW GRADES IN THE NAVY.

(OFFICIAL.)

WAR BULLETIN.

WASHINGTON, May 16.

The skillful and gallant movements of Major-Gen. John E. Wool, and the forces under his command, which resulted in the surrender of Norfolk, and the evacuation of the strong batteries erected by the rebels on Sewall's Point and Craney Island, and the destruction of the rebel iron clad steamer *Merrimac*, are regarded by the President as among the most important successes of the present war. He therefore orders that his thanks as Commander-in-Chief of the Army and Navy, be communicated by the War Department to Maj.-Gen. John E. Wool, and the officers and soldiers of his command, for their gallantry and good conduct in the brilliant operations mentioned.

By order of the President.

Made at the City of Norfolk, on the 11th day of May, 1862. (Signed.)

EDWIN M. STANTON, Secretary of War.

OUR SPECIAL WASHINGTON DISPATCHES.

WASHINGTON, Friday, May 16.

THE PROCLAMATION OF GEN. HUNTER.

Hunter's proclamation excites scarcely any interest in Washington—no one attaching any importance to it, as efficacious to produce the end designed. Martial law is only enforced by martial power, and Hunter has no force at his command adequate to enforce this proclamation. His declaring freedom to all the slaves in three States, when he has no power to free a single one outside of his camp, is regarded in Washington as an act of stultification highly discreditable to any one holding the rank of General, supposed to have ordinary intelligence. If the military power is withdrawn from Hunter's Department before his proclamation is executed throughout those States, it is conceded that the civil power will not complete or countenance what martial law proclaimed, but did not practically execute. Republicans of radical views see the absurdity of Hunter's proceedings, and some of them claim that the proclamation is a forgery. I have heard of not one who indorses it. The President's policy is supposed to be authoritatively settled by his action in Fremont's case, in which all his Cabinet concurred. Fremont freed by proclamation the slaves of all men engaged in the rebellion; Hunter's proclamation frees the slaves of all men in three States, whether they have engaged in rebellion or not—punishing loyalists as well as traitors, and all because he has "declared martial law," where he has confessedly no ability to execute it. It is understood that Hunter took no specific instructions from the President in regard to the management of matters in his department, but was left, as all other military commanders have been, to his own discretion in his attempt to reëstablish the Constitution and laws in the revolted States. It is said that the President will be waited on this evening by gentlemen, to ascertain under what authority Hunter is acting.

The expressed belief of the *Tribune* that Hunter's proclamation will induce any large number of slaves to escape to the Union lines is sufficiently answered by the fact that Fremont's proclamation remained in force at least two weeks, in Missouri, without producing any such result, although the negroes of Missouri have immeasurably better means of learning "Good news" than have those of Carolina and Georgia. The fruits of Fremont's proclamation were two slaves freed.

MAILS FOR NEW-ORLEANS.

The mails for New-Orleans will be made up at New-York, to be forwarded by sea on every steamer which may leave for that port; therefore the communications between these cities will be frequent. Postmasters are requested to forward all mail matter for New-Orleans to the New-York Post-office.

PROBABLE APPOINTMENT OF A MILITARY GOVERNOR IN KENTUCKY.

In consequence of the removal of all National troops from Kentucky to the theatre of war, further South, the Secessionists in Kentucky, numerous in many localities, have become very impudent and lawless. Recruits for Humphrey Marshall have been openly enlisted in some of the central counties, disloyal candidates for civil offices have declared themselves, and plunderings of Union citizens in exposed sections have taken place. Under these circumstances, and in compliance with the request of the Military Board of Kentucky, the National Government will probably send a Military Governor to Kentucky, clothed with such power as Andy Johnson has, to do the duty which Magoffin fails to do, and to visit upon Secessionists four-fold the punishment that they inflict upon Unionists. A force of five thousand soldiers will probably back up this movement. Gen. J. T. Boyle, of Kentucky, who led a brigade at Shiloh, is spoken of as the Military Governor. Kentucky has near forty thousand soldiers in the Union army—ten thousand more than her quota.

THE EXPECTED BATTLE AT CORINTH AND THE PRESS.

On inquiry at the War Department it is ascertained that the order of the Assistant Supervisor of Telegraphs at Cincinnati to the operator at Cairo was not issued by the Military Supervisor at Washington. It was issued by the Assistant Supervisor at Cincinnati [illegible] a misapprehension of the instructions received [illegible] the Military Supervisor, which were intended [illegible] the forwarding from Cairo to the newspapers [illegible] improper military intelligence and sensational [illegible] relating to military matters, such as [illegible] occasions created public anxiety and [illegible], and of which great complaint [illegible]. There has been no change in the orders of the Department, and there is no intention to withhold any authentic information from the public except such as could not be forwarded without embarrassment to military operations and danger to our armies.

EXPECTED RELEASE OF COL. CORCORAN.

The Secretary of War, upon the application of Representative Ely, has ordered the release of Col. W. F. Baldwin, of Virginia, to be exchanged for Col. Corcoran. Capt. Farrell and Lieut. Dempsey, recently released as prisoners of war from Richmond, and who have been a week in Washington, had represented to the President and Secretary of War the necessity and justice of this arrangement on account of Col. Corcoran's health. Aided by Representative Ely, they have succeeded.

THE CASES OF OTHER PRISONERS.

Representative Kerrigan received to-day, through one of the lately returned Union prisoners, a letter from Richmond, dated May 12, which was hid in a piece of soap, urging him to use his political influence to effect the release of Capts. Downey and Griffin, and Lieuts. Underhill and Fay, of New-York regiments. He also received two photographs of the Union hostages as they appeared in Castle Pinckney.

GEN. WOOL PROMOTED.

The Senate to-day confirmed the nomination of Brevet Major-Gen. Wool to be Major-General of the army, for gallant conduct on the 10th of May, in taking the City of Norfolk, and for other gallant services; also of Charles Case, as Postmaster at Winchester, Va.

Among other minor military nominations the following were confirmed. First Lieut. Wm. Kelsey, formerly a page in the Senate; Charles H. Dustan of New-York, Capt. P. T. Schopf of Pennsylvania, Lieut. Montgomery of Rochester, Orson H. Hart and James C. Clark, all Assistant Adjutant-Generals. Benjamin F. Lushbaugh, of Nebraska, is confirmed as Agent for the Pawnee Indians in that Territory.

GEN. SICKLES TO COMMAND THE EXCELSIOR BRIGADE.

Gen. Sickles was to-day ordered to resume command of the Excelsior Brigade, attached to the army of the Potomac.

TEN GRADES OF RANK IN THE NAVY.

The House Naval Committee to-day acted favorably on a bill to establish ten grades of rank in the navy, to wit: Admirals, Commodores, Captains, Lieutenants, Commanders, Lieutenant-Commanders, Lieutenant-Masters, Passed Midshipmen, Midshipmen, Naval Cadets.

CHARGES AGAINST COL. VAN WYCK.

News reached Washington to-day of a painful character respecting Col. C. H. Van Wyck, member of Congress, Chairman of the Investigating Committee, now commanding a regiment in the field. He is said to be arrested by order of Gen. McClellan, and placed under close confinement, for peccadilloes of identically the same character with those of which his committee convicted others—frauds on the Government. I forbear details, with the hope that satisfactory explanations may be made.

THE COMMISSIONER OF AGRICULTURE.

The President has nominated Isaac Newton to be Commissioner of Agriculture, under the new law creating an independent Bureau of Agriculture. Mr. Newton is a practical farmer, and has long been in charge of the Agricultural Branch of the Patent Office. Eli Thayer, of Massachusetts, was a prominent competitor for the place.

WHO TOOK POSSESSION?

Hon. Henry Wilson has received a letter from a field officer of his old regiment, claiming for the Twenty-second Massachusetts the honor of raising the first national flag upon the rebel works at Yorktown at 6 o'clock in the morning of that day, and the Twenty-second relieved Col. Black and the advance guard. Soon after, the rebel works were occupied by Col. Gove, who planted the National flag belonging to his regiment upon the ramparts, where it remained during the day, being the only flag raised upon the works or in the town until the Forty-fourth New-York came up in the afternoon. The officers of the regiment claim that the official record will prove this fact.

THE FUGITIVE SLAVE LAW.

The Fugitive Slave law is being quietly enforced in the District to-day, the military authorities not interfering with the judicial process. There are at least 400 cases pending. It is said that some of the negroes, whose owners or agents from Maryland are here seeking their recovery, mysteriously disappeared this morning.

REVOKED.

Paragraph two of General Orders, No. 102, dated November last, having been revoked, the officers and men transferred to the skeleton regiments, under its operation, will be assigned to their original regiments as fast as vacancies occur.

DEATH OF A SOLDIER.

Sergeant Charles Irvin, Company G, Fifty-fifth New-York Regiment, died this afternoon, at the National Hospital, from wounds received at the battle of Williamsburgh.

[*For Congressional Proceedings see Eighth Page*]

THE NEWLY-OPENED PORTS.

Instructions from the Secretary of the Treasury Regarding Clearances.

WASHINGTON, Friday, May 16.

The Secretary of the Treasury has issued full instructions to the various Collectors, respecting clearances to ports opened by proclamation of the President. These instructions authorize clearances at any time before the 1st of June; but vessels so cleared are not to enter such ports until on or after that date.

TREASURY DEPARTMENT, May 16, 1862.

SIR: I transmit herewith, for your information, a copy of the Proclamation of the President of the 12th of May, 1862, opening the ports of Beaufort, N. C., Port Royal, S. C., and New-Orleans, La., with the regulations of the Secretary of the Treasury, governing the trade with the said ports. In view of the said Proclamation, and in pursuance of the regulations referred to, you are hereby authorized to grant clearances and license to vessels, to proceed to any of said ports, under the following restrictions:

Before granting any such clearance and license, you will require the master of each vessel to exhibit to you a manifest or descriptive statement of his cargo and a list of the passengers and crew, and to verify the same by his oath or solemn affirmation, and you will fully satisfy yourself that said vessel is intended in good faith for a lawful trade, and will in no wise, directly or indirectly, violate the provisions of the aforesaid proclamation and the regulations referred to. You will insert in such clearance the following: —— Master of the ——, of ——, having exhibited to me a manifest or descriptive statement of his cargo and a list of the passengers and crew, and having verified the same by his oath or solemn affirmation, and I having satisfied myself that the said vessel is intended in good faith for a lawful trade, and only for a lawful trade; now, therefore, by the authority of the Secretary of the Treasury, and in pursuance of a proclamation of the President of the United States and the regulations of the Secretary of the Treasury, issued May 12, 1862, permission is hereby granted for the said vessel to proceed to the port of ——, in the State of ——, and to leave said port for any lawful destination, on the conditions hereinafter mentioned, to wit: That the said vessel will convey no persons property or information contraband of war, either to or from the said port, and that the clearance or license shall be exhibited to the Collector of Customs at the said port of —— immediately on arrival, and if required, to any officer in charge of the blockade, and that the master, and all persons concerned in the management and control of the vessel shall faithfully comply with the revenue laws and regulations of the United States and with the conditions of this clearance and license. The violation of any of the conditions of this clearance will involve the condemnation and forfeiture of the vessel and cargo, and the exclusion of all parties concerned from any further privileges of participating in the trade thus opened by proclamation of the President of the United States. The officers of vessels-of-war, and all other persons, will respect this clearance and license, and permit the said vessel to proceed on her lawful voyage unmolested, while prosecuting the same in conformity with its conditions. In all clearances given prior to the first of June, you will insert the further proviso that the vessel so cleared shall not enter any of the said ports previous to the first of June, on penalty of forfeiture of the vessel and cargo.

I am, very respectfully, your obedient servant.

S. P. CHASE, Secretary of the Treasury.

FROM GEN. HALLECK'S ARMY.

Continued Preparations for the Great Battle.

THE ENEMY BUSY FORTIFYING.

A Report of the Capture of Pensacola.

Numerous Desertions from the Rebel Army.

CAMP ON THE CORINTH ROAD, Thursday, May 15.

The following paragraph is from a Field Order just issued:

"Guards will be immediately placed along the line of Chambers Creek. No officers or soldiers will be permitted to pass to the rear, and no citizens to the front of the line, without special authority. Commanders of the army corps and divisions will see their camps are cleared of all unauthorized hangers-on, and any one attempting to evade this will be compelled to work on the intrenchments, batteries, or in the construction of roads."

This is understood to apply to all persons, correspondents included.

Fifty-seven privates, three corporals, and one Sergeant, were captured at Dresden, Tenn., while coming on under a flag of truce.

Col. Jacob Thompson, of Beauregard's Staff, formerly Secretary of the Interior, accompanied by a flag of truce, admits the fall of Norfolk, New-Orleans and Pensacola. He denies the fall of Richmond.

Deserters are coming into camp daily by squads.

They all agree that the rebels are still at Corinth fortifying.

There have been picket skirmishes all day. A half dozen have been wounded on our side.

The weather is very warm.

General Ideas of a Battle—Misconceptions Corrected—The Weather and Inaction—A Small Stampede and its Cause—A Trip to Farmington—Feeling the Enemy—An Ambuscade.

From Our Own Correspondent.

MONTEREY, Thursday, May 8, 1862.

People who have never seen a battle have generally the crudest ideas possible relative to its true character. Nor have the efforts of the immense gang of correspondents done much toward clearing up the mysteries which shroud the "Valley of the Shadow of Death" through which a conflict rages.

One Southern correspondent, in speaking of the battle of Pea Ridge, says, in effect: "Here could be seen where the heavy knives of the Texans did their work—*hair, blood and brains mingled*." Another correspondent, writing at a safe distance from Pittsburgh Landing, in speaking of the battle of Shiloh, says that the muzzle of the Southern rifle was crossed by the Northern bayonets, showing that the conflict was a desperate hand-to-hand struggle, in which the antagonists bayoneted, throttled, gouged and pistoled each other, in a sort of indiscriminate, terrific mob fight.

In regard to these two points, it may be said that both are purely imaginary, or in the case of the first-named, worse than imaginary. There has never been a battle in the West where a hand-to-hand conflict occurred—there has never been a battle in which one party waited to receive a bayonet charge, or did receive a bayonet charge from the other. Thus will result the inference, that if the "heavy knives of the Texans" did such remarkable work in mixing the "hair, brains and blood" of the Yankees, they must have done it to the wounded, to wounded men asking for quarter, and not in any hand-to-hand conflict. And nearly so of the well-rounded phrase relative to the muzzle of the Southern rifle crossed on the Northern bayonet. Such assertions are brilliant efforts on the part of writers to give interest to a subject concerning whose true character they knew nothing.

Another correspondent embellishes his description of the battle with the assertion that during the occasional lull in the thunderous roar of the artillery, the shrieks and execrations of the wounded could be heard rising up from the deep ravines through which had passed the currents of the battle. Very pretty, but all bosh. Wounded men never shriek—never execrate in tones that can be heard any distance. A dozen surgeons have assured me that in all their experience during this war they have never known any such thing as "shrieking"—groans are plentiful, nothing else.

In battles such as we are afflicted with in this section, when the opposing forces reach within forty or fifty yards of each other, one party or the other is sure to yield the ground. The only case of any one killed by a bayonet thrust in the battle of Shiloh, was that of one man found in a tent. He was probably sick or asleep and in that condition was killed by a stab from behind. Thus much for the Cairo war correspondents.

Since my last we have been stationed at this place without having made any changes of importance. One reason of the delay is, that since Sunday noon it has rained as hard and steadily as though it had not rained here before in a century, and is now about to let us have the aqueous accumulations of that period. It rains easily in this country, and with little or no preparation. You retire at tattoo with the crescent moon and myriads of stars looking down calmly through the green leaves from an unclouded sky—an hour later and the rain patters musically against your tent, which it will not fail to continue doing for the next 24 hours.

The country between here and Corinth is composed of high ridges, between which lie bottomless swamps, varying from fifty yards to a full mile in width. Almost impassable at all times, these sloughs are particularly so after a short rain; hence it is that every one has to be bridged before they can be crossed. As our line of battle is not less than seven or eight miles in length, it can easily be imagined that the advance is necessarily of the slowest and most tedious character.

Frequently the various roads are blocked for miles by artillery wagons or provision trains fast in the mud. Starting for a certain point, however near, one is not at all positive when he will reach it—possibly in an hour, quite as likely in half a day. Trains going to the river for supplies needed immediately sometimes return the next day, but quite as frequently do not get back in a week.

Last Saturday afternoon, while the cannonading was going on at Farmington between Gen. Pope and the advance of the enemy, we had quite a stampede at this place. Quite a number of artillery and other officers had congregated at the hospitable quarters of Major Cavender, of the First Missouri Artillery. Everybody had commenced drinking confusion to Beauregard, and had just begun to taste a most excellent article of fluid (whose title is similar to that of the house of Bourbon,) when the heavy detonations of artillery came rolling like a thunder-storm over the woods.

Arms suddenly became rigid, and eyes fixed in astonishment. One gentleman found his voice, and had said as much as "What in ——," when a tremendous volley of small arms broke upon the air, from a ravine not a hundred yards distant.

Away went drinking cups, contents and all, and away, like chaff struck by a whirlwind, went the officers, including your correspondent, who probably untied a mule, mounted it, and had the spurs well at work in less time than similar feats were ever performed during the present war. In next to no time, the officers were all at their posts, batteries were manned, and the expected enemy anxiously looked for.

No enemy came, and the alarm soon subsided. The cannonading was found to proceed from Pope, while the volley turned out to be fired by a regiment of sharpshooters, who went down in the ravine to empty their rifles. Much good Bourbon, and much valuable breath were lost by this unceremonious breaking up of a most social and patriotic gathering.

At present the columns of Gens. W. T. and T. W. Sherman and Hurlburt are some two miles in advance of Monterey—the first-named being on the right, and the last on the left of the advance. Four days' rations are being prepared by the balance of the column of attack, which will probably move forward to-morrow. The advance of this wing (the right) is now within six miles of Corinth; and hence the conflict cannot long be delayed.

FARMINGTON, Friday, May 9.

As matters were getting rather dull on the right wing, I concluded yesterday to take a trip over to the left, and see what is being done by the army under Gen. Pope. The route from the right wing to the left was said to be about six miles in length, and of a character easily traced.

I started after breakfast, with the intention of returning in time for supper, in which laudable design I succeeded to the extent of being able, by hard labor, to reach Gen. Pope's headquarters just before dark. A more horrible road between any two points was never known, and probably never will be.

This morning the whole army under Gen. Pope took one day's rations, and started to "feel" of the enemy. The advance of the forces has been encamped on the Hamburgh and Corinth road, at a point two miles on the east side of Farmington. At the time Pope drove the rebels from this place, he did not occupy it, but withdrew his forces for two miles, leaving pickets close to the town. The rebel outposts were just on the other side, leaving the town a sort of neutral ground, not trespassed upon by either party. For several days things remained in this position, varied, so far as the pickets are concerned, by these gentlemen crawling around the town through the woods to exchange compliments and shots. The conversations were frequent, but not generally either instructive or brilliant, being mostly confined to remarks having a tendency to asperse the geneology of the respective parties. The shooting was quite as destitute of great results as the conversations—breath was wasted in the one case and powder and lead in the other—"nobody hurt."

This morning, soon after sunrise, the Divisions of Stanly, Paine, Granger and Hamilton, started in the direction of Corinth, Granger taking the lead, with about 5,000 cavalry, and Hamilton, with an immense number of batteries and four heavy Parrot siege guns, bringing up the rear as a reserve.

Farmington was reached without adventure, and then the cavalry was started in small bodies in every direction. In the meantime the main body came up and started toward Corinth, Stanly's Division taking the left and Paine's the right, the former going a little south of the direct road to Beauregard's stronghold, the latter going straight at it. Hamilton, at the same time, formed his column of reserves across the east end of the place, with batteries upon every height and supporting infantry behind the brow of every hill, and within the shelter of every piece of timber.

So bad were the roads, and so slow the movements of such a large body of troops, that it was 2 o'clock in the afternoon before the preparations were completed, and the respective bodies *en route* for their various destinations. I do not know what orders were given to the commanders, but suppose that each was in general directed to proceed cautiously forward, feeling for the enemy, in order to obtain at once a knowledge of the country and the positions of the rebels.

A battalion of the Second Iowa Cavalry, (Col. Elliot), under command of Major Lowe, was ordered to proceed down a road which leads nearly southeast from Farmington, and reaches the railroad running from Corinth, at a point some four miles from the former place. The gallant Iowans started off in handsome style, and soon after entered the timber and disappeared. About two hours after, they came back, looking considerably the "worse for wear"—very much, in fact, as a good-looking, well-dressed individual would appear after indulging in a rough-and-tumble free fight, of two hours' duration, with a crowd of Mississippi raftsmen. They came in by squads, some with their heads tied up in handkerchiefs, some with their unprotected locks tossed loosely by the unmannerly winds—all in a plight which indicated that something had happened.

I soon gathered the particulars. After leaving Farmington, they had proceeded along the road they were directed to follow without meeting anybody for some two or three miles. Suddenly they came upon a squad of the rebel videttes, to whom they gave vigorous chase, with a result which showed that, as to wind and bottom, there was but little difference between rebels running and Nationals chasing. Within half a mile of the railroad the pursuing party halted, and, leaving a small party to act as pickets, they retraced their steps toward Farmington.

Entirely unsuspicious of any scurvy tricks upon the part of the chivalry, they were slowly pushing ahead through a muddy bottom, when, suddenly, they were astonished by receiving the contents of some eight hundred rifles and shot-guns from the dense, impenetrable undergrowth which lined both sides of the road.

Such an event, especially if wholly unexpected, is calculated to very seriously disturb anyone's self-possession, and it had precisely that effect in the present case. Such a place is the better the sooner it is evacuated, a fact which Iowa was not slow to perceive, and act upon. Revolvers came out as spurs went in, and then, to music which rang out from pistol and carbine, they hurried from this most undesirable spot.

One Lieutenant was surrounded by the yelling and exultant rebels; in another instant a half dozen of his faithful followers turned, and with their whirling sabres cleared a lane to his side, through which he bounded, and the next moment, followed by a shower of lead, turned a bend in the road and was free.

How many were killed and how many taken prisoners in this little *emeute*, is not yet known. The loss will not probably prove to be as serious as was at first supposed.

The other bodies of cavalry proceeded in various directions, meeting rebels at every turn, and having an interesting and exciting time in chasing them as near Corinth as anticipations of masked batteries and other secession man-traps would permit. The casualties were very few, amounting in all on our side to not more than three killed, among whom, as is rumored, is Major Applet, of the Seventh Illinois Cavalry, shot through the head just below his right eye.

Stanley and Paine proceeded cautiously ahead till they reached within about two miles of Corinth, when they first woke up the enemy in force. Upon a ridge, covered by a peach orchard, the rebels had a four-gun battery, from which they opened fire as Stanley's skirmishers came upon an opposite ridge a short distance away. The main body of the division was led into the ravine, where they comfortably disposed themselves to rest, while the enemy passed the time in vigorously shelling a point some thousand yards or so beyond them. After the character of the ground was well examined, the Division was drawn off and marched back to Farmington. They had scarcely left, when the rebels discovered that they had been firing too high. Accordingly, they altered their range, and five minutes after our troops were out, they commenced dropping shells, with admirable precision, into the very spot occupied by the Nationals, and which they continued doing for two hours after the last Yankee had left the vicinity. The casualties on our side were very few—that of the enemy is of course unknown.

Gen. Payne, on the right of Stanley, also woke up some rebel guns, whose position he ascertained, together with the character of the surrounding country, (composed mainly of bottomless swamps,) and then withdrew, having sustained a very inconsiderable loss.

When the firing first commenced on Stanley's Division, Dr. Thrall, Surgeon of the Twenty-seventh Ohio, returned a short distance to hurry up an assistant with his instruments, after which he was not seen. It is supposed that he was captured by some rebel horsemen, who were not long before seen in the immediate vicinity. He was a very talented man, and will be deeply regretted, both as a gentleman and a surgeon, by every man in his regiment.

This afternoon the telegraph was completed to a house in Farmington, in which Gen. Pope will to-morrow take up his quarters. This evening all the troops have returned to camp except two brigades, which are bivouacked at Farmington.

Several rebel deserters came in to-day, all of whom gave Beauregard's force at about 100,000 men, who, they say, are prepared for a desperate resistance.

The reconnoissance to-day has been successful, so far as giving us an exact knowledge of the country is concerned, while, considering the opposition it encountered, the losses are remarkably small.

Gen. Tyler, of Connecticut, has assumed command of the Second Brigade of Stanley's Division, formerly commanded by Col. John Groesbeck, of the Thirty-sixth Ohio.

The weather here is now delightful. Strawberries are in great abundance and nearly ripe—the peach trees are loaded down with fruit, already half grown. The farmers are planting nothing—many have left their homes, others have remained, but are generally in a thoroughly destitute condition. One family near here, consisting of a man, his wife, two sisters and nine children, represented to Gen. Stanley to-day that they were in a starving condition, not having had a particle to eat in two days. Rations were given them, and as long as the army remains in the vicinity they will be supported by the Government. Every house in Farmington, save one, is deserted, the inhabitants having left for Dixie to escape the dread presence of the Northern Hessians. The whole country is fast becoming a desert, and will become completely so if the rebellion be not speedily ended.

Cotton is found in considerable quantities, for which purchasers are paying the owners from 8 to 10 cents in gold per pound.

GALWAY.

NEWS FROM FORTRESS MONROE.

Another Storm—Distinguished Visitors—Affairs in Norfolk—Trade Regulations There, &c.

FORTRESS MONROE, Thursday, May 15. }
via BALTIMORE, Friday, May 16. }

A cold northeast wind, accompanied with a rain storm, has set in.

In consequence of the storm there is no dispatch to Cherrystone this afternoon.

Secretary Seward and Secretary Welles, and Attorney-General Bates arrived here this morning, and proceeded to Norfolk with Commodore Goldsborough.

Gen. Wool also visited Norfolk to-day. All is quiet there.

Orders have been issued by Gen. Wool prohibiting the sale or distribution of newspapers in Norfolk or the surrounding country; also prohibiting the transportation there of supplies or merchandise of any kind, whether by sutlers or otherwise; and also prohibiting officers, soldiers and citizens from visiting the city except on business connected with the troops belonging to the Department of Virginia.

We understand that the embargo upon travel to Fortress Monroe from Baltimore will soon be removed, and free transit to and fro resumed.

Adams Express Company having secured a location, will open an office in Norfolk to-day.

Lieut. Carncross, one of the most useful members of the Staff of Gen. Wool, has been appointed Assistant Adjutant-General.

DEPARTMENT OF THE SHENANDOAH.

STRASBURGH, Friday, May 16.

A continuous stream of Union residents of the valley are pouring into town, under the mistaken belief that our army is retreating, and a knowledge that detachments of rebel cavalry are visiting every farm-house, impressing all males between fifteen and sixty.

The Secessionists along the route to Harrisonburgh say that Jackson will not attempt to follow us.

Yesterday afternoon a band of about 300 mounted guerrillas made a dash on the railroad guard beyond Front Royal, and killed one and took fourteen prisoners, all belonging to the Twenty-eighth Pennsylvania.

The railroad bridge, 50 feet high and 350 feet long, over the north fork of the Shenandoah was completed to-night. The track will be laid and trains will pass to-morrow forenoon. The work was constructed in forty hours, under the superintendence of G. W. Nagle, Government bridge-builder.

All is quiet in front to-night. It is currently reported that Milroy and Schenk are in occupation of Staunton.

THE BLOCKADING SERVICE.

Prizes Captured on the South Carolina Coast.

WASHINGTON, Friday, May 16.

The Navy Department has information that on the 1st inst., Acting Volunteer Lieut. Nickels, of the *Onward*, dispatched Acting-Master Sleeper in his vessel's launch in chase of the schooner *Sarah*, about 100 tons burden, endeavoring to run the blockade of Bull's Bay on the coast of South Carolina. Her crew thereupon ran her ashore and burned her, themselves escaping.

On the 6th, the United States gunboat *Ottawa* captured the rebel schooner *C. C. Pinckney* from Charleston, for Nassau, with ninety-four bales of cotton, resin, &c.

On the night of the 8th, the *Alabama* ran a schooner on shore at Light-House Inlet. Next day, the *Pocahontas* endeavored to get to her, but could not as she was under protection of the guns of the shore batteries.

LATE EVENTS ON THE PENINSULA.

THE BATTLE OF WILLIAMSBURGH.

A Tribute to the Conspicuous Gallantry of Hooker's and Kearney's Divisions.

DISPATCH FROM GENERAL McCLELLAN.

Interesting Details from Our Own Correspondents.

CAMP 19 MILES FROM WILLIAMSBURGH, May 11.

Hon. E. M. Stanton, Secretary of War:

Without waiting further for official reports which have not yet reached me, I wish to bear testimony to the splendid conduct of Hooker's and Kearney's Divisions, under command of Gen. Heintzelman, in the battle of Williamsburgh. Their bearing was worthy of veterans. Hooker's Division for hours gallantly withstood the attack of greatly superior numbers with very heavy loss. Kearney's arrived in time to restore the fortunes of the day, and came most gallantly into action. I shall probably have occasion to call attention to other commands, and do not wish to do injustice to them by mentioning them now. If I had had the full information I now have in regard to the troops above named when I first telegraphed, they would have been specially mentioned and commended. I spoke only of what I knew at the time, and I shall rejoice to do full justice to all engaged.

GEO. B. McCLELLAN,
Major-General Commanding.

FROM OUR OWN CORRESPONDENTS.

THE VICTORY AT WILLIAMSBURGH—THE PART TAKEN BY HOOKER'S BRIGADE AND THE ELEVENTH MASSACHUSETTS.

CAMP AT WILLIAMSBURGH, Va., Friday, May 9, 1862.

Our victory before Williamsburgh, judging from the accounts in newspapers which have come to hand, as late as May 8, has been by far too lightly estimated. It was no ordinary achievement, and the record to be made will prove that it was a daring, desperate and sanguinary struggle. From the first the engagement promised a victory for the rebel arms, and but for the astonishing perseverance and energy of Gen. Hooker, and the persistency and bravery of his First Brigade, would have so resulted. The delay of a few moments in the advance of our reinforcements would have consummated our defeat.

The march of Sunday from Yorktown, by this gallant Brigade, which was in advance, was not concluded until 11 o'clock at night, when the troops halted in a clearing in the woods, about two miles from the enemy. At daylight, next morning, the march was resumed, and notwithstanding the rain, which had been falling heavily since 2 o'clock A. M., the men sprang to arms with cheerful alacrity at the first summons. At 5½ o'clock we came in sight of the enemy's principal fortification, directly in front of us, and commanding the road, across which it was built, while fort after fort stretched away to the right, to the left, and far into the distant background.

Immediately before us, and stretching away to the right and left of the road, was a large field of felled timber and brush, and beyond a plain extending for miles and checkered with breastworks, forts and rifle-pits. On coming in sight of the enemy, the brigade was deployed into the woods and through the fallen trees to the right of the fort, and were instantly engaged by the rebels. We had no artillery with us, its advance being slow on account of the bad state of the roads. The enemy commenced shelling us soon after coming into the field, and though the iron missiles flew thick and fast, we held our position unflinching and unbroken. It was soon ascertained that the enemy were lurking in the woods and brush in front of us, and skirmishing parties were immediately deployed by regiments, and frequently relieved by others, in order to keep the troops fresh as possible, and to enable us to retain our position until the artillery should come up and reinforcements arrive.

The enemy were found to be in heavy numbers against us in the woods—probably four to one—and when the Eleventh Massachusetts, under Col. Blaisdell, engaged them in the centre, they found themselves subjected to a galling fire from every bush and tree, but with unbroken ranks his brave men followed him, loading, firing and charging with a cool and deliberate calmness. On, on, step by step, this seemingly invincible regiment pressed its way [illegible] unfaltered phalanx, through ditch and swamp [illegible], mounting the enemy's vast barricade, [illegible] before them the skulking foe, with a [illegible] completely overcame all opposition. It was the first of a like series of exploits consummated by this regiment during the day, and the General Commanding took occasion to applaud it on the battle-field.

Suddenly a regiment filed out in front of the advancing Eleventh, bearing a flag of truce. All firing instantly ceased, and the enemy was allowed to approach within speaking distance, when the inquiry was made by them, "What regiment are you?" Without answering the inquiry, the same requisition was made upon the enemy, who replied, "We're the Eighth Alabama." "And we're the Eleventh Massachusetts," was the rejoinder. "Then you're the d—d sons of —— we want!" and the white flag was instantly thrown down, and a volley of musketry poured into them along their whole line, killing and wounding several of our men. The Eleventh, with renewed impulse, immediately charged upon the treacherous horde, and sent them flying into the woods, where they were shot down and bayoneted at our mercy. The Eleventh were soon relieved, and at 9½ o'clock the cheering and shouting of the men in the rear told us our artillery were coming up.

It proved to be Company H, of the regulars, with a battery of six pieces, who immediately advanced to the front, near the open plain, while Sickles' Excelsior Brigade, coming up, deployed into the woods on the left, where they found a numerous enemy endeavoring to turn our left flank. The enemy at the same time were constantly throwing new troops into the field, and were pressing heavily upon the First Brigade at the right—so heavily, indeed, that symptoms of faltering were apparently manifest in one or two regiments; and one, which I will not mention, was retreating rapidly to the rear, when the Eleventh Massachusetts again took position among them, and stayed the tide which was swelling against it, and threatening seriously the fortunes of the day. The Second New-Hampshire, and Twenty-sixth Pennsylvania Regiments, had done fearful execution, and suffered severely, especially the Twenty-sixth Pennsylvania.

For four hours had this Brigade now held in check the enemy, and the bravery displayed has but little rivalry. The odds against them was fearful, and was swelling alarmingly every moment. Col. Blaisdell was sent with a detachment of seven companies of his regiment to request Gen. Sumner, who with a large force, was lying about three miles from the scene of action, and to scour the woods in the rear.

On the approach of our battery the enemy threw out in front of the road a large force of cavalry to charge upon it; but were deterred, probably, through ignorance of the small force we held in reserve. Our guns immediately engaged the fort, and, in [illegible]

The Charleston Mercury.

DAILY PAPER—TEN DOLLARS PER ANNUM, PAYABLE HALF-YEARLY IN ADVANCE. | SPONTE SUA SINE LEGE FIDES JUSTUMQUE COLENTUR. VINDICE NULLO | COUNTRY PAPER—THREE A WEEK—FIVE DOLLARS PER ANNUM, IN ADVANCE.

VOLUME LXXX. | CHARLESTON, S. C., TUESDAY, MAY 27, 1862. | NUMBER 11,457

NEWS BY TELEGRAPH.

IMPORTANT VICTORY IN VIRGINIA—STONEWALL JACKSON RE TAKES WINCHESTER.

RICHMOND, Monday, May 26.—Authentic information has been received here of another victory gained by Stonewall JACKSON at Front Royal, in Warren County. The enemy was routed and a number of prisoners and arms were captured.

(*Second Despatch.*)

The *Examiner* has received the following telegram: "JACKSON and EWELL have taken Front Royal and Winchester. The victory is complete. Four thousand prisoners were taken, and more are still coming in. All the enemy's stores were taken at Winchester. Our loss was 100 killed and wounded."

(*Third Despatch*)

The following official despatch has just been received:

Staunton, May 26.—Gen. JACKSON's forces entered Winchester on Sunday, the 25th inst., capturing all the enemy's commissary and ordnance stores. The Yankees, in their flight, tried to burn the town, but were unsuccessful, because too closely pursued by our advance. At Front Royal, we captured the Yankee First Maryland (bogus) regiment, and the Yankee First Virginia (bogus) cavalry. At Winchester, we captured 2000 more prisoners. Our loss in killed and wounded was about 100. Our forces are still in pursuit of the enemy, who are completely routed.

THE MERCURY.

TUESDAY, MAY 27, 1862.

Foreign Intervention.

The statesmen who control the policy of the British Empire seem at last to be awakening to the terrible disasters, their refusal to recognize the Confederate States, and to disregard the Yankee blockade, have entailed upon their people. They have either been bamboozled by the Yankee Government, with their three months draft on time for our overthrow, and the furnishing of cotton to them from our ports; or they have deliberately put their people under the crucible of suffering in the silly experiment of furnishing themselves with cotton from India. Time, the grand test of wisdom, where the future is involved, is clearly developing the futility of all such expectations; and now the British statesmen seem to be casting about for some way of deliverance from the suffering and ruin their policy has produced on their people.

They must move, however, now, under great disadvantages. The blockade of our ports, which has been hitherto no blockade at all, according to their own authority of the laws of nations, is now more efficient by the occupation of the greater portion of our ports, and the more vigilant supervision of those of our ports which are not occupied, our enemies are able to afford. The Yankees, too, by their late successes, have a better right to demand the non-interference of foreign nations. Under such circumstances, the difficulties are greatly increased to foreign nations of extricating themselves from the evils which their non-action heretofore has produced. Both of the belligerents are less inclined to tolerate it. The Yankees are temporarily stronger, and we are weaker. *They* will repudiate foreign intervention, because they are stronger; and *we*, because we are weaker. The "*uti possedittis*," which is the usual basis of all cessation in wars, will be unendurable to both parties; but especially to the Confederate States. We must have every foot of soil within the Confederate States free of Yankees. Every town, fort or fortress, must be surrendered; and Maryland and Kentucky must be left free, with every Yankee soldier withdrawn from their territory, to choose to which Government, Southern or Northern, they will unite their destinies. Now, what can foreign nations propose to us or the North, as the equivalent to the North, for the surrender of the advantages they now possess in the war? There is but one thing left as the basis of an adjustment; and that is, to propose the re-establishment of the commercial relations heretofore existing between the North and the South—*commercial reconstruction*.

But can France and Great Britain make such a proposition, and cut themselves off from the trade of the South? And, on the other hand, will any statesman of the Confederate States dare listen to such a proposition? We know that, when the war began, reconstructionists, in the Government and out of the Government, were numerous in the Confederate States; and the inactivity of our Government and of our arms was, in no small degree, influenced by this policy. But we trust that this policy is now dead. Although suffering bitterly for the inefficiency and inactivity of our Government, we trust that it has obtained for us one good. The popular rage and hate our sufferings have inspired, will force on our Government the policy of an utter and eternal separation from our Yankee foes, socially, commercially and politically. No foreign intervention—no defeats—no desolations or sufferings, can, we trust, ever induce us to place ourselves, in any degree or form whatever, in the power or under the control of this most detested and detestable people. To us, therefore, considering commercial reconstruction with the North as utterly inadmissible, what benefit can result to us from the intervention of foreign nations? None whatever.

The truth is, situated as the Confederate States are, a peace, upon terms which will secure to them the object of their confederation, is an impossibility. The defensive policy of our Government, if continued in, renders the war eternal. Suppose we were now to drive back every Yankee soldier out of our territory, would we have peace? Certainly not. They have our fortresses on our coast and in our seas in their possession. How are we to compel their surrender? We cannot take them, for they command the seas. We will not buy them by yielding commercial terms, which will compromise our independence and future safety. How then shall we obtain their surrender? By *one* instrumentality—and *one* only—*an aggressive war*. We must not only drive our Yankee foes out of our country, but we must invade theirs. We must be in a condition to give something for something. We must exchange Philadelphia for New Orleans, Cincinnati for Norfolk; and by the sufferings of an aggressive war, real or apprehended, create inducements for peace in our Yankee foes. There never was, from the first, any other way to independence and peace, and until it is entered upon we have no alternative but sternly to reject all offers of mediation or intervention by foreign nations, which are not based upon the acknowledgment of our absolute independence, and all the rights this independence involves.

THE SIEGE OF THE CAPITAL.

(FROM OUR OWN CORRESPONDENT.)

RICHMOND, Saturday, May 24.

Engagements Around the City—Reports About Jackson—Newspaper Generalship—McClellan's Labors—Downfall of "Iron-Clads"—Town Topics, etc., etc.

Yesterday's affair proved to be only a little artillery duel near New Bridge, on the Chickahominy, five or six miles from town. Mr. DAVIS and General LEE rode out to see what was going on, and were complimented with a shell, which passed over their heads. This morning, about 7 o'clock, the early risers were greeted with quite a treat in the way of a cannonade, which lasted some hours. At breakfast time strings of ambulances began to make their way toward the firing, and hence it was supposed that the great battle was about to come off. But now (half-past ten) the firing has ceased, and a friend just from Longstreet's division tells me that Magruder is only interrupting the erection of a Yankee battery on Mrs. Crenshaw's farm, some ten miles off. The papers speak as if the decisive hour had arrived; but, in my judgment, they are mistaken. If attacked, McClellan will retire to his gunboats; if let alone, he will consume time in posting his forces on both sides of the river.

I said yesterday that Jackson and Ewell had joined their commands at Harrisonburg. The statement was based on a letter received by a member of Congress from Jackson. Last night, and again to-day, it is authoritatively rumored that Jackson is at Gordonsville, and that his army will be in Hanover to-morrow evening. What truth there is in this, I know not, but it seems to me that the "counter-irritation" which Mr. Randolph proposed to set up in Maryland would have been the surest defence of Richmond. Officers in Johnston's army say he protested against going to Yorktown; the President insisted, on the ground that we needed time; and the General yielded. But that time could have been gained just as surely by sending a division to aid Magruder in holding the powerful defences he had erected and had already held with 7,500 men, against an assault upon the whole line by McClellan's artillery. Meantime the bulk of Johnston's army might have been sent to the Valley and precipitated upon Maryland. But this would have been "newspaper generalship."

Speaking of McClellan, reminds me of a statement made by a paroled officer, viz: that just in rear of his line of entrenchments, which extended across the Peninsula, McClellan caused a broad ditch to be dug, deep enough to hide cannon and horses. This ditch had a substantial plank floor throughout its whole length, so that his artillery could be rapidly transferred to any point of the line. In addition to this, he had a fine plank road all the way to Fortress Monroe. No wonder Johnston has declared he will never stick another spade into the earth. It is said that Jackson never had but one spade, and the handle of that was broken when he first got it out of the Yankee trenches at Romney. He uses it to cook hoe-cakes on.

We are much elated at the Northern account of the fight at Drury's Bluff. We flatter ourselves that, by the time the "iron-clads" muster courage enough to make us a second visit, we shall have in readiness a "dose" which even the Monitor will be compelled to take. It will not be given in a spoonful of preserves, though it will be something in the nature of *jam jam satis*, for example.

The Episcopal Convention has just closed its sessions in this city. The Baptist General Association of Virginia meets next Thursday. People complain mightily of the high price of provisions. Strawberries and gooseberries have appeared in small quantities. The newspapers advertise the loss of many dogs, negros, pocket books, carpet bags and mare mules. All the criminals condemned in the invaded counties to be hung, have been sent here, to be hung by wholesale shortly. Wind from the east—cold rain falling.

HERMES.

P. S. It is reported the enemy occupied Mechanicsville this morning, and we renewed the fight, intending to dislodge them. Mechanicsville is just the other side of the Chickahominy.

6 p. m.—A rumor, which no one credits, to the effect that we repulsed them, with a loss on their side of 900, and 200 on ours, is flying about the streets.

Magruder is to supersede Lovell, but requests the privilege of remaining here until the fight is over.

THE CAMPAIGN IN THE WEST

(FROM OUR SPECIAL CORRESPONDENT.)

CORINTH, MISS., May 18.

I left Corinth on Wednesday, the 13th, to recruit myself with a few days of necessary quiet. At the date of my departure affairs wore much the same aspect which had led me, in my last, to suppose that the great battle could not be far off. The enemy were in force within a few miles of our entrenchments, our own preparations were complete, and it seemed improbable that two great armies could remain for any time, almost within cannon-shot of each other, without coming to blows. And yet, in spite of this, the common impression when I set out for Columbus was, that a general engagement was a thing rather to be desired than hoped. Before I ventured to risk the loss of my place as a spectator in the grand drama, Beauregard had twice flung down the gage of battle to Halleck, and Halleck had twice declined to take it up. The conclusion, therefore, was that either Halleck was not ready, and was resolved not to fight until he was ready, or that it was his policy to avoid battle altogether, and, if possible, to subdue the place by a regular investment, and the slow process of starvation.

I have not been able to gather at Columbus any information which can be relied on as to the present position of matters at Corinth. A rumor that reaches me to-day is so astounding that I dare hardly venture to give it. It is that Halleck has withdrawn his forces and retired across the Tennessee River. If this be so, the campaign in the West will be indefinitely prolonged, and our hopes of putting an end to it by one brilliant victory are, for the present, rendered vain. But I trust that the rumor is a false one. Everybody must wish the long suspense to come to its close, no matter what that close may be. I myself, if Beauregard can only have a fair field, have little fear of the result. Never since the war began has a Southern army confronted a Northern army so nearly its equal in point of numbers. And when one remembers the character of the material which have swelled Beauregard's host; of the effective regiments of South Carolina and of Georgia, of the brave veterans of Price and Van Dorn, and of late additional reinforcements from Louisiana, one cannot help feeling than an army thus composed ought to be a match for any force that our enemies can send against it.

A very short time ago Columbus must have been one of the quietest, as it is still now one of the prettiest, towns in the Southern Confederacy. From some points it presents the appearance of a vast grove, through which peep here and there cottages and mansions that seem the very abodes of tranquility and peace. A wearied soldier, who looked as if he had been baking for a month past in the hot suns of Pensacola, remarked in my presence that "it was the shadiest place he ever saw." Strolling over the undulating streets of the town, you discover that the houses are surrounded by gardens tastefully laid out, where "flowers of all hues and loveliest of their kind" are arrayed in beautiful profusion.

Yet even into this Eden has the serpent of war entered. There is scarcely one of those houses which does not contain some sick or wounded soldier, taken in by the kind inmate to receive better care than a hospital has to bestow. The "Female Institute," the new hotel, and one or two Churches, have been converted into Hospitals. Manufactories of arms and of all sorts of munitions of war have been established. I have seen some capital sabres which were made here, *here*, where the only instruments which could harmonize with the air and spirit of the place are the plough, the spade and the harrow. But the other day the quiet towns-people were startled by a sound like the peal of cannon. It was the explosion of a small percussion cap factory, by which one man was killed.

The levees on the Mississippi river are broken, and all prospect of a crop in the rich Mississippi bottom lands has been destroyed. The wheat has been almost utterly ruined by the rust. Farmers are cutting it in an unripe state, in the hope of making at least a little indifferent flour. Providence does not appear to be so manifestly on our side as it did at the opening of the Revolution.

I return to Corinth to-morrow. KAPPA.

THE NAVAL BATTLE BELOW NEW ORLEANS—A GRAPHIC ACCOUNT.

The Memphis *Appeal* publishes an interesting letter from an officer of the steam ram *Louisiana*, giving an account of the recent naval engagement below New Orleans. We make an extract:

At half-past three, the bugle sounded the alarm in the forts, and in a few minutes after, the enemy commenced to run the gauntlet with twenty vessels, large steam sloops, and thirteen gunboats. The cannonading was terrific, at least three hundred heavy guns being engaged. I fired the first gun from the Louisiana at a big fellow close aboard. This was the first intimation they had of our existence, and the enemy believing us to be a light gunboat or steamboat, laid us aboard for the purpose of carrying us by boarding, which exposed him to the direct fire of our bow battery, consisting of two 9-inch smooth guns and one 7-inch rifle, the latter much heavier and much more formidable than the "Belmont" or "Lady Polk" guns. Our Captain, McIntosh, divining the object of the enemy, called a number of men on deck to repel, and whilst firing musketry at the ship alongside, he was struck by a grape and severely wounded, losing his right arm, breaking his left, and his right leg. In the meantime the rascal was fast to our bow, about forty feet from us, and poured in a most terrible broadside, driving the hot smoke from his guns into our ports; our metal was too heavy, and he went ahead and came in range of our starboard battery, where I had the pleasure of peppering him with my division of rifles. This settled him, and he dropped off into the stream helpless. Then he fell in with the Manassas, which had been poking and butting in all directions; Warley backed off, and went into our friend full tilt, knocking a hole in his side, which caused him to sink in a few minutes. This was the only close work we had, and that did not last more than ten minutes, if that long, during which we had whipped a first class sloop-of-war. During the balance of the engagement, we stood by our guns, and fired as they passed. In the morning, our upper works were a perfect wreck—cut all to pieces by grape and canister; the steamboat's cabin alongside was literally in splinters, but our iron casemate was unhurt. Two 11-inch shells struck us whilst we were so close, which only made a deep dent in the iron, not starting the wood, and, although I was standing immediately under them, I did not feel the concussion. Warley, in the Manassas, and Huger, in the McRae, covered themselves with glory. Warley seemed to fairly revel in the fight. The Manassas was everywhere. But, unfortunately, the vessels of the enemy were faster than she, and carried twenty guns, whilst she carried but one. The McRae held four of them at bay, and was gallantly fighting both broadsides when Warley came to her assistance. Huger, of the McRae, was mortally wounded. Warley was unhurt.

BUTLER'S OFFICIAL REPORT OF THE OCCUPATION OF NEW ORLEANS.

The *Baltimore American* of the 17th inst., contains BUTLER's official report of the capture of New Orleans. We find nothing to relieve its low narrative, and nothing of interest save the following indications of purpose with which the report concludes:

I propose to so far depart from the letter of my instructions as to endeavor to persuade the Flag Officer to pass up the river as far as the mouth of Red river, if possible, so as to cut off their supplies, and make there a landing and a demonstration in their rear as a diversion in favor of General Buell, if a decisive battle is not fought before such movement is possible.

Mobile is ours whenever we choose, and we can better wait.

I find the city under the domination of the mob. They have insulted our flag—torn it down with indignity. This outrage will be punished in such manner as in my judgment will caution both the perpetrators and abettors of the act, so that they shall fear the "stripes," if they do not reverence the "stars" of our banner. I send a marked copy of a New Orleans paper containing an applauding account of the outrage. Trusting my action may meet the approbation of the Department,

I am, most respectfully,
Your obedient servant,
BENJAMIN F. BUTLER,
Major General Commanding.

The Charleston Mercury.

DAILY PAPER—TEN DOLLARS PER ANNUM, PAYABLE HALF-YEARLY IN ADVANCE. | —VINDICE NULLO SPONTE SUA SINE LEGE FIDEM RECTUMQUE COLENTUR. | COUNTRY PAPER—THREE A WEEK—FIVE DOLLARS PER ANNUM, IN ADVANCE.

VOLUME LXXX. | CHARLESTON, S. C., WEDNESDAY, MAY 28, 1862. | NUMBER 11,458

The Executive Council on the Defence of Charleston.

It has been with great pleasure we have been called upon to lay before the public, in a late issue, the resolutions of the Executive Council of this State, touching the defence of the city of Charleston. Representing in a great degree, as they do at this time, the public authority and dignity of the State, it is but in accordance with their duty, that they should gravely and fearlessly meet the responsibilities of the occasion, so far as it rests in their hands, by a bold and manly declaration in behalf of the honor of the State. The Executive Council has spoken well and timely. The State Convention took similar action some time since. We trust that when the emergency comes, there shall be no occasion to diminish expressions of approbation, and that the will of the people and authorities of the State will be carried out, in action.

But it is only the true and the sterling heart that makes good, in the dark hour of trial, the words of a calmer and brighter season. We want no man to blanch when Charleston is to be fought. 'Tis not the first time she has been fought; and she can be fought again. Is there a man here, with a soul as big as a Guinea-pig's, who would not rather make a Saragossa of Charleston, than to have a Northern ruffian lording it over us with his brutal proclamations, and his inquisitorial proceedings of insolence and outrage upon men and women? Let us turn our eyes to poor Huntsville, and still worse, to New Orleans! If there be a man here whose stomach is strong enough to prefer such scenes, as are there enacted to the fighting of the city to the last, he should be ordered to leave.

Yet, Charleston is in the hands of the Confederate authorities, and not of the State authorities. They have our troops and control our military operations, and it is to them, at last, that we must look. It is to *them* that we must appeal for the preservation of our honor, in whose keeping it has been placed. It is in the hands of the General Commanding. Men who are in earnest in this matter expect from him everything that our ancient honor and present position may demand, even to the last tittle.

THE NEWS OF THE WAR.

THE SIEGE OF THE CAPITAL.

We take the following from the Richmond *Examiner* of Monday:

There was some action on our lines in the neighborhood of Richmond on Saturday. From such reliable particulars as we have, it appears that the enemy made a demonstration in the neighborhood of New Bridge and Mechanicsville on Saturday. At New Bridge two companies of the Fifth Louisiana Regiment were surprised, the enemy having captured the only cavalry picket that was out. We learn that our loss in this engagement was about sixteen killed and thirty wounded. On Saturday afternoon the enemy took possession of Mechanicsville, which is about four miles from the city boundary, on the road which extends from Eighteenth-street. Three pieces of the Washington Artillery were placed across the Chickahominy, but our forces were directed to fall back to the other bank of the stream, which they did after a sharp cannonading. Captain Rosser was wounded in the arm by a fragment of a shell. On occupying Mechanicsville Saturday afternoon the cheers of the Yankee army were vociferous and might have been heard for miles.

Yesterday, there was an entire quiet on our lines, and not a shot exchanged on any portion of them as far as we could learn. In the neighborhood of Mechanicsville, the two armies are distinctly confronted on opposite ranges of hills not more than a mile apart. The enemy's pickets extend to the bridge over the Chickahominy, and our picket lines are not more than six hundred yards apart, a cavalry picket of the enemy being posted directly in the turnpike on the other side of the bridge. Yesterday the enemy were throwing up entrenchments about Mechanicsville, and planting batteries to command the bridge and turnpike. About two or three miles to the north the enemy have possession of the Central Railroad, at what is known as Atlee's Station. The situation is such as keeps the public in constant and daily expectation of a general engagement.

The *Examiner* in commenting upon the situation of affairs in front of Richmond, says:

Throughout this war, our general officers, with one or two exceptions, have been constantly afflicted with the deluded notion that the enemy would do them the favor to commence the attack. Again and again have the most splendid occasions been lost on that ground. When every circumstance indicated that a battle was our best chance, and when the whole army believed that it would be led out to fight on the morrow, "reliable" information was sure to arrive that the enemy was coming to attack us, and consequently we would have all the advantage in waiting quietly behind our redoubts and breastworks to receive him.—The next day and the next pass in expectation; the enemy makes no attack; and having ample time and liberty, does all the manœuvering himself; so that our troops are soon so circumstanced that they are compelled to change their position. This is the history of Manassas, of Yorktown, of Warwick, of Sewell. Let us hope that Richmond will not witness a repetition of the same unhappy concatenation of untoward events.

The defensive system has been followed to the conclusion by the race of little men who have possession of authority in this country. It has affected everything, the generals of the army and their strategy more than anything else. It has brought the Southern Confederacy to the doors of destruction. Since the accidental victory at Manassas a year ago there has not been another general engagement in Virginia, the theatre of the war. All the rest has been skirmish, expectation, and then retreat after retreat. We talk about our want of stores and supplies:—more have been destroyed to effect these retreats than have been consumed by the whole army. We hear of the lack of men: more men have been ruined, demoralized, made sick, and lost by these retreats than twice the whole fighting of the war has touched. The army has been damaged, the country dispirited, the people of Virginia reduced to misery, their lands overrun, their property seized, and the advance of the enemy has never been checked or delayed. The defensive game, in war as in chess, has once more proven the worst of all; impossible of successful execution even by the most adroit hands, and absolutely sure to end in grief if tried on an antagonist of only ordinary skill.

The time has come when the policy of the Southern Confederacy must change. The change must be complete, root and branch. Much wise talk has been heard from the mouths of imbeciles of the necessity of harmony among ourselves, and the propriety of abstinence from criticism and objection to the acts of government while this great struggle against the most hideous and hated of foes is in our hands. Many pretentious commonplace platitudes are repeated, parrot-wise, by one dull man after another, about the evils and difficulties of dissension and disturbance in the midst of an effort, for the success of which all Southern men are earnestly striving. But when it becomes clear that harmony, silence, and passive obedience to Government only serves to ensure our absolute ruin; when we know that a coach we are in is driven along the broad and straight road that leadeth to destruction; when it is evident that the more devotion and union we have upon the present plan of action, the more certain is the doom of ourselves and our country; it is certainly doubtful whether this patience, moderation, unanimity and submission is useful to us—right, patriotic, or sensible. When it is known that the blind lead, the case will not be remedied by hoodwinking the sound eyes of those who are led. When we see that the ship is steered directly on the rocks, and the breakers are becoming closer every moment, the crew that does not cry the danger ahead, and force the helmsman to put the ship about as fast as possible, deserve the drowning. That policy of the Confederate Government has been injudicious throughout, and continues to be so, is not a matter on which difference of opinion is possible, for the results are patent to everybody; hence there is actually no difference of opinion, and the whole population, with the exception of a few officials, hangers-on and aspirants, think alike about it. The time is come when that policy must change. If we gain a great victory here in the next few days, the change will be made with good grace, and for this let us now hope.

MAJOR GENERAL LOVELL AND THE FALL OF NEW ORLEANS.

To the Editor of the Charleston Mercury: The capture of New Orleans very naturally excited great feeling throughout the country, and the people and the newspapers immediately went to work to find a victim upon whose head to wreak vengeance. The failure of a public servant to meet the expectations of those for whom he labors, should not, in case of his failure to do everything with which he is charged, be the signal for his destruction in the public confidence, without it is made manifest that he has been wanting in the vigilance and energy demanded by the position to which he has been assigned.

The fall of New Orleans was a great misfortune. No one knew better the vast importance of holding possession of that city and the lower Valley of the Mississippi than Gen. Lovell; and a fair, cool, candid statement, founded upon personal observation, and upon the official evidence of what was done, is submitted, that the truth may be known, and responsibility of the great misfortune fixed where it properly belongs.

When General Lovell was assigned to the defence of the coast of Louisiana, he immediately discovered that the only serious danger to New Orleans was by an attack of gunboats up the river. He went to work; and with the assistance of the heroic Duncan, soon placed Forts Jackson and St. Philip in as good condition to destroy any fleet that might attempt to pass to the city as the very limited means in his power would permit.

The obstruction of the Mississippi river, at a point near those defences, was deemed essential to the successful defence of the city, and a very short time after he assumed command a raft was moored from one bank to the other of the river, immediately under fire of both forts. This raft was constructed of very large logs with two immense chains passing under and fastening below; and they were likewise secured by riveting large strong slabs across the top. No one for a moment then believed that the combined fleets of the Federal Government could pass up the river.

Upon the night of the 28th of February this immense structure was torn to pieces and swept away by the Mississippi, which is higher than it was ever known before. The writer of this well remembers the energy and dauntless determination with which Gen. Lovell went to work immediately to place another obstruction in the river. It was clearly shown that no raft could withstand the terrific flood that was then passing over the country. An order was issued seizing a large number of ships and schooners, and they were formed immediately, under that gallant, accomplished officer, Col. Higgins, into a line, and anchored with every care and precaution across the river near the forts.

Officers and gentlemen of the highest engineering attainments were confident that this second obstruction could not be carried away. Each vessel was heavily and securely anchored, and immense chains passed from one to the other.—The fragments of the first raft were also again moored and anchored across the river. The Federal fleet was then in the river, but we felt no apprehension; in fact, everybody was more than willing that they should make the attempt against the forts, which were garrisoned by one thousand experienced artillerists.

Right here it is proper to add that there were very few first-class siege guns at either fort; that few we had, Gen. Lovell had procured with great trouble. It is true, he had often called for 10-inch guns, but those having the power to aid him paid but little attention to these demands.

So far as the land defences of the city are in the question, it is only necessary to state that they were of such a character as to have enabled a very small force to hold them against any numbers which the enemy could have brought. Every confidence was felt by men and officers, and universally shared by the community, that the city could not be taken, except the fleet of gunboats succeeded in destroying the defences above Memphis and coming down the river.

Such was the condition when the enemy opened fire, from, as near as could be ascertained, twenty-seven mortar boats. They took their position nearly three miles below Fort Jackson, where but few of our guns could reach them. On Friday night a most violent storm arose; and when the morning came, to the unspeakable anguish of the gallant Duncan and men, it was discovered that the anchors which held the ships and schooners across the river had yielded to the combined pressure of the wind and flood; and the obstruction, upon which so much depended, was destroyed. Prompt measures were taken to repair the damages, but the Federal gunboats opened a tremendous fire upon the men and boats engaged on the work, and they were forced to abandon it.

An open passage to the city was thus before them, through agencies which no power of man could resist. The river was still rising rapidly; the parade ground in Fort Jackson was covered to the depth of fifteen inches with water, and the sharp-shooters, who had been sent to annoy the enemy below the forts, were driven by the water from that position.

The bombardment of the mortar fleet was kept up day and night for a week. They succeeded in getting the range, and the number of shells which fell into Fort Jackson is almost incredible. The wood work of the fort was burned early in the action, and the garrison, up to their knees in water, and without clothes, save what they were wearing when the quarters were destroyed, cheerfully and bravely stood to their guns.

Upon the morning of the 24th of April, about three o'clock, the enemy's fleet of gunboats and frigates was discovered coming up; but owing to the treason of a scoundrel who was on watch below, and whose duty it was to give warning of their approach by sending up rockets, they had reached a point nearly opposite the forts before they were observed. The country knows how the indomitable Duncan fought them; but it was beyond the power of man to hold them in check. On they passed. Gen. Lovell was on an ordinary steamboat (the Doubloon) in the thick of the fight; and, at one time, some of the Yankee fleet were between him and the city. He came up in all haste and ordered well trained artillerists, under Gen. Smith, to the few guns that were at Chalmette—five on one side, and nine 32 pdrs. on the other. It may be asked why there were not more guns at this point? Simply for the reason that Gen. Lovell did not have them. He had been requested to turn over to the naval authorities the guns which he intended for these batteries; and, besides, it was never pretended by any one that any open works, with the river at least four feet higher than the level of the country, could stand the broadsides of a fleet under such disadvantages.

The works at Chalmette held the thirteen large frigates and gunboats about an hour. The last defences having been overcome, the thirteen vessels came up and anchored off the city. General Lovell was in town, and ready and willing to remain with all the troops under his command, which the morning report of that day showed to be about twenty-eight hundred, two-thirds of whom were the volunteer and militia companies which had recently been put in camp, and not one half of whom were respectably armed.

It was the undivided expression of public opinion that the army had better retire and save the city from destruction; and, accordingly, the General ordered his forces to rendezvous at Camp Moore, about seventy miles above New Orleans, on the Jackson Railroad.

A demand was made by Farragut for the surrender of the command, which Gen. Lovell positively refused, but told the officer who bore the message that if any Federal troops were landed he would attack them. Two days after he retired, it was said that the city had changed its purpose, and preferred a bombardment to occupation by the enemy. Gen. Lovell promptly ordered a train, and proceeded to New Orleans, and immediately had an interview with Mayor Monroe; offering, if such was the desire of the authorities and people, to return with his command and hold the city as long as a man and shot was left!

This offer not being accepted, it was decided that the safety of the large number of unprotected women and children should be looked to, and that the fleet would be permitted to take possession. The raw and poorly armed infantry could have done nothing against the fleet. The city would have been destroyed without any corresponding gain; and, if the general commanding had adopted this course, he would have justly been charged with a wanton destruction of life and property.

The impression which prevails, that Gen. Lovell had a large army under his command, is incorrect. He had, since the first of March, sent ten full, splendid regiments to Gen. Beauregard, besides many companies of cavalry and artillery. In fact, the demands for assistance had been so constant, that he was almost stripped of everything. Not a gun had been sent to the Department since he had taken command; but, upon the contrary, as fast as he succeeded in gathering up something in men and materials for the defence of his Department, he was ordered to send it to other fields. He had no control over the navy. It had been urged that all the means of defence should be under his command, but this was refused. A very short time before the fleet passed the forts, he had *implored* the senior naval officer of the station to order the iron-clad steamer Louisiana to be placed below Fort Jackson, which was *refused*. It is confidently believed that if this had been done, New Orleans would have been saved. It is not the intention of the writer of this brief note of explanation to find fault with any one, but the fatal mistake in the management of the Louisiana is no secret. Upon whom the awful responsibility, refusing the assistance which she could have rendered to Duncan in his unequal struggle should rest, *will* be fixed by the proper authorities.

I state, upon any and every responsibility that belongs to a gentleman and a soldier, that General Lovell requested that that iron-clad battery be sent to the Eddy below Fort Jackson, about three quarters of a mile, where she could have engaged the coming fleet, and given the garrison timely notice that the hour of trial had come. How she would have succeeded, may be unquestionably determined by the fact that the enemy failed to make any *impression* upon her *impenetrable* covering of iron, and was only destroyed after the surrender of both forts, to prevent her falling into the hands of the fleet; it being impossible, from the unfinished state of her machinery, to move her.

If General Lovell had had any number of first class guns they could not have been used, as the country was covered with water. As before stated, the river was higher than it was ever known before, and from a few miles below the city to the Gulf was one vast sheet of water, with the exception of the narrow levee on either side, and upon which there was not space enough to manage the guns that could have been effective against ships-of-war.

If any obstruction could have stood the flood of the Mississippi and the furious storm that raged on Friday night, by which the line of schooners was swept away, the city could not have fallen.

The forts were not armed with the largest guns, but they could have destroyed the fleet if it could have been held under their fire for any considerable period. After they succeeded in passing to the front of the city, Gen. Lovell had either to stand a bombardment without the power of replying, and by which the city would have been destroyed, and more than one hundred thousand helpless women and children exposed, or retire and let the enemy take possession. He followed in his decision the wishes of the people; he was ready and willing, and so were his officers and men, to perish in the ruins of New Orleans rather than yield, if such a course had been agreed to by the inhabitants. But it was decided otherwise; and in making this statement no reflection is intended upon the courage and loyalty of that unfortunate city. A truer, braver community never felt the power of the invader; and, to-day, they are proud and defiant in their devotion to the Cause.

I again repeat, but for the storm and flood, which combined to destroy the obstructions in the river, New Orleans would have been saved. General Lovell did all that mortal man could do to save the city; and, it is believed, that the good sense and candor of the people will do him justice. No soldier in the armies of the South has shown stronger evidences of devotion to the cause.

When the revolution commenced, he was a citizen of New York, enjoying a place of great honor and profit, which he could have held; and if he had been disposed to have sided with our enemies, a commission of the very highest grade was at his service. But, abandoning friends, position, fortune and all, he came and offered his great abilities to our people.

Upon the fields of Mexico he had won great honor, and no man of his age ever stood higher in the old army. The *words* of reproach which have been uttered against him, for misfortunes which no human power could have prevented, will not turn the brave soldier and unfaltering patriot from his duty.

He is actively engaged organizing the troops of Louisiana and Mississippi, and the people may rest assured that no clamor, no misrepresentation can make him, for one moment, forget that the present duty is to drive the invader from our soil.

This brief statement is submitted by one entirely acquainted with all the facts, with the conviction that the Southern people will not, when the truth is known, tolerate any wrong or injustice to as true a friend as ever led their sons to battle!

JUSTICE.

The Charleston Mercury.

DAILY PAPER—Ten Dollars per annum, payable half-yearly in advance. | VINDICE NULLO SPONTE SUA SINE LEGE FIDES RECTUMQUE COLENTUR. | COUNTRY PAPER—Thrice a Week—Five Dollars per annum, in advance.

VOLUME LXXX. | CHARLESTON, S. C., THURSDAY, MAY 29, 1862. | NUMBER 11,459

THE SITUATION OF AFFAIRS AT RICHMOND.

RICHMOND, May 28.—All is quiet along the lines to-day, so far as is known here. No cannonading has been heard to-day. It is now raining fast, and this interferes with military operations, as the country bordering on the Chickahominy is swampy, and almost impassable in wet weather.

(*The Latest.*)

Eight o'clock, p. m.—All the sick and wounded in the hospitals at Ashland were brought here this afternoon. The Yankees are reported to be advancing on that place in force. Ashland is a station on the railroad leading towards Fredericksburg, and is about twenty miles from Richmond.

Telegraphic communication between the city and the army has been suspended by military authority.

Soldiers, who arrived on the trains this afternoon, report that a serious engagement took place yesterday near the line of the Central Railroad, between the brigade of Gen. L. O'B. BRANCH and a large force of the enemy. No official intelligence in regard to the affair has been received.

All the efforts of the news agent to obtain late and trustworthy accounts from the army have failed. It is certain, however, that there was no fighting to-day. The city remains quiet.

THE CRISIS AT CORINTH—WHY NO NEWS CAN BE OBTAINED.

MOBILE, May 27.—(*Despatch to Savannah Republican.*)—Gen. BEAUREGARD has issued an order prohibiting the use of the telegraph from Corinth, and requiring all correspondents to retire from the army. This is done because of a telegram to the Memphis *Appeal* by its correspondent, notwithstanding it had been approved by his Adjutant General. I return to Georgia.

The Federals have got one siege gun in position, and are bringing up others.

THE SIEGE OF THE CAPITAL.

(FROM OUR OWN CORRESPONDENT.)

RICHMOND, Monday, May 26.

Thist's Sifting—Preparations for the Great Battle—Jackson and Ewell at Work—Effect on the Programme—Yankee Hunters—Balloons, etc., etc.

If Theophilus Thistle, the successful thistle-sifter, in sifting a sieve full of unsifted thistles, thrust three thousand thistles into the thick of his thumb, then must Theophilus Thistle have been the Richmond correspondent of THE CHARLESTON MERCURY on Saturday last, endeavoring to sift the truth out of a city full of unsifted rumors, reports and "reliables" in regard to the skirmishes of that day. The nearest approach to the truth seems to be this: There were two engagements—one of artillery at Mechanicsville (a blacksmith's shop and a dilapidated tavern are dignified with that name), and another of infantry at the New Bridge, on the Meadow Bridge road, which crosses the Chickahominy a mile and a half or two miles above Mechanicsville. In both of these engagements we were worsted—owing to the inferiority of our forces. Gen. Johnston refused to send reinforcements, his aim being, as many suppose, to draw the enemy over, or to gain time for the completion of certain arrangements by which troops can be rapidly concentrated upon the field of the great battle. General Johnston is too acute to suppose that McClellan, the Cautious, will cross the swamp in force. He will occupy the bridges, while he pushes his men to the head of the Swamp, in the direction of the junction of the Central and Fredericksburg Roads, and there, I feel pretty sure, the great battle will take place. Anderson has already fallen back to the Junction, some of Stuart's cavalry went forward on Saturday, and yesterday a heavy column of infantry marched after them. The rest of the army was engaged in cooking four days' provisions, and this morning the wagons are bringing all the baggage into town. The Petersburg Road is held subject to orders for the transportation exclusively of troops. It is plain, therefore, that the battle is to be no child's play, and that it will take place neither to-day nor to-morrow, as many imagine, but whenever the disposition of the scattered forces can be arranged to the satisfaction of the Generals.

A friend has just this moment come in to tell me of Jackson's despatch to Gen. Lee, about the taking of 2000 prisoners at Winchester, 3000 more at Front Royal, all the baggage, etc., and still pursuing. This may alter the programme to some extent. It sends Shields and McDowell back to Washington, unless there are forces there of which we know nothing—only 3000 were there at last accounts—but McClellan must fight all the same. It will never do for him to go back to Washington again, or even to Fortress Monroe. He must fight where he is, against men inspired by the memories of Williamsburg and the recent victories of Jackson. An acquaintance, who rode through our lines, on the Chickahominy, yesterday, says he was told by Gen. Howell Cobb that the men were much exasperated by Johnston's positive order for them to withdraw from the infantry fight of the day before—our cavalry having just come up to charge the enemy and rout him, as they would almost certainly have done. With this temper among our soldiers, it is not unreasonable to expect excellent results from the great battle.

It seems Ewell did join Jackson last Thursday, as I stated, and both were engaged in the affair at Winchester. Some doubt was entertained about yesterday's telegram concerning the Front Royal engagement, except by those who knew that Jackson had written to Hon. Mr. Boteler to come on, that the time had come when, according to promise made a month or more ago, he would take him home to his house in Jefferson county, not far from Harper's Ferry.

Rather a strange Sunday spectacle was witnessed yesterday, to wit: a party of a dozen young men, armed with very long muskets, very small cartridge boxes and very large haversacks, going out to hunt Yankees. They returned without any game. Not a syllable from Corinth since Thursday last—strange! We are preparing to raise a balloon on Church Hill. As both armies are now bivouacing in the dense woods, this ballooning business does little good except when columns are in motion. If these are moved at night, balloons are of no use except to detect wagon trains. The Examiner has a good article against the defensive policy. The Enquirer says the Yankees are hanging guerillas, and calls for retaliation.

HERMES.

THE MERCURY.

THURSDAY, MAY 29, 1862.

We have glorious tidings from the Border. A Southern Army has, at last, found a fighting leader. Rapid marches, splendid victories in quick succession, a routed and disorganized foe, and booty of inestimable value, tell us that a vigorous and aggressive campaign has at last begun. Stonewall JACKSON has shown himself a true General. In tracing, upon the map, the course of his victorious army, from Staunton to Martinsburg, the rapidity with which he has cleared the rich Valley of Virginia of the invaders seems almost incredible. Having driven BANKS and his army into Maryland, he has struck the line of the Baltimore and Ohio Railroad, effectually breaking up that great thoroughfare of Yankee transportation. We expect to hear next that he is leading his unconquerable battalions through Maryland into Pennsylvania.

The advance of JACKSON puts a new face upon the war. MCCLELLAN must detach a portion of his Grand Army to hasten to the defence of Washington. Meantime, with her own gallant sons of the Old Line pouring in to the rescue, Maryland, we trust, will awake from her slumbers, and Baltimore, throttled as she is by a military despotism, will send forth a new host to swell our advancing columns.

But we will not indulge in anticipations, the realization of which may be more distant than we think. For the present, certainly, the Potomac will again be the theatre of war; and, when that noble river is once more left in the background, we are confident that it will be because the tide of invasion has swept onward towards the Susquehannah.

THE NEWS OF THE WAR.

STONEWALL JACKSON'S VICTORIOUS ADVANCE TOWARDS THE POTOMAC.

The Richmond papers are all jubilant over the recent victories of JACKSON in the Valley of Virginia. The *Examiner* thus comments upon his late successes:

The glorious tidings of General Jackson's victory over Banks, the recovery of Winchester, the capture of four thousand prisoners, the annihilation of the invading army in the Valley, throws the splendor of sunlight over the long lines of the Confederate host. Once more we conquer.—Again the tide sets full in favor of the South.—Jackson's magnificent exploit is enough of itself to illustrate a campaign; but we cannot refrain from the pleasing supposition that it is the forerunner, the noble omen of another battle and another victory, if not more signal and complete, yet on a grander scale and with more decisive results.

But it is not yet known what results Jackson may eliminate from, the wonderful success which his bravery and long toil have fairly won at Winchester. A general expectation has prevailed among his devoted followers that he would soon lead them into Pennsylvania. Lincoln and his comrades at Washington have been, for some time past, in mortal terror that he should rush on their own seat of sin. After his victory over Milroy, the Federal Capital was in such a state of apprehension that packing and preparation for an immediate departure were visible in all the Departments. So far as we know here in Richmond, there is now absolutely nothing to prevent Jackson from doing either the one or the other. Banks' force was the last left capable of resisting him in that region, and, after the tremendous beating it has gotten at Winchester, it must necessarily be for some time quite ineffective. It would, indeed, be a soul-cheering thing if Jackson should now force his way to Washington City and startle the brood of harpies settled there in wait for the carcass of the South.

We may rest satisfied that this great blessing of Providence will be improved by the man to whom it has been vouchsafed. He is not one of those generals who spend their time in camps waiting for somebody else to do something. From the time of his entrance on command up to this moment he has continually marched and fought. If some of his marches were abortive, and if he was often forced to retreat, it shows nothing but the difficulties with which he had to contend. At least, this brave and industrious general was at all times endeavoring *to do*, and not inventing plans and giving reasons *how not to do*. Even his critics have never denied his earnestness, activity, and disposition to fight. These were visible at every step. Entrenched camps, with headquarters in nice houses, have not been heard of in connection with Jackson or Floyd. Those men live on their horses and sleep on the ground. If their troops suffer hardship and run risks, they share the worst with them, and both have gained the devotion of their men and the confidence of the country that has witnessed their ceaseless efforts. With Jackson in the northwest and Floyd in the south, untrammelled by War Departments or "superior officers," Western Virginia will soon be redeemed from the Yankees.

Under the head of "Stop Him," the Richmond *Whig* says:

Stonewall Jackson has marched 250 miles, and won three victories in three weeks. This man must be suppressed. His mind is evidently impaired. He has forgotten the art of war entirely. He has taken it into his head that war means fighting, action, movement, no trench digging, then squalling for reinforcements, then falling back. We shall hear presently that he believes it to be not altogether improper to wound the feelings of the Yankees. After that it is not unreasonable to expect that he will break the only spade he ever had, cross the Potomac, throw away every cartridge, carry Washington at the point of the bayonet, and walk into Philadelphia some fine morning, with his chin at an elevation of 45 degrees—all before the army of the Chickahominy decides whether it will be agreeable to Mr. McClellan not to wait his will and pleasure, even till Doomsday.

This man Jackson must be suppressed, or else he will change the humane and christian policy of the war, and demoralize the Government.—Evidently he has lost his mind. Down with him, or he will establish the independence of the Southern Confederacy.

THE RULE OF THE INVADER AT HUNTSVILLE, ALA.—WANTON AND ATROCIOUS OUTRAGES.

The Knoxville *Register* obtains the following statement from gentlemen who left the vicinity of Huntsville, Alabama, a few days ago. According to this account, General MITCHELL is winning a reputation for infamy only surpassed by that of B. F. BUTLER, in New Orleans:

On the arrival of the Federals in Huntsville, Mitchell sent for the Mayor, told him that he must have food for his men, about 5,000. Mayor Coltart replied that he would consult some of the citizens. Mitchell told him that he would give him to understand he was master, and the food must be provided or it would be taken from the citizens. To prevent outrages on individual citizens, the Mayor provided food at municipal expense. Sundry private citizens were arrested, the first day, and afterwards, without knowing why they were singled out from others who were as much or more in "the rebel" category than themselves, and it is presumed they were pointed out by tories in town. This presumption was confirmed by the fact that squads of Federals showed an extraordinary knowledge of localities by the facility with which they found their way to houses in which Confederate soldiers were or had been staying.

Our informants report that Mitchell appears to take a malicious pleasure in petty annoyances as well as greater outrages upon the people. If he sees half a dozen or more citizens together, he will, in the most haughty and imperious manner, cry out, "Disperse, you d—d rebels!"—knowing well that the balls and bayonets of the myrmidons who back him give him immunity from the penalties due his cowardly insolence, and which outraged freemen would visit upon him if they were unshackled.

The citizens of the town and country have been robbed of bacon, beeves, poultry, corn, fodder, flour, groceries, horses, mules—in short, everything that will replenish the exhausted quartermaster and commissary stores. In some instances they make a pretence to remunerate owners by giving them receipts for the property taken, specifying their own arbitrary unremunerative prices, and telling the owners to present the receipt to the quartermaster; and, when presented, the owner is required to take the oath of allegiance, and if he refuses, payment is refused.—Sometimes Federal scouts will take part of a man's bacon, provender, or other property, and take an inventory of the balance, and if the balance is not forthcoming when called for, the vandals will wantonly destroy almost everything that they can lay their hands on, and perhaps arrest the owner and hold him a prisoner for one or more days, and then release him on parole not to leave certain prison bounds.

The Confederate Marshal, General Ben. Patterson, and his family, left his residence near the city on the approach of the Hessians, and they destroyed his doors, windows, piano, furniture, &c., and carried off his corn, fodder and everything they could make useful. They robbed the grocery store of McCreary, Patton & Sprague, of about $12,000 worth of groceries, and appropriated the house as a sutler's store. They robbed the other grocery stores in like manner, with the exception of one Wm. H. Powers, a Yankee, and they paid him for all they got.

The Federals are greatly incensed by citizens of the country burning bridges, cutting telegraph wires, shooting scouts and pickets, and firing into railroad trains; and prominent citizens, in every neighborhood where such things occur, are arrested, taken to Huntsville, and imprisoned in the court-house, or in law offices, &c., for such times as the caprice of the General or his Provost may direct, and then paroled. Numbers of citizens are thus treated without any apparent reason. When our informant left, some dozen citizens of the town, and thirty odd citizens of the county, were confined. Among the prominent citizens who have thus suffered, we remember the names of ex Governor Clay, ex-Governor Reuben Chapman, Dr. Thomas Fearn, George P. Beirne, and Rev. J. G. Wilson—though nearly every man of any prominence has, at some time or other, experienced this petty despotism.

Ex Governor Clay, who is over seventy years of age and infirm, was ruthlessly taken from his plantation, in Jackson county, twenty miles from Huntsville, carried to town, confined two or three days and released on parole to remain in the city limits;—the alleged ground for this treatment being, that persons had fired on a railroad train containing Federal soldiers, and on a railroad bridge guard, a few miles distant from his plantation. For the same alleged offences, however, they burnt the small village of Camden or Paint Rock, which should have sufficed to satiate their ire. The villages of Woodville and Scottsboro', in Jackson county, on the railroad, were destroyed in like manner, and Mitchell made a speech at Woodville, in which he threatened to burn every house within ten miles, if bridge-burning and bush-whacking did not cease, and he would hang every bush-whacker he caught. The threats have been practically disregarded. Ex-Governor Chapman was taken from his residence two miles from town, confined in town several days, and then returned home on parole, and is kept there under guard. He was an original and decided secessionist, but his special offence was, probably, that General L. Pope Walker and family were his guests when Huntsville was taken.

* * * * * *

Nearly all of the citizens of Huntsville remained true to themselves and their country. The outrages committed on the strong Secessionists had intensified their disunionism and their hatred of the mongrel crew who assail their rights and seek their subjugation; and the hitherto lukewarm were wrought up to a pitch of indignation that only awaits opportunity to rival the most zealous and uncompromising. Some who were half and half—almost, if not quite, Union men—have suffered as much as the most intense disunionist, and, through much tribulation, have reached the conclusion that in disunion alone, permanent and irrevocable, is there any hope of Southern freedom.

A few—half a dozen to a dozen, at most—have demonstrated, beyond all question, their disloyalty and treason to the South. The most prominent of them are Jere Clemens and George W. Lane.

The entire force of Gen. Mitchell is eight thousand—two regiments being at Huntsville, and the remainder scattered from Bridgeport, Alabama, south of the Tennessee river to Athens, near the Tennessee line. The number at most points, bridges and towns, is small, there being only about twenty men at Belfonte, and only three companies at Athens. The Lincoln general complains that it is the first place to which he has been where a house has not been tendered to him, and he is occupying a tent with a strong guard, in front of which is planted one of the Bridgeport cannon. He is reported to stand in constant terror of a visit from Morgan and his men, having lost pickets every night, and one night as many as eight were taken off; in consequence of which he got up a pledge, which he tried to get the citizens to sign, to hang and quarter all engaged in guerilla warfare. Only six signed it, whereupon he seized thirty of the most prominent of them, and told the people that if they did not sign in twenty days, these citizens should be sent to Fort Warren. Two weeks had transpired, yet no one had signed the pledge.

The bank officers succeeded in getting everything valuable out of the way, and burnt all the bills that they had signed. The bank is shut—the newspapers stopped—business stagnant, and the colleges suspended. Gen. Mitchell is reported to have said that if the women did not cease insulting his soldiers, he should not longer attempt to restrain them, but turn them loose to do as they please!

A SEA-GOING MONITOR.

The New York Times states that Captain Ericsson's model of a sea-going Monitor, 340 feet long, has reached the Navy Department. It is similar in construction to its little namesake, now lying in wait for the mailed monster, which is momentarily expected from Norfolk. Like that, it has but one propeller and a single turret. The department inclines to favor two propellers and two turrets for a vessel of this size. A board to examine and report upon the numerous plans and models which have responded to the Secretary of the Navy's advertisement has been constituted.

The Charleston Mercury.

DAILY PAPER—TEN DOLLARS PER ANNUM, PAYABLE HALF-YEARLY IN ADVANCE.

VINDICE NULLO
SPONTE SUA SINE LEGE FIDES RECTUMQUE COLENTUR.

COUNTRY PAPER—THRICE A WEEK—FIVE DOLLARS PER ANNUM, IN ADVANCE.

VOLUME LXXX. | CHARLESTON, S. C., MONDAY, JUNE 2, 1862. | NUMBER 11,462

NEWS BY TELEGRAPH.

RICHMOND, Saturday, May 31.—*Noon.*—There was a violent rain and thunder storm here last evening, which continued for several hours. About nine o'clock the gas works were flooded, leaving the city in total darkness. A skirmish took place, yesterday, on the Williamsburg road, between four companies from the 24th Virginia and 23d North Carolina Regiments, and a Federal Regiment. Our loss was five killed, including Capt. SCARBORO, of North Carolina, and five wounded. A Yankee prisoner taken states that the loss of the enemy was heavy, including a Colonel and Major. A fight is now progressing on the same road, near the Chickahominy river, which is much swollen by the rain of last evening. No reports yet received.

Two o'clock.—The flood in the Chickahominy, caused by the rain, is very heavy. It is reported here that the bridges were washed away, and that three divisions of the enemy were thus caught, unsupported, on this side of the river. Trains of ambulances were sent down from the city at noon. The roar of artillery and musketry can now be distinctly heard here. No courier has yet arrived.

Six o'clock.—The battle has been going on all day near the Chickahominy. All the reports from the field, thus far, are favorable. The engagement is a severe one, and the loss on both sides heavy. Our wounded have been coming into the city for several hours.

Eight o'clock, p. m.—The latest authentic reports from the battle field represent that the enemy had been driven a mile and a half from his position, our forces occupying his camp. We captured three batteries, after most desperate fighting, the enemy being protected by his entrenchments and the woods. Several hundred prisoners are reported taken.

Ten o'clock.—Gen. HILL's division began the fight this morning, RHODES and GARLAND's brigades bearing the brunt of the battle for some time. RAINS' and ANDERSON's brigades also bore a conspicuous part in the engagement, until our reinforcements arrived. The enemy was also reinforced and the fighting continued with great desperation on both sides. The enemy was finally driven from his redoubts and his batteries were turned upon him. Prisoners taken say that Gen. BUELL was in command. President DAVIS and Gen. LEE were on the field, their presence increasing the enthusiasm of our troops. All accounts agree that the Confederates displayed great bravery. The enemy stubbornly contested every inch, whilst giving way before the impetuous charges of our forces. No trustworthy estimate of the casualties has yet been received. A great number of the Confederates were wounded in the arm and hand. Gen. RHODES was slightly wounded. No other general officer on our side hurt as far as known. About seven o'clock in the evening the enemy tried to make a flank movement, but was repulsed by General WHITING's division.

It is belived that the fight will be renewed tomorrow. The community here is in good spirits, and confident of victory.

SUNDAY, June 1, *a. m.*—The battle yesterday took place in the vicinity of Boar Swamp, between the Railroad and the Williamsburg Road, seven miles from the city. The accounts sent yesterday, were, in the main, correct. More cannonading has been heard this morning.

Northern papers of the 28th inst. brought from the battle field state that MCCLELLAN telegraphed to the Yankee Secretary of War that "the battle at Hanover C. H. resulted in the complete rout of the enemy, with a rebel loss of 1000." This, of course, is a Yankee falsehood. The Federal loss on the occasion is admitted to have been 379—killed, wounded and missing. The Philadelphia *Inquirer* says that Stonewall JACKSON's success "has aroused the North," and that "volunteers are pouring in." The confiscation bill has passed the Yankee House of Representative. GEO. F. SHEPLEY, of Maine, is appointed Military Commander of New Orleans, in the absence of BUTLER.

Five o'clock, p. m.—The battle has been progressing furiously to-day—the artillery being chiefly engaged. No definite reports have been received from the field of battle. The general tenor of the statements of wounded soldiers indicates that the Confederates are following up the success of yesterday. Prisoners are constantly coming in. BUELL was not present. MCCLELLAN commanded in person. It is now believed that the larger portion of the Yankee army is on this side of the Creek. Gen. HATTON, of Tennessee, was killed yesterday.

Six o'clock, p. m.—No definite accounts have been received of the result of the battle to-day; but all the reports agree that the enemy has been badly beaten and driven into the swamp. The carnage on both side was dreadful. The Yankee loss was two to our one. Hundreds of wounded are arriving in the city. About five hundred prisoners, in all, have, thus far, been brought in.

[*Note.*—Gen. JOS. R. ANDERSON, formerly of the Tredegar Works, is said to have command of two brigades; his own, of five regiments from Virginia, Georgia, North and South Carolina—the latter consisting of the First Palmetto Regiment, under Lieut. Col. GUS. SMITH, all under command of the Senior Colonel, DANIEL HAMILTON; and Gen. GREGG's brigade, said to consist of North Carolina troops not long in service.]

MOVEMENTS NEAR PENSACOLA.

MOBILE, May 31.—A despatch received here from Pollard, dated May 30, says: A skirmish took place day before yesterday, in which the Simpson Rangers drove the Yankee guard off the O'Bannonsville bridge and burnt the bridge. Our loss was one man and three horses; the enemy's loss unknown. Three citizens of Oakfields have been taked prisoners by the enemy and carried to Pensacola. The Yankee forces are not advancing.

LATEST FROM CORINTH.

The Mobile *Register* learns by passengers by the cars on the 28th, that the reduction of baggage, tents, and camp equipage is being rigidly and systematically enforced at Corinth. Large quantities are sent down to different points, by every train, but no guns or ammunition accompany them.

The Mobile *Tribune*, of Wednesday last, thinks that the great battle at Corinth would begin on that day. It states that Generals PRICE and VAN DORN went out night before last with their commands to try and get between the enemy and the river, and if they accomplished the object, they were to fire signal guns at 3 o'clock, a. m. Firing was heard at that hour, and the whole army was soon afterwards in motion. All of the sick soldiers, women and children—all have been sent away from Corinth. It is therefore, believed, that the great battle has actually commen ced.

The Richmond *Examiner* has reports from Corinth that General BEAUREGARD had succeeded in cutting off HALLECK's supplies by railroad, and his only means of communication was by the Tennessee River, which was falling very rapidly and would soon be unnavigable. It was supposed HALLECK would be compelled to fall back, in which event General BEAUREGARD would attack him.

JACKSON CROSSES THE POTOMAC.

The Richmond *Examiner* says:—Intelligence received in official quarters yesterday leaves no doubt but that *the line of the Potomac has at last been crossed*, and that a portion of General JACKSON's command is now at Williamsport, in Maryland. The army having been once mobilized is in a condition to make rapid marches. It is reported that in Baltimore there were recently but three thousand Federal troops, and scarcely as many in Washington and vicinity.

The Potomac River opposite Williamsport, at this season, is about a quarter of a mile wide, and possibly fordable; if not, rafts and scows are at hand up and down the river. Hagerstown is distant from Williamport about fifteen miles, and Frederick about forty-five miles, both reached by excellent turnpikes. It was the street report yesterday that General JACKSON's vanguard of cavalry had entered Frederick, Maryland; but the report yet needs confirmation. Frederick is, or has been, the subsistence and hospital depot of the Federal Army of the Valley, second in importance to Winchester. Frederick from Baltimore is distant about sixty-five miles by railroad, with two junctions on the Baltimore and Ohio—one at the Frederick Junction, and one at the Washington Junction, at the Relay House, nine miles from Baltimore, where the Washington branch shoots off in a southwesterly direction.

The Relay House is one of the strategic points seized by the Federal Government after the occupation of Harper's Ferry by the Confederates, and before the seizure of Baltimore by Federal authority. A battery of two guns was placed on the road above the junction, commanding the bend in the track from the Avalon Iron Works, and two camps established on the hills, but these have been removed some time since. If the Yankees have not destroyed the track of the railroad in their retreat, there is nothing to prevent Gen. JACKSON, with the aid of ASHBY's cavalry, from taking possession of the railroad from either Harper's Ferry or its Frederick branch to the Relay House, distant sixty-five miles from the ferry and twenty-eight miles from Washington by rail, thus allowing them to operate in either direction.

JACKSON's army is said to consist of some thirty-two thousand picked troops, well armed, and admirably disciplined. His command includes most of the Maryland regiments in the Confederate service; also the Louisiana "Tigers," and other regiments which have already made their mark in this war. Thousands of Marylanders are said to be ready to rise and join JACKSON's column. Many of these gallant men have arms hidden, and those who have none are ready to fight with scythes, sticks or brickbats.

THE MERCURY.

MONDAY, JUNE 2, 1862.

A day of carnage has ushered in the blazing Summer; another bloody Sunday has added its solemn tale to the records of the War. The great struggle for Richmond is at last begun; whether it is yet ended, we know not. But we know enough to assure us that Providence smiles upon our arms in this dread hour of our destiny: that the valor of our soldiers is worthy the sacred Cause for which they fight; and that the fair Capital of Virginia and of the South is still safe from the ruthless hordes gathered for its destruction.

It is well that the great battle has been joined, and a period put to the painful suspense in which the Southern people have so long been held. The two great armies which yesterday met to decide the fate of the campaign in the East—perhaps of the War itself—were ready for the test. The army of the North was as powerful as discipline, equipments, energy and superior numbers can make the champions of a bad cause. We know that our own noble soldiers went forth to the combat nerved with the unalterable purpose to conquer or to die. We are content to leave the issue with the God of Battles, trusting that He, who has so often given us the victory in the early struggles of the Revolution, will not forsake us in this, the hour of need.

But, though we triumph, the glory of to-day is shaded by the certain gloom of the morrow. Before we hail the victors who have won the field, we turn with sadness to the thought of those whose blood and lives have been the costly sacrifice. They have indeed become, willing victims, immolated for their country's good. We deplore their loss and we cherish their memory. Their death has been as glorious as their lives were patriotic, and they have left to their families the proud heritage of a martyr's and a hero's name.

THE GROWING CROP.—The prospect of the growing crop, as seen from the South Carolina Rail Road, between Charleston and Columbia, is encouraging. We recollect, too, to have seen but a single field of cotton, of any extent, along the line. The planters of Sumter have generally pursued this policy, and we learn the prospect for an abundant yield of grain is good.—*Sumter Watchman.*

THE CRISIS AT THE CAPITAL.

(FROM OUR OWN CORRESPONDENT.)

RICHMOND, Wednesday, May 28.

McClellan Tacking—Heavy Skirmishes—Panic in Washington—Captured Stores—Prospective Movements, &c., &c.

A ship running against the wind is compelled to tack. An army coming upon a swamp like the Chickahominy, with a strong force to dispute its passage, is apt to veer. Hence we are not surprised at the increasing severity of the skirmishes toward the head of the Swamp, nor dismayed by the reports of this morning, that BRANCH, of North Carolina, was, worsted yesterday, near the Junction. Johnston must have expected all this. The extent of the mishap has not yet transpired.

A gentleman who left Washington day before yesterday reports a great panic there in consequence of Jackson's performances. Banks was at or near Front Royal, but left in hot haste, with a body guard of 1,000 cavalry, for Harper's Ferry. At last accounts we had taken 13 cannon, a large amount of ordnance stores, several hundred bags of coffee, and as many sacks of salt, and 2,800 prisoners. It is hoped Jackson will destroy the Baltimore and Ohio Railroad and the canal. As to his entering Maryland, opinions differ. There is some talk of his being reinforced for that purpose, while Johnston contents himself with holding McClellan in check. Others say he has been ordered back, via Fredericksburg, on McDowell's rear, and others still declare that Fremont, with the remnant of Milroy's force, and a part of Blenker's division, is hastening to effect a junction with McDowell and Shields on the upper Potomac.

In addition to siege pieces and field artillery protected by entrenchments, McClellan, I am told, has taken pains to command the roads that cross the Chickahominy by felling trees across them. Thus his flanks are protected against attack in time of battle, and pursuit cut off in case he is compelled to retreat; and this strengthens the opinion so often expressed in these letters, that the general engagement will occur at or above the head of the Swamp. At the same time, heavy feints will be made at all the crossings, by which means he disperses our forces along a line of battle fifteen or twenty miles in length, while, with superior numbers, he will press upon our left flank. So, in a manner, we will have a renewal of McDowell's plan at Manassas, the Chickahominy representing Bull Run, and Hanover C. H., or some other point higher up, representing the Stone Bridge and Sudley's Ford. But all these speculations may be knocked in the head by a little dash on the part of Jackson. If he is reinforced, and enters Maryland and menaces Washington, nothing will be left McClellan but to make as good a retreat as he can to his transports, which will hurry him back to the help of Old Abe. I confess it looks to me very much as if it would come to this.

HERMES.

LATEST FROM NEW ORLEANS. THE BRUTALITIES OF BUTLER.

We have received papers from New Orleans as late as Monday, 26th. As we stated recently, Mayor MONROE and the Chief of Police had been sent from the city, and the municipal government was under the control and presided over by Gen. G. F. SHEPLEY, the military commandant. All the old police have been discharged, and Yankees, or men who take the oath of allegiance, are to be put in their places. Permission, however, had been granted to the citizens to elect a "loyal citizen of New Orleans and the United States as Mayor." Here is the essential part of an order in relation to their banks

Ordered:

I.—That the several incorporated Banks pay out no more Confederate Notes to their depositors or creditors, but that all deposits be paid in the bills of the Bank, United States Treasury Notes, Gold or Silver.

II.—That all Private Bankers, receiving deposits, pay out to their depositors only the current bills of City Banks, or United States Treasury Notes, Gold or Silver.

III.—That the Savings Banks pay to their depositors or creditors in Gold, Silver, or United States Treasury Notes, current bills of City Banks, or their own bills, to an amount not exceeding one-third of their deposits, and of denomination not less than one dollar, which they are authorized to issue, and for the redemption of which their assets shall be held liable.

IV.—The incorporated Banks are authorized to issue bills of a less denomination than five dollars, but not less than one dollar, anything in their charters to the contrary notwithstanding, and are authorized to receive Confederate Notes for any of their bills till the 27th day of May instant.

V.—That all persons and firms having issued small notes or "shinplasters" so called, are required to redeem them on presentation at their places of business, between the hours of 9 a. m. and 3 p. m., either in Gold, Silver, United-States Treasury Notes, or Current Bills of City Banks, under penalty of confiscation of their property and sale thereof for the purpose of redemption of the notes so issued, or imprisonment for a term of hard labor.

VI.—Private bankers may issue notes of denominations not less than one, nor more than ten dollars, to two-thirds of the amount of specie which they show to a commissioner appointed from these headquarters, in their vaults, and actually kept there for the purpose of redemption of such notes.

This war on the Confederate currency was producing considerable distress among needy persons. Those who have it in possession are obliged at great depreciation to convert it into what the enemy will take.

The New-York Times.

VOL. XI—NO. 3337. | NEW-YORK, TUESDAY, JUNE 3, 1862. | PRICE TWO CENTS.

SCENE OF THE GREAT BATTLE BEFORE RICHMOND.

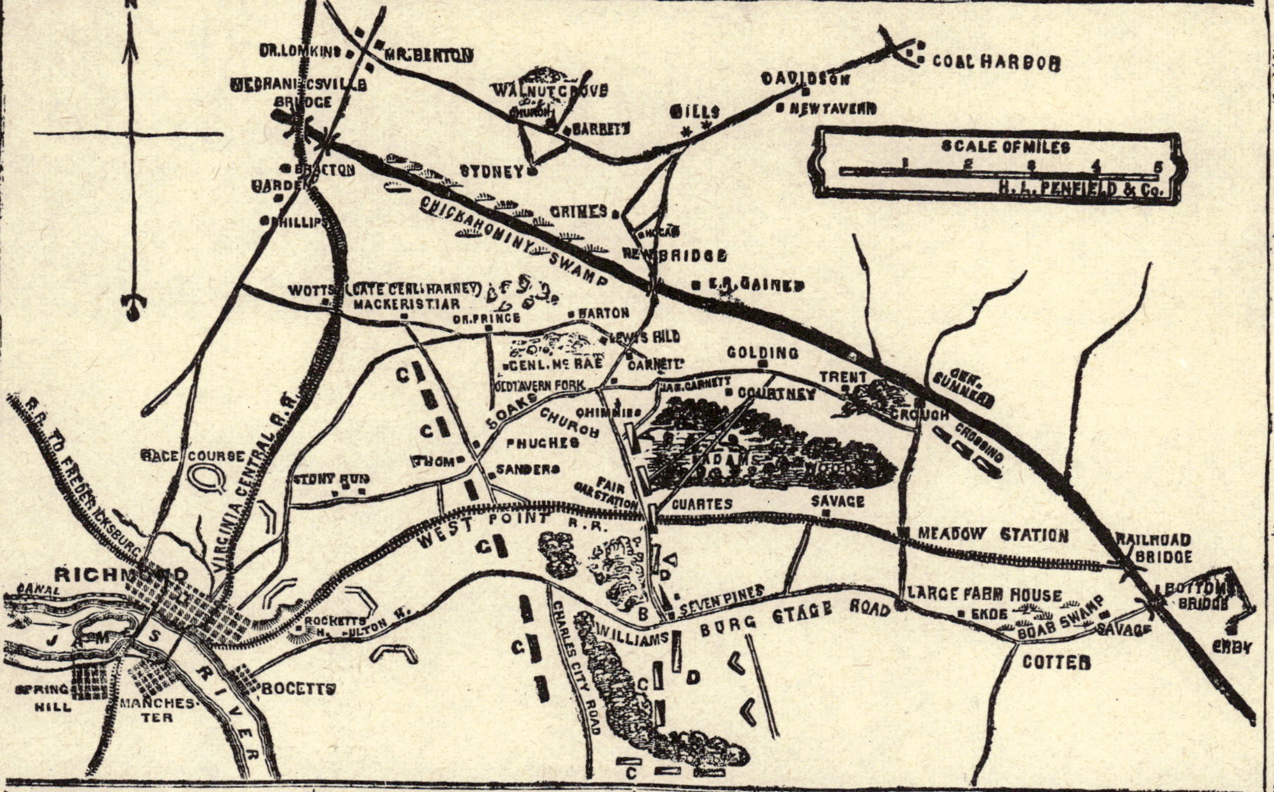

THE GREAT BATTLE.

Full Particulars from Our Special Correspondent.

The Attack on Gen. Casey's Position.

The Temporary Disaster There, with Loss of Artillery and Camp Equipage.

The Divisions of Gens. Kearney and Hooker Brought up.

GALLANT BAYONET CHARGE

The Rebels Driven Back Like Sheep.

The Crossing of the Chickahominy by Our Reinforcements.

DESPERATE NATURE OF THE FIGHTING.

The Great Victory of Our Forces On Sunday.

Our Advance Now Some Distance Beyond the Battle Ground.

FIELD OF BATTLE BEFORE RICHMOND,
Sunday A. M., June 1, 1862.

A battle before Richmond has at last put to the test the rebel boast as to what they would do with Gen. McClellan's army when they should get it beyond the protection of the gunboats. Though the advantage of a sudden movement, against the weakest point in our lines, gave the enemy a temporary success, the final result has not been such as to afford encouragement to their disheartened and demoralized troops, or occasion any fears as to our ultimate possession of the rebel capital.

The attack commenced shortly before 1 o'clock on Saturday, on the left wing of the army, on the further or south side of the Chickahominy, where the advance position was held by the division of Gen. Casey, much the weakest in the army, *composed almost entirely of raw regiments, and reduced by disease to an effective force of some 6,000 men.*

THE POSITION HELD BY GEN. CASEY

Was on the Williamsburgh Stage Road, within six or seven miles of Richmond, and on a line so extended at the front that the troops required to maintain picket guards of sufficient strength, made no slight draft on his weakened forces. The right of the line was held by his First Brigade, under Gen. H. M. Naglee, as brave and vigilant an officer as is to be found in the army of the Potomac. Gen. Naglee's pickets extended across the railroad (running parallel with the Williamsburgh road, about a mile to the right) to near the sixth mile-post from Richmond, and so on further to the right and a little to the rear until within a short distance of a point on the Chickahominy, where Gen. Sumner had thrown a bridge across the stream, and was hourly expected to cross to complete the line of pickets to the river.

The centre of Gen. Casey's position, held by the Second Brigade, Gen. Wassell's, (formerly Gen. Keims',) extended from Gen. Naglee's lines to the left a short distance across the Williamsburgh Road, where it joined the Third Brigade, Gen. Palmer's, stretching some distance further to the left, and joining the lines of Gen. Couch, who guarded the left flank, the main portion of his force being a short distance to the rear of Casey, on the Williamsburgh Road.

THE NATURE OF THE GROUND.

The position occupied by the main body of these two divisions was a clearing of about one mile square, surrounded on the left and the front by a belt of forest, in which Gen. Casey's pickets were stationed. On the right, a wooded swamp divided the clearing from a similar opening in the forest, along the railroad, which was occupied by Gen. Naglee with his brigade. Just beyond the woods to the front were similar clearings with woods on their further side, where the rebels lay concealed, their pickets occupying the edge of the forest, and separated from our pickets by the width of the fields, forming a sort of neutral ground between the two armies, over which each kept close watch lest his neighbor should take possession. The position of Gen. Casey and other Generals, the nature of the ground, etc., will be made clear by reference to the map accompanying this account.

THE ENEMY RECONNOITERING.

Step by step Gen. Casey had pressed on to this point, overcoming such opposition as met him, until it became evident that the rebels had reached the limit of their retreat, and further advance could not be ventured without the risk of a general engagement, for which the plans were not yet ripe. Our proximity to the rebels was evidently annoying to them, and on Thursday, and again on Friday, they made an unsuccessful attempt, with a force of a few hundred, to drive in the pickets and discover what mischief was plotting behind the belt of woods sheltering Gen. Casey from their view. Their attack was resolutely met by the pickets, who fell back on the reserves and held their ground, defeating the purpose of the enemy.

Meanwhile Gen. Casey was actively at work [illegible] ing his position, a large force of men being [illegible] under the skillful direction of Lieut. E. W. [illegible], of his Staff, digging rifle pits and felling trees for abattis. A similar line of defensive works had been commenced and partially completed at Gen. Casey's former position, at the Seven Pines, three miles further to the rear, and just back of these was a line of earthworks, constructed by Gen. Couch, and more carefully finished.

Failing in the two attempts to gather information by forcing back Gen. Casey's pickets, the rebels apparently resolved upon an *advance in force against the left wing of the army*, doubtless determined to drive it beyond the Chickahominy, should the opportunity offer, and put themselves in a position to turn Gen. McClellan's left flank.

THE STORM ON FRIDAY NIGHT.

During the afternoon of Friday, a terrific thunderstorm arose, continuing through most of the night with uninterrupted severity, deluging the earth with rain, converting the spongy soil into a nearly impassable bog, and raising the waters of the Chickahominy so as to carry away one of two bridges Gen. Sumner had prepared for his passage, and somewhat disturb the foundations of the other.

The broad sheets of lightning that night and the camp fires of unusual size, gleaming in the pitchy darkness, seemed to illuminate our position, and may possibly have assisted the rebels in getting an idea of the bearing of things. Just before the storm had reached its fury there was some skirmishing between the artillery on both sides. This commenced again in the morning, several shots flying over our camp, indicating that the rebels had in some way gained a more correct idea of our position.

THE ATTACK ON SATURDAY.

Shortly after noon the grand attack commenced, Gen. Casey's pickets being driven in all along the front, after a spirited resistance, the rebels advancing in force along three roads—the Williamsburgh road, to our left, the railroad, in the centre, and the "Nine-mile Road," as it is called, on the right. With his feeble division greatly weakened by extension, Gen. Casey had no backbone to oppose to this sudden attack. But no thought of yielding his ground entered the mind of the old soldier, scarred with the wounds of Mexico and disciplined to danger by a hundred fights. His troops were immediately formed into position, the three brigades maintaining their relative positions on the right, left and centre, and as thorough preparations were made for resisting the attack as its suddenness would admit of. Regan's New-York Battery was stationed just to the right of the Williamsburgh road, Bates' Battery of Napoleon guns further to the left across the road, and Fitch's Battery three or four hundred yards to the rear, the last sending its shell over the heads of our troops at the enemy beyond. The fourth battery was near the railroad, further to the right.

The vigor with which the enemy pressed forward to the attack indicated the confidence of superior strength. A battalion of two regiments pressed against Gen. Naglee on the right, another fell on Gen. Wassell at the centre, and a third on Gen. Palmer to the left, pouring in at once a fire hot and heavy, and advancing with great resolution in face of the steady fire of canister and grape from the guns in front, and shell from those further to the rear, moving down their ranks in all directions. The rebels had but little artillery, and were evidently disposed to make good the deficiency by pressing to close quarters with their superior force, to bear down at once by weight of numbers the feeble skeleton regiments of three and four hundred men who composed the advanced division.

Most of Gen. Casey's troops were thrown forward to the edge of the woods in front of his position to meet the advance of the rebels, a few regiments being left behind the partially completed rifle-pits, a short distance to the rear. Thus a division, nearly new to warfare, was suddenly exposed, in an open field, to the heaviest of fire from an enemy covered to a considerable extent by the woods through which they were advancing. Terribly the tempest raged, the air almost growing thick with musket balls; officer after officer fell, or was borne from the field a wounded man; the men dropped by scores, and the usual number of weak-jointed ones were falling to the rear. But in spite of the rapid thinning of their ranks, the regiments generally held their ground until the enemy succeeded in rushing around on the left flank, and poured in an enfilading fire from that direction, against which the rifle-pits were no protection. The sixty rounds of ammunition with which they entered the fight were nearly exhausted, and no more was at hand.

ARRIVAL OF REINFORCEMENTS.

Meantime one of Gen. Couch's brigades, commanded by Gen. Abercrombie, was ordered up to the support of Gen. Naglee on the right, Gen. Devens, of the same division, sustaining Gen. Wassell on the center, and Gen. Peck, with the remaining brigade, supporting Gen. Palmer on the left. When Gen. Casey's troops were forced to give way, the rebels fell on these brigades of Couch's Division, who disputed every inch of ground, until sustained by Gen. Kearney, pressing up the Williamsburgh road with reinforcements to meet them, supported by the Division of Gen. Hooker in his rear. Pressing rapidly forward Gen. Kearney advanced along the Williamsburgh road to within a short distance of our original position, where he bivouacked for the night in front of the enemy.

It was along this Williamsburgh road that the main attack was made, and here our troops were forced back for half a mile or more, before the arrival of Gen. Heintzelman's corps, the feeble brigades of Casey's Division, averaging less than 2,000 men, being completely broken up, many, if not most of the officers killed, wounded or missing, and the privates scattered through the woods and along the road. Bravely and well did Gen. Casey do his duty, pressing on to the extreme front and cheering on his men, regardless of the storm of fire and hail that raged about him, cutting down his officers on all sides, but strangely escaping his own person. Bravely and well did most of his officers stand by him, until, one after another, they were borne from the field dead or wounded.

THE LOSS OF ARTILLERY.

Col. Bailey, Chief of Artillery, was shot early in the afternoon, the ball striking him in the head and causing his death after a short period of insensibility. Maj. Van Vaultenberg, the second in command of the First New-York Artillery, was killed, Adj't Wm. Ramsay wounded, while every battery but one lost its quota of men, and some of them lost nearly all their horses. Bates' Battery of Napoleon guns—12-pound brass pieces—which was to the front, thus deprived of locomotion and stuck fast in the mud, was left behind in the retirement of our troops, but not until Gen. Naglee had taken it upon himself to see that several of the pieces were spiked. In addition to this, one 3-inch Parrot gun of Battery H was disabled by a shot, and fell into the hands of the enemy. The Pennsylvania Reserve Battery, of Couch's Division, also lost one of their guns—these eight pieces of ordnance constituting our entire loss, so far as I could learn. We can better afford to spare the pieces than we can afford to have the rebels profit by their gain. They show every indication of being much in want of artillery, and the need is evidently stimulating their efforts to profit by the chances of war to possess themselves of our guns.

GEN. SUMNER'S ADVANCE.

Meantime Gen. Sumner had succeeded in bringing his troops across the Chickahominy, and was advancing on the right to maintain our position there, where less ground had been lost. After several days of labor, Gen. Sumner had thrown two bridges across the creek between Bottom's Bridge and New Bridge, where local reports held it to be impossible to find any foundation for piles to support the superstructures. One of these bridges was some two miles above Bottom's Bridge, the other a mile further up the stream. The lower of these was carried away during the heavy storm of Friday night, and Gen. Sumner was obliged to depend upon a single shaky structure for the passage of his troops, who nearly all, however, succeeded in crossing that night, the head of the column reaching the Nine-mile Road, along which the rebels were pressing our troops, at about 7 o'clock, holding the enemy in check for the night, preventing them from following up in that direction the advantage they had gained during the day.

THE FIGHT ON SUNDAY.

Flushed with their seeming victory of Saturday the rebels awoke with confidence on Sunday to follow up their movements, sure of driving us this time to the Chickahominy and beyond. But they had made the unfortunate mistake of estimating the strength of our reserves by the weakness of our advance. *Most bitterly did they pay for their mistake.* Pressing eagerly forward with confidence of victory, they were met by the trained troops of Heintzelman and Sumner, whose unyielding columns checked their fierce assault, turning the tide of battle everywhere against them, *and forcing them at the point of the bayonet on toward Richmond.* It was their turn now to break and run, and their losses of the Sabbath left them little cause for rejoicing over the trifling gain of Saturday. Terribly did the rebels suffer on this, as well as the previous day, from the well-directed fire of our artillery, *piling the ground with the slain.* Terrible also to them were the frequent charges of our solid columns, pressing them back, step by step, to the last point of endurance, *when they broke and ran*, ingloriously leaving behind them many of their men and officers, as well as privates, prisoners in our hands. The number of these it is not yet possible to ascertain, several days necessarily elapsing after every engagement before a full inventory can be taken.

OUR LOSS IN KILLED AND WOUNDED.

Even of our loss it was impossible to form any correct idea at the time I left the field of battle. The only source of information was the wounded, who gave such particulars, in regard to their respective regiments as they could, as they were borne by from all parts of the field. To the oft-repeated question: "Well, how did your regiment stand it?" I got uniform answers.

"O, Sir, our regiment was all cut to pieces—cut to pieces, Sir; nothing left of it."

I, of course, was able to rely little on such stories from my disabled informants, knowing the tendency, not only among soldiers, but equally among people in civilized life, to magnify their own misfortune into a measure of the public calamity. They took no account of their nimble-footed comrades, who had disappeared without damage to life or limb. It is impossible, so soon after the affair, to give even a rough estimate of the loss in an engagement spread over so great a space of country, and in the confusion which always ensues after a battle. That the loss is very severe, and particularly so in the matter of officers, there is no matter of doubt. The difficulty of rightly estimating our loss is also enhanced by the fact that many of those falling were unavoidably left upon the ground subsequently occupied by the enemy in his first successful attack. The number of these we cannot learn until regimental rolls are compared. It is sincerely to be regretted, in view of the tales we have of the barbarous treatment of our wounded by the rebels, when once they fall into their hands, that necessity should have compelled any to be left upon the field, to receive "the tender mercies of the wicked." That the rebel loss was greater by far than our own I do not doubt. Besides our superiority in artillery, our small arms were much more effective, having all the superiority in fatal power, which the Minié ball has over the round rifle ball. The wounds inflicted by the enemy were mainly by the latter. Had the leaden hail in which our men were obliged to stand so long, been composed of conical instead of round shot, many more Rachels would be mourning over the lost, and many more homes draped in funeral weeds. Your correspondent feels particularly grateful to the blockade, being morally certain that had the ball which lodged so harmlessly in his legging been a Minié, he would have been obliged always hereafter to write standing on one foot—a good figure of speech for Juvenal, but one which he would rather be excused from practically embodying. As it is, the slight abrasion left upon his leg by the ball, after forcing two thicknesses of leather and one of cloth, is sufficiently suggestive of a reward to satisfy his moderate ambition for military adventure.

THE CASUALTIES OF SATURDAY.

Of those who entered into close range of the enemy's guns, scarcely one of the officers that I saw escaped without some mark of the enemy's bullets on clothes or person, when no positive wound was inflicted. Gen. Naglee was struck four times by balls that pierced his clothes, inflicting slight bruises on his person. Lieut. West, Aid-de-Camp to Gen. Casey, who continued constantly under fire while actively discharging his duties, had his clothes badly torn by a piece of shell. Lieut. Foster, who was equally cool and energetic, I heard reported as wounded, but discredit the statement, which I should be sorry to believe true of so efficient an officer. Capt. Smith, Gen. Casey's Assistant Adjutant-General, and Lieut. Harrington Raymond, Aid-de-Camp, were disabled by sickness—Lieut. Raymond fretting upon his sick bed at the thought that he should be compelled to inaction at a time when his services were so much needed by his General.

Of the line officers not positively wounded, Col. C. H. Van Wyck, of the Fifty-sixth New-York Regiment, seems to have met with the most narrow escape, being struck by a spent shell which doubled up his sword-sheath, and severely bruised his left knee. Had the shell been nearer its initial velocity, the Colonel would have lost a pair of limbs, of essential service to a man of his active habits; and had it exploded, Congress would have been minus one of its working members.

All sorts of reports were afloat immediately after the engagement in regard to accidents to prominent officers, in Gen. Casey's Division more particularly. The General himself was reported to me first as wounded, and then as killed, but I was happy to be able to congratulate the brave old soldier on his entire safety before leaving the field with my dispatches.

Gen. Casey's son-in-law, Col. Hunt, received a ball through the fleshy part of his thigh, inflicting a wound more painful than dangerous. Col. Hunt, who is a Captain in the Twelfth United States Infantry, had taken command, only the week previous, of the Ninety-second New-York Regiment, to which he had been appointed. He has seen fifteen years of service in the regular army, and is an officer whose services we can ill afford to spare at this juncture.

NOTICES OF THE DEAD.

Col. Guilford D. Bailey, Chief of Artillery, who fell early in the action, was a graduate of West Point, in the class of 1856, where he maintained an excellent standing, receiving an appointment as Second Lieutenant in the Second Artillery, from which he was promoted to a Captaincy on the 3d of last August, subsequently receiving a commission as Colonel of Volunteers. He was an active young man, of bright and quick intellect, who left a most favorable impression on my mind in the brief intercourse I had with him. I shall not soon forget his bright, cheerful face, which greeted me on the morning of Saturday; nor that other scene, when, on the evening of the same day, I beheld his dead body, covered with blood from the wound which had so suddenly cut short his life.

Col. J. M. Brown, of the One Hundreth New-York, was another valuable officer whose death I regret to report. Energetic and faithful in his duties, he was a man to be relied upon for an emergency, as he had shown but the day before, when, as officer of the day, he directed the pickets of Gen. Casey in their successful resistance to the attempt to break our lines. These two officers were New-Yorkers, Col. Brown being, I believe, a well-known resident of the western part of this State.

Stories were afloat when I left of the death of Brig.-Gen. J. N. Palmer, of Gen. Casey's Third Brigade. I could trace them to no reliable source, though I failed to discover anything of Gen. Palmer before leaving. I have few personal friends whose death I should notice with more regret than that of Gen. Palmer. A thorough patriot, a courteous gentleman, a genial companion he was, at the same time, a faithful soldier, who shrank from no danger into which duty led him.

Col. W. W. H. Davis, of the One Hundred and Fourth Pennsylvania, though bearing a musket-ball in the left arm, I found still actively at work to the last, driving about on horseback with an arm in a sling, seeking for ammunition with which to supply his troops.

Col. Briggs, of the Tenth Massachusetts, who is reported wounded in both legs, is a son of the late Ex-Gov. Briggs, of Massachusetts. He is a thorough soldier.

These hasty personal notices, necessarily incomplete, embrace such only as I was able to gather information. From the most reliable statements to be obtained, I compile the following list of officers killed and wounded, with whose cases I was in many instances personally conversant.

ONE HUNDREDTH NEW-YORK.

Col. J. M. Brown—killed.
Lieut.-Col. Phineas Staunton—wounded.
Maj. C. N. Otis—wounded.
Lieut. Kellogg, Co. G—killed.
Lieut. Brown, Co. E—wounded.
Capt. Daniel D. Nash, Co. A—wounded in the left arm.
Capt. J. Nicholson, Co. C—wounded.
Lieut. Brunck, Co. I—wounded.
Lieut. Kellogg, Co. G—wounded and reported to be left on the field.
Lieut. Mayo, Co. A—slightly wounded in the head.
Corporal Oscar Richards, Co. G—killed.
Corporal Briscoe, Co. G—wounded in the leg.
Corporal Robert Auld, Co. G—wounded.
Corporal John Krofman, Co. G—wounded.

FIFTY-FIFTH NEW-YORK.

Capt. Binsse—wounded in the leg.
Lieut. Israel—wounded.
Lieut. Joseph Arnold—wounded.
Col. Belknap—missing.

EIGHTY-FIFTH NEW-YORK.

Lieut.-Col. A. J. Wellman—wounded in head, not seriously.
Major R. B. King—slightly wounded.
Capt. T. J. Thorp—reported killed.
Capt. Clark, Co. B—wounded.
Capt. Charles Ring, Co. A—wounded.
Lieut. Terwilliger, Co. D—wounded.
Lieut. Munger, Co. C—wounded.

NINETY-SECOND NEW-YORK.

Lieut. Pierce—wounded.
Adjutant C. P. Boswell—shot through the leg.
Capt. Bice, Co. E—wounded in the head.
Lieut. F. W. Smith, Co. H—shot through shoulder.
Col. Hunt—slightly wounded; ball through the fleshy part of the thigh.

ELEVENTH MAINE.

Second Lieut. Price, Co. G—wounded.

ARTILLERY OFFICERS.

Col. G. D. Bailey, Chief of Artillery—killed.
Maj. Van Vaultenberg, 1st N. Y. Artillery—killed.
Adjt. Wm. Ramsey, 1st N. Y. Artillery—wounded.
Capt. Spratt, Battery A, First N. Y. Artillery—wounded.
Lieut. J. H. Howell, Battery H—wounded.

NINETY-EIGHTH NEW-YORK.

Capt. Craig—slightly wounded.
Lieut. Andrews—wounded in leg.
Lieut. Stanton—wounded in shoulder.

TENTH MASSACHUSETTS.

Col. Briggs—wounded in legs.
Capt. Miller—wounded in leg.
Capt. Newell—wounded in leg.

EIGHTY-FIFTH PENNSYLVANIA.

Lieut.-Col. H. A. Purveyance—wounded in leg.
Capt. Geo. Hooker, Co. B—wounded in the arm.
Wm. Howard, private of Co. B—killed while carrying off Capt. Hooker.
Lieut. J. A. Smith, Co. B—wounded.
Second Lieut. Jno. W. Atchison, Co. A—slightly wounded.
Lieut. Hamilton, Co. H—wounded.
Corporal Robt. W. Criswell—wounded.
Private Wm. H. Scott—wounded.
Private Jno. A. McMillen—wounded.
Private Robt. H. Myers—wounded.

ONE HUNDRED AND FIRST PENNSYLVANIA.

Lieut.-Col. Morris, Commanding—severely wounded.
Major Heard—killed.
Lieut. Gaylord—wounded.
Abner Young—wounded.

TWENTY-THIRD PENNSYLVANIA REGIMENT.

Maj. John Ely—fracture of the right leg; doing well.
Adjt. Theo. R. Boggs—severely wounded.
Capt. Edwin Palmer, Co. D—wounded in the left leg.
Capt. Wm. Wallace, Co. E—wounded.
Lieut. Geo. Wood, Co. D—flesh wound.

ONE HUNDRED AND SECOND PENNSYLVANIA REGIMENT.

Col. Rawley—slightly wounded.

ONE HUNDRED AND THIRD PENNSYLVANIA REGIMENT.

Maj. Gozzan is reported to have been seen to fall.

FIFTY-SECOND PENNSYLVANIA REGIMENT.

Capt. Davis, Co. E—lost an arm.
Capt. James Chamberlain, Co. D—wounded.
Lieut. Weidersaul, Co. D—wounded.
Capt. Leonard—wounded.

ONE HUNDRED AND FOURTH PENNSYLVANIA REGIMENT.

Col. W. W. H. Davis—wounded in the left arm.
Maj. John M. Greis—wounded in the thigh.
Capt. Orem, Co. B—wounded.
Lieut. J. P. W. Ransom—killed.
Capt. Burhans—prisoner.

Brig.-Gen. Peck, of Couch's division, had a narrow escape, having his horse shot under him in three places. At the close of Saturday's battle I found him on the field, remounted and apparently good for another fight.

Besides the guns, Gen. Casey lost all his camp equipage, his tents being pitched upon the field of battle in such near proximity to the rebels as to render their loss inevitable in case of the slightest yielding of his troops. The Generals in his division must also have lost their effects, which, fortunately, were of no great value, all the baggage of the officers, as well as the knapsacks of the soldiers, having been some days before ordered to the other side of the Chickahominy, with the wagons, Quartermasters' stores, and everything not absolutely indispensable. So the loss was slight, except in the disappearance of papers of considerable value, which were left in the tents.

No man who knows Gen. Casey can do otherwise than sympathize with him in the misfortunes of disease and disaster which have left him with but the skeleton of a division now able to muster scarcely more, if, indeed, as much, as the strength of a brigade. Occupying the most exposed position on our lines, his raw troops found themselves in the battle of Saturday before they had fairly warmed to their work, subjected to a musketry fire of more than ordinary intensity, the balls pouring in upon them in a constant shower, apparently from all directions, whizzing and buzzing through the air with a murderous spitefulness. Overborne by numbers, failing in support, they gave way, but not until they had held the enemy in check a sufficient length of time to give our reserves an opportunity to press forward to retrieve the fortunes of the day, which they did nobly. All that a brave man could do by personal exertion, Gen. Casey did; and how well he was seconded by his officers, let the list of casualties tell. Gen. Naglee, who escaped with but trifling injury, was everywhere active, encouraging his troops by example and voice, with Gen. Casey pressing to the front and cheering the men to the charge.

PIERREPONT.

REPORT FROM THE PRESS CORESPONDENT.

McClellan's Headquarters,
Monday, June 2—P. M.

Two days of the battle of Richmond have been fought, on both of which our troops have been victorious. The loss on both sides is heavy. The battle was opened by the enemy's making an attack on Gen. Casey's Division encamped near the Seven Pines, on the turnpike leading over Bottom's Bridge, and within seven miles of Richmond. The attack was made about one o'clock on Saturday, by Gen. Hill's Division, composed of five rebel brigades, the

[Continued on Eighth Page.]

General Hancock's brigade at the Battle of Williamsburg

General Hooker's division at the Battle of Williamsburg

Burying the dead and burning the horses at Fair Oaks

The New-York Times.

VOL. XI—NO. 3338. | NEW-YORK, WEDNESDAY, JUNE 4, 1862. | PRICE TWO CENTS.

THE GREAT VICTORY.

Full Details of the Second Day's Fight.

Interesting Letter from one of Our Special Correspondents.

How the Battle was Fought and How the Battle was Won.

The Rebels Driven Back at Every Point with Great Slaughter.

Twelve Hundred of Their Dead Left on the Field.

Distinguished Gallantry of Gen. Sickles.

The Bayonet Charge of the Second Excelsior.

INCIDENTS OF THE BATTLE-FIELD.

BATTLE-FIELD, Monday, June 2, 1862.

The rebel army still occupied the camps of Casey's and Couch's Divisions on Sunday morning, with a strong picket force guarding the road facing Snead's house and the wheat field where our earthworks were thrown up, extending from our extreme left to the railroad, near Fair Oak Station. The distance from the point where our earthworks were located to the edge of the wood could not have been more than four hundred yards. This position the rebels held until day dawned on Sunday morning.

To our right, on the other side of the railroad, the divisions of Gens. Richardson and Sedgwick were found, in a semi-circle, with their left resting on Gen. Hooker's right, at the railroad, and their left flanking the enemy. These divisions were composed of parts of the brigades of Gen. Burns, Gen. French, Gen. T. F. Meagher, with four batteries of artillery.

Gen. Hooker's Division were camped in the wood fronting Snead's house, on the Williamsburgh road, occupying the centre, and a little in advance of our right and left wings. On our left the remaining portions of Couch's and Casey's Divisions rested, with reserves of fresh troops extending to our extreme left, near the middle road, under Gen. Keyes.

Gen. Heintzelman was on the ground at the front as soon as day dawned, accompanied by two Aids. Gen. Hooker met him, and the two Generals sat down at the foot of a tree behind our breastworks, arranging a plan for the day's proceedings.

Gens. Jameson, Keyes and Sickles arrived at the front soon after, and the fight of Saturday was talked over as one of no particular advantage to the enemy, as they had concentrated their main force upon this portion of our front lines, and the effect was more disastrous to them. *Their loss in killed in Saturday's fight exceeded ours two to one*, and of their number wounded it is impossible to form an estimate. Several of their men brought in as prisoners gave their loss in killed and wounded upward of three thousand. They made a desperate attack, it is true, and gained considerable ground, besides a large number of guns, camps, equipage, &c., as trophies, *which they immediately sent to Richmond* to dazzle the eyes of its pent-up inhabitants, who doubtless secretly wish to see the City fall into the hands of McClellan.

PREPARATIONS FOR THE BATTLE ON SUNDAY.

Gen. Heintzelman, at 6 A. M., ordered a reconnoissance to be made by a small force on the left of the wood and to the right, toward the railroad. A Lieutenant with two cavalrymen crossed over the wheat-field behind Snead's house, and was about to penetrate the wood near the Williamsburgh road, when the enemy's pickets appeared at his front. He immediately turned back and reported to Gen. Heintzelman the close proximity of the enemy.

In the meantime, the other parties sent out came in, and reported the enemy in great force in front of our right and left flanks.

Gen. Heintzelman then ordered out Gen. Hooker's Division,—part of which had been left to guard the camp, and a certain position on our extreme left. The regiments Gen. Hooker brought on the field were the five regiments comprising the Excelsior Brigade, under command of Gen. D. E. Sickles, and the Fifth and Sixth New-Jersey regiments; Gen. Heintzelman having resolved to attack the enemy, and drive them from the wood.

THE BATTLE.

It was about a quarter of seven when Gen. Heintzelman ordered Gen. Hooker to attack the rebels in his front, and drive them from the woods. The Excelsior Brigade marched out from their camp in the woods to the Williamsburgh road, the New-Jersey Fifth and Sixth following. The Excelsior Brigade filed in the wheat-field in front of our earthworks, to the right of the road, while the two regiments of New-Jersey troops took a position to the left. As the Second Regiment, Excelsior Brigade, was forming in position to the front of the wood, the rebels opened a rapid and heavy fire upon it, killing two or three privates, and wounding about six. Among those wounded at the first fire of the rebels was Lieut. Lawria (formerly an aid to Gen. Sickles) and Capt. Nolan.

The fire of the enemy immediately became simultaneous along their entire line.

The New-Jersey troops fought splendidly, loading and firing without flinching from their position. Gen. Sickles' regiments did great execution, advancing at every fire upon the rebels masked by the wood. However, it was plainly to be seen the enemy had every advantage, and *it was resolved to clear the woods at the point of the bayonet.*

Gen. Sickles rode along the front of his men, in the midst of an iron hail which the rebels poured in, and gave orders for the Second Regiment, Col. G. B. Hall, to charge bayonets. No sooner was the order given than the men fixed bayonets. Col. Hall gallantly led the charge—*one of the most brilliant ever made in any battle. Not a man shirked or straggled from the ranks.*

The rebels presented a strong front to the gleaming bayonets of our men, not a hundred yards distant.

As the Second advanced on the double quick, cheering and shouting, the rebels held back their fire until our men were hardly one hundred feet from their line, when they fired a murderous volley into the ranks of the Second. It proved too low, and few were killed or wounded.

Immediately after the rebels fired this volley, they broke ranks and fled through the wood. A few of their bravest remained to resist our passage, but they were soon mowed down by the steel front of the gallant Second Excelsior.

Major Herbert, of the Eighth Alabama Regiment, was taken prisoner at this time. His horse had been shot under him, and as he fell he received a shot in his side. He sprang to his feet, however, almost instantly, and seeing several of our men in front of him, mistook them for some of his own regiment.

"Rally once more, boys!" he cried, but they corrected his mistake by presenting their bayonets and demanding him to surrender, which he did with all the grace and finish that an original Secessionist, as he afterwards informed me he was, could do under the circumstances. The rebels made two or three attempts to flank us on the left, after retreating from their centre, but they were beat back with great loss, our troops pursuing them for nearly two miles.

Richardson's Brigade, before the enemy's centre gave way, had a hard fight; the ground was hotly contested by the rebels. The Fourth and Fifth Excelsior Regiments were sent to support one of Richardson's Batteries, but before the battery got in fair working order, the enemy began to show signs of a retreat. The rebel officers could be heard distinctly, urging the men to fight, but they would run away. The Irish Brigade fought splendidly, and routed the rebels at the point of the bayonet.

None of our forces on the left flank participated in the fight. The rebels were defeated and driven back by Hooker's and Richardson's Divisions.

Advance parties scoured the woods on both sides of the Richmond road, and succeeded in capturing nearly two hundred of the rebels, among them three Lieutenants.

At 11 o'clock the firing on both sides ceased. The rebels had fallen back to beyond our original lines, leaving guards stationed to watch our advance and also to bring their wounded off the field.

The enemy were driven from every position they occupied by our troops. The main column rested a mile in advance of their position, at the commencement of the fight.

At about 12 o'clock Gen. McClellan rode up to the front, accompanied by his Staff and body guard, and met Gen. Heintzelman seated at the foot of a tree. Little Mac democratically seated himself at side of Heintzelman, on the ground, when his Staff grouped themselves, resting on stumps of trees and logs. There was the Prince de Joinville, Count de Paris, and the Duc de Chartres, forming a select group of three, conversing quite animatedly in French, and the other members of McClellan's Staff joining in with a little English.

"They fight on Sunday always," said the Duc de Chartres, alluding to the rebels.

Gen. McClellan had been seated probably a half an hour, conversing with Gen. Heintzelman, when Gen. Hooker rode up from the extreme advanced line gained that morning, and as he was dismounting from his horse Gen. McClellan rose from his seat, and, advancing, shook him warmly by the hand, congratulating him and his noble division in terms of the highest praise. A long conversation took place between them. It was plainly seen no further advance was to be made that day, as no troops were ordered up to the front.

At a little after one o'clock Gen. McClellan mounted his horse and rode along the lines of his troops, back and forth, until all the soldiers had a good opportunity of seeing him. Napoleon never was received by his enthusiastic troops with greater manifestation of delight than was McClellan by his army, showing that he possessed the confidence as well as the hearts of his men. They feel that they must ever be victorious under his guidance.

Prisoners continued to be brought in very fast; we had captured nearly five hundred. They were immediately handed over to Provost-Marshal Young, of Gen. Hooker's Division, who sent them properly guarded to Heintzelman's headquarters, at Savage's Station. Many of them were dressed in new clothes, captured in Casey's camp,—a large supply having been sent up to Casey's Division a few days before the battle, but had not been distributed to the men. The result was that the enemy, who had been wearing faded, worn-out home-spun, doffed their forms in our genteel uniforms. This was the cause of many serious mistakes, our men unfortunately mistaking them for our own.

INCIDENTS OF THE FIELD.

Gen. Sickles had several narrow escapes; he was always to be found in the thickest of the fight. Had those gifted Senators who refused to confirm his nomination, but witnessed the enthusiasm of his troops when serving under him, and his military qualification for the office, they would do penance until re-elected.

The rebels during the fight had their sharpshooters posted in trees to pick off our officers—a fact discovered in the early part of the action. One of these sharpshooters had been wounded, and lay down at the foot of a tree; as Gen. Sickles was riding in the wood, he took deliberate aim and fired, but fortunately missed his mark. Some of our men rushed at the wounded rebel, and were about dispatching him with their bayonets, when Gen. Sickles ordered them not to harm him, but take him prisoner.

As I stood watching the regiments of Hooker's Division march in the battle-field, I recognized, marching at the head of his company, Capt. Johnson, belonging to the Third Regiment Excelsior. Capt. Johnson was in the battle of Williamsburgh, where he acted with the most heroic courage, and was wounded badly in the left arm by a minié ball; so dangerously was he wounded, that the surgeons at one time, thought an amputation of his arm would become necessary to save his life. The wound, however took a favorable turn, and he is now in a fair way of recovering. At the head of his company marched this gallant officer, his bandaged arm resting in a sling. As he passed by me smiling, an Aid from Gen. Keyes, who, with his Staff, was on the opposite side of the road, rode up to me and inquired the name of the wounded officer. I gave it to him; he exclaimed, "He is a brave man." If his country rewards her heroes, Capt. Johnson's name will stand among the foremost.

There were many incidents illustrating fully the mettle of our men engaged in this struggle. Many a private displayed deeds of bravery worthy of record. The officers bore themselves well, and shared the dangers in advance of their men.

THE REBEL COMMANDERS.

The rebel Generals, commanding in this engagement, were Gens. Longstreet, Roger A. Pryor, Hill, Branch, Howell Cobb, Rains, Huger and five others whose names I could not learn.

A STAGE AND FOUR HORSES CAPTURED.

A small party of our men reconnoitering, met an omnibus drawn by four fine bay horses, on the New Bridge road, going at a speedy gait toward Richmond, and containing two officers. Driving the horses were two contrabands. Lieut. Lee cried out for them to stop, but no attention was paid to the summons, and he ordered the men to fire. One of the officers jumped out and made good his escape in the woods. The other was shot as he had his head out of the window urging the contrabands to go faster. The driver now held up, and Lieut. Lee mounted the box, first placing the negroes inside, in charge of private Boyd, One Hundredth New-York. The Lieutenant brought the stage safely within our lines. As it made its appearance, emerging from the wood on the Williamsburgh road, where but a few hours ago the enemy were disputing our advance, it created the most intense excitement and curiosity among our men. Many supposed it was sent down by Gen. McClellan, from Richmond, with the news of his occupation of the city. The stage is comparatively new. In size and shape it is about the same as our Broadway stages, perhaps a trifle lighter. From the fact of its being built by "John Stephenson, New-York," (painted on a panel on the inside,) I seriously doubt if John S. has received payment for it. Over the windows, on the outside, "Columbia Hotel" is painted.

THE BATTLE-FIELD.

In company with Gen. Sickles, Col. Graham, Col. Hall and Lieut. Graham, I rode out upon the battle-field on Sunday afternoon at 4 o'clock. The scene witnessed here baffles all description. Caissons, with horses shot dead in their traces, ambulances, wagons, &c., &c., filled the road in front of Casey's camp. There were about two hundred of our wounded still lying where they fell on Saturday. Some of them spoke kindly of the rebels, saying they treated them very well. Dead rebels, as well as our own men, were lying in every part of the field and wood. I counted fifty-seven dead rebels in front of a small piece of woods not forty feet square. One wounded rebel was lying on the ground, unable to move; he was shot in both legs. On each side of him lay some dead rebels. As we passed by, he begged us for God sake to take the dead men away from him. The stench was intolerable.

NUMBER OF GUNS LOST.

We lost 19 guns in the fight of Saturday. Not one of them has been recovered. The rebels ran a train down near Fair Oak Station, and carried away our commissary stores, guns, etc., etc., to Richmond.

The rebels destroyed what they could not conveniently carry away, including the new tents of Casey and Couch's Division.

The two contrabands captured with the stage had left Richmond on Sunday morning, with a party of gentlemen who had chartered the stage to take them out to see the fight. They have furnished the authorities with much information relative to the number and movements of the rebel force, which is highly important. It is not improbable that Gen. McClellan, with his Generals, will dine at Richmond on Sunday next.

I inclose you a list of the casualties, but some days will elapse before a full and perfectly correct list can be obtained.

ACCOUNTS FROM THE PRESS REPORTER.

[The following is the conclusion of the dispatch from Gen. McClellan's headquarters, part of which was published in our morning edition of yesterday. —Ed.]

McClellan's Headquarters, Monday, June 2—P. M.

We have taken some 500 prisoners, among whom are several prominent officers.

On Sunday, as soon as it was light, the fight was renewed by Gen. Sumner with marked success, the fight lasting nearly the whole day. The rebels were driven at every point with heavy loss. The ground gained by Gen. Sumner was about two and a half miles; Gen. Heintzelman on Sunday morning retaking the ground lost the day before by Gen. Casey, after a severe struggle.

Our loss in the two days' engagement, in killed and wounded, will amount to about three thousand. A great number are missing who will probably return, having strayed away.

All of the enemy's killed, and most of their wounded, fell into our hands.

The country in which the battle was fought is swampy, with thick underbrush, and most of the fighting was in the woods. Owing to the nature of the ground very little artillery was used.

Both balloons were up nearly all day yesterday.

All the troops left Richmond, and marched out in the direction of the battle-field.

The railroad has been of inestimable service, the cars running within a mile and a half of the battle-field, bringing forward ammunition and supplies. The wounded were immediately put aboard the cars and sent to the White House.

Gen. McClellan arrived on the battle-field on Saturday evening, where he has remained ever since, directing all the movements in person. His presence among the troops had a most inspiriting effect.

Four separate charges with the bayonet were made yesterday. In one instance, *the enemy were driven a mile, during which one hundred and seventy-three rebels were killed by the bayonet alone!*

Lieut. Washington, Aid to Gen. Joe Johnston, was taken prisoner.

The enemy's dead left on the field, amounted to over twelve hundred.

Gen. Howard was wounded twice in the arm.

Col. Miller, of Eighty-first Pennsylvania, and Col. Ripley, of Pittsburgh, were killed.

Col. Campbell, of Pennsylvania, was wounded in the thigh.

Headquarters, Monday, June 2.

The rebel officers were unable to rally their troops this morning, and have retreated back toward Richmond. Our men have moved forward to Fair Oak, five miles from the city.

Jeff. Davis and Letcher were both at the fight yesterday.

The dead are now being gathered and buried.

Headquarters, Monday, June 2—9 P. M.

Gen. Hooker made a reconnoissance to-day on the Williamsburgh Turnpike to within four miles of Richmond, without meeting the enemy in force. Their pickets kept in sight, but retreated on his approach.

Every one feels sanguine of the fall of the rebel capital when our troops advance for an engagement.

The fight of Saturday and Sunday seals the fate of that city. They threw the main body of the army, composed of the best troops, on our left wing, with a view of crushing it. They were defeated after two days hard fighting, and forced to retreat.

Among the wounded were Col. Hunt, Ninety-second New-York, in the leg; Lieut.-Col. Perry, of the Eighty-fifth Pennsylvania, in the leg, Lieut.-Col. Morris, of the One Hundred and First Pennsylvania, in the leg, and Col. Van Wyck, Tenth Legion, slightly in the leg.

THE KILLED AND WOUNDED.

Headquarters, Tuesday, June 3.

As all the wounded and many of the dead have been sent to Whitehouse by railroad, it is impossible to obtain any correct list of the casualties of the past three days.

ADDITIONAL LIST OF CASUALTIES.

GENERAL WOUNDED.

Gen. Debur, of Mass.

COLONELS KILLED.

Col. Riker.	Col. Miller, 81st Penn.
Col. Ripley, 61st Penn.	Col. Rise—reported.
Col. Bailey, Chief of Artil'y.	Col. Brown, 40th N. Y.

COLONELS MISSING.

Col. Heyman, 37th N. Y.	Col. Howes.

COLONELS WOUNDED.

Col. Van Wyck, 56th N. Y.	Col. W. W. H. Davis, 104th P.
Col. Briggs, 10th Mass.	Col. Hunt, 92d N. Y.
Col. Rawley, 102d Penn.	Col. Campbell, 32d Penn.

LIEUTENANT-COLONELS WOUNDED.

Lieut.-Col. A. J. Wellman, 85th N. Y.	Lieut.-Col. H. A. Purviance, 85th Penn.
Lt.-Col. P. Staunton, 100th N. Y.	Lt.-Col. Morris, 101st Penn.

MAJORS KILLED.

Maj. Culp, —	Maj. King, 85th N. Y.
Maj. Heard, 101st Penn.	Maj. C. Otiss, 10th N. Y.
Maj. Valkenburgh, 100th N. Y.	Maj. Jno. Ely, 23d Penn.
Maj. J. M. Cries, 104th Penn.	

CAPTAINS WOUNDED.

Capt. Chase, 57th Penn.	Capt. Nicholson, 100th N. Y.
Capt. Nolan, 2d Reg. E. B.	Capt. D. D. Nash, 100th N. Y.
Capt. Bailey, 10th Penn.	Capt. Loomis, 56th N. Y.
Capt. Gillespie, 103d Penn. Killed.	Capt. Fuller, 56th N. Y.
	Capt. Burne, 56th N. Y.
Capt. G. B. Leonard, 57d Pa.	Capt. E. Binnse, 56th N. Y.
Capt. Jas Oren, 104th Pa.	Capt. O. W. Craig, 56th N. Y.
Capt. Davis, 52d Penn.	Capt. Parmenter, 85th N. Y.
Capt. Palmer, 23d Penn.	Capt. Miller, 10th Mass.
Capt. Wallace, 23d Penn.	Capt. Newell, 10th Mass.
Capt. Hooker, 85th Penn.	Capt. McConnell, —
Capt. J. Chamberlain, 52d Pa.	Capt. Schorp, 85th N. Y.
Capt. Smith, A. A. G. to Gen. Berry, killed.	Capt. Rice, 92d N. Y.
	Capt. Bartis, — killed.
Capt. Spratt, H. H. N. Y. A.	Capt. Williams, Co. E, 56th New-York.
Capt. W. W. Clark, 85th N. Y.	

ADJUTANTS WOUNDED.

Adj. Boggs, 23d Penn.	Adj. Hancock, —
Adj. C. F. Boswell, 52d N. Y.	Adj. Carlile, 55th N. Y.
Adj. W. Ramsey, 1st Art. N. Y.	

LIEUTENANTS WOUNDED.

Lieut. D. H. Stanton, 98 N. Y.	Lieut. Lauria, 2d Reg. E. B.
Lieut. G. Wood, 23d Penn.	Lieut. Mayo, 100th N. Y.
Lieut. Gaylord, 101st Penn.	Lieut. Munger, 85th N. Y.
Lieut. J. Arnold, 56th N. Y.	Lieut. Howell, Bat. H, N. Y.
Lieut. Terwilger, 85th Penn.	Lieut. Andrews, 98th N. Y.
Lieut. T. L. Andrews, 98 N. Y.	Lieut. Widersalt, 52d Penn.
Lieut. Ballaline, 55th Penn.	Lieut. J. A. Smith, 85 Penn.
Lieut. I. Coukins, 56th N. Y.	Lieut. Runson, killed, 104 P.
Lieut. C. Price, 11th Maine.	Lieut. Hamilton, 85th Penn.
Lieut. F. O. Brunck, 100 N. Y.	Lieut. Anderson, — N. Y.
Lieut. Jas. Pierce, 92d N. Y.	Lieut. Schutt, —
Lieut. H. H. Smith, 92d N. Y.	Lieut. Otto, 103d Penn.
Lieut. Brown, 100th N. Y.	Lieut. B. Leland, 10 M., mor.

SUBALTERNS AND PRIVATES WOUNDED.

W. W. Carpenter, 10th Mass.	Wm. Paxton, Co. K, 5th R., E. B.—killed.
Sergt. J. Mayne, 55th N. Y.	
Chas. McKinsie, 4th R., E. B.	Conrad Wycoff, Co. E, 5th R., E. B.
Felix Gallagher, 2d R., E. B., dead.	
	James Houston, Co. E, 5th R., E. B.
M. Murphy, 2d R., E. B.	
Jacob Bringal, 10th Mass.	Joseph S. King, 81st N. Y.
Rudolph Kessler, Co. B, 2d R., E. B.	Jesse Cumac, 1st L. I.
	Charles Keyser, 104th Penn.
Henry King, Co. F, 4th R., E. B.	A. Huntington, 87th N. Y.
	Richard P. Ogden, 5th E. B.
Wm Cable, Co. E, 5th R., E. B.	Daniel Luther, 5th N. J.
Wm. Anderson, Co. I, 5th R., E. B.	Geo. H. Strasser, 6th N. Y.
	Isaac Kemble, 5th N. J.
Jno. Tuey, Co. I, 5th R., E. B.—killed.	E. P. Zoll, 5th E. B.
	A. Tagge, 1st E. B.
George Thomas, 4th Maine.	Adam Sall, 5th, E. B.
Seth M. Young, 4th Maine.	Geo. Broadwell, 4th E. B.
Sanford Colson, 4th Maine.	W. Beaumont, Co. B, 4th E. B.
Geo. W. Steele, 4th Maine.	Peter Morris, Co. H, 4th E. B.
Simon Higgins, 4th Maine.	Thos Welsh, Co. H, 4th E. B.
John Coner, 4th Maine.	John Boyne, Co. A, 2d E. B.
Thomas Duffy, 1st E. B.	Thos. Weed, 1st E. B.
Henry Homer, 1st E. B.	Jos. W. Kuster, 57th Penn.
C. Sherman, 103th Penn.	S. Wilmouth, 1st L. I.
W. D. Rosenbark, 1st L. I.	James O'Malley, 104th N. Y.
David Smith, 1st L. I.	A. C. Price, 56th N. Y.
R. Hayward, 1st L. I.	A. Richmond, 1st L. I.
Wm. Proud, dead, Co. K, 6th N. J.	Wm. Leroy, 1st L. I.
	G. W. Barnes, 23d Penn.
J. Spencer, 61st Penn.	Wm. Tompkins, 61st Penn.
A. Parker, killed, 4th Me.	Jas L. Howell, 81st N. Y.
J. Knowles, killed, 4th Me.	Geo. H. Williams, 9th N. Y.
Byron McDonald, 5th Mich.	Geo. Helfinch, 23d Penn.
Byron W. Long, 2d Mich.	Geo. H. Fisk, 81st N. Y.
Harvy Utter, 14th Mass.	Joseph Dupue, 8th N. Y.
M. Bardon, 14th Mass.	Fenton Louder, 10th Penn.
A. Swinsen, 3d Mich.	Geo. Kibby, 3d Mich.
Harry Pennington, 1st N. Battery.	Geo. Olmstead, 92d N. Y.
	Isaac Boyle, 23d Penn.
Edwin Baycock, 11th Me.	Jesse Thiber, 61st Penn.
Geo. E. Darling, 81st N. Y.	M. Dugan, 5th Regt. Ex. Br.
Jacob M. Whitman, 23d Penn.	M. Rafferty, 5th Regt. Ex. Br.
Vol. Rosenbaum, 55th N. Y.	John McClung, 103d Penn., dead.
Wm. H. Beckstaff, 101 Penn.	

THE IRISH BRIGADE IN THE BATTLE BEFORE RICHMOND.

Quartermaster Haverty, of the Eighty-eighth Regiment, N. Y. V., (Irish Brigade) telegraphed to the Editor of the *Irish American*, from "Camp at Liters Farm, Va., June 2," that "the Sixty-ninth, (Col. Robert Nugent,) and Eighty-eighth, (Col. Henry M. Baker,) N. Y. V., were engaged yesterday. Lieuts. King and O'Conner, and about thirty privates of the Eighty-eighth were wounded. One man in Company I, Sixty-ninth was killed. The two regiments are highly eulogised by Gens. McClellan and Sumner for their decisive charges. I am busy trying to get rations across the Chickahominy, which is swollen by the rebels turning a canal into it."

The Fort Monroe Telegraph Line and the News.

Washington, Tuesday, June 3.

The telegraph line to Fort Monroe is working well, but the Associated Press and private dispatches are subject to some delay, owing to the immense amount of important official business passing over the wire. The same is true with regard to the military line from Fort Monroe to headquarters. Important Government messages have precedence over all others, and next the Associated Press reports are forwarded, to give the public the earliest possible information. It is impossible for those who are not on the ground to realize the difficulty of obtaining authentic information with regard to the dead and wounded after a great battle has been fought, over a field of many miles in extent, and while all are engaged in taking care of the sufferers, or making preparations for a new contest.

ARMY AND NAVY NEWS.

Brig.-Gen. Silas Casey, whose division broke at the battle of Chickahominy, is an officer of the regular army, and a graduate of West Point. He entered the line after the expiration of his military studies, on the 1st of July, 1830, and is consequently thirty-two years an officer. His first position was that of Second Lieutenant in the Seventh (old) Regiment of Infantry, from which he rose gradually, being promoted for the exhibition of "great soldierly qualities." He was appointed to the Coloncley of the Fourth Regular Infantry in October, 1861, having been previously authorized to act as Brigadier-General of Volunteers. Gen. Casey's reputation as a tactician was always of a high order, and many of his cotemporaries are astonished at the reverse which has suddenly befallen it. He is a native of Rhode Island, to which State his appointment is credited. In the Mexican war the old warrior gave a different account of himself. The rumor about a Court of Inquiry being ordered to investigate the circumstances attending the late battle has not been confirmed.

Several naval officers attached to this station, and a large number of gentlemen interested in the science of artillery, visited Hoboken yesterday, to witness an experiment with a small cannon, recently invented by Mr. R. Rafael, and which is likely to attract serious attention from those who make war their profession. It threw, very accurately, over 60 balls per minute, at distances varying from 500 yards to half a mile. The body of the gun is made of steel, the barrel being three feet long. The ball weighs 524 grains, and 100 grains of powder drive it off. A small carriage, to be drawn, when furnished with from 3,000 to 4,000 rounds, by eight men, moves the piece. The experiments showed that the gun could accurately throw to a distance of half a mile, at least 60 balls per minute, but the number varies according to the distance of the object to be fired at. There are globe sights and open sights attached to the piece.

Commodore Paulding, the commandant of the Brooklyn Navy-yard, was yesterday the recipient of a splendid present from the Government of Nicaragua, for his services during the filibustering career of Walker and others of his disposition. The gift is a magnificent sword, the hilt of which is profusely adorned with gold, the scabbard being also highly ornamented. The deputation, through which the presentation was made in the presence of the officers of the station, entered the navy-yard in carriages at noon. The spokesman, in an appropriate speech, handed the sword to the Commodore, who replied in fitting terms. The sword was manufactured in London expressly for the donors.

The U. S. steam-gunboat *Cayuga*, whose masts were shattered at the battle of New-Orleans, having had new ones put in, was yesterday taken over to the Sectional Dock to have her copper examined and repaired.

The Navy Department has purchased on the Missouri River a vessel called the *Choctaw*, which is to be at once razeed into a ram for war purposes. The work of demolishing her upper works has commenced, and a suitable armament is in course of preparation for her. She will be employed in aiding the gunboats on the Western rivers in their encounters with the rebel rams and floating batteries.

Fire in Galt, C. W.

Galt, Monday, June 2.

A fire here on Saturday night burned the stores of Messrs. Fleming, Robinson, Williams, Frier, and a number of others adjoining. Loss, $75,000—two-thirds insured.

CIVIL RULE IN NORTH CAROLINA.

THE COLORED SCHOOLS BROKEN UP.

Slaves Sent Back—Consternation Among the Fugitives—The Slaveholders Exultant.

Indignation Among the Officers and Soldiers.

H. H. HELPER EXPATRIATED

"NOW, WHAT'S THE NEXT THING?"

Four Hundred More Released Prisoners on their Way to New-York.

From Our Own Correspondent.

Newbern, N. C., Saturday, May 31, 1862.

The experiment of placating the Old North State has commenced, under the rule of the new Governor. The first acts in the drama have the virtue of being intelligible, and pleasing at least to one class of people. As usual, in all attempts to soothe Southern wrath, the negro is thrown in as the offering.

CLOSING THE COLORED SCHOOLS.

The schools established by Mr. Colyer for the instruction of the colored people were suddenly closed on Wednesday evening. It was the first administrative act of the new Governor, since whose advent the military authority seems, to a great extent, suspended.

Hearing that this was to be done, I went early to the Methodist Church on Hancock-street, where one of the colored schools is held. Very few had, as yet, arrived. Sitting at a side door I observed an old couple of at least sixty years of age, each of whom held a little primer, in hand, into which they were intently peering, and by the aid of the dim twilight were endeavoring to master their first lesson in letters. Approaching them, I asked, "How do you get along with your book?" "O, master, we is trying right hard, but git on slow." "Don't you know how to read?" I asked. "No, but we wants to, master, very much; we wants to learn more dan we does to eat a good dinner when we is hungry; we want to learn so dat we can read de Word of God," said the man.

In a few minutes the pupils began to come in. They came—young, old and middle-aged, male and female—and quietly took seats, filling the body of the house, as well as the galleries, and numbering five or six hundred. In front of the altar were sixteen bright and wakeful little boys of from eight to twelve years, ranged on two benches, and confronting the lesson of the evening, which had been written upon a sheet in large letters, and hung over the pulpit:

"Love your enemies; bless them that curse you; do good to them that hate you, and pray for them that despitefully use you and persecute you."—Matt. 5th ch.

When all had become seated, Mr. Colyer gave out the Sabbath school hymn:

"Joyfully, joyfully, onward we move,"

which was sung with earnest pathos by the whole congregation.

During the prayer, when incidental reference was made to the closing of the school, a sob was heard in all parts of the house. That single sentence dashed all hopes and sent a pang to every heart. The Superintendent remarked that during the six weeks the schools had been opened, no disorder had occurred, and not the slightest complaint had been made by the authorities. The schools had been uniformly closed before the hour of guard-mounting, though by this course they had been obliged to assemble at an inconvenient hour, leaving their work at the fortification and on the bridge frequently without their suppers, in order to be early at the school. They had made rapid progress, over one hundred, only a few days since, having been selected as teachers, who could read with facility, and the remainder were able, after a few minutes' instruction, to read the common lesson. He alluded to the fact that three or four hundred of them had been engaged upon one work—the fort—and that no disturbance had occurred, not a fight had taken place among them. Meantime they had lived in most inconvenient places, generally kitchens and outbuildings in the town, crowded together in unhealthy and irritating circumstances.

"These schools," said the speaker, "are now to be closed, not by the officers of the army, under whose sanction they have been commenced, but by the necessity laid upon me by Gov. Stanly, who has informed me that it is a criminal offence, under the laws of North Carolina, to teach the blacks to read, which laws he has come from Washington with instructions to enforce."

The teacher said he hoped that the schools would be closed only for a brief time, and exhorted them to submit patiently to the deprivation like good, law-abiding people, such as they had always proved themselves to be. Those who followed the injunction before them, on the pulpit, and trusted in the Saviour, who had given the command, would not only have this blessing restored to them, but must, ultimately, enjoy even greater blessings than this.

The old people dropped their heads upon their breasts and wept in silence; the young looked at each other with mute surprise and grief at this sudden termination of their bright hopes. It was a sad and impressive spectacle. Mr. Colyer himself could hardly conceal his emotion. A few moments of silence followed, when, as if by one impulse, the whole audience rose and sang, with mournful cadence, "Praise God from whom all blessings flow," and then shook hands and parted.

The school at the Baptist Church, where the more advanced scholars were placed, was closed in a similar manner.

THE SCHOOL FOR THE CHILDREN OF THE CITIZENS.

Mr. Colyer continues the white school for poor children, as usual. This is right. It is better to educate a small part of the rising generation than to neglect the whole. The State raised, during the year 1860–61, for educational purposes, less than $100,000. The sum expended in *powder* during the same period is not stated. Generals Burnside and Reno visited the schools for the whites, and were received by over fifty children—some very pretty—with bouquets of flowers. These they presented to the General, who expressed himself greatly pleased.

SENDING BACK THE SLAVES.

Yesterday the Governor was waited upon by large numbers of the residents, in and out of town, who congratulated him upon the auspicious beginning of his administration. Among others, several persons applied for the restoration of their fugitive property who have sought protection from the tyranny of the plantation within our lines. One Nicholas Bray, living a few miles from town on the Falmouth road, obtained an order to carry off two slave-women. With his wife he proceeded to an old school building where one of them was lying sick abed, he dragged her forth and drove away with her to the plantation. Her sister, a bright mulatto young woman of unusual attractions, hearing of the proceedings, was made almost frantic, and sought asylum at the only place she knew—the headquarters of the poor. Elated at his success, Bray drove up and without ceremony began a search of the premises. Mr. Colyer, at the time was away. Apprised of his coming, Harriet flew with lightning speed, and concealed herself in an out-building almost under the eaves of Gen. Burnside's headquarters. Not finding the object of his search, Bray drove off, probably to renew the search at a more convenient season. Harriet is only about seventeen years of age, and Bray asserts *that he has been offered fifteen hundred dollars for her.*

Bray is a brother-in-law of A. G. Eubank, the Quartermaster of the rebel militia, lately at this place. He is a well known rebel; was mustered into the service, it is said, and only escaped taking part in the battle of Newbern on account of some alleged injury to his back. He *promised* to take the oath of allegiance.

Several other orders were given for the capture and taking away of slaves from the town. Four were reported to have been captured and carried out of our lines yesterday.

FLIGHT OF THE NEGROES.

Frightened at this turn of affairs, a number of the slaves who have congregated in the town had scattered like a flock of frightened birds. Some have taken to the swamps, and others have concealed themselves in out-of-the-way places. A perfect panic prevails among them. The greater part who were employed on the fortifications are so much alarmed at the prospect of being returned to their enraged masters, and being punished, that they are of little use as laborers.

It is believed that many will find their way to the rebel lines, and, in order to make friends with them, will reveal important facts touching the condition of affairs in this department. The slaves express the greatest horror at the prospect of being sent back to their old homes, and say that they will be unmercifully "cut up" for having absconded. One old man of sixty told me to-day that he would rather be placed before a cannon and blown to pieces than go back. Multitudes say they would rather die.

FEELING AMONG THE OFFICERS AND SOLDIERS.

The new administration has fallen upon the officers and soldiers in this place like a wet blanket. Prominent officers, from colonels and quartermasters down to the humblest soldiers in the ranks, speak in terms of the most vehement indignation of the course which the new Governor is pursuing, and I have not met an individual, either officer or soldier, and I have seen a large number, who does not condemn, in the plainest language, the course which has been adopted.

Nevertheless, no whisper of disloyalty to the Government has or will be uttered or tolerated in any quarter. Massachusetts, as well as New-York troops, it is assumed, will conquer their prejudices and execute the behests of the Government, believing that patriotic motives inspire whatever measures are adopted for the putting down of the slaveholding rebellion.

It would be a dereliction of duty on my part, however, to conceal, at the present time, the state of feeling which prevails, and to predict that military force will, before long, be required to assist in compelling the return of fugitive slaves to their claimants.

I have carefully watched in every quarter for the uprising of the Union sentiment in this State, but, unlike the reporters of the *Tribune*, have failed to see it. Hence, I have refrained from misleading the public on that subject. For the correctness of my reports, in this respect, *I appeal with confidence to every officer and soldier in the department.*

Four hundred more of the released Union prisoners arrived here, *via* Washington, last night, on board of the steamer *Virginia*. They are in a deplorable condition, many having scurvy in its worst forms. One man whom I saw, had large scorbutic sores on his limbs, and his flesh turning black and blue. Many have ulcerous gums and loosened teeth, from the constant use of salt, fat pork, and no vegetables. They include the letters G and part of M. Sergeant Matthews, the color-bearer of Col. Corcoran, is on board. They will receive medical attention, some necessary comforts, and sail at once for New-York. —— Morrell, Third United States Infantry, died on board to-day, of dropsy.

ACT THIRD—THE "CRISIS"—MR. H. H. HELPER EXPATRIATED.

The following correspondence explains itself. Mr. Helper, like Gov. Stanly, is a native of this State, and belongs in Rowan County. As his letter states, he has been employed in the army, and also in other important positions of the Government service. He is a brother of Hinton Helper, author of *The Impending Crisis.*

Newbern, N. C., May 30, 1862.

To his Excellency Gov. Stanly:

Dear Sir: I wish you to believe me when I tell you that what I say to you to-day, is said in a spirit of love and kindness,—they are only the words of one man, a son of the State, who heartily desires to become again a permanent citizen.

I enlisted the service a private soldier for the purpose of fighting down the slaveholders' rebellion, and was mustered out of said service on the 1st of February last, on my own application to join this division of the army, in either a military or civil capacity, in the hope that I might be more useful in my native State than elsewhere. This course was by some thought to be impolitic.

I have awaited your arrival with no little impatience, under the expectation that a new era was to be inaugurated by your administration, which would favor my long-cherished hopes of again settling on my native soil, and becoming useful. Without any means of knowing the policy to be adopted by you, upon your arrival, the recent acts of the General Government have led me to expect that you *might* try the effect of an earnest appeal to the people to listen to the gracious offer of the President in his late proclamation, and seek deliverance from the incubus of Slavery, which weighs so heavily upon its industry—an appeal which, backed by the high reputation you have enjoyed in the State for moderation and patriotism, could hardly fail to make an impression upon the people, even in the midst of the wild tumults of war. It had occurred to me, that while you, possibly, thus held out the olive branch to the *few large slaveowners* in the State, whose interest or convenience might temporarily suffer by the change, I might possibly make myself useful among that larger class of non-slaveholding citizens, who have no direct interest in perpetuating the system, and who, I have reason to believe, would be brought, by judicious management, soon to acquiesce in the paternal policy of the President.

Thus much I will reveal to you of my feelings and hopes.

I have had no good opportunity, since you came, to learn what course you proposed to pursue; but your first act, closing the schools which have been established for the instruction of the negroes, has seemed to me to point in quite another direction from that which I had supposed you might pursue.

It strikes me that this is a bad beginning, whether viewed as a stroke of policy or of justice, and my object in this communication is to respectfully inquire—presuming it not to be improper for me to do so, since you observe that you would be glad to hear any suggestions I might offer—whether the course indicated by this first act is to be the line of policy to be adopted by you. If so I shall need no further light, and will prepare as soon as practicable to leave the State, satisfied as I am that I can render the State no service so acceptable to you and them.

I am, Governor, very respectfully, your obedient servant,

H. H. HELPER.

GOV. STANLY'S ANSWER.

Office of the Provost-Marshal,
Newbern, N. C., Saturday, May 31, 1862.

H. H. Helper, Esq.:

Sir: I am instructed by his Excellency the Military Governor of North Carolina, to inform you that he requires you to leave this department in the first vessel going North.

Capt. C. G. Loring, Jr., Assistant Quartermaster, will furnish you with the necessary order for transportation. I am, very respectfully, yours,

DAN MESSENGER, Provost-Marshal.

RETALIATION ON BRAY.

Last night, a party of men, distinguished with the letter "M" on their caps, proceeded to the house of Nicholas Bray, at a distance of two miles from town, and took out the slave woman who was yesterday carried away, and then barred the house. This morning, the wife of Bray appeared before the Governor and made complaint of the facts, and asked again for her negro woman. The Governor calmly advised her to return home, without making any present effort to find her. At last accounts things look mixed.

Though Bray had disregarded the Governor's advice, and armed with the power which had been previously given him, he was still searching the town for his slave.

VESSELS TO BE OVERHAULED.

I am informed that an order has been issued to search closely every steamer or vessel leaving this port, for the purpose of stopping any colored people who may be found on board with the design of getting away to the North. It is also intimated that the names of certain Captains of vessels are on the list of suspicious persons who will be subject to arrest on their arrival here, on charges of carrying away black persons from the State.

Adams & Co.'s Express agents have been waited on and required to show their way-bills for some weeks back, and persons are to be sent to Massachusetts and other places in pursuit of stray *articles of virtu*, sewing machines, &c.

E. S.

The New-York Times.

VOL. XI---NO. 3340. NEW-YORK, FRIDAY, JUNE 6, 1862. PRICE TWO CENTS.

FROM THE POTOMAC ARMY.

Stirring Address of Gen. McClellan to his Soldiers.

A Dispatch from Gen. McClellan to the War Department.

A Correction of his Dispatch Regarding the Battle of Fair Oaks.

The Services of Gen. Sumner Acknowledged.

Effects of the Severe Storm of Wednesday.

Great Rebel Losses in the Late Battle.

AN ARTILLERY FIGHT AT NEW BRIDGE.

WASHINGTON, Thursday, June 5.

The following dispatch was received to-day at the War Department:

NEW-BRIDGE, June 5—10:30 A. M.

To Hon. E. M. Stanton, Secretary of War:

My telegraphic dispatch of June 1, in regard to the battle of Fair Oaks, was incorrectly published in the newspapers. I send with this a correct copy, which I request may be published at once. I am the more anxious about this, since my dispatch, as published, would seem to ignore the services of Gen. SUMNER, which were too valuable and brilliant to be overlooked, both in the difficult passage of the stream and the subsequent combat. The mistake seems to have occurred in the transmittal of the dispatch by the telegraph.

(Signed) G. B. McCLELLAN, Major-General Commanding.

THE CORRECTED DISPATCH.

FIELD OF BATTLE, 12 o'clock, June 1.

Hon. E. M. Stanton, Secretary of War:

We have had a desperate battle, in which the Corps of SUMNER, HEINTZELMAN and KEYES have been engaged against greatly superior numbers. Yesterday, at 1 o'clock, the enemy taking advantage of a terrible storm, which had flooded the valley of the Chickahominy, attacked our troops on the right bank of the river. CASEY'S Division, which was the first line, gave way unaccountably and discreditably. This caused a temporary confusion, during which some guns and baggage were lost, but HEINTZELMAN and KEARNEY most gallantly brought up their troops, which checked the enemy. At the same time, however, Gen. SUMNER succeeded, by great exertions, in bringing across SEDGWICK'S and RICHARDSON'S Divisions, who drove back the enemy at the point of the bayonet, covering the ground with his dead. This morning the enemy attempted to renew the conflict, but was everywhere repulsed.

We have taken many prisoners, among whom are Gen. PETTIGREW and Col. LORING. Our loss is heavy; but that of the enemy must be enormous. With the exception of CASEY'S Division, our men behaved splendidly. Several fine bayonet charges have been made. The Second Excelsior made two to-day.

(Signed) G. B. McCLELLAN, General Commanding.

THE LATEST NEWS FROM HEADQUARTERS.

McCLELLAN'S HEADQUARTERS, Thursday Evening, June 5.

The severe storm which set in Tuesday afternoon lasted during the whole of yesterday. The water in the Chickahominy rose to an unprecedented height. The railroad trains from White House to the late battle-field were detained several hours, and the telegraph line was down in many places.

A contraband, who left Richmond Monday night, states that all the carts, furniture cars, omnibuses and carriages to be found were impressed into the service for the carrying of the dead and wounded from the battle-field; and that the Spottswood and Exchange Hotels, together with a number of public and private buildings, were turned into hospitals. All the information shows that the enemy suffered terribly.

The rebels opened with artillery this morning from five different points opposite New-Bridge, with a view of preventing its reconstruction. Three of our batteries opened on them, causing them to retreat after a hot fire of two hours. Our loss was one killed and two wounded. No further interference took place during the day.

GEN. McCLELLAN TO HIS SOLDIERS.

McCLELLAN'S HEADQUARTERS, Tuesday evening, June 3.

The following address was read to the army this evening at dress parade, and was received with an outburst of vociferous cheering from every regiment:

HEADQUARTERS ARMY OF THE POTOMAC, CAMP NEAR NEW-BRIDGE, Va., June 2, 1862.

SOLDIERS OF THE ARMY OF THE POTOMAC: I have fulfilled at least a part of my promise to you. You are now face to face with the rebels, who are held at bay in front of the Capital. The final and decisive battle is at hand. Unless you belie your past history, the result cannot be for a moment doubtful. If the troops who labored so faithfully, and fought so gallantly, at Yorktown, and who so bravely won the hard fights at Williamsburgh, West Point, Hanover Court-house and Fair Oaks, now prove worthy of their antecedents, the victory is surely ours.

The events of every day prove your superiority. Wherever you have met the enemy you have beaten him. Wherever you have used the bayonet, he has given way in panic and disorder.

I ask of you now one last crowning effort. The enemy has staked his all on the issue of the coming battle. Let us meet him and crush him here, in the very centre of the rebellion.

Soldiers, I will be with you in this battle, and share its dangers with you. Our confidence in each other is now founded upon the past. Let us strike the blow which is to restore peace and union to this distracted land. Upon your valor, discipline and mutual confidence the result depends.

(Signed,) GEO. B. McCLELLAN, Major-General Commanding.

A heavy shower that set in about dark had the effect of again raising the water in the Chickahominy.

Gen. BIRNEY, of Philadelphia, was relieved of his command on the battle-field by Gen. HEINTZELMAN, he having failed to bring his brigade into action when ordered on Saturday.

Reconnoissances made to-day show no material change in the enemy's position.

Further information shows that our troops on Saturday and Sunday engaged six divisions instead of four, making a force of 75,000 rebels.

THE APPROACHES OF CHARLESTON

Map Showing the Position of Stono Inlet, through which the Union Forces are Moving; the Location of the New Fortifications in the Harbor, and the Places of the Blockading Squadron at the Latest Advices.

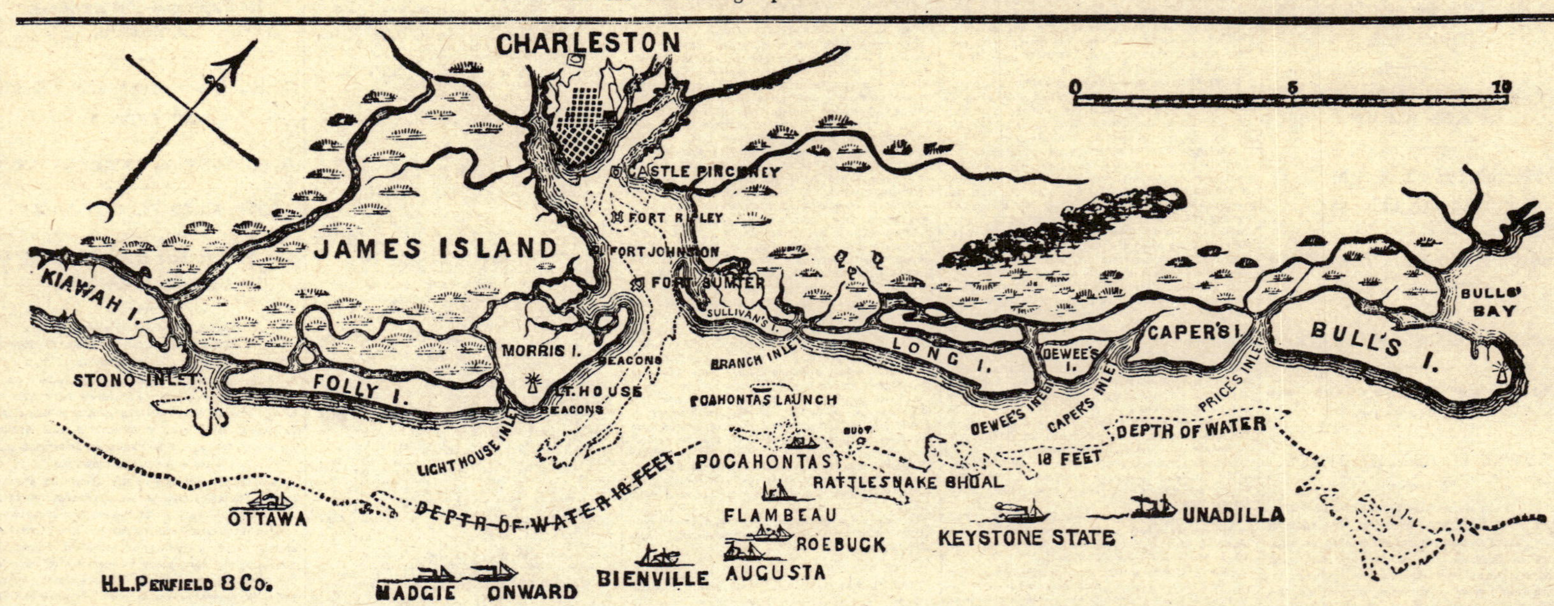

ACCOUNTS FROM RICHMOND.

REBEL REPORT OF SATURDAY'S FIGHT.

CAIRO, Thursday, June 5.

Richmond dispatches of June 1, contained in the Memphis papers, say the Rebels "have thus far driven the Yankees back a mile and a half into the swamp, occupying their camps, capturing their baggage, and over 500 prisoners. Gen. RHODES is wounded. Gen. HALTON, of Tennessee, is killed. The Yankees fought desperately, but they were badly whipped. The carnage was terrible on both sides."

CAIRO, Thursday, June 5.

Memphis papers of the 2d contain dispatches from Richmond of the 1st, of which the following is the substance:

"Gen. HILL'S Division commenced the fight on Saturday morning, RHODES', GARLAND'S RAINS' and ANDERSON'S Brigades bearing the brunt of the battle. Until the arrival of their reinforcements the Federals were driven from their redoubts and their batteries turned on them.

Gen. LEE and President DAVIS were on the field. Their presence increased the enthusiasm of our troops.

The Yankees stubbornly contested every inch of ground, but were compelled to give way before the impetuous charges of our soldiers. A large number of Confederate soldiers are wounded in the arms and legs. Gen. RHODES is slightly wounded.

The enemy tried to make a flank movement about 7 o'clock in the evening, but were repulsed.

On Sunday the battle was resumed chiefly with musketry. Prisoners are constantly coming in. Gen. HATTON, of Tennessee, is killed. The carnage on both sides is dreadful, the Yankees losing two to our one. About 500 prisoners are already taken.

The last dispatch sent on the 1st, says the latest intelligence from the battle-field represents the enemy to be driven back a mile and a half from his position. Our forces now occupy his camps. We captured three batteries, after the most desperate fighting. The enemy were protected by woods and intrenchments.

FROM FORTRESS MONROE.

The Wounded in the Great Battle.

An Unsuccessful Attempt to Exchange the Rebel Privateers.

COL. CORCORAN NOT YET SURRENDERED.

BALTIMORE, Thursday, June 5.

The Old Point boat arrived here about 7 o'clock this morning. Passengers state that three steamers, full of wounded, had arrived at the fort.

FORTRESS MONROE, Wednesday, June 4.

The steamer *C. Vanderbilt* arrived this morning from White House, with 560 wounded soldiers in the recent engagements.

The steamer *Metamora*, which took to City Point Mrs. GREENHOW and party, returned last night. The steamer *Massachusetts*, with the privateers on board, was lying alongside the wharf at City Point. In answer to the notice given of her arrival, a train of three baggage-cars came to City Point from Petersburgh, yesterday forenoon, with two rebel officers on board. They came after the privateers, but not having brought down Col. CORCORAN'S party, the privateers were not given up. Nothing later in relation to the subject had transpired up to yesterday afternoon, when the *Massachusetts* was still awaiting some further communications from Petersburgh.

The Military Commander in Kentucky.

LOUISVILLE, Wednesday, June 4.

Brig.-Gen. J. T. BOYLE, headquarters in this city, assumed command of the National troops in Kentucky this morning. His appointment gives general satisfaction.

THE WAR IN THE SOUTHWEST.

Latest News from Gen. Halleck's Headquarters.

Continued Evidences of the Disorganization of Beauregard's Army.

Several Regiments of Mississippians Disbanded and Gone Home.

Daring Escape of a Party of Railroad Engineers from Memphis.

Vicksburgh Not in Possession of Our Forces.

The Bombardment of Fort Wright Still Progressing.

FROM GEN. HALLECK'S HEADQUARTERS.

HALLECK'S HEADQUARTERS—Midnight 4th, *Via* LOUISVILLE, Thursday, June 5.

A man, who left Grand Junction this morning, says that Memphis and Fort Pillow surrendered to our forces on Friday night.

Several regiments of rebels, Mississippians, have dispersed and gone home. We have captured nine locomotives, partly disabled, and several cars. It is expected, however, they will be in running order in a week.

LATEST REPORTS FROM MEMPHIS.

CAIRO, Thursday, June 5.

Ten Memphis refugees arrived to-day. They were railroad engineers, and say that they ran three locomotives out of Memphis, on the Memphis and Ohio Railroad, to Humboldt, where they switched them off, and brought them north to Trenton, where they found the bridge over the Obion River destroyed. They then ran the locomotives off the track, burned two bridges behind them, and cut the telegraph wires.

They bring the Memphis *Argus* of the 2d, which refers to the so-called Confederate victory at Richmond, but gives no particulars.

FROM THE MISSISSIPPI FLOTILLA.

Renewed Bombardment of Fort Wright—Manœuvres of the Rams—Rebels Captured, &c.

CHICAGO, Thursday, June 5.

Specials from the Mississippi flotilla dated the 4th, say the bombardment of Fort Wright commenced early yesterday, and continued all day, eliciting a brisk cannonade from the enemy. The shells of the latter were quite accurately thrown, but failed to do any damage. At 6 o'clock last evening, three National rams went down to reconnoitre, and were fired on several times after passing Craighead Point, but all returned uninjured. Subsequently the rebel boat *Jeff. Thompson* came around the Point, but being fired on by the *Mound City* and *Cairo*, retired. One shot from the former is said to have taken effect in the wheelhouse of the rebel boat.

Vicksburgh is not yet in the possession of the Nationals.

The Vicksburgh *Evening Citizen* of last Saturday says eleven Union gunboats have gone back down the river, owing, it is supposed, to insubordination and mutiny. Several remain, and on Friday evening shelled the shore several hours. The rebel batteries were being strengthened by having additional guns mounted.

Gen. VILLIPIGNE has asked for reinforcements at Fort Wright.

It was reported at Memphis that Gen. HALLECK had taken Grand Junction.

A meeting of the citizens of Memphis was held at the Mayor's office on Sunday, at which resolutions were adopted that the city never should yield to the enemy voluntarily, and that citizens who do not take up arms are expected to give pecuniary aid to the rebellion.

On Monday a party of our scouts captured the mate and six seamen of the rebel gunboat *Beauregard*, nearly opposite Fulton. They made little resistance.

The bombardment of the fort commenced again on the morning of the 4th, and was going on at the time the steamer left. The rebels reply occasionally.

IMPORTANT FROM ARKANSAS.

A Rebel Gunboat at Jacksonport Destroying Sugar and Cotton.

POCAHONTAS, Ark., Thursday, June 5.

A rebel gunboat came to Jacksonport day before yesterday and destroyed all the cotton and sugar there. She was reported to be on the way here, but we have since learned that she returned down the river, destroying all the cotton and sugar as she went. It is supposed that a very large amount of each has been destroyed. For a time there was much consternation in this vicinity, and troops were under marching orders all Tuesday night. Everything is quiet now.

FROM GEN. FREMONT'S ARMY.

The Movement of the Whole Mountain Department for "Parts Unknown"—Extraordinary March Across the Mountains—A Pontoon Bridge Across the Lower Branch of the Potomac—Junction with McDowell, &c.

From Our Own Correspondent.

WARDENSVILLE, Saturday, May 31, 1862.

For once the secret of the movement of a department of the army, has been withheld from the public, until its communication cannot materially affect the result.

On Sunday, 25th inst., at an early hour, the Mountain Department took up its line of march "to parts unknown," except to the few whose services were necessary to the execution of the plan. Our first destination was Petersburgh. From thence two routes were open, and the army left the town in both directions at one and the same time. *Somewhere*, they came together, and this evening will encamp near Strasburgh, in the Shenandoah Valley. Distance nearly one hundred miles, over mountain passes and through frequent rains, by night and by day. The enemy under the rebel JACKSON, is now before us, with reinforcements variously estimated. He is encamped near Winchester. An engagement apparently cannot be long delayed. Some preliminaries may be necessary, but JACKSON'S retreat and source of supplies is essentially cut off. Our troops are now animated with hope and expectations, and eager to be led forward and into action. Our progress to this place has been conducted with signal energy and spirit, on the part of all those on whom success so much depended. Praise is due to Messrs. CASTLE & WILLIS, for their efficiency in placing the pontoon-bridge (brought from Pittsburgh, Penn.) across the south branch of the Potomac, at a point where the rebels had burnt an important bridge a few months ago. This work was of great value to this movement, as the troops were all passed over safely and without delay, while the stream was swollen and rapid.

The duties of the Quartermaster have been arduous and constant; but Capts. GOULDING and HURTE, who come under my more immediate notice, seem equal to any emergency. A large supply train from New-Creek is now coming up, *just in time.*

This movement has been sudden and most important, and serves to vindicate Gen. FREMONT'S sagacity. Immediately after the evacuation of Yorktown, he is known to have said that if it had been designed by JEFF. DAVIS to leave McCLELLAN before that place without transports, and to make a dash upon Washington, (as at this late day he seems aiming at,) it was one of the greatest strategic plans of the war. Another part of his design indicated by Gen. FREMONT at the same time, was a sudden rush upon Gen. MILROY, resulting in the battle at McDowell, so effectually defeated by Gen. FREMONT'S prompt action in sending Gen. SCHENCK to his relief as we have seen.

When the history of this war shall have been all written, I venture to predict, it will be seen that many of the most valuable suggestions, predictions and plans have emanated from Gen. FREMONT.

P. S.—McDOWELL will reinforce us at Strasburgh, and if JACKSON isn't bagged?—we wait patiently to know the reason why.

NEWS FROM WASHINGTON.

The Official Lists of Killed and Wounded in the Late Battle.

Condition of the National Treasury.

Close of the Debate on the Tax Bill in the Senate.

An Amendment Taxing Slave Property.

OUR SPECIAL WASHINGTON DISPATCHES.

SCARCITY OF NEWS.

WASHINGTON, Thursday, June 5.

No news of importance from any quarter has been promulgated here to-day, and upon inquiring at the War Department I learned that nothing of unusual public interest has been received.

The thrilling intelligence of yesterday from the West is still discussed with enthusiasm, and it is believed in official circles here that the effect of the panic in BEAUREGARD'S army will be so disheartening to the rebels in Richmond, as to give Gen. McCLELLAN the City without another battle. There are, however, not a few who think differently, and look to another severe engagement as imminent. But all of course agree in the certainty of an early and glorious victory.

THE KILLED AND WOUNDED.

We are still without any official record of the killed and wounded at the battle before Richmond. Crowds of the relatives and friends of those engaged are arriving by every train, anxious to obtain correct information, but so far they have come in vain. The answer to the many inquiries at the War Office is that no authentic list of the casualties has been received. It is probable that the Secretary of War will provide that in future the Surgeons of regiments shall report through the brigade and division commanders, as soon as possible after the battles, accurate lists of the killed, wounded and missing.

THE NATIONAL DEBT.

The following is a statement of the particulars of the National Debt the 29th of May, 1862:

Under what Act.	Rate of Interest.	Amount.
Loans, 1842	6 per cent	$2,883,364 11
Loans, 1847	6 per cent	9,415,250 00
Loans, 1848	6 per cent	8,908,311 80
Loans, 1858	5 per cent	20,000,000 00
Loans, 1860	5 per cent	7,022,000 00
Loans, 1861	6 per cent	18,415,000 00
Texan indemnity	5 per cent	3,461,000 00
		$70,104,955 91
Treasury Notes issued prior to 1857	Int'st stopped	$105,111 64
Under act Dec. 23, 1857	Int'st stopped	175,900 00
Under act Dec. 17, 1860	Int'st stopped	221,650 00
Under act June 22, 1860, and February and March, 1861	6 per cent	2,767,900 00
Under act March 2, July 17, and Aug. 5, 1861	6 per cent	111,600 00
		$3,382,161 64
Three years 7.30 bonds	7 3-10 ℔ cent.	120,523,450 00
Twenty years bonds	6 ℔ cent	50,000,000 10
		170,535,450 00
Oregon War Debt	6 ℔ cent	878,650 00
U. S. Notes	No interest	105,880,000 00
Certificates of indebtedness	6 ℔ cent	47,199,000 00
Five and Twenty years bonds	6 ℔ cent	2,699,400 00
		49,898,400 00
Four ℔ cent. temporary loan	4 ℔ cent	5,913,042 21
Five ℔ cent. temporary loan	5 ℔ cent	44,865,524 36
		50,778,566 56
Total amount of Public Debt		$491,448,984 11

Average rate of interest paid on the entire debt, 4 354-1000 ℔ annum.

THE EMANCIPATION BILL.

The substitute of Representative PORTER, which is likely to pass in the form offered, provides for emancipation in the following cases: Of every person who shall hereafter act as an officer in the army or navy of the rebels, or as President, Vice-President, Member of Congress, Judge of any Court, Cabinet officer, Foreign Minister, Commissioner or Consul of the so-called Confederate States; or as Governor of a State, member of a Convention, or Legislature, or judge of any State Court of the so-called Confederate States; or who, having held an office of honor, trust, or profit in the United States, shall thereafter hold an office in the so-called Confederate States; of every person who shall hereafter hold any office or agency under the Government of such Confederate States, or any of the States of such Confederacy; but persons holding State offices, unless appointed since the date of the secession ordinance, or unless they shall have taken an oath of allegiance to such Confederate States; also the slaves of every person not embraced in the foregoing clauses, who, after the passage of this act, being actually, willfully and without coercion or compulsion, engaged in armed rebellion, shall not within sixty days after public warning and proclamation, made at his discretion, by the President, lay down his arms and return to his allegiance.

THE SENATE STILL DEBATING THE TAX BILL.

The Senate was occupied throughout the day in the discussion of the Tax bill. The various sections were disposed of, and the vote will be taken in the morning after a half hour's speech by Mr. FESSENDEN. A motion of Mr. SUMNER'S to remit the tax on paper and pasteboard, which he denominated a tax on knowledge—the paper being used for books and the latter for covers—was rejected. An amendment proposed by the same gentleman, fixing a tax of $2 upon every person claimed for service or labor as a slave, was adopted by a vote of 19 ayes to 15 noes. This is a very ingenious triumph over the Republican prejudice against taxing slaves, and if approved by the House will return a large revenue to the country.

COL. DWIGHT.

Col. WILLIAM DWIGHT, Jr., of the Excelsior Brigade, severely wounded at Williamsburgh, is still at the St. Elizabeth Hospital, in the Government Insane Asylum building. He was visited this afternoon by Col. HOWE, WM. M. EVARTS and R. F. ANDREWS, of New-York, and found to be in excellent spirits. His wounds are rapidly healing, and he hopes to take the field at an early day. It is reported that he will be made a Brigadier-General for gallant service at Williamsburgh, and certainly no one behaved better upon that well fought field. Col. DWIGHT is of a distinguished Massachusetts family. His brother, Maj. WILDER DWIGHT, was taken prisoner by JACKSON at Winchester, and has just reached here on parole. Another brother made the famous cavalry charge at Pea Ridge.

PROMOTED FOR GALLANTRY.

Upon a recommendation of the Secretary of the Treasury, the President has complimented First Lieut. D. C. CONSTABLE, commanding the revenue steamer *E. A. Stevens*, by handing him personally a commission as Captain in the revenue cutter service, in recognition of his gallantry, in leading, with his steamer, the attacking forces in their recent ascent of James River, and bombardment of Fort Darling.

Second Lieut. J. WALL WILSON has also been promoted to a First Lieutenancy for gallant bearing during the same action.

ANOTHER CAPTURE.

The United States steamer *Santiago de Cuba* captured on the 27th, the rebel schooner *Lucy C. Holmes*, just out of the Santee, loaded with cotton. She has been sent to Boston for adjudication.

MAIL FOR PORT ROYAL AND THE GULF.

The United States steamer *Rhode-Island* will sail from Boston on Tuesday, the 10th, taking the mail for Port Royal and both Gulf squadrons.

REGULAR PROMOTIONS OF MAJOR ANDERSON.

Among the regular army nominations pending in the Senate, is one promoting Major ROBERT ANDERSON to Brevet Lieutenant-Colonel for his evacuation of Fort Moultrie and removal to Sumter, and to Brevet Colonel for his gallant defence of the latter fort.

PROPOSALS FOR FIFTEEN GUNBOATS.

The Navy Department has issued proposals for the construction and complete equipment of fifteen gunboats; speed not less than 13 knots, to be delivered within four months; and in conjunction with the War Department proposals are invited for heavy guns for both these branches of public service.

THE SEIZURE OF SPECIE IN NEW-ORLEANS.

The Secretary of State is understood to be engaged on the question brought up by the seizure of the specie found in possession of the Netherlands Consul at New-Orleans.

GEN. PRIM.

Gen. PRIM dined with the Spanish Minister to-day. The Mexican Minister and other members of the *Corps Diplomatique* were present.

COMMODORE WILKES.

Commodore WILKES left for Philadelphia to-night. A sword is to be presented to him there, to-morrow, by the City Councils.

THE REPORT FROM MEMPHIS.

It is reported, as I close this dispatch, that Memphis has been evacuated. This event has been looked for, but it is not certain that any official intelligence has yet been received at the War or Navy Departments.

GOV. STANLY'S INSTRUCTIONS.

It is reliably ascertained that the letter of Secretary STANTON, published this morning, embraces all the instructions to Gov. STANLY.

THE ORDER RELATING TO RECRUITING.

Gen. RUSSELL, the Adjutant-General of Pennsylvania, obtained to-day an order from the War Department which provides that a superintendent be appointed from each State, and that when commanders of regiments report the number of men needed to fill up, officers shall be detailed for recruiting service, with the approval of the Commanding General. The adoption of this plan

[*Continued on Eighth Page.*]

The New-York Times.

VOL. XI—NO. 3363. NEW-YORK, THURSDAY, JULY 3, 1862. PRICE TWO CENTS.

HIGHLY IMPORTANT.

A Reliable History of Events Before Richmond from Our Special Correspondents.

FULL DETAILS TO MONDAY NIGHT.

Five Days of Almost Continuous Fighting.

Repulse of the Enemy Near Mechanicsville on Thursday.

Desperate Battle at Gaines' Hill on Friday.

Retreat of Our Forces Across the Chickahominy.

Repulse of the Enemy in Front on Saturday.

Continuous Skirmishing Along the Rear on Sunday.

Another Desperate Battle in Our New Position on Monday.

OUR GUNBOATS ON JAMES RIVER IN ACTION

The Position of Affairs on Monday Night.

From the Special Correspondents of the New-York Times.

ARMY OF THE POTOMAC, ON THE JAMES RIVER, Monday Evening, June 30, 1862.

Events of the gravest character have transpired within the last five days, touching the condition and prospects of the army on the Peninsula. Acting under the necessity which the Commanding General has long foreseen, the widely-extended lines of the army, with its miles of well-constructed defences, stretching almost from the James River on the left to, and beyond the Chickahominy on the right, have been abandoned, and the army before Richmond has fallen back to a more practicable line of defence and attack, upon the James River. Hither the grand army, with its immense artillery and wagon train; its Commissary and Quartermaster's stores; its ammunition; its cattle-drove, of 2,540 head; in fact, its entire *materiel*, horse, foot and dragoons, bag and baggage, have been transferred. This manœuvre, however—one of the most difficult and dangerous for a commander to execute in the face of the enemy—has been accomplished safely, though under circumstances of difficulty and trial which would have taxed the genius of a Napoleon. *The army has been engaged in constant conflict with the enemy for six days*, during which their highest energies have been taxed to the uttermost. We have had no moment of repose—no opportunity scarcely to properly care for the wounded and to bury the dead. The enemy have closely watched every movement, and, with an army more than double that of our own, have had the ability to constantly launch fresh troops upon our rear, an advantage which they have been quick to discover, and remorseless in improving. Their perfect knowledge of the roads, paths and bridges, and the topography of the country, which has taken us *time* to learn, has placed an immense advantage in their hands. Heaven grant that here, under the shadow of these hills, and with the coöperation of the gunboats, our overtaxed soldiers and officers may have that brief repose which is so essential to them, and to the existence of the army itself.

The interruption of all communication with the Government has, no doubt, convulsed the country with anxiety and alarm. A knowledge of the facts, however, will relieve this feeling, while any effort to conceal the truth will not only be fruitless, but will leave the public to imagine a thousand evils which do not exist.

Beginning with the fight at Mechanicsville on Thursday, our advance forces, while steadily falling back, have had a continuous running fight.

On Friday one of the severest battles which was ever fought on this continent occurred on the right of the Chickahominy, near Gaines' Hill. On Saturday, after our forces had retired in good order across the creek and destroyed the bridges, we were attacked in front of our encampments, but Gen. Smith repulsed the enemy, leaving the ground strewn with his dead.

On Saturday morning, the arrangements having been completed, the wagon train was started on its way to James River, and was followed on Sunday morning by the artillery and Commissary's train.

Meantime the enemy, getting scent of our movement, strongly reconnoitered our front, and finding that several of our positions had been abandoned, pushed in and attacked us vigorously. Gens. Hooker and Richardson drove them back, and Gen. Meagher's Brigade, always on hand at the right time, charged, and captured two of their guns. The rebels paid a dear price for the information which they obtained. The chief struggle was near Savage's Station.

Anticipating a movement on our right flank, the railroad bridge over the Chickahominy was destroyed on Saturday morning. The rebels, supposing we had fallen back on the White House, sent a large force of infantry, cavalry and artillery in that direction, but after a long, rapid and weary march discovered they had gone on a wild goose chase in the wrong direction. They only found a small force of our infantry and cavalry scattered down to guard the rear, who fell back and escaped from White House Landing. The rest was one of those "howling wildernesses", which the rebels intend to leave for us. All the quartermaster and commissary stores had been removed two days before, and the rubbish burned.

Gen. McClellan and Staff left the headquarters at Savage's Station at daylight on Sunday morning, with a body guard of the Fourth United States Cavalry, and halted some five miles out, after crossing the White Oak Creek.

There were, on Saturday, about one thousand of the wounded and sick, chiefly accumulated from the battle of Friday, many of whom it was found impossible to remove, owing to the nature and severity of their wounds, and as a matter of humanity, as well as of necessity, they were left behind. A great many, however, who could walk slowly followed the track of the army, and the ambulances brought away a great many others.

WITHDRAWING FROM THE FRONT.

Gen. Hooker's Division broke camp in the intrenchments at 3 o'clock Sunday morning, and Gen. Sickles' and Grover's Brigades proceeded to the outposts to relieve Gen. Patterson's New-Jersey Brigade. At 5 o'clock A. M. the three brigades fell back to the second line of redouts, where they formed a line of battle with Richardson's and Kearney's Divisions, and remained until 8 o'clock P. M. On discovering that Gen. Hooker had fallen back, the enemy advanced his scouts with two field-pieces, and opened a brisk fire upon his rear, along the line of the railroad. Gen. Meagher's Brigade made a movement on both the enemy's flanks, while the Eighty-eighth New-York charged in front, and captured two of their guns. The enemy then fell back under cover of the wood. None were killed in Hooker's Division. In the Twenty-sixth Pennsylvania three were wounded; the First Massachusetts lost two prisoners. One man lost both legs by a shell. Kearney's and Richardson's Divisions were the last off the field.

On the approach of the rebel force to the Savage's Station, where the hospital was established, a white flag was sent out, and it was met by a Lieutenant-Colonel of the Confederates, who gave assurance that the hospital should be respected. There was no firing, purposely, in that direction, and, if an occasional shell exploded near the house, it is believed to have been accidental.

About 120 rebel prisoners, who were captured on Friday, accompanied us under guard. On Sunday forenoon an advance body of our cavalry, who were reconnoitering in front, discovered a body of rebel cavalry near a small church, and, after a sharp engagement, put them to flight, killing a considerable number of horses, and capturing some twenty-five prisoners, who were added to the group already in hand.

Sedgwick's Division left the front at daylight, and were engaged by the enemy half way to Savage's Station, which they reached at 5 P. M. Here the enemy's infantry, with a battery, came out of the woods on the right, and attacked them.

The First Maine were advanced on the left, with a line of skirmishers in front. They had twelve wounded, three mortally, viz: Smith, Wren and Taylor. C. W. Haskell, Company C, was slightly wounded in the hand by a shell.

Sedgwick's Division crossed the creek at White Oak Swamp about 4 o'clock A. M., Monday. His rear was not annoyed during the night.

Keyes' and Porter's Divisions had already preceded us on the march, and had reached a position on the James River, near Turkey Island, which is about ten or twelve miles above City Point.

The Engineer Brigade of Gen. Woodbury preceded the army, and constructed corduroy roads where they were necessary. At the Four-mile Creek, a bridge was built across the run. At the White Oak Swamp Creek two bridges were also constructed by the same valuable corps. One for the passage of the main army train, and the other to accommodate Gen. Heintzelman's Division, who, with Hooker and Richardson, covered the retreat.

DESTRUCTION OF THE BRIDGES.

As the army resumed its march on Monday morning, information was received, through Gen. Richardson, that the enemy were pursuing, and orders were given to destroy the bridges.

The Engineer Corps was detailed for this duty, and also to defend the approach to the place. A wide space of trees had been felled across the creek, and the brigade was deployed as skirmishers at the right and left of the passage. Ayres' battery of six guns was also left to hold the position, and was stationed on the hill overlooking the swamp.

HOW THE RETREAT WAS CONDUCTED.

The retreat was conducted in the most perfect order. There was no trepidation or haste; no smashing up of wagons by careless or fast driving, and not a single accident of any consequence is believed to have occurred. A drove of 2,500 fat cattle, under the charge of Col. Clark, Chief Commissary, and Capt. E. M. Buchanan, Commissary of Subsistence on Gen. McClellan's Staff, were successfully driven along. They had been brought up from the White House, and narrowly escaped stamping by the rebels.

The country through which we passed contained some of the finest farming lands I had seen in Virginia. Broad farms, with well-grown crops of oats and wheat, were passed along the roads, in which the horses and cattle found abundant forage. The forage of the army had all been consumed the day before, thus relieving the train of an immense burden. Instead of the expected swamps and impassable roads, we found well-traveled country roads in excellent condition, along which the immense artillery and wagon train passed with the greatest ease. After approaching within about five miles of the river, the train was divided, part being sent by each of three roads which converged near the landing. An occasional halt was ordered, to enable the advance to examine the roads and woods in front for a concealed force or masked batteries, but nothing of the kind interrupted our progress. A teamster or some mischievous person would occasionally report that we were attacked in front, which would produce a temporary scare, but beyond this, nothing delayed the movement. The soldiers regarded it as the carrying out of part of a necessary plan—the only dissatisfaction expressed being at the leaving behind of so many of the sick and wounded.

Plenty of provisions and medicines were left for them, however, and if they are permitted to use them their situation for some time to come will be much better there than with the army in the midst of conflict and alarm.

CARE OF THE SICK AND WOUNDED.

At Savage's Station the Government had made arrangements for the sick and wounded as they were brought from the field. It was under the care of Dr. John Swinburne. Dr. Brunot, of Pittsburgh, Penn., arrived on Monday with a corps of surgeons and nurses. How many of these remained with the patients I am not able to state. There is a report that a large part of them ran away when the army left. It was certainly a severe test of their philanthropy to be left in rebel hands. The demand for nursing and surgical attendance was so great that large numbers were obliged to wait for long hours before their cases could be reached. The worst cases were attended to first, but there was and have been a great many who never received attentions at all. The entire area in the back and on both sides of the house was covered with the wounded, and there were also some twenty large tents pitched in the garden at the east of the house, filled with sick and wounded. The stores for Mrs. Harris, the benevolent lady, who, assisted by Mrs. Sampson, are devoting themselves to the sick, were delayed at White House, and if they reached Savage's at all, it is doubtful whether the good things were not appropriated by the rebels as soon as they got possession of the place.

Many poor fellows who were scarcely able to drag themselves along, clung to the skirts of their comrades, or hobbled on crutches, apparently dreading more than death itself, falling into the hands of the rebels. Many became so exhausted that they fell by the wayside, and could only be roused and helped forward by the greatest exertion.

THE APPROACH TO JAMES RIVER.

When an aid of Gen. McClellan rode back and reported that *the way was all open to James River*, a thrill of relief ran through the whole line, and the sight of the green fields skirting its banks was indeed an oasis in the terrible desert of suspense and apprehension through which they had passed. The teams were now put upon a lively trot in order to relieve the pressure upon that portion still in the rear.

Gen. McClellan and Staff rode ahead and took possession of the old estate known as Malvern Hills, owned by B. F. Dew, one mile back from "Turkey Island Bend. It is a large, old-fashioned estate, originally built by the French, and has near it, in front, an old earthwork constructed by Gen. Washington during the Revolutionary war. It has a spacious yard shaded by venerable elms and other trees. A fine view of the river can be had from this elevated position. Gen. McClellan expressed the opinion that *with a brief time to prepare, the position could be held against any force the enemy can bring against us.*

Exhausted by long watching and fatigue, and covered thickly with the dust of the road over which we had passed, many of the officers threw themselves upon the shady and grassy lawn to rest. The soldiers also attracted by the shady trees, surrounded the the house, or bivouaced in the fields near by.

Gen. McClellan immediately addressed himself to the task of preparing dispatches for the Government.

THE FIRE IN OUR REAR.

At 2 o'clock P. M. firing was heard in the direction of White Oak Swamp, where it was supposed Ayres was holding in check the rebel force who were attempting to cross. This continued for nearly two hours, when sudden and heavy firing began further to the left, in the direction of Charles City Cross Roads. At this point an immense body of fresh troop with artillery and cavalry, had made their appearance direct from Richmond, and were engaging our batteries still left to guard the road.

Orders were sent immediately to put the troops in line of battle; and Gens. Porter's and Keyes' commands were soon on the way up the hill, returning from their comfortable encampment beyond Malvern Hills. By 4½ o'clock P. M. the road was thronged with these troops, with artillery and cavalry, hastening to resist the advance of the enemy.

The firing now became more and more rapid, and was evidently approaching our line. The roar of cannon was incessant, and the dust of the contest swept upward and whirled in eddying clouds above the forest trees, which concealed friend and foe from view.

Members of the Staff and messengers hurriedly mounted and rode to and fro with important orders to the commanding officers. The wagons were drawn up on the right of the field as a kind of temporary breastwork, and the troops were disposed in line of battle at the westward, from which direction the enemy were advancing.

THE GUNBOATS BROUGHT INTO ACTION.

The firing now became incessant, the explosion of shells constant and most terrific from both lines, and the roar of musketry, mingled with the shouts and cheers of the contending forces. If we could have seen them, and estimated their strength or number, it would have been some relief, but they were advancing, apparently, to within less than a mile of our position, under cover of woods. It was very evident that *our men were being driven in, and that, too, by an overwhelming force.* At this juncture two of our gunboats, the *Galena* and *Aroostook* moved forward some half a mile and opened fire upon the left with their 54-pounders, the shells exploding in the edge of the woods along the line of hills where it was supposed the enemy would attempt to turn our left. No doubt these terrific missiles had an excellent effect in deterring them from this enterprise, and in retarding their advance. In so long a range there was danger that some of our own men might be hit, and a signal station was established on the top of an old house overlooking the field, and also commanding a view of the river. The firing from the *Galena* was directed in front by these signals. The *Jacob Bell* and also the *Aroostook* fired several shells during the last part of the battle.

During the evening, and while the fight was going on, crowds of dusty men rushed down to the river, and plunged in to bathe. Considering the circumstances of the army, this was hardly the time to adjust one's toilet.

Meantime the contest raged with terrible fury along our whole front and right. Exploding shells filled the air, and rifled shot screamed overhead. So thick was the cloud of dust enveloping the field, it was impossible, except from the sound, to determine which way the tide of battle ebbed or flowed. The gunboats kept up a discharge of their heavy shells upon the enemy's position. Provost-Marshal Porter meantime took charge of the disabled and sick soldiers, and conducted them to the rear. A large number of stragglers filled the road, who seemed to have business in an opposite direction from that in which the enemy was coming.

The Prince De Joinville, with the Duke De Chartres and the Count De Paris, took charge of dispatches for the Government, and Gen. McClellan accompanied them as far as the gunboat *Jacob Bell*, on board of which he bade them a final adieu toward evening. The crew manned the rigging, and cheered as the General returned to headquarters.

The day's contest wound up by a diminuendo of musketry, and by dark all firing, except an occasional shot, had ceased. It was too late to obtain any list of killed and wounded, or in fact to learn definitely the result of the fight. The *Jacob Bell* went down to City Point ordering up the *Southfield*, and all the other vessels lying below.

It should be borne in mind that the wide bottoms along the river separate the gunboats in many places, some two miles from the forces operating on the hills. The gunboats *Galena*, *Maratanza*, *Aroostook*, *Maraska* and *Port Royal*, are near by, and ought to be able to render valuable assistance to the army until it can be placed in position to operate. The indications are that the *enemy will continue to harass our position and give the troops no rest, day or night, until they have been dislodged or compelled to embark.* Should affairs reach the latter crisis, where are the transports to receive such an army on board, with its immense *materiel* of war? There are scarcely vessels enough now in the James River to take on board the wounded and sick, to say nothing of the army.

The *Jacob Bell* having returned from City Point, was dispatched, about 10 o'clock P. M., to Fortress Monroe, with the Prince De Joinville and companions, who, it was understood, carried dispatches to the War Department.

When the steamer left, all was quiet along the river, and it was supposed that our forces were holding their position at Malvern Hills.

The results of this contest are not known. The fight was a most determined one on both sides.

Transports and steamers were proceeding up the river; among them the *Wilson Small*, of the Sanitary Commission. All their vessels will be needed to remove the sick and wounded. Early arrangements will no doubt be made by the Government for the recovery of the wounded from Savage's Station and from the battle-field of Gaines' Hill.

THE BATTLE OF GAINES' HILL.

Full Details of the Desperate Battle of Friday

Had the enemy possessed full information of the purposes of our Commanding General they could not have taken better advantage of our position than they did. The fact that our front gave way at Mechanicsville on Thursday, after making a successful stand, and fell back toward Gaines' Hill, seems to have suggested to them that a general retrograde movement was contemplated; and it became their policy to follow and fight us on the retreat. With the Chickahominy in our rear, it was, of course, impossible for our army to cross, successfully, under the enemy's fire; and there is no doubt but that they expected to overtake and compel us to fight or be cut to pieces at the bridges.

On Thursday nearly all the wagons were sent across, to have them out of the way. This movement was going on all day and night, and, if known to the enemy, must have revealed the fact that our army was either about to retreat or to change its position. This was too valuable an opportunity to be lost, and was improved to the best advantage. Our troops had been engaged in an exhausting contest at Mechanicsville the day before. They had plenty of fresh soldiers, and were near their base of operations, from which whole masses could be drawn at an hour's notice. We were separated from our centre by the bridges of the Chickahominy, from which we could obtain reinforcements only by a comparatively tardy and uncertain process. That they brought nearly their whole force against us on that side of the river shows that a determined effort was to be made to compel us to cross the river, and then to pass to the rear and turn our right.

Foreseeing this plan, and without the necessary force to guard against the movement, *the only expedient left was adopted by the Commander of the Union forces. The enemy were to be held in check as long as possible, to enable him to safely withdraw his whole force to the James River, and take up a new position.* Another day and night would, no doubt, have found our entire right abandoned, and the commands of Porter, McCall and Stoneman withdrawn safely to the left of the Chickahominy, and the bridges destroyed, without a battle. That this was not permitted was owing to the watchfulness of the enemy, or to the treason of some one within our lines who possessed a knowledge of our plans.

A precipitate retreat was out of the question. It would have resulted in the sacrifice of the entire right wing. With our retreating forces massed in front of the Woodbury and Grapevine Bridges, along the river bottoms, a pursuing force commanding the eminence at Dr. Williams' house, would be able to cut them to pieces, or compel a surrender. From the attacking party we here, for the first time, took a position of defence, and accepted the battle which was offered.

THE ATTACK IN THE MORNING.

The enemy's skirmishers made their appearance beyond Gen. Morell's encampment at an early hour in the morning, and were met by the advance pickets of the Ninth Massachusetts, who engaged them sharply, steadily retiring toward Gaines' Hill. During this hour's contest, the Ninth Massachusetts lost a considerable number of their men. They fell back slowly and in good order on the road toward Coal Harbor.

Meantime, McCall's Brigade of Pennsylvania reserves, and Sykes' Brigade of regulars took up a position upon the high land overlooking the valley of the Chickahominy, eastward of and near the roads leading from Gaines' Hill to Coal Harbor. Your correspondent arriving at this place just as the troops were coming up, watched with much care the forming of the line of battle, and the disposition of the troops.

Sykes' Brigade, consisting of the Third, Fourth, Twelfth and Thirteenth United States Infantry, Duryea's Zouaves and Weed's Battery, commanded by Lieut.-Col. R. C. Buchanan, were disposed on both sides of the road leading north from Gaines' Hill, and parallel to the road to Coal Harbor. The Zouaves were drawn up in the open field, facing the line of the enemy's approach, while the regulars were placed to the right, left and rear, in the same field and along the road. Capt. Weed, in anticipation of the attempt of the enemy to push their lines up the Coal Harbor road to our right, found an admirable position for his battery of 3-inch Parrots, in a wheat-field about forty rods to the right of his original position, on a slight eminence which commanded a cross-road intersecting that to Coal Harbor. Here he could sweep a mile of the cross-road, and effectually prevent the passage of any considerable body of the rebels to the right. Experience soon showed that this position was well chosen, for it proved, during the day, one of the hottest in the fight. Capt. De Hart's Battery was posted further to the left, and directly confronted the rebel line, whose position, though not as yet precisely known, was partially revealed by the sound of his artillery and musketry beyond a belt of woods toward Gaines' Hill. Capt. De Hart's Battery consisted of six 12-pounder Napoleon guns, besides which there was a battery of 3-inch rifled guns, of wrought iron, belonging to the reserves. Capt. Eaton's Battery was on his left, and Capt. Kern's further to his left.

This Capt. Eaton, of Drainsville memory, was killed; Capt. Kerns was wounded; Capts. Whiting' Chambliss, Lieut. Sweet killed, and Lieuts. Arnold, Watkins and one other officer were all wounded during the day. Lieut. Hayden, of Edwards' Battery, and Lieut. Piper were also wounded.

McCall's troops came rather wearily into line. They had been fighting nearly all the previous day and night, and did not relish being called so soon to a repetition of the entertainment.

Morell's Division were disposed in the centre and to the left of the hospital, nearly abreast of Gen. Porter's headquarters.

There was now an intermission of the fire beyond the woods lasting for half an hour—an ominous silence,—and all eyes were directed toward the enemy's position to detect, if possible, any movement right or left. The field of conflict about to take place was bounded by the road leading to Coal Harbor, on the west; the meadow or bottom of the Chickahominy on the south and east, and a belt of woods stretching northward nearly parallel with the river. The land is elevated, somewhat undulating, and near the centre contains a thinned growth of pine. Near the north line of this space, and along the road leading to the military bridges are three houses, the first Sally McGee's; the second, Joseph McGee's, at first taken for a hospital, and the third, Dr. Williams' house on the hill, to which all the wounded who were brought off the field were conveyed. Gen. Porter's headquarters was at Adams' house, about a third of a mile distant.

About 10 o'clock the pickets at our right were driven back from the woods skirting the field, and shortly afterward those stationed on the Cross Roads toward the Coal Harbor road, were also driven in. The enemy were silently creeping up to the right. Simultaneously he made his appearance in a green field, directly in front, drawn up in line of battle, and in five minutes their batteries opened on our lines with shell. Following this the enemy had also placed a battery in position, fronting that of Capt. Weed's, and commenced fire—the fire of the two rebel batteries being at an angle of 45 degrees to our position, enfilading the troops. There was a temporary panic among horses, men and servants, who plunged, dodged, scampered and skedaddled to get out of range. Your reporter, perfectly cool himself—of course—was twice tossed nearly out of his saddle or thrown over the horse's head, as he raced uncontrolled about the field. A small party of cavalry disgracefully started down the road to get under cover of the woods, but your reporter hailed and brought them to by a word of gentle admonition. They turned and took a short path out to McGee's. Here we found the rifled shot of the rebels flying overhead, and going nearly a mile beyond, close up to Williams' house. Capt. Weed opened his battery, as did those of Tidball's, which was stationed near the same position. The battery of Capt. De Hart also replied vigorously. The Zouaves, who were drawn up in line nearest to the enemy, stood motionless and stern awaiting the onset, while the regulars occupied the field and road, ready to receive and return the rebel fire as soon as they should get within range. The whiz-z-z of Minié bullets, and scream of shell and shot from a dozen different directions now showed that the work had begun in earnest. The people, old, young, white and black, male and female, occupying the houses near the field, now ran across the field to get under cover of the woods.

The force of the enemy could not be ascertained, as they kept concealed to a great extent, and fired across a small ravine at our line. As they advanced, the Zouaves and regulars also met them, and sturdily maintained their ground.

The position of these batteries and of Sykes' command was not essentially changed during the day. They held their own under a most terrific fire, and to Weed's and Tidball's Batteries is unquestionably due the credit of preventing the flanking of our right.

As the contest thickened, the enemy showed themselves in constantly augmenting numbers. The tide of battle swayed to the left, and finally covered the entire rolling land overlooking the river valley. Details from the Zouaves and other ambulance corps began to bring in the wounded from the field, and soon the hospital was full of the badly wounded. One man whose arm had been torn from his shoulder by a shell, cried with vexation because he could not have time to discharge his musket.

By 2 o'clock, the woods covering the hill were thronged by the two contending armies. The enemy generally advanced in three lines, the first firing and falling down while that behind repeated the same movement. By the time the third line had discharged their pieces, the first had loaded and were ready to rise and fire again.

Thus the battle raged, the enemy at times giving way before the impetuous charges of our men, and again recovering and advancing. The fiercest portion of the fight was near the brow of the hill. Batteries thundered, musketry roared, and the din and noise of the contending forces were terrific.

It was apparent that the rebels were constantly bringing fresh troops upon the field, and there was literally no end to their number.

As soon as it could be done, orders were sent back for reinforcements, and Slocum's Division came over the bridge and marched to the support of our hard-pressed forces. About 5 o'clock the Irish Brigade of Gen. Meagher came upon the field, and with a shout of defiance went in and for a few moments staggered the rebel lines by their persistent and courageous conduct. A few thousand more of such desperate heroes would have turned the tide of battle. The rebels who fell into our hands were furiously drunk, having got a supply of whisky from one of our encampments, where it had been carelessly left by a Commissary.

At this point I find myself obliged to stop writing in order to send forward my copy by my brother reporter. I will finish the account by the next conveyance. E. S.

ADDITIONAL DETAILS.

Graphic Particulars of the Events of Thursday, Friday, Saturday, Sunday and Monday.

ON BOARD THE GUNBOAT STEPPING STONES, JAMES RIVER, Monday, June 30, 1862.

The right wing of our army has at length been attacked by the enemy—an event which was not wholly unanticipated by us. For several days previous to the attack, preparations were being made by the right wing to resist, if possible, to some extent, any advance movement of the rebels from the direction of Hanover or Mechanicsville, but the extent of the preparations were not sufficient to justify the belief that a vigorous stand was to be made on the west side of the Chickahominy.

At the time the enemy first made their appearance to our pickets on the right, which was on the 26th, our force at Mechanicsville consisted of the Eighth Illinois Cavalry, Col. Farnsworth; six companies of the Bucktail regiment, under command of Maj. Stone, and five companies of Pennsylvania Reserves. This force was distributed about the town, also on the road leading to Richmond, the road leading to Ashland, and the road leading to Hanover. The videttes were keeping special watch on the Hanover road.

The Pennsylvania Reserves were guarding the Richmond road, and having received timely information of the near approach of the enemy, returned to camp before the rebels could get between them and it. It was fortunate for Gen. McCall that he had the assistance of the five companies later in the day. They performed their part gallantly, and defended the rifle-pits to the last moment.

At 10 A. M. on Thursday, the 26th, videttes on the Hanover road came into Mechanicsville with the intelligence that the enemy was approaching the town from the direction of Hanover. Three companies of the Bucktail Regiment immediately moved out to a distance of 1½ miles on the road indicated, in order to support the pickets already there. The strength of the enemy was not then known, neither could it be ascertained that he intended anything beyond a reconnoissance.

THE ENEMY'S ADVANCE.

No sooner had the reinforcements reached their destination than it was discovered that the rebels were advancing in considerable force from the direction of Hanover, they evidently having crossed the railroad at Meadow Bridge. The design of the rebels to turn our right could not now be doubted, and as it was clear that our small force would be insufficient to meet the attack, Gen. Reynolds sent back to Gen. McCall for reinforcements.

Meantime, and before the reinforcements could arrive, the enemy had pushed steadily onward and was fast closing in upon Maj. Stone's force. The small command, however, was drawn up in line, ready to receive the rebels, and was determined to do its utmost, even if it lost the life of every man. The cavalry took their position in the rear of the infantry, and remained at their posts until it was evident that the superior number of the rebels would ultimately drive us, when they retired further to the rear, but still within supporting distance of the infantry. Onward came the rebel columns, and firmly stood our small force to combat them. When the rebels had approached within rifle distance, Maj. Stone gave the command to fire, and a volley was poured into the enemy's ranks which told with terrible effect. At this fire a rebel Major was seen to fall.

The enemy returned the fire, and pushed his cavalry to our right, in order to surround our men. They at last succeeded in getting round to the rear, which circumstance placed our men in an exceedingly critical position. Major Stone, observing the importance of immediate action, rode up to his men, and shouted, "Shall we fight or surrender?" "*Fight!*" was the hearty response of the Bucktails; and, after giving one more volley to the rebels in front, wheeled, charged through the cavalry in the rear, and gained a piece of woods, where they took temporary refuge. Here they were again surrounded, and again they cut their way through the rebel cavalry, and proceeded in a direction toward Gen. McCall's camp.

Company K, and a portion of Company B, who were on picket duty on the Ashland road, were too far distant too join their comrades in season to make a retreat with them. It is feared that this portion of the Bucktails were captured by the rebels, as nothing has been heard from them since the commencement of the fight.

THE WESTERLY APPROACHES TO MECHANICSVILLE.

There are two roads leading into Mechanicsville from the west side. The one nearest Hanover we will designate as the upper road, and the other as the lower road. The object of our men was to fall back on the upper road, but the rebels having got possession of the road on the right, our men were compelled to take to the fields and woods.

Gen. McCall's Division was upon the ground, and drew up in line of battle on the west side of a small stream, over which the lower road crosses. A part of the force was placed on the right and a part on the left of the road. The stream referred to is about one mile from Mechanicsville. The First and Second Brigades of Gen. Morell's Division, the former under command of Gen. Martindale, and the latter under command of Gen. Griffin, also arrived upon the ground and took positions at the right and left of the main road leading to the White House, near the junction of the upper Mechanicsville road. Gen. Martindale advanced to the right of the main road, in a direction toward a place called Old Church. Gen. Griffin occupied the woods at the left, and supported the right of McCall's Division.

THE LINE OF DEFENCE.

The space between the Chickahominy and the lower road, the small stream and the upper road, and open field for some distance on the right of the upper road, formed our line of defence. The left was held by McCall's Division, including the Bucktails that fell back from Mechanicsville; the centre by Gen. Griffin's Brigade, and the right by Gen. Martindale's Brigade. We had a rifle-pit on each side of the lines, and a short distance from the stream.

THE POSITION OF THE BATTERIES.

Easton's Pennsylvania Battery occupied positions

[Continued on Eighth Page.]

The New-York Times.

VOL. XI—NO. 3364. NEW-YORK, FRIDAY, JULY 4, 1862. PRICE TWO CENTS.

FROM GEN. M'CLELLAN.

The Great Battle Continued Through Seven Days.

IMMENSE LOSSES ON BOTH SIDES.

Terrific Onslaught of the Rebels on Our New Position.

Final and Overwhelming Defeat of the Enemy.

Death of Stonewall Jackson and Gen. Barnwell Rhett.

Gen. Magruder Reported to be a Prisoner.

Gen. McClellan Safe and Confident in His New Position.

Arrival of Considerable Reinforcements.

OFFICIAL ADVICES FROM GEN. McCLELLAN.

WASHINGTON, Thursday, July 3—3:12 P. M.

A dispatch from Gen. McCLELLAN, just received at the War Department, dated "From Berkley, Harrison's Bar, July 2, 5:30 P. M," states that he has succeeded in getting his army to that place, on the banks of the James River, and *had lost but one gun*, which had to be abandoned last night, (Tuesday,) because it broke down: that an hour and half ago *the rear of the wagon train was within a mile of the camp, and only one wagon abandoned*; that we had a severe battle yesterday (Tuesday;) *that we beat the enemy to-day*, the men fighting even better than before; that all the men are in good spirits, and that *the reinforcements from Washington have arrived.*

ADVICES FROM FORTRESS MONROE.

FORTRESS MONROE, Tuesday, July 1.

A gunboat has just arrived here from the scene of action yesterday, ten miles above City Point.

That division of our army has been fighting five days, and has retreated about 17 miles.

The fight of yesterday was most terrific, the enemy having three to our one.

The battle commenced with our land forces, and after about four hours' fighting, our gunboats got in range, and poured into the rebels a heavy and incessant fire.

This fire the rebels stood about two hours and then retreated.

Our troops have captured, notwithstanding their disadvantages, a large number of artillery pieces and 2,000 prisoners.

Among the prisoners captured is the Rebel General MAGRUDER.

The place where this last action took place is near Turkey Creek.

The retreat of the rebels last evening was with great disorder, and their loss has been very heavy, much greater it is thought than ours.

There is nothing definite, however, in regard to losses.

In the retreat forced upon Gen. McCLELLAN by the superior numbers of the enemy, I learn that he had to spike his siege guns and leave them on the field, after burning the carriages. The nature of the ground rendered it impossible to move them.

[This, it will be seen, is denied by Gen. McCLELLAN himself.]

In the retreat many of our sick and wounded were necessarily left behind. There are, of course, innumerable reports and rumors here, but I send only what appears to be authentic.

FORTRESS MONROE, Tuesday, July 1.

The loss of the enemy in killed and wounded alone yesterday (Monday) is said not to have been less than four thousand, but we hear nothing definite of the loss on either side.

Gen. Shields' army arrived here this morning, and have proceeded up the James River. They came in vessels via Annapolis.

FORTRESS MONROE, Wednesday, July 2,—9 P. M.

The steamer *Daniel Webster* has just arrived here from City Point with upwards of 300 wounded on board.

A gentleman who came down in charge of them informs me that *yesterday was the sixth day that the battle has been going on, with the most terrific fighting the sun ever shone upon.* It has extended the whole length of our line.

We have lost a great many men in killed, wounded and missing, *probably fifteen to twenty thousand.*

He informs me that Gen. McCLELLAN's headquarters are at Hardy's Landing to-day and his lines extend five miles above toward Richmond. This move of the right wing of the army was predetermined upon and planned ten days ago and would have been carried out sooner, but for certain reasons well known in the army, but which it would not be proper to state. The enemy's forces have greatly outnumbered ours in almost every action, *but notwithstanding this they have been repulsed oftener than we have and their loss far exceeds ours.*

Yesterday Gen. McCLELLAN is said to have *captured a whole rebel brigade, and took from them several rifle cannon, and other pieces.*

It is now said that we have lost very few of our siege guns, most of them having been recovered in safety.

There have been a great many wounded prisoners taken on both sides.

Our informant says that Gen. McCLELLAN and his Staff all agree that the present position of our army is *far more advantageous as a base of operations against Richmond than that hitherto occupied.*

The gunboats can now be brought to bear, and materially aid in carrying on the work.

Some of our regiments have suffered terribly, while others have but little. The New-York Fifth suffered terribly. They made a most heroic struggle, and made great havoc among the enemy. About one-half their number are killed, wounded, and taken prisoners. They were in the fight at Cold Harbor, and fought against desperate odds.

Our left wing was engaged yesterday, July 1, up to 2 o'clock, with the enemy, mostly with artillery.

The enemy's force, gathered from prisoners, who were members of Beauregard's Western army, was 185,000 men, whilst our effective force did not exceed 95,000.

The Richmond *Dispatch*, of Monday, announced the death of Gen. "Stonewall" JACKSON, and of Gen. BARNWELL RHETT, of South Carolina.

ADVICES RECEIVED IN THIS CITY.

A person arrived in this City last evening from the field of battle before Richmond, having left there on Tuesday evening, July 1, at 9 P. M.

At that time Gen. McCLELLAN'S advance was three miles northwest of Hardin's Landing, and within fifteen miles of Richmond.

The enemy was terribly repulsed in the battle of Monday, which was sanguinary in the extreme. We were attacked at four different points, and summarily repulsed the enemy three, when they pressed HEINTZEMAN'S left very hard, but SUMNER went to his relief, and they were finally repulsed with great slaughter. HEINTZLEMAN captured eight guns and a whole brigade of rebels, 1,600, including their Colonels—PENDLETON, of Louisirna, ex-Congressman LAMAR, of Georgia, and McGOWAN, of South Carolina.

Our transportation was all safely removed but seventy-five wagons, which were burned in camp.

The enemy's attack, on Monday, was fierce in the extreme. Kearney, Hooker, Richardson, Sedgwick, Smith and McCall participated.

The reserve under McCALL suffered severely, and Gens. McCALL and REYNOLDS were probably taken prisoners, as they were missing Tuesday night. Gen MEADE is severely wounded, and Gens. BURNS and BROOKS slightly.

Stonewall JACKSON is undoubtedly killed. Gen McCLELLAN, after the fullest investigation, credits the report: all the prisoners corroborating it.

The rebel General J. R. ANDERSON was mortally wounded in the action at Savage's Station on Sunday.

On Monday night intrenchments were begun and prosecuted as rapidly as possible. The first boat of reinforcements arrived just as our correspondent left. Supplies were also coming in in abundance.

Our total loss in the whole six days' terrific fighting, from Wednesday up to Monday night, is about twelve thousand, seven thousand five hundred of which were lost in the battle of Friday on the right.

Col. McQUADE of New-York; Col. CASS, of Massachusetts; Maj. PATTERSON, of Pennsylvania, and all the field officers of the Duryea Zouaves heretofore reported killed or wounded and many others, are alive and well.

OUR FORTRESS MONROE CORRESPONDENCE.

CITY POINT, Wednesday, July 2, 1862.

I did not write you yesterday, because the reports were coming in so thick and contradictory, that, without having time to thoroughly sift them, you would be just as likely to receive wrong as right information. What little I am now permitted to tell you is, therefore, reliable; for I have taken pains to obtain it from trustworthy eye-witnesses, or from parties who ought to be thoroughly well posted.

Whatever may be the impression in New-York, there is but one conclusion arrived at here by all intelligent people, in spite of all that the army pedlers and other skedaddling croakers have to say, and that is that the terrific battle which has been raging for the last four or five days has exhibited the most masterly strategy on the part of McCLELLAN, and bravery in himself, his officers and his men. So far from there being anything like defeat in his position, it is eminent success, and the enemy, without intending it, could not have better contrived to play into his hands.

I have just been on board the *George Washington*, which arrived this morning with 821 sick and wounded; among others, Gen. MEADE, and Brig.-Gen. W. A. GORMAN, of SEDGWICK'S Division—the former wounded very severely by the fragment of a shell passing through his body, and the latter prostrate by sickness. I have had a long and interesting conversation with one of the patients—a Captain of the Twenty-third Pennsylvania, and a man of great intelligence—and I was glad to find, not only in the facts he advanced, but in the cheerful and confident view he took of the dreadful struggle now going on, a full corroboration of the opinion so earnestly sustained by the TIMES and its correspondents.

The whole affair is simply this: As soon as McCLELLAN discovered—by the bold raid of STUART near the White House, and other indications—that the enemy had an intent upon that point, he at once come to the conclusion to turn that to account; and, by luring them on to a spot that could be of no ultimate use to them, and too far removed from his own base of operations, concentrated his forces on the James River, where he could have the aid of our gunboats—the terror of the rebels. For this reason—and long before any descent was made upon PORTER'S right wing—Gen. McCLELLAN had caused to be removed [illegible] all the army stores, provisions, &c., from the White House, and all the rest by transports down the York River, leaving but a small portion there (variously estimated at from $5,000 to $50,000, though probably nearer the first sum) to be destroyed, in the event of the enemy approaching sooner than they could remove it.

THE RECENT GREAT BATTLES.

Map Showing Richmond, Fort Darling, the Line of the James River, the Present Location of Gen. McClellan, and the Scene of the Recent Great Battles.

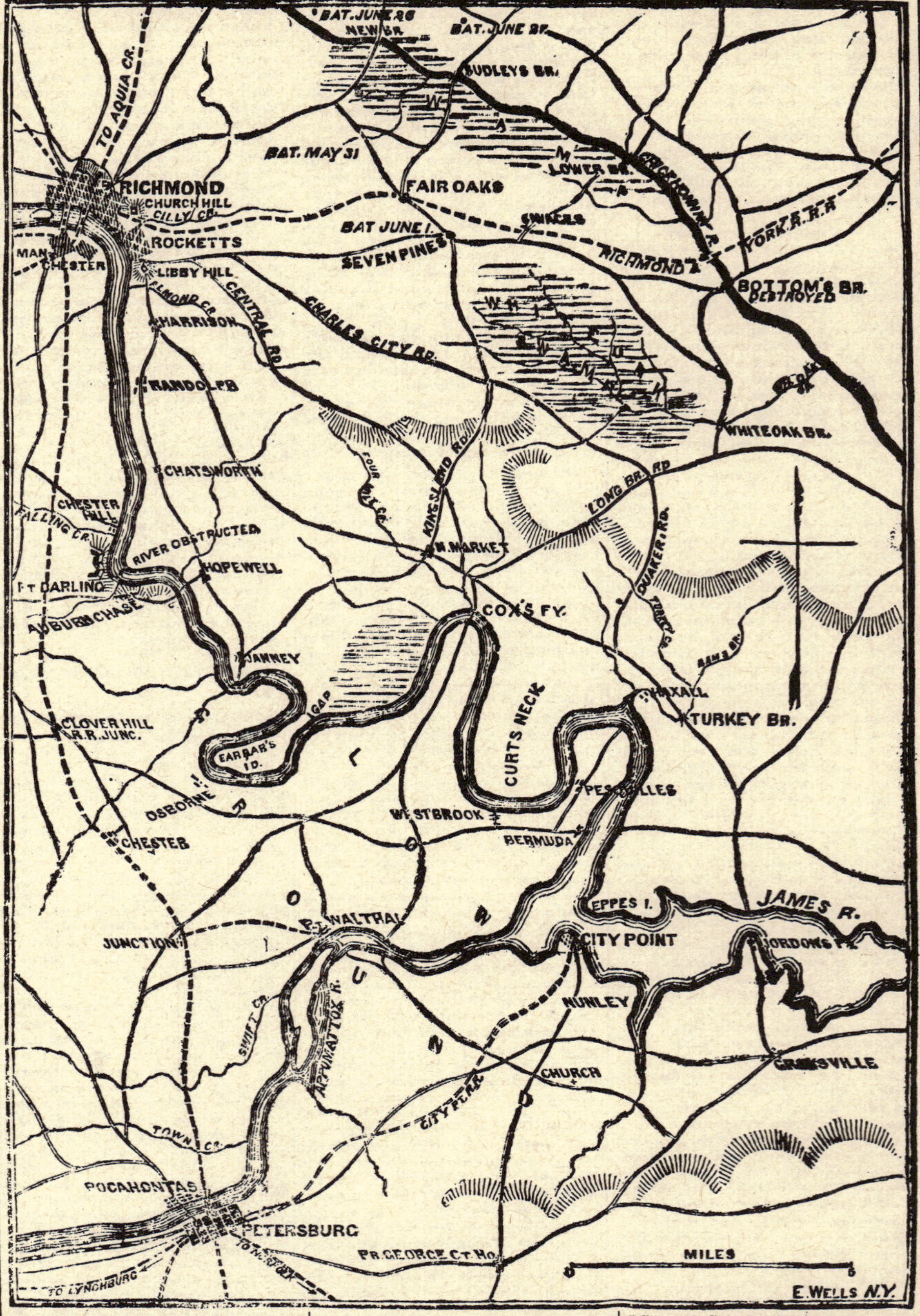

So certain is this, that many days elapsed before there was any demonstration at the White House, loaded vessels were seen coming down the York River and up the James with what intent people did not *then* know, though they do *now*. All this being arranged, orders were given for PORTER'S wing to fall back, and *he was doing so when attacked by the rebels.* The result was that, after great slaughter on both sides, McCLELLAN has reached the very spot he intended on the Jame River, with all his equipments and allowed the rebels to go into the very trap he had prepared for them. Does this look like defeat?

Much excitement prevailed here yesterday (Monday) when news came of the bloody work of the last two days, and the information that our army was on rations which must soon be exhausted. This fear is now, however, entirely removed. Boats, loaded with provisions, are rapidly going up the James River in abundance, and twelve vessels had already unloaded when my informant left, which was at 6 o'clock last evening. I was also informed that Gen. McCLELLAN is in a strong position, under cover from gunboats, and able to hold his own until reinforcements come. The latter we know are rapidly on the way to him—though whence and in what number I am not at liberty to say. Well sustained in the position he now holds, there can be no doubting his success.

Some people here are contemplating not only the possibility but the probability of the rebels venturing down the peninsula as far as Yorktown, and even further. It is almost to be hoped they will have the foolhardiness to do so. They might thereby gain the glory of shedding more human blood, but they will only be rushing on their own destruction. Shut up between the York and James rivers, without a plank afloat to confront our gunboats on them, it is difficult to see how they could either hold anything or sustain themselves there, while every man taken from their forces to go there is only increasing McCLELLAN'S chances of entering Richmond.

It is the province of those of your correspondents who were on the battle-field to give the details of what passed under their own eyes. I am merely giving you impressions derived from those who actually took a part in the fights, and who betray not the remotest symptoms of despondence. They all assured me that never did a General live who commanded more thoroughly the love of his men, and one of them said, with deep emotion, that there was not a man in his army who would not die for him. Should calamity befall our noble young chieftain before Richmond, through lack of strength before overwhelming numbers—and under no other circumstances could he fall—God help the truckling politicians, who will have brought him and his country to such extremity! He has done all that man can do. He has the indorsement of men, both at home and from abroad, who stand high in the ranks of war; and if disaster attends him, the responsibility not only should, but *will* be placed upon other shoulders than his. To know how deeply the army feel upon this subject, one should mix with them, as we correspondents are compelled to do; and you may depend upon it, a long account is being scored up against some political marplots of the Press and Congress.

Among the reports here which I have heard, but know not whether to credit or not, is that Gen. McCALL was wounded in the neck on Sunday, and is now a prisoner in Richmond; also that "Stonewall JACKSON" is killed. Dr. STRONG, Chaplain of the Fourth Michigan, who is unceasing in his attentions to his men, begged me to correct the following mistakes in one of your cotemporaries:

Col. McQUADE, of the Fourteenth New-York, reported as killed on Friday last, was seen yesterday at the head of his regiment in good health.

Col. ROBERTS, First Michigan, also reported killed, is not dead, but only slightly wounded.

Capt. SPALDING, Fourth Michigan, also reported killed, was seen in perfect health yesterday.

Capt. R. G. DEPOT, Company K, Fourth Michigan, was instantly killed on Friday last; also Lieut. T. B. JONES, Company B, Fourth Michigan, in the same engagement.

We are awaiting, with intense excitement, the result of the next two or three days; but unless something worse arrives than we have yet heard, Richmond must and will be ours in a few days.

NEMO.

LIST OF KILLED AND WOUNDED.

The following list of killed and wounded is additional to that published yesterday:

NEW-YORK REGIMENTS.

FIRST NEW-YORK.

T. Ryan, Co. H—hand.
Sergt. P. Stampt, Co. C—arm.
James Higgins, Co. E—hand.
Sergt. S. W. Legoutz, Co. E—finger off.
J. Stansbury, Co. A—arm.

SECOND NEW-YORK.

W. E. Sandford, Co. K—wrist.
J. Post, Co. K—back.
M. Sheckle, Co. C—sick.
C. Wilson, Co. C—sick.
D. Lamb, Co. I—arm.
P. Costello, Co. F—sick.

FIFTH NEW-YORK.

Geo. Cartwright, Co. C—wrist.
C. Albreght, Co. C—head.
E. Momon, Co. B—leg.
G. F. Dorson, Co. I—head.
A. K. Wolomon, Co. I—leg.
J. Fosley, Co. I—leg.
J. W. Brown, Co. I—head.
Thos. Honevan, Co. D—arm.
Andrew Williams, Co. D—thigh.
John Bregan, Co. C—sh'l'r.
James O. Reed, Co. H—mouth.
Sergt. J. W. Sharter, Co. D—arm.
Thomas Murphy, Co. C—shoulder.
Sergt. Geo. A. Mitchel, Co. F—head.
M. Whet, Co. C—rupture.
—— Shreffer, Co. K—arm, (amputated.)
E. C. Tucker, Co. H—foot.
C. Kilsman, Co. E—hand.
M. R. Powers, Co. H—hand.
Jas. Rupert, Co. C—arm.
C. C. Miller, Co. H—hand.
F. Higgins, Co. H—thigh.
C. Snyder, Co. G—hand.
J. A. Shore, Co. A—arm.
Wm. C. Ryan, Co. F—killed.
S. Deely, Co. F—killed.
H. Mandeville, Co. F—killed.
C. O'Neill, Co. F—killed.
Sergt. Phillips, Co. F—wounded and prisoner.
J. H. Stout, Co. F—woun'd.
Geo. W. Leavitt, Co. F—wounded.
Jas. Maloney, Co. F—wounded.
J. W. Neal, Co. F—wounded.
W. Sweeney, Co. F—woun'd.
T. Russell, Co. F—wounded.
Capt. Partridge, Co. I—killed.
C. Allen, Co. E—killed.
A. Berrien, Co. D—killed.

TENTH NEW-YORK.

T. M'Connigal, Co. H—leg.
W. Collins, Co. F—foot.
Jos. Knees, Co. F—head.
M. Bancroft, Co. I—thigh.
H. Seymour, Co. D—hand.

TWELFTH NEW-YORK.

Jas. Kelly, Co. E—breast.
Philip Brady, Co. D.
David A. Byre, Co. B—arm.
Sergeant S. A. Carpenter, Co. H—shoulder.
M. Dogg—arm.
Lt. Oliver, Co. E—wounded.
S't. Richards, Co. E—wounded.
— Wetmore, Co. E—missing.
Corporal Garrison, Co. E—wounded and prisoner.

FOURTEENTH NEW-YORK.

R. Sprague, Co. H—side.
Corp. Sid. Day, Co. I—face.
Sergt. D. R. Butts, Co. I—hand.
A. M. Gennacher, Co. I—head.
J. Beebe, Co. F—shoulder.
N. Mathews, Co. E—hand.
P. Lishlen, Co. E—hand.
Lieut. Skillen—killed.
Major Davis—missing.
Capt. Harra—wounded.

SIXTEENTH NEW-YORK.

Col. Harlan—seriously.
C. H. Hollow, Co. I—hand.
W. Wayne, Co. G—arm.
J. Rawdon, Co. I—arm.
I. Rodger, Co. I—hand.
J. A. Powers, Co. B—arm.
E. J. Sanford, Co. F—hand.
J. O'Connor, Co. C—hand.

EIGHTEENTH NEW-YORK.

S. S. Stevenson, Co. C—neck.
P. Mullen, Co. F—head.
A. King, Co. F—hand.
J. G. Riley, Co. K—left arm.
J. F. Shay, Co. F—forehead.
Sergt. R. Wiscoman, Co. G—arm.
C. C. Starr, Co. H—arm.
E. C. Selden, Co. B—shoulder.
M. Carey, Co. I—neck.
S. L. Stevenson, Co. C—neck.
J. Flynn, Co. C—hand.
Thos. Kerns, Co. F—head.

TWENTIETH NEW-YORK.

S. Solomon, Co. B—leg.
A. Hayes—neck.

TWENTY-FIFTH NEW-YORK.

A. Jack, Co. D—hand.
Sgt. T. Toomey, Co. C—hand.
J. Goby, Co. A—killed.

TWENTY-SEVENTH NEW-YORK.

W. Griffiths, Co. H—shoulder.
G. Lady, Co. H—hand.
F. Driscoll, Co. A—wrist and head.
J. Bonne, Co. E—elbow.
R. M. Hibbard, Co. E—shoulder.
S. Bachman, Co. E—neck.
H. Hammond, Co. C—breast.
Sgt. E. B. Stilsord, Co. E—wounded.
J. K. Barboot, Co. E—w'nd'd.
2d-Lt. J. Webster, Co. E—wounded.
W. Crawford, Co. E—w'nd'd.
E. Butler, Co. E—w'nd'd.

THIRTY-FIRST NEW-YORK.

Jas Kelly, Co. I—neck.

THIRTY-SECOND NEW-YORK.

S. Rosendale, Co. K—arm.
A. J. Formon, Co. C.
Wm. Simpson—arm.
John Deal, Co. D—hand.
J. I. Peck, Co. I—head.

THIRTY-SEVENTH NEW-YORK.

Z. Roden—sick.
L. Martin, Co. D—sick.
John Adams, Co. C—hand.

THIRTY-EIGHTH NEW-YORK.

C. Grobert, Co. C—hand.
F. Hoffmaster, Co. I—breast.

FORTIETH NEW-YORK.

Sergt. J. A. Emory—hand.

FORTY-FOURTH NEW-YORK.

R. H. Burhaus, Co. C—hand.
J. McCowan, Co. G—bruise.

FIFTY-FIFTH NEW-YORK.

Fred. Coppa, Co. C—hand and side.
Ger. Chisholm, Co. B—leg.
Felix Gallrans, Co. C—arm.

FIFTY-SIXTH NEW-YORK.

G. H. Avery.

SIXTY-SEVENTH NEW-YORK.

F. Hays, Co. B—hand.

SIXTY-NINTH NEW-YORK.

J. Quinn, Co. C—died in the hospital.

SEVENTIETH NEW-YORK.

G. Goodall, Co. C—elbow.

SEVENTY-SECOND NEW-YORK.

P. Donnelly, Co. F.

SEVENTY-THIRD NEW-YORK.

J. Wright, Co. H—hand and foot.
H. Hogan, Co. F—leg.
A. J. Hickey, Co. F—arm.

SEVENTY-FOURTH NEW-YORK.

A. Doll, Co. B—finger off.
G. A. Caffon, Co. F—shoulder.

SEVENTY-SEVENTH NEW-YORK.

D. S. Brown, Co. G—side.

EIGHTY-SEVENTH NEW-YORK.

S. E. Honington, Co. C—head.

ONE HUNDRED AND FIRST NEW-YORK.

I. Hall, Company B—hand.

PENNSYLVANIA REGIMENTS.

SECOND PENNSYLVANIA.

Daniel Conner, Co. A.
Corporal Jones, Co. A.
—— Townsend, Co. C—wrist.
W. Goth, Co. C—arm.

THIRD PENNSYLVANIA.

H. Harbaugh, Co. A—arm.
P. F. Holland, Co. A—shoulder.
J. Kocker, Co. A—back.

SEVENTH PENNSYLVANIA.

William H. Schively, Co. I—shoulder.
J. W. Davis, Co. K—shoulder.
Wm. M. Culp, Co. A—arm.
Solomon Saylor, Co. F—arm.
N. S. Horner, Co. A—left shoulder.
J. Grimes, Co. B—shoulder.
Wm. Portsine, Co. B—arm.
Joseph Winters, Co. B—arm.

EIGHTH PENNSYLVANIA.

A. Bane, Co. I—leg.
R. Sayres, Co. I—wounded.
T. Britton, Co. H—leg.

EIGHTH PENNSYLVANIA.

S. M. Drum, Co. G—arm.
Corporal Hugh Gattines, Co. K—thigh.
W. H. Miner, Co. I—breast.
Job Franks, Co. I—arm.
Francis Groton, Co. E—nose.
J. H. Sweeney, Co. H—arm.
H. A. Steward, Co. B—arm.
H. Larkee, Co. G—breast.
E. H. Miner, Co. G—shoulder.
Walter Grubbs, Co. B—leg.
John C. Gray, Co. B—breast.
J. L. Francis, Co. G—thigh.

NINTH PENNSYLVANIA.

Robt. H. Rells, Co. I—leg.
J. W. Donthile—hand.
C. Deitz, Co. B—hand.

ELEVENTH PENNSYLVANIA.

Edward Hoffman, Co. C—face.

THIRTY-EIGHTH PENNSYLVANIA.

D. W. Keever—hip.

FIFTY-SECOND PENNSYLVANIA.

F. Medlin, Co. K—hand.

SIXTY-SECOND PENNSYLVANIA.

Capt. T. B. Monks—wounded and prisoner.
Capt. R. J. Crozier—wounded badly.
Lieut. W. J. Patterson—w'nd.
Lieut. Bell—wounded.
Lieut. Cunningham—w'nd.
Lieut. Lowry, Acting Adjutant—wounded.
Lieut. Seitz, (accidentally burned) Co. B—wounded.
Privates Coursin and Mack, Co. D—killed.
Private Shenan, Co. F—k'l'd.
Private Mintzmer, Co. G—wounded.
Corp. Randolph, Co. F—wounded.
George R. Gaily, Co. F—wounded.
Robert Finnirock, Co. F—wounded.
Capt. F. Brown—wounded and missing.
W. King, Co. K—dead.
L. Eahamiah, Co. F—wn'd.

SIXTY-SECOND PENNSYLVANIA.

R. Erwin, Co. G—wrist.
S. Edwards, Co. G—finger.
T. Ruth, Co. G—left leg.
J. M. Stark, Co. H—shoul'r.
S. Mersaick, Co. A—neck.
J. K. Wilson, Co. F—face.
H. White, Co. F—leg.
W. Closson, Co. A—arm.
Joel Martin, Co. K—face.
C. H. Miersch—leg.
G. B. Gray, Co. F—hand.
A. Fisher—hand.

SEVENTY-SECOND PENNSYLVANIA—BAXTER'S ZOUAVES.

E. Allman, Co. H—finger off.
George Allen, Co. B—foot.
F. Hogg, Co. L—neck.
James Story, Co. I—foot.

EIGHTY-FIRST PENNSYLVANIA.

John Hughes, Co. E—hand.

EIGHTY-THIRD PENNSYLVANIA.

Thos. W. King, Co. C—foot.
F. J. Tsook—chest.
Sergt. J. E. Mozier, Co. H—breast.
John Bovee, Co. B—hips.
Maj. L. H. Nagle—wounded.
O. L. Otis, Co. D—arm.
J. A. Howe, Co. E—arm.
Col. J. W. McLane—killed.
Capts. Zeigler, Morris and Wood—wounded.

NINETY-THIRD PENNSYLVANIA.

H. J. Penrose, Co. B—foot.
F. Kirtz, Co. A—face & hand.

NINETY-FIFTH PENNSYLVANIA.

Col. Gosline—sev'ly wond'd.
Maj. Hobbs—sev'ly wond'd.
Lt. Donohue, Co. C—killed.
Lt. Robinson, Co. E—wounded.
Lt. Luginers, Co. F—wond'd.
D. McCarthy, Co. K—wounded and prisoner.
E. Latham, Co. K—wounded and prisoner.
G. McBride, Co. K—killed.
Corp. McAleer, Co. K—wounded.
M. Pendergast, Co. K—wounded.
A. Stemm, Co. K—wound'd.
J. Shannon, Co. K—wounded and prisoner.
E. L. Eddy, Co. K—wounded and prisoner.
J. Barton, Co. K—wounded and prisoner.

NINETY-SIXTH PENNSYLVANIA.

P. Goslan, Co. I—arm.
W. Strother, Co. G—left leg.
Milton Moyer, Co. D—finger.
J. Divine, Co. I.
D. Woodring, Co. E—head.

FIRST NEW-JERSEY.

Sergt. C. G. Morton, Co. A—head.
J. Ellwood, Co. A—head.

SECOND NEW-JERSEY.

W. H. Warner, Co. A—sick.
W. H. Beens, Co. K—face.
W. Dougherty, Co. I—breast.
J. H. Worden, Co. K.

THIRD NEW-JERSEY.

Patrick Burn (or Brown), Co. B—nose, cheek and shoulder.
Corp. S. Harris, Co. F—neck.
J. G. Lewallen, Co. B—arm.
P. J. Fox, Co. B—arm.
J. Blair, Co. B—shoulder and neck.
F. W. Coull, Co. B—right arm.
W. A. Smith, Co. E—right arm.
E. Prussill, Co. B—left arm.
F. McRaund, Co. G—left wrist.
R. B. McConan, Co. E—shoulder.
C. Bennett, Co. H—breast.
Wm. Kelley, Co. I—left shoulder.
P. Shank, Co. B—mouth.
R. C. Levick, Co. F—knee.
J. Henry, Co. B—finger.
J. Dillon, Co. G—shoulder.

FOURTH NEW-JERSEY.

Col. J. H. Simpson—missing and supposed to be killed.
Lieut.-Col. Wm. H. Hatch—missing and supposed to be killed.
Major Wm. Birney (brother of Brig.-Gen. Birney—missing and supposed to be killed.
Adjt. George H. Sturdiford—missing and supposed to be killed.
Capt. Wm. Mevis—killed.
Capt. Wm. Mulford—killed.
Capt. A. Aaronson—killed.
Capt. Wm. Fetter—killed.
Capt. H. M. Jewett—killed.
Capt. Wm. Nippins—killed.
First-Lieut. Wm. Myer, Co. A.—missing.
2d-Lt. H. Schroder, Co. A—missing.
1st-Lt. E. Wright, Co. D—missing.
2d-Lt. George Bennet, Co. D—missing.
Capt. B. Ridgway—missing.
1st-Lt. T. C. Spear—missing.
G. H. Stubbins, Co. C—wrist.
G. S. Reen, Co. K—stomach.
Sgt. J. E. Doughty, Co. G—head.
Sgt. H. Hopkins, Co. D—elbow.
J. Lanx—shoulder.
Jerome Shields, Co G—arm.
W. Hubert, Co. I—groin.

According to the statement of an officer, this regiment went into the fight with 640 men and only 81 can now be found. The six Captains first mentioned above were all killed within an hour after the fight commenced.

FIRST MICHIGAN.

M. Cotter, Co. G—arm.

FOURTH MICHIGAN.

M. L. Parks, Co. H—w'nd'd.
J. M. Miller, Co. I—w'nd'd.
D. H. Cotterall, Co. F—wounded.
A. D. Clark, Co. I—w'nd'd.
Sgt. J. Plummer, Co. I—wounded.
R. McDonough, Co. I—w'nd'd.
W. Breen, Co. I—w'nd'd.
M. T. Severance, Co. F—wounded.
G. H. Lee, Co. C—wounded.
H. A. Clark, Co. I—wounded badly.
Capt. Depney, Co. I—killed.
Sgt. G. Malts, Co. I—w'nd'd badly.
J. Clag, Co. I—dead.
T. Hogan, Co. I—dead.
W. Ross, Co. E—wounded.
Lt. Smith, Co. E—wounded.
A. J. Deal, Co. I—wounded.
W. R. Balcom, Co. F—w'nd'd.
W. Robinson, Co. I—bayoneted.
C. F. Carris, Co. G—w'nd'd.
C. A. Rouse, Co. D—w'nd'd.
Lts. Jones and [illegible], Co. D—mortally wounded.
J. Fleming, Co. [illegible]—hand.
L. Haviland, Co. [illegible]—arm.
Corp. J. [illegible], Co. K—two fingers off.
A. B. Crane, Co. K—jaw.
H. Petre, Co. K—shoulder.
L. [illegible], Co. K—back.

Entire loss of this regiment is 120.

SIXTEENTH MICHIGAN.

J. Doubleman, Co. A—arm.
S. W. Hilton, Co. C—head.
A. Smith, Co. G—finger.
Sgt. A. Cameron, Co. G—knee.
W. S. Conover, Co. G—right hand.
H. Palmer, Co. I—arm.

SECOND MAINE.

J. Winslow, Co. K.

FIFTH MAINE.

F. C. Bradbury, Co. C—shoulder.
W. H. Everett, Co. C—head.
W. Larraby, Co. C—arm.

SEVENTH MAINE.

E. Irvin, Co. H—hand.

NINTH MASSACHUSETTS.

D. Sullivan, Co. G—arm and breast.
T. Slattery, Co. H—right arm.
Corp. M. Burley, Co. H—right arm.
P. Flynn, Co. H—hand and arm.

ELEVENTH MASSACHUSETTS.

James Browney, Co. C—side.
J. G. Helton, Co. I—contusion.

SIXTEENTH MASSACHUSETTS.

M. Gormley, Co. I—hand.
J. Sullivan, Co. I—foot.

[Continued on Eighth Page.]

The Charleston Mercury.

DAILY PAPER—TEN DOLLARS PER ANNUM, PAYABLE HALF-YEARLY IN ADVANCE. | SPONTE SUA SINE LEGE FIDES RECTUMQUE COLENTUR.—VINDICE NULLO | COUNTRY PAPER—THREE A WEEK—FIVE DOLLARS PER ANNUM, IN ADVANCE.

VOLUME LXXXI. | CHARLESTON, S. C., MONDAY, JULY 7, 1862. | NUMBER 11,493

THE MERCURY.

MONDAY, JUYL 7, 1862.

The Battle of Richmond.

Whether we consider juncture of time, the stake involved, the armies which have met, the conduct of the combatants, or the effect upon the war, the battle of Richmond is a *great battle.* Fought at a critical period—for possession of the Confederate Government's seat, and Capital of Virginia—by the two largest and best disciplined armies ever assembled on this continent—in a series of bloody and desperate engagements—we have reason to rejoice in the issue of the great struggle.

McCLELLAN selected the ground of his approach. He located his powerful works with all the engineering skill of which he he is master. He built them with wonderful energy, almost in his own time. They were covered by a magnificent array of the finest artillery the world has ever seen. They were supported by a regular army, superior in numbers, admirably drilled and disciplined, and supplied with the best arms and all the equipments that money and mechanical resources, after a year of delay and preparation, could furnish. Works and artillery and troops have all failed the North in the trial with the army of JOHNSTON. The onsets of Southern men, accustomed to the use of weapons, bred in the habit of command and with the sentiment of honor, and fighting under the influence of principle and enthusiasm and vengeance, have proved irresistible. The great invading host no longer threatens to overrun the South. Portions are given to carnage, portions to the prison house. Divided and pursued, doubtful escape is the highest hope of the remnants of the Grand Army of the North—happy if they succeed through the mismanagement of their foe and the skill of their retreating general.

But, however we rejoice over the great victory just achieved, it is only a successful defence of Richmond, accompanied by the defeat of the best army of the North. Richmond is not the only place threatened, and there are States and cities already in the hands of the enemy. It is incumbent upon us to redeem these, either by recapture or by the obtainment of equivalents from the enemy: Until we do this, we cannot make a satisfactory peace which will secure us independence, not only in political government, but in commercial relations. Maryland, Tennessee, Kentucky and Missouri have to be redeemed. New Orleans, Memphis, Nashville and Norfolk have to be obtained, and all the ports and harbors on our coasts and rivers now held by the enemy. We, therefore, have a heavy labor yet before us, and one which energy, enterprise and activity on the part of our Government and generals and troops alone can accomplish. We cannot afford to throw away this dear bought opportunity, as we have done several before. We have been sufficiently imperilled by victories, made moral, not material, by hallucinations of prudence and preparation. They have cost us enough of property and life, to fill the land with misery and with mourning. "Masterly inactivity" and "brilliant retreats" are too expensive a species of strategy to be longer tolerated. The people of the Confederate States want action—they want a war of aggressive movement, and this is a moment for inaugurating it in the East and in the West. Rapidity on the part of the Confederate Generals, ere our own victorious army is demoralized, and before the Northern forces can recover from the great disaster they have suffered, can put us in possession of our own, or furnish the means for a satisfactory peace of real independence within a moderately brief period. But every thing depends upon the advantage taken of the late great and bloody victory. Let troops be hurried forward and strike. No breathing time to the enemy. The God of battles favors our cause.

THE NEWS OF THE WAR.

THE BATTLES IN FRONT OF RICHMOND—FURTHER PARTICULARS OF THE DEFEAT OF M'CLELLAN'S ARMY—HIS MASTERLY RETREAT—REMOVING THE DEAD AND WOUNDED, ETC.

More than a week has now elapsed since the opening of the great struggle in front of Richmond. We have already given very full accounts of the fighting up to Saturday, the 28th ult. So far our successes had been plain. Our victory had resulted in driving the enemy from his entire line of defences on the north, and breaking every array of his forces that he opposed to our onset. In the meantime, all communication between McCLELLAN's army and the White House, on the Pamunkey River, had been cut off, General JACKSON holding possession of the York River Railroad; the Chickahominy was in the rear of the enemy, and in front of him were the divisions of Generals LONGSTREET, MAGRUDER and HUGER, leaving him, it was thought, no opportunity of escape, and putting him in a position where victory was to be completed.

It appears, however, that the enemy was imperfectly watched at a conjuncture the most critical in the contest, and that through some omission of our guard, the facts of which have as yet been but imperfectly developed, McCLELLAN succeeded on Saturday night in massing his entire force on the west side of the Chickahominy, and taking up a line of retreat towards the James river.

The Richmond *Examiner* accounts for the various and conflicting statements of the position and movements of McCLELLAN's army by the fact that his forces have been dispersed over such a wide extent of country, and thrown into such confusion, that it has been impossible to follow his movements or reconnoitre his position with precision. We quote from the *Examiner:*

THE POSITION OF M'CLELLAN.

It is believed that that portion of the enemy's forces which are described as in communication with the river, and as having taken their way towards Shirley and Westover, with long trains of wagons, &c., by no means composes the bulk of McCLELLAN's forces, and that a considerable portion of his army is still detained within our line on the roads leading down through Charles City county. The original plan of cutting off the enemy's communication with the river, which was to have been executed by a movement of HOLMES' division between him and the river, was frustrated by the severe fire of the enemy's gunboats, and since then the situation appears to be that of a division or dispersion of McCLELLAN's forces, one portion resting on the river and the other unable to extricate itself from our lines—such a situation in which we would be likely to hear of new dispositions of our forces being made every day, and many confused stories of the nature of operations.

The difficulty in obtaining precise and reliable news from the seat of active operations, besides those which ordinarily exist, is due to the essential nature of the situation itself, in which an immense army of the enemy has shifted his position and scattered his forces to such an extent that even our generals have been able to get but dissolving views in the change of scene and uncertainty of movement which have marked the wonderful retreat of McCLELLAN.

The skill and spirit with which McClellan has managed to retreat are remarkable, and afford no mean proofs of his generalship. At every stage of his retreat he has confronted our forces with a strong rear guard, and has encountered us with well organized lines of battle and regular dispositions of infantry, cavalry and artillery. His heavy rifled cannon have been used against us constantly on his retreat.

THE BATTLE ON TUESDAY.

The battle of Tuesday was perhaps the fiercest and most sanguinary of the series of bloody conflicts that have signalized each of the last seven days.

Early on Tuesday morning the enemy, from the position to which he had been driven the night before, continued his retreat in a southeasterly direction towards his gunboats on James river. At eight o'clock, a. m., Magruder recommenced the pursuit, advancing cautiously, but steadily, and shelling the forests and swamps in front as he progressed. This method of advance was kept up throughout the morning and until 4 o'clock, p. m., without coming up with the enemy. But between four and five o'clock our troops reached a large open field, a mile long and three-quarters in width, on the farm of Dr. Carter. The enemy were discovered strongly entrenched in a dense forest on the other side of this field. Their artillery, numbering fifty pieces, could be plainly seen bristling over their freshly constructed earthworks. At 10 minutes before 5 o'clock, p. m., General Magruder ordered his men to charge across the field and drive the enemy from their position. Gallantly they sprang to the encounter, rushing into the field at a full run. Instantly from the line of the enemy's breastworks a murderous storm of grape and canister was hurled into their ranks, with the most terrible effect. Officers and men went down by hundreds; but yet, undaunted and unwavering, our line dashed on until two-thirds of the distance across the field was accomplished. Here the carnage from the withering fire of the enemy's combined artillery and musketry was dreadful. Our line wavered a moment and fell back to the cover of the woods. Twice again the effort to carry the position was renewed, but each time with the same result. Night, at length, rendered a further attempt injudicious, and the fight, until ten o'clock, was kept up by the artillery of both sides. To add to the horrors, if not to the dangers, of this battle, the enemy's gunboats from their position at Curl's Neck, two and a half miles distant, poured on the field continuous broadsides from their immense rifle guns. Though it is questionable, as we have suggested, whether any serious loss was inflicted on us by the gunboats, the horrors of the fight were aggravated by the monster shells, which tore shrieking through the forests and exploded with a concussion which seemed to shake the solid earth itself.

It must not be inferred from the above account that the slaughter was all upon our side. We have the best reasons to know that the well directed fire of our cannon and musketry, both before and subsequent to our efforts to storm the enemy's position, fell with fatal effect upon his heavily massed forces.

At ten o'clock, p. m., the last gun was fired from our side. Each side held the position occupied when the fight begun, and, during the remainder of the night, each was busily engaged removing their wounded. The rumble of the enemy's ambulances and wagons, in rapid and hurried motion, did not cease even with the dawn. At ten o'clock, Wednesday morning, they were still busy, and discontinued their labors not because their wounded had all been removed, but for fear of our advance. Our wounded were carried from the field directly to the farm houses in the neighborhood, whence, after their injuries had been examined and dressed, they were brought to this city.

During the morning the enemy evacuated his position and retreated, still bearing in a south-easterly direction, and apparently not attempting to lessen the distance between him and his gunboats.

The battle-field, surveyed through the cold rain of Wednesday morning, presented scenes too shocking to be dwelt on without anguish. The woods and the field before mentioned, were, on the western side, covered with our dead, in all the degrees of violent mutilation; while in the woods on the west of the field lay, in about equal numbers, the blue-uniformed bodies of the enemy. Many of the latter were still alive, having been left by their friends in their indecent haste to escape from the rebels.

Great numbers of horses were killed on both sides, and the sight of their disfigured carcasses and the stench proceeding from them added much to the loathsome horrors of the bloody field. The corn-fields, but recently turned by the ploughshare, were furrowed and torn by the iron missiles. Thousands of round shot and unexploded shell lay upon the surface of the earth. Among the latter were many of the enormous shells thrown from the gunboats. They were eight inches in width by twenty-three in length. The ravages of these monsters were everywhere discernible through the forests. In some places long avenues were cut through the tree tops, and here and there great trees, three and four feet in thickness, were burst open and split to very shreds. In one remarkable respect this battle field differed in appearance from any of the preceding days. In the track of the enemy's flight there were no cast-away blue great coats, no blankets, tents nor clothing; no letters and no wasted commissary stores. He had, evidently, before reaching this point, thrown away everything that could retard his hasty retreat.—Nothing was to be found on, this portion of the field but killed and wounded Yankees and their guns and knapsacks. A mute, and to Virginians a most interesting story, was told by these knapsacks. *Upwards of three hundred of them belonged to the famous New York Seventh Regiment*, who were once so feasted and fondled in Richmond. If a remnant of them return to the Empire City they may say with truth that, on Virginia soil they were appropriately welcomed on the occasion of both their visits as friends and as foes.

REPORTED REINFORCEMENT OF M'CLELLAN ON HIS RETREAT.

There are various rumors afloat on Thursday and Friday that McClellan had received large reinforcements on his retreat, which might assist in accounting for the spirit he had displayed in the furious battles of Monday and Tuesday. We are unable to ascertain what truth there may be in these rumors; but are inclined to believe from such information as we have that McClellan was heavily reinforced before the engagements on the Chickahominy commenced from the Federal forces in other parts of Virginia, and that the reinforcements reported to be in the river are from the same resources. The Northern journals are unreserved in the statement that the commands of Fremont, Banks and McDowell have been consolidated into one army, under Major General Pope, with a view of bringing all the Federal forces in Virginia to co-operate with McClellan on the Richmond lines. A portion of this army must have reached McClellan, probably at an early stage of the engagements in the vicinity of Richmond, as General McCall, who was taken prisoner by us, is known to have commanded a division of McDowell's troops. There is little doubt but that we have engaged an army whose superiority in numbers to us was largely increased by timely reinforcements, and with regard to the operations of which the Northern Government had omitted no conditions of success.

THE LATEST FROM THE SCENE OF OPERATIONS.

Thursday night we received reliable information from the neighborhood of the river that General Lee yesterday morning had sent couriers over the whole extent of his lines to ascertain whether the enemy had made any egress, and had carefully reconnoitered his position, and was satisfied that his lines still enclosed a considerable portion of McClellan's forces in the densely wooded and swampy ground in which we described him as having taken refuge. It is supposed that considerable numbers of the enemy who have reached the river have crossed it, retreating towards Norfolk. The enemy enclosed on this side of the river had been stripped of a great deal of his artillery.

It was reported yesterday (Friday) that Jackson has cut off a portion of the enemy's rear guard and taken several thousand prisoners; but we can get no particulars, and find the rumor confirmed only in the circumstance that General Lee had sent an order to the city for prison accommodations for ten thousand men. The reports from the lines yesterday are meagre; but we are informed of an important movement of our troops, the publication of which is not advisable. There are other military topics, which were the subject of a good deal of personal gossip yesterday, to which we think any reference at this time improper and injurious. It is not probable that General Lee will fight the enemy or make any peremptory demand for his capitulation until he has completed the circuit of movements already in progress. Yesterday the Yankee gunboats in the river fired a national salute in honor of the day (Fourth of July).

OUR LOSS IN KILLED AND WOUNDED.

It would be an injustice as well to our brave soldiers, whose efforts have distinguished the last seven days with such great achievements, as to our readers, who expect from us just and intelligent statements of facts, to attempt to underrate the immense loss of our army in killed and wounded. Of course, such an estimate as we must make is founded upon uncertain calculations, but we are assured that we shall not exceed the limits of the facts in making it, since Thursday, June 26, at least fifteen thousand. Although these figures are terrible, we have good reason for believing the loss of the enemy twice as large; for it must be remembered that, although the Confederates have made the attack, the enemy has exposed himself every time in retiring, and whenever his rear has been turned to his adversary he has been pursued with terrible fury, and has tracked the route of his retreat with evidences of the most appalling slaughter.

THE YANKEE WOUNDED.

Since the battle of the Seven Pines, when, though throughout the day of the 31st of May, we drove the enemy before us, occupying his positions one after another, but one hundred and sixty-four of his wounded fell into our hands, we have been convinced that the organization of his ambulance corps had been brought to a point nearly approaching perfection. In the bloody battles recently fought we observe the same extraordinary vigor and success in the removal of their wounded. From every field which they have abandoned, no matter in what haste and confusion, they have borne them off, at least to their rear, and out of our sight. Marking the absence of their wounded and distinguished dead from every field, many of us began to entertain serious fears that their losses were trifling compared with our own. It remained for his repeated defeats, which necessitated his entire abandonment of his positions of the past month, to draw aside the veil from what was becoming a painful mystery, and disclose to our gaze the secret of what became of the enemy's wounded. It was his custom to hurry them to hospitals in the rear, from which they were leisurely, as their condition would permit, sent by rail to the White House. But since his signal defeat at Gaines' farm on yesterday week, and his consequent loss of railway communication, our columns have pressed him so hotly as to necessitate his abandoning many of these hospitals before the inmates could be removed. In this way large numbers of them have fallen into our hands. It is, doubtless, true that the majority of his men wounded since Sunday are either now along with his army, or have been sent ahead down the north bank of James river, in the wagons which observant persons at City Point thought were "empty, because they made such a rumbling noise;" but yet, at least between six and eight thousand have been left in the track of the retreating army. The hospitals of which we speak dot the country at intervals of a mile or two from Dr. Gaines', in Hanover, to Curl Neck, on James river, a distance of sixteen miles. Besides, every farm-house, and every barn and stable have been sought as places of refuge by such of their wounded as were able to walk or crawl!

THE YANKEE DEAD.

From facts which came to light on the morning succeeding the terrific battle of last Tuesday, we feel convinced that in every fight previously the Yankees managed to carry off not only all their wounded but a large number of their dead. It will be recollected that the severest of the battle of Tuesday was fought upon the adjoining farms of Dr. Carter and Mr. Cornelius Crew. On Wednesday morning, when our troops occupied the position just vacated by the enemy, they found in Mr. Crew's garden a thousand dead, as if in preparation to be carried off. Fear of our advance evidently alone led to their abandonment. This removal of the dead, under his present desperate circumstances, can have but one object: to dishearten our men by imposing upon them the belief that they are the greatest sufferers in every renewal of the contest.

The New-York Times.

VOL. XI—NO. 3366. NEW-YORK, TUESDAY, JULY 8, 1862. PRICE TWO CENTS.

GEN. McCLELLAN'S ARMY.

Details of Events to the Afternoon of the Fourth.

The Battles which Followed the One at Gaines' Hill.

Allen's Farm, Savage's Station, Nelson's Farm and Malvern Hills.

Vain Attempts of the Rebels to Force Our Lines.

A SKIRMISH ON THE FOURTH.

Reported Capture of a Thousand Rebel Prisoners and Three Batteries.

LIST OF CASUALTIES.

From the Special Correspondent of the New-York Times.

HARRISON'S BAR LANDING, JAMES RIVER, Friday, July 4, 1862.

The Army of the Potomac rests to-day, after six consecutive and connecting battles, after toils which few armies have ever endured, after a week of continual fighting and marching, leaving behind it thousands of brave men on hard-fought and well-contested battle-fields—after all this, it rests this Independence Day by the side of the beautiful James, to recover strength and proudly tell and retell the story of the memorable movement so happily and yet so sadly accomplished. As I write, my ears catch the unwonted strains of the regimental bands, discoursing patriotic and martial music. Massed around are the solid columns of the great army, forgetful of the toils of the past in the memory of its glory, and the hope of future success. For the first time since last week Thursday, more than a week ago, there is opportunity to pause and collect the events of the week in a continuous story. You have already had full and careful accounts of the great battle of Friday, which strewed the north bank of the insignificant, swampy, pestilential Chickahominy Creek with thousands of the slain and the disabled. I shall, therefore, confine myself to a statement of the events connected with the great military movement, whereby a vast army, in the face of an enemy of superior numbers and intense activity, has *changed its front and defeated every attempt at interference with the plan.*

PREPARATIONS TO FALL BACK.

The great mass of the army, occupying the intrenchments extending for miles from the Chickahominy to the left, were not apprised until midnight of Friday last, after PORTER's hard-pressed corps had partially yielded to the overwhelming force of the enemy, of the intention of Gen. McCLELLAN to change his base from the York to the James River. At that hour orders were received to put everything in readiness for a movement at daylight. Accordingly tents were quickly struck, baggage packed, wagons loaded, and everything prepared for a march, the men meantime getting with alacrity under arms. At 4 o'clock Saturday afternoon the long line of wagons moved down the Williamsburgh and other roads toward the rear—an immense train. The army remained in the intrenchments during the night standing to arms. It commenced moving at 4 o'clock in the morning, just before the appearance of the sun above the tops of the trees to the east, and amid a considerable fog, which threw its kindly obscuring veil over the movement, and blinded the sharp eyes of the enemy. During the evening of Saturday, in various places in the rear of our lines, bonfires had been made of Commissary and Quartermaster's stores, that nothing might fall into the eager hands of the hungry enemy. TURNER's, HEINTZELMAN's and FRANKLIN's corps fell back, nearly simultaneously, at 4 o'clock Sunday morning, a distance of one mile, one hour after drawing in their pickets and taking up their position in line of battle at Orchard Station.

Gen. KEYES' corps had, at about noon of Saturday moved from their line, as the advance toward White Oak Swamp and the Chickahominy, the Engineer corps, the Fiftieth and Fifteenth New-York, the latter under the efficient command of Col. McLEOD MURPHY, whose services in this movement the whole army appreciate, going before to prepare the way and build bridges. The first duty of our troops, after reaching Orchard Station, was to destroy the large quantity of stores which had been gathered there, and which our rebel friends, still ignorant of our movement, had long laid covetous eyes upon. Some ten thousand boxes of crackers, a large number of packages of coffee, barrels of sugar, molasses, beef and other stores, a great quantity of intrenching tools, ammunition and Quartermaster's stores, a rocket battery, powder and shell for siege guns, &c., were burned or otherwise so destroyed as to be of no use to the enemy soon to occupy this ground. This important work done, the smoke and noise it occasioned giving the alarm to the enemy, our brave soldiers stood to arms, awaiting the advance of the rebels, who soon were reported to be rushing in great numbers, with cheers and yells, into our abandoned and beautifully constructed intrenchments, and exploring in vain the deserted camps for booty. There was no chance for loot. Everything was gone.

At nine o'clock the enemy, who had formed into line and commenced the pursuit, made their appearance, to the left of SEDGWICK's Division, driving in the Fifth New-Hampshire, one of Gen. CALDWELL's admirable regiments, and of the brigade which was acting as the advance guard. Our forces were ready for the attack. SEDGWICK's Division held the left, resting on the railroad, joining HEINTZELMAN's right held by HOOKER's Division, RICHARDSON's Division occupying the right of SEDGWICK, these two latter divisions being of Gen. SUMNER's corps. Gen. FRANKLIN's corps occupied the extreme right, thus putting Gen. SUMNER's force in the centre. The firing soon extended along the line, until it reached the left of RICHARDSON's Division. Gen. SEDGWICK soon repulsed the enemy, who had been pouring upon his firm columns a steady galling fire of artillery and musketry. The enemy, then, next appeared opposite Gen. RICHARDSON's centre, opening fiercely with artillery. Capt. HAZZARD's Fourth Regular Battery responded handsomely, assisted by one of Gen. SMITH's batteries, while the Fifty-third Pennsylvania, of Gen. FRENCH's Brigade, opened a heavy fire of musketry upon the rebels, advancing in solid and numerous columns upon us. The firing soon extended through RICHARDSON's Division, continuing with almost unexampled intensity for something like fifteen minutes, when the rebels were driven back. Three times they repeated the attack, and three times were driven back as at first. The ammunition of Capt. HAZZARD's Battery, which had been most beautifully served and doing terrible execution among the enemy, now giving out, Capt. PETTIT's Battery—Battery B, of the First New-York Artillery—came up, got immediately into position, and opened its eight 10-pounder Parrots upon the enemy. Capt. PETTIT almost immediately got the range of the rebels' cannon and soon silenced them. This engagement was fought on ALLEN's farm, and derives its name from that place.

The enemy now discovered the weak place in our lines, endeavoring to get into the gap necessarily left between SUMNER and FRANKLIN. We accordingly fell back in admirable order to Savage's Station, about two miles to the rear, with a view of destroying the material which had been there concentrated, and to make a further stand at that place. The work of destruction was forthwith commenced. A long line of cars loaded with ammunition and stores was blown up, the sound of the grand explosion reaching for miles, the smoke of the burning mass arising in a vast and beautiful column, which soon touched the sky and mingled with the clouds. Along the sides of the railroad, piles of stores were then given to the flames and the work of demolition was completed. Several engines which had been collected were fastened together, steam was gotten up, and they were sent at full speed to plunge into the mud and water of the Chickahominy, whose bridge a few miles below had been previously destroyed.

BATTLE AT SAVAGE'S STATION.

Our forces now took position in the large open field to the left of the railroad, opposite SAVAGE's house, the left occupying the edge of the woods, and the right extending down by the side of the railroad. It was now late in the afternoon; the men had already fought one battle, and been under arms two nights, yet they were ready for battle, and had no thought of yielding to the enemy—troops who never yet had been beaten, nor would be. At about 6 o'clock in the evening, the enemy, who had come down the Williamsburgh Road in pursuit, deployed in the woods to the left, and, in great numbers, opened the attack with artillery and musketry. The columns of Gen. SEDGWICK, posted in the plain to the right of the Williamsburgh Road, were first attacked. A fierce fire soon extended along the whole line of SEDGWICK, working destruction among his men. It was promptly and efficiently responded to by our troops, the rebels suffering terribly. The Eighty-eighth and Sixty-ninth New-York Regiments, of Gen. MEAGHER's Brigade, were now sent to SEDGWICK's support. Meantime, Gen. HEINTZELMAN's Corps had fallen back, taking the road towards White Oak Swamp, and leaving Gens. SUMNER's and FRANKLIN's Corps to carry on the fight. The contest continued until dark—8½ or 9 o'clock—when the enemy were again driven back, having suffered severe loss. We had also lost heavily in the two battles. In this affair, also, PETTIT's and HAZZARD's batteries did splendid service. Our troops, during the morning, commenced to retire towards the James River, FRANKLIN's Corps leaving first, SUMNER's following, RICHARDSON's Division acting as rear guard; Gen. FRENCH, of this division, handsomely executing the difficult task of protecting the extreme rear, and bringing all of his men off. At 12 o'clock, midnight of Sunday, all our forces were moving down the road to White Oak Swamp in good order, the enemy having suffered so severely as to be unable to continue the pursuit that night. The most painful thing connected with this falling back was the imperative necessity which compelled us to leave many of our sick and wounded in the battles upon the field and in SAVAGE's house, in the hands of the enemy. Several physicians and nurses, with hospital stores, were, however, left with them, and they doubtless will be and have been well cared for. Including the wounded of the battles of Mechanicsville and Gaines' Hill, with those of Allen's Farm and Savage's Station, *at least from three to five thousand wounded must have been left in the hands of the rebels.* I hazard much in making this estimate, but think I must fall below rather than exceed the actual number; but I would avoid any exaggeration in this painful matter.

BATTLE OF NELSON'S FARM.

The last of our forces falling back, reached the White Oak Swamp, and crossed the bridge at daylight—5 o'clock—Monday morning. Gen. RICHARDSON bringing up and protecting the rear, succeeded in getting over the bridge a long transportation train, which was in imminent danger of falling into the hands of the enemy, and in collecting and driving forward a large number of stragglers, who had got separated from their regiments during the night. Everything over, he destroyed the bridge, and formed line of battle adjacent to the Swamp, placing his batteries on some commanding hills, his Division taking the centre, SMITH on his right, KEARNEY, HOOKER and McCALL on the left. PORTER and KEYES, who had advanced beyond, moved back and connected to the left of HOOKER. At about 10 o'clock in the morning, the rebels, who had got twelve rifled guns, most of them three-inch bore, opened a terrific fire on Gen. RICHARDSON's Division, who, though sheltered as much as possible by the hills, lost heavily under it—some 200 men—the shell pouring in with terrible intensity for two hours. Capt. HAZZARD's Battery, of RICHARDSON's Division, MOTT's and AYRE's Batteries, of Gen. SMITH's Division, responded shot for shot. MOTT, however, lost one gun, which was spiked, after having been dismounted, and several caissons. Capt. HAZZARD's Battery, after fighting splendidly for three hours, had so suffered in the loss of cannoneers, and its gallant commander himself having been wounded in the leg, that it was obliged to retire. He was relieved by Capt. PETTIT's Battery, which came trotting upon the field, and speedily opened a well-directed fire upon the rebels. This skillful artillerist succeeded in silencing the enemy's guns after some three hours' fire. At Nelson's Farm, our infantry soon became engaged in a fight with the forces of the enemy pressing on in great force.

The rebels opening on HEINTZELMAN at about 3 o'clock, McCALL's, HOOKER's and KEARNEY's Divisions now became actively engaged. The fight continued during the afternoon, with great intensity, the loss on both sides being heavy. Toward evening, the overpowered reserves of Gen. McCALL's Division were evidently wavering, and it looked to an observer as if the battle was going against us. Gen. HEINTZELMAN now sent to Gen. RICHARDSON for help, whereupon Lieut. CHARLES DRAPER, his Aid, brought up to the field of battle, through a most murderous fire, Gen. CALDWELL's already well-tested brigade, and they forthwith plunged into the engagement. At this hour—6½ o'clock in the evening—the roads were lined with exhausted soldiers, and batteries broken and empty of ammunition were hurrying from the field. Gen. CALDWELL did not arrive a moment too soon. Riding rapidly through the clouds of dust and smoke, so thick and heavy that all view of the operations was obstructed, the gallant General led his hardy men on into the fight, every man in order, a column not large, but powerful in courage and will. The tide of battle was soon turned, Gen. MEAGHER bringing his fiery brigade up a little later, and assisting in holding the ground. Night closed in, the enemy again driven back, leaving the field strewn with his wounded and slain, but not yet beaten sufficiently to prevent continued pursuit in the morning.

During the night our forces continued the line of march toward the James River, Gen. FRENCH again covering the retreat. At six o'clock on Tuesday morning they arrived at Haxall's Landing, weary with the exhaustion of five battles and continuous night marches, with little food and scarcely any sleep, unable to understand, and therefore bewildered and partially discouraged by the constant falling back, but not prepared to be beaten, nor exhausted of courage. A portion of the army were already concentrated on Malvern Hills, two miles back of the landing, near the residence and on the place of Mr. DEW, a wealthy Virginia planter, whose sharp-gabled, old-fashioned and eminently comfortable mansion had, during the Revolutionary war, been occupied for a short time by Gen. WASHINGTON as his headquarters, and near by which that General had built a redoubt, commanding with its guns the James River, whose clear waters could easily be seen from the grounds. Here was subsequently fought

THE BATTLE OF MALVERN HILLS.

At eight o'clock Tuesday morning, our forces having been concentrated at this point, the line of battle was formed, Gen. FRANKLIN holding the right, resting on the James River, and Gen. PORTER the extreme left, Gens. KEYES and HEINTZELMAN occupying the centre. Gen. SUMNER's corps was held in reserve. At nine o'clock the rebels opened the battle with a heavy fire of artillery, to which we responded from numerous batteries which had been placed along the hill-sides in commanding positions. The day was a beautiful one, clear and cloudless, unless from the smoke of the incessant artillery fire; the position a fine one; an open country, with rolling ground fringed by thick woods; the James River in sight, and on its waters, cleared for action, two gunboats, the *Jacob Bell* and *Galena*, kindly auxiliaries, whose 100-pounders poured awful missiles of death into the woods above the river, by whose sides rebel reinforcements were coming, in heavy numbers. The fire of the artillery on the hills was kept up during the day, the rebels getting decidedly the worst of it. They, beyond disparagement, fought nobly. We could see several of their batteries pushed out beyond the woods, and almost hear the commands of their officers. Their infantry marched up in solid columns by brigades of ten to the support of the batteries, and would press forward in the face of galling fires toward our artillery, determined to make trophies of our guns. Maintaining their close columns, they pushed forward to receive first our shot and shell, and then drawing nearer, to be mowed down by grape and canister. Facing this as long as they could, they would at length wheel around and march back again in good order, leaving the ground covered with their fallen. *Again and again, with new regiments, this was repeated, and again and again shot and shell, grape and canister gave them awful punishment.* It was too much to be borne, and at last they no longer marched back in columns, but ran hurrying for life from the terrible ministers of death.

At three o'clock in the afternoon the enemy opened a fierce musketry fire upon COUCH, which quickly extended along the line, including KEARNEY and PORTER in its fire. For three hours the battle raged fiercely, the sound of musketry and artillery deafening the ear. Up to six o'clock it was an equal game—if anything, we were getting the worst of it. At 6 o'clock in the evening Gen. PORTER sent word by an aid, who drove hastily up, dust-covered and well-nigh exhausted, to Gen. SUMNER, who, as Senior General, was in command, saying that he must have reinforcements or lose the day. Gen. SUMNER immediately directed that two of RICHARDSON's Brigades—Gen. CALDWELL's and Gen. MEAGHER's—be sent to his assistance. Gen. HEINTZELMAN at the same time sent two of HOOKER's—Gen. SICKLES' Excelsior Brigade and Gen. PATTERSON's New-Jersey Brigade. These new men, fighting with a courage and determination of which the annals of war cannot furnish a superior, drove the enemy until dark, and decided the fate of the Battle of Malvern Hills and the Army of the Potomac. Night coming on, we held the hard-fought and thickly strewn field, having in every engagement during the progress of the movement toward James River beaten and held in check a powerful and superior enemy, at Allen's Farm, Savage's Station, Nelson's Farm and Malvern Hills—a series of battles scarcely paralleled in history. The rebels were so thoroughly beaten that they could no longer pursue with the rapidity or vigor which had characterized their movements, since our movement for a change of position was inaugurated.

TO CAMP ON JAMES RIVER.

The firing of artillery continued until near midnight, at which hour we commenced to fall back on this position. Gen. McCLELLAN having meantime gone forward and selected it, Gen. HEINTZELMAN covered the movement, and at an early hour on Tuesday morning the army was collected here, transportation trains, artillery and troops, welcomed by a beating rain-storm, for which the incessant smoke of the artillery fire was largely responsible. The men were, many of them, exposed for hours, unsheltered, to the beating rain, after they arrived, as they had been during the march; but it was impossible to prevent it. Toward night, however, they had camps arranged, and to-day, after a good night's rest, they marched out to a Fourth-of-July review, as if they had gone through nothing more than a series of sham fights in Washington or on Boston Common.

WE TAKE A BATTERY.

In the afternoon of yesterday, the rebels got a couple of rifled field pieces in position on a hill commanding our camps, and commenced a shelling which did some damage among our crowded wagon camps. The gunboats responded with a few shot, but did not get the range. The little pests must be stopped, and the Fifth Maine undertook the work. Advancing stealthily through the woods they came suddenly upon the battery, flanking it and taking both the guns, and all the cannoneers and their officers. It was a handsomely executed manœuvre, and the Maine men deserve great credit for it. At the battle of Nelson's Farm the Sixty-first New-York captured a splendid stand of colors from the enemy, on which was inscribed "Williamsburgh and Seven Pines." At the battle of Malvern Hills COUCH's Division also captured a rebel flag.

OUR LOSS IN KILLED, WOUNDED AND PRISONERS in all the engagements, Mechanicsville and Gaines' Mill included, can hardly fall far short, or much exceed *twenty-five thousand men*. Our loss in prisoners is heavy, the enemy's cavalry making easy captives of thousands of stragglers who lined the roads in our rear, and besides these we have left thousands of wounded in their hands. Their loss must be at least as heavy, and probably heavier in killed and wounded than our own, but in prisoners it fell far short, though we have taken about two thousand from them. Included in our loss were many of our finest officers, the number of line, company and staff officers killed and disabled, being unusually large. I inclose a list as complete as it is possible to get together, and shall see that the TIMES is soon provided with the whole of the official reports of casualties. Our loss of guns is stated at forty, and we have taken from the enemy perhaps two-thirds that number. To compute the value of the property—stores, cars, ammunition, &c.—destroyed by us in our change of position is impossible, with the scanty data I have at hand, but it must amount to two or three millions of dollars.

THE CHANGE OF BASE

was necessitated by the impossibility of holding our extended lines with the army which Mr. STANTON would grant to Gen. McCLELLAN. Our front extended from Mechanicsville on the right to White Oak Swamp on the left, a distance of fifteen miles. Besides defending this against a greatly superior force of the rebels, to say nothing of satisfying the ambition of the Secretary of War and Congress for an immediate advance, we were obliged to guard some twenty miles of railway, from White House to Fair Oaks. *Gen. McClellan had not enough men to hold this position* after the reinforcement of the rebels by Stonewall JACKSON and others, and he became convinced of this after the dash of Gen. STUART's Cavalry. Our right was constantly subject to the danger of being turned, and our army being surrounded. The rebels knew that this was our weak position, and when they could bring an overwhelming force to bear against it and were sure of success, they made the attempt. Our right wing, held by Gen. PORTER, was turned last Friday, and *the army has only escaped a terrible fate by the masterly accomplishment of one of the most difficult and delicate movements which an army can undertake, the change of its base in face of the enemy by a flank movement.* The glorious success of the movement is the defeat of the rebels, and the order with which our soldiers have gone through it, proves them to be of the very best kind, reliable and worthy of the world's applause. Gen. McCLELLAN owes everything to his soldiers and to some of his leading Generals, for the success which has attended a movement upon which he hazarded the safety of his whole army.

The position which we now occupy is one which our engineers say we can defend against anything JEFF. DAVIS or any other monarch can bring to bear upon us. Our line, instead of being fifteen miles front, with twenty miles of railway to defend, is scarcely five miles long. One of our flanks is the James River, not a railroad to be torn up, nor a highway that may be obstructed, but a sure means of conveying supplies, and easily defended by gunboats. Our other line is readily held by the force we can bring. We occupy the centre of a circle, which greatly facilitates celerity of movement, and are so positioned that no artillery can be brought to bear upon us by the enemy within effective range. If we could only have occupied this same position six weeks ago, instead of the difficult one we took, your correspondent would now be dating his letters at Richmond, instead of twenty odd miles below there. Though further from Richmond than we were last Thursday, in miles and furlongs, in effect we are nearer that stubborn capital, and surer of its capture. I will not venture to name the exact date when we shall exchange the hardships of the camp for such luxuries as Richmond will afford, but the day cannot be far distant, if other coöperative movements are properly conducted. The army is in excellent spirits to-day, and disposed to let off a deal of Fourth of July patriotism and powder. The *Galena*, the *Jacob Bell*, the *Aroostook*, the *Monitor* and other gunboats are with us, and they are welcome visitors. The river is already full of craft, and is rapidly getting to look the same great mart of commerce which distinguished the Pamunkey at White House.

MERITORIOUS OFFICERS.

The number of these is so great that it is impossible to mention any without leaving out many more equally meritorious. Of the Generals great and just praise is accorded to Gens. SUMNER and HEINTZELMAN, Corps Commanders; Gens. Richardson, Kearney, Hooker, Couch, Smith and Sedgwick, to whom, as Division Commanders, the historian of this war and this movement will give such meed of praise as to satisfy the ambition of the most ambitious. Gen. CALDWELL, who, since the battle of Fair Oaks, and the wounding of Gen. HOWARD, has commanded that gentlemanly and Christian officer's Brigade, has demonstrated rare soldierly ability, and won the enthusiastic confidence of his men. His Brigade was in every fight but those of Mechanicsville and Gaines' Hill, and lost perhaps more severely than any other in proportion to the number of men he brought into action. I was personally a witness of the gallantry of Lieuts. DRAPER, MILLER and HURLBURT, of Gen. RICHARDSON's Staff, and Capt. MILES, of Gen. CALDWELL's, and hear a like good tale of the other Staff Officers of the different Generals. Gen. FRENCH receives great and deserved praise for the masterly manner in which he covered the rear of our retreating columns, during the whole of the movement. To Gen. Meagher Gen. Brooks, Gen. Burns, Gen. Dana, and Gen. Gorman, the country cannot accord too much credit.

F. P. C.

CAMP AT HARRISON'S BAR, JAMES RIVER, July 4, 1862.

Worn as the soldiers are after their long continuous marches and severe fighting, they responded heartily to the following order, issued from headquarters early in the morning:

HEADQUARTERS ARMY OF THE POTOMAC, CAMP NEAR HARRISON'S LANDING, July 3, 1862.

CIRCULAR.—I. A National salute will be fired at noon to-morrow, at the headquarters of each Army Corps. Immediately thereafter, the bands will play appropriate National airs.

The General Commanding will visit all the troops during the afternoon, when the troops will be paraded and a Major-General's salute fired in each corps. The troops will be notified of the hour of the visit.

II. Regimental commanders must now see that the sick are taken care of, within the limits of their respective regiments, and not permitted to be sent away, except by orders from these headquarters.

III. The camp of General Headquarters has been removed into the woods, a short distance further up the river, than this morning's camp.

By command of Maj.-Gen. McCLELLAN.

(Signed) S. WILLIAMS, Asst. Adjt.-Gen.

The storm which yesterday drenched many a poor fellow's dusty uniform and chilled his tired frame, and which reduced the clayey soil to that pasty adhesive condition which offends the patience of the pedestrian and tries the nerves of horse and rider alike, passed over during the night, and Independence Day came in with a gladdening sun to cheer the hearts of the army. During yesterday, in spite of mud and rain, the mass of troops which had been poured in here so hastily was reduced to order, and corps and divisions had their definite positions assigned to them, prepared camp grounds, and the men spread couches to enjoy the first real rest which had been permitted them for a week. The long pull of sleep they got last night told on the troops. It was a far happier, brighter, stronger set of men who stood about the camp-fires this morning than that which the day before shivered in the rain. At about noon the bands, such of them as still have musicians and instruments wholly or partially complete, played National airs, which unusual sounds did much to enliven the camps, for months debarred the luxury of music by an imperative order, necessitated by the near proximity of the rebels, who could, from our music, discover our position. A little after noon Gen. McCLELLAN, with his staff, in costumes cleaned of the mud and rust of the long journey, commenced the round of visits to the different corps. The Commanding General looked in excellent spirits, not discovering in the least any appearance of fatigue. He took the different corps in order, reviewing the men, his arrival welcomed in every division by the firing of a Major-General's salute, and he himself received by the troops with hearty cheers, which kept mingling along the whole line, as he passed from brigade to brigade. It was a touching sight to view the thinned ranks drawn up before their General, the warn-worn veterans, no longer the scholar-soldiers whom he reviewed in Washington last November, but heroes of six, eight and ten battles, who had attested their courage and devotion, and won the right to the name of soldiers. Gen. McCLELLAN looked with particular interest on brigades which had suffered very severely in the late battles, and expressed his sorrow at the gaps in their lines, but as Gen. CALDWELL told in answer to such an expression of regret in regard to his Brigade, they died in doing their duty, and the rest were ready to do the same thing. The visit and review of the General occupied nearly the whole of the afternoon, during all which time, the hills resounded with the salutes. The whole ceremony was one of the most impressive and touching that could possibly be witnessed, and cannot be without its good effects upon commander and men. The soldiers on their own part celebrated the Fourth with the popping of guns—forbidden sport—and best of all, by quietly resting and going over the story of the last week's fights.

In the afternoon the enemy had a sharp skirmish with our pickets on the edge of James River, in which we gave them a few artillery reminders, which stopped their demonstrations, but not until they had killed and wounded some twenty of our men. Otherwise, everything is quiet along the lines.

F. P. C.

BATTLE OF CHARLES CITY COURT-HOUSE.

The Most Desperate Conflict of the Week—Final Repulse of the Enemy—Couch and Abercrombie the Heroes of the Day, &c.

From our Own Correspondent.

HARRISON'S LANDING, Wednesday, July 2, 1862.

The most desperate fight attending the withdrawal of Gen. McCLELLAN from the intrenchments, and the opening of communication with James River, took place on Tuesday, July 1, at Charles City Court-house. In this battle the whole of COUCH's Division was engaged. It commenced about 6½ o'clock in the morning, by a cannonade between an immense body of the enemy which had come down from Richmond the night before, and the troops of Gen. COUCH, which had advanced their position in that direction to command the roads. This is the key to the present position of the army.

Many of the regiments engaged had been badly reduced by the previous battles. For instance, the United States Chasseurs, Lieut.-Col. SHALER, had only 300 men; the First Long Island, Lieut.-Col. CROSS, had about 350; the Sixty-first Pennsylvania Volunteers, Lieut.-Col. VALLEE, 306; the Thirty-first Pennsylvania, Col. WILLIAMS, took in 370, and the Twenty-third Pennsylvania, Col. NEILL, had about 400 men. These comprised the whole of ABERCROMBIE's Brigade, of COUCH's Division. When they left Washington they numbered over 4,000, and after the battle of Seven Pines only 2,998.

At about 7 A. M. the First Chasseurs, Lieut.-Col. SHALER, and the Sixty-first Pennsylvania, Col. VALLEE, were advanced to support Gen. HOWE. At 9 A. M., GRIFFIN's Battery was brought into position on the left, and Gen. HOWE was ordered to occupy the centre. His troops were mostly from New-York State, comprising the Sixty-second, Fifty-fifth, and others.

The shelling continued all this time from the enemy, and we were obliged to manœuvre wholly under fire. At 11 o'clock the enemy was seen in large force advancing in an oblique direction, at the same time making a *feint* on our right, but all the time deploying in large bodies with a view to turn our left flank. At about 12:30 the engagement became general, the enemy shelling our reinforcements by a continued cross fire. At 2 o'clock, Gen. COUCH announced to the troops upon the left that a stand of colors had been taken from the rebels by a charge of the Thirty-sixth New-York, which greatly inspirited our men, and they cheered lustily. In fifteen minutes after that, GRIFFIN's Battery captured the colors of a rebel battery—a splendid battle flag of crimson, having a black cross—the battery opposed to them. Gen. COUCH rode up and exclaimed that GRIFFIN's Battery had covered themselves with imperishable honors. Column after column of the Confederates dashed forward to capture the battery, but they were piled in heaps of dead in front of the guns. The enemy pressed up frequently to within one hundred yards, and meeting the deadly discharge of grape and canister, staggered and fell back. They fell like wheat before the reaper's sickle. The enemy here must have lost from three to four thousand men.

The caissons of GRIFFIN's Battery now becoming exhausted of ammunition, they gave way to a battery of KEARNEY's Division, under command of a Lieutenant whose name and battery are not now recollected, which kept up the same murderous fire on the enemy's ranks. Meantime the Sixty-first Pennsylvania and the New-York Chasseurs were ordered to the front. At this juncture the enemy made a desperate charge to capture the new battery, and the attempt was met by the whole of ABERCROMBIE's Brigade, led by Gen. ABERCROMBIE himself, who drove them back beyond their lines into the woods, where a destructive fire was opened upon them. Several batteries were brought into play, comprising some twelve guns. Meantime, ABERCROMBIE's and HOWE's Brigade remained in line of battle, delivering volley after volley of musketry among the staggering ranks of the enemy. They were so numerous at this point that as soon as one regiment gave way, *another, fresh and furious, would take its place as if nothing had happened.*

Night came on, obliging the infantry to cease, but the artillery kept up the same continuous fire as at the beginning, and our wearied and exhausted soldiers retired under the same galling fire which greeted them in the morning. They fell back, led by Gens. COUCH and ABERCROMBIE, who were omnipresent on the field throughout the day. Notwithstanding the severe character of the contest, and the overwhelming numbers of the enemy, the loss of the Union forces, owing to the masterly manner in which the troops were handled, was not large.

The Sixty-first Pennsylvania lost, say 20; the Long Island, 25; the First Chasseurs, 40; the Twenty-third Pennsylvania, 20; and the Thirty-first Pennsylvania about 30. Total, probably about 135.

Capt. N. ELLMAKER, the Brigade Commissary, succeeded in safely bringing off the field the whole of his wagon train and Commissary stores.

The whole force of 60,000 men were withdrawn along the road leading toward Harrison's Landing, and not a man in the division seemed to know that we were retreating.

During the thickest of the fight, while Col. VALLEE's Regiment was lying in front of the enemy in the form of the letter L, an Irish regiment came up on the double quick, and the Colonel addressing VALLEE, asked, "Who commands this regiment?" "I do," said the Colonel. "I want to go through here," said the commander of the advancing regiment. It was now quite dark. "Roll over, boys, and let them through," said Col. VALLEE; and through they went with a yell and a jump, and dashed upon the enemy in the most impetuous manner. This was very timely succor, for many of the guns had become foul from long use, and the balls would not go down in the guns.

E. S.

LIST OF CASUALTIES.

OFFICERS KILLED.

Col Salon H Taggart, 12th Penn Reserves.
Lieut-Col Fisher, 5th Pennsylvania.
Lieut Parker, of Gen Sykes' Staff.
Lieut Adams, 6th Regular Infantry.
Lieut-Col Skillen, 14th New-York.
Capt McGonegal, 72d Pennsylvania.
Col Gore, 22d Massachusetts.
Col Black, 62d Pennsylvania.
Major Rosell, United States Infantry.
Col McLane, — Pennsylvania.
Col Gosline, 95th Pennsylvania.
Major Hobbs, 95th Pennsylvania.
Lieut Donahue, 95th Pennsylvania.
Col Biddle, Gen McCall's Staff.
Col Wyman, 16th Massachusetts.
Lieut Leaton, Berdan Sharpshooters.
Capt Drew, Berdan Sharpshooters.
Lieut Samuel Lowell, 20th Massachusetts.
Lieut-Col Conner, 81st Pennsylvania.
Col Washburn, 4th Michigan.
Lieut Pulford, 5th Michigan.
Capt De Pugh, 4th Michigan.
Capt Carr, 16th Michigan.

OFFICERS WOUNDED.

Capt Irving, Pennsylvania Bucktails—legs.
Capt Jewett, Co D, Pennsylvania Bucktails—back.
Adj Hartshorn, Co K, Penn Bucktails—head.
Lieut Riddel, Co F, Pennsylvania Bucktails.
Maj Clitz, 14th Regular Infantry.
Lieut H A Worth, 6th Regular Infantry.
Lieut Jordan, 2d Regular Infantry.
Lieut Lynn, 6th Regular Infantry.
Lieut Inman, 17th New-York.
Lieut Whiting, Gen Palmer's Aid—arm amputated.
Gen Burns—face, slightly.
Gen Brooks—flesh wound in leg.
Gen Meade.
Lieut Blakeney, Gen Burns' Aid,
Gen Reynolds,
Lieut Scott, Gen Caldwell's Aid.
Capt Hazzard, 4th Regular Artillery—leg.
Lieut Hill, Regular Artillery.
Lieut Roberts, 95th Pennsylvania.
Capt Carroll, 95th Pennsylvania.
Capt Brookbank, Co G, 9th Penn Reserve.
Capt Cuthbertson, Co H, 9th Penn Reserve.
Lieut Winans, 9th Penn Reserve—slightly.
Col Baxter, Baxter's Zouaves.
Lieut-Col Ripley, Berdan's Sharpshooters—leg
Lieut Abbatt, 20th Massachusetts—arm.
Capt Halliwell, 20th Massachusetts.
Col Lee, 20th Massachusetts.
Lieut-Col Miller, 20th Massachusetts—slightly.
Col Cass, 9th Massachusetts—mortally.
Lieut Polton, 20th Massachusetts—leg.
Col Johnson, 81st Pennsylvania.
Col Pierce, 29th Massachusetts.
Col John Burke, 63d New-York.
Major Fairbanks, 57th Michigan.

KILLED AND WOUNDED IN FRENCH'S BRIGADE (RICHARDSON'S DIVISION).

FIFTY-SECOND NEW-YORK VOLUNTEERS.

Theo Meyer, Co B—thigh, slightly.
Louis Herr, Co F—two fingers amputated.

FIFTY-SEVENTH NEW-YORK VOLUNTEERS.

Andrew Miller, Co A—inferior portion left ear.
Geo Boyer, Co A—scalp, slightly.
Capt Chas Mackay, Co F—contusion, left heel.
Philip Romaine, Co F—head, slight.
Owen Moshna, Co F—arm, amputated.
Wm Featherstone, Co K—left foot.
Thos Button, Co I—contusion, left shoulder.

SIXTY-SIXTH NEW-YORK VOLUNTEERS.

John Murphy, Co A—foot, slight.
Johannes Short, Co D—two fingers off right hand.
Geo Meyer, Co E—arm, flesh.
Geo Stevenson, Co E—one finger off.
G Munch, Co G—thigh, flesh.

FIFTY-THIRD PENNSYLVANIA VOLUNTEERS.

Corp Abram H Wiene, Co A—mortally.
Jonas Brickhart, Co A—fracture.
John Nolan, Co C—wounded and missing.
John Test, Co D—wounded and missing.
Sergt C B Wilson, Co D—killed.
Sergt Robert Tate, Co E—slightly.
Wm Stevens, Co E—slightly.
Lyman C Perry, Co G—wounded and missing.
Nelson Crowell, Co G—wounded.
A Jackson Rudel, Co G—fracture, clavis.
Sergt S T Pratt, Co H—thigh, missing.
Harvey Gieger, Co H—contusion, missing.
Theodore Scott, Co H—thigh, flesh.
William Moffit, Co H—hand, slight.
J P Holman, Co I.
J Reese, Co I—hand, slight.
Corporal Wm H Kuhns, Co K—wrist, severe.
Ezra Smith, Co K—slightly.
Henry Kern, Co K—slightly.
Jefferson Lewis, Co K—slightly.

SECOND DELAWARE VOLUNTEERS.

Corporal Frederick Speen, Co F—killed.
William Hipson, Co G—heel, left at White Oak Hospital.
Jacob Bowen, Co K—killed.

SIXTY-FOURTH NEW-YORK VOLUNTEERS.

Albert D Kerr, Co A—slightly.
Jesse Windsor, Co B—right leg broken by shell, prisoner.
Onar Stilwell, Co B—fractured elbow by runaway mule.
Oliver S Benet, Co E—right arm by shell, prisoner.
Smith M Demure, Co G—shoulder, severe.
George W Chandler, Co G—abrasure of hip.
Sergt James J Meservey, Co G—hand and breast, severe.
Sergt Sanfort B McClure, Co I—head by solid shot.
Matthew King, Co I—shoulder and lung, rifle ball.
Total—Killed, 3; wounded, 43.

MISCELLANEOUS.

G H Lee, 14th Michigan—shoulder, severely.
E Starkey, Co D, 22d Mass—side, severely.
G Dale, Co G, 2d Regulars—neck, severely.
S Wilcox, Co G, 8th Penn—shoulder, slightly.
W Guff, Co C, 2d Pennsylvania—arm, severely.
H Brewster, Co G, 5th Penn—side, slightly.
O Crahan, Co E, 9th Mass—neck, slightly.
A B Crane, Co K, 4th Michigan—jaw, shot.
D Simpkins, Co E, 3d New-Jersey—arm, slight.
J A Sawyer, Co A, 3d New-Jersey—side, severely.
H K White, Co F, 62d Penn—leg, slightly.
G L Prentiss, Co G, 10th Mass—foot, slightly.
R Wright, Co G, 14th Regulars—left eye, severely.
Orderly Sergt G Blake, 15th N Y—shoulder, slightly.
O Davenport, Co B, 7th Penn—arm, slightly.
J Mahon, Co D, 31st New-York—hand, slightly.
J Coine, Co I, 16th New-York—hip, slightly.
J Reilly, Co F, 57th New-York—hand, slightly.
Wm Creevye, Co C, 1st Reg Cav.—shoulder, severely.
Frank Howe, Co E, 83d Penn—arm, severely.
R H Ryan, Co. B, 8th Penn—hand, slightly.
Wm P Dean, Co D, 8th Penn—head, slightly.
Peter Meitt, Co E, 6th N Y—arm, severely.
Albert Garnsey, Co B, 4th Mich—hand, slightly.
Harvey P. Compton, Co A, 10th N Y—leg, slightly.
George Whitwell, Co I, 10th N Y—wrist, slightly.
Jacob F Long, Co A, 1st N Y—arm, slightly.
Joseph S Stanbary, Co A, 1st N Y—arm, slightly.
Hugh Chalmers, Co H, 5th N Y—arm, slightly.
John R Finch, Co G, 5th N Y—both arms, slightly.
N D Rodgers, Co G, 5th N Y—knee, slightly.
Francis Higgins, Co H, 5th N Y—thigh, slightly.
James O. Reed, Co H, 5th N Y—mouth, severely.
Patrick Henry, Co G, 14th Reg—both legs, severely.
Thos Crocker, Co G, 14th Reg—left arm, slightly.
Samuel J Gilman, Co A, 5th Me—arm shattered.
Wm Sharp, Co A, 3d Regulars—shoulder, severely.
Joseph S Scanlon, Co B, 9th Mass—hand, slightly.
Thos Quinlan, Co B, 9th Mass—shoulder, severely.
Sergt. G W Fowler, Co A, 2d Penn—right foot, slightly.
William McDonald, Co A, 2d Penn—side and foot, slightly.
A Margins, Co H, 9th Penn—hand, slightly.
J Archland, Co C, 18th N Y—breast, severely.
G M Brown, Co A, 5th Penn—leg, severely.
J G Llywelyn, Co B, 3d N J—arm, slightly.
B Finnigan, Co H, 2d Penn—arm, slightly.
F W Cowell, Co B, 3d N J—arm, slightly.
James Dillon, Co B, 3d N J—arm, slightly.
D Howell, 4th Penn Cavalry—lower jaw, severely.
Hiram M Stephenson, Co H, 5th Penn—shoulder, severely.
John Burk, Co B, 9th Mass—arm, slightly.
Chas E Roberts, Co I, 31st N Y—both hands.
Emanuel Stout, Co G, 6th Penn Lancers—head, severely.
Isaac L Brokaw, Co I, 3d N J—wrist, slightly.
Frank Carpenter, Co K, 14th N Y—hip, severely.
J W Donthill, Co K, 9th Penn—hand, slightly.
Ord Sergt J W Shurter, Co D, 5th New-York—hand, slightly.
Frederick Hare, Co B, 2d Regulars—thigh and hand, severely.
Thos Power, Co C, 2d Regulars—groin, severely.
L Habermold, Co B, 2d Regulars—back, severely.
W Welsh, Co K, 5th Penn—ankle, slightly.
1st Lieut Daniel Connors, Co A, 2d Penn—hand, slightly.
R. Kirkwood, Co A, 2d Penn—neck, slightly.
Sergt Wm Sanders, Co E, 2d Regulars—hand, slightly.
Michael McCarty, Co. B, 2d Regulars—hand, slightly.
Samuel C. Rutherford, Co. I, 95th Pennsylvania—wrist, severely.
Patrick O'Gorman, Co. K, 2d Regulars—hand, slightly.
Charles Brown, Co. B, 12th N. Y.—arm, slightly.
John McLoughlin, Co. A, 9th Mass.—side, severely.
Geo. H. Ward, Co. A, 10th N. Y.—head, slightly.
Andrew Flick, Co. D, 25th New-York—finger off.
Edward Loggre, Co. C, 2d Penn.—leg, severely.
Silas Rosendale, Co. K, 32d N. Y.—arm, slightly.
James Fleming, Co. K, 32d N. Y.—arm, slightly.
Joseph F. Tracy, Co. E, 6th Regular Infantry—leg, severely.
Johnson Dye, Co. K, 8th Pennsylvania—neck.
Mathias Taylor, Co. F, 3d New-York—leg, slightly.
Lawrence W. Mires, Co. D, 12th Regular Infantry—neck, slightly.
George Pearson, Co. D, 12th Regular Infantry—hip, severely.
Arthur C. Kretzler, Co. C, 5th New-York—thigh, severely.
Jas M Van Wagoner, Co I, 5th N Y—back, severely.
Fred Bibbman, Co K, 32d N Y—arm, slightly.
Jeremiah Mahoney, Co F, 12th N Y—wrist, slightly.
Sergt. Wm Crowley, Co L, 3d U S Art—breast, severely.
Edward Rooney, Co I, 5th N Y—arm, severely.
Asa Comstock, Co G, 10th Penn—arm, severely.
Robt D Wilson, Co I, 95th Penn—thigh, severely.
Patrick Flynn, Co H, 9th Mass—arm and fingers, severely.
Jordan M Nesmith, Co G, 8th Penn—thigh, severely.
Corp Frank Peabody, Co A, 3d N J—arm, severely.
Peter McGee, Co C, 8th Penn—leg, severely.
Thomas Slattery, Co H, 9th Mass—arm, severely.
Sergt. Jas W Topin, Co H, 9th Mass—arm, severely.
Wm H Ross, Co E, 4th Mich—head, severely.
Sergt Llywelyn Goodwin, Co F, 5th Me—leg, sev'ly.
Capt Louis D Naserre, Co D, 55th N Y—arm, slightly.
Jacob Kinly, Co I, 1st Penn—hip, severely.
Lieut Wm K Kern, Co H, 12th Penn—leg, slightly.
Sergt H E Cohen, Co H, 5th N Y—hip, severely.
Corp John Fay, Co H, 5th N Y—chin, severely.
Samuel Dunn, Co G, 8th Penn—arm, slightly.
James H O'Brien, Co E, 10th Regular Infantry—leg, severely.
Corp Stephen G George, Co K, 14th N Y—mouth, slightly.
Patrick Lynch, Co H, 9th Mass—breast, severely.
Sergt Chas Lewis, Co K, 14th N Y—leg, slightly.

[Continued on Eighth Page.]

The Charleston Mercury.

DAILY PAPER—Ten Dollars per Annum, Payable Half-Yearly in Advance.

SPONTE SUA SINE LEGE FIDES RECTUMQUE COLENTUR.—VINDICE NULLO

COUNTRY PAPER—Three a Week—Five Dollars per Annum, in Advance.

VOLUME LXXXI. CHARLESTON, S. C., SATURDAY, JULY 12, 1862. NUMBER 11,498

THE SITUATION OF THE ARMIES ABOUT RICHMOND.

For two days we have had no telegraphic advices whatever from Richmond. We have no means of explaining this unusual silence.

The Richmond *Examiner* of Wednesday says: "There were no active operations yesterday on the lines in the vicinity of the river. Of course we are under obligations to give our readers no information of any movements of troops, &c., that may be in progress; and we have invariably respected this obligation, so far as even not to allude to important changes of commands that have at any time taken place in the army, unless at the advice of some authorized representative of the views of the government. The situation of the two armies in the vicinity of Richmond is such as we do not feel at liberty to refer to any thing, beyond incidents which may take place on the lines, or results which have been accomplished or brought within the knowledge of the enemy. We may satisfy the curiosity of our readers, however, by assuring them that there is no immediate prospect of any general action with the enemy, and that it is likely that preparations of great extent will be made on both sides before the conflict will be renewed beyond the point to which it has already been brought."

The Richmond *Enquirer* of the same date says: "The movements of our army, for the past two days, have been entirely strategical. No fighting of importance has transpired, and at least for some days, so far as our advices indicate, none need be expected. It is sufficient for us to know: first, that MCCLELLAN has been defeated before Richmond, and second, that his immediate plans in changing his front have been frustrated through the superior ability of our generals. It will require a herculean effort for him to retrieve his fallen fortunes, an effort which will require time, patience and increasing energy. It is considered a physical impossibility for him to recruit his army in time for an early and earnest resumption of his 'On to Richmond" march. His *status*, at present, though not an idle one, is not and cannot be as active as our own. At no period in the history of the war has the Confederate Government manifested a more dashing and energetic spirit than that which is now permitted to inspire the commanders of our army, although that old temptation, 'foreign intervention,' looms up even more brilliantly and seductively than ever. The war has at length become an earnest one, the Confederate Government has ceased all parley with the rest of the world, and relying upon right and her own resources, is determined to pursue it to the bitter end. It would be imprudent to publish the movements which are now being made by our army. The public must be satisfied that they are wise, practical and essential to the success of the struggle."

We get the following from the Petersburg *Express*, of Thursday: A gentleman who came up yesterday, states that so far as can be discovered by observation on the south bank of James river, no important movements have taken place in MCCLELLAN'S army during the past three or four days. Many of the wagons have disappeared from view, and the tents have extended up the bank of the river almost to the very doors of the family mansion at Berkeley. By the smoke of the camp fires Tuesday evening, it was generally supposed that the enemy had advanced somewhat from the immediate banks of the different water courses by which he was at first almost completely surrounded. It is positively known that heavy reinforcements have reached the Yankee MCCLELLAN, and it is believed that his army now numbers nearly or quite 100,000 men. We have reason to believe that an important movement has been made by a portion of our forces, but the particulars will be known in a few days, and we refrain, for manifest good reasons, from giving them here.

THE MERCURY.

SATURDAY, JULY 12, 1862.

Obedience vs. Individual Judgment and Responsibility.

The foundation of the regulation of armies, is the principle of obedience. The inculcation and example—the theory and practice of military life, is blind, unquestioned obedience to authority. Whether right or wrong, wise or foolish, it does not matter or concern the subordinate. With him responsibility does not rest, save in the fulfillment of his instructions, within his assigned sphere.

But, while surrender of the opinions and judgment and will to the diction of officers of higher grade or older commission obtains in the army, the government under which we live is based upon a principle diametrically the opposite, viz: the exercise of individual judgment in all public matters, and the imposing of a liberal responsibility for results upon all public men. A republic, or republican confederacy, without responsibility to the people, and without the exercise of popular judgment, is republican in name only, and lacks the vital element of such a government.

Since the formation of the Confederate States the people of the South have exhibited a great proneness to surrender their opinions, judgments and wills to their Executive authorities, and an extraordinary zeal to encourage a blind, unquestioning obedience. They have readily acquiesced in being excluded from a knowledge of their own affairs, and in being kept in perfect darkness as to measures and the responsibilities of men. Results alone cannot be concealed. They have passed the responsibility of forming conclusions, and judging of men and measures, and have thrown it upon an untried President and a small Congress sitting in secret, and so subservient to Executive influences and undirected by public criticism. If, therefore, affairs have not been managed with that wisdom and vigor once expected and very desirable, the people must not wholly blame either the Congress for subserviency, or the Executive for dictation and weakness. The people of the South are themselves to blame for violating and setting aside the cardinal principle on which their representative government is constructed. When they have done their part of knowing the operations of their government and forming opinions, and making those opinions felt by their Representatives of the House and Senate and by the chosen Executive head of their government, then they will have done their duty. The responsibility and the blame of failures and disasters and calamities will be thrown from their shoulders upon those to whom it should properly belong, and the power of correction and reform would remedy our evils.

In the meantime, it would be well to ponder on the distinction between military rule and republican government, the principles on which they are respectively administered, and to ascertain which is now in operation and prevailing in the views and conduct of our people towards their government and its affairs.

THE NEWS OF THE WAR.

THE DEFEAT OF M'CLELLAN—FURTHER NORTHERN ACCOUNTS—ABANDONMENT OF WHITE HOUSE LANDING, ETC.

The Northern papers are filled with the details of MCCLELLAN'S late defeat. A correspondent of the New York *Tribune*, writting from White House Landing, Va., 11 o'clock, a. m., June 28, says:

THE EXCITEMENT.

My letters of this morning, which I sent you by the mail boat that left here at 9 o'clock, will have informed you of the general panic which prevailed here up to the time of her leaving.—Shortly after her departure, officers and wagon masters who rode down from the rear of our army, informed us that the enemy had possession of Dispatch Station (which is about midway between the army lines and White House). They also brought the intelligence that Gen. Stoneman, with about 5 000 men, was cut off, and was falling back on White House. This news created the wildest excitement, and a general stampede to the remaining barges and steamers took place. The steam tugs were now seen flying down stream with barges, schooners, and canal boats in tow—the latter crowded with every description of property piled up in the direst confusion, among which were mixed up contrabands, young and old, and of both sexes.

THE PREPARATIONS FOR LEAVING.

Gangs of laborers and fatigue parties from the 93d New York were now set to work at the commissariat, subsistence and forage departments, to pile up the heaps of stores, and prepare them for a grand and stupendous bonfire. Barrels of whisky and turpentine, with loose bundles of hay, were placed all around them. The railroad hands were not idle. The locomotives were seen darting up and down the track, collecting all the cars—most of which were freighted with every kind of stores required by our army—and backing them down toward the river bank. Notwithstanding all these manifestations of immediate skedaddling, a few still lingered, reluctant to leave until the last moment. I now left my tent, and proceeded up the river bank toward the post-office, which is situated near the railroad track, and just on the bank of the river. I passed all the Quartermaster's offices, Provost Marshal's office, the Harbor Master's office. They were all empty. I passed the telegraph tent; they were hastily packing, and just going to leave.

I arrived at the Postoffice; it was empty—everything gone. Continuing on, I soon overtook Perkins, "the Postmaster General of the Army of the Potomac," who, with four contrabands, was conveying a large chest to the Elm City, then the only boat except the Canonicus—which was waiting for Col. Ingalls—which lay above the White House. You must understand. White House Landing extends from a little way above the White House—from which it gets its name—to where the railroad track crosses the river—or rather where it did cross before the rebels burnt the bridge—a distance of about one mile. In a few minutes after the mail was on board, the Elm City steamed down Fortress-Monroe-ward. I looked on for a moment at the preparations making for blowing up the locomotive and burning the long train of railroad cars, and, seeing the workmen retire, I thought I might as well do the same.

The gunboat Currituck, which was up the river about a hundred yards from where I stood, had a lookout on the masthead, while from the quarter deck signals were being vigorously exchanged with our headquarters at the White House. I now felt that I was skedaddling, though I did not like to go until I could see what on earth I was going from; but there were only three boats left, and they were away below the White House; so off I started, soon arriving at the Tribune tent, which was next the mail boat landing. I cast one long, last sorrowful look behind, and then put at a 2:40 pace for the White House, where I passed General Casey and staff as they were dining on the green in front of "the house." Here I learned that General Stoneman, who, with his staff, had arrived at White House—and General Casey had a consultation, at which it was decided that the infantry, numbering some 2000 or more, should be conveyed down the river by the steamers in waiting, while the cavalry and artillery would fall back to Williamsburg. A company of the 93d New-York was now detailed to attend to the blowing up and firing part of the business—their instructions being to make sure work of it.

THE EVACUATION.

The embarkation of troops now commenced, the vessels lying close to the river bank, and some distance below the White House. The C. Vanderbilt, Sanitary Commission boat, had some 250 sick and wounded men on board; to these were added some 100 civilians and 700 or 800 troops; the John Brooks and Knickerbocker to take the rest. The latter was also to take Gen. Casey and staff.

On board the C. Vanderbilt—1.30, p. m.—I am now seated in the stern of the Vanderbilt, from which I have a clear and distinct view of everything in and around White House Landing.

THE CONFLAGRATION.

A great black cloud of smoke and sheets of flame are now seen near the railroad track; still another and another. Now the flames and smoke are seen almost everywhere—up along the plain, on the skirts of the woods, where the sutlers' tents were situated, the flames and smoke have also made their appearance; the whole of the tents, which were occupied by at least three thousand people, and all the goods and effects which they could not remove in the haste and confusion, now lie at the mercy of the approaching flames. Large and commodious frame houses, which had been erected for carpenters, farriers, lumbermen, and the railroad laborers, with steam sawing-machines, &c., all went in their turn.—The park houses sent up a dreadfully black, slowly towering, vast column of smoke. This column, in its appearance, as contrasted with the clear, blue sky, was blacker than the blackest thunder-cloud the eye ever rested on.

THE EXPLOSION.

While all eyes were strained on it, watching its peculiarly slow and winding ascent, a terrific explosion, carrying fear to the hearts of all as it shook the earth, was heard, and a moment after, an immense mass of very white smoke was seen forcing its way up through the dark, rolling mass of black, and, as it developed itself, assumed the shape of a monster balloon. The phenomenon was awfully grand. The lookers-on did not speak, lest they should lose one glimpse of this the grandest scene they ever beheld. Explosions of shells on board our burning barges, which lay up where our wharves were situated, were now frequent, the fragments falling into the river. The red flames shot up at least twenty feet high along the whole length of White House Landing. The White House itself stood calmly looking on, and many were conjecturing what would be its fate. In a few minutes the demon of fire put his head through one of the top windows, and we knew then that all was up with it. It burned steadily for about one hour, when not one inch of it remained, except two tall brick chimneys, to tell the future traveller of its fate.

OUR DEPARTURE.

All being now ready, it only remained to destroy the baggage and ammunition wagons, the ambulances, carriages and stores which had been collected around the headquarters, for a final wind up. These were easily removed to the bank of the river and rolled down the cliff. Great laughter was elicited by this part of the performance. The wagons, heavily laden, were heeled up to the verge, and then the boys let go, all together, and away they went—bang, dash, smash—in some cases turning a complete and well performed summerset. Then nearly a whole company of soldiers competed with each other to see which would pitch bran new shovels, pickaxes, spades, boxes of tea and tobacco, boxes of lemons, oranges, cigars, pickles, iron buckets, &c., furthest into the river. Gen. Casey and Col. B. C. Butler were sitting on the bank of the river while the performance was going on.

7 o'clock, p. m.—All three steamers move out together. Nothing afloat then lay above us but the four gunboats; our engine bell sounded, our wheel went round, and we dropped slowly down the yellow Pamunkey. The last we saw of White House was one mass of smoke, flame and smouldering ruins. We arrived at Fortress Monroe at 7, p. m., on Sunday, having lain at anchor all Saturday night in the Pamunkey, twelve miles below White House. You will notice I did not say one word about our hearing any firing, or seeing any of the much feared Confederates. One hundred thousand dollars worth of property was destroyed. Every one that left White House believes the most of it could have been saved if there was any system adopted by those in authority; but I suppose the amount is so small they thought it hardly worth while to make any effort to save it.

THE WAR IN TENNESSEE—THE THEATRE OF THE WAR IN TENNESSEE—ITS STRATEGIC POINTS, ETC.

As East Tennessee is about to become the theatre of important military operations for its possession by the vandal abolition hordes of the North, a description of this portion of it, extending to the Cumberland Mountains, will not be uninteresting. The following will give the reader an idea of the general nature of the country of East Tennessee, as well as some of the most important points on the theatre of the war:

The physical geography of East Tennessee is very peculiar and intricate in its character, being marked by that extraordinary phenomina of nature which mingles the wonderful with the beautiful and sublime. It is a vast valley of an exceedingly rich agricultural nature, extending from the Cumberland Mountains on the west to the Alleghany on the east. Its remarkable feature consists in the formation of a number of parallel and subordinate valleys, separated by precipitous ridges, and drained by the following rivers respectively: the Powell, Clinch, Holston, and French Broad.

The Cumberland mountains, towards the east, present a sheer precipice, the very base of which rests upon Powell's Valley, one of the most fertile regions of this department. This immense ridge has several depressed indentations, the most famous and practicable of which is Cumberland Gap. Below Cumberland Gap are several other depressions in the mountains, the principal of which are Wilson's Gap, eighteen miles, and Big Creek Gap, thirty-seven miles distant from the Cumberland. Westward from this ridge a vast wilderness of mountains extends for over one hundred and twenty-miles towards Kentucky and Middle Tennessee. The wagon road from Cumberland Gap to Morristown, which is forty miles, runs directly across the valleys of the Powell, Clinch, and Holston Rivers. This road is the great route through which the emigrants from North Carolina first passed to Kentucky, and over which the drovers still make their way from Kentucky to the Atlantic States.

Through the centre of East Tennessee and parallel to the mountains runs the East Tennessee and Virginia railroad, following the valley drained by the Holston, the largest tributary of the Tennessee, and passes through Morristown to Knoxville. The Clinch mountain, which is about eight miles west of Morristown, is the only serious natural barrier to the advance of the enemy's columns during the season when the rivers are fordable, and consequently presents a strong strategic point. Another route from Cumberland Gap is down Powell's Valley, running along the base of the mountain to Jacksboro' and Clinton, where it crosses the Clinch river to Knoxville. This route is nearly double the distance of that above mentioned, but is by far the best for military operations.

Thus it will be seen that to advance upon us the enemy must leave his stronghold at Cumberland Gap, which no longer became a strategical point of importance to us, and fight us on a battle ground of our own selection. Besides, the moment he leaves Cumberland Gap, where it is almost impossible to subsist an army, he loses the advantage of its defence, and, therefore, his present occupation of it is but of small moment.

The Tennessee river, assuming that name after the junction of the Holston and Little Tennessee—which latter flows transversely to the course of the mountainous region of North Carolina—receiving afterwards a large increase from the Clinch river, breaks its way through the Cumberland chain at and below Chattanooga. Consequently, by a glance at the map, it will be seen that Cumberland Gap and Chattanooga are the two great transverse fissures through the continuous ridges of the Cumberland mountains by which East Tennessee may be entered. Another route of military importance at this point is the old road from Knoxville to Nashville, passing through Kingston, which is situated at the junction of the Clinch and Tennessee rivers, and continuing by Sparta, upon the western slope of the Cumberland, passes through Pikeville, McMinnville, and Murfreesboro' to Nashville.

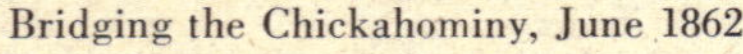

Bridging the Chickahominy, June 1862

Battle of Malvern Hill — General Lee's attack

The retreat from the Chickahominy, June 29, 1862

The New-York Times.

VOL. XI—NO. 3392. NEW-YORK, THURSDAY, AUGUST 7, 1862. PRICE TWO CENTS.

FROM GEN. M'CLELLAN'S ARMY.

Resumption of Offensive Operations.

Important Reconnoissance to Within Ten Miles of Richmond.

Fighting at Malvern Hill and White-Oak Swamp Bridge.

DEFEAT AND FLIGHT OF THE REBELS.

A Heavy Body of Troops Thrown Across the James River.

Porter's Mortar Fleet Gone Up the River.

HEADQUARTERS ARMY OF THE POTOMAC, Wednesday, Aug. 6.

The Army of the Potomac has again assumed the offensive.

The reconnoissance made yesterday, under Gen. HOOKER, to Malvern Hill, White Oak Swamp Bridge, and in the direction of New-Market and Richmond, was in every respect a complete success.

The troops left camp about dark, night before last, arriving at Malvern Hill at 4 o'clock yesterday morning, a distance of ten miles. Here they encountered two regiments of infantry and a battery posted behind earthworks. Fire was immediately opened on them by Capt. BENSON's Battery, and a section of Capt. ROBINSON's.

The infantry was not engaged. The firing lasted about three hours, when the rebels ingloriously fled by the river road toward Richmond, hotly pursued by our troops, who succeeded in taking 100 of them prisoners.

The loss on our side at this point was three killed and eleven wounded. Capt. BENSON had his thigh broken by a piece of shell. The doctors think the leg can be saved. Lieut.-Col. GAMBLE, of the Eighth Illinois Cavalry, was severely wounded in the breast while driving in the enemy's pickets.

Col. AVERILL, with 500 cavalry, took the Quaker road to White Oak Swamp Bridge. There they found the Tenth Virginia Cavalry drawn up to receive them. A charge was immediately ordered, which broke the rebels lines, when they fled. Col. AVERILL followed them three miles, taking twenty-eight prisoners, without losing a man.

Gen. PLEASANTON, with a force of cavalry, took the New-Market Road, on which a portion of the rebels were retreating. He followed them to within a short distance of New-Market, where, meeting two brigades of rebels, he fell back, bringing over thirty prisoners, taken on the way. New-Market is within ten miles of Richmond.

This ended the operations for the day, *when the troops went into camp on Malvern Hill.*

Gen. McCLELLAN, who went to the scene of action early yesterday morning, has not returned.

Three thousand of our prisoners will arrive to-day from Richmond, in exchange for a similar number sent up on Monday.

Everything is quiet on the opposite side of the river.

OUR SPECIAL ARMY CORRESPONDENCE.

Operations on the Lower Side of the James—The Late Important Reconnoissance towards Petersburgh—A Heavy Body of Troops Thrown Across the River—Porter's Mortar Fleet on Hand—The Experiences of a Surgeon in Richmond, &c.

ARMY OF THE POTOMAC, Monday, Aug. 4, 1862.

Yesterday about 2,000 infantry, cavalry and artillery crossed James River at Westover Landing. They remained on guard while the engineers and contrabands felled trees, constructed roads, &c.

At 4 o'clock in the evening firing was noticed from the gunboats off City Point. It was thought at first that the *Richmond* was coming down, but it proved to be our gunboats shelling the woods. Firing in the distance was also heard during the night.

Every evening before dark the gunboats move up from below, and take position within easy distance of City Point.

A force of cavalry will soon make a reconnoissance on the south side of the river, for the purpose of ascertaining the whereabouts of the enemy's line, also of discovering his strong and weak points.

Three large transports, flying a flag of truce, and laden with Union soldiers from Richmond, came down from City Point in the afternoon.

Dr. O. MUNSON, Assistant-Surgeon in the Fifth New-York Zouaves, arrived here on a flag of truce boat last Monday. He was among the Surgeons who remained at Savage's Station, to attend and administer to our wounded, at the time the army fought its way to James' River. He corroborates the statements others have already made, in reference to the brutal treatment our sick and wounded at Savage's received at the hands of the rebels, and adds further that the rapacious fiends did not hesitate to remove for their own use the few subsistance stores that himself and other surgeons had snatched from the burning pile, in order to keep our helpless soldiers from starving. Aware of the perilous condition to which our suffering men were reduced, and the importance of immediate action in their behalf, Dr. MUNSON, accompanied by two other surgeons, mounted his horse and followed the railroad track into Richmond, with the intention of consulting the Confederate Medical Director, and, if possible, making some arrangements by which our sick and wounded could at least be recognized as civilized beings, and not as dogs. Arriving at the Richmond Dépôt, Dr. MUNSON respectfully inquired of a rebel officer the direction he should take to reach the medical headquarters. The officer eyed him for a moment, and replied that he would shortly accompany him and his party thither. The party, not being disposed to await the movements of the officer, and feeling confident that they were entitled to all the immunities usually accorded to the profession, proceeded from the dépôt, determined to ascertain for themselves the object of their search. They had progressed but a few yards, however, when they were halted by the officer, and ordered to return. In about half an hour, the officer announced his readiness to conduct them into town. By this time, the surgeons had discovered that they were regarded as prisoners, and that no respect was paid to their profession. They did not suppose, however, that they would be taken elsewhere than to the office of the Medical Director, and were greatly surprised, upon reaching the Libby Jail, to find themselves marched within its walls. One thousand Union prisoners were already packed into its narrow limits. The uncleanliness of the place, the foul atmosphere, the scanty supply of nourishing food—or, for that matter, of any kind of food—the stringent orders and the barbarous demeanor of the lean, yellow-skinned, heathenish animals acting as guards contributed to make the Libby Jail one of the most frightful places this side of Pandemonium. We have heard related the experience of numerous inmates of that and other prisons in Richmond. The statement of Dr. MUNSON is equally revolting. No wonder that our men shout with joy upon being placed on board a Union transport, after having endured weeks, perhaps months, of the most outrageous treatment ever known or practiced in modern warfare. The excuse offered by the rebels—that they have not the means of properly caring for prisoners—does not furnish them a pretext for acting like savages, and robbing, not only the wounded of their valuables, but the surgeons of their instruments and medical stores. One fellow had the impudence to reproach Dr. MUNSON for not giving more attention to his own wounded. The Doctor retaliated by reminding the fellow of the fact that everything he had in the way of instruments and medicine had been ruthlessly taken from him by the Confederates, and remarked that no one but a fool would suggest his going among the sick and wounded, to tantalize them by informing them that he had not the means of extending aid. Dr. MUNSON finally succeeded in getting a note to the Medical Director, and after the expiration of two days was allowed to embark on board the train for Petersburgh, thence to City Point, where the flag of truce boat was waiting. When in Richmond several more attempts were made to capture his horse. At last he was compelled to apply to Gen. LEE for a document showing that a surgeon could not rightfully be dispossessed of his personal property. But that did not enable him to bring his horse from Richmond, as he was told, at the Petersburgh depôt, that transportation was furnished only for men. By this trick the rebels managed to secure a faithful and valuable animal.

In connection with the foregoing account, the conduct of a Union soldier, named LAMSON, well known to the citizens of Albany, and who was acting as Warden at the Savage Station Hospital, should be held up for lasting detestation by all mankind. The hospital was under the charge of Dr. SWINBURN, of Albany, and under the superintendence of Dr. MUNSON. The rebels having taken away most of the hospital stewards and attendants, left many extra duties to be performed by the surgeons and the few remaining convalescent soldiers—consequently, a few days elapsed before every department could be properly systematized. One of the duties devolved upon LAMSON was to search the pockets of the dead, and deliver the effects to Dr. MUNSON. It appears, that during the press of work, it was the practice of LAMSON to retain a large amount of valuables, and conceal them either in his pockets or his trunk. Suspicion was aroused and his movements were watched, and a favorable opportunity presenting itself, Drs. SWINBURN and MUNSON called upon him at his quarters, and interrogated him as to his proceedings. LAMSON said he came out with between $60 and $70, and upon being asked to exhibit it, did so, remarking, at the same time, that it was all the money he possessed. Upon being pressed to carefully search his pockets for more, he extracted an additional amount of $10. Dr. SWINBURN urged another trial, when out came $10 more. In fact, each pocket contained a sum of money, amounting, in the aggregate, to over $126. He explained the circumstance of his money exceeding the amount as first stated, by saying that he obtained the surplus by exchanging Confederate for United States Treasury Notes with his own comrades.

LAMSON was also forced to produce a gold watch and silver watch-case, which he had taken from the body of Lieut. FISHER, formerly Aid to Gen. BUTTERFIELD. The watch had been hit with a bullet. He also gave up a silver watch and four gold rings. At first he denied having any of those articles in his possession.

Dr. SWINBURN made him hand over $40 of the money, to be appropriated toward a general hospital fund. Of course he had no authority across the line to institute proceedings against him. LAMSON is now at the North. WHIT.

ARMY OF THE POTOMAC, Tuesday, Aug. 5, 1862.

At 5 o'clock Sunday morning, one hundred and fifty men of the Fifth United States Cavalry, and one hundred and fifty men of the Third Pennsylvania Cavalry, the entire force under command of Col. AVERILL, left the mail dock landing and crossed to the opposite side of James River, for the purpose of making a reconnoissance of the district beyond. Three regiments of infantry, which had been sent over the day previous, were stationed half a mile from the river, protecting a fatigue party who were at work felling trees. The cavalry started on the reconnoissance at 9 A. M., and had advanced one mile from the river when they discovered the enemy's videttes in their front. The course taken was in the direction of Petersburgh. After firing a few shots at the advance company, which was commanded by Lieut. McINTOSH, of the Fifth United States Cavalry, the enemy retreated precipitately on the road leading to Petersburgh. Our cavalry gave him hot pursuit, firing upon him at intervals, until they came up to his camp, situated near a Methodist church, and seven miles from the James River. Here our force halted, but the rebels continued in their flight, and nothing more was seen of the party. The rebels numbered about seven hundred. We had one man belonging to the Fifth slightly wounded, and had one horse killed.

Several of our shots took effect among the enemy. We captured three of his men and took two horses. One of the prisoners is named HARRISON, and he is a relative of Dr. COX, formerly Medical Purveyor in Baltimore. He was wounded in the neck, and expressed his pleasure at being taken prisoner; and said that he had been forced into the rebel service.

The cavalry burnt the enemy's camp, camp equipage and baggage; also, a large lot of commissary stores, and considerable miscellaneous property. They returned to James River in the afternoon, bringing with them chickens, green corn, new potatoes, and one or two other camp delicacies, which were a short time previous in possession of the enemy. The cavalry also secured some books, documents and letters which had been left in the camp. On their way to the river, sixty rebel cavalry came upon them from the Suffolk road, but they immediately turned tail when they saw themselves outnumbered.

Some of our men went over to Coggin's Point, where the rebels had pieces stationed on the night of the attack upon our river front. They picked up bandages stained with blood, stretchers, and other things which indicated that the gunboats did some execution.

A considerable force, consisting of infantry, cavalry and artillery, crossed over to the south side of the river yesterday and last night.

Porter's mortar fleet came up during the night, and continued its course up the river.

Artillery firing has been heard this morning at a distance, apparently six or eight miles off, in the direction of Malvern Hill. A heavy force was sent out that way last night to reconnoitre.

We may expect lively times soon. WHIT.

THE NIGHT ATTACK ON SHIPBOARD.

ALARM ON THE UNITED STATES STEAMER CIMERONE—THE MEN AT THEIR GUNS—GOOD PRACTICE—THE ENEMY SILENCED.

Extract of a letter from an officer on board the United States steamer *Cimerone*, Commander WOODHULL:

CIMERONE, Saturday, Aug. 2, 1862.

MY DEAR FATHER: I have passed through another severe battle without injury.

Last night, at 6 P. M., we anchored as usual off Westover, opposite the right wing of the army. At 12 o'clock, night, the watch below, and all hands, were aroused by the roar of cannon and the bustle of preparing the ship for action. We first supposed Gen. FRANKLIN was attacked, but no sooner had our signal officer displayed his lights at masthead, than the shells came whizzing over our rigging, showing the position of the enemy to be opposite, on the south bank of the James River. We soon opened on his batteries with all our guns, being in close range. Commander WOODHULL seeing the signal lights were drawing all the enemy's fire directly upon him, ordered them out.

The *Cimerone* was the only vessel within range of the foe, and so we had the fight all to ourselves. He had twelve pieces bearing on us, and though they were light, compared to our 100-pounder and 9-inch guns, they could be fired much more rapidly, and do good execution at so short distance. For three hours we fought them steadily, throwing not less than 150 shot, shell and shrapnel. During all this time their shot fell around us like rain. The Captain's gig was smashed, the second cutter likewise, the wheelhouse stove, with sundry minor damages, but not a man was struck—not one even by a splinter.

Very soon after our men had fairly got warmed to the work, the rebel fire slackened, and in three hours their guns were silenced. The enemy were probably misled by the lights shown at our masthead. They must have supposed them on deck—as many of their shot passed over us, falling into the small camps on the edge of the river, where five soldiers were killed, including a man attached to signal service. Quite a number also were wounded, and several transport schooners somewhat injured.

I have not before had shot pass quite so near me, and I will acknowledge that I thought my time had come, but found I did not feel the least excitement or loss of self-control.

Commander WOODHULL thanked his officers cordially, and seemed delighted with the conduct of officers and men. I am greatly mistaken if he is not one of the right men in the right place. He appeared cool and collected; it is in such moments that a man's true metal is shown. Gen. McCLELLAN sent a force over to-day, to guard against a repetition.

This morning we started down river to convoy a mail-boat, and had another little affair at Fort Powhattan.

The rebel fleet were seen again to-day. They evidently mean fight. You must be prepared now to hear of hot work. I know of none who wish it delayed.

THE EXCELSIOR BRIGADE.

HOW THE ARMY FEELS ABOUT A DRAFT—A PLAN TO RID THE NORTH OF THE RECREANT SOLDIERS.

Correspondence of the New-York Times.

CAMP NEAR HARRISON'S LANDING, Va., Wednesday, July 30, 1862.

The public has already heard so much of the bloody week during which our line of operations were being changed, that there are perhaps few who would care to read the details of the part taken in those bloody battles by the Excelsior Brigade. Suffice it to say that it did its duty and its whole duty, and established its claim to the title of the "Iron Brigade" still more firmly than ever before.

From the time it fired the first gun, on the 25th, until it fired the last shot on the sanguinary field of Malvern, it did its duty nobly and as of yore. It commenced that fearful series of battles. It ended them by pouring in the last volley upon an enraged but baulked and defeated enemy.

And now "they rest from labors"—and it was rest they needed—the almost constant picket duty of the awful month of June, the malaria of the Chickahominy swamps, the noxious exhalations from the half-buried dead upon the field of Fair Oaks, the dig, dig, dig, in the trenches under a burning sun, had left few men in the brigade fit for any duty; but on the salubrious plains along the James, with the improved rations, and in the enjoyment of comparative rest, the brigade has once more assumed something of its former character.

Yet its ranks have been awfully thinned; not so much by disease as by battle and constant picket skirmishing. It needs fresh men to fill up its ranks to the former standard. Any man may well feel proud to enroll his name as a member of a military organization which *knows no superior.*

It is undeniable that the feeling in the army is unanimously in favor of a draft. The men seem indisposed to await the comparatively slow recruiting. They grumble that large bounties should be paid those who hain't the patriotism to volunteer at first. A vote to-day in the army would almost unanimously indorse an immediate draft and the filling up of the old regiments to the maximum standard, and the promotion to vacant offices of meritorious non-commissioned officers or private soldiers. The latter are decidedly and deservedly popular.

One other thing the army feels bad about. The officers and men who have borne the brunt of the various battles on the Peninsula, who have stood picket at night and dug trenches by day, who have braved death from the enemy's bullets, and the no less dangerous, though more silent, swamp malaria, feel incensed when they see both press and people lavishing honors on those who on one pretence or the other have skulked away, and are now being *fêted* as heroes or promoted to high stations. Such instances are more common than are imagined. Many are the men who have shot off their own fingers who are now loudly vaunting their "valorous" deeds. Many the officer who skulked off under pretence of sickness who now claims honors for gallantry in battles he never saw.

There is but one way to stop this crying evil, for as it now stands cowardice is at a premium, and that is a plain, simple and effectual one. Let the Colonel of each regiment publish in the papers, printed in the section where his regiment was raised, the name of each absentee, the ostensible cause for which he went home, and the length of his leave, thus:

John Smith, ten days' leave—sickness.

Thomas Brown, skulked away from his company—shot his finger off and went home without leave.

Capt. Jones, left his company at battle of Fair Oaks—ostensible reason: sunstroke.

The public would soon find out how severe Capt. Jones' sunstroke was, or how sick John Smith was, while Thomas Brown would be hooted at. As it now is, it pays a man to be a coward, and skulk at the North. Drag forth these skulkers to the light—place them in the pillory of public opinion, and there will be fewer marriages of officers on sick furlough—a less number of able-bodied men rehearsing their pretended valor, and less incentive to cowardice. That alone will abate this crying evil. CEDMA.

Affairs in Albany.

ALBANY, Wednesday, Aug. 6.

The biennial meeting of the Judges of the Supreme Court to revise the rules should have taken place to-day, but no quorum being in attendance those present could not legally act, and therefore adjourned.

The Democratic State Convention Committee will meet at the Delavan House, Albany, Wednesday, Aug. 13, to fix the time for holding the Democratic State Convention.

Gov. MORGAN is at Washington. He is expected to return to-morrow evening, when orders for a draft will probably be issued.

The Persia and the North American Outward Bound.

ST. JOHNS, N. F., Tuesday, Aug. 5.

The weather was very thick on Saturday, and nothing was seen of the *Persia* then due at Cape Race, *en route* to Liverpool.

The *North American*, from Quebec for Liverpool, passed Cape Race this Tuesday evening. Her fog whistle was heard, but she could not be seen or boarded.

NEWS FROM WASHINGTON.

A Great War Meeting Held at the Capitol.

Important Speech of President Lincoln.

His Declarations in Regard to Gen. McClellan and the Secretary of War.

POINTED RESOLUTIONS ADOPTED.

The Government Urged to Prosecute the War with All Possible Vigor.

Traitors in the Departments Should be Weeded Out.

WASHINGTON, Wednesday, Aug. 6.

An immense meeting was held at the east front of the Capitol this afternoon. It was preceded by the ringing of bells, the firing of cannon, and music from the Marine Band. The portico and platform were occupied by many ladies, military, civil and naval officers of distinction.

The Mayor of Washington presided, with thirty-four Vice-Presidents and twenty-two Secretaries.

After a prayer by Rev. JOHN C. SMITH, the following resolutions were read by EDWARD JORDAN, the Solicitor of the Treasury:

Resolved, That we, residents of the District of Columbia, but having among our number citizens of every portion of the country, regard the dismemberment of the Union as an event not to be contemplated in any contingency whatever, it being forbidden alike by our geographical, commercial, social and political condition—by our domestic and foreign interests—by the shame which the world would attach to us, did we suffer its accomplishment, and the worthlessness of what would remain to us afterward; by the mighty interests involved in the Union, and the vast sacrifices which have been made for its defence; by the hopes of the living and the memories of the dead; and we deliberately and voluntarily declare that, rather than witness its overthrow, we would prosecute the present war until the towns and cities should be reduced to ashes. [Applause.] Our fields should be desolated, and we and all that are dear to us should have perished with our possessions. Let the Union be preserved, or the country made a desert. [Applause.]

Resolved, That we have not a doubt that almost the entire population of the loyal States are animated by the same sentiments which we express, and that if there is at the present time any hesitation manifested by them in devoting themselves or their property to the cause of their country, it is owing solely to their misgivings as to the prosecution of the war—[Applause, and cries of "Good"]—to an apprehension that there is, on the part of those who direct our military operations, whether in the Cabinet or in the field, a want of readiness and determination to employ at once, decisively, crushingly, the full power of the nation, which all feel and know to be overwhelming.

Resolved, That profoundly convinced as we are that such is the true cause of the hesitation, we deem it the duty of the President, and therefore most respectfully but earnestly urge upon him to adopt effectual means of assuring the people that he is resolved to prosecute the war on a scale limited only by the resources of the country; and we hail with joy the recent order directing the immediate draft of a large additional force, as cheering evidence of such a resolve. [Applause.]

Resolved, That while there are among us differences of opinion upon minor questions of policy in the prosecution of the war, we are all agreed that the measures adopted should be those which will bear with the most crushing weight upon those in rebellion, whether in arms or not. [Applause.]

Resolved, That, convinced as we are that the leaders in the rebellion will never sincerely return to their allegiance to the Union, or quietly submit to its laws, we are of opinion that they should be regarded as irreclaimable traitors, who are to be stripped of their possessions of whatever character, and either deprived of life or expelled from the country. [Wild applause, and cries of "Good."]

Resolved, That, in our judgment, whenever our armies go within the rebellious States, means should be taken to test the loyalty of the inhabitants, and those who refuse their unqualified adhesion to the cause of the Union, should either be placed under restraint or compelled to go beyond the lines, while their effects should be taken from them, and, so far as available, be converted to the use of the army. [Applause.]

Resolved, That the National Capital is eminently the place where treason should be instantly denounced and punished.

At this point the applause from thousands of voices was deafening, and again three cheers were enthusiastically given, with exclamations: "Read that again—good, good—read it again."

Mr. JORDAN was about to do so when he was interrupted by the heavy and continuous sound of cannon, mingled with the music from the Marine Band, for the President had now made his appearance, and was proceeding to the front of the platform, where a chair had been provided for him in a conspicuous place. Three cheers were given in his honor, and when this pleasant excitement had somewhat subsided, Mr. JORDAN read the entire resolution, as follows:

Resolved, That the National Capital is eminently the place where treason should be instantly denounced and punished, and that the most stringent measures should be adopted by the proper authorities, without delay, to discover and arrest the disloyal men and women who infest the District, and that they should be compelled either to establish, in the most conclusive manner, their fidelity to the Government, or forfeit its protection.

[The reading throughout was greeted with applause.]

Resolved, That we heartily approve of the act of Congress, passed at its recent session, subjecting to confiscation the property of rebels, and declaring free such of their slaves as shall take refuge within the lines of our army; and that we deem it to be the duty of the President, to the utmost of his ability, to give prompt effect to the provisions of that act, and especially that he take the most efficient means within his power to cause full notice thereof to be given to all persons who may be affected thereby. [Applause.]

Resolved, That the Federal Government being the only instrumentality through which the will of the nation can be made effective, that the Government must be sustained, whatever Administration may, for the time being, be in power, and whatever may be the policy within the limits of the Constitution which it may adopt; that he who refuses it his support because of his disapproval of some particular measure of its policy, is false to his obligations to the country—(applause)—that this truth has peculiar force at the present time, when the Government is struggling for its very existence; and that for ourselves, confident as we are in the wisdom and patriotism of the President and members of the Cabinet, we pledge to them an earnest, cordial and determined support in the great work of defending and preserving the Union in which are centered all our hopes, and to the preservation of which we solemnly devote all that we have and are. [Applause.]

Resolved, That we pledge ourselves to make ample pecuniary provision for the families of all citizens of this District who are now in the military service of the country, and who may hereafter enter it during the continuance of the war.

The entire series of resolutions were unanimously and enthusiastically adopted.

Mr. CHITTENDEN, Register of the Treasury, made a stirrring opening speech, in the course of which he said the causes of the quarrel are in the past. Hesitations for compromise and negotiation, delay and timid counsels, are words that belong to the past. The time has come to find out, seize and dispose of every traitor in this country, especially in this city. ["Good, good."] We have suffered men, whose hearts were full of treason, to breathe the same air with us, to sit at our tables, and to fill the offices of Government, and who have availed themselves of the opportunity they enjoy to give information to the enemy. [Cries of "Put them out," "Hang them."] When the war broke out every one of the traitors, who had a speck of honor, removed hence, but those whose natures qualified them for pimps and spies remained. We cannot expect military Governors or Provost-Marshals to look after them. We must do it ourselves. He gave, as an instance, a man who was turned out of office more than a year ago, on the suspicion of disloyalty. This man went to Maryland, was there arrested, and confined in a military prison, but by a mistaken policy, was released, and is now in a public office here, where he can best know the movements of the army, and their sanitary condition.

Voice—What's his name?

Mr. CHITTENDEN replied that he could give it here, but preferred to use it in such a way, privately, as to have the man removed. After some encouraging words as to the prospect of crushing the rebellion, he said: that man is a patriot who sustains the Government, and in conclusion, paid a high compliment to the President and the Cabinet.

He was frequently interrupted by applause.

Three cheers were given for the President, and after the band had played "Hail to the Chief," the President, in response to impatient calls, advanced to the front of the platform and spoke as follows:

THE PRESIDENT'S SPEECH.

FELLOW-CITIZENS: I believe there is no precedent for my appearing before you on this occasion, [applause] but it is also true that there is no precedent for your being here yourselves, (applause and laughter;) and I offer, in justification of myself and of you, that, upon examination, I have found nothing in the Constitution against. [Renewed applause.] I, however, have an impression that there are younger gentlemen who will entertain you better, (voices—"No, no; none can do better than yourself. Go on!") and better address your understanding, than I will or could, and therefore I propose but to detain you a moment longer. [Cries—"Go on! Tar and feather the rebels!"]

I am very little inclined on any occasion to say anything unless I hope to produce some good by it. [A voice—"You do that; go on]. The only thing I think of just now not likely to be better said by some one else, is *a matter in which we have heard some other persons blamed for what I did myself.* [Voices—"What is it]. There has been a very wide-spread attempt to have a quarrel between Gen. McCLELLAN and the Secretary of War. *Now, I occupy a position that enables me to observe, at least, these two gentlemen are not nearly so deep in the quarrel as some pretending to be their friends.* [Cries of "Good."] Gen. McCLELLAN's attitude is such that, in the very selfishness of his nature, he cannot but wish to be successful, and I hope he will—and the Secretary of War is in precisely the same situation. If the military commanders in the field cannot be successful, not only the Secretary of War, but myself for the time being the master of them both, cannot be but failures. [Laughter and applause.] I know Gen. McCLELLAN wishes to be successful, and I know he does not wish it any more than the Secretary of War for him, and both of them together no more than I wish it. [Applause and cries of "Good."] Sometimes we have a dispute about how many men Gen. McCLELLAN has had, and those who would disparage him say that he has had a very large number, and those who would disparage the Secretary of War insist that Gen. McCLELLAN has had a very small number. The basis for this is, *there is always a wide difference, and on this occasion, perhaps, a wider one between the grand total on McClellan's rolls and the men actually fit for duty;* and those who would disparage him talk of the grand total on paper, and those who would disparage the Secretary of War talk of those at present fit for duty. Gen. McCLELLAN *has sometimes asked for things that the Secretary of War did not give him.* Gen. McCLELLAN is not to blame for asking what he wanted and needed, and the Secretary of War *is not to blame for not giving when he had none to give.* [Applause, laughter, and cries of "Good, good."] And I say here, as far as I know, *the Secretary of War has withheld no one thing at any time in my power to give him.* [Wild applause, and a voice—"Give him enough now!"] I have no accusation against him. *I believe he is a brave and able man,* [applause,] and I stand here, as justice requires me to do, *to take upon myself what has been charged on the Secretary of War, as withholding from him.*

I have talked longer than I expected to do, [cries of "No, no—go on,"] and now I avail myself of my privilege of saying no more.

SPEECH OF EX-GOV. BOUTWELL.

Ex-Gov. BOUTWELL, Commissioner of the Internal Revenue, when he announced he came from Massachusetts, said what they proposed to do in this war was to carry it on in sunshine and storm against all odds on this side of the water or the other. They rallied under this banner not for this generation alone, nor for this century, but for all generations and centuries on this side of the Atlantic, until our flag shall wave unpolluted from the great lakes of the North to the Gulf of Mexico; and they meant to take the last man, the last collar, the last hour's labor of the Old Commonwealth, ere these men, with treachery on their lips and treason in their hearts, shall accomplish what they have undertaken. [Applause.] If, to-night, news of disaster should come, every heart, though dismayed for the moment, would be nerved for renewed efforts in the cause of liberty and humanity. The gentleman (CHITTENDEN) who preceded him said he proposed to ferret out the traitors. He would here say, if it had not been for Slavery, there would have been no treason, and when Slavery shall cease to exist, there will be no traitors. [Applause, and cries of "Good."]

OUR SPECIAL WASHINGTON DISPATCHES.

WASHINGTON, Wednesday, Aug. 6.

THE GREAT WAR MEETING.

The most significant feature of the great War Meeting here to-day, was the demand, embodied in the resolutions, forcibly dwelt on by the first speaker, and urged by every one that followed him, and rapturously applauded by the immense crowd whenever alluded to, that rebels and their sympathizers should be weeded out of the Departments and driven from the District. Mr. CHITTENDEN's declaration, that he found the other day a clerk in one of the most important positions in the Government's service, where he had the utmost facilities for learning, at the earliest moment, of the movements of our armies, or orders to Generals, who, a few months ago, had been ignominiously expelled from a similar position for disloyalty, and had subsequently been arrested for traitorous conduct in Maryland, produced profound sensation. The statement was repeatedly made during the meeting that a large number of such persons still retain important positions.

The resolution calling for the expulsion of disloyal persons from the District, had just been read a second time, in response to a demand for re-reading, when the President came in. When the applause over the President's arrival was ended, and the reading resumed, the crowd demanded that the resolution should be read a third time, for the President's benefit, and it was read.

Scarcely less significant was the temper of the crowd on the vigorous prosecution of the war. Every declaration that the time for timid measures was past; that the property of rebels must be confiscated; that the conciliation of traitors must henceforth be abandoned, was applauded to the echo.

ANTICIPATED MOVEMENTS BY THE REBELS.

The call for six hundred thousand men, coupled with some other developments, lead to the belief that the Government is anticipating a formidable aggressive demonstration by the rebels within a few weeks. The fact that the rebels have been so remarkably quiet of late, and that they have made no movements against McCLELLAN, are construed as indicating a preparation for some sudden attack, the plan for which is yet kept secret. The Government is believed to be apprehensive of something of this sort.

JOHN SLIDELL ON SLAVERY.

A member of the Foreign Legations in Washington just arrived from Europe, relates of this distinguished rebel a story which is now widely circulated in this city.

One of his cousins, who holds an office in the Department of the Interior, in France, having been invited to one of SLIDELL's *soirées*, availed himself of the opportunity—first, to see how a Southern rebel looked; second, to know his opinion about Slavery. As it may well be imagined, the French official was the object of the most delicate attention on the part of Mrs. SLIDELL and her husband, who strove to persuade him of the holiness of the Southern cause, and to make him believe in its ultimate success. After having exhausted all their arguments, the Frenchman, politely addressing Mr. SLIDELL, asked whether he was not of opinion that the moral attitude of the North in this contest was an impediment to the success of the South, and if the maintenance of Slavery did not delay the work of its independence. "You are perfectly right," answered Mr. SLIDELL, "Europe is adverse to our institutions and we know it. But please mark; they have not been inaugurated or created, but inherited by us. However, whenever the day marked for the sacrifice of our social privileges will come, the slave-owners in the South will do, I have no doubt, what your ancestors did, nearly an age ago, in the National Assembly of France. They will sacrifice them as a necessary offering to their country's peace and welfare. But now this sacrifice is impossible. It would look as an act of inefficiency on the part of the South to maintain its integrity, and would weaken rather than strengthen us. Be sure, however, that the time is not distant when the institution of Slavery—cause of our present misery—will be forever removed from our statute books. The French Government can greatly assist us in this; if it acts with its proverbial prudence and sagacity, it may place us in the necessity of shortly declaring gradual emancipation at home; an act which would be as satisfactory to many of us as to the spirit of Christianity and civilization abroad."

THE TREATY WITH THE OTTOMAN PORTE.

The treaty of commerce and navigation between the United States and the Ottoman Empire is officially proclaimed. It is marked throughout by much liberality. Tobacco and salt, however, are not included among the articles which our citizens are permitted to import into the Ottoman dominions. But as a compensation for their prohibition, no duty whatever shall in future be levied upon them when exported from the Ottoman Empire by citizens of the United States.

ARRESTS ON THE RAPPAHANNOCK.

Six persons were recently arrested on the Rappahannock, while engaged in shipping salt and other articles in great demand in Richmond across that river for the benefit of our enemies. The prisoners were remanded to the Old Capitol Prison.

Arrest of Editors in Harrisburgh.

HARRISBURGH, Wednesday, Aug. 6.

Gen. WADSWORTH, by direction of the War Department, to-day, arrested the editors and publishers of the *Patriot and Union*, charged with issuing treasonable posters, calculated to retard and embarrass recruiting throughout the State. The whole party left for Washington this morning.

Arrests in Canada.

TORONTO, C. W., Wednesday, Aug. 6.

The Captain and crew of the steamer *City of Madison*, an American boat, partially owned by Canadians, were arrested here, to-day, for inducing British soldiers to desert. Several soldiers of the Thirtieth Regiment have reached Oswego by this boat during the past four weeks.

The City of Washington Outward Bound.

CAPE RACE, Wednesday, Aug. 6.

The steamship *City of Washington*, from New-York on Saturday last, passed this point at 3 o'clock this afternoon, *en route* to Liverpool. She was boarded by the Associated Press news yacht and later news put aboard, as also several messages from the Commercial Agency of GEORGE STOKES, Esq. The weather to-day has been beautifully clear, with a fair prospect of its continuance.

The Asia Outward Bound.

BOSTON, Wednesday, Aug. 6.

The steamship *Asia* sailed at 10 o'clock this morning, with 16 passengers for Halifax, and 114 for Liverpool. She takes out $16,000 in specie.

Lemon Juice Versus Water.

To the Editor of the New-York Times:

The suggestion in yesterday's *Journal of Commerce* relative to the allowing our brave soldiers a few lemons every day, as part rations, merits the attention of those in high places. No one can gainsay but that raw lemon-juice will prove of immensely more benefit to sufferers from that indescribably dreadful thirst than buckets of water, which will cause great distress to the imbibers, without in the least remedying what is sought for, viz., a continued desire to drink. It is a well-known fact that the French applied this remedy with great success during their African campaign, and it was found to be of immense service to the British troops during the Crimean war.

Feeling sure that you will take pleasure in promulgating anything likely to prove beneficial to our brave men, I address the present in the hope that you may find room for same in your valuable journal.

THE SOLDIERS' BENEFACTOR.

Arrivals in the City.

Hon. W. H. Robertson, of Westchester County; E. W. Hinks, of the U. S. Volunteers; J. S. Ames, of Chicopee, Mass.; Dr. R. H. O'Toole, of England; Lieut. D. E. Castle, of the U. S. Signal Corps, from Washington, and Capt. Helm, of the *Ladoga*, and lady, are at the Astor House.

Maj. L. H. Sto[illegible], of the U. S. A.; S. G. Allen, of the U. S. A.; M. N. de Lisle, of Montreal, Canada, and J. G. Sibbald, from New-Orleans, are at the Fifth-avenue Hotel.

Pelatia Perit, from New-Haven; M. de Ayllan, of Havana; R. L. Jenkins, of Philadelphia, and Chas. Allen and M. Fennills, of Washington; C. C. Smith, of Liverpool; J. C. Groome and daughter, of Maryland; H. Hummell, of Boston, and Jules Horvat, of Philadelphia, are at the Brevoort House.

Capt. Jas. Stewart and Capt. J. Aiken, of the U. S. Army, are at the St. Nicholas Hotel.

The New-York Times.

VOL. XI—NO. 3397. NEW-YORK, WEDNESDAY, AUGUST 13, 1862. PRICE TWO CENTS.

FROM GEN. POPE'S ARMY.

Retreat of Jackson's Army Across the Rapidan.

Our Cavalry and Artillery in Pursuit.

Gen. Pope Reinforced by Gen. King's Division.

Further Particulars of the Battle of Cedar Mountain.

Terrible Nature of the Fire on Both Sides.

The Rebels Believed to be Badly Crippled.

Safe Return of the Madison Court-House Expedition.

WASHINGTON, Tuesday, Aug. 12.

The War Department has information from the Army of Virginia in front of Slaughter's Mountain up to yesterday evening. Gen. KING, with his whole division, was then within a few miles of the battle-field of Saturday, and has doubtless joined Gen. POPE ere this. No fighting has occurred in that quarter since Saturday night last.

RETREAT OF THE REBELS ACROSS THE RAPIDAN.

HEADQUARTERS, ARMY OF VIRGINIA, CEDAR MOUNTAIN, VA.—7:30 A. M., Aug 12.

To Maj.-Gen. Halleck:

The enemy has retreated under cover of the night. His rear guard is now crossing the Rapidan towards Orange Court House. Our cavalry and artillery are in pursuit.

(Signed,) JOHN POPE, Major-General.

FURTHER PARTICULARS OF THE BATTLE.

WASHINGTON, Tuesday, Aug. 12.

Accounts from Culpepper, dated yesterday, speaking of Saturday's fight, say that so heavy was the fire to which our comparatively small number of men was exposed, the only wonder is that the entire command was not completely annihilated at the end of half an hour, instead of our bringing off so large a proportion of our force at the expiration of an hour and a half.

The prisoners report that their own troops were mowed down by our fire like grass. Three times were they reinforced by fresh regiments and brigades, and when our troops retired they were too crippled to pursue in the open ground.

The prisoners also report that the heavy guns used by the enemy were of recent English manufacture, with English fixed ammunition.

We lost but one gun, which was left behind in a ditch, spiked, several of the horses having been killed.

The gun was not lost while changing our position for the night, but under the fire of the enemy's sharpshooters.

Col. CHAPMAN, of the Fifth Massachusetts, was shot in the breast, and is probably dead.

Lieut.-Col. STONE fell, with many wounds.

Major BLAKE also fell, and, if alive, is a prisoner.

Adjt. SMITH is wounded or dead.

Major SAVAGE, of the Second Massachusetts, is believed to be killed, as well as many of the Captains and Lieutenants belonging to the regiment.

Dr. LELAND was shot in the eye.

Capt. GEORGE JANNETT, of Gen. PRINCE's Staff, was shot in the breast, and mortally wounded.

The casualties in other regiments have not yet been heard from definitely.

Stragglers from the battle-field to town have been arrested by the orders of Major-Gen. POPE, and by to-morrow a list of the missing will be obtained.

The Twenty-eighth Pennsylvania Regiment escaped without loss, having been detached to guard a signal station eight or ten miles southwest of the battle-field, early in the day. They returned yesterday, escorting safely the signal officers without being compelled to pass near the enemy's pickets.

On Sunday night, about 11 o'clock, while Gen. POPE and Gen. BANKS were in conference in the rear of our advanced batteries, a body of rebel cavalry charged in the most daring manner through the woods on our front upon the group. The discharge of muskets and the whizzing of balls near gave them timely notice of the approach of the rebels. They speedily mounted their horses, and a regiment of infantry fired a volley at the approaching rebels, thus checking their charge, and probably saving both commanders.

Gen. BUFORD with his cavalry command arrived at Culpepper yesterday from Madison.

Previous to Gen. BUFORD's departure, he made a reconnoissance to the Rapidan, where he found a force of the enemy on the south side, but none north of the river.

A telegraph dispatch dated to-day, states that all was quiet last night and this morning.

Col. DONNELLY is still alive but is in a sinking condition.

Other wounded officers are generally doing well.

THE EXPEDITION TO MADISON.

SAFE RETURN OF GEN. BUFORD'S COMMAND.

CULPEPPER, Va., Monday, Aug. 11.

The Cavalry Brigade under the command of Gen. BUFORD made a descent on Madison Court-house on Tuesday last. They found that the rebels had been there, but had left. They made reconnoissances in every direction, and met the rebel pickets on every road.

On the 7th instant, our pickets on the road to Stannardsville had a skirmish, losing one killed and three wounded.

On the 8th instant, the First Maryland Regiment had another skirmish on the Orange Court-house road, in which they lost five killed and four wounded, and about a dozen prisoners. They were then reinforced by the First Michigan, when the rebels were driven back to the Rapidan.

A strong reconnoissance was made the same evening to the Rapidan, on the Orange Railroad. A skir- [illegible] from Gen. BUFORD to return to Madison Court-house.

The party got back at 6 o'clock on the morning of the 9th inst., and found everything ready prepared for a retreat toward Sperryville, as the rebels were approaching from every direction.

The party reached Woodsville in safety, and there camped. Subsequently they pushed on and arrived at Culpepper on Monday night.

The escape of this Brigade is considered almost miraculous, as they were surrounded on almost every side. Many gave it up as lost.

Gen. BUFORD deserves great praise for the very able manner in which he extricated his command from such a perilous condition.

THE ARMY OF THE POTOMAC.

An Explanation of the Affair at Malvern Hill.

Gen. McClellan's Intention to Fight a Battle There.

HOW HE WAS PREVENTED.

FORTRESS MONROE, Monday, Aug. 11.

In regard to the occupation and evacuation of Malvern Hill by the National troops little has been said. Our reconnoitering division took possession on Tuesday, and on that day all the Generals of the army went up, and Gen. MCCLELLAN sent back for the greater part of his army, but the messengers took the wrong road, and thus delayed so long that the troops did not reach Malvern Hill until it was too late, and only a portion of those sent for arrived at all, and those only in season to beat a hasty retreat. This was on Wednesday morning, and on that day a great battle would have been fought had our forces arrived in season. But as some of them were approaching, and in sight of Malvern Hill, there was a very large force of rebels seen coming from Richmond, numbering at least 100,000 men, filling all the roads, passage-ways and vacant lots as far as the eye could reach. A retreat was consequently made to Harrison's Landing.

Gen. MCCLELLAN had planned for a great battle, but the enemy were not asleep, and have taken possession of Malvern with an immense army.

GEN. HOOKER'S DIVISION.

Lieut. W. E. Farwell, of the Massachusetts Eleventh, Drummed Out of Camp upon a False Charge of Cowardice—Indignation of the Men—The Troops on the Alert.

From Our Own Correspondent.

HARRISON'S LANDING, VA., Friday, Aug. 8, 1862.

Ill reports travel fast, and, doubtless, ere this reaches you, the name of an officer, who has sustained throughout the bloody scenes of this Peninsular campaign a reputation for bravery, will have been disgraced far and wide. I allude to Lieut. WM. E. FARWELL, of the Eleventh Massachusetts Regiment, First Brigade, HOOKER's Division, who was this morning drummed through the ranks of that command, in punishment of a charge of desertion. The surprise of the troops, who were at an early hour paraded, was universal. No intimation of the proceedings was given to any one, and it was not until the large column was formed, and the "Rogue's March" struck up, that the brigade knew of his disgrace. The officer made his appearance on the ground, under guard, *fully invested with his insignia of rank*, and a large board upon his back, upon which was inscribed "Lieut. WILLIAM E. FARWELL, deserted his regiment while marching to meet the enemy."

The circumstances which led to this unpleasant exhibition, although reflecting unfavorably upon the performance of his military obligations faithfully, can, in the minds of a majority of our highest military executives, in no wise be construed into so flagrant a character as to warrant strictly the extraordinary and severe measures prosecuted against the offender.

It was advertised on the placard that he had deserted his regiment while marching to meet the enemy. Can this construction be fairly put upon the true circumstances of the case? Lieut. FARWELL was, at the time he is alleged to have committed his offence, (which was on the occasion of the late affair at Malvern Hill,) absent from the division encampment, to which he did not return until too late to join his regiment, and was until then ignorant that a movement had been made. He expressed a willingness and desire to join his company, but the troops were far in the advance, probably at or near their place of attack, and the roads were closed against every one by the rear guard. None were allowed to pass.

This is the immediate cause of punishment, but anterior circumstances have doubtless had important weight with Gen. GROVER in inflicting the severe penalty meted out. Lieut. FARWELL had tendered his resignation, assigning reasons not characterized with strong discretion, and which probably gave offence, aside from the sentiment his document presented. He claimed that the service had become disgusting to him, and that he no longer could maintain his interest in the war, and whatever duty he further performed would be done with reluctance. His previous application for a furlough, and a subsequent resignation of office, had been returned disapproved. Then, in a thoughtless moment, followed the resignation, couched in the above tenor. The sentiment thus strongly expressed, produced an unfavorable effect upon his Generals, and the resolution was formed by his Brigadier to place him in disgrace, and to carry out the punishment without the customary Court-martial deeming the cause sufficient to warrant so irregular and summary a proceeding.

But to the scene. A bewildered feeling dominated the senses of the troops as the strange and rare spectacle of an officer's being drummed through the ranks, moved before their eyes, and not a murmur of pity, indignation or satisfaction broke the stillness of the occasion. Every faculty seemed paralyzed, and complete amazement grasped all thought and nerve as with a grip of iron. All gazed with senseless and stupefied eyes upon the scene. But when it was over—when the sad pageant had passed away—the pride of the soldier awoke within the lines. The facts of the case spread like electricity through the ranks, and tears of pity, murmurs of indignation, and open imprecations against the leaders of this unparalleled proceeding, as they termed it, aroused the senses of every soldier on the field. A universal feeling of sympathy pervaded the mass, and but the sentiment of strongest condemnation actuated their thoughts as they marched to quarters.

The result of this strong measure cannot be easily foreseen; but at present the indignation of the entire brigade is aroused, and has already extended to other commands in the division. Had such a proceeding been anticipated or announced, it is very doubtful if a single officer or soldier would have witnessed the disgrace. If intended as an example, it has entirely failed of beneficial effect. In face of the facts, it is [illegible] boldly denounced as unwarrantable, tyrannical and a disgrace upon the service as well as upon an officer who has, upon every occasion, served his country nobly, faultlessly and bravely. Not a whisper of doubt against his courage and bravery can be raised, and although tacitly disgraced, he still remains a pattern of the true soldier in the hearts of his brigade. With them he is injured rather than disgraced, and his military reputation is all the more exalted and appreciated.

The truth of the whole matter is, the brigade feels the disgrace more—tenfold more—than the gallant soldier selected for punishment. It was this brigade that kept at bay the enemy on the Lower Potomac, through the storms of last Winter. His footmarks are palpable still, hedged in by the soil furrowed up by the missiles of death, and no officer was braver there. It was this brigade that first met the battle-shock at Williamsburgh, and in the human breastwork that flung back the assaults of the foe beat no braver heart than his. At Fair Oaks, Savage's Station, Malvern Hill, and all along the terrible retreat to James River, he was there, brave and fearless as the bravest, although ill and unfit for duty. And even in the shadows of this, to him, eventful morning, he marched disgraced, but lion-hearted, along the lines of his old brigade, manfully braving that humiliation which, more than death, the soldier dreads.

There is one circumstance which creates a doubt whether Lieut. FARWELL is really the officer intended to be thus ignominiously punished. It is this: Gen. GROVER, in conversation with an officer, remarked that the conduct of the Lieutenant would have been more excusable had he not once been Court-martialed for a like offence (cowardice.) Now, it is a fact established by the affirmation of every officer in his regiment, that no such charge has ever been made against him, and that his conduct has never been questioned upon such grounds, but another, bearing the same name, has. He has always been known as a cool, brave, quiet and efficient officer; and, aside from the indiscretion, or offence, contained in his letter of resignation, his record stands as fair as that of any officer in his regiment.

After marching in front of each regiment of the brigade he was conducted to his quarters, under guard, to await further action. An effort is to be made to gain him a hearing. Trial he has had none, and the surprise came upon him simultaneously with that of those who witnessed his disgrace.

Cavalrymen coming into camp from the vicinity of Malvern Hill to-day, report the rebels at that place in force this morning. Unbroken quiet characterizes the army. All are waiting with anxiety the result of recent movements, and the new draft has increased wonderfully the buoyant anticipations of the men. The effect of the news was electric, and even those prostrate with sickness showed strong symptoms of delight. In many instances it had a favorable effect upon their health. New life and animation sprang up everywhere, and a strong desire to have one more brush with the enemy before being reinforced, is uppermost. This is especially the feeling in Gen. HOOKER's Division. With such a leader that hardy and enviable corps would brave heavy odds. The General is proud of his command and the reputation they enjoy and have so nobly sustained. His command is proud of him, and will follow him anywhere. PLEBS.

AFFAIRS AT FORTRESS MONROE.

Important Secret Movements in the Army—Disbanding of our Bands—Argument for and against them—The New Drafting Orders—Lists of Sick and Wounded—Why the Times and other Leading Journals did not have them.

From Our Own Correspondent.

FORTRESS MONROE, Monday, Aug. 11, 1862.

Much movement is now going on, and of the *greatest consequence*, in this part of the country. If I refrain from stating what has come to my knowledge, it is simply because it is of a character that *should not be divulged*. A great number of troops are returning through here from the North—some returned convalescents, or from their leave of absence having expired; while many others are going North for the purpose of recruiting fresh soldiers, and not a few of them to recruit their own exhausted energies.

Among the soldiers going North are a great many bands of the various regiments, an order having been recently issued for dis-banding them—partially, if not totally. Opinions are very much divided in the army respecting the usefulness or uselessness of military bands. Some urge that they are a great and unnecessary expense—a cumbrous appendage to an army—and in time of action worse than useless, as the musicians are generally among the first to scamper off at the appearance of danger. Others, on the other hand, deny this. They say that musicians exhibit as much courage as is expected from them in their position, and that, so far from being useless on the battle-field, they aid very materially in helping the wounded, &c. But, whatever may be the truth respecting military bands in time of action, there can be no doubt whatever that at any other time they are a source of great comfort and exhilaration, if not downright necessity, to our soldiers. Nobody but those who have to endure the long, dreary and monotonous hours too often incident to camp life, can imagine how refreshing it is to hear a band break forth in some well-known air, transporting the hearer instantly among the loved ones at home. The vulgar may laugh at such a notion as visionary, but there is far more truth than poetry in it. Our armies are not composed of senseless boors, but of men the far greater part of whom are refined and intellectual, and to all such, music, under their circumstances, is not only a luxury, but a necessity. At least, all those with whom I have conversed speak very sorrowfully indeed of having to part with their bands.

The proclamation respecting drafting is causing as much flutter here as elsewhere, and the horror at the idea of being drafted will, no doubt, have driven many a volunteer into the army, who had hitherto felt careless if not callous upon the subject. One source of great difficulty will be found in dealing with our three months' men, numbering several thousands. These all say they took up arms for a specific time, and that at the end of the time specified the Government is bound, in good faith, to set them free. How this view will be met, is more than outsiders can determine.

In taking up the TIMES of the last week I have been astonished at finding no list of our sick and wounded—nor in the *Herald*, and other leading papers, (except the *Tribune*,)—although we have had plenty of sanitary vessels arriving here crowded with them. The reason for this was that, in order to obtain accurate lists and save some little trouble to the medical department, all the members of the leading Press here agreed with Dr. GILBERT to leave the sending of lists entirely to the Associated Press, so that we should all fare alike and the public have one reliable channel to depend on. Confiding in the faith of this arrangement, and taking it for granted that no one paper would either seek or be enabled to obtain any advantage over the others I have not, for a short time back, devoted any attention to what was being avowedly performed by others. The system, however, does not seem to work, the New-York *Tribune* having obtained and printed lists of names that, by agreement, were to be intrusted *alone* to the Associated Press, and thus secured an advantage over all its competitors. The TIMES shall not be so caught in future. I shall send you my lists independently, henceforth, unless there is any authority to impede a work that is undertaken out of pure humanity to the friends and relatives of our sick and wounded soldiers. If so, you shall soon hear of it. NEMO.

FROM ANOTHER CORRESPONDENT.

FORTRESS MONROE, Monday, Aug. 11.

Norfolk has been in a state of excitement. A few days since an officer of the provost-guard applied to Gen. MANSFIELD, of Suffolk, for permission to search a house in that city for arms. Authority was given and arms and ammunition to some extent were found in a private dwelling near the General's quarters.

Last night in Norfolk a triple guard was put on duty; this has not been done until many of our guardsmen have been shot at, and some shot down.

It is understood that all the inhabitants of the district in the vicinity of Norfolk, Suffolk and Portsmouth are to be put to the test of either taking the oath of allegiance to the United States or to leave for rebeldom.

The mailboat is just in from Harrison's Landing. The general appearance there is that a move of the whole or a large part of the army is taking place.

Commodore PORTER's mortar fleet still remains at anchor in Hampton Roads.

NEWS FROM WASHINGTON.

The Extent and Significance of the Military Movements in Progress.

Rumors About the Army of the Potomac.

OBFUSCATION OF THE REBELS.

OUR SPECIAL WASHINGTON DISPATCHES.

WASHINGTON, Tuesday, Aug. 12.

THE MEANING OF THE RECENT MILITARY MOVEMENTS.

It is believed here that Gen. POPE's late movements are not without an important connection with the plans on the Peninsula. The real designs for Gen. MCCLELLAN's army have been admirably concealed by feints, and the enemy left at a loss to understand just what is in contemplation. The town, of course, is full of rumors on the subject of a supposed movement. Stories about the army being down at Yorktown, or at other points different from the old location, are afloat.

It is considered certain that highly important army movements are either in progress or completed, but it is not regarded as proper yet to indicate their nature.

Much more cheerful impressions are prevailing concerning Gen. POPE's engagement. JACKSON's retreat is known here to have been a necessity. He had evidently become aware of the trap into which he was being beguiled, and retreated to escape from the danger which the execution of our plans threatened. His eye was on Fredericksburgh as well as Culpepper.

The better opinion here is that all is going well with POPE's army, and that there is no reason for the apprehensions expressed yesterday and to-day. Well-informed persons freely declare that POPE will be in Gordonsville by Saturday at furthest, though perhaps not without fighting, which may be going on now.

THE PRESIDENT AND NEGRO REGIMENTS.

The attempt is making to discredit the well authenticated statement, that the President refused to accept of negro regiments for the present. It is not true, however, that any United States Senator has denied anything of the sort. The sole point in the newspaper controversy here between a Senator and a correspondent, one of your contemporaries, is whether one Senator replied to a remark of the President's that he wished he would resign. It is generally believed here that some reply of that sort was made but this point, at any rate, in no way affects the main result of the interview.

THE NEW GUNBOATS.

The Navy Department has finally decided to withhold the advertisement for proposals for the new gunboats a short time, to give an opportunity for further preparations, and for examining whether some modifications of models may not be necessary in the case of some of them.

OFFICERS OF THE NEW LEVIES.

Some officers of regiments under the new levies arrived to-day, mostly Rhode Islanders. The town is expected to be full of them in a few days.

Hon. E. W. GILPIN and about a dozen more of the delegation from Delaware are here to-day, understood to be on business connected with raising the new levies in their State. They had an interview with the President and Secretary of War to-day, and are to have another to-morrow. The loyal men of Delaware would prefer to have the draft postponed for a month or so in their State, but have no hopes of securing anything of that kind. They deem peculiar regulations, however, necessary for their case.

SPEECH BY CASSIUS M. CLAY.

CASSIUS M. CLAY made a lengthy speech at the Ladies' soldiers' Relief Fair to-night, mainly devoted to his views of the present aspect of our foreign affairs, and to personal matters. He said he was the only one of our Foreign Ministers who had been singled out for abuse in European papers in the interest of the rebels, which he took as a compliment to himself, and an evidence of his fidelity to his country's cause. England, he spoke of as our bitterest enemy with a malignant Press inspired by Government, and which truthfully represented its spirit. France, he insisted, was not unfriendly. Americans had derived unjust ideas on this subject solely by crediting the representations of the British Press. The Emperor was known to be friendly to this country, and semi-official statements in the papers were in our favor. He utterly denied that France desired to interfere, but said that persistent effort had been made by the British Press to make us believe she did. Of Russia, he could hardly find words enough to express his admiration. He spoke of the Czar as one of the greatest and wisest of reigning monarchs; referred to his beneficent emancipation policy, and declared that the United States could rely implicitly on his friendship in any emergency. He asserted, further, that England knew Russia and France to be firm friends to this country, and would therefore not dare to interfere with our efforts for suppressing the rebellion. With reference to our home policy, he urged an earnest prosecution of the war, using every means in our power to crush the rebellion. He was ready to serve the Government here in any way in which his services could be made available; but he would strike only for Liberty, and would never draw the sword for the protection of rebels' slaves.

THE DUTIES OF COMMISSIONER DRAPER.

SIMEON DRAPER, Esq., the War Department's Commissioner to supervise the business of collecting and forwarding straggling soldiers and officers to their respective regiments, has nothing to do with granting discharges and leaves of absence. Letters on that subject should be addressed to the Adjutant-General only.

Mr. DRAPER has received many letters asking him to obtain discharges, leaves of absence, &c. As this is not a part of the business belonging to his office, he has sent them to the Adjutant-General. The great number of such letters prevents their being replied to individually in brief. This is the rule of the Department: A leave of absence not exceeding twenty days may be granted to commissioned officers by the commander of any army or department, or direct when the certificate of a medical officer shall show beyond doubt that a change of location is necessary to save life, or prevent permanent disability. If an officer cannot return to his duty when his leave is out, he need not apply for an extension, as no order will be issued granting one. He must account for his absence by sending to the Adjutant-General and to his regiment commander a proper medical certificate; and when he returns to duty his case will be examined by a proper tribunal to ascertain if he had sufficient cause for absence. No furloughs whatever will be given to enlisted men, and all heretofore given are revoked. They are cared for in United States hospitals.

THE CASE OF GEN. CASEY.

The order calling Brig.-Gen. SILAS CASEY before the Retiring Board has been revoked, and the General assigned to the charge of the new recruits arriving here, who are to be drilled in his improved system of tactics, which has just been adopted by the entire army, with slight modifications.

GEN. BLENKER.

Gen. BLENKER arrived here this morning.

THE GUNBOAT CHIPPEWA.

The gunboat *Chippewa*, under command of Commander BRYSON, which has been for some months on the blockading squadron of Wilmington, N. C., has arrived at the Navy-yard, and this morning her masts were being taken out, preparatory to giving her a general overhauling.

PRISONERS.

Last night about a hundred prisoners were removed from the old Capitol to the new military prison in Georgetown. These were the greater part for desertion.

The prisoners brought up by the *Freeborn* on Sunday, including fifteen negroes captured with the parties, were sent to the old Capitol this morning.

ARRESTED FOR KIDNAPPING.

Messrs. WISE and ALLEN, two well known police officers of this city, were arrested last night by Gen. WADSWORTH on the charge of kidnapping.

CAPTURE OF VESSELS ENGAGED IN THE SLAVE-TRADE.

WASHINGTON, Sunday, Aug. 10.

SIR: The inclosed copy of a dispatch from Her Majesty's Commissioners at Loando, relates to the capture by Her Majesty's ship *Griffin*, on the 27th of March last, of a bark and schooner, without name or colors, fully equipped for the slave-trade, off Black Point, on the west coast of Africa. I have been instructed by Earl RUSSELL to communicate this capture to you as of interest to the Government of the United States, in consequence of the bark in question having been stated to have left New-York on the 1st of December last.

I have the honor to be, with high consideration, Sir, your most obedient and humble servant,

W. STUART.

To Hon. WM. H. SEWARD, &c., &c., &c.

LOANDA, April 1, 1862.

MY LORD: We have the honor to acquaint your Lordship that Her Majesty's ship *Griffin*, Commander PERRY, whilst proceeding to this place with the last mail from Fernando Po, on the 29th ultimo, fell in with a bark and a schooner in company, at Black Point, in lat. 0° 50′ south, and lon. 11° 45′ east. Commander PERRY immediately sent a boat to cut off the schooner, whilst he proceeded in the *Griffin* in the chase of the bark, and having soon come up with her, he found her to be fitted in every respect for the immediate reception of slaves, which, to the number of 800, she was to have shipped the following morning, at Black Point, for the island of Porto Rico. This bark, which was about 400 tons, was destitute of all proofs of nationality; nor were there any papers found on board from which her name could be ascertained; but from a statement from some of the crew it appeared that she had sailed from New-York on the 1st of December last, and touched at Campechie in Mexico, where the necessary equipments were completed. Later in the afternoon of the same day, the officer who had been detained from the *Griffin* in pursuit of the schooner, returned on board in charge of that vessel, having found her abandoned by her crew, and fully equipped for the conveyance. This schooner being small, and incapable of safely undertaking a voyage to St. Helena, Commander PERRY, after causing her to be surveyed, destroyed her by fire, sending the necessary evidence to St. Helena, in order that the case might, with that of the bark, be brought before the Vice-Admiralty Court in that colony for adjudication.

We have, &c.,

(Signed,) EDMUND GABRIEL, H. V. HUNTLEY.

To the Earl RUSSELL, &c., &c., &c.

DEPARTMENT OF STATE, WASHINGTON, Aug. 11, 1862.

SIR: I have the honor to acknowledge the receipt of your note of yesterday, accompanied by a copy of a dispatch from Her Majesty's Commissioners at Loando, to Earl RUSSELL, announcing the capture off Black Point, on the west coast of Africa, by Her Majesty's ship *Griffin*, on the 27th of March last, of a bark and schooner, without name or colors, fully equipped for the Slave-trade.

In reply, I have to thank you for the information thus communicated, which is in every respect entirely acceptable and gratifying.

I have the honor to be, Sir, with high consideration, Your very obedient servant,

WM. H. SEWARD.

To Hon. WM. STUART, &c., &c.

SICK AND WOUNDED SOLDIERS.

By the S. R. Spaulding at Philadelphia.

PHILADELPHIA, Tuesday, Aug. 12.

The following are among the sick and wounded soldiers by the steamer *S. R. Spaulding*, which has arrived here from Harrison's Landing:

Capt. Henry Benson, 4th New-Jersey Artillery—died on board the boat.
G. W. Byrrell, 4th Vermont.
Daniel L. Boyce, 4th Vermont.
Samuel A. Atwood, 4th Vermont.
Chas. Wells, 4th Vermont.
Chauncey B. Lampher, Berdan Sharpshooters.
John E. Wills, Berdan Sharpshooters.
Corp. E. Souper, Berdan Sharpshooters.
Sylvanus L. Brittmore, Berdan Sharpshooters.
B. J. Holbrook, Berdan Sharpshooters.
Nevvill Potter, Berdan Sharpshooters.
Geo. A. Watkins, Berdan Sharpshooters.
E. G. George, Brass Artillery.
Samuel J. Williams, Berdan Sharpshooters.
Benj. F. Warner, Berdan Sharpshooters.
Theo. Wilson, Berdan Sharpshooters.
Corp. Daniel Perry, Berdan Sharpshooters.
Thomas Conners, Berdan Sharpshooters.
Sergt. Orlando Leonard, 4th Vermont.
Wm. E. Bliss, 4th Vermont.
W. H. F. Marsh, 4th Vermont.
W. F. Williams, 4th Vermont.
James Ladd, 4th Vermont.
Martin Rickard, 4th Vermont.
Henry J. Smith, 44th New-York.
Orville de Coblugh, 4th Vermont.
Jacob Dods, 4th Vermont.
Henry Morgan, 4th Vermont.
Harrison Long, Berdan Sharpshooters.
P. A. Reed, Third Massachusetts.
S. L. Lugrin, Third Massachusetts.
George Fisher, Berdan Sharpshooters.
J. F. May, Fifth Massachusetts.
F. B. Washburn, Second Massachusetts.
Corp. John Evans, Fourth Vermont.
Eldridge G. Gibson, Fourth Vermont.
James H. Lewis, Berdan Sharpshooters.
Richard B. Canass, Second Michigan.
Newton R. Johnson, Fourth Vermont.
George Brown, Third Massachusetts.
Wm. S. Weeden, Berdan Sharpshooters.
Charles L. Norton, Berdan Sharpshooters.
Leonard Johnston, Berdan Sharpshooters.
Corp. Abraham Saulsbury, Berdan Sharpshooters.
Corp. Samuel Lusted, Berdan Sharpshooters.
Corp. John Johnston, Berdan Sharpshooters.
Sergt. W. H. H. McCallister, Fourth Vermont.
Corp. E. S. Naylor, Fourth Vermont.
Corp. W. H. A. Brainer, Fourth Vermont.
Corp. C. C. Spalding, Fourth Vermont.
Corp. R. Spaulding, Fourth Vermont.
Corp. J. B. Little, Fourth Vermont.
Sergt. M. Houghton, Fourth Vermont.
Norman Wright, Fourth Vermont.

THE EUROPEAN NEWS.

Arrival of the Scotia and City of Baltimore.

The Prince de Joinville on the Battles Before Richmond.

Earl Russell and the Blockade-Breakers.

They are Requested to "Refrain" from Contraband Trade.

Objects of the French Naval Expedition to the Gulf.

THE LATEST INTERVENTION CANARDS.

CRUISE OF THE TUSCARORA.

THE CANADIAN QUESTION.

MOVEMENTS OF GARIBALDI.

Interesting Correspondence from London and Paris.

The Royal mail steamship *Scotia*, Capt. JUDKINS, from Liverpool at 11½ o'clock on the morning of the 2d, and from Queenstown on the evening of the 3d inst., arrived here yesterday morning.

The screw steamer *City of Baltimore*, Capt. KENNEDY, which sailed from Liverpool at noon on the 30th, and from Queenstown on the 31st ult., arrived here yesterday morning. Her news is anticipated.

The United States sloop-of-war *St. Louis* sailed at Madeira July 22. She was last from Fayal, and was supposed to be bound to Lisbon.

The United States war steamer *Tuscarora*, the sudden departure of which from Southampton caused some excitement under the belief that she was going in pursuit of the Confederate steamer *Merrimac* from Plymouth, arrived at Queenstown on the afternoon of the 21st ultimo.

A new steamer, called "290," sailed from the Mersey for Nassau or Havana on the 29th ult., and was supposed to be intended for the Confederates. After quitting the Mersey, she waited outside for a steam-tug, which conveyed to her a crew of fifty men. She is a powerful steamer, of 1,120 tons. On the 30th July she put into Holyhead, where, for some reason which is not explained, all the men left her. It is supposed that the object of the *Tuscarora's* cruise was to look after this vessel, and not after the *Merrimac*.

The Continental journals continue to propagate mediation rumors. The *Independance Belge* asserts that negotiations had taken place between France, Russia and England, with a view to the recognition of the Confederates and mediation between the belligerents. France and Russia made advances to England, but had not received a final reply.

There is another story that the English Cabinet had dispatched a Special Envoy to President LINCOLN to urge him to take upon himself the initiative of the re-establishment of peace with the South, if he wishes to avoid the offer of mediation by the principal European Powers, which, according to the foreign journals, would lead to a war, if not accepted.

The *Army and Navy Gazette* observes in regard to these rumors, that it is much more probable that for some time to come, English mediation will be confined to such forms as are given to the feelings of the people in the Bishop of Oxford's directions to his clergy. The same journal says that the real reason for the departure of Prince DE JOINVILLE and his nephews was the Mexican war. They knew the French would be avenged, and that this would provoke threats and ill feeling toward France among the Americans.

The Bishop of Oxford had addressed the subjoined letter to the Archdeacons in his diocese:

CUDDESDON PALACE, July 31.

MY DEAR MR. ARCHDEACON: May I request you to communicate to the clergy of your Archdeaconry the following injunction from me as ordinary: That upon the Sunday after the receipt of it, they give notice to their congregations at the conclusion of the Nicene Creed, in these terms: "You are earnestly desired to make your supplications to Almighty God, who is the author of peace and lover of concord, that he will promote peace among our brethren in America, and inspire their hearts with Christian unity and fellowship.'"

To allow of which prayer, a short pause will for the present be made after the suffrage in the Litany, "That it may please thee to give to all nations unity, peace and concord," and also in the prayer "for all sorts and conditions of men," after the words, "we commend to thy fatherly goodness all those who are in any way afflicted or distressed in mind, body or estate." I am, my dear Mr. Archdeacon,

Your faithful friend and brother,

S. OXON.

The *Morning Post* comments upon Gen. POPE's proclamation that his army is henceforth to subsist on the country in which it happens to be carrying on military operations. The *Post* says this means that war is henceforth to be based on rapine, and that in fact it presents the obvious resource of a Government whose credit is failing. The same journal reviews Prince DE JOINVILLE's own account of the circumstances of the departure of the Orleans Princes from America, and says it is really the most unfortunate and deplorable account of the departure which has yet been given, and quite explains the alleged refusal of President LINCOLN to receive the Princes in a farewell audience.

In the House of Commons on the 31st ult., Mr. VILLIERS introduced an additional clause to the bill for the relief of the distress in the manufacturing districts, permitting a resort to loans as well as to rates in aid, and after some debate and amendment the clause was agreed to.

In the House of Lords on the 1st, the Earl of Shaftesbury presented a petition from the Cotton Supply Association, and moved for returns respecting the Godavery. The petition was in favor of opening up the Benares district by a canal system. There was cotton enough there to supply Lancashire for twelve months, and the Madras Irrigation Company were ready to invest their capital, and, after payment to themselves of 12 per cent. thereon, to secure the surplus profit to the Government without any Government guarantee. The Association prayed that private enterprise be allowed free scope in India.

The Duke of Argyle, in thanking the Earl of Shaftesbury for the manner in which he had brought this question forward, said the Government had rejected all schemes for purchasing, growing, or guaranteeing cotton, on the ground that they would thus interfere with private enterprise.

Lord LLANOVER believed that private enterprise was [illegible]

The Charleston Mercury.

DAILY PAPER—TEN DOLLARS PER ANNUM, PAYABLE HALF-YEARLY IN ADVANCE. | SPONTE SUA SINE LEGE FIDES RECTUMQUE COLENTUR. —VINDICE NULLO | COUNTRY PAPER—THREE A WEEK—FIVE DOLLARS PER ANNUM, IN ADVANCE.

VOLUME LXXXI. | CHARLESTON, S. C., FRIDAY, AUGUST 15 1862 | NUMBER 11,527

Battle of Cedar Mountain, August 9, 1862

NEWS BY TELEGRAPH.

NEWS FROM KNOXVILLE.

KNOXVILLE, August 13.—An intelligent prisoner who has just arrived from Nashville, *via* Huntsville and Stevenson, reports that the roads are lined with Federals, and all the bridges strongly guarded. Our guerillas were a constant source of annoyance to the enemy. The preceding train from Huntsville to Stevenson was fired into and three Federals killed.

Perfect desolation reigns outside of Huntsville. The houses are all deserted by the owners and sacked by the enemy, and the fields are laid waste. Gens. BUELL and ROSSEAU have twenty thousand troops in the vicinity of Huntsville, and five hundred negros are engaged in entrenching on the north side of the city. Four hundred negros and a large force of Federals are fortifying Stevenson. The enemy have succeeded in rebuilding all the bridges and broken tracks on the railroad from Nashville to Huntsville and Bridgeport.

FROM THE NORTH.

GRENADA, August 13.—The St. Louis *Republican* of the 7th inst. says that the guerillas continue a vigorous warfare in Missouri. They are crossing to the north side of the Missouri River. On the 4th inst. they attacked and dispersed a body of Federal troops at Taylorsville. Colonel POINDEXTER is reported to be near Hudson with 1200 partizans, threatening the capture of that place. A despatch from Shelbourne reports PORTER, with 2400 men, encamped near Newark. He had bagged two companies of militia there, after a slight reconnoissance, with a large number of horses and guns, and a considerable amount of ammunition.

Up to the 8th inst. 22,000 men were enrolled in the State of New York. Important army movements are anticipated in Washington. No one is allowed to pass MCCLELLAN's lines. Large numbers of negros are being stolen by POPE, near Sanardsville, Virginia. Eleven political arrests had been made at Fairfax C. H., under POPE's late order.

The New York *Commercial* states that an important secret expedition, consisting of one steamer, with a crew of picked men, has left a Federal port, and would soon be heard from.

The news from Gen. POPE's army presents nothing of importance. An advance of an expedition from Culpeper was intimated, the object of which is not stated. Typhoid fever prevails in many of the regiments.

The shooting of Gen. MCCOOK, near Salem, Ala., has led to the burning of every house in the neighborhood of the occurrence, and several citizens have been hung by the Yankees. It is also rumored that the exasperated Unionists in Nashville have shot a number of prominent secessionists.

WM. H. WEBB has entered into a contract with the United States Government to build an iron steam-ram, to be covered with six inch iron, to have two revolving turrets, like the *Monitor*, the bow to be covered with [illegible] iron, and to have a solid iron ram projecting therefrom half the length of the vessel. The price is $1,200,000.

PROGRESS OF THE WAR.

THE BATTLE OF CEDAR RUN—FURTHER PARTICULARS OF STONEWALL'S VICTORY.

From the Richmond papers, of Wednesday, we gather the following additional particulars of the victory gained by Gen. Stonewall JACKSON on Saturday last:

On Friday evening a portion of Gen Jackson's division, consisting of the 1st, 2d and 3d brigades, under the command of Gen. Charles S. Winder, crossed the Rapidan river, a few miles above the railroad, and having advanced a mile into Culpeper county, encamped for the night. Early on Saturday morning, the enemy's cavalry drove in our pickets and fired into our camp. Expecting an immediate attack, our force was drawn up in line of battle, but no attack being made in several hours, they were ordered to march towards Culpeper Court House. In the meantime, several other of our brigades had crossed the Rapidan.

Our men advanced by roads running parallel to, and on the west side of, the Orange and Alexandria Railroad. About four o'clock the enemy's artillery, posted near Mitchell's station, six miles distant from the Rapidan, opened fire upon our advance guard. Our batteries having come up, a terrible artillery fight, of two hours' duration, ensued. Early in the engagement Gen. Winder was struck by a fragment of shell and killed. The effect of the death of this brave officer had, for a moment, a most depressing effect on the whole division, which it required the utmost efforts of the brigade, regimental and company officers to counteract. Between six and seven o'clock our infantry were ordered forward, and the engagement became general. With unsurpassed bravery, our men, for nearly an hour, fought against almost overwhelming numbers. We had but between four and five thousand men, whilst the enemy had at least fifteen thousand. Still, our gallant troops held their own, and, in parts of the field, even drove the enemy before them at the point of the bayonet. The instances of individual and regimental valor were innumerable. Officers who participated in this fight, and who were in the sanguinary battles before Richmond, have since said that they never before saw the Yankees fight with such obstinate desperation.

When the battle was at its fiercest. Gen. Ransom brought reinforcements, which turned the tide in our favor. After a brief show of further resistance, the enemy gave way at all points, and retreated hurriedly. A portion of General A. P. Hill's division, coming up as the enemy gave way, pursued him vigorously to within two miles of Culpeper Court House.

It was confidently stated on the streets yesterday that our troops had entered and still held Culpeper Court House, but from the best information we can obtain, we are inclined to believe that General Hill, on arriving within the short distance mentioned of the Court House, discovered that the enemy had strong entrenchments with heavy siege guns mounted at that point, and that he in consequence fell back a mile or two to await reinforcements.

Our loss in this battle is estimated at eight hundred killed and wounded. The enemy's loss is thought to have been at least three times as great. Among the killed are the following: Lieut. Col. Garnet, of the Forty-Eighth Virginia Regiment, commanding the Second Brigade; Lieut. Col. Richard Cunningham, of the Twenty-First Virginia Regiment; Major Lane, of the Forty-Second Virginia Regiment; and Capt. Wm. H. Morgan, of Company F, Twenty-first Virginia Regiment. Capt. Morgan's company may be said no longer to exist. It carried into action eighteen men, but seven of whom escaped unhurt. These seven have been detailed to attend to their wounded companions.

On Sunday morning our forces were drawn up in line of battle, and as Gen. Jackson rode past, the cheers of the men were most enthusiastic. There was some firing early in the morning, but no engagement took place, the enemy declining to reply, although in sight.

A train left Gordonsville for Richmond on Tuesday afternoon with 120 prisoners, including two or three commissioned officers.

ORDER TO PREVENT THE EVASION OF MILITARY DUTY BY THE YANKEES.

The LINCOLN Government has just issued the following stringent order:

WAR DEPARTMENT,
WASHINGTON, August 8, 1862.

Ordered, 1st. By direction of the President of the United States, it is hereby ordered that, until further orders, no citizen liable to be drafted into the militia shall be allowed to go to a foreign country, and all marshals, deputy marshals, and military officers of the United States are directed, and all police authorities, especially at the ports of the United States on the seaboard and on the frontier, are requested to see that this order is faithfully carried into effect. And they are hereby authorized and directed to arrest and detain any person or persons about to depart from the United States in violation of this order, and report to Major L. C. Turner, Judge Advocate, at Washington City, for further instructions respecting the person or persons so arrested and detained.

2d. Any person liable to draft who shall absent himself from his county or State before such draft is made, will be arrested by any Provost Marshal or other United States or State officer wherever he may be found within the jurisdiction of the United States, and conveyed to the nearest military post or depot, and placed on military duty for the term of the draft; and the expenses of his own arrest and conveyance to such post or depot, and also the sum of five dollars as a reward to the officer who shall make such arrest, shall be deducted from his pay.

3d. The writ of *habeas corpus* is hereby suspended in respect to all persons so arrested and detained, and in respect to all persons arrested for disloyal practices.

EDWIN M. STANTON,
Secretary of War.

CONTEMPLATED "REBEL MOVEMENTS."

A Washington letter writer, under date of the 4th inst., says:

Washington is filled to-night with rumors derived from secession sources by way of Baltimore, that the rebel army at Richmond is now *en route* to make a grand attack upon Washington. This rumor is strengthened by information through similar sources at Fredericksburg, that in less than a week the Federal forces there will be driven out. It is known that the secessionists there have daily and immediate and unrestricted communication with Richmond, and it is regretted that for several days past there have been sent out from that point no scouting parties to ascertain what is going on in front of our position there.

The report from Warrenton to-night that the rebels have actually evacuated Richmond, is not believed, unless they have left their capital for the purpose of attacking Washington. Shrewd military men are of opinion that this is the real and only interpretation of the evacuation, if any has taken place.

It would be a bold and desperate movement, suited to the fortunes of the rebel leaders. They know that it is necessary to strike somewhere before the three hundred thousand recruits shall be brought into the field to overwhelm them. It is known that ever since the seven days' fight in front of Richmond they have been concentrating there all the forces that could be raised in every quarter of the South, and it is believed to be the purpose of the rebel generals to leave in the strong works around Richmond a sufficient force to repulse any attack of Gen. McClellan's army, while an immense army shall be thrown forward, not perhaps down the valley of the Shenandoah, but around it, into Maryland and upon Baltimore and Washington, and thus change the aspect of the war, while Gen. Pope is kept amused with a show of force in his front, until too late to fall back in defence of Maryland from the invaders.

These are the speculations of military men; but they are worthy of consideration, and should stimulate the people of the loyal States to hurry forward their recruits not by scores or hundreds but by regiments and brigades.

IMPORTANT DECISION OF LINCOLN—NEGRO REGIMENTS REJECTED.

The recent proposition of the LINCOLN Government to incorporate negro regiments in the great army by which, it is hoped, the South can be subjugated, has produced so much dissatisfaction, mutiny and desertion among the volunteers from the Northwest, that the Abolition President has found it expedient to back down from his previously expressed resolve. He now disclaims any intention of accepting negro regiments. The following telegraph correspondence of the New York *Herald*, under date of Washington, 4th, will be found interesting:

The efforts of those who love the negro more than the Union to induce the President to swerve from his established policy are unavailing. He will neither be persuaded by promise nor intimidated by threats. To day he was called upon by two U. S. Senators, and rather peremptorily requested to accept the services of two negro regiments. They were flatly and unequivocally rejected. The President did not appreciate the necessity for employing the negros to fight the battles of the country, and take the positions which the white men of the nation, the voters and sons of patriotic sires, should be proud to occupy; there were employments in which the negros of rebel masters might well be engaged, but he was not willing to place them upon an equality with our volunteers, who had left home and family and lucrative occupation to defend the Union and the Constitution, while there were volunteers or militia enough in the loyal States to maintain the Government without resort to this expedient. If the loyal people were not satisfied with the policy he has adopted, he was willing to leave the Administration to other hands. One of the Senators who had preferred this request was impudent enough to tell the President he wished to God he would resign.

The New-York Times.

VOL. XI—NO. 3399. NEW-YORK, FRIDAY, AUGUST 15, 1862. PRICE TWO CENTS.

FROM THE ARMY OF VIRGINIA.

Gen. Pope's Report of the Battle of Cedar Mountain.

A Clear and Comprehensive Document.

DESPERATE CHARACTER OF THE BATTLE.

The Conspicuous Gallantry of General Banks.

Retreat of the Rebel Forces to Gordonsville.

Jackson's Army Swelled to Seventy Thousand Men.

GEN. POPE'S OFFICIAL REPORT.

HEADQUARTERS OF VIRGINIA, CEDAR MOUNTAIN, Aug. 13, 1862—5 P. M.

To Major-Gen. Halleck, General-in-Chief:

On Thursday morning the enemy crossed the Rapidan at Barnett's Ford, in heavy force, and advanced strong on the road to Culpepper and Madison Court-house. I had established my whole force on the turnpike between Culpepper and Sperryville, ready to concentrate at either place, as soon as the enemy's plans were developed.

Early on Friday it became apparent that the move on Madison Court-house was merely a feint to detain the army corps of Gen. SIGEL at Sperryville, and that the main attack of the enemy would be at Culpepper, to which place I had thrown forward part of BANKS' and MCDOWELL'S corps. Brig.-Gen. BAYARD, with part of the rear of MCDOWELL'S corps, who was in the advance, near the Rapidan, fell slowly back, delaying and embarrassing the enemy's advance as far as possible, and capturing some of his men.

The forces of BANKS and SIGEL and one of the Divisions of MCDOWELL'S Corps were rapidly concentrated at Culpepper during Friday and Friday night, BANKS' Corps being pushed forward five miles south of Culpepper, with RICKETT'S Division of MCDOWELL'S Corps, three miles in his rear.

The Corps of Gen. SIGEL, which had marched all night, was halted in Culpepper to rest for a few hours.

On Saturday the enemy advanced rapidly to Cedar Mountain, the sides of which they occupied in heavy force.

Gen. BANKS was instructed to take up his position on the ground occupied by CRAWFORD'S Brigade, of his command, which had been thrown out the day previous to watch the enemy's movements. He was directed not to advance beyond that point, and, if attacked by the enemy, to defend his position, and send back timely notice.

It was my desire to have time to give the corps of Gen. SIGEL all the rest possible after their forced march, and to bring forward all the forces at my disposal.

The artillery of the enemy was opened early in the afternoon, but he made no advance until nearly 5 o'clock, at which time a few skirmishers were thrown forward on each side, under cover of the heavy wood in which his force was concealed.

The enemy pushed forward a strong force in the rear of his skirmishers, and Gen. BANKS advanced to the attack.

The engagement did not fairly open until after 6 o'clock, but for an hour and a half was furious and unceasing.

Throughout the cannonading, which at first was desultory and directed mainly against the cavalry, I had continued to receive reports from Gen. BANKS that no attack was apprehended, and that no considerable infantry force of the enemy had come forward.

Yet towards evening the increase in the artillery firing having satisfied me an engagement might be at hand, though the lateness of the hour rendered it unlikely, I ordered Gen. MCDOWELL to advance RICKETT'S Division to support Gen. BANKS, and directed Gen. SIGEL to bring his men upon the ground as soon as possible.

I arrived personally on the field at 7 P. M., and found the action raging furiously. The infantry fire [illegible]

[illegible] before this change could be effected it was quite dark, though the artillery fire continued at short range without intermission.

The artillery fire at night by the Second and Fifth Maine Batteries, in RICKETT'S Division, of Gen. MCDOWELL'S corps, was most destructive, as was readily observable the next morning in the dead men and horses, and broken gun-carriages of the enemy's batteries which had been advanced against it.

Our troops rested on their arms during the night in line of battle, the heavy shelling being kept up on both sides until midnight.

At daylight the next morning, the enemy fell back two miles from our front, and still higher up the mountain.

Our pickets at once advanced and occupied the ground.

The fatigue of the troops from long marches and excessive heat made it impossible for either side to resume the action on Sunday. The men were, therefore, allowed to rest and recruit the whole day, our only active operation being of cavalry on the enemy's flank and rear.

Monday was spent in burying the dead and in getting off the wounded.

The slaughter was severe on both sides, most of the fighting being hand to hand.

The dead bodies of both armies were found mingled together in masses over the whole ground of the conflict.

The burying of the dead was not completed until dark on Monday, the heat being so terrible that severe work was not possible.

On Monday night the enemy fled from the field, leaving many of his dead unburied and his wounded on the ground and along the road to Orange Court-house, as will be seen from Gen. BUFORD'S dispatch. A cavalry and artillery force under Gen. BUFORD, was thrown forward in pursuit, and followed the enemy to the Rapidan, over which he passed with his rear guard by 10 o'clock in the morning.

The behavior of Gen. BANKS' corps during the action was very fine. No greater gallantry and daring could be exhibited by any troops.

I cannot speak too highly of the coolness and intrepidity of Gen. BANKS himself during the whole of the engagement. He was in the front and exposed as much as any man in his command. His example was of the greatest benefit to his troops, and he merits and should receive the commendation of his Government.

Gens. Williams, Augur, Gordon, Crawford, Prince, Green and Geary behaved with conspicuous gallantry.

AUGUR and GEARY were severely wounded, and PRINCE, by losing his way in the dark, while passing from one flank to another, fell into the hands of the enemy.

I desire publicly to express my appreciation of the prompt and skillful manner in which Gens. MCDOWELL and SIGEL brought forward their respective commands and established them on the field, and of their cheerful and hearty coöperation with me, from beginning to end.

Brig.-Gen. ROBERTS, Chief of Cavalry of this army, was with the advance of our forces on Friday and Saturday, and was conspicuous for his gallantry, and for the valuable aid he rendered to Gens. BANKS and CRAWFORD.

Our loss was about 1,500 killed, wounded and missing, of whom 290 were taken prisoners. As might be expected, from the character of the engagement, a very large proportion of these were killed.

The enemy's loss in killed, wounded and prisoners, we are now satisfied is much in excess of our own.

A full list of casualties will be transmitted as soon as possible, together with a detailed report, in which I shall endeavor to do justice to all.

JOHN POPE, Major-General Commanding.

REPORTS FROM CULPEPPER COURT-HOUSE.

Special Dispatch to the New-York Times.

WASHINGTON, Thursday, Aug. 14.

The following dispatches have just been received from Culpepper Court-house, dated Aug. 13:

The rebels have fallen back to Gordonsville, where it is supposed they will make a stand. Our cavalry to-day entered Orange Court-house. A number of rebel prisoners, stragglers, were captured by them.

A man named MATHEW PEASE, who was identified by some of our men as a bushwhacker, was arrested as a spy while prowling about our camps. He was sent to Gen. SIGEL'S headquarters, in company with other prisoners. The prisoners captured state that JACKSON'S force is 70,000 men. He was heavily reinforced from Richmond the day following the battle. They represent great dissatisfaction as existing among JACKSON'S army, owing to the scarcity of food and raiment. Eleven dead rebels were found in the woods. They were buried by our troops.

Gen. PRINCE, though a prisoner, was not wounded in the late battle. He was taken prisoner while leading a charge with his brigade. The rebel Gen. WINDER was killed by a shell fired from Capt. MCGILVERY'S Sixth Maine Battery. He was partaking of lunch at the time, in a house occupied by the enemy as a signaling post. The shell killed several other officers who were sitting near him. The rebels were commanded by Gens. Jackson, Hill, Stuart and Ewell.

I have sent a list of 300 killed and wounded by mail.

Gen. POPE threatens to make quick work with correspondents, if they do not stop scribbling nonsense. He told me to warn them of that fact.

The rebels are to concentrate at Gordonsville.

WASHINGTON, Thursday, Aug. 14.

Letters from Culpepper contain no news of interest. On Saturday night, after the action, Dr. STEELE, of the Twenty-sixth New-York, while endeavoring to find his way to his regiment, encountered two rebel soldiers, fully armed. He sternly demanded a surrender, and they were so alarmed, apprehensive of their proximity to our forces, that they surrendered, and the doctor marched them into camp as prisoners.

ADDITIONAL ACCOUNTS OF THE BATTLE.

WAR DEPARTMENT, WASHINGTON, D. C., Thursday, Aug. 14, 1862.

The following has been received here from Cedar Mountain, 6 P. M., 13th:

Gen. MILROY and Gen. BUFORD, with their brigades of infantry and cavalry, followed the enemy beyond the Rapidan. Gen. JACKSON'S baggage trains are seen in the distance, and it is said JACKSON will not make a stand this side of Orange Court-house.

Thirty deserters came within our lines this morning. Nearly all of them are from Louisiana and South Carolina regiments. They tell a very pitiful tale of cruelty, starvation, and distress, and say it will be impossible to hold the Southern army together three months longer. They confirm the reports of the prisoners taken in the late battle about the number of the killed and wounded, and say our artillery fire at night was terribly destructive.

Rev. K. P. SLAUGHTER, of Cedar Mountain, on the side at the foot of which the battle was fought, is a strong Union man, and an ardent advocate of the cause of colonization. His library was destroyed by the Rebel soldiers upon discovering among his papers letters favoring the abolition of Slavery.

Scouting parties from Gen. MILROY'S Brigade passed

FROM THE PRESS CORRESPONDENT.

CULPEPPER COURT-HOUSE, Va., Monday, Aug. 11—Midnight.

In an interview with some of our prisoners to-day they stated that the enemy had treated them with kindness; but one instance of gross outrage came under your correspondent's notice. It was that of Capt. O'BRIEN, of the Third Wisconsin Regiment, who was mortally wounded. The rebel Surgeon told him that he had no chance of living, gave him some water to drink, and left him on the field. Some rebel soldiers subsequently came up, took his watch, and cut his pocket out, containing $260, leaving him to die there. He was brought off the field under the flag of truce, but cannot survive the night. I had the statement from the dying man's lips.

The view of the battle-field was a sight never to be forgotten. It was full of horror. For nearly a mile the dead lay scattered or in heaps, many disemboweled, decapitated and mangled by shells. At the point where CRAWFORD'S Brigade twice dashed on the enemy the sight was fearful.

The rebel General, CHARLES WINDER, was killed, and Major SNOWDEN ANDREWS, of Baltimore, of Gen. EWELL'S Staff, mortally wounded.

The advance lines of the enemy extended nearly up to the line of our batteries on the day of the battle.

A reporter of the Press, by missing his way, got further to the rear than laid down by the flag of truce, and was thus enabled to view the location of the enemy's forces. Their batteries, seven in number, occupy nearly the same positions as when they opened on us on Saturday. He learned that the rebel infantry were to the right of their batteries, and that a large rebel reserve was behind the mountain.

One of the rebel Generals told a Union officer he would be in Culpepper to-night, but up to the small hours of the morning he has not attempted to perform his promise.

It is now estimated that our wounded will reach twelve hundred men. Many amputations have been performed, and many have died from their wounds.

The atmosphere in the town is fetid with fever and perspiration.

Most of the wounded are comfortable: Every Surgeon with his assistants, are at their posts, and admirably have they performed their arduous duties. The Division of Medical Directors have managed the whole arrangements in such a manner that it is believed not a single wounded soldier has been unattended to, or left to suffer a moment longer than absolute necessity required.

The following statistics of Gen. WILLIAMS' command on the day of the battle are the only returns obtainable to-day:

GEN. CRAWFORD'S BRIGADE.

Tenth Maine Regiment—Went into the action with two field, twenty-one line officers and two acting Lieutenants. Present to-day: Two field and twelve line officers and 224 men. Capt. Cloudman and Lieut. Folsom are known to be killed. Capt. Adams, Capt. Nye, Lieut. Rankin and Lieut. Freman are wounded. Fifteen men are known to be killed and 140 wounded.

Forty-sixth Pennsylvania Regiment—Col. Knipe, Maj. Mathews, Capts. Eusebius, Luckenback and Brooks, Lieuts. Selheimer, Craig and Scott, wounded; Capts. Foulks and Griffiths, Lieuts. Greatrake, Wilson, Gorman, Selfridge and A. Caldwell, missing. The total in killed, wounded and missing reaches 246. Every company in this regiment suffered in nearly equal proportion.

Fifth Connecticut Regiment—Wounded and probably prisoners: Col. Chapman, Lieut.-Col. Stone and Major Blake. Missing: Capt. Corliss, Lieut. Chaney and Lieut. Doyle. Wounded: Capt. Packer, Capt. Lane, Lieut. Daniels, Lieut. Dutton, Lieut. Whitney, and Adjutant Smith.

Twenty-eighth New-York Regiment—There is no report of this regiment. It is completely broken up and has been removed from the field. The brave and noble Col. DONNELLY is now breathing his last. Lieut.-Col. BROWN suffered the amputation of his arm to-day.

GEN. GORDON'S BRIGADE.

Second Massachusetts Regiment—Went into action with 22 officers and 474 men. Capt. Abbot, Capt. Cary, Capt. Williams, Capt. Goodwin and Lieut. Perkins are known to be dead. One hundred and ten men are known to have been killed and wounded. Eighty are missing. Among the wounded are Lieut. Robertson, Lieut. Grafton, Lieut. Brownin and Lieut. Okey—all of whom are doing well.

Twenty-seventh Indiana Regiment—Went into action with 511 men and 15 officers. One officer was killed, 2 wounded and 1 is missing. Eleven men were killed, 29 were wounded and 32 are missing.

Third Wisconsin Regiment—Lieut.-Col. CRANE and Capt. O'BRIEN are killed; Maj. SCOTT is seriously wounded. Two officers are missing. This regiment went into action with 11 officers and 426 men. It was in the hottest of the battle. Lieut.-Col. CRANE was shot three times. Either of the wounds would probably have been fatal.

COTHRAN'S Battery, attached to this brigade, lost three men.

On Saturday night, when the enemy shelled our camp, this battery fired four shots, which silenced the enemy. A Lieutenant, two men and eight horses belonging to the latter were found dead next morning.

REBEL ACCOUNTS.

The Battle Called by Them the Battle of Southwest Mountain—A Great Victory Claimed, of Course.

From the Richmond Dispatch, Aug. 12.

The prelude to the battle of Saturday evening occurred on Friday, in Culpepper County, beyond the Rapidan River, in a skirmish between the advance of our army and a large force of the enemy. The latter retreated with some loss in killed and wounded, and twenty-one prisoners fell into our hands, including three commissioned officers, who arrived here by way of Lynchburgh, on Sunday night. The pursuit was continued for some distance, and the Yankee forces made a stand at Southwest Mountain, near Mitchell's Station, about six miles beyond the Rapidan. Slight skirmishing was kept up on Saturday morning, and in the afternoon of that day, about 4 o'clock, an attack was made upon the enemy by a portion of the division of Gen. EWELL, and a brigade under Gen. C. S. WINDER. Over 300 prisoners were captured in this engagement, including thirty commissioned officers.

One of the latter admits that a Federal division was cut to pieces while endeavoring to surround the Stonewall Brigade, and the general belief is that the enemy's loss in killed and wounded is at least four times greater than ours. It was while bravely leading on the men under his command that Gen. WINDER was shot through the breast and almost instantly killed. At one moment the fate of his brigade seemed in doubt, when his supports came up, and the enemy was driven back under an impetuous onset. On Saturday night the division of Gen. A. P. HILL was engaged, and the whole Federal force retreated, the pursuit being kept up for a distance of some five miles. Heavy and rapid firing was heard after midnight, and the supposition is that a battle took place immediately on the Rappahannock River, near the line of Fauquier County.

The prisoners were sent back to Gordonsville, whence they were transferred by railroad to Richmond, guarded by a detachment of the First Maryland Regiment, under Capt. WM. GOLDSBOROUGH.

According to the statements of the prisoners, the force under POPE amounts to 40,000 men.

From the Richmond Enquirer, Aug. 12.

The news from JACKSON'S army, which appeared in yesterday's issue, diffused a lively pleasure throughout our city; and well it might, for it told of a very handsome and most cheering victory, and in the right quarter! All honor to the laurel-crowned hero, and his glorious army!

Although "Stonewall" JACKSON was in the front of our new lines, and notwithstanding he was never known to lose time, or to idle away a single hour, yet the amateur Generals had already begun to indulge in heavy censures at the delay. Folly, stupidity, weakness, criminal trifling, &c., were the terms that were coming freely into use, although they fell on JACKSON and his foot-cavalry, whose fame fills the whole Confederacy! The result shows that JACKSON has not been idle. Those preparations and plans, which are as necessary to victory as are skill and courage in the battle itself, had to be completed. To the impatient, the time seemed to be lost; but as the plowman reaps the recompense of his toil in the harvest which follows, so JACKSON is now rewarded by success.

At the time of writing this, we have not received any additional particulars of the battle of Saturday. Such as may reach us before our paper goes to press, will appear in our news column. The battle must have been a hot one, as the heavy roar of artillery was heard in this vicinity for three hours commencing at 3 o'clock Saturday afternoon.

The capture of Gen. PRINCE and the other commissioned officers, will tend to bring the two warring powers to a speedy understanding as to the future policy of the war. LINCOLN will either relieve the hostages we now hold, by revoking his new war policy as set forth in his own General Orders and in those of POPE, or he will respond by counter-retaliation. This will require further action on our part, and the speedy result must be the discarding of all restraints on both sides, and a war of extermination. We hope, however, that our enemies are not so demented and demoniac as to have seriously resolved to force this upon us and upon themselves.

COMMUNICATIONS INTERRUPTED.

The *Dispatch* of the 12th has the following important paragraph, which shows that somebody has been interfering with the rebel communication between Gordonsville and Richmond:

"The city was full of rumors yesterday of a battle on Sunday, but after the most diligent inquiry we could learn nothing definite concerning it. Certain it is that heavy firing was heard in the direction of the Rappahannock, after midnight (Saturday,) and again for a brief period on Sunday morning. No train had arrived from Gordonsville up to a late hour last night, and no intelligence had been received at the War office to confirm the rumors so industriously circulated throughout the day.

"The enemy had 6,030 troops engaged in the battle on Saturday afternoon."

The following is from the *Enquirer* of the same date:

"Accident to the telegraphic wires on yesterday prevents us from giving our readers any satisfactory information from the lines of the army above Gordonsville. At an early hour in the day the line from Gordonsville to Richmond, *viâ* Lynchburgh, became disordered, and the only resort was then to the direct line, but the operator at Gordonsville, fearful of interruption by Yankee operators, as on a former occasion, declined to transmit intelligence, immediately, through that medium. Soon after this the direct line itself became disordered, and nothing more was heard up to last night from that quarter. The only intelligence which was received at all by telegraph during the day was that 'the movements then in progress were *very important*.' It was owing to this fact that the operator on the direct line deemed it prudent to withhold information until certain that the line was clear."

ARRIVAL OF PRISONERS FROM GORDONSVILLE.

From the Enquirer, 12th.

The prisoners taken at the battle of Southwestern Mountain, twenty miles northeast of Gordonsville, by Gen. JACKSON, on Saturday, three hundred and three in number, reached the city at 4 o'clock yesterday morning. They were simply under guard of a competent force, no unusual means having been resorted to for the purpose of keeping them secure. They were perfectly docile. Gen. H. PRINCE was permitted to take up lodgings in the Exchange Hotel, and the remaining officers were locked up with the men in the Libby Prison. The following is a list of the officers who arrived:

Brig.-Gen. H. Prince, United States Army.
Col. George D. Chapman, 5th Connecticut.
Maj. E. W. Cooke, 28th New-York.
Capt. G. B. Halstead, Adj.-Gen. of Augur's Division.
Capt. W. D. Wilkins, Asst.-Adj.-Gen. of Williams' Division.
Capt. H. S. Russell, Co. H, 2d Massachusetts.
Capt. J. H. Vanderman, Co. K, 66th Ohio.
Capt. P. Griffith, Co. A, 46th Pennsylvania.
Capt. E. A. Bowen, Co. D, 28th New-York.
First Lieut. S. J. Widney, 3d Wisconsin.
First Lieut. H. N. Greatrake, Co. K, 46th Penn.
First Lieut. M. P. Whitney, Co. B, 5th Connecticut.
First Lieut. H. C. Egbert, Co. G, 12th U. S. Inf.
First Lieut. A. A. Chinery, Co. E, 5th Connecticut.
First Lieut. T. E. Gorman, Co. H, 46th Penn.
First Lieut. Wm. N. Kenyon, Co. G, 28th N. Y.
First Lieut. J. D. Bedolesey, Co. D, 10th Maine.
Second Lieut. Veala Moses, 109th Pennsylvania.
Second Lieut. Chas. Snyder, Co. D, 8th U. S. Inf.
Second Lieut. J. D. Woode, Co. B, 28th N. Y.
Second Lieut. A. W. Selfridge, Co. H, 46th Penn.
Second Lieut. Otis Fisher, Co. B, 8th U. S. Infantry.
Second Lieut. Wm. N. Green, Co. A, 102d N. Y.
Second Lieut. H. Walker, Co. I, 3d Maryland.
Second Lieut. J. D. Ames, Co. K, 28th New-York.
Second Lieut. Chas. Doyle, Co. D, 5th Connecticut.
Second Lieut. Wm. McAllister, Co. H, 28th N. Y.
Second Lieut. J. Long, Co. A, 28th New-York.

With regard to the treatment of these officers, the *Dispatch* has the following:

"We understand that the officers of POPE'S command, lately taken prisoners by Stonewall JACKSON, professed never to have heard of President DAVIS'S late proclamation with reference to the commissioned brigands of that army, and declared that they had supposed they were engaged in a civilized warfare! This is the coolest thing of the season. A civilized warfare! They burn down our houses, destroy our property, insult our women, arm the contrabands against us, hang and shoot our patriotic guerrillas, throw whole communities of peaceful citizens into jail to be gibbeted in case our guerrillas kill any more of their bands of cut-throats and robbers, and consider all this a civilized mode of warfare. It is only when the same kind of civilization is applied to themselves that they discover their mistake. The truth is, we have borne these horrible outrages so long and so quietly that our moderation and forbearance have been attributed to fear, and to an inward conviction that we are wrong-doers, and deserve all the punishment we are receiving at Yankee hands. They will now discover their mistake. An eye for an eye, a tooth for a tooth, and a life for a life, will be henceforth meted out to these robbers and murderers with the most scrupulous accuracy. It is true that ten thousand lives of such depraved wretches could not atone for the life of one pure, high-minded patriot; but as each of them values his existence as highly as an honest man, the wholesome lesson of retribution will not be without its influence. All the atrocities and horrors that may characterize the war hereafter rest upon the heads of the invaders, who have inaugurated the system of hanging prisoners, and who have manifested in their whole conduct of the war a degree of inhumanity and barbarity which has shocked the moral sense of the world.

We trust most devoutly that Old Stonewall may succeed in capturing the arch fiend and savage, POPE himself. If he were not as fleet of foot as black in heart, we might anticipate a luxury compared with which the capture of a thousand other Yankee Generals would be dull and insipid. POPE and BUTLER! If those two precious miscreants could only fall into Southern hands!

An officer who accompanied to this city the soldiers of POPE'S command who were captured in the skirmish on Friday, says that he inquired of one of the Yankee officers of the party whether he had read the proclamation of President DAVIS and the order of the Adjutant-General with reference to the treatment they were to receive. They promptly replied that their business was to obey orders, and not read the proclamations of JEFF. DAVIS.

From the Enquirer, 12th.

Brig.-Gen. H. PRINCE had the honor of an interview with Gen. WINDER yesterday, who informed him that as soon as arrangements could be made, he should have more appropriate accommodations than he had enjoyed at the Exchange.

Gen. PRINCE was inclined to remonstrate when the idea of a dungeon was suggested; but a decisive allusion to the Pope programme ultimately succeeded in quieting, if it did not confound the Sepoy General.

We find, also, the following paragraph in the *Enquirer*:

"The officers who arrived on yesterday, from Gordonsville, twenty-eight in number, and who were captured by Gen. JACKSON on Saturday, will not be considered prisoners of war, so long as the recent offensive and uncivilized orders of Gen. POPE remain unrepealed. They have all, Gen. PRINCE included, been placed in the Libby Prison, and will, in a few days, be separately confined, to be treated, and finally punished as felons, should the brute Government of the North persist in claiming the right to murder and pillage."

WHO GEN. PRINCE IS.

This officer, who was captured by our forces in the fight at Southwestern Mountain, on Saturday last, is an officer of the old United States army. In the Mexican war he acted as Adjutant-General of the brigade commanded by Gen. STERLING PRICE, whose confidence and esteem he possessed. When the present war broke out, PRINCE was a Captain of dragoons at Fort Leavenworth, and afterward became commandant of that post. In his intercourse with the people of Missouri and Kansas, he is represented to have acted with gentlemanly courtesy, and had the respect of those who opposed the policy of his Government. Such was his leniency toward the Confederates in Missouri, that he incurred the suspicion and ill-will of such tyrants as SIGEL, LANE, &c. These facts we obtain from an officer connected with Gen. PRICE'S Staff during his celebrated Missouri campaign.

THE REBEL GENERAL WINDER.

Brig.-Gen. CHARLES S. WINDER, who was killed in the battle of Southwest Mountain on Saturday, was a nephew of Brig.-Gen. WINDER, Military Commandant of this District. He was promoted from a Colonelcy a few months ago, for distinguished conduct, and was one among the most meritorious young officers, we learn, in the Confederate army.

Arrival of the Arago from Port Royal.

The United States transport *Arago*, HENRY A. GADSDEN commanding, from Port Royal, S. C., 8:15 P. M., Aug. 10, with passengers, mails and ammunition, consigned to Col. D. D. TOMPKINS, Assistant United States Quartermaster-General, arrived yesterday morning.

The *Arago* has 65 first, and 90 second-class passengers. Among the latter there are 33 prisoners, escorted by a guard of 12 men, in charge of Col. J. D. FESSENDEN.

Her cargo consists of 2,495 boxes cartridges, consigned to Maj. R. H. K. WHITELY, Governor's Island.

The *Arago* brought in tow from Hilton Head to New-York the United States steam corvette *Crusader* (engines disabled.)

Died on board Aug. 13, JAMES BRADY, waiter; Aug. 14, RUFUS BARNARD, of Orville, Ashtabula County, Ohio, late a clerk in the Chief Quartermaster's office at Hilton Head.

At 5¼ A. M. Tuesday, Aug. 12, passed steamship *McClellan* towing ship *Planter* hence for Port Royal.

At 10 A. M., Wednesday, Aug. 13, passed steamship *Ericsson*, bound South.

There was nothing new at Port Royal. The health of troops remained good. The rebel ram which was expected down the Savannah River had not made her appearance. Gen. HUNTER and Commodore DUPONT had made all necessary arrangements for her capture.

We are indebted to Purser GRANTEGEIN for prompt delivery of news packages.

Fire in Boston.

BOSTON, Thursday, Aug. 14.

The Lennox Glass Works, in Lennox, were burned on Monday. Loss $20,000.

IMPORTANT FROM HILTON HEAD.

Dashing Attempt to Run the Blockade at Savannah—A Visit to the Prize—Vigilance of Commodore Dupont and his Squadron, &c., &c.

From Our Own Correspondent.

HILTON HEAD, S. C., Friday, Aug. 8, 1862.

A dashing attempt to run the blockade of the Savannah River, with a valuable cargo, selected with especial regard to rebel wants, was made last Sunday night, the 3d ultimo, by the British screw steamer *Ladona*, of Hull, but a well-aimed shot from one of our heavy guns on Tybee struck her on her starboard quarter, just above the water line, and made her retire. The next day the audacious fellow in command pushed his way into Ossebaw Sound, a few miles southward of the Savannah, trusting to find a clear coast and easy passage up the Ogeechee River to the railroad, where he could discharge and send his goods without difficulty to his expectant customers. Circumstances, however, were against him. He fell into a snare. He had never suspected an inside blockade, and he steamed plumply under the guns of the gunboat *Unadilla*, Capt. COLLINS, which was posted at a point commanding the entrances of both the Ogeechee and Vernon Rivers, waiting with spider-like patience any stray fly of the *Ladona's* species.

Let us congratulate the *Unadilla's* officers and crew on their good fortune. At a moderate estimate, and not at secession prices, the prize and cargo are worth $1,000,000—only one-half of which will go into the coffers of Uncle Sam. Brandies of the best brands, cooling claret, genuine gin with Holland labels, dry goods and gentlemen's ready-made garments, boots and shoes, with one item of 3,000 ounces of quinine—more valuable than all the rest to the Medical Department of the rebel army—compose the main part of the assortment, and some say that a few thousand fire-arms are also to be found on board. This latter assertion the officers of the ship deny the truth of.

The prize was brought into Port Royal on Tuesday, and was dispatched hence by Commodore DUPONT, under command of Acting-Master GREEN, of the *Unadilla*, for Philadelphia, where she will be condemned.

I visited the vessel, and found her Captain, a jolly Englishman—a dare-devil sort of fellow, who, I scarcely think, would hesitate at any risk in affording aid and comfort for cash to his rebel customers, and who certainly bore his misfortune with a philosophical composure which was admirable. He was quite cordial and talkative, facetiously endeavoring to convey an impression that he was bound on a legitimate voyage, but having lost his reckoning, found himself at the place where he was captured. The *Ladona* left Falmouth, England, early in June, with a clearance for Tampico, and having a license from our Consul at Hull to visit Port Royal for the purpose of disposing of his goods. Of course, this license was intended as a blind should any of our blockaders chance to meet the vessel prowling along the coast; but it would have proved a blind of such a flimsy sort that the least penetrating eyes must have seen through it. Stopping at Bermuda for coals, the *Ladona* remained some weeks without being able to obtain them, there being none in private hands upon the islands, and she was eventually compelled to leave for Nassau, using the wood of a wrecked vessel for fuel. Having received coals at Nassau, she started late in July for Savannah, her captain being weak enough to suppose that he could pass the batteries at Tybee and Fort Pulaski. I have told of his failure, and I may as well say, for the benefit of other rash Englishmen, that Capt. LUCKEY advises them not to follow his example. He said that the shots fired at him from the Tybee battery were all in line, and he is profuse in his compliments of our gunnery. The third shot—a large rifle projectile—passed through the iron side of the vessel, three-quarters of an inch in thickness, crashing through his cabin, splintering the woodwork, tearing a hole three feet long in an iron bulkhead, making match timber of state-room doors, striking the vessel on the opposite side, and rebounding with a thud upon the floor. I doubt if any one shot ever did greater damage to a vessel's interior arrangements. In spite of this gentle reprimand, Capt. LUCKEY said that he should have continued his course up the river had not his vessel struck the bar, the water on which is shallower than the charts affirm it to be—probably the result of the obstructions which were placed upon it by the Savannahians in the early part of the rebellion.

The supercargo of the *Ladona* is a Mr. PERDU, who had the gay audacity to request Admiral DUPONT'S consent to remain at Port Royal to look after another steamer—the *Peterhoff*—having a more valuable cargo, of which he is also supercargo, and which he significantly said may soon be expected at Port Royal. His services not being considered available for such a purpose, there is no probability that he will be allowed to remain.

Admiral DUPONT bears his new title well. He is just as affable, just as genial, just as much beloved as when he was a Commodore. In fact there is no change in him, and really, if the newspapers had not announced his promotion to the supreme naval grade, I doubt whether anybody would believe such to be the fact. The official notification of his preferment he has not yet received. May he long live to wear his well-deserved honors. His conduct of the blockade of the extensive line of coast, covered by the fleet of the South Atlantic Squadron, has been marked by great ability and most unqualified success. True, here and there a small-sized vessel has sneaked through our lines, but superhuman vigilance could not have prevented that.

In comparison with this blockade, all others heretofore have been insignificant and easy. Let me enumerate the points at each of which the blockade might be broken and goods conveyed to the railroad which runs through the States of Florida, Georgia and South Carolina. Commencing at Georgetown, S. C., the northernmost port which Admiral DUPONT'S cruisers keep sealed, we next have Bull's Bay, then Charleston, and afterward Stono Inlet, and Edisto and St. Helena Sounds. Port Royal is the next point, and then comes, to the southward, Calibogue, Tybee, Warsaw, Ossebaw, Doboy [illegible] Sounds and Brunswick Bay, in Georgia [illegible] ports of Fernandina, Cumberland, St. [illegible] [Au]gustine and others in Florida. All these [illegible] inlets are practically covered at the cost of [illegible] anxiety and literally sleepless vigilance on the part of Admiral DUPONT and the officers and seamen of his command.

And the horrors of the blockading service, I am satisfied, are not fully understood by any except those who are engaged in it. Take the port of Charleston, for instance, where we have twelve vessels stationed. Isolated from the rest of the world, dependent upon a chance vessel for news, getting fresh provisions but once a month, looking each day upon the same dreary coast which the eyes had turned from in disgust the day before, experiencing all manner of personal discomforts, exercising a constant care to escape being run down or fired into by a friend, and to prevent a foe's escape—take these reasons, and add indefinitely to them, and say conscientiously that the life on blockade duty is not the most monotonous and insufferable which humanity may be called to endure and you are more than mortal. H. J. W.

FROM THE REBEL STATES.

Further Reports of Affairs in East Tennessee.

THE EXCHANGE OF PRISONERS.

Agreement in Accordance with which it is Conducted.

THE CASE OF THE STEAMER PLANTER.

Her Former Officers Court-Martialed.

MISCELLANEOUS INTELLIGENCE.

We have received copies of the Richmond *Dispatch* and Richmond *Enquirer* of the 12th inst., from which, in addition to the extracts relating to operations north of the rebel Capital, which we give elsewhere, we take the following matters of interest:

THE BATTLE OF TAZEWELL.

MOBILE, Aug. 11.—A special dispatch to the *Advertiser and Register*, from Knoxville, 9th says: "The enemy's loss in the battle at Tazewell is estimated at 36 killed, 120 wounded, and 60 prisoners. Our loss was 8 killed and 30 wounded, which fell mostly upon VAUGHAN'S Third Tennessee Regiment, who behaved heroically.

Gen. FORREST arrived here Wednesday. Two hundred of the Second Kentucky Regiment, (Federal,) left Rock Island, Tenn., and came over to our lines. Desertions from the Federal army are continually taking place. The Federals have no confidence in the troops in Middle Tennessee. Bull NELSON'S forces are at McMinnville. All the turnpikes between Murfreesboro and McMinnville are strongly barricaded."

A SHORT WAY HOME AGAIN FOR LINCOLN'S RECRUITS.

From the Enquirer.

Our enemies have listed the last of those among them who were willing to fight us for the love of it. At first they all supposed that it would be a short and easy task to conquer us; and there was accordingly a considerable rush of volunteers for the "glory" thus cheaply to be obtained.

Those volunteers have wasted away in the hardships and conflicts of war. New men are wanted to fill their vacant places, and to swell the dimensions of the invading army. For this purpose volunteers have been called, but they have not come. The Federal authority and the States, and the cities and counties, and wealthy corporations and citizens, have concurred, with their separate "bounties," in offering a large sum to those who might thus be persuaded to volunteer. This resource, too, has failed. Nothing is left now but *the draft*. This has been determined upon; and ere now proclamations have gone out, perhaps, in every Northern State, *to drag* men to a war which has become hopeless, and is, therefore, without attraction, and to impel them, to which there is no laudable sentiment.

Of the men thus drafted, most of those who possess the pecuniary ability will doubtless employ substitutes. Of the three hundred thousand drafts, perhaps one-tenth may be able to hire substitutes; though the estimate is, it may be, too large, as the price demanded will be high. The bargain closed, and the money paid, most of the substitutes will desert at the first opportunity, for Patrick and Gottlieb will have no further use for the war;—such at least is Confederate experience, to a considerable degree.

We have heard that already Yankee smartness has discovered a practical evasion by which the draft can be disarmed of its terrors to the unwilling soldier. By the cartel for the exchange of prisoners, captives are entitled to a parole within ten days after being taken. Returning home, they are not allowed to perform military duty of any sort. They thus are at liberty to follow their private business, and at the same time their enlistment entitles them to soldier's pay.

A shrewd Yankee perceives in this a most desirable condition of things. At home with his family—attending to his private business—getting a pension from Government—free from all drafts and compulsions to bear arms—in condition to boast his patriotism because not at liberty to volunteer—how could a man be better suited who wished to shun the fight and escape the reproach?

And to a Yankee captive there would be the promise of permanency as the crowning feature of his good fortune. The Confederate Government has a large balance in its favor in pending the exchange of prisoners. If a Confederate is captured, therefore, he will be quickly released. But there are thousands of paroled Yankees, whose freedom LINCOLN cannot purchase until he shall have captured as many thousands of Confederates. To a new captive all on the existing list would stand as a sort of preferred class. The fortune of war seems, too, to be in favor of the Confederates, and they are constantly adding to the number of unexchanged Federals.

When LINCOLN'S drafted men—his unwilling braves—the men who have "no stomach for this fight," and no interest to urge them—come down to fill his ranks, they have, therefore, two courses before them. One is to fight ferociously, and thus to be killed or mangled. The other is to take the first opportunity to surrender as captives; and, thereupon, to be paroled, sent home, and there dwell in peace, free of all war's alarms, and pensioned by the Government. Conscious that they are fighting in a bad and hopeless cause, and that they can win no glory, it will not be strange if thousands and tens of thousands of LINCOLN'S soldiers, old and new, shall be willing to a trip home by way of Richmond or Vicksburgh. An "On to Richmond" movement of this sort, we shall be ready to welcome them to, and we commend it to them as the speediest, safest and most economical route home.

FEDERAL GUNBOATS AT WEST POINT.

From the Dispatch.

We learn that three Federal gunboats came up York River to West Point on Sunday morning last, and after remaining there a while took their departure. On the same day the Yankees landed a force at Corr's farm, in King and Queen County. The object of these movements is a matter of conjecture, though it is possible that troops are passing by that route from MCCLELLAN'S army to the Rappahannock.

ALLEGED ATROCITIES OF NATIONAL TROOPS.

From the Dispatch.

An intelligent negro, who has been within the lines of the enemy on the Peninsula, gives a truly horrible account of the atrocities perpetrated in Williamsburgh and elsewhere upon our helpless people. He mentions one case, which makes the blood run cold. The daughter of one of the most prominent citizens (whose name has been given us) was seized, disrobed and then whipped by these worse than savages! Her alleged offence was the expression of some "rebel" sentiments that offended the miscreants. Such are the outrages that have been inaugurated since the victories of the South near Richmond! This is their revenge for a fair defeat in an open field!

The negro who brings this intelligence was left behind by his master, a member of the Twenty-first Mississippi Regiment, when our army retired from Williamsburgh, being sick at the time. As soon as he had recovered, and had worked long enough to repay those who took care of him, he found means of getting through the Yankee lines, though he several times narrowly escaped capture. He says he never wants to dwell among Yankees again—he has enough of their brutality toward white and black to disgust him with the race forever.

THE EXCHANGE OF OFFICERS.

From the Enquirer.

The Yankee Generals and other commissioned officers, captured on the Chickahominy, will be sent on, we understand, to-day, in pursuance of the agreement for the exchange of prisoners between the Confederate States and Federal Government. They number about one hundred and forty.

ARRIVAL OF YANKEE PRISONERS.

JACKSON, Sunday, Aug. 10.

Twenty-seven Federal prisoners arrived here to-day from Baton Rouge. The Yankees are visiting the plantations on the Mississippi River, and plundering generally. Several of the thieves have been captured. Confederate guerrillas are very active and successful in Arkansas.

CAPTURE OF THE STEAMER MEMPHIS.

CHARLESTON, Sunday, Aug. 10.

Private intelligence received here announces the

The New-York Times.

VOL. XI—NO. 3400. NEW-YORK, SUNDAY, AUGUST 17, 1862. PRICE THREE CENTS.

NEWS FROM REBELDOM.

More About the Attack on Baton Rouge.

BRECKINRIDGE'S FIRST DISPATCH.

A CONFESSION OF DEFEAT.

A Strike by the Printers in Richmond.

CONFEDERATE COUNTERFEITERS AT WORK

THE WAR ON THE MISSISSIPPI.

THE ATTACK ON BATON ROUGE.

It will be remembered that BRECKINRIDGE, in a dispatch dated "Ten miles from Baton Rouge, Aug. 6," stated that nothing "decisive" had occurred since the previous dispatch. The following is the missing document:

ONE MILE AND A HALF FROM BATON ROUGE, Aug. 5, 1862.

To Gen. Van Dorn:

Receiving a dispatch that the *Arkansas* would coöperate, I attacked Baton Rouge this morning at daylight, with less than 3,000 men. After a struggle of five hours, we drove the enemy from all points to the arsenal and lower, and to the cover of their gunboats, taking a number of prisoners, several flags, and a considerable quantity of property.

My diminished, exhausted force could not take the arsenal and the troops almost perishing for water, we have withdrawn one mile and a half from the city, but hope to resume the attack in half an hour. I think our loss has been as heavy as that of the enemy. Gen. CLARK is mortally wounded. Col. HUNT, of the Fifth Kentucky, and Cols. THOMPSON and ALLEN, of the Fourth Louisiana, and others, severely wounded. The effective force of the enemy, exclusive of the mortarboats, is reported to us as 5,000 strong.

JOHN C. BRECKINRIDGE, Major-Gen. Commanding.

The dispatches dated Aug. 6, stated that the *Arkansas* failed to come to him, and that she was destroyed on that morning. This completes the history of the attack on Baton Rouge, and disposes of the canard which the Grenada *Appeal* and its worthy coadjutor, the Chicago *Times*, have so industriously circulated, that four National regiments had surrendered to BRECKINRIDGE.

GEN. VAN DORN RECOMMENDS PROMPTNESS.

HEADQUARTERS DEPARTMENT OF SOUTH MISSISSIPPI AND EAST LOUISIANA, VICKSBURGH, June 28, 1862.

SPECIAL ORDERS No. 5.—Gen. VAN DORN assumes command in person of the defence of Vicksburgh and surrounding country. Gen. M. L. SMITH will remain in immediate charge of the defence of the city, and will call upon the General Commanding for whatever force he may require from time to time. He will keep him informed of his operations, and of the movements of the enemy on the river in his front.

The General commanding the troops in the field (BRECKINRIDGE'S corps) will make the disposition already indicated by written instructions to him, and will be continually ready for active service. The greatest promptness is essential to success, and it is hoped that all will be actuated by the same spirit to resist to the death, that the citizens of Vicksburgh have manifested by the willing sacrifice of their property.

Lieut.-Col. FERGUSON is charged with observing the movements of the enemy on both flanks of our position. His cavalry should be vigilant, energetic, fearless and untiring. Information must be conveyed promptly to these headquarters. The outpost under command of Gen. COWEN is important, and it is expected that he will do all in his power to guard it well—as well, also, as the post of Col. MILLER.

Couriers should be kept at all headquarters, to convey information to general headquarters. Col. FERGUSON will detail them upon application.

Let it be borne in mind by all that the army here is defending the place against *occupation*. This will be done at all hazards—even though this beautiful and devoted city should be laid in ruins and ashes.

By order of Maj.-Gen. VAN DORN.
M. M. KIMMEL, Major and A. A. G.

AN APPEAL.

HEADQUARTERS, DEPARTMENT SOUTH MISSISSIPPI AND EAST LOUISIANA, VICKSBURGH, July 4, 1862.

To the People of Louisiana and Mississippi:

You will see by General Order No. 10, from these headquarters, that the District Commanders have been directed to assemble together in camps of instruction, and to organize all the troops that can be raised in this Department. They have also been directed to appoint the necessary officers for that purpose, subject to the approval of the President.

I earnestly appeal to you to respond to their call. The object is the defence of your homes as becomes a brave people. The citizens of Vicksburgh have given you an example of what a heroic people may accomplish when they are truly patriotic and brave.

Victory once more sits smiling in the folds of our long drooping banners—the enemy have been driven back in Virginia—he has withdrawn his forces from Charleston Harbor to defend his Capital—is puzzled what to do in North Mississippi and Tennessee, and is still baffled at Vicksburgh. The river is not yet his. One more effort—one more determined blow—and we are free.

EARL VAN DORN, Major-General.
M. M. KIMMEL, Major and A. A. G.

DISLOYALTY NOT COUNTENANCED.

HEADQUARTERS DEPARTMENT SOUTH MISSISSIPPI AND EAST LOUISIANA, VICKSBURGH, July 4, 1862.

GENERAL ORDERS, No. 9.—The General Commanding confidently calls upon all officers, both civil and military, as also the citizens generally, to coöperate with and sustain him in all things necessary for the defence of the country.

Disloyalty must and will not be countenanced. The credit of the Government must be sustained. The seeds of dissension and disaffection shall not be sown among the troops. Speculation and extortion upon soldiers and citizens will not be tolerated; and to these ends the General Commanding orders:

1. Any person who shall trade, or attempt to trade, with the enemy, under any pretence whatever, or who shall give any signal to, or in any manner hold communication with the enemy for the purpose of giving information concerning the Confederate forces, or shall pass into his camps or through his lines without a passport from the proper authority, shall suffer death.

By order, GEN. VAN DORN.
(Signed) M. M. KIMMEL, Maj. and A. A. G.
Official copy:
L. D. SANDIDGE, C. S. A., A. A. A. and Ins. Gen.

A JOKE FROM RUGGLES.

HEADQUARTERS FIRST DISTRICT DEPARTMENT No. 1, TANGIPAHO, La., July 10, 1862.

GENERAL ORDERS No. 5.—1. Commanding officers of troops will take immediate measures to prevent trespass of every kind on the communities of this District.

2. Provost-Marshals will make written applications to officers commanding troops or guards to arrest all offenders, military or civilian, who shall, on any pretence whatsoever, impress, seize or possess horses, cattle, provisions or plantation outfits, in an unauthorized manner, without written instructions for the act from these headquarters.

3. *The General commanding feels constrained to indicate, for the information and guidance of officers and men zealous in our sacred cause, that there is some stock, reputed fine—horses and cattle—at and in the vicinity of Baton Rouge, worth special attention and consideration, for the impressment of which this shall be, and is a good and sufficient order.*

4. The people of Louisiana, whose sons bear her standard aloft on distant fields of glory and victory, whose wives and daughters have been insulted by invaders, debased and infamous, call on every man within her bounds to protect and defend their liberties and firesides, and to hurl the enemy from their soil. This they ask in the name of eternal justice and of the omnipotent Avenger.

By command of Brig.-Gen. RUGGLES.
L. D. SANDIDGE, A. A. G. and Inspector-General.

NON-INTERCOURSE.

HEADQUARTERS FIRST DISTRICT, DEPARTMENT No. 1, TANGIPAHO, La., July 2, 1862.

GENERAL ORDERS No. 2.—1. By authority of the Major-General commanding Department No. 1, and under the existing public necessity, martial law is hereby declared throughout the First District, embracing Louisiana east of the Mississippi River, and the counties of the State of Mississippi bordering on the Gulf of Mexico.

2. All persons, residents and non-residents, within this jurisdiction, will conform strictly to the requirements of this condition of things, and observe such regulations as shall be, from time to time, published under authority from these headquarters.

3. Intercourse with the enemy, by all persons, citizens, non-residents and slaves, will be strictly regulated by the customs of war, and no departure permitted without the special sanction of the Commanding General of the District, or higher authority.

4. All officers in the exercise of official authority, civil and military, are hereby enjoined to require from all persons strict conformity to the existing state of martial law, and to prohibit and prevent all intercourse or traffic with the enemy, or with persons within the enemy's lines, by land or by water, except under a flag of truce, unless otherwise specially authorized from these headquarters.

By command of Brig.-Gen. RUGGLES.
L. D. SANDIDGE, C. S. A., A. A. A. and In. General.

A CAMP OF INSTRUCTION.

GENERAL ORDER No. 1.—Having been assigned to the command of the Camp of Instruction for Eastern Louisiana, it is announced that said camp has been established near the town of Tangipaho, in the parish of St. Helena. All males between the ages of eighteen and thirty-five years, residing in the parishes of West Feliciana, East Feliciana, Washington, East Baton Rouge, Livingston, St. Tammany, Ascension, St. James, St. John, Orleans, St. Bernard, Plaquemine, St. Charles and Jefferson, are hereby ordered to report in person immediately to the undersigned at said camp.

No exceptions will be allowed upon the certificates of physicians, except those who hold commissions as Surgeons in the C. S. Army.

By order of Secretary of War.
J. G. PICKETT, Commanding Camp of Instruction.
TANGIPAHO, La., July 12, 1862.

THE REBEL RAM ARKANSAS.

OFFICIAL REPORT OF LIEUT. BROWN.

HEADQUARTERS THIRD DISTRICT, VICKSBURGH, July 25, 1862.

EDITOR JACKSON MISSISSIPPIAN—*Sir:* I am directed by the Brigadier-General Commanding, to hand you the accompanying communications from Capt. BROWN, of the C. S. gunboat *Arkansas*, for publication.

The first letter refers to the fight in Yazoo River, before the ram entered the Mississippi, where she encountered the whole Yankee fleet.

Whilst everything connected with the recent trip of the *Arkansas* from Yazoo City to this place is interesting to all of us, it is also due to Capt. BROWN and his brave crew that this, not the least brilliant of her noble exploits, should be made public.

Very respectfully, your obedient servant,
J. F. GIRAULT, A. A. General.

STEAMER ARKANSAS, VICKSBURGH, July 15, 1862.

GENERAL: The *Benton*, or whatever iron-clad that we disabled, was left with colors down, evidently aground to prevent sinking, about one mile and a half above the mouth of the Yazoo, (in Old River,) on the right hand bank, or bank across from Vicksburgh.

I wish it to be remembered that we whipped this vessel, made it run out of the fight and haul down colors, with two less guns than they had; and at the same time fought two "rams," which were firing at us with great guns and small arms—this, too, with our miscellaneous crew, who had never, for the most part, been on board a ship, or at big guns. I am, General, very respectfully, your obedient servant,

(Signed) J. N. BROWN, Lieut. Commanding.
To Brig.-Gen. M. L. SMITH, Commanding Defenses at Vicksburgh.
A true copy, J. F. GIRAULT, A. A. General.

C. S. GUNBOAT ARKANSAS, VICKSBURGH, July 23, 1862.

SIR: I beg leave herewith to send a list of names of the killed and wounded of the detachment who so nobly volunteered from the forces of your command, on — June last, to aid in making up a crew for this vessel, to wit:

Killed—John Kane, private, Pinkney's Battalion Louisiana Volunteers; Charles Madden, private, Clinch's Battalion Louisiana Artillery; Henry Shields, Co. E, Antonio Florez, Co. G, and Daniel O'Sullivan, Co. A, of the Twenty-eighth Louisiana Volunteers. Total killed—5.

Wounded—William Alexander, private, Clinch's Battalion Louisiana Artillery; Thomas Lynch, Sergeant, Clinch's Battalion Louisiana Artillery; Bernard Martinez, private, Twenty-eighth Louisiana Volunteers. Total wounded—4. Total killed and wounded—9.

I regret the loss of these men to the vessel and to their country. They fought well. Very respectfully,

(Signed,) J. N. BROWN, Commander C. S. N.
To Brig.-Gen. M. L. SMITH, Comm'g at Vicksburgh.
A true copy, J. F. GIRAULT, Asst. Adjt.-Gen.

A STRIKE IN RICHMOND.

The Richmond *Examiner* denounces a Typographical Union in that City. It says:

"Lately, when the *Examiner* office was already paying five cents more per thousand ems than any other newspaper in the city, this combination sent certain arbitrary regulations to the proprietor of this journal, which he having refused to obey, the "society" ordered the printers in this office to strike. They did strike; the leader of the set having declared that he had no complaint against the office or his wages; but being a member of the "society," he was forced to leave.

The manager of this office then placed in the *Dispatch* an advertisement, stating that a foreman and eight compositors could find employment in this office, and that the highest wages would be given that were given in this city. On yesterday, the morning of its first appearance, it was seen that the *Dispatch* had permitted it to be followed or accompanied in close juxtaposition with this answering notice:

"WANTED—The journeymen printers of all cities and towns in the Confederate States to know—that there is at this time more printers in this city than can find employment. The advertisement of the Richmond *Examiner* for printers is caused by the refusal of the proprietor of that paper to pay his hands for time devoted to his service. N. G. SMITH, President Richmond Typographical Society."

In this advertisement is seen a practical act of this combination. It is a direct, unmistakable attempt to prevent this newspaper from procuring any workmen without submission to the dictation of the conspiracy. If any act by the laws of Virginia, can constitute an indictable offence, this is one. Besides the public misdemeanor, the assertion of this person SMITH, to the effect that the proprietor of the *Examiner* has refused to pay hands for time devoted to his service, being libelous as well as false, constitutes a private injury for which legal proceedings have been commenced against the libeler himself, and the publishers of the Richmond *Dispatch*, the utterers of his libel; and it will soon be ascertained whether the Courts of Justice afford protection to a man engaged in a useful branch of industry against conspiracy and slander directly employed to destroy his ability to carry it on.

Meanwhile, we wish again to inform all honest printers, if there are any in this city or elsewhere who desire employment, that they can find it permanently here at the highest wages per thousand ems paid anywhere, and twenty per cent. higher than is paid in any other office in this city.

The question involved in this "strike" is not whether we will pay the highest wages for a thousand ems, but whether an illegal combination shall extort terms which would render the publication of this newspaper impracticable, by destroying its profits and its organization.

SPIRIT OF THE PRESS.

IMPOSSIBILITY OF SUBJUGATING THE SOUTH.

From the Richmond Enquirer, Aug. 12.

When Gen. GREENE was conducting the war on the part of the colonies, in South Carolina, during the closing years of the Revolution, it was his habit to go into "Summer quarters" during the hot weather, Winter in that climate being much more favorable for military operations than Summer. "The high hills of Santee" were a favorable resort on these occasions. The temperature here for some days past has been such as would do honor to Carolina latitudes, and has probably had some influence on military operations. The Yankees, we trust, felt the full effects of this glowing illustration of the sunny South.

But the seasons of high temperature do not last sufficiently long with us to be permanently debilitating; so that our soldiers will be ready for the long march and the double-quick, and for days of fighting, as soon as the heat descends to a degree that will allow of active exertion. As the campaign is rapidly passing by, it is to be supposed that the Generals on both sides will make diligent use of the remaining months; and we may accordingly expect stirring times in all quarters ere frost settles down upon the earth.

Since the war began a great change has taken place in the ideas of the Northern people. As the Albany *Journal* says, the South has taught them many lessons. They have learned from us the falsity and folly of that delusion which they indulged, to the point of absolute absurdity, that there was a large "Union sentiment" at the South. They have learned that the South is "terribly in earnest," is cordially united, is brave, and is resolved to maintain its separate existence at every hazard and under all circumstances. They have felt the skill of our Generals and the prowess of our soldiers, before whom their own have fled on many a field. They have seen that the hopes which they built as to the weakness of our social fabric are mere imaginings; even THURLOW WEED confessing this, and declaring that our slaves are an important element of our military power.

But the knowledge thus gained seems to have inflamed the passions rather than informed the judgments of our enemies. Instead of enlightening the head, it has embittered the heart. The war is now prosecuted far more from feelings of revenge and hate, and a desire to do us all possible harm, for the gratification of mere malice, than from any remaining hope of accomplishing the purpose with which it was commenced. Petty persecutions of private citizens are not the means of conquest, but the manifestations of chagrin and rage under disappointment and defeat.

There is a reason of selfish interest which, indeed, will bind LINCOLN and his party to hostilities as long as it be possible to wage them. They made the war. Through long years they were kindling its fires, despite all the remonstrances of the wise and patriotic of both sections. They scouted these warnings, and assured the people of the North that the sectional predominance and glory to which they invited them could be usurped and enjoyed in peace, the oppressed section being too weak and spiritless to resist. They thus made the war, and are now responsible for it and for its success. When it shall have ended in failure, as it will, they will be the victims of the popular wrath. Not more surely was King GEORGE's war ministry hurled from place and power by the failure of their endeavor than will LINCOLN and his party be driven into political exile and disgrace when once it is ascertained that the war must end, and the South still unconquered. The legacy of an enormous public debt, and of a national disgrace still more galling, will be the memorials of the Abolition-Republican Party when it leaves the stage, amid the execrations of the populace.

This "evil day" for himself, LINCOLN will put off as long as he can, at whatever cost of human life and treasure. Hence, instead of closing a hopeless war, he stimulates it by new ferocities. He bribes his hired bands to their work by proclamation of license to sack and pillage whatever they can find.

These men have not a single argument, entitled to decent respect, for the war they are now waging. So far as it is intended to gratify their malice, they are doing the express work of the evil one. So far as they cherish a lingering hope that the chances of continued war may develop some now unknown means of accomplishing their evil design, they are seeking a result which they themselves have branded as infamous.

ANOTHER MANASSAS LETHARGY.

From the Richmond Dispatch, Aug. 12.

It has been six weeks since the last gun was fired in the fight around Richmond that sent MCCLELLAN "skedaddling" to the shelter of his gunboats at Westover. Since then a lethargy as deep as that which pervaded the army and the country after Manassas seems gradually settling down upon us. We are, apparently, waiting for the enemy to recruit his exhausted strength, and to come forth in the cool weather that will be upon us in the next sixty days. By that time his regiments will all be filled up, and we shall be assailed by three hundred thousand additional troops. We shall at least escape the chance of attacking him before he is ready. We are giving him all the time he can desire. He can never reproach us with pressing him when he is not prepared. What the consequences will be it is not worth while to anticipate. We saw what they were last year. It is fated, it seems, that we are never to reap the fruits of any victory, no matter how decisive. Manassas was followed by the abandonment of nearly half of Virginia. Shiloh was followed by the entire loss of the Mississippi and the fall of New-Orleans. What is to follow the victories around Richmond we cannot imagine. We have not much more to give up, unless we mean to abandon Virginia altogether.

The people of this country ought to be made aware of the truth before it is too late. We are rapidly giving way to the same delusion that lulled our people into security last year, while the enemy was enlisting and training 700,000 men, and building and preparing 300 vessels-of-war. We are lulled by precisely the same species of delusion. We are still told that England is not only about to recognize our existence, but to take up arms in our behalf, as if it were not plain that she has no intention of doing so, but that France would long since have done it had she not interfered to prevent it. We are told that the North is discouraged, precisely as we were told after Manassas that she could not raise men for the further prosecution of the war. We listen to the song of the syren. We suffer the warm months, when the Yankees, by the mere force of climate, are unable to prosecute their designs, to pass unheeded over our heads. We shall not be awakened until the first white frost, when we shall be aroused by the thundering tread of 300,000 soldiers, come to reinforce those whom we have already beaten, and whom we leave to receive the expected succor before they again take the field. For us the lessons of the past have no instruction; to us reverse and suffering are as though they had never occurred. We apparently love to be deceived. We are sleeping the sleep of Manassas, and it seems as though nothing can break its chain.

THE EXPLOIT AT SUMMERSVILLE.

We copy from the Lexington *Gazette* the following account of the late expedition into Nicholas County, Virginia:

"On Wednesday, the 23d July, the battalion under the command of Maj. R. A. BAILEY, of the Twenty-second Virginia Regiment, composed of the Second Rockbridge Dragoons, Capt. GIBSON, the Charlotte Cavalry, Capt. COCHRAN, and the Valley Rangers, Capt. LACKEY, received marching orders. The command was encamped about five miles east of Union Monroe, and about twenty-five miles from Meadow Bluff, the place where the force under Gen. COOK was encamped.

Maj. BAILEY crossed the Greenbrier River on the first day, and selected a place to encamp for the night, as cautiously as he could, to keep the enemy from discovering his movements, the country being full of Union men. The next morning, (24th,) the battalion proceeded westward through Greenbrier County, crossing the Sewell Mountains, and late in the evening, when we were about to encamp, Maj. BAILEY received intelligence that a force of about 150 Federal troops were stationed at Summersville, the shire of Nicholas County. Before this, I know not where he was going, but this information altered his purpose, and he determined to attack Summersville early the next morning, which was about nine miles distant.

When we started from camp the Charlotte Company was put in front. The second day it came the turn of the Rockbridge Company to march in front; but on the morning of the 25th Maj. BAILEY called upon Capt. GIBSON to draw up his company in front, to lead the charge on Summersville. At about midnight the command moved, and reached Summersville at a little before daylight. The advance guard, composed of an equal number of men from each command, kept a few hundred yards in front. When the guard approached within thirty yards of the Federal pickets it was halted, and commanded to advance one at a time. One of the guard replied that it was the Federal cavalry coming in. The sentinel insisted for one to advance at a time. The advance guard still approaching, saying it was the Federal cavalry, the sentinel said: "By G—, I say halt, or I will shoot." Just then our guard put spurs to their horses, and were fired on several times by the picket. Several balls also passed over the head of the column, when it passed by the picket-post and through the village.

Before we reached Summerville, Maj. BAILEY requested the command to raise a shout on entering the town, and never was a request better responded to. I never heard such a noise from the same number of men. Half a mile of the road on this side of the town was macadamized, and the noise of the feet of the horses in the charge, the shouting of the soldiers, and firing of guns, was enough to wake up the dead. The column advanced quite through the place, to the house where the officers were quartered. The house was entered at once by some of the Rockbridge Cavalry, and all the officers captured. The privates were taken, generally, by the other companies.

After the officers were taken, several soldiers were examining the room, when one, feeling under a couch, caught the leg of a man, and looking under, he said; "Come out, you scoundrel." This fellow was Dr. RUCKER, late of Allegheny, then Provost-Marshal of Nicholas. This fellow, getting into this easy post, fancied he was secure, but we came on him as a thief in the night.

When he was dragged out from under the couch by Mr. JAMES WETHERS, he surrendered, and immediately set about trying to induce the belief that he was on the Confederate side. But all efforts to deceive us failed. He was soon confided to the care and keeping of Mr. WEST PAXTON, of Rockbridge, by Capt. GIBSON.

When the noise of the cavalry was first heard at headquarters the Colonel arose and went out into the porch in his night dress, to see what was the matter. He and a Captain, two Lieutenants, and Dr. Rucker were together. The Colonel and Doctor had little time for reflection. They soon found themselves in limbo.

Some twelve or fifteen shots were fired at us, doing no injury—two men shot through their clothing, but not a man hurt. From our side there were perhaps twenty shots. Three men were killed that I know of, one mortally wounded, and another seriously but not mortally wounded. Some of the prisoners that we took said that there were ten or twelve killed. Six or eight men in the hospital were paroled, and the rest, amounting in all to seventy-three, were brought to the Salt Sulphur Springs.

The route which we had to travel was circuitous, and made a most fatiguing march. We penetrated into the enemy's country at least one hundred miles, in rear of his lines. I doubt very much whether a more daring and dashing feat has been carried through since the war commenced. The enemy had every opportunity to cut us off. We had a most difficult road to pass over. Returning to camp we were loaded with captured articles. Over a hundred Enfield rifles were taken, and as many destroyed by fire.

The prisoners, generally, were pleasant and agreeable. We treated them kindly, and they seemed to be grateful for it. Among the prisoners there was a Lieut.-Colonel, one captain and two lieutenants and seventy privates. The stores destroyed amounted to ten or fifteen thousand dollars, and property captured to probably as much.

COUNTERFEITING CONFEDERATE MONEY.

From the Richmond Examiner, Aug. 12.

The Lynchburgh *Virginian* says that WILSON C. HEWITT, of Liberty, proprietor of the Hewitt House, has been detected in passing counterfeit money on the Bank of Bainbridge, Ga., and the Central Bank of Alabama. The notes were printed in this city, upon the order of ROGER L. MARTIN, purporting to be for the hospital at Liberty, though no such person was ever there. HEWITT, on his own, was agents of the Express Company, and of course received the packages of notes that were sent by express. Information was sent to the Central Bank of the fact that these notes were in circulation, and an officer of the Bank was sent on to investigate the case. He arrived *incog.* at the Hewitt House, and received one of the spurious notes in change. HEWITT was thereupon arrested, and lodged in jail last Friday.

On Saturday his case underwent investigation, and he was sent on for further trial. There were printed $13,500 of the Central Bank notes, of the denominations $2, $3 and $4, signed B. BOX, President, and P. CAM, Cashier. Of the notes of the Merchants' Bank of Bainbridge, $4,000 in all were printed. They are signed J. S. LONG, Cashier. Many of these notes are supposed to be circulating in Franklin, and the people are cautioned against them. It is supposed that HEWITT circulated from $5,000 to $10,000 of the Liberty Savings' Bank notes. These were scarcely less fraudulent upon their face than the others, as no such institution is in existence. HEWITT is now in jail at Liberty.

SIMON STERN and his brother-in-law, ROSENBURG, have been arrested at Columbus, Ga., with $13,070 in counterfeit Confederate money. They acknowledged that they had bought it in Nashville, Tenn., at a low price. They also had $10,000 in unsigned $20 bills. They had been doing an extensive business purchasing cotton at 26 cents with their bogus money. J. JOHNSON, from Montgomery, Ala., who, as he said, has gone to Columbus "to see them hung," was arrested and imprisoned as an accomplice.

HOW NARROWLY RICHMOND ESCAPED

From the Richmond Examiner.

The Yankees are preparing for another desperate effort to capture the City of Richmond, and we may as well make up our minds to meet the issue fairly and squarely. Their chief demonstration, despite all feints in other directions, is, no doubt, to be made from Fredericksburgh, and the Rappahannock as a base. But it is not improbable that what they call their mortar fleet is to second the principal movement by an attack upon Drury's Bluff. Certain it is that the mortar fleet has arrived in the James River: and it is equally certain that it can render no assistance in the grand object of the campaign of the year, except by a ferocious assault upon our works at Drury's Bluff.

But for the barricade that was inserted in the river at that point in the early part of May last, in consequence of the clamor of this newspaper, which it raised in imminent peril of Castle Godwin, Richmond would have been surrendered to the enemy's fleet on the 17th day of that month; and the Confederate Government would have been eking out a migratory existence in some of the upper districts—probably Raleigh, the Company Shops, or Flat Rock—in one or the other of the two Carolinas.

A NEW WORK ON THE WAR.

The following advertisement appears in the Richmond *Examiner*:

NEW FORTHCOMING HISTORY OF THE WAR.

In the preface to *Cause and Contrast*, I stated that if that work met with public favor, it was intended merely to constitute an introduction to a history of the present war.

Through the patriotism of our heroic people, the leniency and generosity of the newspaper Press, and the liberality and friendship of the kindest and most disinterested of publishers, my first historical essay was crowned with unanticipated success. While thus returning thanks of gratitude to all of my patrons, I have to announce my resolution of fulfilling, as soon as possible, the promise made in a moment of doubt and misgiving.

I am not, indeed, unaware of the fact that, to enter on the writing of cotemporaneous annals, is the most difficult undertaking of an historian; but I also know that HERODOTUS, THUCYDIDES and TACITUS accomplished it successfully; and while my sense of inferiority sincerely disclaims even the suggestion of a comparison, which would evidently be humiliating, I can say with reverence—as DANTE did of VIRGIL—that they are my authors, my masters and my guides.

With this view still before me, I have succeeded in collecting a large and invaluable mass of documents and other historical material. I have placed myself in communication with the officials of the several State Governments in the Confederacy, as well as with those of our General Government, each and all of whom have nobly promised to supply me with facts indispensable to complete history. But other information is necessary, and to supply this desideratum I now earnestly solicit the aid of all who feel an interest in putting the gigantic proportions of our struggle on a footing which shall place them fully and fairly in sight of an impartial world; the aid of Generals, all army officers and privates, informing me as to the plans, disposition of forces upon the field, marches, incidents, and results of battles and engagements; the aid of citizens in the vicinities of places invaded by the foe, setting forth such depredations, public wrongs and deeds of darkness as he has perpetrated. These are perishable essentials, if not recorded by the cotemporaneous historian; and as it is my chief ambition to render my enterprise candid, critical, philosophical and complete, every fact bearing upon such subjects will be most thankfully received, and properly acknowledged in the contemplated work. And in this direction, I may add with propriety, while totally dissenting from his views relative to our administration, that the well digested and excellently systematized work of my friend, Mr. POLLARD—*First Year's History of the War*—is inestimably meritorious. Every similar publication should be hailed with pleasure, and I here renew my solicitation to all who feel a desire to promote home literature, to contribute their mite (where he has been lavish) toward my sources of information.

T. W. MACMAHON, Richmond, Va.

GEN. M'CLELLAN'S MOVEMENTS.

As long ago as July 30, the Richmond *Dispatch* published this paragraph:

"The daring exploit of a few members of the Prince George Cavalry, on James River, opposite MCCLELLAN's camp, last Saturday morning, has led to greater watchfulness on the part of the enemy, who seem to fear for the safety of their fleet of transports. All the vessels have been drawn up as near as possible to the northern shore of the stream, where they are protected by gunboats. The belief that a considerable portion of MCCLELLAN's army is being withdrawn for the purpose of reinforcing POPE, gains strength daily. Information has reached us within the past week that large bodies of Federal troops were quietly crossing the Chickahominy and marching down the Peninsula toward Fortress Monroe; but before giving currency to this report, we preferred to await further developments. It is now asserted that observations from the opposite side of James River show that many of the enemy's tents have disappeared, and it is also noticed that the vessels in front of the camp frequently diminish in number during the night. That some important movement is in progress, seems to be well authenticated; and the utmost caution is observed, with the view of preventing the Confederate authorities from learning its object. It is presumed that MCCLELLAN, unwilling to hazard another advance towards Richmond from below, will hold his present fortified position with a sufficient number of men, protected by gunboats, while the business of conquering the "Rebel Capital" will be intrusted to POPE, the idol of the present hour in Yankeedom, who is to have all the men and means necessary to make "short work" of the enterprise.

GEN. WADE HAMPTON.

From the Carolina Times:

In consequence of Gen. STUART having been made Major-General, his fine brigade of cavalry has been assigned to our gallant fellow-citizen, who has the elements of character to prove himself a worthy successor as he will do. He commands now a noble brigade, numbering nearly four thousand men. Among them are the First North Carolina Cavalry, the Cavalry of COBB's Legion, the Jeff. Davis Legion, the Tenth Virginia Cavalry, the Hampton Legion Cavalry, to which two companies from South Carolina have been recently added. We learn that Major M. C. BUTLER, of Williamsburg fame, is now Colonel, and that Capt. FRANK HAMPTON has been appointed Lieutenant-Colonel.

We expect to hear of brilliant doings with such a noble brigade, which has already signalized itself.

A Skirmish—Two Rebels Hung.

KANSAS CITY, Saturday, Aug. 16.

On Thursday morning, Col. PENICK, with a detachment of men, attacked a camp of rebels near Bare. The loss of the rebels is not known. Our loss was two killed and seven wounded.

Two rebels who had been hauling supplies for the rebels for a week or two, and had stated the day before that there was no camp in the neighborhood were taken with arms in their hands, and having Col. PENICK's protection papers on their persons, were immediately hung.

Another Rebel Steamer Coming.

ST. JOHNS, N. F., Saturday, Aug. 16.

The steamship *St. Andrew* arrived last evening and sailed for Quebec this morning. She reports that the steamer *Mercadotte* is advertised to sail from London on the 15th for St. Johns, and private letters received here state that she is a rebel steamer.

From Utah.

FORT BRIDGER, Utah, Thursday, Aug. 14.

A short time since, the Indians stole 150 horses and mules near this place, which belonged to JACK ROBERTSON. The Mormon troops, under Capt. SMITH pursued them 200 miles without success. The troops were without [illegible] a week, and were obliged to

IMPORTANT FROM KEY WEST.

CAPTURE OF ANOTHER PRIZE STEAMER.

Cargo of Armstrong Guns and Enfield Rifles Seized.

PROGRESS OF THE YELLOW FEVER.

ARRIVALS AND DEPARTURES.

From Our Own Correspondent.

KEY WEST, Fla., Saturday, Aug. 9, 1862.

Another English steamer was captured by the United States steamer *Santiago*, Capt. RIDGLEY, on the 3d inst., off the coast of the Bahamas, where the smoke was seen early in the morning, which, upon approaching, proved to be a steamer making all speed for escape, the chase continuing for seven hours. A shot across her bow now brought her to, and boarding, she was found to be the British propeller *Columbia*, from an English port, bound for St. John, N. B. without any register or clearance, which important documents the captain says were inadvertently forgotten, and left. The cargo consists of forty Armstrong guns and carriages ready for mounting; several thousand Enfield rifles, a large quantity of army blankets, lace, tin, and various other articles. The supercargo says the cargo cost $200,000 in England. There were on board six persons as passengers, who are known to be pilots for the Carolina coast, and two persons who were recently discharged at New-York from a condemned prize. The *Columbia*, a new iron propeller of about 400 tons burden, and in good order, is now in port awaiting the action of the Prize Court.

Cases of yellow fever still continue to terminate fatally, notwithstanding the great precaution taken by the authorities. All vessels from Havana or any infected port, are sent into quarantine for thirty days, and the utmost care is taken to guard against every means of infection or contagion on shore. Unacclimated persons are the victims, and since the first appearance of the disease upon the island, which has been traced to a vessel from Havana, (the bark *Adventure*, whose mate died in the hospital on the 1st of July,) there have been about thirty cases that have proved fatal, whilst many have recovered and are doing well. Where the cases are taken early, and judiciously treated, there is small danger of fatal termination, and we may set it down that the disease is not in a violent form, when we consider that the population of the island is about 4,000, which includes soldiers and strangers in large proportion, and mostly Northern men, nearly all of whom are much exposed to the hot sun in their daily avocations.

Reports have been received that the fever is raging quite severely at Havana, and also in a lesser degree at Nassau, N. P.

The only war vessels now in our port are the frigate *St. Lawrence*, steam gunboats *Santiago* Capt. RIDGLEY, *Penguin*, the *Sagamore* and the schooner *Wanderer*. The latter returned from a cruise along the Gulf coast on the 6th, having a prize which they had captured off Cape Sable, and now lies moored near the Custom-house, under the guns of Fort Taylor. The United States mail steamer *Fulton* left our harbor, for New-Orleans, on the 7th; the *Marion*, Capt. PHILLIPS, on the 8th. The transport steamer *Delaware*, from Port Royal, with Gen. TERRY and suite, arrived on the 7th, and have gone to Fort Jefferson on a tour of inspection, and will return here in a few days. Supplies of medical stores and lumber are being sent from here to Port Royal, by order of the Quartermaster.

The steamer *General Meigs*, army transport, arrived from Fort Pickens on the 7th, and is loading up with stores to return to that place. She is to leave this day. The steam transport *Saxon* has just arrived from New-Orleans full of passengers, bound for New-York. She is receiving coal, and leaves this morning. There is no news by her of any importance.

The weather continues very favorable to health. Not a day but there is a cheering breeze, and showers are quite frequent. Vegetation is as fresh and vigorous as at any period of the year, and our island is dressed in all its ordinary garb of beautiful flowers and shrubbery, overhung by the graceful and lofty leaves of the cocoanut in its unvaried and ceaseless supply of health-giving fruit.

The bark *Fanny*, Capt. HERRICK, is now loading with cotton for New-York, and will leave in a few days. Her cargo is Prize Cotton, and sent, by order of the Court, for sale in that market.

F.

AFFAIRS IN KANSAS.

The Africans—Jim Lane—The Raid on Independence, &c., &c.

From Our Own Correspondent.

LAWRENCE, Monday, Aug. 11, 1862.

I think I may as well commence my letter with the Africans, as they seem about the most important class of people in the country—especially in Kansas, and most especially in Lawrence. When I came into this place, a few days ago, I was startled by the clouds of contrabands that met my view. Lawrence has been a sort of Mecca for these poor people, and they have flocked here in great numbers, with every hope of freedom in full bloom, and confident of protection at the hands of their friends. Nor are they wrong. The people of Lawrence, as well as of all Kansas, are true to the noble sentiments which inspire them in their contest with despotism, and have by no means forgotten the dark days when *they* were hunted by the same bloodhounds now on the track of the fugitive black man.

In the welcome that Kansas gives the negro I think there is a good deal of self-denial. Its people have never been negro-lovers; in fact they generally desire that the blacks shall stay away, and this irruption of fugitives is, in a personal point of view, anything but pleasant. As I walked through Massachusetts-street and saw the citizens picking their way through the dusky crowds that filled the sidewalks, I could discover the real feeling of the people to be that this anomalous emigration was a nuisance. Negroes are everywhere; the whole place sounds of negroes, feels of negroes, smells of negroes. They fill to overflowing all the hovels of the town, and literally swarm in the sheds and stables intended for the use of other animals, and yet, so truly chivalric is the impulse of the citizens here, that, although they acknowledge the disagreeable consequences of this influx, yet nothing can be kinder or more patient than the manner in which they treat the poor creatures who have thus complimented them by confiding in their generosity. I am sure that four-fifths of Lawrence would hail the voluntary departure of the negroes with acclamation; and yet, if anyone were wantonly to insult or abuse the lowest of them, every citizen would cry out in indignation. As to kidnappers, and such like gentry, you may rest assured that it would be better for JEFF. DAVIS to go alone into MCCLELLAN's camp than for one of those individuals to venture a turn at his trade in Lawrence.

The negroes, too, are behaving well. Many of them are shiftless and idle; how can it be otherwise, when we consider their education and uncertain prospects? But, in the main, they do their best. Most of them work, in their way; they seem honest, and are overflowing with good nature. The hotels, where they act as servants, waiters, grooms, &c., echo, from morning till night, with the resonant peals of their contagious laughter. Lucky for the inmates if the night itself does not bear impressive testimony to the irrepressible hilarity of their dispositions.

Do not suppose Lawrence the only town whose population has thus been augmented. All the rest have increased in a greater or less degree; and in many instances the rural districts have thus been in part repaid for their contributions to the arms of the Republic.

The "grim chieftian, JIM LANE, is at his work, or rather, I should say, his *works*; for he has on hand several enterprises, either of which would daunt "any other man." He came into Leavenworth the other day, and had a "war meeting" got up to stimulate recruiting. You have heard of the little row that followed; how Mr. PARROTT made answer to his speech, and the crowd turned upon him who had before been their favorite, and could scarcely be brought to listen to his golden eloquence because it seemed calculated to discourage enlistments. I don't think Mr. PARROTT meant it to have that effect; but his animosity against LANE is so great that it blinds his judgment and leads him astray. But LANE thrives under all such attacks; so long as his specialty is to recruit soldiers, all who oppose *him* must incur the odium of opposing enlistments. He is now on a stumping tour through the southeast part of the State, organizing his recruiting enterprise as he goes. He seems endowed with supernatural strength and resolution. The other evening in Lawrence, he spoke two or three hours—carrying with him the crowd which completely filled the street in front of his stand, received his friends during the rest of the night, and started at 4 o'clock in the morning in a hack to meet an appointment the next evening, forty miles away! And this kind of labor he will keep up till Congress meets again. With the work on hand he needs to do so, for he has to *bury* his rival, Gov. ROBINSON, who is dead, but still above ground—fill all the State offices with his favorite friends at the coming election, and organize an army of defence for Kansas in the meantime.

I must not omit to say that LANE is very popular among the blacks. Under his direction they are enthusiastic to enlist and fight. Already about a hundred stalwart fellows are enrolled in Lawrence in two companies, both expected to be filled. I have had the satisfaction several times to see them drilling here in the street, and they march to the music of loyalty with such hearty good will, as makes one wish that the arms now being placed in the hands of the secesh militia of Missouri, were intrusted rather to the black men, in whom is no taint of treason.

LEAVENWORTH, Tuesday, Aug. 12.

I arrived here last evening on my way East, and found the city in a state of excitement that resembled a scare. News had been sent of a raid by HAYES and QUANTRELL upon Independence, and a threatened attack on Kansas City. There were only some six or seven hundred men here, but Lieut.-Col. BURRIS promptly took five hundred of these, put them on the steamboat *Majors*, and started for the scene of conflict. Meantime, some three hundred rebel prisoners were left at the Fort in charge of a third their number of soldiers, and apprehensions were felt that they might embrace so favorable an opportunity to rise and resume their personal freedom, if, indeed, they did not arm themselves, and do a little bushwhacking on their own hook. So the "Home Guards," an institution almost mythical here, was called out and sent up to the Fort on duty. The night was unattended by any disturbance, and the *Majors* has returned from Kansas City with accounts of matters in that vicinity. As you have a correspondent with Col. BURRIS' expedition, who will post you fully, I will only say that the rebels surprised our force at Independence, under Col. BUELL, and captured the whole, except a few killed. Col. BUELL was anxious to surrender, and waved his handkerchief in token of his amiable disposition at the outset. He is believed to be a traitor.

This feat performed, QUANTRELL retired, having paroled the prisoners taken. Col. BURRIS' scouts report no force at Independence; and I think no immediate attack need be feared on Kansas City. The citizens of Independence welcomed the marauders and even *participated in their attack* on our troops. How long will misplaced leniency and ruinous imbecility—not to say treason—be allowed to usurp the places of vigor and loyalty in dealing with these full-fledged miscreants?

Col. JENNISON is placed in charge of the African department of the recruiting service here, by Gen. LANE. I understand that the whole enterprise looks encouraging.

J. H. W.

THE DEPARTMENT OF VIRGINIA.

Arrival of Gen. Burnside at Culpepper Court House.

BOSTON, Saturday, Aug. 16.

A special dispatch to the *Journal* says that Gen. BURNSIDE, with his army, has arrived at Culpepper.

ORDER FROM GEN. POPE.

HEADQUARTERS ARMY OF VIRGINIA, NEAR CEDAR MOUNTAIN, Aug. 11, 1862.

GENERAL ORDER NO. 13.—The Major-General commanding discovers with great dissatisfaction that General Order No. 5, requiring that the troops of this command be subsisted on the country in which their operations are conducted, has either been entirely misinterpreted or grossly abused by many of the officers and soldiers of this command. It is to be distinctly understood that neither officer nor soldier has any right whatever, under the provisions of that order, to enter the house, molest the person, or disturb the property of any citizen whatsoever.

Whenever it is necessary or convenient for the subsistence of the troops, provisions, forage, and such other articles as may be required, will be taken possession of and used, but every seizure must be made solely by the order of the commanding officer of the troops there present, and by the officer of the department through which the issues are made. Any officer or soldier who shall be found to have entered the house or molested the property of any citizen, will be severely punished. Such acts of pillage and outrage are disgraceful to the army, and have neither been contemplated nor authorized by any officers whatsoever. The perpetrators of them, whether officers or soldiers, will be visited with a punishment which they will have reason to remember, and any officer or soldier absent from the limits of his camp, found in any house whatever, without a written pass from his division or brigade commander, will be considered as a pillager, and treated accordingly.

Army Corps Commanders will immediately establish mounted patrols under charge of commissioned officers, which shall scour the whole country for five miles around their camps at least once a day, and at different hours, to bring into their respective commands all persons absent without proper authority or who are engaged in any interruption of citizens living in the country; and commanding officers of regiments or smaller separate commands will be held responsible that neither officers nor men shall be absent from camp without proper authority.

By command of Major-Gen. POPE.
R. O. SELFRIDGE, A. A. G.

Muskets for the Army from the Bridesburgh Arsenal.

PHILADELPHIA, Saturday, Aug. 16.

Messrs. JENKS and MITCHELL, proprietors of the Bridesburgh Arsenal, delivered to the Government to-day the first thousand muskets of the Springfield pattern, made by private contractors. The event was celebrated by seven hundred workmen in raising a flag, firing a salute of thirty-four guns, and speeches.

The arsenal is now turning out a hundred guns a day, and will soon increase its capacity to two hundred and fifty guns a day.

The New-York Times.

VOL. XI—NO. 3112. NEW-YORK, SUNDAY, AUGUST 31, 1862. PRICE THREE CENTS.

HIGHLY IMPORTANT.

Defeat of the Rebels on the Old Bull Run Battle-Ground.

DISPATCH FROM GEN. POPE.

A Terrific Battle on Friday, Lasting All Day.

The Combined Forces of the Enemy Engaged.

The Rebels Driven from the Field.

Our Losses Not Less than Eight Thousand Killed and Wounded.

The Rebel Losses Probably Double.

Important Captures Made by our Forces.

Retreat of the Rebels toward the Mountains on Friday Morning.

PROMPT PURSUIT BY GEN. POPE.

ANOTHER GREAT BATTLE YESTERDAY.

OFFICIAL DISPATCH FROM GEN. POPE.

HEADQUARTERS FIELD OF BATTLE, GROVETON NEAR GAINESVILLE, Aug. 30, 1862.

To Major-Gen. Halleck, General-in-Chief, Washington, D. C.:

We fought a terrific battle here yesterday, *with the combined forces of the enemy*, which lasted with continuous fury from daylight until after dark, by which time *the enemy was driven from the field*, which we now occupy.

Our troops are too much exhausted to push matters, but I shall do so in the course of the morning, as soon as FITZ-JOHN PORTER'S corps come up from Manassas.

The enemy is still in our front, but badly used up.

We have lost not less than *eight thousand men killed and wounded*, and from the appearance of the field, *the enemy have lost at least two to our one*. He stood strictly on the defensive, and *every assault was made by ourselves*.

Our troops have behaved splendidly.

The battle was fought on the identical battle-field of Bull Run, which greatly increased the enthusiasm of our men.

The news just reaches me from the front that *the enemy is retreating toward the mountains*. I go forward at at once to see.

We have made great captures, but I am not able yet to form an idea of their extent.

JOHN POPE, Major-General Commanding.

DISPATCH FROM GEN. McDOWELL.

WASHINGTON, Friday, August 30.

Secretary CHASE received this afternoon through Gen. POPE'S messenger, the following note from Gen. McDOWELL, dated on battle field at 6:15, morning:

"DEAR GOVERNOR—Please telegraph Mrs. McDOWELL that I have gone through a second battle of Bull Run, on the identical field of last year and unhurt. The victory is decidedly ours.

Very sincerely, IRVIN McDOWELL."

ANOTHER BATTLE YESTERDAY.

WASHINGTON, Aug. 30.

Information has reached Washington from private sources that Gen. POPE came up with and attacked the enemy again shortly after nine o'clock this morning.

Gen. FITZ-JOHN PORTER had probably arrived on the field by that time from Manassas, only seven miles distant.

The cannonading was distinctly heard in Washington.

The railroad was regularly run this forenoon from the town of Warrenton to Bristor, so it is already clear that the only damage remaining to be repaired to the railroad is to build the Bull Run and Rappahannock bridges. The former should be completed to-night, and the latter may be in four or five days.

The news received from the army has occasioned the greatest excitement throughout this city.

Orders were issued by the Heads of the different Bureaus, calling upon the employes to repair to the battle-field, for the purpose of attending to the condition of our wounded.

The order required each man to provide himself with two days' rations.

A prompt response was made to the call, and not only the persons employed by the Government, but many others, left the city for the purpose stated.

Although the engagement with the enemy is of a most appallingly sanguinary character, yet such is the confidence of Union men in the skill and strength of our army, that an abiding faith in our ultimate success is everywhere discernible.

THE SECOND BULL RUN BATTLE.

WASHINGTON, Saturday, Aug. 30.

To-day's *Evening Star*, speaking of the battle of yesterday, says:

"The battle was continued by the army corps of Generals HEINTZELMAN, McDOWELL and SIGEL, on our side, against a rebel force believed to number from fifty to sixty thousand strong—that is, against the army corps of JACKSON, and, we presume, a portion of the rest of LEE'S army that had succeeded in making its way down from White Plains through Thoroughfare Gap.

The location of the battle of the day was in the vicinity of Haymarket, and from Haymarket off in the direction of Sudley Church, or, in other words' but a few miles northwest of the scene of the never-to-be-forgotten battle of Bull Run.

HEINTZELMAN'S Corps, if we are correctly informed, came up with the enemy's rear about 10 A. M., seven miles from Centreville, which point he left at day-break.

He found Stonewall JACKSON fighting with McDOWELL or SIGEL, or both, on the right, in the direction of Haymarket, the position they took by going north from Gainesville, to command the entrace to and exit from Thoroughfare Gap.

Our own informant, who left Centreville at 4 o'clock in the afternoon, a cool and clear-headed man, says that, up to that hour, the impression prevailed there that nothing had definitely resulted from the day's fighting, which, though continuous, had not been a very bloody battle.

Persons subsequently arriving, who were on the field of action themselves until 4 P. M., however, represent that the tide of success was decidedly with the Union army, which pushed the rebels successfully on both sides.

An impression prevails that the reserve of LEE'S army, supposed to be from twenty to forty thousand strong, might suddenly appear near the field, and we know that the heavy corps under FITZ-JOHN PORTER was so posted that it could instantly move upon LEE with equal ease, whether attacking McDOWELL, SIGEL or HEINTZELMAN.

The railroad, we are happy to say, has already been repaired quite up to Bull Run, and supplies, etc., are now being transported over it to that point.

By midnight we have every reason to believe that the Bull Run bridge will again be passable, when the trains can again run to Manassas.

Ere evacuating Manassas, the rebels paroled the 700 Union prisoners they had taken since the commencement of the movement for which they are paying so dearly.

The rebels realized that prisoners in their present strait were an elephant in their hands, and wisely thus got rid of them.

These 700 prisoners covered all the stragglers they had taken, as well as the 500 of TAYLOR'S Brigade."

WASHINGTON, Saturday, Aug. 30.

The following is gathered from private sources:

On Wednesday morning, or rather Tuesday night, a report reached Warrenton Junction that JACKSON was again in our rear, and that, instead of making an attack and retiring, as his cavalry did on Friday night last, at Catlett's Station, he had taken up a position on the railroad near Bristor, four miles south of Manassas; had burned two railroad trains, torn up the railroad track, cut the telegraph, and took prisoners all the guards along the road.

These reports prove to have been true, and the events of Wednesday showed his determination not to be easily driven from the neighborhood.

It seems from what can be learned from the rebel wounded in our hands, that JACKSON and EWELL started from the vicinity of Warrenton Springs on Sunday, with three divisions, crossed the Rappahannock some six miles south of the Blue Ridge, and proceeded by way of Orleans and Salem to Bristor, making the distance in about two and a half days.

On reaching this point their first object of attack was the house of Mr. LIPSCOMBE, where ten officers were stopping, and who were on the back porch at the time, smoking.

The house was attacked both front and rear, and the bullet-holes in the wood and plaster, with the fact that none of the party were wounded, showed what poor marksmen these rebel cavalry were. The entire party, however, with the exception of Capt. O. A. TILDENMORE, were taken prisoners.

The names of the officers taken prisoners are as follows:

Lieut.-Col. PIERSON, First New-York Volunteers.

Lieut. ALLEN, and two other Lieutenants of the same regiment.

A Lieutenant of the Fifty-Seventh Pennsylvania Regiment.

First Lieutenant of Company B, One Hundred and Fifth Pennsylvania Volunteers.

A Captain of the Fourth Maine Regiment.

Lieuts. PRENDERGAST and JOHNSON of the Thirty-Eighth New-York Volunteers.

The next attack of the rebels was upon a company of the One Hundred and Fifth Pennsylvania Infantry and some dozen of Pennsylvania Cavalry, left to guard the road, two or three of whom were killed, and the remainder are supposed to be captured.

A train of empty cars then came along from Warrenton, and was fired into by a regiment of infantry and one of cavalry, but escaped without serious injury.

Orders were then issued by JACKSON to tear up the railroad track, which was done, and a second train coming along, ran off the track, and was fired into.

A third train following ran into the second and was also fired into, and some persons on board were taken prisoners.

A fourth train made its appearance, but the Engineer suspected something wrong, stopped at a distance and blew a whistle, and being answered by one of the others, backed and returned toward Warrenton.

The two trains were then fired, under the direction of JACKSON, and entirely consumed, excepting the iron-work.

The rebels then proceeded a mile down the track, burned the bridge at Cattle Run, tore up some thirty feet of the track, and cut the telegraph.

They also burned the bridge across Broad Run, at Bristor.

On Wednesday morning, EWELL'S Rebel Division was placed in position on each side of the railroad, having three batteries, one on the right, one on the left, and the other near the railroad, with infantry and cavalry between, the entire force being concealed behind brush-woods and the [illegible] with an open field in front.

Our troops sent down from Warrenton Junction to attack them consisted of HOOKER'S Division, with a portion of KEARNEY'S, but the latter, it is said, did not get a chance to enter into the contest.

Gen. HOOKER was in command, and not expecting the enemy to be in any large force, ordered a charge through a piece of woods and into the cleared space, when a most murderous fire was opened upon him from the entire line of the rebels, their batteries throwing grape and canister, the most of which, however, went over the heads of our troops; but the fire from the rebel line of infantry was very destructive, and some of HOOKER'S regiments were compelled to fall back to the woods, but on being supported by others rallied, and, after making several bold charges, [illegible] when the rebels broke and retreated, our boys pursuing them, shouting and yelling.

The Third New-Jersey Brigade was commanded by Col. CARR, who had his horse shot under him while urging his men on to an attack. This is the Brigade, though somewhat changed, which so nobly held the extreme left at the battle of Williamsburgh for four hours, sustaining a loss there of over six hundred killed and wounded.

Adjutant BENEDICT'S horse was also shot during the action.

Lieut.-Col. POTTER, of the Second Regiment, Excelsior Brigade, was shot in the hand while leading his men.

The pursuit continued till dark, the enemy retreating towards Manassas.

The result of this action was that the enemy was beaten and driven from the field, sustaining a loss about equal to our own.

Our loss was about fifty killed and over two hundred wounded, a complete list of which was collected, but stolen.

The Second New-York regiment lost about ten officers and some ninety or one hundred killed and wounded.

The Excelsior Brigade suffered severely.

The physicians on the ground (Dr. MORROW of the Second New-Hampshire being the only name I can now recollect) exerted themselves to relieve the wounded; and although the accommodations to operate were very poor, they succeeded during the afternoon and night in attending to all.

Gen. POPE arrived on the ground late in the evening and proceeded towards the scene of action, but the fighting was then over and the enemy in full retreat.

JACKSON had left for Manassas during the day with his division, where he pillaged the place, capturing a large number of prisoners, and burning every building, except the telegraph building and a few shanties, after taking off their own old rags, and putting on our good clothing, and helping themselves to food of all kinds, arms, equipments, and whatever else they could carry away out of the cars, about a hundred of which were at that place, for the greater part loaded with supplies for our army.

The rebels then set fire to all the cars, and they now present a mass of bleached ruins.

On their arrival, they found a portion of two New-Jersey Regiments of Infantry, which had arrived there during the forenoon. They immediately attacked them, our troops defending themselves for some time, but finding the number of the enemy so great, and that they were being flanked, they retreated towards Centreville, and got away with the loss of some forty wounded and about twelve killed. The rebels captured six hundred and twenty-five of them, but they were paroled yesterday morning just before the battle commenced.

The pursuit was continued towards Centreville on Thursday afternoon, and a squadron of the Second Pennsylvania Cavalry, with Gen. BIRNEY, was in the advance, and stopped at Centreville to inquire the route taken by the enemy. While there a woman waved a flag from the back window, at which signal a force of rebel cavalry, about 2,000 strong, under Gen. LEE, emerged from the woods. Our men had scarcely time to mount their horses and escape, coming down the road at full speed, the enemy in swift pursuit. They were followed until they came to where our Infantry were drawn in line of battle on each side of the road, at which point the rebels received a volley which caused them to retreat at more than a double-quick.

Our troops took up the line of march, and followed the rebels during the night on the Gainesville or Warrenton road, and soon came in sight of the old Bull Run battle-ground in strong position, and under cover of the woods.

The action commenced about 9 o'clock, our batteries having been placed in position, and MILROY'S Brigade having the advance, was ordered to charge the rebels through the woods, and to cross toward the railroad switch, when the enemy poured into our troops a perfect storm of grape and canister.

This caused them to fall back, but they soon rallied, and paid the enemy with interest.

The rebels here rose *en masse* behind the railroad track, and again caused our men to fall back, which they did behind HAMPTON'S Pittsburgh Battery, which opened upon the rebels terrifically. The enemy were at the time only about thirty yards distant, and the effect of the fire destroyed at least 600 of them. In this action, however, HAMPTON lost one of his guns. He had to change his position to the left, as he was unable to maintain himself under the fire which the rebels poured into him.

The battle in other quarters raged furiously; the general result of which has already been stated from other sources.

The position of the forces on Thursday night remained about the same as it was at the commencement of the action.

The loss on both sides is heavy.

Gen. DURYEA, while engaged in making a reconnoisance to-day, was wounded in the hand.

The fighting up to 12 o'clock to-day was of a desultory character.

We occupy the ground where the rebels had buried their dead.

FIGHTING STOPPED AT NOON YESTERDAY.

PHILADELPHIA, Saturday, Aug. 30.

The Washington *Star* says:

"At 12½ o'clock this afternoon, the firing that has been heard all day stopped, as we learn from parties just down from Fairfax County. We trust this fact means the surrender of the rebels, and we don't see how it can mean aught else."

The *Star* also contains some severe strictures on the slow movements of Gen. FRANKLIN'S Division which were open to criticism in Washington to-day.

According to the accounts of those last from the battle-field, the belief there was that JACKSON was aiming to get off from POPE in the direction of Aldie.

The *Star* doubts this.

A dispatch is published from Capt. MASSEE, late Commissary in charge at Centreville, announcing his arrival there with 624 paroled prisoners.

The *Star* contains an urgent call for nurses, for whom prompt railroad transmission has been ordered by the War Department.

PREVIOUS NEWS IN WASHINGTON.

From the Washington Star of Friday Evening.

PHILADELPHIA, Saturday, Aug. 30.

We have information that satisfies us that the rebel force that suddenly appeared between the position of the army of Gen. POPE, and at Bristor and Manassas, on Tuesday night last, was the army corps of JACKSON, and STUART'S independent cavalry corps. They consisted of infantry and artillery, and marched about thirty thousand strong from near Waterloo, on the head waters of the Rappahannock, around by White Plains to Manassas, about forty miles in two days, without wagons, tents, blankets, or even knapsacks, thus leaving their baggage of every description to be transported by wagons, with the other army corps of LEE'S following on behind them.

Instead of fighting merely a portion of STUART'S Cavalry at Manassas, on the day before yesterday, TAYLOR'S Brigade were actually confronted by a greater portion of JACKSON'S *corps d'armée*, Maj.-Gens. Jackson, Ewell, Taliaferro, A. P. Hill, and Stuart, and the General-in-Chief, Robert Lee, or his son, Brig.-Gen. FITZHUGH LEE, being present at Manassas during the engagement.

Yesterday, at 1 o'clock P. M., JACKSON'S advance occupied Fairfax Court House in force of cavalry, and had collected their own wounded of the action of the day before with TAYLOR, if not their wounded of the engagement on the same day with HOOKER, and also the prisoners they took from TAYLOR.

In the afternoon, about 800 of this cavalry force under STUART in person, moved down from Fairfax Court-house to Vienna.

HOOKER'S battle, of the day before yesterday, was with EWELL'S division, and was a gratifying success.

Maj.-Gen. POPE, by 9½ o'clock yesterday morning, had concentrated his very large army, so as to sadly interfere with the calculations upon which the rebel Generals must have ventured their bold and extraordinary movement.

At 4 P. M. yesterday an engagement commenced between POPE and JACKSON'S rear or LONGSTREET'S advance, somewhere about Manassas. If with the former, then HEINTZELMAN'S *Corps d'Armée*, or a portion of it, were engaged on our side. If with the latter, then McDOWELL or SIGEL, or both, commenced it. It continued through the balance of the afternoon.

We had gotten McDOWELL'S force, including SIGEL'S probably, between JACKSON'S rear and LONGSTREET'S front, and had also all the rest of his army well up within supporting distance. Thus it continued through the balance of the afternoon.

Facts within our knowledge lead to the impression that in twenty-four hours direct communication will have been established between Washington and Maj.-Gen. POPE'S army; more especially as there are signs that JACKSON'S army corps is endeavoring to proceed northwardly, as though making for the experiment of opposing the reëstablishment of such communication with his immediate front, with POPE'S army practically between him and the other rebel *corps d'armée*.

We may add that Gen. McCLELLAN is disposing of his heavy Union force around Washington and Alexandria, and the fortifications, so as to make it play an important part in the eventful drama of the hour.

In the battle of yesterday, the attack certainly came from our side.

CARE FOR THE WOUNDED.

WASHINGTON, Saturday Aug. 30.

Hundreds of the convalescents of the various hospitals reached their quarters to-day, and will be sent out of Washington to make room for patients from the recent battle-fields, who are already arriving.

The conduct of Maj.-Gen. POPE is highly commended in Government as well as in other quarters.

Between five hundred and a thousand Government Clerks repaired to the battle-field, in compliance with a request from the War Department, not in pursuance of an order, as erroneously stated in a previous dispatch, this afternoon, the report having reached here that the dead and wounded on both sides needed attention.

Col. PULESTON, the military agent of Pennsylvania, accompanied by Majors GILLILAND and PINKERTON, and a number of other Pennsylvanians, left immediately on the receipt of the news for Manassas, with large supplies of stimulants and hospital stores for the wounded.

The Pennsylvania Relief Association also sent off with alacrity quantities of stores in the charge of agents.

Dr. PAGE, of the Columbus Hospital, left this evening for Centreville, in charge of two hundred ambulances and the citizen nurses from the different Government departments.

Dr. WEBSTER, of the Douglas Hospital, also left for the battle-field in charge of a large train of medical supplies and the Citizen Volunteer Surgeons of this District.

Gen. WADSWORTH has taken possession of all the hacks in this city and sent them forward as a train to transport the sick and wounded to this city.

SURGEONS FROM PHILADELPHIA.

PHILADELPHIA, Saturday, Aug. 30.

The city authorities this evening received a dispatch from Col. THOMAS A. SCOTT, that a hard battle had been fought, and that the loss was heavy, and requesting them to have all the surgeons possible sent to Washington to-night.

OUR CORRESPONDENCE FROM THE FIELD

THE GUERRILLA RAID UPON THE ORANGE AND ALEXANDRIA RAILROAD—THE ATTACK NEAR WHITE PLAINS—CAPTURE OF A NEW-YORK BATTERY AT MANASSAS—THE FIGHT AT BULL RUN, &C.

HEADQUARTERS IN THE FIELD, BETWEEN ALEXANDRIA AND BRISTOR STATION, Thursday, P. M., Aug. 28, 1862.

I have fortunately been able to obtain some reliable and interesting details of the transactions during Tuesday night and a portion of yesterday, (Wednesday,) on the line of the Orange and Alexandria Railroad and vicinity. Tuesday evening, between 5 and 8 o'clock, five trains of empty cars were captured and mostly destroyed by a rebel cavalry force on the road between Bristor Station and Manassas Junction, and on the same evening the enemy destroyed the bridge across Broad River, and subsequently the bridges across other small creeks on the railroad. There were stationed at Manassas Junction, Tuesday, the Twelfth Pennsylvania Cavalry, numbering between 500 and 600 men, Col. WHITE, and the First New-York Battery—10 pieces—with about 300 men to serve them. At 5 o'clock, a dispatch was received by telegraph from Warrenton Junction, directing the cavalry to proceed immediately to White Plains, (15 miles,) on the Manassas road, and keep a sharp look out for the enemy, who, it was understood, had crossed the Rappahannock in force on Sunday, and by the way of Jeffersonton and Little Washington, was making his way for some point on the line of the Orange and Alexandria Railroad, with a view, no doubt, to divide our forces and isolate the command of Gen. POPE—a position which the commander of the Union forces desired him to take, and a fatal one to the enemy it is certainly believed to be. The Pennsylvania cavalry left for the point directed, but finding none of the enemy at White Plains, at a late hour the corps started to return to the Junction. When within eight or nine miles of the latter place, they found a corps of about 1,000 cavalry, supposed to be commanded by FITZHUGH LEE, drawn up to dispute their further progress. A brisk skirmish took place, when our cavalry cut their way through the rebel ranks, losing a number in killed, wounded and prisoners. There was a kind of running fight kept up until the Junction was reached, at about 1 o'clock A. M. of Wednesday, when the rebels apparently retired satisfied. The cavalry fell back to a position one mile north of the Junction, known as BEAUREGARD'S Headquarters, and were under arms all night, without knowing what had transpired at the Junction during their absence at White Plains. In this interval the rebels had fallen upon the First New-York Artillery by surprise—the officer in command supposing the approaching force to be our own cavalry until too late—and captured eight of their ten guns. This was not done, however, until after a most sanguinary resistance, resulting in the killing and wounding of quite a number on both sides. A member of the Pennsylvania cavalry, not knowing that the Junction was in possession of the rebels, walked very deliberately to the place at sunrise, and finding himself in a trap, coolly asked the first rebel he met "how things were going," and in reply the rebel soldier said, "All right—we have had lots of fun and plunder." Our soldier then attempted to set loose a number of Government horses tied in a stable, when an officer said, "That is not one of our men—shoot him." At about this time the two guns saved from the New-York Battery commenced throwing shell, and this soldier escaped and reached his own command. It was now 7 o'clock Wednesday morning. The rebels occupied the earthworks near the Junction, but after a time advanced from their position and made an unsuccessful attempt to take the remaining guns of the New-York Battery. A running fight was kept up along the line of the railroad, our troops gradually falling back until near mid-day, when at a point one mile south of Fairfax Station, they were met by a force of infantry and artillery under the command of Brig.-Gen. TAYLOR, of New-Jersey, and the rebels were driven back to Manassas Junction forthwith. A fact especially worthy of notice in this connection is, that upon the person of a prisoner captured was found a copy of the identical dispatch sent by telegraph from Warrenton Junction, between 4 and 5 o'clock P. M. of Tuesday, directing the cavalry at Manassas Junction to leave for White Plains, so that they were enabled to attack the place when the least resistance could be offered. It is believed by many that this dispatch could not have been obtained in any other way than through the agency of some employe of the Government.

Of the fight that took place Wednesday afternoon, with Gen. TAYLOR'S force, on the road between Manassas Junction and Bull Run, and at the latter place, but little reliable information can be obtained at this time. The engagement was a sharp and deadly one—the rebels holding their position at night; but those who ought to know what occurred this morning look very good-natured, and hence we, who are in the dark, draw the inference that the rebels got their desert this morning. The rebel force in action at Bull Run, Wednesday evening, is believed to have been about 5,000 men, principally cavalry and artillery. Our force consisted of ten regiments of infantry, and ten guns. Gen. TAYLOR was so badly wounded in one of his legs, by the explosion of a shell, that the leg was amputated to-day. The Eleventh and Twelfth Ohio Regiments, it is said, suffered the most—the latter having, according to a statement of a member, eighty wounded and twelve killed. The wildest rumors were circulated in Alexandria to-day about the result of the fight yesterday and this morning, but there is no occasion for any alarm. A force of —— men left the vicinity of Alexandria early this morning for the scene of action—a force which, with that under Gen. POPE'S immediate command, is sufficient to crush a very respectable force of the enemy. I shall send forward additional details as soon as anything reliable can be obtained. The excitement was somewhat intensified in Alexandria last night, by the 12th Virginia Cavalry rushing into the city in a panic; and the excitement was again renewed this morning by the return of a train of cars that started for Manassas Junction. The train was fired upon when fifteen miles out, and returned.

I escaped from the Rappahannock just at the right moment. Had I been 20 minutes later on Tuesday night, I should have been captured by the rebels. The train that kept us company all the way up was nabbed. It is supposed that JACKSON had nearly his whole force near White Plains. If so there is no escape for them, so far as I can see. POPE must have 200,000 well-disciplined troops south of JACKSON. There are 75,000 fresh troops encamped about Washington, and then there is an immense force of tried men—say 50,000 men—between this point and JACKSON'S position. Gen. McCLELLAN reached Alexandria Wednesday morning, and was at the telegraph office writing dispatches—orders—nearly all night. He can write with facility with either hand. To-day he is confined to his room by reason of slight indisposition. The rebels captured a saddle of mine at Manassas Junction, and a small bundle of papers and clothing. They were placed on the train just behind the one in which I took passage, by mistake. I hope that HALLECK'S infamous order about correspondents will be modified soon. It is very unsatisfactory to be compelled to obtain information as we do now. The Tenth New-York Cavalry, 750 men (new corps), is now passing to the front. They are the finest set of men, and best mounted, in the service. They elicit the admiration of every one.

New regiments are rolling in upon us here almost every hour in the day—quite as fast as they can be accommodated. Three hundred paroled prisoners, I suppose, left Washington yesterday for Dixie, and Fortress Monroe. But these matters you get by telegraph.

The reports in the *Tribune* of the fighting on the Rappahannock are, for the most part, grossly erroneous.

THE OPERATIONS OF GEN. TAYLOR'S BRIGADE AT BULL RUN AND VICINITY, WEDNESDAY, AUG. 27—JACKSON COMPLETELY CUT OFF ON THURSDAY, BY GENERALS HOOKER AND KEARNEY.

FAIRFAX COURT-HOUSE, Friday, Aug. 29, 1862.

In my last I gave you a correct and somewhat detailed account of the operations of the Twelfth Pennsylvania Cavalry, and First New-York Battery, at Manassas Junction and vicinity, on Wednesday, the 27th inst., down to the time when they were relieved by the arrival of reinforcements. To continue in order as the events occurred, Brig.-Gen. TAYLOR, in command of the New-Jersey Brigade, 1,600 strong—*all infantry*—left Alexandria early on Wednesday morning, to reinforce the command at Manassas Junction. When one mile north of Bull Run Bridge, they found the track obstructed by the *débris* of a destroyed train of cars, and, disembarking, proceeded on foot toward Manassas Junction. Upon arriving in sight of the latter place, they saw the Stars and Stripes flying, and heard the roar of cannon; as the flag was there, and no shots were directed toward Gen. TAYLOR'S column, that officer concluded that our forces were firing upon a force of the enemy beyond, and consequently pressed forward at a double-quick. Too late the discovery was made that the troops at the Junction were rebels, and that the raising of the "Stars and Stripes," and the aiming of their guns in an opposite direction was a ruse of the enemy. When within half gunshot distance, the rebels opened upon Gen. TAYLOR'S command, right, left and front, with the eight 32-pound cannon which they had captured a few hours before from the New-York battery. Their cavalry immediately fired a volley and charged at the same time, which for a moment created a panic in our ranks. Gen. TAYLOR speedily obtained order, and gradually fell back to Bull Run Bridge, having no artillery or cavalry to use against the rebels. At the latter place Gen. TAYLOR was reinforced by the arrival of the Eleventh and Twelfth Ohio Volunteers—the latter a cavalry corps—and quite a brisk fight took place, when the rebels were finally repulsed. Gen. TAYLOR was wounded in the leg while gallantly rallying his men against a superior force of the enemy, composed of cavalry and artillery. Late at night the commander of our forces, learning that the rebels had received large reinforcements, fell back to Fairfax Station, and at 11 o'clock at night moved on to this place, as the advance of a large force which left Alexandria on Thursday morning. The rebels had disappeared.

It is alleged that the Twelfth Pennsylvania Cavalry acted in the most scandalous manner at Bull Run, and the bulk of the regiment made a rapid retreat toward Alexandria. Of the truth of this, however, I cannot vouch.

JACKSON CUT OFF.

The movements on Thursday, the 28th, were more important than any that have taken place on this line during the present campaign. POPE'S strategy is being developed. Gens. HOOKER and KEARNEY, with their thoroughly disciplined commands, advanced upon the rear of JACKSON and have forced him toward Leesburgh, where he is completely cut off, and must, with his whole force, be captured or destroyed, unless some stupendous error is made on our side. JACKSON will probably get into Washington somewhat sooner than he expected, and in a manner less agreeable than he anticipated.

There is heavy firing northwest of this place this morning, and it is supposed that our forces have compelled JACKSON to face about and fight.

IMPORTANT FROM WASHINGTON.

The Significance of the Second Battle of Bull Run.

The Fate of the Bogus Confederacy to be Determined.

THE BULK OF THE REBEL ARMY ENGAGED.

Richmond Almost Deserted.

The Great Struggle Still Proceeding.

Arrangements for the Care of the Wounded.

OUR SPECIAL WASHINGTON DISPATCHES.

WASHINGTON, Saturday, Aug. 30.

THE SECOND BATTLE OF BULL RUN.

The battle of Bull Run substantially began the war—has been the common remark on the streets this afternoon—and the new battle of Bull Run is now ending it. The rebels have staked everything on this die. They know they must defeat us before the new levies become effective, or their last opportunity is gone; and so, abandoning baggage, and with only such rations as they can carry, they have attempted to fight their way into Washington or Maryland. Four days have been spent in this attempt—three of them in hard fighting. They are in a country utterly barren of supplies, and have been too busy to forage for them, if the country did afford them. The rations they carried with them must be exhausted, and the opinion therefore begins to be suggested as probable, in well informed circles, that to-day's battle, or at least to-morrow's, must exhaust their resources and compel either a surrender or a hasty retreat.

Officials likely to be well informed as to the recent progress of affairs express the utmost confidence both as to the results of the engagement thus far, and the prospects for to-morrow. The cannonading continued up to dark, and unless one party or the other retire under cover of the darkness, it must be renewed with dawn.

There are rumors that the rebels have been heavily reinforced, but they probably arise from the pretty well ascertained fact *that the bulk of the rebel army has been engaged.*

The first definite news of yesterday's engagement reached here early this afternoon. The War Department speedily communicated the facts to the different Departments, and made request for volunteer nurses to proceed immediately to the battle-field. Most of the bureaus in several of the Departments were at once left almost destitute of clerks. The following regulations were issued for persons proposing to go down:

Volunteers for attending to the wounded on the battle-field will observe the following directions:

First—The volunteers of each department will be enrolled by one of their own number as chief, and for each division a surgeon will be furnished by the Surgeon-General, under whose direction they will act.

Second—Each volunteer will provide himself with a bucket and tin cup, to supply water, and also a bottle of brandy.

Third—Transportation will be furnished for all as rapidly as possible at the rendezvous, by Capt. DANAS, corner of Twenty-second and G streets. Those who can, should provide their own transportation.

Shortly after these regulations were issued, the Government began impressing the hacks and all other means of conveyance. The Street Railroad Company tendered their omnibuses, recently bought from the late omnibus line, and a large number were accepted. Large numbers of citizens began preparing to go down. Many of them have gone already, and many more start out at daybreak.

Trains are running out to Manassas again, and telegraphic communication is restored.

The wounded have already begun to come in from the battle-fields of the previous days. Provision can be made in the Hospitals already fitted up here for several thousand more—many of the wards having been lately emptied by the return of convalescents to their regiments. Besides these, the hospital accommodations in Baltimore are to be brought into requisition immediately, and some of the wounded have already begun to be sent over. It is also stated that the capitol itself is to be occupied.

THE SOUND OF THE BATTLE.

The *Star* says: "Not only was the sound of the cannonading of the great battle near Centreville today, distinctly heard here, but the smell of the gun powder was quite perceptible at times when the wind freshened from that quarter.

THE COMMAND OF THE ARMY.

It is not true, as stated, that Gen. McCLELLAN has been appointed or placed in command of the National forces in Virginia. Major-Gen. HALLECK is the Commander-in-Chief, and Gens. McCLELLAN, POPE and others are in command of their respective divisions.

AFFAIRS IN RICHMOND.

The French Consul has arrived from Richmond and is now remaining at the French Embassy. It is declared, on what seems good authority, that Richmond is left almost entirely without troops, and that they have nothing there that could prevent a couple of brigades from taking the rebel capital.

THE SEVENTY-FIRST NEW-YORK.

The New-York Seventy-first marched in from its position in the field to-day, and passed down the avenue to the railroad to take a train for New-York. They made a splendid appearance, and are going home in the best possible condition.

THE EXCISE AND TAX APPOINTMENTS.

FOR MISSOURI—First District—Collector, Samuel H. Gardner, of St. Louis; Assessor, Theophile Pasain of St. Louis. Second District—Collector, Joseph Bray, of St. Genevieve; Assessor, Daniel R. Gale, of Washington. Third District—Collector, C. B. Wilkinson, of St. Joseph; Assessor, Jos. A. Hay, of Canton.

The New-York Times.

VOL. XI—NO. 3413. | NEW-YORK, MONDAY, SEPTEMBER 1, 1862. | PRICE TWO CENTS.

ANOTHER BATTLE WEEK.

Desperate Battles on Thursday, Friday and Saturday.

Defeat of the Rebels on the Bull Run Battle-Ground.

Our Losses Not Less than Eight Thousand.

Important Captures Made by our Forces.

The Enemy Heavily Reinforced on Friday Night.

Renewal of the Fighting on Saturday.

Gen. Pope Forced to Fall Back to Centreville.

ARRIVAL OF REINFORCEMENTS.

No Fighting of Consequence Yesterday.

PARTIAL LISTS OF KILLED AND WOUNDED.

HEAVY LOSSES AMONG OUR OFFICERS.

Arrival of a Thousand Prisoners in Washington.

THE GREAT BATTLE OF FRIDAY.

OFFICIAL DISPATCH FROM GEN. POPE.

HEADQUARTERS FIELD OF BATTLE, GROVETON NEAR GAINESVILLE, Aug. 30, 1862.

To Major-Gen. Halleck, General-in-Chief, Washington, D. C.:

We fought a terrific battle here yesterday, *with the combined forces of the enemy*, which lasted with continuous fury from daylight until after dark, by which time *the enemy was driven from the field*, which we now occupy.

Our troops are too much exhausted to push matters, but I shall do so in the course of the morning, as soon as FITZ-JOHN PORTER'S corps come up from Manassas.

The enemy is still in our front, but badly used up.

We have lost not less than *eight thousand men killed and wounded*, and from the appearance of the field, *the enemy have lost at least two to our one*. He stood strictly on the defensive, and *every assault was made by ourselves.*

Our troops have behaved splendidly.

The battle was fought on the identical battle-field of Bull Run, which greatly increased the enthusiasm of our men.

The news just reaches me from the front that *the enemy is retreating toward the mountains.* I go forward at at once to see.

We have made great captures, but I am not able yet to form an idea of their extent.

JOHN POPE, Major-General Commanding.

DISPATCH FROM GEN. M'DOWELL.

WASHINGTON, Friday, August 30.

Secretary CHASE received this afternoon through Gen. POPE'S messenger, the following note from Gen. MCDOWELL, dated on battle field at 6:15, morning:

DEAR GOVERNOR—Please telegraph Mrs. MCDOWELL that I have gone through a second battle of Bull Run, on the identical field of last year, and unhurt. The victory is decidedly ours.

Very sincerely, IRVIN MCDOWELL.

THE SECOND BATTLE OF BULL RUN.

The *Washington Star*, of Saturday evening, in speaking of the engagement of Friday, says:

"The battle was continued by the army corps of [illegible], MCDOWELL and SIGEL, on our [illegible] force believed to number from [illegible]—that is, against the [illegible], a portion of the [illegible] army that had succeeded in making its way [illegible] from White Plains through Thoroughfare Gap.

The location of the battle of the day was in the vicinity of Haymarket, and from Haymarket off in the direction of Sudley Church, or, in other words, but a few miles northwest of the scene of the never-to-be-forgotten battle of Bull Run.

HEINTZELMAN'S Corps, if we are correctly informed, [illegible] with the enemy's rear about 10 A. M., [illegible] Centreville, which point he left at day-[illegible] fighting with McDow-[illegible], in the direction of Haymarket, [illegible] position they took by going north from Gainesville, to command the entrace to and exit from Thoroughfare Gap.

Our own informant, who left Centreville at 4 o'clock in the afternoon, a cool and clear-headed man, says that, up to that hour, the impression prevailed there that nothing had definitely resulted from the day's fighting, which, though continuous, had not been a very bloody battle.

Persons subsequently arriving, who were on the field of action themselves until 4 P. M., however, represent that the tide of success was decidedly with the Union army, which pushed the rebels successfully [illegible] by [illegible] the reserve of [illegible]

An [illegible]

army, supposed to be from twenty to forty thousand strong, might suddenly appear near the field, and we know that the heavy corps under FITZ-JOHN PORTER was so posted that it could instantly move upon LEE with equal ease, whether attacking MCDOWELL, SIGEL or HEINTZELMAN.

The railroad, we are happy to say, has already been repaired quite up to Bull Run, and supplies, etc., are now being transported over it to that point.

By midnight we have every reason to believe that the Bull Run bridge will again be passable, when the trains can again run to Manassas.

Ere evacuating Manassas, the rebels paroled the 700 Union prisoners they had taken since the commencement of the movement for which they are paying so dearly. The rebels realized that prisoners in their present strait were an elephant in their hands, and wisely thus got rid of them.

These 700 prisoners covered all the stragglers they had taken, as well as the 500 of TAYLOR'S Brigade."

THE GREAT BATTLE OF SATURDAY.

WASHINGTON, Friday, Aug. 30.

Information has reached Washington from private sources that Gen. POPE came up with and attacked the enemy again shortly after nine o'clock this morning.

Gen. FITZ-JOHN PORTER had probably arrived on the field by that time from Manassas, only seven miles distant.

The cannonading was distinctly heard in Washington.

The railroad was regularly run this forenoon from the town of Warrenton to Bristow, so it is already clear that the only damage remaining to be repaired to the railroad is to build the Bull Run and Rappahannock bridges. The former should be completed to-night, and the latter may be in four or five days.

The news received from the army has occasioned the greatest excitement throughout this city.

Although the engagement with the enemy is of a most appallingly sanguinary character, yet such is the confidence of Union men in the skill and strength of our army, that an abiding faith in our ultimate success is everywhere discernible.

WASHINGTON, Sunday, Aug. 31—10:55 A. M.

The enemy was heavily reinforced yesterday, and attacked Gen. POPE'S army before the arrival of Gens. FRANKLIN and SUMNER.

The attack was boldly met, and a severe battle followed. The advantage, on the whole, was with the enemy, and Gen. POPE fell back to Centreville with his whole army in good order.

He has been joined at Centreville by FRANKLIN, and SUMNER, was on the march to him last night. He occupies the strongest position in the vicinity of Washington, and is expected promptly to renew the contest and repeat the successes of Friday.

Every effort should be used to hasten the forwarding of the new troops.

THE OPERATIONS OF SUNDAY.

WASHINGTON, Sunday, Aug. 31.

Gen. POPE'S statement that HEINTZELMAN'S Corps would move on the enemy at daylight to-day, is confirmed by the heavy firing heard from that vicinity. Rumors of various successes have reached here, but need confirmation.

Yesterday rebel scouts were seen at Langley's, in the vicinity of Chain Bridge!

Every precaution has been taken to prevent a surprise in that direction.

The impression prevails that the rebels have been entrapped, and the result of the recent manœuvring is looked for with intense eagerness.

WASHINGTON, Sunday, Aug. 31—Evening.

Information received here indicates that there has been but little, if any, fighting to-day.

Our army is well concentrated and the men in good condition and spirits.

REPORTS FROM ALEXANDRIA.

ALEXANDRIA, Saturday, Aug. 30.

There has been heavy firing heard to-day in the direction of Centreville, and the contest of yesterday was undoubtedly renewed this morning.

Telegraphic communication has been reëstablished to Manassas, and the cars are running as far as Bull Run. The bridge and railroad are being repaired with the greatest dispatch, and trains will probably extend their trips to-morrow.

There are still a large number of troops in Alexandria awaiting transportation to the field of battle. A Pennsylvania Brigade, comprising the One Hundred and Twenty-third, One Hundred and Thirty-third, One Hundred and Thirty-fourth and One Hundred and Thirty-sixth Regiments, under Gen. COOK, were to march to-day.

Those who were able to be moved from the Alexandria hospitals have been taken to Washington, to make room for the wounded who are to arrive to-day.

REBEL PRISONERS IN WASHINGTON.

WASHINGTON, Sunday, Aug. 31.

About a thousand rebel prisoners have just arrived in the city, representing nearly all the seceded States.

OUR CORRESPONDENCE FROM THE FIELD.

THE MOVEMENT ON FAIRFAX COURT-HOUSE—A LETTER FROM THE REBEL COL. LEE—CAPTURE OF MASSACHUSETTS SOLDIERS—REBEL SPIES CAPTURED—NO STORES LOST AT RAPPAHANNOCK STATION, ETC.

FAIRFAX COURT-HOUSE, Friday, Aug. 29, 1862.

The troops which had been concentrated at Fairfax Station, yesterday morning commenced a movement upon this place—to find the enemy. In the woods, just above the village, a large force of rebel cavalry was discovered, and skirmishing was at once commenced. The Second New-York Artillery deployed one fire and skedaddled; the Twelfth Pennsylvania Cavalry discharged their duty but little better. The Fourteenth Massachusetts, Col. GREENE, of Essex County, seized two guns of the Eleventh New-York Battery, and then compelled the rebels to retire to cover. The Fourteenth then passed into the woods, occasionally exchanging shots with the enemy, and remained until late at night, when the rebels retired, and our forces were ordered upon another expedition. But few of our men were killed at this point, and only some thirty wounded, so far as known. A rebel corps, under Col. LEE, during the day, captured from the Fourteenth Massachusetts a one-horse hospital wagon, a four-horse ambulance, and the following-named persons, all of whom were at a house used as a temporary hospital.

Surgeon DANA and Assistant-Surgeon MASON, and [illegible], hospital steward.

[illegible] of Lawrence, driver of ambulance; HENRY FOLSOM, of Lawrence, driver of hospital wagon, and JONATHAN FORCE, of Ipswich.

The surgeons and assistant-surgeons were at once sent back, by Col. LEE, who sent a note to Col. GREENE, with his compliments, saying that he (LEE) would have bagged the whole command had not Col. GREENE been so sharp. LEE and GREENE were together at West Point.

During Thursday evening the Fourteenth Massachusetts captured half a dozen spies within their lines, two of whom were in the tops of trees, observing the movement of our troops. They have been sent forward to Washington. The Fourteenth has been stationed for a long time in the fortifications near Harper's Ferry, and although only a few days in the field, it has rendered efficient service, especially in saving Gen. BANKS' baggage train on Tuesday night last. But for the prompt advance of this corps, the whole train, numbering several hundred wagons, would undoubtedly have been lost.

All the bridges on the railroad between Fairfax Station and Warrenton Junction have been destroyed by the rebels within the last two days. At Manassas Junction on Tuesday night they succeeded in destroying a considerable quantity of commissary stores, but elsewhere their raids upon the railroad has not amounted to much. I see that the correspondent of a cotemporary states that a large amount of commissary stores were destroyed by our troops at Rappahannock Station and Bealeton Station, to prevent the rebels from having the benefit of them. This is a mistake. Nearly every article of value was safely removed to the rear from both of the stations named.

As I write there is heavy firing off to the northwest of us, and I must close. *Don't be surprised, however if in my next is recorded the capture of the arch-rebel Jackson.*

Our pickets were attacked last night and driven in at Burke's Station, between Fairfax and Alexandria. There was tall running on both sides and nobody hurt. A man who walked from Warrenton Junction to Fairfax Station to-day, says that he did not catch a glimpse of a rebel.

KILLED AND WOUNDED.

PARTIAL LIST OF THE CASUALTIES.

WASHINGTON, Sunday, Aug. 31.

Gen. SCHENCK arrived to-day, having been severely wounded in the right wrist in the battle of yesterday.

The following are some of the casualties, in the recent actions in Virginia, obtained from unofficial sources:

Capt. McClellan, 101st New-York—wounded in groin.

Capt. W. C. Allen, 101st New-York—ankle by shell.

Capt. E. L. Beckwith, 101st New-York—in breast.

Lieut. Warner, 101st New-York—in hand.

Lieut. Hagadorn, 1st New-York—in shoulder.

FIFTY-FOURTH NEW-YORK REGIMENT.

Lieut. Beer—killed.

Capt. Kemper—wounded in throat.

Lieut. Schenck—in foot.

Capt. Francis Kerneke—in head.

Capt. Vernak—in leg.

Lieut. Anton Grouer—in arm.

SIXTEENTH MASSACHUSETTS REGIMENT.

Lieut. H. B. Banks—killed.

Lieut. Darracott—killed.

Capt. Thomas O'Hare—wounded in leg.

Capt. Donovan—in heel.

Lieut. White—in side.

SEVENTY-SIXTH NEW-YORK REGIMENT.

Capt. Waters—in thigh.

EIGHTY-SECOND OHIO REGIMENT.

Col. Cantwell—killed.

ONE HUNDREDTH PENNSYLVANIA REGIMENT.

Capt. Simon Brown and Capt. Templeton—killed.

Lieut. Curt—stomach and breast.

Lieut. Razen—probably mortally.

Lieut. Parmon—head and arm.

Lieut. Blair—wounded.

Capt. Oliver—in leg.

Capt. Van Gardner—arm off.

Lieut. Spencer—in back.

Col. Leasure—badly in leg.

Major Dawson—in hand.

FORTY-SIXTH NEW-YORK REGIMENT.

Col. Rosa, and Capt. Hold—both wounded.

TWENTIETH INDIANA REGIMENT.

Col. Brown—reported killed.

SIXTY-SECOND PENNSYLVANIA REGIMENT.

Col. Hays—wounded.

ONE HUNDRED AND FIFTH PENNSYLVANIA REGIMENT.

Capt. John Hastings—wounded badly in leg.

Capt. A. C. Thompson—in shoulder.

Capt. Robert Kirk—in shoulder.

Lieut. Craig—in arm.

Lieut. Neil—slightly in breast.

Capt. A. C. Craig, Acting-Colonel—in ankle.

This regiment, it is said, lost half its number at Fair Oakes.

TWENTY-NINTH NEW-YORK.

Col. Soost—wounded in arm.

Adjt. Von Sedlitz—supposed mortally.

Lieut. Rosenberg—in arm.

Lieut. Feidenera—in leg.

FIFTY-EIGHTH NEW-YORK REGIMENT.

Major Henkle—in arm.

Lieut. Wenklebaugh, Adjutant to Gen. Steinwehr—in leg.

Acting-Adjutant, Lieut. Powell, (son of Dr. Powell, of Second Excelsior Brigade,)—wounded.

EXCELSIOR BRIGADE.

Lieut. Franklin—in groin.

Lieut.-Col. Potter—hand and arm; an amputation will not probably have to be made.

Capt. Green—struck by shell.

Lieut. Hoxie—wounded.

Lieut. Donalds—died from effects of amputation.

Lieuts. Murphy, Lowenstrouk, Lewis, and McAlister—all killed.

ANOTHER LIST OF CASUALTIES.

WASHINGTON, Sunday, Aug. 31.

The following casualties are unofficially reported from the late battles in Virginia:

Brig.-Gen. Schenck—right arm shattered by Minié ball. Will require amputation.

Brig.-Gen. Hatch—killed.

Brig.-Gen. Robinson—wounded.

Brig.-Gen. Coulter—killed.

Brig.-Gen. Buford, Illinois—killed.

Gen. Stahl—killed.

Col. Cantwell, 81st Ohio—killed.

Colonel of the New-York Highlanders—wounded.

Col. Henderson, 7th Penn. Reserves—wounded.

Col. Fletcher Webster, mortally wounded and captured.

Col. McDonald, 2d Wisconsin—killed.

Col. Kultz, of Philadelphia—killed.

Col. Roberts, 2d Michigan, successor of Col. Wilcox—killed.

Col. Farnsworth, 8th Illinois Cavalry—wounded.

Adjt. Miller Phelps, 10th Pennsylvania Reserves—shot through left lung.

Capt. J. F. Strong, 56th Pennsylvania—wounded.

Capt. Hueston, 56th Pennsylvania—wounded.

Capt. Carman, 56th Pennsylvania—killed.

Also the following wounded of the 56th Pennsylvania Regiment: Capt. Jack, Capt. Osborne, Lieut. Mumphery, Corp. Retas, John Hartman, E. Rowe and J. Andy.

Col. Sol. Meredith, of Indiana—wounded.

Also the following of the Eighteenth Massachusetts: Lieut. Russell and Sergt. Shaw—killed; Lieut. Meseray, Lieut. Army, Corp. Clifford, Sergt. Parrington, Sergt. Howard, privates Kingsbury, Speer, Perkins, Gibson, Lepham, Stevens, Heason and Bacon—wounded.

WOUNDED BROUGHT TO ALEXANDRIA.

WASHINGTON, Sunday, Aug. 31.

The following is an unofficial list of the wounded in the late battles who have been brought into the Alexandria hospitals:

Albert Walorf, Co. C, 2d Wisconsin.

George Soper, Co. I, 1st New-York Artillery.

Sergt. Christopher Stock, Co. I, 1st New-York Art.

Adjt. John E. Alexander, 11th Ohio Volunteers.

Corp. John H. Toole, Co. I, 3d New-Jersey.

J. M. Conover, Co. G, 3d New-Jersey.

John Conover, Co. D, 71st New-York Volunteers.

Houtly N. Jones, Co. C, 12th Ohio.

Corp. Edw. Van Not, Co. G, 12th Ohio.

Sergt. Pat McGlenn, Co. B, 2d Excelsior.

Thomas McCoorts, Co. D, 12th Penn. Volunteers.

Henry O'Neill, Co. F; Sergt. Denny Brondt, Co. A; Philander Pawner, Co. G, and Lieut. Charles H. Kelly, 50th Pennsylvania.

Lieut. George H. Swan, Co. A, and Sergt. James Hough, Co. E, 16th Michigan.

John Alexander, Co. H; Sergt. Henry Klein, Co. A, and Jno. H. Mill, Co. D, 21st New-York.

M. W. Stetson, Co. A, 35th New-York.

Wm. S. Porter, Co. A, 2d Maryland.

Wm. W. Withrow, Co. C, 1st Virginia Artillery.

Lieut. Henry C. Pratt, Co. F, 38th New-York.

Sergt. John M. Gordon, Co. I, and Frank M. Russell, Co. B, 72d New-York.

Josiah M. Hines, Co. K, 105 Pennsylvania.

Benj. A. Sullivan, Co. F; John Garstenacker, Co. H; Corp. Wm. A. Wheat, Co. F; James Patterson, Co. G, 5th New-York.

Sergeant Chas. E. Bell, Co. C; Corporal John A. Robertson, Co. A, 74th New-York.

Jacob Bancroft, Co. H; John Marcott, Co. C; Jas. Sullivan, Co. D, 2d New-York Volunteers.

Samuel N. Mayne, Co. B; John McCarty, Co. B, 1st Pennsylvania Artillery.

Charles Goolap, Co. E, 22d New-York Volunteers.

Swain Johnson, Co. B, 1st Minnesota.

Wm. Goraborant, Co. K, 2d New-Jersey.

Mathew Cowlin, Co. A, 76th New York.

John J. Kirk, Co. C, 5th Pennsylvania.

Henry Hernles, Co. C, 9th Penn. Reserves.

Nathaniel Trask, Co. F; Wm. Jones, Co. A, 26th New-York.

Andrew Neish, Co. E, 105th New-York.

Henry Fuller, Co. H, 7th Penn. Reserves.

Corp. Ernst Hackinty, Co. K, 1st New-Jersey.

Tale Wield, Co. K, 9th Penn. Volunteers.

John Smith, Co. H, 16th Massachusetts.

Lieut. John S. Hatch, 1st Michigan Volunteers.

George C. Masten and James Castello, Co. F; Corporal Co. C, 20th New-York.

Sergeant Conrad Leiker, Co. D, 4th New-York Cavalry.

Jacob Cunningham, Co. I, 17th New-York.

Thomas Shine, Co. K, Corporal Joseph J. Phillips, Co. F, 28th Massachusetts.

Charles Farber, Co. C, 68th New-York.

In addition to the above, Lieut. Merriam, of the 1st Michigan Cavalry, was wounded and taken prisoner.

Lieut. Morse, of the same regiment, killed.

Col. Roberts and Capt. Pomeroy, of the 1st Michigan Infantry, were killed.

Capt. Parry, commanding the 16th Michigan, was wounded.

Col. Brodhead, of the 1st Michigan Cavalry, was captured.

Lieut. Farnham, of the 22d N. Y., was wounded.

Capt. Lee Perkins, of Co. E, 2d New-York, and Silas German, private, Co. I, 94th Regiment, died of their wounds.

Milton Phelps, Adjutant of the 10th Pennsylvania Reserve, was shot through the left lung.

Lieut.-Col. Fuller, in command of the 14th, (Brooklyn) was wounded in the thigh by a minie ball.

Major C. H. Howe, 1st Michigan Cavalry, was wounded in five places.

Lieut.-Col. Thomas, of the 22d New-York, was wounded in the breast.

MEDICAL SUPPLIES FOR THE FIELD.

WASHINGTON, Sunday, Aug. 31.

Forty-three wagon-loads of hospital supplies left here Saturday evening for the battle-field. Medical Inspector COOLIDGE, Surgeon PAGE, Assistant-Surgeon WEBSTER and other medical officers of the army and private physicians, have proceeded to the same locality.

CARE OF THE CONVALESCENTS.

WASHINGTON, Sunday, Aug. 31.

The following was issued this evening from the Medical Director's office:

MEDICAL DIRECTOR'S OFFICE, MILITARY DISTRICT OF WASHINGTON, Aug. 31, 1862.

All persons who are willing to receive into their houses convalescent soldiers whom it may be necessary to remove from the hospitals in order to make room for the wounded from the recent battles near the city, will please inform this office of their names, residence, and the number of such convalescents they can receive and provide for.

JOHN CAMPBELL, Surgeon U. S. A., Medical Director.

LINT FOR WOUNDED SOLDIERS.

SURGEON-GENERAL'S OFFICE, WASHINGTON, Aug. 30, 1862.

To the Loyal Women and Children of the United States:

The supply of lint in the market is nearly exhausted. The brave men wounded in the defence of their country will soon be in want of it. I appeal to you to come to our aid in supplying us with this necessary article. There is scarcely a woman or child who cannot scrape lint, and there is no way in which their assistance can be more usefully given than in furnishing us the means to dress the wounds of those who fall in defence of their rights and their homes.

Contributions will be received in Boston by Surgeon A. McLaren, U. S. A.; New-York, by Surgeon R. Satterlee, U. S. A.; Newark, Assistant-Surgeon Janeway; Philadelphia, Surgeon Geo. E. Cooper, U.S.A.; Baltimore, Surgeon C. C. Cox, U. S. A.; Washington, Surgeon C. J. Lamb, U. S. A.; Cincinnati, Surgeon Glover Perin, U. S. A.; Louisville, Surgeon J. F. Head, U. S. A.; St. Louis, Assistant-Surgeon C. T. Alexander, U. S. A., or by any other medical officer of the army.

WM. A. HAMMOND, Surg.-Gen. U. S. A.

SURGEONS FOR OUR WOUNDED.

A telegraph was received by Mayor OPDYKE late Saturday evening, to the effect that there had been a very severe battle, and that all the surgeons that could leave New-York should report at once to the Surgeon-General at Washington. Pursuant to this he at once called a meeting of the New-York medical men at the Fifth-avenue Hotel, at 3 P. M., Sunday. On motion of Dr. CHAS. D. SMITH, Mayor OPDYKE was called to the Chair, and Dr. JNO. W. GREENE was elected Secretary. The purpose of the meeting was stated and gentlemen requested to hand in their names to the Secretary.

The following gentlemen at once complied, and most of them left, yesterday, in the six o'clock train for Washington:

Jno. W. Greene,	Peck,	Stone,
Austin L. Sands,	Halleck,	Bouheard,
Chas. D. Smith,	Finnell,	Harris,
W. N. Blakeman,	Porter,	Grissom,
George Lorillard,	Ball,	Maxwell,
Wm. Detmold,	J. M. Markoe,	Little,
Bedford,	Thad's Halstead,	McAllister,
Finell,	Isaac Taylor,	Smith,
Furman,	Briddon,	Bonnaen,
Anderson,	Bulkley,	Tillotson,
Wilson,	Donaghe,	

SURGEONS FROM MASSACHUSETTS, ETC.

A corps of twelve Massachusetts Surgeons, viz.: Drs. W. G. Ereck and Alfred Lambert, of Springfield; F. Hooper, L. S. Davis, P. W. Hartley, W. G. Bennett and assistant, of Fall River; O. E. Brewster, P. L. Miller, P. H. Manning, A. M. Smith and E. V. N. Fisher, of Pittsfield, arrived at the New-England Rooms this morning, and reported to Col. HOWE.

They are *en route* to the seat of war, under special order from the Secretary of War to Gov. ANDREW. Col. HOWE provided transportation south for them, and rendered such other aid as was essential to speed them on their way to the scene of their humane labors.

The ladies of the New-England Rooms have been busily employed all day in packing necessary articles—bandages, lint, medical stores, &c., which have been forwarded by Col. HOWE with the above corps of Surgeons.

PHYSICIANS FROM HARRISBURGH.

HARRISBURGH, Sunday, Aug. 31.

Skillful physicians and surgeons, provided with instruments and all necessary appliances, are being rapidly sent to the relief of soldiers wounded at Bull Run. Six physicians left last night, and others have been invited, by the Governor, and are, no doubt, on their way. Surgeon-General SMITH, with his Philadelphia corps of volunteer surgeons and nurses, also leave to-night.

THE NEWS OF THE GREAT BATTLES

EXCITEMENT IN WASHINGTON.

WASHINGTON, Sunday, Aug. 31.

There is intense anxiety in the hotels and streets to gather incidents of the recent fights, but the reports are so indefinite as, up to this afternoon, not to justify their repetition.

EXCITEMENT IN PHILADELPHIA.

PHILADELPHIA, Sunday, Aug. 31.

The excitement has been intense throughout the city to-day, mingled with a general feeling of depression caused by the meagre accounts of Saturday's battle received to-day.

EXCITEMENT IN BOSTON.

BOSTON, Sunday, Aug. 31.

The excitement in the city to-day has been quite equal to what followed the first battle of Bull Run. Notices appeared in the Sunday papers and were also given from the pulpits, requesting the people to contribute lint, linen, whisky, cordials and other hospital stores necessary for the wounded, and a very large amount of such articles were gathered and sent forward by to-night's train. A large sum of money was also contributed.

Mayor WIGHTMAN, several members of the City Council, a squad of twenty policemen and several physicians, left by the night train also to render aid.

A train of eight double freight cars, filled with hospital stores, contributed by our citizens for the use of our wounded in Virginia, left at 6:30 P. M. The train also had a large corps of volunteer surgeons.

AFFAIRS AT HARPER'S FERRY.

Increased Military Action—Capt. Means' Company—Fight with Guerrillas—Operations of Bushwhackers—Burning of Railroad Train—Twenty-second New-York State Militia—General Hospital Abolished—Col. Washington.

HARPER'S FERRY, Va., Thursday, Aug. 28, 1862.

Affairs in this locality are beginning to wear a decidedly warlike aspect. Troops are arriving; (another New-York regiment, One Hundred and Twenty-sixth, is just in sight,) additional guns mounting, intrenchments completed, and on every side is heard the din of preparation. Nor has this activity been in vain. Should "Stonewall," now that he has so suddenly disappeared, turn up again here, he would certainly meet with a warm reception. Yesterday the village was filled with painful rumors to the effect that Col. MEANS' famous company of Virginia cavalry, numbering one hundred men, had been surrounded by a large band of guerrillas at Waterford, about 16 miles from here, and cut to pieces, only five escaping. The Captain, for whom the Richmond authorities had offered a reward of one thousand dollars, was reported as among the prisoners. Such was the statement brought by one of the members who, being on picket duty, had escaped. All of the cavalry here were sent immediately in pursuit. Toward night, a dispatch was received from Capt. MEANS announcing that he was safe at Point of Rocks. This occasioned great joy, inasmuch as the worst fate was anticipated for him and the immense number of the company who had previously deserted from the rebel service, into which they were impressed. About 10 o'clock in the evening, our cavalry returned reporting that Capt. MEANS' men fought the rebel force until their ammunition gave out, with the loss of one killed and several wounded. None were taken prisoners. The bodies of six dead rebels were found. This was at first supposed to be a part of WHITE'S cavalry force, but it has since been ascertained that they were bushwhackers. These "irregular fighters" are overrunning this part of the State. We hear of their operations in every direction, and during the past week they have become unusually bold. Last Friday a party of them suddenly darted into Smithfield, a small village some twelve miles from here, and captured seventeen out of twenty cavalry who were stationed there. One of them who escaped has shown me a splendid Colt's revolver, which he obtained from the rebels in the *mêlée*. Several of the prominent citizens of the place, who are known to have aided in their capture, have been seized, brought here and imprisoned in the engine house. There is a poetic justice in confining such characters in this place. On the same day the train of cars on the Winchester road were destroyed, about sixteen miles from here—the attacking force consisting of about sixty mounted guerrillas. Obstructions were placed on the track in front, and as soon as the train stopped, in the rear to prevent a back movement. These, together with a volley fired by the enemy, brought it to a halt. Mr. LACOR, the Express agent, was seriously injured. He has since been conveyed to Baltimore. Four soldiers on board were seized, and three in citizen's clothing released. Capt. D'UTASSEY, brother to the Colonel of the Garibaldi Guard, effected his escape in an ingenious manner. Seeing the enemy by the road side as the train approached, he immediately doffed his military coat and belt, buttoning up his linen duster closely around him, and thus passed as a private citizen. One of the rebels seized his equipments lying in the corner, remarking with an oath, that he had secured one Yankee uniform. As soon as all the cars were in flames, they detached the engine from the tender, placed revolvers to the head of the engineer, and threatened to blow his brains out if he did not send his machine adrift. They then decamped with their prisoners. Fortunately, the engine did not run off the track, but sped on in safety, until the motive power was exhausted. Such is the true version of the affair.

Yesterday's afternoon train from Winchester brought some twenty-five guerrillas, who had been captured the day before on the other side of that place. They were clothed in their ragged homespun, presenting a decidedly shabby appearance. Four or five of the number were wounded, and limped along on crutches. They were all forwarded to Fort McHenry. Nine of ASHBY'S Cavalry, captured by the First Vermont Cavalry, were brought here to-day. These numerous demonstrations, which are being made in various quarters, may be but the first ripples which precede the overwhelming rush of the rebel hordes down the Valley.

The Twenty-second N. Y. S. M., which was to have left for home last Sunday, volunteering their services for several days longer, in view of the apparent danger, Gen. WOOL immediately telegraphed a reply requesting them to remain. On Monday, therefore, instead of being *en route* for home, the boys were pulling up stakes, and moving behind the formidable intrenchments built by the contrabands. Companies A, H, G, D and C, to whom several large guns have been assigned, have laid aside their Enfield rifles, and are busily engaged in artillery practice. The remaining companies are detailed to picket the Winchester Railroad track. Should any emergency occur, this gallant regiment will undoubtedly give a good account of itself.

The general hospital here has been abolished, and the patients are to be removed to the Frederick hospitals and elsewhere. Col. MILES is to occupy the grounds hereafter as his headquarters. The Court-martial for this Department, Capt. OTIS, Judge Advocate, has just closed. All of the cases were disposed of. Slaves continue to enter our lines in considerable numbers. LOUIS WASHINGTON, Esq., a rebel Colonel, has lost a large number. His elegant residence, about four miles out of town, has thus far been unharmed. He is the same ignoble descendant of Gen. WASHINGTON whom Capt. COOK arrested at the time of the attack on Harper's Ferry. JOHN BROWN, the leader, lived alone among the thickets of the Maryland heights overlooking the village, while COOK taught school in the vicinity, picking up what information he could of the condition of affairs. This LOUIS WASHINGTON on one occasion had shown him a pair of pistols and a sword which were worn by his immortal ancestor. COOK'S order for his arrest, demanded the surrender of these valuable mementoes. Four hours later JOHN BROWN was to be seen flourishing them as a shibboleth at the head of his men.

Many of the Union people here complain that while their houses are mutilated the elegant residences of rank Secessionists at Charlestown, the county seat, four miles distant, are unharmed. There is some grounds for this complaint. The desolation of war is seen on every hand. It was a favorite theory of PALEY'S that war is a divine institution, established for removing the inequality in numbers which exists between the sexes. What would he say were he living at this time when our young men are falling like leaves of the forest in this unhappy contest.

A DISASTER IN KENTUCKY.

Defeat of Our Forces Under General Manson.

Six Regiments Engaged Against a Rebel Force of 15,000 or 20,000.

RETREAT OF OUR FORCES TO LEXINGTON.

CINCINNATI, Sunday, Aug. 31.

Friday afternoon, the rebels, beyond Richmond, Ky., drove in our cavalry. Gen. MANSON, with the Sixty-ninth and Seventy-first Indiana, moved up, and after throwing a few shells, the enemy retreated rapidly beyond Rogersville, leaving one gun behind. MANSON bivouacked for the night, and, on Saturday morning, advanced with two regiments and four guns, and coming up with the enemy, an artillery fight began, with heavy loss on both sides. The enemy attempted to turn our left flank, when sharp fighting occurred between tee skirmishers.

The Sixty-ninth Indiana advanced through a dense fire of shot and shell, to the relief of our skirmishers, and behaved like old soldiers; but the rebels finally turned our left flank and advanced in full force on our column. Gen. MANSON ordered a retreat; fell back three miles and re-formed in line of battle on high hills, with artillery in position on the right and left flanks.

The firing by artillery was recommenced and kept up by both sides very briskly. After fighting about two hours, the enemy advanced on our right flank, under cover of the woods, and after severe fighting succeeded in turning it. Retreat immediately took place to the original camping ground. Here Gen. NELSON came up, and after great efforts succeeded in rallying the men, and formed another line of battle. Our artillery ammunition was nearly exhausted, and some of the guns were kept without a man to work them—all having been killed or wounded.

Gen. MANSON was wounded at about 3 P. M., when the men again fell back, retreating to Lexington. The enemy's force numbered 15,000 to 20,000. The Federal forces engaged were the Ninety-fifth Ohio, Twelfth, Sixteenth, Sixty-sixth, Sixty-ninth and Seventy-first Indiana, and MUNDY'S and METCALF'S Cavalry. The loss in killed and wounded is heavy on both sides. The number is not yet known.

Lieut. Col. TOPPING, Maj. KEMBLE, of the Seventy-first Indiana, were killed.

Gen. WRIGHT left this morning to take the field. Gen. WALLACE leaves to-night to join him. A large number of regiments are en route to Lexington.

AFFAIRS AT FREDERICKSBURGH.

Gen. Burnside still in Possession of the City.

WASHINGTON, Sunday, Aug. 31.

Private advices from Fredericksburgh, as late as 3 o'clock yesterday afternoon, give contradiction to the current reports regarding the burning of bridges and destruction of property in that locality; there have been no such proceedings. Gen. BURNSIDE had possession of that city certainly at 3 o'clock P. E., yesterday.

THE WAR IN ARKANSAS.

Col. Fitch Denies Hanging Hostages.

HELENA, Ark., Friday, Aug. 22.

To Maj.-Gen. Halleck:

SIR: To-day, for the first time, a letter from Gen. LEE, C. S. A., dated near Richmond, 2d inst., fell under my observation, charging Brig.-Gen. G. N. FITCH with having murdered in cold blood two peaceful citizens. I have no claim to the title, being plain Colonel, but am doubtless the officer alluded to. Some journal lauded me during the late White River Expedition for the alleged hanging of two hostages. Gen. LEE censures me for the same supposed act. The praise and censure are alike undeserved, and the charge in both cases without the shadow of foundation in fact. However many of them may have deserved different treatment, not a man was killed by the troops under my command, except in fair action.

I am, very respectfully, your obedient servant,

G. W. FITCH,

Colonel Forty-sixth Indiana Volunteers Commanding Brigade, and late White River Expedition.

Two Steamers with Disabled Soldiers at Portsmouth Grove, R. I.

PROVIDENCE, R. I., 31st.

Two steamers, with disabled soldiers, arrived at Portsmouth Grove this morning. We have not learned where they came from.

A Prize.

PHILADELPHIA, Sunday, Aug. 31.

Schooner *Mary Elizabeth* arrived to-day. She was captured by gunboat *Stars and Stripes*, on the 24th inst., off Wilmington, trying to run the blockade. She was from Nassau.

Fire in Boston.

BOSTON, Sunday, Aug. 31.

Several wooden tenements and three stables on Thorndike and Forbush streets, Charlestown, were destroyed by fire last night. Twenty families were made homeless. Loss $10,000 to $15,000.

The New-York Times.

VOL. XI—NO. 3414. NEW-YORK, TUESDAY, SEPTEMBER 2, 1862. PRICE TWO CENTS.

THE WAR NEWS.

NO FIGHTING YESTERDAY.

OUR ARMY HEAVILY REINFORCED.

The Union Forces Concentrated at Centreville.

GENERAL BANKS SAFE

Details of the Recent Engagements.

LISTS OF THE KILLED AND WOUNDED.

Commodore Wilkes Demolishes City Point.

Movements of the Western Guerrillas Checked.

THE STATE OF AFFAIRS AT ALEXANDRIA.

CARE FOR THE WOUNDED.

NEWS VIA ALEXANDRIA.

ALEXANDRIA, Sunday, Aug. 31.

According to all accounts Stonewall JACKSON, yesterday, succeeded in forcing his way through the National troops surrounding him, and effected a junction with the remainder of the Confederate forces. This result was not attained without fearful loss on both sides, as the most desperate fighting took place.

From all that can be learned, in the absence of any regular report, the corps of Gens. McDOWELL, HEINTZELMAN, PORTER and SIGEL were engaged, the former having the left, the latter the right, and the others operating about the centre.

The principal part of the fighting seems to have been on the left and centre.

The left was thrown up from Manasses Junction toward Thoroughfare Gap, the right at about Centreville, and the centre on the old Bull Run battle-field out from Manassas.

The action was commenced by the enemy opening his batteries upon our left, between 1 and 2 o'clock in the afternoon.

Their guns were strongly and advantageously posted upon a ridge, while our batteries had to fire from the open plain. Gen. MORELL's Division supported our batteries at this point.

After some severe cannonading, Gen. BUFORD's Brigade of Cavalry, comprising the First Michigan, the First Virginia, and the First Vermont Cavalry, were ordered to our extreme left to reconnoitre, and guard against any attempt to turn our left flank, which movement was threatened by the enemy.

Riding beyond our left, where our infantry were formed close behind our batteries—which were playing with great precision upon the enemy, while our troops were cheering vociferously—our cavalry reached a slight eminence, and were about to send out a detachment to explore, when the enemy were seen coming up in force along the line of the adjacent woods.

A rebel battery was seen to whirl into position, and then came shell thrown into the midst of our cavalry, followed by canister and grape.

Thus was discovered the intention of the enemy to attempt a flank movement.

Long lines of rebel infantry could plainly be seen hurrying up to take position, and soon other rebel batteries were brought up, and opened upon our left.

Our cavalry, forced to retire, retreated behind a low ridge, but the clouds of dust revealing their place of retreat, the rebels continued shelling them, and another change of position was made.

Here a body of cavalry were observed riding toward the spot, and the sabres of our cavalry were drawn to meet the coming foe. The squadron proved to be friends—the Fourth New-York Cavalry. Where they had come from, as Gen. SIGEL was on the right, was and is a mystery. They reported the rebel cavalry under Gen. STUART as about making a charge.

The New-York Cavalry fell in behind Gen. BUFORD's Brigade, the bugles sounded, and over the hill galloped our men to meet the advancing rebels. As our men approached them, the rebel cavalry discharged double-barrelled shot guns and then met us in full charge. Our men broke the enemy's line and pursued them. The rebels rallied in splendid style and dashed forward again to meet the charge. Again their line was broken, and as our cavalry was preparing to charge again the rebels opened fire upon them from their batteries and with musketry, compelling them to retire.

Meanwhile, our left had given way, and was on the retreat, passing the cavalry.

A battery, which had run short of ammunition, was on the point of being captured, but under the determined resistance of our cavalry it was safely brought off.

The troops fell back upon Gen. FRANKLIN's Division, which had just come up, and were formed in line to prevent straggling and anything like a panic.

Had Gen. FRANKLIN's corps arrived two hours earlier upon the field, the result of the day's fighting would have been different.

The fact of Gen. STUART's Cavalry being armed with double-barreled shot-guns is proved by a number of the guns being captured and several of our cavalry having buckshot wounds.

Col. BROADHEAD, commanding the First Michigan Cavalry, was captured.

Lieut. MERRIAM was wounded and taken prisoner.

Lieut. MORSE was killed.

Gen. FRANKLIN's Division retired to Centreville, after preventing confusion and giving our retreating troops time to rally.

During the fight a body of the enemy concealed in the woods annoyed our forces much by their rifle practice. Gen. MARTINDALE's Brigade charged them and drove them from the woods amidst the cheers of our men.

Gen. HARTSUFF's Brigade made a similar charge, but with a different result. They penetrated into the woods, when a deadly fire of grape and canister was opened upon them from a masked battery. At the same time a murderous volley of rifle balls came from one side and a desperate charge of the enemy from the other. Our men fought bravely, but were forced to retire.

The enemy remained upon the battle-field over night.

To-day there has been some skirmishing.

Reinforcements are going up to-day, and a battle is anticipated to-morrow.

The road from Alexandria, extending to Centreville, was densely crowded all this day with wagon trains, ambulances, hacks and private conveyances, on their way to and from the latter place.

The number of wounded sent to Washington was comparatively small.

Not a few persons who had reached Centreville and intermediate points, intending to aid the sick and wounded, were turned back for the reason that the battle-field of Manassas was in the possession of the rebels, and that their services were not needed. Many who had ridden to Centreville have returned to Alexandria on foot.

Pickets had been thrown out all along the road to prevent stragglers from deserting the front.

Four Government employes, who had started from Gen. McCLELLAN's headquarters last night, in company with a mail carrier, (intending to act as nurses,) were arrested at Ball's Cross Roads, on suspicion of being spies, but on being returned to Gen. McCLELLAN's headquarters were discharged.

OUR CORRESPONDENCE FROM THE FIELD.

A DETAILED ACCOUNT OF THE RECENT MOVEMENTS—JACKSON'S TACTICS AND HOW THEY WERE MET—DESPERATION OF THE REBELS.

CENTREVILLE, Va., Sunday, Aug. 31, 1862.

The commencement of the conflict now pending between the National and rebel forces may be said to date from Tuesday, the 26th inst., upon the night of which day Stonewall JACKSON appeared with a large force at Bristor, where he destroyed about fifty cars and two locomotives. He also tore up the railroad track for some distance and burnt two bridges. The cars were on the way to Alexandria, having conveyed a portion of Gen. HOOKER's Division to Warrenton Junction a few hours previous. One of the locomotives was thrown down an embankment and, upon examination, was found to have been pierced with sixty-three rifle shots. The other locomotive, which was remaining on the track, showed marks of having been shot at twenty-five times. One of the engineers jumped from his locomotive and surrendered himself as prisoner, but the rebels did not heed the usage of civilized warfare and shot him upon the spot. At the time of the raid but few persons were aboard the trains, and those were parties employed by the Government to superintend and assist in their running. The cars were empty. The telegraph wire was cut in several places and one of the poles severed.

From Bristor Station JACKSON proceeded to Manasses Junction, two miles below, where he burned about one hundred other cars which were standing upon a side track in readiness to be drawn to Warrenton Junction. The cars destroyed here were heavily laden with subsistence stores, ammunition and saddlers and blacksmiths materials. All, or nearly all the ammunition, consisting of three car loads was secured, and carried away. A few shells had been left in the cars as the fragments of ragged iron found upon the ground testified. All the subsistence stores that he could conveniently dispose of were taken by JACKSON. A half-dozen barrels of hard bread were discovered near the track, also a quantity of hams. At the Junction the rebels burned another bridge, tore up more railroad track and also burned a large bakery and several small buildings in the immediate vicinity of the same. Half an hour before the rebels appeared Gen. STURGIS, who, with his brigade, had been guarding the Junction, was ordered to report with his force to Warrenton. When Gen. STURGIS had left the Junction, six pieces of artillery, belonging to a New-Jersey battery, was left almost entirely unsupported, consequently the rebels found it an easy matter to overcome the artillerists and capture the guns. At about the time the rebels arrived at the Junction, Gen. DANA's New-Jersey Brigade, which was stationed at the railroad bridge over Bull Run, acting upon orders previously received, were advancing to Manassas. The bridge is situated about five miles from the Junction, and, of course, as the Brigade approached that place, they were surrounded by the rebels, and a great many taken prisoners. All the prisoners, however, taken at the Junction by JACKSON were paroled on the following day, he doubtless considering that they might occasion him much trouble before he could get them safely into Richmond.

From the Junction JACKSON proceeded to the railroad bridge over Bull Run and destroyed it. The reflection of the burning cars, bridge and building, could be seen distinctly at Warrenton Junction. The mass continued to burn throughout the night.

Until Thursday morning JACKSON remained in the vicinity of Bristor and Manassas Junction, and dined on Wednesday with a family living near the dépôt, at the former place. When preparing to leave, he ordered his temporary landlord to pack up his wordly goods and make ready to depart with his family into the land of Secessia. The host, however, was too keen to observe the import of the command, and began at once to conjecture how he should escape being forced into the rebel service. He gained permission of JACKSON to go a short distance from his home for the ostensible purpose of procuring a wagon, in which he might convey his family and goods from the Union line; but instead of returning immediately, he remained concealed in the woods until our forces appeared and drove the rebels from the line of the railroad, on the following day.

Although the rebels commenced their depredations early on Tuesday evening, it appears that no effort was made to repel them until the next morning, when HOOKER's Division and one brigade of KEARNEY's, (ROBINSON's,) the whole under command of Gen. HOOKER, were sent from Warrenton Junction down the railroad, to meet and drive away the enemy. The ground in the vicinity of Bristor is undulating, thereby affording good points upon which to plant batteries, and also a fine protection for the men against the enemy's fire. Before reaching Bristor from the Warrenton side, the railroad is lined on each side by dense woods which fringe an open field of many hundred acres in extent. Along the skirt of these woods, JACKSON had posted a portion of his force, while he held the remainder in reserve, and out of sight, behind the hills in the rear. He had two batteries of six pieces each, planted one on either side of the railroad, which the rebels commenced using with destructive effect at the opportune moment. HOOKER ordered his men to advance cautiously and deployed skirmishers through the woods who reported the presence of the rebel pickets at the further end. Soon after, several shots were exchanged by the advance guard on both sides. But instead of moving his troops down the railroad, HOOKER took a sweep round the woods at his left and entered the open field upon the right wing of the enemy's advance. This movement caused the rebels to fall back, and not without confusion, and it being a propitious moment for the Union force to deal a good blow, Gen. HOOKER gave the command to fire, which was followed by a tremendous volley of musketry. More of the enemy fell at this fire than by any succeeding one. Our force suffered mostly from the effect of the batteries stationed on the hills in front of them. The projectile used by the enemy was grape and canister shot. The fight lasted from 3 to 5 o'clock. HOOKER succeeded in forcing the rebels from their position and bivouacked at night on the battle-ground. Our casualties amounted to fifty killed and about one hundred and fifty wounded. The rebels left their dead and over one hundred of their wounded on the field. On Thursday morning the bodies were buried by order of the Commanding-General.

Prisoners captured on this occasion agree in the statement that JACKSON had a force of 30,000 men. They also state that he came to Bristor on the road leading from Centreville to Manassas Gap, and followed the same road on his retreat. He commenced retiring from Manassas Junction Thursday morning, burning all the bridges that he crossed, including the one over Bull Run. KEARNEY and HOOKER closely pursued, and did not stop until the rebels had been driven to Haymarket, and night overshadowed the chase.

It was expected that the rebels would receive reinforcements from Richmond; but, in order to detain the reinforcements as long as possible, KING's Division was sent round to Thoroughfare Gap to oppose the entrance of the rebels. KING's Division took the road leading from Catlett's Station to Manassas. They arrived upon the ground early Thursday evening, and in the course of a couple of hours were engaged with the rebel LONGSTREET, who was endeavoring to force his division through the Gap. The rebels were held in check for some hours, which was a great advantage to POPE, as he had an opportunity to march his troops and properly dispose them.

The attempt of JACKSON to come in upon our rear has evidently been anticipated by POPE for some days before the event actually happened. On Tuesday, the 26th, orders were issued for the troops to proceed to Manassas Junction, and on that same day the line of the Rappahannock was abandoned, with the exception of that portion near Fredericksburgh. During Tuesday night and all day Wednesday the supply and baggage trains were moving towards Manassas Junction, from which place they were sent to Centreville and subsequently to Fairfax Court-house. They were at length concentrated in a valley just outside the limits of Centreville. Three locomotives and about one hundred and fifty cars loaded with the sick and wounded and medical supplies at Warrenton Junction, were waiting at that place for the burnt bridge to be reconstructed and the track relaid so that they might pass on to Alexandria. On Thursday, however, it was deemed advisable to transfer the sick and wounded who could not walk to ambulances, by which means they were conveyed to Alexandria. The medical supplies were placed in wagons. It will be inferred from that movement that the event of the rebels occupying Warrenton Junction was not wholly unanticipated by POPE.

The battles of Friday and Saturday took place upon the old Bull Run battle-ground. On Friday the fight was on our right, which was held by SIGEL in the morning, and in the afternoon and evening by HEINTZELMAN. KING's Division had suffered considerably in the engagement the night previous, and was held in reserve, with the remainder of McDOWELL's Corps.

PORTER's Corps arrived at Warrenton Junction from the Rappahannock on Thursday, and were ordered to proceed to the battle-ground. They took a position on the road leading to Centreville. At the left of the road were stationed McDOWELL's and BANKS' Corps.

At daylight on Friday morning the fight was commenced by the rebels endeavoring to turn our right, or the troops under command of SIGEL. They brought to bear a heavy artillery fire, and received in return one equally as energetic from us. Three times during the morning they advanced in mass upon SIGEL, but were successfully resisted each time. The rebels had the choice of position, and had the advantage of us in that respect. They had woods for cover, and from the rising and falling of the ground, could keep up a rapid and decimating fire, without exposing any large bodies of their troops. SIGEL and his men fought nobly till about 2 o'clock in the afternoon, when they were relieved by KEARNEY and HOOKER of HEINTZELMAN's Corps. The rebels, as is their usual practice, frequently relieved their troops, and had fresh men to meet those of HEINTZELMAN. In the afternoon the fight became desperate, the enemy seeming determined to force back our right. After his usual custom, KEARNEY was at the head of his column, cheering on his men, and throwing defiance at the rebels. HOOKER was equally conspicuous, and fought—as he always fights—with the coolness, judgment and daring of a brave man. The contest lasted till dark, the enemy having been driven a mile from his original position. The loss on both sides was heavy, but it is impossible to make an approximate estimate. SIGEL took 800 prisoners, and captured seven pieces of artillery.

The battle was renewed by us at 7 o'clock on Saturday morning. The disposition of our forces was about the same as on the previous day; HEINTZELMAN held the extreme right; PORTER and McDOWELL the centre, and BANKS the extreme left. SIGEL was held in reserve in the rear of PORTER's corps. The fight was sustained on our part by PORTER's force until afternoon when the enemy concentrated his entire force upon McDOWELL. The engagement was almost entirely with the artillery until 1 o'clock in the afternoon. Up to this time little damage had been sustained on either side. The rebels at length became desperate and charged with solid columns upon PORTER's men. They did not succeed in breaking the line, however, and were compelled to fall back to their original position. The result was in our favor, inasmuch as we drove the enemy, although we suffered severely in so doing. The rebel loss must have been frightful, as our artillerists fired at excellent range.

At 3 P. M. the enemy changed tactics, and moved the major part of his force toward McDOWELL, who was on the left of the centre. At this point we had stationed three batteries—LAPINE's Fifth Maine, of four pieces; THOMPSON's New-York, of six pieces, and HOWELL's Battery, of four pieces. For some reason, LAPINE's battery, which was in the extreme front, was unsupported by infantry. This was certainly a great oversight on the part of McDOWELL. Then again, the troops under McDOWELL were too much scattered to effectually resist an enemy's advance. It was particularly observed that an immense number of stragglers were loafing about the field. Stragglers are a nuisance to an army, and the discipline of troops can be ascertained by observing if many of them leave the ranks during a march.

The enemy charged at first upon LAPINE's Battery and succeeded in capturing it. They then advanced eight columns deep toward McDOWELL's force; but, strange to say, instead of offering any opposition, McDOWELL ordered his men to fall back, which they immediately commenced doing. All three of the batteries were then left unsupported, and, of course, to fall into the hands of the enemy. It is reported, however, that three pieces out of the sixteen were drawn from the field by the artillerists. Soon as McDOWELL's troops commenced retiring, the cowardly stragglers set up a shout and ran pell-mell to the rear. Teamsters and ambulance drivers were the next to follow, and it was feared that another Bull Run flight was about to be inaugurated. The breaking of the line in the centre of course compelled the right and left to fall back. If the movement had been conducted systematically all might have been well, but the fear of being the last man seemed to seize the troops, and they made a rush for Centreville. Before reaching Bull Run they were partially rallied, which had the effect to hold in check the advance of the enemy. Several attempts were made to arrest the flight of the men between Bull Run and Centreville, but they all failed. Men with loaded rifles and fixed bayonets behind a breastwork at Centreville were the only barrier sufficiently strong to keep back the troops.

Darkness soon come on, and it being ascertained that the enemy was not rushing upon them with the celerity of lightning, the men became calm and set about preparing something to eat.

FRANKLIN's entire corps had arrived two miles beyond Centreville when the stampede commenced. They drew up in line of battle at that point and remained there during the night.

The battle of Saturday was a loss to us on account of mismanagement somewhere. McDOWELL is blamed by both officers and men for not standing firm upon the approach of the enemy. His men assert that they will not fight under him again.

Our forces have now fallen back to Centreville. SUMNER's corps passed up from Alexandria to-day. The road from Alexandria is lined with reinforcements. It is doubtless the intention of the rebels to make the next a decisive battle. All their available force is at Manassas. Prisoners state that JACKSON in an address to his men, told them that he would take Washington within eight days or sacrifice his whole army.

The Union and the rebel armies are now face to face with each other. It remains to be seen which side shall conquer. Our casualties in the two days' fight will probably amount to about 5,000 killed and wounded.

WHIT.

THE RECENT BATTLES AS VIEWED FROM WASHINGTON—POSITION OF THE CONTENDING ARMIES, AND THEIR RELATIVE FORCE—WHAT WE MAY EXPECT.

WASHINGTON, Sunday Evening, Aug. 31, 1862.

That the greatest battle of the war has been raging for several days past in the vicinity of Manassas, is row known in Washington, although the information is not allowed to go over the wires. That this fight, up to the present time, has *not* resulted in a success to the National arms, is also now known. The same mail that carries this will convey to you an account of this fearful contest, by one of your special correspondents on the field, and hence I shall not attempt any account in detail; but I will give a few observations from this point of view, and the conclusions to which the intelligent public here has arrived in regard to the present "situation."

When JACKSON threw himself with a comparatively small force, in the rear of POPE, he executed one of those bold inspirations of genius whose very audacity almost insures success. POPE's retreat had been a feat of such astonishing rapidity that he may almost be excused for not conceiving it to be possible for JACKSON to thus overtake and flank him. At the same time, JACKSON's daring subjected him to a terrible risk, but promised brilliant rewards. The risk, thanks to his prompt reinforcement by LEE and LONGSTREET, he has survived, and the rewards he has realized in the capture of immense stores, giving the rebels a welcome supply of ordnance stores and ammunition, as well as of provisions, of which, in consequence of their rapid march, they were destitute.

Had our military leaders, however, possessed the boldness and promptitude of JACKSON, he would inevitably have fallen a sacrifice to his enterprise and courage. Probably he estimated all the chances, as in his raid in the Shenandoah Valley, and the fact shows that his estimate was correct.

Both armies have now been reinforced; JACKSON by a force estimated at from 40,000 to 60,000; POPE by divisions from the corps of McCLELLAN and BURNSIDE. The enemy made an overpowering attack on McDOWELL's corps, when LONGSTREET came up and drove it back with great loss of men and ordnance. The fighting of our men was superb. Since that reinforcement we have been on the defensive, and are now back as far, at least, as Centreville—*perhaps further*. The retreat has been made with entire steadiness, and the men exhibit the utmost coolness and courage. But little fighting has been done to-day; the enemy, *who occupy* the old battle ground of Bull Run, apparently seeking some means of turning our flank. Our Generals are, of course, ignorant of what the morning will bring forth.

In case our troops prove too weak to hold the present line of defence, they will still be able to fall back in good order to the fortifications in front of Washington, *unless the enemy, by some daring flank movement, succeed in occupying them first.* In the former case, Washington is entirely safe till the new levies arrive—in the latter contingency, its fate would seem to be sealed.

I think confidence is lost in Gen. POPE. To-night an officer of some prominence, who was in the fight, announces, after visiting the War Office, that to-morrow morning will see a new Commander in the field. Whom it can be, I can only guess. McCLELLAN has not been in the field at all, nor has BURNSIDE; but there is confidence in the latter, who is now said to be at Centreville, and *must* be the man, if a change is made.

Yesterday afternoon, the War Department invited everybody to go out to the battle-field and assist in tending and nursing the wounded. Washington responded almost *en masse*. From 3 to 7 o'clock the streets swarmed with people and conveyances, armed with blankets and baskets and rolls of lint. A thousand, I should say, went out, and this morning, notwithstanding the rain, a large number more. But at 10 o'clock this morning the order was countermanded and passes were refused, and it turns out that the whole affair was ill-advised, and that very few of those who went were allowed to go far enough to find the wounded they sought. Scarce a hack or omnibus was left in the city; this evening sees them returning. But the affair was not altogether bootless, and the result is very creditable to the loyalty and charity of the citizens of Washington.

The wounded are now arriving in, and are well cared for. Our loss is heavy—probably 15,000 to 20,000 already. We have also some prisoners—1,000 are already in.

On the whole, if our Generals show average *brains*, and the loyal citizens of the country *at once fill up the new regiments*, the war was never in better shape; for though this last kick of the enemy is severe, it is final, and a dying spasm. His present army, all of which is at Manassas, is the *last* he can raise.

J. M. W.

SECURE POSITION OF THE UNION ARMY.

Judge WHITE, of the New-York Supreme Court, telegraphed the *Tribune* from Washington at 3 o'clock yesterday afternoon as follows:

"I have just returned from our army close to the battle-field. Our men are in good spirits and as firm as veterans. They hold Centreville and its vicinity, with part of the old battle-field of Bull Run."

GEN. BANKS SAFE.

WASHINGTON, Monday, Sept. 1.

Dispatches received from Fairfax Court-house, seven miles from Centreville, state that no firing has been heard up to 12 o'clock to-day.

Gen. BANKS' forces were heard from last night, and were in a favorable position for joining Gen. POPE's army.

NEWSPAPER ACCOUNTS.

The Washington correspondent of the Philadelphia *Press*, under date of the 31st, gives graphic descriptions of the battles at Bull Run, from which we select the following:

It will hardly be necessary for me to mention the fact that it was not until yesterday afternoon that the War Department determined to relieve the newspaper correspondents from the restraint placed upon them, in order to prevent them from furnishing any news direct from the army of Virginia. When it was announced that the "embargo" had been taken off, the news spread like lightning, and every one's countenance wore an expression of hope that some reliable information, concerning the details of the recent great battles south of us would be speedily forthcoming in bulletins, extras, and, at the latest, in the Sunday papers.

It is now certain that it was part of the plan of the rebel leaders, JACKSON and LEE, to reach Manassas Junction ahead of us, or drive us out of it and then make it a base of future operations and supply for their armies, as they advanced into Maryland. To this end, LEE ordered LONGSTREET and ANDERSON to move as one column, due north upon the Junction, uniting his forces there with those of JACKSON, advancing from the west. It would seem that the rebel army with which we had to contend in the recent battles, including the grand divisions of JACKSON, LONGSTREET, ANDERSON and HUGER's old command, could not have been less than eighty thousand men.

By some strategy, not yet manifest, the rebels succeeded, about ten days since, in turning our right flank at Warrenton, and marched upon Manassas almost unperceived. As soon as Gen. POPE became assured of this, he ordered HOOKER's Division to march upon Manassas Junction rapidly from Alexandria, with five days' cooked rations, in light marching order, but with a good supply of ammunition.

HOOKER sprang forward with his gallant fighting division, and, meeting the rebels under EWELL, at Kettle Run, several miles southeast of Manassas, gave him a sound thrashing, and drove him from Bristor Station and the railroad, over which our large army, near Warrenton, was being supplied with stores; and although the rebels had made a raid upon Catlett's Station, and destroyed a small portion of the bridge and track at Cedar Creek, this movement of HOOKER prevented LONGSTREET from getting in our rear with a large army, and entirely severing POPE's communication with Washington. Thus the army of Virginia was saved from annihilation or ignominious surrender, which must have followed a want of supplies, as there is no forage in that country.

It will be plainly seen from this that LONGSTREET was at least to hold in check what he supposed to be our entire army at Warrenton, while JACKSON moved through Centreville on to Leesburgh, *via* the turnpike road over Goose Creek, over the Potomac and into Maryland.

LONGSTREET apparently fell back when HEINTZELMAN came up with the balance of his corps to reinforce HOOKER, and upon his arrival at Gainesville opened communication with JACKSON, who is said to have been moving toward Gum Spring, twelve miles Northwest of Centreville, at the time, and informed Stonewall of the condition of affairs, which, being fully appreciated by the latter, he at once turned about and struck for the Warrenton turnpike, intending to join LONGSTREET at Gainesville.

In the meantime Gen. POPE moved his army up from Warrenton as rapidly as possible; McDOWELL, with his own and SIGEL's corps and RENO's Division, moving to the left, through Greenwich, towards Gainesville, which movement, Gen. POPE says, caused the rebels to retreat through Thoroughfare Gap and to return reinforced.

On Friday, after a tedious night advance, McDOWELL, SIGEL and RENO came upon JACKSON, six miles west of Centreville, as he was retreating to Gainesville, and a severe pitched battle took place, which lasted all day, and the field was stoutly contested. This was a drawn battle, but JACKSON's loss was very heavy, and observing the trap that had been set for him, he endeavored to retreat across Bull Run on Friday night, but from some cause he did not get his army entirely over.

Our forces moved after him that night, and by daybreak yesterday morning had driven the enemy over Catharpin Creek. Up to the date of Gen. POPE's dispatch, headed "Groverton, near Gainesville," we had captured all of JACKSON's baggage wagons and camp equipage, and a large number of prisoners.

The fields were said to have been full of rebels overcome with exhaustion, hunger and thirst, who readily gave themselves up. Some of these men state that they started out from Thoroughfare Gap in light marching order, with ten days' rations of very poor quality, and that this had been all consumed. If this be true future victories over him will be easy.

At any rate, I learn that during yesterday the battle continued all day, without any decisive results, the fighting being desultory, and both armies being almost utterly exhausted.

The enemy had now retreated for some distance, and was back of Gainesville. McDOWELL, SIGEL and RENO still held the enemy at bay, and waited anxiously for the arrival of Gen. PORTER's corps of fresh troops from Manassas, but from some unaccountable delay he did not arrive. The probability is that his men have been overtasked with long marches, and want of proper comforts, they having left their camp equipage and overcoats behind.

The city is full of rumors to-day about the battle going on to-day in the vicinity of Bull Run. The excitement runs high on the avenue in consequence of the circulation of these reports. I am happy to say that I have just seen an officer of high rank, this afternoon, who has given me some most important news.

Gen. POPE seems to have met with a temporary reverse to-day. He was successfully driving the enemy during yesterday, whom he supposed to be under command of Gen. JACKSON, but about 4 o'clock a tremendous cloud of dust was seen on the right, and Gen. POPE became convinced that heavy reinforcements for the enemy had succeeded in getting through Thoroughfare Gap, and were marching towards his right, with a view of turning it, and getting in his rear.

He accordingly determined to withdraw his jaded troops from the immediate field of action, which the enemy at once took possession of. It was mortifying for Gen. POPE to do this, but SUMNER and PORTER had not arrived to save the day. Centreville is a most important point, and Manassas Junction is equally so, and no one can fail to see that it is absolutely necessary for us to keep possession of them.

This morning (Sunday) the rebels renewed the battle at daybreak, and it has been raging furiously all day. An attempt was made to turn our right, but the brave SIGEL, with his trusty Germans, and the batteries he knows so well how to manœuvre, was at once ordered to the right, and the enemy was driven back with heavy loss. SIGEL headed a bayonet charge in person, it is said, and in this new position distinguished himself.

Then a bold stroke was made at our centre, which was handsomely repulsed by McDOWELL. After this a desperation was fearfully evident among the rebels, and there soon emerged from the dust a long, solid mass of men coming down upon our poor worn-out army at a bayonet charge on the double-quick. By the description of those who saw this line of bayonets, I am satisfied that in the distance it must have presented a spectacle at once awful, sublime, terrible and overwhelming.

On came the demons, as if emerging from the earth, in well-caparisoned myriads, reaching in solid column as far as the limit of human vision. But we were fully prepared to meet this onset properly, and our men stood, pale but full of courage, awaiting the result, fully determined to die nobly fighting for the Stars and Stripes, if die they must; and they saw no safety in retreat.

Perfectly astonished at the confidence and courage of our men, the rebels came up handsomely within range, and, taking our fire, a semi-orderly commotion was observed in their ranks. While this encouraged our men, Gen. POPE saw what was the intent of it all.

Almost as quick as thought, the bugles sounded the order to the rebel phalanxes, and instantly the huge mass of rebels was hurled against our left wing. The gallant divisions of RENO and SCHENCK—heroes and victors of other fields—stood their ground for a short space, but were soon overpowered and gave way. Setting up a yell of triumph, the rebels pushed over piles of their own dead men and the corpse of many a patriot, using the bayonet at close quarters with our troops.

The rebels were slow in re-forming. They had not driven us back with considerable loss, and they did not make another advance until half an hour after, about noon to-day.

Now everything looks like a great defeat to the arms of the Union, but God has not willed it so. We are never to be defeated at or near Bull Run again. Our reinforcements are in sight at last. SYKES, with his invincible regulars, is in sight.

It is the vanguard of FITZ-JOHN PORTER's corps. they are coming up from Manassas to give the rebels some of the "touches" they applied to them so artistically at Gaine's Mills. His fire is delivered in the enemy's flank, and the rebels stagger back.

The rebels seem three to our one, when cheering is heard in our rear, and the dust rises in clouds seemingly for miles in extent. Half an hour passes by and puts SUMNER, with his augmented and regenerated corps, in the advance. The troops that had fought so hard and so long fall back to Centreville for rest.

Many of them sank right down, and, cooled by the rain that was falling, were soon fast asleep, dreaming of home and all that is lovely and beautiful in life, while the roar of cannon was still ringing loudly in their ears, stupified with the sudden relapse from extraordinary excitement of the past week.

Shortly after noon to-day FRANKLIN's corps moved on from Centreville, and took an advanced position.

It is said that our captures of prisoners and stores, camp equipage, &c., are immense. The various trains returning from the battle-fields are loaded with tons of stores of every description taken in the recent battles.

The army corps of Gen. NATHANIEL P. BANKS is at Manassas Junction. He has rendered most important services, although not actively engaged with the enemy. It is understood that he was anxious to move into the valley and prevent any reinforcements from reaching JACKSON, but it was thought best to leave him to hold the Junction, and keep communication open between our army and Washington.

Persons who have arrived from the immediate vicinity of Manassas to-day report that our loss in killed and wounded is very heavy, and it is generally conceded that 8,000 is too low a figure. But all agree in saying that the enemy's loss far exceeds ours, owing to the superior arms of our soldiers and their determined valor and terrible enthusiasm.

Very triumphantly the rebel hordes advanced. It was evident, at first glance, that they had been heavily reinforced, and it was equally impressed upon our consciousness that we must meet the approaching contest with men wearied enough in body and not a little dampened by the thought that SUMNER and FRANKLIN had failed to come up. But the force under our control was disposed as well as circumstances would allow.

All the officers from the Major-General commanding to the humblest Lieutenant were indefatigable in their exertions to make energy and tact atone for the want of those happy coinciding circumstances which so often materially contribute to decide the issue of a battle. The men stood nobly up to their work.

The day was far advanced. Our men had fought with more than mortal heroism. Inspired valor flushed each eager countenance. We had suffered severely in killed and wounded; but few of our number had been taken prisoners—the fighting was too desperate, and the field too hotly-contested on both sides to prevent any yielding save in death. The bravery of the rebels must be admitted.

Whether they were intoxicated or not, as in the seven-days' battles, I cannot say, but I would not be greatly surprised if such should ultimately prove true. Many of them had thrown aside their coats and jackets, and entered the contest with an Irish dash and recklessness. Many of our men had had not a mouthful to eat since morning, but there was no indication at any point in our line either of wavering or weakness.

It was whispered along the ranks in the pauses of the conflict that FRANKLIN was coming to our aid from Alexandria, and the men were hopeful. Under such circumstances, the order "Fall back! fall back!" came like a thunder-clap to every ear. Each countenance drooped. There was a slacking in our fire, the line wavered for an instant, and the massing of the troops commenced. Sad, indeed, was the massing of such mere fragments.

Regiments were reduced to corporals' guards, and indeed, it is no exaggeration to say that from some brigades it would have been difficult to form a couple of stout companies. But no matter now for regimental forms; the object is simply to get the men into compact form and retreat them safely. Retreat? Palsied be the tongue that dares to call the deliberate backward movement of those wearied men a retreat. If it be retreat to imperil everything that is dear to man for the sake of the National honor—to toil in the excitement of a life-and-death struggle amid every discouragement and actual thwarting—if to hunger, and thirst, and bleed, and fight for two whole days, and then, in presence of overwhelming numbers, to fall back, slowly and orderly, upon reinforcements—if this is retreat, our army *did* retreat.

The intelligence of POPE's reverse, received early this morning, had a visible effect upon the President, and he continued uneasy until Gen. HALLECK informed him of the concentration of our forces beyond Centreville, and our success in *driving the enemy back this afternoon.*

Our Chief Magistrate has the most unbounded confidence in the ability of Gens. HALLECK and POPE, and it was said that he will take occasion to personally thank the Generals who have distinguished themselves in these battles.

This afternoon our whole army is massed ten miles south of Centreville, beyond Bull Run, and notwithstanding that the rebel army has received such great reinforcements, we are driving the enemy at every point, and victory, sooner or later, is considered certain. JACKSON will certainly be driven to the mountains.

He cannot pass through Thoroughfare Gap again, for HEINTZELMAN is guarding the road, and he cannot break through that brave corps, especially with our grand armies at his heels.

RECEPTION OF THE NEWS.

The exciting intelligence given to the people yesterday, but added to the feverish state into which the meagre reports of the papers of the day before had plunged them.

Very many did not hesitate to disbelieve every line of the news; others saw in it but an evidence of darker matter kept away from them, and others again deemed it but an additional excitant to the performance of duty in aiding recruiting, and in hurrying on troops to the aid of our armies in Virginia.

Little business was attended to. Every man waited for additional word from the seat of war, and as extra after extra doled out its half column of news, they were bought up quickly, read hastily, and thrown aside for the next. Public opinion was in this, as on all other matters, divided.

The rumors concerning the action and possible displacement of Gen. McCLELLAN, aroused his friends to vigorous argument in his behalf, they urging that more troops should be sent on, and that had he been let alone his plans would ere this have been crowned with success. Others thought that it was high time for his removal from all command, and that a rigid settlement be made with him. Indeed, if possible, the rumors concerning him caused a greater excitement than did the report of POPE's retreat to Centreville.

Discussion ran high, and the report that a news paper, which had deemed it wise to give currency to the Anti-McClellan stories, had been suppressed by the Government, but added fuel to the already towering flame of excitement.

The later hours of the day brought no additional news, save that POPE was resting and receiving reinforcements. This was partially reassuring, and people generally concluded that as regiments of troops are hourly arriving at Washington, there will soon be such an army gathered there as will enable our Generals to fight with successful result.

On the whole the popular mind was unsettled—it could with difficulty understand the dispatches of McDOWELL, of POPE, and of the correspondents. They could not reconcile the terms "glorious news," and "retreat," "we have the advantage," and the appeals for succor.

But a universal belief in the desire of the Government to do what it could, was met by a general determination on the part of the people to re-strengthen the hands of the President to reinforce the armies, that again they may attempt, and this time with no uncertain result, the annihilation of the enemy.

THE KILLED AND WOUNDED.

WASHINGTON, Monday, Sept. 1.

The following is a list of some of the killed and wounded in the recent Bull Run battle:

Lieut. Thos. J. Little, 13th Massachusetts—wounded in the leg, cheek and arm.

Capt. Ward, 2th N. Y. M.—wounded severely.

Col. Roberts, 2d Maine—reported killed.

Col. O'Connor, 2d Wis.—reported killed.

Major May, 19th Indiana—reported killed.

Col. Rose—wounded severely.

Col. Coltes, 73d Pennsylvania—killed.

Col. Conwell, 82d Ohio—killed.

Lieut. Riff, Co. F, 61st Ohio—wounded in the thigh.

Col. Garvin, 7th Indiana—musket ball through the right breast.

Capt. Robinson, 7th Indiana—knocked down and bruised.

Sergt. Fred. Schneapper, Co. A, 58th N. Y.—hand.

J. F. Strong, Co. F, 56th Pennsylvania—arm.

Sergt. John Volkhardt, Co. A, 58th New-York—collar bone broken.

Adjt. M. M. Phillips, 10th Pennsylvania Reserves—right breast, seriously.

John Knapp, Co. A, 56th Penn.—face, slightly.

C. L. Stimson, Co. H, 30th New-York—leg.

Andrew Cassiday, Co. I, 14th N. Y.—left hand.

L. E. Rimons, Co. A, 30th N. Y.—hand, slightly.

E. Ranch. Co. F, 56th Penn.—hand, slightly.

Jacob Hartman, Co. F, 56th Pennsylvania—arm.

Col. Hayes, 63d Pennsylvania—feet.

Lieut. S. A. Craig, 105th Pennsylvania—arm.

The two latter officers have arrived in this city.

PHILADELPHIA, Sunday, Aug. 31.

A special dispatch from Washington to FORNEY's *Press* says in addition to Gen. SCHENCK, Gens. HATCH, PATRICK, DURYEE and TOWER, are slightly wounded. Col. KELTZ, Seventy-third Pennsylvania; Lieut.-Col. McLEAN, Eighty-eighth Pennsylvania; Col. O'CONNOR, Second Wisconsin; Col. CANTWELL, Eighty-second Ohio; Capt. FRANCIS SHELLINGAIR, Twelfth Pennsylvania Reserves, were all killed.

Gens. BUFORD, STAHL, HATCH and COULTER are all reported killed.

FROM OUR SPECIAL CORRESPONDENT.

The following wounded in the recent battles came in the ambulance train to-day from Centreville, and are at College Hospital, Fourteenth-street:

M. J. Hill, Co. G, 2d Regulars; W. Brown, Co. E, 2d Regulars; Chas. Newton, Co. C. 3d Regulars; Capt. Owen Leonard, Co. D, 6th Regulars; Edward Simpson, Co. I, 4th Regulars; Sergt. Chas. Pitgree, Co. E, 1st New-York Vol.; Peter Fraley, Co. C, 1st New-York; Lieut. W. Hoffman, Co. I, 5th New-

[*Continued on Eighth Page.*]

The Charleston Mercury.

DAILY PAPER—TEN DOLLARS PER ANNUM, PAYABLE HALF-YEARLY IN ADVANCE

SPONTE SUA SINE LEGE FIDES RECTUMQUE COLENTUR — VINDICE NULLO

COUNTRY PAPER—THRICE A WEEK—FIVE DOLLARS PER ANNUM, IN ADVANCE

VOLUME LXXXI | CHARLESTON, S. C., FRIDAY, SEPTEMBER 5, 1862 | NUMBER 11,546

NEWS BY TELEGRAPH.

THE LATEST FROM THE SEAT OF WAR—PARTICULARS OF THE BATTLE OF SATURDAY—THE CASUALTIES, &c.

MANASSAS, August 30 (*via* RAPIDAN, September 4).—The second Battle of Manassas has been fought on precisely the same spot as that of the 21st July, 1861, with the difference that our forces occupied many of the positions which were held by the enemy at that time, and that the enemy fought upon the ground that had been held by us. Several of our regiments entered the field just where McDOWELL's divisions did a year ago. The fight began about three o'clock in the afternoon, near Groveton, on the Warrenton turnpike. LONGSTREET was on the right and JACKSON on the left, their line being in the form of a broad V, with the enemy within. The enemy made their first advance by endeavoring to turn JACKSON's flank, but were repulsed in great confusion—a battery of twenty pieces of artillery, commanded by Col. STEPHEN D. LEE, of South Carolina, mowing them down by scores. LONGSTREET at once threw forward HOOD's and BRYSON's brigades, and advanced his whole line, which was in a short time separately engaged. JACKSON now gave battle, and the enemy was attacked on every side. The fight was fiercely contested until after dark, when the Yankees gave way and were driven in disorder for a distance of three miles. Their force consisted of McDOWELL's, SEIGEL's, BANKS', MORELL's, SICKLES', MILROY's, McCLELLAN's, and POPE's divisions. The loss of the enemy exceeds that of the Confederates in the ratio of five to one. Their dead literally cover the field. Our men captured a number of batteries, numerous regimental colors, thousands of prisoners, and from six to ten thousand stand of arms. We might have taken more of these last; but the men could not be burdened with them. One Yankee Brigadier General is now lying dead at the negro *Robinson's* house, where the Yankee bodies are so thickly strewn that it is difficult to pass without stepping upon them. Generals EWELL, JENKINS, MAHONE and TRIMBLE, are wounded. Colonels MEANS, MARSHALL and GADBERRY, of South Carolina, are killed. Colonels BENBOW, MOORE and McGOWAN, of the same State, are wounded. Major D. C. KEMPER is severely wounded in the shoulder; Captain TABB and Captain MITCHEL, of the First Virginia (the latter a son of JOHN MITCHEL, the Irish patriot), are wounded. Adjutant TOMPKINS, of the Hampton Legion, and Adjutant CAMERON, of the Twenty-Fourth Virginia, were both wounded. About fifty Yankee "citizens of Washington," who had come out to witness the show, have been bagged by our forces

RICHMOND, September 3.—No official despatches have been received from the seat of war in Northern Virginia to-day. The reports brought by passengers all indicate that our victory over the Yankees was complete, and that our troops are in pursuit of the routed enemy.

FROM THE WEST.

JACKSON, MISS., September 3.—(*To the Mobile Advertiser.*)—An official despatch received here, dated Natchez, September 2, says that fourteen Yankees landed there and began pillaging under the hill. About thirty men went down and attacked them. The pillagers were mostly all either killed or drowned. Only three were seen to return to their boats. They fired shell, grape and canister at us as we came up the hill. None of our men were killed. Three children were killed and one wounded by a shell from the gunboats. Both gunboats have gone up the river, it is supposed to get a better range. They shelled the town two hours, without giving time to move the women and children. The officers expressed their determination to join the upper fleet. The *Essex* hoisted the black flag as she went down.

TUPELO, September 3.—Intelligence from the front of our lines is to the effect that the enemy's reports confirm the defeat of the Federal army at Manassas, and announces the Yankee loss to include 3,000 prisoners. The same information states that the defeated armies were falling back on Arlington Heights, where a stand was to be made.

FROM CHATTANOOGA.

CHATTANOOGA, September 4.—Arrivals from Winchester, Tennessee, confirm the rumor of the Yankees having evacuated Huntsville. They were, at last accounts, passing Winchester in a rapid retreat, desolating the entire country in the line of their march.

The Nashville *Dispatch*, of the 30th inst., received here, contains the following telegram, dated Alexandria, Va., August 29: "McCLELLAN has visited Washington, and accepted the command of the Army of Virginia. POPE is beyond Manassas, cut off from Washington. BURNSIDE is with him. A large force of Confederates are at Leesburg, and it is thought they intend to cross into Maryland by Walker's Ford."

The Yankees also report having three fights with SCOTT's La. cavalry at Crab Orchard and Mount Vernon, on Wednesday, Thursday and Friday. Of course they whipped them.

THE NEWS FROM RICHMOND.

(CORRESPONDENCE OF THE MERCURY.)

RICHMOND, Tuesday, September 2.

Another Day of Manassas—Pope and McClellan Routed—Anxiety about our Losses—Gen. Lee—The Extension of the Conscription Law—Gens. Beauregard, Johnston and G. W. Smith—Vizitelly, the Artist, etc., etc.

The plains of Manassas have been again dyed in blood, perhaps more deeply than before, and this time there has been no rain to swell the Potomac, no lack of transportation, no army of PATTERSON to come from Harper's Ferry to defend Washington; and now, shall we cross the Rubicon? The master of Arlington Heights must answer this question.

All we know, up to the present moment, is that McClellan and Pope have been routed, and that our boys are pursuing the fragments of the two armies towards the Occoquan—it is believed—for all seem to agree that McClellan landed there. A part of McC.'s army (five or six thousand men) had not left Fortress Monroe on Saturday, the day of the decisive battle; and we hear nothing of Burnside, who has been at Fredericksburg, and is now, doubtless, *en route* to McClellan. Hence we see that there are still some veteran troops to encounter, in addition to the raw recruits now at Washington. Still, we ought to be able to advance.

We look anxiously for the train this evening, to hear what losses we have sustained. They have been heavy, unquestionably. Pope admits a loss of 8,000 in Thursday's fight, which Lee speaks of as an affair of small moment.

There is wailing in all New England,
And by Schuylkill's banks a knell.

Yes, and there is sorrow enough in all the South.

Gen. Lee will probably head the army of invasion, or, at least, of deliverance to Maryland. That he has been meditating work in and beyond his present vicinity, was inferred weeks ago from an expression of impatience which escaped him at hearing that some of our guerillas had again broken up the Baltimore and Ohio Railroad. "It will be invaluable to us," said he.

Much dissatisfaction is expressed against the course pursued by Congress in regard to extending the Conscript Law and making adequate preparation for the new Yankee levies. But Job is in Congress as well as in the Chair of the Executive, and Job is timid and afraid to look a coming danger in the face. De Quincy, considering murder as a Fine Art, says that a man who begins with murder may gradually rise to the high crime of procrastination. In our case, just at the present time, procrastination is not paradoxically worse than murder—it is murder of the direst proportion—national murder.

The Examiner, always urgent in its appeals to the people and the Government to make timely preparation, came out yesterday morning in a lengthy leader in behalf of the Conscript extension. The article is said to have been dictated by Jno. M. Daniel himself, whose wound has been well, or nearly so, for some weeks. But his arm and hand will be of no use to him for many months to come.

Congress appears timid in the matter of retaliation. Why, Pope's late back-down ought to encourage them. By the way, I am glad to hear from a friend, just from the departments, that we have captured Gens. Blenker and Thomas, of Pope's army. The common sense of the country long since called for retaliation, and the success which has attended even its semblance, as given in General Order No. 54, ought to induce our legislators to put more trust in the sense of their fellow countrymen.

I hear that Gen. Beauregard has been assigned to the command of the Atlantic coast, with his headquarters at Charleston. Gen. J. E. Johnston takes charge of the Trans-Mississippi Department, with Gens. Price, Magruder and Holmes under him. Gen. G. W. Smith retains command here, and has taken a house not far from the President's.

Frank Vizitelly, a well known artist of the London Illustrated News, has been at the Spotswood for some weeks, having a gay time with a number of young bloods of the army and navy. Vizitelly had to run the underground railroad to get to our side; after being with the Yankee army of the Potomac for a year, no wonder they refused him a pass to our lines. He has made a number of sketches of scenes in and around Richmond.

The weather has been singularly cool to-day.

HERMES.

THE SECOND BATTLE OF MANASSAS.

The Richmond *Examiner* has accounts from passengers, from Manassas, of the mortal wounding of Generals POPE and McDOWELL, and the capture by our army of seven or nine thousand prisoners. The same journal contains the following account of the battle of Saturday last:

The battle was fought on the Plains of Manassas, our forces occupying the identical positions occupied by the enemy at the beginning of the ever memorable battle of the twenty first of July, eighteen hundred and sixty-one, and the enemy occupying the positions held by us on that occasion.

On Monday, General A. P. Hill moved down from Salem along the Manassas Gap railroad, and on Tuesday took possession of Manassas Junction, capturing several hundred prisoners and eight or ten guns. General Ewell followed Gen. Hill, and General Taliaferro, commanding General Jackson's old division, followed General Ewell. General Taliaferro reached Manassas Wednesday evening, just as the troops of Ewell and Hill were evacuating that position and falling back towards Bull Run in the direction of Centreville. General Taliaferro occupied Manassas, and made a show of throwing out heavy pickets towards the enemy, who was at Bristow Station, on the Orange and Alexandria railroad, five miles distant in a southwesterly direction; but shortly after nightfall, calling in his pickets, he also fell back towards Centreville, and took a position near Groveton, where he remained all night. His position was to the right of Generals Hill and Ewell. At dawn the next (Thursday) morning, occasional reports of cannon and musketry began to be heard towards the left, which were kept up at intervals until evening. Still no enemy had yet been seen on the portion of the field occupied by General Taliaferro's division. But about five o'clock, p. m., they were suddenly borne down upon by several heavy columns of the enemy, numbering, it was estimated, twenty thousand men. The fight was opened on both sides with artillery; at first at long range, but gradually the enemy drew up his batteries to our lines. By six o'clock the distance between the combatants had been reduced to musket range, and the fight along the whole line of Taliaferro's, Ewell's and Hill's divisions became general. The enemy fought with great obstinacy, being inspired, it is thought, by the supposition that they had caught General Jackson in small force, and had an opportunity of crushing him. But as often as they charged our lines they were driven back with thinned ranks, without being able to move us from our position. Finally, night closed over the scene, and the enemy retired from the conflict. The battle was, however, kept up until nine o'clock by the artillerists on both sides. Our men rested on their position that night, and on Friday morning moved forward a mile in the direction of the enemy.

Our loss in this battle is estimated at between eight hundred and a thousand killed and wounded. The enemy's is known to have been more than double that number. Among our casualties were the following: Gen Ewell, leg shattered, rendering amputation necessary; Gen. Taliaferro, slightly wounded in the foot, neck and arm; Gen. Jenkins, wounded in chest and leg; Gen. Trimble, shot in head; Gen. Field, in thigh; Col. Skinner, of First Virginia, mortally wounded; Major M—y, Twelfth Virginia, killed; Col. Neff, Thirty-Third Virginia, killed; Major Terry, of —— Virginia, wounded in arm; Major Lawson Botts, Twenty-Second Virginia, shot in head; Col. Baylor (commanding Stonewall Brigade), killed; and Lieut. Col. Fleury, of Seventh Virginia, wounded. The wounded have all been removed to hospitals established near Aldie, in the county of Loudoun.

It was stated last night, upon apparently good authority, that after their defeat on Saturday the enemy fled towards Edwards', on the Potomac, near Leesburg, whither they were pursued by a portion of our victorious troops. Another report prevailed to the effect that a portion of our army were in Alexandria.

General John Pope

General Irvin McDowell

The Charleston Mercury.

DAILY PAPER—TEN DOLLARS PER ANNUM, PAYABLE HALF-YEARLY IN ADVANCE

VINDICE NULLO
SPONTE SUA SINE LEGE FIDES RECTUMQUE COLENTUR

COUNTRY PAPER THRICE A WEEK—FIVE DOLLARS PER ANNUM, IN ADVANCE

VOLUME LXXXI | CHARLESTON, S. C., SATURDAY, SEPTEMBER 6, 1862. | NUMBER 11,546

NEWS BY TELEGRAPH

IMPORTANT FROM THE NORTH.

THE YANKEE ACCOUNTS OF OUR LATE VICTORIES.

GREAT LOSSES OF THE ENEMY.

RICHMOND, September 5.—A despatch from Harrisonburg, Virginia, dated yesterday, says: The Provost Marshal at New Market writes today that the Yankees evacuated Winchester night before last, burning all their stores and blowing up their magazine. They also burned one whole square in the town. We hear from the same source that late Baltimore papers report the death of General McCLELLAN.

We have Baltimore papers of the 1st and 2d instants. They report the Federal loss in the battle on Friday to be not less than 8000 killed. They claim, however, the victory on that day. In alluding to Saturday's fight the *American* says: "The advantage remained with the rebels." The *Sun* styles it "an utter rout." The Yankee losses up to Friday night were estimated at 17,000. Generals BUFORD, HATCH, TAYLOR and PATRICK were killed. Generals SCHENCK, TOWER, KEARNEY and SEIGEL, were severely wounded. Col. FLETCHER was killed. Col. FARNSWORTH was wounded. The Baltimore *American* has a list of more than 150 officers killed. POPE's report admits a loss of 8000 on Friday. The *American* contains an account of the fight at Richmond, Kentucky, in which it admits that the Yankees were defeated with immense slaughter, and driven to Lexington, Gen. BULL NELSON was severely wounded. Gen. McCLELLAN retains command only of the Army of the Potomac. He was not sent, as reported, to take command over POPE.

CASUALTIES.

RICHMOND, September 5.—(*Private Despatch*).—I am just from Greensville. Amid conflicting rumors, I am unwilling to cause needless distress by unreliable information. The following list of casualties is obtained from an eye witness:

GREGG'S BRIGADE.

Killed.—Lt. JOHN MONROE, Carolina Light Infantry.

Sergt. E. DARBY, Carolina Light Infantry.
Private FLEETWOOD, "
Sergt. A. SMITH, Richland Rifles.
Private THOS. WILLIAMS, Butler Sentinels.
Corporal C. N. GARDNER, "
Private JASPER HOLLY, "

Wounded.—Private CHAS. ATWELL, Carolina Light Infantry.

Private T. SHEPPARD, Carolina Light Infantry.
Captain C. D. BARKSDALE, "
Private E. EDWARDS, Richland Rifles.
Sergeant T. F. WILLIAMS, Butler Sentinels.
Private W. H. HOLLOWAY, "
Private M. W. WHATLER, "
T. M. BRANSON, "
T. C. LOMPKINS, "
W. THOMPSON, "
JOHN H. KING, "

Privates SMITH, Marion Volunteers.

THOS. McCRADY, Irish Volunteers.

Major EDWARD McCRADY, commanding regiment.

Ex Governor MEANS was certainly killed. He died on Monday morning from the effect of a shell in the breast.

Later.—The following list is reliable. I will not send rumors:

Spartan Rifles, Palmetto Sharpshooters.—Killed: H. A. McSWAIN, T. L. CAPERS, JAMES PALMER, WHITEFOORD SMITH. Wounded: HIRAM MITCHELL, S. WALDEN, WM. WALDEN (slightly), JOHN HOLT, ALTMAN KIRKLAND, JNO. E. WALKER (slightly).

Cols. GADBERRY and GLOVER are killed. Col. MOORE is wounded through the lungs.

R. W. BARNWELL.

GORDONSVILLE, September 4.—I am slightly wounded in the breast and painfully wounded in the left arm. CATER SEABROOK, Adjutant of the Brigade, is killed.

M. JENKINS.

RICHMOND, September 4.—(*To the Columbia Guardian.*)—Among the casualties of the late battle are the following:

Palmetto Sharpshooters, Co. D.—Killed—DAVID MOORE. Wounded—Lieut. R. A. SNODDY, slight contusion in foot; Serg't F. V. LANDRUM, slight; Corp'l G. W. HOWELL, seriously; RICHARD BARNETT, slight; M. C. WINGO, seriously.

Palmetto Sharpshooters, Co. K.—Killed—Serg't H. A. McSWAIN, Corp'l JAS. J. PALMER, D. T. BEARDEN, T. L. CAPERS, WHITEFOORD SMITH, R. A. WATSON. Wounded—Serg't H. H. MITCHELL, dangerously, in head; Corp'l F. WALDEN, in leg; NAHUM CANNON, seriously, in leg; G. A. KIRKLAND, severely, in face; A. McDONALD.

Col. Glover's Regiment, Co. H.—Killed—Lieut. NESBITT and Sergeant TEAGUE. Wounded—D. THOMAS, Corporal SHANDS, H. M. SPILLERS, W. J. RHODES.

A DAY OF PRAYER AND THANKSGIVING.

RICHMOND, September 5.—President DAVIS has issued a proclamation, setting apart Thursday, 18th instant, as a day of Prayer and Thanksgiving to Almighty God, for the great mercies vouchsafed to our people, and more especially for the triumph of our arms at Richmond and Manassas.

THE MERCURY.

SATURDAY, SEPTEMBER 6, 1862.

Manassas.

Slowly the smoke is clearing away from the famous field of Manassas, and, while we can learn but little of the later movements of the opposing forces, it is easy to see that the struggle of Saturday was, indeed, for us, "a signal victory." Already the sounds of wailing and lamentation come echoing from the North. Thousands upon thousands of the invading host have gone down before the valor of our veteran troops; the third Grand Army which had been marshalled upon Virginia soil for the subjugation of that noble State, is beaten, and has fled "in utter rout;" Maryland, from her eastern shore to the Blue Ridge, is throbbing with the hope of an early deliverance, and sits uneasy in her chains; while Washington, the centre of official falsehood and corruption, is quaking at the approach of the very army that the Yankee leaders were lately so confident of crushing and driving "to the wall."

But new blows must be struck and new victories won before the enemy can be brought to his senses. The army of KIRBY SMITH must press forward from Lexington until the tramp of its brigades shall startle the people who dwell beyond the Ohio. Our victorious troops in Virginia, reduced though they be in numbers, and shattered in organization, must be led promptly into Maryland, before the enemy can rally the masses of recruits whom he is rapidly and steadily gathering together. When the Government of the North shall have fled into Pennsylvania, when the public buildings in Washington shall have been razed to the ground, so as to forbid the hope of their ever again becoming the nest of Yankee despotism, then, at last, may we expect to see the hope of success vanish from the Northern mind, and reap the fruit of our bloody and long continued trials.

PROGRESS OF THE WAR.

NEWS FROM THE ARMY OF NORTHERN VIRGINIA.

Our intelligence of the great battle fought last Saturday on the Plains of Manassas is still meagre and unsatisfactory. The few facts we have are obtained through the Richmond *Examiner*, from an officer of LONGSTREET's division, who was wounded about the close of the engagement. His knowledge, however, extends little beyond the occurrences in his own immediate brigade.

The battle was begun about three o'clock in the afternoon. JACKSON having command of the left wing, rested his extreme left on Bull Run, at Union Mills; LONGSTREET in the centre, faced Manassas Junction; while our left, under A. P. HILL, stretched away towards Thoroughfare Gap. The battle was begun on the left, but in a few moments became general, and raged with unexampled fury until near nightfall, when the enemy giving way, were pursued on all sides with great slaughter. Having retreated a distance of two miles, the enemy suddenly and very unexpectedly halted, and poured such murderous volleys of artillery and musketry into our lines, that our advance was checked. At this juncture, darkness coming on, there was an end of the conflict. Our troops occupied that night the ground they had taken from the enemy. The next morning the combat was renewed and lasted for two hours, but with what result we have been unable to learn. Our loss in the fight of Saturday is loosely estimated at ten thousand men. The enemy's is thought to be double that number. Our informant says that the two miles over which we pursued the enemy were red with dead and wounded Zouaves. We took several thousand prisoners, all of whom are said to have been paroled the next morning, and allowed to proceed through our lines to Washington. Among these prisoners were some raw recruits who had only been in the service ten days. Our informant thinks the forces of the enemy outnumbered us two to one. The enemy retreated towards the Potomac in the direction of Occoquan.

The following glowing version of the battle is given by the Lynchburg *Republican* of Wednesday:

But few additional particulars of the battle on Saturday last, upon the plains of Manassas, were received last night. That our victory was a most signal one, and the rout of the enemy total and complete, admit of no doubt. But that this glorious result was attained at a fearful cost of life and the loss of many of the noblest and bravest spirits of the Southern army, is, alas! but too true.

On the side of the enemy, General McDowell is said to be mortally wounded, General Seigle killed, as also the infamous Sickles. Pope and McClellan are also reported wounded, but we know not with what truth.

Our losses in the fight of Saturday, it is supposed, will reach at least ten thousand, and of these three thousand were killed. Our informant, an officer, who participated in the fight, says the ground was covered with the dead. In many places they lay in heaps; and in one particular spot, in an open field, through which our men charged upon a battery of the enemy, he could walk over the dead for the space of fifty yards.

On the enemy's side, the losses are supposed to be at least twice as great as ours, exclusive of prisoners, whom the officer above mentioned thinks did not exceed four thousand, taken during the fight, though they were being captured each moment in their flight. He was in the battle of the 21st of July, and describes the rout of the enemy on Saturday as far more disastrous than that. Our cavalry charged them at every step in their retreat, and slaughtered them until it became a butchery. Night put an end to the bloody scene, and our men bivouacked in the open field to renew the pursuit on Sunday morning.

The retreat of the enemy was being urged towards Luray, every other avenue of escape being cut off. But little chance, it was thought, was open to them on the route, and our informant thinks that before this, in all probability, the army of Pope has ceased to exist, and the larger portion of it is killed or captured.

The number of cannon captured was under-estimated yesterday. It is stated that Pope had about one hundred and fifty guns, and it is not thought that he saved twenty of them. They, however, were many of them rendered unfit for use before being abandoned by the enemy. The whole battle field was strewed with small arms of every description, and overcoats and blankets almost innumerable. The fight, as we stated yesterday, was near the Sudley Church, and nearly upon the same ground of the memorable conflict of last year. When our informant left, on Saturday night, having been wounded, our men were in glorious spirits, and there was not one who did not anticipate that before the week closed, the last of the invaders would be driven from our State, and our victorious legions be pouring into Maryland to rescue her from the oppressor's grasp.

There were rumors of more severe fighting on Monday, but we place no credence in them whatever. From all accounts that have reached us, Pope's army was too much cut up and demoralized to have made a stand so soon, and we are reliably informed that on Sunday our troops were sixteen miles from the battle field, on the Leesburg road, still pursuing the enemy, who were in detached squads and without any show of organization.

By the latest reports from the army we learn that Gen. EWELL, having suffered amputation of his leg, is doing well. POPE was wounded in the thigh, and SICKLES certainly killed. We are believed to have captured over eighty pieces of cannon—many of them rifle pieces. Another battle is thought to have been fought on Wednesday in the neighborhood of Manassas.

General Sigel's corps at the Second Battle of Bull Run, August 29, 1862

The New-York Times.

VOL. XI—NO. 3429. NEW-YORK, FRIDAY, SEPTEMBER 19, 1862. PRICE TWO CENTS.

THE GREAT BATTLES.

The Fighting Continued Through Wednesday.

The Advantages on the Side of the National Army.

THE BATTLE NOT RENEWED YESTERDAY.

Great Extent and Magnitude of the Struggle.

The Entire Rebel Army in Maryland.

A Dispatch from the Gallant General Hooker.

He Claims a Great Victory on Wednesday.

DREADFUL CARNAGE ON BOTH SIDES

Our Losses Estimated at Ten Thousand Killed and Wounded.

DISPATCH FROM GEN. HOOKER.

CENTREVILLE, Md., Wednesday, Sept. 17.

A great battle has been fought, and we are victorious. I had the honor to open it yesterday afternoon, and it continued until 10 o'clock this morning, when I was wounded, and compelled to quit the field.

The battle was fought with great violence on both sides.

The carnage has been awful.

I only regret that I was not permitted to take part in the operations until they were concluded' for I had counted on either capturing their army or driving them into the Potomac.

My wound has been painful, but it is not one that will be likely to lay me up. I was shot through the foot.

J. HOOKER, Brig.-Gen.

NEWS BY WAY OF HARRISBURGH.

HARRISBURGH, Penn., Thursday, Sept. 18.

The news received during last night indicates that the result of yesterday's fight was decidedly in our favor; but still another battle is necessary to determine who shall finally be the victor.

It was expected that the battle would be again renewed this morning, but no firing has been heard, and it is supposed that burying of the dead is the order of the day.

Gen McCLELLAN's headquarters are at Sharpsburgh.

Surgeon-Gen. SMITH dispatched a special train to Hagerstown yesterday to attend our wounded.

The number of wounded in Gen. McCLELLAN's army is very large; most of them will probably be brought into Pennsylvania.

The rebel prisoners taken have been sent to Fort Delaware.

HARRISBURGH, Thursday, Sept. 18—P. M.

Information received here this morning direct from the battlefield, represented that the battle would undoubtedly be resumed to-day, but up to this hour no firing had been heard at Hagerstown. The forces remain about in the same position as in yesterday's fight.

Preparations are now being made here for receiving the sick and wounded from the late battle. Citizens are anxious to do all in their power for the comfort of those who are fighting for the support of the National Government.

Troops are still coming in by thousands and are immediately forwarded.

The Government having complete control of the road to Chambersburgh and Hagerstown. The regular trains to these points were suspended to-day, but will be resumedd in a few days.

NEWS BY WAY OF PHILADELPHIA.

PHILADELPHIA, Thursday, Sept. 18.

A special dispatch, dated Hagerstown, yesterday, to the *Press*, says of the fight on Tuesday:

"The battle raged with great spirit. The firing on either side was very heavy, until toward sundown, when the rebels were flanked by HOOKER and PORTER, and severely punished. Their fire became desultory, and it was evident that their ammunition was giving out.

This morning the battle was renewed by the rebels with renewed vigor. They acted as if they had been reinforced and furnished with fresh ammunition. The battle lasted until 4 o'clock this afternoon, when the rebels retreated, leaving Gen. LONGSTREET and the remnant of his division in our hands as prisoners.

The entire rebel army will be captured or killed. There is no chance left for them to cross the Potomac, as the river is rising and our troops are pushing them continually and sending prisoners to the rear.

Six batteries of artillery belonging to Gen. LONGSTREET's Division were captured yesterday and to-day, and it is said that we taken nearly 15,000 prisoners since Sunday.

Stonewall JACKSON's army is with Gen. LEE and other distinguished officers will be forced to surrender within a day or two at furthest.

Our immense army is in motion, and our Generals are certain of ultimate and decisive success.

Stores for our army are coming by way of Harrisburgh and Baltimore.

Gen. BURNSIDE has retaken the position of Harper's Ferry, and is advancing on a special mission with his troops.

NEWS BY WAY OF BALTIMORE.

BALTIMORE, Thursday, Sept. 18.

I was on the battle-field up to 10 o'clock yesterday morning, and left with confidence that all was going on right. It was a grand battle—the most severe of the war—every division of the rebel army being on the field.

From Harrisburgh dispatches and other movements, I think there has been some change in the position of the armies at the close of the day, but have no doubt all is well. Army trains were moving forward from Frederick this morning.

OUR DISPATCHES FROM WASHINGTON.

WASHINGTON, Thursday, Sept. 18.

A special dispatch from Fredericksburgh states that fighting has been desperate at Sharpsburgh, and that among the wounded are Gen. HOOKER, Gen. MEAGHER, and Col. HINKS of the Nineteenth Massachusetts, and the Surgeon of the Twelfth Massachusetts reported killed.

The churches in Frederick are all taken for hospital uses. A great many rebel prisoners have been captured.

WASHINGTON, Thurday, Sept. 18—10 P. M.

The rebel prisoners captured by our scouts near Leesburgh, were brought into the city last evening. They say that the rebel force under Gen. HOOD, lately stationed at Leesburgh, left that place on Monday morning for Williamsport, for the purpose of reinforcing LONGSTREET. The prisoners were unable to accompany their regiments on the march to Williamsport, on account of exhaustion. HOOD's force was about 5,000 men.

A great many straggling and wounded soldiers from the battle-fields in Maryland had arrived at Leesburgh. The prisoners say they all concurred in the fact that the hardest fighting of the war is now going on in Maryland; that LEE was getting badly whipped, and that he would be annihilated unless reinforcements speedily came to his assistance.

A division lately encamped at Waterford had also left to reinforce LEE. It numbered about 6,000 men.

The prisoners state that the whole of the rebel army is in Maryland.

WASHINGTON, Thursday, Sept. 18th—Midnight.

We have no reliable news from Gen. McCLELLAN to-day, though the city is full of rumors. The general belief is that our army has not gained any decisive advantage, though still acting on the offensive. Apprehensions are felt that JACKSON may succeed in executing some dangerous flank movement with fresh troops, which will imperil our forces, but with Pennsylvania in their rear, constantly sending on reinforcements, he will scarcely venture to place himself between them and McCLELLAN.

The continued silence of the Government adds greatly to the disposition of the public to apprehend disaster to our arms.

FROM ANOTHER CORRESPONDENT.

WASHINGTON, Thursday, Sept. 18.

The latest information received here up to 11 o'clock to-day, was dated from the seat of war at 11 o'clock last night, when it was telegraphed thot Gen. McCLELLAN had a severe engagement throughout the day, *resulting in gaining the position for which our army faught.*

Information from a point within four miles of the battle-ground, up to 9 o'clock this morning, says nothing of the engagement having been renewed previous to that hour. It merely states that a thousand rebel prisoners were taken yesterday, and that they were being marched to the rear past that point under a guard.

A reconnoissance in force, made yesterday, has demonstrated that *there are no rebel troops between Washington and Bull Run*, while our scouts yesterday reported that they were in full force at Drainesville on Tuesday evening.

NO BATTLE FOUGHT YESTERDAY.

HARRISBURGH, Thursday, Sept. 18—Evening.

Advices just received at headquarters, from Hagerstown, confirm the report that no fight had taken place to-day; that the rebels are supposed to be short of ammunition, and that the fight would probably commence at daybreak to-morrow.

Our troops are said to have behaved nobly, and talk confidently of gaining a great victory to-morrow.

Gov. CURTIN had arrived safely at Hagerstown, together with Col. J. A. WRIGHT, Surgeon-General SMITH, and his corps of Surgeons. Gov. CURTIN and staff are using every exertion in preparing for the comfort of the wounded brought into that place.

A telegraph line is being extended to Boonsboro, thus bringing us much nearer to Gen. McCLELLAN's Headquarters. It will be completed to-morrow.

DETAILS OF THE BATTLE OF TUESDAY.

HEADQUARTERS ARMY OF THE POTOMAC, Tuesday Evening, Sept. 16, *Via* FREDERICK, Thursday, Sept. 18.

To the Associated Press:

During this afternoon information was received at headquarters showing that the enemy were recrossing the river, and concentrating their forces on the ridge of hills outside of the town of Sharpsburgh to within three miles of the main body of our army. JACKSON left Harper's Ferry this morning, his troops commencing to arrive during the afternoon, when it became evident that LEE was disposed to engage our forces in battle at this point.

Gen. McCLELLAN sent for FRANKLIN's Corps and COUCH's Division, who were about seven miles distant, on the other side of Elk Ridge.

FIELD OF THE LATE AND PENDING BATTLES.

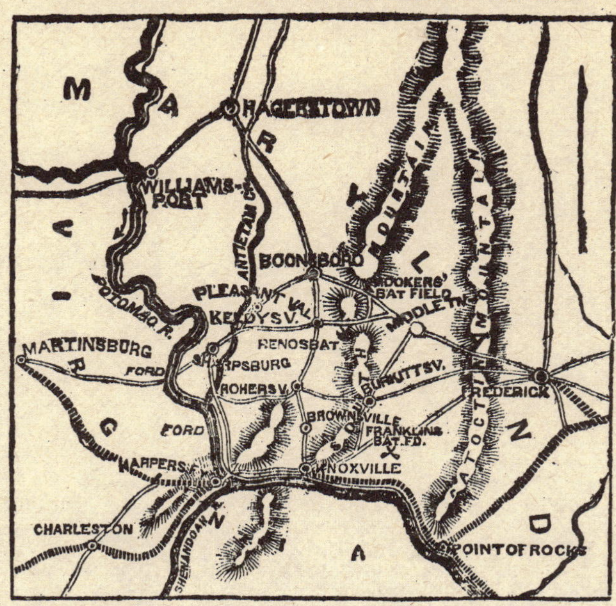

THE GREAT BATTLES IN MARYLAND.

The accompanying map will give a succinct view of the scene and localities of the great battles of the present week, and of the course of the rebel movements from the time they crossed the Potomac until Wednesday night. On Friday evening last, one week ago to-day, our army entered Frederick, having driven the rebel forces up to and beyond that place, from the point at which they crossed the Potomac, above and below the Point of Rocks. Our forces followed the retreating rebels from Frederick across the Catoctin Mountains, and on Sunday HOOKER and RENO came up with their rear guard at the gap in South Mountain, indicated in our map, (incorrectly called "Hagerstown Heights,") while Gen. FRANKLIN engaged another body of them on the same day, at a point to the southeast. Of these battles, the TIMES on Wednesday and Thursday gave by far the fullest and best accounts that have been published. The different bodies of the rebels seem to have then swept around southwesterly on Monday from these localities and from Hagerstown—skirmishing briskly as they retired—until on Tuesday all their forces were concentrated in the neighborhood of Sharpsburgh, at a point east of Antietam Creek, and probably at the intersection of the roads leading from Middletown to Sharpsburgh, and Rohersville and Williamsport. Here was fought the great but indecisive battle of Tuesday; and during the day's fighting, we drove the rebels south and west for some distance—our army at night occupying the ground where the battle closed. The tremendous engagement of Wednesday was fought closer to Sharpsburgh, or between Sharpsburgh and Rohrersville; and though we do not definitely know the course and result of the battle, we know that at night we occupied Rohrersville, and that Gen. McCLELLAN had destroyed the aqueduct at the mouth of the Antietam Creek, and the bridge across that creek upon the road leading to Sharpsburgh. So that from all we can gather, it would appear that the rebel army is now collected in the great bend of the river, (see map,) which will be observed as running some ten miles north from the junction of Antietam Creek with the Potomac. There are mountain ridges on both sides of the creek, and the whole country in this vicinity is thickly covered with hills, so that it is necessarily slow work pursuing the rebels, and they are able to contest many points. One dispatch asserts that the greater part of the rebel army, instead of being west of Antietam, has retreated southward in the direction of Harper's Ferry. When it is considered, however, that Gen. BURNSIDE, with a large force, holds Harper's Ferry, and that other troops, under Gen. SIGEL, are moving in this direction from Washington, it would seem that wherever the rebel army may be placed, or in whatever direction it may be retreating, it will find escape a difficult matter if our troops are thrown upon it with skill and vigor. There will likely be another, and a decisive, battle fought speedily on this part of the line of the Upper Potomac; and on the space covered by our little map is, very probably, located the ground which will see the death, as it is now seeing the dying, struggles of this great rebellion.

There was considerable artillery firing during the day on both sides, resulting in our having about forty men killed and wounded. Among the seriously wounded was Major ARNDT, of the First New-York Artillery, who was struck in the side by a piece of shell.

The disposition of the troops for the impending battle was as follows: Gen. SUMNER's corps, with Gen. BANKS' division to occupy the centre. Gen. HOOKER's corps, with the Pennsylvania Reserves and FRANKLIN's corps on the right. Gens. PORTER and BURNSIDE on the extreme left, with the view of turning the enemy's right flank. Gen. PLEASANTON supported the centre with 2,500 cavalry hnd four batteries.

Gen. HOOKER, in the afternoon, crossed Antietam Creek, and took a position on the hills facing Sharpsburgh, and three miles to the east of Keetsville. His troops got into action about dusk. The battle lasted two hours, during which the enemy were driven about half a mile with considerable loss. The Pennsylvania Reserves who were in front suffered much.

The night was occupied in getting the troops in their respective positions, while ammunition trains and ambulances were forwarded to the different commands.

DETAILS OF THE BATTLE OF WEDNESDAY.

HEADQUARTERS ARMY OF THE POTOMAC, Sept. 17, *via* Frederick, Sept. 18.

This has been an eventful day in the history of the rebellion. A battle has taken place, in which the army of the Potomac has again been victorious, and which exceeded in extent any battle heretofore fought on this continent.

At the dawn of day the battle was resumed on the centre and right. by HOOKER and SUMNER, who, after a sharp contest of two hours, drove the enemy about one mile. The rebels rallied shortly afterward, and, with terrible loss, regain much of the ground. At this time the fearless and indomitable HOOKER received a shot in the ankle, and was carried from the field. The command of his troops now devolved upon SUMNER.

Gen. RICHARDSON, commanding a division, was severely wounded at the same time. Gen. SUMNER, determined to take the lost ground, ordered the troops to advance, which they did with a will, driving the rebels before them with great slaughter. They not only retook the ground, but drove drove them a quarter of a mile beyond.

In this action Gen. MANSFIELD was shot through the lungs, and died soon after.

During this time the troops under BURNSIDE and PORTER had not been idle. They drove the rebels from the line of Antietum Creek, on the main road to Sharpsburgh, built a bridge, (the old one having been destroyed, and occupied the opposite bank. The loss here was considerable. The troops now held both banks of the creek. To get possession of the ridge of hills on the right and left hand sides of the road, from which the rebels were thundering away with artillery, was a task not easily accomplished. SYKES' Brigade, with the assistance of SUMNER, carried the ridge on the right hand side after considerable trouble and loss, the rebels running in all directions.

It is now 4 o'clock, and all the enemy's positions have been carried except the one on the left hand side of the road. To do this duty BURNSIDE was assigned. The artillery opened and the infantry advanced. The point was carried, but we were forced to retire before a superior force. Knowing that if they lost this ridge, a complete rout of their army would be the result, they fought with great desperation.

Darkness now overlooked the two armies, and hostilities ceased as though by mutual consent.

The battle lasted from 5 o'clock in the morning till 7 at night without a moment's cessation.

The conduct of all the troops, without exception, was all that any General could wish. Several regiments of new troops, who were in action for the first time, behaved admirably.

Hundreds of Marylanders were present to witness the battle, which could be seen from many of the surrounding hills. The sharp rattle of fifty thousand muskets, and the thunders of a hundred pieces of artillery is not often heard, nor the consequent excited movements of such armies witnessed.

It is impossible at this writing to form any correct idea of our loss, or that of the enemy. It is heavy on both sides; ours will probabaly reach in killed and wounded ten thousand. That of the enemy will not exceed it.

The enemy's dead, which nearly all fell into our hands, were thickly strewn over the fields, in many places lying in heaps.

Our wounded were immediately carried from the field, and the best possible attention given them.

When Gen. HOOKER fell, Gen. McCLELLAN immediately proceeded to the right, where he was enthusiastically received, and by his presence added much to our success in recovering the ground lost. He was in the centre and on the left as well, anxiously watching the progress of the battle, and giving directions as to the manner of attack. He is in his tent to-night for the first time since he left Frederick City.

We took some 1,500 prisoners during the day, while the enemy obtained but few.

The following officers were among the killed and wounded:

Gen. Hartsaff, wounded.

Gen. Duryea, wounded.

Gen. Sedgwick, wounded in the shoulder.

Col. Childs, Eleventh Connecticut, seriously wounded.

Lieut.-Col. Parisen, Fifty-seventh New-York, killed.

Capt. Andenreid, Aid to Gen. Sumner, wounded.

Maj. Sedgwick, killed.

Col. McNiel, of the Bucktails, and Lieut. Allen were killed.

Col. Polk, Second United States Sharpshooters wounded.

Maj. Burbank, Twelfth Massachusetts, wounded.

Several other prominent officers were reported killed and wounded, but nothing positive is known concerning them.

A FIGHT AT LEESBURGH.

A Reconnoissance from Gen. Sigel's Force.

Rebel Force Driven Back at Leesburgh at the Point of the Bayonet.

WASHINGTON, Thursday, Sept. 18th—9 P. M.

A force, consisting of artillery, infantry and cavalry, under command of Lieut.-Col. KILPATRICK, left Gen. SIGEL's headquarters, yesterday morning, on a reconnoissance toward Leesburgh.

On arriving at Goose Creek, the passage of that stream was disputed by a squadron of rebel cavalry, who, however, were soon put to flight by our artillery.

Our force then proceeded to Leesburgh, which place they found occupied by one regiment of rebel infantry and a battalion of cavalry. After a short engagement the enemy were driven out of town with considerable loss. Our loss was slight.

We captured the regimental flag of the enemy, a number of guns and a number of prisoners.

The Tenth New-York Regiment behaved with great gallantry, driving the enemy through the town at the point of the bayonet.

SECESH REPORTS IN BALTIMORE.

WASHINGTON, Thursday, Sept. 18—10:20 P. M.

By a special dispatch from the TIMES correspondent in Baltimore we learn that orders have been received there to prepare for the arrival of a number of wounded to-morrow.

The Secessionists in Baltimore claim to be in receipt of private intelligence from the seat of war favorable to the rebel cause, and are in excellent spirits.

THE TWELFTH NEW YORK MILITIA.

BALTIMORE, Thursday, Sept. 18.

The Twelfth New-York Militia, paroled at Harper's Ferry, leave for New-York to-night. None of the regiment were injured. The officers retain the side arms and personal effects.

Col. MILES' body arrives here this afternoon.

LIEUT.-COL. DWIGHT WOUNDED.

BOSTON, Thursday, Sept. 18.

A private dispatch states that Lieut.-Col. DWIGHT, of the Second Massachusetts Regiment, was badly wounded in the late battle.

OUR SPECIAL CORRESPONDENCE.

LETTER FROM BOONSBORO.

The Rear-Guard of the Rebels Overtaken on Monday—An Artillery Duel—Commencement of the Great Battle of Sharpsburgh on Tuesday—The Rebels Driven Back at all Points, &c.

BOONSBORO, Md., Tuesday, Sept. 16, 1862.

The pursuing Union army came up with the rear guard of the rebel forces in Pleasant Valley yesterday. The enemy made a stand, for the evident purpose of gaining time for their advance to cross the river, and erected batteries upon the heights two miles beyond Boonsboro. Gen. SUMNER's corps, with BANKS' command, occupied the advance, and shelled the rebels steadily during the afternoon. There was no infantry engagement, and but slight loss on ou side. Our guns, however, seemed to tell with good effect, and soon silenced the rebel batteries, and they pushed on toward the river, whither our forces pursued them to within five miles of the Potomac, skirmishing all along the way.

The rebel troops took advantage of the confusion existing in their ranks, and concealed themselves by hundreds in the woods, awaiting the approach of our troops, when they would come out and give themselves up. They seem thoroughly disgusted and tired of fighting. They do not manifest any leaning toward the Union cause, but simply wish to get out of a bad scrape. A squad of seven hundred of them will be sent to the rear, under a strong guard, to-night. I incline to the belief that the well-known character of Gen. BURNSIDE for clemency in the treatment of his prisoners has had a powerful effect upon the rebel army, and is fast depleting their ranks. They seem to regard him with a feeling almost akin to veneration.

RENEWAL OF THE CONFLICT TO-DAY.

About 8½ A. M., our batteries, supported by Gen. BANKS' column in the centre, began to shell the enemy, who had crossed Antietam Creek, a stream about as large as the Monocacy, and at a point about five miles from the Potomac. The cannonading was continued up to 2½ o'clock P. M. without bringing on any general engagement. The enemy appears to have expended his stock of shells, and uses principally round shot. One of their missiles struck near the root of a tree where a group of our men were sitting, and killed and wounded three or four. There had been no great loss, apparently, on either side, up to the time above-named. *The enemy, however, were steadily dislodged and driven back from every place where he made a stand,* and it was reported at the front, at 2½ o'clock, that the rebels were skedaddling in disorder. "*Sauve qui peut*" had become the cry in the rebel ranks, and each man, on his own hook, was making for the river. I cannot vouch for the correctness of the report. A heavy firing wound up the day.

Gen. McCLELLAN's headquarters are now at the extreme front. His presence inspires the troops with emulation and enthusiasm.

The reports from Harper's Ferry have been conflicting. I have seen some soldiers belonging to the Maryland Brigade, who assert that Col. MILES surrendered Maryland Heights to the rebel forces yesterday morning. That he held out in expectation of reinforcements, but failing to receive them, gave up the position, after spiking the guns and throwing some of the heavier cannon down the precipice. It is also reported that the whole force, some 8,000 strong, were paroled and dismissed, Gen. LONGSTREET taking possession of the Heights.

On the contrary, the report to-day at headquarters is that Col. MILES had three times repulsed the rebel troops, and still held out. In the midst of so many conflicting rumors, it is difficult to decide what is true and what false. I shall press forward in that direction in the morning.

PHELPS' Georgia Legion and COBB's Legion have suffered heavily by desertions since they came into Maryland. They do not seem to relish a return to Virginia, with the prospect of another long Winter campaign before them, and the State wasted by the ravages of war, and destitute of crops and subsistence for the troops.

There are now strong indications of an easterly storm—perhaps we are about to have the usual equinoxial storms, in which case the chances of the rebels escaping across the Potomac, swollen by heavy rains, will be very poor indeed.

B. S.

P. S.—Our loss at the battle of Crampton's Gap was not heavy. I have not yet heard the report of the numbers killed and wounded, but judge it does not exceed 75 or 100. Some dozen of the wounded were last evening sent to Middletown, where they ought not to have been sent, considering the already crowded condition of the town.

LETTER FROM BALTIMORE.

The Secessionists Still Confident—How They Interpret the Retreat of the Rebel Army.

BALTIMORE, Wednesday, Sept. 17, 1862.

The reports of McCLELLAN's victories over the rebel army do not seem greatly to disconcert the Secessionists in this city. The evident exaggeration in some of the details of our successes give them encouragement to doubt the substantial results of the whole story of their discomfiture, Harper's Ferry being regarded as an offset for all our apparent gain. Rumors are rife among them of Confederate victories at other points along the Potomac, when fabulous legions have sprung up in the track of our advancing army, "cutting to pieces" this or that division, and throwing themselves in the rear of the main body, to devour it at leisure. It is their plan, they hint, to entice McCLELLAN as far as possible into the mountains, where he can be destroyed or kept engaged, while Washington is assailed.

Full assurance that the rebel campaign in Maryland is at an end will bring grief and despondency to the Secessionists here, who, in spite of their seeming apathy, have been as busy as bees with their little plots, which they have been watching their opportunity to execute. Taking advantage of the supposed demoralization of our army, and the confusion in our councils at Washington, following the discomfiture of Gen. POPE, the rebel army pushed boldly into Maryland, where they could at least save themselves from starving, while they arranged for the capture of Washington, drawing our armies away from there by a foray into Pennsylvania.

The details of this plan were, of course, too dependent on McCLELLAN's movements to be arranged fully beforehand; and though their leaving it may have been modified by circumstances, the Confederates here do not acknowledge its defeat or abandonment. In the retirement of the rebel forces they see only a plan to entangle McCLELLAN among the mountains, to enable them to elude him and pass into Virginia at Harper's Ferry, crossing at some lower ford, to throw themselves between the army and Washington, while their friends here reenact the programme of April 19, 1861, by cutting off railroad communication with the North, and raising a hubbub generally.

Some such plan has been, undoubtedly, brewing, from which we are to be saved by the skill and promptitude of McCLELLAN's movements. Though his success in driving the rebels has been so marked up to to-day, having Harper's Ferry against us, the rebels claim that the balance is in their favor, so far as prisoners and the capture of *materiel* is concerned, and that they have no cause for discouragement. With Harper's Ferry in rebel hands, our Generals have still need to be wary; least with POPE they find while advancing, that "disgrace and disaster lurk in their rear."

I give you in this the secession view of things. If it be true, as reported to-day, that BURNSIDE has retaken Harper's Ferry with 5,000 prisoners, I do not know what the rebels will have to say to the different complexion this little circumstance will put upon affairs. Their faith is wonderful, and I have yet to learn what discomfiture is equal to its total overthrow.

PIERREPONT.

AFFAIRS AT HARRISBURGH.

The Battle Near Sharpsburgh—Attempts of Rebel Sympathizers to Discourage Our Men—Forces Hurrying on to Chambersburgh—Arrival of Rebel Prisoners and a Spy.

From Our Special Correspondent.

HARRISBURGH, Wednesday, Sept. 17, 1862.

Before this is in print, intelligence will in all probability have reached us that will fill the whole country with rejoicing, or the reverse. Authentic information has reached this place that a desperate battle is at this moment being fought in what is called the Middletown Valley—between the South Mountain and Coshacton Hills, and some two miles from Sharpsburgh, Md.

I was at headquarters last night as late as 10½ o'clock, endeavoring to get information, but nothing could be learnt except that a battle had been raging the whole afternoon. Up to that hour, and later yet, the indefatigable Gov. CURTIN was at his post, surrounded by anxious inquirers, receiving and answering dispatches, replying to a thousand different questions upon all subjects, and yet as affable and courteous to every one as if he were at his own peaceful fireside, free of all care whatever.

The news, up to the time of posting my letter, is that the fight was renewed this morning at 6 o'clock, that matters were going on bravely and our men in the highest spirits. Information has just reached headquarters here that LONGSTREET is killed, but as it came through stragglers and unofficially, nobody knows whether to believe it or not. There are, also, some ugly speculations about Harper's Ferry—people supposing that the rebels would never have dared to unite their forces on this side of the Potomac, unless they knew they could hold themselves there, and there is no other apparent stronghold of the kind but Harper's Ferry. In the meantime, Gov. CURTIN is keeping his eye upon any emergency that may arise, and is hurrying on regiment after regiment, just as fast as the trains can carry them.

Some temporary dissatisfaction has been caused among the new recruits by rebel sympathizers getting among them and persuading the weak-minded that, although enlisted for only three months, if they once cross the border they become amenable to the National Government for the *whole term of the war*. But this weak device of the enemy will fail. The authorities here have an eye upon some of the leading rascals who are thus trying to breed dissension among the brave and honest fellows so nobly responding to the call of their country; and it is to be hoped that when any of the said rascals are fairly detected at work, Gov. CURTIN's kindly nature will not prevent him from making public examples of them. The laws of Pennsylvania absolutely prohibit the Governor from calling out the militia for more than three months, and Gov. CURTIN is not the man to break faith with his own people, even if he had the power to do so.

Not less than five regiments of infantry and a battery left this city yesterday for Chambersburgh. Among them was a regiment of Home Guards from Philadelphia, very well disciplined and splendidly equipped. Five thousand more are expected to-day from Philadelphia.

A batch of secesh prisoners, numbering 130, were brought here yesterday by a squad of the First Pennsylvania Militia. They were captured by a squad of our cavalry on the Hagerstown Road. A more miserable, ragged and dirty set of beings I never saw than these rebels,—accustomed as I am to the scenes at Fortress Monroe. They were, for the present, taken to Camp Curtin, whence they will soon be probably removed to taste the temporary hospitalities of Fort Delaware. Among these rebels was a traitor named FITZHUGH, captured on Monday last near Williamsport, Md. This scoundrel was actually in Harrisburgh only two or three days before his capture,—doubtless obtaining all sorts of information to take to the enemy. He belongs to this State, and comes from Franklin County. They have him at present in irons, in the guard-house at Camp Curtin, but what will be further done with him nobody knows. Hanging is far too good for a villain who can turn spy and traitor against his own people in a crisis like this, and a few examples are certainly required, to deter others of his stamp who are doubtless skulking among us.

NEMO.

The Charleston Mercury.

VINDICE NULLO
SPONTE SUA SINE LEGE FIDES RECTUMQUE COLENTUR

VOLUME LXXXI | CHARLESTON, S. C., THURSDAY, OCTOBER 2, 1862 | NUMBER 11,567

THE BATTLE OF SHARPSBURG.

THE GREATEST BATTLE OF THE WAR—RELATIVE STRENGTH OF THE ARMIES—DISPOSITION OF THE FORCES—THE BATTLE GROUND—M'CLELLAN'S STRATEGY—THE CRISIS OF THE CONFLICT—A TERRIBLE SCENE—A. P. HILL, THE BLUCHER OF THE DAY—THE RESULTS OF THE FIGHT, &c., &c., &c.

(Correspondence of the Savannah Republican.)

SHARPSBURG, MD., Sep. 18.

The fiercest and most hotly contested battle of the war was fought here yesterday. It commenced at early dawn, the enemy being the attacking party, and lasted, with occasional breathing intervals, until it was quite dark. Whether we consider the numbers engaged, the fierceness of the assault, the dogged courage of the Confederates, or the almost unparalled duration of the fight, it must be regarded as one of the most extraordinary battles of modern times. In no instance, since the revolution was inaugurated, has either party had engaged as many as 100,000 men at any one time. At Richmond, each side had, all counted, perhaps as many as 100,000; but in no one of the series of battles fought around that city was anything like that number engaged, either on the part of the Confederates or the Federals. I had estimated the force of the enemy here at too high a figure, probably; but if it be reckoned at 125,000 men, and our own at two thirds of that number—say 80,000—we have two tremendous armies, such indeed as have not been seen on any battle field in this war. The enemy had brought up the last man he could get. The coasts of Virginia, North Carolina, South Carolina and Georgia had been stripped of the troops sent to desolate them. Northwestern Virginia had been abandoned by Cox and his command, and all the new volunteers, except enough to garrison the works about Washington, had been sent to McClellan. These, with the army he brought with him from the Peninsula, now recruited and prepared for fresh labors, and Burnside's seasoned corps, gave him an army formidable alike in numbers and material.

His artillery was on a scale commensurate with the great army he commanded. It was really superb, whether we regard the number of batteries engaged and the range and calibre of the guns, or the splendid manner in which they were handled. The men fought well, too—better in fact than the Federals have ever done before, except at Shiloh; and the new volunteers did about as well as the older troops. They are of a better class of men, and make up in spirit and intelligence, what they lack in drilling and discipline. There can be no doubt upon this point; since we took some of them prisoners and know they fought well before they yielded.

McClellan commanded in person the enemy's right (our left), besides exercising a general supervision over the whole field; Burnside on the left, and Sumner in the centre. On our side Longstreet commanded the right wing, Jackson the left, and D. H. Hill the centre—the whole being under the calm and watchful eye of Gen. Lee. This order of battle brought McClellan and Jackson face to face, Longstreet and Burnside, and Hill and Sumner. Thus pitted and matched, the battle was opened as soon as there was sufficient light to point a gun, and continued for fourteen long and weary hours. It was dry and dusty beneath, but cloudy and pleasant above. The enemy had availed himself of the darkness of the preceding night to post his batteries at commanding points. This he was the more able to do, since he had subjected us to a heavy cannonade the day before, and thus forced us to develop our lines and positions.

The battle ground was along the banks of the Antietam River, just in front of Sharpsburg.—This lovely stream runs due south along the foot of the Blue Ridge, and empties its crystal waters into the Potomac a short distance above Harper's Ferry. The Confederates held the western side of the river, except for a short distance on the left and above, where the enemy's lines crossed it, and the Federals held the eastern side next to the mountain. Indeed, the general configuration of the country, and as well as the positions of the two armies, recalls to mind the Chickahominy and the James River, and the position of the combatants in front of Richmond, except that the enemy had the Blue Ridge at his back here, whilst his lines were thrown forward across the Antietam on our left instead of our right as on the Chickahominy. With this exception, the lines of the enemy closely hugged the east bank of the river, which is shallow, easily fordable except for artillery, and not more than thirty feet in width. On the swelling elevations between the stream and the Blue Ridge the Federal batteries were planted, whilst ours occupied the hills on the Sharpsburg side. The distance from Sharpsburg across to the base of the mountain does not exceed a mile and a half, and the river is about midway between the two. On our right was a wide stone bridge, which it was important that we should hold. The ground was mostly open, but very uneven.

The respective positions of the two armies were equally strong, except in this, that the enemy had his back against the Blue Ridge, which would, under almost any circumstances, prevent a rout on his part, or pursuit on ours.

The battle was opened by McClellan both with artillery and small arms on our left, where a fierce and nearly successful assault was made upon Jackson. Column after column was brought up and hurled against the Stonewall corps, which had been marching and fighting almost daily since it left Richmond; and for two hours or more our ranks were slowly forced back by the overwhelming numbers brought against them. Jackson reached his position the night before when it was quite dark, and, consequently, was entirely ignorant of the topography of the field. The old Stonewall brigade yielded the ground inch by inch, and Ewell's division, now commanded by Lawton, the best officer probably under Jackson, fought desperately. This division embraces some of the best regiments in the army, including the unconquerable Twelfth Georgia. Our ranks suffered terribly, and many a brave spirit was made to bite the dust. Among others, I may mention Brigadier General Lawton, who received a painful wound in the leg, and Col. Marcellus Douglass, of the Thirteenth Georgia, commanding Lawton's old brigade. Seeing he was mortally wounded, Douglass refused to be removed, preferring, as he said, to die upon the field. His body was subsequently recovered and taken to the Virginia side.

Meanwhile, and almost simultaneous with the attack on the left, Sumner opened a terrific fire on our centre, which was followed by a like assault on our right by Burnside's corps. It was an indescribably sublime scene when the tide of fire and smoke swept slowly and majestically from the left down the valley past the centre, and on to the extreme right. The solemn Blue Ridge formed an appropriate back ground to the awful spectacle.

The elevations upon which the batteries were planted, were crowned with wreaths of smoke of most fantastic shapes, nearly concealing "the valley of death" below, where the infantry were engaged in a fearful struggle. Each party had, probably, as many as two hundred pieces of artillery on the field, though but little over half that number was brought into action at the same instant, either by the Confederates or Federals. But think of two hundred cannon of every available calibre engaged in deadly conflict at short range! The Federals directed their pieces chiefly at our batteries, and sometimes the latter were so enveloped in smoke from their own discharges, and the bursting shells from the enemy's guns, that they were completely lost to sight. Our own pieces, on the contrary, were pointed at the infantry columns of the Federals, by special order of Gen. Lee. Artillery duels, so called, accomplish little, except to enable the parties to display their gunnership. In the present instance, the departure from the old rule was productive of most beneficial results, in that the enemy's assaulting columns were repeatedly repulsed by the well directed fire of our artillerists.

The great object of McClellan was to reach the Potomac on the left—distant not more than a mile and a half from the Antietam—and thus to close us, as it were, in a *cul de sac*. The two streams make a sudden curve towards each other at this point. Knowing that we would hardly attempt to cross the Antietam, along the banks of which, with slight exceptions, the two armies were engaged, he had massed an enormous column on the left and another on the right. Owing to the great inequality of the forces engaged, Jackson found it necessary to yield the ground he held at the beginning of the fight, and to call for assistance. Fortunately, McLaws' division had arrived from Harper's Ferry some time during the previous night, and was sent to the relief of Jackson about 9 o'clock. It arrived just in the nick of time. The enemy, already badly worsted by Jackson, were compelled to fall back with great slaughter before the impetuous charges of the fresh regiments, until the parties occupied their original positions in the morning. The fighting, however, was continued until night, with occasional intervals, though without any particular advantage to either side.

Battle of Antietam

The conflict along the centre was severe, but, owing to the nature of the ground was confined chiefly to artillery. Indeed, the artillery took an unusually prominent part in the battle in every part of the field. The small arms were not warmly engaged for some time, early in the day after a few volleys, except on the left. The Washington Artillery behaved splendidly, and so did Cutts' battalion. The former is attached to Longstreet's corps, the latter to D. H. Hill's. The other batteries, and the heavy reserves under Gen. Pendleton, performed their parts handsomely also.

The most formidable assault on the right was made about 9 o'clock, and continued until after two. The object of the enemy was to gain possession of a stone bridge just in front of Toombs' division; which occupied the extreme right in Longstreet's corps. The Second and Twentieth Georgia, Lieut. Col. Holmes and Col. Cumming commanding, belonging to Toombs' old brigade, and now commanded by Col. Benning, were entrusted with the duty of defending the bridge. The regiments were very much reduced, but they discharged their duty most heroically. Regiment after regiment, and even brigades, were brought up against them; and yet they held their ground, and the bridge too, until they had fired their last cartridge. The men were clamorous for fresh ammunition; for it had now become a point of honor with them to maintain their ground, even if it cost the life of the last one of them. But owing to the furious onslaught made against the entire right wing, it was found impossible to supply them in time; and consequently they had to retire, with the loss even of McIntosh's battery. This was fifteen minutes after 2 o'clock, when a strange silence, broken only by a random shot, ensued for the space of two hours along the whole front of the army. The accomplished and chivalric Holmes of the Second fell pierced through the body a few minutes before the firing ceased, and died instantly. An effort was made to remove his body, but the persons who attempted it were wounded and compelled to leave it on the field. Maj Harris assumed the command, and with Col. Cumming of the Twentieth, displayed great coolness and valor. The enemy lay in heaps in front of the bridge, as they did on the left in front of Jackson. An officer who examined the ground over which McLaws and Jackson drove them, says the enemy's dead lay so thick at one place, over an area of three acres, that he could walk over every yard of it on the bodies of the slain!

The silence which followed at a quarter past two o'clock, was all the more profound and impresssive from the stunning fire that had raged so furiously since early dawn. Was the enemy content with the possession of the bridge and the ground in front of it? Had both combatants had enough of the bloody work? Or did they stop by mutual consent, in order to allow the exhausted fighters time to recover their breath? For hours the Confederates had been turning their eyes wistfully towards the Potomac, in hopes of seeing the head of A. P. Hill's advancing column. Would the Blucher of the day come up in time?

At length, about 3 o'clock, Hill made his appearance, and his brigades were quietly distributed along the lines where they were most needed. The enemy were hardly aware of his arrival; for his forces were advanced behind hills and thickets to their proper positions. Everything being ready, the Confederates renewed the conflict at 4 o'clock, and from that hour until night it raged without interruption. The Fifteenth and Seventeenth Georgia, commanded by Col. Milligan and Capt. McGregor, and a portion of the Eleventh Georgia, which had just been brought up from the rear, where they had been on detached duty, united in the charge. Colonel Milligan addressing his men, told them to follow their officers, and, if they fell, to march forward over their bodies—an injunction that was literally fulfilled, for the brave Colonel was killed, and his command dashed over him as if nothing had happened. Toombs had dismounted and placed himself at the head of his small forces, and led them like a captain to the the encounter. He and they soon placed themselves in front of the remainder of the line, and, dashing forward in the most impetuous manner, soon re-captured McIntosh's battery, and drove the enemy pell-mell across the bridge. The ground was strewn with the Federal dead, but our own loss in this charge was not very heavy, owing to the furious rate at which the men moved. The conflict of infantry on the right at this point, as on the left early in the day, was unusually severe—probably as severe as any that has occurred since the war. Pinder's and Fields' brigades of A. P. Hill's division, and other forces, co-operated gallantly in the charge.

It was now near night. The combattants, with slight exceptions in our favor, occupied the positions they did in the morning; and when it had become quite dark, the firing ceased on both sides.

It is probable that the enemy would not have renewed the contest at 4 o'clock, had the Confederates remained quiet. Many of the houses in Sharpsburg were riddled by the enemy's balls, which passing over the heads of our men, entered the buildings on the rising ground behind. Many of the women and children had sought refuge in the cellars and behind the stonewalls of the houses and enclosures; others had fled to the country on horseback behind husbands and parents; whilst others had boldly stood it out, saying their Federal friends were not ignorant of their sentiments, and would spare them as far as possible. Some of the houses, and many hay-ricks and stacks of wheat straw, were set on fire, and added no little to the sublimity and fearfulness of the scene.

The results are easily summed up. It was McClellan's battle. He made the attack, and was repulsed with very heavy slaughter. His losses are variously estimated at from 15,000 to 20 000 killed, wounded and missing; ours at from 5,000 to 10,000. These figures may be wrong; I am disposed to think they are too flattering to our own side, and offer them as rough estimates of others. We took but few prisoners—not more than six or seven hundred. The enemy captured as many, as you will see hereafter. Indeed, it was nearly a drawn battle—the enemy having the advantage in position and numbers, we the superiority in fighting, and in repulsing his assault. The only prisoner of distinction we took was Col. Palfrey, of Massachusetts, who was wounded and fell into our hands. But I must close for the present. I write at a hospital, in the midst of the wounded and dying, amputated arms and legs, feet, fingers, and hands cut off, puddles of human gore, and ghastly, gaping wounds.

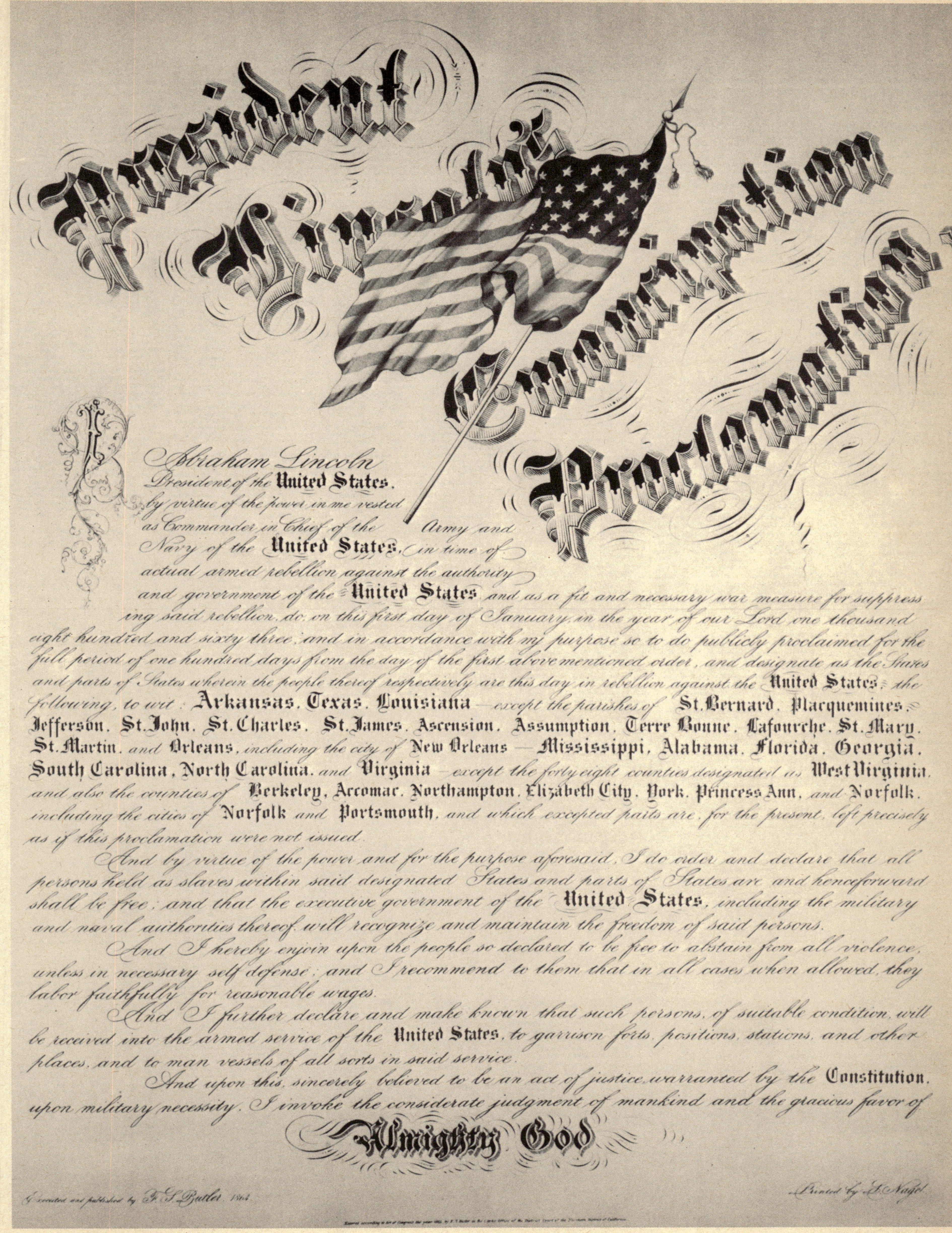

President Lincoln's Emancipation Proclamation.

I, Abraham Lincoln, President of the United States, by virtue of the power in me vested as Commander in Chief of the Army and Navy of the United States, in time of actual armed rebellion against the authority and government of the United States and as a fit and necessary war measure for suppressing said rebellion, do, on this first day of January, in the year of our Lord one thousand eight hundred and sixty three, and in accordance with my purpose so to do publicly proclaimed for the full period of one hundred days from the day of the first above mentioned order, and designate as the States and parts of States wherein the people thereof respectively are this day in rebellion against the United States, the following, to wit: Arkansas, Texas, Louisiana — except the parishes of St. Bernard, Placquemines, Jefferson, St. John, St. Charles, St. James, Ascension, Assumption, Terre Bonne, Lafourche, St. Mary, St. Martin, and Orleans, including the city of New Orleans — Mississippi, Alabama, Florida, Georgia, South Carolina, North Carolina, and Virginia — except the forty eight counties designated as West Virginia, and also the counties of Berkeley, Accomac, Northampton, Elizabeth City, York, Princess Ann, and Norfolk, including the cities of Norfolk and Portsmouth, and which excepted parts are, for the present, left precisely as if this proclamation were not issued.

And by virtue of the power and for the purpose aforesaid, I do order and declare that all persons held as slaves within said designated States and parts of States are, and henceforward shall be free; and that the executive government of the United States, including the military and naval authorities thereof, will recognize and maintain the freedom of said persons.

And I hereby enjoin upon the people so declared to be free to abstain from all violence, unless in necessary self defense; and I recommend to them that in all cases when allowed, they labor faithfully for reasonable wages.

And I further declare and make known that such persons, of suitable condition, will be received into the armed service of the United States, to garrison forts, positions, stations, and other places, and to man vessels of all sorts in said service.

And upon this, sincerely believed to be an act of justice, warranted by the Constitution, upon military necessity, I invoke the considerate judgment of mankind and the gracious favor of

Almighty God

Executed and published by F. S. Butler, 1864. Printed by L. Nagel.

The New-York Times.

VOL. XI—NO. 3432. NEW-YORK, TUESDAY, SEPTEMBER 23, 1862. PRICE TWO CENTS.

HIGHLY IMPORTANT.

A Proclamation by the President of the United States.

The War Still to be Prosecuted for the Restoration of the Union.

A DECREE OF EMANCIPATION

All Slaves in States in Rebellion on the First of January Next to be Free.

The Gradual Abolition and Colonization Schemes Adhered to.

Loyal Citizens to be Remunerated for Losses, Including Slaves.

WASHINGTON, Monday, Sept. 22.

By the President of the United States of America:

A PROCLAMATION.

I, ABRAHAM LINCOLN, President of the United States of America, and Commander-in-Chief of the Army and Navy thereof, do hereby proclaim and declare, that hereafter, as heretofore, the war will be prosecuted for the object of practically restoring the constitutional relation between the United States and the people thereof in which States that relation is, or may be suspended or disturbed; that it is my purpose, upon the next meeting of Congress, to again recommend the adoption of a practical measure tendering pecuniary aid to the free acceptance or rejection of all the Slave States so called, the people whereof may not then be in rebellion against the United States, and which States may then have voluntarily adopted, or thereafter may voluntarily adopt, the immediate or gradual abolishment of Slavery within their respective limits, and that the efforts to colonize persons of African descent with their consent, upon the Continent or elsewhere, with the previously obtained consent of the governments existing there, will be continued.

That on the first day of January, in the year of our Lord one thousand eight hundred and sixty-three, all persons held as slaves within any State, or any designated part of a State, the people whereof shall then be in rebellion against the United States shall be then, thenceforward, and forever, free; and the Executive Government of the United States, including the military and naval authority thereof, will recognize and maintain the freedom of such persons, and will do no act or acts to repress such persons, or any of them, in any efforts they may make for their actual freedom.

That the Executive will, on the first day of January aforesaid, by proclamation, designate the States and parts of States, if any, in which the people thereof, respectively, shall then be in rebellion against the United States; and the fact that any State, or the people thereof, shall on that day be in good faith represented in the Congress of the United States by members chosen thereto at elections wherein a majority of the qualified voters of such State shall have participated, shall, in the absence of strong countervailing testimony, be deemed conclusive evidence that such State and the people thereof have not been in rebellion against the United States.

That attention is hereby called to an act of Congress entitled "An act to make an additional article of war," approved March 13, 1862, and which act is in the words and figure following:

"Be it enacted by the Senate and House of Representatives of the United States of America in Congress assembled, That hereafter the following shall be promulgated as an additional article of war for the government of the army of the United States, and shall be obeyed and observed as such.

ARTICLE—All officers or persons in the military or naval service of the United States are prohibited from employing any of the forces under their respective commands for the purpose of returning fugitives from service or labor who may have escaped from any person to whom such service or labor is claimed to be due, and any officer who shall be found guilty by a Court-martial of violating this article shall be dismissed from the service.

SECTION 2. And be it further enacted, that this act shall take effect from and after its passage."

Also to the ninth and tenth sections of an act entitled "An act to suppress insurrection, to punish treason and rebellion, to seize and confiscate property of rebels, and for other purposes," approved July 17, 1862, and which sections are in the words and figures following:

SEC. 9. And be it further enacted, that all slaves of persons who shall hereafter be engaged in rebellion against the Government of the United States, or who shall in any way give aid or comfort thereto, escaping from such persons and taking refuge within the lines of the army; and all slaves captured from such persons or deserted by them and coming under the control of the Government of the United States, and all slaves of such persons found on (or being within) any place occupied by rebel forces and afterward occupied by the forces of the United States, shall be deemed captures of war and shall be forever free of their servitude and not again held as slaves.

SEC. 10. And be it further enacted, That no slave escaping into any State, Territory or the District of Columbia, from any of the States, shall be delivered up, or in any way impeded or hindered of his liberty, except for crime or some offence against the laws, unless the person claiming said fugitive shall first make oath that the person to whom the labor or service of such fugitive is alleged to be due, is his lawful owner, and has not been in arms against the United States in the present rebellion, nor in any way given aid and comfort thereto, and no person engaged in the military or naval service of the United States shall, under any pretence whatever, assume to decide on the validity of the claim of any person to the service or labor of any other person, or surrender up any such person to the claimant, on pain of being dismissed from the service.

And I do hereby enjoin upon and order all persons engaged in the military and naval service of the United States, to observe, obey and enforce, within their respective spheres of service, the act and sections above recited.

And the Executive will in due time recommend that all citizens of the United States who shall have remained loyal thereto throughout the rebellion, shall (upon the restoration of the constitutional relation between the United States and their respective States and people, if the relation shall have been suspended or disturbed,) be compensated for all losses by acts of the United States, *including the loss of slaves.*

In witness whereof, I have hereunto set my hand, and caused the seal of the United States to be affixed.

Done at the City of Washington, this Twenty-second day of September, in the year of our Lord one thousand eight hundred and sixty-two, and of the Independence of the United States the eighty-seventh.

ABRAHAM LINCOLN.

By the President.

WILLIAM H. SEWARD, Secretary of State.

GENERAL NEWS FROM WASHINGTON.

OUR SPECIAL WASHINGTON DISPATCHES.

WASHINGTON, Monday, Sept. 22.

THE PRESIDENT'S PROCLAMATION.

The great event of the day here is the proclamation of the President ordering the execution of the war measures of the last Congress, and promising freedom to the slaves in all States that persist in the rebellion against the Government. This act, so long expected, so long delayed, bids fair to simplify at once the issues of the war, and immediately to array against each other the unconditionally loyal and the rebellious of all shades and grades. If the cause of the Union and free institutions is strongest, this test will show it, and the only question of its triumph will then be the power in the Government to execute its policy with courage and vigor.

THE NEWS FROM KENTUCKY.

A special private dispatch, just received from Cincinnati, announces that BRAGG is marching on Louisville, Ky., and that Gen. NELSON has ordered the women and children to leave the city. BUELL is believed to have been outgeneraled, and to be several hours behind. The dispatch closes—"A General wanted for the West."

THE OLD ISSUE OF TREASURY NOTES.

I have the following statistics in regard to the old issue of United States Treasury Notes, receivable for duties, of the $60,000,0000 issue: $28,420,000 have been returned to the Department and burned; $43,000 have been returned, and are not yet burned; $4,000,000 have been redeemed, but not yet returned to the Department, leaving $27,537,000 yet outstanding. As only about half the whole issue has yet been redeemed, and as the Government will be able to get no gold in payment of duties, so long as any of these notes remain in possession of the public, it is plain that the specie required to pay the interest falling due on Oct. 1—$4,000,000—as well as that falling due Jan. 1—$5,000,000—must be procured by the Government by purchase or loan.

Thirty thousand dollars of small currency notes were to-day paid out at the Treasury Department, and were all taken within an hour.

CONDITION OF GEN. HOOKER.

Gen. HOOKER is now with his friend, Dr. NICHOLS, at the United States Insane Asylum Hospital, near Washington. His wound is a rifle ball through the left foot. Although the wound is painful, it is not considered dangerous; yet it is sufficient to disable him for active service.

THE CONVALESCENT CAMP.

The Convalescent Camp, under the regulations of Gen. BANKS, is becoming an institution of very great utility. All stragglers and convalescents are immediately sent there, as are officers who have been absent without leave, or have overstayed their leave under circumstances that entitle them to lenity. Soldiers are classified according to the corps to which they belong, and are placed in charge of officers belonging to the same corps, who subject them to the daily drill of camp instruction. When the accumulation becomes sufficient to justify their removal, they are sent to their regiments and commands.

PENSIONS.

The Commissioner of Pensions has commenced making appointments of surgeons to make examinations and give certificates in cases of applications for pensions. The fees will make the offices desirable. The following are the appointments already made: Cincinnati, James H. Oliver; Indianapolis, Geo. W. Mears; Leavenworth, Kansas, Selden W. Jones; New-Philadelphia, Ohio, Wm. G. Smith; Terre Haute, Ind., Geo. W. Clippinger; Lafayette, Ind., O. L. Clark; Boston, Geo. S. Jones; Bangor, Me., Ralph J. K. Jones; Rochester, N. Y., Harvey F. Montgomery; Oswego, N. Y., Chas. C. P. Clark; Lyons, N. Y., Nelson Peck; Norridgewack, Me., Uno Robbins, Jr.

ACTING REAR-ADMIRALS.

The following naval officers have been made Acting Rear-Admirals and assigned to the command of the following squadrons, respectively: C. H. BELL, Pacific Squadron; CHAS. WILKES, "Flying Squadron;" T. L. LARDNER, Eastern Gulf Squadron; C. H. DAVIS, Mississippi Flotilla.

From Salt Lake.

SALT LAKE, Monday, Sept. 22.

CHARLES MCBRIDE, from Virginia City, arrived here yesterday, one of a party of fifteen bound for the States. He says:

"The party were attacked by the Snake Indians at the City of Rocks, on the Humboldt route, 150 miles north. They fought the Indians for 20 miles, losing six killed and two wounded, and all of their outfit. JOHN CONNER, JOHN SHAFER, BENJAMIN WHITE, JAMES SHAW, WM. DAVIS and MR. GOODMAN were killed. JOHN FOSTER and SAM. KELLY had their arms broken."

Reports of Indian depredations northward are coming in daily, and much trouble is expected to emigration.

THE LATEST WAR NEWS.

A Raid of Stuart's Cavalry Across the Potomac at Williamsport.

NO DAMAGE DONE.

The Reoccupation of Maryland Heights by Our Forces.

THE REBELS CONTINUING THEIR RETREAT

No Further Collisions at Last Accounts.

LATEST REPORTS FROM HEADQUARTERS.

HEADQUARTERS OF THE ARMY OF THE POTOMAC, Saturday Evening, Sept. 20, 1862.

The firing heard last evening in the direction of Williamsport, turns out to have been a raid of STUART's rebel cavalry. He crossed the Potomac on Friday night into Maryland, at that point, with his cavalry, one regiment of infantry, and seventeen pieces of artillery. The force sent up to drive him back, arrived near the town late in the afternoon. The firing heard was principally from the rebel guns. During the night they recrossed into Virginia and this morning they had disappeared from the opposite shore. No one was hurt.

The work of burying the dead is still continuing. They average about one thousand per day. To-morrow will probably finish it.

The Maryland Heights were yesterday occupied by a National force.

The indications are that the rebels are continuing their retreat into Virginia, leaving the line of the Potomac.

Divine worship was held at headquarters this evening, Bishop WHIPPLE, of Minnesota, officiating.

HEADQUARTERS, ARMY OF THE POTOMAC, Monday Evening, Sept. 22.

The following is the official report of loss in SUMNER's corps at the battle of the Antietam:

GEN. RICHARDSON'S DIVISION.

Killed	212
Wounded	899
Missing	24

GEN. SEDGWICK'S DIVISION.

Killed	335
Wounded	1,577
Missing	321

GEN. FRENCH'S DIVISION.

Killed	293
Wounded	1,321
Missing	203

Total loss in Gen. SUMNER's Corps	5,208

The loss in missing may be somewhat reduced by stragglers returning.

A train of cars crossed the Monocacy this morning. The road is now open to Harper's Ferry, where there is a sufficient Federal force for all purposes.

The rebels, in their hasty retreat from Maryland, left between 1,100 and 1,200 wounded between Sharpsburgh and the river. They are being paroled.

Twenty-six stands of colors were taken during the battle of the Antietam, and have been received at headquarters. Seven more are known to have been captured, and are in the hands of the different regiments which captured them.

OUR LATEST WASHINGTON DISPATCHES.

WASHINGTON, Monday, Sept. 22.

A special dispatch from Frederick states that some surgeons, just arrived from the army, report rebels still falling back from the Potomac. Not even their pickets are now to be seen.

Another dispatch states that our losses in the last fight are not nearly as great as at first reported, especially in SUMNER's Corps. In the California Regiment only one commissioned officer was killed (Lieut. WILSE) and one hundred and fifty privates killed and wounded.

The last reports from headquarters represented "All quiet along the lines."

THE WAR IN MARYLAND.

Another Account of the Great Battle of Antietam.

LETTERS FROM THE BATTLE-FIELD.

The Strong Position Chosen by the Enemy—How the National Forces were Arranged—Desperate Character of the Fighting—The Results, &c.

ON THE FIELD NEAR SHARPSBURGH, MD., Wednesday Evening, Sept. 17, 1862.

This day will be memorable for one of the bloodiest fought battles on the American Continent. The combined forces of the enemy, under JACKSON, LEE, LONGSTREET, and the whole rebel set, have made a stand near Sharpsburgh, and all day long, from 5 o'clock in the morning until now, (8 o'clock P. M.,) have been contesting with the Union Army under MCCLELLAN, led by BURNSIDE, HOOKER, SUMNER, KEYES, and the other heroes of the war. Nothing, I am sure, since the battle of Pittsburgh Landing, can compare with this day's fight, either in its collossal proportions, or in the bloody character of the struggle. Our advance overtook the rebel forces, apparently in full retreat toward the Shepherdstown ford of the Potomac, yesterday morning, and a temporary halt was ordered near Kedysville, a little village three miles north from Sharpsburgh. The enemy had taken possession of the Antietam Hills, on the right of the creek by that name, with Sharpsburgh in their rear. They were attacked yesterday by our batteries across this creek, for the purpose of occupying them until our whole force should come up, but no general engagement ensued. The rebels were evidently preparing for a last desperate stand, before the final attempt to cross the Potomac. Their failure to check our advance here they knew would be fatal to their whole army, for they could not escape safely into Virginia with our artillery and infantry assailing their rear.

The day closed without any decisive results, except that in every encounter our artillery practice was found to be too accurate and terrible for them, and they doggedly yielded every position which they took up.

Meantime, LONGSTREET, who had succeeded in obtaining possession of Maryland Heights the day before, having forced the entire force found there, (excepting the cavalry, which cut their way through and escaped,) abandoned the position, and was hurrying forward to reinforce the rebel troops at this point.

Thus the two armies, wearied by a harassing march over mountain ranges, and of four days' running fight from beyond Frederick, came together on this memorable field.

The enemy having chosen a strong position on the hills just beyond Kedysville, began a sharp cannonade at 5 o'clock in the morning. He found our boys wide awake, who replied firmly and steadily to the attack.

Gen. FITZ-JOHN PORTER had thoroughly examined the field on the previous day, and a council of the Generals had made a disposition of the various army corps for the grand contest. It will be sufficient, for the present purpose, to state that Gen. BURNSIDE took command of the extreme left, while the other Generals occupied the enemy's front and right. BURNSIDE, with Gens. RODMAN, WILCOX, COX and STURGIS Brigades, extended his lines as far as to the southeast of Sharpsburgh, with the stone bridge across the Antietam Creek in his front. Between their position and that of the enemy, who lay toward the village at the northwest, is a succession of hills running nearly north and south, the highest and most abrupt of which is that rising from the bed of the creek. Gens. HOOKER's and SUMNER's corps have been conspicuous throughout the bloody day, the early part of the fight being over their part of the field, while a fierce and protracted struggle was going on at the Stone Bridge, where Gen. BURNSIDE commanded in person. In the latter place we lost, in the forenoon, several brave officers and men. Gen. HOOKER is reported wounded; Lieut. Col. THOMAS BELL, of the Fifty-first Pennsylvania Volunteers, was mortally wounded while leading his men to the attack at this place, and died soon after. Lieut. BEAVER, of the same regiment; Capt. MALCOLM WILSON and Sergeant HARRY H. STEWART, of the Second Maryland Regiment, Co. A, were also killed. Col. KINGSBURY, of the Eleventh Connecticut, was mortally wounded; and Adjutant ANDREW FOWLER, of the Fifty-first New York, is dead. Sergeant DAVIS, acting Lieutenant in the Twenty-first Massachusetts, had a leg badly shattered; Capt. MARTIN, Co. E, Second Maryland, lost a leg; and Color Sergeants OSBORN and HOOVER, of the Second Maryland, are both severely wounded; also Capt. NEILL, Thirty-fifth Massachusetts. I saw all these lying at a barn near the Stone Bridge, while the battle was progressing, having visited the spot for the purpose of obtaining a list (which is only partial,) of the killed and wounded.

I also saw lying dead on the field the following privates: James Kirby, Co. A, Second Maryland; Peter Daily, Co. I; Wm. Kelly, Co. H; Sergt. Jas. Clark, Co. H; John Q. Adams, Co. C; Daniel Fisk, Co. F, Sixth N. H.; Corp. Chas. M. Noyes, Co. K, Ninth N. H.; S. H. Case, Co. B, Seventeenth Mich.; Sergt. Howard Rand, Co. K, Sixth N. H.; Michael Boland, Co. G, Second Md.; —— Connerty, Co. G, Fifty-first N. Y.; Corp. Keefe, Co. I, Fifty-first N. Y.; Thomas N. Stockwell, Co. I, Fifty-first N. Y.; Robert C. Dale, Co. G, Fifty-first N. Y.; Geo. Summerlock, Co. A, Fifty-first Penn., and Thos. Davis, Co. I, Fifty-first Penn. I saw some half-dozen others on the east side of the bridge, whose names I could not learn, lying on the field. It was not safe to cross the bridge, but I was told several others lay on that side. It is impossible, in the present state of affairs, to obtain anything like an estimate of the numbers killed and wounded, but our losses have been very heavy.

The Irish Brigade, Gen. MEAGHER, in SUMNER's corps, occupied a very prominent position, and the brave General, I am told, had a horse shot under him. Some report him killed, but I cannot now learn that it is true. He rode in front of his brigade, and waving his flashing blade in the air, beckoned on his men to the attack. Wherever they made a charge the rebel lines were seen to waver and fall back.

The rebels kept as much as possible under cover of the ravines, and seldom advanced to the attack, but there has never been a battle, probably, where there was so little of woods for the rebels to conceal themselves in. The fighting has been mostly in the open field, with the exception of the sharp contest at the stone bridge, where woods (not dense) line both sides of the stream—and a considerable block of trees occupying nearly the centre of the right, where HOOKER was engaged.

The rebels have been driven back at least two miles since the fight began, so that Sharpsburgh has been, during the afternoon, about the centre of the rebel lines.

Three times the rebel caissons have been blown up by our shells. Five different conflagrations have occurred on the field of barns and houses which were set on fire by exploding shells, or purposely fired by the enemy. While I write the whole heavens are lighted up by burning barns and wheat stacks. It is an immense conflagration.

I made the following memoranda of events while overlooking the field:

Capt. COOK's Parrot Battery, Eighth Massachusetts, occupies the east hill opposite Sharpsburgh and the bridge, and does excellent practice on the enemy's position. Lieut. BENJAMIN, in charge of CARLISLE's Battery, also doing splendid execution. Twice the enemy's battery of six guns had been silenced or compelled to withdraw from the opposite hill.

The musketry firing down at the stone bridge, where WILCOX and STURGIS are engaged, is sharp and continuous. At 11 o'clock squads of rebels are seen "getting up" the hill. Our batteries are playing on them, which hurries their time. Shells burst, and solid shot plow up the ground all around them. Cheers from the ravine. The Seventeenth Michigan (new regiment and all brave boys) are charging down to the help of WILCOX. Our infantry are seen charging up the hill, and our batteries are ordered to cease firing to avoid hitting them. They are turned on the rebel batteries, which now open on the hill to the right of Sharpsburgh. Our infantry advance, and are shelled by the rebel batteries, and compelled to lie down and finally retire under cover of the next ravine. Our 20-pounder Parrots upset the rebel guns. Splendid shots by BENJAMIN. The Forty-fifth New-York come to the rescue, and are pressing by us toward the bridge. Gen. BURNSIDE has just sent orders for Gens. WILCOX and COX to cross the bridge with their brigades and occupy the hills south of the town. Our troops again advance, and as soon as they show themselves a new rebel battery of four guns, on the hill at the left opens upon us. At 12 o'clock a rebel caisson is blown up, the third one since morning.

Sharpsburgh is now the centre of the action in our front, while HOOKER is actively at work on the right. The firing in that part of the field is terrific and unceasing. The rebel lines are seen drawn up along the ravines at the northwest, and occasionally attempting to advance. In each instance they are met and driven back.

At 1 o'clock the fighting at the Stone Bridge has ceased, and WILCOX and COX have all passed over. We now have a large force on the hills confronting the rebel lines. They keep up a constant cannonade upon the Union troops. At 1½ P. M. a squad of seventeen rebels are brought to Gen. BURNSIDE as prisoners, who orders them sent to the rear. The spokesman of the party says: "I don't think there is a man of us who doesn't want to get out of the fight." Gen. COX is ordered to move up and occupy the hills south of Sharpsburgh. At 2½ P. M. there is a temporary lull of the firing, but it is very short. At 4½ P. M. our troops push up the hill (the rebels always continue to have us on the down-hill side of the fight) and a large force appears at their extreme left, advancing toward them over the hill. A perfect storm of shot and shell now greet the advance of our boys from a half dozen different batteries at once. On the right of our advance our troops push up toward the rebel lines and are met half way, at a ravine, where a fierce musketry fight continues for half an hour. The balls strike up the dust in the plowed fields in all directions. The fight ... and so many batteries are in play, from so many different quarters, it is difficult to distinguish friend from foe. Dull ... [illegible]

On the left of the town the Union forces have now gained the crest of the hill, the rebels giving back under their steady fire, and cheers and shouts ring along the line. The rebel flag waves sulkily in the heavy air, in close proximity to the cheerful Red, White and Blue, borne into the thickest of the fight by our brave boys. The Union troops hold their position at the Sharpsburgh road for half an hour, while a deadly contest is going on. Our artillery, which has crossed the bridge, now takes up a position at the left, to check the advance of the rebels, who are trying to flank us, and open a brisk fire. On come the rebel hosts in overpowering numbers, to flank the force on the hill, and WILCOX's Brigade, which has stood their ground for over an hour, now retire part way down the hill. A tremendous onset was now made from the south, the enemy apparently having received reinforcements, and our left is pressed back. The sun has set, but the contest only thickens with the close of the day. The enemy's shell begin to burst over our hospital near the bridge, and the horses at BENJAMIN's Battery are shot at the guns. He is ordered by Gen. BURNSIDE to withdraw them. Stragglers come in from the field, some wounded, some *tenderly* escorting comrades who are wounded—it generally takes two or three to perform this service for one man, and all hands wear a gloomy countenance and limp. Gen. BURNSIDE orders them back to their regiments, with a sharp reprimand. Among these delinquents is a Lieutenant of the Sixteenth Connecticut Regiment, whom the General reprimands, and orders his name to be taken. He goes limping, and says a ball hit him in the leg. "But you walked all the way from the field—why did you come here to exhibit your cowardice? You had better remained at home," said the General sharply. At the same instant a youth, not over fifteen, who had his arm torn by a shell or ball, came up, holding the bleeding member in his other hand. "Look at that boy, Lieutenant, he has some excuse for leaving the field," but you have none. Shells now began to hum and burst all over the ground where we stood, and your correspondent began to think there might be danger in remaining longer in *that* place, so he *quietly* mounted his horse and *slowly* moved to the rear.

The rebels received a check soon after dark, and the contest ended for the night. It has been a most sanguinary fight. Our dead lie mingled with the rebel corpses on every part of this wide field—over a space of three or four miles. Many a poor fellow will lie on the cold, damp earth to-night, and pray for death to relieve him of his sufferings.

I shall endeavor to send fuller particulars of the fight than I am now enabled to do, as soon as they can be procured.

Both armies encamped on the field. To-morrow the dead must be buried, and possibly a renewal of the contest be had.

We shall have reinforcements of COUCH's Division this evening, from Harper's Ferry. E. S.

Events Succeeding the Great Battle—The Rebel Retreat Foreseen—Heavy Losses—Some of the Killed and Wounded—Incidents, &c.

ON THE FIELD, NEAR SHARPSBURGH, Md., Thursday, Sept. 18, 1862.

There has been no engagement to-day—only occasional firing between the pickets, who continue to confront each other on substantially the same field where the contest closed at sundown yesterday. The body of the enemy—if there be any body remaining—are at least three miles further toward the river than they were at the beginning of the battle yesterday morning. Competent judges, with whom I have conversed, among whom is Gen. GRIFFIN—a careful observer, and well versed in the ways of the rebels—believe that they are merely amusing us by these exhibitions of force, while the army proper is really on the retreat to the river, and should this hypothesis prove correct, we shall have a most mortifying result for all the labor, loss and bloodshed of this Maryland campaign. The rebel leaders have drawn after them from Washington an immense army, with its enormous train, which has marched, toiled, fought, and been dragged for fifty miles, over three mountain ranges, at an untold outlay of strength, expense and suffering; they will have supplied their starving army with all it needed; slaughtered and wounded thousands of our brave Union soldiers, and then have escaped back to Virginia to laugh in their sleeve at our laggard way of following up our successes. The old-fashioned way of waiting for the rebel army to make the first move to attack: to choose their own field of operations to fight us; lie still or retreat as suits *their convenience*, seems to be the humor of the hour.

What motives of "strategy" or mysterious plans requiring *time for* development, explains this failure to attack the rebels to-day, a mere novice in warfare has no right to draw in question. But one thing seems apparent to me, the Union army are eager to be "up and at them," and make an end of this rebel *canaille*, and of the rebellion, while we have them and it in our power. The humblest Union soldier will feel the mortification of permitting this ragged and whitish lazaroni to escape our clutches, by crossing again into Virginia.

In order to ascertain the number of the killed and wounded, as near as might be, so soon after the battle, and to obtain such names of prominent persons who have suffered, I passed over the field to-day, and went to nearly all the hospitals where the wounded are being gathered in.

While the wounded are still on the field, and no official returns are made, it is, of course, impossible to obtain anything like a correct list of the killed and wounded. Lists will soon be prepared, however, and full accounts be sent forward. Every house and large barn contiguous to the field, is occupied by the wounded, where, I am happy to say, provision has very promptly been made for dressing wounds and rendering them comfortable.

The troops in HOOKER's, SUMNER's and RICHARDSON's corps have suffered greatly. Some officers of the General Staff estimate the number of wounded at 13,000, and say there are 5,000 on the field. My own judgment, after going pretty well over the ground is, that this estimate is greatly exaggerated, and that they do not amount to half that number, while the killed is very small in proportion to the wounded. I think six to eight hundred will cover the *killed*, and twenty-five hundred to three thousand the wounded, making a total of not to exceed *four thousand of killed and wounded.*

Gen. Rodman was shot through the body, the ball passing through the lung. Gen. Mansfield was instantly killed. Gen. Hooker was wounded in the foot. Gen. Hartsuff, of Rickett's Division, wounded in the right iliac region; a serious wound. Col. Beal, 10th Maine, in the thigh. Col. Richard Oakford, of Scranton, Penn., (132d Penn. Vol.) was killed. Robert A. Abbott was seriously wounded in the lower jaw. Lieut. Jno. C. Dolan, injured in the hip by a shell. First Lieut. Sawyer, 7th Maine, killed, and about 100 privates of the same regiment wounded. Lieut.-Col. Fillebrown was thrown from his horse and injured, but not seriously. Gen. Max Weber was wounded seriously in the arm, and amputation may be rendered necessary. The Lieutenant-Colonel of the 49th New-York Volunteers, was dangerously wounded. Col. Kingsbury, of the Eleventh Connecticut, who was shot through the body twice and wounded in both feet, died this morning. Col. Childs, of the 4th Pennsylvania Cavalry, was killed while leading a charge on the right of the field. Gen. Richardson was wounded, and Gen. Hancock takes his command. Capt. Kelley, of the 8th Illinois Cavalry, was badly wounded on Monday in the mountain ... [illegible] ... command, this cavalry did ... [illegible] ... battery of horse artillery lost several other officers and men, whose names I cannot now obtain.

In Gen. King's Division the loss has been heavy. Col. H. A. V. Post, of the Second United States Sharpshooters, was wounded; also, Lieut. Chas. B. Gould, Co. E, 23d New-York; Lieut. Wildman, Co. B, had his leg shot off—dead; Capt. Myers, Co. I, 14th Brooklyn—dead; Capt. O'Brien, Co. I, 14th Brooklyn—dead; Adgt. Parmele, 2d U. S. Sharpshooters—dead; Lieut. Seabury, 2d U. S. Sharpshooters—wounded; Lieut. Guest, 2d U. S. Sharpshooters—wounded; Capt. Chase, Co. A, 2d U. S. Sharpshooters—wounded; Sergeant-Major Short, 2d U. S. Sharpshooters—wounded.

In Caldwell's Brigade the loss was severe. The Fifth New-Hampshire Regiment have 119 killed and wounded, among which are fourteen officers. Some of these wounded are the following: Col. Cross, wounded in the head, slightly; Capt. Long, Co. G, wounded in the arm; Capt. Randlet, Co. E, wounded in the thigh; Lieut. Graves, Co. H, forearm, slight; Lieut. Bean, Co. H, severely; Lieut. Gay, Co. H, mortally; Lieut. Parks.

KILLED IN MICHIGAN SEVENTEENTH REGIMENT.

Phelix Randall, Co. B.	Israel Colf, Co. C.
Andrew Salier, Co. C.	John A. Troy, Co. C.
Samuel Hunt, Co. D.	S. H. Hadley, Co. B.
Martin V. Moore, Co. D.	Daniel McMartin, Co. B.
Benjamin Ward, Co. D.	Almeron Palmeter, Co. D.
H. A. Smith, Co. D.	Henry Tomlinson, Co. E.
Wm. Woodward, Co. E.	Alex. McKinnon, Co. F.
Robert C. Irvin, Co. E.	Corp. Miron Hawley, Co. H.
Ephriam Micks, Co. F.	Silas Gardner, Co. D.
Deloe Vandeberg, Co. H.	Mason Kasner, Co. I.
Frank Belknap, Co. I.	Wm. Clay, Co. K.
Oliver Cheeney, Co. K.	Leonard Ives, Co. K.
David D. Tompkins, Co. K.	Total, 26.

Mr. Ives, of Providence, an Aid of Gen. Burnside, received a severe flesh wound in the thigh by a piece of shell. Probably not mortal. Mr. Ives is a brother of Capt. J. Peyton Ives, who commanded the Picket in North Carolina, under Gen. Burnside.

The Seventh Maine regiment (Third Brigade, Smith's Division,) commanded by Major Hyde, went into the fight with 175 men and 14 officers, and came out with only 65 men and four officers unhurt.

Lieut. Butler, Co. A, was wounded and is missing; Capt. Jones, Co. B, wounded slightly; Adjt. Haskell was shot through both legs and his horse was killed; Lieut. Beason, Co. C, wounded in leg; Lieut. Goodman, Co. D, killed; Lieut. Emery, Co. E, wounded slightly; Lieut. Shorey, Co. F, wounded in the leg; Lieut. Warren, Co. H, wounded and missing; Capt. Cook, Co. I, wounded in leg; Lieut. Brown, Co. I, supposed killed; Capt. Cochran wounded in foot; Major Hyde wounded in hand and horse shot under him—not serious.

This regiment is now the body-guard of Gens. Franklin and Smith. The loss in this regiment is said to have been heavier than any regiment engaged, in proportion to numbers, since the beginning of the war. Their colors with "Williamsburgh" inscribed on them, were riddled with bullets. Capt. J. W. Channing has three bullet-holes through his clothes, and both he and Major Hyde came off the field with their clothing all bespattered with the blood of their comrades.

THE TURNER RIFLES.

Officers Killed.

Capt. Gustav A. Loreng, Co. C.
First Lieut. Jacob Pabot, Co. D.
Second Lieut. —— Krano, Co. G.

Some of the Wounded.

Capt. Robert Meikle, Pauls (?) Frick, —— Lohman, Capt. Weber, Lieut. Voelker.

Of enlisted men, there were twenty-six killed and eighty wounded.

THE FIRST DELAWARE—*Complete.*

Killed.

Capt. Watson, Co. A.	Corp. John Brierly, Co. A.
Capt. Leonard, Co. B.	Benjamin Lee, Co. A.
Capt. Richards, Co. C.	Mims J. Nelson, Co. E.
Ed. Mosley, Co. A.	Thomas Oakins, Co. A.

Wm. McCoy, Co. D—shot in both hands.
Emanuel Delasse, Co. F—left elbow.
Thos. G. Chance, Co. F—right knee.
Sergt. Chas. F. Holland, Co. E—right side.
Sergt. J. Spearsley, Co. H—left foot.
James E. Clark, Co. K—right thigh.
John Marshall, Co. A—left leg.
H. L. Savage, Co. G—little finger and right hand.
Geo. R. Ellis, Co. E—left leg.
Thos. Y. McCullen, Co. B—right shoulder.
Clarkson Cloud, Co. K—right shoulder.
Jos. Windser, Co. A—left leg.
Robt. Brierly, Co. A—abdomen.
James P. Dickerson, Co. F—abdomen.
Perry Wright, Co. D—right hand.
Wesley Freeman, Co. G—ball through right shoulder.
Wm. Porter, Co. H—bayonet thrust in hip.
Jesse Hurd, Co. K—struck by shell in the breast.
James Forgsum, Co. I—ball through right leg.
James Hilleyard, Co. F—right hand.
James Ross, Co. F—hand.
Ed. Ingham, Co. A—spent ball in breast.
Albert Nelson, Co. A—ball in back.
Corp. Geo. Camperson, Co. D—left knee.
Thos. Thornton, Co. I—flesh wound in left arm.
Corp. Patrick McClusky, Co. C—arm.
Jesse D. Farls, Co. A—wrist.
Sergt. J. Martin, Co. A—hand.
J. J. Kerbaugh, Co. A—right hand and one thumb amputated.
David M. Johnson, Co. E—left shoulder.
Henry Morris, Co. F—leg.
Patrick McGarraty, Co. C—right eye.
Corp. Henry Vinning—spent ball.
Jos. Fitzsimmons, Co. F—hip and back.
John Barton, Co. F—flesh wound in leg.
Thomas Workman, Co. F—neck.
Wm. Veach, Co. A—flesh wound in hand.
H. S. Chaffer, Co. I—flesh wound in left ear.
Sergt. M. Hill, Co. C—right foot.
Lieut. C. Tanner, Co. H—breast.
Jno. Walker, Co. H—left leg.
Jno. Curry, Co. H—left hand and right thigh.
Corp. Jos. Booth, Co. H—groin and leg.
Anthony Cheevers, Co. H—shoulder and leg.
Color Corp. Lewis Corell, Co. H—flesh wd. finger.
Daniel Reed, Co. H—flesh, left shoulder.
Jno. Shepherd, Co. A—left shoulder.
Wm. Wahl, Co. G—flesh wound in finger.
Patrick O'Brien, Co. E—flesh wound in left breast.
C. Platt, Co. A—hit by butt of a musket in breast.
Corp. Duley, Co. H—head and breast.
John Sweeney, Co. A—left side.
Jasper Calhoun, Co. A—left wrist.

In Gen. Burnside's Corps there has been severe losses in officers and men. The great conflict culminated on the left, where he commanded, and a desperate effort was made to outflank Wilcox and Cox's Divisions, which had gained the summit of the hills, and were fast turning the tide of battle. The contest here was desperate and bloody. To-day I can see our dead scattered over the hill side up which our gallant boys fearlessly charged the enemy. Nothing in modern warfare could exceed the steadiness and courage of the troops, who fought on this part of the field. To-day they occupy the hill, only a quarter of a mile in rear of the position which they took yesterday. The enemy's batteries of seven guns on the left of Sharpsburgh and about the same number on the right of the town continue to threaten our front lines. No material change has occurred since last evening in the position of the forces, but *we occupy the field of battle.*

Gen. Burnside and Staff have remained constantly on or near the field, watching intently every movement of the rebels, who keep themselves habitually out of sight. We ought to learn a lesson from them in this respect. This afternoon the General and his Staff and his Aids might all have been seen lying on the ground, under the shelter of a large wheat stack during a heavy rain. Let those who covet the glory and labors of the battle-field follow the march, and share the toils of our *working Generals*, and they will soon have enough of war.

On the right, in the extreme front, I found General Cochrane, this morning, with his entire brigade engaged in picket service. Two hundred yards in advance of where he and Adjutant Rooke were, our lines of sharpshooters were lying along the ground, within short rifle range of the enemy's pickets. Every two or three minutes the sharp crack of rifles, and the "him-m-m" of the bullet was heard, in some cases, passing directly overhead or on either side. Behind them, in a large plowed field, the rebel dead lay very thickly scattered about, in every conceivable position; while muskets, bayonets and the *debris* of the previous day's battle covered the ground. Beside the fence of a small square burying-ground I counted

[*Continued on Eighth Page.*]

The effects of the proclamation — freed Negroes coming into Union lines in North Carolina

The Cabinet considering the Emancipation Proclamation

The New-York Times.

VOL. XI—NO. 3435. NEW-YORK, FRIDAY, SEPTEMBER 26, 1862. PRICE TWO CENTS

Editorials

A POLICY AT LAST.—The President's proclamation, suspending the writ of *habeas corpus* in certain cases, excites quite as much disgust in the minds of the opponents of the Administration as did the Proclamation of Emancipation. The latter was pronounced objectionable because immediately impracticable, and as tending to provoke the augmented animosity of the South. The former is represented to be a return of the Administration to the policy of restricted speech and summary imprisonment, which excited so much popular discontent last Winter.

Both papers, however, are free from the defects complained of, while they possess others for which the entire country has been clamorous. The Government has lacked a determined policy. It has assumed no fixed relation to the Slavery difficulty. And whatever may be the view taken of the expediency of the emancipation measure at the present moment, it certainly has the merit of placing the Administration in an intelligible and entirely definite position before the country, so that the standing charge of indecision ceases to be applicable. So with the proclamation touching arrests. Heretofore they have been made without regard to any fixed principle. Sentiments and acts which were in one locality indulged with perfect impunity, in another involved a prompt consignment to Fort Lafayette. And while the bench generally declined to interpose the *habeas corpus* to discharge the prisoner, judges were found always ready to issue that great prerogative writ. It is not, therefore, to introduce a new system of espionage and arrest, that the recent declaration is issned; but to restrain and define and mitigate the operation of a system which is already in active use. With the present rescript before the public, the requirements of the public service will be better comprehended; the good citizen will know how distant danger is from the path of straightforward loyalty; and the bad citizen will be warned of the limit to which his evil-doing and saying may safely proceed. So far as these remarkable documents thus tend to define an administrative policy, they are therefore important and valuable. But are there not other sinuosities of that policy which equally need straightening?

Chief Justice Roger Brooke Taney, who challenged Lincoln's arbitrary seizure of citizens under war powers

Lincoln and his Cabinet reviewing artillery batteries and cavalry regiments in Washington

The New-York Times.

VOL. XII—NO. 3445. NEW-YORK, WEDNESDAY, OCTOBER 8, 1862. PRICE TWO CENTS.

THE VICTORY AT CORINTH.

The Enemy Intercepted in their Flight by Gens. Hurlbert and Ord.

Another Battle of Seven Hours' Duration.

The Rebels Driven Back Again Toward Corinth.

They Are Again Attacked by Rosecrans and Completely Routed.

Everything Thrown Away in Their Flight.

HEADQUARTERS OF GENERAL GRANT, JACKSON, Tenn., October 6, 1862—12:20 o'clock.

To Major-General Halleck, General-in-Chief:

Generals ORD and HURLBERT came upon the enemy yesterday, and General HURLBERT having driven in small bodies of the rebels the day before, after seven hours' hard fighting, drove the enemy five miles back across the Hatchie towards Corinth, capturing two batteries, about three hundred prisoners, and many small arms.

I immediately apprised Gen. ROSECRANS of these facts, and directed him to urge on the good work. The following dispatch has just been received from him:

CHEVALLA, Oct. 6, 1862.

To Major-Gen. Grant:

The enemy are totally routed, throwing everything away. We are following sharply.

W. S. ROSECRANS, Major-General.

Under previous instructions, Gen. HURLBERT is also following. Gen. MCPHERSON is in the lead of Gen. ROSECRANS' column. The rebel Gen. MARTIN is said to be killed.

U. S. GRANT, Major-General Commanding.

(The rebel General MARTIN, who is reported in the above dispatch as killed, is probably Brig.-Gen. JAS. G. MARTIN, a North Carolinian, who was a Captain and Brevet-Major in the Quartermaster's Department of the United States Army when the war broke out. He lost an arm in Mexico. Some years ago he was stationed at the United States Arsenal in Philadelphia.)

SOME DETAILS OF THE FIGHTING.

CAIRO, Tuesday, Oct. 7.

As yet we can only state the general results of the fighting at Corinth. Skirmishing commenced Tuesday last, and there has been more or less fighting every day since. The rebel loss is about 800 killed and from 1,500 to 1,800 wounded. We have 1,800 prisoners at Corinth and 300 on the Hatchie River and more constantly coming in.

We have taken several thousand stand of arms thrown away by the rebels in their flight. They are mostly new and of English make.

Our loss, it is believed, will be 300 killed and 1000 wounded.

Many houses in the town were badly shattered by shot and shell.

On Sunday Gen. ORD drove the enemy five miles, over hills, and through woods and valleys, the rebels taking advantage of every wood for their infantry, and every hill for their artillery. The fight lasted seven hours.

The rebel Gen. ROGERS was killed. Gen. OGLESBY has died of his wounds. Gen. ORD is slightly wounded.

Prisoners taken say their effective force in the vicinity is 65,000 men. This is probably an over-estimate, but it is certain that they have outnumbered us two to one.

IMPORTANT FROM KENTUCKY.

The Rebels Believed to be Retreating to Hall's Gap—A Stand to be Made There.

LOUISVILLE, Tuesday, Oct. 7.

Gen. GILBERT with his corps is at Lebanon. It is supposed here by military men that the whole rebel force is retreating to Hall's Gap, a few miles south of Crab Orchard, where they intend to make a stand.

The bridges at Shepherdsville will be completed by Sunday. Nearly all the bridges between us and the rebels have been burned by them, and some three weeks will elapse before they can be reconstructed.

The story of the capture by the rebels, near Elizabethtown, of three companies of Ohio cavalry last week, is untrue.

LEXINGTON BEING EVACUATED.

LOUISVILLE—Midnight.

Lexington is mostly evacuated by the rebels, there being only 100 remaining. They took and sent to Camp Dick Robinson 7,000 barrels pork from CHENAULT & Co., packed on their own account and for other parties, mostly Secessionists.

They also took $9,000 worth of jeans and linseys from OLDHAM, SCOTT & Co., which they have manufactured into clothing. The rebels paid for these goods in Confederate scrip, unless owners refused to receive it, in which event no consideration was given.

Reliable individuals from Lexington, who have conversed with rebel soldiers, are confident that a battle must ensue before the rebels leave Kentucky. Rebel soldiers tell them they prefer being killed, or captured and paroled, rather than march over the mountains again. This seems to be the conclusion of the whole rebel crew.

THE SITUATION IN KENTUCKY.

From the Indianapolis Journal, Oct. 4.

Dr. CHITTENDEN, Surgeon of the Sixteenth Regiment, returned from Kentucky yesterday, leaving Richmond on Monday and Lexington on Tuesday. He has been attending our wounded, and in constant contact with the rebels, and is therefore able to speak intelligently of their strength and the events of the past few weeks. He says that about three weeks ago our Gen. MORGAN, on his way from the Gap to the Ohio, near Manchester, captured KIRBY SMITH's ammunition train, and all the supplies he had there. He also seized all the salt and flour which had been stored there by the rebels. This news, which we have not heard before, was learned by Dr. C. from the rebels themselves, and is doubtless correct.

About two weeks ago the guerrilla [illegible] started out with 800 cavalry to disperse a band of Home Guards near Irvine, but was completely defeated, and his men came back terribly demoralized and disordered. A number of wounded were brought to Richmond, and several young men belonging to Richmond, who had joined the rebel force, were killed. The Doctor saw this himself, and heard the rebels talk of their discomfiture repeatedly.

On Friday of last week heavy and continuous cannonading was heard in the vicinity of Irvine, so far as could be judged by the sound, and a bloody battle between KIRBY SMITH and Gen. MORGAN was believed to be going on. At that time nearly the entire rebel force had left Richmond. On Saturday night the Doctor saw a large number of the rebel wounded brought to Richmond. They filled the African church with them. On last Monday evening, while at Lexington, to which place our wounded were taken, he saw a number of rebel stragglers coming in, and heard from the citizens that they admitted they had been badly whipped by MORGAN, and had lost all their artillery, but one gun. This news comes directly, and we have no doubt is true. Nothing has been said of it because nothing definite has been learned of it either at Cincinnati or Louisville. The Doctor says that Gen. WRIGHT had some intimations of such news, but it was so uncertain that he would allow no publication of it made.

Of the Union feeling in Kentucky, and the conduct of the loyal citizens, the Doctor speaks in enthusiastic terms. He says that as our ambulance train entered Lexington, the citizens cheered the soldiers openly and heartily. Both BUCKNER's and KIRBY SMITH's Staffs were on the corner of the street, by the Phœnix Hotel, and the windows above, and on all sides of them, were crowded with ladies, displaying Union flags. Over three hundred ladies met the train at the hospital, to take care of the wounded, and supply them with everything they needed. Every delicacy that money could get was furnished in profusion. No men were ever more nobly cared for. The Doctor says our soldiers express the deepest gratitude for the generous treatment they received from the Lexington people and especially the ladies. At Paris, the Union feeling was exhibited with great enthusiasm. At Richmond, the citizens came for miles in carriages to take our wounded from the hospitals to their homes, and 300 of them were kept by the people for four weeks without a cent of compensation. The wealthiest and most refined ladies of the neighborhood almost made their homes in the hospitals, working at whatever was found necessary for the comfort of the men, no matter how hard or unpleasant.

An amusing incident is related by the Doctor of a Union lady near Paris. As the train of wounded came up, she came out to the gate with a Union flag and waved it and cheered with all her might. While she was in the midst of her enthusiastic welcome one of our guards who happened to have on a rusty grey suit, very like the rebel uniform, rode up, and asked the lady to give him that flag as he wanted to keep it. She took him to be rebel, and said, "Sir, I thought you were a Union soldier. I see you are a rebel. You shan't have this flag." And she tore it all to rags before his face. The Union feeling in Kentucky, the Doctor says, is in no way affected by the President's proclamation. The people say they want the Government and they will preserve it, let what will perish in doing so. The Doctor speaks with special gratitude of the kindness of Mrs. Judge GOODLOE, Mrs. Col. HOLLOWAY, Mrs. Judge EMBRY, Mrs. GREEN CLAY, Mrs. CASSIUS M. CLAY, Mrs. Dr. SMITH, and Mrs. Dr. LYMAN.

A VICTORY IN MISSOURI.

Gen. Schofield Whips 15,000 Rebels at Newtonia.

The Advantage Followed Up.

ST. LOUIS, Tuesday, Oct. 7.

Dispatches received at headquarters bring intelligence to the effect that on Saturday morning Gen. SCHOFIELD advanced upon the rebels at Newtonia, a small town about fifty-four miles south of Springfield, and after a two hours' engagement the rebels broke and fled in all directions. The force of the enemy is estimated at 15,000 men. Our loss is

Dispatches intercepted after the fight acquainted Gen. SCHOFIELD of the intention of the enemy to concentrate their whole force at a point twelve miles distant from Newtonia, to which point he was pushing rapidly with the expectation of renewing the battle on Sunday.

No further particulars have been received.

AFFAIRS AT NORFOLK.

A Stricter Code of Regulations Established by Gen. Viele.

HEADQUARTERS OF THE MILITARY GOVERNOR, NORFOLK, Va., Oct. 6, 1862.

No more passes or permits will be issued to take supplies into the country, except a certificate from the Clerk of the Market, that the persons applying for the permit actually brought supplies to town. Supplies will only be allowed for the family use of those who take them.

The pickets and sentinels will be instructed not to allow any person or vehicle to pass out of the lines, with the exception of market carts or wagons, each containing but one person.

Physicians will be allowed to pass on the same conditions as heretofore.

No person or vehicle, unless for market purposes, will come into the lines, with this exception, that should the person have came from a distance, having no knowledge of this order, they will be allowed to pass in, and their names and residences reported at the headquarters, where instructions will be given as to allowing them to return to their homes.

A picket will be placed at the Marine Hospital immediately, and no boat allowed to land there with or without a pass.

No boats except lighters with wood or supplies, will be allowed to pass the draw-bridge, going up or down.

Until further orders the daily passenger boat will not return to Fortress Monroe, and no passes will be given to go there by other Government vessels, except return passes or to officers on duty or with leave from Suffolk. The ferry to Portsmouth will run every half hour only during the day, unless a more frequent use shall be required for military purposes.

These orders will continue in force until a more general good faith is exhibited toward the Government. Unless the attempts to violate the military laws necessarily established here shall be discountenanced and suppressed by the citizens themselves, they must blame themselves alone for the consequences.

All persons are solemnly warned against attempting to pass the lines, for any purpose whatever, without authority. Ignorance of military law, in this respect, will not hereafter be accepted as an excuse for its violation. By order of

Brig.-Gen. EGBERT L. VIELE, Military Governor.

The Eleventh Ward Homicide.

CONCLUSION OF THE CORONER'S INQUEST—VERDICT OF THE JURY.

The inquest in the case of the Eleventh Ward homicide, was continued last evening at the Eleventh Precinct Station House, before Coroner WILDEY. WILLIAM HENRY MUMFORD (colored) was examined at some length, his evidence being corroborative of that published in the *Times* of yesterday. He stated that the parties under arrest were in the habit of carrying knives, and identified a murderous looking weapon, which, he knew, was carried by CROWSON. This knife had a blade twelve inches in length, and two inches in width.

STEPHEN SHORTLE, a detective policeman of the Eleventh Precinct, who was on hand three minutes after the alarm was given, stated that he arrested SUSANNA REID, (the party accused of murdering DONNELLY,) and that REID admitted there had been trouble, and that he struck deceased in the breast, though not with a knife.

Dr. BEACH gave his evidence relative to the *post-mortem* held on the body of deceased, and stating that death was the result of a stab made by some sharp instrument.

Mrs. DONNELLY, wife of deceased, was in the room a few moments during the inquest, but left soon after the proceedings opened. About one hundred citizens of the Ward were also present.

After an hour's deliberation, the jury returned the following

VERDICT:

That deceased came to his death with a knife in the hands of SUSANNA REID, on the 5th of October.

REID was examined, and in reply to questions, said he was 21 years of age, was a cartman by occupation, and not guilty of the crime. He was remanded to the Tombs by Coroner WILDEY.

FROM THE ARMY OF THE POTOMAC.

AN IMPORTANT CAPTURE.

An Entire Wagon Train, with Supplies of all kinds, Secured.

Pursuit of a Body of Rebels up the Great Cacapon River.

BALTIMORE, Tuesday, Oct. 7.

The *American* has received the following special dispatch from Cumberland:

IMBODEN's entire wagon train, embracing supplies of all kinds, two pieces of artillery, 100 small arms, and 50 prisoners were captured, and Col. MCREYNOLDS is in pursuit of him up the Great Cacapon River.

(NOTE.—IMBODEN is a noted rebel artillery officer.)

AN IMPORTANT GENERAL ORDER.

HEADQUARTERS ARMY OF THE POTOMAC, CAMP NEAR SHARPSBURGH, Md., Oct. 7.

GENERAL ORDER, No. 163.—The attention of the officers and soldiers of the Army of the Potomac is called to General Orders, No. 139, War Department, Sept. 24, 1862, publishing to the army the President's Proclamation of Sept. 22. A proclamation of such grave moment to the nation officially communicated to the army, affords to the General commanding an opportunity of defining specifically to the officers and soldiers under his command the relation borne by all persons in the military service of the United States toward the civil authorities of the Government. The constitution confides to the civil authorities legislation, judicial and executive, the power and duty of making, expounding and executing the Federal laws. Armed forces are raised and supported simply to sustain the civil authorities, and are to be held in strict subordination thereto in all respects. This fundamental rule of our political system is essential to the security of our Republican institutions, and should be thoroughly understood and observed by every soldier. The principle upon which, and the objects for which armies shall be employed in suppressing the rebellion must be determined and declared by the civil authorities, and the Chief Executive, who is charged with the administration of the National affairs, is the proper and only source through which the views and orders of the Government can be made known to the armies of the nation. Discussion by officers and the soldiers concerning public measures determined upon and declared by the Government, when carried at all beyond the ordinary temperate and respectful expression of opinion, tend greatly to impair and destroy the discipline and efficiency of troops by substituting the spirit of political faction for that firm, steady and earnest support of the authority of the Government, which is the highest duty of the American soldier. The remedy for political errors, if any are committed, is to be found only in the action of the people [illegible] tween the soldiers and the Government, the General Commanding merely adverts to an evil against which it has been thought advisable during our whole history to guard the armies of the Republic, and in so doing he will not be considered by any right-minded person as casting any reflection upon that loyalty and good conduct which has been so fully illustrated upon so many battle-fields. In carrying out all measures of public policy, this army will of course be guided by the same rules of mercy and Christianity that have ever controlled its conduct toward the defenceless. By command of

Maj.-Gen. MCCLELLAN.

JAMES A. HARDIE, Lieut.-Col. and Aid-de-Camp, and A. A. A. G.

FROM HARPER'S FERRY.

The Reconnoissance to Charlestown on Monday—The Rebels Found there in Considerable Force—Evidences that the Bulk of the Rebel Army is Moving Southward—The Loyalty of Martinsburgh, &c.

HARPER'S FERRY, Va., Monday, Oct. 6, 1862.

An important reconnoitering force, consisting of the Fifth and Sixth Cavalry, (Regulars,) and two batteries, are just starting out for Charleston, with the design of ascertaining definitely how many rebs occupy this place. A previous reconnoissance waked up a rebel battery in the vicinity, which will be engaged by our guns to-day. Owing to the watchfulness of the Confederates, whose numerous pickets are constantly on the alert, our scouts and spies have found it almost impossible to penetrate their lines, still we are enabled to determine their movements to some extent from other sources.

I learn from the servant of Dr. FERGUSON, Eighth New-York Cavalry, who escaped last week, that *a considerable body of them have moved Southward.* This negro, whose statements can be relied upon, was seized at the time of the taking of Harper's Ferry, hurried off with the contrabands, and made driver of a Quartermaster's wagon. On the first day (Monday), he, among others, was employed in conveying the captured muskets to a short distance beyond Charleston, where they were deposited in barns, and corn-cribs, and afterward taken on to Winchester. On Wednesday they returned to Harper's Ferry for ammunition, which they conveyed to Winchester, which was full of sick and wounded soldiers. Thursday they drove down to HENRY COMER's, on the Shenandoah River, and secured several loads of corn which were taken to Martinsburgh. They remained at Martinsburgh until Saturday. When reaching Charleston, *en route* for Winchester, word came that MCCLELLAN's forces were upon them, and one half hour was given the soldiers and citizens to pack up and be over. This was on the Saturday succeeding the battle of Antietam, and shows what results might have been attained had we followed up the successes of that day. On the following Saturday Sept. 27, no enemy appearing, they were sent from Winchester to Martinsburgh with five loads of the captured guns, 200 to a load, for five hundred new recruits there from Staunton, and as many more who were expected in a few days. When in the vicinity of Bunker's Hill they were met by a courier who ordered them to turn about, as the army were moving back that way. They did so, and by the time they reached Charleston the rebel army overtook them and continued passing from an hour before sunset until 10 o'clock, the time at which he escaped. *He saw full thirty thousand men and fifty cannon pass by, and they were still coming when he left.* He overheard one officer ask another, "Where are we going?" "Don't know, *but we must hurry back, because they are flanking Richmond,*" was the reply.

That the rebels have withdrawn most of their forces from between Charleston and Martinsburgh is also shown by the result of the reconnoissance to the latter place last week, when no rebel infantry were to be seen. This being the case, we have reason to expect that MCCLELLAN will cross the Potomac at Sharpsburgh Dam No. 4 and Williamsport, and occupy Martinsburgh, Shepherdstown, and the surrounding country. Should he, however, send a superior force, made up largely of cavalry, directly from this place to Charleston, I am confident he could cut off and capture all the forces above who are carrying on their depredations and impressing the citizens. They could not escape through Western Virginia or Maryland.

Several Union men, who had come away from Martinsburgh with our reconnoitering party, reached Williamsport while I was there. Among them was N. D. KNISTEN, one of the most influential and loyal citizens of the place, who was brought away outside of one of our caissons. They represent the place as filthy and full of vermin from the three weeks of Confederate occupancy. Many rebel wounded were taken there from the battle-field of Antietam. Gen. STEWART held command of the place and vicinity. Their headquarters are at Gushman's Mills, four miles out on the Yuscarora Road, which are kept running night and day. BELLE BOYD, recently released from Fort McHenry, has returned home, and is "around." Immediately on our forces entering the village, Adjt. SLADE, of the Twelfth Illinois Cavalry, who escorted the lady from Winchester last June, *en route* for Baltimore, calling to see her, was informed by her younger sister that she had gone out with Mrs. FAULKNER. Mr. FAULKNER remains quietly at home most of the time, appearing desirous of occupying a neutral position in the present contest. The rebels have destroyed little private property, but everything belonging to the Government save hotel buildings. *All the culverts and bridges on the Baltimore and Ohio Railroad, for several miles each way, have been blown up.* The people have exhibited no signs of wavering, but continue, as before, loyal to the old flag. Supposing that our forces had come to occupy the place permanently, the citizens mounted Union Hill, and welcomed them with shouts of joy. What was their disappointment, on seeing them retire after the lapse of an hour or more. Berkley County, of which Martinsburgh is the county seat, gave a majority of 795 against secession. It is a shame that her loyal, faithful people have so often been left to the mercy of the rebels.

The mail bearer is here for the first time to-day. The temporary railroad bridge over the Potomac has been completed and cars are run over to the village. A pontoon bridge has also been thrown across the Shenandoah. The weather is very mild and beautiful.

LATER—2 o'clock P. M.—The force sent out on a reconnoissance have just retired, the enemy were found in large numbers at Charleston. They took one captain prisoner. Two members of Company D, Sixth Cavalry, (Regulars,) were killed, JOHN EWEN and DAVID JAMES.

J.

REBEL OFFICERS PAROLED.

HARPER'S FERRY, Monday, Oct. 6.

Lieut.-Col. RUTHERFORD and First Lieut. DWIGHT, of the rebel army, were paroled by Gen. SUMNER, to-day. Transportation to Baltimore was furnished to them.

FROM BEFORE WASHINGTON.

Movements of the Rebels on This Side of the Rappahannock.

Their Pickets Within Sixteen Miles of Centreville.

A DIVISION STATIONED AT WARRENTON.

By a special dispatch from the TIMES' correspondent with Gen. SIGEL, dated this morning, we learn some interesting facts in regard to rebel operations in our front. His information is obtained from statements of rebel prisoners and deserters and from Government scouts.

Gen. JO. JOHNSON's corps, as before stated, is between Warrenton and Culpepper, apparently acting as an army of observation. Three divisions are at Culpepper Court-house, two of them commanded by Gens. HARLAND and GUSTAVUS SMITH, all raw troops. MUMFORD's Brigade is between Warrenton and Sulphur Springs, consisting of nine hundred to one thousand men. Gen. MUMFORD is reported to have said that Gen. JOHNSON has been ordered to the command of the Western Army, BRAGG having been relieved.

A large force of rebels is reported at Gordonsville.

The railroad bridge over the Rappahannock has been repaired, and trains run daily between Culpepper and Bristow. JO. JOHNSON's force is moving leisurely across that stream, one division being now at Warrenton.

The rebel pickets are again advanced to within sixteen miles of Centreville. Night attacks upon the Union lines are becoming frequent.

Within the last eight days the number of rebel soldiers captured by Gen. STAHL amounts to two thousand.

The rebel Generals are now beginning to return to us deserters from our army, perhaps in the hope of securing the adoption of the same policy by our Government. Forty were thus returned with the last batch of paroled prisoners.

One of Gen. LONGSTREET's Orderlies at the battle of Antietam states that the officers of the Confederate army put their loss at 10,000 in all, of which 4,000 are deserters. Before the battle they were reinforced by 800 cavalry and 2,000 infantry, of whom 600 were from Pennsylvania.

LEE is believed, by deserters, to have 180,000 men at Winchester and vicinity. The old regiments are being filled up by conscription.

MASSACHUSETTS POLITICS.

The People's Union Convention of Massachusetts.

BRIGADIER-GENERAL DEVENS NOMINATED FOR GOVERNOR.

BOSTON, Tuesday, Oct. 7.

The People's Union Convention, called to meet in Faneuil Hall to-day to nominate a State ticket, is very largely attended in numbers, but the State appears only partially represented.

Hon. LINUS CHILD, of Boston, presided, assisted by a large number of Vice Presidents.

The greatest enthusiasm prevailed.

The Convention have nominated Brig.-Gen. DEVENS, of Worcester, for Governor, by acclamation.

BOSTON, Tuesday, Oct. 7—2 P. M.

The People's Union Convention of Massachusetts is now quite largely attended, delegates having arrived from all parts of the State. Two hundred and ninety-nine towns are represented.

The following is the complete State Ticket nominated by the People's Union Convention of Massachusetts:

For Governor—Gen. CHARLES DEVENS, of Worcester.
For Lieutenant-Governor—THOMAS F. PLUNKETT, of Pittsfield.
For Secretary of State—OLIVER WARNER, of Northampton.
For State Treasurer—HENRY K. OLIVER, of Salem.
For Auditor—LEVI REED, of Abington.
For Attorney-General—HENRY W. PAINE, of Boston.

The Ticket was greeted with tremendous cheers by the Convention.

The Convention was addressed by LINUS CHILD, the President, Judge J. C. ABBOTT, Judge PARKER, of Cambridge, LEVERETT SALTONSTALLS and others.

Resolutions were adopted calling upon the people of all parties to support the Administration and put down the rebellion, classifying with the most infamous criminals the authors and promoters of the rebellion against the most beneficent Government on earth, and declaring and trusting that the people will never consent that one star be stricken from the constellation upon the old flag, or one pillar be removed from the temple of liberty; recognizing ABRAHAM LINCOLN, the Chief Executive Magistrate of the Nation, whose rightful authority and power ought always to be rigorously and religiously guarded and preserved; that he, the President, must answer to us, the nation, to posterity, and above all, to God. We make, therefore, no captious criticisms of his acts and declarations; we burden him with no party or partisan policy; we offer no conditions to our patriotism; we resolve that Massachusetts, with all her heart and soul, and mind and strength, will support the President of the United States in the prosecution of this war to the entire and final suppression of the rebellion.

The last two resolutions are as follows:

Resolved, That we offer the thanks of this Convention to the loyal States of the Border, for their devotion to the Union, Constitution and the flag. We know what they have suffered. We know against whom they contended. We know the strength of their patriotism. It is firm and true; when hostile armies encamp upon their soil and desolate their homes, and we brand as false and wicked the imputation of fanatics and partisans, that their loyalty is doubtful, and therefore their counsel should be spurned. God bless Maryland for the last proof of her fidelity; God help the brave State of Kentucky, cursed to-day by the tread of the rebel army. Her people are our people; her cause is our cause, and it is our proud confidence that she will pass through the present trial with her fair fame untarnished, and while she routes those who have invaded her, will confound those who have slandered her.

Resolved, That Massachusetts responds with full heart to the acclaim with which the army received the appointment to its command of Major-Gen. GEORGE B. MCCLELLAN. Let all irregular and irresponsible intermeddling with his command of the army, whether in high places or in low, by letters written in camp or Governors in Convention, anywhere and everywhere, henceforth cease.

IMPORTANT FROM THE LOWER POTOMAC

Another Attempt to Establish a Blockade.

A Rebel Battery Destroyed at Cockpit Point.

WASHINGTON, Tuesday, Oct. 7.

Capt. JOB RUARK, of the schooner *Statesman*, who arrived here to-day, reports that the rebels had succeeded in placing a battery at Cockpit Point on the Potomac River, and that just before sunset yesterday one of our gunboats ran into the Point and shelled the battery, entirely destroying it. He thinks there must have been a considerable quantity of combustible material in the immediate vicinity of the battery, as a large fire was burning nearly all night.

The Captain of the schooner *Eliza Ann Johnson*, which arrived this morning, states that he spoke a schooner below Cockpit Point, which warned him not to go too near in, as the steamer *Georgia* had been fired upon, and was told our gunboats had run in and shelled the rebels out, setting the place on fire. The captain had heard firing during the afternoon, and as he came up he saw three of our gunboats lying out from the Point, and a large fire burning on shore.

No one [illegible] Triennial General Episcopal Convention, now in session in this City, can have failed to perceive the singular omissions, inaccuracies, misstatements and absurdities contained in the reports of their debates in some of the City newspapers. As one of the Lay Deputies from this diocese, I have not hitherto been inclined to attempt the correction of these numerous errors, preferring to await the full and authentic report, which will doubtless appear after the close of the Convention. The *Evening Post* of last evening, however, contains a misstatement so monstrous and so injurious, that I cannot allow it for a moment to go unnoticed.

In advocating the postponement until the next Triennial Convention of the movement yesterday made by Dr. VINTON, to rebuke the Diocese of Alabama for its recent consecration of a Bishop, without the consent of the Northern Dioceses, that journal reports, that "Mr. RUGGLES *denounced* the war as *horrible, dastard and unholy*."

I now distinctly deny, that either then or ever, I "denounced" the war at all; but, on the contrary, aver that in the debate in the Convention yesterday, while admitting the horrors of slaughtering brethren heretofore united by the ties of churchmanship, of which a most affecting instance had just been narrated in the Convention, I expressed my most earnest wish that the pending war might be prosecuted with the utmost vigor, and with the whole military and naval power of the Republic, until every State now in rebellion should be reduced to submission to the constituted authority of the Government. Expressing also my confident hope that such result would be attained before the next meeting of the General Convention, I urged upon the body the expedience of postponing the pending measure until that happy restoration of peace, when the reunited Church could adjust this and all other ecclesiastical differences with the Southern Dioceses in the renewed spirit of fraternal Christian union.

The City Press surely owes it alike to its own respectability and sense of justice, not only to make the present correction, but so long as it shall profess to report the debates of the Convention, to make at least some slight approach to their true language and spirit.

SAMUEL B. RUGGLES.

NEW-YORK, Wednesday, Oct. 8, 1862.

People's Union Central Committee.

At a regular meeting of the People's Union Central Committee, held at their headquarters, No. 8 Union-square, Oct. 6, 1862, the following call was adopted:

Resolved, That the several People's Union District Associations of this City shall meet at the headquarters of said Associations in their various Assembly Districts, on Thursday, the 9th of October, 1862, at 7½ P. M., for the purpose of choosing delegates to the following Conventions, viz.:

A County Convention, to nominate a candidate for Surrogate and one supervisor.

A Congressional Convention in each of the Congressional Districts in this City.

An Assembly Convention in each of the Assembly Districts in this City.

The County Convention shall consist of three delegates from each Assembly District.

The Congressional Convention shall be composed of five delegates from each of the Wards composing such Districts.

The Assembly Convention shall consist of nine delegates from each Assembly District. The election of delegates shall be conducted in the manner that may be prescribed by the several Assembly Union District Associations.

The County Convention shall be held at headquarters, No. 8 Union-square, on the 10th day of October, 1862, at 7½ P. M.

The several Congressional Conventions shall meet on the 13th of October, 1862, at 7½ P. M., as follows, viz.:

The Fourth at the Dupont House, corner of Hudson and Laight streets.

The Fifth at Humboldt Hall, Nos. 65 and 67 Forsyth-street.

The Sixth at southwest corner of West Tenth-street and Sixth-avenue.

The Seventh at the headquarters of the Assembly District Association in the Seventeenth Ward.

The Eighth at No. 8 Union-square.

The Ninth at the Mason House, corner of Sixth-avenue and Forty-fourth-street.

The several Assembly District Conventions shall meet on the 14th of October, 1862, at 7½ P. M., at such places as may be designated by the various Assembly District Union Associations.

WALDO HUTCHINS, Chairman.

SAMUEL C. REEL, LORENZO TRAUB, } Secretaries.

DEPARTMENT OF THE SOUTH.

Beauregard Promises to Retake Fort Pulaski in Thirty Days.

The Rebel Salt Works at Bluffton Destroyed.

A DARING EXPEDITION UP THE SAVANNAH.

The Expedition to St. John's River, Fla.

The steamer *Star of the South* arrived here yesterday with Port Royal dates of the 4th instant. Among her passengers are Maj.-Gen. HUNTER's Staff.

The *New South* pronounces as untrue the report at the North that Fort Sumter had been assailed.

Deserters from Savannah report the arrival there of Gen. BEAUREGARD, who had made a speech to his troops pledging that he would retake Fort Pulaski in thirty days. The *Fingal* and other batteries would be ready in two weeks.

Col. BARTON with part of his Forty-eighth New-York Regiment, had destroyed the extensive salt works at Bluffton.

Two gunboats had shelled the rebel battery at Cranston's Bluff on the Savannah River.

OUR PORT ROYAL CORRESPONDENCE.

The Expedition to St. John's—Popularity of the Emancipation Proclamation in the Army—A Skirmish—Educating the Blacks for Freedom, &c.

PORT ROYAL, Friday, Oct. 3, 1862.

I was sorry to find that New-York papers of the 27th ult. published information of a projected expedition to the St. John's River, Florida, near the mouth of which the rebels have erected a battery that has given some annoyance to the blockading vessels. There is always uncertainty about the time when expeditions set out, and particularly so in cases where troops have to be transported by water, therefore it is better to say nothing publicly of such matters until a fair start has been made, if you would avoid giving the enemy an advantage. Acting upon this belief, I omitted to send you word of the contemplated movement, and circumstances prove the wisdom of my course. It was intended to hurry the expedition away ten days before it started, and the troops had embarked for the enterprise, when an interval of heavy weather set in, making it impossible for the transports to cross the shallow bar at the mouth of the river, and, consequently, the departure was delayed until last Tuesday, the 30th ult. The postponement, though so evidently necessary, was disheartening to the eager soldiers, but the weather on the morning they got away made ample amends for all [illegible] North-with all the pomp of flaunting banners, and the "circumstance of war," embarking [illegible] Boston, amid enthusiasm from a crowd of [illegible]. Just before the transports left the wharf, Gen. MITCHEL rode down, accompanied by his Staff, and made the soldiers a brief, vigorous and pointed address, incidentally alluding to the "Decree of Emancipation,"—which, by-the-by, has been received with very general satisfaction here, not having caused a single officer's resignation, as far as I know,—and expressing a wish that he could be young again, that he might have the privilege of seeing its glorious effects upon coming ages; and as he ceased, the air was rent with cheers and shouts of exultation. A few days must bring the result of the expedition.

There are further signs of the electricity now charging this Department. Col. BARTON, at Gen. MITCHEL's suggestion, with a detachment of his regiment, the Forty-eighth New-York, now stationed at Fort Pulaski, took the boats *Planter* and *Starlight*, both heavily armed, and made a descent upon Bluffton, on the "main," last Tuesday, the 30th, to destroy the salt-works there, from which the rebels are said to have derived extensive profit. The force, led by Capt. STRICKLAND, landed and drove the pickets, and the boats ascended the river. The rebels had two companies of cavalry at the village, but no resistance was offered, and Col. BARTON accomplished his object without any loss. The next day the Colonel, with a company of his regiment, under Capt. LENT, and of the Third Rhode Island Artillery, under Capt. GOULD, with the same boats, ascended the Savannah to within about two miles of Fort Jackson, and broke up a working-party who were sinking stone obstructions in the channel. The six steamboats which had allowed their fires to go down came in for a fire of another sort, hot and peppery, and, as quickly as possible, made for shelter beneath the guns of Fort Jackson. A battery at Carsten's Bluff opened upon Col. BARTON's party, but the replying fire silenced it after six shots from the rebels of too short a range for damage. Our boats then recoiled before the excitement they had themselves caused, so great that the housetops of Savannah were distinctly seen, sprinkled with spectators, rousing the floating battery, which descended, and which is now anchored so much lower down, that it is no longer safe for another adventure with such small boats.

Of matters at headquarters there is little to say. The present negro quarters—a long row of partitions into which are crowded young and old, male and female, without respect either to quality or quantity, such has thus far been the necessity—having become a sort of Five Points, half stye, half brothel, the Major-General has ordered to be removed outside, and accordingly a piece of ground has been selected near the Drayton Plantation, about two miles off, for a negro village. The negroes are to be made to build their own homes, and as it is thought to be high time they should begin to learn what freedom means by experience of self-dependence, they are to be left as much as possible to themselves, of course, for a time, under proper supervision, in preparation for the advance of the army, when they will be intrusted with the entire charge of the islands. A teacher has been provided for them—since they have as yet had none upon this island—who will be paid from the Quartermaster's Department. Should the General see fit to extend this policy, it ought to meet with approval, for education is an "institution of police," and therefore too important to be shifted upon private associations, however public-spirited and zealous. Gen. MITCHEL is just the man to bring this complicated department to system; administration is his *forte*, however, we trust, he may soon be permitted to illustrate his ability upon other forts—Sumter, for instance.

European Steamers Arrived.

SANDY HOOK, Wednesday, Oct. 8.

Steamship *City of Washington* will be up at 2½ A. M. News anticipated.

SANDY HOOK, Wednesday, Oct. 8—1:45 A. M.

The steamer *Saxonia* will be up at 3 o'clock.

Missouri Politics.

ST. LOUIS, Tuesday, Oct. 7.

FRANK P. BLAIR was unanimously nominated for Congress in the First District, by the Union Emancipation Convention yesterday.

Advance of the Federal troops on Corinth — General Hurlbut's division forcing their way through the mud

The New-York Times.

VOL. XII—NO. 3446. NEW-YORK, THURSDAY, OCTOBER 9, 1862. PRICE TWO CENTS.

THE VICTORY AT CORINTH.

Desperate Assault Upon the Place by Fifty Thousand Rebels.

The Battle Continued Through Two Days.

The Final Repulse of the Enemy with Terrible Slaughter.

The Rebel Losses Much Heavier Than Ours.

PROMINENT OFFICERS KILLED.

CORINTH, Miss., Sunday, Oct. 5.

The correspondent of the St. Louis *Democrat* has the following details of the battle at Corinth:

"On the morning of the 3d, our outposts were attacked by the enemy in force, about six miles northeast of Corinth, and before 9 o'clock the engagement became general and fierce, and a sanguinary battle was fought.

Our men under ROSECRANS stood up manfully, and fought with great coolness and bravery; but regiment after regiment, and brigade after brigade poured in upon us, and we were forced slowly backward, fighting desperately. The rebels pushed forward with determined obstinacy, and held every foot of their advantage ground.

They outflanked our inferior force and were forming in the rear, and we were obliged to fall back still further to prevent this movement from being accomplished. The enemy were now inside our breastworks pushing us backward toward the town when darkness put an end to fighting that day.

During the day's fight our loss was heavy, but that of the enemy must have largely exceeded ours.

Three pieces of the First Missouri Battery were captured after having stood for hours before the enemy's fire. Brig.-Gen. HACKLEMAN fell mortally wounded at the head of his men, and died the same evening. Gen. OGLESBY was shot in the breast.

About 4 o'clock A. M. of the 4th, the enemy opened on the town with shot and shell. Our batteries replied, and for an hour or more a heavy cannonading was kept up. At the expiration of that time, two rebel guns had been disabled, and, shortly after daylight, their battery of seven guns was captured.

A portentous quiet soon occurred, and it was evident that some movement was being made by the enemy. The Western Sharpshooters, under Col. BURKE' were ordered forward as skirmishers, to feel the enemy. At 9½ they met him three-quarters of a mile in advance of our line of battle, advancing rapidly in heavy columns upon the town. Immediately a murderous fire was opened on this heavy line by our skirmishers, who slowly began to retire, returning the fire of the enemy with effect.

The woods seemed alive with rebels, and it appeared impossible for this gallant regiment to escape destruction in their retreat over the three-quarters of a mile of open ground which intervened between them and our temporary works of defence.

In a few moments the engagement became general; our batteries opened a destructive fire on the exposed ranks of the rebels, mowing them down like grass. Their slaughter was frightful, but with unparalleled daring and recklessness they pushed impetuously forward.

They charged our works desperately, broke our lines of infantry, and captured a small fortification, in which a battery of the First Missouri was planted. All seemed lost, and a temporary panic seized our men, and the rebels once more marched into the streets of Corinth; but new batteries opened on them, and our men, under the direction of a few courageous officers, and stimulated by their example, fought desperately, and the advance of the enemy was checked.

They wavered, and then fell back. Our lost battery was regained, and once more it hurled destruction into their ranks. The day was saved, and the enemy was in full retreat.

Our loss was comparatively small during this charge. That of the enemy *was fully twenty to our one killed.*

Among the rebels killed and left on the field were Brig.-Gen. RODGERS, of New-Orleans; Col. and Acting Brig.-Gen. JOHNSON, of Mississippi, and another Colonel commanding a brigade, whose name was not learned.

The enemy was commanded by VAN DORN, PRICE and VILLIPIQUE, with their respective army corps' which swelled their forces to 50,000 men.

It is impossible now to give a list of the casualties. Our proportion of officers is thought to be large. We lost but four taken prisoners.

Heavy Losses Among the Rebel Officers.

CHICAGO, Wednesday, Oct. 8.

The Chicago *Tribune's* Cairo special says that the rebel Cols. JOHNSON, ROGERS, ROSS, MORTON, McLAINE and Major JONES were killed, and Cols. DALY and PRITCH were severely wounded in the late battle at Corinth.

THE WAR IN ARKANSAS.

The Numbers and Locations of the Rebel Forces.

HELENA, Ark., Saturday, Oct. 4.

A correspondent of the Missouri *Republican* says:

We have late and very reliable intelligence from the rebel forces in this State, which is regarded by military men here as worthy of confidence. It is as late as the 18th and 22d ults., and seriously modifies many reports we have heard, some of which have reached the country. According to this information, the rebel forces in Arkansas number and are encamped as follows:

Gen. HINDMAN, at Austin, 25 miles north of Little Rock, with 5,000 men and one battery.

Gen. ROAN, at White Sulphur Springs, near Pine Bluffs, on the Arkansas River, 50 miles southeast of Little Rock, with 5,000 men, two regiments of whom are conscripts, (one unarmed;) also, a Texan regiment, and one battery, consisting of three 6-pounders, (iron,) one 12-pounder, (brass,) and one siege piece mounted.

Gen. McRAE is on the Arkansas River, thirty miles west of Napoleon.

Gen. RAINS is at Cross Hollows with a reported force of from 4,000 to 5,000 men, mostly conscripts.

Gen. HOLMES, Commander-in-chief of all the forces is at Little Rock, with about 2,000 men and two batteries, one of two 12-pounders and three 6-pounders, the other of two rifled 6-pounders and two 12-pounder howitzers.

Gen. McBRIDE is at Batesville with about 2,000 men, only 1,500 of whom are effective.

Most of their cavalry force is dismounted, and at present it is not believed that they have more than 2,300 cavalry in the State.

At Arkadelphia, 80 or 100 miles southwest of Little Rock, the rebels manufacture munitions of war, and have removed there all the State records and papers.

Though the rebel Generals boast of their intention to invade Missouri, it is not believed by intelligent men in their camps that they intend to do so. If they save the capital of their State, it is all they desire at present, and perhaps more than they expect.

THE WAR IN KENTUCKY.

Gen. Morgan's Forces Occupying Frankfort.

LOUISVILLE, Wednesday, Oct. 8.

A reliable report, just received, says that Gen MORGAN'S advance reached Frankfort at 1 o'clock this afternoon, and that 3,000 more of his men are rapidly approaching that place. Our troops had left Frankfort for Lawrenceburgh, Ky.

On Saturday, near Hardensville, SCOTT'S rebel Cavalry cut off and dispersed Co. A Ninth Kentucky Cavalry, under Lieut. MORRIS. The Company has not since been heard from. It is reported that Lieut. MORRIS and two privates were shot after capture by the rebels.

Gen. DUMONT'S Division is still at Shelbyville.

An Exciting March from Louisville to Mount Washington—Skirmishing with the Flying Enemy, &c.

From Our Own Correspondent.

MOUNT WASHINGTON, SEVENTEEN MILES EAST OF LOUISVILLE. Thursday, Oct. 2, 4 o'clock P. M., 1862.

This has been rather a stirring day with our men. We left camp, twelve miles this side of Louisville, at 8 o'clock this morning, the Brigade, commanded by Col. BEATTY, leading the advance. The First Ohio Cavalry and the Fourth Indiana Cavalry went in front. We knew that the rebels, in scouting and skirmishing parties, were all along the route, and that their guerrilla bands infested every hill and hollow. Capt. DRURY'S Third Wisconsin Battery of Parrot guns, preceded us, feeling the way with an occasional shot that made it unpleasant for the rebels. The two regiments—the Ninth Kentucky and Nineteenth Ohio—which had been on picket all night, fell into line one mile from camp, and our whole corps, led by Gen. CRITTENDEN in person, moved forward in splendid order, and with buoyant feelings, anticipating an engagement with the rebels [illegible].

We had proceeded but about two miles when brisk musketry was heard between our advance cavalry and the enemy's pickets. We were now near Floyd's Fork, at which place the rebels were reported in considerable force. Gen. CRITTENDEN rode along the lines of the entire corps, and showed by his looks the highest confidence in his gallant men.

Shortly came the order to keep the ranks closed and to "fire low," in case we met the enemy. The breeze of battle began to snuff quite strongly. A little on ahead we reached a beech grove; a very brief halt was ordered, the canteens were filled with fresh water, and every gun loaded. Here we left the turnpike, turning to the left and ascending an elevated hill that overlooked the valley of Floyd's Fork.

Again the rattle of musketry was heard in front. Then followed the reports of cannon in rapid succession. We galloped to the front, where we found Capt. DRURY, of the Third Wisconsin Battery, with his guns planted upon an eminence that projected into a curve of Floyd's Fork, and commanded the turnpike to our left, and quite an area of country around. Two hundred rebel cavalry, just this side the creek, were making their way in hot haste for the ford, to avoid our advance. Capt. DRURY was pouring his Parrot pills at them in fine style. These rebels were all in their shirt sleeves, but were apparently well mounted. They succeeded in effecting their escape across the river, pursued and harassed by our cavalry. Two of their men were killed by our firing.

Our advance now drew up in line of battle upon the eminence referred to, while the cavalry were sent across the creek to ascertain the position of the flying enemy. Very soon Gen. VAN CLEVE came riding up and ordered us forward. Col. BEATTY, the acting Brigadier of the Eleventh Brigade, which had the advance, had in the meantime inspected our position with a lorgnette, and, with the quick eye of a regular veteran officer, pronounced it admirable. The cavalry on the opposite bank of the creek had sent back for infantry and artillery, and when the order was given it was obeyed with alacrity. We proceeded cautiously, but steadily, down the steep declivity into the bottoms of Floyd's Fork, preceded by DRURY'S Battery, with our cavalry, the First Ohio and Fourth Indiana in advance of it. The turnpike bridge across the creek had been burned by the rebels. It was a two-span wooden structure. The creek, being not much over our shoe-tops, the burning of this bridge was a piece of wantonness and foolery. Our men and artillery turned a little to the right and crossed the creek, making their way through a field of heavy corn without obstruction.

It was reported that the rebels, after leaving the creek in such haste, would make a stand at Mount Washington, and that they would be reinforced at that point. Immediately after crossing the creek, as we ascended the hill, two rebel horses were found lying in the road. One of them was in a dying condition, his nostrils distended, and blood flowing from them copiously. The prints of the rowels of the spur were visible in his sides. The other was quite dead, quantities of blood having come from his nose. They were both evidently run to death.

Just as we had reached the top of the hill, boom came the sound of the rebel cannon in our front. The firing became more rapid, and our men were, in a double-quick, ordered into line of battle. These cannon were fired from Mount Washington, two miles ahead. DRURY'S Battery hurried up the road, unlimbered, and took a position to our right. The guns then let loose upon Mount Washington and High Grove, where the rebels had just been encamped. Hoarsely and loudly they thundered, as the balls and shells went screaming through the air, cutting limbs and tops from the trees. All now was eagerness, and every round we expected a reply from the enemy. They did not reply, however.

Presently we saw a man coming toward us from Mount Washington with a white flag. With Maj. MANDISON we galloped forward to meet him. The bearer proved to be Capt. CHURCH, of Col. BAYLES' Kentucky Cavalry, who being at home at Mount Washington when the rebels came there, had been forced to conceal himself till the sound of our cannon proclaimed his deliverance. We now learned that the rebels had left Mount Washington, as they had done Floyd's Creek, and fallen back toward Salt River. The rebels which have been here and along the road are FORREST'S Cavalry. They number near twelve hundred. The rebels expected to make a stand at this point. All the fences have been torn away to assist in cavalry movements. They had two brass six-pounders, which they withdrew on our approach. So rapid was their flight from this place, that slice bacon was found on their camping ground, and wood gathered for fires which had not been kindled. The rebels are reported as being extremely destitute of clothing and food. The hotels and the citizens here have been entirely stripped of all they had.

The rebels are represented as being in strong force and with a large amount of artillery at Salt River. We are four miles from Salt River, and about eighteen from Bardstown. We push forward in the morning.

P. S.—As I close this, heavy cannonading is going on in the direction of Salt River. We may have hot work in a short time. Two rebel prisoners have just been brought in, captured at Mount Washington.

THE ARMY OF THE POTOMAC

FROM ANTIETAM.

Rebel Demonstrations—Winter Quarters in Prospect—Sentiment of the Army—Impatience of Delay—Visitors at Headquarters—The Order of Gen. Burnside on the Death of Gen. Rodman, &c.

From Our Own Correspondent.

ANTIETAM IRON WORKS, Md., Monday, Oct. 6, 1862.

The rebels made their appearance yesterday, in small force opposite this place, for the evident purpose of—showing themselves. They were mounted, and numbered two hundred or less. As they seemed anxious to attract attention, a section of a Parrot battery was brought up, and a few shells were sent after them across the river. Of course, they made tracks.

The best information that can be derived from Virginia confirms the theory I have already put forth, that the body of the rebel army, which lingered for a time on the south bank of the Potomac, retired up the Valley from the direction of Martinsburgh *over a week ago.* They succeed, however, in keeping up the semblance of a force along the Potomac, for their own purposes. Thus this splendid Fall weather, with its invigorating air and excellent roads inviting to activity, will soon give place to storms and muddy thoroughfares, which will forbid us to move. By the time the Potomac has been swollen by rains, which will secure "My Maryland" against another rebel raid, the roads, by the same natural agencies, will have been rendered impassable. We shall then be ready, I suppose, to go into Winter quarters, where the army will waste away by sickness and inaction, and be ready (?) for active operations *in the Spring.*

There is nothing the soldiers desire so much as to have the war brought to a close. With them *time* is everything. They are tired of the business and want to go home. This is as true of the rebel soldiers as of our own; and with a certain class—not, I hope, by any means the best or largest—every hour's delay makes them more and more indifferent as to *how* the fighting ends, so that it *ends.* Remove the *legal* restraint which holds the army together, and half of them would go home to "see their parents" to-morrow—the other half would vote to send Commissioners to Richmond, or to welcome propositions from the rebels for winding up the struggle—rather than drag through another Winter campaign in the swamps of the Chickahominy, or in any other part of Virginia. But give them the word "Forward," and with the needful leaders and reinforcements, they will not stop until they have chased the rebels into the Gulf.

There is nothing the soldiers so much dread as this eternal delay, and the prospect of an indefinite prolongation of the war. "Let us whip or get whipped, and have an end of it," is the language of every man I meet and talk with on the subject. The officers (who are worth a copper) would say the same thing if they possessed the independence of those in the ranks, and would speak their minds. I mention these things, not willingly, but for the purpose of showing the *temper of the army,* and the absolute necessity of *keeping their energies employed* and *their minds easy.*

New recruits for the old regiments continue to arrive, and twenty-six came, only a day or two since, for the Ninth New-York, (HAWKINS' Zouaves.) The excellent band of this regiment also arrived here a few days since, and has added much to the spirit of this noble young corps.

Those well-known and patriotic citizens, Mr. WM. H. ASPINWALL and Mr. CUTTING, of New-York, are here to-day, the guests of Gen. McCLELLAN. This afternoon the Chaplain of the Ninth New-York, held religious services at Headquarters, the band of the same regiment attending, and adding greatly to the interest and pleasure of the occasion. Several of the members of the late Gen. RENO'S Staff have returned after accompanying homeward the remains and, attending the funeral of their beloved chief. Among them is Capt. NEILL, his Adjutant-General, than whom no one has labored with a more disinterested energy in the prosecution of the war. I am not yet informed as to who will succeed to the command of Gen. RENO'S corps, though the prevailing opinion is, that that excellent soldier and gentleman, Gen. PARKE, now chief of Gen. BURNSIDE'S Staff, will be the man.

I send, herewith, a general order touching the death of Brig.-Gen. RODMAN, of Rhode Island. The truth, as well as the beauty of the tribute paid to him, will be appreciated by every one who knew the man.

I send, also, a few other names of those who have died in the Keedysville hospitals. E. S.

HEADQUARTERS NINTH ARMY CORPS, ANTIETAM, Md., Oct. 5, 1862.

GENERAL ORDERS, No. 18.—The Commanding-General announces to the Third Division the death of their late Commander, Brig.-Gen. RODMAN, caused by a wound received at the battle of Antietam.

One of the first to leave his home at his country's call, Gen. RODMAN, in his constant and unwearied service, now ended by his untimely death, has left a bright record of earnest patriotism undimmed by one thought of self.

Respected and esteemed in the various relations of his life, the army mourns his loss as a pure-hearted patriot and a brave devoted soldier, and his division will miss a gallant leader who was always foremost at the post of danger.

By command of Major-Gen. BURNSIDE.
(Signed,) LEWIS RICHMOND, Lieut.-Col. and Asst. Adjt.-Gen.

DEATHS IN THE KEEDYSVILLE HOSPITALS.

Dr. STONOW reports the following deaths in the hospitals under his charge up to Oct. 3:

BRICK-STORE HOSPITAL.

David Perkins, Co. H, Fourth Pennsylvania Reserves, of erysipelas, after amputation of leg, Oct. 2.

Corp. Wm. T. Cosman, Co. F, Ninth New-York State Militia, of pyæmia, Oct. 2.

Henry Allyn, Co. H, Second Wisconsin Volunteers, of pyæmia, Oct. 2.

BROWN-STONE HOSPITAL.

Charles W. Crawford, Co. A, One Hundred and Fourth Pennsylvania Volunteers, died after amputation of leg, Oct. 2.

DOUBLE-BRICK HOSPITAL.

Walter Rourke, Co. I. Ninety-seventh New-York Volunteers, gunshot wound of chest, involving subclavian artery, received 17th, died of exhaustion Oct. 3.

LIST OF WOUNDED CONFEDERATE OFFICERS CAPTURED AT ANTIETAM.

Second Lieut. W. J. Muse, Co. I, 1st Tennessee—thigh.
Second Lieut. J. J. Kimbrough, Co. I, 6th Ala.
Adjutant J. W. Rentz, 13th Ala.
First Lieut. W. M. Hardwick, 48th Ala.—foot.
First Lieut. T. P. Samford, Co. M, 1st Texas—back and leg.
First Lieut. A. J. McKean, Co. A, 4th Texas.
Second Lieut. J. M. Alexander, Co. K, 5th Texas.
Third Lieut. J. P. Drake, Co. I, 5th Texas.
Capt. E. M. Morrison, Co. C, 15th Virginia—arm amputated.
First Lieut. G. P. How, Co. I, 15th Va.—shoulder, severe.
Second Lieut. G. W. Berry, Co. H, 15th Va.—leg amputated.
Lieut. James Anderson, Co. G, 30th Va.—died.
Third Lieut. J. N. Hume, Co. B, 37th Va.—arm.
Col. John E. Penn, 42d Va.—thigh amputated.
Third Lieut. J. V. Shelton, Co. E, 13th Mississippi—thigh.
First Lieut. C. H. Wilson, Co. F, 16th Mississippi—thigh amputated.
First Lieut. T. J. Williams, Co. K, 17th Mississippi—thigh.
First Lieut. J. McNutt, Co. C, 17th Mississippi—thigh amputated.
Second Lieut. J. M. James, Co. B, 17th Mississippi—chest.
First Lieut. W. B. Stinson, Co. —, 18th Miss.—hip.
Capt. J. Howard, Co. B, 2d North Carolina—shoulder and thigh.
Second Lieut. R. L. Withrington, Co. F, 2d North Carolina—head and foot.
Lieut. W. Quince, Co. —, 3d North Carolina—brought in on litter dead.
Second Lieut. W. A. Threadgill, Co. C, 14th N. C.
Lieut. H. H. West, Co. H, 20th N. C.—shoulder.
First Lieut. J. Y. Whitted, Co. G, 27th N. C.
Lieut. James H. McBride, Co. —, — Louisiana—head, shell, died.
Second Lieut. M. V. B. Swan, Co. B, 2d Louisiana—shoulder and breast.
Col. J. M. Williams, 2d Louisiana—lung.
Lieut. R. H. Slaughter, Co. F, 8th Louisiana.
Second Lieut. Wm. E. Cooke, Co. A, 8th Louisiana—thigh and leg—tetanus.
Capt. V. St. Martin, Co. K, 8th La.—both thighs.
Lieut. Arnge Bozier, Co. —, 9th Louisiana.
Capt. C. B. Marmillion, Co. G, 10th La.—thigh.
First Lieut. Chas. Knowlton, Co. B, 10th Louisiana.
Lieut. S. Herrero, Co. G, 10th Louisiana.
Capt. M. D. Robinson, Co. —, 13th Alabama.
Capt. W. P. Harper, Co. H, 7th La.—abdomen.
First Lieut. A. E. Knox, Co. H, 7th Louisiana—fracture lower jaw.
Lieut. —— Chandler, Co. —, 48th Virginia—died.
G. W. Chadbourne, 9th Louisiana—neck, died.
Lieut. J. B. Blackman, Co. H, 12th South Carolina—left thigh amputated.
Total .... 42.

THE ARMY OF VIRGINIA.

IN FRONT OF WASHINGTON.

Rumors from Rebel Sources—A Deserter's Story—What a Scout Reports, &c., &c.

From Our Own Correspondent.

FAIRFAX C. H., Tuesday, Oct. 7, 1862.

Yesterday and to-day the camp has been fairly alive with rumors—principally from rebel sources, however—some of which, if true, are important, but, for the most part, are only interesting because new. Instead of obtaining our information from reliable contrabands and reliable gentlemen, as has been usually the case, we now have a flood of information from rebel deserters, rebel prisoners and conscripts. Some of their stories agree in important particulars, but for the most part they are as wide apart as truth and falsehood.

First, we had yesterday come into our lines Lieut. ROBERTS, of Mississippi, whose statement was to the effect, that he had had a quarrel with the Major of his regiment and shot him. Rather than be served the same way himself, by order of a drum-head Court-martial, he made tracks for our lines, and is now beyond rebel rule. According to his story, the whole rebel army is in a very demoralized condition, and, to keep the men from deserting, requires an immense rear guard on every march and at every camping place; notwithstanding all these precautions, however, a large number of soldiers manage to escape every day. In confirmation of a portion of his statement, the fact should be mentioned, that rebel soldiers, who profess to be deserters, come into our lines daily. He alleges that LEE exercises the most despotic rule over his command, and predicts that if the Government forces make no further demonstrations, the rebel army cannot not be kept together another year. This Lieut. ROBERTS is a smart, shrewd fellow, and will bear watching.

By the kindness of Lieut.-Col. ROBINSON, Provost-Marshal, I have had an interview with a rebel deserter who gave himself up to one of our pickets yesterday. His statement, as taken from his own lips, is as follows: "My name is HENRY LOGAN. I was born in Ohio, and joined the rebel army at New-Orleans, in April, 1861, and was transferred to the Second Virginia Cavalry (from which corps he deserted) in June, 1861. The Second Virginia Cavalry is commanded by Col. STEWART, the brigade is commanded by Gen. MUMFORD, and is now stationed between Warrenton and the Springs. The brigade moved from Leetown one week ago last Sunday, and arrived at Berryville (Clarke County) same day. On Monday it moved to Leesburgh; on Tuesday, to within four miles of Aldie. At this point I left the regiment, to wait upon a brother who was wounded at Manassas. He died last Saturday evening. I then left Aldie for the National lines on Monday, Oct. 6, at 9 o'clock A. M. There are from 30 to 40 wounded men at Aldie.

MUMFORD'S Brigade has from 900 to 1,000 men. There are three divisions of rebel troops at Culpepper Court-house, commanded by Gen. GUSTAVUS SMITH, Gen. HARLAN, (I think,) and the other division commander I don't know. Two of these divisions are composed of new troops, who have never been in action. The corps is commanded by Gen. Jo. JOHNSON. I heard Gen. MUMFORD say that Gen. Jo. JOHNSON had been ordered to take command of the Department of the West, to supersede BRAGG, who has been relieved from duty.

I saw a young man from Richmond on Saturday who says there is a large rebel force at Gordonsville. I was with the rebel army in Maryland, and heard the officers say that their loss was 16,000 in killed, wounded and missing—4,000 being deserters; that the army was then reinforced by 800 cavalry and 2,000 infantry, 600 of whom were from Pennsylvania. I understood that LEE has 180,000 men under his command at Winchester and vicinity, and reinforcements are constantly going forward, and the old regiments are being filled up by conscripts. At the battle of Manassas the officers admitted they were whipped on Friday. I acted as Orderly for Gen. LONGSTREET at the battle of Antietam."

A captured rebel soldier—a smart and intelligent fellow, and a rebel all over—was brought in yesterday. He reports that one brigade of Jo. JOHNSON'S command is at Warrenton Junction, and that the whole of JOHNSON'S force is gradually moving across the Rappahannock. The bridge at Rappahannock Station has been repaired and rebel trains now pass over the road daily, between Bristol and Culpepper.

RETURN OF A SCOUT.

A scout who has been absent several days, returned yesterday. He had been within a few miles of Culpepper, but saw no large force of the enemy at any one point. He believes there is yet a large force of rebels at Culpepper. The conscript law is everywhere being enforced, and citizens are daily leaving their homes for some place of concealment, to avoid being forced into the rebel service.

Saturday morning a force of rebel cavalry attacked one of our pickets near Centreville. Several shots were exchanged, wounding two of our men, when the rebels took their departure. The rebel pickets are now within 16 miles of Centreville. These night attacks have become so frequent of late, that our picket force has been enlarged at every point.

Five hundred rebel prisoners, recently captured near Centreville, were paroled to-day. Not less than 2,000 rebel soldiers have been captured by Gen. STAHL'S command within the last eight days.

A reconnoissance in force is being made to-day, and doubtless by to-morrow we shall have another large batch of rebel prisoners.

The rebels are beginning to return deserters from our army, doubtless in the hope of inducing the Government to reciprocate the favor, and thereby deter men from deserting the rebel cause. In one lot of paroled soldiers sent into the Union lines, there were forty marked as men who had come into the rebel lines as deserters.

Gov. ANDREWS, of Massachusetts, with a party of friends, reached here this morning. I have not been able to ascertain the special object of this visit just at this time. P.

NEWS FROM FORTRESS MONROE

Advices by Flag of Truce from Richmond.

Postponement of the Adjournment of the Rebel Congress.

Rumors of a Fight at St. John's River, Florida.

FORTRESS MONROE, Tuesday, Oct. 7.

The steamboat *John A. Warner* (flag of truce) returned from Aiken's Landing to-day, arriving at Fortress Monroe at 1 o'clock. She brings down none of our prisoners in charge for the State prisoners sent up. I learn from Major R. W. BOSTWICK, of the One Hundred and Thirty-fifth Pennsylvania Volunteers, officer in charge, that the Commissioner, Major OULD, of the Confederate Government, refused to exchange the prisoners of State belonging to Virginia, on the ground that they were taken on territory belonging to the Confederacy.

The Richmond *Examiner* of Oct. 6 contains the Military Exemption Act, passed Oct. 4, 1862, which exempts police for sections of country having dense negro population; secures the liberty of the Press by exempting editors and such help as they require in their business; exempts employes of transportation and telegraph companies; ministers of the Gospel; physicians; shoemakers; tanners; blacksmiths; wagon-makers; millers; superintendents and employes in hospitals, and wool, cotton and paper mills; employes on Government works; overseers of plantations, and one man to every five hundred head of cattle. The Exemption Act passed April 21 is repealed.

The *Examiner* says: "Congress has serious business on its hands at present. The subject of revenue and finance is now before Congress. The bill provides that every citizen give to the Government one-fifth of his gross income, and receive in acknowledgement eight per cent. bonds. "Of all laws eight per cent. is the worst; of all taxes twenty per cent. on gross income is the most oppressive. By this project Congress strikes a heavier blow at our credit thrn the public enemy. The Government has committed financial blunders enough to ruin its credit if the confidence of the public were not so well supported."

Congress has postponed adjournment till Oct. 13.

PATRICK McGOWAN and JOHN KILLAHER were shot at Camp Lee, on Saturday last, for desertion. OWEN McGUIRE received fifty lashes for the same offence.

The *Examiner* has also a dispatch, dated Savannah, 4th, which says the Federals attacked our batteries on St. Johns, on the 1st, and after an hour's engagement were repulsed.

The Nationals subsequently landed at Greenville Point in force, and marched a mile to the rear of our battery, where a fight commenced at 10 o'clock A. M. No particulars received.

The Episcopal Convention.

IMPOSING PENITENTIAL SERVICES AT TRINITY CHAPEL.

The session of the Episcopal Convention, which met in St. John's Chapel, as usual, at 9 o'clock A. M., yesterday, was very brief, all interest centering upon the services in token of fasting, humiliation and prayer, for which the day was set apart by the House of Bishops.

At 11 A. M., the hour fixed for morning service, Trinity Chapel was thronged, the Bishops and clergy, with other members of the Convention, occupying the ranges of pews along the middle aisle.

In accordance with the special occasion, the 130th Psalm, *De Profundis Clamavi,* was chaunted instead of the *Venite Exultemus.* The lessons were the 40th chapter of Isaiah and the 9th of St. Luke, commencing with the 20th verse. The reading of the Litany on the theme "unity, peace and concord" was extended with the words "and especially into this nation now afflicted by civil war." After the special prayers the Choir sang the 32d Psalm:

"Thy chastening wrath, oh! Lord restrain."

The Epistle and Gospel appropriate for Ash Wednesday followed, and the Eightieth Hymn, "Almighty God, before thy throne," was chaunted.

Right Rev. Bishops McCROSKY, of Michigan, HOPKINS, of Vermont, McILVAINE, of Ohio, WHITTINGHAM, of Maryland, KEMPER, of Wisconsin, and SMITH, of Kentucky, conducted the services, which were in the highest degree imposing, although the music was stripped of superfluous ornament, and subdued to an extent befitting the penitential character of the occasion.

After an Offertory and a *Benedictus* by Bishop HOPKINS, the congregation retired from the chapel.

Capt. Duffy against Fernando Wood for Congress.

NEW-YORK, Oct. 7, 1862.

HON. FERNANDO WOOD—*Dear Sir:* I have been informed by parties whose word in the matter I consider entirely reliable, that, at a recent meeting of prominent political leaders like yourself, who met for the purpose of healing the difficulties of the Democratic Party, in a manner satisfactory to themselves only, a meeting very numerously attended, the proceedings and dicta of which may exercise this community to some extent, you, on your own responsibility, made the statement, substantially, that I had told you personally that I had withdrawn from the contest, or that I was not a candidate, for the position of representative of the Fifth Congressional District in this City.

If you stated that I had withdrawn from the contest, you stated a falsehood—a malicious, unblushing falsehood.

If you stated that I told you that I had withdrawn from the contest, or any words to that effect, you stated a falsehood—a malicious, unblushing falsehood.

If you stated that I had informed you that was I not a candidate for the position of Representative of the Fifth Congressional District, in the City of New-York, or words to that effect, you stated a falsehood—a malicious, unblushing falsehood.

If it be possible that you can have the audacity to leave the District in which you reside, and with the intention of foisting yourself on this constituency as a candidate for Congress, to enter this District, to represent citizens whose fidelity to the Union has been sealed with blood on every battle-field during the present struggle, while you were fulminating treason and secession, and covertly and cowardly aiding, abetting and comforting the enemies of our country—if the loyal people of this District submit to the yoke which a self-convicted demagogical traitor imposes on them in his own election to one of the most important offices in the nation—if they be content, by electing such a man as you to embarrass the Administration in its efforts to preserve the Union—then all the blood that has been shed has been shed in vain.

Now, Sir, know you what you knew before, that I am a candidate for the position of Representative of the Fifth Congressional District in the City of New-York. Very respectfully,
CAPT. JOHN DUFFY.

Municipal Election in Baltimore.

BALTIMORE, Wednesday, Oct. 8.

The unconditional Union candidate for Mayor JOHN LEE CHAPMAN, was elected to-day, by a majority of 7,694 over FREDERICK FICKY, Independent.

BALTIMORE, Wednesday, Oct. 8—P. M.

The city election passed off very quietly. A very small vote was polled. CHAPMAN, the regular Union candidate, received 8,877 votes, and FICKEY, Independent Union, received 1,183. The entire regular council ticket was elected, except in one instance.

The Michigan Democratic State Convention.

DETROIT, Wednesday, Oct. 8.

The Democratic State Convention which met in this city to-day, adopted the nominees of the Union Convention, held at Jackson on the 2d inst., as candidates for State offices.

IMPORTANT FROM THE GULF.

Preparations for an Attack on Galveston.

The United States bark *A. Houghton,* NEWELL GRAHAM, Acting Master, commanding, arrived yesterday from Pensacola, after a passage of 18 days. She brings home invalids from the Western Gulf Squadron.

At Pensacola all was quiet, and the health of the troops good. A part of the mortar fleet sailed for Galveston on Sept. 16, and the remainder with the gunboats were to sail the next day to make a combined attack upon Galveston.

LIST OF OFFICERS.

Newell Graham, Acting Master, commanding.
W. C. Hornford, Executive officer.
George B. Clifton, Acting Master's Mate.
James Treadwell, Acting Master's Mate.
C. C. Walden, Paymaster of the United States steamer *Westfield,* attached temporarily.

Drafts on the Canal Department Protested.

A QUARREL BETWEEN TREASURER LEWIS AND AUDITOR BENTON.

ALBANY, Wednesday, Oct. 8.

Several drafts on the Canal Department of the State Government have within the past few days, been protested for non-payment.

The difficulty arises from a quarrel between State Treasurer LEWIS and Auditor BENTON. The Auditor claims the right, in drawing a warrant on the Treasurer, to specify on what bank the Treasurer shall draw his check. The Treasurer refuses to recognize the right of the Auditor to make such directions. He therefore draws checks on such banks having canal deposits as he deems proper. When these checks are not drawn on banks specified in his warrant, the Auditor refuses to countersign them, and hence the protest of drafts.

An application was made by the Auditor to remove the State Treasurer, but the Governor is understood to have refused to interfere.

Since Gov. MORGAN'S absence from the city an effort has been made to induce Lieut.-Gov. CAMPBELL to exercise the functions of Governor, and suspend Treasurer LEWIS, but without success.

Treasurer LEWIS remains firm in his determination to resist the claim of Auditor BENTON to control the canal deposits.

Massachusetts Democratic State Convention.

BOSTON, Wednesday, Oct. 8.

The Democratic State Convention, held at Worcester to-day, was fully attended. EDWIN C. BAILEY, of the Boston *Herald,* presided. A motion to adopt the People's ticket, nominated at the Faneuil Hall Convention, was discussed with considerable warmth.

Resolutions were read, pledging support in the use of all legitimate means to suppress the rebellion, urging the President to stand by the Constitution; repudiating the meeting of Governors; eulogizing Gen. McCLELLAN; sympathizing with the families and friends of those who have fallen; that the province of the Goverement is to save the Union, and not to save or destroy Slavery;—That we are opposed alike to secession and abolitionism and there can be no permanent Union where these exist; tendering sympathy to the loyal men in the border States; recommending making no nominations, but expressing a willingness to unite with conservative men of all parties; regretting that the President, forgetful of his obligations, has issued his Emancipation Proclamation, and protesting against it and against the suspension of the writ of *habeas corpus,* and calling on the President to restore the trial by jury, giving freedom of speech and the Press.

Judge WELLS moved to amend, by recommending the adoption of the Faneuil Hall ticket.

The Convention adjourned amid great confusion and without clearly leaving any record of its action.

Great Trotting Match on Fashion Course, for $2,000.

The great trotting match, mile heats, best 3 in 5, for $2,000, between SIMMONS' Hambletonian brown stallion, to sulky, and the black gelding *Gen. Butler,* to saddle, took place yesterday, on the Fashion Course. There were, probably, between 3,000 and 4,000 persons present, a large number of whom—including many ladies—occupied the new stand and windows and lawn of the Mansion House. The horses started from the old stand, which was well filled. The capability of *Gen. Butler* for making such fast time as in the present race, was an entire secret from all those not immediately interested in him.

The betting was in favor of the Hambletonian, at 100 to 40, and found plenty of takers among the friends of the gelding, who were in a decided majority on the course, and very demonstrative in expressing their opinion of the merits of their favorite.

Previous to the start, which did not take place till nearly 4 o'clock, the horses trotted over the course several times, and both looked in splendid condition. The brown horse was driven by HORACE F. JONES, and was accompanied in his trial trots by *Old Rube,* a celebrated four-mile racer, in whose company he has been wont to take his breathings. *Butler* was mounted by the Boston driver, DAN MACE. JONES had the inside.

First Heat—MACE commenced the worrying game for the first three attempts. JONES pulled up on the fourth, and the word was given on the fifth, with *Butler* a length in advance, who took the track and entered the turn two lengths ahead, increasing it to four lengths at the quarter pole, which was passed in 35 seconds, and the half mile in 1:10. Increasing his lead on the last turn, the stallion reducing the gap by a fine burst of speed down the home stretch; *Butler* passing the Judges' stand only two lengths in advance, in 2 minutes 21½ seconds.

Second Heat—The brown horse led by half a length, but *Butler* led him two lengths, in going around the turn, HORACE lapping him at the quarter pole in 35 seconds, and leading him by half a length at the half mile again in 1 min. 10 sec. Just as they reached the new stand *Butler* hopelessly broke up, and JONES came over the score, an easy winner, in 2 min. 24¾ sec.

Third Heat—An even start, and *Butler* led by half a length at the ¼ pole, in 36 seconds, increased it to two lengths at the half mile, in 1:11. *Horace* reduced the daylight by a length at the new stand, and ran lapped round the turn and down the homestretch, amidst the utmost excitement—*Butler* winning by a head only, in 2:23.

Fourth Heat—*Butler* led by a length, and came over the score by only half a neck in 2:27. Mutual recriminations took place, JONES saying that MACE run his horse 100 yards on the back-stretch, and MACE claiming that although he broke up, he did not gain by it, and that JONES had lashed him with his whip. The judges having examined the persons sent round the track, announced that they all agreed that there was nothing but fair and square trotting by both horses, and therefore *Butler* had won the heat and race.

RECAPITULATION.

Gen. Butler	1	2	1	1
Simmons' Brown Stallion	2	1	2	2

Time—2:21½; 2:24¾; 2:23; 2:27.

It is now likely that SIMMONS' horse and *Patchen* will be matched for a trot during the present season.

Terrific Fire at Oil Creek.

OIL CITY, Penn., Wednesday, Oct. 8—9 P. M.

A terrific fire in the oil wells at Oil Creek, on BLOOD & TAR'S farms, is now raging. Several refineries and 30,000 barrels of oil have been burned, besides a great many buildings. The fire extended over half a mile. Loss from $100,000 to $200,000.

Damage to the Port Dalhousie Light-House.

TORONTO, C. W., Wednesday, Oct. 8.

The light-house at Port Dalhousie took fire this morning, and is so badly damaged that it cannot be used for the present.

TO THE FIFTEENTH WARD REPUBLICAN AND UNION ELECTORS.—The Union and Republican voters of the Fifteenth Ward are particularly requested to be on hand at the meeting to be held this evening, at Wright's, corner of Eighth-street and Broadway, at 7½ o'clock, to protect their rights, and see that the Ward is *fairly* represented in the Nominating Committees then to be chosen, and how a primary election is conducted.
GEO. W. BLUNT.
ORISON BLUNT.
JOHN T. DENNY.

MR. GOTTSCHALK'S CONCERTS.—This evening Mr. GOTTSCHALK gives his last concert at Irving Hall, previous to his departure for the Eastern States. Mr. GOTTSCHALK will be assisted by Mrs. JENNY KEMPTON, Mr. HARRY SANDERSON, Mr. J. R. THOMAS, Mr. H. C. TIMM, and Mr. THEODORE THOMAS.

Ambrose E. Burnside, Commander of the Army of the Potomac, November, 1862, to January, 1863

General McClellan surrendering the command of the Army of the Potomac to General Burnside

President Lincoln at McClellan's headquarters at Antietam after the battle. McClellan stands fourth on the left of the President. October, 1862

The New-York Times.

VOL. XII—NO. 3473. NEW-YORK, MONDAY, NOVEMBER 10, 1862. PRICE TWO CENTS.

IMPORTANT NEWS.

Gen. McClellan Relieved of the Command of the Army of the Potomac.

Gen. Burnside Appointed in his Place.

The Order of Displacement Delivered on Friday Night.

A FAREWELL ADDRESS TO THE SOLDIERS

General McClellan on his way to Trenton, N. J.

How the News was Received in Washington.

HEADQUARTERS OF THE ARMY OF THE POTOMAC, SALEM, Va., Saturday, Nov. 8—12 o'clock, noon.

The order relieving Major-Gen. McCLELLAN from the command of the army of the Potomac was received at headquarters at 11 o'clock last night. It was entirely unexpected to all, and therefore every one was taken by surprise.

On its receipt, the command was immediately turned over to Gen. BURNSIDE.

Gen. McCLELLAN and his Staff will leave to-morrow for Trenton, where he is ordered to report.

The order was delivered to him by Gen. BUCKINGHAM, in person.

His last official act was the issuing of an address to his soldiers, informing them in a few words that the command had devolved on Gen. BURNSIDE, and taking an affectionate leave of them.

THE NEWS IN WASHINGTON.

Special Dispatch to the New-York Times.

WASHINGTON, Sunday, Nov. 9.

The removal of Gen. McCLELLAN, and the significant fact of his being ordered to report to his family at Trenton, have produced some excitement here to-day. At the hotels, crowds have been discussing the subject, and occasionally the feelings of some have found expression in language disrespectful to the President and disloyal the Government. The truly loyal and more sensible of Gen. McCLELLAN's friends, however, whilst they regret his removal, acquiesce ie the action of the President, as the friends and admirers of other Generals have done on like occasions. It is certain that Mr. LINCOLN never performed a duty which gave him so much pain as did the removal of McCLELLAN just at this time; but facts recently presentod in an official shape by the General-in-Chief made it clear to the President that he had but one course to pursue, and when these facts are given to the public, as they will be soon, all true supporters of the Government will not hesitate to concede the wisdom of the act, whilst those who are blinded by prejudice, and those animated by a spirit of disloyalty, will, of course, seize this occasion as an opportunity for renewing their expressions of hostility to the Administration

A few gentlemen, wearing shoulder straps, have been rendering themselves to-day, fit subjects for the Old Capitol Prison, by talking loudly against the act of relieving McCLELLAN of his command. A Lieutenant-Colonel said publicly, to-night, that if by fighting another hour he could put down the rebellion, he would not do so.

It is understood that Judge HOLT has written a long letter to a gentleman of your City, strongly condemnatory of Gen. McCLELLAN's course, which it is said will be made public.

Dispatch to the Associated Press.

WASHINGTON, Sunday, Nov. 9.

The first information the public received of the relief of Gen. McCLELLAN from the command of the Army of the Potomac, was through the telegram published this morning. It affords a general theme of conversation and comment, and excites surprise, the event occurring unexpectedly. The cause of the Executive action in the premises does not appear to be known outside of official circles, and hence the absence of facts gives rise to conflicting speculations.

Gen. McCLELLAN, it is said, passed through Washington to-day, on his way to Trenton.

THE ELEVATION OF BURNSIDE.

REJOICING IN PROVIDENCE.

PROVIDENCE, Sunday, Nov. 9.

By order of Gov. SPRAGUE, a salute of 100 guns is to be fired here to-morrow noon, in honor of the appointment of the Rhode Island-General, BURNSIDE, to the command of the Army of the Potomac.

THE NEWS IN PHILADELPHIA.

PHILADELPHIA, Sunday, Nov. 9.

The removal of Gen. McCLELLAN has caused much excitement throughout the city, and is the universal topic of conversation. Among the rumors as to the cause, it is said that some instructions from the General-in-Chief were not followed, and that the escape of LEE followed as a consequence.

FORNEY's *Press* of to-morrow, in speaking of the removal, says:

It was purely a military act, and was the result of a military consultation and decision, although recommended to the President and approved by him some time ago. It was only finally resolved upon after the change became inevitable. No act of the present Administration, we might say no Executive act since the beginning of the Government, has been the subject of more careful deliberation.

GENERAL McCLELLAN.

Letter from Gen. Halleck to the Secretary of War Concerning Gen. McClellan's Complaints of Lack of Supplies.

HEADQUARTERS OF THE ARMY, WASHINGTON, Oct. 28, 1862.

HON. E. M. STANTON, Secretary of War—*Sir:* In reply to the general interrogatories contained in your letter of yesterday, I have to report:

First—That requisitions for supplies to the army under Gen. McCLELLAN are made by his Staff officers on the Chiefs of Bureaus here; that is, for Quartermaster's supplies by his Chief Quartermaster on the Quartermaster-General; for commissary supplies by his Chief Commissary on the Commissary-General, &c. No such requisitions have been to my knowledge made upon the Secretary of War, and none upon the General-in-Chief.

Second—On several occasions Gen. McCLELLAN has telegraphed to me that his army was deficient in certain supplies. All these telegrams were immediately referred to the heads of Bureaus with orders to report.

It was ascertained that in every instance the requisitions had been immediately filled, except one, where the Quartermaster-General had been obliged to send from Philadelphia certain articles of clothing, tents, &c., not having a full supply here. There has not been, so far as I could ascertain, any neglect or delay in any Department or Bureau, in issuing all supplies asked for by Gen. McCLELLAN or by the officers of his Staff. Delays have occasionally occurred in forwarding supplies by rail, on account of the crowded condition of the dépôts or of a want of cars; but, whenever notified of this, agents have been sent out to remove the difficulty. Under the excellent superintendence of Gen. HAUPT, I think these delays have been less frequent and of shorter duration than is usual with freight trains. An army of the size of that under Gen. McCLELLAN will frequently be for some days without the supplies asked for, on account of neglect in making timely requisitions, and unavoidable delays in forwarding them, and in distributing them to the different brigades and regiments. From all the information I can obtain, I am of opinion that the requisitions from that army have been filled more promptly, and that the men, as a general rule, have been better supplied than our armies operating in the West. The latter have operated at much greater distances from the sources of supply, and have had far less facilities of transportation. In fine, I believe that no armies in the world, while in campaign, have been more promptly or better supplied than ours.

Third—Soon after the battle of Antietam, Gen. McCLELLAN was urged to give me information of his intended movements, in order that, if he moved between the enemy and Washington, reinforcements could be sent from this place. On the 1st of October, finding that he purposed to operate from Harper's Ferry, I urged him to cross the river at once and give battle to the enemy, pointing out to him the disadvantages of delaying till the Autumn rains had swollen the Potomac and impaired the roads. On the 6th of October he was peremptorily ordered to "cross the Potomac and give battle to the enemy, or drive him south. Your army *must* move now while the roads are good." It will be observed that three weeks have elapsed since this order was given.

Fourth—In my opinion, there has been no such want of supplies in the army under Gen. McCLELLAN as to prevent his compliance with the orders to advance against the enemy. Had he moved to the south side of the Potomac, he could have received his supplies almost as readily as by remaining inactive on the north.

Fifth—On the 7th of October, in a telegram in regard to his intended movements, Gen. McCLELLAN stated that it would require at least three days to supply the First, Fifth and Sixth Corps; that they needed shoes and other indispensable articles of clothing, as well as shelter tents. No complaint was made that any requisitions had not been filled, and it was inferred from his language that he was only waiting for the distribution of his supplies. On the 11th, he telegraphed that a portion of his supplies, sent by rail, had been delayed. As already stated, agents were immediately sent from here to investigate this complaint, and they reported that everything had gone forward. On the same date (the 11th) he spoke of many of his horses being broken down by fatigue. On the 12th he complained that the rate of supply was only "150 horses per week for the entire army there and in front of Washington." I immediately directed the Quartermaster-General to inquire into this matter and report why a larger supply was not furnished. Gen. MEIGS reported on the 14th, that the average issue of horses to Gen. McCLELLAN's army in the field and in front of Washington, for the previous six weeks, had been 1,459, per week, or 8,754 in all. In addition, that large numbers of mules had been supplied, and that the number of animals with Gen. McCLELLAN's army on the Upper Potomac was over thirty-one thousand. He also reported that he was then sending to that army all the horses he could procure.

On the 18th, Gen. McCLELLAN stated in regard to Gen. MEIGS' report that he had filled every requisition for shoes and clothing: "Gen. MEIGS may have ordered these articles to be forwarded, but they have not reached our dépôts; and unless greater effort to insure prompt transmission is made by the Department of which Gen. MEIGS is the head, they might as well remain in New-York or Philadelphia, so far as this army is concerned." I immediately called Gen. MEIGS' attention to this apparent neglect of his Department. On the 25th he reported as the result of his investigation, that 48,000 pairs of boots and shoes had been received by the Quartermaster of Gen. McCLELLAN's army at Harper's Ferry, Frederick and Hagerstown; that 20,000 pairs were at Harper's Ferry dépôt on the 21st; that 10,000 more were on their way, and 15,000 more ordered. Col. INGALS, Aid-de-Camp and Chief Quartermaster to Gen. McCLELLAN, telegraphed on the 25th: "The suffering for want of clothing is exaggerated, I think, and certainly might have been avoided by timely requisitions of regimental and brigade commanders." On the 24th he telegraphed to the Quartermaster-General that the clothing was not detained in cars at the dépôts. "Such complaints are groundless. The fact is, the clothing arrives and is issued, but more is still wanted. I have ordered more than would seem necessary from any data furnished me, and I beg to remind you that you have always very promptly met all my requisitions so far as clothing is concerned. Our dépôt is not at fault. It provides as soon as due notice is given. I foresee no time when an army of over one hundred thousand men will not call for clothing and other articles."

In regard to Gen. McCLELLAN's means of promptly communicating the wants of his army to me or to the proper Bureaus of the War Department, I report that in addition to the ordinary mails, he has been in hourly communication with Washington by telegraph.

It is due to Gen. MEIGS that I should submit herewith a copy of a telegram received by him from Gen. McCLELLAN. Very respectfully, your obedient servant,

H. W. HALLECK, General-in-Chief.

UNITED STATES MILITARY TELEGRAPH.

(Received Oct. 22, 1862—9:40 P. M.)

FROM McCLELLAN'S HEADQUARTERS.

To Brig.-Gen. Meigs:

Your dispatch of this date is received. I have never intended in any letter or dispatch to make any accusation against yourself, or your department, for not furnishing or forwarding clothing as rapidly as it was possible for you to do. I believe that everything has been done that could be done in this respect. The idea that I have tried to convey was, that certain portions of the command were without clothing, and the army could not move until it was supplied.

(Signed.) G. B. M'CLELLAN, M. G.

ARMY OPERATIONS IN VIRGINIA.

Stuart Again Defeated by Gen. Pleasanton.

Three Pieces of Artillery and Several Officers Captured.

The Bridge Across the Rappahannock Held by Gen. Bayard.

THE STRUCTURE UNINJURED.

Details of Recent Skirmishes During the Advance.

HEADQUARTERS, WARRENTON, Sunday, Nov. 9.

Gen. PLEASANTON yesterday, in a skirmish with STUART, near Little Washington, captured three pieces of artillery, also a Captain, Lieutenant and five privates. No loss has been reported.

Gen. Bayard yesterday occupied and now holds the railroad bridge across the Rappahannock. The bridge is not injured.

The bridge across Broad River has been destroyed.

There is nothing new up to this writing from the front at the Rappahannock.

The weather is clear and cold.

OUR CORRESPONDENCE FROM THE ADVANCE.

LETTER FROM THE EXTREME FRONT.

FORTY-FIVE MILES FROM THE POTOMAC, AND FIVE BEYOND MARKHAM, Wednesday Evening, Nov. 5, 1862.

The Grand Army moves with lightning speed. Such rapid marching as we have performed during the past four days is truly wonderful, and indicates a zeal and vigor on the part of our generals hitherto unknown.

My last letter to you left Gen. PLEASANTON at Uniontown, Sunday noon, driving STUART's Cavalry before him. Soon after they received reinforcements, but to no purpose. Our cavalry and artillery continued pushing them back, until they reached their infantry force at Upperville, a little village, situated on the direct turnpike from Winchester to Alexandria. Yet there was no rest for the wicked. National guns continued their shower of shot and shell, and cavalry and infantry alike skedaddled. The former took the road leading in a southwesterly direction to Piedmont, a small station situated on the Manassas Gap Railroad. Our cavalry still pursued them, shelling them from every new position they occupied. They continued their flight toward Markham, another small station, five miles in the direction of the Gap. A spirited engagement took place here yesterday afternoon, resulting in the death of sixteen rebels and the wounding of several of our own men. In about the centre of the village, where the road turns, is a hill with a gradual ascent. Behind this the rebels planted two of their guns, intending to open on our men as they came up. Pickets were thrown out in order to make known our approach. The Lieutenant who was stationing them presented a conspicuous mark, and four balls, shot from the distance of one hundred and fifty yards, tumbled him dead from the saddle. He lies buried by the wayside.

No sooner had the position of the rebel guns become known, than it was determined to storm them. Lieuts. ASH and HASTINGS, of the Fifth Regulars, with half a squadron of men, dashed forward on the hazardous undertaking. Steadily they galloped onward through the fields, turning neither to the right or left, and had nearly reached the coveted prize, when suddenly a high stone fence presented an insurmountable barrier to their further advance. The bold movement, however, alarmed the rebels, and the guns were moved on to another position. Here we were more successful, and a second charge of our men resulted in the capture of Confederate cannon. The small force were not properly supported, however, and the enemy succeeded in recapturing them. Once more the identical guns were taken by a charge, but once more lost on account of the smalless of the charging force. The following men were wounded in these encounters, all belonging to the Fifth Regular Cavalry:

Michael Clary, Co. D—leg, by solid shot; since amputated.

John Jennings, Co. D—forearm, by ball, flesh wound.

Martin Sharp, Co. E—leg, slight.

Thomas Lindell, Co. H—brain, dangerous.

—— Graham, Co. H—scalp, slight.

James M. Guion, Co. J—chest, not dangerous.

In the skirmishes of the day previous, the following men of this regiment were also wounded:

Conrad Rasnor—a toe, by rebel pistol-shot.

Michael Carey, by ball from revolver, not dangerous.

Thos. Cauldfield—lung, dangerous.

The solid shot which took off CLARY's leg passed clean through the body of his horse. Chief Bugler KLINE knocked the revolver from the hands of a rebel, after he had discharged it at him five times. SHARP's Lieutenant afterward killed the Confederate who inflicted a wound on him. Some fourteen prisoners were taken. We had about a dozen horses killed.

Following our last charge, the enemy continued their flight in the direction of the Gap. Our forces tarried for a short time, selecting what was formerly a tavern-stand for a hospital, where the wounded are now being kindly provided for. Markham is a place of some eight or ten houses. I found here the most intelligent man I have yet met in the Old Dominion, a Mr. MARSHALL, owner of a splendid plantation, well stocked with slaves. Though strongly Southern in his sentiments, he yet extended to us the hospitalities of his mansion, and exhibited those characteristics which mark the Christian gentleman. He conversed freely concerning the war, its causes and probable results. He had perused the speeches of SEYMOUR and JOHN VAN BUREN at the Cooper Institute, and was disappointed at finding two such Southern sympathizers advocating a prosecution of this war. It would terminate, he was confident, in nothing save a further alienation between the two sections.

Pursuing the enemy, we overtook them not far from the village, and again opened with our batteries. By this time they had received reinforcements, and we were compelled to fall back for a time. This morning, however, the chase was renewed, the enemy retiring before us, though contesting every inch of ground as they retired. When about four miles and a half from the village they pushed forward, barricaded the road with wagons, timber, &c., and planted guns on hills to the right and left. As our men came up they opened upon them, when detachments of the Eighth Illinois, Eighth Pennsylvania and Third Indiana deployed out on both sides of the road for a charge, which was made in splendid style. The Eighth Illinois acted most gallantly, charging right up to the cannon's mouth, routing the enemy and capturing several prisoners. Among the number was one Captain, who was injured by his horse falling upon him, which had been shot through the shoulder. It was a noble steed, and the owner appeared to regret its death more than his own capture. He was conveyed to an adjoining farm-house, used as a hospital, and seemed very thankful as well as surprised at the kind attentions which he received from our men. A corporal in Company B, Eighth Illinois and a private in Company E, were killed. There were also several wounded, whose names will be forwarded you to-morrow. They bore up under their wounds most heroically. One injured very severely in one leg came in laughing, and exclaiming, "I can walk one leg yet." Another, on being asked if he was severely hurt, replied, "Yes; but I don't care anything about that, as long as we have whipped the rebels." Side by side lay a National and a Confederate horseman, who had shot one another dead. After the engagement, pickets were thrown out, and Gens. PLEASANTON and AVERILL are to-night waiting the arrival of PIATT's Brigade of Infantry. The contest will be renewed on the morrow. It is the general impression that this force of cavalry, to-day increased to three brigades, is covering the retreat of the rebel forces. No one appears to, and probably no one does know, save the commanding Generals, if it be true that the Confederate forces are retiring. Gen. McCLELLAN undoubtedly intends to pursue and attack them before they have time to fall back and occupy some chosen position. The rapid hurrying forward of the infantry can mean nothing else, unless it be that the bulk of the rebel army is still in the Shenandoah Valley, and a flank movement is determined upon. Should this be the case, it has already been accomplished, for we have got in the rear of Winchester, Berryville and Bunker Hill, and Ashby's and Snicker's Gap are occupied, thereby preventing their crossing the mountain and getting between us and our base of supplies. The ease with which they gave up these important Gaps inclines me to the former belief, viz: that they have retreated. If this be so, the forces which they left in the Shenandoah to deceive us by threatening Harper's Ferry, will certainly find it difficult to escape. All goes well whichever hypothesis is true. Gen. McCLELLAN's headquarters to-night are at Rectortown, about ten miles from Upperville. About all of our force, save those left to hold the Gap, are on this side of the latter named place, encamped for the night in the vicinity of Markham, Piedmont, Rectortown and adjoining places. The men are in the best of spirits, and think they can see their way clearly to Richmond this time.

The County through which we are passing is very thinly settled, dwellings appearing but occasionally on the road. A few elegant residences are seen, which are built according to Southern custom.

J.

NEWS FROM FORTRESS MONROE.

FORTRESS MONROE, Friday, Nov. 7.

Steamship *S. R. Spaulding* arrived early this morning from Alexandria, bringing the Twenty-second Maine Regiment.

A severe northeast storm has been raging here since early last evening, and in consequence no boat has arrived from Yorktown to-day.

The mail-boat *Louisiana*, from Baltimore, arrived at 9½ o'clock, and brings rebel prisoners from Fort McHenry to be sent by next flag of truce to Aiken's Landing for exchange. Among them are several majors and doctors.

HORATIO SEYMOUR AT UTICA.

What He Says About the Result of the Election.

The Democrats of Utica had a "time" on Thursday evening over the result of the election, and Mr. SEYMOUR being in the city, was called out for a speech. A synopsis is thus given in the Utica *Herald:*

"His address was mostly congratulatory of the fact of his election. He thanked the electors for their verdict on the aspersions that had been cast on his principles and loyalty. The decision of the ballot-box he regarded as a sufficient justification of his antecedents. The victory had been won not alone by the votes of democrats, but by those of conservative men of all parties. It was due largely to the letters of soldiers who had written home, entreating their friends to support the Democracy. The victory would carry joy through the whole nation. From this time henceforth it would be seen there is a great Union party all through the South, who desire to cooperate with a party they know to be ready to welcome them back into the Union. The success of the Democracy would bring back the country to the position of years ago, when the Constitution was the supreme law, and the laws were impartially administered. Henceforth the laws were to be obeyed, and constitutional authority respected. The Democracy would offer no opposition to the legal actions of the President. It was not their intention to obstruct any constitutional measures of the Administration; on the contrary, it would be sustained in every constitutional demand for the prosecution of the war. There must be no more 'higher laws,' but only the law of the Federal compact. He denied the charge that the Democratic party were not loyal to the Government. They opposed the Government only because it failed to fulfill the promises with which it assumed the reins of power."

A synopsis of the speech, given in the *Telegraph*, is as follows:

"Hon. HORATIO SEYMOUR was called for with all the vigor with which nearly 2,000 throats could utter simultaneously the name of SEYMOUR. The Governor soon appeared, and though still laboring from hoarseness, which he apologized for in a measure, by saying that none of his Republican friends were troubled that way, he spoke about half an hour, with all his accustomed energy. Among other things which the late elections have taught, was the lesson that laws are to be respected, the Constitution preserved, and the authorities obeyed. There must be no higher law-ism. The country is to be brought back to the principles established by the founders of the Government. The fears entertained by some, that the Democracy were disloyal, are groundless. We have been sneeringly called 'Union-savers,' and other opprobrious epithets have been applied. No, we love the Union, and, instead of weakening and embarrassing the Government, we intend to sustain it in all its constitutional acts. It has failed to carry out the promises with which it started, therefore, it has been rebuked. When the grand news reaches all parts of the Union, new confidence will spring up, and new hopes will animate the people. You have saved the country—our country—and it will now be carried back to the original plan. Respect for the laws will be restored: the integrity of the Constitution be maintained. We will re-erect the structure of the Union upon the great principles our fathers established. Renewed vigor, glory and greatness will spring from the elections just passed, and we will sing hosannas over the rescue of our land."

The State Assembly.

The Albany *Journal* of Saturday has the following in regard to the political character of the Assembly:

"The political complexion of the Assembly is changed for the better, by the election of E. W. BOSTWICK, Union, from the Second District of Columbia County by a majority of ten, and CHAUNCEY M. DEPEW, from the Third District of Westchester County, by a majority of sixty. As corrected, our table now stands, Union 65, Democrats 63.

IMPORTANT FROM THE SOUTHWEST

Gen. Grant's Army Pressing Toward Holly Springs.

The Rebels Preparing to Evacuate.

AN EXPEDITION FROM HELENA, ARK.

CAIRO, Saturday, Nov. 8.

Gen. GRANT has made his headquarter at La Grange, near the Mississippi line. The railroad from Jackson to that place is in running order.

A telegram from Col. LOWE, from Fort Henry to headquarters here, says there is no doubt about Gen. ROUSSEAU's having had a fight with the rebel WOODWARD's command in the vicinity of Garrettsburgh. Reports from various sources indicate the rout of the rebels. We have nothing definite, however.

A letter from Memphis says that 500 guerrillas are in the vicinity of Colliersville, enforcing the conscription.

Gen. SHERMAN issued an order prohibiting the importation of liquors to Memphis, except by gentlemen citizens or officers, for the exclusive use of themselves or families, or by regular apothecaries for medical purposes, to be retailed on physicians' prescription, by keepers of hotels, licensed saloons in limited quantities, not exceeding at any one time one month's supply.

The Grenada *Appeal*, of the 5th, says there was a great fire in Augusta on the 4th, which burned cotton warehouses, &c., valued at $500,000.

GEORGE N. SAUNDERS has returned from his European mission, and brings most gratifying assurances of a speedy recognition of the Confederacy. The people of the South greatly rejoice thereat. Belgium is to take the initiative.

In the Memphis *Bulletin* of the 7th, it is said: "A large Federal army passed South from Grand Junction on Tuesday last." It further learns from a gentleman who lives in De Soto County, Miss., that for 20 miles out on the Pigeon Roost road the rebel cavalry have entirely disappeared. The same gentleman says for several days past the rebels at Holly Springs have been moving back all their prisoners and stores. This was understood to be preparatory to evacuating that place. It is believed they will fall back on Grenada.

On Wednesday last an expedition left Helena for Cotton Plant, where it was understood a rebel force 2,500 strong had gathered. They took five days' rations. Nothing has been heard from them. A cavalry force also crossed from Helena into Mississippi to punish rebel bands, who have recently given great annoyance by forays on National pickets.

THE GUERRILLAS IN KENTUCKY.

A Fight with a Rebel Force Under Fowler—Fowler Killed and his Gang Routed.

CINCINNATI, Sunday, Nov. 9.

A special to the *Commercial* from Indianapolis says: Wednesday night a battalion of Col. SHACKLEFORD's Eighth Kentucky Cavalry was attacked by a large force of guerrillas under Col. FOWLER, on Pond River, eleven miles from Madisonville, Ky.

The attack was gallantly met, and the rebels compelled to retire. Their loss was eight killed, including Col. FOWLER, and a large number of wounded and prisoners.

NEWS FROM WASHINGTON.

OUR SPECIAL WASHINGTON DISPATCHES.

WASHINGTON, Sunday, Nov. 9.

FACTS DENIED AND FACTS PROVED.

The correspondents of some of your cotemporaries seem to have been principally employed, during the last two or three days, in attempting to discredit certain statements of facts, their first knowledge of which appears to have been derived from this column. The denial of these facts, however, injures only the credit of those who make it. That a special meeting of the Cabinet was held on Wednesday last is now well known, as is also the contemplated retirement of at least one member of that Council, while our announcement of impending military changes is already verified by the removal of the General lately commanding the Army of the Potomac. In regard to the French dispatches, we said nothing about intervention or recognition, and their reality is admitted in some journals that deny it in their telegraphic columns.

THE DEMOCRATIC MEMBERS OF CONGRESS.

Mr. STEELE, of New-York, and other Democratic Congressmen elect, who are here, declare their purpose of supporting the President and his Administration in all measures for the speedy suppression of the rebellion.

GEN. BANKS.

Gen. BANKS arrived here this morning, and has been occupied most of the day in consultation with the President and Secretary of War. The destination of his expedition is not yet positively known, but that he is to leave soon in charge of an important command, is certain.

TO THE ASSOCIATED PRESS.

WASHINGTON, Sunday, Nov. 9.

THE INTERNAL REVENUE.

Acting Commissioner of Internal Revenue BOUTWELL has addressed a letter to Mr. J. D. VERMILYE, Chairman of the Committee of the New-York Clearing-House Association, in which he states that the Government now have increased facilities for supplying internal revenue stamps, and all orders now in this office of the kind already engraved, will be filled before the 15th inst. Within a very short time, plates for every denomination of the different kinds of stamps will be finished and all orders will be proptly supplied. When this can be done, an order will emanate from this Department, giving notice that after a certain day stamps must be used, or the penalty will be enforced in all cases where stamps can be promptly furnished by the Government on application.

GEN. HOOKER.

The friends of Gen. HOOKER say he has sufficiently recovered from his wound to resume his duties in the field.

GEN. HUNTER.

Maj.-Gen. HUNTER will in a few days return to the Department of the South.

THE MONITOR.

The *Monitor* left the Washington Navy-yard yesterday evening, and passed down the Potomac River.

TERRIBLE DISASTER.

Destruction of the Brooklyn Roman Catholic Orphan Asylum by Fire.

TWO CHILDREN BURNED TO DEATH

Several Hundred Turned Into the Street—Meeting in Behalf of the Unfortunates, &c.

About 2½ o'clock, Sunday morning, a fire broke out in the extensive building on Bedford-avenue, between Willoughby and DeKalb-avenues, Brooklyn, occupied as an Asylum for Roman Catholic orphan boys, and resulted in its complete destruction, together with the loss of two lives. The structure is of brick, 150 feet front by 100 in depth, and five stories in height. The grounds attached comprise fourteen lots, and extend from Bedford-avenue to Spencer-street, affording ample space for exercise in fine weather. About 150 feet in the rear is a wooden shed about 30 by 75 feet in extent, which is designed for a play-house in inclement weather. The main building is divided into apartments for the accommodation of the Superintendents and Assistants, and conveniences are provided for 350 children. The second, third and fourth floors were used as sleeping apartments. Heat was furnished by means of furnaces, two of which were located in the basement under the north wing, and two under the south wing. The main entrances in front and rear of the centre building, the halls and stairways, were all of wide dimensions, and to this feature, together with the presence of mind and the activity displayed by those in charge, it is mainly owing that the conflagration did not result more disastrously—*for*, as near as could be ascertained, two children only, out of 248, lost their lives.

The fire was caused by the overheating of a flue leading from one of the furnaces of the south wing. The floors and other wood work inside, being of pitch pine, ignited with great rapidity and the flames speedily extended upward until the whole was enveloped.

The teachers were aroused from their slumbers by one of the lady assistants, and immediately proceeded to save the children. In this they were fortunately most successful, having, in a very short time thereafter, conducted them to the play-house. It was supposed at the time that no one was missing, and the police and firemen were so informed. The efforts to suppress the flames were then redoubled, but without avail, and the firemen were compelled to leave the building to its fate.

Some two hours thereafter Mr. JAMES GILL, of Hose Company No. 13, discovered the crisped body of a child on one of the upper floors; and Messrs. BRADY, of Engine No. 9, and WALDRON, SEARY and COLYER, of Truck No. 3, found another, and conveyed them to the Ninth Ward Station-house. The children had doubtless become bewildered, and ascended to the upper floors, instead of coming down stairs.

Nearly all the books and papers were consumed. A record of the names of the children was saved, and, on calling the roll, all answered but two, named MICHAEL CARRICK and DANIEL McMAHN.

At the time of the fire the wind was blowing strongly from the northwest, and the rain was falling in torrents. The ground was covered with snow and slush, and through this the children were compelled to wade, barefoot and in their night-clothes, to the play-house on Spencer-street, which proved a temporary place of refuge from the elements. Subsequently they were conducted to the neighboring residences, and everything possible was done (with one exception) by all to relieve the little ones of their sufferings.

In consequence of the early hour and the disagreeable state of the weather, comparatively few citizens gathered about the scene of disaster. The duty of saving the inmates therefore, devolved almost exclusively upon the Superintendent and his assistants.

The President of the Brooklyn City Railroad Company placed the cars on the several routes, as well as all the old stages, at the disposal of the officers of the institution. The children having all been provided with shoes by Mr. McNALLY, who keeps a store in Myrtle-avenue, near Bedford, were collected together and conveyed to the Roman Catholic Girl's Orphan Asylum in Congress-street, where they will be provided for until other arrangements can be made.

The Roman Catholic Orphan Asylum for Boys was erected in 1856, at a cost of $25,000. Last year some necessary improvements were made at an expense of $5,000. The loss, including contents, amounts to about $35,000, upon which there is an insurance of $15,000 in the Montauk, Lafayette, Firemen's, Mechanics', Brooklyn, and Nassau Companies.

The Institution is in charge of the Roman Catholic Orphan Asylum Association of the City of Brooklyn, of which the Right Rev. Bishop LOUGHLIN is President. It is supported by contributions collected in the different city Catholic Churches.

Those in immediate charge are Mr. THOMAS BRADY, Principal; ALEXANDER J. ROONEY, JAMES P. BARRY, WALTER HOYLE and fourteen female assistants—Sisters of Mercy.

The fact that the building was on fire was discovered by a little boy seven years of age, who is sick with intermittent fever. He went to the bedside of one of the Sisters and told her he could not sleep as he was sure there was fire somewhere. She ordered him back to bed and then took the precaution of looking out into the hall, and was made aware of the fact that but little time remained to save the inmates. Every one was aroused, and all, with two exceptions, saved.

The furnaces and flues in the building had recently been introduced, and Saturday last fire was used for the first time. It is, therefore, evident that there was some defect in the flues.

Coroner MORRIS will hold an inquest on the bodies to-day.

The names of the unfortunate victims of this catastrophe are MICHAEL CARRICK and DANIEL McMANN.

The Association having in charge the Asylum, held a meeting at St. James Cathedral in Jay-street, yesterday afternoon. F. G. TURNER, Esq., Vice-President, occupied the chair. The object was stated to be to make arrangements for obtaining contributions, and to take other measures with the view of collecting money to rebuild the structure.

Contributions can be left at the house of Bishop LOUGHLIN, No. 180 Jay-street.

A Committee of five was appointed to make arrangements for a public lecture at the Academy of Music, and to solicit RICHARD O'GORMAN, Esq., to deliver said lecture. Time to be fixed hereafter.

Resolutions requesting each member of the Society to solicit subscriptions were passed.

A vote of thanks was tendered to the Brooklyn City Railroad Company for furnishing conveyances, and for offers of money for the relief of the children, after which the meeting adjourned.

It is understood that the children will be transferred to the Convent corner of Willoughby and Classon avenues, in a day or two.

The Letter of Gen. Dix.

The Albany *Evening Journal* publishes the following letter, written by Gen. DIX in reply to one asking permission to use his name as the Democratic candidate for Governor. Mr. WEED gives it as part of the evidence which led him to believe that Gen. DIX would be a very proper candidate for the Union Convention to nominate:

FORT MONROE, Va., Sept. 7, 1862.

MY DEAR SIR: As the time approaches for the meeting of the Democratic State Convention, I am more strongly confirmed than ever in the opinion I have heretofore expressed that *this is not the time to reorganize the Democratic Party*, and that I ought not to abandon my position in the field for any civil office, unless it be one directly connected with the prosecution of the war. That of Governor of New-York is not such a place; and while appreciating fully the distinction it would confer, while I am grateful to my friends for their favorable opinion, I am sure they will not press on me, when the country is bleeding at every pore, and when the services of every citizen, who can be spared from home, is needed in the field, a position I do not want, and which I feel I cannot take without infidelity to more sacred duties. There is only one condition, (and that in the existing state of things is an impossible one,) which would, in my judgment, justify me in relinquishing my military post—a general call from the people of New-York to become their Chief Magistrate *for the purpose of carrying more vigor, if it be possible, into the conduct of the war*. And you will allow me to add, that, if in this crisis of public calamity—the greatest that has ever fallen upon any people—we cannot rise above all party considerations and rally around the Chief Magistrate of the Union for the maintenance of our nationality, there will be little left for us in the future but disaster and disgrace. I am, sincerely, your friend,

JOHN A. DIX.

Hon. EDWARDS PIERREPONT.

Cartoons
Harper's Weekly
November 1, 1862

"MY MARYLAND!!!"

CONFEDERATE LIBERATOR. "We come to free you all, my friend, from the Iron Heel of LINCOLN and his hordes! We take nothing without paying for it! Your hour of freedom has come. Be Happy! be Happy!"

DEVOTED SECESH. "Yes! oh, yes! Our feelings, and all that sort of thing, are with you. But, good gracious! haven't you got a *Green Back* or two? How the d——l am I going to fill up again with this trash!!!"

JOHN BULL'S NEUTRALITY.—A DISTINCTION WITH A DIFFERENCE.

JOHN BULL (*solus*). "A few more Pirates afloat, and I'll *get all the carrying trade back into my hands.*"

THE RAILROAD IN BROADWAY.

THE CELEBRATED PIG "LIVE OAK" (*grunts*). "Ugh! You may drive me off now, but I've rooted up *two miles* of Broadway already. I'll root up the rest, *or die!*"

The Charleston Mercury.

PAPER—Ten Dollars per annum, payable half-yearly in advance. — VINDICE NULLO —SPONTE SUA SINE LEGE FIDES RECTUMQUE COLENTUR. — COUNTRY PAPER: Three a week—Five Dollars per annum, in advance.

VOLUME LXXXI. CHARLESTON, S. C., FRIDAY, DECEMBER 5, 1862. NUMBER 11,622

TELEGRAPHIC NEWS.

DIRECT NEWS FROM THE NORTH.

THE LATEST WAR INTELLIGENCE.

MESSAGE OF PRESIDENT LINCOLN: &c., &c., &c.

We have been placed in possession of the New York *Herald* of *last Saturday*, November 29. The news is quite interesting.

The Yankee correspondents account for the inaction of BURNSIDE, by the statement that he is waiting for his pontoon bridges, and not very patiently either, since he was about to arrest the parties responsible for the delay. The rebels are stated to be busily and continuously erecting earthworks on the heights around Fredericksburg, within plain view of the Yankee forces. The railroad from Acquia Creek to BURNSIDE's headquarters, on the Rappahannock, has been completed, and trains began running on Friday last. The Philadelphia *Inquirer* remarks knowingly, that "the Army of the Potomac will win "Richmond on the Rappahannock, but the Army "of the James will occupy Richmond." The *Herald* abuses the *Inquirer* for having given "aid and comfort to the enemy" in this statement.

An arrival from Port Royal brings intelligence that the ravages of the Country fever among the invaders have ceased. The formation of the brigade of "contrabands" was still going on under direction of Gen. SAXTON, and the correspondents gloat over the recent barbarous raid of a portion of that brigade against the defenceless town of St. Mary's and in Doboy Sound. The *Herald* gravely assures us that "Gen. BEAUREGARD has pronounced Charleston indefensible" and that "the inhabitants are moving their property from the city." Abolition accounts from the North Carolina coast state that 4000 rebels under Gen. MARTIN had attacked Eewbern but were effectually repulsed.

The *Herald* contains some additional European news. The London *Post* (Government organ), says the best and shortest summary of RUSSELL's despatch, in reply to NAPOLEON's proposition, is "*Not yet!*" England, adds the *Post*, strongly feels that she cannot interfere *on the invitation of only one of the belligerents*. But, when the Peace Party shall have established its power at the North, England will be ready, on the most indirect hint, to join with the maritime Powers in furthering the work of pacification. The London *Times* thinks that the moral effect of the discussion that has taken place between the three Powers will be as great as if they had actually infered. The London *Herald* (DERBY organ) is very bitter in its comments upon the position taken by the British Ministry.

Later dates from Nassau had been received in New York. The Nassau *Guardian*, of November 22, announces that the Confederate steamer *Antonica* (formerly British steamer *Herald*) and the steamer *Leopard* had arrived from Charleston the previous Thursday. Also, that a Southern schooner, bound for Nassau, had been captured, about a week before, by a Yankee gunboat, between the western main of Abaco and Allan's Carp. Admiral WILKES was in trouble again with the British officials at Nassau and Abaco, and the Nassau papers teem with complaints in regard to his conduct.

Thanksgiving day (November 27) at the North was the occasion of the release of nearly all the State prisoners confined in Fort Warren. Mayor BROWN, of Baltimore, and the other gallant Marylanders who have so long languished in that Bastile, were among those unconditionally restored to liberty. PIERRE SOULE and Sheriff MAZEREAU, of New Orleans were also released from Fort Lafayette.

The Democrats carried the city election at New Haven, Connecticut. FITZ JOHN PORTER was on trial by Court Martail at Washington, and BUELL and McDOWELL were both before Courts of Inquiry. The *Herald* says that McNIELL, who butchered the ten Missouri patriots, is only a Militia General, commanding a portion of the Missouri Home Guards. As he is not "a regular U. S. Army officer" the *Herald* presumes that President DAVIS, on learning that fact, will at once withdraw his retaliatory order. Great alarm prevails at Memphis, owing to repeated and desperate efforts that are being made to burn the city. On Sunday week there were ten different incendiary attempts, and fourteen on the following Monday.

Gold in the Northern markets continues to fluctuate in the neighborhood of 129¼.

(*The Latest—By Telegraph.*)

PETERSBURG, Thursday Night, December 4—The N. Y. *Times*, of the 2d instant, has been received here.

LINCOLN's Message was read before his Congress last Monday. It is a very sorry document. It opens by saying that "Since the last assembling "of Congress another year of health and bountiful harvests has passed. While it has not pleased "Almighty God to bless the United States with "the return of peace, we (the Yankees) can but "press on, trusting that, in God's good time, all "will be well." He calls his famous proclamation "compensated emancipation."

A Captain of a Texas Regiment and a Clerk in the Quartermaster's Department, at Richmond, deserted near Fredericksburg, on Friday night. As is usual in such cases, they make all kinds of astonishing disclosures.

A Washington despatch says that it is no longer a question that the Army of the Potomac owes its failure to cross the Rappahannock promptly on its arrival there, to inexcusable delay in furnishing means of transportation. It is rumored that General MEIGS has been removed, and General WOODBURY arrested for causing this delay.

It is stated, on good authority, that 180,000 soldiers are now absent from the Yankee army without leave.

Gen. BLUNT, after a forced march, is said to have routed 8000 rebels on the 20th ult, at Cane Hill, Arkansas. The battle lasted several hours and the Yankees claim a complete victory, 60 rebels being killed and the same number wounded.—BLUNT thinks that the rebels will not again venture north of Boston Mountain during this winter.

The *Hibernian* had brought Liverpool dates to the 20th ult. Another Confederate steamer had left Liverpool, and still another was nearly ready. There is no news in regard to the mediation *projet*.

The N. Y. *Herald* of the 2d is also received, but it contains nothing of special interest. The rebels were reported still fortifying at Fredericksburg, and showing no signs of retreat.

SITUATION OF AFFAIRS IN VIRGINIA—LATEST REPORTS FROM RICHMOND.

RICHMOND, Thursday Evening, December 4.—All is quiet at Fredericksburg. Passengers express the opinion that the enemy is going away perhaps to Port Royal.

HAMPTON's cavalry, yesterday, captured a Yankee picket guard, consisting of a Lieutenant and five men, at Stafford Store, north of Fredericksburg.

The report that BURNSIDE has been superseded by HOOKER is revived, with a show of truth. A person who ran the blockade, says that he saw it in a Northern paper.

A Yankee gunboat came up to West Point, on the York River, on Tuesday, and destroyed two small vessels there.

In a skirmish in Hampshire county, a few days ago, Gen. ROSE, a Yankee brigadier, was killed by IMBODEN's Rangers.

The Petersburg *Express*, of to-day, mentions a report of a severe skirmish which occurred last Tuesday, on the Blackwater River, between DODGE's New York Mounted Riflemen and Capt. WRIGHT's Rocket Battery. Our men were forced to retire, losing one section of their battery and sixteen killed and wounded. The Yankee loss has not been ascertained.

THE MERCURY.

FRIDAY, DECEMBER 5, 1862.

The Situation on the Rappahannock.

The news from the North, which we publish this morning, is of a later date than has yet reached us over the wires from Richmond. BURNSIDE, it appears, is still in command of the army at Fredericksburg, and still intent upon an advance on Richmond, by that route, at the earliest practicable moment. The lack of pontoon bridges is the alleged cause of his delay. This want cannot detain him long.

This information is important, for, however we dread the carnage of a great battle-field, such as this must be, yet, so far as the great cause is concerned, we have reason to entertain high hopes of the result, and of its effect upon the duration of the war. The army under General LEE is the oldest and best we have. We are informed that, owing to the recent great efforts, it is getting pretty well provided with shoes and clothing. It is in high spirits and in excellent fighting trim. The army under BURNSIDE has been repeatedly worsted by this Confederate army. It has just been filled up with untried recruits. It has just lost its favorite General, and is commanded by one who has never evinced any particular miliary ability. His army must be more or less demoralized, from all the circumstances under which this move must be made. Our troops at Sharpsburg fought and repulsed, with slaughter, more than three to one, and they were weary, half starved, half shod and clothed, and short of ammunition. Now, our position can be selected; full time has been allowed for the concentration of all our available forces, and there can be no difficulty about either ammunition or food. Everything considered, we take it that the battle will be fought under happy auspices, and that, to us, victory is almost certain. We trust victory may be the utter ruin of the United States army. Such an action we believe would be the harbinger of early peace. We therefore feel mingled anxiety and confidence as to the result of this great impending conflict. The God of battles must be our Judge and Arbiter, and to Him let us earnestly make our appeal.

CAPTURE OF YANKEE GUNBOATS IN NORTH CAROLINA—INTERESTING PARTICULARS.

The "terrible" gunboats are meeting with disaster after disaster. It is clear that they cannot operate in narrow rivers, whose banks are inhabited by bold and determined men. Two cases have occurred in North Carolina. In one, Capt. NEWKIRK's cavalry, with a piece of artillery, captured an iron steamer in New River, N. C., and in the other, Capt. WHITFORD's Rangers captured a gunboat and her entire crew in Bay river, N. C. Of the first capture, a correspondent of the Wilmington (N. C.) *Journal* gives an interesting account. The steamer entered New River, in Onslow county, on the morning of the 24th ult. The letter says:

Her arrival was duly noticed and promptly reported by Capt. Ward's pickets to the proper authority, when Capt. Newkirk, with a detachment of the Rebel Rangers, together with Lieut. Latham, with one piece of the Kennedy Artillery, proceeded to the mouth of New River to pay her their respects. They arrived on the morning of the 25th, just as she was returning from Jacksonville, where she had taken the mail and what papers she could find, in the meantime appropriating to her especial use some boxes of clothing deposited there by the patriotic ladies of Onslow for the use of our brave soldiers in the field. And just here, for their consolation, let me inform them that, although they failed to reach their proper destination, yet they never gave warmth to their enemies, as they were destroyed with the steamer. As she was quietly proceeding down the river, on her way out, apparently in no hurry at all, Lieut. Latham opened upon her with his rifled piece, checking her progress, throwing her out of the main channel of the river, and causing a general confusion on board.

So soon as she recovered from her shock she opened upon him a terrific fire of shell and canister, but he heeded not her reply, and continued to pour upon her a rapid fire, causing her iron sides to ring. But 'twas a play at ball with no equality on our side, for, having but the one piece to contend with, she was able to direct her three heavy guns at us, while Lieut. Latham's balls failed to enter her iron sides, and it was not until he found he could not sink her did he leisurely, and in the best of order, retire, while grape was firing thick and fast in every direction. The steamer continued to shell the woods to find out the whereabouts of the artillery, and shying around the place where she knew it had been she stuck fast on a sand bar, and could neither get over nor back away from it. Capt. Newkirk, the officer in command, immediately despatched a courier to the artillery camp for one more gun, which arrived the night of the 25th, under command of Captain Adams. It was then determined to renew the attack by daylight.

Positions were chosen, and next morning, an hour before day, all parties were ordered to their respective places. Capt. Newkirk superintended the movements. Everything was now ready, and there ensued for a few moments a perfect stillness, which was broken by the rifled shell of Captain Adams, which went thundering forth; then another made her ring, then came Lieut. Latham's shot, which did its errand well; then replied the steamer with her would be murderoes grape, while both pieces of artillery kept up a rapid fire; just then a boat was seen going down, and just as it touched the water, Lieuts. McClammy and Spicer, with their detachments, stood ready to dispute their passage to the land, but that boat had business elsewhere; they made towards a schooner which lay well towards the inlet, and though the artillery threw shot near enough to them to throw the water in their boat, it failed to sink them. Just as a shell from the artillery made an entrance into the cabin, a light was discovered, and Captain Nerkirk proclaimed the day ours.

Very soon the wood work of the steamer was in a light blaze, and the attention of all was directed to the schooner, which bore them away as a stiff breeze carried them fast down the river. Had it been calm, the entire crew would have been ours; but let us rest content with what was done. They left in the utmost confusion, leaving everything they had, their rifles, cutlasses, books, caps, shoes, and even their beef and crackers half done. Whether any of them were killed is not known. The shell fell all around her. On her passage up the river she was fired into by Capt. Simmons and his picket, with what effect is not known. She accomplished nothing at all. Our pickets burned the schooner that was ready for sea. All the papers the steamer got at Jacksonville must have been lost. She, luckily for herself, stole a schooner in which to make her escape, and was forced by forty five men to abandon her element of power. The officers and men engaged are deserving of especial praise. Her cannon, magazine, chests, water tanks, boiler, and a vast quantity of iron, have been saved. Many things of value were found, among them a lot of newly-invented shackles for the feet, together with handcuffs in abundance.

Union troops attempting to cross the Rappahannock

The New-York Times.

VOL. XII—NO. 3503. NEW-YORK, MONDAY, DECEMBER 15, 1862. PRICE THREE CENTS.

IMPORTANT FROM VIRGINIA.

The Great Battle Fought on Saturday at Fredericksburgh.

Storming of the First Line of the Enemy's Works.

FAILURE TO CARRY THE POSITION.

TERRIFIC FIGHTING UNTIL DARK.

Splendid Success of Gen. Franklin on the Left.

Stonewall Jackson Driven Back About a Mile.

Several Hundred Prisoners Captured.

A Number of Our General Officers Killed and Wounded.

NO GENERAL ENGAGEMENT YESTERDAY.

THE OPERATIONS OF SATURDAY.

HEADQUARTERS OF THE ARMY OF THE POTOMAC, Saturday, Dec. 13, 1862. IN THE FIELD—11 o'clock, A. M.

The great battle, so long anticipated between the two contending armies, is now progressing.

The morning opened with a dense fog, which has not entirely disappeared.

Gen. REYNOLDS' Corps, on the left, advanced at an early hour, and at 9:15 A. M., engaged the enemy's infantry. Seven minutes afterward the rebels opened a heavy fire of artillery, which has continued so far without intermission.

Their artillery fire must be at random, as the fog obstructs all view of almost everything.

Our heavy guns are answering them rapidly.

At this writing, no results are known.

HEADQUARTERS OF THE ARMY OF THE POTOMAC, Saturday Dec. 13—11 P. M.

The fog began to disappear early in the forenoon, affording an unobstructed view of our own and the rebel positions.

It being evident that the first ridge of hills, in the rear of the city, on which the enemy had their guns posted behind works, could not be carried, except by a charge of infantry, Gen. SUMNER assigned that duty to Gen. FRENCH'S Division, which was supported by Gen. HOWARD'S.

The troops advanced to their work at ten minutes before 12 o'clock at a brisk run, the enemy's guns opening upon them a very rapid fire. When within musket range, at the base of the ridge, our troops were met by a terrible fire from the rebel infantry, who were posted behind a stone wall and some houses on the right of the line. This checked the advance of our men, and they fell back to a small ravine, but not out of musket range.

At this time another body of troops moved to their assistance in splendid style, notwithstanding large gaps were made in their ranks by the rebel artillery. When our troops arrived at the first line of the rebel defences, they "double quicked," and with "fixed bayonets" endeavored to dislodge the rebels from their hiding places. The concentrated fire of the rebel artillery and infantry, which our men were forced to face, was too much for them, and the centre gave way in disorder, but afterwards they were rallied and brought back.

From that time the fire was spiritedly carried on, and never ceased until after dark.

Gen. FRANKLIN, who commanded the attack on the left, met with better success. He succeeded, after a hard day's fight, in driving the rebels about one mile. At one time the rebels advanced to attack him, but were handsomely repulsed, with terrible slaughter and loss of between four and five hundred prisoners belonging to Gen. A. P. HILL'S command. Gen. FRANKLIN'S movement was directed down the river, and his troops are encamped to-night not far from the Massaponox Creek.

Our troops sleep to-night where they fought today. The dead and wounded are being carried from the field.

The following is a list of officers killed and wounded as far as yet known:

Gen. JACKSON, of the Pennsylvania Reserves, killed.

Gen. BAYARD struck in the thigh by a shell, and afterward died.

Gen. VINTON wounded in the side, but not seriously.

Gen. GIBBON wounded in the hand.

Gen. KIMBALL wounded in the thigh.

Gen. CALDWELL wounded in two places, but not seriously.

Col. SINCLAIR, of the Pennsylvania Reserves, wounded seriously.

Capt. HENDERSON, commanding the Ninth New-York State Militia, wounded seriously.

The following is the loss of officers in the Fifth New-Hampshire Regiment:

Col. CROSS, wounded in the abdomen.

Major STURTEVANT, killed.

Adjutant DODD, killed.

Capt. MURRAY, killed.

Capt. PERRY, killed.

The firing of musketry ceased about 6 o'clock this evening, but the Rebels continued throwing shell into the city until 8 o'clock.

The position of the rebels was as follows:

Gen. LONGSTREET on the left, and holding the main works.

Gen. A. P. HILL and "Stonewall" JACKSON were in front of Gen. FRANKLIN, with JACKSON'S right resting on the Rappahannock, and HILL'S forces acting as a reserve.

The troops are in good spirits and not the least disheartened.

FROM ANOTHER CORRESPONDENT.

HEADQUARTERS ARMY OF THE POTOMAC, Saturday, Dec. 13—10 P. M.

Last night our troops were rapidly pushed across the river, and every preparation made for a battle. Gen. FRANKLIN'S Division crossed two miles below the city, while Gen. SUMNER'S troops occupied a portion of the town. Gen. FRANKLIN'S line was moved forward at sunrise, with his right resting on Fredericksburgh, his centre advanced a mile from the river, and his left resting on the river three miles below.

Skirmishing commenced on the left about daylight. Soon after a rebel battery opened on our lines, and the Ninth New York Militia was ordered to charge, but after a fierce struggle was compelled to retire. The remainder of the Brigade, under Gen. TYLER, then charged the enemy's guns, when the fight became general on the extreme left.

Gen. MEAD'S and Gen. GIBBON'S Divisions encountered the right of Gen. A. P. HILL'S command.

The cannonading was terrific, though our troops suffered but little from the enemy's artillery. Gradually the fight extended around to the right. Gen. HOWE'S division went in, and then Gen. BROOKS' division. About 10 o'clock A. M. Gen. SUMNER'S troops engaged the enemy back of the city, since which time the battle has raged furiously along the whole line. The enemy, occupying the woods and hills, had a much more advantageous position, but were driven back on their right a mile and a half early in the day.

About noon Gen. GIBBON was relieved by Gen. DOUBLEDAY, and Gen. MEAD by Gen. STONEMAN. Afterward Gen. NEWTON'S Division moved round to the support of the left, when the firing ceased in that portion of the field for a short time, and broke out with greater fierceness in the centre, where our troops were exposed to a plunging fire from the enemy's guns and earthworks from the hills.

Along the whole line the battle has been fierce all day, with great loss to both sides. To-night each army holds its first position, with the exception of a slight advance of our left. Cannonading is still going on, and the musketry breaks out at intervals quite fiercely.

Gens. GIBBON, VINTON, BAYARD and CAMPBELL are wounded. Gen. BAYARD was struck in the hip by a solid shot, while conversing with Gen. FRANKLIN and his Staff, and cannot survive. His right leg has been amputated, but the operation will only serve to prolong his life a short time.

Several hundred prisoners have been taken, who report that Gen. LEE'S entire army is in the immediate vicinity. Gen. HILL'S troops were withdrawn this morning and started down the river, but afterwards returned. Gen. FRANKLIN is to-night opposed to Stonewall JACKSON.

It is impossible to form an accurate idea of the loss on either side, as the firing is still going on, rendering it extremely difficult to remove the killed and wounded.

The city suffered terribly from the enemy's artillery, and is crowded with our troops, the front extending but a short distance beyond.

The balloon has been up all day. During the morning but little could be seen, owing to the dense fog; but the afternoon was remarkably clear.

This evening the rebels have been shelling Fredericksburgh, endeavoring to drive our troops out of the place, but without success.

THE OPERATIONS OF SUNDAY.

HEADQUARTERS ARMY OF POTOMAC, Dec. 14—11:30 A. M.

There is no fog to-day, the sun shining brightly, with a strong breeze. At daylight this morning there was a heavy fire of artillery and infantry in front of the first line of works, where Gens. SUMNER and HOOKER were engaged yesterday. The fire slacked about an hour afterward, and was heard only at intervals until now. The same occurred in front of Gen. FRANKLIN'S Division down the river. The object of both parties was evidently to feel the other.

During last night and this forenoon the rebels have considerably extended their works and strengthened their position. Large bodies of troops are now to be seen where but few were to be seen yesterday.

Our dead which were killed yesterday, while charging in front of the enemy's works, still remain where they fell. When attempting their removal last night, the rebels would open fire with infantry, but the wounded have all been removed from the field, and all the dead obtained are now being buried.

The indications are that no decisive battle will be fought to-day, unless the rebels should bring on the engagement, which they will not probably do.

REPORTS BY WAY OF WASHINGTON.

WASHINGTON, Sunday, Dec. 14.

It is thought here that about 40,000 of our troops were engaged in yesterday's battle.

From information received early this morning, preparations were making all night for a conflict to-day, Gen. BURNSIDE remaining on the field, giving orders, looking to the position and condition of his forces.

Additional surgeons, and everything which the necessities of the wounded require, have been dispatched from Washington to the battle-ground.

It is proper to caution the public against hastily crediting the many unsupported rumors concerning yesterday's battle. Some of them here prevalent have no other basis than surmise, and are mere inventions in the absence of facts. Rebel sympathizers are responsible for not a few of these fictions.

Gentlemen in high public positions repeat the assertion, as coming from Gen. BURNSIDE, that *he has men enough, and, therefore, desires no further reinforcements.*

OUR SPECIAL ARMY CORRESPONDENCE.

Details of Operations to Saturday Morning.

The Crossing of the Rappahannock—The Movement Splendidly Performed—Preponderance of the Union Forces—Condition of Fredericksburgh, &c., &c.

CAMP OPPOSITE FREDERICKSBURGH, Saturday, Dec. 13, 1862.

Affairs are rapidly culminating here, and the crisis of battle, the grandest—probably the most decisive—of the war, approaches apace.

The nation may well pause and hold its breath, in the terrible suspense now impending. The prelude of the conflict has passed. The taking of the town by assault, and after a determined fight with the enemy's sharpshooters and skirmishers, and the crossing of the river by a considerable portion of the Union force, are fast bringing the two great armies face to face. To-day—to-morrow at farthest—must witness events which will long live in history. May we hope that the battle will be as decisive as it now promises to be bloody and terrible.

The events of yesterday may be briefly summed up as follows:

Gen. SUMNER'S Corps, the Right Grand Division, were across and occupied the town; one Division took possession the first night, and the remainder of the column passed across the upper bridges in the morning. They filled the whole length of Caroline or Main-street to the lines of the railroad, and by degrees extended their front to Commerce-street, and the streets running up from the river, until the body of the town was filled up. They remained under cover of the houses, the streets running nearly North and South being parallel to the line of the enemies' batteries behind the town. The completion of a second pontoon bridge during the first night greatly facilitated the passage of the troops. The first artillery thrown across were the Napoleon batteries attached to Gen. SUMNER'S Division.

The enemy's pickets stubbornly occupied the outskirts of the town, and a fusilade between them and our own advance pickets was kept up during the day. The remainder of FRANKLIN'S column crossed their two pontoon bridges during the forenoon, two miles below the centre of the town. Their passage, as well as that of Gen. SUMNER'S Corps, was disputed by occasional but not very persistent firing from the rebel batteries, which are chiefly to the South and rear of the town, so as to command the line of the railroad, and also the Bowling Green.

Gen. REYNOLDS' First Corps brought up the rear of FRANKLIN'S column, and occupied the broad plateau South of the town, extending for miles down the river.

Gen. HOOKER'S Grand Division, which had been on foot since Thursday, when they broke camp, remained with the head of its column pointed toward the upper bridges, but up to 3 o'clock awaited Gen. BURNSIDE'S orders to advance.

Three times during the day the enemy's battery commanding this crossing opened fire upon the troops which came down, their shells exploding with uncomfortable accuracy just at the hither end of the bridge, on the slope of the hill, and even beyond on the level plain by which they approached.

Shortly after 3 P. M. HOOKER'S column began to move down the river, as if with the design of crossing on the bridges below, where FRANKLIN crossed. Up to a late hour, however, they had not gone over. It is believed they passed the river during the night.

This change in the line was no doubt occasioned by the extraordinary activity displayed by the rebel batteries southeast of the town.

At 2½ P. M. the whole semi-circle of batteries in that direction opened fire upon the pontoon bridges, and upon the lower part of the town, where our troops were quartered. Their other batteries, north of the plank-road, and toward Falmouth, simultaneously poured in their contribution upon the upper crossing, and that part of the town lying in front of it.

Five separate batteries below, working ten or twelve guns, and four above, with eight or ten, kept up a fire of shot and shell until near sundown. Many of their shells fell short, but some took effect in the town, and near the river. What damage they did to the troops I could not learn at that late hour.

Several shells burst near the Lacey House, and one close by the north end of the building while I was getting the names of the wounded lying in that place. One man, a few minutes afterward, was brought in with his arm terribly shattered by a piece of shell. A considerable body of cavalry and infantry were partially sheltered behind these buildings, which are of brick. It being used as a hospital, and occupied by the rebels in common with the Union wounded soldiers is a guarantee (?) that it will be respected. Its position being only a little to the left of the crossing, and nearly in line of one of the main rebel batteries, probably accounts for these shells bursting so near it.

We must presume that they were accidental shots, as I believe there is no well authenticated instance of their intentionally firing upon a hospital. It is situated only two hundred yards north of Lieut. MILLER'S battery, which is protected by earthworks, and very prominent on the high land below the house. These circumstances render the place unsafe, and it will only be used as a temporary hospital. The wounded will, for the present, be carried to the rear, where tents have been established for their accommodation.

The main body of the rebel army is believed to be in position some five or six, perhaps ten miles west, with a strong rear guard for coöperating with and supporting their batteries.

If estimates which I have heard be correct, we have an aggregate of over sixty thousand men more than the estimated strength of the rebel army. Our artillery figures up over five hundred guns. Considering the difficulties of the situation, the completion of six pontoon bridges, and the crossing of such an army in twenty-four hours, is worthy of all military achievement. The events of the last two days have increased the enthusiasm of the whole army toward its Commander, and strengthened confidence in the Generals leading the Grand Divisions. With town and river behind we must fight—there is no backing out.

THE TOWN—ITS CONDITION.

Our shot and shell have riddled a great many of the houses in town; and most of the churches, from foundation to steeple, have been *accidentally* perforated by the storm of missiles which were sent into the town. As the monuments and representatives of a priesthood and people thoroughly baptized in treason, they deserved no exemption from the common doom, but being larger than any other buildings, and very prominently in the range of our fire, they naturally received their full share of the iron storm. The clock in the steeple of the Episcopal church was untouched, and continues to toll off the eventful hours, for the benefit of the Union forces in the town.

In spite of prompt and general efforts to guard the houses from intrusion and pillage, by the establishment of guards, a good many residences have suffered more or less spoliation. Household articles, such as cooking utensils and crockery, pickles, sweetmeats and flitches of bacon, were observed among the troops, as I passed through the different streets. The latter, taken from the meat houses of the first families, no doubt, were generally transfixed on the end of bayonets, and carried in triumph on their shoulders.

There has been, as yet, no general pillaging of the town, and it will not be permitted. The principal stores have each a strong guard to protect the small stock of goods left behind in the flight of their proprietors.

Not over twenty houses all told, have been burned, and the total damage to the place, by the bombardment and flames, I estimate at not over two hundred thousand dollars.

The few dead who were shot in the streets, have been buried, necessarily in the town, near where they fell. Considering all the terrible circumstances of provocation, the preservation of the town from total destruction, and its wholesale pillage by the army, are in the highest degree creditable to the Union troops, and to their discipline. [illegible] killed and wounded as far as ascertained.

In haste to send the mail. E. S.

LIST OF CASUALTIES.

Killed and Wounded at the Battle of Fredericksburgh.

TWENTIETH MASSACHUSETTS.

Capt. Chas. Cabot—killed.
Corp. C. Light—right leg.
Sergt. A. Rice—right hip.
E'g'ne Connor—right arm.
J. F. Murphy—right cheek.
A. C. Parker—groin.
Alex. Winthrop—knee.
John Driscoll.
James McGuiness.
Peter Kittz.
John Devine.
Michael Sullivan.
Donald McPhee.
E. F. Briggs.
Richard S. Gardner.
Col.-Sergt. Charles Hunt.
William Durfee.
Thomas J. Russell.
James Barrett.
Sergt. Frederick H. Schoff.
James Berry.
Patrick Morrisey.
Richard Hawkins.
John Duscall.
James McGrives.
William Casey.
J. O'Connor.
J. P. McVey—cheek.
Capt. Allen Shepherd.
Lieut. A. R. Curtis.
Lieut. H. E. Wilkins.
Capt. Richard Hawkins.
Sergt. Horace Devey.
Sergt. Pat'k J. Champion.
J. Day.
A. Holbrook.
J. Wells.
O. Murphy.
B. F. Bumpus.
David G. Chapman.
P. O. Horn.
William Forthib.
John McIntyre.
John Leezson.
William Powers.
Daniel Murphy.
E. A. Wardard.
Daniel Crow.
J. J. Johnson
J. Dorsey.
A. Sieffins.
S. Allen.
A. R. Curtis.
H. E. Wilkinson.

FIFTY-NINTH NEW-YORK.

Capt. Patrick Lalley.
George H. Harris.
Michael Powers.
Edward Kearney.
Philip Smith.
Lieut. James Peacock.
L. Parick.
H. Seymour.
Henry Heitman.
Richard Todd—right thigh.
Wm. Bickford—left arm.

NINETEENTH MASSACHUSETTS.

J. T. Jordan.
G. Dew.
H. Orr.
D. Jewett.
C. R. Bartlett.
James Smith.
Walter Williston.
Corp. Stephen Noyes—right thigh.
James Boyle—right arm.
George W. Bradley—left leg.
J. W. Morrison—right cheek and neck.

SIXTY-SIXTH NEW-YORK.

Lieut.-Col. J. H. Bull, mortally—since dead.
Capt. Dodge, mortally—since dead.
C. H. Major.

EIGHTY-NINTH NEW-YORK.

J. H. Rode.
J. D. Walker.
C. D. Ernest.
Willie Hill.

FIRST NEW-YORK.

Mike Conoha.
J. Paine.

SEVENTY-FIRST PENNSYLVANIA.

Wm. H. Cressee.

SEVENTH MICHIGAN.

Foster Blakeley—right leg.
A. Hayes.
James Roslyn.
Thomas Caldwell.
H. E. Palmer.
C. H. Baxter.
D. Dorn.
George W. Vaughn.

FIFTY-SEVENTH NEW-YORK.

Capt. Reynolds.
Patrick Cassady.
M. S. Cassett.
Alexander Smith.
William Mallon.

THE DEAD.

Seventeen privates of the Union army were shot in the streets of the town, who were gathered together and buried in a house lot at the corner of Caroline and Wolf streets yesterday forenoon. On account of the confusion, their names have not yet been obtained.

REBEL OFFICERS AND SOLDIERS WOUNDED AT THE LACEY HOUSE.

Capt. T. W. Shurman, Co. D, 13th Mississippi—right leg amputated.

J. D. Hubbard, private 8th Florida—left thigh shattered; says he was forced in by conscription.

J. G. Sumrall, Co. D, 13th Miss.—thigh broken.

Corp. E. Calhoun, Co. F, 13th Mississippi—knee.

GEN. HOWARD'S DIVISION HOSPITAL.

J. Franklin, Surgeon in charge.
Justin Drowelle, Surgeon of Hospital.
G. Hayward, operating Surgeon.
S. Rizer, operating Surgeon.

THE LOSSES OF SATURDAY.

KILLED.

Gen. Jackson, of the Pennsylvania Reserves.

Gen. Bayard.

Lieut.-Col. Dickinson, commanding battery Fourth United States Artillery.

WOUNDED.

Gen. Thomas Francis Meagher is reported by Col. Nugent shot through the leg.

Gen. Vinton, in the side, but not seriously.

Gen. Gibbon, in the hand.

Gen. Kimball, in the thigh.

Gen. Caldwell, in two places, but not seriously.

Col. Nugent, 69th New-York, badly wounded. Has been brought to Acqua Creek, and is on board the steamer *Rockland*.

Col. Sinclair, of the Pennsylvania Reserves, seriously.

Major Jennings, 26th New-York.

Capt. Hendrickson, commanding 9th New-York State Militia.

Capt. Cameron, 9th New-York.

Capt. Muche, 9th New-York.

Capt. Carpenter, 94th New-York.

Capt. Hart, Assistant Surgeon-General to Gen. Tyler.

Capt. Hendrickson, commanding the Ninth New-York State Militia—seriously.

Capt. Andrew Mahoney, Co. E, 19th Massachusetts—arm and breast.

Capt. M. Dunn, Co. D, 19th Massachusetts—thigh.

Lieut. Newcomb, 19th Massachusetts—both legs.

Lieut. J. F. Hazett, Co. E, 106th Pennsylvania—arm.

Lieut. A. R. Benedict, of the Regulars, dangerously wounded.

Sergt. G. Pitcher, Co. G, 59th New-York—cheek.
Sergt. R. C. Steward, Co. B, 4th New-York—arm.
Sergt. B. McManus, Co. G, 69th New-York—sh'ldr.
Sergt. H. I. Carr, Co. G, 19th Massachusetts—leg.
Corp. J. E. Douglass, Co. H, 19th Mass.—wrist.
Corp. J. Cumming, Co. F, 20th Massachusetts—leg.
Jas. Porter, Co. H, 29th Massachusetts—hand.
A. B. Rogers, Co. B, 10th Michigan—arm.
Henry Crum, Co. D, 7th Michigan—leg.
Henry Marback, Co. I, 7th New-York—shoulder.
Patrick Manning, Co. K, 20th Mass.—leg amputated.
Randolph Colwell, Co. B, 19th Massachusetts—side.
P. I. Campbell, 20th Massachusetts—arm amputated.
T. Harrington, Co. E, 19th Massachusetts—arm.
Geo. Danforth, Co. E, 19th Massachusetts—arm.
H. O. Shifferdecker, Co. B, 20th Mass.—breast.
L. J. C. Dodge, Co. D, 19th Massachusetts—breast.
H. G. Wagman, Co. B, 19th Massachusetts—leg.
Andrew Dougherty, Co. B, 69th Penn.—head.
R. Knapp, Co. I, 42d New-York—face.
Chas. Hanna, Co. B, 18th New-York—hand.
C. F. Barrett, 20th Massachusetts—head.
L. C. Richards, 20th Massachusetts—hand.
Henry Vocal, 24th New-York—hand.
E. F. Briggs, 20th Massachusetts—hip.
John Driscoll, 20th Massachusetts—wrist.
John Devine, 20th Massachusetts—elbow.
Jas. Cochran, Co. E, 20th Massachusetts—wrist.
Michael Holgan, 15th Massachusetts—hand.
Owen Herle, 20th Massachusetts—arm.
Andrew Kirby, Co. H, 20th Massachusetts—head.
Morgan Sweeny, Co. G, 20th Massachusetts—ear.
Jas. McGinnis, Co. G, 20th Massachusetts—groin.
John Riley, Co. F, 20th Massachusetts—leg.
J. H. Barrett, Co. F, 20th Massachusetts—foot.
A. Atkins, Co. F, 4th New-York—hip.
P. Kelty, Co. H, 20th Massachusetts—wrist.
Wm. H. Edwards, Co. H, 57th New-York—arm.
Daniel Martin, Co. D, 69th New-York—shoulder.
E. McManus—arm.
Wm. Humphreys, Co. D, 72d Pennsylvania—elbow.

ADJT. DODD ALIVE.

We understand that a dispatch has been received from Adjt. DODD, of the Fifth New-Hampshire Regiment, stating that he is alive and uninjured. His name has been reported among the killed.

THE LEFT GRAND DIVISION.

Details of the Crossing of Gen. Franklin's Command Below Fredericksburg.

BERNARD'S PLANTATION, ONE MILE AND A HALF BELOW FREDERICKSBURGH, Friday Evening, Midnight, Dec. 12, 1862.

At sunset last evening the first troops of the left wing of the army crossed to this side of the Rappahannock. Gen. NEWTON'S Division came over, the second Rhode-Island being in the advance and moving in "double quick." It was a most beautiful and imposing sight, and the cheer after cheer which arose from those in the rear as their comrades passed the river in safety, made us forget that this is indeed war.

Gen. NEWTON'S Division had been over but a short time before an order was received from Gen. BURNSIDE, directing them all to return with the exception of the First Brigade, which remained. This brigade is commanded by Brig.-Gen. DEVIN, of Massachusetts, and consists of the following regiments: Seventh Massachusetts, Col. RUSSELL; Eleventh Massachusetts, Col. EUSTISS; Second Rhode-Island, Brig.-Gen. WHEATON; Thirty-sixth New-York, Col. BROWNE; and Thirty-seventh Massachusetts.

Very early this morning, Gen. FRANKLIN'S entire command, consisting of BURK'S and REYNOLDS' corps, commenced crossing. Gen. BURK'S force came over first, all reaching this side before 9 o'clock. By noon all of Gen. REYNOLDS' command was also over. The ground occupied consists of a wide plain, stretching out for two miles or more, bounded on the north by Fredericksburgh, east by the Rappahannock, south by a small stream emptying in the Rappahannock, and west by the range of hills occupied by the enemy. The ground, marshy in some places, ascends gradually from the river for nearly half a mile, when there is considerable of an elevation.

At sunrise this morning, Company A, Twenty-third Pennsylvania, were thrown out as skirmishers. They were relieved by the Sixth Vermont, Col. LONG, after the expiration of two hours. Though considerable firing took place, no one was injured on our side. The enemy's skirmishers fell back on our advance.

About 9 o'clock, a portion of Gen. BURK'S Corps were drawn up in line of battle, facing to the west, Gen. PRATT'S Brigade being on the extreme left, which extended to the building where I am now writing. The force moved forward gradually, offering battle to the enemy, if any there should be. As Gen. REYNOLDS' Corps came over, Gen. GIBBONS' Division proceeded to the left, and were formed in line of battle, facing to the south. Skirmishers were here thrown out in front, also, who gradually moved southward, but found no enemy save a few skirmishers, who, after delivering a few volleys of musketry, disappeared. Gen. DOUBLEDAY'S [illegible]'s Division remained in the rear [illegible] river also, also the First, Second and Third Vermont Regiments, Vermont Brigade, HOWE'S Division, BURKES' Corps. About 11 o'clock, the first man on our side was wounded, JOHN S. HEAVEM, Company H, Thirty-third New-York. A stray ball from the enemy's sharpshooters struck him in the right leg, and, fracturing the bone, made amputation necessary. This was the only casualty on our side during the forenoon. Our batteries were planted, two on the extreme right, facing the enemy's intrenchments, above Fredericksburgh; one on the west, another to the south, while the remaining guns belonging to this division were located on the plain, at different points, ready to return the fire of the rebels, should they open upon us. About 2½ o'clock, the Second Regiment Pennsylvania Reserve were moved down across the stream below, where it took position for the day, prepared to resist any attempts of the enemy to approach in that direction and destroy the bridges. About the same time, the enemy opened from several guns in their intrenchments on our batteries facing in that direction, which immediately limbering up, moved several yards further to the front, and returned the fire. Several of our guns on the opposite side of the river also returned the fire. The artillery duel was kept up for some time, resulting in the wounding of four of our men. Gen. BURNSIDE rode out among the troops just before dusk, and was received with tremendous cheering by the troops, who are in the best of spirits. The Fifteenth New-York Engineers commenced laying a third bridge near this point about 3 o'clock, but were called off to throw one across the river near Fredericksburgh. The two bridges already completed are guarded by the Seventh Indiana, Col. GAVIN; Seventy-sixth New-York, Col. WAINRIGHT; Fifty-sixth New-York, Lieut.-Col. HOFFMAN; and Ninety-fifth New-York, Col. BIDDLE. The forces to-night occupy the following positions: Gen. BURKE'S corps, to the front and right; Gen. NEWTON'S division resting on the river; and Gen. REYNOLDS' corps to the rear and southward. This mansion is occupied by a wealthy Secessionist—BERNARD, by name—who is now a prisoner here. It is occupied as a hospital for General SMITH'S division, and in charge of Drs. BALLOU and HALL. It is the general impression that the enemy have proceeded in the direction of Richmond, leaving a small rearguard to dispute our advance. A rumor to the effect that Fort Darling has been taken, occasions much joy among the men, who are disposed to give it credence.

REBEL ACCOUNTS FROM FREDERICKSBURGH.

FORTRESS MONROE, Saturday, Dec. 13. Via Baltimore Sunday, Dec. 14.

The Richmond *Inquirer*, of the 17th, has the following:

"Heavy firing is going on at Fredericksburgh. LONGSTREET'S troops are engaged. The cannonading is severe. On Thursday last, our batteries stationed below the town opened fire on the gunboats anchored in the stream, consisting of the *Freeborn, Anacosta, Live Yankee* and *Resolute*.

The firing lasted an hour and a half, and was very heavy and rapid. Eleven houses were struck, and four completely riddled—the best in the village. No notice was given of an intention to shell. After the bombardment, the gunboats dropped down the river some miles. The people of the town, like those of Fredericksburgh, are now scattered in the farmhouses and cabins of the adjacent country.

Truly, the Yankees are waging a war of extermination. ABRAHAM LINCOLN is a fit compeer for NENA SAHIB."

IMPORTANT REBEL NEWS.

Movements of the National Forces in North Carolina.

An Attack Expected at Weldon and Petersburgh.

The following important items of news are from the Richmond *Dispatch* of the 12th inst.:

Important movements are on foot in Eastern North Carolina. Twelve regiments left Newbern on Saturday. Some think their destination is Wilmington. The more general belief is, that they design an attack on Weldon and Petersburgh. On Sunday two transports and five gunboats ascended the Chowan River, and a land force of ten thousand were seen in motion from Suffolk, indicating a movement on Weldon.

The Raleigh *Progress* announces the landing of a large Federal force in Gates County. If this be true, an immediate attack on Weldon may be expected.

JEFF. DAVIS AT KNOXVILLE.

KNOXVILLE, Tenn., Thursday, Dec. 11.

President DAVIS made a speech here this morning. He thinks the Toryism of East Tennessee exaggerated.

GOODS SEIZED IN GEORGIA.

Governor BROWN, of Georgia, acting under the authority of the Legislature of that State, has seized from $300,000 to $400,000 worth of goods in Augusta, for the use of the soldiers, to be paid for, of course, at reasonable rates. It has caused great excitement.

REBEL EMISSARIES.

Col. LUCIUS M. LAMAR will visit Europe accompanied by Col. L. Q. C. LAMAR, of Mississippi, who goes with instructions to Messrs. SLIDELL and MASON.

Arrivals in the City.

Gen. McClellan returned to this City on Friday evening last, at a very late hour. He was recognized upon his arrival at the Jersey City Dépôt by the crowd, who manifested their appreciation of his presence by vociferous cheering. The General acknowledged the recognition in a quiet manner, after which he proceeded across the river to Cortlandt-street, and was driven directly to the Fifth-avenue Hotel. He was accompanied home by Lieut.-Col. Hudson, one of the members of his Staff.

Hon. Daniel S. Dickinson, Albany; Hon. C. C. Chaffee (Ex-Member of Congress), from Byetown, Mass., and Maj. Warberg, U. S. A., are registered at the Fifth-avenue Hotel.

Hon. Chauncy Vibbard, from Schenectady; J. E. Williams, New-Orleans, and Charles E. Willis, Philadelphia, are stopping at the St. Nicholas Hotel.

Col. Hardin, of the Penna. Reserves; H. L. Whiting, U. S. Coast Survey; Lieut.-Col. W. J. Wentworth, of the Twenty-seventh Maine Regiment; Wm. Gillespie, U. S. Navy; and Dr. J. Homans, Jr., U. S. Army, are at the Astor House.

M. J. McAuliff, Liverpool; Dr. Potter, U. S. A.; A. Adamson, U. S. N., and C. G. Greeley, Boston, are at the Lafarge House.

Jas. Macdonald Jeffries, of the steamship *Kangaroo*; E. Churchill and family, Portland, and C. E. H[illegible], Wisconsin, are at the New-York Hotel.

Assault on Marye's Heights at Fredericksburg

Capture of the heights of Fredericksburg

Pontoon bridge across the Rappahannock

The New-York Times.

VOL. XII—NO. 3504. NEW-YORK, TUESDAY, DECEMBER 16, 1862. PRICE THREE CENTS.

FROM THE ARMY OF THE POTOMAC.

No General Engagement on Sunday or Yesterday.

Desultory Skirmishing Along the Advanced Positions.

The Position of the Two Armies Unchanged.

Continued Preparations for the Second Great Conflict.

Removal of the Wounded to the Washington Hospitals.

Over Seven Hundred Prisoners Captured by Us.

Engagement Between the Gunboats and a Rebel Battery.

HEADQUARTERS OF THE ARMY OF THE POTOMAC, MONDAY MORNING, Dec. 15, 1862—11 o'clock.

There was considerable firing yesterday, between the advanced troops of the two armies.

At one time the rebels showed a disposition to move upon Gen. FRANKLIN's forces.

Occasionally the rebels would throw a few shells among our troops, just to remind us that they were still there.

With these exceptions, everything was quiet.

There is some skirmishing this morning, with considerable artillery firing.

The body of Gen. BAYARD left for Washington to-day. He was to have been married next Wednesday.

HEADQUARTERS, Monday, Dec. 15—P. M.

The weather to-day has been clear and warm, with a strong southerly wind. The roads are in very good condition.

The position of the two armies remain nearly the same. There was not much artillery firing this afternoon by either party. Those shots the rebels did fire were thrown into the city.

The enemy, who are in plain view, are not idle, but busily employed in strengthening their position.

Most of the wounded, to-day, were removed from the [illegible] as on the renewal of the battle the rebel guns would likely cause its destruction.

Over seven hundred prisoners have been taken since our army crossed the river.

REPORTS FROM WASHINGTON.

WASHINGTON, Monday, Dec. 15.

A large number of the wounded from Fredericksburgh are expected here to-night or early to-morrow. A number of steamers have been dispatched to Aquia Creek for that purpose. The hospitals here are being rapidly depleted of such as are able to bear removal, to make room for the fresh comers.

Gen. VINTON, who is severely, but not dangerously, wounded in the side, is here under the care of his father, Rev. Dr. VINTON, who came on this morning.

GUNBOAT FIGHT ON THE RAPPAHANNOCK

WASHINGTON, Monday, Dec. 15.

On Wednesday evening, our gunboats at Port Royal, about twenty-seven miles from Fredericksburgh, were fired into by a rebel battery from the shore, supposed to number twenty heavy guns.

One of the rebel shots struck a coal schooner, wounding Capt. SIMMONS, who has since died.

Another shot struck the *Currituck* on the larboard side, pushing into the engine-room and wounding H. F. SMITH, of Rhode Island, who has since died; also, wounding JEREMIAH DAILY dangerously, and two others slightly.

The firing was very rapid and continued, until sundown, when the rebel batteries were silenced.

Two schooners, at the commencement of the fight, were lying directly in range of the rebel guns, near the shore, but were brought off safely by the *Teaser*. Our gunboats laid off the shore until morning, when they again opened upon the rebel battery, but met with no response.

THE OPERATIONS OF FRIDAY.

Continual Skirmishing Throughout the Day—About Two Hundred of our Men Killed and Wounded, &c.

From Our Special Correspondent.

FREDERICKSBURGH, Va., Friday, Dec. 12, 1862.

As I stated in my last letter, the National troops occupy the town of Fredericksburgh. During the preceding night FRANKLIN's and a portion of SUMNER's Grand Divisions passed over the river and bivouacked on the opposite bank. Skirmishers were sent to reconnoitre the several streets, and met with much opposition from the rebel sharpshooters, who were posted behind buildings, chimnies and fences. The night was quite dark, and it was with considerable difficulty that the rebels could be discovered in their hiding-places. The skirmishers, however, understood their duty, and displayed much courage in ferreting out the foe. They finally gained their point, and drove the rebels out of the town. As may be naturally supposed, our loss in casualties was not light. Numbers of our men were shot dead, and a great number, considering the nature of the fight, wounded. During the day and evening our casualties were about 200 killed and wounded. The rebel loss cannot be estimated, as they removed their killed and wounded before we got possession of the place.

This morning our troops were massed on the two principal streets of the town running parallel with the river. The upper portion of the town was occupied by the skirmishers, while just at the outside the pickets were stationed. Our force has not made any material change in position to-day. FRANKLIN's troops are bivouacked at the lower end of the place. The troops have not as yet ventured far to the upper end of Fredericksburgh, in consequence of the rebel sharpshooters being in position some five hundred yards distant.

This morning, while the rear of SUMNER's column was passing over the upper pontoon, the rebels opened fire from guns in their second tier of earthworks. The shots were well directed, but fortunately our men escaped injury. After firing a few rounds, the rebels ceased. Our batteries near Falmouth replied, and possibly had much to do in silencing the enemy's guns. Nearly all of our batteries, which were planted along the river bank yesterday, were taken across the bridges to-day. They were not, however, excepting those which accompanied FRANKLIN's troops, placed in position, but remained upon the streets, their commander awaiting orders.

This afternoon HOOKER's troops appeared at the upper bridge for the purpose of crossing. The rebels immediately opened a heavy fire upon them. The order was at length countermanded and the troops were marched down to the vicinity of the lower bridge upon which FRANKLIN crossed, and upon which they will cross early to-morrow morning.

To-day, Gen. FRANKLIN sent out artillery and skirmishers to the left of the rebel fortifications. They were met with a vigorous fire from the rebel guns, and made but little progress toward an advance.

Four companies of the Eighth Illinois Cavalry, under Major BEVERIDGE, made a reconnoissance toward the rebel earthworks. They went sufficiently near to count the guns—eight in number—in one battery. The rebels did not offer to fire upon them, probably from the fact of their being unable to depress their guns to the proper degree.

Lieut KERNES, of the Sixth United States Cavalry, with four men, forded the river just above Fredericksburgh. The water was ascertained to be four feet deep, which rendered the crossing of artillery and supply wagons by the same means impracticable. It is decided that the entire army must cross the river over bridges. There are now four bridges constructing, two at the upper and two at the lower end of the town.

The appearance of Fredericksburgh after the severe cannonading it received yesterday can be readily imagined. Hardly a house stands that has not been penetrated by more or less shots. In the midst of all the shelling, however, some of the citizens remained in their houses, taking refuge in the cellars. Among the citizens I notice a few women. No reliable information could be obtained from the inhabitants in regard to the position and strength of the rebels. As near as I could learn the town was defended yesterday by two Mississippi Regiments, one of which was the Seventeenth.

The number of prisoners taken yesterday and to-day amount to over two hundred. A deserter came in this morning. He reports that the rebels have their lines of earthworks extending a distance of two miles. They are so built as to command every street leading from the river.

Our next movement [illegible] the rebels [illegible] Gen. BUTTERFIELD has issued orders to his Staff, to-night, to prepare themselves with five days' rations, it being the intention to pursue the enemy until he is forced to fight or surrender. This order would imply that it is not impossible that the enemy may evacuate his position before morning. It is considered a singular circumstance that he has not opened upon us with more continuous and vigorous fire. It is the intention to cross Gen. HOOKER's Grand Division in the morning. The three Grand Divisions will then be across the river. To-morrow a strenuous effort will be made to take the rebel earthworks. If the rebels stand we shall certainly have a terrible conflict.

WHIT.

THE KILLED AND WOUNDED.

From different sources we have the following names of those killed and wounded in Saturday's engagement: for the most part additional to those already published.

KILLED.

Maj. Ed. S. Sturtevant, 5th New-Hampshire.
Capt. Jno. Murray, 5th N.H.
Capt. Jas. B. Perry, 5th N.H.
Lieut. Geo. Dickenson, 4th U. S. Artillery.
Lieut. Birdsall, Co. D, 59th Pennsylvania.
Lieut. Hightman, Co. D, 59th Pennsylvania.
Capt. Reynolds, 59th Penn.
Maj. Pitcher, 4th Maine.
Capt. P. Egan, Co. C, 9th N.Y.
Lieut. Hirst, Co. C, 9th N.Y.
Lieut. Layton, Co. C, 9th N.Y.
Corp. C. F. Tyson, Co. C, 9th New-York.
F. J. Binner, Co. F, 9th N.Y.
A. Arnold, Co. B, 9th N.Y.
L. Tower, Co. I, 9th N.Y.

WOUNDED.

Capt. Hunt, Assistant Surgeon-General to Gen. Tyler.
Chas. Hanna, Co. B, 15th N.Y.
R. Knapp, Co. I, 42d N.Y.
Sergt. G. Pitcher, Co. G, 69th New-York.
Sergt. B. McManus, Co. G, 69th New-York.
D. Martin, Co. D, 69th N.Y.
E. McManus, Co. —, 69th N.Y.
Capt. Jos. D. Morch, Co. B, 83d N.Y., (9th State Mil.)
Capt. John Hendrickson, 83d N.Y., (9th State Militia)—Commanding Regiment.
M. Holgan, Co. —, 15th Massachusetts.
Capt. Mercena Dunn, of Boston, Co. D, 19th Mass.
Capt. Andrew Mahoney, of Boston, Co. E, 19th Mass.
Lieut. Edgar M. Newcomb, of Boston, Co. —, 19th Mass.
Sergt. H. J. Carr, Co. G, 19th Massachusetts.
Corp. J. F. Douglass, Co. H, 19th Massachusetts.
Randolph Colwell, Co. B, 19th Massachusetts.
Timothy Harrington, Co. E, 19th Massachusetts.
L. J. C. Dodge, Co. D, 19th Massachusetts.
F. G. Wayman, Co. B, 19th Massachusetts.
Corp. John Cumming, Co. F, 20th Massachusetts.
J. Porter, Co. H, 20th Mass.
P. Manning, Co. K, 20th Mass.
P. I. Campbell, Co. —, 20th Massachusetts.
H. O. Shifferdecker, Co. B, 20th Massachusetts.
Capt. Angus Cameron, Co. F, 83d N.Y., (9th State Mil.)
Capt. L. Carpenter, Co. —, 94th New-York.
Sergt. R. G. Steward, Co. B, 94th New-York.
A. Atkins, Co. F, 94th New-York.
Hy. Vosal, Co. —, 94th N.Y.
A. Dougherty, Co. B, 68th Pennsylvania.
Wm. Humphreys, Co. D, 72d Pennsylvania.
Lieut. J. F. Hazett, Co. E, 106th Pennsylvania.
C. F. Barrett, Co. —, 20th Massachusetts.
L. C. Richards, Co. —, 20th Massachusetts.
E. F. Briggs, Co. —, 20th Massachusetts.
John Driscoll, Co. —, 20th Massachusetts.
John Devine, Co. —, 20th Massachusetts.
James Cochran, Co. E, 20th Massachusetts.
O. Heric, Co. —, 20th Mass.
A. Kirby, Co. H, 20th Mass.
M. Sweeny, Co. G, 20th Mass.
James McGinness, Co. G, 20th Massachusetts.
J. Riely, Co. F, 20th Mass.
J. H. Barrett, Co. F, 20th Massachusetts.
P. Kelly, Co. H, 20th Mass.
A. B. Rogers, Co. B, 7th Michigan.
Henry Crum, Co. D, 7th Michigan.
Henry Marback, Co. I, 7th Michigan.

FROM AQUIA CREEK.

The following names of killed and wounded were gathered at Aquia Creek:

FIFTY-SEVENTH NEW-YORK REGIMENT.

Col. A. B. Chapman—breast, slightly.
Capt. J. H. Bell, Co. C—shoulder, slightly.
Capt. H. H. Mott, Co. I—thigh and arm.
Lieut. H. M. Brewster, Act. Adjutant—arm.
Lieut. Thos. C. White, Co. B—foot, slightly.
Lieut.-Col. Bull, 66th N.Y.—killed.
Wm. Osborne, Co. K—hand.
Jas. Cleary, Co. K—killed.
H. J. Hinton, Co. C—leg, slightly.
Joseph A. Lothrop, Co. B—neck.
Wm. Cahan, Co. D—leg.
Patrick Morgan—leg.
James Hunter, Co. D—arm.
Richard Tayler, Co. D—leg.
Aug. Geising, Co. H—knee.
W. H. Edwards, Co. H.
Jas. Larkins, Co. A—ankle.
Sergt. John Niles, Co. I—head, slightly.
Andrew Baker, Co. K—side, slightly.
Earl Park, Co. D—shoulder.
Theo. Batcher, Co. I—foot.
David H. Paine, Co. D—arm.
Thos. Donnell, Color Corp.—breast.
Aaron Clark, Co. I—chest, fatally.
Patrick Cassidy, Co. I—ankle, severely.
Martin C. Crosset, Co. D—arm amputated.
John Murlin, Co. D—knee.
James Carroady, Co. D—shoulder.
Michael Kennedy, Co. F—head.
Orderly Serg. Thos. Fritton, Co. I—leg.

SIXTY-SIXTH NEW-YORK REGIMENT.

Capt. P. Dodge, Co. D—killed.
Michael Shields—foot.
Lieut. Switzer, Co. D—thigh, slightly.

MISCELLANEOUS.

Major Wright, 119th Penn.—shoulder.
Major Jennings, 26th N.Y.
Capt. Hart, Assistant Adjutant-General to Gen. Taylor—breast.
Capt. J. M. Kent, Co. K, 8th Penn.—shoulder.
Capt. Hendrickson, com'd'g 8th Pa. R.—leg and ankle.
Fr. Kennedy, 57th Pa.—leg.
Lieut. F. A. Worth, Co. H, 86th Penn.—face.
Lieut. F. C. Basger, Co. G, 46th New-York—hand.
Lieut. W. T. Bliss, Co. E, 46th New-York—head.
Lt. E. Mulkins, Co. I—hand.
Lieut. Stevens, 16th Maine.
Lieut. Austin—side.
Sergt. Forster, Co. A.
Sergt. Williams, Co. A.
Sergt. McAllister, Co. G, 4th Vermont—leg.
Sergt. Miller, Co. K, 11th Pennsylvania.
Sergt. Demming, color bearer, 94th N.Y.—side.
Sergt. Wheeler, Co. B, 121st Pennsylvania—thigh.
Sergt. Hasell, Co. C, 88th Pennsylvania—arm.
Sergt. Bowenn, Co. I, 9th New-York—face.
Sergt. Knipe, Co. I, 9th New-York—leg.
Sergt. Marchant, Co. B—leg.
Corp. Carlton, Co. C, 9th New-York.
Corp. Skinner, Co. C, 9th New-York.
Corp. Culhian, Co. C, 9th New-York.
Corp. Harriet, Co. D, 9th New-York—foot.
Corp. Preuss, Co. G, 9th New-York.
Capt. Musche, Co. B.—9th New-York—leg.
Capt. Lovitt, Co. E, 16th Me.
Capt. Carpenter, Co. H, 94th New-York—head.
Capt. Cameron, 9th N.Y.
Lieut. Penten, Co. K, 11th Penn.—arm.
Lieut. Foster, Co. C, 68th Penn.—leg.
Lieut. Shorter, Co. A, 68th Penn.—leg.
Lieut. Frink, Co. A, 9th N.Y.
Lieut. Crocker, (rebel,) 19th Tennessee—leg.
Lt. Layton, Co. C, 9th N.Y.
Sergt. Cook, Co. C, 9th New-York—leg.
Sergt. Congy, Co. C—breast.
Sergt. Osgood, Co. D.
Sergt. Page, Co. F—wrist.
Sergt. Pierce, 4th Vermont—arm.
Sergt. Jacobs, Co. G, 9th N. York.
Corpl. Van Valkenburg, Co. D, 9th New-York.
Corpl. Grams, Co. D, 9th New-York.
Corpl. Durborn, Co. D, 9th New-York.
Corpl. Johnson, Co. A, 9th New-York.
Corpl. Hodgkinson, Co. A, 9th New-York.
Corpl. Shange, Co. C, 9th New-York.
Corp. Davis, Co. C, 9th N.Y.
Corp. Power, Co. G, 9th New-York—hand.
Corp. Gauther, Co. B, 88th Pennsylvania—leg.
Corp. Baker, Co. C, 49th New-York—hip.
Corp. Alkin, color bearer, 4th Vermont—arm.

PRIVATES.

Beckwith, Co. A, 9th N.Y.
Delany, Co. A, 9th N.Y.
Winnie, Co. A, 9th N.Y.
Ellison, Co. A, 9th N.Y.
J. Butler, Co. D, 9th N.Y.
Vanseeklin, Co. D, 9th N.Y.
Wall, Co. D, 9th New-York.
R. White, Co. D, 9th N.Y.
Leslie, Co. D, 9th N.Y.
Arkwith, Co. D, 9th N.Y.
Fargo, Co. D, 9th N.Y.—side.
Lewis, Co. D, 9th N.Y.—slightly.
McCreary, Co. C, 9th N.Y.—arm.
Malone, Co. C, 9th N.Y.—leg.
Morgan, Co. C, 9th N.Y.—leg.
Terry, Co. C, 9th N.Y.—leg.
R. Colemans, Co. I, 4th Vt.—hand.
D. C. Grindle, Co. K, 16th Maine—leg.
R. M. Jones, Co. K, 26th N.Y.—arm.
J. Rogers, Co. E, 11th Penn.—head.
S. Sydney, Co. F, 26th N.Y.—head.
A. Cobb, Co. H, 8th Penn.—arm.
A. B. Titus, Co. B, 2d Vermont—knee.
M. Mullen, Co. B, 4th Vermont—arm.
J. Yourdon, Co. C, 26th N.Y.—head.
J. Riley, Co. E, 3d Vt.—face.
E. L. Barker, Co. F, 16th Maine—head.
M. Colley, Co. D, 4th Vermont—arm.
P. Helpin, Co. I, 2d Vt.—hand.
P. Holden, Co. I, 2d Vt.—hand.
H. Brady, Co. C, 9th N.Y.—leg.
J. F. Bockett, Co. C, 10th N.Y.—leg.
C. A. Seargent, Co. B, 4th Vt.—leg.
J. Hess, Co. K, 136th Pa.—leg.
J. M. Barclay, Co. K, [illegible]—arm.
A. McBride, Co. K, 99th Pa.—thigh.
W. Wheeler, Co. E, 16th Me.—foot.
J. Gyer, Co. B, 9th N.Y.—side.
J. M. Carlton—[illegible]
N. Skellon, Co. B, 121st Pennsylvania—thigh.
J. [illegible], Co. I, 9th N.Y.
S. G. Paul, Co. I, 9th New-York—arm.
J. P. Jawdon, Co. I, 9th New-York—mouth.
W. Briston, Co. I, 9th New-York—arm.
F. Brueths, Co. I, 9th New-York—leg.
J. Campbell, Co. I, 9th N.Y.
W. Durent, Co. I, 9th New-York—leg.
A. Gerike, Co. I, 9th New-York—leg.
J. Geyer, Co. I, 9th New-York—side.
J. Heborn, Co. I, 9th New-York—leg and arm.
G. W. Washburne, Co. G, 9th New-York, groin.
J. Beargen, Co. I, 9th N.Y., arm.
J. B. Lythe, Co. I, 9th N.Y., arm.
H. McCourt, Co. I, 9th N.Y., shoulder.
J. Walsh, Co. H, 9th N.Y., head.
J. E. Smith, Co. H, 9th New-York, leg.
J. Holmes, Co. H, 9th N.Y., arm.
J. Brian, Co. C, 9th N.Y.
P. Brophey, Co. D, 9th New-York.
J. Osborne, Co. D, 9th N.Y.
W. W. Earling, Co. D, 9th New-York.
P. Marvin, Co. D, 9th N.Y.
A. W. Mins, Co. D, 9th N.Y.
A Vashage, Co. D, 9th N.Y.
Bickerton, Co. D, 9th N.Y.
Coleman, Co. D, 9th N.Y.
Jacques, Co. D, 9th N.Y.
Mosher, Co. D, 9th N.Y.
Street, Co. D, 9th N.Y.
S. T. Farnam—leg and side.
J. F. Robinson, Co. E, 16th Maine—shoulder.
M. Hilsen, Co. F, 26th N.Y.—leg.
H. Ramshill, Co. G, 16th N.Y.—shoulder.
M. Thagon, Co. H, 43d N.Y.—leg.
G. E. Bigelow, Co. C, 13th Mass.—thigh.
J. Ayres, Co. H, 136th Penn.—head.
W. W. Darling, Co. D, 9th New-York—hand.
J. Vansant, Co. A, 11th Penn—thigh.
W. Sturm, Co. K, 7th Wisconsin—head.
W. Wilson, Co. B, 4th Vt.—leg.
J. Stafford, Co. H, 43d N.Y.—leg.
J. S. Hands, Co. H, 43d N.Y.—leg.
J. M. Stow, Co. K, 26th N.Y.
P. Crance, Co. H, 4th Vermont—arm.
J. Berlin, Co. K, 11th Penn.—shoulder.
J. W. Clarke, Co. B, 4th Vermont—leg and chin.
E. M. Sprout, Co. B, 4th Vermont—leg.
L. Layard, Co. I, 5th Vt.—foot.
N. Robinson, Co. G, 5th Vermont—hand.
A. J. Harbot, Co. H, 8th Pa., leg.
J. Eliott, Co. K, 11th Pa.—head.
S. Bayer, Co. H, 11th Pa.—side.
A. Boyndon, Co. B, 4th Va., leg.
[illegible]
[illegible] Tower, C[illegible] Me.—hand.
R. Christy, Co. B, 4th Me.—side.
J. Bake, Co. K, 11th Pa.
S. [illegible] Pennsylvania.
L. Hull, Co. K, 11th Penn.
P. Kelly, Co. I, 9th New-York—leg.
J. Nesely, Co. I, 9th New-York—wrist.
J. Windon, Co. I, 9th New-York—wrist.
J. High, Co. B, 88th Pennsylvania—ankle.
D. McNeil, Co. B, 88th Pennsylvania—leg.
G. Arnard, Co. B, 88th Pennsylvania—arm.
J. Brown, Co. G, 9th N.Y.
S. Donelson, Co. G, 9th New-York.
F. H. Monday, Co. G, 9th New-York—leg.
J. G. Weaver, Co. G, 9th New-York—arm.
W. Payne, Co. H, 9th N.Y., thigh.
J. H. Dawes, Co. C, 9th N.Y.
H. T. Patrick, Co. C, 9th N.Y.
W. H. Pedley, Co. C, 9th N.Y.
G. F. Seybold, Co. C, 9th N.Y.
J. R. Brady, Co. C, 9th N.Y.
H. G. Bradley, Co. C, 9th N.Y.
— Craig, Co. D, 9th N.Y.
— Connor, Co. D, 9th N.Y.
C. Skinner, Co. D, 9th N.Y.
J. Bell, Co. D, 9th N.Y.
M. Murray, Co. D, 9th N.Y.
A. B. Bailey, Co. D, 9th N.Y.
J. Simpson, Co. D, 9th N.Y.
J. Johnson, Co. D, 9th N.Y.
W. O. Brian, Co. H, 9th N.Y.—leg.
J. Larkins, Co. H, 9th N.Y.—thigh.
D. D. Simmons, Co. F, 9th New-York.
W. Rinkum, Co. F, 9th N.Y.

Capt. Shepard, 20th Massachusetts; Lieut. A. R. Curtis, 20th Massachusetts; Lieut. H. E. E. Wilkins, 20th Massachusetts; Lieut. T. M. McKay, 20th Massachusetts—all wounded; none dangerously.

M. Shepard, Co. F, 9th N.Y.—hand.
Sergt. Thos. Owens, Co. I, 15th Connecticut.
M. Neptent, Co. K, 52d New-York.
F. D. Rock, Co. F, 48th Pennsylvania.
Jacob Chad, Co. C, 13th New-York.
G. Vanhousten, Co. C, 107th New-York.
J. Fitzgerald, Co. H, 21st Connecticut.
M. McLoughlin, Co. C, 48th Pennsylvania.
D. C. Rary, Co. A, 21st Mass.
Geo. Gaither, Co. K, 27th Connecticut.
Wm. Seigel, Co. C, 1st Mich.
J. G. Gerrolf, Co. D, 3d Mass.
Sergt. John Dean, Co. A, 26th New-York.
B. Buttell, Co. D, 52d N.Y.
B. J. Cushing, Co. G, 53d Pennsylvania.
E. Laurel, Co. A, 7th N.Y.
E. Ullman, Co. E, 66th N.Y.
J. Murchy, Co. E, 37th N.Y.
J. L. Gilman, Co. A, 11th New-Hampshire.
W. Harrison, Co. C, 5th N.H.
P. Rondan, Co. I, 10th N.H.
J. Good, Co. C, 4th N.Y.
H. H. Hoyt, Co. H, 10th New-York.
C. Detwelin, Co. K, 81st Pa.
Henry White, Co. F, 51st Pa.
Hugh McDaid, Co. I, 12th R.I.
Serg.-Maj. Manchester, 7th Rhode Island.
Serg.-Maj. McCormick, 145th Pennsylvania.
Corp. W. J. Mason, Co. C, 5th Massachusetts.
O. P. Robinson, Co. K, 35th Massachusetts.
Second Lieut. Wilber, Co. E, 7th Rhode Island.
A. W. Samison, Co. G, 4th R.I.
O. D. Cancer, Co. K, 35th Mass.
Ord.-Serg. S. Wilson, Co. H, 145th Pennsylvania.
C. J. Sikweder, Co. D, 61st New York.
O. Light, Co. F, 12th R. I.
R. Bammer, Co. K, 13th N.Y.
O. Kennedy, Co. K, 63d Pa.
S. Topping, Co. B, 17th N.Y.
R. F. Pelan, Co. E, 8th R. I.
C. Mott, Jr., Co. I, 7th R. I.
J. Surgeon, Co. M, 62d Pa.
T. A. Take, Co. G, 4th R. I.
J. P. Huber, Co. D, 118th Pa.
D. E. Powell, Co. D, 25th N.J.
Ell Ward, Co. G, 25th N. J.
J. Ranney, Co. C, 25th N. J.
L. L. Robinson, Co. G, 25th N.J.
C. Gorkeil, Co. D, 25th N. J.
W. J. Giles, Co. C, 25th N. J.
T. A. Barber, Co. E, 49th N.Y.
A. Wills, Co. I, 25th N. J.
L. G. Lindsey, Co. E, 25th N.Y.
— Bohlinger, 103d N.Y.
J. Delk, Co. D, 25th N. J.
W. Mecomber, Co. A, 108th N.Y.
C. H. Lancaster, Co. C, 11th Mass.
M. Boyston, Co. C, 9th Mass.
R. Evans, Co. F, 35th Mass.
N. Matthews, Co. H, 52d New-York.
T. Bennett, Co. B, 163d N.Y.
G. Oswig, Co. K, 52d N.Y.
Sergt. A. Nathrop, Co. I, 21st New-York.
Sergt. G. H. Bean, Co. H, 21st Massachusetts.
M. V. B. Metcalf, Co. D, 14th Connecticut.
W. Akerly, Co. K, 145th Pennsylvania.
Sergt. W. H. Alain, Co. H, 27th Connecticut.
J. T. Maynard, Co. D, 22d Massachusetts.
J. Daggan, Co. K, 26th Mass.
F. M. Higgins, Co. B, 5th New-Hampshire.
N. W. Sprague, Co. I, 57th New-York.
Capt. B. Drallin, Co. A, 8th Pennsylvania.
S. W. Prentiss, Co. I, 21st Ct.
J. Shirlas, Co. I, 69th N.Y.
Capt. J. Dwinell, Co. G, 21st Massachusetts.
Corp. E. Kuhn, Co. A, 7th New-York.
J. M. Bunell, Co. K, 53d Pa.
W. H. Heck, Co. K, 53d Pa.
D. Conrey, Co. F, 5th N. H.
M. Shein, Co. A, 2d Md.
A. J. Guados, Co. A, 53d Mass.
J. A. Merritt, Co. A, 21st Massachusetts.
M. Harop, Co. C, 7th R. I.
J. Sunderland, Co. E, 48th Pa.
W. H. McMaster, Co. H, 145th Pennsylvania.
Serg. Otto Kosack, Co. K, 2d Maryland.
R. Logan, Co. F, 51st N.Y.
Serg. T. Punkett, Co. E, 21st Massachusetts.
A. Hutchinson, Co. C, 11th New-Hampshire.
H. Gallagher, Co. E, 21st Mass.
B. F. Hahn, Co. K, 13th N.Y.
Maj. S. Willard, 35th Mass.
M. Keen, Co. D, 7th R. I.
O. H. Godfrey, Co. A, 2d Maine.
Lieut.-Col. Connor, 44th N.Y.
John Beale, Co. D, 51st Pa.
J. Harwood, Co. C, 25th N.J.
Sergt. Titus, Co. E, 51st Pa.
F. Stillman, Co. B, 27th N.J.
Corp. Ludlow, Co. F, 7th N.J.
Wm. Farden, Co. I, 7th N.J.
W. B. Shaw, Co. D, 7th N.J.
Daniel Cain, Co. I, 7th N.J.
And. Ricker, Co. B, 20th Me.
D. H. White, Co. F, 25th N.J.
J. R. Giddings, Co. C, 44th N.Y.
B. F. Sewell, Co. B, 25th N.J.
J. R. Green, Co. A, 7th R. I.
H. B. Bridgman, Co. K, 13th N.Y.
R. Mosely, Co. H, 5th N.Y.
Ser. F. Atwood, Co. C, 18th N.Y.
J. Norton, Co. K, 61st N.Y.
Ser. Wiseman, Co. C, 155th Pa.
H. Noiler, Co. E, 13th N. H.
H. Hitchson, Co. G, 25th N.Y.
J. P. Jones, Co. H, 21st Mass.
— Coleman, Co. D, 25th N.J.
P. S. Gillett, Co. I, 22d Mass.
P. Dillon, Co. F, 10th N. H.
[illegible], Co. F, 16th N. H.

W. Van Vleit, 89th N.Y.
J. Pfeiffer, Co. C, 13th N.Y.
W. Sallby, Co. A, 89th N.Y.
D. Coons, Co. A, 14th N.Y.
J. H. Daniels, Co. I, 21st Conn.
J. Graves, Co. C, 62d Penn.
E. Cornella, Co. E, 25th N.J.
Dennis Pang, Co. E, 22d N.J.
Corp. J. Vogt, 27th Conn.
Corp. A. R. Schell, 129th Pa.
C. Campbell, Co. D, 10th New-Hampshire.
A. J. Cole, Co. C, 44th N.Y.
R. Love, Co. F, 13th N.Y.
C. F. Layard, Co. K, 12th New-York.
G. W. Sawing, 9th N. H.
2d Lieut. Knott, Co. I, 10th New-Hampshire.
Capt. Knott, Co. I, 10th N.H.
R. Brown, Co. C, 25th N.Y.
W. H. Gilford, Co. E, 2d Delaware—hip.
Geo. Simpson, Co. B, 2d Delaware—eye.
Geo. McNeil, Co. C, 2d Delaware—side.
Ernest Graw, Co. H, 2d Delaware—finger.
Sergt.-Maj. McMenvasy, 2d Delaware—shoulder.
C. B. Hammer, Co. K, 2d Delaware—left leg.
Joel Taggert, 2d Del.—arm.
Chas. Wier, Co. G, 2d Delaware—arm.
G. Yule, Co. E, 2d Del.—arm.
F. Hanscom, Co. D, 2d Delaware—eye.
Color-Sergt. Wier, Co. D, 2d Delaware—arm.
F. Nourse, Co. H, 2d Delaware—arm.
F. Lynch, Co. I, 2d Delaware—leg.
R. Ritchie, Co. H, 2d Delaware—groin.
— McLean, Co. H, 2d Delaware—neck.
David S. Hawkins, Co. A, 21st Connecticut.
Lieut. E. L. Melkins, Co. F, 63d New-York.
John Crappe, Co. I, 69th New-York—foot.
Dan. Green, 7th R. I.—thigh.
Col. Heenan, 116th —, arm broken.
Lieut.-Col. Mulholland—arm broken.
O. Kilduff, 69th N.Y., both legs.
Peter Garrison, 69th N.Y., head.
J. McDermott, Co. G, 69th N.Y., killed.
Capt. Bonohan, Co. G, 69th New-York, right arm.
Lieut. Callahan, 69th New-York, right arm and left thigh.
Lieut. Burke, 69th N.Y., right arm.
Capt. Leddy, 69th N.Y., shoulder.
Major Kavanagh, 69th N.Y., thigh.
Capt. Bell, 81st Penn., killed.
Capt. Stewart, 81st N.Y.
Lieut. Buckley, 61st N.Y.
Lieut. Schoonmaker, 51st New-York.
Lieut. Keene, 51st N.Y.
A. Kelly, Co. F, 10th N. H.
F. F. Maury, Co. F, 25th N.J.
R. Jamieson, Co. G, 25th N.J.
J. S. High, Co. F, 25th N.J.
Geo. Fisher, Co. F, 7th R. I.
W. A. Morell, Co. E, 52d N.Y.
P. Envery, Co. A, 103d N.Y.
Corp. Amilia, Co. F, 10th N.H.
John Keefe, Co. D, 69th N.Y.
W. B. Humphreys, Co. C, 89th New-York.
J. Callahan, Co. F, 10th N.H.
Oliver Barnes, Co. F, 10th New-Hampshire.
J. Mantustuk, Co. D, 163d New-York.
P. Cosey, Co. D, 163d N.Y.
J. H. Bruce, Co. I, 7th R. I.
R. Possell, Co. H, 51st Pa.
Corp. Brown, Co. H, 51st Pa.
— Bunnet, Co. C, 2d Delaware—eye.
Col. W. P. Bailey, 2d Delaware—slightly in foot.
Capt. Winnie, Co. I, 2d Delaware—arm.
Lieut. James, Co. I, 2d Delaware—shoulder.
Lieut. Reynolds, 2d Delaware—shoulder.
Lieut. Bird, Co. E, 2d Delaware—eye.
— McKnight, 2d Del.—leg.
Wm. Kingston, Co. C, 2d Delaware—thigh.
J. Campbell, Co. F, 2d Delaware—leg.
Major Ricketts, 2d Delaware—hip.
Major Burdel—in hand.
Major O'Neil, 63d New-York—shot in two places.
Capt. Hart, of Meagher's Staff—wrist.
Capt. Burke, 88th —.
Adjt. Young, 88th —.
John Fay, Co. A, 69th New-York—shoulder.
Sergt. McManus, Co. G, 69th New-York—arm.
— Kelley, 69th New-York—leg.
Corp. Delaney, 69th New-York—right thigh.
John Clare, 69th New-York—hip.
Edgar Hamilton, 69th New-York—severely.
John Kane, 69th New-York—right leg.
Lieut. O. Donovan, 69th N.Y., five places.
Major Harghan, 88th N.Y., killed.
Lieut.-Col. Sayles, 7th R.I., by shell in body, torn to pieces.
Lieut. Dickerson, Battery E, 4th U. S. Art., killed.
Capt. Casey, (Gen. Sturgis' Staff,) head.
Orderly Sergt. Donohue, (Gen. Sturgis' Escort,) scrotum.
Major Babbitt, 7th Rhode Island, seriously.
Major Willard, 35th Mass., groin.
Lieut. Butler, 51st N.Y.
Lieut. A. F. Walcott, Gen. Ferrero's Staff—wrist.
Lieut. McKibbin, Gen. Ferrero's Staff—wrist.

FOURTH NEW-YORK.

— Sheridan, Co. I—killed.
Col. McGregor—arm.
L. Scribner—side.
J. Palmer, Jr.—hand.

SEVENTH NEW-YORK.

Capt. Masbury—killed.
Capt. Belcher—wounded.
Capt. Herring—wounded.
Lieut. Windor—wounded.
Lieut. Foulkt—wounded.
Lieut. Bokenhein—wound'd
Lieut.-Col. Gable—wounded

FROM WASHINGTON.

The following names have been received at Washington:

Jas. King, Co. H—81st Penn.—leg.
John McFadden, 81st Penn.—thigh.
J. T. Jones, Co. H, 81st Penn.
Sergt. Peters, Co. G, 81st Pa.
Sergt. [illegible] Pennsylvania—arm.
Sergt.-Major Williams, 81st Pennsylvania.
Sergt. Menyon, Co. [illegible], 81st.
[illegible], Co. I, 4th Mich.
[illegible] Walters, 88th Penn.
J. S. English, 134th Penn.
Fred. Jacobi, 7th New-York.
Lieut. Smith, 88th Penn.
Lieut.-Colonel McKean, 81st Penn.—in side and foot.
Capt. Connor, Co. I, 81st Pa.—though left lung, probably mortal.
Lieut. J. W. Pryor, Co. G, 81st Pennsylvania.
Laurence Brewer, Co. G, 81st Pennsylvania.
Jno. Andrews, Co. K, 81st Pennsylvania.
Peter Heddinger, Co. I, 81st Pennsylvania.
Conrad Baker, Co. I, 81st Pennsylvania.
Daniel Washburn, Co. I, 81st Pennsylvania.
John Bruner, Co. G, 81st Pennsylvania.
Geo. Washington, Co. K, 81st Pennsylvania.
M. Haggerty, Co. I, 64th New-York.
John Hickey, Co. B, 64th N.Y.
Lieut.-Col. Brooks, 64th N.Y.—through left shoulder.
Jas. Bryden, Co. E, 64th N.Y.
M. G. Atwater, Co. E, 64th N.Y.
A. Opdyke, Co. E, 64th N.Y.
W. Porter, Co. B, 64th N.Y.
L. Ryan, Co. I, 64th N.Y.
Lt. Parker, Co. C, 64th N.Y.—breast, seriously.
P. Devine, 61st New-York.
Wm. McNally, Co. A, 64th New-York.
George Pelton, Co. D, 64th New-York.
George Herbey, 64th N.Y.
John Moore, 81st Penn.
Wick Morgan, Co. A, 64th New-York.
John Yoke, Co. A, 64th N.Y.
C. Babcock, Co. G, 64th N.Y.
E. W. Johnson, Co. E, 64th New-York.
George Van Attis, 7th N.Y.
A. Howe, 5th N. Hampshire.
Samuel F. Pease, Co. F, 64th New-York.
Serg. Underwood, Co. A, 130th Pennsylvania—head.
— Foster, Co. A, 130th Pa.—arm.
J. S. Forrest, Co. C, 130th Penn.—slightly in head.
Lieut. Levi Haverstick, Acting Adjutant 130th Penn.—both legs and arm shot off.
Lieut. Marshall, Co. H, 130th Penn.—slightly in hand.
Daniel L. Smith, Co. C, 130th Penn—hand.
Jacob Laferse, Co. C, 130th Penn.—slightly in hand.
John Staley, Co. D, 130th Penn.—head.
— Steward, Co. F, 130th Pa.
— Keller, Co. F, 140th Pa.
Alfred Sites, Co. C, 130th Pa.—thigh.
H. Cole, Co. H, 136th Pa—head.
James Bridgehouse, Co. H, 130th Pa.—slightly.
D. H. Kauffman, Co. H, 130th Pennsylvania.
R. Gilen, Co. H, 130th Pennsylvania—hand.
Sergt. Hood, Co. A, 130th Pennsylvania—neck.
Patr'k Herrerty, 81st Penn.
Nathan Doney, 81st Penn.
Thos. Dunn, 81st Penn.
Michael Carroll, 81st Penn.
Samuel Wirt, 81st Penn.
[illegible] Witt, 81st Penn.
Geo. Jackson, 81st Penn.
Corpl. H. Keenan, Co. D, 81st Pennsylvania.
M. McManus, Co. D, 81st Pa.
Lieut. George Barton, 81st Pennsylvania.
Corpl. D. Gallagher, Co. G, 81st Pennsylvania.
Sergt. G. W. Landon, Co. D, [illegible]
Sam'l Steinmetz, Co. D, 81st Pennsylvania.
N. Roberts, Co. D, 81st Pa.
Sergt. Thos. Burns, Co. D, 81st Pennsylvania.
Gen. Caldwell, in hand.
Capt. Cauldwell, Adj. Gen. on Gen. Caldwell's staff—leg.
H. Wheat, Co. H, 61th N.Y.
C. F. Paine, Co. F, 64th New-York.
E. Russell, Co. F, 64th N.Y.
A. Gaultz, Co. G, 64th N.Y.
N. Alexander, Co. D, 64th New-York.
W. Starkweather, Co. D, 64th New-York.
H. Thompson, Co. E, 64th New-York.
J. Sherman, Co. A, 64th N.Y.
Sergt.-Maj. J. Savage, Co. A, 64th New-York.
Cornelius Sullivan, 61st N.Y.
Col. Miles, 61st N.Y.—chin and neck.
Geo. Miller, Co. G, 64th N.Y.
M. Bordway, Co. A, 64th N.Y.
Geo. Miller, Co. G, 61th N.Y.
Geo. W. Kimball, 5th N. H.
A. Gallagher, Co. C, 64th N.Y.
B. F. Crandall, Co. G, 64th New-York.
Chas. Meyers, Co. A, 64th N.Y.
A. J. Bannister, Co. D, 61th New-York.
C. Van Dusen, Co. D, 64th New-York—killed.
Col. H. J. Zinn, 130th Penn.—shot through head.
Capt. Laughlin, Co. E, 130th Penn.—had head blown off by shell.
John Fetzen, Co. F, 130th Penn.—head blown off by shell.
Capt. Jenkins, Co. C, 130th Penn.—slightly in the arm.
Sergeant Major Bosler, 130th Penn.—arm.
James Miller, Co. E, 130th Penn.—wrist broken.
Corp. Landis, Co. E, 130th Pa.—back by piece of shell.
Keller Roth, Co. F, 130th Pa.—arm.
J. Steigelman, Co. F, 130th Pennsylvania—leg.
Serg. Geo. Farrer, Co. F, 130th Pennsylvania—hip.
Joseph Forney, Co. F, 130th Pennsylvania—head.
William White, Co. F, 130th Pennsylvania—hand.
— Culbertson, Co. F, 130th Pennsylvania—arm.
— Lamberton, Co. F, 130th Pennsylvania—breast.
George McCauley, Co. I, 130th Pa.—hip.
Thomas J. Collins, Co. I, 130th Pennsylvania—hip.
Eli Meyers, Co. K, 130th Pennsylvania—body.
— Kroll, Co. K, 130 Pa.—head.
Charles Meddaugh, Co. H, 64th N.Y.—shot thro' brain.
Lieut. Davis, Co. A, 81st Pa.
Col. Cross, 5th New-Hampshire—reported killed.
Serg. Kirby, Co. E, 61st N.Y.
Corp. Bixby, Co. K, 61st N.Y.

WOUNDED RECEIVED AT CLIFFORD HOSPITAL, WASHINGTON.

S. D. Bates, Co. D, 26th N.Y.—dyspepsia.
Horace Fenton, Co. C, 12th Penn. Reserves.
Hewit Bartholomew, Co. E, 40th New-York.
M. Welch, Co. E, 40th N.Y.
M. Roach, Co. I, 9th Mass.
M. Casey, Co. F, 13th N.Y.
L. Caney, Co. C, 13th N.Y.
J. Gisley, Co. C, 13th N.Y.
D. W. Chapman, Co. E, 13th New-Hampshire.
J. McMahon, Co. I, 88th N.Y.
Gabriel McElravey, Co. C, 2d New-York Militia.
T. Walter, Co. G, 127th Penn.
Owen McDermott, 88th N.Y.
P. Wagner, Co. F, 7th N.Y.
Arnold Groshat, Co. D, 7th New-York.
Louis Hebner, Co. D, 7th New-York.
Robert Schoan, Co. F, 7th New-York.
Christian Magog, Co. F, 7th New-York.
H. Bernhard, Co. F, 7th New-York.
Wm. Bomacker, Co. I, 7th New-York.
Anton Koca, Co. I, 7th N.Y.
J. O. Edwards, Co. B, 57th New-York.
Thomas Mullen, Co. A, 25th New-York.
A. Bentley, Co. A, 12th N.Y.
Aaron Baker, Co. H, 1st Pa. Reserves.
Michael Mullen, Co. G, 13th New-York.
P. O'Conner, Co. E, 40th New-York.
J. Tack, Co. F, 7th N.Y.
W. Macumber, Co. A, 108th New-York.
M. S. Ellis, Co. H, 23d N. J.
Jas. Moore, 7th Penn. Res.
J. Bennet, Co. A, 5th Penn. R.
D. S. Foster, Co. A, 5th Pa. R.
R. Brinson, Co. C, 25th N. J.
M. McLaughman, Co. C, 48th Pennsylvania.
L. Washburn, Co. D, 7th U. S. Infantry.
Thos. Mahoney, 88th N.Y.
August Graff, Co. F, 7th New-York.
L. Cronomeyer, Co. F, 7th New-York.
Wm. Shoar, Co. G, 7th N.Y.
E. A. Heath, Co. E, 105th New-York.
Wm. W. Sprague, Co. I, 57th New-York.
Henry Frank, Co. I, 7th New-York.
Mich. Smith, Co. F, 7th N.Y.
Pat'k Feeney, Co. B, 1st Pa. Reserves.
Wm. A. Turner, Co. A, 99th Volunteers.
D. C. Ray, Co. A, 21st Mass.
Henry Vandber, Co. C, 38th New-York.
B. Keiler, Co. F, 7th N.Y.
Francis McKenna, Co. C, 63th New-York.

SUPPLIES FOR THE WOUNDED.

WOMAN'S CENTRAL RELIEF ASSOCIATION, BRANCH OF THE U. S. SANITARY COMMISSION, Dec. 15, 1862.

Pressing telegraphic dispatches have been received at this office, making demands on us to which we are utterly unable to respond. The emergency caused by the recent battle at Fredericksburgh calls for very large supplies of shirts, drawers and woolen socks. The stock both here and in Washington is exhausted, and we earnestly ask the prompt assistance of all interested in our cause. Contributions of flannel will be most acceptable from those who cannot send us ready-made clothing, as many persons are now offering their labor who have not the means to furnish the material.

Contributors will have the satisfaction of knowing that their gifts to suffering men will be forwarded direct to the battle-field. Prompt and kindly aid for the wounded will inspire new courage in those who are left to struggle through the coming fight, and who must win success over the bleeding bodies of their fallen comrades.

It is desirable that one thousand shirts, drawers and socks should be forwarded to Washington within the present week.

MRS. W. M. FELLOWS,
MISS. GERTRUDE STEVENS,
Committee for New-York and Brooklyn.

RELIEF FOR CONNECTICUT WOUNDED.

NEW-HAVEN, Ct., Monday, Dec. 15.

Hon. Mr. Coe, of Waterbury; Dr. Townsend, of New-Haven; Dr. S. S. Salisbury, of Plymouth; and Mr. Hodge, of Colebrook—a Committee appointed by the General Assembly of Connecticut, to make provision for wounded soldiers in Virginia—left New-Haven this evening for the camp at Fredericksburgh.

REBEL REPORTS FROM FREDERICKSBURGH.

The Events of Thursday Last.

From the Richmond Dispatch of Friday.

Early yesterday morning intelligence was received in this city that the ball had opened in earnest at Fredericksburgh, and that, from the fight, there was little room to doubt a general engagement would ensue. Throughout the day anxiety was evinced to hear from the conflict, and as usual, rumors of every variety were most industriously circulated.

Passengers by the Fredericksburgh train last night report that the enemy attempted simultaneously to cross the Rappahannock at three different points—the railroad bridge at the town, Knox's Mill, and Deep Run. The attempt was made about 5 o'clock A. M. At the two former places they were repulsed with great slaughter by our sharpshooters, who, from the defences of their rifle-pits, poured a galling fire into the ranks of the enemy, who fell back in confusion, after having sustained a heavy loss.

Our loss is reported to be only five killed and seventy-five wounded. At Deep Run the enemy were more successful. Under the protection of their heavy batteries they succeeded in crossing—in what force we were unable to ascertain. Our men fell back in good order. It is stated that our batteries completely sweep the plateau at this point, and that so far from having secured any advantage by the passage of the river, they have placed themselves in exactly the position our commanding General wishes them.

Exasperated at their warm reception, the enemy wantonly shelled the town, killing a Mr. GROTZ, an old citizen, and mortally wounded his brother. The residences of Messrs. GEO. P. KING and [illegible] were fired by the shells [illegible] engaged in the [illegible] of yesterday, and that nearly all the loss sustained was in that corps.

The latest advices received are contained in a dispatch dated 6 o'clock, which states that a large force of the enemy had succeeded in effecting a crossing, and that it was expected that the fight would be renewed again this morning.

From the Examiner of Friday.

At an early hour [illegible] rumor was [illegible] that the long expected action at Fredericksburgh had at last commenced, and that we were engaged with the enemy in force. The authorities were, as usual, both costive and dilatory in giving out anything to gratify public curiosity; and it was intimated at the War Department, with obvious propriety, that it would be advisable for the newspapers to await the official dispatches, and not plaster their bulletin boards with hasty and sensational reports.

The following is an epitome of all the intelligence received at the War Department in the shape of official dispatches up to a late hour last night.

The dispatches of Gen. LEE relate that the fight began at Fredericksburgh at 5 o'clock in the morning. At that hour the enemy attempted the passage of the Rappahannock at three different points by means of pontoon bridges. At two points they were repulsed. At the third it is presumed that they effected a passage, as the dispatches stated that they had got under cover of their guns and could not be interrupted in their construction of a bridge. At last accounts, dated about noon, the fight was progressing on the southern side of the Rappahannock.

FURTHER PARTICULARS, INCIDENTS, ETC.

It is understood that the point at which the enemy effected a passage of the Rappahannock was at Deep Run, about two miles below Fredericksburgh. The Yankees are said to have secured a landing there on a low cape, and our guns were in a position to sweep their ranks on their reaching the table land extending toward Fredericksburgh.

The passenger train which reached here last evening left its station, three miles this side of Fredericksburgh, about 1½ o'clock in the afternoon, and brought a number of persons who profess to have had close and minute observation of the morning's part of the action.

The description of the carnage which we have from these sources are frightful. At one point we are said to have cut the line of the enemy's pontoon bridges, and pouring in deadly showers of grape, to have filled the air with the legs, arms and disjointed members of the Yankees.

When the fire was opened on our lines, several women and children were remaining within the limits of Fredericksburgh, and their consternation is said to have been most pitiful. We have, from different sources, the report that two women were certainly killed by the enemy's fire. We could not obtain the names of the unhappy victims.

From the best information we can obtain it appears that LONGSTREET's Division was the portion of our force actively engaged yesterday.

The rumor was circulated in the streets last night that the town had been fired by the incendiary shots of the enemy. The rumor up to a late hour had obtained no confirmation in anything received at the War Department.

The general conclusion from what we learn up to the hour of writing are, that the enemy had effected a passage of the Rappahannock, probably in considerable force; that the action of yesterday was without any important fruits or prefatory to a more important action now impending; and that to-day will witness a large and important, but, perhaps, indecisive battle on the disputed lines of Fredericksburgh. As confirmatory of this prospect, *an order was received last night at the Medical Purveyor's office, for all the ambulances and stretchers that could possibly be sent from this city. These are the gloomy indications of the work to-day.*

LATER ACCOUNTS.

By through passengers who arrived here last night from Fredericksburgh, we learn that simultaneously with his attempt to throw his pontoon bridges across the Rappahannock, the enemy bombarded the town. The few inhabitants still remaining there began to leave immediately and make their way toward Hamilton Station on the railroad. A number of the houses in the town were struck, and two of them, Mr. JOHN C. KING's, near the dépôt, and a Mr. SCOTT's, were burned. One of the church steeples was also struck, and some say knocked down. The number of casualties to citizens are variously stated. Some accounts say that only one man, JACOB GROTZ, was killed, and another wounded. But persons, who were among the last to leave the town report that there were six citizens killed, among whom were Mr. J. GROTZ and his brother GEORGE, and a woman and her infant.

Heavy cannonading and the occasional fire of skirmishers was heard at the dépôt from 5 o'clock A. M. until 11, when a perfect silence ensued all along the lines, and continued unbroken until 1 o'clock. P. M., the hour of the departure of the train for Richmond. Persons who came down on this train knew nothing of the movements going on except such as they obtained from the flying inhabitants of Fredericksburgh, who knew nothing more than that their town was being shelled over their heads, and that their safety depended on a hasty evacuation. The account, however, brought by them does not differ in the main from that obtained from more reliable sources. They say that at 5 o'clock A. M. the enemy attempted to throw across pontoon bridges at three points, the old railroad bridge about the centre of the town, and above and below Deep Run, a stream three miles lower down the Rappahannock; that at the first of these two points the bridge-builders were driven from their work by our sharpshooters, but that at the point below the creek mentioned, the ground being low and open for a considerable space on this side, his artillery, posted on the opposite heights, had dispersed our sharpshooters, and enabled his men to perfect the bridge. At last accounts our artillery had been brought into a position covering and completely commanding the open space upon which the enemy's troops would deploy in crossing.

THE BANKS EXPEDITION.

Reported Landing of the Forces at Winton, N. C.

Operations Against Weldon, Petersburgh and Richmond.

Special Dispatch to the Philadelphia Press.

WASHINGTON, Sunday, Dec. 14.

During the day the City was filled with rumors in regard to BANKS' expedition. Some reported that it had been landed at the head of York River, and all agreed that it had not gone South of Hatteras.

I have just received information from good authority that Gen. BANKS has landed with twenty thousand men at Winton, N. C., near the headwaters of the Chowan River.

Gen. NATHANIEL P. BANKS has assumed command of the Army of the Blackwater, consisting of three *corps d'armée*, forming a grand division of the army.

Gen. FOSTER will command the left wing—three divisions, forming a *corps d'armée*.

Gen. PECK will command the right wing, forming a *corps d'armée* of three divisions.

Gen. AUGAR will command the entire corps of three divisions.

Gen. EMORY will command the reserve troops, composed of twelve trusty regiments, three batteries of artillery, and two squadrons of cavalry.

Gen. BANKS is already advancing, having formed a junction with our troops at Suffolk. Gen. FOSTER's army has joined him by this time.

It may be that Weldon will be taken immediately, but Petersburgh must fall in a few days, while BURNSIDE is driving LEE back upon Richmond, to receive the "last toss of the fork" from Gen. BANKS as he endeavors to retreat to Lynchburgh or Danville.

Gen. BANKS has full possession of the Seaboard and Roanoke Railroad, and his future supplies will reach him by two other routes besides this one.

Thus far the movement may be considered a great success, and, while its demoralizing effects upon the enemy will be very great, the effect upon the spirit of the Northern people will be most salutary.

Expect stirring news from the Army of the Blackwater hourly.

E. A. W.

NEWS FROM FORTRESS MONROE.

Plymouth, N. C., Destroyed by Fire.

[illegible] SUFFOLK.

PHILADELPHIA, Monday, Dec. 15.

A Fortress Monroe letter of the 14th instant, says that Plymouth, North Carolina, had been destroyed by fire, but by what division of the Federal army was [illegible]

A scouting party from Suffolk had a skirmish on Friday at Joiner's Ford, and captured two Captains and fifteen privates.

FORTRESS MONROE, Sunday, Dec. 14.

A British sloop-of-war arrived here this forenoon, and anchored in the Roads.

A scouting party from Suffolk had an engagement on Friday with the rebels at James Roads, on the Blackwater, and captured two Captains, one Sergeant and fourteen privates.

Lieut. JOHN ROBINSON, of the Sixth Massachusetts, was killed. The rebels retreated.

The *Colorado* is coming up the Roads.

Release of 270 National Prisoners.

FORTRESS MONROE, Saturday, Dec. 13.

The flag of truce steamboat *New-York* arrived here, this morning, from City Point, in charge of Capt. E. MULFORD, of the Third New-York Regiment. He brought down 270 released Union prisoners, among whom are Mrs. JAMESON and Mrs. WEBSTER. It will be recollected that the husband of the latter was hung by the rebels as a spy.

Mrs. J. R. ANDERSON and Mr. MOORE, British Consul, also came as passengers in the *New-York*.

FORTRESS MONROE, Saturday, Dec. 13.

The British frigate *Cadmus* arrived and anchored in the Roads this morning.

The steamboat *New-York* leaves here this afternoon for New-York, with the released Union prisoners she brought away from City Point.

New recruits continue to arrive at Newport's News, but it may turn out that they are establishing a Military School at that place for the Winter.

ANOTHER RAID INTO MARYLAND.

WHITE'S REBEL CAVALRY AT POOLESVILLE.

WASHINGTON, Monday, Dec. 15.

Last night, about 8 o'clock, rebel cavalry, under Maj. WHITE, about three hundred and ninety-five strong, made a raid into Poolesville, Md. They found there thirty-five men of Co. L, SCOTT's Nine Hundred, quartered in a wooden building. After a brief but determined struggle, and when the building was on fire, Lieut. SMITH, and seventeen men of Co. L, surrendered and were paroled.

On our side the loss was one killed—Lieut. STILES—and two wounded—namely, Lieut. SMITH and Corp. BERRY. The rebels lost two killed and thirteen wounded. Of course, they took everything valuable from the men they paroled, and thoroughly stripped the body of Lieut. STILES, who was, according to the testimony of Col. JAMES B. SWAIN, one of the bravest men that ever served his country. He had been ten years in the regular service.

CITY MORTALITY.—The City Inspector reports that 351 persons died in New-York last week; 84 men, 77 women, 112 boys and 78 girls—an increase of 31 upon the mortality of the previous week, and a decrease of 40 as compared with the mortality of the corresponding week of 1861. Of the deceased, 170 were children under five years of age. The mortality by the principal diseases was as follows: Consumption, 46; croup, 38; diphtherite, 17; infantile convulsions, 17; inflammation of the brain, 16; infantile marasmus, 15; scarlet fever, 13; dropsy in the head, 10; inflammation of the bowels, 8; disease of the heart, 6; death from external causes, 35; among which are reported 6 premature births; 1 suicide; 1 drowned; 8 killed by accidents. There were 28 interments in Potter's Field, and 33 deaths in the Institutions.

—Brig.-Gen. A. Pleasanton, commanding the cavalry attached to the Army of the Potomac, has officially recommended Major Chapman, of the Third Indiana Cavalry, for promotion to a Colonelcy.

Union soldiers in the streets of Fredericksburg

The Charleston Mercury.

VINDICE NULLO
PONTE SUA SINE LEGE FIDES RECTUMQUE COLENTUR

VOLUME LXXXI. | CHARLESTON, S. C., TUESDAY, DECEMBER 23, 1862. | NUMBER 11,637

THE MERCURY.

TUESDAY, DECEMBER 23, 1862.

Treatment of Slaves Returning from the Enemy or Captured.

During the seven years' war of the Revolution, the British sought to injure our people and cause by enticing slaves to run away, and go within the lines of their armies. In South Carolina twenty-five thousand slaves are estimated to have been drawn off from their owners to the enemies of their masters. A heavy loss was thus inflicted on the patriots. A portion of these slaves were transported to the West Indies, and sold into the less humane servitude which there prevails. And a considerable portion perished from starvation and hardship on the islands of our coast, where they had followed the retreating armies of Great Britain, and were left to a wretched fate. Their bones, for years, whitened the sands of Otter Island, Fenwick's Island, and other localities. At that day the negros were, to a considerable degree, "new"—many of them recent importations from Africa, semi-barbarous, and not bound to their American masters by a lifetime relationship as slaves. They were accustomed to a sterner discipline, and were less assured and trustful than the slaves of our day.

In this second war of independence the Yankees are doing all they can to injure our people and cause, by enticing slaves to run away and go within the lines of their armies. The malign efforts of the Southern masters' foes are cloaked under the specious pretence of their being, *par excellence*, the friends of his slaves. The lure of "freedom" is held out. The vicissitudes of war and the hardships of the blockade create doubt and depression in the minds of this ignorant and feeble race, shaking their loyalty. The liberty of the Abolition United States and Canada are agreeably shadowed out. They may also receive accounts of provision made for a transfer to South America—land of promised freedom, idleness and abundance. The negro's imagination is affected, his mind is overpowered, and, in credulity or indecision, he yields to the varied temptations and evil influences brought to bear upon him by the enemy. He little comprehends that, at the North, besides the words of fanatical haters of his master, there is nothing for him but sharp competition, in a few menial callings, against the close, active, unsympathising, selfish Yankee—that it is a climate whose severity is fatal to his constitution—that he will be left to his own feeble shifts—and that starvation and destruction alone await his race. He does not understand that colonization and emigration mean dispersion in Cuban slavery; or want, misery, barbarism and probable extinction in the forests and sands of South America. He does not know enough to perceive that the Yankee invader is actuated, more by his real hate for the master than by his affected friendship for the slave, and is the enemy of both alike, seeking the subjugation of the former, while luring the latter to an inevitable doom. The negro is tempted; they are a feeble folk; they fall away from their allegiance and abscond; or, as in the great majority of cases in this State, they remain passive, governed by local attachments and uncertitude of mind, rather than by any premeditated disloyalty. Thus, to the number of some fourteen thousand, they have fallen into the hands of the enemy, and are for the time under his control. Here some opportunity is afforded, if not of discerning the future which is before them, yet of observing the character of those professed friends, and of gaining some little experience. This first and brief acquaintance is often sufficient to open their eyes. Instead of the promised leisure, license and plenty, they find task-masters and short allowance. They see shiploads sent off to an unknown country and an unknown fate. Many at once discover their mistake. The greater proportion, if permitted by the Yankees, would, we believe, be happy to return, with any certainty of being restored to their former condition. Some have effected their escape, and others may find opportunity. But, being under strict military surveillance, the difficulties are great.

How these runaways to the enemy should be treated, when returning or taken, is a question of both authority and of expediency. We think that all due allowance should be made for the position in which these slaves have been placed by the public enemy, considering the temptation to which they have been subjected, and their own natural weakness. The presence of the Yankee invader, is not the work of the slave. To run away, is no public offence in South Carolina. It is a matter for the master, an offence exclusively within his jurisdiction, and for the exercise of his judgment. It is an offense against his authority; and to him the discipline has heretofore been left, and should still be left. His discretion will, as a rule, be the best law and best policy. In our opinion, therefore, these runaways should be treated like ordinary runaways. They should be turned over to their masters, with the single condition of being immediately removed into the interior, from the temptations and influences of contiguity with the enemy.

Such is the course we would recommend in regard to runaways. But, besides absconding from his master, a slave may be guilty of *crime*. When detected in crime, of course he becomes a public offender, liable to public penalties, and these penalties of a broken law it would be proper to inflict, now as heretofore, on runaways as well as on others.

Theft, robbery, housebreaking, arson and murder are punishable respectively by whipping, imprisonment and death, and the law should be executed.

It is a law of this State, that white men carrying off slaves are punishable with death. Runaway negros detected in enticing and aiding other slaves to escape to the enemy, are guilty of a similar offence, and should be liable to the same punishment. Several have, in cases tried within the year, suffered capitally. The crime is one needing severity for the sake of prevention and security, and the effect should be thoroughly tried.

Runaway negros taken in the act, or proved to have acted, as spies or guides in the service of the enemy, forfeit their lives as public enemies and traitors, according to military law, and should suffer accordingly.

If, hereafter, any runaways become insurgents, or are taken with arms in their hands, or it is proved that they have been in arms, of their own choice, their crime is one against the State, and they must be punished with death.

In these cases and in all others, the law should be executed. It should not be altered. Nor should runaways be outlawed or left without protection. There is no renunciation of authority on the part either of the master or the State. The master is still the friend of his slave, and the public authorities should still temper the administration of justice with mercy. Discretion should be exercised in the administration of justice to those guilty of public crime; and those whose offence, is running away, should, according to circumstances, be received with kindness, and some measure of indulgence should be mingled with the master's discipline.

We are happy to know that the views here expressed, are such as will meet the general approval of our military authorities.

LETTER FROM RICHMOND.

(CORRESPONDENCE OF THE MERCURY.)

RICHMOND, Wednesday, December 17.

Nothing Later from Fredericksburg—General Lee Jubilant—Anecdote—General Gregg's Remains—Palmerston and the British People—The Mercury's Distinction—Cold Weather, etc., etc.

Nothing from Fredericksburg since Gen. LEE's brief despatch announcing BURNSIDE's disappearance from his front. Reported last night that we had taken the enemy's pontoon bridges and his siege guns, but this is not confirmed. LEE's official report appears in the morning papers—a remarkable instance of promptitude. General Lee, I learn, is jubilant, almost off his balance, and seemingly desirous of embracing every one who calls on him. As this is a fine bracing morning, and as we have news of another victory and "change of base" at Kinston, I will tell you an anecdote about Lee. At Sharpsburg he hailed one of the many stragglers, and inquired:

"Where are you going, sir?"
"Goin' to the rear."
"What are you going to the rear for?"
"Well, I've been stung by a bung, and I'm what they call demoralized."

This was enough. Gen. Lee had not the heart to say more to an innocent who had been "stung by a bung"—meaning perhaps that he had been stunned by a bomb.

Gen. Gregg's remains were escorted yesterday to the depot by the City Battalion, and a large concourse of citizens and officers. The Examiner says truly that the body of this "brave soldier and accomplished gentleman," as Gen. Lee styles him in his report, ought to have been deposited in the Rotunda of the Capitol. It was not from want of respect, I am sure, that it was not placed there, but from want of forethought—a distinguishing characteristic of the people of this city.

The distinction drawn by THE MERCURY between Palmerston's Cabinet and the British people is favorably commented upon in official circles here. There is no doubt that the people of England are heartily, and by a large majority, on our side. This is stated bitterly in a letter from Adams to Seward, which will be published to-morrow. Adams says that, from the day of his arrival in England, the current has been setting steadily in favor of the Confederacy and against the United States, and Russell is compelled to acknowledge the fact. In this same letter Adams says, what we have long suspected, that Lord Lyons has been doing his utmost to prevent recognition and to keep Palmerston true to the neutrality programme. It is not improbable that ere long there will be a "change of base" in the British Cabinet, and then we shall see that the people who have already sent us all the arms, munitions, supplies and clothing that we have received, who have advocated our cause in many of their ablest papers, and who have, in the practical English way, done and said more for us than all other nations combined—Louis Napoleon was not hampered by a Cabinet of Abolitionist dotards. While we do full justice to Louis Napoleon, let us by no means neglect to encourage the good will of the English.

Old men predicted that the aurora seen on Sunday night was the forerunner of cold weather; and so it has turned out. To-day it is very sharp, and the wind is high and cutting. HERMES.

RICHMOND, Thursday, December 18.

Not a "Repulse" but a Terrible Defeat—Jackson at a Council of War—Numbers Engaged—Enemy Used Up—Treatment of the Wounded—Youthful Officers—Freezing Weather, etc., etc.

How terrible was that defeat at Fredericksburg which our General modestly heralded as a "repulse"! From many points we hear that the enemy's loss was from 18,000 to 20,000. Three thousand of his dead he left unburied, after laboring hard all Saturday night and all day Sunday in the sad work of interment and the removal of the wounded. Leesburg has been re-enacted on a grand scale, as we shall learn ere long, although Washington papers of the 16th received this morning, do not admit even a defeat, but declare that General Burnside is "perfectly satisfied with the result of Saturday's fight." "I shouldn't wonder"—as the showman remarked when asked if the Siamese twins were brothers.

I learn, on good authority, that Gen. Lee was so confident that the battle would be renewed on Monday, that he had disposed his forces to meet the shock in a manner that would have horrified those who thought they tested the whole rebel strength on Saturday. A story is floating about to the effect that Jackson, who generally goes to sleep at councils of war, was quite excited on Saturday night, and insisted that the Yankees should be driven into the river forthwith, without waiting for morning. My information is that near 200,000 of the enemy were more or less actively engaged, against only 22,000 on our side—14,000 of Jackson's corps and 8000 of Longstreet's.

All the talk of the town is about the great victory which we achieved almost without knowing it, and I could fill a dozen letters with the accounts, all joyous, of parties who have come down from Fredericksburg. But everybody seems to be at a loss in regard to the next move of the enemy. Reports say he has gone down the left bank of the river, but there is not a point between Fredericksburg and the mouth of the river where he would be likely to fare any better than he has done. He is, to the best of everybody's knowledge and belief, a "used up man," and we have made a long step towards independence. Government authorities say Burnside will go home, and his army return to Washington. We shall see.

The Examiner has some statements about the treatment of the wounded, which conflict with those made in a recent letter of mine; but the mass of evidence shows that there is more system and attention than heretofore.

A singular feature in this war is the youthfulness of many of our distinguished artillery officers. The "gallant Pelham," as Gen. Lee calls him, is an Alabamian about 20 years old; Pegram, of the Purcell Battery, is hardly 21; Latimer, the Captain of the Letcher Artillery, is only 17; and Dearing, of Latham's old battery, is not above 22 or 23.

Clear freezing weather. We will get plenty of ice. HERMES.

FROM THE NORTHERN PAPERS.

THE BATTLES BEFORE FREDERICKSBURG.

We have received the Washington *Chronicle* of Tuesday last, the 16th instant. It contains a very full account of operations before Fredericksburg; but, as the paper is entirely under the control of the administration, the narrative is shaped with a view to conceal, as far as possible, the extent of the disaster. The only editorial allusion to the battle is a brief paragraph, which says "General BURNSIDE is entirely satisfied with the result of Saturday's fight, as are all the general officers, and the whole army is in excellent spirits. More than this we do not know, and any speculation on the movements of the army would be merely idle." The following are the words of BURNSIDE's despatch to LINCOLN:

HEADQUARTER'S ARMY POTOMAC,
4, A. M., 14th December.

THE PRESIDENT: I have just returned from the field. Our troops are all over the river, and hold the first ridge outside the town and three miles below. We hope to carry the crest to-day. Our loss is heavy—say five thousand.

A. E. BURNSIDE,
Major-General Commanding.

Negro refugees pass into northern lines after the Confederate victory at Bull Run

1863

The Charleston Mercury.

VOLUME LXXXII. | CHARLESTON, S. C., TUESDAY, JANUARY 6, 1863. | NUMBER 11,647

TELEGRAPHIC NEWS.

RETREAT OF BRAGG'S ARMY FROM MURFREESBORO'—THE OFFICIAL DESPATCHES.

CHATTANOOGA, January 5.—The following despatch has been received from Gen. BRAGG:

TULLAHOMA, January 5.

Unable to dislodge the enemy from his entrenchments, and learning of reinforcements having reached him, we withdrew from his front night before last. He has not followed. My cavalry are close on his front.

(Signed) BRAXTON BRAGG.

Despatches from Wartrace state that the enemy had not occupied Murfreesboro' this morning. Reports were still coming in that the enemy was returning to Nashville. Parties just from the front report that MORGAN had met and routed a force of the enemy at Gallatin.

RICHMOND, January 5.—The following official despatch was received this morning:

CHATTANOOGA, January 5.

To Gen. S. Cooper:—We retired from Murfreesboro' in perfect order. All the stores were saved. About 4000 Federal prisoners, 5000 stand of small arms and 24 cannon, brass and steel, have already been received here.

(Signed) B. S. EWELL, A. A. G.

THE BATTLE OF MURFREESBORO'—THE LATEST NORTHERN ACCOUNTS.

PETERSBURG, VA., January 5.—We have received Northern papers of Saturday last, January 3.

There is no doubt of the result of the battle in Tennessee. On Friday HALLECK received the following telegram, dated "Murfreesboro', January 1:"

"A terrible battle took place yesterday. At the latest advices from the field (up to noon) the rebel centre had been broken, and things looked favorable. The losses on both sides are reported to have been enormous. Generals STANLEY, ROUSSEAU and PALMER were wounded. The rebel Generals CHEATHAM and RAINS were killed."

A telegram to the Northern press, dated "near Murfreesboro', December 31," says: "Our whole line suffered terribly this morning. Four regiments of regulars lost half their men and all their commanding officers. General ANDERSON'S troops suffered severely. We are advancing our whole line, General ROSECRANS personally superintending the movements. One shot killed two of his staff officers. The 15th Wisconsin lost seven captains."

A despatch, dated Louisville, January 1, says: "General ROSECRANS captured Murfreesboro' on Tuesday morning, and now occupies it, the rebels having retreated to Tullahoma. The rebels made but little resistance, though ROSECRANS lost a train of wagons following him, which was captured by the rebels under Colonel MORGAN." The New York *Herald* says that the foregoing despatch is evidently false.

A despatch from Brigadier General J. T. BOYLE, at Louisville, on the 2d, reiterates the statement that ROSECRANS had occupied Murfreesboro'.

A despatch from Nashville, dated the 2d, says: "The Federal forces encountered the rebels on the 30th near Stewart's Creek. After heavy skirmishing the rebels were driven back, with the loss of 150 prisoners and many killed and wounded. The fight continued until 1, p. m., on the 31st ult., at which time we (the Yankees) had maintained our position. The Union loss is extremely heavy. Among the killed are General SILL; Col. GARESCHE, ROSECRANS' Chief of Staff; Gen. WILLICH, of Ind.; Col. KELLY, of the 2d Ohio; Colonel SHEFFER, acting Brigadier General; Col. FARMER, of the 15th Kentucky; Colonel JONES, of the 24th Ohio; Colonel COTTON, of the 6th Kentucky; Colonel JONES, of the 39th Indiana; Col. CARPENTER and Colonel McKEE, of the 15th Wisconsin. Among the wounded were General KIRK, of Illinois; General WOOD, of Indiana; Gen. VANCLIVE and Major General ROUSSEAU, of Kentucky, with many other general officers. The 21st, 25th and 35th Illinois Regiments lost two-thirds of their men; the 15th and 38th Ohio half their number. Other regiments lost heavily. The total number of killed and wounded is estimated at 2500. The rebel loss was much heavier. We have captured 500 prisoners.

Latest from Murfreesboro'.—We (the Yankees) occupy Murfreesboro'. The rebels are in full retreat. The *Herald* makes no editorial comment upon the battle.

Gold in New York had advanced to 135, Exchange to 148, and Cotton to 68 cents.

BUTLER and staff reached New York on Friday morning. MORGAN is reported to have been defeated by Gen. REYNOLDS at Killing Fork, Ky.

THE LATEST NORTHERN NEWS—A NEW PROCLAMATION FROM LINCOLN.

RICHMOND, December 5.—6, p. m.—Northern dates of the 2d have been received.

LINCOLN has issued his proclamation declaring, as a fit and necessary war measure for suppressing the rebellion, that all persons held as slaves in certain designated States and parts of States are, and henceforward shall be, free. He further declares that such persons will be received into the armed service of the United States. Upon this act, sincerely believed to be an act of justice, and warranted by the Constitution as a military necessity, he invokes the considerate judgment of mankind and the gracious favor of Almighty God.

The Washington correspondent of the New York *Tribune* states that the latest foreign news confirms the belief that the French Emperor designs to persist in the mediation scheme, even if he has to proceed alone.

Beast BUTLER arrived in New York on the 1st. No mention is made of any public reception. He proceeded to Washington on Friday.

THE END OF THE "MONITOR."

PETERSBURG, January 5.—By a flag of truce at City Point, it is ascertained that the famous Yankee iron-clad gunboat *Monitor* foundered off Hatteras a few days since, and carried down with her 30 souls. Another account says that all on board perished. The *Galena* narrowly escaped, after having thrown overboard her armament and ammunition. These iron clads are supposed to have been *en route* for Wilmington.

THE MERCURY.

TUESDAY, JANUARY 5, 1863.

Political Economy.

"A wholesome public opinion should restrain bargaining within the bounds of decency and prevent cruel exactions." But the principle of free trade and no monopoly, in its widest sense, is a doctrine of sound political economy and practical wisdom on the part of communities. The temporary effect, under peculiar circumstances, sometimes is to enhance prices by competition caused in consequence of the wants of persons. But it is a self-adjusting rule in practice. In the long run and final result, it is assuredly wise in policy. The principle of private interest is made to combat and regulate private interest to the certain and infinite benefit of the public. Laws against extortion are almost invariably mischievous in their consequences. They stop production, or are evaded and inoperative. Laws can hardly be made to prevent men from making good bargains. They will buy and sell where the profits are great and the transactions are fair and open. Those who observe the laws quit a business whose profits are curtailed; and others find means of escaping the penalties of laws which they consider unjust and unwise. The public at large gains little by the effect of such laws. But where capital and enterprise are attracted by the great profits into any line of business, competition in supplying the public necessities is sure to be produced. This active competition in production reduces prices to the point of ordinary legitimate profits. The increased manufacture of salt and the rapid fall in price is an apt illustration of the great cardinal rule of political economy.

The City of Charleston.

With all their blathering about Richmond, we believe that the capture of Charleston would afford even more exquisite delight to the Northern heart than the downfall of Richmond. It is true that the latter is the Confederate Capital; but its capture, except in name, would prove a barren victory. If they could take Richmond, that event would be probably foreseen by this Government in time to remove from the Capital everything of value. Virginia and the South abound with natural facilities for manufacturing purposes, and the workshops already in existence in the interior would be increased and multiplied to an indefinite extent. The Government archives could be transferred to another locality without any difficulty, and, in the language of President Davis, the war could be carried on in Virginia for twenty years. After the first inconveniences of the loss of Richmond, our national defence would proceed with fresh energy, and we should still possess the only means of transporting supplies we have ever had—the railroads—for our rivers have been, and still are, of use only to the enemy. Moreover, the frequent discomfiture which the Yankees have met in their "on to Richmond," and the increasing improbabilities of accomplishing that object, are beginning to make the grapes somewhat sour in the estimation of those amiable foxes. But the Charleston grapes still hang in tempting clusters, and the grudge they owe South Carolina is older and more venomous than that towards Virginia. Their journalists never refer to Charleston without styling it that "adder's nest of treason," and breathing forth a burning desire to measure conclusions between their feet and the bite of the "adders." South Carolina committed the unpardonable crime of lighting the flames of this "unholy rebellion," and of first causing the United States flag to trail in the dust. Moreover, she is an old offender, having for thirty years been chafing in her chains, and loathing with intense and unconcealed disgust her compulsory companionship with Yankee Doodledom. Besides all this, her proud and pure character is a standing affront to inferior natures which can never be forgiven. How they would delight to humble her in the dust, to tread her in the mud, to jump, and halloo, and whoop over her prostrate form. The condition of New Orleans would be an Elysium compared to that of Charleston if it should fall into Yankee hands. There is no indignity its people would not be made to suffer; no atrocity its enemies are not capable of perpetrating. It would be better that not one brick should be left standing upon another in Charleston; better that its whole population should be driven out houseless and homeless to the interior, than surrender to the Yankees, and be governed probably by Butler the Beast, who might be sent there as the most efficient agent to make Charleston drink to the dregs the bitter cup which the Yankees have prepared for her lips. But we have no fears of any surrender. If Charleston should be destroyed, it will be only the loss of a few acres of Carolina soil, leaving intact the strength and independence of the State. We are satisfied, however, that Charleston will drive back the invaders in ignominious confusion, and come out of the conflict with all her banners flying. There is in command of that coveted city an old acquaintance of the Yankees: he who made Fort Sumter bend its proud head, and who first sent the Yankees to the right about at Manassas, with a velocity unparalleled in the annals of war. He is a man whose heart burns with an intensity of patriotism, more than equal to the ardor of their fanatical passions, and whose military genius is equal to any emergency of the war. With Beauregard at the head of Carolina's chivalry, there will be such an entertainment ready for the Yankees at Charleston which will satisfy their appetites for invasion for generations to come.—*Richmond Dispatch.*

THE BATTLE OF MURFREESBORO'.

[*From the Chattanooga Rebel.*]

The engagement of Wednesday, from every advice which reaches us, was one of the bloodiest of the war. It might well be so. The troops brought against us by the enemy were the flower of his army. The General commanding was one of the ablest of its officers. Two thirds of the army of Bragg are Tennesseeans. Much traduced by the passionate, the ignorant and the ill-tempered, these men have only desired and waited a fair field, and a competent leader. Making due allowance for the prejudices entertained against Gen. Bragg, the soldiers under his command must have entered the fight with faith in a great conclusive triumph. It was at their door-sills. The very eyes of the loved ones of home were on them. The fight was a defence of hearth stones and chimney corners, which men are most loath to sacrifice in winter time. No wonder, therefore, that the close of Wednesday witnessed a great victory—four thousand prisoners, thirty-one pieces of artillery, two Generals of Brigade, stores and munitions of war to a large amount. The fight was a free fight. It was an open field fight. The ground over which the shock of battle passed is familiar to us—a rolling level of semi-undulating land, of corn fields and meadows, with sparse groves of timber, semi-circled by the winding, zig-zag course of Stone's river. Our fortifications were merely temporary earth works and rifle pits, if, indeed, we had any at all. Theirs must have been even less. One advantage, however (and a very considerable one), had we. It was this: The sun, bright, clear and dazzling, shown directly in their face during two thirds of the day, whilst it fell upon our rear. So long as the present geographical positions are continued, this decided piece of advantage will be on our side when the sun shines.

The completion of this victory is only needed to set the Western campaign on its legs, and to place us of Tennessee on a secure footing. If we drive the swollen ranks of Rosecrans—ranks of fresh troops, ranks of veteran troops, ranks too of Western troops—back upon Nashville, the result may restore us our capital, and will give us substantial occupation of the entire region of country lying within the embrace of the Cumberland, Duck and Tennessee rivers, south, east and west of Nashville.

Battle of Murfreesboro, Tennessee

The New-York Times.

VOL. XII—NO. 3518. NEW-YORK, THURSDAY, JANUARY 1, 1863. PRICE THREE CENTS.

A BATTLE AT MURFREESBORO.

A General Advance of Rosecrans' Army on Monday.

The Enemy Pushed Back Seven or Eight Miles.

A Sharp Brush on the Nolinsville Road.

A Rebel Gun and Caisson Captured.

Our Army Sweeping Down all the Roads on Tuesday.

A GENERAL ENGAGEMENT IMMINENT.

CINCINNATI, Wednesday, Dec. 31.

The *Enquirer* has advices from Nashville, stating that ROSECRANS' army had moved on the enemy, driving them before him with considerable heavy skirmishing. The Federals are in high spirits and anxious for a fight. On Monday ROSECRANS' advance was in sight of Murfreesboro, with the enemy in full view, drawn up in line of battle. A battle was expected on Tuesday.

A DISPATCH FROM THE ARMY.

CINCINNATI, Wednesday, Dec. 31.

The following is a special dispatch to the *Commercial*:

NEAR MURFREESBORO, Tenn., Tuesday, Dec. 30.

The Fourteenth Army Corps made a general advance yesterday, and pushed the rebels back seven or eight miles. COLLINS' Brigade, of Gen. McCOOK's Corps, had a sharp brush with the enemy just beyond Nolinsville. Cannonading took place for an hour, the enemy wasting considerable ammunition. Our troops reserved their fire, until advancing briskly, by a dexterous flank movement, the One Hundred and First Ohio captured one gun and a caisson. We lost one killed, and three wounded.

A general engagement is imminent. Our army is sweeping down all the roads to Murfreesboro. Heavy artillery firing is now heard on the Nolinsville Road, where Gen. McCOOK is engaging the rebel HARDEE. The weather is damp and the ground very heavy.

A LATER DISPATCH.

CAMP, TEN MILES FROM MURFREESBORO, Wednesday, Dec. 31.

Gen. CRITTENDEN reports the enemy drawn up in line of battle on the east side of Stone River, menacing Gen. ROSECRANS. He is ordered to form in line of battle, two divisions in front, one in reserve and covering his flanks, and Gens. NEGLEY and ROSSEAU to close up.

Gen. McCOOK also reports his command on Wilkinson's Creek, seven miles from Murfreesboro. The enemy is in line of battle on Stone's River, from Murfreesboro to Franklin Pike. A similar disposition of McCOOK's forces is ordered, as on Gen. CRITTENDEN's line.

It now appears that a great battle will be fought on Stone's River to-morrow, in front of Murfreesboro.

LATEST REPORTS FROM LOUISVILLE.

LOUISVILLE, Wednesday, Dec. 31.

All is quiet south of here, as far as headquarters are advised.

FROM CORINTH AND OTHER POINTS.

CAIRO, Wednesday, Dec. 31.

Information from Corinth to Saturday night states that the garrison at that place were on half-rations. Foraging parties, however, were able to supply the deficiency.

Col. LEE, with a large cavalry force, is still in pursuit of VAN DORN.

Trains are running from Corinth to Jackson, and from Jackson to Holly Springs. The road is also repaired from Jackson to a point nine miles north of Trenton. Every station-house and all the bridges between Trenton and Moscow, within twelve miles of Columbus, are burned. All the bridge-timber along the route is also destroyed, and much of the tracks torn up.

A National force, to the number of 3,000, which had left Trenton in the direction of the Tennessee River, on a reconnoissance, had not returned when the information left.

A construction train left Columbus yesterday. It went as far as Union City without meeting any obstacle. Two regiments and a battery left to-day to assist in putting the road in order. The rebels have evidently left the road. It will be repaired in a week.

FROM ALBANY.

Arrival of Gov. Seymour—Preparations for the Inauguration, &c.

ALBANY, Wednesday, Dec. 31.

Gov. SEYMOUR and Lieut.-Gov. JONES arrived to-day. A large number of prominent citizens of the State are in the City, to witness the ceremonies of the Inauguration, to take place in the Assembly Chamber at 11 o'clock to-morrow. New-Year is [illegible] expected.

The Court of Appeals adjourned to-day. In the Forest divorce case, judgment was affirmed. [illegible]

The Missouri Legislature.

JEFFERSON CITY, Tuesday, Dec. 30.

Both Houses of the Legislature completed their organization to-day by the election of all the Emancipation candidates.

There seems to be a general desire that Congress should lead off in the Emancipation movement, and there is no doubt that a prompt, liberal tender of compensation would greatly facilitate the Emancipation measure in the Legislature.

There is a strong prospect that the Senatorial question will be disposed of this week. Under the Constitution of this State a simple majority only is required to pass any bill over the Governor's veto.

FROM THE ARMY OF THE POTOMAC.

An Important Reconnoissance in Force.

A Portion of the Rebel Army Supposed to Have Moved up the Rappahannock.

HEADQUARTERS ARMY OF THE POTOMAC, Wednesday, Dec. 31.

A reconnoissance in force went out yesterday morning, which will probably be heard from in a few days.

It is believed here that a considerable portion of Gen. LEE's army has moved from its late position in our front, and gone up the Rappahannock. Its destination, however, is not known.

It has been ascertained by flag of truce that Capt. SWEARENGEN, of the late Brig.-Gen. JACKSON's Staff, who was reported killed in the battle of the 13th, was only wounded and captured. He is now doing well at a farm-house about four miles in the rear of the enemy's front.

Lieut. REDY, ordnance officer of Gen. WHIPPLE's Staff, is a prisoner in Richmond. He was unhurt on the battle-field.

LETTER FROM DUMFRIES.

Stuart's Raid at Dumfries—A Failure—He is Forced to Retire—Gallant Conduct of the Union Troops—How the Rebels Escaped—Their Programme—The Killed and Wounded—No Government Property Captured or Destroyed.

DUMFRIES, Va., Monday Evening, Dec. 29, 1862.

I have already sent you a brief account by telegraph, of the attack upon this place, Saturday, by a force of rebel troops under Gen. STUART, and should have forwarded another dispatch last night had not Gen. STUART cut off the telegraph wire between this point and Fairfax Station.

From all that we can learn, STUART, with 6,000 cavalry—embracing FITZHUGH LEE's Brigade, HAMPTON's Legion and STUART's own command—with six pieces of artillery, crossed the Rappahannock at Kelly's Ford, about six miles east of the Orange and Alexandria Railroad, some time during Friday night, and marched directly to Stafford Church, which is back several miles from the river road, and some twelve miles southeast of Dumfries. At this point, after a brief rest, he divided his command into three columns, each having two pieces of artillery, and in this order proceeded toward Dumfries, arriving within sight of the place at about 11 o'clock A. M., Saturday. Dumfries is surrounded by high hills, thickly covered with pine—the former affording excellent positions for artillery, and the latter almost complete protection to troops from any fire that can be brought to bear. At this time there were only three regiments of infantry, 400 cavalry and two pieces of artillery in Dumfries of Gen. SLOCUM's Corps, all under the command of Col. CANBY.

As soon as the rebels had taken a position, they commenced shelling the town, and for about five hours, rely upon it, the missiles of war were scattered about in a very reckless manner. The rebel force, greatly outnumbering ours, and having decidedly the advantage of position, the wonder is that our whole force was not either captured or destroyed. The troops under Col. CANBY, however, kept up good spirits, and manifested a degree of enthusiasm scarcely ever equaled before under such adverse circumstances, and let no opportunity pass to harrass the enemy. The two pieces of artillery were in constant use for about five hours, and whenever the rebels exposed themselves in front of the timber behind which they were most of the time concealed, they were speedily forced under cover again by our infantry. At about 5 o'clock, the enemy retired—doubtless hearing the approach of a force in the rear—without having gained a single advantage. It is surmised that they supposed Gen. SIGEL occupied the town, for the building where he recently made his headquarters seemed to be the special object of their hate, and it was completely riddled with balls. Several other prominent buildings in the place were also made targets of, and badly riddled. Our loss is five men killed, and nine or ten wounded. The rebels left 16 dead behind them, and 15 wounded. They succeeded in capturing about twenty of our cavalry before reaching Dumfries, who were patrolling the country, and we captured thirty of their men after the fight commenced. The Union troops, almost without exception, conducted themselves in the most gallant manner, obeying all orders promptly, and with a spirit evincing that their heart was in the work before them.

It seems that when STUART retired, he marched directly to Burke's Station, on the Orange and Alexandria Railroad, cut the telegraph wire, and took up the railroad track in several places; captured the telegraph operator at Burke's Station; then crossed the little pike road one mile east of Fairfax Court-house; had a skirmish with a portion of Gen. STOUGHTON's Vermont Brigade; was repulsed; then passed on through Vienna toward Drainesville, and, taking a short turn to the left, passed through Aldie, and, it is supposed, passed through Ashby's Gap, and crossed the Shenandoah at Berry's Ford. STUART had one man wounded and one horse killed near Fairfax, by Gen. STOUGHTON's troops.

One special object of this raid was, no doubt, to capture the Government stores at Fairfax Station, and in this respect it was a most signal failure. He did not succeed in capturing or destroying a dollar's worth of Government property, except what the 20 cavalrymen captured by him had with them, and all he obtained was a few sutlers' teams. These, however, were just from Washington, and were well loaded with all kinds of delicacies. The wagons were burned on the road near Occoquan, and the contents were disposed of by the rebel soldiers on the spot. A man who passed over the little pike road this morning, says he saw a fine assortment of old boots and empty bottles lining the roadside for miles.

News from Fortress Monroe.

FORTRESS MONROE, Tuesday, Dec. 30.

The British frigate *Petrel* left Fortress Monroe recently, and has gone to Charleston, S. C. The [illegible] left for Bermuda.

In Norfolk, last evening, MILES TAYLOR was stabbed by [illegible], who was immediately arrested.

[illegible] five rebel prisoners arrived here this morning from Fort McHenry. They came upon the Baltimore mail-boat *Georgiana*, and will soon be sent to City Point for exchange.

MISS BATEMAN AT THE BROOKLYN ACADEMY.—We have space only to state that Miss BATEMAN's reappearance at the Brooklyn Academy was a complete success. The house was well filled by an intelligent and fashionable audience, whose greeting of the fair actress was most [illegible]. Messrs. WALLACK, ADAMS and DAVENPORT ably supported Miss BATEMAN, who was called before the curtain after each act. To-night, with a capital cast, "The Lady of Lyons."

THE WAR IN ARKANSAS.

The Expedition of the Army of the Frontier to Van Buren.

The Rebel Camp Shelled Across the Arkansas.

HINDMAN DECLINES A BATTLE.

A Large Amount of the Enemy's Stores Captured and Destroyed.

Hindman's Army Greatly Demoralized.

The Return of the Expedition to Prairie Grove.

ST. LOUIS, Wednesday, Dec. 31.

Gen. BLUNT telegraphs to Gen. CURTIS, under date of Van Buren, Ark., Dec. 28, as follows:

"My long range guns are now shelling the rebel camp across the river, five miles below here. If the enemy does not retreat during the night, I shall endeavor to cross my troops in the morning, and offer them battle.

Among the property captured, are four steamers, three of them partly loaded with supplies, a ferry-boat and a large amount of ammunition.

Quite a number of the enemy were killed."

RETURN OF THE EXPEDITION.

FAYETTEVILLE, Ark., Wednesday, Dec. 31.

Additional particulars of the expedition to Van Buren have been received. Our army was ten miles this side of Van Buren yesterday morning, and would bivouack on the mountain top last night, and expected to reach Prairie Grove again to-day. Gen. SCHOFIELD joined them a few miles beyond the foot of the mountains.

The steamers *Nolet*, *Rose Douglass*, *Frederick Notrebe*, *Erie No. 6*, and *Van Buren*, with their cargoes of grain and provisions for the rebel army, were burned; also, a large amount of army stores. The rebels burned their arsenal and ferry boat at Fort Smith, to prevent their falling into our hands, also a large quantity of provisions on the opposite bank of the river. A general conflagration was in progress when our forces left.

Many deserters came into our lines, who report that two regiments of Missourians stacked arms, a few days ago, crossed the river and went home. Another regiment of Missourians left a short time afterward, taking their arms with them. Two regiments of Texans also stacked arms and started for home. A regiment of cavalry was sent in pursuit, but, instead of arresting, they joined the runaways. Everything goes to show that the rebel army of the Trans-Mississippi is completely disorganized.

The Arkansas River is at a boatable stage, and the country bordering on the river, from a point twenty-five miles below Van Buren to Little Rock, is well provided with forage and food to subsist an army.

Our troops are in splendid spirits, having accomplished the most daring and successful raid, without the loss of a single life.

AFFAIRS ON THE FRONTIER.

The Exploits of the Army Under Gens. Blunt and Herron—The Battle of Prairie Grove—Probable Capture of Fort Smith, &c.

From Our Own Correspondent.

CAMP HENNING, FORT SCOTT, KANSAS, Tuesday, Dec. 23, 1862.

The arrival yesterday at this post of a train of 150 wagons, with a large number of rebel prisoners and over 100 contrabands, from Rhea's Mills, Washington County, Ark., is the first direct communication we have had in Kansas with Gen. BLUNT and the Army of the Frontier, except the telegraphic dispatches announcing the battle and its results, since the splendidly-contested field of Prairie Grove added new lustre to our thrice victorious arms on the Southwestern Border. These victories come in rapid succession, and although not contests upon which seem to rest the fate of the nation, yet they are brilliant episodes, made more glorious by the gloom which the disaster at Fredericksburgh cast about us. Newtonia, old Fort Wayne, Cane Hill, and, lastly, Prairie Grove, all fought against the odds of four to one, and all of them decisive defeats of the rebel forces.

From a letter from a friend with the First Brigade of the First or Kansas Division, under date of Dec. 11, I learn that the army was then encamped between Prairie Grove, six miles south of Fayetteville and Cane Hill, 26 miles southeast, while Gen. BLUNT's headquarters are at Rhea's Mills, and Gen. HERRON's near the Grove. The latter is simply a place where a school-house, church and store makes a point of interest to the neighborhood farmers. The Army of the Frontier is now about 25,000 strong, the Second and Third Divisions from Springfield, under HERRON, by whom the earliest and main portion of the battle at the Grove was fought, numbering some 17,000 men. These regiments are principally Illinois, Indiana, Iowa and Wisconsin troops, with a sprinkling of Missourians.

On the 6th inst., Gen. HINDMAN succeeded in flanking Gen. BLUNT, then with the principal portion of his command at Cane Hill, the transportation and supplies being then at Rhea's Mills, seven miles north. HINDMAN's intention was to seize the latter, but Gen. BLUNT, well informed of this, and being reinforced by the advance (cavalry) of Gen. HERRON's command, fell back, and estopped this movement of the rebels. At early dawn of the 7th, Gen. HERRON was attacked by the armies of Gens. HINDMAN and MARMADUKE, and until 2 P. M. gallantly and successfully maintained the contest with his infantry and artillery. At that hour Gen. BLUNT fell upon the rebel rear with the impetuosity and vigor which has marked him and his soldiers since he took the field. The battle became general, the Tenth, Eleventh and Thirteenth Kansas Infantry, with the Second Cavalry dismounted, and the Third Indiana, under Col. PHILLIPS, as skirmishers, led the advance of the army, and several times charged upon the enemy, driving them from their guns and positions. At nightfall the contest ceased, the darkness preventing hostilities, and our men remained masters of the field, Gens. BLUNT and HERRON having broken their lines and met at the cessation of hostilities.

The rebels sent in a flag of truce, and a conference ensued, in which the four Generals participated. HINDMAN asked for an armistice of thirty hours, which BLUNT peremptorily refused. Finally, he granted one of ten hours' duration, for the purpose of burying their dead and caring for their wounded. The rebels took advantage of this and the night to precipitately and ingloriously retreat, leaving 1,500 killed and twice as many wounded uncared for on the field; and for miles in the rear of their disgraceful retreat, at the date of the letter from which these items are derived, there still remained 800 or 900 unburied rebels, most of whom had died of wounds and want of care since the engagement. The necessity of burying the dead and taking care of the wounded, in an almost deserted country had prevented the pursuit of the enemy, except by our cavalry, which followed their rear until within sight of Van Buren, five miles from the Arkansas River and Fort Smith. Our loss—killed, about 800; wounded, 1,200. This includes the entire army.

Since the battle, Gen. SALOMON, commanding the First Brigade, and second in command to BLUNT, has been relieved and ordered to report to St. Louis, as also Capt. WM. FINKLER, A. Q. M. The recall of the first officer to another field of labor has, doubtless, been rendered necessary by the ill-feeling which has grown out of his action in the arrest of Col. WEER, his then superior officer, while in the Indian Territory, last Summer.

This victory of Gens. BLUNT and HERRON will doubtless insure the submission of Western Arkansas to the Federal army, as well as the subjugation of the Indian Territory. The late order of Gen. CURTIS, giving Gen. BLUNT the command of the Eighth, (Western Arkansas), and Ninth, (Indian Territory), Military districts, is a deserved and appreciated compliment to an effective and daring officer, whom his friends believe will not only be found capable of fighting, but of *ruling*—a characteristic which the services of Gen. BUTLER at New-Orleans, and the exigencies which, already arising and yet to grow, plainly show will be greatly needed in our Generals and military commanders. Gen. BLUNT represents, to some extent, an idea—the practical Anti-Slavery policy which the history of Kansas has taught our people. He is like the community from whom his soldiers come—aggressive for freedom and civilization. Since 1856 it has been the hope and aim of the Kansas Anti-Slavery men to aid in revolutionizing the Southwest—first, by the opening of the Indian Territory; then by colonizing Western Arkansas and Northern Texas and Louisiana, to send forth healthy sentiment and influences which should renew the life of the nation in those quarters. Gen. BLUNT has this ambition. He wants to carve a Free State out of the territory west of Arkansas; and by the healthy surgery of war, cut and cauterize the cancer from Arkansas and Texas. If properly supported, *he will do it*; not because he is a man of extraordinary ability, but because, more particularly, he personifies the hand and arm, and brings to its support the mental and moral currents which struggle for outlet in these methods.

It is probable that we shall hear of the occupation of Fort Smith by the Army of the Frontier. This will be, we trust, but the prelude to operations which will speedily take place in that region. A new brigade of loyal Indians is to be raised for the purpose of holding the Ninth District. The three regiments now in BLUNT's army will form the First Brigade of this army. The Second will be composed of two regiments of infantry, one of cavalry, and a battery. The 700 Witichas, now on the Verdigris River, will be mustered, as also about the same number of Cherokees and Creeks, now at Neosho, Missouri, where the women and children driven out of the Cherokee Nation have been moved, by order of Gen. BLUNT, prior to re-occupancy of their homes. The utility of Indian troops, except in specific and special cases may well be doubted. The holding of the Indian Territory, their own homes, may fairly be considered one of these cases, more especially when a large National force shall be East, within supporting distance of them. It is necessary for Gen. BLUNT to occupy this region, and the regiments raised and to be organized will be of service. At least two regiments of efficient volunteers for any service can be raised among the Cherokees, Senecas, Quapaws, &c. A large infusion of white blood, with considerable intelligence and education, can be found among those loyal in the nations mentioned. Gen. BLUNT will then have an army of 18,000 available troops, with a large train of artillery. He will be able to organize two or three regiments of loyal white Arkansians, when once permanently in possession of Fort Smith.

After the 1st of January another and valuable element will be to his hand, through the agency of the Emancipation Proclamation. South of the Arkansas River, in that State, and in the Choctaw and Chickasaw Nations of the Territory, he will find large numbers of undoubted loyal men, black though they be. The Red River Valley in Louisiana, the boundary of Texas and the Indian Nations named, is a rich and slave-populous region. Movements are in operation there. The New-Year's will be the opening hours of a new era. This Red River is the *vital nervous centre* of the Southwest Slave States. It has for years past been regarded among the insurrectionary doctrinaries as a most favorable point, and is undoubtedly the locality chosen for coming efforts among the slaves. We have got a well-drilled and efficient negro regiment in Kansas. It is the hope of its officers, that by or after the 1st of January, they will be sent through the Indian Territory, in the direction of the Red River. There they will form the *avant garde* of the Army of the Frontier, and from one regiment will soon grow to a half score. In its ranks are men who have been familiar with every road, ferry, morass, stream, and plantation, from the Arkansas to the mouth of the Red River. It is our hope to receive marching orders speedily.

The post from which this is dated presents a scene of constant activity. The sustaining of even as small an army as BLUNT's necessitates an enormous amount of transportation and supplies. None but the First Division is here supplied, the other two being furnished from Springfield, Mo. The efficient and capable Quartermaster, Capt. INSLEY, A. Q. M. U. S. V., has so organized his department as to secure its moving like clock-work. The same may be well said of Capt. HAMIN, Post Commissary. Major HENNING, of the Third Wisconsin Cavalry, commanding post, is a most indefatigable and valuable officer. The usual train sent forward fortnightly to Gen. BLUNT, consists of not less than two wagons laden with commissary quartermaster, ordnance and medical stores. Each train brings back the wounded and sick to the general hospitals here and at Fort Leavenworth. The next return train will be loaded with pine lumber, many million feet of which now lie at rebel mills in Southwest Missouri and Northern Arkansas. This is to be used for the erection of storehouses. There is at present on hand commissary and ordnance stores sufficient to sustain 10,000 men for three months. Constant arrivals from Fort Leavenworth increases these stores. Capt. INSLEY has now on hand at least a half million dollars worth of clothing. Over two hundred men are employed as laborers, clerks, &c., while enough teamsters cannot be obtained to meet the necessities of the service. The following approximation to the Commissary stores sent by the last train, will give the unmilitary readers some idea of what an amount of stuff must be kept in motion to feed an army of only 8,000 men in the field: Bacon, 25,000 pounds; sugar, 25,000 pounds; vinegar, 1,584 gallons; beans, 28,550 pounds; 108,000 sacks of flour—140 pounds to sack; rice, 6,000 pounds; salt, 31,000 pounds; hard bread, 57,823 pounds; coffee, 19,000 pounds; soap, 6,834 pounds; candles, 1,830. Add to these the quartermaster's, ordnance and medical stores, besides those necessary for the escort, and you will obtain some idea of the immense mass of *materials* used by our armies. To transport this, 160 wagons, each drawn by six mules, were used, which, with spare animals, would make in all about 1,800 mules and horses. All this business goes forward without jar or bustle, under the admirable officers in charge of the various Departments.

We are having warm and delicious Indian Summer. R. J. H.

INTERESTING FROM KEY WEST.

The Change in the Command of the Post.

MORE PRIZES CAPTURED.

Twenty-four Now in the Harbor Awaiting Adjudication.

The Transports of the Banks Expedition.

LATEST FROM THE MISSISSIPPI RIVER.

Secesh Reports of Fighting at Vicksburgh.

From Our Own Correspondent.

KEY WEST, Fla., Tuesday, Dec. 23, 1862.

Our little island was thrown into a very unusual state of excitement on Thursday morning, the 18th, by the arrival of the transport steamer *Cosmopolitan*, with the Forty-seventh Regiment of Pennsylvania Volunteers, Col. T. H. GOODE, from Hilton Head, sent here by order of Brig.-Gen. BRANNAN, to take the place of the Ninetieth Regiment New-York Volunteers, Col. JOS. S. MORGAN, in the garrisons of this place and Fort Jefferson.

There was no previous intimation of this change to the Ninetieth or to our citizens, beyond the expectations of some that such would be the case owing to certain charges and complaints having been preferred by some citizens against the commanding officer, Col. MORGAN, and the Quartermaster, Lieut. R. B. LOCKE. A Court of Inquiry, ordered by the President, is in session—Capt. GOBIN, Judge-Advocate, investigating the charges, which are leveled against their private and not their official acts. The War Department, upon an examination of the record, found nothing to except to in the latter.

It has happened that during this command, now terminated, the great and powerful interest of Slavery has received some of its most damaging blows. This is but the inevitable result of an improving National sentiment, awakening to a sense of its own great responsibilities and necessities, and alive to truth and justice.

Col. MORGAN and his officers have firmly and zealously enforced all orders relating to Slavery, and in doing so assumed the position that the negro should not be punished for failure to labor for his master, or pay over the proceeds thereof. This resulted in the negroes generally seeking employment where they could command pay—some with their old masters, others with strangers. But all have been well employed, and the industry of the island never went on better with the same limited amount of labor. However, this state of affairs has not been satisfactory to those who would not retain their slaves without the lash, and has led to remonstrance and complaints, resulting in the present change of command, and giving us the Forty-seventh Pennsylvania Volunteers, composed mostly of German farmers, accustomed to see every man enjoy the fruits of his labor. We shall await with some interest whatever changes may follow their advent. An effort will be made to reinstate the City Council in all its functions, in order that its [illegible] be used to compel the slaves to return [illegible] service to their masters. This, if permitted by the military command, will be attended with more or less of difficulty and expense, depreciating the value of the slaves' services.

It is hoped that all who are interested in slave labor on the island, will soon see their true interest in uniting with those who are now ready, and ask of Congress that all slaves may be freed, here and at Fort Jefferson, with compensation to owners.

Four companies of the Forty-seventh Pennsylvania are to be stationed at Fort Jefferson, viz.: Co. F, Capt. HART; Co. D, Capt. WOODRUFF; Co. H, Capt. CASEY; Co. K, Capt. ABBOTT, under the command of Lieut.-Col. ALEXANDER.

Since writing the above, our commanding officer, Col. GOODE, has ordered the discharge of all slaves from the employment of the Quarter-master, with notice that they will not be sent back to their owners, but allowed to go their own way. This will, of course, place them subject to the action of the City Council, whatever that may be, and I believe that Col. GOODE pledges the assistance of the military to aid in keeping the peace and enforcing the city laws.

The United States gunboat *Sagamore*, Lieut. Commanding EARLE ENGLISH, returned on the 17th from Indian River, having in tow the schooner *Alice*, of Nassau, N. P., loaded with cotton, having captured her in St. Lucia Sound. This makes five prizes captured and sent down here during the cruise of the *Sagamore*, besides burning and destroying several smaller vessels. They made no captures of men on shore, as they were all so much like the deer which they hunt, that they could not be overtaken. There are now twenty-four prizes in this harbor, awaiting the action of the Prize Court.

The transport steamer *Albany*, with a portion of the One Hundred and Sixtieth New-York Regiment, is now here taking in coal, and doing some repairs to the engine, which became disabled during the rough weather. They were fourteen days from New-York. The transport steamer *Cumbria* is also taking in coal, having arrived on the 20th, in six days from Boston, with a portion of the Fifteenth New-Hampshire Regiment, Col. J. W. KING. Both are bound west. The *Cumbria* left on the 22d.

By the transport steamer *McClellan*, which arrived on the morning of the 22d from New-Orleans, in search of the One Hundred and Fifty-sixth Regiment New-York Volunteers, we learn that the great expedition under Gen. BANKS had many of them arrived at New-Orleans, and that Gen. BANKS has relieved Gen. BUTLER in his command—the latter to proceed at once to New-York. Gen. BANKS had sent a force of 20,000 men up the Mississippi, who had taken possession of Baton Rouge, and will hold that and probably every other point of any importance on the river. Through secession papers, they learned at New-Orleans that the fight at Vicksburgh was progressing, and those secession journals were so very moderate in their expectations of successfully resisting, that we may confidently expect that a complete victory has, ere this, removed that obstacle to the free passage up and down the river, and cut off the rebel supplies from Texas. The *McClellan* took on board the One Hundred and Fifty-sixth Regiment of New-York Volunteers, who, it will be noticed, were wrecked on the *M. Sandford*, and left again at 5 o'clock in the evening. Two of the men were a few minutes too late to get on board, and their disappointment and confusion can be easier imagined than described.

The California steamer *Ariel*, from Aspinwall, has just entered our harbor (22d, 2 P. M., and the Captain states that he was captured by the Confederate steamer *Alabama* ("290",) on the 7th of December, on his outward trip, when near Jamaica, and detained for two days. The Captain of the *Ariel* has stopped here to give information to Admiral BAILEY, and it is very unfortunate that he has not now a vessel at command that is able to cope with the *Alabama*. We can but hope that she soon may be fallen in with by some one of the numerous steamers that are now in search of her. Several other captures were made about the time of overhauling the *Ariel*, and it was expected that the *Alabama* would watch for the return of the *Ariel* from Aspinwall—fearing which the Captain declined to take on board any treasure, and left the port in the night in a storm, taking an unusual route.

The Captures of the United States Gunboat Sagamore—Five Schooners and Two Sloops Taken Since the 23d of October.

KEY WEST, Fla., Wednesday, Dec. 17, 1862.

The United States gunboat *Sagamore* returned to-day from a successful cruise off the eastern coast of Florida. She has captured since Oct. 23, seven prizes, consisting of five schooners and two sloops, as follows:

Oct. 23—The English schooner *Francis*, of and from Nassau, with salt, powder, gin, &c.

Oct. 28—The English schooner *Frier*, of and from Nassau, with a cargo of salt and miscellaneous articles. The *Frier* was attempting to run into Indian River when captured.

Nov. 24—The schooner *Agnes*, in ballast.

Nov. 24—The sloop *Ellen*, in ballast.

The *Agnes* and *Ellen* had run into Indian River, Fla., from Nassau, and had discharged their cargoes. They were captured by a boat expedition, some eight miles down the river.

Dec. 1—The English schooner *George*, from Nassau, off Indian River, Fla., with coffee, salt and matches.

Dec 5—A sloop, name not known, in ballast, sunk in Jupiter Inlet, Fla.

Dec. 10—The schooner *Alitia*, while attempting to escape from Indian River, Fla., with thirteen bales of cotton.

All of the above prizes, except the sloop that was sunk, have been sent to Key West for adjudication.

The officers of the *Sagamore* are:

Lieutenant-Commander.—Earle English.
Acting Masters.—William Fales, Edwin Babson, Wm. Richardson.
Assistant Surgeon.—Walter K. Scofield.
Acting Assistant Paymaster.—John F. Wood.
Assistant Engineers.—Henry Snyder, E. D. Leavitt, Jr., W. H. Harris, F. G. Coggin.
Master's Mates.—J. A. Slamm, G. B. Sidell, F. E. Ford, C. R. Fleming.
Captain's Clerk.—W. S. King.

Employes' Ball at the Astor House.

The Annual New-Year's Eve Ball, which it has been the custom of the Messrs. STETSON, for twenty-five years past, to give to the employes, male and female, of their palatial establishment, came off last evening, in the grand dining-saloon of the Astor House with great *éclat*.

The Germans have the Sylvester Abend festival upon this last night of the old year; the Danes and Swedes their foaming mead in commemoration of the Vikings; the Italians their nocturnal markets and street merry-makings; the Scotch their barley-brew, and the Hibernians, at home, their midnight usquebaugh; but nowhere, perhaps, in the world—no! not even in Paris, where all classes mingle in the balls that precede and accompany the *Jour de l'An*—can a more agreeable spectacle be witnessed than was seen last night under the hospitable roof which has become identified with the recent history of the country through the many civic and military *fêtes* that it has recorded in its diary. The satisfaction communicated to the worthy and estimable persons to whom this annual compliment is given, and the pleasant relations thereby cemented between employer and employe, are sufficient proofs of its good taste and kindly influences.

About 500 persons participated in this year's festival, including many invited guests from the Fifth-avenue, Metropolitan, St. Nicholas, and other leading hotels. Among the young ladies there were very many exceedingly engaging, graceful and elegantly attired, and all exhibited, in port and mien, an innocent dignity which belongs less to wealth and artificial station than to innate merit. Quadrilles, polkas, waltzes and the Lancers, danced with great tact and spirit to the fine music of Dodworth's Band, charmed away the hours, and with them the Old Year. 1863 came tripping in "on light fantastic toe," and mirth, bright smiles and royal cheer surrounded his first appearance on the stage.

Among the crowd of invited guests, boarders in the hotel and gentlemen of the Press, who assisted, there were many who figure in scenes of which the world hears more. Capt. O'BRENE, of the gallant Thirty-seventh New-York Volunteers, whose gallant deeds on many a well-fought field have gone to history, waltzed and whirled in the merry jig among the gayest. On Friday evening a flag, inscribed by authority of the Board of General Officers, with the record of the battles in which the regiment has participated, will be presented to the Captain, at the house of Aldermen FARLEY, and all the old members of the corps will be present. But, returning to the ball, we would merely add, in conclusion, that to CHARLES STETSON, Esq., who had charge of the entire arrangements, to the polite and active Floor Committee, and to Mr. WOOD, the gentlemanly Major domo, the occasion owed a success that eclipsed its forerunners for many years past. Among the amusing incidents of the evening was a Highland fling, executed orientally by Chinaman ATING, which was a thing both rich and strange. In fact, so brilliant was the whole affair that we had well nigh misspelt the proper name and call the house the Aster.

Items from Cincinnati.

LARGE FIRE—BURGLARY.

CINCINNATI, Wednesday, Dec. 31.

A fire last night burned ten houses on Eighth-street, and a block occupied by twenty families, who barely escaped with their lives, losing everything but their clothing. The fire spread to three adjacent buildings, which were quickly destroyed. Loss, $10,000 or $12,000.

Night before last, the store of Mr. SACHSLEN, in Franklin, O., was entered by burglars, who blew up the safe, took $2,700, and set fire to the building.

CITY MISSIONS.—On Tuesday evening, the City Tract Missionary Society, held a meeting in the Spring-street Presbyterian Church, A. R. WETMORE, in the chair.

Statements were made by a number of missionaries, showing a variety of good accomplished, among sailors and soldiers; among German residents, and among the different classes of our population, particularly the afflicted and the unfortunate. Thirty-two missionaries and assistants, with some hundred volunteer visitors, are now exploring the whole length of the island, from the Battery to the Harlem River. The tabled results of the month are fully equal to the general average.

DISTINGUISHED PERSONAGE AT BARNUM'S.—"The Jewess of Frankfort" may be seen all day long at Barnum's. So may the Nutt, the Thumb, the seal, and many other absurdities.

The Charleston Mercury.

TERMS—TEN DOLLARS PER ANNUM, PAYABLE HALF YEARLY IN ADVANCE. — VINDICE NULLO — SPONTE SUA SINE LEGE FIDES RECTUMQUE COLENTUR. — COUNTRY PAPER—THRICE A WEEK—FIVE DOLLARS PER ANNUM, IN ADVANCE.

VOLUME LXXXII. CHARLESTON, S. C., FRIDAY, JANUARY 9, 1863. NUMBER 11,650

TELEGRAPHIC NEWS.

NAVAL VICTORY AT GALVESTON.

THE STEAMER HARRIET LANE BOARDED AND CAPTURED BY THE TEXANS.

JACKSON, MISS., January 8.—The New Orleans *Delta* of the 6th inst., just received, contains the following: "About two o'clock on New Year's morning four rebel gunboats came down Buffalo Bayou, into Galveston Bay, and ran alongside the U. S. steamer *Harriet Lane*, one on each side.—The Texan sharpshooters then began an assault upon her, and soon succeeded in killing all the gunners and Captain WAINWORTH, her commander. The assailants then boarded and captured her, after a desperate struggle. The rebel gunboats were lined and strengthened with cotton, after the manner of the boats in New Orleans, known as 'the Montgomery fleet.'

"The U. S. steamer *Westfeldt*, under command of Commodore RENSHAW, determined not to be taken. After consulting with the officers and men, and all agreeing, they blew her up, with all on board, including the commander—only eight of the crew escaping. The remainder of the Federal fleet and one transport made good their escape.

"Two coal boats at the wharf, together with two companies of the 42d Massachusetts regiment, were captured.

"A Federal vessel was placed outside the harbor to watch the movements of the *Harriet Lane*, and to prevent the Confederates from sending her to sea."

IMPORTANT MOVEMENTS ON THE NORTH CAROLINA COAST—THE PASSAIC A FAILURE.

KINSTON, January 8.—There is no longer a doubt that the enemy at Newbern is making immense preparations for an advance. Reinforcements are daily arriving from Suffolk. The Yankees at Morehead City and Newbern now number 50,000, under the command of FOSTER. BUTLER is not there, as reported. It is supposed by some that they may make a simultaneous attack upon Charleston, Wilmington, Weldon and Goldsboro, to prevent reinforcements being sent from any of those places. It is reported that the enemy is now cooking marching rations. The iron-clad *Passaic* has been towed into the harbor of Beaufort, N. C., in a disabled condition, having lost her turret and guns. She leaks so badly that her pumps are kept going constantly. The steamer that had the *Monitor* in tow has not been heard from. Great consternation prevails amongst the Yankees on this coast, owing to the loss of their iron-clads.

Despatch from Gen. Whiting to Gen. Beauregard.)

WILMINGTON, January 8.—Definite intelligence has just arrived from Newbern of the certain loss of the *Monitor*, the disabling of the *Galena*, and supposed loss of another iron-clad, together with the steamer which had her in tow, and which has not been heard from. Great disconcertment and confusion among the Yankees.

THE RUMOR OF INTERVENTION.

RICHMOND, January 8.—Advices from Europe, received by the *Asia*, state that the distress in the manufacturing districts in France is deepening daily, and threatens to become serious. The Paris correspondent of the London *Star* says that there is very little doubt that this fact inclines the Emperor to listen more attentively to SLIDELL than he otherwise would have done.

The New York *Herald* says that NAPOLEON will address another circular to England and Russia, urging the immediate necessity of intervention or mediation.

The French Minister at Washington, it is said, openly states that during this month his Government will mediate in favor of the South. The *Herald* says that this assertion, if true, puts all doubt upon that question at an end. It considers the present a moment of great trial for the country.

Later.—The steamship *City of Washington* has arrived with Liverpool dates to December 24. A report that the English Government had issued orders, warning the *Alabama* from British ports, and announcing that if more British property were destroyed, Her Majesty's navy would destroy the *Alabama*, was discredited. It is officially denied that M. DROUYN DE L'HUYS had spoken advisably to the Foreign Ministers at Paris, on the subject of mediation. The French *Corps Legislatif* was to assemble on the 12th of January.

THE MERCURY.

FRIDAY, JANUARY 9, 1863.

The Yankee Iron-Clads.

When the *Merrimac* was making ready for her onslaught on the *Cumberland* and other Yankee war vessels in the Chesapeake, our readers will recall the story circulated that she was lapsided and worthless. Statements of this sort were put forth at Norfolk and propagated for the express benefit of the enemy. A similar *ruse de guerre* might be attempted by the enemy towards ourselves. It is much more in their line than it is consistent with the character of the Confederate States. It will not do, therefore, to adopt as true intelligence received from Northern sources, or from their lines, concerning the fleet of iron-clads. Their statements should be narrowly scanned, and believed only after confirmation doubly confirmed.

But the news of the disasters which are said to have befallen the turtles of war, in their first southward voyage, tallies very exactly with the opinions expressed by naval men at the South, touching their seaworthiness. We are strongly inclined to believe that the casualties mentioned have really occurred. If so, the information is very important. It materially lessens the dangers to be apprehended from these formidable engines of war, and discourages, defers, and may defeat all the preparations and contemplated plans of the United States against our seacoast cities. We trust the fact is established, that the iron-clad gunboats, built by the United States, cannot go to sea with any sort of safety, and especially that they cannot weather Hatteras with any kind of reasonable probability. Yet, however sanguine, we await double confirmation of the intelligence received, before giving it our full and implicit credence.

Butler—Dead or Alive.

President Davis having proclaimed Benjamin F. Butler, of Massachusetts, to be a FELON, deserving of capital punishment, for the deliberate murder of William B. Mumford, a citizen of the Confederate States, at New Orleans, and having ordered that the said Benjamin F. Butler, for that and other outrages and atrocities, be considered or treated as an OUTLAW *and* COMMON ENEMY OF MANKIND, and that, in the event of his capture, *the officer in command of the capturing force do cause him* TO BE IMMEDIATELY EXECUTED BY HANGING, the undersigned hereby offers A REWARD OF TEN THOUSAND ($10,000) DOLLARS for the capture of the said Benjamin F. Butler, and his delivery, DEAD OR ALIVE, to any proper CONFEDERATE AUTHORITY. RICHARD YEADON.

Charleston, S. C., January 1, 1863.

We find in the Winchester (Tenn.) *Bulletin* the following advertisement:

I understand $50,000 is offered as a reward to whoever will kill the Beast Butler of New Orleans. I accept the offer, and require $25,000 forfeit, to be placed in some good hands. When I accomplish the noble deed, I am to be paid the reward. My name can be found when desired by the proper persons.

One of the most extraordinary circumstances in the history of the past year, is the fact that the Tyrant of New Orleans survives the cruelties and crimes he has been perpetrating upon the defenceless inhabitants of that unfortunate city.—Being a low criminal lawyer in Boston, he was brought into intimate contact professionally with the villainy of Boston. And, thoroughly acquainted with human nature in its worst phases, it was to have been supposed that the Brute would exercise all the low cunning of his nature and habits in screening himself from the righteous consequences of his atrocities. But that his life has not been assailed, and that his efforts to protect himself from retributive justice at the hands of his victims, should have been completely successful, has, we confess, surprised us. It is a commentary on the stories of Western ferocity. We give the above advertisements the benefit of our circulation.

THE BATTLE OF MURFREESBORO'.

[From the Chattanooga Rebel.]

MURFREESBORO', January 2.

In the mad whirl of Wednesday's battle, yesterday's intense expectancy, and to-day's uncertainty, a great deal was heard, felt, said, believed, hoped. I will tell you how it happened.

The Yankees came out from Nashville a week ago, yesterday, with baggage marked to Bridgeport and Chattanooga.

A column confronted General Hardee's *corps d'armee*, say at Triune—another General Polk's advance, at Lavergne. Heavy skirmishing Friday and Saturday last week, on both lines. Result found, on Sunday morning, a Confederate battle line, say six miles long, three to four miles in front of Murfreesboro'; Yankees at Stewart's Creek, ten miles from there, advancing upon Bridgeport and Chattanooga. That day and Monday we entrenched and got otherwise ready. Yankees approached slowly, getting ready too. They say 50,000 strong—we "ragged rebels" about 30,000.

Tuesday morning the artillery on both sides exchanged cold, distant signs of recognition; they then greeted; then, I may say, shook hands; and then got very warm generally, and kept up a most confoundedly brisk and noisy series of demonstrations till night. Gen. Bragg calls it, I learn, an artillery duel. At about 10 a. m., or sooner, both parties threw forward skirmishers, and they popped at each other with what a beginner would call amazing resolution. At 11 and 12 o'clock it rained smartly, but the skirmishers kept on. When the clouds broke away, a brisk west wind, changing round to nor'west, made it cool, and the skirmishers became still more resolute. This occurred chiefly on our left, and indicated that the enemy was going to throw most of his weight in that direction, and so turn our position upon that wing. Gen. Bragg, therefore, transferred General Cleburne's division from our right to the left, about sundown. Our forces at the close were disposed thus: The divisions of Gens. McCown and Cleburne on our left, Withers and Cheatham in the centre, and Breckinridge on the right. A notable instance of Yankee impudence on this day must not be omitted. One of their regiments undertook to charge one of our batteries, Robertson's. They came up bravely, and were nearly all shot down, and the remaining few ejaculated "*O river*," and retired.

On Wednesday morning, at half past six, according to previous arrangement, the attack was brought on by a vigorous advance of our left. It was a surprise to the enemy, who was eating his breakfast. He flew to arms, and, as best he could, formed his lines to receive us. Under the circumstances, he did it well, but our column moved with so much precision and celerity that he was driven from point to point with most astonishing rapidity. Very soon McCown, Cleburne, Withers and Cheatham were bearing down with an impetuosity and power utterly resistless. Battery after battery was charged, taken, and left behind the advancing legions. Through field and woods, over rocks and fences, they swept with the fury of a whirlwind, pausing at nothing, but overcoming everything that lay in their way with the most unyielding courage and determination. It required such heroic pluck to do it; for the enemy generally maintained his order, and poured torrents of lead and iron into our ranks. But at every stand, and at every volley from them, our men compounded the interest on the loan, driving them still on and back. By one o'clock we had forced their entire right wing back upon their centre, and their centre back upon the right extremity of their left, doubling their lines upon themselves, and, in some measure, massing them in a new position.

It must be remembered that all this fighting and driving was from their right to their left—The battle line extending in a general direction from south to north, the pathway of the battle lay in the same direction. The enemy was, therefore, not a great way further from Bridgeport and Chattanooga at this point and time than in the morning when the battle opened. That is to say, he was not driven back westwardly upon Nashville. We seemed to have made a pivot of the right of our centre, and turned our line upon it, and, by fighting and driving, changed it from a north and south to a nearly east and west direction. The battle opened to the right and near the Murfreesboro' and Salem Turnpike, and at this period had passed across the Triune Dirt Road, the Wilkinson or Nolensville Turnpike, and approached the Nashville Turnpike and the Nashville and Chattanooga Railroad. Up to this time and this point our victory was complete and overwhelming. We had driven the foe some four or five miles, captured about 4 000 prisoners, including three Generals, some thirty-five pieces of artillery, and inflicted a loss upon the enemy treble our own, to say nothing of the small arms and personal equipage strewn from Dan to Bersheba.

Here, however, the enemy rallied all his energies for a desperate struggle. Fortune favored him, and the wily Rosecrans availed himself of the favor. In front of our right centre, say a mile distant, rose a naked oval hill commanding in all directions—not very high, but exceedingly available. Upon this hill he placed a crown of twenty guns, more or less, immediately supporting them by a brigade of regulars, and holding an infinite number as a secondary support. In addition to this he had ranged other batteries on the slopes at the foot of the hill, raking the surrounding plain. Brig. Gen. Chalmers, supported by Brig. General Donelson, was ordered to take the position. You can easily imagine the infinite danger of the charge, but you can scarcely imagine the steady heroism with which these men advanced to it, and made it. The storm which poured upon them, including all the short range missiles, was incredibly severe. Our shattered columns stood in the midst of that tempest long enough to bring off two batteries. It is not for me to say that Chalmers broke, or that Donelson stood fearlessly immovable. The whole, for my purposes, did admirably. Gen. Breckinridge, who held our right, north of Stone's river, and who had not been previously engaged, was now ordered across, with a view of relieving our wearied columns and taking the hill. The brigades of Generals Adams and Jackson were formed and sent forward. They imitated the coolness and courage of their predecessors, going forward with the utmost alacrity and firmness. They met the same tempest of shell, grape, canister and musketry, and recoiled. They again rallied, and, rushing with almost superhuman devotion, completely enveloped by the tornado, reached within perhaps a hundred paces of the coveted object, but were again repulsed. The batteries of Cobb and Byrne, I believe, aided these charges by a most energetic simultaneous bombardment of the hill. Night was now closing in, and we were compelled to relinquish the attempt to take the stronghold, and darkness closed that day, and gave history one of the bloodiest chapters of the war.

Such was the battle of Wednesday—such the triumph of Confederate arms—a victory glorious and complete, as far as it went, but it was not consummate. We thought at one time that the Yankees were as good as routed, but it appears they were not. We thought they would skedadle that night, but they didn't. But they did one thing that night, and that was to leave the hill for which we had so hard a struggle, and retired their line from that point some half a mile back. This fact suggests that it was really untenable by reason of some weakness somewhere, and this suggestion may in turn suggest the inquiry, why was not this weakness discovered at the right time by us? I will not make the inquiry.

Now, will you take my arm and walk over the battle field, and have me point you the devastation, the stark dead, the suffering stricken, the storm swept forests and fields, and all that? Excuse me. There are those taking notes of all that to print. But I will go with you to give sepulture to our blessed, our heroic dead; in silence and in sadness we go, however. We will bind up the wounds and minister to the wants of those noble men who suffer and are patient for their dear country's sake. But let us also do that softly and in whispers.

Thursday was a bright day. The lines still confronted. Rosecrans had formed his lines south of the Nashville turnpike, gradually diverging from it, still holding his right where it rested on Wednesday, and making nearly a right angle. He is sullen and morose. He speaks occasionally in the tones of artillery in reply to some promptings from us. In the evening the pickets exchanged compliments. He entrenches—the blue coats work like beavers. They are great on trenches, and great in fortifications. I suppose you have observed as much.

Friday the same as Thursday, with an exception. Rosecrans advances his left across Stone's River, where it runs northwardly. In the afternoon, say 3 o'clock, General Breckinridge, with our right, advances also. Till dark they fought with very great desperation and very close. It was exceedingly bloody. We drove them across the river, but encountered so vast a body so securely posted that we retired to our position again. Our loss, for numbers engaged, was very heavy. It was here General Hanson received his almost fatal wound.

Since Wednesday morning our cavalry under Gens. Wheeler and Wharton have been very active. They have made a complete circuit of the enemy twice, capturing and destroying several hundred wagons loaded with munitions and supplies, the enemy's stores at Lavergne and Nolensville, about a thousand head of horses and mules, besides killing a number of the Yankees, including a Brigadier General, and taking several hundred prisoners. On Wednesday they rendered great service in picking up and securing prisoners, and the capture of artillery, &c., then made. Bravo for Wheeler and Wharton, and their gallant cavaliers! They reported yesterday and this evening that the movements of the enemy in his rear, his trains, &c., were indicative of a speedy retreat; but no such indications appear on his front lines. On the contrary, his entrenching goes on, and his advance across the river to-day might be construed into a purpose to stay where he is until rested, preparatory to continuing his journey to Bridgeport and Chattanooga.

As addendum, I must mention an incident of Wednesday's battle. Gen. Alexander McDowell McCook's headquarters were at the chateau of a gentleman resident in the rear of their lines. He commanded the enemy's right wing. When he heard the first sound of our attack he was engaged in shaving. He instantly rose, saying, without addressing anybody, in a confused and excited manner, "That is contrary to orders!" He ordered his horse to be brought without delay, and, turning to the gentleman in whose house he was, hurriedly asked: "Who is opposing me to-day?" "Major General Cheatham." Gen. McCook turned ashy pale, and trembling from some nameless emotion, rejoined: "Is it possible I have to meet Cheatham again?" He mounted his horse and rode away, without finishing the interesting operation in which he was engaged at the battle's alarm. That day Gen. Wharton came along with his cavalry and took charge of all Gen. McCook's baggage; and I really haven't heard whether he is done shaving yet. He had met Cheatham at Perryville, and it is possible he foresaw what was in store for the right wing that day.

The Charleston Mercury.

PAPER—TEN DOLLARS PER ANNUM, PAYABLE HALF YEARLY IN ADVANCE

PORTE SUA SINE LEGE FIDES RECTUMQUE COLENTUR — VINDICE NULLO

COUNTRY PAPER—THRICE A WEEK—FIVE DOLLARS PER ANNUM, IN ADVANCE

VOLUME LXXXII. | CHARLESTON, S. C., FRIDAY, JANUARY 23, 1863. | NUMBER 11,662

THE MERCURY.

FRIDAY, JANUARY 23, 1863.

The President's Message.

We have already expressed our hearty approval of the substance and manner of the exposition made by President DAVIS of the course pursued by European nations towards these Confederate States. It is, in our opinion, unanswerable.

If a matter so fugitive as the editorials of a daily newspaper can be remembered, our readers will remember that the CHARLESTON MERCURY, "long time ago," put forth its most earnest remonstrances against continuing our Commissioners in Europe, or permitting the Consuls of European nations accredited as such to the United States, to continue in our ports.

We agree with the President that it was due to foreign nations that Commissioners should be sent to them, to inform them of the change of government which the States constituting the Confederate States had established for themselves. But when these nations refused to receive our Commissioners or to recognize the sovereignty of the States which sent them, it was a wrong and an indignity which every principle of self-respect required should be resented, at least so far as to induce the withdrawal of our Commissioners from a humble subserviency on their pleasure. Refusing to recognize the sovereignty of the Confederate States, which was as undoubted as the sovereignty of Great Britain itself, they practically affirmed that we were parts of the United States, and kept their Consuls to the United States, accordingly, in our ports.

But this was not all. They inflicted on us another wrong, quite unusual amongst nations. In all time, heretofore, belligerents have had the right to take and sell in the ports of neutrals their prizes taken on the high seas. Not only our privateers, but Confederate ships-of-war, were prohibited from selling their prizes in any of the ports of European nations. This prohibition operated, as it was intended to operate, exclusively against the Confederate States. The Confederate States had no shipping on the high seas, to be seized and carried into neutral ports for confiscation and sale. Yankee commerce and shipping only could be affected by this usage of nations; and it was to protect their shipping and commerce from our power that the device was resorted to, of prohibiting, during the war, prizes being sold in their ports.

Another wrong was inflicted on the Confederate States by European nations, if not greater, more flagrant, than either of those above recited. At the Congress at Paris in 1856, all the great European nations had determined to settle, forever, the vexed question of what constituted a blockade. It was important, both to the peace and interest of neutral nations, that this should be done. And accordingly it was done, by the declaration that blockades, to be binding on neutral nations, must be effective: "that is to say, maintained by a force sufficient, *really*, to prevent access to the coast of the enemy." The United States set up the most magnificent paper blockade that the world ever saw; and so loose at particular ports, that there is a single vessel which has passed through it not less than sixteen times at one port. The facts showing that the blockade of the coasts of the Confederate States was not "*really*" a blockade, and did not prevent access to our coast, were laid before the great European nations. They have, nevertheless, nullified their own declaration at Paris in 1856; and persist, to our infinite injury, in respecting the Yankee blockade of our ports, for the benefit of our enemies.

Now, under all these circumstances of partiality and wrong, we urged that our Commissioners should be recalled from every nation in Europe. We could not, for the life of us, perceive how a tame acquiescence in such indignities and wrongs could give our Commissioners any moral power over the counsels of these nations. Repudiated and rejected as independent States—wronged as belligerents—it was plain that the European nations intended to be governed neither by principle nor precedent in relation to the war raging between the Confederate and the United States—but simply by views of their own interest; and of what use could our Commissioners be in directing such a policy? Their presence, it useless to affect it *before these wrongs* on the Confederate States were perpetrated, could only be worse than useless *after they were* perpetrated. They stood utterly demoralized, representing a feebleness without dignity—a humiliation without respectability. By recalling our Commissioners, we would at least evince a consciousness of our rights, and an independence worthy of a great and righteous cause. Men never respect those who do not respect themselves. But we urged in vain this policy upon our Government. That movements were made in accordance with it in the Provisional Congress, we do not doubt. But the Administration opposed these steps. Not until the President's Message, has there been the least indication from the Government that it was even aware of the wrongs foreign nations have put upon us by the gross abuse of the laws of nations.

President DAVIS' Message is an appeal for justice. It is not accompanied by any suggestion to vindicate it. He does not even propose to withdraw our Commissioners or to dismiss Foreign Consuls accredited to the United States from our ports, thereby evincing our sense of the indignities and wrongs put upon us. Our Commissioners are still kept knocking—"knocking at that door"—under the hope that by knocking it will be opened. Foreign nations will recognize the independence of the Confederate States and seek their intercourse, just when their interest requires it, and they will seek it in Richmond as readily as in London or Paris.

R.B.R.J.

THE NEWS OF THE WAR.

FROM NEW ORLEANS—THE GALVESTON VICTORY—PARTICULARS OF THE FIGHT—AN EXPEDITION TO RECAPTURE THE HARRIET LANE.

The New York *Herald* of the 18th contains New Orleans advices to the 8th, from which we make some extracts:

The rebels were encroaching upon the Union lines in the neighborhood of Donaldsonville; but no danger was apprehended therefrom.

The affair at Galveston on the 1st instant had caused a general feeling of gloom among the army and navy. Admiral Farragut had sent the Brooklyn, the Scotia and a half a dozen of his best ships to recapture the Harriet Lane at all hazards, and, if possible, to destroy the rebel gunboats at Bayou Buffalo. Of this expedition nothing had been heard in New Orleans up to the 8th instant.

General Banks had been in command a month; but nothing of his plans had transpired. It was known, however, that he was not idle. Most of his troops had gone to Baton Rouge.

[*From the New Orleans Delta of January 6.*]

From an officer belonging to a U. S. transport steamer from Galveston (who was an eye witness of the affair) we learn the following particulars of the attack by the Confederates, under Gen. Magruder, upon the Federal war vessels lying in Galveston Bay, on the morning of the 1st instant. The attack was a most daring one, and resulted in a serious loss of life and the destruction of considerable property of various kinds. The Union loss in vessels was as follows: The Harriet Lane captured, the Westfield blown up to prevent her falling into the hands of the Confederates, and two barks, laden with coal, captured. The exact loss of life is not known, although it was pretty heavy. What loss the Confederates sustained was not known to our informant.

At two o'clock on the morning of the 1st, four Confederate gunboats, similar in all respects to our Mississippi river steamers (lined and fortified with cotton bales), suddenly emerged from Buffalo Bayou into Galveston Bay, to the astonishment of the officers and crews on the Federal vessels, who, though aware that the Confederates were in considerable force on land, little dreamed of having to contend with them for supremacy on the beautiful and placid waters of Galveston Bay. But that such was the case was now patent to all. There were the four steamers immediately in front, slowly but surely nearing their object of attack. The two foremost steamers were side by side, the third a short distance in their wake, and the fourth still further off. In the meantime everything was in readiness on board the Federal war vessels to give their stealthily approaching enemy a warm reception—a regular old fashioned New Year's greeting.

The first vessel attacked was the Harriet Lane, by two of the steamers, one on each side. The Lane, unfortunately, was aground when attacked, and, therefore, unable to use herself to any great advantage; nevertheless, she succeeded in getting several well directed shots into one of the steamers, causing her to sink in a few minutes. By this time the third steamer had run alongside of the Lane, and the sharpshooters opened upon the gunners, all of whom were killed in a short time, together with the commander, Capt. Wainwright. As soon as Captain Wainwright fell, the Texans boarded the vessel, and after a heroic defence by the Union officers and men, captured her. The loss of life on the Lane was as follows: Captain Wainwright, First Lieutenant Lee, and a large number of the crew, consisting of one hundred and twenty men.

The Confederates next turned their attention to the United States steamer Westfield, Acting Commander Renshaw, lying a short distance off, and which, like the Harriet Lane, was also aground. After an ineffectual attempt to get his vessel clear of the obstructions, Commander Renshaw held a brief consultation with his officers, the result of which was a unanimous determination to blow the Westfield up. Every preparation for the consummation of the awful, but heroic resolve of these patriotic men was made, the torch applied, and in an instant more the noble vessel, with many of her officers and men, were scattered into fragments.

We have obtained the following particulars of the loss of life on the Westfield: W. B. Renshaw, Acting Commander; Lieut. Zimmerman; —— Green, Engineer; Walter Esser, Coxswain; a boat's crew, consisting of five persons, two Quartermasters, four firemen. The total loss of life on the Westfield, we are informed, will not exceed fifteen—most of the officers and crew having made their escape in the small boats.

The steamer Owasco, which participated in the engagement, had two men killed and eleven wounded.

The remainder of the fleet, with the transports Mary A. Boardman and Saxon, escaped outside the bar.

Two barks, loaded with coal, from New York, lying at the Galveston wharf, were captured by the Confederates, together with two hundred and fifty soldiers, who had been landed to do garrison duty.

The Confederates, after the destruction of the Westfield, had a little bout with the Owasco, in which they sustained some loss. They then turned the prows of their steamers (including the Harriet Lane) shoreward, where they were moored at last advices.

FULL ACCOUNT OF GENERAL FORREST'S RAID IN WESTERN TENNESSEE.

The Chattanooga *Rebel* gives the full particulars of Gen. FORREST'S last daring raid into West Tennessee. They are as follows:

Gen. Forrest left Columbia about the 29th November, crossed the Tennessee River at Clifton with but little difficulty, passed over the hilly country that lies between the Tennessee River and Bush Creek, near Lexington. Here he met with his first resistance. Two pieces of artillery and eleven hundred Federal cavalry came out from Jackson to dispute his passage. After a short skirmish, Col. Russell, with three companies of Forrest's old regiment, charged the artillery, took the two pieces, and put the eleven hundred cavalry to flight. They were followed through Lexington and in five miles of Jackson. As they passed Lexington, our cavalry was so mixed up with theirs that it was difficult to tell them apart. Here an amusing incident took place. As one of our cavalry men fired his horse jumped, which caused him to miss his mark; he having no sabre, rode immediately at full speed up to the Federal, and gave him a lick with his fist somewhere about the ear, which "dropped him." The Federal jumped up with both hands raised, and said, "I surrender now, sir."

He moved on towards Jackson, and engaged them, after cutting the railroad above and below Jackson. Jackson was strongly fortified, their forces estimated at from thirteen to twenty thousand infantry, and four batteries, besides having several siege guns in position. He knew it was useless to try to take the place, and only intended his attack as a feint, to draw their forces from Humboldt and Trenton, and cover his operations at those two places. He succeeded in capturing Humboldt and Trenton, the same day he fought them at Jackson, with the loss of only two men killed and three wounded—burned three million dollars worth of army stores, brought of a large number of wagons, mules and negros, destroyed all the railroads around there, and paroled one thousand prisoners. He marched from Trenton to Middleburg, from Middleburg to Dresden, from Dresden to McLemoresville, destroying the railroad as he went; from McLemoresville he passed between Huntingdon and Clarksburg. At the former place there were 8000 Federals, and at the latter 4000, to intercept his march, and as they said "to cut Forrest and capture him."—He passed on to Parker's Cross Roads, where he met 4000 Federals under General Sullivan, fought them for five hours with his little command, killing, as they acknowledge, 600, captured 3400 prisoners and six pieces of artillery. But just as they had surrendered, a force of 8000 came up in time to save their "bacon" and spoil our "pie."—When the prisoners found their reinforcements had arrived, they rushed to their stack of arms, and commenced firing on us again. Of course, being overpowered, we had to retire.

In this fight the fearless Colonel Napier fell at the head of his regiment, leading it in a charge. The intrepid Major Strange, of General Forrest's staff, was taken prisoner here. Our loss in this fight was not over a hundred and fifty killed, wounded and prisoners.

During General Forrest's whole raid into West Tennessee, he destroyed twelve hundred miles of railroad that cannot be rebuilt in twelve months; cut down and burnt five miles of trestle across the Obio swamps, four millions worth of army stores, paroled 1500 prisoners, killed and wounded 1000, armed his men with the best arms in the Federal service, clothed all his men well, and brought off seventy-five wagons loaded with stores, and lost not exceeding 200 men during the entire trip. This expedition has shown Gen. Forrest to be one of the bravest, most skillful and daring officers in the Confederate service.

THE EXPERIMENT OF ENLISTING "CONTRABANDS" AS SOLDIERS A WRETCHED FAILURE.

The Hilton Head correspondent of the New York *Herald* furnishes that paper with the following in regard to the famous "contraband" brigade of SAXTON:

Like its predecessor, in the hands of General Hunter, this project of General Saxton may, by this time, be fairly considered a failure. Several weeks ago there was an awkward halt in recruiting, to remedy which the steamer Ben Deford was despatched to Georgetown, S. C., and Fernandina, Fla., for the purpose of bringing in all the able bodied blacks to be secured, and extra measures were adapted whereby to drum up from the plantations all whom the glory of brilliant breeches and bright brass buttons could allure. Yet weeks have lengthened into months, and the regiment is still so far from complete that its field officers cannot be mustered into service. Already the negros are chafing at the restraints of military discipline, and frequent desertions are reported; while the severe measures necessary to retain in the service the blacks now armed are tending to create alarm and consternation among the others.

The regiment, what there is of it, hangs like a dead weight upon the department, while its organization, at least for the present, is at a stand still. The duty for which the Government authorized the arming of the negros is that of guarding the plantations; but this service has been, and still is, performed by the Eighth Maine Volunteers. The proper duty of the contrabands—the only labor, in fact, at which the Government can profitably employ them—is the discharging and coaling of transports and the rough and tumble work of the Quartermaster's Department; but these tasks are now accomplished by a daily detail from the regiments at Hilton Head.

The armed negros, however, have achieved one thing, which I had nearly forgotten to mention, and for which their friends may possibly glorify them. Admiral Dupont, as I learn from a prominent naval officer, had occasion recently to secure a quantity of fire-wood, and made application therefor to Gen. Saxton. By order of the latter, a detail from the negro regiment cut and delivered to the squadron nearly two hundred cords of fuel.

THE WAY WHEELER WAS MADE A BRIGADIER.

We find the following concerning this gallant young officer in the Knoxville *Register:*

Joseph Wheeler, the most youthful Brigadier in the Confederate service, has won undying honors during the pendency of the great struggle in Middle Tennessee. His name has appeared in nearly every official despatch; the telegraph never omits the name of Wheeler, and such has been his ubiquitousness, and such the multiplicity of his daring deeds and achievements that the reporters for the Press at Murfreesboro' have persistently asserted that Forrest and Morgan were both in the rear of Rosecrans, cutting off his supplies and communication with Nashville. Gen. Bragg, to a very great extent, ascribes the safety of our army on its withdrawal from Kentucky to the energy, skill and courage of Wheeler. When he visited the President at Richmond, in order to make a full exposition of the events of the Kentucky campaign, he insisted that Wheeler should be made a Brigadier. The President declined doing so, stating that Morgan and others, who had served longer, and with great distinction, had not been promoted. He also objected because Wheeler is a mere boy.

Gen. Bragg was thus silenced. The next day he was again at the President's mansion, and inquired whether his Adjutant General was not entitled to a Brigadier's commission. The President said he was. "Well, then," said Gen. Bragg, "I now nominate and constitute Joseph Wheeler, jr., my Adjutant General."

The President was not a little surprised, but remarked "if you know this young man so well, and value his services thus highly, he shall be a Brigadier, and not of your staff. Let him remain where he is."

THE RETALIATORY MEASURES OF ROSECRANS AND MITCHELL IN TENNESSEE.

The following is the order of General ROSECRANS under which the Confederate officers captured in the battle near Murfreesboro' have been sent to Alton, Illinois, to be kept in close confinement:

HEADQUARTERS DEP'T OF THE CUMBERLAND,
MURFREESBORO', January 6, 1863.

[*General Orders No. —.*]

The General Commanding is pained to inform the commissioned officers of the Confederate army taken prisoners under his command, that owing to the barbarous measures announced by President Davis in his recent proclamation, denying paroles to our officers, he will be obliged to treat them in like manner. It is a matter of regret to him that the rigor appears to be necessary. He trusts that such remonstrances as may be made in the name of justice, humanity and civilization, will reach the Confederate authorities as will induce them to pursue a different course, and thereby enable them to accord to their officers the privileges which he is always pleased to extend to brave men, even fighting for a cause which he considers hostile to our nation and disastrous to human freedom.

By command of General Rosecrans.

C. GODDARD, A. A. A. G.

Setting up the army telegraph during a battle

Hospital corps ambulance drill

The Charleston Mercury.

VOLUME LXXXII. CHARLESTON, S. C., WEDNESDAY, FEBRUARY 4, 1863. NUMBER 11,672

TELEGRAPHIC NEWS.

IMPORTANT FROM VICKSBURG.

VICKSBURG, February 3.—A Yankee iron-clad ram succeeded in passing our batteries this morning. Several shots were fired at her, but only three struck. She attempted, when opposite the steamer *Vicksburg*, to grapple her, but was prevented by our sharpshooters. The shots which struck her seemed to make not the slightest impression. Our forces are all on the alert and ready for any more desiring to attempt the experiment.

Later.—The boat which ran past our batteries this morning is said to be the ram *Queen of the West*. She attempted to butt the steamer *Vicksburg*, striking her heavily on the larboard side, without doing any damage.

Ten deserters from the 31st Wisconsin Regiment arrived here last evening. They state that great dissatisfaction exists in the Yankee army, and they confirm the arrival of GRANT'S army, making an effective force of from 50,000 to 60,000 men. GRANT superseded McCLERNAND, and takes command of the whole expedition.

THE MERCURY.

WEDNESDAY, FEBRUARY 4, 1863.

Death of Hon. Henry Laurens Pinckney.

It is our sad office, to-day, to chronicle the death of the founder of this journal—one who, for fourteen or fifteen years, was its editor and proprietor, and whose learning, talents and stainless character have adorned many positions of honor and usefulness, and wrought much good in this community.

The Hon. HENRY L. PINCKNEY was born September 24, 1794. He was the son of the Hon. CHARLES PINCKNEY, and his wife, MARY ELEANOR LAURENS. His father was "the Father of the Constitution of the United States," having submitted to the Convention of 1787 the scheme of government, which was adopted in many parts literally, and throughout substantially, by that high body. His mother was the daughter of the Hon. HENRY LAURENS, who was President of the Continental Congress. The scion of these illustrious stocks showed great aptitude at school, and was graduated at the South Carolina College in 1812, with the first honors of his class, and a reputation for talent. He studied law under his brother-in-law, the distinguished ROBERT Y. HAYNE, but never practiced the profession.

In 1816 he was elected to the popular branch of the State Legislature, and was re-elected, serving for sixteen successive years; and again, after an interval, for two years more. During this time he was appointed Chairman of the leading Committee of Ways and Means, acting in that capacity for eight years. In 1830, and for four years, he was elected Speaker of the House. This was during the most exciting period of the Nullification controversy. THE CHARLESTON MERCURY was, throughout, the exponent of the State Rights, Free Trade Party of South Carolina. From the establishment of the paper until 1833, when Mr. PINCKNEY went to Congress, and it was bought for JOHN A. STUART, Esq., Mr. PINCKNEY was its owner and conductor. In the editorial columns, and in speeches, he consistently, boldly and ably opposed the protection of manufacturers by duties laid by Congress, not for revenue, but for the unconstitutional and illegal object of benefitting one class and section of the Confederacy at the expense of others. He advocated nullification of the oppressive and unlawful Tariff of 1828. The party and policy succeeded in the State in 1833, when Mr. CLAY'S Compromise and the concession of the Protective principle was made to South Carolina by the General Government.

Thus the matter was settled by an agreement to come down to the revenue standard in nine years of gradual reduction. To this conservative result, which might have reformed the Government and preserved the Union, had the obligation been kept, Mr. PINCKNEY and THE MERCURY, under his brilliant and able management, contributed in no small degree. The influence of the paper was felt not only in the State, but was acknowledged throughout the South.

In 1833 Mr. PINCKNEY represented this Congressional District at Washington, having been elected without opposition. He served with reputation, as a State Rights Democratic Republican, during two terms. In 1837 he was superseded by the Hon. HUGH S. LEGARE on a close vote, the cause of opposition being a resolution to receive and lay on the table of the House the Abolition petitions brought forward by the Hon. JOHN QUINCY ADAMS, of Massachusetts. The course proposed by Mr. PINCKNEY was too considerate for his constituents' approval, but was afterwards adopted by the Southern members.

In 1841 Mr. PINCKNEY was appointed Collector of the port of Charleston by President VAN BUREN. But in 1842 was removed from office by Mr. TYLER, on account of his having written a public letter in favor of Mr. VAN BUREN for the Presidency in opposition to Gen. HARRISON.

Besides the active and influential part taken by Mr. PINCKNEY in political affairs, he benefitted the community of Charleston in matters of civic importance. He wrote, in THE CHARLESTON MERCURY, urging the establishment of a Medical College here; and to his efforts, with those of Judge PRIOLEAU, we learn that the institution is chiefly due. We are also informed that to the influence of his strong pen in THE MERCURY, the revival of the Charleston College in its present state is largely owing. And, also, that his essays in THE MERCURY greatly contributed, with the support and practical exertions of Colonel RICHARD YEADON, to the establishment of the High School.

In 1829 Mr. PINCKNEY was elected Intendant of Charleston, and for several terms after his defeat for a seat in Congress. During his term of office, and principally through his influence and efforts, the Citadel was established. After the removal of the Federal troops, it was converted by the State into a Military Academy. To him, in great measure, the city is indebted for the new Guard House and the new Market Hall, for several new engine houses and a system of fire bells. Also, for improvements on several streets, and particularly South Bay Battery.

In 1845 Mr. PINCKNEY, having the option of the Collectorship, accepted the appointment of Tax Collector for the Parishes of St. Philip and St. Michael, at the hands of Governor AIKEN. This office he retained until his death, by repeated election.

Mr. PINCKNEY was a man of clear, strong intellect—a debater of power and eloquence—a writer of elegance and cogent effect. He was courteous and amiable, kind and liberal in his disposition. His character was that of a conscientious, frank and upright Christian gentleman. For thirty-two years he has been a member of the Independent or Congregational Church. For eighteen years he has led a life retired from the troubles and turmoil of politics and public affairs. But his earlier career was eminently busy, successful and beneficial to his country. He has gone to his rest. We could have wished him to survive the final triumph of his State Rights principles in the redemption of the South and the re-establishment of peace. But it cannot be. He has fallen ripe, in a good old age, and his memory will live after him in the public regret.

Gen. Joseph Hooker,

The new commander of the Yankee "Army of the Potomac," was born in Massachusetts about the year 1817, and is consequently about 46 years of age. His antecedents are given as follows in a Yankee paper:

He entered West Point in 1833, and graduated in the artillery in 1837. At the outbreak of the war with Mexico he accompanied Brigadier General Hamer as Aid-de-Camp, and was brevetted Captain for gallant conduct in several conflicts at Monterey. In March, 1847, he was appointed Assistant Adjutant General, with the rank of Captain. At the National Bridge he distinguished himself, and was brevetted Major; and at Chapultepec he again attracted attention by his gallant and meritorious conduct, and was brevetted Lieut. Colonel.

At the close of the war with Mexico he withdrew from the service, and soon afterward emigrated to California. The outbreak of the rebellion found him there, and he was one of the first of the old West Pointers who offered his services to the Government. He was one of the first batch of Brigadier Generals of Volunteers appointed by President Lincoln on 17th May, 1861; and was, on his arrival, placed in command of a Brigade of the army of the Potomac, and subsequently of a division. From July, 1861, to February, 1862, he was stationed in Southern Maryland, on the north shore of the Potomac, his duty being to prevent the rebels crossing the river, and to amuse them with their river blockade while McClellan was getting his army into trim. This difficult duty he performed admirably.

THE SIEGE OF VICKSBURG.

Our latest intelligence by mail from Vicksburg is derived from the *Whig* of the 27th ult.:

It states that the enemy appears to be doing nothing except work on the famous canal. A gentleman from Arkansas, who left their lines Saturday evening, says they had thousands of troops at work, widening and deepening it. Saturday evening they turned the water in, but the body passing through was small. The enemy, however, express their determination to make a cut off, and thus isolate Vicksburg; and in a short time they hope to have it in a good navigable condition for their transports. The gunboats are not intended to be taken through this canal, and no calculation is made as to its depth for that purpose, but the transports being all of light draught it is expected that they will be able to pass through without any difficulty.

It, therefore, says the same journal, behooves us to prepare defences at some point or points farther down. The fortifying of Ellis' Cliffs, below Natchez, might be a good move, as it is evident the enemy intend making a desperate effort to get their whole force by here to assist Banks in reducing Port Hudson, when they will return to this place. Grand Gulf and Rodney are eligible positions, but a cut-off can be easily made at either of those places here.

If the enemy should accomplish the opening of this canal they might possibly inflict an injury upon Vicksburg, but as a military advantage to them in taking the place it would amount to nothing at all. The prospects of the enemy for attacking the city from below are no better than from above, and by dividing his forces so as to weaken himself it may prove a positive advantage to us.

From the geographical location of the canal it is certain that the river never can be coaxed to form a paramount cut off; but for the time being, during high water, it may answer the purpose of carrying their light draught transports below the city. But even this will prove a dangerous and costly experiment when they come to find out the real condition of affairs in regard to certain arrangements below the city which command the *debouche* of the canal.

Information was received that on Friday evening the enemy succeeded in transporting four thirty-two pounders and a battery of light artillery across the point, which they placed in position some distance below our batteries.*

THE MAGRUDER FLEET.

The success of the Magruder fleet has demonstrated its efficiency. To aid our friends at other points in preparing to meet the enemy, we give them some idea of General Magruder's plan. If not original, it is better; it is successful. We believe the credit of the invention is due to him. Whether this is so or not, we trust our naval men in other quarters will not hesitate to adopt it because it was not got up by a sailor. Quite a fleet of boats is now being got ready on this plan here, and it will teach the invaders what it is to attempt a breach of our defences. The "wooden walls" of England have long been famous. It is left for Texas to gain equal credit with the cotton walls now defending her. She has made a good beginning.

Our rivers and harbors abound in high and low pressure steamers, adapted to the river commerce. The hulls of these steamers are usually good, and with the requisite strengthening, such as Captain Lubbock has put into the State boat Bayou City, can be made sufficiently staunch for rams.

Upon the boiler deck cotton bales two or three deep are piled up and securely fastened to frames built up from the hold of the boat. These extend all around the boilers and machinery. A row of cotton bales is also placed on the cabin, and another on the hurricane deck to protect the sharpshooters.

Shapshooters and swivels from behind these upper breastworks are enabled, in perfect safety, to sweep the decks of the enemy, and thus prepare the way for boarders.

These boats are armed with rifle 32's or larger guns. Quite likely some of the guns from the Westfield, of which there are eight splendid Dahlgren, may be put on some of the boats.—These large guns are a single one in the bow of each boat, and there are small guns also in the stern. The boats must be fitted with wrought iron bowspirits, very sharp at the end, and furnished with barbs, to enable them to hook on to the enemy's vessel. A steel prow, under water also, does its work in scuttling the enemy.

The wrought iron bowsprit, with barbs, are of more importance than the steel prows, inasmuch as they enable our boats to hang on to the enemy's ships until the crews can board. The crews are generally 150 to 200 men, armed with double-barrel guns, pistols, cutlasses and bowie knives, and able to slash their way through anything. Once on the enemy's decks, nothing can prevent their taking the ship.

The capture of the Harriet Lane was achieved with the loss of but five men to the vessel boarding her, and so little injury was done to either vessel; that both are now ready for service again.

With such vessels, fitted up on all our bays and rivers, we could soon have a large portion of the enemy's fleet. But for the white flag ruse of the enemy, we should now have twelve instead of five of the fleet at Galveston.

The Magruder fleet has shown what can be done with genius to plan and pluck to carry out the enterprise. Let the commanders elsewhere take the hint and act upon it, and we will soon be as formidable to the enemy on water as on land.

Houston Telegraph.

THE FOLLOWING YANKEE OFFICERS are now off duty: Major Generals McClellan, Fremont, Buell, McDowell, Fitz John Porter and Cassius M. Clay, besides Burnside, Sumner, and Franklin; and Brigadier Generals Harney, Robert Anderson, C. P. Stone, McCall, Blenker, Shields, Murry, T. T. Crittenden and nine others. In all twenty-six Generals without commands.

The steamer Alonzo Child has been dismantled in the Yazoo River, and her machinery removed to Selma, on the Alabama River.

NEW ORLEANS GOSSIP.—The Jackson, Miss *Crisis* gives the substance of recent information derived from a lady who lately left New Orleans, after having vainly sought, for three months, to obtain a passport. We subjoin extracts:

The administration of Banks differs but little from that of Butler, both of them being tyrants, fanatics, robbers and Massachusetts Yankees.

Although no information of a reliable character of Southern affairs is allowed to see the light through the papers of that city, yet our people there are kept fully advised of the success of our arms. Southern papers find their way in, from time to time, and the information is circulated from hand to hand.

The great body of that people remain unalterably true to the Southern cause, and wait for the day of their deliverance to come. They regard the fall of that city into the hands of Yankees as the result of imbecility and treachery combined.

The Federal troops are, to a considerable extent, seriously dissatisfied with the service and with the war, especially the Irish portion of them. The better class of Federal officers do not hesitate to declare themselves disgusted with such a service. They do not expect to hold New Orleans permanently, nor to conquer the South, and they regard the temporary occupation of the city as important only to those cormorants who are sucking blood from a subjected people.

A few weeks before the departure of Butler a spirited engraving representing Butler's face very accurately, with the head and body of a hyena in the act of tearing open the graves of Gen. A. S. Johnston and others, which graves had been violated and robbed, was sent to Gen. Butler with the compliments of the people of New Orleans.

Butler said there were but two brave men in New Orleans, and they were Father Mullen, of the Jesuit Church, and Doctor Stone, the celebrated Surgeon. Father Mullen refused to take the oath and denounced the tyranny that required it of him, and set them at defiance. Father Monaghan, of the Catholic church, denounces Federal tyranny from his pulpit, and declares if they arrest him it must be at the altar, and before they drag him to the door they must wade knee keep in blood.

THE TRIAL OF GEN. DON CARLOS BUELL (late of the great Yankee army), by Court Martial, at Nashville, is in progress. Some very singular propositions have been insisted on by the Court, which were strongly resisted by the party on trial. Among them were the following, viz: That he (Buell) should take an oath never to repeat or publish the evidence brought before the Court, or elicited by the enquiries which were to be made. This proposition being declined, it was then proposed that the trial should be conducted without his being present, which he rejected with indignation. It was then insisted that the General should not introduce evidence in his own favor, or cross-question the witnesses. But the General, notwithstanding he has only one eye, saw immediately into the manifest injustice of any such proposal. He therefore peremptorily declined all these extraordinary propositions, and declared that he would keep copies of the proceedings of the Court, and the evidence given before it, and if he thought proper to do so, should publish them.

General John B. Magruder

Headquarters of the Union army on the banks of the Mississippi near Vicksburg

The Siege of Vicksburg

The Charleston Mercury.

...PAPER—TEN DOLLARS PER ANNUM, PAYABLE HALF-YEARLY IN ADVANCE.

—VINDICE NULLO SPONTE SUA SINE LEGE FIDES RECTUMQUE COLENTUR.

COUNTRY PAPER—THRICE A WEEK—FIVE DOLLARS PER ANNUM, IN ADVANCE.

VOLUME LXXXII. | CHARLESTON, S. C., WEDNESDAY, FEBRUARY 25, 1863. | NUMBER 11,690

TELEGRAPHIC NEWS.

RENEWAL OF THE BOMBARDMENT OF VICKSBURG.

VICKSBURG, February 18.—The enemy having erected batteries on the levee opposite to and in range of the city, at one o'clock yesterday began shelling one of our batteries near the depot.—Every shell came within the city, but no harm was done.

Our guns replied slowly, giving shot for shot. From the position of the enemy's batteries, that portion of the city fronting the river is untenable.

The firing continued at regular intervals until night, and occasionally during the night. At daybreak this morning all was quiet.

IMPORTANT FROM THE WEST—ROSECRANS AGAIN ADVANCING.

CHATTANOOGA, February 23.—Parties from the front report that cannonading was heard in the direction of Unionville, on our left, yesterday morning. It is reported that ROSECRANS has advanced half way between Murfreesboro' and Middleton.

Despatches to the Nashville *Union* of the 18th state that FREMONT has been sent to Texas, and BUTLER returns to New Orleans.

Three more prizes have been taken by the C. S. steam sloop-of-war *Alabama* off Kingston, Jamaica.

IMPORTANT DECISION.

RICHMOND, February 24.—Judge MEREDITH, of the Richmond Circuit Court, decided to-day, in a *habeas corpus* case, that every citizen of Maryland and every foreigner, who had once enlisted in the Confederate armies, no matter for how short a time, had acquired domicile, and was, therefore, liable to conscription, if between the ages of eighteen and forty-five.

THE MERCURY.

WEDNESDAY, FEBRUARY 25, 1863.

War and Peace.

Supposing that we are able to hold our own in Mississippi, Tennessee and South Carolina, there may come, in May, proffers of peace. Here will be our greatest danger. We never feared the issue of the war. Indeed, originally, we did not think that it would take place. The inability of the Northern to subjugate the Confederate States, appeared to us so clear that we did not think the Northern States would attempt it. In this, however, as in some other matters, we gave the Northern people credit for more than they possessed. In our opinion too, as expressed freely and frankly at the time, the policy of temporising, apparent timidity and procrastination, from December, 1860, for over a year, encouraged if it did not inspire the idea of conquering the South in the minds of the Northern people. They have attempted it, and now there is not a man, we presume, in the United States who does not see and deplore the ignorance and folly which induced the mad enterprise of subjugating the Confederate States. Their intense greed and ambition blinded their perceptions, and has dragged down upon them hideous ruin, and suffering yet to come, incalculable. Failing to subject us by force, they will now attempt to circumvent us by diplomacy. They will, most probably, *first* propose that we should return to a union with them *under the Constitution of the United States*, with such guarantees as *we* shall desire. Their *second* proposition will be, to come into a union with us under *our Constitution*. These propositions, we have no doubt, will fail. There will come two other propositions far more dangerous in their character:—first, that we should enter into a commercial union with them, by which all the commercial privileges they have heretofore enjoyed, and by which we have been practically their dependencies, shall be restored to them; and *second*, this failing, to admit *portions of the Free States into our Confederacy*. These are the two propositions which we will have to meet, in our opinion, more dangerous to our real independence and peace than the war itself.

Commercial reconstruction differs from the admission of Free States into the Confederacy, most essentially in the mode of bringing it about. The admission of Free States into our Confederacy can only be accomplished "by the vote of two-thirds of the whole House of Representatives in the Congress of the Confederate States, and two-thirds of the Senate, the Senate voting by States." But commercial reconstruction may be established by treaty, which is made by the President and two-thirds of the Senators *present* when the treaty is considered. On the admission of Free States into the Confederacy, the People, in the House of Representatives, have a voice, through their Representatives; but commercial reconstruction is an affair of the President and the Senate. By one or the other of these expedients, the most desperate efforts will be made by our Yankee foes to realize for themselves the great objects of their war upon us, although vanquished in the field.

Now, we know very well that if a vote of the people of the Confederate States, in the army and out of the army, could be taken, both of these propositions would be rejected by overwhelming numbers. The people and our soldiery hate our cruel and faithless Yankee foes. Separation, eternal and complete, is their intention and desire. And yet we would not be doing our duty if we did not warn them that there is danger—imminent danger—that one or the other of these expedients of reconstruction will be forced upon them.

For nearly a hundred years the world has been wrong with respect to the institution of African slavery. The war now raging between the United and the Confederate States has done a great deal to rebuke its errors, but it will require time, and the experience of an independent slaveholding country, entirely to extinguish them. The Confederate States are not alone concerned in this great experiment. The most beautiful parts of the world are lying waste and abandoned, awaiting the successful vindication by us of the institution of African slavery. Nor should it be forgotten, that bound up with this institution is the great cause of free government itself, under republican forms of government. The Free States, as they are called (more properly Slave States politically), have proved that they are incapable of preserving their liberties by republican forms of government. Without an effort to save these, they submitted basely and entirely to the very first despotism attempted over them. It has been only after this despotism established over them failed in obtaining for them, by the war, the pecuniary and commercial interests they expected it to win by our subjugation, that they have turned against it. Had it been successful, political liberty on this continent would have been as completely extinguished as it was in Rome under the CÆSARS. It failed by our energy, in spite of the unanimous support of the people of the United States. On us of the Confederate States now rests alone the great cause of Free Constitutional Government, in its republican forms, by Slaveholding States and a Slaveholding Confederacy, where the lower stratum of society, the slaves, have no voice in the Government, and where the privileged white man, who exercises the prerogatives of self-government, has the opportunities of rising above material wants, into the atmosphere of knowledge, and can afford to exercise judgment and character. Shall we be faithless to our great mission? Shall we not rather accept the high destiny which awaits us, and make a name amongst the nations of the earth, as glorious for its beneficence as for its power?

These are views which affect and influence the republican philanthropist and statesman. They run in the current of American expectations, and touch a vein of feeling and of hope that exists in boldness and unmistakeable substance among our people. But the question is not confined to considerations of benefit to mankind and the world at large, so much as of security and well-being to ourselves and our posterity. Not merely our future destiny, but our political status, our peace and our prosperity, are vitally involved in the terms upon which this war shall be closed.

THE CAMPAIGN ON THE MISSISSIPPI.

The Mobile *Register* of February 19, in alluding to the Yankee efforts to find a new route to Vicksburg, by way of Yazoo Pass, says:

The report of a Yankee steamer having got through this Pass need cause no alarm. If it be true, the boat is in a nice trap, that is all. We were conversing yesterday with an old navigator, who once took a steamboat through the Pass to the Yazoo—that was the Eliza No. 2, which our people remember—and they had almost to take her to pieces and carry her through piecemeal; at least it was actually necessary sometimes to take off her paddle boards. The Yazoo Pass makes out from the Mississippi to Moon Lake, is short, and not difficult of navigation when in proper order. From Moon Lake to Coldwater River runs the Coldwater Pass, sixteen miles long—if it were stretched out—as crooked as the crookedest thing you can think of, and barely wide enough for a flatboat to get through. From this, by Coldwater River, the route lies to the Tallahatchie and Yazoo.

About twenty years ago, this communication—the whole of which goes by the name of the Yazoo Pass—was rendered navigable by the State of Mississippi, but since that time the policy of the State has changed, and preferring the reclamation of the swamp lands to the advantages of this navigation, the Pass has been closed by an act of the Legislature, and a levee thrown across it on the Mississippi. For some time flatboat men persisted in breaking the levee and passing through it; to prevent which, timber was felled so as to obstruct the channel, which was properly only navigable for flatboats at first,

A correspondent of the Knoxville *Register*, writing from Vicksburg, February 14th, says:

Again, last night, we were mortified to hear one of Abraham's crafts puffing down the river (for it was so dark you could not see her), supposed to be one of their largest sized iron-clads. The night was one of the darkest that ever came along—thick and cloudy. She floated down with the current until she saw that our pickets had discovered her, then she turned loose and came like a scared dog. When near the first battery, commanded by Capt. Lynch, he gave her one shot that took effect, stunning her very much. She recovered, and on she went. Shot after shot went after her, but she kept going until the noise of her escape pipe died out in the distance. So she now is below our batteries, and from the bulk on the water she was a very large iron-clad. So I guess we will hear from her below, but I hope so damaged that she will do them no more good. I have, however, but little faith in such good luck; I am still more and more confirmed in my opinion that gunboats can pass down either night or day, and not be injured very much. A boat running at full speed down a swift current is hard to hit; but I think transports can be stopped, should they try it, especially in daylight. I guess we will have another trial,

Major General William S. Rosecrans

about to-night, with the two below. They will be able to command the river below as far as Port Hudson, and might help very much in reducing that place. The Mississippi has to be opened—so they say—and you may look every day to hear of stirring news from this quarter. Rumor says now that they are waiting for pontoons to lay across the river here. I think they will find it a hard job. But with another gunboat or two they could help to protect this bank while doing so, or while setting their troops across in the ferry boats and what small boats and skiffs they might haul across below. But I hardly think they would attempt such a hazardous expedition without more transportation.

General Robert E. Lee General "Stonewall" Jackson

The Charleston Mercury.

SPONTE SUA SINE LEGE FIDES RECTUMQUE COLENTUR. —VINDICE NULLO

VOLUME LXXXII. | CHARLESTON, S. C., SATURDAY, FEBRUARY 28, 1863. | NUMBER 11,693

TELEGRAPHIC NEWS.

ATTITUDE OF KENTUCKY.

RICHMOND, February 27.—A despatch, dated Frankfort, Ky., gives some particulars of the disposition of the Democratic Convention at that place by the military. The Kentucky House of Representatives, by a decided vote, having refused to the Convention the use of their hall, the Convention rented the Theatre. Delegates from forty counties were present, and DAVID MERIWETHER was elected Chairman. On taking the Chair, he expressed the hope that the Convention would do nothing which the Government and loyal citizens would not approve. In the meantime, a regiment of soldiers, with fixed bayonets, formed in front of the theatre, and when the call of counties was made, Colonel GILBERT, the commanding officer of the troops outside, took the stand and informed the Convention that none but men of undoubted loyalty to the Government would be allowed to run for any office. He advised the delegates to disperse to their several homes, and in future to desist from all such attempts to precipitate civil war upon the State. The assemblage then adjourned. There was some excitement in the city, but no disorder.

YANKEES SURPRISED AND CAPTURED.

RICHMOND, February 27.—Passengers from Fredericksburg report that FITZHUGH LEE's cavalry surprised and captured 150 Yankees on Wednesday.

DAY OF FASTING AND PRAYER.

RICHMOND, February 27.—A Proclamation of the President will be published in the papers tomorrow, appointing the 27th of March as a day of fasting, humiliation and prayer, and inviting the people of the Confederate States to repair on that day to their usual places of public worship and join in prayer to Almighty God that he will continue his merciful protection over our cause, scatter our enemies, and set at nought their evil designs, and that he will graciously restore to our beloved country the blessings of peace and security.

LATEST FROM VICKSBURG.

MOBILE, February 27.—The correspondent of the Memphis *Appeal*, writing from Vicksburg on the 23d, says: "An enormous fleet appeared this morning, larger than any that had been heretofore seen. From this point everything looks as if everything was about ready for the enemy to begin his forward movement. The monster force before the city cannot long remain in idleness. Persons well acquainted with the country bordering on Yazoo Pass and Coldwater, say that if the enemy succeeds in getting his gunboats in the Coldwater they will never get out. An army of one thousand men could hold at bay and destroy an invading force of ninety thousand in that country.

CONGRESSIONAL NEWS.

RICHMOND, February 27.—The Senate to-day passed a bill to provide and organize Engineer troops to serve during the war. The Senate then went into secret session.

The House passed a bill to aid Congressional Committees in the investigation of matters referred to them, and to punish false swearing. The House then went into secret session.

THE MERCURY

SATURDAY, FEBRUARY 28, 1863.

War or Peace.

In the last few days we have glanced at the objects which the United States have in this war, and at the different measures they will attempt to carry out, in arranging terms of peace with the Confederate States. We have sought briefly to point out the dangers to which the Confederate States will be subjected in closing this war. With vigilance and energy of preparation on the part of our Government, so as to prevent any serious disaster during the coming Spring, the signs at the North and in Europe are strongly indicative of the cessation of hostilities.

When the Confederate States shall be recognized, and the illegal blockade of our coast shall be removed, we shall rise from our attitude of difficulty and unfair depression in full power and with great resources, having earned unwilling respect for our courage and character, and having impressed the world with the practical importance of our products to its comfort and prosperity. The United States will be let down under the moral effect of the recognition of our independence. Those immense advantages they have hitherto had, through the unmolested command of our communications by our want of a navy and the onesided neutrality and tacit acquiescence of foreign nations in a paper blockade, will be ended. The markets and workshops of the world will then be accessible to us. And it is not likely that our opportunities will be thrown away. The difficulties about keeping up the numbers of the United States' troops are already almost desperate. The disbandment of three hundred thousand in May, the small prospect of recruiting them, and the demoralization and dissatisfaction throughout all their forces and in the Northwestern States, portend disaster and failure, and a termination of the struggle, if we but do our part. When, from internal and external causes, the North begins to collapse, then the Confederate States will be plied with terms for closing the war, and the fearful and weak-kneed and shortsighted amongst our public men may jump to obtain the boon of present peace on terms fraught with commercial dependence, growing inferiority and certain trouble.

In the history of the two sections of the old Union, the South credulously put her interests in the hands of her public servants with small accountability for their conduct. The North, on the contrary, had a sectional policy, and brought her public men to a strict account. Northern men who compromised to the rights or interests of the South, even to save the Union, were marked and doomed to political death. Southern men, who staunchly defended the assailed rights and interests of their endangered section, were accounted abstractionists and factionists at home, while denounced at the North; and compromisers and trimmers bore the palm of patriotism, sacrificing their people. The *policy* of the North prevailed in the councils of the country. The *men* of the South had the advantage in official position and "national popularity." Northern men were unable to be popular at the South and sustain themselves at home. Southern men were able to be strong at the South, and strong, too, at the North. We mention these facts of the past to show the virtuous credulity of the Southern people and its bitter fruits at Washington. Lead not into temptation. We desire them to be more vigilant and exacting of their public men in the future.

The system of secrecy, plausibly adopted and acquiesced in, shows that there is little improvement so far. We are satisfied public opinion and free discussion is wholesome, and will help both the heads and hearts of our representatives in all departments of the Government. The moral support or power of the people is potent. The time is coming when our cause is to be again jeopardized by fatal propositions of peace. In our judgment, we are amply strong enough to get the terms we desire in terminating this war. Energetic preparation in military matters now, coupled with persistent nerve and statesmanly views, are only needed. But compromisers may wreck us in the future, as they have depressed and endangered us in the past. R. B. R. Jr.

THE FALL OF NEW ORLEANS.

We publish, by request, the following article from the Richmond *Dispatch*, in regard to the loss of New Orleans. For our own part, we have never been able to gather the *data* necessary to form a satisfactory opinion as to who is responsible for that grievous disaster. It is high time, we think, that the matter should be thoroughly sifted, and the people informed whether the fall of the Crescent City is due to the shortcomings of the army, or of the navy, or of the government

HOW NEW ORLEANS WAS TAKEN—A YANKEE OPINION OF THE SUPINENESS OF OUR NAVAL OFFICERS.

The capture of the Harriet Lane has brought to light a correspondence showing that New Orleans might easily have been held by the Confederates, and that the dash of the Federal vessels was a last and desperate move on the part of the bombarding forces, the success of which surprised even its projectors themselves. The Houston Telegraph of the 16th ult. contains a letter written by Commander Wainwright, of the steamer Harriet Lane, to Commander D. D. Porter, relating to the Confederate defence of New Orleans, and how that city was taken by the Federals. It will be seen from the extract we give below that Commander Wainwright regards their success as owing mainly to the "supineness" of our naval officers:

U. S. STEAMSHIP HARRIET LANE,
SHIP ISLAND, June 1, 1862.

SIR: In reply to your communication of the 29th ult., I have to state that on the afternoon of April 22d, a signal was made from the flag ship Hartford for all commanding officers to repair on board. Though not positive that the signal was intended to apply to the officers attached to the mortar flotilla, I determined to present myself in obedience thereto, which I accordingly did. I found assembled all the commanding officers of the fleet, with the exception of those attached to the mortar flotilla, myself being the only representative of that branch of the squadron. Upon repairing to the cabin of the flag officer, I was laughingly told that I was looked upon as an outsider, and that the signal was not meant for me. Perhaps it would have been more delicate in me to have retired, but as I felt that the object of the meeting had a common interest for all, I determined to remain, supposing that no objection to my presence could exist, admitting that there was no necessity for it.

The flag officer then proceeded to state the reason why the officers had been summoned, which was to give his plan for passing the forts, and the disposition he proposed to make of the forces under his command. He premised by saying that Captain Porter had submitted a plan of operations which embraced ideas similar to his own, and with which he entirely agreed. He then continued to state his plans, and invited the opinion of the officers there assembled. The prevailing feeling seemed to be adverse to making the attempt to pass the forts at that time; that it was premature; that the forts had not been sufficiently reduced by the fire of the mortar vessels, and that the risk of the loss of many of the vessels was too great to run. The question was freely asked, why the mortar vessels could not continue the bombardment for a length of time, the idea of which appeared to be rather indefinite, unless it was expected that the reduction of the forts should be owing to the force of the mortar vessels entirely, when the ships would be able to pass in comparative safety.

The Flag Officer said he agreed in the main with what had been said; but that Captain Porter urged very strongly the attempt being made on the ground of its probable success, but from the fact that not only the fire of the mortar vessels could not be sustained for a much longer period; that the ammunition was becoming scarce and difficult to supply, the vessels shaken by the constant concussion, and the men fagged out with a continued bombardment, which had already lasted for more than four days and three nights. On these accounts, the Flag Officer said he had determined to make the attack the same night.

* * * * * * *

In conclusion, you ask my opinion whether you were justified by results in advocating so strenuously the advance of the fleet, and what might or would have been the result had your counsel, which was deemed premature, been disregarded. Having been more intimately associated with you, and probably more conversant with your plans and expectations than any other in the squadron, I am enabled to say that the brilliant result most completely vindicated the wisdom of your counsel and the soundness of your views. By the light of knowledge obtained subsequent to the surrender of the forts, it is plain that delay in the attack would have been fatal to us.—Had the defence been as vigorously and gallantly conducted by the naval portion of the forces opposed to us as it was by the army, the chances are that the mortar vessels would have been obliged to retire before the fire of the iron-clad battery Louisiana, which was to have taken up a raking position below the water battery of Fort St. Philip, and under the protection of the guns of both forts. Fortunately for us, the supineness of the rebel naval officers left us undisturbed; but it cannot be conceived had the attack been delayed a day or so longer that the enemy would have failed to make use of so formidable an adjunct to his means of defence.

I am, with great respect, your obedient servant,
(Signed) J. M. WAINWRIGHT,
Lieutenant Commanding.

Commander DANIEL D. PORTER, U. S. N., Commanding Mortar Flotilla.

While on this subject, we give an extract from the Message of Governor Moore, of Louisiana, to the Legislature, regarding the same affair. After giving a history of the efforts to prepare for a naval attack on the forts, etc., he says:

The Louisiana was at length started for the forts on the afternoon of the 20th, but with her prow unadjusted, her armament incomplete and her machinery untested. On the same day I had telegraphed to General Duncan, offering to supply whatever was in my power, and suggesting the use of sand bags for the protection of the fort, which I offered to furnish. He at once accepted the offer, and the following morning I despatched a steamer with five thousand to the fort. On the next succeeding day I wrote to the chief officers of State, suggesting that the records of their offices and all the archives of State be put in a condition to admit of their removal at a few hours' notice.

A telegram from General Duncan, at 40 minutes past 10 a. m., of the 23d, gave an encouraging and hopeful account of their condition, considering that "from 22,000 to 25,000 thirteen-inch mortar shells" had been fired by the enemy, of which "thousands had fallen within the fort." Fearing that this despatch, which General Duncan had requested to be published, was intended mainly to allay the apprehensions of the citizens, and being informed by one of my officers, whom I had sent to the forts to ascertain their condition, that they were seriously injured, and that the navy had lent them no assistance, I immediately telegraphed the General a request to inform me "of the exact condition of things." His answer at 6 p. m., of the same day, was, "the navy has lent me no assistance whatever up to this hour, and we cannot get them to place the Louisiana in position. They say they will do so to-morrow night. I am much obliged for your kindly offer, but we want nothing. The fear we have is that in a general engagement some of the vessels may get by. "To-morrow night" was too late. Ten hours after that despatch was received, the fear that some of the vessels would get by was realized.

UNCLE ABE: "Hello! Ben, is that you? Glad to see you!"
BUTLER: "Yes, Uncle Abe. Got through with that New Orleans job. Cleaned them out and scrubbed them up! Any more scrubbing to give out?"

The Charleston Mercury.

DAILY PAPER—TEN DOLLARS PER ANNUM, PAYABLE HALF-YEARLY IN ADVANCE. — VINDICE NULLO / SPONTE SUA SINE LEGE FIDES RECTUMQUE COLENTUR. — COUNTRY PAPER—THRICE A WEEK—FIVE DOLLARS PER ANNUM, IN ADVANCE.

VOLUME LXXXII. | CHARLESTON, S. C., MONDAY, MARCH 2, 1863. | NUMBER 11,694

THE MERCURY.

MONDAY, MARCH 2, 1863.

A Remonstrance.

Our Northern enemies, says the Richmond *Enquirer*, have certainly used, without reserve or compunction, the advantage they possess in shutting us out, almost entirely, from the outside world. They have had the ear of mankind, and have poured into it what tale they please. They have had the telling of our story, as well as their own; and unhappily that "military necessity," which excuses everything in these days, has imperatively required them to rouse the indignation of the universe against us by a continuous system of falsehoods. * * * * * *

The special case in which the magnanimous Yankee nation is now bellowing forth the falsehood, while the truth is prudently blockaded, muffled and garrotted, is the matter of the exchanges of prisoners of war under the cartel, and the determination announced by our President in his message to retain—or deliver over to the several State authorities—such Federal commissioned officers as may be for the future made prisoners in arms within those States and parts of States embraced in Mr. LINCOLN's Emancipation Proclamation. On these points it will be well to put on record a few facts. Our words, though frozen up by blockade at present, will be audible when the thaw comes.

On July 22d, 1862, we having then many more Yankee prisoners than the enemy had of Confederate, and this fact having disposed them, for the first time, to treat us as belligerents—a cartel for exchange of prisoners was agreed on by Gen. DIX, Federal, and Gen. D. H. HILL, Confederate. The fourth article of the cartel has these words: "All prisoners of war to be discharged on parole in ten days after their capture, and the prisoners now held, and those hereafter taken, to be transported to the points mutually agreed upon at the expense of the capturing party."

By another article citizens were only to be exchanged for citizens, as soldiers for soldiers, rank for rank. By still another, "Local, State and militia rank, held by persons not in actual military service, were not to be recognized, the basis of exchange being the grade actually held in the naval and military service of the respective parties."

Under the cartel, Commissioners of Exchange were appointed by the two parties, and parole and exchange of prisoners regularly proceeded. On our part the conditions of the cartel were strictly complied with. It soon become known, however, through many channels, to our Commissioner, that large numbers of Confederate prisoner, in the hands of the enemy, who were entitled to be paroled, and many of them already paid for with Federal prisoners, were still kept in military prisons. That there has been a gross and constant violation of the cartel by the enemy, is a matter which will need to be not only asserted, but proved, and the proofs are at hand.

On the 4th October, 1862, Mr. Commissioner OULD, of Richmond, represented a number of these cases, by letter, to Col. LUDLOW, the Federal Commissioner, and urged fulfilment of the contract. He received no reply, and no satisfaction was given.

Again, on the 20th November, Mr. OULD called the attention of the Federal Commissioner to the facts and grievances stated in his former communication, and added other instances, especially the cases of a number of officers and men (specifying names, ranks and regiments) of the Louisiana troops—men actually paroled, but afterwards seized by BUTLER and confined in prison—and still more especially the case of MUMFORD, a citizen executed for "treason" in New Orleans, although by the terms of the cartel citizens held by either party "for disloyalty or other civil offences" were to be exchanged for other citizens. To these repeated applications for specific fulfilment of the cartel no answer was returned, and it became known to our authorities that hundreds of our Confederate soldiers and officers were languishing in dungeons all over the enemy's country—many of them in irons.

For the sake of accuracy we give some names: Capt. MORRISON, of the 15th Virginia, captured at Antietam; Capt. CHARLES COOPER, Lieut. MILAN and Capt. MARBURY, all of 5th Tennessee, captured at Harrodsburg in October last. These four officers are *now* confined in Fort McHenry. Lieut. Col. WRIGHT, Col. BENTON, Capt. FAULKNER, all of 37th Mississippi, with thirteen other officers captured at Perryville and Harrodsburg, *now* at Camp Chase; Capt. HARRIS, 5th Tennessee; Lieut. BUTLER, 1st Tennessee; Capt. TAYLOR, 37th Tennessee: all captured at Perryville, *now* at Harrodsburg; Capt. MARKS, of the Confederate States Commissary Department, captured on the steamer *Union*, *now* in prison at Key West; WM. GLASS, arrested at Hopkinsville, Ky., *now* in Camp Chase; Col. POINDEXTER, confined at St. Louis; Col. J. C. MOOREHEAD, Lieut. JAMES BAKER, and Lieut. WM. GARNETT, arrested between Hernando and Memphis last June, *now* confined at Jackson's Island in Lake Erie. Every officer and soldier in this list (which we have materials to make much longer) was long since *exchanged* by the agreements between the Federal and Confederate Commissioners, and ought to have been, are now, in our active service again.

These things were becoming multiplied and aggravated, when our President, in December last, felt that something must be done in justice to our devoted soldiers, then pining in foul dungeons, counting the hours and gazing wearily out through their bars over the Yankee clearings of Ohio or the gray waters of the Canadian Lakes. Their equivalents in exchange (though far from their equivalents in any attribute of manhood) were long ago blazing again in blue and gold, and marching to the subjugation of *their* homes and country! This could not go on.

Accordingly, after Commissioner OULD had made his last representation, and furnished his last list, requiring a satisfactory adjustment in fifteen days—and, after twenty-five days had elapsed, and no adjustment and no answer—the President, evidently with reluctance, yielded for the first time to the pressure of public opinion in these States, and to his own feeling of the hard necessity of the case, and made proclamation, on December 23d, that in view of the numerous and grievous breaches of all the laws of war, and of express and positive agreements, the commissioned officers of the enemy thereafter to be taken should not be *paroled* for exchange.

They could still be, and they still have been, exchanged *per capita*, or, man for man, in actual presence on the lines; but our Government was taught by painful experience that if we sent off our captives without payment in hand, the enemy would make pretexts to throw some of their prisoners into dungeons, or even neglect or decline to admit them to parole, without any pretext at all. In dealing with our Yankee brethren, we cannot altogether expect to be treated on the principles which regulate the usages of honorable war, or peace either, amongst other nations of the earth.

Interior of a Confederate fortification

The next event in order, is the Proclamation of President LINCOLN, declaring that all our slaves are free, plainly inviting them to revolt and murder their masters, and commanding officers and soldiers of the United States to aid such insurrection and slaughter. (We do not give the words, but this is the *thing*.) Now let the human imagination try to conceive any atrocity so diabolical as this attempt. * * * * Future ages will hereafter point to the Proclamation of Mr. LINCOLN, that the warning may never be lost to the human race, when parents shall tell their incredulous children to what extremities philanthropy and "military necessity" once drove the Yankee nation.

Officers and soldiers, after that LINCOLN Proclamation, making war in the Confederate States under its instructions, are instigators of negro insurrection, and therefore *felons* by the laws of all the States. Accordingly, our President in his Message, read to Congress a few days after, announced that he should, *if authorized by Congress*, deliver up such criminals (being commissioned officers) to the authorities of the States respectively in which they should be taken in the perpetration of that crime—there to be dealt with according to law.

This was right, and was the only right thing, as we shall take occasion to demonstrate another day. *Congress, however, has not yet acted upon it.*

As the case stands now, however, something has already been gained by the President's Proclamation of December 23. The Federal Commissioner has now agreed to deliver up all those Confederate officers and soldiers who had been wrongfully detained previous to the Proclamation—whether belonging to the regular Confederate army, or to irregular organizations—also all non-combatants—also the officers detained by BUTLER, and such soldiers as have been tried by their military tribunals and sentenced. In short, all those cases which provoked the President's Proclamation are now to be redressed; and if the Yankees act in good faith, every Confederate soldier and citizen confined in their prisons (except officers captured since the Proclamation) will be delivered within three weeks. This will include the brave and unfortunate ZARVONA. Mr. Commissioner OULD, who has indefatigably negotiated this arrangement, will, however, do well to hold on to *his* prisoners until there is an actual delivery of the other.

So it stands with respect to all prisoners taken on either side before the President's Proclamation of 23d December. The future begins a new score; and it demands the most anxious attention of the President and Congress. It may be interesting to know that the enemy has at this moment almost or quite as many officers of ours in their hands as we have of their officers. But of privates, we hold a much larger number than they. We shall again ask the reader's attention to the matter; in the meantime we give the foregoing statement by way of a formal protest and remonstrance against the attempt being now made by the Yankee nation to persuade the world that we have broken faith with them.

CAPTURE OF THE QUEEN OF THE WEST.—From the Jackson *Mississippian* of the 21st, we get the following particulars of the capture of the Federal gunboat *Queen of the West*:

On Wednesday of last week the Queen ran past Natchez and anchored two miles below. The DeSoto followed her, stopping just above the landing, where she destroyed several flat boats and skiffs. From one of the flats she took three boys prisoners, who were raised in Natchez. The Queen of the West remained at anchor in protecting distance while these depredations were carried out by the DeSoto. They both then steamed away together, the boys having been placed on the Queen of the West. The two vessels proceeded down the river, entered Red river, and at or near the mouth of the Atchafalaya Bayou, the Era, No. 5, with a load of corn for Port Hudson, was captured. They were fired upon at the mouth of the Atchafalaya, by a light battery, when the Captain of the Queen was killed. In revenge, they steamed down the Bayou, and utterly destroyed six plantations by shelling them. They pressed the pilot of the Era No. 5, who deceived them as to the location and strength of our batteries. One of the boys captured at Natchez heard Colonel Ellett repeatedly assert that before he would surrender, he would blow the boat up, but when he was fired upon by our batteries his feather immediately wilted and his only anxiety was the safety of his precious person. He was afterwards seen floating down the river on a bale of cotton.

The Natchez Courier has the following report of the affair: The engagement lasted above one hour, when twenty-five of the crew were taken prisoners—ten or twelve were drowned—and Col. Ellett, who was in command of the Queen, cowardly forsook his boat and floated down the stream on a cotton bale. His own crew shot at him for his cowardice. The Queen had on board six heavy guns. The De Soto was scuttled and sunk by her crew, as well as the coal boat in tow. The Era No. 5, being in possession of the Federal guard below the scene of action, she soon put out to the Mississippi River, bringing with her our informant, Thomas O'Brian, who was afloat in the river on a cotton bale, and who brings us this intelligence. About ten miles below Natchez the Era No. 5 met the Federal gunboat Indianola, carrying four 11 inch guns and about 200 men. Here both boats came to an anchor, and our informant made his escape.

Young O'Brien and two others were kept on board the Queen of the West as prisoners, during the attack of our batteries. He says that every shell from the Confederate batteries carried destruction to the boat and crew. The first shell completely cleared the gun deck of her men, and the second or third came crashing through her engines, cutting her steam pipe in twain, and completely disabling the gunboat. She will soon be got off for repairs. On the Era, when taken, were two Confederate officers and twenty-five privates. The privates were paroled. The victory on Red River was complete. The amount of stores taken is large.

The Charleston Mercury.

DAILY PAPER—TEN DOLLARS PER ANNUM, PAYABLE HALF-YEARLY IN ADVANCE.

VINDICE NULLO—SPONTE SUA SINE LEGE FIDES RECTUMQUE COLENTUR.

COUNTRY PAPER—THRICE A WEEK—FIVE DOLLARS PER ANNUM, IN ADVANCE.

VOLUME LXXXII. | CHARLESTON, S. C., WEDNESDAY, MARCH 4, 1863. | NUMBER 11,696

THE MERCURY

WEDNESDAY, MARCH 4, 1863.

Lincoln Dictator.

The Black Republican Congress of the United States goes out of power to-day. The new House of Representatives elect have a right to their seats should an extra session be called. But it is not at all probable that the President will assemble them, or that they will exercise any legislative functions, until the regular session of December next, which may not be avoided. Before vacating their seats, the party of Mr. LINCOLN has taken care to put large powers into his hands—besides great appropriations of money, the right to call out and officer the whole militia of the United States, and to suspend the *Habeas Corpus*, and imprison at discretion. It remains to see whether the people of the North are prepared, for the sake of better attempting the conquest of the Confederate States, to yield every vestige of liberty to a Military Dictator. An issue is now upon the Northern Democrats which, it appears to us, must decide their fate, no less than their country's. If they acquiesce in the execution of the powers recently conferred upon the President, they are likely to be crushed out. Mr. LINCOLN then controlling the army, will master the country. Notwithstanding the New York *Herald*, we judge that the discontent and demoralization already existing at the North, will not be soothed by the bold attitude assumed by the Abolition party. Nothing but some great and early military success can enable the Yankee President to use these extraordinary powers.

Lincoln

Beauregard.

There is something in the deportment of Gen. Beauregard, in all the various positions that he has filled, which endears him to the masses of the people, no less than to the soldiers who more directly have been thrown in contact with him. There is a certain air of romance attached to his character, which makes every one wish that he could be more prominently brought forward, and a certain sympathy felt, that altogether he has not had a proper showing in the great drama of the war. A very large number of the people of the Confederacy feel a strong attachment to him through the fame that he has achieved for our country. At the first battle fought in the beginning of the war, when he commanded at Fort Sumter, he won fame for ability, and a modest deportment even in the first flush of triumph to our unfledged arms. Called subsequently to the army of the Potomac, he found a chaotic mass of raw and undisciplined troops, whom he soon taught to move like regulars, and won their love by his superior intelligence and kind urbanity. Soon thereafter he led them against the serried hosts of the foe, moving down in all the pride of equipment and confidence, and by his well matured plans he caused such a route as has not been equalled since in two years of a great war. That he is the hero of Manassas, we have the testimony of Gen. Joe Johnston, when serenaded lately in Mobile, and addressed as the hero of that battle. "Gentlemen," said he, the hero of Manassas is now in command at Charleston." This tribute to Gen. Beauregard is just, and shows that Gen. Johnston has no disposition to let his friends claim for him the merit due to another. General Beauregard is held in great estimation by his admiring countrymen, and we find it expressed by all classes of people whenever he is the subject of conversation. He possesses that magnetic attraction which forms the chain that binds him to all hearts, and the enthusiasm of the soldiers who have served under him shows how strong is his hold on the hearts of the nation.

The Generals who are his cotemporaries, entertain great affection and admiration for him, and we have never heard of any other opinion being expressed of the great chieftain by any of them. "Stonewall" Jackson, we are credibly informed, "entertains an unfaltering affection and admiration for Gen. Beauregard," and that it is reciprocal, we have lately seen, in the present sent to the former by the latter. Deep seated in the hearts of the people, Gen. Beauregard will find in their affection a reward for the arduous devotion he has shown to the cause of our country. We doubt whether any other General would command a greater ovation than will be awarded to him when peace once again smiles over our land. We have never met with Gen. Beauregard, and in giving expression to the above views we simply put upon record our estimation of the man, which we believe is shared by nine-tenths of the people. Long may he live to enjoy in peace the laurels with which this war has already crowned him.

Lynchburg Republican.

SAVANNAH, March 3—2, p. m.—The enemy opened the attack on Fort McAlister, at Genesis Point, at 8 30 this morning. Three iron-clads and two mortar boats are keeping up a constant fire upon the fort. An eight-inch Columbiad in the fort has been dismounted. The only casualties on our side, thus far, are two men slightly wounded. The firing continues very heavy.

LATEST FROM THE UNITED STATES.

RICHMOND, March 3.—Northern dates of the 27th have been received here.

"Long live ABRAHAM, our President! LINCOLN, temporary Dictator!" Under this head the New York *Herald* declares that the measures lately passed by Congress, and others that will become laws, will practically invest President LINCOLN with all the powers of a Dictator; but that there is not the slightest danger of any abuse of power on his part, for ambitious purposes.—"Accepting the plea of imperious necessity, we cheerfully assent to the transformation of the President into a temporary Dictator."

By an arrival from Port Royal the *Herald* has further information respecting the difficulty between HUNTER and FOSTER. HUNTER had peremptorily ordered the staff of FOSTER to leave his Department, and put Gen. STEVENSON under arrest for disparaging the negro troops.

CHARLES CARROLL HICKS, late second officer of the privateer *Retribution*, is now confined in the old Capitol, Washington, and will be tried as a spy.

The Negro Soldier Bill has not passed the Senate.

DAILY PAPER—TEN DOLLARS PER ANNUM, PAYABLE HALF-YEARLY IN ADVANCE.

VINDICE NULLO—SPONTE SUA SINE LEGE FIDES RECTUMQUE COLENTUR.

COUNTRY PAPER—THRICE A WEEK—FIVE DOLLARS PER ANNUM, IN ADVANCE.

VOLUME LXXXII. | CHARLESTON, S. C., WEDNESDAY, MARCH 18, 1863. | NUMBER 11,707

THE MERCURY.

WEDNESDAY, MARCH 18, 1863.

Superior Power of the North.

The presses of the United States still rely upon the superior physical power of the North to subject the Southern States. In their view, our conquest is a simple affair of arithmetic. As eighteen is greater than eight, therefore eighteen millions of people must subdue eight. They ignore all moral influences. They ignore God. Material and sensual, they regard a struggle for liberty and independence as an affair of mechanics, in which a longer lever or a stronger pulley will lift the load. So corrupted are they by the prosperity which they wrung from the South, that they seem to have forgotten history—their own history, and the history of the people they are striving to subdue. FREDERICK the Great, with but five millions of inhabitants in Prussia, in a seven years' war, beat back Austria, Russia and France combined—each of them being five times as great numerically as Prussia. In the Revolution of 1776 we were but two millions and a half of people, against the most powerful nation, by land and sea, at that time in Europe. Since this war began we have repulsed the Northern armies in every pitched battle, although they have had their own time for their preparations and superior numbers. Yet they still argue that, because they are numerically greater than we are, they must subdue us.

BONAPARTE very truly observed that the *morale* of an army is three-fourths of its strength. An army is not the mere bones, flesh and blood which compose it. It consists of men—with all the passions, feelings, and motives which actuate men. Men may enter an army simply to obtain bread, which is the case with one-half of the present army of the United States; and when brought into battle they will fight, perhaps, under circumstances, very bravely. Men may enter an army on a speculation of robbery. They want the country they invade either as a source of future gain or of present occupancy. A large portion of the United States army really believed, when they invaded the South, that they were only going down to select fat farms; another portion came to coerce us as their future tributaries. But there is one thing all robbers prefer to robbery—and that is life. In the game of robbery, there is a reasonable limit to all adventures. But what are these motives for conquering us, compared with those which must actuate the people of the Confederate States in defending themselves? The land invaded is their land. The property to be appropriated is their property. The homes to be desecrated, or given to the flames, are their homes. The butchery and murder to be perpetrated is of them and their children. Country, property, home, all we love or live for, is put up at every battle as the price of victory. Is it at all surprising that, in such a contest, the Southern people should be invincible? Why should any man in the South survive one day the subjugation of the South to Yankee domination? Death is a thousand times preferable to the doom which awaits him and his. Our ruthless and bloody foes have left us in no doubt as to their designs. They have written them upon their Statute Books; they have proclaimed them to the world. The deeds of BUTLER and MITCHELL are but faint glimmering shadows of the horrible and unspeakable atrocities they meditate for our torture and humiliation, should they succeed in subjugating us. How can the motives of the robber or mercenary arm him with the same intrepidity and desperation in battle, which, under such circumstances, must nerve the arm of the Southern man?

Whilst ignoring all moral influences, our savage foes also ignore God. It is true that we sometimes see proclamations from their authorities, setting apart certain days for thanksgiving and praise to God for some successful murder of our people. There can be no more striking repudiation of the Deity than a denial of His attributes. How can a God of justice and holiness accept the thanksgiving and praise for the success of the robbers and murderers of an unoffending, innocent people? But in their presses they make no reference to God whatever in their meditated slaughter of us. Victory is a simple affair—of so many *more* men against so many *fewer* men.—God, with them, does not reign; but Mammon and Moloch. Material, infidel and bloody as they are—it is our task to scourge them from our land, and make them the hissing scorn and detestation of the world.

FROM PORT ROYAL—A CHAPTER ABOUT THE MONITORS.

We make some interesting extracts from the Port Royal correspondence of the New York *World*:

PORT ROYAL, S. C., February 25.

We have been waiting since the 1st instant for the iron-clads to arrive. Two more only are now due. Our iron-clad navy will soon have full and complete control of Charleston harbor. The health and spirits of the troops are good, and everything indicates success.

The requirements of the public service, in addition to my own desire not to say anything which may conduce, however remotely, to the benefit of the rebels, prevent my giving your readers a full description of the iron-clads now in these waters. Our antagonists have shown an amount of prudence and inventive capacity in this war for which few were, until lately, disposed to credit them; and although it is almost an impossibility to imagine any engine of destruction more nearly perfect in all that constitutes offensive and defensive strength than our Monitors, yet a chance remains of the enemy's discovering a Roland for our Oliver, and meeting us with tricks which have not been foreseen in our calculations. Hitherto what they have not possessed themselves, or have failed to invent, they have obtained from the sympathy or cupidity of Europeans; and we may rest satisfied that nothing would cause greater satisfaction to our revilers across the Atlantic than to see our iron fleet worsted and sunk in the harbors of our Southern ports. The time cannot be far distant, however, when this check of secrecy will be removed; and the triumph of American ingenuity will then be all the more appreciated when the means are fully made known which have led to so victorious a result.

But there is much in the internal economy of a "Monitor" which will be interesting to the public, even though it be in a non military point of view. It is not relevant to my purpose to argue whether Ericsson or Timby be the inventor of that now famous "Yankee cheese-box," the turret; apart from that grand feature in these vessels, a Monitor possesses qualities bordering on the marvellous, an adaptability of means to the end unexampled in naval construction. From stem to stern she is crammed with strange devices; she combines strength with lightness, buoyancy with solidity, space with but limited capacity. And to these *semi invisibility!* Standing on the pier at Hilton Head, it is well-nigh impossible to make out any one of these vessels across the harbor, whilst a miserable fifty ton schooner, or leg-of-mutton sail boat, stands up perfectly defined to the naked eye. When in motion, the spectator on shore sees nothing but a tower and smoke-stack following each other on the water; the hull is down even in smooth weather; and if the Monitor approach inland, a slight, straight line of foam or ripple—similar to that on the edge of a shoal—is all that marks the iron hull trailing its way as it were over the surface of the water. It will be hard work to strike such an object, moving at eight knots an hour, through the smoke and noise of a score of batteries.

A chief triumph of construction in the Monitor is the surprising manner in which so much is packed in so small a space. Ten separate and distinct steam engines work out their duties noiselessly within the hull—not a crank, lever or pipe raising itself above the water line. The provinces of these ten engines are as follows: two work the propeller, two ventilate the ship, two condense water for the crew, two turn the turret, and two function the pumps. Sitting in the Captain's cabin, or standing on the deck, no one would suppose that any machinery is on board; all the ten engines perform their several duties with an entire absence of noise, and mile after mile is traversed without any of the motion so palpable in other vessels. When frigates like the Wabash and Minnesota roll unpleasantly in the sea, the iron box Monitor floats solidly in the waters, her decks lovingly embraced by the caresses of Neptune.

Ventilation has always proved a difficult question on shore as afloat. The art was lost with the ancient Romans. Ericsson has found it. No house on a hill is better ventilated than the close metal chests called Monitors; in hot weather they are cool, in cold, warm—a genial, equable temperature permeating the atmosphere throughout. This will appear the more astonishing when it is understood that not a ventilator is needed on the deck other than the turret; the latter is but twenty-one feet in diameter, the deck is two hundred feet long, and as hermetically sealed as solid iron can make it. The revolving fans, turned by machinery, exhaust the foul air from the vessel, throwing it out by the smoke-stack; while the pure air rushes in to supply the vacuum through the roof of the turret, and enters the body of the ship by registers placed in the floors. A hundred men may smoke below, and yet no odor of tobacco will be present, for the fumes are immediately sucked out, so to speak, by the ventilators, and discharged through the smoke-stack. Seventy men sleep in the small apartment called the "berth deck," so small that they have to pack themselves in layers of three, one over the other; yet the atmosphere is so pure and fresh that it is hard to believe any persons are sleeping therein. How few of our bed-rooms are thus well ventilated!

A round tower, a smoke stack, and a raft—such is a Monitor externally. Not a protuberance on deck, simply a plain flat surface of iron from stem to stern; a turret, modeled after a "Yankee cheese box"—the den of two monsters—and a little tower above, where the captain directs his ship, and prays devoutly that fate will throw in his way a few of those so-called "Merrimacs" or "Rams," which pounce at night time upon "paper gunboats" like the poor little Mercedita. Rams, indeed! Three Monitors could "eat" Fort Sumter to pieces without firing a shot at it, if there were only water sufficient for them to get at its walls.

But I must check myself, for I am here unintentionally entering upon the subject of "muscle." Suffice it to say, one of these Monitors may run at the top of her speed, that is eight or nine knots an hour, against a solid rock without danger. She would damage the rock, but the bows and hull would come off scatheless. The disaster which occurred to the Weehawken, namely, the breaking in two of her cylinder in consequence of strains received by her machinery in the gales of January, will not delay her entry into active service. Immediately on the facts becoming known to the department a new cylinder was ordered and forwarded to Port Royal. The plates of the deck have been raised and the defects remedied, and I hear that the vessel will be in as good trim as ever by the end of the present week.

The Hunter-Foster imbroglio has at length been settled, but it required the presence here of Assistant Adjutant General Townsend to effect this result. Foster, as you doubtless have heard ere this, returns to his department of North Carolina, while Hunter retains the troops composing the late expedition, and supervises the preliminaries of the approaching campaign. I think we may safely put down the entire of the proceedings in relation to this affair as the masterpiece of blundering during the war. More than all, it is a cruel injustice to two officers—Generals Hunter and Foster themselves. If Hunter was capable of administering the Department of the South, why send Foster here to gather laurels which belonged to him alone; and if it were not intended for Foster to remain, why rob him of the flower of the North Carolina army? I am informed that he brought with him here the best regiments under his command—regiments like the Tenth Connecticut and Ninth New Jersey, the heros of Roanoke and Newbern—whose history is inseparably connected with victory in the Old North State. Again, some of the regiments are split up—part being here at Port Royal, part at the Neuse River, whilst the force remaining at the latter place is reduced to numbers which render offensive operations next to impossible. What has Foster done that he should thus be started on a fool's errand; and why was it attempted to supplant Hunter at the very moment when his military abilities could be made useful?

A late gunboat reconnoissance in the direction of Fort Sumter showed that the rebels had removed their lower tier of guns, and placed them *en barbette*, doubtless with the intention of destroying our iron-clads by means of plunging shot. All these manœuvres have been foreseen, and others also to which it would not be proper to refer. Torpedoes, sunken ships, piles, rock and all the curious gear used to close harbors will be of little avail. You will discover, within the next two or three weeks at farthest, that this delay in commencing operations has been very usefully employed by at least one branch of the service; but this is certainly no reason for the delay having occurred. Charleston, anyhow, will fall; but it ought to be in our hands at the present moment.

The news of the Ninth Army Corps being at Fortress Monroe has led many to expect the appearance here of Gen. Burnside. His appointment to command the forthcoming operations would hugely please both the army and navy, and quickly lift the former from its present depression.

The New-York Times.

VOL. XII—NO. 3600. NEW-YORK, WEDNESDAY, APRIL 8, 1863. PRICE THREE CENTS.

THE SIEGE OF VICKSBURGH.

The Yazoo Pass Expedition Still in Front of Fort Pemberton.

Gunboat Reconnoissance of Haines' Bluff.

TWO IMPORTANT EXPEDITIONS UNDER WAY.

CINCINNATI, Tuesday, April 7.

A special dispatch from Helena, dated the 3d inst., says that advices from Gen. QUIMBY's Expedition to the 30th ult., state that no progress had been made in the reduction of Fort Pemberton, at Greenwood.

Our forces were still in front of the enemy, and there had been considerable skirmishing between the pickets on shore. The rebels were improving the time by greatly increasing the strength of their works. They have received and mounted more heavy guns, and are well supplied with ammunition.

The country along the Tallahatchie is occupied by two regiments of Confederate cavalry, and swarms with guerrillas.

One of our Musquito boats captured five rebel raftmen at the mouth of the Coldwater River, and indications of attempts to place torpedoes in the channel have been discovered.

The first reconnoissance of Haines' Bluff by gunboats was made by Admiral PORTER. The object was one of reconnoissance only. They proceeded within range of the rebel batteries, and fired shots over at them, but the shots were not returned.

CAIRO, Tuesday, April 7.

The steamer *Gray Eagle*, from Memphis, has arrived. From passengers we learn of two important expeditions, the objects of which are not to be made public.

Reports in regard to the Yazoo Pass Expedition are still conflicting. The preponderance of evidence is that it is not abandoned. Last week, while the steamer *A. D. Hine* was passing down Cold Water, it was fired into by guerrillas. Several deck hands and one engineer were killed. The Captain was mortally wounded.

In retaliation for firing into the gunboat *St. Clow*, on the Cumberland, Tuesday last, Capt. FITS, with a gunboat, went to the town of Palmyra on Saturday, and, after giving the inhabitants time to leave, they burned the entire town.

Another skirmish occurred Saturday, near Nancouat. The National pickets, numbering fifteen, were attacked by BLYTHE's Cavalry. The latter were repulsed. Loss unascertained. Our loss was two wounded, and two taken prisoners.

LATER FROM NEW-ORLEANS.

Reported Evacuation of Port Hudson by the Rebels.

The United States steam transport *Eastern Queen*, Capt. COLLINS, arrived at this port last evening, from New-Orleans March 29, and Key West on the 1st inst., with passengers, to United States Assistant Quartermaster. She brings about sixty discharged soldiers from Gen. BANKS' Division. Capt. COLLINS reports that while at Fort Phillip, Southwest Pass, his vessel was boarded by the United States boarding officer, who reported having received a telegram from New-Orleans, stating that the rebels had begun to evacuate Port Hudson.

FROM THE ARMY OF THE POTOMAC.

Splendid Condition of the Army—Reviews by Gen. Hooker—The Roads Rapidly Improving—The Rebels Constantly Reinforced.

From Our Own Correspondent.

FROM THE LEFT WING OF THE ARMY, Saturday, April 4, 1863.

During the past week the roads have improved rapidly, and will soon be in fine condition, if the weather continues to remain favorable. Several hours are devoted daily to drilling by the various commands, which are scattered over hill and through dale as far as the eye can reach. It is the universal testimony of all the officers with whom I have conversed, that the army never was in so good fighting trim as now.

Yesterday Gen. HOOKER reviewed the Sixth Army Corps, commanded by Gen. SEDGWICK. Gens. NEWTON's and BROOKS' divisions were reviewed on an open field not far from headquarters and Gen. HOWE's, on what is known as the "Balls' Farm." This estate is situated near the Rappahannock, below Falmouth, and commands a fine view of the rebel encampments on the crest beyond. The enemy could witness the evolutions of our troops. Gen. HOOKER appeared upon the ground about 1 o'clock, accompanied by his entire staff and a cavalry escort. He was dressed in full military suit, and mounted upon a magnificent white charger. A lady rode by his side. There were also upon the field Gens. SEDGWICK, SLOCUM, SICKLES, HOWE, BROOKS, PRATT, PATRICK, RUSSELL and NEILL, accompanied by their staffs. The presence of so many Major and Brigadier-Generals gave considerable *éclat* to the occasion. The division being drawn up, Gen. HOOKER galloped down in the front of the line, saluting the various regimental colors as he passed, and returning in the rear of the regiments. The artillery were inspected in a similar manner, after which the General assumed a stationary position, and the several brigades filed in review before him. After passing him, the Vermont troops obliqued round a muddy spot, to the displeasure of their brigade commander, Col. GRANT, who remarked, "You can make soldiers face the cannon's mouth, but never march through a mud puddle." The review over, Gen. HOOKER, accompanied by Gens. SEDGWICK, SLOCUM, SICKLES, and others, repaired to Gen. HOWE's headquarters to partake of a repast prepared for them.

Everyone present was struck with the splendid *morale* of the troops. Robust, active, full of life—a finer body of men were never seen. If I mistake not, the sanitary condition of the Sixth is better than that of any of the other corps comprising the Army of the Potomac. For the past few months it has steadily increased in size, the number of returning convalescents more than balancing the number discharged from sickness. The corps, therefore, comes out of its Winter quarters larger than it was last Fall. Of the divisions, Gen. HOWE's is in the best condition physically—which is to be attributed to the skill and care of the surgeons. The Medical Inspector pronounces the division hospital the best conducted of any of the field hospitals in the lines. I visited it yesterday and was struck with the neat and tidy appearance of the various wards, and the regard for the comfort and ease of the patients displayed in the surroundings. Among other things, I observed on the green in front of the hospital a bower of cedars for the invalids to lounge in on these warm balmy afternoons. The officers in charge of the hospital are: Surgeon D'ESTAING DICKERSON, Thirty-third New-York, Director; Surgeon H. A. ALLEN, Fourth Vermont, Assistant.

The published reports to the effect that the enemy are about abandoning Virginia create considerable amusement here. Instead of falling back the enemy are daily increasing their forces around Fredericksburgh. Intelligence was received yesterday that Gen. LEE is now hurrying forward all his troops in anticipation of an immediate attack from us. J.

DEPARTMENT OF THE CUMBERLAND.

Particulars of the Defeat of Morgan by Gen. Stanley.

The Rebels Driven from Three Separate Positions.

ANOTHER DASHING CAVALRY AFFAIR.

CINCINNATI, Tuesday, April 7.

Dispatches from Murfreesboro give the following account of the fight near Snow Hill:

On the 2d inst. Gen. STANLEY, with two thousand cavalry, and Col. MATTHEWS' infantry brigade, started to capture MORGAN's and WHARTON's Eighth regiment of infantry and cavalry at Snow Hill.

Beyond Auburn they drove in the rebel pickets. The Seventh Pennsylvania cavalry turned the rebel right, while MINTY's and PALMON's cavalry brigade, with NEWELL's battery, moved up in front. The enemy fled.

The enemy's pickets were then encountered west of Liberty, and a considerable force of rebels were posted on the bluffs on the opposite side of Smith's Ford. They resisted and were driven back and formed again on Dry Fork, from whence they were again driven.

The rebels then formed a third and stronger line on Snow Hill. The Second and Fourth Ohio cavalry were sent to the enemy's rear. They charged with sabres in hand and broke the line of the rebels, when the fight ended in the flight of the rebels.

The rebel loss was from fifteen to twenty killed, a number wounded, and sixty prisoners.

Gen. STANLEY also captured thirty horses and mules and a quantity of bacon and wheat, and destroyed considerable forage.

The position of the rebels defeated Gen. STANLEY's intention to surround and capture them. They escaped with their guns.

Our loss was one private of the Seventh Pennsylvania cavalry, and two slightly wounded.

Gen. STANLEY returned to Murfreesboro by way of Lebanon, capturing six prisoners at the latter point.

It is reported that the gunboat *Lexington* and some other boat shelled the town of Florence, Alabama, on the 2d inst., and drove away a company of rebel cavalry stationed there.

REPORT FROM GEN. ROSECRANS.

WASHINGTON, Tuesday, April 7.

The following has been received at the headquarters of the army here:

MURFREESBORO, Monday, April 6.

To Maj.-Gen. Halleck, General-in-Chief, Washington:

Gen. STANLEY has returned from his scout, bringing in some forty or fifty prisoners, and three hundred serviceable horses and mules. He drove MORGAN's cavalry from the Peninsula, whipping them from their stronghold, Snow's Hill, north of Smithville, and but for their precipitate retreat, and the difficult nature of the country, would have had a force in their rear, and captured their artillery and animals. The enemy left quite a number of dead, and fled toward McMinnville, losing many horses, saddles and guns. W. S. ROSECRANS.

ANOTHER DASHING CAVALRY AFFAIR.

NASHVILLE, Tenn., Tuesday, April 7.

Gen. ROBERT B. MITCHELL, with 350 cavalry, went out yesterday on the Lebanon Pike to Green Hill, and dashing into a rebel camp, where there was a large number of conscripts, on the sabre charge, he took 15 prisoners, killed 5, and captured all their arms, horses, equipments, &c. The rebels were composed of parts of MORGAN's and McCOWN's bands. Among the prisoners are Capt. BRADY, of the Eighteenth (rebel) Tennessee regiment, and a Lieutenant of MORGAN's cavalry. A still-house containing 40 casks of liquor was destroyed. The place had been used as a conscripting rendezvous. One man was wounded on our side. Gen. MITCHELL's command made a march of 55 miles in twelve hours.

THE BRITISH WEST INDIES.

The Cornubia Runs the Blockade at Wilmington—Affairs in Barbados, Demerara, Jamaica, Antigua, &c.

The Bermuda *Royal Gazette*, of March 24, has been received.

The British neutral blockade runner *Cornubia* arrived at St. Georges from Wilmington, N. C., on the 22d of March, with a cargo of 314 bales of cotton, 29 casks of tobacco and two casks of turpentine.

The British schooner *St. George* also arrived on the 23d of March, from the same port, with 145 bales of cotton, 160 bbls. of resin, and 65 boxes of tobacco.

BARBADOS.

The shipping of the new crops had commenced, causing a revival of business.

A bill has passed the Legislature, extending to other mail steamers bringing letters from Europe or America to Barbados the same privileges as are granted to the Royal Mail Steamship Packet Company.

DEMERARA.

Trade is stagnant.

Large numbers of Africans have been imported here from St. Helena. Seventy-four females, seduced from there by promises of a Captain, were much disappointed, and the Governor refused to pay their passage.

Gold has been discovered in the Cuyum River.

ANTIGUA.

Small pox is raging fatally at Antigua.

GRENADA.

A joint stock company has been started, in which the Lieutenant-Governor is a large stockholder.

JAMAICA.

Emigrants from the East Indies continue to arrive, 284 having just reached Jamaica from Madras.

The hull, spars, etc., of the wrecked Boston ship *Colombo*, were advertised for sale by auction at St. Georges, Bermuda, on the 24th of March. Her cargo was also to be sold on the 26th.

The Steamer S. R. Spaulding.

BALTIMORE, Tuesday, April 7.

The steamer *S. R. Spaulding*, from Hilton Head, arrived at Fortress Monroe yesterday.

CHARLESTON.

The Sailing of Our Gunboats and Iron-Clads from Port Royal on Wednesday Last.

The Rebels on the Rappahannock in Possession of Bad News.

WASHINGTON, Tuesday, April 7.

It is officially known here that the United States fleet of gunboats and iron-clads *left Port Royal on Wednesday last and would probably reach the scene of operations Thursday evening.* Up to 3 o'clock this afternoon nothing further was known of their movements.

REPORTS FROM THE RAPPAHANNOCK.

HEADQUARTERS, ARMY OF THE POTOMAC, Tuesday, April 7.

There are indications, but nothing of a definite character, that the enemy on the opposite of the river are in possession of information from some point, unfavorable to them. *They are unusually careful to prevent any of their papers from getting into our lines.*

THE STORY OF AN ALLEGED REFUGEE.

WASHINGTON, Tuesday, April 7.

No flag of truce crossed the Rappahannock today—consequently we are without advices from Charleston through the Richmond papers. The hotels are digesting the story of an alleged refugee from Charleston, who has had communication with the Government, and sorrowfully assured it that 116,000 troops occupied the city and its fortifications; that two thousand cannon were in position; that Sumter was clad in Palmetto logs, and sheathed outside of these with 4½ inch iron; that the harbor and the river were paved with torpedoes of monstrous quality, and that the channel was barricaded. This refugee, venerable for his white hairs and his family name, predicted failure and disaster in the several Departments in which he has recited his desponding story. In one he was silently voted to be an emissary and a spy, sent to effect a delay of the doom of Charleston, and was audibly encouraged with the request to keep up his spirits for a few days, when he would surely have the happiness of seeing that city an ash-heap.

DEPARTMENT OF THE SOUTH.

Capture of the Schooner Expeditious—Capts. Allen and Vernon, of the Forty-seventh New-York, Taken Prisoners.

Correspondence of the New-York Times.

PORT ROYAL, Tuesday, March 31, 1863.

The dispatch steamer *Mattano* arrived this afternoon from Fort Pulaski, bringing information of the capture yesterday morning of the schooner *Expeditious* in the Savannah River. The vessel was from Nassau, N. P., with a cargo of 340 sacks of salt, and attempted to run past Pulaski up to Savannah. In the darkness she missed the channel and went into Calibogue Sound, where she was discovered at daylight. A detachment of the Forty-eighth Regiment was at once put on board the *Mattano* and dispatched to secure her, which was soon accomplished. Had the Captain of the prize been a good pilot he could have escaped before the steamer reached him, as it was blowing fresh and fair up the river. This was a novel sort of prize for soldiers to make.

The *Mattano* also brings a rumor of the capture of Capts. ALLEN and VERNON, of the Forty-seventh Regiment, and three men by the rebels. The party left Fort Pulaski some days since in a small boat, intending to reach their encampment on the Ogeechee Sound by passing through Lazaretto Creek. They have not since been heard of, and the supposition is that they encountered a rebel picket boat in Warsaw Sound. With them were lost the mail for the regiment brought down on the last trip of the *Arago*, and official dispatches from the headquarters to Lieut.-Col. VAN BRUNT, commanding the post at the Ogeechee.

Here is the last General Order:

HEADQUARTERS DEPARTMENT OF THE SOUTH, HILTON HEAD, PORT ROYAL, S. C., March 30, 1863.

GENERAL ORDERS No. 28.—It having been unanimously certified to the Major-General Commanding by the Colonel, Lieut.-Colonel, Major and Surgeon of the One Hundred and Seventy-sixth Regiment of Pennsylvania Militia, that they consider Capt. DAVID SCHAAD, commanding Company "D" of said regiment, "a very disloyal officer, and a traitor to his country;" and they unanimously recommending, (in which recommendation their Brigade Commander joins,) that Capt. DAVID SCHAAD be summarily dismissed the service, without pay or emoluments;

It is hereby ordered that the said Capt. DAVID SCHAAD, Company "D," One Hundred and Seventy-sixth Regiment Pennsylvania Militia, be dishonorably dismissed the service of the United States, without pay or emoluments, subject to the approval of His Excellency the President of the United States.

By command of Maj.-Gen. D. HUNTER.
CHAS. G. HALPINE, Lieut.-Col. and A. A. G., Tenth Army Corps and Department of the South.
(Official.) ISRAEL SEALY, First. Lieut., 47th N. Y. Vols., A. A. A. G.

IMPORTANT FROM FLORIDA.

THE CITY OF JACKSONVILLE EVACUATED AND DESTROYED—RETURN OF THE NEGRO BRIGADE.

From the New South.

The news from the St. John's River by the latest arrival is important. On the 26th ult., Col. MONTGOMERY, of the Second South Carolina Volunteers with two companies of his regiment, embarked on the transport *General Meigs*, Capt. WATKINS, and pushed up the river as far as Orange Grove, where they anchored for the night. On the following day they proceeded to Palatka, where the *Meigs* ran up to the wharf and landed her troops, who immediately took possession of the town. While lying at the wharf a volley of musketry was fired from the village, and Capt. WATKINS and Judge LATTA, who were conversing together near the pilot-house, narrowly escaped, the bullets whizzing close to them, and lodging in the woodwork all about them. Lieut.-Col. LIBERTY BILLINGS was shot through both hands, and one or two of the negroes were also wounded. Meantime, Col. MONTGOMERY ordered the town to be shelled, while he went beyond it and captured a Lieutenant and 14 men of a rebel company stationed there. The next day the *Adams* came up with orders for the forces to return, and nothing further was accomplished at Palatka.

At Jacksonville the rebels succeeded in creating some commotion by placing a section of artillery upon a platform car, and running it to the edge of the city, whence they threw a number of shells, without effecting any serious results, however. One shell entered the dwelling of a Union man, passing through the room where himself and wife were sleeping, and penetrated the rocking-chair on which their clothes were piled. One soldier of the Eighth Maine regiment, we learn, was killed, and another was wounded. In retaliation for the conduct of the rebels, Col. RUST, when the order to evacuate was received, burned the town and brought away with him the families of the Union people. Our forces left Jacksonville on the 31st.

The United States Bark Restless in a Storm

SHE IS COMPELLED TO THROW HER BATTERY OVERBOARD.

The United States bark *Restless*, Acting Master WM. S. BROWN, commanding, from Boston Feb. 28, bound to Port Royal, has come to this port in distress, having experienced a succession of heavy gales since leaving Boston. On the 4th inst., lat. 71° 30′, lon. 37° 30′, encountered a cyclone, commencing from northeast, which blew with great violence for 48 hours, and during which the vessel labored badly; was compelled to throw the battery, consisting of four long 24s, overboard, to save the vessel. On the 6th inst., on the edge of the Gulf Stream, passed a quantity of hay, lumber, and broken spars, also pieces of bulwarks.

The following is a list of the officers:

WM. R. BROWN, Acting Master, commanding; Morris Degard, Acting Master, Executive Officer; H. Esson, Acting Ensign; Jas. J. Russell, Acting Ensign; Chas. M. Hicks, Acting Ensign; Wm. J. Cushman, Acting Assistant Paymaster; Chas. H. Page, Acting Assistant Surgeon; J. Walter Mackie, Acting Master's Mate; Wm. B. Brown, Acting Master's Mate.

BREAD RIOT IN RICHMOND.

Three Thousand Hungry Women Raging in the Streets.

Government and Private Stores Broken Open.

BALTIMORE, Tuesday, April 7.

Col. STEWART, of the Second Indiana Regiment, one of the fourteen United States officers just released by the rebels, and who has just arrived here, makes the following statement:

On Thursday last he saw from his prison window in Richmond a great bread riot, in which about three thousand women were engaged, armed with clubs, guns and stones. They broke open the Government stores and took bread, clothing and whatever else they wanted. The militia were ordered out to check the riot, but failed to do so. JEFF. DAVIS and other high officials then made speeches to the infuriated women, and told them they should have what they needed. They then became calm, and order was once more restored.

All the other released Union officers confirmed this statement.

The Methodist Conference.

GEN. WOOL ON THE WAR—LIST OF APPOINTMENTS.

In pursuance of an invitation extended by the Chairman, (Bishop BAKER,) Gen. WOOL, Judge BETTS, of the United States Court, and Hon. M. F. ODELL, of the Congressional Committee on the Conduct of the War, were present at the proceedings of the New-York East M. E. Conference, at the South Second-street Church, Brooklyn, Eastern District, yesterday.

After the usual routine business had been transacted, loud calls were made for Gen. WOOL, who was reluctantly compelled to make a speech, in the course of which he referred to the letter he had written to Secretary CASS, calling his attention to the importance of taking prompt steps to stifle the rebellion, which was then in an inchoate state. He urged CASS to use his influence with President BUCHANAN, and endeavor to get him to use his power in assisting its accomplishment. In that letter, Gen. WOOL said he predicted certain things which must and would happen, and which had already taken place. He then alluded to the present condition of the war, which he thought hopeful. The Southerners had no plea under heaven for seceding but to perpetuate the institution of Slavery, and to protect the slave-trade. If he had time, he could prove it to them. He would never be contented until the Union was restored. He deprecated the idea of some men to dismember the Union. Where shall we draw the line? It was no matter where or how we drew the line, trouble was sure to follow. The Northwest must have an outlet, and so with the other sections of the country. Some talked about putting New-England out of the Union. ["Amen! Amen!"] He was for keeping the country together, ["Amen,"] and therefore he was opposed to a separation of any kind; he was opposed to all and any lines of demarkation, and wanted nothing but the whole country. [Vehement applause, which lasted some moments, during which Gen. WOOL resumed his seat.]

Hon. M. F. ODELL then made a few patriotic remarks, in which he assured them that success must ultimately crown our undertakings. He was very severe upon the Peace party men, and showed what we had done to convince them, or those who believed we had done nothing, that we had done something.

The following is the

LIST OF APPOINTMENTS.

New-York.

John-street—J. M. Carroll.
Forsyth-street—John Pegg, Jr.
Allen-street—John A. Roche, John S. Mitchell.
Alanson Church—John E. Searles.
Willett-street—Wm. McAlister.
Second-street—R. H. Loomis.
Seventh-street—Francis Bottome.
Ninth-street—A. H. Mead.
Seventeenth-street—G. R. Crooks.
Twenty-seventh-street—S. A. Seaman.
Thirty-seventh-street—Daniel Curry.
Beekman's Hill—James Floy.
Sixty-fifth-street—To be supplied.
Second-avenue—John L. Peck.

Brooklyn.

Sands-street—L. S. Weed.
York-street—W. H. Boole.
Washington-street—W. F. Watkins.
Centenary Church—C. E. Glover.
Warren-street—A. S. Francis.
Eighteenth-street—S. Rushmore.
First-place—A. S. Hunt.
Pacific-street—F. S. De Hass.
William-street Bethel—M. N. Olmstead.
Fleet-street—R. M. Hatfield.
Hanson-place—G. W. Woodruff.
Carlton-avenue—F. C. Hill.
Washington-avenue—C. B. Sing.
De Kalb-avenue—R. C. Putney.
N. Bangs Church—W. F. Hatfield.
Union-place and East New-York—W. E. Smith.
Flatbush and Flatlands—To be supplied.
Cook-street—J. Henson.
Janes Church—W. H. Simmson.
South Fifth-street—C. D. Foss.
South Third-street—B. Pilsbury.
Gothic Church—G. Taylor.
South Second-street—J. W. Horne.
North Fifth-street—H. F. Pease.
Greenpoint—J. F. Booth.
Astoria—H. Cooke.
Flushing—E. S. Janes.

A Prize.

The prize schooner *Sue*, of Nassau, N. P., arrived yesterday, Acting Master RICHARD HUSTACE, in charge. She reports that she was 15 miles to the southward and eastward of the Highland Lights on the evening of the 3d inst., when she was hailed by the pilot-boat No. 9 for a pilot, and one came alongside, but on learning that the vessel was a prize, refused to take her into port, saying he got no pay for piloting such vessels. Being unable to get a pilot, the *Sue* was driven in the late gale 90 miles to sea. On the afternoon of the 6th, managed to get a pilot from No. 1, when to the northward of Barnegat.

The Pirate Alabama Spoken on March 23.

BOSTON, Tuesday, April 7.

Capt. SCOTT, of the British schooner *Roderick Random*, which arrived here on the 31st ult. from Miragoane, makes the following report:

"On March 23, in latitude 22° 30′, longitude 73° 32′, spoke the privateer *Alabama* and exchanged longitude with her."

The Steamship America Disabled.

SHE PUTS INTO HAMPTON ROADS.

BALTIMORE, Tuesday, April 7.

The steamship *America*, from Central America, with 700 passengers, put into Hampton Roads yesterday, disabled. Eighty of her passengers arrived here to-day in the Baltimore boat.

Court of Appeals.

ALBANY, Tuesday, April 7.

The following is the calendar of the Court of Appeals for Wednesday, April 8: Nos. 26, 27, 29, 30, 22, 32, 33, 34, 35, 36.

THE SUFFERING POOR OF IRELAND.

The Knights of St. Patrick at the Academy of Music.

An Enthusiastic Assemblage—Speeches by Gen. McClellan, Archbishop Hughes, Judge Daly, John McKeon, Richard O'Gorman, Gen. Meagher, and Others.

The meeting at the Academy of Music last night in aid of the suffering poor of Ireland, was an immense success, both in point of numbers and enthusiasm. At 7½ o'clock the entire edifice was filled with beauty and fashion. On the stage were the officers of the Society known as the Knights of St. Patrick; Mayor OPDYKE, who presided over the meeting; His Grace Archbishop HUGHES; Rev. Messrs. O'REILLY, MOONEY, SCHNEIDER, Hon. Judge DALY, Hon. Recorder HOFFMAN, Brig.-Gen. MEAGHER, Very Rev. Dr. STARRS, Vicar-General; Rev. THOMAS QUINN of Rhode Island, Rev. Mr. MORAN of Newark, Mayor KALBFLEISCH of Brooklyn, and several other distinguished gentlemen, both of the lay and clerical orders.

The proceedings were opened by His Honor Mayor OPDYKE assuming the Chair, when the New-York Harmonic Society, who were seated on the stage, sang "Hail to Our Nation," by KELLER. This having been concluded, the orchestra struck up "Hail to the Chief," and Gen. McCLELLAN and lady entered a private box. The General was received with loud cheers, and having been called upon for a speech, he came to the front of the box and spoke as follows:

SPEECH OF GEN. M'CLELLAN.

MY FRIENDS: I came here to-night as a listener and spectator—not to participate in the proceedings of the evening. I came to hear the ablest and best of the friends and sons of Ireland plead her cause. In doing so, I departed from my usual course, which is to avoid vast assemblies, and I did so because I knew that this one had no party or political purpose, but that you were to assemble for the noblest of all purposes—to manifest charity toward suffering brethren in a distant land. [Loud applause.] I came here simply to evince my sympathy in your cause; for I feel that I have strong and peculiar reasons to feel intense sympathy and interest in all that relates to Ireland and the Irish. [Loud applause.] I sprang myself from a kindred race. I have often seen the loyalty of the Irish to their Government and to their General proved. I have seen the green flag of Erin side by side with our own Stars and Stripes amid the smoke and din of battle. I have witnessed the chivalry and bravery of the Irish race, when a boy, upon the fields of Mexico, and in maturer years I have seen these qualities again displayed on the fields of Maryland and Virginia. [Prolonged applause.] It has often been my sad lot, but pleasant withal, to watch the cheerful, smiling faces of the Irish, when suffering from painful and ghastly wounds. I have always, under all circumstances, found the Irish heart warm and true; and, as I have already said, I feel that I have a peculiar right to sympathize with your cause. It is most unfortunate that there are so many in Ireland who need our sympathy and assistance; but we should, at least, thank God that He has given us the means to extend our hands to them and aid them. It is unfortunate, perhaps, for Ireland, that laws, with the making of which her people had so little to do, and a Government in which they have been so little represented, should have compelled so many of them to leave their native land, and seek refuge in foreign climes; but the loss of Ireland has been the gain of America. [Loud cheering.] It has given us some of the brightest intellects that have adorned our history, countless strong arms which have developed our resources, and soldiers immeasurable who on every field, from those of the revolution to those of the present sad rebellion, have upheld the honor of their adopted country. [Great cheering.] Therefore, I say, we have gained what Ireland has lost. One thing more before I close. Although, as I said before, we have come here to-night for no political purpose, yet no true friend of his country in the present crisis can express altogether the thoughts that will crowd upon his brain. What is it that enables us now to extend our hands in succor to your brethren across the Atlantic? What is it that our fathers worked for, and for which we too have worked and are working now? To establish upon this broad continent one nation, one free government, that might be a refuge for all from foreign lands. I know, then, that I express the sentiments of all who listen to me, when I say that all our energies, all our thoughts, all our means, and, if necessary, the last drop of our blood must be given to uphold that unity, that nationality. [Great cheering.] I do not rise to make a speech, but simply to express my warm and most cordial thanks for the greeting with which I have been honored. I will, therefore, thank you again, and then make way for abler and more eloquent men, who will plead the cause of your country to-night.

[Enthusiastic applause again and again renewed, in the midst of which Gen. McCLELLAN sat down.]

Gen. McCLELLAN having concluded his remarks, after a short address from Mayor OPDYKE, WM. F. LYONS, Esq., Secretary of the Knights of St. Patrick, read the address prepared by a committee of that organization, appealing to the generosity of the American people on behalf of Ireland, which was received with great enthusiasm. His Honor the Mayor then introduced His Grace Archbishop HUGHES, whose appearance was the signal for loud and long-continued applause. He spoke as follows:

SPEECH OF ARCHBISHOP HUGHES.

LADIES AND GENTLEMEN: If I stand up to speak under the honorable introduction of the Mayor of New York, you will anticipate not so much a speech as an apology for the absence of it. It would be very strange, indeed, if all the feelings of my heart were not intensely entwined in sympathy with the purpose and the object of this great meeting. [Applause.] I shall not now enumerate the reasons why they are so, but I suppose that every one can appreciate them. It is but too well known that many of the Irish people are suffering for want of food and raiment, and that fact alone is a substitute for eloquence, if I were master of it. We cannot think of it patiently; you cannot bear it; I cannot bear it. It is a terrible fact that fellow-beings, many of them related to us directly or indirectly, are slowly dying of starvation. I have said that you cannot bear it, and your presence here to-night is a proof of it; human nature cannot bear it—it is too bad. God permits it, no doubt, as he permits many things that we may regret, not reproving him; but under the pressure of this state of things upon every Christian heart, I conceive that eloquence does not now consist in words, but in action. [Loud cheering.] I have given my little mite towards this object, $250; and, as they would say in Wall-street, I felt 250 per cent. lighter of heart as soon as it was given. I will not occupy your time long. I do not stand here to preach a charity sermon. In the pulpit I have done so, and may do so again, for such is my office; but a work like this which you have so generously taken in hand is not to be accomplished by a charity sermon. The work is a great one; it is prompted by generosity, by humanity, and by charity, and extends to all, without distinction of creed or party. [Applause.] Even from the Pagans we learn the maxim, that where humanity suffers, every man who has a stake in that humanity ought to suffer with it—by sympathy at least. Ours is sympathy indeed; but sympathy without help is nothing. You must put your hands to the wheel. You have a noble example in what was done during a former famine in Ireland. There is nothing in history that can compare with the universal uprising of human sympathy and relief for the sufferers upon that occasion. Since the last famine in Ireland, that poor country has been dodging on in her usual way. The things of which I speak now have not come under my own actual observation, but I have every reason, and I am sorrowfully bound to believe in the existence of the distress of which we have heard. I said awhile ago that I would not spoil this undertaking of yours, by talking to you as if I were preaching a charity sermon, and I will not. I merely wish to say a few words to you in a simple way. I may say, however, that when I have spoken upon such occasions, I have never failed to meet a sympathetic response. I have been delighted by the magnificent spirit of charity manifested in this City toward the suffering operatives of Manchester. A suffering man in Manchester is not exactly what a suffering man in Ireland is. The former is surrounded and almost swamped by wealthy capitalists; but the Irish poor, if they were to forget themselves so far as to assert and carry out their will and purpose to help themselves, (which, after all, is the right of the starving man everywhere,) [loud applause,] they would find around them nothing but poverty like their own. Yet I cannot refrain from complimenting and being proud of the people of the City of New-York for the liberal contributions they have made in aid of the English workingmen. They have done honor to themselves; they have heaped coals of fire upon heads that did not understand what the meaning of heat was—heat of that character. I am afraid, ladies and gentlemen, that there is a temptation in the atmosphere which prolongs my observations beyond their intended limit, but I must close. This matter has been nobly taken up by gentlemen of the lay order, and being a clergyman, I have felt some delicacy as to whether I ought to be present; but I could not withhold my approval of their efforts. They are gentlemen of influence and means, and I know that they are not deficient in that eloquence which, coming from them, will stir up every feeling of charity, generosity and humanity in your bosoms. It only remains for me to repeat what I have already said, that I go with the movement heart and hand.

Hon. Judge DALY was the next speaker. He illustrated the present condition of Ireland by comparing it to the regard which Joseph evinced for the sufferers in his own land after he had been raised to power and position in Egypt, and appealed to the audience, both native and Irish born, to act the part of Joseph in extending their charity to the Irish people, who now send to us across the Atlantic a cry for aid.

RICHARD O'GORMAN, Esq., followed in a speech, in which he depicted the wrongs of Ireland in terse and vigorous language, and portrayed the extent of the present famine there, showing how essential it was that immediate relief should be extended the people of that unhappy country.

Hon. JOHN McKEON was then introduced, and spoke in feeling terms of the miseries which the poor Irish were now suffering from a lack of food. He considered it the duty of Americans to contribute toward alleviating the sufferings of a people who had ever been our warmest friends, and who had done so much toward making our country prosperous beyond any other nation on earth. Let us show, said he, that our sympathy is as bright in war as in peace. If each one would contribute a little, the aggregate would be millions, and we should have the consolation of knowing that we have done our duty in the cause of humanity.

P. J. MEEHAN, Esq., editor of the *Irish-American*, WM. E. ROBINSON, Esq., and Brig.-Gen. MEAGHER then addressed the assemblage, after which the Harmonic Society sang "Where Liberty dwells is my Country." Hon. HORACE GREELEY was loudly called for, and coming forward, moved a resolution counseling the various Irish societies throughout the country to carry forward the good work so auspiciously commenced to-night. He supported this resolution by a few appropriate remarks, which were well received.

Mr. P. J. MEEHAN announced that BRYAN LAWRENCE, Esq., had contributed $1,000 towards the relief fund, which announcement was received with loud cheers.

A letter was read from Rev. Dr. CUMMINGS, of St. Stephen's Church, stating that indisposition prevented him from attending the meeting, and inclosing $50 as his donation to the cause.

A Committee to solicit subscriptions was appointed for each Ward, after which the meeting adjourned.

THE CONNECTICUT ELECTION.

HARTFORD, Tuesday, April 7.

We have returns from every town in the State except Hampton. The vote on Governor foots up: BUCKINGHAM, 38,304; SEYMOUR, 35,836. BUCKINGHAM's majority will be 2,500.

The Senate stands 14 Union and 7 Democrats; the House, 139 Union and 94 Democrats, with two towns a tie.

For Congress—DEMING, BRANDEGEE and HUBBARD, Union, and ENGLISH, Democrat, are elected.

Other State and Municipal Elections.

IN MICHIGAN.

DETROIT, Mich., Tuesday, April 7.

Partial returns indicate the success of the Republican State ticket by an increased majority over last Fall's election.

IN MASSACHUSETTS.

BOSTON, Mass., Tuesday, April 7.

The vote in the State, yesterday, upon repealing the Two-year Amendment law relating to the naturalization of foreigners, was very light. The repeal was carried by a considerable majority.

IN OHIO.

CLEVELAND, Ohio, Tuesday, April 7.

The Unionists carried the city, yesterday, by a handsome majority.

CIRCLEVILLE, Ohio, Tuesday, April 7

This place has gone Democratic.

Zanesville and Steuben have gone Union.

In Portsmouth the Democrats have elected their Mayor. A majority of Union men are elected to the Councils.

IN MISSOURI.

ST. JOSEPH, Mo., Tuesday, April 7.

The election yesterday resulted in the reëlection of the present incumbents, with the exception of Councilmen. The Unconditional Union ticket was carried throughout by a large majority.

KANSAS CITY, Tuesday, April 7.

The municipal election yesterday resulted in the entire success of the unconditional Union ticket by a majority of 300 votes.

IN KANSAS.

LEAVENWORTH, Kansas, Tuesday, April 7.

At the city election yesterday, ANTHONY, the Radical Republican candidate, was elected Mayor by 700 majority over ATWOOD, the Conservative Republican candidate, who was supported by the Democrats. The whole Republican ticket was elected. The city has heretofore been Democratic.

LAW REPORTS.

Court Calendar—THIS DAY.

SUPREME COURT—CIRCUIT.—*Part I.*—Nos. 1643, 1681, 1685, 1695, 1699, 1705, 1709, 1711, 1713, 1715, 1719, 1721, 1723, 1725, 1727, 1729, 1731, 1733, 1745, 1747. *Part II.*—Nos. 2426, 2518, 2522, 2524, 2530, 2534, 2538, 2540, 2542, 2544, 2546, 2548, 2550, 2552, 2554, 2556, 2558, 2560, 2566, 2568. *Part III.*—Nos. 1704, 1055, 1578, 2326, 142, 2056, 837, 1467, 485, 525, 577, 583, 611, 712¼, 715½, 747, 747½, 768, 758.

SUPREME COURT—SPECIAL TERM.—Demurrer No. 19. Issues of Law and Fact.—Nos. 241, 217, 224, 225, 226, 227, 228, 229, 230, 231, 232, 233, 234, 236, 237, 238, 239, 240, 242.

SUPERIOR COURT—TRIAL TERM.—*Part I.*—Nos. 1845, 1871, 1919, 1939, 1745, 837, 1815, 1969, 1761, 1789, 1803, 1829, 1849, 1857, 1743. *Part II.*—Nos. 1742, 784, 1722, 1152, 1496, 1514, 2096, 2106, 2108, 2110, 2112, 2114, 2116, 2118, 2120.

COMMON PLEAS—TRIAL TERM.—*Part I.*—Nos. 1434, 1435, 1436, 1437, 1438, 1439, 1440, 1441, 1442, 1443, 1444, 1446, 1447, 1448, 1206. *Part II.*—Nos. 1379, 966, 1424, 1365, 1206, 1369, 1284, 1449, 1450, 1451, 1452, 1453, 1454, 1455, 1456.

Administrators of the Estate of Robert T. Haws—Mr. Haws Died Intestate.

SURROGATE'S COURT.

Before Surrogate Tucker.

Matter of the Estate of Robert T. Haws.—Mr. Haws having died intestate, Messrs. John H. Williams, of Queens County, James H. Pinckney and William Allen, of this City, have been appointed Administrators of his estate, with the usual powers in such cases.

Mr. Williams is understood to be the brother-in-law of Mr. Haws, and Mr. Allen to have been his late Chief Clerk while Comptroller of the City.

Decisions.

SUPREME COURT—CHAMBERS.

Before Justice Barnard.

Van Wyck et al. vs. *Schultz*; *Gebhard* vs. *Geer*; *Merrill et als.* vs. *Condy*; *Brainard, Receiver*, vs. *Alexander*; *Adair* vs. *Wood*; *Braynard* vs. *Braynard*.—Motions denied.

Hewlett et als. vs. *Lewis et al.*; *Hoffman* vs. *Valkenburgh et als.*; *Lockwood* vs. *The New-York Central Railroad*; *Beecher* vs. *Cox*; *Hawkins et als.* vs. *Hayman et als.*; *Devlin et al.* vs. *Hastings et als.*; *Ruggles* vs. *Reynolds et als.*; *Cauldwell* vs. *McCann et al.*; *Cheesbrough et al.* vs. *Benson et al.*; *Mutual Life Insurance Company* vs. *McCullough et al.*; *The Same* vs. *Tomlinson et al.*; *Whitney* vs. *Merritt et al.*; *Kimberly* vs. *Hayman et al.*; *Mutual Life Insurance* vs. *Van Rayden et al.*; *Hedden* vs. *Tracy et al.*; *Devlin et al.* vs. *Hastings et al.*; *Hancock* vs. *Lyle et al.*; *Brooklyn Fire Insurance Company* vs. *Stewart et al.*; *McVean* vs. *Waterbury*; *Grant et al.* vs. *Smith*; *Fritz* vs. *Borcheit et al.*; *Importers' and Traders' Bank* vs. *Adams*; *Judah* vs. *Ferrett et al.*—Motions granted.

Terbell et al. vs. *Wells et al.*; *Coursen* vs. *Woodruff*.—Motion granted, and reference ordered to hear, &c.

Lewis et al. vs. *Bryant*.—Motion granted, with $10 costs.

Losee vs. *Lynch*.—Motion granted, with stay.

Taylor et al. vs. *McNamee et al.*—Motion granted; stay for thirty days.

Hurd vs. *De Forest*.—Motion granted; five per cent. ordered.

Webb vs. *Van Zandt*.—Motion granted, and five per cent. ordered.

In the matter of McKain, an infant.—The writ discharged, and the child remanded to the custody of the grandmother.

The Charleston Mercury.

DAILY PAPER—TEN DOLLARS PER ANNUM, PAYABLE HALF-YEARLY IN ADVANCE. | VINDICE NULLO SPONTE SUA SINE LEGE FIDES RECTUMQUE COLENTUR. | COUNTRY PAPER—THRICE A WEEK—FIVE DOLLARS PER ANNUM, IN ADVANCE.

VOLUME LXXXII. | CHARLESTON, S. C., WEDNESDAY, APRIL 8, 1863. | NUMBER 11,723

THE MERCURY.

WEDNESDAY, APRIL 8, 1863.

The Attack on Charleston Opened.

At last, the long period of doubt and delay is at an end; and this goodly city, girdled with the fiery circle of its batteries, stands confronted with the most formidable Armada that the hands of man have ever put afloat.

The first scene in the novel drama of the war, which, we trust, is to add new lustre to the fame of Charleston, has closed. Let us render thanks to the Lord of Hosts that the result, thus far, has been one of proud triumph to our country. As yet, however, we have but entered upon the ordeal. It will be for the next few days to tell the tale of our sad disaster, or complete success.

In view of the reticence which (for reasons of military policy) has heretofore marked our allusions to the presence of the iron clad fleet, a brief review of the events of the week will not be out of place. About noon on Sunday last the first intelligence was flashed to the city from Fort Sumter, that the turrets of the far-famed Monitor gunboats were looming up against the southeastern horizon. During the afternoon the entire fleet hove in sight. Eight Monitors, besides the frigate *Ironsides* and twenty-seven wooden war vessels, took up their position just beyond the bar. As the news became bruited about the city, very many of our non-combatant population (previously incredulous of danger) made hasty preparations to depart; and every train that has left the city since has gone heavily laden with the eleventh-hour refugees and their effects.

Sunday night passed quietly by. Monday morning brought us reports of the movements of transports up the Stono River, and the debarkation of a considerable force of Yankee troops on Cole's Island. But throughout Monday and Monday night, the armored fleet held its position beyond the bar. On Tuesday morning it was observed that another Monitor had arrived, making a force of no less than ten iron clad vessels, including the *Ironsides*.

At two o'clock on Tuesday afternoon a despatch from Fort Sumter announced that these ten vessels had crossed the bar, and were cautiously steaming inward—the foremost one having at that time reached a point about three thousand yards from the Fort. The next news was brought to us, an hour later, by the dull detonation of the first gun from Fort Moultrie, which was immediately answered by a heavy report and a cloud of white smoke from the turret of one of the Monitors. At ten minutes after three, the enemy having come within range, Fort Sumter opened her batteries, and, almost simultaneously, the white smoke could be seen puffing from the low sand hills of Morris and Sullivan's Islands, indicating that the Beauregard Battery on the left, and Battery Wagner on the extreme right, had become engaged. Five of the iron-clads, forming in line of battle in front of Fort Sumter, maintained a very rapid return fire, occasionally hurling their 15 inch shot and shell against Fort Moultrie and the minor batteries, but all directing their chief efforts against the east face of Fort Sumter. Gradually, but visibly, the distance between the attacking vessels and the Fort was lessened, and as the enemy drew nearer the firing became hot and almost continuous.

About half-past four o'clock the battle became fierce and general. The scene at that hour, as viewed from the Battery promenade, was truly grand. Battery Bee had now mingled the hoarse thunder of its guns in the universal din, and the whole expanse of the harbor entrance, from Sullivan's Island to Cumming's Point, became enveloped in the smoke and constant flashes of the conflict. The iron-clads kept constantly shifting their position, but, whichever way they went, their ports, always turned towards the battlements of Sumter, poured forth their terrible projectiles against the walls of that famous stronghold. Ever and anon, as the huge shot went ricochetting towards the mark, the water was dashed up in vast sheets of spray, towering far above the parapet of the Fort, while the wreaths of smoke constantly ascending from the barbette guns showed how actively the artillerymen of the post were discharging their duties. In the foreground, our own staunch little iron-clads, the *Palmetto State* and *Chicora*, could be seen steaming energetically up and down their chosen fighting position, evidently impatient to participate in the fray.

Up to this time the frigate *Ironsides* had born a very conspicuous part in the fight. Her long hull lay at the distance, apparently, of a mile from our batteries, and her tremendous broadsides were more than once fitly answered by broadsides from the Fort. It soon became apparent that she was unable to stand the severe fire directed against her. Steaming rapidly southward, she gave Fort Sumter a few parting shots and withdrew from the action. The *Keokuk*, a double turretted Monitor, soon after followed her example; and before five o'clock the firing had evidently begun to slacken. The remaining Monitors, however, still kept up the bombardment and our forts and batteries replied with undiminished alacrity. At quarter after five, p. m., the Monitors began to retire, and at half past five the enemy fired the last shot of the engagement.

Gratifying as were the general results of the fight, the late hour at which it closed precluded the possibility of our receiving the full details from the Forts. A despatch from Fort Sumter informs us that the *Ironsides* and *Keokuk* were both very roughly handled, and retired seriously injured. The *Keokuk* had her flag shot down, her boat shot away, three holes in her smoke stack and a portion of her bow shot off. The practice of our gunners was most creditable. Nearly every shot struck some one of the iron clads, but with what effect is not known. Fort Sumter was struck thirty-four times. One of our guns was dismounted, but otherwise the Fort is in good condition. Fort Moultrie was uninjured. The casualties at Fort Sumter were a drummer boy, named AHRENS, mortally wounded; two men severely wounded, and three others slightly injured. At Fort Moultrie, one man was accidentally hurt by a fall from the flagstaff, on which he was replacing our flag, which had been shot away. We learn that he afterwards died. Two small houses on the back beach of Sullivan's Island were demolished by the enemy's fire.

After their withdrawal from the action, the enemy's iron-clads anchored off Morris Island where they now lie. Many think that the fight will be renewed at daybreak this morning; but up to the time at which we write (3 a. m.) all is quiet. The reports we get from the Stono River say that the enemy's transports still remain in the stream. Doubtless the Yankee Generals intend, before venturing upon a land attack, to await the issue of the struggle between their ships and our batteries.

THE FIGHT AT PORT HUDSON.

A correspondent of the Jackson *Appeal*, writing from Port Hudson, La., under date of March 15, gives the annexed account of the Yankee attack on that place:

The long expected contest between the Yankee fleet took place before daylight this morning, the first shot being fired at ten minutes past twelve o'clock, and the last one at twenty minutes past two. It was short, sharp and decisive.

Six vessels were to complete the expedition, divided into two divisions. The vanguard was to consist of the flag ship Hartford, a first class steam sloop-of-war, carrying twenty-six 8 and 9 inch Paixhan guns, leading, followed by the Monongahela, a second class steam sloop, mounting sixteen heavy guns, and the Richmond, a first class steam sloop-of-war, of twenty-six guns, principally 8 and 9 inch Columbiads. The rear guard was composed of the first class steam sloop Mississippi, twenty-two guns, 8 and 9 inch, and the gunboats Kinnes and Genesee, each carrying three Columbiads and two rifled 32 pounders. The Mississippi was a side wheel steamer. All the others were screw propellers. The vanguard was commanded by Admiral Farragut in person, on board the Hartford. The rear guard was under the command of Captain Melancthon Smith, flying his pennant from the Mississippi. They were to proceed up stream in single file, the prow of one following close upon the stern of another, and keeping their fires and lights well concealed, until they should be discovered by our batteries, when they were to get by the best way they could, fighting their passage, and once above, they believed they would have the rebel stronghold on both sides—their guns covering every part of the encampment. Besides this, the Essex and mortar boats anchored at the Point, and supposed to have already acquired our range, were expected to play no mean part in the affair.

Shortly before midnight the boats, having formed the line of battle as described, their decks cleared for action, and the men at their quarters, the Hartford led the way, and the others promptly followed her direction. At the moment of their discovery a rocket was to be sent up from the Admiral's flag-ship, as the signal for the Essex and her accompanying mortar boats to commence work. So dark was the night, and so slightly had the armed craft nosed their way up, that the flag-ship had passed some of our guns, and all the fleet were within easy range before their approach was known. Almost at the same time a rocket from our Signal Corps, and a discharge of musketry by an infantry picket, aroused our line. Quick as a flash, while the falling fire of our alarm rocket was yet unextinguished, there shot up into the sky, from the Hartford's deck, another. Then came one grand, long, deafening roar that rent the atmosphere with its mighty thunder, shaking both land and water, and causing the high battery crowned cliffs to tremble. Every gun on the fleet and every mortar at the Point joined in one simultaneous discharge. Relying greatly upon the suddenness and vigor of their attack to disconcert and confuse the defenders of our cliffs, the roar of their first discharge had not died away upon the ear before it recommenced, and when the quick and irregular but unceasing volleys and broadsides showed that the crews of each Yankee ship were vieing with each other in celerity. The sheets of flame that poured from the sides of the sloops at each discharge lit up nearly the whole stretch of river, placing each craft in strong relief against the black sky. The noise was stunning to the ear, but they knew not yet the position of our batteries, and the shot and shell, fired at random, had no material effect.

Now commenced the battle in all its terrible earnestness. Outnumbered in guns and outweighted in metal, our volleys were as quickly repeated, and the majority of them unerring in their aim. As soon as the enemy thus discovered our batteries, they opened on them with grape and canister, which was more accurately thrown than their shells, and threw clouds of dirt upon the guns and gunners; the shell went over them in every conceivable direction except the right one. The Hartford, a very fast ship, now made straight for up the river, making her best time, and trying to divert the aim of our gunners by her incessant and deafening broadsides. She soon outstripped the balance of the fleet. Shot after shot struck her, riddling her through and through, but still she kept on her way. Every craft now looking out for itself, and bound to make its very best time to get by, the fleet lost its orderly line of battle, and got so mixed up it was difficult, and sometimes impossible, to distinguish one from another. It was speedily apparent to the enemy that the fire was a great deal hotter and more destructive than had been expected, and all the ships except the Hartford undertook to put about and return the way they came. For this purpose the Richmond sheered close in to the left bank, under the batteries, and then circled round, her course reaching nearly up to the opposite point. In executing this manœuvre she gave our batteries successively a raking position, and they took excellent advantage of it, ripping her from stern to stern. From the crashing of timbers plainly heard during every brief interval of the din, and from the view had of shots that struck her, it was plain that her doom was sealed. It was reported among a crowd of observers on the bluff that a voice from her deck had called out; "We surrender! we surrender!" If this was said, it was not probably spoken by her commander, who, however, appealed to our batteries to cease firing upon her, as the ship was sinking. As she was evidently drifting down in an unmanageable condition, and apparently settling, the batteries let her alone, and turned their attention to other craft. Whether or not she sank I do not as yet know.

The Mississippi undertook to execute the same manœuvre of turning round and making her escape back to the point she started from. She had rounded and just turned down stream, when one of our shots tore off her rudder, and another went crashing through her machinery. Immediately after came the rushing sound of steam escaping from some broken pipe, and the now unmanageable vessel drifted aground directly opposite our crescent line of batteries. Her range was quickly gained, and she was being rapidly torn to pieces by our missiles, when the commander gave the order for all hands to save themselves the best way they could. At the same time fire broke out in two places. At this time her decks were strewn with dead and wounded, according to one of her crew, with whom I have conversed, who thought that one half her complement of men were included in the list of casualties.

The three larger vessels had occupied most of the attention of the batteries, but the other craft had not by any means been overlooked. Two had turned round and started down stream. One of them apparently escaped without serious disability, but the other, which was probably the Kinnes, floated down past the batteries in an unmanageable condition, receiving our volleys without being able to return them; and from the confusion of voices, and the mingling of oaths, execrations and orders heard from her deck, it was evident that great slaughter must have been made among her crew, else that the boat herself was in a critical predicament. A vessel, which was either the Tennessee or Monongahela—most probably the former—slipped by in the confusion, and joined the Hartford up the river. Some fifty-five or sixty persons saved themselves by jumping overboard and swimming or wading from the Mississippi to the shore. Of these, the Major and Captain of Marines and Assistant Engineer, with forty five sailors and marines, have been arrested by our cavalry, and brought across during the day. Some few others are reported to be hiding themselves in the swamps. The dead and wounded were left upon the Mississippi, which soon floated off and started down with the current.

When the burning Mississippi reached the point where the mortar boats and other craft lay, she created a perfect panic among them. At five minutes past 5 o'clock, when the Mississippi was probably within five miles of Baton Rouge, a sudden glare lit up the whole sky. The cause was well known to be the explosion of the magazine. After a considerable interval of time, a long rumbling sound brought the final proof that the Mississippi, one of the finest vessels of the United States navy, which had earned an historic fame before the commencement of the present war as the flag ship of the Japan Expedition, was a thing of the past.

Such are the particulars of this morning's fight at Port Hudson. For the time it lasted it was one of the most desperately contested engagements of the war. Our success is to be attributed to the coolness, gallantry and skill of the officers and men engaged. If the country is not satisfied with the Port Hudson fight, then it must, indeed, be unreasonable. Under all the circumstances, the result has been as surprising as it has been gratifying. The relative loss of life is one of the most significant features of the affair. The loss on board the enemy's vessels must amount to at least 250 killed and wounded. On the Mississippi, alone, the loss was over 150. The loss in our batteries was one Lieutenant, of the 1st Alabama, slightly wounded, and one man, of the 1st Tennessee battalion, severely wounded.

Bombardment of Fort Sumter, April 7, 1863

The Charleston Mercury.

DAILY PAPER—TEN DOLLARS PER ANNUM, PAYABLE HALF-YEARLY IN ADVANCE.

VINDICE NULLO
SPONTE SUA SINE LEGE FIDES RECTUMQUE COLENTUR.

COUNTRY PAPER—THRICE A WEEK—FIVE DOLLARS PER ANNUM, IN ADVANCE.

VOLUME LXXXII. | CHARLESTON, S. C., SATURDAY, APRIL 11, 1863. | NUMBER 11,726

TELEGRAPHIC NEWS.

LATEST FROM VICKSBURG.

VICKSBURG, April 8.—Everything quiet here. Two more transports left this afternoon, bound up the river. A number of transports are still in sight.

LATEST FROM PORT HUDSON.

PORT HUDSON, April 9.—All quiet here. The enemy's fleets, above and below, have disappeared. The former is above Bayou Sara. Forty exchanged and paroled prisoners from New Orleans arrived here yesterday. Our troops at this point are in excellent spirits, and are vigilantly watching the Yankee vessels.

We have trustworthy information from St. Joseph's, La., to the effect that HARRISON'S pickets are skirmishing with the enemy. Three flats, loaded with Yankees, came down the Tensas a few days ago.

THE LATEST FROM TENNESSEE.

CHATTANOOGA, April 9.—The enemy occupies Lebanon with a division, under Gen. REYNOLDS. The Yankees are also in force at Carthage. The news we get from Kentucky is cheering. The Louisville *Democrat* spurns the tyranny of the Union Democratic Convention and its platform. All is quiet at Columbia. Twenty more prisoners reached here yesterday. We have advices from Memphis that the enemy is preparing more empty boats as "cotton-clad," for the purpose of landing troops at Vicksburg. The Yankee boats had returned from Steele's Bayou, badly damaged. More families have been exiled from Memphis on account of "rebel" raids on the railroad.

VAN DORN'S Cavalry has succeeded in capturing one gunboat and two transports on the Cumberland River, near Palmyra, which were burned. A grand review took place yesterday at Tullahoma.

THE FOOD QUESTION AND THE SPECULATORS.

RICHMOND, April 10.—The President will issue his Proclamation to-morrow morning, urging the people to direct their agricultural labor mainly to the production of food crops. He takes an encouraging view of the present position of affairs, and urges the raising of food for man and beast, as the means of averting the only danger that the Government regards with apprehension. He administers a rebuke to the speculators.

REPULSE OF THE ENEMY IN FLORIDA.

PALATKA, FLA., March 31.—On Friday, the 27th inst., the large transport steamer *Ben DeFord* landed at this place for the purpose of occupying the town. A fine cavalry corps stationed here, under command of Capt. J. J. DICKISON, met them very handsomely. We fired upon them with Enfield rifles, at a distance of about one hundred yards, killing and wounding a great many, the notorious Colonel MONTGOMERY, the Kansas "jayhawker" and outlaw, among the number. They immediately fled to their boat, and did not return the fire until they were out in the stream. It is almost a miracle that we had only one man wounded from the amount of shell and grape thrown. They retreated across the river, and took on board two companies of negros whom they had there engaged plundering and stealing. They then steamed off down the river, and we have not heard from them since. We have just received a despatch which states that they have burnt Jacksonville and left the river.—*Savannah News.*

THE MERCURY.

SATURDAY, APRIL 11, 1863.

Notes of the Fight of the 7th at Fort Sumter.

At two o'clock p. m., just as the officers had seated themselves for dinner, the first advance of the iron-clad fleet was announced to the commandant of the post. Their anchorage had been within the bar of Ship Channel, off the southern end of Morris Island, some four miles from Sumter. Upon inspection, it was judged that good time would be allowed for the conclusion of the meal, and, after communicating the movement by telegraph to Headquarters in Charleston, dinner was comfortably dispatched. At half past two o'clock, after examination of the approaching armament from the terreplein, the order for the "long roll" was issued. The whole garrison knew that the hour of trial was at hand, and the greatest enthusiasm and alacrity prevailed. The men rushed to their guns with shouting and yells of exultation. The regimental band was ordered to the rampart. The garrison flag (the Confederate States) was already flying defiantly from the staff at the northern apex of the pentagonal fortress. The blue and white banner of the Palmetto State was given to the wind on the southwest corner of the work, and the elegant black and white color, of the First Regiment South Carolina Artillery (Regulars), was run up at the southeast angle, in the face of the coming foe. A salute of thirteen unshotted guns was fired, and the band broke forth with the stirring strains of "Dixie."

It was determined to permit the fleet to come well within range before opening fire. Lieutenant Colonel JOSEPH A. YATES, who that morning reported for duty, was assigned to the special command of the barbette batteries. Major ORMSBY BLANDING was assigned the special command of the casemate batteries. They were both at their posts, with officers, men and guns ready, and awaiting the order to begin the engagement. Colonel ALFRED RHETT, the commandant of the post, stood on the parapet watching the progress of the doughty iron-clad dogs of war. Every heart beat high. Every face was flushed with calm excitement, properly incident to such a moment. On they came, steaming slowly north-eastward—seven Monitors, their hulls sunk down to the water level, showing only a black line on the surface and a projecting turret and smoke stack each—the *Ironsides*, looming up from the sea a formidable looking monster, and the *Keokuk*, her hull more distinctly visible than the Monitors, and with two turrets, the most dreaded of all the nine.

In front, a Monitor, supposed to be the *Passaic*, commanded by DRAYTON, pushed forward a long raft, forked and fitting her bow, intended to catch, by suspended grappling irons, any entanglements, or to explode any torpedoes, which might lie in the path of their hostile advance. Next followed, in approximate *echelon*, another Monitor, bearing a pennon, and conjectured to be the flag ship of the commanding officer of the fleet. This was succeeded, in the same order, by two others of similar kind, only distinguishable by slight differences in the adornments of red or white paint upon their generally black turrets and smoke stacks. These constituted the first line or division. After an interval of space came the *Ironsides*, of much larger proportions, her sleek and glistening black sides rising high and frowning above the water. She occupied a central position, and was followed, at some distance, by the three remaining Monitors and the *Keokuk* in the rear. These four formed the other line or division of battle.

At three o'clock, when the leading gunboat had got east southeast of Sumter, at a distance of about fourteen hundred yards, Fort Moultrie fired the first gun. The band was hushed at Sumter, the musicians were dispatched to their pieces, and the order was issued to open fire, carefully and by battery.

At 3.03 min. the guns belched forth their fierce thunders upon the foremost monster. Within two minutes there was a response. His shots were directed against Sumter, and the strife was inaugurated. The east and northeast batteries, *en barbette* and in casemate, were those only engaged, together with a mortar battery on one of the ramparts, which fired for a short time. It may be improper to publish, at this juncture, the garrison of the fort, but we may mention that the east barbette battery was officered, as we understand, by Captain D. FLEMMING, Lieut. F. D. BLAKE, Lieut. JONES, and Lieut. JULIUS RHETT (a volunteer, absent from PRESTON'S Battery Light Artillery on sick leave). The northeast barbette battery was officered by Capt. HARLESTON, Lieut. MOM. KING and Lieut. W. S. SIMKINS. The mortar battery was for a time manned and was officered by Capt. MACBETH and Lieut. JULIUS ALSTON, who were subsequently transferred to one of the casemate batteries engaged. The other, the largest casemate battery engaged, was commanded by Capt. W. H. PERONNEAU and Lieut. FICKLING, while a third small battery was in charge of Lieut. GRIMBALL.

For thirty minutes the guns of Fort Sumter were concentrated on the leading vessel, irrespective of the answering cannon of the others. The garrison fought with eagerness and impetuosity. They had to be restrained, and after trial, firing by battery, it was found that, from the small size of the object at a distance of 1100 to 1400 yards, and its constant and alternate moving and stopping, it was difficult to keep the guns trained to shoot simultaneously with accuracy. The method was changed, with apparent advantage, during the course of the engagement. The gunboats fired deliberately, at intervals. The smoke stack of the pioneer boat was riddled with balls. The turret was repeatedly struck and impressions distinctly visible. At 3.25 a flat headed bolt of chilled iron, projected from a Brooke gun (rifled and banded 7 inch), struck with manifest damage. A volume of steam was seen to issue from the creature, and it turned off on a curve toward the east and southeast, steaming out of range and out of the fight. Meantime, the three other Monitors of the first line had bestowed their attentions upon the fort with impunity. They now, after the retirement of the supposed *Passaic*, received each, for a brief season, sundry acknowledgments. That bearing the pennon, at 3.37 had its emblem of command cut down by a well directed shot. Its turret and hull were indented. Several shot were visible, driven and sticking in the iron. The smoke stack was repeatedly pierced through. And at 3.45 this invulnerable man-of-war also drew off, followed by the two that had accompanied it.

The *Ironsides* seemed shy of the contest. She fired a few shots at a distance of not less than 1400 yards, and perhaps as much as 1800. Three balls were seen to strike her in return. She soon headed off out of range, and was counted out.

The Monitors of the second line were under a concentrated fire, each a few minutes. All were hit, but apparently with no special injury. The longer the fight continued, the more accurate the firing proved with the gunners of that gallant and admirably trained corps.

The *Keokuk* now boldly advanced, bow on, to 850 yards of the east side of Fort Sumter. This was the shortest distance attained by any of the fleet, no other venturing so near. Colonel RHETT now requested Lieutenant-Colonel YATES to take charge of a Brooke gun for a few shots, and to sight it carefully himself. The first shot entered the open port hole of the foremost turret, apparently silencing the boat.

The next ball was a centre shot upon the turret. The third penetrated the bow, some ten feet from the stem, making a large opening at the water line; and a fourth also struck the hull. During this time a concentric fire was poured into the monster from all the guns that could be brought to bear. The fire of the fort had been reduced by order to one gun from each battery every five minutes, and was exceedingly precise and effective. For many minutes the boat drifted, lifelessly with the tide, under a terrific hail, being torn in different places, and having shot plainly imbedded in the iron armor. It was strongly hoped that it would be so disabled as to surrender, falling into our hands by capture. But, after being under punishment forty minutes, it managed to crawl feebly off and escape, giving a parting salute as it was getting out of range, to show that the will was there to fight. The following morning it settled down some five hundred yards to sea from the beach towards the south part of Morris Island.

This was the end of the fight. After a short engagement of two hours and twenty-five minutes, an unprotected brick fort, by the use of its cannon, assisted by Fort Moultrie and the guns of one or two sand batteries, employing few guns, repulsed a fleet of nine of the boasted iron-clad gunboats. The *Keokuk* was sunk. The *Passaic* has disappeared from view, probably sent or towed to Port Royal for repairs. And the flag-boat has been undergoing the mending process in plain sight. The prestige of their invulnerability is gone. The question is reduced to the relative powers of destruction of the fort and the assailing fleet. It is a question of pluck and survivorship in a square stand-up-fight for victory. Iron-clad fleets can be destroyed as well as forts. Fort Sumter, although somewhat pitted, to-day is, we believe, as strong as it was when this fight begun. We deem that, if the attack is renewed as before (and there is good reason to believe it will be), the six Monitors left and the *Ironsides* will come out the defeated party, with worse results than those obtained in their first attempt. *Nous verrons.*

The enemy fired about eighty shots—mostly 15 inch and steel pointed shells—at Fort Sumter. This estimate was made from Sullivan's Island. Forty only struck the work. One 10-inch gun was temporarily disabled by a shot. One Columbiad of old pattern burst. One 7 inch rifled gun dismounted by recoil, and one gun was disabled for a few moments by fracture of the elevating screw through recoil.

Not a person was killed in Fort Sumter from any cause. Sergeant FAULKNER, and Privates CHAPLIN, MINNIX and PENN, Company B, were injured by a shower of bricks thrown from a traverse on the rampart by a large shot of the enemy. A drummer boy, AHRENS, was struck on the head by the explosion of a shell over the parade. A negro laborer was also wounded. All, we learn are doing well, and there is no danger of losing a life or a limb. The wounded were dressed by Surgeon MOORE, of the post, and sent out of the way to a hospital in the city, where they now remain.

The regimental ensign was pierced near the centre by a ball. The Confederate flag was also perforated.

THE BATTERIES OF SULLIVAN'S ISLAND.

FORT MOULTRIE opened the engagement. At three o'clock, the head of the grim procession of Monitors having come within reasonable range, the word was given, and the first shot of the battle went whizzing at the iron fleet. In a very few minutes the batteries of Sumter, with the earth works of Morris and Sullivan's Islands, were mingling their deep voices in the chorus of the fray. During the entire fight the batteries of Fort Moultrie maintained a well directed fire against the Monitor that happened to be nearest, and the frequency with which the Yankees turned from their main effort against Fort Sumter to give a spiteful shot to Fort Moultrie showed how effectively and accurately the men at the latter post were hurling their metal on the foe.

There was but one casualty at Fort Moultrie. A shot from one of the Monitors cut away the flag staff, a few feet above the parapet, and the staff fell upon Private LUSBY, Company F, 1st S. C. (regular) Infantry, inflicting injuries, from the effects of which he soon died.

The garrison of Fort Moultrie it would not be proper to enumerate. It consists of the First South Carolina (regular) Infantry. The commandant of the post is Colonel WM. BUTLER, of the same regiment, and the companies during the action were severally commanded by Captain T. A. HUGUENIN, Captain B. S. BURNET, Capt. CONSTANTINE RIVERS, First Lieut. E. A. ERWIN and Captain R. PRESTON SMITH—the last named officer having special charge of the mortar battery. The closest range into which the enemy ventured was estimated by the officers of the fort at about 1200 yards. The flagstaff has been replaced, and as no other portion of the fort sustained any damage whatever during the engagement, the post is in excellent condition to join in another trial of strength with the turreted armada.

BATTERY BEE, on Sullivan's Island, just opposite Fort Sumter, was commanded by Lieutenant Col. SIMKINS, of the 1st S. C. (regular) Infantry, and manned by companies of that Regiment. The Captains commanding the companies at this post engaged, were Captains ROBERT DETREVILLE, WARREN ADAMS, and W. T. TATUM. The battery was the recipient of occasional shots from the enemy, but was not in any way injured, nor were there any casualties amongst the men. During the fight Gen. RIPLEY was present at Battery Bee. Whenever the enemy may choose to renew the attack, if his object should be to dash into the harbor, Battery Bee will have a far more important part to play.

The BEAUREGARD BATTERY, with three of its guns, also took part in the general melee of heavy artillery, and twice received a broadside from the enemy. This battery, commanded by Captain J. A. SITGREAVES, 1st Regiment S. C. (regular) Artillery, is situated on the Sullivan's Island beach, northeast of Fort Moultrie, a little beyond the Moultrie House, and is manned from the 1st Regiment S. C. (regular) Artillery, 1st Lieutenant ERWIN commanding, and Co. B, 1st Regiment S. C. (regular) Infantry, Captain WARLEY commanding. The battery was in no respect damaged, although many of the Yankee round-shot fell upon the sand in the immediate neighborhood.

The forces on Sullivan's Island (which is a portion of the subdivision commanded by Brigadier-General TRAPIER) were under the immediate command of Colonel L. M. KEITT, of the 20th Regiment S. C. V. Both General TRAPIER and Colonel KEITT were on the Island at the time of the action, and during the firing were moving from battery to battery.

The New-York Times.

VOL. XII—NO. 3621. NEW-YORK, SUNDAY, MAY 3, 1863. PRICE FOUR CENTS.

FROM THE ARMY OF THE POTOMAC.

Details of Operations to Friday.

A Stirring and Significant Address from Gen. Hooker.

The Operations Thus Far Brilliantly Successful.

The Enemy's Defences of no Service to Him.

The Choice of Flight, or a Battle on Ground of General Hooker's Choosing.

The Fifth, Eleventh and Twelfth Corps Complimented.

A Brisk Artillery Duel on Thursday Below Fredericksburgh.

LITTLE DAMAGE DONE ON OUR SIDE.

A LIST OF CASUALTIES.

From Our Special Correspondent.

TWO MILES BELOW FREDERICKSBURGH, Thursday, April 30—11 o'clock A. M.

The following inspiring address is being read to the various troops, amid tremendous cheering and other demonstrations of delight:

HEADQUARTERS ARMY OF THE POTOMAC, NEAR FALMOUTH, VA., April 30, 1863.

It is with heartfelt satisfaction that the General Commanding announces to the army that the operations of the last three days have determined that our enemy must ingloriously fly, or come out from behind their defences and give us battle on our own ground, where certain destruction awaits him.

The operations of the Fifth, Eleventh and Twelfth Corps have been a series of splendid successes.

By command of Maj.-Gen. HOOKER.

S. WILLIAMS, Adjutant-General.

I learn from Gen. SEDGWICK's quarters that this success of the corps consists in the fact of their having succeeded in getting in the rear of the enemy's works. Heaven grant that it may be so, and give to us a glorious victory. The steady rain which set in yesterday afternoon and continued all night, served to dampen our ardor to some extent; but this announcement of the success on the right has changed the aspect of affairs, and I never have witnessed such enthusiasm and *elan* as prevails at this moment. Scattering over the plain, in every direction, can be seen regiment after regiment, cheering vociferously, and tossing their hats in the air, while the bands discourse national airs.

Brig.-Gen. PRATT, Commander of the "Light Division," whose resignation was accepted several days since, but who remained to participate in the coming fray, took his departure this morning, having been summoned home by urgent business.

The following is his farewell address

HEADQUARTERS LIGHT DIVISION, SIXTH CORPS, NEAR FALMOUTH, VA., April 30, 1863.

The General commanding the Light Division, announces to his troops that his connection with them has ceased. It is with the deepest regret that he parts with this command, and it is enhanced by the fact that the army is about to enter upon a brilliant campaign. Your experience, equipment, discipline and courage clearly indicate your future history, and he feels assured that no demand will ever be made upon your constancy, courage and patriotism, that will not be responded to. You were among the first troops in the field. The history of the Army of the Potomac is your history. You have participated in every battle save one in which this army has been engaged.

Your record is a proud one—your cause is just—it will succeed. I leave you only because circumstances render it imperative.

To that portion of the command whose term of service is about to expire, (Thirty-first New-York,) and with whom I have been more particularly identified from the commencement, I may be permitted to say a word.

Two years of active service in the field have made you *soldiers*—hence your services are most valuable to your country. I hope to see you as a regiment once again in the field, and shall take pride in watching your future course, as I have ever regarded you with pride and satisfaction in the past.

CALVIN E. PRATT, Brigadier-General.

Gen. PRATT left New-York as Colonel of the Thirty-first Regiment, in the month of June, 1861. He received a severe wound while gallantly leading his regiment forward, and was promoted to a Brigadiership on the 14th of September, 1862. Col. HIRAM BURNHAM, of the Sixth Maine, succeeds to the command of the division. Our skirmish line has advanced considerable distance this morning without opposition. The enemy's line, which last night rested along the Richmond Road, about half a mile from the Rappahannock, has, as far as I can judge from this side of the river, fallen back some distance. No firing has taken taken place as yet between the lines, though within rifle shot of each other.

Half-past Eleven O'Clock.—The balloon is just going up in the rear of Gen. ——'s quarters, which has attracted some of the soldiers, one of whom remarked: "That aint so big a thing as there is over on those heights." The clouds are breaking away, which will enable the balloon to make satisfactory observations. Rapid artillery firing has just opened on the extreme left. Owing to the mist we are not able to determine whether it is our own or the enemies.

The troops have had their shelter tents up since yesterday, which have protected them from the rain. The white tents of the enemy can be seen distinctly scattered along on the summit and side of the opposite range of hills. The smoke from their camp fires is also plainly visible, rising above the tops of the trees and floating away to the southward. The rebels have, thus far, maintained the same mysterious silence which characterized them during the hours preceding the battle in December. It may be their policy to reserve their fire until our forces are all across, and advanced to a point where they can open a cross fire upon them. Their heaviest guns at the last battle were located on the part of the hills immediately to the rear of Fredericksburgh. At the height of the engagement one 32-pounder opened a cross fire on our lines, but, wrote the London *Times* correspondent at the time, exploded on the third discharge. The trains have been kept running constantly on the Richmond road since we advanced here. Two engines with cars attached are just leaving from a point below as I write. It is the supposition that they are bringing up LONGSTREET's corps from below. The abandonment of the siege of Washington by this portion of the army was undoubtedly for the purpose of cooperating with the forces on the Rappahannock. A prisoner taken yesterday states that Gen. Stonewall JACKSON is in command—Gen. LEE being absent from some cause. This may or may not be true; as a general thing but little reliance can be placed upon the statements of rebel prisoners.

TWO MILES BELOW FREDERICKSBURGH, Thursday Evening, 9½ o'clock, April 30, 1863.

A severe artillery engagement has closed the operations of to-day on the left. In the afternoon casual shots were exchanged, when suddenly, at 5½ o'clock, a Whitworth gun threw a 12-pound shell with wonderful accuracy—it being planted four miles away, on the side of the crest opposite the river. Ten 10-pounders immediately followed, throwing their shell at our infantry, who were drawn up on the opposite bank of the Rappahannock. The force consisted mainly of regiments belonging to —— division, formerly commanded by Gen. ——. The first shell from the 10-pounders struck fairly in the gully where Gen. ——'s headquarters were located, but fortunately killed no one. The second fell directly into Co. K, Ninetieth Pennsylvania, seriously wounding six men. Their firing now became very rapid, and was replied to by Capt. TAFT's Parrots; Battery F, First Pennsylvania Reserve, Capt. RICKETS; Independent Pennsylvania Battery, Capt. THOMPSON and First New-Hampshire, Capt. EDGELL. The rebels had obtained their range at the former battle of Fredericksburgh, and threw shell from their 20-pound Parrots with the same accuracy which characterize the Whitworth. Our infantry were soon ordered to fall back for protection under the bank of the river, which they did quietly; the shell bursting all around them. About 6½ o'clock the firing became very hot on both sides, many of the rebel missiles ricocheting and struck in the vicinity of the —— Division Hospitals, located at the Fitzhue House, full two miles on this side, causing the ambulance to move, and many of the spectators to change their position. It was feared for a time that the Whitworth gun (a proof of British neutrality,) which annoyed us most would be turned upon the hospital, around which large crowds were congregated, but fortunately the rebels did not do so. The firing continued until 7½ o'clock, when it became too dark to distinguish objects, we throwing the last shell.

The following were the casualties on our side:

Lieut. A. C. Lindsey, Co. F, 136th Pennsylvania.
Capt. Bush, 13th Massachusetts—killed.
Lieut. Wm. Cordewell, Co. F, 13th Massachusetts, wounded in head—since dead.
George Beck, Co. K, 90th Pennsylvania—wounded.
Frank Fretchy, Co. K, 90th Pennsylvania—wounded.
Wm. G. Loyd, Co. K, 90th Pennsylvania—wounded.
Corp. S. Jackaway, Co. K, 90th Penn—wounded.
Samuel R. Miller, Co. K, 90th Penn—dying.
Thomas Critchet, Co. I, 12th Massachusetts.
John Duyer, Co. I, 104th New-York.
Corp. John Fay, Co. F, 13th Massachusetts.
Hugh Sterling, Co. F, 90th Pennsylvania.

Strange to relate, our batteries escaped unharmed through the terrific firing to which they were exposed. One Whitworth shell burst immediately under one of Capt. THOMSON's guns; another just missed the caisson in the rear.

Capt. RICKETS fired 49 shots; Capt. THOMSON fired 50; Capt. EDGELL fired 40, and Capt. TAFT about the same number.

For prudential reasons I omit to give the bore of these respective guns. Suffice it to say that they all fired with rapidity and accuracy.

It is believed by many that this attack by the enemy is to cover an evacuation to-night, owing to our success on the right. Firing is heard from that direction as I write. The air is mild and balmy to-night, and the troops in the best of spirits.

TWO MILES BELOW FREDERICKSBURGH, Friday Morning, May 1.

A heavy mist enshrouds us this morning, rendering it impossible to discover the position of the enemy. Yesterday afternoon they were extended in a long line of battle, on the identical ground occupied by them in December. With a glass they could be seen distinctly in the tree-tops and on the neighboring heights, watching our movements. No demonstrations have yet taken place, this morning,

D. W. J.

Correspondence of the Philadelphia Press.

AQUIA CREEK, Thursday, April 30.

On Monday night, our engineers made a selection for a point at which our pontoon bridges could be laid in safety, and the work of their construction was immediately commenced, and carried on without serious interruption. On Tuesday morning, two bridges were completed, and Gen. MEADE's army corps prepared to cross the river.

I am informed that the first regiment of the Union troops to cross the Rappahannock River on this occasion was the gallant 119th Pennsylvania Volunteers. Upon arriving on the south bank of the stream, they were at once deployed to the right and left through the wooded skirtings of farms to observe the movements of the enemy. In this advance the Colonel of the regiment received a second honorable wound, which it is said will not prove a serious one. Before night on Tuesday five pontoon bridges had been completed, and our entire army was crossing.

As our troops advanced, during yesterday, the rebels fell back, skirmishing with our advance guard. It was soon discovered that the enemy had withdrawn his main column from the line of the Rappahannock, and contrabands informed Gen. HOOKER positively, that there were no troops, in great force, anywhere in our front, for a distance of twenty miles south.

Falling back through the vale of the Matapony, the enemy destroyed the bridges over this stream and its tributaries, but did not appear disposed to dispute our continued advance very stoutly. During yesterday a large number of prisoners were captured, but they consist, for the most part, of men who could not keep up with their fellows in their retreat, and dropped along the roads and by-paths from sheer weakness.

I learn that Gen. HOOKER and staff crossed the river yesterday, and that to-day our troops are marching forward, driving the rebels back from every point as they proceed. There has been no heavy fighting yet, and no cannonade, except the firing of shells at the enemy occasionally, to discover his whereabouts.

Every one here seems delighted with the news from the advance, and predict a great and decisive victory for Gen. HOOKER and his excellent army. The Government officers are especially good-natured, and seem to think that the people will take this as another proof of the determination and ability of our rulers to push on rapidly toward Richmond.

It is reported that the City of Fredericksburgh was occupied yesterday with a strong garrison under the direction of Provost-Marshal-General PATRICK, and the railroad to Richmond is being rapidly repaired. It is also believed that Port Royal, on the Rappahannock, has been occupied by our troops, and will be used as a landing for stores.

It is not thought that Gen. HOOKER will advance much further south just at present. I will not say why, because it is unnecessary to allow the enemy to obtain any idea of our future movements. Communication with another corps of our army will be opened in a few days, when the real merits of the present grand movement will begin to develop themselves, and some discoveries may be made that will surprise the public considerably.

Thus far, fortune has certainly favored our arms in this movement. Our troops have been engaged in skirmishing all day, but no battle has taken place, and it is thought that our losses have been slight. We are entirely prepared for the enemy, and when the great battle is fought, we shall be the victors, especially if we are attacked by the enemy in the progress of our advance.

Gen. STONEMAN's light division has advanced to Culpepper. The railroad has been repaired, and Government trains are running to that point. The reports from this column are encouraging, and we hear nothing of the complaints of inefficiency in any particular, so common in other campaigns.

Some 1,500 rebels were captured yesterday, it is said, in the rifle pits beyond Fredericksburgh. About 300 have been sent to Washington for examination, as they desire to take the oath of allegiance to the Government of the United States.

ARRIVAL OF PRISONERS IN WASHINGTON.

WASHINGTON, Saturday, May 2.

Another detachment of prisoners have reached here. They number one hundred and forty-four, and include several commanding officers. Others are expected in the course of the day. The prisoners were all sent to the Old Capitol Prison. All of them were comfortably clothed, although their garments were coarse.

THE WAR IN WESTERN VIRGINIA.

Our Forces Under Gen. Mulligan Defeated at Fairmount.

His Loss Said to be 250 Men Taken Prisoners.

The Rebel Force Believed to be 12,000 Strong.

WHEELING THE POINT AIMED AT.

Extensive Damage to the Baltimore and Ohio Railroad.

The latest information from Western Virginia, up to Friday afternoon, received through private sources, is, that the Union forces under Gen. MULLIGAN were repulsed near Fairmount, and that the Baltimore and Ohio Railroad bridge at that point was entirely destroyed by the rebels.

A large force of rebels now occupy Morgantown.

The Baltimore and Ohio Railroad has suffered severely.

The bridge at Fairmount and Cheat River was blown up.

NEWS RECEIVED IN PHILADELPHIA.

PHILADELPHIA, Saturday, May 2.

Intelligence from Western Virginia has been received. All of Maj. SHEWALTER's command of the Sixth Virginia regiment—600 men and four pieces of artillery—arrived at Pittsburgh in a special train from Uniontown, *via* the Connellsville road, at 2 o'clock this morning. They left immediately for Wheeling by boats.

The military authorities seem convinced that Wheeling is the object of attack, and troops are being concentrated there.

The reports state that MULLIGAN lost 250 men taken prisoners, but escaped with his artillery.

The rebels at Fairmount are said to be 12,000 strong.

THE BALTIMORE AND OHIO RAILROAD.

BALTIMORE, Saturday, May 2.

We are now able to report positively that the crisis with the Baltimore and Ohio Railroad is past. The Confederates have all left it, moving southward, and our military forces, in great strength, are following and endeavoring to intercept them.

The extent of the injury done to the road is now known. The line is intact, from the Monongahela River, three hundred miles distant, to Baltimore. The damage to the main stem is confined to the large iron bridge, one mile east of Fairmount, and to five unimportant bridges within thirty miles west of it. Three bridges on the Parkersburgh branch, within twenty miles of Grafton, were also destroyed. The track is uninjured, except at these bridges.

The telegraph lines are all fully restored and in use. The bridges will all be renewed within five days—temporarily, but effectively.

It is expected that all the regular passenger trains will be resumed on Monday next, and the freight trains also. The passengers and freight will possibly have to be transferred, for two or three days, at the Monongahela bridge. It is thought that the Parkersburgh line can be put in full order by Tuesday or Wednesday next.

FIGHT AT GREENLAND GAP.

The following dispatch was received on Tuesday from Gen. KELLEY by Lieut.-Col. CHESEBOROUGH, of Gen. SCHENCK's Staff:

GREENLAND GAP, HARDING CO., VA., Tuesday, April 28, 1863.

To Lieut.-Col. Cheseborough, A. A. G.:

The affair at this place on Saturday was one of the most gallant since the opening of the war. Greenland Gap is a pass through the Knobley Mountain only wide enough for the road and a small mountain stream. This gap was guarded by Capt. WALLACE, (Twenty-third Illinois,) with a detachment of Company G, Twenty-third Illinois regiment and a small detachment of Company H, Thirteenth Virginia infantry, Capt. SMITH, in all between seventy and eighty men.

Capt. WALLACE occupied a large church at west end of and near the mouth of the gap and Capt. SMITH held a log house about a hundred yards distant, both position commanding the gap. JONES was compelled to capture or dislodge the little band before he could pass. His troops made three gallant charges, but were each time repulsed with great loss especially of officers. The fight commenced at 5 P. M., and lasted till after dark. The rebels, availing themselves of the darkness, approached and fired the church, but the gallant Irish boys would not even then surrender till the burning roof fell in. The killed and wounded of the rebels outnumbered our whole force engaged. Five of the officers out of eight commanding the leading battalion which made the first charge were either killed or wounded. Among the latter, Col. DULANY, commanding. Capt. WALLACE and SMITH had only two men killed and four wounded. I counted to-day eighteen dead horses within musket range. I most earnestly request the Major-General commanding to apply to the Secretary of War to have every officer, non-commissioned officer and private engaged in the fight presented with a medal, in recognition of the gallantry displayed.

[Signed,] B. F. KELLEY, Brig.-Gen.

Gen. SCHENCK has promptly recommended the participants in this gallant defence to the special attention of the Secretary of War.

More about the Rebel Raid—Movements of Imboden.

From the Wheeling Intelligencer, April 29.

Monday night, at a late hour, news reached here that a heavy force of rebel cavalry had occupied Morgantown, during the afternoon, and were believed to contemplate an advance on Wheeling. The intelligence was confined to a few, and while it occasioned great activity in some quarters, the city was comparatively quiet. The morning train, which came down from Washington, brought a confirmation of the news. Col. BOYERS, Deputy Marshal, who lives about two miles from Morgantown, had arrived there in the night. He reported that a cavalry force of 1,500 under IMBODEN had occupied Morgantown about 3 o'clock on the preceding afternoon. Their appearance was very sudden and unexpected. The Court, which was in session, had barely time to escape. Senator WILLEY got away. Col. BOYERS says their horses were very much jaded. It seems pretty certain that this force is the one, in part at least, that was at Oakland the day preceding, they having come across by Kingwood. They burned the bridge over Yough River, about a mile west of Oakland, also the station at Cranberry Summit.

Col. BOYERS had gone to Washington, under belief that he could telegraph from there, but upon finding himself mistaken in this, he proceeded at once to Pittsburgh to try to procure arms and aid.

Early in the day, yesterday, it was reported that the force at Morgantown had advanced to Waynesburgh, Penn., which is nearly equi-distant from Morgantown and this city. This looked like an advance on Wheeling. Not long after, communication was lost with Fairmount, and it was believed that place had fallen into rebel hands.

In the afternoon communication was again opened with Grafton. About two o'clock it was represented that the rebels, instead of going to Waynesburgh, had moved up from Morgantown and were approaching Fairmont; that a company of militia had been sent thither from Mannington, and that a part of MULLIGAN's force was moving in the same direction. Dispatches were received, stating that two or three bridges had been burned near Mannington by guerrillas from the surrounding country. Later in the evening communication was had with MULLIGAN at Grafton and WILKINSON at Clarksburgh. Col. WILKINSON expressed a good deal of incredulity at the news from this point.

Col. MULLIGAN said his position at Grafton was secure, and that he had sent force sufficient to make Fairmont safe, although it was threatened. Doubts were felt as to the genuineness of these dispatches, and some were inclined to believe that the rebels had possession of the line and were answering.

Late in the evening a lot of engines which had been lying at Cameron came in. Some of the citizens who came on them reported a great deal of excitement there, occasioned chiefly by reports from this city that the enemy were at Waynesburgh. They reported, however, that a bridge was burned this side of Burton, where a few cavalry were seen, about 20 miles east of Cameron.

Still later a dispatch was received from Pittsburgh, stating that a force of rebel cavalry had come into Uniontown, Fayette County, where they were tearing up the Pittsburgh and Connellsville Road. This is presumed to be the force from Morgantown, and, if true, it is difficult to reconcile it with the statement that Fairmont is threatened by the same force, as the two places are not very near together.

The indications at a late hour last night were that there was a good deal more scare than danger about the situation of affairs at Grafton and Fairmont. The operators at these two places got scared and packed up and left. That was why no communication could be had with those points—but the cause not being understood here it occasioned a good deal of anxiety. At 9 o'clock last night the operators here were conversing with these points. The fine bridge over the Monongahela was untouched. The bridges burned between here and Grafton are not important, and can soon be repaired.

We shall not be surprised if it turns out that there has been a good deal of unnecessary alarm.

STILL LATER.

At 10 o'clock a dispatch from Grafton announced that at 2 o'clock P. M. a rebel force estimated at 4,000 suddenly appeared at Newburgh, a station 13 miles east of Grafton, burnt the fine company shops there, and came down to Independence, a mile below, destroyed the bridge there over Three Forks, and disappeared in the direction of Morgantown. Whither they were really going was a matter of conjecture.

MOVEMENTS ON THE MONONGAHELA.

From the Wheeling Intelligencer, April 30.

The remainder of the cavalry scout which went out in the direction of Waynesburgh on Monday returned last evening. Three of their number proceeded to Poplar Spring, within four miles of Waynesburgh, when, learning that the rebels had not been there, they went over to Cameron, and returned thence to the city. From intelligent parties at Poplar Spring, they learned something of the capture of Morgantown, and the subsequent movements of the enemy. They were told that about four companies of militia were at Morgantown when the enemy came in, and undertook to defend the place. They took refuge in houses and fired from them, but the rebels shelled them out and set the houses on fire, and they were then gobbled up. Seven of them were killed. The rest were taken off in the direction of Dixie, as prisoners. The estimate of the force put it at four thousand, which is without doubt a great exaggeration.

The rebels proceeded from Morgantown to Uniontown, where they committed some depredations and returned by way of Blacksville towards Fairmont, passing within thirteen miles of Waynesburgh. There was a good deal of alarm at Waynesburgh, and the cashier of the bank there destroyed $60,000 of the bank's issue, for fear of its falling into their hands.

This, in view of the fact that the rebels now occupy Fairmont, gives us a tolerably intelligent idea of the movements of this force.

It is claimed that they have artillery, but if so it must be very light to be moved with such facility.

AN IMPORTANT BRIDGE DESTROYED.

About 11 o'clock last night, we learned from official sources that dispatches had been received, announcing that the rebels at Fairmont had attacked Col. MULLIGAN's forces, which, together with 17 companies of militia, were guarding the splendid iron bridge across the Monongahela, a mile east of that place, had beaten them off and destroyed the bridge. It was also believed they had captured the artillery which Col. MULLIGAN had planted to defend it.

THE NORTHWESTERN VIRGINIA RAILROAD THREATENED.

At 1 o'clock yesterday morning, dispatches were received by the authorities here, from Col. WILKINSON, at Clarksburgh, stating that a force of guerrillas (infantry) were approaching Weston from the direction of Sutton. They were led by WM. L. JACKSON, formerly a Judge at Parkersburgh. There was another force west of there, said to be under command of IMBODEN. [Query: How can IMBODEN be in so many places, at such great distances apart, at the same time?] Col. WILKINSON was of opinion that these forces were heading toward West Union, the capital of Doddridge County, with a view of destroying the railroad bridge there, over the Middle Island River. If they succeeded in this, he thought they might then drift down in the direction of Clarksburgh.

FROM HAVANA.

Later Intelligence from Mexico.

French Confessions of Bloody Work at Puebla.

MOVEMENTS OF BLOCKADE RUNNERS.

HAVANA, Monday, April 27.

The reports which I sent you in my last letter, in regard to affairs in the Mexican Republic, have not been confirmed by the French steamer *Louisiana*, which arrived at Santiago de Cuba on the 22d inst.

The *Prensa*, of this city, published on the 22th inst. the following:

"We have just received a telegraphic dispatch by way of Puerto Principe, dated the 24th inst., at 5:55 P. M., in which we are told the *Louisiana* has arrived from Vera Cruz, with dates to the 16th inst. The battle at Puebla was becoming very bloody, and the losses on both sides were heavy."

The rebel steamer *Nita* left on the 25th inst., but returned on the 26th.

The English steamer *Labuan*, from Matamoras for Liverpool, with cotton, put in here on the 24th inst., for provisions.

12. M.—A rebel steamer is just coming in. She is supposed to be the *Eugenia*, loaded with cotton.

THE LOSS OF THE ANGLO-SAXON.

ST. JOHN, N. F., April 30, *via* PORT HOOD, May 2.

The following is the Purser's list of the cabin passengers lost on the *Anglo-Saxon*:

Capt. Stoddert, Miss Arkwright,
Miss Malley, Alice Wilson,
Mr. Fisher, Mr. Pemberton,
Mr. Scott, Mr. Mills,
Mr. Haughton, Mr. Rogers,
Mr. Christian and child, Mr. James and child,
Lieut. Clark, and two persons unknown.

It is reported from Cape Race that twenty-five bodies have been recovered and buried.

FROM SAN FRANCISCO.

Terrible Steamboat Disaster—Forty Persons Killed—Twenty Wounded.

SAN FRANCISCO, Friday, May 1.

The small steamer *Ada Hancock*, employed in carrying passengers from the wharf at San Pedro to the steamer *Senator*, which anchors in deep water, five miles from the landing, exploded her boiler on the 27th of April, killing forty out of sixty passengers and wounding all the balance, with the exception of seven.

Among the killed are the following; Capt. Seelay, Wm. T. B. Sanford, Fred. Keerlin, a son of the late Albert Sidney Johnston, Dr. H. M. Myles, Wm. P. Ritchie, Hiram Kimball, the Mormon missionary; Capt. Joseph Bryant.

The markets generally are dull. There is a speculative movement in bagging, and the concentration of the stock has caused an advance of 20 per cent.

Atlantic Currency Exchange is at the rate of 33 to 40 per cent. premium for gold, on New-York.

Sterling Exchange is unchanged.

Legal Tender Notes sell at 64@66.

Special despatch to the Merchants' Exchange and News Room.

SAN FRANCISCO, Saturday, May 2.

The steamship *Constitution*, Capt. WATKINS, sailed this forenoon at ten o'clock for Panama. She takes 700 passengers and $730,000 in treasure for England, and 250,000 for New-York.

[The above dispatch came through in one hour.]

FROM NEW-ORLEANS.

ARRIVAL OF THE CREOLE.

The Reported Successes of Gen. Banks Confirmed.

Washington and Opelousas in His Possession.

Capitulation of the Rebel Fortifications at Butte la Rose.

The steamer *Creole* has arrived here with New-Orleans dates of the 23d and Havana of the 27th of April.

There is no later news from Gen. BANKS, except that on the 21st of April he occupied Opelousas and Washington, and that the column was resting for the day at the latter place.

The want of horses for cavalry was being supplied from the country round about. Seven hundred horses had been brought into Opelousas.

The brig *St. Mary*, at New-Orleans, reports, "April 8, off Passa l'Outre, was followed into shoal water by a schooner having the appearance of, and supposed to be a pilot-boat, and got ashore. The schooner then kept away."

A correspondent of the *Era*, writing from Brashear City under date of the 20th of April, states that the plantations in the neighborhood of Bayou Lafourche were all submerged. The levee had broken down near Thibodeauxville, and the water was rushing furiously over the whole vicinity. The flood was doing great damage at the railroad. It was fast undermining the sluice-ways, walls and the stringers, flowing over the track, rendering it dangerous for trains to travel over it.

The same correspondent states that the Confederate fort at Butte a la Rose, on the Atchafalaya, sixty miles north of Brashear City, capitulated on the morning of the 20th of April.

A Crevasse—The Capture of Butte a la Rose.

Correspondence of the Era.

BRASHEAR CITY, April 20, 1863.

Yesterday I returned once more to this military depot, which circumstances have rendered quite important.

As the regular passenger train crossed Bayou Lafourche, I noticed that the neighboring farm-yards were all afloat. Upon inquiry I found that the levee had broken down near Thibodauxville, and a great flood of water from this high banked bayou was rushing furiously over the whole vicinity. In some instances the water had reached the lower floors of the houses, and hens and pigs were swimming wildly about, while small boys perched on planks and logs were paddling around to collect the scattering property. At the railroad the flood was doing great damage. It was fast undermining the sluice-ways, walls, and the stringers, flowing over the track, rendering great caution necessary in passing the trains over it. It may interrupt the trains for a day or two.

Still the ball is moving. Every day brings tidings of a new victory by our advancing hosts. The rebels are giving up all hope of holding this portion of the State, so that each contest with them results in easy triumph. The capitulation of the rebel fort at Butte a la Rose, or Rosy Hill, this morning, is a fair proof of the last remark. This place is on the Atchafalaya river, sixty miles north of Brashear City, and commanding the river. It is now almost an island, a wet swamp lying where the river does not surround it. Even the inside of the fort has a flooring of thick mud. The prisoners taken there were really delighted to leave what one of them termed the "last hole of hell." The same person remarked that we captured about four thousand musquitoes to every square inch when we took the place, besides an indefinite quantity of fleas and mud. A man died there recently by the measles, the Surgeon said, but the men swear that it was by musquito bites. At a late hour in the forenoon, the gunboats *Clifton*, *Calhoun*, *Arizona* and *Estrella* reached this place. Coming within range, a shot was fired at the boats from the fort. The boats replied, and after one more shot had been fired from the *Mary T.*, lying near by, and another from the fort, down went the banner of stars and bars that had floated over the enemy's works. The *Mary T.* at once steamed off, pursued by the *Clifton* and *Arizona*. From the other boats a landing was made, and the fort was at once surrendered.

By taking this place we secured over a hundred rounds of artillery ammunition, several hundred pounds of powder, a number of small arms, one 32-pound cannon, and one 24-pounder, and 56 prisoners.

Opelousas and Washington Occupied.

From the Picayune, April 23.

We understand advices have been received in this City, dated at Opelousas, Tuesday, that Gen. BANKS, on that day, occupied Opelousas and Washington, and that the column was resting for the day at the latter place.

It is stated that the want felt by the advancing column for an increase of the cavalry force has been supplied from the region round about; and that as many as seven hundred horses had been brought into Opelousas.

The Result of Gen. Banks' Operations.

The New-Orleans *Picayune* has a long review of Gen. BANKS' operations in the Teche Country, which concludes thus:

"The force of the Confederates is not certainly ascertained. Gen. TAYLOR is known to have been in command, with at least three brigades, among them those of Gens. SIBLEY and MORTON. They were known to have had reserves at New-Iberia and at St. Martinsville and Opelousas. Yet they do not appear to have been thrown forward to the assistance of their main body. It has been said that Gen. MAGRUDER was marching from Texas upon New-Iberia with a large force, but they cannot have arrived, for the retreat was continued through that place in as hurried a manner as when it first commenced near Centreville. The Confederate force, with the reserves included, has been reported as high as 25,000 men, but this can hardly be the case under existing circumstances, for with that force they would certainly have at least attempted to hold the army of Gen. BANKS in check by a strong rear guard, until their main body could have reached a point where a stand could have been made.

As soon as the Federal army reached New-Iberia, a force was sent to take possession of the celebrated salt works. The possession of these alone is of great importance, and a severe blow to the Confederates, for they were the source that supplied, in a great measure, the want of that necessary article in this section of the country. How far Gen. BANKS will continue his advance remains to be seen. He was reported day before yesterday at Opelousas, having met with opposition only at Vermillionville. His march has been exceedingly rapid, and his blows have been struck with great vigor and well followed up. He has, in a campaign of one week, possessed himself of one of the richest countries in the whole South, a country that will yield an immense amount of produce, and an admirable one for keeping his army during the warm months of the coming Summer. To dispossess him will require greatly augmented forces and vastly superior Generalship to what the Confederates have recently had in that country; for at New-Iberia it is but a short distance from the sea-marsh on one side to the bayous on the other. Thus are both his flanks protected, and he can intrench and fortify in a manner to effectually resist a greatly superior force that may be brought against him.

It is also said that Bute la Rose has fallen before the Federal advance. This is very possible, for a panic once created in an army, and there is no telling where it is to stop. Gibraltars sometimes fall through this cause, when a handful of determined men could have held them against an army of thousands. The influence of this short campaign of Gen. BANKS will be felt far and wide; it will be most cheering to the people of the North, and directly the opposite, of course, to the people of the South; and if the operations, commenced so vigorously, are followed up in the same manner, they will be of more importance than any attempted during the present war. It is undoubtedly a heavy blow against Port Hudson—heavier, indeed, than if it had been struck directly against that strongly fortified position, for it is aimed at the great depot of supplies;—cut these off and there is no telling what the result will be. With Admiral FARRAGUT at the mouth of Red River, and a powerful army in Western Louisiana, the great highway to Texas is closed, and will remain so long as they have the ability to maintain their positions. To sum up the entire affair, it is safe to say that it has been a most disastrous ten days for the Confederates in this section of the country, and most fortunate for the forces of the United States.

The events of the next month in this State will be most interesting as well as exciting, for it will be determined in that time which party is to hold possession of this State during the next few months. That part now in possession of the United States forces gives them almost the entire control of the Louisiana seaboard, there is nothing left of it worth having, and an army at New-Iberia is as near its base of supplies as if it were at New-Orleans.

"Such a brief outline of what has been accomplished in a few days' time by activity and energy. The navy has also done its share and accomplished the destruction of vessels that might have made an entire change in the present aspect of affairs, and turned a great victory into a most disastrous defeat. It has been a movement the success or defeat of which hung upon a chance, this time the chance was with the forces of the United States, and they have followed up the advantage gained in a manner that reflects upon them the highest credit an army or navy can obtain.

Capture of the Steamer Fox by the Rebels.

ANOTHER STORY—TREACHERY OF THE CAPTAIN.

From the New-Orleans Era, April 20.

About a week ago, the towboat *Fox*, Capt. WALKER, was sent by Capt. SHIPLEY down to the Southwest Pass with orders to assist the steamship *Fulton* off the bar. It has since transpired that the Captain, instead of going to Southwest Pass, as directed, went down to Pass-a-l'Outre, and the next we hear of him and his boat, they have been captured by a Capt. ANDERSON, who seems to have been conveniently near the Pass-a-l'Outre bar, with a small boat full of men. The circumstance looks very suspicious on the part of Capt. WALKER, and we have little doubt that he has been guilty of an act of treachery. It is thought there were a number of passengers on board the *Fox*.

The *Fox* was a very useful towboat, and was captured from the rebels some time last May, in one of the bayous near the Gulf. She was loaded with cotton at the time of her capture by our fleet, and it was thought she was preparing to run the blockade. She has been very serviceable in towing ships to and from the bar since she was taken, but has latterly been in the employ of the Government.

This WALKER was Captain of the *Lewis Whiteman* at the time of the collision, and was subsequently brought before the Military Commission to answer some very grave charges in connection with that disaster. The trial was interrupted by a change in the officers of this Department. WALKER was released on bail, and finally intrusted with the command of the *Fox*. He has not disappointed any one who knew him by taking the steamer into Mobile.

In a subsequent issue the *Era* says:

"WALKER stood before this community charged with an enormous crime—that of wilfully sinking the *Lewis Whiteman*, with a large number of our dead and wounded from the battle-field of Baton Rouge on board. Instead of being kept in confinement until he could be convicted or acquitted, we find him out on bail, and soon in command of a boat in the Government employ. Of course he acted according to his treacherous impulses, and betrayed the trust.

They are competent steamboat-men, of known loyalty, who might, we presume, be employed to command river steamers, without taking such men. And while we are on this subject, we may as well allude to another little matter of a similar nature. In our correspondence from Brashear City, published on the 19th, it is said that after the capture of the steamer *Cornie*, the engineer, THOMAS HARKINS, and the pilot, CHARLES SIMMONS, still retained their situations on board. These two men are represented to us to be notorious and original secessionists, and if they are kept in their responsible positions on the *Cornie*, we shall expect shortly to hear that she has been either blown up or smashed up by coming in collision with another boat or a snag. It is possible that these officers on the *Cornie* have been superseded by others of known loyalty before this; but, if not, they should be, and that at once."

An Exciting Scene in the Varieties Theatre.

From the Picayune April 23.

Last night was the occasion of a complimentary benefit to Mr. GEORGE RYER, one of the leading actors of the company. The play announced was "Richelieu," and there was a very fair house. The dress circle and parquette were filled, and the galleries presented nearly the usual audience. The first act, which, by the way, was played very well, terminated with the fall of the drop scene, when, as if by a concerted movement, from various parts of the house loud cries were raised for "Hail Columbia." These cries, at first imperfectly understood by the majority of the audience, who supposed that the beneficiary was called to appear before the curtain, became sufficiently evident when the call was more distinctly made—"Play Hail Columbia."

The orchestra had not yet appeared, and, the noise and confusion increasing, several ladies and those accompanying them left, or attempted to leave the house. A person then stood up in the parquette and stated generally that the citizens had liberally patronized the theatre during the season, and they had a right to call for the national airs. The manager then appeared on the stage, and we understood Mr. BAKER to say that he could not comply with the request of those who called for "Hail Columbia," from the fact that not four weeks since he had been instructed not to play national or airs having a political tendency. "It's a lie," was shouted out in various parts of the house. Mr. IVES, who holds a position in the acting Mayor's office, and who was in one of the private boxes, stepped upon the stage and apparently corroborated the statement of Mr. BAKER. In the almost indescribable din and confusion, his answers to one or two questions from the house were clearly discernible. Thus: "Do you mean to say that the military authorities will not allow the national airs to be played in this theatre?" Mr. IVES: "I do." "As a representative of the acting Mayor," (who is absent from the city,) "do you say that you will not allow 'Hail Columbia' to be played by the orchestra?" "I will not."

More confusion—one man "put out" amidst much screaming of ladies, and loud calls for the air. Messrs. BAKER, IVES and BOWERS in vain attempted to say something to the audience, and finally the manager seemed to signify to the leader of the orchestra that the air might be played.

At all events it was played. The house, much thinned by absentees, subsided to comparative quiet, and the play proceeded and was finished, we believe, without further demonstration or interruption.

Prisoners Taking the Oath of Allegiance.

From the Era, April 23.

We shall publish on Friday morning, 24th inst., a list of such of the prisoners of Louisiana regiments, captured mostly in Mississippi, Tennessee and Louisiana, and confined in the Gratiot-street prison, at St. Louis, as have been released on taking the oath of renunciation and allegiance. The men who have thus thrown off the yoke of JEFF. DAVIS & Co., and gone back to their proper allegiance, are mainly from the Thirteenth, Sixteenth, Twentieth and Twenty-first regiments. These regiments were largely recruited in this city.

Killed.

From the Picayune, April 22.

We learn that Col. JAMES REILY was killed on the second day of the battle on the Teche. He was the senior Colonel, and in command of SIBLEY's brigade; was a brother-in-law to Hon. L. D. CAMPBELL, of Camp Chase, Ohio, and by marriage a nephew of HENRY CLAY, of Kentucky—a gallant and brave officer. In his death the Confederates have suffered a great loss. His wife and daughter accompanied the troops from the commencement of the war to the time of his death, and have since retreated with the forces.

Chased by a Privateer.

From the Picayune, April 23.

Capt. DUNHAM, of the brig *St. Mary*, on the 16th March, off Tortugas, was spoken by brig *Emily Fisher*, from Fortune Island, W. I., bound to Boston with a cargo of salt, who reported having been chased and run ashore by a privateer on Inagua, and was compelled to throw overboard the cargo to get the vessel off.

Arrival of Gen. Ullman and His Brigade.

From the Era, April 22.

Gen. ULLMAN, having completed the preliminary organization of his brigade, left New-York on the 10th, in the steamer *Matanzas*, with the officers of his command, and arrived here on Monday.

Custom-House Regulations.

CUSTOM-HOUSE, NEW-ORLEANS, April 23, 1863.

The permits heretofore granted to parties having business with the internal trade of the State have, in many instances, been so greatly abused by the trader, sutler and military subordinates, that I have determined to refuse all applicants who do not comply with the following rules:

First—All requests for permits must be made in writing, inclosed in an envelop, giving the name of the shipper and consignee, with the precise destination.

Second—No sutler's request will be recognized unless indorsed by the commanding officer of his station, and that indorsement made upon the face of the order or memorandum of articles required.

It is my desire that the system of blackmail and monopoly of business by sutlers and their associates, which are so prevalent, should be abolished.

CUTHBERT BULLITT,
Special Agent of the Treasury Department and Acting Collector of Customs.

Sailing of the Jura.

PORTLAND, Me., Saturday, May 2.

The steamship *Jura* sailed at 4 o'clock for St. John, Londonderry and Liverpool.

The New-York Times.

VOL. XII—NO. 3623. NEW-YORK, TUESDAY, MAY 5, 1863. PRICE THREE CENTS.

FROM THE ARMY OF THE POTOMAC

Details of the Important Operations to Sunday Night.

Letters from Our Special Correspondents.

Terrible Battles Fought on Saturday and Sunday at Chancellorsville.

Unsuccessful Attempt of Stonewall Jackson to Turn General Hooker's Right.

A Terrific and Successful Night Attack upon the Enemy.

A Fierce Battle of Six Hours' Duration on Sunday.

A FAIR STAND-UP FIGHT.

The Results in Our Favor, but Undecisive.

THE OPERATIONS AT FREDERICKSBURGH.

The Two Ridges Behind the City in Our Possession.

OUR FORCES ADVANCED FOUR MILES

About Four Thousand Prisoners Captured

TERRIBLE LOSSES OF THE ENEMY.

Chancellorsville, Va., Ten Miles West by South of Fredericksburgh, Saturday, Midnight, May 2, 1863.

I.

The military operations which have been in progress on the line of the Rappahannock for a week past, have to-day culminated in what, if not precisely a great battle, only escapes that designation because we all feel that greater, by far, remains behind.

Gen. Hooker, by a series of brilliantly audacious manœuvres and movements, of a celerity wholly unmatched in this war, has succeeded in crossing the Rappahannock River, and gaining for his army a position ten miles west by south, and in the rear of Fredericksburgh.

Gen. Lee, at first completely surprised by this move, and utterly puzzled as to his antagonist's intentions, has, however, had time to recover himself, and with a hand almost equally bold in the grand game of strategy—abandoning his position in Fredericksburgh, and the line of twenty miles down the Rappahannock which he has held for months—has changed his front, and stands opposite us in the horrid gage of battle.

We have secured a strong position, *completely turning the line of rebel defensive heights in the rear of Fredericksburgh*, against which our army on the 13th of last December madly dashed itself. This, as Gen. Hooker expresses it in his inspiriting order of Thursday, gives us the advantage of compelling the enemy to fight us on ground of our own choosing.

Figure to yourself a huge triangle or redan, one leg of three miles long, resting on the south side of the Rappahannock, above Fredericksburgh, and between Banks and United States Ford, and the other on Hunting Creek, an affluent of the Rappahannock, with the apex at Chancellorsville, and you have, in epitome, the situation as it now stands. This position, naturally strong, has been rendered doubly stronger by breastworks and abattis thrown up in front to cover the troops.

Imagine, now, the enemy massed in front of this position—front to front, and flank to flank—and you have the rebel situation. Take into account, also, that the enemy have strengthened themselves by the same appliances adopted by us.

These relative positions were assumed three days ago, and the history of that period is that of skirmishing along the advance line, developed in front of both armies—we feeling the enemy at various points, the enemy feeling us at various points.

This afternoon and evening, however, the enemy was emboldened to depart from these minor operations, and make a bold *coup*, by attacking our right flank in force, and attempting to double us up. About 6 o'clock this evening, Jackson—you will recognize as I go on the operations and all its circumstances as one quite in his style, and the affair will recall to you Cedar Mountain and other memories—with his whole corps of forty thousand men, threw himself impetuously on our extreme right, formed by the Eleventh Army corps, under command of Major-Gen. Howard. The assault was one marked by all the dash and audacity that characterize his mind, and as it was made precisely at our weakest point, and on a corps which Jackson has already several times beaten, it was well calculated to succeed.

That he only *partially* succeeded in turning our flank was not owing to the conduct of the Eleventh Army Corps, which was disgraceful, but to the superb generalship of Hooker, who promptly threw reinforcements on our right to stop the enemy's advance. Such changes in our position as circumstances dictated are to-night being made—I must not at present mention what they are—and there is little prospect that the enemy will succeed in his purpose of either breaking our line or cutting our communications, while a vigorous offensive will probably in a few hours be assumed. The rebels will do one of two things: either abandon their position here and seek to make good their retreat to Gordonsville—the only line now left them, as Fredericksburgh has been abandoned, and their line of communication with Richmond *is in all probability by this time cut*—or they will remain here and give us battle.

It is, of course, impossible for me to predict which alternative Gen. Lee will adopt; but a few hours will develop; and if the hopes of our leaders and our own do not prove deceptive, you may expect soon to hear of the greatest victory of the war.

To make the battle of to-day intelligible in all its relations, it is absolutely necessary that I should take a brief retrospect of the operations of the entire week. You have already received from your correspondents current accounts of events as they have transpired; but as it was inevitable that these should be written without a full appreciation of the meaning and relations of the movements and manœuvres, it will be necessary to go back and trace the development of the situation from the start. Let me add that owing to the accumulation of material, I must abandon all hope of entering into a *descriptive* account, as my note-book would fill several pages of the Times, and must, to the sacrifice of artistic effect, treat it purely in its military relations.

II.

It is Monday morning, (April 27,) and the army is all in motion. The vast area it covers of miles and miles in extent is an animated scene of bustle and stir. The camps are "broken," and the comfortable log huts and Winter-quarters, in which the men have been lodged for months, are abandoned. Columns of troops are moving on this road and that, and on a dozen different roads—carefully concealing themselves from the enemy's view by marching through the woods and behind the knolls and ridges of the broken ground along the Rappahannock. Long trains of artillery, pack mules and ambulances add their own features of the imposing and the picturesque to the scene.

The movement would many days ago have been inaugurated but for these fickle April skies, which have left but brief intermissions of fine weather, and during the rest of the time have been deluging the country with rain, and ruining these treacherous Virginia roads. At length, however, operations are actually begun, and a new life and vivacity stir the men.

The army, in all its aspects, material and moral, is in splendid condition.

The army is larger than it was ever before materially. The health of the troops is better than it ever was before. From the first day Gen. Hooker took command, it was felt that a directing brain animated the mass. *Mens agitat molem.* Great mobility has been secured by prodigiously cutting down the amount of transportation, and by employing pack mules, which go anywhere in all weathers, instead of our heavy wagons, which are always stuck in the mud. But two wagons are allowed to a regiment. The army is no longer encumbered with that ponderous impediment which used to be the marvel of all who beheld it. In fact, we now approximate the French standard, which enables an army to carry fourteen days' provisions without a wheel behind it.

The moral transformation is not less complete. It may be in the recollection of some of your readers that I had occasion two months ago to give a minute dissection of the condition of the Army of the Potomac as it was at the time of the last bungling campaign on the Rappahannock. I was accordingly much interested, after an absence of a couple of months, to make a comparative study of the internal change that had come over it in the interval under the new military *régime*. The metamorphosis could hardly have been more complete, and I have often had difficulty in convincing myself that that army, where general croaking, jealousies, disaffection, desertion and universal demoralization prevailed, is the same with this in which a new vitality animates the men, system, harmony and organization are seen, and a true military spirit pervades the troops.

Nothing in this line of phenomena struck me more than the admirable secresy that existed in regard to the proposed plan and movements of the opening campaign. It was a new and somewhat tantalizing sensation; for any one who has followed the movements of the army in the field will bear me out when I say, that hitherto projected operations have always been known and discussed by nearly everybody—even the negro servants in the camps—for days and weeks before they took place. In this case absolute ignorance prevailed. Not even the corps commanders knew what was intended, and had only their specific individual order for the day.

Accordingly, early in the week every one was rubbing his eyes, and asking where is the army? No one could tell. Here was a column moving up, another moving down, and the column that was up yesterday proves to be down to-day. I confess I was heartily glad of the general bewilderment, though it was rather puzzling for a correspondent to observe movements along a line twenty-five or thirty miles in length. In this case, it was the spectators of the great game of chess that were blindfolded. The master player alone had his eyes open.

In the great game of war, time and space are the elements with which the General has to deal. Celerity (and for that purpose the greatest possible *mobility*) with secresy are the indispensable conditions of all military combinations. The mind of Gen. Hooker is one that will put forth all the resources of these elements.

By Tuesday morning, however, an acute eye might begin to take in a rough outline of a plan from the dispositions then made of the troops. Three of the seven *corps d'armée* composing the Army of the Potomac—namely, the First Corps, (Maj.-Gen. Reynolds,) the Third Corps, (Maj.-Gen. Sickles,) and the Sixth Corps, (Maj.-Gen. Sedgwick,) had been moved from their camps the night before and had taken up their positions at the same point of the Rappahannock where Gen. Franklin had his crossing at the time of the battle of Fredericksburgh—namely, two miles below that city—and covered from the enemy's view by the curtain of hills that fringe the Rappahannock. While these movements are going on, other columns, consisting of the corps of Gen. Meade, (the Fifth,) and Gen. Slocum, (the Twelfth,) are moving on different roads, and have taken up positions up the Rappahannock, in the neighborhood of Banks' and United States fords, which are respectively eight and eleven miles above Fredericksburgh, and are, it will be remembered, the places selected by Gen. Burnside for his crossing on the occasion of the mud campaign.

These circumstances made it probable that operations would be inaugurated at both points, though it still left one entirely doubtful as to *where* the main attack would be, whether below or above, and the more so, as—albeit the general disposition of the troops was as indicated—Gen. Hooker still held the balance of power in his hand, ready to throw large reinforcements either up or down. It was fair to suppose, however, that the operations at one point would be merely of the nature of a demonstration, while the real attack would be made at the other. The points being fifteen miles apart, and out of supporting distance, it was not to be presumed that he would thus divide his army, and give the rebel commander (who held the centre position on the *chord*, while we occupied the *arc*,) this opportunity of falling upon and beating us in detail.

Before dawn of Tuesday the pontoon boats had been taken from the wagons, a couple of miles below Fredericksburgh, and under cover of a very heavy fog, were carried noiselessly down on men's shoulders to the river's brink and deposited in the water. They were immediately manned by the troops of Russell's brigade, (Brookes' division, Sixth Army corps,) and rapidly pushed over, in the manner taught us by Gen. Hunt at the time of the crossing in December. The rebels here, as at every ford for forty miles up and down the river, were posted along the river's margin in double lines of rifle pits, containing, perhaps, a couple of hundred men each. At the lower crossings, however, they made but a feeble resistance, and in a few moments our men were in possession of both lines of rifle pits, with the loss of half a dozen men. Indeed, a rebel Lieutenant captured here, a disingenuous young man, told us that they had been expressly instructed not to offer very serious resistance. This being accomplished, the whole of Brookes' division was passed over the three pontoon bridges which were immediately constructed under charge of Chief-Engineer Benham, to hold the position and the bridge-head.

A mile and a half below the position of Gen. Sedgwick's bridges, at an estate called Southfield, Reynolds' command was also instructed to effect a crossing. In doing this, however, they were not quite so lucky as those above them. Daylight had come while the engineers were still endeavoring to get the pontoon boats down to the water, but the fire from the rebel sharpshooters, who were placed in rifle-pits which had been thrown up opposite them, also succeeded in delaying operations so much, that it was 10 o'clock in the forenoon before they could be got into the water. To silence the fire of the sharpshooters, Col. Warner, commanding artillery on the extreme left, under the able Chief of Artillery, Gen. Hunt, brought forty guns to bear upon them. This completely "corraled" them, for they were afraid of leaving their pits and exposing themselves to the murderous fire of the artillery. This detained them until a force was able to push over in boats, when, charging up the hill, they captured all the men in the first row of rifle-pits, numbering about one hundred and fifty. Immediately after the crossing of this force, a couple of pontoon bridges were built, and Gen. Wadsworth's division of Reynolds' corps was thrown over. Gen. Wadsworth himself, however, did not wait for the completion of the bridges, but while his men were crossing in the open boats, plunged in on horseback and swam his horse over to the other side.

Thus far, it is to be noticed that but *one* division of each of the two army corps had been sent across the river—the remaining *four* divisions stayed on the other side. But they were not idle. They were put in motion on the hill-slope on one side of the river, and in plain view of the enemy were marched along the crest of the ridge and down, as though to the crossing. But, instead of crossing, they were quietly drawn up *back* through a gully, round the rear of the ridge, and round again on its top. They made the appearance of an army of at least a hundred thousand men, and must have presented the appearance of a *massing* on our side, preparatory to a passage of the river under cover of the night. The same "circusing" was performed by the artillery, the same by the wagon trains.

Was this a *ruse de guerre?* It could hardly be anything else—and yet to any one but a careful observer, even on *our* side, the deception could not have been detected.

The effect on the rebels was prompt. Two hours afterward their columns began moving up the Bowling-green road from down the river. Here a considerable force, including the whole of Jackson's corps—first, Trimble's brigade, down opposite Port Royal, then coming up successively, A. P. Hill's brigade, D. H. Hill's division, and Ealy's brigade—had been posted as a corps of observation. The Bowling-green road is at this point a sunken road; but we soon began to detect at various points the rebel column moving up—we were removed say a couple of miles—the bayonets glistening in the sun.

Were the same plains that witnessed the savage fight last December to see a renewal of it to-day? There was certainly every appearance of it. Our main force was massed here; a hundred and fifty guns were in position on the heights on our side, and the two divisions across the river were busily engaged strengthening the rebel rifle pits now occupied by them.

In the afternoon I passed over to the old battle-ground. It was now covered with a beautiful carpet of green; while the brilliant peach and hawthorn blossoms scented the air and delighted the eye. It is a superb plain for a review—several miles in length and one and a half in width—where *both* armies of the Potomac might march and countermarch; but a horrid place for a battle. At the rear of the plain the ridges rise, forming a perfect amphitheatre of hills around, thickly studded with rebel batteries, affording a hideous converging and enfilading fire on any troops attempting to pass across it. In the mind's eye one might see that battle raging and its fierce antagonisms painted on a cartoon of air.

History, it is said, repeats itself; but I knew too well Gen. Hooker's ideas on throwing troops against fortifications, when the resources of strategy enable one to circumvent them, to think for a moment that he would repeat that horrid episode. Maugre all the array, therefore, I firmly held to the impression that this was, after all, but a demonstration, and that the hot work would be elsewhere.

Passing up the river we have fresh confirmation of this. During Sunday and Monday, Howard's corps, (the Eleventh,) Slocum's corps, (the Twelfth,) and Gen. Meade's, (the Fifth,) had been moving to the upper fords of the Rappahannock. On the night of Tuesday, between 10 P. M. and 2 A. M., Howard's entire corps crossed the Rappahannock on the pontoon bridge at Kelly's Ford, twenty-seven miles above Falmouth. At day-light Gen. Slocum's corps followed, and during the forenoon Gen. Meade's corps was thrown across.

This movable column then struck direct for Germania Ford on the Rapidan River, distant twelve miles, one of the main affluents of the Rappahannock, into which it empties at United States Ford. Gen. Meade, however, instead of taking this direction on passing the river, struck a road diverging eastward, and made Ely's Ford on the Rapidan, eight miles nearer than Germania Ford, to the *embouchure* of that stream into the Rappahannock. At Germania Ford, a force of about a hundred and fifty rebel pioneers was discovered building a bridge. These, by a well executed manœuvre, were all captured.

Celerity of movement being the chief desideratum, it was resolved immediately to put the troops over by wading—an affair not very easy of execution, for the waters of the Rapidan, even at the ford, come up to a man's shoulder, and the current is very rapid. The men, however, plunged in, many of them stripping and carrying their clothes and cartridge boxes on their bayonets—and waded over, up to their armpits, amid Homeric scenes of laughter and gayety—a cavalry picket being placed below to catch those that were carried away by the current. In the meantime a foot bridge had been constructed on the abutments already placed there by the rebels, and during the night the whole remaining force was passed over, the piers being lighted up with huge bonfires. While this was going on at Germania Ford, Meade's troops were crossing at Ely's Ford. Both columns now moved as ordered, for Chancellorsville, at the junction of the Gordonville turnpike with the Culpepper and Orange Court-house plank road—communication being kept up between the two movable columns by a squadron of Pleasanton's cavalry, while another part of the same horsemen moved on the right flank of the outer column to protect it from rebel cavalry attacks. This manœuvre having uncovered United States Ford (which lies between Kelly's Ford and Falmouth—twelve miles from the latter,) Couch's corps, which had, for three days, been lying at that point, was passed over the Rappahannock by a pontoon bridge on Thursday, without any opposition or indeed any demonstration more formidable than a brass band playing Hail Columbia. This force also converged toward Chancellorsville and on Thursday night four army corps—namely, Howard's, Steven's, Mead's and Couch's were massed at this point. That same night Gen. Hooker and staff reached Gordonsville and established his Headquarters in the only house here.

III.

I think you will readily agree with me that there are few examples in history of a military movement of such proportions, executed with such celerity and success. To have marched a column of seventy-five thousand men, laden with sixty pounds of baggage, together with artillery and trains, thirty-six miles in two days, to have bridged and crossed two streams along a line which a vigilant enemy undertakes to observe and defend, with a loss of perhaps half a dozen men, one wagon and two mules, is an achieve which assuredly has had few parallels.

Remember how enormously difficult the task of crossing the Rappahanock proved last December, how two days were spent in the attempt after we had our force massed on the river's edge, and with what loss it was finally accomplished, and you will have the means of duly appreciating it.

There is no miracle about this result. It is simply the work of a planning and directing brain, with the most utter secrecy and the greatest possible celerity. But these qualities produce results which, in their *ensemble*, appear almost miraculous.

I remember, in my military reading, but one operation of precisely the same kind. It is the operation of Prince Eugene against the French, who held the line of the Adige. Eugene, by a series of skillful manœuvres, induced the French commander to scatter his troops along the line of the river; then, by dexterous feints, he entirely deceived his adversary as to the direction of his march, and the latter was suddenly surprised with the news that the line of the Adige was forced, and a detachment of his forces wholly routed at Carpi.

Lee's surprise could not have been greater when he heard that the Union army was across the river and had turned his flank. And, indeed, we have not merely material proof of this—such as that, when we were across the Rapidan the enemy was yet picketing the Rappahannock—but we have documentary evidence of it in a letter from Gen. Lee himself, which was found in the house at Chancellorsville.

This letter, signed by Gen. Taylor, Lee's Chief of Staff, was written to the rebel officer commanding the post at Chancellorsville, and was dated from Lee's headquarters at 4:29 o'clock P. M., of the day we arrived. It stated, in substance that "*the General had at that moment heard that the Federal force was across Ely's Ford*" (we had been across eighteen hours)—"*that Gen. Anderson*" (who commanded at United States Ford with a couple of brigades) "*knew nothing of our arrival*"—and asked him "*to come down immediately and consult with the Commanding General!*"

The order which the commanding General issued on Thursday, after the achievement of this position, is the key to the situation, and to the expectations of the commander. I repeat it here for its relations with the recital:

Headquarters Army of the Potomac, Near Falmouth, Va., April 30, 1863.

It is with heartfelt satisfaction that the General Commanding announces to the army that the operations of the last three days have determined that our enemy must ingloriously fly, or *come out from behind their defences, and give us battle on our own ground*, where certain destruction awaits him.

The operations of the Fifth, Eleventh and Twelfth Corps have been a series of splendid successes.

By command of Maj.-Gen. HOOKER.
S. Williams, Adjutant-General.

The significance of the emphasized words will be seen from a glance at the map of the country. It will be seen that the position gained at Chancellorsville, which is ten miles west by south of Fredericksburgh, *completely turns the line of rebel defences on the series of ridges in the rear of Fredericksburgh*, and in fact there was now but one alternative: the enemy *must* either retreat along the line of the railroad toward Richmond, while that line was yet uncut, (for there was no other line of retreat, the communication with Gordonsville being threatened by our hold on that line,) or else come out and "give us battle on our own ground." Lee had been completely outgeneraled, and in a strategic point of view had suffered a defeat before we had fired a single shot. It was in this sense, and not in the meaning that they were actually destroyed, albeit he anticipated nothing less than that, that Gen. Hooker on the night of our arrival at Chancellorsville proudly exclaimed, "The rebel army is now the legitimate property of the Army of the Potomac."

Gen. Lee seems to have felt himself strong enough to pursue the latter alternative, and he took prompt measures to carry his plan into execution. There is very little doubt that he had been heavily reinforced with troops from the South. We are at the present moment fighting Charleston. For, like the attack on Fort Donelson, that movement had been made too soon. A month had passed since that attack, and its result had emboldened Lee to call up the great portion of the force in South Carolina. The troops for the defences of Charleston numbered fifty-five thousand men, and he could afford to feel able to draw on forty thousand of that number. In addition, Longstreet's force had been recalled from North Carolina. Furthermore, it is the universal testimony of all the prisoners, (numbering several hundred taken during the past week) that their army has been heavily reinforced. What that force is, it is, of course, impossible to say. I think it would be unsafe to estimate it at less than *eighty thousand*, and there are those having good means of knowing who carry it to a *hundred thousand*.

Occupying, too, the interior line, Lee's facilities for a change of front were, of course, very great; and our army had hardly gained its position when a rebel column was marching up to confront it.

On Saturday, two prisoners were brought in from the Twenty-third North Carolina, belonging to Hill's division, of Jackson's corps. Their testimony (I heard them keenly questioned by the able chief of the secret service, who knows the position of every rebel regiment) showed that that division started from below Hamilton's crossing, in the *rear* of Fredericksburgh, at 3 A. M., of Friday, and that they were portions of the same column which we saw moving up the Bowling Green road, *below* Fredericksburgh, two days before. I mention this circumstance as a slight clue to the great game which was now being played between the two able leaders of the respective armies.

On Thursday night we were massed in the vicinity of Chancellorsville, simply covering the approaches.

On Friday morning, Gen. Hooker began the strategic disposition of his force. As the enemy has since been engaged with us all along this line, and as the disposition has, since then, been altered, there can be no objection to state that it formed a line of battle of a triangular or redan shape, resting with its wings respectively on the Rappahannock between Banks and United States fords and Hart's Creek, and having its apex at Chancellorsville.

The day was occupied with operations along the skirmish line, and reconnoissances for the purpose of feeling the enemy.

The night previously, Col. McVicar, of the Sixth New-York cavalry, had pushed out on the Spotsylvania road; but having, in the ardor that characterized him, got far beyond the point intended by the General, Fitz-Hugh Lee, with two brigades of cavalry and a battery of horse artillery, got on a cross road between him and us. He had two hundred men, and there was but one course for him—to pierce through the enemy's line, leading the assault, sabre in hand, and he fell at the first charge. I knew him well. He was a Scotchman and gallant soldier, and he died as he would have wished—cutting his way through the enemy. The intrepid band left fifty of its number behind.

At noon of Friday Sykes' division of Mead's corps, occupying the extreme left, was sent out on a reconnoissance on the Banks' Ford road. They pushed the enemy steadily for an hour, gaining a mile of ground, which was in itself important as giving us possession of two successive heights, from which the enemy would annoy us with artillery. This accomplished, the order was given to fall back. There were those who were disposed to be captious at this, but the mind that took in the totality of operations knew well what he did. In itself the position was valuable; but it could not, without weakening us, have been made available in the general line.

In like manner a portion of Slocum's command was thrown out about three miles on the Fredericksburgh plank road, and other advances of the same kind were made on the right.

These "feelers" had the obvious purpose of causing the enemy to develop his force; but they had also another purpose, not so obvious, namely: that of a topographical survey, as existing maps are enormously defective. Gen. Hooker, with the chiefs of the Topographical Department, busied himself all day in making himself thoroughly acquainted with the ground.

It will not be out of place for us here briefly to do the same. The situation of Chancellorsville is in the middle of a clearing in the woods, which takes the form of an irregular elipse, about a mile in length and half a mile in width. The solitary house that makes up Chancellorsville stands almost in the middle of this opening.

The ground in the region between here and Fredericksburgh is broken and wooded, there being occasional clearings in the forests. It rises as it nears Fredericksburgh, when it develops into bold heights. Its strategic importance, as already indicated, is derived from the fact that it covers the Fredericksburgh turnpike and the Culpepper and Orange Court-house plank road, and threatens the line of Gordonsville.

IV.

The military situation on Saturday morning, therefore, stands as follows: Our main force holds the position at Chancellorsville, confronting the main rebel army now massed opposite us. Howard's corps has the extreme right—then a division of Sickles' corps—then Slocum—then Couch—then Meade on the left, Humphrey's division of Meade's corps holding the extreme of the left. Working parties have been employed during the whole night in throwing up breastworks, and the woods have resounded with the strokes of a thousand ax-men felling trees for the purpose of constructing abattis. We hear the rebels, not half a mile distant, at work with the same view, and in the morning both armies are well entrenched. It will now be who will come out and give battle. Hooker is determined to put forth all the resources of the craft of which he is a consummate master, to tempt them out.

So much for the Right. Another, though minor force, is working on the left, independently, yet with its definite strategic bearings on the main operation. This subordinate operation is at Fredericksburgh. Balloon reconnoissances show clearly that the enemy have taken their main force from the heights of Fredericksburgh and the line down the Rappahannock, and massed it against us at Chancellorsville. They have also removed the greater bulk of their artillery with the same end; and Gen. Sedgwick, who commands the left, thinks himself strong enough to carry the heights. The Commanding General assents, if there be good prospect of success; for it is of the utmost importance not to *anticipate* the golden moment to strike.

Still another coöperative *rôle* is assigned the powerful cavalry expedition under Gen. Stoneman. This is nothing less than to cut the railroad bridges that cross the two affluents of the Pamunkey—namely, the North and South Anna—less than twenty miles from Richmond. The bridge over the North Anna is a hundred and fifty feet long and eighty feet high, and cannot possibly be reconstructed in less than a fortnight. You can see how tremendously this will embarrass the rebels.

Whether Stoneman has by this time actually performed his task, is not yet reported. I have followed him only as far as Rappahannock Station, south of Culpepper, through which he dashed on Thursday night.

This rapid survey will indicate how colossal is the plan of campaign which Gen. Hooker has marked out for the army. It contemplates nothing less than the destruction of the entire rebel force in Virginia. It is stupendously daring; but Hooker is a man who thoroughly understands that, in war, to greatly gain one must greatly dare.

V.

The active operations of Saturday comprise a series of attempts in force on the part of the rebels to break our line at various points, which were in one case partially successful, in another completely successful, and in all the others completely unsuccessful.

In the morning, as we stood on the balcony of Chancellor's house, the attention was aroused by a sharp rattle of musketry coming from a column of rebels coming up by the main Fredericksburgh plank road, directly in front of us. Knapp's battery, however, which was planted directly in front of the position, opened upon them, and after a few rounds caused them to retire.

Immediately afterwards a battery opened from the height which I have mentioned as having been gained by Sykes, yesterday, and then abandoned by us. The position was rather upwards of a mile distant from the cleared space, and its object was to damage our ammunition train which was visible to the rebels from the tops of trees on the height. One of our batteries was, however, immediately opened in reply. The third shot blew up one of the caissons and a subsequent shot blew up another, and this settled their account.

Subsequently a reconnoissance was sent, on our part, consisting of the Twenty-sixth Pennsylvania Volunteers, (Carr's brigade, Berry's division, Sickles' corps,) on the same road by which the rebels had approached in the morning, for the purpose of feeling their strength. They went out on the plank road, deployed on both sides in the form of a letter V, chaced the rebel skirmishers a couple of miles, till they came to a heavy double line of battle, with artillery in position, when they retired, bringing us *that* piece of intelligence.

Another reconnoissance was next sent out on our right, consisting of Berdan's sharpshooters. They met the enemy's pickets, drove them handsomely, and at 4 o'clock returned with fifty prisoners of the Twenty-third Georgia.

At 4 the rebels are moving down in force on the plank road, where we had a little before made the reconnoissance. Geary's division of Slocum's corps is sent in on the double quick into the woods—their bayonets flashing in the sunlight. A sharp contest ensues, and in a few minutes they come back in disorder. A portion of Kane's brigade, composed of raw troops, had broken, and thrown the column into confusion.

An Aid from Slocum comes to ask Gen. Hooker if he can have reinforcements. "No! he *must* hold his own. Howard will, of course, support him from the right. Let Geary's division, however, be thrown to the right of the road, so that the artillery may be able to sweep the enemy on the left." This treatment presently repaired the damage, and checked the hope of the rebels being able to pierce our centre.

Foiled in this, they now prepared to make a still

Continued on Eighth Page.

The New-York Times.

VOL. XII—NO. 3624. NEW-YORK, WEDNESDAY, MAY 6, 1863. PRICE THREE CENTS.

FROM HOOKER'S ARMY.

Letters From Our Special Correspondents to Monday Morning.

Further Details of the Great Battles of Saturday and Sunday.

The Storming of the Heights at Fredericksburgh.

Prodigies of Valor Performed by Our Troops.

THE PRISONERS AND GUNS CAPTURED.

Unsuccessful Attempt of the Rebels to Recapture the Heights.

Gen. Lee Said to be Calling for Reinforcements.

Fitzhugh Lee Reported a Prisoner in Washington.

RUMORS ABOUT STONEMAN

A Partial List of Casualties on the Left.

HEADQUARTERS IN THE FIELD, NEAR CHANCELLORSVILLE, Sunday Evening, May 3, 1863.

At this hour of writing, it is impossible to estimate the loss in to-day's battle on either side. We know that ours is heavy—heavier than ever before in a battle of so short duration. We further know that the loss of the enemy is admitted by themselves to be perfectly frightful. We had the advantage in artillery, and our shells and canister tore and mangled their ranks fearfully. The prisoners are silent as to the loss of prominent officers, but some of the Alabamians in A. P. HILL's division say that he was killed early in the day, and that Gen. RAYNOR is now in command of the division.

THE BATTLE-GROUND.

Probably no battle was ever fought upon ground more unfavorable for the manœuvring and deploying of troops. Nearly the whole country in this vicinity is covered with dense forest, much of it being of the same character as "The Wilderness," lying only a short distance west of this point. The timber is mostly dead, and still very dense; then, to make the forest still more impenetrable, there is a denser growth of dead underbrush, so that it is hardly passable for man—certainly not for beast—and the worst place conceivable for handling troops. Yet a very great part of to-day's terrible battle was fought in this almost impenetrable jungle, and many dead and wounded on both sides still lie there, concealed in the gloomy depths of "The Wilderness." The only open ground upon which the battle was fought, was the plain on the south side of the plank-road, near Chancellorsville, half a mile long, and perhaps three hundred yards wide. The only open ground in our present position is a semi-circular crest, extending from the left of Gen. SYKES' position to the right of Gen. HOWARD's. Immediately in front of this are dense woods, concealing our skirmishers and those of the enemy. This crest is our artillery position, and here guns enough are massed to blow to atoms the armies of a dozen Southern Confederacies. The enemy seem to have a proper appreciation of the courtesies in waiting for them from this position. Twice to-day they have essayed out of the woods toward our guns, and twice have those guns sent to their earthly doom untold numbers of desperate wretches. The artillery at this point is in charge of Capt. WEED, Chief of Artillery of the Fifth Army Corps.

PRISONERS.

The exact count of prisoners thus far taken, during the battle of Sunday, is not yet known, but it must be, all told, *nearly, if not quite, two thousand*. They were brought in singly, in squads, in companies and by regiments; and our men say that they could have taken many more, "but for the trouble of bothering with them on the field of battle." They would rather shoot than capture. Two regiments were taken entire—the Twenty-third Georgia and the Fourth Alabama—the former yesterday and the latter to-day. Then there are detachments from fifty or sixty other regiments, including many North and South Carolina, Virginia, Mississippi and Louisiana regiments. The enemy has undoubtedly taken several hundred of our men, mostly wounded, with some from the Eleventh Corps, who couldn't run fast enough to get away.

THE ELEVENTH CORPS.

The unaccountable and inexcusable conduct of a large portion of this corps, was the means of turning to ashes a grand victory almost within our grasp, while the position was only retrieved by the superb generalship of the Commanding General. A portion of the troops, the brigades of Cols. BUSHBECK and McLEAN, stood their ground manfully until overpowered by vastly superior numbers. Gen. BARLOW's brigade was absent with Gen. SICKLES.

The manner in which Gen. HOOKER proposed to checkmate the rear attack of JACKSON strikingly illustrates the bold and daring character of our commander. Finding that JACKSON was marching by the old Catharpin road past our right front, Gen. HOOKER promptly ordered Gen. SICKLES to attack that impudent column on the flank. This was not more quickly conceived than vigorously executed. In one hour and a half from the time the movement began the head of Gen. BIRNEY's division was engaging the enemy, and our force and vigorous attack were so great that the enemy's left flank was speedily turned, his columns doubled back one upon the other, and his men seized with demoralization and panic. WILLIAMS' division ably assisted this dashing movement, while Gen. GEARY attacked sharply on our centre front, and the prospects were cheering indeed. The Eleventh Corps was strongly intrenched. Its position ought to have been held, and *somebody* is to blame for this disgraceful affair which smote us so sorely, just as we were about to reap rich fruits from the boldest move yet projected since we crossed the river. And to remedy the effect of this disaster, we have spent this day in fighting which only puts us in our former condition, and the enemy once more in our front. Albeit we have inflicted on LEE a murderous loss, and so shattered his columns that he must have time and reinforcements to enable him to fight again as savagely as he fought to-day. Beside, his position is now such that he must inevitably attack our strong position, or retreat. Retreat in his case, with our swift-marching army after him, is most surely disastrous. He may precipitate his whole force upon SEDGWICK, who can retire to the Heights of Fredericksburgh, and wait for HOOKER to follow up in his rear. Two or three times Gen. HOOKER has said that he would compel the rebels to come out of their fortications and attack him on his own ground. It is brilliant generalship, indeed, that has so faithfully fulfilled this promise. To-day the enemy literally leaves his fortifications, and stands before our intrenched camp, essaying its capture.

The question of supplies must now be of great moment to the enemy. His communication by rail, if not totally severed by our cavalry, must be seriously interrupted by the presence of our forces in the vicinity of Hamilton's Crossing, five miles below Fredericksburgh, which has been the rebel supply depot during the Winter. The prisoners taken to-day had nothing to eat, and some of them say no rations had been issued to them for three days.

SPIRIT OF OUR TROOPS.

Our men never behaved more magnificently. Cool, confident and brave, they fought with splendid valor, and were even complimented by the prisoners who fell into our hands. The demoralization of the Eleventh Corps did not affect the rest of the army in the least. Some how or other they looked upon it as a matter of course. Gen. HOOKER's appearance on the field, under severe fire, created tumultuous enthusiasm among the men, and he was cheered to the echo time and again. When it became known that he had been struck by a piece of spent shell, (although uninjured,) the cheers grew louder still.

To the indefatigable efforts of Major-Gen. HOWARD, commanding the Eleventh Corps, is due the fact that before daylight this morning this corps was so far reorganized as to be placed on duty again in an important position. Gen. HOWARD is one of our bravest and best officers. His emotions at the conduct of some of the brigades cannot be described. Had he been longer in command of these men, undoubtedly this stampede would not have occurred.

OUR OWN SUPPLIES.

When the army started on its present movement, the troops took eight days' rations in their haversacks and knapsacks. The prospect of having to carry this amount of food on a long march was not very palatable to the troops, and mutterings were loud and frequent. But the eight days' rations are just what has enabled the army to do so much and march so far in so short a time. The rations will be used up to-morrow, and large amounts are already coming forward in supply trains to United States Ford, and on the backs of pack mules from that point hither. The mules carry the boxes of hard bread on their pack-saddles, while the meat ration is fresh beef, driven on foot.

RETURN OF GEN. AVERILL.

Gen. AVERILL, with his cavalry command, returned to United States Ford to-day, and reported in person to Gen. HOOKER this afternoon. Gen. A. has been out 23 days, and been as far south as Rapidan Station, on the Orange and Alexandria Railroad, where he destroyed the bridge and track of the road. During his trip, he drove LEE and STUART out of Culpepper, and captured there about five thousand dollars' worth of salt and bacon belonging to the rebel Government, which he did not destroy, but distributed among the poor and suffering people of that vicinity. This made Gen. A. very popular, and hereafter the people there will prefer his visits to those of LEE and STUART.

Gen. AVERILL has received instructions for more important work, and our communications may be considered entirely safe so long as his force is in reach.

HEADQUARTERS.

The headquarters of the Army of the Potomac in the field are to-night under a large tree, just in the rear of the front line of rifle-pits and abattis. Gen. HOOKER has just dined on hard tack and cold ham. The gentlemen of the Staff are looking for their "pack mule." L. L. CROUNSE.

THE FIGHTING AT FREDERICKSBURGH.

HEIGHTS ABOVE FREDERICKSBURGH, Monday Morning, May 4, 1 o'clock.

Yesterday was a proud day for the Union arms. The boasted heights of Fredericksburgh were stormed by our brave boys, and the Stars and Stripes now wave triumphantly over this Gibraltar of America. Whatever may have been the result of the fighting on the right, on the left has crowned our arms with imperishable renown. This crest of hills, wrote the London *Times'* correspondent, after the battle in December, constitute one of the strongest positions in the world—impregnable to any attack from the front. Yesterday's achievements have again demonstrated, for the twentieth time, that what is impossible with John Bull becomes possible with Jonathan.

The going down of the sun on Saturday found our troops of the left scattering out on both sides of the river, some two miles below the city. The Fiying division had advanced to the old Richmond road, Gen. BURN's command lay back, nearer to the river. Gen. HOWE's and Gen. NEWTON's forces were on the plain opposite. To mention where the other troops were would not be prudent.

Under cover of night Gens. HOWE and NEWTON crossed over the river. (Gen. NEWTON's division is now temporarily commanded by Gen. WHEATON, he having assumed command of Gen. SEDGWICK's corps.) About 2 o'clock in the morning orders came to move at once on the enemy. The greater portion of the forces moved quietly up the Richmond road winding down through the gully just below the city reached the outskirts of Fredericksburgh, between 4 and 5 o'clock. Gens. HOWE and NEWTON's divisions were in the advance, then followed the "flying division," or "light brigade," and Gen. BROOKS' forces were extended on the extreme left. Meantime companies of the Fiftieth New-York engineers had constructed pontoon bridges directly across to the city, both above and below the Lacey House, and the Forty-second New-York, Nineteenth and Twentieth Massachusetts, Fifty-ninth New-York and the One Hundred and Twenty-seventh Pennsylvania, constituting HALL's—DANA's old brigade, Second corps—together with three other regiments, including the Second New-York and Fifteenth Massachusetts, crossed on the upper bridge and deployed out along the bank above the city. Batteries were also brought up and planted close to the city; among them HARNE's, MARTIN's, Battery B, Second Rhode Island, Lieut. BROWN; Battery G, Eighth Rhode Island, Capt. ADAMS, and Battery D, Second artillery. The First Maryland and "HEXAMERS" Pennsylvania Battery were posted on the plain further below, where they could deliver a fire either up or down the range of hills. The object of this movement to the city was to storm the first line of rebel earthworks above, which Gen. SUMNER attempted in vain to take, last December, losing 7,000 men in the effort. Nor did the idea of again charging against those formidable intrenchments appear so insane to the troops as one might think. So buoyant and hopeful were the boys that they felt as if they could go anywhere and surmount any and every obstacle. The reader will remember that this line of earthworks is about one-third of a mile from the city, extending close along the monument erected to MARY, the mother of WASHINGTON, which is erected on a sort of natural bluff. Beneath runs the famous stone wall and a road leading off in the direction of Richmond. Between this road and the city is an open plain commanded by the rebel works. Across this plain and over the stone wall the charging column had to advance before reaching the fortified bluff. About 5½ o'clock in the morning COCHRANE's old brigade, (NEWTON's division,) now commanded by Col. SHALER, and led by him in person, charged over the plain, and succeeded in nearly reaching the stone wall, but were obliged to fall back. The Sixty-second New-York, it is said, endeavored to storm the works before this hour of the morning. The rebels kept up a constant fire of musketry from behind earthworks, buildings and rifle pits, while the guns from above rained down a perfect storm of grape and canister on the troops. Gen. BROOKS' division, which was on the extreme left, suffered least, though fired at the most, owing to the fact of most of the enemy's missiles passing over the heads of the troops. It was now 11 o'clock, continuous fighting had been going on for full six hours, and the rebels still held their works. Gen. SEDGWICK now determined on having the "light brigade" charge the heights. Col. BUNHAM commanding moved his forces along under the protection of abandoned earthworks, and the hill-side formed by the sloping down of the plain near the city, until he had arrived directly in front of the most formidable position, known as the "Slaughter pen." Knapsacks and any article of clothing which might impede their rapid movement were cast aside by the men, and they were deployed out in the following order: one half of the Fifth Wisconsin, Col. ALLEN, as skirmish line; Thirty-first New-York, Col. JONES, on the left; Sixth Maine, Lieut.-Col. HARRIS commanding, and the remaining portion of the Fifth in the rear of, and supporting the Thirty-first at the same time. At the same time a force consisting of the Forty-third New-York, and Sixty-first Pennsylvania, and one or two other regiments were sent up the road at the right of the stone wall. Going on to the regiments of the Light Brigade, prepared for a charge were the Thirty-sixth New-York, and Seventh Massachusetts, and still further on other regiments. At twenty minutes past eleven the lion-hearted men rose from their feet. Every one of the thousand spectators on the hills in the rear held their breath in terrible suspense, expecting to see them all the next moment prostrate in the dust. "Forward!" cried the General, and they dashed forward on the open plain when instantly there was poured upon them a most terrific discharge of grape and cannister. Many lay dead, but not one faltered. Full 400 yards must be passed over before gaining the stone wall. As they press forward, delivering the battle-cheer, which is heard above the roar of artillery. The rebel gune further to the left are turned upon them. But they falter not. A moment more they have reached the stone wall, scaled its sides, are clambering the green bank of the bluff, and precisely as the City clock struck, they rush over the embrasure of the rebel guns and the Heights are ours. The enemy, with the exception of the cannoniers, fled in wild confusion, secreting themselves in the houses, woods and wherever a place of concealment was afforded. The guns captured proved to be the Washington Artillery, the battery so highly complimented by Gen. LEE in his report of the last battle of Fredericksburgh, and which has figured more or less since the outbreak of the rebellion. "What men are these," was the interrogatory of one of the astonished and terrified members, as our brave boys appeared over the ramparts. "We are Yankees, —— —— you; do you think we will fight now," was the response from one of our men. "Boys," remarked the Commander of the Battery, "You have captured the best battery in the Confederate service." The Sixth Maine were the first regiment to reach the scene. Lieut.-Col. HARRIS, with unparalleled bravery, rushed right up to the mouth of one as it was belching away, and through the mist and smoke his form could just be discerned as he cheered his men forward. He, together with Capt. FURLONG, were the first to lay hold of the rebel pieces.

The rebels succeeded in getting one gun away to some distance, when the force which had gone round to flank the battery perceived it, and immediately starting in hot pursuit, captured it with seventy-five prisoners. A wagon train was ahead which they might have secured, had they not received orders to proceed no further. On the Washington Artillery being surrendered the other batteries to the right did not make much resistance, but fled hastily before our charging forces. Gen. MILLS' Brigade consisting of the Seventy-seventh New-York, Twenty-first New-Jersey, Forty-ninth New-York, Thirty-third New-York, and Second New-York, made a very gallant charge.

The Rhode Island batteries at the right of the road kept up an animated fire during the storming of the works. The rebels on the extreme left, in front of the Barnard House, retreated up the hills when we obtained possession of the city.

The following are some of the casualties which occurred.

Col. Spear, 61st Pennsylvania—killed.
Maj. Hancock, 61st Pennsylvania—wounded.
Capt. Gray, 61st Pennsylvania—killed.
Capt. Ballinger, 61st Pennsylvania—killed.
Capt. Irwin, 61st Pennsylvania—killed.
Capt. Burk, 61st Pennsylvania—killed.
John H. Spencer, Co. G, 23d Pennsylvania—killed.

SIXTH MAINE.

Corp. Gilman Swett, Co. K, 6th Maine—dead.
Maj. Haycock, 6th Maine—dead.
Sergt. Holmes, Co. A, 6th Maine—dead.
Sergt. Ginn, Co. E, 6th Maine—dead.
George Perry, Co. D, 6th Maine—wounded.
Alonzo Merrill, Co. H, 6th Me.—mortally wounded.
——— Skinner, Co. H, 6th Maine—wounded.
——— Sutherland, Co. I, 6th Maine—wounded.
——— Moore, Co. E, 6th Maine—wounded.
——— Blackman, Co. C, 6th Maine—wounded.
——— Jennis, Co. I, 6th Maine—wounded.
——— Gould, Co. I, 6th Maine—wounded.
A. McRegan, Co. D, 6th Maine—wounded.
Cummings, Co. H, 6th Maine—wounded.
Hugh Mangum, Co. K, 6th Maine—wounded.
R. Welch, Co. K, 6th Maine—wounded.
Sergt. McKabe, Co. C, 6th Maine—wounded.
Sergt. Braddish, Co. G, 6th Maine—wounded.
Wm. Lincoln, Co. F, 6th Maine—wounded.
Ord.-Sergt. Whittaker, Co. H, 6th Maine—badly wounded.
Sergt. Frank Holmes, Co. A—killed.
J. E. Fogg, Co. A—killed.
John Rivers, Co. A—killed.
—— Ward, Co. D—killed.
Hiram Croxford, Co. I—killed.
George Emerson, Co. I—killed.
John George, Co. C—mortally wounded.
George Smith, Co. A—mortally wounded.
Chas. O. Randall, Co. H—killed.
Chester Lancaster, Co. H—killed.
Sergt. Merrill, Co. H—mortally wounded.
Gilbert Swift, Co. K—killed.
Edward R. Philips, Co. B—killed.
Albert A. Dow, Co. B—killed.
Chas. V. Dudley, Co. E—killed.
Sergt. —— Quinn, Co. E—killed.
Wm. Honey, Co. B—mortally wounded.
Sam. Merrill, Co. E—mortally wounded.
G. H. Philbrook, Co. G—killed.
Hannibal H. Leighton, Co. G—killed.
Enoch H. Wood, Co. G—mortally wounded.
John Willett, Co. G—mortally wounded.
Stephen Connick, Co. F—mortally wounded.

FIFTH WISCONSIN.

Maj. Wheeler—wounded.
Capt. Lurner—killed.
Capt. Strong—mortally wounded.
John Frawley, Co. H—killed.
Myron Tripp, Co. H—died since.
Sergt. C. J. Kavanagh, Co. B—killed.
Wm. Kelley, Co. B—killed.
George Adam, Co. B—died.

THIRTY-FIRST NEW-YORK.

Ord. Sergt Joyce, Co. G—killed.
Henry Von Haughton, Co. I—killed.
Patrick Brady, Co. I—killed.
——— McFlim, Co. B—killed.
Thos. McNamara, Co. I—killed.
Lieut. Juvesbury, Co. F—killed.
Jas. Dorsy, Co. G—killed.
Wm. Tibbetts, Co. H—killed.
Lieut.-Col. Newman—wounded in foot.
Corp. Sloan—leg.
Lieut. Ruess—killed.
Capt. Knickerbocker, 43d New-York—killed.
Lieut. Coons, 43d New-York—killed.
Thos. Lindsey, bugler, 7th Michigan—shot in head.
Lieut. McKinley, 6th Maine—wounded in legs.

D. W. JUDD.

[A hasty postscript to our correspondent's letter announces that a considerable body of rebels had made their appearance below Fredericksburgh, marching toward that place, to gain a position in the rear of Gen. SEDGWICK's corps, which had meantime advanced on the road toward Gen. HOOKER's position. Our correspondent judged the force to be LONGSTREET's corps, coming up from below. Whatever it was, it appears from the dispatches that the attempt to retake the heights was unsuccessful.—ED. TIMES.]

THE CAPTURES AT FREDERICKSBURGH.

One of our correspondents, writing from headquarters, near Falmouth, gives the following facts concerning Gen. SEDGWICK's captures at Fredericksburgh:

"Among the prisoners taken are the Sixteenth and Eighteenth Mississippi, of BARKSDALE's brigade, who have usually defended the river passages during the past Winter.

There is also a whole company of the famous Washington Artillery, of New-Orleans, and a more aristocratic and intelligent lot of Southern chivalry I have never seen. The officers are Capt. SQUIRES, Lieut. GALBREATH, and Lieut. EDWARD OWEN, formerly of Cincinnati. A fine-looking young man introduced himself to me as Private MORGAN E. HARRIS, formerly of Cincinnati, and desired that his friends should know where he was. Most of them appeared much chagrined at their capture, and said it was the first misfortune of the kind. Four of their guns were taken; also two of ALEXANDER's battery. These were all the guns captured, I believe."

THE FIGHTING ON SATURDAY AND SUNDAY.

REPORTS TO THE ASSOCIATED PRESS.

WASHINGTON, Monday, May 4.

The city is intensely excited, to-day, by the reports from the Army of the Potomac. The news is regarded thus far as favorable and encouraging. But, at the same time, there is naturally much solicitude as to further and future developments.

The arrival of about 1,100 prisoners since Saturday, certainly shows that our army has not been idle in making captures, and it is reported that others will soon arrive.

A gentleman connected with army operations, who arrived here early this morning, says there was skirmishing all day Saturday on the left, and on Sunday our batteries crossed over to Fredericksburgh on pontoons at the foot of the Lacy House, or at a point where some of our forces passed over previous to the former battle. There was some opposition from the rebels, but it was soon ended, and a few were killed. The movement was completed about 5 o'clock in the morning.

The rebel intrenchments were, not long after this, shelled from the vicinity of Fredericksburgh and in front. Meanwhile, our troops on the left made a flank movement, and, gaining the enemy's rear, gallantly and impetuously attacked them, driving the rebels from their positions and causing them swiftly to retreat at least two miles further back.

The result was the capture of eleven 12-pounders, and a large number of killed, wounded and prisoners fell into our hands. The enemy succeeded in moving off their other guns, which had been kept on wheels.

The gentleman from whom the above information is obtained, witnessed the fighting from an eminence near Fredericksburgh, and while the contest was raging, crossed over, and not long thereafter visited the deserted fortifications.

The absence of cavalry was a misfortune. Had there been a force of that arm of the service the enemy must have been badly cut up in his flight. The enemy were slain in heaps before that stone wall, which so well answered the purpose of their defence at the former battle of Fredericksburgh.

This information says that while our troops were driving the enemy, firing was heard far back in their rear.

The men were in splendid spirits, and all of them had the utmost confidence in Gen. HOOKER.

PHILADELPHIA, Tuesday, May 5.

The Washington *Chronicle* of to-day has the following:

A gentleman who left Falmouth early yesterday morning, reports that early Sunday morning, simultaneously with the commencement of the battle on the right, our batteries on the left opened on the rebel defences of Fredericksburgh, which were replied to smartly by the rebels, but their fire gradually slackened off. Our Infantry immediately moved forward under the direction of Gen. SEDGWICK. The men had bayonets fixed, and presenting a firm front, moved on steadily until they reached within a few hundred yards of the famous stone wall. Here they met with a most murderous fire of infantry, while grape and canister plowed through their ranks. Still they pressed onward to within a few feet of the goal. The wall was cleared and the ridge gained. The brave boys with a cheer pushed onward toward the second line of intrenchments, but an order reached them to return, which was complied with, but not without a great deal of reluctance. The opinion gained ground that it was not necessary to drive them much further, as this would prevent our forces on the right reaching their rear.

So great was the panic of the rebels that they abandoned cannon, arms, knapsacks and everything else that would in the least impede them in their flight. The works were held all day without any desperate efforts on the part of the enemy to drive our forces from them. They kept up a pretty sharp skirmish, and occasionally made sallies out of their second and third lines of entrenchments, but they were invariably driven back. Upwards of 1,300 prisoners were taken in this engagement, mostly belonging to Mississippi, Georgia and Virginia regiments. A large number of officers, from Colonels down to Third Lieutenants, were also taken prisoners.

It is rumored that the rebels yesterday made, or were preparing for, an attack on our forces within the works, but it is quite clear to every one, independently of the high authority we have for the opinion, that even if they have been successful it will amount to nothing at all. The main fighting has been transferred to some other point, and in the operations which are now progressing, as we hope, to a successful completion, the occupation of Fredericksburgh is not of the slightest consequence. If the rebels have attacked us there it is probably a mere feint, and will only amount to a useless expenditure of life and ammunition.

WOUNDED.

Capt. Sherwood, Co. I, 86th New-York.
Lieut. Woodward, Co. I, 86th New-York.
Capt. Lansing, 86th New-York.

ACCOUNTS FROM THE WASHINGTON PAPERS.

From the Republican of Monday Evening.

In consequence of the reported dashing operations of Gen. STONEMAN on the line of railroad to Richmond, Gen. LEE could not "ingloriously fly," but was compelled to "come out from behind his defences" and fight on HOOKER's "own ground," selected near Chancellorsville, about ten miles southwest of Fredericksburgh. The battle lasted most of the day on Saturday, and continued with great fierceness until two o'clock on Sunday morning, when hostilities ceased for two hours.

At 4 o'clock the ball opened again, and lasted until 10 o'clock yesterday forenoon, when the enemy's batteries became silent, and the wildest cheering commenced on our extreme right, and ran along the whole line. When our informant left the prevailing opinion was that the enemy's ammunition was exhausted, or they had been attacked by HOOKER's left wing, the force under Gen. SEDGWICK, which crossed below Fredericksburgh.

Our informant says that before he left the field at Chancellorsville, the general result was completely successful to our arms; that a large number of prisoners had been captured. He hastened from the field as soon as the firing stopped, and recrossed the river at Banks' Ford, and proceeded to Falmouth, opposite to which (Fredericksburgh) a desperate battle was raging.

Another gentleman, who was with our forces in Fredericksburgh, says Gen. SEDGWICK succeeded in reaching the key to the whole line of monster rebel works in Fredericksburgh before the day dawned Sunday morning.

The rebels immediately opened a most terrible fire. At the first shock some of the regiments wavered at seeing their commanding officers—Colonels, Majors and Captains—falling around them, but the skillful and dashing Col. SHAILER, by his cool daring and personal example, rallied the staggering column and led it into the rebel works, carrying the key, and with it the whole line at the point of the bayonet, with a wild yell that was heard above the shock of arms.

One gun on the right of the key was very annoying to our advancing forces. An order was given to take it, and in three minutes afterward, says our informant, the rebel gunners and their infantry support were in full retreat, and their own gun, which had been captured by our men, was sending death into their ranks.

As soon as the principal work (the key) was carried, about 11 o'clock yesterday forenoon, the whole rebel force in and about Fredericksburgh made a precipitate retreat out upon what is known as the plank-road toward Chancellorsville, in the direction of LEE's main army.

The capture of the City of Fredericksburgh and the works surrounding it was complete. The killed and wounded on our side in Fredericksburgh was comparatively small, but the rebel rifle pits were said to be filled with killed and wounded rebels.

The slaughter at Chancellorsville is estimated to be large on both sides. Among the killed on our side is Gen. BERRY, of Maine. Gen. HOWARD was wounded in endeavoring to rally the German regiments, which wavered on Saturday before the heavy masses of the enemy thrown against them.

We captured many large guns, ammunition, stores, and, up to yesternoon, about two thousand prisoners.

The last report from Gen. STONEMAN, who is in the advance toward Richmond, received last night, was that he had cut LEE's railroad and telegraphic communication with Richmond and captured Gordonsville, but for that we cannot vouch.

Postscript.—Our advices from the field of operations up to noon to-day are that the victory of Gen. HOOKER's army is a more complete one than was first supposed. All that the most sanguine could hope for has been realized, if we except the awful slaughter, which, for the present, we forbear to enter upon.

The *Republican* also says:

"Eight hundred and thirty prisoners of war arrived in this city this morning, having been captured at Fredericksburgh yesterday by Gen. HOOKER. Among the number captured are 100 officers, ranging from colonels, lieutenant-colonels, majors, captains, down to sergeants. The Twenty-third Georgia regiment was captured entire.

P. S.—Since writing the above Capt. TODD, Provost-Marshal of this city, has received a dispatch that 600 more prisoners of war will arrive here this evening from Fredericksburgh. This makes a total of 1,500 prisoners arrived to-day."

The *Republican* has likewise the following:

"A gentleman up from the army to-day says it was understood at Falmouth that LEE attacked HOOKER, near Chancellorsville, just after midnight, this morning.

If true, it was nothing more or less than a military death struggle, which it was necessary for LEE to make in order to hold his men in trim and to keep them ignorant of the fact that they are surrounded and must surrender if they cannot cut their way out."

From the Washington Star of Monday Evening.

It appears that while HOOKER was occupying the attention of the Confederates near Chancellorsville, SEDGWICK, early on Sunday morning, crossed at Fredericksburgh, and, after a sharp contest, a good deal of it over the same ground that BURNSIDE occupied in his fight, carried the heights and drove the rebels (such of them as were not bayoneted on the spot) pell mell from the intrenchments.

In this attack upon the fortifications of Fredericksburgh our men got in the rear of the celebrated stone wall that so effectually protected the rebels in the disastrous attack under BURNSIDE.

This morning the Confederates made a desperate attempt to retrieve the position at Fredericksburgh, but were again repulsed.

The fighting has been desperate, with heavy losses on both sides.

We regret to say that the gallant Gen. BERRY, Second Army corps, was killed yesterday morning in the desperate fight near Chancellorsville, where his division was gallantly engaged retrieving the ground temporarily lost by Gen. HOWARD's division on the preceding evening, under the attack of an overwhelming force of the enemy. He was struck by a Minie ball, which pierced the lungs and probably the heart.

It is rumored that a telegram from the rebel Gen. LEE to the authorities at Richmond has been intercepted, in which he calls for reinforcements, and announces his entire inability to hold out two days longer unless they are sent.

STONEMAN's cavalry appears to be doing effective work in the rebel rear, and is stated to have cut the Virginia Central Road, and also the Fredericksburgh and Richmond Road at a point near Milford Station, southwest of Chancellorsville, tearing up some five miles of the track, and thus cutting off LEE's communication with Richmond. STONEMAN is also said to have captured a Confederate supply train at that point.

We have not heard of the trestle-work nearer to Fredericksburgh being destroyed, but if any considerable extent of rail has been removed, it will cut off the communication between Fredericksburgh and Richmond sufficiently long to answer HOOKER's purpose, we take it.

From the Chronicle of Yesterday.

ARRIVAL OF WOUNDED.

The first installment of wounded soldiers, two hundred and sixty in number, arrived at the foot of Sixth-street last evening about ten o'clock. A great majority of them were only slightly wounded. The most desperately were left at improvised hospitals at Falmouth and Aquia Creek. Those who arrived here last evening were distributed around the different hospitals.

The body of Gen. BERRY reached this city yesterday morning. It is being embalmed, and will be sent home either to-day or to-morrow.

ARRIVAL OF PRISONERS.

Upward of fourteen hundred prisoners arrived in the city yesterday. A large number of officers were among the number. A further lot consisting of nearly fifty rebels, including two officers of the Nineteenth Mississippi, were brought into the Central Guard-house. The officer who had them in charge informed us that before he left Aquia Creek a dispatch had been received there announcing that *four thousand more* were on the way to the Creek.

The *Chronicle* editorially announces that Gen. FITZHUGH LEE had been taken prisoner, and had arrived in Washington.

OUR LATEST WASHINGTON REPORTS.

WASHINGTON, Tuesday, May 5.

The steamer *Hero* arrived to-day, with over eight hundred rebel prisoners—among them forty-eight officers of all grades, below Lieutenant-Colonel. Several officers appear to have lately been uniformed, but a large majority of officers, and all the men, are the same hard-looking set we have been in the habit of seeing. They were escorted by a detachment of the Thirty-ninth Massachusetts to the Cliffburne Barracks, Twenty-first-street. Some of these prisoners say that they have been here before, and express the hope that they may be treated as well this time as formerly.

The *Juniata* brought up one hundred and twenty-five prisoners belonging to a Louisiana regiment.

This afternoon President LINCOLN sent down, by his little son, a beautiful bouquet of rare and fragrant flowers, and a wreath of evergreens decked with flowers, to be placed upon Gen. BERRY's coffin. Lieut.-Col. FREEMAN, of Gen. BERRY's Staff, will accompany the remains to New-York. Capt. GREENHAIGH, also of his Staff, will take charge of the remains from that point.

For two hours the heaviest downfall of [illegible] this rainy Spring has been steadily falling. [illegible] creeks and rivers in Northern Virginia must [illegible]ately be affected by it.

WASHINGTON, Tuesday, May 5.

A son of Ex-Senator A. G. BROWN, of Mississippi, is among the rebel prisoners. More than three thousand are now here.

The National Typographical Union.

CLEVELAND, Monday, May 4.

At a meeting of the National Typographical Union held here, to-day, the following officers were elected: President, EUGENE VALETTE, of Philadelphia; First Vice-President, GEORGE K. McLUKES, of St. Louis; Second Vice-President, J. A. SPENCER, of Cleveland; Secretary and Treasurer, THOMAS J. WALSH, of New-York; Corresponding Secretary, WM. F. MOORE, of Detroit.

IMPORTANT FROM MISSISSIPPI.

Some of the Results of the Great Cavalry Raid.

Destruction of the Jackson and Meridian Railroad.

The Communications with Vicksburgh Severed

Failure of the Attempt to Occupy Grand Gulf.

Preparations to Attack Vicksburgh Above and Below.

LANDING OF GEN. SHERMAN ABOVE THE CITY

Gen. Grant on the Eastern Side of the Mississippi

CHICAGO, Tuesday, May 5.

The Jackson *Appeal* of the 28th of April, says of Col. GRIERSON's Federal raid, that besides tearing up the railroad, he has destroyed two bridges, each 150 feet long, seven culverts, burned twenty-eight freight cars, blown up two locomotives, and burned the railroad depot and two commissary buildings at Newton. He also destroyed the telegraph line by destroying five miles of wire, and captured two trains.

Special dispatches from Cairo say that the report that the Federal troops have occupied Grand Gulf is premature, the rebels having planted batteries on the hill, and repulsed our troops.

IMPORTANT FROM VICKSBURGH.

Preparations for an Attack on the Rebel Stronghold.

CHICAGO, Tuesday, May 5.

A special dispatch from Cairo says the steamer *Lady Franklin* has arrived from Vicksburgh on Thursday night last. She reports that on that morning Gen. SHERMAN, with a fleet of transports, accompanied by gunboats, passed up the Yazoo and made an attack on the rebel batteries. In the afternoon several more transports followed with troops aboard.

It was reported that Gen. SHERMAN landed precisely in the same place he landed when he made the former attack.

Cannonading and musketry were distinctly heard at Young's Point, on Thursday, till long after nightfall.

A gentleman who left New Carthage on Wednesday last, states that a very heavy force of Gen. GRANT's army has been landed on the eastern side of the river, eight miles above Grand Gulf, and that our gunboats had been shelling the latter place for several days.

IMPORTANT FROM SUFFOLK.

Two Reconnoissances Across the Nansemond on Monday.

The Enemy Driven Out of Their Intrenchments.

Rumored Capture of a Battery of Eight Guns.

Hasty Departure of Rebel Troops on Monday Afternoon.

SUFFOLK, Va., Monday, May 4.

At 9 o'clock, yesterday morning, Gen. PECK sent a force of infantry, cavalry and artillery across the Nansemond River at Suffolk to make a reconnoissance. They advanced cautiously up the old Petersburgh turnpike, and when two miles out, encountered the enemy's rifle pits which were thoroughly manned.

The Eighty-ninth New-York and Thirteenth New-Hampshire regiments made a spirited and successful charge upon the rebel works and carried them after a heavy resistance, when the enemy retreated, and fell back out of range, leaving their dead and some wounded on the field.

During this time the drawbridge battery and our army gunboat *Smith Briggs*, Capt. LEE, were playing upon the enemy, doing good execution among the sharpshooters secreted in the woods.

In the afternoon our troops came upon a rebel masked battery situated two and a half miles north of Suffolk, and at 4 o'clock DAVIS' Massachusetts battery and the gunboat *Smith Briggs* commenced shelling it out. After thirty minutes the rebels returned fire, which was kept up on both sides until sunset, when the enemy's battery was silenced.

Col. RINGOLD, of the One Hundred and Third New-York, was shot while leading his regiment in front, and died during the night.

The Chaplain of the Twenty-fifth New-Jersey was wounded.

Dr. SMITH, of the One Hundred and Third New-York, was shot severely by an insane officer yesterday.

While the above skirmishing was in progress, Gen. GETTY crossed the Nansemond, four miles below Suffolk, and encountered the enemy; and it was rumored and believed that he had succeeded in capturing a rebel battery of eight guns and a large number of prisoners. This needs confirmation.

Scouts were sent out from Suffolk yesterday on the Somerton and Eatonton roads, but discovered nothing of the enemy; and after going about six miles, they returned.

The enemy's rifle pits on the South Quay Road and in our front were vacated yesterday afternoon, and the troops left in great haste, taking their baggage with them, evidently having more important business elsewhere.

From Bermuda.

By the brig *Ocean Traveler*, we have Bermuda papers to April 28. They contain little news.

The steamers *Robert Lee*, with 620 bales of cotton, besides pitch, turpentine, resin, &c., and *Cornubia*, with 370 bales of cotton, had arrived at St. George's from Wilmington. The former cleared on the 24th on her return voyage.

Arrived at Hamilton, Bermuda, April 20, bark *Eliza Barss*, COOPER, New-York; April 21, brig *Col. Penniman*, FLEEKITT, New-York.

Cleared, April 20, brig *Henrietta*, DOE, New-York; April 22, ship *Gertrude*, WHITMAN, Shanghai: April 23, schooner *Hound*, PEARMAN, Baltimore.

The Charleston Mercury.

DAILY PAPER—TEN DOLLARS PER ANNUM, PAYABLE HALF-YEARLY IN ADVANCE. | VINDICE NULLO—SPONTE SUA SINE LEGE FIDES RECTUMQUE COLENTUR. | COUNTRY PAPER—THREE A WEEK—FIVE DOLLARS PER ANNUM, IN ADVANCE.

VOLUME LXXXII. | CHARLESTON, S. C., FRIDAY, MAY 8, 1863. | NUMBER 11,749

TELEGRAPHIC NEWS.

FROM THE RAPPAHANNOCK—FURTHER DETAILS OF THE LATE BATTLES.

RICHMOND, May 7.—The correspondent of the Richmond *Whig* gives some further details of the battles of Chancellorsville and Fredericksburg.

HOOKER accomplished the capture of Marye's Heights by a ruse. On Saturday evening he moved several heavy columns of troops towards the right of his line. During the night, however, he recalled them, and threw them rapidly across the river on pontoons.

The battle began at daylight. BARKSDALE'S brigade of Mississippians, by desperate fighting, held the enemy in check for some time. The fight opened with volleys of musketry, but the combatants soon closed with the bayonet, many of our men encountering the enemy with clubbed muskets. Finally, the Mississippians were compelled to fall back before overwhelming numbers, but not until the ground had been piled with the slain Yankees. Our loss was about one hundred. All of the 10th Mississippi, excepting two companies, were captured. Colonel GRIFFIN and Adjutant STUART were killed, and Major CAMPBELL was wounded. All but seven of Company A, Washington Artillery, were made prisoners, including Captain SQUIRES. The Yankees showed "no quarters" to the rebels. The guns of the Washington Artillery were not retaken.

Most of our casualties in the battles around Chancellorsville consisted of slight wounds in the hand or arm. Few, comparatively, were killed.

The loss of the enemy was equal to that which he sustained in any previous battle of the war. The field was literally strewn with his dead.

The prisoners captured were mostly two years and nine months' men, whose term of service would soon expire. They say they were put in front by HOOKER at every point. The main body of the enemy, being driven to the river, remain hemmed in by our army, afraid to advance and yet fearing to attempt to re-cross.

Gen. LEE has remarked that the present position of affairs in the field is quite satisfactory to him.

GUINEA STATION, May 5.—The 12th regiment South Carolina Volunteers have not been engaged in the fight. It was detached to guard prisoners. Corporal ELLIS, Company E, of Lancaster District, was wounded in a skirmish severely.

JOHN L. MILLER.

RICHMOND, May 5.—Lieut. PROCTOR lost his leg; Lieutenant COTHRAN, wounded in hand; MCLAUGALIN, mortally; Lieut. DUBOSE, 1st regiment, killed; Maj. MILLER, slightly wounded; Lieut. ROBINSON, 4th regiment, seriously.

R. W. BARNWELL.

The following South Carolina casualties are announced:

Killed—Col. James M. Perrin, Captain C. Boyd, Capt. T. C. Perrin, Lieut. Pinckney Seabrook.

Wounded—Arthur Wardlaw, seriously; General Edwards, Gen. McGowan, Colonel J. L. Miller, slightly; Capt. Cuthbert, severely; Captain A. C. Haskell, painfully in foot.

THE WAR IN VIRGINIA.

We make up from our Richmond exchanges of Tuesday a summary of such additional intelligence of the recent movements of the campaign in Virginia as had been received up to Monday night:

THE BATTLE.

The scene of the battle is in Spotsylvania county, between the Wilderness and Chancellorsville. The latter is a place with only one dwelling, a large brick house, formerly a tavern, and latterly a boarding school. It is about ten miles west of Fredericksburg. The Wilderness we suppose to be indicated by "Wilderness Creek," a small stream running into the Rappahannock, about four or five miles from Chancellorsville; the country adjacent and widening out towards Chancellorsville is the Wilderness, out of which the enemy came at the bidding of Jackson. The United States Ford is on the Rappahannock, eight miles above Fredericksburg, and two miles below the mouth of the Rapidan. Ely's Ford is on the Rapidan, four miles above its mouth. The enemy having crossed into Spotsylvania, presented himself on the left of our line in front of Fredericksburg. But our sagacious Commander had taken proper measures, it may be inferred by the result. Longstreet and his command were recalled in good time, and by the best routes for an opportune junction with our main line, while the strategy for getting in rear of the enemy was matured. This decisive movement was conducted by that warrior who never fails, and on Saturday (as we understand) the enemy, to his dismay, found Jackson thundering upon his rear. Driven from his position towards Chancellorsville, he got out of the frying pan into the fire by encountering Longstreet. His rout was complete, as we are officially informed by General Lee.

Brigadier General E. F. Paxton, of Rockbridge county, Va., whose fall in battle is announced, was formerly Gen. Jackson's Adjutant General. He commanded a brigade in Jackson's corps, and it is sufficient praise to say of him, that he commanded Jackson's affectionate confidence.—Green grow the turf over his grave, and undying be his fame!

A letter dated Guinea Station, Sunday, 2 p. m., says:—"The latest news from the battle field represents our prospects as brilliant. The Yankee infantry are fighting badly. Their artillery, however, is handled very skilfully.—This is the only thing in our way. Our Generals thought we would finish the enemy to-day."

THE YANKEE RAID TOWARDS RICHMOND.

The Yankee forces lately engaged in raids upon the railroads were composed of twenty-eight regiments, all under General Stoneman, a force of at least 15,000 men. The detachment of so large a body of troops upon such an expedition, while a battle like that just fought in Spotsylvania was in actual delivery, will remain one of the inexplicable manoeuvres of Yankee strategy. Fifteen thousand cavalry is a most formidable force, and, judiciously used on the battle field, might have caused us irreparable loss. But Hooker has seen fit to expend this formidable force, not upon the battle field, but upon the undefended railroads—and what damage has he done?

From all we can gather, three engines have been partially destroyed, the rails torn up at several points on the lines, creating a delay of transportation of possibly two or three days. The exact amount of the injury done to the railroads has not been ascertained, and the rumors and reports are so conflicting and contradictory that it is folly to repeat them. We learn from a gentleman who was captured by them at Ashland, and whose horse was taken, that no damage was done to the cars, except, perhaps, to the engine; that the force was expecting to be captured; that a Colonel Davis, commanding the force, so expressed himself; that hungry, dispirited and jaded, many of the men expressed openly a desire to be captured. Their main object was avowed to be the destruction of the Central Railroad bridge over the Chickahominy, which they accomplished. Not being gratified by being captured, they are said to have crossed the Chickahominy at Meadow Bridge, and gone over the Pamunkey at Old Church, and to be making their way either to Gloucester Point or the Rappahannock.

Another party under Col. Windham passed through Louisa county towards Columbia, on the canal, and being followed by Gen. W. H. F. Lee, were overtaken and dispersed with the loss of thirty prisoners and six killed. The destruction or injury of the canal was prevented by Gen. Lee, who was unable to follow them upon their retreat from the blown and jaded condition of his horses.

We have further intelligence of the attack on Ashland, and of the raid on other points, which may be summed up as follows:

The enemy, about five hundred strong (cavalry), entered Ashland about half past four o'clock on Sunday afternoon, and piled up a number of logs on the railroad track, to obstruct the passage of the down train, which soon after appeared. As it came up they took possession of it, set fire to the engine and several of the cars, after robbing the mail cars of about a peck of miscellaneous letters (none of any importance), and, detaching a portion of the train containing about two hundred sick and wounded Confederates, a part of whom escaped, the rest were paroled. They tore up some twenty five feet of the track at Ashland Station, and performed a similar "feat" some half a mile below, besides breaking into a small wooden culvert, which latter was the principal damage done on the road. The engine of the material train, which they also captured, they ran off the track, but did not injure it. Their last achievement was the burning of Mrs. Crenshaw's barn, in the vicinity. The whole amount of damage will be repaired by to-day.

From Ashland they proceeded to Atlee's, on the Central railroad, which they reached yesterday morning, where they tore up a portion of the track, and came down to the Chickahominy and destroyed the bridge. An old locomotive, the "Augusta," which was recaptured from the enemy last year, was sent up with several persons on board to ascertain damages, and reached Atlee's just in time to be taken, the passengers escaping by taking to the woods. The engine was set agoing by the Yankee, and ran into the Chickahominy at the bridge, which they had caved in. The damage done here was very slight, the bridge being a small concern, and the rest of the damage hardly worth mentioning.

Another party, acting in concert with these, visited Hanover Court House and burned the depots, doing no other injury worthy of note. They then proceeded down the north bank of the Chickahominy, directing their course towards Williamsburg. There were many rumors afloat as to their movements after their operations at Atlee's, which we deem unnecessary to mention, there being no truth in them.

Above is to be found all that approaches reliability as to the injury done by these raids.

The Examiner of Tuesday says: "The nearest approach to this city ever made by hostile Yankees was accomplished on yesterday morning. When McClellan beleaguered the Capital of the Confederacy, twelve months ago, and "On to Richmond" was the watchword of his numberless legions, five miles was the least distance ever between him and the object of his hopes and ambition. But on yesterday morning, at 9 o'clock, three hundred Yankee cavalry visited the farm of Mr. John B. Young, on the Brooke turnpike, two miles from the corporate limits. Their stay, it is true, was brief, but they enjoyed one of the finest views of the spires and housetops of the city."

SEIZURE OF A CONFEDERATE GUNBOAT AT LIVERPOOL—A SHIPYARD UNDER SURVEILLANCE.—Considerable excitement was created in Liverpool on the 6th ult., by the seizure of the gunboat *Alexandria* by the Custom House authorities, on suspicion that she was intended for the service of the Confederates. A Liverpool letter in the London *Daily News* gives the following particulars of the seizure:

It had been well known for some weeks past that one gunboat, if not more, was fitting out in some of the minor docks in Liverpool, and those employed about them made no secret of the destination for which they were intended. On the facts coming to the knowledge of Mr. Dudley, the United States Consul at Liverpool, he at once communicated with the American Minister in London, and the result was that inquiries were instituted into the whole of the proceedings bearing upon the building of the vessel seized. These inquiries appear to have been so far successful that the British Government sent down orders to seize the vessel, and at an early hour yesterday morning (April 6th) Mr. E Morgan, one of the Customs Surveyors, went on board the Alexandria—that being, like "290," the first christening of the gunboat, as no doubt had she got clear off she would have undergone a rechristening—and took possession of her.

The Alexandria is a wooden screw steamer of about one hundred and twenty tons, and a very fine model. She was built by Messrs. Miller & Co., of the South End, for Messrs. Fraser, Trenholm & Co., of Liverpool, the 'depositaries' in Liverpool (in conjunction with Mr. James Spence) of the Confederate Government. At the time the vessel was seized she was lying in the Toxteth dock, a quiet, out of the way place.

An iron ship building firm, near the builders of the Alexandria, have a large iron gunboat, of about twelve hundred tons, on the stocks for the Confederate Government; but it is now stated that our Government has issued instructions to the officials here that in all cases where there is the slightest suspicion that ships are being built here for other than neutral powers, they are to seize such vessels and await the decisions of the legal authorities.

Since writing the above we have heard that, although there was every appearance of fitting up for guns, there were actually no guns on board the Alexandria. The vessel, however, is now in charge of Government officials, and no doubt the investigation which is to take place will elucidate whether there were guns on board or not. The excitement among the gentlemen of Southern proclivities is very great.

LAIRD'S famous shipyard, at Liverpool, where the *Alabama* was built, it would seem from the following paragraph of a Liverpool letter, published in the Manchester *Guardian*, is also to be watched:

The Government, in addition to the seizure of the Alexandria on the Liverpool side of the Mersey, are about, if they have not already done so, to put the building yard of Messrs. Laird & Brothers, at Birkenhead, under a kind of surveillance, as it is no longer doubted in Liverpool that the two gunboats now in course of construction at the Birkenhead Iron Works are intended for the Confederate Government. Information, we know, has been received in Liverpool of the above intention of the Government.

Battle of Chancellorsville, May 2, 1863

Battle of Chancellorsville, May 1, 1863

The New-York Times.

VOL. XII—NO. 3626. NEW-YORK, FRIDAY, MAY 8, 1863. PRICE THREE CENTS.

FROM HOOKER'S ARMY.

Abandonment of the South Side of the Rappahannock.

NO BATTLE ON TUESDAY.

The Withdrawal Commenced on Tuesday Night.

Our Losses in the Great Battles Estimated at Ten Thousand.

GEN. STONEMAN HEARD FROM.

All the Railroads and Telegraphs Communicating with Lee's Army Cut.

Our Cavalry Within Five Miles of Richmond.

Important Movements in Other Directions.

Interesting Reports from the Richmond Papers.

Our intelligence this morning puts beyond doubt the fact that Gen. Hooker's army has again retired to the north side of the Rappahannock. From various sources we collect the following facts in regard to the movement.

There was no fighting on Tuesday of any consequence, and the rumors to that effect were founded on a misapprehension.

The sharpshooters were quite active, and the artillery opened occasionally, but results were unimportant. The enemy had evidently massed his army on our right.

About 5 o'clock in the morning it commenced raining. The water fell in torrents over an hour, deluging the roads, tearing up the corduroys, sweeping away bridges, and threatening the destruction of the pontoons. The river rose with great rapidity, and soon overflowed the ends of the pontoons, rendering crossing impracticable. The upper pontoon was taken up, and used in lengthening out the others, and after several hours of very hard labor the bridges were once more ready. It was soon evident that Gen. Hooker, seeing his position was rendered temporarily untenable by the storm, had determined to cross over again to this of the Rappahannock. On Tuesday the order was given to retreat. New roads were cut. The trains and reserve artillery were sent back, and the evacuation was commenced.

Pine boughs were spread upon the pontoons to prevent the noise of crossing, and at 10 o'clock Tuesday night the troops commenced falling back. The First Corps (Couch's) was the first to cross. The Fifth (Meade's) Corps remained in the intrenchments to cover the retreat. The Sixth Corps also recrossed the United States Ford, and are marching back to Falmouth. At 3 o'clock on Wednesday morning wagon and mule trains and the artillery had all passed, and the infantry was crossing on two bridges at United States Ford. Couch's corps was in the advance. The retreat was covered by the Fifth, Meade's corps. By dark, the wagons, extra caissons, pack mules, &c., were at Falmouth. The wounded were hastily removed from the hospitals, and sent to Washington, leaving nothing on the other side except our infantry and artillery.

After fighting the severe battle of Sunday morning, Gen. Hooker continued to strengthen his lines, throwing up double lines of rifle pits, and constructing abattis along the entire line of his camp. The enemy continued to make demonstrations along the works, driving in the pickets, and delivering volleys of musketry at men most exposed.

Sedgwick, at Fredericksburgh, was overwhelmed by numbers, and pressed hard on both front and rear, and was hardly able to make good his escape near Banks' Ford. Fredericksburgh and the heights beyond have been reoccupied by the enemy.

Sedgwick has lost in killed and wounded about 5,000 men. His artillery and trains were safely brought over on Monday night.

Richmond papers of the 5th, state that Stoneman's cavalry had completely severed all Lee's communications with Richmond, and that the only reports of the fighting were received there from mounted messengers. These journals also state that Gen. Peck's forces were pressing on after the rebel forces, which had abandoned the siege of Suffolk; and that Keyes' corps at Yorktown was also moving.

Reports are said to have been received in Washington that, after cutting the railroad lines leading into Richmond, Stoneman deployed his forces along the road leading from Lee's army to Gordonsville. It was also said that troops were arriving at the latter point, *en route* to Lee's army, but that they came from Lynchburgh, and not from Richmond.

The most intelligent estimates place our losses during this brief campaign at not more than 15,000. The rebel army is thought to have lost at least one-third more, as they charged upon our batteries in masses, and were fearfully slaughtered by our artillery.

Our correspondent with the left wing alludes to a rumor that Gen. Sickles had fallen in the fight on the right. The report lacks confirmation, however.

We subjoin the letters of our correspondents detailing the important movements which transpired previous to Gen. Hooker's withdrawl from the south bank of the Rappahannock. The lists of casualties, so far as they have been received, are also given.

A SEMI-OFFICIAL STATEMENT.

From the National Intelligencer of Yesterday.

Official information received last evening at the War Department authorizes us to state that Gen. Hooker, after waiting in vain near Chancellorsville, on Tuesday last, for a renewal of the battle by the enemy, recrossed the Rappahannock on the evening of that day, influenced by prudential motives, springing, doubtless, in part, from the great and sudden rise of the Virginia rivers, in consequence of the recent heavy rains.

We do not learn that Gen. Hooker was apprized, before making this retrograde movement, of the success which is alleged to have attended the operations of Gen. Stoneman in breaking the enemy's communications with Richmond. If this fact had been known to him, (assuming it to be a fact,) it may be doubted whether Gen. Hooker would have deemed it necessary to take a step which must tend to deprive him of some, at least, of the advantages resulting from Gen. Stoneman's coöperative expedition.

Among events which have not transpired officially, but of which there are rumors having the appearance of truth, it may be stated that Gen. Sedgwick, in endeavoring, on Monday last, with the greater part of his command, to effect a junction with Gen. Hooker's army near Chancellorsville, encountered the enemy in force and met with a serious reverse, the particulars of which are not yet known.

LATEST NEWS FROM THE ARMY.

Washington, Thursday, May 7.

It is ascertained from the front that the Army of the Potomac has arrived, with all its material, at their old camps at Falmouth.

The demonstration of Gen. Hooker has proved no disaster, but simply a failure, owing to the impracticability of the position which the army had gained with so much skill and energy. Less than three-eighths of the whole force was engaged as could be engaged, the ground being covered with forest, and being without any practicable roads.

Our entire loss in killed, wounded and missing does not exceed 10,000. The enemy's loss must have been double of this—honorably to the army, but lamentably for the country, the greatest proportion of them in killed and wounded.

Our loss of prisoners does not exceed 1,700. We have received 2,450 prisoners of the enemy.

We lost eight guns, and took the same number of pieces from the enemy.

The relinquishment of the position was made simply because it afforded no field for the manœuvreing of the army, and not from any reverse or injury sustained by it. The General and the entire army are in excellent heart and ready for a new movement. We will probably not know where this is to be made after it has been commenced.

Richmond papers show that Stoneman's corps went within two miles of Richmond and effected many captures and a great destruction of property. At least a part of all this gallant force has reached Gloucester, in Keyes' command, opposite to Yorktown, on the York River.

There can now be no impropriety in saying that the President and Major-Gen. Halleck visited Gen. Hooker and the army yesterday, and returned to the city to-night.

At nearly 1 this morning information was received that Gen. Stoneman has safely arrived at Rappahannock Station, with the remainder of his force. He has cut the railroad connections of the enemy in all directions, and thus won a noble distinction.

THE NEWS IN WASHINGTON.

Washington, Wednesday, May 6.

The news that Hooker and his army had recrossed the Rappahannock, flashed through Washington about 5 o'clock this afternoon. The impression produced by it was profound. Men's minds were cast down from the congratulatory cheerfulness with which all had for three days discussed the events which succeeded the brilliant passages of the Rappahannock and the Rapidan. The fact that our army had recrossed was all-sufficient. Scarcely any interest was excited by the details attempted here and there of the restoration of headquarters at Falmouth—of intrenchments thrown up in the rain—of this measure for security or that measure.

It made men silent and thoughtful beyond anything I have ever seen in Washington.

And yet what is the fact? The immense downfall of rain had swollen the Rappahannock so deep and so rapid as to endanger the existence of Hooker's bridges. One statement is, that the water rose seven feet in 24 hours.

A Council of War is said to have unanimously agreed that the army should be transferred to the other bank of the river in anticipation of the loss of the bridges, and it was accordingly transferred. The artillery crossed at 3 o'clock this morning. The infantry followed.

All who have come from Fredericksburgh, and from the upper fords to-day, unite in unstinted praise of the heroic fighting done by Sickles' and Sedgwick's corps. Birney's, Berry's and Whipple's divisions—particularly Birney's—covering themselves with glory. The sad losses we have sustained fell principally on these brave organizations. The large captures made were mostly made by Sickles' regiments. Experienced witnesses of the panoramic contest at Fredericksburgh agree in their estimate that Sedgwick's fifteen thousand fought at least twice the number of the rebels.

The losses at Chancellorsville and Fredericksburgh are about even on each side. The numbers of killed and wounded are about even, and of prisoners captured, and of guns lost and taken; and justice requires me to say that the fighting of the two armies was equal. Each walked right up to the muzzles of the other's guns.

Washington, Thursday, May 7—11:15 P. M.

Brig.-Gen. Stoughton arrived to-day from Richmond, exchanged. He says that on Monday morning the neighboring farmers rushed into Richmond, bringing the startling news that Stoneman, with his cavalry and artillery, was at the suburbs of the city; that they had destroyed all the railroads and public property, and were gobbling up everybody as prisoners.

The alarm spread like wildfire. The bells were rung, and the news carried from street to street. A fearful consternation ensued. All business was immediately suspended, and families who could do so packed up their property to leave. The military guard at Libby Prison were ordered off to the fortifications, and the clerks in the departments were put in their places.

The panic continued throughout the day and night, and not until it was known that Stoneman was on his way down the peninsula was quiet restored.

Gen. S. thinks that a detachment of Stoneman's force struck the Richmond and Fredericksburgh Railroad, above Chesterfield, north of the junction of the Gordonsville road going South; destroyed the bridges over the North and South Anna, Chickahominy, and other streams, and tore up the road at frequent points to within two miles of Richmond. Second detachment destroyed portions of the Gordonsville Railroad, and crossed it, striking the James River at Columbia, breaking the canal banks, and passing down the river, burned considerable property at Goochland, within twenty miles of Richmond, and joined the first detachment near Richmond.

The whole force threw aside worn out horses and took fresh ones wherever they could find them, and appropriated property available for the expedition. They captured two rebel trains, and paroled many prisoners. They got within sight of the Richmond churches, and citizens riding out in barouches encountered our cavalry with Union flags, and went marching back, shouting that the Yankees were upon them, that Lee's army was defeated, and Richmond summoned to surrender.

The intrenchments surrounding the city were very weakly garrisoned, if at all. Gen. Stoughton thinks there were no troops in Richmond except a battalion of 400 men. One of our officers and two men were taken within a mile and a quarter of the town.

Gen. S. heard it reported that "Stonewal" Jackson was wounded, and had his left arm amputated.

ESTIMATES OF LOSSES.

Washington, Thursday, May 7.

The *Evening Star* says:

"Gen. Hooker, it is understood, estimates his losses in the late battles at about ten thousand, all told, killed, wounded and missing; also, that he brought all his material away safely from his late position; and that while we were so unfortunate as to lose some artillery, we have taken at least as many pieces as we have lost."

ACCOUNTS FROM WASHINGTON PAPERS

From the Washington Star, April 6.

Stoneman's force was divided into three columns, one of which, that moving in the direction of the Richmond and Fredericksburgh railroad, he commanded in person, though the havoc worked from Hanover Junction down to within five miles of Richmond, was made by a subdivision under the command of Col. Davis.

One of the three columns, commanded by Brig.-Gen. Averill, after crossing the Rappahannock at Kelly's Ford, pushed on to Brandy Station, where it met the enemy's pickets and drove them back in a short skirmish. It then pushed on direct to Culpepper Court-house, where Gens. Fitzhugh and William Henry Lee were found with a rebel force of perhaps 500 cavalry, which fled precipitately back across Cedar Mountain.

At Culpepper Court-house Gen. Averill captured a lot of rebel Government flour, and then pushed on after the retreating Lees, following them to Rapidan Station, where they burned the railroad bridge, over which they retreated, after a smart fight, in which they lost Col. Rosser, (late of the United States Army,) who commanded one of their brigades. Our loss there was inconsiderable, and they lost several killed besides Col. Rosser and also thirty-one prisoners, whom Gen. Averill brought back with him. The object of Averill's expedition seems to have been to destroy this (Rapidan) bridge, which the enemy in their panic did for him. After proceeding as far as Orange Court-house, he returned with his force to the main army, joining it at Chancellorsville on Sunday last.

Another column of Stoneman's force, under command of Gen. Buford, which left the Rappahannock at the same time, pushed on directly toward Gordonsville, and positive information has just been received announcing its success in cutting the Central Railroad between Gordonsville and Richmond, and also between Gordonsville and Charlottesville, thus (with the achievements of the column in destroying the railroad between Fredericksburgh and Richmond) completely stopping rail communication in any direction out from Lee's main army, and breaking up for the time being the enemy's facilities for forwarding supplies or reinforcements to it from any direction.

According to the Richmond papers of yesterday, Longstreet, in person, joined Lee some days ago, but was accompanied by none of the troops with which he had been operating before Suffolk.

We regret to have to say that Brig.-Gen. A. W. Whipple, who was wounded in the recent engagement in which Gen. Berry was killed, died yesterday at 2 P. M.

The latest information from the field states that the aggregate rebel loss in the four days' fighting has been far larger than ours—which is natural enough, as they were necessarily in every case the attacking party, and followed their old practice of massing their troops very heavily against the points they selected to assail, thus presenting numerous opportunities for our artillery to mow them down in great numbers.

The Richmond papers of yesterday claim that Lee took in the engagement of Saturday 5,000 of the Eleventh Army Corps as prisoners. This is the corps that behaved so badly on Saturday, but the number of prisoners taken from it is nothing like this number.

It is but fair to the Eleventh corps to say that they retrieved their reputation measurably by good conduct on Monday and yesterday, showing that their bad behavior previously was from one of those panics that will sometimes overtake the best troops.

OUR SPECIAL ARMY CORRESPONDENCE.

MOVEMENTS ON THE LEFT.

Falmouth, Va., Tuesday, May 5, 1863.

Yesterday two terrible battles were fought by the Sixth corps, Gen. Sedgwick, resulting in fearful carnage on both sides. Owing to the sudden appearance of the enemy in rear, I was unable yesterday to complete my account of Sunday's operations, and will now go back and refer briefly to them. After the charge of the flying division on the Washington Artillery, portions of Howe's charged up the hill further to the right, under a most galling fire, capturing four guns. They were taken by Mills' brigade and the Vermont ——, which suffered the most. One brass twelve-pounder was charged and taken by the Thirty-third New-York, Col. Taylor—which afterward, together with the Seventy-seventh New-York, pushed on after the fleeing rebels, who, getting under the protection of woods, returned a hot fire. They stood, however, but a short time and then fled. The earthworks were stormed, twelve guns captured, and the stars and stripes planted.

The various divisions of the corps (Sixth, Gen. Sedgwick's) moved rapidly forward up the Gordonsville turnpike, to the distance of four miles, skirmishing all the way, where they found the enemy in force, when another battle ensued, in which Brooks', Newton's, and the Flying division, were engaged—the first suffering severely. The rebels were in a woods, and, as we advanced to it, opened a galling fire. Russell's brigade, composed of the Ninety-fifth and One Hundred and Seventeenth Pennsylvania, and One Hundred and Twenty-first New-York, made a charge, and suffered severely, the Ninety-fifth being almost annihilated. While the battle was progressing, the enemy suddenly commenced firing on our left to the rear, and Brooks' division was obliged to change front. The battle lasted till dark without any decisive results being obtained on either side. During the night the woods took fire, and it is feared that many of the wounded on both sides perished in the flames. Monday morning the rebels suddenly made their appearance on the hills to the left of Fredericksburgh, and coming down rapidly, occupied the city, thus getting in the rear of the corps. Your correspondent happened to be in a farm-house at the point where they descended to the plain, and you can judge of his astonishment on looking out of the window to see this large force advancing in the field in front of the house. Most of the supply trains, ambulances, mules and soldiers in the vicinity were taken. A fleet horse saved me from capture. A serious blunder was perpetrated in pushing our forces on so rapidly without ascertaining whether or not there were any rebels on the woody heights to the left of the city. One whole corps came down and forming in line of battle immediately marched after the corps. The only way of retreat lay by Brooks' Ford, five miles above the city. Gen. Sedgwick was signaled from this side of the river of the condition of affairs and immediately turning about formed a line of battle facing this way, holding the rebels in check, and working down toward the ford. The lines of battle remained in this condition until about the middle of the day, when the rebels attacked us, and were gallantly repulsed—Howe's division capturing 300 prisoners. The rebel reinforcements had fought none, while our troops had been fighting more or less since the previous Tuesday night. For a time it was feared that the corps could not make communication at Banks' Ford, and that the whole of it must be captured. But by noon, a connection was made, and Gen. Sedgwick sent for supplies. Meantime the wounded in Fredericksburgh were being taken across the pontoons to this side, all of them being got away on the sudden appearance of the enemy on the outskirts above. The Doctors, supposing, of course, that the enemy would come down and take them, made all the arrangements for being taken prisoners; but for some reason, either through fear of our forces above or siege guns on this side of the river, the enemy did not advance into the town. The positions of the respective armies were then as follows: Our main force on the north, then the main force of the enemy, the Sixth Corps below, corps of rebels still lower, and our heavy guns on this side—a most extraordinary sandwiching of opposing forces together.

Skirmishing occurred along the whole line until 5½ o'clock in the evening, when the rebels attacked us from two ways. The Union forces were at the time arrayed in an arc, both wings resting on the river, the right at Banks' Ford. They were arrayed as follows:

Flying Division.	Brooks'.
Howe's.	
	Newton's.
2d Div., 2d Corps.	
	Together with the Vt. Brigade.
River.	River.

We were arranged in two lines of battle. The enemy attacking, the Second division of the Second corps and Howe's at first approaching them diagonally from Fredericksburgh and the country directly beyond. Gen. Mills' brigade, consisting of the Thirty-third New-York, Seventy-seventh New-York, Twentieth New-York, Forty-ninth New-York, together with the Vermont brigade and Seventh Maine, bore the brunt of the charge, repulsing the enemy handsomely. The Vermont brigade were on the left of Gen. Mills. Gen. Mills' brigade and other troops made a counter charge; but reinforcements coming up to the enemy, we were not able to drive them. The Seventy-seventh acted nobly, but the Twentieth New-York behaved very disgracefully, as it did at White Oak Swamp, and falling back, brought a cross fire on the Thirty-third. Their Colonel, however, conducted himself most bravely. The other lines of battle were now attacked by overwhelming numbers and obliged to fall back to the river. While the battle was raging terribly our siege guns on this side of the river opened a rapid fire on the enemy from behind, but they advanced so far in driving our forces that the shell, after a short time, failed to reach them. Our forces were pursued back steadily, musketry and artillery firing continuing all night. Our guns made terrible havoc among the enemy, as they charged repeatedly upon them in solid column. The artillery reserved their fire until the charging parties came within a few rods, and then poured the shot and canister into them at a fearful rate. Having broken the column they would fall back to a new position, and prepare to receive another column. Gen. Hayes, of Louisiana; Gen. Berry, of Early's division, and Col. McDowell, of the Fifty-fourth North Carolina, were killed, among many other rebels.

Gen. Brooks, on our side, was wounded.

Gen. Mills is killed or wounded, and Col. Taylor has command of brigade.

Lieut.-Col. Corning ——, Thirty-third New-York, wounded.

Lieut.-Col. Martindale, Twenty-sixth New-Jersey, killed. And many other valuable officers killed and wounded.

The Vermont Brigade suffered very severely, as well as many other commands.

An officer from Banks' Ford this morning informs me that the Second Corps, together with 20 pieces of artillery, crossed over the pontoons at Banks' Ford early this morning, and covered the retreat of the Sixth Corps as it came back over this side of the Rappahannock. But the artillery firing which is now going on in the rear of Fredericksburgh inclines me to doubt the statement, and believe that the corps is still on the other side, trying to fight its way to the river. Last evening the rebels opened artillery on the bridges, and damaged one of them considerably, but it was repaired by our engineers. One bridge cannot, I think, be reached by their guns. Our artillery on this side kept up a rapid fire on the rebel guns during the night. The ambulances have been bringing in the wounded all night. It is reported that Gen. Sickles has been killed on the extreme right. D. W. J.

Falmouth, Va., Wednesday Morning, May 6, 1863.

The Sixth Army Corps succeeded in cutting its way through the enemy, reaching this side of the river yesterday morning. The rebels made herculean efforts to surround it, but were foiled in their endeavors. They had succeeded in getting on three sides of the force, and then opened a battery on the bridge which served for a retreat. How it got away in so good a condition, is a great mystery to all of us. Yet the corps suffered severely, having been subjected to the ordeal of four heavy battles within 36 hours, fighting the last two against overwhelming odds, and when hope of escape seemed well nigh gone. Prior to this disaster, the Sixth Corps was the finest in the Army of the Potomac. During these seven days' battles, it has done the work on the left, from the very first, constructing three of the bridges, doing all the skirmishing, storming the Fredericksburgh Heights, and rushing on to the support of the right. Who is responsible for this successful flanking of the force, I am unable to say. One thing is true, however. After taking the heights, the corps pushed rapidly on up the river, regardless of heavy firing from guns planted in the wood crest at the left of the city, and as we moved on in our rear, the road from this crest was unguardedly left open, and when the overwhelming force of the enemy appeared, there was not a Corporal's Guard, in comparison, to resist them.

Up till this time everything was working admirably. We were both in the front and rear of the enemy, and had we been content to rest on the Fredericksburgh Heights without pushing on, we should have had the rebels in a tight place. All this advantage is now lost. The Heights have been recovered and operations suspended by us on the left. The history of Sunday, Monday and Tuesday would furnish volumes of incidents. The wounded in Fredericksburgh, medical stores, &c., were saved by some one organizing the stragglers in the streets into a picket line facing the Heights taken possession of, thereby causing the enemy to think we had a considerable force both in the city and on this side, which was far from the case. Dr. Foor, of the Eighty-second Pennsylvania, left a wounded man he was dressing, snatched a musket, and rallied several of the men.

These pickets, or skirmishers, kept up a fire on the rebels until all our wounded and stores were got across the river.

The remains of Capt. Strong, Fifth Wisconsin; Capt. Knickerbocker, Forty-third New-York; Capt. Robinson, Sixty-first Pennsylvania; Lieut. Coons, Forty-third New-York, were interred in the yard of G. H. Rowe, and Sergt. Hinman, of the Sixty-fifth New-York, together with several others of Newton's division, in Robert T. Hunter's yard.

The bridges opposite the city were taken up at daybreak yesterday. The last soldier to leave the city was Alex. Camel, of the Twenty-third Pennsylvania, who, delaying, or being left until after the bridges were taken up, stripped off his clothes and pushing them on a boat before him, swam across.

Sergt. Frank. E. Holmes, of the Sixth Maine infantry, a nephew of Vice-President Hamlin's, was killed in the charge on the enemy's works, on Monday night.

Companies F and C, of the Forty-third New-York, Col. Baker's, were taken prisoners while on picket, and if I mistake not, all of the picket line of the Flying division. The Forty-third has only about 200 men left.

Lieut.-Col. Hamilton, son of Dr. Frank Hamilton of New-York, distinguished himself by the gallant manner in which he led the Sixty-second New-York, in the absence of its Colonel.

The grape shot taken from the foot of Lieut.-Col. Newman, of the Thirty-first, is full an inch and a third in diameter; one of the most remarkable cases on record that this large ball or missile should have remained so long in his foot without making its presence known. It was not removed until Monday afternoon, the wound having been received in the Sunday's charge. He is now doing well.

The Sixteenth and One Hundred and Twenty-first New-York, have suffered very severely; in fact both the First and Second Brigades of Gen. Brooks' division, are badly cut up. The Sixty-second New-York has lost very heavily, both in officers and men. Had our forces not been so outnumbered by those of the enemy we should have administered a terrible punishment to them when they attacked and drove us towards the river, since we had the advantage of position, being on higher ground. We had such a long line, however, to defend, that the various regiments had to be shifted from point to point to resist fresh attacks of the enemy. We captured a large number of prisoners though compelled to leave most of our wounded on the field. Nearly one whole brigade, consisting of one General, 20 Captains, 30 Lieutenants and 2,000 privates, which charged upon us, were, I am informed, ensnared into our lines and taken prisoners. I trust the information may not prove untrue. We certainly killed the Colonel, Lieutenant-Colonel and Major of the Seventh Louisiana, and the Lieutenant-Colonel and Major of the Fifth Louisiana. There is no question as to our having mowed the rebels down by whole regiments when they charged upon our batteries. They lay in heaps upon the battle-field. Not a gun was taken, though so many charges upon them were made. The corps retired in good order across the river, saving their camp equipage, mule trains, &c., with the exception of a few which were gobbled up in the momentary panic which ensued when the enemy first made their appearance in our rear above Fredericksburgh. The road was filled with ambulances, (which had been conveying the wounded all night to the city from the battle-field of Sunday evening,) pack mules and vehicles. A part of them fled back to the city, and a part on to the force beyond. While storming the heights, a shell from one of our siege guns planted on this side of the river exploded a rebel caisson behind the redoubts, and killed sixteen horses. The shell struck the first two in line behind the caisson, after exploding it, and hurled the fourteen others down the steep precipice in the rear, into the deep, yawning chasm beneath. They presented a hideous sight, as they lay at the bottom, dead and dying.

Col. Taylor, of the Thirty-third New-York, reported killed in the fight of Monday evening, is unharmed. Lieut.-Col. Corning was wounded in the arm. Maj. Platner had both of his horses shot. Capts. Cole and Root, and Lieut. Porter, of the same regiment, were wounded. Sunday morning it numbered 500 men. It is estimated that not more than 200 are left. Too much praise cannot be awarded to this regiment, the Thirty-first, Col. Jones, and other two years' regiments, whose time is up within two weeks, for the gallant manner in which they have conducted themselves in the various fights. The brave boys were beginning to count the days which intervened between the period of their departure for home.

Yesterday considerable picket-firing took place above Falmouth, and heavy fighting on the extreme right.

About noon our heavy siege guns commenced shelling the heights above the city, and kept it up at intervals during the afternoon. A fearful rainstorm set in about 4 o'clock in the afternoon, which must have caused the river to rise rapidly. A little stream which I stepped over easily at 3 o'clock, I was compelled to wade three hours later, on returning, doffing my wearing apparel and carrying it in my hand. The storm continued all night, and the weather is very cold and chilly this morning, occasioning some discomfort to the wounded. Very heavy artillery firing has been going on at the right, for the last hour, and if there is a corresponding amount of musketry, another fierce battle is going on.

MOVEMENTS OF THE RIGHT.

Headquarters in the Field,
Three Miles from U. S. Ford,
Monday, May 4, 1863.

There has been very little of interest transpiring to-day. A portion of the army has been engaged in constructing rifle-pits and abbatis in divers and various places. The larger part of the army has been resting after the severe labors of the last week. Marches and countermarches, skirmishes, combats and battles, have thoroughly wearied the men and the horses. But, to-day, they are comparatively at rest. Better than that, long trains of pack-mules are winding their way along the crooked wood-roads, and into every camp. The haversacks of the men are being freighted with three days' rations of bread, meat, coffee and sugar. The men are in excellent spirits, and confident that they shall whip the rebels.

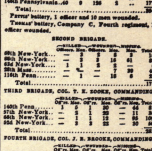

Early this morning the rebels succeeded in bringing a battery to bear upon the wooded bluffs north of the Rappahannock, near United States Ford. Their shell were intended for our wagon train, but by reason of the fact that a body of rebel prisoners had been halted for the night where they supposed the wagon train to be, they troubled their friends more than they did their enemies.

The following is the loss in Gen. Hancock's division, (First division, Second corps):

FIRST BRIGADE.

	Killed. Mounted Men.	Wounded. Off'rs.	Wounded. Men.	Missing. Off'rs.	Missing. Men.	Total.
5th New-Hampshire	1	5	27	..	15	48
81st Pennsylvania	3	4	39	..	62	109
61st New-York	1	2	12	1	15	31
148th Pennsylvania	40	9	126	2	..	177
Total						364

Pettis' battery, 1 officer and 10 men wounded.

Thomas' battery, Company C, Fourth regiment, 1 officer wounded.

SECOND BRIGADE.

	Killed. Officers.	Killed. Men.	Wounded. Officers.	Wounded. Men.	Missing. Men.	Total.
69th New-York	—	3	2	8	3	16
88th New-York	—	3	3	15	61	83
63d New-York	1	1	2	2	—	6
28th Mass	—	[illegible]	—	7	39	46
116th Penn	—	1	—	18	6	25
Total						176

THIRD BRIGADE, COL. T. K. ZOOKE, COMMANDING.

	Killed. Off'rs.	Killed. Men.	Wounded. Off'rs.	Wounded. Men.	Missing. Off'rs.	Missing. Men.	Total.
140th Penn	1	5	1	30	—	44	81
57th New-York	—	2	1	22	—	11	36
66th New-York	—	1	1	12	—	95	109
52d New-York	—	3	3	22	—	30	58
Total							282

FOURTH BRIGADE, COL. J. R. BROOKE, COMMANDING.

	Killed. Off'rs.	Killed. Men.	Wounded. Off'rs.	Wounded. Men.	Missing. Off'rs.	Missing. Men.	Total.
2d Delaware	—	1	4	21	2	62	90
53d Penn	—	1	1	7	—	12	21
64th New-York	—	16	2	16	—	16	50
145th Penn	—	1	2	5	6	119	133
27th Conn	Not yet known.						
Total							294

WOUNDED OFFICERS.

Gen. Couch—slightly.
Col. Beaver, 148th Pennsylvania—seriously.
Col. Frank, 52d New-York.
Col. McKeen, 81st Pennsylvania.
Lieut.-Col. McCreery, 141st Pennsylvania—missing, supposed killed.
Maj. Cross, 5th New-Hampshire.
Maj. Patten, 145th Pennsylvania.
Maj. Fairland, 148th Pennsylvania—slight.
Capt. Overton, 14th infantry—leg.
Lieut. Wells, 17th infantry—leg.
Capt. Lynch, 63d New-York.
Adjt. Dodge, 66th New-York.
Lieut. King, 66th New-York.
Lieut. McEwen, 140th Pennsylvania.
Lieut. Van Dyke, 140th Pennsylvania—seriously.
Capt. Bible, 148th Pennsylvania—killed.
Capt. Egan, 88th New-York—killed.
Lieut. Davis, 2d Delaware—supposed killed.
Capt. McCullough, 2d Delaware—badly.
Lieut. Jordan, 2d Delaware—badly.
Lieut. Huff, 53d Pennsylvania.
Capt. Darby, 64th New-York.
Lieut. Roller, 64th New-York.
Lieut. Kirby, commanding battery—severe.
Lieut. O'Donohue, of Thomas' battery—killed.
Capt. D. B. Logan, 11th New-Jersey—slightly.
Capt. J. H. Meyer, 11th New-Jersey—arm.
Capt. T. J. Halsey, 11th New-Jersey—thigh.
Capt. Luther Martin, 11th New-Jersey—slight.
Lieut. John Lowter, 11th New-Jersey—slight.
Lieut. C. S. Newberry, 11th New-Jersey—hand.
Lieut. Lott, Bloomfield, 11th New-Jersey—killed.
Lieut. Edw. Kelly, 11th New-Jersey—killed.
Capt. Gallbrath, 20th Indiana—arm.

Many gallant deeds were performed by the Staff Officers of the various Generals. At the right of the Chancellor house, a battery of six guns was abandoned, the men and officers being killed and wounded. Gen. Hancock directed his Staff to bring them off. Through the exertions of Major George W. Scott, Lieut. W. P. Wilson, and others of the Staff, the guns were dragged off by hand and saved.

Hancock's division was under a cross fire from three directions, and was the last to leave that portion of the field. Gen. H. had his horse shot under him, as did his Aid, Lieut. Mitchell, and his Orderly Daniel O'Rourk, Sixth New-York cavalry. Two of his orderlies were wounded.

Gen. Couch had his horse shot under him, was slightly wounded, and his clothes were twice struck.

To-day all the Generals are praising the gallantry of Col. Miles, of the Sixty-first New-York, who behaved so gallantly and was wounded so severely yesterday. He is said to be one of the best officers and bravest soldiers in the army. He had command of several regiments upon the lines near the Chancellor house, and with his skirmishers repulsed several strong attacks without their being able to reach his line of battle. If he should live, he will certainly be promoted. Every officer whom I have heard speak of the matter has spoken with great enthusiasm of the Colonel's conduct, and expressed a wish that he may live to wear the honors he has so justly earned.

I was very sorry to learn that Gen. Whipple, while sitting in his tent, was severely wounded to-day by a chance ball from a rebel sharpshooter. Our Generals, with a bravery entirely unparalleled hitherto in the history of this war, have had their headquarters, day and night, in the advance, among their troops, and in every instance within reach of shot and shell. This has done much to inspire the troops with confidence; but in Gen. Whipple's case has resulted disastrously to himself.

This afternoon there was another dash upon our lines near Hooker's headquarters, but a few rounds of canister made them glad to take French leave.

Battery K, Fourth United States artillery, did most excellent service at the battle. It lost 48 men killed and wounded. Sergt. Marrion had three horses shot under him in a few minutes. The battery having suffered so severely in men and horses, has gone to the rear to recuperate. Capt. F. W. Seeley, commanding, says that in three days he can be ready for service again, and is anxious to go to the front as soon as possible.

We have heard guns in the direction of Sedgwick this afternoon. Z. W. B.

Casualties at Chancellorsville.

THE ELEVENTH CORPS.

Below we give a complete list of the casualties in the New-York regiments in the Eleventh Army corps, at Chancellorsville, on May 2:

STAFF.

Killed.

Capt. Francis A. Depuner.

Wounded.

FIRST DIVISION.

Brig.-Gen. Charles Devans, in foot.
Major Frenaff, slightly, in arm.
Capt. Powers, McLean's Staff, severely, in hand.
Capt. Orto Weber, A. D. C., arm amputated.

ONE HUNDRED AND FIFTY-SEVENTH NEW-YORK VOLUNTEERS.

Killed.

Sgt W C Miner, Co A	Sgt E P Ford, Co E
M F Brown, Co A	Corp R W Hall, Co F
D Hyland, Jr, Co A	H J Preston, Co F
Audrew Mochler, Co B	

Wounded.

Lieut M L Hunt, Co A	Corp E Graves, Co B—head
Corp C D Burdick, Co A	H H Whitman, Co B—missing
D C Clark, Co A	J Seabrook, Co B—missing
E Curtis, Co A	O A Nichols, Co B—missing
S H Davis, Co A	John Wright, Co B—head
M J Hyland, Co A	S A Ruggles, Co B—head
W W Long, Co A	B Harp, drum'r, Co B—side
R Knightengale, Co A	Lieut J A Coffin, Co C
E Tucker, Co A	Corp O Courtney, Co C
D Van Hovenburg, Co A	Corp J P Smyth, Co C
Corp C S Herd, Co B—missing	W W Chapel, Co C
Arthur B Fox, Co C	Nath Wagoner, Co D, arm
Russell Rice, Co C	Geo E Douglas, Co E, groin
Orson A Strobeck, Co C	A Shafer, Co E, ankle
Jay Vanslyke, Co C	W Davis, Co E
Smith Cooper, Co C	R D Ballard, Co E, slight
Lieut S Z Miner, Co D, slight	A Baker, Co E, slight
Corp Z M Blashfield, Co D, arm	Franklin Parschurst, Co F
W G Owens, Co D, badly	Wm M Cady, Co F
C H Sweet, Co D, badly	Corp J E Berry, Co F, neck
John Shafer, Co D, badly	J W Clark, Co F, leg
T T Peters, Co D, badly	J Snyder, Co F, flesh
John Bisbee, Co F	Frank M Curley, Co F, arm
Wm Barney, Co F	John Pfikener, Co A
Henry Whitney, Co A	Sergt C Launay, Co A
Corp D Baker, Co A	C F Baker, Co A
J W Card, Co A	—— Hackett, Co A
W Perry, Co A	B Schemerhorn, Co A
W H Bacon, Co D, hand	H Toppein, Co A

[Continued on Eighth Page.]

The Charleston Mercury.

DAILY PAPER—TEN DOLLARS PER ANNUM, PAYABLE HALF-YEARLY IN ADVANCE. | SPONTE SUA SINE LEGE FIDES RECTUMQUE COLENTUR.—VINDICE NULLO. | COUNTRY PAPER—THRICE A WEEK—FIVE DOLLARS PER ANNUM, IN ADVANCE.

VOLUME LXXXII. | CHARLESTON, S. C., MONDAY, MAY 11, 1863. | NUMBER 11,751

THE BATTLES ON THE RAPPAHANNOCK.

A week has passed since the defeat of HOOKER, and, as yet, no full or consecutive account of it has been obtained. The main facts, however, are now known. The Richmond *Examiner* thus briefly sketches the movements of the two armies:

Hooker's first object in crossing the Rappahannock above the town was to get in the rear of Fredericksburg. His second aim was to prevent a flank attack on the left by the Confederates, who, he supposed, would march up the bank of the river to cut his army at the fords. Hence, he determined to cross the Rappahannock above the confluence with the Rapidan, to march through a portion of Culpeper, and passing the latter river at Germanna and Ely's, to keep his communication behind him, the Rappahannock on his left flank, and the Confederate army and Fredericksburg always in front of him. On Tuesday week his troops were drawn up in full array on the hills of Stafford, in view of the town, pontoons were thrown over, and a strong detachment sent across at Deep Run. This first step was a mere feint to distract the attention. Next day his army disappeared, and the detachment was withdrawn, while the main body passed the rivers above in the order stated. Still believing that Lee's onset would be made close to the river, and on his left flank, he rapidly strengthened that part of his line with field works, and then swung the rest forward to Chancellorsville.

It appears, however, from the despatches of the Confederate General, that his ways were not as the ways of Hooker, nor was his attack made in the manner which Hooker had decided he should make it. The Confederate operations were aimed at the right wing—that reaching to Spotsylvania Court House—of the Federals. General Jackson did flank them, after all, but it was the *right* flank—that nearest Richmond—not the left flank, which Hooker had carefully guarded with a river and field works. General Jackson appears to have turned the Yankee line somewhere beyond the Court House, and penetrating to the Wilderness, a creek between Culpeper and Spotsylvania, got partly in their rear. Attacked by the rest of the Confederates in front, while Jackson's corps came down from the Wilderness, the finest army on the planet, commanded, though it was, by General Judas Hooker, was shortly defeated with great slaughter, dislodged from all the positions around Chancellorsville, doubled up on itself, and pressed down in confusion to the banks of the Rappahannock. In this condition their rout and annihilation were nearly certain, could the attack have been continued as commenced.

But the Confederate victory appears to have been marred by the news from Fredericksburg. A part of the army, supposed to have been sufficient, had been put to guard the old heights back of the town. Hooker had left a large force—said to have been two full corps—on the opposite hill, under an old regular officer, General Sedgwick. His important part in the play was to pass the river and "carry the crest," if possible, while Lee had his hands full of Hooker, and then rush upon his rear. After a long delay, he crossed the river, and did actually get possession of Marye's Hill. Sedgwick was now in Lee's rear, and the event might have been fatal to that General if Hooker had held his own in front. But Hooker was already beaten, and at that time helpless. Lee, therefore, could turn on Sedgwick with safety. He did so, whipped him at once, sent him back to Stafford, and re-occupied Fredericksburg. It is reported that he then went to finish Hooker.

It was too late! The Yankee General had gotten his beaten army in a very defensible position, supported by the Rapidan and Rappahannock, and had erected strong works in front. The Confederate General might well pause before he attacked him there without necessity.

These who know the character of those rivers need not be told that there is no necessity to attack an army which depends on their fords for every particle of supply. It is possible to defend such a position as that which Hooker is said to have assumed; but impossible to remain in it. This is the season of heavy showers. One of these converts those streams in an hour from insignificant creeks into terrible torrents, which would sweep off Pharoah's host. No pontoon could live a minute on its flood. Hooker had the choice, to come out and fight forward, or get back to the northern bank as soon as possible. As his army is a beaten army, we were not surprised to hear that he has chosen the latter alternative, and retreated while still able.

DETAILS OF THE BATTLE.

The correspondent of the Richmond *Enquirer* writes from Fredericksburg, May 6th, as follows:

The battle seems to be over, and from all I can gather a glorious victory has crowned the Confederate arms. I propose to give you a history of the whole fight, beginning with the crossing below town on Wednesday morning last and bringing it down to the brilliant charge of Monday evening, when the enemy were driven in confusion across the river, their midnight cry being *"retreat to Banks' Ford."*

The first movement of the enemy, *i. e.* the crossing below town, can hardly be said to have been a feint. It would be perhaps more proper to speak of it as a movement designed to co-operate with the main attack at Chancellorsville, or it is possible that this force was left in front of Fredericksburg to prevent a rear movement on our part, which, if successful, and the river once crossed by our troops, at a point near town, their access to the railway could have been cut off and their base of supplies rendered useless to them. To guard his rear and protect his base, the force, which afterwards operated offensively, was at first intended to act defensively, in all probability.

How it afterwards acted on the offensive, and succeeded in carrying by storm "Marye's Heights," can probably be explained by the fact that Hooker had been hard pressed and whipped in the fight of Saturday and Sunday morning at Chancellorsville, and made this in order to create a diversion, and enable him to cover his retreat.

Chancellorsville having been the real point of battle it will be most fitting to treat of it first. On Thursday evening Gen Anderson, who was holding a position in front of the United States Mine Ford, twelve miles above Fredericksburg, ascertained that the Yankees, numbering five army corps, with at least eighty thousand men, crossed the Rapid Ann at Kelley's and Germanna Fords, having previously crossed the North Fork of the Rappahannock at Easley's Ford, in Culpeper county, and were advancing down the plank road. General Anderson at once fell back to Chancellorsville, and took up a line of battle in front of the plank road, and extending to the river, and reaching over towards the old Catherine Furnace. General Anderson, however, having too small a force to hold the enemy at this point, fell back to a position some four miles below Chancellorsville, and fronting the old mine road. On Friday morning General Anderson was reinforced on the right by General McLaws, and on the left by General A. P. Hill. At this period General Jackson took command, and ordered an advance, himself leading it, and succeeded during the day in driving the enemy back, they making but slight resistance. On Friday night our forces rested fully two miles beyond the ground occupied by the Yankee forces on the previous evening. The forces principally engaged thus far in this quarter, belonged to Semmes' brigade of McLaws' division, and Mahone's brigade, of Anderson's division.

Saturday morning wore away without important results. There was some artillery firing and a little skirmishing, but the engagement did not become general until about five o'clock in the afternoon, from which hour the fight raged furiously until about eight o'clock. Jackson, at this time, had thrown a force on their upper flank, and was driving them fiercely down upon our lower line, which, in turn, was hurling them back, and rendering futile all their efforts to break through our lower lines, and making it necessary for them to give back towards the river.

There was an intermission in the firing from eight o'clock until about nine. But from nine until long past midnight the sound of artillery and small arms was well nigh deafening. The explanation was ready. Jackson was pressing them with a night fight. Our boys drove the Yankees, who stoutly held their ground, until near day; and at early dawn on Sunday the fight began on both ends of the line, and by eleven o'clock the firing had ceased. On the upper end of the line, near Chancellorsville, the Yankees were badly whipped, and were in full retreat towards the river. On the lower line, near Fredericksburg, however, they had succeeded in carrying Marye's Heights, and were rioting in the wild excess of joy. They had stormed, they said, the Gibraltar of America, and their route to Richmond was plain and easy, little remembering that they had hurled a column of fully ten thousand upon one regiment in front, and thus gaining the rear of the rest of Barksdale's brigade.

But "the best laid schemes of men and mice gang aft agree," and whilst the Yankees were felicitating themselves on their splendid successes, and in imagining themselves to be in the rear of our army, General Lee was so manœuvering as to meet the enemy, who were now throwing themselves forward from the town on the Plank Road. About four o'clock on Sunday evening McLaws' division, including Wilcox's brigade of Anderson's division, met the advance column of the Yankees, under General Sedgwick, at Salem Church, four miles beyond Fredericksburg, on the Plank Road, and our line of battle was formed at right angles with the Plank Road. The battle here raged for about two hours, but the Yankees were repulsed with considerable loss, including some five or six hundred prisoners. Our line on the telegraph road meantime had been formed at Smock's, about three and a half miles out from town. Early on Monday morning Lawton's old brigade, now General Gordon's, supported by General Smith and General Hayes, all of Early's Division, advanced towards Marye's Heights, and charged them without the firing of a gun, driving the enemy from a position from which less than twenty-four hours before he had dislodged Barksdale's gallant Mississippians, after a most heroic resistance, in which the enemy's loss was quite considerable. In this condition matters remained until about five o'clock in the evening, when a general advance was ordered. At the firing of a signal gun, General Early moved upon the enemy from the right, and Generals Anderson and McLaws from the left. The enemy, who held a position on the Plank road, extending up and down, were quickly dislodged and driven with great loss from the field. Their resistance was slight. The charge was grand. Early's men, and especially the Louisianians, under Hayes, walked over the enemy as giants over pigmies, while from above, the men of Anderson and McLaws, who had been constantly marching and fighting for five days, showed no signs of relaxation, but marched boldly and fearlessly up to their appointed work. The result was the enemy was driven in confusion towards Banks' Ford, across which he succeeded in making his way during the night—not, however, without serious loss in killed, wounded and prisoners. General Hoke, of the North Carolina brigade, in Early's division, was wounded in this charge. Whilst this was going on, Barksdale's men were holding the stone wall, Marye's Hill and the heights commanding the Plank Road, so as to prevent a movement on our rear out from Fredericksburg. But this was hardly necessary. Yankee desire for a general advance had been satisfied, and by nightfall the Yankees had begun to prepare for the third and last time to evacuate Fredericksburg—and by day-break our pickets were in the town, which is once again in the hands of Barksdale's men.

Though the enemy at Chancellorsville did not recross the river at the United States Ford until to-day, there has been no general engagement since Sunday—only some occasional skirmishing and feints of attack to cover up their retreat across the river. Hooker, though having the choice of position, did not act offensively after crossing, but fortified and threw himself on the defensive, thus forcing our men to contend against him in this fight against vastly superior numbers, aided by breastworks, fortifications and obstructions of all sorts. But they were of little avail; Jackson turned their flank and fell upon their rear. And Jackson's boys did their work with all their might and main. They charged faster over the battle field than they marched to it, and their cheering as they drove the enemy before them, broke upon the air with fine, inspiring effect, and told too plainly that our men were terribly in earnest.

The battle field, which reaches from Fredericksburg to a point above Wilderness, some twelve miles up from town, and out to the river, with the exception of about two miles between Salem and Zoar churches, attests the skillful aiming and deadly destruction of our artillery. The Yankee dead and wounded are strewn over the entire country. Yet had it not have been one of the most thickly wooded sections of land in Virginia the Yankee loss would have been far greater. Over this same field of battle are scattered, in immense quantities blankets, overcoats, canteens, knapsacks, haversacks, cartridge boxes, and any quantity of rifles, muskets, and various other equipments of the soldier. Our boys, however, found but little to eat. The Yankees had well nigh devoured the commissariat, still a good quantity of hard tack, with some good cooked meats and coffee, were found in the Yankee haversacks. We also captured some freshly slaughtered meats, and some corn and oats; all of which are quite valuable, and just the articles we needed.

Fredericksburg, on this occasion, did not suffer severely as she did before, though the Yankees managed to steal a good deal. Private houses, I believe, were in no instance entered, where the families were present, and the town was not shelled, nor were any citizens arrested or carried off in the town. A few were arrested outside, but in every instance I believe they were rescued by our own soldiery.

Hooker commanded in person at the Chancellorsville fight, and occupied a position near that place during the fight. Hooker has made a good fight. He has manœuvred well, and done better than any other Yankee General; but Hooker is not the equal of Lee. He has so manœuvred and combined as to surround the Yankees twice, and drive them back to the river, when they supposed, on both occasions, that they had gotten into his rear, and were about to surprise him; whilst General Jackson has outdone himself, and exhibited the highest characteristics of a strategist and skillful General, fully confirming all his past renown, and adding new laurels to the many already won in the service of his country.

Our losses are fully 5000, whilst those of the Yankees are confessed to be fully 25,000, and about thirty pieces of artillery. We have captured very near 8000 prisoners, and have lost, I suppose, about 1000 prisoners. These results of the fight point most conclusively to a most brilliant Confederate victory.

THE CASUALTIES.

Gen. T. J Jackson, wounded; Gen. Paxton, killed; Gen. McLaws, struck, but not much hurt; Gen. A. P Hill, contusion, has resumed his command; Gen McGowan, slightly, but painfully, wounded; Brig. Gen. Heth, not much hurt, still in command; Col. J. Q A. Nadenboush, 2nd Regiment Infantry, slightly wounded; Capt Fulton, of the 4th Virginia Volunteers, lost a leg; in the 5th Virginia Volunteers Lieut. Bell was killed, and about 150 killed and wounded; Col. Edmundson, of the 27th Virginia Volunteers, lost an arm; in the 10th Virginia Volunteers (from Rockingham), Col. Warren, commanding the brigade, was shot through the right shoulder (not serious); Lieut. Col. S. W. Walker, killed; Maj. Stover, shot three times and killed. Nine out of eleven commandants of companies were killed, wounded and prisoners; Col T. S. Garnett, of the 48th Virginia Volunteers, commanding the brigade, was wounded, and is believed to be dead.

Maj. Rodgers (artillery) wounded; Col. F. M. Mallory, reported killed; this is doubted. Capt. Boswell, Chief of Engineers, on Jackson's staff, killed. Maj Price of Richmond, killed. Capt. Forbes, of A. P. Hill's staff, killed; all the staff of A. P. Hill either killed or wounded. Capt. Duncan McKim killed. Conway Howard of A. P. Hill's staff killed. In the 18th Virginia Volunteers, Capt. Field and Lieut. Morehead killed, and thirty killed, wounded and missing. In the 58th Virginia Volunteers, Lieut. Col Casey prisoner; seventy killed, wounded and missing. Col. Stafford, 14th Louisiana, wounded. Gen. Hope, of North Carolina, lost 120 men. Lieut. Bell, 5th Virginia Volunteers, was killed. This makes nine out of twelve in this family killed in that regiment. Lieuts. Calhoun and Ryan lost each a leg. Capt. Van Borsch, of Gen. Stuart's staff, a gallant Prusian officer, killed.

Rhode's brigade suffered severely, it is reported, in officers—one-third of whom were either killed or wounded—the proportion being ten wounded men to one killed.—In the 1st Washington Artillery, Captain Squires, Lieutenant Galbraith and Lieutenant Owens were taken prisoners. Lieutenant DeRussey, P. H. Von Cotton, Otto Frank, Barton Kirk and —— Vallentine were wounded. Sergeant Wm. West, Corporal Lewis and Robt. Many were killed. In the 51st Georgia Regiment, Col. Slaughter and Lieutenant Colonel Patton were killed; Colonel Mallory, of the 55th Virginia, Major Miles Selden, aid to Gen. Heth, Capt. Greenlee Davidson, Letcher Battery, Captain Edward Branch, of Richmond Grays, Capt Banks, of the Petersburg Grays, and Major Channing Price, of General Stuart's staff, were killed; also, Col. Purdy, of 18th North Carolina, and Capt. Paine, of Gen. Lane's staff.

DAILY PAPER—TEN DOLLARS PER ANNUM, PAYABLE HALF-YEARLY IN ADVANCE. | SPONTE SUA SINE LEGE FIDES RECTUMQUE COLENTUR.—VINDICE NULLO. | COUNTRY PAPER—THRICE A WEEK—FIVE DOLLARS PER ANNUM, IN ADVANCE.

VOLUME LXXXII. | CHARLESTON, S. C., WEDNESDAY, MAY 13, 1863. | NUMBER 11,753

Jackson.

Seldom, indeed, has a people manifested so deep and universal a sorrow as that which has spread over the land with the announcement of the loss of the loved and trusted leader, whom both hemispheres had learned to know and admire as "Stonewall" JACKSON. General LEE's sublime tribute to his services in the late battles, his profound and sincere sympathy for his sufferings previous to their fatal termination, leaves us at a loss which to admire and love most—the author or the receiver of the letter, in which this magnanimity and manly sorrow are conveyed. "How gladly would I have borne, in my own person, the serious loss you have sustained, for to you, and to you alone is due the victory we have achieved." To this effect is LEE's letter. Who, asks the Richmond *Whig*, is not proud to live in the same day and to belong to the same race with such men? Together, they make up a measure of glory which no nation under Heaven ever surpassed. The central figure of this war is, beyond all question, that of ROBERT E. LEE. His, the calm, broad military intellect that reduced the chaos after Donelson to form and order. But JACKSON was the motive power that executed, with the rapidity of lightning, all that LEE could plan. LEE has been the exponent of Southern power of command; JACKSON, the expression of its faith in God and in itself, its terrible energy, its enthusiasm and daring, its unconquerable will, its contempt of danger and fatigue, its capacity to smite, as with bolts of thunder, the cowardly and cruel foe that would trample under foot its liberty and its religion.

But, though Stonewall JACKSON is dead, his fiery and unquailing spirit still survives in his men. He has infused into them that which cannot die. The leader who succeeds him, be he whom he may, will be impelled, as by a supernatural impulse, to emulate his matchless deeds. JACKSON's men will demand to be led in "Stonewall JACKSON's way." The leader who will not or cannot comply with that demand, must drop the baton quickly. JACKSON's corps will be led forever by the memory of its great chieftain.

The New-York Times.

VOL. XII—NO. 3626. NEW-YORK, FRIDAY, MAY 8, 1863. PRICE THREE CENTS.

FROM HOOKER'S ARMY.

Abandonment of the South Side of the Rappahannock.

NO BATTLE ON TUESDAY.

The Withdrawal Commenced on Tuesday Night.

Our Losses in the Great Battles Estimated at Ten Thousand.

GEN. STONEMAN HEARD FROM.

All the Railroads and Telegraphs Communicating with Lee's Army Cut.

Our Cavalry Within Five Miles of Richmond.

Important Movements in Other Directions.

Interesting Reports from the Richmond Papers.

Our intelligence this morning puts beyond doubt the fact that Gen. Hooker's army has again retired to the north side of the Rappahannock. From various sources we collect the following facts in regard to the movement.

There was no fighting on Tuesday of any consequence, and the rumors to that effect were founded on a misapprehension.

The sharpshooters were quite active, and the artillery opened occasionally, but results were unimportant. The enemy had evidently massed his army on our right.

About 5 o'clock in the morning it commenced raining. The water fell in torrents over an hour, deluging the roads, tearing up the corduroys, sweeping away bridges, and threatening the destruction of the pontoons. The river rose with great rapidity, and soon overflowed the ends of the pontoons, rendering crossing impracticable. The upper pontoon was taken up, and used in lengthening out the others, and after several hours of very hard labor the bridges were once more ready. It was soon evident that Gen. Hooker, seeing his position was rendered temporarily untenable by the storm, had determined to cross over again to this of the Rappahannock. On Tuesday the order was given to retreat. New roads were cut. The trains and reserve artillery were sent back, and the evacuation was commenced.

Pine boughs were spread upon the pontoons to prevent the noise of crossing, and at 10 o'clock Tuesday night the troops commenced falling back. The First Corps (Couch's) was the first to cross. The Fifth (Meade's) Corps remained in the intrenchments to cover the retreat. The Sixth Corps also recrossed the United States Ford, and are marching back to Falmouth. At 3 o'clock on Wednesday morning wagon and mule trains and the artillery had all passed, and the infantry was crossing on two bridges at United States Ford. Couch's corps was in the advance. The retreat was covered by the Fifth, Meade's corps. By dark, the wagons, extra caissons, pack mules, &c., were at Falmouth. The wounded were hastily removed from the hospitals, and sent to Washington, leaving nothing on the other side except our infantry and artillery.

After fighting the severe battle of Sunday morning, Gen. Hooker continued to strengthen his lines, throwing up double lines of rifle pits, and constructing abattis along the entire line of his camp. The enemy continued to make demonstrations along the works, driving in the pickets, and delivering volleys of musketry at men most exposed.

Sedgwick, at Fredericksburgh, was overwhelmed by numbers, and pressed hard on both front and rear, and was hardly able to make good his escape near Banks' Ford. Fredericksburgh and the heights beyond have been reoccupied by the enemy.

Sedgwick has lost in killed and wounded about 5,000 men. His artillery and trains were safely brought over on Monday night.

Richmond papers of the 5th, state that Stoneman's cavalry had completely severed all Lee's communications with Richmond, and that the only reports of the fighting were received there from mounted messengers. These journals also state that Gen. Peck's forces were pressing on after the rebel forces, which had abandoned the siege of Suffolk; and that Keyes' corps at Yorktown was also moving.

Reports are said to have been received in Washington that, after cutting the railroad lines leading into Richmond, Stoneman deployed his forces along the road leading from Lee's army to Gordonsville. It was also said that troops were arriving at the latter point, *en route* to Lee's army, but that they came from Lynchburgh, and not from Richmond.

The most intelligent estimates place our losses during this brief campaign at not more than 15,000. The rebel army is thought to have lost at least one-third more, as they charged upon our batteries in masses, and were fearfully slaughtered by our artillery.

Our correspondent with the left wing alludes to a rumor that Gen. Sickles had fallen in the fight on the right. The report lacks confirmation, however.

We subjoin the letters of our correspondents detailing the important movements which transpired previous to Gen. Hooker's withdrawl from the south bank of the Rappahannock. The lists of casualties, so far as they have been received, are also given.

A SEMI-OFFICIAL STATEMENT.

From the National Intelligencer of Yesterday.

Official information received last evening at the War Department authorizes us to state that Gen. Hooker, after waiting in vain near Chancellorsville, on Tuesday last, for a renewal of the battle by the enemy, recrossed the Rappahannock on the evening of that day, influenced by prudential motives, springing, doubtless, in part, from the great and sudden rise of the Virginia rivers, in consequence of the recent heavy rains.

We do not learn that Gen. Hooker was apprized, before making this retrograde movement, of the success which is alleged to have attended the operations of Gen. Stoneman in breaking the enemy's communications with Richmond. If this fact had been known to him, (assuming it to be a fact,) it may be doubted whether Gen. Hooker would have deemed it necessary to take a step which must serve to deprive him of some, at least, of the advantages resulting from Gen. Stoneman's coöperative expedition.

Among events which have not transpired officially, but of which there are rumors having the appearance of truth, it may be stated that Gen. Sedgwick, in endeavoring, on Monday last, with the greater part of his command, to effect a junction with Gen. Hooker's army near Chancellorsville, encountered the enemy in force and met with a serious reverse, the particulars of which are not yet known.

LATEST NEWS FROM THE ARMY.

Washington, Thursday, May 7.

It is ascertained from the front that the Army of the Potomac has arrived, with all its material, at their old camps at Falmouth.

The demonstration of Gen. Hooker has proved no disaster, but simply a failure, owing to the impracticability of the position which the army had gained with so much skill and energy. Less than three-eighths of the whole force was engaged as could be engaged, the ground being covered with forest, and being without any practicable roads.

Our entire loss in killed, wounded and missing does not exceed 10,000. The enemy's loss must have been double of this—honorably to the army, but lamentably for the country, the greatest proportion of them in killed and wounded.

Our loss of prisoners does not exceed 1,700. We have received 2,450 prisoners of the enemy.

We lost eight guns, and took the same number of pieces from the enemy.

The relinquishment of the position was made simply because it afforded no field for the manœuvreing of the army, and not from any reverse or injury sustained by it. The General and the entire army are in excellent heart and ready for a new movement. We will probably not know where this is to be made after it has been commenced.

Richmond papers show that Stoneman's corps went within two miles of Richmond and effected many captures and a great destruction of property. At least a part of all this gallant force has reached Gloucester, in Keyes' command, opposite to Yorktown, on the York River.

There can now be no impropriety in saying that the President and Major-Gen. Halleck visited Gen. Hooker and the army yesterday, and returned to the city to-night.

At nearly 1 this morning information was received that Gen. Stoneman has safely arrived at Rappahannock Station, with the remainder of his force. He has cut the railroad connections of the enemy in all directions, and thus won a noble distinction.

THE NEWS IN WASHINGTON.

Washington, Wednesday, May 6.

The news that Hooker and his army had recrossed the Rappahannock, flashed through Washington about 5 o'clock this afternoon. The impression produced by it was profound. Men's minds were cast down from the congratulatory cheerfulness with which all had for three days discussed the events which succeeded the brilliant passages of the Rappahannock and the Rapidan. The fact that our army had recrossed was all-sufficient. Scarcely any interest was excited by the details attempted here and there of the restoration of headquarters at Falmouth—of intrenchments thrown up in the rain—of this measure for security or that measure.

It made men silent and thoughtful beyond anything I have ever seen in Washington.

And yet what is the fact? The immense downfall of rain had swollen the Rappahannock so deep and so rapid as to endanger the existence of Hooker's bridges. One statement is, that the water rose seven feet in 24 hours.

A Council of War is said to have unanimously agreed that the army should be transferred to the other bank of the river in anticipation of the loss of the bridges, and it was accordingly transferred. The artillery crossed at 3 o'clock this morning. The infantry followed.

All who have come from Fredericksburgh, and from the upper fords to-day, unite in unstinted praise of the heroic fighting done by Sickles' and Sedgwick's corps. Birney's, Berry's and Whipple's divisions—particularly Birney's—covering themselves with glory. The sad losses we have sustained fell principally on these brave organizations. The large captures made were mostly made by Sickles' regiments. Experienced witnesses of the panoramic contest at Fredericksburgh agree in their estimate that Sedgwick's fifteen thousand fought at least twice the number of the rebels.

The losses at Chancellorsville and Fredericksburgh are about even on each side. The numbers of killed and wounded are about even, and of prisoners captured, and of guns lost and taken; and justice requires me to say that the fighting of the two armies was equal. Each walked right up to the muzzles of the other's guns.

Washington, Thursday, May 7—11:15 P. M.

Brig.-Gen. Stoughton arrived to-day from Richmond, exchanged. He says that on Monday morning the neighboring farmers rushed into Richmond, bringing the startling news that Stoneman, with his cavalry and artillery, was at the suburbs of the city; that they had destroyed all the railroads and public property, and were gobbling up everybody as prisoners.

The alarm spread like wildfire. The bells were rung, and the news carried from street to street. A fearful consternation ensued. All business was immediately suspended, and families who could do so packed up their property to leave. The military guard at Libby Prison were ordered off to the fortifications, and the clerks in the departments were put in their places.

The panic continued throughout the day and night, and not until it was known that Stoneman was on his way down the peninsula was quiet restored.

Gen. S. thinks that a detachment of Stoneman's force struck the Richmond and Fredericksburgh Railroad, above Chesterfield, north of the junction of the Gordonsville road going South; destroyed the bridges over the North and South Anna, Chickahominy, and other streams, and tore up the road at frequent points to within two miles of Richmond. Second detachment destroyed portions of the Gordonsville Railroad, and crossed it, striking the James River at Columbia, breaking the canal banks, and passing down the river, burned considerable property at Goochland, within twenty miles of Richmond, and joined the first detachment near Richmond.

The whole force threw aside worn out horses and took fresh ones wherever they could find them, and appropriated property available for the expedition. They captured two rebel trains, and paroled many prisoners. They got within sight of the Richmond churches, and citizens riding out in barouches encountered our cavalry with Union flags, and went marching back, shouting that the Yankees were upon them, that Lee's army was defeated, and Richmond summoned to surrender.

The intrenchments surrounding the city were very weakly garrisoned, if at all. Gen. Stoughton thinks there were no troops in Richmond except a battalion of 400 men. One of our officers and two men were taken within a mile and a quarter of the town.

Gen. S. heard it reported that "Stonewal" Jackson was wounded, and had his left arm amputated.

ESTIMATES OF LOSSES.

Washington, Thursday, May 7.

The *Evening Star* says:

"Gen. Hooker, it is understood, estimates his losses in the late battles at about ten thousand, all told, killed, wounded and missing; also, that he brought all his material away safely from his late position; and that while we were so unfortunate as to lose some artillery, we have taken at least as many pieces as we have lost."

ACCOUNTS FROM WASHINGTON PAPERS

From the Washington Star, April 6.

Stoneman's force was divided into three columns, one of which, that moving in the direction of the Richmond and Fredericksburgh railroad, he commanded in person, though the havoc worked from Hanover Junction down to within five miles of Richmond, was made by a subdivision under the command of Col. Davis.

One of the three columns, commanded by Brig.-Gen. Averill, after crossing the Rappahannock at Kelly's Ford, pushed on to Brandy Station, where it met the enemy's pickets and drove them back in a short skirmish. It then pushed on direct to Culpepper Court-house, where Gens. Fitzhugh and William Henry Lee were found with a rebel force of perhaps 500 cavalry, which fled precipitately back across Cedar Mountain.

At Culpepper Court-house Gen. Averill captured a lot of rebel Government flour, and then pushed on after the retreating Lees, following them to Rapidan Station, where they burned the railroad bridge, over which they retreated, after a smart fight, in which they lost Col. Rosser, (late of the United States Army,) who commanded one of their brigades. Our loss there was inconsiderable, and they lost several killed besides Col. Rosser and also thirty-one prisoners, whom Gen. Averill brought back with him. The object of Averill's expedition seems to have been to destroy this (Rapidan) bridge, which the enemy in their panic did for him. After proceeding as far as Orange Court-house, he returned with his force to the main army, joining it at Chancellorsville on Sunday last.

Another column of Stoneman's force, under command of Gen. Buford, which left the Rappahannock at the same time, pushed on directly toward Gordonsville, and positive information has just been received announcing its success in cutting the Central Railroad between Gordonsville and Richmond, and also between Gordonsville and Charlottesville, thus (with the achievements of the column in destroying the railroad between Fredericksburgh and Richmond) completely stopping rail communication in any direction out from Lee's main army, and breaking up for the time being the enemy's facilities for forwarding supplies or reinforcements to it from any direction.

According to the Richmond papers of yesterday, Longstreet, in person, joined Lee some days ago, but was accompanied by none of the troops with which he had been operating before Suffolk.

We regret to have to say that Brig.-Gen. A. W. Whipple, who was wounded in the recent engagement in which Gen. Berry was killed, died yesterday at 2 P. M.

The latest information from the field states that the aggregate rebel loss in the four days' fighting has been far larger than ours—which is natural enough, as they were necessarily in every case the attacking party, and followed their old practice of massing their troops very heavily against the points they selected to assail, thus presenting numerous opportunities for our artillery to mow them down in great numbers.

The Richmond papers of yesterday claim that Lee took in the engagement of Saturday 5,000 of the Eleventh Army Corps as prisoners. This is the corps that behaved so badly on Saturday, but the number of prisoners taken from it is nothing like this number.

It is but fair to the Eleventh corps to say that they retrieved their reputation measurably by good conduct on Monday and yesterday, showing that their bad behavior previously was from one of those panics that will sometimes overtake the best troops.

OUR SPECIAL ARMY CORRESPONDENCE.

MOVEMENTS ON THE LEFT.

Falmouth, Va., Tuesday, May 5, 1863.

Yesterday two terrible battles were fought by the Sixth corps, Gen. Sedgwick, resulting in fearful carnage on both sides. Owing to the sudden appearance of the enemy in rear, I was unable yesterday to complete my account of Sunday's operations, and will now go back and refer briefly to them. After the charge of the flying division on the Washington Artillery, portions of Howe's charged up the hill further to the right, under a most galling fire, capturing four guns. They were taken by Mills' brigade and the Vermont ——, which suffered the most. One brass twelve-pounder was charged and taken by the Thirty-third New-York, Col. Taylor—which afterward, together with the Seventy-seventh New-York, pushed on after the fleeing rebels, who, getting under the protection of woods, returned a hot fire. They stood, however, but a short time and then fled. The earthworks were stormed, twelve guns captured, and the stars and stripes planted.

The various divisions of the corps (Sixth, Gen. Sedgwick's) moved rapidly forward up the Gordonsville turnpike, to the distance of four miles, skirmishing all the way, where they found the enemy in force, when another battle ensued, in which Brooks', Newton's, and the Flying division, were engaged—the first suffering severely. The rebels were in a woods, and, as we advanced to it, opened a galling fire. Russell's brigade, composed of the Ninety-fifth and One Hundred and Seventeenth Pennsylvania, and One Hundred and Twenty-first New-York, made a charge, and suffered severely, the Ninety-fifth being almost annihilated. While the battle was progressing, the enemy suddenly commenced firing on our left to the rear, and Brooks' division was obliged to change front. The battle lasted till dark without any decisive results being obtained on either side. During the night the woods took fire, and it is feared that many of the wounded on both sides perished in the flames. Monday morning the rebels suddenly made their appearance on the hills to the left of Fredericksburgh, and coming down rapidly, occupied the city, thus getting in the rear of the corps. Your correspondent happened to be in a farm-house at the point where they descended to the plain, and you can judge of his astonishment on looking out of the window to see this large force advancing in the field in front of the house. Most of the supply trains, ambulances, mules and soldiers in the vicinity were taken. A fleet horse saved me from capture. A serious blunder was perpetrated in pushing our forces on so rapidly without ascertaining whether or not there were any rebels on the woody heights to the left of the city. One whole corps came down and forming in line of battle immediately marched after the corps. The only way of retreat lay by Brooks' Ford, five miles above the city. Gen. Sedgwick was signaled from this side of the river of the condition of affairs and immediately turning about formed a line of battle facing this way, holding the rebels in check, and working down toward the ford. The lines of battle remained in this condition until about the middle of the day, when the rebels attacked us, and were gallantly repulsed—Howe's division capturing 300 prisoners. The rebel reinforcements had fought none, while our troops had been fighting more or less since the previous Tuesday night. For a time it was feared that the corps could not make communication at Banks' Ford, and that the whole of it must be captured. But by noon, a connection was made, and Gen. Sedgwick sent for supplies. Meantime the wounded in Fredericksburgh were being taken across the pontoons to this side, all of them being got away on the sudden appearance of the enemy on the the outskirts above. The Doctors, supposing, of course, that the enemy would come down and take them, made all the arrangements for being taken prisoners; but for some reason, either through fear of our forces above or siege guns on this side of the river, the enemy did not advance into the town. The positions of the respective armies were then as follows: Our main force on the north, then the main force of the enemy, the Sixth Corps below, corps of rebels still lower, and our heavy guns on this side—a most extraordinary sandwiching of opposing forces together.

Skirmishing occurred along the whole line until 5½ o'clock in the evening, when the rebels attacked us from two ways. The Union forces were at the time arrayed in an arc, both wings resting on the river, the right at Banks' Ford. They were arrayed as follows:

Flying Division. Brooks'.

Howe's.

Newton's.

2d Div., 2d Corps.

Together with the Vt. Brigade.

River. River.

We were arranged in two lines of battle. The enemy attacking, the Second division of the Second corps and Howe's at first approaching them diagonally from Fredericksburgh and the country directly beyond. Gen. Mills' brigade, consisting of the Thirty-third New-York, Seventy-seventh New-York, Twentieth New-York, Forty-ninth New-York, together with the Vermont brigade and Seventh Maine, bore the brunt of the charge, repulsing the enemy handsomely. The Vermont brigade were on the left of Gen. Mills. Gen. Mills' brigade and other troops made a counter charge; but reinforcements coming up to the enemy, we were not able to drive them. The Seventy-seventh acted nobly, but the Twentieth New-York behaved very disgracefully, as it did at White Oak Swamp, and falling back, brought a cross fire on the Thirty-third. Their Colonel, however, conducted himself most bravely. The other lines of battle were now attacked by overwhelming numbers and obliged to fall back to the river. While the battle was raging terribly our siege guns on this side of the river opened a rapid fire on the enemy from behind, but they advanced so far in driving our forces that the shell, after a short time, failed to reach them. Our forces were pursued back steadily, musketry and artillery firing continuing all night. Our guns made terrible havoc among the enemy, as they charged repeatedly upon them in solid column. The artillery reserved their fire until the charging parties came within a few rods, and then poured the shot and canister into them at a fearful rate. Having broken the column they would fall back to a new position, and prepare to receive another column. Gen. Hayes, of Louisiana; Gen. Berry, of Early's division, and Col. McDowell, of the Fifty-fourth North Carolina, were killed, among many other rebels.

Gen. Brooks, on our side, was wounded.

Gen. Mills is killed or wounded, and Col. Taylor has command of brigade.

Lieut.-Col. Corning ——, Thirty-third New-York, wounded.

Lieut.-Col. Martindale, Twenty-sixth New-Jersey, killed. And many other valuable officers killed and wounded.

The Vermont Brigade suffered very severely, as well as many other commands.

An officer from Banks' Ford this morning informs me that the Second Corps, together with 20 pieces of artillery, crossed over the pontoons at Banks' Ford early this morning, and covered the retreat of the Sixth Corps as it came back over this side of the Rappahannock. But the artillery firing which is now going on in the rear of Fredericksburgh inclines me to doubt the statement, and believe that the corps is still on the other side, trying to fight its way to the river. Last evening the rebels opened artillery on the bridges, and damaged one of them considerably, but it was repaired by our engineers. One bridge cannot, I think, be reached by their guns. Our artillery on this side kept up a rapid fire on the rebel guns during the night. The ambulances have been bringing in the wounded all night. It is reported that Gen. Sickles has been killed on the extreme right.

D. W. J.

Falmouth, Va., Wednesday Morning, May 6, 1863.

The Sixth Army Corps succeeded in cutting its way through the enemy, reaching this side of the river yesterday morning. The rebels made herculean efforts to surround it, but were foiled in their endeavors. They had succeeded in getting on three sides of the force, and then opened a battery on the bridge which served for a retreat. How it got away in so good a condition, is a great mystery to all of us. Yet the corps suffered severely, having been subjected to the ordeal of four heavy battles within 36 hours, fighting the last two against overwhelming odds, and when hope of escape seemed well nigh gone. Prior to this disaster, the Sixth Corps was the finest in the Army of the Potomac. During these seven days' battles, it has done the work on the left, from the very first, constructing three of the bridges, doing all the skirmishing, storming the Fredericksburgh Heights, and rushing on to the support of the right. Who is responsible for this successful flanking of the force, I am unable to say. One thing is true, however. After taking the heights, the corps pushed rapidly on up the river, regardless of heavy firing from guns planted in the wood crest at the left of the city, and as we moved on in our rear, the road from this crest was unguardedly left open, and when the overwhelming force of the enemy appeared, there was not a Corporal's Guard, in comparison, to resist them.

Up till this time everything was working admirably. We were both in the front and rear of the enemy, and had we been content to rest on the Fredericksburgh Heights without pushing on, we should have had the rebels in a tight place. All this advantage is now lost. The Heights have been recovered and operations suspended by us on the left. The history of Sunday, Monday and Tuesday would furnish volumes of incidents. The wounded in Fredericksburgh, medical stores, &c., were saved by some one organizing the stragglers in the streets into a picket line facing the Heights taken possession of, thereby causing the enemy to think we had a considerable force both in the city and on this side, which was far from the case. Dr. Foor, of the Eighty-second Pennsylvania, left a wounded man he was dressing, snatched a musket, and rallied several of the men.

These pickets, or skirmishers, kept up a fire on the rebels until all our wounded and stores were got across the river.

The remains of Capt. Strong, Fifth Wisconsin; Capt. Knickerbocker, Forty-third New-York; Capt. Robinson, Sixty-first Pennsylvania; Lieut. Cooms, Forty-third New-York, were interred in the yard of G. H. Rowe, and Sergt. Hinman, of the Sixty-fifth New-York, together with several others of Newton's division, in Robert T. Hunter's yard.

The bridges opposite the city were taken up at daybreak yesterday. The last soldier to leave the city was Alex. Camel, of the Twenty-third Pennsylvania, who, delaying, or being left until after the bridges were taken up, stripped off his clothes and pushing them on a boat before him, swam across.

Sergt. Frank. E. Holmes, of the Sixth Maine infantry, a nephew of Vice-President Hamlin's, was killed in the charge on the enemy's works, on Monday night.

Companies F and C, of the Forty-third New-York, Col. Baker's, were taken prisoners while on picket, and if I mistake not, all of the picket line of the Flying division. The Forty-third has only about 200 men left.

Lieut.-Col. Hamilton, son of Dr. Frank Hamilton of New-York, distinguished himself by the gallant manner in which he led the Sixty-second New-York, in the absence of its Colonel.

The grape shot taken from the foot of Lieut.-Col. Newman, of the Thirty-first, is full an inch and a third in diameter; one of the most remarkable cases on record that this large ball or missile should have remained so long in his foot without making its presence known. It was not removed until Monday afternoon, the wound having been received in the Sunday's charge. He is now doing well.

The Sixteenth and One Hundred and Twenty-first New-York, have suffered very severely; in fact both the First and Second Brigades of Gen. Brooks' division, are badly cut up. The Sixty-second New-York has lost very heavily, both in officers and men. Had our forces not been so outnumbered by those of the enemy we should have administered a terrible punishment to them when they attacked and drove us towards the river, since we had the advantage of position, being on higher ground. We had such a long line, however, to defend, that the various regiments had to be shifted from point to point to resist fresh attacks of the enemy. We captured a large number of prisoners though compelled to leave most of our wounded on the field. Nearly one whole brigade, consisting of one General, 20 Captains, 30 Lieutenants and 2,000 privates, which charged upon us, were, I am informed, ensnared into our lines and taken prisoners. I trust the information may not prove untrue. We certainly killed the Colonel, Lieutenant-Colonel and Major of the Seventh Louisiana, and the Lieutenant-Colonel and Major of the Fifth Louisiana. There is no question as to our having mowed the rebels down by whole regiments when they charged upon our batteries. They lay in heaps upon the battle-field. Not a gun was taken, though so many charges upon them were made. The corps retired in good order across the river, saving their camp equipage, mule trains, &c., with the exception of a few which were gobbled up in the momentary panic which ensued when the enemy first made their appearance in our rear above Fredericksburgh. The road was filled with ambulances, (which had been conveying the wounded all night to the city from the battle-field of Sunday evening,) pack mules and vehicles. A part of them fled back to the city, and a part on to the force beyond. While storming the heights, a shell from one of our siege guns planted on this side of the river exploded a rebel caisson behind the redoubts, and killed sixteen horses. The shell struck the first two in line behind the caisson, after exploding it, and hurled the fourteen others down the steep precipice in the rear, into the deep, yawning chasm beneath. They presented a hideous sight, as they lay at the bottom, dead and dying.

Col. Taylor, of the Thirty-third New-York, reported killed in the fight of Monday evening, is unharmed. Lieut.-Col. Corning was wounded in the arm. Maj. Platner had both of his horses shot. Capts. Cole and Root, and Lieut. Porter, of the same regiment, were wounded. Sunday morning it numbered 500 men. It is estimated that not more than 200 are left. Too much praise cannot be awarded to this regiment, the Thirty-first, Col. Jones, and other two years' regiments, whose time is up within two weeks, for the gallant manner in which they have conducted themselves in the various fights. The brave boys were beginning to count the days which intervened between the period of their departure for home.

Yesterday considerable picket-firing took place above Falmouth, and heavy fighting on the extreme right.

About noon our heavy siege guns commenced shelling the heights above the city, and kept it up at intervals during the afternoon. A fearful rainstorm set in about 4 o'clock in the afternoon, which must have caused the river to rise rapidly. A little stream which I stepped over easily at 3 o'clock, I was compelled to wade three hours later, on returning, doffing my wearing apparel and carrying it in my hand. The storm continued all night, and the weather is very cold and chilly this morning, occasioning some discomfort to the wounded. Very heavy artillery firing has been going on at the right, for the last hour, and if there is a corresponding amount of musketry, another fierce battle is going on.

MOVEMENTS OF THE RIGHT.

Headquarters in the Field,
Three Miles from U. S. Ford,
Monday, May 4, 1863.

There has been very little of interest transpiring to-day. A portion of the army has been engaged in constructing rifle-pits and abbatis in divers and various places. The larger part of the army has been resting after the severe labors of the last week. Marches and countermarches, skirmishes, combats and battles, have thoroughly wearied the men and the horses. But, to-day, they are comparatively at rest. Better than that, long trains of pack-mules are winding their way along the crooked wood-roads, and into every camp. The haversacks of the men are being freighted with three days' rations of bread, meat, coffee and sugar. The men are in excellent spirits, and confident that they shall whip the rebels.

Early this morning the rebels succeeded in bringing a battery to bear upon the wooded bluffs north of the Rappahannock, near United States Ford. Their shell were intended for our wagon train, but by reason of the fact that a body of rebel prisoners had been halted for the night where they supposed the wagon train to be, they troubled their friends more than they did their enemies.

The following is the loss in Gen. Hancock's division, (First division, Second corps):

FIRST BRIGADE.

	Killed. Enlisted Men.	Wounded. Off'rs.	Wounded. Men.	Missing. Off'rs.	Missing. Men.	Total.
5th New-Hampshire..	1	5	27	..	15	48
81st Pennsylvania....	3	4	39	..	62	108
61st New-York.......	1	2	12	1	15	31
148th Pennsylvania..	40	9	126	2	..	177
Total................						364

Pettis' battery, 1 officer and 10 men wounded.

Thomas' battery, Company C, Fourth regiment, 1 officer wounded.

SECOND BRIGADE.

	Killed. Officers.	Killed. Men.	Wounded. Officers.	Wounded. Men.	Missing. Men.	Total.
69th New-York...	—	3	2	8	3	16
88th New-York...	—	3	3	16	61	83
63d New-York....	1	1	2	2	—	6
28th Mass.........	—	—	—	7	39	46
116th Penn.......	—	1	—	18	6	25
Total..............						176

THIRD BRIGADE, COL. T. K. ZOOKE, COMMANDING.

	Killed. Off'rs.	Killed. Men.	Wounded. Off'rs.	Wounded. Men.	Missing. Off'rs.	Missing. Men.	Total.
140th Penn.......	1	5	1	30	—	44	81
57th New-York..	—	2	1	22	—	11	36
66th New-York..	—	1	1	12	—	95	109
52d New-York...	—	3	3	22	—	30	58
Total..............							283

FOURTH BRIGADE, COL. J. R. BROOKE, COMMANDING.

	Killed. Off'rs.	Killed. Men.	Wounded. Off'rs.	Wounded. Men.	Missing. Off'rs.	Missing. Men.	Total.
2d Delaware.....	—	1	4	21	2	62	90
53d Penn.........	—	1	1	7	—	12	21
64th New-York..	—	16	2	16	—	16	50
145th Penn.......	—	1	2	5	6	119	133
27th Conn........Not yet known.							
Total..............							294

WOUNDED OFFICERS.

Gen. Couch—slightly.
Col. Beaver, 148th Pennsylvania—seriously.
Col. Frank, 52d New-York.
Col. McKeen, 81st Pennsylvania.
Lieut.-Col. McCreery, 141st Pennsylvania—missing, supposed killed.
Maj. Cross, 5th New-Hampshire.
Maj. Patten, 145th Pennsylvania.
Maj. Fairland, 148th Pennsylvania—slight.
Capt. Overton, 14th infantry—leg.
Lieut. Wells, 17th infantry—leg.
Capt. Lynch, 63d New-York.
Adjt. Dodge, 66th New-York.
Lieut. King, 66th New-York.
Lieut. McEwen, 140th Pennsylvania.
Lieut. Van Dyke, 140th Pennsylvania—seriously.
Capt. Bible, 148th Pennsylvania—killed.
Capt. Egan, 88th New-York—killed.
Lieut. Davis, 2d Delaware—supposed killed.
Capt. McCullough, 2d Delaware—badly.
Lieut. Jordan, 2d Delaware—badly.
Lieut. Huff, 53d Pennsylvania.
Capt. Darby, 64th New-York.
Lieut. Roller, 64th New-York.
Lieut. Kirby, commanding battery—severe.
Lieut. O'Donohue, of Thomas' battery—killed.
Capt. D. B. Logan, 11th New-Jersey—slightly.
Capt. J. H. Meyer, 11th New-Jersey—arm.
Capt. T. J. Halsey, 11th New-Jersey—thigh.
Capt. Luther Martin, 11th New-Jersey—slight.
Lieut. John Lowter, 11th New-Jersey—slight.
Lieut. C. S. Newberry, 11th New-Jersey—hand.
Lieut. Lott, Bloomfield, 11th New-Jersey—killed.
Lieut. Edw. Kelly, 11th New-Jersey—killed.
Capt. Gallbrath, 20th Indiana—arm.

Many gallant deeds were performed by the Staff Officers of the various Generals. At the right of the Chancellor house, a battery of six guns was abandoned, the men and officers being killed and wounded. Gen. Hancock directed his Staff to bring them off. Through the exertions of Major George W. Scott, Lieut. W. P. Wilson, and others of the Staff, the guns were dragged off by hand and saved.

Hancock's division was under a cross fire from three directions, and was the last to leave that portion of the field. Gen. H. had his horse shot under him, as did his Aid, Lieut. Mitchell, and his Orderly Daniel O'Rourk, Sixth New-York cavalry. Two of his orderlies were wounded.

Gen. Couch had his horse shot under him, was slightly wounded, and his clothes were twice struck.

To-day all the Generals are praising the gallantry of Col. Miles, of the Sixty-first New-York, who behaved so gallantly and was wounded so severely yesterday. He is said to be one of the best officers and bravest soldiers in the army. He had command of several regiments upon the lines near the Chancellor house, and with his skirmishers repulsed several strong attacks without their being able to reach his line of battle. If he should live, he will certainly be promoted. Every officer whom I have heard speak of the matter has spoken with great enthusiasm of the Colonel's conduct, and expressed a wish that he may live to wear the honors he has so justly earned.

I was very sorry to learn that Gen. Whipple, while sitting in his tent, was severely wounded to-day by a chance ball from a rebel sharpshooter. Our Generals, with a bravery entirely unparalleled hitherto in the history of this war, have had their headquarters, day and night, in the advance, among their troops, and in every instance within reach of shot and shell. This has done much to inspire the troops with confidence; but in Gen. Whipple's case has resulted disastrously to himself.

This afternoon there was another dash upon our lines near Hooker's headquarters, but a few rounds of canister made them glad to take French leave.

Battery K, Fourth United States artillery, did most excellent service at the battle. It lost 46 men killed and wounded. Sergt. Marrion had three horses shot under him in a few minutes. The battery having suffered so severely in men and horses, has gone to the rear to recuperate. Capt. F. W. Seeley, commanding, says that in three days he can be ready for service again, and is anxious to go to the front as soon as possible.

We have heard guns in the direction of Sedgwick this afternoon.

Z. W. B.

Casualties at Chancellorsville.

THE ELEVENTH CORPS.

Below we give a complete list of the casualties in the New-York regiments in the Eleventh Army corps, at Chancellorsville, on May 2:

STAFF.

Killed.

Capt. Francis A. Depuner.

Wounded.

FIRST DIVISION.

Brig.-Gen. Charles Devans, in foot.
Major Frenaff, slightly, in arm.
Capt. Powers, McLean's Staff, severely, in hand.
Capt. Orlo Weber, A. D. C., arm amputated.

ONE HUNDRED AND FIFTY-SEVENTH NEW-YORK VOLUNTEERS.

Killed.

Sgt W C Miner, Co A
M F Brown, Co A
D Hyland, Jr, Co A
Andrew Mochler, Co B
Sgt E P Ford, Co E
Corp R W Hall, Co F
H J Preston, Co F

Wounded.

Lieut M L Hunt, Co A
Corp C D Burdick, Co A
D C Clark, Co A
E Curtis, Co A
S H Davis, Co A
M J Hyland, Co A
W W Loug, Co A
R Knightengale, Co A
E Tucker, Co A
D Van Hovenburg, Co A
Corp C S Herd, Co B—missing
Arthur B Fox, Co C
Russell Rice, Co C
Orson A Strobeck, Co C
Jay Vanslyke, Co C
Smith Cooper, Co C
Lieut S Z Miner, Co D, slight
Corp Z M Blashfield, Co D, arm
W G Owens, Co D, badly
C H Sweet, Co D, badly
John Shafer, Co D, badly
T T Peters, Co D, badly
John Bisbee, Co F
Wm Barney, Co F
Henry Whitney, Co A
Corp D Baker, Co A
J W Card, Co A
W Perry, Co A
W H Bacon, Co D, hand
Corp E Graves, Co B—head
H H Whitman, Co B—missing
J Seabrook, Co B—missing
O A Nichols, Co B—missing
John Wright, Co B—head
S A Ruggles, Co B—head
B Harp, drum'r, Co B—side
Lieut J A Coffin, Co C
Corp O Courtney, Co C
Corp J P Smyth, Co C
W W Chapel, Co C
Nath Wagoner, Co D, arm
Geo E Douglas, Co E, grein
A Shafer, Co E, ankle
W Davis, Co E
R D Ballard, Co E, slight
A Baker, Co E, slight
Franklin Parschurst, Co F
Wm M Cady, Co F
Corp J E Berry, Co F, neck
J W Clark, Co F, leg
J Snyder, Co F, flesh
Frank M Curley, Co F, arm
John Pilkeger, Co A
Sergt C Launay, Co A
C F Baker, Co A
—— Hackett, Co A
B Schemerhorn, Co A
H Toppein, Co A

[*Continued on Eighth Page.*]

The Charleston Mercury.

DAILY PAPER—TEN DOLLARS PER ANNUM, PAYABLE HALF-YEARLY IN ADVANCE.

VINDICE NULLO
SPONTE SUA SINE LEGE FIDES RECTUMQUE COLENTUR.

COUNTRY PAPER—THRICE A WEEK—FIVE DOLLARS PER ANNUM, IN ADVANCE.

VOLUME LXXXII. CHARLESTON, S. C., SATURDAY, MAY 30, 1863. NUMBER 11,768

THE MERCURY.

SATURDAY, MAY 30, 1863.

A Defence of the People of Charleston.

We see, from the newspapers in various quarters, indications of dissatisfaction with the people of Charleston, in consequence of the foreign commerce carried on by her merchants. The running of the blockade—exporting cotton and importing goods—is regarded as unpatriotic, and injurious to the interests of the Confederacy. By this means, it is said, we supply Great Britain (who refuses to enforce the laws of nations touching blockade) with a necessity, which, if kept from her, will at least make her feel *our* power and *her* dependency. It is said to be even worse than this. We supply our enemy with cotton, and consume many goods in return; for who in the Confederate States can control the trade at Nassau, and determine that the Yankees shall not purchase our cotton when sold there, or return us their goods in payment therefor?

The State of Georgia, doubtless actuated by such reasons, has taken action upon the subject, and we find in the proceedings of the Senate in Congress the following statement:

SENATE—MONDAY, April 27, 1863.—Mr. Johnson, of Georgia, presented a preamble and resolutions adopted by the Legislature of Georgia, in favor of the passage of a law to prevent the running of the blockade, either by land or water, during the existence of the present war, by any person whatever, except under the direct control and for the exclusive benefit of the Government of the Confederate States.

The resolutions were referred to the Committee of Finance.

Now, we beg leave to submit a few facts upon this subject. The people of Charleston, at the opening of this war, were as much opposed to the exportation of our great staples to foreign nations as any people in the Confederacy. Indeed, they exhibited their opposition in a way that we believe no other people in the Confederacy manifested. They objected to permit a ship loaded with cotton to leave her berth, and induced her owners to unload, until it became distinctly understood that the Messrs. JOHN FRASER & Co. intended to send all their cotton to Liverpool, and to import regularly and heavily for the Government arms, powder, saltpetre, ammunition, medicines, soldiers' shoes, cloths, &c., only completing their return cargos with other goods. To this day these gentlemen have followed strictly their intention, and their blockade running has been of immense service to the cause of the South. But to this day the Government has put no limit or restrictions to exporting cotton and importing Yankee goods, notions and luxuries. Other parties have not been so particular, and some cargos entirely of assorted goods have come in. It is known that the matter was considered in the Provisional Congress, and that that Congress, and every other Congress which has sat, has refused to prohibit it. In the Provisional Congress a bill was reported from the Committee on Foreign Affairs distinctly prohibiting the exportation of cotton, tobacco, naval stores and other commodities for private purposes. The Government, and the adherents of the Government in that Congress, *opposed it, and defeated the effort to take it up and consider it.* When the Executive Council of South Carolina undertook to prohibit the exportation of cotton from the ports of South Carolina, the Secretary of the Treasury promptly interposed, and denounced the act as unconstitutional, because Congress had the "power to regulate commerce." Whether the action of the Council was within their legal competency, we will not now consider; but we do not hesitate to affirm that the State of South Carolina can put upon *her citizens any* penalty she pleases, for contravening *any policy within her limits* she deems injurious to *her* liberties or safety, the opinion of the Secretary of the Treasury to the contrary notwithstanding. The Council repealed their order, and nothing has been done in Congress to regulate or prohibit this trade.

The cotton trade, even in Yankee goods across the Rio Grande in Texas, was at one time prohibited by military authority. We are informed that Gen. MAGRUDER obtained instructions from Richmond to repeal the prohibition. Consequently a great business is going on steadily there.

How then stands the matter? It is the law of the Confederacy that cotton shall be exported, and goods, English or Yankee, *ad libitum*, shall be imported into the ports of the Confederate States. This law embodies the policy of the Administration and of the majority in the Congress of the Confederate States. The people of Charleston have been opposed to it; and *some* of their Representatives have striven in vain in Congress to alter it. They have failed in their opposition. The fixed policy of the Government is, the exportation of *everything*, and the importation of *everything*.

If blame or censure is due any where, is it not due to the Administration of the Government, and the majority in Congress who support the Administration in adopting this policy? Why do not those who disapprove of it, turn on the Administration, or on their Representatives in Congress who ordain it? Why assail the people of Charleston, who do no more than carry out the laws, and the policy of the Government, distinctly declared, in conducting the war? Let Congress overthrow this policy, and nowhere in the Confederate States will there be a more prompt and cordial submission to its behests than in the city of Charleston. Our views of unregulated blockade running in our great agricultural productions during the war, are known. If it is the prevailing notion which possesses the country to support whatever measure or policy seems good to the President, and without criticism to approve his direction of the legislative power of the country, then let all now endorse and sustain as much exportation of cotton and as much importation of goods as can be carried on. At any rate, let not Charleston or the merchants of Charleston be made the scapegoats of sins according with the impeccable policy of the Government.

As to the extent of the exportations of cotton, we have obtained from the Charleston Custom House the following figures in round numbers:

Bales of cotton exported in year 1862............23,000
Bales of cotton exported 1st quarter 1863............9,800

We are also told that all the steamers running the blockade at this port have willingly agreed, of late, to import for the Government one-third of each return cargo.

The proportion of cotton going to Liverpool and that sold at Nassau, we have not ascertained. But many of the purchases of goods made at Nassau are paid for in sterling exchange.

[illegible]

THE YANKEE ARMY IN JACKSON.

The following, with some abridgment, is the account given in the *Mississippian extra* of the occupation of Jackson by the Yankees:

But a short time elapsed after our troops passed through before the enemy's cavalry came dashing into town. Their infantry soon followed, and the Yankee ensign was displayed from the capitol amid the shouts of the enemy.

Their forces camped in and around the city to the number of at least ten thousand. The officers assured the citizens that their persons and all private property should be protected; that nothing but government property should be destroyed, &c., but that their army was greatly excited, and they feared would be hard to control. A provost guard was posted throughout the city, and for a time matters proceeded quietly enough, under the circumstances. But no sooner had their troops arranged their encampments than the soldiers came pouring into the city by hundreds. Then commenced a scene of pillaging and wholesale robbery, the parallel of which has probably not been known, in a city so small as Jackson, since the war commenced. The guard could not prevent it, even had they been inclined.

Stores were first entered, and soon the effects of liquor were evident. Bands of drunken ruffians then began their rounds, and continued roving from dwelling to dwelling, first, generally, demanding something to eat, and then appropriating everything conceivable. Safes, drawers, desks, bureaus, wardrobes, etc., were broken open and their contents either carried off, destroyed or scattered around the premises. This continued nearly or quite all the night.—Some few families called for guards for their dwellings, which in no case was refused, so far as we have learned, and, to "give the devil his due," all such dwellings escaped.

But on the next Friday morning destruction on the grandest scale commenced by orders. The railroad tracks were utterly demolished for between two and three miles in all directions, including Pearl River Bridge, and the depot buildings and platforms burnt. Then the torch was applied to the Government shops and factories—Phillips' wagon manufactory, Green's cotton factory, Stephens' iron foundry, the Government storehouses, Bailey's cotton shed, which contained an immense quantity of cotton, sugar and molasses; all the sugar and molasses deposited in the vicinity of the depots, both public and private, shared the general destruction.

All the flour, meal and provisions of all kind that could be found anywhere (and we think they found it all, save what was in the hands of families, and some of these did not escape,) were consumed or scattered in the streets. Every grist mill in town was burnt.

Gen. Steele took his headquarters at Col. Mabry's, but his presence was no protection. Every room was pillaged, and every mouthful of provisions taken from him. Brigadier General Tuttle made his headquarters at the residence of Mr. F. T. Cooper, editor of the Mississippian where they destroyed the fences, despoiled the smokehouse, burnt up all the papers and books, and when they were about to depart set fire to the house in three places, but through the importunities and strategic representations of two faithful old servants, the fire was put out and the building saved. The negros pleaded that it was the only home they had, and they were too old to move away. "For *your* sake," said the Yankee General, "the house is saved, but if we get hold of the damned rebel editor, it will be very different with him."

The State and city public buildings were spared, except the Penitentiary, which was used by the Government for manufacturing purposes. The convicts had been released (save a few desperate ones, who were transferred to the Alabama Penitentiary) and put in the ranks.

All the cattle, horses and mules in the city and vicinity were carried off. Many negro men and women voluntarily left, but most that are missing were forced off. Some have already escaped and returned.

About 10 o'clock on Saturday the Yankee army commenced evacuating the city in haste, but in good order, taking the direct road to Vicksburg. At the moment of leaving, to crown their vandalism, the Confederate House and the new hotel opposite, with the buildings adjoining, all the property of R. O. Edwards, were set on fire and burnt to the ground. This was done, the Yankees said, because Mr. Edwards refused to entertain General Prentiss and his officers as they passed through here as prisoners from the field of Shiloh.

The Mississippian office was turned inside out, the type thrown into the street, three fine presses demolished, stands broken, &c. With the exception of two presses and a quantity of new type which we were fortunate enough to have removed South, the Mississippian establishment is no more. We were generously informed, by "hand writing on the wall," that, "We don't burn this building because it would cause the burning of the whole block."

We print this bulletin at the office of the Mississippi Baptist, which was also materially injured.

The Yankee army had scarcely left before Capt. Wm. Yerger's Company of Confederate cavalry, of Adams' regiment, retired from an opposite direction. Col. Cromwell, of the 47th Illinois, who had galloped back, after the army had left, to take, we suppose, a farewell drink in Jackson, was hailed just as he had started back to rejoin his command, and ordered to surrender. He refused, and in attempting to draw his pistol, was shot dead. His body was taken to the Bowman House, and buried decently and with honor on Sunday evening, in the coffin prepared for the remains of Col. McGavock, 10th Tennessee, killed at Raymond.

When Captain Yerger entered the city he immediately spread the Confederate flag on the dome of the capitol, and his company then hung about the rear of the enemy and took a large number of Yankee prisoners.

REVIEW OF THE LATE CAMPAIGN ON THE RAPAHANNOCK.

GENERAL HOOKER'S OPERATIONS AT CHANCELLORSVILLE AND FREDERICKSBURG—STRANGE COURSE OF THE COMMANDING GENERAL.

The following remarkable letter, which affords positive information with reference to the movements of HOOKER in the battles of Chancellorsville and Fredericksburg, appeared in the New York *World* of the 18th. It will be observed that the writer asserts it as a fact that HOOKER had exact information of the strength of our forces, giving the location and effective strength of every regiment. The letter proceeds:

By his administration of army matters since he took command, General Hooker had acquired its confidence in him. No one, therefore, doubted our success in the movement about to take place, and there never was a time when the Army of the Potomac was in more effective condition. On the 28th of April General Hooker had nothing left to desire; he had men enough and means enough; he was sustained to the fullest extent at Washington, and had the heartiest support of the army. Information (obtained I know not how, but which General Hooker and General Butterfield insisted was reliable beyond question), furnished the exact strength of the rebel army opposite, giving the location and effective strength of every regiment. This information was furnished corps commanders. They were assured that it was obtained from sources and by means entirely reliable. According to this information the total strength of the force on the other side was 49,800 men, composed of Jackson's corps, 35,100, and two divisions of Longstreet's, numbering, 14,700 men. This force was distributed along the Rappahannock, from Port Royal to United States Ford; the bulk of it, however, was below Fredericksburg. General Hooker's plan was to cross with the principal part of his army at Kelly's Ford and United States Ford, to move down upon the left of the enemy, force him to give battle outside of his entrenchments, or else fall back rapidly on Richmond. In either event the left wing of Hooker's force, consisting at first of three corps (First, Third and Sixth), under Sedgwick, was to cross below Fredericksburg, and vigorously pursue down the Bowling Green Road and the Telegraph Road, capturing, destroying, &c., &c.

The main purpose, however, to be accomplished on the left, was to retain as large a force as possible in front of Sedgwick. If this purpose failed, and they detached any considerable number of troops, an attack was to be made to obtain possession of their works and of the telegraph road, cutting off their retreat from in front of Hooker.

On the morning of the 29th Sedgewick effected a crossing, sending one division of the 6th corps across two miles below Fredericksburg, and one division of the 1st corps across about one mile further down. On the following day the 3d corps (Sickles') was detached from his command and ordered to join Gen. Hooker near Chancellorsville, crossing at United States Ford. The enemy still continued in front of our left in sufficient force to hold his works there and render an attack unadvisable, but at the same time troops were moving almost constantly from the direction of Richmand and passing towards our right. The General commanding having been informed that these troops were doubtless reinforcements from Richmond, replied by telegraph that he hoped they were, as the greater would be our success! Up to the 2d of May matters on the left remained unchanged. On that day the 1st corps (Reynold's) was ordered to march at once and join Gen. Hooker at Chancellorsville. There had been no general battle on the right. It seems that Hooker took position near Chancellorsville; the enemy felt his line on Saturday, and finally attacked Howard, who commanded Siegel's corps on the extreme right. A panic among the Dutchmen was the result. The stampede was checked, some of the guns captured from Howared were recovered, and the line re-established before night. In the evening of May 2d Sedgwick was ordered, first to cross his entire corps and capture Fredericksburg and everything in it; second, to puruse the enemy by the Bowling Green road with his entire force. Hooker then stated that the enemy was flying, endeavoring to save his trains. A third, received at 11 o'clock that night, directed him to cross at Fredericksburg and march out on the plankroad toward Chancellorsville until he connected with the right under Hooker, to destroy any force he might meet upon the road, and to be in the vicinity of the commanding General by daylight the following morning.

In the execution of the two first he had already crossed to the Fredericksburg side. He accordingly moved at once on the Bowling Green road and entered the town shortly before daylight, having skirmished the entire way.

He found the works on the heights in rear of the city strongly occupied, but carried them splendidly by assault, losing one thousand men before it was accomplished. He then pushed on as directed, the enemy making what resistance he could at every favorable point. In the afternoon he came upon the enemy, reinforced by Wilcox's brigade from Banks' Ford, and McLaw's division from the rebel main body, strongly posted on commanding ground near Salem Chapel, about half way to Chancellorsville. He attacked at once and continued the attack until dark, but failed to dislodge the enemy in front of him. During the day (May 3) Gen. Hooker had one corps, and only one, engaged for a short time in the morning; but during the rest of the day he did nothing. Sedgwick's guns were thundering in his ears—the very rattle of the musketry reached him; he knew that Sedgwick was coming to his relief, that the enemy were sending heavy reinforcements from his front to resist Sedgwick's advance, yet he never fired a gun to encourage him, although on the night of the 3d (Sunday) Sedgwiok was within five miles of his lines. From 10 o'clock on Sunday night until we recrossed the river he remained in his entrenchments idle. On Monday morning a force of the enemy from below Fredericksburg re-occupied the heights, cutting off Sedgwick's communications with the town, and threatening his flank and rear. The force Sedgwick had failed to dislodge the day before was still in position at Salem Chapel.

He formed line of battle to the front and rear and repulsed an attack from the direction of Fredericksburg, intended to cut him off from Banks' Ford, which was now his only line of retreat. Hooker sent word that he had contracted his lines and was safe; he hoped the enemy would attack him; that Sedgwick must not attack, but must look to the safety of his corps, falling back upon Fredericksburg or re-crossing the river at Banks' Ford. Sedgwick remained all day in his position fighting more or less, his line forming three sides of a square, or nearly so, his extreme left resting on the river about midway between Banks' Ford and Fredericksburg. Reinforcements were constantly coming to the enemy from Hooker's front, and in the afternoon Lee arrived in person. A desperate attack was immediately made upon the left of Sedgwick's line by McLaw's, Anderson's and Early's divisions in echelon of battalions and in column. This assault, one of the most formidable and determined of the war, was handsomely checked by Howe, who held his own until nightfall. During the night the corps fell back upon Banks' Ford, and took position there, as directed by General Hooker, who telegraphed that it was of vital importance for Sedgwick to hold some position on the right bank until the next day. Before morning he ordered Sedgwick across the river. As soon as the crossing was made the order was countermanded. It was too late to go back, and the corps went into camp on the left bank. The following day the main body crossed and returned to their old camps, having lost more men and material than McClellan did in the seven days, and so ended the first (and I trust the last) campaign under "Fighting Joe." The feeling in the army is one of bitter disappointment and intense disgust. Among the officers of the regular army not one of any position has the slightest confidence in Hooker. Not even a plausible explanation of the strange conduct of the Commanding General has been furnished.

No one can tell why he did not attack on Friday morning with his whole force. It was evident from papers captured at Chohcellorsville that he had surprised Lee, and that up to that time no provision had been made to resist him. He had three corps on the ground, and two others, Couch's and Sickles', on the march to join him. No one can explain why he did not attack with every available man when he heard Sedgwick's guns on Sunday afternoon. No one has yet attempted to account for his inactivity on Monday when he knew that Sedgwick was pressed by overwhelming numbers in front, flank and rear. The fight on Monday afternoon was within six miles of Hooker's lines, yet he never fired a gun. Lastly, no one can tell *why he re-crossed the river!* He went over there to fight, and came back without a battle. He selected the ground and chose the time. The weather could not have been better adapted to military operations, and there seemed to be nothing but his own indecision to defeat him. You can well imagine, without my going into details, what the feeling is in the army. The desire for McClellan's return, which has never abated since his departure, has now become more outspoken than ever. Men talk of it as possible, probable, certain; and rumors of every description constantly prevail.

It is taken for granted that there must be a change.. For my part, I fear that if there is, it will not be the right one. Meanwhile, Hooker talks boldly of further movements and another crossing. He is in this position: Another failure, no matter how disastrous, cannot place him personally in a worse position than he now occupies. A lucky venture may restore his fallen fortunes.

He has everything to gain, nothing to lose, by another effort, no matter how rash. Under the circumstances, it is easy to foretell what course a man of his character and training will adopt. Unless something is done, and that speedily, to restrain him, he will send his army to destruction. The President has been here, and as usual, is infatuated, believing everything is well. The only hope is that by exposing the facts the radicals or semi-radicals may, in order to save themselves, do something to save the old Army of the Potomac from another awful sacrifice. Confidential agents from New York are now with the army to ascertain the state of feeling. One of them, a prominent Tribune man, spent a couple of days with the army and went away much astonished. It is stated that after a long interview with the General commanding one of the corps, he asked, "In case Hooker is relieved who is the proper man to command the army." The General answered emphatically, "George B. McClellan." The other replied, "But he is, of course, out of the question; can't you name some one else." The General answered yes; "William B. Franklin; and aside from these two men, I know of no one fit to lead this army."

The New-York Times.

VOL. XII—NO. 3655. NEW-YORK, THURSDAY, JUNE 11, 1863. PRICE THREE CENTS.

GREAT CAVALRY FIGHT.

The Engagement at Beverley's Ford and Brandy Station.

Full Details from Our Special Correspondents.

Desperate and Gallant Fighting by Our Forces.

THE REBELS DRIVEN BACK THREE MILES.

THEIR CAMPS CAPTURED AND OCCUPIED

Two Hundred Prisoners and One Stand of Colors Taken.

Highly Important Information Gained.

Stuart Proposing to Start on his Great Raid Yesterday Morning.

His Force 12,000 Cavalry and 16 Pieces of Artillery.

Our Losses About 400 Killed, Wounded and Missing.

THE REBEL LOSS MUCH HEAVIER.

IN BIVOUAC AT BEALETON, VA., ORANGE AND ALEXANDRIA RAILROAD, Tuesday Evening, June 9, 1863.

This has truly been an exciting day. An hour since I sent you the mere skeleton of the day's operations, which scarcely affords any idea of the extent or character of our achievements. I informed you by letter on Monday what might be expected to-day, and I have now the result to record.

About the middle of last week, information of a pretty positive character was received at headquarters, concerning the massing and drilling of a large force of the enemy's cavalry in the vicinity of Culpepper. Numerous reports had been received before, but they were more or less conflicting, especially that portion of them which concerned the movement of the rebel infantry forces in a westerly direction. In my letter of Monday I gave in substance such information as I had concerning the strength and character of the enemy's augmented cavalry force. It was in the main correct; but, in the light of to-day's operations, I can give you the details as specifically as you can desire, for, beside defeating the enemy in a severe battle, we have ravaged his camp, ascertained his strength to a figure, and frustrated a bold plan, the execution of which *was* to have begun to-morrow morning at daylight.

The bold reconnoissance across the Rappahannock on Friday last, below Fredericksburgh, which we rightly thought would startle the indifferent public, had more than one object. Its first object was to discover the exact whereabouts of the rebel army, which was accomplished Saturday morning. Its second object was to remain where it was as a diversion, while we hastily gathered together a force to feel of, and if prudent, to attack this threatening mass of cavalry opposite our extreme right flank.

Gen. HOOKER conceived the whole plan very quickly, and caused its execution to be begun with that rapidity and secrecy for which he is noted.

Saturday evening the composition of the force was determined upon, and all the cavalry that could be made immediately available was detailed for the work under command of Gen. PLEASANTON, (Gen. STONEMAN having been relieved,) assisted by Gens. BUFORD and GREGG, and Col. DUFFIE, as subordinate commanders. In addition, two small brigades of picked infantry, under Gen. AMES, of the Eleventh corps, and Gen. RUSSELL, of the Sixth corps, were detailed to accompany the expedition. A detail of artillery was made in the proportion of one battery to each brigade, the horse-batteries, with the cavalry, being in charge of Capt. ROBERTSON, chief of artillery on Gen. PLEASANTON's Staff.

The infantry force selected challenged particular admiration. The regiments were small, but they were *reliable*—such for instance as the Second, Third and Seventh Wisconsin, Second and Thirty-third Massachusetts, Sixth Maine, Eighty-sixth and One Hundred and Twenty-fourth New-York, and one or two others of like character.

The force, when completed, did not, by several thousand, reach the reported number of the enemy, from twelve to fifteen thousand, but then as far as cavalry was concerned we sent all that could be spared, and as far as infantry was concerned the sequel proved that fully as much was sent as could be used to advantage. And then there was a strong supposition that the force of the enemy had been exaggerated.

General PLEASANTON's cavalry rendezvoused during Saturday and Sunday at Catlett's Station and Warrenton Junction, getting supplies of forage and food from both places, by the Orange and Alexandria Railroad. Gen. AMES' infantry moved Saturday evening to the Spotted Tavern, and on Sunday to near Bealeton Station. Gen. RUSSELL's brigade moved on Sunday to Hartwood Church, and on Monday to Kelly's Ford. The plan was to rendezvous the command at the two points on the Rappahannock, Beverly's Ford on the right, and Kelly's Ford on the left, the two being six miles apart, and then move the column forward toward Culpepper, on roads converging at Brandy Station, where a junction of the forces was to be formed, or sooner, if necessary.

On Monday evening, therefore, Gen. BUFORD's column left Warrenton Junction, and followed by Gen. AMES from Bealeton, bivouacked for the night near the Bowen Mansion, about one mile from Beverly's Ford. Gen. GREGG, taking his own and Col. DUFFIE's command, moved to the left from the Junction, and encamped for the night in close proximity to Kelly's Ford, where Gen. RUSSELL had already arrived. No fires were allowed, and a vigilant watch was kept to prevent disturbances or anything which might give any indication of our presence.

The orders were to arouse the command at 2 A. M., and to make the passage of the river as soon as it was daylight.

At dawn Gen. BUFORD's command was in motion. Col. DAVIS' brigade, led by two squadrons of the Eighth New-York, and supported by the Eighth Illinois and Third Indiana, had the advance. The morning was cool and pleasant, a thick mist hung over the river, and objects on the other side were rather indistinct. Our cavalry soon reached the river, dashed in, dashed up the bank, and were well on the opposite side before the rebels in their fortifications were aware of their presence. The suddenness of the movement completely surprised them, and they at once broke for the first friendly timber, which was about one-fourth of a mile in their rear. Our cavalry followed rapidly, and in these woods the first severe skirmish occurred, in which we speedily lost one of the most valued officers of the command, Col. B. F. DAVIS, of the Eighth New-York cavalry, and captain in the First Regular cavalry, and the same gallant officer who led the gallant charge out of Harper's Ferry last Fall, and captured LONGSTREET's ammunition train. When the rebels, who were dismounted reached the woods, they began to skirmish, and detained our force there long enough to give the alarm to JONES' brigade, they being encamped just beyond in the outer edge of the woods. Though their horses were grazing in the fields, yet they speedily fell in, and in a very short time two or three squadrons came charging down the road and through the timber. Hurling their force upon the Eighth New-York, they broke it and forced it back, and killed and wounded quite a number. Col. DAVIS, who was gallantly leading the advance, turned to rally them, and waiving his sword to the Eighth Illinois, shouted, "Come on boys," when a rebel rode out in front of him, and fired three shots from his pistol at him, the last one taking effect in his forehead, and inflicting a mortal wound. Quick as thought, Lieut. PARSONS, acting A. A. General to Col. DAVIS, was at the side of the rebel, and raising, in his stirrups, with one well directed blow of his sabre, he laid his head open midway between eyes and chin, and the wretch fell dead in the dust at his horse's feet. PARSONS is but a youth; his adversary was a strong, athletic man, yet the former, though young in years and slight stature, nobly avenged his Commander's fall.

By this time the gallant Eighth Illinois, though meeting with a hot reception, in which Capt. CLARK and Capt. FORSYTH were both wounded, had charged upon the rebels, and driven them back upon the main body of the enemy, who were now engaged in deploying and forming in the rear of the woods, and just beyond their camp, nearly two miles from the river.

Maj. WHITING's command now came up to the support of the Illinois and Indiana troops. Gen. AMES also brought his infantry over, and deployed them on the left of the road as skirmishers, and then pushed them out in line of battle to the edge of the woods, in front of which the enemy was drawn up by squadrons, with artillery at the intervals, which omitted no opportunity to shell everything in sight that had motion to it. Thus far the enemy evidently had but one brigade at hand, and a few prisoners taken said they belonged to the Sixth, Seventh and Twelfth Virginia cavalry, of General JONES' brigade. When asked if he was "JONES, the guerrilla," they indignantly denied the imputation. Nevertheless he was. Gen. PLEASANTON now directed Gen. BUFORD to make preparations to charge this force in the flank, while the infantry and artillery engaged it in front. It was desirable to do this as soon as possible, as the enemy might be getting reinforcements at any moment. Gen. BUFORD having driven the enemy's pickets and skirmishers in the open fields on the right of the road, sent in the Sixth Pennsylvania, supported by the Fifth and Sixth regulars, to charge this line on the flank. The Pennsylvanians came up to their work in splendid style. This is the regiment formerly known as the "Lancers," and they had a matter of pride to settle in this charge. Steadily and gallantly, they advanced out of the woods, in excellent order, and then dashed across the open field in an oblique direction toward the enemy's guns. They went up almost to their very muzzles, through a storm of canister and shell, and would have taken them, when suddenly there dashed out of the woods on their right flank, in almost the very spot from which they themselves had issued, two whole regiments of the enemy, on the full charge. Retreat was almost cut off, but the regiments, now subjected to a fire in front, and on both flanks, charged back, cutting their way out with considerable loss. The Sixth regulars came to the rescue, but the fire was so severe that even these veterans could not stand it, and they fell back with some loss. In this charge we lost about the only prisoners captured by the enemy during the day. Maj. MORRIS, of the Sixth Pennsylvania, was seen to fall from his horse, and is probably wounded and a prisoner. Capt. DAVIS, of the same regiment, was killed. Capt. LIEPER was wounded, and Maj. HAZELTINE had his horse shot under him. Capt. DAHLGREN, of Gen. HOOKER's Staff, a model of cool and dauntless bravery, charged with the regiments, and his horse was shot in two places. He describes the charge as one of the finest of the war.

The enemy was now being reinforced very rapidly, and in a short time Gen. PLEASANTON found that BUFORD's small division was opposed by three strong brigades of rebels, with artillery to match.

After the repulse of the Sixth Pennsylvania, the rebels made two rapid attempts to gain our rear and the approaches to the ford, both on our right and on our left, but particularly on the right. But they were handsomely foiled by BUFORD, and for two hours there was very sharp skirmishing, rapid shelling and admirable manœuvering by both sides, in the open and undulating fields on our extreme right. A brigade of the enemy's cavalry came down the road which branches off to the right from Beverley's, and made a dash for the ford. But they were too late. A couple of squadrons and a section of artillery interposed. They never got nearer than a mile to the point, and during the two hours that they remained in position they suffered severely from our shells and skirmishers.

At this stage of the engagement, Gen. PLEASANTON plainly saw that the division under Gen. BUFORD was far outnumbered, and much anxiety was expressed to hear from Gen. GREGG, whose column was considerably stronger than BUFORD's. Word had been received from him at 8 o'clock, saying that he had crossed with scarce any opposition, and that he was driving the enemy before him, but his guns had not yet been heard. Matters thus remained *in statu quo* until twelve o'clock, nothing being done save some artillery pratice, which was pretty accurate on both sides. We dismounted one gun of a section that the enemy had on the extreme right, and compelled the enemy to move the other. During this interem the skirmishers of each party would frequently become very annoying. Gen. AMES formed his skirmish line, and they picked off the rebel officers without mercy. Although our infantry were masked by the timber, yet the enemy seemed to know what we had, and always refused to meet them, save by dismounted cavalry as skirmishers against skirmishers. They were very profuse of their shells and canister, however, and opened whenever any of our cavalry approached near enough. Many of our men were wounded by canister shot, a thing almost heretofore unknown in cavalry fighting.

At one time, on the left of Gen. AMES' brigade, the rebel cavalry skirmishers had advanced and concealed themselves in some bushes, where they were annoying a body of the Ninth New-York. Major MANNING, of that regiment, was finally ordered to take a squadron and drive them out. This he most gallantly did, though it was right in the teeth of the enemy's artillery, and he was met by a perfect storm of canister. He captured fifty prisoners, but owing to the severity of the enemy's fire, could bring but a portion of them away. The gallant Major was himself wounded in the shoulder.

About 1 o'clock BUFORD again began to press the enemy, and this time he showed evident signs of uneasiness, and soon withdrew his force from our right flank as though he had a fire in the rear. About the same time we heard GREGG's guns, and some prisoners taken from ROBINSON's North Carolina brigade just then reported Gen. RUSSEL's infantry advancing through the woods on their right flank and rear. Gen. GREGG, from the sound of the firing, was evidently in the vicinity of Brandy Station. PLEASANTON now pushed forward, but the rebels soon gave way, and fell back rapidly. They were in a bad predicament—for GREGG was almost directly in their rear, RUSSELL was on their right flank, and BUFORD on their front. They therefore made a hasty retreat, abandoning their old camp entirely, part of which we had already occupied, and two regiments were very near being cut off, as KILPATRICK moved off toward the right, to make connection with BUFORD. They had but a narrow strip of land, not covered by our force, through which to escape.

Gen. PLEASANTON's headquarters were moved forward to where the rebel Commander's had been, and the lines of the two columns were soon connected.

Gen. GREGG reported that his two brigades, under KILPATRICK and WYNDHAM, had been hotly engaged all the morning, but had driven the enemy uniformly from the river back to Brandy Station. Our troops, especially the First New-Jersey, First Maine and Tenth New-York, fought most gallantly, and repulsed the enemy in repeated charges, though losing heavily themselves. The artillery with Gen. GREGG also suffered considerably, and the Sixth New-York battery was almost totally disabled. It did excellent service, however. In the charges by Gen. GREGG's column, a stand of colors and over one hundred and fifty prisoners were taken. Col. WYNDHAM's brigade captured the heights commanding Brandy Station, and there discovered rebel infantry being brought up by the cars. A portion of it drew up and fired a volley at our cavalry. Another correspondent will give you further particulars about the gallant fighting of this column. Col. WYNDHAM was shot through the calf of the leg by a bushwhacker, but his wound is not serious, and he still keeps the saddle.

While a junction was being effected with GREGG's column on the left, BUFORD and AMES were pushing out on the right, and, with VINCENT's battery, BUFORD had by 2 o'clock carried all the crests occupied by the enemy during the forenoon, and had forced him back over three miles from the river. In these exploits the regulars, especially the Second and Fifth regiments, distinguished themselves by their intrepidity. The Third Wisconsin skirmishers also won praise by the accuracy of their fire, which was fatal to many a rebel.

The fact that the enemy were now falling back upon strong infantry supports, and we being already numerically inferior to them, induced Gen. PLEASANTON to consult with his subordinates, and it having been left discretionary with the former to advance or return, it was finally deemed prudent to return, and at 4 o'clock our forces began falling back. The enemy was not inclined to "pick a fight" on the return, and, save some slight skirmishing, we were not molested. BUFORD's division fell back to Beverley Ford, and GREGG's division to Rappahannock Ford, a mile and a half below. We brought off all our dead and wounded, and also some of the enemy's, while many of the latter were still remaining on the field when we retired. By dark our forces were all over the river, and the wounded of BUFORD's division all loaded in the cars and on the way to Washington. The loss in his division is about one hundred and eighty, and in GREGG's about the same. The rebel prisoners report their loss as heavier than ever before, and express admiration of the gallantry of our cavalry. The total number of prisoners taken is about two hundred and twenty-five, and we lost about fifty.

Though our force was not large enough to thoroughly defeat the rebels, yet they received a sound thrashing, and it will result in postponing their "grand raids" into the North for some time, if not indefinitely; for, beside chastising them, we have gained full information of their strength, character and designs. Witness the following letter captured on the battle-field, which I have copied from the original *verbatim*:

CAMP NEAR BRANDETH STATION, CULPEPPER COURT-HOUSE, June 8, 1863.

DEAR BROTHER: We have made another change of base. We left Dayton one week ago to-day, and after five days of marching, we encamped at this place. We have had two grand reviews of *five brigades of cavalry, about 12,000 in number*, under Gen. STUART. The first took place on Saturday, when we were inspected by STUART; and I have just now returned from the second, when we were inspected by Lieut-Gen. ROBERT E. LEE, in person. He was a fine looking man, but very gray haired. We are now in a battery *numbering about sixteen pieces*, under the command of Major BECKHAM. *Longstreet's division passed us on Saturday.* The Wise artillery was along. You can look out for some *small* fighting *before a week*. We are now about two miles from the Rappahannock, at Beverley's Ford. I expect, from the preparations that is being made, that *we are going to make a grand raid toward the Potomac, as soon as the valley is cleared.* * * * *

You must excuse the shortness of this letter, as I have just returned from the review, and I feel tired from riding so much. Direct your letter to CHEW's battery, JONES' cavalry brigade.

Please write immediately, *as we may leave in a couple of days.*

Your affectionate brother, J. M. D.

I leave the name blank for the sake of the writer. This confirms all the information we previously had. FITZHUGH LEE, W. F. LEE, G. W. JONES, ROBINSON, of North Carolina, and FIELD, of Virginia, commanded the brigades. In the latter's brigade is all the mounted infantry they had—reported at 800 men.

An order was found from Gen. STUART, dated June 6, ordering the commands to be held in readiness to move at fifteen minutes' notice.

A Captain, who was taken prisoner, said *they were under orders to move on Wednesday morning at daylight.* They moved a day sooner, and backward at that.

The prompt manner in which these plans of the enemy have been baffled will elicit the admiration of every one. *A day longer, and it would have been too late.* Their plans are now known, and we can prepare accordingly. Pennsylvania and Maryland will awake to the importance of the occasion, and make all needful preparations to receive this horde of raiders. They will probably only defer, not abandon, their designs' and such a body of cavalry once loose in a defenceless State they can take the whole of it. But Gen. HOOKER has unmasked them, and given time for preparation. Shortly he will be fully ready himself to take them thoroughly in hand.

L. L. CROUNSE.

THE CASUALTIES.

My associate, Mr. PAUL, has made up the following list of casualties, which comprise nearly all of those in Gen. BUFORD's column, and a few from that of Gen. GREGG's:

KILLED.

Col. B. F. Davis, 8th New-York cavalry, commanding brigade, Buford's division.
Lieut.-Col. Irvin, 10th New-York cavalry.
Capt. Foote, 8th New-York cavalry.
Capt. Davis, 6th Pennsylvania cavalry.
Capt. Canfield, 2d regular cavalry.
Lieut. Cutter, 8th New-York cavalry.
A. J. Supplee, Co. A, 6th Pennsylvania cavalry.
James Evans, Co. L, 8th Illinois.
John Lasson, Co. A, 8th New-York.
Daniel Crimmings, Co. C, 5th regulars.
John S. Smith, Co. D, 8th New-York.
Chas. Ford, Co. D, 8th New-York.
Charles Richards, 9th New-York.

WOUNDED.

Col. Wyndham, 1st New-Jersey cavalry, commanding brigade, Gregg's division—left leg, slight.
Lieut.-Col. Broderick, 1st New-Jersey—wounded and missing.
Maj. Shellmire, 1st N. J.—wounded and missing.
Maj. Morris, 6th Pennsylvania cavalry—wounded and prisoner.
Capt. Lieper, 6th Pennsylvania—head.
Lieut. Reeves, Co. C, 8th New-York—side.
Lieut. Phillips, Co. I, 6th New-York—left leg amputated.
Lieut. Lessure, 2d United States—seriously.
Lieut. Madden, 6th U. S.—back, not serious.
Lieut. Greenlee, Col. Wyndham's Staff—knee.
Lieut. Brooks, 1st New Jersey—arm.
Lieut. Lucas, 1st Pennsylvania—head.
Lieut. G. S. Taylor, 3d Indiana—leg.
Lieut. D. P. Smith, 4th Pennsylvania—bruised.
Lieut. G. Urban, Co. B, 5th United States—leg.
Lieut. F. N. Dickinson, Co. D, 5th United States—head, slight.
Lieut. J. W. Houston, Co. D, 124th New-York infantry—thigh.
Lieut. Ether, 8th New-York—stomach.
Capt. George A. Forsyth, 8th Illinois—thigh.
Capt. Clark, commanding regiment, 8th Ill.—hand.
Maj. Martin, 9th N. Y.—shoulder, not dangerous.
Capt. D. J. Hynes, Co. G, 8th Illinois—foot.
L. L. Crounse, Correspondent NEW-YORK TIMES—left shoulder, slight.
Lieut. R. Lennox, 2d U. S. cavalry—neck.
Lieut. P. Quirk, 2d U. S. cavalry—left leg.
Adjutant Ellis, 6th Pennsylvania cavalry—left leg.
Lieut. Luther Herrick, 8th New-York cavalry—right thigh.
Lieut. C. M. Loeser, 2d U. S. cavalry—side.
Lieut. E. B. Wells, 2d U. S. cavalry—abdomen.

Sixth Pennsylvania Cavalry.

Corp. Wm. O'Meara, Co. L—shoulder.
Sergt. C. L. Bumer—foot.
Thompson Carson—left hand and knee.
John B. Smith, Co. K—head.
Henry McGovern, Co. L—right side
Edmund Barry, Co. K—left foot.
Thomas Evart, Co. F—foot.
Sergt. Keyser, Co. G—foot.
Sergt. James Naylor, Co. K—hand.
John Shields, Co. K—face.
John McQuaid, Co. K—leg.
John D. Schmearer, Co. K—head.

Eighth Illinois Cavalry.

James O'Brien—right foot.
Judson W. Farrar—knee, by a shell.
James McCarty—side and back.
Capt. A. Clark—in hand, in command of regiment, in the first charge.
Charles Slyter—back.
Geo. Huff, Co. K—sprained.
W. Cosman, Co. H—left arm.
Isaac M. Brooks, Co. H—right hand.
M. Crossman, Co. A—arm.

Eighth New-York Cavalry.

Geo. McBinney—left breast.
Chas. Geer, Co. B—left leg.
John Smith, Co. B—left leg.
G. W. Clark, Co. A—shoulder.
Henry Smith, Co. B—right foot.
Milton Culver, Co. M—breast.
Wm. H. Stigleman, Co. A—left arm.
Risley Lowe, Co. H—right shoulder.
R. B. W. Falkner, Co. A.
John Shroeder, Co. A—right shoulder.
Frank L. Thompson, Co. D—left foot.
Corp. Geo. D. Scott, Co. K—right foot.
Charles Church, Co. D—side and finger.
E. Water, Co. E—left shoulder.
Sergt. Daniel Haskell, Co. F—head.
Sergt. J. J. Brown—left foot.
E. H. Cox, Co. K—left leg.
—— Stickerman, chief bugler—arm.
S. H. Bell, Co. B—back.
H. Burroughs, Com. Sergt.—three sabre cuts.
Wilson Cruthers, Co. M—leg.
John Byers—left breast.

Third Indiana Cavalry.

John Walters, Co. H—neck.
D. W. Kirkpatrick, Co. A—wrist.
David Schumaker, Co. D—hip.
Eugene Page, Co. B—thigh.

Second United States Cavalry.

E. M. Adams, Co. F—right leg.
John Henderson, Co. B—head.
James Campbell, Co. D—sabre wound in head.
F. Lorens, Co. L—shoulder and leg.
W. Cooper, Co. F—face.

Ninth New-York Cavalry.

Henry Gibbs—left leg.
Major Martin—right shoulder, not serious.
Isaac Benham, Co. A—right leg.
John G. Dixon, Co. M—left leg.

Fifth Regular Cavalry.

Richard Hanlon, Co. C—thigh.
Sergt. Jacob Buck, Co. C—shoulder.
Corp. Felix Collins, Co. C—head, slight.
Sergt. Grothem—right arm.
Sergt. Kane, Co. K—left thigh.
Julius Goldwig, Co. A—left foot.
Mike Doherty, Co. G—abdomen.
A. Speigle, Co. K—neck.
Charles Olens, Co. K—back.
John Marshall, Co. D—breast.
Corp. Wilson, Co. D—head.
Wm. Mackler, Co. B—left leg.

Sixth Regular Cavalry.

John P. Kinney, Co. I—cheek.
Wm. Williams, Co. D—left leg, above knee.
Wm. Lutzinger, Co. C—testicles.
Fred. Taro, Co. C—right foot.
Corp. Charles F. Meller, Co. F—left breast.
Herman Groff, Co. C—left leg.

Miscellaneous.

Thomas Day, Co. K, 1st U. S. Artillery—head.
O. S. Hire, 8th Illinois—elbow.
C. W. Stanton, 2d United States—side.
George Mills, 8th Illinois—head.
Wm. Shutliff, 8th Illinois—foot.
M. Fifer, 2d U. S.—leg.
B. H. Bowman, 33d Massachusetts Infantry—arm.
A. J. Ham, 2d U. S.—leg.
H. Coates, 6th U. S.—cheek.
Sergt. Wm. Colt, Co. G, 6th New-York—instep.
Wm. L. Colt, Co. G, 6th New-York—foot.
J. Chamberlain, 8th New-York—head.
Patrick Kelly, Co. M, 6th New-York—foot.
B. Dingman, Co. E, 6th United States—hip.
E. N. Foster, Co. I, 3d Wisconsin—side.
Joseph Attwood, Co. I, 8th New-York—arm.
Geo. Woodruff, Co. C, 8th Illinois—hand.
O. Richard, Co. N, 6th Pennsylvania—thigh.
James Lewin, Co. K, 6th Pennsylvania—side.
E. D. Hughes, Co. A, 6th Pennsylvania—side.
H. Huff, 86th New-York—back and arm.
Lees Jones, Co. D, 6th United States—breast.
H. Burns, 6th United States—side.
C. Miller, 6th United States—side.
M. Arnold, Co. A, 9th New-York—breast.
John E. Dewitt, Co. A, 9th New-York—head.
Sergt. M. Summy, Co. A, 9th New-York—leg.
Geo. C. Welton, Co. C, 9th New-York—slight.
C. Van Epps, Co. A, 9th New-York—rib broken.
John Eusten, Co. K, 9th New-York—ankle.
J. Clemens, Co. H, 8th Illinois—arm.
Chas. Minor, Co. G, 8th New-York—hip.
E. Mason, Co. D, 2d Massachusetts—knee.
David Lowers, 124th New-York Infantry—ankle.
John Kirser, Co. G, 6th Pennsylvania—leg.
Felix Collins, Co. C, 5th United States—head.
J. W. Ross, Co. A, 5th Virginia, (rebel.)
John H. Kendrick, 33d Mass. infantry—cheek.
Sergt. D. McGregor, Co. H, 9th New-York.
P. Herrigan, Co. E, 2d U. S.—right shoulder.
Geo. Hawins, Co. E, 13th Wisconsin infantry—right shoulder.
G. Evans, Co. B, 13th Wis. infantry—right arm.
S. B. Conkright, Co. A, 9th New-York—head.
C. W. Van Ness, Co. A, 9th New-York—head.
James Hopes, 2d U. S.—right breast.
L. J. Powers, 2d Mass. infantry—foot amputated.

Eighty-sixth New-York Infantry.

Corp. Henry H. Cole—hand.
Corp. Charles R. Cappell—left hand.
Charles L. Odell, Co. B—head.
Albert Silsbee, Co. D—face.
Edward Stuart, Co. F—left shoulder, shell.
Myron M. Seeley, Co. F—head.
Sergt. Jere Ryan, Co. A—six ball wounds in legs.
Sergt. E. B. Camp, Co. E—left leg.
John Hanley, Co. F—left thigh.
Sergt. E. B. Kemp, Co. E—left leg.
A. J. Marvin, Co. B—forefinger.

One Hundred and Twenty-fourth New-York—Infantry.

—— Callis, Co. D—slightly wounded.
James N. Hazen, Co. F—fingers, slightly.
W. H. Callister, Co. B—shell wound in shoulder.
John Raymond, Co. D—thumb of right hand.
James Jones, Co. A—side.
Daniel A. Nierman, Co. A—finger, right hand.
Ed. Sharpe, Co. F—right arm.
Sanford Gordon, Co. F—hip.

Third Wisconsin—Infantry.

V. Clarno, Co. C—left leg.
G. L. Harrison, Co. I—side.
Henry Fuller, Co. C—thigh.
James Golder, Co. C—face.
Joseph H. Ames, Co. E—finger.
James Parrett, Co. E—thigh.
Wm. Steffen, Co. E—right arm.
Hans Berryman, Co. E—feet.

THE SIEGE OF VICKSBURG.

AFFAIRS PROGRESSING FAVORABLY.

Our Total Loss thus Far Not Over Seven Thousand.

Arrival of Admiral Farragut with Additional Gunboats.

AN ALMOST CONSTANT BOMBARDMENT.

CINCINNATI, Wednesday, June 10.

The *Commercial* has advices from Vicksburgh through an officer of the Forty-eighth Ohio Volunteers.

The condition of affairs there was favorable.

The troops were impressed with the idea that Vicksburgh must fall, and have no idea of failure.

Our losses are greatly exaggerated.

The total loss since the crossing of the Mississippi will not exceed 7,000.

THE LATEST CAIRO DISPATCHES.

Dispatch to the Missouri Democrat.

CAIRO, Sunday, June 7—10 P. M.

The steamer *Alice Dean*, Capt. PEPPER, bringing Vicksburgh dates to Thursday, and Memphis dates of yesterday P. M., arrived this evening.

An officer of the *Alice Dean* reports everything progressing as usual in the rear of Vicksburgh. The sappers and miners were still burrowing the hillsides. The gunboats and mortar-boats are still operating in front, and new siege guns had opened fire on Thursday, as had been anticipated, but with what success was not ascertained.

Our sharpshooters still command the rebel works in the rear, and the rebels are not allowed to show their heads without becoming targets for hundreds of rifles.

The general position of GRANT's army remains unchanged. The advanced regiments are being daily relieved, and fresh ones take their places. Gen. OSTERHAUS is at Big Black River, to hold JOE JOHNSTON in check, should he attempt a movement. JOHNSTON's force, it is supposed, is not over 10,000 reliable fighting men; but he is reported to have 20,000 conscripts, of all ages, at Eutaw, Miss., and about the same number near Jackson.

Deserters report the rebels in the besieged city as reduced to one ration per day, consisting of thirteen ounces of meat and meal, and greatly demoralized in other respects.

The sanitary condition of GRANT's army is good.

The *Alice Dean* took down goods. Her Captain says they have no more room for hospital stores, for the sick and wounded have more than needed. Nearly all the wounded having been taken up to Memphis, they are well supplied with everything.

DETAILS OF THE SIEGE.

The Weather—Heat—Sinking of the Cincinnati—Busy Times at Vicksburgh—Admiral Porter—Farragut on hand—A Fast Day in Vicksburgh.

From Our Own Correspondent.

IN REAR OF VICKSBURGH, Saturday, May 30.

The weather, which for the last month has been as cool as one could expect, has suddenly become as hot as the furnace prepared for the three uncompromising Hebrews. The air is tremulous with heat; the dust-covered leaves droop and wither; thunders go growling and roaring over the sky toward evening, but bring us no rain, only hot lightnings and hypocritical clouds; the nights are stale with polished skies and a bright moon that instead of light glow with and reflect back the heat which the earth has absorbed during the day. Where yesterday there was a green, placid bayou, there is to-day only a natural canal, on whose steep banks lie rotting dogs and unshapely driftwood, and whose bottom is covered here with oozy, bubbling slime, and there with yawning cracks that seem to open down to the centre of the earth.

Standing upon any one of the higher hills between Haines' Bluff and Vicksburgh, the entire position of our army, its movements and the passage of teams can be correctly guessed at by the spectator, by watching the lines of dust that rise above the ocean of verdure whose leafy swells and hollows stretch away illimitably before him.

The Southern Summer—that Summer with its sweltering heats, its dried-up streams, its nights dripping with unhealthy dews, its dust-malaria, discomforts and death—is upon us.

We are making some progress toward the capture of Vicksburgh, although, just now, operations are so multifarious and extended, that it puzzles one to keep track of them all, and at the same time to catch other bearings upon the main object of the present undertaking. MOWER, with his brigade, is skirmishing with rebels at Haines' Bluff; BLAIR, with a small army, has struck up in the direction of Yazoo City; other troops are leaving various portions of our line of investment, and moving in converging lines toward some point between Yazoo City and Big Black River; and then there is our army digging around Vicksburgh; a fleet of mortar-boats thundering away in front; a reinforcement of gunboats from below by FARRAGUT, and of land forces by BANKS—making, in all, as broad a field of operations as a correspondent can well keep watch of.

Day before yesterday several gunboats from below, and the *Cincinnati* from above, made a combined attack upon the river defences of Vicksburgh, which resulted in the withdrawal of the former and the sinking of the latter, with a loss of thirty-one men killed and wounded. The fight did not last long, and resulted in adding strength to the conclusion that ironclads are inferior to strong earthworks placed on an eminence, so that the latter have the other under a plunging fire. Fort Donelson, Fort Pillow, Fort Pemberton, Port Hudson, No. Ten, Grand Gulf, Haines' Bluff and Vicksburgh have proved this fact beyond dispute. The gunboats claim to have silenced the batteries at Grand Gulf; they silenced them to the extent that the rebel gunners ceased firing, but not to the extent of disabling the guns, as is shown in the fact that when, two or three hours afterward, the transports ran by, every gun save one was in working order.

At Haines' Bluff the gunboats have again and again tried their metal without ever having effected the slightest damage upon the impregnable fortifications; and yet, after GRANT, by a march of 150 miles, and fighting five bloody battles, had secured a position in rear of Haines' Bluff, and forced its evacuation, the Admiral runs up, lands his forces, and in two minutes after nineteen rebel guns bear the announcement that they were "captured by the U. S. naval squadron, May 8, under Rear-Admiral A. D. C. PORTER, at Haines' Bluff, Miss."

The *Cincinnati* received a shot through her bow, close to her water-line. She commenced sinking, but was run into a slough or small bayou on the opposite side of the river before she sank too far to become unmanageable. She will not prove a loss, as she is only partially submerged, and can, with no great labor, be raised and made as good as new in a short time.

The eight mortar-boats seem to be doing very efficient service. Within the last two days they have blown up choice magazines in town, and besides causing much other perceptible damage, have kept the inhabitants in a constant state of alarm and wakefulness. Deserters, of whom there is a continuous stream, inform us that soldiers, citizens and everybody else, live night and day in ditches, outside of which there is not an instant's security of life. Wednesday was determined upon as a fast-day, with the double purpose, probably, of propitiating Providence and economizing their limited rations. In the evening one of the Pastors, during a lull in the firing, got a few of his flock together, and took possession of one of the churches, for the purpose of having a quiet season of prayer and penitence. Scarcely, however, were they in full progress ere a shell from one of the mortars crashed through the roof, beneath which was gathered the secession supplicants, and blew one entire end of the building into a pile of brick, dust and shattered timbers. Of course this interruption put an end to the prayer meeting, and instanter the pious rebels betook themselves to the security of their ditches. To a superstitious mind, the advent of the shell at that particular moment and place might indicate that Providence was not listening with a willing ear to their petitions for the success of treason; but, whatever conclusions they may derive from this incident, it is more than likely that hereafter their matutinal orisons, as well as their vesper supplications, will not be put forth in places liable to the visitation of our 200-pound shells.

Deserters also state that they have sufficient provisions to sustain life for three weeks by reducing the issue to half and quarter rations. They say that their force consists of from 15,000 to 20,000 men, but that the ceaseless cannonading kept up from our lines has worked them out by keeping them constantly on the alert, and preventing them from sleeping. They continue to hold out under the hope that they may yet receive assistance from beyond Big Black River.

Yesterday morning the mortars, gunboats and all the batteries on land opened simultaneously soon after daylight, and kept up the fire until each gun had expended fifteen rounds; the whole being devised to annoy the rebels, for which purpose the guns were all shotted, and to celebrate the anniversary of our march into Corinth. Undoubtedly, the rebels derived far less gratification from the jubilation than we—particularly as their side of the celebration occurred *before* the muzzles of the guns, while ours took place at the breech—a trifling difference in position which, as I have frequently noticed, makes a vast difference in a man's feelings.

FARRAGUT reached here yesterday with five additional gunboats, which added to those already below makes our naval force in that vicinity reach the respectable number of thirteen. Whether this formidable fleet will be able to silence the river batteries is more than is known. I do not even know that they will attempt it. Probably, however, so large a force will not be kept idle, and if they do make a united assault upon the place it will be one of the grandest bombardments of the whole war.

Yesterday, a rebel dispatch bearer came to the headquarters of Gen. GRANT, and gave him a letter, which had been intrusted to him by Gen. PEMBERTON, to deliver to Gen. JOHNSTON. The letter informed JOHNSTON that unless within ten days he attacked GRANT with at least 30,000 men, Vicksburgh would have to fall. It is thought by some that the whole operation is a *ruse* on the part of the Confederates; but even supposing the letter to be of that character, I do not see what the rebels would gain by it.

Last evening, the anniversary of the taking of Corinth, was again observed along our entire line. I do not believe that heavier salutes ever shook the air than on this occasion. It was an operation whose fullness, resonance and rapidity would have delighted the most fastidious of anniversary observers, and it was, probably, as satisfactory to us as it was annoying and ominous to the rebels.

GALWAY.

FROM GEN. HOOKER'S HEADQUARTERS.

Our Force Still Across the River Below Fredericksburgh.

A Brief Cannonade, but No Damage Done.

WASHINGTON, Wednesday, June 10.

The latest news from the Rappahannock is as follows:

Yesterday afternoon the enemy opened several of their crest batteries upon our ranks and the forces on the plain west of the river and south of Fredericksburgh. They also threw several shells on this side of the river. Our batteries replied to them. There was no loss on our side. The cannonading lasted only a few minutes. This was the first time the enemy have opened their guns on our new position.

The respective lines remain the same as yesterday morning. It is said the enemy has but one corps opposed to our front below the town.

ITEMS FROM THE SOUTH.

Reported Imprisonment of Vallandigham by the Rebels.

CINCINNATI, Wednesday, June 10.

The *Gazette* has a dispatch from Murfreesboro', dated the 9th inst., which says:

"Refugees who have arrived here from the South report that Mr. VALLANDIGHAM has been imprisoned by the rebels."

The *Gazette* publishes the following Southern items:

JACKSON, Miss., Friday, June 5.

There is not a rumor to-day from Vicksburgh or Port Hudson. Heavy firing continues at the former place.

Dispatches from Jackson, to the 3d inst. to the Mobile *Tribune* say that Port Hudson is closely besieged. The news from that quarter is conflicting. It is believed that the accounts heretofore reported of fighting there are greatly exaggerated. The Yankees have abandoned the New-Orleans and Jackson Railroad. They burned the Manchac bridge, and destroyed the fortifications there.

Pascagoula dispatches say that Gen. SHERMAN had arrived at New-Orleans, and had his leg amputated, but that afterward he died.

The election returns from Virginia indicate the election of Gen. WILLIAM SMITH as the Governor of that State.

The Recent Captures by the Alabama.

HALIFAX, Wednesday, June 10.

The English papers received by the *Africa* contain only a mere mention of the fact of the capture by the pirate *Alabama* of the vessels mentioned in the dispatch of yesterday. No particulars are given.

Messrs. CRAWSHAW & Co., English merchants, publish a letter in the papers of the 22d ult., complaining of the destruction by the pirate of the ships *Nora* and *Louisa Hatch*.

The steamer *Norwegian*, from Quebec, arrived at Liverpool on the 28th ult., and the steamer *St. Andrew*, from Portland, arrived on the same day.

The New-York Times.

VOL. XII—NO. 3672. NEW-YORK, WEDNESDAY, JULY 1, 1863. PRICE THREE CENTS.

THE REBEL INVASION.

Important Intelligence Regarding the Movements of Lee.

Sudden Withdrawal of His Forces from Before Harrisburgh.

Hurried Evacuation of York and Other Places.

Probable Concentration of the Rebel Army at Shippensburgh.

The Army of the Potomac Pressing it Closely.

A Great Battle Expected in the Cumberland Valley.

Pleasonton's Outer Pickets Reported Near York.

A Cavalry Fight and Defeat of the Rebels at McConnellsburgh.

MARTIAL LAW IN BALTIMORE.

SPECIAL DISPATCHES FROM WASHINGTON.

WASHINGTON, Tuesday, June 30.

Advices received here this evening indicate that LEE is at last thoroughly aroused to the peril of the position in which he has entangled his army. He is drawing in his forces to the neighborhood of Shippensburgh, *where a great battle will probably be fought.*

The position of our army cannot be stated, but the public may rest assured that it is rapidly forcing conclusions with the enemy. Its present numbers, and moral and physical condition are such as to give informed parties here to-night the most sanguine expectations. The tide has turned to-day, and will hardly flow again in the enemy's favor.

TELEGRAMS FROM HARRISBURGH.

HARRISBURGH, Tuesday, June 30—1 o'clock P. M.

The city is now as quiet as though it was Sunday.

There is no excitement in the city.

The soldiers are all at their posts.

Yesterday 400 cavalry, belonging to Col. PIERCE's command, late MILROY's, had a fight with IMBODEN's cavalry at McConnellsburgh, defeating them and driving them through the town.

The rebels had three killed. On our side two men were wounded. We took thirty-three prisoners.

The rebel division of Gen. EARLY left for York this morning, taking the road to Carlisle.

Gen. LEE is now concentrating his army in the valley between Shippensburgh and Chambersburgh, evidently anticipating an attack from the Army of the Potomac.

Gen. EWELL's rebel corps is still in front of Harrisburgh, and may commence the attack at any time.

THE REBELS RETIRING.

HARRISBURGH, Tuesday, June 30.

All is quiet. The rebels have retreated beyond Carlisle.

TELEGRAMS FROM COLUMBIA, PENN.

COLUMBIA, PENN., Tuesday, June 30.

S. S. BLAIR, Trainmaster on the Northern Central Railroad, left York at 8 o'clock this morning. The rebels had all left, except their rear-guard, which was beginning to move off when he left.

The rebels are supposed to be moving toward Harrisburgh. They left unexpectedly, and in a hurry.

It was reported that Gen. PLEASANTON's outer pickets had been seen within four miles of York.

The total demand on York by the rebels, amounted to three hundred thousand dollars.

The citizens raised $30,000 in cash and subsistence, and the rebels allowed them twenty days to raise the balance.

No private families were molested. The citizens were all treated with respect.

The railroad property was not disturbed, with the exception of about thirty old cars that were at the shops awaiting repairs.

The railroad south of Glen Rock was not injured in any way.

The rebel force at York was not over 8,000, with eighteen pieces of artillery.

The rebel force at Wrightsville was 3,000, with five pieces of artillery.

TELEGRAMS FROM PHILADELPHIA.

PHILADELPHIA, Tuesday, June 30—2 P. M.

Intelligence has been received here to-day that Gen. LEE and his Staff were at Carlisle last night.

A rebel infantry force was seen this morning, about fourteen miles from Harrisburgh, marching toward that city. They may come up to our forces some time this afternoon. An engagement is then expected to take place, although it may be postponed until the morning.

The telegraph wires are uninterrupted along the whole line of the Pennsylvania Railroad. The trains are running also, but slowly and cautiously, so as to avoid surprises.

The Reading *Adler*, the organ of the Democrats and generally known as the Berks County "Bible," has come out with a stirring appeal to the farmers to quit their fields and rally for the defence of the State. A camp has been formed, and it is expected that there will be 20,000 men assembled there immediately.

PHILADELPHIA, Tuesday, June 30—3:15 P. M.

A dispatch from Harrisburgh, received this morning, states that the authorities at Harrisburgh have information, apparently reliable, that EWELL's corps, with portions of HILL's and LONGSTREET's, will move this day toward Harrisburgh.

They number about forty thousand men.

The report that several companies of Col. THOMAS' regiment had been captured is incorrect. They have arrived safe, with but small losses.

PHILADELPHIA, Tuesday, June 30.

Fifty rebel prisoners from Harrisburgh arrived here to-day.

TELEGRAMS FROM BALTIMORE.

PHILADELPHIA, Tuesday, June 30—9½ A. M.

A special dispatch to the *Inquirer*, from Baltimore, says:

"A train came in this morning from Union Bridge, the western terminus of the Western Maryland Railroad, having passed through Westminster. No rebels had appeared anywhere along the route.

It is ascertained that a large body of National cavalry reached Gettysburgh, took possession of the town, and captured quite a number of rebels. Our army is gradually moving in that direction.

The train on the Northern Central Railroad run this morning to Parkton, twenty-six miles from Baltimore.

Several bridges have been destroyed north of Parkton.

No apprehensions are felt for the Baltimore and Washington Railroad, as it is strongly protected. The same may be said of the Philadelphia, Wilmington and Baltimore Railroad.

The gunboats are in each of the gun-powder rivers, and at Havre de Grace and at Bush River.

The defences of Baltimore are now very strong.

All the negroes that can be found, without distinction, are impressed into the service and made to work in building fortifications.

The cars from Baltimore to Frederick, this morning, were obliged to return after reaching Sykesville, where a large force of rebel cavalry were seen tearing up the track and burning bridges.

The train narrowly escaped being captured.

BALTIMORE, Tuesday, June 30.

The *American*, this morning, publishes the following paragraphs:

A portion of the First Delaware cavalry regiment, which were stationed at Westminster, twenty-eight miles from the city, were attacked, yesterday, by rebel cavalry, and a running fight ensued, in which our cavalry were chased to within seven miles of the city, but few of the detachment reporting at headquarters.

Later in the evening it was reported that a considerable force of rebel cavalry were advancing toward the city on Reister's town road. The preconcerted signal was immediately given, and the members of the Union Leagues promptly assembled at their different headquarters, received their arms and marched to the barricades. The promptness with which the call was answered was highly creditable to their patriotism and courage.

The *American* also says:

We are gratified to be able to announce that the Army of the Potomac is in rapid and successful motion under its new commander, Maj.-Gen. MEADE. The character of this movement is such as will satisfy the country of the vigor, skill and good judgment of the new commander. We feel that we ought not to explain the grand movement in its present stage, but we assure our readers that it will give great satisfaction.

BALTIMORE, Tuesday, June 30.

The following definite information relative to the rebel cavalry force which crossed the Potomac River at the Point of Rocks on Saturday night, has been received by the *American*, in a letter from a Methodist clergyman residing at Brookville, Md.:

Very much to the astonishment of the citizens the rebels came in there on Sunday evening about 6 o'clock.

Gen. STUART was with the rebel force, and took possession of the Reverend gentleman's house.

The rebels had with them captured wagons, prisoners, contrabands and mules, besides other plunder.

On Monday morning the rebels left, going northward, as is learned from another source.

The Reverend gentleman says he entertained five of the National prisoners (officers) at breakfast, among them Major DUANE and Capt. MECKLING, of the United States Engineers.

This was doubtless the same rebel force which struck the Baltimore and Ohio Railroad yesterday morning.

It is equally certain that it is the same rebel force which passed northward of this city last evening, in the direction of Westminster, doubtless aiming to reach their forces at York or Gettysburgh, which gave rise to the alarm here last night.

BALTIMORE, Tuesday, June 30.

The *American* says:

"The response of the Union Leagues of this city last night to the call of Gen. SCHENCK for the public defence, was most prompt and enthusiastic. Old and young flocked to the armories to obtain arms, and the supply was not sufficient for one-half of those who presented themselves. By previous concert each company marched to its post at the barricades, and stood guard during the night.

"We learn from citizens of Westminster, who arrived here this morning, that the First Delaware cavalry made a most splendid fight, and fought with sabres and revolvers when first attacked, and until the enemy appeared in overwhelming numbers. The enemy came up on the Washington road, and at the time our cavalry were [illegible] and preparing for a scout [illegible]. They captured two or three horses and men at a blacksmith's shop at the end of the town, when the balance charged on them in an effort to recover the prisoners. A fierce fight ensued, in which a number were wounded on both sides.

"While the fight was going on about 300 more rebel cavalry came in sight, when a retreat was ordered, and they passed through the length of the town, skirmishing and fighting the whole distance, in which one of the rebels was shot by a citizen. [illegible] more than sixty of the Delaware cavalry in the engagement, and it is feared that the greater portion of them were killed, wounded or captured. Not more than fifteen out of 110 in the command have arrived here.

"Commodore DORNIN has, at the request of Gen. SCHENCK, placed two gunboats near the end of Broadway, and one at the bridge on the western side of the city, in an admirable position to bear upon the city and its approaches.

[illegible]

MARTIAL LAW PROCLAIMED IN BALTIMORE.

BALTIMORE, Tuesday, June 30.

The *American* contains the following:

HEADQUARTERS MIDDLE DEPARTMENT, EIGHTH ARMY CORPS, BALTIMORE, June 30, 1863.

The immediate presence of a rebel army within this Department and in the State of Maryland requires, as a military necessity, a resort to all the proper and usual means of defence and security. This security is to be provided against known hostilities and opposition to the lawful and National Government, from every quarter and in every form. Traitors and disaffected persons within must be restrained and made to contribute to the common safety, while the enemy in the field is to be met and punished [illegible].

Martial law is therefore declared and hereby established in the City and County of Baltimore, and in all the counties of the western shore of Maryland. The Commanding General gives assurance that this suspension of the civil Government within the limits defined shall not extend beyond the necessities of the occasion. All the civil courts, tribunals, and political functionaries of State, county and city authority, are to continue in the discharge of their duties, as in time of peace, only in no way interfering with the exercise of the predominant power assumed and asserted by the military authority.

All peaceful citizens are requested to remain quietly at their homes and in the pursuit of their ordinary avocations, except as they may be possibly subject to calls for personal services, or other necessary requisitions for military purposes or uses hereafter.

All seditious language or mischievous practices tending to the encouragement of rebellion are especially prohibited, and promptly be made the subject of observation and treatment. Traitors and disaffected persons must expect to be dealt with as the public safety may seem to require.

To save the country is paramount to all other considerations. When the occasion for this proclamation passes by, no one will be more rejoiced than the Commanding General that he can revoke his order and return to the normal condition of a country at peace and a Government sustained by a united and loyal people.

(Signed) ROBERT C. SCHENCK, Major-Gen. Commanding.

EXCITEMENT AT OXFORD, PENN.

OXFORD, Chester County, Penn., Tuesday, June 30.

The excitement at this point is increasing. The merchants are moving away their goods. Rebel scouts have been seen passing down the banks of the Susquehanna River, on the Harford side, and they have been reported as far down as Peach Bottom.

OUR HARRISBURG CORRESPONDENCE.

The Report of a Spy—His Adventures in Carlisle and Vicinity—Ewell's Corps There, Numbering 20,000 Men—Lee's Movements—The Work of the Copperheads—Information to the Enemy—The Rebel Intentions, &c.

HARRISBURGH, Monday, June 29, 1863.

I have just had an extremely interesting conversation with a young man whose name I dare not mention, because if the rebels should ever catch him they would surely shoot or hang him as a spy—for such he was. He voluntarily went within their lines, and traversed all their camps in the vicinity of Carlisle, with which country he is entirely familiar. While in Carlisle he met an old friend now in the rebel army, and through him was introduced to several of the rebel Generals, who talked with him very freely. They said he could not get out of town, and they did not care how much they told him. He is brave, adventurous, and as cool as a man can be, though he is but a mere boy. He made his escape over the South Mountain, though the rebel soldiers were in pursuit of him, and he arrived in Duncannon at 2½ o'clock this morning. He walked twenty miles in three hours and a half, having left Carlisle at 11½. He arrived here in the 12 o'clock train.

Nearly the whole of EWELL's corps is at and about Carlisle, and it numbers about 20,000 men. Gen. EARLY left yesterday, with a considerable body of troops, for Gettysburgh. All the expeditions hereabouts have been made from this corps. Gen. ANDERSON's corps is close behind at Chambersburgh, and advancing. Gen. LEE passed through Chambersburgh yesterday, on his way to Gettysburgh. He holds the centre, which is composed, in part at least, of LONGSTREET's corps. EWELL is on the left, and A. P. HILL, who is now at Hagerstown, on the right. The whole rebel army is on this side of the Potomac, and most of it in Pennsylvania. It consists, probably, of not far from one hundred thousand men.

The information of the rebels is very full and accurate. They showed my informant a complete map of the fortifications here, and told him of fords on the river. They know as well as we do the number of men that we have, and their character. They say that our militia won't be able to stand two volleys of musketry, and that they are not afraid of as many as we can bring against them. There are plenty of Copperheads, who furnish them all the information they want, and point out to them the places where goods are hidden. While they use these men, they despise them. "There," said a rebel officer to my informant, "do you see that man?" (pointing to one of these sympathizers.) "Well he is a —— rebel; and if I were in the place of you people that are loyal, I would hang him as soon as we get away from here." The individual alluded to felt the force of the remark, and left. The rebels concurred in saying they honored an open enemy, but despised a snake. The more I think of it, the more I wonder that a Northern man can be found who will aid the rebels while invading the Free States. That some Southern people retain their loyalty to the Union, and their affection for the old flag, is not surprising, but a traitor to the Union in the Free States is an anomaly.

Gen. EWELL said he should encamp in front of Harrisburgh to-night, and would have done so last night but that he preferred not to travel on Sunday, where it could be avoided. Several of the other Generals said the intention of the rebel army was to capture Harrisburgh at all events, and then march on Philadelphia. They all appear to be in the greatest spirits, particularly the officers, who have of late had very superior quarters to those they are accustomed to. The privates are many of them better clad than the wretched tatterdemalions who are brought in as prisoners; but they seem to feel very well, and marched through the streets of Carlisle singing "Dixie" at a great rate. They are very rude and unfeeling in their conduct toward our prisoners, tantalizing and abusing them when they are taken through the camps. They told my informant that HOOKER had retreated to Washington and that GRANT had been repulsed at Vicksburgh, both of which statements they profess to believe.

A great many desert from the rebel army. The mountains are full of deserters, and they come into Harrisburgh every day. The picket guard has been doubled in order to prevent this. I apprehend Gen. LEE will find a good deal of trouble on this score. Thousands of the privates are tired of fighting and have no heart in the cause. Now that they have got into a Free State and having a good chance, if they once get beyond the pickets, of escaping North, many will leave and regain their freedom. After the first great fight, when the usual precautions to catch deserters are necessarily somewhat intermitted, the rebel army will unquestionably lose heavily in deserters and stragglers. Heretofore, if they escaped, they could only go south. Now the case is quite different. The most of them, however, are very plucky. They say they are fighting for their rights, and that if they can only succeed in staying North during the Summer they are sure to be recognized.

They make requisitions on the inhabitants for all they want. They made one requisition on Carlisle yesterday morning for 1,500 rations, and later in the forenoon another for 500 barrels of flour. They strip the stores, but touch nothing in private dwellings, and they are courteous and polite to citizens, particularly ladies. I am happy to be able to say, also, that our ladies do *not* follow the example of Southern ladies in their treatment of the rebel soldiers.

Thus, while we of the North have been quibbling, grumbling and criticising, instead of aiding the Government—maneuvring for the next President instead of fighting for our country, and quarreling about our Generals instead of following them cheerfully, a powerful, desperate and determined foe has invaded our soil and driven our citizens from their homes. While our peace Democracy have been advocating an armistice, and resisting all our preparations for men, the character of the issue has changed, and now we are obliged to fight or be conquered. Why don't FERNANDO WOOD go down to Gettysburgh and ask LEE if he won't consent to an armistice? I think Mr. LEE would say, if he deigned to answer him at all, that he would talk about that when he should get to Philadelphia. Even now, appalling as the danger is, I hear from all quarters, both high and low, scarcely less vindictive denunciations of the War Department and the Abolitionists than of the rebels. "Why don't the President send up 10,000 men from HOOKER's army," they whine, "and defend Harrisburgh." As though any one would think of such a thing as dividing the army, which is our only hope, to save such a contemptible little village as this. People have got so into the habit of blaming and finding fault that it seems as though they could do nothing else. They are doing better now, however, than they yet have. The whole population is ready to take up arms; very many are formed into companies. The veterans of 1812 have taken their muskets and cartridge boxes. Two companies of negroes were armed yesterday and marched through the streets, strange to say, without being insulted. The thought seemed to impress itself on every mind that there was bone and muscle even if the skin was black. The darkies themselves are highly delighted. They polish up their muskets and stuff their cartridge boxes full, laughing and chatting all the time as merrily as possible—tickled as a child with a new toy. These men have never been drilled much, and are officered by colored men, but I am inclined to think they will fight as well as the militia. When we consider the *fearful risk they run* we must acknowledge that it requires a high order of courage for a negro to enlist.

The fortifications are finished, and there are now a great many troops to defend them. They are impregnable, if well defended, and I hope the rebels will find cause to change the contempt they feel for our militia into admiration, when once they test their mettle. I do not suppose the great battle will be fought here; but I have very little doubt of their intention to take Harrisburgh if they can do it. Though they made no use of the capture, it would be a great thing to say that they had taken the capital of Pennsylvania. It would be worth five thousand men to them. If, however, they mean to stay in the North the whole Summer, they could not do better than to occupy Harrisburgh permanently. In the meantime, a few days longer will explain the whole plan up to the first battle.

The Philadelphia *Age* published on its bulletin-board to-day that there were no rebels near Harrisburgh. A message was sent to Gen. COUCH that the statement was believed in many quarters, and that it had the effect which was undoubtedly intended—to stop enlistments—and asking for the facts. He answered that the rebels were within four miles of Harrisburgh and advancing, and that an attack was hourly expected.

Col. COPPEE is relieved of his onerous duties, and his place is filled by WAYNE MCVEIGH, Esq., who is an old newspaper man, and will, I hope, be able to give us more news than we obtained from Col. COPPEE.

There was a slight skirmish over the river to-day. Nobody hurt, but some a good deal frightened. The Seventy-first New-York was engaged; also, SPENCER MILLER's battery. The rebels were about one hundred and fifty cavalry. They have made no advance this afternoon, so far as heard from. A detachment was seen at a point about thirty miles north of Harrisburgh, on the river, but no report has yet come of their operations.

The bridge company at this place keep an account of all the soldiers and teams that cross the river, and intend to present their bill to the State or the National Government, whichever they think will be fool enough to pay it. Patriotic!

THE SITUATION

just at present, seems to be this: LEE's whole army is in Pennsylvania and the borders of Maryland. LEE himself is at the centre, at or near Gettysburgh, with LONGSTREET's corps. A. P. HILL is on the right, and EWELL on the left. The latter corps is much the strongest, and numbers, according to information received by Gov. CURTIN, *thirty-seven thousand men*. Other accounts place it at thirty-four thousand. LONGSTREET's corps is said to be only ten thousand, but this, it seems to me, must be a mistake. ANDERSON's corps is in reserve, and is now at Chambersburgh. The whole rebel army must number at least one hundred thousand men.

EWELL's corps, which consists largely of cavalry and mounted infantry, and were the first to advance into the Cumberland Valley, is charged with the double duty of watching our movements and making excursions to various points for the purpose of plunder, and also to break our railroad connections. IMBODEN is advancing on Bloody Run, probably to capture MILROY's remnant, at the same time a force is at Perryville, thirty miles north of Harrisburgh, and will probably cut the Pennsylvania Railroad at some important point. A force is also at York, and has laid that unfortunate city under contribution to the amount of $150,000 in money and a large amount of flour and other edibles. These points are at least one hundred miles apart. A large force is threatening Harrisburgh, and all these detachments are parts of EWELL's corps. I think the other corps, LONGSTREET's, A. P. HILL's and ANDERSON's, are to be held in hand, while EWELL's does the work of burning bridges and cutting off our communications with the North, East and West, and at the same time collects together horses and supplies for the main army. I can no longer doubt that the rebels intend to carry on the Summer campaign in the North. It is a desperate movement, but it is their only hope. They must neutralize our victories in the West if they can. If we can beat them the rebellion is crushed, for whether we capture and destroy their army, or whether we only drive them back to Richmond, they cannot live through another Winter. The "black cloud" is gathering in the Southwest. A counter fire is gathering in the Northeast. When the fire and the cloud meet, the bolt that falls will destroy the last vestige of the rebellion. The people of the North must realize the fact that the rebels have actually attempted their conquest, for such is the fact. They trust to the machinations and schemes of their friends here to succeed. May this be discouraged and foiled now and forever.

Gen. COUCH has issued an order forbidding all newspaper correspondents to cross the river.

The Enemy Quiet—Speculations as to Their Intentions—The Army of the Potomac, &c.

HARRISBURGH, Penn., Monday, June 29, 1863.

The day has passed, and the enemy has not made an attempt to capture the city. The present quiet state of affairs was certainly not looked for by the inhabitants this morning. Everyone expected to hear the sound of musketry and the roar of cannon sometime during the day. It is asserted by the best authority that the enemy is in force at Carlisle, having arrived there at noon yesterday. Carlisle is distant from here 18 miles, and if the enemy had been inclined he could have reached our outer pickets without any difficulty, as far as traveling is concerned, this afternoon. Perhaps, after all, the rebels do not intend to occupy Harrisburgh. In fact, some people begin to think the rebels could not be bribed to come here. To be sure, there is a difference of opinion among the citizens, and while some assert that the rebels will be walking the streets in 24 hours, others are equally confident that the capture of the city will not be attempted. Judging from the position of affairs at the present moment, it would seem that the enemy wished to avoid Harrisburgh and strike for Baltimore. We have intelligence that he is at York in heavy force, having retired from Wrightsville last night. The rebel General commanding at York, this afternoon, levied a contribution upon the citizens of $150,000 in money, 150 barrels of flour, 40,000 pounds of beef, 50 bags of coffee, and large quantities of other stores. If such acts of robbery are not sufficient to awaken the ire of all Pennsylvanians, then what will? In order to save the State, the people must rally to its defence. If the enemy had attacked the fortifications to-day, who knows but their superiority in numbers alone would have given them success. It is true that to-morrow our forces will be augmented, but there cannot be a surplus of soldiers on this occasion.

There are some in our midst who rely wholly upon the Army of the Potomac to rout the invaders. The news received this evening that Gen. MEADE had opened communication with Gen. COUCH created much joy with those people, and nothing could convince them that the game was not up with the rebels. They now walk the streets with comparative ease and smoke costly segars without concern or remorse. They should not forget, however, that rumors have, at times, little to do with truth, and, perhaps, after all, they may wake up some bright morning, and find themselves bodily in possession of the rebels.

The remnant of Col. JENNINGS' regiment came in from Gettysburgh last night. Only about ninety men out of over four hundred returned. The remainder are struggling through the country. All the privates were paroled, but the officers were ordered to Richmond, to await an exchange.

The cars on the Pennsylvania Central Road have been running very irregularly since the advance of the enemy to Wrightsville. Only one train went out from here to-day. The surplus locomotives and cars belonging to the roads going East have been taken to points of safety. The rolling stock remaining can be got away in fifteen minutes' time.

Thirty-three prisoners captured at Mount Union were brought into town this morning. They were taken to the Court-house yard, where they were gazed upon by hundreds. WHIT.

THE ARMY OF THE POTOMAC.

The Contrast Between Maryland and Virginia—Sugarloaf Mountain—The Occupation of Frederick by Our Forces, &c.

From Our Special Correspondent.

"MY MARYLAND," Saturday, June 27, 1863.

Following the example of the enemy, your correspondent has concluded to "invade." The transition from the soil of traitorous Virginia to that of loyal Maryland is quite as pleasant to me as to the rebels. We leave barren wastes and desolate ruins for well-tilled fields, quiet villages, and well-filled lardres—only I fear to leave some of these as barren and as desolate as some we have mourned over in other regions.

Riding yesterday from Washington, on horseback, to a point well up toward Harper's Ferry, I could not help feeling a sense of intense relief in viewing the scenes of rural beauty and domestic quietude, spread profusely on every hand, and all so very different from the scenes which have been before our eyes in ravaged Virginia for the past ten months.

We feel that we are not in an enemy's country. Sour looks, frowns and scoffs, are less frequent. Smiles even pervade the faces of some. Hospitalities are frequently tendered. Charges are moderate—a strange thing so near Washington. Questions are civilly answered, and information volunteered in many cases.

[illegible] haven't any news to write this morning. I am campaigning on my own hook for a day or two, with headquarters in the saddle in the daytime, and my blankets spread this night not a thousand miles from the top of Sugarloaf Mountain, and no pesky cavalry near to steal my horse.

For the present I know nothing about the Army of the Potomac. I feel pretty sure it isn't fighting, and if it clears up soon, we shall find some signals somewhere, and direct our march accordingly.

Sugarloaf Mountain is one of our old haunts. Signal men have a partiality for it. Last Fall a signal officer, with one orderly and an electric battery, drove the rebels out of it, and gallantly held the position until MCCLELLAN reinforced him—about a week. From the top we can signal to Frederick, Loudon Heights, Catoctin and Bull Run Mountains.

Not being in communication with Harrisburgh, I have, of course, nothing about EWELL, with his forty thousand men. (I suppose EWELL would not have forty thousand and one, if he could, because "Stonewall" always had just that number.) I have ascertained the exact strength of the rebel army. I took all the reports of one day from Harrisburgh, and footing up the number of rebels positively said to be at each place named, I find it to be *two hundred and twenty thousand*. This, however, does not include the corps of LONGSTREET and A. P. HILL, which are to be added to the footings. This will make the total strength of the enemy not less than five hundred thousand men. One Harrisburgh dispatch, to the effect that the rebels have four thousand pieces of artillery, I think is slightly exaggerated. I do not think the number will exceed thirty-five hundred!!!

Campaigning in Maryland is delightful, by contrast with Virginia. For breakfast, ham and eggs and coffee; lunch, bread and milk; dinner, chickens; dessert, cherries—and no guerrillas, no bushwhackers, *no cavalry to steal your horse.*

SATURDAY—4 P. M.

A heavy force of National cavalry occupied Frederick last night. Further intelligence of important movements has been received during the day, but under existing circumstances I cannot give them to the public. Correspondents have again been enjoined that now, more than ever, is the time for holding their tongues with reference to the movements of our forces. So I communicate only such as are perfectly apparent to the enemy—and leave the rest to be noted when results follow.

The heavy rain of Thursday night and yesterday has no particular effect in raising the streams. Neither advance, retreats, nor pursuits will be affected by the wet weather so far.

The Quakers of Loudon County averred yesterday that LONGSTREET's corps was still encamped under the shadows of the Blue Ridge. But I don't know that the Quakers are any wiser than some other folks. All the evidence goes to show that the rebels have been very strict in prohibiting communication over the Blue Ridge. L. L. CROUNSE.

The Position of the Army of the Potomac.

BALTIMORE, Tuesday, June 30.

The *American* says:

"We are not at liberty to give the precise present position of the Army of the Potomac. Suffice it to say that both railroad and telegraphic communication was resumed this morning with Frederick and Harper's Ferry, and that the rebels raiders, who occupied Montgomery County yesterday and Sunday, found it necessary yesterday afternoon to make a rapid move from those localities. They also disappeared from Marriottsville and Sykesville, on the Baltimore and Ohio Railroad, yesterday afternoon, and there was no enemy last night between the Frederick Road and the Potomac.

Gen. MEADE, so soon as he took command of the army, issued orders for a general movement, and in a few hours relieved both Baltimore and Washington of all present fear of rebel invasion. We apprehend there is not a rebel in arms within thirty miles of Baltimore, and none on this side of the Potomac within a similar distance of Washington.

The Baltimore and Ohio Railroad was repaired last night. The bridge over Piney Run has been restored, and the train which left this morning for Frederick and Harper's Ferry has gone through without interruption. The telegraph was repaired half an hour after the rebels disappeared, and in a few hours the bridge track was laid and the rails replaced.

The rebel cavalry, which yesterday attacked a company of the First Delaware cavalry at Westminster, and drove them toward this city, was doubtless the advance guard of FITZHUGH LEE's cavalry leading the way across the country, through Baltimore County, to enable them to join the main rebel army in the vicinity of York and Gettysburgh. They had found that longer delay on the line of the Baltimore and Frederick Turnpike and Railroad would not be safe, in view movement of Gen. MEADE, and were making a rapid march across the country.

It is supposed by many that the alarm given last night, of the approach of an enemy toward the city in considerable force, was merely a ruse to test the earnestness of our citizens in behalf of a vigorous defence. This, however, was not the case. Signal pickets, twenty miles out, announced the movement in the neighborhood of Westminster, of a large cavalry force of the enemy. This was undoubtedly FITZHUGH LEE's cavalry, which crossed the Potomac on Sunday morning and occupied the line of the Baltimore and Ohio Railroad yesterday.

The movement of Gen. MEADE's army made hasty departure necessary, but they were rather getting away from the city than coming toward it. We are still in hopes that they were intercepted during the night by the portion of Gen. PLEASANTON's cavalry sent in pursuit of them.

FROM CENTRAL KENTUCKY.

Threatening Demonstrations on the Cumberland.

Fifteen Thousand Rebels Preparing to Enter the State.

CINCINNATI, Tuesday, June 30.

The *Commercial*, of this city, has a dispatch from Central Kentucky, which says:

"Matters on the Cumberland River wear a threatening aspect.

The rebels are represented to be in force at Albany. They are said to number 15,000 men.

The rebels are commanded by PEGRAM and MARSHALL, who are preparing to advance into Kentucky from the Walker and Cumberland Gaps.

The advance of the rebel force entered Columbia yesterday.

The character of the rebel movement is not yet fully developed, but those in command of our forces are confident of their ability to repel any attack the enemy are likely to make.

DEFENSIVE PREPARATIONS IN OHIO.

A Conference Between the Military and Civil Authorities—Suspension of Business at Columbus—Address by Gov. Tod—Information about the Rebels.

CINCINNATI, Tuesday, June 30.

A Committee of the City Councils and citizens had an interview with Maj.-Gen. BURNSIDE last night, in relation to the defences of the city. The Committee adjourned without action, to meet again this morning.

There was a general suspension of business at Columbus yesterday.

A meeting was also held at the State House, which was addressed by Gov. TOD, who said that he had information that it was the design of the rebels to enter Ohio within the next month.

A Committee of citizens were then appointed to adopt a plan of action, and to raise volunteers for home defence.

ORGANIZATION OF STATE TROOPS.

Thirty Regiments to be Organized Immediately in this City and Brooklyn.

ALBANY, Tuesday, June 30.

Gov. SEYMOUR has ordered Inspector-General MILLER to go to New-York immediately, and organize thirty regiments in that City and Brooklyn. They will be drilled in artillery as well as infantry practice, with the view of placing them in fortifications.

The Obsequies of Admiral Foote.

NEW-HAVEN, Conn., Tuesday, June 30.

The ceremonies attending the burial of Admiral ANDREW HULL FOOTE in this city, to-day, were the most imposing ever witnessed in this State. The principal military companies of the State, the Governor and Staff, the State officers and members of the Legislature, together with the civic authorities of the Cities of New-Haven and Hartford, and the officers of the National Government, participated in the solemn pageant. The stores of the city were closed and mostly draped in mourning, as were many of the private residences.

The remains lay in state in the State House—from 10 until 2 o'clock, when, escorted by a company of marines, they were borne to the Centre Church, where Dr. LEONARD BACON, assisted by Drs. DUTTON and CLEVELAND, conducted the exercises.

At 4½ o'clock the military, commanded by Maj.-Gen. RUSSELL, and the civic procession, in charge of BENJAMIN NOYES, Esq., formed in line on Temple-street, where some 10,000 citizens had assembled. The pall-bearers—Admirals GREGORY, SMITH, STRINGHAM, DAVIS and STEWART, and Capt. SIMPSON—bore the remains to the hearse; and the procession, after passing through a few of the principal streets, conveyed, amid the sound of tolling bells and booming cannon, the hero to the City Cemetery. At the grave Prof. HARWOOD read the burial service, when the last volleys were fired, and the chieftain's form passed from mortal sight.

Government Finances.

PHILADELPHIA, Tuesday, June 30.

The Government Subscription Agent reports the sale of Five-Twenty Bonds to-day to the amount of $1,805,000, at the agencies in Boston and Philadelphia. The receipts from the West have been delayed by the non-arrival of the mail. This mode of disposing of the loan has proved so successful—the sales having reached over $140,000,000—that the Secretary of the Treasury will most probably continue, for a brief period, the sale of the loan through the present popular medium of sub-agencies. Should he determine to do so the announcement will be duly made to-morrow.

The Missouri State Convention.

JEFFERSON CITY, Mo., Tuesday, June 30.

Great confusion and excitement have prevailed in the Convention for the past few days. Nothing has been done except the rejection of a large number of amendments to the Emancipation Ordinance. It is thought something definite will be accomplished to-morrow, but it is doubtful whether the action of this Convention will be accepted by the mass of the people.

Trial Trip of the Shenandoah.

BOSTON, Tuesday, June 30.

The new sloop-of-war *Shenandoah*, from Philadelphia the 25th, on her trial trip, arrived here this afternoon. She easily made 12½ knots, without canvas, and her officers consider her equal if not superior, to any war vessel afloat. Capt. D. B. RIDGLY is in command, J. S. SKERRETT is Lieutenant-Commander, and E. M. GUILD Paymaster. Her complement of seamen will be made up at this port.

Amusements.

WINTER GARDEN.—At this establishment, on Thursday evening, Mr. W. R. FLOYD takes his benefit, on which occasion DAN BRYANT, celebrated in negro minstrelsy, will make his "first appearance" with a white face as *Handy Andy*, in the Irish comedy of that name.

Gen. THUMB and his wife, and their friends, the Nutt and the Warren, continue to be the attractions at BARNUM's. On the Fourth they will give entertainments every hour.

Court of Appeals.

ALBANY, Tuesday, June 30.

The following is the Calendar of the Court of Appeals for Wednesday, July 1: Nos. [illegible]

The New-York Times.

VOL. XII—NO. 3673. NEW-YORK, THURSDAY, JULY 2, 1863. PRICE THREE CENTS.

THE REBEL INVASION.

Highly Important from the Army of the Potomac.

Defeat of Stuart's Cavalry in Three Fights.

The Rebels Driven from Westminster to Hanover by Gen. Gregg.

Their Defeat at Hanover by Gen. Kilpatrick.

Another Defeat of the Rebels at Hanover Junction.

Their Loss Four Hundred Men and Six Pieces of Artillery.

A Supposed Heavy Battle Between Gens. Meade and Lee.

Rapid Cannonading Heard at Harrisburgh Last Evening.

Probable Position of the Main Rebel Army.

Special Dispatch to the New-York Times.

Headquarters Army of the Potomac, Tuesday Evening—8 P. M.

I am just in from the front, and send by a messenger to Frederick a brief dispatch of the occurrences of yesterday and to-day. The rebel force which made the raid on the Baltimore and Ohio Railroad consisted of Stuart's whole force, with eight pieces of artillery. On Monday night they arrived at Westminster and interrupted the Western Maryland Railroad. They threw out strong pickets, and shot two citizens who attempted to escape and give us information. Early this morning, Gen. Gregg attacked Stuart and drove him all the way from Westminster to Hanover, Pennsylvania—a distance of eighteen miles. During the forenoon Gens. Kilpatrick and Custar drove Stuart out of Hanover after a splendid fight, and they are still pursuing him; part of his force going toward Gettysburgh and part toward York.

During the day Gen. Buford drove a regiment of rebel infantry out of Gettysburgh, who also retired in a northeasterly direction.

You may expect to hear of brilliant news.

The whole army is in splendid spirits.

The rebels are reported to have burned Cashtown, Penn., yesterday. It is between Gettysburgh and Chambersburgh.

Headquarters Army Potomac, Wednesday, July 1, 1863—8 A. M.

Gen. Kilpatrick captured fifty prisoners, including a Lieutenant-Colonel and a Lieutenant yesterday afternoon. They belonged to Fitzhugh Lee's cavalry brigade. The rebels retreated by way of the road to York, which is the nearest route to Harrisburgh. The column of infantry which was driven out of Gettysburgh, also fell back east toward York by way of Berlin and Abbottsville. This looks like a concentration of their forces near Harrisburgh.

LATER.

Wednesday, 12 M.

From the best information we can obtain the rebels appear to be concentrating their forces on a line running from Cashtown to Berlin. Longstreet and A. P. Hill were near Cashtown yesterday. They are ripping, stripping and stealing everything. Citizens report that they burned twenty-five houses in Shippensburgh a couple days ago. In Gettysburgh they took everything that was left—most of the goods having been sent away in advance.

Our cavalry received a glorious welcome in Gettysburgh.

It looks at this hour as though the rebels were preparing to clear from the State with their plunder, or else to concentrate and give us battle.

York, Penn., was evacuated by the enemy last evening. L. L. CROUNSE.

DISPATCHES FROM WASHINGTON.

Washington, Wednesday, July 1.

Letters of to-day's date have been received from the Army of the Potomac, in which the following facts are stated:

Our last movements have been characterised by a marked willingness on the part of the soldiers to undergo any fatigue within the bounds of human endurance.

The rebels recently sent only a small scouting or reconnoitering party to the vicinity of Frederick. Sharing in the general belief that there is no force of the enemy between that city and Hagerstown, the stage proprietor this morning sent out his team from the former for the latter place. This fact is stated to show that the intervening distance is now believed to be safe to travelers.

A portion of our forces surrounded Emmettsburgh on Monday, and captured without conflict a battery—the only reble force there.

Notwithstanding various reports to the contrary, our pontoon bridges at Edwards' Ferry have been taken up and safety secured by the Engineer brigade.

Gen. Stahl was relieved from his cavalry command by Gen. Hooker on Sunday, and Gen. Kilpatrick appointed in his place.

Brigadier-Gen. Copeland has been assigned to other duty, and his late command has been reorganized.

The very best spirit pervades the army, and the hope of an early and decisive battle is the prevailing sentiment of the troops.

The portion of Maryland occupied by our army is teeming with rich agricultural products, affording large supplies. The most friendly disposition is evinced toward us by the inhabitants generally, and every precaution is taken to prevent the wanton destruction of property.

The following circular has been issued:

Headquarters Army of the Potomac, June 30, 1863.

The Commanding General requests that previous to the engagement soon to be expected with the enemy, corps and all other commanding officers address their troops, explaining to them the immense issues involved in the struggle. The enemy is now on our soil. The whole country looks anxiously to this army to deliver it from the presence of the foe. Our failure to do so will leave us no such welcome as the swelling of millions of hearts with pride and joy at our success would give to every soldier of the army. Homes, firesides and domestic altars are involved. The army has fought well heretofore. It is believed that it will fight more desperately and bravely than ever if it is addressed in fitting terms. Corps and other commanders are authorized to order the instant death of any soldier who fails to do his duty at this hour.

By command of Major-Gen. MEADE.
S. Williams, Assistant Adj.-Gen.

Our cavalry is actively scouting in every direction, and no fears of surprise are for an instant entertained by any one.

Washington, Wednesday, July 1.

Official advices from the Army of the Potomac state that a portion of our cavalry under Gen. Kilpatrick had a handsome fight yesterday with the enemy's cavalry at Hanover. We captured a battle-flag, Lieutenant-Colonel, a Captain, and 45 privates. Fifteen or twenty of the enemy were killed.

MOVEMENTS OF THE ENEMY.

Special Dispatch to the New-York Times.

Washington, Wednesday July 1.

Parties arriving to-night assert that Lee is nearer Frederick than we supposed this morning, and that the relative positions of the two armies is more complicated than indicated in yesterday's dispatches.

Lee is believed to be striving to make headway in a south-east direction.

An extended reconnoissance made beyond the fortifications of Washington develops no signs of the enemy. All have left for more northern regions.

TELEGRAMS FROM HARRISBURGH.

Harrisburgh, Penn., Wednesday, July 1.

Everything is quiet.

There is no news from any quarter this morning.

Gov. Curtin leaves at 1 o'clock for Philadelphia. He will stop at the Continental Hotel, and return here at 10 o'clock.

Gov. Curtin desires to see the citizens, that they may know and appreciate the danger which they have been so loth to believe, that they may not relax their efforts until the danger is over.

Harrisburgh, Wednesday, July 1—9:30 P. M.

A battle took place yesterday afternoon at Hanover Junction, between Pleasanton and the rebel cavalry. It lasted nearly the whole afternoon. The result was that the enemy lost 400 killed, wounded and prisoners, besides six pieces of artillery. Our loss is reported at 200.

It is believed that the main body of Lee's army is between Gettysburgh and Chambersburgh.

The indications are, that a battle has been fought to-day between Lee and Meade, but to what extent and with what result is unknown; nor is it likely to be known to-night.

Heavy firing has been heard here the whole evening in the direction of Carlisle. It is a long way off and at times very rapid. The river banks are lined with persons listening and discussing the probable results.

OUR FORCES AT HANOVER JUNCTION.

The Lancaster *Express*, of Tuesday evening, publishes the following important intelligence:

"We have just learned from a reliable source that Gen. Meade has taken Hanover Junction, thus cutting into the rebel lines, and turning their right. Gen. Early has retreated from York, and Ewell from in front of Harrisburgh.

The position of our army is such now that Lee must either beat a hasty retreat at great disadvantage, or give battle to Gen. Meade on his chosen ground. In either event it is of the utmost importance that the new levies be pushed on as rapidly as possible. Now is the hour in which to strike the decisive blow."

TELEGRAMS FROM WASHINGTON.

NO REBELS WITHIN TEN MILES.

Washington, Wednesday, July 1.

It was ascertained by our scouts yesterday, who completed a circuit extending ten miles from the city, that there was not a single rebel soldier to be seen.

Our scouts are confident that there are no rebel soldiers anywhere between Frederick and the Potomac.

Washington to-day is remarkably quiet.

DISCIPLINE OF THE SEVENTH REGIMENT.

Baltimore, Wednesday, July 1.

The discipline which is exercised in the New-York Seventh regiment is marked by such discrimination and prompt punishment, that that organization fully maintains its character. The regimental bulletin board at Fort Federal Hill to-day contained the following notice:

[*Extract from General Order.*]

Private W. E. Kidder, of Co. A, having violated his pledge to return on the expiration of his furlough, is hereby dishonorably dismissed from further duty, and will not be allowed to rejoin his Company during their present term of service.

OUR SPECIAL ARMY CORRESPONDENCE.

Our Scouts in Hagerstown—The Departure of Gen. Hooker—Rapid Marches of our Troops—Gen. Meade's Staff—Doings of the Rebel Cavalry—No Telegraphic Communication with Washington, &c.

Army of the Potomac, Monday, June 29, 1863.

A party of Col. Sharpe's gallant scouts, only nine in number, headed by Sergt. M. W. Kline, dashed into Hagerstown this morning, in the very rear of the enemy, and captured ten prisoners and a large rebel mail, which was on its way from the South to Lee's army.

Gen. Hooker, accompanied by Maj. Lawrence and Capt. Russell, his two personal Aids, left Frederick at noon, to-day, having been delayed by supposed trouble on the Baltimore and Ohio Railroad. His departure was entirely private.

The day has been wet and the roads heavy, but the troops are performing great feats of marching. They press forward with great vigor. When the history of this march is written people will be startled by the feats of endurance which our troops daily sustain.

I am very happy to say that the retirement of Gen. Hooker has involved no material delay in the movement of the army. Gen. Meade steps in vigorously, and applies himself with great energy to the task before him.

The entire Staff, save Gen. Hooker's personal Aids, remains as heretofore for the present. Gen. Meade adds three Aids, however, in the persons of Maj. Biddle and Capts. Jay and Meade.

I should not be surprised if a great battle is fought on the Fourth of July, possibly sooner.

This is the important week of the war.

The Army of the Potomac will do its duty.

Middleburgh, Carroll Co., Md., Tuesday, June 30.

The presumption here is that the public are having a nice little excitement over the doings of the rebel cavalry in the rear of Washington. As that point is not exactly in my department, I cannot give you the particulars about the rampaging rebels down in that vicinity. We heard last evening that the rebel cavalry moving toward Annapolis, had struck and destroyed the Washington Branch of the Baltimore and Ohio Railroad at Laurel Factory, sixteen miles north of Washington. Where they went to from that point we have not fully learned, but an impression prevails that they steered for Ellicott's Mills on the main line, only ten miles distant by pike from Baltimore, and about fifteen by railroad.

Washington, we know, is not in telegraphic communication with us, and the only railroad in operation to-day is the Western Maryland Railroad, from Union Bridge to Baltimore. I sent a special messenger by that last evening, and he arrived in Baltimore safely.

The Frederick Road was not in operation. The regular morning train from Frederick, as also the special train with Gen. Hooker, Gen. Marston, Col. Hardie and others, were delayed at Monocacy Junction until after 12 o'clock, and I do not know that they left then. The telegraph line was not in operation and the road was being reconnoitered by a couple of engines, but with what success I did not learn.

The fact that Washington is absolutely cut off excites little sympathy in this army. If Nero could fiddle while Rome was burning, it is believed he finds his counterpart in the Commander-in-Chief, who cat-hauls the Army of the Potomac while the rebels are positively knocking at his own doors.

We have very little information from the enemy. The great distance between the two armies, and the rapid movement of both, have tended to lessen reports from the enemy. We shall, however, have definite information from the enemy in a day or two, and possibly a battle by the close of the week.

I am indebted to Capt. Dahlgren, formerly of Gen. Hooker's Staff, but now volunteer aid to Gen. Pleasanton, for late Richmond and Charleston papers, which I forward herewith.

The dash into Hagerstown, yesterday, by Sergeant Cline and eight scouts, was a very daring thing. They took more prisoners than they had men in their own party.

The public may be laboring under excitement now, because of recent bold movements of the enemy; but by the close of the week, if signs and plans do not fail, there will be cause for far greater perturbation of the public pulse. We all hope it may beat freer with the tidings of victory.

LATER.

Tuesday, June 30—10 A. M.

The Western Maryland Railroad is also stopped, and the Army of the Potomac is without either telegraphic or railroad communication with Washington, or any other point. Blissful moment.

Rumors of a fight at Westminster prevailed last evening, but they proved to have been induced by the advance of our cavalry, some of them being taken for rebels by the citizens.

A few Baltimore papers of Monday have reached us, giving accounts of the rapid advance of the enemy along the Southern border of Pennsylvania, and the interruption of the Northern Central Railroad at York and Wrightsville. These things excite lively comment among the troops, and sharpen their appetites for the coming contest. We earnestly hope they will not fail to cross the Susquehanna and move on Philadelphia.

I sent a Times messenger by the Baltimore and Ohio Railroad from Frederick yesterday, but I am not at all sure that he got through. He had a full account of Gen. Hooker's removal, and the causes thereof. I send another to-day through the country on horseback, and hope he will not fail. Communications are decidedly precarious.

If it will assure the public at all, I can say that the Army of the Potomac is in good position, full of spirit, and nerving itself for the great work before it. A feeling, based upon what it *can* do, pervades the army—that the time has now come for a change of the score from defeat to victory.

L. L. CROUNSE.

DEPARTMENT OF NORTH CAROLINA.

Rebel Knowledge of Gen. Foster's Movements—Patriotism of the Nine Months' Men.

Newbern, N. C., Saturday, June 27, *via* Fortress Monroe, Tuesday, June 30.

The Wilmington *Journal* gives full accounts of our movements here, naming the regiments that were departing, and giving their destination before anything had been sent North about it for publication.

The *Journal* thinks that the remarkable celerity of Gen. Foster's movements is a just cause for grave apprehension, and says he is the nimble antelope that will step into Richmond, while the Confederates are napping, unless he is well watched.

Though the time of the nine months' men in the Department of North Carolina had about expired, they cheerfully volunteered to serve during the present emergency, however long it might last.

NEWS FROM BERMUDA.

The Rebel Steamer Lady Davis and other Blockade Runners—Arrival of Vallandigham.

We have the Bermuda *Royal Gazette* of June 23.

The rebel steamer *Lady Davis* arrived at St. Georges on the 22d from Wilmington. She is reported to belong to the rebel Government and to have brought important dispatches from that Government to the British Government.

There were twelve blockade runners at Wilmington on the 16th. Two of them left in company with the *Lady Davis*, which passed close to the blockading squadron on her way out of Wilmington. The *Lady Davis* was formerly the *Cornubia*.

The steamer *Harriet Pinckney* had arrived from England and the *Lord Clyde* had cleared for Nassau.

The steamer *Marion*, from Nassau, bound to England, had called for coal, but not being able to get supplied she proceeded to Halifax.

A line of steamers is about to be established between Bermuda and Liverpool.

The *Gazette* says:

"Mr. Vallandigham.—This gentleman, who has caused so much excitement in the Northern States, and who was banished to the Southern States for a stated period, arrived here in the Confederate steamer *Lady Davis*, from Wilmington, on Saturday last. It is reported that Mr. V. is on his way to Canada, and there to await coming events."

Arrived at Hamilton, Bermuda, June 18, schooner *E. A. Willard*, Conly, Bangor.

GEN. ROSECRANS' MARCH.

Full Details from Our Special Correspondent.

Manœuvres and Counter-Manœuvres of the Two Armies.

The Fighting at Hoover's Gap and Other Points.

THE REBELS FALLING BACK.

ESTIMATED FORCE OF BRAGG'S ARMY

PROSPECTS OF ACTION.

Headquarters Army of the Cumberland, In Bivouac at "Big Spring Branch," on Murfreesboro and Manchester Pike, 8 miles southeast of Murfreesboro, Thursday, June 25, 1863.

I fear that no map which you either have access to or can publish will enable you to fix the point at which headquarters are now established, and which I have localized as best I can in the heading of this letter.

The army had barely got into motion yesterday morning when a warm, soaking harvest rain began to fall. We had hoped that it might clear up by the time we should start in the afternoon, but our hopes were vain. It poured and pelted all the afternoon and evening, and our ride from Murfreesboro to this point was amid rain and mud. The road on which we were moving was the route assigned to the centre column—Gen. Thomas' corps—namely, the Murfreesboro and Manchester Turnpike; and we passed on our way the teams, and trains, and artillery, and the hearty fellows trudging along with their rubber-blankets wrapt round their shoulders and muskets. The General and Staff found shelter on the balcony of the solitary house at this point, and here we waited till well on toward midnight before the wagons came up, and with them our tents, our blankets and our supper.

Courier-lines were by-and-bye established; orderlies and messengers came in from the several commanders, and it became possible to take a general view of the result of the day's operations.

The column of the right, commanded by Gen. McCook, moved down by the Murfreesboro and Shelbyville road, skirmishing commencing about six miles south of Murfreesboro, at the point where our outer vedettes have been posted. Johnston's division had the advance, and drove the rebels handsomely till well on in the afternoon, when we had pushed them back to "Liberty Gap," twelve miles south of Murfreesboro. Liberty Gap is an opening through one of these isolated sporadic knobs which form the western outposts of the great East Tennessee range. It is an excellent point for defence, and we had expected that the rebels would make a stand here and contest the pass. We were not disappointed. Johnston found the force strongly posted, with artillery at commanding positions. He drove them, however, and with nightfall succeeded in holding the outer rim of the Gap.

Hardee's corps of Bragg's army seems to have had the advance, and covering the whole front of the rebel line, as we found his troops opposite our right, centre and left.

The force in the vicinity of Liberty Gap consisted of about 800 Arkansas troops, and at the time of our advance they were out harvesting.

Johnston's loss in the day's running fight was about 90 men in killed and wounded. We lost no prisoners. I have no information of the rebel loss; but we took about twenty prisoners, who were eager to be taken, and thinking that our advance was only a slight demonstration, were anxious to be taken to the rear lest they should be recaptured.

The flank of our extreme right was covered by Mitchel's division of cavalry, who moved out on Salem and Versailles, threatening Middleton.

Our centre, composed of Thomas' corps, moved out by the same road which I have indicated as our line of advance. He found no enemy up to the point where headquarters are now established. Eight miles in advance of this point we met another of those spurs of highland, the opening through which is called "Hoover's Gap." Some distance this side of that point, Reynolds' division, which had the advance, encountered the enemy, who were prepared to contest this pass also. By night he had succeeded in pushing the enemy back and into the Gap, which is three miles long. He had penetrated it for about a mile, holding the first ridge and commanding the road which crosses the middle of the Gap.

You will observe that the knob through which Hoover's Gap passes is about four miles east of that through which Liberty Gap passes. The interval is covered by a kind of natural curtain. There is, therefore, no danger of the enemy penetrating between our right and centre.

In this contest we had a slight loss, and we succeeded in taking about thirty prisoners. Crittenden moved still further to our left, and last night established his headquarters at Bradyville.

Such was the situation last night. Operations were resumed early this morning along the whole line, but we have as yet no reports of operations.

It continued to rain all last night, and this forenoon up to the present hour of writing, (11 A. M.,) the rain still continues.

I regret not to be able to enter into the strategic relations of this march of manœuvre, but the mail agent waits while I write.

Headquarters, Army of the Cumberland, Big Spring Creek, Friday, June 26, 1863.

I.

GENERAL VIEW OF THE SITUATION.

The third day of the advance of the Army of the Cumberland finds us at about midway of the interval between the positions lately held by the two forces, whose headquarters have been respectively at Murfreesboro and Shelbyville. Our front sweeps across a stretch of fifteen miles from Liberty Gap, where our right rests, to Lumley's Station, and where our left rests. Beyond these, on either side, our cavalry sweep a swarth on flank and front.

Although the main front of the enemy has been along the line of the Duck River, they have yet held a secondary front up to within half a dozen miles of our position at Murfreesboro, the interval being held by forces of observation and occupation. These outposts of the enemy—the surf of the tide-wave—have been pushed steadily backward, as we have pushed steadily forward, till at length they have found *points d'appui* on the lateral group of mountain ridges (the outer sentinels of the great Cumberland range) through which the gorges, styled respectively Guy's Gap, Liberty Gap and Hoover's Gap, run. Backed on these strongholds they have turned at bay, and have for two days been able to prevent this army from debouching into the country southward.

It is barely possible that Gen. Rosecrans was partly consenting to their occupation of these points. At least no very vigorous effort has been made to drive them out. The problem before this army at the outset of the campaign was not simply that of a march as rapid as possible on the shortest line between two given points, say Murfreesboro and Shelbyville. It was a much more difficult, more complicated, more hazardous task. Marches of manœuvre have this differentiating them from mere marches of concentration, that they have strategic bearings, and wield a great, often even a decisive, control over the issue before battle, or even without battle at all. It is necessary to manœuvre so as to deceive the enemy as to our real intentions—to make feints and demonstrations in various directions—while our real point of concentration is, in fact, *another*. It will be plain to any one who will examine the map of this region, with an eye even slightly instructed in the military relations of topography—who will look at the position and line of retreat of the rebels—*that our only hope of bringing on a decisive engagement was to manœuvre so as to flank the rebel right by a turning movement on Tullahoma.*

The army has now reached that point, where it is within easy communicating distance, and whence it can depart to execute the ultimate design of the commanding General. The passage of the Gaps, whether they shall be carried by assault, or be turned by making detours, is, therefore, only a secondary question. The main issue being settled, the other will be of comparatively easy execution; and the advance is down on the programme for to-day.

Viewed in its whole scope, the movement of the army has, thus far certainly, been attended with remarkable success. There is good evidence to show that the advance—if not the mere fact of the advance, which of course the rebels are constantly expecting, yet its direction and development thus far—has taken the enemy by surprise, and it is evident that Bragg does not yet penetrate the real nature of the movement. He appears to be massing on our right, with a view of covering Shelbyville, while we are massing on *his* right, with the design of seizing Tullahoma and the Chattanooga Railroad. The plan of Gen. Rosecrans is no less bold than to plant his army on the rear of Bragg's, compelling him to change front and fight a battle with his back to the Duck, and we between him and his line of retreat.

In manœuvres of this kind, however, everything depends on rapidity of movement, for all offensive operations must perforce be either on the front or one of the flanks. Of course, if any considerable time is allowed, the adversary has time to recover his surprise, test by reconnoissances which is feint and which is reality, and make his dispositions accordingly. When an advance is once fairly begun, a point is presently reached where the commander must clearly settle his ultimate object and the means by which he proposes to accomplish it; and when once determined, he cannot move too rapidly on its execution. I have seen more than one campaign fail by a want of decision and vigor at this critical point.

In our own case this delay, which has lasted now for two days, has been unavoidable, first because it was necessary that the right and left wings, after making their detours and unmasking the gaps, should concentrate on the centre for the purpose of making the final march in mass; and then because these operations have been retarded by the rain which has been falling almost continuously ever since we started out. The three main roads on which the three great columns are moving southward are excellent pikes, and are little injured by the rain; but the country roads connecting these, and by which the wings have to move on the centre are greatly cut up and all movement is exceedingly slow and toilesome. To-day will, we hope, however, see the columns through the gaps, and massed for the final march.

The statements of the rebel prisoners with respect to the positions of their forces are necessarily conflicting at a time when there is movement over the entire theatre of operations. But, with respect to the total strength of Bragg's army, the statements we get are encouraging if they can be relied on. An intelligent Arkansas Lieutenant puts their entire force before us at thirty-five thousand in all arms. He acknowledges the transfer of portions of the army to Mississippi, but says the deduction has been partly made up from reinforcements elsewhere. Gens. Clayton and Churchell, he says, with five thousand men, joined Bragg from Mobile a fortnight ago. Gen. Polk, with his command, has been engaged at Tullahoma, erecting fortifications which, if completed, would be of great strength. We will be likely to disturb the benevolent designs of the Right Reverend General.

If we shall be successful in the turning movement on the rebel right wing, the intelligence we receive from Gen. Burnside of the operations of Carter's cavalry force on the railroad of East Tennessee—and which you also have doubtless received and published—is of immense importance. It appears that Col. Saunders destroyed the Richmond and Chattanooga Railroad all the way from Lenoir to Knoxville, tearing up the rails and destroying three bridges. The first of these, Stalesbridge, is 312 feet long; the second, Strawberry Plains Bridge, 160 feet long; the third, Mossy Creek Bridge, is 325 feet long. If the destruction has been as complete as official authority represents, it will be impossible for the rebels to use this great artery of communication between their forces in the centre zone and those in the left zone. Of course it cuts off Bragg from all hope of reinforcements from Virginia. If then we shall be able to bring the rebel force to battle, it will certainly make the chances of *decisive* action much brighter than they have yet been.

We can now enter into some details of movements on the right, centre and left.

II.

OPERATIONS ON THE RIGHT WING.

In my yesterday's letter I mentioned the general scope of Mitchell's operations, who, with his division of cavalry, has been operating on the extreme right of our right wing. As his operations have been on a field removed from us here by fifteen or twenty miles, it was, of course, impossible for me to give any details. But reports which come in from the chief of cavalry, show that his work of Wednesday and Thursday was spirited and successful in the highest degree. He left Triune at 8 A. M. of Wednesday—struck the rebel pickets half a mile south of Eagleville, and continued heavy skirmishing, driving them to Rover, where he met the enemy in force. Here he formed a line of battle, pushing the enemy a quarter of a mile beyond the town. At this point the rebels opened with a battery of six guns, supported by a regiment and a battalion of infantry. Pushing on, however, he drove them to their rifle-pits within half a mile of Unionville. Twenty-seven horses were found killed, and the same number of men dead and wounded. At this point Gen. Mitchell received orders from the Chief of cavalry to attack Middleton. This he immediately proceeded to do, driving the enemy with loss of sixty horses. The rebels now took refuge in the houses, from which they fired on our approaching cavalry. A vigorous shelling, however, soon compelled them to evacuate a town which was presently in flames. Having achieved this handsome bit of work, he fell back with his command to Gen. Stanley's camp. Our entire loss in the expedition was twenty killed and wounded.

In the programme of operations on the right, it was arranged that Gen. Granger, with his force of reserves, should make vigorous demonstrations on the right of our right wing, for the purpose of engaging the enemy's attention in that direction. On Wednesday he had moved down as far as Fosterville, and yesterday he sent down Col. Patrick, with his cavalry command, as far as Guy Gap, on a reconnoissance. He found the enemy at the Gap, with a battery of artillery and three or four regiments of infantry. It is a strong position, and can be turned only by a long detour.

The operations of Gen. McCook's column were confined yesterday to pushing the enemy through Liberty Gap. Early in the day the rebels came up through the gap evidently for the purpose of feeling our line. Having become somewhat troublesome, Gen. Johnston, with his division, had permission to make the attack. This he did in good style, pushing the rebels clear through the gap, the whole length and both openings of which we now hold. Our loss in this encounter is fifty killed and wounded; and among the mortally wounded is Col. Miller, a valuable brigade commander.

III.

OPERATIONS OF THE CENTRE COLUMN.

Yesterday afternoon I accompanied Gen. Garfield, the Chief of Staff, to the extreme advance of our column on this road, ten miles south of headquarters. We found Gen. Thomas' corps holding Hoover's Gap, almost up to its end, which was still occupied by the rebels.

The gap is three miles in length—the opening being from two hundred yards to half a mile in width. Near the southern end of the gap it is crossed laterally by a small stream named Garrison Fork, which bisects the ridge, thus forming two knobs on the southern extremity of the ridge. When the advance of Gen. Thomas pushed the rebels through the gap, they took up position here, and they have been able to retain it up to the present time. They thus prevent our troops from debouching, and have been able to arrest the advance of the centre column for two days.

The driving of the enemy through Hoover's Gap—performed by Wilder's brigade of mounted infantry, which had the advance of Thomas' command—is the most spirited and successful bit of work that has been done since the present campaign began. The whole length of the pass is marked by positions admirably fitted for a vigorous defence, and it was further strengthened by rifle-pits and works. About half-way through, the rebels had a couple of well-made lunettes, flanking the road on each side. Wilder, however, got the rebels handsomely on the run, and he chased them vigorously almost to the end of the gap where Garrison Fork crosses. At this point a road strikes off to Fairfield. This portion of the enemy's front was held by Stuart's division—composed of the brigades of Bates, Beach and Johnston—the force being posted at Fairfield, on the Fairfield road up to the gap and the gap itself.

The advance of the centre corps seems to have taken the rebels quite as much by surprise as that of the flanks. When we came up the rebel force was having a gala time, and that portion which was on the Fairfield road, near the gap, was holding a review. The apparition of Wilder brought them promptly to think of more serious business. The long roll was forthwith sounded, and the rebels hastily massed to meet our advance. On coming into action, the mounted infantry, as you know, are wont to dismount, the horses of each set of four being held by the fourth men, while the others form to engage the enemy. The rebels greatly outnumbered Wilder's force, for he had pushed on half a dozen miles beyond the head of the column; but he boldly engaged them. While thus employed the rebels sent a column round on his right, with a view to make a turning movement on that flank. They were able to come round under cover of a ridge, but Wilder had detected the movement, and detached one of his regiments to check it. Both forces, in fact, were ascending opposite slopes of the hill at the same time, and had come to very close quarters before encountering each other. The rebels had all the advantage of position and of powerful supports to fall back upon; but our men had the advantage in arms. The mounted infantry are armed with the Spencer rifle, a breech loader, which enables them to fire with great rapidity. For example, after the first mutual volley, our men were able to fire twice while the rebels were loading—an operation very demoralizing to the rebel mind. They got a severe punishing. In the meantime the enemy had sent *another* force to attempt a flank movement, by making a greater detour. Wilder, finding himself thus endangered, fell back on the infantry—the head of the column having by this time reached the entrance of the gap. Reynolds' division, of Thomas' corps, having come to his assistance, the rebels were again chased back.

The loss to the enemy in this gallant little brush was quite heavy. We found twenty-three of their dead on the field. Others they had carried off. Their wounded numbered between two and three hundred, and we took fifty prisoners. In addition, we got a train of nine wagons, which we burnt. Our own loss was ten killed and about twenty wounded.

Little was done by the centre corps than hold the position in Hoover's Gap gained on Wednesday, as above described. The rebels continued, and up to the hour of writing continue, to hold the southern extremity of the Gap. Brisk firing was kept up during the day on the skirmish line, and our advance batteries were engaged with the rebel artillery. The enemy has on this position twelve guns, two of which, however, we succeeded in dismounting, and, by "pegging away at them," have compelled the enemy to shift them from point to point.

It would probably not have been a very difficult task to have by a vigorous assault in force, compelled the rebels to abandon this position. The plans of the commanding General have, however, limited Gen. Thomas to holding the gap until the movements of McCook and Crittenden become more developed.

And it was in fact to counsel with Gen. Thomas (in whose sound, sagacious judgment Gen. Rosecrans places much confidence,) touching a proposed strategic manœuvre of the three corps, that the Chief of Staff rode out to the front.

Orders were sent out early this (Friday) morning to Gen. Thomas to carry the head of the gap, and although we have as yet no reports from him, Gen. Rosecrans is of the opinion that he has taken it. If so the rebels must have abandoned the position during the night, as we have heard no firing at the front (distant ten miles) this morning. The next position which the rebels will take up on the Manchester Pike, will probably be at "Matt's Hollow," about four miles beyond Hoover's Gap. This is a very narrow defile—so narrow, in fact as to be a mere cañon. The rebels have rifle-pits and earthworks at its head, and will be able to make it a strong *tête-de-pont*. The probability is that Col. Wilder will make a detour, coming in on the southern opening of the defile, and if the rebels remain in it they will be apt to find themselves "corraled."

IV.

OPERATIONS OF THE LEFT WING.

With the exception of slight outpost skir[illegible]mishing, Gen. Crittenden's command has met with [illegible] no resistance on its march. The bad condition [illegible] of the roads has, however, retarded his progress [illegible] much that he is full a day's march behind whe[illegible] he should have been. His headquarters are at [illegible] Lumley's Station, but portions of his troops a[illegible] still back of Bradysville.

While I write the te[illegible] being struck, and we [illegible] miles south. [illegible] at headquarters here are [illegible] move to Beach Grove, ten [illegible]

W. SWINTON.

The New-York Times.

VOL. XII—NO. 3674. NEW-YORK, FRIDAY, JULY 3, 1863. PRICE THREE CENTS.

VERY IMPORTANT NEWS

Further Particulars of the Battle Near Gettysburgh on Wednesday.

Gen. Reynolds' First Army Corps in the Advance.

An Attack by Longstreet and Hill.

THE ATTACK SUCCESSFULLY RESISTED.

CESSATION OF THE BATTLE AT 4 P. M.

The Whole Army of the Potomac on the Field on Wednesday Evening.

THE REBEL ARMY NOT CONCENTRATED.

Reported Capture of a Large Number of Prisoners.

2,400 OF THEM IN BALTIMORE.

Desultory Fighting All Day Yesterday.

THE DECISIVE BATTLE EXPECTED TO-DAY.

Repulse of a Rebel Attack on Carlisle.

EVACUATION OF MARYLAND HEIGHTS

BALTIMORE, Thursday, July 2—11 P. M.

I shall send you soon an account from the battle-field near Gettysburgh of yesterday's battle, *which is very favorable.*

Meanwhile, the cheering announcement has been made of *the capture of a large number of prisoners,* some of whom have arrived here and others are on the way. The number is stated at 6,000; but this may be an exaggeration. Gen. SCHENCK has just announced at the Eutaw House that 2,400 of them have already arrived.

LATEST FROM THE FRONT.

BALTIMORE, Thursday, July 2.

The *American* learns from parties who left Gettysburgh at noon to-day that everything was progressing favorably for the ultimate success of our arms. Up to that time they assert that 6,000 prisoners had been captured and sent to the railroad terminus at Union bridge, for transportation to Baltimore. The Seventh regiment have just gone to Bolton depot to take charge of 800, already arrived, and Gen. SCHENCK has just announced from the Eutaw House that he then had in Baltimore and at the Relay House 2,400 in his possession.

We learn that nearly 1,000 of these prisoners were captured on Wednesday, by the Eleventh Army Corps, in their gallant charge on LONGSTREET'S corps. They are said to have at first slightly faltered, but when Gen. HOWARD cried to them to "Remember Chancellorsville," they rushed into the fight like infuriated demons, and the whole line of the enemy gave way before them.

During the early part of to-day, up to noon, when our informant left, there had been no general battle, though heavy skirmishing had been going on all the morning, resulting in a heavy loss to the enemy, and the capture of over 5,000 more prisoners. In all these skirmishes, which were conducted under the direction of Gen. MEADE, our arms were entirely successful; but the enemy studiously avoided any general engagement, and it was thought there would be none before to-day, when it was said to be the intention of Gen. MEADE to press the enemy along the whole line.

The prudence and skill displayed by Gen. MEADE in the management of his army, and the strategy evinced by him in coping with LEE, had already won the confidence of his troops, and his presence drew forth the strongest demonstrations of attachment.

The army evinced the determination to win at all hazards, and had been strongly impressed by the officers with the dreadful consequences that would ensue to them and the country if disaster should occur to our arms in the coming conflict.

The enemy was rapidly concentrating troops yesterday, and Gen. MEADE'S whole army had reached the field of battle.

Gen. COUCH was expected to press down through the Cumberland Valley on the enemy.

Eleven o'clock P. M.—Eight hundred and thirty rebel prisoners have just passed down Baltimore-street under guard. Among the number are Gen. ARCHER and seventy other officers.

BALTIMORE, Thursday, July 2.

The Baltimore *American* has the following in regard to the battle of Wednesday:

The body of Maj.-Gen. JOHN F. REYNOLDS, killed in the battle near Gettysburgh, arrived here this morning and was taken to the residence of his brother-in-law, Mr. GILDERSLEEVE.

We regret to learn from officers who brought down the body of Gen. REYNOLDS, that Brig.-Gen. PAUL was killed in the same fight in the south of Gettysburgh.

Gen. PAUL commanded the Third brigade of the First army corps.

Col. STONE and Col. WISTAR were both wounded and taken prisoners.

Col. WISTAR commanded the Bucktails—a Pennsylvania regiment.

Col. STONE also commanded a Pennsylvania regiment in the Second brigade of the First army corps, and was Acting Brigadier-General of the Second brigade.

Gen. NEWTON took command of the First Army Corps on the fall of Maj.-Gen. REYNOLDS.

LATER.

We learn from the officers of Maj.-Gen. REYNOLDS' Staff that our forces passed through Gettysburgh at 10 o'clock yesterday morning, and when a quarter of a mile west of the town, encountered Gens. LONGSTREET and HILL, who attacked the corps of Gen. REYNOLDS, which was in the advance.

This corps stood the force of the attack until it was relieved by the Third corps, and a commanding position secured.

The rebels made a strong attempt to flank the position we had gained, but were repulsed in the attempt.

Gen. REYNOLDS and Gen. PAUL fell under a volley from the rebel infantry. Both officers were mounted and at the head of their troops.

In the course of the conflict we fell back before superior numbers to a stronger position, and the fight ceased for the day at 4 o'clock.

At the close of the evening the whole Army of the Potomac had reached the field, and Maj.-Gen. Meade had all the corps strongly posted for a renewal of the battle this morning.

The loss of the enemy was considered fully equal to ours.

The Army of the Potomac is in fine condition and very enthusiastic.

Our loss of officers is severe.

Cols. WISTAR and STONE were wounded when they fell into the hands of the rebels.

Our army is regarded as better concentrated than that of the rebels for the events of the day.

OFFICIAL DISPATCHES FROM GEN. MEADE.

WASHINGTON, Thursday, July 2.

The latest dispatches received from Gen. MEADE are dated last night. They state that the corps engaged with Gen. EWELL'S army were Gen. REYNOLDS' and Gen. HOWARD'S. Gen. PLEASANTON succeeded in inflicting severe injury upon STUART'S cavalry. Gen. REYNOLDS was killed.

The reports received from all quarters are encouraging.

SPECIAL DISPATCH FROM WASHINGTON.

WASHINGTON, Thursday, July 2.

At the present hour, 9 P. M., no reliable advices have been received here from the Pennsylvania battle-field. It is generally felt that this is the crisis of the war. Intense anxiety prevails. The earliest information of yesterday's battle received here was L. L. CROUNSE'S dispatch to the TIMES.

Profound sensation is excited here by the death of Gen. REYNOLDS, whose brilliant qualities as a soldier, and unvaried success as a brigade, division and corps commander, marked him for present and future distinction. The President, it is well known, hesitated long between the choice of him or Gen. MEADE as successor to Gen. HOOKER. Priority of rank finally determined the matter.

Eleven P. M.—At 10:30 P. M. no news had been received from the battle-field.

WASHINGTON, Thursday, July 2—Midnight.

Up to this hour the Government has not received any official details of yesterday's fight near Gettysburgh. The fact of its not being in immediate telegraphic communication with the Head-quarters of the Army of the Potomac will explain the non-receipt of dispatches.

It is very likely that our army has been engaged in combat with the enemy to-day, although if this be true, the War Department has no official notification of such fact.

JEFF. DAVIS IN PENNSYLVANIA.

PHILADELPHIA, Thursday, July 2.

A dispatch to the *Inquirer* says JEFF. DAVIS is at Greencastle.

TELEGRAMS FROM HARRISBURGH.

Special Dispatch to the New-York Times.

HARRISBURGH, Thursday, July 2.

There has been no fighting of moment between Gen. SMITH'S forces and the enemy to-day. I left Carlisle at 2 P. M., and since arriving here have seen some parties who left there later. Gen. SMITH occupies the town. The enemy has apparently gone in the direction of Gettysburgh. Our scouts are in pursuit.

Yesterday several houses were struck by rebel shells. Mr. J. H. YOUNG and others, of the United States Sanitary Commission, were with the troops, and gave aid to the wounded. The Dickinson College was used as a hospital. Our loss yesterday was one killed and sixteen wounded. After the fight at Oyster Point sixteen dead rebels were counted.

Annexed is the list of casualties:

Robert Walter, Co. I, 30th Penn. militia—killed.
Robert Wiley, Co. D, Blue Reserves—knee.
Morris Hunter, Co. B, 28th Penn.—contusion.
George McNult, Co. C, Blue Reserves—right leg.
Stuart Patterson, Co. A, 1st Philadelphia artillery—hand.
Lieut. W. Provost, Co. K, 37th New-York—hand.
H. C. Mecklen, Co. C, 37th New-York, knee.
J. Cowly, 37th New-York—contusion.
B. W. Walter, Co. H, Gray Reserves—face.
—— Ashmead, 1st Philadelphia artillery.
—— Blackinston, Co. D, Gray Reserves.
F. Croft, Co. H, 30th Pennsylvania—slight.
A. S. Hibbard, Co. K, 37th New-York—scalp.
P. Garrett, Co. G, Gray Reserves—slight.
C. W. Collady, Co. D, Gray Reserves—right leg amputated.
Ed. Colwell, Co. A, 1st Phila. artillery—ankle.
W. Scott, Co. A, 1st Philadelphia artillery—head.

There are under treatment a few cases of exhaustion.

WHIT.

HARRISBURGH, Thursday, July 2.

The last of the rebels left Carlisle yesterday morning, and the town was occupied in the afternoon by a portion of our forces under Gen. SMITH.

About 5 o'clock in the evening the rebel cavalry appeared in large force, having come in on the York road.

A rebel officer sent in a flag of truce to Gen. SMITH, demanding the surrender of the town, which was refused.

The rebel officer, on receiving Gen. SMITH'S reply, opened on the town with their artillery.

The rebel fire was promptly responded to by our forces.

The firing continued with intervals until about 10 o'clock, when the rebels fell back in the direction from whence they came.

The rebels burned the barracks, gas works and one dwelling.

Many buildings in the place also suffered from the rebel artillery.

The Court-house was struck several times.

When the rebels opened their fire on the town, the excitement among the citizens was very great.

The women and children fled in all directions, and hid themselves in cellars.

Our loss was three killed and eleven wounded.

The rebel loss is not known.

Previous to the retirement of the rebels they sent in another flag of truce, notifying the citizens to leave, as they intended to renew the attack to-day.

This morning the rebel pickets are again in sight.

HARRISBURGH, 12 o'clock noon.

Up to this hour no news has been received of a renewal of the attack on Carlisle by the rebels.

The barracks and gas-works which the rebels have burned are located a short distance outside of the town, which accounts for their being burned.

There is no news from any other quarter.

HARRISBURGH, Thursday, July 2.

Information received here shows that there is no enemy in Loudon or McConnellsburgh nor in that section of the country. They left this morning in the direction of Chambersburgh, taking a large amount of stolen property which they had collected.

The rebels in the neighborhood of Carlisle have all fallen back in the direction of LEE'S army.

Heavy firing was heard to-day in the direction where Gen. MEADE'S and LEE'S armies are supposed to be.

As LEE'S army is between here and the Army of the Potomac, we are not in a position to learn early news.

TELEGRAMS FROM PHILADELPHIA.

PHILADELPHIA, Thursday, July 2.

The *Bulletin* has the following special dispatch regarding the rebel attack on Carlisle:

HARRISBURGH, Thursday, July 2.

A demand was sent for an unconditional surrender of Carlisle by Gen. W. H. F. LEE.

Gen. SMITH promptly refused to give up the place, when the rebels placed a battery of six pieces in position to the left of the barracks and commenced to shell the town.

Gen. SMITH replied from his guns which were mounted in Main-street, near the centre of the town.

During the shelling the rebels made a detour around the railroad and fired the barracks.

The gas-works were also fired, sparks from which are said to have burned several lumber-yards, one private dwelling and several barns.

Some citizens are known to be injured.

The Court-house was damaged, and several shells fell upon the College building and grounds.

Gen. LEE then sent in another flag of truce, notifying the women and children to leave the town by 10 o'clock this morning.

Every confidence is had in Gen. SMITH'S ability, not only to hold the place, but unless the rebels rapidly retire, his flanks and rear will be obstructed, and his force probably captured.

The citizens in the vicinity give Gen. LEE'S force at 3,000 cavalry, and one battery of six guns, light 12-pounders.

TELEGRAMS FROM COLUMBIA.

PHILADELPHIA, Thursday, July 2.

The *Press*, of this city, has the following special dispatch:

COLUMBIA, Penn., Wednesday, July 1.

The Fifth New-York, the First Vermont, the First Virginia and the Eighteenth Pennsylvania cavalry regiments left Frederick on Saturday and moved forward to Hanover.

They arrived there on Tuesday morning, when they were charged upon in the rear by the rebel cavalry of STUART.

The National forces numbered about 1,800, and the rebel force was nearly or quite 6,000.

The battle commenced at 9 o'clock in the morning, and continued until 7 o'clock in the evening.

The contest was a succession of charges, recharges, advances and repulses.

Our troops fought with desperate gallantry and daring, and gained a brilliant triumph.

We captured all the First South Carolina regiment except thirteen. The rebels, in turn, took but sixty prisoners.

A piece of artillery belonging to the First South Carolina is among our trophies.

The rebels lost beside one field-piece and one breech-loading steel rifled piece.

Our cavalry had no artillery.

TELEGRAMS FROM LANCASTER, PENN.

LANCASTER, Penn., Wednesday, July 1—11 P. M.

There is no news of importance to communicate.

Col. FRANKLIN has communication with our forces at McCall's Ferry and Peach Bottom by a line of couriers.

The last message received from him at 10 o'clock last night says that there are no signs of rebel forces in that vicinity.

TELEGRAMS FROM BALTIMORE.

BALTIMORE, Thursday, July 2.

The *American*, this afternoon, published the following:

HEADQUARTERS OF THE MIDDLE DEPARTMENT, July 2, 1863.

Until further orders the citizens of Baltimore City and County are prohibited from keeping arms in their possession unless enrolled as volunteer companies for the defence of their homes.

In accordance with the foregoing order the dwellings of citizens are now being visited by the Provost-Marshals and the police to obtain the arms in their possession.

We learn from a gentleman who was at Westminster and a prisoner in the hands of the rebels during their sojourn in that town, that Gen. STUART with his cavalry force reached there about 5 o'clock in the afternoon, and did not leave until daylight the next morning. The rebel party which had a fight with the Delaware cavalry was Gen. STUART'S advance guard, and numbered about three hundred. The rebels lost in that fight two Lieutenants killed, and fully a dozen wounded. One of the wounded was an officer, who was shot by a citizen who took part in the fight, and is reported to have since died. Col. MULFORD, the commander of the rebel advance guard, admitted to the citizens that the charge of the Delaware cavalry was most brave and dashing, but he thought very rash, in view of the disparity of numbers. The rebels admitted that their loss in killed and wounded was greater than ours. Our loss was two privates killed, and twenty-eight taken prisoners. The rebels also captured Lieut. BOWMAN and the Provost-Marshal of Westminster, with ten of his men.

The rebel sympathizers at Westminster are charged with having given information as to Union citizens, though the rebels in their levy on store keepers treated all alike.

FITCH'S dry goods store was completely gutted; BOWEN & GEER, commission merchants, at the depot, lost heavily, and MEXELL & ORNDERFF suffered to the amount of $700 in flour and feed.

The rebels stole all the horses along the roads they traveled, as well as those in the town, but they were in too much of a hurry to scour the side-roads.

The rebel officers visited the houses of rebel sympathizers, and Gen. STUART took tea at the house of JOHN C. FRYEDE, Cashier of the Westminster Bank, where he was received with all the honors.

The rebels left on Tuesday morning early, and a few hours afterward a division of the National army reached the town, causing great rejoicing among the loyal citizens. The National soldiers were welcomed with every demonstration of joy, and houses were thrown open to dispense their hospitality.

The rebel force was from 4,000 to 5,000 cavalry.

PRISONERS ARRIVED AT BALTIMORE.

BALTIMORE, Thursday, July 2.

Over eight hundred rebel prisoners have just passed down Pratt-street under guard. More are expected to-night.

MARYLAND HEIGHTS EVACUATED.

From the Baltimore Sun, July 2.

It was publicly announced yesterday that Maryland Heights had been evacuated by the Federal troops, a large number of whom were from this State and city. The evacuation was successfully accomplished on Monday night and Tuesday, the troops all being away from there before 12 o'clock on Tuesday night. All the Government property incidental to a large encampment was removed, together with all the guns, (with the exception of a few of the larger ones, which were destroyed,) ammunition, &c. The fortifications were all destroyed. A gentleman who witnessed the dismantling of the latter states that the wreck was very thorough.

The wooden portions of the Harper's Ferry railroad bridge were removed both from the Maryland side and the Potomac side, leaving the iron spans, lately constructed, and forming the centre of this important bridge, intact. This was done to prevent the Confederates from blowing up the iron structure, which it will now be impossible for them to accomplish, and also to prevent them from using the bridge across the Potomac in that vicinity.

Gen. FRENCH'S forces, lately at Maryland Heights, will now take an active part in the present important campaign. A brigade of his troops are all Marylanders, and are commanded by Brig.-Gen. KENLY, of this city. Their movements or their present whereabouts cannot be made public at present.

Gen. BAYLOR'S Confederate cavalry appeared in and around Harper's Ferry on Tuesday evening, but remained but a short while, retiring toward Charlestown, Va., where, it was stated, a force of Confederates are encamped.

Several Confederate scouts have been seen in the several days past on the Virginia side of the Upper Potomac, (Loudon County,) but none of them have attempted to cross to the Maryland side.

LEE'S GENERAL ORDER FOR THE INVASION.

HEADQUARTERS ARMY NORTHERN VIRGINIA, June 21, 1863.

GENERAL ORDERS No. 72.—While in the enemy's country, the following regulation for procuring supplies will be strictly observed, and any violation of them promptly and rigorously punished.

No. 1. No private property shall be injured or destroyed by any person belonging to or connected with the army, or taken, except by the officers hereinafter designated.

No. 2. The Chiefs of the Commissary, Quartermaster, Ordnance and Medical Departments of the army will make requisitions upon the local authorities or inhabitants for the necessary supplies for their respective departments, designating the places and times of delivery. All persons complying with such requisitions shall be paid the market price for the articles furnished, if they so desire; and the officer making such payment shall take duplicate receipts for the same, specifying the name of the person paid, and the quantity, kind and price of the property, one of which receipts shall be at once forwarded to the chief of the department to which the said officer is attached.

No. 3. Should the authorities or inhabitants neglect or refuse to comply with such requisitions, the supplies required will be taken from the nearest inhabitants so refusing, by the order and under the directions of the respective Chiefs of the Departments named.

No. 4. When any command is detached from the main body, the Chiefs of the several Departments of such command will procure supplies for the same, and such other stores as they may be ordered to provide, in the manner and subject to the provisions herein prescribed, reporting their action to the Heads of their respective Departments, to which they will forward duplicates of all vouchers given or received.

No. 5. All persons who shall decline to receive payment for property furnished on requisitions, and all from whom it shall be necessary to take stores or supplies, shall be furnished by the officer receiving or taking the same with a receipt specifying the kind and quantity of the property received or taken, as the case may be, the name of the person from whom it was received or taken, the command for the use of which it is intended, and the market price. A duplicate of said receipt shall be once forwarded to the chief of the department to which the officer by whom it is executed is attached.

No. 6. If any person shall remove or conceal property necessary for the use of the army, or attempt to do so, the officers hereinbefore mentioned will cause such property, and all other property belonging to such person that may be required by the army, to be seized, and the officer seizing the same shall forthwith report to the chief of his department the kind, quantity and market price of the property so seized, and the name of the owner.

By command of Gen. R. E. LEE.
H. H. CHILTON, A. A. and I. G.
Lieut.-Gen. R. S. EWELL, Com'g 2d Army Corps.

A REBEL ADDRESS.

GEN. EARLY TO THE CITIZENS OF YORK.

YORK, Penn., June 30, 1863.

To the citizens of York:

I have abstained from burning the railroad buildings and car shops in your town, because after examination I am satisfied that the safety of the town would be endangered, and, acting in the spirit of humanity which has ever characterized my Government and its military authorities, I do not desire to involve the innocent with the same punishment of the guilty. Had I applied the torch without regard to consequences, I would have pursued a course that would have been fully vindicated as an act of just retaliation for the unparalleled acts of brutality perpetrated by your own army on our soil. But we do not war upon women and children, and I trust the treatment you have met with at the hands of my soldiers will open your eyes to the odious tyranny under which it is apparent to all you are groaning.

J. A. EARLY, Major-General, C. S.

CALL FOR NEW-YORK TROOPS.

ALBANY, Thursday, July 2.

A telegram is just received from Gov. CURTIN, addressed to Gov. SEYMOUR, stating that the battle near Gettysburgh was not decisive, and asking him to send on all the troops he can raise without delay; that the need of them is pressing.

ANOTHER CALL ON NEW-JERSEY.

TRENTON, Thursday, July 2.

Gov. PARKER has received a dispatch from Gov. CURTIN asking for more troops, and says he cannot magnify the importance of the demand.

A State battery of four guns arrived from Rahway this evening.

MILITARY MEETING IN TRENTON.

TRENTON, N. J., Thursday, July 2.

A large meeting of citizens was called by the ringing of the City Hall bell to-day, and addressed by the Mayor upon the importance of sending troops to Pennsylvania. A committee was appointed to wait on Gov. PARKER, who appeared and addressed the meeting, urging the volunteering of men at once. Resolutions were adopted urging the Council to raise a bounty for men. Several speeches were made, and several rolls for men were opened, and the signing commenced briskly.

OUR HARRISBURG CORRESPONDENCE.

Ewell's Corps Withdrawn from before the City—The Danger Not Over—Where the Cumberland Valley Leads—The Importance of Defending Harrisburgh—Our Duty.

HARRISBURGH, Tuesday, June 30, 1863.

The crisis is past for the present. EWELL'S corps has been withdrawn from the immediate vicinity of Harrisburgh. A column, 10,000 strong, was seen to pass through Carlisle, on the Baltimore turnpike, on the road to Gettysburgh, where LEE and LONGSTREET are both supposed to be. They have also left Mechanicsburgh and York, the latter, however, only after having collected the tax levied upon its inhabitants. The telegraph will have informed you of this fact. The withdrawal is generally attributed to the fact that MEADE is in their rear and moving. There is a rumor at headquarters, not confirmed, that PLEASANTON has captured three miles of LEE'S wagon train at some point between Hagerstown and Gettysburgh. There seems to be little doubt that MEADE is moving.

But if the people of the North think that the danger to Harrisburgh is over, they will be very much mistaken. If LEE should beat MEADE, or should even not be driven out of the Valley, as the result of the impending battle, our troubles will only have begun. The battle which will prevent the Southern army from invading the North, and running riot on our soil as we have on theirs, is to be fought at Harrisburgh, unless LEE is immediately driven out. The Valley of the Cumberland is an open door to the North. The same valley continues to Westchester County in New-York. The roads are all good. The flanks of a marching army would be easily protected. The subsistence is ample for a large army a long time. The farmers of this valley are wealthy, and often have on hand two crops of wheat at a time. Cattle, hogs, hay, and pasturage abound. Gen. GRANT subsisted his army for many a month off the miserable and wasted country of Northern Mississippi. Certainly LEE could do the same for a year in Pennsylvania and New-York; and if LEE beats MEADE and takes Harrisburgh, he will do it. So Harrisburgh is the point to defend. The fortifications here are nearly impregnable—quite so, if properly defended. There is no ford on the Susquehanna that could be of any use to an army within twenty-five miles north, and none at all south, notwithstanding Gen. EWELL'S boast that he knew a dozen fords. They are only practicable at low water, and for cavalry and infantry, not for artillery. Besides, they are easily defended. The enemy might cross above here, but in order to reach Harrisburgh they must control the pass at Clark's Ferry, about twelve miles north, and that can be easily made impregnable. The position at Harrisburgh commands the approach to the North.

Moreover, it is of great importance, in view of the southern part of the valley, Chambersburgh, Gettysburgh and Baltimore are all from seventy to eighty miles from Harrisburgh. Suppose LEE beats MEADE; a large army here will be ready to pounce upon him at either of those points—and some of them we must occupy—and would at the same time prevent his marching North. Suppose the fight between MEADE and LEE should result in a drawn battle, a large force here would be of the greatest use in cooperating with MEADE, and crushing LEE. On the other hand, suppose MEADE beaten and Harrisburgh taken, the remnants of MEADE'S army must be withdrawn to protect Washington, which will be isolated. Some may be sent here, but a large force will have to remain about Washington. Then from Harrisburgh LEE has absolutely nothing to prevent his marching to Philadelphia and New-York, to say nothing of Baltimore. This is no fancy sketch. History shows how a small invading army, when led by a great General, can conquer a large amount of territory, and dictate terms to the inhabitants, especially when there is no large well-organized army to resist the invasion. Prudence dictates to us that we take immediately the precautionary measure of raising, equipping and organizing a great army which shall not only defeat the intentions of LEE, but shall sweep through the entire South like a besom of destruction. With ROSECRANS' success, which is almost certain, and GRANT'S, which is already achieved, the small remnant of the rebel armies will be crushed between the black cloud of the Southwest and the free and loyal millions of the North.

Every effort should be made in the North to raise men. The crisis of the war is at hand. The rebels have commenced to carry the war into Africa, and invasion is now their motto. If their attempt is nipped in the bud the rebellion is crushed. But if they once get the tremendous vantage ground afforded by the possession of Harrisburgh we shall stand on the defensive; nobody can tell how long the South will be enriched with the plunder taken from us, and the rebellion will have a new lease of life. Enlistments should, therefore, go on as rapidly as possible. The greatest efforts should be made to induce men to avail themselves of the bounteous offer of the Government to those who reënlist. The honor of the country is at stake, and no one ought to hesitate a moment. The first rebel flag has been hoisted on Northern free soil. That sore and humiliating sight has been witnessed in Pennsylvania. Unless the people of the North awake to the importance of the emergency they will soon find the emblem of treason floating over many a free and powerful city.

A WARNING TO COPPERHEADS.

GEORGE BOOKER, State Senator, who lives at Pagestown, about nine miles from Harrisburgh, has been visited by his friends from Dixie. He is known as one of the most violent Copperheads in the Legislature. He was the leader in the movement to forbid Senator WRIGHT and ANDY JOHNSON from speaking in the Capitol last Winter, and has never made any concealment of his hostility to the war against the rebellion and his sympathies with the South. When he heard the rebels were coming, he said he did not care—they were *gentlemen*, and respected private property. They collected in front of his house and he came out and made a little speech. He said, so I am informed from several sources, that he sympathized with them, that the rebellion was justified and the war unjust, that it was all the Abolitionists, &c., &c., &c., in the usual style of Copperheads. Whereupon the rebels immediately proceeded to give him a benefit. They took all his horses and cattle, all the flour and grain from his mill, which is a large one, and was, unfortunately for him, very well stocked, and, in fact, "cleaned him out" most completely. So much for Buckingham. On the other hand, the Governor says to-day that they did the same for that grand, brave old hero, THAD. STEVENS, and even more effectually. They destroyed everything, his houses, workshops, furnaces, fences, crops, and everything. Mr. STEVENS is now a poor man. He has paid the penalty of his patriotic, and, thank God, successful efforts to support the Government in the last Congress. Clearly the rebels are no respecters of persons.

Adjutant-Gen. THOMAS was here to-day, and had long consultations with Gov. CURTIN and Gen. COUCH. He expects to leave to-morrow. He is the guest of Hon. SIMON CAMERON.

CARLISLE.

A gentleman just arrived from Carlisle, says that the rebels behaved remarkably well in regard to the College grounds in that city. Some of them said they were graduates of the University, and others that their fathers had graduated there. They camped in the College grounds, and were even careful to build their fires on the gravel walks and not on the grass plots. This gentleman, who is a Professor in the College, describes the discipline of the army as being perfect.

TROOPS

Are pouring in faster than they are wanted. The country is at last alive. Some counties that were called upon for only 90 or 100 men, have responded with five or six companies. The surplus will be sent back to harvest the crops.

In the skirmish which occurred this afternoon at Mechanicsburgh, our militia are said to have behaved very well. They are getting into the work.

The Rebels Retiring—Gen. Knipe upon the Rear of the Retreating Column—The Havoc Committed by the Rebels—The Copperheads.

HARRISBURGH, Wednesday, July 1, 1863.

The rebels are still retiring, some taking the road to Chambersburgh and others moving in the direction of Gettysburgh. They commenced leaving Carlisle yesterday morning. A citizen who left that place at 12 M. yesterday, says only 250 rebels were in the town at that time. Another citizen, who left three hours later, reported the same number there then. It is believed that Carlisle is free from the enemy this morning, although no direct intelligence has as yet been received from there. Gen. KNIPE, with a small force of infantry and cavalry, and a few pieces of artillery, is following them up. He is necessarily obliged to advance cautiously, as the enemy may at any time reinforce his rear-guard and then give battle. Last evening a skirmish took place just beyond Mechanicsburgh. On our side the Twenty-second and Thirty-seventh New-York regiments and a section of a Philadelphia battery were engaged. The enemy had cavalry, one regiment of infantry and four pieces of artillery. The rebels drew up in line and waited the advance of our forces, and at the proper range opened with two pieces. Our men behaved nobly, not flinching in the least. A number of shot struck directly in their front, but without causing a panic or doing any great amount of injury. Our pieces then returned the fire and in a short time the infantry advanced. The rebels perceived the movement and fell back two miles, evidently with the intention of drawing the Union forces nearer to their main support. Lieut. ABBY, of the Thirty-seventh, was wounded in the neck, and a drummer-boy, named LAWSON, in the calf of the leg.

This morning Gen. KNIPE was reinforced, but the main body of the troops will not leave the immediate front of the Harrisburgh fortifications, until it is ascertained beyond doubt that the Capital is free from danger. The movements of the rebels are to be carefully watched, for at any moment they may sweep down on the right or left flank, with a view of either surrounding Gen. KNIPE, or capturing the city, or doing both.

The amount of havoc committed by the rebels in the various towns through which they have passed is represented by the citizens to be immense. They took whatever they wanted, and when so disposed, offered in payment Confederate scrip. A boot and shoe dealer in Mechanicsburgh was completely cleaned out of his entire stock, and all he had to show for it was $4,000 in worthless rebel currency. At Carlisle the people were made to furnish rations to 1,500 men. As would be naturally supposed, it did not take long to reduce the supply of provisions in that place to a small quantity. All the horses, cattle, sheep and swine in a vast section of country have been led away or slaughtered. It is related that a Copperhead resident of Mechanicsburgh, who has heretofore been loud in his assertion that the rebels were chivalrous, and would never think of disturbing private property, was especially sought after by them, and his house and furniture damaged to a heavy extent. His neighbors have an idea that perhaps he has learned to distinguish the difference between his friends and foes. If the rebels have only served all Copperheads they have come across in the same manner, the loyal people will be grateful to them. There are a few of this contemptible race of outcasts who continue to live and pollute the atmosphere of Harrisburgh. Let such take warning that they are not only the loathed of the loyal, but the despised of the open enemy.

Company after company of volunteer militia has been arriving in the city, in response to the Governor's proclamation. The people are at length aroused to the danger that threatens them, and are now prepared to sustain their own and the country's reputation to the last. The following special order has been issued by Gov. CURTIN:

HARRISBURGH, June 30, 1863.

All persons, residents of the City of Harrisburgh or vicinity, unattached to any military organization, to whom arms and ammunition or either have lately been issued from the State Arsenal, or who are in possession of arms belonging to the State, will immediately attach themselves to a military organization, to report to these headquarters, or return the arms and other State property in their hands to the Arsenal. By order of

A. G. CURTIN,
Governor and Commander-in-Chief.
A. S. RUSSELL, Adj.-General, Pennsylvania.

Forty-five prisoners taken by Col. PRICE'S command at McConnellsburgh, were brought here last night. They will be removed to Philadelphia to-day.

WHIT.

Major-Gen. John F. Reynolds.

We have information by telegraph of the death Major-Gen. JOHN FULTON REYNOLDS, U. S. A., late commander of the First Corps of the Army of the Potomac, from a wound received on Wednesday in the battle near Gettysburgh, between the First and Eleventh corps and the rebel forces under Gens. LONGSTREET and HILL. Major-Gen. REYNOLDS was born in Pennsylvania about the year 1821, and entered the Military Academy at West Point in 1837. In 1841 he graduated and received his first commission as Brevet Second Lieutenant of the Third artillery. He served with distinction in the war with Mexico, being breveted Captain for gallant and meritorious conduct at Monterey, and again Major at Buena Vista. In 1852 he served as Aid-de-Camp on the Staff of Maj.-Gen. WOOL, and in 1855 received his rank as Captain. The following year he was sent to Oregon Territory, where he distinguished himself in several severe conflicts with the Indians, near Rogue River.

When the rebellion broke out Gen. REYNOLDS warmly espoused the cause of the Government, and, on the organization of the Pennsylvania Reserve Corps, he was appointed by Gov. CURTIN one of the brigade commanders. He took part with the Army of the Potomac in nearly all its actions, and so valuable were his services that the people of the State acknowledged them by the presentation of a sword.

At the commencement of the present year Gen. REYNOLDS was promoted to the Major-Generalship and command of the First Army Corps. After the removal of Gen. BURNSIDE from the office of Commander-in-Chief of the Army of the Potomac, the name of Gen. REYNOLDS was prominently mentioned for the succession, and again after the battle of Chancellorsville; but his own preferences were in favor of Gen. MEADE.

He fell while bravely leading his men, like LYON in Missouri, STEVENS and KEARNY at Chantilly, WILLIAMS at Baton Rouge, and other kindred spirits have nobly fallen. The country at large, as well as his associates in the army, will lament his death, but no one will feel a more poignant sorrow at this fortune of war than Maj.-Gen. MEADE, the new Commander of the Army of the Potomac. The deceased and he were bosom friends, and in the arduous and difficult duties that now devolve upon him he must have counted largely upon the aid and skill of the soldier who possessed his full confidence.

The body of Gen. REYNOLDS was yesterday taken to Baltimore.

The Militia Law of Ohio to be put in Force.

THE ENROLLMENT DIFFICULTY IN SULLIVAN COUNTY, IND., ENDED.

CINCINNATI, Wednesday, July 1.

At a special meeting of the City Council last night, it was resolved to put the State Militia law in force at once.

All citizens, between 18 and 45 years of age, not physically disabled, are to be organized into companies on the 4th of July, and are subject to the Governor's call for duty, in such numbers as he may think necessary.

Large war meetings were held at Columbus, Ohio, and Indianapolis, Ind., last night.

The difficulty in regard to the enrollment in Sullivan County, Ind., is ended, and the military will return to Indianapolis to-day.

Naval Intelligence.

EASTPORT, Maine, Thursday, July 2.

The schooner *Germ*, Capt. LEONARD, arrived here this morning from Pictou. She reports that she was boarded by the officers of the United States schooner *Sarah Burton*, off Liverpool, Nova Scotia, June 30, which was in search of the bark *Tacony*. Two American steamers, at the same time, were also in sight.

The Maine Twenty-third Regiment.

BOSTON, Thursday, July 2.

The Maine Twenty-third regiment passed through Boston to-day for home, its term of nine months having expired.

Fire at South Wayne, Me.

PORTLAND, Me., Thursday, July 2.

A shovel handle factory at South Wayne was burned at noon yesterday with forty other buildings, stores, factories, mills, &c. Loss, $40,000.

The New-York Times.

VOL. XII—NO. 3675. NEW-YORK, SATURDAY, JULY 4, 1863. PRICE THREE CENTS.

THE GREAT BATTLES.

Our Special Telegrams from the Battle Field to 10 A. M. Yesterday.

Full Details of the Battle of Wednesday.

No Fighting on Thursday Until Four and a Half, P. M.

A Terrible Battle Then Commenced, Lasting Until Dark.

The Enemy Repulsed at All Points.

The Third Battle Commenced Yesterday Morning at Daylight.

THE REBELS THE ATTACKING PARTY.

No Impression Made on Our Lines.

The Death of Longstreet, and Barksdale of Mississippi.

Other Prominent Rebel Officers Killed or Wounded.

A LARGE NUMBER OF PRISONERS.

Gen. Sickles' Right Leg Shot Off.

OTHER GENERAL OFFICERS WOUNDED.

Special Dispatches to the New-York Times.

Battle-Field near Gettysburgh, Thursday 4:30 P. M. *Via* Baltimore, Friday A. M.

The day has been quiet up to the present moment. The enemy are now massing a heavy force on our left, and have just began the attack with artillery. The probability is that a severe battle will be fought before dark.

The rebel sharpshooters have been annoying our batteries and men all day from the steeples of the chnurches in Gettysburgh.

We hold the Emmettsburgh and Baltimore roads. L. L. Crounse.

Battle-Field near Gettysburgh, Friday morning July 3,—three A. M. *via* Baltimore, one P. M.

At the close of my last dispatch at 4½ P. M. yesterday, the enemy had just opened a heavy attack by artillery on our left and centre. The tactics of the enemy were soon apparent—a massing of their main strength on our left flank, which covered the Frederick road, with the determination to crush it. So intent were the enemy on this purpose, that every other part of the lines was left alone.

The fighting was of the most desperate description on both sides. Our gallant men fought as they never fought before. We had against this great onslaught of the enemy three corps—the Second, Third and Fifth. The Third and Fifth joined hands, and fought heroically. The Second ably supported them, and at the same time held its own position. One division of the First was also engaged.

The fighting was so furious that neither party took many prisoners. We captured about 600 in one or two charges.

The losses, considering the duration of the conflict, are more than usually heavy on both sides. Many of our most gallant officers have fallen. Gen. Sickles' right leg was shot off below the knee. Amputation has been performed, and he is doing well.

Late in the evening, Gen. Meade called a council of his corps commanders, and it was resolved to continue the fight so long as there was any one left to fight. L. L. Crounse.

Baltimore, Friday, July 3. *Via* Washington, Friday, July 3.

Your correspondent has just arrived from the battle-field at Gettysburgh, having left there at 3 o'clock this morning. The reports of the occurrences in that vicinity, as thus far rendered in the Philadelphia and Baltimore papers, are almost totally incorrect. A brief and candid statement of the situation up to this morning is this:

In Wednesday's fight we were repulsed, simply because we were overpowered and outflanked. We fell back to the rear of Gettysburgh, and held that position. The action was not general, and was not intended to be by Gen. Meade. It was brought on by Gen. Reynolds, under the impression that his force exceeded that of the enemy.

There was no fighting yesterday until 4½ o'clock, P. M. A bloody engagement was then fought, lasting until dark, *resulting in a substantial success to our forces, the enemy being repulsed with great loss.* The particulars I have already sent you by a special courier.

Neither Gens. Wadsworth, Van Steinwehr nor Doubleday are wounded.

The total number of prisoners taken up to this morning was about fifteen hundred—eight hundred and fifty on Wednesday, and six hundred on Thursday. This is reliable.

The enemy made the attack yesterday. *It was terrific, and they threw their whole force into it, but they were finally repulsed with great slaughter.*

At daylight this morning the battle was renewed, the cannonading being rapid and heavy. *It was the determination of our Generals to fight to the bitter end.* L. L. Crounse.

OFFICIAL DISPATCHES FROM GEN. MEADE.

Washington, Friday, July 3.

An official dispatch was received this afternoon from Maj.-Gen. Meade, dated Headquarters Army of the Potomac, July 2, 11 o'clock P. M., which says:

"The enemy attacked me about 4 P. M. this day, and, after one of the severest contests of the war, was repulsed at all points. We have suffered considerably in killed and wounded. Among the former are Brig.-Gens. Paul and Zook, and among the wounded Gens. Sickles, Barlow, Graham and Warren, slightly. We have taken a large number of prisoners."

SECOND DISPATCH.

Washington, Friday, July 3.

A later dispatch has been received from Maj.-Gen. Meade, dated 8 o'clock this morning, which says:

"The action commenced again at early daylight upon various parts of the line. The enemy thus far have made no impression upon my position. All accounts agree in placing their whole army here. Prisoners report that Longstreet's and A. P. Hill's forces were much injured yesterday, and had many general officers killed. Gen. Barksdale, of Mississippi, is dead. His body is within our lines. We have thus far about 1,600 prisoners, and a small number yet to be started."

THE BATTLE OF WEDNESDAY.

Special Dispatch to the New-York Times.

Battle-Field near Gettysburgh, Thursday, 12 M., July 2, via Frederick, July 3.

The engagement yesterday was quite severe, though confined to our advance, the First and Eleventh corps; the action being mainly fought by the First corps, under Gen. Reynolds, who was killed by a sharpshooter early in the fight. We first attacked the enemy's advance just beyond Gettysburgh, and repulsed it, when the whole corps became engaged, and subsequently the Eleventh corps, which came up to support by the Emmetsburgh road. The opposing forces were the rebel corps of Hill and Ewell. Our men gallantly sustained the fight, holding their own until 4 o'clock, when they retired to a strong position just to the eastward and southward of Gettysburgh. This was maintained until the arrival of reinforcements at night, and our lines are now well formed.

No general engagement has yet taken place, but the probability is that a great battle will be fought this afternoon or to-morrow. The enemy is in great force. Our troops are now all up and well in hand.

The battle yesterday was sanguinary in the extreme. Wadsworth's division sustained the early portion of it with great valor, charging the enemy and taking a whole regiment of prisoners with Brig.-Gen. Archer. We have taken fully one thousand prisoners and lost many, most of them being wounded and in Gettysburgh, the greater portion of which the enemy now hold.

The rebels occupy Pennsylvania College as an hospital. Robinson's division and one brigade of Doubleday's supported Wadsworth with great gallantry. The Eleventh corps, most of it fought well, and redeemed the disgrace of Chancellorsville. Among the general officers we lose beside Maj.-Gen. Reynolds, Gen. Paul killed, and Gen. Barlow wounded. Gen. Schimmelfennig is a prisoner. An estimate of yesterday's casualties cannot now be made.

Gettysburgh was injured by shells to a considerable extent. Most of the inhabitants remain in the burgh; many got away yesterday. It is a beautiful place, surrounded by a beautiful open and rolling country.

There has been more or less skirmishing all the morning, but no engagement of dimensions. Both parties are preparing for the great contest before them. Our troops are in splendid condition and fight like veterans.

Among the casualties in yesterday's engagement were the following:

Lieut. Bayard Wilkeson, commanding battery G, Fourth regular artillery, son of Saml. Wilkeson, Washington Correspondent of the Times, right leg shot off below the knee while gallantly fighting his battery against an eight gun battery of the enemy enfilading his position; believed to be prisoner.

Col. Stone, One hundred and Forty-ninth Pennsylvannia, commanding brigade, badly wounded.

Col. Root, Ninety-fourth New-York, wounded and prisoner.

Col. Tilden, Sixteenth Maine, taken prisoner.

Capts. Hovey and Thomas of Gen. Robinson's Staff, wounded.

Col. Muhler, Seventy-fifth Pennsylvania, dangerously wounded.

Col. Lockman, One Hundred and Nineteenth New-York, wounded.

Adjt. Dodge, One Hundred and Nineteenth New-York, wounded and captured.

Lieut.-Col. Arrowsmith, One Hundred and Fifty-seventh New-York, killed.

The following is a list of losses of officers in Gen. Sol. Meredith's brigade, Wadsworth's division, First army corps, in yesterday's fight:

Gen. Meredith, bruised on top of the head by a fragment of shell. His horse was shot under him and fell upon him, bruising and injuring him internally.

Lieut. G. W. Woodward, Aid-de-Camp to Meredith, wounded in right arm.

NINETEENTH INDIANA.

Lieut.-Col. Dudley, killed.

Major Lindley, slightly wounded.

Capt. Halloway, in leg.

Capt. Shafer, in arm.

Captains Jones, Hart and Ives, wounded.

Lieut. Jones—killed.

Lieut. Patrick—wounded in both legs.

Lieut. Schlagle—mortally, Gioe, Whittemore, Branson, Patrick, Nash, and Campbell—wounded.

Sergt.-Major A.W. Blanchard—killed.

SIXTH WISCONSIN.

Capt. Jno. T. Yekner—killed.

Lieutenants Rennington—in left shoulder; Beally—in arm; Pruin—in left hand; Harris—in neck; Mander and Merchant—wounded; Chapman—killed.

SECOND WISCONSIN.

Col. Fairchild—left arm amputated, doing well.

Lieut.-Col. Geo. H. Stevens—mortally wounded.

Maj. John Mansfield—wounded in leg and hip.

Lieut. W. S. Winnegar—killed.

Capts. Perry and Parsons, wounded.

Lieuts. Schowalter, Jameson, Lee, Morrison, and Dailey, wounded.

Sergt.-Major Leggett, wounded.

SEVENTH WISCONSIN.

Lieut.-Col. John Callis, wounded.

Capts. Hobart, Bean and Pond, wounded.

Lieut. Bruce, killed.

Lieuts. Johnson, Weeks, Compton, Estes, Gibson, Kidd, and Fulks, wounded.

TWENTY-FOURTH MICHIGAN.

Col. H. A. Merrow, slightly wounded.

Lieut.-Col. Flannegan, leg amputated.

Major Wright, slightly in right eye.

Capt. Bexford, Acting Adjutant, severely wounded in leg.

Capt. O'Donnell, killed.

Capts. Dillon, Speed, Hoyt and Hutchinson, wounded.

Lieuts. Whiting, Safford, Wallace, Buhl, Dodsley and Sprague, wounded.

Lieuts. Shattuck, Humphreyville and Dickey, killed.

EIGHTY-THIRD NEW-YORK.

One private killed, 3 officers and 15 men wounded, 2 officers and 81 men missing.

Of Gen. Baxter's Staff—Lieut. T. Thomas, Acting Inspector, killed; Lieut. D. P. Weaver, A. A. G., wounded; Lieut. R. C. Knoggs, A. D. C., missing.

The wounded of this brigade are all prisoners, at present, having been taken into houses near Gettysburgh and left there, as they could be better cared for.

Col. Bates, of the Twelfth Massachusetts, is wounded badly, but retains command of his regiment. The entire loss of the Second brigade is 658. They took into the fight 1,130 men.

ONE HUNDRED AND FOURTH NEW-YORK.

Lost, Capt. Wiley, Capt. Fisher, Lieut. Greggs, Lieut. Rose, Lieut. Richardson, Lieut. Dow, Lieut. Keam. All wounded. Capt. Starr, Lieut. Weed, Lieut. Lamson, Lieut. Snider, Lieut. Starks, Lieut. Tuthill, Lieut. Dickson, Lieut. Stevens, Lieut. Daily, Lieut. Steele, missing.

NINETY-FOURTH NEW-YORK.

Lost, Capt. White, Capt. Parsons, Lieut. Mesler, wounded. Col. R. Root, Capt. White, Lieut. Sears, Lieut. Parker, Lieut. Locklin, Capt. McMahon, Capt. Whiteside, missing.

1,057 killed, wounded and missing from First brigade, Second division, First corps.

Major Lemons, Third Indiana cavalry, killed.

Among other casualties of the day were Maj.-Gen. Reynolds, commanding First army corps, shot through the head by sharpshooter while on extreme front arranging line of battle.

Gen. Paul, severely wounded in leg, since dead.

Gen. Barlow severely wounded and prisoner.

Gen. Schimmelfennig captured.

Col. Robinson, Eighty-second Ohio, wounded; Lieut.-Col. Boobel, Twenty-sixth Wisconsin, and Maj. Baltz, of the same regiment, wounded.

In the Seventh Wisconsin, partial lists, now in, already foot up twenty-five enlisted men killed and ninety-seven wounded. Many more names are yet to come in.

In the Sixth Wisconsin, partial lists show seventeen killed, one hundred and twenty two wounded, ten missing; in the Second Wisconsin, partial lists show eighteen privates killed and one hundred and twenty-two wounded.

In the Nineteenth Indiana there were nineteen killed and eighty-eight wounded. In the twenty-sixth Wisconsin, sixteen killed and one hundred and forty-four wounded. L. L. CROUNSE.

REPORTS FROM PHILADELPHIA.

Philadelphia, Friday, July 3.

The *Evening Bulletin* learns from parties who have arrived in this city the following particulars:

The fight opened at Gettysburgh on Wednesday, when our forces were about half a mile beyond the town.

But one brigade of the corps of Major-Gen. Reynolds was in position to do service at the opening of the struggle.

Gen. Reynolds gallantly pushed that brigade to a commanding position on Seminary Hill, and endeavored to hold it until the rest of the corps could come up.

Reinforcements were, however, delayed, and our forces subsequently fell back of the locality called Seminary Hill.

About 10,000 of our men in this fight were engaged with 30,000 of the enemy.

The last position taken by the Union forces was held up to the latest dates.

Gen. Reynolds was killed very early in the action, while placing the brigade in position.

During Wednesday night, about seventy-five thousand of Gen. Meade's troops came up and took favorable positions for reopening the battle on Thursday morning, while at that period some twenty-five thousand other Union troops belonging to the Army of the Potomac were so near at hand as to be immediately available for the conflict.

The rebels had mainly concentrated their forces near Gettysburgh on Wednesday night, and there was but little doubt that the great battle of yesterday would involve every available man of both armies.

FURTHER DETAILS OF THE BATTLE.

Correspondence of the Philadelphia Inquirer.

On Battle-field near Gettysburgh, Wednesday Evening, 8 P. M.

To-day, and on Pennsylvania soil, has been fought one of the most desperate and bloody battles of this accursed rebellion.

This morning early the First and Eleventh corps, which had been during the night encamped near Emmettsburgh, advanced, the First corps marching in the following order: First division under Gen. Wadsworth; Third division, Gen. Doubleday; these followed by five full batteries, under Col. Wainwright; bringing up the rear was the really splendid division of Gen. Robinson; this corps having been in the advance during the whole time of our march from Falmouth, were the first force of infantry to reach Gettysburgh, and to come up with and fight the enemy.

During the day this corps had been under the direction of Major-Gen. Doubleday, Gen. Reynolds being in command of the right wing, comprising the First, Third, Eleventh and Twelfth corps.

When some three miles from town, and while quietly marching along, the sound of heavy and rapid cannon firing was heard, coming from the direction beyond Gettysburgh. Almost at the same instant Capt. Mitchell, Aid upon Gen. Reynold's Staff, came dashing down the road, with orders to the various division commanders to push forward their divisions as rapidly as possible. The order was given to "double-quick," which was instantly obeyed, and kept up until the intervening space, where our batteries were engaged, was passed over. These batteries, two in number, were a part of the artillery belonging to Gen. Buford's division, and were stationed some half a mile to the south of the Gettysburgh Theological Seminary, while the opposing force were stationed and strongly intrenched upon the east side of Marsh Creek, and at about the same distance from the Seminary as were our own forces.

The latter was the first to open fire, and were for a time compelling our batteries to retire from their position. This they were quietly doing and in good order, when the division of Gen. Gadsworth came to their support, the two able regiments, the Second Wisconsin and Twenty-fourth Michigan regiments rushing up and driving from in front of them the infantry force who were making desperate efforts to capture the pieces. When these supports arrived the batteries again took up a commanding position, which they were enabled to hold during the day.

In rear of the position so taken up, and to the right, the Division of Gen. Wadsworth were drawn up in line of battle, with the division of Gen. Robinson holding the second line. At the moment that these formations were completed, the rebels, emboldened by their partial success in driving from position the batteries, attempted another charge, with the object of seizing the pieces, when the brigrdes of the Second division, with fixed bayonets, made a charge upon them, and such as were not killed were taken prisoners. Two entire regiments—a Tennessee and Missouri regiments—were then "bagged."

Immediately after the arrival and going into position of the First Corps, the Eleventh, under Gen. Howard, who had been in the rear and marching on the same road as the First, made their appearance, marched directly through the town, and at once formed a line of battle on the right of the Chambersburgh road, and some half a mile west of the College, which is located at the extreme end of the town. After some three hours of artillery duelling the rebels commenced retire. There were massed the two infantry corps, and in this formation a pursuit of their retreating column was commenced. After driving them back toward the mountain, something over a mile, soon after four o'clock it was discovered that with an extensive force of infantry and cavalry they were endeavoring to turn our left flank, with a view, probably, to get between us and our supply trains. Upon this being noticed, and it being evident that our reinforcements, the Third and Twelfth Corps, who had been anxiously inquired after during the entire day, were not yet up, no other alternative was offered us than to retire to the east of the town and take up a better position upon the top of a hill, and along the line of road leading to Emmettsburgh. This was done, but in admirable order, no unusual haste being apparent, while, at the same time, all ammunition and supply wagons which were up to the front were sent to the rear.

A little after 4 o'clock, the Third corps, under command of Gen. Sickles, came upon the field, and went into position upon the right of that held early in the morning by the First corps; the Twelfth, under Gen. Slocum, as well arrived about the same time, and were stationed upon the right of the Eleventh corps. After those two corps, as well as those who "had borne the heat and burden of the day," were formed in "battle array," they made an advance, and, with but little resistance, succeeded in driving the rebels from the town and back into the positions they occupied early in the morning. In this manner and in these locations both armies are resting for the night.

The Second, Fifth and Sixth corps are moving this way, and by morning will be up and ready to do battle with us.

While the latter mentioned movement was being made, the enemy kept up a continual rain of shot and shell upon the town, and when ceasing, their cavalry dashed through the town, capturing all stray parties there congregated, together with the wounded who were occupants of, and the surgeons and nurses who were in attendance in, the many hastily organized hospitals there located. While the firing was in progress some few buildings were set on fire, but the town not being compactly built, only such buildings as were struck by the shells were consumed.

OUR CASUALTIES.

Among the prominent officers killed is found the name of Gen. Paul. Gen. Wadsworth is severely wounded, Gen. Robinson, for the third time, had a horse shot from under him, while among the names of officers of less rank who are more or less wounded, are found the names of Col. Bates, of the Twelfth Massachusetts; Col. Leonard, of the Thirteenth Massachusetts; Col. Fairchild, of the Second Wisconsin; Col. Root, of the Ninety-fourth New-York; Capt. Robert Williams, of the Twelfth Massachusetts; Lieut. Thomas, Acting Aid to Gen. Baxter, and Capt. Chas. Hovey, of the Twelfth Massachusetts, a valuable and efficient Aid to Gen. Robinson, occupying upon the Staff the position of Inspector-General; Adjutant Weaver, Lieutenant of Nineteenth regiment of your city.

Among those captured are the names of Dr. Nordquist, Medical Director of Gen. Robinson's division, and Captain Fred Gerker, of your city, the Commissary of same division.

In the confusion and excitement occasioned by the charge of cavalry, and our approach to the many hospitals being cut off, it is impossible at the present writing to obtain anything like a correct list of casualties. Our losses, though, are enormously heavy, especially among field and line officers; neither are we warranted in guessing how seriously the rebels have suffered.

THE DOINGS OF THE FIRST CORPS.

Upon reaching the scene of the engagement, this corps found the cavalry division, under Gen. Buford, drawn up in line on the Chambersburgh road, about three miles from Gettysburgh, with their batteries in the position as before stated.

Gen. Reynolds, then being in command of the entire right wing, immediately rode to the front, for the purpose of making a reconnoissance and learning the position of the opposing force, when he was struck with the missile that ended his life. The command of the corps then devolved upon Gen. Doubleday, who immediately hurried up to the front. In the meantime the cavalry kept the enemy's infantry fully employed, until the corps was well in position.

The First and Third Divisions first reached the front, and after being placed in position, the Second, still keeping up its double-quick, coming immediately up to the right of the line. Soon after, the rebels advanced and opened fire along the entire line. Meredith's brigade, all Western troops, dashed forward, and, with fixed bayonets and a good solid Union cheer, succeeded in capturing near six hundred prisoners. The first and Third Divisions holding their own, and finding no impression could be made upon them, the enemy turned their attention to the splendid division under command of Gen. Robinson. This division being situated upon a ridge, and having no support, was obliged not only to fight the front, but protect his flank.

Suddenly a strong column of rebels came upon this division's front. Volley after volley was poured into them, but steadily they advanced. Finding the rifle balls had no effect upon them, a recourse was had to cold steel. The brigade under the gallant Baxter was ordered to charge bayonets upon them, and so well did they obey this order that the rebels were compelled to retire with a loss, in prisoners taken alone, of some four hundred and eighty men.

At this juncture the rebels were seen advancing in force on the right flank of the division. But finding himself hard pushed in that direction, he sent for the excellent brigade under command of Gen. Paul, who immediately came up but not a moment too soon, as the rebels were found to be coming out of the dense woods on both flanks, as well as in front, and in immense force; again did the Second repel them. It was while bravely leading the latter charge that the noble Gen. Paul received the fatal wound.

All this time the First and Third divisions were being hard pushed, but still held their ground, the Second division doing the hard work, requiring frequent changes and prompt decisions in its commanding officer. So rapid and frequent had they been firing that at this time they were completely out of ammunition, and were compelled to get that then very useful article from the cartridge boxes of their dead and wounded comrades.

While the fight was progressing and the firing the hottest a Lieutenant of the Eighty-eighth Pennsylvania came up to Gen. Robinson, after saluting, in an impromptu speech presented the flag of the Sixteenth Alabama. Another flag was captured by the Ninety-seventh New-York.

So rapidly were the rebels reinforced with fresh troops in those attempts to turn the First's left, that it obliged the order to be given to fall back a distance of perhaps a mile, fighting the whole time.

The Second division went into the fight at 11 o'clock A. M., and there remained all the time, subject to a galling fire, without support or reinforcements, until 5 o'clock.

The Staff attached to Gen. Robinson's command was all actively engaged, and exhibiting a bravery seldom met with under such peculiarly distressing and harrassing circumstances. Among the wounded of the Staff are Capt. Charles Hovey and Lieut. James Mead, the latter of your city, though but slightly wounded, being able to attend to his duties. The amiable Dr. Nordquist and the agreeable Capt. Gerker are now doubtless entertained by the rebels.

THE BATTLE OF THURSDAY.

Special Dispatch to the New-York Times.

Battle-field near Gettysburgh, Penn., *Via* Baltimore, Friday, July 3.

My brief dispatches regarding the desperate engagement of yesterday have hardly conveyed a true idea of its magnitude and character. We have now had two days' fighting. Nearly the whole of Wednesday was thus employed by the First and Eleventh Corps, with varying success, they finally being obliged to fall back before greatly superior numbers.

This morning there were strong premonitions of an early engagement with the enemy in force, but as the day wore away and no positive exhibition was made by the enemy, We began to think that perhaps there would be no immediate battle after all. We were hardly in a condition to give battle, as all our dispositions had not been made, Gen. Meade not having arrived on the ground until 2 o'clock in the morning. The position of our forces after the fight of Wednesday was to the eastward and southward of Gettysburgh, covering the Baltimore Pike, the Taneytown and Emmittsburgh roads, and still being nearly parallel with the latter. The formation of the ground on the right and centre was excellent for defensive purposes. On our extreme left the ground sloped off until the position was no higher than the enemy's. The ground in front of our line was a level, open country, interposed here and there with an orchard or a very small tract of timber, generally oak, with the underbrush cut away. During the day, a portion of the troops threw up temporary breastworks and an abattis. Gen. Meade's headquarters were at an old house on the Taneytown road, immediately in rear of the centre.

Our line was not regular in shape. Indeed the centre protruded out toward the enemy so as to form almost the two sides of a triangle. Before sundown Gen. Mead's headquarters proved to be the hottest place on the battle-field, so far as careless shelling was concerned.

Gen. Howard occupied, with his corps, a beautiful cemetery on a hill to the south of Gettysburgh. Cannons thundered, horses pranced, and men carlessly trampled over the remains of the dead. From this hill a beautiful view could be obtained of the valley, and also of a goodly portion of the enemy's line of battle.

Our forces had all been concentrated on Tuesday night, save the Fifth and Sixth corps. The former arrived during the morning, and the latter soon after noon. They were all massed immediately behind our centre.

Whether or no it was Gen. Meade's intention to attack, I cannot say, but he was hardly ready for it before the afternoon of yesterday. The day had become almost dull. Skirmishing was now and then brisk, and the sharpshooters in the steeples and belfreys of the churches persistently blazed away at officers and artillery horses. It was by a sharpshooter in a barn just opposite Wadsworth's Division, yesterday, that Capt. Stevens, of the Fifth Maine Battery, got hit. A bullet passed through both legs below the knee, inflicting a severe, but not dangerous wound.

At 3½ o'clock, Gen. Meade had received sufficient assurances to justify him in the belief that the rebels were concentrating their forces on our left flank, which all felt to be secure under the protection of the invincible Third corps. Our line was immediately strengthened on that flank, Gen. Sickles' corps being sent to its support, and several batteries from the reserve being brought out and placed in position.

At about 4½ o'clock P. M., the enemy sent his first compliments by a salvo of artillery, his first shells falling uncomfortably near Gen. Meade's Headquarters. From this hour forth to 8½ o'clock, occurred by all odds the most sanguinary engagements yet chronicled in the annals of the war, considering its short duration. The artillery attack which was made by the enemy on the left and centre was rapidly followed by the advance of his infantry. The Third corps received the attack with great coolness. The rebels at once made for our flank, and kept moving heavy columns in that a direction. This necessitated support, which was quickly given by the Fifth Corps. The division of Gen. Barnes being sent to the right, and that of Gen. Ayres, regulars, to the left, with Gen. Crawford in reserve.

The battle now became perfectly fearful. The armies engaged each other at very short range, and for three long hours the war of musketry was incessant. I have heard more noise, louder crashes, in other battles, but I never saw or heard of such desperate tenacious fighting as took place on this flank. The enemy would often bring up suddenly a heavy column of men, and force our line back, only to be in turn forced back by our own line of glittering steel. Our gallant columns covered themselves with glory over and over again. They fought a superior force in numbers. The dispositions of the enemy were very rapid, for look where you would on that field a body of rebels would be advancing. Our dispositions were equally rapid, and the enemy found more than their equal in such gallant veterans as Sickles and Birney and Humphreys. At half-past six Gen. Sickles was struck in the right leg by a piece of shell, and borne from the field. The injury was so great that amputation became necessary, and it was performed successfully—the limb being taken off below the knee.

The struggle grew hotter and hotter. The Second corps was called on for aid, and though its own position was strongly threatened, yet the First division, formerly Gen. Hancock's flung themselves into the fight with desperation, and after a long and obstinate conflict the enemy slowly and sullenly gave way. In this last charge the brigade of Gen. Caldwell, Second corps, and that of Col. Switzer, from the Fifth corps, won great honors. The charges made by our men deserve mention, but want of time forbids. The rebels made frequent attempts to capture our artillery, and at one time had Watson's battery in their possession, but it was retaken in a furious charge by Birney's division.

The battle lasted till fully 8½ o'clock, when the enemy fell back to his old position, and left our veterans the ensanguined victors of that field. Our pickets were thrown out, and our lines covered most of the field, including a great number of the enemy's dead and wounded.

I visited some portions of the line by moonlight and can bear personal witness to the terrible ferocity of the battle. In front of some of our brigades, who had good protection from stone walls or fences, the rebel dead laid piled in lines like winrows of hay. In front of Gen. Webb's—the Philadelphia—brigade, they lay so thick as to literally cover the ground.

Not far from here was found the body of Gen. Barksdale, that once haughty and violent rebel, who craved as a dying boon a cup of water and a stretcher from an ambulance-boy. He is literally cut to pieces with wounds, and must die.

A great and magnificent feature of this fight is the splendid use of artillery. Though our line of battle was only a mile and a half long, yet almost every battery belonging to the Army of the Potomac was more or less engaged. Every one of the reserve batteries was brought into action, the positions for use being numerous. The enemy also used artillery largely, but not to near so great an extent as we did. From this they suffered immensely, and specially on the left, where canister was largely used. I believe we lost no artillery, unless it was two or three disabled pieces, though it was very wonderful we did not. L. L. CROUNSE.

YESTERDAY'S BATTLE.

Our Special Telegrams from the Battle Field.

Gettysburgh, Friday, July 3.

The third day's battle began this morning at 4 o'clock. It is now 7 o'clock, and a circle of fire of musketry and artillery on the south side of Gettysburgh describes the field of contest. The musketry fight is wholly within the woods; the artillery occupies the eminences shorn of timber.

The attack was commenced by the rebels on our right. The fight there has been unceasing, and the irregularity of the fire—slack and scattering for a while, and then heavy and continuous—indicates reinforcements of both sides.

The men at this hour are in the best of spirits, and the general officers feel confident of the result. The battle has been planned and thus far fought by Gen. Meade with equal prudence (ably and energetically assisted by Gen. Butterfield, who has not left the Army of the Potomac) and courage.

The day is now overcast, and the air damp and cool. The sky threatens rain, and a fog already obscures the outer edge of the field of battle.

Quarter of Eight, A. M.

Gen. Barksdale, of Miss., wounded yesterday, is lying dead within our lines. The rumor of the death of Longstreet, brought by rebel prisoners yesterday, is confirmed by prisoners taken this morning. Longstreet's and Hill's corps are said to be fighting on the right; Ewell's in front.

10 O'Clock A. M.

Sixteen hundred prisoners, thus far during the engagement, have been sent to the rear, and more are here.

What the result may be to-day cannot now be predicted. Hancock, Howard, Slocum, Warren, Gibbon and all the general officers have given the highest evidence to-day of capacity, energy and spirit.

Important dispatches have been captured by Capt. Dahlgren and the gallant scout Kline, from Jeff. Davis and Cooper to Gen. Lee. They indicate anxiety for the position of Richmond. Both decline to send Lee the reinforcements from Beauregard he asked for. WILKESON.

THE ASSOCIATED PRESS DISPATCHES.

REPORTS FROM HARRISBURGH.

Harrisburgh, Friday, July 3.

There is great excitement here to know the result of the battle fought yesterday and last night between Gen. Meade and Lee's army.

Persons at Columbia and Bainbridge, and in the neighborhood of York, heard distinctly the roar of artillery. At times it was rapid and heavy.

At daylight this morning it was again renewed. The battle must have been in the neighborhood of Gettysburgh.

Telegraphic communication has been reopened with Baltimore, by way of the Northern Central Railroad.

There have been no movements in this Department worth mentioning.

Harrisburgh, Penn., Friday, July 3.

The city is in the greatest state of suspense. All rebel infantry and detachments of cavalry, under Jennings, Imboden and Fitz Hugh Lee, have disappeared from the front, and travel has been resumed between this city and Carlisle. Nothing is yet known as to the result, but the impression prevails that the great decisive battle of the campaign has been fought in the neighborhood of Cashtown.

Philadelphia, Friday, July 3.

A special dispatch to the *Bulletin* from Harrisburgh says:

Nothing is yet known as to results, but the impression prevails that the great decisive battle of the campaign, has been fought in the neighborhood of Cashtown, between Gettysburgh and Chambersburgh.

It is believed that we have suffered heavy losses in officers and men, but Lee is so crippled as to be placed on the defensive.

Yesterday Gen. Meade assumed the offensive. The day before Lee had attacked Meade, and was repulsed with heavy loss.

Lee holds a gap in South Mountain near Chambersburgh, through which he hopes to escape if defeated. A guard stationed at Bridge eighty-four on the Northern Central Railroad, heard firing in that direction like that of flying artillery, whence it is believed that Pleasanton is again at work with his dashing cavalry, fighting for the possession of the Gap.

Harrisburgh, Friday, July 3—Midnight.

A prominent citizen of Gettysburgh, who left there yesterday morning on a pass issued by Gen. Ewell to go to Heidleburgh, met Stuart, Fitzhugh Lee and Wade Hampton, with what he estimated at 10,000 cavalry, who were moving in the direction of Gettysburgh.

Their officers told him that Lee had no intention of leaving Pennsylvania, but was going to remain here until his army was destroyed or victorious. He arrived here this evening, the enemy making no effort to detain him.

Two militia men from Susquehanna County were killed this evening at Camp Curtin by lightning.

A dispatch from London this morning states that

[*Continued on Eighth Page.*]

Major General George Gordon Meade (seated at center) and his staff

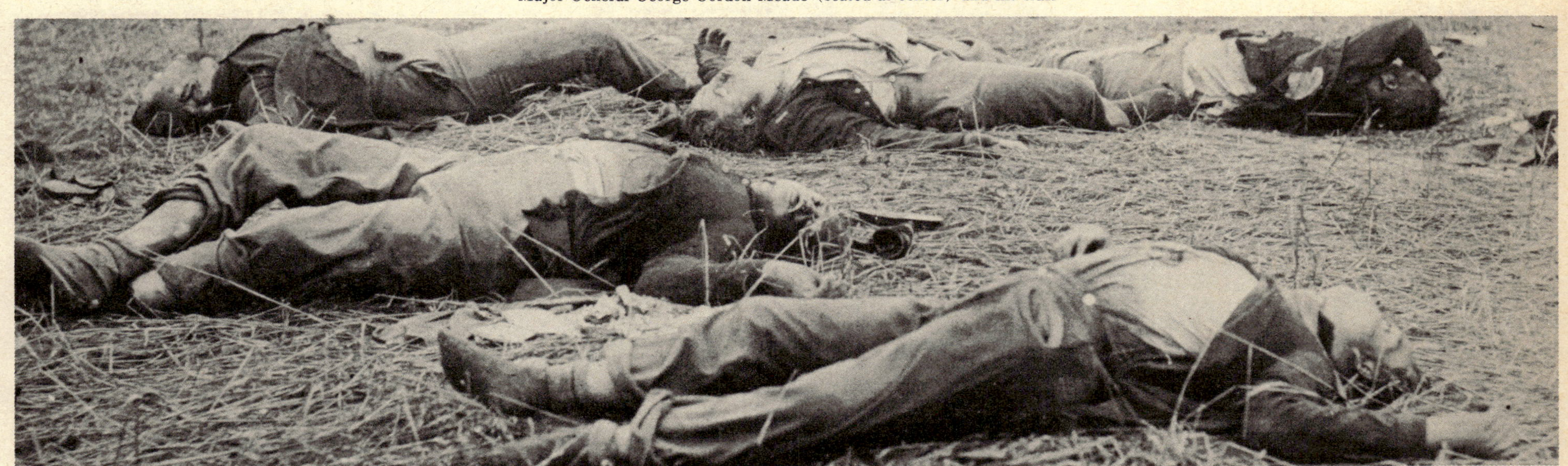
Victims of the Battle of Gettysburg

Battle of Gettysburg, July 1-3, 1861

The New-York Times.

VOL. XII—NO. 3676. NEW-YORK, MONDAY, JULY 6, 1863. PRICE THREE CENTS.

THE GREAT BATTLES.

Splendid Triumph of the Army of the Potomac.

ROUT OF LEE'S FORCES ON FRIDAY

The Most Terrible Struggle of the War.

TREMENDOUS ARTILLERY DUEL.

Repeated Charges of the Rebel Columns Upon Our Position.

Every Charge Repulsed with Great Slaughter.

The Death of Longstreet and Hill.

Our Cavalry Active on the Enemy's Flank.

THE REBEL RETREAT CUT OFF.

Chambersburgh in Our Possession.

Advance of the Militia under Gen. Smith to Important Positions.

The Rebel Pontoon Bridge at Williamsport Destroyed.

The Contents of the Captured Dispatches from Jeff. Davis to Lee.

A Peremptory Order for the Rebel Army to Return to Virginia.

OFFICIAL DISPATCHES FROM GEN. MEADE.

WASHINGTON, Saturday, July 4—10:10 A. M.

The following has just been received:

HEADQUARTERS ARMY OF POTOMAC, NEAR GETTYSBURGH, Friday, July 3—8½ P. M.

Major-Gen. Halleck, Genneral-in-Chief:

The enemy opened at 1 P. M., from about one hundred and fifty guns, concentrated upon my left centre, continuin without intermission for about three hours, at the expiration of which time, he assaulted my left centre twice, being, upon both occasions, handsomely repulsed, with severe loss to him, leaving in our hands nearly three thousand prisoners.

Among the prisoners is Brig.-Gen. ARMSTEAD and many Colonels and officers of lesser rank.

The enemy left many dead upon the field, and a large number of wounded in our hands.

The loss upon our side has been considerable. Maj.-Gen. HANCOCK and Brig.-Gen. GIBBON were wounded.

After the repelling of the assaults, indications leading to the belief that the enemy might be withdrawing, a reconnoissance was pushed forward from the left and the enemy found to be in force.

At the present hour all is quiet.

My cavalry have been engaged all day on both flanks of the enemy, harassing and vigorously attacking him with great success, notwithstanding they encountered superior numbers both of cavalry and infantry.

The army is in fine spirits.

GEORGE G. MEADE,
Maj.-Gen. Commanding.

WASHINGTON, Sunday, July 5—4 P. M.

The latest official dispatch received here, up to this hour, from Gen. MEADE, is dated at Headquarters Army of Potomac, 7 A. M., July 4, which merely states that the enemy had withdrawn from his position, occupied for attack, on Friday. The information in the possession of Gen. MEADE, at that hour, did not develop the character of the enemy's movement, whether it was a retreat or a manœuvre for other purposes.

Reliable information received here to-day asserts that Gen. LEE'S Headquarters were at Cashtown yesterday afternoon, and further represents that the rebels were fortifying at Newman's Cut, in the South Mountains, apparently to cover a retreat.

Later official dispatches are expected this evening.

SECOND DISPATCH.

HEADQUARTERS ARMY OF POTOMAC, July 4—Noon.

Maj.-Gen. Halleck:

The position of affairs is not materially changed since my last dispatch of 7 A. M.

We now hold Gettysburgh.

The enemy has abandoned large numbers of his killed and wounded on the field.

I shall probably be able to give you a return of our captures and losses before night, and a return of the enemy's killed and wounded in our hands.

GEORGE G. MEADE, Major-General.

THIRD DISPATCH.

HEADQUARTERS ARMY POTOMAC, July 4—10 P. M.

To Maj.-Gen. Halleck:

No change of affairs since my dispatch of noon.

GEO. G. MEADE, Major-General.

FOURTH DISPATCH.

WASHINGTON, Monday, July 6—12.30 A. M.

The following is the latest official dispatch:

HEADQUARTERS ARMY OF THE POTOMAC, Sunday, July 5—8:30 A. M.

MAJOR-GEN. HALLECK: The enemy retired under cover of the night and the heavy rain, in the direction of Fairfield and Cashtown.

Our cavalry are in pursuit.

I cannot give you the details of our captures in prisoners, colors and arms.

Upward of twenty battle-flags will be turned in from one corps.

My wounded and those of the enemy are in our hands. GEO. G. MEADE, Major-General.

THE PRESIDENT TO THE COUNTRY.

WASHINGTON, D. C., July 4—10:30 A. M.

The President announces to the country that news from the Army of the Potomac, up to 10 P. M. of the 3d, is such as to cover that army with the highest honor; to promise a great success to the cause of the Union, and to claim the condolence of all for the many gallant fallen; and that for this, he especially desires that on this day He, whose will, not ours, should ever be done, be everywhere remembered and reverenced with profoundest gratitude.

(Signed) A. LINCOLN.

THE GREAT BATTLE OF FRIDAY.

Our Special Telegrams from the Battle-Field.

NEAR GETTYSBURGH, Saturday, July 4.

Another great battle was fought yesterday afternoon, resulting in a magnificent success to the National arms.

At 2 o'clock P. M., LONGSTREET'S whole corps advanced from the rebel centre against our centre. The enemy's forces were hurled upon our position by columns in mass, and also in lines of battle. Our centre was held by Gen. HANCOCK, with the noble old Second army corps, aided by Gen. DOUBLEDAY'S division of the First corps.

The rebels first opened a terrific artillery bombardment to demoralize our men, and then moved their forces with great impetuosity upou our position. HANCOCK received the attack with great firmness, and after a furious battle, lasting until 5 o'clock, the enemy were driven from the field, LONGSTREET'S corps being almost annihilated.

The battle was a most magnificent spectacle. It was fought on an open plain, just south of Gettysburgh, with not a tree to interrupt the view. The courage of our men was perfectly sublime.

At 5 P. M. what was left of the enemy *retreated in utter confusion*, leaving dozens of flags, and Gen. HANCOCK estimated *at least five thousand killed and wounded on the field.*

The battle was fought by Gen. HANCOCK with splendid valor. He won imperishable honor, and Gen. MEADE thanked him in the name of the army and the country. He was wounded in the thigh, but remained on the field.

The number of prisoners taken is estimated at 3,000, including at least two Brigadier-Genera s—OLMSTEAD, of Georgia, and another—both wounded.

The conduct of our veterans was perfectly magnificent. More than twenty battle flags were taken by our troops. Nearly every regiment has one. The Nineteenth Massachusetts captured four. The repulse was so disastrous to the enemy, that LONGSTREET'S corps is perfectly used up. Gen. GIBBON was wounded in the shoulder. Gen. WEBB was wounded and remained on the field. Col. HAMMELL, of the Sixty-sixth New-York, was wounded in the arm.

At 7 o'clock last evening, Gen. MEADE ordered the Third corps, supported by the Sixth, to attack the enemy's right, which was done, and the battle lasted until dark, when a good deal of ground had been gained.

During the day EWELL'S corps kept up a desultory attack upon SLOCUM on the right, but was repulsed.

Our cavalry is to-day playing savagely upon the enemy's flank and rear. L. L. CROUNSE.

FROM ANOTHER CORRESPONDENT.

GETTYSBURGH, Friday, July 3.

The experience of all the tried and veteran officers of the Army of the Potomac tells of no such desperate conflict as has been in progress during this day. The cannonading of Chancellorsville, Malvern and Manassas were pastimes compared with this. At the headquarters, where I write, sixteen of the horses of Gen. MEADE'S staff officers were killed by shell. The house was completely riddled. The Chief of Staff, Gen. BUTTERFIELD, was knocked down by a fragment of case-shot. Col. DICKINSON, Assistant Adjutant-General, had the bone of his wrist pierced through by a piece of shell. Lieut. OLIVER, of Gen. BUTTERFIELD'S Staff, was struck in the head; and Capt. CARPENTER, of Gen. MEADE'S escort, was wounded in the eye.

While I write the ground about me is covered thick with rebel dead, mingled with our own. Thousands of prisoners have been sent to the rear, and yet the conflict still continues.

The losses on both sides are heavy. Among our wounded officers are HANCOCK, GIBBON and a great many others whose names I feel restrained from publishing without being assured that they are positively in the list of casualties.

It is near sunset. Our troops hold the field, with many rebel prisoners in their hands. The enemy has been magnificently repulsed for three days—repulsed on all sides—most magnificently to-day. Every effort made by him since Wednesday morning to penetrate MEADE'S lines has been foiled. The final results of the action, I hope to be able to give you at a later hour this evening.

S. WILKESON.

DISPATCH TO THE ASSOCIATED PRESS.

HEADQUARTERS ARMY OF THE POTOMAC, Friday, July 3—6 A. M.

The enemy's guns opened on our left wing at daylight, apparently to feel our position. They found us "at home," and soon suspended operations. They also endeavored to push forward their front on our right, but were driven back with loss.

9:40 *A. M.*—An hour ago, the enemy made a strong infantry attack on our right, and endeavored to break our line. The Twelfth corps, which formed our right, steadily drove them back for half an hour, when the enemy were reinforced, and a portion of the Sixth corps was sent to its support.

Failing in this, the enemy opened a heavy cannonade all along the line. The attack on the right is believed to have been a feint to cover a more formidable flank movement on the left. The cannonading is now heavy in that direction, and appears to be extending.

The Third Corps suffered greatly yesterday. The number of wounded is heavy, with a large number of officers. No estimate can be formed of the killed at this writing.

Heavy musketry has opened now on our right again and cannonading on our left is slackening. The enemy are fighting with the greatest desperation. Nothing can surpass the vigor and precision of our artillery.

Yesterday, the rebels took two of our guns, for want of horses and infantry support, but the division (HUMPHREY'S, I think,) rallied and recaptured them. We took one from the enemy.

Comparatively few prisoners have been taken on either side up to this hour.

Ten o'clock A. M.—The cannonading has slackened.

Rebel prisoners say when their infantry charged our left-wing batteries yesterday, the massacre was beyond parallel. Some of the guns were masked, and did not open until the enemy were within canister range.

IMPORTANT SEMI-OFFICIAL DETAILS.

HEADQUARTERS ARMY OF THE POTOMAC, July 3, 1863.

The decisive battle has been fought to-day, and the enemy have been repulsed with terr[illegible] loss.

At daylight LEE'S right wing batteries opened upon our left, and shortly after those of his centre followed. After half an hour's cannonading, doing but little damage to us, the fire slackened, and only occasional shots were exchanged.

Shortly afterward the enemy's left, composed entirely of infantry and sharpshooters, made an attack on our right wing. So sudden and impetuous was it accomplished that our skirmishers and front line were driven back from their intrenchments; but, by the aid of the batteries in the rear, and the indomitable bravery of the Twelfth corps, we regained the first position, capturing a considerable number of prisoners.

Several hours of ominous silence followed this repulse. At 1 o'clock the enemy fired two shots, apparently as signals for the grandest artillery fight ever witnessed on this continent. Before a moment had elapsed it is estimated that at least eighty guns opened upon us. Our batteries returned the compliment with interest. *The air seemed literally thick with iron*, and for more than an hour it seemed impossible that man or beast could live through it. Strange to say the enemy's accuracy of range, as exhibited on the two previous days, was wanting on this occasion. Most of their shells exploded far in the rear of our front, and generally missing our batteries.

Under cover of this *feu d'enfer*, LEE advanced his columns of infantry from the covers, and made several desperate attempts to carry the lines by assault; but each successive attempt was repulsed with terrible havoc to their ranks.

After an hour's incessant cannonading the fire grew less intense for a short time, but was again renewed for a little while, with great spirit. During this period, some of our batteries whose ammunition was expended and the men exhausted, ceased to fire, and on the approach of the reserve batteries, withdrew to the rear. The enemy only seeing the batteries withdrawing, and mistaking this for a retreat, made a massed infantry charge up the hill, and obtained a position in our lines, cutting to pieces and almost annihilating the small infantry supports; but before they had time to rejoice at their imaginary success, the fresh batteries poured in a deadly fire of canister and case-shot. The infantry reserves joined on either flank of the gap, charged them, and added [illegible] to their destruction. They were completely surprised; and *hundreds of them threw down their arms and asked for quarter.* Nearly the entire brigade of Gen. DICK GARNETT surrendered, and GARNETT himself, wounded, barely made his escape.

Longstreet was mortally wounded and captured. He is reported to have died in an hour afterward.

About 4:30 P. M. the artillery of the enemy slackened and had entirely ceased at 5, the last shots which they fired being far beyond their original position, and the infantry columns had withdrawn to their covers.

We took upward of three thousand prisoners. The enemy captured but few if any of our men.

The rebel prisoners report that *Gen. A. P. Hill was killed outright upon the field*, and that their officers suffered far greater casualties than in any previous engagement.

So terrific was the enemy's fire that the small house where Gen. MEADE and Staff were quartered, was perforated by several shots. Many of the Staff horses were killed around the house.

Gen. BUTTERFIELD was struck in the breast, and it is feared internally injured, by a piece of shell which exploded in the building. Lieut.-Col. JOSEPH DICKINSON, of the Staff, had his left arm perforated by a flying fragment of shell, and it seemed a miracle that no greater damage was done to life or limb.

Several of our general officers were wounded in the engagement. Gen. HANCOCK was wounded in the leg. Gens. GIBBON, WARREN and HUNT were wounded. In consequence of the excitement and difficulty in ascertaining their locations, the names of many prominent officers reported as killed or wounded cannot be ascertained to-night.

Too much credit cannot be given to our artillerists, who for hours stood to their guns under a broiling sun, and surrounded by the missiles of death, retiring only to give their positions to others, when their caissons and limbers were exhausted of ammunition. The infantry engaged also nobly did their duty, and the enemy to-day at their hands *has received the greatest disaster ever administered by the Union forces.*

All officers award the highest honors to Gen. MEADE for the able generalship he has displayed since he assumed command, and particularly for his coolness, decision and energy on this memorable 3d of July.

Last night, believing it to be his duty to the cause, and to learn how far he would be supported in the approaching conflict, he summoned his corps and division commanders for consultation.

DETAILS FROM OUR SPECIAL CORRESPONDENT.

HEADQUARTERS ARMY OF POTOMAC, Saturday Night, July 4.

Who can write the history of a battle whose eyes are immovably fastened upon a central figure of transcendingly absorbing interest—the dead body of an oldest born, crushed by a shell in a position where a battery should never have been sent, and abandoned to death in a building where surgeons dared not to stay?

The battle of Gettysburgh! I am told that it commenced on the 1st of July, a mile north of the town, between two weak brigades of infantry and some doomed artillery and the whole force of the rebel army. Among other costs of this error was the death of REYNOLDS. Its value was priceless, however, though priceless was the young and the old blood with which it was bought. The error put us on the defensive, and gave us the choice of position. From the moment that our artillery and infantry rolled back through the main street of Gettysburgh and rolled out of the town to the circle of eminences south of it. We were not to attack but to be attacked. The risks, the difficulties and the disadvantages of the coming battle were the enemy's. Our were the heights for artillery; ours the short, inside lines for manœuvreing and reinforcing; ours the cover of stonewalls, fences and the crests of hills. The ground upon which we were driven to accept battle was wonderfully favorable to us. A popular description of it would be to say that it was in form an elongated and somewhat sharpened horseshoe, with the toe to Gettysburgh and the heel to the south.

LEE'S plan of battle was simple. He massed his troops upon the east side of this shoe of position, and thundered on it obstinately to break it. The shelling of our batteries from the nearest overlooking hill, and the unflinching courage and complete discipline of the army of the Potomac repelled the attack. It was renewed at the point of of the shoe—renewed desperately at the southwest heel—renewed on the western side with an effort consecrated to success by EWELL'S earnest oaths, and on which the fate of the invasion of Pennsylvania was fully put at stake. Only a perfect infantry and an artillery educated in the midst of charges of hostile brigades could possibly have sustained this assault. HANCOCK'S corps did sustain it, and has covered itself with immortal honors by its constancy and courage. The total wreck of CUSHING'S battery—the list of its killed and wounded—the losses of officers, men and horses COWEN sustained—and the marvellous outspread upon the board of death of dead soldiers and dead animals—of dead soldiers in blue, and dead soldiers in gray—more marvellous to me than anything I have ever seen in war—are a ghastly and shocking testimony to the terrible fight of the Second corps that none will gainsay. That corps will ever have the distinction of breaking the pride and power of the rebel invasion.

For such details as I have the heart for. The battle commenced at daylight, on the side of the horse-shoe position, exactly opposite to that which EWELL had sworn to crush through. Musketry preceded the rising of the sun. A thick wood veiled this fight, but out of its leafy darkness arose the smoke and the surging and swelling of the fire, from intermittent to continuous, and crushing, told of the wise tactics of the rebels of attacking in force and changing their troops. Seemingly the attack of the day was to be made through that wood. The demonstration was protracted—it was absolutely preparative; but there was no artillery fire accompanying the musketry, and shrewd officers in our western front mentioned, with the gravity due to the fact, that the rebels had felled trees at intervals upon the edge of the wood they occupied in face of our position. These were breastworks for the protection of artillerymen.

Suddenly, and about 10 in the forenoon, the firing on the east side, and everywhere about our lines, ceased. A silence as of deep sleep fell upon the field of battle. Our army cooked, ate and slumbered. The rebel army moved 120 guns to the west, and massed there LONGSTREET'S corps and HILL'S corps, to hurl them upon the really weakest point of our entire position.

Eleven o'clock—twelve o'clock—one o'clock. In the shadow cast by the tiny farm house 16 by 20, which Gen. MEADE had made his Headquarters, lay wearied Staff officers and tired reporters. There was not wanting to the peacefulness of the scene the singing of a bird, which had a nest in a peach tree within the tiny yard of the whitewashed cottage. In the midst of its warbling, a shell screamed over the house, instantly followed by another, and another, and in a moment the air was full of the most complete artillery prelude to an infantry battle that was ever exhibited. Every size and form of shell known to British and to American gunnery shrieked, whirled, moaned, whistled and wrathfully fluttered over our ground. As many as six in a second, constantly two in a second, bursting and screaming over and around the headquarters, made a very hell of fire that amazed the oldest officers. They burst in the yard—burst next to the fence on both sides, garnished as usual with the hitched horses of aids and orderlies. The fastened animals reared and plunged with terror. Then one fell, then another—sixteen laid dead and mangled before the fire ceased, still fastened by their halters, which gave the expression of being wickedly tied up to die painfully. These brute victims of a cruel war touched all hearts. Through the midst of the storm of screaming and exploding shells, an ambulance, driven by its frenzied conductor at full speed, presented to all of us the marvelous spectacle of a horse going rapidly on three legs. A hinder one had been shot off at the hock. A shell tore up the little step of the Headquarters Cottage, and ripped bags of oats as with a knife. Another soon carried off one of its two pillars. Soon a spherical case burst opposite the open door—another ripped through the low garret. The remaining pillar went almost immediately to the howl of a fixed shot that WHITWORTH must have made. During this fire the houses at twenty and thirty feet distant, were receiving their death, and soldiers in Federal blue were torn to pieces in the road and died with the peculiar yells that blend the extorted cry of pain with horror and despair. Not an orderly—not an ambulance—not a stragger was to be seen upon the plain swept by this tempest of orchestral death thirty minutes after it commenced. Were not one hundred and twenty pieces of artillery, trying to cut from the field every battery we had in postion to resist their purposed infantry attack, and to sweep away the slight defences behind which our Infantry were waiting? Forty minutes—fifty minutes—counted on watches that ran! Oh so languidly. Shells through the two lower rooms. A shell into the chimney that daringly did not explode. Shells in the yard. The air thicker and fuller and more deafening with the howling and whirring of these infernal missles. The chief of staff struck—SETH WILLIAMS—loved and respected through the army, separated from instant death by two inches of space vertically measdred. An Aide bored with a fragment of iron through the bone of the arm. Another, cut with an exploded piece. And the time measured on the sluggish watches was one hour and forty minutes.

Then there was a lull, and we knew that the rebel infantry was charging. And splendidly they did this work—the highest and severest test of the stuff that soldiers are made of. HILL'S division, in line of battle, came first on the double-quick. Their muskets at the "right-shoulder-shift." LONGSTREET'S came as the support, at the usual distance, with war cries and a savage insolence as yet untutored by defeat. They rushed in perfect order across the open field up to the very muzzles of the guns, which tore lanes through them as they came. But they met men who were their equals in spirit, and their superiors in tenacity. There never was better fighting since Thermopylæ than was done yesterday by our infantry and artillery. The rebels were over our defences. They had cleaned cannoniers and horses from one of the guns, and were whirling it around to use upon us. The bayonet drove them back. But so hard pressed was this brave infantry that at one time, from the exhaustion of their ammunition, every battery upon the principal crest of attack was silent, except CROWEN'S. His service of grape and cannister was awful. It enabled our line, outnumbered two to one, first to beat back LONGSTREET, and then to charge upon him, and take a great number of his men and himself prisoners. Strange sight! So terrible was our musketry and artillery fire, that when ARMSTEAD'S brigade was checked in its charge, and stood reeling, all of its men dropped their muskets and crawled on their hands and knees underneath the stream of shot till close to our troops, where they made signs of surrendering. They passed through our ranks scarcely noticed, and slowly went down the slope to the road in the rear.

Before they got there the grand charge of EWELL, solemnly sworn to and carefully prepared, had failed.

The rebels had retreated to their lines, and opened anew the storm of shell and shot from their 120 guns. Those who remained at the riddled headquarters will never the crouching, and dodging, and running, of the Butternut-colored captives when they got under this, their friends, fire. It was appalling to as good soldiers even as they were.

What remains to say of the fight? It staggled surlily on the middle of the horse shoe on the west, grew big and angry on the heel at the southwest, lasted there till 8 o'clock in the evening, when the fighting Sixth corps went joyously by as a reinforcement through the wood, bright with coffee pots on the fire.

I leave details to my excellent friend and associate Mr. HENRY. My pen is heavy. Oh, you dead, who at Gettysburgh have baptised with your blood the second birth of Freedom in America, how you are to be envied! I rise from a grave whose wet clay I have passionately kissed, and I look up and see Christ spanning this battle-field with his feet and reaching fraternal and lovingly up to heaven. His right hand opens the gates of Paradise—with his left he beckons to these mutilated, bloody, swollen forms to ascend.

INCIDENTS OF THE BATTLE.

Capt. CUSHING, Company A, Fourth Regular artillery, was killed, and his battery suffered severely. The gallantry of this officer is beyond praise. Severely wounded early in the afternoon, he refused to leave his post beside his guns, but continued to pour grape and canister into the advancing columns of the rebels until they had reached the very muzzles of his pieces, and sure of their capture, were attempting to turn them upon our forces, when they were driven off by our infantry. At this moment Capt. CUSHING received his death wound, and fell lifeless to the earth. Heaps of corpses and wounded in front of his battery this morning, told a terrible tale of the effectiveness of its fire.

None of the company were taken prisoners by the rebels. After the battle but one gun of this battery remained uninjured—the rest having been dismounted or destroyed by the terrible fire of the enemy, which for the time was concentrated upon the batteries on this part of the field. In front of this position fell dead the rebel Gen. DICK GARNETT, who was courageously leading his men in this charge upon our batteries on Crow Hill. The rebel Gen. ARMSTEAD was also wounded here while advancing at the head of his brigade.

About fifty yards in front of our batteries was a stone wall, running from our centre in a southwesterly direction, behind which laid several of our regiments, picking off the enemy as they advanced up the slope of the hill. Notwithstanding the terrible fire poured into their ranks from our guns, so impetuous was the charge of the rebels that they drove our men from their position, and were advancing upon our batteries, several of which they captured, but the capture was only temporary. Gen. GIBBON'S division, composed of Gens. WEBB'S, HARRELL'S and HALL'S brigades, at the point of the bayonet, drove them back over the stone wall into the plain below.

Gen. GIBBON'S division captured fourteen stand of colors and a large number of prisoners. Twenty-eight stands of colors in all were captured by the Second corps.

Gen. ARMISTEAD, when taken prisoner, asked immediately for Gen. MEADE, who was his classmate at West Point.

Col. WARD, of the Fifteenth Massachusetts, was killed.

Corp. HAYDEN, of the First Minnesota, was captured,—escaped, seized a musket and seized a rare opportunity, and actually made ten rebels surrender. While marching them to Gen. GIBBON'S quarters, a rebel behind a tree on the way drew a bead on him with his rifle. HAYDEN saw him in time to bring his piece to a level, and cry out, "Surrender." The fellow actually threw down his gun and joined the cavalcade, and HAYDEN came in with eleven captives.

Wounded prisoners taken in Gettysburgh this morning report that Gen. BRADLEY L. JOHNSON, of Maryland, was killed in Thursday's attack on our right. He was struck by a shell while charging our lines at the head of his division. Gen. HOOD is also reported to have had his leg shot off, and from the effects of which he has since died.

Rebel officers with whom I have conversed frankly admit that the rebuff of the last two days has been most disastrous to their cause, which depended, they say, upon the success of LEE'S attempt to transfer the seat of war from Virginia to the Northern Border States. A wounded rebel Colonel told me that, in the first and second days' fight, the rebel losses were between ten and eleven thousand. Yesterday they were greater still. In one part of the field, in a space not more than twenty [illegible] cumference, in front of Gen. GIBBON'S [illegible] I counted seven dead rebels, three of [illegible] piled on top of each other. [illegible] spot not more than fifteen feet [illegible] "graybacks," stretched in death. [illegible] adventurous spirits, who in the face of the [illegible] stream of canister, shell and musketry, [illegible] fence wall in their attempt upon our batteries. Very large numbers of wounded were also strewn around, not to mention more who had crawled away or been taken away. The field in front of the stonewall was literally covered with dead and wounded, a large proportion of whom were rebels. Where our musketry and artillery took effect they lay in swaths, as if mown down by a scythe. This field presented a horrible sight—such as has never yet been witnessed during the war. Not less than one thousand dead and wounded laid in a *space of less than four acres* in extent, and that, too, after numbers had crawled away to places of shelter.

The enemy's infantry, saving a small force of sharpshooters, was wholly out of sight at daylight on Saturday morning. There was talk on Friday night, after the battle, of organizing a column of pursuit.

Before the fighting was over—before sunset, considerably—the Signal Officers reported that an immense train of army wagons was going out of Gettysburgh northwest, on the road to Cashtown. Oh! that they could have run against the stonewall of the Harrisburgh army.

PARTIAL LIST OF KILLED AND WOUNDED.

Lieut. Dayton L. Card, commanding Co. E, 108th New York, was killed instantly by a shell. His body presented a ghastly sight. He was struck in the middle of the breast by a missile which exploded and tore him literally in two. Half of his face was also torn away by a fragment of shell.

Charles P. Leclear, Co. E, 108th N. Y.—killed.
J. Wickham, Co. E. 108th N. Y.—wounded.
Sergeant A. B [illegible], do. do.,—wounded.
Sergt. M. C. Bryant, Co. E. 108th N. Y.—wounded.
J. D. Ansirk, Co. E. 108th New-York—wounded.

Cowan's New-York Battery—Killed.

Privates James Gray, Otis C. Billings, Jacob Y. McIlroy, Edmund P[illegible].

Wounded.

Lieut. Wm. P. Wright—right breast, probably mortally.

[*Continued on Eighth Page.*]

The New-York Times.

VOL. XII—NO. 3676. NEW-YORK, MONDAY, JULY 6, 1863. PRICE THREE CENTS.

Editorial

The Triumph of the Army of the Potomac.

The Army of the Potomac, under its new leader, has won its greatest victory. The tremendous actions of the first three days of the month of July at Gettysburgh have been followed by the complete discomfiture of the entire rebel army, which so audaciously and exultingly crossed the Potomac, and planted itself on Pennsylvania soil less than a fortnight ago. Entertaining not a doubt of triumph, it advanced with flying banners, defiant shouts, and steady tread. From the Rappahannock to the Blue Ridge, from the mountains to the Potomac, from the Potomac to the Susquehanna, they swept unmolested over a distance of two hundred miles; and at the beginning of last week, were just preparing to consummate their triumphant campaign. They contemned the Army of the Potomac, sneered at its late leader, and boasted that they could kick him and his army around the continent. Their commander had already led them in five great campaigns, two of them in their inception offensive, two defensive, and one what Jomini styles offensive-defensive; and all of them they regarded as victorious. There were but three things more needed to insure their final success, and these were—to route the Army of the Potomac, capture Washington, and hold their army on our soil until they could dictate terms of peace and enforce the recognition of the Southern Confederacy. By the seizure of Philadelphia, and Baltimore, they could also thoroughly humiliate us, and after the fashion they established at York, could fill the coffers of the Confederacy, and gratify their army with plunder. Their task was simple and their assurance unbounded.

So at least it appeared last Monday. So it appeared on the first day of the month of July.

But their lately exultant and defiant army of invasion—where is it, and what is it now?

Defeated in the very opening of the campaign. Defeated in three great battles in which their whole force of infantry, cavalry and artillery was engaged. Defeated by the Army of the Potomac. Defeated by Gen. Meade, who then fought his first battle at the head of the army. Defeated with tremendous loss in killed and wounded, in prisoners and in artillery; and defeated when defeat was destruction. Defeated after struggling for three days with a fury more than mortal and an energy madder than that of despair.

Thus it stood on Friday night, and thus upon our army rose the Fourth of July, ghastly but glorious—gloomy as death for the rebellion, but bright with hope for the country.

We are not yet informed what has become of Lee and the remnant of his army since Friday night. We know that they have fled somewhere among the mountains, and are probably trying to make their way to the Potomac, over which they would now be glad to bear drooping the banners which but late they bore to this side proudly flaunting. We know that our army holds Gettysburgh, Chambersburgh—that an expedition has been sent out from Hagerstown, which has destroyed the pontoon bridge over the Potomac at Williamsport, and that the river has risen—perhaps so high as to make a sudden and successful fording of it impossible. We can only hope that our reserve force, the Pennsylvania militia and the troops of Gen. Heintzelman will consummate the work so gloriously executed by Gen. Meade, and see that this insolent army of invasion never gets back to Richmond or offers us any more trouble.

Through the brief campaign Gen. Meade's genius has shone resplendent. Taking the army at the most inauspicious moment, and under the most inauspicious circumstances, he has, within four days of that on which he assumed command, achieved these results. It is the work of eminent military genius—of genius such as has not heretofore been displayed in this war. His adversary was a good soldier, who had the prestige of past success—though we have never seen any reason to class him as a great military chief, as some have been so hasty to do. But his strategy on this occasion was bold, and was only defeated by the more masterly and heroic combinations of Gen. Meade. The choice of the President and the officers of the army has been amply confirmed and approved by the result of this great battle. He also had able cooperation in his corps, and division and brigade commanders, and every one of them achieved undying honor, and proved himself worthy of his position.

The Army of the Potomac too, will now, more than ever, receive the admiration of the country. Its struggles for two years have been unparalleled, and often unsuccessful. But it has never lost its faith nor its valor, nor its inflexibility of purpose. It has been willing ever to serve and to struggle, to fight always, everywhere, and under all circumstances, to the death. To all its other and perhaps greater claims to admiration, it now adds that of the most honorable and complete success. Its heroic struggle during the three first days of July will forever adorn the annals of war, and of the American Republic.

Battle of Gettysburg

The New-York Times.

VOL. XII—NO. 3679. NEW-YORK, THURSDAY, JULY 9, 1863. PRICE THREE CENTS.

GEN. LEE'S RETREAT.

The Main Force of the Rebels Between Hagerstown and Williamsport.

Their Army Completely Enveloped by Our Cavalry.

The Enemy Forming a Line from Funkstown to Falling Waters.

A Portion of Early's Command Reported Cut Off in the Mountains.

Havoc Among the Rebel Wagon Trains.

Ewell's Train Nearly Destroyed by Kilpatrick.

THOUSANDS OF PRISONERS CAPTURED.

Ten Feet of Water in the Potomac at Williamsport.

ANOTHER GREAT BATTLE PROBABLE.

SPECIAL DISPATCHES FROM FREDERICK.

FREDERICK, Md., Tuesday, July 7—9 P. M.

The latest intelligence from the front places LEE's headquarters at Hagerstown to-day. The prospect of another conflict ere crossing the river is not promising. LEE secured the short line of retreat by seizing the Waynesboro Gap.

The weather is very wet, and the roads heavy, yet the troops are doing well.

The total number of prisoners captured, reported at the Provost-Marshal General's Office up to last night, including the wounded, is in the vicinity of eleven thousand. There is no truth in the stories of great amounts of artillery captured by us. It is possible that we took one battery, but even this is not certain. The reason is apparent enough,—we fought the battle entirely on the defensive, and did not pursue the enemy beyond the contested ground.

About two-thirds of the burial parties sent out to bury the rebel dead have made returns. The number reported by them is thus far twenty-six hundred and eighty. The total cannot fall under three thousand five hundred, not including those of Wednesday's fight, which the enemy himself buried.

Our losses, as to-day reported semi-officially, foot up seventeen thousand, killed, wounded and missing. The Third corps loses forty-four hundred; the Fifth corps, two thousand three hundred and forty-nine; the Twelfth corps, seven hundred and fifty; the Second corps, four thousand eight hundred. The balance I have not yet obtained.

FREDERICK, Tuesday, July 7—10 P. M.

Intelligence from the front, just received, informs us that LEE's forces are crossing the Potomac at Williamsport in two flat boats, leaving their wagons behind. This is reliable.

Our cavalry have done great service within the past week. Yesterday KILPATRICK sent in fifteen hundred prisoners, whom he had captured with the trains on Sunday evening. On that day he destroyed four hundred wagons; to-day he destroyed sixty more, and sent in three hundred horses and mules. The cavalry under BUFORD and KILPATRICK had a severe fight with the enemy's infantry yesterday, while getting out of their lines. Capt. CLARK, of the Eighteenth Illinois, was killed. Maj. WADILL was severely wounded.

In Gen. GREGG's fight last Thursday, both WADE, HAMPTON and JENKINS were wounded. The former had two sabre cuts on his head.

KILPATRICK says the rebel cavalry Gen. ROBERTSON is among the prisoners to-day, with the insignia of his rank torn off. Our cavalry have done brilliant service, and are in the highest spirits. Their losses are heavy.

FREDERICK, Tuesday, July 7—11½ P. M.

STILL LATER.—The following dispatch has just been received from Mr. E. A. PAUL, your gallant cavalry correspondent with Gen. KILPATRICK.

SOUTH MOUNTAIN, Md., Sunday, July 5, 1863.

Gen. KILPATRICK's command left its position near Gettysburgh on Saturday, July 4, and started across the Mountain by way of Monterey Gap, passing through Emmittsburgh, Fountaindale, to Monterey Gap, Waterloo, Redgeville and Smithburgh, Md., where the command made a temporary halt. The train of Gen. EWELL's corps was struck near its centre where the pike crosses the Monterey road on the westerly slope of the Mountain. Before arriving at this place the command had captured four miles of wagon trains, between 1,500 and 2,000 prisoners, cavalry and infantry, about 200 officers, and 2,000 horses and mules—in fact, the entire train of EWELL's command, which was strongly guarded by both cavalry and infantry. Among the prisoners are a large number of Gen. EARLY's division.

Having written so much, I started with a scout and Capt. ESTES to reach Gen. PLEASANTON's headquarters, and we were chased four miles by rebel cavalry. I send this by a scout, MCCULLOUGH. We are surrounded, and expect a fight every moment. *We shall win.*

E. A. PAUL.

FREDERICK, Md., Wednesday, July 8.

It is again necessary to caution the public against estimating the results of the late battle too highly. The number of prisoners captured, including the wounded, is now about 12,000, but we have taken no cannon.

The rain is still falling heavily, and while it may fill the Potomac, yet it will retard our own movements. The roads are very heavy. Our columns are pushing ahead, however.

A portion of LEE's force is known to be across, but we shall be up with the balance in time to get some more prisoners, at least.

FREDERICK, Md., Wednesday, July 8—12 M.

Official information, just received from the front, places LEE's main force on the rapid passage from Hagerstown to Williamsport. Yesterday our cavalry completely enveloped the enemy, and harassed him on front, flanks and rear.

LEE has now thrown out one corps of infantry toward Boonsboro, forming a line from Funkstown on their left to Falling Waters on their right. This commands the Hagerstown and Sharpsburgh, and Boonsboro and Williamsport turnpikes. Behind this road the enemy are pushing back as rapidly as possible. It was in forcing our cavalry back to form this line that a severe fight occurred yesterday, in which we met with considerable loss in the unequal contest with their infantry.

A portion of Gen. EARLY's command is reported cut off in the mountains.

There is ten feet of water in the Potomac at Williamsport.

L. L. CROUNSE.

SPECIAL DISPATCH FROM WASHINGTON.

WASHINGTON, Wednesday, July 8—11 P. M.

The impression to-night is that the rebels, baffled in their endeavors to recross the Potomac, will intrench themselves at and about Antietam, and there await battle, with every advantage of position and shelter.

A portion of their infantry are actually across the river, but the passage was made hesitatingly, and seemingly with a fear to put on the other side any force that might be needed on this.

It is almost certain that LEE has already thrown up works that stretch from Williamsport to Antietam.

FROM ANOTHER CORRESPONDENT.

WASHINGTON, Wednesday, July 8.

Messages for the Associated Press, received from Frederick, Md., to-night, say:

"Information which can be relied upon comes from the front this morning, of the following purport: The rise in the Potomac has checked the passage of the rebel army. A small portion of LEE's transportation has been crossed on rafts at Williamsport and Shepardstown, and his stock swam over. His ambulance trains, with wounded, have also crossed, but his supply trains, artillery, infantry and cavalry are reported to be nearly all on this side. His first line of battle has been formed on the Antietam Fields." Should this prove true, and it is certain that he cannot receive reinforcements, he will be compelled to trust the fate of his army to the arbitrament of a bloody field. Our forces are gradually concentrating in that direction. The hopes and prospects of annihilating the entire army of Virginia are bright. The best possible spirits animate the officers and men. At the last advices, LEE was concentrating his forces by every available route. Fearing an attack, he yesterday morning planted his batteries on every road by which we were likely to approach.

BUFORD and KILPATRICK, with the cavalry division, made a demonstration in the direction of Williamsport, but were unable to penetrate LEE's lines. Many citizens of Hagerstown, Funktown, Williamsport and Clear Spring, have left their homes, believing a battle imminent. Some of them have arrived in Frederick, and think that LEE only placed his guns in position to keep us in check while his fordes were crossing.

The reports as to the existence of rebel bridges at Williamsport are contradictory, but the general impression at Frederick is that none have been built. A scout, who was there on Tuesday, says preparations were in progress to build one. This may have been frustrated by the sudden and heavy rise in the Potomac.

Gen. MEADE and Staff have arrived at Headquarters, having ridden thirty-five miles from Gettysburgh. Several corps are understood to be nearer the point desired. A considerable force has probably reached the vicinity of Williamsport to-night. In the meantime our cavalry are on the enemy's left flank and rear, and make frequent attacks. Our scouts are frequently heard from, and their reports add confirmation of LEE's endeavors to recross the Potomac.

NEWS RECEIVED IN HARRISBURGH.

HARRISBURGH, Penn., Wednesday, July 8.

News received here to-day by telegraph, by way of Loudon and Bedford, shows that the main body of Gen. LEE's army is between South Mountain and Hagerstown.

Gen. LEE will probably select a place between Hagerstown and the Potomac to give Gen. MEADE battle, as it is considered utterly impossible for him to reach Virginia.

Gen. IMBODEN is at Williamsport with from 7,000 to 10,000 troops, protecting the rebel supply trains.

Gen. LEE's wagon train is at that point, to the number of 4,000 to 5,000, making their way into Virginia as fast as their limited means will admit.

Gen. LEE evidently sees that there is no escape for his army, and is preparing himself to give Gen. MEADE another battle, which will probably take place on Friday or Saturday.

The rain poured down in torrents last night, and has continued to do so until 12 o'clock to-day.

The present flood would destroy any pontoon bridge on the Potomac, even if the rebels had one, and it is positively known they have nothing of the kind.

The authorities are throwing troops up the valley as fast as possible.

Gen. MEADE's army and the troops under Gen. COUCH, are moving as rapidly as the roads will admit.

NEWS RECEIVED IN BALTIMORE.

BALTIMORE, Wednesday, July 8.

The *American's* special Frederick letter, dated this morning, says:

"It is no longer a question whether the Potomac is fordable, but whether any bridge the rebels may have would stand before such a flood.

It speaks of active army operations. Our cavalry are continually picking up prisoners and send them in by the hundred; also capturing or burning rebel trains. The rebels are abandoning their wounded, whom they placed in wagons taken from farms along the road. If LEE is detained at the river *his case will be most desperate if not hopeless.*"

BALTIMORE, Wednesday, July 8—10 P. M.

The *American's* special, dated Frederick, Wednesday noon, July 8, says:

"The position of the rebels and their condition have been definitely ascertained. Their infantry line is drawn across from Funkstown, Maryland, to Falling Waters, and behind this line they are using almost superhuman exertions to get their trains, such as they have saved, and their artillery and ammunition across the river. The best military authority here doubts—I might almost say is convinced—that they have no pontoon train beside that destroyed at Falling Waters; and that with such canal-boats as they had not previously burned, and with timber felled in the vicinity of and at Martinsburgh, they are endeavoring to supply the deficiencies of their Engineer corps. It is known that two days ago they had troops felling timber. They also attempted to cross some wagons on flat boats, but the impetuous current of the river rendered the attempt futile. They are now crossing their horses on boats and leaving their wagons on this side, probably intending to take them to pieces, and thus transport them on the canal-boats.

I have heard the opinion expressed in a very high military quarter that the rebels will probably secure the most defensible line in front of Williamsport, entrench themselves, and endeavor to hold our army at bay, while they secure the means of crossing. The position of the rebels is much more desperate than I had allowed myself to think heretofore. Of course they may get away; but it looks much less probable now than it did 24 hours ago.

The cavalry of Gen. PLEASANTON have been operating with magnificent success during the last three days. It is a positive fact that while the rebels were retreating we had cavalry in their front and rear, and on both flanks. Its presence and bold dashes greatly aided in increasing the demoralization of the rebels, and their discipline has been greatly relaxed.

LEE's Headquarters are definitely ascertained to be at Hagerstown to-day, and his troops are mainly on the road between there and Williamsport, which is only seven miles distant.

Gen. EARLY's rebel command is to-day reported to be cut off in the mountains, near Greencastle, by our cavalry. This is, of course, at present only a rumor; but it is credited to some extent, in view of the knowledge of the purposes of Gen. PLEASANTON's present movements.

It is the opinion at headquarters, that our cavalry have taken not less than 6,000 prisoners, including wounded rebels who had been picked up everywhere along the road, and in farm houses, where they had been abandoned by their friends. Among the captured is Brig.-Gen ROBINSON. He had torn off the insignia of his rank, and was dressed in citizen's clothing. Brig.-Gen. TRIMBLE, of the 19th of April and Philadelphia Railroad fame, is also a prisoner. He was found in the farm house of Mr. DAVID WISTER, near Gettysburgh, with his left foot blown off by a shell.

The damage done the rebel trains by the dashes of our cavalry is almost incredible. Everywhere they were captured, cut off and burned. Gen. KILPATRICK dashed into the middle of Gen. EWELL's train, and burnt between 200 and 300 wagons, and run off the horses. To-day he captured 60 more wagons, and 300 horses and mules. Our cavalry (I think KILPATRICK's division) had a fight yesterday at Hagerstown with a rebel infantry division. Their position was at one time dangerous, but they got out finally without serious loss.

Our army is moving steadily. Of its direction and disposition I shall say little, though the former may be readily guessed at from what is said of the position of the enemy. If LEE remains this side of the river, there is a probability of another battle within the next forty-eight hours.

As I close the heavy rain-storm is over, the sun breaking through the clouds. Forward is the word along the whole line.

GEN. JONES AND 1,000 PRISONERS.

BALTIMORE, Wednesday, July 8.

Nearly one thousand rebels, captured by Gen. KILPATRICK, arrived here this morning, including Brig.-Gen. JONES, a cavalry officer, and 51 commissioned officers.

THE REPORTED FIGHT AT WILLIAMSPORT.

WASHINGTON, Wednesday, July 8.

No information has been received from Williamsport to 2 o'clock to-day. It is not believed there was a fight there yesterday, although it is probable Gen. SEDGWICK has done the enemy's rear much damage.

THE FRESHET IN THE POTOMAC.

PHILADELPHIA, Wednesday, July 8.

There is a heavy rain-storm here. The constant rain which has been falling for the last three days west of Harrisburgh insures a lasting freshet in the Potomac River for a week at least.

THE SECOND VERMONT BRIGADE.

Of the Second Vermont brigade, commanded by Gen. GEORGE J. STANNARD, the Thirteenth, Fourteenth and Sixteenth regiments were engaged in the battles of Thursday and Friday. They fought like old veterans, captured a battery and three stands of colors from the enemy. Their loss in killed and wounded is reported at 300. Gen. STANNARD was wounded in the leg while leading his command.

CONGRATULATORY ORDER FROM GEN. DOUBLEDAY.

HEADQUARTERS THIRD DIVISION, FIRST CORPS, July 6, 1863.

The Major-General commanding the division desires to return his thanks to the Vermont brigade, the One Hundred and Fifty-first Pennsylvania Volunteers and the Twentieth New-York State militia for their gallant conduct in resisting in the front line the main attack of the enemy upon this position, after sustaining a terrific fire from seventy-five to one hundred pieces of artillery. He congratulates them upon contributing so essentially to the glorious and—it is to be hoped—final victory of yesterday.

By command of Maj.-Gen. DOUBLEDAY.
EDWARD C. BAIRD, Captain and A. A. G.

OUR SPECIAL ARMY CORRESPONDENCE.

Further Details of the Battle of Gettysburgh—Characteristics of the People of the Town—Interesting Incidents, &c.

GETTYSBURGH, Tuesday, July 7, 1863.

The history of the great battle cannot now be either fully or truthfully written. The ignominous retreat of the enemy, and the pursuit of our own forces, renders the gathering of facts and lists of casualties very difficult. A thousand and one incidents remain untold, and they are all of the most interesting character. I have a dozen themes, all pressing for mention in this letter, and scarcely time for doing justice to one of them.

One of the most important is the extent of our losses. There are all sorts of wild estimates, some of them too, I am sorry to say, by gentlemen of the medical profession, who ought to know better. I have carefully culled all the reports yet in, and though the fighting *was* the severest of the war, yet I do not see how the actual casualties can exceed seventeen thousand, and probably will not go above fifteen thousand. Several thousand men are counted among the missing, but they are not prisoners—they are on a grand straggle, and the country from Frederick to Westminster, to Hanover, to Gettysburgh, and back again to Frederick, swarms with loose men away from their commands—luxuriating among the farm-houses as long as their money lasts, and safe from the gobble of provost-guards, of which, by the way, nobody has seen any lately.

The country must not over-estimate the results of the victorious contests of last week. True, people were famishing for a success at the hands of the Army of the Potomac, and having got it, they applaud to the skies. It is already better than Antietam, and it may be a great deal better, but let not false reports be born only to be extinguished in bitter disappointment.

And to our captures. Whoever is so sensational as to pen the deliberate falsehoods with reference to the number of prisoners and guns captured, should at once be compelled to wear a straight-jacket. Either thing could be easily verified—the first by going to the Provost-Marshal-General, and the second by going to the chief ordnance officer. I applied at the former's office last evening, and learned that the number of prisoners, including rebels wounded, thus far reported, was nearly eleven thousand. I know now that we captured no artillery whatever, and the enemy none from us.

But there is one thing the country cannot have too much of—sympathy for the fallen—or cannot give too much—aid for the wounded, and unstinted praise for the valorous ones, whose steady and unflinching courage have turned the tide of successive disaster into a sweeping and surging victory—let a nation be truly thankful.

And *apropos* to this, let me make it a matter of undeniable history that the conduct of the majority of the male citizens of Gettysburgh, and the surrounding County of Adams, is such as to stamp them with dishonor and craven-hearted meanness. I do not speak hastily. I but write the unanimous sentiments of the whole army—an army which now feels that the doors from which they drove a host of robbers, thieves and cut-throats, were not worthy of being defended. The actions of the people of Gettysburgh are so sordidly mean and unpatriotic, as to engender the belief that they were indifferent as to which party was whipped. I will give a few instances.

In the first place the male citizens mostly ran away, and left the women and children to the mercy of their enemies. On their return, instead of lending a helping hand to our wounded, and opening their houses to our famished officers and soldiers, they have only manifested indecent haste to present their bills to the military authorities for payment of losses inflicted by both armies. One man yesterday presented a Captain with a bill for *eighteen rails* which his men had burned in cooking their coffee! On the streets the burden of their talk is their losses—and speculations as to whether the Government can be compelled to pay for this or that. Almost entirely they are uncourteous—but this is plainly from lack of intelligence and refinement. Their charges, too, were exorbitant—hotels, $2 50 per day; milk, 10 and 15 cents per quart; bread, $1 and even $1 50 per loaf; *twenty cents for a bandage for a wounded soldier!* And these are only a few specimens of the sordid meanness and unpatriotic spirit manifested by these people, from whose doors our noble army had driven a hated enemy. I wish it to be understood that the facts I have stated can be fully substantiated by many officers high in rank, as well as by what I personally saw and experienced. This is Adams County—a neighbor to Copperhead York, which is still nearer to the stupid and stingy Berks.

Of course there were some bright exceptions to this conduct, and one or two that came to my notice I desire to allude to here, for they richly deserve it, having interspersed a bright oasis in this desert of shameless indifference and discourtesy—a shalessness which refused Miss DIX and her lady nurses board, because they "didn't want to be troubled with boarders."

In honorable contrast to this sordidness was the conduct of Prof. STOEVER and his amiable wife. As many as twelve wounded Union soldiers at once lay upon his dining-room floor, receiving from himself and Mrs. STOEVER constant care. His spacious yard was for days a free ordinary, where our men ate their fill, without money and without price not only, but with that hearty and cheerful welcome which so reanimates the weary. In his cellar he concealed three Union officers for three days while the town was in possession of the rebels—anxiously determined to save them from arrest and the Libby Prison. His wife fed them stealthily during that time. This generous man encountered Mr. WILKESON while searching for his son's body, and overcame him wholly with his tender outpouring of sympathy and offers of service. He subsequently sought him out and compelled him to come to his home and take food. The next day, as Mr. WILKESON was passing the Professor's door to an undertaker's, he placed his little son on the watch for him, and as Mr. W. returned he went out and tenderly forced him in, and showed him a room prepared for his use so long as he should stay in Gettysburgh, and then insisted upon his sitting down to a tea table generously and elegantly spread for him and five other strangers.

Squire SAMUEL DONBORROW, living near Two Taverns, five miles east of Gettysburgh, for days fed scores of men and officers, including Gen. MEREDITH wounded; kept his wife and servants cooking constantly, and provided large amounts of food for the wounded, and for all this he refused compensation. He has a noble son in the army, who he would have thus done by. He came home to see his father, and that father blessed him as they parted, and said, "My son, I wish to save your life if I can; don't expose yourself to needless danger, but reflect credit upon your family—*do your duty.*" And that son, now two years a soldier in the Reserves, does his duty.

In Maryland, I am happy to say, there were few cases of extortion. The contrast between the two States was marked. Articles of food were generally freely provided and sold at a very moderate price. The towns of Middlebury, Taneytown, Liberty, Union Bridge and others, will long be remembered by our soldiers.

A few more incidents of the battle may be interesting here.

JOHN BURNS, a resident of Gettysburgh, about fifty years of age, took his own shot-gun and joined in the battle on Thursday, in defence of his home. He fought very bravely, as was shown by his receiving five wounds, none of them serious, however.

On the evening of the second day's fight, the rebels charged on Battery B, First Pennsylvania artillery. A rebel Lieutenant jumped over the works, and demanded of the Captain the surrender of the battery. The Captain responded by knocking him down and taking 40 of his men prisoners.

The First New-Hampshire battery was located on a rise of ground, with a small grove of timber close in the rear. When the rebels were advancing across the open plain the men left their pieces, heavily shotted, and secreted themselves in the grove. The rebels perceiving this, supposed the pieces deserted, and came on at a rapid rate. When within short range the men rejoined their pieces, and opened a terribly destructive fire upon them, which caused them to break and fall back precipitately, with large numbers killed and wounded. The Nineteenth Massachusetts, Col. DEVEREUX, took three stand of colors, the Fourteenth, Nineteenth and Fifty-third Virginia regiments. A portion of the battle field, the importance of which was immense, and the contest for which has not been fully described, was the extreme left flank, which the enemy endeavored to turn with so much desperation. When the Fifth corps was put into position, it, in fact, supported the Third corps, in part relieved it, and was extended out on the left, to lengthen our line, and checkmate the enemy's flanking attempts. AYRES' division was on the left of the Third corps, and the Third brigade of the First division, (then commanded by Gen. BARNES, the brigade of Col. VINCENT) was detached and sent to guard the extreme left flank. Here some of the most desperate fighting of the day occurred. Col. VINCENT, a brave and highly accomplished officer, was seen mortally wounded, and taken from the field. The command of the brigade then devolved upon Col. JAMES C. RICE, of the Forty-fourth New-York. The command had hardly gotten into position, and thrown out a heavy line of skirmishers, before two brigades of Texas and Alabama troops made a desperate charge against their position, with the purpose of passing between our line and the mountain (Wolf Hill) immediately on our flank. They made five or six desperate attempts to accomplish this purpose, pressing up to within fifty yards of the line of our gallant brigade, which fought with great desperation—slaughtering the enemy by hundreds. But Col. RICE saw the great importance of the position and determined to hold it—a determination in which that fire-proof brigade sustained him most gallantly. Not a man or officer was allowed to flinch; ammunition got low, but was quickly re-supplied; the struggle became more and more deadly; many officers were falling, when Col. RICE sent to Gen. SYKES for reinforcements, so that he could advance and take possession of the mountain, a third of a mile to the front beyond. *Five regiments of* CRAWFORD's *Reserves* came under Col. FISHER. They were placed in a strong position and Col. RICE then ordered the Twentieth Maine, Col. CHAMBERLAIN, to advance and take possession of Wolf Hill, which he gallantly did, taking twenty-five prisoners, including several officers.

The brigade took, altogether, over three hundred prisoners, including two Colonels and fifteen commissioned officers, over four hundred stand of arms, saved all of our own dead and wounded and those of the enemy, and held at night his entire ground. One-third of the brigade was killed and wounded. Col. RICE's disposition of the troops in action, and his ordering the advance so that we rested our flank on the mountain, were highly praised by his superior officers. Fifty dead rebels were buried in front of the position of the Twentieth Maine and Forty-fourth New-York, and the Eighty-third Pennsylvania brought in nearly a hundred of the enemy's wounded.

This brigade has an old fighting reputation. And such commanders as RICE and CONNER, of the Forty-fourth New-York, WELCH, of the Sixteenth Michigan, CHAMBERLAIN, of the Twentieth Maine, and WOODWARD, of the Eighty-third Pennsylvania, will nobly sustain it.

Great grief is expressed at the loss of Col. VINCENT, whom they all admired and respected as an accomplished gentleman and gallant soldier. He was wounded in the groin, and though still living, is not expected to survive many hours.

L. L. CROUNSE.

FURTHER LIST OF CASUALTIES.

First Brigade, Regular Infantry. Second Division, Fifth Corps.

Killed.

Second Lieut. S. A. Miller, 12th infantry.

Wounded.

Capt. S. Van Rensalaer, 12th infantry.	Lieut. Geo. Williams, 4th infantry.
Capt. H. W. Freidley, 3d in'y	Lieut. E. L. Alston, 12th infantry.
Capt. J. M. Locke, 14th inf'y.	Lieut. Edward Liscum, 12th infantry.
Lieut. D. Parker, 3d inf'y.	Lieut. W. O. Douglas, 12th infantry.
Lieut. Geo. B. Batter, 3d infantry.	Lieut S. Morton, 3d inf'y.
Lieut. S. T. Crowley, 4th infantry.	

Total casualties—392 killed, wounded and missing.

Returns of Casualties, July 2, 1863, Second Brigade, Second Division, Fifth Corps.

First Lieut. Goodrich, 2d infantry—killed.	Lieut. H. Rockford, 11th infantry—killed.
Maj. A. T. Lee, 2 infantry—wounded.	Capt. J. M. Goodhue, 11th 11th in—hand, slightly.
First Lieut. McLaughlin, 2d infantry—wounded.	Lieut. M. Elder, 11th in—leg, severely.
Second Lieut. F. E. Lacey 2d infantry—wounded.	Lieut. A. A. Harback, 11th in—hip, slightly.
Second Lieut. D. W. Burke, 2d infantry—wounded.	Lieut. L. Peter, 11th infantry—ankle, severely.
First Lieut. W. F. Miller, 7th infantry—killed.	Lieut. O. H. Healy, 11th infantry—neck, severely.
First Lieut. R. B. Crawford, 7th infantry—left arm amputated.	Lieut A. Barber, 11th infantry—leg severely.
First Lieut. R. R. Comba, 7th inf.—hand, slightly.	Capt. G. W. Edgerton, 11th infantry—back, slightly.
1st Lieut. E. C. Woodruff, 7th inf'ry—knee, slightly.	1st Lt. W. H. Chamberlin, 17th infantry—killed.
1st Lieut. W. J. Fisher—10th infantry—killed.	Capt. S. Dana, 17th infantry—leg.
Capt. Wm. Clinton, 10th in.—right leg, slightly.	Capt. D. H. Chase, 17th infantry—slightly.
Capt. E. G. Bush, 10th in.—hand, slightly.	Capt. W. G. Mooreland, 17th infantry—leg.
1st Lieut R. G. Wells, 10th infantry—leg, not known.	1st Lt. T. H. Carpenter, 17th infantry—leg.
2d Lieut. M. C. Boyce, 10th infantry—abdomen, sev'y.	1st Lt. W. H. Walcott, 17th infantry—leg amputated.
2d Lieut. G. Hamilton, 10th—right leg, slightly.	1st Lt. H. A. Swartwout, 17th infantry—leg.
Capt. T. O. Barri, 11th in'y—killed.	1st Lt. D. S. Montgomery, 17th infantry—arm.
Lieut. H. Kenaston, 11th infantry—killed.	1st Lt. G. W. Green, 17th infantry—leg, slightly.
1st Lieut. G. W. Green, 17th infantry—leg, slightly.	2d Lieut. E. S. Abbott, 17th infantry—mortally.
1st Lieut. R. P. Wilson—17th infantry—hand.	2d Lieut. J. H. Bradford, 17th infantry.
1st Lieut J. S. Knapp, 17th infantry—leg.	2d Lieut. W. Ewing, 17th infantry—dangerously.

Total—killed, 73; wounded, 371.

Casualties in Third Brigade, Second Division, Fifth Army Corps, July 2 and 3, 1863.

OFFICERS KILLED.

Gen. S. H. Weed, Commanding Third Brigade.
Col. P. H. O'Rorke, 140th New-York Vols.

OFFICERS WOUNDED.

Capt. Spiers, 140th New-York Vols.—mortally.
Capt. Starks, 140th New-York Vols.—severely.
Capt. Sibley, 140th New-York Vols.—in both legs.
Lieut. McGraw, 140th N. Y. Vols.—severely, leg broken.
Lieut. Cline, 140th N. Y. Vols.—flesh wound, thigh.
Capt. S. A. McKee, 155th Penn. Vols.—slightly.
Lieut. J. H. Foster, 155th Penn. Vols.—slightly.
Lieut. D. E. Lyon, 155th Penn. Vols.—slightly.
Lieut. J. S. Donnell, 91st Penn. Vols.—contusion.
Capt. Jas. E. Jenkins, 146th N. Y. Vols.—seriously.

Third Brigade—First Division.

EIGHTY-THIRD PENNSYLVANIA.

Capt. J. M. Sell—leg shot off.	Col. Strong Vincent—mortally wounded.

TWENTIETH MAINE.

Lieut. W. L. Kendall—killed.	Capt. S. F. Kean—side.
Capt. C. W. Billings—knee.	J. B. Fitch—thigh.
Lieut. J. B. Stanwood—leg.	Lieut. R. H. Limcott—leg.

SIXTEENTH MICHIGAN.

Lieut. Butler Brown—killed.	Lieut. W. V. Bergman—wounded.
Lieut. W. H. Borden—killed.	Lieut. A. J. Cameron—wounded.
Lieut. W. Jewett—killed.	

FORTY-FOURTH NEW-YORK.

Lieut. Dunham—killed.	Lieut. Thomas—wounded.
Capt. Larrabee—killed.	Adj. Herendeen—wounded slightly.
Capt. Munger—wounded.	
Capt. Bourne—wounded.	

The Forty-fourth New-York lost 2 officers and 24 men killed, and 5 officers and 73 men wounded.

The Twentieth Maine lost 6 officers wounded, and 29 men killed, and 92 men wounded.

The Sixteenth Michigan lost 3 officers and 18 men killed, and 2 officers and 31 men wounded.

The Eighty-third Pennsylvania lost 10 killed, and 35 wounded.

First Brigade. First Division, Fifth Corps.

ONE HUNDRED AND EIGHTEENTH PENNSYLVANIA.

Capt. R. W. Davids—killed.	Lieut. J. B. Inmann—hip, seriously.
Lieut. J. B. Wilson—side.	

Two men killed, 15 wounded.

FIRST MICHIGAN.

Col. Abbott—wounded.	Lieut. Randall—severely.
Capt. Spence—severely.	Lieut. Woodruff—slightly.
Capt. Bradish—slightly.	Lieut. Ladd—killed.
Lieut. Merritt—severely.	

TWENTY-SECOND MASSACHUSETTS.

Lieut. Rock—both legs.	Lieut. Look—slightly.
Lieut. Knowles—severely.	

EIGHTEENTH MASSACHUSETTS.

No officers injured.

THE DEATH OF COL. HUSTEN.

From the following dispatch to Sheriff LYNCH, we learn of the death of Col. HUSTEN, formerly of the Second regiment N. Y. S. M., and recently appointed Colonel of the Eighty-second regiment New-York Volunteers:

BALTIMORE, July 5, 1863.

Sheriff James Lynch, New-York:

Col. JAMES HUSTEN, of the Eighty-second New-York Volunteers, late of the Second New-York State Militia, was killed yesterday in battle. The body will be forwarded. (Signed,) E. L. SPROUT. A. Q. M., Gettysburgh.

Col. JAMES HUSTEN, long known as an officer of the New-York State Militia, left this City with his regiment, May 1, 1861, as Captain of Company E; was promoted Lieutenant-Colonel, in which capacity he commanded the regiment at the battles of Fredericksburgh and Chancellorsville, and has since been commissioned by Gov. SEYMOUR as Colonel.

His energy and zeal in encouraging his regiment to stand firm against the repeated attacks of EWELL's corps, exposed him to the sharpshooters of the enemy, and he fell pierced by three shots at the head of his columns, while giving his commands.

His noble regiment did not long survive him. It is reported that of three hundred and sixty-five rank and file, but three officers and fifty-seven men remain of the Second New-York State Militia, (Eighty-second New-York Volunteers,) "the oldest Militia regiment in the State, and the first to volunteer for the war."

His bereaved widow and his numerous friends in this City, have the sympathy of the community in their irreparable loss. His remains are expected to arrive here this week.

WHERE GEN. REYNOLDS FELL.

Capt. W. H. WILCOX, Aid-de-Camp, of the late Gen. REYNOLDS' Staff, says, in a card to the Philadelphia *Inquirer*:

"I notice in the papers very erroneous statements regarding the manner of Maj.-Gen. REYNOLDS' death—allow me to correct them. He was riding along the line of skirmishers, endeavoring to rally and urge forward some Western troops (of well-tested courage) who had broken from the terrible fire to which they were subjected, when he received the mortal wound which in fifteen minutes after deprived the army of one of its most gallant and able commanders. This was about 9½ in the morning, a short time after the action commenced, and *not* in the afternoon. The place of his death was about where the "College" or Seminary is located on the map, (this building was only about quarter of a mile out of town,) and *not* where marked as being on the side of the city opposite to the place of action. The First corps did *not* retire *before* the General died, but some two hours after. As I was the Aid who rode by his side at the time he was wounded, I am enabled to give you thus briefly the facts."

OUR HARRISBURG CORRESPONDENCE.

The News from the Army of the Potomac—The Passes—Enormous Number of Deserters—Gen. Couch's Troops.

HARRISBURGH, Monday, July 6, 1863.

Everybody here is in high spirits at the glorious news from the Army of the Potomac. The telegraph has anticipated me of course, but it may be as well to say that confirmation of the best possible reports is hourly arriving. Wounded officers and citizens are arriving from Gettysburgh continually, and report everything favorably. The army is in splendid spirits at the great victory. This is the first time the Army of the Potomac has actually chased the army of Virginia, and sent it flying before them. I remember well what a soldier said to me after the battle of Chancellorsville. "I don't understand these victories," he remarked. "I only know that I have always been chased, and that I should like to do a little chasing myself now." Unless he is numbered among the fallen he has his ambition gratified. For the rebel army is in full retreat, and our forces fresh and inspirited by their victory, are rapidly following them. The South Mountain—a continuation of the same range that runs down into Maryland, spreads out between Carlisle and Chambersburgh into a series of rugged and almost impassable hills.

There are three passes, one at the extreme east this side of Carlisle, which is not practicable for the rebels, both because it is far out of their road of retreat, and because it is secured by our troops under Gen. COUCH. The next pass is the Mount Holly pass. This is a mile or two long and very easily defended. I presume our troops are there also. They were on their way yesterday, but were temporarily detained by the rising of a small stream which carried away a bridge about five miles this side. This obstacle can easily be removed, and the belief here is that a sufficient force to hold the gap arrived there this morning. The third pass is at the south end of the mountain, directly on the road from Gettysburgh to Chambersburgh. We have no news from that point and it is entirely probable that the pass has been secured by LEE. I presume, however, that there is no doubt that our forces occupy Chambersburgh, for I know that orders have been issued to furnish all the telegraph offices between Carlisle and Chambersburgh, with operators, and the remnant of MILROY's force, which has been at Bedford and Bloody Run, has started for that place, and is said to have arrived there yesterday. The rebel army is evidently endeavoring to make its way to the Potomac at or near Williamsport, being ignorant of the destruction of their pontoon bridge at that point. The result of the whole thing seems to be that LEE's army is completely hemmed in, and every line of retreat cut off. There is no doubt, too, that it is greatly disorganized. I have mentioned before the large number of deserters who took advantage of being in a Free State to escape, even though no enemy was within reach, and considerable vigilance could easily be exercised by the guards and pickets, and I ventured to predict that after the first great battle, whether favorable or unfavorable to them, the rebel soldiers would desert by thousands. My prediction is verified. Thousands of rebel soldiers, separated from their commands, fill the mountains. Some have arms and some have none. Most of them are very ready to be taken. In fact, it is their only salvation from starvation. The rout is, I verily believe, complete. Straws show which way the wind blows, and the hundred stories that are flying about of LEE's surrender, LEE's shooting himself, and all that sort of thing, would never be concocted unless there was some substantial foundation to rest them upon.

The great question, of course is, will there be another battle? It seems to me there must. MEADE must divide his forces in order to cut off LEE's retreat. He has already done so, in fact. There are many places on the line of retreat where a stand can be made, and it is hardly to be supposed that LEE is going to die without a struggle. The desperation of some of the charges of the rebels on the last day of the battle exceeded anything in the history of the war. Some of them fell dead close to the wheels of our batteries. Certainly nothing has equaled this save, perhaps, the charges on our heavy batteries at Corinth, when the ditch in front of the works was filled to the top with rebel dead. This battle was even more important to them than that, and if there is a possible chance of their retrieving themselves in the Valley of the Cumberland, even in the slightest degree, they will make an attempt to do so. The end is not yet.

The latest news to-night is encouraging. It will be sent by telegraph. We must not place too much reliance on COUCH's forces. They are not to be trusted in battle. Most of them were never in action, and all that can be expected of them is to hover on the flank of the rebels, capture stragglers, and, in the event of another battle, compel the detachment of a considerable force to watch them. I am authorized to say that there are at least 20,000 militia now close to the rebels or doing efficient service in some other part of the theatre of war. I see by some of the New-York papers that Gen. MEADE is said to have remarked that if COUCH was ready to attack at the right time his victory was certain. It is not probable that Gen. MEADE said any such thing for he knows per-

[*Continued on Eighth Page.*]

Charge on Cemetery Ridge

The Charleston Mercury.

VOLUME LXXXIII. CHARLESTON, S. C., SATURDAY, JULY 11, 1863. NUMBER 12,[illegible]

TELEGRAPHIC NEWS.

FROM GENERAL LEE'S ARMY.

MARTINSBURG, VA., July 9.—The army is all at Hagerstown. All is quiet there to-day. A cavalry skirmish took place yesterday. We have no information of the movements of the Yankee army. Maryland Heights have been re-occupied by a small force of the enemy. An ordnance train has just passed through, on its way to General LEE, who is awaiting its arrival.

RICHMOND, July 10.—All the papers this morning give more cheering accounts from our army in Maryland. The uneasiness which prevailed yesterday has given place to a feeling of confidence in the ability of General LEE to resume the offensive. The Martinsburg correspondent of the *Dispatch* says that all the news of the battles of Gettysburg, which had been received there, was brought by Major HAWKS, of EWELL'S Corps, who left Gettysburg on Saturday morning. He says that our loss in the first two days' fighting was not very great. On Friday it was heavy, especially in PICKETT'S Division. General TRIMBLE lost a leg, and General HOOD an arm. Wounded officers who arrived in Richmond yesterday say that our army fell back with the greatest order and deliberation. There was no demoralization. It was generally understood that the falling back was caused by the difficulty of obtaining supplies through so long a line of communication. The men were in fine spirits, ready for another fight.

It is reported that the enemy advanced from the south end of Morris Island upon Battery Wagner, and heavy fighting (artillery and infantry) occurred this morning. The enemy was finally driven back, and is now behind the sand hills at the lower end of the Island. The Monitors have drawn off at long range from Battery Wagner, and are not replying.

2, p. m.—Heavy skirmishing continues on the Clinton road. The enemy is slowly working around our left. The attack may not become general before morning, though the enemy is still pressing forward. We have lost but few men as yet. The enemy must be suffering for water, as all the cisterns and tanks have been destroyed. Thermometer 92.

FROM GENERAL JOHNSTON'S ARMY.

JACKSON, MISS., July 9—4, p. m.—The enemy is still advancing slowly, shelling our cavalry. They are now within four miles of our works. There will probably be no engagement before morning.

9, p. m.—A regular artillery duel has been going on for the past hour, three miles off. The Yankees are moving up slowly but steadily. Warm work is looked for at daylight.

RICHMOND, July 10.—A despatch from Martinsburg, dated yesterday, says that a heavy cavalry skirmish took place the day before. We drove the enemy seven miles, capturing a number of prisoners. The army is quiet at Hagerstown.

LATEST FROM THE UNITED STATES.

RICHMOND, July 10.—The Baltimore *Gazette* of the 7th says: "What we really know in reference to the recent battles before Gettysburg amounts simply to this: The Confederates were attacked on Wednesday by two army corps, which they drove back with great slaughter, capturing many prisoners. On Thursday afternoon the whole Federal force was attacked by the Confederates, and, after a sanguinary conflict, repulsed them. On Friday the battle was renewed, and lasted through the day. It resulted in a more signal repulse of General LEE than on the day before. The losses on both sides were extraordinarily heavy. The Federal loss in general officers was beyond all precedent.

On Saturday night LEE fell back towards the mountains, and what has occurred since, is, with us, almost entirely a matter of conjecture; but it is now admitted that LEE holds the passes of South Mountain, and will fight or retire as circumstances may decide. The pontoon bridge over the Potomac at Williamsport have not been destroyed.

European dates to June 24, have been received. French mediation rumors were again prevalent. ROEBUCK and LINDSAY, of the British Parliament, have had an interview with NAPOLEON, who assured them that his views in regard to the American war were unchanged. He decided again to interpose his good offices, in conjunction with England. At a Cabinet meeting, in which NAPOLEON presided, it was resolved to renew the French proposal to the English Government for joint diplomatic action in America.

Gold in New York 138@139. Nothing had yet been heard there of the fall of Vicksburg.

THE MERCURY.

SATURDAY, JULY 11, 1863.

Our Situation.

Charleston is untaken, and we judge that if our people rise up at once to the emergency, it will not be taken. But to save it prompt, daring and desperate valor are now essential; and this must be backed and supported by as much ready labor as can be employed in securing, upon the spot, fruits of the most vigorous operations against the enemy. In the present situation on Morris Island, time is our enemy, and the position of affairs should, we conceive, be changed in the shortest possible time, at any cost of life and labor. Upon this, all may depend for Charleston and the State. The cost of circumspection and delay at this juncture is likely to be ultimately tenfold that of bold aggression. Does it not put our cause upon the hazard of scientific engineering and gradual approach? Let us learn from the foe, by the style of gallant attack upon the battery at Secessionville last year, how the Yankees, as yet without works, may be driven from Morris Island. While the opportunity lasts, and ere it is too late, we venture to throw out this suggestion for what it may be worth. Could we retake the south end of Morris Island, and quickly build proper works, it would be better than staking our safety solely on Fort Wagner.

THE SIEGE OF VICKSBURG—STRENGTH OF GRANT'S POSITION.

We copy below from the army correspondence of the Augusta *Constitutionalist* a letter from Jackson, Miss., which, viewed in connection with the fall of Vicksburg, will be found deeply interesting. This letter is from an officer in Gen. JOHNSTON'S army, and makes revelations which are as astounding as they are unexpected and novel:

I wish I had some good news to give you. I have not. People away from here expect a great deal, and I am satisfied a great deal too much from Gen. Johnston. There is no room for generalship in this case. Physical obstructions, such as Johnston will have to overcome, will quell and oppress the genius of any man. Grant has entrenched himself around Vicksburg as strongly as Pemberton has in it. The hills are in many places nearly perpendicular, with but little room on their tops, and high enough to permit a very small party to prevent the ascent of as many men as can be got to them. This almost interminable succession of steep hills and deep valleys for miles and miles around Grant's camp has been fortified with all the skill that the devilish ingenuity of these rascals could secure. The hills are crowned with heavy guns, and every gorge is ready to belch forth destruction.

He has devastated the country all around him, for 20 to 30 miles, leaving nothing that could contribute to the support of an army advancing on him, and has obstructed all the roads leading towards him in every possible way for many miles. You will perceive that it would be no easy job for Johnston to get to him. Besides, Grant has from 70 to 80,000 men—Johnston not half so many. (I am afraid to commit to paper the strength of this army.) Grant's communications are open; his facilities for receiving stores, supplies and reinforcements are unbounded, while Johnston has to work hard to buy every mouthful his army eats, and then is obliged to haul it many miles—sometimes 40 or 50—and the farther he goes towards Vicksburg, the farther he must wagon his supplies.

Now, with these facts before you, work out the problem. If Grant, with all he has and all the means he wants or asks for, can't take Pemberton in Vicksburg, with 13 or 15 000 men, how is Johnston, with only all the men he can get, to destroy or subdue Grant in a fortified camp equally strong, with 80,000 men to defend it? This is the proposition; work it out; put "Q. E. D." at the end and send it to me, for I would like mightily to see it.

In all this I do not undervalue nor underrate the elements at Gen. Johnston's command, nor his great ability. His army (I will state *entre nous*) not as high as 30,000 fighting men, is composed of the very best fighting stock on the continent, and if Johnston could only get Grant into the field, would maul a much larger force "till they should think the very devil himself had come from hell." They are anxious to fight, and have every confidence in the General, and will do what men can do—yet this is not enough to overcome the immense disadvantages under which he labors.

I do not write this to discourage you, for I know no more of Gen. Johnston's plans than you do, perhaps not so much. I hope that he will be let alone, however, and not driven by taunts, and innuendoes, and abuse, to sacrifice an army which is confessedly the only barrier that at present protects, in any considerable degree, the States of Mississippi, Alabama and Georgia.

OUR CAVALRY IN MARYLAND.—The New York *Tribune* has a number of letters describing the performances of STUART'S cavalry around Washington. Our correspondent thus describes the rich haul our men made of an immense train of wagons near Rockville:

* * * One passing on our way we came up with the rear of a long wagon train, comprising 150 vehicles, each drawn by six mules, driven by a very black and picturesque negro. This train must have been at least two miles long, for by the time we had reached the other end, riding leisurely, we were within a mile or two of Rockville. Here, just as we had passed the last wagon, an excited horseman, coming from the direction of Rockville, halted our party, and in a somewhat confused voice gave us the pleasing intelligence that about 400 rebel cavalry were close at his heels. A short consultation of war resulted in the making up our minds to retreat. This conclusion was scarcely arrived at when two more men came full tilt past us, shouting that the rebels had fired on them and were close behind. Then came a cavalry soldier, one of the six who formed our paltry guard, leading a riderless horse, whose master (another of our guard) had just been shot. Then came thundering along a second trooper, much excited, and evidently charged with some important mission. He immediately halted all the mule teams, ordering them to turn back. And now commenced a scene of excitement and confusion which none but a maniac could properly describe. Wagons upset by their drivers in abortive attempts to turn them round, others locked together, mule teams inextricably snarled up, and through this jam and mess some twenty or thirty horsemen (your correspondent among the number) galloping like mad. Had the devil been behind us it would have been impossible to go faster; as fast as the frightened horses could lay their legs to the ground they went, knicking up stones and earth with their heels in the most exciting manner.—Two scared farmers led the retreat on powerful horses, and so long as they galloped it was impossible to stop any of the other horses. At last we got sufficiently far from the train to deem ourselves safe, and as the farmers had got out of reach, we pulled up and reconnoitered. Away far back on the road we could distinguish smoke from the burning teams. They were doubtless all destroyed. All the mules were captured, and two ambulances containing officers, were likewise gobbled up.

Another correspondent writes of the operations of our cavalry in the same vicinity:

The rebels, in their recent raid at Rockville, Maryland, captured Chief Justice Bowie, and after marching him on foot for six miles, allowed him to return to his family. They also arrested Postmaster Bailey, Provost Marshal Moulden, the United States enrolling officer, and examining surgeon. Stuart commanded the rebels in person, and was introduced to several of the rebel sympathizers in Rockville. The rebels took every horse within four miles of Rockville, whether the owner was Unionist or traitor.

THE WAR IN LOUISIANA.

The steamship *Morning Star* left New Orleans on the 27th June, and reached New York on the 3d of July. The New York *Herald* says rumor was current at New Orleans on the morning of the *Star's* departure, that Port Hudson had been taken by General BANKS, but this was not confirmed by telegraph at the Belize at a later period of the day. The following is the *Herald's* correspondence:

NEW ORLEANS, June 26.—As I feared would be the case when writing my last letter, we have lost Brashear City. The enemy succeeded in capturing it on Monday morning last, and with it all the troops that were there, all the camp equipage, artillery, ammunition, and, in fact, everything—no means being at hand to remove, and no time given to destroy the valuable property there stored. An order was issued yesterday by the Provost Marshal General directing the different newspapers of this city to say nothing whatever regarding military movements in this department. This in itself proves that all is not well with us. Were it otherwise, everything going on would be given without hesitation to the public. It is certain, however, that we have lost everything west of the Mississippi river, and have gained nothing as yet east of it. Our troops have fallen back from Latourche Crossing, having first burned the bridge, and I am under the impression that our outposts do not extend beyond Butte Station—twenty miles from the city.

It will be very evident to those who have studied this department that we are in a worse condition than ever regarding this State. We do not possess, by many square miles, as much territory as we did three months ago, and I see no prospect whatever of any change for the better. Our army is dwindling away rapidly from every cause, while that of the enemy is becoming stronger every hour. Although the papers are prohibited from saying anything about the military movements, still it does not require anything more than the following extract from the Era's monetary and financial article of this morning to fully understand the situation. It says: "The total stock of produce from the interior is too limited for operations of magnitude, and transactions in financial circles are consequently on very limited scale. The total available stock of sugar in the country is extremely small, and the present prospects for a crop this season are of a most unfavorable character, while the indications are that what little may be produced will be very inferior in quality." The above paragraph speaks volumes, and we better understand by its language the condition of affairs than if a full account had been given of the assaults upon Port Hudson, affairs in the Attakapas country, and a correct list of our losses. It requires almost the use of a microscope now to discover what portion of Louisiana still remains in our possession.

Smother the news as much as possible, yet enough leaks out among the populace of New Orleans to give them every reason to believe our reverses much worse than they really are. Hence the bad policy of not publishing the true state of the case at once. I saw more evidences yesterday in the streets of this city of the true state of feeling in the community than ever before since I have resided here.—The ladies did not hesitate to display their secession colors in every manner; their red, white and red fans and bonnet ornaments were conspicuous in every direction, excepting among those who were in mourning, and the men showed their feelings by crowding the grogshops and talking of large purchases of rope of the proper size, not stating, however, for what purpose it was intended, but leaving that to the imagination.

As a further proof of how near the enemy are in another direction, I give you the following:—For some time a force of workmen have been engaged in repairing the railroad bridge over Pass Manchac. A locomotive and a few cars have been used for the purpose of running material and conveying the workmen and their tools to and fro. The bridge being about completed, the cars were sent out yesterday for bringing back the men, but they never returned, and this very naturally led to suppose that they, with the party of workmen, have been "gobbled," and are now on on their way to Jackson or some other part of Dixie. The bridge has not yet been destroyed by our force, but I have no doubt it will be, in order to prevent any attempt to cross it in that direction. As far as New Orleans is concerned, it is to-day as secure as ever. No force the enemy could bring to bear would ever be successful in reaching a point nearer the city than they now are. The guns of the fleet command every approach, and General Emory has so disposed his command as to effectually defend every point. The city is to day as safe as New York or Boston, and must remain so. Its geographical position renders it a place easily defended by a small number of men against an army of large proportions, as it cannot be approached in force, except by water, which the enemy have no means whatever of doing. We feel perfectly secure, notwithstanding the people generally have every hope in a few days of once more seeing the secesh flag over the City Hall, the squadron of Admiral Farragut annihilated, and the General commanding and Admiral on their way to Richmond.

The news from up the river is of the same character as when I last wrote. We hear rumors almost every hour of "forlorn hopes," and desperate fighting; but nothing has occurred of any importance since the assault of the 14th instant. The enemy is hovering in our rear at Port Hudson with small parties of cavalry, annoying us whenever the opportunity offers; but we have no positive evidence of their being in force within striking distance. The bombardment still continues, and the last advices state that another assault is to take place between now and Monday evening next. This assault has been promised us every day and night for ten days past. When it occurs we can speak more fully of it. As matters stand now we consider its coming off exceedingly doubtful. Good authority says that the trouble is with the nine months men. They will not fight, preferring to go home rather than be shot, especially now that their term of enlistment is nearly over. The storming columns heretofore have been three years New York and Western regiments, supported by nine months' men; and when the stormers reached the parapet and looked round, the supporters were nowhere to be seen. Consequently a "falling back" was considered the most prudent move that could be made in order to save the few remaining of the column from capture or destruction. The river transports now go fully armed, in order to repel any attack by parties along the river bank. We have not heard of any being fired at in the last few days, the enemy having probably concentrated all his force to accomplish fully the capture of Brashear City and the Opelousas Railroad.

Imagine the sufferings of the poor negros, those who have been enticed and driven away from their comfortable homes, and promised protection by our forces. Over two thousand of them were retaken when Brashear City was lost, besides the thousands of others who were on the government plantations. All they have ever suffered in their lives before will be but a tithe of what they will have to undergo at the hands of the men who now have them in charge. Better to have left them where we found them, if unable to provide for their safety, than to have the poor creatures placed in the position they now are in. You will understand very readily how exasperated the planters of Western Louisiana are against us when you know that nearly every negro had been taken from them by our army. Then, again, they feel that the negros, in the late attacks upon Port Hudson, killed, beyond doubt, many of their friends, and possibly some relatives. All these things combined render their hatred [illegible] us beyond all bounds, and when we again attempt to recover Western Louisiana we will have far more men and much more desperate fighting to encounter than we had in the last advance, when the people were more or less friendly to us. Had we respected the private property of the people of the country when we passed through it, and not taken everything we could carry, even to the little fancy articles that composed part of the furniture of a gentleman's drawing room, we would have far less enemies than we now have. We cannot expect a man to feel at all friendly towards us now who has lost everything at our hands, although friendly to our cause at the time of the robbery.

It is all folly to attempt to speculate upon what is to be the result of the present state of affairs. A very few days will decide if Port Hudson is to fall or not. If not, the army will fall back to this point, and will remain here until the heat of summer is over, for it will be impossible to send our men into the swamps of this State until cooler weather sets in. They need resting, many of them are invalids, and should be in a hospital rather than in the field. The nine months men will be going North, and the three years regiments will have to try and fill up their depleted ranks. Four months must elapse before we can hope to resume active operations and take the offensive once more. In that time I hope that fifty thousand men will be assembled here, ready to make our operations short and successful. It is to be hoped that whatever troops are sent here for the campaign of next winter will be men who do not require three months drill before being able to take the field. We want no more nine months men in this department: nothing but soldiers for the war and disciplined troops. Give us these, and our Generals will have tools with which they can work in a proper manner, and accomplish results that will be satisfactory to the Northern people. We have had proof enough of the value of nine months men during the past month, and we want no more of them.

The New-York Times.

VOL. XII—NO. 3683. | NEW-YORK, TUESDAY JULY, 14, 1863. | PRICE THREE CENTS.

THE MOB IN NEW-YORK.

Resistance to the Draft---Rioting and Bloodshed.

Conscription Offices Sacked and Burned.

Private Dwellings Pillaged and Fired.

AN ARMORY AND A HOTEL DESTROYED.

Colored People Assaulted--An Unoffending Black Man Hung.

The Tribune Office Attacked---The Colored Orphan Asylum Ransacked and Burned---Other Outrages and Incidents.

A DAY OF INFAMY AND DISGRACE.

The initiation of the draft on Saturday in the Ninth Congressional District was characterized by so much order and good feeling as to well nigh dispel the forebodings of tumult and violence which many entertained in connection with the enforcement of the conscription in this City. Very few, then, were prepared for the riotous demonstrations which yesterday, from 10 in the morning until late at night, prevailed almost unchecked in our streets. The authorities had counted upon more or less resistance to this measure of the Government after the draft was completed, and the conscripts were required to take their place in the ranks, and at that time they would have been fully prepared to meet it; but no one anticipated resistance at so early a stage in the execution of the law, and, consequently, both the City and National authorities were totally unprepared to meet it. The abettors of the riot knew this, and in it they saw their opportunity. We say abettors of the riot, for it is abundantly manifest that the whole affair was concocted on Sunday last by a few wire-pullers, who, after they saw the ball fairly in motion yesterday morning prudently kept in the back ground. Proof of this is found in the fact that as early as 9 o'clock, some laborers employed by two or three railroad companies, and in the iron foundries on the eastern side of the City, formed in procession in the Twenty-second Ward, and visited the different workshops in the upper wards, where large numbers were employed, and compelled them, by threats in some instances, to cease their work. As the crowd augmented, their shouts and disorderly demonstrations became more formidable. The number of men who thus started out in their career of violence and blood, did not probably at first exceed threescore. Scarcely had two dozen names been called, when a crowd, numbering perhaps 500, suddenly made an irruption in front of the building, (corner of Third-avenue and Forty-sixth-street,) attacking it with clubs, stones, brickbats and other missiles. The upper part of the building was occupied by families, who were terrified beyond measure at the smashing of the windows, doors and furniture. Following these missiles, the mob rushed furiously into the office on the first floor, where the draft was going on, seizing the books, papers, records, lists, &c., all of which they destroyed, except those contained in a large iron safe. The drafting officers were set upon with stones and clubs, and, with the reporters for the Press and others, had to make a hasty exit through the rear. They did not escape scatheless, however, as one of the enrolling officers was struck a savage blow with a stone, which will probably result fatally, and several others were injured.

From the above it will be seen that the drawing by Provost-Marshal JENKINS did not commence punctually at 9 o'clock, as was intended. Intimations had been received that a riot was probable, and Acting Assistant Provost-Marshal-General NUGENT was applied to for a force which would be sufficient to preserve the peace. At 10 o'clock, however, no other response had been made to this application than the arrival of a dozen policemen, and Provost-Marshal JENKINS decided to resume the drawing. The wheel was placed prominently upon the table, the blindfolded man stood beside it, the man whose duty it was turn the wheel was ready, and Mr. JENKINS announced that the draft, which was begun on Saturday, would be concluded. At this time there were about two hundred persons present, and, during the twenty minutes before the riot was inaugurated, they freely made use of excited and threatening language. These ruffians did not hesitate at all about joining the main body of the rioters as soon as they arranged themselves before the building, and their exit was the signal for the attack, which commenced with a volley of stones. When the office had been cleared of the officers and other persons, many of the more excited of the rioters rushed in and played instant havoc with the machinery, and demolishing the furniture and papers. The books, lists, records, and blanks were dragged into the street, torn into fragments, and scattered everywhere with loud imprecations and savage yells. The men seemed to be excited beyond expression, and in their futile efforts to wrench open the iron safe, which contained the names of the drafted, gave themselves wholly to devilish rage and fury.

The destruction of the material in the office was hardly accomplished when smoke was discovered to be issuing from the rear of the room, and this evidence of the building being on fire was received with vociferous shouts, and other indications of delight. As the flames gradually increased, the passions of the mob grew deeper, and their yelling and brandishing of clubs, and threatening of everybody connected with the enforcement of the draft was more emphatic. Some of the crowd supposed that the Enrolling officers had secreted themselves in the upper part of the building, and notwithstanding the fact that women and children were known to occupy the upper floors, the cowardly wretches threw stones and other missiles into the windows.

Fearing that these poor people would either be burned to death or maimed by these projectiles, Deputy Provost-Marshal EDWARD S. VANDERPOEL bravely stepped to the front, and assuring the rioters that they had utterly destroyed all the drafting paraphenalia, requested them to withdraw, or to do something to prevent the destruction of the helpless women and children. Suspecting from his uniform that he was one of the drafting officers, one of the rioters seized him and struck him. Mr. VANDERPOEL merely shook off his assailant, and in a pacific manner renewed his request; [illegible] attracted the attention of the [illegible] and a number of them [illegible] him with their hands [illegible]

could not resist them, he withdrew to the place where the police were posted. The rioters followed him with great clubs, and the men, who were desperate, beat him upon the body and head. His head was so badly bruised that blood flowed profusely, when he was thrown down and kicked. He afterward escaped by the aid of the police and one or two of his friends; but the rioters followed him, striking him with clubs. He is so badly injured that there is but little probability of his recovery.

Meantime the fire spread from the enrolling office to the adjoining buildings, and the entire block was consumed.

ATTACK UPON SUPERINTENDENT KENNEDY.

Soon after the rioting began Superintendent KENNEDY hurried to the scene in a carriage, and as he alighted a portion of the crowd recognized him, greeting him at first with uncomplimentary epithets and afterwards with blows. A score or more of the ruffians fell upon him, and dealt heavy blows upon his head, face and body, injuring him severely. They doubtless would have killed him outright had not a strapping fellow in the crowd felt some compunction at the brutality of the rest and dashed in to the rescue. By vigorous blows he kept a clear space about Mr. KENNEDY's prostrate body until two policemen gathered up their Chief and removed him to a place of safety. In addition to his painful cuts and bruises, Mr. KENNEDY was also a sufferer in the loss of his watch, spectacles and gold-headed cane. The ruffians in this as in many other instances made plunder a part of their programme.

The rioters soon betook themselves to other places, apparently with no concerted plan but bent on fresh depredations.

THE ATTACK ON THE ARMORY IN SECOND-AVENUE.

At about 4 o'clock the crowd proceeded from the scene of their exploits in Lexington-avenue and Forty-fourth-street, to the armory situated on the corner of Second-avenue and Twenty-first-street. The building was a large four-story one, and was occupied for the manufacture of rifles and carbines for the Government. In the early part of the day the Police authorities had placed in the building a large number of Policemen, consisting principally of the Broadway Squad. Their instructions were to protect the building and the property therein, and to resist with force any attempt of the invaders to enter the premises. The mob on Second avenue, Twenty-first and Twenty-second streets rapidly increased, and at the time the first attempt was made to force the doors of the building, it amounted to from three to four thousand, the greater part of whom were boys. At this time some 18 or 20 men, followed by scores of youngsters, made an attempt to force the doors of the armory on Twenty-first-street. The doors were burst open by means of heavy sledges, and the crowd made a rush to enter the building. Those in charge of the building, acting under instructions, fired upon those who were entering, and four or five were wounded. One man, named MICHAEL VANEY, was shot through the heart, and died immediately. VANEY was a mechanic, and worked in the Morgan Iron Works. He was about 40 years of age, and resided in Twenty-third-street, between Avenues A and B. The other persons who were shot are not regarded as being seriously injured.

The shooting of VANEY, who was one of the ringleaders of the party making the attack, was the signal for a general onslaught upon the armory. Loud and deep were the curses uttered against the officers who had shot their leader, and for the next hour the paving-stones flew thick and fast, and not until the last pane of glass in the windows of the building had been broken, did they desist. It is proper to remark that nearly all those who threw the paving-stones were boys under twelve years of age. During all this time efforts of a desperate character were being made to fire the building. The doors on Second-avenue were finally forced open, and an excited multitude tried to effect an entrance. They were promptly repelled by those inside. Very soon they received reinforcements and again they made the attempt to enter, some of them with lighted torches in their hands. Meantime a dispatch was received by the officers of the Broadway Squad in charge of the building, from Police Headquarters, to the effect that inasmuch as it was impossible to reinforce them, and the attacking party so greatly outnumbered them, they must retire in the best manner they could. In a short time, they were all safely outside the building, with the exception of two of their number who were pelted on the head with brickbats; one of them was very seriously injured. The excitement against all policemen, at this time, ran so high that it was regarded a most hazardous undertaking for one to show himself to the excited populace. The fact that there was a private entrance in the rear was a most fortunate circumstance for them.

The police having vacated the premises, the mob found it comparatively an easy task to enter and fire the building. In fifteen minutes from the time the crowd had undisputed possession of it, the entire structure was a mass of flame. About half a dozen men remained inside as a sort of forlorn hope, and when all escape for them by the ordinary ways had been cut off by the flames, the poor fellows let themselves down from the windows of the third story in the best manner they could. One took hold of the window sill, and another slid down to his feet and then dropped to the pavement. In this way they all managed to escape; but two of them had each a leg broken, one had his skull so much fractured that he is not expected to recover, and another was so bruised and injured that when he was taken into a neighboring drug store life seemed extinct. Amid the excitement and confusion our reporter was unable to obtain the names of any of those who were thus injured.

SCENES BY AN EYE-WITNESS.

At 11 A. M. word reached the Park Barracks of the disturbance, and Lieut. REED and a detachment of the Invalid corps immediately repaired to the scene of the riot. They went by the Third avenue route, the party occupying one car. On the way up, crowds of men, women and children gathered at the street corners, hissed and jeered them, and some even went so far as to pick up stones, which they defiantly threatened to throw at the car. When near the scene of disturbance, Lieut. REED and command alighted, and formed in company line, in which order they marched up to the mob. Facing the rioters the men were ordered to fire, which many of them did, the shots being blank cartridges, but the smoke had scarce cleared away when the company (which did not number more than fifty men, if as many,) were attacked and completely demoralized by the mob, who were armed with clubs, sticks, swords and other implements. The soldiers had their bayonets taken away, and they themselves were compelled seek refuge in the side streets, but in attempting to flee thither several, it is said, were killed, while those that escaped, did so only to be hunted like dogs, but in a more inhuman and brutal manner. They were chased by the mob, who divided themselves into squads, and frequently a single soldier would be caught in a side street, with each end blocked up by the rioters. The houses and stores were all closed (excepting a few liquor shops, which had their shutters up, but kept the back door open,) no retreat was, therefore, open for him, and the poor fellow would be beaten almost to death, when the mob becoming satiated and disgusted with their foul work, he would be left sweltering in blood, unable to help himself.

Elated with success, the mob, which by this time had been largely reinforced, next formed themselves into marauding parties, and paraded through the neighboring streets, looking more like so many infuriated demons, the men being more or less intoxicated, dirty and half clothed. Some shouted, "Now for the Fifth-avenue Hotel—there's where the Union Leaguers meet!" Others clamored among themselves for the muskets which they had taken from the soldiers. The streets were thronged with women and children, many of whom instigated the men to further work of blood, while the injured men left the crowd, and found seats up the street corners, at one of which the reporter heard the following conversation between an intoxicated youth, who was badly wounded in the head, and an elderly excited woman, probably his mother:

Youth—"An' bedad, if it hadn't been for this lick, which the son of a —— guv me, I'd a belabored him 'afor this. And bedad I wud."

Woman—"Musshanuilusha, ye betters mind yer own biseniss."

Youth—"No, if SAM. GARRIGAN [or Galligan—REP.] had a' dun the business browner, it wud be all right."

From this it may be inferred that the Sam. Garrigan, or Galligan, mentioned in the conversation above, is the ringleader, of which there can be little doubt, as the reporter frequently heard Garrigan's or Galligan's name cheered and called the "Bully boy." Garrigan or Galligan, we believe, is a well-known wire-puller of the Ward, and from conversations between the men, we gleaned the following, which may be taken for what it is worth: 1. That Garrigan or Galligan is the ringleader. 2. That the mob, numbering about 500 men, assembled this morning at Central Park, armed and equipped, *i. e.*, with clubs and sticks, and from there proceeded to the [illegible] office, where they commenced [illegible]

considerably augmented, for, as yet, the workmen had not all gone to their day's work. As soon as the Provost-Marshal's Office had been gutted of its contents, and the adjoining building—a wheelwright's shop, in which there was much combustible material—had been fired, the telegraph wires were cut. Parties and bands of men and boys then visited the various workshops in the vicinity, and compelled the men to leave their work and join, threatening them with death unless they complied with their demands. It is said word was now sent by the rioters to Brooklyn, Jersey City and Albany of the outbreak, and a message, it is rumored, was received from the 'longshoremen of this City, stating that they would be up in the evening, armed to the teeth, to assist them.

By this time the Fire Department of the District arrived on the ground, and were preparing to work on the fire; but were prevented from doing so by the mob, who threatened them with instant death if their orders were disobeyed. The cars were stopped from running either way; the horses in several instances were killed, and the cars broken to pieces; the drivers were threatened with violence if they attempted to move on, as, by this means the City authorities would hear of the outbreak.

The fire, which had now consumed the wheelwright's shop, had extended to the Provost-Marshal's office, which was soon enveloped in flames, from which issued a large and dark volume of smoke.

The rioters meantime danced with fiendish delight before the burning building, while the small boys and "Rocks" and "Softs" sent showers of stones against the office, smashing in the doors and windows, the fire seeming to do the work too tardily to suit them. The murky atmosphere and the heavy black clouds which lined the horizon, formed a strange, weird spectacle, which was made the more complete by the demoniac yells of the mob.

It now became evident to the firemen that if the flames were not subdued the whole block would be consumed; and, accordingly, several attempts to operate on the fire were made, but without success, as their apparatus was seized by the mob, and the firemen themselves were severely beaten. At this stage of the proceedings, Chief-Engineer DECKER, or some other high official of the Fire Department, appeared amongst the crowd, and after much persuasion and talking, finally succeeded in quieting the rioters. The military, however, soon appeared on the ground, which aroused the ire of the mob, who renewed their violence with increased numbers.

To resume the thread of our report, the military being immediately routed, they fled to the side streets, where, as we have shown, they were shamefully maltreated. After this the mob concentrated and returned to the fire, where they found their friends awaiting them, with nourishment in the shape of liquors, which, as may be supposed, only added fuel to the fire already kindled: whisky soon accomplished its mission; the men became quarrelsome and squabbled amongst themselves. Some boasted of what they had done, one man boasting that he had nearly killed two soldiers, and wounded many more. Another, an obese, small, villainous-looking Irishman, who carried the butt of a bayonet, boasted that he had "done for" a nigger. Others, suffering from the wounds they had received, consoled themselves by exclaiming: "Never mind, SEYMOUR and WOOD are around, and will help us!" and "Old ABE will pay $300 to keep quiet," and the like. All vehemently protested against the "$300 clause," and were willing to be drafted, if the rich man would be made to shoulder the musket the same as they. Those who had done the most in routing the military, such as chasing a soldier until he fell from sheer exhaustion, and then beating him till he was near dead, were cheered and petted by their friends, who, both men and women, gathered around them by dozens.

During the row a man, said to be an officer or policeman in undress uniform, shot a horse purposely, it is stated, because had the animal moved, it would be at the risk of the life of those standing around him; the owner (the horse was attached to a dray) endeavored to clutch the man, who dodged him and run up a flight of stairs in a house near by, with the probable intention of getting on to the roof to escape the mob, who were so infuriated at the deed, which they, of course, interpreted to be a retaliatory act on his part; he was pursued and dragged down stairs with his skull broken, when he was pitched to the mob, who, it is said, literally tore him to pieces. At this point a policeman who had become separated from his companions, who were stationed on a corner near by, in attempting to rescue the wounded man, found himself surrounded by the rioters, who commenced to pound and beat him shamefully; he drew his revolver and shot one man. The influence of this was electric; they rushed upon the unfortunate policeman, whom they deprived of his arms, struck him with their clubs and pelted him with stones. His companions, observing this, quickly formed in a line, but their attempts to make a stand were abortive; overpowered by superior numbers, they were utterly routed, several of their number being badly injured. The rest fled through the side streets, where they were chased by the infuriated mob; some jumped fences and hid in the corners of uncultivated lots, where they were found and maltreated shamefully. Two cases of the most painful description came under the reporter's observation: A policeman, having eluded their vigilance for several blocks, unable to run away further, threw himself down and begged for mercy. But his entreaties were unheeded; he was pelted with stones and beaten with clubs until his features could not be distinguished for the blood; even then their persecutions were continued, until, abandoning himself to his fate, the policeman feigned death; then, through the exertions of a few of the more humane of the rioters, he was left alone; friends soon rushed to his aid, and conveyed him to the Station-house. Another was beaten until his eyes were so clotted with blood that he could not see.

BURNING OF THE ORPHAN ASYLUM FOR COLORED CHILDREN.

The Orphan Asylum for Colored Children was visited by the mob about 4 o'clock. This Institution is situated on Fifth-avenue, and the building, with the grounds and gardens adjoining, extended from Forty-third to Forty-fourth-street. Hundreds, and perhaps thousands of the rioters, the majority of whom were women and children, entered the premises, and in the most excited and violent manner they ransacked and plundered the building from cellar to garret. The building was located in the most pleasant and healthy portion of the City. It was purely a charitable institution. In it there are on an average 600 or 800 homeless colored orphans. The building was a large four-story one, with two wings of three stories each.

When it became evident that the crowd designed to destroy it, a flag of truce appeared on the walk opposite, and the principals of the establishment made an appeal to the excited populace, but in vain.

Here it was that Chief-Engineer DECKER showed himself one of the bravest among the brave. After the entire building had been ransacked, and every article deemed worth carrying away had been taken—and this included even the little garments for the orphans, which were contributed by the benevolent ladies of this City—the premises were fired on the first floor. Mr. DECKER did all he could to prevent the flames from being kindled, but when he was overpowered by superior numbers, with his own hands he scattered the brands and effectually extinguished the flames. A second attempt was made, and this time in three different parts of the house. Again he succeeded, with the aid of half a dozen of his men, in defeating the incendiaries. The mob became highly exasperated at his conduct, and threatened to take his life if he repeated the act. On the front steps of the building he stood up amid an infuriated and half-drunken mob of two thousand, and begged of them to do nothing so disgraceful to humanity as to burn a benevolent institution, which had for its object nothing but good. He said it would be a lasting disgrace to them and to the City of New-York.

These remarks seemed to have no good effect upon them, and meantime the premises were again fired—this time in all parts of the house. Mr. DECKER, with his few brave men again extinguished the flames. This last act brought down upon him the vengeance of all who were bent on the destruction of the asylum, and but for the fact, that some firemen surrounded him, and boldly said that Mr. DECKER could not be taken except over their bodies, he would have been dispatched on the spot. The institution was destined to be burned, and after an hour and a half of labor on the part of the mob, it was in flames in all parts. Three or four persons were horribly bruised by the falling walls, but the names we could not ascertain. There is now scarcely one brick left upon another of the Orphan Asylum.

ATTACK ON THE TRIBUNE OFFICE.

During the greater part of the day, a crowd, composed principally of overgrown boys, amused themselves by going around to the various newspaper offices down town, cheering the bulletins which announced the progress of the riot in the upper part of the City, groaning the editors of such journals as were deemed obnoxious by the mob, and chasing and beating every person of color who chanced to make his appearance. The *Tribune*, as a matter of course, came in for the principal share of the groans, and it is but fair to add, that the *Daily News* monopolized the cheers. Various hints were given out by the rioters that the *Tribune* would be attacked in the evening, but they were not credited, or if they were, no preparations appear to have been made to repel it. About 7 o'clock, however, the crowd of boys began to be swelled by a different class of roughs, who appeared on the ground with clubs in their hands, and from their appearance, had evidently been engaged in the more bloody work up town. They immediately gathered around the *Tribune* office and commenced a series of the most unearthly groans and demoniac yells. In a few moments one of the more forward among them commenced an attack upon the door of the publication office, which was locked, but which soon gave way to the pressure of the mob, who, amid the crashing of broken doors and windows, rushed in [illegible]. In a moment more files of the *Tribune* were thrown out to the crowd and torn and scattered to the winds. In less than five minutes the office was completely gutted, and the desks and counters upset and broken. At length a platoon of the First Ward Police came rushing up Nassau-street, and on seeing them the mob, which numbered not less than four hundred men and boys, ran like so many sheep, leaving Printing-house-square, in less than three minutes, almost as clear of people as it is of a Sunday morning. It was a striking illustration of the cowardice of a mob when confronted by a handful of determined officers of the law. Several shots were fired by the policemen at ringleaders of the mob—but, so far as is known, none of them took effect. One of the policemen was also shot at by a rioter, the ball taking effect in the back. The wound is serious, but it is thought not dangerous. Before leaving the office, the rioters set fire to the building, but it was extinguished by a policeman before much damage was done.

OUTRAGES UPON COLORED PERSONS.

Among the most cowardly features of the riot, and one which indicated its political *animus* and the cunningly-devised cue that had been given to the rioters by the instigators of the outbreak, was the causeless and inhuman treatment of the negroes of the City. It seemed to be an understood thing throughout the City that the negroes should be attacked wherever found, whether then offered any provocation or not. As soon as one of these unfortunate people was spied, whether on a cart, a railroad car, or in the street, he was immediately set upon by a crowd of men and boys, and unless some man of pluck came to his rescue, or he was fortunate enough to escape into a building he was inhumanly beaten and perhaps killed. There were probably not less than a dozen negroes beaten to death in different parts of the City during the day. Among the most diabolical of these outrages that have come to our knowledge is that of a negro cartman living in Carmine-street. About 8 o'clock in the evening as he was coming out of the stable, after having put up his horses, he was attacked by a crowd of about 400 men and boys, who beat him with clubs and paving-stones till he was lifeless, and then hung him to a tree opposite the burying-ground. Not being yet satisfied with their devilish work, they set fire to his clothes and danced and yelled and swore their horrid oaths around his burning corpse. The charred body of the poor victim was still still hanging upon the tree at a late hour last evening.

Early in the afternoon the proprietors of such saloons and other places of business as had negroes in their employ, were obliged to close up for fear that the rioters would destroy their premises. In most of them the negroes were compelled to remain over night, not daring to go home lest they be mobbed on the way.

COURAGEOUS ACTION OF THE POLICE.

At about five o'clock a large body of rioters, differently estimated from one hundred to three hundred,—the latter much the nearer figure—marched down Broadway with a banner, inscribed "No draft" with the American flag, and with every conceivable diabolical weapon. They amused themselves *en route* by cheering and groaning at will, and occasionally killing or maiming every "nigger" they met. When below Fourteenth-street they avowed their determination of entering the La Farge House and seizing every colored servant there. Fortunately they were met at Amity-street—unexpectedly to them—by a body of Police some two hundred strong, under Inspector CARPENTER and Sergeant COPELAND. The Police instantly formed company front, and, with Inspector CARPENTER far in advance, at once charged on the "double quick." The fight for a few moments was savage and terrific. Men fell by the dozen under the sturdy blows of the Police, who had orders to "make no prisoners," and in five minutes naught was left of the lawless horde but the bodies of those ruffians who were knocked senseless lying on the ground. Too much credit cannot be awarded to the Police for their behavior on this occasion. They did not know whether one hundred or five thousand of the lawless were their adversaries, nor did they wait to ascertain. On they charged, and in five minutes were masters of the situation. Capt. CARPENTER was far ahead of his men, with reckless courage, rushing into the midst of the mob, and handling his club against fearful odds. It is a wonder he was not killed. This charge, and its success, must have had a salutary effect, being the first regular fight with the organized mob, and showing them that the Police are their superiors.

The Police, at the time they met the mob, were on their way to Mayor OPDYKE's house, in Fifth-avenue, which it was rumored was to be attacked. None of the Police were seriously injured in the encounter, while at least two of the rioters were killed, and ten or fifteen more were so badly used up that they will not be likely to take a hand in another riot at present.

THE ATTACK ON THE MAYOR'S RESIDENCE.

A short time previous to the fight above described, the mob had paid a visit to the residence of Mayor OPDYKE, No. 79 Fifth-avenue. Their number was estimated at about 500. As the police had not yet arrived upon the ground, it seemed a foregone conclusion that the Mayor's house would share the fate of others, and be pillaged and burned by the mob. While the rioters were about preparing for the attack, Judge BARNARD made his appearance, and by a well-timed speech persuaded them to desist from their purpose. While the Judge was addressing them, the ardor of the more violent roughs had time to cool, and on the conclusion of his remarks, they took up their line of march in another direction.

MEETING OF EX-OFFICERS AT THE ARMORY OF THE SEVENTH REGIMENT.

In accordance with the call of Gen. SANDFORD, the ex-officers now in the City, to the number of some two hundred or more, met at the armory of the Seventh regiment last evening, for the purpose of taking some action with reference to make their services of avail in the present emergency. In the absence of Gen. SANDFORD the meeting was organized by appointing Col. JULIUS W. ADAMS, late of the First Long Island volunteers, Chairman, and Capt. W. C. CHURCH, late of Major-General CASEY's staff, Secretary. On motion of Col. BAIRD, the officers present, willing to render service, were requested to record their names with the Secretary. It was also voted that the field officers present be appointed a Committee to devise a plan of operations. Gen. SANDFORD arriving in the meantime, the meeting resolved itself into a crowd, who gathered about him while he explained what action had been already taken to suppress disturbance, and what further measures were proposed to that end. He advised the officers representing different regiments to form a *nuclei* for as complete a reorganization of their several regiments as the exigency would permit. Officers of volunteer regiments were requested to enroll themselves under Col. J. M. DAVIES, late of the Harris Light cavalry, who would proceed immediately to perfect a regimental organization. All ex-officers of volunteer regiments now in the City are accordingly requested to report to Col. DAVIES, at the Armory of the Seventh regiment, at 8 o'clock this morning. They will come prepared to report the number of men they can procure to assist in quelling the riot. Discharged soldiers, citizens or others, organized or unorganized, willing to render service, are requested to report at the same time and place. They will be furnished with arms and equipments, and at once set to work.

CHARACTER OF THE MOB.

In the early part of the day yesterday, there were a number of respectable workmen and persons engaged in different occupations in the City, who were momentarily seduced from their labors and their work-shops, and went with the crowds in the street. But they at once saw the horrible character of the mob and the atrocious work they had on hand; they heard their threats and saw their shocking brutalities, and were only too glad to get out from among them. At last the mob or mobs were composed of only the vilest men in the City, and there was not a crime conceivable, from firing houses to hanging negroes, of which they were not capable. The reign of ruffianism was short, but it at last became a reign of the true article.

ROVING RIOTERS.

Some of the scenes in the side streets of the City, during the day were painful in the extreme, and humiliating to human nature. In the streets running north from Canal-street, where many colored people reside, mobs of foul-looking boys and men scoured up and down in the afternoon and evening, in pursuit of negroes, who were assailed wherever found; and our reporter observed in one gang, several women armed with sticks, rushing to and fro with the vile and cowardly crowd; but it is only justice to say that the voluble tongues of these women gave vent to their thoughts with an accentuation which was never acquired on this side of the Atlantic ocean. It was almost impossible to look down any street in that part of the City, or any other, without seeing a crowd roving hither and thither, or standing still in heated conversation. They seemed to have no special object in view. They appeared to have had no evil-defined atrocity to perpetrate. They were rather on the look out for something upon which to wreak their bad passions.

APPREHENDED ATTACK ON THE POLICE HEADQUARTERS.

At 1½ o'clock this morning, Inspector CARPENTER, at the head of 300 Policemen, marched from the Police headquarters to take down the body of the negro who was hung to a tree in Clarkson-street. They had gone but a short distance before they were recalled to repel an apprehended attack on the headquarters. No attack had been made when our paper went to press. The headquarters were guarded by 500 Policemen and 58 soldiers from the regular army, brought from Forts Hamilton and Lafayette.

THE HOUSES BURNED IN LEXINGTON-AVENUE.

Two fine brown-stone private residences in Lexington-avenue, between Forty-third and Forty-fourth streets, were entirely destroyed. One of them was occupied by a mechanic named WM. TURNER; the other one was believed to be the dwelling of a Deputy Provost-Marshal, who was connected with the enrolling and drafting office in Broadway, between Twenty-eighth and Twenty-ninth streets.

DESTRUCTION OF A BLOCK ON BROADWAY.

The drafting office for the Eighth Congressional District is located in Broadway, near Twenty-eighth-street. Here, under the direction of Provost-Marshal MANIERRE, the drafting was opened at 9 o'clock, and conducted without interruption until 12, when the announcement was made that further proceedings would be suspended until to-day. The mob soon afterward paid a visit to this place, sacked it, and then set it on fire. It was totally consumed, as well as the remainder of the block.

BULL'S HEAD HOTEL.

This famous hotel, for many years past kept by Mr. ALLERTON, and situated on Forty-fourth-street, between Lexington and Fifth avenues, shared the fate of so many other fine buildings in that part of the City. It was entirely destroyed, together with several barns, sheds and other out-houses on the premises. We do not understand that the cause of its destruction was owing to the fact that Mr. ALLERTON, or any one other person immediately interested in the establishment, was specially odious to the incendiaries. The mob entered the hotel in large numbers and demanded liquor. They took all there was in the house, and many of them drank to excess; they also took all the cigars they could find. Many of them then ransacked the house and took everything they could lay their hands upon. In a short time flames were discovered bursting from the second story windows, and before a single fireman was on hand the building was past all hope of being saved.

A STATION-HOUSE AND THE RESIDENCE OF THE CITY POSTMASTER BURNED.

About 9 o'clock, the rioters in strong force assembled at the Twenty-third Precinct Station-house, near Yorkville, and set fire to the building before their intentions could be frustrated. The books and records of the Precinct were saved by one of the Sergeants. The house of Mr. ABRAM WAKEMAN, Postmaster of the City, was also visited by the mob, and totally destroyed by fire.

THIEVES AND PICKPOCKETS.

This industrious class of our population availed themselves of the confusion to ply their arts, and in every instance with great success. Indeed the chief notice of a large portion of the rioters in joining the mob seemed to be the opportunity that would be offered them for promiscuous pillage and plunder. Many instances were reported of men being robbed of watches, pocket-books, breast-pins, &c., and all the houses that were burned were first plundered of their valuables by the mob.

THE POLICE.

The events of the day resulted in a great many casualties—a few fatal and many severe—among the Police. We have been able only to obtain a few names.

Officer SWAINSEE, Twenty-ninth Precinct, struck in the head and badly cut; HOLMES, Twenty-ninth, cut in the head severely; MORRISON, Twenty-ninth, dangerously wounded; CHARLES B. LAW, Eighth, seriously; NOLAN MCCARTY, Twenty-ninth, not expected to live; NOLEN WALSH, Eighth, badly cut; SUTHERLAND, Fifteenth, seriously cut and bruised.

PREPARATIONS FOR TO-DAY.

At 2 o'clock this morning the City was apparently quiet. A heavy rain fell about midnight which helped greatly to disperse the rioters. The preparations to meet the outbreak to-day, if it is renewed, we are assured are such as will prevent the recurrence of such scenes as were enacted yesterday. The rioters had it pretty much their own way yesterday, but if they resume their demonstrations to-day a good share of them will come to a bloody and well-deserved end of their career.

WHAT WAS DONE IN BROOKLYN—THE POLICE—THE NAVY-YARD—THE FIRE DEPARTMENT—THE PROVOST-MARSHAL'S OFFICE IN THE THIRD DISTRICT, ETC., ETC.

The riot in New-York has created an intense excitement in this city, and large numbers of persons crossed the river to see what was going on.

Capt. S. B. GREGORY, Provost-Marshal of the Third Congressional District, on hearing of the proceedings in New-York, packed up all his papers and transported them to a place of safety. There is nothing now in the building of the least importance to any one.

The draft, which was fixed for Wednesday morning, has been suspended for the present. Further notice will be given when the drawing will take place.

The number of persons enrolled in the different Wards comprising the District, and the number to be drafted, is as follows, all of the first class:

	No. Enrolled.	No. to be Drafted.
First Ward	707	180
Second Ward	944	257
Third Ward	1,057	340
Fourth Ward	1,367	369
Fifth Ward	1,960	551
Seventh Ward	1,374	373
Eleventh Ward	3,378	1,050
Thirteenth Ward	1,869	528
Fifteenth Ward	866	235
Nineteenth Ward	686	169

Of the second class about 11,000 persons are enrolled, making in all of both classes nearly 30,000.

Chief Engineer CUNNINGHAM, in view of the present exigency, ordered last night that in case of fire, the bells shall ring three rounds, designating the district, and then the general alarm. This is for the purpose of assembling all the firemen, so as to extinguish any fire that may occur. These orders will be in force until further directions.

The colored people are having a hard time of it. They are attacked everywhere and beaten. They crowded about the police stations last night, asking for protection, being prevented from going to their homes, or even walking the streets.

The police to the number of 100 went to New-York, in charge of Inspector FOLKES.

There was great commotion in the Navy-yard. The walls were manned and mounted with guns. Thirteen 18-pounders are mounted on the Flushing-avenue side, so as to sweep everything. Two 32-pounders command the main entrance, and all the vessels have been hauled into the stream, the guns shotted, and everything ready for any emergency.

Several companies of Marines, with 60 rounds of cartridges, and 12 boat-howitzers, rifled cannon, with ammunition-boxes, loaded with percussion shells, shrapnell, canister, and grapeshot, were sent to New-York toward evening. The Marines were accompanied by 300 sailors, armed with cutlasses and revolvers.

Some guns were taken from the State arsenal in Portland-avenue on Sunday night, which gave rise to the rumor that it had been attacked. The facts are that two companies of artillery, belonging to the Seventieth regiment militia have been ordered to Fort Hamilton, and the guns were taken for their use. They were placed on vessels at the foot of Little-street and transported to the fort. There are no arms in the building at present.

A Call to the Veteran Volunteers!

The veterans who have recently returned from the field of battle have again an opportunity of serving, not only their country, but the great emporium of New-York from the threatened dangers of a ruthless mob.

The Commanding-General of the Eastern Department trusts that those who have exhibited so much bravery in the field of battle, will not hesitate to come forward at this time, to tender their services to the Mayor, to stay the ravages of the City by men who have lost all sense of obligations to their country, as well as to the City of New-York.

JOHN E. WOOL, Major-General.

P. S.—These men are requested to report to Maj.-Gen. SANFORD, corner Elm and White streets, on Tuesday, July 14, at 10 A. M.

CALLS FOR MILITIA TO MEET THIS MORNING.

The following calls were issued last evening:

NATIONAL ZOUAVES—ATTENTION!—The officers and members of the Tenth regiment New-York volunteers, who are willing to assist in the enforcement of the laws, are requested to meet at No. 590 Broadway, Armory of Thirty-seventh New-York State Guards, as early this day as possible, in full uniform.

JOHN E. BENDIX, Colonel.

HEADQUARTERS EIGHTH REGIMENT N. [illegible] The members, ex-officers and members [illegible] ment in the City, including troops are requested to meet at the Armory to-morrow, July 14, at 8 o'clock A. M. By order of Maj. LEANDER BUCK.

D. B. KEELER, Jr., Adjutant.

NINTH REGIMENT N. Y. N. G.—A meeting of the members and ex-members of this regiment will be held at the Mercer House, corner of Broome and Mercer streets, at 9 o'clock this morning, for the purpose of assisting in maintaining the State and City authorities in suppressing the riot. The call is signed by Lieut.-Col. ROTHERFORD, Maj. DIGGS, Capt. PICKETT, Capt. LANSING and Lieut. STRONG.

The following order was issued last evening by Gen. BROWN, commanding United States troops in this City:

HEADQUARTERS NEW-YORK, July 13, 1863.

ORDERS No. 1.—In obedience to the orders of the Major-General Commanding the Eastern Department, the undersigned assumes command of the United States troops in this City.

Lieut.-Col. FROTHINGHAM and Capt. REWOLLS are of the Staff of the undersigned, and will be obeyed accordingly.

HARVEY BROWN, Brig.-Gen. Commanding.

TWENTY-SECOND REGIMENT N. G. S. N. Y.—All members of the Twenty-second regiment are requested to meet at the Regiment Armory, this morning, at 8 o'clock.

BOARD OF ALDERMEN.

The Conscription Act and the Riot—Alderman Farley's Opinion of both—Alderman Hall's Plan to Relieve Poor Conscripts.

The Board of Aldermen met by special call at 1½ o'clock yesterday afternoon, "to take action in such business as might come before them." The call was signed at about 9 o'clock in the morning, before the riot up town had begun, and the real object of the meeting was to authorize the Corporation Counsel to associate such eminent counsel with him as he might choose, and take steps to test the constitutionality of the National Enrollment Act, under which the draft is being made. Alderman FARLEY was the prime mover in the matter. The whole plan failed, however, for want of a quorum. A quorum failed to appear because of the excited state of feeling in the community, consequent upon the riot up town. It was at first designed to carry out Alderman FARLEY's idea, but the excitement that soon became alarming in the streets, led several of the Democratic members to the conclusion that it would be impolitic to take any action on the subject of the draft till quiet should be restored. Hence, when the Board met, only five members answered to their names—Messrs. HENRY, REED, JEREMIAH, HARDY and FARLEY.

Alderman JEREMIAH was called to the Chair, to fill the place of President WALSH. The roll being called, and a quorum not appearing, the Chair asked the pleasure of the Board. Alderman FARLEY arose and said:

ALDERMAN FARLEY'S SPEECH.

Alderman FARLEY—Mr. President, I much regret that there is not a quorum present. I had hoped that the Board would be able to take some action to-day in regard to the General Government act for making a draft. In my district, I understand, the officers engaged in making the draft have been driven from their duty, and a serious riot is in progress. I regret that a disturbance of the kind should be initiated in the City in my district, because the people there will be wrongly charged with the responsibility of it. But the fault is not theirs, for they are as orderly and law-abiding as any community in the whole country. The persons creating the riot, and who are responsible for its consequences, came from New-Jersey. They crossed the river this morning from Weehawken and Guttenberg in crowds and proceeded to the place in the Ninth Congressional District, where the draft was in progress. They marched along the streets in a body, and on their way they forced workmen wherever they could from their labors to join them in resistance to the draft. You can, therefore, understand, Mr. President, that the fault of opposition to the draft, originating in my district, was wholly owing to the fact that the enforcement of the Conscription act was begun there. To this fact alone may be attributed the unfortunate circumstance of the first open opposition to the law being shown in my district. The persons who incited the trouble no doubt had been organized for the occasion, and a riot would have been set on foot by them in any other locality in the city, had the enforcement of the draft been first attempted elsewhere than in the district I have the honor to represent in this Board. I must repeat my regret at the absence of a quorum of this Board, for I had hoped that every member would rise in his seat and talk peace. The people are excited, and it is necessary that their excitement should be calmed down to a degree of respect for enacted laws. Then let them resort to the Courts to decide their grievances. The impression is strong that the Drafting act is unconstitutional, and until the question of its legality is decided by the proper judicial tribunals, they will regard any attempted enforcement of it as harsh and arbitrary. We should, therefore, talk and counsel peace, and quiet and aid the people to ascertain whether the law, which is so generally regarded as offensive and undemocratic, is in legal harmony with the fundamental law of our organization as a nation and Government. I suppose the question could be reached by any conscript getting out a writ of *habeas corpus*. I have a paper in my hand proposing a method whereby we should speedily test the question of the legality of the law. I had designed to offer it at this meeting, but it is of no use now. I hope, however, that every member of this Board will preach up peace. Let it be understood that the citizens of New-York are for law and order, and in favor of a just test of every measure that is obnoxious to them. The event of the riot to-day is unfortunate, because it will affect the reputation of the city, and possibly be a pretext for a declaration of martial law here. It affords the excuse probably desired by the Administration, for supplanting the civil by the military law in this Democratic City. The enactments of Congress and the acts of the Administration are already sufficiently burdensome to us, without recourse to such a sweeping assumption of authority as that. But we cannot say to what extent our rights may be interfered with. Perhaps those in a position to seize upon such an authority would be only too glad to have some sort of pretended excuse for prohibiting us from meeting here.

Adjourned.

No other remarks were made, and the President *pro tem.* declared the Board adjourned for want of a quorum, till the first Monday in August.

The paper to which Alderman FARLEY referred contained the following preamble and resolutions.

Whereas, It is apparent to all who are in any way conversant with the feelings and opinions of the population of this City, that a deep-seated and irradicable opposition pervades all classes against the provisions of the act of the late Congress of the United States, known as the "Conscription act;" and

Whereas, It is equally apparent that such opposition is taking form and shape, and will manifest itself at an early day in open armed resistance to the attempt of the authorities of the General Government to force citizens of this State, against their convictions and against their will, out of the limits or jurisdiction of their State; and

Whereas, The mutterings of the coming storm imperatively demand that the authorities of this City should take some steps to allay the excitement now daily and hourly increasing, and by mild and salutary measures to assist in abating the popular indignation against the manifest injustice about to be inflicted upon our citizens, consequent upon an enforcement of the provisions of the aforesaid act of Congress: be it therefore

Resolved, That the Counsel to the Corporation be and he is hereby authorized and directed immediately to take the necessary legal measures to test the legality of the act of the late Congress of the United States, known as the "Conscription Act," with reference to its application to this State.

Had it not been understood beforehand that there would in all probability be no quorum, Alderman HALL would have been on hand to offer the following as a substitute for Alderman FARLEY's paper:

Whereas, It is apparent that the three hundred-dollar clause in the National Enrollment act of the late Congress is calculated to inflict great privations upon the poorer classes of our citizens: therefore, be it

Resolved, That the Committee on National Affairs be and they are hereby instructed to report to this Board a plan whereby an appropriation can be made to pay the commutation of such of our poorest citizens as are likely to be most sorely affected by the enforcement of a conscription.

This plan was submitted by Alderman HALL to several of the Democratic members, and all who were consulted about it unhesitatingly declared themselves favorable to it.

It is not improbable that the Board will hold a meeting at an early day to consider it.

The Draft in the Eighth Congressional District, New-York City.

In the Eighth Congressional District, comprising the Eighteenth, Twentieth and Twenty-first Wards, the draft was yesterday morning commenced, under the direction of Hon. [illegible] MANIERRE, Assistant Provost-Marshal, at the headquarters, No. 1,190 Broadway. This is about the largest Congressional District in the City, and the number of names to be drawn will exceed 3,000.

The building was filled to its utmost capacity, except the space occupied by the Commissioners, and the vicinity of the table occupied by the reporters, which were [illegible] police force. A powerful force [illegible] the outside of the building [illegible] off with the [illegible]

The New-York Times.

VOL. XII—NO. 3684. NEW-YORK, WEDNESDAY JULY, 15, 1863. PRICE THREE CENTS.

THE REIGN OF THE RABBLE.

Continuation of the Riot—The Mob Increased in Numbers.

DEMONSTRATIONS IN THE UPPER WARDS

Encounters Between the Mob, the Metropolitans and the Military.

Large Numbers of the Rioters Killed.

COLONEL O'BRIEN MURDERED AND HUNG.

Streets Barricaded, Buildings Burned, Stores Sacked, and Private Dwellings Plundered.

Gov. Seymour in the City—He Addresses the Mob and Issues a Proclamation.

Increased Preparations on the Part of the Authorities.

The Mercantile Community Aroused—Citizens Volunteering en Masse.

REPORTED SUSPENSION OF THE DRAFT.

The reign of the mob which was inaugurated on Monday morning has not yet ceased, although to-day will probably witness the end of its infamous usurpation. All Monday night the rioters, unchecked, prosecuted their depredations, and yesterday morning found the lawless spirit not a whit abated. On the contrary, the malignant originators of the disturbance grew bolder at the impunity with which they were necessarily permitted to indulge in their first day's career, and at one time more serious consequences than any which have yet occurred were threatened. Happily, however, the military and police authorities early in the day recovered from the partial paralysis into which the sudden demonstrations of the mob had thrown them, and in sufficient force were able to contend with the truly formidable organization of lawless men. A few wholesome but severe lessons were administered to the rioters during the day wherever they showed themselves most turbulent, and toward evening there seemed to be unmistakable indications that the supremacy of law would soon be acknowledged even by the most rabid of the offenders. Perhaps, however, the mere fact that a score or more of the rioters were killed in the various conflicts with the military and the police was not solely the cause of this abatement of the spirit of violence. The proclamation of Gov. HORATIO SEYMOUR, and the announcement, made early in the afternoon, that President LINCOLN had ordered the draft in this City to be suspended, may also have had something to do with restoring the malcontents to reason. At any rate, after nightfall the streets were comparatively quiet.

There is no question that the rioting yesterday was engaged in by vastly larger numbers than on Monday, and the spectators of the disorderly scenes were increased also by many thousands. This may be accounted for by the fact that all the large manufacturing establishments were closed, labor on the docks and at the ship-yards was suspended, and every branch of business was arrested, leaving thousands of persons at liberty to participate in the excesses, either passively as spectators, or in an active manner.

In the movements of the mob yesterday, moreover, there was no mistaking the fact that pillage was the prime incentive of the majority. "Resistance to the draft" was the flimsiest of veils to cover the wholesale plundering which characterized the operations of the day.

Our reporters record their observations and the incidents they have been able to collect, as follows:

The Riot in Second-avenue.

EIGHTEEN PERSONS REPORTED KILLED, SEVERAL FATALLY INJURED.

Between 12 and 1 o'clock yesterday, the rioters commenced their attack upon the Union Steam Works, situated on the corner of Twenty-second-street and Second-avenue. The guns taken from the armory on Monday were stored in this building, and the most active efforts were made by the insurgents to secure them.

The rioters turned out in large force, numbering from 4,000 to 5,000 people—including children. The shops and stores for half a mile around were closed, and the streets were filled with crowds of excited men, women and children.

At 2 P. M. three hundred Policemen, under the command of one of the Inspectors, arrived upon the ground. The rioters had in the meantime taken possession of the building, and, when the officials made their appearance, they attempted to escape by the rear windows; but too late the escape the notice of the Police. Finding themselves caught in a tight place, they made an attack on the Police. This assault the Officers met by a volley from their revolvers, and five of the mob were shot.

About twenty rioters remained in the building; there was but one way for them to make their exit. The police filled the door, and each had, in addition to his usual weapons, a loaded revolver. The mob became desperate and made a deadly assault upon the police; they in turn used their weapons so effectually that fourteen of the mob were almost instantly killed. A scene, which defies all powers of description then followed. Men, women and children rushed through the streets in the most frantic state of mind, and as the dead and wounded were borne from the place, the wild howlings of the bereaved, were truly sad to hear.

Four persons were killed and quite a number were injured by jumping from the second story windows of the building.

When the rioters were dispersed, the Police took possession of the Union Steam Works building, and at a late hour last night they still held the place. A collision between the authorities and the mob is liable to take place at any moment. The Police and military are fully prepared to meet them.

THE RIOTERS IN THE SECOND-AVENUE.

At about 8½ o'clock yesterday morning a telegraphic dispatch was received that a large crowd of rioters were gathering all along the Second-avenue, in the neighborhood of Thirty-fourth-street, threatening all the houses along that thoroughfare. A strong force of police, about 200, were immediately detailed under Inspector CARPENTER to break up the crowd. The rioters had gathered in formidable numbers, and for a time committed no overt act. It was then ascertained that Col. H. F. O'BRIEN, of the Eleventh New-York Volunteers, who lives in the immediate neighborhood, had tendered his services, and those of his command, for the purpose of suppressing the riot. The mob becoming incensed, proceeded to the residence of the Colonel and warning his family to leave, completely gutted the entire house. They were about to set it on fire, but finding that the house was not his property, they desisted. The police, under Inspector CARPENTER and Capt. COPEL then marched from the Central office, preceded by the Broadway Squad, to the Bowery, where they took possession of a sufficient number of the Third-avenue cars, and proceeded up the avenue. On arriving at Thirty-second-street, the railroad track was found obstructed, and the police then formed in a solid column and marched down to the Second-avenue. They were met by the assembled mob with silence. When the whole force had got in the block between Thirty-fourth and Thirty-fifth streets, they were closed in upon by the mob and assailed by a thick shower of bricks and stones, which rained from the houses and windows in the neighborhood. For some moments the men wavered and the peril was imminent, when the reassuring voices of the officers in command recalled them, who then returned the shower of stones with their revolvers. The order was then given to charge, and a most furious onset was made on the rioters, driving them into the houses, the officers chasing them all over the buildings and driving them into the street, where they were scattered by a most vigorous application of clubs. All the side streets were then cleared, and the police marched over the battle-ground victorious. The police then marched through the infected district, meeting nothing but lowering looks, the mob being thoroughly beaten. While marching through the Third-avenue, they met a detachment of the Eleventh regiment N. Y. S. V., headed by Col. O'BRIEN, and a couple of field-pieces, under command of Lieut. EAGLESON, coming down the avenue on a trot. They formed a junction with the police force, and then countermarched through the Second-avenue.

THE DEATH OF COL. O'BRIEN.

After the detachment of military under Col. O'BRIEN had succeeded in dispersing the mob, they fell back at some distance from the Colonel, who went forward near the crowd, having his sword and a revolver in his hands, when he was immediately set upon, surrounded, and so dreadfully maltreated that he expired in a short time after. His body lay dead on the sidewalk for some time, and some of the more fiendish in the crowd amused themselves by firing several pistol-shots at his head, after which the body was strung up to the nearest lamp-post, where it remained for some time. It was afterward taken down and thrown again in the street, and had not been moved up to 8 o'clock last night. The reasons given by some of the rioters for such treatment were that the military had shot a mother and her child.

Doings of Gov. Seymour.

Gov. SEYMOUR arrived in this City yesterday morning, and at 12½ o'clock addressed a large crowd of men and boys, numbering 800 or over, from the steps of the City Hall. On taking the stand he was greeted with vehement and prolonged cheers. He said he had come from his quiet home to this scene of excitement to do what he could to preserve the public peace.

A VOICE—We want you to stay here.

GOVERNOR—I am going to stay here, my friends.

He implored the men whom he saw before him to refrain from all acts of violence and from all destruction of property. They owed it to themselves and to the Government under which they lived to assist with their strong arms in preserving peace and order. If they would only do this and refrain from further riotous acts, he would see to it that all their rights were protected. [Cheers.] He was their friend, and the friend of their families. He would say a word about the draft; and first, he would state that on Saturday last he sent his Adjutant-General (SPRAGUE) to Washington to ask the Government to stop the draft in this City for the present. [Prolonged cheers.] There was no occasion for resistance, for the draft had not yet been enforced. If they would now quietly disperse to their homes and abstain from further acts of violence, he would promise them that no injustice should be done in the matter of the conscription, and that the rights of themselves and their families should be fully protected. [Great applause, during which the Governor retired within the City Hall.] Before the Governor commenced speaking a company of armed soldiers, with fixed bayonets, from the Park Barracks, were drawn up in his rear on the steps of the City Hall. While marching up the steps the soldiers were groaned and hooted by the crowd in the wildest manner, to which they paid no attention, and none of them were otherwise molested.

While in the City Hall, the Governor held consultation with the City and Military authorities. The subject of proclaiming Martial law was broached, and the Governor dissented from the opinion of some of the other authorities as to its necessity. He admitted the necessity of putting down the riot speedily and effectually, but did not think that Martial law should be proclaimed until all other means had failed. During the consultation Mayor OPDYKE sent to the Police Commissioners asking for a detail of 50 men for the City Hall, stating that Gov. SEYMOUR was in consultation with the authorities, and a large crowd surrounded the Hall. The men were immediately sent and remained at the Hall during the day. Their services were often required to disperse the crowds which continued throughout the day to hover around the Park and in the square fronting the *Tribune* office. Many prominent citizens, besides the authorities, joined in consultation with the Governor, and among other things it was agreed that places should be at once designated as rendezvous for citizens wishing to volunteer to preserve the peace. The following places were agreed upon and hand-bills announcing the same and signed by the Governor were speedily issued:

City Assembly Rooms—Gen. Ward B. Burnett, in command.

Seventh Regiment Armory—Gen. Duryea and Major Pinckney.

Centre Market—Col. McGregor, Charles E. Cornell, Capt. Ottiwell.

Thirty-second-street and Broadway—Col. J. Mansfield Davis, Col. Smedburg and Capt. Thos. Murphy.

City Hall—Col. Shannon and Capt. Rynders.

No. 220 Third street—Capt. H. Sower, F. Repper.

Before leaving the City Hall the Governor issued the following proclamation:

To the People of the City of New-York:

A riotous demonstration in your City, originating in opposition to the conscription of soldiers for the military service of the United States, has swelled into vast proportions, directing its fury against the property and lives of peaceful citizens. I know that many of those who have participated in these proceedings would not have allowed themselves to be carried to such extremes of violence and of wrong except under an apprehension of injustice; but such persons are reminded that the only opposition to the conscription which can be allowed is an appeal to the Courts.

The right of every citizen to make such an appeal will be maintained, and the decision of the Courts must be respected and obeyed by rulers and people alike. No other course is consistent with the maintenance of the laws, the peace and order of the City and the safety of its inhabitants.

Riotous proceedings must and shall be put down. The laws of the State of New-York must be enforced, its peace and order maintained, and the lives and property of all its citizens protected at any and every hazard. The rights of every citizen will be properly guarded and defended by the Chief Magistrate of the State.

I do therefore call upon all persons engaged in these riotous proceedings to retire to their homes and employments, declaring to them that unless they do so at once, I shall use all the power necessary to restore the peace and order of the City. I also call upon all well-disposed persons not enrolled for the preservation of order, to pursue their ordinary avocations.

Let all citizens stand firmly by the constituted authorities, sustaining law and order in the City, and ready to answer any such demand as circumstances may render necessary for me to make upon their services; and they may rely upon a rigid enforcement of the laws of this State against all who violate them.

HORATIO SEYMOUR, Governor.

NEW-YORK, July 14, 1863.

During the afternoon the Governor addressed a large concourse of people in Wall-street. His speech there was the same in substance as that delivered from the City Hall steps. He said he had sent to Washington to ask that the draft in this State might be suspended until the Courts could decide upon its legality. To the decision, when it came, all owed obedience. If they decided it to be legal, he would use every exertion to make it as equal as possible upon all citizens. The Governor's remarks were well received.

Subsequently, the Governor addressed the people in the upper part of the City—the tenor of his remarks being substantially the same.

PROCLAMATION FROM THE MAYOR.

Mayor OPDYKE issued the following proclamation during the afternoon:

MAYOR'S OFFICE, NEW-YORK, July 14, 1863.

It is highly important to the peace of the City and the suppression of the existing riot, that the rioters shall not be allowed to furnish themselves with arms and ammunition, and I do hereby accordingly enjoin upon all persons who keep arms and ammunition for sale, that they will at once cease selling to private persons, and close their places of business.

GEORGE OPDYKE, Mayor.

Doings of the Military.

At an early hour the military began to assemble at Police Headquarters, and were in readiness to proceed to the performance of any duty to which they might be assigned. A company of United States regulars from Governor's Island, under the command of Lieut. WOOD, formed in line in front of the Headquarters.

At 10½ o'clock this company was sent to the Seventh Ward, where the rioters had begun to tear down a number of buildings, and were also setting them on fire. The following order was issued by Gen. SANDFORD:

NEW-YORK, July 14, 1863.

The whole military force now at the Police Headquarters will forthwith return to the Seventh-avenue arsenal and report to Maj.-Gen. SANDFORD.

CHAS. W. SANDFORD, Major-General.

HEADQUARTERS DEPARTMENT OF THE EAST, NEW-YORK, July 13, 1863.

SPECIAL ORDER.—All the troops called out for the protection of the City are placed under command of Maj.-Gen. SANDFORD, whose orders they will implicitly obey.

C. T. CHRISTIANSEN, Assistant Adjutant-General.

In pursuance of these orders all the available military force, with the exception of Lieut. WOOD's company of United States regulars, were sent to Thirty-fourth-street, where the mob was carrying on their work of destruction, tearing down buildings and setting them on fire. About 10 o'clock, the military were drawn up in line, and orders given to fire.

The orders were promptly obeyed, many persons being wounded, and a large number (it is reported) were killed. The muskets were loaded with Minie balls.

About the same time, Lieut. WOOD's company encountered a large crowd in Delancy-street, which attempted to obstruct their passage, and made an attack upon the soldiers. The brave fellows, however, were not to be frightened, and Lieut. WOOD immediately gave the order to fire, which was obeyed with the greatest promptitude. A large number of the mob fell, some killed and others seriously wounded. Those who escaped the galling fire of ball scattered, and the soldiers were left in possession of the field.

At about 10½ o'clock yesterday morning, as a Company of United States infantry from Forts Lafayette, Hamilton and Richmond, under command of Lieut. WOOD, were marching through Pitt-street, they were assailed with volleys of bricks and stones, and at length, having been ordered to disperse the rioters at all hazards, fired upon the crowd, and several persons are said to have been killed.

In Thirty-fourth-street, at about the same time, three detachments of United States Marines, one company of Zouaves, and one company of regulars from Fort Schuyler, together with a company of artillery, and two pieces of ordnance from Staten Island, arrived on the ground where the mob had strongly posted themselves. Col. O'BRIEN had command of these forces, and marched his men straight through the crowd down the Third-avenue. He also fired his revolver into the crowd, which resulted in death to some and wounded many.

The crowd, continuing to increase, the two howitzers were placed in position on the corner of Thirtieth-street, and three rounds of blank cartridge were fired among the rioters. This dispersed them but for a few moments, for they again shortly after appeared in full force, menacing the military with threats of speedy retaliation. Many of them had, by this time, obtained arms, and threatened to overpower the troops.

Col. O'BRIEN, of the Eleventh New-York, was afterward beaten to death by the crowd on Second-avenue, and then hung.

At the Seventh regiment Armory a guard of 400 men were stationed, under Lieut. KEMPE. They had two howitzers loaded with grape and canister.

Col. HENRY E. DAVIES was busily engaged during the day in organizing a volunteer force at the same armory. Volunteering seemed to go on briskly. And the Colonel expected to have a force of 10,000 men organized before morning.

At the Eighth regiment Armory there were over 100 men guarding the premises.

Col. JARDINE, of the old Hawkins Zouaves, was engaged in reorganizing the old regiment of the Hawkins Zouaves.

At the Arsenal and the Division Armory cannon were trained and ready for use, and any attack upon them would be repulsed with great loss to the rioters.

The military force under the command of Gens. BROWN and SANDFORD, were strongly posted at the arsenal in Thirty-seventh-street.

The Division Armory, at the corner of White and Elm streets, is the rendezvous of the returned soldiers now in this City. Nearly two hundred men of the Tenth regiment—which was ordered to the seat of war, but was detained here—are in charge, with 100 men of other regiments and a company of artillerists. Col. ALLEN, of the First regiment of National volunteers; Col. TAYLOR, of the Fourth New-York volunteer regiment; Major WALES, of the Seventeenth Chasseurs, and Col. HOWARD, of the Twelfth Heavy artillery, make their headquarters at the Division Armory.

The Custom-house and other public buildings are also garrisoned. It is the intention of the Government to protect all public property.

In accordance with orders from Gen. SANDFORD, the reserve force of the City regiments assembled at their various armories at 12 M., to await orders.

Reinforcements are expected from the Eastern States, and the rioters may soon expect to be outnumbered, and quelled by superior force.

Gen. BROWN sent to Riker's Island for five hundred men, under Col. LANSING.

He gave orders to the men under his command to start with loaded arms, and if they saw the crowd, to fire without awaiting orders.

A meeting of the members and ex-members of the old Ninth regiment was yesterday morning called together. Lieut.-Col. RUTHERFORD was called to the Chair, and Lieut DRAPER acted as Secretary. There was a very full attendance and a long list of names were enrolled to do duty.

By an order from Lieut.-Col. ASHLEY, the members of the Thirty-seventh regiment N. Y. N. G., now in the City, were requested to meet at the Armory, in uniform, at No. 506 Broadway.

At 11 o'clock a messenger came to Police Headquarters bringing the intelligence of the result of a charge which was made on a mob in Pitt-street. Lieut. WOOD, wherever he went with his men, succeeded in driving the crowd, scattering them like chaff and sending them flying in dismay in every direction.

By this charge five of the rioters were killed; unfortunately two of the victims were children. The crowd was encountered in Pitt-street, and came rushing upon the soldiers, the leader carrying an American flag. As they came up they attempted to hold a parley with the soldiers, and finding that they could not drive them back, began making demonstrations, threatening to beat them with clubs and otherwise injure them.

While this was going on (it all transpired in about three minutes) a number of shots were fired by the mob at the soldiers. The order to fire over the heads of the crowd was then given, which was obeyed. This made the mob more audacious than before, and the rioters made a movement as if to charge on the soldiers. Lieut. WOOD then ordered his men to fire. The soldiers leveled their muskets and fired, with the result given above. The crowd then dispersed as rapidly as possible.

About one hundred of the Invalid corps and a deputation of the sailors and marines from the Navy-yard are in Worth-street, between Church-street and West Broadway, in readiness for any emergency.

APPEALS TO THE LOYAL CITIZENS OF NEW-YORK.

To the Loyal Citizens of New-York:

All persons who wish to enroll themselves for temporary duty, to assist in suppressing the present disgraceful riot, are requested to report themselves at either of the following places, to the officers detailed for the purpose of organizing them, viz.:

Park Barracks, Broadway.
Lafayette Hall, No. 597 Broadway.
Cooper Institute.

JOHN E. WOOL, Major-General.

ATTENTION OLD THIRTY-EIGHTH REGIMENT.

NEW-YORK, July 15, 1863.

In accordance with the request of Maj.-Gen. WOOL, commanding Department of the East, the officers and members of the old Thirty-eighth regiment (Second Scott Life Guards) are requested to meet at Central Hall, corner of Grand and Centre streets, this morning, at 9 o'clock, for the purpose of tendering our services for the protection of United States and State property. All old soldiers of other regiments are invited to join with us. By order of

ROBERT F. ALLASON,
Lieut.-Col. Thirty-eighth N. Y. S. Vols.

ATTENTION COMPANY A, THIRTY-EIGHTH REGIMENT NEW-YORK STATE VOLUNTEERS.

You are requested to be at Central Hall this day at 9 o'clock A. M., for the purpose of arming for the defence of United States and State property. Our friends of other Companies are invited to join us.

J. LEONARD,
Late Capt. Co. A, Thirty-eighth N. Y. S. Vols.

HAWKINS' ZOUAVES.

Col. JARDINE earnestly requests the officers and men of the old "Ninth," and other volunteer regiments, to meet at the Headquarters, No. 510 Broadway, at 9 o'clock this (Wednesday) morning.

THIRTY-FIRST NEW-YORK VOLUNTEERS.

The members will assemble, without delay, at the Arsenal, corner of Thirty-fifth-street and Seventh-avenue. Ex-members are requested to report as above.

FRANK JONES,
Colonel Thirty-first New-York Volunteers.

HEADQUARTERS SECOND DIVISION N. G. S. N. Y.,
BROOKLYN, July 15, 1863.

All active and exempt members of this division now in the City, are requested to report to Capt. THORNE, at the City Armory, this morning, at 9 o'clock.

Maj.-Gen. H. B. DURYEA.

CITY ARMORY, BROOKLYN, July 15, 1863,
Thirteenth regiment, N. G. S. N. Y.

All members of this regiment, now in the City, are hereby ordered to assemble at the armory, and report to the officers of their respective companies, at 9 o'clock, this morning, in accordance with orders from Maj.-Gen. DURYEA.

Capt. R. V. W. THORNE, Jr., Commanding.

Miscellaneous Movements.

BARRICADES ON THE FIRST-AVENUE.

Late in the afternoon the rioters commenced to barricade First-avenue, near Eleventh-street, and First-avenue, near Fourteenth-street. The telegraph poles, which they had torn down, were used for these barricades, together with numerous carts, which had been picked up in the adjacent streets. At Thirteenth-street two street-sweeping machines, which had been captured the previous evening were burned amid the shouts of the men, women and boys who thronged the avenue. The especial spite the rioters had against these machines was that they were labor-saving, and to their ignorant minds, they appeared their prime enemies. The moving spirit in this riotous conduct was a man who announced himself a returned soldier, but who declared that his sympathy had been aroused for the South by the emancipation of the "niggers." He made excited speeches to crowds of people, and seemed particularly desirous of stirring up a fight with any one who should have the hardihood to combat his sentiments. He and others inveighed bitterly against grain-elevators as labor-saving machines—as inimical to the poor man, and intimated a purpose to destroy them as they had destroyed the street-sweepers. Upon the adjacent tenement houses were numbers of men, some of them armed with guns in anticipation of an attack by the soldiers. A gun-store in Fifth-street near Avenue A had been broken open in the morning and completely gutted of its contents. The mob were in a great state of fear lest the militia should make their appearance, the false alarms of mischievous boys causing a general scampering.

ATTACK ON THE MAYOR'S RESIDENCE.

Early in the morning the rioters had assembled *en masse* on Fifth-avenue, in front of the residence of Mayor OPDYKE, and commenced a violent assault upon his house, and succeeded in forcing the front door, and in breaking the costly plate glass in the second and third story windows. One of the lamps on the front stoop was entirely demolished. The riot here was mainly conducted by boys between the ages of eighteen and twenty years.

Col. B. F. MANIERRE seeing that things were likely to take a serious shape, organized a few friends into a platoon, and with clubs and revolvers succeeded for a time in holding the rioters in check. They were finally relieved by a strong detachment of police, who held the position unmolested until they in turn were relieved by a detachment of United States soldiers from Governor's Island, under command of Capt. WILKINS. This detachment numbered 84 men and four Sergeants, and now hold the place without opposition. It will be necessary to keep a strong detachment of police or military around the house of Mayor OPDYKE, as it is, if possible, the sincere intention of the rioters to gut and burn the building.

Before we left this scene of action a man named PETER DOLAN, who lives in the upper part of the City, was arrested and taken into custody by the police on the charge of being one of the ringleaders in the assault upon Mayor OPDYKE's house.

STOPPAGE OF CITY CARS.

The cars on most of the City railroads suspended their trips early in the day, so that it was found difficult to obtain access to different parts of the City. The Third-avenue cars did not run at all during the day, a portion of their track up town having been torn up by the mob on Monday. The Fourth-avenue ran cars till noon, when they were obliged to stop from the same cause. The Sixth and Eighth-avenue cars also ran during the forenoon, but stopped early in the day. The reason of the mob tearing up the railroad tracks is said to have been to prevent the cars from conveying troops up town. The track of the Hudson River Railroad, between Fifty-third and Fifty-ninth street, was torn up by the rioters early in the morning. The horse cars of this road were stopped during the morning at the corner of Twenty-sixth-street and Eleventh-avenue, probably for the purpose of plundering the passengers, but after being detained awhile, they were permitted to pass on. Some of the City railroad lines stopped running on account of the mob threatening the drivers and conductors. They also threatened to burn the depots unless the roads suspended their trips.

Many of the stages running through Broadway, were taken possession of by the Police Commissioners to be used in transferring the Police from place to place. One of the drivers of these stages having taken it into his head that he would not carry Policemen, his place was very summarily filled by a member of the force, and himself turned loose upon the street.

BUSINESS GENERALLY SUSPENDED.

The rioters, in large numbers, at early morning went to the docks and ordered the longshoremn to join them, under threats of violence. The New-Orleans and other lines of steamers have in consequence been compelled to cease loading. Jewelry stores, money brokers' offices and other establishments containing property of a valuable character, were not opened at all, and after 3 o'clock, as a general thing, all business places were shut up. The Custom-House and Assay-office were closed at an early hour in the afternoon.

BURNING OF A GAS-HOUSE AND FERRY-HOUSE.

After perpetrating several acts of brutality in the vicinity of the North River, the mob proceeded to the gas house on Forty-second-street, and in a few moments the building was in flames. They then went to the ferry-house at the foot of Forty-second-street, North River, and after meeting with some opposition by the police, which proved of no avail whatever, they set fire to the building, and it is now in ruins. The crowd at this point was probably the largest ever seen in this City congregated in one place. It may be safely asserted that there were over 6,000 people assembled in that neighborhood. Some were armed with clubs, some with pistols, and a few muskets. The police were powerless, and were obliged, from sheer exhaustion, to let the rioters for a time take their own way.

BURNING OF CAPT. DUFFY'S HEADQUARTERS.

About 1 o'clock yesterday morning the headquarters of Capt. DUFFY, Provost-Marshal of the Fifth Congressional District, corner of Grand and Ridge streets, was surrounded by a mob of about five hundred persons, who applied the incendiary torch and burned it to the ground.

The papers and documents had, however, been previously removed.

THE RIOTORS IN CATHARINE-STREET.

About 10 o'clock, last evening, a barber-shop and a shoe-store in Catharine-street, near East Broadway, were set on fire by a mob of about 500 men and boys. The buildings were entirely destroyed. The large clothing store of BROOKS BROTHERS, situated in the same street, was also visited by the insurgents. A great amount of plunder was secured by the mob in the shape of clothing, boots and shoes, and goods from a grocery adjoining the burned buildings.

ONSLAUGHT ON NEGRO DWELLINGS.

At Thirty-fifth-street there are a number of negro dwellings. An onslaught was next made upon them; fortunately, however, all the negro women and children had been secretly conveyed by the Police to the Twentieth Precinct Station-house, where they were made secure in the cells. Learning this, and with a purpose, if possible, not to lose their prey, the rioters next made a charge on the Station-house, but by the untiring exertion of Capt. WALLING and his brave men they were prevented from gaining admission. They were at last dispersed by the military, who, firing upon the crowd, soon set them to flight.

ORGANIZATION OF MINUTE MEN.

The organization of Minute men by Col. DAVIS, under order of Gen. SANDFORD, proceeded yesterday with great vigor at the Seventh Regiment Armory at the Tompkins Market. A complete regiment was raised and command given by Col. DAVIS to Col. CLEVELAND WINSLOW, Duryee's Zouaves. A large number of the old regiment volunteered their services. The organization of Minute men will be continued to-day at the same place by Col. DAVIS. A brigade will probably be completed by this evening. It is the duty as well as the immediate interest of every citizen to organize. The services of the members of the old regiment are particularly desired to command drill the new levies. All law-abiding citizens are most urgently requested to report at the Seventh Regiment Armory without a moments delay, when every man will be immediately equipped. Every man in arms to-day will be worth ten to-morrow.

CONTEMPLATED ATTACK ON GEN. WOOL'S HEADQUARTERS.

At 4½ o'clock in the afternoon, large gatherings collected in Amity-street, the object of which could not be definitely ascertained. It was thought, however, that they intended to make a descent upon Gen. WOOL's headquarters in Bleecker-street, where the business of the Department of the East is carried on. Ample preparations were made by the authorities to counteract their intentions, whatever they may have been, and when the mob beheld a body of soldiers marching toward them, they beat a retreat as quickly as possible.

THIRTY-FOURTH-STREET—SECOND-AVENUE.

At about 3 o'clock in the afternoon, this part of the City presented a very excited appearance, and large bodies of rioters had congregated at the different corners. It is stated that the crowd were charged on by the military, and that two or three of the ringleaders were shot. The rioters presented a very formidable appearance, but the action of the military had the effect of deterring them from carrying out their wicked designs in the destruction of property. They were armed with sticks and bludgeons.

RUMORED ATTACK ON A COAL-YARD.

A report was current that after being foiled in their purposes at Thirty-fourth-street and Second-avenue, the mob had repaired to the corner of Thirtieth-street and Seventh-avenue, for the purpose of demolishing the extensive coal-yards of Messrs. LUDLOW, YOUNG & Co. One of our reporters visited the place late in the afternoon, and can positively contradict this rumor, as up to that time no attempt had been made to injure the premises of these gentlemen, nor had any crowds appeared in the locality.

THE ELM-STREET ARMORY.

At this armory three field-pieces of artillery are in readiness to be brought into play at any moment when ordered. They are under the command of Col. HOWE and a fine sturdy set of fellows of the Thirteenth Heavy Artillery. Two of them are 6-pounders, and the other a 4-pounder. If called into operation they will do dreadful havoc. The armory is well filled with troops of the Thirteenth and Tenth Infantry. Besides the soldiers, there are upward of one hundred citizens in the armory who have volunteered to assist the military if called upon. Col. BENDIX is in full command of the armory.

THE SEVENTH REGIMENT ARMORY.

This armory is in complete readiness to carry out the desires of the authorities, and is well furnished with troops. The men express a strong desire to have an encounter with the rioters, and are very anxious to get the word of "Up guards and at them."

THE BURNING OF HART'S HOTEL AND OTHER BUILDINGS.

About 3½ o'clock yesterday morning, the shed attached to Mr. HART's hotel, corner of One Hundred and Twenty-seventh-street and Third-avenue, was deliberately set on fire by a party of rioters. It was subsequently extinguished. The same party then proceeded to One Hundred and Twenty-ninth-street, and there set fire to the premises of Mr. HANSON, occupied as a turning and planing mill.

The flames soon spread to adjoining buildings occupied by Mr. Vandever, A. D. Meyers, Mrs. Smith, C. J. Sutton, Francis Martin, Jane, Martin, C. Kempton, Mr. Brenners and T. Tookers. All these buildings were destroyed. The loss is estimated at over $35,000.

The colored boarding houses Nos. 74 and 76 Rosevelt-street, and No. 20 Vandewater-street, were attacked about 6 P. M. last evening, and the inmates driven out. The house on Rosevelt-street was set on fire.

THE MARINES FIRE UPON THE CROWD.

In the Seventh and Thirteenth Wards the riot and confusion raged furiously during the forenoon. At length a detachment of United States Marines arrived, and after making every effort to subdue the mob on the corner of Delancey and Pitt streets, were at length compelled to fire; their aim was directed low, and their fire effectual. We learn that the result was that twelve of the rioters were left dead on the spot. This had its due effect; the crowd was dispersed, and everything in that vicinity was quiet.

RECAPTURE OF ARMS.

On the corner of Third-avenue and Twenty-second-street is a gun and pistol manufactory. This building the rioters had succeeded in breaking open at 11 o'clock, and securing to themselves about 200 carbines and pistols. While quarreling among themselves for the possession of these weapons, they were suddenly pounced upon by the Police, who made a desperate charge into the crowd, but at first did not succeed in making any impression upon them. The Police being only armed with their clubs, were met by the rioters with the butt ends of the muskets they had taken, and for a time the contest seemed doubtful as to its issue. By the timely arrival of a reinforcement, however, the victory was secured to the police, who, in addition to dispersing the crowd, succeeded in disarming many of the rioters and taking possession of the weapons. The arms taken from the rioters are now all secured at the Police headquarters in Mulberry-street.

At the Police headquarters about one thousand specials were sworn in, and armed with clubs. They were all most respectable-looking people, anxious to lend their aid for the preservation of law and order.

THE NINTH REGIMENT IN THE FIELD WITH A BATTERY.

A meeting of the members and ex-members of the old Ninth regiment (Militia) was held at 9 o'clock yesterday morning. The majority of the members of this regiment, it will be remembered, volunteered for the war during the Summer of 1861, and were mustered into the United States service as the Eighty-third New-York Volunteers. The meeting was called to raise a force to be offered to the Major General of the First District, to aid in putting down the present riot. Lieut.-Col. RUTHERFORD was called to the Chair, and Lieut. DRAPER acted as Secretary. The meeting was very fully attended, and a long list of names were enrolled, pledged to do duty during the present emergency. A Committee was appointed to wait on Maj.-Gen. SANDFORD, who will supply the regiment with arms. Adequate measures were taken to notify all members of the regiment now in the City of the call; after which the meeting adjourned. A battery of artillery is already secured for the regiment, to be commanded by Ex-Capt. MORRISON, of Company A.

DESTRUCTION OF BUILDINGS IN YORKVILLE AND ELSEWHERE.

The residence of Col. NUGENT, in Eighty-sixth-street, between Third and Fourth avenues, was destroyed at an early hour yesterday morning. The mob, before setting fire to the house, plundered it of all the valuables. From this place the crowd went to the residence of ABRAM WAKEMAN, which, after they had sacked and plundered, they burned to the ground. From thence the rioters visited Washington Hall, at Harlem, which was plundered and burned.

Mr. MOLTERS' house, on the corner of Eighty-sixth-street and Third-avenue, was pillaged, everything in the shape of furniture being thrown into the street, and the house burned.

The bridge over McComb's Dam was destroyed early yesterday morning. The tracks of the Fourth and Third-avenue Railroads were torn up in the neighborhood of Yorkville, and the telegraph wires cut.

About 10 o'clock yesterday morning the mob visited a porter-house on Fifth-avenue, near Ninety-first-street, and called for something to drink. Upon being refused, they set fire to the building, and in a short time it was totally destroyed.

DOINGS OF GEN. BROWN.

Brig.-Gen. BROWN, of the regular army, was nearly all day at the Police Headquarters in Mulberry-street, rendering every assistance in his power to the Police Commissioners. He was in constant communication with his officers at the scenes of action. The General appeared perfectly cool, and he and Mr. THOMAS ACTON, one of the Police Commissioners, expressed the utmost confidence in the final quelling of the mob.

CUTTING TELEGRAPH WIRES.

The Police and Fire Telegraph wires were cut during the afternoon in the First-avenue, and also on Ninth-avenue, between Thirty-fifth and Forty-eighth-streets, and all communication with headquarters had to be made by special messenger.

LOSSES BY PLUNDER.

It is impossible to estimate the losses sustained by individuals from the promiscuous plunder and robbery of the mob during the last two days—all of which the City will be compelled to pay for. From all parts of the City we hear of stores, jewelry shops, private residences, &c., being entered by the rioters, and their contents carried off or destroyed, and in many instances the owners shamefully maltreated and beaten. The latest that has come to hand is the clothing store of P. BECK & BROTHER, No. 556 Third-avenue, which was visited by the mob last evening, and plundered of its entire contents, valued at $1,600.

DEFENCE OF THE PARK AND PRINTING-HOUSE-SQUARE.

The preparations for the defence of the City Hall and the buildings around Printing-House-square, last evening, were such as almost to cause a regret in the breasts of law-abiding people that the mob did not make their appearance in that quarter. The TIMES office was brilliantly illuminated, so as to afford them a good chance to see and be seen. Inasmuch as they did not see fit to honor the neighborhood of the Park with a visit, it is hardly worth while to tell them what pains had been taken to receive them; further than to say that we overheard an old army officer say that he had got batteries so placed at various points around the Park that he could sweep off bodies of evil-disposed men, who should attempt to intrench upon his premises, at the rate of 75,000 every ten minutes. What a pity the "left wing of LEE's army" (so a Loyal-League man calls this mob) did not give him a chance.

GREAT CROWD IN ROOSEVELT-STREET.

In Roosevelt-street, near Pearl-street, about 4 P. M., an immense crowd reassembled, and it was evident that they required but a spark to enkindle the most angry passions. The character of the population in that vicinity is one well calculated to take the most active and energetic part in the general riot. Several negro habitations have been entirely demolished in that neighborhood, and the poor tenants turned into the streets helpless. Many have taken shelter in the Station-house. The poor creatures look perfectly bewildered—they are unable to discriminate between friend or foe. Many have lost all they ever had in the world, and some of them may become charges on the county. The crowd carried away the weather boards, and every part of the negro habitations that can be detached to make firewood of.

A GUARD AT THE MAYOR'S OFFICE.

A communication was received from the Mayor asking for a guard of fifty men for his office. Mr. ACTON ordered the required number to be sent.

Sergt. YOUNG, of the Detective force, has been acting as Commissary General. He has ransacked all the provision stores in the neighborhood, and has now about twenty barrels of crackers, cheese in an unlimited quantity, three hundred pounds of smoked beef, four hundred hams, and bread in loaves uncountable.

One of the men killed in the charge of the regulars this morning, was named PATRICK DOUGHERTY, and resided at the corner of South and Jackson streets.

At 1½ o'clock yesterday morning, the packing house of Mr. ROSS, corner of Washington and Houston streets was set on fire by the incendiaries. The building was entirely destroyed; also the lumber yard of Messrs. BAKER & WELLS. The damage is very great.

ATTACKS FRUSTRATED.

It was expected that an attack would be made on the House of Detention for Witnesses. Sergeant FOLGER, however, was dispatched with a special squad to take charge of the building, and it is now considered perfectly safe from attack.

An attack was also meditated upon the dwelling of D. D. FIELD in Gramercy Park, but ample means have been taken for its defence by the Police.

INTENTION TO ATTACK COLUMBIA COLLEGE.

During the day a large body of rioters proceeded to the Columbia College grounds, evidently intent on attacking that ancient seat of learning. Why they should wish to meddle with such an institution no one could conjecture, unless it was the fact that the President of the College, CHAS. KING, has acted as President of a Loyal League. Fortunately the rioters were met on the grounds by a Catholic priest, who addressed the mob and persuaded them to desist from their purposes.

DEFENCE OF THE SUB-TREASURY BUILDING AND WALL-STREET.

Col. BLISS has raised a battery of the following officers, for the purpose of protecting the Sub-Treasury and Wall-street generally: Lieut.-Col. MANCHESTER, Capt. SWEET, Capt. RAYNOR, Capt. HYSLOP, Lieut. TURNER, Lieut. E. LEFFERTS; Gunne F, Lieuts. DOUGLAS, WM. BARTON, JOSEPH LAMB and others.

AN INCIDENT OF MONDAY'S LAWLESSNESS.

Alderman MCCOOL, in the afternoon, returned to the City from a drive in the suburbs, and was stopped up town by a crowd of men and boys, who seized the reigns of his horse, and demanded to know who he was. He replied "My name is JOHN MCCOOL." "McCool," echoed some of the crowd, followed by the speculative remarks of "Who the devil is McCool?" "What are you?" "What do you do?" The alderman answered that he was the alderman of the Fifth Aldermanic District. "Alderman be ——," the crowd responded; "we want something to drink." The alderman smiled pleasantly, and thinking discretion to be the better part of valor in his situation, searched his pockets for some money. He could only find a five dollar bill. This he handed over to a stalwart fellow near him, and then he was permitted to proceed without further hindrance. The alderman tells the story himself, and regards the affair as a big joke on one of the City Fathers by a deputation of the unruly municipal children.

ACTION OF DOWN-TOWN MERCHANTS.

A large number of the merchants, brokers, and others, doing business in the lower part of the City, met yesterday afternoon, at 1 o'clock, at No. 111 Broadway, to devise measures for assisting the authorities to restore order in the City.

Mr. F. L. W[illegible] presided, and Mr. W. M. VERMILYE was appointed Secretary.

The Chairman having stated the object of the meeting, Mr. WM. E. DODGE then offered the following resolutions:

Resolved, That when treason against the Government is rampant, when rebellion against the City authorities is defiant, when the residence of our Mayor is sacked by a mob, and orphan asylums and private dwellings are robbed by a rabble and given to the flames; the men of this City and State who prize Government, respect law, and love good order, should rise in their might, and, at any price of blood and treasure, crush the traitors and outlaws, and restore the supremacy of the law.

Resolved, That in the present crisis, it is the duty of every citizen to stand by and assist the Municipal authorities, also the duty of every able-bodied man to render his services for that purpose.

Resolved, That the merchants, bankers and others of this city be requested to furnish every facility for their employes to render such assistance in the present emergency as may be practicable.

Resolved, That this meeting recommend to the proper authorities the consideration and the propriety of declaring martial law in this city.

Mr. CHAS. PARTRIDGE spoke of the necessity of proclaiming martial law, and moved that the meeting adopt a resolution in favor of it. The subject, however, was not pressed.

Mr. JOHN A. STEVENS, Jr., then proposed the following, which were adopted:

Resolved, That the merchants and bankers be requested to close their stores and offices at 3 o'clock this day.

Resolved, That when this meeting adjourn, it adjourn to meet in Wall-street, on the south side, in companies of one hundred, to report to the authorities.

Subsequently there was a large assemblage in Wall-street, the thoroughfare being blocked from Nassau to William. Speeches were made and several companies of volunteers were organized.

MEETING AT THE PRODUCE EXCHANGE.

Immediately after business at the Produce Exchange had closed, a meeting of the members of the Commercial Association was organized by the election of Mr COLEMAN as President, for the purpose of considering the disturbed state of the City and for the enrollment of volunteers to aid the authorities in enforcing the laws. There was much determination to carry out the design of the meeting, and a large number of merchants, salesmen, clerks and others enrolled themselves.

THE SPECIAL POLICEMEN ENROLLED AT HEADQUARTERS.

In pursuance of the proclamation of Mayor OPDYKE, calling upon all good citizens to report themselves at Police Headquarters, and enrol themselves as special Policemen, a large number of men appeared at an early hour yesterday morning at the appointed place, all of them anxious to do what they could to protect the City from the ravages of the rioters.

So great was the number of applicants, that many of them were compelled to wait there for hours before they could enroll their names and be sworn in according to law. The number enrolled up to 7 o'clock last evening, amounted to over twelve hundred. The enrolling at Police Headquarters will be continued to-day, and the organization of the volunteer companies under proper officers, will be made as fast as possible.

THE POLICEMEN INJURED.

The following named Policemen were seriously injured during the day and night of Monday:

EIGHTH PRECINCT—Sergeant Ellison; officers Andre, Law, Palmer, Nildeberger, Hart, Van Buren, Barclay, McCaul, Maggsuppl.

FIFTEENTH PRECINCT—Sergeant McCredie, Tr[illegible]

[Continued on Eighth Page.]

The New-York Times.

VOL. XII—NO. 3685. | NEW-YORK, THURSDAY, JULY 16, 1863. | PRICE THREE CENTS.

ANOTHER DAY OF RIOTING.

CONTINUATION OF MOB RULE.

A PROCLAMATION FROM THE MAYOR.

A Morning and an Evening Fight—The Streets Raked with Canister.

A Large Number of Rioters Killed.

Several Soldiers Killed and Wounded.

THE EVENING MOB ARMED WITH RIFLES.

They Pick Off the Soldiers from the Housetops.

Citizen Volunteers Killed—Col. Jardine Wounded.

MORE NEGROES HUNG.

The Contagion Spreading—Riotous Demonstrations in Westchester County, Brooklyn, Jersey City, Staten Island and Jamaica.

Increased Preparations by the Authorities.

INCIDENTS, CASUALTIES, &c., &c.

The ravages of the mob which commenced its diabolical career on Monday are not yet ended, and it is impossible to say at the hour of going to press this morning whether the worst has yet been seen. All through Tuesday night marauding bands of plunderers in greater or less numbers, continued to commit their depredations in various parts of the City, but at daylight yesterday morning they had generally dispersed, and there was a fair prospect of a speedy restoration of quiet and order. The authorities, both State and military, appeared to consider the riot as substantially subdued, and after a consultation early in the forenoon, between Mayor OPDYKE, Gov. SEYMOUR and Gen. WOOL, at the St. Nicholas Hotel, the following proclamation was issued from the Mayor's office:

PROCLAMATION OF THE MAYOR.

To the Citizens of New-York:

I am happy to announce to you that the riot which for two days has disgraced our City, has been in good measure subjected to the control of the public authorities. It would not have interrupted your peace for a day but for the temporary absence of all our organized local militia. What now remain of the mob are fragments prowling about for plunder; and, for the purpose of meeting these, and saving the military and police from the exhaustion of continued movements, you are invited to form voluntary associations under competent leaders, to patrol and guard your various districts. With these exceptions you are again requested to resume your accustomed daily avocations. This is as necessary to your personal security as to the peace of the City.

The various lines of omnibuses, railways and telegraphs must be put in full operation immediately. Adequate military protection against their further interruption will be furnished on application to the military authorities of the State.

Fellow-citizens, the laws must and shall be obeyed; public order shall not be broken with impunity. Our first duty now is to restore the public peace and preserve it unbroken, and to pursue and punish the offenders against the majesty of the laws.

GEORGE OPDYKE, Mayor.

The Mayor also gave to the public, through the newspapers, the following

DISPATCH FROM SECRETARY STANTON:

WASHINGTON, July 14, 1863.

To Hon. George Opdyke, Mayor:

Five regiments are under orders to return to New-York. The retreat of LEE, now become a rout, with his army broken and much heavier loss of killed and wounded than was supposed, will relieve a large force for the restoration of order in New-York.

Intelligence has just reached here of the auspicious commencement of Gen. GILMORE's operations against Charleston.

All but one fort on Morris Island have been captured, and that will speedily be reduced, after which Sumter must follow.

EDWARD M. STANTON,
Secretary of War.

Our citizens, on reading the foregoing proclamation and the accompanying dispatch from the Secretary of War, felt a double pleasure in the prospect of an utter rout of the army of LEE on the Potomac, and his sympathetic band of coadjutors and thieves in this City, at one and the same time. How far these pleasant self-congratulations were warranted by the facts, our telegrams from the Potomac, published in another column, and the reports which follow of the doings of the mob up to a late hour last night, must determine.

A Morning Riot in Thirty-second-Street.

THE MILITARY FIRE UPON THE MOB.

Late on Tuesday night a raid was made by the mob on a number of negro dwellings situate on Thirty-second-street, between Sixth and Seventh avenues; these buildings were almost entirely demolished and several attempts were made to fire the whole vicinity.

An unfortunate negro, who made an attempt to fly for his life from the fury of these persecutors, was caught and severely beaten with stones and bludgeons; the infuriated mob not satisfied with thus brutally mangling their victim, slipped a rope around his neck and hung him to a tree in the neighborhood, where he remained until quite an early hour this morning.

About 9 o'clock yesterday morning, Capt. MOTT, of the United States artillery, having been sent with a strong force to cut down the unfortunate negro, was met by the mob with the most persistent opposition. After requesting them to disperse, and being still menaced by the crowd, he ordered his men to fire; three rounds of grape were poured into them with fearful effect. When they dispersed, it was ascertained that upward of twenty-five had been killed and a number seriously wounded.

Another negro was also hung by the mob in the forenoon, in Thirty-sixth-street, between Sixth and Seventh avenues.

The following is a partial list of the killed and wounded in the fire of the military upon the rioters in Thirty-second-street:

Michael Ryan, Eleventh-avenue, killed.
Daniel Kiernan, Eleventh-avenue, killed.
Patrick Garvey, Eleventh-avenue, killed.
John Grey, Forty-second-street, killed.
John Kearney, Eleventh-avenue, killed.
Patrick Quinn, Eleventh-avenue, killed.
James Garrett, Eleventh-avenue, killed.
Mrs. Thornton, Eleventh-avenue, shot through the heart.
Child of Mrs. Thornton, Eleventh-avenue, shot through both legs.
Patrick Casey, Eleventh avenue, killed.
Mrs. Lawrence, Eleventh-avenue, killed.
Two Germans, names unknown, Forty-second-street, killed.
Two Germans, names unknown, Forty-third-street, killed.
Mrs. Lawrence and child, Eleventh-avenue, killed.
Mrs. Kirtland, Eleventh-avenue, killed.
Richard Stafford, Eleventh-avenue, killed.
C. Larkin, Eleventh-avenue, killed.
Woman, name unknown, killed.
Lawrence Ryan, Eleventh-avenue, killed.
Mr. Ackley, Eleventh-avenue, killed.

The above twenty-three names are all that could be obtained up to the hour of going to press, but it is known that several others were mortally wounded. The greatest consternation prevails in the neighborhood, the women and children filling the air with their cries and lamentations, while the men who were happily spared from the dreadful fate of their friends and companions sat mournful and sullen.

An Evening Riot in the First-avenue.

THE RABBLE IN CONFLICT WITH CITIZEN-VOLUNTEERS—THIRTY OR FORTY PERSONS KILLED.

A messenger brought information to the Seventh regiment Armory, at 6 o'clock last evening, that the mob was in great strength in the First-avenue, between Eighteenth and Nineteenth streets, apparently organizing, preparatory to moving upon a marauding expedition. Col. WINSLOW, of the Fifth regiment, (Duryea Zouaves,) then in command at the Armory, immediately ordered a detachment of volunteers under arms, consisting of three companies, comprising an aggregate of 150 men, and a battery of two howitzers. Placing himself at the head of this force, and taking with him Major ROBINSON and Col. JARDINE, of the Tenth regiment (Hawkins' Zouaves)—the latter in command of the battery—Col. WINSLOW led his command at the double quick to the scene of the disturbance. Passing down Nineteenth-street, the howitzers were brought into position, promptly unlimbered, and trained up and down the First-avenue, while the infantry formed in line to support them. The locality abounds in tenement-houses, where the class of persons live of which the mob is composed, and into these buildings the mass of the rioters took refuge on the appearance of the soldiers. From the roof and windows of every house the mob at once opened an attack, delivering a brisk and persistent fire upon the military of musketry and pistols, as well as a volley of bricks and other missiles. To this assault the soldiers replied, and the howitzers raked the avenue up and down with canister, of which ten rounds were discharged. It is estimated that this fire killed as many as thirty persons, and the effect was a partial dispersion of the rioters, although some of the more bold among them lurked behind the corners of the buildings, whence they would sally out, discharge their guns, and again go to cover.

The infantry force, meanwhile, although uniformed, and just enrolled for the emergency, stood gallantly up to the work, loading with rapidity and firing with precision at the rioters, wherever they showed themselves, at window, or upon roof, or at the street corners. The mob, in this instance, however, clearly had the small force of soldiers at an advantage. Col. WINSLOW had not men enough to make a charge upon the buildings, and as many as ten of his little command, after twenty minutes' fighting, had already fallen—several being killed outright. He reluctantly, therefore, ordered a retreat, which was conducted with veteran coolness, notwithstanding the fact that as the soldiers marched through Nineteenth-street they were followed for some distance by the howling mob, which were left masters of the field. Unfortunately Col. WINSLOW found it impossible to bring away all the killed, and a few of the bodies were left in the hands of the frenzied mob. Among the dead were a Captain and Lieutenant, both of whom had served with the Duryea Zouaves, and Col. JARDINE was wounded in the thigh. He was taken to the house of a surgeon in Nineteenth-street, whose door it was necessary to force, and there left to be taken care of.

The mob in this instance seemed to be remarkably well organized, firing at the word of command.

About 11 o'clock the riot in Nineteenth-street and First-avenue was renewed. Capt. PUTNAM and Capt. SHELBY, of the United States army, with two field pieces and 150 men, repaired to the scene. They were assaulted with stones and brickbats from the tops of houses and from windows. They fired upon the mob and cleared the streets. The brickbats came so thick from the houses that it became necessary to give the order to turn the fire on the buildings. Five rounds of grapeshot were fired, with destructive effect. It is impossible at this late hour to give the number killed. The troops remained on the ground until 12½ o'clock, at which time perfect quiet reigned in the neighborhood.

The wounds received by Col. JARDINE, at the fight in the early part of the evening, are more severe than was at first anticipated, and are likely to prove fatal.

FACTS AND INCIDENTS OF THE RIOT.

At a late hour on Tuesday night the mob, numbering 4,000 or 5,000, made an attack upon the clothing-store of Messrs. BROOKS BROTHERS, in Catharine-street, corner of Cherry. Sergeant FINNEY, of the Third Precinct, while in the discharge of his duty in endeavoring to protect the property of this establishment, was knocked down, beaten on the head and body with clubs, and afterward shot in the hand by a pistol by one of the rioters. He was subsequently conveyed to the Station-house, where his wounds were dressed. He is very severely injured, and no hopes are entertained of his recovery. Officer DANIEL FIELDS, of the same Precinct, was knocked down and brutally beaten about the head and face at the same time.

A man named JOHN MATZEL was shot and instantly killed. It is reported that he was one of the leaders of the mob, and that the ball which pierced his heart came from a revolver in the hands of one of the officers of the law. He was in the act of entering the clothing-store at the time he met his death.

Plunder seems to have been the sole object with the marauders in their attack upon the store of the Messrs. BROOKS. The fine ready-made clothing therein was tempting. Fortunately, the Police and the employes of the establishment successfully repelled the invaders before much property had been stolen. Three or four persons, whose names could not be ascertained, lost their lives at this place, and many others were badly injured.

An unoffending citizen named VAN R. FITCH, was quietly walking through Warren-street, about ten o'clock on Tuesday night, when he was knocked down and beaten in a shocking manner by some unknown parties. After the infliction of this outrage they left the man in the middle of the street, evidently believing him to be dead, and made good their escape. Mr. FITCH was picked up by some citizens and taken to a neighboring drug store, where his wounds were dressed. He was afterwards conveyed to his residence in Eleventh-street, in a dying condition.

THE MURDER OF COLORED PEOPLE IN THOMPSON AND SULLIVAN STREETS.

At a late hour on Tuesday night the mob made an attack upon the tenement houses, occupied by colored people, in Sullivan and Thompson streets. For three hours, and up to two o'clock yesterday morning there was what may be truly said to be a "reign of terror" throughout all that portion of the City. Several buildings were fired, and a large number of colored persons were beaten so badly that they lay insensible in the street for hours after. Two colored children at No. 59 Thompson-street were shot and instantly killed. Men, women and children, in large numbers flocked to the Eighth Precinct Station-house for protection. Over one hundred of them were there accommodated with temporary shelter.

THE SACKING OF BUILDINGS IN AVENUES B AND A.

Late in the afternoon of Tuesday the hardware-store of AARON HAXTER, situated at No. 78 Avenue B, was attacked by the rioters. The front doors were burst open, the windows of the building were all smashed with stones and brickbats, and all the goods and valuables were taken away. The store was completely stripped, nothing of value being left.

From this place the mob repaired to the lock and gunsmith store of JOHN WAGNER, No. 86 Avenue A. This was also broken open, sacked and robbed of the contents, and afterward the property was distributed among the rioters.

Late on Tuesday night the tailoring establishment of THOMAS EGAN, on Avenue A, was forced open by the mob, the doors and windows were all destroyed, and the place completely stripped of its contents.

A COLORED MAN BEATEN TO DEATH IN LEROY-STREET.

In the forepart of the day on Tuesday, a colored man was set upon by a party of men and boys in Leroy-street, and beaten on the head, face and breast with large clubs, until life appeared to be extinct. They then stripped him of his raiment and left him for dead. A few citizens afterward conveyed him to the residence of a benevolent lady, where his wounds were dressed by a Surgeon, and everything possible was done to make the injured man comfortable. His injuries are so serious, however, that it is impossible for him to recover.

THE RIOTERS IN THE SEVENTH PRECINCT.

A colored man, named PETER HUESTED, 63 years of age, came to the Seventh Precinct yesterday, suffering from severe injuries received at his residence, No. 74 Roosevelt-street. His head and face were horribly mangled, and several of his ribs were broken. His house was burned down and all of his property stolen. He was conveyed to Bellevue Hospital in a dying condition.

A colored man, named THOMAS LEWIS, aged 33 years, was conveyed to Bellevue Hospital in a dying state from the effects of a fracture of the skull and other injuries received by the mob at the corner of Market and Monroe streets.

Officer NIXON, of this Precinct, conveyed to Bellevue Hospital, a boy named KELLY, aged 14 years, who was shot in the lower part of the abdomen. The wound is believed to be fatal.

The grocery-store of HENRY SCHLOS, situated on the corner of Water and Gouverneur streets, was attacked by the mob, late on Tuesday night. After the plunderers had robbed it of all its contents, they set it on fire. Fortunately, the flames were extinguished by the firemen before they had communicated to the adjoining buildings.

DOINGS OF GOV. SEYMOUR.

Gov. SEYMOUR has established his Headquarters at the St. Nicholas Hotel, where Gen. WOOL resides, and he spent most of the day yesterday in consultation with the General and with the City authorities as to the speediest mode of restoring the public peace. He feels confident that the mob has no organization, and regards them as roving bands of lawless desperadoes bent on plunder. He is anxious that the people should follow the instructions set forth in his proclamation of Tuesday, and organize themselves into armed squads in their respective neighborhoods to protect their property and the peace of the City. The following letter, written by the Governor on Monday, may be of interest:

NEW-YORK, 13th July, 1863.

MY DEAR SIR: I have received your note about the draft. On Saturday last I sent my Adjutant General to Washington for the purpose of urging a suspension of the draft, for I know that the City of New-York can furnish its full quota by volunteering. I have received a dispatch from Gen. HALLECK that the draft is suspended. There is no doubt that the conscription is postponed. I learn this from a number of sources. If I get any information of a change of policy at Washington, I will let you know. Truly yours,

HORATIO SEYMOUR.

Hon. SAMUEL SLOAN, President of the Hudson River Railroad Company, New-York.

The conjectures of the Governor contained in the above as to the postponement of the draft, were confirmed yesterday by the following note received from Assistant Provost Marshal NUGENT:

THE DRAFT.

NEW-YORK, July 15, 1863.

The draft has been suspended in New-York City and Brooklyn.

ROBERT NUGENT,
Colonel and Assistant Provost-Marshal-General.

AN ATTACK ON MR. GREELEY'S BOARDING-HOUSE—GREAT AMOUNT OF PROPERTY DESTROYED.

Late on Tuesday night, the rioters visited the house of Mr. SINCLAIR in Twenty-ninth street. They had been informed that this was the residence of Mr. HORACE GREELEY, and the threats of vengeance which were uttered were many and loud. Mr. GREELEY had formerly boarded at this place, and the rioters believed the premises were his. The mob, numbering about a thousand, made a fierce attack on the building, but for a time all their efforts to force the doors were useless. Meantime a young man named HYDE mounted the front stoop and addressed the crowd. He said, "I am a good Democrat, and am bitterly opposed to the draft; but I do not wish to see private property destroyed. Mr. GREELEY does not reside here, and it is hard to see the private property of unoffending citizens wantonly destroyed. It is unjust to plunder and burn this residence simply because Mr. GREELEY once boarded here."

The mob could not understand the justness of this speech, and young HYDE was at once seized by the leaders, hurled to the pavement and beaten by men, women and children in the most cruel and inhuman manner. Just at the time when HYDE was believed to be expiring, a man named WILSON, residing in Twenty-ninth-street, aged about 50 years, was pointed out as Mr. GREELEY. The cry of "GREELEY" rapidly spread through the crowd, and the man WILSON was forthwith seized, his clothes entirely torn from his person, and he was most cruelly beaten upon the head and body until he became unconscious. At this point in the tragedy, Mrs. WILSON, the wife of the victim, ran out from a house opposite, and with uplifted hands, and agony of voice truly pitiable to hear, she implored the mob for Heaven's sake to desist and not to kill her husband. This wild appeal caused a lull among the rioters, and in the meantime three men caught up the body of WILSON and conveyed it to his residence. The crowd finding themselves foiled in reference to GREELEY alias WILSON, immediately turned their attention to HYDE, whom they swore they would hang and burn if caught. In the midst of this excitement the Police made their appearance and scattered the rioters, not, however, until Mr. SINCLAIR's house had been sacked and robbed of everything of value.

THE GAS HOUSES.

The mob has made several demonstrations upon the gas houses which they seem very anxious to destroy in order that they may the better carry out their schemes of plunder under cover of the universal darkness that would follow such a catastrophe. Frequent threats were made yesterday that they should be burned last night, but the authorities early saw the importance of securing the safety of these establishments, and ample preparations have been made to repel any force that can be brought to bear against them. Still the riot has not been without serious effect in reference to the supply of gas, owing to large numbers of the workmen employed in the gas houses (under the influence of threats from the rioters or from some other cause) leaving their post, as will be seen from the following note from the engineer of the Manhattan Gas Company:

To the Editor of the New-York Times:

Will you please request our citizens to use the gas as sparingly as possible for a couple of nights; our men having been taken away, the supply of gas is limited.

Yours, &c., JOS. A. SABBATON,
JULY 15, 1863. Engineer.

THE RIOT IN THE TENTH PRECINCT.

A boy, 11 years of age, was brought to the Station-house of this Precinct late on Tuesday night. Some citizens from the corner of Pitt and Delancey streets found him dead in the street. He had been stabbed with a bayonet in four different parts of his body. His name was subsequently ascertained to be WM. H. THOMPSON. He resided with his parents at No. 38 Sheriff-street.

Nearly one hundred colored persons sought refuge in this Station from the infuriated mob.

THE PLUNDERING OF STORES IN THE ELEVENTH PRECINCT.

The dry goods store of Messrs. GOLDSCHMIDT & SOLINGER, No. 17 Avenue C, was broken open and sacked by a mob numbering at least a thousand, the most of whom were boys. The entire contents, valued at $40,000, were stolen.

The lumber-yard of OGDEN & Co., corner of Avenue C and Fourteenth-street, was set on fire, and the contents, valued at $50,000, entirely destroyed.

ANOTHER STATION HOUSE BURNED.

About midnight the mob proceeded to the Eighteenth Precinct Station house in Second-avenue and set fire to the building. The fire continued for upwards of two hours. The attack was so unexpected that no resistance could be offered with any prospect of success.

OTHER OUTRAGES.

An attempt was also made to sack the colored church in Lexington-avenue, but by the timely interference of the Police, any violence on this building was prevented.

The Thirteenth Ward was the scene of great excitement during the night. Bands of thieves, taking advantage of the occasion, joined themselves with the rioters for the purpose of plunder. They went into a lager-bier saloon, on the corner of Governeur and Division streets, and demolished the premises.

They also demolished another lager-bier saloon in Suffolk-street, between Grand and Hester streets, and drove a number of negroes who resided in the rear of the premises into the street. The colored people, however, took timely refuge in the Tenth Ward Station-house.

Throughout Grand-street the scene was almost all night one of intense excitement. Many of the stores were broken into, and the mob helped themselves to whatever they wanted.

The women and children which accompanied the mob, supplied themselves freely, and then the citizens of the ward, seeing no chance of any assistance from the City authorities, although there were soldiers in the Station-house near by, straightway held a meeting and resolved to take the law into their own hands. Accordingly, about fifty citizens, armed with all conceivable weapons, attacked the party while they were pillaging the boot and shoe store corner of Grand and Pitt streets, and completely dispersed the thieves, capturing five men and one boy.

Several of the rioters were severely wounded, but they, with the balance of their gang, made good their escape. This drama had hardly been ended, and the citizens retired to their houses, when a large military force made its appearance. Too much praise cannot be rendered to the citizens of the Thirteenth Ward for the fearless and energetic manner in which they disposed of these rowdies.

Yesterday morning the Post-Office in this City was threatened, but ample means have been taken to protect it—it is strongly garrisoned, and is supplied with a heavy armament.

A strong detachment under Capt. WILKES, acting under orders of Brig.-Gen. BROWN, were yesterday morning sent to protect the Forty-second-street Gas-house. Everything in that neighborhood is considered safe.

Yesterday morning a strong mob assembled in front of the residence of Judge WHITE, of the Superior Court of this City, and commenced demonstrations of a lawless character. The Judge put out his flag, which the mob ordered him to pull in again; this was refused, and as a consequence, several windows were broken. The crowd, however, were finally arrested by the police.

THE BODY OF COL. O'BRIEN.

It is now ascertained that the body of Col. O'BRIEN is at the dead-house. His murderers, after beating him in the most merciless manner with stones, bars of iron, bludgeons and slung-shots, grabbed him in several parts of his body and then dragged him through the gutters by a cord around his neck, then threw him into an area way and stood guard over him. His body was at length removed and conveyed by two priests to the dead-house at Bellevue Hospital. He was almost naked and terribly mangled.

WAREHOUSES GUARDED.

There are three warehouses in the City, one in Worth-street, another in Franklin street, and another in White-street, which contain Government stores and munitions. These have been strongly guarded. The Old City Guard, under command of Col. BURTNETT, Capts. JONES and MCNEAL, are strongly posted in at the building in Franklin-street. Col. ROWE is in command of a strong force of regulars in Worth-street, and Col. VREGREBACK is in command of a strong force on White-street.

These were all placed in position on Tuesday night. Assistant Provost-Marshal N. J. GLASSEY, under the direction of Gen. WOOL, had the entire management and disposition of the men, and posted them to the best advantage. Everything in these quarters is quiet.

SOME OF THE KILLED AND WOUNDED.

The four Coroners of this City were very busily engaged all day yesterday in holding inquests upon the victims of the riot. Coroner NAUMANN held an inquest upon the body of MARTIN HALEY, who was shot through the heart by a pistol in the hands of a Mr. SMITH, at the shoe-store No. 159 Greenwich-street.

Also, on the body of W. C. WILLIAMS, a book-keeper, residing at No. 87 Clinton avenue, Brooklyn. The deceased was a young married man, of very peaceable habits, and took no part in the riot. He was shot through the heart at the burning of the Armory in Second avenue and Twenty-First-street.

The same Coroner held an inquest on the body of JANE BARRY, 10 years of age, who was killed by furniture which was thrown upon her at the burning of the Colored Orphan Asylum, in Fifth-avenue.

Also, on the body of JULIA HENNESSEY, a married woman, aged 35 years, who was shot in her house at No. 209 East Twentieth-street. The woman had fifteen minutes before been confined with an infant. The shot passed through her heart and also killed the child, which was lying beside her.

An inquest was held on the body of PATRICK FLANNIGAN, who was shot in the neck, in Broadway, near Twenty-ninth street, yesterday morning.

THOMAS RILEY came to his death from being beaten with clubs at No. 253 East Twenty-first-street. He was about forty-one years of age, and was one of the leaders in the riots of Monday and Tuesday.

JOHN MARTIN was clubbed to death at No. 30 Hamilton-street by the mob. He was a respectable man, and took no part in the riot.

An inquest was held upon VALENTINE HEUTTLIN, a German, aged 39 years, who was shot at the burning of the Armory in Twenty-sixth-street. He was one of the ringleaders of the riot.

Coroners RANNEY, COLLIN and WILDEY were also engaged during the whole day in different portions of the City in holding inquests, but owing to the great number of dead, no returns had been made at the office at a late hour last evening.

POLICEMEN SHOT.

The following officers of the Twenty-fifth Precinct (Broadway Squad) were shot on Tuesday night while on duty between Ninth and Tenth avenues: ALBERT D. ROBINSON, EDWARD DIPPLE and JOHN HODGSON. They were taken to the New-York Hospital, where their wounds were dressed. They are regarded as being in a very critical condition.

THE RIOT AT HARLEM.

A great many erroneous reports have been circulated about the depredations committeed by the mob at Harlem. There is no truth in the report that any of the bridges there have been burned or even molested. The only damage done has been the burning of Mr. HANSIN's factory early Tuesday morning. Small bands of the rioters, composed in great part of boys, have amused themselves by prowling about the streets shouting, singing and drinking, and a great many threats have been made, but no violent acts committed except the above. The demonstration in Harlem did not commence till Monday night, after the news of the down-town riot had got generally circulated, and by Tuesday night the citizens had fully organized themselves and were prepared to defend themselves and their property. A knowledge of this fact by the rioters probably deterred them from entering on a general system of plunder. Most of the men who joined in the prowling gangs are well known there and will brought to justice at the proper time.

RIOTOUS DEMONSTRATIONS ON STATEN ISLAND.

A mob, consisting of men and boys, are going around the different towns and villages in Richmond County, armed with clubs, and at every place their number is increased. They have possession of the arms that were in the Lyceum, and they say it is their intention to go to the County Jail and get a negro, who is confined there, and hang him.

They are also going to Fort Richmond to get possession of the arms at that place; they also have several houses in view, which they intend to destroy, among them that of JOHN C. THOMPSON. A small force of military, if on hand, could easily put down this mob.

AT YORKVILLE.

The vicinity of Yorkville was also haunted on Tuesday night with the mob, and there being no military or police force on the spot at the time, they had undisputed sway for nearly all night. Several houses were torn down, and a vast amount of irreparable mischief perpetrated. The house of Mr. GRAY, of Yorkville, was fired no less than four times, by the marauders, and they at last succeeded in getting it in a full blaze. A reign of terror prevails among the population of this vicinity, many of them have packed up whatever of value they can carry with them in a hasty flight, and have left for the country. The upper part of the town was almost the entire night in complete possession of the mob.

A WORD FOR OUR FIREMEN.

The firemen of this City deserve the heartiest thanks and gratitude at the hands of the citizens of our metropolis.

Notwithstanding the fact that they have run great risks in attempting to extinguish the conflagrations kindled by the mob, they have been fearless and prompt in the execution of their duties.

In many places where they have been called upon to extinguish the flame of the marauders, they have met with some opposition from the crowd, yet they have persevered fearlessly in the performance of their duties, and have worked untiringly to save property from destruction.

The citizens cannot be too grateful to this highly useful class in our community. They deserve the best thanks and gratitude of all true and law-abiding men.

DEFENCES OF THE TIMES OFFICE.

Last night the TIMES Office again presented itself in a state of the most formidable defence. It appeared able to withstand a long siege before it would surrender to the mob.

Pursuant to the following order, Lieut. CHARLES B. SMITH took command of the defences of this building.

PRINTING HOUSE SQUARE, July 15, 1863.

Lieut. Smith:

SIR: In my absence you will attend to the defences of this post as now arranged, and are authorized to call upon the troops under command of Capt. GREYTENSON, and the Light battery for support in the event of attack.

(Signed,) J. W. ADAMS,
Col. Commanding.

Lieut. SMITH had under his command about thirty regulars and one hundred and fifty volunteers; in addition to this, he had two cannon posted—one commanding Spruce and Nassau streets, the other commanding the range of Park-place.

Lieut. SMITH had most judiciously posted sentries along the street, from Spruce-street to Tammany Hall, and from Park Row to Nassau-street, fronting the TIMES Office.

These were relieved about 4 o'clock this morning by fresh sentries, and the utmost good order prevailed during the entire night.

THE TIMES AGAIN ILLUMINATED.

The partial illumination of the TIMES Building on Tuesday night had the intended effect of annoying the thieves and scoundrels whose deeds alone befit the darkness. Last night, therefore, for the especial benefit of the mobocracy, the illumination was repeated, but on a more extensive and splendid scale. Our front on Printing House-square not only cast bright rays far out toward Chatham and Centre streets, eliciting the admiration of all good citizens, but on the Park-row side also the immense flaming eagle, holding the fiery scroll of Union, gazed fiercely at the blazing arch of light above, that figured in letters of gold the name of the NEW-YORK TIMES. Even from Broadway through the softening foliage of the trees in the Park, the illumination was charming enough to all who saw it, save to the scoundrels but for whose threats it would not have been made.

REINFORCEMENTS FOR THE MOB.

The scoundrels and roughs—the Blood Tubs and Plug Uglies of Baltimore, and the Schuylkill Rangers and other rowdies of Philadelphia—are reported to have come to the City in large numbers to make common cause with the Dead Rabbits, Mackerelville, and other leading spirits of the riot in their work of carnage and plunder. The scoundrels cannot afford to miss this golden opportunity of indulging their brutal natures, and at the same time serving their colleagues the Copperheads and secesh sympathizers.

ARRIVAL OF TROOPS.

The Seventh regiment New-York National Guard arrived last evening from Harrisburgh, also the Sixty-fifth (Buffalo) regiment, with a battery. They reported to Gov. SEYMOUR. Other regiments will arrive to-day.

THE COMMON COUNCIL ON THE DRAFT.

A special meeting of both Boards of the Common Council was held yesterday, and $2,500,000 appropriated to pay $300 exemption to poor men who may be drafted. See official report in another column.

THE NATIONALITY OF THE RIOTERS.

The *Tribune* of yesterday morning has the following: "It is a curious fact, that of all the arrests made, every one is Irish." However this may be, it is a fact, patent to every one who has seen anything of the mob, that it is composed almost exclusively of Irishmen and boys. In view of this fact, the following appeal from the distinguished prelate whom the Irish particularly revere, and whom everybody respects, is timely and appropriate:

An Appeal to the Irish Catholics from Archbishop Hughes.

In the present disturbed condition of the City, I will appeal not only to them, but to all persons who love God and revere the holy Catholic religion which they profess, to respect also the laws of man and the peace of society, to retire to their homes with as little delay as possible, and disconnect themselves from the seemingly deliberate intention to disturb the peace and social rights of the citizens of New-York. If they are Catholics, or of such of them as are Catholics, I ask, for God's sake—for the sake of their holy religion—for my sake, if they have any respect for the Episcopal authority—to dissolve their associations with reckless men, who have little regard either for Divine or human laws.

†JOHN,
Archbishop of New-York.

RIOTERS IN WESTCHESTER COUNTY.

On Tuesday morning a band of about 70 or 60 coarse-looking men passed along the Harlem Railroad, from Mott Haven to the junction with the New-Haven road, a mile or so above Williams' Bridge, and tore up the track at several points. Going up they passed through the suburbs of Morrissania, and through the village of West Farms, going along with clubs, but with quite orderly demeanor, offering no one any indignity. It was understood from them that they were bent on obstructing the railroad, fearing that it might be used to bring troops over from the East. The crowd came in part from New-York, it was believed, and in Westchester County they were joined by a considerable number of the railroad laborers and others. At Williams' Bridge they tore up the track three different times, and it was twice relaid by a section of workmen, who twice fled from the rioters. Exasperated at the prompt manner in which the track was relaid, they set to work to burn the passenger depot at Williams' Bridge, but were dissuaded from this purpose on being assured that it was private property, belonging to the man who keeps a refreshment saloon in it. They broke open the ticket office, however, and threw the papers and tickets outdoors, scattering and destroying them by tearing them up. They then destroyed the telegraph apparatus, and afterward broke down the telegraph and cut down three or four of the poles. When they proceeded up the track, news of their progress reached the village of Mount Vernon, three miles distant, on the New-Haven Railroad. It was supposed they were going there to destroy the cartridge factory of Messrs. DOW & JOHNSON, who recently located there. The firm took every precaution to disappoint the rioters, if they came there. The hands were all dismissed for the day. These are chiefly young girls. The stock of powder and other material was then removed to the magazine, which is located some distance off, in an out-of-the way place. The report that rioters were likely to visit the village created much consternation. Some families left their houses, and went to others considered more secure. In consequence of the cars not running, many of the male residents, who mostly come to the City daily, were at home, and steps were taken to defend private property from damage. The rioters did not come near the village, but went on up the Harlem road. Had they visited Mount Vernon they probably would have met with a damaging repulse, the citizens being determined to resist them and to put them down. On Wednesday morning the track was all in good order on both roads, the brakes having been repaired, but no cars were running, in consequence of the disturbed state of affairs in the City. Persons who felt obliged to come to the City came in private conveyances and on foot. In going back all sorts of means were resorted to. Conveyances were scarce, and exorbitant prices were in general asked for them. In many cases even ladies walked from Harlem Bridge out from one to ten miles, rather than pay the excessively high prices charged for wagons. The people living out of town, and doing business in the City, at least those who daily travel over the Harlem and New-Haven Railroads, have suffered great inconvenience this week. One train went out on each road on Monday night, from Mott-Haven, but on Tuesday morning the trains were all running right again. Tuesday afternoon no trains ran, nor did any run yesterday. Every night this week, persons going to Mount Vernon and above there have been from two to five hours in making the journey.

DOINGS IN BROOKLYN

The city continues quiet, and there is no apprehension that the peace of the community will in any way be disturbed. The draft having been suspended for the present, there can be no pretext whatever for inaugurating scenes of disorder.

The exempt members of the different regiments now absent have effected organizations, and the Arsenal and City Armory are guarded night and day.

The Mayor was requested by prominent citizens to call a public meeting, but in consequence of the present excitable state of the public mind it was deemed advisable not to do so.

The Sheriff of Kings County has issued the following appeal to the citizens:

The undersigned, Sheriff of the County of Kings, congratulates the inhabitants of said County upon the peace and good order which have been hitherto maintained in their midst, notwithstanding the violence and excitement prevalent in the adjoining City. He earnestly exhorts all citizens to render prompt and entire obedience to the laws, and to abstain from all acts, assemblages and words tending to any breach of the peace. And he suggests that all citizens may render essential service in the maintenance of law and order by enrolling themselves in companies, and designating proper persons for the purpose of communicating with the undersigned, that in case of violence they may be forthwith summoned as a posse, in aid of the authorities, in maintaining good order. He suggests the Station-houses of the Police in the various precincts as convenient and proper places for such enrollment, and that the Police will extend all reasonable facilities for such purpose.

ANTHONY F. CAMPBELL, Sheriff.

Dated, BROOKLYN, July 15, 1863.

Several persons were brought before Justice PERRY, yesterday, on the charge of stealing from BROOKS BROTHERS clothing store, in New-York, during the sacking of that establishment on Tuesday. They were arrested at Catharine Ferry, having in their possession bundles of clothing, consisting of coats, pants, vests, collars, boxes of buttons, thread and trimmings, amounting in value to about $150. The accused gave their names as ANN MOORE, THOMAS SMITH, ANTHONY SMITH and RICHARD BALENSBERGH. Mr. BROOKS was sent for and identified the goods, and the parties were committed to jail for further examination.

EXCITEMENT IN JAMAICA—A NUMBER OF STORES ROBBED.

The disorderly proceedings originating in New-York have spread to the village of Jamaica, in Queens County, and has resulted in the sacking of several stores. It appears that on Tuesday about 1,000 men appeared in the streets, and after sacking the Provost Marshal's office, attacked the stores and helped themselves to such things as they wanted. [illegible] Their [illegible] familiar [illegible] the old [illegible]. There being no force to preserve order, the mob had it their own way. A meeting of citizens was [illegible] and several companies [illegible]. Mr. AARON A. DEGRAW was [illegible] to go to New-York for arms, in which he succeeded, and a sufficient number of muskets [illegible] to [illegible] [illegible] by morning. They [illegible] amply prepared for any emergency. The [illegible] [illegible] a number of mounted citizens [illegible] [illegible] as they marched along, but [illegible] of the way as soon as they could. The [illegible] promise the [illegible] a warm reception should they again make their appearance. [illegible] uniforms were in the Marshal's office. Of these about thirty were [illegible] in the streets and set on fire. The uniforms and accoutrements which were saved, were brought to the Navy-yard last night for safe keeping.

THE BOARD OF SUPERVISORS.

The Board met at the Alms-house [illegible]. A number of bills were [illegible] [illegible] was offered appropriating [illegible] toward paying exemption fees for such poor men with large families who may be drafted. The subject was laid over for one week.

DESTRUCTION OF GRAIN-ELEVATORS IN THE ATLANTIC DOCK BY FIRE—GREAT DESTRUCTION OF PROPERTY.

Two of the immense grain-elevators in Atlantic Dock Basin were destroyed by fire last night, involving great loss of property. They were set on fire by a mob consisting of about [illegible] men, supposed to be grain-shovelers formerly employed by the owners of the elevators, who, since the strike, had made threats that they would destroy them. The mob made their appearance shortly after 11 o'clock, and crossing four vessels, which lay between the dock and the Centre pier Elevator, commenced throwing stones. Only four men were present, and feeling themselves unable to resist, barricaded the doors, and made their escape into a small boat. A barrel of pitch, taken from HARP's storehouse was placed in the elevator and ignited. The flames spread rapidly, and it was present, but soon enveloped. The mob then set fire to the floating elevator, owned by Mr. B. BARBER, that also was soon in flames, and they then turned their attention to a mud-scow belonging to the Atlantic Dock Company, which shared a similar fate. The incendiaries then left, and were seen no more in the neighborhood. They threatened, on leaving, that other elevators in Erie Basin would next be attended to. The firemen were promptly on hand, but were unable to do more than to protect the neighboring vessels, all of which were hauled to a safe distance as fast as practicable. The elevators and scow was burned to the water's edge. The police and Mayor of the City were all was quiet. There was not a sign of disorderly conduct. Everything transpired peaceably. The incendiaries having accomplished their object, kept at a distance. The Central Pier Elevator was owned by SMITH, FANCHER & Co., and was constructed at a cost of $60,000. The Floating Elevator was the property of W. B. BARBER, and worth $25,000. The scow is valued at $5,000. Everything was destroyed. The reserved military were in readiness to act, if occasion should require, but their services were not needed.

DOINGS IN WILLIAMSBURGH.

The excitement in Brooklyn (E. D.) is subsiding. During Tuesday night and yesterday it ran pretty high in the Fourteenth Ward of the city, but the announcement that the draft has been suspended by the authorities has produced a most happy effect. Citizens are rapidly enrolling in volunteer companies, and are doing that is necessary to maintain the good order of the city.

On Tuesday evening a meeting of those partially disaffected took place in the open air, at which it was resolved to organize for a resistance of the draft until it should have been decided by the Courts. Col. EDWARD TAYLOR addressed the crowd, and all was orderly and quiet.

At Jamaica, on Tuesday evening, a mob of 50 persons broke into a store, and taking therefrom $3,000 worth of soldiers' uniforms, burned them.

RIOTOUS PROCEEDINGS IN JERSEY CITY.

On Tuesday night a few hundred persons, mostly boys, assembled at the railroad crossing in Jersey City; but, through the efforts of Father KELLY, Sheriff MCANALLY and Chief of Police REILY, they committed no acts of violence further than hunting negroes, &c. Yesterday, toward evening, they began to show a restless spirit, and the negroes nearly all left the city for the country. Threats were made to burn the Bethesda Baptist Church, and also to destroy the property of prominent citizens.

MORE MILITARY ORGANIZING.

ORGANIZATION OF THE FIRST N. Y. CAVALRY.

There will be a meeting of the old members of the First New-York Cavalry, now in the City, at 9 o'clock this morning, in the arsenal, corner of Thirty-Fifth-street and Seventh avenue, to organize a cavalry company for duty in the present emergency. The company will be immediately equipped by the City authorities. The call is made by Capt. ADAMS, Capt. BATTERSBY, Lieut. LAVERTY and Lieut. LEVORSEE, and all members now in the City are earnestly invited to attend.

"ATTENTION," OLD THIRTY-EIGHTH REGIMENT.—New-York, July 16, 1863.—In accordance with the request of Major-Gen. WOOL, commanding Department of the East, the officers and members of the old Thirty-eighth regiment, (second Scott Life Guard,) are requested to meet at Central Hall, corner of Grand and Centre streets, this morning, at 10 o'clock, for the purpose of tendering our services for the protection of United States and State property. All old soldiers of other regiments are invited to join us.

JAS. D. POTTER, late Lieut.-Col. 38th N. Y. V.
ROBT. F. ALLASON, late Lieut.-Col. 38th N. Y. V.
Capt. GEO. M. DENNETT, late of Co. D.
Capt. JACOB LEONARD, late of Co. A.
Capt. ROBT. S. WATSON.
Capt. CURVISLIER.

SEVENTEENTH REGIMENT NEW-YORK VOLUNTEERS.—The old members of this regiment are requested to assemble at headquarters, No. 200 Broadway, and enroll themselves into companies to repress the insurrection. Members of the old regiments now in the City are invited to join. Arms and ammunition will be issued.

WM. T. C. GROWER,
Colonel Commanding.

HEADQUARTERS SIXTH REGIMENT NEW-YORK VOLUNTEERS, WILSON'S ZOUAVES, CAMP SPRAGUE, July 15, 1863.—By order of Gov. SEYMOUR, I hereby assume command of the State and Volunteer forces on Staten Island for the purpose of suppressing riot and maintaining law and order. I call upon all good citizens to report at once for military duty, and all members and friends of the Sixth regiment New-York volunteers, are requested to rally round their old commander. They will report to Maj. BURGESS, at No. 639 Broadway, New-York, for transportation, or at the Camp, New-Dorp, S. I.

First Lieut. JAS. ENTWISLE is appointed Acting Assistant Adjutant-General, and will be obeyed and respected accordingly.

WM. WILSON,
Colonel, Commanding Troops on Staten Island.

ORDER FOR A MEETING OF THE NINTH REGIMENT.—HEADQUARTERS, NINTH REGIMENT N. Y. S. N. G.—In compliance with peremptory orders from Major-Gen. SANDFORD, the members and ex-members of this regiment will assemble this morning, July 16, at the City-Guard Armory, No. 654 Broadway, at 10 o'clock, in full fatigue dress. Those members not having uniforms will appear in citizen's dress, as the emergency requires the presence of every man. By order of

Capt. JOHN W. DAVIS, Commanding.

CHARLES R. BRAINE, Acting Adjutant.

THE EAGLE ENGINE COMPANY.—The members of Eagle Engine Company No. 13 held a meeting at their house last evening, and formed themselves into a Home Guard to protect the property in their neighborhood from the rioters.

CALL FOR MOUNTED PATROLS.—It has become a matter of vital importance in the present disturbed condition of the City that the streets should be properly patrolled, that speedy information may be thus obtained of the first signs of gatherings of disaffected persons.

To this end the sons of gentlemen, merchants and others who own, or can control, the use of horses for the purpose, are invited to report mounted to the

[Continued on Eighth Page.]

The New-York Times.

VOL. XII—NO. 3684. NEW-YORK, WEDNESDAY JULY, 15, 1863. PRICE THREE CENTS.

Editorials

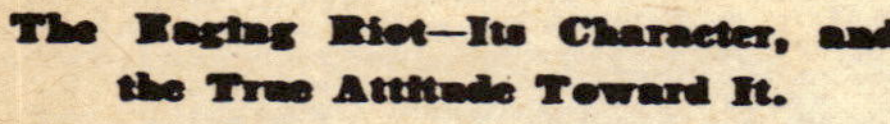

The Raging Riot—Its Character, and the True Attitude Toward It.

The mob in our City is still rampant. Though the increasing display of armed force has done something to check its more flagrant outrages, it is yet wild with fury, and panting for fresh havoc. The very fact of its being withstood seems only to give it, for the time, new malignity; just as the wild beast never heaves with darker rage than when he begins to see that his way is barred. The monster grows more dangerous as he grows desperate. More than ever, everything depends on the energy and vigilance of the authorities, and the sustaining coöperation of all true men. Official duty and public spirit should supremely rule the hour. The man in public place, or in private place, who falters in this dread crisis should stand accursed.

We trust that Gov. SEYMOUR does not mean to falter. We believe that in his heart he really intends to vindicate the majesty of the law, according to his sworn obligations. But, in the name of the dignity of Government and of pub'ic safety, we protest against any further indulgence in the sort of speech with which he yesterday sought to propitiate the mob. Entreaties and promises are not what the day calls for. No official, however high his position, can make them, without bringing public authority into contempt. This monster is to be met with a sword, and that only. He is not to be placated with a sop; and, if he were, it would only be to make him all the more insatiate hereafter. In the name of all that is sacred in law and all that is precious in society, let there be no more of this. There is force enough at the command of Gov. SEYMOUR to maintain civil authority. He will do it. He cannot but do it. He is a ruined man if he fails to do it. This mob is not our master. It is not to be compounded with by paying black mail. It is not to be supplicated and sued to stay its hand. It is to be defied, confronted, grappled with, prostrated, crushed. The Government of the State of New-York is its master, not its slave; its ruler, and not its minion.

It is too true that there are public journals who try to dignify this mob by some respectable appellation. The *Herald* characterizes it as the people, and the *World* as the laboring men of the City. These are libels that ought to have paralyzed the fingers that penned them. It is ineffably infamous to attribute to the people, or to the laboring men of this metropolis, such hideous barbarism as this horde has been displaying. The people of New-York and the laboring men of New-York are not incendiaries, nor robbers, nor assassins. They do not hunt down men whose only offence is the color God gave them; they do not chase, and insult, and beat women; they do not pillage an asylum for orphan children, and burn the very roof over those orphans' heads. They are civilized beings, valuing law and respecting decency; and they regard with unqualified abhorrence the doings of the tribe of savages that have sought to bear rule in their midst.

This mob is not the people, nor does it belong to the people. It is for the most part made up of the very vilest elements of the City. It has not even the poor merit of being what mobs usually are—the product of mere ignorance and passion. They talk, or rather did talk at first, of the oppressiveness of the Conscription law; but three-fourths of those who have been actively engaged in violence have been boys and young men under twenty years of age, and not at all subject to the Conscription. Were the Conscription law to be abrogated to-morrow, the controlling inspiration of the mob would remain all the same. It comes from sources quite independent of that law; or any other—from malignant hate toward those in better circumstances, from a craving for plunder, from a love of commotion, from a barbarous spite against a different race, from a disposition to bolster up the failing fortunes of the Southern rebels. All of these influences operate in greater or less measure upon any person engaged in this general defiance of law; and all combined have generated a composite monster more hellish than the triple-headed Cerberus.

It doubtless is true that the Conscription, or rather its preliminary process, furnished the occasion for the outbreak. This was so, simply because it was the most plausible pretext for commencing open defiance. But it will be a fatal mistake to assume that this pretext has but to be removed to restore quiet and contentment. Even if it be allowed that this might have been true at the outset, it is completely false now. A mob, even though it may start on a single incentive, never sustains itself for any time whatever on any one stimulant. With every hour it lives, it gathers new passions, and dashes after new objects. If you undertake to negotiate with it, you find that what it raved for yesterday, it has no concern for to-day. It is as inconstant as it is headstrong. The rabble greeted with cheers the suppliant attitude of Gov. Seymour, and his promises with reference to the Conscription law, but we have yet to hear that they thereupon abandoned their outrages. The fact stands that they are tonight, while we write, still infuriate, still insatiate.

You may as well reason with the wolves of the forest as with these men in their present mood. It is quixotic and suicidal to attempt it. The duties of the executive officers of this State and City are not to debate, or negotiate, or supplicate, but to *execute the laws*. To execute means to enforce *by authority*. This is their *only* official business. Let it be promptly and sternly entered upon with all the means now available, and it cannot fail of being carried through to an overwhelming triumph of public order. It may cost blood—much of it perhaps; but it will be a lesson to the public enemies, whom we always have and must have in our midst, that will last for a generation. Justice and mercy, this time, unite in the same behest:—*Give them grape, and a plenty of it.*

Draft riots in New York — Ruins of the Provost-Marshall's office

The Conscription Must be Enforced.

Not only must this infamous and dastardly mob be put down, but it must be balked in the object for which it was gotten up. It was ostensibly to defeat the enforcement of the Conscription. The Conscription is a necessity; the Conscription is a law; the Conscription is just. It is demanded for the suppression of the Southern rebellion; it is needed to fill up our heroic but shattered regiments; the country called for it, and acquiesced in its passage; the army is a unit in urging its enforcement. It is the justest mode of raising an army—just to the people of every class and condition, poor and rich, black and white. No class or order of citizens is exempt from its operation—even poor clergymen, if drafted, being compelled to shoulder their musket.

This mob should in no way be allowed to interfere with its enforcement. If a few hundred desperadoes, backed up by a few thousand misguided and deceived men, may violently nullify a law of such grand and wide-spread scope and value as this—if they are permitted to nullify and violently overthrow any law of the land, then all law everywhere and finally is at an end. We have not only no Union, but no Government, no society, no civil order. We have anarchy in its most frightful form. We have the condition of things which this great City has suffered from for the last two days made permanent. We shall have faction giving battle to faction, class warring upon class, sect fighting sect, interest contending with interest, knavery with honesty, lawlessness with legality—not in the old arenas, not on the forum and through the Press, with the weapons of reason and justice, but with ball, bayonet, bowie-knife and slung-shot, amid blood, carnage and rapine.

We cannot afford to yield the Conscription to this mob. The mob is an additional argument for its enforcement. The Government cannot afford to suspend a general law, intended to apply to the whole country, because of a local riot sprung by a few bad schemers in this City. The Conscription has already been enforced in Massachusetts, Rhode Island and Connecticut; and it is in the order of enforcement in every State of the Union. Can a scheme so extensive as this, so generally accepted everywhere, be thwarted by such a mob as has disgraced this City for two days?

We are astonished that Gov. SEYMOUR should hold out hopes that this will be the case. We are grieved that he should so far justify the mob as to admit that it will prove successful in its lawless object. In each of his three short speeches in the City yesterday he put forth that this would be the case. Gov. SEYMOUR is false to his responsibilities, to his duties, and to his office, in paltering with the mob in this way. He is false to the country of which he is a citizen, to the laws of which he is the constituted upholder, to public order of which he is the guardian. Such talk is an encouragement to this mob; it is an encouragement to all mobs. Coming from a man in his position, it foretokens no good to the City or the country. His duty is to enforce law, and especially when there are organized attempts to overthrow it by violence.

The conscription, we repeat, cannot be abrogated in this City because of the mob. Its temporary suspense for a few days, until order is restored, is, of course, necessary. But, on the restoration of order, its execution must here be proceeded with at all hazards, as it has been successfully executed elsewhere.

The Charleston Mercury.

DAILY PAPER—Twenty Dollars per annum, payable half-yearly in advance. | SPONTE SUA SINE LEGE FIDES RECTUMQUE COLENTUR.—VINDICE NULLO | COUNTRY PAPER—Thrice a Week—Ten Dollars per annum, in advance.

VOLUME LXXXIII | CHARLESTON, S. C., MONDAY, JULY 27, 1863. | NUMBER 11,817

THE MERCURY.

MONDAY, JULY 27, 1863.

The Riot in New York Successful.

The cause of the late riot in New York was the Conscription Law, and its object was to get exemption from its operation. The riot has ceased. Armed troops have been placed in the city, and the conscription is ordered to go on. This gives the appearance sought to be produced, that the conscription will be carried out and that conscripts forced into the service will swell the army of the United States.

This is a Yankee lie, or it may turn out to be a Yankee fraud. The people of New York are not as conscripts, to be added to the Yankee army. Here is the truth. The City Council of New York appropriates two and a half millions of dollars to purchase the exemption of the conscripts drawn under the Conscription Law. The appropriation will secure the exemption of over 8000. The entire number of fresh levies required of the city, by the last call of the President of the United States, is supposed to be 22,000. Of these the 8000 exempts purchased by the appropriation of the city, it is expected, will cover all those who cannot afford to pay the exemption money. The rest have the means to buy themselves from the service, and will do so. The few troops, if any, which the Conscription Law will put into the army, will practically be volunteers. Under such circumstances the people allow the forms of the Conscription Law to go on,—as it is become only a financial expedient to raise money for the United States Government, which takes little from them, and with which they have practically, little to do. This is the result of the riot. It is successful.

The Government of the United States is nothing now but a despotism. No despotism can afford to be openly defied and baffl[illegible]d. Its principle is force; and when its force is successfully resisted, the foundation on which it exists is shaken. A precedent is displayed—an example is set, that threatens its discontinuance. Force meets force successfully, whilst all the passions and interests which have stirred up resistance, are fomented by the conflict. Yielding cannot save a despotism. It must always be predominant, or it must be overthrown.

The tyrants at Washington understand this very wel[illegible]. Hence they seek *the appearance* of enforcing the Cons[illegible]iption Law in the city of New York. They trust those in other localities, where the people are not as brave or as earnest in resistance as the people of New York, the appearance will also be the reality. But it must be a hazzardous experiment. The people in other localities must see through the veil. The people of New York are practically not conscripted—why should they be? The Government is not only a despotism, but a partial despotism, which demands the blood of some for its support, whilst others stay at home and are free. Even if they are the most abject subjects, conscripts put into the army under such circumstances must be opposed to the war and the service.

We know full well that it is difficult to reason as to Yankee toleration. They have submitted so patiently to the overthrow of their liberties by a daring despotism, that all reasoning from any of the higher impulses of our nature must be erroneous. They are slaves, because they wish to be successful robbers; but even robbers require equality. The people of the United States thrust into the army to fight against the Confederate States, are the mere tools of political knaves or commercial speculators, to win consideration or money. Their liberties are torn from them,—a Government of force is established over them, and more now are driven to the battlefield to be slaughtered, or, if they survive, to serve their masters. Will not the gross, material interests which such a policy destroys, rise up and resist it?

TELEGRAPHIC NEWS.

NEWS FROM RICHMOND.

RICHMOND, July 26.—A proclamation of President DAVIS will be published to-morrow appointing August 22 as a Day of Fasting, Humiliation and Prayer.

An official communication from General LEE to Adjutant General COOPER contradicts MEADE'S statement that he captured a brigade of infantry, etc., as the Confederate army retired to the south bank of the Potomac, with only a few stragglers.

The train on the Virginia Central Railroad resumed its regular trips to-day. It brought this evening from Gordonsville 350 prisoners captured in the fight on Friday at Snicker's Gap. The Yankees attempted to prevent our troops from passing through the Gap, but A. P. HILL'S corps charged the enemy, cleared the road, and captured the prisoners above mentioned.

(*The Latest.*)—RICHMOND, July 26.—LINCOLN has removed from active service and placed on the retired list, Generals WOOL, HARNEY and HARVEY BROWN.

In the House of Commons, on the 10th instant Sir J. FERGUSON urged that, considering the character of the American war, it would be impolitic to resume the discussion of the recognition of the South. He therefore moved the adjournment of the debate. PALMERSTON seconded the motion in order to add his request to ROEBUCK to drop the debate, which stood for Monday. Events of the utmost importance now taking place in America shewed that they would not be able to resume the discussion. He submitted, also, that an interview between two members of the House and a foreign sovereign would hardly be a fit subject for debate in the House. Such a discussion might end in preventing the Emperor of the French, in future, from giving a courteous reception to Englishmen of distinction. LINDSAY complained of attacks upon his veracity by the ministerial organ, declaring that all that ROEBUCK had stated respecting the interview was true. CUNNINGHAM was prepared to show that the sympathies of the working classes were all in favor of the Northern States now struggling against the rebellion in the slave power. GREGORY believed that if ROEBUCK persisted in his motion it would be rejected by a large majority, which action would be construed as opposition to the Confederacy, whereas the fact was that a vast number of members were Southern, heart and soul, but did not wish, in the face of events now pending, to pronounce a premature discussion. FORSTER expressed the hope that the debate would go on, and that England would no longer display the amount of cowardice which she had hitherto done whenever the American question had arisen.

ROEBUCK said that he would reserve his motion and the adjournment was withdrawn.

A Negro is hanged in Clarkson Street

Charge of the police on the rioters at the *Tribune* office

The surrender of Vicksburg — View of the city from the river bank, showing part of the river batteries

GENERAL GRANT AND STAFF.

GENERAL PEMBERTON AND STAFF.

The surrender of Vicksburg — Confederate troops marching out

The Charleston Mercury.

DAILY PAPER—Twenty Dollars per annum, payable half yearly in advance.

SPONTE SUA SINE LEGE FIDES RECTUMQUE COLENTUR. —VINDICE NULLO

COUNTRY PAPER—Thrice a Week—Ten Dollars per annum, in advance.

VOLUME LXXXIII | CHARLESTON, S. C., THURSDAY, JULY 16 1863. | NUMBER 11,808

FROM GEN. LEE'S ARMY—THE BATTLE OF GETTYSBURG.

[*Correspondence of the Richmond Dispatch.*]

MARTINSBURG, July 6.

The wounded are arriving constantly, but there is a singular dearth of details amongst them. They all concur in the statement that the battle of Gettysburg will hereafter take rank amongst the celebrated battles of the world, from the numbers engaged, the obstinacy of the contest, and the loss of men. The Yankees, in places, fought with desperation, having been persuaded by their officers that Lee was fighting under the black flag. In one instance, after we had a brigade surrounded, they refused to surrender, and our troops were compelled to massacre six hundred of them before the remainder would ground their arms. The prisoners said they had been told that we were fighting under the black flag.

I have been unable to learn as yet the part borne by the different portions of our army in this grand fight. Military nomenclature is so strange to me, and the repetition of brigades, of divisions, and the regiments of brigades, with the names of their several commanders, hurried through by the reciter, who is familiar with them, confuses my attention, and when the speaker has done, I have an imperfect idea of marchings by the left and right, by the flanks and centre, and scarcely aught else. I have given you a general account of the fight on Wednesday and Thursday, when we drove the enemy to their fortifications. Hill twice drove the enemy's right from their works, but their centre remained unbroken, and he retired—not driven back—but because he would not advance so far as to expose his flank. Ewell also drove the enemy's left from their entrenchments, but for the same reason he retired. Their centre held an almost impregnable position upon the top of a hill, so steep that our troops could not advance in order of battle, but had to struggle up as best they could, by companies, and were entirely exhausted by the labor of climbing. When they reached the heights it was in numbers so small, from the nature of the ground, that but a trifling force could be brought to bear. The consequence was they were obliged to retire. It is positively asserted, however, that a brigade of Louisianians, 900 strong, did successfully storm a battery of sixty of the enemy's heaviest guns, losing all but eighty men out of their number. They could not hold the position after capturing it. From what I can learn there was little fighting on Saturday. On yesterday (Sunday, 5th) the enemy were again attacked, and we learn it here that they were driven three miles, with the loss of an immense number of prisoners. I have gathered no particulars of this day's engagement. General Anderson passed through town this morning, but stopped only a very short time, and I did not see him. He said that Lee would hold his position. Anderson's brigade lost heavily. I have been unable to learn the names of the officers killed. It is stated that Colonel Burgwyn, of North Carolina, was killed; and also Captain West, in command of the 5th North Carolina.

There seemed to be a general understanding in both armies that this fight was to decide the contest, and each side contended with desperation. From every source, and from every rumor, thus far received, we believe that Lee is master of the situation.

WINCHESTER, July 8.

Perfectly authentic news from the battle field at Gettysburg has come no later than up to Friday night. I will not attempt now a full description; it will be time enough when the fighting there is over. As you have doubtless learned ere this, our troops under Gen. A. P. Hill crossed the Potomac at Williamsport, and advanced towards Gettysburg, took a position Wednesday about three miles from the town, and near a range of hills, which intervened between him and the town.

After desultory skirmishing, which continued most of the day until 1 o'clock p. m., he moved on the enemy in front. Gen. Ewell, who had been at Carlisle, came up from that direction, and reached a position on our extreme left. Soon after, Gen. Hill advanced to the attack. Here Gen. Ewell encountered a large body of the enemy, who had apparently come up from the rear of Gettysburg, and who afterwards constituted the extreme right of the enemy. With two of his divisions—Rodes' and Early's—he engaged the enemy in his front simultaneously, with Gen. A. P. Hill in the centre. While this was progressing Gen. Longstreet swung around his column to the right, and on Thursday morning appeared on the enemy's extreme left. Such was the position of our lines in the first day's engagement. The result of the fighting that day was the complete repulse of the enemy from his position, followed by Gen. Hill's and part of Gen. Ewell's corps, who drove them across the range of hills between us and the town, through the town, and to a point about half a mile beyond, where they occupied a mountain, a splendid and almost impregnable position, which they fortified and bristled with artillery, their line holding this mountain and extending to the right and left of it.

Thursday the events of the day opened as on Wednesday, heavy skirmishing commencing at an early hour, and continuing until about 1 o'clock p. m., when General Longstreet, whose corps constituted our right wing, advanced to the attack, and succeeded in driving before him the enemy's left, after hard fighting for the remainder of the day and during a portion of the night.

On Friday Longstreet again opened the fight on the right, which extended to the left, Ewell driving in the enemy's left before him. Thus our whole line surrounded three sides of the mountain, the enemy within; but such was the strength of their position that to take it by assault was almost a hopeless undertaking. Nevertheless, our infantry, preceded by heavy fire of artillery, charged it several times during the day, and, though almost uniformly successful in capturing batteries, were compelled, owing to the heavy fire of artillery concentrated on them, to fall back to the position whence they started. The charge had to be made across an open and gradually inclined plain, without any protection whatever from the observation of the enemy on the mountain. With over one hundred pieces of artillery we kept up an incessant fire on the enemy, frequently dislodging them from their strong positions, and slaughtering great numbers. The musketry and cannonading is described as most terrific by all who participated, and exceeding in rapidity and severity any previous battle of the war. Notwithstanding, our gallant men boldly "faced the music," and could not be restrained. Not a man or a regiment flinched. The enemy, too, who raised the rallying cry, "You are fighting for your homes, now, boys," fought unusually well. The loss on both sides is heavy, that of the enemy roughly estimated at from two or three to one of ours killed and wounded. At this date, though, it is impossible to obtain anything like a correct estimate. It may be observed, though, that four-fifths at least of our casualties are from wounds, and those principally in the hands and limbs. Very few severely wounded have yet reached here. Over 2000 wounded have reached here since the first day's fight, and as many more are on the way. Among the wounded officers here are Major-Generals Pender, Heth, Brigadier-Generals G. T. Anderson, of Georgia, Scales, of North Carolina, and Jenkins. General Hood was severely wounded in the arm by the fragment of a shell, but fortunately the wound does not endanger the arm. He was struck while going into action on the right, Thursday. General Trimble lost the leg in which he was once wounded before. None of these officers, I am pleased to state, are seriously wounded. Generals Garnett, Kemper, Armistead and Barksdale are undoubtedly killed. The three first belonged to Pickett's division, which suffered most severely in general and field officers, and men—particularly in the second.

I have said that we have no established information from the battle field since the close of the day's operations on Friday. But one report has prevailed, however, of the proceedings Saturday and Sunday, and all who have left the field since Saturday morning agree in the statement. Such is the uniformity in this that it is believed to be reliable. The report is that Gen. Lee, desiring to draw the enemy from his strong position on the mountain and avoid an unnecessary sacrifice of his men in taking it by storm, effected a retreat towards the Potomac, preceded by his wagon trains. The Yankees, believing it a genuine falling back to this side of the river, came down from the height and followed, when, at a distance of two or three miles, they encountered our picket line, which fell back towards the main body. Hill and Longstreet turned upon them and repulsed them with great slaughter. Meantime their retreat to the mountain again was intercepted. General Ewell, who had also fallen back from his position on the left, concealed his men from the observation of the enemy, and when Hill and Longstreet commenced driving them back, moved so as to get in their rear—Jackson-like—and cut off their retreat to their fortifications on the mountain, capturing over 50 regiments and 30 pieces of artillery. Though no official confirmation has yet been received here of this report, it obtains very general credence.

The enemy attacked our wagon train and convoy near Williamsport, Monday evening, but were repulsed, with the loss of one hundred prisoners, after two hours or more hard fighting by General Jenkins. The enemy numbered a brigade and eight pieces of artillery. We had three pieces of the Washington Artillery. These attacks on our wagon trains are of almost daily occurrence, and unless they are strongly convoyed the passage from the river to the army is dangerous. Stuart (Gen. Jeb) has penetrated almost within sight of Washington, and intercepted and captured about 180 wagons and 1,100 mules.

The destruction of our pontoon bridge below Williamsport was owing to carelessness. It was guarded by an inadequate body of men, and they without arms. Lee, however, seems to have little use for it at present.

WINCHESTER, July 9.

Of the rumor I mentioned in my last, concerning the successful ruse of Gen. Lee at Gettysburg, Sunday—the cutting off of a large number of prisoners, the capture of the fortified mountains, &c.—there is no positive confirmation or denial. The disadvantages of our position may be understood by saying it was decidedly worse than the respective positions of the hostile forces at the first battle of Fredericksburg reversed. It is generally believed and conceded that we have gained a victory. Our loss, at first greatly exaggerated, has dwindled down most astonishingly. Late Yankee papers, it is said, acknowledge a defeat and heavy loss. At any rate the invasion has done much towards disposing the minds of the people of Pennsylvania for peace. According to latest intelligence there has been no fighting since Sunday. A seemingly well authenticated report prevails, to the effect that the enemy are falling back towards Washington, and that Gen. Lee's force, at various points, is moving in the same direction. Another great pitch battle will be fought soon, and that on the soil of Maryland, of which I hope to be wholly or in part an eye-witness.

Detachments (several hundred strong) of our soldiers arrive here almost daily, and are forwarded, under command of some field officer, to the army. But for this moving in bodies many of our men would be cut off and captured by the Yankee cavalry. The Potomac, lately swollen several feet by the heavy rains, is again, as I am informed, in fordable condition. Several crossed by fording at Williamsport yesterday.

Most of our slightly wounded have arrived here, and are being forwarded, with all dispatch, as far as possible to the rear. Few of the badly wounded have yet arrived.

A large hotel on Main-street—Taylor's—is filled with Milroy's wounded ragamuffins captured in the late storming of the works commanding the city. Near ten thousand prisoners are on their way here from the late battle field. It is understood that many, or all, of those taken the first day were released on account of some emergency which would not then allow the detailing of a guard to bring them off.

Not having yet reached the vicinity of the battle field, I am unable to give you particulars of the bloody contest, but will close with some authentic details of the operations of General Imboden, the "Guerilla Chief," prior to the invasion, and which have not yet appeared in print. On the 9th of June he left Churchville, and with his command marched 159 miles. At his approach to Romney the Yankees were seized with a panic, and fell back from every point they occupied in that region to New Creek, where they had over 3,500 men. Pushing matters, and losing no time, he destroyed utterly and beyond repair two splendid iron bridges over the north and south branches of the Potomac. They were of Finks' patent, and, except the bridge at Fairmont, the best and finest by far of any on the Baltimore and Ohio Railroad. One was 400 feet in length, the other 533. They were shot down with artillery, and fell thirty odd feet below, presenting such a wreck as never was seen.

He then burnt the railroad bridges over Little Caper, over Potomac Creek, Chesapeake and Ohio Canal, and over Everett's Creek, near Cumberland; made two crevasses in the Chesapeake and Ohio Canal that can't be filled in two months; burnt all the depots, water tanks and stationary engines between Caper and Cumberland, captured thirty or forty prisoners, sixty or seventy horses, and sent out over five hundred fat cattle.

On the 17th, Col. George, of Imboden's command, drove a Yankee battalion out of Cumberland by shelling them in the streets, and the Mayor surrendered the city to "our boys." Kelly, commander of the Yankee cavalry, was there, but made his escape on an engine which was stopped about eight miles from town by a break in the road made by our men. Citizens state that here he jumped off and took to the bushes on foot.

On the night of the 17th General Imboden camped in Alleghany county, Md., twelve miles from Cumberland, but recrossed into Virginia the next morning. This movement was prompted by a rumor that Kelly was moving to attack Imboden at daybreak on the 19th. As there were no railroads, mails or telegraphs in these parts of the General's visit, it is inferred that his command were ignorant of what was progressing in the rest of the world.

THE FALL OF VICKSBURG.

[*Correspondence of the Mobile Advertiser.*]

JACKSON, July 8.

Vicksburg is lost to us, and that stronghold has passed into the possession of the enemy. The hour of misfortune has come, and let us rise above the storm cloud and battle more resolutely than ever. General Johnston could not by possibility, with the means at his command, have relieved Vicksburg. All that skill, energy and zeal could do, has been done, although his efforts have not resulted as we fondly anticipated. He had to create an army and all its appliances before he could move with any reasonable hope of success, and to have moved at an earlier day without adequate preparation for the emergency of the conflict, would have been but to expose his army to the blows of the enemy, with the certainty of its defeat; for to have attacked Grant would have resulted in the sacrifice of the only army which remains for the protection of the interior, while this sacrifice would not have saved Vicksburg.

Grant occupied a country with double our numbers, over which an enemy could not have been marched in line of battle if there were no foe to meet and dispute its advance. I hinted this fact to you in previous letters. This position was obtained, fortified and defended in every possible way, before Johnston had an army with which he could commence offensive operations.

The root of the disaster is two-fold. First, Grant's flank movement by way of Port Gibson, which should have been checked at all hazards. This might have been done with competent and prompt action. It was not done, neither was it attempted. Grant was suffered, with but a feeble resistance by inadequate numbers, to move where he pleased, and secure all he desired. The second cause of disaster was, that Vicksburg had been supplied with but one month's scant rations to stand the siege with! This was the preparation of a year! All accounts, however, previous to the unfortunate capitulation, went to insure the belief that the garrison was amply supplied with provisions for a long time, and believing these assertions to be true, I so telegraphed and wrote.

The garrison was starved out, and our glorious boys staggered from utter exhaustion when they left the trenches. What in Heaven's name has the commissariat been doing? I am reminded that last winter the garrison at one time were reduced to but four days' rations, and the "Southern Crisis" was so severe with its lash that an alarm prevailed, but which soon subsided when it was made known that provisions were being sent forward. That there has been a crying incompetency in the antecedent management of affairs is apparent to all. With the credit of the Government at command, an ample supply of provisions in the land, when speculators were brushed out of the way, I am at a loss to account for the shortness of supplies within the fortifications. Would to God the sugar and molasses crop had been sunk in the Mississippi River before ever it had been moved by way of Vicksburg.

Major General George E. Pickett

That Gen. Pemberton is disloyal to our cause no sensible man believes, and none will so assert who knows anything about him or the affairs of the country. He has certainly done the best he knew how—if he lacks capacity it was his misfortune and not his fault. The appointing power must take the responsibility before the country with respect to Vicksburg and the Trans Mississippi Department. Our ablest men believe that we have magnified the importance of Vicksburg far beyond its intrinsic importance to the Confederacy in any military point of view.

The army of Vicksburg is not lost to us, and in a few days these brave men will again be in our ranks; and the question of resisting Lee on the part of the enemy, and of our strengthening Bragg must be settled. Those who calmly survey the field—whose nerves do not sway like the aspen—are to-day as hopeful, firm and confident of our glorious ultimate success and independence as at any time during the struggle.

* * * * * *

When the history of the siege of Vicksburg shall have been written, then, and not till then, will all the noble sufferings and endurance of the garrison be known. Who has not wept over the stirring play of "The Siege of Lucknow," when all the art of man was brought into requisition to portray the sufferings of that garrison? But it is not worse than that of Vicksburg, though clothed in burning poetry. I have conversed with some of the officers who have come out, and they say that when the men rose from the trenches where they had been for *thirty-eight days without ever being relieved*, and marched out to stack their arms, that one third of them reeled and staggered like drunken men from famine and exhaustion, and many of them fell to the ground unable to rise again; but when the color bearers marched up to lay their tattered and worn banners upon the stacks, then, and not till then, did they seem to know and feel that all that they had struggled and suffered for for many long and dreary days and weeks was lost. All had been in vain; and men with famine written upon their faces, to which was now added despair, turned away and wept like children at the sight of the banners they had followed so long and so well doomed never again to flutter above them, the ensign of freedom and hatred of tyranny.

I gladly turn from the sickening picture presented to the causes that rendered it necessary to surrender a post upon which so much depended, together with an army of twenty thousand of our bravest and best troops.

Of course, there will be an endless amount of crimination and recrimination, each trying to shield his favorite, even though at the expense of truth and justice. That Gen. Pemberton has nobly redeemed his promise to Grant to hold Vicksburg to the last, and made the best defence possible under the circumstances, there can be no doubt. But aside from other grave mistakes—to give it the kindest name—that he has made, was that of allowing himself to be invested without a sufficient supply of subsistence and ordnance stores, when the whole country was open to him, instead of allowing himself to be cut off, with less than sixty days' rations and but little ammunition. But this is no time to discuss this question, and in my next I will proceed to show that the responsibility rests with persons a thousand miles away to the east, from which the light is breaking that will relieve the darkness in the west.

Gen. Johnston had reached the Big Black, and would have crossed at daylight on Monday morning, but at ten o'clock Sunday night he received information that Vicksburg had fallen, and that Grant was on the opposite bank to dispute the passage of the river. He immediately fell back to ——, closely pursued by Sherman's corps, who were constantly skirmishing with our cavalry.

The New-York Times.

VOL. XII—NO. 3687. NEW-YORK, SUNDAY, JULY 19, 1863. PRICE FOUR CENTS.

THE FALL OF PORT HUDSON.

News via New-Orleans, by the Steamer Locust Point.

PARTICULARS OF THE SURRENDER.

Five Thousand Prisoners, Fifty Pieces of Artillery, Numerous Small Arms, &c.

The Garrison in a Ravenous Condition.

THE LAST MULE EATEN.

Details of the Siege to the Date of the Surrender.

The *Locust Point*, from New-Orleans on July 11, arrived at this port yesterday morning.

The New-Orleans *Era* has the following announcement of the fall of Port Hudson:

"The great stronghold of the Mississippi surrendered to the forces under Gen. BANKS at 7 o'clock on the morning of the 9th. GARDNER, the commander of the rebel fortress, had sent a flag of truce asking terms. The response was an unconditional surrender, and he was allowed twenty-four hours to consider. He did not take so much time, and at 7 o'clock on the morning of the 9th, unconditionally surrendered the stronghold, with all it contained. There were 5,000 prisoners.

The moment the surrender was completed, the enemy sent out a request that six thousand rations should immediately be sent in, as the garrison had *eaten its last mule*. This was found to be literally the fact. The last mule at Port Hudson had been devoured.

The good old ship *Hartford* and the *Albatross* came down below Port Hudson at once, and were greeted with much enthusiasm after their glorious work.

The *Tennessee* is the flag-ship of Admiral FARRAGUT. She came down with a bearer of dispatches from Gen. BANKS to Gen. EMORY, and made the trip from Donaldsonville in *four hours and a half*. She reports all quiet in the river.

ADDITIONAL PARTICULARS.

The *Era* of the 11th inst. says, on Wednesday, the 8th, at 2 P. M., Gen. GARDNER, the rebel commander of Port Hudson, surrendered unconditionally to Maj.-Gen. BANKS. The rebel army was drawn up in line, stacked arms, and Gen. BANKS took possession of the place. Five thousand prisoners, fifty pieces of artillery, and all small arms, &c., have fallen into our hands.

A dispatch to the *Era*, dated on the morning of the 8th, from Port Hudson, says: "At 2 o'clock a parley was sounded from the fort, and being replied to, inquiry was made about the news from Vicksburgh. On being assured that it had fallen, Gen. GARDNER promised to surrender to-day. We entered the place at noon. The glorious event has filled our army with the wildest enthusiasm."

A subsequent account states that GARDNER sent a flag of truce, on the 8th, asking for terms, and Gen. BANKS responded, "Unconditional surrender," with twenty-four hours to consider. At 7 A. M., on the 9th, GARDNER unconditionally surrendered. The moment the surrender was completed the rebels sent a request for 6,000 rations, as the garrison had eaten its last mule. This was found to be literally true—they had devoured their last mule.

The news was brought to New-Orleans by the flag-ship *Tennessee*. One hundred guns were immediately fired by Gen. EMORY. The loyal citizens of New-Orleans were to have a torchlight procession, illumination, and a general joyful jubilation on the night the steamer sailed. The Secessionists in that city are represented as rather gloomy in countenance.

NATHANIEL HODD, of Boston, gunner of the *Tennessee*, died of apoplexy.

The news of the capture of Vicksburgh, reached Port Hudson on the 7th, occasioning the greatest enthusiasm.

OUR PORT HUDSON CORRESPONDENCE.

The Approaching Fourth of July—Rebel Raid at Springfield Landing—Disgraceful Conduct of the Rhode Island Cavalry—Gallantry of the Blacks—A New Battery—A Rebel Explosion—Deserters—The Medical Department.

MAJ.-GEN. AUGUR'S HEADQUARTERS, REAR OF PORT HUDSON, Friday, July 3, 1863.

To-morrow ushers in the Fourth July. Whether or not we shall, as we have been hoping, see the old flag waving upon the ramparts of Port Hudson on that eventful day, is what the next few hours—pregnant, it may be, with so much good or evil to our cause—will certainly determine.

In taking a comprehensive view of all that is passing around me, I confess that at this moment of writing—3 o'clock P. M.—I see and hear nothing at all to indicate an aggressive movement on our part to-night or to-morrow. But it will not do for me to judge by the appearances of things around me, Gen. BANKS is one of those men who keeps his own secrets so profoundly, that I should not be surprised at any moment to hear the order given for an advance. We can have very little more to do now in the way of approaching the enemy, for in some cases we are actually upon him.

THE SPRINGFIELD LANDING AFFAIR.

We had quite a day of excitement yesterday, the 2d inst., caused by an impudent raid of the rebel cavalry upon our depot at Springfield Landing, on the river below Port Hudson. When it is remembered that Springfield Landing is not only our chief depot for the transportation of all commissary stores, troops, ammunition, &c., but, as it were, the principal back door left open to us between here and New-Orleans, you can imagine what a commotion it made when we heard that the rebels had actually got in there.

At early dawn I was aroused from slumber in my tent, near the road, by the loud tramping of horsemen, and rising up to see what it was, found a large squad of our cavalry passing, and going along the Springfield road. This was the first indication we had that "something was up." Presently, we saw lots of empty wagons returning, the riders and horses fairly buried in dust, and each one—as is usual in all such cases—big with the most portentous intelligence of every sort of disaster, and each rebel, of course, magnified into at least twenty or thirty men in buckram.

Hurrying to headquarters as the best place to obtain correct information, I found that the wild rumors had reached there also. Our Generals were in close confab, couriers were constantly dashing up with information or being sent out in search of it, squads of cavalry were galloping off, and uninitiated individuals like myself had only to look on and wonder. When everybody was hurrying *from* Springfield Landing with hobgoblin stories, to go *to* it in search of news was even more enterprise than I thought you would require of your correspondent, and so I remained in the good company in which *I* found myself.

For two or three hours in the morning there was manifestly no little apprehension observable on the part even of those who tried to laugh the matter off as unimportant. But toward noon the affair began to clear up, and after it had been shorn of all exaggerations and fear-begotten coloring, this last piece of rebel impudence and daring turned out (for the *present*, at least) far more harmless than anybody had imagined. Here is Brig.-Gen. DWIGHT's official report, which puts the whole thing in a nutshell, and will spoil any capital that the rebels and their Northern emissaries may try to make out of it.

HEADQUARTERS SECOND DIVISION, NINETEENTH ARMY CORPS, NEAR PORT HUDSON, July 2, 1863.

Lieut. Col. Irwin, A. A. Gen.:

SIR: I have the honor to report that, in my opinion, the dash at Springfield Landing this morning was accomplished by the enemy through the disgraceful negligence of the guard at the landing, and the faulty disposition of his forces made by the officer in charge there. That the panic and alarm which existed was caused by the disgraceful cowardice of the officers and soldiers of the Second Rhode Island cavalry, who were sent out expressly to prevent this alarm, and to cut off the enemy, should he attempt to do what he accomplished.

The same dash would have been made against our stores, at the cross roads in rear of my old headquarters, had it not been prevented by the vigilance of Capt. GODFREY and his cavalry pickets. They prevented that dash and gave me such information that you sent the Rhode Island cavalry here. The Rhode Island cavalry were ordered to drive back the enemy where last seen by our pickets, and to proceed to Springfield Landing to see that the road was clear. They hesitated, and had to be positively ordered before they would go.

To this disgrace they have added that of having fled the moment they got sight of the enemy, (who did not outnumber them,) without showing the least intention of fighting, and finally spreading the most absurd and exaggerated rumors to give the greater alarm. Indeed, the last thing they were guilty of was running and increasing the panic and spreading the report that the rebels were advancing on my old headquarters, at the sight of a Lieutenant of the Sixth Michigan, a forage-master and one of our own wagon-masters, who were galloping back to assure them that there were no rebels on the road. Had the Rhode Island cavalry obeyed orders boldly and strictly, they must have fallen on the rear of the rebel force which visited the landing.

The damage done at Springfield Landing is very slight. The rebels were in too much haste to dismount, and therefore accomplished little. What was burned at the landing was done by the officers or men of Gen. ULLMAN's command. Very respectfully, your obedient servant, WM. DWIGHT, B. G. C.

P. S.—I am informed that the conduct of the officers of Gen. ULLMAN's brigade, during the panic near my old headquarters, was particularly disgraceful, as a rule, while the black soldiers of that command, on being supplied with muskets and ammunition by my ordnance officer, (Lieut. DICKEY, Sixth Michigan Volunteers,) were easily formed in line, and did not, in the least, yield to the panic about them. W. D., B. G. C.

These strictures of Gen. DWIGHT, severe as they are, do not come up to half what I heard of the disgraceful conduct of some of our cavalry—the men upon whom, above all others, we have to depend in our present position for safety from surprises by the enemy. It is lucky for us that this is not to be taken as a rule but an inglorious exception. While those men were covering themselves with lasting dishonor, the Second Louisiana (Capt. GODFREY's) cavalry proved themselves men of the true metal.

They were out on picket duty—only ten of them, under Sergts. BURSALL and BURGER—when they met the affrighted and stampeding Rhode Islanders. Instead of joining the flying body, the Second Louisiana men boldly stood their ground, and two privates among them, ROBERT ELLIOTT and LEMUEL COLLINS, (be sure and not mistake these names,) actually had the bravery to rush forward in advance to encounter the enemy, whom they kept employed until their companions coming up, quickly followed by other reinforcements, the enemy thought fit to skedaddle.

From all I can learn, this marauding force could not have far exceeded one hundred men. Coming upon our sleepy, if not sleeping men at the Landing, they bagged some few prisoners, and killed and wounded some four or five of our people, losing as many, if not more, themselves.

As far as the affair goes, it was a shameful trifle in itself; but it is no trifle that the enemy should have been permitted, so near to us, to reconnoitre our position, and to get off scot free with his information. The only good offset is that, emboldened by what he saw and did, he may be induced to make the attempt again—in which case he will be likely to find us a little better prepared.

Your readers will not fail to notice the compliment officially paid to the *black* soldiers by Gen. DWIGHT's letter, in contrast to their *white* officers. After a few more of such unsought examples, perhaps some of your Northern negro-haters will begin to acknowledge the value to the nation of our black friends down here. I can only tell you that without *their* aid in this department—in every conceivable way, from the handling of a spade to the shouldering of a musket—from the detection of hidden dangers to the confronting of them at the cannon's mouth—we might long ago all have packed up and gone home. This is no flattering confession for "Caucasians," but I defy any man who has watched events here to honestly disprove my assertions.

NEW BATTERY.

We are gradually tightening the reins upon the enemy. Within a day or two, a new battery has been erected across the river, and played with such accuracy upon their river front that we have already, with one of our 30-pound Parrots, disabled one of their large 100-pounders.

HOIST WITH HIS OWN PETARD.

Last night a terrific explosion, or rather series of explosions, were heard in the enemy's works, accompanied by fearful groans, opposite Gen. GROVER's. It appears they had accumulated a number of hand-grenades, or other explosive missiles, to throw among our men, when one of them, having prematurely exploded, set fire to the others, causing a terrific noise and an amount of mortality that we have, as yet, no means of ascertaining.

DESERTERS

Continue to come among us, and each day only aggravates the stories they bring of the horrible life from which they have just escaped. One man told me, to-day, that he and his companions—nine others—had had no meat for two days. Beans and molasses are all that now remain for them,—and GARDNER says he has enough of that to last a month—*i. e.*, if the men can or *will* stand it. The Arkansas men, they say, will fight us to the last; but the others would be *heartily glad to see us take possession of the fort.*

THE MEDICAL DEPARTMENT.

In my letter which appeared in your issue of June 13, describing the gallant action of our colored troops, I made some strictures respecting the lack of provision for ambulances for the wounded on that occasion. While withdrawing nothing of what I actually saw, and the complaint I actually heard from the men themselves, I would be sorry, indeed, for my remarks to be construed into any blame of the Medical officers in this Department, who, I know, are applying, to the utmost limits, every means at their disposal, and to whom, in the very same letter, I endeavored to pay a marked and well-deserved compliment.

I repeat, that I never knew any army in which greater care and attention are paid to the sick and wounded than in this Department; and the small list of mortality in this—the most dangerous of climates, by common repute,—is direct proof of the skill and exertions employed.

Dr. R. H. ALEXANDER, the Medical Director of the Department of the Gulf, is himself a man of unsparing energy, and he is ably seconded in his efforts by the following gentlemen under him: Surgeon T. B. REED, Medical Director of GROVER's division; Surgeon M. D. BENEDICT, Senior Surgeon of WEITZEL's brigade; Dr. HARTWELL, Acting Medical Director of PAINE's division; Dr. RAUON, Medical Director of AUGUR's division; Dr. E. F. SANGER, Medical Director of DWIGHT's division; and Dr. JAMES L. FISHER, Surgeon at Springfield Landing, who has charge of all transportation of the wounded, medical stores, &c., from the army to Baton Rouge. Among the minor officers I can scarcely mention any without appearing invidious; but my accidental position enables me to see so much of the skill and unswerving devotion of Dr. COGGSWELL, of the Fiftieth Massachusetts, and Dr. HUTCHINS, of the One Hundred and Sixteenth New-York, that I am bound to speak of them as men unsurpassed by any in the whole medical fraternity of the Department.

On the occasion especially alluded to, respecting the lack of ambulances, Dr. HARTWELL was the officer in charge. I had before noticed so much of this gentleman's humane and untiring exertions, especially on the 14th June, at Paine's Hospital, which I mentioned distinctly to his credit in a former letter, that I would be the last to say anything to his disparagement. I am informed, and am glad to believe, that the ambulances I noticed as lacking were soon forthcoming, and that Dr. HARTWELL, although the colored regiments had never reported to him as Medical Director of that division, had sent them two ambulances, (all at his disposal,) placed his medical stores for the use of their Surgeons, and aided them in every manner that humanity could suggest.

The Fourth of July at Port Hudson — A Novel and Aventurous Celebration—Loyalty and Treason Face to Face—Bad Weather—The Storming Party—Another Deserter—A Countermine.

GEN. AUGUR'S HEADQUARTERS, REAR OF PORT HUDSON, Sunday, July 5, 1863.

The Fourth of July came and went without seeing us in possession of Port Hudson. In the morning I was aroused by loud and continuous cannonading quite near us, which sounded like an attack, but it soon turned out to be only a national salute in honor of the day. Soon the other batteries took up the hoarse music along the whole length of our line, and in the distance came booming the thunder notes of the great guns from the fleet. The same salutes were fired—34 guns each—at noon and at evening.

I took a ride round to Gen. BANKS' headquarters, and was glad to find him quite recovered from a severe cold which had, for some days past, taken away his voice almost entirely. The General must have an iron constitution to withstand the fatigue he is now undergoing, both mentally and bodily. It is a common thing for him to be in the saddle two or three nights in succession, examining the works along our whole lines, and not returning till 4 or 5 o'clock in the morning, to snatch a few hours' sleep.

CELEBRATION OF THE FOURTH.

Beyond these salvos, and a little symptom of *stolen* conviviality, noticed here and there—especially toward evening—there was nothing, of a public character, to mark our natal day. It was my lot, however, to be present at a little spontaneous sort of celebration, which was probably the first—and may it be the last—one of the kind ever seen in this country.

I was seated in the tent of Maj. G. B. HALSTED, Gen. AUGUR's Acting Adjutant-General, when an Orderly came up and handed him the following note:

HEADQUARTERS SECOND VERMONT BATTERY, NEAR PORT HUDSON, July 4, 1863.

MAJ. HALSTED—*Sir:* I have the honor to request that, if convenient, you will be present in the battery at 12 M. to-day, and read the Declaration of Independence to my command; after which I will fire a salute of thirty-four guns—each of which *shall deposit a shot in the enemy's works.*

Please invite Mr. —— (your humble servant "Nemo") to be present.

I am, Sir, very respectfully, your ob't servant, P. E. HOLCOMB, Captain Second Vermont battery.

To this the Major at once dispatched the following reply:

AUGUR'S HEADQUARTERS, 19TH ARMY CORPS, LEFT WING, July 4, 1863. In Camp before Port Hudson, La., at present a nest of black-hearted traitors against the best Government the sun shines on.

Captain P. E. Holcomb, Second Vermont Battery:

DEAR CAPTAIN: I have just received your very patriotic request for me to be present in your battery, at 12 o'clock to-day, and read the Declaration of Independence to your command.

Thanks, many thanks, Captain, for the high honor intended. Nothing could afford me more pleasure, on this recurrence of our nation's natal day, here under the very flash, sound, smoke, and smell of rebel powder and whistle of rebel bullets—within 300 yards of their breastworks—to perform the pleasing task you have solicited of me.

I shall send immediately to try and procure a copy of that immortal work—"The Declaration." If found—which I much fear cannot be in this traitorous region—I will be with you at the hour named, to perform the pleasing task, which I know will afford equal pleasure to the audience—officers and men—patriots gallant and true, of the Second Vermont battery.

Mr. —— returns his sincere thanks for your invitation, and will accompany me.

With kindest wishes for yourself and all your command, believe me, most admiringly and respectfully, Your obedient servant, GEORGE B. HALSTED, A. A. G., U. S. Volunteer army.

"The Union must and shall be preserved."

A copy of the "Declaration" was found, and at the appointed time I set out on horseback with Major HALSTED, accompanied by no one but his orderly. Leaving our horses tied in the woods, at some little distance from the battery, we threaded our way cautiously among the brushwood until we got past the exposed portion of the road, and passing behind the cotton bales, which screened us from the enemy's bullets, we soon found ourselves standing within HOLCOMB's famous and formidable battery.

The Captain was in his tent, trying to get a little repose, for the midday sun was almost intolerable; and both parties seem instinctively to come to a truce about noon, when the heat is fiercest. After partaking of a little lemonade, and drinking to the toast, "May this be the most unhappy Fourth of July ever seen in the United States!" Capt. HOLCOMB collected his men, and Major HALSTED, standing in the midst of that noble group—facing the enemy, but three hundred yards from us—addressed them as follows:

"FELLOW-CITIZENS—FELLOW-SOLDIERS: Are we not proud of these titles? A citizen of this great Republic may boast, as in the palmy days of Rome it was the proudest boast of one of her sons, 'I am a Roman citizen.'

Two years since I had the honor of reading the Declaration of Independence in presence of that patriot, Admiral STRINGHAM, his officers and crew, on the deck of the United States ship *Minnesota*, then at anchor in Hampton Roads, Va., where traitors claimed jurisdiction, but despite them, that glorious flag—the Stars and Stripes—waved as defiantly there as on this battery.

I consider the incident of being invited to read the Declaration of Independence here to-day, in Louisiana, within easy musket-range of traitor breast works, no less flattering to myself and the gallant men before me.

I was told, on the occasion above alluded to, by old officers present, that it was the first time they had heard "The Declaration" read on the deck of a United States ship. I think we may take it for granted that the pleasant celebration in which we are now uniting never had its parallel—at least under such circumstances. God grant it may be the last!

I am proud to be the humble instrument of thus recalling the glorious past, the noble patriots of '76, and hope we may all so live and act in this hour of our country's trial, that our names may be classed (if far below in glory) with that band of worthies.

While this, we trust, is our position, fellow soldiers, for others—with shame be it said—there are parallels of depravity in a class of men who endeavor to embarrass the Government we love, in its struggle with traitors. I mean *Copperheads of to-day*—worthy compeers of *Tories of the Revolution*.

Let us, fellow-soldiers, try to do our duty despite all opposition. Let us show that patriots of '63, like those of '76, can cope with their enemy in arms and their Copperhead allies in council.

I know well I do not talk to deaf ears or cold hearts in "Holcomb's battery." "*Like Commander, like Men*," is encomium enough for me to speak.

I proceed to the pleasing task to which you have invited me, with the single request that you will examine upon what grave and oft-repeated injuries and neglect our revolutionary fathers rebelled. It will excite no wonder. Then recall, if you can, any wrongs of omission or commission by the Federal Government, warranting the traitors whom we are fighting, in their rebellion against and efforts to destroy that Government.

I have been unable to find any cause for this rebellion, and view as sacrilegious the efforts which traitors, their aiders, sympathizers, and abettors, make to enforce a parallel, by saying: "The Patriots of the Revolution were rebels, we are no more." True, they were called rebels, but for good and sufficient cause, while it is equally true that these are traitors without cause, but *solely to carry out the darling wish of their hearts to establish in this nineteenth century, on this Continent, an aristocratic Government, having for its chief corner-stone Slavery.*

Our forefathers would have indignantly scouted any such idea in their day, we but do our duty to them and to ourselves, in resisting this effort in our time. It never can, it never *shall* be done. 'The Union must and shall be preserved.' Slavery must die, for it is dangerous to that Union."

Major HALSTED then read in a loud and distinct voice, the Declaration of Independence, amid the deepest interest of his stalwart auditors, some grouped around him, and some leaning against their cannons.

At the conclusion, Capt. HOLCOMB thanked the Major for his presence in a few pertinent words, and then said that the best echo we could hear for the sentiments expressed, was from the voice of his cannon. The word was scarcely uttered, when one piece thundered forth its approbation, then another, and another, in rapid succession, until the national salute of thirty-four was complete.

The enemy, having now fairly roused up from their midday siesta, began to retaliate, and the whistling bullets came flying over and about us with a rapidity that would have been very unpleasant but for the five or six feet thickness of cotton bales behind which we were located. It reminded one of a hornet's nest, into which some unwary schoolboy had poked his stick, so thickly were they buzzing about.

The Major waited, at my especial request, until the gentleman seemed cooled down a little, before we again ventured to run the gauntlet in reaching our horses, which we did in perfect safety—Capt. HOLCOMB accompanying us that far.

These are brave fellows—perpetually undergoing privations and dangers that we civilians can only now and then glance at—whom your Northern Copperheads speak of as engaged in an inglorious work, little short of murder—men who are insulted by being told that their brave comrades have died uselessly by their sides. I tell you many of your Northern politicians terribly mistake the feelings of our armies, if they think the latter can listen coolly to such atrocious things. There was not one man of that crowd yesterday, but who, on hearing such scandalous principles uttered, would long to sieze the speaker by the throat and strangle him on the spot.

BAD WEATHER.

In the afternoon of the 4th we had the most severe storm of rain, accompanied by thunder and lightning, which we have yet encountered here, and which lasted nearly through the night. It did much to mar, if not entirely break up, any patriotic demonstrations that might have been on the tapis.

Just before it began I heard, for the very first time out here, the strains of martial music. As they came sweetly floating through the woods, the effect was so thrilling and refreshing, that I really wondered that music is not more considered for its cheering effect upon our men. We did two very silly things—in the estimation of most sensible officers, both of the army and navy, with whom I have conversed—first, when we curtailed the bands in our army, and second, when we cut off the sailor's grog. There were many *real* abuses, both in army and navy, to be attended to before either of those fictitious ones.

I believe the intention of this band was to have regaled us at headquarters, in the evening, with music; but the very heavy storm put an effectual damper upon the proceeding.

THE STORMING PARTY.

I have the pleasure in adding to the list of names already sent you the following, who have joined the glorious band—all from the Second Louisiana regiment (white):

Corp. Jacob Stall, Co. H.	Francis McGahey, Co. I.
Patrick Garrity, Co. H.	Edwin Rice, Co. I.
Louis Icks, Co. H	James E. Marriner, Co. I.
John Eldridge, Co. H.	Thomas Blakeby, Co. I.
John E. Phillips, Co. E.	

Besides these, I now forward a complete "roster" of the first and second battalions; showing the names of all the officers engaged in this noble undertaking, the number of men supplied by each regiment, &c. This list will prove valuable, not only to the friends of these heroes, but for future reference to the scroll of honor. With Col. BIRGE and Staff, you will see that the number required is already complete.

ANOTHER DESERTER

came in to-day, and gave us more important intelligence than perhaps any who preceded him. He is a very intelligent fellow—formerly a printer of Dubuque, Iowa—who was forced, as usual, into the rebel army, some three months ago. I am not at liberty to tell what he said, beyond the fact that it is to our advantage and the enemy's discomfiture. As his testimony has been carefully received at headquarters, I have no doubt that Gen. BANKS will see how to turn it to the best account. Among other things, the deserter told us that we should very soon hear of a whole company of the Third Arkansas deserting in a body.

A COUNTERMINE.

Yesterday the enemy stole a march upon us, by countermining an intrenchment we were making upon them at our right, and blowing up our works, but fortunately with no damage to any one. But this is a mere trifle, easily repaired, and counts as nothing in a siege to which we can apply fifty pairs of black arms to their one.

News of the Surrender of Vicksburgh.

TUESDAY, July 7, 1863.

I reopen my letter, to say that Lieut. EMERSON, of Gen. BANKS' Staff, has just arrived here, and set us all in the wildest uproar of joyous excitement, by news of the capitulation of Vicksburgh. A gunboat came down with a naval officer bearing the thrilling fact. Already the glad tidings have spread like wild-fire along our lines, and cheers after cheers from thousands of voices came reverberating through the woods, mingled with the strains of music. GARDINER will learn the cause soon enough, for the men in our trenches are within speaking distance of those on his ramparts. God grant I may soon have to send equally good news of Port Hudson!

An Intimation of the Fall of Port Hudson.

JULY 8, 1863—7 A. M.

I open my letter a second time to send you some news that promises gloriously. Gen. GARDNER this morning at 2 A. M., sent in a flag of truce, which turned out, as we expected, to have a deep significance.

The following dispatch has just arrived from headquarters, to Gen. AUGUR:

SIR: By direction of the commanding General, I have the honor to inform you that Gen. GARDNER has offered to surrender Port Hudson, and that a Commissioner has been appointed to draw up the terms, to meet at 9 o'clock this morning.

Active hostilities will entirely cease until further orders. You will keep the troops well within the works. Very respectfully, your obedient servant, R. B. IRWIN, A. A. G.

You will thus see that we are *all but in* Port Hudson, which can scarcely now be delayed beyond a few hours. I send this on to Baton Rouge by a trusty hand, so as to make sure of the boat, and when we fairly get in I will send the joyful postscript flying after. NEMO.

OUR NEW-ORLEANS CORRESPONDENCE

The Celebration of the Fourth—Gen. Emory's Order Modified—The Guerrillas Still Active.

Correspondence of the New-York Times.

NEW-ORLEANS, Saturday, July 11, 1863.

The Fourth July (Independence Day) was ushered in by salvos of artillery and the ringing of bells, but the great feature of the day was the collation given by the Collector of the Port, CUTHBERT BULLITT, Esq. His residence, opposite Lafayette-square, was festooned with flags most artistically arranged, with the busts of Gen. ANDREW JACKSON and HENRY CLAY, of Kentucky. Mr. BULLITT's house was the centre of attraction, where all met and exchanged freely their sentiments. In the evening the great demonstration of Union feeling was continued in Canal-street, where three stands were erected.

T. J. DURANT, Esq., opened the exercises with a speech, and was followed by Col. T. B. THORPE in his happy style at stand No. 1. Nos. 2 and 3 were well represented by Judge WHITE, of Jefferson City, and others.

The steamer *Sallie Robinson* came in yesterday. She had the bark *Scotland* lashed on one side, and the three-masted schooner *Russell* on the other side. She was convoyed below Donaldsonville by gunboats, and as all was considered safe, they left her; but at College Point the rebels opened on them, and the bark *Scotland* is perfectly riddled. A shell exploded on the deck of the steamer, treating *Miss Sallie Robinson* rather badly—(a fine wooden full-length carved statue of her being on the upper deck.) A shell carried away her breastworks and head. The *Sallie Robinson* brought to the city 125 National prisoners, part of 1,100 (eleven hundred) taken by the rebels at Brashear City. The other boats, the *Zephyr*, &c., will bring in the rest.

The important order of Gen. EMORY, issued to take effect 5th of July, has been modified as follows:

HEADQUARTERS, DEFENCES OF NEW-ORLEANS, NEW-ORLEANS, July 6, 1863.

GENERAL ORDERS, No. 21.—So much of General Order No. 18, as prohibits peaceable citizens from being out after 9 o'clock P. M., is hereby rescinded, provided they are not in parties of more than three. By command of Brig.-Gen. EMORY. W. D. SMITH, Lieut.-Col., A. A. A. G.

To-night a grand torchlight procession is to come off in honor of the recent victories and the opening of the Mississippi. The market here already feels the influence of the anticipated Western trade. Sugars have advanced, and holders of large lots have withdrawn them from the market.

The mortuary report for the week ending 5th of July, shows 185 deaths; 41 of diarrhœa and dysentery and 25 from fevers. GILBERT.

THE SURRENDER OF VICKSBURGH.

An Account from Another of Our Special Correspondents.

VICKSBURGH, Miss., Sunday, July 5, 1863.

I send greeting to all the loyal readers of the TIMES. No longer obliged to date my letters "above," "below," "opposite" or "near Vicksburgh," I salute them from the very Court-house—the heart and centre of the rebel Gibraltar on the Mississippi. Yes, Vicksburgh, with its accumulation of forts, traverses, rifle pits and magazines; its guns, large and small; its "whistling dicks" and "whispering jimmys;" its shattered and roofless houses; its skeleton walls and prostrate chimneys; its barricaded streets, dirt, rubbish and filth, its starved and vermin-devoured garrison—all are ours.

Twenty-eight thousand prisoners, including 8,000 to 10,000 in hospitals and convalescent camps;

Fifteen Generals and their Staffs;

Fifty thousand stand of arms, rifles and muskets;

Over one hundred siege guns;

Immense quantities of ammunition;

Sixty-three field pieces in the outer line; and

Fifty field pieces in the inner lines. Total, 113.

Four large foundries and machine-shops, literally full of shot and shell, all manufactured in the town—everything except provisions and the means of subsistence, are the trophies of this most desperate and protracted siege.

The entire army had been reduced to the greatest straits for food. There were twelve days' rations for the army inside when Gen. GRANT invested the place. These have been made to feed the stomachs, or rather to furnish mere subsistence, *for forty-five days.*

True to their declared purpose, the rebel army were subsisting upon mule meat when the act of surrender was signed. I saw one of the rebel officers—a very intelligent and apparently truthful man—not an hour ago, who told me that he had several mules slaughtered in his own command. I saw with my own eyes delicate rib pieces of mules lying about the streets, which had evidently been rejected by rebel stomachs and thrown away.

A woman living opposite a large rebel rendezvous, in Walnut-street, assured me that she had often seen the soldiers take *rats* from a trap, which had been caught for the purpose over night, and skin, fry and eat them for breakfast. As the mules and rats were giving out, the dogs were beginning to fall victims to insatiate rebel maws. Dog meat was getting high on the street, and good fat curs were in demand. I myself observed a great scarcity of the canine race; cats were also scarce in the town. But seriously, there probably was never seen a hungrier crowd of men than that which surrendered to the Union forces on the 4th of July. This was the last day of grace allowed by Gen. GRANT, and had not the surrender taken place the General would have "immediately moved upon their works."

THE SURRENDER.

The preparations for the combined assault were complete. Our mines had been pushed entirely under some of the strongest rebel works, and all were looking for a final and bloody struggle on that day.

Weakened by the sickness and death of so many men, without food to eat, and despairing of receiving succor from without, is it strange that there were serious misgivings as to the result inside the rebel lines? They had only *five hundred gun caps left*, though many of the soldiers had, besides good Enfield rifles, an extra musket loaded with buck and ball. The rebel works had been completely invested, and our troops were waiting the explosion of our mines to make a rush for the possession of the first line of works. One Alabama regiment would have been wholly annihilated had not the surrender taken place as it did. Five barrels of powder were deposited directly under their fort.

Shortly before 10 o'clock A. M. a flag of truce was sent out to Gen. SMITH. It reached our headquarters, accompanied by Gens. BOWEN, PEMBERTON, PRICE and Major McGOWANS, who talked over the terms. The surrender was unconditional, but it was agreed that they should be paroled, subject to exchange. Each officer of the Staff was allowed to have his side arms and a horse each. Thirty teams were also allowed them to remove their own supplies, but inasmuch as they had none, they were to be generously furnished with sufficient to last them to their camps in Georgia and Alabama.

Only one division—that of Gen. LOGAN—entered the city to take formal possession.

Gen. McPHERSON was placed in command of the District of Vicksburgh, and Lieut.-Col. KENT, of the Twenty-ninth Illinois, was made Provost-Marshal-General.

He has his hands full. The paroling is done by companies, each man giving a separate parole and signature. Ten regiments were disposed of yesterday, and probably forty will be to-day.

The Generals, Field and Staff officers were all paroled yesterday.

three rebel Generals were killed during the last attacks, viz.: MARK, GREEN, TILGHMAN, and another, whose name I could not learn.

Gen. GRANT and Staff only spent half an hour inside the enemy's intrenchments, and he then turned and followed the bulk of his army, which had already been dispatched to overtake and attack JOHNSTON.

Probably there never were so many hungry men gathered in one place before—and so hungry Officers and men rushed towards our soldiers, earnestly imploring for food. Our boys immediately emptied their well-filled haversacks to supply their present wants. The meat and bread thus dispensed were devoured with ravenous appetites, and then they called for more. During the two days since the surrender, the soldiers declare they have fared better than at any time since they left home. Every hour seems to make the men better acquainted with each other. They mix freely, walk together, converse and discuss matters in the most good-natured fashion.

Those who have the best opportunity of judging of the temper and feeling of the paroled soldiers say that not one-third of them will ever follow their leaders out of our lines. This statement came from a gentleman prominent in Gen. GRANT's Staff. Those who are within traveling distance of their homes are clamorous to be passed out of the lines, and be permitted to leave the service, of which they have had enough. The prisoners are all detained within the lines, either in the trenches outside, or are scattered through the town in the vacant houses and stores. The jail and yard where our own officers and men were but recently crowded together is now filled by Confederates, who peer through the gratings of the windows, or gather in groups before the large holes made by our shells in the prison walls. I do not see the justice or the propriety of restraining these poor soldiers—many of them most unwilling tools in the hands of bad men—and permitting the officers to ride their horses, in uniform and with side-arms, unrestrained, about the town. As a general thing, I notice that there is no particular restraint exercised over the prisoners, who go where they please inside of our lines.

In one hospital I visited—that of Gen. BALDWIN's division—I found about 300 sick and wounded. The Surgeons were very courteous, and stated that they were very short of medicines and other hospital supplies. The condition of these sick and wounded was pitiable in the extreme. They admitted the fall of Vicksburgh was a great blow to the Confederacy, and with the fall of Port Hudson, must give us the possession of the Mississippi and cut their Confederacy in twain. The war, however, would be prosecuted, and when they were driven to it, they would take to the woods and fire upon us from the corners of the fences. All of which, I conceded, was eminently proper, and expressed the hope that they would prosecute the "corn-fence" war as long as they found it agreeable and profitable. As we were just getting our hand in, I remarked, we should not be able to follow any other business for the next five years.

BARRICADES.

At the intersection of the river streets with Walnut-street, perfect barricades have been constructed with plank abutments on the up-hill side and a deep ditch below. These were to protect the place from assault in front, and to furnish shelter for riflemen. This system has completely blocked up the streets, except those running parallel with the river at and above Walnut. Parties of contrabands have been busy for two days in leveling these barricades and restoring the ancient landmarks.

Very few houses in the compact part of the town have escaped injury to some extent from our shot and shell. The Court-house, being a very prominent building, has received particular attention, having several large holes through its sides; and a shell which fell through the roof has torn a large opening in the ceiling of the first floor. The chief damage, however, has been from fire, which has left the charred and blackened walls of many formerly fine buildings, in nearly every street in the town. Immense holes in the earth in many places mark the places were our mortar shells have fallen and burst. Missiles of every description, from the 12 and 20-pounder Parrott shell to the 9-inch shell and 100-pounder Parrott shot and shell, can be found in every street. They are too common for trophies and too heavy to transport as curiosities.

HOLES IN THE GROUND.

A most ingenious device for escaping the effect of our shot and shells was adopted by the citizens and soldiers. The cellars afforded no protection, but in many parts of the town the streets are cut through a ridge of fine hard clay, leaving bulkheads fronting the streets as steep as the side of a house, and some twenty-five feet deep. Into the sides of these tough, clayey knolls, the rebels had excavated caves of various dimensions, but generally large enough to admit and comfortably contain from six to twenty persons. The doors are generally from four to five feet in height, tapering at the top in Gothic style, and wide enough to admit one person, and the bottoms on a level with the streets. Whenever our shells began to fly, these places were resorted to by both soldier and citizen. In some cases, whole families moved into these caves, carrying in their beds, and remaining until the storm was overpast. They would then emerge from their skulking places, and be ready to retreat to them when the next bombardment commenced. These catacombs, where the living have so long immured themselves as if among the dead, will remain for years, if not disturbed, as among the remarkable marks of the siege of Vicksburgh.

Now that peace once more, with heavenly wing, broods over the devoted city, families begin to return to their deserted homes. All day yesterday I observed carts loaded with household furniture coming into the town, and women and children, at once the earnest and proof of civilization, are beginning to return and give a civilized aspect to the streets. The wealthy rebels, who are not prepared to take the oath of allegiance to the "best Government the sun ever shone upon," will continue to make themselves scarce. So mote it be. Good Union men, who deserve protection and the prosperity which the position holds out, should be encouraged to locate and start business here. The opening is inviting.

The shore batteries, their location, size of guns, their number, &c., must form the staple of another letter. It may suffice here to say that these river batteries are composed of the heaviest guns known to modern warfare, both smooth bores and rifled, and all the most formidable projectiles were made in the town. They gathered up all the shot and fragments of shell we threw into the place, and recast them for their own heavy guns to throw back at us. They had buried many guns, which are being constantly discovered and dug up.

STILL ANOTHER FOURTH OF JULY VICTORY—VALOR OF THE NEGRO TROOPS IN ARKANSAS.

The steamer *New National*, Capt. GRANT arrived here this afternoon from Cairo, bringing supplies for the fleet, and a most welcome mail. The dates from New-York are to June 26. We learn by Capt. GRANT that another most decisive Union victory crowned our arms on the 4th of July in Arkansas, rendering the day illustrious. It seems that the Union forces under PRENTISS at Helena, Ark., was attacked by a greatly superior army under PRICE, who came down on the place intending a surprise. We had not to exceed four thousand, about one-half being black troops. The gunboat *Tyler* being present did the heavy business, throwing about one hundred and eighty shell and shot. Our troops were protected by intrenchments and fought with the most determined valor. I have not learned how long the contest raged, but the result was a total repulse of the rebels, with a loss of two hundred killed and four hundred prisoners who fell into our hands, with a considerable amount of arms and ammunition. *The negro troops stripped off everything but pants, and fought with the most persistent courage.* It is said that they could with difficulty be restrained from breaking out of the intrenchments and pursuing the enemy in the open field. PRICE's force was estimated all the way from five thousand to fifteen thousand men. The day is not a lucky one for the rebel cause. It is supposed that this force was on the way to reinforce, Vicksburgh. It is remarkable that this rebel stronghold during the battle at Helena had already surrendered to Gen. GRANT with its entire garrison and *materiel* of war.

A considerable number of steamers have arrived from above to-day, and added to the already large fleet which had accumulated at the Vicksburgh wharves gives to the place a most lively and business-like aspect. At night I can count over fifty transport steamers; five or six tin-clads, light armed steamer; two naval-store ships, and seven iron-clad gunboats. The latter occupy the channel way at anchor, or are moored alongside the opposite bank of the river, where the officers and crew may be seen curiously inspecting the shot-battered and shell-plowed city. DE SOTO.

The Charleston Mercury.

DAILY PAPER—Twenty Dollars per annum, payable half-yearly in advance. | SPONTE SUA SINE LEGE FIDES RECTUMQUE COLENTUR.—VINDICE NULLO | COUNTRY PAPER—Three a Week—Ten Dollars per annum, in advance.

VOLUME LXXXIII | CHARLESTON, S. C., THURSDAY, JULY 23, 1863. | NUMBER 11,814

THE MERCURY.

THURSDAY, JULY 23, 1863.

Charleston Must not Fall!

When General PEMBERTON proposed to the Government at Richmond that he should abandon all the defences around the Bay of Charleston, he received, in response, a very decided declaration, that these defences and the City of Charleston itself should be held and defended to the last extremity. All the reasons which induced this determination then, operate with tenfold force now. Vicksburg and Port Hudson had not then fallen. Our army on the Potomac had not made a fruitless march on Pennsylvania, and returned to Virginia after a disastrous battle. The more endangered a cause becomes in any contest, the more resolute must be the course of its defenders. The strong may waver or yield, and no serious injury to their cause may ensue; but those who have an impaired or imperilled cause to support can yield nothing. Every step must be contested with the sternest resistance.

But, independent of the circumstances which now environ us, there are reasons affecting the whole Confederacy, which demand that Charleston should be held at any hazard or cost. Better that the whole city should be destroyed, than that it should be surrendered. Vicksburg having fallen, the attention of the world is called to the siege of Charleston. Our enemies stigmatize it as "the nest of the rebellion;" and their hate has singled it out for vengeance and destruction. The signal and bloody repulse of the foe at Secessionville lent distinction to our cause. The gallant defence of Fort Sumter, in beating off and crippling their iron-clads, has been the theme of discussion and praise throughout the civilized world. The brave deeds of our valiant troops have inaugurated and rendered this struggle in our defence more illustrious. So much greater will be the shame of our defeat. The honor of every soldier (ever dearer than life) is put up on the issue, and is lost or won according to the issue.—With the time we have had to prepare, it is impossible but failure must be disgrace. Confidence in the Government, and our cause itself, will be shaken by the fall of Charleston. When, in the Revolution of 1776, our fortunes were at their lowest ebb, the defence of Fort Moultrie and the discomfiture of our British foe, lifted up the spirits of our ancestors, and aroused them to renewed energies for the attainment of their liberties. Shall not the same results be produced in the great contest in which we are now engaged, and in the Bay of Charleston? We trust that it will; and that renewed claims to the gratitude of the Confederacy will cluster around the brows of the officers who have in charge our destinies. Let us support them, then, with all our power, and carry out with alacrity and cheerfulness all orders and every measure for our defence. Let us, one and all, rise to the great emergency, and meet the duties of the present with a brave, unshaking, devoted and hopeful spirit.

THE SIEGE AND FALL OF VICKSBURG.

BY ONE OF THE GARRISON.

On Sunday, the 17th of May, the Confederate army fell back from their position east of Big Black, their breastworks having been stormed by the enemy on that morning, and about eight o'clock on Sunday night reached the city of Vicksburg, where they were immediately reorganised and placed in the following positions: Gen. Smith's division on the extreme left, Maj. Gen. Forney in the centre, Maj. Gen. Stephenson on the right, and Brig. Gen. Bowen's division of Missourians held in reserve. At about two o'clock on Monday afternoon the enemy's skirmishers came in sight and opened fire on our line of works, without doing any damage whatever to the Confederate army; by seven o'clock that night they had placed several batteries in position about three hundred yards from the breastworks, but abstained from firing. On Tuesday morning before daylight they opened fire from their batteries, our guns responding immediately and with fine effect, compelling the enemy to shift their batteries several times. At the same time the enemy endeavored to throw forward a body of sharpshooters, but were prevented, by the fire of our men, from so doing. The artillery duel and sharpshooting continued for about three hours, when Gen. Pemberton rode up and ordered our men to cease firing, as he desired no artillery duels! In obedience to the order our men ceased firing, and the result was that next morning the enemy, emboldened by our silence, approached one hundred yards nearer than they were before, without any opposition.

On Tuesday the enemy made their first assault on the line of works held by Brigadier-General Shoup's Brigade of Louisianians. They marched up in one solid column, our men withholding their fire until the Yankees had approached within thirty yards of the lines, when they opened a terrific volley of musketry. The enemy wavered a moment then marched forward, they were again met by another volley, when they broke and fled under cover of the hills. This was the only attempt made on that day to force our lines, and the attempt was evidently made more with the intention of "feeling" our lines than with any serious idea of storming them. The days intervening from the 19th to the 22d, were spent in one continued bombarding and sharpshooting during the day, in the night they generally ceased firing. On the morning of the 22d the enemy opened a terrific fire with their Parrott guns, and continued it till about eleven o'clock, when the bombardment ceased, and heavy columns of the enemy could be seen forming in line of battle. Our forces were all ready for them and eager for their advance. At about a quarter to twelve the columns of the Yankee army advanced all along the lines in splendid order, and with a loud cheer dashed up to the works. They were gallantly responded to by our brave boys, and the first charge repulsed On the extreme right of our lines the nature of the ground prevented the enemy from making any heavy attack, but on the right of the centre, the centre, and the left of the centre, the assault was desperately made and gallantly met—but once did our lines break, and that was in Lee's brigade; the enemy gained a temporary footing on the rifle pits, but Lee quickly rallied his men, and after a desperate hand-to-hand fight drove them out and re-captured the lines. The engagement at this point and the right of the line, held by Brigadier-General L. Herbert, was of a terrible nature, the Yankees having thrown their best troops on these works. Five times did they charge, and each time were repulsed.

The last charge on the right of Brigadier General Herbert's lines was made by an Irish regiment, (the 17th Wisconsin) carrying the green flag of Erin. They came at a double quick up the hill, each man in the front rank furnished with a ladder to reach the works. Three times they essayed to plant their ladders, but were prevented by the obstinate resistance offered by the consolidated 21st and 23d Louisiana regiments. At the third charge they came within ten yards of the line, but two volleys of buck shot from the shot guns of our forces compelled them to make a precipitate retreat from the front of our works. At about two o'clock they made their last charge, and were again repulsed, when they retired, and did not attempt any further demonstration that day. The loss of the enemy on that day is estimated, by competent parties, at not less than from 5,000 to 10,000, while our loss was between 800 and 1,000 in killed and wounded. To describe the battle would be an impossibility. The cannonading appeared like one continuous peal of thunder, and the sharp crack of thousands of rifles lent a grandeur to the scene that defies description. Thursday was no doubt the heaviest and most desperate assault on a line of breastworks that has ever been attempted during this war. No higher praise can be given to our troops for repulsing the enemy than the acknowledgment that the Yankees fought with a valor worthy of a better cause, and the frank acknowledgement of Gen. Grant that the troops that kept him out of Vicksburg for forty-seven days on one quarter rations were the bravest men he ever saw, and men that could have kept him out as long as they had provisions. On the 22d we lost some noble men, among whom were Colonel Herrick of the 21st Louisiana, Captain Gomez, of the same regiment, and other gallant and chivalrous Southern men.

From the commencement of the siege to the 26th of May, the Yankees had only fired during the day, but from Tuesday the 26th they kept up one continued fire night and day. The mortars on the peninsula opposite Vicksburg opened fire on the 25th of May, and continued an unceasing fire until the surrender of the city. Each day new batteries were erected, and a larger amount of guns brought to bear upon the town. It is estimated that as many as 6000 mortar shells alone were thrown into Vicksburg every twenty-four hours, and on the line in the rear of the city as many as 4000 per day.

After the grand attack on the 22d of May, the enemy evidently perceived the hopelessness of taking Vicksburg by storm; they then commenced mining our works. To give an idea of why they ventured to mine our lines, we would state that our men, having to obey the order of Gen. Pemberton, did not "waste any ammunition on the enemy," but allowed them to come within fifty yards of our line of breastworks, when they commenced throwing up works and erecting forts; this they were allowed to do without any further molestation than the occasional throwing of a few hand grenades, in many cases the enemy flinging them back to us. From the 22d of May to the 25th of June, no attempt was made of any serious nature, with the exception of the attack by the turreted iron-clad gunboat Cincinnati to silence one of our land batteries. The engagement lasted about fifteen minutes, when the Cincinnati commenced sinking, having been pierced several times by the Brook gun known as "Whistling Dick." This was a spirited and exciting engagement, and the result appeared wholly unexpected by the Yankees, as they confidently anticipated the destruction of the battery by their vaunted iron-clad. During the engagement a number of the enemy congregated on the banks of the river opposite Vicksburg, while Sherman with his entire corps rested on their arms waiting for the destruction of the works, when he would "enter Vicksburg without any trouble." As soon as it became evident that the boat was sinking, she was run ashore and set on fire. She now lies like a dismantled wreck immediately above the city on the Mississippi shore.

From the commencement of the siege to the 25th of June our loss in officers had been very large: Lieut. Col. Rogers, of the 17th Louisiana, and Major Hoadly, of the heavy artillery, killed; Col. Patton, Lieut. Col. Steever, Col. Marks, Col. Harrison, Brig. Gen. Baldwin, Capt. Bruisle and others wounded, all belonging to the field and staff. Col. Garrott, commanding an Alabama regiment, was killed at the breastworks; also Capt. Emanuel, Chief of Artillery for Herbert's Brigade, and a most promising young officer. For about five days after the siege commenced the troops were allowed full rations. At the expiration of that time they were gradually reduced to the following amount of food: 4 ounces flour, 4 ounces bacon, 1½ ounces rice, 2 ounces peas (the latter not eatable), and 8 ounces sugar—making a total of 14½ ounces of food per day. From the small number of our forces it took every man to defend the lines, so that the men had no time whatever to rest. Occasionally a company would be permitted to go out to wash their clothes, taking their arms with them, and receiving strict orders at the first sound of musketry to hurry back to their position. Whole companies would lie back of the breastworks for three weeks without leaving the line for a moment.

It had been previously known that the enemy were undermining our works, particularly the fort on the immediate left of the Jackson road, and occupied by the Third Louisiana Regiment, of Herbert's brigade. At about half past four or five on Thursday, the 25th of June, a terrific explosion took place, caused by the blowing up of the above mentioned fort. Luckily, most of our forces occupying that fort had been withdrawn to an inner line of entrenchments, erected by our forces in anticipation of the fort being blown up, so that only a few men were wounded by the explosion. As soon as the fort was destroyed, a column of the enemy advanced, as if with the intention of storming the line, but were met by the Sixth Missouri, under Col. Eugene Erwin. A desperate struggle for mastery now took place. Col. Erwin was the first to ascend the parapet. As soon as he had mounted, a shot from the enemy's sharpshooters pierced his heart, and he fell dead. He was a grand-son of Henry Clay, and one of the most ardent supporters of Southern rights. The Sixth Missouri, enraged at his death, and aided by the Third Louisiana, sprung on the dismantled fort, and after a severe combat, drove the enemy from their position. Our loss on this occasion was heavy being no less than eighty-six killed and wounded. The loss of the enemy was estimated between 800 and 400. They were severely punished in their first attempt at "blowing up" our works.

We now have to record an event of a most melancholy nature. On the 27th of June, Brig. Gen. Green, of Missouri, was shot in the neck by a minnie ball. He lingered for about an hour when he died. He was an aged man, beloved by all who knew him, for his devotion to our cause, his intrepid valor, and his genial and amiable qualities; he was a quiet and unassuming man; the meanest private in his command had free access to his presence, and he was looked upon by his men, not as a General, but a father to his brigade. Many noble sons of Missouri have fallen during this war, but none of her martyrs in our war of independence will be spoken of in more glowing terms, or more deserved praise, than "the man" who fell in defence of Vicksburg. His wish was gratified—he lived not to see Vicksburg fall!

During the siege many instances of daring took place.—Several times our forces sallied out, taking prisoners.—Among them were one Lieut. Col. Cann, of an Illinois regiment, with a good many subaltern officers and privates. On the 22d May the 2d Texas, of Moor's brigade, captured a stand of colors from the enemy in the following manner: The enemy charged up the hill towards our works; as soon as they had arrived about thirty yards from our line of breastworks, the color bearer of the Yankee regiment rushed forward and planted the United States flag on the edge of our works. One of the men of the 2d Texas quickly jumped out of the rifle pit, shot the color bearer, and taking away the flag, returned to our lines. Many other instances of individual heroism occurred during the siege, too numerous to narrate. Our forces, buoyed up with the hope of a speedy relief, determined never to permit the enemy to cross the line of works. Repeated assurances were given to the men that succor would soon arrive. Couriers arriving from Johnston brought most exaggerated reports of the strength of the army under his command—many placing it as high as 80,000 effective men.

While these events were transpiring at the breastworks around the town, the enemy were not idle on the peninsula opposite. One constant stream of mortar shells was poured into the devoted city, the enemy exhibiting a refinement of cruelty in throwing their shells at the hospitals particularly, aware that the men who were now well and hearty were perfectly indifferent to the storm of shot and shell poured like hail upon them. They fired into buildings on which the yellow flag waved, killing and wounding several of the inmates. Whether General Pemberton offered any remonstrance at their doing so has not been ascertained. If he did, no regard was paid to his complaint. The women and children remaining in town suffered severely, no less than three having been killed and twelve wounded during the siege. In spite of which, with all the heroism that characterizes our Southern women, those remaining well declared their willingness to run the risk of being killed rather than lose Vicksburg. Among the ladies wounded are Mrs. Hazzard, Mrs. O. W. Petus, Mrs. H. H. Clements, Mrs. Major T. B. Read, Miss Lucy Rawlings, and Miss Maggie Cook, the most of these ladies being well known in the State of Mississippi. The firing on the city was not marked with the same regularity and precision observed on the front of our breastworks, the mortar shells falling in every direction over the town, as if no particular object was aimed at. After the surrender of the town, the Yankee artillery officers stated that the mortars and Parrott guns opposite the city were manned by fresh troops, and were placed there for a double purpose: first, to annoy us in the city, and to practise themselves in that arm of the service; and gave that as their excuse for our hospitals being struck so often. The enemy's sharp-shooters were all splendid shots, and after the first few days of the siege it was a very dangerous thing for any one to look over the breastworks. So accurately did they aim, and in such numbers were they, that a hat placed on a stick and held above the fort for two minutes was pierced by fifteen minie balls.

On the 29th of June, the enemy succeeded in blowing up the same portion of our line again. We lost several men of the 3d Louisiana from the explosion. The enemy, however, made no attempt to charge the work, being apparently contented with the occupation of one portion of the ruined fort.

Tremendous cannonading continued during the remaining few days of the siege, with but little damage to the Confederates. The men were all in good spirits, and appeared satisfied to live on the meagre allowance of rations given them, rather than yield the city they had defended gallantly for so long a period. Not a murmur was heard among them—all were inspired with the greatest enthusiasm and devotion to their cause, and the word "surrender" was never broached among them. Five or six days previous to the surrender of the city "mule meat" was tried and found of good quality—the meat being equal to the finest venison, and was liberally eaten by the soldiers and citizens alike.

An attempt was made by our forces to countermine the enemy, but the attempt signally failed—as from the position of the enemy's works they could not be mined.

On Friday morning, the 3d of July, Gen. Pemberton sent out a flag of truce, and a short time afterwards himself and Brigadier General Bowen were seen leaving our lines. As soon as they left the works the men conjectured that the object of his going to Grant in person was to treat for a surrender of the city. There was soon considerable excitement observed among the soldiers, not one of whom favored such a course; the excitement was partially allayed by the statement that General Pemberton had gone to Grant for the purpose of getting his consent to our removing the sick and wounded and the women and children from the town. After remaining at Grant's headquarters for about two hours, Generals Pemberton and Bowen returned. An armistice had been declared till ten o'clock that night. The firing had ceased, and nothing but the voices of soldiers in angry and indignant conversation could be heard.

At half-past six on Friday evening a meeting of all the Generals took place at General Pemberton's headquarters, and at ten o'clock a messenger went into the Federal lines with despatches from Pemberton.

On Saturday morning a circular from the Lieut. General commanding announced the surrender of the city, and the terms of capitulation, as follows: The entire force of Confederate troops were to surrender as prisoners of war to the United States army, under General Grant; the whole army, including the Generals, were to be immediately paroled and sent into our lines; all officers were to retain their arms; all mounted officers to have the privilege of riding out; private property to be respected, and all parties, whether citizens or not, connected in any manner with the army, were to be allowed the privilege of leaving the Federal lines on parole. All ammunition, stores, field artillery and siege guns were to be surrendered to the United States army, as well as all small arms in our possession.

On Saturday morning, at half past eleven o'clock, the men having stacked their arms, marched from the breastworks they had stood behind with such heroic valor for nearly two months. Soon after the Yankee army commenced pouring into the town—in the space of fifteen minutes the city was crammed with them—and then began a scene of pillaging. Houses and stores were broken open and the contents appropriated by the Yankees. In justice to General Grant, I would say that as soon as complaint was made to him, a guard was placed at the buildings that had been broken open. Soon after entering the city, the stars and stripes were hauled up on the spire of the court house, amid the exulting shouts of the Yankee soldiers, and the deepest feeling of humiliation on the part of the Confederates.

The Confederate army remained in the city for one week, during which time repeated fights took place on the streets between our men and the Yankees—many of whom were very insulting and full of taunting remarks on the downfall of our Gibraltar.

On Saturday, the 11th July, at about 12 o'clock the Confederate army, having all been paroled, took up its line of march from Vicksburg, and arrived at Big Black that evening. It was a solemn and imposing departure. Tears were seen coursing the cheeks of many of our troops, and ever and anon the men would turn back to take one last look at the city they had so well and nobly defended. On Tuesday morning the troops commenced arriving at Brandon, where it is anticipated they will remain for a few days.

Thus fell the city of Vicksburg after an obstinate and heroic defence of forty-seven days, forty-two of which the Confederate army had subsisted on one-quarter rations. The city is now in the hands of the invaders, yet its fall adds not one single laurel to their wreath of victory. Starvation succeeded in doing what the Yankee army could never have done, and though the result was a reverse to the Confederate arms, when future historians shall speak of the siege of Vicksburg, the memory of the gallant men who bared their bosoms with unflinching firmness to the storm of shot and shell poured upon them, will shine with a lustre of unsurpassed magnificence. All honor to them! Nobly have they sustained the Southern name, and in their fall robbed the enemy of a single claim of victory!

As a few remarks on certain facts may not be deemed inappropriate, I would state that on the Sunday evening that our army entered Vicksburg there was but fifteen days' rations in the town; for five days the men got full rations, and the remaining forty-two days subsisted on ten days' rations. The question has been asked, "Could not the Commissary of Subsistence get the corn to purchase?" He could. Six months ago the planters offered the Government corn from their plantations free of charge, if the authorities would only send and haul it. The reply to the offer was: "If it is hauled into town we will pay for it, but we cannot send for it." The result was, that when the enemy occupied the country west of the Big Black, he found enough corn and bacon to have supplied our army for twelve months. To substantiate my assertion, I would state that among the planters who offered their corn free of charge were Colonel Benson Blake, Dr. J. C. Newman, Col. Auter, and Dr. P. H. Cook. All these are men of well known standing in their State.

Let the gentlemen who had the provisioning of Vicksburg come forward and account for the cause of only fifteen days' provisions being in the town. Until they bring forward abundant proof that it was no fault of theirs, the people of the Confederate States must hold them from the General Commanding to the Commissary of Subsistence to strict accountability for their shameful and culpable neglect of duty. Before the investment of Vicksburg, had the press called attention to the fact of there being no provisions in the city, and the city been afterwards taken, people would have said that the papers had invited the assault by their imprudence, in letting the enemy know of it; and by keeping silent those in authority were allowed to continue their course without anything being said to them.

It has been said that Lieut. Gen. Pemberton stated that he always "believed that a large supply of provisions was stored away in Vicksburg." Believed! Section 818 of the Army Regulations is worded as follows: * * * "He (referring to the General Commanding) studies the works and the exterior within the radius of attack and investment, the strength of the garrison, the artillery, munitions of war, subsistence and supplies of all kinds, and takes immediate measures to procure whatever is deficient." In what manner did the Lieut. Gen. Commanding the Department of Mississippi and East Louisiana perform these duties laid down in the regulations? Why was it that all during the fall of 1862, when the river from Port Hudson to Vicksburg was in our possession and boats were trading up and down, not one single boat load of provisions ever arrived? Did the Confederate Government get all the sugar and molasses brought up to Vicksburg? Or is the assertion that certain commissaries and quartermasters were speculating with Government money correct?

Our fortifications were pronounced by the Yankee officers to be the "most miserable" they had ever seen, and it was a matter of great surprise to them that, with fifteen months' time, we had not erected works that could have defied an army of 200,000 men. The works were so badly made that the damage done to them by the enemy's fire in the day could scarcely be repaired by a large force of men working all night. Our engineers only existed in name; in fact there was not one man among them that understood his duty. The fortifications were so poor that General McPherson, after riding over the line, is said to have exclaimed, "Good Heavens! are these the boasted fortifications of Vicksburg? It was the rebels alone, and not their works, that kept us out of this town."

The amount of prisoners captured at Vicksburg was about 23,000 altogether. Among them were three Major Generals and nine Brigadier Generals. About ninety pieces of artillery were captured, of which several are unfit for use; forty thousand stand of arms and between thirty-five and forty stand of colors were taken by the enemy. The amount of ammunition surrendered is immense, there being not less than six months' supply stored away in the magazines. There was a useless saving of ammunition during the siege. Had our men been allowed to keep up a fire on the Yankee lines, they could never have approached to within thirty yards of our lines, much less have erected forts that close to us.

Taking a view of the whole campaign, we can only come to the conclusion that Gen. Pemberton was out-generaled in the most glaring manner by General Grant. The neglect to reinforce Gen. Bowen at Grand Gulf; the battle at Baker's Cree, where our army slept the night previous within forty yards of the enemy without knowing they were there; and the day of the battle when nearly the whole of our artillery was captured without firing a shell; the battle of Big Black, and the retreat into Vicksburg, was sufficient proof of Gen. Pemberton's incompetency. A great deal has been said of his "gallant defence." This is simply ridiculous. Had the soldiers been solely under the command of that General, the city of Vicksburg would have been evacuated the Sunday night that our forces fell back into the town.

The men had not the slightest confidence in General Pemberton, and since the surrender of Vicksburg express their determination of deserting rather than serve under Pemberton after they are exchanged. The very Major Generals and Brigadier Generals have got the poorest opinion of General Pemberton's capacity; and of his unpopularity General Pemberton is well aware. It is not correct to hastily pass judgment upon the merits or demerits of military men, but in a case of this kind, when there are so many proofs of incapacity, it is the duty of a free people to demand that such men be removed from command, and competent men placed in their stead. Let this reverse at Vicksburg be ever so much smoothed over by those who desire military patronage, to all sensible men it must be painfully apparent that if censure is to fall on any one for the loss of Vicksburg, it must naturally rest on the man who held command.—*Mobile Advertiser.*

The Charleston Mercury.

DAILY PAPER—TWENTY DOLLARS PER ANNUM, PAYABLE HALF-YEARLY IN ADVANCE.

VINDICEM NULLO SPONTE SUA SINE LEGE FIDES RECTUMQUE COLENTUR.

COUNTRY PAPER—THRICE A WEEK—TEN DOLLARS PER ANNUM, IN ADVANCE.

VOLUME LXXXIII | CHARLESTON, S. C., MONDAY, JULY 20, 1863. | NUMBER 11,8[illegible]

THE MERCURY.

MONDAY, JULY 20, 1863.

The Struggle for Charleston.

The result of the tremendous bombardment and desperate assault of Saturday is exceedingly gratifying—not more from the glorious and bloody defeat of the enemy's designs, than from the small loss sustained by us in men and by the unimpaired condition of Fort Wagner. Let us not, however, deceive ourselves by the pleasing illusion that we have accomplished anything further than inflicting a heavy loss on the enemy and gaining time. So long as Monitors and the wooden gunboats are allowed to approach, the work is still exposed to a concentric fire of nearly half a circle by sea and land from the heavy artillery of the foe. His sharpshooters, too, are in occupation of rifle pits only some six hundred yards off. Renewed assaults at times and in ways of his own selection, it is still in his power to attempt. New batteries and new guns are likely to be put in position—perhaps means of reducing the fort other than either bombardment or assault may be tried. It is plain that men, materials, scientific labors and military contrivances will be exhausted by the active, scientific and ambitious commander of the Yankee forces in this Department. Either great exertions will have to be used to enable Battery Wagner to fight the battle of Charleston—to cope with the foe and beat him off successfully as long as he sees fit to attack, or the fight for the possession of Charleston harbor must be made elsewhere than on Morris Island, and by prompt and vigorous preparations. These questions, of course, we leave to the wisdom and experience of our military authorities to decide and meet. We wish merely to let our people see where we are, and the value of the great and glorious engagement of the 18th instant. While rejoicing with gratitude to God for this victory, we should not encourage false hopes and expectations. We should rather, by a knowledge of the truth, stimulate to every exertion for the lasting preservation of Charleston.

Oaths of Allegiance, Pledges and Promises.

In the late General Orders from the War Department at Washington, very adroitly issued on the 3d of July, just in time to nullify such paroles of sick and wounded prisoners as General LEE had granted on the field, and to embarrass him with the necessity of guarding through a long march the numerous other prisoners in his hands, the following declarations are embraced, which meet the cases of thousands of Confederate citizens upon whom the detestable oath of allegiance to the Yankee Government has been imposed by "ill usage and cruelty" or the fear of them, which is the same thing. According to these declarations all oaths taken, and all pledges and paroles given to avoid incarceration or secure release from imprisonment, or to protect property, or avoid any other sort of ill usage, are to be held as "not binding." The passages read as follows:

Any pledge or parole of honor extorted from a prisoner by ill usage or cruelty is not binding.

The obligations imposed by the general laws and usages of war upon the combatant inhabitants of a section of country passed over by an invading army close when the military occupation ceases, and any pledge or parole given by such persons, in regard to future service, is null and of no effect.

The Late Colonel DeSaussure.

Colonel WILLIAM DAVIE DESAUSSURE, 15th Regiment S. C. V., was killed on the 2d of July 1863, at the battle of Gettysburg. Descended upon both the paternal and maternal sides from Revolutionary ancestry, he fell a martyr to the cause of Southern Independence. He was a grandson of the late Chancellor DESAUSSURE, and the eldest son of Honorable WILLIAM F. DESAUSSURE, and SARAH, daughter of the late General WILLIAM DAVIE, and was born in Columbia, South Carolina, in 1819. He graduated at the South Carolina College in December, 1838, and after the necessary preparatory study was admitted to the bar. The Mexican war called into practice his strong military predisposition, and he raised a company for the Palmetto Regiment. From Vera Cruz to Garita de Belin he shared in the hardships of the campaign, and participated in every battle in which the Palmetto Regiment was engaged. Upon the close of that war he returned home, and was elected a member of the Legislature for Richland District. He then applied for and obtained a commission as Captain of Dragoons in the United States service. He was assigned to the 2d Regiment, and, with his command, was engaged in the Utah Expedition. While serving in the West he formed the acquaintance of General JOSEPH E. JOHNSTON, who conceived of him a favorable opinion as an officer, and expresses of him cordial feeling as a friend. At the time of the secession of his native State he was stationed near the Rocky Mountains, but as early as he learned what had occurred promptly resigned his commission, and by an arduous journey of over five hundred miles through the snow, returned to South Carolina. By Governor PICKENS he was appointed Major of a squadron of cavalry, and actively engaged in enlisting what now constitutes Major LUCAS' Battalion. Desirous of more active service than then appeared probable with that battalion, he resigned his commission, and sought to unite himself with another organization. In September, 1861, he was elected and commissioned Colonel of the 15th Regiment S. C. V. At the battle of Port Royal his regiment was the infantry support of the garrison. After several months of service on the sea coast of South Carolina his regiment was sent to the Army of the Potomac, and with that army he shared in the arduous campaign into Maryland, and was an active participant in the battles of Boonsboro and Sharpsburg. In this second campaign he is believed to have fallen.

Colonel DESAUSSURE was an amiable man. He was a firm friend, and a devoted brother, son, and husband. A high regard for truth was one of his eminent characteristics; and he scorned all that was dishonorable. He was constitutionally a brave man, and his spirit instinctively revolted at injustice or oppression.

THE NEW CALL FOR TROOPS.

The following is the proclamation of the President, extending the call under the Conscript Act, to embrace all residents of the Confederacy, between 18 and 45 years, not legally exempt. Under the terms of the proclamation and rulings of the Confederate Courts, foreigners, who are actual residents, will be called upon to do military service in defence of the country in which they reside:

PROCLAMATION BY THE PRESIDENT.

Whereas, it is provided by an act of Congress, entitled "an act to further provide for the public defence," approved on the 16th day of April, 1862, and by another act of Congress, approved on the 27th September, 1862, entitled "an act to amend an act entitled an act to provide further for the public defence, approved 16th April, 1862," that the President be authorized to call out and place in the military service of the Confederate States, for three years, unless the war shall have been sooner ended, all white men who are residents of the Confederate States, between the ages of eighteen and forty-five years, at the time the call may be made, and who are not, at such time, legally exempted from military service, or such part thereof as in his judgment may be necessary to the public defence.

And whereas, in my judgment the necessities of the public defence require that every man capable of bearing arms, between the ages aforesaid, should now be called out to do his duty in the defence of his country and in driving back the invaders now within the limits of the Confederacy:

Now, therefore, I, Jefferson Davis, President of the Confederate States of America, do, by virtue of the powers vested in me aforesaid, call out and place in the military service of the Confederate States, all white men residents of said States between the ages of eighteen and forty five years, not legally exempted from military service; and I do hereby order and direct that all persons subject to this call and not now in the military service, do, upon being enrolled, forthwith repair to the conscript camps established in their respective States of which they may be residents, under pain of being held and punished as deserters in the event of their failure to obey this call, as provided in said laws.

And I do further order and direct, that the enrolling officers of the several States proceed at once to enroll all persons embraced within the terms of this proclamation, and not heretofore enrolled.

And I do further order, that it shall be lawful for any person embraced within this call to volunteer for service before enrollment, and that persons so volunteering be allowed to select the arm of service and the company which they desire to join, provided such company be deficient in the full number of men allowed by law for its organization.

Given under my hand, and the Seal of the Confederate States of America, at the city of [SEAL] Richmond, this fifteenth day of July, in the year of our Lord one thousand eight hundred and sixty-three.

(Signed) JEFFERSON DAVIS.

By the President,

(Signed)

J. P. BENJAMIN, Secretary of State.

THE INVASION OF PENNSYLVANIA—THE BATTLE OF GETTYSBURG—THE RETREAT TO HAGERSTOWN.

The Richmond *Examiner* furnishes us with the following extract of a letter from an officer of the Army of Northern Virginia. It contains the only connected and intelligible account that has yet been given to the public of the movements of General LEE from his crossing of the Potomac to his return to Hagerstown, after the battle of Gettysburg.

THE GREAT PENNSYLVANIA CAMPAIGN.

"The advance of the Second corps crossed into Maryland on Thursday, June 18th, near Shepherdstown. Gen. Rhodes had already crossed below Martinsburg, and was occupying Hagesrtown. General Jenkins was at Chambersburg, and Imboden about Cumberland The Second corps (excepting Rhodes' division) occupied the battle-field of Antietam the 20th, 21st and 22d of June, and marched beyond Hagerstown on the 23d. The reception of these gallant victors of Winchester all through the lower valley was refreshing, and at Shepherdstown fair ladies crowded the streets, and welcomed the soldiers with flowers and smiles. Sharpsburg was black Union, but Hagerstown turned out wild with joy at our approach. On the 24th the corps pushed on through Greencastle to Chambersburg. I should say here that Early bore off to Waynesboro', and was at York when the rest occupied Carlisle.

"At Greencastle and Chambersburg the stores were taken possession of by the Quartermaster, the contents seized, so far as they were useful to the army (*i. e.* to the Quartermaster) and appropriated according to an accurate distribution by Chief Quartermasters and Sub-Quartermasters. A Major General got a hat, but as to the rest, hats, shoes, boots, calicoes, whisky, for the most part, that great unfathomable sponge, the active Quartermaster's Department, got them. At Shippensburg the track of the railroad was torn up and a bridge burned. The citizens, who turned out in large numbers to witness the passage of the rebels, were generally quiet. Occasionally you found a spirited girl, or a spunky parson. But, if one fact was more remarkable than any other, it is this: That portion of Pennsylvania which our army occupied was completely subjugated, very few having the courage to raise their heads. Foraging thrived. For a little Confederate note, and often for nothing, a soldier could get quantities of onions, apple butter, cow butter, ham, good Dutch loaves, cheese, and every delightful thing in the grand category of the productions of the great Cumberland Valley.

"On Friday, 26th, we took up the line of march through Chambersburg, on the Harrisburg road. The splendid band in the 4th Louisiana brigade, Colonel Williams, preceded the column, playing "Dixie" and the Marseillaise, whilst our red-cross banners flaunted proudly over the dark columns of our gallant troops. The scene subjugated that town. We passed through Shippensburg to the sound of martial music again, and went on to Carlisle. The troops were not allowed to plunder. Horses were taken and receipted for by authorized agents. So with cattle and flour. Foraging was tolerated, but the soldiers were expected to pay for their supplies. It was thought, and perhaps rightly, that licensed plundering would demoralize the army, and render it useless for great achievements. But this was occasionally carried to absurd lengths. We overheard an officer, with lachrymose countenance, deprecating the destruction of a cherry tree by some hungry rebels The burning of rails was at first prohibited, but after a day or two it was generally permitted.

"We staid long enough at Carlisle to get what we wanted. Harrisburg was in a panic—and some of our engineer officers went to the banks of the Susquehanna, and found them fortifying the enormous heights on the southern side. Early and Jenkins were at York, and beyond, seeing after the bridges up as far as the river, all of which were destroyed. On the 30th Johnson marched back from Carlisle to Fayetteville, leaving Rhodes at Carlisle. On Wednesday, July 1st, A. P. Hill marched from South Mountain to the neighborhood of Gettysburg, followed by Johnson. Early reached the same vicinity on the same day from York, and Rhodes from Carlisle. Meade's advance of three or four army corps disputed the occupation of the town, giving battle to the north and east of the town from 10 a. m. to about 5 p. m. The result was a glorious victory to the Confederates. The invincible and gallant Early drove the force opposed to him for miles, and occupied the town. The 11th Corps, of Chancellorsville memory, gave themselves up by thousands. Gordon's brigade made what is regarded a most brilliant charge. It could but be successful with such men and such a leader. The Fayetteville Road was "cleaned out" by Hill. Rhodes swept down the Carlisle Road, and Early down the York turnpike. The loss of the Confederates in killed and wounded was probably 600. The Yankee loss in killed probably reached 400 and his wounded 2000.—We captured most of his wounded and 5280 additional prisoners.

"Gettysburg is in Adams county, Pennsylvania, somewhere near eight miles from the South Mountain which is the eastern boundary of the Cumberland Valley. It is a beautiful town of some 5000 inhabitants, and the centre of the following roads: A road from Baltimore; a road from Frederick, both on the southern side of the town, and the three roads just mentioned; between these two former roads and about three-quarters of a mile from the town were two tall hills, one wooded and detached, the other the front of a range that swept backward to the south. These positions boldly commanded the town and vicinity, and Meade occupied them Wednesday, heavily entrenching during the night. On Thursday morning, Ewell's corps lay beneath the first eminence and near the Baltimore road; A. P. Hill occupied a position to the west of the town and near it. Longstreet was not yet up. During the morning, occasional artillery and infantry skirmishing alone broke the silence that hung over the expectant hosts. The day was warm and beautiful. The enemy's cavalry stretched up to the south of the York road, threatening our rear, but was closely watched by the indefatigable Stuart, whose recent seven days and nights march from the vicinity of Washington was the most wonderful cavalry achievement of the war.

"At last Longstreet having passed to the south of A. P. Hill, opened at four p. m., followed by Hill and Ewell. Then ensued undoubtedly the fiercest cannonade of the war. This terrific fire lasted till night. About dark Ewell charged the position on the wooded hill. The enemy had several lines on this eminence and cannon in position, with abattis and planted sticks in rows to prevent our advance. The sides of the hill were rocky and precipitous to almost an inaccessible degree. Our lines, however, gallantly marched up under a fearful fire of musket balls and grape. A partial advantage was gained by Johnson's troops, and lost by accident. But it was beyond mortal endurance to stand before that terrific blast of shot, and the men were withdrawn, after suffering heavy loss. During the afternoon, the other corps had attacked the positions on the south without success. On Friday, July 3d, the battle was renewed early in the morning, and, with the exception of a lull from ten o'clock a. m., to one o'clock p. m., lasted all day. The Confederates did not succeed in holding any of the crests, although one or two were reached; and night again closed on the smoke-wrapped field. From 3½ to 5 p. m., General Stuart succeeded in driving back, very handsomely, the enemy's cavalry threatening our rear. The fight was quite severe and loss unknown.

"Thus ended the great battle of Gettysburg, the most remarkable conflict of the war. The loss of the enemy was probably 25,000 men—perhaps 30,000 during the three days. He was severely handled—for it is believed that he fell back with the greater portion of his force on Friday night, towards Boonsboro'. When I turn from this to our own loss my heart sickens. It was frightful. The loss in general officers was remarkably great. I believe the following to be correct:

"Brigadier General Garnett, killed; Major-General Trimble, leg amputated and captured; Brigadier General J. R. Jones, severely wounded; Brigadier-General Jones, of the cavalry, captured; Brigadier-General Archer, wounded and prisoner; Brigadier General Armistead, wounded and prisoner; Brigadier General Barksdale, mortally wounded and left; Brigadier General Kemper, killed; Brigadier General Jenkins, slightly wounded.

"The list of Colonels and other field officers lost is enormous. The field officers of the First Maryland battalion were severely wounded. All of the field officers of Pickett's division, except the commander and one Lieutenant-Colonel, are killed and wounded. This division was almost destroyed in one brilliant charge; and, as the gallant commander looked over the pitiful remnant of his brave boys, he bowed his head and wept like a child.

"All our wounded that could be transported were removed beyond the Potomac. Those severely wounded had to be left. The Confederate loss in killed, wounded and prisoners (of which there are few) must be *twenty thousand.*

"All day long of July 4th our army lay in line of battle, in a new position overlooking the town. Scarcely a picket shot disturbed the day-long quiet. Meade was withdrawing, but we did not know it. Our trains were quietly moving back to Williamsport, and are now safely packed there, with the loss of but twenty vehicles, of various kinds, and teams! This was brilliantly executed.

"On the night of the 4th the army began quietly to fall back by Fairfield towards Hagerstown. The march back to Hagerstown, some twenty-four miles, occupied three days. The army took one road most of the way, and marched quietly and with dignity back. No defeat to the Confederates was shown in that proud, invincible tread, that spirited and bold heart, that grieved but proud and fierce array of freemen. The *morale* of our army was utterly unaffected; but Meade dare not say so much, as he points to his terrible loss and his enforced retreat. One word here as to his greater loss. It may be said that the attacking army, especially when assailing such a position, must suffer more than the other. But the Yankees were crowded on their hills, and when our eighty cannon opened on them the slaughter was terrific. So when Johnson's division attempted the crest, nearly every shot of our men told among their compact ranks.

"Our army is yet numerous, and perfectly defiant. Witness even this fact: A few days ago the Yankees with three pieces of cannon attacked our park at Williamsport. Imboden, with his men, armed the teamsters and charged the enemy. The wagoners fought like devils, and took two pieces of artillery, and the enemy fell back.

"General Stuart, glorious, unconquerable Jeb, fought the Yankees yesterday morning a few miles from Hagerstown, on the Boonsboro' road, and drove them back after a furious fight, gaining a very handsome victory.

"The rear of our army was feebly attacked as far as South Mountain, eight miles from Gettysburg, on its retirement; but Meade has shown no disposition to trouble us with his main army.

"The battle of Gettysburg was a most remarkable conflict. It is strange that Lee attacked Meade where he was, when he had it in his power to choose his own position and compel Meade to fight him. As far as we can see (which isn't far) the battle as projected and executed on the 2d and 3d was a great military blunder. If Meade had been soundly defeated, as he would have been on even ground or when he had attacked our heights, his army could have been cut to pieces and dissipated before he could reach Baltimore or Washington. The Monocacy could be his only hope, and this was too far off. As it is, we may yet beat him. Most persons adhere to the notion that we shall cross the river, but I cannot, will not believe it. The proud army of Northern Virginia will terminate this bloody campaign within the halls of the Federal Capital.

"We saw many a Pennsylvanian tired of the war. We met several Knights of the Golden Circle. One intelligent farmer told me that "we ought to be unsuccessful in the war unless we captured Abe Lincoln this trip, and that our advent in Pennsylvania was hailed with hearty joy by three million Northern Democrats.' Take this for what it is worth. There is truth somewhere in it.

"You all complain of 'respecting private property.' Such was the order from headquarters, and attempted to be faithfully executed. But take your horse and follow the track of our army up the Cumberland Valley, thence to Gettysburg and thence to Hagerstown. You will find the route marked by the devastating trail—destroyed bridges, burnt fences, beat down wheat and rye fields, devoured clover fields, ransacked stores, horseless and cattleless farmers. At Gettysburg four houses were burnt, three large brick buildings, during the battle of the 1st by the explosion of shell. The vicinity of the city is desolate and trampled and cut up—being, I believe, the most *marked* field of the war. There has been no tendency to outrage. Our forces have not plundered, except in unauthorized squads, and these were few. Order has been enforced as much as possible, and well for us—but still there is the necessary, inevitable *trail*, which a great army leaves in its own country.

"Chambersburg or Carlisle should have been burnt by authority in retaliation for the ruthless destruction of Darien. Such destruction does not demoralize an army—whilst it gives the foe a wholesome lesson by which we vastly profit. How long will our Government pursue this weak-kneed policy of supinely receiving the enemy's cruelty and inhumanity and admitting it within the pale of civilized warfare by the sanction which this failure to retaliate inevitably carries with it? Burn! but by authority. Destroy! but through official proclamation and always with reference to some desecrated home or ruined city that once adorned a sunny landscape in the South. *Au revoir.*"

The Charleston Mercury.

DAILY PAPER—Twenty Dollars per Annum, payable half-yearly in advance.

VINDICE NULLO SPONTE SUA SINE LEGE FIDES RECTUMQUE COLENTUR.

COUNTRY PAPER—Thrice a Week—Ten Dollars per annum, in advance.

VOLUME LXXXIII. | CHARLESTON, S. C., WEDNESDAY, JULY 22, 1863. | NUMBER 11,813

THE SIEGE AND FALL OF PORT HUDSON—INTERESTING PARTICULARS.

An officer who succeeded in passing out from Port Hudson while the surrender was taking place on Thursday, the 9th instant, furnishes the Mobile *Advertiser* with the following very interesting details of the progress and results of the siege of Port Hudson:

The initiatory steps of the siege may be reckoned from the 20th of May, when Gen. Auger advanced from Baton Rouge. His approach being reported by our cavalry, on the 21st Gen. Gardner sent out Col. Miles, with 400 cavalry and a battery, with orders to proceed to the Plain Store, six or seven miles from Port Hudson, and reconnoitre.—About four miles from Port Hudson he encountered the enemy, and a severe action ensued of two and a half hours' duration, with a loss of thirty killed and forty wounded on our side. At night, in pursuance of an order of recall from Gen. Gardner, our forces fell back within the fortifications. At the same time Col. Powers' cavalry, some 300 strong, were engaged on the Baton Rouge and Bayou Sara road, a mile and a half or two miles from Col. Miles. No communication has been had with them since, and their loss is unknown.

On the morning of the 22d the enemy pushed his infantry forward within a mile of our breastworks, and at the same time it was reported by the cavalry scouts that General Banks, who had recently completed his Teche campaign, was landing troops at Bayou Sara (12 miles above) and moving in the direction of Port Hudson. From Saturday the 23d to Tuesday the 26th inclusive, the enemy was engaged in taking his position for the investment of our works. This being completed, on the morning of the 27th he advanced with his whole force against the breastworks, directing his main attack against the left, commanded by Colonel Steadman. Vigorous assaults were also made against the extreme left of Colonel Miles and General Beale, the former of whom commanded in the centre, the latter on the right.

On the left the attack was made by a brigade of negros, comprising about three regiments, together with the same force of white Yankees, across a bridge which had been built over Sandy Creek on the night of the 25th. This force was thrown against the 39th Mississippi Regiment, commanded by Col. Shelby. About 500 negros in front advanced at double-quick within 150 yards of the works, when the artillery on the river bluff and two light pieces on Colonel Shelby's left, opened upon them, and at the same time they were received with volleys of musketry from five companies of the 39th. The negros fled every way in perfect confusion, without firing a gun, probably carrying with them, in their panic flight, their sable comrades further in the rear, for the enemy themselves report that 600 of them perished. If this be so, they must have been shot down by the Yankees in the rear, for the execution we did upon them did not exceed 250; and, indeed, volleys of musketry were heard in the direction of their flight. Among the slain were found the bodies of two negro Captains with commissions in their pockets.

The 1st Alabama, Lieutenant Colonel Locke, and the 10th Arkansas, Colonel Witt, engaged the enemy outside the works, in the thick woods, and fought most gallantly, but were compelled by the heavy odds brought against them to fall back across the creek and within the works. Colonel Johnson, with the 15th Arkansas regiment, numbering about 300 men, occupied a hill across Sandy Creek, which he had been fortifying for the previous week. About 5,000 of the enemy came against this position, moving down a very narrow road, and many of them succeeded in gaining the breastworks, but they were repulsed and compelled to fall back into the woods, leaving 80 or 90 dead in front of the works. On General Beale's left, consisting of the 1st Mississippi and the 49th Alabama, the enemy advanced in strong force, and were driven back with great slaughter. The repulse on Colonel Miles' left was decisive.

About 8 o'clock the Yankees, true to their knavish national instinct, raised the white flag, and under it attempted to make a rush with their infantry. This being reported to General Gardner, he sent orders to the different commanders not to recognize any white flag unless sent by the Federal commander himself. At sunset the firing ceased, after a hotly contested engagement of twelve hours, during the whole of which our men had behaved with unflinching gallantry, and had completely repulsed the enemy at every point. Every man along the entire line had done his duty nobly. While this assault was going on, all the gun and mortar boats kept up an incessant firing upon the lower batteries, but without inflicting any damage.

On the 28th, General Banks sent a flag proposing a cessation of hostilities, for the purpose of burying the dead, which was granted. About 8 o'clock, p. m., the truce ceased, and the enemy, in heavy force, made a furious attack upon the 1st Alabama, which was gallantly repulsed.

From this time till June 13th, heavy skirmishing was constantly kept up, the men were behind the breastworks night and day, and one could scarcely show his head an instant without being made the mark of a sharpshooter. Many were sick from exposure to the sun and other causes. The enemy were, meanwhile, engaged in digging ditches, erecting batteries, and advancing their parallels. The gun and mortar boats kept up a continual fire by night and day, it would seem, more for the purpose of exhausting the garrison by wakefulness than from any hope of direct advantage.

Monday, the 13th of June, a communication was received from General Banks, demanding the unconditional surrender of the post. He complimented the garrison and its commander in high terms. Their courage, he said, amounted almost to heroism, but it was folly for them to attempt to hold the place any longer, as it was at his will, and he demanded the surrender in the name of humanity, to prevent the sacrifice of lives, as it would be impossible for his commanders to save the garrison from being put to the sword when the works should be carried by assault. His artillery, he said, was equal to any in extent and efficiency, and his men outnumbered ours five to one. He knew to what a condition they were reduced, as he had captured Gen. Gardner's courier sent out with despatches to Gen. Johnston. As these despatches were in cipher, it is probable that Banks exaggerated the amount of information he had derived from them.

Gen. Gardner replied that his duty required him to defend the post, and he must refuse to entertain any such proposition.

On the morning of the 14th, just before day, the fleet and all the land batteries which the enemy had succeeded in erecting at 100 to 300 yards from our breastworks, opened fire at the same time. About daylight, under cover of the smoke, the enemy advanced along the whole line, and in many places approached within ten feet of our works. Our brave fellows were wide awake, and opening upon them with "buck and ball" drove them back in confusion, a great number of them being left dead in the ditches. One entire division and a brigade were ordered to charge the position of the 1st Mississippi and the 49th Alabama, and by the mere physical pressure of numbers some of them got within the works, but all those were immediately killed. Every regiment did its duty nobly, but this was the main attack. After a sharp contest of two hours, the enemy were everywhere repulsed and withdrew to their old line,

Bombardment of Port Hudson — A mortar schooner at work

but heavy skirmishing was kept up most of the day.

After this repulse Gen. Banks sent no flag of truce to bury his dead, which remained exposed between the lines for three days. At the end of that time Gen. Gardner sent a flag to Banks, requesting that he would remove them. Banks replied that he had no dead there. Gen. Gardner then desired Gen. Beale to send a flag to Gen. Auger and request him to bury the dead of his division, which lay in front of the 1st and 49th. Auger replied that he did not think he had any dead there, but he would grant a cessation of hostilities to ascertain. Accordingly parties were detailed to pass the dead bodies over to the Yankees, and 260 odd were removed from this portion of the works, and with them one wounded man, who had been lying there three days without water, and was fly-blown from head to foot. It was surmised that Banks was unwilling that his men should witness the carnage which had been committed, but if that were the case he only made matters worse by this delay, for much exasperation was manifested at the sight of the wounded man, and a great many were heard to say that if that was the way the wounded were to be treated they wanted to be out of the army. A great many of the dead must have perished during the three days' interval. In front of Johnson, Steadman, and elsewhere, none were buried, and the bodies of the slain could be seen from the breastworks on the day of the surrender, twenty-six days after the fight.

During the rest of the month there was heavy skirmishing daily, with constant firing night and day from the gun and mortar boats, and the works were generally drawn close to our line, which, it may here be remarked, was about three miles in extent, and in the centre some three-fourths of a mile from the river. Batteries of Parrott guns had been erected across the river, which were well served by the United States regulars, and maintained a continuous and very effective fire upon our river batteries, disabling many of the guns. On the land side a formidable battery of seventeen 8, 9 and 10-inch columbiads was established 150 paces from our extreme right, one of seven guns in front of General Beale's centre, one of six guns in front of the 1st Mississippi on the Jackson road, and seven guns and mortars were planted in front of Colonel Steadman. From these a fire was maintained day and night, doing but little damage to our men, but as the siege continued, most of our artillery was disabled, only about 15 pieces remaining uninjured at the time of the surrender.

During the siege of six weeks, from May 27th to July 7th inclusive, the enemy must have fired from fifty to seventy-five thousand shot and shell, yet not more than twenty-five men were killed by these projectiles. They had worse dangers than these to contend against, but against them all they fought like heros, and did their duty cheerfully. Several buildings were burned by the enemy's shells, among which was the mill, entailing a loss of two or three thousand bushels of corn.

About the 29th or 30th of June the garrison's supply of meat gave out, when General Gardner ordered the mules to be butchered, after ascertaining that the men were willing to eat them. Far from shrinking from this hardship, the men received their unusual rations cheerfully, and declared that they were proud to be able to say that they had been reduced to this extremity. Many of them, as if in mockery of famine, caught rats and ate them, declaring that they were better than squirrels. At the same time the supply of ammunition was becoming exhausted, and at the time of the surrender there were only twenty rounds of cartridges left, with a small supply for artillery.

The hardships, privations and dangers of the situation were diversified by many exciting incidents. One day our men were rolling ten inch shells over the rampart to explode against the enemy's works, which were not more than fifteen feet off, when a rush was made at our breastworks by about 200 of the enemy. Two companies were hurried to the spot, and they were driven back. Of some sixteen who had gained the interior of our works, every one was killed. Mining was resorted to by the enemy; and after the surrender they said that they had a charge of 8000 pounds of powder already laid under the lower river battery. This, in fact, consisting of a single pivot gun, was the key to the whole position, as it commanded both the river and the land approaches, and against this the heaviest guns of the enemy, and their most vigorous efforts by land and water were directed. Their story, however, is somewhat doubted. But if the enemy mined, the garrison countermined, and succeeded in blowing up the works in front of the 1st Mississippi.

Some time between the 20th and 30th of June a singular circumstance occurred one night about 11 o'clock, after a heavy fire. The water commenced running up stream, and in half an hour rose six feet. In one place about twenty feet of the bluff disappeared, carrying away one of our river batteries. The roar of the water could be heard like distant thunder. If this were an earthquake—and it is difficult to give any other explanation—it must have "rolled unheededly away," so far as the enemy was concerned, for no notice of it has appeared in any of the Yankee papers. We are obliged to omit incidents generally, including this brilliant sortie and spiking of the enemy's guns, but merely remark that the story about Banks' capturing fifteen prisoners on that occasion, and sending them back, for whom Gardner liberated a like number of Yankee prisoners, is merely a Yankee romance.

On Tuesday, July 7th, salutes were fired from the enemy's batteries and gunboats, and loud cheering was heard along the entire line, and Yankees who were within conversing distance of our men told them that Vicksburg had fallen. That night, about 10 o'clock, Gen. Gardner summoned a council of war, consisting of General Beale, Colonels Steadman, Miles, Lyle and Shelby, and Lieut. Colonel Marshal J. Smith, who, without exception, decided that it was impossible to hold out longer, considering that the provisions of the garrison were exhausted, the ammunition almost entirely expended, and a large proportion of the men sick, or from exhaustion unfit for duty. A communication was sent to Gen. Banks stating what had been heard from the men, asking for official information as to the truth of the news, and stating if it were true, that Gen. Gardner was ready to negotiate terms of surrender. General Banks' reply was received just before day, enclosing a letter from General Grant announcing the fall of Vicksburg. General Banks asked General Gardner to appoint commissioners to arrange with those on his part the terms of surrender, and Colonels Miles and Steadman and Lieut. Col. Smith were appointed.

General Banks demanded an unconditional surrender, as in the first instance, but finally agreed that officers and soldiers should retain their private property (in which negroes were not included). A demand for a parole of the garrison was refused. General Banks said he would grant such terms with the greatest pleasure, but the orders of the Secretary of War forbid it. The surrender was fixed to take place at 7 o'clock on the morning of the 9th. At 6 o'clock the garrison were drawn up in line and two officers of General Gardner's staff were sent to conduct the Federal officer deputed to receive the surrender. This was General Andrews, who entered the lines shortly after 7 o'clock on the Clinton road. General Gardner met him at the right of our line and delivered up his sword, observing that he surrendered his sword and his garrison since his provisions were exhausted. General Andrews replied that he received General Gardner's sword, but returned it to him for having maintained his defence so gallantly.

Meanwhile the enemy's infantry moved down in front of our line, both wings resting on the river, and completely encircling the little garrison, as if to cut off any attempt to escape. About that time our informant succeeded in passing through the lines and evading the enemy's outposts. A great many of the garrison—probably several hundred—had made an attempt to escape the previous night, but the guard of the enemy was so strict that they could not pass out. The number of the garrison which surrendered was between 5000 and 6000, of whom there were not more than 2000 effective men for duty. During the siege about 200 had been killed and 300 wounded, besides several deaths from sickness. Among the officers killed were Colonel Pixley, of Arkansas, Captain Boone, of Louisiana, and Lieutenant Simonton, of the 1st Mississippi, besides a few others with whose names our informant was not familiar.

The universal feeling in the garrison is that General Gardner did everything in his power to foil the enemy and protract the siege, and only succumbed to the direct necessity. The garrison, too, have made a noble record. Even the enemy's accounts, upon which we have been entirely dependent for nearly two months, bear testimony to heroism unsurpassed during this war; but much yet remains to be told, and not a word of it but will reflect the greatest honor upon these devoted men.

The Charleston Mercury.

DAILY PAPER—Twenty Dollars per annum, payable half-yearly in advance.

VINDICE NULLO
SPONTE SUA SINE LEGE FIDES RECTUMQUE COLENTUR.

COUNTRY PAPER—Three a Week—Ten Dollars per annum, in advance.

VOLUME LXXXIII. CHARLESTON, S. C. SATURDAY, JULY 25, 1863. NUMBER 11,816

TELEGRAPHIC NEWS.

FROM THE ARMIES OF GRANT AND JOHNSTON.

MORTON, Miss., July 2?.—A citizen who has just come out states that the Yankees have totally destroyed the city of Jackson, Miss. The State House was blown up. There are none of the enemy this side of Pearl River.

FROM NORTH CAROLINA.

GOLDSBORO', July 24.—We have nothing from below. 160 negros, recaptured, and 12 Yankee prisoners arrived here this morning. Some negro children were drowned by the Yankees crossing Otter Creek.

FROM RICHMOND—NEWS FROM THE NORTH AND EUROPE.

RICHMOND, July 24.—The city is very quiet today. We have no military news from any quarter. The Central Railroad train, due this evening, has not yet arrived, having been detained by an accident. The weather is oppressively warm. The silence of the press correspondents with LEE's army indicates that movements are in progress which may again bring it into collision with the army of MEADE.

The latest European advices are to the 12th instant. The brief telegraphic summary in the Baltimore *American*, of the 21st instant, reports a statement in the London *Post*, that LINDSAY would give, on July 12, a detailed account, in the House of Commons, of his interview with NAPOLEON.

We have no explanation of the rise of gold in New York on Tuesday. It may be that private advices by the last arrival from Europe caused the advance. The next arrival from Europe will bring us the result of ROEBUCK's motion. If the position of the Ministry be sustained, self-respect will demand the immediate recall of our Commissioners to Great Britain. This is the general opinion here.

The Department of State has received the manifesto of Gen. FOREY on taking possession of the City of Mexico. While tendering the aid of France to the Mexicans for the free exercise of the popular will, in establishing a government. FOREY speaks of this as a task imposed upon him in which he seeks the aid of the Mexicans. There are not wanting indications of a purpose to establish a monarchy.

A party of Yankee cavalry, 150 strong, visited Warrenton on Tuesday. On the same day about 10,000 appeared at Manassas, and were scouting as far as Brentville. They were probably receiving reinforcements from Centreville.

LETTER FROM RICHMOND.

(CORRESPONDENCE OF THE MERCURY.)

RICHMOND, Tuesday, July 21.

Riot Suppressed—Draft Enforced—Lee and Meade—Enemy Operating on our Railroad Lines—The Victory at Wagner—Affairs in Mississippi—Citizens in Arms, etc.

As we foresaw, the riot has been put down in New York and the draft is being enforced at the cannon's mouth. SEYMOUR has lent himself as a tool to LINCOLN, who glories in the opportunity to display and strengthen his power. So, then, more men will be raised, and we must make ready for them. To do this, we must strain every nerve that God has given us.

News from Lee's army is very indefinite. The enemy appears to be contesting his passage east of the Blue Ridge; but if he knows the gaps as well as Jackson, Meade will come to grief, as Fremont and Shields did. It is not likely that Lee will be able to reach Culpeper without a battle; indeed it is not believed that he desires to do so. Another Manassas may be in store for us.

Availing himself of the weakness of certain lines from which Lee has been reinforced, the enemy has been pushing his cavalry upon our railroads, but as yet with trifling success. At Wytheville he was severely punished by raw troops, a lesson to other parts of the country, if they will learn it. What damage has been done to the Petersburg and Weldon road we do not know. Some think the late attack on Charleston and the simultaneous movement of gunboats up James river, was part of a plan to get possession of the Southern road. It was said yesterday that the enemy had denuded the Peninsula of troops for this purpose.

Sympathizing fully with you in the pride you must feel in the signal repulse of the desperate night assault on Wagner, we are nevertheless compelled to look with anxiety to the issue of the struggle for that apparently vital post. In Mississippi, Johnston is retreating for lack of men to oppose Grant's large force, and Pemberton's army, straggling over the whole country, unable or unwilling to take the arms that have been sent them. The case is too serious to admit of concealment. The people must arouse themselves to a sense of their great and imminent danger.

Our citizens, old and young, rich and poor, are drilling every day. Is every other city, town, and village doing the same thing? Cloudy and hot.

HERMES.

THE SIEGE OF CHARLESTON.

FULL AND INTERESTING YANKEE ACCOUNTS FROM MORRIS ISLAND.

We have received the last issue of the *New South*, the Yankee sheet published at Port Royal. It is filled with accounts of the enemy's operations on Morris Island, from which we make full extracts. Our readers will remember that the facts, as narrated, are not without the usual admixture of fiction, found in every Yankee narrative of the war:

[*From the New South, July* 18.]

THE ADVANCE ON CHARLESTON—CAPTURE OF THE GREATER PART OF MORRIS ISLAND—A TERRIFIC BOMBARDMENT—SPENDID CHARGE BY STRONG'S BRIGADE—CAPTURE OF ELEVEN BATTERIES—ONLY TWO FORTS REMAINING—DISASTROUS CHARGE ON FORT WAGNER—FULL AND AUTHENTIC ACCOUNT.

We have obtained from reliable sources a full account of our victory at Morris Island. We are obliged, for want of space, greatly to condense the details, but we give all the essential facts.

Since Gen. Gilmore's arrival in the Department the greatest activity has prevailed, but all movements were made with such judicious secresy and caution, that no suspicion was excited among the rebels or at the North that the Department of the South was to be distinguished by an active campaign.

Brigadier General Vogdes was relieved as Post Commandant at Folly Island by Brig. Gen. Seymour. Brig. Gen. Strong was placed in command of a fine brigade; guns and ammunition were transferred to Folly Island by night, and the plan of building batteries on this end of Folly Island, where nothing but our own troops and vessels could ever come, was changed for one of batteries at the front, where we could defend against attack or assume the offensive.

Large fatigue parties, consisting sometimes of six regiments, were set at work each night, building batteries under the direction of General Vogdes, with General Seymour, also supervising, and Lieutenants Suter, Wilson and Maguire, of the Engineers, to attend to details, we had admirable topographical advantages. The point was surrounded by a range of sand bluffs, and covered by a dense growth of wood and chaparral. While our men worked, erecting impregnable defences, and mounting batteries which they could not withstand, with all their prepartion, the rebels supposed we had only a small picket force there, and amused themselves by wasting shell in the woods where they supposed our pickets to be located. The arrangements had been made for an attack on the morning of Thursday, July 10th, but Providence had ordered it otherwise, and decreed that Friday should be the rebels' unlucky day. It had been arranged that General Stevenson's Brigade, and Colonel Montgomery's colored brigade, should go up on transports, on Wednesday night, to join Terry's Division, which had an important part to perform on James Island. During the night a gale arose, there was a high wind and a heavy sea, and the transports were obliged to lay off the bar till morning. So the attack was postponed for a day, and the plan sufficiently changed to ensure success in case the original one had been discovered.

THE PLAN OF ATTACK.

The principal features of the plan of attack were as follows: A general bombardment of the rebel works from all the batteries at Camp Seymour, on the front of Folly Island. Co-operating with the navy, in bombarding the forts at the other end of Morris Island. An attack with boat howitzers on the rebel rifle pits protecting the exposed flank of their works. Capture of the rifle pits by a charge with four companies of the 7th Conn. Storming of all the works by the remainder of Strong's brigade, landing from Folly River. Occupation of a portion of James Island by a strong force under Gen. Terry, to operate farther at the proper time, under verbal instructions.

All these features of the plan were most successfully executed, without a single failure in any particular. We have the orders containing these plans, but they are too lengthy for our columns. The brigades outside the bar came in on Thursday, and the movements accordingly all came off that night. The attack commenced at five o'clock on Friday morning from Camp Seymour, where we had forty-four guns, commanded and manned as follows: On right of first line, Co. I, 3d R. I. Artillery, Captain Brayton, four three inch Dyer guns; on left of first line, Co. M, 3d R. I., Capt. J. J. Comstock, Jr., four ten inch mortars; in the centre of first line of works, Captain Hamilton's Battery E, 3d U. S. Artillery, commanded by Lieut. Myrick, six ten inch Parrott guns, and detachment 1st U. S. Artillery, under 1st Sergeant Lee, Co. C, three thirty pound Parrotts; and also in the first line, Co. I, 3d R. I. Artillery, Capt. C. G. Strahan, four twenty pound Parrotts; Co. B. 3d R. I. Artillery, Capt. Albert Green, six ten inch mortars, and Co. D, 3d R. I. Artillery, Capt. Richard Shaw, eight 30 pound Parrotts. In the second line, commanded by Major Bailey, 3d R. I., were five eight inch mortars, worked by detachment of Co. M, 3d R. I., Lieut. Holbrook; and four Weird guns, under command of Lieut. Burgemeyer, 3d N. Y. Artillery.

THE FIGHT OPENED.

The first shot disabled a prominent rebel gun, and as piece after piece opened on them, the air about them was full of deadly missiles. The Monitors, too, opened on them, sending fifteen-inch shells, with other shot and shells, among them. They were taken completely at surprise, and while at roll call. They did not mistrust the existence of batteries, or the intention of attack, but were rather occupying themselves with plans for taking Folly Island. They soon replied with a few guns, but it took a long time to get the range, or to find out where to take us; their shells at first went far over the camp, bursting in the marsh, and when they began to fall behind and on the works, hurt nobody. We had only one man killed from their fire, and two Rhode Islanders badly wounded (each losing both arms and receiving other bad wounds), by a premature discharge of one of our own guns. These were all the casualties.

For nearly two hours this one-sided artillery duel went on. In the meantime, Lieut. Bunce, Executive Officer of the Pawnee, came up toward Light House Inlet with four boats mounting howitzers, and peppered the rebel rifle pits. The rifles and howitzers responded, giving Lieutenant Bunce's and General Strong's forces, (who had come thereafter in boats) a hot fire. Only one casualty occurred before the landing. A shell struck a boat full of troops, and took a 6th Connecticut man's leg off. With his other leg and his hands he succeeded in swimming to another boat, but bled to death in a few minutes.

At half past six Lieut.-Col. Rodman, of the 7th Conn., (battalion consisting of Cos. I, A, B, and K,) landed from a creek below, with Capt. Chamberlain and twenty men, and finding no batteries as had been anticipated, skirmished up and reconnoitered the rifle pits. He then landed with his whole battalion, charged gallantly on the rifle pits and took them, losing five or six men, and killing the enemy in heaps.

CHARGE OF STRONG'S BRIGADE.

Gen. Strong then landed with the 6th Connecticut, at Light House Inlet, took them up the beach and went back for the rest of the brigade. The whole force then charged furiously up the bluffs to the rebel works, Gen. Strong leading the main column in person. They made a splendid charge, sweeping everything before them, and capturing fifty prisoners in one batch. As they trailed up at double-quick, they shouted, waved flags, and the men in camp Seymour responded. It was a splendid affair. Gen. Strong inspired his troops at the landing by rushing to the front, waving a flag, and crying, "come on my men—I'll lead you." The whole brigade charged down the bluffs to where they terminate, and are succeeded by a less rugged, but still very uneven surface. They captured many prisoners, and at the termination of the bluffs got possession of the last of the rebel batteries except Point Cummins and Fort Wagner. They then skirmished down under heavy fire from the forts, to which the gunboats replied, to a marsh it was impracticable to occupy, General Strong leading them all the way, and pleasing his men beyond measure. They are as proud of their General as any Brigade in the army, and will follow him anywhere.

General Strong disposed his men with especial regard to their safety as well as efficiency, and all who could be spared were sent back to the rebel encampments to seek that rest they so much needed. The rebels continued shelling our works, and the Catskill, (Commodore Dahlgren's flag-ship), Weehawken, Montauk, Nahant went up and gave it to them at short range, drawing the fire of Forts Sumter, Wagner, Point Cummings (or Battery Bee). The Catskill was struck over fifty times, but not seriously injured. The top of her pilot house was smashed, and one of the flying bolts came very near the Admiral's head. The only casualty was the injury of one man, who was leaning against a turret in one of the Monitors, when a shot struck the outside, and the concussion from a bolt paralized him. At five o'clock, without capturing Fort Wagner, the Monitors withdrew.

YANKEE VIEWS OF THE IMPORTANCE OF BATTERY WAGNER.

A plan was then decided on to surprise and take the fort by storm. It was very important to take it, for that once in our hands, Cumming's Point battery must fall, and with possession of Cumming's Point we are sure of Sumter. So desperate measures were justifiable. Gen. Strong was confident that his gallant troops, any of them, would stand any ordinary fire with reasonable prospect of achieving a success. Lieut. Col. Rodman, of the intrepid 7th Conn. battalion, volunteered, with his four companies, to act as the advance, promising that if properly supported he would take any fort in South Carolina. Gen. Strong selected as the support two fine regiments, which he had been very gallant in the morning, and in which had great confidence, the 9th Maine, Colonel Emery, and the 76th Pa., Colonel Strawbridge. The regiments appeared much pleased with the honor of being selected for this duty, and the prospects were very favorable.

THE ASSAULT ON BATTERY WAGNER.

Soon after midnight all the regiments in camp were silently aroused and formed in line of battle. The storming force advanced to within half a mile of the fort, and waited the time for the assault. At the last moment it was learned that Colonel Strawbridge, of the 76th, in whom the regiment have great confidence, and who was to take the right of the support, was severely ill and could not come out. This dispirited the regiment somewhat, but Major Hicks, a popular and brave officer, took command, and there were no signs of failure. Henry's Battery moved down to the front to co-operate, and in the dusk of the morning, just before three o'clock the battalion and two regiments moved on. General Gilmore and several of his Staff were where they could see the assault, and General Strong, with his Staff, and Colonel Turner, the efficient Chief of General Gilmore's Staff, all mounted, accompanied the troops toward the fort. At two hundred yards from the fort the pickets were encountered and driven in. General Strong rode up to the advance and said in an impressive manner, "fire low, and put your trust in God! Forward the Connecticut Seventh!" They gave a loud cheer, just as a round of canister and grape swept over their heads; they did not flinch, nor did the second round, which took off some of their brave men, cause them to stagger; a third round came, and many more fell, but still the noble men kept on, regardless of danger, cheering, clambering over moat and ditch, heroes in courage and devils in impetuosity. Hand grenades were showered among them, but they heeded them not. Up over the parapet they went, and replied to a volley of Minie balls by a shout of triumph, for they supposed the support was at hand and victory certain. But the support had wavered. When the fearful fire mowed down their ranks, the 76th halted, but advanced again like brave men trying to face certain destruction. The fire was terrible, and when round after round played through them, those in the rear became demoralized, the advance were left alone, the 9th Maine became infected, and when Colonel, Rodman, wounded mortally, as he supposed, in the side, but still waving his sword on the parapet, as blood rushed from his mouth, turned to look for his support, he saw only a fleeing crowd of routed men, and exclaimed, in very despair, "That's a d—d pretty support—see how the cowards run!" Major Hicks and a few brave fellows pressed directly up to the front and mounted the breastworks, or were slaughtered in the ditch.—The Seventh were almost alone, and there was nothing left but to retreat. Over two hundred muskets and rifles were thinning their ranks, and the survivors reluctantly left off bayoneting gunners to turn their backs on the foe. But now came the worst of the slaughter. As the troops retreated they could be more distinctly seen, and the volleys came with fatal precision. Colonel Rodman had his leg shattered, and was the only wounded man brought off from the front. His men would not have deserted him, had they all perished in trying to rescue him. Little more was done during the day, except that working parties were busy constructing batteries and entrenchments.

THE YANKEE LOSSES.

Our losses on the first day were fourteen killed, one missing and ninety odd wounded, some fatally. In the storming party of Saturday morning the 7th Conn. had 103 killed, wounded and missing. The missing are all prisoners or killed; many are known to be killed or wounded. The total loss of the whole day, reported in Strong's brigade, were 334 killed, wounded and missing, but of the missing many are stragglers from the 76th Penn. and 9th Maine, who will yet turn up.

A "REBEL" STEAMER BURNED.

On Sunday a rebel force of negros and others was dicovered building flanking works on Morris Island in the direction of Fort Johnson. Hamilton's Battery went down to a convenient place and opened fire on them. They were speedily captured, and a steamer which was lying at the landing was disabled at the first shot, one man being killed. Shortly after the steamer was blown up by a shot through her boilers. On Monday she was burned by our troops. During Monday the rebels shelled our pickets and advance, and were in turn shelled by the gunboats, both the monitors and wooden ones, the principal fire being directed at Fort Wagner.

A TROUBLESOME GUN.

During the day one of the captured Keokuk's guns, which our navy should have looked after, was pointed from Fort Sumter, towards the camp, three miles distant, where General Gilmore's headquarters were, and immense elongated shells were thrown into it. Nearly every one burst in the immediate vicinity of headquarters. One man was killed and several wounded; we hear of no other casualties there; but at the front some were wounded. Tuesday all was tolerably quiet, with the exception of some shelling on both sides.

YANKEE ACTIVITY, ETC.

We are rapidly constructing batteries and defences, principally by night, and are succeeding admirably. Among the prisoners we captured, was Lieut. Bee, cousin of the rebel General Bee; Capt. McCelter, son of the Mayor of New Orleans, and nine other commissioned officers, with 113 privates.

General Terry's Division is on James Island, having landed from Stono river. They have had no fight as yet, but in a slight skirmish the pickets killed two rebel cavalry. They will be heard from in due time.

The Charleston Mercury.

DAILY PAPER—TWENTY DOLLARS PER ANNUM, PAYABLE HALF-YEARLY IN ADVANCE.

VINDICE NULLO—SPONTE SUA SINE LEGE FIDES RECTUMQUE COLENTUR.

COUNTRY PAPER—THRICE A WEEK—TEN DOLLARS PER ANNUM, IN ADVANCE.

VOLUME LXXXIII. | CHARLESTON, S. C., TUESDAY, JULY 28, 1863. | NUMBER 11,818

VICKSBURG AFTER THE SURRENDER.

The following interesting description of scenes in Vicksburg, after the surrender, is copied from a letter in the New York *Tribune*, dated the 5th instant:

What a near view of Vicksburg would disclose, after being so long subjected to a rain of shot and shell, has been a theme of much speculation in our army and elsewhere. Those who have witnessed the siege cannot fail to be surprised that there is anything left of the town but ruins. But we have, it seems, yet something to learn of the endurance of a town as well as of men. But few buildings in Vicksburg are totally demolished. None have been completely ruined by the bombardment. On one of the principal streets near the river, and running parallel with it, there are remains of a block of buildings which were burned about the time of the fight at Champion Hills. In the block was a mill and a storehouse, in which were stored a considerable quantity of flour—two hundred barrels and upward—which was burned at the same time. The buildings were fired by a crowd of incensed rebel soldiers and citizens, as a punishment due to some heartless and extoritonate speculators who had bought up the flour to be enabled to get siege prices for it.

There are a few other houses scattered about that are but heaps of rubbish. The great majority of the buildings, both public and private, can be by repairs made "as good as new."

The streets are barricaded to a limited extent, and have been ploughed up by shells. In walking along the pavements one must be careful not to tumble into a pit dug for him by a projectile from a 13-inch mortar or from a Parrott gun. The yards, gardens and open lots are also cut up with shell holes. A profusion of beautiful shrubbery has heretofore rendered Vicksburg a very handsome town, but the broken and torn fencing, and havoc incident to the presence of an army anywhere, have greatly diminished the beauties of the place. Nearly every gate in the city is adorned with unexploded 13-inch shells placed atop of each post. The porches and piazzas (nearly every house has one) are also adorned with curious collections of shot and shells that have fallen in the yards. It is said that there are some houses in the city that have escaped untouched; but in my rambles through the streets I could not find them.

I entered, perhaps, twenty buildings in all, and found frightful looking holes in the walls and floors of every one. The house occupied by General Pemberton as his headquarters has a hole in the first room you enter on the left side of the hall, which a mule could crawl through without difficulty. The publisher of the Vicksburg Citizen invited me into his residence and interspersed his remarks, while showing me around, with frequent cautions not to tread here and there, for fear a shattered piece of flooring would let me through into the cellar. And so it is all over the place. The northern portion of the city suffered most, and I cannot convey any idea of the damage sustained better than by saying it has been smashed.

Notwithstanding the evidence everywhere visible of the terrible ordeal through which the people and city have passed, the Vicksburgbers persistently assert that they have not been *much* damaged; that shells are comparatively innocent things—"nothing when you get used to them;" that they could have held out a year if they had had provisions, &c. They also claim to have learned how to dodge shells, and say that those fired from the mortars had become favorites with the people. Shots from Parrott guns were not so popular.

The most noticeable feature of the city is the group of caves on every hill side. In these caves the women and children were sheltered during the nights, and occasionally in day time when the firing was very severe. The excavations branch out in various directions after passing the entrance. I should not imagine them very desirable bed chambers, but they seem to have answered a very good purpose. In one or two instances shells entered them, and two women and a number of children were thus killed during the siege.

THE MERCURY.

TUESDAY, JULY 28, 1863.

Manufacturing History.

The *Sentinel*—the Government organ in Richmond—is busy manufacturing history. In its issue of the 21st instant, is an editorial headed "Idle Alarms," in which it speaks of the Presses which have ventured to criticise the follies of the Administration, financial and military, as "the *one* or *two* really bad *treasonable* sheets in our Confederacy that have surrendered themselves to personal prejudices, and to the sentiment of opposition to the Administration," and then, in face of the terrible disasters of the fall of Vicksburg and Port Hudson, and the retreat of the army of the Potomac from Maryland with the loss of twenty or thirty thousand men—a vast complication of incompetency and folly, by which our cause has received the heaviest blows inflicted since the war—it asserts that President DAVIS "conducts our affairs with *transcendent ability*, and fills his high station with honor to himself and to his country." If President DAVIS had *listened to remonstrances*, and had sent the twenty or thirty thousand men whom we have lost in the campaign in Maryland to General BRAGG or General JOHNSTON, to save Vicksburg and Port Hudson, and the valley of the Mississippi, from the results of incompetency, and had kept kept the army of the Potomac where it now is—on the defensive—he would have displayed some "ability," and would have secured to us peace in the fall. But our object is not now to show the evil consequences of the policy of the Administration in the East and West, but to expose the "history" of the *Sentinel*. It says:

And yet we are bold to say, that probably there was never less cause for the most unfounded accusation, than for this: that never were charity and justice more outraged than by the suspicion that President Davis contemplates any *trespass* on the laws of his country, and *any enlargement* of the *limits* of his power. His whole Administration has manifested a signal respect for the laws, even under difficult circumstances, and when they were such as to embarrass the public defence. Let those who feel it a luxury to find fault with him, point to *one act of disregard of law*. Let those who are ready to suspect him of all possible and impossible usurpations, and of a licentious will, point to some *single instance* in which he has *overborne* the Constitution, or *grasped doubtful powers*; or else let them confess that their accusations are ungenerous and unfounded, and worthy only of the public disgust.

Now there are two stubborn facts to meet these bold assertions, that the *Sentinel* can hardly suppress from history:

1. President DAVIS, in imitation, we presume, of President LINCOLN, undertook, in direct violation of the laws of the land, to suspend or abrogate them all, by proclamations establishing martial law in the Confederacy. General VAN DORN, in the West, by his authority, extended it over whole States, and President DAVIS himself proclaimed it over Richmond, Virginia, and the military district including it. Martial law not only suspends the writ of *habeas corpus*, by which the liberty of the citizen is secured against illegal and arbitrary arrests, but all the other guaranties of liberty, trial by jury—free discussion—and the freedom of the press, are held at the will of the President. The power of the President to proclaim or establish martial law, was resisted and tested before the courts in Richmond; and the courts having declared that the exercise of such a power was against the laws and the Constitution, it was abandoned.

2. Nor has President DAVIS shown himself more regardful of the rights of property, than of the personal rights of the citizen—the two grand corner stones of liberty. He arbitrarily, and without law, undertook to seize and appropriate the property of the citizens of the Confederacy. Here again he was checked by the legal tribunals of the country. They pronounced his seizures unconstitutional and void, and ordered release and retribution for his illegal acts.

Now, if the *Sentinel* can show that these acts of President DAVIS did not take place, it can consistently, with truth, assert that he has never "trespassed on the laws of the country"—has never contemplated "any *enlargement* of the *limits* of his power"—has manifested "a signal respect for the laws"—has never, "in a *single instance*, overborne the constitution or *grasped doubtful powers*." But if the facts we have stated really took place, then let it cease its fulsome flattery and its vain attempts to "manufacture history." At any time such bold enterprises would be of no use to the administration. Under present circumstances they are as disgusting as they are untrue.

A Lesson from History—Let us Remember it.

King EDWARD, of England, at the head of a well appointed army of near one hundred thousand men, in the month of June, 1314, invaded Scotland. To meet this large force, ROBERT BRUCE could raise but thirty thousand men. But determined to conquer or perish with the liberties of their country, they met the English at Bannockburn, on the 23d June, 1314, and achieved a signal victory. The slaughter was immense—twenty-seven barons, two hundred knights, seven hundred esquires, and thirty thousand of the common file filled up the fatal roll. Sir WALTER SCOTT, from whose history of Scotland the above facts are taken, closes his tenth chapter as follows:

But if, in a strategetical point of view, the field of Bannockburn was lost on the part of the Scottish nation, they derived from it a lesson of pertinacity in national defence which they never afterwards forgot during the course of their remaining a separate people. They had seen, before the battle of Bannockburn, the light of national freedom reduced to the last spark, their patriots slain, their laws reversed, their monuments plundered and destroyed, their prince an excommunicated outlaw, who could not find in the wilderness of his country a cave dark and inaccessible enough to shelter his head: all this they had seen in 1304; and so completely had ten years of resistance changed the scene, that the same prince rode over a field of victory a triumphant sovereign, the first nobles of the English enemies lying dead at his feet, or surrendering themselves for ransom. It seems likely that it was from the recollection of that extraordinary change of fortune, that the Scots drew the lesson, never to despair of the freedom of their country, but to continue resistance to invaders, even when it seemed most desperate. * * * And the Scots may have the pride to recollect, and other nations to learn from their history, that to a brave people one victory will do more to sustain the honorable spirit of independence than twenty defeats can effect to suppress it."

THE WESTERN CAMPAIGN.

[*From the Atlanta Confederacy.*]

JACKSON, MISS., July 16.

The movement for the relief of Vicksburg commenced on the 1st inst. On that day Breckinridge, Loring, French and Walker moved their divisions from their camps near this place and Canton, to unite with troops near Big Black, where it was expected the whole army would cross the river The 4th was spent in bivouac from seven to ten miles from Big Black. On the afternoon of 5th the whole line was moved within a few miles of the river, and it is said that orders had been issued to the various division commanders to cross at midnight. During the night intelligence of the fall of Vicksburg was received, and at an early hour on the next morning the whole army was in full but orderly retreat towards Jackson. Breckinridge brought up the rear and arrived at Jackson late in the afternoon of the 7th inst.

The troops remained in bivouac during the next day resting, cooking rations, and preparing for Grant's expected arrival. Before daylight on the 9th the army was ordered into line, Loring's right resting on Pearl river above the town, Walker in the centre, and Breckinridge completing the line, his left reaching the river below Jackson. French and the remainder of our force constitute the reserve, except our cavalry and a sufficient number of infantry to line east bank of the river for miles above and below the town. Jackson's cavalry division contested Grant's advance with the usual spirit of our men, and the roar of their guns could be heard at intervals on Thursday, but it only served to enliven our troops who were hard at work strengthening old and constructing new fortifications.

Early on Friday, the 10th, our skirmishers were driven in and the enemy appeared in front of Fort "Johnston" on the Clinton road. At ten minutes past ten the first gun was fired from the fort. The day was spent in skirmishing with a few artillery duels. The sharpshooters too commenced annoying our line, especially Evans' S. C. brigade.

Skirmishing and artillery firing commenced along the whole line on the 14th, and the enemy made a vigorous attack upon a fort on Moody's Hill, but they met a bloody repulse from Buford's brigade. Our loss in this affair was near eighty, principally in the 7th and 8th Kentucky regiments. Gist's Georgia and Helm's Kentucky brigade were ordered to Buford's support, but were not needed. Helm then moved to "Fort Jennie Withers;" thence to the left, having lost but six men during the day. Forts "Breckinridge" and "Lady Gracey," are located in the centre of Breckinridge's line, a short distance apart, and are occupied by the Washington (La.) Artillery and Cobb's (Ky.) Battery.

On Sunday about noon the enemy threw seven regiments of picked men against these forts. The charge was a short but bloody one. The enemy must have lost fully 800 men, in killed wounded and prisoners. The artillery did splendid service, while Stovall's brigade of Georgia, Florida and North Carolina troops, did their whole duty. Among the trophies were three stands of colors. Cobb lost eight men (six by an accident), and Stovall twelve. This covers our entire loss. The 2d and 9th Kentucky Regiments were ordered to Stovall's support, but did not fire a gun, so short was the fight. As soon as the firing ceased our Infirmary Corps hastened to the relief of the wounded Yankees, when their sharpshooters opened a brisk fire upon them. They held up their litters, and in many ways indicated their mission of mercy, but it all availed nought, and after losing several men the corps was compelled to retire within the trenches, despite the groans and piteous appeals for water and help from the wounded and dying Yankees.

Forty-eight hours after the engagement Gen. Johnston sent a flag of truce, offering to bury the dead. The offer was accepted, the work accomplished, and our men relieved from the terrible stench. But two of our men were found on the field—one dead, the other reclining against a stump, keeping the flies from his wound with a brush. He coolly remarked when the burial party found him, "I have been expecting you."

A number of heavy skirmishes have occurred along the line, but I have not been able to gather the details. As I write—at noon—the rattle of musketry and roar of artillery in that direction would indicate a heavy assault upon Loring's centre. Skirmishing and artillery firing continue night and day. The enemy's shells have done some little damage to the buildings in Jackson. Yesterday a house in the centre of the town was fired by one.

A number of ladies have remained here, and they are truly to be pitied. When the shells commence flying too fast for safety, whole families can be seen running for the river bank, while many seek protection there night and day.

General Pemberton and his troops are at Brandon, where a Parole Camp has been established. The *morale* of Johnston's army is fine. Our gallant commander may evacuate Jackson to-night, and retreat to Meridian or Selma, or any other point, without impairing the unlimited love and confidence of his troops, except a very few cowardly wretches who swear they will never leave Jackson—the meanest place or thing on earth, except themselves. These same fellows are in the habit of abusing Kentucky, Missouri, Maryland, and even Tennessee.

THE FALL OF FORT PULASKI.

As a subject of interest at the present juncture, and in order to assist our preparations, we republish the accounts of the bombardment of Fort Pulaski with its results, as first published in Savannah. The following is the *Republican's* account:

Yesterday morning the most terrible bombardment of the siege commenced soon after daylight. The guns were louder and more rapid than at any time previous, and the windows of the city shook as if rocked by an earthquake; indeed the very earth trembled with the fierce cannonade. Such was the fire that even the confident began to feel uneasy for the fort. The bombardment of Sumter was no approach to it, either in the number of guns or the size and weight of the shot. At 2 p. m., the firing ceased altogether.

Later.—We learn that Fort Pulaski, after a most gallant defence, against guns vastly superior to its own, surrendered to the enemy at 2 o'clock p. m., yesterday. Corporal Law, of the Phœnix Riflemen, stationed at Thunderbolt, brings the information direct. He reached the fort at 5 o'clock a. m., yesterday, and started on his return trip immediately after the flag was struck. The surrender was unconditional. Seven large breaches were made in the south wall of the fort by the battery of *eight Parrott guns at King's Landing;* all the barbette guns were dismounted, and three casemate guns, leaving but one gun bearing on that point. Three balls had entered the magazine, and a clear breach had been made in it. The balls were conical and steel pointed, and propelled with such force as to pass entirely through the wall at nearly every fire. No lives were lost during the terrible bombardment of the fort. Four men only were wounded—three have lost a leg and one an arm, each—all privates:—one of the Wise Guards, one of the Mongomery Guards, and two of the Oglethorpe Light Infantry. No names are given. The Oglethorpes occupied the most exposed portion of the Fort. Lieut. Hussey was stunned, but not seriously hurt. Col. Olmstead attempted to signalize to Causton's Bluff yesterday morning, but such was the fire that no human being could stand on the ramparts for even a moment. Nearly a thousand shell, of the largest size, were thrown into the Fort from the Federal batteries. Though much exhausted, all the garrison are well except the four wounded men. This account may be relied on as correct. It is corroborated by another witness, a signal man, who went down and returned in company with Corporal Law.

From the account of the surrender, which appeared in the Savannah *News*, we take the following:

A courier arrived in the city last night, from whom we learn that the Fort was breached in several places by the *heavy rifled Parrott guns twelve of which were in the King's Point battery, distant about a mile and a quarter from the Fort.* Early in the day all the guns in the barbette except two were dismounted or otherwise disabled by the fire of the enemy's batteries, and seven of the casemated guns bearing on the batteries disabled. The shot and shell of the enemy's batteries having made extensive breaches in the walls of the Fort, their fire was directed towards the magazine, the location of which they had doubtlessly learned from deserters, and which was in imminent danger of being exploded, having been breached in three places. The fort having become untenable under the terrific fire of the heavy guns of the enemy, nearly all our guns that could be brought to bear against their batteries having been disabled, and the magazine being in imminent danger, a longer resistance was deemed hopeless, and the fort was surrendered about two o'clock in the afternoon. Our informant states that the effect of the enemy's batteries on the walls of the fort was utterly demolishing, and that the strong masonry heretofore deemed almost impregnable, offered but a feeble resistance to the steel-pointed shot of the immense Parrott guns.

The Charleston Mercury.

DAILY PAPER—TWENTY DOLLARS PER ANNUM, PAYABLE HALF-YEARLY IN ADVANCE. | VINDICES NULLO SPONTE SUA SINE LEGE FIDES RECTUMQUE COLENTUR. | COUNTRY PAPER—THRICE A WEEK—TEN DOLLARS PER ANNUM, IN ADVANCE.

VOLUME LXXXIII. CHARLESTON, S. C., TUESDAY, AUGUST 11, 1863. NUMBER 11,830

TELEGRAPHIC NEWS.

NEWS FROM THE WEST.

MOBILE, August 10.—Persons who have lately come out of Vicksburg report that GRANT has gone to supercede MEADE in the command of the Yankee Army of the Potomac. General MCPHERSON takes GRANT'S place in the West. Gen A. J. SMITH is in command of the post at Vicksburg.

MORTON, Miss., August 9.—Colonel LOGAN was again at work a few days since. He attacked the enemy, 700 strong, near Jackson, East Louisiana, and routed them completely, killing a large number, and capturing 200, with three pieces of artillery.

AUGUST 10.—We have no news of interest in front. SHERMAN'S quarters are near OSTERHAUS' old quarters, about two miles from the bridge over the Big Black. Two divisions have been moved back of the Big Black, to escape the contagion which still prevails te a frightful extent. STEEL'S division is in picket this side of the Big Black, but none venture as far as two miles from the river. We hear daily accounts of the preparations of the enemy. One Mrs. ANDERSON, of Natchez, has been hung because she refused to disclose the whereabouts of her husband. The Confederate authorities have re-opened the Post-office at Jackson, Miss.

BRANDON, Miss., August 8.—LOGAN encountered at Jackson, La., 500 Yankee infantry, 200 cavalry and two pieces of artillery. He killed and wounded a number, capturing the artillery, 200 Yankees, and two commissary wagons.

NEWS FROM MEADE'S ARMY.

GORDONSVILLE, August 9.—An intelligent gentleman arrived to-day from Middleburg, from which place he fled on Wednesday last. The Yankee raiders in that section are burning the wheat, destroying everything and carrying off all the citizens they can capture, including two little boys. They are also taking all the horses, cattle and sheep. MEADE'S headquarters are said to be at Catlett's Station, and SEDGEWICK'S at Warrenton. PLEASANTON'S cavalry are at Warrenton Junction. It is stated that MEADE has sent North a certain number from every company in his army for the purpose of gathering conscripts to fill up his ranks.

MILFORD, VA., August 10.—It seems confirmed that the Yankees are in some force in Stafford county. We have nothing new here.

LATEST FROM RICHMOND.

RICHMOND, August 10.—We have no news to-night. Weather intensely hot.

NEWS FROM THE UNITED STATES.

RICHMOND, August 10.—Late Northern papers received here contain the following items of news:

The steamer Ruth was burned on the night of the 4th, at Island No. 1, Mississippi river. About thirty lives were lost, and the cargo, embracing 400 tons of commissary stores, and several paymaster's boxes, containing $260,000 in greenbacks, were destroyed.

At Louisville, Bramlett (Union) received 3,467 votes, and Wickliffe (Democrat) 1,270.

The London Times regards the New York riots as little short of insurrection.

Articles in the New York and Washington papeas represent war with Great Britain to be imminent.

In the late advance of Grant's army upon Jackson, Miss., letters were captured fully confirming the treason of Ex President Buchanan. His replies to the letters of Jeff. Davis confirm General Scott's accusation.

A serious collision took place on the 1st inst., at Keokuk, between the Democrats and Unionists. One Democrat was killed and two others died of their wounds. The Democrats were driven from the place. Subsequently, however, they were reinforced to the number of 1500 and were hourly receiving fresh accessions, all fully armed for the fight. The Sheriff of Keokuk had gone to Davenport for military assistance. Similar disturbances had taken place at Columbus, Ohio.

Hong Kong newspapers give an account of a terrible earthquake which occurred at Manilla on the 3d of June. Half the city was destroyed and two thousand lives lost.

In the House of Lords on the 23d instant, Lord Palmerston denounced the practice of the Yankee Consuls in receiving bonds that cargoes of specified vessels are not intended for the Confederates. He declared such a course to be a violation of international law. Remonstrances, he said, had been made, and the Federal authorities had promised to stop the proceeding, but he feared that they had not done so. He hoped, however, that fresh remonstrances would prove more effectual.

A gentleman who left Washington on last Wednesday states that 50,000 negro troops are now being organized there. The Lincoln Government is conscribing all blacks, slave or free, in the State of Maryland. Since the battle at Gettysburg twenty-one new batteries have been erected at Baltimore, and three thousand negroes are still engaged fortifying around the city. The people of Maryland are in despair, being subject to the most unrelenting tyranny and suspicion.

New York, New Jersey, and the New England States are buying their conscripts out of the army. Large bodies of troops have been sent to New York and New England to preserve order. The enrolment is going on quietly, but trouble is looked for when the men are actually called out.

A terrific storm had taken place around Reading, Penn., doing immense damage to the crops. Emmettsburg, Md., has been almost destroyed by fire.

Vallandigham is still at the Clifton House, Canada.

Major General George Gordon Meade

THE MERCURY.

TUESDAY, AUGUST 11, 1863.

The Duty of the People.

Every man sees and knows that the great cause of the Confederate States, but a few weeks since strong and prosperous, by a series of the most matchless blunders has been reduced to a condition of imminent peril. What course ought the people to pursue to meet their present disastrous condition?

1. In the first place, every man, who is physically able to do so, should step into the service of the Confederacy.

2. In the second place, every effort made by the Confederate Government to redeem our disasters, should be supported with all zeal and energy.

3. In the third place, all officers put over our forces, who have not forfeited our confidence by their ruinous incompetency and self-sufficiency, rendering confidence impossible, should be supported and upheld with all our power.

4. And, in the fourth place, we should search out and expose the true causes of our disasters, in order that they may not be repeated, and thus render all our efforts to recover our lost security and success vain and futile.

These are very plain principles of duty. The first two the Government organs uphold with great unanimity. The third they except to, as being supervisory of the Administration. The competency or incompetency of the officers put over us is an affair of Mr. DAVIS'S, with which the people have nothing to do. Their business is to believe him infallible. But the fourth and last they absolutely cry out upon. It is right down treason—playing into the hands of the enemy—to assert the fact, or to prove or believe it, that the President of the Confederate States has grossly abused the appointing power, by substituting private likes and dislikes for the rule of combined honesty and competency as tests of fitness for office in Cabinet, Bureaux, and army commands—by thrusting away ability and character, and keeping dependents of favor like MALLORY, and BENJAMIN, and NORTHROP, and MYERS about him, and by putting such men as Generals PEMBERTON and HOLMES over the armies of the Confederacy, whilst such men as Generals PRICE and GUSTAVUS SMITH are driven out of the service; and when it is still further asserted that to President DAVIS, by his silly disposition of the troops of the Confederacy, all our disasters are attributable, they lift up their hands in patriotic amazement and horror, and cry unanimity is essential—deliver us from faction!

Our readers are perfectly aware that when President DAVIS, after the first battle of Manassas, refused to concentrate troops and advance on the enemy as the commanders desired and advised (a fact adroitly denied then, but now indisputable from proofs in our possession), we lost all confidence in him as a statesman or a strategist. He was either aiming at a reconstruction of the Union, and on that account deprecated all fighting, or he was totally unfit to direct the conduct of our armies. Events soon after confirmed our estimation of him. The fall of New Orleans and Fort Donelson were proofs of the most lamentable incompetency. Whilst the whole country was deceived with the representations of the military resources furnished to these places, the Government was not deceived. The retreat of SIDNEY JOHNSTON'S feeble army, and the disclosures before the Court of Inquiry held on General LOVELL, prove a full knowledge of the true state of things, and the grossest neglect and fatuity.

Yet, after these great disasters, our indomitable soldiery held up our cause. Whether thrown on fortified redoubts or in the field, they vanquished our enemies. Our cause went on and went up, until recognition by foreign nations and peace seemed almost within our grasp. Suddenly, by one of those stupendous blunders which TALLEYRAND says are worse than crimes, our cause is again prostrated by President DAVIS. The follies of 1862 at New Orleans and Fort Donelson, are re-enacted. Whilst Port Hudson and Vicksburg are beleaguered, instead of sending troops to relieve them from the Army of Virginia, he enters on the desperate enterprise of invading Pennsylvania in the *white cravat* style. Discomfiture and defeat overwhelm us everywhere. Now, if we follow the course of the Administration organs, where is the mischief this flagrant incompetency and perversity produces to end? If we still continue to look to President DAVIS as "Our MOSES," what security have we that, when again we beat down our foes, he may not again do as he has twice done before—blast our prospects by another exemplification of stupendous folly? The base subserviency of the Press and Congress has brought upon us the evils and dangers which now oppress us. The true cause of all evils must be exposed and resisted, or they cannot be rectified. If President DAVIS had been checked in his incompetent appointments to office, in the Cabinet and in the Army, by the exercise of the constitutional right and duty of the Senate to confirm or not confirm—if Congress had persisted in passing the bill President DAVIS vetoed, appointing a military head of the army at Richmond, responsible for its movements—if the Press had spoken out the truth, instead of plastering over his deficiencies and follies—and, by the Press and Congress, a powerful enlightened public opinion had been organized to sustain and enforce a vigorous prosecution of the war through competent agents and efficient measures, the Confederate States at this day would have been one amongst the nations of the earth, and we would have had peace. But a self-blinded man-worship has been the order of the day among the people. They have been unwilling to hear the truth because unpleasant. They have preferred to flatter themselves in credulity. And Congress, with its secret sessions, has bowed down and humbled itself in the dust before the idol. The Press has gone with the current. Congress and the Press, vacating their proper functions, their delinquencies have been popular and profitable. As it is, we will win our independence; but it must be through more rivers of blood. Let us be taught by the past, and not stupidly profess a confidence which no man of sense can feel, but bravely carry out the principles of the Government we have established, and bring all our officials, high and low, to the stern test of a rigorous accountability. By this means we will make the Government in practice what it is in theory, and achieve our independence. Not money-making, but a credulous and unreasonable man-worship, is the curse under which we suffer grievous dispensations. This, we believe, is the crying sin that is rife among the people of the Confederate States. Sinful gain is confined to a most insignificant fraction of our population. Baseless credulity and flattery and self-abandonment to a single department of the Government, and to one man, has been a raging moral epidemic.

OPERATIONS ON JAMES RIVER—REPULSE OF THE YANKEE GUNBOATS—A TORPEDO EXPLOSION AND ITS RESULTS.

The latest accounts represent the Yankee flotilla of monitors and gunboats as having disappeared from the James River, and all was quiet along that classic stream. The Richmond *Dispatch* of Saturday brings us the following particulars of the recent repulse of the gunboats:

On Tuesday evening, about four o'clock, the three gunboats and the monitor passed Varina, coming up the river. They were all connected by lines, and were towing each other, the monitor being second from the front. They commenced shelling along the shore to rouse up a Confederate battery, but the shelling was in vain, no reply from Confederate guns being elicited, if any of our artillery was in the neighborhood. They continued on up the river.

About 6 o'clock they turned a bend, near which a torpedo lay in the channel of the river. The operator on shore exploded the torpedo. The explosion, which was terrific, took place a few seconds too soon and before the foremost boat had gotten her bow over the deadly engine, which, had it been beneath her, would have scattered her to atoms. The water was thrown up from the bed of the river to a height of sixty feet, lifting the bow of the approaching steamer high in the air, and tearing from it quantities of planking and gearing. In falling the great mass of the water fell on the vessel, tearing open her upper works and doing further damage. Those who, from the shore, witnessed this unexpected water spout describe it as a grand spectacle. The negro spectators were greatly astonished, one of them running to his master's house with the astounding intelligence that "de ruver had done gone up in de ar."

The scene after the explosion was one of terror on board the Yankee fleet. On the foremost vessel screams and calls for help filled the air. "For God's sake bring up a boat" was the most frequent cry from the first steamer to her companions in the rear. On all the steamers the seamen were running about in the wildest confusion, and it was some time before order enough could be restored to allow of aid being given their distressed companions. The first that went to her aid was the Monitor, which ran up along side, and after that all hands on the fleet were engaged in repairing damages. Had a battery of artillery been on shore at the time the explosion occurred and opened a brisk fire on them, there is very little doubt that at least two of the boats might have been captured.

Fractured pieces of the bow, chains, sailors' caps, and planking floated ashore during Wednesday. The vessel which was so badly damaged was nearly square, with the ends slightly pointed, and our informant thinks was an iron-clad gunboat, or an old ferry boat sheathed with iron. The fleet, after the accident, sailed further up the river, where it lay Wednesday night, and Thursday morning, about 5 o'clock, passed Varina again going down the stream.

At Deep Bottom, a mile below Varina, they were destined to receive another surprise. The artillery and infantry which had been sent there and placed in position the night before, about 1 o'clock, opened upon them briskly, to the utter astonishment of those on board. Some effort was made to return the fire. The monitor backed up the river a little distance to get the range and delivered several shots, but finding it useless, put on steam and went down as fast as she could move. After the fleet passed Deep Bottom, the artillery was limbered up, and, with the infantry, went at a double-quick down to Turkey Island. They had arrived there about five minutes, and the guns had just been gotten into position when the fleet hove in sight, coming slowly down. This time one of the gunboats was being towed, having been so damaged by the fire at Deep Bottom that she was unable to make her way through the water. Her engines were not working; a shot hole through her wheelhouse was visible. As they came in range they were received with a galling fire, which was continued until they passed out of the reach of our guns.

As they passed City Point the Monitor was flanked by a gunboat on either side, with another wooden craft following in her wake, but attached by a tow line. Large holes could be seen in the hindmost steamer, and great pieces of canvass could be seen over the sides of the one next to the southern shore of the river, all indicating pretty rough treatment.

There is little doubt that these gunboat raids up James river are intended for the purpose of ascertaining the location and effecting the removal of the torpedoes suspected to be in the river, and this anxiety to have the river clear may be deemed as proof that the next "on to Richmond" will be made by two routes—one of them being the Peninsula.

We learn that our land forces had several wounded, but none killed, in the fight with the gunboats. They fired a number of shots, but their shot and shell were thrown at random, and fell wildly about the country.

The Charleston Mercury.

DAILY PAPER—TWENTY DOLLARS PER ANNUM, PAYABLE HALF-YEARLY IN ADVANCE. | VINDICEM NULLO SPONTE SUA SINE LEGE FIDES RECTUMQUE COLENTUR. | COUNTRY PAPER—THRICE A WEEK—TEN DOLLARS PER ANNUM, IN ADVANCE.

VOLUME LXXXIII. | CHARLESTON, S. C., FRIDAY, AUGUST 14, 1863. | NUMBER 11,833

THE MERCURY.

FRIDAY, AUGUST 14, 1863.

Planters, Engineers and Overseers—The Supply of Labor.

We are informed that some of the owners of negroes at work on the fortifications are threatening to take them away, on account of losses chargeable to remissness and indifference of the subordinate officers to whom the slaves are entrusted.

The commanding officer of this Department is striving, to the best of his ability, to hold these subordinates to a strict accountability for any delinquencies and carelessness manifested in the watchful care of this important species of property. Efforts are made by the Engineer of the Department to detect negligence, and to guard against heedlessness, and to make officers know and feel their responsibility for the valuable private property put into their hands. Of this we are assured.

Perfect success may not be obtained. There may be instances of inattention, worthlessness and offensive indifference. Offences must needs occur, and we do not wonder that planters are sometimes indignant. But these furnish no real ground for taking away, at this great crisis, the means of saving Charleston and South Carolina. If Charleston falls for the want of the labor of these negroes, the owners may only gain a further and entire loss. Interest, no less than a high sense of duty, urges the continuous supply of slaves, even at a sacrifice of property and feeling. Some things we must overlook. This is no time for petty motives or actions less than patriotic. The country has a claim upon all that we have. It is the country's hour.

MISFORTUNE REPAIRED.

[*From the Richmond Whig.*]

It is very true that in times of great public trouble nothing should be done to weaken the confidence or abate the hope of the people. This will be the argument of those who, in view of the fall of Vicksburg, believe the first duty of the press and the people will be to renew their assurances of confidence in the Administration, and thereby, in the hackneyed language of the sycophant, "strengthen the hands of our authorities." Superficially, this is plausible; radically, it is most false and dangerous.

Misfortunes, like diseases, can be treated successfully only by a thorough and fearless examination of the causes which produced them. If the investigation reveals a want of head or of heart in any official, however conspicuous, it should nevertheless be fully exposed. To conceal these deficiencies is to leave the cause of the misfortune untouched, and necessarily to prolong it. Hence, no radical treatment, no permanent cure of the evil; temporary expedients, mere palliatives alone are possible. The time for palliatives in this Confederacy is past. We are to strike at the root of our troubles or we are lost.

The causes of the fall of Vicksburg are threefold—the scattering of forces, the prejudice against men of proved ability, and the partiality for men of proved incompetency. Unless these causes are removed, disasters will continue to befall our arms as surely as night follows day.

If all the troops now or until lately scattered far and wide, under Bragg, Pemberton, Holmes, Magruder and Kirby Smith, had been concentrated in one great army, and that army placed under the command of a General of proved ability—and such an one has been left in idleness for nearly a year—it cannot be doubted that affairs in the Southwest would have worn a very different aspect. Pemberton, while at Charleston, proposed to dismantle Forts Sumter and Moultrie, and to destroy them utterly. The President and General Lee disapproved of this singular plan of defence, and the former promoted him to the office of Lieutenant-General. Neglecting to fortify Grand Gulf properly, and being entirely inexperienced in the field, he, with fifteen or twenty thousand men, offered but a feeble resistance to Grant with eighty or one hundred thousand. With the loss of nearly all his field artillery, he was driven into Vicksburg, where he has made a stubborn defence. It is not easy to perceive what else he could have done under the circumstances; yet he has been so much praised that he will again be entrusted with the command of men in the field and the conduct of a campaign.

As for Holmes, he is so nearly imbecile, if not idiotic, that he may be dismissed as a nonentity, except so far as he was able, acting under instructions from the War Department, to keep Price from doing any thing.

Counting Pemberton's paroled army, Johnston's forces and others, there are now on both sides of the Mississippi at least 150,000 men. Whether they can ever be got together, we do not know. Whether the President thinks the country has suffered enough at the hands of his favorites, it is impossible to say. But if he thinks the gratification of his evil passions and his fantastical preferences, or if he supposes the persistence in his system of divided forces, under pet Lieutenant Generals, of more consequence than the independence of the Confederacy, then we need no longer doubt what fate is in store for us.

RETURNING CONFIDENCE.

Judging from the general tone of the press in all portions of the Confederacy, as well as from the tenor of popular sentiment and feeling, we think there is no room to doubt but that a healthy reaction is taking place in the public mind relative to our national affairs. That the gloomy shadow of despondency had settled upon the hearts of many of our people immediately after our late reverses, it is needless to deny.—But such is always the effect of the first shock of misfortune. Very soon the buoyancy of hope, and the elasticity of the human heart, coupled with physical energy, surmount all opposing obstacles, and what was at first the slough of despond becomes the limpid stream of faith, which teaches us the wholesome lesson that misfortunes are often blessings in disguise.

The same despondent feeling seized upon the country immediately on the fall of Fort Donelson and New Orleans, but through the energy and patriotic ardor of the people, confidence was soon restored, and our armies went into action with a renewed determination to conquer or die. Failure was not for a moment contemplated, nor did the dread or fear of it paralyze the arms or blast the hopes of those who know how to hate tyranny and love liberty. And so it is now. It is only the coward who dreads to meet the enemy in battle array, or the weak kneed croaker who hopes to save his property in the event of subjugation, who now show the most evident signs of despondency. Poor creatures; they seem incapable of imbibing lessons of wisdom from observation and experience. They forget that the only means of preserving their property as well as their honor and their liberty, is by overcoming the armies of the foe. The conduct of the enemy in the subjugated portions of Virginia, North Carolina, Tennessee and Louisiana teaches them this fact. Neither oaths nor sycophantic fawning have saved the people in these sections, and it is the wildest fatuity for others to suppose that they will meet with any more favor in the event our country is overrun.

Our people are beginning to realize these truths, and, like Hercules, are beginning to put their own shoulders to the wheel. When this is the case there can be no such thing as despondency or despair. A brave, proud, and self reliant people can never long be kept under a cloud. Whatever strokes of misfortune may befall them, a returning sense of confidence and self-reliance will rapidly recuperate their energies, and push them forward in the acomplishment of the ends they have in view.

The South to-day is far richer in resources, both as to men and means, than was Greece when she resisted, nobly and successfully, the invasion of the Persian hosts under Darius and Xerxes. Our people surely have as high an appreciation of the blessings of liberty and independence as had the Greeks, and if they do not maintain them at every hazard, they will go down to their graves in ignominy and disgrace, and forever receive the bitter curses of their posterity.—*Appeal*

A REACTION.

Courage and faith, under the inspiration of a great cause, are now asserting their power over the public mind, and as was the case after the depression following the disasters at Forts Donelson and Henry, we look for a great reaction in the public mind, culminating in a glorious revival of the war spirit. God grant it! It is all we need to insure victory. Once more to the breach—one more brave, strong and steady pull all together, and the foe is vanquished and the haven reached. We believe this religiously, and it is because we are so powerfully impressed with the conviction, that the thought so often falls from our pen. Nothing stands between us and our freedom but the troops of the enemy now in the field. Their number is largely estimated at 350,000, and these are divided and spread over territories of vast expanse. Beat them and drive them from the soil, and Lincoln can find no more to put in their places. Now, have we the power to beat them? Yes! as with the besom of a resistless tempest, the people of this invaded land can rise and scatter them like chaff, or doom them to destruction. Ask any General in our service—ask Lee, or Johnston, or Beauregard, or Bragg, and each will tell you that if 100,000 men could be suddenly added to our arms in the field, they would guarantee that before the first frost not a Yankee foeman would stand in arms upon your soil. If Lee had had 20,000 more men to guard his long line of communication and his train and rear, he would to-day have been at Washington and Baltimore. Give Bragg 25,000 more bayonets and Rosecrans must abandon Tennessee. If when Johnston reached Jackson three months ago he had found his present army with 25,000 men added to it, Grant's whole campaign would surely have been broken up; he would have been beaten to his gunboats, and Vicksburg this day would be reposing in her heroic mantle under the folds of the Confederate flag. To-day we believe Lee is strong enough to drive the rash and rapid Meade from Virginia; but, give him 25,000 more men and the belief would become a certainty. In truth, we have arrived at a point where we can almost reach and grasp within our hands victory and freedom. A few more men, one more hearty and consentaneous lift, another effort, comparatively small, and the thing is done, the great prize is won. We belong to the class of the unwavering in faith as to the end of the war. Bad news is not more agreeable to us than others—it produces its momentary depression, it causes sadness to think of the prolongation of the war, with its sufferings and sacrifice. But it never shakes our confidence in the final result. We hold constantly to one proposition as unalterable, impregnable—the Yankees cannot conquer this country. The glorious end is sure, and we believe it is nearer than most men suppose.

Mobile Register.

HOW THE YANKEES DROVE THE NEGROS TO SLAUGHTER AT PORT HUDSON.

[*Correspondence of the New York Express.*]

NEW ORLEANS, June 23.—The report in question gives a somewhat different version of the conduct of the negros in the assault made on the 27th to that given by eye witnesses of their heroism, determination and daring. Of their possession of these qualities there appears to have been some doubt, and, to force them to maintain their position in front and prevent a sudden "change of base," a Connecticut regiment was placed in their rear. From this it would seem that "they made, during the day, three charges upon the batteries of the enemy," more as a matter of necessity than of choice. They were sent forward as sappers and miners, without arms, but with the implements and means of preparing for the advance of the white troops. Before them was an unseen enemy; behind them glistening bayonets in the hands of their professed friends. That they became desperate under such circumstances is by no means surprising. They rushed forward upon sudden destruction, as a horse is said to dash into the devouring flames.

As to the batteries upon which the negros charged, a word of explanation is necessary. The enemy had placed one or two, perhaps more guns, as a decoy, in a position that was exposed not only to a front but an enfilading fire. This decoy battery was the one upon which the negro regiments made their desperate charges, to be repulsed with a heavy loss. What was left of them were afterwards sent to bring off the wounded, when they were again exposed to a terrific fire. The result was, as reported by eye witnesses, that only six or seven hundred out of nearly two full regiments of negros escaped slaughter. But few of their wounded were rescued, and that few saved themselves, not being disabled in their lower limbs.

One of the members of the Connecticut regiment stationed to protect the negros in the rear, says he fired a number of times during the day, and on neither occasion did he aim at the rebels. This fire in the rear may have had the effect of goading on the "sable soldiers" to such feats of desperate heroism.

Previous to the assault upon his works, Gen. Gardner sent under a flag of truce, to inquire whether the negros were to be pitted against his forces? The reply of Gen. Banks was, that the negros were United States soldiers, and must be treated and respected accordingly. On the receipt of this answer, those who witnessed the assault report that it appeared as though every available gun on the works or within them was brought to bear upon the two negro regiments. This may have been what was expected of them. If so, Gen. Banks was justified in saying of the negros "they answered every expectation." If there is any glory in being thus substituted for breastworks and being sacrificed for the protection of others, the negros have covered themselves all over with that dear-bought commodity. Since then this terrible slaughter of the negros who were rushed forward at the point of the bayonet, unarmed, upon certain destruction, is used to excite the negros to rush to arms and avenge the death of their comrades.

The accounts of desperate hand to hand struggles between the furious rebels and savage negros, in which the latter freely used, having no other weapons, their feet, hands, head and teeth, are purely imaginary. No such contests took place. Why would the Confederates come from their breastworks, when they were mowing them down by the hundred? Men of common sense would not be thus prodigal of their lives, and the correspondents who write such stuff must entertain a very mean opinion of the intelligence of their Northern readers. White men of the South would not even thus acknowledge the equality of the negro. They only kill them as a matter of necessity.

In the second assault the negroes are reported to have suffered a loss of six or eight hundred, but as no account appears to have been kept of them, the public will never know how many of them are thus emancipated for all time to come upon the battle field. The destruction of slavery appears to be the prime object of the war, and it would seem that the authorities have become tired of the slow and somewhat uncertain process of emancipation, and have determined to adopt the more summary mode of putting the males, all that are able bodied, in the front rank, and thus get them killed off, while the women and children are huddled together in unhealthy localities, and left to die of disease and want. This is Northern philanthropy.

THE YANKEE ARMY IN BRANDON—TERRIBLE DESTRUCTION OF PROPERTY.

[*From the Brandon (Miss.) Republican, July 22*]

On Thursday night last Gen. Johnston evacuated Jackson, and on Friday his army passed through Brandon, on its way east, but to what particular point we are not advised. On Saturday a small force of the enemy crossed Pearl river, but were driven back by our cavalry. On Sunday morning they crossed in considerable force, generally estimated at 15,000, and advanced on Brandon. When within two miles of the town they met our cavalry under Gen. Crosby, who skirmished with them about an hour and then fell back through the town, followed by about four or five thousand Yankees. They reached the Academy square a little before sundown, where they encamped for the night. In ten minutes from the time the head of the column reached the academy every back yard in the place was filled with a gang of thieves, who broke open smoke houses, dairies, pantries, fowl houses, etc., and emptied them of their contents. In most instances, where the families remained at home, the private residences were not entered, though in some cases they were, and robbed of clothing, jewelry, wines, cordials, pickles, preserves, etc. Many families did not have provisions enough left for breakfast the next morning. Meat, sugar and molasses were all taken, and there are not chickens enough left in town to warn us of the approach of daylight. We have not heard of a single family who escaped.

Every store was entered and the contents carried off or scattered over the floor. About nine o'clock the large block of buildings on the south side of the public square, owned by Richardson & Robinson, was fired and entirely consumed, with all its contents. This building embraced the store room of Block & Hart, J. J. Thornton, Richardson & Willis, and the Post Quartermaster's Department, besides a number of rooms up stairs, occupied by the telegraph office and a number of single gentlemen as bed rooms. From this building the flames communicated to the large store house of Maxcy & Falls, and from there to Cohen's barber shop, Dick Shield's residence, and a small house belonging to Mrs. W. C. Anderson, all of which were entirely consumed. The flames also spread across the street to the store of H. F. Shelton, Fox's grocery, C. H. Meadow's store and residence, T. P. Ware's law office, and the large brick building of Lombard & Ware, which was occupied by the Post Office and B. M. D. Mason. All of these buildings were entirely destroyed, together with almost everything they contained. The thieving scoundrels entered our office, threw our types over the floor and into the street, tore up our paper and demolished everything it contained, and then were about to stick fire to the building, when Miss Estes and Mr. Harris persuaded them from it on the ground that it would burn their residences, which are on either side of us. Luckily we had hid a portion of our type in the woods, which enables us to continue the publication of our paper.

We would like to give a detailed account of the losses sustained by each individual, but we have not the time or space to do it; suffice it to say that there is scarcely a horse, mule, fat cow, or hog, bushel of corn, pound of meat or sugar, bottle of wine or cordial, or jar of preserves left in town. The heaviest losers among our merchants were C. H. Meadows, Col. J. T. Thornton, and H. F. Shelton, all of whom lost everything in their stores, and Col. Thornton lost eight negros, and Messrs. Shelton and Meadows each two horses.

Almost every negro in town and a great many from the country were persuaded off with them—none that we have heard of were forced off. Many ladies in town are now compelled to do their own cooking, who have probably never before cooked a meal of victuals.

All the plantations on the line of their march are utterly ruined—fences torn down and burned up—stock turned in the corn fields, all horses and mules taken, farming implements broken up and all gin-houses burned. We have heard of but one private residence being burned, that of Mr. J. C. Bruce. A. P. Miller and Joseph Hudnall were very heavy losers. Mr. Hudnall lost over sixty negros and all of his horses and mules, and Mr. Miller had nearly all his fences destroyed around his three large farms, his gins burned, a large quantity of wheat burned, and all his stock driven off. He also lost about thirty negro men several days before the Yankees reached this place. Jesse Norrell lost every negro he had. Joe. Todd lost four; Mr. Whittington lost everything except the clothes he had on his back; Amos Green lost six negro men M. Bourns six, J. Whitfield fifteen, and almost every other planter in the surrounding country lost from one to ten or fifteen.

On Monday morning, about eight o'clock, the Yankee army moved out to the depot, stacked arms, set fire to the depot, and went to tearing up and burning the railroad track. They destroyed the road out a short distance east of the depot, but from there to Jackson, we are informed, they have destroyed the whole of it. In the afternoon they left in the direction of Jackson, which place they reached Monday night. Persons who left Jackson on Tuesday say they were engaged destroying everything connected with the Southern and New Orleans and Canton Railroads, undermining the capital for the purpose of blowing it up, and burning up private dwellings generally. They are evidently going to evacuate the place, and will most probably fall back to Big Black, leave a small army to hold Vicksburg, and then proceed to Mobile. We don't expect them around here again until the corn is gathered.

Jackson's cavalry is now between Brandon and Jackson, watching the movements of the invaders, and as long as they remain there this section of the State is secure from the raids of the enemy. If our citizens see them skedaddling they may know there is danger and prepare to get out of the way.

The Charleston Mercury.

DAILY PAPER—TWENTY DOLLARS PER ANNUM, PAYABLE HALF-YEARLY IN ADVANCE.

VINDICE NULLO
SPONTE SUA SINE LEGE FIDES RECTUMQUE COLENTUR.

COUNTRY PAPER—THREE A WEEK—TEN DOLLARS PER ANNUM, IN ADVANCE.

VOLUME LXXXIII. | CHARLESTON, S. C., THURSDAY, SEPTEMBER 17, 1863. | NUMBER 11,8[illegible]

TELEGRAPHIC NEWS.

REPORTS OF THE PRESS ASSOCIATION.

FROM GEN. LEE'S ARMY—THE ENEMY ADVANCING.

Orange C. H., Va., September 13.—The enemy, with artillery, infantry and cavalry, crossed the Rappahannock this morning at Starke's and Kelly's Fords, co-operating with the force which for some time has been encamped this side of the river. At the railroad bridge the enemy attempted to surprise us, but failed. Our cavalry and artillery made a stand at Brandy Station, and fought them, but were forced to give back. The enemy held Culpeper C. H. Our cavalry are still falling back. Our loss is not over thirty, as far as heard from. Nearly everything was removed from Culpeper C. H., before the enemy got possession. This advance of the enemy is believed to be a reconnoissance in force. Fighting was still going on at four o'clock.

Later.

Richmond, September 14.—The report brought from Fredericksburg of a threatening attempt on the part of a force of Yankees to cross the river at that place is not true.

Nothing additional has been received from the Upper Rappahannock, except a report of the renewal of the fight at Culpeper to-day. It is understood that the exchange of prisoners at City Point will be renewed in a few days.

The Virginia Legislature has passed an act authorizing the reception of all issues of Confederate notes at the State Treasury in payment of taxes and other State dues.

The subject of the punishment of desertion from the army is now under consideration. The Senate has already passed a bill to punish persons harboring deserters with a severe penalty. Another bill is pending to outlaw deserters.

Richmond, September 15.—In the fight at Brandy Station, on Sunday, Gen. Stuart lost two pieces of horse artillery.

The enemy has advanced to the Rapidan. Skirmishing was going on all day yesterday between the cavalry and sharpshooters on either side. It is thought that a final engagement may occur to-day near Orange C. H.

The Latest.

Richmond, September 15—8, p. m.—All has been quiet along the Rapidan to-day. The prospect of an engagement is diminishing. We lost 23 killed and wounded in the artillery duel at Raccoon Ford.

THE MERCURY.

THURSDAY, SEPTEMBER 17, 1863.

Our Fate, if We Fail.

The Yankee papers publish a long letter, written by Mr. Whiting, Solicitor of the War Department at Washington. It is generally supposed to enunciate the policy of Lincoln. What that is, will be seen by the following synopsis of its positions:

1. Every citizen residing in the seceded States is a public enemy, whether loyal or disloyal, Unionist or Secessionist.

2. The people of the South do not cease to be public enemies upon the close of the war.

3. "Civil war obliterates all lines of States or counties."

4. The people of the Southern States must be governed in their domestic concerns by the will and pleasure of the North.

5. Seceded States, with their Constitutions unaltered, cannot be allowed to resume State powers.

6. The rebels must come back as a conquered people, but not as our equals.

7. The Southern people can only form themselves into States by abolishing slavery.

8. Conquered districts must be kept under military government—or, in other words, the war must continue until State Governments are established in the South prohibiting slavery.

9. The conquered districts are to be held to all their obligations under the laws, but it is for us to dictate what privileges they will enjoy.

The radical papers of the North are delighted with this scheme of oppression and rapacity, which, they assume, represents the purpose of the Yankee Administration. We have no doubt that they are right; and the reason why the same principles have not been sooner announced may be found in the doubtfulness of the struggle until recently. The enemy now assumes that the South is conquered, and secrecy in respect to its fate is no longer necessary.

This semi-official exposition of the purposes of our deadly foes needs no comment from us. We commend it to the attention of those amongst us—if any such there be—whose spirit has for a moment quailed under the accumulation of disasters which have recently befallen our cause.

THE NEWS FROM TENNESSEE—MOVEMENTS OF BRAGG AND ROSECRANS.

We gather from our North Georgia exchanges some very interesting details of the highly important campaign now progressing in East Tennessee and along the Tennessee and Georgia boundary line. The Marietta *Rebel* of Friday evening last has the following:

CHATTANOOGA OCCUPIED BY THE ENEMY.

From the latest reliable intelligence from "the front," there seems to be no doubt that Chattanooga is in the possession of the enemy. All of our stores have been removed to Dalton and below. Our army is centred about Lafayette, in Catoosa county. The impression prevails that the enemy will endeavor to retire upon Chattanooga, and there form a junction with Burnside, who is reported to have advanced down the East Tennessee and Virginia Road, from Knoxville, as far as Cleveland. The enemy's advance in the Wills' Valley is reported motionless, and we are without means of ascertaining whether our army is inactive or not. No skirmishing reported this morning.

The Marietta Confederate of the same date says. There are so many conflicting rumors from above, that we can gather very little reliable information. We learn from a telegraph operator, who reached here by the 1 o'clock train this a. m., that the enemy did not occupy Chattanooga until Wednesday night, and then only in small force, who are said to have crossed the river about the point where the Lookout Mountain touches it. The mass of Rosecrans' army was believed to be in Wills' Valley, Ala., and it was rumored to be falling back on Chattanooga. The enemy had not reached Ringgold last evening. A small cavalry force may have come as far as Chickamauga. The enemy's advance from Cleveland were reported to be at Red Clay Station, between Cleveland and Dalton. Some of our cavalry were at Dalton. It would be improper to publish what we hear of the position of other forces. Everybody from the front is still sanguine of victory, if a battle be fought, and only fear that Rosecrans may fall back across the river, and avoid a battle.

A BATTLE IMMINENT.

The Atlanta *Appeal* of Saturday evening, says

We have information through a gentleman who left General Bragg's headquarters at an early hour yesterday morning, that a battle was then expected to take place during the day. The enemy appeared to be in force at the eastern base of the mountains in Walker county, or rather in a gap, and at four o'clock our forces were disposed in line of battle in his front, four miles west of Lafayette. Our informant, however, thinks no fight occurred, as he heard no cannonading during the day. The Yankee force in front of Gen. Bragg was in all probability only sufficient to hold the gap, and placed there for that purpose. We are still under the impression that Rosecrans will give no fight in that quarter, and that the column against which attention seems to be wholly directed is only a small portion of his army.

We have pretty reliable information that a cavalry skirmish occurred a few miles above Dalton yesterday, in which General Forrest was very slightly wounded. No results were reported beyond this. The enemy had advanced south below Tunnel Hill, and had burned the eating house at Catoosa. The force of the enemy moving down the State road is estimated to be three or four thousand strong.

COMMENTS OF THE PRESS ON THE SITUATION OF AFFAIRS.

The *Rebel* of Friday evening says:

The impression prevails to-day from information received through various reliable sources from "the front," that the enemy are falling back or rather flanking toward Chattanooga, and have withdrawn, or are withdrawing their advance from the Wills Valley to that point. The town was evacuated by our people Sunday, and the last straggling soldier left it on Monday night. The last issue of the Rebel (Army Gazette) appeared on Sunday morning. The edition for Tuesday morning was in type, but was not printed off, the printers moving off with the material, accompanied the military caravan, and came down to Chickamauga Station. It is possible Rosecrans may entrench himself at Chattanooga, and having accomplished all that was contemplated and desired by the Yankee War Department for the present fall campaign, in the occupation of East Tennessee, may endeavor to hold it. The enemy does now hold the "key to the back door of the Confederacy."

General Braxton Bragg

It behooves our commanders, if they design the accomplishment of anything at all, before the winter sets in, to move on him quickly. Our necessities imperatively demand that we should immediately advance and give battle. The lack of men can no longer be urged as an excuse. If the enemy has gained an advantageous position we must dislodge him by force. He must be driven across the river. Who can tell in how short a time the gallant defenders of Charleston may need assistance? It is useless to mince matters about newspaper indiscretions; it is worse than folly to keep shut up in silence like sheep led to the shambles, through the ignorance or vacillation or negligence of those in power, without sounding the alarm; we cannot longer be lulled into fancied security by the stereotyped song of twenty-one thousand men coming from this point or that.

We are losing valuable moments. We have abandoned the line of communication *via* Knoxville to the east, and if Charleston fall, as fall it may, what is to prevent the enemy from advancing forty miles farther to reach our only remaining railway line of communication with the Capital, at Branchville? We do not believe that Charleston will be taken, but that question must be made a certainty. We believe that General Bragg intends to fight Rosecrans, but to insure the success of such a movement, surely the attack ought to be made before the enemy shall have had time to construct his depots of subsistence, and have planted pontoons across the Tennessee, sufficient to render the stream not the slightest impediment to his retreat. We grow impatient under the seeming hesitancy if it is not real delay. We long to hear the echo of the guns, for we cannot but believe that a speedy battle will be the most expedient.

Much in the same strain are the following editorial remarks from the Atlanta *Appeal* of Saturday evening:

The situation of affairs in front is day by day becoming more interesting, if not even a little ticklish. The Intelligencer of this morning has information, which it deems reliable, that Rosecrans, with sixty thousand men, is at Sand Mountain, Alabama, and that our forces are in the right place to meet them.

Could the truth of this intelligence be established and assurances given that Rosecrans will give battle to Gen. Bragg, we should feel perfectly easy on the subject. But we have our doubts and misgivings as to whether or not the wily Dutchman will hazard a general engagement.—Our opinion is that he has accomplished what he designed by sending a heavy column down Wills' Valley—the evacuation of Chattanooga, of which he has taken possession, and which he will soon fortify and hold against all efforts to reoccupy it. This will become the base of his future operations, and all he has to do now is to guard the lines of his railroad communications, leading both to Nashville and Memphis, by means of which he will in a short while be enabled to provision the place with six or twelve months' supplies, combined with what he would be enabled to gather from Middle and East Tennessee. To protect these lines we suspect that the main body of the Federal forces will be withdrawn from this side the river, while immense raiding parties will operate through the States of Georgia and Alabama from their base at Chattanooga.

We know the opinion prevails that the evacuation of Chattanooga can be forced by the destruction of these lines of railroad, but Rosecrans has a wonderful facility of keeping his base of supplies along with him. We doubt not that even now he has at least a twelve months' supply of both ordnance and commissary stores accumulated this side of Murfreesboro'. It is not presumable that he has been idle since March last, and, knowing what he had to perform, we are justified in the belief that he has amply provided for every emergency. Of one thing we feel assured—it will require a most energetic and vigorous campaign to frustrate his designs or thwart his purposes, and we very much fear he will spend his winter in Chattanooga, and be prepared in the spring to fall with destructive violence upon the Gulf States.

This, we admit, is rather a gloomy picture of the situation as it at present presents itself, but looking at what has transpired since the commencement of the war, and more particularly within the past six months, we are justified in taking this view of it. The enemy has never been known to yield a single important point he has once wrested from us, nor have we ever yet been able to see or appreciate the immense advantages we have derived from that strategy or policy which prompts evacuation after evacuation, and the surrender of territory which it is vital to us to hold. We greatly fear, that like the advance of General Lee into Pennsylvania and of Morgan into Ohio, this evacuation of East Tennessee and Chattanooga in particular, will prove a blunder rather than a wise strategical movement. That we may be disappointed in this is our most ardent hope. We know that General Bragg has a good army—an army composed of the very best material that the country affords—and whatever can be done we feel assured it will do to retrieve the ground we have lost. If properly handled it will accomplish wonders, and no one would be more delighted than we to see General Bragg guilty of one grand *coup de guerre* that would astonish the country, and draw down upon him and his noble troops the choicest blessings of a grateful people. The whole country is looking, with commingled hope and fear, to the *denouement* of the present campaign. The army itself is not only hopeful but confident as to the result.

The Marietta *Rebel* of Saturday evening says:

The army is at Lafayette, and extended from there to Graysville and beyond. Both armies are believed to be within six miles of each other.—Yesterday Wheeler, in front of Lafayette, encountered the enemy and was driven back, and Forrest, at the same time, with his own and a portion of Morgan's command under Col. Johnston, met the enemy at Ringgold, and after a sharp combat fell back to Tunnel Hill. At last accounts he was covering Dalton, from which point all the stores have been ordered to the rear. A well known officer from the front writes that Buckner was ordered to open the fight to-day.—We are of opinion, however, that several days will intervene before a general engagement takes place, if it be had at all. It is the general impression that Rosecrans will endeavor to avoid a battle, and fall back upon Chattanooga.

Generals Scott and Pegram, with their respective commands, had gotten in on the right, and had taken their positions.

The Chattanooga postoffice and telegraph office are removed to Kingston.

The New-York Times.

VOL. XIII---NO. 3744. NEW-YORK, WEDNESDAY, SEPTEMBER 23, 1863. PRICE THREE CENTS.

THE GREAT BATTLES.

IMPORTANT DETAILS.

Substantial Successes for the Union Army.

HEROIC FIGHTING OF OUR TROOPS.

THE BATTLE ON SUNDAY.

Fierce Assaults on Our Left and Centre.

Repulse of the Enemy at all Points.

Our Army in Position at Chattanooga.

Casualties and Captures.

Special Dispatch to the New-York Times.

WASHINGTON, Tuesday, Sept. 22.

Shortly after noon to-day a dispatch was received here from an officer in command at Chattanooga, speaking in most encouraging terms of the general result of the actions of Saturday and Sunday last, wherein, according to his representations, the Union army achieved a substantial success instead of being beaten—the enemy being more damaged in killed, wounded, &c. On Sunday night Gen. ROSECRANS changed the position of his army to points near Chattanooga, with Gen. THOMAS' command still occupying the front, which shows how much less that officer's corps was crippled than the first newspaper accounts alleged. Our total loss in prisoners was but 2,000, while 1,300 rebel prisoners had been sent to the rear when the dispatch in question left Chattanooga, and more were being expected in from the front. The army is in excellent spirits, and the brightest anticipations are entertained.

REPORTS FROM WASHINGTON.

WASHINGTON, Tuesday, Sept. 22.

According to official dispatches received here, dated as late as 5 o'clock yesterday afternoon, Gen. ROSECRANS had information that LONGSTREET's corps had reinforced BRAGG before the battle of Saturday; and it was subsequently stated by deserters from the rebel army that EWELL's corps had also come to his assistance.

A prisoner, taken from BRAGG's army, says that Mobile has been stripped of troops for BRAGG's army, and that some troops have been sent to him from Charleston; also that troops from LEE's army were in the late fight; in fact, that the whole Confederacy seemed concentrated there for that attack on ROSECRANS.

A rebel dispatch has been intercepted on the extreme front of the Army of the Potomac, wherein the rebel commander of the Army of Northern Virginia is informed from Richmond that BRAGG engaged ROSECRANS on Saturday and Sunday, capturing 20 pieces of artillery and 500 prisoners.

The *Star* and *National Republican*, in their late editions this afternoon, have accounts evidently derived from official sources. The longer one, from the *Evening Star*, is as follows:

On Saturday, the 19th, a demonstration was made by the rebels in strong force, which appears to have been repelled by the force under Gen. THOMAS, with the advantage on the Federal side.

On Sunday an engagement commenced late in the morning. The first gun was fired at 9 A. M., but no considerable firing took place until 10. Previous to 10 o'clock, Gen. ROSECRANS rode the whole length of our line. Soon after the battle commenced, Gen. THOMAS, who held the left, began to call for reinforcements. About 12 o'clock, word came that he had been forced to retire.

The second line of reinforcements were then sent to him, and MCCOOK's whole corps, which was on the right, and as a reserve in the centre, was sent to his assistance. Gen. WOOD, of CRITTENDEN's corps, and VAN CLEVE, who held the front centre, were also ordered to the left, where the fury of the cannonade showed that the enemy's force was massed.

Their places were filled by DAVIS and SHERIDAN, of Gen. MCCOOK's corps. But hardly had these divisions taken their places in the line, when the rebel fire, which had slackened, burst out in immense volleys upon the centre.

This lasted about twenty minutes, and then VAN CLEVE, on THOMAS' right, was seen to give way, but in tolerable order; soon after which the lines of SHERIDAN and DAVIS broke in disorder, borne down by the enemy's columns, which are said to have consisted of POLK's corps.

These two divisions were the only divisions thrown into much disorder. Those of NEGLEY and VAN CLEVE were thrown into confusion, but soon rallied, and held their places—the first on the left, and the second on the right of THOMAS' corps. DAVIS and SHERIDAN, late in the day, succeeded in rallying about 8,000 of their forces, and joined THOMAS.

Gen. THOMAS finding himself cut off from the right, brought his divisions into position for independent fighting, his line assuming the form of a horse-shoe along the crest of a wooded ridge. He was soon joined by GRANGER, from Rossville, with a division of Gen. MCCOOK, and Gen. STEADMAN's division, and with these forces firmly maintained the fight until after dark.

Our troops were as immovable as the rocks they stood on. The enemy repeatedly hurled against them the dense columns which had routed DAVIS and SHERIDAN in the morning; but every onset was repulsed with dreadful slaughter. Failing first on one and then on the other point of our lines, the rebels for hours vainly sought to break them. Gen. THOMAS seemed to have filled every soldier with his own unconquerable firmness, and Gen. GRANGER, his hat torn by bullets, rode like a lion wherever the conflict was thickest. Every division commander bore himself gloriously, and among them Gens. TURCHIN, HAZEN, and PARKER, especially distinguished themselves.

TURCHIN charged through the rebel lines with the bayonet, and being surrounded, forced his way back again. PARKER, who had two horses shot under him, Saturday, forming his men in one line, made them lie down until the enemy was close upon them, when suddenly they rose and delivered their fire, with such effect that the assaulting columns fell reeling back in confusion, leaving the ground covered with killed.

When night fell this body of heroes stood on the same ground occupied by them in the morning, their spirits being unbroken. Their losses are not yet estimated.

Gen. THOMAS telegraphs (Monday forenoon) that the troops are in high spirits. He brought off all his wounded. Of the sick and wounded at Crawfish Spring, including our main hospital, nearly all had been brought away.

The number of prisoners taken by the enemy will hardly surpass 2,000, besides the wounded, of whom not more than 1,000 could have fallen into their hands.

Of rebel prisoners we have sent 1,300 to Nashville. Most of our losses in artillery were occasioned by the killing of all the horses.

Gen. THOMAS retired to Rossville on Sunday night, after the battle had closed. Gen. ROSECRANS had issued orders for all his troops to be concentrated with the forces at Chattanooga.

In the last two assaults our troops fought with bayonets, their ammunition being exhausted.

The latest information that has reached this city is from Chattanooga last evening, and was to the effect that ROSECRANS would concentrate on Chattanooga last night. THOMAS had been engaged with the enemy prior to 5 P. M. yesterday, and it was therefore questionable whether he would be able to reach Chattanooga last night. There were indications that the army was contemplating a demonstration on another part of our line last evening.

FURTHER PARTICULARS OF THE CONFLICT.

[The following appeared in a part of our yesterday's edition.—ED. TIMES.]

CHATTANOOGA, Tuesday, Sept. 22.

The battle on the 19th resulted well for us, we having held our own as established on our left, and concentrated our forces during the day; and on Sunday morning we held a handsome line, with our right on a ridge of hills and our left protected by rude works of logs thrown up during the night. Our left rested on the east side of Rossville and Lafayette, about four miles south of Rossville.

In the fight of the 19th we had lost about 600 killed and 2,000 wounded, and were ahead three pieces of artillery; and the men were in splendid spirits.

The engagement was resumed at 9 o'clock on the morning of the 20th by attempts of the rebels to storm Gen. THOMAS' left and front. They were severely repulsed several times with heavy loss to them and very little to us. This fight lasted an hour and a half, and was the most terrific of the war, a continuous fire of musketry and artillery being kept up with deadly effect.

During this fight our right and centre were not engaged—our skirmishers keeping up a halting fire.

The enemy, finding their assaults vain, manœuvered to the left with the intention of throwing a force on the Rossville road and attacking THOMAS on the left flank. At this juncture THOMAS ordered Gen. BRANNAN, who had one brigade in reserve and two with REYNOLDS, holding the key of the position, which was THOMAS's right, to move to the left of the line, to protect the flank of Gen. ROSECRANS, and at the same time sent DAVIS and VAN CLEVE from the right and centre to support BRANNAN in the effort to hold the line to Rossville, and protect THOMAS's right.

On seeing the withdrawal of the skirmishers in front of the division, which was moving from the right and centre, the enemy made a vigorous attack on that part of the line, piercing the centre, cutting off DAVIS and SHERIDAN from the left, and driving the centre into the mountains, both right and centre being much scattered, without very serious loss in killed or wounded.

The right and centre gone, THOMAS' right became exposed to a most terrific flank attack, and REYNOLDS and BRANNAN, and the right of THOMAS' line was swung around. His extreme left being as at first, this also fell back a short distance on the Rossville road.

Parts of the centre were gathered up and reported to THOMAS, who made several stands, but was unable to check the rebel advance until the arrival of reinforcements. At 1 o'clock, Gen. GRANGER, with one division of reserves, came up, and was at once thrown into the centre, driving the enemy handsomely from his position on a strong ridge, with heavy loss. The fire from one of GRANGER's batteries mowed them down like grass.

This fight lasted about half an hour, with slight loss to us. Capt. RUSSELL, Gen. GRANGER's Adjutant, was killed before we had been ten minutes in the fight. After this bloody repulse the enemy remained quiet until 4 o'clock, persisting, however, in manœuvering on both flanks. Their full and correct information regarding this country enabled them to do so with great facility.

Having gotten again on our flank the enemy made a vigorous attack, and a fight ensued, which has no parallel in the history of this army.

Col. HARKER's brigade and Gen. WOOD's division distinguished themselves in the fight.

Gen. WOOD, Col. HARKER and Gen. GARFIELD were present, and with the remnant of Gen. JOHNSON's division held the left, and covered himself with glory.

On the right and centre, Gens. BRANNAN, BAIRD, REYNOLDS and PALMER, with parts of their divisions, fought most gallantly, while Gens. STEDMAN and GRANGER held the reserve, and drove the enemy at every point where they went in.

At 5 o'clock, Gen. THOMAS was still triumphant, and on the left held his line of the morning, but with the right of the enemy nearly back to his line, nearly at right angles with that of the morning. Two lines of retreat were open to Gen. THOMAS to Chattanooga, one of which he fell back to—to Rossville—during the night. Our losses have necessarily been heavy but the list of killed will be surprisingly light, and in the two days' engagement we have not suffered more in men than the enemy. In the charge by Gen. THOMAS, on the first day, the enemy lost as many in killed as we did in the whole day. What the losses in prisoners and material are cannot now be reported. Our killed will reach 1,200; our wounded will amount to 7,000—most of them slight wounds.

Among the general officers killed are Gen. LYTTLE, Col. KEY, Col. KING, commanding brigade, and Col. Bartleton, of the One Hundred and First Illinois. Among the wounded are Gen. Morton, of Gen. Rosecrans' Staff; Col. Craxter, Fourth Kentucky; Col. Frankhouse, Ninety-eighth Illinois; Lieut.-Col. Mudge, Eleventh Michigan; Lieut.-Col. Hunt, Fourth Kentucky; Col. Bradley, commanding brigade in Sheridan's division; Col. Chas. Anderson, Sixth Ohio; Maj. Mildman, Eighteenth Kentucky; Lieut.-Col. Tripp, Sixth Indiana; Lieut.-Col. Bryan, Seventy-fifth Indiana; Col. Armstrong, Ninety-third Ohio; Maj. Johnston, Twenty-second Illinois, and Lieut.-Col. Maxwell, of the Second Ohio—all slightly wounded.

Lieut.-Col. Vaughan, of the Seventh Kentucky; Col. Stanley, of the Eighteeth Ohio, and Maj. Dawson, of the Nineteeth Infantry, were all slightly wounded.

Gen. John H. King is reported wounded and a prisoner.

We have captured Gen. Adams, of Texas, and 1,300 of his men.

CONFIRMATORY REPORTS.

WASHINGTON, Tuesday, Sept. 22.

The official information received from Gen. ROSECRANS' army, which is several hours later than that published in this morning's papers, confirms the leading points in the printed telegrams.

The fact that Gen. ROSECRANS was not sooner reinforced, is certainly not the fault of the Government; but there is no doubt that every effort is now making to increase his strength by reinforcements from more than one direction.

NEWS FROM WASHINGTON.

OUR SPECIAL WASHINGTON DISPATCHES

WASHINGTON, Monday, Sept. 22.

NO DRAFT IN OHIO.

It may be considered finally settled that there will be no draft in Ohio. The State is deficient eight thousand men only, which number will be readily made up by volunteer enlistments under the ample bounties that the Provost-Marshal General is able to offer.

REBEL TRICKERY.

The flag-of-truce boat which left Fortress Monroe on Saturday for City Point has not been heard from since. It is believed that the rebel authorities have detained her to prevent officers of the Sanitary Commission, who have been prisoners in Richmond, and were on their return, giving information regarding the rebel movements.

ABUSES TO BE INQUIRED INTO.

A military Commission has been ordered to meet at Chicago on the 1st of October, to examine and report upon the alleged abuses in relation to the supplies of hospitals at that place; and also the abuses in regard to the pay received for soldiers discharged, and in supplying artificial limbs.

M'CLELLAN TESTIMONIALS.

Subscriptions for McClellan testimonials are passing through the Army of the Potomac. One of these, proffered to an officer, was headed by Gen. SYKES with a subscription for $20.

MONEY FOR THE SOLDIERS.

Warrants for twenty millions have been passed at the Treasury for funds wherewith to pay soldiers in the field.

DISPATCHES TO THE ASSOCIATED PRESS.

WASHINGTON, Tuesday, Sept. 22.

SEÑOR CORTEZ.

The importance of the visit of Señor CORTEZ to Washington has been highly exaggerated. He was a General in the Mexican liberal army, and comes here merely as a private gentleman, without any credentials or official mission whatever.

CAPTURE OF GUERRILLAS.

Several days ago officers COLE and MEARS, of the local loyal cavalry, crossed Harrison's Island to Leesburgh, and captured fourteen of WHITE's rebel partisans in the vicinity. Four of them were at the time engaged in making cider.

A CHARGE RESPECTING TRAITORS.

Judge FISHER, in his charge to the Grand Jury at the opening of the Criminal Court to-day, said: "The readiness with which you have each taken the oath of loyalty prescribed by the act of June 17, 1862, leads me to rely, gentlemen, with full confidence and faith upon your determination to bring to condign punishment, so far as you can, any traitor, if there shall be any in our midst, who has by his acts and conduct made himself obnoxious to the provisions of those statutes which have been enacted for the punishment of treason—the highest crime known to the law.

From Boston.

THE CASE OF A CONSCRIPT.

BOSTON, Tuesday, Sept. 22.

SAMUEL L. CROCKER, Jr., a member of the Suffolk bar, has been arrested for desertion, he having been drafted and failed to report in due form to the Board of Enrollment of the Third District.

When Mr. CROCKER was notified to appear at the headquarters of the Provost-Marshal, he went there with a substitute; but because he refused to comply with what he considered the improper exactions of the Provost-Marshal, the substitute presented was not accepted.

This provoked Mr. CROCKER, and he appealed to the authorities in Washington to protect him in his rights, and defied the Board of Enrollment to hold him, as they would not accept of his substitute.

The War Department subsequently sustained the action of the Board of Enrollment, and Mr. CROCKER, some time after the time given him to report had expired, was notified of this, and requested to call at the office of the Provost-Marshal; but he neglected to do so, and was arrested.

On examination by the Board of Enrollment, Mr. CROCKER was declared to be able-bodied, and was ordered into the service; but as a matter of leniency he was allowed a furlough until Wednesday, when he will have to go into camp, as by the decision of the War Department his privilege to furnish a substitute or to pay the commutation money is now cut off.

Mr. CROCKER is the son of Hon. SAMUEL L. CROCKER, of Taunton, formerly a Member of Congress, and brother-in-law of Maj.-Gen. COUCH.

Fair at Kingston, C. W.

KINGSTON, C. W., Tuesday, Sept. 22.

The Provincial Fair opened to-day with nearly 5,000 entries. The horse show is fine. There are 400 entries of horses, 500 of sheep, and 400 of cattle. The weather is fine.

FROM CHARLESTON.

Temporary Cessation of Active Operations.

THE NAVY DOING NOTHING

Beauregard Perfecting His Defences.

Our Forces at Folly Island Threatened.

THE RUINS OF FORT SUMTER.

The transport *Fulton*, from Charleston Bar Sept. 19, and the *Mississippi* from Hilton Head Sept. 18, arrived at this port yesterday.

The *Mississippi* reports passing Charleston at 8 A. M. on Sunday, and heard heavy firing.

The *Fulton* reports that the work of mounting guns on Battery Gregg was very slow, in consequence of the annoyance received from the rebel Battery Bee and Fort Moultrie, by shot and shell which were fired at intervals of about twenty minutes.

Among the passengers by the *Fulton* from Port Royal was the late Surg.-Gen. HAMMOND, who has been on a visit of inspection to the Department of the South.

MORRIS ISLAND, S. C., Saturday, Sept. 19, 1863.

From Our Special Correspondent.

Nothing has transpired worthy of note since the date of my last letter. In fact, it is not very evident that anything will occur for some weeks to come. The navy does not manifest the first sign of activity. The army is ready to put in a blow when the proper time arrives.

It seems as though another attack by the navy on any of the rebel works was not to be dreamed of for a moment. Consequently the enemy is strengthening his works with the utmost vigor, and it would not be a surprising event if the harbor of Charleston was nearly if not completely secure against any effort the iron-clads may make to force an entrance.

It was thought the other day that it was not impossible to remove the obstructions in the channel if the work was prosecuted with determination. It was even planned to commence operations in that quarter on a specified night. But for some reason the matter has been allowed to dwindle into vain speculation, and instead of witnessing an attempt to break through the chains, we have been entertained with accounts of what might have been done under certain and peculiar circumstances. The September gales are upon us, and, of course, the vessels cannot be managed in a rough sea. But two nights ago we were visited with a fearful storm, which threatened to drive all the vessels on the beach and sweep the tents from off the island. Such storms are frequent at this season of the year.

An attack on our forces at Folly Island was not unlooked for a few nights ago. Regiments were called out, batteries placed in position, and every preparation made to give the rebels a warm reception. After all this trouble, however, the rebels were mean enough to stay away.

All the rebel prisoners captured during the late skirmishes and engagements, have been sent from the island. Some are at Hilton Head, others have been sent North. It is reported that the enemy has removed a large number of his prisoners from Richmond to Charleston, to prevent Gen. GILLMORE from shelling the latter city.

A deserter lately came into our lines with a statement to the effect that Savannah was almost in a defenceless state. The troops had been called to Charleston, leaving only a small garrison in the forts.

The deserter is confident a small body of troops could easily take Savannah. The stories of deserters are not always to be relied upon, however, and that is particularly the case at the present time, when the enemy is or has been in such close quarters.

Capt. C. R. BRAYTON, of the Third Rhode Island artillery, is on his way home to accept the appointment of Lieut.-Colonel of a colored artillery regiment now forming in that State. Capt. J. J. COMSTOCK, Jr., has also gone North to accept the appointment of Major in the same regiment. They are both valuable officers, and distinguished themselves in the late bombardments.

WHIT.

Our correspondent sends us the following extract:

FORT SUMTER.

From the Charleston Courier, Sept. 16.

No point connected with the defence of Charleston is of more interest to the public, not only of our own State, but of the entire Confederacy, than Fort Sumter. Associated as it has been in the past with pleasant memories, and in the present with heroic deeds, it has become as it were an heir-loom of our whole people; and from the hour when it fell into our hands, as the first victorious offering of South Carolina to the Confederacy, until the present moment, it has been defended and protected as "the apple of our eye." At last it has been laid in ruins—its fair proportions, its noble walls, its threatening tiers of guns, all demolished by the ruthless demon of war. Yet there the stately old pile still stands, proud and defiant as in her palmiest days—crushed but not conquered, wrecked but not reduced—every foot of her massive sides written all over with the tributes of the foe to the patriotism, skill and courage of those who have been her defenders.

It is not our purpose to enter into a descriptive detail of the present condition of the fort, since it would be manifestly imprudent to state what is not known to the enemy, but there are a few facts which may be interesting and proper to mention.

There is nothing in the entire range of facts or fancy to which the ruins of Sumter can be likened that would convey an idea of their external appearance. On the sea face scarcely a brick is to be seen. Bushel by bushel, cart-load by cart-load, the wall has been chipped off, until nothing is left but a gray, ragged mass of mortar, from which project the outlines of former casemates, heavy beams and iron bars. The berme or base is literally covered with the *débris*, amid which, at every step as you climb over the great fragments of stone and brick that have fallen from the parapet, you tread on broken projectiles of the enemy, scattered in pieces whose weight varies from an ounce to a hundred pounds. The Sullivan's Island face is less shattered, but even here the pits are deep, and huge piles of material torn from the edge of the parapet by the over-shot balls have fallen on the rocks below. On the Morris Island face the spectacle baffles all description. For a distance, roughly guessed, of thirty yards, the wall is little less than a steep hill that descends from the parapet to the water's edge. This, too, is a ghastly pile of the once magnificent shape, from which stand out, in almost sickening aspect, fragments of guns, gun-carriages, masses of machinery, balls, bolts, rammers, sponges, all bound and mixed together with the iron, brick and mortar, in lumps and in dust, that have been wrenched from their long time-honored places. Here, too lie the myriad fragments of projectiles.

On the parapet as you glance around the pleasant walk that has been the scene of so many social episodes, eagerly remembered by our fair ones, you observe that the demon of destruction has likewise laid his heavy hand. One solitary gun, looming high above all else, keeps its lonely watch, and this has been partially covered by the dirt dashed over it in the passage of a shot. Other guns broken in every conceivable manner lie around, their carriages in splinters, and every vestage of their former use destroyed.

Russian Frigates.

STONINGTON, Conn., Monday, Sept. 21.

Two large steam-frigates, probably Russian, are now lying off here waiting for pilots, evidently bound westward. Wind fresh and northwest.

Government Loan.

PHILADELPHIA, Tuesday, Sept. 22.

The sale of Five-twenties to-day amounted to $538,650. Deliveries of bonds are made to Sept. 17.

FROM NEW-ORLEANS.

Arrival of the United States Steamer Continental—Low Stage of Water in the Mississippi River—Return of Gen. Grant to Vicksburgh—The Ammunition Used at Vicksburgh.

The United States steamer *Continental*, Capt. MARSHMAN, from New-Orleans in six days and twelve hours, arrived at this port last evening, bringing passengers, mails, and a cargo of merchandise.

We are indebted to the Purser of the *Continental*, S. E. CRAFT, Esq., for files of New-Orleans papers.

The Mississippi River was nearly fourteen feet below high-water mark, being lower than it had been in any season for the past twelve or fifteen years. There had been no rains, and the feeding streams must be low throughout the entire length of the valley. There were no symptoms of a rise, but rather of a still lower fall.

On the afternoon of the 14th, Gen. GRANT found himself so far recovered from his injury received on the 5th, by his horse coming in collision with a carriage, that he started for his headquarters at Vicksburg, accompanied by Gen. THOMAS and their respective staffs. Among the prominent military gentlemen present at the levée, to say adieu to the distinguished hero of Vicksburgh, were Gens. BANKS, ORD, FRANKLIN, STONE and RANSOM.

Col. DUFF, Chief of Artillery of the army of Major-Gen. GRANT, has furnished the following statement of the whole number of cannon shots fired during the campaign, commencing with the affair near Port Gibson, on the Mississippi, and ending with the capitulation of Vicksburgh:

"From the time of crossing the Mississippi River, May 1, till the surrender, July 4, 18,889 solid shot, 72,314 shell, 47,897 case, 2,723 canister, were expended, making a total of 141,823. They were used in the several engagements as follows: 3,960 at Port Gibson, 82 in the pursuit from Port Gibson, 620 at Raymond, 476 at Jackson, 3,422 at Champion Hill, 1,297 at Big Black River, 9,598 on the 19th of May, (really the first day of the siege,) 10,754 on the 22d of May, and 111,614 during the remainder of the siege—an average of 653 shots for each cannon used. These are cannon-shots, the reader will remember. Add to these the musketry, and some idea may be formed of the immense amount of ammunition consumed."

THE ARMY OF THE POTOMAC.

The Advance to Culpepper—Interesting Particulars of the Skirmishing.

The following private letter from one who accompanied the Second New-York Cavalry in the recent advance upon Culpepper, gives some interesting particulars of the skirmishing preceding the occupation of that place:

NEAR RAPID ANN RIVER, Va., Monday, Sept. 14, 1863.

KILPATRICK's division moved Saturday morning. We arrived at Kelly's Ford in the evening, and lay by our horses in marching order during the night. Between 3 and 4 there came up one of the most drenching showers I ever experienced. The rain fell in torrents, and we were soon standing in pools of water. At daylight we crossed, capturing the enemy's picket. Our advance was rather slow and cautious till we reached the forest bordering on the old Brandy Station battle-field. Here we first struck the enemy in some force. A rapid charge ensued. The First brigade, under Col. H. E. DAVIES, which had the advance, kept it throughout the day, led the charge at a gallop. We soon emerged on the old Brandy Station battle-field. Here the sight was grand in the extreme. The Second New-York Cavalry (Harris Light) had the advance of the brigade, and were charging over the plain supported by the other regiments, Col. DAVIES leading everything. Off in the distance we could see Gens. GREGG and BUFORD bringing up their column at a gallop. In the far advance charges were being made, and skirmishers were circling over the hills like the advancing waves of a flood tide. Prisoners and wounded began to come in. The plain was soon cleared of the enemy, and soon our force disappeared in pursuit. Now commenced a running fight, till we reached the vicinity of Culpepper—the Harris Light still keeping the advance, and giving the enemy not a moment's rest. Whenever they made the slightest pause, an impetuous charge from this regiment would start them again. For two miles before reaching Culpepper, the Harris Light was exposed to a very severe artillery fire, as great trees broken off and shattered clearly proved. The enemy finally planted their guns up a high hill, at the entrance of the town. It was a very commanding position. The enemy must be dislodged, and that right speedily, too. The Harris Light were ordered by Gen. DAVIES to do the work. Maj. MCIRWIN led the charge, accompanied by Capts. DOWNING and MITCHEL, and Lieut. JONES, and supported by two batteries. Gen. CUSTER, whose irrepressible gallantry led him far ahead of his command, came up and went with them. Down the hill they went at a gallop—a perfect avalanche of shot and shell crashing above them, and ploughing the ground around them. Dressing the line for a moment at the foot of the hill on which the battery was, they charged up with such impetuosity that everything gave way before them. With great rapidity they dashed around in the rear of the guns, and in a moment they were ours. After the guns were captured Gen. COSTAR came up armed only with his riding whip, compelling many a man to surrender at discretion. Capt. MITCHEL ordered a rebel to help limber up the guns. He replied with perfect coolness that he was not going to help the Yankees capture their guns. He again received the order and again refused. MITCHEL then drew his sabre and said, "Now do as you are ordered." This final ponited argument prevailed, and the rebel said, "Well, if I must. I suppose I must."

Perhaps the incident contains a moral. Capt. MITCHEL then rallied the men and charged through the town, which, in a few minutes, was ours also. We would have captured a train of cars loaded mainly with contrabands, but Gen. COSTAR's flank movement was delayed by a deep and almost impassable ravine. At one point Capts. HASTY and MITCHEL fought the enemy, they having five to our one. After taking Culpepper we drove the enemy till night—KILPATRICK's division encamped on Stony Mountain, on the extreme left.

We had a hospital at Brandy Station and Culpepper. While at the latter place Dr. HACKLEY, the Division surgeon requested him to find some bed-ticking, if possible, for the wounded. I was fortunate enough to discover within twenty yards of the hospital a lot of stuffed mattrasses and ticking, and abundant provisions for the hospital. It was a rebel storehouse—a sort of sanitary commission. A young lady in town had her leg taken off by a shell. I saw two ladies on the porch of one house that had four or five shells through it. In one house off to the left both father and son were killed by a shell. KILPATRICK said our regiment never did so well before, which is saying a great deal. Col. KARHOUSE, who commands the regiment manœuvred it ably. Col. DAVIS handled his brigade splendidly, as all remarked and as the result proved.

We encamped at night on Stony Mountain, in a drenching shower of rain, and slept soundly on the wet ground. Dr. KINGSTON, our surgeon, showed himself a brave and skillful man, and our wounded got the best of attention.

Acting Brig.-Gen. W. R. Brewster.

The following extract, taken from Maj.-Gen. HUMPHREY's report of the battle of Gettysburgh, will be read with interest by the many friends of that brave and meritorious officer, Col. W. R. BREWSTER, who has served since the organization of the "Excelsior brigade," as Colonel of the Fourth regiment, better known as the Second Fire Zouaves. May he soon be a full Brigadier:

Extract from Maj.-Gen. Humphrey's (Chief of Staff, Army of the Potomac,) Official Report of the Battle of Gettysburgh.

* * * * * * *

"The fine qualities of many officers were brought out conspicuously. In some instances their gallant conduct fell under my own observation. I wish particularly to recommend to notice the cool courage, determination and skillful handling of the Excelsior brigade by Col. WM. R. BREWSTER, and First brigade by Gen. CARR.

Musical.

Mr. MARETZEK publishes his first official announcement of the coming season at the Academy of Music, in another column, to-day. It is brief, and states nothing different to what we have already mentioned. The most important feature is that the subscribers will have a chance of looking after their boxes, &c., to-morrow, and as the season, so far as they are concerned, is limited to twelve nights, the quicker they take advantage of this fact the better. The boxes are far more limited in number than those who wish to obtain them.

VISIT OF GEN. SICKLES TO THE HOSPITALS.—Gen. SICKLES visited the hospitals hereabouts yesterday, to see the sick and wounded who had served under him. He was accompanied by a number of personal friends.

The War in Arkansas and Mississippi.

EVACUATION OF LITTLE ROCK.

From the Mississippi Journal, Sept. 26.

The steamboat *Kentucky* arrived last evening from Helena, with news of interest from Arkansas. The news we have had of the evacuation of Little Rock was correct. The National troops hold the country from Duvall's Bluff on White River to Little Rock on the Arkansas. Arkansas people have said for the last six weeks that Little Rock would be given up as soon as seriously threatened; they also said the Confederate troops in the State would all be marched to Texas. The result has justified these statements. Arkansas is now more in the power of its legitimate authorities than any other conquered State. She is left exhausted and prostrate, and will probably readily become good, loyal ground. The enemy's "trans-Mississippi Department," which includes Missouri, is getting small by degrees and beautifully less. The giving up of Little Rock is the surrender of Arkansas. We now turn to Texas; thither the struggle must retire, and there it can have no opportunity of distinct military existence. The possession of a few posts in that sparcely populated State will hold the whole.

The *Emerald* had come up the river as the flag-ship of Gen. SMITH; on her way from Vicksburgh to Helena she was fired upon on Monday when near Island No. 68, twenty-five miles below Helena, from the Arkansas side. Some dozen shots were fired, but fortunately no person on board was injured.

We had the pleasure of conversing last evening with a shrewd Memphis merchant, an old resident, who has a wide acquaintance in the surrounding country. He had been last week at Austin, Commerce and other towns and plantations along the river. The conversation of the people was generally in favor of a return to the Union, as the only relief from the troubles of the past two years. They generally stated that if treated as gentlemen and some reliance placed in their honor, they will behave with strict loyalty, and clear out the mischievous guerrillas. They ask but courteous dealing and time to show that they will act in good faith. If this is the sentiment it does honor at least to the discernment and foresight of those who entertain it.

Arrival of Cavalrymen from Fort Delaware.

From the Philadelphia Inquirer, Sept. 22.

Yesterday morning about two hundred and eighty rebels, who had been captured at the battle of Gettysburgh, and subsequently confined in Fort Delaware, arrived at Arch-street wharf direct from the fort, having been conveyed thither in the steamer *Reybold*. They marched through several streets, and were finally entertained at the Cooper Shop refreshment saloon, at the foot of Washington-street. They were originally captured rebels who took the oath of allegiance, and were then received into the United States service. They look happy, and as though they had been well cared for since their sojourn at the fort.

Among the noted ones among them was a bugler, who, it was stated, was originally in the service of FITZHUGH LEE's cavalry. They are intended for the Third Maryland regiment, which, on their arrival at Baltimore, where the regiment is recruiting, will swell their numbers to about 800 men. The names of the officers are as follows:

Col. C. CARROLL TEVIS in command; Lieut.-Col. De Vere, Capt. Gregory, Capt. A. J. Pemberton, Maj. Wm. Kesler, Capt. H. E. Clask and Capt. Welsh.

All the officers and men have seen service and are anxious to enter the field once more, where they may be able to aid in advancing the Union cause.

They presented an appearance quite favorable to them, and when in conversation they expressed themselves willing to do all in their power to defeat the rebels. They were anxious, however, not to come in contact with the rebel Gen. LEE, and hoped that they would be assigned to a position that would prevent such an occurrence.

Capt. PEMBERTON, whose name has been mentioned in connection with those in command, is a brother to the rebel Gen. PEMBERTON. The men, after spending the day in this city, left in the Baltimore train in the evening. Their appearance on the streets attracted large crowds of spectators. There were representatives among them from North and South Carolina, Indiana, Illinois, Virginia, Maryland, Pennsylvania, New-York and Connecticut. Most of the men had been in the army from the commencement of the war, and a large number were the unwilling subjects of the Southern rebellion, having been pressed into the service.

Fashion Course Trotting.

The fifth heat of the *Butler* and *Prince* trotting match came off yesterday, and terminated in favor of *Butler*. An even start was effected, and *Prince* led round the turn a length in front of *Butler*, who broke at the quarter-pole, and fell off a couple of lengths before he recovered again; he was soon lapped on *Prince*, and was neck and neck at the half-mile, and just headed *Prince* as they were approaching the stand, when the latter broke up and *Butler* led two lengths before *Prince* caught again, *Butler* breaking badly and yawing across the track as he entered the three-quarter turn, but recovering in time to prevent HORACE JONES from passing him with *Prince*, and kept his lead to the score, with *Prince* breaking again as he approached the distance-stand. *Butler* won the heat and race in 2:29½.

Previous to the start a discussion was had as to who should take the money bet on *Fillingham* in the pools sold by TOMMY JOHNSON, the pool auctioneer. It must be understood that, by the postponement, all bets and pools are expressly declared off by the racing rules, and the money ought to be returned to the betters, but it was said that those who bet on *Fillingham* had lost their money in any event, and the question was who would be entitled to the money; some said the winner; some said, suppose they divide the $1,000 prize between the owners of *Butler* and *Prince* by compromise, would the owners have a right to divide *Fillingham's* pool-money? and others again urged that the horses had nothing to do with it if the *Fillingham* party did not get back their money, but that those who had bet their money in the pools on the winning horse ought to be entitled to it, if any were.

The owner of *Prince* settled the point for himself before the race, by disclaiming any right to it; and thus it remained until the close of the race, when Mr. GENET notified JOHNSON that he should hold him responsible for the large amount in his hands, and claimed it as owner of the winning horse; and requested him to select three men to decide the question. Mr. VAIL, President of the Hartford Horse Association, suggested that it be left to Mr. GEORGE WILKES, of *Wilkes' Spirit*, and said that his was the only recognized organ for such matters, (except the *Clipper*, which had given some attention lately.)

DAN MACE here interposed by telling JOHNSON that he had better select three good horse men himself, and so the matter remained—JOHNSON determining to select three men to decide a very novel and knotty point among betting men. Mr. WILKES would have been the most proper person to have established a precedent, as, from the character of his paper and sporting circles, there would have been a guarantee of responsibility about the matter; but if the parties who bet the money on *Fillingham* are not to get it back, it cannot for a moment be supposed that the owner of *Butler* can claim a prior right to it over the betters on *Butler* in the pools; therefore it is suggested that, in the absence of a more satisfactory way of settling the affair, that the money be divided among the members of the Association, under the supervision of Messrs. GENET and JOHNSON, two of the most active members, or invested in several gold medals for the next Ladies' Saddle Race.

The race announced for to-morrow, between *Fillingham* and *Butler*, will not take place in consequence of indisposition of *Fillingham*.

The Bombardment of Port-au-Platte.

BOSTON, Tuesday, Sept. 22.

A private letter states that 100 lives were lost in the bombardment of Port-au-Platte, St. Domingo. The loss of property is also quite heavy. The American Consul remained at his post. The other Consuls took refuge on board of vessels in the harbor.

Deserters Sent Back.

WASHINGTON, Tuesday, Sept. 22.

Three hundred and eighty deserters were yesterday sent from the defences south of the Potomac, where they have been at work for some time, to Provost-Marshal TODD, who will return them to their various regiments.

Railroad Collision and Loss of Life.

TOLEDO, Tuesday, Sept. 22.

A collision took place near here this morning, on the Dayton and Michigan Railroad, between a passenger and a wood train. Two persons were killed and seventeen wounded.

Departure of Canadian Blockade Runners.

QUEBEC, Tuesday, Sept. 22.

The steamer *Bowmanville* went to sea last night, clearing for Havana, but it is expected that she will take a cargo from Nova Scotia and run the blockade. The steamer *Caledonia* leaves to-day on similar business.

The Charleston Mercury.

DAILY PAPER—Twenty Dollars per annum, payable half-yearly in advance. | SPONTE SUA SINE LEGE FIDES RECTUMQUE COLENTUR. —VINDICE NULLO | COUNTRY PAPER—Three a Week—Ten Dollars per annum, in advance.

VOLUME LXXXIII. | CHARLESTON, S. C., FRIDAY, SEPTEMBER 25, 1863. | NUMBER 11,865

THE VICTORY AT CHICKAMAUGA.

HIGHLY INTERESTING DETAILS.

We have gleaned from our Atlanta exchanges a deal of interesting information concerning our great victory at Chickamauga, which has not reached us by the wires. We make up a summary:

THE GENERAL RESULT.

The Atlanta *Appeal* thus sums up the events and result of the fighting:

In the absence of all official statements the public will be satisfied with the intelligence that all our brave troops covered themselves with glory, and all vied with each other in their efforts on the field. The battle was general—the whole force of both armies present participated; and the result is that the superior spirit and determination of our troops, contending against superior numbers, has won the most decisive victory of the war. This can be safely said—indeed, we believe we would be correct in saying the battle of Chickamauga is the only really decisive conflict that has yet taken place. The enemy has been completely routed; his loss, in killed, wounded and prisoners, will not be less than 25,000; he loses half of his artillery, with large quantities of munitions; his dead were left unburied, and his wounded on the field; and, to day, instead of threatening an invasion of two of the States of the Confederacy, he is seeking safety for the remnant of his hosts in ignominious flight, with a victorious and jubilant army pressing upon his rear. Such, in brief, is the result upon which the people of the Confederacy can congratulate themselves, and for which they are indebted to the bravery of their own sons and brothers.

As remarked, the defeat of Rosecrans is complete. We speak with great certainty of the correctness of our information, when we say that the Federal army, or what is left of it, has recrossed the Tennessee. The belief in official circles in front, at the latest moment, was that after burning Chattanooga, with all his stores accumulated south of the river, Rosecrans crossed at that point and other points below, destroying his pontoons to avoid pursuit, on Monday night and yesterday morning. The most careful reconnoissance failed to discover any Federal force this side of the river yesterday afternoon, and in the evening an engine was started on a reconnoitering expedition to Chattanooga, which went through and returned.

Rosecrans, we suppose, will attempt to reorganize his shattered army near the river, and await reinforcements from Burnside and elsewhere. There are rumors of his rear communications, north of the river, having been disturbed, but these need confirmation. Whether Gen. Bragg is in possession of the means of crossing or not, we are not prepared to say, but it is to be hoped he is. If so, the spirit of his army is such that the enemy will not be allowed to rest and recuperate; he can be driven still farther back, and Middle and East Tennessee, if not Ketucky, be again re-occupied by our armies. Such a consummation will crown with everlasting laurels the heroes that may achieve it.

OUTLINES OF THE BATTLE.

The *Appeal's* Dalton correspondent gives the following sketch of the battles on Saturday and Sunday:

The fight on Saturday commenced on this side of the Chickamauga River, extending from the right of Lee and Gordon's Mills to what is known as the New Bridge, across that stream, a distance of about five miles, with a flanking force well out on either wing. During the day the fighting was all on this side of the river, but in the evening the Yankees retreated across that stream, burning the New Bridge behind them—the river dividing the two armies for the night.

Sunday morning, before day, the banks were dug down on each side of the stream just below the point where the bridge had been burned, and our forces forded the stream and drew up in line of battle and commenced the advance about 8 o'clock. One mile and a quarter from the stream the enemy were found intrenched behind rifle pits, and other temporary fortifications, that they had thrown up during the night. The engagement opened all along the line about 9 o'clock, and was kept up with increasing fierceness until about 11, when the enemy fell back from their rifle pits, the centre making another stand about a half mile to the rear, while the two wings continued to be forced back.

Affairs continued in this condition till about 3 o'clock, when a desperate charge was made upon the centre, and it gave way, though without panic and in good order, recovering itself when it had reached a point on a line with the two wings. Continued and heavy firing was kept up all along the lines at short range, until late in the evening, when the infantry rested upon their arms, and the artillery kept up a heavy fire upon the position of the enemy all night to prevent them from throwing up new lines of fortifications.

In the morning it was found that the enemy had retreated during the night, and although pursuit was commenced at a very early hour, it was found that they were too nimble of foot to be caught. Late Monday evening heavy firing was heard, as stated above, between McFarland's Springs and Chattanooga, and it was supposed that Longstreet and Breckinridge, who were in the front, had caught up with their rear; certainly, it is thought not more than a mile or mile and a half from Chattanooga.

Monday evening orders were given to bring forward the commissary trains to McFarland's Springs and this morning all the wagon trains started forward.

Another correspondent, in describing the battle of Sunday, says:

Our forces were engaged along the whole line, reaching from near Chickamauga Station nearly to Lafayette. Both wings of the enemy gradually gave way before the impetuous valor of our forces; but the centre maintained a steady position. With a view to break the centre, if possible, our forces were concentrated about 2 o'clock, and a terrible charge made upon that portion of the enemy's lines. On this portion of the line, at this time, the battle is said to have raged with unprecedented fierceness. Many of Hood's division (Longstreet's corps), who arrived here wounded this morning, say they never saw such fighting in all their Virginia campaigns. It was absolutely, in many places, a hand to hand engagement in its literal sense, in which superior determination and nerve, even against superior numbers, were victorious, and about 4 o'clock Rosecrans' centre wavered, and trembling under the weight of our determined columns, gave way, falling back something near four miles between that time and six o'clock, at which time my informant left the field.

BRECKINRIDGE'S DIVISION IN THE FIGHT.

The Atlanta *Confederacy* says:

On Saturday morning Gen. Breckinridge's Division was on the extreme left of our line of battle, and was not extensively engaged. As the day advanced the battle grew fiercer on the right, and this division was ordered to the support of the right wing on Saturday evening. On Sunday morning the general engagement of the day commenced, and the battle raged through the greater portion of the day without a decisive result. In the evening three lines were formed—Breckinridge's being in the rear. The first line advanced on the enemy, pouring a concentrated fire into his ranks, and, when their assault had accomplished all it could, those who had not fallen lay down to allow the second line to advance, which likewise made a gallant charge. But the enemy contested the ground with powerful resistance, and finally Breckinridge's line advanced over the bloody ground and charged the enemy with an impetuosity which overcame his stubborn resistance, and some time after dark succeeded in driving him completely from the field, and the division slept a mile beyond the position which the enemy had held by the most desperate fighting. This most gallant charge completed the work of the day, and the field and the victory was ours, but the thinned ranks of those who fought, and the long lists of killed and wounded, especially in Breckinridge's division, will tell how dearly the victory was obtained. The deeds of Breckinridge at Shiloh, Baton Rouge, Murfreesboro and Chickamauga are all of the same character. No more desperate charges, or deeds of greater daring have been performed during the war.

OPERATIONS OF FORREST'S CAVALRY.

A correspondent of the *Appeal* writes:

On Friday Gen. Forrest, with two brigades of cavalry, on a reconnoissance in front, met a heavy force of the enemy on West Chickamauga Creek, between Ringgold and Lafayette, and about ten miles from the former place. Engaging the enemy in front with his cavalry, he soon found that they were too strong, when an infantry reserve was ordered forward, the cavalry, in the meantime, falling back before the pressure of the heavy columns of the enemy. Elated with their apparent victory, the Federals were pressing forward with the utmost confidence, when the cavalry, filing right and left, exposed them to a heavy line of our infantry, supported on either flank by the cavalry, which the enemy had supposed up to this time was the only force in their front. The result, it is hardly necessary to say, was a bloody repulse of the enemy, with small loss on our side; the details of which I find it impossible to obtain, as men arriving from the immediate front seem to have general ideas of everything, instead of minute ideas of anything. The enemy were pursued about four miles, when our pursuing columns were recalled, flushed with victory.

On Saturday morning Gen. Forrest made another reconnoisance, with Morgan's forces, now under the command of Col. Johnson, when a short engagement demonstrated the superior force of the enemy, and Forrest was reinforced with two batteries of artillery. Of the result of this engagement I am not fully advised. Other demonstrations were evidently made at the same time, as artillery firing was heard far to the left of Forrest, in the direction of Lafayette, which continued at intervals up to half past three or four o'clock in the afternoon.

On Sunday morning Forrest's cavalry moved to the front, and met the enemy near Lee's mills, on Chickamauga creek. After some slight skirmishing, the engagement was commenced by our cavalry charging the enemy's lines of cavalry, utterly dispersing them and pursuing some two and a half miles. As the move had been made in the morning, before the stock were fed, the cavalry were now dismounted, corn gathered from the fields, and the horses furnished with their morning "rations." While things were in this condition, the Yankee lines of infantry skirmishers were seen approaching, when Gen. Forrest called his forces into line as dismounted troopers, and again charged the enemy's lines, driving the advance back upon their reserves. As it had been supposed that the movement would result in a general engagement, and as it was thought the strongest effort of the enemy would be made against our left, our heavy infantry columns had been massed upon that wing. On driving the advance upon their reserves, however, Gen. Forrest found the enemy too heavy for his cavalry, and commenced falling back slowly, at the same time despatching for reinforcements. Buckner's corps was soon brought up, but they were still unable to oppose a barrier to the steady advance of the enemy, and were followed in their order by Walker, Cheatham and Hood.

Battle of Chickamauga

The New-York Times.

VOL. XIII—NO. 3747. NEW-YORK, SATURDAY, SEPTEMBER 26, 1863. PRICE THREE CENTS.

FROM GEN. ROSECRANS' ARMY.

INTELLIGENCE TO THURSDAY NIGHT.

The Position Considered Impregnable.

The Enemy in Mass at Chickamauga Creek.

FURTHER DETAILS OF THE BATTLE

General McCook Said to be Responsible for Our Defeat.

IMPORTANT AND SUCCESSFUL RECONNOISSANCE

Anxiety Respecting Burnside's Army.

REPORTS FROM WASHINGTON.

WASHINGTON, Friday, Sept. 25.

A telegram from Gen. ROSECRANS, dated last night, says he made a reconnoissance in force along the enemy's lines yesterday afternoon and found him in force. The enemy did not resist the advance of our reconnoitering column, which returned to its quarters after having accomplished the object of the movement, which proved to be of considerable importance.

WASHINGTON, Friday, Sept. 25.

Telegrams up to 2 o'clock, yesterday afternoon, from Gen. ROSECRANS, give additional assurance that his position can be assailed only by regular siege.

The purpose of Gen. ROSECRANS seems to be to resume offensive operations as soon as the reinforcements, including Gen. BURNSIDE's troops now on the way, reach him.

The mass of the rebel infantry are in Chickamauga Creek valley.

A division of rebel cavalry advanced yesterday or the day before from Stevens' Gap threatening a Union regiment guarding one of our signal stations, whereupon the regiment in question retired from its isolated position in the extreme front before it could be attacked.

Gen. HALLECK expresses the earnest wish that Gen. BRAGG will venture a prompt attack upon him, but is of opinion that it will not be made.

All was quiet along his lines at 2 P. M. yesterday.

Special Dispatch to the New-York Times.

WASHINGTON, Friday, Sept. 25, 1863.

It appears now that all three of ROSECRANS' Grand Divisions were engaged in the battles in front of Chattanooga, two of which were driven back in considerable disorder.

Gen. ROSECRANS, in his dispatches, imputes the loss of the battle to disobedience of orders on the part of Gen. MCCOOK, who failed to occupy an important position assigned him by ROSECRANS. Had he done as ordered, Gen. ROSECRANS' opinion is that the battle would have resulted in a splendid Union victory. By extending his forces too much, the enemy were enabled to penetrate Gen. ROSECRANS' lines.

Great anxiety is felt here in army circles for the safety of BURNSIDE. In order to reinforce ROSECRANS, his only safe course would be to cross the Tennessee River and move down between the river and mountains, or to penetrate to some of the gaps and move down behind the mountains. The opinion of military men seems to be, that if he attempts to move down this side of the river, he will run great risk of being cut off.

DETAILED ACCOUNTS OF THE BATTLES.

In the course of the 17th, already unmistakable signs indicated that the enemy had discovered the weak points of our position, and were massing their forces in front of our left centre and left, for the manifest purpose of crushing those parts of our lines, or getting between them and Chattanooga. A corresponding movement by the left flank was thence made by the whole army further down the West Chickamauga, so that on Friday morning our extreme left rested at Gordon's Mill, at the crossing of the Chickamauga by the Lafayette Pike, about 12 miles southwest of Chattanooga. On the morning of the 18th, (Friday,) a portion of the expected reinforcements, consisting of two brigades of the reserve corps, respectively commanded by Cols. MCCOOK and MITCHELL, made their appearance near Chattanooga, and were immediately ordered to make a reconnoissance toward Ringgold, and develop the intentions of the enemy from that quarter.

They came upon the advance of LONGSTREET's corps, pushed it back for some distance, took a number of prisoners from it, and fully established the anticipated concentration of the enemy in front of our left. All day Friday the cavalry, covering our front, skirmished with different bodies of the enemy issuing from the various gaps of the Pigeon Mountains and advancing upon and again retiring from our line. No serious collision however, occurred. It was evident the rebel Generals meant to create a false impression as to the points of our line against which they proposed to strike a blow with concentrated power. But Gen. ROSECRANS was not deceived. The reports from the front all tended to confirm his previous impression that an effort in overwhelming numbers was contemplated upon our left flank, and that it had to be met by a still further shifting of the line toward Chattanooga.

Accordingly on Friday night the divisions of BRANNAN and BAIRD, formerly commanded by Gens. ROUSSEAU and REYNOLDS, of THOMAS' corps, together with JOHNSON's, of MCCOOK's corps, moved from the centre to the left of CRITTENDEN's corps. They were in their new positions at daybreak. The two other divisions of MCCOOK's corps, DAVIS' and SHERIDAN's, were to move into the position abandoned by THOMAS' corps, but had not time to assume it fully before the commencement of the action on the next morning. On the morning of Saturday our line then appeared as follows: On the extreme left BRANNAN, next BAIRD and REYNOLDS, with JOHNSON in reserve in the centre, PALMER on the right of REYNOLDS, and VAN CLEVE on his left. The line, as already stated, was to be completed by DAVIS' and SHERIDAN's divisions, faced a little east of south. The scene of all the movements on the 17th and 18th was McLEMORE's Cove, previously described as the valley formed by the Missionary and Pigeon Mountains. The valley is washed for its greater part by the West Chickamauga, and traversed by two roads, one leading from Rossville, and the other from Chattanooga direct to Lafayette. The two roads run about two miles apart, and west of the Chickamauga, where the battle of Saturday was fought.

The section of the valley bordered by the two roads is almost a plain, covered with thick woods, which rendered the field unfavorable for the effective use of artillery. The line proper, as given above, rested nearly at the base of the Missionary Mountains, some distance in advance of its right. Gordon's Mills, the point of intersection of the road from Chattanooga to Lafayette, and the Chickamauga aforementioned, was still held on Saturday morning by WOOD's division of CRITTENDEN's corps, supported by NEGLEY's of THOMAS'. Their position was a strong one; but at an angle with the line proper, exposed like a dangerous extension of the latter, and was proved such by subsequent events. It was meant to secure our right against turning manoeuvres, but officers of good judgment entertained the belief that both greater compactness from closer concentration and perfect security of the right might have been obtained by posting the latter on the eastern abutments of Missionary Ridge. The brigades of MCCOOK and MITCHELL of the reserve corps were ordered back to Rossville, on Friday afternoon, for the protection of our communication with Chattanooga, and hence were not to participate in the struggle of Saturday. The night had been frosty, and the troops not being permitted to kindle bivouac fires, the discomfort they experienced, together with the fatigue from marching and want of sleep, put them in a physical condition by no means as vigorous as it should have been for the severe work before them. Fortunately the sun rose clear, and, with its cheering rays, did much to revive the spirits of the army.

The early forenoon passed away without forewarning of the approaching conflict; but shortly before 11 o'clock the storm that had been brewing all the morning above the rebel camp burst forth in the expected direction. At that time a long mass of rebel infantry was seen advancing upon BRANNAN's division on the extreme left. It first came upon the Second brigade, Col. CROXTON commanding, and soon forced it back despite its determined resistance. The two other brigades of the division at once came to its assistance, and succeeded in checking the progress of the rebels and driving them back; but their column being in turn strongly reinforced, they advanced again with wild yells. So powerful was this assault, that they pushed BRANNAN back to and beyond his position in the line, and thus uncovered the left of BAIRD's division. Making prompt use of their advantage, they changed their course to the left, and speedily enveloped SCRIBNER's and KING's brigades—the latter of Regulars. They were almost surrounded, but managed to disentangle themselves after fearful loss.

The crushing rebel masses next came upon JOHNSON's division, and rolled it upon REYNOLDS', which also became speedily involved in the desperate struggle. The stubborn resistance of these divisions, however, and the sweeping fire of seven batteries posted under the personal supervision of Gen. ROSECRANS, arrested at last their sweeping advance.

The divisions of BRANNAN and BAIRD having been rallied, Gen. THOMAS ordered a general advance of the right, and soon the tide of battle was decidedly turned in our favor. With cheers our line advanced, halting only at times to shatter the rebel columns by volleys. Several times the latter's retreating line stopped and valiantly tried to retain their gained ground; but steadily they were driven from position to position, and by 4 o'clock all the ground lost was nearly recovered. Several batteries belonging to Gen. BAIRD's and BRANNAN's divisions, whose horses had been killed and supports were swept away, were retaken, and several hundred prisoners captured. The enemy left all their dead and nearly all their wounded on the field. There were at least 500 of the former. The rebel troops engaging THOMAS belonged to BUCKNER's and LONGSTREET's commands.

At the time the struggle was turning in our favor on the left, BRAGG's army proper, consisting of the corps of POLK and HILL, (formerly HARDEE's,) moved to a most determined and well-executed attack upon PALMER's and VAN CLEVE's divisions in the centre. Its object was obviously to relieve the defeated rebel right. PALMER and VAN CLEVE soon found themselves overpowered and their divisions breaking. Their complete rout was imminent, when DAVIS' division came to their support on VAN CLEVE's right. The timely reinforcement at first had the effect of checking the enemy and restoring our line; but the rebel attack was speedily renewed with greater numbers, and the centre again compelled to yield. DAVIS was forced to the right and VAN CLEVE to the left, and the enemy advanced through the opening made in our line, threatening to take the centre and right by their flanks, as they had done on the left. At this critical juncture, SHERIDAN's division appeared, and was at once thrown upon the enemy. It stood its ground gallantly for a while, but becoming soon exposed to a destructive flank fire, was also compelled to fall back. Fortunately, the divisions of Gens. WOOD and NEGLEY, that had been easily withdrawn from Gordon's Mills when the rebel attack on the left threatened to be successful, now came to the rescue. After a brief contest, the rebels found themselves at last matched and commenced giving way in their turn, REYNOLDS having also been sent to the assistance of the centre.

After the repulse of the rebel right an advance was ordered, and the original position regained about sunset.

About dark the enemy made another demonstration with a heavy artillery and musketry fire upon the centre, but, eliciting a lively response, they soon abandoned this last effort of the day. Thus ended the battle of the 19th. It had been a defensive one on our part, and although we lost no ground, and probably less men and material than the enemy, its result could hardly be claimed as a triumph of Union arms. No substantial advantage had been won, and a large portion of the army was badly shattered. That the enemy, with his numerical superiority, would be able to offer again battle on the following day, could well be supposed. Gen. ROSECRANS anticipated a renewal of the struggle, and prepared for it.

During the night the disposition of our forces was changed. The line was made to rest along a cross-road running northeast and southwest, and connecting the Rossville and Lafayette Roads. By this disposition our extreme right was made to rest on Missionary Ridge. The new line was a mile shorter than that of the day before. The different divisions were disposed in this order: From right to left, one brigade of Negley's, Johnson's, Baird's, Palmer's, Reynold's, two brigades of Negley's, Wood's, Sheridan's and Davis'. Brannan's and Van Cleve's formed the reserve. The mounted brigades of Wilder and Minty covered the right flank.

Sunday morning broke upon the hostile armies as fair as that of the preceding day. Contrary to the universal expectation on our side, the enemy again allowed the early hours, so well suited to offensive manoeuvres, to pass away undisturbed by the sounds of battle. The adaptation of their plan of attack to our new line, doubtless, necessitated this. About 9 o'clock a few shots were heard at various points of our front. But it was only at little before 10 that the report of whole volleys announced the resumption of the fight in good earnest. The firing that had begun upon our left, at once assumed the fiercest character. The enemy repeated the tactics of the previous day by throwing themselves first upon our extreme left, formed by Gen. BEATTY's brigade of NEGLEY's division. It stood the onset for some time, but finally retired.

Desiring to unite the two portions of Gen. NEGLEY's command, Gen. ROSECRANS ordered Gen. WOOD's division to take the position of the two brigades stationed further to the right. The rebels, perceiving the withdrawal of NEGLEY, and believing it to be a retreat in good earnest, quickly also moved upon the centre, and the action speedily became general. Finding themselves unable to make an impression on WOOD, the enemy, after the lapse of an hour or so, seemed to concentrate their main strength upon the centre, now again commanded by THOMAS.

During the night our troops had constructed along the line barriers of logs and fence-rails, and thus comparatively sheltered, they kept a continuous, murderous musketry fire upon the enemy. Our artillery was planted upon higher ground in the rear, and fired over the infantry. Destructive as our fire from small-arms and cannon was, it did not stay the advance of the rebels. At times they staggered, but only to rally and push again forward toward our line. With frantic yells, LONGSTREET's and HILL's corps both came rolling steadily on, in columns by battalions. Our centre, weakened to the extent of almost one-third, was not strong enough for success in this unequal contest. Closer and closer approached the shouting hostile masses, and at last forced BRANNAN's division to yield its position.

Meantime, as Gen. REYNOLDS was severely pressed, Gen. WOOD was ordered to march instantly by the left flank, pass BRANNAN, and go to his relief. DAVIS and SHERIDAN were to shift over to the left, and thus close up the line. As the occasion was urgent, Gen. WOOD drew in his skirmishers with considerable haste, and the rebels for the second time, mistaking a withdrawal for a flight, pressed forward like a torrent, and poured musketry, canister and grape into the flank of the division, moving upon the double-quick. The men endeavored for a time to keep their files in order, but as the pitiless storm of lead and iron continued to be hurled against them, the regiments began to spread out like a fan wider and wider until finally they were torn to flinders. This was especially the case with the brigade commanded by Col. BUELL. PARKER's brigade alone passed on to its destination comparatively intact.

The battle now entered upon its most critical phase. The breach, temporarily caused by the shifting of divisions from one point of the line to another, was promptly perceived and turned to advantage by the enemy, that they proved fatal, and cost the loss of the day. DAVIS' division, coming up to take WOOD's position on the extreme left, was taken with great suddenness and fury by the left flank, and pushed to the right in utter disorder. Simultaneously the weak remnants of VAN CLEVE's and PALMER's divisions, exposed by the withdrawal of DAVIS', were attacked with equal vehemence on the right, and forced back in great confusion. The rout of the left and the right was now complete, and even the exertions of Gen. ROSECRANS and his Staff, who, with drawn swords, attempted to restore order, were of no avail. Streams of demoralized, uncontrollable men, fleeing toward the rear, were all that remained of a large portion of the army.

After that fatal break, our line of battle was not again to be formed during the day. The army was, in fact, cut in two, MCCOOK, with DAVIS, SHERIDAN and WILDER, being thrown off to the right; CRITTENDEN's, except one brigade of WOOD's, being broken in pieces, and THOMAS, with his indomitable corps, and JOHNSON's division of MCCOOK's, remaining alone upon the left. THOMAS' divisions—NEGLEY's, BRANNAN's and BAIRD's—had been fearfully shaken and much scattered by the fight over the log works, and REYNOLDS' was the only one that retained its compactness. The retreat was now the only resort left, and the whole, disorganized mass of our right and centre took the road to Rossville. Crowds of stragglers, in mob-like disorder, made good speed toward Chattanooga, with the exception of SHERIDAN, DAVIS and WILDER, who, cut off from the centre, still struggled as best they could.

On the right the divisions of BAIRD, REYNOLDS, NEGLEY and BRANNAN, and HARKER's brigade of WOOD's division, alone retained their unbroken cohesiveness, and held a strong position at the base of Missionary Mountains, where the Rossville road debouches from them, for another fight. The line was formed so that the left rested upon the Lafayette road, and the right at the gap represented an arc of a circle, and a southeast hill about its centre formed the key to the position. Between 2 and 3 o'clock the enemy appeared on the Lafayette road, and, moving by the left flank, soon formed for another attack.

At first they directed a heavy fire of musketry and artillery upon our position, as though meaning to dispirit its defenders before coming to an assault, but the 10,000 or 12,000 men that confronted them felt that the fate of the Army of the Cumberland and, in a great measure, that of the Union, depended upon the repulse of the enemy, and when the rebel lines finally rose repeatedly to the attack, they advanced but to recoil with severe loss. Our troops were formed in two lines upon the crest, and firing one after the other, they kept up an unbroken fusillade with telling effect. The enemy, consisting of POLK's corps, were not only repelled, but thrown into such disorder that TURCHIN's brigade charged upon them, was followed, and took several hundred prisoners. Toward sunset the enemy drew back to the position they took when first on the Lafayette road, and abandoned the contest.

While THOMAS' divisions were most sorely pressed during the afternoon, and it looked at one time as though they would again have to succumb to superior numbers, they were gladdened and encouraged by the advent, on the right, of MITCHELL's and WHITAKER's brigades, of the reserve corps, under the command of Gen. GORDON GRANGER, himself. With the accession of strength, our ability to maintain our position was no longer doubted. Soon after Gen. GRANGER had reported to Gen. THOMAS, his two brigades were sent out on the road, under command of Gen. STEADMAN, to retake an ammunition train that had fallen into the hands of the enemy. They came upon a large rebel force, and after a severe conflict, drove them away.

While Gen. THOMAS was making his gallant fight, SHERIDAN and DAVIS had managed, after being much cut up, to work their way to the Rossville Road with the remnants of their divisions, and fallen back in the direction of Chattanooga. At night Gen. THOMAS fell back to Rossville, four miles from Chattanooga, after bringing away all the wounded, transportation, and other material within reach.

While the struggle of Saturday ended in a drawn battle, that of Sunday resulted in a disastrous defeat. The failure of the first day was partly due to the greater numerical strength of the enemy, and partly to the deficient formation of our line of battle. That of the second is justly ascribed to improper tactics on the battle-field, and above all to the absence of command. The inspiring example set and influence exercised by the Commander-in-Chief at Stone River were wanting—he having been compelled to leave the field and return to Chattanooga before the action was over.

The early disappearance of two corps commanders from the field also made a demoralizing impression. The loyal people certainly have cause for self-congratulation that the Army of the Cumberland was not completely destroyed, and owe profound gratitude to Gen. THOMAS and those under him that saved it. Our losses are great. That in killed, wounded and missing will probably reach ten thousand. Of artillery, we are less some fifty pieces, mostly lost on Sunday. Of wagons, loaded with ammunition and supplies, ambulances, &c., we have also lost a great number. They were abandoned in the retreat on Sunday.

Gen. ROSECRANS and his lieutenants were busily engaged on Monday in strengthening their position by field works, and reorganizing their commands. While the army itself may be considered safe enough, it is most certain that if the enemy have the advantage of greater numbers, flanking movements will compel ROSECRANS to retreat across the Tennessee, in case reinforcements should not promptly reach him.

REPORTS FROM LOUISVILLE.

LOUISVILLE, Friday, Sept. 25.

Scraps of information from passengers just arrived, lead to the belief that SHERMAN's corps of GRANT's army joined ROSECRANS on Tuesday or Wednesday, and that BURNSIDE's corps has more recently effected a junction at Grapevine.

Reports prevalent to-night on the street say that BURNSIDE's force has been captured; but nothing has passed over the wires to-day indicating such an event, and it is undoubtedly false.

A DISPATCH FROM GEN. GARFIELD.

Special Dispatch to the Chicago Evening Journal.

LOUISVILLE, Wednesday, Sept. 23.

Gen. GARFIELD telegraphs from Rossville at 8:40 P. M. on the 20th:

"THOMAS has left BAIRD's, BRANNON's, REYNOLDS', WOOD's and PALMER's divisions in good order, and has maintained almost the exact position occupied in the morning, except that the right has swung back.

LYTLE fought a most terrific battle, and has damaged the enemy badly. Gen. GRANGER's troops moved up just in time, and fought magnificently. The fighting was far fiercer than I ever saw. Our men not only held the ground, but at many points drove the enemy splendidly. LONGSTREET's Virginians have got their bellies full.

Nearly every division in the field exhausted its ammunition.

TURCHIN charged the rebel line and took five hundred prisoners, became enveloped, swept around behind their lines, and cut his way out in another place, but abandoned his prisoners.

Another brigade was attacked just at the close of the fight, and, its ammunition being exhausted, it 'went in' with the bayonet, and drove the enemy, taking two hundred prisoners, and have them yet.

On the whole, THOMAS and GRANGER have done the enemy fully as much injury to-day as they have suffered from him, and successfully repelled repeated combined attacks most fiercely made by the rebel army, frequently pressing the front and both flanks at the same time.

Gen. MITCHELL left Crawfish Springs with his trains safe with him."

THE ARMY OF THE POTOMAC.

Reports for the Present to be Kept Back.

In compliance with a suggestion of the War Department, urging the advisability of preserving a strict silence at this time respecting present and prospective movements of the Army of the Potomac, we cheerfully withhold all reports of movements in Virginia. It is thought that the publication of anything now might prove adverse to our arms.

ANOTHER PRIZE.

Capture of the Steamer Juno.

The prize steamer *Juno*, (British,) Acting Master FRANKLIN HOPKINS commanding, a prize to the United States gunboat *Connecticut*, arrived at this port last evening.

The *Juno* was captured Sept. 22, off Wilmington, N. C., after a chase of four hours, during which the *Connecticut* fired thirty rounds of shell and solid shot. The *Juno* threw overboard part of her cargo of cotton. She is an iron vessel of 120 tons burden, side-wheel, built at Bristol, Eng., and is ten years old; her engines are oscillating and are about 400-horse power. The cargo consists of 200 bales of cotton, 3 tons of tobacco, and a small quantity of turpentine, and is valued, together with the vessel, at $100,000. She is bound to Boston, but put into this port for a supply of fuel.

The National Horse Exhibition.

NEW-HAVEN, CONN., Friday, Sept. 25.

The managers of the National Horse Exhibition at Hamilton Park, which opens on Tuesday next, have made ample preparation for a large attendance. The grounds comprise 50 acres, with a splendid half-mile track, buildings for the reception and entertainment of ladies and gentlemen, and seats for several thousand persons. Members of the press will be provided with a tent, and an extra stand has been erected for their accommodation. The horses can be accommodated on the grounds, the box stalls, sheds and barn room being amply sufficient for the purpose.

From San Francisco.

SAN FRANCISCO, Cal., Thursday, Sept. 24.

Trade is exceedingly quiet, causing general complaint amongst importers who exhibit a growing disposition to realize at current rates.

Sailed, ship *Aracan* for Cork, carrying 1,750 sacks of beans, 36,000 hides, 9,000 horns, 118 tons old iron, 580 sacks of mustard seed, 418 casks whale oil, 2,000 bales of wool, 8,000 casks of California wine, and 3,100 sacks of copper ore—all valued at $230,000.

Also sailed, ship *Lizzie Oakford* for Callao.

Dr. H. M. GRAY, formerly of New-York, died to-day.

From Fortress Monroe.

FORTRESS MONROE, Thursday, Sept. 24.

The flag-of-truce boat *New-York*, Capt. CHISHOLM, arrived last evening from City Point, with 800 prisoners of war.

Col. MICHAEL S. DONOHUE, of the Tenth New-Hampshire regiment, received orders yesterday to proceed to Concord, N. H., and look after the transportation of conscripts.

Government Loan.

PHILADELPHIA, Friday, Sept. 25.

The sales of five-twenties to-day amounted to $481,550. Deliveries of bonds are made to Sept. 17.

Arrival of Steamer Bavaria.

The Hamburg steamer *Bavaria*, Capt. MEIER, arrived yesterday morning from Hamburg, *viâ* Southampton the 10th inst. She brings 42 cabin and 216 steerage passengers. Was detained one day at Southampton on account of heavy gales in the North Sea. She had adverse winds most of the passage, and was three days off Cape Race in a dense fog. In the channel when off Pentland, passed Bremen steamer *Bremen*, for Southampton. The *Bavaria* arrived off the Hook at 2 o'clock yesterday morning.

Marine Disaster.

The Norwegian ship *Louisiana*, hence for Antwerp, Sept. 3, was abandoned on Sept. 14. Her officers and crew were taken off by the Danish schooner *N. M. Harboe*, and six of the crew (Americans) were subsequently transferred to the Russian steam frigate *Alexander Newsky* and brought to this port.

The Wounded at Chattanooga.

U. S. SANITARY COMMISSION, No. 823 BROADWAY, NEW-YORK, Sept. 25, 1863.

To the Editor of the New-York Times:

Dr. J. S. NEWBERRY, our Secretary of the Western Department, telegraphs us that twenty additional agents of the Sanitary Commission have gone to Chattanooga; that stores are going forward in large quantities, and that everything possible is doing to alleviate the sufferings of our wounded.

Respectfully yours,

HENRY W. BELLOWS, President.

AMERICAN INSTITUTE.

Premiums Awarded at the Thirty-fifth Annual Fair of the American Institute.

As yesterday was the last of the American Institute Fair, there was a large attendance of visitors notwithstanding the inclement weather, and the scene of beauty and comfort inside of the Academy of Music was in brilliant contrast to the cloudy and rainy prospect without.

At 4½ P. M. the list of awards, which we give below and exclusively, was read aloud by Dr. JNO. B. RICH, of the Board of Managers.

The President of the Board then made a brief but happy address, alluding to the flattering prospects of the Institute and the advance of American cultivation, invention and manufacture in all their branches, notwithstanding the troublous nature of the times. Throughout the evening a very large concourse of guests, the majority of whom were ladies, were regaled by the music of the fine band and of amateur performers on the splendid pianos exhibited, and feasted their gaze and fancies upon the beautiful marvels displayed around them. At 10 o'clock, the signal was sounded, and in a few moments the fairy scene was dark and silent.

We are glad to learn that, in despite of numerous unusual drawbacks, the Institute has, upon this occasion, reaped a fair success, the receipts amounting sometimes to as much as $600 per diem. The various commodities were excellent in quality and not meagre in number. In the Horticultural Department the display of fruit, including the splendid importation from France was the finest ever seen in this country. The Board of Managers were untiring in their efforts to secure success, and were ably sustained by the exertions of their courteous Secretary, Mr. CHAMBERS.

MECHANICAL DEPARTMENT.

AGRICULTURAL IMPLEMENTS.

John Vanderbilt, No. 23 Fulton-street, for a collection of Agricultural Implements—Silver medal.

E. H. Reeves, No. 185 Water-street, for a collection of Agricultural Implements—Silver medal.

R. H. Allen & Co., No. 191 Water-street, for a collection of Plows—Silver medal.

S. S. Hickok, Marlboro, Monmouth County, N. J., for the best Potato Digger—Bronze medal.

E. H. Bennett, Nos. 42 and 44 Greene-street, for an easy working, compact and durable Horse-power—Bronze medal.

Sandford & Mallory, Harlem Railroad Buildings, for the best Hemp and Flax Dresser—Silver medal.

John T. Foster, Wayne-street, Jersey City, for a model Seed Sower, Harrower and Roller combined—Diploma.

Haines & Pell, No. 27 Cortlandt-street, for a Hay and Straw Cutter—Diploma.

R. H. Allen & Co., No. 189 Water-street, for a Store Truck—Diploma.

L. Bolles & Co., South Oxford, Chenango County, N. Y., for Cast Steel Hoes—Diploma.

A. M. Halsted, Rye, Westchester County, N. Y., for a Cultivator and Seed Drill combined, (Silver medal has been before awarded)—Diploma.

Miles Manufacturing Company, No. 328 East Twelfth-street, for Meat Cutters—Diploma.

J. B. Brown & Co., Peekskill, N. Y., for a Dog-power—Diploma.

Fleming & Davidson, No. 67 Nassau-street, for Horticultural Implements—Diploma.

WASHING MACHINES AND CLOTHES WRINGERS.

J. Johnson & Co., No. 457 Broadway, for the best Washing Machine—Bronze medal.

A. G. Heckrotte, No. 431 West Thirty-sixth-street, for the second best Washing Machine—Diploma.

Metropolitan Washing Machine Company, R. C. Browning, Agent, No. 347 Broadway, for the best Wringing Machine—Bronze medal.

Haley, Morse & Boyden, S. Hawes, Agent, No. 498 Broadway, for the second best Wringing Machine—Diploma.

SEWING MACHINES.

Wheeler & Wilson Manufacturing Company, No. 505 Broadway, for the best Double-threaded Sewing Machine, being the most perfect and simple in its construction and working points—A gold medal having been before awarded—Diploma.

Sloat Elliptic Sewing Machine, Mrs. A. H. Suplee, Agent, No. 537 Broadway, for the second best Sewing Machine—Silver medal.

Wilcox & Gibbs, No. 508 Broadway, for the best single-threaded Sewing Machine, for stillness of its running and perfection of work—Gold medal.

Wheeler & Wilson Manufacturing Company, No. 505 Broadway, for a Button-hole Machine, for novelty and perfection of its work—Gold medal.

Madame Demorest, No. 473 Broadway, for a Sewing-machine Attachment for tucking—a valuable attachment to Sewing Machines—Silver medal.

Daniel Barnum, No. 130 West Twenty-fifth-street, for a Self-sewer—Diploma.

DENTISTRY.

J. Allen & Son, No. 22 Bond-street, for superior specimen of Mounted Continuous Gum Teeth—Silver medal.

Samuel S. White, Philadelphia, Penn., and No. 685 Broadway, N. Y., for the best Artificial Teeth—Silver medal.

John D. Chevalier & Sons, No. 639 Broadway, for section Blocks for Rubber, the best in form, translucency and general life-like appearance—Bronze medal.

E. A. L. Roberts, No. 56 Bond-street, for an Improvement in Heaters for Vulcanizing—Bronze medal.

J. L. McDermut, No. 130 West Twenty-fifth-street, for an excellent Heater for Vulcanizing—Diploma.

John D. Chevalier & Sons, No. 639 Broadway, for superior Dental Instruments—Bronze medal.

John D. Chevalier & Sons, No. 639 Broadway, for a Dentist's Lathe—Diploma.

Samuel S. White, Philadelphia, Penn., or No. 658 Broadway, N. Y., for the best Dentist's Chairs, "Perkins"—Bronze medal.

O. F. Harris, Worcester, Mass.; S. S. White, Agent, No. 658 Broadway, New-York, for the second best Dentist's Chair—Diploma.

LAMPS AND GAS FIXTURES.

Geo. A. Jones, No. 569 Greenwich-street, for the best Mechanical Lamp—Silver medal.

Savage & Co., No. 202 Fulton-street, for the "No Chimney Burner" Lamp—Bronze medal.

J. E. Ambrose, No. 255 Pearl-street, for the second best House Lamp—Diploma.

B. R. Sturges, No. 102 Nassau-street, for Lamps with Improved Slides—Diploma.

J. G. Leffingwell & Co., Newark, N. J., for the best Gas Governor—Bronze medal.

Sterling & Co., No. 505 Broadway, for a Gas Governor—Diploma.

Geo. Burgess, No. 254 Broadway, for the best Gas Burners—Diploma.

PIANO-FORTES.

Wm. B. Bradbury, No. 427 Broome-street, for the best piano-forte—Gold medal.

J. B. Peck, No. 252 Ninth-avenue, for the second best piano-forte—Silver medal.

M. Dücker, No. 19 West Houston-street, for a grand piano-forte—Bronze medal.

E. H. Hass, No. 95 West Thirty-second-street, for an upright Piccolo piano-forte—Bronze medal.

Mathushek & Kühner, exhibited by Bristow & Hardenbrook, No. 765 Broadway, for a piano of new and elegant shape—Bronze medal.

ORGANS AND TRIOLODEONS.

Mason & Hamlin, Boston, Mass., Mason & Bros. Agents, Mercer-street, New-York City, for the best cabinet organs, silver medal having been before awarded—Diploma.

M. Dücker, No. 19 West Houston-street, for a superior triolodeon, a large silver medal having been before awarded—Diploma.

MATHEMATICAL AND PHILOSOPHICAL INSTRUMENTS.

C. C. Harrison, No. 458 Broadway, for Globular Lenses—Silver medal.

A. Hass, No. 567 Sixth-avenue, for the best Electrotypes—Gold medal.

E. Kendall, New-Lebanon Spa, for Aneroid Barometers—Bronze medal.

G. Tagliabue, No. 298 Pearl-street, for superior Barometers, (Silver medal having been before awarded)—Diploma.

Jerome Kidder, No. 545 Broadway, for the best Electro Magnetic Machine—Diploma.

Samuel Clark, No. 219 Centre-street, for Hatters' Conformeters—Silver medal.

B. H. Horn, No. 212 Broadway, for model of a Steam Engine—Diploma.

John Matthews, No. 437 First-avenue, for Electro-metallurgical Deposits—Silver medal.

E. Holms, No. 252 Broadway, for a Burglar or House-Alarm Telegraph—Bronze medal.

Jerome Kidder, No. 545 Broadway, for Galvanic Insoles—Diploma.

The London Stereoscopic Company, No. 579 Broadway, for exhibition of Stereoscopes and Views—Bronze medal.

BLANK BOOKS AND STATIONERY.

J. H. Duyckinck, No. 164 Pearl-street, for the best Blank-books—Diploma.

Thaddeus Davids & Co., Nos. 127 and 129 William-street, New-York, for Sealing-wax, Mucilage, Ink and Wafers—Bronze medal.

Victor E. Mauger, No. 115 Chambers-street, for Direction-tags and Labels—a useful article—Diploma.

W. H. Swartwout, No. 137 Broadway, for Metallic Paper-fasteners—Diploma.

ENGRAVING.

American Bank Note Company, corner Wall and William streets, New-York, for the best Bank Note Engraving—Silver medal.

Wm. E. Marshall, Boston, Mass., for the best Portrait in Line Engraving—Bronze medal.

A. H. Ritchie, No. 442 Broadway, for the best Mixed Style of Engraving—Bronze medal.

F. F. Hewitt, No. 339 Broadway, for the best Card Engraving—Diploma.

T. N. Hickok, No. 280 Pearl-street, for Stencil Plates and Punches, and Steel Dies—Bronze medal.

Wm. Schaus, No. 749 Broadway, for beautifully carved Frames—Diploma.

MARINE ARCHITECTURE.

Augustus Walker, Buffalo, N. Y., for a model of a Seagoing Monitor—Silver medal.

R. G. McDougall, No. 96 Maiden-lane, for a model of a Floating Battery for Harbor Defence—Bronze medal.

Jeremiah Simonson, Greenpoint, L. I., for five models of Naval Architecture—Silver medal.

John Englison, foot of Tenth-street, East River, New-York, for a model of the United States revenue cutter *Ashuelot*—Bronze medal.

E. T. Darling, Port Jefferson, N. Y., for a model of a Yacht—Diploma.

W. H. and J. S. Darling, No. 371 South-street, for a Pleasure Barge—Bronze medal.

PENMANSHIP.

Mrs. E. M. Bassett, New-York, for a specimen of Penmanship—Diploma.

J. D. Williams, Bryant & Stratton's College, for the best off-hand and business Penmanship—Silver medal.

B. F. Brady, No. 169 Elm-street, for superior specimens of Ornamental Penmanship, a Silver medal having been before awarded—Diploma.

H. Grelling, No. 56 Myrtle-avenue, Brooklyn, for beauty of design and execution of a piece of Penmanship—Diploma.

GAS AND SODA-WATER APPARATUS.

Walker & Eppstein, No. 133 Fourth-avenue, N. Y., for a Portable Apparatus for Generating Carbonic Acid Gas for family use—Silver medal.

G. D. Dows, No. 525 Washington-street, Boston, for Ice Cream Soda-water apparatus—Silver medal.

John Matthews, No. 437 First-avenue, for a display of chaste and elegant Soda water Fountains—Silver medal.

William Gee, Nos. 6 and 7 New-Haven Railroad Building, for Soda-water Apparatus—Bronze medal.

BOOTS AND SHOES.

John L. Watkins, No. 667 Broadway, for specimens of Boots and Shoes—Diploma.

BUILDING MATERIALS.

W. J. Fryer, Jr., Albany, N. Y., for the best Chimney Flues made of stone ware—Bronze medal.

Wm. Osmond, No. 92 First-avenue, for an improved Sand Screen—Diploma.

A. Derrow, Paterson, N. J., for a Portable Sectional Building—Bronze medal.

A. M. Cochrane, No. 442 West Thirty-fifth-street, for an Iron Window Blind Fastening, simple and useful—A bronze medal having been before awarded, Diploma.

A. Klaber, No. 109 East Thirteenth-street, for a Marble Mantel-piece—Diploma.

PUMPS, GUAGES, ETC.

Sewell & Cameron, corner Second-avenue and Twenty-second-street, for the best Steam and Hand-pump combined—Silver medal.

Brinckerhoff & Springsteen, Nos. 427 and 429 Tenth-street, for the best Hand Force-pump—Bronze medal.

J. D. West, No. 179 Broad street, for the second best Hand Force-pump—Diploma.

G. C. Cary, No. 2 Astor House, for the best Rotary Power Pump, a Gold medal having been before awarded—Diploma.

Hart & Co., Utica, N. Y., for the second best Rotary Pump—Bronze medal.

R. H. Allen & Co., Nos. 189 and 191 Water-street, for a Cephydriac—Diploma.

Abner Van Horn, No. 624 Fifth-street, for the best Steam Valve—Bronze medal.

ARTIFICIAL LIMBS AND SURGICAL APPLIANCES.

Wm. Selpho, No. 516 Broadway, for the best Artificial Limbs—Silver medal.

J. M. Weston, No. 491 Broadway, for Metallic Corrugated Legs—Bronze medal.

Marsh & Co., No. 2 Vesey-street, for Supporters and Surgical Appliances, a Silver medal having been before awarded—Diploma.

Marsh & Co., No. 2 Vesey-street, for an instrument for the purpose of extending the leg or thigh—Bronze medal.

Haggerty Bros., No. 10 Platt-street, for Mattison's Syringes—Diploma.

FURNITURE, SHOW CASES, ETC.

Lorenz & Cone, No. 13 North William-street, New-York, for the best Show Cases—Silver medal.

J. H. Fraser, corner of Reade and Hudson-street, New-York, for well-made Show Cases—Diploma.

John Dagmer, No. 39 Mercer-street, for a shut-up Table and Chairs combined, an ingenious piece of work—Diploma.

George P. Sloat & Co., Philadelphia, Penn., Mrs. H. C. Suplee, Agent, No. 537 Broadway, New-York, for an elegant Rosewood Cabinet—Diploma.

Fischer & Bro., No. 126 Macdougal-street, for a black and gilt Lady's Writing Table and Pedestal—Diploma.

HOUSE FURNISHING GOODS.

H. H. Cary, — Broadway, New-York, for an assortment of House Furnishing Goods—Silver medal.

E. D. Bassford, Cooper Union Building, for an assortment of House Furnishing Goods—Silver medal.

Wheeler & Wilson, Sewing Machine Company, No. 505 Broadway, for Foote's Patent Umbrella Lock-Stand—Silver medal.

J. R. Browne, No. 212 Broadway, for Metallic Weather Strips—Bronze medal.

Stephen W. Smith, 498 Broadway, New-York, for Patent Locomotive Cantering Horses—Bronze medal.

L. Tibbals, No. 512 Broadway, for a Spring Hobby Horse—Diploma.

D. S. Plume, No. 59 Duane-street, for Balsley's Patent Step Ladder—Diploma.

Vincent Fountain, Jr., Staten Island, N. Y., for a Step and House Ladder combined—Diploma.

S. Bissicks, No. 294 Bowery, for a Wash and Water Stand combined—Diploma.

Steele & Co., No. 3 Park-row, for Ostrich Feather Dusters—Bronze medal.

Jas. Murtagh, No. 1,335 Broadway, New-York, for a Dumb Waiter—Bronze medal.

E. T. Woodward, No. 43 Gold-street, New-York, for Tea-kettles and Boilers—Diploma.

John G. West, No. 4 Liberty-place, for a Mangle—Diploma.

Hiram Young, No. 20 John-street, for the best Silver-plated Ware—Silver medal.

E. D. Bassford, Cooper Union, New-York City, for second best Silver-plated Ware—Diploma.

BURIAL CASES, ETC.

W. J. & A. E. Lyman, East Hampton, Mass., for Indestructible Burial Cases and Indicating Ventilators—Silver medal.

Wm. G. Lord & Co., No. 37 Park-row, for the best Bier for burying the dead, (Fitzgerald's patent,—Bronze medal.

Wm. G. Lord & Co., Newark, N. J., for a Patent Bier for burying the dead, (Scarlett's patent,—Diploma.

HARDWARE, ETC.

H. Getty, No. 55 Willow-street, Brooklyn, for the best Pipe Wrench—Bronze medal.

H. F. Read, Nos. 55 and 57 First-street, Brooklyn, for the second best Pipe Wrench—Diploma.

C. B. Rogers, Norwich, Conn., for Blondin Skates—Diploma.

American Spiral Spring Hinge Company, W. W. Hayes, Agent, No. 198 Broadway, New-York, for Spiral Spring Hinges—Diploma.

John Russell, Williamsburgh, L. I., for a Patent Dressing Case—Diploma.

SIGNS, GRAINING, SHOW CARDS, ETC.

Chromo-Fulgent Print Company, No. 156 William-street, New-York, for Gelatined Pictures and Show Cards—Silver medal.

Albert B. Waldron, Nos. 155 and 157 Broadway, for Medallion Show Cards—Diploma.

Ashe, Dayton & Co., Nos. 159 and 161 Mercer-street, for an excellent Sign—Diploma.

Cyrus Griffith, No. 49 East Twelfth-street, for Sign Painting and Gilding on Glass—Diploma.

Barney & Stiles, No. 40 Hudson-street, for Lettering on Glass—Bronze medal.

E. Y. Clark, No. 278 Spring-street, for Lettering on Wire Shade—Bronze medal.

A. Warnesson, No. 416 Sixth-avenue, for Metallic Sign—Bronze medal.

Stewart S. Bannon, No. 148 East Thirty-sixth-street, for specimen of Graining—Diploma.

SADDLERY.

Peck Brothers, No. 61 Chambers-street, for an Improvement in Saddles—Bronze medal.

MILLINERY.

Isaac Binns, No. 309 Hudson-street, for the best Millinery—Bronze medal.

Mrs. A. A. Binns, No. 551 Broadway, for the second best Millinery—Diploma.

Mrs. Wm. Simmons, No. 637 Broadway, for specimens of Millinery—Diploma.

PHOTOGRAPHS.

J. Gurney & Sons, No. 707 Broadway, for the best

[*Continued on Eighth Page.*]

The New-York Times.

VOL. XIII—NO. 3794. NEW-YORK, FRIDAY, NOVEMBER 20, 1863. PRICE THREE CENTS.

IMPORTANT FROM EAST TENNESSEE

The Rebels Advancing upon Knoxville.

THE PLACE COMPLETELY INVESTED.

HEAVY SKIRMISHING YESTERDAY.

The Position Very Strongly Fortified.

THE REBEL FORCES UNDER LONGSTREET.

KNOXVILLE, Thursday, Nov. 17.

The enemy began skirmishing from their position on Kingston Road, at 10 this morning. Our advance alone, composed wholly of mounted infantry and cavalry, occupied the position, under command of Gen. SANDERS, and each man fought like a veteran. At noon the enemy opened with artillery at short range, their battery protected by a large house. BENJAMIN's battery was the only one which replied, occupying the chief fortification, half a mile in front of and to the right of the town. A desperate charge was made by the enemy about 3 P. M. Our men were protected by rail barricades on the crest of the hill. Gen. SANDERS was severely wounded, and was borne from the field.

We yielded the position, and fell back about a third of a mile to a stronger one. We have lost about one hundred, one quarter of whom were killed. The enemy had completely invested the place, but Gen. BURNSIDE will defend it to the last man, and it is believed successfully. The troops are in the best spirits. Every important point is fortified, and confidence prevails that we shall whip the enemy out.

A MORE DETAILED ACCOUNT.

KNOXVILLE, Tenn., Tuesday, Nov. 17.

Gen. LONGSTREET, after crossing the Tennessee on Saturday morning, 14th inst., was attacked in the afternoon by Gen. BURNSIDE, who drove the advance guard back to within a mile of the river's edge by nightfall.

LONGSTREET crossed the remainder of his troops during the night, and on Sunday morning advanced in force.

Gen. BURNSIDE, finding it impossible to cope with him with the small force at his disposal, fell back to Lenoir, the rear guard skirmishing heavily with the enemy through the day.

Three desperate charges were made upon our positions during Sunday night, but they were handsomely repulsed.

On Monday morning Gen. BURNSIDE evacuated Lenoir, but owing to the energy with which the rebel pursuit was kept up, determined to give them a decided check, and accordingly came into line of battle at Campbell's Station, when a fight ensued, lasting from late in the forenoon until dark. Our first position commanding the road from both sides, the infantry deployed in front of this, and were soon attacked by the enemy, who made several gallant charges, and finally succeeded, by outflanking our men, in driving them to the cover of the batteries, which now opened a terrific and destructive fire. The rebels retired before it, gave way, and eventually fell back to the river.

It was now three o'clock in the afternoon. The rebels showing a desire to renew the attack, and having brought three batteries to their assistance, Gen. BURNSIDE fell back to a more desirable position and again gave them battle. The contest continued, closing at nightfall, with our troops in possession of their own ground.

The object of the fight having been attained, and as the detention of the rebels had enabled our trains to get all in advance, our troops fell back during the night and early Tuesday morning reached Knoxville, where a great battle is expected to be fought to-morrow.

Yesterday the rebel advance guard attacked our outposts upon the Loudon and Clinton roads and heavy skirmishing continued all day.

This morning the attack was resumed when the fog which set in during the night had lifted. The rebels finding it impossible to drive our men with infantry, brought several guns into position, and poured in a flanking fire.

In the afternoon they brought forward a heavy force of infantry once more, and, after a brief skirmish, charged our position. A terrific hand to hand conflict occurred—both sabres and revolvers being used on both sides. Our men fought with the greatest gallantry, but at last were compelled to fall back about a third of a mile, to a strong line, which they hold to-night.

We have to regret the wounding of Gen. SANDERS and Capt. SIMES, of the cavalry, who commanded the outpost. His condition is critical. Lieut.-Col. SMITH, of the Twentieth Michigan, was killed at Campbell's Station. Our loss in that fight was between two and three hundred. Our loss to-day will not exceed one hundred and fifty.

Our men are in the best of spirits and perfectly confident of success to-morrow.

LATE FROM CHATTANOOGA.

Correspondence of the New-York Times.

CHATTANOOGA, Monday, Nov. 16, 1863.

The stream of deserters from the enemy continues to increase. Among them are some of the Vicksburgh paroled prisoners, who are much exercised regarding their *status*. From information which they bring it is now rendered certain that LONGSTREET is operating against BURNSIDE in East Tennessee.

The weather for the past few days has been very fine, and the roads are in excellent condition.

REPORTS FROM REBEL SOURCES.

ATLANTA, Friday, Nov. 13.

Nothing from the front this morning. A party of Georgia State troops and Indians killed the notorious BRYSON and thirty-four of his men, a short time since, on the line between Georgia and North Carolina.

A special to the *Register*, dated Sweet Water, Nov. 12, says: "*The Federals have removed all their supplies to Knoxville for safety*, and are living on half rations. Several deserters, recaptured, were executed here yesterday."

A special to the *Intelligencer* says: "Two Yankee officers who deserted and came into our lines, report that GRANT expects soon to assault Lookout. His army is on half rations.

THE ARMY OF THE POTOMAC.

Cavalry Skirmish at Germanna Ford—Great Scarcity of Contrabands—The Army Being Paid Off.

WASHINGTON, Thursday, Nov. 19.

The intelligence received to-night from the Army of the Potomac is to the effect that a cavalry skirmish between 200 rebels and part of the Eighteenth Pennsylvania cavalry took place yesterday morning at Germanna [illegible] on the Rapidan. The rebels crossed the river, [illegible] our men fell back [illegible] pickets, [illegible] loss was small. [illegible] were captured. [illegible] reviews and division drills, the country and weather being favorable for such purposes.

Hundreds of contrabands could be profitably employed in the army as drivers, teamsters, &c. In one artillery brigade alone, a sufficient number of soldiers are employed as wagoners and teamsters, to man a six-gun battery, for want of negroes.

Yesterday evening some cannonading was heard in the direction of the Rapidan south of Culpepper, but no particulars had been received when the messenger this afternoon left the army.

No sutlers have yet been granted right of transportation for their stores to the army. A few occasionally succeed in passing goods, but they are liable to arrest and confiscation.

Paymasters are busily at work in the discharge of their duties in almost all, if not all, the army corps.

THE HEROES OF JULY.

A Solemn and Imposing Event.

Dedication of the National Cemetery at Gettysburgh.

IMMENSE NUMBERS OF VISITORS.

Oration by Hon. Edward Everett—Speeches of President Lincoln, Mr. Seward and Governor Seymour.

THE PROGRAMME SUCCESSFULLY CARRIED OUT.

The ceremonies attending the dedication of the National Cemetery commenced this morning by a grand military and civic display, under command of Maj.-Gen. COUCH. The line of march was taken up at 10 o'clock, and the procession marched through the principal streets to the Cemetery, where the military formed in line and saluted the President. At 11¼ the head of the procession arrived at the main stand. The President and members of the Cabinet, together with the chief military and civic dignitaries, took position on the stand. The President seated himself between Mr. SEWARD and Mr. EVERETT after a reception marked with the respect and perfect silence due to the solemnity of the occasion, every man in the immense gathering uncovering on his appearance.

The military were formed in line extending around the stand, the area between the stand and military being occupied by civilians, comprising about 15,000 people and including men, women and children. The attendance of ladies was quite large. The military escort comprised one squadron of cavalry, two batteries of artillery and a regiment of infantry, which constitutes the regular funeral escort of honor for the highest officer in the service.

After the performance of a funeral dirge, by BIRGFIELD, by the band, an eloquent prayer was delivered by Rev. Mr. STOCKTON, as follows:

O God, our Father, for the sake of the Son, our Saviour, inspire us with thy spirit, and sanctify us to the right fulfilment of the duties of this occasion. We come to dedicate this new historic centre as a National Cemetery. If all the Departments of the one Government thou hast ordained over our Union, and of the many Governments which Thou has subordinated to the Union be there represented; if all classes, relations and interests of our blended brotherhood of people stand severally and thoroughly apparent in Thy presence, we trust it is because Thou hast called us, that Thy blessing awaits us, and that Thy designs may be embodied in practical results of incalculable, imperishable good. And so with thy holy Apostle and with the Church in all lands and ages, we unite in the ascription: Blessed be God, even the Father of Our Lord Jesus Christ, the Father of Moses, and the God of all comfort, who comforteth us in all our tribulation, that we may be able to comfort them which are in any trouble by the comfort wherewith we ourselves are comforted of God. In emulation of all angels, in fellowship with all saints, and in sympathy with all sufferers, in remembrance of Thy works, in reverence of Thy ways, and in accordance with Thy word, we love and magnify Thy infinite perfections, Thy creative glory, Thy redeeming grace, Thy providential goodness, and the progressive, richer and fairer development of thy supreme, universal and everlasting administration. In behalf of all humanity, whose ideal is divine, whose first memory is thy image lost, whose last hope is thy image restored; especially in behalf of our own nation, whose position is so peerless, whose mission is so sublime, and whose future is so attractive; we thank Thee for the unspeakable patience of thy compassion and for the exceeding greatness of thy loving kindness. In contemplation of Eden, Calvary and Heaven, of Christ in the God on the cross, and on the throne—nay, more—of Christ as coming again in all-subduing power and glory; we gratefully prolong our homage by this altar of sacrifice, on this field of deliverance, on this mount of salvation, within the fiery and bloody line of these mountains and rocks, looking back to the dark days of fear and of trembling, and the rapture of relief that came after, we multiply our thanksgivings and confess our obligations to renew and perfect our personal and social consecration to thy service and glory. O, had it not been for God! for our enemies, they came unresisted, multitudinous, mighty, flushed with victory and sure of success; they exalted on our mountains; they reveled in our valleys; they feasted, they rested, they slept, they awakened, they grew stronger, prouder and bolder every day; they spread abroad, they concentrated here; they looked beyond this horizon to the stores of wealth, to the haunts of pleasure and the seats of power in our Capital and chief cities; they prepared to cast the chain of Slavery around the form of freedom, and to bind life and death together forever. Their premature triumph was the mockery of God and man. One more victory, and all was theirs. But behind these hills was heard the feebler march of a smaller but still a pursuing host; onward they hurried, day and night, for their country and their God; footsore, wayworn, hungry, thirsty, faint, but not in heart; they came to dare all, to bear all, and to do all that is possible to heroes. At first they met the blast on the plain, and bent before it like trees; but then led by Thy hand to the hills, they took their stand on the these rocks, and remained as firm and immovable as they. In vain were they assaulted; all art, all violence, all desperation failed to dislodge them. Baffled, bruised, broken, their enemies retired and disappeared. Glory to God for this rescue! But, Oh! the slain, in the freshness and fullness of their young and manly life! with such sweet memories of father and mother, brother and sister, wife and children, maiden and friend. From the coasts beneath the Eastern star; from the shores of Northern lakes and rivers; from the flowers of the Western prairies; from the homes of the midway and the border, they came here to die for us and for mankind! Alas! How little we can do for them! We come with the humility of prayer, with the pathetic eloquence of venerable wisdom, with the tender beauty of poetry, with the plaintive harmony of music, with the honest tribute of our Chief Magistrate, and with all this honorable attendance; but our best hope is in Thy blessings. O Lord, Our God, bless us. O, Our Father, bless the bereaved, whether absent or present. Bless our sick and wounded soldiers and sailors. Bless all our rulers and people. Bless our army and navy. Bless the efforts to suppress this rebellion, and bless all the associations of this day, and place, and scene, forever. As the trees are not dead, though their foliage is gone, so our heroes are not dead though their forms have fallen. In their proper personality they are all with thee, and the spirit of their example is here. It fills the air, it fills our hearts, and as long as time shall last it will hover in these skies and rest on these landscapes, and pilgrims of our own land and of all lands, will thrill with its inspiration, and increase and confirm their devotion to liberty, religion and God.

Mr. EVERETT then commenced the delivery of his oration, which was listened to with marked attention throughout. [The oration of Mr. EVERETT will be found on our second page.]

[The oration of Mr. EVERETT will be found on our second page.]

Although a heavy fog clouded the heavens in the morning during the procession, the sun broke out in all its brilliancy during the Rev. Mr. STOCKTON's prayer and shone upon the magnificent spectacle. The assemblage was of great magnitude, and was gathered within a circle of great extent around the stand, which was located on the highest point of ground on which the battle was fought. A long line of military surrounded the position taken by the immense multitude of people.

The Marshal took up a position on the left of the stand. Numerous flags and banners, suitably draped, were exhibited on the stand among the audience. The entire scene was one of grandeur due to the importance of the occasion. So quiet were the people that every word uttered by the orator of the day must have been heard by them all, notwithstanding the immensity of the concourse.

Among the distinguished persons on the platform were the following: Governors Bradford, of Maryland, Curtin, of Pennsylvania, Morton, of Indiana, Seymour, of New-York; Parker, of New-Jersey, and Tod, of Ohio; Ex-Gov. Dennison, of Ohio; John Brough, Governor Elect, of Ohio; Charles Anderson, Lieutenant-Governor of Ohio; Major-Generals Schenck, Stahel, Doubleday, and Couch; Brigadier-General Gibbon; and Provost-Marshal-General Fry.

PRESIDENT LINCOLN'S ADDRESS.

The President then delivered the following dedicatory speech:

Fourscore and seven years ago our Fathers brought forth upon this Continent a new nation, conceived in liberty and dedicated to the proposition that all men are created equal. [Applause.] Now we are engaged in a great civil war, testing whether that nation, or any nation so conceived and so dedicated, can long endure. We are met on a great battle-field of that war. We are met to dedicate a portion of it as the final resting-place of those who here gave their lives that that nation might live. It is altogether fitting and proper that we should do this. But in a larger sense we cannot dedicate. We cannot consecrate, we cannot hallow this ground. The brave men, living and dead, who struggled here have consecrated it far above our power to add or detract. [Applause.] The world will little note nor long remember what we say here, but it can never forget what they did here. [Applause.] It is for us, the living, rather to be dedicated here to the refinished work that they have thus so far nobly carried on. [Applause.] It is rather for us to be here dedicated to the great task remaining before us, that from these honored dead we take increased devotion to that cause for which they here gave the last full measure of devotion; that we here highly resolve that the dead shall not have died in vain; [applause] that the Nation shall under God have a new birth of freedom, and that Governments of the people, by the people and for the people, shall not perish from the earth. [Long continued applause.]

Three cheers were then given for the President and the Governors of the States.

After the delivery of the addresses, the dirge and the benediction closed the exercises, and the immense assemblage separated at about 4 o'clock.

About 3 o'clock in the afternoon, the Fifth New York regiment of heavy artillery, Col. MURRAY, was marched to the temporary residence of Gov. SEYMOUR, where they passed in review before the Governor, presenting a handsome spectacle. Upon the conclusion of this ceremony, which attracted quite a crowd of sight-seers, Gov. SEYMOUR presented a handsome silk regimental standard to the regiment, accompanying the gift with the following speech:

GOV. SEYMOUR'S SPEECH.

SOLDIERS OF NEW-YORK: We love our whole country, without reservation. But while we do so, it is not inconsistent with that perfect and generous loyalty to love and to be proud of our own State. This day, when I took part in the celebration that was to consecrate yonder battle-field, while I felt as an American citizen, proud of my own country, and proud of the gallant services of her citizens, in every State, nevertheless my eye did involuntarily wander to that field where lie the glorious dead of our good and great State, and when I returned, to see marching before me your manly and sturdy columns, not knowing you belonged to New-York, my heart did quicken and my pulse tingle, to learn that you were acting commissions issued by myself; I am most proud and most happy that I have have this opportunity, on behalf of the merchants of the great commercial City of New-York, to present to you this glorious banner, which has been sent as a token of their confidence in your loyalty and your courage, and your fidelity in the hour of danger. Sergeant, I place these colors in your hands in the firm confidence that they will be borne through every field of triumph, of toil and of danger, in a way that will do honor to yourselves, to the great State which you represent, and the still greater country, to which we all belong. My God bless you as you serve your country in the distant field of danger. We find in those glorious fields you left behind you are not indifferent to this conflict; are not indifferent to the welfare of the whole Union. I do not doubt, therefore, that when you shall return from your dangerous fields of duty, you shall bring back this standard to place among the archieves of our State with honorable mention of the services her sons have performed. I do not doubt that though it may perhaps be returned torn and stained, yet it will be still more glorious, and with glorious recollections clustering around it. In concluding these remarks, I ask in return of the men of New-York, to give three cheers for the Union of our country, and three cheers for the flag of our land.

Gen. SCHENCK followed in a short speech.

A subscription of $280 was made by the Marshals attending these ceremonies, to be devoted to the relief of the Richmond prisoners.

In the afternoon, the Lieutenant-Governor elect of Ohio, Col. ANDERSON, delivered an oration at the Presbyterian Church.

The President and party returned to Washington at 6 o'clock this evening, followed by the Governors' trains. Thousands of persons were gathered at the depot, anxiously awaiting transportation to their homes; but they will probably be confined to the meagre accommodations of Gettysburgh till to-morrow.

DEPARTMENT OF THE GULF.

ARRIVAL OF THE CREOLE FROM NEW-ORLEANS.

The Attack upon Gen. Washburn's Column.

Our Entire Loss Six Hundred and Seventy-seven.

The steamship *Creole*, Capt. THOMPSON, arrived yesterday morning from New-Orleans, bringing dates to the 10th inst. Further accounts from the Teche country concerning the attack on WASHBURN's column represents our whole loss in killed and wounded and taken prisoners at 677. The Indiana Sixty-seventh was captured almost entire; the Sixtieth Indiana and Ohio Ninety-sixth lost largely. The rebel force was as five to one. We only excelled them in artillery, by means of which, at short range, it is thought, we killed a large number of the enemy. It is reported that the Thirteenth army corps, now in the Teche country, is ordered back to Memphis.

The attack was made by the enemy in force of 5,000 upon our rear guard, only 1,800 strong. The enemy captured two pieces of artillery, but one of them was subsequently retaken. The fight took place at Buzzard Prairie, on the east side of Bayou Teche.

Gen. PRICE was reported at Alexandria with 15,000 men, and for this reason, as well as the impossibility of getting supplies, it was deemed best to fall back.

Gens. THOMAS and WADSWORTH arrived in New-Orleans on the 10th inst.

THE DELAWARE ELECTION.

The Union Ticket Overwhelmingly Successful—Smithers, for Congress, Walked the Course.

WILMINGTON, Thursday, Nov. 19.

The election in this State passed off quietly. The Copperheads, seeing defeat staring them in the face, abandoned the contest. BROWN did not withdraw, but the leaders, knowing they would be compelled to proclaim themselves loyal men in order to vote, gave the key-note for the whole party to stay at home. SMITHERS walked the course. Newcastle County gives SMITHERS 4,014 votes, and BROWN 6 votes. In six Districts of Kent County, SMITHERS has 1,275 votes, BROWN none. In five Districts of Sussex County, SMITHERS has 844 votes, and BROWN 7 votes, showing a gain for SMITHERS over FISHER's vote of last year in this county.

J. T. HEALD,
Chairman State Committee.

GREAT BRITAIN AND AMERICA.

Welcome to Rev. Henry Ward Beecher.

Demonstration at the Brooklyn Academy of Music.

A GREAT SPEECH:

His Impressions of British Feeling Toward America.

An immense audience assembled at the Academy of Music, Brooklyn, last evening, to welcome and hear the Rev. HENRY WARD BEECHER. The meeting was under the auspices of the War Fund Committee, the entire proceeds to be devoted to the Sanitary Commission. Rev. Dr. STORRS made an eloquent address of welcome to Mr. BEECHER, who, on his appearance, was most enthusiastically greeted. When quiet was restored Mr. BEECHER spoke as follows:

MR. BEECHER'S ADDRESS.

I will not attempt to disguise the deep feeling with which your generous kindness, expressed in the words of my brother, affect me. I am more touched and more stirred by this sympathy than by all that I have seen and by all that I have experienced in the whole of my travel abroad; and I speak the simple truth, which has the witness in your hearts, that it is here in this city more than anywhere else that I desire to be so greeted. For as, when in England, it was my pride to be an American, so when I am in America, it is my pride to be a citizen of Brooklyn; and I accept your generous confidence, and this affecting testimony of it, in so far as it relates to me personally, with profound sensibility and with deep gratitude. I thank you; and yet I should be vain if I supposed that this was meant for me in my simple individuality. I am myself the effect of American institutions; I am made by them and if I have done any service to the public worthy of your regard, I owe it to this very public and the institutions which enrich it the power to do it any service. And I am glad that it is so—so deep are my feelings of patriotism, so profoundly am I impressed with the grandeur of this latest and ripest development of civil life, that I am more than willing to be sunk myself if my decadence and disappearance could add anything to the glory of my country. I would fain be as the oil in the lamp that gives its life, that the light may be bright which consumes it. And that which is my feeling is your feeling, and I know I bear your sympathy with me in this simple and artless expression of my feelings to-night. I am glad that you asked me to be present; and I am proud that it shall go abroad that when I came back to America, having witnessed as I could in Europe for the truth of our cause, the first place to greet me was my own home, where I am best known. It is, indeed, a wreath which I shall wear none the less because it is invisible. I went abroad, as you know, simply as a private citizen. It was tauntingly asked me, on my arrival in England, why, in the very height and paroxysm of our national agony, I abandoned the field to go abroad. I did not answer, but I now do answer. I foresaw that the Autumn and the Winter would require labors even greater than any period previous, and the excitement and the excessive labors of the two and a half years, or three years preceding, had not destroyed my health nor destroyed my constitution; but certainly I was jaded, and I feared to go into the labor of the Autumn and Winter, which required the best powers of every man, without my full strength; and since I could do nothing in the Summer, I took that opportunity, upon the generous invitation of my own people, to go abroad and rest, that I might come back to labor more assiduously. Allow me to say that this generosity of my own dear people was a comfort to me everywhere, and that in Great Britain—not because I disesteemed their kindness or undervalued their hospitality, but because it was something that I cherished with a secret pride—I refused to received their hospitality or, in the remotest degree, compensation in any form. I said to them, my own people sent me abroad, and it is their pleasure that I shall stand upon them for support, and I will not take one penny from the hand of an Englishman. [Applause.] You will not misunderstand me; it was not because I disdained their kindness, but because I valued yours. It was also said that I had come abroad sent by our Government. That would have spoiled it all. I had no official character, and would not have had one. I went simply as a private citizen, and I was there merely and only as an American citizen. And when, unsought and, indeed, against my feelings, if not against my judgment, I entered upon the labor of the past few weeks of my sojourn in England, I assumed the responsibility, I cannot say with trembling, for I am not accustomed much to tremble; but I assumed the responsibility with the gravest sense of what it was. I have felt the inspiration of nationality often, but I never before was placed between two such great people, where I saw them both in prospective, both in their present relations and in their future. I never before felt so much as I felt all the time, waking or dreaming, night or day, what it was to stand and plead for the unity of these two great nations, for the sake of struggling mankind; and it was at once an excitement to me and a support. But, after all, I did not know how my countrymen would regard my efforts. If you had disapproved, I should have been sorry that you disapproved, but not sorry for what I had done. I did the best I knew how to do, every time, everywhere disinterestedly, for the love I bear to the cause and to the principles which underlie it, and I had no word, could not have, from home whether my representations of policy, and of fact, and of history, and of the tendencies of things, would accord with yours, or whether I should not be caught up in the whirl of conflicting parties, my reasonings traversed, my arguments denied—not till I landed in Boston did I hear one whisper—and then I learned for the first time that my services had been accepted by my countrymen. [Applause.] But to-night I meet you a citizen returned among his friends, profoundly thankful that the labor and the service which I attempted for the public good have the seal of their approbation. It is my purpose not to trespass any further upon your time in matters that are personal to myself. I know that you will not think me vain for what I have said, and I desire now this evening to speak upon that which you all have come to hear—namely, my impressions and experiences in respect to the condition of things in Great Britain, as they relate to this struggle and this country. Among the wise things said by that wisest of modern political writers, DE TOCQUEVILLE, is this: "That it is impossible to judge of the affairs of one country by applying to them the experiences and the rules of another one." There are many reasons why one would have presumed beforehand that it was easy to understand British feeling and British policy. There was a similarity of institutions and a sameness of radical principles; but that very similarity, since it begets, by different institutions and different vehicles, different policies in the end, is liable to deceive us, and we are liable to come to many conclusions, because, upon the face, things look like those to which we are accustomed at home. I myself have experienced that, for I had judged of the condition of England from the impressions produced upon me by my first four weeks' tarry there in the Summer. I should have judged very wrongly, as judged by my present convictions. Nor do I feel myself now adequate to analyze or state either the causes or the results of my feeling. I am quite aware that I am imperfect in my views in many directions. Nor can I presume to say that I present you opinions. My nature gives intensity to my expressions, and yet I wish beforehand to ask you to consider that the statements that I make are impressions liable to mistake, subject to corrections that may afterward be made in them. And with these preliminary remarks I will tell you what I saw and found. You are aware that the original expression of our people was almost universal that in Great Britain we should find a sympathizer, ready and prepared. One thing we counted sure, and that was, that if all the other nations stood aloof, there was one that would stand by us in the hour of our peril, and that was Great Britain. And the sharpness of our retaliatory complaints was acuminated by that very disappointment of a very confident conviction. When I was asked in Great Britain why the American Press so severely inveighed against England, and was almost silent in respect to France, I said: "Because we in our deepest hearts care for England, and not much for France." [Applause.] "Because under anger, and lower down than prejudice, when you strike the deeper feelings, the Americans know that they have an English origin, and they are proud of their history; when it gets back further than the present generation, [laughter;] and it was this growing affection and sympathy in the best natures and in the best parts of the best natures—it was this that made the disappointment of public expectation so sharp and so hard to be borne when Great Britain foiled our expectations and gave us no sympathy. We never asked for help. We never asked that she should lend us anything or stretch out so much as the little finger of her right hand. We did ask simply the generous confidence and generous moral sympathy and that was all, and that we did not get, and we felt sharply, the conduct of England. The expression of public feeling had an effect of throwing her moral weight against the North and for the South. So I told them. I carefully discriminated between the intention and the result. What men intend has much to do with judging of their moral character; but what men do does not depend always on their intention. And when, therefore, the British people disclaimed sympathy with the South, or a disposition to go against their own principles as represented by the North, I said to them, "What your intentions are you can best judge, but what the effect of your attitude is we on the other side can best judge," and we know that the moral influence of Great Britain has substantially gone for more than two years to help the rebellion of the slavocracy of the South, and to hinder the progress of free institutions in the North. And if there is rescue or relief—if there is redemption finally, Great Britain must stand aside, and it must be said: "The nation that boasted of her free institutions and her sovereign sympathy with the welfare of the common peoples has had no part nor lot in the great work." [Applause.] The denial of moral sympathy in Great Britain was only interpreted by the active exertions of certain parts of the British people on behalf of the South, so much so that it, I think, will scarcely be denied by any man that if the shipyards, and foundries, and looms, and shops of Great Britain had refused their succor to rebellion, the rebellion would have died out in the nation long ago. I said in private what it did not seem altogether judicious to say in public, that in some sense I might bring this war and lay it at the feet of the British people, and say, not that you intended it, but that the course of conduct pursued, legal or illegal, was such that, but for you, the rebellion would have perished almost in the beginning of it. [Applause.] And no man but knows that there was also in England an extraordinary spectacle of men who, from sheer hatred of war, by misjudgment and mistake were left to foment it. There never was a misposition more signal than that of the British public, as represented in their leading intelligent classes, in this conflict. There never was a case where a nation, by its upper classes, went so unquestionably in favor of slavery at the same time that they occupied themselves in the intensest denunciations of slavery—that went against free society at the very time they were particularly praising free society and arrogating to themselves its highest claims and honors. Under such circumstances we were, you recollect, drifting right toward war. I told the British people that war was not our choice, and yet terrible and cruel as it was, there was something in this struggle so near to us, and so indispensable to national life, that rather than that there should be interference, rather than there should be disruption and dismemberment, rather than that this republican free Government should fail, we would stand war with Great Britain, with France, with Europe. [Applause.] It would have been difficult to say this without the appearance of threat; but that difficulty was itself dissolved by the iterated and reiterated charges brought against me of having been bellicose in my own country, and of having threatened all manner of desolation to Great Britain; and my reply was this, that I felt a part, and full part in proportion, of the deep indignation which my own people felt against Great Britain, and that I had never desired war, and abhorred it, but that I held the great principles of free Republican Government to be so precious that we would not give them up, not even at the threat nor infliction of war, no matter who brought it upon us. This being the cruel disappointment that we experienced in our expectation of sympathy from Great Britain, you will ask me, "What did you find to the facts and condition of things?" I found, in the first place, on going there, that every man I met was a Southern man, not literally born in the South, but this is the division they have themselves made. These are the terms applied. They are Southerners and Northerners even more than we are here. I found that on the railways, on the boats, in the hotels, wherever there was a traveling public, there was a public that sympathized with the South, and adverse to the North. It was not an uncommon thing to hear a gentleman who had talked freely and kindly with me on other matters say as the news was discussed, "Bad news we have got by the last steamer." "Ah, what is the news?" being a little troubled. "I understand," he would reply, "that MEADE has driven LEE entirely out of Pennsylvania." [Laughter.] "God send us much more bad news, then," said I. But coming from communities enthusiastic and almost homogeneous on this subject, it was strange to my ears to hear well-dressed and well-read men congratulate themselves on disasters to the North, and rejoicing in the success of the South; and such is the case. Nor will there return to your side one young man has been traveling that will not bring back to you this substantial account; that wherever he went almost every man whom he met, without exception, was against the North and in favor of the South; and you can well imagine the impression that would be made on the mind of such. They would say "There is no question about this matter—the whole British nation is against us." Go where you will, up or down, you will find it all the same, and that was the effect impressed upon my mind. On still further inquiry, I was disappointed to find that that body to which I myself belonged—the Congregationalists, known as Independents in England. I had supposed, since they are set for a testimony for freedom and have been arrayed almost invariably on the side of struggling peoples and struggling liberties, I supposed I should find them right, I did not. I do not mean that there is not a very large part of that power whose principles are right. They will be included under the head which I shall mention by and by, but I am sorry to say that I did not find the influential and leading clergymen of that denomination, nor the influential and leading laymen on our side. They said that they sympathized with liberty. Yes, they sympathized with liberty just exactly as the icicles sympathize with sunlight and Summer. [Laughter.] It chills you to come near them; and I said to them, I want no such sympathy, and I want nothing if it cannot come from enthusiastic hearts, it does no good and we do not want it. I found also the most profound ignorance of our affairs and of the operation of our institutions, and that, too, in quarters where I had a right to expect more intelligence. I found the most active and unscrupulous efforts made by Southern men to stir up animosity toward our country. And let me say that the bad cause was better served than a good one there, as to some extent it has been in our own land, for I am sure that the South, for a bad cause, has more nearly put forth every particle of strength that it has to put forth than we have for a good cause. And as it is at home, it was abroad. Where we sent one man to England to influence public opinion, they sent a score; where we print one book of information, they a library; where we touched one spring, they touched a hundred. They seemed to pervade England, and they seemed, with the unerring instinct of selfishness and despotism, to know just where to undermine the generous and better feelings—just where to invoke the influence of ignorance—just where to touch men so that principle should fail and profit take its place. [Applause.] You may then imagine the surprise and skepticism with which, under these circumstances, I received the assurance of friends on every side that the great heart of the British nation was on our side. I had found nobody except unconditional friends of emancipation in whose society I was thrown—I had found almost nobody that spoke kindly of us or that seemed to be in sympathy with us, and yet my ears were filled with these assurances day and night. "You are mistaken, you are mistaken, this great English people are sound at heart." I said where under heavens do the English people keep their hearts, then? [Laughter and applause.] And if I had spoken in my early visit to England in June, I could not have spoken as I now do and shall. Neither on my first return from the Continent in September could I have understood and felt what I understand now, in some measure, and entirely believe that they were right, and that, after all, the great heart of the British nation is with us of the North. [Great applause.]

Let me take up, then, one part of society after another, and state, as I understand them to be, the facts. First, there is the great commercial class of England, those that are making money and those that have made it; if you please, call them the plutocracy. They are against us. In the first place there is a large class of men that are actively employed in supplying the South with all its necessaries—except principle, [laughter,] and they are making on suppose that they are making large fortunes. We cannot doubt which side they take. The next is a very large class of men who, for precisely an opposite reason, somehow are opposed to the North and in favor of the South; namely, those who have been accustomed to make money, but found this interrupting war has stopped their profits; and men that want to make money, but do not; they are opposed to us. And between these two classes lies an intermediate one of men, who are bewildered and perplexed, and see that business is more or less affected, as it is over the whole continent, by its sympathetic relations with this continent. They say when will this war end? and as the offensive is on the northern side, they feel as though whenever the North will stop *aggressing* the Sout the war will stop. So in the main they are against us. It may be lowered down to this: that while there are very noble exceptions here and there all through England—men that stand out of their class above and against it, not speaking comprehensibly, the commercial class of England are against the North, and in favor of the South. I have spoken of the religious people. It is very difficult for me to analyze the causes that have turned both the established churchmen and the dissenters in respect to their most influential men against us. I do not think so in respect to the laymen; but the influential laymen and the influential clergymen, I think, are adverse to us as a body. The ground usually taken is this: that the North is not sincere; and secondly, that the war is a great sin. And nowhere else in this world is there so tender a conscience on the subject of the war as Great Britain—when she is not waging it herself. [Great applause.] She has, I believe, only three wars on hand now—in China, Japan, and, I believe, in Australia—no matter where it is, it is somewhere; and the rest of her leisure she occupies with a profound regret and horror for this American war. If it was for but a ship on the sea, she was ready to go to war with us; if it was for the territory of a remote island in the Antartic Ocean, she was ready to go to war with the savages; if it was but to beat down the cities of Japan, she had no objection to burn the seat of 160,000 inhabitants in it; but when a people are making war for their own life, for everything that dignifies humanity, they stand throwing out their hands that men will make war. [Laughter.] But I am sorry to say that, while from the Friends, who have always maintained as against their own countrymen a consistent testimony against war, it should have been expected, from those men, that had no particular objection to the Crimean war, none to the opium war in China, and none to the war that they now have, if not on their hands, on the tips of their fingers. I told them to their faces, in Exeter Hall, there was not a land on the face of the globe against which they had not dashed their bloody prows and that their flag was a symbol of their history—a cross inscribed on a field of blood. [Great applause.] The English nobility, as a class are also against us. I shall read some very noble exceptions by-and-by. But these exceptions do not alter the general statement that the nobility as a class are against us. For the most obvious reason we are not accustomed to estimate the effect of our example upon European institutions. When he takes his walk abroad, it is not the elephant that weighs and measures its own gravity as he treads on the field-mouse's tail. It is the mouse that meditates. [Laughter.] A gigantic nation as this, on such a continent as this, while we are treading on the steps of accomplishing history, we are not feeling the jar that we ourselves are making; but they that have thrones and aristocratic privileges do; and they are the best interpreters of the reactionary influence of American ideas and American institutions. And it was the *Saturday Review*, that scholarly, keen, brilliant, unprincipled paper of England; it was that paper that had the frankness to say that Americans must not think that their remarks were because they disliked us, but it was because they found our ideas and our example working in Great Britain, and they were obliged in order to defeat these ideas in England to attack us in America. They are there, fighting home battles; for there is an unerring instinct—there is this feeling—that if a Government can be so efficient, covering such a continent, and so ludicrously cheap, how can we maintain our expensive and complicated Government in our sphere? Lest they should not think of it themselves, millions of common people, who are being taxed perpetually, suggest it to their attention. Do you suppose they do not know it? Do you not know that the effect of our Revolution was to send revolution all through Europe? The causes of it were all prepared. It was the torch of our Revolutionary war that set fire to the trains that burned all over Europe. They don't forget it. They dread the reactionary influence of American ideas. Such prosperity—such power and at so little expense—with so few monopolies and prerogatives to the favored classes. Therefore, when they oppose us, it is not to be construed as malignant opposition to us—it is nothing more than another form of self-love, for it is self defending itself. If you had been born with a coronet on your head, you would have done just so. [Laughter.] In Parliament, if a vote were taken to-day according to the private thoughts, sympathies and wishes among members, I suppose they would vote five to one against the North and in favor of the South. It is believed, too, by those well informed, that at least a portion of the Government have been entirely willing to go into a rupture with the North, and that but for the unflinching restraints they would have done so long ago. It is the impression throughout the realm that the Sovereign of Great Britain has been from the first our judicious but our steadfast friend. [Prolonged applause.] It is believed and so represented to me that her never rightly estimated and lamented consort was our fast friend, and that among the last acts of his life were those which erased from documents presented to him sentences that would have inflamed the growing anger. [Renewed applause.] He died with the blessing upon his head, "Blessed are the peacemakers." [Applause.] All through in the British Government, as at present constituted, (and I shall read you their names bye-and-bye,) there are several that are known to be warm and disinterested in their regard for the North, as there are others in that Government who, it is known in England—at least it was so represented to me by those who ought to know—who would not hesitate to plunge the Continent in a war for the sake of disrupting this nation. And if you ask me what is the great underlying influence that has been at work upon the upper class of England, I answer thus:

1. Commercial interest and rivalry therein.
2. Class power and the fear of contagion and American ideas.
3. (I know not how I shall say it so that it shall be the least offensive to our friends on the other side, but they have not come and you have not come to the bottom of the conduct of Great Britain until you have touched that delicate and real foundation cause.) We are too large and strong a nation. [Laughter.]

This is, in my judgment, the right of the whole matter. A distinguished clergyman of London, personally kind and friendly to me, said to me in these very words: "Mr. BEECHER, you may just as well have it said to you; you have been growing so strong that we have felt for a good many years that we had got to take you down, and we were very glad when the job was taken from our hands by your own people." [Laughter.] When Mr. ROEBUCK—whose speech it was my great privilege to hear—[laughter]—declared that same fact in Parliament, it was cheered immensely, but reprobated in the *Times* and in the other presses that sympathized with the South, not because he had not spoken the truth, but because it was a truth not best to be spoken. [Laughter.] It is said (and I intended to have brought here to-night to have read) in one of their recent publications—and it was the immediate cause of one of my speeches there—that we were a lawless and arrogant set of men; were proud of our sudden growth; and it is said that even Mr. BEECHER himself was regarded as a specimen of what they should have to deal with in the nation supposed to be composed of men breathing that sort of threats. [Laughter.] Now when men make such lamentable mistakes as to suppose that such a peaceful man as I am is so dangerous, [laughter] is it to be supposed that they would not make a mistake in estimating the whole nation? [Renewed laughter.] It is the sun that makes the seeds grow. It is the light that stimulates the seeds into growth; but under all this is the dunghill that makes the heat that causes the seeds to spring up under the genial influences of the sun. And it is just exactly that hot bed at the bottom, underneath, that works up and turns aside what would be otherwise insufficient to do so, the natural sympathies from the North. It is just that which has prepared them for this, that and the other prejudice and misinformation. With this state of facts you will ask how is it then that the English people have been restrained? How is it that they have not gone into overt belligerency? That is the very question that I propose to answer and in the statement that the English heart is on our side. [Applause.] The nobility is against us; the Government is divided and a part is against us. I think I may say that while the brains that represent progress in Great Britain are in our favor, yet the conservative intelligence of Great Britain is against us, and that all there is on the surface of society representing its dignities, its power and intelligence is Anti-American. And the question I propose to you is how with the papers, magazines and universities—how with their titled estates opposed to us, that they have been restrained from manifesting this in open hostility? It is because there is a great underlying influence that restrains them—it is the influence of that underlife, and to a very great extent of the non-voting English who have produced this effect. It is a thing I could not understand at first, and which it is very difficult for us to understand—for whenever in our country there is a majority of the votes there is sure to be a direction of affairs. But it is not so in England. I learned that the men who could not vote where they were united and determined had the power to control the men who do vote. This is not an anomaly, then. It would be in our institution, but it is not in English institutions—among other reasons, because in a nation where one class have a preeminence and privilege and the underlying class have none, all the instinct of self-preservation teaches this favored class never to goad that great underlying class into madness. There is always that dragon of of revolution coiled up that they are afraid to arouse. Therefore it is, that when the great under class of England is determined in one direction, they always carry their point; first or last, the upper classes have to give way. Men whose fortunes are made—men whose only thought of the future is to carry the rich freights of the present along into their future—that class are generally against us. Men who have no fortunes—men having very little in the present to care for, who are struggling for better fortunes for themselves and children—that class are on our side. They are in our favor, but they are a class who have not much voice—have very little expression, and they are therefore little heard. Their report is not wafted across, but their influence is felt on the other side of the sea. It seems to me that it is peculiarly fitting that we, who believe in the common people, should find ourselves opposed by the titled and strong, but should find our allies and fast friends in the emergency have been

[Continued on Eighth Page.]

The New-York Times.

VOL. XIII—NO. 3802. NEW-YORK, MONDAY, NOVEMBER 30, 1863. PRICE THREE CENTS.

Editorials

The Danger of Over Confidence.

It may not be amiss to caution the public against over-sanguine estimates of the recent victories of the Union arms. There seems to be no doubt that GRANT has achieved a very brilliant success, and has defeated BRAGG's army, which was the main strength of the rebellion in that quarter. It is not yet certain, however, that he has so routed and broken it as to prevent it from taking the field again, though it is not likely that its old strength can ever be renewed. BURNSIDE is still in a position of danger, though our latest advices indicate his ability to hold his ground until aid can reach him. MEADE, moreover, has commenced a movement against LEE, from which we may reasonably anticipate the best results, though it is well to remember that LEE is a much more formidable opponent to deal with than BRAGG.

If these movements are crowned with complete success, the back-bone of the rebellion will unquestionably be broken. We shall have seen the beginning of the end. But the end itself will not have been reached. Very much will remain to be done before resistance on the part of the rebels will cease, and the supremacy of the Constitution will be restored. There will still be elements of force scattered throughout the South powerful enough to require the presence and active efforts of a very large Union army, and to draw largely, for some time to come, upon the resources and the patience of the Government. For a long time, certainly for months and possibly for years, it will be necessary to maintain strong National garrisons in every part of the rebel States,—not only for the purpose of enforcing the authority of the National Government, but for the preservation of domestic peace. Our conquest, however complete, will leave society in the Southern States in a state of chaos and confusion. Its peace has rested hitherto solely on force,—on a system of repression more perfect in its details, and more rigid in its rule, than prevails in any other part of the world. This whole system will be overthrown, suddenly and by violence, and nothing is left to take its place. This lack must for a time, at least, be supplied by the National Government. The presence of very powerful Union armies will be absolutely essential in the Southern States for a long time after active hostilities against the National authority shall have ceased.

It must not be supposed, therefore, that the patriotic efforts of the friends of the Government can safely be relaxed. Every exertion must still be made to fill up the ranks of our armies. The volunteer movement should be pushed forward with steady and unremitted energy. The country will still have need of all the men it has called for. It must still expend enormous sums of money, and call upon the country for the largest contributions of men and means, to insure the complete and final overthrow of the rebellion.

The Union Victory in Georgia.

In the history of the military operations that have thus far marked the progress of the war, Gen. GRANT's operations of last week stand out in distinct relief as the one example, on either side, *of a victory followed up, and rendered decisive by the complete rout of the enemy.* It is this unique fact which forms the most striking characteristic in a success so magnificent in all the features of its planning and execution. Indeed, in the estimate of the great weight of debt under which Gen. GRANT has laid the nation by this victory, it is not easy to say whether we should set most by the material gain to the Union arms of this great blow inflicted on the enemy, or by the moral gain to the whole country of this inspiring example of unwonted military vigor and power. At a stroke, Gen. GRANT has brushed away the cobwebs of military pedantry, (dignified by the name of prudence,) which would make us believe that the pursuit of a defeated foe has become an impossibility; and in a country which accumulates in itself every condition unfavorable to pursuit (thus making it the more glorious), has ground to powder and scattered to the winds a great army of the rebellion, a week ago intrenched in a position so formidable by nature and art as to seem absolutely unassailable.

Gen. GRANT's victory has been so completely won "on the wing" that hardly a moiety of his captures in men and material have been made in battle. Indeed there has been throughout the week's operations, properly speaking, no great battle at all. GRANT caught BRAGG in the act of preparing for retreat, flung himself impetuously on the mountain lair, which the rebel Commander turned savagely to defend, routed him from it, and has since hung on his flanks and rear with the tenacity of a bloodhound. The first day's action, that of Monday, was for the enemy's advanced position, directly fronting Chattanooga, which was carried with trifling loss. Tuesday gave us the possession of the north slope of Lookout Mountain, carried by Gen. HOOKER, and the north slope of Mission Ridge, carried by Gen. SHERMAN. During the night of Tuesday, the rebels evacuated Lookout Mountain, and thereby the valley of Chattanooga. On Wednesday Gen. SHERMAN assaulted the rebel position on Missionary Ridge, and was repulsed, but a general advance of the whole line carried the Ridge. As the result of these three operations, between four and five thousand prisoners and forty pieces of artillery were taken. BRAGG's whole line, broken and shattered, fled during the night. "I believe," writes Gen. GRANT, "I am not premature in announcing a complete victory over BRAGG."

A General of the ordinary stamp would have rested abundantly satisfied with these three days' magnificent work. But GRANT is not a General of the ordinary stamp. Inspired with the Napoleonic maxim that nothing is done till all is done, *pursuit* presented itself as the next thing in order. "We will pursue the enemy in the morning," he writes on Wednesday night. Flying columns accordingly were promptly dispatched after the broken battalions of the enemy—HOOKER toward Ringgold, SHERMAN toward Redclay, and other corps wherever the enemy was to be found. This completed the work. It had been a defeat; it now became a rout, with all its attendant exhibitions. "It is a singular thing," says MARMONT, "the different impression produced upon the soldier when he looks the enemy in the face, and when he turns his back upon him. In the first case, he only sees what really exists; *in the second, his imagination increases the danger.*" All the powerful effects of this subtle metaphysical influence are fully displayed in the details which reach us of this wonderful flight and pursuit, continued for four days and perhaps not yet ended. Artillery, ammunition, caissons, wagons, arms, knapsacks, everything, in fact, that impeded their flight, was thrown away. "Wherever we reach portions of the rebel army," writes an eye-witness, "they instantly throw down their arms and scatter like frightened sheep. What is now left of BRAGG's boasted army is but a panic-stricken mob." The captures already have been immense—in men reaching probably ten thousand, in artillery at least sixty pieces.

We have said before that last week's work stands out in the history of the war as our sole example of a defeat, turned, by a vigorous pursuit, into a total rout. We may add that there are few examples in military history of a pursuit that will match it. There is, however, one case so analogous to it, that the description of each might almost stand for either indifferently. The instance is BLUCHER's pursuit of NAPOLEON's army after the defeat of Waterloo, and the details are thus indicated by VENTURINI:

"The furiously pursued mass of the fugitives fled with wild rapidity a distance of about two leagues, and came at last to Genappes, where they fancied they would be able to pass the night. They hastened to drag together some wagons to serve as a protection against cavalry, barricaded the entrance of the chief street, and placed a few pieces in battery in order to hold in check the pursuing enemy. Scarcely had this been done when the Prussian bugle-horn was heard. All started up, and the flight began with greater disorder and confusion than before. The cannoniers abandoned their pieces, the soldiers of the train cut the traces of their horses and raced away. Infantry, cavalry, all the different arms, promiscuously mingled, fled across the fields. Here and there separate crowds had massed themselves, following involuntarily those whom accident had placed at their head. Wherever they endeavored to withstand they were cut down or taken prisoners. The mournful flight had lasted during the whole night, throughout which the terror was so great that numerous mobs of cavalry and infantry allowed themselves to be captured without resistance. When the day dawned the remnants of the army reached, some Charleroy, others Marchienne, and hastened to make their way over the Sambre, the army going to pieces spontaneously."

Whether the blow which GRANT has inflicted on the army of BRAGG is to be counted as crushing as that which BLUCHER dealt the legions of NAPOLEON, can only be known when we are able to grasp the full scope of what has already been done, and when the work itself shall have been finished, which it is not as yet. There is every present appearance that when Gen. GRANT gets through with the business, the great rebel army of the Southwest will have ceased to exist: not, necessarily, that he will have "bagged" or butchered the whole host; but that its losses in men and material shall be so great, its disintegration and demoralization so complete, as to render it no longer available as an independent, effective army. The budget of rebel losses may show greater or less; but this, we believe, will be the net result. In doing this Gen. GRANT has done what no other Commander on either side has done during this war, and what has not very often been done in any wars.

President Lincoln, General Hooker and their staffs reviewing the Army of the Potomac

The New-York Times.

VOL. XIII—NO. 3799. NEW-YORK, THURSDAY, NOVEMBER 26, 1863. PRICE THREE CENTS.

GLORIOUS VICTORY!

GEN. GRANT'S GREAT SUCCESS.

Bragg Routed and Driven from Every Point.

SUCCESSFUL BATTLE ON TUESDAY.

Gen. Hooker Assaults Lookout Mountain and Takes 2,000 Prisoners.

General Sherman Finally Carries Missionary Ridge.

Gen. Thomas Pierces the Enemy's Centre.

Forty Pieces of Artillery Taken.

Five Thousand to Ten Thousand Prisoners Captured.

Flight of the Rebels in Disorder and Confusion.

Probable Interception of the Rebels at Rossville.

SPECIAL DISPATCH TO THE N. Y. TIMES.

WASHINGTON, Wednesday, Nov. 25.

Dispatches giving details of recent operations before Chattanooga were received to-night from Gen. GRANT. He is in happy spirits and confident of success.

Atlanta he declares to be a prize already within his grasp.

DISPATCHES TO THE ASSOCIATED PRESS.

CHATTANOOGA, Wednesday, Nov. 25.

We are completely victorious. The enemy is totally routed and driven from every position. Our loss is very small and the enemy's is heavy in prisoners. Finding Gen. HOOKER so successful in his movements against Lookout Mountain, the enemy evacuated that position during the night.

Gen. HOOKER took possession early this morning. The enemy moved south and got on Missionary Ridge on the battle-field somewhere near Chickamauga. He is expected to intercept the flying foe. Gen. HOOKER is said to have captured 2,000 prisoners in his magnificent assault of Lookout Mountain.

Gen. SHERMAN being all prepared to begin an assault at 8 A. M. to-day, upon the strong position of the enemy at the north end of Missionary Ridge. He had the day before taken a hill near the position of the enemy, but commanded by their artillery. He had to descend into a valley, and he then made another ascent to the position held by the enemy. Two unsuccessful assaults were made by Gen. SHERMAN, but, with the coöperation of the centre, he ultimately gained the position, and completed the great victory.

The brigade of Gen. CARSE, with a portion of Gen. LIGHTBURN'S brigade, composed the storming party in the first assault. They were repulsed with quite a heavy loss after an attack persisted in for an hour; but being reinforced they were enabled to hold a part of the hills. In this attack Gen. CARSE was wounded quite severely in the thigh. The Thirty-seventh Ohio and Sixth Iowa and One Hundred and Third Illinois regiments were in the attack. A second assault was made at 1½ o'clock, in which MATHIAS', LOOMIS' and RAUL'S brigades were engaged. The force reached within twenty yards of the summit of the hill and the works of the enemy, when they were flanked and broke, retiring to their reserves.

In this assault Gen. MATHIAS was wounded and Col. PUTNAM, of the Ninety-third Ohio, killed, their persistent efforts compelled the enemy to mass heavily on his right in order to hold the position of so much importance to him. About 3 o'clock Gen. GRANT started two columns against the weakened centre, and in an hour desperate fighting, succeeded in breaking the centre, and gaining possession of the ridge in which the enemy was posted, the main force was driven northward toward Gen. SHERMAN, who opened on them, and they were forced to break, and seek safety in disordered flight down the western slope of the Ridge, and across the western ridge of the Chickamauga. We have taken not less than 5,000 prisoners and perhaps 10,000. Gen HOOKER will probably intercept the flying enemy in the vicinity of Rossville and the region east of it.

There are reports that we have taken a whole corps.

Among the casualties are Lieut.-Col. ESPY, of the Sixty-eighth Indiana regiment; Major MCCAWLEY, of the Tenth Iowa; Col. OMANS, of the Ninetieth Illinois; Lieut.-Col. STUART, of the Ninetieth Illinois; Major WALKER, of the Tenth Missouri; Major WELSH, of the Fifty-sixth Illinois; Major INNISS, of the Sixth Iowa, wounded; Major LEWIS, of the Sixth Iowa, killed.

Full reports of the killed and wounded cannot be obtained, as most of the killed were in Gen. SHERMAN'S corps, and remained at dark in the hands of the enemy. The list will be telegraphed to-morrow. The prisoners say that BRAGG was on the Ridge just before they were taken.

The successful storming parties consisted of WOOD'S and BAIRD'S divisions on the left centre and JOHNSTON'S and SHERIDAN'S on the right centre. Some of our wounded were left in the hands of the enemy after Gen. SHERMAN'S unsuccessful assault, but were ultimately recovered.

CHATTANOOGA, Wednesday, Nov. 25—10 P. M.

The captured artillery is reported at about forty pieces. Gen. HOOKER captured five boxes of new muskets on Lookout Mountain.

We are in entire possession of the field. We have control over the railway and river to Bridgeport. Two boats came through this morning. Our loss will not amount to more than 300 killed and 250 wounded in the three days operations. The success has been most brilliant.

The enemy is reported to be bivouacking two miles beyond Missionary Ridge. Col. PHELPS, of the Thirty-eighth Ohio, and Major GLASS, of the Thirty-second Indiana, are killed. Gen. JOHN E. SMITH is reported wounded. Col. AVERY, of the One Hundred and Second New-York, lost a leg, and Major ELLIOTT is the same as dead.

REPORTS FROM WASHINGTON.

WASHINGTON, Wednesday, Nov. 25.

The following was received here this afternoon from a responsible source:

CHATTANOOGA, Wednesday, Nov. 25—11 A. M.

We have had a brisk engagement this morning, and have driven the enemy entirely off Lookout Mountain, a considerable portion of which they held up to this morning. We have also taken Missionary Ridge from him this morning, and the troublesome rifle-pits, in possession of which yesterday's engagement left them at the close.

All firing has ceased for a sufficient time to warrant the conclusion that BRAGG has retreated certainly, leaving all the ground and strong points in our possession for which we have been fighting for the last three days.

It is too early yet to enable me to state the casualties on either sides, which are not yet known. Our army is in glorious exultation indeed, over their series of victories.

WASHINGTON, Wednesday, Nov. 24.

Information has been received to-night at the War Department from Gen. GRANT of a great battle fought to-day, resulting in a complete victory over the rebels.

Our army has carried at the point of the bayonet Lookout Mountain Top, Missionary Ridge, and all the intrenchments and rifle-pits around Chattanooga. The bravery exhibited in this great contest by our troops has never been surpassed.

OFFICIAL REPORTS FROM GEN. THOMAS AND GEN. GRANT.

WASHINGTON, Wednesday, Nov. 25.

The following official dispatch from Maj.-Gen. GRANT has been received at the headquarters of the army here:

CHATTANOOGA, Tenn., Tuesday, Nov. 24—12 M.

Major-Gen. H. W. Halleck, General-in-Chief:

Yesterday, at 12½ o'clock, Gen. GRANGER'S and Gen. PALMER'S corps, supported by Gen. HOWARD'S, were advanced directly in front of our fortifications, drove in the enemy's pickets, and carried his first line of rifle-pits between Chattanooga and Citer's Creek.

We captured nine commissioned officers and about 100 enlisted men.

Our loss is about 111.

To-day Gen. HOOKER, in command of Gen. GEARY'S division, Twelfth corps; Gen. OSTERHAUS division, Fifteenth corps, and two brigades, Fourteenth corps, carried the north slope of Lookout Mountain, with small loss on our side, and a loss to the enemy of 500 or 600 prisoners; killed and wounded not reported.

There has been continuous fighting from 12 o'clock until after night; but our troops gallantly repulsed every attempt to take the position.

Gen. SHERMAN crossed the Tennessee River before daylight this morning, at the mouth of the South Chickamauga, with three divisions of the Fifteenth corps and one division of the Fourteenth corps, and carried the northern extremity of Missionary ridge.

Our success so far has been complete and the behavior of the troops admirable.

GEORGE H. THOMAS, Major General.

SECOND DISPATCH.

CHATTANOOGA, Tuesday, Nov. 24—6 P. M.

Maj.-Gen. Halleck, General-in-Chief, Washington:

The fighting to-day progressed favorably.

Gen. SHERMAN carried the end of Missionary Ridge, and his right is now at the Tunnel, and his left at Chickamauga Creek.

The troops from Lookout Valley carried the point of the mountain, and now hold the eastern slope and point high up.

I cannot yet tell the amount of casualties, but our loss is not heavy.

Gen. HOOKER reports 2,000 prisoners taken, besides which a small number have fallen into our hands from Missionary Ridge.

U. S. GRANT, Major-General.

REPORTS FROM REBEL SOURCES.

FORTRESS MONROE, Wednesday, Nov. 25.

The Richmond *Dispatch*, of Nov. 24, has the following:

MISSIONARY RIDGE, Monday, Nov. 23.

The enemy massed a heavy fire on our right this morning, and advanced at 2 o'clock, driving in our pickets. It is not certain yet whether they intend an attack in force, or to advance their lines.

There are various rumors of the occupation of Knoxville by our forces, but nothing official, however.

Two thousand Yankees passed Rogersville, and five regiments through Jacksborough, *en route* for Kentucky. Our forces are active in front.

President DAVIS arrived at Orange Court-house on Saturday. He is stopping with Gen. LEE.

MISSIONARY RIDGE, Nov. 23.

To Gen. Cooper:

We hold all the roads leading into Knoxville, except the one between Holston and French Broad Rivers. Gen. JONES' cavalry might close that. The enemy's cavalry is most broken up. WHEELER cut off his train between Cumberland Gap and Knoxville.

(Signed,) BRAXTON BRAGG.

EXTENSIVE FIRE IN MULBERRY-STREET.—Between 11 and 12 o'clock last night a fire broke out on the third floor of the tenement house No. 35 Mulberry-street, occupied mostly by Italian organ-grinders. The flames soon extended to No. 37, same street, and before the fire could be extinguished these two buildings were nearly destroyed. The latter building was a large tenement house, and was occupied by many families. Building No. 35 is owned by the Valentine estate, and is damaged to the amount of about $1,500. The loss to the inmates could not be ascertained. Several of them barely escaped with their lives.

CAPT. MAURICE W. WALL A BRIGADIER-GENERAL.—A private dispatch from Washington states that Capt. MAURICE W. WALL, late acting as Adjutant-General of the Irish brigade, has been appointed a Brigadier-General of Colored Volunteers, to report immediately to Maj.-Gen. SCHOFIELD, of St. Louis, Mo. Capt. WALL is a veteran, having been in every engagement from Bull Run [illegible] Gettysburg.

FROM KNOXVILLE.

GEN. BURNSIDE'S POSITION SATISFACTORY

The Investment of the North Side of the Town Close.

Details of Three Days' Operations Before Knoxville.

CINCINNATI, Wednesday, Nov. 25.

The situation of Gen. BURNSIDE at Knoxville is perfectly satisfactory.

There was heavy firing west of the town on Saturday.

The investment of the north side of the town is close, but the south side is open.

Gen. BURNSIDE is confident of final success.

KNOXVILLE, Sunday, Nov. 22, 1863.

Thursday morning revealed a line of rifle-pits which the enemy had thrown up during the night. A house near our works was occupied by their sharpshooters, to the annoyance of our men, until our batteries shelled them out. During the day the rebels opened with a battery beyond the railroad depot, and threw a *few* shells. It was silenced by our guns.

On Friday a desultory fire was kept up between the skirmishers. Toward dusk the enemy opened with a new battery of six pieces and again threw a few shells. On the right a brilliant and successful sortie was made to burn a house on the Loudon road, which interfered with our range. The rebels were driven from their rifle-pits and the house burned, when our men came back, shelling them as they did so.

On Saturday a rain-storm set in, lasting nearly all day. The operations of the day were confined to skirmishing.

To-day skirmishing has been constant along the whole line. A few shots have been exchanged between the batteries. The enemy have invested the city with batteries. Their rifle-pits are quite close to our works, and sharpshooters occasionally pick off a man.

NEWS FROM WASHINGTON.

OUR SPECIAL WASHINGTON DISPATCHES.

WASHINGTON, Wednesday, Nov. 25.

ARMY OF THE POTOMAC MUD-BOUND.

Intelligence from the front to-night, is that the rains have rendered the roads almost impassable, and that the army is as completely mud-bound as it was at any time last Winter or Spring. Well informed officers hint that active operations of magnitude are at an end for this season. The ardent and hopeful persuade themselves that the mud will soon dry up. The natives of the sacred soil say there will be no more marching weather till next May.

THE NEW-YORK CUSTOM-HOUSE.

There is already shadowed a searching investigation, by a Committee of the House, of the administration of the New-York Customs Department, and particularly into the business of seizures and forfeitures. It is predicted that one of its results will be the refusal by the District Court, in a large number of cases, of the certificate of probable cause so customarily granted to the Collectors.

ANOTHER RAILROAD WANTED.

The present price of coal, sixteen dollars a ton, is made the basis of a demand already active, that Congress shall give a charter to somebody to construct a new line of railroad northward from Washington till it meets cheap fuel, and, incidentally, cheap food.

PERSONAL.

Senator NESMITH, of Oregon, arrived here to-day from Chattanooga. He was present at the last battle of Chickamauga, and says, after careful examination of the topography of the region, that if the rebels risk a fight on the first battle ground, they will not only be whipped but annihilated. He represents GRANT'S army in splendid fighting condition.

FURLOUGH TO VETERANS.

The Twelfth Illinois cavalry, which has been in the Army of the Potomac for nearly two years, to-day left in a body for Chicago, on thirty days' furlough. The entire regiment has reënlisted for three years.

GEN. MEREDITH WILL NOT BE RELIEVED.

The report that Gen. MEREDITH has been relieved as Commissioner of Exchange, travels faster than the policy of the War Department. He will be retained so long as OULD is retained. The present determination of the Government is to make no more exchanges until the military *status* and rights of our colored troops are definitely settled.

A CURIOUS PROCEEDING.

For several days past, Capt. SCHUTZ'S Detectives have been on the track of a notorious rebel ordnance officer named LENOSTAY, who came from Richmond to Washington to collect money rents, perhaps for renegade "Washingtonians" now in Dixie. His mission was successful. He gathered $150,000 and was on his way South *viâ* Baltimore, where he was arrested by the Detectives. Col. FISH, Provost-Marshal of that city, sent him South *viâ* Harper's Ferry, with all the money on him. There is much desire to know here why a rebel army officer with so large a pile is sent to a destination he desires to reach at our Government's expense.

COMMISSARY-GENERAL HOFFMAN

has returned from his tour of inspection in the West. He visited Johnson's Island, Camp Chase, Helena, Ark., and all other places in the West where rebel prisoners are confined. He reports that rebel prisoners are in excellent condition—well clothed, well fed, in good quarters, and enjoying every comfort that they could desire—contrasting strangely with the condition of our prisoners in Richmond.

At Helena, Ark., buildings are being erected for the accommodation of such of the Southern chivalry as may be captured in the Southwest. The buildings are designed to accommodate 10,000 men.

AT PAROLE CAMP.

There are now at the Parole camp at Annapolis and Camp Chase, Ohio, fourteen hundred paroled Union prisoners, enlisted men, paroled since the 1st of September last. The last declaration of exchange by our Government included only those prisoners paroled to that date. Why our Government does not declare these men exchanged is not known, as the rebels have declared all those captured by GRANT to be exchanged. Official figures show that the rebels are greatly in arrear in these exchanges.

THE LAND OFFICE.

During the month of October the cash sales at the United States Land Office at Marquette, Mich., (in the upper peninsula,) amounted to upward of $24,000, which shows that cash land sales are reviving.

SILVER AT LAKE SUPERIOR.

The General Land Office has received information to-day of large discoveries of silver in the neighborhood of Marquette, on Lake Superior.

DISPATCHES TO THE ASSOCIATED PRESS.

WASHINGTON, Wednesday, Nov. 25.

SOME OF MOSBY'S MEN CAPTURED.

[illegible] of MOSBY'S guerrillas, captured by Col. LOWELL in the skirmish on Monday, and several of WHITE'S battalion have arrived here, and were sent to the Old Capitol Prison, together with seven prisoners of State.

FROM THE ARMY OF THE POTOMAC.

The only information from the Army of the Potomac, to-night, is that all is quiet and nothing of a public character worth communicating going on. The roads are still in a bad condition.

NAVAL ORDER.

Lieut.-Commander WM. T. TRUXTON has been detached from the Navy-yard at Philadelphia, and ordered to the command of the *Tacony*.

WHOLESALE DISMISSION OF OFFICERS.

Maj.-Gen. THOMAS has issued General Orders dishonorably dismissing one Colonel, two Majors, fifteen Captains, twenty-six Lieutenants and one Surgeon, for various offences, including drunkenness, feigning sickness, spreading false rumors, permitting men to plunder, misbehavior in face of the enemy, shameful cowardice, gross disloyalty, dishonest practices, and conduct unbecoming officers and gentlemen.

Course of the National and State Authorities Concerning Colored Volunteers.

LETTER FROM GOV. SEYMOUR.

The "New-York Association for Colored Volunteers," formed at a meeting called by Peter Cooper, Gen. Sickles, Wm. C. Bryant, Gen. John Cochrane, Henry J. Raymond, Wm. Curtis Noyes, Wm. E. Dodge, David Dowd, David Dudley Field, and many other citizens—of which meeting Gen. WM. K. STRONG, late of the army, was President—took prompt measures for ascertaining the views of the National and State Governments concerning the conditions on which colored troops might be enlisted under the President's Proclamation for more volunteers. Gen. STRONG was requested to telegraph the War Department, and Mr. JAMES RODGERS went to Albany to learn the views of Gov. SEYMOUR on the subject.

The callers of the meeting said: "If we allow our citizens to be drawn away by superior inducements offered by other States, we lose them in making up our quota, and the draft will fall heavily upon those who are left; or, if we raise men by volunteering at the last hour, we shall have to pay large bounties and heavier taxes. Let us move in this matter without delay. Other States are fast taking our men to fill their quotas—especially our colored men. Several thousand of these may be added to the strength of our army, and also *saved to the quota of our State*, by a prompt and vigorous movement. Our country's interest and self-interest here unite."

The General Committee of the Association, in their letter to Secretary STANTON, dated Nov. 21, said: "This application to the National Government results from the refusal of certain State functionaries to recognize *colored* men in the call for *volunteers*, notwithstanding the fact that the President's Proclamation makes no discrimination in color, and the additional fact that that class of citizens are subject, like white men, to *a draft*."

And, in their representations at Albany it was added that "justice and patriotism alike require that all men who are subject to draft shall have equal privilege in volunteering under the President's Proclamation"—it being desirable, also, "that our white fellow-citizens shall be measurably relieved from drafting by allowing colored citizens to volunteer for the war—in the course of which war the colored troops have evinced discipline and bravery worthy of the noble cause of National self-defence."

Answers have been received from Washington and Albany. Under date of the 24th the Secretary of War says: "On application, by suitable persons, special authority will be granted to raise colored troops in New-York, according to the rules and regulations relative to organizing and raising colored troops. The troops so raised *will be credited to the State*. Until Congress shall authorize it no bounty can be paid, and the pay is limited by act of Congress to ten dollars a month. The department will recommend that, in this respect, the act be amended so as to make the pay the same as for other colored soldiers. They will be enrolled as *United States Volunteers*, and the officers be appointed and commissioned by the President." (Signed EDWIN M. STANTON, Secretary of War.)

Gov. SEYMOUR replies thus to the inquiry made through Mr. RODGERS:

STATE OF NEW-YORK, EXECUTIVE DEPARTMENT, }
ALBANY, Nov. 24, 1863. }

SIR: In answer to your inquiries about the enlistment of blacks and the organization of regiments and companies, I have to say:

First—That, under the State laws, the bounty is paid to all, without distinction, who are mustered into the service of the United States, of whom credits are given to New-York, under the President's call for troops.

Second—As to new organizations, I have no power to authorize any, either for blacks or whites, which will be entitled to the benefit of the bounty given by the General Government. The object at Washington is to fill up the ranks of the regiments in the field. If any new organizations, for either white or black troops, are made, they *must be authorized by the War Department*, to entitle those who join them to the benefit of the money paid to volunteers.

Yours, &c., HORATIO SEYMOUR.

These answers are published for the information of the Association and all others interested, and the coöperation of all loyal citizens is earnestly invoked in furtherance of the objects above mentioned.

By order of the General Committee.

HENRY O'RIELLY, Secretary.

Rooms of the Association, No. 26 Pine-street, Nov. 25, 1863.

THE WAR IN SOUTH CAROLINA.

Dispatches via Richmond—Vigorous Shelling Continued.

FORTRESS MONROE, Wednesday, Nov. 25.

The Richmond *Dispatch*, of the 24th, contains the following from Charleston:

CHARLESTON, Monday, Nov. 23.

There was no shelling of the city last night, but a slow fire on Sumter.

The second dispatch says there has been a vigorous fire kept up between the enemy's batteries and ours all day. The enemy has not shelled the city to day, but divided his attention between Sumter, Moultrie, Johnson and Simkins. They also threw a number of shells on James Island; 290 shots were thrown in Sumter last night.

The Northwestern Convention of War Democrats.

CHICAGO, Ill., Wednesday, Nov. 25.

The Northwestern Convention of War Democrats organized this morning.

The business was transacted with closed doors.

None but accredited delegates were admitted.

All the States named in the call were represented.

Gen. JOHN A. MCCLERNAND was chosen President of the Convention.

A Committee of nine, of which Judge LOVERIN, of Indiana, was selected as the Chairman, has been appointed to frame a platform or a call.

The Draft in Baltimore—Three Newspaper Reporters Drawn.

BALTIMORE, Wednesday, Nov. 25.

The draft is progressing in a most orderly manner. Three newspaper reporters were so fortunate as to be drawn this morning—one from the *American*, one from the *Clipper* and one from the *Daily Gazette*.

Quota in New-Hampshire.

A dispatch from Concord states that New-Hampshire is rapidly filling up her full quota of men by volunteers.

Sailing of the Asia.

BOSTON, Mass., Wednesday, Nov. 25.

The steamer *Asia* sailed to-day at 10 o'clock, taking 37 passengers for Liverpool and 23 for Halifax; also, $55,042 in specie.

Sale of Five-Twenties.

PHILADELPHIA, Wednesday, Nov. 25.

The Subscription Agent reports the sale of five-twenties to-day at $911,800.

Items from Boston.

BOSTON, Wednesday, Nov. 25.

Commodore WILLIAM S. WALKER, U. S. N., died in this city yesterday at the advanced age of 76 years.

Five of MOSBY'S guerrillas that were lately captured in the vicinity of Washington have reached Fort Warren for safe keeping.

The steam frigate *Niagara* is shortly expected at Charlestown Navy-yard to have her armament changed. The 200-pound Parrotts on the spar deck are pronounced too heavy, and guns of less calibre will be substituted for them. The *Tacony* [illegible] the Dry Dock.

THREE DAYS LATER FROM EUROPE

ARRIVAL OF THE ARABIA AT HALIFAX.

Opposition to the Proposed Peace Congress.

The Matter Considered Impracticable.

AMERICAN TOPICS AGAIN DISCUSSED.

The French Government Unchanged Respecting Southern Recognition.

MISCELLANEOUS CONTINENTAL NEWS.

Serious Illness of the King of Denmark.

FINANCIAL AND COMMERCIAL INTELLIGENCE.

HALIFAX, Wednesday, Nov. 25.

The steamer *Arabia*, Capt. COOK, left Liverpool at 10:30 on the morning of the 14th inst., and Queenstown on the evening of the 15th, and arrived at this port on the 25th, at 7 P. M., *en route* for Boston. She had on board 16 Halifax and 32 Boston passengers. She brings three days later news.

The *Arabia* sailed for Boston at 2 o'clock A. M.

The steamer *Hammonia*, from New-York, arrived at Southampton on the 12th.

The steamship *Scotia*, from New-York, arrived at Liverpool on the 13th.

On the 14th she passed the ship *Far West*, bound in. Off Fastwell passed a Galway steamer, bound in; 10 A. M., latitude 46°, longitude 48°, *Adriatic*, bound east.

The steam frigate *Phantom*, on the North American station, has been ordered to Charleston.

The extraordinary treble murder in a London cab, and the subsequent suicide of the murderer, resulted a verdict of *felo de se* on the body of the latter and he was buried at midnight without funeral rites.

The Official Board of trades enquiring into the accident to the steamer *Africa* resulted in the suspension of Capt. STONE'S certificate for 6 months for neglecting either to slow his engines or use the lead. The examination of the *Africa* shows no material damage. It was merely confined to the dead wood forward.

The London *Times*, expatiating on the disaster to the *Anglia* at Galway, and the shortcomings of the Galway Line in general, says the affair is a dead failure, and the question cannot be evaded, and whether the experiment has not been tried long enough. A survey of the *Anglia* shows but little damage, but the vessel is so strained that she is ordered to Liverpool to be Dry-docked.

AMERICAN TOPICS.

ANOTHER REBEL WAR VESSEL.

THE GOVERNMENT LOOKING AFTER HER.

From the London News, Nov. 11.

The Glasgow Emancipation Society lately sent a memorial to Earl RUSSELL, Secretary of State for Foreign Affairs, regarding an iron screw steamer at one time named the *Canton*, but now named the *Pampero*. The memorial stated that this vessel had lately been launched from the building-yard of Messrs. JAMES & GEORGE THOMSON here, and was being rapidly fitted out in Glasgow harbor; that she was currently, and the memorialists believed truly, reported to have been constructed for the Confederate Government; that she was of a similar construction to the *Alabama*, and, like her, intended to prey upon the merchant ships of the Northern States; that she was fitted up with gun-ports, ring-bolts for guns, &c., although the gun-ports had since been filled up and the fittings removed, and these things disguised as much as possible; and that the Society, therefore, requested his Lordship would cause a satisfactory investigation to be made into the character, ownership and destination of this vessel, with the view that, if found to be of the description and for the purpose they believed her to be, she might be prevented from leaving Britain. The following reply has been received from Earl RUSSELL.

FOREIGN-OFFICE, Nov. 7, 1863.

GENTLEMEN: I am desired by Earl RUSSELL to acknowledge the receipt of the memorial dated the 4th inst., and signed by you on behalf of the Glasgow Emancipation Society, requesting the interference of Her Majesty's Government to prevent the departure from that port of the steam-vessel *Canton* until an investigation has taken place as to her character, ownership and destination, and I am to acquaint you in reply that the attention of Her Majesty's Government has already been directed to this matter.

I am, gentlemen, your most obedient humble servant, E. HAMMOND.

W. SMEAL, Esq., and AND. PATON, Esq., Secretaries Glasgow Emancipation Society.

PROJECT FOR PEACE.

The London *Times* publishes a project for peace in America, by a Northern gentleman writer. He says if the war is to go on for a time, from mere momentum, perhaps, it must be let alone; but it should be turned as soon as possible from a war of attempted conquest to a war for limits and terms of settlement. He suggests that negotiations be opened at once with the Richmond Government for such settlements, and for making a more formal recognition. One of the matters for discussion—the Confederates of course to be recognized *de jure*—must be the navigation of the Ohio and Mississippi; and in the event of Maryland joining the South, the Susquehannah and Chesapeake are to be free, with a common tariff for the two Confederacies.

THE PROPOSED PEACE CONGRESS.

It is rumored that DROUYN DE LHUYS is drawing up an explanatory document, comprising the different questions which the Emperor intends to submit to Congress; in the meantime the English journals appear to be generally taking a view adverse to Congress. The *Globe*, Ministerial, opposes it. The *Daily News* and *Morning Herald* also oppose it, and agree that if it is held unfavorable results will ensue. The *Times* inquires what England will have to do in the Congress, should it ever prove more than an ideal conception, and points out that there is no place for England in it, all the honors being monopolized by France. The English Cabinet held meetings to consider upon the subject. The result has not transpired and other meetings is fixed for the 16th.

The Madrid *Correspondencia* says the Spanish Government has resolved to send representatives to the Congress, but some Spanish journals look cooly on it.

It is asserted that Austria will give no answer till the resolution of England is known.

FRANCE.

The Bank of France, on the 12th, raised the rate of discount to 7 per cent. The monthly returns of that institution show a decrease of cash in hand of 67 millions of francs. Bourse pretty steady; Rentes 67c.@35c.

POLAND.

Affairs remain unchanged in Poland. The withdrawal of the Grand Duke CONSTANTINE from the Governorship is confirmed. An additional taxation is imposed on Poland by the Russian Government, and a forced loan by the National Government of Prussia.

PRUSSIA.

The Chamber of Deputies elected Herr VON GRA- now President. In his speech he pointed out that the King's desire for a solution of pending differences would be fulfilled if the Constitution were interpreted and stated in its obvious spirit.

DENMARK.

The King is ill with erysipelas and a slight fever. The Danish Regsraad adopted the Government project for a Constitution for Denmark and Schleswig.

Commercial Intelligence per Arabia.

LIVERPOOL PROVISION MARKET.

The PROVISION market is quiet and steady. BIGLAND, ATHYA & Co., and GORDON, BRUCE & Co. report BEEF inactive, PORK quiet and steady, BACON still declining.

LIVERPOOL PRODUCE MARKET.

The Produce market is quiet and steady. BUTTER firm. LARD quiet, at 39s.@40s. TALLOW easier, at 42s.@43s. 6d. SUGAR was buoyant at the opening, but closed quiet. COFFEE very dull. RICE firm. ASHES steady. LINSEED OIL dull. COD OIL steady, at 51s. RESIN inactive, at 30s. SPIRITS TURPENTINE quiet and steady. PETROLEUM flat and irregular; refined, 1s. 9d.@1s. 10d.; £15 9s. for Crude ₩ ton.

LONDON MARKETS.

LONDON, Saturday, Nov. 14.

BREADSTUFFS firm. IRON steady. SUGAR firm, and advanced 6d.@1s. COFFEE easier and irregular. TEA steady. RICE quiet. LINSEED CAKES dull. LINSEED OIL still declining. SPIRITS TURPENTINE steady, at 85s. PETROLEUM dull. SPERM OIL quiet. TALLOW dull, at 43s. PROVISIONS inactive. BUTTER still advancing. SPIRITS TURPENTINE firmer. RESIN steady. AMERICAN SECURITIES steady; sales small. CONSOLS for money 92¾@92⅞.

LIVERPOOL, Saturday, Nov. 14.

COTTON—Sales of the week, 33,000 bales. The market opened to-day at an advance of ¼d.@½d., but subsequently lost, closing irregular. The sales to speculators reached 8,000 bales, and exporters 6,000 bales. The sales to-day foot up 5,000 bales, the market closing quiet. Of the above, speculators and exporters took 2,000 bales. The following are the authorized quotations: Orleans Middling, 28⅝d.; Mobile, 28¼d.; Uplands, 28d.

The stock of Cotton in port is stated at 182,000 bales, of which 28,000 are American.

TRADE REPORT.

The advices from Manchester are unfavorable. Market flat and still declining.

The Breadstuffs market is steady.

RICHARDSON, SPENCE & Co. WAKEFIELD, NASH & Co., and others report: FLOUR steady at 19s.@23s. WHEAT firm; Red Western, 7s.@8s. 5d; Red Southern, 8s. 6d. @8s. 9d. CORN steady at 28s. 3d.@28s. 6d.

The Bullion in the Bank of England has decreased £338,000.

LATEST VIA LIVERPOOL.

LIVERPOOL, Saturday, Nov. 14—Evening.

COTTON flat; sales 2,000 bales, of which speculators and exporters took 1,000.

BREADSTUFFS quiet and steady. SUGAR buoyant.

Consols for Money 92⅞@92⅞.

Illinois Central Shares 19½@18½ discount, Erie 65@67.

Latest by Telegraph to Queenstown.

The Bank discount is unchanged.

The English journals generally oppose NAPOLEON'S Congress.

The Paris Bourse was flat. Rentes closed at 67f. 25c.

The French Government had informed Mr. DAYTON that their views on the American question were unchanged. They had not recognized the South, and consequently had not signed the treaty for the acquisition of Texas and Louisiana as reported.

BERNE, Sunday, Nov. 15.

The Juarez Government had addressed a note to the Federal Council, protesting against the modification of the Republican Constitution by French invasion, hoping for the sympathy of Switzerland.

COPENHAGEN, Sunday, Nov. 15.

The King of Denmark is seriously ill, at Flucksburgh, with tupplas, attended by fever, delirium and want of sleep.

MADRID, Sunday, Nov. 15.

A marriage is spoken of between the Infanta ISABELLA and the Count of Paris.

The steamship *America*, which sailed from Londonderry on Friday last, put back to Moville this morning, disabled.

LIVERPOOL, Saturday, Nov. 14—Evening.

The leading journals to-day continue their arguments against the proposed Congress. The *Times* treats the subject as a very unreal proposition, and says it may possibly turn out that the proposal was something in the nature of a fire-escape—the expedient of a man determined to come down some door from an untenable position. The Emperor may have made the proposition without desiring the Congress itself, and England, by declining to join it, may be doing the Emperor the greatest possible service.

A Paris letter says a cold shoulder is all that is to be seen with regard to the Congress, and the matter is drifting into an abyss of impracticability.

WM. CORNELL JEWETT publishes a long pamphlet in advocacy of mediation in America, in which he maintains that the American question is designed to come before the proposed Congress as the most important matter affecting the peace and prosperity of Europe, and urgently appeals to England to support NAPOLEON.

A movement has been inaugurated among the shipping men of Liverpool to appeal against the sentence of Capt. STONE, of the *Africa*. A meeting will be held to-day on the subject.

Money is rather easier.

PERNAMBUCO, Sunday, Nov. 1.

Exchange, 28. SUGAR—Whites, 3‖000. COTTON, 18‖000@20‖000.

RIO JANEIRO, Saturday, Oct. 24.

Exchange on London 27¼@27½. Coffee—Good firsts 6‖900@7‖00. Shipments—73,900 bags; stock, 13,000. Freights 35s. 6d.@40s.

BAHIA, Thursday, Oct. 29.

Exchange 27¾@27⅞. Sugar—Whites, 2‖200@2‖560; Browns, 1‖600@1‖800. Cottons, 24‖000@26‖000.

Union Officers Imprisoned in the South.

To the Editor of the New-York Times:

Having many letters of inquiry as to officers confined with me in the jail at Columbia, S. C., I inclose for publication in your columns the names of all who were there on the 6th inst., when I left for Richmond and City Point.

Respectfully, yours,

H. CLAY TRUMBULL,

Chaplain Tenth Connecticut Volunteers.

HARTFORD, Conn., Nov. 24, 1863.

ARMY OFFICERS.

Lt.-Col. John Bedel, 3d N. H. V., captured July 18.
Maj. John H. Filler, 55th Penn. V., July 18.
Capt. D. B. Hogeland, 76th Penn. V., July 11.
Capt. V. B. Chamberlain, 7th Conn. V., July 11.
Capt. Jerome Tourtellotte, 7th Conn. V., July 11.
Capt. Louis S. Payne, 100th N. Y. V., Aug. 3.
1st Lieut. and Adjt. H. W. Camp, 10th Conn. V., July 19.
1st Lieut. W. E. Phillips, 7th Conn. V., July 11.
1st Lieut. D. J. West, 6th Conn. V., July 18.
1st Lieut. C. L. Bittinger, 76th Penn. V., July 11.
2d Lieut. E. C. Jordan, 7th Conn. V., July 11.
2d Lieut. Rudolph Kost, 6th Conn. V., July 18.
2d Lieut. John King, 6th Conn. V., July 18.
2d Lieut. Elton W. Ware, 9th Maine V., July 11.
2d Lieut. F. J. O'Sullivan, 67th Ohio V., July 18.
Chaplain J. H. Fowler, 1st S. C. V., (col'd,) Sept. 13.

NAVAL OFFICERS.

Lieut.-Com. E. P. Williams, *Wissahickon*, captured Sept. 9.
Flag-Lieut. S. W. Preston, *Wabash*, Sept. 9.
Lieut. E. T. Brower, *Housatonic*, Sept. 9.
Lieut. G. C. Remey, *Canandaigua*, Sept. 9.
Ensign B. H. Porter, *New Ironsides*, Sept. 9.
Acting Ensign E. G. Dayton, *Wissahickon*, Sept. 9.
Acting Ensign M. W. Tillson, *Thos. A. Ward*, Oct. 20.
Acting Master's Mate C. P. Hovey, *Powhatan*, Sept. 9.
Acting Master's Mate C. S. McCarty, *Canandaigua*, Sept. 9.
Third Asst. Engineer J. H. Harmany, *Housatonic*, Sept. 9.
1st Lieut. R. L. Meade, (U. S. Marines,) Sept. 9.

Assistant-Surgeon JOHN T. LUCK, of the *Ottawa*, taken July 19, and Acting Master E. L. HAINES, of the *Powhatan*, taken Aug. 4, confined for a time at Columbia, were removed to the Libby Prison, Richmond. All the above-named officers were in good health at latest dates.

Distressing Accident in the North River—Seven Russian Sailors Drowned.

Last evening soon after 8 o'clock, a boat containing twelve men from one of the Russian war vessels in the harbor, was run down by the ferry-boat *Jersey City*, of the Cortlandt-street line, while she was nearing the slip. All the sailors were thrown into the water and seven of them are believed to have been drowned. The other five were rescued by the crew of the ferry-boat.

The Charleston Mercury.

DAILY PAPER—TWENTY DOLLARS PER ANNUM, PAYABLE HALF-YEARLY IN ADVANCE. | VINDICE NULLO SPONTE SUA SINE LEGE FIDES RECTUMQUE COLENTUR. | COUNTRY PAPER—THREE A WEEK—TEN DOLLARS PER ANNUM, IN ADVANCE.

VOLUME LXXXIII. CHARLESTON, S. C., MONDAY, NOVEMBER 30, 1863. NUMBER 11,922

THE BATTLE OF LOOKOUT MOUNTAIN—FURTHER PARTICULARS.

The latest North Georgia papers that have come to hand contain scarcely a line of interest in regard to the disaster to our arms at Lookout Mountain. We copy the successive despatches of the army correspondent of the Savannah *Republican*, from the scene of action:

MISSIONARY RIDGE, November 24.—Hostilities have been resumed here in earnest. The enemy assaulted Lookout Mountain from the west side, at 11 o'clock, a. m. to-day, in great force, and the battle is still raging. Our force engaged is comparatively small, very many of the troops having been sent to other parts of the line. General Stevenson commands the Confederates on the mountain, and has been forced back to a point east of Craven's house. We shall probably abandon Lookout altogether, it being of but little value to us in a strategic point of view since the loss of Lookout Valley beyond. The enemy is now throwing a considerable force across the Tennessee River at the mouth of Chickamauga Creek, and pressing round upon our right. The weather is unfavorable—raining.

(*Later.*)

MISSIONARY RIDGE.—November 24—9, p. m.—The battle still rages on Lookout. The enemy has moved round to the north face of the mountain, and is slowly pushing the Confederates back. Our force on the mountain is small. We can see the flashes of the muskets on the mountain, but the fog has been so dense all day that it has been impossible to see clearly the movements of the two armies, and our artillery, in consequence, has been rendered useless.

The enemy has massed a formidable army here under able leaders, and changes in our position may become necessary. The importance of the mountain ceased with the loss of the valley.

(*Latest.*)

CHICKAMAUGA STATION, November 25, 9, m.—General Bragg abandoned Lookout Mountain last night, as no longer tenable or important, and massed his army on Missionary Ridge. Our right extended well up to the mouth of Chickamauga Creek, where the enemy had sent heavy forces. Hardee commanded the right wing and Breckinridge the left.

The battle opened fully by 12 o'clock, having commenced at 10 o'clock on the right. General Hardee repulsed the enemy's assault with great slaughter, capturing seven flags and some prisoners. But the enemy succeeded in gaining the ridge near our centre, from which he enfiladed our lines. Our men, supposing that the enemy were successful at other points, gave way on the left, when the Federals occupied that part of the ridge. Seeing this. General Bragg withdrew our whole army at night fall, and are now crossing the Chickamauga. There are no roads by which we can bring off our artillery, and consequently in some places several guns were lost and some prisoners. Our loss in killed and wounded in the day's engagement was slight. The enemy's forces were two to our one.

A correspondent of the Knoxville *Register* furnishes the following notes of the battle at Missionary Ridge:

The morning of the 25th came very thick and foggy. During the night our forces had evacuated Lookout Mountain, and withdrawn to the right of Chattanooga Creek. About 8 o'clock, a. m., the fog cleared and revealed an immense force of Yankees along the base of Missionary Ridge. Gen. Bragg had vacated his quarters during the night, hence, when the enemy opened their terrific cannonading on that point, they found no game.

The fight continued furiously during several hours, when comparative quiet reigned. We could not perceive the result, but from the fact that that point is only four and a half miles from Chickamauga Station, and that the enemy had not made any demonstration on that place, they could not have gained much advantage over our left.

At 9 o'clock heavy cannonnading was heard on our extreme left. Soon the battle raged furiously. General Cleburne had taken position during the night on the extreme right of Missionary Ridge, and massed the greater portion of his forces near the Tunnel. At this point Swett's battery was posted, and during the entire day it kept up its continuous music.

The Yankees marshalled their forces in long and broad columns from Chattanooga, and the various positions along the Citico Creek, advancing like the cloud on the unflinching heroes of Cleburne's and Cheatham's commands. Sherman's Corps, supposed to number 35,000 men, advanced to the assault, and made assault after assault against the impregnable position.

During the hours between 11, a. m., to 5, p. m., the firing of musketry and cannon was incessant. We have never heard it equalled on any field on which it has been our lot to do battle. But their charges were unavailing. They were beaten back time and again. At one time they came within fifteen feet of Swett's battery, when the 5th Arkansas, with a yell and a volley, that echoed high above the din of war, drove them back. Numbers of the men finding their guns so fouled as to be useless, cast them away and threw rocks into the faces of the foe.

One Irishman, whose left hand was so shattered that he could not hold his gun, threw stones until he was exhausted, and came back swearing that while old Pat was there the boys could whip all the damned Yankees they could bring against them.

The Second Tennessee also was supporting this battery, and, for infernal stubborn fighting, it has never been surpassed.

One more assault at 4, p. m., and Sherman's corps received a terrific punishment, that made them turn and fly down the hill, and soon they were lost to view in the stinking murky clouds of war. Our forces pursued them rapidly, and the last accounts we had from the foe was, that they had crossed the Tennessee, and we had destroyed their pontoons at the mouth of the Chickamauga.

At half-past 4, p. m., an attack was made some distance down the ridge towards our centre, and, judging from the terrible and rapid firing of musketry, our forces were slowly retiring over the crest of the ridge. The continuous and heavy firing was heard at half-past 5, p. m., when the train left.

We can form no estimate of our loss, though we know a large number of wounded were received at the field and general hospitals. But the Yankees turned their pale and bloody faces to the setting sun on the western slope of the ridge by so many hundreds, that we are satisfied that hell had one of its grandest jubilees over its accessions from their ranks. The slaughter in the path of our batteries was awful and immense, but not one assault on us proved successful.

General Ulysses S. Grant

Grant (*left*) at Lookout Mountain

Confederate troops shelling Union camps at Lookout Mountain

The New-York Times.

VOL. XIII—NO. 3801. NEW-YORK, SUNDAY, NOVEMBER 29, 1863. PRICE FOUR CENTS.

GRANT'S VICTORY.

Detailed Official Report of the Operations.

Dispatch from Gen. Meigs to Secretary Stanton.

Graphic Accounts of the Three Days' Fighting.

The Preliminary Movements a Surprise to the Rebels.

The Best Directed and Best Ordered Battle of the War.

GLORIOUS CONDUCT OF OUR TROOPS.

Our Entire Loss Officially Reported at about Three Thousand.

OUR SPECIAL WASHINGTON DISPATCH.

WASHINGTON, Saturday, Nov. 28.

An official statement of our losses in the recent battles at Chattanooga was received here this morning. Our casualties in killed and wounded on the 23d, 24th and 25th, were but little over three thousand at the storming of Lookout Mountain, and at the assault upon Missionary Ridge about two hundred.

The report of our losses on the 26th is not yet received.

Our wounded are all under cover and well cared for. Hospital and all other supplies are abundant.

DETAILND OFFICIAL DISPATH.

HEADQUARTERS, CHATTANOOGA, Nov. 26, 1863.

Edwin M. Stanton, Secretary of War:

SIR: On the 23d instant, at 11½ A. M., Gen. GRANT ordered a demonstration against Mission Ridge, to develop the force holding it. The troops marched out, formed in order, and advanced in line of battle, as if on parade.

The rebels watched the formation and movement from their picket lines and rifle-pits, and from the summits of Mission Ridge, five hundred feet above us, and thought it was a review and drill, so openly and deliberately, so regular, was it all done.

The line advanced, preceded by skirmishers, and at 2 o'clock P.M. reached our picket lines and opened a ratl ng volley upon the rebel pickets, who replied and run into their advanced line of rifle-pits. After them went our skirmishers and into them, along the centre of the line of 25,000 troops which Gen. THOMAS had so quickly displayed, until we opened fire.

Prisoners assert that they thought the whole movement was a review and general drill, and that it was too late to send to their camps for reinforcements, and that they were overwhelmed by force of numbers. It was a surprise in open daylight.

At 3 P. M., the important advanced position of Orchard Knob and the lines right and left were in our possession, and arrangements were ordered for holding them during the night. The next day, at daylight, Gen. THOMAS had 5,000 men across the Tennessee, and established on its south bank, and commenced the construction of a pontoon bridge about six miles above Chattanooga.

The rebel steamer *Dunbar* was repaired at the right moment, and rendered effective aid in this crossing, carrying over six thousand men. By night-fall, Gen. THOMAS had seized the extremity of Missionary Ridge nearest the river, and was entrenching himself. Gen. HOWARD, with a brigade, opened communication with him from Chattanooga, on the south side of the river. Skirmishing and cannonading continued all day on the left and centre. Gen. HOOKER scaled the slopes of Lookout Mountain, and from the valley of Lookout Creek drove the rebels around the point. He captured some two thousand prisoners, and established himself high up the mountain side, in full view of Chattanooga. This raised the blockade, and now steamers were ordered from Bridgeport to Chattanooga. They had run only to Kelly's Ferry, whence ten miles of hauling over mountain roads and twice across the Tennessee on pontoon bridges brought us our supplies.

All night the point of Missionary Ridge on the extreme left and the side of Lookout Mountain, on the extreme right, blazed with the camp-fires of loyal troops.

The day had been one of dense mists and rains, and much of Gen. HOOKER'S battle was fought above the clouds, which concealed him from our view, but from which his musketry was heard.

At nightfall the sky cleared and the full moon, "the traitors doom," shone upon the beautiful scene, until 1 A. M., when twinkling sparks upon the mountain side showed that picket skirmishing was going on. Then it ceased. A brigade, sent from Chattanooga, crossed the Chattanooga Creek and opened communication with HOOKER.

Gen. GRANT'S headquarters during the afternoon of the 23d and the day of the 24th, were in WOOD'S redoubt, except when, in the course of the day, he rode along the advanced line, visiting the headquarters of the several commanders, in Chattanooga Valley.

At daylight on the 25th the Stars and Stripes were descried on the peak of Lookout. The rebels had evacuated the mountain.

HOOKER moved to descend the mountain, and striking Mission Ridge at the Rossville Gap, to sweep on both sides and on its summit.

The rebel troops were seen as soon as it was light enough, streaming regiments and brigades along the narrow summit of Mission Ridge, either concentrating on the right to overwhelm SHERMAN, or marching for the railroad, and raising the siege.

They had evacuated the valley of Chattanooga—would they abandon that of Chicamauga?

The twenty-pounders and four and a quarter-inch rifles of WOOD'S redoubt, opened on Mission Ridge. Orchard Knob sent its compliments to the Ridge, which, with rifled Parrotts answered, and the cannonade thus commenced continued all day. Shot and shell screamed from Orchard Knob to Missionary Ridge, and from Missionary Ridge to Orchard Knob, and from WOOD'S redoubt over the heads of Gens. GRANT and THOMAS and their Staffs, who were with us in this favorable position, from whence the whole battle could be seen as in an amphitheatre. The headquarters were under fire all day long.

Cannonading and musketry were heard from Gen. SHERMAN, and Gen. HOWARD marched the Eleventh corps to join him.

Gen. THOMAS sent out skirmishers who drove in the rebel pickets, and chased them into their intrenchments, and at the foot of Mission Ridge SHERMAN made an assault against BRAGG'S right, intrenched on a high knob next to that, on which SHERMAN himself lay fortified. The assault was gallantly made.

SHERMAN reached the edge of the crest, and held his ground for (it seemed to me) an hour, but was bloodily repulsed by reserves.

A general advance was ordered, and a strong line of skirmishers, followed by a deployed line of battle, some two miles in length. At the signal of leaden shots from the headquarters on Orchard Knob, the line moved rapidly and orderly forward. The rebel pickets discharged their muskets and ran into their rifle-pits. Our skirmishers followed on their heels. The line of battle was not far behind, and we saw the grey rebels swarm out of the ledge line of rifle-pits, in numbers which surprised us, and over the base of the hill. A few turned and fired their pieces, but the greater number collected into the many roads which cross obliquely up its steep face, and went on to their top. Some regiments pressed on and swarmed up the steep sides of the ridge, and here and there a color was advanced beyond the lines. The attempt appeared most dangerous, but the advance was supported, and the whole line was ordered to storm the heights, upon which not less than forty pieces of artillery, and no one knew how many muskets, stood ready to slaughter the assailants. With cheers answering to cheers, the men swarmed upwards. They gathered to the points least difficult of ascent, and the line was broken. Color after color was planted on the summit, while musket and cannon vomited their thunder upon them.

A well-directed shot from Orchard Knob exploded a rebel caisson on the summit, and the gun was seen galloping to the right, its driver lashing his horses. A party of our soldiers intercepted them, and the gun was captured with cheers.

A fierce musketry fight broke out to the left, where, between THOMAS and SHERMAN, a mile or two of the ridge was still occupied by the rebels.

BRAGG left the house in which he had held his headquarters, and rode to the rear as our troops crowded the hill on either side of him.

Gen. GRANT proceeded to the summit, and there did we only know its height.

Some of the captured artillery was put into position. Artillerists were sent for to work the guns. Caissons were searched for ammunition.

The rebel log breastworks were torn to pieces and carried to the other side of the ridge, and used in forming barricades across.

A strong line of infantry was formed in the rear of BAIRD'S line, hotly engaged in a musketry contest with the rebels to the left, and a secure lodgement was soon effected.

The other assault to the right of our centre gained the summit, and the rebels threw down their arms and fled.

HOOKER coming in favorable position, swept the right of the ridge and captured many prisoners.

BRAGG'S remaining troops left early in the night, and the battle of Chattanooga, after days of manœuvring and fighting, was won. The strength of the rebellion in the centre is broken. BURNSIDE is relieved from danger in East Tennessee. Kentucky and Tennessee are rescued. Georgia and the southeast are threatened in the rear, and another victory is added to the chapter of "Unconditional Surrender GRANT."

To-night the estimate of captures is several thousands of prisoners and thirty pieces of artillery.

Our loss for so great a victory is not severe.

BRAGG is firing the railroad as he retreats towards Dalton. SHERMAN is in hot pursuit.

To-day I viewed the battle-field, which extends for six miles along Mission Ridge and for several miles on Lookout Mountain.

Probably not so well directed, so well ordered a battle has been delivered during the war. But one assault was repulsed—but that assault by calling to that point the rebel reserves, prevented them repulsing any of the others.

A few days since BRAGG sent to Gen. GRANT a flag of truce, advising him that it would be prudent to remove non-combatants who might be still in Chattanooga.

No reply has been returned, but the combatants having removed from this vicinity, it is probable that non-combatants can remain without imprudence.

N. C. MEIGS, Quartermaster-General

GEN. BURNSIDE'S SITUATION.

Interesting Statements by Col. Leisure.

Col. LEISURE, of the Roundhead (Pa.) regiment, who left Knoxville on Nov. 11, has given the Pittsburgh *Chronicle* the following interesting information regarding BURNSIDE'S situation.

"That General says that BURNSIDE has been all along aware that a movement was to be made against him, and that the late fight at Campbell's Station, and other points between Loudon and Knoxville, was not so much to allow his trains to get off as to afford his outlying posts, &c., to concentrate at Knoxville. This has been successfully done, and BURNSIDE'S force now amounts, we are glad to say, to full 20,000 men. This includes, however, several new levies of East Tennesseeans, who, although individually brave, are ignorant, badly drilled, and generally unreliable when hard pressed. BURNSIDE has plenty of guns and ammunition, and can hold Knoxville against four times his numbers. Some of the best batteries in the service, including one of 20-pound Parrotts, is with him, while the formidable fortifications stretching in a semi-circle a couple of miles from the town, and constructed by the rebels against us, have been materially strengthened under directions of Col. POE.

It is a mistake to suppose Knoxville closely invested. LONGSTREET is only on the north side, while the south and all the region across the Holston River is open to us. This district is full of forage, corn, wheat, &c. BURNSIDE has all the mills. He has also fortified the heights immediately across the river, and his batteries command for four miles the only practicable roads of approach to the city on that side.

It is by this route BURNSIDE'S telegraph to Cumberland Gap runs, by which he communicates with GRANT, and it is by this route he could retreat to Cumberland Gap if the rebels pressed him too hard. The most reliable troops with BURNSIDE are the Ninth army corps, now numbering about twelve thousand men. He has abundance of cavalry, under Gen. SHACKELFORD, the commander who chased MORGAN through Ohio, and altogether is able to give LONGSTREET a hard tussle.

Gen. LEISURE states that not only has BURNSIDE entire confidence in his position, but that his whole army have entire confidence in *him*, and will hear of his being relieved with great regret. It is probable that by this time the railroad between Cleveland and Loudon, by which LONGSTREET came, and must get all his supplies, has been cut either by GRANT'S or BURNSIDE'S cavalry; and if this be the case, LONGSTREET will have a 'very hard road to travel.' He has already been punished severely, and it will be a singular thing if, between SHERMAN and BURNSIDE, he be not caught in a trap which will finish his campaign for some time to come.

The troops which were probably intended to reinforce LONGSTREET from LEE, *via* Lynchburgh and Jonesboro, have doubtless been recalled to Gordonsville, by MEADE'S threatened advance. MEADE is waiting on the banks of the Rapidan, to strike at LEE whenever that General shows any symptoms of weakening himself to strengthen either BRAGG or LONGSTREET, so that the situation appears to be satisfactory all around. LONGSTREET'S force is composed chiefly of Alabamians and Georgians, but with the exception of HOOD'S division, the rest are not the best troops in the South. Besides, even supposing his railroad communications uncut, he will have to wagon all his supplies over most wretched roads for over thirty miles. This he cannot do long, so that if he be not overwhelmed, we may soon expect to hear of his speedy retirement.

A DISPATCH FROM PARSON BROWNLOW.

The following dispatch appears in the Cincinnati *Gazette*:

CAMP LOUDON, Ky., Wednesday, Nov. 25.

Gen. BURNSIDE still holds Knoxville, and has held his position for ten days, against great odds. He is a moral and military hero, and has endeared himself to the Union men of East Tennessee as no man ever did, and deserves the honor and confidence of the whole country. My family are in Knoxville, and I am on my way to Cincinnati—advised to leave by the military authorities. I shall return by Chattanooga.

W. G. BROWNLOW.

NEWS FROM WASHINGTON.

WASHINGTON, Saturday, Nov. 28.

THE PRESIDENT GETTING BETTER.

The condition of the President, who has been confined to his chamber for several days by sickness, seemed to be much improved to-day, and to promise an early recovery of health. There is nothing in the symptoms of his ailment to excite the fears of his friends.

THE IRON-CLAD SANGAMON.

A commission of competent engineers has, by direction of the Secretary of the Navy, made a thorough examination of the iron-clad *Sangamon*, now lying at Washington Yard, and pronounced her in all respects seaworthy.

INCREASE OF THE TAX ON DISTILLED LIQUORS.

The Commissioner of Internal Revenue has concluded to recommend in his report to the Secretary of the Treasury a large increase in the excise tax on distilled spirits, the present tax being considered absurdly low as compared with that levied by other Governments, while in England it yields twenty per centum and upward of the gross internal revenue of that country. In our own it yields less than ten per centum. As it is deemed necessary to increase taxation to make the law meet the expectations of Congress, there is no article on which it can be better levied than on this. Therefore, the Commissioner will ask that the tax be increased to fifty or sixty cents, probably to the later sum.

THE PROVOST-MARSHAL OF ALEXANDRA.

Some idea may be formed of the immense amount of business transacted at the office of Lieut.-Col. W. H. WELLS, Provost-Marshal for the defences south of the Potomac, Alexandria, Va., by reference to the following statement:

Number of prisoners arrested or forwarded from June 1, 1863, to Nov. 15, 1863, 2,245.

Number of passes issued to citizens from June 1 1863, to Nov. 15, 1863, 59,194.

Number of permits to take out supplies issued from June 1 to Nov. 15, 1863, 5,115. [This item may vary somewhat.]

The number of horses and mules captured from June 1, 1863, to Nov. 15, 1863, 362.

NOTE.—A very large amount of miscellaneous goods have been captured and turned over, the value of which we have no means of estimating, and a schedule of which would be very voluminous.

PRIZE SCHOONERS.

Prize schooner *Arctic*, captured off Wilmington, and schooner *Geo. Chisholm*, off Sankee River, each with cargoes of salt, from Nassau, have arrived at Washington.

ESCAPE OF JOHN MORGAN.

The Noted Horse-Thief and Six of his Officers Break Out of Columbus Jail.

COLUMBUS, Saturday, Nov. 28.

Maj.-Gen. JOHN MORGAN and six of his officers—Capts. BENNETT, TAYLOR, SHELDON, HAINES, HOCKERSMITH and MAGEE—escaped from the Ohio Penitentiary this morning between 2 o'clock and daylight.

JOHN MORGAN, on retiring, changed with his brother DICK from the top cell to the lower tier. The floor of the lower cell is two and a half inches thick, in which a hole was cut, under the bed, leading down into a two and a half foot sewer, running to the main wall around the Penitentiary. This wall was cut under, and the party escaped into the open country. The night was dark, with heavy rain. All efforts are being made by the authorities for his recapture.

CINCINNATI, Friday, Nov. 28.

JOHN MORGAN and six of his officers, viz.: Capts. BENNETT, TAYLOR, SHELDON, HAYNES, HACKERSMITH, and McGEE, escaped from Columbus Penitentiary last night, by digging through the floor of their cell to a sewer leading to the river. One thousand dollars reward is offered for the arrest of MORGAN. ■

A BRITISH STEAMER SEARCHED.

Passengers by the Corsica Examined—A Confederate Mail and Rebel Funds Found.

On the arrival of the British steamship *Corsica*, on Friday, from Havana and Nassau, she was boarded by the Custom-house officials in force. Every passenger on board was thoroughly searched in their persons and baggage, when a large amount of specie and Confederate money, also a large Confederate mail, was found. We did not hear of any of the passengers being detained in custody.

From Fortress Monroe.

FORTRESS MONROE, Saturday, Nov. 28.

About two thousand boxes and packages arrived here yesterday by Adams' Express, *en route* for National prisoners in and about Richmond, from their friends at the North.

The steamer *Conqueror* sailed for Newberne, N. C., at 3 o'clock this afternoon.

The Prize-Steamer Herald at Boston.

BOSTON, Saturday, Nov. 28.

The British steamer *Herald*, in charge of Acting Master KING, from Port Royal, S. C., arrived here this morning. She was captured Oct. 25, by the gunboat *Tioga*, on the Bahama Banks, while on the passage from Savannah to Nassau. She has 261 bales of cotton on board.

Bounty in Erie County.

BUFFALO, Saturday, Nov. 28.

The Board of Supervisors have to-day adopted a resolution appropriating five hundred thousand dollars for bounties in Erie County, each recruit to receive three hundred dollars.

Sailing of the North American.

PORTLAND, Me., Saturday, Nov. 28.

The steamship *North American* sailed at 4:30 P. M. to-day for Liverpool.

Additional from the Bermudas.

THE PIRATE SUMTER.

From the Newark Advertiser, Nov. 27.

Mr. ABRAM VAN WINKLE, of this city, who, with his wife, was a passenger on the *Harvest Queen*, which arrived at New-York from St. George, Bermuda, on Wednesday evening, has given us some information from that Anglo-rebel island—the chief resort of the blockade-runners.

The steamer *Gibraltar*, formerly the noted privateer *Sumter*, arrived at Hamilton on Sunday, the 15th inst., in four days from Wilmington with 350 bales of cotton, having succeeded in eluding the vigilance of our blockading squadron. She was coaling there and would leave in a day or two for Liverpool. It was understood among the Southerners there that she would receive an armament and resume her old occupation as privateer.

The Clyde steamer *Herome*, of 160 tons burden, reached Hamilton on Friday, the 13th. She is one hundred and eighty feet long, can carry three hundred bales of cotton, draws but three feet nine inches water, and on the trip from St. George to Hamilton ran *nineteen miles an hour*. She was being painted lead color when Mr. VAN WINKLE left, and was intended for running the blockade. The steamers *City of Petersburgh*, from Greenock, Scotland, and *Ceres*, from London, each loaded with very valuable cargoes of merchandise, had reached Hamilton, intending to run the blockade. Both vessels are also very fast.

There was quite a fleet of blockade-runners in the harbor, all of which were being painted lead-color. They are low, long vessels of great speed, and hardly discernible in the night. These vessels clear from Hamilton for Nassau, but as soon as they get out to sea sail straight for Wilmington: if caught by our West India squadron their Nassau clearance is made a pretext for release. Recent trips have, however, been very unfortunate, five of seven blockade runners having been caught by our cruisers off Wilmington. New and faster vessels are, however, constantly arriving and running their chances.

Among the passengers on the *Harvest Queen* was the widow of Ex-President TYLER, who had run the blockade from Wilmington.

GEN. BANKS' DEPARTMENT.

Arrival of the George Washington from New-Orleans.

Operations in Texas Still Successful.

Surprise of the Enemy in Western Louisiana.

Attempt of the Rebels to Interrupt River Navigation.

The U. S. mail steamer *George Washington*, Capt. WILLETS, from New-Orleans, arrived yesterday evening, bringing dates to the 21st inst. She has a full passenger list, the mails, and a large and valuable cargo.

To Mr. E. S. ALLEN, the Purser of the ship, we are again indebted for full files of papers and the prompt delivery of our correspondence.

Correspondence of the Associated Press.

NEW-ORLEANS, Saturday, Nov. 21, 1863—7 A. M.

News from Gen. BANKS in Texas continues good. He has captured Corpus Christi and several smaller places. The Texans are exhibiting strong evidences of Unionism wherever the army marches—so much so that arms and equipments for them, particularly for the cavalry service, are being sent from here.

From Western Louisiana there is news of a very well managed reconnoissance and surprise of the enemy. On the 20th, cavalry were sent out on the Abbeville road, and the Vermillion road, a mile in the rear of Camp Pratt, supported by infantry and artillery. They took the enemy completely by surprise, capturing the whole of the Sixth Texas, (with the exception of 25 men,) commanded by Col. BAGLEY. The Lieutenant-Colonel and Major were absent and escaped. They also dispersed the Second Louisiana cavalry (rebel) and returned with slight loss.

The British brig *Dashing Wave* arrived here on the 20th, a prize to the gunboat *New-London*. She was captured going into the Rio Grande. She had on board a cargo of clothing and medicines and $70,000 in gold.

Reports from the Mississippi River are that a rebel force ranging from 5,000 to 10,000 men are trying to concentrate at some point on the river not far above Port Hudson, to impede navigation. On the 18th the steamboat *Emerald* was attacked by a section of this force having four pieces of artillery. They fired several shots at her, one of which went through the pilot-house. She was struck also by a shell in the boiler deck. There being a heavy fog, she escaped further injury. No lives were lost. There is a report, which is authentic, of a strong rebel force gathering at Clinton, La., and another at Woodville, Miss. The rebels are very active all along the river from Baton Rouge to the Mississippi State line, and all their movements look to preparations for concentrating at some point on the river in heavy force, and planting batteries to obstruct the commerce of the Mississippi. Their plans will be developed shortly.

The steamer *White Cloud* arrived last night, bringing 3,000 barrels of flour.

The steamer *Sunny Side*, from Memphis for the Ohio River, with [illegible] bales of cotton and a number of passengers, was destroyed by fire, several lady passengers being burned to death or drowned.

THE VERY LATEST.

By Telegraph to the Southwest Pass.

NEW-ORLEANS, Saturday, Nov. 21.

On the 17th inst. our forces attacked Aransas City, Texas, and it surrendered. We captured 100 prisoners and three guns.

THE ARMY OF THE POTOMAC.

No News of the Advance—Our Cavalry on Friday near the Chancellorsville Battle-Ground.

WASHINGTON, Saturday, Nov. 28.

No intelligence respecting the Army of the Potomac has been received to-day at army headquarters, up to 2 o'clock this afternoon.

The *Star* says that yesterday morning our cavalry pushed forward as far as Locust Grove, where they met the advance of the rebel cavalry, and the latter were driven across Russell Creek, or river, and afterwards across Mill Run. A body of rebel infantry was posted between that point and Orange Court-house, and the whole rebel force moved off in the direction of the latter place.

Locust Grove is four miles south of Germanna Ford, in Orange County, and within a short distance of the wilderness where HOOKER fought his battle.

Mill Run is two miles from Locust Grove, and from thence to Mountain River, where the rebel Gen. EARLY, with EWELL'S old corps, is said to be in force, is about six miles. Orange Court-house is eight or ten miles further on in a southwest direction.

A Steamer Burned at Port Hudson with 3,500 Bales of Cotton—Price of Cotton at Memphis.

CAIRO, Ill., Saturday, Nov. 28.

A steamer from Natchez, bound for New-Orleans, laden with 3,500 bales of Cotton, was entirely consumed by fire at Port Hudson last week.

On the 25th instant, Cotton was in better demand at Memphis than for several days previous. Factors generally were holding the higher grades for better prices. Over 400 bales were sold at prices averaging from 35c.@75c.

Seven hundred bales of Cotton passed Cairo yesterday, *en route* for Cincinnati.

The Cherokee Indians Asking for Relief, etc.

SPRINGFIELD, Mo., Saturday, Nov. 18.

A delegation of Cherokee Indians, headed by Capt. CHRISTY, Acting Chief, paid their respects to Gen. MCNEIL, to-day, by order of their National Council.

It is reported that CHRISTY recounted the sufferings of the Indians from roving banditti; asked for protection against their depredations: desired authority to raise a regiment of cavalry, and to adopt guerrilla warfare as the only means of ridden themselves of mounted marauders. Also, that they asked that the districts allotted for their settlement should be better protected by the United States authorities, so as to enable the Indians to cultivate the soil and secure more comfortable homes.

Gen. MCNEIL replied that he represented the condition of the Indians to the proper authority, recommending some measures for their improvement, and that he would afford them all the protection in his power.

From San Francisco.

SAN FRANCISCO, Thursday Nov. 26.

Business is generally suspended and to-day is devoted to Thanksgiving.

The Sheriff of Los Angelos proposing yesterday to arrest the members of a vigilance committee who had hung five horse thieves and murderers, a cavalry company of United States Volunteers from San Pedro marched to the town, when the Sheriff stopped the proceedings.

SAN FRANCISCO, Friday, Nov. 27.

The Nevada Constitutional Convention has adopted an article compelling all children between six and fourteen years of age to attend school,

EUROPEAN NEWS.

ARRIVAL OF THE ARABIA'S MAILS.

THE SITUATION OF THE FRENCH EMPIRE.

The Polish, Mexican and American Questions.

FULL TEXT OF THE EMPEROR'S LETTER.

VIEWS OF THE PROPOSED CONGRESS.

The mails by the *Arabia* arrived at this port yesterday morning. In our files we find the following interesting and important details of the news, of which we have already had a full synopsis by telegraph:

FRANCE.

SITUATION OF THE EMPIRE.

From Galignani, Nov. 12.

The official statement of the situation of the Empire, composed of reports sent in from the various Ministerial departments, has been distributed to the members of the Two Chambers. As the financial explanations are to be presented separately, nothing is said for the moment of that branch of the service. For Foreign Affairs, the account published commences in these terms:

THE POLISH QUESTION.

At the opening of the last session of the great bodies of the State, the Emperor's Government congratulated itself on the general situation of Europe. If some difficulties existed on different points of the Continent, there was nothing to lead to the anticipation of speedy complications, and in particular nothing to announce that the Polish question was on the eve of again forcing itself on the attention of the Cabinets.

For the last two years a certain degree of agitation prevailed in Poland, but no project of a rising manifested itself; everything, on the contrary, appeared to show that a recourse to arms no more entered into the calculations of the men invested with the confidence of the country than into the wishes of the people. The recruitment, transformed into a measure of proscription, drove to despair those whom it threatened to affect, and conflicts broke out simultaneously on several points.

The question, however, did not present itself except under the auspices of a purely local movement caused by a determinate cause of complaint. The convention signed at St Petersburgh on Feb. 8, by which, under pretext of maintaining order on the frontier, Prussia bound herself toward Russia to cooperate in a certain degree in the repression, gave to the struggle an international character, and obliged the Cabinets to occupy themselves with it.

The Polish question is essentially European, for it cannot put itself forward without involving the most important interests. France signed the documents under the protection of which Poland has been placed, and French sympathies have never been wanting to that nation in her former trials. It is a tradition which the Emperor's Government could less avoid deferring to than any other.

England had the same rights and the same reasons for interfering. The French Government therefore applied to that Power, to come to an understanding, in order to represent in concert to the Cabinet of Berlin, the danger of her intermeddling in an affair of which she was so unfortunately extending the importance. We moreover were aware that Austria regarded the engagements concluded at St. Petersburgh in the same light as ourselves. The Emperor's Government made known to her its intentions. The Cabinet of Vienna had already expressed its sentiments to Prussia and to Russia, when they solicited her adhesion to these arrangements. The proceedings adopted with the Prussian Court had for result to obtain explanations which lessened the fear which had been entertained of seeing her take an active part in the hostilities.

When we had to make known our views at Berlin, we took care to avoid any isolated action, and also to avoid any false interpretation. The nature, however, of our relations with Russia, authorized and induced us at the same time to attempt with her the plan of personal efforts and friendly counsels before coming to official communications and a combined action.

The French Government had not waited, in order to give prudent advice, to be constrained to it by urgent necessity. In 1857, His Majesty wishing to avail himself, in the interest of order and of peace, of the confidence which so happily united the two Cabinets, felt himself induced by the sincerity of his esteem and of his friendship for the Emperor ALEXANDER, to recommend the state of Poland to the solicitude of the Court of Russia. Such language was worthy of being understood by the Sovereign who was about to give, in the emancipation of serfs, so striking a proof of his prudence. Facts have since too strongly shown the opportuneness of those suggestions, and testify every day how much it is to be regretted that they were not listened to.

His Majesty's Government, in presence of the conjunctures which have justified its previsions, considered it as a duty not to conceal its anxieties from Russia. It pointed out with unreserved frankness our perplexities in the midst of events of which the public opinion of the country, as well as the general interests of Europe, would not allow us to remain indifferent spectators. The French Ambassador was instructed to point out, in terms the most conformable to the friendly relations of the Governments, the advantages of a policy of reparation and of progress.

The English Government, in a dispatch addressed at that time to its representative at St. Petersburgh, recommended a general amnesty and the restitution of the privileges granted to the Poles by the Emperor ALEXANDER I. The French Cabinet could not but approve of the applications, which to a certain point entered into the more general order of ideas which it also entertained, but in order to leave to Russia the merit of entire spontaneousness, it abstained from directly supporting them. The English Cabinet having afterward proposed to invite the parties who signed the general Treaty of Vienna to express similar wishes, the Government of His Majesty announced its intention of adhering to that proposal only in case of obtaining the consent of the other Powers.

We had pointed out to the Russian Cabinet the interest it had in anticipating diplomatic representations by resolutely assuming the initiative. But we had not obtained any promises—any assurance that would allow us to hope for a satisfactory result from a longer personal pressure. It became necessary to adopt another course.

The Government of her Britannic Majesty had preceded us in its communications to the Russian Cabinet. Austria, without viewing events in the same light as England, continued to observe a well-disposed neutrality as to the Poles. The Emperor's Government accordingly flattered itself with the hope of forming between the three Courts an understanding which would insure to their measures the European character required by the nature of the interests at stake, and at once unite all the guarantees of moderation and force.

The Cabinet of London, in its first communication, had taken the treaties of 1815 as a starting-point. Russia has made a precise reply by contesting the interpretation given to them by the principal Secretary of State: she confined herself, as a method of pacification, to speaking of an amnesty after the war, and promising not to withdraw any of the concessions she had made. The French Government doubted the success of any measure based exclusively on those treaties, and thought that matters should be viewed from a higher ground. The acts of 1815 assuredly conceded precious advantages to the Poles, in reviving the Polish name, in stipulating for her national institutions, and in establishing certain links between all the parts of the kingdom as it existed before the first partition. But those arrangements have not prevented the recurrence of commotions which periodically menace the repose of Europe. Without denying that the treaties offered to the Cabinets a legal motive of intervention, the French Government thought that it would be proper to invoke principally the interests of European order common to all the Powers.

The two Cabinets appreciated these considerations; and the Emperor's Government made them the subject of a dispatch to the French Ambassador at St. Petersburgh. The dispatch concluded by signalizing the opportunity of considering the means of placing Poland in the conditions of a durable peace.

Austria, whilst alleging special interests as a Power conterminous and more exposed to the influence of these disturbances, held a language similar to our own. England, without abandoning her first argument on the treaties, reproduced, in a briefer form, the ideas which we had developed. The greater part of the States of Europe gave their adhesion to them, and thus stamped the communications of the three Courts with the character of a veritable European manifestation.

Russia appeared to receive these overtures with favor. Although she endeavored to cast the responsibility of the Polish movement on encouragements from without and revolutionary intrigues, she recognized the extent of the evil, and the inefficacy of the measures adopted up to that time to provide a remedy. She neither contested the general interests engaged in the Polish question, nor the special interests of conterminous States. She did not decline the competence of the Governments who signed the final act of the Treaty of Vienna, but appeared, on the contrary, to accept their assistance for a deliberation, the bases of which she invited the three Powers to communicate.

England was of opinion that the negotiations should be preceded by an armistice, in spite of the difficulties which its execution might encounter. The idea of stopping as soon as possible the effusion of blood was too conformable to the feelings of the French Government not to obtain its approbation; and whilst itself acquiesced, it recommended the same to the Court of Austria.

The Cabinet of Vienna, on its part, drew up a programme in six articles, the principal object of which was to claim for Poland institutions similar to those of Galicia. Judging these data insufficient, the French Government introduced notable modifications in them, and for the sake of a good understanding agreed to admit the programme, but only as a starting-point for the conferences. We had, besides, attached much value to an appeal made to the whole of Europe to participate in the negotiations. France has constantly declared that she will always be found ready to enter on such discussions in the full light of day.

The three Courts, in the communications which they a second time directed to their Ambassadors, had not succeeded in avoiding certain shades of expression which could not escape the attention of Russia. It might have been foreseen that that Power would seek to derive profit from the apparent diversity of views. In order to parry that danger as much as possible, the French Government made to the Vienna and London Cabinets a proposal to consolidate the accord by taking, in the form of a convention or a procotol, an engagement to pursue in concert a regulation of Polish affairs, by diplomatic methods, or otherwise, if necessary. Such an engagement, besides the immediate advantage of exalting the authority of the language of the allied Courts, would have offered to that Power whose position required most consideration the guarantees of a complete solidarity in all eventualities. We were persuaded that the surest method of preventing complications was to show ourselves ready to meet them with all the firmness required, and that conflicts between Governments took their origin not so often in bold resolutions as in protractions and hesitations that allowed difficulties to become aggravated. Our proposition was not accepted. The Russian Court replied to the programme of the three Powers by an absolute refusal. She promised to take the six points into consideration, but only when the insurrection was suppressed. She rejected all idea of a supension of arms, and declining the competency of the Powers which signed the General Act of 1815, which she had previously admitted, she proposed to open with Austria and Prussia, as participating Powers, a separate negotiation.

The Vienna Cabinet rejected that proposal without hesitation, as being contrary to her duties to the two other Powers, and gave explanations at St. Petersburgh with a spontaneousness and a frankness which did honor to her sincerity.

The French Government at the same time expressed at London and Vienna the painful impression it had felt on receiving the replies of Russia. The three Cabinets addressed fresh communications to St. Petersburgh, the conclusions of which were conceived in identical terms. They unanimously declared Russia to be responsible for the consequences which might arise from a refusal to take their representations into account, and from the prolongation of the troubles in Poland. The last dispatches of Prince GORTSCHAKOFF are well known.

Notwithstanding the little success of the diplomatic intervention of the three Powers, the Emperor's Government has the satisfaction of knowing that it has, from the moment in which the Polish question was brought forward, in the measure of its rights and its duties toward England, neglected nothing to arrive at a solution. Ever attentive to the painful spectacle of the struggle which is going on in Poland, it loses sight of none of the interests which are connected with that conflict. It will maintain its accord with England and Austria, and it cannot believe that the union of the Cabinets, in an affair so worthy of their solicitude, must remain sterile.

We have not, however, the pretension to impose our solutions on the Powers interested, as much or even more directly than ourselves in the settlement of the existing difficulties. In a question essentially European, it is neither in conformity with our obligations or our rights to incur alone a responsibility which it is the duty of all to partake.

The Danish dispute, Rome and Italy, the relations with Turkey, and the situation of MONTENEGRO are touched up, and then the

AMERICAN QUESTION

is discussed as follows:

"The sad previsions suggested by the exasperation of the struggle carried on during three years in the United States, have been but too much realized. Blood has continued to flow, whilst the respective situations of the belligerents do not allow us to anticipate a period of this terrible crisis. In presence of such an accumulation of ruins, and such a sacrifice of life in a struggle hitherto fruitless, *we have felt profound regret that the proposition which we made at London and at St. Petersburgh, to unite in provoking an armistice, was not accepted.* Compelled to renounce that project by a double refusal, we have, however, declared that our desire to contribute to the reëstablishment of peace in any form would not be the less lively and sincere. We have given proof of this by suggesting the idea of substituting for the project of an amicable intervention of the Maritime Powers, the expedient of direct messages between the Government of the United States and the Confederates of the South. This new attempt has not been more fortunate than the preceding.

From that time we have nothing left but to follow out the line of conduct adopted ever since the beginning of this war by the Government of the Emperor. This we have striven to do with scrupulous care under all circumstances. We have remained neutral and well disposed; although it has often been difficult for us to reconcile this part with our duties toward our fellow-countrymen. Independently of the sufferings, which, in our departments, are the consequence of the American crisis, hostilities on the territory of the Union itself have occasioned considerable detriment and loss to French residents. They have often had occasion to make just complaint of the abusive proceedings of the civil and military authorities. Our countrymen must understand that their interests, like those of other foreigners, cannot claim an exceptional security in the midst of the tumult of arms, and that in such cases all ordinary guarantees necessarily lose something of their efficacy. Moreover, a state of war imposes inevitable fetters on the commerce of neutrals. If the progress of liberal doctrines tends to relax them, it cannot wholly suppress them.

The Cabinet of Washington has been able to satisfy itself that we have made, in our reclamations, a large allowance for these difficulties. But the Government of the Emperor cannot disguise its pain at seeing so many aggrieved interests, well deserving of its care, making a vain appeal for protection."

MEXICO.

The object which the French Government aimed at in Mexico is declared to be very near its final accomplishment. The following is the language used:

"The Emperor's Government is on the point of attaining the object which it proposed to itself when it displayed the flag of France on the shores of Mexico. The success of our arms, by rendering the country free to dispose of itself, has confirmed the hopes which we founded in the good sense of the Mexican nation. The capture of Puebla has become a new title of glory for our heroic army; and the acclamations which greeted it in entering Mexico have loudly testified that our soldiers were received there as liberators. The Assembly of Notables has pronounced that Mexico could only expect regeneration from a monarchical institution. It also at the same time designated to the Mexican nation the Prince whom political circumstances approved to ourselves to indicate as most preferable. The expression of these wishes, inspired by a just confidence in the high and brilliant qualities of him to whom they were addressed, has been favorably received, with the sole reserve that the whole nation should be called on to ratify the patriotic and spontaneous impulse which decided the sending of the mission charged to offer the crown of Mexico to the Archduke MAXIMILIAN. This is how we, on our part, had understood the bearing of the resolutions of the Assembly.

Whatever might be the authority of the influential men who composed it, their decisions, in our opinion, to become definitive, must receive from the populations a more explicit sanction. We congratulate ourselves on seeing our ideas shared by the eminent Prince whom Mexico calls to inaugurate its new destinies.

The fortune of France and the blood of her soldiers belong to France only. An evident and imperious French interest could therefore alone determine the Emperor's Government to engage in an undertaking of which it had beforehand weighed the sacrifices and difficulties. It had, moreover, foreseen the salvation of Mexico as a possible consequence of the military expedition to which it was constrained. The public feeling of the country and the wisdom of the Archduke MAXIMILIAN justify all our hopes in this matter.

In an early future we expect to receive from the new Government of Mexico the guarantees which have been wanting to our interests under all the Governments which preceded it. For the moment, important questions necessarily remain to be settled as concerns ourselves; for the military result of our expedition has only prepared the ground for ulterior

The Charleston Mercury.

DAILY PAPER—TWENTY DOLLARS PER ANNUM, PAYABLE HALF-YEARLY IN ADVANCE.

VINDICE NULLO—SPONTE SUA SINE LEGE FIDES RECTUMQUE COLENTUR.

COUNTRY PAPER—THREE A WEEK—TEN DOLLARS PER ANNUM, IN ADVANCE.

VOLUME LXXXIII. | CHARLESTON, S. C., WEDNESDAY, DECEMBER 2, 1863. | NUMBER 11,924

THE BATTLE OF MISSIONARY RIDGE.

ARMY OF TENNESSEE,
Chickamauga, November 25—Midnight.

The Confederates have sustained to-day the most ignominious defeat of the whole war—a defeat for which there is but little excuse or palliation. For the first time during our struggle for national independence, our defeat is chargeable to the troops themselves, and not to the blunders or incompetency of their leaders. It is difficulty for one to realize how a defeat so complete could have occurred on ground so favorable, notwithstanding the great disparity in the forces of the two hostile armies. The ground was more in our favor than it was at Fredericksburg, where Gen. Longstreet is said to have estimated that Lee's army was equal to 300,000 men. And yet we gained the battle of Fredericksburg and lost that of Missionary Ridge.

But let us take up the painful narrative at the beginning, and see how this great misfortune, if not this grievous disgrace, has befallen the Confederate arms.

Lookout Mountain was evacuated last night, it being no longer important to us after the loss of Lookout, or Will's, Valley, and no longer tenable against such an overwhelming force as General Grant had concentrated around Chattanooga. Gen. Bragg abandoned, also, the whole of Chattanooga Valley, and the trenches and breastworks running along the foot of Missionary Ridge and across the valley to the base of Lookout, and moved his troops up to the top of the ridge. It was found necessary to extend his right well up towards the Chickamauga, near its mouth, in consequence of the heavy forces which the enemy had thrown up the river in that direction. The Tennessee and Missionary Ridge approach nearer to each other as one goes up, or rather down, the valley—the width of which, at some points, does not exceed one-fourth of a mile. Across this valley, now almost an open plain, varying from a fourth of a mile to two miles in width, the Federals advanced to the assault, their ranks exposed to our artillery fire from the ridge, while in the plain, and to the infantry fire when they attempted the ascent of the hill or mountain.

The only objection that can be urged against our line was its length and weakness, the latter being the result of the former, and the former the result of circumstances beyond our control, it being necessary for us to guard the passes in the Ridge and to conform to the length of the line presented by the enemy. The Ridge varies in height from four to six hundred feet, and is crossed by several roads leading out from Chattanooga. The western side next to the enemy was steep and rugged, and in some places almost bare, the timber having been cut away for firewood. Our pickets occupied the breastworks below, while the infantry and artillery were distributed along the crest of the Ridge from McFarlan's Gap almost to the mouth of the Chickamauga, a distance of six miles or more. In addition to the natural strength of the position, we had thrown up breastworks along the Ridge wherever the ascent is easy.

The Federal army was marshalled under Grant, Thomas, Hooker and Sherman, and did not number less than 85,000 veteran troops. The Confederate army under Bragg, Hardee and Breckinridge, did not number half so many. Longstreet's Virginia divisions and other troops had been sent to East Tennessee. Had these been present, with their steady leader at the head of them, we should have won a victory quite as complete as our defeat has been. As it was, we ought to have won the day, and should have done so if our men had done as well as usual. Possibly a mistake was committed when Longstreet was sent away, and possibly it would have been better not to have accepted battle to-day, but have retired last night. General Bragg thought, however, that there was not time, after the loss of Lookout, to get his army safely over the Chickamauga last night, and that it would be better, occupying so strong a position, to fight it out. But what could he expect from battle where the odds were so much against him? Not only did Grant have nearly three to one in numbers, but the geographical configuration of the ground, in manoeuvering an army, was as favorable as he could desire. Nature had provided an ample protection for his flanks and rear, and rendered his front almost impregnable. He possessed the additional advantage of being able to manoeuvre his army upon the chord of a semi-circle, while Bragg could move only upon the arc.

But let us proceed with the battle, the strangest, most singular and unsatisfactory conflict in which our arms have been engaged.

Grant deployed his immense masses in two heavy lines of battle, and sometimes in three, supported by large reserve forces. The spectacle was magnificent as viewed from the crest of Missionary Ridge. He advanced first against our right wing, about 10 o'clock, where he encountered that superb soldier, Lieutenant General Hardee, who commanded on the right, whilst Major General Breckinridge commanded on the left. Hardee's command embraced Cleburne's, Walker's (commanded by General Gist, General Walker being absent), Cheatham's and Stevenson's divisions. Breckinridge's embraced his old division, commanded by Brigadier General Lewis Stewart's, part of Buckner's, and Hindman's, commanded by Patton Anderson. The enemy's first assault upon Hardee was repulsed with great slaughter, as was his second, though made with double lines supported with heavy reserves. The wave of battle, like the waves of the sea when it dashes against a rock-bound coast, beat, and hissed, and struggled in vain, for the brave men who guarded our right were resolved never to yield one foot to the hated invaders. The odds against which they contended were fearful; for while the enemy advanced in two and even three massive lines, their own army consisted of only one long and weak line, without supports. Yet they not only repulsed every attack, but captured seven flags, about 300 prisoners, and remained masters of the ground until night, when they were ordered to retire, carrying off all their guns, losing no prisoners, and but a small per centage of killed and wounded. The whole command behaved well, and especially that model soldier, Major General Cleburne, a true son of the Emerald Isle, and his heroic division. General Hardee saved the army from a disastrous rout, and added fresh laurels to his brow.

The attack on the left wing was not made until about noon. Here, as on the right, the enemy was repulsed: but he was obstinate, and fought with great ardor and confidence, returning to the charge again and again in the handsomest style, until one of our brigades near the centre, said to be Reynold's, gave way, and the Federal flag was planted on Missionary Ridge. The enemy was not slow in availing himself of the great advantages of his new position. In a few minutes he turned upon our flanks and poured into them a terrible enfilading fire, which soon threw the Confederates on his right and left into confusion.—Under this confusion the gap in our lines grew wider and wider, and the wider it grew the faster the multitudinous foe rushed into the yawning chasm. The confusion extended until it finally assumed the form of a panic. Seeing the enemy in possession of a portion of the heights, the men hastily concluded that the day was gone, and that they had best save themselves. Just at this time the alarm was increased by an artillery battery which rushed down the hill to the river for a fresh supply of ammunition; the men, however, supposed they were flying from the field, and that all was lost. Nearly the whole left wing eventually became involved, and gave way—a portion of it retiring under orders, but the greater part in an unmitigated rout.

Gen. Bragg did all he could to rally the fugitives, and reform the broken line. He exposed himself in the most unguarded manner; and, at one time, it looked as if he would certainly be killed. His staff officers were also conspicuous in their efforts to restore our line. They and their chief were the last to leave the ridge.

The day was lost. Hardee still maintained his ground: but no success of the right wing could restore the left to its original position. All men—even the bravest—are subject to error and confusion; but to-day some of the Confederates did not fight with their accustomed courage. Possibly the contrast between the heavy masses of the Federals, as they rolled across the valley and up the mountain ridge, and their own long and attenuated line, was not of a character to encourage them.

Our casualties are small—very small—too small, indeed, to be recorded along with so complete and humiliating a defeat. Included among our losses are some of our best guns—perhaps as many as thirty or forty. The infantry supports in some instances fled so precipitately that there was no time left to remove the guns. There were but few roads down the mountain by which they could retreat, and this occasioned further loss.—All the artillery behaved well. The men in Cobb's battery stood their ground after their supports had fled, and though they lost their guns, they fought them to the last; and when they could use them no longer on account of the steepness of the descent, they hurled hand-grenades at the foe as he crawled up the mountain beneath the muzzles of the guns.

The enemy's loss must have exceeded ours ten to one. Our dead and some of the wounded were left on the field.

But it is late and bitter cold, and I must close. We cross the Chickamauga to-night, and then proceed to Dalton. I write under the greatest possible disadvantages.—*Cor. Savannah Republican.*

Battle of Missionary Ridge

The Charleston Mercury.

DAILY PAPER—TWENTY DOLLARS PER ANNUM, PAYABLE HALF-YEARLY IN ADVANCE. | VINDICE NULLO SPONTE SUA SINE LEGE FIDES RECTUMQUE COLENTUR. | COUNTRY PAPER—THREE A WEEK—FIVE DOLLARS PER ANNUM, IN ADVANCE.

VOLUME LXXXIII. | CHARLESTON, S. C., THURSDAY, DECEMBER 17, 1863. | NUMBER 11,936

THE MERCURY.

THURSDAY, DECEMBER 17, 1863.

Lincoln's Message.

The message of ABRAHAM LINCOLN is to be found in this journal this morning. So much curiosity exists relative to this document, and so much of the information which it contains is important to the right understanding of the present phase of the war, that we have published it nearly entire, to the exclusion of much other matter.

In style, remarks the Richmond *Examiner*, it is bare as a leaf from a ledger. Such derisive laughter has been excited by the Hoosier's previous attempts at fine writing, that he has no longer spirit to show himself. The tone is subdued; the language dry and plain; the exposition is brief as arithmetic. But all reflection upon the general characteristics of this "State Paper" is forgotten in wonder over the conclusion at which it arrives, and the proclamation appended thereto. After re-affirming the universal abolition of slavery, without compensation, in the broadest manner, ABRAHAM LINCOLN offers a "pardon" to all persons in the Confederacy, under the rank of Colonel, and who have not held any civil office—executive, judicial, legislative or diplomatic—in the Confederate States, who will give themselves up, and swear oaths of allegiance to the United States, which contains an obligation to accept the proclamation emancipating the slaves. When one tenth of the population of any State has sworn this oath, the said tenth shall constitute a State Government, and send members to Congress at Washington. On condition of such submission, the creatures who make it shall be permitted to crawl on the face of the earth and possess property, with the exception of slaves. These are to be enrolled in the army of the United States and quartered over the conquered States, where negro soldiers will be billeted in every house, and negro Provost Marshals lord it in every village.

Such are the first terms of peace offered by the United States to the people of the Confederate States. These terms are joined with many vague intimations that they may be withdrawn or modified as occasion requires. "Those laws and proclamations are enacted and put forth," says the shallow knave, "for the purpose of aiding in the suppression of the rebellion." But in vain is the trap set in sight of any bird. Even geese would scorn the chaff with which it is baited, and shun the snare which shows the noose on the surface. The Proclamation of Pardon will have as much, and no more, effect than the Proclamation of Emancipation, and the Proclamation "to disperse," which began the war.

This document has, however, one trait of real importance. It reveals the decline of the mania for war in the United States. LINCOLN represents his people now as he did two years ago. Then, all was bloody. Confiscation, subjugation, extermination, were the only measures he and they thought or spoke of. Great is the distance between those days and these. Instead of "crushing the rebellion" in "sixty days" by a gigantic "Union army," the chief hope now rests in a juggle. There is a time for all things. A time for fighting, and that time is nearly past; a time for cheating, and that time is nearly come.

LATEST FROM THE NORTH.

LINCOLN'S ANNUAL MESSAGE—ANNUAL COST OF THE WAR—A PLAN FOR THE RECONSTRUCTION OF THE "UNION"—PROPOSED AMNESTY TO ALL "REBELS" BELOW COLONELS IN THE ARMY AND CAPTAINS IN THE NAVY, ETC.

The annual message of ABRAHAM LINCOLN was read in the Yankee Congress on Wednesday. We give a synopsis of the document as far as it will interest our readers. He says that "another year of health and of sufficiently abundant harvests has passed." The United States remains at peace with foreign powers. The following is his allusion to this fact:

The efforts of disloyal citizens of the United States to involve us in foreign wars, to aid an inexcusable insurrection, have been unavailing. Her Britannic Majesty's Government, as was justly expected, have exercised their authority to prevent the departure of new hostile expeditions from British ports.

The Emperor of France has, by a like proceeding, promptly vindicated the neutrality which he proclaimed at the beginning of the contest. Questions of great intricacy and importance have arisen out of the blockade and other belligerent operations between this Government and several of the maritime Powers, but they have been discussed, and, as far as was possible, accommodated in a spirit of frankness, justice and national good will.

THE FINANCES OF THE NATION.

The operations of the Treasury during the last year have been successfully conducted. The enactment by Congress of a National Banking law has proved a valuable support of the public credit, and the general legislation in relation to loans has fully answered the expectations of its favorers. Some amendments may be required to perfect existing laws; but no change in their principles or general scope is believed to be needed. Since these measures have been in operation all demands on the Treasury, including the pay of the army and navy, have been promptly met and fully satisfied. No considerable body of troops, it is believed, were ever more amply provided and more liberally and punctually paid; and it may be added that by no people were the burdens incidental to a great war more cheerfully borne.

The receipts during the year, from all sources, including loans and the balance in the Treasury at the commencement, were $901,125,674.86, and the aggregate disbursement $895,796,630.65, leaving a balance on the 1st of July, 1863, of $5,329,044.21.

Of the receipts, there were received from customs, $69,059,642 40; from internal revenue, $37,640,787 95; from direct tax, $1,485,103.61; from lands, $167,617.17; from miscellaneous sources, $3,046,615.35, and from loans, $776,682,361.57—making the aggregate $901,125,674.86. Of the disbursements there were for the civil service $23,253,922,08; for pensions and Indians, $4,216,526.59; for interest on public debt, $24,729,846.51; for the War Department, $599,298,600.83; for the Navy Department, $63,211,105 27; for payment of funded and temporary debt, $181,086,635 07—making the aggregate $895,796,630.65; and leaving the balance of $5,329,044.21.

But the payments of the funded and temporary debt having been made from moneys borrowed during the year, must be regarded as merely nominal payments, and the moneys borrowed to make them as merely nominal receipts; and their amount, $181,086,635 07, should therefore be deducted both from receipts and disbursements. This being done, there remains, as actual receipts, $720,039,039.79; and the actual disbursements, $714,709,995 58, leaving the balance as already stated.

The actual receipts and disbursements for the first quarter and the estimated receipts and disbursements for the remaining three-quarters of the current fiscal year, 1864, will be shown in detail by the report of the Secretary of the Treasury, to which I invite your attention.

It is sufficient to say here that it is not believed that actual results will exhibit a state of the finances less favorable to the country than the estimates of that officer heretofore submitted, while it is confidently expected that at the close of the year both disbursements and debts will be found very considerably less than has been anticipated.

THE WAR REPORT.

The report of the Secretary of War is a document of great interest. It consists of—

First—The military operations of the year, detailed in the report of the General-in-Chief.

Second—The organization of colored persons into the war service.

Third—The exchange of prisoners, fully set forth in the letter of Gen. Hitchcock.

Fourth—The operations and the act of enrolling and calling out the national forces—detailed in the report of the Provost Marshal General.

Fifth—The organization of the Invilid Corps. And

Sixth—The operations of the several departments of the Quartermaster General, Commissary General, Paymaster General, Chief of Engineers, Chief of Ordnance and Surgeon General.

MISCELLANEOUS RECOMMENDATIONS AND AFFAIRS.

Arrangements have been made with the Emperor of Russia for a telegraph line through his territory on this continent. Immigration is to be encouraged. The steam navy is to be greatly increased. The number of seamen in the navy has increased from 7,500 to 34 000. The Postoffice Department lacks $150,000 of paying its expenses. A novel and important question, involving the extent of the maritime jurisdiction of Spain in the waters which surround the Island of Cuba, has been debated without reaching an agreement, and it is proposed, in an amicable spirit, to refer it to the arbitrament of a friendly power. A convention for that purpose will be submitted to the Senate.

THE REBELLION.

When Congress assembled a year ago the war had already lasted twenty months, and there had been many conflicts on both land and sea, with varying results. The rebellion had been pressed back into reduced limits; yet the tone of public feeling and opinion at home and abroad was not satisfactory. With other signs the popular elections, then just passed, indicated uneasiness among ourselves, while, amid much that was cold and menacing, the kindest words coming from Europe were uttered in accents of pity that we were too blind to surrender a hopeless cause. Our commerce was suffering greatly by a few armed vessels—built upon and furnished from foreign shores—and we were threatened with such additions from the same quarter as would sweep our trade from the sea and raise our blockade. We had failed to elicit from European Governments anything hopeful upon this subject.

THE EMANCIPATION PROCLAMATION.

The preliminary emancipation proclamation, issued in September, was running its assigned period to the beginning of the new year. A month later the final proclamation came, including the announcement that colored men of suitable condition would be received in the war service. The policy of emancipation and of employing black soldiers gave to the future a new aspect, about which hope, and fear, and doubt, contended in uncertain conflict. According to our political system, as a matter of civil administration, the Government had no lawful power to effect emancipation in any State, and for a long time it had been hoped that the rebellion could be suppressed without resorting to it as a military measure. It was all the while deemed possible that the necessity for it might come, and that, if it should, the crisis of the contest would then be presented. It came, and, as was anticipated, was followed by dark and doubtful days.

THE CONTRABANDS IN SERVICE.

Eleven months having now passed, we are now permitted to take another review. The rebel borders are pressed still further back, and by the complete opening of the Mississippi the country dominated by the rebellion is divided into distinct parts, with no practical communication between them. Tennessee and Arkansas have been substantially cleared of insurgent control, and influential citizens in each, owners of slaves and advocates of slavery, at the beginning of the rebellion, now declare openly for emancipation in their respective States. Of those States not included in the Emancipation Proclamation—Maryland and Missouri—neither of which three years ago would tolerate any restraint upon the extension of slavery into new Territories, only dispute now as to the best mode of removing it within their own limits. Of those who were slaves at the beginning of the rebellion, full one hundred thousand are now in the United States military service—about one-half of which number actually bear arms in the ranks; thus giving the double advantage of taking so much labor from the insurgent cause and supplying the places which otherwise must be filled with so many white men. So far as tested, it is difficult to say they are not as good soldiers as any. No servile insurrection and tendency to violence or cruelty has marked the measures of emancipation and arming the blacks. These measures have been much discussed in foreign countries, and contemporary with such discussion the tone of public sentiment there is much improved. At home the same measures have been fully discussed, supported, criticised and denounced; and the annual elections following are highly encouraging to those whose official duty it is to bear the country through this great trial. Thus we have the new reckoning.

THE CRISIS PAST—A PROCLAMATION.

The crisis which threatened to divide the friends of the Union is past. Looking now to the present and future, and with a reference to a resumption of the national authority in the States wherein that authority has been suspended, I have thought it proper to issue a proclamation, a copy of which is herewith transmitted. On examination of the proclamation, it will appear (as believed) that nothing is attempted beyond what is amply justified by the Constitution. True, the forms of an oath is given, but no man is coerced to take it. The man is only promised a pardon in case he voluntarily takes the oath, The Constitution authorizes the Executive to grant or withhold the pardon at his own absolute discretion, and this includes the power to grant on terms, as is fully established by judicial and other authorities. It is also proffered that if in any of the States named a State government shall be organized and guaranteed by the United States, under it the State shall, on the constitutional conditions, be protected against invasion and domestic violence.

THE PROPOSED RECONSTRUCTION.

The constitutional obligation of the United States to guarantee to every State in the Union a republican form of government, and to protect the State in the cases stated, is explicit and full. But why tender the benefits of this provision only to a State Government set up in this particular way? This section of the Constitution contemplates a case wherein the element within a State favorable to a republican government in the Union may be too feeble for an opposite and hostile element, external to, or even within, the State; and such are precisely the cases with which we are now dealing. An attempt to guarantee and protect a revived State Government, constructed in whole or in preponderating part from the very element against whose hostility and violence it is to be protected, is simply absurd. There must be a test by which to separate the opposing elements so as to build only from the sound; and that test is a sufficiently liberal one which accepts as sound whoever will make a sworn recantation of his former movements. But if it be proper to require as a test of admission to the political body an oath of allegiance to the United States, and to the Union under it, why not also to the laws and proclamations in regard to slavery?

THE OATH.

Those laws and proclamations were enacted and put forth for the purpose of aiding in the suppression of the rebellion. To give them their fullest effect there had to be a pledge for their maintenance. In my judgment they have aided, and will further aid, the cause for which they were intended. To now abandon them would be not only to relinquish a lever of power, but would also be a cruel and astonishing breach of faith. I may add, at this point, while I remain in my present position I shall not attempt to retract or modify the emancipation proclamation, nor shall I return to slavery any person who is free by the terms of that proclamation or by any of the acts of Congress. For these and other reasons it is thought best that support of these measures shall be included in the oath; and it is believed that the Executive may lawfully claim it in return for pardon and restoration of forfeited rights, which he has a clear constitutional power to withhold altogether or grant upon the terms he shall deem wisest for the public interest. It should be observed also that this part of the oath is subject to the modifying and abrogating power of legislation and supreme judicial decision.

THE REVOLUTION IN THE LABOR SYSTEM.

The proposed acquiescence of the national Executive in any reasonable temporary State arrangement for the freed people is made with a view of possibly modifying the confusion and destitution which must at best attend all classes by a total revolution of labor throughout whole States. It is hoped that the already deeply afflicted people in those States may be somewhat more ready to give up the cause of their affliction, if to this extent this vital matter be left to themselves, while no power of the national Executive to prevent an abuse is abridged by the proposition.

The suggestion in the proclamation as to maintaining the political framework of the States, on what is called reconstruction, is made in the hope that it may do good without danger of harm. It will save labor and avoid great confusion. But why any proclamation now upon this subject? The subject is beset with the conflicting views that the step might be delayed too long, or be taken too soon.

In some States the elements for resumption seem ready for action, but remain inactive, apparently for want of a rallying point— a plan of action. Why should A adopt the plan of B, rather than B that of A? And if A and B should agree, how can they know but that the General Government here will reject their plan? By the proclamation a plan is presented which may be accepted by them as a rallying point, and which they are assured in advance will not be regretted here. This may bring them to act sooner than they otherwise would.

The objection to a premature presentation of a plan by the National Executive consists in the danger of committal on points which could be more safely left to further developments. Care has been taken to shape the movement so as to avoid embarrassment from this sourse, saying that on certain terms certain classes will be pardoned, with rights restored. It is not said that other classes or other terms will never be included, saying that reconstruction will be accepted if presented in a specific way. It is not said it will never be accepted in any other way. The movements by State action for emancipation in several of the States not included in the emancipation proclamation, are matters of profound gratulation.

APPEAL TO CONGRESS—THANKS TO THE ARMY AND NAVY.

And, while I do not repeat in detail what I have heretofore so earnestly urged upon this subject, my general views and feelings remain unchanged; and I trust that Congress will omit no fair opportunity of aiding these important steps to the great consummation. In the midst of other cares, however important, we must not lose sight of the fact that the war power is still our main reliance. To that power alone can we look for a time to give confidence to the people in the contested regions that the insurgent power will not again overrun them. Until that confidence shall be established little can be done anywhere for what is called reconstruction. Hence our chiefest care must still be directed to the army and navy, which have thus far borne their harder part so nobly and well; and it may be esteemed fortunate that, in giving the greatest efficiency to these indispensable arms, we do honorably recognize the gallant men, from commander to sentinel, who compose them, and to whom, more than to others, the world must stand indebted for the home of freedom disenthralled, regenerated, enlarged and perpetuated. ABRAHAM LINCOLN.

December 8, 1863.

THE PROCLAMATION.

The following is the proclamation referred to in the message:

Whereas, in and by the Constitution of the United States it is provided that the President shall have power to grant reprieves and pardons for offences against the United States, except in cases of impeachment; and whereas a rebellion now exists whereby the loyal State Governments of several States have for a long time been subverted, and many persons have committed and are now guilty of treason against the United States; and, whereas, with reference to said rebellion and treason, laws have been enacted by Congress declaring forfeitures and confiscation of property and liberation of slaves, all upon terms and conditions therein stated, and also declaring that the President was thereby authorized at any time thereafter, by proclamation, to extend to persons who may have participated in the existing rebellion in any State, or part thereof, pardon and amnesty, with such exceptions, and at such times, and on such conditions as he may deem expedient for the public welfare; and, whereas, the Congressional declaration for limited and conditional pardon accords with the well established judicial exposition of the pardoning power and, whereas, with reference to the said rebellion the President of the United States has issued several proclamations with provisions in regard to the liberation of slaves; and, whereas, it is now desired by some persons heretofore engaged in the said rebellion to resume their allegiance to the United States, and to reinaugurate loyal State Governments within and for their respective States:

Therefore, I, Abraham Lincoln, President of the United States, do proclaim, declare, and make known to all persons, who have directly, or by implication, participated in the existing rebellion, except as hereinafter excepted, that a full pardon is hereby granted to them and each of them, with restoration of all rights of property, except as to slaves, and in property cases where the rights of third parties shall have intervened, and upon the condition that every such person shall take and subscribe an oath, and thenceforward keep and maintain said oath inviolate, and which oath shall be registered for permanent preservation, and shall be of the tenor and effect following, to wit:

"I do solemnly swear, in the presence of Almighty God, that I will henceforth faithfully support, protect and defend the Constitution of the United States, and the Union of the States thereunder, and that I will in like manner abide by and faithfully support all acts of Congress passed during the existing rebellion with reference to slaves, so long and so far as not reported, modified, or held void by Congress or by decision of the Supreme Court, and that I will in like manner abide by and faithfully support all proclamations of the President made during the existing rebellion having reference to slaves, so long and so far as not modified or declared void by decision of the Supreme Court. So help me God."

The persons excepted from the benefits of the foregoing provisions are all who are or shall have been civil or diplomatic officers or agents of the so-called Confederate Government, all who have left judicial stations under the United States to aid the rebellion; all who are or shall have been military or naval officers of said so-called Confederate Government, above the rank of Colonel in the army, of Lieutenant in the navy; all who have left seats in the United States Congress to aid the rebellion; all who resigned commissions in the army or navy of the United States, and afterwards aided the rebellion; and all who have engaged in any way in treating colored persons, or white persons in charge of such, otherwise than lawfully as prisoners of war, and which persons may have been found in the United States service as soldiers, seamen, or in any other capacity. And I do further proclaim, declare, and make known that whenever, in any of the States of Arkansas, Texas, Louisiana, Mississippi, Tennessee, Alabama, Georgia, Florida, South Carolina and North Carolina, a number of persons not less than one tenth in number of the votes cast in such States at the Presidential election of the year of our Lord 1860—each having taken the oath aforesaid, and not having since violated it, and being a qualified votor by the election law of the State existing immediately before the so called act of secession, and excluding all others—shall re-establish a State Government which shall be republican, and in nowise contraveuing said oath, such shall be recognized as the true Government of the State, and the State shall receive thereunder the benefit of the constitutional provision which declares that "the United States shall guarantee to every State in this Union a republican form of government, and shall protect each of them against invasion, on application of the Legislature, or of the Executive when the Legislature cannot be convened, and against domestic violence."

And I do further proclaim, declare, and make known, that any provision which may be adopted by such State Government in relation to the freed people of such State which shall recognize and declare their permanent freedom, provide for their education, and which may yet be consistent as a temporary arrangement with their present condition as a laboring, landless, and houseless class, will not be objected to by the National Executive. And it is engaged as not improper that, in constructing a loyal State Government in any State, the name of the State, the boundary, the subdivisions, the constitution, and the general code of laws, as before the rebellion, be maintained, subject only to the modifications made necessary by the conditions hereinbefore stated, and such others, if any, not contravening said conditions, and which may be deemed expedient by those framing the new State Government.

To avoid misunderstanding, it may be proper to say that this proclamation, so far as it relates to State Governments, has no reference to States wherein loyal State Governments have all the while been maintained. And for the same reason it may be proper to further say that whether members sent to Congress from any State shall be admitted to seats, constitutionally rests exclusively with the respective Houses, and not to any extent with the Executive; and, still further, that this proclamation is intended to present to the people of the States wherein the national authority has been suspended and the loyal State Governments have been subverted, a mode in, and by, which the national authority and loyal State Governments may be re-established within said States, or in any of them; and, while the mode presented is the best the Executive can suggest with his present impressions, it must not be understood that no other possible mode would be acceptable.

Given under my hand, at the City of Washington, the 8th day of December. A. D. 1863, and of the independence of the United States of America the eighty-eighth.

ABRAHAM LINCOLN.

1864

The Charleston Mercury.

SPONTE SUA SINE LEGE FIDES RECTUMQUE COLENTUR. — VINDICE NULLO.

COUNTRY PAPER—THRICE A WEEK—EIGHT DOLLARS, FOR SIX MONTHS—PAYABLE IN ADVANCE.

VOLUME LXXXIV. | CHARLESTON, S. C., SATURDAY, JANUARY 16, 1864. | NUMBER 11,960

THE MERCURY.

SATURDAY, JANUARY 16, 1864.

Taxes on Profits of Blockade Running.

The Special Committee on Finance, in their bill proposed to Congress, lay a tax on profits in trade and business made since the 1st January, 1862, of *thirty-three* per cent., with an *additional* tax of *twenty-five* per cent. on the excess over twenty-five per cent. of the "profits of incorporated and joint stock companies, made in any of the years since the war." The main object of this tax is to appropriate to the use of the Government the profits resulting from running the blockade on our coasts established by our enemies.

1. And first, we would observe, that whether good or bad (and our readers know that we thought it bad), the policy of importing goods and exporting cotton and other agricultural products by merchants and companies, *was the policy of the Government.* Those who entered into this trade, and braved its dangers for its profits, distinctly understood that they were carrying out the policy of the Government of the Confederate States. When the Council of South Carolina undertook to prohibit the exportation of cotton, excepting, we believe, by the Confederate Government, Mr. MEMMINGER, the Secretary of the Treasury, immediately interposed, and denied their power to pass such an ordinance, on the ground that it was a regulation of commerce, and to Congress, by the Constitution of the Confederate States, it was given "to regulate commerce." It is notorious that, in the Provisional Congress, a bill was introduced to prohibit the exportation of cotton and other agricultural productions, excepting by the Confederate Government, and it was defeated by the active opposition of the Government. Under such circumstances, many mercantile men in Charleston and elsewhere deemed it not only a fair matter for mercantile adventure, to export cotton and import foreign goods, but that patriotism required it. The Government wanted arms and munitions of war, and the people clothing. They accordingly entered on the enterprise. It seems, now, by this proposition, that they are to be treated as criminals, and one-half of their gains are to be wrested from them.

2. In the second place, we would remark that all *ex post facto* legislation is necessarily fraudulent. When this trade was encouraged by the Government and entered into by our merchants, they could not have anticipated that this Government would tax them retroactively to the amount of one-half of their profits. If they had understood this, they might not have entered on the enterprise at all. So far from understanding this, they had a right to suppose, as one of the elements of their calculations, that it would be as free of any extraordinary taxation in the future as it had been in the past. Least of all could they have anticipated that, after these profits had been for months and years applied and vested, a law would be passed, with a retroactive efficacy, appropriating one-half of the fruits of their enterprise and daring.

3. It matters not what you call their gains—"profits in trade" or any thing else—they are now the *property* of those who earned them, and vested in various ways. This property is like all other property fairly earned, and the Government has no right to tax it *higher than any other property.* It is entitled to be exempted from taxation exactly as all other property is exempted, and to be made to contribute to the support of the Government exactly as all other property contributes. All *special* legislation, looking to a higher exaction from it than is imposed on other property, is partial and unjust, and inconsistent with that general equity which should govern all nations towards their citizens.

4. All taxes, to be just, should be *prospective.* The citizen should be able, in his pursuits of industry, to know what the Government requires, in order that no wrong may be done to him in his contracts, investments and enterprises. Suddenly to interfere and force into his contracts and money operations an unexpected burden, in the shape of taxation, is necessarily a wrong—and often ruin. Last February a heavy tax bill passed Congress, operating on property then owned and on profits to be acquired in the future. This was just. The bill now proposed in Congress is accumulations of that bill—and far beyond that bill—not in its exactions for the future—for that, however heavy, would not be unjust; but reaching both to *past* and *closed* transactions, and making them the pretext for exorbitant and partial exactions. This is wretched statesmanship. It is oppression.

What Subjugation Means.

"Oppressed nationality" shall never, by God's blessing, be a designation for the States of this Confederacy; and, while we stand in armed and defiant resistance, it may even be thought gratuitously offensive to enter upon an account of that interesting class of communities, as if it could have any possible relation to us and our destinies. Yet, in order that we may all, with one heart and mind, continue to resist to the triumphant end; in order that none of the very cowards amongst us may ever dream of laying down those arms, in the delusive hope of peace, until a glorious independence has been achieved, it may be well to keep before our eyes the miserable, shameful, but too sure alternative. Nothing can be more certain than that we have before us either a complete military success in this war, or else the full measure of Poland's and of Ireland's grinding oppression and emaciating humiliation.

Some weak-minded persons, we are sorry to learn, still soothe themselves with the idea that, if the worst should come, we should but be reduced to the present condition of Kentucky or Missouri; in which there has been as yet no sweeping confiscation of estates nor absolute extermination of people; and they fondly imagine that, even if the country should fall entirely under the power of the Yankee nation, still the property and the rights of *them* (the weak minded persons) might still be, somehow, saved harmless by some sort of base oaths and pledges of "loyalty" to the new masters. So dreamed many of the Irish before the capitulation of Limerick and disbandment or exile of the national forces. It was not till after that event, when the island lay really in the condition of a conquered country, that the code of "penal laws" began to be enacted. There was then no army in the field to which men, goaded by oppression, could fly for refuge and for vengeance. The war was over, and only its fruits remained to be gathered.

Now, the Yankee enemy has hitherto forborne from applying the law of conquest to Kentucky and other border States simply because he knows that those States are not yet conquered. The war (thank God) is not over. Our Confederate armies are still on foot, and on the banks of the Rapid-Ann, and in the gap of Chickamagua, not only guard Virginia and Georgia, but also postpone indefinitely the fate of Kentucky and Maryland. If the enemy should now prematurely put in force the policy of confiscation and proscription in those States, the effect would be only to send their young men trooping to Gen. LEE and Gen. JOHNSTON. It must be only after the submission of the whole land—if our eyes should ever see that evil day—that the Yankee nation can begin to parcel it out as reward for the soldiers. No matter what might be the guaranties, treaties, amnesties, capitulations, under which we should have laid down our arms, pretexts would be instantly found for evading them all, as in the case of the Vienna and Limerick treaties. *No* treaty between victor and vanquished ever binds the former; and unless we are to suppose in the Yankee nation some superhuman virtue, some angelic purity and benignity, some grandeur of soul heretofore unexampled, we may be sure that they would proceed generally as the Russians and the English did; with, perhaps, some ingenious additions; for our neighbors are an inventive people. They would need all their ingenuity, however, if they wished to improve much upon the methods elsewhere tried with such success. The grand object to be obtained in such cases is always uniform; it is to appropriate the lands and goods of the subject people, and to make their industry subservient to the profit of their masters. The means, therefore, are tolerably uniform also; the means are to invent ever new and more and more humiliating tests and oaths, such as cannot fail to excite local insurrections and conspiracies—then to crush these with brutal rigor, and afterwards reap the harvest in plunder. To carry out this process with safety it is needful to take the pluck out of the subject people by disarming them carefully, and thus killing in them the spirit of men. Also, to take into the hands of "government" the whole education of the young, in order that the school-books given them to read may carefully conceal the fact that they once had a country, and how it was lost. Here, in the case supposed, our school-books and teachers would come all from Massachusetts and Connecticut; and they would teach our children that they ought to be proud of living under the glorious Stars and Stripes; if the "rebellion" were ever mentioned at all in their historical readings, it would be with execration upon the unhappy miscreants who, in those years, criminally sought to destroy the best government in the world. Under the Irish system of penal laws, in the reign of George I, Irish children were forbidden to be educated at all, except by English Protestant schoolmasters; and as the Catholic gentry of the country then adopted the practice of sending their children to be educated in France and Spain, another act was speedily passed:—"That if any Catholic child were sent abroad without license, it was presumed by law that he was sent to be educated in a foreign seminary, by which a forfeiture of his personal, and of the income of his real estate, was incurred." The personal and the real estate was the main point; but, in order to clutch it, all education had to be controlled, all history perverted, and the spirit of the rising generation denationalized in its very spring.

It may be imagined that the cases of Poland and Ireland are scarcely applicable to any possible state of affairs amongst us, inasmuch as in both those countries much of the persecution was occasioned by religious intolerance. The Irish and the Poles were Catholics; and Great Britain and Russia were resolved to crush out that religion, and establish, in the one country, Anglican Protestantism; in the other, the Greek Church. Yes, but in both cases religion was only the pretext, and any other pretext would have done as well. The grand object was the real and personal estate. If the people had really become converted, under that sort of severe proselytism, why, some other pretext would have had to be invented, that is all. In these States one could easily contrive cunning tests and oaths quite as hard to swallow, and quite as sure to yield a crop of confiscation, as any subscription to a religious creed. Besides, are we sure that the Yankees are not provided with the very same religious machinery of plunder? Is it forgotten that all the Churches in America (save one) are irreconcilably divided upon a great moral question—that the Northern branch of each communion holds it abominable to teach that Christianity countenances slavery, while the Southern branch renounced all connection with Yankee Christianity upon that very question? The Churches are divided upon the very question upon which the States seceded. Conquest of the Southern States would be conquest of the Southern Churches: they would instantly become schismatic, heretical, accursed; and the zeal and *odium thelogicum* of Yankee Christians—not without an eye to the "real and personal"—would soon not only cover them and their pastors and communicants with evil repute, but also provide penal laws against the "negro-drivers' Church," the "Church of the blood mongers," &c., which, if it did not produce conversions, would, at least, produce confiscations; and that would be quite as good, or much better.

Colonel CZYRMA, whose work on the religious policy of Russia in Poland is of high authority, has given an account of the measures taken by the Emperor NICHOLAS to force the United Greeks or Basilians—about three million of people—into the regular Greek Church.

"In most of the parishes," says Czyrma, "a strong opposition was offered by the clergy, but all in vain; the recusant priests were expelled their parishes and deprived of their livings. Many were sent off to schismatic monasteries, and there incarcerated, with no food but bread and water: some had even that denied them, but remained in cold, dark dungeons," &c.

As for the method of dealing with the laity, take two extracts from the same writer. After a forced recantation, relapse was thus provided against:

"As to apostates, an ukase of the 21st of March, 1840, declares, besides the punishment already provided by law, that their *real and all other property* shall be confiscated; they cannot employ any orthodox peasantry, nor sojourn where orthodox people live. Their children shall be taken from them and brought up in the orthodox church," &c.

Again—

"Up to the 6th January, one hundred and seventy of the clergy had fallen victims of inhuman treatment. The younger portion, who would not turn schismatics, had their heads shaved, and were sent as recruits to the Caucasian army."

The nature of the penal code in Ireland is, perhaps, sufficiently well known. A Catholic turning Protestant was to take the fee-simple of his father's estate, avoiding all settlements made by his father, and turning his father into a tenant for life. Catholics were prohibited from taking land by lease for a longer period than thirty-one years; prohibited from purchasing any of the forfeited estates; prohibited from exercising the office of mayor, sheriff, bailiff, alderman, burgess, town clerk or common councilman in any corporate town. A Catholic could not legally own a horse of five pounds value; and if any Protestant discovered a Catholic possessing such a quadruped, he had nothing to do but get a constable, break open the stable door, bring the horse before a magistrate, and then and there paying down five pounds five shillings, take and keep such horse "as if bought in market overt." All Catholic clergymen, of every rank, were ordered to depart the kingdom before the 1st of May, 1698; and those who should return were to be hanged without benefit of clergy. It would be tedious to narrate the long and curious elaborate code which was in force in Ireland for nearly a century. The point to be remarked is, that the atrocity of this code only made the people of Ireland more attached to their church and clergy; and this had been foreseen and intended; for, thereby, the real and personal estate of that kingdom came by degress into the hands of orthodox believers. The very obstinacy of the Catholics was the profitable circumstance; and, if they had allowed themselves to be converted, that would have defeated the whole scheme, and another scheme would have become necessary.

We do not do our very ingenious neighbors at the North the injustice of supposing that they can be at any loss for an efficient system of appropriating real and personal estate with such plain examples before them. Indeed, it seems almost certain that the religious machinery we have suggested would be worked with the most decisive effect; because a murderous fanaticism is more easily excited in that direction than in any other. The Southern schismatic churches could be easily designated as the enemies, and indeed, calumniators of God himself—men who falsify the Bible and pretend that the Saviour of the world was a slave driver. Out of this controversy could not fail to come much real and personal estate. Dr. MINNEGERODE and Dr. HOGE, with other schismatics, might have their heads shaved and be sent to work on the Pacific Railroad; while their parishioners, who should sympathize with them, or hear them preach, or refuse to renounce their heresies—or should relapse, or refuse to teach their children the Yankee catechism—would be simply stripped of all they have and turned out to beg.

This is the principle, and this is the method. If any reader do really believe that the Yankees are invading us with any other motive than that of entering into the land to possess the land—or imagine that they will be more delicate or forbearing than other nations in the like exigency—then the innocence of such reader is admirable, but we cannot compliment him on his understanding.

Other details remain to complete the picture of a subjugated people. It is still to be shown how the dominant nation proceed in the matter of education and of arms, both of which subjects always need to be strictly regulated by methods most offensively inquisitorial, but quite indispensable to the main design. The more revolting all these details may be, so much the better; we shall not spare one hideous feature of them; because all Confederates ought to know them, and to think of them, and ponder on them, until

"——— the thought thereof
Doth, like a poisonous mineral, gnaw their inwards."

Richmond Examiner.

The New-York Times.

VOL. XIII—NO. 3914. NEW-YORK, SATURDAY, APRIL 9, 1864. PRICE THREE CENTS.

FROM WASHINGTON.

The Anti-Slavery Amendment to the Constitution.

Passage of the Joint Resolution in the Senate.

SLAVERY TO BE TOTALLY ABOLISHED.

An Interesting Discussion in the House.

Views of One of Mr. Vallandigham's Friends on the War.

The Election Key-note of the Democratic Party.

SPECIAL DISPATCHES TO THE N. Y. TIMES.

WASHINGTON, Friday, April 8.

THE SHIPMENT OF SPIRITS FOR EXPORTATION.

The Treasury Department is about to issue a circular giving instructions in relation to the shipment of distilled spirits for exportation. They provide that whenever a distiller or owner desires to transport spirits, subject to an excise duty from a distillery or bonded warehouse, to a port of entry for exportation, without payment of duties thereon, he shall make an application in writing to the Collector of Internal Revenue in the district in which said distillery or bonded warehouse may be situated, for a permit to do so, the spirits having first been duly inspected by a United States Internal Revenue Inspector, who shall ascertain the quantity thereof, and make an entry of the same, together with the inspection and marks and numbers of packages. Application will be accompanied by an oath or affirmation of the distiller or owner, setting forth that he desires a permit to transport said spirits for exportation and for no other purpose whatever. Upon receipt of this application, duly verified by the oath or affirmation of the distillers or owners of spirits, the Collector will exact from them a transportation bond, with good and sufficient sureties, in at least double the amount of duties upon said spirits.

GEN. SEDGWICK'S TESTIMONY.

Gen. SEDGWICK testified to-day before the Committee on the Conduct of the War. He justified the conduct of Gen. MEADE at the battle of Gettysburgh, and was very severe on Gen. HOOKER in regard to the battle of Chancellorsville. In reply to the question why Gen. HOOKER recrossed the river, he said he could give no reasons to justify such a step. He only did so after positive orders from Gen. HOOKER, which he exhibited to the committee. He also laid before the committee many other important orders in connection with that movement, which have never been made public.

THE OPERATIONS OF SUBSTITUTE BROKERS.

The proposed Congressional action designed to stop swindling operations of substitute brokers has been deferred, under the opinion that the local State laws were potent enough to effect that object.

THE REBEL DIPLOMATISTS IN EUROPE.

Advices received by the last steamer from Europe represent that the functions of the rebel diplomatists have materially changed within the past two months. MASON is in dignified retirement—a perfect anchorite—having shut himself out of sight of even his own cotemporaries.

SLIDELL is speculating, and has already obtained a notoriety among the gamblers of the Bourse. He has made money; but he never touches Confederate securities, and, like SLIDELL, so are all his co-adventurers. It is noticeable that the rebel diplomats are far more successful as speculators than they were as plenipotentiaries.

MINISTER TO GUATEMALA.

The President sent in to-day the nomination of WILLIAM KELLOGG, ex-member of Congress from Illinois, as Minister to Guatemala.

THE RELIEF OF NAVAL CONTRACTORS.

Naval engine contractors have a hope of relief extended to them, through the agreement of the Naval Committee to report a bill authorizing the Secretary of the Navy to act in the premises as may to him seem just and reasonable. The reason for this action is that a large portion of the burdens of which contractors complain were forced upon them by the alteration of plans for machinery after the contracts were made.

THE AD VALOREM TAX ON BUSINESS.

The Ways and Means Committee to-morrow will take up the proposition of Mr. ODELL to impose an ad valorem tax on all sales of merchandise, real estate, stocks, bonds, and incorporated companies.

THE SUBSISTENCE OF THE CAPTURED INDIANS IN NEW-MEXICO.

The number of captive Indians in New-Mexico that have to be fed by the Commissary, until the Department of the Interior can purchase or send them food, is so great that it is found necessary to diminish the ration of bread and meat issued to troops at the military posts in that department. The value of the deficiency will be paid to the soldiers in cash. The captive Indians will be allowed, if practicable, one pound of flour or corn meal, or of wheat or corn, to every individual, and one pound of fresh meat per day. When "small rations" are issued, they will be in lieu of bread or meat.

DISPATCHES TO THE ASSOCIATED PRESS.

WASHINGTON, Friday, April 8.

THE CASE OF MAJ. MCLEAN.

Inquiry was made some time ago in relation to the case of Maj. N. H. MCLEAN, of Ohio, to which the Secretary of War has replied that that officer was ordered to Vancouver because it was deemed expedient to the service that he should go there, and that it has never been the practice of the department to furnish copies of charges affecting the capacity or fidelity of its officers previous to taking action upon their cases. The Secretary says it is not deemed compatible with the public interests to make further answer.

NINE-MONTHS' MEN AND MILITIA.

It appears from an official report of Assistant Adjt.-Gen. TOWNSEND, that the number of nine-months' men under the act of July, 1862, was 18,884 volunteers and 65,300 militia. The bounty paid volunteers was $25 each. The volunteers were all from Pennsylvania, having been raised by Gov. CURTIN. Bounty has been paid to 3,934 Vermont nine-months' men without the authority of the Department, owing to a mistake of the mustering officers and paymasters.

THE DUTIES ON WOOL.

The Committee on Manufactures have made a report relative to duties on wool. They say that the expectation that low grades of wool would not compete with domestic products has not been realized. Seven-eights of all importations last year were invoiced below the minimum of 18 cents per pound, the whole averaging less than 17 cents. This has defrauded the Treasury and done great injustice to wool-growers. The entire duties of last year did not produce more than half a million dollars. The committee recommend that the duty of 5 per cent. on wools under 18 cents be changed to a specific duty of 3 cents per pound, and an ad valorem duty of 20 per cent.; on wools costing over 18 and not over 24 cents, a specific duty of 6 cents per pound and an ad valorem duty of 20 per cent.; on wools costing over 24 cents, 9 cents per pound and 20 per cent. ad valorem, at the port where the duty is paid. The total amount of wool imported during the last fiscal year was 71,882,123 pounds, costing $12,290,630.

PROCEEDINGS OF CONGRESS.

SENATE.

WASHINGTON, Friday, April 8.

THE FOREIGN AND COASTING TRADE.

Mr. MORRILL, of Maine, (Union,) introduced a bill to regulate the foreign and coasting trade on the northern, eastern and northwestern frontiers of the United States, and for other purposes, which was referred to the Committee on Commerce. It prescribes that the coasting vessels shall be enrolled and licensed by the Secretary of the Treasury. No certificate of registry is required, but each shall be subject to all the regulations and penalties applying to registered vessels. A compensation of $1,000 per year, with fees under the Treasury regulations, and 3 per cent. on collections, is proposed for Collectors of Customs at Pembina, Chicago, Milwaukee, Sault Ste. Marie, Detroit, Miami, Sandusky, Cuyahoga, Presque Isle, Erie, Dunkirk, Buffalo, Niagara, Genesee, Oswego, Cape Vincent, Oswegatchie, Champlain and Vermont, provided that the salaries shall not exceed $25,000; the Collectors' bonds to be approved by the Commissioner of Customs.

RELATING TO EXECUTIVE SESSIONS.

Mr. TRUMBULL, of Illinois, (Union,) reported from the Judiciary Committee the proposed amendment to the rules of the Senate, requiring nominations to be acted upon in open Senate, with a recommendation that it do not pass. The report was adopted.

ANOTHER NATIONAL BANK.

Mr. SHERMAN, of Ohio, (Union,) introduced a bill to provide for a national currency, secured by the pledge of United States stocks, and to provide for the circulation and redemption thereof. The bill is that proposed by Mr. HOOPER in the House without material change. Referred to the Committee on Finance.

RELIEF FOR INDIANS.

Mr. HARLAN, of Iowa, (Union,) introduced a bill for the relief of certain friendly Indians of the Sioux nation in Minnesota. Referred to the Committee on Indian Affairs. It appropriates $10,000 to make provision for the welfare of such Indians as periled life in saving from the massacre many whites in 1862.

JURISDICTION OF DISTRICT COURTS.

Mr. MORRILL, of Maine, (Union,) introduced a bill extending the jurisdiction of the District Courts, which was referred to the Committee on Commerce. The bill gives the same jurisdiction to such courts over actions concerning coasting vessels on lakes and rivers as they now have over vessels on the high seas, and repeals the Act of February, 1845.

THE LAND GRANTS TO THE PERE MARQUETTE RAILROAD.

Mr. HOWARD, of Michigan, (Union,) introduced a joint resolution to extend the time for reversion to the United States of the lands granted to the Père Marquette Railroad, which was referred to the Committee on Public Lands.

THE ARREST OF CAPTS. FERGUSON AND STODDARD.

On motion of Mr. NELSON, of Massachusetts, (Union,) the Secretary of War was directed to communicate information touching the arrest of Capt. C. B. FERGUSON, Quartermaster United States Army, and Capt. WILLIAM STODDARD, Assistant Quartermaster, lately in charge of the military depot at Alexandria, Va.

PROFESSORS IN THE NAVAL ACADEMY.

On motion of Mr. ANTHONY, of Rhode Island, (Union,) it was resolved that the Committee on Naval Affairs be instructed to inquire into the expediency of placing the Professors of Ethics, of Spanish and of Drawing, in the Naval Academy, on the same footing with the other Professors.

THE TITLE TO PROPERTY AT ROCK ISLAND.

Mr. HOWARD, of Michigan, (Union,) introduced the bill to acquire a title to certain property at Rock Island, Illinois, for the purpose of building an arsenal thereupon for the United States.

The bill occasioned some debate, during which the morning hour expired.

THE TRANSFER OF SEAMEN FROM THE ARMY TO THE NAVY.

By unanimous consent Mr. HALE called up the bill to repeal the first section of the joint resolution of Feb. 24, 1864, relating to the transfer of persons from the military to the naval service, which was passed.

THE AMENDMENT TO THE CONSTITUTION.

The Senate then proceeded to the consideration of the joint resolution amending the Constitution.

Mr. SUMNER, of Massachusetts (Union,) said that the first thought that would strike an angel from the skies, or a stranger from another place, if either could be permitted to visit this earth, with surprise, after viewing the extent and resources of our people, would be the fact that there are four millions of human beings held in the most abject bondage, driven by the lash like beasts, and deprived of all rights, even that of knowledge and the sacred right of family. The stranger's astonishment would be doubly increased when he was pointed to the Constitution as the guardian of this many-headed wickedness. He would interpret the Constitution in its true sense, and say that Slavery could not exist by its positive text. He (SUMNER) contended that the words "slave" and "Slavery" did not appear in the Constitution, and if the pretension of property in man lurks anywhere in the Constitution, it was under a feigned name. He considered the preamble the key to open the whole instrument to freedom. He would call attention to those chain-breaking words, "No person shall be deprived of life, liberty or property, without due process of law." Scorning all false interpretations and glosses, which may have been fastened upon the Constitution as a support of Slavery, he would declare there was nothing in the text on which the hideous wrong could be founded. In dealing with this question in the past, it has not been the Constitution so much as human nature which has been at fault. Let the people change, and the Constitution would change also, for the Constitution was the shadow, while the people were the substance. Under the influences of the present struggle the people have changed, and in nothing so much as Slavery. Old opinions and prejudices have dissolved and the traditional foothold which Slavery once possessed has been weakening gradually, until now it scarcely exists. Naturally this change must show itself in the interpretation of the Constitution, and it is already visible in the concession of powers which were formerly denied, and the time has come when the Constitution, so long interpreted for Slavery, may be interpreted for Freedom. He contended, among the concessions for power over Slavery as a military necessity. Many join with PATRICK HENRY, who, in the Virginia Convention, declared the power of manumission was given to Congress in the Constitution, and argued against it on that ground. Slavery, receiving no support in the Constitution, he contended, was clearly under the control of Congress, under the giving Congress power to "provide for the common defence and general welfare." To all who would deny the power of Congress over Slavery, he referred to the words of PATRICK HENRY, when he said that on that subject the Constitution "speaks to the point." He contended that under the war power no one could deny its complete efficiency in enfranchising the soldiers-slave and his family. In the words of SHAKSPEARE, when he makes *Harry*, on the eve of the battle of Agincourt, say to his men to encourage them: "For he, to-day, that sheds his blood with me shall be my brother; be he ne'er so vile, this day shall gentle his condition." He contended also that the clause guaranteeing a Republican form of Government to each State made it our plain duty to abolish Slavery, considering the essential elements that constitute it, as understood by our fathers. The clause that no person shall be deprived of life, liberty, or property, without due process of law, throws protection over every person without regard to color, class or condition. He held that this was not only a guarantee against, but a prohibition of Slavery. On the very face of the Constitution Slavery was an outlaw, and in its express provisions he had shown from sources of power, which, if executed, rendered it impossible. Nothing but hesitancy and delay in eradicating Slavery was unconstitutional. Slavery was not only a nuisance, but a public enemy and traitor in the rebellious States, lending succor to them, and holding out blue lights to encourage and direct their operations, and it must be abolished. In reference to the question of compensation, founded on the shameful assumption that there was property in man, there was a time when he was willing to pay money for emancipation. But it was as a ransom, and not compensation. Money was no longer needed for the purpose. The time had come for the old tocsin to sound, "Millions for defence; not one cent for tribute." Millions of dollars and strong arms to defend our country against slave masters; not one cent for tribute for them. Every dollar for compensation paid should go to the slave. He contended that the pretension to compensation for the renunciation of a system too disgusting to picture or detail, was odious. Slavery must be overthrown; first, by the courts declaring and applying the true principles of the Constitution; second, by Congress in the exercise of the powers which belong to it, and that by the people by amending the Constitution to that end. As the courts had failed to do their duty, Congress, by a single brief statute, will sweep Slavery out of existence. If Congress may not do this, let the Fugitive Slave Law be repealed and all others conflicting with the right of colored persons. But beyond all, the people must put the capstone on the glorious structure by an amendment to the Constitution. While he was desirous of seeing the great rule of freedom which we were about to ordain embodied in a text which should be like the precious casket to the more precious treasure, he was consoled by the thought that the most homely text containing such a rule would be more beautiful far than any passage of poetry or eloquence of words, and would be read with gratitude when the rising dome of this Capitol, with the statue of liberty which surmounted it, had crumbled into dust.

The discussion was further continued by Messrs. POWELL and DAVIS.

Mr. SAULSBURY, of Delaware, (Dem.,) proposed lengthy amendments and a substitute securing the liberty of the press and free speech, and reëstablishing the principles of the Missouri Compromise, which were rejected.

Mr. SUMNER withdrew his amendment, heretofore offered as a substitute, as he did not desire the committee's amendment in its passage.

Mr. MCDOUGALL, of California, (Union,) said that the vote he should give against the measure was not from want of philanthropy to the slave, or from hatred to freedom. He had been the teacher of philanthropy to some of those who were now so blatant for freedom. He denied that the question of emancipation was germane to the present war, and had, therefore, declined to take part in it, believing that it tended to aggravate, rather than heal our wounds. Any effort to antagonize the blacks and whites must result in disaster to the former. As a true friend of the black race, he should vote against the measure.

The amendments, as reported from the Judiciary Committee, as a substitute for the original bill of Mr. HENDERSON, were then adopted.

YEAS—Messrs. Anthony, Brown, Chandler, Clark, Collamer, Conness, Cowan, Dixon, Doolittle, Fessenden, Foot, Foster, Grimes, Hale, Henderson, Howard, Howe, Johnson, Lane of Indiana, Lane of Kansas, Morgan, Morrill, Nesmith, Pomeroy, Ramsay, Sherman, Sprague, Sumner, Ten Eyck, Trumbull, Van Winkle, Wade, Wilkinson, Wiley, Wilson—38.

NAYS—Messrs. Davis, Hendricks, McDougall, Powell, Riddle, Saulsbury.

The following is the joint resolution as passed:

Be it Resolved, by the Senate and House of Representatives of the United States of America, in Congress assembled, two-thirds of both Houses concurring, that the following article be proposed to the Legislatures of the several States, as an amendment to the Constitution of the United States, which, when ratified by three-fourths of said Legislatures, shall be valid to all intents and purposes, as a part of the said Constitution, namely:

ARTICLE XIII, SECTION 1. Neither Slavery nor involuntary servitude, except as a punishment for crime whereof the party shall have been duly convicted, shall exist within the United States, or any place subject to their jurisdiction.

SEC. 2. Congress shall have power to enforce this article by appropriate legislation.

The Senate then adjourned until Monday.

HOUSE OF REPRESENTATIVES.

WASHINGTON, Friday, April 8.

THE CASE OF MR. LOAN, OF MISSOURI.

Mr. GANSON, of New-York, (Dem.,) from the Committee on Elections, made a report, accompanied by a resolution, declaring that BENJAMIN F. LOAN is not entitled to a seat in this House, as a member from the Seventh Congressional District of Missouri, and another resolution that JOHN P. BRUCE, the contestant, is also not entitled to the seat.

Mr. UPSON, of Michigan, (Union,) from the same committee, submitted the views of the minority, with a resolution that Mr. LOAN is entitled to retain his seat.

Mr. GANSON desired to fix a day for the consideration of the subject, but the Speaker said it could be called up at any time.

AD VALOREM TAXES ON BUSINESS.

On motion of Mr. ODELL, of New-York, (Dem.,) it was resolved that the Committee of Ways and Means be instructed to inquire into the expediency of reporting a bill laying ad valorem taxes on all sales of bonds, stocks, specie, merchandise of all descriptions, and on the receipts of railroads, coal, gas and all other incorporated companies.

DISTRICT OF COLUMBIA MATTERS.

The House resumed the consideration of the bill to erect a penitentiary, jail and house of correction in the District of Columbia.

A PERSONAL MATTER.

Mr. PATTERSON, of New-Hampshire, (Union,) said the gentleman from Illinois, (WASHBURNE,) yesterday charged him with voting for a swindle. To answer the elegant frenzy of the gentleman, a person's brains ought to lie in his mettle to do it.

Mr. WASHBURNE asked from what the gentleman read?

Mr. PATTERSON replied—The House report in the *Chronicle*.

Mr. WASHBURNE said what he uttered would be found in the columns of the *Congressional Globe*.

[NOTE.—The *Globe* report represents Mr. WASHBURNE as saying "the people of Charlestown saw the purchase of grounds to extend the Charlestown Navy-yard to be a swindle, and sent a committee here to expose it;" and remarking "the gentleman from New-Hampshire would not go with me in my vain attempt to get the committee to strike it out, but he voted, if I rightly remember, to keep it in the bill. It was a little thing, only $135,000—a mere bagatelle—and 'I grew eloquent over it,' as the gentleman would say, [and he refused to vote against the appropriation. I opposed the appropriation on the ground that the sum named was enormous and extravagant, and in fact, that it was reported to be a swindle, as it had turned out to be since."]

Mr. PATTERSON said that other members understood the gentleman's (WASHBURNE'S) remarks as he did, and that the Chairman of the Committee on Naval Affairs had promptly denied that it was a swindle. If he (PATTERSON) voted for a swindle of $135,000, he had very good company on both sides of the House. It was hardly courteous in any member to accuse another of voting for a swindle. Was it necessary for the gentleman (WASHBURNE) to misrepresent the facts?

Mr. WASHBURNE said that he did not cast reflections on any member of this House. He had referred to the gentleman from New-Hampshire (PATTERSON) as voting for an approproriation which he thought outrageous, and was astonished that the gentleman should think it was a reflection upon him when it was not.

Mr. PATTERSON said as the gentleman (WASHBURNE) disclaimed charging him with a design of voting for a corruption fund he exonerated him fully.

Mr. WASHBURNE replied that the gentleman had never heard him use the words "corruption fund."

Mr. PATTERSON said the gentleman used the word "fraud."

Mr. WASHBURNE further explained that he had said that the gentleman had voted for a matter which had since been charged to be a swindle.

Mr. MORRILL, of Vermont, (Union,) said the subject of this purchase had been pending several years, and the property was sold for the same amount that was given for it. The Committee of Ways and Means had a conference with Admiral SMITH a well-known honest man, and he recommended the appropriation in view of public interests.

The House recommitted the pending bill, with instructions to inquire into the expediency of reporting one merely providing for building a house of correction in the District of Columbia.

REIMBURSEMENT FOR LOSSES DURING MORGAN'S RAID.

The House passed the bill authorizing the Postmaster-General to allow the Postmaster at Harrison, Ohio, $523, that being the amount of money and postage-stamps taken from the office by MORGAN'S rebel force, during his raid in July last.

GRANTS OF LAND FOR AGRICULTURAL COLLEGES.

The House proceeded to the consideration of the Senate bill extending the time for States to accept grants of land for agricultural and mechanic college purposes.

Mr. HOLMAN, of Indiana, (Dem.,) offered an amendment providing that any State or Territory may appropriate the revenue derived from lands donated to them for the education of orphans, soldiers and sailors.

Mr. MORRILL, of Vermont, protested against diverting the act from its original purpose.

Several other gentlemen took a similar position.

Mr. HOLMAN defended his amendment, which was subsequently rejected.

The bill passed with an amendment including the State of West Virginia in its provisions.

THE PRESIDENT'S MESSAGE.

The House went into Committee of the Whole on the State of the Union, and took up the President's Annual Message.

Mr. LONG of Ohio, (Dem.,) made an hour's speech, in the course of which he said aid and comfort were not given to the enemy by those who were opposed to the Republican party, but by that party and the Administration, who by their Confication Acts, and Proclamations of Emancipation and Amnesty, and other extraordinary and unconstitutional measures, were strengthening the hands of the South, and weakening the Union feeling in that section. He quoted from BENTON, LINCOLN, SEWARD, EVERETT, JOHN QUINCY ADAMS, FILLMORE, and others, to show that coercion could not be successful under our republican system, and that the last three years had proved the truth of the proposition. He agreed with the gentleman from Pennsylvania (STEVENS) that the Confederates are an independent power *de facto*; that they maintained their declaration three years by the force of arms; and while they have cut asunder all the ligaments which bound them, they have separated from all the obligations which held them under the Constitution. He accepted this as true, and if a charge of disloyalty should be made against him for this opinion, he would take shelter under the broad mantle of the distinguished leader of the Republican party. He would make any reasonable sacrifice to bring back the seceded States, but not use force, for the Union could only exist in the hearts, and with the consent of the people. If the Democratic party were now in power, they could not restore the union of the States. There were only two questions: First, the recognition of the Confederacy; and, second, the continuation of the war for the subjugation of the South. Of the two he preferred the former. He believed the Democratic party were for peace, and would be placed in a false position if they nominated a war candidate.

Mr. LONG'S hour having expired he asked a few minutes longer to conclude his speech.

Mr. WASHBURNE, of Illinois, (Union,) said—I hope the gentleman will be allowed to finish his speech, as it is the key-note of the Democratic party for the coming election.

Cries of "Order, order," from the Opposition side of the House.

Mr. WASHBURNE—It means the recognition of the Southern Confederacy by foreign Powers, and peace on the terms of disunion.

Mr. LONG gained permission to finish his speech.

Mr. GARFIELD, of Ohio, (Union,) said he remembered when two armies stood face to face in the West, that under a white flag he went up to the man in the uniform of the Confederacy, and reached out his hand and told him he respected him as a brave and honest man. Though he wore the emblems of disloyalty and treason, under his vestments he beheld a brave and honest soul. He (GARFIELD) would reintroduce that scene, with a change only of person. Were there a flag of truce, he would extend his right hand, and ask the member who had just addressed the committee to meet him, and let him shake hands with him, because he honored his bravery and honesty, and because he believed what had fallen from his lips, were the honest sentiments of his heart; and in his uttering them, he had made a new epoch in the history of the war. He had done a new thing under the sun, a braver thing than most men can perform. He would now ask that the white flag be taken away, while he returned to the Union lines and spoke of what his colleague had done, what the member said might be pictured by "Paradise Lost." When Satan, who had rebelled against the glory of God, was hurled down from Heaven, he suddenly lifted up his head, exclaiming: "Which way I flee is hell." And like Satan, his colleague, might have added; "Myself am hell." During the Revolutionary War, Lord FAIRFAX, after deliberation, decided to go over to the Mother Country, and went over grandly and solemnly. But there was another man who had joined his fortunes to the struggling country, and remained with it till the war was well-nigh done; but, as in the darkness which precedes the morning, that man hatched treason, to surrender to the enemy all that had been gained. And that man was BENEDICT ARNOLD. When the present war commenced some men hesitated as to what they should do, while others went over to the enemy. ROBERT E. LEE, who sat at his home at Arlington, hesitating and doubting, at last went over almost tearfully. But now, when hundreds of thousands of brave soldiers have ascended to God, under the shadow of the banner which now waves over us, and when thousands more have gone into a state of decrepitude—when three years of terrific war have been raging, and our arms have pushed back the rebellion—and now, when the uplifted arm of majestic power is ready to let fall the lightnings of vigorous execution, here in the quiet of this hall, rises the dark purpose of BENEDICT ARNOLD, which would surrender the nation, its flag, and honor and glory to the bitter curses of the traitors of our country. For the first time in the history of the war it is proposed to give up the struggle and abandon the war, and let treason run riot in the land.

Mr. GARFIELD then controverted his colleague's positions. The issue was now made up. We should use the common weapons of war. If with these we should not succeed, he would take measures as he would against the savage who attacked himself or family. He would resort to any element of destruction; and, if necessary, he would fling all constitutional sanctions to the winds, rather than lose his country.

Mr. ELDRIDGE, of Wisconsin, (Dem.,) asked him whether he had not sworn to support the Constitution.

Mr. GARFIELD replied he had, and he was glad the gentleman had asked the question. He recollected that the Constitution declared the purposes for which it was framed; it was for the general welfare and public defence. And on that ground he swore to support it, regretting that he had not a sword in his uplifted hand at the time to show a determination to interpose all means to overthrow this cursed rebellion. He said that when he was in the military service a spy brought to him two letters addressed to JOHN C. BRECKINRIDGE. They contained commendations of the bearer who desired a place in the ranks to fight the Abolitionists. One of them was written by a man who lately held a seat on this floor, and was from Indiana.

Messrs. HOLMAN, (of Indiana,) C. A. WHITE, (of Ohio,) and others on the Opposition side, called for the name of the writer.

Mr. GARFIELD replied he had the letter and was understood to say that he would give the name at the proper time. He then alluded to the Knights of the Golden Circle, with their secret signs and pass-words. Such organizations came up before the American people under the lead of the party over the way. This will be the signal for throwing up blue lights at the Capitol at Richmond. This he believed to be the elevated banner, the signal to be answered by traitors all over the land.

Mr. LONG replied that he said very distinctly, when he commenced his remarks, that he spoke for himself, and that he was alone responsible for his utterances. He was well aware of all he did say. He said it deliberately, because his conscience told him it was right and his judgment approved it. He said it, because when he approached the front of the desk and held up his hand to swear to support the Constitution before Heaven, he intended to maintain the solemnity of the obligation. And so help him God, fearless of all charges which could be made by that gentleman or others, in spite of all the means of power in the land, he never would violate that oath, nor shrink from the responsibility he assumed on the first day of the session. He never belonged to a party which took the oath with a mental reservation. He remembered the district of country from which his colleague hailed. The resistance to the Fugitive Slave Law, and the setting at defiance of the most solemn acts of Congress and the decision of the Supreme Court, occurred there. He had never been guilty of that. If the gentleman charged him with being a traitor, he ought to remember the authorities from which he (Mr. LONG) quoted to support his position. They were the opinions of the leaders of his own party, who had advocated the doctrine which he had promulgated to-day. Secretary CHASE had advocated the identical doctrine. If this was treason, all those men were traitors. If this was treason, they might make the most of it. He was willing to abide the consequences and take the responsibility. He had no knowledge of the Knights of the Golden Circle. With God's help, he would never be connected with that order.

Mr. GARFIELD said he did not charge his colleague with being connected with it; but that it was under the patronage and protection of the Democratic party.

Mr. LONG repeated that he made his speech because it met the approbation of his judgment. He believed that there was no power under the Constitution to coerce the sovereign States.

Mr. GARFIELD explained that he would leap over the Constitution in order to preserve the national existence; but it would be into the arms of the people who made the Constitution.

Mr. LONG said while his colleague would leap over the Constitution, he himself would bear being called a traitor for supporting the Constitution. He would stand by this position, if he stood alone. He would not retract one syllable. He hurled back the charges of traitor. The men who were destroying this fair fabric of liberty were the first who declared that the Union could not exist part slave and part free. They started the ball which had produced the present condition of affairs. He believed our fathers were as good as we were. They were as good Christians and patriots. They would not push from the communion-table those who held slaves. God prospered them. What our fathers had provided was good enough for him and his children. He was ready to make any sacrifice to restore the Union. But this was not to be done by such exhibitions as they had recently had in this Hall. Applause to the echo had been given to the sentiments of those who had always been trying to sunder the bonds which united us. He would prefer having liberty in the little State of Ohio, or in Greece, or in Switzerland, than to live under a despotism like that of Austria, with bayonets constantly pointing at him.

Mr. HOLMAN wished to ask the name of the Indianian alleged to have written the treasonable letter, but general consent was not given.

At 6:15 the committee rose, and the House adjourned.

Russian War Vessel off the Hook.

SANDY HOOK, Friday, April 8.

A Russian sloop-of-war is now outside of the bar, bound in.

Navigation of the Penobscot.

BANGOR, MAINE, Friday, April 8.

The ice left the Penobscot to-night.

PROCEEDINGS OF THE LEGISLATURE.

SENATE.

ALBANY, Thursday, April 7.

AFTERNOON SESSION.

The bill authorizing a change in the location of the proposed Central Railroad Bridge at Albany, was discussed at length, and progress was reported.

Maj.-Gen. SICKLES, in response to an invitation of the Senate, appeared within the bar, and was welcomed in a neat complimentary speech by Lieut.-Gov. JONES, who took occasion to denounce the rebellion as the most monstrous known to history.

Gen. SICKLES replied, alluding to the wicked character of the rebellion, the generous and honorable part New-York had taken in the efforts made to suppress it, and expressing the belief that the war would close this year.

BILLS ADVANCED TO A THIRD READING.

Relative to the Utica City Railroad.

Incorporating the Musical Mutual Protective Union of New-York.

For a special County Judge in Monroe County.

Relative to the Church of Intercession of New-York.

Adjourned.

ALBANY, Friday, April 8.

BILLS ADVANCED TO THIRD READING.

Amending the Charter of the Home Insurance Company; incorporating the Dime Savings Bank of Williamsburgh; incorporating the Iowa and Minnesota Homestead Company.

Mr. LAIMBEER asked consent to introduce a bill authorizing the Commissioners of Emigration to sell unclaimed property. Objected to.

Mr. MURPHY made a minority report on the Soldiers' Voting Bill. The minority bill provides that the Governor and Comptroller shall appoint twelve voting agents to visit all the regiments from this State, collect the vote in locked bags, bring them to Albany, where they shall be assorted and sent in packages to the respective election districts, to be canvassed; also that all soldiers from this State be registered. Adjourned.

Incorporating the Musical Mutual Protective Union of New-York.

BILLS ORDERED TO A THIRD READING.

The Albany Bridge Bill.

Amending the charter of the Hudson and Harlem River Canal Company.

Mr. HASTINGS, in alluding to the personal passage between himself and Mr. FIELDS yesterday, remarked that he regretted the occurrence.

Mr. FIELDS replied that he had not tasted ardent spirits during the entire day, and that his reply to the slander against him was the only one that a gentleman could make. Recess.

ASSEMBLY.

ALBANY, Friday, April 8.

BILLS PASSED.

Relative to the Lebanon Springs Railroad.

To amend the charter of the Security Fire Insurance Company.

To amend the charter of the New-York Medical College for Women.

Relative to the Excelsior Insurance Company of Brooklyn.

Regulating the use of the wharves and piers leased to the Delaware and Raritan Railroad.

To amend the charter of the Citizens' Fire Insurance Company.

To amend the charter of the New-York Market Savings Bank.

To amend the charter of the Phœnix Fire Insurance Company of Brooklyn.

To amend the charter of the Home Insurance Company.

Incorporating the Erie Basin Dock Company of Brooklyn.

Relative to divorces. Recess.

EVENING SESSION.

ALBANY, Friday, April 8.

BILLS REPORTED.

Relative to the weight of butter, lard and cheese packages; to extend the operation of general incorporation laws; incorporating the Loan Exchange Warehouse Company.

BILLS PASSED.

Relative to the Rochester Police; to incorporate the Rondout and New-York Steam Navigation Company; declaring the Erie basin at Buffalo a part of the Erie Canal.

On motion of Mr. BURKE, the privileges of the floor were extended to MILES O'REILLEY. Adjourned.

The Jefferd Case.

ALBANY, Friday, April 8.

In the case of CHARLES M. JEFFERD, convicted of the murder of MATHEWS, killed at the same time with WALTON, the conviction has been affirmed by the Court of Appeals. A reargument was ordered last December, but the decision is now unanimous.

From Fortress Monroe.

FORT MONROE, Thursday, April 7.

Two steamers, the *New-York* and *Express*, left to-day under flag-of-truce for City Point, to bring down all the Federal officers and soldiers, now prisoners of war at Richmond, about 1,000 in number.

The underwriter's boat *Atlantic*, attempted to visit Cape Henry to-day to look after the wrecks, but the weather was so rough the boat returned.

The Baltimore boat arrived at 3 P. M., eight hours late.

Lookout Lighthouse Destroyed by Rebels.

FORTRESS MONROE, Friday, April 8.

The steamer *Spaulding*, just arrived from Newbern, reports that Cape Lookout Lighthouse was partially destroyed by the rebels, and there will probably be no light there for a week.

Lieut.-Col. W. T. JOHNSON, United States Army, Medical Inspector of this department, arrived on the *Spaulding*.

Railroad Accident.

LOUISVILLE, Thursday, April 7.

The upward morning passenger train from Nashville ran off the track at Cave City this afternoon, which will cause about ten hours' delay. Only one person was injured, and he but slightly.

BILLIARDS.

Play of Friday Afternoon.

PETER D. BRAISTED, JR., AND WILLIAM FREEMAN—100 POINTS UP, FRENCH THREE-BALL GAME—FOR $500.

As the time of playing this game was unannounced, it came off in private, before a few personal friends of the parties. It proved to be quite a skillful bout, the contestants going along quite evenly until near the close of the game, when BRAISTED went ahead, and came out winner by 21 points. Mr. BRAISTED then handed over $50 to Mr. PHELAN, to add to the fund for the working women.

Friday Evening.

MICHAEL PHELAN AND DUDLEY KAVANAGH—100 POINTS UP, SHOVE SHOTS BARRED—THE LOSER TO PAY $100 TO THE FUND OF THE SANITARY COMMISSION—A SUPERB DISPLAY.

About five hundred persons were present this evening, presenting one of the most respectable and intelligent audiences imaginable. The contrast with the assemblage of the previous evening was remarkable. There was no betting on this occasion, the parties having come together to witness the science and beauties of the game of billiards, as demonstrated by two of its most expert masters.

Before commencing, H. P. CARR, Esq., arose and stated that the receipts of the evening were to be paid over to the Working Women's Relief Association; and as one worthy gentleman had set a capital example, he trusted others would do likewise. That was, that the gentleman had handed Mr. PHELAN a donation of $10 for the fund. Those who desired to "follow the leader," could do so by calling at the box-office.

The game commenced at 8¾ o'clock, Kavanagh winning the lead. The first call was Phelan, 155; Kavanagh, 73. The second, Kavanagh, 105; Phelan, 179. Third, Phelan, 246; Kavanagh, 146. Fourth, Phelan, 301; Kavanagh, 190. Fifth, Kavanagh, 208; Phelan, 309. Sixth, Phelan, 401; Kavanagh, 267. Seventh, Phelan, 509; Kavanagh, 369. Eighth, Phelan, 618; Kavanagh, 390. Ninth, Kavanagh, 403; Phelan, 537. Tenth, Kavanagh, 506; Phelan, 687. Eleventh, Phelan, 713; Kavanagh, 515. Twelfth, Kavanagh, 601; Phelan, 778. Thirteenth, Phelan, 815; Kavanagh, 682. Fourteenth, Kavanagh, 736; Phelan, 844. Fifteenth, Kavanagh, 800; Phelan, 852. Sixteenth, Phelan, 909; Kavanagh, 867. Seventeenth, Kavanagh, 903; Phelan, 909. Phelan made game on the 119th innings, winning by 34 points. Time, 3 hours 40 minutes. The game not closing until after midnight rendered it impossible to give a full report this morning.

THE WAR IN THE SOUTHWEST.

A Rebel General's Order on the Repulse at Paducah.

WEST KENTUCKY TO BE HELD.

MISCELLANEOUS INTELLIGENCE.

CAIRO, Thursday, April 7.

The Cairo *News* has been furnished with an order issued by Gen. BUFORD, commanding the Second Division of FORREST'S cavalry, congratulating the troops on the success of their Kentucky campaign. He praises their conduct during the attack on the fort at Paducah and alludes feelingly to the loss of Col. THOMPSON, commanding the Third Brigade.

He asserts that they silenced the guns of the fort, and compelled one of the gunboats to withdraw from action. The rebel loss is set down at 50 killed, and 40 wounded, and the Federal loss at 27 killed, and 76 or 80 wounded. He concludes by informing the division of his intention to hold Western Kentucky.

The actual loss of the Federal forces was fourteen killed and forty-two wounded. Rebel prisoners admit a loss of three hundred killed, and three times as many wounded.

The latest Memphis advices report nothing later from FORREST or GRIERSON. It was rumored that the former was preparing to attack Memphis.

Confiscated goods to the amount of $49,000, consisting mostly of cotton and sugar, were sold here to-day by order of the United States District Court. Eighteen hundred bales of cotton yet remain to be sold. Two hundred and two bales mixed and inferior quality, in bad condition, sold at auction at 41c. @57½c.

Over one hundred bales of cotton have been brought up by the naval dispatch boat *New National*, from Red River, as have also two 9-inch Dahlgren guns, being part of the armament of Fort De Russey. These guns are part of those taken from the *Harriet Lane* and *Indianola*.

It was the steamer *Joe Jayes* and not the *Carrie Jobs*, that was sunk by the *Gen. Anderson*, as mentioned in a previous dispatch.

The steamer *Forsyth* has been released, and left for Memphis. Several thousand dollars' worth of contraband goods were found in her hold. The first clerk is held for examination.

The election returns received indicate that L. HUMMICK, Republican, has been probably elected Judge of the Thirteenth Circuit.

In the Memphis Cotton market rates for low qualities are unchanged; the better qualities tend upward. Receipts, 366 bales. Ordinary to good 55c.@56c.; low middling, 57c.@58c.; good middling, 62c @63c.; fair, 66c.

The Rebel Forrest Leaving Kentucky.

PHILADELPHIA, Friday, April 8.

A special Cincinnati dispatch to the *Bulletin* says:

Notwithstanding the rebel BUFORD'S assurance that he intends to remain permanently in Kentucky, it is reported that FORREST is manœuvering to get out of the State by dividing his forces into small detachments and slipping them off by byways.

Large Amounts of Cotton Captured.

ST. LOUIS, Friday, April 8.

The *Democrat's* Alexandria, La., dispatch says a large amount of cotton is being captured along Red River. It was reported that several naval officers had been captured while confiscating cotton.

Admiral PORTER had issued a circular to Captains and owners of steamboats in the employ of the rebel Government as transports, stating that if they will deliver the boats to him he will afford them every opportunity to recover their property, while, if they burn them they will be a total loss.

THE LAST LOST REBEL RAM.

Sinking of the Great Iron-clad Rebel Ram Tennessee off Mobile.

The great rebel ram, off Mobile, which, according to Southern accounts, was to sink our whole fleet, has been sunk by a squall.

From the New-Orleans Era, March 29.

WEST GULF SQUADRON, Sunday, March 20, 1864.

On March 1 the *Kennebec* steamed up to Dauphine Island, to communicate with the vessels in the Sound. Several rebel gunboats, the *Tennessee* among them, were seen lying near Grant's Pass.

The day was squally, and at about 3 o'clock in the afternoon, the lookout on board the *Kennebec* sung out, "The *Tennessee* is sinking!" All the officers on deck immediately looked toward the place where the *Tennessee* was lying, and, sure enough they saw her go down.

At the same time signals were seen on board the *Octarora*, lying in the Sound, and said signals interpreted, read: "The rebel ram *Tennessee* sunk."

It appears that a squall struck her, and, she being very low in the water, keeled over and went down.

Two feet of her smoke-stack can now be seen above the water, at the spot where the great ram once lay at anchor.

The *Tennessee* ran down from Mobile when we first began bombarding Fort Powell, and rebel deserters said she was expected to sink our whole fleet.

She was an extremely powerful vessel, her armor plates being six inches in thickness. She was very short in the hull, but had a long, projecting spear, or ram, which was entirely under water. Her excessive weight made her slow and hard to handle, being too much for her engines; and she would not, therefore, have proved a very formidable opponent for our fast cruisers.

Her armament is the greatest loss to the enemy. It consisted of six 100-pounder rifled Parrott guns, three in front and three astern. I believe there were three or four smaller pieces also on board.

From California.

SAN FRANCISCO, Monday, April 4.

Arrived, ships *Swallow* from Boston; *Franklin* from New-York.

The Legislature adjourns finally at 12 o'clock to-night. The only act passed of interest, outside of California, is one whereby the State engages to pay the interest on a million and a half of the Central Pacific Railroad Company's bonds for twenty years. In approving this act, the Governor expressed the belief that any future Legislature will have the power to repeal it.

SAN FRANCISCO, Tuesday, April 5.

Arrived ship *Hornet*, from New-York. She reports having spoken April 1, in lat. 30 north, ship *Enterprise*, from New-York for San Francisco.

Lieut.-Col. GEO. H. RINGGOLD died yesterday. A military funeral will be given him from St. Mary's Cathedral to-morrow.

The Legislature adjourned at midnight, not to meet again for two years. Many bills of local interest were vetoed or retained in the Governor's possession.

The bill submitting to a vote of the people a proposition to issue $500,000 of State bonds to the Western Pacific Railroad Company, and $1,500,000 to the Central Pacific Railroad Company, was vetoed on the ground of unconstitutionality.

Under another bill the Central Company has the interest on $1,500,000 of its bonds paid by the State for twenty years, as reported yesterday.

The Charleston Mercury.

DAILY PAPER—Fifteen Dollars, for Six Months—Payable in Advance.

SPONTE SUA SINE LEGE FIDES RECTUMQUE COLENTUR.—VINDICE NULLO

COUNTRY PAPER—Three a Week—Eight Dollars, for Six Months—Payable in Advance.

VOLUME LXXXIV. | CHARLESTON, S. C., WEDNESDAY, APRIL 13, 1864 | NUMBER 12,031

THE MERCURY.

WEDNESDAY, APRIL 13, 1864.

Weakness of the Governments, North and South.

It is perfectly plain that the United States were never so badly prepared, at the opening of the spring campaign, as they are now, for assailing the Confederate States. This, we suppose, is attributable to two causes: 1. A large portion of their armies are going out of the service, in consequence of the expiration of their term of enlistment; and 2d, the difficulty of getting troops in consequence of the growing discontent from the continuance of the war. If their old troops had freely re-enlisted, there could have been no necessity of any vast increase of their armies. They probably, at the close of the fall campaign, outnumbered our troops two to one. The call for seven hundred thousand men by conscription (five for the regular service, and two for reserves), is a palpable proof of weakness. It shows the immense drain their armies have sustained, by desertions and the expiration of enlistments. The universal and extensive conscription of negroes, is also a proof of their failing resources, in soldiers, to carry on the war. The Government dare not and cannot force the native population, by conscriptions, into their armies. Hence the importation of Germans and Irishmen, and the conscription of negroes, to fill up their depleted ranks. The frontier States are to be held down by their negroes, whilst the white soldiery are to march upon the Confederate States. This is not exactly what Kentucky and Maryland bargained for, when they submitted to the tender embraces of the Yankee. But like most romantic people, they must pay for their misplaced affections. Their fate, however, foreshadows the fate of the Confederate States, if they should ever fall under Yankee domination.

In contrast to the seething discontent and desperate resorts of our enemies, stands the Confederate States. We have our troubles, it is true. The Confederate Government, both in its financial and military operations, has not met the expectations of a vast portion of the people. In integrity and efficiency, it has fallen far below the high standard of principles which originated the Confederacy. Yet no one, or very few at least, in the Confederate States will, on that account, fail to support, cordially, all the efforts of the Confederate Government to carry on the war. Their cause of discontent is not that the war has been waged too sternly or uncompromisingly, but that it has been waged too weakly. They are for war, relentless war—war forever—rather than submission to the hated and hateful Yankee.—They disclose and express their dissatisfaction, not to weaken the Government in carrying on the war, but to induce a wiser and more energetic course in conducting it. They expose the baleful influence of the Beaureaucracy at Richmond, not to paralyze our armies, but to give them more efficiency and success. The greatest soldiers of ancient or modern times—CÆSAR or NAPOLEON—could not sit down in Richmond and carry on successfully such a war as we are now waging, by ordering all the campaigns and directing the movements of our armies. The busy patronage of the Government over all the little Lieutenants in the army, and its absurd policy of directing and controlling, over so vast a country, all the Commissaries and Quartermasters of our armies, rendering them independent of the General of the armies they are to serve, and responsible only to some Bureau in Richmond, is a monstrous source of imbecility and insubordination. Yet, if the Government will not be corrigible, and will persist in its damaging absurdities—it will be supported. Our campaigns may be most absurdly planned—our troops may be sent upon the most unintelligible raids—divided *here*, when they ought to be united—thrown *there*, where they are not wanted—Commissaries and Quartermasters may kill off our cavalry, and starve our armies, and defy the Generals in command, and luxuriate in the smiles of Executive favor—still the war will be supported. We are in mortal combat; and although our faithless sword breaks at the hilt, we will seize the blade, and close in with it on our enemy. These discontents—(malcontents as Government dependents call them)—are the very last men who will fail the Government in carrying on the war. Unlike the Peace Democrats of the North,—unlike the opponents of "Miscegenation"—they do not seek to weaken or overturn the Government. They are the deadliest foes to a re-construction, commercial or political, of our former union with our Yankee enemies, and they will stand by the Government as long as it will fight. Discontent in the South, is the strongest support;—in the North, the most fatal weakness to the Government.

Advance on Shreveport, Louisiana — Crossing Cane River

ATROCITIES OF THE ENEMY IN NORTH ALABAMA.

The darkest chapter in the history of this cruel war, if not in any other war, will record the atrocities of the Yankees wherever, in the Confederate States, they have been permitted to march their thieving brutal hordes. Their deeds, so in violation of all the rules of civilized or humane warfare, entitle them to a place in history with the Goths and Vandals who overrun and laid waste Southern Europe. Intent upon their barbarous errand, they have shown themselves entirely wanting in the instincts of common humanity, much less possessing any of the traits of a civilized or humane people. They have not been satisfied to take possession of a portion of Confederate territory, they must needs make it a waste, howling wilderness, by destroying the provisions, buildings, fences, agricultural implements, stock, etc., and driving defenceless old men, women and children into the woods, in many instances setting fire to their houses over their heads. We take from the Montgomery *Mail* the following account of their atrocities in North Alabama:

In no portion of the Confederatee States have they acted more barbarous and cruel than in the Nortern portion of Alabama. A journey through parts of Jackson, Madison, Limestone and Lauderdale counties would recall to mind the descriptions of Greece through which the Turkish fire and sword had gone, or the utter destruction of whole sections of Poland by the Russian hordes. We have been lately put in possession of the facts in detail of certain Yankee atrocities in Limestone and Lauderdale counties, which it is well to put on record for the information of the world. In the former county, the outrages were committed by the 9th Illinois Regiment, commanded by Lieut. Col. Jessee J. Philips, of Belville, Illinois.

On January 25th General Roddy, with a small portion of his command, attacked the forces of Lieut. Col. Phillips, who were encamped near and in the grove of Mrs. Coleman, the widow of Judge Daniel Coleman, deceased. The enemy's pickets were driven into the encampment, when they, with those of the forces who were in camp, took shelter behind the dwelling house of Mrs. Coleman. They fired a few rounds and fled in perfect consternation.

One of our secret scouts, who was in the enemy's lines a day or two after the raid, says that the treatment of Col. Phillips' men to Mrs. Coleman and family was unparalleled in the history of the war. Our men, having accomplished their purpose, were scarcely out of sight, when the Yankees rushed back to their encampment perfectly infuriated because of their defeat. To avenge themselves, they rushed into the house of Mrs. Coleman with fire brands, and built up a large fire in one of the handsomest parlors. The mother and daughter implored them not to burn the house, but they heeded not their entreaties. They pushed them violently out of the house, drawing pistols on them both. In a few hours that portion of the command which was on a scout at the time of the attack by Gen. Roddy, which was commanded by Major Kuhne, returned to camp. They rushed into the house of Mrs. Coleman, and commenced plundering. Mrs. Coleman appealed to Major Kuhne to control his men and to give her his protection as a defenceless female. He ordered her from his presence, saying: "Woman, go away, I have no protection for you. Men, pitch into her house, and sack it from bottom to top."

The vandals needed no encouragement from their officer, but immediately obeyed his order to do their work of destruction. Mrs. Coleman had with her two little boys, her only protection, she having lost in this cruel war two as noble and brave sons as mother ever had, and her oldest son is now absent in the service of his country. Her little boys were torn from her in the night, put under guard, and carried to the jail. Their mother plead with the Colonel for their release, when he added to her already unutterable anguish by saying that he would have to send the older one of the boys to Northern prisons. He, however, relented in a few days after torturing their mother sufficiently, as he thought, and released the boys from their imprisonment. Mrs. Coleman and daughter were driven from their home in the night to seek refuge in the town of Athens, which was about one mile distant. The furniture, which was of the finest rosewood, was split up. The marble slabs to the bureaus and washstands were broken into pieces, mirrors were shattered, handsome Brussels carpets cut up into saddle blankets, beds dragged out into camp with all the bed clothing, including the finest blankets and Marseilles quilts.

The portrait of Judge Coleman, also that of Mrs. Coleman, were so pierced by their bayonets that they could not be recognized. All of the table ware and several pieces of silver were taken out into camp. Several handsome silk dresses and other articles of clothing belonging to the family were taken. A little trunk which Mrs. Coleman prized more than anything else, because it contained the mementoes and letters of her noble sons, who had given their precious lives to their country, was broken open, and their precious contents destroyed by their infamous hands. The books of a large and select library were scattered through the camp and destroyed. All of Miss Coleman's music was taken. After the completion of their work of destruction, the officers, Major Kuhne and others, took possession of the house and are now quartered in it. Mrs. Coleman, daughter, and two sons, were ordered out of the Yankee lines. Mrs. Coleman's health would not admit of her coming out, hence her order was recinded. Miss Coleman and her two little brothers are now exiles in our lines.

Col. Phillips took Mr. Crenshaw, a respectable citizen of Limestone, into his tent and demanded his money. Crenshaw handed his pocket book and some loose change he had in his vest pocket. Colonel Phillips asked if that was all. Mr. Crenshaw replied no, and Phillips demanded the balance, and took from his person five thousand dollars belted around his person. This man is trying to equal Butler, the Beast, and is the representative of the Lincoln Government.

In Lauderdale County the conduct of the enemy has been as bad as in Limestone. This county is continually ravaged by bands of tories, who have been armed by the enemy. They are stealing all the horses, mules and cotton.

On the 21 February John Wesson, a tory, shot and killed Lewis C. Moore, an aged and highly respectable citizen, a member of the Commissioner's Court. Wesson is a young man, and had been reared in Moore's neighborhood, and Moore was in the act of shaking hands with him when Wesson shot him.

WHAT IF GRANT SHOULD FAIL?—The New York *Herald* says, editorially:

If Grant, who has never failed in the past, should fail in the future, it will be because there is treachery in Washington. It will be because in that spirit of partisan fury that forgets all else but its object the Washington men have determined to employ all their power to ruin another man who stands high with the people. At this hour the energy and ingenuity of the adherents of the President are intensely concentrated on the game for the next presidency. No scheme that can make capital for them is forgotten. Wires are pulled in legislative halls, in custom houses, postoffices, and in contemptible county conventions. No one can fail to see how indefinitely more advantageous and grand is that field upon which a successful soldier like Grant may work for the Presidency in the campaigns of this summer; and the public may well believe that, while the politicians work in their mole-like way at the North, they will not fail to damage to the extent of their power the chances of the man who has this nobler field. But let them take care. If Grant fails through their treachery, it will not conduce to the success of Lincoln. It will initiate a Northern civil war. It will, perhaps, destroy the public confidence in Grant; and the people thus cast loose from another faith, confusion and anarchy of the worst description must ensue; or if public order is still kept, the hopes of the people will once more fall upon General McClellan, and a grand tide of popular enthusiasm will carry that hero to the Presidency.

VICTORY ON RED RIVER.

RICHMOND, April 12.—An official despatch from Mobile says that the Surgeon General of BANKS' army admits that the Yankee forces had been repulsed with great loss at Shreveport, and that six steamers have been destroyed by our torpedoes in Red River, besides one transport which was captured by the Confederates.

FARRAGUT is reported to be preparing to attack Mobile.

NEWS FROM NORTHERN GEORGIA.

DALTON, GA., April 12.—Miss MARY E. WALKER, Assistant Surgeon of the 52d Ohio Regiment, was captured by our pickets and brought here yesterday. She is quite sprightly, and says that she only wished to deliver letters to our pickets, and had no idea of being arrested.

It is reported on good authority that GRIERSON attacked FORREST at Summerville, Miss., on the 8th instant, but was handsomely repulsed.

HOWARD relieves GRANGER in the command of the Fourth Yankee Army Corps; SCHOFIELD takes command of the Twenty-third.

The New-York Times.

VOL. XIII—NO. 3920. NEW-YORK, SATURDAY, APRIL 16, 1864. PRICE THREE CENTS.

THE BLACK FLAG.

Horrible Massacre by the Rebels.

Fort Pillow Captured After a Desperate Fight.

Four Hundred of the Garrison Brutally Murdered.

Wounded and Unarmed Men Bayoneted and Their Bodies Burned.

White and Black Indiscriminately Butchered.

Devilish Atrocities of the Insatiate Fiends.

FROM CAIRO.

CAIRO, Thursday, April 14.

On Tuesday morning the rebel Gen. FORREST attacked Fort Pillow. Soon after the attack FORREST sent a flag of truce demanding the surrender of the fort and garrison, meanwhile disposing of his force so as to gain the advantage. Our forces were under command of Major BOOTH, of the Thirteenth Tennessee (U. S.) Heavy Artillery, formerly of the First Alabama Cavalry.

The flag of truce was refused, and fighting resumed. Afterward a second flag came in, which was also refused.

Both flags gave the rebels advantage of gaining new positions.

The battle was kept up until 3 P. M., when Major BOOTH was killed, and Major BRADFORD took command.

The rebels now came in swarms over our troops, compelling them to surrender.

Immediately upon the surrender ensued a scene which utterly baffles description. Up to that time, comparatively few of our men had been killed; but, insatiate as fiends, bloodthirsty as devils incarnate, the Confederates commenced an indiscriminate butchery of the whites and blacks, including those of both colors who had been previously wounded.

The black soldiers, becoming demoralized, rushed to the rear, the white officers having thrown down their arms.

Both white and black were bayoneted, shot or sabred; even dead bodies were horribly mutilated, and children of seven and eight years and several negro women killed in cold blood. Soldiers unable to speak from wounds were shot dead, and their bodies rolled down the banks into the river. The dead and wounded negroes were piled in heaps and burned, and several citizens who had joined our forces for protection were killed or wounded.

Out of the garrison of six hundred, only two hundred remained alive.

Among our dead officers are Capt. BRADFORD, Lieuts. BARR, ACKERSTROM, WILSON, REVEL and Major BOOTH, all of the Thirteenth Tennessee Cavalry.

Capt. POSTON and Lieut. LYON, Thirteenth Tennessee Cavalry, and Capt. YOUNG, Twenty-fourth Missouri, Acting-Provost-Marshal, were taken prisoners.

Maj. BRADFORD was also captured, but is said to have escaped; it is feared, however, that he has been killed.

The steamer *Platte Valley* came up at about half-past 3 o'clock, and was hailed by the rebels under a flag of truce. Men were sent ashore to bury the dead, and take aboard such of the wounded as the enemy had allowed to live. Fifty-seven were taken aboard, including seven or eight colored. Eight died on the way up. The steamer arrived here this evening, and was immediately sent to the Mound City Hospital, to discharge her suffering cargo.

Among our wounded officers of colored troops are Capt. PORTER, Lieut. LIBBERTS and Adjt. LEMMING.

Six guns were captured by the rebels, and carried off, including two ten-pound Parrotts and two twelve-pound howitzers. A large amount of stores was destroyed or carried away.

The intention of the rebels seemed to be to evacuate the place, and move on toward Memphis.

LATER.

CAIRO, Thursday, April 15.

Two negro soldiers, wounded at Fort Pillow, were buried by the rebels, but afterward worked themselves out of their graves. They were among those brought up in the *Platte Valley*, and are now in hospital at Mound City.

The officers of the *Platte Valley* receive great credit from the military authorities for landing at Fort Pillow, at eminent risk, and taking our wounded on board, and for their kind attentions on the way up.

REPORTS FROM ST. LOUIS.

ST. LOUIS, Friday, April 15.

The correspondent of the *Union*, who was on board the steamer *Platte Valley* at Fort Pillow, gives even a more appalling description of the fiendishness of the rebels than our Cairo dispatches.

Many of our wounded were shot in the hospital. The remainder were driven out, and the hospital was burned.

On the morning after the battle the rebels went over the field, and shot the negroes who had not died from their wounds.

Several of the guns captured by FORREST at Fort Pillow were spiked before falling into his hands. Others were turned upon gunboat No. 7, which, having fired some 300 rounds and exhausted her ammunition, was compelled to withdraw. Although a tin-clad, she received but slight injury.

Gen. LEE arrived and assumed the command at the beginning of the battle. Previous to which Gen. CHALMERS directed the movements. FORREST, with the main force, retired after the fight to Brownsville, taking with him the captured funds.

While the steamer *Platte Valley* lay under flag of truce, taking on board our wounded, some of the rebel officers, and among them Gen. CHALMERS, went on board, and some of our officers showed them great deference, drinking with them, and showing them other marks of courtesy.

Many of those who had escaped from the works and hospital, who desired to be treated as prisoners of war, as the rebels said, were ordered to fall into line, and when they had formed, were inhumanly shot down.

Of 350 colored troops not more than 56 escaped the massacre, and not one officer that commanded them survives. Only four officers of the Thirteenth Tennessee escaped death.

The loss of the Thirteenth Tennessee is 800 killed. The remainder were wounded and captured.

Gen. CHALMER told this correspondent that, although it was against the policy of his Government to spare negro soldiers or their officers, he had done all in his power to stop the carnage. At the same time he believed it was right.

Another officer said our white troops would have been protected had they not been found on duty with negroes.

While the rebels endeavored to conceal their loss, it was evident that they suffered severely. Col. REED, commanding a Tennessee regiment, was mortally wounded. There were two or three well filled hospitals at a short distance in the country.

FROM LOUISVILLE.

LOUISVILLE, Thursday, April 14.

Col. PRATT, commanding at Paducah, telegraphs that he is informed that Paducah has been attacked, and the town is full of rebels.

FURTHER FROM PADUCAH.

CAIRO, Friday, April 15.

No boats have been allowed to leave here for points below Columbus since the first news of the Fort Pillow affair.

The attack on Paducah yesterday proved to be a mere raid for plunder, made by a couple of hundred men, who were shelled out by the fort and gunboats after occupying a position of the city in squads.

About noon they left, taking away a number of horses and considerable plunder, and leaving behind about six of their wounded. No one was hurt on our side.

THE WAR IN ARKANSAS.

News from Gen. Steele to April 7—The Rebels Twice Defeated—A Junction to be Made with the Forces from Fort Smith.

LITTLE ROCK, Thursday, April 14.

Advices from Gen. STEELE to the 7th inst. are received.

His expedition had then reached a point five miles south of Ekin Ferry, on the Little Missouri River, and about 25 miles from Camden, where he expected Gen. THAYER, with the force from Fort Smith to join him the next day.

On the 2d the rebel Gen. SHELBY attacked Gen STEELE's rear guard, under Gen. RICE, with 1,200 cavalry and two pieces of artillery, and was repulsed, with the loss of 100 killed and wounded. Our loss was 44 killed and wounded and 15 prisoners.

On the 4th, the rebel Gen. MARMADUKE attacked Gen. STEELE with 3,000 or 4,000 cavalry and five pieces of artillery, on the south side of the Little Missouri River, and after five hours' fighting, was repulsed, with the loss of four killed and twenty-three wounded. Our loss was twenty-three wounded.

There is a large force of rebels five or six miles in advance, but it is not expected they will make a stand.

Nothing had been heard by Gen. STEELE of Gen. BANKS or the gunboats on Red River.

FROM ALBANY.

The Bank Question—A Spicy Discussion—The Senate Refuses to Print the Majority Report—Passage of the Chenango Canal Extension Bill.

Correspondence of the New-York Times:

ALBANY, Friday, April 15, 1864.

The bank question has again been sharply debated in the Assembly to-day. Four thousand copies of the minority report were ordered printed, and upon this Mr. ANDRUS desired to call up the majority report. The House permitted him to do so, and he proceeded to read a carefully prepared and temperate speech, setting forth the reasons which governed the majority of the committee in making their report. His remarks were complimented by members who did not agree with his views, as in contrast with the style of the report which he supported. Several members replied, assailing the majority report as disloyal, and the debate became animated and exciting. The principles and language of the report were severely criticised, and denounced in unmeasured terms by prominent members. At the conclusion of the debate, a resolution which provided that no more than the usual number of copies of the majority report should be printed was lost by a decided negative vote. The Speaker ruled that a refusal to adopt this resolution was equivalent to declining to print any copies of the report, and members voted upon the resolution with this understanding.

The Assembly adjourned at an earlier hour than usual to-day in order to grant the use of the Assembly Chamber to a delegation of gentlemen from New-York, who desired to be heard in regard to taxation in that City. Judge J. W. EDMONDS is addressing the Committees on Affairs of Cities and many members of the Legislature beside upon this subject.

The bill providing for the extension of the Chenango Canal passed the Senate this morning by a vote of 21 to 9.

PROCEEDINGS OF THE LEGISLATURE

SENATE.

ALBANY, Friday, April 15.

BILLS REPORTED.

To provide an armory for the Eighth Regiment National Guard.

Against the bill relative to the West Shore Railroad in Rockland County.

In favor of the Assembly bill to regulate the passenger and freight tariff on the Hudson River Railroad—a majority report.

Messrs. ANGEL and HOBBS dissented from the report.

The President presented a report from the New-York Tax-Payers' Committee, asking to be heard before the Senate.

The report was laid on the table.

Mr. STRONG introduced a bill to incorporate the Manhattan and Long Island Improvement Company.

BILLS PASSED.

Providing for an extension of the Chenango Canal, and appropriating $150,000 for the present year.

For the improvement of the Champlain Canal. This appropriates $65,000.

BILLS ORDERED TO A THIRD READING.

For the improvement of Third-street, Brooklyn.

For the relief of the town of New Lotts, King's County. Recess.

EVENING SESSION.

The Flushing Railroad Bridge Bill, and the bill authorizing the authorities of New-York to convey certain premises on Ward's Island to the society for the protection of destitute Catholic children in New-York, were ordered to a third reading.

Adjourned.

ASSEMBLY.

REPORTS.

To amend the charter of the Harlem and Hudson River Canal Company. Complete.

To amend the charter of the New-York Warehouse and Security Company. Complete.

For the use of dummy engines on railroads.

To incorporate the National Savings Bank.

The New-York Court-house Bill.

Authorizing the Second-avenue Railroad Company to extend their track.

Amending the act relative to the New-York Department of Charities and Corrections.

For a public market in Brooklyn.

The Printing Committee reported against printing extra copies of the majority report of the Bank Committee against the act enabling the State banks to form under the National Banking Act.

The committee say that the report of the Bank Committee is characterized by semi-disloyal language towards the General Government, and especially towards the Secretary of the Treasury, Mr. CHASE.

The report continues: "That at this peculiar crisis the Government needs the support of every loyal citizen, and he that criticises the acts of the Government in language not favorable to the Government, which in times of peace might be justifiable in a party view, becomes a criminal."

The committee add that they think the majority report of the Bank Committee is subject to the charge of "disloyalty."

The committee then conclude by recommending the printing of 4,000 extra copies of the minority report of the Bank Committee.

The previous question was ordered on agreeing to the report of the Printing Committee, and it was agreed to by yeas 65, nays 32.

The question was then taken as stated by the Speaker, "whether any copies of the majority report of the Bank Committee should be printed."

The question was decided in the negative by the following vote: yeas 42, nays 62.

The Assembly here took a recess to hear counsel from New-York for the New-York tax-payers, on the Tax-levy Bill.

Judge EDMONDS spoke at length on the bill, urging a reduction of the items. Recess.

EVENING SESSION.

The New-York and Brooklyn Passenger and Baggage Bill was ordered to a third reading.

A bill was reported to facilitate the acquisition of land for the extension of the Croton Water Works. Adjourned.

FROM WASHINGTON.

SYNOPSIS OF THE NEW TAX BILL.

Passage of a Bill for Ocean Steam Service to Brazil.

The Gold Speculation Bill in the Senate.

Passage of the Bill for Postal Money Order System.

The Disagreement on the Montana Territorial Bill.

SPECIAL DISPATCHES TO THE N. Y. TIMES.

WASHINGTON, Friday, April 15.

THE MASSACRE AT FORT PILLOW.

Up to this evening no account whatever had been received at the War Department of the reported massacre at Fort Pillow. The report is not generally credited in military circles. [In spite of the fact that the Government don't know anything about it, there is every reason to believe it to be entirely true. —ED. TIMES.]

AN EFFORT TO PASS THE GOLD BILL.

An effort will be made to-morrow, by Mr. STEVENS, of the Ways and Means Committee, to pass the new gold bill. The Senate have had it under discussion all day, and will get a vote to-morrow. It will pass.

THE TARIFF BILL.

The committee decided to take up the Tariff Bill, and proceed from day to day without until completed. It will conform to the new Revenue Bill just reported.

THE BANK BILL.

Mr. HOOPER will endeavor to put the Bank Bill through the House to-morrow under the previous question. There is a large delegation here, representing the State banks, opposing its passage.

THE NEW COINAGE OF CENTS.

The Ways and Means Committee had under consideration to-day the Senate bill providing for the coinage of one and two cent pieces out of the new combination material. The committee are opposed to the measure.

THE MISSOURI CONTESTED SEAT.

The House Committee on Elections have a meeting to-morrow for the purpose of considering the Missouri contested election case of BLAIR *vs.* KNOX.

The committee are understood to be about equally divided upon the question.

LAND SALES AT CHILLICOTHE.

During the month of March, $16,256 was received for cash sales for land at Chillicothe, Ohio, and $2,966 in scrip.

GEN. GRANT.

Lieut.-Gen. GRANT returned to the front to-day.

DISPATCHES TO THE ASSOCIATED PRESS.

WASHINGTON, Friday, April 15.

SYNOPSIS OF THE NEW TAX BILL.

The new Internal Revenue Bill is a complete revision of the act now in force, and retains the same machinery with such improvements as experience has rendered necessary. It contains one hundred and seventy-three sections, forty-seven of which are devoted to general provisions.

There is one provision which exempts from distraint the tool or implements of a trade or profession, one cow, arms, and provisions, household furniture kept for use, and the apparel necessary for a family.

Amongst the prominent features of the bill are the following:

In addition to duties payable for licenses, there is to be paid on all spirits distilled, and sold and removed for consumption or sale, if first proof, prior to the 1st of July next, a duty of sixty cents per gallon; on and after that date, to the 1st of January, 1865, one dollar; on and after January 1, 1865, one dollar and twenty-five cents; provided, the duty on all spirits shall be collected at no lower rate than the basis of first proof, and shall be increased in proportion for any greater strength than of first proof.

All distilled spirits and refined coal oil, upon which an excise duty is imposed by law, may be removed without payment of duty; *provided* these articles, so removed, shall be transferred directly from the distillery or refinery to a bonded warehouse.

All beer, lager bier, ale, porter, and other similar fermented liquors, by whatever name called, are to pay a duty of one dollar per barrel of not more than thirty-one gallons.

All bankers are taxed as follows: Using and employing capital not exceeding the sum of $50,000, one hundred dollars for each license; when using or employing capital exceeding $50,000, for every additional thousand dollars in excess of $50,000, two dollars.

When goods, wares and merchandise are sold by the manufacturer or producer, or agent thereof having charge of the business, the following deductions only may be allowed: 1. Freight from place of deposit at time of sale to place of delivery; 2. The actual commission paid, but not exceeding three per centum, and no commission shall be deducted when the sale is made at the place of manufacture or production.

On all mineral coals, except such as are not known in the trade, as pea coal and dust coal, a duty of five cents per ton is imposed.

On lard oil, mustard seed oil, and on all animal or vegetable oils not exempted or provided for elsewhere, whether pure or adulterated, five cents per gallon.

Gas, illuminating, made of coal wholly or in part, or of any other material, when the product shall not be above 500,000 cubic feet per month, pays a duty of 20 cents per 1,000 cubic feet; when the product shall be above 500,000, and not exceeding 5,000,000 cubic feet per month, 25 cents on 1,000 cubic feet; when the product shall be above 5,000,000 cubic feet per month, 30 cents per 1,000 cubic feet; provided that the coal-tar produced in the manufacture of illuminating gas and the products of the redistillation of the coal-tar thus produced shall be exempt from duty.

Illuminating oil and naptha, benzine and benzoil, refined, produced by the distillation of coal, asphaltum, shale, peat, petroleum or rock oil, and all other bituminous substances used for like purposes, a duty of twenty cents per gallon; provided that such oil, refined and produced by the distillation of coal exclusively, shall be subject to pay a duty of 12 cents per gallon; on spirits of turpentine 20 cents per gallon; ground coffee, and on all ground substances for coffee, or preparations of which coffee forms a part, and on all unground substitutes for coffee, a duty of one cent per pound; ground pepper, ground mustard, ground pimento, ground cloves and ground clove stems, ground cassia and ground ginger, and all imitations of the same, 1 cent per pound; molasses, syrup of molasses, concentrated molasses or melado and cistern bottoms, produced directly from sugar cane juice, a duty of 5 per cent ad valorem; brown or Muscovado sugar, not above No. 15, Dutch standard in color, produced directly from the sugar cane, and not from sorghum or imphee, other than those produced by the refiner, 1 cent per pound. All clarified or refined sugar above No. 15, Dutch standard, in color, produced directly from the sugar cane and not from sorghum or imphee a duty of 2 cents per pound; on the gross amount of sales of sugar refiners, including all the products of their manufactories or refineries, 1½ per cent. ad valorem; sugar candy and all confectionery made wholly or in part of sugar, valued at not exceeding 20 cents, a duty of 2 cents a pound; exceeding 20 and not exceeding 40 cents per pound, 4 cents per pound; when exceeding 40 cents a pound or sold otherwise than by the pound, 10 per cent. ad valorem; chocolate and cocoa, prepared, 1½ cents per pound; saleratus and bicarbonate of soda a duty of 5 mills per pound; made of corn or wheat a duty of three mills per pound; made of rice or any other material, a duty of 1 cent per pound; on white lead, a duty of 35 cents per 100 pounds; on oxide of zinc, a duty of 35 cents per 100 pounds; on sulphate of barytes, 12 cents per 100 pounds; on all printers and painters colors, dry or ground, in oil or in paste, or with water, not otherwise provided for, 5 per cent. ad valorem.

Glue and cement, made wholly or in part of glue to be sold in the liquid state, 40 cents per gallon.

Clocks and time-pieces, and clock movements, when sold without being cased, 5 per cent. ad valorem.

Umbrellas and parasols made of cotton or silk, or other material, 5 per cent. ad valorem.

Gold leaf, 18 cents per pack, containing not more than twenty books of 25 leaves each.

Paper of all descriptions, including pasteboard, binders board, and tarred paper for roofing or other purposes, 3 per cent. ad valorem.

Soap, castile, palm oil, erasive, and soap of all other descriptions, white or colored, except soft soap, and soap otherwise provided for, valued not above 5 cents per pound, a duty of 2 mills per pound; soap fancy, scented, honey, cream, transparent, and all descriptions of toilet and shaving soap, 5 cents per pound; soft soap, 5 per cent ad valorem. All uncompounded chemical productions not otherwise provided for, 5 per cent. ad valorem. Essential oils of all descriptions, 5 per cent, ad valorem.

Pickles and preserved fruits, vegetables, meats, fish and shellfish in cans, kegs or air-tight packages, five per cent. ad valorem.

Billheads, printed cards, five per cent, ad valorem.

All printed books, magazines, pamphlets, reviews, and all other similar printed publications except newspapers, five per cent. ad valorem.

All repairs of engines, cars, carriages, or other articles, when such repairs increase the value of the article repaired, ten per cent., or over three per cent. on such increased value.

On hulls, as launched, of ships, barks, brigs, schooners, sloops, sail-boats, steamboats, canal-boats, and all other vessels or water craft, not including engines or rigging hereafter built, made or constructed, 2 per cent ad valorem.

Slate, freestone, sandstone, marble, and building-stone, any other description, when dressed, hewn or finished, 3 per cent. ad valorem.

On marble gravestones and other monumental stones, whether with or without inscriptions, 5 per cent. ad valorem.

Lime and Roman or water cement, 3 per cent. ad valorem.

Masts, spars, ship or vessel blocks, 2 per cent. ad valorem.

All furniture and other articles made of wood sold in rough or unfinished state, 5 per cent. ad valorem.

On salt, 6 cents per 100 pounds.

On sails, tents, shades, awnings and bags made of cotton, flax or hemp, 5 per cent. ad valorem.

Pig iron, $1 per ton. Blooms, slabs or loops, whether made in forges or bloomeries, $1 50 per ton. Railroad iron—on rolled $1 50 per ton. On all iron advanced beyond blooms, slabs or loops, and not advanced beyond bars or rods, and band, hoop and sheet iron not thinner than No. 18 wire gauge; and plate iron not less than one-eighth of an inch in thickness, a duty of $3 per ton. On band, hoop and sheet iron thinner than No. 18 wire guage, plate iron less than ⅛ inch thick, and cut and wrought nails and spikes, and horseshoe nails when wrought by hand, not including nails, tacks, brads or finishing nails, usually put up and sold in papers and otherwise, nor horseshoe nails wrought by machinery, a duty of $3 50 per ton.

Stoves and hollow ware and castings of iron, exceeding ten pounds in weight for each casting not otherwise provided for $3 per ton.

On rivets exceeding ¼ inch in diameter, nuts less than 2 oz. each in weight, and bolts not less than 4 oz. each in weight, $4 per ton.

Steel in ingots, bars, sheets or wire, not less than ¼-inch thick, valued at 7 cents per pound or less, $5 per ton; valued at above 7 cents per pound and not above 11 cents per pound, $10 per ton; valued at above 11 cents per pound, $12 50 per ton.

Steam engines, including locomotives and marine engines, three per cent. ad valorem.

Gold, silver and quicksilver produced from quartz mines, from beds of rivers, from the earth, or in any other way or manner; copper and lead ingots, pigs or bars, and spelter and brass, three per cent. ad valorem.

Patent enamelled and Japanese leather and skins of every description, 5 per cent. ad valorem.

On leather of all descriptions, tanned or partially tanned in the rough, 5 per cent. ad valorem; curried or finished, 5 per cent. ad valorem.

Wine made of grapes, 5 cents per gallon. All other wines, or liquors known and denominated as wine, or produced by being rectified and mixed with other spirits, or into which any matter whatever may be infused to be sold as wine, or by any other name, and not otherwise provided for in this act, 25 cents per gallon.

Furs of all descriptions, when made up or manufactured, 5 per cent. ad valorem.

Cloth, and all textiles or knitted and felted fabrics of cotton, wool or other materials, before the same has been dyed, printed or bleached, and all cloth painted, enamelled, shined, tarred, varnished or oiled, 5 per cent. ad valorem.

Ready-made clothing, boots and shoes, caps, hats and bonnets, and other articles of dress for the wear of men, women or children, five per cent. ad valorem.

Cotton, upon which no duty has been levied, collected or paid, or which is not exempted by law, two cents per pound, which shall be and remain a lien thereon until said duty shall have been paid in the possession of any person or persons whomsoever.

All manufacturers of cotton, wool, silk, worsted, flax, hemp, jute, India rubber, gutta percha, wood, willow, glass, pottery ware, leather, paper, iron, steel, lead, tin, copper, zinc, brass, gold, silver, horn, ivory, bone, bristles, wholly or in part, or of other material not in this act otherwice provided, 5 per cent. ad valorem.

PROCEEDINGS OF CONGRESS.

SENATE.

WASHINGTON, Friday, April 15.

DISTRICT OF COLUMBIA MATTERS.

Mr. HOWARD, of Michigan, (Union,) introduced a bill to amend the statutes in force in the District of Columbia; repealing the saving clause in favor of pension beyond lives in the old Maryland laws; for the limitation of certain actions for avoiding suits at law; the administration of justice in testamentary affairs, &c.

TAX ON THE MANUFACTURE OF AGRICULTURAL IMPLEMENTS.

Mr. DOOLITTLE, of Wisconsin, (Union,) presented the memorial of the Legislature of Wisconsin, asking that a tax be placed only upon profits of money invested in the manufacture of agricultural implements, instead of three per cent. on all sales. It represents that these manufactures are five times the value of the capital invested, equal to fifteen per cent. on the capital; that they have greatly benefitted the West, and without them the development of agricultural resources would be retarded. The memorial was referred to the Committee on Finance.

THE GOLD SPECULATION BILL.

Mr. SHERMAN, of Ohio, (Union,) called up the bill prohibiting speculative transactions in gold, &c., as published in yesterday's proceedings. He said the object of the bill was to prevent gambling in gold. The committee thought that at this time it had an injurious effect, and that the sale of gold by a party who had no gold to sell was an offence, was being daily committed by parties when they had not a cent to sell. He presented the following letter from the Secretary of the Treasury on the subject. In a letter to Mr. FESSENDEN, Chairman of the Finance Committee, under date of the Treasury Department, April 12, 1864, the Secretary of the Treasury says: "SIR, notwithstanding the diminished amount of United States notes in circulation, and our gradual withdrawal from use as currency of interest bearing United States notes made a legal tender for their face, the price of gold continues to advance. This effect can only be attributed to one or two causes, and is probably due in part to each. First, the increase of the notes of local banks, and secondly, the efforts of speculators. I have already submitted, through you, to the consideration of the Committee on Finance, a bill intended as a remedy for the first evil. I now beg leave to submit to its consideration a bill intended as a remedy for the second. The first bill, if it becomes a law, will have, I doubt not, the most salutary consequences. The effects of the second will probably be more immediate, though, perhaps, not of such permanent importance. I ask for both a candid consideration, and, if approved, the favorable action of Congress. It must not be thought, however, that I regard either or both of these measures adequate remedies for financial disorder. Nothing short of taxation of one-half of the amount of our current expenditures and a reduction of those expenditures to the lowest point compatible with efficiency, will insure financial success to the Government, and without military success, all measures will fail.

Very respectfully yours, S. P. CHASE.

Mr. SHERMAN said that although the Committee on Finance were not certain that the evils sought to be remedied by this bill would be; so he was certain, however, that the bill might do good, and could do no harm. The true remedy for our evils, as all knew, was the success of our armies.

Mr. FESSENDEN, of Maine, (Union,) advocated the bill, and said it might tend to cure an evil which existed because of the desire of some persons to make money at any expense to the country; and again, as he was sorry to say, because there were many among us who cultivated a hostility to the currency because they sympathized with our enemy. In a great commercial city like New-York it was impossible to repress this entirely, but he thought the bill would accomplish good.

Mr. COWAN, of Pennsylvania, (Union,) opposed the bill as useless and doubtful legislation. He did not believe our currency had so depreciated as to require such a means to bolster it up. He denied that these speculations had the least effect on the price of gold. The price of gold depended upon its intrinsic material value, and, if there was an article in the world which had a regal right to be called king, it was gold. He quoted at length from THIERS' *History of the French Revolution*, giving a history of the assignats issued at that time, and drew a parallel between that era and this.

Mr. COWAN moved to strike out the clause requiring the manual delivery of United States notes or national currency in all gold transactions. He said the bill will have no better effect than the Gold Bill passed recently, when gold went up five per cent. the day after its passage. He opposed the bill as useless and impracticable.

His amendment was rejected—as follows:

YEAS—Messrs. Buckalew, Clark, Collamer, Harding, Hendricks, Howe, Johnson, Nesmith, Powell, Saulsbury and Wright—14.

NAYS—Messrs Anthony, Brown, Chandler, Conness, Dixon, Doolittle, Fessenden, Foster, Hale, Harris, Lane of Indiana, Lane of Kansas, Morgan, Morrill, Pomeroy, Ramsey, Sherman, Sprague, Sumner, Ten Eyck, Trumbull, Van Winkle, Wade, Willey and Wilson—25.

Mr. CHANDLER, of Michigan, (Union,) supported the bill. It was well known that there were in many of our large cities persons of disloyal opinions, who used all kinds of methods to break down the confidence in the Government and its currency. In New-York City, to-day, JEFF. DAVIS would get a larger vote than a loyal man. These gold gamblers were nearly all sympathizers with the rebellion. He believed the people had confidence in our securities, as for every dollar the Government issued there was a mortgage on the solid wealth of the country. One reason of the great demand for gold was the extravagance of the people. There was what was called the "Gold Ring" in New-York, who were sympathizers with the rebellion, and this bill would have an effect on them and upon similar combinations. When our armies should march to victory, the speculators would be the ones to suffer.

Mr. JOHNSON, of Maryland, (Union,) made a legal argument to show that it was not competent for Congress to undertake to regulate this matter, as it was a matter solely belonging to the States. If, as alleged, it was a crime to gamble in gold, it was to be punished by the laws of the States. He denied our authority to regulate State Banks under the Constitution. Gold had become an article of trade and contract, and as such the laws of the States should regulate it. This bill further proposed to regulate foreign exchange. If we had power in Congress to do this, why not extend it to bonds, stocks, promissory notes, &c., and thus regulate the entire business of the State. The bill would not be a success permanently, because these speculators, instead of having their places in the street, would continue under one roof and exert the same influence they now did. We wanted additional taxation and a vigorous and successful prosecution of the war. With this the people would allow the debt to be trebled.

THE DISAGREEMENT ON MONTANA.

A message was received from the House, announcing their non-concurrence in the report of the Committee of Conference on the disagreeing vote on the bill creating a Territorial Government for Montana, and stating that they had appointed a new committee, with instructions asking the appointment of a similar one by the Senate.

Mr. FESSENDEN and others, while expressing a willingness to recede, condemned the manner in which the House made the request. He was tired of seeing the Senate continually getting on its knees to the House.

On the motion of Mr. COLLAMER, of Vermont, (Union,) the Senate refused to accept the proposition of the House, coming in the form it had.

THE GOLD BILL AGAIN.

A motion by Mr. COLLAMER to strike out the second section, forbidding the purchase or sale of gold at other than the ordinary place of business of the seller or purchaser, was rejected. Adjourned.

HOUSE OF REPRESENTATIVES.

WASHINGTON, D. C., Friday, April 15.

NIGHT SESSIONS.

Mr. WILSON, of Iowa, (Union,) again asked, but failed to obtain, consent to offer a resolution providing for night sessions for the transaction of business.

INVALID PENSIONS.

Mr. WHALEY, of West Virginia, (Union,) from the Committee on Invalid Pensions, reported a bill, which was passed, supplementary to the law of 1862.

THE DISAGREEMENT ON MONTANA.

Mr. BEAMAN, of Massachusetts, (Union,) from the Conference Committee on the disagreeing amendment to the bill providing a temporary government for the Territory of Montana, made a report recommending a concurrence in the Senate amendment, striking out the qualification of "white" voters, and substituting "every male citizen of the United States and those who have declared their intention to become such."

Mr. BEAMAN said that he would not, at this time, make any remarks. He believed that the subject was well understood by every gentleman, and therefore moved the "previous question."

Mr. HOLMAN, of Indiana, (Dem.,) moved to lay the report on the table.

Motion to lay on the table lost, by yeas, 66; nays, 67.

The House then disagreed to the report by a vote of 53 against 83.

Mr. HOLMAN moved that the House "adhere" to its amendment.

Mr. BEAMAN moved that the House "insist," and ask another Committee of Conference.

Mr. WEBSTER, of Maryland, (Union,) moved the following instructions: "And that the Committee of Conference agree to no report which authorizes to vote any other than "free white male citizens, and those who have declared their intentions to become such."

The question was taken on the instructions of Mr. WEBSTER, and they were agreed to by yeas, 75; nays, 67.

Mr. BEAMAN's motion for another Committee of Conference was then adopted, with the instructions as above.

THE UNEMPLOYED GENERALS.

The joint resolution to dispose of the unemployed Generals was postponed for ten days.

OCEAN STEAM MAIL SERVICE TO BRAZIL.

Mr. ALLEY, of Massachusetts, (Union,) from the Committee on the Post-office and Post Roads, reported a bill authorizing the establishment of ocean mail steamship service between the United States and Brazil.

Mr. ALLEY showed the importance of the measure.

Mr. PRUYN, of New-York, (Dem.,) expressed the hope that this would receive the unanimous support of the House, as it would show that we were well disposed to cultivate the good feeling of Brazil toward us, and further increase the benefits of commercial communication between the two countries.

Mr. STEVENS, of Pennsylvania, (Union,) thought they had abandoned the system of subsidies. We tried it with the Collins line and abandoned it, leaving everything open to competition, as it should be. If it were ever profitable it seemed to him that we should not resort to it at this time when gold was at a premium, ranging from 50 100 per cent., and when the public expenses were three millions of dollars a day.

Mr. ALLEY said the gentleman misapprehended the bill. It proposed to give for the service not exceeding $150,000 per annum, provided Brazil would pay an equal amount. There was no subsidy. No particular line was selected; but the service was open to fair competition.

Mr. KASSON, of Iowa, (Union,) remarked that the bill did not merely provide for cultivating postal and commercial communications with Brazil, but with intermediate points, and he briefly showed the advantages of the bill.

Afterward, further proceedings took place, when Mr. STEVENS moved that the bill be laid upon the table.

This was disagreed to—80 against 37.

The bill was then passed.

The bill authorizes the Postmaster-General to unite with the Post-office Department of Brazil in establishing mail communication between the two countries, by means of a monthly line of first-class sea-going steamers, of not less than 2,000 tons each, of sufficient number to perform twelve round trips per annum between a United States port north of the Potomac River and Rio Janeiro, touching at St. Thomas, in the West Indies, and at Bahia and Pernambuco, provided that the expense to the United States shall not exceed $200,000 per annum.

The Postmaster-General is authorized to advertise for proposals for such service sixty days in one or more newspapers in Washington, Baltimore, Philadelphia, New-York and Boston, such contract to go into effect on or before Sept. 1, 1865.

RAILROADS MUST CARRY THE MAILS.

Mr. ALLEY, from the Postal Committee, reported a bill compelling all railroad corporations to carry the mails for such compensation as may be provided by law.

The bill was passed.

THE POSTAL MONEY-ORDER SYSTEM.

Mr. ALLEY called up the bill to establish a postal money order system, and it was passed.

This bill specifies that no order is to be issued for less than one dollar, or more than thirty.

MR. DONOHUE WANTED.

Mr. ROLLINS, of Missouri, (Union,) from the Committee on Public Expenditures, reported a resolution authorizing the Speaker to issue his warrant to the Sergeant-at-Arms for the arrest of JOHN H. DONOHUE, of New-York, who has refused to appear and testify in relation to the affairs of the New-York Custom-house.

The resolution was passed.

RELIEF OF POSTMASTERS WHO HAVE BEEN ROBBED BY GUERRILLAS.

The House passed a resolution for the relief of Postmasters who have been robbed of stamps, money, &c., by the rebel forces or bands of guerrillas.

The House adjourned at 4:30 o'clock.

DEPARTMENT OF THE GULF.

Arrival of the Continental and George Washington from New-Orleans.

ALL QUIET AT ALEXANDRIA.

Gen. Banks Moving Up the Red River.

Our Land and Naval Forces Still Advancing.

AFFAIRS IN TEXAS.

THE CONSTITUTION CONVENTION IN SESSION.

THE "IRON-CLAD" TEST OATH OF LOYALTY.

The steamer *Continental*, from New-Orleans on the 8th instant, arrived at this port yesterday morning. The *George Washington*, with New-Orleans dates to the 9th, also arrived yesterday. We are under obligations to Purser ALLEN for the prompt delivery of our files. The news is of only ordinary interest. Alexandria dates of the 5th instant report that Gen. BANKS and staff proceeded up the river and were reported to be at the Grand Ecore. All was quiet at Alexandria, and ample precaution taken against surprise by the enemy.

For the present Grand Ecore will be the headquarters of Gen. BANKS. The *Black Hawk*, on returning to Alexandria, when about twenty-five miles below Grand Ecore, was fired at by a party of about thirty guerillas, wounding Maj. E. GIFFORD, Paymaster United States army, the engineer, and a negress. Neither of the three was seriously injured, although Maj. GIFFORD had a narrow escape. He was struck in the arm by a buckshot, and a minie ball passed through and cut off some of his whiskers. The *Black Hawk* sustained but trifling injuries. Red River had fallen six feet at Alexandria, and was still receding. The heavy iron-clads had dropped down to Fort de Russy. There was still sufficient water for the gunboats and transports to cross the falls. The streets of Alexandria were barricaded in case of raids by the rebels. Some five hundred of the people have taken the oath under the President's Amnesty Proclamation. A Union meeting was held on the 4th inst.

The steamer *Luminary*, before reported destroyed, was above the Falls, uninjured.

The reports of a rebel attack on Alexandria are untrue.

OUR NEW-ORLEANS CORRESPONDENCE.

The News from Gen. Banks—The Union Feeling in the Red River Region—History of the Parish—Tableaux Vivants—Cotton from the Red River.

NEW-ORLEANS, Saturday, April 9, 1864.

The news from Gen. BANKS is cheering, and everything is progressing finely, so far as the movements of the army are concerned. His command is above Natchitoches, and up to this time there has been no battle between us and the rebel forces, printed rumors and "authentic details" to the contrary notwithstanding. There is constant skirmishing, however, between our advance guard and the rear of DICK TAYLOR's force, and things promise that there may be a collision at Shreveport, for that is the important point, as the gate of Texas into Louisiana. A number of prisoners have been taken, though it would seem as if these people straggled off for the sake of being captured. This idea is confirmed by the fact that Capt. TODD, an own cousin of Mr. LINCOLN, surrendered himself and expressed his willingness to take the oath of allegiance, and said he was sick of the war.

The most significant thing in this connection is the uprising of the Union people in Rapide Parish, the court-house town of which is Alexandria. Rapide is called from its size and immense production the "Empire Parish," and it contained, before the breaking out of the rebellion, the largest cotton farms, and the richest planting population in this part of the country. The people were always distinguished for their intelligence and liberality. The leading citizens were staunch friends of Mr. CLAY, and always conservative in their politics.

It is, therefore, not surprising that the first favorable opportunity that occurred for the people to return to the Union should be taken advantage of. The gentlemen engaged in the movement are all old residents of the parish, not new comers, and are, therefore, more to be admired for their patriotism. Prominent among the gentlemen who took the oath of allegiance were citizens of the highest character, social and political. LEWIS TEXADA, Esq., is a lawyer and planter, and has for years been a member of the State Legislature. J. K. ELGEE is a distinguished lawyer and a wealthy planter. He is one of the most accomplished gentlemen in the country; was a member of the secession convention and signed the infamous ordinance. Since DICK TAYLOR has had command of the rebel forces in western Louisiana, Mr. ELGEE has been much of his time his companion and civil adviser. His abandonment of the renegade son of "Old Zack" has a significance. The cause of the rebels must be bad indeed on Red River.

So far we have been disappointed as to the receipts of cotton from Red River. Comparatively very little cotton has been received. It is stated that some thousands of bales, seized by Com. PORTER, of the gunboats, will be sent to Memphis. I heard a story of "Jack" seizing the staple, that shows an eye to business not ordinarily credited to the sailor. They had orders to seize no cotton not marked "C. S. A.;" so they went ashore, in many instances, with marking-pots in their hands, and first marked "C. S. A." on a bale, and then crossed off the offensive initials and put underneath "U. S. A.," and with this new christening seized it as lawful prize, and tumbled it on board of the gunboats.

COTTON REPORT FOR THE WEEK ENDING APRIL 8, 1864, BY RUTSON MAURY, JR., COTTON BROKER.

Middling, 72@73; Strict Low Middling, 70; Low Middling, 68@69; Good Ordinary, 64@65; Ordinary, 60@62.

Sales this week, 26,000; exports this week, 27,000; estimated stock, about 6,000 bales.

Remarks.—The market has been freely met by buyers, at an advance of fully 3c.@4c. over quotations of last week. A larger business would have been done if the stock offering had been more liberal and of suitable quality.

The accounts from Red River continue discouraging regarding future receipts from that quarter.

On Tuesday next comes off the exhibition of *tableaux vivants* at the Opera House, the proceeds to be expended for the benefit of the soldiers, their wives and children, of the Department of the Gulf. The spirit that the ladies have displayed in the affair cannot be sufficiently admired.

East and West—The Wounding of Col. Sargent—The Delegate Election—The Constitutional History of Louisiana—Henry Clay's Monument in New-Orleans.

NEW-ORLEANS, Saturday, April, 2, 1864.

It cannot be denied that there existed some time ago a good deal of sectional prejudice between the

The New-York Times.

VOL. XIII—NO. 3923. | NEW-YORK, WEDNESDAY, APRIL 20, 1864. | PRICE THREE CENTS.

THE WAR IN LOUISIANA.

Reported Defeat of the Union Forces.

A Severe Battle at Pleasant Hill, La.

The Cavalry and Two Divisions of Infantry Repulsed.

The Rebel Advance Checked by the Nineteenth Army Corps.

Our Loss Two Thousand—Rebel Loss Heavy.

General Banks' Army Falling Back to Grand Ecore.

CHICAGO, Tuesday, April 19.

The *Journal's* letter from Grand Ecore, 10th inst., says:

"Our cavalry has been driving the enemy for two days, but in the forenoon of the 8th, sent back word for infantry supports. Gen. RANSOM, in command of the Third and Fourth Divisions of the Thirteenth Corps, was ordered to send forward a brigade, and he did so. At noon, he followed with the Fourth Division. After advancing about five miles from where the Third Division of the command and the Nineteenth Corps were encamped, the rebels made a stand, and our line, consisting of only 2,400 infantry, formed in a belt of woods with an open field in front, and the enemy in the woods on the other side. Gen. STONE, of Ball's Bluff fame, chief of Gen. BANKS' staff, was on the field, and took direction of the movements.

Gen. RANSOM was in favor of advancing only in force, but his wish was disregarded. After a skirmish across the open field for about an hour, the enemy advanced upon us in overwhelming numbers, estimated at 10,000 strong. Gen. RANSOM got all the available troops to the front and opened on them. The enemy lost heavily, but advanced steadily.

Soon all of the cavalry gave way, and the infantry fell back. In a few moments the enemy pressed us closely. The panic of the cavalry so demoralized the army that the retreat became a rout. The General did all in his power to rally the men, but finding it impossible without reinforcements, made every effort to save the artillery. While endeavoring to get the Chicago Mercantile Battery off safely, Gen. RANSOM was severely wounded in the leg. Capt. CYRUS E. DICKEY, his Adjutant, was instantly killed."

Our loss was large, probably 2,000.

The Mercantile battery lost all its guns. Capt. WHITE is a prisoner, Lieuts. THROOP and MCBRIDE were killed. The loss of the battery in killed and captured is thirty-one. One hundred and ten of them returned to camp after the disaster.

While the Fourth Division was falling back in disorder, the Third Division, numbering only 1,600 men, came up and was immediately routed.

Finally, the Nineteenth Army Corps, with 7,000 men, came up and formed in line. They checked the enemy, and held them until we got all the trains off, except that of the cavalry.

The whole army is falling back here, where it must wait to reorganize before proceeding further toward Shreveport.

REBEL REPORTS.

We find the following curious dispatch in late Southern papers, which may or may not be connected with the above affair:

MOBILE, April 11.

To Gen. S. Cooper, A. and I. General:

The following report was received at Baton Rouge, on the 3d inst., from the Surgeon-General of BANKS' army: "We met the enemy near Shreveport. Union force repulsed with great loss. How many can you accommodate in hospitals at Baton Rouge? Steamer *Essex* or *Benton* destroyed by torpedoes in Red River, and a transport captured by Confederates."

FARRAGUT reported preparing to attack Mobile. Six monitors coming to him. The garrisons of New-Orleans and Baton Rouge were very much reduced for the purpose of increasing BANKS' forces.

D. H. MAURY, Maj.-Gen. Commanding.

REPORTS VIA ST. LOUIS.

ST. LOUIS, Tuesday, April 19.

The *Democrat* has several dispatches from the Red River, containing nothing, however, of special importance. Little had occurred except skirmishing.

BANKS' army left Grand Ecore on the 6th, and the boats last out of Red River reported the fleet within 100 miles of Shreveport, and the men expected to reach there on the 12th.

Several hundred rebel prisoners had reached our fleet from New-Orleans to be exchanged for a like number of Federal.

Hundreds were taking the amnesty oath.

It was reported that Capt. CARTHWAIT, of the gunboat *Chilicothe*, was killed on the 4th inst. by a shot from the shore.

A prominent Frenchman of New-Orleans predicts a treaty of friendship between the Confederates and MAXIMILIAN, backed by NAPOLEON.

The French Commander-in-Chief has ordered Admiral BORSE to make an effective demonstration against CORTINAS.

SANTA ANNA has returned to St. Thomas.

From the Mississippi.

CAIRO, Ill., Tuesday, April 18.

The steamer *Lady Pike*, from Memphis, on the 16th inst., passed here, to-day, with 800 bales of cotton, of which 160 bales are for Evansville, and the remainder for Cincinnati.

On the 4th inst., Capt. PHELPS, of gunboat No. 26, captured a rebel mail carrier near Crockett's Bluff, Ark., with five hundred letters from Richmond and other points, and 60,000 percussion caps for Gen. PRICE'S army. The letters contained official communications for Shreveport, and a considerable sum of Federal money.

A squad of rebel cavalry captured Representative CLARK and the Sheriff of Kansas County, Ark., and carried them off. They also burned a lot of cotton and arrested seven cotton buyers. The latter they let go after robbing them of several thousands of dollars.

The Case of the Malden Murderer.

BOSTON, Tuesday, April 19.

The arraignment of EDWARD W. GREEN, the late Postmaster of Malden, took place in Lowell to-day, before Judge HOAR, of the Supreme Judicial Court. The indictment charged the willful murder of FRANK E. CONVERSE, late Teller of the Malden Bank, to which GREEN pleaded guilty. He was remanded for sentence.

Movements of President Lincoln.

BALTIMORE, Tuesday, April 19.

President LINCOLN returned to Washington this morning. He expressed himself as much gratified with his visit to Baltimore.

THE MASSACRE AT FORT PILLOW.

Details of the Butchery—A Walk Through the Fort Under Flag of Truce—Scenes and Incidents.

Correspondence of the Missouri Democrat.

CAIRO, Thursday, April 14, 1864.

Before leaving Memphis Tuesday afternoon, we heard a report that Fort Pillow was captured, and at 5 P. M. we proceeded up the river in the *Platte Valley*, loaded down with passengers, and with the gunboat *Silver Cloud*, No. 27, under Acting Master FERGUSON, in tow. We designedly proceeded slowly, and arrived near the fort at 8 A. M., where the gunboat cast off, and steamed up toward the fort. We were about three miles below the fort, and could see mounted pickets on the shore. After the gunboat got within reach she opened on the fort with shell, but met with no reply. She continued slowly until she got in near the fort and near the shore, where she fired a shot or two and then stopped. We had followed her at a distance, and now, about 10 A. M., came up abreast and passed her and the fort. As we came up, we saw fire and smoke proceeding from the shore, which proved to be some buildings and some hay on the levee. We also, for the first time, saw people moving about, some on foot and some on horseback, behind the smoke; and soon several persons came to the bank of the river with a white flag. The gunboat sent a skiff ashore, which returned in about twenty minutes, and then the gunboat landed. We, at this time, were a mile above, and being signaled by the gunboat, returned and landed by the boat. While returning near the shore, we saw numerous dead bodies strewed along the river and on the sides of the bluff. We found, on landing, quite a number of Confederate officers; among them Brig.-Gen. CHALMERS with his Staff, and Maj. C. W. ANDERSON, of Gen. SMITH'S staff, and others of the rebel officers whose names I did not learn. Arrangements were made to parole all the wounded, and men were detached to bring them in. An agreement for truce till 5 P. M., was agreed upon, and permission freely given to visit the fort and grounds. Escorted by Capt. LINDSEY, formerly of Natchez, now in the rebel army, your correspondent visited the fort and adjacent grounds—the scene of action the day preceding. On the way up—about three miles below the fort—we were signalled by a flat-boat on the Missouri shore, and took on board a colored corporal and three wounded men, and received our first account from them of the fight.

THE ASSAULT AND CAPTURE OF THE FORT.

We have gleaned the facts of the fight from authentic sources, and they may be relied upon as truthful. The rebels, under FORREST, appeared and drove in the pickets about sunrise on Tuesday morning. The garrison of the fort consisted of about two hundred of the Thirteenth Tennessee Volunteers and four hundred negro artillery, all under command of Major BOOTH; the gunboat No. 7 was also in the river. The rebels first attacked the outer forts, and in several attempts to charge were repulsed. They were constantly reinforced, and extended their lines to the river on both sides of the fort. The garrison in the two outer forts were at length overpowered by superior numbers, and about noon evacuated them and retired to the fort on the river. Here the fight was maintained with great obstinacy, and continued till about 4 P. M. The approach to the fort from the rear is over a gentle declivity, cleared and fully exposed to a raking fire from two sides of the fort. About 30 yards from the fort is a deep ravine, running all along the front, and so steep at the bottom as to be hidden from the fort, and not commanded by its guns. The rebels charged with great boldness down the declivity, and faced without blanching a murderous fire from the guns and small arms of the fort, and crowded into the ravine where they were sheltered from fire by the steep bank which had been thus left by some unaccountable neglect or ignorance. Here the rebels organized for a final charge upon the fort, after sending a flag of truce with a demand for surrender, which was refused. The approach from the ravine was up through a deep, narrow gully, and the steep embankments of the fort. The last charge was made about 4 P. M., by the whole rebel force, and was successful after a most desperate and gallant defence. The rebel army was estimated at from two thousand to four thousand, and succeeded by mere force of numbers. The gunboat had not been idle, but guided by signals from the fort, poured upon the rebels a constant stream of shot and shell. She fired 260 shells, and as testified to by those who could see, with marvelous precision and with fatal effect. Maj. BOOTH, who was killed near the close of the fight, conducted the defence with great coolness, skill and gallantry. His last signal to the boat, was, "We are hard pressed and shall be overpowered." He refused to surrender, however, and fought to the last. By the uniform and voluntary testimony of the rebel officers as well as the survivors of the fight, that the negro artillery regiments fought with the bravery and coolness of veterans and served the guns with skill and precision. They did not falter nor flinch until at the last charge, when it was evident they would be overpowered, they broke and fled toward the river, and here commenced the most barbarous and cruel outrages that ever the fiendishness of rebels have perpetrated during the war.

REBEL ATROCITIES.

After the rebels were in undisputed possession of the fort and the survivors had surrendered, they commenced the indiscriminate butchery of all the Federal soldiery. The colored soldiers threw down their guns and raised their arms in token of surrender, but not the least attention was paid to it. They continued to shoot down all they found. A number of them finding no quarter was given, ran over the bluff to the river, and tried to conceal themselves under the bank and in the bushes, were pursued by the rebel savages, and implored them to spare their lives. Their appeals were made in vain, and they were all shot down in cold blood and in full sight of the gunboat, chased and shot them down as they would dogs. I passed up the bank of the river and counted fifty dead strewed along. One had crawled into a hollow log and was killed in it, another had got over the bank in the river, and had got on to a board that run out into the water. He lay on it on his face, with his feet in the water. He laid there when exposed stark and stiff. Several had tried to hide in crevices made by the falling bank, and could not be seen without difficulty, but they were singled out and killed. From the best information I could get, the white soldiers were, to a very considerable extent, treated in the same way. One of the Thirteenth Tennessee on board—D. W. HARRISON—informs me that after the surrender he was below the bluff, and one of the rebels presented a pistol to shoot him. He told him he had surrendered, and requested him not to fire. He spared him, and directed him to go up the bluff to the fort. HARRISON asked him to go before him, or he would be shot by others, but he told him to go along. He started, and had not proceeded far before he met a rebel, who presented his pistol. HARRISON begged him not to fire, but paying no attention to his request, he fired and shot him through the shoulder, and another shot him in the leg. He fell, and while he lay unable to move, another came along and was about to fire again, when HARRISON told him he was badly wounded twice, and implored him not to fire. He asked HARRISON if he had any money. He said he had a little money and a watch. The rebel took from him his watch and ninety dollars in money, and left him. HARRISON is, probably, fatally wounded. Several such cases have been related to me, and I think, to a great extent, the whites and negroes were indiscriminately murdered. The rebel Tennesseans have about the same bitterness against Tennesseans in the Federal army, as against the negroes. I was told by a rebel officer that Gen. FORREST shot one of his men and cut another with his sabre who were shooting down prisoners. It may be so, but he is responsible for the conduct of his men, and Gen. CHALMERS stated publicly, while on the Platte Valley, that though he did not encourage or countenance his men in shooting down negro captives, yet that it was right and justifiable.

INCIDENTS OF THE FIGHT.

The negro corporal, JACOB WILSON, whom we picked up below Fort Pillow, had a narrow escape. He was down on the river bank, and seeing that no quarter was shown, stepped into the water so that he lay partly under it. A rebel coming along asked him what was the matter; he said he was badly wounded, and the rebel, after taking from his pocket all the money he had, left him. It happened to be near by a flat boat tied to the bank, and about 3 o'clock in the morning. When all was quiet WILSON crawled into it and got three more wounded comrades also into it, and cut loose. The boat floated out into the channel, and we found it ashore some miles below. The wounded negro soldiers we have aboard feigned themselves dead until we came along. Capt. YOUNG, Twenty-fourth Missouri, Provost-Marshal at the fort, was captured, and was out on his parole. He was at the boat, and while there the *Lady Pike*, from St. Louis, came up, with his wife aboard. He was allowed to go into the boat to see her, and then returned to his captors. Major BRADFORD was also captured, and at large on his parole. The rebel officers denounce him for breaking his parole, and say that during Tuesday night he escaped. It is believed that the rebels killed him, and that the charge of breaking his parole is a mere pretence to conceal his murder.

Capt. LINDSAY, rebel officer, to whom I am indebted for courteous attention, admitted to me that Gen. FORREST was slightly wounded, and had a horse killed under him, but another rebel officer informed a friend of his, who was on the boat with us, that Gen. F. was twice wounded, and badly, by the bursting of a shell.

The rebels claim to have but only ten killed and thirty wounded, but Capt. YOUNG, who had been to their camp, says that they have two hospitals well filled, and he thinks their killed and wounded exceed ours.

When I visited the fort, the guns had all been taken away. The huts scattered around had been mostly burned up. In one of these were bodies of colored soldiers partly burned, but whether or not by design I cannot state.

Dr. FITCH, Surgeon of the fort, was taken prisoner, and through the influence of some rebel Surgeons was released on his parole and came up with us. He confirms, from his own personal observation, the butchery of our soldiers by the rebels. He informed me, that after the fort was taken the soldiers ran down the bluff to the river, throwing away their arms, holding up their hands, and crying out that they surrendered, but the rebels continued to fire on them from the bluff without the least regard to their cries. Dr. FITCH says he saw twenty white soldiers paraded in line on the bank of the river, and when in line the rebels fired upon and killed all but one, who ran to the river and hid under a log, and in that condition was fired at a number of times and wounded. He says that Major BRADFORD also ran down to the river, and after he told them he had surrendered, more than fifty shots were fired at him. He then jumped into the river, and swam out a little ways, and whole volleys were fired at him there without hitting him. He returned to the shore, and meeting, as the Doctor supposes, some officer, was protected, but he heard frequent threats from the rebels that they would kill him. It was a subject of considerable remark that Capt. YOUNG was treated by the rebels with so much favor—and it is said that his brother, who has been in the rebel army, kept a grog shop at the fort, and was a rebel sympathizer.

DISGUSTING TOADYISM.

Two or three Federal band-box officers on board the *Platte Valley*, one of them with his young bride, made themselves conspicuous in fawning around the rebel officers. They brought Gen. CHALMERS and several subordinate cut-throat looking officers on board the *Platte Valley*, drank with them, introduced them to their wives, and invited them to dinner. They made room for them at the ladies' table, and they sat down to dinner; but it happened, either by accident or from a just idea of the fitness of things on the part of our high spirited Captain, that at that moment the signal bell for moving was heard, and the rebel officers, leaving their soup untouched, skedaddled. Gen. CHALMERS, soliloquizing as he hurried past your correspondent that he had learned to run as well as to fight. In the conversation preceding the dinner, Gen. CHALMERS said he did not countenance or encourage his soldiers in killing captive negro soldiers, but it was right and justifiable. A Federal officer who will so disgrace himself and his country, ought to be dismissed the service.

The rebel officers were generally well clad, but had very little to distinguish them from the privates. Gen. CHALMERS had simply a black feather in his hat, and the other officers stripes on their collars.

FROM THE SOUTH.

The Armies of Lee and Longstreet—A Fast Day in Virginia—Markets, Prices, &c.

THE WAR IN VIRGINIA.

DAY OF FASTING IN LEE'S ARMY.

ORANGE COURT-HOUSE, Thursday, April 7.

Gen. LEE has issued a General Order directing the observance of to-morrow as a day of fasting, humiliation and prayer; directing the due preparation of all the departments to anticipate the wants of the several commanders. All military duties, unless absolutely necessary, are to be suspended, and the chaplains are desired to hold divine service in their regiments and brigades. Officers and men are requested to attend.

It is reported that a scouting party of the enemy appeared on the heights of Stafford, opposite Fredericksburgh, yesterday.

Great activity is visible in the Yankee camps.

AFFAIRS IN THE VALLEY.

From the Richmond Dispatch, April 12.

From all we can hear from the Lower Valley, the enemy are particularly zealous in guarding the Baltimore and Ohio Railroad of late. The inference is, that they are transporting troops over that road to reinforce the Army of the Potomac.

About a week ago a battalion of negro soldiers visited Winchester, where they remained several hours, but did no damage during their stay. A gentleman who saw them says they seemed to be dejected, and looked more like prisoners under guard of the few white soldiers who accompanied them, than soldiers with arms in their hands.

The report that Messrs. CONRAD and WILLIAMS had been carried off by them is without foundation.

LONGSTREET'S ARMY.

Correspondence of the Richmond Dispatch.

BRISTOL, Monday, April 4, 1864.

There is no news in this department that would be proper to publish. Where LONGSTREET is going or what he intends to do no one knows, and ought not to tell it if he did. One thing, however, I can write which is gratifying, and that is, notwithstanding the gloomy weather of the past two weeks, attended with snow, mud and rain, the troops are all in fine spirits and ready for anything that may "turn up." The same enthusiasm that prevailed at the beginning of the war seems to have burst forth anew, and, I sincerely hope, to be properly directed. What has produced it is hard to say; whether the recent legislation in Congress, showing for the first time on the part of our rulers some appreciation of the magnitude of the contest, or the apathy on the part of our enemies, evincing a weariness of a hopeless war, or mere probably an increasing disgust for them produced by their cruelties and barbarism.

Every Southern soldier now feels that there is no hope for him but to fight on, and there are few in the army who would consent to any compromise short of an eternal separation from the roundhead fanatical Abolition despotism that rules the North. They are long since convinced that Mr. LINCOLN intends our utter subjugation, and the destruction of the last vestige of our society, and if every State in the Confederacy should offer to lay down their arms and ask to be allowed to go back in the Union, the offer would be spurned. The Abolition crew who rule there, not only intend, if possible, to make us the slaves of our slaves, but say our sisters and daughters shall intermarry with our negroes.

It is rumored that Gen. LONGSTREET has given Gen. MORGAN permission to "go somewhere," and I am sure it will be a great relief to his men if it should turn out to be correct. All of them, both officers and men, that I have seen, express themselves as heartily tired of their inactivity.

FROM THE SOUTHWEST.

Correspondence of the Richmond Dispatch.

DALTON, April 7, 1863.

Gen. HARDEE'S sham battle of to-day was witnessed by a large number of ladies, soldiers and citizens, and was a very agreeable affair. The Yankees also had one in front of Ringgold. Their fire was distinctly heard there. All quiet in front.

In Bristol, Tenn., on Saturday night of last week, some two hundred members of Gen. WARFORD'S Georgia Brigade, being dissatisfied with the quality of the rations drawn by them that day, determined to right themselves. They accordingly marched down in a body to the store of the post commissary, which they violently broke open and plundered of about seventy-five sacks of flour, seven hundred pounds of bacon, ten casks of bran, and fifty or sixty pounds of candles, which they proceeded to carry off with them. Meantime, the alarm was given, and the provost guard, some twelve in number, having arrived, and vainly endeavored to arrest the rioters, fired upon them, killing one (a Lieut. REYNOLDS) on the spot, and wounding five or six more, one or two of them, it is said, mortally. The rest made their escape with their plunder. That night and the next day a number were caught and placed under arrest. Swift and sure punishment will be sure to follow. The men were not armed, except with stones, a few bushels of which they left in the storehouse. It is not pretended that they were driven to commit the act by hunger. Their day's rations had been served out to them that morning.

MARKETS IN THE SOUTH.

From the Richmond Dispatch, April 8.

The markets remain almost entirely unchanged. Many merchants continue to take the old currency at the rate of three for two, with the exception of fives, which are held on the same footing with the new currency. A few merchants offer slight inducements in favor of the new currency. The markets have not had sufficient opportunity as yet to recover from the retarding effects of the recent rains, which kept many articles of necessity away. It is confidently expected that in a few days things will be more plentiful, and prices more inclined to fall.

Already, under the influence of the new currency, prices have taken rapid strides downward in several leading Southern States. Corn is selling in Atlanta, for example, for seven dollars in the new currency; flour, one hundred dollars; Irish potatoes, fourteen; sweet, fifteen; corn meal, seven; peas, molasses, fourteen to fifteen; rice, new, thirty-five cents; old, twenty; bacon, two dollars and seventy-five cents; lard, the same; sugar, three and a half to four dollars. It is time some like steps were taken by the merchants of Richmond, which, unlike Atlanta, is almost entirely free from the presence of an army.

We observe, also, that in Montgomery, Alabama, bacon and lard have fallen to $3 25 a pound, and in Mobile $6 a bushel is the current price for corn, when a few days ago it was $12, and fodder, which was $20 and upwards, sells now at $5 per cwt.

On yesterday, we regret to say, the speculators of this city exhibited a most cruelly avaricious disposition. At an auction sale, sugar was run up to $9 a pound, molasses to $51, and several other necessary articles were advanced in similar proportion. The practice of producing petty panics at the auctions, should be frowned down by all respectable persons, merchants or citizens, and whenever exorbitant bidding is attempted, the party or clique guilty of it should be hissed, if not kicked out of the house.

FROM WASHINGTON.

Suspicious Movements of the Rebel Army.

A New Disposition of the Invalid Corps.

THE INTERNAL TAX BILL IN THE HOUSE.

Earnest Speeches by Messrs. Morrill and Stebbins.

The Pacific Railroad Bill Reported in the Senate.

SPECIAL DISPATCHES TO THE N. Y. TIMES.

WASHINGTON, Tuesday, April 19.

RUMORED MOVEMENT OF GEN. LEE.

It is rumored here to-night that LEE is moving a portion of his army to this side of the Rapidan, near Madison Court-house. Nothing, however, reliable. Information has been received of the presence of a considerable rebel cavalry force near Leesburgh. Measures have been taken to check their advance in case they should attempt it.

CAPTURE OF GEN. LEE'S SCOUTS.

WASHINGTON, D. C., Tuesday, April 20.

Two of LEE'S scouts were captured, a day or two since, at Culpepper. A third made his escape. They were disguised as teamsters. A halter awaits them.

THE INVALID CORPS.

It is reported that Lieut.-Gen. GRANT has decided to make some practical use of the Invalid Corps, by pushing to the front such men as are able to bear arms, and returning to their homes those disabled from active service in the field. The corps has become a convenient refuge for triflers and idlers, and its dismemberment will return to the ranks many hundreds of able-bodied soldiers.

THE INTERNAL TAX BILL.

The speech of Mr. STEBBINS, to-day, in the House, was the ablest yet delivered on that subject during the session. Secretary CHASE was on the floor during its delivery, and was among the first to congratulate Mr. STEBBINS after he had concluded. The speech made a decided impression, especially on the Democratic side of the House.

THE BANK BILL.

The Senate Finance Committee to-day heard a Committee of New-York Bankers opposed to the passage of the new Bank Bill. The contest between the friends of the State and National Banks in the Senate promises to be animated.

THE REPEAL OF THE FUGITIVE SLAVE LAW.

The failure of the passage of SUMNER'S bill to repeal the Fugitive Slave Law, after the adoption of SHERMAN'S amendment, in the Senate this afternoon, seemed to take its author, as well as every one else, by surprise. Just after it had passed a third reading and seemed to have been fully ventilated, and had been put upon its passage, FOSTER desired to speak, but MCDOUGALL moved an adjournment, and the passage of the bill was defeated to-day.

THE TRANSFER OF SEAMEN FROM THE ARMY TO THE NAVY.

The Secretary of War has revoked Circular No. 23, of March 9, in relation to the transfer of enlisted men from the army to the naval service. Department and Army Commanders are ordered to cause to be transferred as speedily as possible to the nearest Naval station all enlisted men who desire to enlist in the navy, and who fulfill the conditions required in General Orders No. 91, without regard to the restriction in said orders as to reduction of regiments and companies below the minimum organization, which restriction is removed.

RARITAN AND DELAWARE BAY RAILROAD.

The Raritan Bay Railroad question, by consent of both parties, has been postponed for two weeks. This is regarded here virtually as an abandonment of the enterprise.

THE NAVAL INVESTIGATION.

The Naval Investigation Committee are preparing their report. They will recommend radical changes in the present mode of purchasing naval supplies.

ILLNESS OF A TREASURY OFFICER.

Dr. SOLGER, Assistant Register of the Treasury, was struck with paralysis last week, and has been speechless since.

DISPATCHES TO THE ASSOCIATED PRESS.

WASHINGTON, Tuesday, April 19.

THE TEN-FORTY LOAN.

The subscriptions to the Ten-forty Loan reported at the Treasury to-day amounted to $2,400,000.

THE TAX BILL.

No further general debate will take place on the Internal Tax Bill, but amendments will be discussed in five-minute speeches.

INDIAN AGENTS.

The Secretary of the Interior has recommended to Congress the appointment of an Indian Agent for the Kioway, Apache and Camanche Indians.

THE ARMY RATION.

A pamphlet has appeared, by Prof. HORSFORD, of Cambridge, upon the army ration. His suggestions contemplate the increased comfort and mobility of troops with an estimated reduction in the cost of subsistence for the current year of one hundred millions of dollars.

PROCEEDINGS OF CONGRESS.

SENATE.

WASHINGTON, Tuesday, April 19.

THE PACIFIC RAILROAD.

Mr. HOWARD, of Michigan, (Union,) from the Committee on the Pacific Railroad, reported Mr. SHERMAN'S bill with important amendments. No United States bonds are authorized, but the several railroad companies may issue their own bonds in sums of $1,000, payable thirty years after date, bearing 6 per cent. interest, payable in gold or silver coin semi-annually, at the rate of twenty-four for each mile completed and equipped to the eastern base of the Rocky Mountains; 96 for each mile for 150 miles west of said base and eastwardly from the western base of Sierra Nevada; 48 for each mile between the mountain sections, and 24 for each mile west of the base of Sierra Nevada. On these bonds the Secretary of the Treasury shall indorse payments of interest for nineteen years, and pay absolutely the first year's interest in gratuity. It authorizes the construction of bridges over the Mississippi and Missouri Rivers, not less than ninety feet above low water mark, nor more than forty feet above high water.

Mr. GRIMES reported from the Committee on the District of Columbia, the bill to incorporate the inhabitants of the District of Columbia. Passed.

Mr. ANTHONY moved that the Committee on Printing be authorized to inquire into the expediency of printing a limited number of documents for sale.

Mr. LANE called up the House bill to amend the Enrollment Act, so as to raise the rank, pay and emoluments of the Provost-Marshal-General to those of a Brigadier-General. After a short debate it was passed.

THE DISAGREEMENT ON MONTANA.

A message was received from the House, announcing their adherence to the disagreement on the bill establishing a Territorial Government for Montana, and asking for a committee of conference.

Mr. SHERMAN, of Ohio, (Union,) explained that however much he might be disposed that the Senate recede, he thought it necessary for one reason to appoint a committee to meet that of the House. The difficulty with the bill was that in its present shape persons from Canada could come into the Territory, without declaring their intention to become citizens, and vote. This should be provided against in the bill.

Mr. DOOLITTLE, of Wisconsin, (Union,) thought the question for which the Senate contended was an abstract one. There was not now, nor would there be, any number of negroes in Montana, and we were legislating against an emergency which would never occur in the history of the Territory.

THE GENERAL APPROPRIATION BILL.

The Senate then proceeded to the consideration of the Legislative, Executive and Judicial Appropriation Bill.

An amendment offered by Mr. ANTHONY was adopted providing for the publication of the laws in localities contiguous to the rebellious States, that their dissemination among them be the better secured.

After a few unimportant amendments the bill was passed.

THE REPEAL OF THE FUGITIVE SLAVE ACT.

Mr. SUMNER, of Massachusetts, (Union,) called up the bill to repeal all acts for the rendition of persons to service or labor.

The bill passed to a third reading without debate. The yeas and nays were called for on its passage.

Mr. SUMNER said he did not intend to say a word about the bill. It was as plain as the multiplication table, a diary or the Ten Commandments. [Laughter.]

Mr. HENDRICKS, of Indiana, (Dem.,) did not think that there should be such an amendment to the Constitution as this. It might be as plain as the multiplication table, but it was doubtful to him whether the high morality of the Ten Commandments would sanction its passage. It was decided in 1793, and again in 1850, to be lawful and expedient. The Fugitive Slave Law had been decided to be constitutional by every court of the United States, and had been reaffirmed by the people. Now, while the Constitution remained unchanged with all its provisions obligatory upon us as members of Congress, it was proposed to repeal it. While he was not a member from a Slave State, he would vote against the bill so long as the oath he had taken to support the Constitution was upon his conscience.

Mr. SHERMAN, of Ohio, (Union,) always thought the law of 1850 was unconstitutional, and had no objection to its repeal now. He doubted the propriety of going back as far as 1793. He would give the loyal people of the South all their rights.

Mr. SUMNER wanted to make a clean sweep while we are at it, and wipe out the barbarous code from our statutes.

Mr. SHERMAN would vote against the bill, because he did not wish to extend the repeal back to the law of 1793. The States, to a great extent, in which the law of 1793 was operative, were for themselves rapidly perfecting measures of entire emancipation. He moved to amend the bill by inserting "except the act, approved Feb. 12, 1793, for the rendition of persons from service or labor."

Mr. SHERMAN'S amendment was then adopted by a vote of 24 yeas against 17 nays, as follows:

AYES.—Messrs. Buckalew, Carlile, Collamer, Cowan, Davis, Dixon, Doolittle, Foster, Harris, Henderson, Hendricks, Howe, Johnson, Lane, of Indiana, McDougal, Nesmith, Powell, Riddle, Saulsbury, Sherman, Ten Eyck, Trumbull, Van Winkle, Willey—24.

NAYS—Messrs. Anthony, Brown, Clark, Conness, Fessenden, Grimes, Hale, Howard, Lane, of Kansas, Morgan, Morrill, Pomeroy, Ramsay, Sprague, Sumner, Wilkinson, Wilson—17.

Mr. CONNESS said he could not vote for the bill as amended, and, as he could not explain his views now, he moved to lay the bill on the table.

His motion was rejected—31 yeas, 9 nays.

A motion of Mr. DAVIS to adjourn was lost, 27 to 13.

Mr. FOSTER desired to discuss the bill, and was willing to do so this evening.

For a few moments he gave way, on a motion of Mr. MCDOUGAL to adjourn, which was carried.

HOUSE OF REPRESENTATIVES.

WASHINGTON, Tuesday, April 19.

THE FORT PILLOW MASSACRE.

The House concurred in the Senate amendment to the House resolution, so as to read that the Committee on the Conduct of the War inquire into the truth of the rumors attending the recent attack on Fort Pillow, and whether that fort could not have been sufficiently reinforced, and report the facts as soon as possible.

THE INTERNAL TAX BILL.

The House went into committee, Mr. WASHBURNE, of Illinois, (Union,) in the Chair, and proceeded to the consideration of the Internal Tax Bill.

Mr. MORRILL, of Vermont, (Union,) explained the provisions of the measure. The war having continued longer than was anticipated, it was now necessary to revise our estimates so as to cover all deficiencies. The demands upon the Treasury are unprecedented, but our resources are equal to any emergency, good or bad. The receipts from this bill and from foreign importations will pay the ordinary expenses of a hundred millions of people, and are much greater than would pay the interest on a debt of three thousand millions of dollars, with a most respectable sinking fund besides. If we pass this bill it will show we will maintain our financial credit at all costs. We have, under the present law, received forty or fifty millions more than last year. Even now the revenue from the internal tax, as was anticipated, is more important to the treasury than the revenue from imports, and both are equal to any ordinary expenditure in time of peace. If we pass this measure without curtailing the rates we shall furnish proof that we cannot only pay the interest on the public debt and ordinary expenditures in time of peace, but shall contribute handsomely to keep our expenditures within moderate limits. We shall show the people of the United States we not only have the means to pay every dollar we now or ever will owe, but the principal and interest of the public debt, in coin. He repeated that the public faith will be maintained at all hazards. The Government is now supplied with more gold than is sufficient for its purposes, and is actually begging its creditors to receive payments in advance, in order to be relieved from the plethora of gold which is blocking up the commerce of the country. Let it be known that if the war shall be closed in 1865, we will be able not only to support the Government, but to pay our national debt in little more than ten years! Let it also be known that the present large annual expenditures are not equal to our annual increased wealth. When the war commenced we had only a hundred vessels; now we have over six hundred, constituting one of the finest navies of the world. We have added great quantities of the most approved appliances of war at a vast expense. With the dash of the General who never fails, we must anticipate crushing results to the enemy. But let us set our house in order financially, and with military success we shall be victorious over all ills. Let us show that we are stripping for the fight. He trusted that every member will consent to make large sacrifices for the good of the country. Let us have taxes and loans, lessen the amount of legal tenders and increase the pay of the soldiers. It is hoped that the internal and import taxes will enable the Secretary of the Treasury to obtain all the funds he wants, and reduce the legal tender issues. The freedmen will contribute much more to the national wealth than their friends claim. They are largely increasing the amount of production, to which they were limited by unpaid and forced labor. He examined this subject in an economical light, and not to present a theory. Our faith is to give them shelter and protection.

Mr. MORRILL, of Vermont, (Union,) then explained at length the prominent features of the bill, stating that even through its machinery they might obtain a larger sum than is now proposed. It will yield over $250,000,0000 when fairly in operation, to which may be added $90,000,000 from the tariff, and $40,000,000 internal revenue, annually.

Mr. STEBBINS, of New-York, (Dem.,) said that the preservation of the country demands the passage of this bill, and taxation sufficient for our demands both during and after the war. It was the point on which the struggle in which we are now engaged, must eventually turn. The Government, under the Constitution, is putting forth its power to preserve the national life, and performing its solemn duty in devising the means for the accomplishment of the great work. Our means are far more ample than ever before existed, and more extensive than those of any country on the face of the globe. This he proceeded to show by reference to official records. The war, he said, though requiring so many millions of expenditures had been carried on at the expense of less than the agricultural products of the country, while the resources have not been diminished to the extent of a single dollar. Furnishing the means of war within ourselves will tend to develop still more our industry and show the overwhelming power of this nation. This bill was a part of the great chain forged by this Congress to hold the nation together. From the struggle of eight millions of people to preserve their social institutions, he could not doubt that the war will be of long continuance, and terminate only when the rebels shall submit themselves to the Constitution and the laws. Therefore, the nation should place itself in the strongest position and guard against every possible approach of exhaustion. Mr. STEBBINS reviewed the recuperative energies of the British, drawing a striking contrast between them and our own, which are vastly superior, and give us the power and ability to overcome our energies. In the course of his remarks, he said the National banks must take the place of the State banks, as they could not coexist, and expressed himself in favor of a tax on sales of gold and sterling exchange as a source of revenue. The nation, he remarked, was destined to cover the continent, bound together by diffusive intelligence and industry, with an unlimited policy of internal improvement, consolidated in one nationality and directed by the sovereign will of the people. Pass the Tax Bill, the bill to prevent gambling in gold and the National Bank Bill, and he believed that Congress would receive the blessings of the people.

Mr. BROOKS, of New-York, (Dem.,) remarked: While listening to the glowing accounts of the gentleman from Vermont (MORRILL) and to his colleague, (STEBBINS,) he had imagined that he was wandering in the picture galleries of Versailles, or among the sculptures of the Vatican, where men were represented in armor and depicting war, but without the actual scenes of battle. He (BROOKS) had almost come to the conclusion, from the remarks of the gentlemen, that war is a blessing, and debt a divine institution. The gentleman from Vermont (MORRILL) had mentioned the fact that this bill will produce two hundred and fifty millions, while his colleague (STEBBINS) placed the amount at three hundred millions of dollars, with ninety millions from foreign imports, adding three hundred and forty millions to the public revenue, annually. His colleague (STEBBINS) had held up for imitation the British system of debt and taxation, a system which had driven the subjects of the kingdom of Great Britain, of Ireland and of Scotland to our shores. Taxation does not always produce the desired revenue. All the inflation of prices since December last from the smaller articles of consumption, tea and coffee, to the largest, beef, pork and bread, has been occasioned by the addition, by the Secretary of the Treasury, of two hundred and forty millions of currency beyond what he promised at that time. He (BROOKS) said that unless the currency is curtailed and the expansion lessened, we will approach a crisis from which no army can rescue the property and labor of the country. There is no crime so great as an unnecessary increase of paper money. It is robbery in the worst form, and serves to corrupt the morals of the people. The only way to reduce importation is to check the expansion of the currency. The necessity of ending the war is apparent. He did not believe with his colleague (STEBBINS) that we can endure a war indefinitely without bankruptcy. The main object of his (BROOKS) arguments was to produce a curtailment of the currency.

Mr. KASSON, of Iowa, (Union,) in alluding to the remarks of Mr. BROOKS, said that he (BROOKS) had been a Whig, then a Know-Nothing, and now was a Democrat. The gentleman from New-York (BROOKS) had defended the Irish, which was not in accordance with his former Know-Nothing principles.

Mr. BROOKS denied that he had ever belonged to the Know-Nothing party, and he had never been in a Know-Nothing Lodge.

Mr. KASSON then pointed to the sentiments of the *Express*, of which the gentleman (BROOKS) was part proprietor.

Mr. BROOKS replied that he was in Europe when that party was organized. He never had anything to do with the Know-Nothing party.

Mr. KASSON said that the gentleman (BROOKS) being a "foreigner," he (KASSON) could not, of course, hold him responsible. Mr. KASSON then briefly defended the Secretary of the Treasury from the charge that the latter had inflated the currency. The inflation was by the State Banks in New-York, as the premium on Saturday on the National currency, as contrasted with the State issues, demonstrated.

Mr. FERNANDO WOOD, of New-York, (Dem.,) assumed that the present bill was to meet the immense expenditures which grew out of this war, and therefore it was legitimate to discuss every question pertaining to the war. He was in favor of giving a liberal support to the Government. In this emergency he was not prepared to criticise too closely the administration of public affairs. He believed that the Administration had undertaken a task for which no man or set of men were competent. Hence there should be the greatest generosity for the mistakes which had been made. Mr. WOOD then proceeded to examine the financial question, reviewing the acts of the Secretary of the Treasury in this connection in condemnation. He said this was the first time in the history of the world when any people or government had departed from the common-sense principles of finance to sustain a government and prosecute a war. The pending bill was full of errors. He (WOOD) wanted a measure that was equitable and fair to all the interests that contributed to taxation.

The Committee here rose, when

Mr. GARFIELD, of Ohio, said: In my response to my colleague (LONG) a few days since, I asserted that many leaders of the Democratic party in the North were in correspondence with the rebel leaders, and I promised to produce the letters to which I then referred. We found that some of our regiments in the Army of the Cumberland were being corrupted and induced to desert by politicians at home, and sent secret-service men North to find out who was doing it. One young man went to Indiana, and by representing himself as friendly to the rebels, obtained these letters and brought them to me. I did not know the writers, but called several Indiana officers to examine them, and found out from those who knew the handwriting the history of the writers. I took tracings of the letters, and sent the scout with the originals through the lines.

Mr. GARFIELD then read the following letters:

ROCKVILLE, Ind., July 14, 1863.

Major-Gen. John C. Breckinridge:

DEAR SIR: I take great pleasure of recommending to your favorable acquaintance the bearer, Mr. ———, of Greencastle, in this State. He wishes to visit the South, and not be subject to any danger from such a visit. Mr. ——— was connected with the army for some months as a Quartermaster of the —th Indiana Volunteers, but resigned immediately after the evacuation of Corinth by our forces, and has had no sympathy or connection with the army since. Any duty he may agree to perform, you may rely upon it that it will be faithfully done. Any favor shown him will be reciprocated by me whenever any opportunity offers.

I am, General, yours, with much respect,

JNO. G. DAVIS.

GREENCASTLE, Ind., July 1, 1863.

DEAR SIR: I take this method of introducing to your favorable consideration Mr. ——, a resident of this place. Mr. —— wishes to enter the service of the South in some capacity so that he can be of some assistance to your cause. I can safely recommend him to you as an energetic and faithful man in any capacity you may place him, and I know that he can be of valuable assistance to you. Mr. —— was for some time connected with the Union army, but became disgusted with the party in power, and resigned in consequence thereof. Any favor that may be shown him will, I am satisfied, never be betrayed.

I am, General, very respectfully, your obd't serv't,

D. R. ECKLES.

To Gen. J. C. BRECKINRIDGE, C. S. A.

ECKLES was a judge in Utah under BUCHANAN. DAVIS was a member of the Thirty-second, Thirty-third, Thirty-fifth and Thirty-sixth Congress, and the predecessor of the member from the Terre Haute district, (Mr. VOORHEES.) Both were his constituents, and leading lights in the Democratic party.

Mr. VOORHEES replied: What the gentleman from Ohio (GARFIELD) had produced were not original letters, but only what purported to be copies. He would say to Mr. GARFIELD that Mr. DAVIS is one of the most distinguished men in Indiana, and perhaps, at this time, is dying on a bed of sickness. There was nothing traitorous about him. He (VOORHEES) might pronounce those letters false and spurious.

Mr. GARFIELD replied that he wished the gentleman (VOORHEES) would.

Mr. VOORHEES said in reply that as it would not suit him to do so he would not pursue that course.

It being now 4¼ o'clock, the House took a recess until 7 o'clock this evening.

EVENING SESSION.

THE RARITAN AND DELAWARE BAY RAILROAD.

The Raritan and Delaware Bay Railroad Bill was taken up, when

Mr. WILSON, of Iowa, (Union,) offered a substitute therefor, namely: That for the better regulation of commerce among the several States, every railroad company in the United States whose road is operated by steam, be and is hereby authorized to transport freight and passengers from one State to another, anything in the law of any State to the contrary notwithstanding.

On motion of Mr. YEAMAN, of Kentucky, (Union,) the consideration of the bill was postponed for two weeks.

RAILROAD BRIDGE OVER THE OHIO.

The House passed the bill authorizing the construction of a railroad bridge over the falls of the Ohio, near Louisville.

A NATIONAL STATUARY HALL.

Mr. RICE, of Maine, (Union,) reported a bill setting apart the old Hall of Representatives as a National Statuary Hall, the several States being invited to send thither statues in marble or bronze, not exceeding two in number, for each of their most illustrious civic or military men. The bill appropriates $24,000 for the necessary arrangements.

Mr. MORRILL, of Vermont, (Union,) said the old Senate Chamber has been assigned to the use of the Supreme Court, but the old hall is an unappropriated waste, draped with cobwebs. He urged that from its grandeur of style and its legislative associations, it could be appropriated to no more fitting and patriotic purpose.

The bill was passed.

RECONSTRUCTION.

The House resumed the consideration of the bill reported from the Select Committee, providing for the reconstruction of overthrown or rebellious States.

Messrs. JAMES C. ALLEN, (Dem.,) of Illinois, and SMITHERS, (Union,) of Delaware, spoke at length, the former in opposition, and the latter in favor of the bill.

At 10 o'clock the House adjourned.

Sentence of a Swindler.

BOSTON, Tuesday, April 19.

In the Superior Court to-day, EDWARD P. JEFFRIES was sentenced to two years' hard labor in the State Prison. The case will be remembered as one of extensive swindling. JEFFRIES occupied a high social and business position, and for a time was reputed very wealthy.

The Charleston Mercury.

DAILY PAPER—FOURTEEN DOLLARS, FOR SIX MONTHS—PAYABLE IN ADVANCE. | VINDICE NULLO SPONTE SUA SINE LEGE FIDES RECTUMQUE COLLENTUR. | COUNTRY PAPER—THREE A WEEK—EIGHT DOLLARS, FOR SIX MONTHS—PAYABLE IN ADVANCE.

VOLUME LXXXIV. CHARLESTON, S. C., SATURDAY, APRIL 23, 1864. NUMBER 12,013

THE STORMING OF FORT PILLOW—A YANKEE ACCOUNT.

A Yankee naval officer, named N. D. WHITMORE, writes to the Memphis *Argus* a long account of the capture of Fort Pillow by FORREST. The following are the main points of his narrative:

The combined forces of Major-Generals Forrest, Chalmers, McCulloch and Bell, numbering seven or eight thousand, made an assault on our fortifications at about 6, a. m., on the 12th. Our forces consisted of two hundred and fifty whites and three hundred and fifty blacks.

The United States steamer New Era, lying off the fort, shelled the rebels and drove them from their position, which they had gained on the South side of the fort. They again assaulted our works from the North side. Owing to the timber, it was impossible for the guns of the New Era to dislodge them, though a continued shower of shell and shrapnel was rained down on them. The garrison was so small and the rebel force so overwhelming, that the enemy carried our works about 3 80 p. m., and the gallant few who were left alive, taken prisoners. The guns of the fort consisted of two 12-pounder howitzers, two 20-pounder rifled, two 10 pounder Parrott—six pieces in all.

Major Booth and two Captains of Sixth U. S. Artillery (colored) were killed early in the fight, also two Lieutenants of the Sixth severely wounded. Capt. Bradford and Harter, Adjutant Seymour, and Lieut. Barr, of the 13th Tennessee Cavalry, were killed, and some others who could not be identified. Maj. Bradford, commanding the post, was taken prisoner, and reported by the rebels as having been paroled with the liberty of their camps, and violated it by escaping last night; but I was told that he was taken out and shot late in the evening. Capt. Young, Provost Marshal, was slightly wounded and taken prisoner, and paroled with the liberty of their camps and allowed to see his wife. He says our forces behaved gallantly throughout the whole action. Our loss in killed exceeds two hundred. He also states that Gen. Forrest shot one of his own men for refusing quarter to our men.

Lieutenant Commander Thos. Patterson, commanding Naval Station at Memphis, sent the steamer Platte Valley, with U. S. steamer Silver Cloud in tow, with ammunition to Fort Pillow. When we arrived in sight of the fort the commissary and other public buildings, with some twelve stores of private property, were in flames, and the rebels were seen moving about applying torches to barracks, stables and huts. We threw shells, &c., for thirty minutes at detached squads. A flag of truce appearing, we ceased firing and sent a boat ashore. It presently returned with a communication from Gen. Forrest, saying that a large number of wounded were suffering for want of proper care, and that he would allow us to bury our dead and remove our wounded under flag of truce, but that we could not remove anything from the battle field. Captain Ferguson knowing that our shells would explode among our wounded, causing greater loss of life, agreed to the proposal.

Major Anderson, aid to General Forrest, drew up the agreement, giving us possession of fortifications and landing till five p. m.—the flag of truce to end at that hour. The rebels were efficient and aided as much as possible our work.—The wounded who were able to walk, generally came down the bluff road, supported on either side by a rebel soldier.

He then appends a list of wounded sent to Cairo by the Platte Valley, and remarks: I know that, in storming a fort, where such desperate resistance is offered as was here offered, that many must fall, but in this instance it looks to me more like indiscriminate butchery than honorable warfare. Now that the excitement is over, the thought of those charred bodies, together with the nausea, caused by the stench of roasting human flesh, and two hundred or more dead bodies, mangled, dying, pleading for quarters, with distorted faces, broken skulls, &c., I am sick and can write no more.

Massacre at Fort Pillow

The New-York Times.

VOL. XIII—NO. 3926. NEW-YORK, SATURDAY, APRIL 23, 1864. PRICE THREE CENTS

Editorials

Justice at Last—The Taxes Coming.

The people will breathe the freer now that there is the prospect of good stiff taxation. Their faint-hearted representatives at last understand that longer evasion of their duty will not be tolerated, and are fairly buckling to the work. They are showing, too, an independence in resisting the appeals of lobbyists for special favor, that is worthy of praise. It seems to be well apprehended that it is a public wrong to comply with these appeals, however plausible. If the House sticks to the interests of the people in this style for a week longer, it will excite the liveliest astonishment and gratitude.

The reluctance which the House has evinced to take up the tax bill has been owing to a shameful distrust of the people. The feeling has prevailed that the people would become disaffected with the war, if their burdens were increased; and that it was the true policy to make things as pleasant for the time as possible, even at the cost of any amount of suffering after the war is over. As new Congressional elections are soon to come, Congressmen have had a nervous apprehension, too, that if they taxed, the people would fly into dudgeon, and snuff them out of existence.

Now all this is delusion. The people are not the dolts they have been taken for. They have not been deceived in the least by these attempts to make the war seem dog-cheap. It was an insult to them to imagine that they require to be reconciled in any such fashion to the continuance of the war. The people from the beginning have been more determined than the public men—have been more earnest, more patient, more ready for any effort or any sacrifice. It is not the politicians that have so upheld their patriotism, but their patriotism that has upheld the politicians. From the first uprising, the people have been foremost. The self-styled leaders have not been leaders at all; they have only followed. The public condition is so different from the ordinary political life of the country, that politicians even yet find it the most difficult thing in the world to adapt themselves to it. They are constantly running away with the old idea that the people require managing—that they are best managed by humoring them—and that the science of politics is simply the art of cajoling. In the "weak, piping time of peace," politicians, it must be confessed, practice upon this theory with considerable success. But in a crisis like this, it is absurdly out of place. It is ridiculous presumption for any public men to imagine that they must wheedle the people in order to hold them to the war, or to suppose that in any degree the war spirit is a political manufacture.

This war against the rebellion is the people's war, just as the rebellion itself strikes at the people's government. Having accepted the war, the people are prepared to accept all its sacrifices, whether they be of blood or of money. They well understand that it would be just as foolish to attempt to keep up the war by sham battles as by sham money; and that all paper money is sham unless it draws vitality from living, present, values. Taxation on actual property, they know, is the vital source of all national credit; and it has been with mingled pity and indignation that they have so long borne with the efforts of their representatives to evade this palpable truth. They have paid dear for that patience. In lack of the revenues that ought to have been provided for in the first and second years of the war, the Government has been obliged to meet its wants by loans and by unduly large emissions of paper money; and the consequence has been that the currency of the country has lost nearly half of its producing power, and that all the expenses of the war, as well as all private expenses, have been made nearly double what they otherwise would have been. Thus a vast national debt has been accumulating, which will weigh terribly upon our children, and that too without really lightening our own burdens for the time; for our comparative freedom from taxation has been more than counterbalanced by the evils of a depreciated currency. It was absurd in our Government to imagine that, because taxation is ordinarily an unwelcome thing, therefore the people would be glad to escape taxation in a way that recoiled upon themselves and their children in this style. The people are too sensible and practical to put up with any such penny-wise and pound-foolish policy. They are immovably determined to prosecute this war to its successful consummation; and they are just as fully prepared to meet any liability that justly belongs to it.

The Government has not shrunk from setting before the people the financial necessity in all its true proportions. Secretary CHASE has declared that taxation to the extent of one-half the current expenditures is needful for the solid credit of the Government. The Tax Bill that he has submitted, through the Committee of Ways and Means, is calculated to meet that requirement—estimating the yearly expenses of the Government at eight hundred millions, which, with a properly regulated currency, ought to be the extreme limit. The bill, if allowed to stand substantially as reported, will raise at least three hundred million dollars, and that, too, without imposing any appreciable burden upon any of the necessaries of life, or in any way injuring the productive energies of the people. This amount, added to the hundred million yielded by the tariff, will secure the credit of the Government beyond all contingencies, whether the end of the war comes soon or late.

Members of the House may rely upon it that the bill which they have so dreaded to touch, is welcome to the people; and that they cannot possibly commend themselves better to their loyal constituents than by putting this measure through in the same earnest spirit which they now seem to be displaying. It will be found, when the next elections occur, that the favorite popular test of fidelity to the war will be the staunchness with which this bill is supported. Acts speak louder than words, and a single vote here will be taken as a ten thousand times better proof of the stuff of which a Congressman is made than any amount of buncombe. Humbug does not thrive on bloody soil. The men in the Capitol cannot too well understand this.

Bunkum Speeches.

Mr. VAN WINKLE, of Western Virginia, on Thursday, in the Senate, when the bill for the repeal of the Fugitive Slave law came up for consideration, opened the debate by saying that, "The remarks he would make, though not particularly applicable to the bill under consideration, would not be inappropriate." He then proceeded to make a speech, in which he discussed the loyalty of the Border States; the absurdity of the Copperheads; the constitutionality of the admission of Western Virginia to the Union, and the circumstances attending that event; the extent to which the new State had contributed men to the army; the consequences that would have followed her failure or refusal to do so; and it was only at the close of his long speech, if we are to judge from the summary, that he found time and opportunity to say a few words upon the subject before the Senate. That "these remarks were not particularly applicable to the bill under consideration," so far from being a matter of no great moment, as Mr. VAN WINKLE seems to think, did, in fact, render them peculiarly inappropriate; and the erroneous notions of the nature and objects of parliamentary discussion, which he seems to entertain, are so widespread, and are just now doing so much mischief, that we seize this opportunity of protesting against them. Congress is not a debating club, in which discussions are carried on for the sake of discussion. It is an assembly for the prosecution of serious and important business—just now the most serious and important that was ever laid before any deliberative body. There are a great number of questions before it, all of them of the highest moment, and each of them, every time it comes up, demands the serious and undivided attention of every member present. This cannot be given, and will not be given, as long as anybody who has possession of the floor is permitted to make long, rambling speeches upon everything that comes into his head, except the subject that is legitimately before him. The waste of time which this practice causes, the restless, scatter-brained, indolent style of thinking which it inevitably produces, the extent to which it protracts the debates on every measure, are just now evils of the first magnitude, and something ought to be done to put an end to them. The practice itself is a legacy bequeathed to us by the old times—for they are now old times—before the war, when the one subject of discussion was Slavery—and when everybody knew so well what everybody else would say about it, that it made little difference what he said, particularly as Congress had little else to do than to listen to him. As there was plenty time, and no other means of keeping himself before the public, every member felt it his duty to give, at least once in every session, a full history of the Slavery controversy from the foundation of the Government down to the year 1850; then to castigate his opponents severely, and finally to expose the immorality, cruelty and waste of slaveholding, ending with some caustic remarks upon the trouble and dismay that would be caused amongst the European aristocracies, by the prospective growth of the Republic.

We need not tell any of our readers how much change there has been since then. If not a word were uttered in Congress for the next four months, except upon the bills now before it, and if every member was in his place every time they were brought up, and gave each of them, as it came before him, his sole and undivided attention, the larger number of them would still be very unsatisfactorily framed, very imperfectly debated and very improperly understood. We cannot impress too strongly upon the members of both branches the fact, that a large proportion of them are very ill-qualified for their work, have a very limited acquaintance with many of the subjects with which they have to deal, and that they have consequently not a minute to spare from their study of them.

The wickedness and causelessness of the rebellion; the goodness of the United States Government; the ambition and unscrupulousness of JEFF. DAVIS and his confederates; the powers and resources of the North; and the rascality of England and France, are now the favorite themes of Congressional spouters. No matter what is before either House, few members feel easy till they have delivered themselves of a large quantity of "perilous stuff" on these points. We respectfully suggest, that we have now had enough of it from that quarter, and that declamation on these tempting topics had better, in future, be left to the newspapers, and that the National Legislature occupy itself solely and exclusively with such bills as the payment of the national debt, the subjugation of the South, the maintenance of a large army and navy, and the care of the emancipated blacks. We promise faithfully to find other very enticing subjects for "orations" when these matters have been satisfactorily settled, but we confess we do not believe our ingenuity will be tested for a long time to come.

THE SWORD.—The great sword contest will close to-day. It has been as entertaining as meaningless, and as profitable as exciting. It has brought close upon twenty thousand dollars to the treasury of the fair, and to the relief of sick and wounded soldiers. The fact that one person could cast as many votes as he pleased, by simply paying a dollar for each, rendered the voting worthless in the way of ascertaining the popular preference between the two Generals who were in nomination. But still, the plan was a good one; for the primary object of the whole thing was to raise money for the cause, and not to learn who was the greatest General in popular estimation.

Let the friends of MCCLELLAN and the friends of GRANT walk up to the polls to-day and vote. Vote early and vote often. Vote for one or the other, or vote for both. Every vote will be the means of soothing a soldier's pangs, drying a patriot's tears, cheering a wounded spirit; and for every vote, or rather for what each vote will be the means of procuring, the blessings of the brave will be given.

THE FORT PILLOW BUTCHERY.—There is now an overwhelming and painfully minute mass of proof of the truth of the first reports of the rebel massacre of our troops, black and white, at Fort Pillow. We have had, and have given, the evidence of eye-witnesses, the evidence of victims offered in their last moments, the evidence of persons who visited the scene of the butchery immediately after it, and we have had other evidence not less conclusive, such as the arrival at Cairo of some of the bodies, which bore upon them marks of the worst barbarities charged against the rebels. It now only requires the official statement of the officers appointed to investigate the matter, to furnish irrefragable proof for history. It was superserviceable labor on the part of any one to deny the massacre, in behalf of the rebels. JEFF. DAVIS officially proclaimed this to be his policy, and he was backed up in his ferocious proclamation by the whole rebel press. To deny that the rebels would carry out their measure is preposterous to the perception of all of us who know that, atrocious as rebel threats have been, their deeds have always been more bloody than their threats. We have not yet had the Southern defense of the massacre and their jubilations over it; but their organs in the North have already justified it as a perfectly proper act of war.

The New-York Times.

VOL. XIII—NO. 3926. NEW-YORK, SUNDAY, APRIL 24, 1864. PRICE FOUR CENTS

THE WAR IN NORTH CAROLINA.

The Union Disaster at Plymouth Confirmed.

Probable Surrender of the Town and Garrison.

THE REBEL RAM AT WORK.

The Gunboats Bombshell and Southfield Sunk.

CAPTAIN FLUSSER, OF THE MIAMI, KILLED.

Communication Interrupted and the Ram in Possession of the River.

A FLEET OF GUNBOATS SENT TO DESTROY HER.

Arrival of Refugees at Roanoke Island.

From our Special Correspondent.

NEWBERN, N. C., Wednesday, April 20, 1864.

Advices just received from Plymouth warrant the conclusion that it has fallen into the hands of the enemy. It was attacked by a heavy land force on Sunday evening, (the 17th,) in connection with an iron-clad ram which came down the Roanoke River. In the engagement, the ram sunk the *Southfield*, (gunboat,) and a small vessel which has frequently been on expeditions up the Roanoke, called the *Bombshell*. It also partially disabled the gunboat *Miami*. The ram getting below Plymouth, it is thought impossible for reinforcements to reach the place. The enemy numbered some ten to twelve thousand, and only took the place, if at all, by a most desperate effort. They were repulsed in four distinct charges, with great slaughter, and the attack, which commenced on Sunday night, continued until Tuesday morning, when the firing ceased. It is supposed that Gen. WESSELLS, with his brave garrison, surrendered; but nothing definite is known as yet, none of our vessels having been able to reach them since Sunday. Our force numbered about 2,000.

Of the casualties I have been able to learn nothing definite, except that Capt. FLUSSER, of the *Miami*, and the senior officer of the navy at that place was killed by the recoil of a shot from one of his own guns. This officer is spoken of universally as one of the bravest of the brave. His loss is felt very much.

Thus, while GRANT is preparing for his great campaign against Richmond, the enemy are making good use of the advantage which they have always had of us in this struggle, that of being within the ring.

While our forces are assembling for an advance on the rebel capital, they have time to send against us in North Carolina a strong detachment, which can do much injury here and return in due time for service there. In view of this fact, it is strange that this department should have been left so destitute of troops; and, if finally the rebels are forced to leave Virginia, the points we now hold in this State will be of great value to them; and it will not be possible to withstand their desperate efforts to take them without a larger force than we have at present.

The ram, though small and mounting but two guns, is said to be so heavily armored that all the shot which struck her either broke into fragments or rolled off like hail. It seems strange to a looker-on that this ram with one on the Tar and Neuse Rivers respectively, should have been so long expected to make their appearance, and yet we have no vessels of the kind to destroy them when they come. Had we one or two light draft iron-clads to move in the sound and these rivers, we should feel some security. Without them it is impossible to estimate the damage we may suffer. The positions which we hold in this State should either be abandoned or a sufficient land and naval force placed here to protect us from such known contingencies. ELIHU.

ANOTHER ACCOUNT.

A gentleman who left Roanoke Island on Thursday morning, arrived in this City last night, and favored us with the following particulars:

Plymouth was attacked by a large force of rebels on Sunday afternoon. They made several assaults on Sunday and Monday, all of which were repulsed. On Tuesday morning, about 3 o'clock, an iron-clad ram came down the river, passing the batteries unobserved, and attacked the gunboats *Southfield* and *Miami*. The ram was not seen until it was close upon the gunboats, and, passing across the bow of the *Miami* struck the *Southfield* under the guard, the prow penetrating nearly to the magazine. Capt. FLUSSER a moment before the ram struck ordered both boats to be put under full steam, but they could not be got under way in time to avoid the blow. The *Southfield* filled and sunk within five minutes. Capt. FLUSSER was killed by the explosion of a shell fired from the *Miami*, which rebounded from the ram.

The *Miami* being injured, fell back to the mouth of the river, and was there found by the gunboat *Whitehead*, which escaped the ram by passing through the Cashie river. The gunboat *Ceres* being disabled by the fire from the enemy's batteries, came over to Roanoke Island on Tuesday evening, bearing the body of Capt. FLUSSER, and information of the disaster to the *Southfield*. The rebel ram had full possession of the river in front of the town, and during Tuesday was shelling the town and the works. It is believed to carry three or four Whitworth guns of small calibre.

On Wednesday morning the transport *John Faron* carried up from Newbern two regiments, numbering in all about 800 men, commanded by Col. WARFORD. It is not known whether they succeeded in reaching Plymouth. The transport was seen passing down toward Newbern early on Thursday morning, but our informant could not ascertain whether the troops were still on board. The mailboat *Gen. Berry*, which left Roanoke Island at four o'clock on Thursday morning, passed the propeller *De Witt Clinton*, carrying women and children from Plymouth, having left there Wednesday morning. The persons on board said fighting was still going on, but the place must soon be surrendered.

The armed vessels at the mouth of the Roanoke on Wednesday were the *Miami*, *Whitehead* and the new "double-ender" *Tacony*, the latter having gone up on Wednesday morning.

The rebel ram is described by persons who saw it on Tuesday as being about 125 feet long and 40 feet beam, with an iron-plated casemate similar in construction to that of the *Merrimac*. It is very low in the water, not showing more than six feet above the water line. It is very slow, and could probably be destroyed by the gunboats, if it ventured into the open sound.

Several hundred refugees, principally women children and negroes were at Roanoke Island. The steam transports *Thos. Collyer* and *Massasoit* were plying between the Island and Plymouth.

It was feared at the Island that an attack might be made upon the canals between Roanoke and Elizabeth River, but the *Gen. Berry*, which left on Thursday morning, came through without interruption. The line of the canal is strongly guarded and fortified.

REPORTS FROM BALTIMORE.

BALTIMORE, Saturday, April 23.

The following highly important intelligence was received from Fortress Monroe this morning:

On Sunday last the rebels assaulted our works at Plymouth, N. C., and were twice repulsed.

On Monday morning, at 1 o'clock, the gunboat *Bombshell* ran up the Roanoke River to look out for the iron-clad ram, reported coming down.

Soon after passing our works, the *Bombshell* was fired into by a rebel battery and sunk.

About three o'clock, the rebel ram came down, ran past our batteries and then run into the gunboat *Southfield* and sunk her.

The gunboat *Miami*, a very strong vessel, lay close to the ram, and Capt. FLUSSER, one of the most gallant men in our navy, cleared her decks for action and fired nine-inch shells at the rebel ram, which rebounded from her sides, exploded and killed Capt. FLUSSER.

The *Miami* was then immediately run down the river out of danger.

The rebel ram, so far as heard from, has not fired a shot, and now has possession of the river below Plymouth.

Our garrison at Plymouth is cut off from all communication.

The post, however, is well garrisoned, and has plenty of provisions, ammunition and arms.

Gen. BUTLER is confident that it will withstand any further assault that the rebels can make.

Advices from Newbern say that Little Washington is also threatened by the rebels.

Gen. BUTLER has sent a fleet of gunboats into the Sound, to open communication with Plymouth and aid the navy vessels to destroy the rebel ram.

Admiral LEE has also sent a gunboat to replace the *Southfield*.

DESTRUCTION OF THE GUNBOAT SOUTHFIELD.

WASHINGTON, Saturday, April 23.

The Navy Department has received the following information of the destruction of the gunboat *Southfield*:

About 5:30 P. M., April 17, Fort Gray, above Plymouth, was attacked by the rebels from the battery of six field pieces on a sand bank some thousand yards up the river.

Lieut.-Commander FLUSSER dispatched the *Ceres* to communicate with the *Whitehead*, which was doing picket duty up the river. In passing by the rebel battery she received a shot through her port gangway, killing two and wounding seven men. The firing on the fort ceased at about 9 o'clock; the *Ceres* returned about that time. At early dawn of Monday the enemy charged upon Fort Gray and were repulsed. The *Bombshell*, an army gunboat, in command of Ensign THOMAS B. STOKES, steamed up the river to communicate with the fort. She returned and sunk at the wharf. Later in the day the enemy appeared in force in the rear of the town, and at sunset commenced a vigorous attack on Fort Williams and Fort Wessell, at which time the *Miami* and *Southfield*, previously joined together, were cast loose. The *Southfield* steamed up the river to protect Fort Wessell, while the *Miami* dropped down and shelled the enemy in front of Fort Williams.

During the evening the enemy assaulted Fort Wessell, and were repulsed three times, the *Southfield* throwing shell among them. About 10:30 P. M. the *Southfield* dropped down the river, and reported to Lieutenant-Commander FLUSSER, who ordered the vessels to be lashed together with hawsers, the *Southfield* being on the port side of the *Miami*. About midnight the *Whitehead* came down the Cachie, and came alongside the *Miami*, and reported the ram coming down.

At 3 A. M. on Tuesday, the ram dropped down alongside the *Miami*, under cover of the shade of the trees, and when near, ran obliquely across into the starboard bow of the *Southfield*. The vessels had been firing all the previous evening at the enemy on shore, and were loaded with shell, which there was not time to draw. The Lieutenant-Commander fired the first shell, and on its bursting, some fragment either from that or the *Southfield's* shells, rebounded, which caused death, the fragments piercing his chest and skull, also wounding the following officers and men: Acting Ensign Thos. G. HARGIS, Acting Third Assistant Engineer HARRINGTON, and some six or eight men—none mortally. Upon the approach of the ram, the *Southfield* fired at her. The prow of the ram running into the *Southfield*, caused her to fill with water, and she sunk inside of fifteen minutes. The forward lashings were parted by the pressure of the ram between our vessels and the after ones were cut, and as many as could get on the *Miami* did so, when the *Miami* retired, and was pursued a short distance by the ram, which was considered slow, making but four knots per hour, the *Miami* throwing solid shot at her as she retired. Some of the men of the *Southfield* took to small boats, and were picked up by the *Whitehead* and *Ceres*.

The *Ceres* was dispatched to Newbern immediately with the body of Commander FLUSSER.

The officers missing of the *Southfield* were:

Acting Master Wm. B. Newman.
Acting Ensign Thos. B. Stokes.
Acting Second Assistant Engineer Wm. T. Goff.
Acting Third Assistant John A. Stileby.
Acting Master's Mate Geo. W. Pratt.
Paymaster's Clerk Geo. W. Brown.

Some of the officers and men of the *Southfield* may have been captured, but most have escaped. Few or none were probably lost. The *Miami* is uninjured. The ram is thought not to have used her guns whilst under the bows of the *Miami* and *Southfield*, nor could our guns then bear on her. The shell fired at her was when she approached.

THE ARMY OF THE POTOMAC.

Review of the Second Army Corps and Artillery Reserve—Capture of Guerrillas.

WASHINGTON, Saturday, April 23.

Advices from the Army of the Potomac to-day state that the Second Army Corps, Major-Gen. HANCOCK commanding, was reviewed yesterday by Gens. GRANT and MEADE. Gens. SEDGWICK, WARREN and SHERIDAN, with their Staffs, were present. The discipline of the troops was highly praised by the Generals, as well as by all who witnessed the spectacle. This is the largest corps in the army, and the scene presented as they passed in review with bands playing and colors flying was magnificent.

The artillery reserve also passed in review, after which the Generals proceeded to witness the evolutions of the Nineteenth and Twentieth regiments Massachusetts Volunteers in an entirely new drill, which was much admired. The reviewing party afterward partook of refreshments with Gen. HANCOCK at his headquarters.

Yesterday a party of six guerrillas were captured near Morrisville. They had attacked a picket station and killed a man a short time previous.

Two Men Shot at Fort Warren for Desertion.

BOSTON, Saturday, April 23.

CHARLES CARPENTER and MATTHEW RILEY, alias JOHN ROACH, were shot yesterday afternoon, for desertion, at Fort Warren.

The iron-clad *Canonicus* sailed last night under convoy of the steamer *Osceola*.

THE RED RIVER EXPEDITION.

Arrival of the Mississippi and the Evening Star.

DETAILS OF THE RECENT BATTLES

Heavy Losses Sustained by Our Forces at Sabine Cross Roads.

Complete Discomfiture of the Rebels at Pleasant Hill.

Partial List of the Killed and Wounded.

Correspondence of the New-York Times:

DEPARTMENT OF THE GULF, NEW-ORLEANS, Saturday, April 16, 1864.

The history of the rebellion has had another fearful page added to its record. The gallant soldiers of the East and the West have, side by side, emulated each other in devotion to their country's cause; they have fallen side by side as they have together triumphed over the common enemy, and throughout all time the fire-side stories of the homes of those who live in the Upper Mississippi Valley will be details of how their fathers fought shoulder to shoulder for freedom along with their brothers of New-England homes.

No information has reached this city, of an official character, but there are continual arrivals of wounded, of prisoners, and intelligent persons attached to the steamers in the Red River trade. From all these witnesses have been gathered such particulars as we have of the battles of the 7th, 8th and 9th. The account published in the New-Orleans *Era*, of the 14th inst., from my most intimate acquaintance with the country where the battles took place, seems to be justly entitled to precedence, and from that source I am almost entirely indebted for the details of the battles.

The country lying between Grand Ecore, which is the river landing of Nactchedotches and Shreveport, one hundred miles in extent, is not alluvial but level land, broken by slightly elevated ridges, bisected in places by bayous, which empty into Red River. The distance between the Shreveport road and the river varies from five to ten miles, which intervening land is almost entirely composed of impenetrable swamp. It is therefore perceivable that the gunboats are useless to the army after it leaves Grand Ecore. The whole distance from Nactchedotches to Shreveport is more or less a low sandy ridge, broken by straggling forests of pine and scrub oaks. Crump's Mills consists of one or two miserable houses, and there are no settlements, the plantations that once existed having been long abandoned, until you get to Pleasant Hill, which is a little village situated on a low ridge, containing in peace times probably 300 inhabitants. Just beyond the town are still the marks of the track of a hurricane that, some two years ago, nearly destroyed every house in the place. This drift is lower than the ridge on which the town is built; it is very dense, the road having been cut through the fallen timber and the sand-hills, which were thrown up by the roots of the trees. On the left of Pleasant Hill, and on the right, up to the edge of the "drift," are abandoned plantations, here and there covered with groups of low, second growth pine. Passing on, you come to WILSON's plantation—a place of cleared land on each side of the road, surrounded by dense woods. Just beyond are Bayou de Paul and the old Sabine Road, which make the place by nature a strong military position. Two miles beyond WILSON's is Mansfield, the shire town of De Soto Parish, a very pretty place, containing 800 inhabitants.

Our army broke up its encampment on the 6th inst., and marched along the Shreveport Road twenty-one miles, the cavalry in advance, resting at Crump's Mills, the supporting infantry some four miles in the rear, on a pleasant bayou, famous for affording good spring water in its vicinity. On the morning of the next day, the 7th, at daylight, the cavalry started, and ere it had gone two miles, commenced heavy skirmishing with the enemy. This running fight was kept up for fourteen miles, until our cavalry passed through the drift above Pleasant Hill, and reached the open fields, known as WILSON's plantation. Here was a heavy body of rebel infantry, 2,500 strong, deployed along the edges of the woods, by which disposition our men were, to avoid them, compelled to charge over the abandoned fields. The only Union soldiers that had advanced far enough to take part in the fight, which was inevitable, was the cavalry brigade of LEE's corps, commanded by Col. HARAI ROBINSON. As he had either to attack or be attacked, he decided to take the initiative, and he led his men in with such a dash and vigor, that at last the enemy was completely whipped and driven from the field. This engagement lasted two hours and a half, and our losses amounted to about forty killed and wounded, the enemy's being at least as many. Col. ROBINSON pursued the retreating rebels as far as Bayou du Paul, where he found they had received heavy reinforcements, including four pieces of artillery, and were again in line of battle waiting attack. As it was nearly dark, and the risk was too great in again attacking with his small force, he placed his men in the most advantageous position available, and awaited the progress of events.

Early on the following morning, the 8th, the cavalry, supported by a brigade of infantry, under Col. LANDRUM, resumed its march. The enemy was discovered to be on the alert, and a battle almost instantly commenced. Col. LANDRUM's infantry brigade was on the right of the road, and Col. LUCAS' cavalry brigade on the left. The skirmishing was very fierce, and every foot of ground won from the enemy had to be taken by hard knocks, but at two o'clock in the afternoon our forces had compelled the enemy to retreat beyond Pleasant Hill. Our loss, as well as the enemy's, was very severe during this time. Lieut.-Col. WEBB, of the Seventy-seventh Illinois, shot through the head and instantly killed, and Capt. BREESE, commanding Sixth Missouri Cavalry, severely wounded in the arm, being among the casualties on our side.

From the constantly increasing severity of the fighting, it was evident that a large force of the enemy was near, as it was subsequently ascertained that Gens. DICK TAYLOR, MOUTON, GREEN, and PRICE were present with a command of not less than 18,000 men, while our force by comparison was nothing. The rebels occupied a strong position in the vicinity of Sabine Cross Roads, concealed in the edge of a dense wood, with an open field in front, the Shreveport road passing through their lines. Gen. RANSOM, arriving on the field with his command, formed his line as well as circumstances would permit, after reconnoitering and feeling the rebel position. Col. EMERSON's brigade, of the Thirteenth Corps, was stationed on the left of the line, with NIM's Massachusetts Battery. Col. LANDRUM's forces, parts of two brigades on the right and centre, with RAWLE's Battery G, Fifth Regulars, and a battery of the First Indiana Artillery in rear of his right and centre. Col. DUDLEY's brigade of cavalry, of LEE's corps, supported the left and held itself in readiness to repel any attempt to flank; while LUCAS protected the right flank. Col. ROBINSON, with his brigade, was in rear of the centre, protecting the wagon train which was on the Shreveport road.

Gen. BANKS and Staff rode upon the field by the time this disposition of our forces was effected, and word was sent back to Gen. FRANKLIN to make all speed for the scene of the momentarily expected battle. It was the design of Gen. BANKS to remain quiet until the remainder of his army came up, and then open the battle himself; but KIRBY SMITH, knowing his own superiority of numbers, began the conflict before they could arrive.

About 5 o'clock the firing between the skirmishers become very hot, and in a short time our skirmish line was driven back upon the main body by an overwhelming force. The whole strength of the enemy was then advanced and heavy and repeated volleys were discharged and replied to on our right and centre. Soon this portion of our line became heavily engaged, and all our available strength was required to prevent their being crushed by the masses of the enemy. Our left, which was now, also, hotly fighting, was necessarily much weakened, and it was observed that a strong body of the enemy was massing in a dense piece of woods, preparatory to dashing down and flanking this end of our line. The danger was plain and imminent, but there was no remedy. Gen. STONE ordered Gen. LEE to have NIM's battery withdrawn, although it was doing great execution, in order that it might not become a prize to the enemy, and Gen. LEE sent his Aid-de-Camp, Col. J. S. BRISBIN, to withdraw the battery. On reaching the point, its removal was found impossible, nearly every one of the horses having been killed. In a few moments more a solid mass of the rebels, under command of Gen. MONTON, swept down upon the spot and four of the guns were taken, the other two being dragged from the field by hand. The havoc made in the ranks of the enemy at this point of the action is represented as appalling, the whole six guns belching forth double charges of grape and canister; and some five or six rounds were fired between the time the rebels left the woods until the artillerymen were forced from their pieces. As the rebels were in mass, the execution such a shower of missiles caused can be easily imagined. MONTON fell mortally wounded. The two senior officers of NIMS' battery were wounded, Lieut. SNOW mortally, he having since died.

The fighting on all parts of our line was now at short range, and to use the expression of one of the participants, "we were holding on by the skin of our teeth only." It was known that FRANKLIN's troops had been sent for, and anxious and wistful were the glances cast to the rear. Gen. CAMERON, with his brigade came up, and going at once into action on the right, where the battle again waxed hottest, created the impression that the veterans of the Nineteenth had arrived, and a glad and exultant shout went up from our wearied and desperately situated little band. This belief was strengthened by the arrival of Gen. FRANKLIN, who dashed boldly into the thickest of the fray, cap in hand and cheering on the men. Gen. BANKS, too, seemed ubiquitous, riding wherever the men wavered, and by personal example inciting them to renewed deeds of daring and reckless valor. Cols. CLARK and WILSON, with other members of the staff, sabre in hand, mixed with the soldiers on foot and horseback, and cheered and encouraged them to continue the unequal fight.

But human beings could not longer withstand such fierce and overpowering onslaughts as our men were bearing up against, and our line finally gave way at all points, and the men fell back fiercely contesting the ground they yielded. Unfortunately a sad mishap befell them at this time. The large and cumbersome wagon train blocked up the way; the frightened horses dashed through the infantry lines, entangled themselves with the artillery, and created a momentary but unfortunate confusion. This gave the rebels, who were rapidly pressing us, possession of several pieces of artillery.

The enemy followed our men step by step for three and a half miles, but he was advancing to meet a fearful retribution. The Nineteenth Army Corps had been ordered to stop and form its line of battle—the retreating Union troops passed through this line and formed in the rear. The rebels thinking they had repulsed our whole army, dashed impetuously on, and thought the line, but half visible in the woods before them, was another feeble but desperate stand of a few men.

Gen. EMORY commanded this force, consisting of two full brigades, and he ordered the fire to be reserved until the rebels were within short range, when from both infantry and the artillery posted thickly along his line, a storm of iron and lead was hurled upon the foe that literally mowed them down. The rebels halted in amazement, but still they fought and bravely. Volley after volley was discharged from each side full into the ranks of their opponents, but neither gave signs of yielding, and night charitably threw her mantle over the ghastly scene, and enforced a cessation of hostilities.

The two divisions, under command of Gen. A. J. SMITH, belonging to the Sixteenth and Seventeenth Army Corps, had reached Pleasant Hill, and were there halted. Gen. BANKS determined to withdraw his army to that point, for the sake of the advantageous position which he could there occupy, knowing that the enemy would follow what they supposed to be a demoralized army. In accordance with this plan of operations, all our men were quietly withdrawn from the enemy's front, and the line of march taken up for Pleasant Hill. This conjunction of his forces was satisfactorily effected, and the result confidently awaited. So well was the movement conducted that although the first body started at 10 o'clock, and the remainder were not under way until nearly day, the rebels had not the slightest suspicion of what was going on.

Gen. FRANKLIN was conspicuous during this part of the day, rallying his men, and two horses were killed under him; Capt. CHAPMAN, of his staff, had both feet taken off by a round shot, and the horse of Capt. FRANKLIN was killed at the same time.

THE THIRD DAY'S FIGHT.

At 7 o'clock on Saturday morning our forces were all at Pleasant Hill, and the rebels were advancing, cavalry in front, endeavoring to discover our position. Col. O. P. GOODING, with his brigade of LEE's cavalry corps, was sent out on the Shreveport road, to meet the enemy and draw him on. He had gone about a mile, when he came upon the rebel advance. Skirmishing immediately ensued, and according to the plan he slowly fell back. The fight was very sharp between these cavalry bodies, and GOODING lost nearly forty men killed and wounded, inflicting, however, as much damage as he received. Among his casualties are Capt. BECKER and Lieut. HALL, of the Second New-York Veteran Cavalry. Lieut. HALL has since died of his wounds. Col. GOODING made a narrow escape, a ball passing through and tearing out the crown of his hat, and grazing the skin. The brigade behaved very gallantly, covering Gen. EMORY's front until his line was formed.

The battle-field of Pleasant Hill, as we have already described, is a large, open field, which had once been cultivated, but is now overgrown with weeds and bushes. The slightly-elevated centre of the field, from which the name Pleasant Hill is taken, is nothing more than a long mound, hardly worthy the name of hill. A semi-circular belt of timber runs around the field on the Shreveport side. Gen. EMORY formed his line of battle on the side facing these woods, Gen. MCMILLAN's brigade being posted on the right. Gen. DWIGHT's on the centre, and Col. BENEDICT's on the left. TAYLOR's Battery, L, First Regulars, had four guns in rear of the left wing, on the left of the Shreveport road, and two on the road in rear of Gen. DWIGHT's line. HIBBERD's Vermont battery was on the right.

In the rear of EMORY, and concealed by the rising ground were Gen. SMITH's tried troops, formed in two lines of battle fifty yards apart. All his artillery was in the front line, a piece, section or battery being on the flank of each regiment, the infantry lying between them. The Thirteenth Corps was in reserve in the rear under Gen. CAMERON—Gen. RANSOM having been wounded the day before. Gen. SMITH was Commander-in-Chief of the two lines back of the crest, while Gen. MOWER was the immediate Commander of the men. The Commander of the right brigade in Gen. SMITH's first line was Col. LYNCH; the left brigade was Col. SHAW's. The second line also consisted of two brigades—the right under control of Col. ———, and the left commanded by Col. HILL. CRAWFORD's Third Indiana Battery was posted on the right of the Eighty-ninth Indiana Infantry, and the Ninth Indiana Battery on the right of the line of battle. The Missouri Iron Gun Battery, and others whose names and numbers we could not ascertain, were also in this section of the battle.

The skirmishing was kept up with considerable vigor until about 5 o'clock in the afternoon, when the rebels had completed their arrangements for the attack. At about this hour Gen. EMORY's skirmish line was driven in on the right by the rebels, who appeared in large force, coming through the timber above-mentioned. They soon reached the open ground, and moved on to the attack in three lines of battle. Our batteries and infantry opened with terrible effect, doing great slaughter with grape and canister, while the enemy's artillery, being in the woods and in bad position, did scarcely any damage.

Col. BENEDICT's brigade on the left was first engaged, soon followed by DWIGHT's and MCMILLAN's. The fighting was terrific—old soldiers say it never was surpassed for desperation. Notwithstanding the terrible havoc in their ranks, the enemy pressed fiercely on, slowly pushing the men of the Nineteenth Corps back, up the hill, but not breaking their line of battle. A sudden and bold dash of the rebels on the right, gave them possession of TAYLOR's Battery, and forced our line still further back.

Now came the grand *coup de main*. The Nineteenth, on arriving at the top of the hill, suddenly filed off over the hill, and passed through the lines of Gen. SMITH. We must here mention that the rebels were now in but two lines of battle, the first having been almost annihilated by Gen. EMORY, what remained being forced back into the second line. But these two lines came on exultant, and sure of victory.

The first passed over the knoll, and all heedless of the long line of cannons and crouching forms of as brave men as ever trod mother earth, pressed on. The second line appeared on the crest, and the death signal was sounded. Words cannot describe the awful effect of this discharge. Seven thousand rifles, and several batteries of artillery, each gun with an extra load of grape and canister, were fired simultaneously, and the whole center of the rebel line was crushed down as a field of ripe wheat through which a tornado had passed. It is estimated that one thousand men were hurried into eternity or frightfully mangled by this one discharge.

No time was given them to recover their good order, but Gen. SMITH ordered a charge, and his men dashed rapidly forward, the boys of the Nineteenth joining in. The rebels fought boldly and desperately back to the timber, on reaching which a large portion broke and fled, fully two thousand throwing aside their arms. In this charge TAYLOR's Battery was retaken, as were also two of the guns of NIM's Battery, the Parrott gun taken from us at Carrion Crow last Fall, and one or two others belonging to the rebels, one of which was considerably shattered, besides, 700 prisoners. A pursuit and desultory fight was kept up for three miles, when our men returned to the field of battle.

INCIDENTS OF THE BATTLE.

The accounts from all quarters agree in stating that Gen. BANKS, during the entire contest, showed the greatest possible daring and valor, as did Gen. FRANKLIN, and the staffs of each. They will reap their reward in the grateful hearts and prayers of the American people, and in the increased devotion and love of their soldiers.

Gen. RANSOM, when wounded, was directing the firing of the Chicago Battery, standing among the men, and he had scarcely been removed when the rebels were in possession of the spot on which he fell. This gallant officer, the youngest of his rank in the army, has been, I believe, now three times wounded. He is one of the men chosen by Gen. GRANT to give his celebrated unconditional surrender order. He now lies at the St. Charles Hotel, shot through the leg with a musket ball. He will most certainly recover.

Col. BRISBIN, of Gen. LEE's Staff, had his horse's head blown off while riding across the field, by a shell, and would have been taken had not some of the men pulled him out. He succeeded in capturing a rebel horse and leaving the field on his back. Col. BRISBIN lost in his trunk, in the baggage train, the sash taken from Gen. BARKSDALE on the field at Gettysburgh, which had been made a present to him, and Gen. VILLEPIGUE's sabre, taken from him in Virginia.

Col. ROBINSON, while defending the wagon train on the first day, was shot in the hip, but refused to leave the field for two hours after. It was supposed he would lose his leg in consequence, but the surgeons now think it can be saved. Among the most regretted of the slain is Col. BENEDICT of the One Hundred and Sixth-fifth New-York.

Partial List of Casualties.

Col. Vance, of 96th Ohio, wounded and left on the field.

Col. Webb, 77th Illinois, and Lieut.-Col. Cowen, 19th Kentucky, wounded and prisoners.

Lieut. Stone, C. S. of the Third Brigade, is among the missing.

Lieut. Miller, 6th Missouri Cavalry, missing.

Capt. Morse, 1st Louisiana Cavalry, severely wounded.

Lieuts. Brown and Gorman were also severely wounded.

Lieut. Graham, 87th Illinois, wounded.
Lieut. Meedower, 87th Illinois, wounded.
Capt. McCullough, 11th Illinois, missing.
Lieut. Stevenson, missing.
Capt. Stearn, missing.
Lieut. McCullough, 11th Illinois, missing.
Lieut. Wyman, 11th Illinois, missing.
Lieut. Douane, 14th New-York Cavalry, missing.
Capt. Morse, 16th Indiana, severely wounded.
Lieut. Jones, 16th Illinois, killed.

Capt. Marklan, 14th New-York Cavalry, slightly wounded.

Lieut.-Col. Green, wounded in arm.

Capt. King, 8th New-Hampshire, wounded and left on the field—supposed his wound is a mortal one.

Lieut. Troop, Mercantile Bat.—wounded.
Lieut. Stack—slightly wounded.
Maj. Mann, 19th Kentucky—slightly wounded.

Lieut. Saunderson, Bat. 8, 1st Regiment—mortally wounded.

Capt. Mahler, 1st La. Bat.—severely wounded.
Maj. Reed, 113th Illinois—missing.
Lieut.-Col. Lindsay, 48th Ohio—killed.

165TH NEW-YORK (2D DURYEA'S ZOUAVES.)

Lieut.-Col. Carr—flesh wound in the right arm.
Lieut. D. T. H. Thomas—ankle.
Lieut. Andrew Napier—right leg.

30TH MAINE.

This regiment suffered severely, losing about 70 men in killed, wounded and missing. The color staff was struck twice and shattered. The Color Sergeant was shot in the leg; but he bravely stood by the flag and held it up until relieved by another Sergeant.

Major Royal E. Whitman, flesh wound in the hip.
Lieut. Strout, Co. E, killed.

Capt. Randall, Co. E, shoulder, slightly; kept the field.

Col. Emerson, wounded and left in the hands of the enemy.

FIRST LOUISIANA CAVALRY.

Col. HARAI ROBINSON, while gallantly leading his command into action, was wounded severely in his hip, but continued to urge his men onward with undiminished zeal.

The loss of the First Louisiana Cavalry in killed, wounded and missing, so far as has been ascertained, is 5 officers and 23 men. Their names are as follows:

Col. Robinson, wounded.
Capt. Andrew Morse, wounded.
Capt. Thos. Maher, dead.
Private Ed. Sullivan, Co. A, 1st La.
Private Aug. Phillip, Co. B, 1st Louisiana.
Private Barney Grimes, Co. B.
Private John H. Landfer, Co. E.
Private August Schormwald, Co. G.
Private Wm. Button, Co. I.
Private Martin Ford, Co. B.
Private James Jones, Co. D.
Private D. ?. Rae, Co. L.
Private Jules Michel, Co. I.
Sergt. Augustus Letton, Co. C.
Sergt. J. Adams, Co. B.
Sergt. Thomas Welch, Co. I.
Sergt. Peter Quinn, Co. E.
Corp. Thomas Kelly, Co. I.

EIGHTY-SEVENTH ILLINOIS.

Lieut. John Graham, Co. G.
Lieut. P. S. Meader, Co. A.
Sergt. James Bridwell, Co. B.
Sergt. John M. Simpson, Co. K.
Private M. Cramer, Co. D.
Private Elias Smith, Co. D.
Private Geo. Burnhard, Co. F.
Private D. J. Collins, Co. A.
Private Geo. W. Carey, Co. A.
Private Harrison Frances, Co. B.
Private Thos. Eaton, Co. E.
Private Geo. M. Chamber, Co. B.
Private J. M. Doherty, Co. I.
Lieut.-Col. Webb, Seventy-seventh Illinois, killed.

Capt. Breese, Sixth Missouri Cavalry, wounded in the arm.

Lieut. Snow, Nim's Massachusetts Battery, killed.

Capt. Chapman, of Franklin's Staff, had both legs shot off.

Capt. Becker, Second New-York Veteran Cavalry, wounded.

Lieut. Hall, Second New-York Veteran Cavalry, killed.

Deaths of Returned Prisoners.

BALTIMORE, Saturday, April 23.

The following returned prisoners died at Jarvis Hospital to-day: Sergeant JOHN CLINE, Company K, 89th Ohio Regiment; JOHN R. ROBINSON, private Company E, 45th Kentucky Regiment, and M. L. OSTRANDER, Company B, 5th Michigan Cavalry.

THE WAR IN THE FAR WEST.

The Vote in Arkansas upon the Constitution.

DISPOSITION OF THE REBEL FORCES.

AFFAIRS IN NORTHERN TEXAS.

MILITARY MOVEMENTS.

ACTIVITY OF THE GUERRILLAS.

From Our Own Correspondent.

FORT SMITH, Ark., Wednesday, March 30, 1864.

The vote upon the Free State Constitution and for loyal State Officers of the *Free State* of Arkansas is now known to your readers. In this county (Sebastian) the vote was large. For the Constitution, it stood, 1,080—the same aggregate being given for Gov. ISAAC MURPHY. This is the vote of five precincts. Other points and the soldiers' vote, still unknown, will certainly increase this vote to 1,200. As the vote in this county before the war was about 2,400, it will be readily seen how large a portion have continued loyal and how many are despairing of the rebel cause.

The following telegram received here from Little Rock gives a general summary of the vote. Its aggregate is quite encouraging:

LITTLE ROCK, March 23, 1864.

The votes have not been counted. Not more than half the poll books are in yet. The vote as far as heard from is over 8,000. Batesville and the Helena District to hear from, and most of the Arkansas troops. The vote will be over 10,000. ROGERS elected to Congress from the Second District.

ISAAC MURPHY.

But two persons who voted refused to vote for the Constitution. Col. J. M. JOHNSON is undoubtedly reëlected to Congress from the Third District; Lieut. E. D. PERKINS, of the Thirteenth Kansas, who was placed on the track against him three days before the election, has received several hundred votes. It was not presumed that he would be elected when his candidacy was announced. Lieut. PERKINS is now in Washington as delegate from the Provisional Government of the Choctaw Nation. Lieut. PERKINS is a talented, energetic young officer, who at the time of being commissioned in the Thirteenth Kansas, was a sergeant in the artillery service United States Army. Since being stationed here he has married a very fascinating young widow, who by a slight admixture of Indian blood, is the representative of the chief family in the Choctaw Nation. Lieut. PERKINS has used the influence this has given him well and wisely for the restoration of the Federal authority among the Choctaws.

The calling of a convention to resume relations of fealty and to accept the generous spirit of the Amnesty was through the influence of Lieut. PERKINS. Of that convention your correspondent has already written. It is hoped and believed that the mission of Delegate PERKINS will be of benefit to the Indian Territory and the interests of the Government therein. Responses have been received to its action from leading Choctaws, whom circumstances precluded from attendance. The Provisional Governor has issued a proclamation recalling the tribe to their allegiance.

The name of Gen. COOPER brings to mind the fact that the Interior Department is now in possession of a large quantity of papers belonging to the affairs of the Superintendency of Southern Indians. It will be remembered that ELIAS RECTOR, of this place, was, at the time Arkansas seceded, Indian Superintendent. D. H. COOPER was Agent for the Choctaws. A large amount of Government funds was appropriated as reported, for the benefit of the Confederate Government, but, as was shrewdly suspected, for the individual use of the two worthies named. Major RECTOR had a fine farm close to this place. He was a leading rebel, his son and son-in-law, Gen. CABELL, being in the army. When Gen. BLUNT occupied Fort Smith, RECTOR with most of the prominent citizens fled to Texas.

Through information received from negroes, the papers before spoken of were exhumed from their grave on the Rector farm. They were found to consist of the records of superintendency from 1839 to the Summer of 1861; also, the papers of the Confederate Receiver for sequestrating the property of Northern aliens, as we were termed. The private correspondence of RECTOR, COOPER, and others was extremely interesting. From these papers it appears that $80,000 in gold, belonging to the Indian Bureau, was appropriated and divided among the faithless and traitorous officials in this region.

Gen. THAYER, with the Kansas division, is now at Booneville, fifty miles southeast of this place. He has with him three brigades, two of infantry and one of cavalry. The first brigade, commanded by Col. CHARLES W. ADAMS, Twelfth Kansas, consists of that regiment, the First (Col. J. WILLIAMS) and Second (Col. CRAWFORD) Kansas Colored Volunteers, and the First Arkansas Battery, Capt. SEARL. The Second, commanded by Col. EDWARDS, Eighteenth Iowa, consists of that regiment and the First and Second Arkansas Infantry, with RABBS' Indiana Battery. The Cavalry Brigade consists of the Second Kansas, Lieut.-Col. BASSETT, three battalions of the Fourteenth, Lieut.-Col. BROWN, and six companies of the Sixth, Lieut.-Col. CAMPBELL, with a howitzer battery. Col. BASSETT has been in command of this brigade. The arrival of Col. CLOUD, of the Second, will place him in command. These regiments are all full, at least the minimum. They make an aggregate of 6,500 men. Gen. BLUNT, on whom the command of this army properly belongs, is left here, with scarcely troops enough to hold the garrison walls here and at Fort Gibson.

There is one result to proceed from this, which is much to be deplored. The people of this section, relying upon the faith of the Government, have accepted in truth the conditions of amnesty, and on the 14th of this month voted to make Arkansas a Free State, and thus resume her relations to the Union. In doing this they are entitled to the fullest and amplest protection—a protection which shall extend not only to preventing the Confederate *armies* from retaining any hold upon the State, but to crushing out the marauding bushwhackers, who have cursed Missouri. The loyal citizens, those who have voted under the Amnesty Proclamation, should be guarded in the exercise of all their rights. Western Arkansas could now be cleared of bushwhackers, if a vigorous policy were pursued. Not only that, but the people could go to work, with comparative safety, on their farms. *Unless this section be cultivated* it will be *almost impossible for either army or citizen to remain here next Winter and Spring.* To enable this to be done requires a considerable force of cavalry, as well as infantry for post duty. There are hundreds of miles of telegraph and mail routes to keep open as well. One regiment of infantry, and barely one of cavalry, with four guns, are all that is left to hold, occupy, and preserve order in this region and north of the river.

We have late intelligence from PRICE's headquarters, Washington, Hempstead County, about one hundred miles south. A party of ladies arrived here under flag of truce going North. They brought with them copies of the Washington (Ark.) *Telegraph*, of

The Charleston Mercury.

VINDICE NULLO
SPONTE SUA SINE LEGE FIDES RECTUMQUE COLLENTUR

VOLUME LXXXIV. | CHARLESTON, S. C., SATURDAY, MAY 21, 1864. | NUMBER 12,067

THE MERCURY.

SATURDAY, MAY 21, 1864.

Reasons for Yankee Lying.

It is important to General GRANT that disgrace from failure should be avoided as long as possible, and that he should get the benefits of time, even though brief, in order to redeem his affairs by all practicable efforts. It is important to the tottering finances of the Yankee Government at Washington to conceal, as long as possible, the failure to crush LEE's army and take the Confederate Capital. It is important to the credit of the Yankee nation abroad that such a failure should not be known. It is important to the interests of many of the financial bulls in Wall street. It is important to the tone and spirit of the army operating against Gen. JOHNSTON in Upper Georgia.

To lie accords with the habit and principles of the Yankee Government, and it has had great success in the practical effect hitherto produced—at least in Europe.

General Johnston's Strategy.

We have experienced, (says the Atlanta *Confederacy*,) in more than three years of defensive warfare against the United States, that whenever an invading campaign of the Yankees is programmed, it is usually correctly foreshadowed through the leaders or the army correspondence of more than one of the Northern newspapers. The last illustration has been afforded in SHERMAN's advance upon Dalton. Weeks before that exciting event was put into execution, an intimation slipped into the Yankee newspapers, and thence through the lines, announcing that all was in readiness, and the advance would soon commence, in three colums, *via* Lafayette and Cleveland, on the wings, with an advance upon the centre in front of Dalton.

The last information of the movements of the enemy in front, estimates the Federal force at upwards of one hundred thousand, advancing in separate columns, one by the Lafayette road, aiming to strike the line of railroad at Resaca, and the other from Cleveland by Spring Place and the old Federal road to East Tennessee, to strike the railroad at Cassville.

With this view of the situation the manœuvres in our front are no longer inexplicable or mysterious to military *savants* in the rear, nor to those even unlearned in the science of strategy and high tactics.

The plan was evidently to advance upon JOHNSTON in three columns, converging towards the rear of Dalton. The orders were issued and the heavy machinery was put in motion. SHERMAN with the centre column tries Rocky Face Ridge, and feels and avoids it, and goes through the gap nearest Resaca and the railroad. He might, it is true, have been checked at this gap, but would have accomplished the end anyway, by flanking farther to the left.

Gen. JOHNSTON was, of course, fully advised of all these movements of the enemy. That his course was most judicious, under the circumstances, in anticipating SHERMAN, and thwarting the design to entrap him, is admitted, while all will agree that the entire retrograde movement was admirably conceived and skillfully carried out, with but little risk or loss, and with disastrous effect upon the Yankees. The Federal commander, no doubt fully advised of JOHNSTON's strength, concludes that he must give fight at Dalton, and is unprepared for a retrograde movement on the part of his sagacious adversary, which disconcerts his whole plan and throws all his movements into confusion. The leaders of the separate columns are too far apart for immediate consultation before the design is detected, and JOHNSTON master of the situation.

Thus the situation appears to the uninitiated, and the impression is general now that JOHNSTON will hurl his forces upon the enemy at some point between his present line of battle and the Etowah River, upon the result of which, with our knowledge of that army and its great commander, we are willing to stake our hopes.

HOW SLAVES ARE ENLISTED IN MARYLAND.—The correspondent of the Philadelphia *Press* writes to that paper, from Washington, May 2d:

Colonel S. M. Bowman came here to-day, a shadow of his former self, worn nearly to death in the vast labor of enlisting every male slave in Maryland of fighting age and qualifications. He has cleaned "My Maryland" out, and knocked Bishop Hopkins' divine institution into limbo. He raised in forty days two full regiments of as fine black troops as can be found on the earth. He left no slaves fit for military duty in Maryland. He overran with his squads every county; they visited almost every farm. The boats ran up every stream, until masters were obliged to hide their slaves in the woods, conceal them in boats, and confine them in jails and houses. He opened the jails even. He has not drawn one dollar from the treasury, and his three thousand black troops have not cost the government five per cent. of what the same number of white troops cost. But in doing this work he laid aside all style, all form and ceremony, and went into negro churches nights, Sundays, whenever he could get an audience, and always addressed them on this, the great day of their salvation. Bowman is a Western jury lawyer, and he pleads this case with the negroes of Maryland almost individually. His hours of labor were from 8, a. m., to 11, p. m. He personally inspected every recruit, and mustered the whole in squads and singly administered the oath, and always spoke to them noble words about their duties.

THE WAR IN THE FAR WEST.

BATTLES OF MANSFIELD AND PLEASANT HILL.

[*From the Houston Telegraph, April 22.*]

MANSFIELD, LA., April 15

Little did I think when I bade you farewell in Texas that I should so soon have to record two of the most bloody battles which have been fought during this eventful war.

The battle of Mansfield was fought two and a half miles from the little city of the same name. The battle had been preceded by some heavy skirmishing, but the general battle commenced on the 8th of April, about 10 a. m., General Taylor in command. Major General Green commanded the left wing, Brigadier General Mouton the right, General Walker's division on the right of Mouton, and two cavalry regiments on the extreme right of Walker. General Green commenced the attack with a portion of his dismounted cavalry. The enemy pressing the left wing heavily, General Green then ordered Mouton's division to advance, and the fighting was terrible along the lines of both combatants. The battle raged fiercely for five hours, when the enemy broke and fled, having been forced back two miles, where commenced a general route.

Gen. Churchill's division did not arrive in time to participate in this action, but were in the battle of the following day. Gen. Mouton fell early in the action, while receiving the surrender of a large body of the enemy. He fell but a few feet from the muzzles of their guns. He is reported to have acted gallantly, and his noble division lost heavily in both officers and men, and covered themselves with glory. Col. Phil. Herbert was here wounded, and Col. Buchel mortally—since dead. It was here, too, that the lamented Chancey B Sheppard, of Gen. Green's staff fell, and the gallant Major J. D. Sayres wounded.

The fruits of the victory consisted in capturing 2500 prisoners, 200 wagons loaded with stores, 1400 mules, 30 ambulances, with immense medical and other stores. In this battle the enemy fought three army corps, viz: the 13th, 19th and famous 16th, formerly commanded by Gen. Sherman, and which had so often boasted that it had never known defeat. The loss of the enemy in the two engagements will not be less than 6000 killed, wounded and prisoners.

The enemy commenced their retreat as soon as routed, in the direction of Pleasant Hill, some eighteen miles from the battle field of Mansfield.

Our army having pursued, the line of battle was formed about 4 p. m. of the 9th of April, and the contest was more bloody than on the preceding day. General Green's Division, under his command, was posted on the extreme left; Mouton's Division, under command of Brigadier General Polignac, on Green's right; General Walker, on Polignac's right; General Churchill's Division of Arkansians and Missourians, having arrived, on the extreme right; the Valverde Battery opening the battle and losing the majority of their horses, but few men injured; General Churchill, with his division of infantry, then moved forward, and the battle commenced furiously along the whole line. The enemy pressing Churchill in overwhelming numbers, he was compelled to fall back. Generals Walker and Polignac then moved forward and broke the entire line of the enemy, and threw them into a general rout, and night put a stop to the carnage. They fell back to Rambiere Bayou, some twenty miles, Green's cavalry in hot pursuit, who followed them to the river. General Walker was slightly wounded. So was General Scurry.—(General Polignac was not wounded, as first reported.)

Gen. Waul was in command of a brigade, and every man, both officers and privates, acted like heroes. Col. Debray (since promoted to Brigadier General) is reported to have behaved very gallantly. He had his horse killed under him. Our loss was very heavy. General Scurry took 1200 men in the fight, and lost 400, killed and wounded. Our loss in the two battles is estimated to be 1400, killed and wounded, and about 150 prisoners.

We captured in the two battles 32 pieces of artillery, and small arms beyond computation, and about 4000 prisoners—many officers among them. These are the greatest battles fought west of the Mississippi, and, of all the battles, the most fruitful. The invasion of Texas is no longer to be thought of, and probably the complete evacuation of Western Louisiana by the enemy, besides relieving the pressure on Arkansas, which General Price may be enabled to regain. I should here state that General Taylor fought these battles contrary to the opinion of others, and he has eclipsed the fame of his father, old "Rough and Ready."

This is a sad night in camp. A few rods from where I am writing lies the corpse of Maj Gen. Thos. Green, the Napoleon of the West. Many a heart in Texas will mourn the loss of our hero. Just promoted, having never known defeat when he commanded, enjoying the confidence of his troops to a degree unsurpassed, and very rarely equaled, with a constitution of iron and a will like adamant, Gen. Green leaves a void in the armies of the Confederacy which will remain unfilled, and future generations of Texas will tell of the heroic deeds of the man who first led our cow boys to board and capture vessels of war.

Maj. Gen. Green was killed instantly, about 5 o'clock on the evening of the 12th instant, at Blair's Landing, on Red River, about 35 miles from this place, while directing an attack with 1000 men on five gunboats and five transports, the latter loaded with troops, the former ironclads. He was standing near the edge of the bank, which, at that place, is about 30 feet high. While encouraging his men under a terrific fire from the gunboats, he was struck over the right eye by a charge of grape shot—the whole top of his head was carried away, and death of course instantaneous. His body was brought to the camp the next day, and will be sent to Texas by Major J. H Beck, Quartermaster of the cavalry corps.

The tent is lighted up and guarded by a detachment of Texas cavalry. The sensation caused by his death it is impossible to describe. Generals Polignac, Waul and Scurry shed burning tears when they heard of it. Every one seemed to have lost a near and dear relative and friend. General Taylor was overwhelmed with grief, for Green had always been his true and staunch friend. I am told that he said when his officers remonstrated against his going into the fight himself, that he wouldn't if he had his old brigade, but some of the troops were new and he must go. The troops engaged were Wood's and Gould's regiments, and Parson's brigade. We lost 75 men killed and wounded. The slaughter of the enemy on board the transports was fearful, as our men were only thirty or forty yards from them, and one of the gunboats was completely silenced and about to surrender, when three others came to her assistance; none were captured.

Had General Green lived no one doubts but what he would have captured all the transports. The engagement lasted about half an hour after the General fell, when the officer who took command withdrew the troops. Such is the statement of officers who were there.

NEAR GRAND ECORE, April 17.

It would be contraband for me to state the force of the army of Louisiana; and I have seen large armies before, but this surpasses all I have yet seen. Skirmishing is going on daily, and a few prisoners brought in. They all admit that they were badly whipped the other day, and say the "Texas fellers" fought like tigers. A number of their officers told me that they had never seen such bravery as displayed by the Texans; the 16th Army Corps had never before met such a number of Texans, and they all say they now believe the stories they have so often heard of the Texans' fighting qualities. The prisoners all lay the defeat on Gen. Banks—say he is no General, &c. We fought the flower of the United States army, and I must say that the Western men acted bravely, but they could not stand the Texas yell and fearful charge. The loss of the enemy in officers is very large—many being among the wounded. I visited the battle fields of Mansfield and Pleasant Hill a few days ago.

The field of Mansfield was a plantation, skirted with woods and composed of small hills and valleys. It contains some 300 or 400 acres of land, but much of the hardest fighting took place in the timber where the enemy were. The fences had been level[illegible] the enemy upon hearing of General Taylor's [illegible], expecting to take us by surprise and slaughter our troops on the open plain. The annals of history do not record a harder contested field. Thousands of dead horses are strewn over the field, and the stench is horrible. I was forced to run my pony at the height of his speed over many portions. The majority of our troops who fell were buried in the city cemetery, while those of the enemy [illegible] buried upon the field. They were buried in trenches side by side as decently as possible.

When our cavalry pursued, after their rout, hundreds were cut down, and all along the road to Pleasant Hill, 20 miles, is strewn with the carcasses of dead horses and occasionally a new made grave is seen by the road side. The battle field of Pleasant Hill extends for the distance of a mile from the town. The enemy had made a stand on the top of a high hill, one mile from the town. Planting their batteries, they awaited the approach of our pursuing forces. As soon as their scouts gave warning that our cavalry were in range, they opened a brisk fire in every direction. Our batteries having got into position, the old Valverde opened and soon silenced their main battery, killing nearly all their horses, while De Bray at the head of his regiment, charged up the hill, followed by Buchell—the enemy turning and retreated. The Arkansians and Missourians, under Gen. Churchill, the Louisianians under Polignac and the cavalry of Green, threw them into a complete rout.

The enemy's line of battle extended several regiments deep along the whole line of battle, and when our batteries opened, the slaughter was horrible. The battle was fought on ground much like that of Mansfield, but they had many advantages; ditches had been cut by the owner of the plantation for the purpose of drainage, and the enemy used them as rifle pits; but they were soon driven from them by the desperate assaults of the infantry. The last of the series of those hills and ditches extended up to and was part of the town. But few horses, comparatively, were killed here, but the slaughter of the enemy was fearful. The dead are buried together in scores, and it was an awful sight to view the scene. I could trace with my eyes the spots where the most desperate carnage had taken place.

The road, after leaving Mansfield to this place, is strewn with dead horses which fell by the pursuit of our cavalry. Many of the stately residences along the route are blackened ruins, the fences destroyed by fire, and a scene of desolation and devastation is seen on every side. I wondered what the object was for an army and people who professed to belong to a Christian nation, to thus devastate the land they profess to come to save—oh shame! where is thy blush? I had formerly believed that many of the stories of the burning of dwellings, robberies of churches, &c., were exaggerated, but after seeing these things with my own eyes I am now satisfied they are true. A Catholic Church in the Spanish settlement near Double Bayou bridge was sacked, and the church ornaments carried away, even the window curtains were taken. This cannot be denied.

In the knapsack of one of the 10th army corps was found the jewelry of a young lady. Ear rings, breast pins, and even her underclothing was there. I will do the enemy the justice to say that the orders of their Generals severely punish outrages of this kind, but many of the inferior officers encourage their men to do these acts, and even share with them in the spoils.—These incidents are no bombast or misrepresentation. I can vouch for their truth.

The New-York Times.

VOL. XIII—NO. 3938. NEW-YORK, SUNDAY, MAY 8, 1864. PRICE FOUR CENTS.

THE BATTLE.

IMPORTANT NEWS FROM VIRGINIA.

A Great Battle Begun on Thursday.

Lee Confronts Grant with His Whole Army.

Severe Engagement Between Hancock and Longstreet.

HEAVY LOSS ON BOTH SIDES.

The Fifth Corps also Partly Engaged.

The Battle Renewed on Friday Morning.

Gen. Burnside's Corps on the Ground for Support.

STUART'S CAVALRY ROUTED BY SHERIDAN

The Troops Enthusiastic to a High Degree.

HIGHLY IMPORTANT FROM BUTLER'S ARMY

Very Successful Landing at City Point.

THE REBELS COMPLETELY SURPRISED.

Cavalry Expedition to Destroy the Richmond and Petersburgh Railroad.

Full Particulars from Our Special Correspondent.

WASHINGTON, Saturday, May 7.

The statements which were received here to-day, and which are entitled to belief, are that Gen. Lee made a tremendous and violent attack to pierce our centre, hoping thereby to divide our forces and to secure a victory; but Gen. Hitchcock's corps came to the relief, and, amid a murderous fire, formed in line of battle, and thwarted the designs of the rebels. The loss was heavy on both sides.

Gen. Sheridan was profitably engaged in another part of the field, and sent the Chief in command a message that he had routed Stuart's cavalry.

The attack of Lee was on our advancing columns, who doubtless anticipated a victory by his onslaught, before the main body could advance to the field of battle.

The appearances on Thursday were that the hostilities would be renewed on Friday.

A Battle Begun on Thursday—Grant Confronted by Lee's Whole Force—Severe Engagements Between Portions of Each Army—Hancock Engages Longstreet—The Battle-Ground near Chancellorsville.

From the Tribune.

UNION MILLS, Va., Friday, May 6—9 P. M.

The grand Army of the Potomac crossed the Rapidan on Wednesday. The Second Corps moved on Tuesday to the Mills, opposite Ely's Ford. On Wednesday morning, at 4 o'clock, the cavalry crossed and drove the rebel pickets from the opposite heights, meeting with no opposition.

A position was gained and the corps moved on at 7 o'clock, taking the road to Chancellorsville, at which place Gen. Hancock would establish his headquarters.

The Fifth and Sixth Corps crossed at Germanna Ford in the course of the day, taking the road to the Wilderness.

On Wednesday night Gen. Warren's headquarters were at the Wilderness, Gen. Sedgwick on his right, and the general headquarters at Germanna Ford.

On Thursday morning the rebels pressed our pickets, and appeared to be in strong force on our right. The Fifth New-York Cavalry, skirmishing on the Orange Court-house road, near Perkins' tavern, were driven in with a severe loss, leaving many wounded on the field. Gen. Griffin's division was marched forward on our right about 11 o'clock to feel the enemy's position, and were met by the rebel Gen. A. P. Hill, supported by Gen. Ewell.

A severe action took place, in which we captured about 300 prisoners, though it is reported that we lost two guns. Meantime, Gen. Hancock marched his corps to the right to connect with Warren, and had hardly got into position, his left resting on or near Chancellorsville, when he was attacked by Longstreet with his full corps, and a part of Ewell's.

Gen. Hancock, with the assistance of Getty's division of the Sixth Corps, held his position under musketed fire of two and a half hours duration, in which his command suffered severely, inflicting much injury upon the rebels.

Other developments showed Lee to have his whole force in our front.

This knowledge of their position was, of course, highly important, and was thus obtained only by the greatest skill in the handling of our troops. It not being the purpose of Gen. Meade to advance upon the enemy, he ordered the line of battle to be held till morning.

The position of our troops on Thursday night was parallel with and a little in advance of the road from Germanna Ford to Chancellorsville, the two flanks resting on those points, and general headquarters at the Wilderness.

Meanwhile, in the afternoon the advance of the 9th Corps crossed Germanna Ford, taking position on our right flank.

Gen. Burnside's rear arrived this forenoon.

It was understood that a general attack was to be made this morning, and heavy firing had commenced on our right when I had left, at 5 o'clock.

Heavy cannonading was heard when I passed Kelly's Ford, about 9 o'clock this forenoon, which leads me to believe that we had driven them to their defences, as no heavy guns could be brought into action on the former position.

There ought to be no doubt that there has been a grand victory, as Gen. Meade showed his strength yesterday by a stubborn and gallant defence without using half the command that he has undoubtedly brought into the action to-day. The troops are in a high state of enthusiasm.

Reports from Washington—Doubtful Rumors—A Three Days' Battle Reported.

WASHINGTON, Saturday, May 7.

The *Republican* has the following:

"The Government has information this morning, whether from official sources or other we are unable to learn positively at the moment of going to press, that on Wednesday at daylight Gen. Grant's whole army was entirely across the Rapidan. It marched to a plain a little beyond, and near the Chancellorsville battle-ground, when Lee was forced out of his works and offered battle, which was at once accepted. The fight became fierce, and lasted until dark, the enemy being forced back some distance, with great loss, leaving most of his killed and wounded in our hands.

The two armies lay on their arms all night Wednesday, and at daylight on Thursday the battle opened again, and raged with the greatest fury on both sides until dark, when it was found that the enemy had been forced back in the two days' fight about two miles and a half, leaving heaps of dying, killed and wounded on the field to be buried and taken care of by our troops. We have heard various estimates made of the number slaughtered, but at this moment it is useless to speculate on the subject. Everyone knows that it must have been terrible, and will speak to the senses when the facts are known.

On *Friday* morning, at 5 o'clock, the forces were marshaling for another conflict, Gen. Grant moving on Lee's works.

Up to this time Gen. Burnside's corps, numbering 30,000 men, had taken no part in the battle, but at half-past five was marching into position to engage in the bloody contest of the third day's battle.

Of the result of this day's battle we have no report up to the moment of going to press. The battle commenced at 6 o'clock in the morning. Unless Lee received reinforcements equal to Burnside's corps, the battle of Friday must have proved terribly disastrous to him.

The fact that we have received no news of yesterday's fighting leads to the belief that Lee is endeavoring to get away to Richmond, and Grant is in pursuit.

It is evident that the rebel forces about Richmond cannot be spared to reinforce Lee, as they have discovered ere this that they have enough to attend to there, probably from two attacks upon the city by Gen. Butler's force.

[The above dispatch is so extravagant in its statements, and corresponds so poorly with other and more reliable advices, that it is doubtless entitled to very little credit.—ED. TIMES.]

From Washington—Intense Excitement in the City—All Sorts of Reports, Rumors, &c.

WASHINGTON, Saturday, May 7.

The city has been intensely excited all day with the news from the Army of the Potomac, the early publications serving to excite the public curiosity concerning the military movements.

The bulletin boards of the newspapers attracted throngs of readers. Inquiries were repeatedly made of all who were supposed to have items of intelligence, while extra newspapers continued to be cried by the newsboys, and purchased in abundance.

Rumors of defeat and brilliant victories prevailed to a limited extent, but both classes of reports required authenticity to gain general belief.

The thoughtful, however, came to the conclusion that a single encounter would not determine the contest, and a series of battles may have to be fought before there can be any decisive result.

It was telegraphed hence by the Independent Telegraph Line, but refused by the other lines, doubtless for prudential reasons, that a great victory was achieved by Gen. Grant on Wednesday and Thursday, he driving the rebels two and a half miles with immense loss, and that he was following up that victory on Friday morning by an assault on the rebel works.

The *Star*, in noticing a similar statement of an afternoon cotemporary, remarks:

"We should be very glad to be able to confirm this news, but have to say, after diligent inquiry, we are satisfied that the Government has received no such information, or any information of more decisive results than that furnished by the *Tribune* dispatch, elsewhere."

The fact that Gen. Meade was able to stand the brunt of the Confederate onset with a portion of his command is considered a hopeful indication, and we hope soon to be able to announce a decisive victory; but we shall not trifle with our readers by manufacturing bogus victories for an hour's sensation."

The above contradiction of the *Star* is believed to be based on reliable information.

During the day many inquiries were made of officers of the Government, but without the satisfaction naturally desirable on the part of those who have impatient desires for early and complete success, and who forget that the work must be necessarily stubborn, heavy and persistent on both sides, owing to the great importance to each of the result.

The fragmentary information received from time to time shows nothing decisive, but serves to contradict many rumors and speculations concerning the whereabouts and designs of the rebels which were so confidently asserted.

Further from Washington—No Later News Received by the Government up to 5 o'clock Last Evening.

WASHINGTON, Saturday, May 7.

Up to 5 o'clock this afternoon the Government had received no information of more decisive results than was furnished by dispatches published this morning. Therefore, the reports of a great victory achieved by Gen. Grant on Wednesday and Thursday, and the pursuing of the enemy on Friday, etc., are, to say the least, not reliable.

WASHINGTON, Sunday, May 8—1 o'clock A.M.

It is said to-night that Gen. Hays was killed in the fight on Thursday, and that several other generals were wounded.

Reported Casualties—Death of Brig.-Gen. Alexander Hays—Brig.-Gen. J. J. Bartlett and Col. Gurney Wounded.

PHILADELPHIA, Saturday, May 7.

A special dispatch to the *Evening Telegraph*, from Washington, says:

Gen. Alexander Hays was killed on Thursday, while deploying his troops as skirmishers.

Gen. Bartlett and Col. Gurney were severely wounded.

Gen. Hays was a native of Pittsburgh.

The Forward Movement.

From the Washington Star, of Friday Evening.

We have information that up to 7 P. M. of Wednesday evening last no firing was heard in the direction taken by our Army of the Potomac the night before, and we have reason to believe that it was definitely known to Gen. Grant that Lee had left his former positions before our advance took place. That up to this hour it is not known here by telegraph from Fortress Monroe, that Lee has attacked or confronted Maj.-Gen. "Baldy" Smith's force, strikes us as embracing substantial proof that Grant's pursuit commenced very shortly after Lee's movement—so soon after, as that, if he did move against our troops on the Peninsula, he could hardly open upon them before Grant can attack his rear. But every succeeding hour of the absence of intelligence of a battle in that quarter strengthens the probability that Lee's movement was simply a retreat to get behind the Richmond fortifications; as by this time Grant, if not seriously opposed, could have marched to within thirty or forty miles, at most, of the rebel capital, or to within supporting distance of where Gen. Smith's army must be by this time, unless its advance has been delayed by the appearance of Lee in his front; in which case, Grant's route to his support would be shorter than if his advance had been unopposed. Twenty-four hours at most must, however, solve all the so interesting questions as to what has happened in that quarter up to this time.

We have no fear of the success of any possible effort of Lee to attack and defeat Gen. Smith's force before it can be amply sustained by the main army under Grant, as we know many facts going to show that among Gen. Grant's purposes is surely that of guarding against any disaster to Smith's army that might otherwise result from Lee's movement.

THE COMBINED MOVEMENTS IN VIRGINIA.

Map Showing the Lines of Operation on the Rapidan, the North Anna and the James Rivers, where Grant and Butler, Lee and Beauregard are Manœuvering; and their Relations to Richmond.

GEN. BUTLER'S COLUMN.

Movements on the James River—A Complete Surprise—Our Forces Landed and Pushing Forward.

FORTRESS MONROE, Friday, May 6, via BALTIMORE, Saturday, May 7.

On Tuesday night, the 3d inst., about one-half of the large fleet of transports that have been lying in the Roads for some time were ordered to Yorktown, and commenced embarking troops on Wednesday.

The rest of the fleet went up and took the remainder of the troops on board and came back here.

The whole fleet then proceeded up the James River, passing here last night.

The movement was conducted with the greatest secrecy and with all possible quietness.

The fleet advanced up the James River, preceded by the army gunboats, under the command of Gen. Graham.

During to-day and last night a very successful landing has been effected, and no resistance had been met with up to 4 o'clock this morning, at which time the steamboat *Thomas Powell* left with dispatches in charge of Capt. Pfeiffer.

No casualty had occurred beyond the killing of a colored soldier and the injury of two others by being caught between two boats.

Our movements were evidently a complete surprise.

At last advices, our forces were being rapidly landed and pushed forward.

We have landed at Wilson's wharf, Fort Powhatan, Landen, Bermuda Hundred, above the Appomattox River, etc.

Our monitors and gunboats are all over the bar at Harrison's Landing and above City Point.

The operations of the fleet have been characterized by great energy and success.

OUR SPECIAL CORRESPONDENCE.

The Expedition up the James—The Start from Fortress Monroe—The Occupation of Fort Powhatan and Wilson's Wharf—The Successful Landing at City Point—Surprise of the Enemy—Important Cavalry Expedition from Suffolk.

STEAMER GRAYHOUND, OFF FORT POWHATAN, JAMES RIVER, Va., Thursday, May 5, 1864.

The movement of the Union army in this direction, which, for weeks past, has been vaguely expected, commenced this morning. The obligation to keep silence respecting the hostile preparations, which, for prudential reasons was imposed, is now removed; and here, under the shadow of the commanding fortification, erected by the rebels in 1862 for the purpose of interrupting McClellan's water communications after his reverses before the rebel Capital, known as Fort Powhatan, I commence the record of the campaign. Premising that up to this point every circumstance has been auspicious, and that not the slightest symptom of resistance on the part of the enemy to our advance in the direction of Richmond has been encountered, either from guerrillas, torpedoes or any other source, I shall go back a few weeks, and briefly trace from its conception the enterprise which, to the present point, in all its details, has been a wonderful success.

THE PLAN.

To Major-Gen. Butler, I am told, is exclusively due whatever credit shall result from the inception and execution of the plan. When, four weeks since, Lieut.-Gen. Grant, the actual commander of the armies of the United States, visited Fortress Monroe, it was for the purpose of ascertaining the views of Gen. Butler respecting an advance upon the rebels by way of the Peninsula, to be carried out in cooperation with the Grand Army of the Potomac. Gen. Grant had considered the various plans proposed with this object in view, but had committed himself to none, and was inclined, therefore, to listen attentively to what Gen. Butler might suggest. The sequel proves that the proposition of Gen. Butler fully commended itself to the judgment and acquiescence of the Commanding General, and measures were at once taken to put it in execution.

Briefly, the project was to advance upon Richmond by the James River; get a foothold as near the city as possible, on the south bank of the stream; seriously interrupt the communications of the rebel Capital southward, and eventually compel the evacuation by Lee's army of their strongly-fortified position on the Rapidan, thus forcing the rebels to give Grant battle, or press rapidly rearward to the walls of their Capital. This plan will be generally admitted to be both bold and comprehensive, while the arrangement of its preliminaries has been marked by the rarest shrewdness and military sagacity.

THE ORGANIZATION.

The first step toward organization was made some weeks since, by the concentration at Yorktown, from the various posts in the Department of North Carolina and Virginia, the great bulk of the Eighteenth Army Corps. To the command of these troops was assigned Maj.-Gen. W. F. Smith, whose glorious career under Grant at Lookout Mountain and Mission Ridge has won for him the confidence of the army and the gratitude of the country. In addition to these war-worn heroes from the coast of North Carolina and the posts in Virginia, nearly all the brave and gallant fellows of the Tenth Army Corps, (under Maj.-Gen. Gillmore,) fresh from the bloody field of Olustee and the more remote and scarce less bloody sands of Morris' Island, were sent to Gen. Butler to participate in the movement, forming their encampment at Gloucester Point, opposite Yorktown.

That Yorktown and Gloucester Point, both at the mouth of the York River, should have been selected for the rendezvous of these troops, naturally led to the supposition that the advance was intended to be made up the Peninsula by the route which proved so fearfully disastrous to McClellan. But this show of force was merely a stupendous *ruse de guerre*, and circumstances indicate that it succeeded admirably in deceiving the rebels. Their journals have constantly spoken of these troops as destined to follow the path of 1862, and that the assurance of their deception might be made doubly sure, a brigade of Union troops was dispatched by Gen. Butler even as late as yesterday to West House Landing, where, at sunset, when we last heard from them, they were sedulously engaged in felling timber and constructing a wharf, as if preparing to facilitate the landing of a large army. To aid in this scheme of mystification, all the light-draft steamers were kept until the last moment at Fortress Monroe, whence, early yesterday morning, they were dispatched to the York River, and the work of embarking the troops, whose arrangements for the purpose had been already made, was begun promptly. Soon after the shades of evening closed over the camping-ground, the last tent was struck and the troops were all on board.

Gen. Butler's order to his subordinate Generals, made it incumbent for them to repair to Hampton Roads, as quickly as possible after dark, where they were to anchor for the night. At day-break the order commanded an advance of the troops up the James River, convoyed by three army gunboats, under Brig.-Gen Graham, and a naval force, consisting of five monitors and eleven gunboats, under Rear-Admiral Lee.

THE PLAN FOR THE CAVALRY.

The cavalry branch of the expedition is commanded by Brig.-Gen. A. V. Kautz, who has just received his stars, but who is pretty well known as the Colonel of an Ohio cavalry regiment, that last year, after a wearying chase, stopped the rapacious career of the guerrilla General Morgan, by a handsome charge upon the immensely larger force of the marauder, as they attempted to cross the Ohio River into Kentucky. Kautz, with a fine body of several thousand white troopers, left Suffolk, Va., also at daylight yesterday morning. The point at which he aims primarily to strike is Hickford, a town on the Petersburgh, Richmond and Weldon Railroad. A ride of about eighty miles, by the Surrey and Sussex roads, allowing him time to pay his compliments to the people as he passes along, would bring him to Hickford to-morrow evening. The railroad bridge there, which is a strong one, about three hundred feet long, will be destroyed, if possible; and then the dashing horsemen will do other damage to the enemy's means of supply as far as they can find opportunity. Gen. Kautz has received a roving commission, and if not too hardly pressed by the rebels, he may penetrate as far South as Weldon, N. C., returning when it suits his convenience. We may not hear of him for a month, but meanwhile it is expected that he will make a good record.

Starting up the Peninsula from Williamsburgh, another cavalry force, somewhat smaller, command by Col. West, also set out at daybreak. Their object was to create a diversion in our favor by keeping the rebels excited and attack on guerrillas and the garrisons of the outposts. Col. West would try to cross the Chickahominy at Bottom's bridge and make his way to the main body on the James. Taking it for granted that the cavalry started at the proper time and are now having a good time and a glorious gallop, I must return to

THE ADVANCE OF THE MAIN FORCE.

As on every occasion when a large piece of machinery is put in operation, there is certain to be more or less friction of the parts, so this complex machine of a gallant and mighty army did not move smoothly according to the programme. The Eighteenth Corps (Gen. Smith's,) having the advance, was promptly up to time, down finding all the steamers used in its transportation steaming by Newport's News into the mouth of the James River. But the steamers of the Tenth (Gen. Gillmore's) Corps were still quietly at anchor off Fortress Monroe. Here was an unexpected source of detention. Gen. Butler had every reason to suppose that the sailing-orders were perfectly understood, and would be implicitly followed by his Corps Commanders. It was easy to perceive that he was both distressed and annoyed at the delay. He had hoped to reach his intended point of debarkation (City Point, fifteen miles below Richmond,) at three o'clock in the afternoon. This he expected to accomplish, even in case that the possession of two points on the way up the river, viz.: Wilson's Wharf and Fort Powhatan, should be contested by the enemy, as it was very likely would be done. There was nothing for it, then, but to learn the cause of this dilatoriness of the Tenth Corps, and to hasten the vessels forward. This was done.

The fleet new steamer *Grayhound*, the flagboat of the expedition, on board which Gen. Butler, with his staff, had come at midnight, went back from Newport's News to Fortress Monroe. Gen. Gillmore was sent for, and made satisfactory explanations, I believe, to Gen. Butler. This accomplished, off we started at 8 o'clock up the river.

The scene in the hazy light of the beautiful Spring morning was picturesque and animated. Crowded steamboats labored heavily through the still water, pontoon trains and lumbering canal barges, to be used in disembarking, were in tow of the swifter transports. The long low lines and wedge-like shapes of those naval nondescripts, the monitors, with their high cylindrical turrets amidships, gave variety to the scene. The swift *Grayhound* flits among the slow-moving craft and slackens her speed an instant as she comes abreast each vessel, allowing Gen. Butler from the hurricane-deck to order them to advance with all the celerity possible. "Give her all the steam you can, Captain," shouts the General, with upraised cap, and as the crowds of blue-coats recognize him they burst out vociferously in cheers. The scene, as we pass up the river, is charming in the extreme. The high wooded banks of the stream present us every variety of delicate foliage with which the Spring delights to clothe the earth in vernal beauty. Occasionally a house is visible over the bluffs, and a man appears, beyond doubt very much amazed at the sudden appearance of so large a fleet of invading Yankees. The trip up the river is unbroken by any sign of war.

Taking the advance, Gen. Butler's boat reaches Wilson's Wharf, a point about 35 miles below Richmond. Here a regiment of Gen. Wilde's negro brigade have effected a landing, and are busily engaged in making preparations to hold the place. From this point up the river to Fort Powhatan is a clear straight reach of seven miles, which it would never do to leave in command of the enemy, who could fortify the bluffs and play the mischief with our water communications. So Gen. Butler takes possession of both these strong positions. The stalwart Africans gaily run up the bluffs, and are soon at work swinging axes with a will, and the giant trees fall with a mournful crash under their sturdy strokes. Soon a wide space of woods on the high banks are cleared away, and rebels approaching from toward Richmond must come within the sweep of our batteries. Bye-the-bye, there can be nothing mentioned, I think, which better shows the perfect surprise of this movement to the rebels, than the fact that, according to their own admission, they have a strong force at Charles City Court-house, six miles inland from Wilson's Wharf, engaged in collecting negroes together for work on the Richmond fortifications. It is strange if this force was aware of our approach that they did not come up and give us a few shots from a field battery. But no welcome of this left-handed sort greeted us. It is quite likely that our negroes may repair *vi et armis* to the Charles City rendezous, and so reverse the kind of work their brethren have been assembled to perform on the strongholds of Richmond. The boat is just now leaving Powhatan, where a strong sable garrison has been landed, having little to do in the way of securing their position, but mount the ordnance in the works which the rebels two years ago so laboriously constructed.

The bell rings for the boat to move off for City Point. This place to us is of the first strategic importance, but the indications now are that we shall peacefully occupy it. I must, therefore, stop this hurried writing and go with the other passengers on deck to watch with anxiety the approach of our fleet to its proposed destination.

OCCUPATION OF CITY POINT.

There is a splendid chance for exultation here, and we are all devoutly thankful. City Point has become ours without a struggle. The Union forces are securely planted in a splendidly advantageous position within fifteen miles of the rebel capital. Our troops are landing as rapidly as possible. The negro soldiers, always in the advance, to-day are streaming up the steep bluffs like ants toward an ant-hill. It is now three o'clock, and before nightfall the greater part of this immense army will have disembarked. Our line will stretch across this narrow strip of land, the left resting upon the James River, and then passing over the little River Appomattox, the prolongation of the line will reach to the James again, holding that almost insular position called the township of Bermuda Hundred. Intrenched here, with both flanks of the army protected by gunboats, we can bid defiance to Lee's cohorts, if Grant's sharp pressing drive them down upon us. The position is considered admirable for seriously threatening Richmond. Lee's army is now between two fires, and should our cavalry raid seriously impair his communications south, starvation will be added to his other troubles. Before we left Fortress Monroe a dispatch from the War Department was received by Gen. Butler, announcing Grant's safe passage of the Rapidan. We suppose that Lee ere this has given him battle or has hastened to the Richmond defences. In either case he must be at this time in a peculiarly unpleasant position. His army certainly was never in such an ugly place before. We are very thankful and joyous here at the perfect ease with which the entire plan of this expedition has been carried out.

THE SCENE AT CITY POINT.

The *Grayhound* having been delayed quite a while at Fort Powhatan, some of the transports went by and arrived at City Point just before her. I forgot to mention that three army gunboats, under command of Brig.-Gen. Graham, led the advance the entire distance up the river, keeping a few miles ahead of the naval vessels. As we in the *Grayhound* came in view of the commanding bluffs of the Point, we

Continued on the Eighth page.

The New-York Times.

VOL. XIII—NO. 3939. NEW-YORK, MONDAY, MAY 9, 1864. PRICE THREE CENTS.

GLORIOUS NEWS

Defeat and Retreat of Lee's Army.

TWO DAYS BATTLE IN VIRGINIA

Lieut.-General Grant Against Gen. Lee.

The Struggle of Thursday and of Friday in the Wilderness.

IMMENSE REBEL LOSSES.

Lee Leaves His Killed and Wounded in Our Hands.

OUR LOSS TWELVE THOUSAND.

GEN. BUTLER'S OPERATIONS.

Capture of City Point and Reported Occupation of Petersburgh.

Railroad Communication Destroyed.

Gen. Sherman's Movements in Georgia.

ADVANCE TO TUNNELL HILL.

Retreat of Joe Johnston's Army Toward Atlanta.

DISPATCHES FROM THE WAR OFFICE.

FIRST DISPATCH.

Gen. Grant Successful—Lee Reported to be Retiring—Gen. Sherman Advancing—Tunnel Hill Occupied.

To Gen. John A. Dix, New-York:

WASHINGTON, Sunday, May 8—9 A. M.

We have no official reports from the front, but the Medical Director has notified the Surgeon-General that our wounded were being sent to Washington, and will number from six to eight thousand.

The Chief Quartermaster of the Army of the Potomac has made requisition for seven days' grain, and for railroad construction trains, and states the enemy is reported to be retiring.

This indicates Gen. GRANT's advance, and affords an inference of material success on our part.

The enemy's strength has always been most felt in his first blows, and their having failed, and our forces not only having maintained their ground, but preparing to advance, lead to the hope of full and complete success, for when either party fails, disorganization by straggling and desertion commences, and the enemy's loss in killed and wounded must weaken him more than we are weakened.

Nothing later than my last night's dispatch has been received from Gen. BUTLER.

A dispatch from Gen. SHERMAN, dated at 5 o'clock P. M. yesterday, states that Gen. THOMAS had occupied Tunnel Hill, where he expected a battle, and that the enemy had taken position at Buzzard Roost Pass, north of Dalton. Skirmishing had taken place, but no real fighting yet.

Nothing later from Gen. BANKS.

You may give such publicity to the information transmitted as you deem proper.

It is designed to give accurate official statements of what is known to the department in this great crisis, and to withhold nothing from the public.

EDWIN M. STANTON, Secretary of War.

SECOND DISPATCH.

No Fighting on Saturday—The Wounded at Rappahannock Station—Severe Fighting by Gen. Butler's Army—The Richmond and Petersburgh Railroad Destroyed.

WASHINGTON, Sunday, May 8—5 P. M.

Major-Gen. John A. Dix, New-York:

We are yet without any official dispatches from the Army of the Potomac, except those referred to this morning from the Medical Director and Chief Quartermaster, and nothing additional has been received by the department from any other source. It is believed that no fighting took place yesterday.

A part of the wounded arrived in ambulances this morning at Rappahannock Station, and are on the way in by railroad. The department will probably receive dispatches by that train, which will arrive to-night.

A dispatch from Gen. BUTLER, just received, and which left him yesterday, states that a demonstration had been made by his forces on the railroad between Petersburgh and Richmond, and had succeeded in destroying a portion of it, so as to break the connection; that there had been some severe fighting, but that he had succeeded. He heard from a rebel deserter that HUNTER was dangerously wounded, PICKETT also, and JONES and JENKINS were killed. Nothing has been heard from Gen. SHERMAN.

EDWIN M. STANTON, Secretary of War.

SPECIAL DISPATCHES TO THE N. Y. TIMES

FRIDAY'S BATTLE.

FIRST DISPATCH.

WASHINGTON, Sunday, May 8, 1864.

The latest news from the army received here is up to seven o'clock yesterday evening, at which time GRANT fully maintained his position. The fighting on Thursday and Friday was very severe, with skirmishing only on Saturday. LEE's first onset was made upon our left, but failing he then fell upon our centre and finally upon our right, where the hardest contest took place. Here the rebels charged upon our lines twice, but were repulsed each time with severe loss. HANCOCK's corps charged back twice, and at one time entered that portion of the enemy's entrenchments commanded by A. P. HILL, but were at length compelled to fall back. SEYMOUR's division of HANCOCK's corps was badly cut. Gens. WADSWORTH and BARTLETT were badly wounded, the former having been knocked off his horse by a spent minie ball. The rebels were reported retreating yesterday morning. The number of wounded is reported at about ten thousand; the killed at two thousand. The loss of the enemy exceeds this. He left his dead and disabled on the field, in our hands. The Ambulance Corps, with its admirable organization, is working up to its full capacity, carrying the wounded to Rappahannock Station. Sixteen trains of cars, dispatched from Alexandria to-day, will receive them. It is expected that they will return, with their bruised and mangled freight, about daylight. Several car-loads of ice were also sent down for the comfort of the wounded. The Sanitary and Christian Commissions are on the field, with a full force of assistants, and with plentiful supplies of everything necessary for the wounded. The Government has hospital accommodations here for thirty thousand, which will probably meet all demands.

SECOND DISPATCH.

WASHINGTON, Sunday, May 8—Midnight.

Your special correspondent, writing from headquarters at Wilderness Tavern, Friday evening, May 6, gives the following intelligence of the great battle on Friday:

The day has closed upon a terribly hard-fought field, and the Army of the Potomac has added another to its list of murderous conflicts. LEE's tactics, so energetically employed at Chancellorsville and Gettysburgh, of throwing his whole army first upon one wing and then upon another, have again been brought to bear, but I rejoice to say that the army of the Potomac has repulsed the tremendous onslaught of the enemy, and stands to-night solidly in the position it assumed this morning. The first attempt was made upon HANCOCK, upon the right, somewhat weakened in numbers by the battle of yesterday; but the iron old Second Corps nobly stood its ground; then the enemy hurled his battalions upon SEDGWICK, and once or twice gained a temporary advantage, but our veterans were nobly rallied, and the rebels repulsed with awful slaughter. About half-past four P. M., LEE made a feint attack upon the whole line, and then suddenly fell, with his whole force, upon SEDGWICK, driving him back temporarily, but the advantage was soon regained, and the rebels hurled back with great loss. Night had now come on, and it is believed at headquarters, at this hour, that LEE has withdrawn from our front. Although the nature of the ground has been of a terrible character, most of it being so thickly wooded as to render movements all but impossible, and to conceal entirely the operations of the enemy, yet he has been signally repulsed in all his attacks, and nothing but the nature of the battle-field has prevented it from being a crushing defeat. The loss on both sides has been very heavy, but at this hour of hasty writing, I cannot even give an estimate.

THURSDAY'S BATTLE.

FULL DETAILS.

WASHINGTON, Sunday, May 8.

The special correspondent of the Rochester *Democrat*, with the army, has arrived in Washington with the following account of operations up to Friday morning:

GEN. GRANT'S HEADQUARTERS, GERMANNA FORD, Wednesday, May 4—7 P. M.

The whole Army of the Potomac to-day effected the passage of the Rapidan. Gen. WILSON's cavalry division forded the river at Germanna Ford, and Gen. GREGG's division at Ely's Ford, eight miles below, at daybreak. The few mounted pickets of the enemy that were watching the two points, scampered off before them. Double pontoon bridges were at once thrown across the river, and the infantry that had marched to the Ford during the night commenced crossing over at about 8 A. M. Gen. HANCOCK's corps and the reserve artillery crossed at Ely's Ford, and Gen. WARREN's at Germanna. SEDGWICK's corps followed the latter. The passage of the river continued all day at both points. All the troops are over at this hour. The trains will cross during the night. Gen. HANCOCK is encamped on the Chancellorsville battle-ground. Gen. WARREN is at the old Wilderness Tavern, and Gen. SEDGWICK at the tavern and Germanna Ford. Both Gen. GRANT and Gen. MEADE's headquarters are at this point for the night.

Not a shot was fired during the crossing. Immediately after reaching the south bank, Gen. WILSON's and Gen. GREGG's cavalry pushed forward, the former to Parker's Store, the latter some distance beyond Chancellorsville. They discovered nothing of the enemy but weak parties of cavalry, developing the fact that there was no strong rebel force south of us. About a dozen prisoners were taken by our cavalry, among whom were several couriers. One of the latter carried a dispatch from Gen. RHODES to Gen. EWELL, informing him that the Yankees had crossed in force at Germanna and Ely's Fords. There is absolutely nothing known of the movements of the enemy at headquarters to-night. It is supposed, however, that LEE is concentrating, and that we will meet him in force to-morrow. Efforts will be made, at all events, to ascertain his whereabouts. The army will be pushed southwestwardly to the open country beyond the Wilderness, provided developments in regard to the enemy do not necessitate a change of this purpose. The movements to-day were made in fine order, and with creditable precision. There was hardly any straggling, notwithstanding the hard work during the night and day. The troops are full of spirit; the most auspicious weather favors the advance. Gen. BURNSIDE's command, consisting of four (4) divisions, commanded by Gens. POTTER, FERRERO, WILSON and CRITTENDEN, is expected to come up with the army to-morrow afternoon.

GEN. GRANT'S HEADQUARTERS, May 5—8 P. M.

As expected, last night, the army came up with the enemy to-day. A battle has been fought between parts of it and the whole rebel army, but, as at Gettysburgh, the bloody scenes of this day were only a prelude to the bloody work, and it is to be hoped more auspicious results, to-morrow. Reveille was sounded at 3 A. M., and the whole army was again in motion at daylight. According to the order of the day, Gen. HANCOCK's corps was to march upon Chancellorsville, southwestwardly on the Pamunkey road to Grove Church, Gen. WARREN's from Old Wilderness Tavern to Parker's Store, on the Orange Court-house plank road. SEDGWICK's corps was to follow behind WARREN's.

Gen. SHERIDAN was to concentrate the whole cavalry corps at Piney Branch Church, a few miles south of Chancellorsville, and start upon a general hunt after STEWART's cavalry, the main body of which was reported to be concentrating for a fight. The different bodies had been in motion but a short time, when, at about 6 o'clock, reports came in from both turnpike and plank-road running almost parallel from this vicinity to Orange Court-house, that the enemy were advancing with infantry and artillery toward us from near Old and New Verdiersville. The evidence accumulating in the course of the next two hours that strong rebel columns were moving upon us from the directions mentioned, Gens. GRANT and MEADE came up from Germanna Ford, and orders were issued to halt the various columns of infantry, concentrate and form them for battle at this point. Commanding ridges running from the northwest to the southeast across both roads over which the enemy were advancing, about half a mile to the west of this point, offered a fine position for the formation of a battle front, and was selected for this purpose. SEDGWICK was ordered to take the right, WARREN the centre, and HANCOCK was expected to come up on the left. WARREN and SEDGWICK got into line about 11 o'clock, and soon after skirmishing was heard on the front. About noon Gen. WARREN was ordered to push GRIFFIN's division forward to the right and left of the turnpike, and ascertain what the enemy were about. BARTLETT's brigade moved up the left, and AYRES' regulars to the right of the road—SWEITZER's following in reserve. After advancing about three-quarters of a mile, they suddenly found themselves confronted by a well-formed and strong rebel position on a thickly wooded ridge. A severe fight ensued. Our two brigades held their ground against evidently greater numbers for nearly an hour, but the enemy succeeded in overlapping AYRES' regular brigade, and forcing it back precipitately. The flank of BARTLETT's brigade being exposed, it was also soon forced back for some distance. Two pieces of the Third Massachusetts Battery had to be left behind in consequence of the killing of nearly all the horses, and fell into the hands of the enemy. SWEITZER's brigade, and WADWORTH's, of ROBINSON's division, were ordered forward, and relieved the two brigades. The enemy soon attacked these, but were held at bay. Brisk musketry and artillery firing were kept up for an hour longer, when the enemy drew off from that part of the line. Our loss in this affair was quite severe—AYRES' and BARTLETT's brigades principally suffering. No definite figures can now be given. But the total will probably not exceed six hundred in killed, wounded and missing.

Among the wounded are Gen. BARTLETT, slightly; Col. HAYES, Eighteenth Massachusetts, slightly; Col. GWYN, One Hundred and Tenth Pennsylvania; Col. GUINEY, Ninth Massachusetts; Col. LOMBARD, Fourth Michigan. We took about three hundred prisoners.

HANCOCK's corps had been ordered to turn off the road he had started out on, and march over a cross-road as rapidly as possible for this point, to complete the formation of the line of battle. About 3 o'clock in the afternoon, after the fight on the centre had closed, a movement by the enemy was discovered, evidently meant to throw a force between HANCOCK and the remainder of the army. GETTY's division of SEDGWICK's corps was ordered at once to stay this dangerous demonstration. HANCOCK's advance, MOTT's division, arrived just in time to form with GETTY's, to the left and right of the plank road leading directly from Chancellorsville to Orange Court-house. Gen. GRANT ordered them to attack the advancing enemy, in order to give the remaining divisions of HANCOCK's time to come up and form. They did so, and became at once hotly engaged in woods so thick that it was almost impossible to advance in line. BIRNEY's division of the Second Corps soon came up, and quickly formed on the right of GETTY. BURLOW's and GIBBONS' divisions formed a second line as they came up. The enemy in vast force pressed energetically and repeatedly upon the front, and a most furious musketry fight continued for nearly two hours. The heavy timber and dense undergrowth rendered the use of artillery impossible, and only a few rounds from heavy pieces were fired on either side, but as to violence, the musketry surpassed everything in the history of the Army of the Potomac. Our line steadily held its ground until the whole corps was forward, when nightfall prevented an advance on our part, and put an end to the fight. WADSWORTH's division and a brigade of ROBINSON's division, under command of Gen. ROBINSON, were ordered to take the enemy in front of HANCOCK by the right flank, but darkness also prevented the full execution of this fight. The loss on our left will probably reach one thousand, including Gen. ALEXANDER HAYS, killed; Cols. S. S. HICKS, CARRALL and TYLER among the wounded.

HANCOCK's men behaved most admirably. The Fifth New-York Cavalry, in advance on the road to Parker's Store, was attacked by superior force in the morning and driven back with considerable loss. Gen. SHERIDAN sent a message to Gen. MEADE in the evening, to the effect that he had met part of STUART's cavalry and was driving them in every direction. Gen. LEE made two attempts to cut our army in two, both on the right and left, by getting between the river and WARREN's and SEDGWICK's corps, with only part of BURNSIDE's across on the one side and between HANCOCK's corps and the remainder of the army on the other. That he was foiled in both purposes and that the army has been concentrated, notwithstanding his two well conceived attacks, constitutes a most substantial success for Gen. GRANT. Not quite one-half of the army was engaged to-day. To-night every corps is in proper position, BURNSIDE's being fully up and Gen. GRANT has at his command a force sufficient and will make a general attack upon the enemy at daylight. There was heavy firing on SEDGWICK's part of the line after dark, but it was of short duration. It is understood that it was brought about by an advance on our side to clear our front.

WASHINGTON REPORTS.

Speculations, Rumors, &c.—Everything Looking Bright—The Success of Butler and Sherman.

WASHINGTON, Sunday, May 8.

The *National Republican* has the following:

We are glad to be able to state that the result of the fighting on Thursday and Friday is all that the most sanguine friends of the Government can desire. The dawn of day on Saturday exhibited no evidence of the presence of the enemy. Gen. GRANT with great promptness took advantage of the fact and ordered a forward movement. It is proper to say here that in consequence of such movement nothing has been heard directly from Gen. GRANT. He has more important duties to perform. It is believed by those who have the best means of knowing, that LEE is hastening to the works of Richmond, not only to save the remnant of his own army, but to rescue, if possible, the rebel capital from falling into the hands of that dreaded chieftain, Gen. BUTLER. There is little doubt that LEE will have to make good time to prevent such a disaster to DAVIS' rebel dominions. There are many things known to the Government, all of a cheerful tendency, which it is not proper to state at this time. For instance, it would not be proper to state what we know about the operations on the Peninsula, up James River, &c.; but at the same time, in general terms, it is not improper for us to state that everything is progressing successfully. We are in possession of information that the rebel authorities at Richmond, seeing the fate which awaits the city, have taken measures to remove everything of value to them from the city. The ten thousand wounded men upon the field mentioned in our last extra to-day, some of which have at this writing probably reached Rappahannock Station, *includes the wounded on both sides*. The list of killed and wounded have not reached the city yet, and probably will not before to-morrow or next day, as the time of every one is employed in rendering relief to the unfortunates.

Further details are momentarily expected of the two days' battles, but it is doubtful if anything is received from Gen. GRANT until the retreat and pursuit terminate.

It is sufficient to say that all the dispatches from the advancing armies under SHERMAN, HOOKER, SCHOFIELD and WASHBURN are as encouraging as could be asked for.

SECOND REPORT.

WASHINGTON, Sunday, May 8.

The *Star*, in its extra this morning, says:

The only official information from the Army of the Potomac is derived from dispatches of the Medical Director and Chief Quartermaster to their respective Bureaus.

The wounded, numbering from 6,000 to 8,000, have been sent from the battle-field to Rappahannock Station, there to be forwarded to Washington. A portion of them have arrived at Rappahannock.

The Chief Quartermaster has made a requisition for grain for the animals. This imports an advance by Gen. GRANT.

Gen. INGALLS says: "We have fought two days. The enemy are said to be retiring."

There seems to be no doubt that although nothing decisive has yet occurred, the enemy has been foiled in his confident expectation of driving Gen. GRANT back before his operations could be fully developed, and that LEE has been compelled to give way. The tactics of the enemy have uniformly been to strike his heaviest blow at the outset, and to this their success has always been owing. This has now failed.

The casualties reported are Gen. HAYS killed, and Gens. GETTY and GREGG, and Col. HAYES and Gen. OWENS are reported wounded.

Gen. HANCOCK is reported to have received a slight wound, while rallying his men to resist A. P. HILL's onset.

Two of Gen. BURNSIDE's Staff are reported killed, while carrying dispatches.

There seems to be no doubt of the death of Gen. HAYS, of Pittsburgh, Penn. He held the position which bore the brunt of A. P. HILL's attack, and fell at the head of his command, just at the moment that support had been ordered forward to reach him.

THIRD REPORT.

WASHINGTON, Sunday, May 8—2 P. M.

Reports received from the front up to 11 o'clock on Saturday morning, say there had been two days' severe fighting on Thursday and Friday, and that it was believed that the enemy were retreating.

Our wounded were being sent to the rear, showing that we had lost no ground in the fighting.

It is believed that our forces were pressing forward.

Nothing further has been heard from Gen. BUTLER.

Reports from Chattanooga, dated at 5 o'clock yesterday (Saturday) afternoon, say that Gen. SHERMAN was then at Tunnel Hill, the enemy at Buzzard Roost Gap and our Gen. MCPHERSON was operating against the enemy's communications with Rome through Vilanan and Resaca.

The *Star* says: "Were we at liberty to mention facts within our knowledge, we think we could demonstrate that LEE has real occasion to dread the strategy of our military operations, as well as the vigor with which they are pressed. We believe that JEFF. DAVIS finds to-day, in reality, what has sometimes been talked about, that 'it thunders all round.' The line of attack by LEE, in the fighting of Thursday and Friday, nearly at right angles with GRANT's line of advance, and from the direction of Orange Court-house, indicates that LEE made the latter point his base and headquarters. The forced march of a day and night by BURNSIDE, from Manassas, by which he got his troops to GRANT's support on Thursday night, is said to have surpassed his brilliant forced marches in East Tennessee, by which he surprised the enemy there. Probably LEE has by this time had occasion to feel their presence with GRANT."

Gen. WEBB was killed in the battle of Friday.

Our loss was stated at 6,000 to 8,000 killed and wounded.

FOURTH REPORT.

WASHINGTON, Monday, May 9—2 A. M.

A dispatch received this evening by a distinguished member of the Cabinet, from Fortress Monroe, states that Gen. BUTLER has succeeded in destroying the railroad between Richmond and Petersburgh.

No wounded from the front had arrived here up to half-past one o'clock this morning.

The Government, up to ten o'clock to-night, had not received any particulars of Friday's engagement. This is the report of those who made special inquiry.

Three thousand of our wounded, whose injuries are slight, are to be cared for where they now are, while the others are to be brought to Washington.

It was feared in Alexandria, to-day, that some injury had been inflicted on the railroad by MOSBY's guerrillas.

The train is not yet in.

THE PENINSULAR MOVEMENT

Capture of Petersburgh—The City Burned by the Rebels—Gunboat Commodore Jones Blown up by a Torpedo—Handsome Achievements by Colored Cavalry.

FORTRESS MONROE, Friday, May 6—8 P. M.

Our troops, under Major-Gen. BUTLER, are in possession of Petersburgh, Va.

LATER.

NEW-YORK, Sunday, May 8—6 P. M.

By the arrival at this port of the steam transport *Western Metropolis*, Capt. MILTON, from Fortress Monroe, Capt. MILTON reports that, on leaving, he gained the following information:

"On the 6th inst. our forces, who had landed at City Point, moved on Petersburgh, when the enemy immediately set fire to the place and abandoned it.

On the morning of the same date, the United States gunboat *Commodore Jones*, while on picket duty in the James River, near Turkey Bend, was blown up by a torpedo, one of the cigar-shaped infernal machines, and several of her officers and men killed, and some forty wounded. The rebel who had charge of the torpedo was shot, and two of his companions made prisoners.

On the 5th inst. the First and Second regiments of Colored Cavalry, under Col. WEST, made a dash across the Chickahominy River, and two companies dismounted and charged into the camp of the Forty-sixth Virginia Cavalry, killing 30 men and capturing 35 horses. The horses were immediately mounted by our troops, who pursued the rebels to within ten miles of Richmond."

Official Dispatch from Gen. Butler to Gen. Grant.

OFF CITY POINT, Va., May 5, 1864.

Lieut.-Gen. Grant, Commanding Armies of the United States, Washington, D. C.:

We have seized Wilson's Wharf Landing. A brigade of WILD's colored troops are there. At Fort Powhatan Landing two regiments of the same brigade have landed. At City Point HINKS' Division, with the remaining troops and battery, have landed. The remainder of both the Eighteenth and Tenth Army Corps are being landed at Bermuda Hundreds, above the Appomattox.

No opposition experienced thus far. The movement was apparently a complete surprise. Both army corps left Yorktown during last night. The monitors are all over the bar at Harrison's Landing and above City Point. The operations of the fleet have been conducted to-day with energy and success. Gens. SMITH and GILLMORE are pushing the landing of the men. Gen. GRAHAM, with the army gunboats, led the advance during the night, capturing the signal station of the rebels.

Col. WEST, with eighteen hundred cavalry, made several demonstrations from Williamsburgh yesterday morning. Gen. KUNTZ left Suffolk this morning with his cavalry, for the service indicated during the conference with the Lieutenant-General.

The *New-York*, flag-of-truce boat, was found lying at the wharf, with four hundred prisoners, whom she had not time to deliver. She went up yesterday morning.

We are landing troops during the night—a hazardous service in the face of the enemy.

BENJ. F. BUTLER, Maj.-Gen. Comd'g.

A. F. PUFFER, Captain and A. D. C.

OUR SPECIAL CORRESPONDENCE.

The Expedition up the James—The Start from Fortress Monroe—The Occupation of Fort Powhatan and Wilson's Wharf—The Successful Landing at City Point—Surprise of the Enemy—Important Cavalry Expedition from Suffolk.

STEAMER GRAYHOUND, OFF FORT POWHATAN, JAMES RIVER, Va., Thursday, May 5, 1864.

The movement of the Union army in this direction, which, for weeks past, has been vaguely expected, commenced this morning. The obligation to keep silence respecting the hostile preparations, which, for prudential reasons was imposed, is now removed; and here, under the shadow of the commanding fortification, erected by the rebels in 1862 for the purpose of interrupting MCCLELLAN's water communications after his reverses before the rebel Capital, known as Fort Powhatan, I commence the record of the campaign. Premising that up to this point every circumstance has been auspicious, and that not the slightest symptom of resistance on the part of the enemy to our advance in the direction of Richmond has been encountered, either from guerrillas, torpedoes or any other source, I shall go back a few weeks, and briefly trace from its conception the enterprise which, to the present point, in all its details, has been a wonderful success.

THE PLAN.

To Major-Gen. BUTLER, I am told, is exclusively due whatever credit shall result from the inception and execution of the plan. When, four weeks since, Lieut.-Gen. GRANT, the actual commander of the armies of the United States, visited Fortress Monroe, it was for the purpose of ascertaining the views of Gen. BUTLER respecting an advance upon the rebels by way of the Peninsula, to be carried out in co-operation with the Grand Army of the Potomac. Gen. GRANT had considered the various plans proposed with this object in view, but had committed himself to none, and was inclined, therefore, to listen attentively to what Gen. BUTLER might suggest. The sequel proves that the proposition of Gen. BUTLER fully commended itself to the judgment and acquiescence of the Commanding General, and measures were at once taken to put it in execution.

Briefly, the project was to advance upon Richmond by the James River; get a foothold as near the city as possible, on the south bank of the stream; seriously interrupt the communications of the rebel Capital southward, and eventually compel the evacuation by LEE's army of their strongly-fortified position on the Rapidan, thus forcing the rebels to give GRANT battle, or press rapidly rearward to the walls of their Capital. This plan will be generally admitted to be both bold and comprehensive, while the arrangement of its preliminaries has been marked by the rarest shrewdness and military sagacity.

THE ORGANIZATION.

The first step toward organization was made some weeks since, by the concentration at Yorktown, from the various posts in the Department of North Carolina and Virginia, the great bulk of the Eighteenth Army Corps. To the command of these troops was assigned Maj.-Gen. W. F. SMITH, whose glorious career under GRANT at Lookout Mountain and Mission Ridge has won for him the confidence of the army and the gratitude of the country. In addition to these war-worn heroes from the coast of North Carolina and the posts in Virginia, nearly all the brave and gallant fellows of the Tenth Army Corps, (under Maj.-Gen. GILLMORE,) fresh from the bloody field of Olustee and the more remote and scarce less bloody sands of Morris's Island, were sent to Gen. BUTLER to participate in the movement, forming their encampment at Gloucester Point, opposite Yorktown.

That Yorktown and Gloucester Point, both at the mouth of the York River, should have been selected for the rendezvous of these troops, naturally led to the supposition that the advance was intended to be made up the Peninsula by the route which proved so fearfully disastrous to MCCLELLAN. But this show of force was merely a stupendous *ruse de guerre*, and circumstances indicate that it succeeded admirably in deceiving the rebels. Their journals have constantly spoken of these troops as destined to follow the path of 1862, and that the assurance of their deception might be made doubly sure, a brigade of Union troops was dispatched by Gen. BUTLER even as late as yesterday to White House Landing, where, at sunset, when we last heard from them, they were sedulously engaged in felling timber and constructing a wharf, as if preparing to facilitate the landing of a large army. To aid in this scheme of mystification, all the light-draft steamers were kept until the last moment at Fortress Monroe, whence, early yesterday morning, they were dispatched to the York River, and the work of embarking the troops, whose arrangements for the purpose had been already made, was begun promptly. Soon after the shades of evening closed over the camping-ground, the last tent was struck and the troops were all on board.

Gen. BUTLER's order to his subordinate Generals, made it incumbent for them to repair to Hampton Roads, as quickly as possible after dark, where they were to anchor for the night. At day-break the order commanded an advance of the troops up the James River, convoyed by three army gunboats, under Brig.-Gen GRAHAM, and a naval force, consisting of five monitors and eleven gunboats, under Rear-Admiral LEE.

THE PLAN FOR THE CAVALRY.

The cavalry branch of the expedition is commanded by Brig.-Gen. A. V. KAUTZ, who has just received his stars, but who is pretty well known as the Colonel of an Ohio cavalry regiment, that last year, after a wearying chase, stopped the audacious career of the guerrilla General MORGAN, by a handsome charge upon the immensely larger force of the marauder, as they attempted to cross the Ohio River into Kentucky. KAUTZ, with a fine body of several thousand white troopers, left Suffolk, Va., also at daylight yesterday morning. The point at which he aims primarily to strike is Hickford, a town on the Petersburgh, Richmond and Weldon Railroad. A ride of about eighty miles, by the Surrey and Sussex roads, allowing him time to pay his compliments to the people as he passes along, would bring him to Hickford to-morrow evening. The railroad bridge there, which is a strong one, about three hundred feet long, will be destroyed, if possible; and then the dashing horsemen will do other damage to the enemy's means of supply as far as they can find opportunity. Gen. KAUTZ has received a roving commission, and if not too hardly pressed by the rebels, he may penetrate as far South as Weldon, N. C., returning when it suits his convenience. We may not hear of him for a month, but meanwhile it is expected that he will make a good record.

Starting up the Peninsula from Williamsburgh, another cavalry force, somewhat smaller, command by Col. WEST, also set out at daybreak. Their object was to create a diversion in our favor by keeping the rebels excited and attacking guerrillas and the garrisons of the outposts. Col. WEST would try to cross the Chickahominy at Bottom's bridge and make his way to the main body on the James. Taking it for granted that the cavalry started at the proper time and are now having a good time and a glorious gallop, I must return to

THE ADVANCE OF THE MAIN FORCE.

As on every occasion when a large piece of machinery is put in operation, there is certain to be more or less friction of the parts, so this complex machine of a gallant and mighty army did not move smoothly according to the programme. The Eighteenth Corps (Gen. SMITH's,) having the advance, was promptly up to time, dawn finding all the steamers used in its transportation steaming by Newport's News into the mouth of the James River. But the steamers of the Tenth (Gen. GILLMORE's) Corps were still quietly at anchor off Fortress Monroe. Here was an unexpected source of detention. Gen. BUTLER had every reason to suppose that the sailing-orders were perfectly understood, and would be implicitly followed by his Corps Commanders. It was easy to perceive that he was both distressed and annoyed at the delay. He had hoped to reach his intended point of debarkation (City Point, fifteen miles below Richmond,) at three o'clock in the afternoon. This he expected to accomplish, even in case that the possession of two points on the way up the river, viz.: Wilson's Wharf and Fort Powhatan, should be contested by the enemy, as it was very likely would be done. There was nothing for it, then, but to learn the cause of this dilatoriness of the Tenth Corps, and to hasten the vessels forward. This was done.

The fleet new steamer *Grayhound*, the flagboat of the expedition, on board which Gen. BUTLER, with his staff, had come at midnight, went back from Newport's News to Fortress Monroe. Gen. GILLMORE was sent for, and made satisfactory explanations, I believe, to Gen. BUTLER. This accomplished, off we started at 8 o'clock up the river.

The scene in the hazy light of the beautiful Spring morning was picturesque and animated. Crowded steamboats labored heavily through the still water, pontoon trains and lumbering canal barges, to be used in disembarking, were in tow of the swifter transports. The long low lines and wedge-like shapes of those naval nondescript, the monitors, with their high cylindrical turrets amidships, gave variety to the scene. The swift *Grayhound* flits among the slow-moving craft and slackens her speed an instant as she comes abreast each vessel, allowing Gen. BUTLER from the hurricane-deck to order them to advance with all the celerity possible. "Give her all the steam you can, Captain," shouts the General, with upraised cap, and as the crowds of blue-coats recognize him they burst out vociferously in cheers. The scene, as we pass up the river, is charming in the extreme. The high wooded banks of the stream present us every variety of delicate foliage with which the Spring delights to clothe the earth in vernal beauty. Occasionally a house is visible over the bluffs, and a man appears, beyond doubt very much amazed at the sudden appearance of so large a fleet of invading Yankees. The trip up the river is unbroken by any sign of war.

Taking the advance, Gen. BUTLER's boat reaches Wilson's Wharf, a point about 35 miles below Richmond. Here a regiment of Gen. WILDE's negro brigade have effected a landing, and are busily engaged in making preparations to hold the place. From this point up the river to Fort Powhatan is a clear straight reach of seven miles, which it would never do to leave in command of the enemy, who could fortify the bluffs and play the mischief with our water communications. So Gen. BUTLER takes possession of both these strong positions. The stalwart Africans gaily run up the bluffs, and are soon at work swinging axes with a will, and the giant trees fall with a mournful crash under their sturdy strokes. Soon a wide space of woods on the high banks are cleared away, and rebels approaching from toward Richmond must come within the sweep of our batteries. Bye-the-bye, there can be nothing mentioned, I think, which better shows the perfect

Continued on the Eighth page.

The New-York Times.

VOL. XIII—NO. 3943. | NEW-YORK, FRIDAY, MAY 13, 1864. | PRICE THREE CENTS.

THE GREAT CAMPAIGN.

The Gigantic Struggle on the Rapidan and the Po.

Comprehensive and Authentic Account.

The Strategy, Fighting, Gains and Losses.

Full Details from Our Special Correspondent.

THE BATTLE OF THURSDAY, MAY 5.

TODD'S TAVERN, Va., Sunday, May 8, 1864.

The details of the wonderful three days' battle of the Wilderness, which closed last night just as the blood-red sun went down behind the margin of the Rapidan, will have given you some idea of the labyrinth of action through which its course ran, and the maze of tactics out of which it was evolved; but the battle of the Wilderness must remain, for the present, undescribed, for the reason that it is really indescribable. I remember a pregnant observation of Gen. ROSECRANS, that with us war is only "bushwhacking on a large scale." Now, if this is true of the kind of ground on which many of our battles have been fought, the analogy holds still more forcibly in the wild, tangled pine woods in whose thickets and along whose margins the prodigious Indian fight of Thursday, Friday and Saturday raged.

No man can claim that he saw this battle, and although undoubtedly it had a line and formation of its own, it would puzzle even the Commanding General to lay it down on the map. There is something horrible and yet fascinating in the mystery shrouding this strangest of battles ever fought—a battle which no man could see—and whose progress could only be followed by the ear. It is, beyond a doubt, the first time in the history of war, that two great armies have met, each with at least two hundred and fifty pieces of artillery, and yet placed in such circumstances as to make this vast enginery totally useless. Not a score of pieces were called into play in the whole affair, and I may mention it as a fact strikingly illustrative of this battle, that out of the three thousand wounded in the hospitals of HANCOCK's command alone, not one of the wounds is a *shell* wound. In like manner our cavalry has been totally useless, *as* cavalry. In all their engagements the men have been compelled to dismount and fight on foot, and the horse, except for locomotion, has been a hindrance rather than a help. In such circumstances, in the utter impossibility of manœuvering or effecting any grand combination, the difficulty of generalship is enormously increased. It will also be inferred, from the circumstances in which the battle of the Wilderness was fought, that it was quite impossible for it to be decisive in its results. The combat lasted three days, but it might have been prolonged a fortnight longer and still have left the issue undecided. Now that it is ended by the withdrawal of the enemy, though we are hardly justified in calling the result a *victory* in the positive sense of the word, yet, if it be considered that the enemy was signally foiled in the purpose with which he sought battle in the Wilderness, that he was compelled to fall back, discomfited, and that we are in vigorous pursuit, under circumstances that give us the shorter line of advance on Richmond, even the most cautious and skeptical will admit the gross and scope of the action to be a most substantial advantage to our arms.

When GRANT, on Wednesday night and Thursday morning, threw his army across the Rapidan at Germanna and Ely's Fords, and the labor of a twelvemonth brought to nought. The chief consideration that the enemy's fortified position was turned, prompted the flanking movement on the enemy's right rather than on his left, was, doubtless, that a successful movement by the former direction would uncover for us water communications by Aquia Creek and Urbana—an advantage not to be overlooked, and, indeed, indispensable in any protracted march toward Richmond. The disadvantage is, that the line of march southward from the points of crossing leads through a region in which no General would seek to fight a battle. I mean, of course, the "Wilderness," a wild tract of barren country, overspread with a thick growth of stunted pine, extending from Chancellorsville up to Mine Run. By changing front by the right, LEE had it in his power, using the Orange and Chancellorsville turnpike and the Orange and Chancellorsville plank-road, to strike us at right angles. The only escape would be to make our passage of the Rapidan a surprise—a conception which was very happily carried out. The march to the river having been made during the night of Wednesday, Thursday morning found the whole army planted safely on the south side of the Rapidan, and well in hand. So complete indeed seems to have been the surprise, that even after the whole army had passed the river, our signal officers reported the rebels still busy on their works on the Rapidan.

But, of course, it was not long before LEE became fully aware of the situation, and he promptly changed front, and pushed out to strike us by the two roads already named, which, as you will observe, runs from west to east, and strike the road on which we must advance, (the Germanna and Chancellorsville plank-road,) precisely at right angles. This was a masterly movement, for it obliged GRANT to halt, form line of battle, and dispose his force in such a way as to cover the fords, by which all our teams were yet to pass, and which it was absolutely necessary to keep open in order to preserve our line of communication.

This, then, was how it came, strategically, that we were compelled to fight the battle of the Wilderness—an encounter which I am very sure both Gen. GRANT and Gen. MEADE would gladly have avoided, had it been possible to do so. This much credit at least is due to Gen. LEE, whose manœuvre was one of great boldness and rapidity. Whether Gen. LEE intended merely to delay our advance and gain time for the new combinations necessitated by our successful crossing of the Rapidan, or whether he chose this line as one on which to try the gage of a decisive battle, in the hope of defeating us in the same way as he did in the same region (Chancellorsville) at the same period of last year, is a question which I have no means of determining, although the desperate vigor of the three days' attack would give strong color to the probability of the latter design. And it must be confessed his advantages were great. He crowded us into a restricted triangle, densely wooded, with few roads, which we knew imperfectly, and with the whole of our vast trains yet to be brought over the river. On the other hand, the enemy knew the country; with fifty thousand men he could here do as much as we with a hundred thousand, and he had the strong line of Mine Run, six miles in his rear, to fall back upon in case of repulse. When I say that after three days' fight, in which he with desperate fury threw himself repeatedly against every point of our line—right, left and centre—in the hope of breaking through and rolling us up, he has been compelled to retire discomfited, the sum and substance of the story is told.

Thursday morning found WARREN's corps (the Fifth) at Old Wilderness tavern, on the Germanna and Chancellorsville plank-road, five miles south of the ford, and SEDGWICK in his rear, on the same road, and extending down to the river. HANCOCK's corps, on the same day, crossed the river at Ely's Ford, five or six miles further down the river, under orders to move to Shady Grove Church. BURNSIDE's corps was to remain behind for twenty-four hours at Culpepper, and then join the main column. The manœuvre of the enemy compelled Gen. MEADE to form line of battle north and south, and this was done about a mile west of the Germanna plank-road and parallel to it, SEDGWICK's corps forming the right and resting on the river at Germanna Ford, and WARREN joining his left. Finding the enemy was determined to make a stand here, the order to HANCOCK to move to Shady Grove Church was countermanded, and he was directed to diverge by what is called the "Brock road," swing round, come up and form the left of the line.

The disposition above given will have shown that there must be for a considerable time a great interval between our centre (WARREN) and our left (HANCOCK)—an interval which could only be filled by HANCOCK swinging round and connecting with WARREN. The attempts of the enemy were mainly directed to getting possession of the plank-road, and planting himself between the two halves of the army. In this he was completely foiled, for WARREN and SEDGWICK held the front firmly until HANCOCK in the afternoon arrived, and completed the line. This was not done without severe loss, especially on the part of WARREN, two of whose divisions, namely, those of WORDSWORTH and GRIFFIN, lost each a third of its numbers.

From Chancellorsville, where HANCOCK had bivouacked on Thursday night, he advanced to the intersection of Brock road and the Orange and Chancellorsville plank road, where he found GETTY's division of the Sixth Corps. Forming line of battle he attacked at 4 o'clock, and fought very severely until 8, engaging HILL's corps. The enemy held a strong position behind improvised breastworks and was already formed in line of battle, while HANCOCK had great difficulty in getting in as he was marching by the flank to mass, but he stoutly held his position at the cross-roads, from which all the efforts of the enemy could not drive him.

The engagements of Thursday were so far successful that they defeated the purpose of the enemy to advance up the Orange road and penetrate between HANCOCK and WARREN. It was, however, only by the utmost skill and vigor that this was effected, for had the rebels been able to penetrate a mile further they would have achieved their end.

THE BATTLE OF FRIDAY, MAY 6.

Unwilling to remain on the defensive, Gen. GRANT, on Thursday night, ordered a general attack along the whole line for 5 o'clock the next morning. BURNSIDE, who had been hitherto in reserve was ordered in, and HANCOCK, who, as was realized had a severe part to perform, was strengthened by four divisions taken from the Fifth and Sixth Corps, so that he now commanded nearly one-half the army.

Promptly at the hour the flame of battle burst forth all along the line, which, from SEDGWICK's right to HANCOCK's left, had an extent of about seven miles.

On the right SEDGWICK attacked, engaging EWELL, who, however, showed a strong front. The two divisions WARREN has left, namely, those of GRIFFIN and CRAWFORD, badly handled yesterday, content themselves with repulsing the rebel attack. WADSWORTH, connecting with HANCOCK's right, puts forth a desperate valor, leads in person several charges at the head of his division, has two horses shot under him, and is then himself shot in the head and left in the hands of the enemy, but whether dead or alive is not yet known. BURNSIDE, somewhat tardy, is only skirmishing as yet, and has had no serious business. HANCOCK, on the left, attacked promptly at 5 o'clock and gallantly drove the enemy about a mile and a half, taking the rebel line of rifle-pits and five colors. In their turn the rebels attack vigorously, and the ammunition of HANCOCK's men being exhausted, they are forced back to their original line at 11 o'clock. The enemy even turns the extreme left, formed by FRANK's brigade of BARLOW's division, which broke in considerable confusion down the road. This, however, was promptly repaired, and the enemy prevented from following up his advantage. After this all remained quiet with HANCOCK until 4 o'clock in the afternoon.

Hitherto HANCOCK had met only the corps of HILL, but at 4 in the afternoon, LONGSTREET's corps, which had marched twenty-five miles to get into the fight, came up, and LEE prepared to hurl the main weight of his force, with a view of doubling up our left flank, and rolling us back on the enemy. The rebel attack was made at precisely 4½, and was made in four lines, the left on the plank road. It was marked by the greatest vigor, and succeeded in breaking our lines. Part of our breastworks got afire, and a portion of the Third and Fourth Divisions broke. GIBBON's division was, however, promptly formed in rear of the break. The brigade of CARROLL (who conducted himself with distinguished gallantry, and though shot through the arm, would not leave the field,) forming by the left; the brigade of BROOKS by the right. This was effectual in checking the rebel advance, and after forty-five minutes of most desperate fighting, the crisis had passed. The heroism and skill of HANCOCK, and the valor of his command had saved our army. Failing on the left, the rebels repeated their usual tactics by a night assault on our right, and they succeeded in rolling up the brigade of Gen. T. SEYMOUR, who was himself captured, but the break did not extend to the other portions of the line, and though some confusion was inseparable from a night assault, the rebels had gained nothing after all.

LOCALITIES OF THE LATE BATTLES ON THE RAPIDAN AND THE PO.

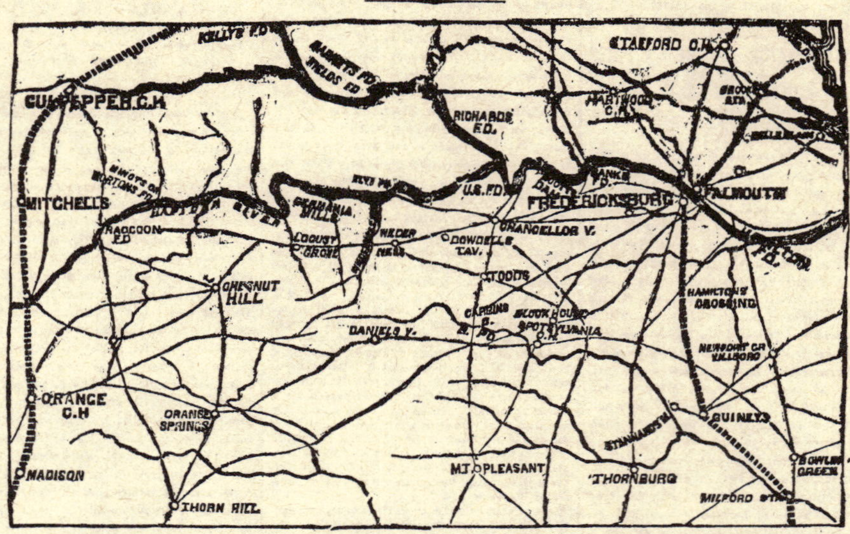

GRANT's position prior to the advance was at Culpepper Court-house; LEE's position was at Orange Court-house. The Wilderness south of the Rapidan, and Spottsylvania Court-house on the Po, will be seen above. Richmond is about fifty miles south of Spottsylvania Court-house.

The rebels expended their utmost strength in the battle of Friday, and failed to accomplish any decisive results. It was obvious that they were in very great strength, for they showed a full line along our whole front, extending beyond our right and overlapping our left.

SKIRMISHES OF SATURDAY, MAY 7.

It was, therefore, difficult on Friday night to say whether the enemy would resume the attack or retire. In case of the former alternative, a new and stronger line, considerably contracted, was selected on Friday evening. The attack, however, was not resumed in the morning, and reconnoissances and skirmishes made during the day along the whole line, though developing on the part of the enemy a strong skirmish line, left little doubt that the main portion of his army was retiring.

In this state of facts, Gen. GRANT formed the determination of throwing forward this army by a rapid night march toward Spottsylvania. Accordingly a march of 15 miles was made during the night, and this morning finds the whole army massed at Todd's Tavern. We shall doubtless, to-day, feel forward toward Spottsylvania Court-house, where we shall probably find the enemy in position.

Although we have no reliable returns of our losses in the three days' fight, it is probable they will reach 15,000. The loss of the enemy cannot vary much from that figure, and we have taken 2,000 prisoners.

THE BATTLE OF SUNDAY, MAY 8.

NEAR SPOTTSYLVANIA COURT-HOUSE, Va., Monday, May 9—2 P. M.

I have this morning returned from our advanced line of battle, which lies within two and a half miles of Spottsylvania Court-house, the enemy confronting in force. Our army reached this position yesterday morning, WARREN's corps having the advance, and heavy fighting took place during the day. It was hoped that we could have reached Spottsylvania before the enemy would be able to make that point; but in the foot race which the two armies ran on Saturday night, from the battle ground of the Wilderness, the rebels beat us. LONGSTREET, it appears, started at 11 P. M. of Saturday; our advance left at 10 P. M. The two columns marched by parallel roads, but LONGSTREET's corps had time to arrive and form line of battle, and when our force was thrown out to feel the enemy this morning, he was found in position. Our first attack was made by BARTLETT's brigade of GRIFFIN's division, on the right of the road, with ROBINSON's division on his left. BARTLETT had been ordered by Gen. WARREN to attack in column, under the belief that only rebel cavalry would be found. Instead of this, however, he ran on the whole of LONGSTREET's corps, and his brigade, already reduced by the fearful losses of the three days' battle of the Wilderness, was frightfully cut up. One of his regiments, the First Michigan, went in a hundred strong and came out with but twenty-five, having lost three-fourths of its numbers in fifteen minutes. ROBINSON's division, which held the left, was also roughly handled, and broke in disorder. Seeing this, Gen. WARREN seized the division flag and rallied the men in person. Fresh troops were thrown in, and after fighting from 8 A. M. till 12 M., our troops had gained the object sought—an open space up to the woods in which the rebel line was formed. In this engagement Gen. ROBINSON was severely wounded in the leg, and will have to lose his limb.

At 6 P. M., two fresh divisions, namely, those of CRAWFORD, (Fifth Corps,) and GETTY, (Sixth Corps,) were thrown in, and after a severe engagement lasting for an hour and a half, CRAWFORD carried the rebel position, took their first line of breastworks and captured over a hundred prisoners. This ended the action of yesterday. For the numbers engaged, our losses were extremely severe, and will count up to 1,500.

This morning found our line established two and a half miles this side of Spottsylvania Court-house, and securely intrenched. LONGSTREET has also been strengthened by the arrival of EWELL's corps. The rebel line lies on a ridge a mile in front of the Court-house, and it will be a position somewhat difficult to carry, should it be decided to make a direct attack.

It will be observed on the map that our present position carries us many miles south and in the rear of Fredericksburgh, whose famous fortified heights are in our possession without the need of firing a shot. It will be used as a depot and for hospitals, and several thousand of our wounded were, yesterday, sent there. A small army of 2,500 greybacks have also just been marched by headquarters en route to the same point. They are generally hearty-looking fellows, and rather better clad and shod than I have before seen them.

Everything thus far has gone on satisfactorily, although it would doubtless have been better had we been able to find an opportunity of fighting a decisive battle.

The Army of the Potomac is in superb condition and spirits—in fact, was never before in any such condition. We are going on to Richmond, depend upon it; at least, some more formidable obstacle than has yet appeared will have to present itself to stop us. BUTLER, we see by the Richmond papers of yesterday, is between Petersburgh and Richmond; SIGEL and AVERILL are in the right place, and you will presently hear from the cavalry corps of this army, under the bold and energetic leadership of SHERIDAN, in a way that will throw all previous raids into the shade.

The headquarters of the Lieutenant-General and Gen. MEADE, are always established near each other, and in action the two Generals and their staffs are always together. Gen. MEADE retains the immediate command of this army, while Gen. GRANT exercises a general supervision over the movements over the whole field. In regard to the operations of this army, the two Generals are in constant consultation, and it would, I think, be hard to say how much his own practical share in the actual command is. Perhaps I may say that Gen. GRANT indicates the strategic moves and combinations, while Gen. MEADE takes charge of their technical execution.

The rebel papers acknowledge a loss of two general officers killed and two mortally wounded, while it is now positively ascertained that LONGSTREET also is wounded.

P. S.—We have this moment been shocked by the announcement that Gen. SEDGWICK, Commander of the Sixth Army Corps, has just been killed by a shot through the head. He was standing up with his staff in his advanced line of breastworks, and was picked off by a rebel sharpshooter, perched in a tree. The ball entered the face a little below the eye, and came out at the back of his neck. He lived for half an hour after being struck, and then expired. His body has just passed headquarters in an ambulance. It will be embalmed and sent North. The profoundest grief is felt at the death of the lion-hearted chieftain, and it is felt that we could better afford to lose a whole division of the army than one whose valor, illustrated on so many fields, we can ill spare at this time. He never fought so well as in the arduous three days' fight in the "Wilderness," and it was a matter of general remark how splendidly SEDGWICK had been doing. It is presumed that Gen. WRIGHT will take the vacant command of the Sixth Corps.

SKIRMISHES OF MONDAY, MAY 9.

[In order to make our account continuous from day to day, we insert again a part of a letter given yesterday.]

IN FRONT OF SPOTTSYLVANIA COURT-HOUSE, Va., Tuesday, May 10, 1864.

The military situation at this hour (Tuesday, 12 M.) finds the line of the army drawn around Spottsylvania Court-house in the arc of a circle, the concave toward us. The enemy is in force at that point, and seems determined to dispute the passage. I mentioned in my letter of yesterday that the two armies ran a race from the Wilderness for Spottsylvania, but unfortunately the enemy won the race. This should not be interpreted as conveying any censure on the Army of of the Potomac, which has marched with new inspiration and a rapidity never before seen in its history. But the very necessities of our condition as the invading party, with our old base abandoned and a new one not yet opened, obliges us to take immense trains, which, of course, retard the general movement of the army; the rebels constantly falling back on their base, and favored by their very poverty, can readily beat us on an equal start. It would certainly have been a great point gained had we been able to make Spottsylvania Court-house in advance of the enemy. An inspection of the map will show you that it is an important strategic point, being the point of divergence of the roads leading southward, both to the right and left. The enemy's command of it enables him to cover the withdrawal of his trains and at the same time bars our further advance, unless on the condition of an assault—which, in the country in which we are now fighting, is very destructive of life—or of a turning movement. It is probable that to-day will decide the question; and if, as we hope, it gives us Spottsylvania Court-house, we shall then be out of the Wilderness, and have a clear road on to Richmond.

Yesterday was intended to be a day of quietude, during which the army, fatigued by five days incessant marching and fighting, would have an opportunity to recuperate and renew the supplies of rations. Little occurred to interfere with this programme, although the rebels made an attack on WILCOX's Division of BURNSIDE's Corps, early in the afternoon. They were, however, handsomely repulsed, and BURNSIDE has the extreme left of our line, within a mile and a half of the Court-house.

About 6 o'clock last evening, Gen. HANCOCK, holding the right of our line, crossed Po Creek and seized the Block House Road, the direct line from Parker's Store to Spottsylvania Court-house. Immediately afterward, WARREN, who now has centre, advanced his line of battle, drove the rebels for half a mile, and took up a strong position. Up to the present hour, the situation remains as here described.

The rebels have as yet shown no disposition to assume the offensive at this point. It was confidently expected on Sunday night that an attack would take place on HANCOCK's front, toward the Catharpen Road, and on a line with the Brock Road. The troops showed great diligence in throwing up breastworks, and a brigade was advanced out for a mile or more from the main front over some cleared land. About an hour before sunset this attack was made. Immediately upon the retirement of the advance brigade, the enemy charged toward our line, but never reached it. They put a few guns in position, and shelled the woods for a while, but did no harm. A small number of Gen. BIRNEY's troops, on whom the attack was principally made, were wounded by the enemy's musketry before they withdrew, having received more harm than they had done. Before this attack, our advance could see HILL's Corps marching south to join the main body, opposing our progress in front on the branch of the Po. As it was necessary to hold this position until it was certain the enemy were gone, Gen. HANCOCK did not stay the progress of the men engaged in forming breastworks, but added another line in the open ground around Todd's Tavern, a regiment of heavy artillery working all night to finish them. It was a very pretty sight. The lanterns of the workmen hung to the blossoming cherry-trees, and picturesque groups of soldiers digging and erecting the works, while batteries stood harnessed up, their cannoniers lying on the ground around the carriages, in wait for any emergency. At sunrise scouts advanced and found the enemy in small force; and about noonday Gen. HANCOCK left Gen. WARD's brigade to hold the position, and advanced with his corps toward the River Po, which by night he had, after considerable resistance, passed. Gen. BURNSIDE pushing out on the extreme left, advanced to a place in front of SEDGWICK's (now WRIGHT's) corps. A reconnoissance by two regiments was made. These advanced some distance without meeting much resistance. At the same time the cannonade along some portions of the front was quite brisk between ours and the rebel artillery.

The prisoners we have are in apparent good condition. One fellow, who was taken with much trouble, explained his determined efforts to avoid capture, on the ground that it was currently reported that we should massacre all our prisoners, in revenge for the slaughter of our negro soldiers.

We have fewer stragglers than usual, though not so few as might be. It is not easy to straggle in a country where there is no communication, and guerrillas loaf around the army to pick up any waif or estray sleeping in the woods. The Provost-guard has all it can do, to keep the lingerers up to their duty.

Gen. PATRICK had quite a brigade of them one day, and I believe had serious thoughts of making a charge with them.

The same intolerable heat which we have had ever since this movement commenced still continues, and numerous cases of *coup de soleil* happen every day. It is, however, one compensation for the heat that it keeps the roads in excellent traveling condition, saving and excepting the dust, which is here of a most malignant type.

Gen. WRIGHT, who formerly commanded a division of the Sixth, is now in command of that Corps so grievously deprived of its head by the death of the beloved SEDGWICK, the details of which I yesterday sent you. The grief at this sad event intensifies as it becomes known throughout the army. An effort was at first made to keep the sad fact from the knowledge of his men. Gen. WRIGHT is an excellent soldier, and will command the Sixth well.

The road which our troops faced runs from Orange Court-house to Fredericksburgh, and is forty-one miles long. It crosses no river. Proceeding from Orange Court-house, we come at a distance of ten miles to Verdiersville; ten miles further brings us to Parker's Store, six miles further to Wilderness; five miles further to Chancellorsville; ten miles more to Fredericksburgh.

Just as I close this letter a heavy cannonading has commenced in the front, for which I leave immediately.

THE BATTLE OF TUESDAY, MAY 10.

WASHINGTON, Thursday, May 12.

The following dispatch has just come to hand:

HEADQUARTERS ARMY OF THE POTOMAC, NEAR SPOTTSYLVANIA C. H., Wednesday, May 11.

My dispatch dated 6 P. M. yesterday gave an outline sketch of the operations of that day down to the hour named, and included the announcement of the turning of our right flank [This dispatch has not yet come to hand.—ED. *Times.*] I would gladly have avoided leaving the situation suspended in this perilous condition, but the messenger by whom I had the opportunity to send my dispatch left just as the courier bearing the tidings arrived. I hasten to add that the menacing break was speedily repaired, and that the army holds at present a position not differing greatly from that we have held for the past two days, with the exception that our right is somewhat more strengthened.

Yesterday's operations now assumed the character of the most bitter and perhaps the most bloody of the series of battles which have been fought since we crossed the Rapidan. Knowing, as we do, that our cavalry force has been working havoc with LEE's communications, that his supplies are almost exhausted, that the lines of investment are being drawn around Richmond, and that echoes of disaster reach his ear from afar-off Tennessee, and presage the downfall of the fabric of the rebellion, we are left to infer that the attack of yesterday was a desperate, and, let us hope, final attempt to retrieve the rebel fortunes by dealing a crushing blow at this army. It is enough to say that it failed, and though he inflicted a severe loss of life upon us, he suffered not less himself, and we still hold a position against which the rebel fury may dash itself in vain. It would seem to have been the policy of LEE in the series of battles which he has delivered during the past week, to contest the advance to Richmond at every available point, to wear us away by degrees, and then, perhaps, to fall upon the Union forces under BUTLER, and endeavor to annihilate them. This plan he has carried into execution with a masterly skill, inspired by a fury perfectly diabolical.

We are steadily pressing the rebels southward. The enemy have been greatly favored by the nature of this country, in whose dense woods and tangled chapparal the lithe and wary are much more at home. Fortunately, if we once carry the position which they now hold in front of Spottsylvania Court-house, we shall be out of the "Wilderness" and reach open country.

The operations of yesterday were opened by a reconnoissance on the left by BURNSIDE's corps, which developed the fact that the enemy was in no force there—nothing but cavalry disputing the advance. This caused the division of MOTT to be withdrawn from its position on the extreme right and it was sent to the left to connect with BURNSIDE. The rebel position now very much resembled ours at Gettysburgh, a curved interior line, well protected by breastworks, with the additional defence of a marshy run in front. Holding us at bay in the centre, they discovered the weakness of the right, now held by BARLOW's division. This division of HANCOCK's command, as I yesterday mentioned, had made the passage of the Po, throwing out skirmishers on the east bank. This gave it a coigne of vantage, from which it not only enfiladed the entire rebel position, but commanded the road on which their trains were passing. At the same time, however, it isolated it from the rest of the army—a false position, of which the rebels could hardly have failed to take advantage, and of which they did take advantage, as we shall presently see.

Gen. WARREN's corps held the centre of the line. [illegible] it was resolved that a vigorous assault sh[illegible] made there, while HANCOCK and BURNSIDE endeavored to assail and turn the two flanks of the enemy. With this view, two divisions of the Second Corps were thrown over to connect with the right of WARREN and support him. In execution of the projected design, WARREN's corps moved forward during the day, pressing the rebels through the woods to an open space behind, close to the enemy's breastworks. This was attended by very heavy shelling from the enemy, and it was three or four o'clock P. M. before the woods were cleared. After this, the corps advanced to assault the breastworks. In this, however, it did not succeed, although the attempt was gallantly made. CARROLL's brigade went in on the charge and lost eight hundred men.

Gen. MEADE realizing the critical position in which the extreme right of our line (BARLOW's division,) was placed, had ordered it to draw back. The rebels had, however, anticipated us, and making a detour came in on its rear, making it a matter of considerable difficulty to withdraw; supports coming up, however, it was successfully accomplished. A general attack was ordered along the line, to take place at 5 o'clock, but owing to the tardiness of some of the Commanders to get into line it was postponed, first to 6 o'clock, and then to half-past. A furious cannonade from our artillery preceded the charge. The worst of it was that the lateness of the hour prevented its being perfectly successful.

Gen. WRIGHT advanced the flower of the Sixth Corps. Nobly and well they sustained their reputation. UPTON's brigade leading, they advanced rapidly upon the enemy's breastworks without

Continued on the Eighth Page.

The Charleston Mercury.

VINDICE NULLO — SPONTE SUA SINE LEGE FIDES RESTUMQUE COLLENTUR.

VOLUME LXXXIV. CHARLESTON, S. C., MONDAY, MAY 23, 1864. NUMBER 12,068

THE WAR IN VIRGINIA—INTERESTING DETAILS.

We received yesterday an avalanche of back Richmond mails, with some N. Y. papers of May 14. We glean from them such accounts of affairs in Virginia as we can make room for in this issue.

A YANKEE ACCOUNT OF THE BATTLE OF MAY 12—THE CAPTURE OF GENERALS STUART AND JOHNSON.

We make some interesting extracts from the despatches (dated May 12) of the correspondent of the New York *Times*, at GRANT'S Headquarters:

SIX O'CLOCK, A. M.—At midnight, last night, Hancock, with his corps, changed from his position on the extreme right, and went in on the left of the line, between the Sixth Corps and Burnside's, where there had been a gap. At 5 o'clock, this morning, he assaulted the enemy's position, carried their second line of breastworks, and turned the right flank of the rebels. It was a complete surprise, favored by a mist, which concealed our movements. He has taken 3000 prisoners and three Generals, namely: Gen. Stuart, commanding a brigade in General Johnson's Division of Ewell's Corps; Major General Johnson, Commander, and another General Johnson, commanding a brigade. This is entirely reliable, as I have just heard the despatch conveying the joyful intelligence read aloud by the Chief of Staff.

Everybody is in the best of spirits. The enemy had not been expecting an attack on their right, as our reconnoissance of yesterday on the left seemed to indicate that as our point of assault.

Hancock's glorious success, if sustained, will solve a very difficult problem, as the rebels had fortified their powerful position in front of Spottsylvania Court House so strongly that an attempt to carry it in front must have been attended with immense loss of life. The intelligence from Sheridan's cavalry raid, brought by a scout last night, shows that he has had the most complete success. He destroyed ten miles of the Orange and Gordonsville Railroad—the line on which Lee has been mainly dependent for his supplies—and destroyed three trains of cars and a large amount of supplies. He took several pieces of artillery and recaptured five hundred of our prisoners—among them two Colonels, whom the rebels were lugging off to Richmond.

SIX THIRTY A. M.—The magnitude of Hancock's victory rolls up, as its full proportions become known. He has captured Major Gen. Johnson's entire division of Ewell's corps, numbering 3,000 men, and he has also taken twenty or thirty cannon up to this hour.

SEVEN A. M.—A most interesting scene is now going on at Headquarters. Maj Gen. Johnson, who, with his whole division, was captured this morning, has just been brought up, under charge of an officer, to headquarters in the woods, where Gens. Grant and Meade and their staffs are seated around a bivouac fire. Gen. Meade, who had been an old friend of Gen. Johnson, shook hands with him and introduced him to Gen. Grant.

"Formerly of the Sixth Infantry?" inquires the Lieutenant-General. "Yes," replies the rebel General, "You were of the Fourth, and we were both in the same brigade." Of course, military etiquette precluded any other inquiries than those of a purely personal character. To the question whether General Wadsworth was dead, he replied that such was his belief, though he was not positive. Our Generals, Seymour and Shaler, who were captured in the battle of the Wilderness, he had yesterday seen at Lee's headquarters. Longstreet he reports as severely but not mortally wounded. Almost all the staff appear to have been old friends and acquaintances of Johnson, and numerous mutual inquiries in regard to old army comrades are being made.

Gen. Hunter, Chief of Artillery, when he met him, had a mind to make a set speech, but the old familiar formula, "ED., I'm glad to see you," came out in a salutation to which Johnson replied: "Well, Hunt, under the circumstance, I am not glad to see you." He spoke of the abomination of such a country as the Wilderness to fight in; spoke of the capture of his division, but said, with a quiet, good natured manner, that we would have a hot time of it yet. Johnson is a stout built fellow, with a strong, rough face, but his dress is in bad condition, and his slouched hat, with his brownish grey hair sticking out through an aperture at the top, is such as even a New York dead rabbit would scorn to sport.

An aid who has just come in from Gen. Hancock's headquarters says that when the captured General Stuart (G. H.) was brought in, Hancock extended his hand, but the high born captive drew back, saying that "his feelings would not allow him to shake hands"—an incident which has just created a merry laugh at headquarters.

TEN A. M.—The whole line is now engaged, including the corps of Warren's Fifth, of Wright's Sixth, of Hancock's Second, and of Burnside's Ninth. From the present position of headquarters, which is near enough to be under fire, we can distinguish Burnside's and Hancock's line of battle in our front, and Wright and Warren stretched off to the right. It is too densely wooded to see the manœuvres, or even the line of battle, but we mark the line by the margins of smoke rising up above the trees, and the flashes of the artillery.

ELEVEN O'CLOCK.—There is a lull along the line, with the exception of a vigorous cannonading, which continues. The rebels have been fighting with an obstinacy that challenges the name of sublime, and Lee has been putting forth his best powers. The situation at this hour leaves our line holding all the ground they have gained; but they are not now advancing. The men are excessively fatigued, and it is now somewhat doubtful whether the issue can be decided in to-day's battle.

TWELVE M.—The rain has ceased and the sun just has burst forth. May it be another sun of Austerlitz. Burnside, who has hitherto had but one division (Potter's) of his corps engaged, is ordered to make an attack with his whole force. The left has been the cardinal point ever since Hancock's turning movement.

ONE, P. M.—As Warren's attack on the right did not succeed, our right wing is being retired or drawn back, and Meade is massing more on the left, where a vigorous attack is again being made with very heavy musketry and artillery fire. Hancock has turned a number of the rebel captured guns against the enemy.

TWO P. M.—It has been impossible yet to dislodge the rebels, who hold their position most stubbornly. Lee has repaired his left on a strong position, and his line is covered all along by breastworks. A tremendous cannonade is now being made for the purpose on the enemy's position. Though victory now appears highly probable, you must not be surprised if the final result is not achieved to-day.

The rebels will fight to the last, and have already, in the wonderful eight days' Battle of the Wilderness—of which this is but a continuation—made good all the boasts ever made of their prowess. They will really die in the last ditch, and only then. Of our losses thus far during this day's severe battle it is impossible to form anything like an accurate estimate; but they must be extremely heavy. The losses of officers is also very great.

AN AUTHENTIC ACCOUNT OF GRANT'S ALLEGED VICTORY OF MAY THE TWELFTH.

We get from the Richmond *Examiner*, of Monday the 16th, the following clear and interesting account of the bloody battle of the 12th inst., over which GRANT has crowed so lustily:

When the last number of this journal went to press, authentic news had been obtained of an assault in force on Lee's breastworks, continued through the whole of Wednesday, and repulsed with tremendous punishment of the enemy. Rumors were circulated of a renewal of the same desperate effort on Thursday, but unsupported by evidence. We now know that these rumors contained nothing that was not true.—Grant had received a full corps of fresh troops—kept back up to the moment to defend the trenches of Washington—and risked with the recklessness of a true gambler on the cast of the dice. He attempted no manœuvre. He relied on main strength—bringing up his ten lines at a run, each one close behind another, and dashed them like the waves of the sea against the rocks, on the breastworks of the South. By these tactics, either a perfect victory is won or an attacking army is lost. The first rush was successful on one point. The enemy broke through the blaze of the living volcano upon Johnson's men, leaped the works, took two thousand prisoners and sixteen guns. But reserves were ready, and a charge of greater fury than their own drove them out in a brief time. On all other parts of the line they were entirely unsuccessful. They were utterly repulsed; with scarcely any loss to the Confederates, who fired with the advantage of rest, aim, and cover; but with a slaughter of the foe which is represented by universal testimony to have been the most terrible of modern warfare.

In these two battles the Army of Northern Virginia has enjoyed, for the first time, the advantages of firing into the enemy with grape and rifle balls from lines of substantial breastworks; and if one may judge, from the high spirits and unbounded confidence of the wounded men who have come to this city from the battle, it has been highly gratified by the new position. "We just mowed them every time,"—such is the only account they give of the struggle.

The Confederate loss, killed, wounded and missing, in all these battles, beginning with the Wilderness and concluding with that of Thursday last, at Spottsylvania Court House, was under fifteen thousand. The Washington Chronicle, the organ of Lincoln, that sees all things in the rose's color, announces the "depletion" of Grant's army by the battle of the Wilderness, and "other causes," to have been, on Tuesday evening ascertained, thirty-five thousand. To this awful figure must now be added the two days of unsuccessful assault on the breastworks of Spottsylvania—assault without manœuvre, full in front, with deep columns, each forcing the other on the muzzles of the guns—wherein the carnage and loss must, in the necessity of things, have been many times greater than in the open battles of the Wilderness and succeeding days. Putting the two data together, it is impossible to doubt the deduction that Grant's "depletion" by killing, wounding, and "other causes"—that is to say, by straggling, desertion, etc.,—has surpassed seventy thousand. The disproportion of numbers between the antagonists was very great when the Federal General crossed the Rapid Ann, and it is probable that he has since received the troops originally retained to defend Washington; but that disproportion was wonderfully reduced when the sun went down on Thursday afternoon.

The capture of a brigade and sixteen cannon from our lines is certainly a disagreeable circumstance; but that the victory on Thursday was indubitable and complete, and immense in effect upon the enemy, is proven beyond cavil, by the fact that he laid still behind his own trenches all Friday without firing a shot. Considering that he had commenced the work on Wednesday morning and continued it with unabated vigor till long after sunset—that he has begun where he left off on Thursday at the break of light, and rushed, charge after charge, upon General Lee, throughout the day—this fact, that the next dawn found him still and silent, is most significant. General Lee announces, in the despatch received last night, that he *himself* was in condition to resume the offensive on Saturday, and made a partial attack with brilliant success.

Nevertheless, we have no idea that Lee and Grant have yet settled their accounts in full.—Grant will get up the last rakings of the Northern army and try again. He is said to have made everybody about him understand that he will not re-cross the river while he has a living man under his orders. There are butchers of humanity to whom the sight of their fellow-creature's blood affords an intoxicating pleasure; they are indifferent whose blood it is, so that it does not come from their own veins; and Grant is one of these charming individuals. His Government and his brother Generals will not baulk him in the present instance. A large part of the army now in his hands is composed of the regiments enlisted for three years, and their term expires in this coming summer. They have resisted every inducement to re-enlist; and have formally notified the Secretary of War that they will obey orders so long as they are legally given, but no longer. The Government is entirely willing that Grant should save it the trouble and mortification of giving the discharge to these veterans.—He will use them—and he is using them.

The question occurs, will these men submit thus to be put in the shambles again and again? We answer, yes. Considered as individuals, they are no braver now than when they ran away at Manassas. But they have been drilled in arms for three years. They are entirely bound by the magic of military discipline. When ordered to go into the fire, however little they like it, they cannot resist the spell—they will go and stand up until shot down. But if Grant will only continue the tactics of Wednesday and Thursday, they will soon be relieved from the inconvenience. We only fear that he will now depart from that favorite game, and think twice before he forces assaults with seven and ten lines of men on the army of Northern Virginia, ensconced in trenches. It might do very well against an army that could be scared—but the army of Northern Virginia cannot be scared. Instead of marching up to the breastwork again, the last account represents him changing his position; and while he will not confess defeat by re-crossing the Rappahannock, he may yet go down the river and re-appear in the Peninsula.

THE BATTLE MONDAY NEAR DREWRY'S BLUFF—DETAILS OF BEAUREGARD'S VICTORY.

As expected and already stated, the great battle near Drewry's Bluff was joined Monday. The plan of battle was conceived and decided upon on Sunday night by the gallant BEAUREGARD, and as daylight broke, the work commenced. A Richmond papers thus refers to it:

Almost before the grey of morning, our forces on the left, under the command of Gen. Ransom, marched out against the enemy, and gave him battle. The enemy occupied a strong position, and was strongly entrenched in some fortifications that had been evacuated by us on Friday last, with a view of drawing the enemy on and inducing him to venture an assault on our inner line of fortifications. This was the enemy's right and our left, and perhaps about a mile or so from Drewry's Bluff. No sooner were our men up than they charged upon the enemy with a perfect yell. The fighting grew severe, and the battle for a time, wavered. But the onset of our men was too much. In a moment our men swept over the fortifications like an avalanch, and the enemy was soon in rapid flight, leaving our men in full possession of the fortifications and the captors of four stand of colors and one battery. This movement on our left was most handsomely executed, and all accomplished by seven o'clock in the morning.

Driven from these fortifications, the enemy fell back upon his own entrenchments and a general advance was ordered along the lines. The victory on the left was quickly followed up. The enemy was no sooner within the fortifications than an order was given to charge him. Our men advanced to the charge, but his fire was so terrific that certain regiments broke in confusion. Here was the trying point—the enemy must be dislodged. In an instant some of those men who stormed the memorable heights of Gettysburg were ordered up, and a second charge was made. The enemy's fire was terrible—making wide gaps in our lines—but steadily our men moved on. As they approached, the enemy poured into them a most galling fire—seemingly reserving his fire until our men were well up—sweeping them down by rows—but not a cheek blanched or an arm faltered. Through a perfect sheet of fire they marched up to the fortifications, and with a shout of victory leaped over the breastworks and captured the greater portion of the enemy's force—General Heckman and over eight hundred privates.

While this was going on along our left our centre and left were also pressing the enemy with great success. A change had been made upon his centre, across the turnpike, by Gen. Hoke, and he had been driven back from each of his positions. Here the enemy had no regular fortifications, but was well protected by abattis formed by felling trees and other temporary defences. Our artillery was used against him with great effect. The Washington Artillery, supported by Hagood's South Carolina brigade, who acted most gallantly throughout, succeeded in silencing a battery of the enemy's, consisting of three 20 pounder Parrotts and two 12 pounder Napoleons. One of the Parrotts was turned upon the enemy, and contributed to putting him to flight.

The following note tells of the noble action of HAGOOD'S Brigade:

"ON THE FIELD, May 16.

Captain Owens, Washington Artillery:

"I am instructed by General Hagood, whose brigade captured two 12 pounders, Napoleons, and three Parrott guns, to request a guard over them until they can be marked. I shall request Colonel Waddy, of General Beauregard's Staff, to give them to you. Please report when they are together, and I shall be at General Hagood's headquarters.

"Very respectfully,

"EDWARD MAZYCK,

"Hagood's Brigade."

Up to this time the enemy had fought well and with great stubbornness, but, driven from his fortifications and pressed on all sides, he began to fall back rapidly. Our victory now became easy. Dispirited and discomfited, the enemy showed but faint resistance, and the retreat was but a step removed from a rout. In charging upon them a whole regiment threw down their arms and rushed into our lines. From a dozen sources we have reports of their demoralization. On official authority we learn that several hundreds of prisoners captured in the retreat expressed the greatest alacrity to come on to Richmond, saying that their time was nearly out—that they were tired of the war—and that if they would "only show them the road to Richmond, they would come over without any guard being placed over them."

The retreat once began and the enemy gave way rapidly. Our army continued to press him, and up to 4 o'clock yesterday we had driven him two miles and a half. Our forces kept well on his heels, and captured a good deal of artillery, stores, arms and ammunition which he had strewn along the way. Several hundred prisoners were picked up in squads, and many of them were under the influence of liquor—showing that Butler, like Grant, had plied his men with whiskey before going into battle. This is confirmed by dozens of person from the battle field, and admits of no doubt.

It is impossible to state just now the fruits of our victory, but there is no doubt that our army won yesterday, under the gallant Beauregard, a most brilliant success. The fight was commenced yesterday with the enemy posted in his fortifitions, but by seven o'clock our army had dislodged him, and before the setting of the sun he had been repulsed and driven back to Proctor's creek, a distance of two miles or more. The number of prisoners taken is not yet known, but it may be put down considerably over a thousand—a Brigadier General among the number—and, perhaps later accounts may swell it to several thousand. We captured, also, a great deal of artillery some say as much as twenty six pieces—besides a quantity of stores, ammunition, &c. It may be a day or two before we can know the extent of our success, but in the meantime let us be content with the assurance that our army, under the invincible Beauregard has won a great victory.

The following despatch was received from General BEAUREGARD:

"*To General B. Bragg:*

"DREWRY'S BLUFF, May 16, 8.30, a. m.

"Our progress is very satisfactory. General Ransom turned the enemy's James River flank early this morning, and driving him towards our right. We hold still on the right, and are pressing the enemy back in front of our centre, disabling and capturing some artillery. General Ransom stormed the breastworks, took four stand of colors, and about three hundred prisoners. Our losses, on the whole, appear not to be heavy. G. T. BEAUREGARD."

Sketch of a Confederate soldier

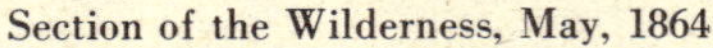

Section of the Wilderness, May, 1864

Photograph of General Grant probably taken at the time of the fighting in the Wilderness

Major General Wadsworth fighting in the Wilderness

The Charleston Mercury.

VINDICE NULLO
SPONTE SUA SINE LEGE FIDES RECTUMQUE COLLENTUR.

VOLUME LXXXIV. | CHARLESTON, S. C., TUESDAY, MAY 24, 1864. | NUMBER 12,069

THE FIGHTING IN VIRGINIA.

The Great Battle of the 12th of May---Full and Highly Interesting Details.

The following letter from Mr. P. W. ALEXANDER, the well known army correspondent, gives a graphic sketch of the great battle of May 12, claimed by GRANT and his trumpeters as a Yankee victory. Our readers will find this account full of interest:

SPOTTSYLVANIA C. H., May 13

On yesterday was fought in front of this modest little village—henceforth to be known through all coming time—one of the fiercest and most obstinate battles of modern times. It commenced at daylight, and raged and roared with tremendous fury until 2 o'clock in the afternoon, when the enemy retired from the bloody conflict.—Grant made the attack again, as he did at the Wilderness, and gained a considerable advantage by the suddenness and vigor of the assault early in the day, but with this exception, he was repulsed with a loss that will carry mourning to thousands of Northern and European hearthstones, and dismay and confusion to the tyrants and demagogues whose hosts he leads. The Confederates failed at one point only—partly from accident, partly from mistake, and partly I fear, from lack of spirit, but on all other parts of the field they were victorious, and as firm and resolute as ever. The enemy was beaten, but not routed or driven from the field.

The battle was fought on the North side of Spottsylvania Court House, on the undulating ground, diversified by fields, pine thickets, and patches of woods. Our line is crescent shaped, or perhaps it would be more correct to say that it is nearly in the form of a horse shoe, and extends around the Court House or village on the north and northwestern side, so as to cover all the approaches from those quarters. Slight entrenchments had been thrown up along our entire front, extending from near the Shady Grove (or Catharpen Road continued) on the west, around to and beyond the Fredericksburg Road on the northeast side of the village. At one point on the right is an eminence a few hundred yards in advance of the general direction of our line, and in order to prevent the enemy from getting possession of it for his artillery, a sharp angle was projected so as to include the hill within our entrenchments. The result shows that this was an unfortunate piece of engineering.—Past the foot of the hill, on the north side, sweeps a ravine which presents a convex line to the hill, the two approaching each other like circles that touch but do not cut each other. The enemy availed himself of this ravine in his assault upon the angle, which was the weakest point in our lines, being considerably in advance of the general line, and beyond the reach of support from the forces operating on the right and left.

Information was received night before last that Grant was retiring in the direction of Fredericksburg and Germanna Ford; a report to this effect was noised abroad throughout the army, though subsequent events show that it was without the least foundation. Through a mistake, which I cannot trace to its source, but which grew out of this mischievous report, the artillery which had been posted on the hill in the angle alluded to above, was withdrawn during the night. This left Major-General Johnson, of Ewell's corps, whose division, heretofore considered one of the best in the army, occupied this part of the line, without any artillery support. He communicated this fact to his corps commander at midnight, with the additional intelligence that the enemy was massing a heavy force in his immediate front for the purpose, as he believed, of assaulting him next (yesterday) morning. These guns or others were sent back, and were just moving into the angle at 4 o'clock yesterday morning, when the force which Johnson reported to be massing in his front made a vigorous assault upon his position and carried it.

The assaulting force had been assembled in the ravine at the foot of the hill, was very strong, and advanced, one report says, in column of regiments. It had rained the evening before, and considerable fog prevailed, under cover of which the attack was made. One or two guns were got into position and fired, but the horses attached to the other pieces were shot down before they could be unlimbered, and most of the cannoneers captured. Jones' Virginia brigade, whose commander was killed in the Wilderness, the Stonewall and other brigades belonging to the division [illegible] becoming involved, soon followed, and the last [illegible] was seen of General Johnson he was standing almost alone with a musket in his hand, contesting the ground single-handed with the multitudinous foe. The brigades composing this division are the Stonewall, J. M. Walker and Jones' brigades, both of this State, Stewart's brigade of Virginians and North Carolinians, and Stafford's brigade of Louisianians. Jones and Stafford fell at the Wilderness; Walker was wounded yesterday; Stewart and Johnson, the commander of the division, were taken prisoners; and the Colonel commanding Jones' brigade is reported killed, with many other officers. The guns left on the field, but which neither party has been able to move on account of the fire of the other—some eighteen or twenty—are said to belong to Cutshaw's and Page's battalions. 1000 or 1200 prisoners were lost at the same time.

This occurred at a very early hour in the morning. If Jones' brigade had not given way, it is possible, though not probable, that Johnson would have been able to maintain his ground.—He is one of the best officers in the army, and the sublime spectacle he presented when battling alone with the enemy, though deserted by his command, should excite our admiration rather than provoke criticism. But it should not be imagined that the enemy gained the hill without opposition, sudden and vigorous as his assault was. He was received with volley after volley, and the ground was covered with his slain; but he had massed such a heavy force upon a single exposed point, some distance in advance of the general line, and incapable of being instantaneously supported, that it was found impossible to repulse him. It is but just to add, too, that the enemy's charge was as spirited as it was successful, and reflects no little credit upon his troops. He was aware of the weakness of the point from its comparative isolation, having effected a temporary lodgment in the angle two days before, and it would have been a wonder if he had not been successful, with the preparation he had made.

The Confederates suffered severely as they retreated across the intervening space to our second line, or rather to the line which extends the angle, and which may be considered the base of the triangle covering the hill. Even this line is somewhat in advance of the direction of the general line. But the broken division did not stop here; they continued their retreat far to the rear. Fortunately, the gallant Gordon, commanding Early's Division, was in reserve, and swept to the rescue in a manner that excited the admiration of every beholder, including General Lee. The enemy swarmed over the hill and rushed against the lines to the right and left, but Rhodes and Gordon and Wilcox were there to meet them.

The battle was soon fully joined, and for nine hours it roared and hissed and dashed over the bloody angle and along the bristling entrenchments like an angry sea beating and chafing against a rock-bound coast. The artillery fire was the most sustained and continuous I have ever heard for so long a time, averaging thirty shots to the minute or 1,800 to the hour, for six hours. The rattle of musketry was not less furious and incessant. At 10 o'clock, when the din and uproar were at the highest, an angry storm cloud swept over the field, and thus to the thunders of battle was added "the dread artillery of the skies." It was now manifest that Grant's real assault, as Gen. Lee had believed, would be launched against our right wing, and to that point the opposing forces gravitated from all parts of the field, just as when a cloud surcharged with electricity forms in the heavens, all the lesser clouds and racks drift to it, and are swallowed up in the swelling, angry mass.

Grant strove hard to hold us to other parts of the field, and prevent this concentration of force, and for that purpose he engaged Anderson on our left, and Early, who had been sent to the extreme right. He made three separate assaults against the former, but was repulsed each time with frightful loss by Fields' Division, formerly Hood's. Early, at the head of Hill's Corps, hurled him back, as a mad bull would an incautious mastiff caught upon his horns, as often as he advanced upon him.

But it was against Ewell, who held the right of the original line, that Grant expended his greatest efforts and made his most desperate assaults. Having gained a foothold in the angle or centre of Ewell's position, he brought up line after line and hurled it with tremendous violence, at one time against Rhodes, at another against Gordon, and then against both. Wilcox was brought up and placed on Gordon's left, and Wofford and Humphreys, of Kershaw's Division, and Jenkins' Brigade, of Fields', Anderson's Corps, were sent to the assistance of Rhodes. Additional batteries were sent in the same direction. Heth went to the right, and all of Anderson's old division but Wright followed him. And thus the whirling, remorseless maelstrom drew everything into its angry vortex. The enemy exhibited a courage and resolution worthy of a better cause; Grant seemed to have breathed into his troops somewhat of his own spirit and indomitable energy. But if the Federals fought well, the Confederates fought better. From early dawn until far in the afternoon, with steady hands and unblanched cheeks, they faced the leaden hail that was rained upon them without intermission. At some points the two armies fought on opposite sides of the entrenchments, the distance between them not being more than the length of their muskets. Again and again would Grant marshal his men for the onset, and right valiantly did they respond; but as often as they returned to the assault so often were they repulsed, as if they had rushed against a wall of iron. At no point of the line, and at no time during the long and terrible and exhausting conflict, did the heroic children of the South falter or waver for a moment. Each man knew that he was fighting the battle for the possession of Richmond—the battle, indeed, for the independence of the Confederate States—and the thought of yielding to the foe never once entered his mind.

During one of the assaults, Gordon inflicted very heavy loss upon the enemy by moving around and striking the assaulting column in flank. The enemy was thrown into great confusion, and retired rapidly to the rear, leaving many dead and wounded on the ground.

The most important movement against the enemy's flank, however, was executed by Mahone's and Lane's brigades on the extreme right, under the direction of General Early. The expedition was intended to operate, not against the flank of the assaulting column, but against the flank of the Federal army, and thus afford relief to our

Officers of Mosby's Rangers

centre and left wing, both of which were hard pressed. The two brigades were placed under command of Mahone, who passed around to the Fredericksburg Road, and was about to engage the enemy, when he met the latter coming out, probably to take us in flank. An engagement ensued immediately, and resulted in the defeat of the enemy, who retired back to the main army, where considerable commotion was produced by the fresh danger with which it was threatened. A division operating against our left, supposed to belong to Burnside's corps, was withdrawn and double-quicked across the field to check Mahone. Just before it reached the scene of action, it came within full view of Pagne's and Pegram's guns, and not more than 1200 yards distant. Twelve pieces were brought to bear upon it in less time than it requires to describe this brilliant episode in the battle. The enemy stood their ground for a moment, then staggered back, and finally broke in the wildest disorder. What with Mahone's fire in front and the artillery ploughing great gaps in their ranks, their loss was severe. This movement afforded instantaneous relief to our left, and from this time the assaults of the enemy grew more and more feeble along the whole line, and finally they ceased altogether, at 2 p. m.

Our men were anxious to follow up the enemy when he was repulsed, but General Lee's plan was to act on the defensive, and not to strike until the right time came. The Federal army far exceeded his in numbers, they had entrenched themselves as his had done, and common sense, as well as military science, would teach the propriety of patiently waiting rather than rashly making the attack. The result has shown the wisdom of the policy adopted. Grant has already well nigh exhausted himself, whilst Lee's army remains almost intact, ready to assume the offensive or to continue to act on the defensive, as occasion may require.

Our loss in the rank and file is remarkably small, the men being well protected by the entrenchments. The casualties, however, has been unusually heavy among field officers who were unprotected, and had to move frequently from one point to another, under the terrible infantry and artillery fire of the enemy, which swept every part of the field in rear of our entrenchments.—The ground is torn and ploughed up by the direct and cross fire of the Federal guns as if it had been prepared by the farmer for the reception of spring seed. Three assistant surgeons were killed in the discharge of their duty on the field; and Captain Owen, of Texas, who carried the news to General Lee at Chancellorsville that Sedgwick was moving on his rear from Fredericksburg, was severely wounded early in the morning whilst on his way to the Richmond Howitzers to hold prayers. Including the battle of the Wilderness, we have lost the following general officers. Killed, Brigadier Generals Stafford, of Louisiana; Jones, of Virginia; Jenkins and Perrin, of South Carolina; and Daniel, of North Carolina. Wounded: Lieutenant General Longstreet of Alabama, and Brigadier Generals Hays, of Louisiana; Benning, of Georgia; McGowan, of South Carolina; Ramseur and Johnson, of North Carolina; and James M. Walker, (Stonewall Brigade.) H. H. Walker and Pegram, of Virginia. Captured: Major General Edward Johnson, of Georgia, and Brigadier General George H. Stewart, of Maryland.

General Lee made more than one narrow escape, his clothing being covered with mud thrown upon him by bursting shells. He will persist in staying near the point of greatest danger. The whole country, with one voice, should protest against such rash exposure of a life in which we are all so deeply interested, and upon the preservation of which so much depends. Gen. Taylor, his Adjutant General, had his horse shot. Gen. Ramseur's wound is slight. Many valuable field officers were killed and wounded.

The two armies, led by the most renowned chieftains on the Western Continent, if not in the world, have now been wrestling with each other for the mastery for eight days. Thank God, that ours has been so marvelously successful, and has suffered comparatively little loss, except in officers; whilst the larger, being the wrong doer, has been punished beyond all precedent in this war. His dead and many of his wounded still remain on the ground, being too near our entrenchments to be moved, and they tell their own melancholy tale. If half that prisoners report of their losses in battle, and from desertion, straggling and demoralization be true, then the enemy's casualties are indeed frightful. The loss in prisoners here has been about equal—say, 1500 on each side. This gives us the advantage of 3000, including those taken at the battle of the Wilderness. Of the prisoners captured here, two or three hundred were taken by Mahone, and four colors and one guidon, when he moved on the flank of the enemy.

Last night we rectified our lines near the angle which has given so much trouble, retiring it somewhat, and locating it where it should have been run originally. The enemy still retains possession of the angle, but has not been able to remove the guns left by Cutshaw and Page, nor have we, sharpshooters on either side preventing it. We brought away from the Wilderness 12,000 captured rifles and muskets.

Both armies have rested from the strife to-day. The dead have to be buried, the wounded have to be cared for, shattered regiments and brigades have to be reorganized, and fresh plans to be devised. This requires time, and the men require rest. There can be no doubt that Grant's troops were well supplied with liquor before they entered the battle; many of the prisoners, including more than one Colonel, were in a state of intoxication when taken.

May 14.—There has been a good deal of shelling and picket firing to day, and at one time a renewal of the strife seemed imminent. We hear that the movement upon Richmond from City Point and the Peninsula has failed to accomplish its purpose; that being true, what can Grant hope to gain by pressing further in this direction? It is said he started with 93,000 muskets: if he can muster 50,000 of these now, he is more fortunate than prisoners, both officers and men, represent him to be.

The Charleston Mercury.

VINDICE NULLO
SPONTE SUA SINE LEGE FIDES RECTUMQUE COLLENTUR.

COUNTRY PAPER—THREE A WEEK—EIGHT DOLLARS, FOR SIX MONTHS—PAYABLE IN ADVANCE.

VOLUME LXXXIV. CHARLESTON, S. C., THURSDAY, MAY 19, 1864. NUMBER 12,065

THE MERCURY.

THURSDAY, MAY 19, 1864.

The Glorious News.

The news which we publish to-day is eminently satisfactory. The enemy, repulsed with terrible losses in all his advances on General LEE's army, is necessarily much enfeebled and too demoralized to fight well in any further movements projected against Richmond, however GRANT may attempt to redeem his failure. In Upper Georgia, General JOHNSTON also has selected his ground. He seems master of the situation, has a fine army, confident in his high capacity for grand tactics, and has repulsed the foe with slaughter in the first attack. In Louisiana, although BANKS has escaped with a fraction of his army, the greater portion of his troops have surrendered as prisoners of war. Thus far this year our successes have been great and unbroken. Let us still manfully bend every effort to the thorough accomplishment of our independence, and the smiles of Providence will rest upon us.

HIGHLY INTERESTING FROM GENERAL JOHNSTON'S ARMY.

FULL DETAILS OF THE BATTLE OF RESACA.

From our North Georgia exchanges we get a mass of interesting details of the news from General JOHNSTON's army. It is evident from all accounts that there has already been much hard fighting, and that there is to be a great deal more before the fight is over. Our loss is considerable and that of the Yankees is very heavy.

About one thousand or fifteen hundred of our wounded from the late battles in front reached Atlanta Monday afternoon. They were promptly cared for. All the citizens have been requested to send their men servants to the Provost Marshal's office every morning.

Our army left Resaca Monday morning in good order and without any serious losses of any kind. The railroad bridge over the Oostenaula river was burned after our forces were placed in position on the south side. Our army retired to Calhoun without any confusion or disorder, and General JOHNSTON still commands all the roads leading to Atlanta.

Only two divisions participated in the late engagements. Lieut. Gen. HARDEE had his horse killed under him by a shell. One of his staff was slightly wounded. Our line of battle now extends about twenty-eight miles.

The Yankees hold Snake Gap, and are fortifying it rapidly. General KILPATRICK, the celebrated Yankee cavalry raider, has been wounded mortally. No one knows what General JOHNSTON's future plans are. He keeps them all to himself. His army has the greatest confidence in him, and will follow him anywhere.

Reports were current in the streets of Atlanta on Monday night that a Federal force advancing on Rome was repulsed by a force of Confederate cavalry stationed there, or *in transitu* for some other point. It is stated that General FORREST was at Chattanooga. This is rather improbable, although not impossible. At last accounts FORREST was at Tupelo, Miss. In order to reach the place he is said to be in, he must have made some extraordinary forced marches.

We devote a large portion of our space this morning to copious extracts from our Atlanta exchanges. The following account of the Battle of Resaca is from the *Confederacy*:

OPENING THE FIGHT.

From intelligent soldiers, among the wounded who came down Sunday afternoon, we learn that the fight was opened about 10, a. m., on Saturday, and continued fierce and general along the lines until night. Our men, with the brief period allowed them before the enemy attacked, threw up temporary breastworks of logs and rails, from behind which they repulsed every assault. Our cannoneers were so much exposed to the enemy's sharpshooters and so close to the Yankee lines, that they loaded their guns in a recumbent position.

The Yankees fought with a desperate valor, worthy of a better cause. They tried to charge several times during Saturday evening, but every time they came up our boys poured the leaden hail into them, and they turned and fled in confusion before the wrathful storm. Our men were not permitted to pursue. The time has not come for that.

SPIRIT OF OUR TROOPS.

Whenever the Yankees advanced to the charge our boys wound breast the works and sing out, "fix bayonets," when a clangor of metal would ensue which was ominous of death. The wounded veterans who have reached Atlanta state that their comrades in front are in the finest feather, and as full of pluck as ever. They say the Yankees may come up in swarms, and they will meet every charge, even to the point of the bayonet and the club of their Enfields. There is no disposition to fall back, and an order to that effect, even from General Johnston, whom they all revere, would be obeyed reluctantly.

The enemy, towards evening on Saturday, attempted to turn our right, but, instead of accomplishing this, found their left turned by General Hood, who charged and drove them back three quarters of a mile, and was still driving them when night closed the operations of the day.

"We'll fix these things to-night," exclaimed the soldiers of Bate's division, pointing to the insecure breastworks, and the word was caught up all along the lines. Accordingly, at night the rifle was temporarily laid aside for the "shovel and the spade," and our defences were materially strengthened before the Sabbath sun had ushered in another day of battle.

POSITION OF THE LINES.

On the enemy's line McPherson and Hooker are on their right wing, but we could not learn who commanded their left. Up to Friday evening Sherman's headquarters were at Tunnel Hill, but he has of course moved down since to field headquarters. On our line, Polk is in command of the left wing, Hardee in the centre, and Hood on the right. Walker's Division was on our extreme left Saturday evening, in the direction of Calhoun. We understood that Loring's and French's Divisions are at Rome. On Friday, the enemy's lines extended from the Oostenaula at a point two miles below Resaca, to within a short distance of the railroad, the position they had held for three days previous. One of our correspondents at the front went with a scouting party along the whole front of the enemy but could learn nothing definite as to his force. They, however, report themselves from 30,000 to 40,000 strong.

PRELIMINARY MOVES.

Some of our dismounted scouts sent to the enemy's right and rear on Friday reported a column of 25,000 strong moving slowly toward Resaca, through Snake Creek Gap, fortifying as they come. Colonel Grigsby charged a regiment capturing sixty, and would have captured the horses of the entire command but from the fear of being flanked and surrounded.

Saturday afternoon our line was formed in the shape of an inverted A, the apex towards the enemy, our left extending in the direction of Calhoun and our right beyond Resaca. Bates' Division and the Kentucky brigade were near the apex of the A, and of their part in the action, we have received the following accounts:

(FROM OUR CORRESPONDENT.)

BATTLEFIELD, 9 P. M., May 14.

The enemy massed their strength in front of the portion of our works manned by Hindman and Bates' divisions, and commenced the assault by a direct charge this evening at fifteen minutes past one o'clock. Permitting them to approach within short gun shot range before firing, we poured a murderous withering fire into their deep ranks, and they broke and fled like cowards.

Three successive times fresh lines were put in, and they attempted with heavy battalions to carry our works by storm, and, at every effort, they were signally, gloriously sent reeling back—their men flinging their guns away in their craven flight. Two Yankee flags lay within gun range of our works, and the enemy have failed in every effort to get them. We will send for them to night. I have not heard the casualties elsewhere than our immediate position of the line—only general result. The orphan boys of Kentucky, led by General Lewis, and Tyler's brigade, led by Col. Tom Smith (of the 20th Tennessee Regiment), fought with the valor and vim of desperation. They were everywhere waving their hats in a tempest of bullets, and cheering their men to fight for home.

I can now only recall among the wounded Capt. Pickett, Engineer Corps; Captain Blanchard, 37th Georgia Regiment, and Lieutenant Rawley, 20th Tennessee Regiment.

NEAR RESACA, GA., May 14

Yesterday was the most exciting day that we have had since the enemy advanced upon our position. At fifteen minutes past 8 o'clock, a. m., on the 13th, the enemy entered Dalton, our cavalry, under General Wheeler, retiring slowly and sullenly before his masses of infantry. General Wheeler formed his line of cavalry three miles this side of Dalton, in a ridge, upon the Resaca road, and gave them a very severe check, evidently inflicting heavy loss upon them. Confident in his overwhelming columns, he still pressed, and we fell back again to take a new position.

Our wagon train at Tilton was ordered to move rapidly to Resaca. It reached there just in time to receive a furious shelling from the Yankees, who made the air hideous with their hissing missiles. Teamsters and wagons made better time through town than we have ever seen made before. Late yesterday noon we had another severe engagement with them, but lost none killed. The Yankees were entirely around us at one time.

OUR POSITION SUNDAY.

Our usually well posted correspondent "Paxton" writes us Sunday morning from Resaca: "The left wing of the enemy rests near this place, while the right extends to the river. A reconnoitering force crossed the river Monday afternoon, but at great sacrifice. They recrossed it last night. In Monday's fight we neither gained nor lost ground—both Johnston and the enemy occupy their same lines as in the commencement of the engagement."

The same correspondent writes: "Our loss thus far is comparatively small. It is reported that the enemy's loss is very heavy in killed—but few were taken prisoners. If Johnston succeeds in turning their left wing he will bag the whole of them, as they will then be completely hemmed in by the river on one flank and Johnston on the other."

THE FIGHTING SUNDAY

was general along the lines all day, though it could be scarcely considered a general battle in which the results could have been decisive. Our men were engaged repelling the enemy at various points at intervals. With the exception of a lull about 9 o'clock on Sunday morning (occasioned, it was believed, by the fog and smoke) there was a running fire from sunrise until dark. Bates' and Cheatham's divisions were under heavy fire during the day.

OUR POSITION ON TUESDAY.

Our lines Tuesday, according to the most accurate information we can gather, extend nearly parallel with the railroad, and our troops are on both sides of the Oostenaula, the railroad bridge over which is still in our possession, notwithstanding repeated efforts of the enemy to take it. The enemy have also made frequent attempts to cross the Oostenaula at a ford, in order to reach our rear, by Calhoun, but have every time been repulsed.

We believe the enemy may attempt the passage of this river at the old Indian Ford about five miles below Calhoun, and that they will mass their forces in Springtown Valley, where it is likely a decisive battle may occur. They have constantly attempted to flank, and as constantly leaving their own flank exposed.

THE FIELD

Is described by those who took part in the action thereon, as very similar to that of Shiloh, a broad level, cut up into ravines and thickly wooded at various points.

Battle of Resaca, Georgia, May 14, 1864

The New-York Times.

VOL. XIII—NO. 3963. NEW-YORK, MONDAY, JUNE 6, 1864. PRICE THREE CENTS.

THE ARMY.

STEADY PROGRESS.

Grant Moving on the Enemy's Works.

LEE NARROWING HIS LINE.

HEAVY LOSSES.

LARGE REINFORCEMENTS

SHERMAN PUSHING SOUTHWARD.

[OFFICIAL.]

WASHINGTON, Sunday, June 5—1 P. M.

To Major-Gen. Dix:

A dispatch from Gen. GRANT'S headquarters, dated 8:30 o'clock last night has been received. It states that about 7 P. M. yesterday, (Friday, 3d of June,) the enemy suddenly attacked SMITH'S brigade, GIBBONS' division. The battle lasted with great fury for half an hour. The attack was unwaveringly repulsed. SMITH'S losses were inconsiderable.

At 6 P. M., WILSON, with his cavalry, fell upon the rear of a brigade of HETH'S division, which LEE had thrown around to his left, apparently with the intention of enveloping BURNSIDE. After a sharp but short conflict, WILSON drove them from their rifle-pits in confusion. He took a few prisoners. He had previously fought and routed GORDON'S brigade of rebel cavalry.

During these fights he lost several officers, among them Col. PRESTON, First Vermont Cavalry, killed; Col. BENJAMIN, Eighth New-York Cavalry, seriously wounded; Gen. STANNARD, serving in the Eighteenth Corps, was seriously wounded yesterday, (Friday.)

Our entire loss in killed, wounded and missing during the three days' operations around Cold Harbor, will not exceed, according to the Adjutant General's report, 7,500. This morning, (Saturday, June 4,) the enemy's left wing, in front of BURNSIDE, was found to have been drawn in during the night.

Col. CESNOLA, in command of 5,000 men, arrived here yesterday, having marched from Port Royal, [on the Rappahannock.]

Telegraphic communication between Cherryston and Fortress Monroe continues uninterrupted.

A dispatch from Gen. SHERMAN, dated yesterday June 4, 8 A. M., thirteen miles west of Marietta, reports that his left is now well around, covering all roads from the south to the railroad about Ackworth. His cavalry has been in Ackworth and occupies in force all the Allatoona Pass. No other military intelligence has been received by the department.

EDWIN M. STANTON, Secretary of War.

A Battle on Friday—Combined Assault on the Rebel Works—No Decisive Advantage Gained—The Rebels Driven Within their Works.

[SATURDAY'S OFFICIAL DISPATCH.]

WASHINGTON, June 4, 1864.

To Major-Gen. Dix:

Dispatches from Gen. GRANT'S headquarters, dated 3 o'clock yesterday, have just been received. No operations took place on Thursday. Yesterday, at 4:30 o'clock A. M., Gen. GRANT made an assault on the enemy's lines, of which he makes the following report:

"We assaulted at 4:30 A. M., driving the enemy within his intrenchments at all points, but without gaining any decisive advantage. Our troops now occupy a position close to the enemy, some places within fifty yards, and are remaining. Our loss was not severe, nor do I suppose the enemy to have lost heavily. We captured over three hundred prisoners, mostly from BRECKINRIDGE."

Another later official report, not from Gen. GRANT, estimates the number of our killed and wounded at about three thousand. The following officers are among the killed:

Col. HASKELL, Thirty-sixth Wisconsin.

Col. PORTER, Eighth New-York Heavy Artillery.

Col. MORRIS, Sixty-sixth New-York.

Among the wounded are Gen. R. O. TYLER—seriously—will probably lose a foot; Col. MCMAHON, One Hundred and Sixty-fourth New-York; Col. BYRNES, Twenty-eighth Massachusetts—probably mortally; and Col. BROOKE, Fifty-third Pennsylvania.

EDWIN M. STANTON, Secretary of War.

FROM GEN. BUTLER.

Rebel Stories—Arrival of Prisoners at the White House.

FORTRESS MONROE, Saturday, June 4.

A rebel Major came into Gen. BUTLER'S lines at Bermuda Hundreds yesterday, who says that the federal forces are at Secessionville, and threatening Charleston. The commander has telegraphed the rebel authorities for reinforcements, saying unless he receives them immediately Charleston is lost.

The steamer *Manhasset*, from White House, reports that the cannonading which had been heard very distinctly for nearly three days closed yesterday afternoon, and was not renewed this morning, at 8 o'clock.

One thousand prisoners had arrived at the White House, captured by Gens. SMITH and BURNSIDE.

The steamer *Thomas Powell* arrived from Bermuda Hundred at 4 P. M. There have been no active operations there since the last account.

The steamer *May Flower* was fired into, going up the James River, this morning. No damage was done.

Heavy cannonading was heard in the direction of Richmond, last night.

The Fight of Thursday—The Rebels Make a Dash at our Rifle-pits—How the Dash Was Circumvented and the Rebels Captured.

From Our Own Correspondent.

IN THE FIELD, BERMUDA HUNDRED, Friday, June 3, 1864.

We had quite a "brisk little time" here yesterday morning. The enemy made a dash at our pickets, with the intention of gaining possession of the entire line of rifle-pits, wherein our sentries "hide" themselves, as the rebs say. It will be remembered that they gained possession of a portion of these pits when they made their first attack on our position, but on TERRY'S front they were unsuccessful. It seems they have, ignoring the commandment to the contrary, secretly coveted these pits from the very hour they were so decisively repulsed, and, if possible, determined to have them or, well, do something else. With this determination they attacked our lines yesterday morning, throwing forward their entire picket. Little did they dream of the treatment in store for them. That such an attack was expected at some time, is evident from the disposition made to meet it. The pickets of the right wing, holding the pits, were ordered to hold their position while the left should fall gradually back. It was hoped that the enemy, feeling exceedingly certain of bagging our retreating pickets, would not notice the gap which would thereby be caused in their line. And so it proved. On their left rushed, never noticing that the right had been checked, and they were not only detached, but gradually getting further and further within our lines. When they had got well into the trap, a part of the picket reserve slipped through the gap in behind the advancing foe. When fairly surrounded, they appreciated their danger, and tried to cut their way out, but 'twas no use. Their Colonel and many of his men having been killed, the remainder surrendered.

They proved to be a portion of the Twenty-second South Carolina Volunteers, Col. DANTZING. The men who so neatly executed this well-devised plan, were dismounted cavalry, partly of the First District of Columbia Regiment. These men were armed with rifles shooting sixteen shots before they require loading.

Our loss was small—one killed, sixteen wounded; number of prisoners I have been unable to get.

After visiting all places of local interest, Mrs. Gen. BUTLER returned to Fortress Monroe to-day, by the steamer *John A. Warner*.

From Bermuda Hundred.

FORTRESS MONROE, Friday, June 3.

The enemy attacked Gen. BUTLER'S lines of defence, above Bermuda Hundred, on Wednesday evening, at 9 o'clock, and made a charge with the evident intention of capturing our Parrott guns, but were repulsed with heavy loss. The fighting continued until near Thursday morning, when the enemy were driven back. Our loss was very slight.

FROM GEORGIA.

A Fierce Battle on May 25.

CINCINNATI, Sunday, June 5.

The Cincinnati *Commercial* has accounts from SHERMAN'S army up to May 31.

There was a sharp and bloody fight, on the 25th of May, between HOOKER'S corps and the rebel Gen. HOOD'S command, near Dallas. The battle began at 5 o'clock in the afternoon. The Second Division, under Gen. WILLIAMS, drove the enemy from their first line of works for a distance of two miles.

This division was soon relieved by the First and Third Divisions, under Gens. GEARY and BUTTERFIELD, who advanced steadily, under a terrible musketry fire, and proceeded within forty yards of a concealed battery, which opened upon them a sudden and murderous discharge of grape and canister.

The First Division, in this charge, lost 900 men. The battery was finally silenced, and the enemy driven away. Few prisoners were taken on either side. Our loss was probably greater than the enemy's and amounted to about 1,500.

The substantial fruits of the day's work were the gain of two miles of ground, a favorable position, two pieces of artillery, and a better arrangement of our line for subsequent operations.

On the 26th a general engagement was expected, but Gen. MCPHERSON'S corps did not come up.

There was a good deal of skirmishing with musketry and artillery firing.

Prisoners report that reinforcements had increased JOHNSTON'S army to 70,000 men.

On the 27th there was a severe fight on the left. WOOD'S division and SCRIBNER'S brigade of JOHNSON'S division lost 400 men.

On the 28th there was heavy picket firing.

On the 29th the rebels made a night attack, but were repulsed with heavy loss.

On the 31st HOOKER and MCPHERSON were moving their troops to the left of our position, their right resting on Dallas and left near the railroad, eight miles from Alatoona.

The following is a partial list of our casualties:

Brig.-Gen. Johnson, wounded.
Col. Patrick, Fifth Ohio, killed.
Col. Payne, One Hundred and Twenty-fourth Ohio, missing.
Col. McDougal, 123d Penn—lost a leg.
Col. John Grimes, 13th New Jersey—slightly wounded.
Col. McGroaty, 61st Ohio—slightly wounded.
Col. Neibling, 21st Ohio—lost an arm.
Lt.-Col. Hurst, 11th Ohio—slightly wounded.
Lt.-Col. Thompson, 82d Ohio do do
Major Hamsen, 124th Ohio—killed.
Major Stinson, 5th Maine—dangerously wounded.
Major Farmer, 123d Penn.—slightly wounded.
Capt. M. H. Todd, 111th Pennsylvania—killed.
Capt. J. A. Moore, 147th Penn.—severely wounded.
Capt. Cheesebore, 46th Pennsylvania—killed.
Capt. Craig, 46th Pennsylvania—slightly wounded.
Capt. Stephens, 107th N. Y.—severely wounded.
Capt. Hartley, 28th Pennsylvania—severely wounded.
Capt. Phillips, 46th Pennsylvania—killed.

The Battle at Resaca—Bravery of Hooker's Troops—The Advance to Cassville.

Correspondence of the New-York Times:

CASSVILLE, Geo., Sunday, May 22, 1864.

For the past fifteen days the army under Gen. SHERMAN has been fighting its way into the heart of Georgia with unvarying success. It is now within sixty miles of Atlanta and about seventy from Chattanooga. The most obstinate resistance against our advance was made at Resaca, fifteen miles south of Dalton. JOHNSTON had fortified the heights northward from the town with great care, and having been joined by POLK'S corps, was confident of success. The people were told that the "Yankee" army would here be signally defeated and its further progress rendered impossible. GEARY'S division had, a few days before, attacked the enemy at Mill Gap, an impregnable position to the west of Dalton, and engaged their attention while MCPHERSON had passed through Snake Gap in the Chattoogata Mountains, seven miles south, without opposition, and taken a position in their rear. Retreat became imperative, and accordingly JOHNSTON evacuated Dalton and fell back to Resaca. SHERMAN did not pause long before attacking the enemy at Resaca, and such was the vigor with which the Union troops assailed the rebel intrenchments that, one after another, they fell into our hands with comparatively small loss. The battle lasted for three days, but was at no time general. On the third and last day HOOKER'S corps attacked their strongest position with great fury, and such was the enthusiasm of the troops under him that it was difficult to restrain them properly. No other troops were engaged on our side this day, and the larger portion of our splendid army held the position they had before gained and looked quietly on while the "Potomac men," as HOOKER'S corps is called, were exhibiting their fighting qualities in a manner to excite the admiration of all. It was reserved to HOOKER'S corps to carry their strongest position, and nobly was it done.

The battle-field was a succession of steep hills and intermediate ravines, densely wooded and almost impervious to the eye or foot of man. On the summits of the ridges the enemy had prepared formidable breastworks, with artillery planted on the commanding positions. A consultation was held in the morning by the leading Generals, among whom I saw Hooker, Howard, Scofield, Sickles, Williams, Geary, Ruger and Knipe, all sitting upon the trunk of a prostrate pine, and arranging the plan of battle. There were four double stars, and four single, all names that have become familiar in the history of the war.

Soon the columns of the Twentieth Corps were in motion, and with quiet yet energetic movement, entered the forest toward the rebel lines. All was hushed and the air seemed heavy with silence. The divisions of WILLIAMS, GEARY and BUTTERFIELD took their assigned positions as nearly as they were able, and the work of blood began. The enemy opened on us heavily with canister and musketry, but our men advanced steadily in columns of battalions, and with well directed volleys soon sent the enemy flying from their first line of works to the shelter of their artillery and supplementary lines. Immediately in front of BUTTERFIELD and GEARY, was a battery of four guns masked behind a thick undergrowth of scrubby oaks and protected by an earthwork. It annoyed us seriously.

Directly behind it, within fifty paces, was a rifle-pit on a slight elevation, which completely covered the guns and gunners. To capture this battery was very desirable, and the task was undertaken alternately by the men of both divisions. The contest was sharp and bloody. Our troops advanced to the roughly made fort and gained the base of the parapet, but as they showed their heads above it and endeavored to reach the guns, they were shot down by the men in the rifle-pits behind the batting. Thus the four brass pieces remained between the contending parties, inaccessible to either without almost certain death. Our men could put their hands upon the muzzles of the guns as they protruded through the embrasures, but no more. It was equally hazardous for the enemy to undertake to approach. Our forces just under and around the fort, were commanded by Col. COBHAM of GEARY'S division, as brave an officer as ever drew a sword. Things remained in this condition for several hours until darkness approached. Col. COBHAM then consulted with Gen. GEARY, and was told that he must secure the guns at all hazards, but with as little loss as possible. A plan was devised by which the men dug away the earth on each side of the embrasures, and made an opening sufficiently wide to pass the guns out to the front. Ropes were attached to them, and some time after midnight they became ours. About this time the enemy gave us a parting volley, and their whole force retreated under cover of the night.

Our losses were considerable, particulars of which have doubtless reached you by telegraph.

Lieut.-Col. LLOYD, One Hundred and Nineteenth New-York Volunteers, was killed; and Col. IRELAND, commanding Third Brigade, GEARY'S division, was severely but not dangerously wounded. Capt. WOLTON, One Hundred and Eleventh Pennsylvania Volunteers, was killed in the charge upon the battery.

When daylight came our whole force started in pursuit. We entered and passed through the town and station of Resaca, capturing considerable material and many prisoners. The enemy had burned the railroad bridge over the Oostanaula, but our men were quickly at work rebuilding it. The Oostanaula is a stream of about the same volume as the Rappahannock at Kelly's Ford. It is fordable at certain points at this season of the year. Our whole army was quickly crossed over—some by the various ferries above and below Resaca, and others fording the stream.

The Twentieth and Twenty-third Corps moved on the left flank some distance east of the line of the railroad, while the Fourth and Fourteenth Corps were in the centre and on the right. We were fast penetrating into the more cultivated portions of Georgia, leaving the mountains behind us. Most of the inhabitants had fled. A few of the wiser remained to meet us, and hailed our advance with joy. Fine farms and plantations greeted our vision, with stately mansions surrounded by shady groves and disciplined shrubbery. From Resaca to Kingston it was a running fight of several days. The bulk of the rebel army was in front of the Twentieth and Twenty-third Corps. Approaching Cassville we found the enemy had made preparation for a determined resistance, and our arrangements were made to attack with vigor. There was considerable fighting on the 20th, but in the course of the night the enemy again fell back, and are now said to be fortifying the line of the Etowah.

Our battle of the 20th was in and around Cassville, the shire town of Cass County. It is a very pretty village, containing a college, several fine churches, hotels, &c. The town has suffered much from the battle in and around it. It lies in a beautiful valley, between two ranges of hills, and before war had laid its blighting hand upon it, was, doubtless, a pretty country village. There are several very fine private residences, giving evidence of former wealth and luxury. Rome, Kingston and Cassville, all lying on nearly the name parallel, are now in our possession, and our course is Gulfward. Our losses during the series of battles since we left Chattanooga, do not exceed 5,000 in the aggregate. Reinforcements are constantly coming up, and our army has largely increased since the commencement of the campaign.

We repair the railroad as we advance, and the trains keep close upon us with all needed supplies.

People in this vicinity have never seen a Union army before, and the national colors have not been unfurled to their astonished gaze for nearly three years. As they look upon our glorious old banner, their recollection of the prosperity and happiness they formerly enjoyed under its protection comes vividly before them, and many hail it with tears of joy.

"Remain with us," said an intelligent planter, and let your flag and the bayonets of your men protect us from those who have worked our ruin." When the rebels evacuated Cassville and Kingston, our troops entered with colors flying and bands playing familiar patriotic airs. The surrounding hills seemed to rejoice as they echoed the music of the Union. Other hills and valleys southward are waiting for the advent of the starry flag of old, and the patriotic hearts that bear it onward. They shall not wait long.

NICKAJACK.

Gen. Sherman's Campaign.

The following extract from a private letter written by a Boston boy, an officer in a Western regiment under Gen. SHERMAN, contains some facts of interest:

SIX MILES EAST OF KINGSTON, Ga., Friday, May 20, 1864.

We have had a hard campaign thus far, to be sure, but it has been very pleasant, nevertheless. We are now in one of the finest parts of the country I have ever seen. Everything looks fresh and luxuriant excepting the people, and the few who have ventured to await the coming of the Yanks are mostly of the "poor white trash" description. A more ignorant and slavish set one never desires to see. All the educated class, who ought and do know what lies their stories about Yankee ferocity are, have fled before us. All the negroes have been run South, except an occasional old worn-out negro or some very small children. The best informed of the inhabitants have told their stories of Yankee barbarity so often to keep the "poor trash" in arms, that at last they have come to believe them themselves, and they are nearly scared to death. Judging from the appearance of the country since we left Nashville, and more particularly since we left Chattanooga, the country below us must be pretty well filled with refugees, white and black. A few months ago there were thousands of negroes on the plantations in this country, and now you can hardly find fifty in the country.

We have had considerable light fighting every day since we left Ringgold, and quite a battle at Resaca, but not half so hard a one as we should have had if the rebels had not become frightened. They had a very strong position and were well fortified, but their hearts failed, I suppose, and they ran away.

The weather has been delightful, and the country is in its Summer dress. Flowers are abundant and beautiful. With a really civilized population this would be paradise itself. The scenery is grand, and the soil good. I could ask no better country to live in, if it were not for the miserable race of degraded beings, white and black, which now inhabit it. Those of the so-called higher class who stay in their houses until we come, have "book-learning enough to be highly educated," but they have not, apparently, an idea outside of their books, but negroes and "snuff-dipping." If we are successful in this campaign, I shall apply for a leave of absence to come come home and see you in June or July. You know we can say nothing about military matters, and so all I can say is that *I expect to get home within the coming three months.*

FROM NASHVILLE.

From Nashville to Chattanooga—A Costly Road and Perilous Route—Wasting War, and Restoring Nature—The Tennessee River—What Chattanooga has Gained from the Rebellion—Bragg's Hospital—Lookout Mountain and its Mirabilia—Chattanooga Cemetery.

From Our Own Correspondent.

NASHVILLE, Tenn, Wednesday, June 1, 1864.

Chattanooga is one of the names which the rebellion has made specially prominent. It is connected with some of the most marked and memorable events of the war. For months a rebel stronghold deemed impregnable, its capture by our forces, demonstrated the certain progress of the Union arms southward, foreshadowing the downfall of the rebel power. The Union grasp upon this place has been unrelaxing, as it usually is everywhere. And since the stars and stripes have waved above it and the surrounding hills, the circumjacent region has echoed again and again with the thunder of artillery, and been trampled by opposing hosts encrimsoning the soil in conflicts as fierce as they were frequent.

I returned, a day or two since, from my first visit to this historic battle-ground, or bloody ground, as it might be termed without much hyperbole. Starting from Nashville at 2.30 P. M., we made the journey of 150 miles in 16 hours, arriving at Chattanooga at 6.30 of the following morning. This is hardly Hudson River Railroad speed, but is considered creditable speed, under present circumstances, in traveling the distance between these two points. The road is rather ricketty, and the vast freights which its trains constantly carry, consisting of multitudinous soldiers and countless tons of military supplies, with the risk of interruption by rascally guerrillas, renders special circumspection in running essential to safety. All along the route lie wrecks of cars from former disasters, condemned iron, splintered ties, and other palpable evidences of the destructive wear and tear to which this road has been subjected, as well as of the ceaseless and indomitable energy of the Government in keeping the road in repair. Three trains—a passenger, a hospital and a freight train—usually start at the same hour, with suitable intervals between; and several of these, in this order, go forward in the course of twenty-four hours. Returning, as the track is single, the trains, to avoid the danger of collision, make the route by way of Huntsville, Ala., branching off at Stevenson. This route is now open, though guerrillas have greatly infested it of late, taking advantage of the withdrawal of our main army for the great work it is doing in Georgia. Three of these gentry had been taken near Huntsville, and incontinently hung, by order of Gen. LOGAN, on the very day we passed through the region. It is a fitting doom with which to visit so desperate and murderous a class of miscreants.

The road runs straight through the famous battle-field of Stone River, and of ROSECRANS' glory. In the bright bloom of the laughing Spring, few marks strike the eye of the terrific and sanguinary struggle which, less than a year and a half ago, strewed these plains with the mangled and dead. A massive monument, apparently about fifteen feet square, built of the gray stone of the region, records the valor of the heroes of Murfreesboro, whose blood was poured out here for their country, and whose remains consecrate the spot. When completed it will be an imposing structure, and will speak eloquently to the passers-by of coming times of what the country owes to the noble men who died to save it.

Murfreesboro is not pretty, as seen from the cars, whatever of beauty it boasted at any time, having vanished at the scowl of war. Its fortifications are elaborate and striking. It is a strong military position,—science and art, with their many-handed appliances, having made it truly formidable. The country around Murfreesboro is beautiful. It forms one of the most fertile portions of Tennessee. It looks far less war-ravaged than Virginia. Cultivation was going on more widely than I expected to find it. Large tracts of rich and mellow soil were smiling with their incipient burdens of corn and cotton. Though three weeks of May had hardly passed, corn six inches high was basking in the sun, while broad fields of oats, and the superb blue grass of the region, with rye and wheat already in ear, cheered the eye, and reminded one strongly of the fairest portions of the Middle States. The young cotton, just above ground, looking as we were whirled by, something like the cucumber, with its drills stretching over fields occasionally of sixty or eighty acres, appeared fresh and promising. Tennessee is in truth a noble State, physically, if I may repeat what I have said in other letters. The Union cannot produce richer soils than certain portions of this, at present, war-scathed State. Let peace be restored, and under the hand of skillfull and educated tillage, she will develop resources that will astonish herself.

We reached the mountain region, in which Chattanooga lies, before day; and when the dawn came, we were rushing along amid wild and picturesque mountain scenery, with the noble Tennessee River stretching on our left, for miles in view. It is a far finer river than the Cumberland—broader, deeper, with bolder and more variegated banks, which for miles and miles are fringed with a dense growth of forest trees, many of them of superb stature, throwing their branches far over the stream. Where the road runs along the Tennessee from Stevenson to Chattanooga, the view is charmingly varied and surpassingly beautiful, but I have no room for description. One needs beauty on the road to reconcile one to the deformity at the journey's end, when the famed Chattanooga bursts upon you in all its naked ugliness and desolation.

It was little more than a village of a thousand people or so, in its palmiest days, and apart from its situation and surroundings, never could have been pretty. In peaceful times, however, a profusion of trees and shrubbery, hid, in summer, much of what was unsightly and common place, as we see everywhere through the country, all prodigal nature covering up the architectural defects and beautifying what man has had neither taste nor means to adorn. The war here has stripped off every comely garment. The dense woods, which embosomed the place once, have been swept away for miles around. All fences have disappeared; walls have fallen in; buildings have been burned, leaving blackened ruins. Others, partially dismantled and wholly marred, serve as sutler's stores, or places where adventurers ply their various traffic. The most commodious buildings the Government has taken to meet its imperative and never-ceasing demands. The Commissary, Quartermaster, Medical Purveyor and Medical Director occupy what quarters they have been able to procure. The Sanitary and Christian Commissions are here, of course, dispensing from the most unpretentious of storerooms, benefactions which fall noiseless as the dew, and refresh and gladden as widely. Tents gleam on every side. Patrols, tramping troops, the clatter of hoofs, the ceaseless rolling of countless wheels, the hot haste, the noisy activity, the clouds of dust, the incessant scream and thunder of railroad trains, form sights, sounds and experiences which those at Chattanooga now find more striking than agreeable.

On a hill, toward the right, as you leave the depot stands Bragg's Hospital, a series of high, narrow, whitewashed buildings, forming, at present, the only general hospital of the place. It was overflowing with the wounded from Georgia; many tents having been reared around the main buildings to accommodate the numbers coming in from the front. From 1,500 to 2,000 wounded and sick were here on Tuesday last—nearly as many at the field hospital, at the foot of Lookout Mountain, the whole number in the place being not far from 5,000. They were still arriving with every train from Resaca, and going forward also with every train leaving for Nashville.

I saw a train of twenty cars, filled with wounded men, set out for the latter place on Monday—the men sitting on the bare cars, which, in several cases, had no covering whatever. They were all very slightly wounded; able to walk and in some sort help themselves. The numbers needing to be moved forward, make it indispensable at times to use anything in the shape of a car for transporting soldiers to hospital. To the wounded, the journey from the field to the hospital, is, at the best, a sore sorrow, very often a bitter agony. Deep as our sympathy may be with these sufferers, there is no alternative between their encountering the grim journey, or remaining on the field or near it, with few of the comforts that a well-arranged city hospital will give them. Most choose the latter, willing to run every risk to reach it.

Lookout Mountain rises grandly toward the west, seemingly about two miles from Chattanooga depot. I found it every furlong of five miles to reach the top. The road up the mountain is circuitous, and somewhat rough. Had it been smoother, and had fewer trees been cut down on its sides, I would have recognized strong points of resemblance to that leading to Pine Orchard. As it was, I could without much violence, fancy myself traversing the romantic region where RIP VAN WINKLE slept, and woke after many years. Immense boulders lie grimly on the roadside from point to point, beneath one of which, and far within the bowels of the rock, gushes a spring of crystal water, very refreshing to those who were footing it from Alp to Alp, beneath a sultry sky, on the day in question. Arrived at the crowning plateau at length, you find the remains of the rebel encampments. You gaze with delightful astonishment from an elevation of 1,460 feet above the Tennessee, at the superb panorama that stretches before you. You advance a mile to the extreme point of the mountain, and look toward the north—a deep valley on the right and left, flanked on the one hand by Missionary Ridge, on the other by Raccoon Mountain, while the majestic Tennessee, creeping amid sweet fields and luxuriant covert growths, for miles in its sinuous course, makes a sudden bend at the very base of the mountain, and stretches northward, till in the far distance, it dwindles and is lost. The first line of rifle-pits which our brave boys took lies far below the point. Another line is half a mile back on the summit. It is marvelous that a place of such natural strength could have been taken. But for HOOKER'S flanking operation all efforts to assail it successfully in front must have proved abortive. The battle above the clouds, and its triumphant issue for our arms, must remain among the prodigies of Union prowess and achievement.

At the extreme point of the mountain is planted a telegraph station, with its appurtenances; while an enterprising photographist—of the universal Yankee nation stripe, I may safely venture to assert—has erected his shanty amid magnificent scenery, which has few parallels in the whole country. Here the cunning artist takes various views of the mountain and ambitious physiognomies of visitors, at prices only three or four times greater than those ordinary mortals ask who act and work with their fellow-mortals on the common level of mother earth. It is costly, in more senses than one, to be lifted among the clouds.

Lookout Mountain has been for years a fashionable resort for Southerners in the Summer months. A commodious though not large hotel, with a score of smaller buildings around it, some of them cottages, owned once by people of wealth, were wont to shelter a gay and amusement-seeking society of the *élite* of Tennessee and some of the adjoining States. Deliciously cool nights and mornings, days not inordinately hot, the finest air and water, and most splendid scenery in the world, must have made the sojourn here cozy, comfortable, charming. Uncle Samuel's war-worn heroes, whom wounds have made invalid, find it eminently so now. Some five hundred of them find themselves snugly perched on Lookout's accessible peaks, or *roosted*—to be very metaphorical—in the shady cottages of this "Buzzard's Roost," which they find a much more hospitable shelter than their comrades did the other roost that conducted into Dalton. Of this number 123 are, or were a few days since, officers, who speak rapturously of the elevated privileges which this lofty place affords; while the remainder, being privates, proclaim that they have found nothing so delightful in all their travels through the South. May they all enjoy and grow strong upon the sweets they have suffered so much to procure. Dr. L. R. HARLOW, the efficient surgeon in charge, is laboring to make this a permanent hospital; but the labor and expense of dragging invalids and all the supplies they need up this mountain make it doubtful whether the "powers that be" will favor the enterprise. It is more than probable that Lookout Mountain Hospital will have to "come down" among its unpretending sisters of the lowlands—a leveling process which this war has exemplified in a great many ways since it began.

Chattanooga Cemetery must have a closing word. It is an area of 100 acres, a mile south from the town. Its form is slightly conical, with a circular plateau at the top 100 yards in diameter, on which an imposing mausoleum, to be seen from afar, is designed at some future period to be reared. A massive wall is to surround the grounds, the foundations of which are now laid. It is artistically designed and laid out, though everything thus far is incipient and crude. The remains of three thousand of our honored dead already repose there, and Chaplain VAN HORN, of an Ohio regiment, long in charge of the grounds—through whose energy, aided by the liberality and good will of the military authorities, the enterprise has its present shape—is sparing no pains to gather into this hallowed inclosure the remains of all our soldiers who have fallen upon the various battle fields of this whole region. The spot will have a pensive interest for all the nation, and draw pilgrims, to view with swimming eyes, that sanctuary where

Sleep the brave, soft laid to rest,
With all their country's honors blest.

C. V. S.

FROM THE MISSISSIPPI.

Rebel Guerrillas Active.

ST. LOUIS, Sunday, June 5.

Dispatches received by Gen. EWING from Col. ROGERS, commanding at Cape Girardeau, state that the enemy is unusually active just now in that portion of the State.

Col. MCLEAN reports on the night of the 2d inst., that there were 200 guerrillas in camp near Pittston, at a mill, where they were busy grinding corn, and he sent a force of 200 men to look after them.

A force of guerrillas is reported on Cave Island, and another band at Doneghan. Col. ROGERS thinks the movements of the guerrillas are intended to cover an attack upon some important point, and that MCRAE will probably make demonstrations on Patterson.

A message from Capt. EWING, at Bloomfield, says the guerrillas destroyed the telegraph line near Charleston, and swore they intended to keep it down.

A dispatch from Col. ROGERS, dated Cape Girardeau, June 3d, says: "The whole company of guerrillas crossed the river and swamp and were within eight miles of here last night. They have cut the telegraph line to New-Madrid."

The presence of these bands of guerrillas is accounted for by the abandonment of Batesville and Jacksonport by the Union troops, which leaves the country open to the rebels of Arkansas.

SOUTH AND CENTRAL AMERICA.

IMPORTANT FROM PERU.

The Spanish Admiral Backs Water.

Rumored Assassination of Spaniards in Bolivia.

INTERESTING FROM PANAMA.

The Spanish Agent and French Consul Mobbed.

MUTINY ON BOARD THE OCEAN QUEEN.

$250,846 in Treasure.

The *Ocean Queen*, from Aspinwall on the 27th of May, arrived at this port at 2 o'clock P. M., yesterday. The *Ocean Queen* brings a large number of passengers. The following is her specie list:

Order	$17,604	Schoble & Bros	30,000
A. S. Rosenbaum & Co	80,700	A. Rich & Bros	9,500
Jennings & Brewster	9,000	J. Z. Parker & Son	3,500
J. B. Newton & Co	22,366	Duncan, Sherman & Co	37,676
H. Cohu & Co	20,800	Wells, Fargo & Co	36,500
H. Cohu & Co	32,700		
Total			$250,346

From Our Own Correspondent.

PANAMA, Friday, May 27, 1864.

The British steamship *Talca* arrived at Panama from Valparaiso and intermediate ports, on the evening of the 20th, bringing very interesting news from the South Coast. Dates from Valparaiso and Santiago de Chili are to the 1st, and from Callao and Lima to the 14th instant. The *Talca* brought only $130,000 in specie, with the usual number of passengers; also freight, consisting of copper, indigo, cotton, wool, cocoa, bark, &c., principally for Europe.

PERU.

Since my last, the Spanish Commissioner and Admiral PINZON, seem to have taken alarm at the warlike and determined attitude of all the South American States, as respects Spanish fillibustering on this Continent, and have abated largely the pretensions set forth in their previous manifestos. Admiral PINZON addressed a note to the Peruvian Minister of Foreign Affairs, in which the right of revindication of the Chincha Islands by Spain is no longer insisted on, and now alleges that the seizure of the Chinchas had no other object than to force the Government of Peru to make reparations for the injuries inflicted on Spain. "My instructions," says Admiral PINZON, "authorize me to hostilize the ports of Peru, in case the mission of the Special Commissioner should lead to no favorable result; but I have preferred to seize the Chincha Islands, in order that the Government of Peru and not its citizens, should be the loser."

The Spanish agents having thus shown a disposition to retreat from their first position, a meeting of the diplomatic corps was held at Lima on the 4th, at which it was resolved to send a deputation to the Chinchas to propose an amicable settlement with the Peruvian Government. On the next day H. B. M. sloop-of-war *Sheerwater* conveyed the Chargés from England and France, and the Minister from Chili to the islands, who remained there three days. In the new declaration made by the Spanish agents, resulting from this meeting, they say that Spain has no intention to hold the Chinchas, if the Peruvian Government will pay the claims of the Spanish Government, and leave the doubtful claims of private individuals to be settled by a mixed commission. The Ministers returned to Callao with this declaration on H. B. M. war-ship *Leander*, which vessel had the Peruvian war-steamer *Iquique*, seized by Admiral PINZAN, in tow, the Admiral having given her up voluntarily. On this, the Lima *Comercio* remarks:

"We learn that these voluntary negotiations have been unattended by any satisfactory result, and that the Peruvian Government will enter into no negotiation with the agents of Spain until they withdraw from the occupation of its territory. Consequently, we have refused to receive the *Iquique*, brought from the Chincha Islands to Callao by the foreign diplomatic agents, in tow of a British man-of-war."

Señor SALAZAR Y MAZZAREDO, the Spanish Minister, returned in the vessel of the diplomatists, and took passage on the *Talca* for Panama, where he arrived on the 20th, and embarked the next day for Europe from Aspinwall, and thus the matter rests. The following notes will place the readers of the TIMES *au courant* with the whole affair:

To the Peruvian Public:

The events which happened at the Chincha Islands on the 14th of April have been explained in documents already known to the public.

The representatives of the Queen have always trusted that the moderation of Peruvians and their natural calmness of spirit will at last bring this question to a satisfactory settlement.

At present when the diplomatic body residing at Lima has deigned to send to the Chincha Islands a commission, composed of the Ministers of Great Britain, France and Chili in order to confer on the actual situation, the undersigned declare again spontaneously, that Spain does not wish to meddle with the form of Government of the Peruvian Republic, and that the occupation of the Chincha Islands by way of reprisal, until Her Majesty's Government decide the matter, was preferable to other acts of hostility, which, causing effusion of blood, would render the arrangement of pending affairs difficult.

The Representatives of the Queen have not placed the least impediment in the way of the merchants of of Peru or its officers in the transaction of their business; and they have expressly prohibited since the first day, that vesseles without license of the authorities of Callao should load guano. The Peruvian authorities may also legalize in conformity with existing instructions all documents of the captains before they leave for the port of their destination.

Desirous to give a proof of their good wishes, the undersigned request the Ministers of England, France and Chili also to inform their colleagues that the bark *Iquiquen* will be given up.

The Spanish squadron will remain on the defensive so long as it is not forced to do otherwise, and it will grant a term of forty-eight hours to the respective authorities, if it finds itself compelled to act in a hostile manner toward any port of the republic.

Her Majesty's Government, according to the verbal communication to the chiefs of the foreign naval stations, will not claim the payment of any private debt which is not of Spanish origin, and based on actual rights of Spanish subjects.

All doubtful claims of private persons will be submitted to a mixed commission.

And, finally, the rumors that Spain wishes to establish in Peru, or in any other of the not recognized republics of America, European dynasties, are without the least foundation.

LUIS H. PINZON.
E. DE S. MAZARREDO.

ROADSTEAD OF THE CHINCHA ISLANDS, on board the frigate *Resolution*, 7th of May, 1864.

Señor SALAZAR Y MAZARREDO, Her Majesty's Commissioner to Peru, and her Minister to Bolivia, desires to inform the public that he sacrifices his *amour propre*, in view of the importance of the questions discussed between Spain and Peru, resigning by the last mail his appointments, which he owes to the confidence of the Queen, as he believes that in grave conflicts all men respecting themselves must, in the nineteenth century, place their Governments in a position to overcome without difficulty, and with a high spirit of impartiality, all questions presenting themselves, abnegating individuals, but always adhering to principles.

All over Peru, the excitement, in consequence of these events, has been intense. The *Comercio* says:

"The attitude assumed by the country is worthy of the cause to be defended. Government receives daily from all parts of the Republic the most ardent manifestations of patriotism, and political parties have laid aside their differences for the sake of unity; now we have but one party—that for the defence of

The New-York Times.

VOL. XIII—NO. 3952. NEW-YORK, TUESDAY, MAY 24, 1864. PRICE THREE CENTS.

THE GRAND CAMPAIGN.

The Situation in Virginia, Louisiana and Tennessee.

The Great Flank Movement Against Lee.

Our Army Rapidly Pressing Southward.

THE ADVANCE SOUTH OF THE MATTAPONY

Gen. Sherman Again in Pursuit of Johnston.

LATER FROM THE RED RIVER.

THE FLEET AND THE ARMY ALL SAFE.

How the Army is Being Reinforced and Supplied.

DISPATCH FROM SECRETARY STANTON.

Arrival of Admiral Porter at the Mouth of the Red River—The Fleet all Safe—Gen. Banks at Semmesport—Sherman Again in Pursuit of Johnston—The Way the Armies are Being Reinforced and Supplied.

[OFFICIAL.]

WASHINGTON, May 23.

Maj.-Gen. Dix:

Dispatches from Maj.-Gen. CANBY, dated mouth of the Red River, at midnight, May 15, state that "Admiral PORTER has just arrived. The remainder of the gunboats will arrive to-night. Gen. BANKS will probably reach Semmesport, on the Atchafalaya to-morrow."

A dispatch from Admiral PORTER, dated on board the flagship *Black Hawk*, mouth of Red River, May 16 states that the portion of the squadron above the falls at Alexandria have been released from their unpleasant position, owing to the indefatigable exertions of Lieut.-Col. BAILEY, Acting Engineer of the Nineteenth Army Corps, who proposed and built a tree dam of six hundred feet across the river at the lower falls, which enabled all the vessels to pass in safety, the back-water of the Mississippi reaching Alexandria, and allowed them to pass over all the shoals and the obstructions planted by the enemy, to a point of safety. Lieut.-Col. BAILEY will be immediately nominated for promotion, for distinguished and meritorious services.

An unofficial report from Cairo, dated May 22, states that the army and gunboats were all safe at the mouth of the Red River and Semmesport.

Maj.-Gen. SHERMAN, by a dispatch dated 8:30 P. M. last night, reports that he would be ready by the morning to resume his operations. Returned veterans and regiments, he says, have more than replaced all losses and detachments.

We have no official reports since my last telegram from Gen. GRANT or Gen. BUTLER.

Official reports of this department show that within eight days after the great battle of Spottsylvania Court-house, many thousand veteran troops have been forwarded to Gen. GRANT.

The whole army has been amply supplied with full rations of subsistence.

Upward of twenty thousand sick and wounded have been transported from the fields of battle to the Washington hospitals, and placed under surgical care.

Over eight thousand prisoners have been transported from the field to prison depots, and large amounts of artillery and other implements of an active campaign brought away.

Several thousand fresh cavalry horses have been forwarded to the army, and the Grand Army of the Potomac is now fully as strong in numbers and better equipped, supplied and furnished than when the campaign opened.

Several thousand reinforcements have also been forwarded to other armies in the field, and ample supplies to all.

During the same time over thirty thousand volunteers for a hundred days have been mustered into the service, clothed, armed, equipped, and transported to their respective positions.

This statement is due to the chiefs of the army staff and bureau, and their respective corps, to whom the credit belongs.

EDWIN M. STANTON,
Secretary of War.

THE FLANK MOVEMENT.

Lee's Right Flank Effectually Turned—Our Advance Eighteen Miles South of Spottsylvania on Saturday—Lee Falling Back—Hard Fighting Expected.

From Our Special Correspondent.

GUINEA'S STATION, Saturday, May 21—7 P. M.

The Army of the Potomac is again on the march toward Richmond. During the night, HANCOCK's corps, which had held the left of our lines in front of Spottsylvania Court-house, took up its march, moving on the road parallel with the Ny River. Early this morning it reached Guinea's Station, on the Fredericksburgh and Richmond railroad, twelve miles due south of Fredericksburgh. Thence it pushed onward, following the railroad, and to-night finds the head of HANCOCK's column at Bowling-green, eighteen miles south of Fredericksburgh. The other corps have been to-day following the same general line, and the Fifth is now passing the point at which this dispatch is dated. You will observe from these indications that the Commanding General has *effected a turning movement* on the right flank of LEE, who is now hastily falling back to take up a fresh defensive position. It is expected that his next stand will be on the South Anna River, although he may endeavor to hit us while moving by the flank, just as he did when outflanked in his lines on the Rapidan.

Heavy firing, in fact, is this moment heard across the Ny, where one of our columns is moving. A mile south by west of Guinea's Station is the point of confluence of the Po and Ny Rivers, and at this point the stream is crossed by Guinea's Bridge, which is in our possession. The river south of the junction of the Po and the Ny is called by the inhabitants of the country the "Mattapony," although the Mat and Ta, its other two affluents, do not enter it till we reach a point a dozen miles south of this.

Our army is now all gone from the front it has held before Spottsylvania Court-house for the past two weeks, and the lines of Spottsylvania pass into history. They are associated with fighting as desperate as was ever made by embattled foes, and by the greatest valor on the part of both armies. Its woods sepulchre thousands of bodies of brave men, perished in the great cause for which this army marches and fights and suffers.

You will notice by the map that our present front, while it puts us in a very advantageous position in regard to the enemy, at the same time perfectly covers our communications, which are by way of Fredericksburgh and Acquia Creek. The railroad will soon be open from Acquia Creek to Fredericksburgh, and will doubtless be put in order south of that point as we advance. There are also several available points of water communication by the Rappahannock, as at Port Royal, &c., which will probably be used.

I should misrepresent the conviction of the soundest heads in this army if I should convey the impression that our progress is to be now only a triumphal march. We shall be met by the most obdurate resistance which skill and courage on the part of the enemy can command. But Gen. GRANT has given you the key-note of the sentiment of this army: we shall go through with this business, "if it takes all Summer to do it." SWINTON.

GEN. BURNSIDE'S CORPS.

The Ten Days' Struggle—The Roads—The Prisoners—Reinforcements.

Correspondence of the New-York Times:

IN CAMP, NY RIVER, Monday, May 16, 1864.

After ten days' fighting, more terrible than the fighting on the Peninsula, at Antietam, or at Gettysburgh, we have driven the enemy to the heights lying on the north and northeast of Spottsylvania Court-house. But the struggle has cost us dear. One-third of the Army of the Potomac is *hors du combat*, and for a few days, before we again deliver battle, our brave and inspirited soldiers must be allowed to rest. Supplies also must be brought up from Belle Plain through Fredericksburgh, before the army can again move.

We have taken 18 guns from the enemy, 8,000 prisoners, and have inflicted on them a loss probably equal to our own. The military character of the Lieutenant-General, in this campaign at least, seems to be that of a man of untiring energy and of invincible determination. By dint of desperate fighting he intends to cut his way to Richmond.

The spirit of the army is high and confident. During the last three days I have talked constantly, by the roadside, around the camp fires, in the batteries and rifle-pits, in the hospitals, with hundreds of soldiers. "We are sure to win this time," are the words I have always heard. Their severe marching and fighting have not lessened, scanty rations and the pelting rain, have not diminished their assurance of final complete success.

This is the first clear day since the 11th. Daily rains have made almost impassable our roads of supply, the turnpike and the plank road to Orange Court-house, and the road to Spottsylvania Court-house. No one can form a correct notion of the condition of the highways except from personal observation. Even as I write, by the wooded roadside at headquarters, three horses of six, which are harnessed to an army wagon, are lying on their sides in the mud. The teamster is wading about, trying to unharness them; the roadmaster is helping him by giving contradictory orders, and by very loud and very vigorous cursing. Dead horses and broken down army wagons and ambulances one meets with nearly every mile, as well as occasionally the half-engulphed body of a mule, which, getting cast in the traces, has been suffocated in the mud before he could be rescued. The soil of this portion of Virginia is sand or loam, and the three or four thousand army wagons which compose our supply train cut up the roads and the fields by the roadside whenever rain falls for a few hours. But on the other hand, the soil is porous, and two or three days of pleasant weather will enable our large train to bring up abundant supplies of hard bread, salt pork and salt beef.

At Fredericksburgh I chanced to see two thousand prisoners marching under escort to Belle Plain. They were a motley crowd, scantily dressed, and ununiformed. But I saw nothing in their countenances or in their movements which indicated lack of food in the rebel army. They were as vigorous and healthy in appearance as our own troops. I have made particular inquiries from our soldiers respecting the condition of the rebel prisoners when they were first taken. The result of these inquiries has convinced me that LEE has thus far been able to supply his army with sufficient food.

To-day the Ninth Army Corps lies about four miles from Spottsylvania Court-house. Batteries guard the crests of the ridge on which we lie. From a section of the battery of the Eleventh Massachusetts, whose guns are three-inch Parrotts, taken from us at the first Bull Run battle, and retaken by us at Bristoe Station, I have just looked over a portion of our extended lines. Sharpshooters lie in the edge of the woods which bound the horizon, and which conceal the rebel fortifications. The crack of their rifles is incessant. The rebel riflemen are equally on the alert. But casualties are few. Two wounded men of our own and one wounded man of the rebels, is the result, thus far, of the incessant picket-firing directly in our front. Within easy shelling range of the enemy's batteries, in a dense wood of pines and hemlocks, the headquarters of the Ninth Army Corps have been pitched. We change them, I trust, to-morrow. Not a hundred feet from the shelter-tent of Gen. BURNSIDE, a dozen cattle have been slaughtered for the use of the army. The offal lies festering in the sun, and last night the odor, blown through our camp, was exceedingly offensive.

On the left of our lines, just beyond our rifle-pits and in plain view, lie the bodies of several rebels, who were killed during the great battle of the 12th. One is the body of an officer. His gray coat is ornamented with gold lace, but the badges of his rank have been taken from his coat by our soldiers, as trophies or as mementos.

In the operations of the Ninth Army Corps the Third New-Jersey Cavalry, Col. MORRISON, have taken an arduous part. The duty assigned to this regiment was, and still is, to patrol the country on both sides of the Rapidan, from near its junction with the Rappahannock to Germanna Ford. On the 11th and 12th hourly reports were sent from the patroling lines to Gen. BURNSIDE. It was the assurance which these reports gave, that no enemy was in his rear, that enabled him to throw his whole force into the battle of the 12th. For the thorough manner in which this regiment did its duty on these days, Gen. BURNSIDE, in the presence of his staff, warmly thanked Col. MORRISON.

The army is cheered to-day with the news that reinforcements, large enough to fully supply our losses, have been landed at Belle Plain. In a few days we shall resume our advance. God give us a complete and final victory! H. B.

FROM FREDERICKSBURGH.

Ewell's Attack Upon Our Right—Desperate Fighting of the Heavy Artillery Regiments.

From Our Own Correspondent.

FREDERICKSBURGH, Friday, May 20—6 A. M.

Yesterday our forces were massing on the left, and the enemy made a show of massing in the same direction by exposing their columns moving past Spottsylvania Court-house. Toward night a large force, said to be EWELL's whole corps, made a demonstration upon our extreme right, and for a time cut off all communication between the army and Fredericksburgh. Our forces in that vicinity, composed largely of artillery, acting as infantry, were at first repelled, but upon receiving reinforcements from the Ninth Corps, promptly rallied, and in less than an hour the enemy was handsomely repulsed. Our loss was heavy, and so was that of the enemy, who made a desperate attempt to cut our communications.

Guerrillas hover on the road between Belle Plain and Fredericksburgh, and also between the latter place and the army. A party attacked some straggling teamsters night before last near Gen. HOOKER's old headquarters, two miles from Falmouth, and beside capturing several horses, shot a teamster and then cut his throat. The Provost-Marshal of Fredericksburgh is arresting all citizens to-day, upon the supposition that they have furnished the enemy with information which led to the attack last night.

Lists of Casualties—Slaughter of the Rebels.

FREDERICKSBURGH, Saturday, May 21.

Inclosed you will find a pretty full list of men killed and wounded during Thursday evening, 19th, when EWELL attempted to flank us on the right. Most of the men who resisted this formidable attack never were in a fight before—artillerymen from the forts about Washington acting as infantry.

Our loss in that fight, which lasted about an hour and a half, will probably reach 1,000. But the enemy were fairly slaughtered. Some persons believe that they had as many killed as our total loss. The line has been advanced one and a half miles.

E. A. PAUL.

Losses in the Fight of Thursday Evening, May 19.

CASUALTIES IN TYLER'S DIVISION.

FIRST MASSACHUSETTS HEAVY ARTILLERY, COMPLETE—COL. TENNATT, COMMANDING.

Officers Killed.

Major F A Rolfe. | Lieut Graham, Co K.
Capt W G Thompson, Co E.

Officers Wounded.

Major N Shatswell—head. | Lieut C W Peasley, Co A.
Capt E A Andrews, Co I—thigh. | Lieut W Stacy, Co B—arm.
Capt W F Martin, Co L—thigh. | Lieut Atkinson, Co C—groin.
Capt W Preston, Co K—leg. | Lieut F Davis, Co I—breast.
Capt A A Davis, Co C—knee. | Lieut P D Smith, Co G—hand.
Lieut F F Spilford, Co I—3 wounds in thigh. | Lieut Noyes, Co G—hip.
Lieut C Carroll, Co H—both shoulders.
Lieut Roundy, Co B—ankle.

COMPANY A.

Killed.

J Briant. | L T Jewett.
J A Foster. | C. McCarter.
J Gordon.

Wounded.

H N Andrews—hand. | C H Leach—ankle.
G E Benson—hand. | A McGregor—thigh.
J W Clark—hand. | J Poland—arm and abdo'n.
J J Fowler—wrist. | B A Phippen—hand.
J Hopkins—wrist and side. | C H Phippin—hand.
[illegible]—hand. | W P Ross—thigh.
A M Keene—bowels. | R W Shurley—both legs.
J A Leonard—shoulder. | W Sit[illegible]—leg.

COMPANY B.

Killed.

Capt F C Mason. | George Harington.
James Allen. | Edward Gage.
A[illegible] Parker. | Harvey Gould.
George W Brickett. | L D Jackman.
Henry Colby. | C H Remick.

Wounded.

Sergt P H Waldo—wrist. | John Heath—side.
Sergt C H Ayer—ankle. | G[illegible] Howard—shoulder.
Sergt Chas [illegible]—hand. | B W Jones.
Sergt S D [illegible]—foot. | G E [illegible]—hand.
Sergt [illegible]—head. | H Sample—head.
Corp Sidney [illegible]—thigh. | Thomas Martin—hand.
Corp H J [illegible]—hand. | A [illegible]—hand.
Corp Daniel Kelley—leg. | J [illegible]—head.
Corp A M Bartlett—ankle. | W E Miller.
E C Allen—side. | [illegible]—stomach.
Charles [illegible]—leg. | [illegible]—hand.
S F Coolidge—face and arm. | H C Richardson—hip.
J [illegible]—foot. | [illegible] Sargent—hand.
Wm Cesick. | [illegible]—wrist.
Wm H Daniels—leg. | [illegible] Smith—groin and ankle.
[illegible]—face. | [illegible]—arm.
[illegible] Fitzgerald. | [illegible]—hand.
H S Forbes. | J A White—leg.
A Forbes—back. | F Webster—foot.
B [illegible]—hand. | F Woodsume—head.

COMPANY C.

Killed.

Michael Fitzgerald. | Andrew J Kenny.
Charles J Jarvis.

Wounded.

Capt A A Davis—knee. | Geo W Kent—hand.
Lieut B C Atkinson—arm and leg. | P Linehan—leg.
Sergt C H Atherton—arm and side. | A W Lewis—leg.
Sergt O H Widger. | Geo [illegible]—hip.
Sergt Henry Magee—leg. | C J Nason—ankle.
Corp E P Bruce—leg. | C Neale—leg.
J S Arnold—arm. | H J Poland—shoulder.
Wm Belger—ankle. | F C Poland—leg.
S R Bond—arm and breast. | Wm H Perry—leg and spine.
C Batchelder—legs. | Robert Phillips—leg.
Abel Gates—arm. | F Parrott—thigh.
C P Bliss—leg. | E P Rowell—thigh.
J G Chapman—lungs. | Geo W Rea—arm.
D Curran—hand. | F E Rose.
S C Fairfield—arm and foot. | J F Smith.
Wm H Flowers—leg. | —— Shepardson.
David Graves—foot. | E F Pratt—thigh.
Porter Homan. | J S Tarbox—thigh.
Ebenr Howard—both legs and arms. | Fred Shannon—foot.
Stephen Kenrick—back. | Rich Totton—leg.
M Tower—leg.
J Wells—testicles.

Missing.

Corp H B Phipps. | Wm H Tarbox.
C T Mills. | T Twisder.
C H Parish.

COMPANY D.

Killed.

E W Burrell—head. | A A Henrick—bowels.
F Gardner—head. | J W Woodbury.

Wounded.

Sergt J P Withey—groin. | W S Howard—internal.
Corp W S Rogers—hand. | R Pederick—leg.
Corp W A Cushing—arm. | N Pitman—leg.
Corp C A Warner—leg. | E W Reeves—foot.
D C Becket—back. | C E Ricker.
H B Demeret—leg. | J C Stackney—wrist.
G P Plurgerron—leg. | C Thomas—leg.
L M Goldthwaite. | E A Walton—shoulder.
C W A Goudey—leg.

COMPANY E.

Killed.

H T Webster. | H M Uunkins.

Wounded.

Corp O E Burham. | B F Leck.
Corp L W Farar. | N G Spafford.
J H Brown. | J T Merrill.
D B Burnham. | J McDonald.
A F Chaples. | H A McCann.
D Davis. | E A Ring.
W P Eddy. | T P Ray.
H S Eaton. | N J Rittle.
Lewis Hinger.

COMPANY F.

Killed.

Eleazer Washburn.

Wounded.

Sergt L A Stevens—hand. | Geo W Bickwell—hip.
Corp W Kennedy—shoulder. | Jerry Short—leg.
C H Parshley—forehead. | J A Guild—arm.
Patrick Cline—hand. | Jas Bailey—breast.

COMPANY G.

Killed.

W H Joshron. | Wm Tindly.
E C Staples. | R McCurley.

Wounded.

Corp N Tucker—hand. | Wm Laybee—hip.
Corp B F Aborn—head. | W F Luscomb—leg.
Corp A N Deland—foot. | F Magee—arm.
E F Chapman—back. | J D Pierce—leg.
B Downing—head. | J Roundey—hand.
T Foley—back. | B F Swasey—hand.
C [illegible] Filebrown. | S O Getchel—leg.
W B Bawford—hand. | J[illegible]—head.

Missing.

J Graham. | Corp W Bing.

COMPANY H.

Killed.

Sergt Edward Farmer. | Sam'l Aeking.
James Eastes. | James Rothwell.
Jona A Holt. | G K Cutler.
Chas W Ridley.

Wounded.

1st Lt C Carroll—shoulders. | Francis W Edwards—leg.
Sergt J B Sargent—hand. | Henry L Lovejoy—face.
Corp G E Pike—shoulders. | James Findley—arm.
Corp M B Townsend—neck. | Edward O'Hara—arm.
Chas H Bell—arm. | John Hays—hand.
David B Gilcreast—neck. | Charles Mears—arm.

Missing.

Chas P Barnard. | Sam'l Cheever—prisoner.
Jas Costello—shoulder. | Edwin J Pendleton—leg.
L G Hatch—abdomen. | Henry M Knox—abdomen.
Andrew J Hatch—hip. | James Cunningham—leg.
J Cusick—breast and legs. | David B Morgan—shoulder.
P C Lavalette—leg amp. | John Hardy—hand.
Aug K Russell—foot. | Geo E Hayward—abdomen.
Charles Cummings—head. | Chas F Trull—hip.
Michael Mahoney—breast. | Edward P Abbott—hand.
E E Bryant—leg and arm. | Malachi Nolan—leg.
Wm E Jennings—foot. | Wm Craig—arm, slight.
Sam P Farnham—arm. | T R Baily—foot, slight.

COMPANY I.

Killed.

Geo S Wilier.

Wounded.

A Brown—neck. | O Parkman—head.
G D Batchelder. | S Murey—hand.
A Sinclair. | W W Wilson—leg.
T Sheehan. | G H Yound—head.
J E Hallis—head. | H Byrnes.
J M Coffin—hand. | W K Werrill—hand.
J C Evans—arm. | O B Burton—hand.
O F Curtis—arm. | E F Fuller—leg.

COMPANY K.

Killed.

Capt. F. La Baris. | A T McGowen.
R Atkinson. | S Smith.
R Crosby. | H A Stodard.
S Murphy. | F Rafferty.
A. Holt.

Wounded.

Sergt N M Bartlett—leg. | J E Woodbury.
Sergt W W Wallace—back. | T McDool.
Sergt G F Cutler. | E R Holt.
Sergt E R Boardman. | A Preston.
Corp R Morse—breast. | J Hendricks.
J Bradley—foot. | A Williams.
J Batchelder. | L Wilder.
N Brinley. | J Murphey.
Uriah Blake—hand. | O Springer.
W Smith—arm. | W J Rooman.
G W Marrony. | W J Stephens.
C Hall—breast and leg. | J S Lyman, Jr.
A R Hobbs. | L P Littlefield.
E W Healy—mouth. | J B Flint.
J Williamson. | C Getchel.
A Shaw. | R Marsall—foot.
H Humphrey. | A Southwick.
J Marron. | E Kelley.
J Scott. | G Handy.

Missing.

Asa Rowe. | Sam Melvin.

COMPANY L.

Killed.

Sergt J Noyes. | J Kelly.
Capt A J Tuttle. | T Shenan.
P J Parker. | W Paris.

Wounded.

Sergt J S Eastman—ankle. | D W Davis.
Wm T Porter. | Y A Byron—breast.
D L Dickinson. | J P Willard.
J Murtle. | N Hill—neck.
H E Boynton. | C F York.
R Willis. | P Holbrook.
H Haskell. | E Town.
W W Bryant. | W J Mansfield.
J B Dodge. | N Horn.
A N Jewett. | L M Blaisdell.
J Dunbarey. | Wm Dufly.
J E Robinson.

Missing.

Sergt J W Hart. | E W Rand.
Capt G W Ransome. | S G Burnham.
J O'Connor. | C W Cross.
Geo Tarr. | J Wood.

KILLED AND WOUNDED IN OTHER REGIMENTS.

Capt V Brubecker, 1st Md Vet Vols. | John Wilson, K, 4th N Y—thigh.
John Collins, E, 1st Md—shoulder and arm. | Jas S Evans, M, 7th N Y Artillery—shoulder.
E W Lindsay, 10th Penn—hip. | Capt Morris, C, 7th N Y A'y—killed.
Geo Ferguson, 1st Mass A'y—hand. | G[illegible] Hiscock, E, 1st Me Artillery—thigh.
Maj [illegible], 1st Mass Artillery—killed. | [illegible], H, 1st Me Art'y—leg and arm.
Capt L W Farrar, E, 1st Mass Artillery—thigh. | Chas Crell, E, 1st Me Art'y—thigh.
Wm W Wilber, D, 7th N Y Artillery—side. | Capt Parker—killed.
Capt McCulloch, D, 7th N Y Artillery—killed. | Lieut Vickery—killed.
Jacob Peters, [illegible], 15th N Y Artillery—foot. | [illegible], 2d N Y Art'y—both legs.
Henry Crandall, 2d N Y Art'y. | John Ratzeber, 4th Md—back.
Jas Kane, C, 1st Maine Art'y. | [illegible] Chamberlin, E, 1st Maine Artillery—head.
—— Smith, Capt Maine Artillery—killed. | J [illegible], 1st Maine Artillery—killed.
—— [illegible], 1st Maine Artillery—killed. | Wm Graver, E, 1st Maine Artillery—foot.
A [illegible], N Y—killed. | P O'[illegible], 2d N Y Artillery—breast.
[illegible], H, 1st Md Infantry. | W[illegible], 2d N Y Artillery—[illegible].
Sergt Wm N [illegible], 1st Me Artillery—leg. | Sergt [illegible], 1st Maine Artillery—[illegible].
L[illegible]—killed. | [illegible], 1st Maine Artillery.
A [illegible]—killed. | [illegible], 1st Maine Artillery—killed.
W[illegible], 1st Maine Artillery—side. | [illegible], Maine Artillery—[illegible].
T [illegible], 1st Maine Artillery—[illegible]. | J A [illegible], 1st Me Art.
Capt Parker, 1st Maine Art—killed. | [illegible], 1st Me Art.
C F Hays, 1st Maine Art. | [illegible], 1st Maine.
—— [illegible], 1st Maine Art—killed. | [illegible], 1st Me Art.
Lieut Noes, 1st Maine Art—killed. | [illegible], 1st Me Art.
J W Smith, 1st N Y Art'y—[illegible]. | [illegible], 1st Me Art.
C F Winston, 1st N Y Art'y. | [illegible], N Y Art'y.
J Quess, [illegible] N Y Art'y. | [illegible], 1st Me Art'y.
L E [illegible], 1st Me Art'y. | A [illegible], 1st Me Art'y.
G Dunham, 1st Me Art. | [illegible], 1st Me Art'y.
L Nichols, 2d N Y Art. | A [illegible], 1st Me Art'y.
E Owen, 20th Indiana. | J W [illegible], 2d N C.
S [illegible], 1st Maine Art. | L B Shaw, 1st Maine.
H O Spring, 1st Maine Art. | [illegible], 1st Penn.
A J Douglass, 1st Me Art. | E F Smith, 1st Maine Artillery.
M [illegible], New-York. | Wm L De Wolf, 1st Maine.
D D [illegible], 8th New-York Artillery. | J L Brown, A, 1st Maine.
D W Barrett, A, 1st Maine. | J O Hughes, A, 1st Maine.
J M Colt, A, 1st Maine. | F McLoughlin, A, 1st Me.
E Bowley, A, 1st Maine. | R [illegible], A, 1st Me.
S A Simmons, A, 1st Maine. | S Flanders, A, 1st Maine.
A Lancey, A, 1st Maine. | J[illegible], 1st R I—sick.
Geo Patt[illegible], A, 1st Maine. | —— Holliday, 4th Ohio.
William H Campbell, A, 1st Maine. | [illegible] Williams, 6th Me Inf.
C E Wells, A, 1st Me. | A B Shea, A, 1st Maine.
R Howes, A, 1st Me. | A McKnight, 63d New-York.
Geo Curtis, 20th Mass. | O Dennison, A, 1st Me.
S Christian, 20th Mass. | Capt [illegible], A, 1st Me.
O H West, A, 1st N Y. | H Hardy, A, 1st Me.
B F Buzzell, A, 1st Me. | C M Weymouth, A, 1st Me.
Geo Durkee, 12th N Y. | J A [illegible], A, 1st Me.
Wm J Darbey, 22d N Y—fatally. | Lieut R V Moore, A, 1st Me.
Capt J Kellaher, 20th Mass—arm and cheek. | Geo Crump, A, 2d N Y.
Lieut Griffin, 20th Mass—leg. | A. G. Sawyer, A, 1st Me.
J Finn, 1st Maine. | A Holt, A, 1st Maine.
Lt Rollins, A, 1st Me—thigh. | Lieut A F Warnell, 4th Michigan—sick.
Capt E [illegible] Hersey, A, 1st Me—ankle. | W J Lavender, 9th N H—wounded.
Lt Geo W Gout, A, 1st Me. | Sergt [illegible] Salsbury, A, 1st Me.
Lt B Frazier, A, 1st Maine—thigh. | C T[illegible], A, 1st Maine.
D B Wiggin, A, 1st Maine. | John Couse, 4th New-York Artillery.
T M Pierce, A, 1st Maine. | E [illegible] Cleveland, A, 1st Maine.
Wm Guest, 6th New-York Artillery. | M Kelly, A, 1st Maine.
J Chapman, 1st Maine Art. | C George, A, 1st Maine.
E B Slauson, 2d N Y Art. | J Mitchell, A, 1st Maine.
J E Robbins, 1st Maine Art. | Lt Isaac W Magor, A, 1st Me Artillery.
J E Grim, 1st Maine Art. | B W Abbott, 1st Maine Art.
John Slater, 2d N Y Art. | J L Emery, 1st Maine Art.
A Green, 2d N Y Art. | J M Moore, 1st Maine Art.
Geo S Stanwood, 1st Me Art. | Peter Smith, 6th N Y Art.
F Knapp, 4th N Y Art. | N St Pere, 1st Maine Art.
S F Douglass, 1st Me Art. | A Morrison, 1st Maine A.
H A Gernon, 6th N Y Art. | Wm Treshue, 14th N C.
F K Clark, 1st Me Artillery. | M O'Connor, 7th New-York Artillery.
J H Smallwood, 26th Ind. | H C Hutchinson, 1st Me Art.
J L Crocker, 1st Me Art. | Wm L Holmes, 1st Me Art.
W S Averill, 1st Me Art. | B F Hiller, 4th N Y Art.
W H Jones, 1st Me Art. | L Doane, 1st Me Artillery.
Wm Dougherty, 1st Me Art. | Sergt C H Getchell, 1st Me Art.
A Mason, 1st Me Artillery. | A Heldohnum, 15th N Y Art.
H W Pomeroy, 1st Me Art. | Gottlieb Fecti, 15th N Y Art.
Peter Lee, 7th N Y Artillery. | D I Darby, [illegible] N Y Art.
Sergt G A Watson, 1st Me Art. | J Doherty, 1st Me Art.
F Obermank, 62d New-York.

THE PIRATE FLORIDA.

Steering for the Track of Vessels from America to England.

The rebel steamer *Florida* sailed on the 14th from Bermuda, after landing an officer who was sick, and stood to the northward. She reported having burned a New-York ship from Callao about three weeks previous, and sent her crew to England on a foreign vessel.

From Newbern.

The North Carolina *Times* of the 21st is received. There is nothing very new in it.

The rebels in Little Washington set fire to the town on the 11th, destroying all but about twenty houses, and robbed all the women and children in the place.

GEN. BUTLER'S ARMY.

THE REBELS ASSUME THE OFFENSIVE.

Our Rifle Pits Seized—Part of Them Retaken.

Particulars of the Capture of the Rebel General Walker.

From Our Own Correspondent.

IN CAMP, BERMUDA HUNDRED, VA., Friday Night, May 20—10 P. M.

BEAUREGARD will not "let us alone." After the fighting last Monday, as you already know, Gen. BUTLER brought his forces down in good order to their present position in the intrenchments, a few miles this side of the railroad, but the active little French creole sharply followed with his cohorts. Why could he not have stayed in peaceable possession of Fort Darling and the long line of its outer defences? We had given them a fair trial and found them too hard a nut to crack while a part of our strength was necessarily expended elsewhere. But, Mr. BEAUREGARD, like all other unfeeling rebs., seems not to care a snap of his finger for our convenience, for even while I am writing this, the stillness of the night is continually broken by the heavy boom and sharp rattling reverberations of artillery as the woods sheltering his misguided cohorts are vigorously shelled. Indeed, there has been very lively fighting all day in front of Gen. GILLMORE's lines, and the enemy, as long ago as yesterday, began to develop himself in force in our front. The old saying that the wicked find no peace may, with great propriety, be applied to this entire command, for not only have the vile among us, but likewise the righteous, been kept in a tense strain of activity in their various spheres—Generals down through all the grades to drummer boys—ever since the occupation of this choice strip of Virginia territory.

I have been riding about considerably to-day to learn what I might of the fighting, and have just arrived in camp from Gen. GILLMORE's headquarters, which are probably two miles from here, provided one happens to take the direct road. But, unfortunately, these pesky roads are full of blind and intersecting paths, whose shady depths are beguiling to strangers, but strayed into, are found to lead nowhither, like the labyrinth of classic fable. Into one of those I diverged, and here I am at last, pretty thoroughly fatigued by a long and patient effort to thread my own way out. It may interest some to know that I was materially aided in the consummation by a telegraph wire which I happened finally to strike upon in the forest. It was moonlight, and discovering this voiceless messenger of the military authorities, whose running between the various headquarters I hope it is not contraband to mention, I followed its guidance gratefully to our encampment.

But excuse this long prologue. I have more important matters to communicate. I have seen to-day the wounds, the mangled forms, the shocking as well as the noble incidents of horrid war—and of the savage fighting out of which they result I must give some account.

Long after midnight the enemy began to demonstrate heavily upon that portion of our line held by Gen. AMES, being the Third Division of the Tenth Corps, and also with scarcely less fierceness upon the left of the First Division (Gen. TERRY's) connecting with AMES. The night was moonlight and misty, and altogether favorable for the assault. The rebels, therefore, made a desperate effort to drive back the centre of our line, which they supposed to be the weakest, hoping to cut us in two. The assault upon our works was gallantly repulsed by both TERRY and AMES, with scarcely any loss whatever to us, but it is said at a severe cost to the enemy. The sudden firing of artillery and musketry at the dead hour of night, of course, disturbed the encampments everywhere and there was a hasty sending out of mounted orderlies to ascertain its meaning. Less than half an hour of tumult passed, however, when matters again subsided into stillness. The weary troops, lying in the rifle-pits, again roll themselves snugly in their blankets, and clasping their trusty muskets to their hands, are soon once more asleep after the rude, disturbing episode.

The remainder of the night passed in quietness. Gen. GILLMORE and his staff rode out at daybreak and made such dispositions of his forces as was thought best to meet another expected assault; and the ever watchful and soldierly SMITH, who knows intuitively precisely what is required for any possible military emergency, and anticipates every movement of the enemy by making the necessary counter preparations to thwart it, had the Eighteenth Corps ready for whatever might occur.

At 9½ o'clock the enemy again made demonstrations in force against the centre of our line, driving in, in some confusion, the pickets, and getting possession of our rifle-pits in front of AMES, about 1,200 yards from our works—making it necessary, also, for Gen. TERRY to withdraw his picket line connecting with AMES' left.

It was absolutely necessary to retake the line of rifle-pits thus unfortunately lost, and to keep possession of which the enemy has obstinately contended. To this end there has been stubborn fighting all day, and from the front of TERRY the rebels at nightfall had been dislodged, but AMES had not recovered all his line.

Among the incidents of the day, the Thirteenth Indiana were sent out by Gen. AMES to recover the last position. The enemy met them with a blasting musketry fire, and the loss was very large. Among the officers of this regiment wounded and missing are: Lieut.-Col. WILSON, in the shoulder; Capt. ROTHROCK, Company C, mortally; Capt. HUNTER, Company I, and Lieut. HENDRICKS, Company F missing—having been left on the field between two fires; Lieut. VANCE, Company B. Probably no more noble incident has happened during the war than one of which Sergt. JOHN REAM, of Company B, this regiment, is the hero. Lieut.-Col. WILSON had fallen wounded on the field. The regiment was retreating hastily under the fire. The wounded officer, in his helplessness, recognized Sergt. REAM as he passed. He called him: "Carry me off the field, Sergeant," said the Colonel. The noble fellow stopped, regardless of the whizzing balls, and throwing away his musket, gently lifted Col. WILSON upon his back and coolly walked off the field, exposed every step of the way to instant death, never dropping his burden until he had regained the shelter of the intrenchments.

In the afternoon a charge was made upon the rifle-pits by the Ninety-seventh Pennsylvania Regiment under Maj. PENNYPACKER. It was a deadly movement to the boys of the Keystone State. There seems to have been a misapprehension of the order. They were told or expected to advance upon the enemy under shelter of the woods, but instead of doing so, charged madly across an open field between our works and the pits. They were slaughtered like sheep by the concentrated fire of a field battery. Below I give a partial list of the wounded—the officers suffered greatly.

The line in front of Gen. TERRY was recovered by Col. HOWELL's brigade, assisted by the One Hundred and Forty-second New-York, Col. CURTIS, and the Eighty-ninth New-York, Col. FAIRCHILD. In this effort the rebel Brig.-Gen. WILLIAM S. WALKER, commanding the South Carolina brigade, was captured. He was reconnoitering the left of the enemy's line, when Col. HOWELL dashed upon him at the head of his brigade. WALKER at first thought our men were his own, but soon discovering his error, put spurs to his horse to get away. A volley brought him down. He received one wound in the left arm and another shot tore off part of his leg. He was quite cool, brave and insolent when Col. HOWELL approached him. The latter is also brave as JULIUS CÆSAR, and as perfect a gentleman as ever breathed. His soft reply to the angry rebel officer turned away his wrath completely. A litter was procured, and he was tenderly conveyed to Gen. GILLMORE's headquarters, himself requesting that no operation should be performed on him until he was taken out of the range of the shells. He also asked to see Gen. "Baldy" SMITH and Gen. TERRY, having known the former before the war, when he was an honored officer of the old army, and having met Gen. TERRY several times in the progress of the South Carolina campaign. WALKER commanded the forces at Pocotaligo when Gen. O. M. MITCHELL attempted to cut the railroad. Dr. CRAVEN, Medical Director of the Tenth Corps, gave up his tent to the wounded man, and there I saw him a little while since, moaning in agony, and so weak from loss of blood that the amputation of his limb, though necessary, had to be postponed until such time as he should rally. There seems to be little chance of his recovering. He dictated a letter, last night, to Gen. BEAUREGARD, stating the circumstances of his capture, describing his injuries, and expressing his acknowledgments of the courtesy and kindness he had received, requesting that the communication might be sent by flag of truce.

Our losses yesterday were considerable. The enemy, however, suffered incomparably more. Our batteries played havoc with them as they were massed in the woods. The One Hundred and Forty-second New-York and Eighty-ninth New-York both suffered severely. Companies B and G of the former regiment kept two rebel regiments at bay, and lost 16 in killed. The Eighty-ninth lost about 150, of whom 30 were killed. Maj. N. G. AXTELL was wounded twice, but not seriously. Lieut.-Col. JACKSON's horse was shot as he was getting SAGER's and the Fourth New-Jersey Battery in position.

P. S. Saturday morning, 6 o'clock.—The firing was renewed about an hour since, at the place where the rebels demonstrated yesterday. H. J. W.

WOUNDED IN THE NINETY-SEVENTH PENNSYLVANIA.

Lieut Isaac Falk, D—groin and foot. | Corp J Daubman, A—both legs.
Major G Pennypacker—arm. | Robert Gizenbler, A—lung.
Capt J M C Savage, B—foot. | R Fenn[illegible], E—leg.
Capt J Price, C—thigh. | Sergt E B Moore, C—shoulder.
Lieut Geo A L Meister, H—arm. | Wm J Smith, E—leg.
Capt D C Lewis, F—missing. | Corp N R Cowen, A—leg.
Lieut Thos Cosgrove, F—missing. | Wm Given, A—neck.
Lemuel McBride, D—leg. | Sergt C L Smith, E—hand.
John Goodwin, D—thigh. | Frederick Sellon, A—arm.
Jacob Putnall, D—head. | Sergt Wm H. H. Gibson, I—knee.
Richard Walrein, I—head. | E Fright, C—hand.
Saml A Marsh, I—foot. | E Broutzman, I—thigh.
E Brown, C—scalp. | A K Wright, I—leg.
C B Musgrove, B—sh'lder. | Henry Kerr, B—leg.
A McKenney, K—hip. | Geo Groce, E—scalp.
J Clark, B—hip. | F A Connell, K—foot.
Ord Sergt F Guest, F—mortally, since dead. | Corp J M Boyd, F—breast.
H Brower, F—wrist. | H Loud, F—breast.
W Agg, C—head. | Sergt M Brosirs, K—sh'dlr.
E W Anderson, H—thigh. | W P Moon.
Ord Sergt J H Walton, H—hand. | Corp W S Green, I—leg.
W H Smith, E—hand. | S Tierney, F—breast.
T C Huntsman, F—hand. | H Rogers, I.
J McClune, F—shoulder. | W McDonald, H.
W. Bennett, H.
S G Scott, F.
E Cole, I.
D Faber, K.
F A Hoopes, G—side.

FOURTH NEW-HAMPSHIRE.

Lieut Stearns, C—abdomen. | W Bateman, G—shoulder.
Lieut Brewster, B—leg. | D Welch, G—hip.
A Pottnoe, D—hip. | C Wilson, C—side.

All Quiet on Saturday—Both Armies Digging—Night Attacks—The Wounded—The Rebels Repulsed at Fort Powhatan.

IN CAMP, BERMUDA HUNDRED, VA., Sunday Morning, May 21, 1864.

Yesterday there was very little fighting. For the first time since our coming here, the expression "all is quiet along the lines," might have been truthfully used. Early in the morning there was a brisk picket skirmish in front of TERRY's division, for the purpose of pushing forward a short distance; and occasionally during the day, the gunboats on our flanks, in the Appomattox and the James, relieved the silence by sending a few shells into the woods to disturb working parties of the enemy. On both sides, as far as I could discover, the troops are vigorously digging to make their respective positions impregnable. Passing along our lines in the afternoon, and looking upon the busy scene where spades and axes were the implements of warfare, my unprofessional eye was satisfied that I need no longer feel alarmed about spending a cheerless Summer in the Libby. Mr. BEAUREGARD would find it, I think, a difficult matter to drive us out of here or "gobble" us. His army in front of us, from the best information given by deserters and prisoners, is estimated at *thirty thousand* men. Their object seems to be, from the way in which they are piling up earthworks, to keep Gen. BUTLER penned in here, away from the railroad and turnpike, the loss of which last week was quite damaging to their military schemes.

Since retiring to this point the charge of our defences has been assigned to Brig.-Gen. GODFREY WEITZEL, whose reputation as an engineer is first-class. The Second Division of the Eighteenth Corps, (Gen. SMITH's) which WEITZEL has splendidly led in all the fighting since we came here, was yesterday turned over to Brig.-Gen. MARTINDALE, who will ably fill WEITZEL's place.

A night attack upon Gen AMES, (Second Division of the Tenth Corps,) was the chief incident of the last twenty-four hours. It was made at 11 o'clock, and lasted until midnight, when all became quiet again. There is something very exciting connected with these sudden assaults which the enemy often makes. For instance, last night when the furious storm of war burst over us, the camp of Gen. BUTLER's headquarters was changed in a second of time from the quiet of a grave-yard to the bustle and animation of a market-place. A sloping meadow, whereon a canvas city picturesquely stands bathed in silvery moonlight—where the solemn hush is scarcely broken by the footsteps of the sentinels—is transformed in the twinkling of an eye to a place where the noisy accessories of war have full play. The silent tents are alive with men, who swarm out hastily, half-dressed, yet, like true soldiers, thoroughly and instantly awake at the first report of the artillery, and ready for any duty. Horses, fully equipped in their showy and lumbersome military trappings, appear magically from the rear, and orderlies, with clanking sabres and jingling spurs, come out and hold their fretting steeds ready to dash madly away wherever they shall be sent. In the meanwhile there is an incessant rattling of musketry and a quick thundering of artillery over the woods scarcely two miles away, with an occasional vivid flash caused by a shell too highly aimed exploding above the tree-tops. Suddenly there is a prolonged and ringing cheer, which never comes from other throats than those of Union soldiers. This announces to us that the enemy's assault has been re-

Continued on the Eighth Page.

The Charleston Mercury.

DAILY PAPER—[illegible]

VINDICE NULLO — SPONTE SUA SINE LEGE FIDES RECTUMQUE COLETUR

COUNTRY PAPER—Three a Week—Forty Dollars, for Six Months—Payable in Advance.

VOLUME LXXXIV. | CHARLESTON, S. C., THURSDAY, JUNE 9, 1864. | NUMBER 12,083

Great Battle of May Twelfth at Spottsylvania Court House.

The Conflict, as Described by an English Correspondent.

Mr. HEWSON, the correspondent of the London *Herald*, is writing a series of very interesting letters for that journal, descriptive of the operations of the spring campaign in Virginia. We regret that the pressure upon our columns will not allow us to publish these letters in full. We must content ourselves with reproducing the most interesting portion of his last, giving a minute and graphic account of the great conflict of the 12th of May:

RICHMOND, May 25, 1864.

* * * * * *

On the 12th of May the battlefield lay, before dawn, enveloped in a heavy fog. At 4 o'clock in the morning of that day the hostile lines burst, as under the sudden bidding of an electric wire, into a fierce cannonade. An explosion in its suddenness, it raged from the first moment of its opening in the full depth of its fury. The metalic peal of the solid shot, the sharp clap and the flat crash of the shell rose from side to side with rapidity. They seemed to shake the very earth with their thunders. That terrific storm, while undiminished in depth, underwent immediately after its first outburst a change in character, for the sharper peals of shot and shell were succeeded in a moment by the duller thuds that hurling forward grape and canister, told of a struggle deepened into the sternness of close quarters.

The suddenness of the thunders with which the artillery rent the air was not greater than that with which the deafening storm burst from the infantry. The musketry that followed immediately after the very first gun, was so great in volume from its opening that it bespoke clearly the presence of large masses of men. Rising in a deep roll one and unbroken, its blended ringing clared that the hostile thousands from whom it swelled up must have met in conflict, hand to hand. The peals in quick succession of the artillery, did not drown its voice; but on it went distinctly, a flowing roar that rose to Heaven, like the constant outcry of a rushing river. Divination was not necessary with all those evidences to tell me, as I rose from my blanket in the rear, that, as in the case of our own conflict at Inkerman, an attack, prepared with deliberation, in close proximity to the Confederate lines, had moved suddenly from the cover of the morning fog.

The field works that protected Ewell's right on the morning of the 12th extended through a wood. They occupied the line of a low ridge and, by what appears to me to be a grave error, lay somewhat down its reverse slope. An enemy approaching them could not be seen from some part of the works until he had appeared over the rise in their immediate front. Retreating from them, he received, once behind that swell of the ground, protection from the fire of part of those defences. The course of the breastworks followed that of the ridge, and accordingly formed, at one place, a salient with an angle so small as to be almost acute. They consisted of two lines which ran one parallel with the other; and containing between both, a space sufficiently wide for a line of battle, would be decribed by military engineers as a "double sap." Epaulments were placed in support of the whole at several points of the line, and at the salient, sufficient for so many as twenty guns. A general understanding of the position may be obtained from this description, after, it has been stated that the sides of the salient, subject, as they were, in the event of an attack, to enfilade from its apex, were protected for some distance down the line, with a series of short traverses.

General J. M. Jones' brigade occupied the salient. On the left of Jones' men were formed the Stonewall, under Walker; and next in order of the line of battle, the Louisianians under Hays. The right of Jones—who, be it recollected, held the salient—rested on the brigade of Stuart. Such was the distribution on the morning of the 12th, behind the breastworks of Ewell's right wing, of the men constituting the division of General Edward Johnston. On the right of this division was an unoccupied part of the works about two hundred yards in length, and further on that staunch brigade of Wilcox's division—Lane's, Jones' brigade had sent one of its best regiments, the 31st Virginia from the salient, to cover the gap between Stuart and Lane as skirmishers. Two others were also sent out of the works in the same capacity, with the view of protecting the angle of the position from sudden attack. But three regiments of the brigade remained to defend a weak point that had been held previously by six. Of twenty guns that had been planted in the salient, sixteen had, under an expectation entertained during the night of an attack upon the extreme right, been withdrawn. Such was the array and strength of Ewell's right on the morning of the 12th.

Johnston, informed at three o'clock a. m., that the enemy was massing in his front, sent off in hot haste for guns to replace those that had been removed from his works during the night.

In the meantime the signs in the front began rapidly to take the definite form of attack. His skirmishers came in short notice; and the forest behind them impressed the senses with the feeling that, wrapped as it was in fog, it was swarming with masses of human life. Page's battalion of artillery had, in response to the demand of General Johnston, come up to the salient in a trot, but a tremendous column of the enemy having at that moment emerged from the haze, it had arrived only to have its horses shot dead in their traces, and its men mowed down in the act of unlimbering. So terrible was the fire of the enemy that but one of the guns was brought into action. Captain W. Carter had, with great devotion, succeeded, unassisted, in making that ready for work, and, standing at it, heroically alone, continued, until his capture, to fire it, charged with grape and canister, into the Federal ranks.

General Johnston had no sooner become aware of the exact point of the attack than he rushed towards the salient. He was too late. The column that had burst from the fog upon that weak point, held it already in possession. The three regiments which had been left in line for its defence, had fled before the storming mass, without firing a shot, Johnston, caught in the rush of friend and foe, was made a prisoner; and was thus left, by the bad conduct of some of his own men, to waste his brave spirit ingloriously in prison. His bravery is of the antique. His conduct as a general officer was marked by constancy and address. A great favorite with Lieutenant General Ewell, he was known amongst the rank and file, in affectionate recognition of his courage and obstinacy, as "Old Blucher."

The salient carried, and one-half of Jones' men killed, wounded or captured, the enemy poured through the Confederate line in immense force. The Stonewall Brigade, on the immediate left of the gap thus opened in the Confederate ranks became exposed on the right flank. Gen. Walker, its chief, attempted immediately to swing that wing around; but, while in the act, was disabled by a very severe wound in the side. Pressed hotly by the Federal advance, that movement became then, after even the brief delay consequent on that accident, impossible. The pressure upon its flank having commenced, many of the men forced into disorder were killed, wounded or captured; but several of the regiments wheeling into position behind the short traverses running back from their breastworks, disputed every foot of the ground they held with a steadiness worthy of their traditions. Colonel Terry, while holding, with unflinching firmness, one of those short fronts, received a severe wound. The Stonewall Brigade, however, overborne by the movement upon its flank, was finally forced back; and what of it was neither captured, wounded nor killed, found protection behind the battle array of the brigade that had been in line on its left—Hays' Louisianians.

Stuart's brigade, on the right of the regiments that had occupied the salient, was taken by the surging masses of the Federalists in flank. Those of them who were neither captured, killed nor wounded, found shelter behind the brigade that had been in line upon their right—Lane's of Wilcox's division. Engaged in front with a heavy column of the enemy, Lane, on learning of the miscarriage at the salient, became alarmed for his left flank; and having immediately swung his line around almost squarely with its original position, encountered the enemy's triumphant advance. Charging in fine style, he drove it back after a contest that must have cost it dearly. His North Carolinians thus won the glory of being the first to stem the tide of Federal victory on the right.

While the Stonewall Brigade fought and fell back, the next on its left—Hays'—had time to swing round. Colonel Monagan, its senior Col. being in command, it confronted the rushing advance to the left. Standing behind a traverse that extended perpendicularly from the original position of the brigade, it presented a front as firm as a ledge of rock. The wave of the enemy's triumph surged up to that barrier; but, having broken upon it in mere spray, left the honor of the arrest of its overflow on that side of the field to those houseless, landless warriors of Louisiana.

Between Hays' men on the one side and Lane's on the other, the Federalists had driven all opposition from their path. For a width of a mile they had swept the works of their defenders, but though complete masters within that limit, were confronted by an impassable barrier on the one hand and on the other. Pouring through the gap they had made, their masses formed rapidly from the right and from the left, with the view of turning the line of Hays on that side, and of Lane on this, by pressure on those officers' exposed flanks.

Apprehension of attack during the night on the front of Hays, had led to the transfer to its support of the fine brigade of Pegram. The other brigades of the division under the command of Gordon—two—were, at the time of the assault upon the salient, half a mile to the left. Springing forward without orders, Gordon moved at "double quick" in the direction of the fire that had burst upon the dawn in sudden thunders. Rushing into the fog, he could see neither friend nor foe, but guided by the instincts of a soldier, still sped forward rapidly under the bidding of the battle's hoarsest roar. The thick haze into whose unknown depths he drove on, soon lit its murderous terrors, as he closed into the conflict, with lurid flashes; and, in the next moment, flung out a sheet of lightning that hurled about the ears of his advancing ranks a very tempest of bullets.

Gordon had come up in column. General R. D. Johnston's Brigade first upon the field, he threw rapidly into line, and launching it against the enemy through the fog, checked the advance. Having arrested, thus, at one point, the surging ranks of the foe, he sought to stop him as they swept around his right. The torrent streaming rapidly in that direction, he was about to be borne back by the flank, when, bringing up his own brigade, its firm line presented to the riverlike rush an additional width of barrier. The living flood of Federal triumph dashing against it in vain, swept still farther around, again threatening the Confederate right with destruction under a rapid movement upon its flank. Gordon having by that time brought up his third brigade—Pegram's—formed it under the command of Colonel Huffman, somewhat detached from the others, across the new front of the enemy's advance.

The whole line then delivered a murderous volley into the dim masses of human life that stood before its shrouded—and very, very many of them winding-sheeted—in that morning fog. Instantly seizing the colors of the centre regiment of his own brigade, Gordon spurred forward under a storm of bullets, ordering a charge His men rushed upon the misty ranks that they had just cut gashes through with their deadly fire. Their fury bore down all resistance. The charge had become a chase. Huddling the Federalists in headlong flight over the breastworks that had been held during the night by Stuart, that murderous race was continued for half a mile beyond. Opposition had disappeared before the pursuit: still, however, it held its way in unabated fury. Starting out suddenly from the fog upon a hostile force in line, Gordon's demand for surrender having, in the confusion of his sudden appearance, obtained no reply, the Federalists fell where they had but a moment before stood in lusty life, a battle array of dead and dying.

The enemy still held the ground he had won on Stuart's left. Gordon falling therefore back, occupied the works he had carried so gloriously. His charge had cost the Confederates the services for a time, of Brigadier General R. D Johnston. That gallant officer was disabled by a wound, that is, however, not very severe. Col. Jones, a soldier of high promise, lay upon the field mortally wounded. Lieutenant Colonel McArthur, and Colonel Garrett, both officers of ability, gave up upon that field their life blood in manly assertion of the liberties that have been handed down to them from our common ancestors of the days of Runneymeade. Terribly, however, were the Confederate lives, lost in that movement, avenged. For a width of three hundred yards the Federal slain were scattered over a length of three-quarters of a mile; and, in all the open fields included in that space, lay in a sickening slaughter. Four guns that had been taken at the time of the enemy's advance were, during the charge, recaptured, and in the absence of horses, sent by manual labor for some distance to the rear.

The Federalists continued to hold their ground in the salient, and along the line of works to the left of that angle, within a short distance of the position of Monaghan's (Hays') Louisianians, Ramseur's North Carolinians, of Rodes' division, formed, covering Monaghan's right, and ordered to charge, were received by the enemy with a stubborn resistance. The desperate character of the struggle along that brigade front was told terribly in the horseness and rapidity of its musketry. So close was the fighting there for a time that the fire of friend and foe rose up rattling in one common roar. Ramseur's North Carolinians dropped from the ranks thick and fast, but still he continued with glorious constancy to gain ground foot by foot. Pressing under a fierce fire, resolutely on, on, on, the struggle was about to become one of hand to hand, when the Federalists shrunk from that bloody trial. Driven back, they were not defeated. The earthworks being at the moment in their immediate rear, they bounded to the opposite side, and having thus placed them in their front, renewed the conflict. A rush of an instant brought Ramseur's fellows to this side of the defences, and, though they crouched close to the slopes, under enfilade from the guns of the salient, their musketry rattled in deep and deadly fire on the enemy that stood in overwhelming numbers but a few yards from their front. Those brave North Carolinians had thus, in one of the very hottest conflicts of the day, succeeded in driving the enemy from the works that had been occupied during the previous night by a brigade which, until the 12th of May, had never yet yielded to a foe—the Stonewall.

The Confederate line had been re-established by Ramseur to the position held during the night by Gen. J. M. Jones' left, it had been restored by Gordon to the point occupied during the same time by Jones' right. The gap originally made remained however, still in the possession of the enemy, and with it all the guns—with the exception of the four retaken by Gordon—that had been captured at the time of the rush into the salient. Through that the Federal masses swept out between the flank of Gordon—of Pegram's brigade—on the one hand, and of Ramseur on the other, endeavoring, by movements to the right and to the left in conjunction with heavy attacks in front, to give the unrecovered space greater width. They still protruded from the open interval between the flanks of those officers and continued to press still forward with the view of preventing their connection by an intervening array of battle. Moving out in tremendous force with the ultimate purpose of driving them still farther apart and of turning their lines, they were encountered by the stern front of Battle's Albamians of Rhodes' Division.

Battle met the crushing weight of the advance unaided. He sought to insert his line between Gordon's left—Pegram's men—and the right of the brave fellows under Ramseur. Receiving the shock of the forward movement as a rock hurls back a wave of the sea, he pressed after the recoil, foot by foot. Closing in on it slowly, he succeeded, after a severe struggle, in pressing it back into the breastworks of the salient—for a part, be it recollected, a "double sap"—under a fire of musketry that exceeded anything I ever heard in its rapidity and volume. It roared unceasingly, a very river of death. Forcing his way on with heroic resolution; now straining forward; then standing in obstinate resistance; and next, for a moment, yielding stubbornly, as the mortal struggle swayed from side to side, Battle kept, with indomitable courage, laboring onward, inch by inch. Aided by the fire of Ramseur's men on the left flank of the Federalists, he succeeded, finally in driving them from a part of the works on that officer's right.

The gap in the Confederate array had been reduced to a small extent by Battle's left. The other part of his line continued to swing heavily backwards and forwards as the tide of battle rolled from side to side. Shattered terribly by the severity of the contest, he was reinforced by Harris' Mississippians, of Anderson's division, and McGowan's South Carolinians, of Wilcox's division. The heaviness of the fire at the point where these brigades went into action was terrible. Two young oaks, each upwards of twelve inches in dameter, pierced so often across their trunks, were thus actually cut down, to the serious injury of some of McGowan's men, by minnie bullets.

Fresh troops being put in continually, in front of Harris and McGowan, the contest grew in fierceness. Reeling to and fro, for the width of a brigade front, it surged now to this side, then to that, over a bloody space of over two hundred and fifty yards. The guns that had been captured in the salient by the rush of the first attack, lay, during the fierce struggle in their original position—at one time within the onward roll of the Federal lines, and at another closed within the surging ranks of the Confederates. Major Cutshaw, a gallant officer of the battalion of artillery, whose pieces lay thus between the ebb and flow of battle, hung devotedly in their immediate rear, and watching the moment that saw them included in the advancing array of the Confederate infantry, sprang forward from his lair in the thicket to load them with canister and grape.—Bang! bang! bang! he plied them in hot haste; and thus tearing the ranks of the enemy at close quarters into shreds, he continued, with rare steadfastness, hurling his thunders until the line of his supports had begun once more to yield.—Retiring again and again as the tide of strife rolled back upon him, he continued, on each occasion, to watch his opportunity in patient resolution, and whenever the battle surged onward, bounded to his guns to work them with the same ardor and with the same havoc.

McGowan behaved, in the struggle for the works at the salient, gloriously. He fell, in its progress, painfully, but I hope not dangerously wounded. Several of his best officers yielded up their lives on that field of blood. General Harris set a brilliant example in the stern strife, to his brigade, but though he escaped accident in the tempest of bullets which swept on the wings of death around him, he lost heavily. His losses in officers includes some men of high promise. Colonel Baker and Lieutenant-Colonel Feltus, of the 16th Mississippians, and Colonel Hardin, of the 19th, are not amongst the least of the gallant soldiers who fell dead from the Confederate lines in that murderous salient. South Carolinians and Mississippians continued, however, to rival each other in their persistent striving to recover the captured works; and finally obtained firm possession of them still further in advance of the foothold that had been secured in them previously by Battle. Consolidating within the defences thus far recovered on the left of the salient, the strife was renewed in their front—and very often so close to the muzzles of their rifles as the opposite slopes of the breastworks behind which they crouched under enfilade from the apex of the salient.

Perrin's brigade of Anderson's division, sent up to reinforce Battle, formed behind some light works in the rear. Ordered to charge into the salient, its chief, as he rode at the head of its left wing, received a Minnie bullet in the thigh.—The femoral artery cut, he had hardly time to say "carry me back, boys," when the poor fellow had bled to death. Two of his regiments had been, at the time, rushing at the works on the right, under the direction of a gallant and promising young officer, now commanding the brigade, Colonel J. C. Saunders. They succeeded in making a lodgment in the defences on the left of Gordon. The other three regiments, bounding on to the left as Perrin fell, swept also without opposition into the breastworks on the right of the men of Harris and McGowan. The width held by the enemy at the salient had thus been reduced to about one hundred yards, but, included within it, at the appex, a battery of artillery that, captured in the morning, swept both sides by enfilade.

continued on next page

THE MERCURY.

THURSDAY, JUNE 9, 1864.

continued—

Captain Wynne, the Adjutant General of Perrin's brigade, attempted to communicate with the Colonel commanding; but, venturing recklessly with that view across the immediate rear of the salient—where nothing human could apparently survive—returned to the left, after having run the gauntlet of the enemy's skirmishers, with a painful wound in his arm. Saunders, in the meantime, threw out some of his Alabamians as sharpshooters; and by the accuracy of their aim, succeeded in silencing the guns that had been hurling shell into his ranks in deadly enfilade. Opening again from time to time, they burst upon him repeatedly; but in a moment afterwards the hands by which they had been worked fell under his unerring rifles, stiff in death. The enemy's grasp upon the "double sap" at the angle of the salient, still undisturbed, Col. Saunders maintained his ground in this way on both sides of it, with admirable resolution.

From four o'clock in the morning until half-past one, the struggle within the salient had raged in terrible fierceness. At the expiration of that time it sank into a comparative lull. The roll of the heavy skirmish-shooting went on without intermission, however, around that angle of blood, and awaited, after a brief break in the main contest, into the furious roar of a renewed attack. The restored front on each side of the salient burst into thread like flashes; and from two o'clock, throughout the evening until nightfall, and from nightfall until midnight, and from midnight until the approach of dawn of the 13th, a close and rapid fusillade rushed up in commingled roar from the contending ranks. At one time bursting through the gap on Gordon's right, and endangering his flank; at others raging up to the face of the very works held by that officer, by Saunders, by McGowan, by Harris, by Battle, by Ramseur, the conflict raged furiously until the enemy repelled firmly at all points of his attack, it settled, long after midnight, into the sharp and venomous whizzings of the skirmishers.

The four guns that Gordon had recaptured still remained two hundred yards in his rear. They could not be removed under the terrible fire that swept over the ground they occupied. Fourteen guns remained in possession of the enemy, and, with those four, constituted substantially the only object of continuing the murderous struggle for the salient. The conditions of that contest had changed Lee's policy of defence for that of attack, and had thus made a further maintenance of it highly inexpedient. A material advantage, of some importance to the enemy, lay in the possession of the height on which the salient stood, but even this did not, in the opinion of the Commander-in Chief justify an avoidable waste of the lives of his men.

Before dawn, on the morning of the 13th, a line of works had been thrown up by the pioneers of the 2d corps, under Major Green, half a mile in rear of the point to which the contest of the day had been narrowed, and, connecting the original defences on the right with those on the left, by a route considerably shorter, presented a favorable position for return to the policy of defence. Covered by skirmishing, the gallant fellows who had fought their way so stubbornly over the bloody ground within the salient, into the works that had been captured by the enemy in his rush of the morning of the 12th, retired before day on the 13th to that new line.

In the battles of the Ny, no officer earned such glory as General Gordon. His admirable flank movement at the Wilderness, his repulse of the enemy's rush through the position of Dole, and his dash and skill in stemming the Federal torrent from the salient on the 12th, won the admiration of the army. General Lee acknowledged, on the field, publicly, the great services of that officer, and informing him at the time that he should ask for his promotion, has had him rewarded with the rank of Major General.

The battles, ending with the morning of the 13th, had closed. A more stubborn contest than that of the 12th has not been witnessed during the war. The losses of the Confederates, during these struggles, include between two and three thousand prisoners, eighteen guns, and from six to seven thousand killed and wounded. Those of the enemy in the conflicts of the 10th and of the 12th, including as they do the disaster at the hands of Early's flanking force, of the murderous repulses from the front of Field, and from that of Dole, and the terrible havoc of Gordon's charge on the right of the salient, cannot have been less, in killed and wounded, than from twenty to thirty thousand. The rotting dead found unburied on the ground the Federalists occupied during those contests presented a spectacle utterly horrible in the immensity of their number. During the campaign the losses in Ewell's corps, according to an official statement of the chief of its medical staff—Dr. Hunter Maguire—does not exceed in killed and wounded, after summing the losses of each of its brigades up to the 13th of this month, 3,500.

With this basis of approximate estimate, and the further fact that the number of wounded that had been sent to the rear up to the 19th, by those devoted men, the Richmond committee for the relief of the wounded, had not reached, including those disabled by sickness, ten thousand, there can be very little doubt of the conclusion that Lee's total losses, in killed and wounded, inclusive of the battle of the 12th, have not overrun, at most, eleven or twelve thousand. About three thousand five hundred prisoners added to that, the depletion of his forces by the battles of the campaign, up to this time, is fully represented, I should think, by fourteen or fifteen thousand men. Grant's army has shown, in the increasing feebleness of, and longer intervals between his attacks, in his change from offence to defence, from fighting to manoeuvring, unmistakeable evidence of the crippling unavoidable, under losses that, including about four thousand prisoners, must certainly amount to fifty, but that all, in all probability, not much short of sixty thousand.

Defeated in forcing the roads covered by Lee at the battle of the Wilderness, and again at that of the Ny, Grant slid a second time upon our front. Moving off from his position before Spotsylvania Court House, at an angle forty degrees to the east of the line to Richmond, he marched fourteen miles to a place called Bowling Green. By way of Port Royal on the deep waters of the Rappahannock, he might have reached that village, if it had been in the route of his first intention, without firing even a shot. Once there, however, he has admitted that the original plan of his campaign has been abandoned, and that having ceased to contemplate the inland route, he has settled down on the adoption of that attempted in vain by McClellan.

Lee had maintained his original line of defence—that of the Mattapony—unbroken. The offensive having brought the contest within the limits of tide-water, the Confederate chief was, therefore obliged to adopt a policy in keeping with those new conditions; and for that purpose, crossing the North Anna, placed in his front the navigable depths of the Panunky. He thus, covered Richmond and his own rear from any attempt at a coup de main. His front adapting itself to Grant's change of base is now swinging around to the eastward. The federal commander has crossed the Chickahominy, and is now within a few miles of the White House. He has, therefore, reached a position which he might have occupied, by having had the courage to adopt McClellan's route without any serious opposition, whereas, that by which he has done so has cost his army seriously in morale, and even terribly in its numerical forces. Shorn of his strength, he yet may—if Lee did not find it expedient to take the offensive—give a color, by his position near Richmond, to electioneering at the North. I think it very probable that he may not take the aggressive until after the meeting at Baltimore of the Black Republican Convention for nomination of a candidate for the Presidency.

The danger of the opening campaign in Northern Virginia is now virtually passed. If that in Georgia should not turn out unfortunately, in the face of my reasonable anticipations, and thereby arouse the war spirit at the North I think we have arrived at the beginning of the end. Last August, you will recollect, I ventured to condition the return of peace during this coming August, on the miscarriage of the heavy and quick blows that I looked for during Spring, and now that these have taken a form which leads to the conclusion of their total failure. I find some justification in them, and even now, somewhat bold speculations touching peace, in the fact that regiments, whose term of service have expired, have already commenced to stream from the army of General Grant homeward.

Struggle for Salient, near Spotsylvania

General John Sedgwick,
who was killed at Spotsylvania

Stevens' battery at Cold Harbor

Battle of Spotsylvania, May 8-21, 1864

The Charleston Mercury.

VINDICE NULLO
SPONTE SUA SINE LEGE FIDES RECTUMQUE COLENTUR

VOLUME LXXXIV. | CHARLESTON, S. C., SATURDAY, MAY 28, 1864 | NUMBER 12,073

THE MERCURY.

SATURDAY, MAY 28, 1864

The President and the Habeas Corpus Act.

In reply to a resolution of Congress, enquiring of the President, if the public safety requires the continuance of the suspension of the Writ *Habeas Corpus*, the President affirms that "the "effects of the law have been *most salutary;* and "*to that law,* in a *considerable degree,* are we in-"debted for the *increased efficiency of the military* "*preparations,* which have enabled our armies to "beat back the invader's forces which still threat-"en us."

In what way, the suspension of the Writ of *Habeas Corpus*, has increased "the efficiency of our military preparations, which have enabled our armies to beat back our invaders," the President does not explain. When he urged upon Congress the suspension of the *Habeas Corpus* Act, it was affirmed in vindication of his recommendation, that he might have reasons for it, which the public at large could not and ought not to know. It was darkly hinted, that some secret treason might exist, which the prompt despotism which the suspension of the writ of *Habeas Corpus* would establish, could alone be competent to disclose and suppress. But since the law has passed, suspending the writ of *Habeas Corpus*, who has heard of any treason it has suppressed? Indeed, who has heard of any good this wanton attack upon the liberty of the citizen has done any where? Fortunately for the truth, the President comes from behind the clouds of conjecture and points to a distinct benefit, which, he alleges, it has produced. We have now something tangible. It has given "efficiency he thinks to our military preparations." "Military preparations" are not impalpable things. They are open acts in open day. What military preparations have been made efficient by the suspension of the Writ of *Habeas Corpus*? We know of but two with which the *Habeas Corpus* Act has had anything to do—the enforcement of the conscription law—and the enforcement of the law abolishing substitutes. It was this latter law which occasioned the denunciations by Mr. BROWN, Senator from Mississippi, of the State Judges, and the proposition to evade the law, with a suspension of the Writ of *Habeas Corpus* to enforce it. But, it so happens, that with respect to both of these two millitary preparations for the increased efficiency of our armies, the suspension of the Writ of *Habeas Corpus* Act has had simply nothing to do. On the contrary, the questions under these laws, were made by the *exercise*, not the *suspension*, of this very Writ, before the Courts of the States of the Confederate States. In Georgia, a Judge below, did determine, about two years ago, that the conscription law was unconstitutional, but on appeal to the Courts above, the law was affirmed to be Constitutional. So in Virginia, Alabama, and other States, the judicial tribunals of the States, affirmed the Constitutionality of both of these laws; and thus, by their decrees, proved most palpably, that it was totally unnecessary to suspend the Writ of *Habeas Corpus*, to enforce either of these military preparations, to enable our armies to beat back our invaders. The truth is, there never has been any good cause for suspending the Writ of *Habeas Corpus*. The ordinary operation of the laws, with a proper enforcement of military authority within its legitimate sphere, has been ample for our protection; and the suspension of the Writ of *Habeas Corpus*, has put a stain upon our cause, which the most energetic military preparations or military successes can never wipe out.

FROM GENERAL LEE'S ARMY.

(LETTER FROM "P. W. A.")

SPOTTSYLVANIA C. H., May 18.

The calm which has prevailed along the lines since the great battle of the 12th was broken at an early hour this morning. At dawn of day, before any of us but the brave men who keep watch in the trenches had left our blankets, the enemy opened a furious artillery fire upon Major General GORDON, of EWELL's corps. Of course, General LONG, formerly of General LEE's staff, and now commanding the artillery of EWELL's corps, was not slow in returning this early morning salutation of the Federal army. For nearly two hours the cannonade equalled that at Gettysburg. The enemy seemed to have massed his heaviest and best guns on that part of the lines which he had assaulted successfully on the 12th, and all supposed that another death struggle for the mastery was about to occur. Fortunately, the precautions taken by our great chief were so wise, and his dispositions so admirable, that all the brave Confederate soldier had to do, when he rose from his dreams on the ground behind the entrenchments, was to reach out for his trusty musket.

As you were informed by my letter of the 16th and by Gen. Lee's official despatches, the enemy moved a portion of his forces to the east bank of the Ny, in the direction of the Richmond and Fredericksburg railroad. The opinion prevailed at the time that Grant was trying to throw his army to the east side of the Mattaponi, and that he would probably move down the stream to Bowling Green, and possibly to West Point, where he would form a junction with Butler and Smith. Doubtless he desired to produce this impression upon General Lee, as in that event he might reasonably "calculate" that the latter would make a corresponding movement to the east. It is not yet time for me to say precisely what General Lee did do. This much, however, may be safely published now, viz: That he did exactly what was best for the army and worst for the enemy. Accordingly, when Grant commenced the assault this morning upon what was formerly our right wing but is now our left, he found Ewell and Gordon just where he left them on the 12th. His stratagem had failed to accomplish its purpose. Lee did not move his whole army to the right and away from the battle field, and thus leave the way open to an advance, as he had hoped he would do. The truth is, Grant, while a bold leader and an able commander, is no more a match to our great captain in tactics and strategy than his motley followers are to the bronzed veterans of the South in the qualities of the soldier. He may march his army one way in the day time and countermarch it another way at night; but at the end of all his labor and trouble he will find no one so much surprised as himself.

But let us return to the battle—the last, let us hope, of the battles of Spottsylvania Court House.

The attack was begun as soon as it was light enough for the enemy to see how to train his splendid guns upon our position. The fire was very heavy, and was kept up without intermission from near four o'clock until six, when the infantry were brought forward to carry the works. The assault by the latter, however, was very feeble, the enemy at no time coming nearer than seventy-five yards from our entrenchments. At many places they kept at the respectful distance of two and three hundred yards. The artillery fire was renewed at seven o'clock for half an hour or more, and again at nine, and fresh and earnest efforts were made to bring the infantry up to their work, as on the 12th, but all to no purpose. They would advance, but would not fight as heretofore, being easily repulsed, in many instances by our sharpshooters and skirmishers alone. No attack was made upon other parts of the lines.

A few prisoners were taken, who report that the assaulting column consisted of 8000 men from the Second and Sixth Corps, who, in response to a call from General Grant, had volunteered their services in the attack. If the Federal army has reached a point of demoralization where it becomes necessary to call for volunteers to assault our works, and if the volunteers when they come forward do no better than those did to-day, then the struggle here is approaching its end. But there is a homely but wise maxim which teaches us not to shout until we get out of the woods.—After all, these movements on the right and feeble attacks on the left may have a meaning which we do not yet fully understand.

The prisoners report, also, the arrival of a division yesterday under Gen. Augur, composed of the sweepings of the hospitals, jails, and provost guard houses. These are believed to be the last reinforcements that can be sent to Grant, unless a portion of the forces operating in North Georgia and against Richmond from below are recalled. It is not improbable that the arrival of Augur's division, and intelligence of the defeat of Butler by Beauregard, may have influenced Grant to order the attack. Augur's troops, like Burnside's "black spirits and white," will be worth but little in the hour of trial.

To show you how the Yankees are keeping up the agony, I send herewith Meade's congratulatory order to his troops after the great battle of the 12th. It is as follows:

HEADQUARTERS ARMY OF POTOMAC,
May 19, 1864

SOLDIERS: The moment has arrived when your Commanding General feels authorized to address you in terms of congratulation. For eight days and nights, almost without intermission, in rain and sunshine, you have been gallantly fighting a desperate foe, in position naturally strong, and rendered doubly so by entrenchments. You have compelled him to abandon his fortifications on the Rapidan, to retire and to attempt to stop his onward progress, and now he has abandoned his last entrenched position so tenaciously held, suffering a loss in all of 18 guns, 24 colors, and 8000 prisoners, including two general officers. Your heroic deeds and noble endurance of fatigue and privation will ever be remembered. Let us return thanks to God for the mercy thus shown us, and ask earnestly for its continuance.

Soldiers, your work is not over. The enemy must be pursued and, if possible, overcome. The courage and fortitude you have displayed render your Commanding General confident your future efforts will result in success.

While we mourn the loss of many gallant comrades let us remember the enemy has suffered equal if not greater loss. We shall soon receive reinforcements, which he cannot expect. Let us, then, determine to continue vigorously the work so well begun, and, under God's blessing, in a short time, the object of our labors will be achieved. GEO. G. MEADE, Maj. Gen.

Official: S WILLIAMS.

Last night about sundown the enemy, about one hundred strong, dashed into Guiney's Station and burnt it. During the day of yesterday the enemy are reported to have landed from their gunboats at Port Royal, after first shelling the woods for an hour or more.

OUR CAPTURED OFFICERS.—The Yankee papers claim to have captured the following officers in the late Virginia battles:

Major General Edward Johnson, Brig. General Geo. H. Stuart; Colonel Pebbles, of Georgia; Col. Davidson, of New Orleans; Colonel Hardeman, of Georgia; Colonel Harrell, of North Carolina; Col. Fitzgerald, of Virginia; Colonel Parsley, of North Carolina; Colonel Davant, of Georgia; Major Carson, of Georgia; Major Enett, of North Carolina; Major Wilson, of Louisiana; Major Warnum, of Louisiana; Colonel Vandervender, of Virginia; Colonel Cobb, of Virginia; Colonel Haynes, of Virginia; Major Nash, of Georgia; Major Perkins, of Virginia, and Major Anderson, of Virginia.

THE BATTLE OF NEW MARKET.

A correspondent of the Richmond *Sentinel* gives the annexed account of the late great victory of Gen. BRECKINRIDGE at New Market, Va.:

All things considered, I do not hesitate to pronounce General Breckinridge's brilliant victory at New Market one of the most remarkable achievements of the war. Now, that it is over, it may not be uninteresting to give a statement as briefly as possible of the movements preceding this affair, and the means by which Staunton has been saved, and Siegel driven in confusion down the Valley. On the 5th of May General Breckinridge was at Dublin Depot, the headquarters of the department of West Virginia. A force was threatening his front, while it was known that Siegel was preparing to move upon Staunton. The importance of this point to the security of General Lee's line was apparent, and considered as paramount. It had to be defended. General Lee, daily expecting an attack, could not weaken his numbers, and no force was nearer elsewhere than that of General Breckinridge. He was, therefore, ordered to march to Staunton and resist the advance of Siegel, then known to be at Winchester accumulating troops for movement.

Accordingly, on the evening of the 5th, General Breckinridge started from Dublin. Thence to this point is one hundred and forty miles by the route selected, through Giles, Monroe and Alleghany counties. The command marched to Jackson's River Depot, whence but a portion being able to get transportation by rail, the larger part marched to this point—General Breckinridge coming the greater part of the way on horseback, accompanied by part of his staff only. The remainder being left on duty with the portion of the command left in his department, arrived here on the night of the 8th, in advance of his command. He found Siegel already giving indications of movement. To meet him it was necessary to be prompt. And there was no delay. The reserves of several counties were called out, and the corps of cadets summoned. All had arrived on Thursday, 12th. On Friday, 13th, the column moved down the Valley, on the Harrisonburg road. Brigadier General Imboden was opposing, with his cavalry force, Siegel's advance, but was falling back slowly, and had retired above Woodstock. The command marched to Mount Crawford, eighteen miles, and encamped. The weather was very inclement. It had been raining for several days, and the troops were drenched on the march and in camp at night.

On Saturday, 14th, they marched through the rain seventeen miles and camped at Lacey's Spring, where they cooked two days' rations. While there, Gen. Imboden, whose headquarters were at New Market, came to meet Gen. Breckinridge for consultation, reporting the enemy pressing him and his force retiring. It had been proposed to march at daybreak, but at ten o'clock p. m., Gen. Imboden announced that the enemy occupied New Market, nine miles distant, in force. Gen. Breckinridge at once determined to make an early attack. Accordingly, the command was ordered to move at one o'clock a. m. The night was dark and rainy. The troops had had a fatiguing march with wet clothes over a hard turnpike road, rendered peculiarly trying to the feet of the soldiers from the softening of the leather by the excessive rain. The troops, however, who had showed the most cheerful spirit from the start, were promptly in motion, and daylight found them near New Market in rear of Imboden's picket line.

A line of battle was formed just two miles and a half from New Market; but the enemy showing no disposition to advance, his pickets, on the contrary, retiring before ours, the troops were moved up in full view of the town. The line was then formed with the right resting on the pike and the left extending over the range of hills running parallel with the road. General Imboden, with the cavalry, was put upon the right flank, it being more open to attack than the left. General Breckinridge, feeling that everything depended upon celerity of movement, opened with his artillery and began to move his line at nine and a half o'clock. The enemy responded, and for an hour or two the firing was very heavy. Then began the movement which resulted in success. The troops were moved forward as rapidly as the nature of the ground would admit, there being ploughed fields deep in mud, the artillery keeping its relative position, firing and limbering up as the line advanced.

Up to this time, our line having reached the town of New Market, where, amidst the screaming of shells, their deliverers were greeted with welcome by the undaunted ladies, the enemy had only developed a heavy line of skirmishers, which had fallen back with slight resistance, when pressed. Now, however, could be seen, about a mile below New Market, dark lines of infantry, with heavy bodies of cavalry on the flank. General Breckinridge, after thorough personal reconnoissance close to the enemy's skirmishers, massed the greater part of his artillery on the extreme right of his infantry, and ordered an advance.—Our line moved in fine order, notwithstanding the difficult ground at times. The field was perfectly open, without woods or fences. The enemy were strongly posted on an elevated position, to reach which we had to advance up a gradual ascent, swept by his batteries. It was not long before the opposing forces were engaged along the whole line, amid heavy artillery firing, the enemy used canister freely as we neared him. It was a trying time to our troops, and enough to make any recoil. A slight quaver was made in the first line as the canister told; but being well sustained by the second line, and the artillery on the right, under the immediate direction of Gen Breckinridge, being converted with an oblique fire upon their guns, together with the steadiness of our brave troops, was too much for them.—The enemy's line wavered, a shout went up from ours; we pressed on, and the fight was won.

At the critical moment, when our lines was momentarily checked, the enemy's cavalry started to charge over ground fearfully favorable to success; but a few shell, made them halt and retire, some fifteen or twenty only reaching our lines. Half of these had their saddles emptied before they reached us, and the rest passed to the rear as prisoners. It was now raining in torrents; but, fatigued as the troops were, they even pressed on until the enemy apparently halted for a stand at Rood's hill, a very strong position, three miles beyond. A halt was made to replenish the artillery chests and cartridge boxes, when the line being adjusted, moved forward, the interval being occupied with a lively cannonade. On reaching the top of Rood's hill, the rear of the enemy's line was seen in the distance, hurriedly retreating.—Our artillery opened upon them, but shortly after the last man crossed the bridge over the north fork of the Shenandoah, and immediately it was fired.

Night was now setting in. The stream was swollen past fording or swimming, and we were forced to quit pursuit. Our troops camped where they halted, and sought on the wet earth the rest and repose called for by almost thirty-six hours' continuous labor. Not, however, until they knew from the testimony of citizens that their boastful enemy had been disgracefully routed, and had fled in disorder and confusion, never equaled since the First Manassas.

In reviewing the action, we will briefly add this summary: General Breckinridge, with a body of mixed troops, whose numbers it is not necessary to state, except that he had enough for the work before him, engaged Siegel, who commanded in person, with 8000 infantry and 1500 cavalry.

In order to do so he had come 180 miles in less than nine days, and had made fatiguing marches, chiefly over bad mountain roads, through drenching rains; and in the last thirty-six hours had marched his troops thirty six miles, ten of which he was fighting, without any save an hour or two's rest. When the magnitude of the stake is considered, the great danger which threatened Staunton, and the almost forlorn hope of averting it, in conjunction with the rapid movements and great unflagging energy of the Commanding General, the result cannot be over estimated in importance. By a campaign of four days in the Valley, Gen. Breckinridge has driven the enemy in rapid flight back to the point whence he started, cleared Lee's left flank of all danger, given confidence to our troops and people, and destroyed the prestige of Siegel, whom the Yankees have trumpeted as the ablest of their Generals.

As the minor results of the battle we have about five hundred prisoners and six pieces of artillery.

The loss of the enemy in killed, wounded and captured, is estimated at fifteen hundred.

THE CAPTURE OF STEELE'S WAGON TRAIN.—Extract of a letter from Captain E O. MORSE, commanding Company D, 5th Kansas Cavalry, dated Pine Bluffs, Ark., April 28th, 1864, to a friend:

Yesterday a terrible disaster happened to our army. One of General Steele's wagon trains, of over 240 wagons, was returning from Camden, with an escort of about 2000 men, consisting of detachments from the 77th Ohio, 33d and 36th Iowa, 43d Indiana infantry, 1st Indiana cavalry, 7th Missouri cavalry, 5th Kansas cavalry, and 2d Missouri artillery. When forty miles from Pine Bluffs, where the roads were bad, and the train had scattered along for six miles, we were attacked by a rebel force of 6000, and kept up a hard fight for four hours, till our ammunition was exhausted and the infantry were fighting with clubbed muskets. The first and second officers in command were killed. The enemy had taken our cannon and turned them upon ourselves. Then the cavalry rallied for a final assault and cut its way through, all but fifty or sixty arriving at Pine Bluffs.

The New-York Times.

VOL. XIII—NO. 3960. NEW-YORK, THURSDAY, JUNE 2, 1864. PRICE THREE CENTS.

GRANT'S ARMY.

The Fighting of Monday and Tuesday.

Hancock's and Warren's Operations.

The Rebels Make a Night Attack on Hancock.

They Are Repulsed, With the Loss of Many Prisoners.

The Brilliant Cavalry Battle of Saturday.

THE ENEMY ADMIT A SEVERE DEFEAT.

News to 10 O'Clock Tuesday Morning.

The Battle of Monday Evening—Hancock Drives the Enemy from their Rifle Pits—The Rebels Attempt to Surprise Him at Night and meet with a Bloody Repulse—Our Lines Generally Advanced on Tuesday Morning—Rebel Admissions of Defeat.

Special Dispatch to the New-York Times.

GEN. GRANT'S HEADQUARTERS, ONE MILE SOUTH OF HAWES' STORE, Monday Night, May 30—8:30 P. M.

Our lines have advanced and moved to the left to-day. The enemy resisted the movement but feebly till about three hours ago, when he suddenly threw a strong force along and on both sides of the Mechanicsville road, upon CRAWFORD's division of WARREN's corps, and forced it back slightly. Rebel prisoners give information that the force was a reconnoissance made by RHODES' division of EWELL's corps, with two brigades of cavalry sent out to feel our position. As soon as WARREN was apprised of this movement of the enemy, he sent reinforcements to that part of his line, whose timely arrival prevented the enemy from turning his flank. The engagement was severe and lasted nearly an hour, resulting in the discomfiture of the rebels, who were driven back in disorder, and left most of their dead and wounded and a number of prisoners in our hands. WARREN's line remains where it was at noon. The enemy's cavalry force engaged in this reconnoissance advanced from Mechanicsville by a road nearly parallel with that taken by their infantry, and 1½ miles to the east.

Old Church Tavern cross-roads was held by TORBETT's division of our cavalry. It is about two miles from the Pamunky. The rebels drove in our pickets at this point, and pressed up to the main line. The first charge by TORBETT's men routed them, and they retired in confusion, leaving about a hundred killed and wounded on the field. They were pursued about two miles, to the vicinity of Cold Harbor. Our loss was two officers and five men killed, and three officers and seventy men wounded. As soon as word was brought to Gen. MEADE of the enemy's attack on WARREN's left, he ordered an advance of the whole line to relieve him. Gen. HANCOCK alone received the order before dark, and he drove the enemy from their first line of rifle-pits, which he still holds. Our loss was small. We captured about one hundred prisoners.

LATER.

Tuesday, May 31—10 A. M.

The rebel papers of yesterday claim that FITZ HUGH LEE and HAMPTON met the whole of our cavalry corps in Saturday evening's fight. In fact we had only GREGG's division and one of TORBETT's brigades engaged. They admit a defeat and a loss of one thousand, and that they were obliged to leave their dead and wounded in our hands. They own to a loss of one hundred and sixty-four in the Sixth South Carolina alone.

At midnight, last night, the enemy attempted to surprise HANCOCK, and threw a heavy force upon him. They were repulsed after a sharp fight, and left four or five hundred prisoners in our hands. It will be remembered he was occupying their rifle-pits from which he drove them just at dark last evening. During the night it was determined to advance the whole line as far as HANCOCK's front, and the movement began soon after daylight. It is still going on. There is considerable firing of musketry and artillery, and the enemy is evidently making some resistance. As yet there are no indications of a general engagement.

LEE's army holds a naturally strong position, which he has strengthened by steady work during the last few days, on the north bank of the Chickahominy. We are threatening his right, but he does not show any signs of giving up his position, and is apparently as ready to assume the offensive as he was while on the North Anna.

It is considered certain that BRECKINRIDGE has joined LEE with his forces, and prisoners say BEAUREGARD is joining him. WILLIAM SWINTON.

Details of Recent Movements—The Brilliant Cavalry Operations of Saturday and Sunday.

OLD TAVERN CHURCH, Va., Tuesday, May 30.

Our forces were withdrawn from the north side of the North Anna River last Thursday and Friday.

Gen. SHERMAN, with Gen. TORBETT and GREGG's division of cavalry, marched all night, and Thursday morning the forces on the Pamunky were in our possession.

At Dabney's Ferry, BAKER's North Carolina Brigade opposed our advance, and resisted when we laid our pontoon bridge. CUSTER and DAVIS's brigades drove them off to Hanover Court-house, killing many and capturing a large number of prisoners.

The Sixth Corps was soon at our heels. Then came the Second, Eighth and Ninth. LEE was doomed to disappointment. His elaborate fortifications would not serve him. GRANT was on his right flank, and he must away to Richmond.

Saturday morning GREGG's division of cavalry was fired into near HAWES' Shop. DAVIES' brigade was in the advance. The woods seemed alive with rebels, and they soon began to resound with the sharp volleys of our carbines. In a short time DAVIES' entire brigade was fighting in earnest. Col. GREGG was ordered to DAVIES' support, and the remainder of the division was hotly engaged. FITZ HUGH LEE commanded in person. His cavalry corps was all fighting, assisted by a brigade of mounted Fire-eaters from South Carolina, commanded by Col. BUTLER. These men had just arrived from the seaboard, and admit the warmth of the reception which our troops gave them. Conspicuous in the battle were the Fourth and Sixteenth Pennsylvania, First New-Jersey, Sixth Ohio and First Massachusetts. For a long time these men held FITZHUGH LEE back. All the cavalry engaged behaved with valor.

We found the rebels strongly entrenched in this woods, with heavy guns in position; but with every advantage upon their side they were badly beaten, flying from the field in great confusion, leaving their dead and wounded in our hands, and over one hundred prisoners.

GREGG maintained the contest from noon till 2 P. M., when CUSTER came up, formed his squadrons into line, and charged their works. GREGG's command advanced at the same time with a cheer. Many a brave fellow fell in this daring assault. The works were ours. Not an armed rebel could be found for three miles.

The Thirteenth and Sixteenth Pennsylvania, and the Fifth and Seventh Michigan suffered a heavy loss. Capts. ROBBINS and SWAN, of the Sixteenth, were wounded. Of the Tenth Pennsylvania, Capt. JOHN KLINE was killed, and Capt. P. KANE, Lieuts. STEIN and MCDONALD were wounded, also Lieut. BOWEN, of the Fourth Pennsylvania.

Too much praise cannot be given to this brigade which fought with unprecedented coolness amid that storm of grape and canister.

Our loss will amount to 350 killed, wounded and missing. The rebels used grape and canister profusely.

Our infantry was all up that evening. Long and strong lines of fortifications were erected. If LEE crossed our path we were prepared. He did not.

Next morning the newly-made breastworks were abandoned. The column moved on toward Richmond.

MONDAY, May 30.—Major DEVLAND had two squadrons of the Seventeenth Pennsylvania Cavalry on picket. He held the road leading from Cold Harbor to Old Church Tavern. About noon his pickets were driven in. The enemy appeared in heavy force. Col. DAVIN sent the Ninth and Sixth New-York to reinforce Major DEVLAND.

A heavy engagement ensued. JOHN ANGLIN, Quartermaster of the Seventeenth Pennsylvania, was killed while fighting in the skirmish line.

Gen. MERRITT soon arrived with his brigade, trained a battery of brass Napoleons on the rebels and opened fire. The Sixth Pennsylvania was sent in on the left of the line and charged the rebel flank. Capt. LIEPER was wounded and Lieut. MARTIN killed.

CUSTER next entered. A general charge was ordered, and the rebels were swept from sight. They fled, leaving a large number of dead and wounded on the field.

Lieut. BLUNT, Sixth New-York, and Capt. TICE, Seventeenth Pennsylvania, were wounded, and CHAS. W. HORNER, Sixth Pennsylvania, and THOMAS WHALLEY, of the same regiment were killed.

STUART came through this road two years ago. FITZHUGH LEE was thus baffled and foiled in his attempt to stop our communication with the White House.

Our advance is near Mechanicsville. On the left WARREN was using his cannon freely all day. He drove in the rebel pickets about four miles.

LEE's army occupy the trenches about Meadow and Bottom Bridges.

This day communication with the White House was opened. The Pamunkey is full of transports and gunboats.

We expect Gen. SMITH to join us with his command in two days.

HANCOCK made an effort last night about dusk to relieve WARREN, who had been slightly pressed during the afternoon.

Our loss is very trifling.

Lieut.-Gen. Grant in Communication with the White House—Intelligence from Richmond—The Rebels Beginning to Appreciate Grant.

FORTRESS MONROE, Tuesday, May 31.

Lieut.-Gen. GRANT's communication with the White House is complete, and all works well.

Richmond papers of Monday, the 30th ult., have been received here. They have changed their views with regard to the military ability of Gen. GRANT, and say that they have been underrating him. They say that he is smarter than they had dreamed of, and manifest some fears in regard to the safety of LEE, or rather as to his success in repelling the Yankee army.

A messenger from Gen. GRANT reports that on Monday morning our army had reached Mechanicsville with but little opposition.

Gen. SHERIDAN had routed the enemy's cavalry at all points and captured many prisoners.

Heavy cannonading was heard in the direction of Mechanicsville.

FROM GEN. SMITH'S COMMAND.

The Movement of the Eighteenth Army Corps up the Pamunky—A Torpedo Incident—Arrival at White House.

PAMUNKY RIVER, Va., Monday, May 30, 1864.

I wrote you yesterday that an expedition, under command of Major-Gen. W. F. SMITH, composed of troops detached from Gen. BUTLER's army, was moving down the James River. The date of this dispatch shows you that we have steamed around to the north side of the famous Virginian Peninsula. Our destination is White House Landing—MCCLELLAN's base during his disastrous campaign of 1862. As I write, there is a picturesque and very singular scene before me. A long line of river transports, looking like gigantic beehives with their swarming freights of blue-coated heroes, is stretched in S shaped form on the waters of the crooked Pamunky. We are down toward the river's mouth, where there is a broad sweep of marsh on either side of the narrow stream, and the marsh is bounded by wooded bluffs, which rise from the sedges as perpendicularly as a wall. Some of the steamers are heading North, some South, others East and others West, yet they are all bound up stream, are steaming fast and keeping close in each other's track. Except round our own boat there is no water to be seen, and if I didn't know any better, I should explain this marsh-navigating phenomenon where steamers are playing such an odd game of cross purposes, by saying that a miracle had been worked on land to admit the passage of our army on boats, as in olden time the Red Sea was divided to make a way for the hosts of the chosen people of the Lord.

We did not expect, on setting out from the James River, that we should get up the Pamunky to White House unmolested by the rebels or their infernal works. At Fortress Monroe, however, Gen. SMITH got news authoritatively that GRANT's army had crossed the river on Saturday at Hanover Ferry, several miles further up and this lessens our chances of being attacked. But there is still sufficient spice of danger to give zest to the advance. We have heard of torpedoes and have learned of late that such things are not "weak inventions of the enemy." At Fortress Monroe there are harrowing stories afloat of these infernal inventions being scattered about the Pamunky by our Southern brethren without the slightest regard to economy, and we are fast approaching places where we shall test the truth of these suspicions. Ours is the second boat in the line; but if there is any nervousness it finds on board no expression in words. Gen. SMITH and several members of his Staff are on the forward deck, within a few feet of me, conducting themselves very nonchalantly in view of what might happen. By the by, I think Gen. SMITH errs in one thing. He is always at the post of danger. The vicinity of the pilot-house, experience teaches me, is not the safest place in passing suspected localities. The river at this point is very narrow. It is like a stream running through a mountain gorge. The bank on the left hand is perpendicular and nearly a hundred feet high. On the crest are two embrasures for rebel guns shoveled out of the stiff red clay.

The gunboat *Morse* is a length ahead of us. She is our escort up the river, and by right leads the fleet. She is commanded by Lieut.-Commander BABCOCK. Her bell rings now to slacken speed. Here is a splendid place for mischief, if any is intended, either from guerrillas or torpedoes. If we are not bothered here, I hope to finish this letter in peace. The brave boys of the *Morse*, who have been standing all the trip at their grape-charged guns, ready to blaze away at the first moment, relinquish their stations and seize muskets. The rest of the transports close in upon us. A few moments of suspense, in which I suppose everybody shares, all the fleet again moves slowly forward, without a show of molestation, either from land or water. Henceforth I expect we shall advance less warily.

One of the General's Staff has just told an incident connected with torpedoes on the James River. It is new to me and I will relate it here as showing the little sense of honor which some of our chivalrous enemies possess. The inventor of these torpedoes is HUNTER DAVISON, who was formerly in the United States Navy. Under his supervision the machines which destroyed the *Commodore Jones* and the *Shawsheen*, the other day, were put in the James River. Not long after these disasters, Admiral LEE penetrated the river considerably above where they happened. DAVISON was putting down more of his devilish contrivances when the gunboats came upon him, and in his small torpedo-boat he took refuge in a tributary of the James, called Four Mile Creek. The gunboats went further on, and DAVISON must either run the gauntlet of them or remain in the creek all night. A cunning thought. He would hoist a flag of truce, visit Admiral LEE, and inquire into the alleged violation of that sacred emblem by Gen. BUTLER, when our troops first landed at Bermuda Hundred. The idea was carried out and succeeded. With plausible tongue DAVISON represented to the high-minded and unsuspecting Admiral, that he was commissioned to visit him, and departed, stroking his flowing beard, and laughing gaily in his sleeves at his dishonesty. The trick was soon discovered, and Admiral LEE notified Mr. DAVISON that in no way hereafter would he be treated with the courtesy of war. There is a rod in pickle for him, to be surely used if he falls into the hands of the insulted navy.

Our boat is now passing a finely located plantation house. A beautiful locust grove spreads a delightful shade over its spacious lawn. A lonesome white woman watches us closely from the piazza. We have passed many houses before on the trip, but this is the first white face I have seen. Indeed, a dozen persons have not been developed by the closest scrutiny of our party, whose glasses are constantly in use, and whose discoveries are duly announced, even though they be no greater than an unsuspecting cow in the pasture, or a pig industriously foraging. Three times my attention has been called to a white-wooled negro, standing on the bank and energetically waving his ancient hat. Each of these negroes looked and acted vastly like the other, and I begin to question whether they are not one and the same person. It would not be difficult for a moderately active fellow, even though he hobbled on crutches, to get across lots over one or two of these dovetailed river-bends faster than a swift steamer winds round by the stream.

Here is another incident, and it is likely to be the last ere we get to White House Landing, for we are nearly to the end of the trip. A wide dugout is just ahead, containing an old fisherman whose shriveled features are brown enough to make him pass for a mulatto, if it were not for a white boy sturdily wielding the paddles who calls him father. They are ordered on board after our boat stops, but don't seem to comply cheerfully. Both are greatly terrified. Gen. SMITH questions them about torpedoes, and they plead ignorance. Their anxiety, however, to get away appears so great that he is determined to detain them that we may have sympathizers in our desire to avoid these contrivances of their friends for the remainder of the trip. The old man plaintively pleads that his fresh fish will spoil and his wife will suffer anxiously for his safety; but Gen. SMITH won't be moved by his entreaties, and as everybody distrusts the old codger, he don't get any sympathy.

But White House or rather its ruins are in sight. We see the partly destroyed railroad bridge across the Pamunky. The quiet of desolation seems to rest here, as everywhere, on this war-ravaged land. The signs are auspicious for a peaceful debarkation. This afternoon I shall add something to these disconnected jottings of the uneventful trip. H. J. W.

The Landing of the Corps—White House—A Speedy Junction with Grant—Repairs to the Railroad.

From our Special Correspondent.

WHITE HOUSE, Va., Monday, May 30, 1864—P. M.

The landing of troops has been going on expeditiously and uninterruptedly for the past three hours. The remains of one of the wharves, built in MCCLELLAN's time, served as a foothold for debarkation purposes, and engineering skill and activity have speedily patched up the ruins into serviceable shape. Other wharves are improvised out of old canal boats brought along for the purpose; and the soldiers, each of whom carries a well-filled knapsack, blankets and extra rations, are trotting gaily ashore and form by regiments on the plain. The scene is very animated as viewed from where I write, beneath the shade of a noble old apple tree near the ruins of the house which was situated on the spot where WASHINGTON courted the Widow CUSTIS. The river is alive with steamers and the land is covered with moving masses of men. On the luxuriant green sward around the desolate chimney stacks, which now are all that remain of the Custis homestead, soldiers are grouped in all sorts of attitudes, enjoying apparently with keen zest the delicious breeze and shade, and revelling in the fragrant grass. There are evidences of SHERIDAN's visit here ten days since, in plenty of empty "hardtack" boxes, and a couple of dead horses, whose speedy burial would be very desirable. [After finishing the last sentence I gathered myself up from the grass to brush off the little green bugs, which were proving a pest, and discovering a stout stake loosely thrust into the earth, a few feet off, I attempted to pull it up for a seat. My eye glanced down, and I was saved a piece of sacrilege. The post marked a grave. Its badly written inscription in ink told that "Sergt. JOHN JASSTON, Company I, Eighth Illinois Regiment," died in May, 1862, and was buried there.

If ever the loose earth had been shaped into a mound over the body, there is no sign of it now, and the sergeant's last resting-place will soon be unknown, like thousands and thousands of others, which make Virginia soil indeed "sacred"—a very Golgotha of honored dust.]

Gen. SMITH has just been riding about to establish his lines. He tells me of a cavalry man from GRANT, who has just come in. This man says that GRANT's cavalry crossed at Hanover Ferry on Saturday and the infantry yesterday. There had been fighting, and hard fighting, ever since. Even now I hear the boom of heavy guns, and suppose, from the rapidity of the reports, that a hard battle is raging. GRANT's headquarters are not more than fifteen miles from us, and to-morrow, at daybreak, if the unloading of supplies and munitions is finished, we shall start on the march to meet him.

This point will be made secure as a base of supplies, and the indications at present are that the entire Army of the Potomac will be dependent on it, for a time at least.

Capt. FARQUHAR, of the Engineer Corps, has given orders for the repair of the railroad bridge at this point, and Lieut. TALFER, with a sufficient force, has got it nearly into a condition for service. The crew of the gunboat *Morse* have enthusiastically aided in this work.

I have just heard of a sad accident. The report comes by one of the transports, that Lieut. HUNT, commanding Battery L, Fourth United States Artillery, was drowned by falling overboard on the passage up the river. HUNT was considered one of the best artillery officers in the service. It is hoped that the report of his death will prove untrue. H. J. W.

GEN. BUTLER'S ARMY.

The Attack of the Rebels on Monday—What was it for—Reports of Deserters—The Railroad Between Petersburgh and Richmond Fully Repaired.

From Our Own Correspondent.

BERMUDA HUNDRED, Monday, May 30, 1864.

This is the first day of many on which anything of a startling nature has occurred to break the monotonous silence which has reigned supreme. Toward evening some new batteries, known to our people only from the reports of deserters, opened heavily on our works. To say the fire was brisk would be to give but an imperfect idea of the rapidity with which the guns of the enemy were served. It was one continuous roar of cannon, the discharge of the guns being only equaled by the incessant flight and explosion of projectiles. Our gunners were not long in concluding what action to take in the premises, and were very soon busily returning their compliments to the enemy with compound interest. The fight lasted about one hour, not one person being hurt on our side that I have heard of. It is not known what instigated the enemy to make this sudden and furious artillery onslaught. One proposition is that they wished to get the range of the guns in this new battery, but the correct theory is probably that, believing we have sent away large numbers of men to the assistance of Gen. GRANT, it must necessarily have so weakened us that it would be an easy matter to carry our works. If the promptitude with which our fire was returned and maintained is any criterion from which to judge, they have probably concluded that their impressions regarding the decrease in our strength was erroneous. No infantry was engaged.

While the fighting was going on in our front, heavy artillery firing was distinctly heard coming from the direction of Richmond. The impression of many officers was that it was probably an engagement between our gunboats and some shore batteries of the enemy. I believe, with others, that it was GRANT's artillery. The firing was too continuous and was kept up until too late an hour of the night to be any other than field batteries desperately engaged.

From two deserters who came to our lines to-day, we learn that the communications between Petersburgh and Richmond are fully restored, and trains are constantly passing to and fro. Gen. BEAUREGARD has imperative orders to protect it from further damage at all hazards. These deserters also report that Gens. H. B. JOHNSON and HOKE are still with BEAUREGARD, but that HOKE's troops have left. They even heard a conversation betwen the Colonel and Major of the picket, wherein the statement was made by the Colonel that SHERMAN had been defeated by JOS JOHNSTON, and that LEE was fighting to-day. Secessionville, it was reported, had been flanked and captured. They complained bitterly of the scarcity of food in the army. A ration of only two-thirds of an ounce of bacon and thirteen ounces of meal were allowed daily. Many more had intended to follow him from the rebel camp, and we might expect them at any moment.'

I very nearly forgot to mention that they asserted the rebel force in the works before us to be very small—scarcely large enough to man the entire line.

A strange phenomenon in the way of a balloon-shaped cloud was to be witnessed last evening. It was first seen soon after the firing on our front had ceased, and moved from the direction of the rebel works over ours toward the landing. Being twilight, the illusion was not discovered until the cloud commenced breaking up. It was actually thought by many to be a balloon sent up by the rebels on a reconnoissance, which had broken the guy ropes, and thus escaped.

TUESDAY, May 31—1 P. M.

No more fighting has been done at our front. Some heavy cannonading has been heard, though, from about the same point whence the heavy firing of last evening seemed to come.

From Fortress Monroe—Sanitary Order—Death of Soldiers in Hospital.

FORTRESS MONROE, Tuesday, May 31.

The following order has been issued by Gen. BUTLER:

In accordance with orders from the War Department, and for sanitary reasons, no bodies will be disinterred in this department until the 1st of October.

By order of Major-Gen. BUTLER.

Capt. J. B. LAWRENCE, Ninth New-Jersey Volunteers, and private GEORGE A. BROWN, of the Eighth Maine Volunteers, died to-day in the Chesapeake Hospital. Privates JOHN BARRY, Second New-Hampshire, JEFF. GEDDES, One Hundred and Eighty-eighth Pennsylvania, and E. F. HALL, Eleventh South Carolina (a prisoner,) died, and Sergeant F. A. FLETCHER, of the Second New-Hampshire, wounded in the arm, was admitted in the McClellan Hospital yesterday.

All Quiet at Bermuda Hundred—Grant's Forces at Mechanicsville—Cavalry Skirmishes—Cannonading Heard.

FORTRESS MONROE, Tuesday, May 31—4 P.M.

The steamer *Thomas Powell* has just arrived from Bermuda Hundred. All was quiet with Gen. BUTLER's forces to-day.

The steamer *C. W. Thomas*, with a bearer of dispatches from Gen. GRANT, has arrived from the White House.

A portion of Gen. GRANT's forces arrived at Mechanicsville yesterday morning and had not encountered the enemy in force up to that time.

Gen. SHERIDAN's cavalry had had several skirmishes with the enemy and completely routed them.

Heavy cannonading was heard yesterday in the direction of Mechanicsville.

The highest hopes are entertained by those competent to judge of the situation.

The Arguelles Case.

WASHINGTON, Wednesday, June 1.

The President, in response to an inquiry, to-day, sent to the Senate all the papers in the Arguelles case on file in the State Department, and also a letter of Secretary SEWARD, in which the latter says: "By the act of Congress of May 15, 1820, the African slave-trade is declared to be piracy; and by the treaty of 1842 with Great Britain, it is stipulated that they will invite and urge upon all Powers the propriety and duty of effectually at once and forever closing all African slave markets." The Secretary says, there being no treaty of extradition between the United States and Spain, nor any act of Congress directing how fugitives in the Spanish dominions shall be delivered up, the extradition in the ARGUELLES case is understood by the State Department to have been made in virtue of the law of nations and the Constitution of the United States. Although there is a conflict of authorities concerning the expediency of exercising comity toward a foreign Government, by surrendering at its request one of its own subjects charged with the commission of crime within its territory; and although it may be conceded that there is no national obligation to make such a surrender upon a demand therefor, unless it is acknowledged by treaty or statute, yet a nation is never bound to furnish asylum to dangerous criminals who are offenders against the human race; and it is believed that if in any case the comity could, with propriety, be practised, the one which is understood to have called forth the resolution of inquiry of the Senate furnished a just occasion for its exercise.

Our Consul at Havana writes to Secretary SEWARD on May 23, that on the arrival of ARGUELLES he was immediately lodged in jail, and the next morning was conveyed to Moro Castle, where he still remained.

FROM ARKANSAS.

Murder of Union Men by Guerrillas—Horrible Atrocities—Reported Attempt to Invade Missouri.

ST. LOUIS, Wednesday, June 1.

A telegram to headquarters from Rolla, Mo., May 30, states that a train of Union refugees from Jacksonport, Arkansas, under escort of seventy men of the Second Wisconsin Cavalry, was attacked at Salem, Arkansas, by three hundred guerrillas. The entire train was burnt, and eighty men and some women killed.

On Friday last, ten men of a detachment of the Second Wisconsin Cavalry, out on a scout from Rolla, becoming separated from the main body, were surrounded by guerrillas, and five killed, the others making their escape. Returning in larger force, they found the bodies of those killed stripped, and their throats cut.

A gentleman just arrived from Little Rock, represents all quiet in the vicinity.

JOE SHELBY had left Brownsville about two weeks ago, with a force estimated at 1,500 to 3,000, for Southwest Missouri. Gen. WEST, with several companies of cavalry, had been sent against him. SHELBY is represented to be well mounted, and to have been joined by MCRAE, with 500 cavalry, in addition to his own force.

FROM NEW-ORLEANS.

Late Southern News—Death of T. Butler King—Affairs in Mobile—News from Mexico.

ARRIVAL OF THE CAHAWBA.

The U. S. steam transport *Cahawba*, Capt. BAKER, commanding, arrived here at 2 A. M. yesterday, from New-Orleans the 25th ult., at 5 P. M., and the Bar at 1 A. M. 26th, with mails. She also brings the Fifty-sixth Ohio Veteran Volunteers, Capt MANNERING, commanding. The vessel is consigned to U. S. Quartermaster.

DEATH OF THOMAS BUTLER KING.

From the New-Orleans Picayune, May 25

We learn from our Mobile files that the Hon. THOMAS BUTLER KING died at his residence in Waresboro, Ware County, Ga., on the 10th inst. His disease was pneumonia. Mr. KING was a native of Pennsylvania, but moved to Georgia some years ago, when quite a young man. He married the daughter of the late Col. PAGE, of St. Simond's Island, and settled in Glynn County, which he represented for several successive years in the State Legislature. He was a gentleman of liberal education, enlarged views and of the State Rights school of politics. When the Nullification question arose, he allied himself to the State Rights party of Georgia, and in 1838 was elected, with the entire ticket of the party, a member of the United States House of Representatives, to which he was reelected during several successive terms, identifying himself with the Whig party in the Harrison-Tyler Presidential campaign.

In Congress Mr. KING was very useful, especially in connection with naval affairs and ocean steam navigation. On the accession of Gen. TAYLOR to the Presidency, Mr. KING was appointed Collector of the Port of San Francisco, in which office he continued about two years. During his whole career he was devoted to the cause of internal improvement, and he exercised much influence in the councils of the State, and also of the nation. On the secession of Georgia, he was sent by the State as Commissioner to Europe, and his correspondence in that capacity was marked by great ability and practical acquaintance with the laws of trade, and the rules for international dealing. Mr. KING was from the first a zealous adherent of the Southern secession movement.

AFFAIRS IN MOBILE.

From the Picayune, May 20.

We have a few late Mobile papers from which we gather the following *resumé* of affairs in the "Gulf City:" CHARLES C. RIDDLE, an engineer on the iron-clad *Tennessee*, has been committed for trial for the murder of THOMAS QUINN, a fireman on the same craft. The *Tribune* says that the interruption of telegraphic communication with Richmond had caused considerable anxiety on the part of those having relatives and friends in the Virginia army. The ship-yards are busy building steamboats and schooners for private parties and for the Confederate Government. "There are but few idlers in the city; the mechanics and laboring classes are all employed. The plow and the hoe have made their marks in hundreds of gardens in the suburbs, while repairs and improvements have been steadily going on in the city. Government works, etc., having given employment to many who are exempt from military duty." The markets show but little change. "Flour is selling at $90 per sack, while corn has advanced some little; it is quoted at $5 50 to $6 per bushel, which is due to the reported advance in other States, which has caused planters to advise their merchants to hold for higher rates. The scarcity of money being so keenly felt, produce must fall to meet the circumstances of the people."

The *Register* says that "the sunken *Tennessee* may yet raise herself from the bottom of the bay, where the Federal fleet saw her sink."

The ladies have given several suppers at Odd Fellows' Hall for the purpose of raising funds for the benefit of the maimed and disabled soldiers of the war. The money market is tight, and loans on call or short time readily command a heavy premium. On Friday, TONY, a slave, was hung for the crime of burglary. The slave population, as a class, are under good discipline, and are sufficiently submissive; but there are a goodly number who require strict watchfulness—not more so, however, than in ordinary times.'

LATER FROM MEXICO.

From the Picayune, May 25.

We are indebted to Gen. D. DOMINGO DE GOICOURIA for the perusal of private letters from Matamoros, from which we extract as follows:

MATAMOROS, Saturday, May 7, 1864.

It seems that some Frenchmen coming from Tampico conspired to take the life of CORTINA. Two of them attacked one of the Governor's aids, one of them shooting but missing him, whereupon the Governor killed that Frenchman. The other Frenchman was tried, sentenced and executed, all before 12 o'clock in the day.

We have letters from Monterey, of the 4th, which state that an expedition was to have started out with 6,000 men under CARRAJAL the Mozravieff of the French expedition, on the 10th. (The writer does not state from whence or for what purpose.)

We doubt this very much, as our advices show a disposition to concentrate their forces near Mexico, with a view to the early approach of MAXIMILIAN.

MATAMOROS, Friday, May 13.

I am assured that there are 2,000 Confederates at Davis' Ranch, (Ringold Barracks, one hundred miles above Brownsville,) and that they design occupying the latter place. The mere accusation of this by one of CORTINA's officers, caused the Licenciados (counsellors) Vilasco, Barando, Aguado, and Rojas and D. Antonio Garcia Chapa, to be enrolled as common soldiers of the regiment of riflemen. They were sent out to be drilled in the (dry) laguna back of the city in the presence of an immense crowd. These soldiers of the new levy had been talking about our State authorities. They were subsequently released with a reprimand, which gave them to understand that worse treatment would be their lot if they were wanting in respect to authority.

From California, &c.

SAN FRANCISCO, Tuesday, May 31.

Arrived bark *Nomautum*, from New-York.

Parties just in from Arizona bring favorable reports concerning the silver ledges near Colorado River.

The lumber mills, foundry and machine-shop at Port Madison, Puget Sound, were burned May 27.

A meeting has been called at Virginia, May 28, by parties in favor of a paper currency, strongly denouncing the project, which is probably dead.

The crop prospect in California continues improved.

The flour and grain markets are flat. The *Cora* is to sail for Sydney with a cargo of breadstuffs valued at $140,000.

Very few mining corporations are forming now.

The Cleveland Convention.

EVENING SESSION.

The committee not being prepared to report, a meeting was organized by selecting Mr. ALDEN for Chairman, and, on invitation, PARKER PILLSBURY addressed the audience at some length, expressing extreme radical Anti-Slavery views.

Mr. GILBERT reported the following as the National Central Committee:

EDW'D GILBERT, N. Y.	D. GREINER, N. J.
WALTER H. SHUPE, N. Y.	J. W. BARKER, Penn.
FRED'K KAPP, N. Y.	WEND'L PHILLIPS, Mass
B. B. CHAPMAN, Ohio.	J. P. FREKBOLD, Iowa.
E. H. PRETORIOUS, Mo.	WM. SMETHER, Md.
CHAS. E. MOSS, Mo.	CHARLES POST, Ind.
JAMES TAUSSIG, Mo.	CASPER BUTZ, Illinois.
JAS. F. LEGGETT, Kansas	

Mr. GILBERT also reported the names of the "Radical Democracy," which was adopted by the convention.

Mr. SMETHER moved that a committee of five be appointed to wait upon Gens. FREMONT and COCHRANE, and inform them of their nominations.

Carried, and Messrs. Smether, Moss, Gilbert, Butz and N. P. Sawyer were appointed.

After remarks by S. S. FOSTER, of Massachusetts, the convention adjourned *sine die*.

Maine Democratic State Convention.

PORTLAND, Wednesday, June 1.

The Democratic State Convention met at Portland to-day. Four hundred delegates were present. Every county but Aroostook was represented. The following delegates at large to the Chicago Convention were chosen: Hon. GRAHAM L. BOYNTON, of Bangor; WILLIAM P. HAWES, of Biddeford; JOHN W. DALA, of Fryeburgh; RICHARD D. RICE, of Augusta.

Affairs in Colorado.

DENVER CITY, C. T., Wednesday, June 1.

The Relief Committee for the sufferers by the late flood have raised nearly $5,400. About the same amount is to be raised in the mountain towns.

Groceries and provisions are exorbitantly high here. The following are wholesale prices: Sugar, 38c.@40c.; Coffee, 62c.@75c.; Flour, $16@$18 ℔ 100 lbs.; Bacon, 40c Other things in proportion.

The mining prospects are good, but operations are restricted by the great scarcity of labor.

The Pittsburgh Sanitary Fair.

PITTSBURGH, Penn., Wednesday, June 1.

Business was suspended this afternoon on the opening of the Sanitary Fair. There was a grand military and civic procession, the largest ever known. The streets on both sides were crowded in the whole line of the procession, from the Monongahela Hotel, in Pittsburgh, to the fair ground in Allegheny City. Gov. CURTIN delivered the oration, which was enthusiastically received. The Hyatt Cadets, from the West Chester Military Academy, excited considerable interest.

Queer Robbery.

ALBANY, Wednesday, June 1.

The office of the District Attorney of Rensselaer County, JOHN H. COLBY, was entered by burglars at an early hour this morning, the safe pried open, and a large number of indictments found against criminals, stolen. Among the indictments thus destroyed was one against WILLIAM CULVER for murder. The prosecution of the criminals will have to be suspended for a time in consequence of the robbery.

Re-Election of Senator Anthony.

NEWPORT, R. I., Wednesday, June 1.

The General Assembly to-day elected HENRY B. ANTHONY to the United States Senate for six years from March 4, 1865. The vote stood: ANTHONY, 75; GEORGE H. BROWN, Democrat, 27; scattering, 1.

The Recent Fire in St. Louis.

ST. LOUIS, Wednesday, June 1.

The total loss by the burning of the warehouse of C. H. BELL yesterday was about $160,000; insurance, $5,000.

Serenade to Miss Major Pauline Cushman

SHE MAKES A SPEECH.

A large number of citizens gathered on the sidewalk in front of the Astor House, about 11 o'clock last evening, to testify their appreciation of the eminent services of Miss Major CUSHMAN, the gallant Union scout and spy, [whose daring and skill have elicited the warmest commendations of ROSECRANS, GARFIELD, and other Union officers. A fine band was in attendance, and greeted the fair Major with several patriotic airs. Miss CUSHMAN appeared at a window in the second story and was introduced to the assembly by Mr. F. W. B. HIBBARD, Esq., of this City. She was received with three cheers. As soon as the crowd became quiet, she spoke as follows:

GENTLEMEN: I trust that you will in kindness pardon the brevity of my remarks, as this evening I am truly to be ranked with the Invalid Corps. I am at a loss for words to express my heartfelt gratitude for this testimonial of your appreciation of my humble efforts to aid in the glorious work of restoring the union of our once happy States; and, believe me, that I am ever with you in heart and soul for the success of our cause. I am no orator, and make no pretence to eloquence; but as our gallant Gen. GRANT, when called upon to make a speech, I can say, "I can fight for my country." My sufferings at the hands of those who are now arrayed against the flag of our Republic have been far more than requited by the privilege of seeing the cause of justice triumph. To-night our noble troops are besieging the capital of treason; and with them and you I unite my feeble voice in the cry, "Long live the Union!"—the Union cemented by the blood of so many gallant sons of New-York. Good night, and God bless you all.

After the conclusion of these brief remarks, Miss Maj. CUSHMAN, who was suffering from a severe indisposition, retired, saluted by the cheers of the assemblage.

ANNUAL MEETING OF THE STOCKHOLDERS OF THE NEW-JERSEY RAILROAD.—The annual meeting of the stockholders of the New Jersey Railroad and Transportation Company was held yesterday at the depot, in Jersey City, and was quite largely attended. The following is an abstract from their annual report: The receipts for the year ending Dec. 31, 1863, was $1,286,600 12; total expenses, $591,685 74. Increased receipts over the year 1862, $175,513 37, and increase in the expenses $132,723 31. The cost per mile run for 1862, was 89 58-100ths cents, while for 1863 it was 104 18-100ths cents. Amount of Government tax paid was $40,020 13. The stockholders were reëlected.

The New-York Times.

VOL. XIII—NO. 3962. NEW-YORK, SATURDAY, JUNE 4, 1864. PRICE THREE CENTS.

THE SITUATION.

No News from Gen. Grant Since Wednesday.

The Telegraphs in Virginia Destroyed by a Storm.

A Battle Believed to Have Been Fought on Thursday.

Heavy Cannonading Heard at White House.

Full Details of Movements Up to Tuesday Evening.

DEMONSTRATIONS AGAINST GEN. BUTLER.

Important Movements of Gen. Sherman.

THE ADVANCE UPON ATLANTA

NO FURTHER NEWS FROM GEN. GRANT

Telegraph Communication Interrupted by a Storm—Important Movements of Gen. Sherman.

[OFFICIAL.]

WAR DEPARTMENT, WASHINGTON, June 3—10 P. M.

To Maj.-Gen. Dix:

A dispatch dated yesterday at 7½ P. M., has this evening been received from Gen. SHERMAN. He reports that on Wednesday, June 1, MCPHERSON moved up from Dallas to a point in front of the enemy a New Hope Church. On Thursday, June 2, SCOFIELD and HOOKER, having been shifted to the extreme left, pushed forward toward Marietta. At the same time STONEMAN'S and GARRARD'S cavalry were sent to Allatoona Pass, which they reached and held possession of. These movements, the dispatch says, have secured the pass, which was considered a formidable one. Movements are reported by the dispatch as in progress which are not proper now for publication.

Nothing has been heard from Gen. GRANT since his dispatch dated at 7 o'clock yesterday morning. Telegraphic communication has been delayed by a violent storm on the Peninsula yesterday evening and last night, and cannot be reëstablished before sometime to-morrow.

EDWIN M. STANTON, Secretary of War.

DETAILS OF OPERATIONS.

Special Dispatch to the New-York Times.

HEADQUARTERS ARMY OF THE POTOMAC, IN THE FIELD, NEAR HANOVERTOWN, Tuesday, May 31, 1864.

By one of those odd coincidences of which the history of the Virginia campaigns is so full, Gen. GRANT'S headquarters are this morning at the very point which formed the extreme right wing of the Army of the Potomac in the Peninsular campaign two years ago. HARRIS' shop, near which we now are, and four or five miles southeast of Hanover Court-house, was then occupied by the Fourth Regular Cavalry as an outpost, and it was here, just two years ago, that STUART, moving from Hanover Court-house to make his raid around MCCLELLAN'S line, struck our right flank.

Draw a line five or six miles in length from the Pamunky, near Hanover Court-house, where our right now rests, almost due south across Totopotamoy Creek, three miles south of Hanovertown, and you will have our line of battle as it now stands. Five miles west of our line runs that famous stream, the "Chickahominy." Along that river, in front covering the Virginia Central Railroad, from Atlee's Station to Shady Grove, five miles north of Richmond, the rebel front is formed. Midway of the interval that divides these two points of mighty opposites, the skirmish lines of two armies meet, and to our ears the morning air brings the crackle of musketry like the spluttering of some hell cauldron, while now and then comes the boom of guns, whose reverberations are easily heard in the Capital of the rebellion. Gaines Mill and Mechanicsville are within an hour's ride. Fair Oaks you can reach in a two hours' trot. Richmond is ten miles off. 'Tis thus that history repeats itself.

The present position of this army is the result of that fine turning movement, which, commencing on Thursday last, in two days planted our corps across the Pamunky River, rendered useless the elaborate rebel defences of the South Anna, and secured us communication with York River, the Chesapeake, and the ample resources which these waters float. Of this movement I have sent you such reports as it has been possible to send with such infrequent opportunities of communication as are afforded. I fear, however, that no reports which you can have received are at all adequate to set forth the true presentation of this great operation in strategy. Your readers would require better maps than can possibly be accessible to them, and would need to bring to them an amount of study of which you are capable in order to grasp its relations and its reality. Enough that it has planted this army twenty miles nearer Richmond, that it has foiled the plans and purposes of the wily enemy, and has brought us in easy communication with a secure and perfect base. I must not, however, forbear to emphasize one point. It appears to be conceived that this movement is understood to be a following up of the enemy, who is supposed to have fallen back from his lines between the North and South Anna—a conception which does injustice to the generalship of our Commander.

It was not LEE but GRANT that took the initiative. LEE would gladly have remained in his lines along the South Anna, and would willingly have awaited battle there, but he was forced out of his cherished position, just as he was compelled to evacuate the lines of Spottsylvania, by an offensive movement threatening his communications—a movement bold in conception and masterly in execution. ("There are," says the Arch-Duke CHARLES, "battles which are already won by the mere direction of the strategic line of advance.") In a like sense it can fairly be claimed that by a couple of days' marching this army has gained a victory more substantial than a week's hard pounding could in the situation we have won; and that we are entitled so to regard this great flank movement is confirmed by the tone of mingled mortification and braggadocio in which the Richmond press treats it.

"GRANT," says the *Examiner* of Saturday, the 28th, "has definitely declined battle at Hanover Junction. Perhaps we should say that his army has saved him the trouble of declining. It is certain that both armies are once more moving. Two stories have lately prevailed of the direction in which GRANT is going—one account represented a large body of Yankees at Negro Foot, in the upper part of Hanover, but it has not been confirmed and is unlikely. The more probable statement is that GRANT put fortifications along his line before the junction to prevent an attack from Gen. LEE, and then returning to the northern bank of the North Anna, pushed down the Pamunky to Hanovertown, a few miles above the "Piping Tree," the point to which boats can come here. He is said to have crossed the river with the greater part of his forces. If GRANT has really landed there he may be said to have already reached the destination predicted for him since his check at Spottsylvania, the York, and the Peninsula. His next base will be the Pamunky and York, the White House and West Point. Unable to remove the obstacle on the threshold of his proposed campaign, nothing was left but to abandon it, and make his way down the valley of the Rappahannock to the head waters of the York, a monstrous circuit, to reach a point where he might have landed on the first of May, had not his head been addled by his victories over PEMBERTON and BRAGG."

This is the tone of men who nowing the prodigious labor expended in fortifying a chosen position, see themselves compelled to forfeit its advantages and seek elsewhere, and ominously nearer their capital, a new line of defence. Certainly if the Richmond journalists find any satisfaction in the monstrous circuit this army has made the to point at which it has aimed, this army is in a condition to share the sentiment. The line of march, I dictate with above extract, as taken up by this army, is quite correct. After the recrossing of the North Anna, on Thursday night and Friday morning, the corps were directed on parallel roads down the course of the Pamunky to the town of Hanover, in the vicinity of which two divisions of cavalry crossed the river at 6 o'clock in the morning, and three hours afterward "RUSSELL'S" division of the Sixth Corps, after a beautiful march of 23 miles, made the passage.

The enemy, apparently not expecting the crossing to be made so far down the river, had only a cavalry force in observation at this point. The party was easily driven off, sixty being captured, and the fords were uncovered for the passage of the army, which was effected during the day. It is quite certain that it was not until this movement was fairly under way that LEE commenced the manœuvres necessary to meet it. "GRANT," says a correspondent of one of the Richmond papers, writing on Friday, "last night commenced rapidly moving toward our right with his whole force, and corresponding movements are now on foot on our side to meet those of GRANT." The movement necessary on the part of the rebels was a simple change of front and retrograde march due south along the railroad, and ten miles would bring them to the Chickahominy. For us, on the contrary, it was necessary to give a great development to our left, so that to reach the same point which the enemy could make in a ten miles' march, it was necessary for us to march something like thirty miles—that is, we had to move in a southeasterly direction to effect the passage of the river, and then move westward, for the purpose of striking the enemy or meeting his advance. This detour, or "monstrous circuit," as the Richmond writer terms it, was necessitated by two different considerations. First, because a flank march of the kind determined upon, is one which is always somewhat hazardous in the face of a vigorous and energetic opponent; and secondly, because it was a prime desideratum to open up a water base—our communications having been abandoned when this move was initiated. This was secured yesterday, when a cavalry force was sent to White House, and to-day our water transportation is reported at that point.

The work of the past three days has been a steady pressing forward of the force from Hanovertown to westward, on the lines leading to the Chickahominy, and the Virginia Central and Fredericksburgh and Richmond Railroads. The advance of GREGG'S division on Saturday developed the enemy, with the entire cavalry force and a portion of infantry, covering those roads, and brought on an engagement, which, from the losses on both sides, ranks among the heaviest cavalry fights of the war. GREGG'S division lost over three hundred and fifty men and forty officers, but drove the enemy, and during Sunday and yesterday our front has been steadily advancing. Yesterday (Monday, 30th) found our line stretched from the Pamunky immediately in front of Hanover Court-house, where our right rested. Along the direct road from Hanover Court-house to Richmond, our left stretched beyond Totopotamoy Creek, about ten miles from the rebel capital. The enemy showed in our front a line of battle and a skirmish line, formed by part of the corps of EWELL and HILL. During yesterday only skirmishing took place, we feeling the enemy's line. Early in the morning, CRAWFORD'S division of WARREN'S corps moved in support of Gen. GRIFFIN'S division, which was moving out the road toward Pole Green. It was directed by Gen. WARREN to support GRIFFIN'S left as he advanced. The road to Mechanicsville ran along parallel to the road upon which it was advancing, and was held firmly by the enemy's cavalry and some infantry.

CRAWFORD determined to push for this road, cross it if possible, and advance toward Mechanicsville. Accordingly, he ordered Col. HARDIN forward with the First Brigade, directing him to advance the picket line in his front, support it closely, and move for the Mechanicsville road.

It was nearly three-quarters of a mile from our left flank. HARDIN pushed in and soon found the enemy's cavalry, which he drove across the road, occupying it. Forming here, he was slowly advancing, when the enemy advanced his line of battle directly on his flank. CRAWFORD sent two regiments to his support, but the enemy attacked him upon both flanks, and finding the force hotly engaged, he moved to the field with his whole division, the enemy having flanked HARDIN when he arrived. CRAWFORD hastily threw FISHER'S brigade to hold the right, and advanced Col. KITCHEN'S, with two regiments, to support the line on the left, but was too late, and he ordered the line to fall back to the crest of a hill. Here he extended it, and ordered the men to throw up intrenchments. Old rails, logs, and whatever was handy, were used, and a breastwork soon prepared, after which FISHER'S brigade was thrown across a ravine on the right, and two pieces of artillery were planted on top of the ravine. Hardly were the men in position, when the rebels advanced their line of battle directly upon our line. Awaiting their coming until they were within one hundred yards, the Pennsylvania *Reserves* opened a very heavy fire. Thrice the rebel colors were shot down, and the last time they were not raised again. Whoever had them crawled away with them. Twice they rallied their line and advanced. Each time they were driven back, until the men laid down, when they commenced running back, and our line marched out of their works, and took 70 prisoners. Among them were six or seven officers. A very large number of the enemy was killed; among them a Colonel and five officers, and 300 dead were left lying in our front, inside of the line of skirmishers. CRAWFORD lost a considerable number of men. Brig.-Gen. RAMSEY was left on the field, as reported, killed. Col. W. H. KENT, of the Sixth Regiment, was shot through the hand. Capt. WATERS, of the Sixth, was also wounded. Col. TYRELL is killed. Sergt. THOMPSON, of the Bucktails, who captured the battle-flag of the Fifteenth Georgia at Gettysburgh, was wounded and made prisoner.

When this attack was made upon WARREN, HANCOCK was ordered at 7 o'clock last evening to make a diversion in his favor; the order was vigorously executed, and for a couple of hours a heavy cannonade was kept up on the rebel position by several batteries and six Cohorn mortars.

This morning finds our line in much the same formation as it had yesterday. The Sixth Corps, "WRIGHT'S," holds the right, then comes the Second, HANCOCK'S, then the Fifth, WARREN'S, and then the Ninth, BURNSIDE'S, which holds our left.

The only portion of our forces thus far engaged to-day is HANCOCK'S corps, from whose front I have just returned. The division of BIRNEY on the right and BARLOW on the centre, while I remained on the ground, advanced about six hundred yards, carrying the enemy's first line, which was held by a strong skirmish force. BIRNEY captured forty prisoners, who proved to belong to BRECKINRIDGE'S command. There is hardly a doubt, however, that the position now held by the rebels in our front is but an advanced line, which they will hold as long as possible, for the purpose of gaining time to perfect their defences on the Chickahominy. On that historic line, it is now fully expected that we shall ere long deliver battle.

I need not say that in the relative position of the opposing forces this is the only field fight we are likely to have outside of Richmond, and that its result must decide whether the rebel capital can be carried by a *coup de main* or whether it is destined to be come the object of a Summer's siege.

SWINTON.

A Battle Going on Thursday—Heavy Cannonading Heard at White House—The Fight of Tuesday—Repulse of Rhodes and Early.

WASHINGTON, Friday, June 3.

The steamer *Keyport* arrived this afternoon having left the White House at noon yesterday. Parties who came up on her state that heavy cannonading was heard there when they left, indicating that an engagement was in progress.

A cavalryman, who came in from the front to the White House, reported that the Sixth Corps was engaged, having brought it on by a rapid and sudden movement from the left to the right.

Several regiments of negro troops, doubtless a portion of Gen. BUTLER'S forces, were being landed at the White House when the *Keyport* left.

The hospital steamer *Connecticut* was engaged in taking on the wounded that had been brought down from the front.

WASHINGTON, Friday, June 3.

A dispatch from the Army of the Potomac, dated on Tuesday night, says:

"The day before the Fifth Corps, advancing from Hawe's Store toward Bethesda Church, drove the enemy about two miles. At sunset, while our men were engaged in digging rifle pits, RHODES and EARLY'S divisions made an attack on WARREN'S right flank, causing him to fall back from his first line. The enemy then advanced and charged the second line. KITCHEN'S brigade of heavy artillery was posted there and opened a heavy fire in conjunction with batteries on both flanks, which nearly demolished the rebel column of attack. The enemy fell back in terrible disorder, and left their dead and wounded behind them on the field."

Not Very Late News—A Successful Skirmish—Fifty Prisoners Captured.

WASHINGTON, Friday, June 3.

A dispatch from the Army of the Potomac, dated 5 o'clock Tuesday afternoon, says: This morning Gen. BIRNEY'S division advanced against a breastwork held by BRECKINRIDGE'S corps on the south side of Totopatamoy Creek, on a high eminence, a very strong position, and one which might have been easily held against a vastly superior force. The enemy, after firing a round or two, and seeing a determination to take the place, evacuated and retreated to the woods.

Our loss was about twenty-five. We took about fifty prisoners, mostly belonging to BRECKINRIDGE'S command, some of whom said they were in the valley in the fight with Gen. SIGEL, but did not have to fight as stubbornly as they did here.

Capt. ROWE, of the Sixteenth Massachusetts, and Adjt. JACKSON, Second New-York, were among the wounded, this morning—the latter having had his leg amputated.

The attempt made to turn our left, last night, and to cut us off from the White House and new base of supplies, was defeated, with considerable loss on both sides.

FROM FORTRESS MONROE.

Repulse of the Rebels by Gen. Butler—Reported Capture of Fitzhugh Lee and 500 Rebel Cavalry.

FORTRESS MONROE, Thursday, June 2, Via BALTIMORE, Friday, June 3.

The steamer *John A. Warner*, from Bermuda Hundred at 4 o'clock last evening, has arrived. At 7 o'clock yesterday morning (1st) the enemy attacked Gen. BUTLER'S left wing, and a spirited fight with musketry and artillery was kept up until 9 o'clock, when the enemy were again repulsed. Thirty rebel soldiers came into our lines yesterday morning and surrendered. Our loss was very slight. The enemy's loss has not been ascertained.

The steamer *George Washington*, from the White House at 7 o'clock this morning, has arrived here.

It is reported that Gen. FITZHUGH LEE, and 500 of his command (cavalry) were captured last night while attempting to make a raid in the direction of the White House. Gen. SMITH'S forces made the capture.

[Gen. GRANT'S official dispatches dated June 2, 7 A. M., make no mention of this capture, and the report may therefore be regarded as unfounded. Eds. TIMES.]

There is no later news from Gen. GRANT'S army.

A prize steamer, name not ascertained, arrived in Hampton Roads this evening.

Wounded from Bermuda Hundred.

FORTRESS MONROE, Thursday, June 2.

The following wounded men arrived from Bermuda Hundred, yesterday, and were admitted into the McClellan Hospital:

Adjt. Charles Higgins, 47th New-York—foot.
Lieut. C. A. Kinsbuley, 112th New-York—head.
Lieut. Edward Charlton, 112th New-York—side.
Lieut. Newton Baldwin, 7th Connecticut—back.
J. M. Carter, 97th Pennsylvania—shoulder.
P. S. Hector, 1st United States Artillery—breast.
Daniel Wilcox, 67th Ohio—hand.
B. F. Sealy, 7th New-Hampshire—arm.
J. F. Brown, 3d New-Hampshire—leg.
Peter Denant, 3d New-Hampshire—leg.
John D. Fenner, 48th New-York—knee.
N. Doughty, 48th New-York—shoulder.
J. M. Thompson, 48th New-York—leg.
Andrew Banning, 13th Massachusetts—knee.
Thomas McKay, 6th Connecticut—shoulder.
Frank Bussey, 6th Connecticut—arm.
David Avery, 6th Connecticut—side.
John Plumb, 6th Connecticut—hip.
Chas. Hodge, 6th Connecticut—ribs.
Samuel Porter, 6th Connecticut—hip.
W. A. Hammond, 76th Pennsylvania—hip.
Wm. Bell, 13th Indiana—hip.
Geo. F. Woods, 24th Massachusetts—foot.
A. M. Perkins, 40th Massachusetts—hip.
A. M. Askell, 40th Massachusetts—knee.

The following deaths in the McClellan Hospital took place May 31 and June 1:

John Morrison, 142d New-York Volunteers.
Charles O. Leonard, 40th Massachusetts.
John Sellers, 5th United States Cavalry.
J. W. Jayroe, 25th South Carolina (prisoner.)
Jacob Bennett, 47th New-York.
Henry D. Rose, 8th Connecticut.
Levi Fuller, 118th New-York.
Joseph Lama, 98th New-York.
Joseph S. Sickles, 9th New-Jersey.
George H. Smith, 2d Virginia, (prisoner.)
Richard W. Bateman, 4th New-Hampshire.

In the Chesapeake Hospital:

Lieut. R. P. Wheeler, 23d Massachusetts, June 2d, He was aid-de-camp to Gen. HECKMAN.
George A. Brown, 8th Maine, June 1.

THE WAR ON THE MISSISSIPPI.

Engagement at Gaines' Landing—The Rebels Driven Off—The Steamer Lebanon Burned—Bold Rebel Movements in Arkansas, Etc.

MEMPHIS, Tuesday, May 31.

The tin-clads *Marmora*, *Juliet*, and *Prairie Bird*, recently engaged the rebel batteries at Gaines' Landing, and succeeded in driving them away. The *Prairie Bird* was struck thirty times, and the Marmine Brigade boat *Delta* had her donkey engine shot overboard, and the engineer killed.

MARMADUKE, who is reported to be in command of the rebels, had taken twelve pieces of artillery.

He captured and burned the steamer *Lebanon*, and carried the crew and passengers off as prisoners.

The boats from the White River report the rebels to be thick, but the boats are not molested.

A heavy force of rebels is reported to be within twenty-five miles of Duval's Bluff marching on that place. They are supposed to number 15,000.

The rebel Gen. SHELBY captured Dardanelis last Monday, taking 200 prisoners. After the capture he crossed the Arkansas River, and it was supposed that he intended to strike the Little Rock Railroad.

Guerrillas are represented as unusually active in Arkansas.

It appears to be the intention of the rebels to force the Union troops to evacuate all the State except Little Rock and Helena.

Jacksonport and Batesville have been evacuated by our forces.

Eight Steamers Burned at New-Orleans, &c.

CAIRO, Thursday, June 2.

The steamer *Pauline Carroll*, from New-Orleans 27th ult., has arrived.

The news is unimportant.

The officers report that when some distance from the city, they noticed a large light, supposed to be at New-Orleans. On arriving at Baton Rouge, they learned that a dispatch had been received stating that eight steamboats had been burned at New-Orleans. No particulars had reached Baton Rouge.

Favorable news from New-York had given an upward tendency to the New-Orleans cotton market; the supply was light and there was not much doing. Sugar was dull and drooping, with small sales of fair to good at 17c.@18c., and fully fair at 19c.@20c. Nothing doing in molasses, and quotations nominal.

The Eighteenth Indiana Volunteers, Col. WASHBURNE, came up on the *Carroll* from Baton Rouge, en route home on furlough.

The portion of the Eighteenth Illinois which has not reenlisted, has arrived from Little Rock, en route to Springfield, to be mustered out of the service by order of Gen. CANBY.

Capt. JOHN G. KLINCK, Acting Quartermaster, has been assigned to duty as General Superintendent of the Land and Water Transportation, within the Division of West Mississippi. The officers and owners of all steamboats plying on the Mississippi River and its tributaries south of Cairo, are ordered to report to him at headquarters, which is at Natchez, and give the names of their boats and barges of every description, their tonnage owners, and the trade in which they are engaged.

A Convention of Unconditional Unionists to elect delegates to the Baltimore Convention, from the Western District of Tennessee, assembled at Memphis on the 30th ult., and resolutions were adopted indorsing the Administration, and pledging themselves to support ABRAHAM LINCOLN for President, and ANDY JOHNSON for Vice-President.

FIRE AT MOUND CITY, MO.

Loss Half a Million of Dollars.

MOUND CITY, Wednesday, June 1.

A large, valuable naval wharf-boat was burned at 8 o'clock this evening. The fire was first discovered in the paint and oil room, supposed to have originated from spontaneous combustion. The fire was not discovered until it had spread beyond control. The progress of the flames was so rapid that nothing could be saved. Many persons on board narrowly escaped with life; the smoke and flames rendered egress by stairway impossible; many escaped by roof. No lives were known to have been lost. Paymaster BOGGS, of the United States Navy, was seriously burned, and came near being suffocated while attempting to save his funds and papers. The entire loss is said to be one-half million of dollars or more, consisting principally of naval stores, including Paymaster DAVIS' safe, containing $200,000, and another $11,000. There was no ordnance stores or provisions on board.

From California.

SAN FRANCISCO, Wednesday, June 1.

Another large Christian Commission meeting was held last night.

There was a large gathering of alumni at Oakland yesterday, on the occasion of the graduation of the first class of the College of California. EDWARD STANLEY, Dr. BELLOWS and Gen. WRIGHT were present and spoke. A strong Union feeling prevailed.

A large quantity of confiscated Chinese opium, which was smuggled into this port, is to be sold by the United States Marshal.

Stock of all kinds much depressed. General trade dull.

The ship *Nesutan* is now discharging four 15-inch and two 10-inch guns for harbor defence.

There have been no arrivals or departures of note

THE NEW-YORK YACHT CLUB

Fifteenth Annual Regatta.

The day could hardly have been more pleasant, or the wind more favorable, for the Fifteenth Annual Regatta of the New-York Yacht Club, which took place yesterday. At an early hour the pier at the foot of Twentieth-street, North River, was thronged by people anxiously awaiting the arrival of the steamers which were to accompany the yachts "down the river." Before 10 o'clock, the hour designated for the departure of the fleet, the steamer *Matteawan* was crowded by members of the club, and their lady friends, and shortly after that hour the boat swung into the stream leaving the press to await the arrival of the *Meta*. This petty manifestation of exclusiveness was fully appreciated by the Reportorial Corps, and considered a special dispensation in their favor—the society on board the *Meta* being quite as agreeable, and possibly as select as those on board the *Matteawan*.

At 10½ A. M. the yachts entered for the regatta sailed from the flag-boat abreast the Club House at Hoboken, in this order:

1st. Sloops.	2d. Sloops.	3d. Schooners.	4th. Schooner.
Narragansett,	Nettie,	Julia,	Magic.
Richmond,	White Wing,	Juniatta.	
Annie.	Geraldine.		

The sloops *Alarm*, *Nautilus* and *Plover*, which were entered, failed to take their places—thus losing their chances in the race.

The following is an official classification of the boats:

SLOOPS—SECOND CLASS—MEASURING 900 FEET AND UNDER.

(Allowance of time—one second and thirty-five hundredths per square foot.)

No.	Name.	Owners.	Area.	No of Crew.	Start. M. S.
1	Narragansett.	F. G. Dexter.	740.6	8	3:31
2	Richmond.	J. Van Schaick.	763.6	8	1:54
3	Annie.	L. Livingston.	805.4	9	1:05

SCHOONERS—SECOND CLASS—MEASURING 1,500 FEET AND UNDER.

(Allowance of time—one second and thirty-five hundredths per square foot.)

No.	Name.	Owners.	Area.	No of Crew.	Start. M. S.
1	Julia.	H. S. Fearing, G. T. Gandy and S. Dalton.	1,182.2	15	—
2	Juniatta	J. W. Grigg.	—	—	—

SLOOPS—1ST CLASS—MEASURING OVER 900 FEET.

(Allowance of time—one second per square foot.)

No.	Name.	Owners.	Area.	No. of Crew.	Start. M. S.
1	Nettie.	L. D. Senate & others.	934.02	10	5:40
2	White Wing.	R. Stuyvesant.	1,004.4	11	4:37
3	Geraldine.	J. S. Dickerson.	1,277.5	13	—

SCHOONERS—1ST CLASS—MEASURING OVER 1,500 FEET.

(Allowance of time—one second per square foot.)

No.	Name.	Owners.	Area.	No. of Crew.	Start. M. S.
2	Magic.	W. H. McVicker.	1,670	21	—

The terms "second class" and "first class" are arbitrary, and refer to the comparative sizes of the vessels.

The "measurement" of the vessels refers to the area on the water-line, and the "allowance" named is deducted from the time of the trip.

The "No." column in the table defines the order of placing the vessels side by side.

The "area" is accounted for in the explanation of measurement.

The statement of minutes and seconds in the last column defines the aggregate difference of time which must be allowed.

The course, according to the rules of the club, commenced from the flag-boat, stationed off the Elysian Fields, the yachts passing to the north and west of the flag boat at Robin's Reef Light; thence easterly to a flag-boat off Owl's Head, Long Island, passing it to the north and east; thence around the buoy of the Southwest Spit, passing it from the north and east.

Returning, they first passed the flag-boat anchored off Owl's Head, Long Island, to the south and east; thence to the flag-boat off Robin's Reef Light, to the south and west; thence to a flag-boat off Governor's Island, to the south and east; thence to the flag boat abreast of the Club-house, Hoboken, passing it to the westward.

In going and returning, all the buoys on the west bank, viz.: Nos. 11, 13 and 15, were passed to the eastward.

When the signal for the departure was given the wind was very light and there was a prospect of a calm. Before, however, the sloops first named had reached a point nearly opposite the Battery, a breeze sprang up and all fears of a dull day were dispelled. The race was for a time exciting, the contest between the *Annie*, the *Richmond*, and the *Narragansett* being at first exceedingly close, but on the home stretch the question as to which boat would win the prize was settled in favor of the *Annie*, which seemed to fairly fly away from her competitors.

The following is the official report of the time made by the different vessels entered for the race:

GOING DOWN.

Annie passed buoy at Southwest Spit, 1.21:30; *Richmond*, 1:30; *White Wing*, 1.38:10; *Nettie*, 1.40:52; *Geraldine*, 1.45:05; *Magic*, 1.45:34; *Julia*, 1.54:54; *Juniatta*, 2.08:24.

RETURN.

Annie, 3.59:20; *Magic*, 4,07:01; *Narragansett*, 4.11:26; *Richmond*, 4.11:52; *Nettie*, 4.15:26; *White Wing*, 4.15:28; *Julia*, 4.17:56; *Geraldine*, 4.18:15; *Juniatta*, 4:26.

During the race a large number of vessels not entered accompanied the yachts going down and returning, many of which were from the Brooklyn Club. On board the *Meta*, a fine collation was served at 1 o'clock. Mr. C. H. HASWELL, Jr., presided, and the entertainment was gotten up under the able management of Mr. C. K. BRANT.

The *Annie*, being the first vessel to round the flag-boat on the home stretch, was heartily welcomed by the spectators of the race.

The following are the present officers of the New-York Yacht Club.

Commodore, EDWIN A. STEVENS; Vice Commodore, Ambrose C. Kingsland; Secretary, Hamilton Morton; Treasurer, Robert S. Hine; Measurer, Charles S. Haswell; Surgeon, Dr. G. F. Woodward.

George, the Count Joannes, Seeketh a Value for His Wounded Honor.

COURT OF COMMON PLEAS.

Before Justice Cardozo.

George, the Count Joannes vs. John Clancey.—The plaintiff in this case brings an action against the editor and proprietor of the New-York *Leader* for an alleged libelous and defamatory article published in that paper against his good name and character. The article was headed "Count, No-account," and insinuated that the world-renowned author, poet and actor, George, the Count Joannes, is only a Count by the courtesy of those who have a mind to call him so. The eminent nobleman appears in person in this action and claims the sum of $20,000, as the exact amount of damages to his wounded honor.

A motion was made yesterday, on the part of the defendant, to compel the plaintiff to file security for his costs, and the motion was supported by an affidavit of JOHN CLANCY, in which he set forth that GEORGE JONES, by which name he calls the noble Count, was a non-resident, and, moreover, was not pecuniarily responsible. In answer to this, the Count related how he lived in a big hotel in this City and paid his bills too, which he offered for the inspection of the Court, with the receipts attached.

His Honor declined to receive them as evidence, and said that he would reserve his decision upon the question of security. The Count placed his beaver upon his noble head, and departed to "his hotel."

THE PRIVATEER FLORIDA AT BERMUDA.—The Bermuda *Gazette* of the 17th ult., thus notices the arrival of the privateer *Florida* at Hamilton:

"The far-famed *Florida* paid us another visit on Thursday last, this time only a flying one, as she did not enter St. George's harbor at all, but remained for the few hours, three, we believe, of her stay, in Five Fathom Hole. She merely touched here in order to pick up late newspapers and letters for her officers, &c., from sweethearts and wives—her officers and crew having been without any news for a month and more. Her intelligence is devoid of any particular interest. She reports having overhauled a large number of Federal vessels, but as they had all availed themselves of the usual resource, and in effect changed their flag, she was obliged to let them go."

The Young Men's Christian Association.

BOSTON, Friday, June 3.

The convention of the Young Men's Christian Association for the United States and Canada to-day took an excursion in the harbor, visited Fort Independence and the Farm School, and, by invitation of the Mayor, the city institutions on Deer Island, where they were formally received by the City Government. A collation was furnished, addresses of welcome were made, and GEORGE H. STUART, President of the Christian Commission, responded for that institution. The meetings of the convention have been very fully attended, and large delegations from abroad were present.

The Charleston Mercury.

COUNTRY PAPER—Thrice a Week—Eight Dollars, for Six Months—Payable in Advance.

VINDICE NULLO — SUA SINE LEGE FIDES RECTUMQUE COLLENTUR.

VOLUME LXXXIV. CHARLESTON, S. C., SATURDAY, JUNE 4, 1864. NUMBER 12,079

THE MERCURY.

SATURDAY, JUNE 4, 1864.

The Unconstitutionality of the Act Suspending the Writ of Habeas Corpus.

Amidst the exciting troubles of the times, we know that cold arguments upon the Constitution will be read by very few of our readers; but we deem it nevertheless due to the country, as well as to ourselves, briefly to state a few views on the constitutionality of the late act of Congress suspending the Writ of *Habeas Corpus*.

The Writ of *Habeas Corpus*, in *form and substance*, is prescribed by the Statute 31, CHARLES II. This statute has been made of force in South Carolina, and we believe has been incorporated into the laws of every State in the Confederacy. In no other statute of Great Britain is this writ prescribed; and it has remained unaltered from the time of its passage to this day. The words and directions of this statute have been followed in every Writ of *Habeas Corpus* which has been issued in Great Britain or in this country since it originated.

The first question which arises under the Constitution with respect to this writ is this: Does the Constitution, when it speaks of "the *privilege* of the Writ of *Habeas Corpus*," refer to the Statute of CHARLES II. or not? The words are "The "*privilege* of the Writ of *Habeas Corpus* shall not "be suspended, unless when in case of rebellion "or invasion the public safety may require it." Those who think that the late Act of Congress is *unconstitutional* maintain that, to know what "*privileges*," by the Writ of *Habeas Corpus*, Congress may suspend, we must look into the Act of CHARLES II. That Act is very clear on this point. The "*privilege*" extends only to cases "of *commitment for criminal or supposed criminal matters*." To this effect was the answer of the Judges of England to certain questions propounded to them in BACON'S Abridgment, 3 vol., 438. The question was also made in the Supreme Court of the United States, in the case of *ex parte* WILSON, 6 CRANCH 53, and the Court determined that "the Courts of the United States could not issue a Writ of *Habeas Corpus* in any case of arrest under *civil powers*, and refused to award the writ." If these views are correct, the late law of Congress must be unconstitutional; for this law, authorizing the President to suspend the Writ of *Habeas Corpus* not only in cases "of commitment for criminal or supposed criminal matters," but in all cases of arbitrary arrest by the President or his officials for any cause whatever.

Other clauses of the Constitution seem also to support the position, that Congress can suspend the Writ of *Habeas Corpus* only in cases of arrests and commitments of crimes. In the 15th clause of the 9th section, 1st article, it provides that "the right of the people to be secure in their "persons against unreasonable seizures *shall not* "*be violated*, and *no warrants* shall issue, but "on probable cause, *supported by oath or affir*"*mation*, particularly describing the persons to "be seized." Now, if the person has already been seized by warrant duly issued on a charge of *crime* supported by oath or affirmation, (which is the case provided for by the Statute of Charles II.)—the suspension of the writ of *Habeas Corpus* thus limited, does not militate at all with this clause of the Constitution. Both clauses—the one providing for the protection of the citizen against arbitrary arrests, even for crime, by requiring reasonable cause to be shown and oath to be made—and the other, authorizing the suspension of the writ of *Habeas Corpus* against him, after his crime may be presumed and he is under arrest, with all the guarantees of the Constitution exhausted to protect him against a wrongful seizure—are fully carried out. Consistency in the Constitution, and harmony in its provisions, seem to demonstrate that its framers must have had in view the Statute of Charles II. when it ordained that "the privilege of the writ "of *Habeas Corpus* shall not be suspended un"less when in case of rebellion or invasion." When suspended in rebellion or invasion, a criminal committed for treason, or conspiracy, or other crimes—State or civil—shall not be brought up before a court for investigation or release by the Writ of *Habeas Corpus*. This is all the Constitution means. To take any other view than this, throws the Constitution in conflict with itself, and in fact annihilates it. If the President and his officials can, of their mere volition, by the suspension of the Writ of *Habeas Corpus*, seize any man and cast him into prison and keep him there, then the right of the people to be secure in their persons against unreasonable seizures is violated, and they are arrested by warrants issued by the Executive for no cause shown, and supported by no oaths or affirmations, and the Constitution itself is practically annihilated. Its sole great end—the liberty of the citizen—is destroyed.

This view of the limited power of the Confederate Government to control the liberty of the citizen is also in keeping with the character of the whole Government. It has no citizens. Every citizen in the Confederate States is the citizen of a State, which alone is his sovereign. Whatever doubts existed on this point under the Constitution of the United States, no longer exist under the Constitution of the Confederate States. The sovereign States composing the Confederacy are perfectly competent to supply, by their action, any deficiency of means they have conferred on their agent—the Confederate Government—to carry out the objects for which they created it. To argue, therefore, that any power in the Confederate Government is incomplete or deficient, is to argue to no purpose. This Government, by its very nature, is a limited Government, and the States to which it belongs may have intentionally conferred only a limited power over its citizens. They stand possessed of all other powers, to control their citizens and to protect themselves.

The upholders of despotic authority in the Executive urge various objections to these views. We have before us the late "opinion of Judge HALYBURTON," Judge of the District Court of the Confederate States in Virginia adjudicating that the Act of Congress suspending the *Habeas Corpus* Act *is constitutional*. We propose to state the chief grounds of his opinion.

Judge HALYBURTON admits that the Statute of CHARLES II. grants the *privilege* of the Writ of *Habeas Corpus* only in cases of persons *committed for crimes*. If, therefore, the Constitution when it provided, that "the *privilege* of the Writ "of *Habeas Corpus* shall not be suspended unless "when in case of rebellion or invasion," had reference to this Statute, he [illegible] the unconstitutionality of the Act of Congress. But he contends, that even before and after the passing of the act in England, "*by the common law of En*"*land*, the Writ of *Habeas Corpus*, may be "issued to relieve those who were in any way "unlawfully imprisoned, or under illegal restraint, "whether charged with crime or no." Hence, he argues, that the Constitution has reference to the common law of England, not to the Statute of CHARLES II., and as by this law, the *Habeas Corpus* Act was applicable to all cases of imprisonment, the suspension of it by Congress, has the same scope, and all prisoners by Executive authority, are stripped of its privileges.

In coming to this sweeping conclusion, the learned Judge admits, that in the case of *ex parte* WILSON, the Supreme Court of the United States determined directly contrary to them; but then he adduces a decision in the case *ex parte* ROBERT B. RANDOLPH, 2 BROCKENBROUGH, Reports, wherein the District Judge of the United States for Virginia, Judge PHILIP P. BARBOUR, decreed in conformity to his views, and Chief Justice MARSHALL assented to it.

Now, in the *first* place, it is rather a new doctrine that a District Judge of a single State can overrule the decisions of the Supreme Court of the United States. It does not appear that an appeal from Judge BARBOUR'S decision was carried up to the Supreme Court of the United States. It is, therefore, simply a decision on circuit, which is worth nothing as authority against the decisions of the Supreme Court of the United States.

But, in the *second* place, every one knows the proneness of the United States Courts to support usurped power. Even if the decision of Judge BARBOUR had been affirmed by the Supreme Court of the United States, it should weigh but little in the Confederate States. We all know that this Court affirmed the alien and sedition laws to be constitutional. But where this Court determines against assumed power, the case should be considered as conclusive against such power.

In the *third* place, we would submit, with all deference, that *the common law* of England is not of force in these Confederate States. The first Congress under the Confederate States passed a law, making of force in the Confederate States all the *statute laws* of the United States; but they passed no law adopting either the *statute law* or *the common law* of England by the Confederate States. We do not suppose, if Congress had not passed the law adopting the statute laws of the United States, Judge HALYBURTON would have allowed any of these laws to be read before him, as authority for his decisions. By what process of reasoning he now holds *the common law* of England any more than the civil law, or the Code NAPOLEON, to be of force in the Confederate States, we are a loss to determine.

Judge HALYBURTON next refers to the Judiciary Act passed by the Congress of the Confederate States, to support his views. This Act is the Judiciary Act of the United States, adopted by the Confederate States. It simply provides that "both "the District and Supreme Courts, and the Judges "thereof, shall *have power to issue writs of Habeas* "*Corpus*." The Judge argues that this Act does not limit the power to issue writs of *Habeas Corpus* to those cases alone which are authorized by the Statute of CHARLES II, it is therefore unlimited. We do not see the correctness of this inference. Laws are made to carry out the Constitution. That it is consistent with the Constitution of the Confederate States that its Judges should have the power of issuing Writs of *Habeas Corpus* in certain cases, no one will deny. The Judiciary Act simply authorizes them to issue such Writs in such cases. It does no more. It does not define what these cases are. It leaves that to the Constitution. The law appears to us to be proper as it is, and is no way to be a commentary on the Constitution.

But the learned Judge sees great inconvenience to result, unless his views are sustained. Cases under civil proces may arise, which might produce monstrous hardships, unless the courts of the Confederate States could issue Writs of *Habeas Corpus*. He states the case of a person arrested and imprisoned by a Marshal of the Confederate States District Court, after bail had been given or no bail was required. Here is no case of criminal offence; yet there would be monstrous injustice if the Court could not release the party from imprisonment by the Writ of *Habeas Corpus*.

We reply, in the *first place*, that the Marshal of a District Court is an officer of the Court, and therefore always amenable to a summary accountability, by a simple rule of Court. By this means, he may be compelled to bring up before the Court any prisoner he has illegally detained in custody, and the prisoner may be discharged. But we are not content to meet the argument on mere technicalities. For the sake of the argument, we will admit, that there may be some cases of illegal imprisonment, which cannot be reached *by the Courts or Judges of the Confederate States*, according to our construction of the Constitution. But they may not be remediless on that account. The Judges and Judicial tribunals of the States are in existence, fully competent to make the Writ of *Habeas Corpus* adequate to the protection of their citizens from all oppression or illegal arrests. Let their central agency—the Confederate Government—keep within the limitations they have prescribed in the Constitution. It is their affair, to take care of their people. It is their business, to see that their liberties are not infringed. As they made the Confederate Government, and gave it all the power it possesses—they must be presumed to be competent by the exercise of their Sovereignty, either in conjunction with other Sovereigns in the Confederate Government, or by their separate action, to protect the liberties of their people. Any other presumption must be false to our whole system of Government.

MR. REEVES, of Virginia, in his late speech in the Congress of the Confederate States, advocates the suspension of the Writ of *Habeas Corpus*, and pushes still further the *argumentum ab inconvenienti*. He says "the suspension of the Writ of "*Habeas Corpus necessarially* carried with it the "suspension of the kindred rights and remedies "secured in other clauses of the Constitution, or "such suspension would be *nugatory* and *absurd*."

Here, as the logicians say, is a begging of the question, with suppositious evils alleged. We deny that, by the Constitution, the suspension of the Writ of *Habeas Corpus* necessarily carries with it a suspension of any of the kindred rights or remedies secured by the other clauses of the Constitution. We deny that the sovereign States of the Confederacy have given to the Congress of the Confederate States the power to suspend a single right or privilege possessed by any free citizen under their sovereignty. They have given to Congress only the power to suspend the Writ *Habeas Corpus with respect to criminals—persons already deprived of their personal liberty in prisons on account of their crimes*. In other cases they have reserved the suspension of this writ to themselves. They never intended that the grand series of prohibitions and guarantees for liberty contained in the 12th, 13th, 14th, 15th, 16th, 17th, 18th and 19th clauses of the 9th Section of the 1st Art. of the Constitution, should rest on the volition of Congress, and that Congress should have the power, at any time, *by a mere majority*, to abolish them all and establish a Military Dictatorship in their stead over them and their people. With great respect, we submit *that prohibitions in the Constitution cannot be upset by grants of power*. If they are inconsistent, the prohibitions ought to prevail, because it is not reasonable to suppose that the States intended to grant what they prohibited. To infer the contrary, would indeed be that huge dislocation of the Constitution, which Mr. REEVES so pointedly condemns, and charges the Vice President with doing. That construction of it, which leaves all its prohibitions and grants of power acting harmoniously together, is preserving, not dislocating, the Constitution. It is in conformity with that cardinal rule for construing all instruments—that it shall be so construed as to give if possible efficacy to all its provisions. But to construe one clause so as to destroy all the rest, is one of those huge and unreasonable dislocations and usurpations, which we might have supposed we never would have heard of in our day, after having got rid of Yankee rule and Yankee profligacy. Nor would the suspension of the Writ of *Habeas Corpus*, according to the limitations of the Statute of CHARLES II, "be nugatory and absurd." If so, then this world-wide renowned statute is itself "absurd." But it is not "absurd." It is worthy of all the admiration that for centuries has been offered to it by the descendants of Englishmen. The "*privilege*" it secures against arbitrary and tyrannical imprisonment is of inestimable value; and the Constitution of the Confederate States rightly prescribes that this privilege shall not be suspended by Congress "unless when in case of rebellion or invasion the public safety may require it." It is a sad omen of the times, and a strong proof of the falsity of any argumentation put forth in defence of the Government, that it becomes necessary to depreciate this noble guarantee of liberty, in order that its despotic policy may be maintained. It is a still sadder omen, in the midst of a gigantic struggle for liberty, to find able men striving to educe out of a Constitution framed to establish it, the right to destroy it and to build up a despotism over the Confederate States.

PROGRESS OF THE CAMPAIGN IN VIRGINIA.

STEIN'S FARM, VA., June 2.—HAMPTON fought WILSON'S division of Yankee cavalry, near Ashland, yesterday, defeating and pursuing it over three miles, and capturing 500 horses and some [illegible] prisoners. Our loss is estimated at 75, killed and wounded.

Yesterday the enemy assaulted our lines at various times, in front of HETH'S division and in front of ANDERSON'S corps, but were handsomely repulsed each time.

About dark last evening, three divisions of the Sixth Yankee Army Corps assaulted HOKE'S Division, causing CLINGMAN'S North Carolina brigade for a moment to give way. Colonel TUTT'S Georgia Brigade, however promptly came to its assistance, and recovered nearly all the ground lost by CLINGMAN. We captured 60 prisoners. Our loss is not over 200. Many of our men are missing, but it is supposed that they will presently come in.

This morning the enemy was found to have abandoned the front of A. P. HILL'S corps, stretching from Atlee's around to the Mechanicsville Pike. WILCOX'S skirmishers pushed forward and brought in about 100 prisoners.

About four o'clock this afternoon, EWELL flanked the enemy's right on the Mechanicsville Pike, capturing over 500 prisoners, including ten commissioned officers, mostly from the 2d, 9th, 11th, 12th and 14th regiments of regulars in the Fifth corps. At seven o'clock p. m., EWELL had taken three lines of the enemy's breastworks.—Our loss was not heavy; but amongst the killed was the brave Gen. BOOLES, of Georgia.

The New-York Times.

VOL. XIII—NO. 3964. NEW-YORK, TUESDAY, JUNE 7, 1864. PRICE THREE CENTS.

THE GRAND CAMPAIGN.

The Battle of the Chickahominy.

THE GREAT ACTION ON FRIDAY.

Gen. Grant's Object in the Movement.

Brilliant Assault on the Rebel Works.

The Enemy's Lines Carried in Front of Hancock and Wright.

The Rebels Rally and Retake Them.

TEN MINUTES OF HISTORY.

THE LOSS OF OUR KEY POSITION.

Incidents of the Afternoon's Work.

REBEL NIGHT ATTACK

THE RESULT OF THE DAY'S OPERATIONS.

Full and Thrilling Details of the Battle from Our Special Correspondent.

HEADQUARTERS, ARMY OF THE POTOMAC, COLD HARBOR, NEAR THE CHICKAHOMINY, Friday, June 3—10 P. M.

I.

GENERAL VIEW OF THE BATTLE.

Judged by the severity of the encounter and the heavy losses we have experienced, the engagement which opened at gray dawn this morning and spent its fury in little over an hour, should take its place among the *battles* of the war; but viewed in its relations to the whole campaign, it is, perhaps, hardly more than a grand reconnoissance—a reconnoissance, however, which has cost us not less than *five or six thousand* killed and wounded.

The object of the action was to force the passage of the Chickahominy, on the north side of which, and covering the roads to Richmond, the rebels had planted themselves in a fortified line. What we have done is to *feel* this line by a vigorous attack, in which, though gaining some temporary successes, and at one or two points actually carrying the enemy's works, we have, on the whole, reached the conclusion that any victory that could here be won must cost too much in its purchase. I do not say this as speaking with any authority, but only as recording the general conviction of the army. Such conviction, however, when the common judgment of such men as have to-day led their lines against the enemy, is apt to be of itself *authority*, and hence I think I may safely predict that there will be *no renewal of the assault on the lines of the Chickahominy*; that we must look to the resources of strategy to plant this army in a position where, being at less of a disadvantage, its valor will have a better promise of adequate reward.

It is in this view that the action of to-day assumes to me the aspect of a great reconnoissance. But it might easily have been more. Were prudence not as much a characteristic of Lieut.-Gen. GRANT's mind as pluck, did he not know as well how and when to cry a halt as to order an advance, he might have pushed the action from a reconnoissance to a bloody battle; but to me it is clear we should have had only another Fredericksburgh and its useless slaughter. Gen. GRANT is not so poor in resource that he need do this; and I think already his eyes are turned away from the Chickahominy to lines and combinations more bold than any yet essayed.

II.

STRATEGIC OPERATIONS FROM THE PAMUNKY TO THE CHICKAHOMINY.

To gain a clear view of the present situation, of the relations of the contending forces, and of the purposes of to-day's action, it is necessary to glance for a moment at the series of strategic operations which, after crossing the Pamunky, have drawn our lines in their present position and formation. After the passage of the river at the town of Hanover on Saturday last, our line of battle was formed almost due north and south, and our front thrown forward due west, for the purpose of again gaining a point of contact with the enemy, from whom we had for a day or two been separated by the flanking operation, which swung the army from the North Anna around and across the Pamunky. This formation was necessitated by the obligation of covering the fords and bridges over the Pamunky, by which our supplies, trains, artillery, etc., had to pass. On pushing out on Sunday and Monday we found the enemy also forming line of battle north and south, directly in front of the Virginia Central Railroad, and extending from Atlee's Station (with cavalry thrown out to Hanover Court-house,) south to Shady Grove, ten miles north of Richmond. In this position LEE covered both the Virginia Central and the Fredericksburgh and Richmond Railroads, as well as all the roads leading to Richmond, west of and including the Mechanicsville pike. This formation had been imposed upon the enemy by a similar motive that prompted the front we took up, namely: The duty of covering the lines by which his trains and material would pass in the change of front necessitated by the turning movement which compelled LEE to abandon the line of the South Anna.

In this situation, our right, the Sixth Corps (WRIGHT) fell back near Hanover Court-house; our left, held by the Fifth Corps, (WARREN,) rested across Totopatamoy Creek. HANCOCK had the right centre; BURNSIDE the left centre. During Monday, energetic reconnoissances were pushed forward on the right and left, which developed the enemy in full force. On the left, WARREN made a vigorous effort, the full details of which you have received from me, to carry the Mechanicsville pike, but failed. Meanwhile the cavalry had been distributed on the flanks of the army—the division of WILSON on the right flank; the divisions of GREGG and TORBETT on the left.

No serious impression having been produced on the enemy's line by Monday's operations, the Commanding General resumed his favorite tactics of developing the left flank. This manœuvre appears to be characteristic of him, as he adopted it both at Spottsylvania and on the North Anna. The mode of executing this ingenious movement is as follows: The corps holding the extreme right of the line is, under cover of night, withdrawn *behind the line of battle* of the other corps, (the picket line of course being left to conceal the movement,) and carried to the extreme left of the line, where it intrenches. The next corps to the right is then withdrawn in like manner, and connects in the same way with the new left, forming a prolongation of its line. In this manner, in the course of a couple of days, a complete reversion of position of the corps has taken place: what had been the extreme right forming the extreme left, and what had been the extreme left forming the extreme right; and thus the army finds itself drawn to the left by the length of its whole line of battle—say eight or ten miles.

During Tuesday night the Sixth Corps, (WRIGHT,) which had held the right of the army, was in this way moved down the Hanover Court-house road, and on Wednesday morning, took position near Cold Harbor, on the left of the left. Here it was joined by the reinforcements, (the Eighteenth Corps with part of the Tenth,) brought by Gen. W. F. SMITH, from White House. This column had been ordered by Gen. GRANT from White House to *New Cold Harbor*, but by an error in the telegraph the dispatch named the point *Newcastle*. The mistake was corrected, but not until he had neared the latter place, so that this corps was compelled to make a fatiguing march of five and twenty miles, and arrived at Cold Harbor on the afternoon of Wednesday, just in time to take part along with the Sixth Corps, in a severe engagement that ensued. As no accurate account of this affair has yet been given, a brief sketch of it will not be out of place.

III.

WEDNESDAY'S FIGHT AT COLD HARBOR.

I have already mentioned that the Cavalry Divisions of GREGG and TORBETT had been placed so as to cover the left of our line, held by WARREN, from whose corps they were separated by an interval of four miles. On Tuesday evening they met the rebel cavalry near Cold Harbor, and whipped them most completely.

On the following morning (Wednesday) they renewed the fight, once more punished the rebels severely, but presently found out that the enemy had, during the night, brought up strong infantry supports, so that SHERIDAN was compelled to await the arrival of WRIGHT and SMITH, then on their way up.

While writing of this affair, I have chanced to receive a copy of yesterday's Richmond *Inquirer*, (Thursday, June 2,) and find in it an account of Wednesday's cavalry affair. It is as follows:

"About 3:30 A. M., yesterday, artillery was opened upon the enemy on the Chickahominy, and by 8 o'clock heavy skirmishing occurred along a considerable portion of the lines. HOKE's division commenced an advance at an early hour for a position near Cold Harbor, when it was met and attacked by a largely superior force of the enemy. The division sustained itself against the shock which ensued, but *was compelled to fall back*. McLAWS' division coming to HOKE's support joined in the fray, when HOKE returned to the conflict and drove the enemy back a distance of a mile and a half, capturing some 300 prisoners and otherwise severely punishing his forces. Other portions of LONGSTREET's corps were engaged. The battle raged hotly for several hours, quieted down somewhat between 10 and 11 o'clock, and closed about 1 o'clock."

Now, what is amusing in this recital is, that the rebel writer either did not know or had not the honesty to acknowledge that in this affair the rebel divisions named (the divisions of HOKE and McLAWS and "*other portions of Longstreet's" corps*) were fighting nothing but *cavalry*, who, dismounted, and with their carbines were able to punish the rebels, breaking one entire division, and after retiring were able to hold in check the whole of LONGSTREET's corps until WRIGHT and SMITH got up. Of the sequel the rebel writer says nothing: that remains to be told. Having arrived, in the afternoon, the corps of WRIGHT and SMITH formed in line of battle, WRIGHT in four lines, and SMITH in a single line on the right of the Sixth.

In front of our line was an open space of two-thirds of a mile in width, beyond which in a piece of pine woods, the enemy was in force, intrenched. Across this opening Gen. SMITH ordered a charge, which was brilliantly executed by DEVINS' division, (brigades of DRAKE and BARTON.) The division, though moving at the *pas de charge*, suffered very heavily from the artillery of the enemy which had a clean sweep of the field. DRAKE's brigade especially had been much cut up, its leader had fallen mortally wounded, and on reaching the rebel ranks began to waver. BARTON's brigade, however, emerging from the woods on its right, dashed forward with a yell, cleared the abattis, and gained the enemy's works, taking about 300 prisoners. RICKETTS' division of the Sixth Corps, which was formed on the left of DEVINS', behaved with equal gallantry, carried the rebel rifle-pits, and also took several hundred prisoners. The enemy, however, still held his position on the right of SMITH, in front of the division of BROOKES. With the view of dislodging him from this position, HENRY's brigade, of BROOKES' division, was ordered forward, and succeeded in taking the rifle-pits. Here, however, he was swept by the fire from a redoubt in his front, and MARTINDALE, who was ordered to support, not having been able to effect his dispositions in time to do so, HENRY was compelled to fall back, the enemy following him to the skirt of the woods. The position thus carried was, as will presently be seen, one of cardinal importance, though it was purchased at a loss of two thousand killed and wounded. The rebel loss cannot have been less, as we took nearly six hundred prisoners, and the enemy left many hundred dead and wounded within our lines.

IV.

COLD HARBOR—ITS MILITARY IMPORTANCE.

The operations of Wednesday, though they had cost us dearly, had won a point of the very highest value, and this not merely tactically and with regard to operations on our immediate front, but strategically, and in relation both to present and prospective movements. Cold Harbor is the point of convergence of all the roads radiating whether to Richmond—our objective point, or to White House—our base of supplies. Until we gained this point, indeed, we had no line of communication with our base, except by making an immense detour to the north of the Pamunky. The importance of this point was, no doubt, appreciated by the rebels, and one of the Richmond papers, several days ago, and before we had begun moving in this direction, said in a witty prophecy in reference to GRANT's favorite tactics, that "GRANT has grown so enamored of his left flank that he will probably work his way down toward the James River, and *we shall have another decisive battle of Cold Harbor*." By this, the writer means what we term the battle of Gaines' Mills—that having been the position held by the corps of FITZ JOHN PORTER in the battle of 1862, while Cold Harbor was held by Stonewall JACKSON. In the battle of to-day the relations were just reversed—we holding Cold Harbor, while the rebels hold Gaines' Mills. Why, in recognizing the commanding importance of the point to us, LEE did not make preparations to hold it at all hazards, is a question which he will find difficult to answer with entire satisfaction. Discovering on the night of Tuesday that the Sixth Corps was retiring from the front of his left wing, (held by LONGSTREET's command,) he rapidly countermarched LONGSTREET to anticipate us in the possession of Cold Harbor; and there is little doubt that he would have been able to seize it in advance of us had it not been for the admirable tenacity with which our cavalry held on to it until it was relieved, and the position was secured beyond a peradventure, by the arrival of the columns of SMITH and WRIGHT.

V.

BEFORE THE BATTLE.

Cold Harbor being secured by the action of Wednesday, Gen. GRANT determined to give battle the day following, for the purpose of essaying the passage of the Chickahominy. Accordingly, during the night, HANCOCK's corps, which, by the previous withdrawal of the Sixth Corps, held the right of the line, was moved and took position on the extreme left; and early on Thursday, the headquarters of Gens. GRANT and MEADE, which had been in the rear of the right, were transferred to the rear of the left and established at Cold Harbor. It had, as I have said, been designed to give battle on Thursday; but HANCOCK was compelled to fight his corps into position, and his formation was not completed until afternoon. The attack was then ordered for 5 o'clock in the afternoon; but a thunder-storm as heavy as that which swelled the Chickahominy on the day before Fair Oaks, set in, and the order had to be countermanded.

The hour of attack was then fixed for 4:30 o'clock this morning. Had Gen. LEE, under these circumstances, emulated the conduct of that Union General whose chief glory is to be thought well of by the rebels, and planted his army astraddle the Chickahominy, as McCLELLAN did, the storm which swelled that stream yesterday afternoon might have given Gen. GRANT an opportunity which you may depend upon it he would have improved. But while the rebels *praise* McCLELLAN they do not *imitate* him. LEE had his entire force north of the Chickahominy, and the only result of the delay in attack caused by the rise in the river was to give the enemy, who had by this time discovered the disposition of our troops, the hours of night during which to perfect his defensive preparations.

VI.

THE SITUATION AT 4 A. M., FRIDAY.

In saddle at 4 o'clock in the morning, the gray light of dawn is struggling through a thick envelope of clouds, and a light pattering rain is falling. Our men still lie behind their breastworks, worn out with the work of the night; the rebels, too, lie behind their intrenchments, and only the sleepless pickets peer with wary eyes forward through the dusk of the woods. All is still as the grave, yet in thirty minutes the storm of battle will burst forth along a stretch of six miles. There is but time to take a glance at the lines: Here on the left wing of the army is the corps of HANCOCK, (the Second;) connecting with him on the right, and forming the left centre, is WRIGHT's, (the Sixth;) then SMITH's, (the Eighteenth,) which holds the centre; next comes WARREN's, (the Fifth,) which forms the right centre, and then BURNSIDE's, (the Ninth,) which holds the extreme right. Our line runs almost parallel with the Chickahominy and from one and a half to two and a half miles north of it. On the left wing we approach nearest the river, on the right we are somewhat refused. HANCOCK, holding the left wing, rests across the Dispatch Station road, (that is, the road leading from Cold Harbor to Dispatch Station;) our right is across the Totopamoy. The rebel front is formed immediately in front of the Chickahominy, in three lines, (two lines of battle and a skirmish line,) on an irregular line to conform with the woods and ridges and swamps of the ground. Between the two armies is a low, swampy region, whose dark hollows will soon be lit up with the fires of death. Suddenly from behind the rude parapet there is an upstarting, a noiseless springing to arms, the muffled commands of officers forming the line. The attack was ordered for 4:30, and it may have been five minutes after that, or it may have been ten minutes, but it certainly was not later than 4:45 when the whole line is in motion. Skirmishers are thrown out, and presently meet the enemy's pickets as we learn by the smart fusilade you hear; our artillery opens, the rebels respond, and in a moment the deadly conflict is joined.

VII.

TEN MINUTES OF HISTORY.

The metaphysicians say that time is naught, is but a category of thought; and I think it must be so, for into ten mortal minutes this morning was crowded an age of action. Ten minutes of the figment men call time, and yet that scant space decided a battle! There are a thousand details, ten thousand episodes, but the essential matter is this, that that first rush of advance carried our whole front but up against a line of works, which we were unable to break through, or, breaking through, were unable to hold. Conceive of this in the large—the fierce onslaught amid deafening volleys of musketry and the thunder of artillery, and the wild, mad yell of battle, and see the ranks mown down, and the lines break here and there, and the sullen, obstinate retreat, every inch contested, and we shall then be able to descend to some of the points of action as they individualize themselves along the line.

VIII.

THE LEFT—HANCOCK'S CORPS.

HANCOCK held the left of the whole line of battle; and of his three divisions, that of BARLOW held the extreme left of the army, that of GIBBON was drawn on the right of BARLOW's, while BIRNEY's division was held in reserve. Of the four brigades of BARLOW's division, BROOKS had the left and MILES the right—each brigade in double line of battle. SMITH, commanding the Irish Brigade, was placed in support. The left was protected by refusing it—the Third Brigade being disposed so as to cover that flank.

The formation of GIBBON's division on the right of BARLOW was similar, TYLER's brigade (heavy artillery) holding the right, SMITH's the centre and OWEN's the left—McKEAN in rear of TYLER's centre, in two lines. On HANCOCK's line there were but few places where artillery could be used with effect.

BARLOW had directed that his attacking brigades should, previously to the assault, be moved out, and formed just in rear of the picket line. From this point they advanced for half a mile through woods and over open intervals, under a severe fire, square up to the enemy's works. That portion of his front where the right of MILES' brigade joined with the left of BROOKS'—the same brigades that so brilliantly carried the famous salient in the lines of Spottsylvania—succeeded in a similar splendid *coup* here; they got over and into the enemy's parapet, capturing his guns, (four light 12-pounders,) his colors and five or six hundred prisoners, about 300 of whom were secured by promptly passing them to the rear. The storming column, in fact, were just turning the enemy's guns on the retreating rebels, when powerful reinforcements from the second rebel line appeared advancing. The first rebel line was held by BRECKINRIDGE's troops and was carried, but LEE is too good a General to leave a point so important thus weakly defended. BRECKINRIDGE's men were placed in the fore-front to receive the baptism of fire, but behind these lay the veterans of HILL's corps, and it is these we now see dashing forward to retrieve the honors we had snatched. BARLOW's brigades—stout hearts not used to pale before the greatest odds—could have held their own under conditions the least short of desperation, but the situation in which they now found themselves, o'erleaped its limits. It was not merely the overwhelming front that came pressing down upon them, of that they had no fear, but the position they had gained placed them in advance of the whole line of battle, and gave the rebel artillery the opportunity for a deadly enfilading fire. Beside this, they had lost the directing heads of two of the chief commanders. BROOKS and BYRNES, "souls of courage all compact," fell mortally wounded, and all the organizations had suffered fearfully from an unparalleled loss of officers. In this state of facts they fell back, bringing with them the prisoners they had taken and a captured color, but not the guns. They fell back, but not to their original position; to a position far in advance of that they had held, and at different points not more than fifty yards from the enemy. Here they intrenched, and here I leave them to pass on to GIBBONS' division of the same corps on the right, and which was engaged at the same time.

GIBBONS' advance was simultaneous with BARLOW's, but in moving forward, he came upon one of the swamps of the Chickahominy, which had to be turned or overpassed, in the process of which it became very difficult to establish the connection between different parts of his line. This overcome, however, his troops pressed forward with the same vigor that marked the conduct of their companion division on the left. Parts of the brigades of TYLER and OWEN gained the rebel works, but for reasons identical with those that forced back BARLOW's troops, they also were compelled to give up what they had won. GIBBONS' division, too, lost very heavily. Gen. TYLER, before reaching the works, was carried off the field, shot in the ankle. One of his regimental commanders, Col. PORTER, of the Eighth New-York Heavy Artillery, was killed: immediately after, the Lieutenant-Colonel (BATES) fell dead. Another of his regimental commanders, Col. McMAHON, of the One Hundred and Sixty-fourth New-York, was struck while planting his colors on the rebel works, and was left a prisoner in the enemy's hands—his troops not supporting him after he was wounded. OWEN's brigade lost two entire companies taken prisoners inside of the enemy's intrenchments. In giving way, GIBBONS' division also was far from losing all the ground it had gained. It took up an advanced position, close to the enemy, and just over the crest, the rearward slope of which was held by the rebels. This position it has retained during the day, and McKEAN's brigade has held all day a position within *fifteen yards* of the enemy's works.

IX.

THE KEY-POINT OF THE BATTLE, AND HOW IT WAS LOST.

Not until the splendid attack of HANCOCK's Corps had been made, not till after its blood-bought victory had been wrested from our hands, was he or any man in this army aware of the supreme importance of the position this morning carried and lost. The key-point in the battle of Gaines' Mills, two years ago, it is strange and mortifying that no one should have appreciated its value. This position is a bald hill, named "Watts' Hill," dominating the whole battle-ground, and covering the angle of the "Dispatch road." Along this ridge the rebel works formed a salient, and in front of it was a sunken road. Of this road HANCOCK got possession, and the brigades of MILES and BROOKS actually struck and carried the work directly on the salient! Had we held this point we would have had a position whence the entire rebel line might have been enfiladed; and I think it is not too much to say that the day would have been ours, and LEE pushed across the Chickahominy. Had we even known in advance its commanding importance, very different dispositions for attack would have been made: we would have massed on the left, and made the victory a certainty. These considerations certainly inspire bitter regrets; but who does not know that it is on precisely such contingencies that the fate of battles often hangs?

X.

THE LEFT CENTRE AND CENTRE.—WRIGHT AND SMITH.

Simultaneously with the attack of the Second Corps, the Sixth, under WRIGHT, connecting on the left with HANCOCK, made a general advance at a quarter before five o'clock—each division assaulting on the entire line. Of this corps, the Second Division, (McNEILL,) held the right, the Third Division, (RICKETTS,) the centre, and the First Division, (RUSSELL,) the left. Five batteries, under charge of the Chief of Artillery of the Second Corps, Col. TOMPKINS—namely: Adams' First Rhode Island Battery, Cowan's First New-York, (Independent,) Hahn's Third New-York, (Independent,) McCurtin's First Massachusetts, and Rhode's First Rhode Island, were planted in good positions and did effective service in covering the advance. The assault of the Sixth Corps was made with the utmost vigor, and succeeded in carrying the first line of rebel rifle-pits along its entire front, and got up within two hundred and fifty yards of the main works. SMITH's Corps, connecting on the right with the Sixth, had advanced in conjunction with it; but the left division, that of MARTINDALE, who led the attack in heavy, deep columns, got disarranged, and was repulsed. Gen. SMITH made three different attacks to relieve MARTINDALE, but his last supports did not get up in time to allow him to hold on. The effect of this repulse on the left of SMITH had a disastrous effect on the position of WRIGHT. It uncovered the right flank of the Sixth, and exposed RICKETTS' Division, which was stoutly holding the advanced position, to a savage fire on the prolongation of its line. In this state of facts, to retain possession of a position somewhat in advance of his point of starting, was the utmost Gen. WRIGHT could possibly do.

XI.

OPERATIONS ON THE RIGHT AND RIGHT-CENTRE—WARREN AND BURNSIDE.

Operations along the fronts of WARREN and BURNSIDE were of an importance quite subordinate to that of operations on the left. No results were achieved except the carrying of the line of rifle-pits occupied by the rebel skirmishers. The Fifth and Ninth Corps nowhere struck the enemy's main work. BURNSIDE kept up a furious cannonade for some hours; but it was nothing—*vox et preterea nihil*. From the tenor of one of BURNSIDE's morning dispatches, it was at one time hoped that he would be able to turn the enemy's left; but this hope also was doomed to disappointment.

XII.

A LONG LULL—INCIDENTS OF THE DAY.

Returning from the ride along the lines at 8 A. M., I found that Gens. GRANT and MEADE had established their personal headquarters in advance of that occupied during the night, and had taken their station on the site of Cold Harbor, where Gen. WRIGHT's headquarters were fixed—he himself, however, having gone forward with his corps. The rain of the early morning ceased, and the sun was struggling through the clouds.

The fate of the day was like the aspect of the heavens above—mingled light and shade, a clear issue nowhere. The first terrible climax of the battle was over. Would the assault be renewed?

To those looking into the face of GRANT for an answer to this query, there was no legible response. His is a face that tells no tales—a face impassive in victory or defeat; face of stone; a sphinx face! Not of him can it be said, as Lady Macbeth to her lord: "Thy face, my thane, is as a book, wherein one may read strange things." Rather is it a *palimpsest*, whose obscured characters escape the scrutiny of the keenest-eyed searcher.

Nothing, indeed, could be more striking than the contrast presented by the two commanders, as they stood in consultation on that bare hill, with their faces turned Richmond-ward. The small form with the slight stoop in the shoulders, sunken grey eyes, still, reserved demeanor, impassive face and chin as of a bull-dog or close-set steel trap—that is GRANT; the tall figure, with the nervous, emphatic articulation and action, and face as of antique parchment—that is MEADE—and the antipodes could not bring together a greater contrast.

Whether it was that Gen. GRANT himself was in doubt as to the path which should be pursued, or that he felt the need of seeing for himself the actual situation—for from our point of vision everything was hid by a veil of woods—I know not, but he suddenly mounted his horse, and rode rapidly down (an occasional shot or shell passing over his head and falling around us at headquarters) to the headquarters of Gen. HANCOCK, and afterward to those of Gen. WRIGHT; and when he came back it was plain there would be no renewal of the battle, for we all rode leisurely back to the old camp occupied the night before.

This was noon; and though the white heat of battle had died out, there were still spirts of fight along the line, and vigorous interchange of fire from the hostile batteries. Such rencounters were inevitable from the unparalleled closeness of the opposing lines. This was particularly the case on the left, where there were points at which the rebels and our own men were divided but by a narrow neutral interval of fifty yards. As the possibility of our troops occupying a line in such proximity to the enemy's works may not be clear, I will offer a word of explanation. The rebel intrenchments in front of BARLOW's and GIBBONS' divisions had, with a fault of engineering of which the rebels are not often guilty, been drawn on the *rearward* slope of the crest and thrown too far back, so that after the repulse of our men, the moment they had fallen back over the ridge, they were partially under cover, and here the sharpshooters were able to keep the rebel heads down long enough to allow portions of our line to protect themselves with improvised parapets, which they held all day.

This explanation is the more needed, because

Continued on the Eighth Page.

ONE WEEK LATER FROM EUROPE.

Arrival of the Viginia and Etna at this Port--The China at Halifax.

The News of General Grant's Operations Received.

Profound Sensation---Views of the Press.

A Decline of Five to Six per Cent. in the Rebel Loan.

The Laird Rams Purchased by the British Government.

THE GERITY PIRATES DISCHARGED.

Aspect of the Schleswig-Holstein Question.

FINANCIAL AND COMMERCIAL INTELLIGENCE.

The steamship *Virginia*, from Liverpool May 24, via Queenstown May 25, and the steamship *Etna*, from Liverpool May 25, via Queenstown May 26, arrived at this port yesterday. The *China* also arrived at Halifax yesterday, with advices to the 29th of May, making a total of one week's later news.

THE NEWS BY THE VIRGINIA AND ETNA.

THE WAR IN AMERICA.

RECEPTION OF THE NEWS IN ENGLAND.

The news of the great battles in Virginia, received by the steamship *Europa*, caused a profound sensation throughout England, and the people were astounded at the magnitude of the losses. The probable result of the bloody combat was eagerly canvassed on all sides.

The Confederate Loan recovered three per cent., and cotton became weaker under the news.

The *Times* says:

"GRANT has fully justified his reputation for unconquerable tenacity. If he has not achieved absolute success he has bid for it more desperately, and approached it more nearly than any of his predecessors. It is true the intelligence from the field of battle reached us through Federal sources, and is, perhaps, colored somewhat favorably for the North. It is hard to discern the inclination of the balance, so evenly do the scales appear to be weighed. LINCOLN's proclamation and STANTON's bulletin speaks of the Federal success in terms so qualified as to express anything rather than confidence, while the premium on gold, which was 73 when GRANT began his march and which fell to 69 at one period, has risen to 77; it was 75½ at the departure of the mail. The successive retirements of the Confederate Commander was but so many judicious and preconcerted operations of the campaign. In none of these movements was there the slightest confusion or the evidence of inferiority. The whole road to Richmond, be it remembered, is a series of positions which have long been studied and strengthened by the Confederates, terminating in a capital fortified by all the defences which modern art could devise, through a period of three years. LEE, if he falls back, is only falling back from one strong post to another, till he finds himself in the strongest post of all. GRANT, if he falls back ever so little, gives up the game, while if he persists in advancing, he discovers harder work than ever before him at the end of each day's march, and separates himself from his supplies in the same proportion."

From the London Times, May 25.

The details of the great battles in America are calculated rather to enhance than diminish the sensation with which the telegrams were received. There has been no exaggeration, no overstrained description of the conflicts or the carnage. If, indeed, it be recollected that even the long reports of furious fighting, which we yesterday published, still leave two days of sanguinary action unaccounted for, it must be allowed that war has never come before us in a shape so appalling. Perhaps the Americans may be proud of the pre-eminence, but they have certainly fought more desperately, for a longer time, and with more dreadful slaughter than any nation before them. It would not be impossible to match the results of any one day's battle with stories from the wars of the Old World; but never, we should think, in the history of man, were five such battles as these compressed into six successive days. It is hard to conceive how nature could have supported the exhaustion and the strain. We have been told that after a single day's hard fighting the lassitude and reaction in even a victorious army are such that any fresh force might snatch its laurels from it; whereas here are two armies hotly engaged in the work of slaughter from the morning of Thursday till the night of Tuesday with scarcely the intermission of an hour. On every day except Saturday there was a pitched battle, contested with the utmost fury; and even Saturday was devoted to marching and fighting on the march. Nor were these prodigious operations divided among immense numbers brought into action by relays. Neither army numbered apparently over one hundred thousand men, and of these every man seemed to have been engaged in every battle. Indeed, we are expressly told that the Federal "reserves" were brought up on the very first day.

The desperate ferocity of the fighting may be inferred from the fact now reported that the slaughter was produced without the aid of artillery. No rifled guns or murderous shells did execution among crowded masses. The great battle of Friday, which is said to have cost the Federals alone upward of 10,000 men, was a hand-to-hand fight. The Confederates were posted in the well-known woods in the vicinity of Chancellorsville, where HOOKER once received so bloody a repulse, and so dense was the thicket that cannon could not come into play. Regiment against regiment, and man against man, the combatants fired and hacked at each other in this tangled wilderness till night closed in; and an intercepted report from Gen. LEE actually tells us that, on his side, the heaviest loss was in men killed outright, and that he had comparatively few wounded. If this be a correct version of the dispatch, it gives a a more impressive idea of the fury of the conflict than any other of the incidents reported. It is clear, indeed, that whatever may be said of the composition of the Northern armies, and of their inferiority in this respect to the patriot legions of the South, they have fought in this campaign with a valor as obstinate as that of their enemies. No mere indifferent or disaffected mercenaries could have been led from a battle like that at Wilderness to three more such battles at Spottsylvania. Be the impulse what it may, the Federals are fighting in stern reality, and with a spirit as resolute as that of their adversaries.

Except that Gen. LEE more than once surprised the Federals with a sudden attack in mass, and that his positions were always occupied with admirable skill, there appears to have been little display of strategy. On Thursday LEE attacked, and with a result which at one moment looked very like success. On Friday GRANT attacked, and LEE repulsed him. On Sunday and Monday GRANT attacked again, with no better result; on Tuesday LEE appears to have been once more the assailant. But in all these battles there was more fighting than manœuvring, and more loss than result. Now that the outlines of the earlier telegrams have been filled up by detailed reports, the contest appears even more indecisive and the issue more obscure than before. For the Confederates, it may be said that they have never actually lost a battle. On the first day LEE only failed to inflict a complete defeat on the advancing Federals. On the second day he himself claimed the victory, and his enemies hardly denied it. On the fourth and fifth days he repulsed every attack, and held his position; while on the sixth day he was strong enough and confident enough to refuse his adversary the respite he desired. As we are told, on the authority of Secretary STANTON himself, that GRANT did not design to renew the attack on Tuesday, whereas we know that the fighting on that day was the most desperate of all, it follows that the battle must have been provoked by LEE, so that as the curtain falls on this first act of the dreadful drama the Confederates are assuming the offensive, and compelling

The Charleston Mercury.

VINDICE NULLO
SPONTE SUA SINE LEGE FIDES RECTUMQUE COLETUR.

VOLUME LXXXIV. CHARLESTON, S. C., WEDNESDAY, JUNE 8, 1864. NUMBER 12,082

THE GREAT BATTLE OF LAST FRIDAY ON THE BANKS OF THE CHICKAHOMINY.

[From the Richmond Dispatch, June 4.]

The roar of artillery is still ringing in our ears as we sit down to record the most tremendous slaughter that has ever taken place on this continent—a slaughter as far exceeding that of Thursday, the 12th, as the slaughter of Thursday, the 12th, surpassed every other field of carnage.

The battle commenced yesterday morning for the possession of the Grape Vine, or, as it is sometimes called, McClellan's Bridge, over the Chickahominy. It is the same by which McClellan withdrew his troops when they were defeated in the double battle of Cold Harbor and Gaines' Mill. Had Grant succeeded in obtaining possession of this bridge, he might have passed the Chickahominy and established himself in McClellan's old fastnesses on this side. It was the object of General Lee to prevent him, and he accordingly took possession of and fortified the position formerly held by McClellan. The ground on which the battle was fought was the same with that on which the battle of '62 was fought. But the positions were reversed, we holding McClellan's and Grant holding Lee's. According to the accounts of prisoners Grant on the night of Thursday caused a quart of whiskey to be distributed to each of the soldiers, and about four o'clock yesterday morning, having primed them well for the work, commenced an assault upon our works. Repulsed again and again, with unprecedented slaughter, he constantly renewed the attack with fresh troops, sending his men up in columns ten deep, and, in great part, so drunk that they knew not what they were about, and pressed on with the most reckless audacity. Nothing could exceed the coolness with which they were received by our troops, who, standing behind their breastworks and suffering but little, shot them down by thousands, with as much deliberation as though they were firing at so many marks. At 1 o'clock the action ceased along the whole line, our troops having repulsed the enemy, who left several thousand behind him, dead or wounded, on the field. General Lee afterwards rode over the field, and declared that the slaughter far exceeded that of the 12th of May. Many of the Yankees were so drunk that they tumbled over our breastworks, and were either killed or made prisoners; others after firing their guns could not reload them. In a word, the drama of the 12th of May was repeated to the letter. Our lines were considerably advanced in consequence of our success yesterday. Doubtless the enemy will seek to drive us back, and another general battle may ensue. We have not heard how many prisoners and guns were taken. In a battle of this sort, where it is the object of one party to defend breastworks, and of the other to capture them, many prisoners are not usually taken. We saw about a thousand, however, pass down the street yesterday.

The most marvellous thing about this battle is the small loss of our army. At 12 o'clock, we learn from undoubted authority, Longstreet's corps had not lost a hundred men in killed and wounded. A few hundreds will cover our whole loss. Since New Orleans, when Gen. Jackson said, "scarce a sprig of cypress was mingled with the wreaths of laurel," there has been nothing like this. When the Yankees occupied those same lines from which we have just repulsed them with such terrible slaughter, we drove them from them. At that time they were much stronger than they are now. This fact alone would be sufficient to show which are the best troops. Devoutly thankful should the whole Confederate States be to that Providence which has watched over us in this great crisis, and under Him to that brave army, and that great General, who have turned our day of trial into one of joy. Especially ought we to hold the latter dear, for the skill which has continued to accomplish such a mighty enterprise with so little loss.

LATEST NEWS FROM VIRGINIA.

BATTLE GROUND, NEAR GAINES' MILL, June 6.—Last evening GRANT sent a flag of truce into our lines, proposing that, in the intervals of the fighting, unarmed parties should be permitted to bury the dead and to care for the wounded. This proposal General LEE is understood to have declined, intimating, however, his willingness to entertain regular flags of truce for these purposes. This morning GRANT sent in another flag of truce to say that he would avail himself of the understanding, to send out unarmed parties to bury the dead and to care for the wounded. Gen. LEE promptly replied, showing that GRANT has misunderstood his answer of last evening. There the matter rests.

There was heavy firing last night, but it amounted to nothing. Last night the enemy abandoned our front on the left, and along part of the centre, apparently in great haste. EARLY has followed them ten miles to-day, capturing sixty prisoners, who say that GRANT has gone to the White House, because his men won't fight.

The impression here, however, is that GRANT is making for the James River, intending to cross to the Southside. There has been some sharpshooting on our right to day.

RICHMOND, June 7.—General LEE's despatch of last night merely confirms the enemy's withdrawal from our left and from part of our centre.

We have nothing from the Valley this morning. General W. E. JONES was killed in a fight near Staunton on Sunday. All our trains were brought off safely to Waynesboro'.

All citizens paroled prior to May, and all soldiers delivered at City Point up to the present time, are declared exchanged.

The sale of guarantied bonds is again postponed until the 21st inst., the sale to take place at Columbia.

THE LATEST NEWS FROM NORTH GEORGIA.

RIGHT WING NEAR ANDERSONVILLE, SIX MILES N. N. E. FROM MARIETTA, June 6.—A heavy force of the enemy drove in our pickets this morning on our right. After brisk skirmishing with WILLIAMS' Kentucky brigade and WHEELER's cavalry, the enemy occupied Big Shanty Station, nine miles north of Marietta.

Our line of battle has been changed to confront the enemy. Our right rests towards Andersonville, and our left on Pumpkin Vine Creek, near PICKET's house, fifteen miles northwest from Marietta.

It is rumored that CHALMERS' cavalry has destroyed three wagon trains near Calhoun.

General Robert Edmund Lee

Military bridge across the Chickahominy

The New-York Times.

VOL. XIII—NO. 3965. NEW-YORK, WEDNESDAY, JUNE 8, 1864. PRICE THREE CENTS.

GRANT'S ARMY.

Intelligence Up to Tuesday Morning.

Three Rebel Night Assaults Repulsed.

A MIDNIGHT ATTACK ON BURNSIDE.

A FOGGY ATTACK ON HANCOCK.

The Enemy Driven Back with Heavy Loss.

GRANT BESIEGING LEE'S LINES.

Flags of Truce for the Care of the Dead and Wounded.

Late News from Gen. Grant—An Attack on Burnside Repulsed—Exchange of Flags of Truce in Reference to the Killed and Wounded—Grant Besieging Lee in his Lines.

[OFFICIAL.]

WAR DEPARTMENT, WASHINGTON, June 7—10:15 P. M.

Major-Gen. Dix:

Dispatches from headquarters, Army of the Potomac, dated 9 o'clock this morning, have been received. An assault was made on BURNSIDE about midnight, and successfully repulsed. In the preceding afternoon, a hundred picked men of the enemy made a rush to find out what was the meaning of HANCOCK's advancing siege lines. Nine of the party were captured, and the rest killed or driven back.

Several letters have passed between Gen. GRANT and Gen. LEE in respect to collecting the dead and wounded between the two armies. Gen. GRANT in the closing letter, regrets that all his efforts "for alleviating the sufferings of wounded men left on the field, have been rendered nugatory."

Two rebel officers and six men, sent out to search for the wounded of their commands, were captured in consequence of the enemy not delivering Gen. LEE's letter until after the hour he had named had expired. Gen. GRANT has notified Gen. LEE that they were captured through a misunderstanding, and will not be held as prisoners, but will be returned.

No other military intelligence has been received.

EDWIN M. STANTON, Secretary of War.

BATTLE OF SUNDAY.

Special Dispatch to the New-York Times.

NEAR COLD HARBOR, Sunday Evening, June 5.

The enemy appear to be exceedingly anxious to break up our lines, particularly on the left, so as to cut off all communication with White House Landing. During the last three days they have made several assaults, but in each instance were repulsed with fearful loss. The last attempt of this kind was made just after dark this evening in front of SMYTHE' brigade, late CARROLL's, of GIBBONS' Division, Second Army Corps. The weather was peculiarly favorable for the movement, as the rain of last night was succeeded by a hot murky day, and, in consequence, the whole lower strata of atmosphere was a dense mist. Under cover of this impenetrable fog the enemy advanced a strong line of battle, and succeeded in reaching a point within pistol range of our works before discovered by the advanced pickets. No sooner did the outpost give the alarm than one sheet of fire belched forth from our ranks in front and on both flanks of the enemy. In about half an hour he fell back, leaving the ground covered with his dead and wounded.

At a little later moment there was apparently a similar demonstration about to be made in front of RUSSELL's Division of the Sixth Corps, but that was speedily checked.

These night attacks have got to be so frequent that they cease to create an alarm, for the whole army is always on duty, ready at any moment to meet any emergency. Gens. GRANT and MEADE are constantly on the alert, so that a surprise is practically an impossibility.

But while these attacks at night create no alarm there is something romantically interesting about them. It is a pyrotechnic display of gigantic proportion. The continued explosions of thousands of rockets would be no comparison.

The loss on our side in this last assault was small owing to the fact that the men were behind earthworks.

Lieut. MCCUNE, Fifth Excelsior, of Gen. HANCOCK's Staff, had his leg shot off while standing near Gen. HANCOCK's headquarters.

The Second Cavalry Division, Gen. GREGG, gained an important position to-day on the left.

E. A. PAUL.

OPERATIONS OF SATURDAY AND SUNDAY.

Special Dispatch to the New-York Times.

ARMY OF THE POTOMAC, Sunday, June 5—P. M.

There has been no material change in the position of the Army of the Potomac since the close of the hard battle on Friday. On the left of our line, the Second Corps (HANCOCK's) still holds the ground, stretched along the road leading to Dispatch Station, and protected on the flank by SHERIDAN, whose dashing cavalry pickets the intervening region on the bank of the Chickahominy.

Our right wing is along the line of the Bethesda church road, and gradually pressing toward the left, thus rendering the army compact and firm.

WILSON's cavalry division, watchful and adventurous, covers the flank in this direction.

Our lines have moved forward a very little since Friday's costly struggle. Indeed the advance might be counted by inches.

The enemy, snugly covered inside his high breastworks, makes a vigorous defence to all our assaults, and shows no signs of yielding.

On our side, especially in front of the Sixth and Eighteenth Corps, the attack is sharp and urged onward with a full determination to win. By dint of pluck and sheer power of endurance, our lines have been pushed ahead inch by inch, almost solely by the use of the spade, the musket being simply an auxiliary, until at some points in front of MARTINDALE's Division of the Eighteenth Corps, they are not more than one hundred yards apart. This digging is done solely at night, and as the sappers advance, large numbers of the bodies, both rebel and our own, of those who fell on Friday, are reached and buried.

On both sides sharpshooters—fairly entitled to the name—perched in trees or hidden in pits, take grim delight in sending a bullet into any luckless individual whom incaution or duty exposes. This fact has been brought home to us quite painfully during the past few days by the loss of several excellent officers. Even this morning I was speaking to Capt. P. REED, Assistant Adjutant-General of the Staff of Brig.-Gen. BROOKS. Five minutes afterward a rebel rifleman, stationed nearly a mile distant to the right, succeeded in planting a minie ball in the Captain's leg, as he walked across the field in front of Gen. SMITH's Headquarters. These sharpshooting pests have disabled, at a low estimate, one hundred men per day, since Friday, in both the Sixth and Eighteenth Corps, while other organizations of the army have also not been exempt from their annoyance.

But the fighting has not been entirely confined to sharpshooting. There has been several artillery episodes, to vary with hoarser sounds, the lively, but not continuous, bang, bang on the skirmish line.

At 9½ o'clock last night, the rebels in front of the Eighteenth Corps attempted to thwart Gen. SMITH's settled purpose of relieving his troops in the rifle-pits. To do this they suddenly unmasked a battery about a mile distant from corps headquarters, sending their screeching vetoes through the air for a few minutes, with a rapidity that was quite demoralizing to everybody who listened, except, of course, the seasoned soldiers, to whom such harsh-voiced messages are familiar. The cannonade was accompanied by several sharp volleys of musketry, scattered shots of which clicked unpleasantly in the trees of the picturesque grove where Gen. SMITH has chosen to pitch his tents, causing leaves to fall in gentle showers. Capt. ELDER, Chief of Artillery of the Eighteenth Corps, speedily rebuked this presumption of the enemy. He massed his batteries on their position and blazed away so fiercely for a while that the very ground shook as he thundered. Silence thus secured, the remainder of the night passed away without disturbance.

There have been one or two animated artillery passages to-day also, in each of which Capt. ELDER grandly put a stop to the rebel demonstrations, by massing his pieces and firing with magnificent rapidity. The enemy lost his morale, and withdrew crestfallen. The few shots sent by the rebels were not, however, altogether harmless. There were three regiments in line near the edge of a piece of woods, about half a mile in the rear of our breastworks. These must have been observed, and doubtless drew the enemy's fire. Four of the shots went hing, screeching overhead and cutting off tree-tops af they passed beyond. The fifth struak in the ranks of the Tenth New-York Heavy Artillery, completely disemboweling one man and injuring four others. A chance shot to-day also worked some misbhief in the Second Rhode Island Regiment. The term of the regiment has expired, and it was going from the front bound for home. Having got, as was supposed, well out of range, the order was given to halt, and a moment after came the rushing ball bringing its death message to two poor fellows who, after faithful service, having escaped all the dangers of the fight, were full of joyful anticipations at the speedy prospect of being home again. Their fate was doubly shocking.

About 7 o'clock to-night there was a furious fire suddenly opened on the left. For twenty minutes the rattling of musketry and roaring of artillery was kept up with a steadiness that is seldom equalled. Persons at a distance interpreted it into a determined attack by the rebels, with the view of turning HANCOCK's position. The indications certainly pointed to something desperate, and the weakhearted made preparations for a skedaddle. Investigation has not made it precisely clear why so much noise was made. Some declare that the enemy attacked in force, attempting to break SMYTH's brigade of the Second Corps, while others insist that a scare was got up in the darkness, without any justification whatever. At any rate, our lines were preserved intact, and I must wait the developments of the morning for the facts.

Brig.-Gen. BARNARD was to-day assigned to duty as Chief Engineer of the Army of the Potomac.

H. J. W.

CASUALTIES.

First Sergt A D Brooks, A, 8th Connecticut.
Jas Straw, A 12th N H
Second Lt Scott, 14th N Y.
J P Randall, F, 1??th N Y.
C M Tuttle, I, 81st N Y.
Danl Anderson, B, 2d N H.
A C Bedell, F, 139th N Y.
S Lapier, G, 118th N Y.
O F Wallace, H, 12th N H.
Sergt W F Dunham, F, 81st New-York.
G Hebot.
D O'Connell, E, 20th Mass.
First Sergt G K Hughes, K, 12th N H.
N Pierce, K, 4th N H.
Lieut J H Darn, 117th N Y.
S Johnson, G, 115th N Y.
Serght A K Blake, A, 12th New-Hampshire.
R G Sanford, E, 81st N Y.
Chas H Pelton, 25th Mass.
Lieut A R Blondin, D, 12th Indiana.
Wm Blodin, F, 98th N Y.
Sergt A Mackey, H, 47th New-York—arm.
A Cole, I, 47th N Y—thigh.
A Mann, C, 47th N Y—abdomen.
P Carroll, B, 47th N Y—foot.
Sergt I Riley, A, 47th N Y—leg.
J Meyers, 47th N Y—arm.
J Buckard, B, 47th N Y—arm.
Lieut H Matthews, G, 25th Mass.
J M Hickoc, A, 98th N Y.
C Guyer, B 81st unknown.
J Babcock, I, 188th Penn.
First Lieut Jas Knott, I, 10th New-Hampshire.
R B Joice, K, 98th N Y.
Corp J E Hujar, K, 81st N Y.
M McMahon, E, 25th Mass.
Lieut-Col Perry, 139th N Y.
J W Pearson, C, 139th N Y.
Lieut J G Johnson, 139th N Y
E H Combs, 27th Mass.
F Kohrl, G, 25th Mass.
Corp C W Truax, F, 13th Indiana.
J Reynolds, F, 13th N Y.
Sergt Jas M McKee.
P P Cutter, D, 25th Mass.
M Carlink, K, 117th N Y.
J L Davis, A, 10th N H.
Sergt J Wilson, B, 47th N Y—killed.
I Agen, K, 47th N Y—head.
M Cancey, B 47th N Y—arm.
W Lyons, I—arm.
Sergt E West, A, 47th N Y—shoulder.
Sergt Bens, I, 47th New-York—killed.
— Smith, I, 47th N Y.
— Cunningham, I, 47th New-York.
W H Cook, I, 47th New-York—finger.

June 5.

G Lammis, K, 48th N Y—leg.
Corp J F Lewis, K, 48th N Y—head.
G Yorks, E, 58th N Y—face.
A Horton, B, 48th N Y—leg amputated.
Corp J J Johnson, B, 48th N Y—elbow.

Additional names of killed and wounded of BARTON's brigade, from June 1 to June 3:

D Harmaker, C, 48th N Y—killed.
P Dillan, C, 48th N Y—killed.
J Clancy, W, 48th N Y.
F Muller, W, 48th N Y—hand.
Corp C Emory, G, 48th N Y—killed.

WOUNDED.

[illegible]

DIED FROM WOUNDS RECEIVED IN ACTION—JUNE 3.

[illegible]

The following is the official report of the number of casualties in the First Division of the Sixth Corps on the 2d and 3d inst.: Commissioned officers—killed, 9; wounded, 38; missing, 4; total, 51. Enlisted men—killed, 162; wounded, 861; missing, 142; total, 1,164.

The following are the names of officers killed and wounded and missing in the actions of June 1, 2 and 3:

[illegible]

Lieut F Lowe, 121st N Y.
Lieut J C Paradis, 5th Me.
Adjt J T Hammond, 49th Pa.
Lieut B F Crane, 5th Wis.
Capt J H Cook, 5th Wis.
Capt E Williams, 6th Me.
Adjt W H Conn, 6th Me.
Capt A B Hutchinson, 49th Pennsylvania.
Capt A W Wakefield, 49th Pennsylvania.
Lieut J P Smith, 49th Penn—missing, supposed prisoner.
Maj B J Hickman, 49th Pa—killed.
Lieut C B Hatch, 2d Conn heavy artillery.
Maj A I Daggett, 5th Me.

THE BATTLE OF FRIDAY.

Further Particulars—The Gallantry of Gibbons' and Barlow's Divisions—List of Casualties.

From Our Special Correspondent.

NEAR COLD HARBOR, Friday, June 3—3 o'clock P. M.

Since my dispatch of 9 o'clock A. M., I have gathered some additional particulars of the contest this morning. Compelled to leave the field to get off that dispatch at the early hour I did, and not foreseeing that our troops might be compelled to give up a portion of the works they had won against such odds, makes my first account under present circumstances rather exaggerated; that is, the object of the movement on the left was not fully accomplished. True, the cavalry on the left of our line rests upon the Chickahominy, and this morning all felt confident that the left of the infantry line would certainly hold that position, by doing which the enemy, taken in flank, would have had their whole line on this side of the Chickahominy rolled up like a piece of parchment, and the entire demoralization of the enemy must have been the result. As it was, the success was only partial. Our extreme left (BARLOW's division of the Second Corps) advanced to within three-quarters of a mile of the river—an advance of nearly one mile. Of this gallant movement I wish to speak more in detail. Gen. BARLOW's division occupied the extreme left of the line—of the army, in fact; Gen. GIBBON's next, while Gen. BIRNEY's division was held in reserve. The movement was inaugurated by the advance of one-half of the first-named division. Gen. MILES' brigade, composed of the Fifth New-Hampshire, Sixty-first New-York, Eighty-first Pennsylvania, One Hundred and Fortieth Pennsylvania, One Hundred and Eighty-third Pennsylvania, Twenty-sixth Michigan and Second New-York Heavy Artillery, of BARLOW's division, occupied the extreme left; while BROOKS' brigade, of the same division, composed of the Fifty-third, One Hundred and Forty-fifth, One Hundred and Forty-eighth Pennsylvania, Sixty-sixth and Sixty-fourth New-York, Second Delaware and Seventh New-York Artillery, moved up on the right. The movement was commenced at precisely 4½ o'clock A. M. The One Hundred and Forty-eighth Pennsylvania, Col. BEAVER, deployed as skirmishers. At first the ground over which the command moved was covered with trees and an undergrowth of bushes, passing through which the command emerged into an open space, in full view of the enemy. At this moment a terrific fire was opened upon the devoted patriots—but they quailed not. Continuing to advance, one-half the command charged upon and obtained possession of the enemy's works. A battery of six guns was in our hands, and just as Col. MORRIS, of the Second New-York Artillery, was in the act of turning the guns upon the foe, they advanced in overwhelming numbers, and the braves of the Union were compelled to fall back. The enemy did not then and have not since been able to use these guns. Our men (One Hundred and Forty-eighth Pennsylvania, Col. BEAVER,) hold a position within thirty-five yards, and every man is shot who attempts to approach the guns. The enemy, composed of HILL's and BRECKINRIDGE's troops, are behind a line of earthworks, on the crest of a roll of land, while our boys hold a similar position in a depression of the land, having thereby a little advantage as to position, as the reader will readily perceive, for to aim at our men a rebel must raise his head so far above the earthworks as to look down a hill, while ours look up at an angle of perhaps thirty degrees; the enemy's flag floats defiantly over the parapet, and has been frequently shot away; when this is done the boys banter the enemy to raise their "rag" again. Not a head or the least portion of a man's person can be exposed but what a dozen guns are instantly fired by our men; and various are the expedients resorted to to induce some of the enemy to make a show of hands; some of these which have been successfully used a number of times, are to give the word of command as though our men were to advance, about to be relieved, or reinforced; being within within a few paces, the enemy hearing every word distinctly, in large numbers peer over their works to take advantage of the supposed order. Scores of them to-day have forfeited their lives by serving a bad cause with such alacrity. In the charge upon the works, Corp. TERRANCE BIGLER, Company D, Seventh New-York Heavy Artillery, snatched the State flag of the Twenty-sixth Virginia Infantry, from the hands of the bearer within the enemy's works, and carried it off triumphantly to the rear. The different temperament of men under the excitement of battle is strongly illustrated by the following incident: The Colonel of the Twenty-sixth Virginia was bayoneted on the spot by one of our men, while a Captain at his side was taken prisoner by another—all the work of a moment; 15 commissioned officers and 215 non-commissioned officers and privates were captured by this division.

GIBBON's division, as I have before said, was at the right of Gen. BARLOW. His command also had a desperate conflict, assaulting the enemy's works several times, and gaining some ground and capturing about 150 prisoners. MCKEAN's, OWEN's, SMITH's and TYLER's brigades were all in the fight. A portion of one brigade got so far within the enemy's works that it could not go either way, and there it remains at this moment. The men will be got out to-night.

Among the casualties in these two divisions were the following:

Lieut. B. Y. DRAPER, Aid-de-Camp to Col. T. A. SMITH, Third Brigade, Third Division.

Col. JOHN R. BROOKE, commanding Third Brigade, First Division, had a shrapnel ball strike a breast button of his coat, wounding one finger, and making a slight contusion on his stomach.

Col. O. H. MORRIS, Sixty-sixth New-York, killed. He was instantly killed, having been shot through the heart.

Col. R. BYRNES, commanding brigade, mortally wounded—shot through the spine with a rifle ball.

Capt. J. D. BRADY, Brigade Inspector, Fourth Brigade, of Sixty-third New-York, wounded in breast and arm by same ball.

Lt D S Munn, 66th N Y.
Lt S Piricus, 66th N Y.
Lt West, 28th Mass. (This regiment lost every Field Officer and Captain.)
Lt Ludwig, 53d Pennsylvania—shoulder.
Lt Kenny, of Gen Tyler's Staff.
Capt W L Palmer, Ordnance Officer—thigh.
Col McMahon, 164th N Y—wounded and a prisoner.
Capt H A Hall, Inspector—foot.
Lt Owen, Aid to Gen Tyler—arm.
Capt Schuyler, Aid to Gen Tyler—leg.
Capt Somerhays, 20th Mass—wrist.
Lt Holland, Adjt 20th Mass.

Capt. PARKER, of Gen. HANCOCK's Staff, had his horse killed. Of the operations of the Eighteenth and Sixth Corps you will receive accounts from another correspondent. The enemy, endeavoring to create a diversion, made an assault upon the Ninth Corps on our right, but were repulsed with heavy loss. Last night, also, Gen. WILSON's Third Cavalry Division had a severe fight with GORDON's command near Bethesda Church. The enemy was forced to retire.

GEN. RUSSELL'S DIVISION, SIXTH CORPS.

Wounded.

Lieut Paradue, 5th Maine.
Lieut Camp, 2d Conn.
Lieut Gordon, 95th Penn.
Simon Peters, E, 1st New-Jersey—shoulder.
Wm Hughes, B, 1st N J—arm.
John Sailor, D, 1st N J—fatal.
H H Patten, E, 1st N J—fatal.
Sergt M B Stull, D, 1st N J—mouth.
J O'Hara, B, 1st N J—hip.
Col Wm Henry, 1st N J—side
Lieut Melner, 1st N J—arm.
Jas Denton, F, 1st N J—hip.
J Barkley, B, 1st N J—shoulder.
J T Willetts, B, 1st N J—leg.
D Kane, A, 1st N J—arm amputated.
Thos Edlard, K, 1st N J—arm.
Dan Nutt, K, 1st N J—leg amputated.
Lieut J N Bullfish—scalp wound.

NATIONAL UNION CONVENTION.

The Assembling at Baltimore Yesterday.

Six Hundred Delegates in Attendance.

Dr. Breckinridge, of Kentucky, Temporary President.

Governor Denison, of Ohio, Permanent President.

ENTIRE HARMONY AND ENTHUSIASM.

Speeches of Rev. Dr. Breckinridge, Senator Morgan, Governor Denison and Parson Brownlow.

BALTIMORE, Tuesday, June 7.

The National Union Convention assembled this morning in the Front-street Theatre.

The building is tastefully decorated and fitted up for the occasion. The galleries are festooned with flags and the interior stage is thrown open. This was done by the City Council of Baltimore.

The President's chair is on an elevated platform at the extreme end of the stage, under a canopy of flags.

There is a numerous staff of pages in attendance, who are decorated with tri-colored badges.

There is also a considerable number of telegraph messengers in attendance, whose duty it is to convey dispatches direct from the reporters' tables to the telegraphic instruments in the lobbies.

The doors of the theatre opened at 11 o'clock, and the building soon commenced filling up with delegates and spectators—the latter being admitted only to the galleries.

The Dress Circle is reserved for the ladies.

There are nearly six hundred delegates present, including many from the remote Territories.

New-Mexico has sent a delegation consisting of Hons. JOHN S. WATTS, FRANCIS PEREA and JOSHUA JONES, Jr.

1 o'clock, P. M.

The band of the Second United States Regiment, from Fort McHenry, is stationed in the gallery, and at noon they opened with the performance of a grand overture.

The building is now densely packed, from the lower floor to the ceiling.

Hon. EDWIN D. MORGAN, of New-York, Chairman of the National Union Executive Committee, called the Convention to order; and spoke as follows:

MEMBERS OF THE CONVENTION: It is a little more than eight years since it was resolved to form a national party, to be conducted upon the principles and policy which had been established and maintained by those illustrious statesmen, GEORGE WASHINGTON and THOMAS JEFFERSON. A convention was held in Philadelphia, under the shade of the trees that surround the Hall of Independence, and candidates (FREMONT and DAYTON) were there nominated who had espoused our cause and were to maintain it. But the State of Pennsylvania gave its electoral vote to JAMES BUCHANAN, and the election of 1858 was lost. Nothing daunted by defeat, it was determined to fight on "on this line," not only "all Summer," but four Summers and four Winters, and in 1860 the party banner was again unfurled, with the names of ABRAHAM LINCOLN and HANNIBAL HAMLIN inscribed thereon. This time it was successful; but with success came the rebellion, and with the rebellion, of course, war, and war, terrible and cruel war, has continued up to the present time, when it is necessary, under our Constitution, to prepare for another Presidential election. It is for this highly responsible purpose that you are to-day assembled. It is not my duty nor my purpose to indicate any general plan of action by this convention; but I trust I may be permitted to say that, in view of the dread realities of the past and what is passing at this moment, the fact that the bones of our soldiers are bleaching in every State of the Union, and with the further knowledge of the further fact that this has all been caused by Slavery, the party of which you, gentlemen, are the delegates and only representatives, will fall short of accomplishing its great mission, unless among its other resolves it shall declare for such an amendment of the Constitution as will positively prohibit African Slavery in the United States. [Prolonged applause, followed by three cheers.] In behalf of the National Committee, I now propose for temporary President of this convention, ROBERT J. BRECKINRIDGE of Kentucky, [applause,] and appoint Gov. RANDALL of Wisconsin, and Gov. KING of New-York, as a committee to conduct the President pro tem to the chair.

Three cheers were proposed for the "Old War Horse of Kentucky," and they were given.

As soon as silence was restored, Mr. BRECKINRIDGE returned his thanks for the honor conferred upon him in a brief and eloquent speech as follows:

GENTLEMEN OF THE CONVENTION: You cannot be more sensible than I am that the part which I have to perform here, to-day, is merely a matter of form; and acting upon the principles of my whole life, I was inclined, when the suggestion was made to me from various quarters, that it was in the minds of many members of the convention to confer this distinction upon me, to earnestly decline to accept it. Because I have never sought honors, I have never sought distinction. I have been a working man, and nothing else. But certain considerations led me to change my mind. [Applause.] There is a class of men in the country far too small for the good of the country. These are the men who by their example, by their pen, by their voice, try to do good, and all the more in perilous times, without regard to the reward that may come. It is given to many such men to understand, by the distinction conferred upon me, one of the humblest of their class, that there are men whom the country will cherish and who will not be forgotten. There is another motive relative to yourselves and to the country at large. It is good for you—it is good for every nation and every people, every State and every party, to cherish all generous impulses, to follow all noble instincts, (and where are men more noble, more generous?) to purge yourselves of all self seekers and betrayers, and to confer offices, if it be only in mere form, upon those worthy to be trusted, and ask nothing more. [Applause.] Now, according to my convictions of propriety, having said this, I should say nothing more. [Cries of go on.] But it has been intimated to me from many quarters, and in a way which I cannot disregard, that I should disappoint the wishes of my friends, and perhaps the just expectations of the convention, if I did not as briefly, and yet as precisely as I could, say somewhat upon the great matters which have brought us here. Therefore, in a very few words, and plainly as I can, I will endeavor to draw your attention to one and another of these great matters in which we are all engaged. In the first place, nothing can be more plain than the fact that you are here as representatives of a great nation—voluntary representatives, chosen without forms of law, but as really representing the feelings and principles, and, if you choose, the prejudices of the American people, as if it were written in their laws and already passed by their votes. For the man that you will nominate here for the Presidency of the United States and ruler of a great people, in a great crisis, is just as certain, I suppose, to be become that ruler as anything under Heaven is certain before it is done, [prolonged cheers,] and moreover, you will allow me to say, though, perhaps, it is hardly strictly proper that I should, but as far as I know your opinions, I suppose it is just as certain now as before you utter it—whose name you will utter, and which will be responded to from one end to the other of this nation, as it will after it has been uttered and recorded by your Secretary. Does any man doubt that this convention intends to say that ABRAHAM LINCOLN shall be the nominee? [Great applause.] What I wish, however, to call your attention to, is the grandeur of the mission upon which you are met, and, therefore, the dignity and solemnity, earnestness and conscientiousness with which, representing one of the greatest and certainly one of the first people of the world, you ought to discharge these duties. [Applause.] Now, beside the nomination of President and Vice President, in regard to which sacred office I will say nothing, because I know there is more or less difference of opinion among you, but beside these nominations, you have other most solemn duties to perform. You have to organize this party throughout the United States. You have to put it in whatever form your wisdom will suggest, that will unite all your wisdom, energy and determination to gain the victory, which, I have already said, was in our power. More than that, you have to lay down with clearness and precision the principles on which you intend to carry on this great political contest, and prosecute the war which is underneath them; and the glory of the country which lies before us if we succeed; plainly not in a double sense, briefly not in a treatise, with the dignity and precision of a great people, to utter by its representatives the political principles by which they intend to live, and for the sake of which they are willing to die, so that all men everywhere may understand precisely what we mean, and lay that furrow so deeply and clearly, that while every man who is worthy to associate with freemen may see it and pass over it, every man who is unworthy, may be either unable to pass it, or may be driven far from it. We want none but those who are like us to be with us. [Applause.] Now, among these principles, if you will allow me to say it, the first and most distinct is that we do not intend this nation to be destroyed. [Applause.] We are a nation, no doubt a peculiar one, a nation formed of States, and no nation except as these States form it; and these States are no States except as they are States in that nation. They had no more right to repudiate the nation than the nation has to repudiate them. None of them had even a shadow of a right to do this, and, God helping us, we will vindicate that truth, so that it shall never be disputed any more in this world. [Applause.] It is a fearful utterance that is set before us, but there are great compensations for it. Those of you who have alluded to this subject know that from the foundation of the present Government, before and since our present Constitution was formed, there have always been parties that had no faith in our Government. The men that formed it were doubtful of its success, and the men that opposed its formation did not desire its success; and I am bold to say, without detaining you on this subject, that for all the outcry about our violations of the Constitution, this present living generation and this present Union party are more thoroughly devoted to that Constitution than any generation that has ever lived under it. [Applause.] While I say that, and solemnly believe it, and believe it is capable of the strongest proof, I may also add that it is a great error which is being propagated in our land to say that our national life depends merely upon the sustaining of that Constitution. Our fathers made it, and we love it. I intend to maintain it. But if it suits us to change it, we can do so; [applause;] and when it suits us to change it, we will change it. [Applause.] If it were torn into ten thousand pieces, the nation would be as much a nation as it was before the Constitution was made—a nation always—that declared its independence as a united people, and lived as a united people until now—a nation independent of all particular institutions under which they lived, capable of modeling them precisely as their interests require. We ought to have it distinctly understood by friends and enemies that while we love that instrument, we will maintain it, and will with undoubted certainty put to death friend or foe who undertakes to trample it underfoot; yet, beyond a doubt, we will reserve the right to alter it to suit ourselves, from time to time, and from generation to generation. [Applause.] One more idea on that subject. We have incorporated in that instrument the right of revolution, which gives us, without a doubt, the right to change it. It never existed before in the American States, and there is no need of rebellion, insurrection, or civil war except upon a denial of the fundamental principles of all free Governments that the major part must rule, and there is no other method of carrying on society except that the will of the majority shall be the will of the whole, or that the will of the minority shall be the will of the whole. So that in one word, to deny the principles I have tried to state is to make a dogmatic assertion that the only form of government that is possible with perfect liberty, and acknowledged by God, is a pure and absolute despotism. The principles, therefore, which I am trying to state before you, are principles which if they be not true, freedom is impossible, and no Government but one of pure force can exist, or ought to endure among men.

But the idea which I wished to carry out as the remedy for these troubles and sorrows, dreadful as they are, is this: This fearful truth runs through the whole history of mankind that whatever else may be done to give stability to authority, whatever else may be done to give perpetuity to institutions, however wise, however glorious, practical and just may be the philosophy of it, it has been found that the only enduring, only imperishable cement of all free institutions has been the blood of traitors. No Government has ever been built upon imperishable foundations, which foundations were not laid in the blood of traitors. It is a fearful truth, but we had as well avow it at once, and every lick you strike, and every rebel you kill, every battle you win, dreadful as it is to do it, you are adding, it may be a year, it may be ten years, it may be a century, it may be ten centuries to the life of the Government and the freedom of your children. [Great applause.] Now, passing over that idea, passing over many other things which it would be right for me to say did time serve and were this the occasion, let me add—you are a Union party. [Applause.] Your origin has been referred to as having occurred eight years ago. In one sense it is true that you are far older than that. I see before me not only primitive Republicans and primitive Abolitionists, but I see also primitive Democrats and primitive Whigs, primitive Americans, and if you will allow me to say, I myself am here, who all my life have been a party to myself. [Laughter and applause.] As a Union party I will follow you to the ends of the earth, and to the gates of death, [applause;] but as an Abolition party, as a Republican party, as a Whig party, as a Democratic party, as an American party, I will not follow you one foot. [Applause.] But it is true of the mass of the American people, however you may divide and scatter while this war lasts, while the country is in peril, while you call yourselves as you do in the call of the Convention, the Union party, you are for the preservation of Union and the destruction of this rebellion, root and branch. And in my judgment, one of the great errors that has been committed by our administration of the Federal Government, the Chief of which we are about to nominate for another term of office—one of the errors has been to believe that we have succeeded when we have not succeeded, and to act in a manner which is precisely for those who have succeeded. You will not, you cannot succeed until you have utterly broken the military power of this people. [Applause.] I will not detain you on these incidental points, one of which has been made prominent in the remarks of the excellent Chairman of the National Committee. I do not know that I would be willing to go so far as probably he would, but I cordially agree with him in this. I think, considering what has been done about Slavery, taking the thing as it now stands, overlooking altogether either in way of condemnation or approval, any act that has brought us to the point where we are, but believing in my conscience, and with all my heart, that what has brought us where we are in the matter of Slavery is the original sin and folly of treason and secession. Because, you remember that the Chicago Convention itself was understood, and, I believe, it virtually did explicitly state, that they would not touch Slavery in the States. Leaving it, therefore, altogether out of the question how we came where we are on that particular point, we are prepared to go further than the original Republicans themselves were prepared to go. We are prepared to demand not only that the whole territory of the United States shall not be made slave, but that the General Government of the American people shall do one of two things—and it appears to me that there is nothing else that can be done—either to use the whole power of the Government, both war power and peace power, to put Slavery as nearly as possible back where it was, (for, although that will be a fearful state of society, it is better than anarchy,) or else to use the whole power of the Government, both of war and peace, and all the practical power that the people of the United States will give them to exterminate and extinguish it. [Prolonged applause.] I have no hesitation in saying for myself, that if I were a Pro-Slavery man; if I believed this institution was an ordinance of God, and was given to man, I would unhesitatingly join those who demand that Government should be put back where it was; but I am not a Pro-Slavery man. I never was. I unite myself with those who believe it is contrary to the brightest interests of all men and of all government, contrary to the spirit of the Christian religion, and incompatible with the natural right of man. I join myself with those who say, away with it forever, [applause,] and I fervently pray God that the day may come when throughout the whole land every man may be as free as you are, and as capable of enjoying regulated liberty. I will not detain you any longer. One single word you will allow me to say in behalf of the State from which I come, one of the smallest of the thousands of Israel. We know very well that our eleven votes are of no consequence in the Presidential election. We know very well that in our present unhappy condition it is by no means certain that we are here to-day representing the party that will carry the majority of the votes in that unhappy State. I know very well that sentiments which I am uttering will cause me great odium in the State in which I was born, which I love, where the bones of two generations of my ancestors and some of my children are, and where very soon I must lay my

Continued on the Eighth Page.

The New-York Times.

VOL. XIII—NO. 3966. NEW-YORK, THURSDAY, JUNE 9, 1864. PRICE THREE CENTS.

PRESIDENTIAL.

Lincoln & Johnson.

Proceedings of the National Union Convention Yesterday.

Unanimous Renomination of President Lincoln.

Gov. Andy Johnson, of Tennessee, for Vice-President.

THE LOYAL PLATFORM.

Slavery Must Perish by the Constitution.

Emancipation, the Monroe Doctrine, Economy and the Pacific Railroad.

Enthusiastic Scenes at the Nomination.

THE FINAL ADJOURNMENT

BALTIMORE, Wednesday, June 8.

The Convention reassembled at 10 o'clock this morning, President DENISON in the Chair.

A prayer was offered up by Rev. Mr. GADDIS, a delegate from Hamilton County, Ohio.

The hall was, if possible, more crowded than on yesterday, every nook and corner being occupied.

REPORTS OF COMMITTEES.

The President called for reports from the Committees.

The Committee on the Order of Business by its Chairman, Mr. DAY, of Connecticut, reported a set of rules to control the convention in the transaction of its business, which were read, amended and adopted.

THE COMMITTEE ON CREDENTIALS.

PRESTON KING, of New-York, said: The Committee on Credentials, after a patient hearing of the representations made by gentlemen who have appeared as delegates to this convention, wherever there has been a question of their right to a seat here, from whatever cause that question may have arisen, have come to conclusions, which they report as the report of the committee, upon the main questions of which there has been entire unanimity. But upon some points there will be a minority report. There will also be two or three points upon which I differ from the report, but desiring that it should be regarded as the report of the committee, I concluded to agree to it as such, but to move to amend the report on my individual responsibility as a member of the convention. The report of the majority of the committee was in substance, as follows:

First—That the delegations from the States of Maine, New-Hampshire, Massachusetts, Connecticut, Vermont, Rhode Island, New-York, New-Jersey, Pennsylvania, Delaware, Maryland, Ohio, Kentucky, Indiana, Illinois, Iowa, Minnesota, Oregon, California, Kansas and West Virginia are all regular, and are admitted to seats with the rights and privileges of members, except one district of Pennsylvania, which had elected four instead of two members. The committee admit the two who received the largest number of votes as delegates, and the other two as alternates.

Second—That there being two delegations from the State of Missouri claiming seats, the committee recommend that those styling themselves the Union Radical delegation be awarded the seats. [Applause and cheering.]

Third—That the delegates from Virginia, Tennessee, Louisiana and Arkansas be admitted to all the privileges of the floor, except that of voting.

Fourth—That the persons presenting themselves as delegates from the State of South Carolina are not entitled to the rights of delegates on the floor.

Mr. KING then asked that the convention receive the report of the minority of the committee, after which he would make his motion to amend the report.

Mr. E. STEVENSON, of West Virginia—I desire to state that this minority report was prepared very hurriedly this morning. The committee deliberated until long after midnight, and I have not been able to obtain the signatures to report that I expected to obtain.

The minority report was then read as follows:

The undersigned concur in the report of the majority of the Committee on Credentials, except that portion which proposes to exclude from the privilege of voting in the convention the delegates from the States of Virginia, Louisiana, Arkansas, Tennessee and Florida, and from the Territories of Colorado, Nevada, New-Mexico, Dakotah and Montana; therefore, the undersigned recommend that the delegates from the said States and Territories be entitled to vote on all questions brought before the convention,

Which is respectfully submitted,

W. E. STEVENSON, West Virginia.
HIRAM SMITH, Oregon.

PRESTON KING—I am informed that the minority were not entirely agreed, but that the member from Kansas desires also to submit a minority report. I ask that he be allowed to submit that report.

A. H. INSLEY, of Kansas, presented the following minority report:

The undersigned respectfully desires to present a minority report from the Committee on Credentials, of which he is a member, in relation to the admission of the delegates from the Territories of Nebraska, Colorado, and Nevada, to seats and votes in this convention. Differing with the majority of the committee only on this point, it is fitting that I present my reasons for the course herein urged. The first and foremost is the fact that the three Territories named are about to pass from the territorial condition of dependence on the General Government, to that of State Sovereignties, subordinate only to the supreme law and necessities of the nation. The present Congress having passed enabling acts whereby these Territories receive a pledge of admission into the Federal Union, provided only they come clothed in the robes of freedom, and the people of those Territories having gladly accepted the supreme condition, are even now engaged in the work of State organization, with a fair prospect of completing the same in time to wheel into line with the other loyal States, and by voting for the nominees of the Union party, and politically as they have already done materially and by arms in the establishment of the national authority and securing the perpetuity of the Union.

Secondly—The recognition of the delegates from these Territories by the Convention will very materially aid the party of nationality and freedom in these communities. Our interests lie with the movements now being made under the authority of Congress for their organization and admission. It is our duty, both as loyal men seeking the supreme good of the nation, and as members of a great party, having that end for its primary purpose, to give all the aid and strength we legitimately may for the furtherance of that object. It is believed that the recognition of these delegates will materially benefit our cause as well as the State movements now pending. The loyalty of these Territories none can question. Nebraska has sent her citizens to the field, and from Donelson to Chattanooga their courage and sacrifices have been freely offered. Colorado makes the proud boast of never having had a Copperhead in her Territorial Legislature. She has a prouder boast than this in that New-Mexican campaign, where her volunteers won such imperishable honors, saving thereby the immensely important mountain Territories of the far West from being overrun by the Texan rebels, and securing uninterrupted our communication with the Pacific. For Nevada, let the Treasury of the Sanitary Commission speak in praise. Under the wise rule of Gov. NYE that distant Territory is emerging as not only one of the richest, but one of the most loyal of States. For this reason I urge the admission of these gentlemen with all the rights of delegates into this convention. Let me refer you as a precedent for such action to the course taken in relation to that State (Kansas) which I have the honor in part to represent here. The Republican Convention of 1856 admitted its delegates to seats and votes. It was then seeking admission into the Union under what was known as the Topeka Constitution. Again at Chicago, in 1860, was the same course adopted. Its admission was pending before Congress, nor was it recognized as a State until the party of freedom, under the lead of ABRAHAM LINCOLN, obtained power. It will not do in this hour, with this precedent, with the facts before us, and strong probability presented by these Commissioners of being enabled to swell the vote of the next President of the United States, ABRAHAM LINCOLN, by the welcome addition of three members to the Electoral College, to ignore the claims of Nebraska, Colorado and Nevada.

Mr. PRESTON KING—There was scarcely a proposition in the report of the majority of the committee from which some member did not dissent. There were three propositions on which I dissented, and I move to amend the report, to substitute for the proposition of the majority report, that the delegation known as the Unconditional Union Delegation from Missouri, be admitted as delegates with the Radical Union Delegation from that State; that when the delegates agree they cast the vote to which the State is entitled, and when they do not agree the vote of the State shall not be cast. The majority report proposes to admit the delegates without voting, and in my amendment I propose also to give all the delegates admitted the rights and privileges of delegates without any exception, but that the District of Columbia and the territories shall be entitled to two votes only, and that no State, or District, or Territory, be allowed to cast more votes than they have delegates present in the Convention, or in any case more than they are entitled to under the rules of the Convention. I move this proposition as a substitute for the report of the Committee on these subjects.

A member requested that the amendment should be divided so as to take a motion upon the different propositions separately.

Mr. KING—I prefer that they should be taken together. But any member of the Convention has a right to call for a division.

Mr. SCHOLES, of Wisconsin—In order that we may have a properly constituted convention, I would suggest that, before we proceed to vote upon these disputed questions, that portion of the report of the committee which is unanimously presented, be adopted by this convention. That will admit as delegates all who come here without question, and will give us the power to vote upon any questions that may arise.

The President stated that there was a pending question, which he ruled to be susceptible of division.

Mr. REEDER, of Pennsylvania—I suggest to the Chairman of the committee to withdraw his motion to allow the report of the majority, as far as it is unanimous, to be adopted, so that we delegates from uncontested States may be admitted, that we may know who shall be entitled to vote should there be a call of the States making. I prefer not to withdraw this motion, but I will modify my own motion so as to make that the first clause of my amendment.

The majority report, so far as it related to uncontested States, was adopted by the convention.

Mr. KING—The second portion of my amendment is to that portion of the report relating to the State of Missouri, which determines that the Radical Union delegation from that State shall be admitted, and they only, as the delegates to be from that State. The original clause is this: That the delegation known as the Radical Union delegation from Missouri be admitted as the delegates to represent that State. My motion is to amend by substituting that the delegation from Missouri be admitted with the delegates of the Radical Union delegation, and that where the delegations agree, they shall cast the vote of the State, and where they do not agree, the vote of the State shall not be cast. I think that the suggestion of this proposition is all that is required by this convention. Unless this suggestion is such as meets their approbation, no argument could carry it through. I make the motion in the spirit of brotherhood, and union and harmony, and in the determination to strike down every common enemy, and to strike down nobody else. I suppose it was wisest and best to admit these delegates as brethren. I would not have offered this proposition that I have made in ordinary times. I do not propose that it shall be a precedent. I hope we shall never again be in a condition of affairs in this country, and I do not believe we ever shall be, when an action now may be quoted as a precedent. This is my proposition. I will not debate it. There is a right and a wrong in that case. There is a delegation here duly accredited, and there is but one, and it is the duty of the convention to ascertain which of these contesting delegations is that duly credited delegation holding credentials from an organized party association in that State. I aver from facts which none will dispute, that the radical delegation is the only true delegation here, and that the Unconditional Union delegation has no constituency in that State embracing any considerable element in the natural history of that State. The Radical delegation represent the only Republican organization which existed at the time the Convention was called to send delegates to this National Convention. There was no other organization except a rebel organization existing in the State of Missouri.

Mr. BRECKINRIDGE—I wish to move an amendment to the amendment to suit both parties, that the rule be that they shall divide. I move to amend the amendment offered by the gentleman from New-York, to the effect that, instead of silencing both parties from Missouri, when they cannot agree, that they may then divide the vote.

VOICES—"Question," "question."

Dr. BRECKINRIDGE—The gentleman from Connecticut has made a statement of facts at second-hand, and he has no personal knowledge of them except as they were told to the committee, of which he was a member. I also live remotely from Missouri. But Kentucky is a great deal nigher Missouri than Connecticut, and I suppose he will admit that Kentucky and Missouri thought not exactly alike, are more alike than Missouri and Connecticut. I therefore suppose that my knowledge is as good as his. With the greatest possible respect, both for his statements of facts and his statements of inference, I have not a particle of doubt, but say to you to-day, if I were in the profession of the law, I would risk my head upon making twelve of you find everything he has stated is either unfounded or wrongly considered. If you pursue the course undertaken to be recommended by that gentleman, you will get Missouri into a condition, if possible, worse than it has already been in. But for compromise sake, if you choose to admit both delegations without asking whether this or that is radical, then it appears to me that as it is perfectly certain that one or the other is entitled to vote, it is absurd in us to undertake to silence a State that is truly represented here by somebody, and that the proper course will be for them, if they will, to agree to take half of the vote of the State from each delegation. I think this is the only way to do under the circumstances. My object is, if you let both in, not to silence both, but to let them divide this vote so that we can get the votes of the State; for undoubtedly the State is entitled to representation by somebody.

Mr. DORSEY, of Ohio, said—I want simply to call attention to the fact that this convention for the purpose of deciding questions which could not be decided in mass convention, appointed a Committee on Credentials, because they knew they could better judge of facts which would be presented by a small number of men to such committee than a mass convention could judge of the same facts. Under the lead of its excellent chairman, the gentleman from New-York, that committee had a prolonged session of many hours, and had brought before it gentlemen representing both sides of the contest in the State of Missouri, and with great deliberation they weighed the arguments of both contesting parties. The result from the deliberations of that committee, based upon the statements of the contesting parties, the convention has, in the report of the majority, and I beg leave to say to this convention, with all respect for the honorable chairman, and without violation of any of the proprieties of that committee rule, that the very same proposition presented here before the convention this morning, was presented before that committee and voted down. Why so? Is it proper then to present the same question to this convention? The question having been decided in the committee ought not to be brought up here.

The Committee voted down the very proposition which the honorable Chairman now proposes to the Convention.

Mr. BRECKINRIDGE, of Missouri, was announced as having the floor.

Mr. LANE, of Kansas—Who is Mr. BRECKINRIDGE, of Missouri?

VOICES—He is not a delegate.

[Mr. BRECKINRIDGE was one of the excluded delegates.]

Mr. CURTIS, of New-York—I submit that this convention is at present composed only of those delegates who are here without any contest.

The Chair said that the gentleman from New-York was correct.

Mr. CURTIS said the Missouri question was no new question either to this convention or to the country. It is a question which is almost coeval with that of the most profound reverence for our eminent friend from Kentucky (BRECKINRIDGE,) which is well known and understood all over the country. The Missouri question is one which must be met and settled, and nowhere can it be so well met and conclusively settled as in this National Convention of Union men. [Applause.] We yesterday appointdd a committee, as the gentleman from Ohio has so well stated, for the purpose of making these inquiries of details which it was impossible for this convention to make. We have the report of that committee, which is unanimous, with the exception of my honored friend from New-York, that the Radical delegation from Missouri shall be admitted, with the privilege of voting and with every other privilege. The question has been settled and reported on by that committee, why should we admit the Radical delegation? I take my words from the mouth of my most honored friend from New-York, who here introduced this question. It is because we wish to strengthen the Union sentiment of the country. [Applause.] It is because we wish to strengthen the brave men who have bared their breasts in battle and who have stood firm since the outbreak of this war. It is for that reason that I implore you to give no uncertain sound. My most eminent friend says we have also been true. I freely confess we have not had the bitter sufferings they have had in the Border States, but that we may be strengthened at home and that the army all along the line with SHERMAN and GRANT may hear of no uncertain sound from us at the rear. As a practical contest there is no man in this convention who does not know that the admission of the Radical delegates from Missouri is the practical settlement of this question, and the practical adhesion of the great national party of this country to the policy and measures which will save the country.

Mr. MACE, of Indiana, moved that the proposed amendment be laid upon the table.

Mr. SMITHERS, of Delaware—I call for the previous question.

Mr. STEVENS, of Pennsylvania—Do I understand the previous question to be called upon the whole proposition, or only upon this amendment.

VOICES—Only on the amendment.

Mr. STEVENS—Then Pennsylvania seconds the amendment.

VOICES—Read the amendment.

CHAIRMAN—The amendment is that where two sets of delegates from Missouri cannot agree, that instead of not voting at all they shall divide the vote.

The question on the amendment to the report was lost.

CHAIRMAN—The question now is on adopting the report of the majority on the Missouri question.

After further debate Mr. BRANDAGE moved the previous question on the Missouri case.

Yeas—Maine, 14; New-Hampshire, 10; Vermont, 10; Massachusetts, 24; Rhode Island, 8; Connecticut, 12; New-York, 88; New-Jersey, 14; Pennsylvania, 49; Delaware, 6; Maryland, 14; Kentucky, 21; Ohio, 42; Indiana, 26; Illinois, 32; Michigan, 16; Wisconsin, 16; Minnesota, 8; California, 10; Oregon, 6; Western Virginia, 10; Kansas, 6.

Nays—Pennsylvania, 3; Kentucky, 1.

Total—Yeas, 440; Nays, 4.

Then said the President, the Radical delegation of Missouri are admitted as full delegates to the Convention. The question is now upon the second clause of the amendment.

Mr. KING—The second clause is that the delegates from Virginia, Tennessee, Louisiana, Florida, Arkansas, and from all the Territories and the District of Columbia, who shall be admitted to this Convention shall be allowed all the privileges of delegates, including that of voting. But that the Territories and the District of Columbia shall be allowed two votes, and no State, or Territory, shall be allowed to cast more votes than it has delegates here, or more than it is entitled to under the rules of the Convention.

Mr. STEVENS, of Pennsylvania, moved the previous question, and the main question was ordered to be taken.

Mr. KING—The remainder of the report, which has not been adopted, is as follows: That the delegations from Virginia, Tennessee, Louisiana, Florida and Arkansas be admitted with all the rights and privileges of delegates to this committee, except that of voting; that the delegation asking admission from South Carolina be not admitted to the convention; that the delegations from the organized Territories and the District of Columbia be admitted to the convention, with all the rights and privileges of delegates, except that of voting.

Mr. LANE, of Kansas, asked for a division of the question, so as to take the vote separately upon Tennessee, Arkansas, Louisiana, Nebraska, Colorado and Nevada.

Subsequently he modified his demand for a division, so that the question should first be taken on the three States—Tennessee, Louisiana and Arkansas.

Mr. ELDEN, of Indiana, demanded a further division, so as to take the vote on Tennessee separately.

The question was stated to be upon admitting the delegation from Tennessee.

A call for a vote by States was made and the House voted, Yeas 310, Nays 153, as follows:

YEAS—Maine 3, Vermont 2, Rhode Island 2, Connecticut 10, New-York 66, New-Jersey 14, Pennsylvania 31, Delaware 1, Maryland 1, Missouri 19, Kentucky 4, Ohio 42, Indiana 24, Illinois 32, Michigan 2, Wisconsin 15, Iowa 9, Minnesota 1, California 10, Oregon 6, West Virginia 10, Kansas 6.

NAYS—Maine 11, New-Hampshire 10, Vermont 8, Massachusetts 24, Rhode Island 6, Connecticut 2, Pennsylvania 21, Delaware 4, Maryland 13, Missouri 3, Indiana 2, Michigan 14, Wisconsin 1, Iowa 7, Minnesota 7.

Mr. LANE, of Kansas, now moved that Kansas and Louisiana be admitted by acclamation.

Mr. STEVENS, of Pennsylvania, objected.

The question was stated to be upon admitting the delegation from Arkansas and Louisiana, with the right of voting.

Mr. STEVENS demanded that the vote be taken by States, and the demand was seconded. The vote resulted—ayes, 307; nays, 167.

The question was then taken upon that portion of the report as amended, and it was agreed to.

The question was stated upon admitting the delegations of the Territories of Colorado, Nebraska and Nevada, with the right of voting.

That portion of the report was then agreed to as amended.

Mr. SCAMMON, of Illinois—What is to be done with Virginia, South Carolina and Florida?

PRESTON KING—The only portion of the report which remains is that which relates to admitting the delegates from Virginia and Florida, without the right of voting; the rejection of the delegation from South Carolina, and admitting the delegates of the territories other than those already passed upon, and of the District of Columbia without the right to vote.

The remaining portion of the report was agreed to, amid great applause.

THE PLATFORM.

Mr. RAYMOND, of New-York, from the Committee on Resolutions, reported the following resolutions:

Resolved, That it is the highest duty of every American citizen to maintain against all their enemies the integrity of the Union, and the paramount authority of the Constitution and laws of the United States, and that laying aside all differences and political opinions, we pledge ourselves as Union men, animated by a common sentiment, and aiming at a common object, to do everything in our power to aid the Government in quelling by force of arms the rebellion now raging against its authority, and in bringing to the punishment due to their crimes the rebels and traitors arrayed against it. [Prolonged applause.]

Resolved, That we approve the determination of the Government of the United States not to compromise with rebels, or to offer any terms of peace except such as may be based upon an "unconditional surrender" of their hostility and a return to their just allegiance to the Constitution and laws of the United States; and that we call upon the Government to maintain this position and to prosecute the war with the utmost possible vigor to the complete suppression of the rebellion, in full reliance upon the self-sacrifices, the patriotism, the heroic valor and the undying devotion of the American people to their country and its free institutions. [Applause.]

Resolved, That as Slavery was the cause, and now constitutes the strength, of this rebellion, and as it must be always and everywhere hostile to the principles of Republican Government, justice and the national safety demand its utter and complete extirpation from the soil of the Republic; [applause,] and that we uphold and maintain the acts and proclamations by which the Government, in its own defence, has aimed a death-blow at this gigantic evil. We are in favor, furthermore, of such an amendment to the Constitution, to be made by the people in conformity with its provisions, as shall terminate and forever prohibit the existence of Slavery within the limits or the jurisdiction of the United States. [Applause.]

Resolved, That the thanks of the American people are due to the soldiers and sailors of the army and the navy, [applause,] who have periled their lives in defence of their country and in vindication of the honor of the flag; that the nation owes to them some permanent recognition of their patriotism and their valor, and ample and permanent provision for those of their survivors who have received disabling and honorable wounds in the service of the country; and that the memories of those who have fallen in its defence shall be held in grateful and everlasting remembrance. [Loud applause.]

Resolved, That we approve and applaud the practical wisdom, the unselfish patriotism and unswerving fidelity to the Constitution and the principles of American liberty with which ABRAHAM LINCOLN has discharged, under circumstances of unparalleled difficulty, the great duties and responsibilities of the Presidential office; that we approve and indorse, as demanded by the emergency and essential to the preservation of the nation, and as within the Constitution, the measures and acts which he has adopted to defend the nation against its open and secret foes; that we approve especially the proclamation of emancipation and the employment as Union soldiers of men heretofore held in slavery [applause]; and that we have full confidence in his determination to carry these and all other constitutional measures essential to the salvation of the country into full and complete effect.

Resolved, That we deem it essential to the general welfare that harmony should prevail in the national councils, and we regard as worthy of public confidence and official trust those only who cordially indorse the principles proclaimed in these resolutions and which should characterize the administration of the Government. [Applause.]

Resolved, That the Government owes to all men employed in its armies, without regard to distinction of color, the full protection of the laws of war. [applause] and that any violations of these laws, or of the usages of civilized nations in the time of war, by the rebels now in arms, should be made the subject of full and prompt redress. [Prolonged applause.]

Resolved, That the foreign immigration which in the past has added so much to the wealth and development of resources and increase of power to this nation—the asylum of the oppressed of all nations—should be fostered and encouraged by a liberal and just policy.

Resolved, That we are in favor of the speedy construction of the railroad to the Pacific.

Resolved, That the national faith pledged for the redemption of the public debt must be kept inviolate, and that for this purpose we recommend economy and rigid responsibility in the public expenditures, and a vigorous and just system of taxation: that it is the duty of every loyal State to sustain the credit and promote the use of the national currency. [Applause.]

Resolved, That we approve the position taken by the Government that the people of the United States can never regard with indifference the attempt of any European Power to overthrow by force or to supplant by fraud, the institutions of any Republican Government on the Western Continent; [prolonged applause;] and that they will view with extreme jealousy, as menacing to the peace and independence of this our country, the efforts of any such Power to obtain new footholds for Monarchical Governments, sustained by a foreign military force in near proximity to the United States. [Long-continued applause.]

The reading of the resolution elicited the wildest outbursts of enthusiasm, especially the emancipation and Anti-Slavery sentiments enunciated.

The mention of the name of ABRAHAM LINCOLN was received with tremendous cheering, the whole house rising and waving hats and handkerchiefs.

The resolution indorsing the Monroe doctrine was also received with great applause.

On motion of Mr. BUSHNELL, of Connecticut, the resolutions were adopted by acclamation.

THE NOMINATIONS.

Mr. DELANO, of Ohio—I move that this convention now proceed to the nomination of candidates for President and Vice President of the United States.

The Chairman stated the motion.

Mr. CAMERON—I move the following as a substitute for the motion of the gentleman from Ohio.

The Chairman directed the Secretary to read the resolution.

Resolved, That ABRAHAM LINCOLN, of Illinois, be declared the choice of the Union party for President, [applause,] and HANNIBAL HAMLIN, of Maine, be the candidate for Vice President of the same party.

Cries of "No, no."

A VOICE—Divide the resolution.

Mr. CRESWELL, of Maryland—I call for a division.

Mr. STONE, of Iowa—I ask if I can make an amendment to that resolution.

The Chairman said the resolution of Mr. CAMERON was now the question before the convention.

Mr. STONE—I move to lay it on the table. Carried.

Mr STONE—I now move that ABRAHAM LINCOLN, of Illinois, be the unanimous nominee of the convention.

Cries of "Question" and great confusion.

The CHAIRMAN—Will the gentleman listen for one moment. The gentleman from Iowa moved that a resolution offered by the gentleman from Pennsylvania (CAMERON) be laid on the table. That has been carried. The Chair then recognized Mr. COOK, of Illinois, as having the floor.

Mr. STEVENS, of Pennsylvania—I called for the vote by States before the vote was declared to the House.

Mr. STONE, of Iowa, claimed the floor.

Mr. STEVENS—I have not yielded the floor.

The CHAIRMAN—Does the gentleman from Pennsylvania insist upon a call of the States, upon the motion to lay on the table the resolution of Mr. CAMERON?

MANY VOICES—State the question.

The CHAIR—The gentleman from Iowa moved to lay upon the table the substitute offered by Gen. CAMERON, of Pennsylvania, and Mr. STEVENS informs the Chair that before that motion was put to the convention he moved a call of the States under the rules. Before the announcement of a vote, a delegate has a right to move a call by States, that being so the convention will now come to the question of laying on the table the substitute offered by Mr. CAMERON. Upon that the States were ordered to be called.

Mr. CRESSWELL, of Maryland—I call for a division of the question.

Mr. GOLDSBOROUGH, of Maryland, also called for a division.

The CHAIRMAN—The question is shall the resolution offered by Gen. CAMERON as a substitute be laid upon the table. The Secretary will proceed with the call.

Mr. BRECKINRIDGE—I wish to make a motion concerning the whole of this subject, and I hope the house will hear me for one moment. I want to modify it so as to lay the resolution on the table for the purpose of declaring ABRAHAM LINCOLN the nominee by acclamation.

Mr. STEVENSON, of Indiana—I desire to know what has become of the vote to lay, the substitute of Mr. CAMERON on the table.

The CHAIRMAN—That is now before the convention. The Secretary will call the roll of the States for the purpose of knowing whether it will be laid upon the table.

Mr. LANE, of Kansas—I appeal to the gentleman from Pennsylvania, with the consent of the convention, to withdraw his resolution. It places us in a very awkward predicament. I hope Gen. CAMERON, consulting the best wishes of the country, will withdraw his resolution. Let us vote upon the motion put by the gentleman from Iowa.

Mr. STONE, of Iowa—Hurrah for LINCOLN.

Mr. CAMERON—To save all this trouble to gentlemen who seem to wish to show their hands here I will withdraw it. [Applause.]

The CHAIRMAN—Mr. COOK, of Illinois, has the floor.

Mr. CAMERON, of Pennsylvania—I will withdraw it, or amend by moving that this convention nominate by acclamation ABRAHAM LINCOLN for a second term.

Mr. STONE, of Iowa—The gentleman is cheating me out of my motion; I object.

Laughter—Cries of "order," "order," "question," "question."

Mr. LANE, of Kansas—Hurrah for STONE.

The CHAIRMAN—Mr. CAMERON's motion to amend is not in order. It must be an absolute withdrawal, or none at all. Does he withdraw his resolution.

Mr. CAMERON—I will modify my resolution to make it "nominate ABRAHAM LINCOLN by acclamation."

Mr. STONE, of Iowa—That won't do. You must withdraw.

The CHAIRMAN—The gentleman from Pennsylvania has not answered the question of the Chair. Has the resolution been withdrawn or not?

Mr. CAMERON—I want to modify.

The CHAIRMAN—That is not a definite answer, and cannot be recognized as such by the Chair. The question before the convention is upon the resolution offered by Mr. CAMERON. A call of the States is demanded.

Mr. RAYMOND, of New-York—I understand that the question before the convention is the substitute offered by Gen. CAMERON for one which he offered and afterward withdrew, and that the motion now is that ABRAHAM LINCOLN be nominated for the Presidency. I desire to say one word upon the manner in which it is proposed to be done. I believe that there is no man in this convention who will not, however the vote may be taken, give his vote in just one way. It can therefore, be from no apprehension of the result of the vote that this particular way of taking it should be proposed, therefore, we may as well look to other considerations in deciding how we will take it. It is very well known that attempts have been made, though with no very great success, to create the impression that the nomination of ABRAHAM LINCOLN has to be pushed through this convention by some demonstration that will not look to the exercise of individual influence. Is it wise under these circumstances to take a vote by acclamation? It cannot possibly change the result. It can add no weight whatever to its earnestness, and it may give rise to false impressions. I suggest, and will move as a substitute a resolution embodying my view. I suggest that the wisest course would be to allow the roll of the States represented in this convention to be called, and let every delegation declare its vote. I believe there will be a unanimous vote from every delegation precisely to the same effect. I think the effect of that vote will be greater than one taken by acclamation. It can be reinforced, as it will be reinforced, by this convention, and throughout the country by the loud acclamations of the American people; and now I move, as a substitute for the motion of the gentleman from Pennsylvania, that the roll of the States be called, and that each delegation be called upon to record its vote. [Applause.]

Mr. CAMERON—I accept the modification.

Mr. COOK, of Illinois—Mr. President, the State of Illinois again presents to the loyal people of this nation, for President of the United States, ABRAHAM LINCOLN—God bless him!

Mr. CAMERON—I desire to accept the modification of the gentleman of New-York.

Cries of "Roll, roll," "Question," &c.

The CHAIR—The gentleman from Ohio moved that this convention proceed to the nomination of candidates for President and Vice-President. Upon that a resolution was offered by Gen. CAMERON that has been discussed. Upon that the gentleman from New-York (RAYMOND) moves we proceed to the nomination of a candidate for President alone. I ask the gentleman from Ohio whether he accepts that as a substitute for his motion.

Mr. DELANO—It was in full comprehension of the necessity of having an individual expression of opinion in favor of ABRAHAM LINCOLN that I made my motion, and that there should be no misapprehension, and no claim that he had been nominated by clamor, that public sentiment had been suppressed, that I desired the nomination as indicated by my resolution. For no man desires his nomination more than I. I accept the resolution offered by the gentleman from New-York as a substitute for my own.

The Chair stated that the question was to proceed to a nomination for President by a call of the States.

After further debate, and great confusion, the question was put on Mr. RAYMOND's substitute, which was adopted.

The convention then proceeded to ballot for President, which resulted as follows:

For Mr. Lincoln—Maine, 14; New-Hampshire, 10; Vermont, 10; Massachusetts, 24; Rhode Island, 8; Connecticut, 12; New-York, 66; New-Jersey, 14; Pennsylvania, 52; Delaware, 6; Maryland, 14; Louisiana, 14; Arkansas, 10; Tennessee, 15; Kentucky, 22; Ohio, 42; Indiana 26; Illinois, 32; Michigan, 16; Wisconsin, 16; Iowa, 16; Minnesota, 8; California, 10; Oregon, 6; West Virginia, 10; Kansas, 6; Nebraska, 6; Colorado, 6; Nevada, 6. Total, 497.

For Gen. Grant—Missouri, 22.

On motion of Mr. HUME, of Missouri, the vote was declared unanimous.

The enthusiasm was perfectly indescribable, the whole convention being on their feet, shouting, and the band playing "Hail Columbia."

After the nomination the Chairman read a dispatch from the Secretary of War, giving the good news from Gen. HUNTER, which was received with great cheering.

The convention resolved to proceed to vote for a candidate for Vice-President.

The following names were presented:

DANIEL MACE, of Indiana, presented the name of ANDREW JOHNSON, of Tennessee.

Mr. STONE, of Iowa, seconded the motion.

Mr. CAMERON, of Pennsylvania, offered the name of HANNIBAL HAMLIN.

Mr. TREMAINE, of New-York, in behalf of a portion of the delegation, presented DANIEL S. DICKINSON.

Mr. MAYNARD, of Tennessee, advocated the claims of ANDREW JOHNSON.

Mr. TREMAINE, of New-York, made an eloquent appeal in favor of the nomination of DANIEL S. DICKINSON. His remarks were received with great enthusiasm.

Great impatience was manifested to vote.

The President announced the following names as being before the convention:

ANDREW JOHNSON, of Tennessee.
HANNIBAL HAMLIN, of Maine.
L. H. ROUSSEAU, of Kentucky.
DANIEL S. DICKINSON, of New-York.

The House then proceeded to ballot.

Maine, New-Hampshire, Vermont, Connecticut, New-York, New-Hampshire, New-Jersey, Pennsylvania, Delaware, Maryland, Louisiana, Arkansas, Missouri, Kentucky, Ohio, Indiana, Illinois, Michigan, Iowa, California, Oregon, West Virginia, Kansas, Nebraska, Colorado and Nevada voted entire for Johnson. Massachusetts voted Johnson 21; Dickinson 3. Rhode Island, Johnson, 7; Dickinson, 1. Wisconsin, Johnson, 2; Dickinson, 10; Hamlin, 4. Minnesota, Dickinson, 3; Hamlin, 5. The total vote was Johnson, 492; Dickinson, 17; Hamlin, 9. Previous to the vote being announced, Johnson had 200; Dickinson, 113; Hamlin, 145; Butler, 28; Rosseau, 21; Burnside, 2; Colfax, 6; Col. Colt, 2; Tod, 2, and King, 1; but the States changed their votes before the announcement was made.

The Chair announced the next business in order was the election of a National Committee, and the States were called to name the same, as follows:

NATIONAL COMMITTEE.

Maine, Samuel F. Hersey; New-Hampshire, John B. Clark; Vermont, Abraham B. Gardner; Massachusetts, William Claflin; Rhode Island, Thomas G. Turner; Connecticut, N. J. Sperry, New-York, H. J. Raymond; New-Jersey, Marcus L. Ward; Pennsylvania, not appointed yet; Delaware, N. B. Smithers; Maryland, H. W. Hoffman; Virginia, W. H. Wallace; Florida, Calvin S. Robinson; Louisiana, Cuthbert Bullit; Arkansas, Jas. S. Johnston; Missouri, S. H. Boyd; Tennessee, Jos. S. Fowler; Kentucky, R. K. Williams; Ohio, G. V. Senter; Indiana, J. D. Defrees: Illinois, Burt C. Cook; Michigan, R. Giddings; Wisconsin, S. Judd; Iowa, D. B. Stubbs; Minnesota, Thomas Simpson; California, not named yet; Oregon, Erasmus D. Shattuck; West Virginia, A. W. Campbell; Kansas, James H. Lane; Colorado, James P. Taylor: Nebraska, W. H. H. Waters; Nevada, H. D. Morgan; Dacotah, S. M. Binney; New-Mexico, John W. Kerr; Montana, N. P. Lankford; Washington, Arthur A. Denin; Idaho, W. H. Wallace; Arizona, James S. Turner; District of Columbia, James T. Combs.

Mr. KING, of New-York, offered a resolution returning thanks to the President and officers of the convention for the able and satisfactory manner in which they had performed the duties assigned them.

The resolution was adopted.

A resolution was also adopted returning thanks to the Mayor and City Council of Baltimore for the excellent arrangements they had made for the accommodation of the convention.

On a motion for a final adjournment being made, the President in a few eloquent remarks congratulated the convention on the happy conclusion of their labors, and returned his thanks for the complimentary resolution that had been passed.

The convention then adjourned *sine die*.

The Union National Committee.

BALTIMORE, Wednesday, June 8.

The Union National Committee appointed by the convention met at BARNUM's hotel, this evening.

On motion of Gen. LANE, of Kansas, HENRY J. RAYMOND, of New-York, was elected Chairman, and E. MCPHERSON, of Pennsylvania, Secretary.

The committee adjourned to meet in Washington on Friday.

Mass Meeting in Baltimore.

BALTIMORE, Wednesday, June 8—Evening.

A great mass meeting to ratify the nominations is now being held in Monument-square. The Mayor of the city is presiding, and Messrs. MAYNARD and BROWNLOW, of Tennessee; GADDIS, of Ohio; Ex-Mayor SWAN, and others, are the speakers. Resolutions were adopted cordially indorsing and ratifying the nomination of President, and commending the same to the loyal voters throughout the country.

THE DRAFT.

Report of Provost-Marshal-General Fry—Recommendation that the $300 Clause be Repealed.

WASHINGTON, Wednesday, June 8.

The following was laid by the Speaker before the House to-day, and was referred to the Committee on Military Affairs:

To the Senate and House of Representatives:

I have the honor to submit, for the consideration of Congress, a letter and inclosure from the Secretary of War, with my concurrence in the recommendation therein made.

(Signed) ABRAHAM LINCOLN.

WASHINGTON, D. C., June 6, 1864.

WAR DEPARTMENT, WASHINGTON CITY, June 7, 1864.

To the President:

SIR: I beg leave to submit to you a report made to me by the Provost-Marshal-General, showing the result of the draft now going on to fill the deficiency in the quotas of certain States, and recommending a repeal of the clause in the Enrollment Act, commonly known as "the three hundred dollar clause." The recommendation of the Provost-Marshal-General is approved by this Department; and I trust that it will be recommended by you to Congress.

The recent successes that have attended our arms leads to the hope that by maintaining our military strength and giving it such increase as the extended field of operations may require, an early termination of the war may be attained. But to accomplish this it is absolutely necessary that efficient means be taken with vigor and promptness to keep the army up to its strength and supply deficiencies occasioned by the losses in the field.

To that end resort must be had to a draft. But ample experience has now shown that the pecuniary exemption from service frustrates the object of the Enrollment Law by furnishing money instead of men.

An additional reason for repealing the exemption clause is, that it is contemplated to make the draft for comparatively a short term. The burden of military service will therefore be lightened. But its certainty of furnishing troops is an absolute essential to success.

I have the honor to be your obedient servant.

(Signed) EDWIN M. STANTON, Secretary of War.

WAR DEPARTMENT, PROVOST-MARSHAL-GENERAL'S OFFICE, WASHINGTON, D. C., June 6, 1864.

To Hon. Edwin M. Stanton, Secretary of War:

SIR: In accordance with the amended Enrollment Act, approved Feb. 24, 1864, and your orders on the subject, I am now conducting a draft in various sub-districts for their respective deficiencies on quotas of troops heretofore assigned. The results of this draft, so far as showing the reports to this date, are worthy of attention. They are briefly as follows:

Number of drafted men examined.............14,741
Number exempted for physical disability.......4,374
Number exempted for other causes..............2,632
Total number exempted.........................7,616
Number paid commutation money.................5,050
Number who have furnished substitutes.........1,416
Number held for personal service..............1,259

The last includes some who may yet pay commutation money.

Total not exempted............................7,725

These reports come from sub-districts in eight different States.

I invite your attention to the small proportion of soldiers being obtained under the existing law. I see no reason to believe that the army can be materially strengthened by draft so long as the $300 clause is in force; nor do I think it safe to assume that the commutation paid by a drafted man will enable the Government to procure a volunteer or substitute in his place.

I do not think that large bounties, by the United States, should be again resorted to for raising troops.

I recommend that the $300 clause, as it is known, be repealed.

I am, Sir, very respectfully, your obedient servant,

(Signed) JAMES B. FRY, Provost-Marshal-General.

Turf Record.

THE PATERSON, N. J. RACING MEETING—SECOND DAY—WEDNESDAY.

The brilliant success which attended the opening of the Spring meeting of the Passaic County Agricultural Society on Tuesday found no abatement yesterday. All the leading patrons, both of the running and trotting turf, were again present in full force, whilst those who have no direct interest in racing, but love it simply for the gratification that the keen contests of that noblest of animals—the horse—affords them, were nearly as largely represented as on the previous, the Derby Day. The 8 and 10 o'clock A. M. trains brought down ample living freights of sporting humanity, and the 11:45 special was literally jammed throughout its lengthy proportions; whilst the delightful ride over the fine turnpike road from Hoboken tempted numbers to adopt that method of reaching the course, and there was a splendid display of fast teams, buggies, barouches, tandems, four in hands, &c., mixed up with the humbler vehicles ordinarily met with on the Jersey roads.

The ladies, who in other lands are enthusiastic patrons of the sports of the turf, were, as on the previous day, present in large numbers.

Too much praise cannot be awarded to the Executive Committee of the Passaic Club—its energetic Chairman, Mr. COLT, and indefatigable Secretary, Mr. CHRISWELL—for the truly admirable manner in which all the arrangements of the meeting have thus far been carried out; the strictest punctuality in the time of starting has been observed—the strictest decorum preserved, and absolute exclusion of all improper or obnoxious characters stringently adhered to—detectives traveling with each train, and immediately sending back to New-York any persons whose presence would not be desirable or agreeable to the respectable classes of society. The course is kept absolutely free from intrusion during the running of the different races—no gambling has been permitted either on the track or its vicinity.

COPY.

PASSAIC COUNTY AGRICULTURAL SOCIETY, Wednesday, June 8, 1864.

MEETING OF EXECUTIVE COMMITTEE.

It appearing there has been collusion and fraud in relation to the running of the colt *Norfolk*, in the Jersey Derby, perpetrated by JAMES L. EOFF, with the knowledge, or by the collusion of CHARLES MARSH. It is unanimously resolved that the said JAMES L. EOFF, *be ruled off this track forever*; that CHARLES MARSH be censured for his complicity in the affair, and that the colt *Norfolk* be not allowed to start again on this track until the further order of this committee.

E. BOUDINOT COLT, Chairman Executive Committee.

R. B. CHISWELL, Secretary.

WEDNESDAY'S RACING.

The sports of the turf commenced to-day with the *Underwood*, a one-mile dash, for all ages, named in honor of Dr. UNDERWOOD, a gentleman whose name and fame are patent on every race course, North and South.

SUMMARY.

WEDNESDAY, June 8.

PREMIUM—The Underwood gift of $200, for all ages, one mile dash.

Mr. W. H. RENFRO, enters b f sister to *Tipperary*, 4 years old..........1
Mr. JOHN HUNTER, enters b c *Copeck* by *Lexington*, dam *Rosette* by imp. *Yorkshire*, 4 years old......2

The betting was all in favor of the filly, viz.: 100 to 80 on her. She had the inside place and was admirably ridden by "Honest old Abe," GILPATRICK tooling *Copeck*. In a good start the filly had a slight advantage, and took a decided lead as she rounded the turn, increasing it past the quarter to the half-mile, where *Copeck* vainly struggled to get up to her. The filly continued her lead round the turn, and up the home stretch was never approached in the run in, and won as she pleased, by two or three lengths.

Time—Quarter, 0:26¼; half-mile, 0:51¾; mile, 1:47¼.

SECOND RACE—SUMMARY.

SAME DAY.—The Nursery Stakes, a sweepstake premium of $200, for two-year olds; $100 entrance, $50 forfeit; three-quarter mile dash; to carry 90 pounds; four or more nominations to fill. Entries to be made on or before January 1, 1864. Free to all colts or fillies foaled in 1862. Closed with the following entries:

1. Mr. John Hunter enters ch. c. Waxlight by Colossus dam Waxwing by Wagner..........dr.
2. Mr. John Hunter enters b. f. Alexandria by imp. Sovereign, dam Miss Duke by imp. Glencoe dr.
3. Mr. John Hunter enters blk. f. La Noir by imp. Knight of St. George, dam Blonde by imp. Glencoe..........1
4. Mr. John Hunter enters ch. c. by imp. Knight of St. George, dam sister to Tangent by Wagner. dr.
5. Mr. James S. Watson enters b. c. by Lexington, dam Miss Julia by imp. Glencoe..........dr.
6. Mr. James S. Watson enters br. f. by Slasher, dam Pasta, by Revenue..........2

This race was reduced to a match between the pick of the two stables, Mr. HUNTER selecting his black filly, *La Noir*, and Mr. WATSON his *Revenue* filly—that excellent colored rider, ABE, having justly the mount on the black; and, as will be seen, again defeating his white rival, Jockey GILPATRICK, on Mr. WATSON's nomination, which was thought to be so good a thing that in the betting, $100 to $50, and ultimately 100 to 40 was freely laid on her. The story of the race is soon told. In a good start *La Noir* was first on her legs, and soon took a lead of a length, which she increased to two on reaching the quarter; from this point she opened the gap wider and wider to the turn into the home stretch, which she came up pulling hard, and passing the score the easiest of winners by four lengths. Time, 1.23. The first quarter was ran in 0.52¾, which is the fastest quarter ever done on this track.

THIRD RACE.

SAME DAY.—Premium of $400 for all ages; three-mile dash.

Mr. James S. Watson enters b. c. Capt. Moore, by imp. Bairownie, dam Jenny Rose, by imp. Glencoe..........Walked over.

FOURTH RACE.

SAME DAY.—Selling race of $300, for all ages, one and a quarter mile dash. Horses entered to be sold for $1,500, (no entries for a higher price,) to carry their proper weights; those entered to be sold for $1,000, allowed 7 pounds; if for $600, 14 pounds; if for $300, 21 pounds. The winner to be sold at auction immediately after the race. All over the price named in the entry to go to the society. The owner to retain his horse if he should not bring the price named in the entry. No penalties for other races won.

1. Mr. T. O. Smith enters b. h. Bill Davis, dam Rally, by Trustee, 5 years old. Price $600.... 0
2. Messrs. Bewie & Hall enter ch. h. by Red Eye, dam Sciene, 5 years old. Price $1,000.......... 0
3. Mr. W. H. Strong enters ch. h. Punch, by Mahomet, dam by Yorkshire, 5 years old. Price $600.......... 3
4. Mr. James S. Watson enters br. f. Miss Hays, by Lexington, dam Kate Hays, by imp. Albion, 4 years old. Price $600.......... 2
5. Mr. H. Hogans enters Zig-Zag, by Rurie, dam by Zenith, 4 years old. Price $1,300.......... 0
6. Mr. John Hunters b. c. Copeck, by Lexington, dam Rosette, by imp. Yorkshire, 4 years old. Price $1,000.......... 1

Time—2:18¼. The first quarter was done in 00:27¼, and the last mile in 1:51¼.

To-day, the last of the meeting, three races are on the cards, which are likely to be prolific of first-class running. In the post stake the renowned *Thunder* meets *Captain Moore* and *Fleetwing*.

From Fortress Monroe.

FORTRESS MONROE, Tuesday, May 7.

Lieut. PAYSON, Aid-de-Camp to Gen. DEVENS, arrived at Chesapeake Hospital last evening, wounded.

The steamer *Metamora* arrived at 1 P. M. from the White House with a few "sick" officers. They had not been in the front for several days, and brought no news whatever.

4 *P. M.*—The steamer *John A. Warner* Capt. CONE has arrived from Bermuda Hundreds. She reports no fighting was reported there.

No news had been received from Gen. GRANT. No cannonading had been heard.

DEATHS IN THE CHESAPEAKE HOSPITAL JUNE 5, 1864.

David Noakes, 13th Ind.	Wm A Goddard, 9th Maine.
James Goodrich, 14th N Y.	Henry M Park, 40th Mass.

DEATHS IN THE HAMPTON HOSPITAL, JUNE 5.

Corp Dan C Storrs, 11th Ct.	John Sellers, 96th Penn.
Thos D Cook, 11th Me.	Martin Russell, 118th N Y.
John Smith, 97th Penn.	Wm H Jones, 7th South Carolina—rebel.
Chas H Smith, 4th N H.	Robert Rozier, 11th South Carolina—rebel.
Clark Eastman, 3d N H.	
Wm Hull, 67th Ohio.	

JUNE 6.

Albert E Littlefield, 25th Massachusetts.	James A Mager, 115th N Y.
Sergt James H Harman, 9th Maine.	Chas McNab, 117th N Y.
Daniel Beaman, 11th Me.	Isaac McHamer, 55th Pa.
	Corp Lewis Hengle, 188th Pennsylvania.

Shot by a Soldier.

ALBANY, Wednesday, June 8.

A young man named JAMES MURRAY, of Brooklyn, was shot by a soldier at the depot in East Albany this evening, while getting off the cars.

The New-York Times.

VOL. XIII.—NO. 3983. NEW-YORK, WEDNESDAY, JUNE 29, 1864. PRICE THREE CENTS.

THE GREAT CAMPAIGN.

News from Gen. Grant to Monday Evening.

General Wilson Tearing Up More Railroads.

Gratifying News from General Hunter.

The Complete Success of his Expedition.

Immense Destruction of Railroads and Supplies.

IMPORTANT FROM SHERMAN.

An Attack on the Rebels at Kenesaw Mountain.

Our Troops Repulsed with a Loss of 2,500.

THE ENEMY'S POSITION VERY STRONG.

WASHINGTON, Tuesday, June 28.

To Major-Gen. Dix:

A dispatch from Lieut.-Gen. GRANT, dated yesterday, the 27th, at 3:30 P. M., at his headquarters, reports no operations in front except from our own guns, which fire into the bridge at Petersburgh from a distance of two thousand yards. The dispatch gives the following intelligence from rebel papers. A Petersburgh paper of the 25th inst. states that Gen. HUNTER is striking for Jackson River depot, about forty miles north of Salem, and says that if he reaches Covington, which they suppose he will do with most of his forces, but with loss of material, he will be safe.

The same paper accuses Gen. HUNTER of destroying a great amount of private property, and stealing a large number of wagons, horses and cattle.

The same paper also states that Gen. WILSON destroyed a train of cars, loaded with cotton and furniture, burned the depot buildings, &c., at Burkesville, and destroyed some of the track, and was still pushing South. All the railroads leading into Richmond are now destroyed, and some of them badly.

A dispatch from Gen. SHERMAN, received this morning, reports that yesterday, June 27, an unsuccessful attack was made by our forces on the enemy's position, which resulted in a loss of between two and three thousand. The following particulars are given.

Pursuant to my orders of the 24th inst. a diversion was made on each flank of the enemy especially down the Sandtown road. At 8 A. M. Gen. MCPHERSON attacked at the southwest end of Kenesaw, and Gen. THOMAS at a point about a mile further south. At the same time the skirmishers and artillery along the whole line kept up a sharp fire. Neither attack succeeded, though both columns reached the enemy's works which are very strong.

Gen. MCPHERSON reports his loss about 500, and Gen. THOMAS' about 2,000.

The loss is particularly heavy in general field officers. Gen. HARKER is reported mortally wounded; also, Col. DAN. MCCOOK, commanding a brigade; Col. RICE, Fifty-seventh Ohio, very seriously. Col. BARNHILL, Fortieth Illinois, and AUGUSTINE, Fifty-fifth Illinois, are killed.

Gen. MCPHERSON took one hundred prisoners and Gen. THOMAS about as many, but I do not suppose we inflicted a heavy loss on the enemy, as he kept clear behind his parapets.

No other military intelligence has been received by the department.

EDWIN M. STANTON,
Secretary of War.

GEN. HUNTER'S EXPEDITION.

[OFFICIAL.]

WASHINGTON, June 28, 1864—4 P. M.

Major-Gen. Dix:

The following dispatch has just been received from Gen. HUNTER:

"I have the honor to report that our expedition has been extremely successful, inflicting great injury upon the enemy, and victorious in every engagement. Running short of ammunition, and finding it impossible to collect supplies while in the presence of an enemy believed to be superior to our force in numbers, and constantly receiving reinforcements from Richmond and other points, I deemed it best to withdraw, and have succeeded in doing so without serious loss to this point, where we have met with abundant supplies of food. A detailed report of our operations will be forwarded immediately. The command is in excellent heart and health, and ready after a few days rest for service in any direction."

Nothing later than my telegram of this morning has been received from Gen. GRANT, or Gen. SHERMAN.

EDWIN M. STANTON,
Secretary of War.

From Gen. Grant's Army.

HEADQUARTERS OF THE ARMY OF THE POTOMAC, Monday, June 27—5 o'clock A. M.

An attack was made on BURNSIDE's line at about 11 o'clock on Saturday night, with the intention of driving back a working party who were engaged in digging intrenchments toward the enemy's front, so as to gain a better position in which to place guns to more effectually cover the rebel works. The firing was very brisk for about an hour, resulting in our men holding their ground and continuing their labors without any loss of consequence.

The usual amount of picket firing took place yesterday, it being a little more persistent in front of the Ninth Corps than at any other point.

It is usual to relieve picket line shortly after dark, and the rebels being generally on the alert at the least noise, invariably open fire in hope of being able to pick off some men while the change is being made.

It is seldom any harm results from these attacks, as the men have become so careful to screen themselves that it is next to impossible for the rebel sharpshooters to get a range on them.

The health of the troops is in the main good, considering the oppressively hot weather they have had to endure since their arrival here, and the scarcity of water in this section.

The Eighteenth Corps seem to have the greatest number of men in the hospital from the effects of the weather.

The colored troops are reported as being unaffected by the heat. Surgeon JACKSON, in charge of the Fourth Division Hospital, Ninth Corps, reports, that in that division only forty men out of four thousand were unfit for duty when they were put in front on Tuesday last to relieve the Second Corps. This tends to show how much better they can endure the scorching rays of the sun than white troops.

Appearances yesterday afternoon indicated that we should have a shower of rain. Black clouds appearing in the west, accompanied with a good deal of thunder, but we were disappointed. The storm passed off to the northeast, only a few drops falling in this vicinity.

FROM FORTRESS MONROE.

Sheridan's Passage of the James River.

FORTRESS MONROE, Monday, June 27.

The steamer *Highland Light* arrived here at 6 o'clock, from City Point.

She reports that all is quiet in front.

Gen. SHERIDAN's command met with a slight loss in an engagement with the enemy's forces at Wilson's Landing, but punished the enemy to a greater extent than our loss.

Gen. SHERIDAN will complete his crossing over the James River at sun-down to-night, which is being accomplished entirely by transports, and not by pontoons, as heretofore erroneously reported.

FORT MONROE, Sunday, June 26.

Mr. WILCOX, army correspondent of the New-York *Tribune*, arrived at Chesapeake Hospital yesterday, sick with typhoid fever.

The Fifty-eighth Pennsylvania Regiment left for home on thirty days' furlough this morning.

JAMES O. MELIS, of the Tenth New-Hampshire, died in the Chesapeake Hospital on the 25th.

ADMITTED IN HAMPTON HOSPITAL, JUNE 25.

Capt John F Kerrington, 117th New-York.	Capt J H B Smith, 139th New-York—wounded.
Lieut F P Johnson, 10th New-York.	Lieut Henry Churchill, 13th New-Haven—wounded.
Lieut J W Sourtleef, 5th U S Cavalry—wounded.	Capt D J Cary, 169th N Y—wounded.
Lieut Thos Mulchay, 139th New-York—wounded.	Capt C H Lawrence, 169th New-York—wounded.

DEATHS IN HAMPTON HOSPITAL—JUNE 26.

J J Mitchell, 11th Pennsylvania Cavalry.	Henry T Marsh, Peterboro battery—(rebel.)
H B Marcy, 11th Penn Cav.	H Johnson, 7th N H.
R Robushba, civilian.	R M Alden, 134th Ohio.
Geo Granger, 5th U S Cav.	J N Leonard, 1st Me Art.
Geo W Hayes, 26th Va (reb.)	F Debaigne, 2 Penn (brought dead.)
W Thompson, 100th Penn.	

Operations in Virginia.

From the Washington Republican, June 27.

Gen. HUNTER's movements have been carried on upon a grand scale, and so far as known down to this morning, have been highly successful, notwithstanding all the efforts of LEE to overtake and defeat him.

It is known in official quarters that Gen. HUNTER has adhered to the Virginia and Tennessee Railroad with a pertinacity unparalleled. He produced a consternation at Lynchburgh that the rebels in that vicinity will never forget.

While one portion of his force was engaged in tearing up the railroads, the other portion fought the enemy. HUNTER then pushed on westerly to Liberty, on the same road, destroying the Big and Little River Railroad bridges, the rails and sleepers on the road, and rebel supplies. From there he moved along the same road to Salem, where he destroyed a large number of bridges, including the railroad bridges over the branches of the Staunton River. At this point he turned northward toward Fincastle, and, at last accounts, his command was out of the reach of any forces sent against him by LEE. He has performed a great work. He has not done it, of course, without hard fighting and losing some men; but he has done his work and has done it well.

Gen. WILSON has reached Burkesville, *the junction of the railroads leading from Danville and Lynchburgh to Richmond and Petersburgh,* and destroyed a large portion of both roads.

The cutting of this communication, the accomplishment of which is acknowledged in the Richmond papers, is one of the most important achievements now going on around Richmond.

This, together with the results of HUNTER's expedition, cuts all of LEE's communications with the South and Southwest, and is the beginning of the great work of investing the rebel capital.

FROM THE SOUTHWEST.

A Fight Near the Mouth of White River—Defeat of the Rebels.

CAIRO, Sunday, June 26.

Memphis papers say, on the morning of the 22d inst., a detachment of Gen. MAGRUDER's command, 600 strong, attacked two companies of the Twelfth Iowa Infantry, stationed near the mouth of the White River.

After severe fighting the rebels were repulsed, with a loss of twenty-four killed and wounded.

Our loss was one killed and five wounded.

The removal of the gunboat *Tyler* from that station probably emboldened the rebels, and but for the fortunate arrival of the gunboat *Lexington*, the result might have been unfavorable to us.

Our forces fought desperately, repelling several charges of the rebels, and driving them from the field.

Gen. Marmaduke Reported Moving on Little Rock, Ark.

MEMPHIS, Thursday, June 23. Via CAIRO, Sunday, June 26.

Rebel deserters who have surrendered to our gunboats below, say that Gen. MARMADUKE is moving on Little Rock, Ark., to attack Gen. STEELE and capture that city if possible.

GEN. PILLOW DEFEATED.

An Attack upon Lafayette—The Rebels Repulsed.

CHATTANOOGA, Saturday, June 25.

Yesterday, at 5 o'clock in the morning, a flag of truce was sent into Lafayette, in the name of Gen. PILLOW, demanding the immediate surrender of the town, and threatening to burn it if the demand was not complied with.

The rebels were 3,000 strong, and had completely surrounded the town, and on the refusal of Col. WATKINS, who had only 400 men, to surrender, the rebels advanced from all directions.

At 9 o'clock they occupied three-fourths of the town, when Col. JOHN T. CROXTEN, of the Fourth Kentucky, came up and captured about 70 rebels.

Col. WATKINS lost about 50 killed and as many wounded.

Gen. PILLOW left 100 dead and wounded on the field.

Col. FALKNER, of the Seventh Kentucky, was captured in an attempt to make a charge upon the rebels.

Destruction of the Seneca Mills by Fire.

OSWEGO, Tuesday, June 28.

The Seneca Mills, at Minetto, the largest flouring mills in this State, were destroyed by fire early this morning, together with 1,800 barrels of flour, 15,000 bushels of wheat, 1,800 tons of feed, and some 20,000 empty flour barrels. Loss on the buildings, $200,000; insurance on buildings and stock, about $100,000. The buildings were owned by E. G. & M. MERRICK.

The Fifth Maine Regiment at Home.

PORTLAND, Me., Tuesday, June 28.

The Fifth Maine Regiment, Col. EDWARDS, arrived home from three years' service this afternoon. The City Government and the military escorted the veterans through the principal streets, and they feasted at Barnum's Hotel.

The Twelfth Massachusetts Regiment.

WASHINGTON, Tuesday, June 28.

The Twelfth Massachusetts Regiment, Col. BATES, arrived in town this morning en route for home, their term of service having expired.

Arrest of Col. Wolford.

LOUISVILLE, KY., Monday, June 27.

Col. WOLFORD was arrested at Lebanon this morning, by order of Gen. BURBRIDGE, and brought to this city to-night.

From New-Orleans.

CAIRO, Monday, June 27.

The steamer *Sultana* has arrived from New-Orleans, 21st. There has been a slight advance in sugar and molasses. Operations in cotton are limited and quotations nominal.

Fire in Brantford, C. W.

BRANTFORD, C. W., Monday, June 27.

The machine shop of the Buffalo and Lake Huron Railway was burned yesterday. The loss amounts to $50,000.

Bailed.

BOSTON, Tuesday, June 28.

The Secretary of the Navy has consented to release the Messrs. SMITH from Fort Warren on bail of $20,000 each.

Boston Bank Statement.

BOSTON, Tuesday, June 28.

The following is the weekly statement of the condition of the banks of this city:

Capital Stock	$38,381,700
Loans and Discounts	69,691,000
Specie	6,470,600
Due from other Banks	12,872,600
Due to other Banks	12,260,600
Deposits	30,865,600
Circulation	9,068,700

The Fire at Rockaway.

THE MARINE PAVILION AND OTHER BUILDINGS BURNED.

From the Long Island Farmer, June 27.

On Saturday last, June 25, at 12 o'clock M., a fire broke out in the Pavilion, at Rockaway, completely consuming that far-famed hotel, with most of the furniture, and extending to and destroying several other buildings, viz.: WM. CLEARY's Beach House and stables; Mr. BAINBRIDGE's cottage, adjoining the Pavilion; Mrs. BULL's stables and the extensive barns belonging to the Pavilion.

We are informed that there is insurance on the Pavilion of $20,000. The policy on the furniture for $8,000, expired only a few days since and had not been renewed. The furniture belonging to Mr. BAINBRIDGE, which, together with some very valuable paintings, was destroyed with the exception of the parlor furniture; that was saved. There were but few boarders in the house, as yet, and we do not hear that they lost any of their effects. WALBRIDGE & Co. were the lessees of the hotel this Summer. Mr. WALBRIDGE was in the city on Saturday, and heard of his misfortunes in the afternoon at Jamaica.

Mr. CLEARY, the owner of the Beach House, estimates his loss at $10,000—is insured $4,000 on his house and $1,500 on his furniture, in the Tradesmens' Insurance Company, New-York. We have not been able to ascertain the amount of Mrs. BULL's loss.

It is not known how the fire originated. Singularly enough, it was first discovered running up, and inside one of the large columns that supported the north side and rear of the hotel, and extending directly to the roof; the flames, driven by a stiff breeze, in a very short time enveloped the whole building. The high wind carried the fire over and beyond several buildings, which escaped destruction, to the Beach House, that was situated a considerable distance from the Pavilion.

The Marine Pavilion was a large and splendid edifice. The corner-stone was laid June 1, 1833. When first erected the main building was 230 feet front, three stories high, with wings extending rearward, one 75 and the other 45 feet long. It was erected by an association of gentlemen of the City of New-York, at a cost of $43,000, including land and standing furniture. It was subsequently sold, in May, 1836, to STEPHEN WHITNEY and CHARLES A. DAVIS, Esqs., for $30,000. About ten years since, Mr. DANIEL SMITH, builder, of Jamaica, added one hundred feet to each end of the main building, so that at the time of the fire it had a front of about 450 feet on the Ocean side. The largest front and finest piazza of any hotel in this country, designed and used as a Summer resort. This noble structure was swept away by fire, in about one hour and a half.

This fire will lessen the travel very materially to Rockaway this Summer. Hundreds were on their way to this famous resort on last Saturday afternoon, but when they heard, at Jamaica, that the Pavilion was destroyed, their routs were changed; many continued on east, and many returned to the heated city.

This fire will also entail considerable loss upon several of our enterprising business men. Messrs. J. S. REMSEN, B. W. CURTISS and JACOB SMITH, had made extensive preparations for carrying passengers to and from Rockaway this season.

There will be without doubt another and even a nobler Pavilion built on Rockaway Beach.

The Stoppage of the World and Journal of Commerce.

LETTER FROM GOVERNOR SEYMOUR TO DISTRICT ATTORNEY HALL, OF NEW-YORK.

EXECUTIVE CHAMBER, ALBANY, June 25, 1864.

A. Oakey Hall, Esq., District Attorney of the City and County of New-York:

SIR: In the matter of the seizure of the offices of the *World* and *Journal of Commerce*, the Grand Jury, in disregard of their oaths "to diligently inquire into and true presentment make of all such matters and things as should be given them in charge," have refused to make such inquiries, and declare that "it is inexpedient to examine into the subject referred to in the charge of the Court," with respect to such seizures. It becomes my duty under the express requirements of the Constitution "to take care that the laws of the State are faithfully executed." If the Grand Jury, in pursuance of the demands of the law and the obligations of their oaths, had inquired into the matter given them in charge by the court and the public prosecutor, their decision, whatever it might have been, would have been entitled to respect. As they have refused to do their duty, the subject of the seizure of these journals should at once be brought before some proper magistrate. If you wish any assistance in the prosecution of these investigations, it will be given to you.

As it is a matter of public interest that violations of the laws of the State be punished, the views or wishes of the parties immediately affected must not be suffered to influence the action of public officers. If through fear, or other motives, they are unwilling to aid you in getting at facts, it will be your duty to compel their attendance as witnesses in behalf of the people. Respectfully yours,

HORATIO SEYMOUR.

FATAL MISTAKE AT SARATOGA—DEATH OF A YOUNG LADY.—SUSAN W. SHEPARD, a young lady 21 years of age, daughter of S. SHEPARD, formerly of the American Hotel, Troy, died at Saratoga on Saturday, from the effects of a wrong dose given by a physician. Her funeral took place from the Fifth-street Baptist Church, in Troy, on Monday morning. The *Saratogian* gives the following particulars of this sad affair:

Miss SHEPARD and her mother were visiting the family of JOHN BENEDICT, of this place, and during Saturday afternoon Miss S. was taken somewhat ill. Her mother called upon Dr. S. S. STRONG to prescribe for her daughter. A prescription was prepared by him, and handed to Mrs. SHEPARD, who returned and administered the potion. Miss SHEPARD was soon affected, complained of a singular sensation in her head, and jocosely remarked that if she ever had hysterics she should suppose she was going to have them. Her eyes were observed to dilate unnaturally, and within a few minutes she became completely prostrated. Dr. STRONG, whose residence is but a square distant, was promptly summoned, and hurried to the scene. At first the doctor could not believe that the medicine had produced the effect, and to show his confidence, took a spoonful of it himself. But on more closely observing the peculiar symptoms, the cause was revealed to his mind, and he frankly stated that he must have given a medicine he did not intend to, and that in her condition there was danger it would prove fatal. Immediate efforts were made, however, to relieve her of the fatal potion, and to counteract its effects, but without avail. She lived only about an hour and a half after the medicine was administered. Dr. STRONG was intensely affected, and expressed a willingness to take the place of the young lady if that would restore her. In explanation of the mistake, he states that there are two bottles standing near together on his shelves labelled respectively "Geranium" and "Gelseminum," the contents of which are similar in appearance. He intended to give the "Geranium," but was deceived in looking at the label, and inadvertently gave the "Gelseminum." The mistake, it will be seen, was one of the eye, deceived by the similarity of the words in appearance, the beginnings and terminations being exactly alike. The "Gelseminum," tends to produce nervous prostration, and in small doses, such as was inadvertently given to this young lady, would not ordinarily have a fatal effect. Delicate females are frequently given from three to four small doses a day. But in the case of Miss SHEPARD, her nervous system was peculiarly susceptible to the prostrating influence of the drug. Dr. STRONG, himself, owing to the mental depression following the termination of this sad case, was affected by the dose he had taken, and recourse was had to stimulants to aid in relieving him from the unpleasant effects. Many absurd rumors have been set afloat respecting his condition, for which there are no foundations in truth."

Maryland a Free State.

From the Baltimore American, June 27.

The Twenty-third article of the Bill of Rights, reads as follows:

"Hereafter, in this State, there shall be neither Slavery nor involuntary servitude, except in punishment of crime, whereof the party shall be duly convicted; and all persons held to service or labor as slaves, are hereby declared free."

This article, after a protracted debate in the Constitutional Convention, in the course of which it was sustained in a masterly manner by the advocates of Anti-Slavery, was passed, as our readers have already learned, by a vote of 53 yeas to 27 nays.

There is no single act in the history of Maryland that can compare in importance with the passage of this article. As we gaze through the long vista of coming years, and contemplate the changes that will be wrought by this measure, we are overwhelmed with the immeasurable significance of an act so wondrous in its simplicity.

The reception of this news hardly creates a ripple upon the current of our tranquillity. It was a foregone conclusion, and our minds were long ago made up in regard to its realization. We are not taken by surprise, and we do not hurrah with wild excitement. We simply enjoy the calmer and the higher satisfaction that springs from the consciousness of duty done. We understood the nature of the obstacles to be overcome, and we knew at the same time how to remove them. We rejoice quietly in the hour of consummation, and in our inmost hearts we are exceeding glad at the success which has crowned our efforts.

The members of the convention will look back upon that day as one laden with precious memories. Should it be the only public act in the life of any one of them, that life will not have been lived in vain. It is not granted to every man to gild the evening of his declining days with such a reminiscence.

The regeneration of a commonwealth like ours is not an everyday occurrence. It is hard to estimate this work at its full value. But we shall see and know it better hereafter. All we know now is that the vestiges of a great evil are cleared away; that the canker of a great iniquity is extirpated, root and branch; that to our posterity no compromise is bequeathed which may be a fruitful source of discord hereafter. Races are forgotten and humanity is honored. We have joined the train of rejuvenated States in the march of Freedom. We have torn away the mask from the deformity of Slavery, and we have wrenched the rod from the oppressor. We look to the future with hearts full of hope and trust, confident that Providence in its own good time will work out for us a brighter destiny.

We offer our hand to our sister States and ask their congratulations. We ask them to join us in the prayer, God preserve the Commonwealth of Maryland. They have watched our course with approving smiles, and cheered us with words of encouragement, and in this hour of joy we shall not forget the thanks we owe to them.

Three of Morgan's Guerrillas in Fort Lafayette.

The United States steamer *Newbern* recently brought to this port thirty-one prisoners, captured on board the prize steamer *Thistle*, in the attempt to violate the blockade of Wilmington. These prisoners made affidavits that they were British subjects, and twenty-eight of them were discharged by Marshal MURRAY, under the instructions of the Navy Department relating to foreign subjects violating the blockade. The remaining three, whose names were ascertained to be JAMES CROWDERS, CHARLES DRAKE and J. D. ALLISON, were discovered to be Kentuckians, formerly belonging to the guerrilla band of Gen. MORGAN. They had been captured and confined at Camp Chase, Ohio, but contrived to make their escape into Canada, whence they proceeded by way of Halifax to Nassau. From Nassau they sailed in the blockade-runner *Thistle*, for Wilmington, with the avowed purpose of rejoining Gen. MORGAN. The capture of the *Thistle* produced an awkward derangement of their plans, and brought them into the custody of Marshal MURRAY. These facts were elicited by a long and close examination. As the prisoners appeared to be possessed of considerable shrewdness and ability, the Marshal transferred them yesterday to Fort Lafayette, under a guard provided by Gen. DIX, whence they will find it a more difficult job to escape than it was to undermine the walls of Camp Chase.

Celebration of the Fourth.

The Joint Special Committee of the Common Council, appointed to make arrangements for celebrating the coming Fourth of July, met and organized yesterday. Alderman MASTERSON was elected Chairman, and E. W. TAYLOR was appointed Secretary. Sub-committees on fireworks, stands, printing and music were appointed, and then the committee adjourned to meet at the call of the Chairman.

The committee, it is understood, will make no further arrangements for the celebration than to give the customary display of fireworks by the Messrs. EDGE, with music at each exhibition, at the following places:

City Hall; junction of East Broadway and Grand-street; Madison-square; Tompkins-square; junction of West Broadway and Franklin-street; junction of Broadway and Forty-third-street; Jackson-square; Battery; Mount Morris-square; junction of Tenth-avenue and King's Bridge-road; junction of Marion and Spring streets; Thirty-fourth-street, between Eighth and Ninth avenues; junction of Market and Monroe streets; Randall's Island.

The chief piece at the City Hall will be of special design and large size. The Randall's Island exhibition, of course, is for the children—those under the charge of the Commissioners of Charities and Correction.

The resolution authorizing the committee to act left the amount of appropriation blank, but they will not exceed an outlay of $10,000. The customary display of pyrotechnics will cost much more, owing to enhanced prices, than it has heretofore.

Onions for the Potomac Army.

NEW-YORK, Monday, June 27, 1864.

To the Editor of the New-York Times:

Inclosed please find $5 toward furnishing onions to our gallant soldiers, to whom we owe the immunity we enjoy of eating not only our onions, but everything else. Yours, &c.,

EX-SOLDIER
Of the Army of the Potomac.

EXTENSIVE FIRE IN CHATHAM-STREET—DAMAGE ESTIMATED AT OVER $60,000.—Soon after three o'clock yesterday afternoon, flames were discovered issuing from the windows of the fifth floor of the large brick building, known as Nos. 138 and 140 Chatham-street, corner of Baxter. The premises were mainly occupied by Mr. E. KINGMAN, manufacturer and dealer in cabinet furniture. The fire originated in the varnish room, where one of the men was at work at the time. The cause of it is, however, unknown at present. The Fire-Marshal is engaged making an investigation as to its origin. The three upper floors were entirely destroyed, and all the lower portion of the buildings badly damaged. Mr. KINGMAN's loss on furniture, fixtures, &c., by fire and water will not fall far short of $40,000. He is insured for $30,000 in the North River, Lenox, Tradesmen's, Atlantic, St. Mark's, New-York, Equitable, Firemen's, Astor and other insurance companies. Mr. T. THOMPSON occupied the corner store as a porter-house. His damage to stock and fixtures by fire and water is about $600; insured for $1,500 in the Jefferson Insurance Company. Mr. L. ST. JOHN, who kept a broker's office on the first floor, was damaged to the amount of $200; no insurance. Mr. R. HUTCHINSON occupied a small store under the buildings on the Baxter-street side as a second-hand clothing establishment. A portion of his stock was removed, but he has sustained a loss of about $300. The buildings were owned by Mr. H. B. HOFFMAN. The loss on them is between $12,000 and $15,000; said to be fully insured in City companies. Capt. JOURDAN, with his men of the Sixth Precinct, and also platoons from the Third, Fourth and Twenty-seventh Precincts, were on hand promptly and rendered valuable assistance in saving property.

WAR ITEMS.—An army letter from Petersburgh says that during the fight on Friday one of our boys, either becoming short of ammunition or in the hurry of the engagement, fired the ramrod of his gun from his musket. On the subsequent capture of the works two rebels were found dead and completely transfixed with the iron shaft.

THE PRESIDENCY.

ACCEPTANCE OF MR. LINCOLN.

Address of the Committee Appointed at Baltimore.

NEW-YORK, June 14, 1864.

HON. ABRAHAM LINCOLN—*Sir:* The National Union Convention, which assembled in Baltimore on June 7, 1864, has instructed us to inform you that you were nominated with enthusiastic unanimity for the Presidency of the United States for four years from the 4th of March next.

The resolutions of the convention, which we have already had the pleasure of placing in your hands, are a full and clear statement of the principles which inspired its action, and which, as we believe, the great body of Union men in the country heartily approve. Whether those resolutions express the national gratitude to our soldiers and sailors; or the national scorn of compromise with rebels, and consequent dishonor; or the patriotic duty of union and success; whether they approve the Proclamation of Emancipation, the constitutional amendment, the employment of former slaves as Union soldiers, or the solemn obligation of the Government promptly to redress the wrongs of every soldier of the Union, of whatever color or race; whether they declare the inviolability of the pledged faith of the nation, or offer the national hospitality to the oppressed of every land, or urge the union by railroad of the Atlantic and Pacific oceans; whether they recommend public economy and vigorous taxation, or assert the fixed popular opposition to the establishment by armed force of foreign monarchies in the immediate neighborhood of the United States, or declare that those only are worthy of official trust who approve unreservedly the views and policy indicated in the resolutions—they were equally hailed with the heartiness of profound conviction.

Believing with you, Sir, that this is the people's war for the maintenance of a Government which you have justly described as "of the people, by the people, for the people," we are very sure that you will be glad to know, not only from the resolutions themselves, but from the singular harmony and enthusiasm with which they were adopted, how warm is the popular welcome of every measure in the prosecution of the war, which is as vigorous, unmistakable and unfaltering as the national purpose itself. No right, for instance, is so precious and sacred to the American heart as that of personal liberty. Its violation is regarded with just, instant, and universal jealousy. Yet in this hour of peril every faithful citizen concedes that, for the sake of national existence and the common welfare, individual liberty may, as the Constitution provides in case of rebellion, be sometimes summarily constrained, asking only with painful anxiety that in every instance, and to the least detail, that absolutely necessary power shall not be hastily or unwisely exercised.

We believe, Sir, that the honest will of the Union men of the country was never more truly represented than in this convention. Their purpose we believe to be the overthrow of armed rebels in the field, and the security of permanent peace and union by liberty and justice under the Constitution. That these results are to be achieved amid cruel perplexities, they are fully aware. That they are to be reached only through cordial unanimity of counsel, is undeniable. That good men may sometimes differ as to the means and the time, they know. That in the conduct of all human affairs the highest duty is to determine, in the angry conflict of passion, how much good may be practically accomplished, is their sincere persuasion. They have watched your official course, therefore, with unflagging attention; and amid the bitter taunts of eager friends and the fierce denunciation of enemies, now moving too fast for some, now too slowly for others, they have seen you throughout this tremendous contest patient, sagacious, faithful, just; leaning upon the heart of the great mass of the people, and satisfied to be moved by its mighty pulsations.

It is for this reason that, long before the convention met, the popular instinct had plainly indicated you as its candidate; and the convention, therefore, merely recorded the popular will. Your character and career prove your unswerving fidelity to the cardinal principles of American liberty and of the American Constitution. In the name of that liberty and Constitution, Sir, we earnestly request your acceptance of this nomination; reverently commending our beloved country, and you, its Chief Magistrate, with all its brave sons who, on sea and land, are faithfully defending the good old American cause of equal rights, to the blessing of Almighty God.

We are, Sir, very respectfully, your friends and fellow-citizens,

WM. DENNISON, Ohio, Chairman.
JOSIAH DRUMMOND, Maine.
THOS. E. SAWYER, New-Hampshire.
BRADLEY BARLOW, Vermont.
A. H. BULLOCK, Massachusetts.
A. M. GAMMELL, Rhode Island.
C. S. BUSHNELL, Connecticut.
G. W. CURTIS, New-York.
W. A. NEWELL, New-Jersey.
HENRY JOHNSON, Pennsylvania.
N. B. SMITHERS, Delaware.
W. L. W. SEABROOK, Maryland.
JOHN F. HUME, Missouri.
G. W. HITE, Kentucky.
E. P. TYFFE, Ohio.
CYRUS M. ALLEN, Indiana.
W. BUSHNELL, Illinois.
L. P. ALEXANDER, Michigan.
A. W. RANDALL, Wisconsin.
A. OLIVER, Iowa.
THOMAS SIMPSON, Minnesota.
JOHN BIDWELL, California.
THOMAS H. PEARNE, Oregon.
LEROY KRAMER, West Virginia.
A. C. WILDER, Kansas.
M. M. BRIEN, Tennessee.
J. P. GREVES, Nevada.
A. A. ATOCHA, Louisiana.
A. S. PADDOCK, Nebraska.
VALENTINE DELL, Arkansas.
JOHN A. NYE, Colorado.
A. B. SLOANAKER, Utah.

Reply of Mr. Lincoln.

EXECUTIVE MANSION, WASHINGTON, June 27, 1864.

Hon. William Dennison and others, a Committee of the Union National Convention.

GENTLEMEN: Your letter of the 14th inst., formally notifying me that I have been nominated by the convention you represent for the Presidency of the United States for four years from the 4th of March next, has been received. The nomination is gratefully accepted, as the resolutions of the convention—called the platform—are heartily approved.

While the resolution in regard to the supplanting of Republican Government upon the Western Continent is fully concurred in, there might be misunderstanding were I not to say that the position of the Government in relation to the action of France in Mexico, as assumed through the State Department and indorsed by the convention, among the measures and acts of the Executive, will be faithfully maintained so long as the state of facts shall leave that position pertinent and applicable.

I am especially gratified that the soldier and the seaman were not forgotten by the convention, as they forever must and will be remembered by the grateful country for whose salvation they devote their lives.

Thanking you for the kind and complimentary terms in which you have communicated the nomination and other proceedings of the convention, I subscribe myself,

Your obedient servant,
ABRAHAM LINCOLN.

CITY MORTALITY LAST WEEK.—The deaths in the City for the past week were 447, being 27 more than during the previous week, and 40 more than in same week of 1863. The deaths were of men, 100; women, 103; boys, 131, and girls, 113. Two hundred and ten of the children were under five years of age.

EUROPEAN NEWS

Arrival of the City of London and Hibernian with Dates to June 17

The Pirate Alabama Repairing at Cherbourg.

Burning of the Ships Tycoon and Rockingham.

Capt. Semmes Defends His Piratical Exploits.

Fresh Instructions from the British Government Regarding the Treatment of Prizes.

Forged Confederate Bonds in Circulation.

INTERESTING MISCELLANEOUS INTELLIGENCE.

FINANCIAL AND COMMERCIAL.

The *City of London* arrived at this port yesterday. She brings the summary of the *Sidon*, which left Liverpool June 14.

The steamship *America*, from New-York, arrived at Southampton on the 15th inst.

The Cunard screw steamer *Hecla* would leave Liverpool for New-York simultaneously with the *Arabia*, on the 18th of June, to accommodate the cargo intended for the *Persia*.

The United States steamer *Kearsage* was in Flushing Road on the 12th of June, and passed Deal June 13, bound west.

The United States corvette *St. Louis* sailed from Algesiras on the 3d of June, for the westward.

The steamship *Hibernian*, from Liverpool June 16, via Londonderry 17th, was boarded off Cape Race at 6 o'clock, Monday morning, on her way to Quebec.

The news is one day later than the *City of London's*.

The steamship *Westminster*, from New-York, arrived at London on the 17th.

The steamship *Caledonia*, from Quebec, arrived at Glasgow on the 17th.

AMERICAN TOPICS.

THE ALABAMA.

The notorious rebel cruiser *Alabama* arrived at Cherbourg, France, on the 11th of June, and was admitted to free *pratique*. She landed 40 prisoners—the crews of the ship *Tycoon*, Capt. AYRES, from New-York, bound to San Francisco, destroyed by the *Alabama*; and of the ship *Rockingham*, previously reported destroyed.

Capt. SEMMES has requested the *Times* to insert the reasons why the Confederate cruisers burn their prizes and his suggestion for a remedy. The communication, which the *Times* of course publishes, fills two columns and a half of the paper. He says it was his intention to have sent all his prizes for adjudication into the ports most convenient for the parties concerned, but this intention was frustrated by British order in council. Capt. SEMMES asks was it expected that he would abandon the right of capture altogether, or that he would be guilty of the child's play of capturing the enemy's ships with one hand and releasing them with the other? Further, he inquires what inconvenience to Great Britain, for example, could possibly have grown out of the fact of the captured vessels lying quietly in the port of Liverpool in charge of a ship-keeper and prize-agent until she could be adjudicated, and if she should be condemned, why should she not have been sold as quietly as if she had been seized and sold under any execution for debt. Capt. SEMMES takes credit to himself and his officers for every ship set on fire, insomuch as they sacrifice their chances of prize money to the good of the Confederate States.

The *Times* replies to Capt. SEMMES' arguments relative to the burning of ships, and shows them to be fallacious and judicially unsound.

BELLIGERENT CRUISERS.

IMPORTANT INSTRUCTIONS TO GOVERNORS OF COLONIES.

The following instructions have just been sent by Her Majesty's Government to Governors of Colonies respecting the treatment of prizes captured by Federal or Confederate cruisers if brought into British waters:

DOWNING-STREET, June 2, 1864.

SIR: I think it well to communicate to you the decisions at which Her Majesty's Government have arrived on certain questions which have arisen respecting the treatment of prizes captured by Federal or Confederate cruisers if brought into British waters.

1. If any prize captured by a ship-of-war of either of the belligerent Powers shall be brought by the captors within Her Majesty's jurisdiction, notice shall be given by the Governor to the captors immediately to depart and remove such prize.

2. A vessel which shall have been actually and *bona fide* converted into, and used as, a public vessel-of-war, shall not be deemed to be a prize within the meaning of these rules.

3. If any prize shall be brought within Her Majesty's jurisdiction through mere stress of weather, or other extreme and unavoidable necessity, the Governor may allow for her removal such time as he may consider to be necessary.

4. If any prize shall not be removed at the time prescribed to the captors by the Governor, the Governor may detain such prize until Her Majesty's pleasure shall be made known.

5. If any prize shall have been captured by any violation of the territory or territorial waters of Her Majesty, the Governor may detain such prize until Her Majesty's pleasure shall be made known.

Her Majesty's Government have not thought it necessary to make any addition to the instructions already given with respect to cargoes—viz., that Her Majesty's orders apply as much to prize cargoes of every kind which may be brought by any armed ships or privateers of either belligerent into British waters as to the captured vessels themselves. They do not, however, apply to any articles which may have formed part of any such cargoes if brought within British jurisdiction, not by armed ships or privateers of either belligerent, but by other persons who may have acquired or may claim property in them by reason of any dealing with the captors.

These rules are for the guidance of the executive authority, and are not intended to interfere in any way with the process of any court of justice.

I have, &c.,
(Signed) EDWARD CARDWELL.

FEDERAL RECRUITING.

From the Oldham Chronicle.

The Mumps Railway Station has, on two or three occasions recently, presented a rather animated appearance, consequent on the departure of "factory workers" for America. It seems that a party representing himself to be from America has come to Oldham at intervals to engage weavers and self-actor minders for factories in the Northern States. Inquiries are particularly made for females, but it has been remarked that men are most frequently engaged; in fact, only a very slight proportion of women find acceptance. On Monday last, out of 17 who took their departure, there were only two females. The party by whom these engagements are made is said to be unquestionably a Yankee. He is accompanied by a "clerk," and comes to Oldham with a first-class return ticket. He alleges that he could stand at his own door and count no less than seven factories at a stand-still for want of hands. Under these circumstances it is scarcely to be wondered at if he gets numbers of credulous and blinded men to hurry away from home, leaving, in many cases, wives and families behind them. Anti-

The Charleston Mercury.

SPONTE SUA SINE LEGE FIDES RECTUMQUE COLENTUR. — VINDICE NULLO

COUNTRY PAPER—THREE A WEEK—EIGHT DOLLARS, FOR SIX MONTHS—PAYABLE IN ADVANCE.

VOLUME LXXXIV. CHARLESTON, S. C., THURSDAY, JUNE 30, 1864. NUMBER 12,10!

THE CAMPAIGN IN VIRGINIA.

Petersburg is in possession of our forces. An outer line of entrenchments, two miles from the town, was stormed by General Smith on the 15th instant, and the town was occupied by Generals Hancock and Smith the next day.

The fact that General Grant has been able to get Petersburg so cheaply may doubtless be accepted as an evidence that his passage of the James River had taken General Lee by surprise. Had General Lee contemplated the passage of the river as a possibility he would have thrown a large force, if not his whole army, into Petersburg during the two days in which Grant was making his way to the river. He had ample time to reach Petersburg, and it was certainly the point for him to hold. His army is of more consequence to the Confederacy than Richmond is, and he might better have risked that now worthless city on a single battle than to risk the very existence of his army in the attempt to hold a nominal capital, hopelessly isolated from its whole territory and from all means of support and supply.

Lee's failure to hold Petersburg is a satisfactory evidence of his inability to cope with Grant. Campaigning in the well beaten track from the Rapidan to Richmond, and in the well measured and well tried country on the Chickahominy, Lee did very well; but the moment that a grand and new idea comes into the struggle he fails.

If Lee is to hold Richmond, Fort Darling will be the next point of interest. But the despatch from Mr. Stanton states somewhat obscurely that Lee is preparing to hold the west bank of the Appomattox. Near Petersburg the Appomattox runs from west to east, and if we are to understand that Lee is holding the north bank we may, perhaps, infer that he is holding a point on which to rest his left wing in an attempt to retreat towards Danville.—*N. Y. Herald, June* 18.

THE CAPTURE OF PETERSBURG.

It is impossible to escape the conviction, from the facts in possession of the public, that Lee has been outgeneraled and taken at a disadvantage by the recent change of base effected by General Grant's army. It is inscrutable why Lee did not attack Grant, on flank and rear, while crossing the peninsula; and, failing in that, it is equally inexplicable why, having the interior line, he did not throw a sufficient force into Petersburg to hold it against the attack of Gen. Grant's advance. The secret of this last oversight may be in the fact that Petersburg was captured by General Smith's forces, which were sent around to Bermuda Hundred, from West Point, on transports; and hence Lee, in watching and timing the movements of various corps of the Army of the Potomac, did not take into account the possibility of a movement of any of the corps by water. The sudden capture of Petersburg, before the change of base was effected, is a very marked instance of the rapidity with which General Grant executes his movements, and reminds one of the sudden march of General Sherman's corps toward Jackson, Mississippi, the day after Vicksburg fell.

The capture of Petersburg is undeniably of very great importance; in renders unavailable the great Southern Railroad by which Richmond is connected directly with Wilmington, Charleston and Savannah, and indirectly with the whole South. Doubtless full one-half of the supplies which reach the rebel capital come by this route. With the disablement of the Virginia Central and the Gordonsville Roads, which has been pretty thorough, there remain but two sources of supply to Richmond—the Danville Road and the James River Canal. It was the intention of the Sheridan raid, among other useful objects, to have made the canal useless to the rebels.

While it is undoubtedly true that General Grant is in a better position for striking a deadly blow at the rebel capital than he has ever been before, it would be well not to be too sanguine of immediate results. There is a vast deal yet to do to capture Richmond and defeat the rebel army. Fort Darling will have to be taken—a job of itself of no small magnitude; the south side of the rebel capital must be invested, and, more important than all, the Danville Road must not only be reached, but held. The country must prepare, therefore, for possible disappointment. Fort Darling may be more difficult to capture than has been conjectured. And the investment of Richmond may prove a tedious operation.

As for the Danville road, Lee's whole army will doubtless be engaged in guarding it, and, if he is allowed time to throw up entrenchments, the eventual possession of the road may cost numerous and bloody struggles. Hence, though the news is cheering, and promises to yield fruit in due season, it will not do for the country to jump to the conclusion that Richmond is already captured. We discredit entirely the rumors that the rebel capital has been, or is to be, evacuated. We believe that the rebels will hold on to it to the last extremity, and that Lee's army, instead of being cooped up in the city, will be employed to keep open communication with it by way of the Danville and other roads. The nation, however, has cause to be truly thankful for the splendid success which Gen. Grant has achieved in changing his base.—*N. Y. World, June* 15.

Johnson's Mill, Petersburg, Virginia

Mortar dictator, Petersburg, Virginia

The New-York Times.

VOL. XIII.---NO. 4001. NEW-YORK, THURSDAY, JULY 21, 1864. PRICE FOUR CENTS.

PEACE NEGOTIATIONS.

Rebel Propositions to Return to the Union.

The Rebel Terms and Conditions.

The Union Conditions and Terms.

Semi-Official Interview Between Confederate Commissioners and Mr. Greeley.

HOW IT ORIGINATED AND TERMINATED.

STILL FURTHER ON THE MATTER.

An Independent Commissioner to Richmond.

Rev. Col. Jaques Has an Interview With Jeff. Davis.

What He Tells and What He Withholds.

The following important dispatch from Niagara Falls to the Rochester *Democrat*, was telegraphed to a private party in this City, last evening. We do not vouch for its accuracy.

NIAGARA FALLS, Wednesday, July 20.

Two weeks ago, GEO. N. SANDERS, C. C. CLAY, of Alabama, JACOB THOMPSON, of Mississippi, and J. P. HOLCOMB, of Virginia, arrived at the Clifton House, just across the river from this place. Their arrival was duly announced in the public press, and the object of their mission was understood to be to consult with the Democratic leaders of the North in reference to the Chicago Convention.

Results proved, however, that they had a double purpose in view, which was first developed to HORACE GREELEY by GEORGE N. SANDERS, who wrote to Mr. GREELEY, stating that Messrs. CLAY, THOMPSON and HOLCOMB were duly recognized Commissioners of the Confederate Government, and desired to know what terms could be made for terminating the war between the two sections. He added, however, that these Commissioners were not specially authorized to negotiate for a cessation of hostilities or a restoration of the Union, but that they would like to have an informal conference with such persons as the United States Government might indicate to meet them. These facts having been presented to Mr. LINCOLN, he requested Mr. GREELEY to act in the matter as he thought advisable under the peculiar circumstances, and stated that he (Mr. L.) should at any time be pleased to receive propositions from those who had been in arms against the Government for a return to their allegiance and duty as citizens of the Union. He also stated that he should be pleased to see the Union restored upon any terms consistent with the present and future safety, welfare and honor of the Government. Mr. GREELEY having settled all preliminaries with Mr. LINCOLN, proceeded to this place, reaching here last Monday morning, and took up quarters at the International Hotel. A correspondence was at once opened with the commissioners, and, as a final result, they made the following proposition, and gave it as their opinion that the Richmond Government would approve and ratify the same. The restoration of the Union in *statu quo* upon this basis:

First. All negroes which have been actually freed by the war, to be secured in such freedom.

Second. All negroes at present held as slaves to remain so.

Third. The war debt of both parties to be paid by the United States.

Fourth. The old doctrine of State rights to be recognized in reconstructing the Union.

This proposition was laid before Mr. LINCOLN by Mr. GREELEY. The President at once telegraphed to Mr. GREELEY the terms upon which he would propose a settlement and reconstruction, to wit:

The full and complete restoration of the Union in all its territorial integrity; the abandonment of Slavery by the seceded States, under conditions which should, while respecting the property-rights of all loyal men, afford ample security against another war in the interest of Slavery.

After considerable correspondence between the parties, it was concluded to refer the whole matter back to the two Governments for reconsideration. All negotiations having been terminated, Mr. GREELEY, in company with Mr. HAY, Private Secretary of Mr. LINCOLN, called upon the Commissioners at the Clifton House, on the Canada side, where a protracted and pleasant interview was held, and the various questions under consideration were discussed at length. Mr. GREELEY left the Falls for New-York on this afternoon's train. It is understood that the commissioners with SANDERS and JEWETT, who are both, are to remain and carry on negotiations with the Democrats. A letter is to be prepared for the Chicago Convention, in which the commissioners will hold out strong assurances of a restoration of the Union under Democratic auspices. The whole movement is regarded by many as a mere scheme to entrap the Administration into a false position before the country and the world, for the benefit of the disunion Democrats.

A MISSION TO RICHMOND.

Special Dispatch to the New-York Times.

WASHINGTON, Wednesday, July 20.

An individual, fresh from Richmond, not as a released prisoner, but an honored guest, entertained three days in the capital of the Southern Confederacy, feasted by JEFF. DAVIS, BENJAMIN and their compeers, having around him the romance and the mystery of an unknown mission, and knowing the secrets of the rebel prison-house, is *rara avis* enough to make a sensation even amid the leaden and languid heat of a Washington Summer's day. Such a personage, bringing with him all the experiences enumerated, arrived here to-day direct from Richmond by way of Gen. GRANT's headquarters. His name is Col. JAMES F. JAQUES, of the Seventy-third Illinois Volunteers, Colonel, but parson also, being a minister of the Methodist Episcopal Church. Though neither envoy nor ambassador, Col. JAQUES had a mission of his own, clothed with no authority to speak for either President or Government, he appears to have had authority enough of some kind to command a hearing from the principalities and powers that sit in Richmond; in fine, without being a plenipotentiary, he seems to be endowed with a certain species of power behind the throne that caused him to be attentively listened to and kindly treated by the chiefs of the rebellion.

CHARACTER OF HIS MISSION.

Of the real object and end of Col. JAQUES' mission, I am requested by himself not now to speak. It is perfectly proper to state, however, that it is in no respect official in its character, and that he had no warranty whatsoever to enter into any negotiations between this Government and the rebel authorities. Any statement that would convey a different impression is false. Secondly, it may be stated that though Col. JAQUES' mission contemplates results of the highest importance; these results are ulterior rather than immediate. Finally, it is warrantable to say that though his mission was one of peace, it was not a peace mission. Col. JAQUES belongs to the church militant and believes most heartily in dealing the rebellion what HUDIBRAS calls "apostolic blows and knocks." Yet he has faith that the time will come, and is rapidly coming, when an agency of reconciliation which he believes to be of immense power, can be used.

Animated by this sentiment, he succeeded in so impressing his views upon Mr. LINCOLN that the President, without according him the smallest official recognition or authority, was willing, believing his honesty of purpose, that he should try the experiment of a visit to Richmond. Accordingly, he gave him a personal recommendation to Gen. GRANT to pass him through the lines, or otherwise forward his views.

COL. JAQUES GOES TO RICHMOND.

Thus aided, Col. JAQUES, accompanied by Mr. EDWARD KIRKE, made his way from Gen. GRANT's headquarters by the north side of the James River, and passing the rebel lines, reached the Confederate Capital. Here they remained for three days—Saturday, Sunday and Monday last. While in Richmond, Col. JAQUES, at his own request, was placed under guard; but he had the entire freedom of the city, and put up during his visit at the Spottswood House, the "crack" hotel of Richmond.

INTERVIEWS WITH THE REBEL PRESIDENT.

The Colonel, during his three days' stay, visited the various Confederate authorities, as well as the prisons and hospitals in which our captives and wounded are confined. He had two prolonged interviews with President DAVIS in his office in the Custom-house; and although the nature and subject matter of the conversations between himself and the rebel President are not proper for present publication, yet it is understood that Col. JAQUES met with considerable success in impressing his views upon Mr. DAVIS. When taking his leave, DAVIS took the Colonel's hand in both his, shook it warmly and cordially, and stated that, leaving out of view the present struggle, he had the highest respect for his character and aims.

HOW THE COLONEL WAS ENTERTAINED.

The Colonel, while a guest at the Spottswood House, fared sumptuously, being fed on chicken, turkey, mutton and all the viands of a well-appointed hotel, and entertained with fine brandies and costly wines. His bill would have amounted to more than $500 in Confederate money, but he found it impossible to induce his entertainers to accept any return for the hospitality he had received.

HE VISITS VARIOUS DIGNITARIES.

Col. JAQUES also had interviews with Mr. BENJAMIN, Secretary of State, Mr. OULD, Commissioner of Exchange, and other Confederate dignitaries and authorities.

THE REBEL PRISONS.

The Colonel was permitted to visit the Libby and Belle Isle Prisons, and reports that he was agreeably disappointed by the comparatively comfortable condition in which he found our Union captives therein confined. The wounded, also, though only the more desperate cases are retained in the hospitals of Richmond, he found as well cared for as could be expected.

HOW RICHMOND LOOKS.

The streets of Richmond are almost deserted, few others being seen than soldiers, women, negroes and cripples. Many of the stores, however, remain open, and there is some business activity.

THE REBEL PRESIDENT.

Col. JAQUES describes JEFF. DAVIS as hale and hearty in appearance, his health being much better latterly than it had been, and, though thin in face and person, the tough and wiry constitution of the rebel chieftain presents no likelihood of his giving out during the natural life of the rebellion.

CHARACTER OF COL. JAQUES.

Extraordinary though Col. JAQUES' story, his mission and all belonging thereto, may appear, there can be no doubt whatever of his thorough honesty; and with this quality he appears to be credited both by our own and the rebel authorities. Of his wisdom there may possibly be more question.

GEN. SHERMAN'S ARMY.

Official Report of the Passage of the Chattahoochee.

Our Cavalry Sent to Operate on the Railroad Between Atlanta and Augusta.

Everything Progressing Satisfactorily.

WASHINGTON, Wednesday, July 20.

The latest official information from Gen. SHERMAN, is that his army crossed the Chattahoochee in several different places north of the railroad bridge. The movement was made with such celerity as to take the enemy by surprise, and therefore the resistance to his advance was feeble on the part of the rebel cavalry.

Our cavalry was at once sent to operate on the railroad east of Decatur—one of the objects being to cut off communication between Atlanta and Augusta—thus preventing the removal of stores to the latter place and the reinforcement of JOHNSTON.

Our main army was within ten or twelve miles of Atlanta.

All the operations of our army were progressing in the highest degree favorably.

FROM LOUISVILLE.

LOUISVILLE, Ky., Wednesday, July 20.

The Nashville *Union*, of yesterday, editorially, says:

"The report of the capture of Atlanta, Ga., by our forces are all premature, though our whole army is in motion, and we expect to hear of its capture in a few days."

FROM CINCINNATI.

CINCINNATI, Wednesday, July 20.

The *Commercial*, of this city, has advices from Gen. SHERMAN's army to the 16th instant.

Nearly our whole force had crossed the Chattatooche River and occupied a position on the south side.

A portion of our troops had advanced two miles toward Atlanta, but they encountered nothing but small bodies of rebel cavalry.

Gen. BRAXTON BRAGG had arrived at Atlanta, and would, it was supposed, exercise a personal supervision over the movements of the rebel army.

GUERRILLAS ON THE CUMBERLAND RIVER.

Burning of the Steamer St. Louis by Guerrillas—Four Rebel Prisoners to be Shot.

LOUISVILLE, Ky., Tuesday, July 19.

The steamer *St. Louis*, hence for Nashville, laden with Government stores, was burned, yesterday, by guerrillas at the Sailor's Rest, on the Cumberland River.

Four rebel prisoners have been selected from our military prison, to be sent to Mitchellsville and Clarksville, to be shot, in retaliation for the murder of two Union men near those places.

THE WAR IN MISSOURI.

A Call From Gen. Fisk—Five Thousand Men Wanted to Put Down the Guerrillas in Northwestern Missouri.

ST. LOUIS, Wednesday, July 20.

Gen. FISK, commanding at St. Joseph, has issued an appeal calling for five thousand loyal men to rally for the protection of life and property, and assist him in exterminating the guerrillas in Northwestern Missouri.

Guerrilla Operations in Ray County—Refugees—Intended Raid in Kansas—How the Rebels are Subsisted, Concealed and Encouraged.

ST. LOUIS, Wednesday, July 20.

Private letters from Lexington say that from three to nine hundred bushwhackers are in Ray County. Some Federal troops had a fight with them on Sunday, near Richmond, in which six or eight of our men were reported killed.

About three hundred guerrillas were at Elkhorn on Monday.

About thirty bushwhackers killed nine citizens in Carroll County, robbed the mail-coach and passengers, and did considerable promiscuous thieving, last week. All the persons murdered had been in the military service, and were prominent Union men.

The St. Joseph *Herald*, of yesterday, says the city is full of refugees from the lower counties, and hundreds have gone to Leavenworth and other places. The panic extends throughout the whole country. All the business houses of Weston are closed, and the citizens are in constant fear of a raid.

About fourteen buildings were burned at Platte City by the Federal troops, including the Platte *Sentinel* office, and a few other houses belonging to Union men. Col. FORD tried to save the *Sentinel* office, but the fire was under too great progress.

A letter, without date, signed by "THORNTON H. TODD, Commanding," was found at Platte City Station. The rebels were about ready to concentrate their army; asked for the state of things; acknowledged the receipt of the name of friends, and saying they would cross the Missouri River below Parksville Ford, and the Kansas River west of Wyandotte, and accomplish their trip through Kansas.

This letter shows that they intended, after a few days' plundering, to join the rebel army of the South, effecting their escape through Kansas.

THORNTON had been in Platte and Clay Counties about eight months, and recruited 1,200 men; and during this time had been aided, protected, concealed and subsisted by the citizens of those counties.

The steamer *War Eagle*, on her way down the Missouri River, was fired into by guerrillas at Rockport, but no one was injured.

ANOTHER DISPATCH.

ST. LOUIS, Tuesday, July 19.

A special dispatch from St. Joseph to the *Democrat* says:

"The city and country are wild with rumors and excitement. It is reported that Col. FORD attacked THORNTON's guerrillas at Arnoldsville on Sunday, and the fighting was kept up all day, but the result was unknown.

Another body of guerrillas, from 300 to 600 strong, are encamped on GORDON's farm, in Platte County.

Official information states that 200 more of the paid raw militia of Platte and Clay Counties have joined THORNTON's guerrillas.

A collision occurred in Chisan County, to what extent is not known.

The people are constantly flocking into St. Joseph from the surrounding counties, and many are departing for other points, leaving the grain unharvested, in consequence of which much suffering is apprehended in these localities.

ST. JOSEPH, Mo., Tuesday, July 19—P. M.

It appears that Col. FORD left bands of guerrillas, numbering nearly two hundred, in his rear, who are committing all manner of depredations in the southern part of this county.

A large scouting party sent from here this morning have not since been heard from.

Every train from Weston brings large numbers of refugees from Platte, Clay and Ray Counties. Many of them stop here, while others go eastward.

It is said that the entire militia of Andrew, Holt, and Atchison, who are not away, and of other counties in Northwest Missouri, will be immediately called into service.

Operations of the Guerrillas—Platte City Captured and Burnt By Federal Troops—One Half the Town Destroyed—Several Men Burned to Death—Battle at Camden Point.

From the St. Joseph Herald, July 16.

From passengers who arrived last night from below, we learn Platte City was almost destroyed yesterday morning by the Federal troops. Not over half the houses were left standing. The Methodist Church, a fine building, the *Sentinel* printing office, and the three-story brick block in which it was located, together with many business and dwelling-houses are all in ashes. Thus has vengeance, swift and dire, been visited upon a people who not only basely and cowardly surrendered themselves to THORNTON's thieves and murderers, but who also welcomed the villains with every demonstration of affection and delight.

The town was a nest-hole of treason. Not over a half dozen Union families residing there. Desolation and destruction have swept over it, and if the report brought us be true, the work has been most thoroughly performed. While we fear the few Union men of the place have been caused to suffer in property, and perhaps in life, we have not the slightest sympathy with the rebels.

It was rumored in Weston when the train left, that JESSE MORIN had been burned in his own house, that CLINT COCKRELL had joined the guerrillas and been killed in a skirmish, and Mr. F. A. COX, the venerable editor of the *Sentinel*, was killed. The two former were regarded as secession sympathizers, while the latter was a sound, honest, true Union man. One passenger informed us that he had heard Mr. COX was sick at his home, and had not been disturbed. We hope the latter story is true, for we should mourn the loss of so pure and good a man.

The report was also brought into Weston that the troops were going south toward Parkville, from Platte City, and that they had declared their intention of showing no quarter to any rebel who should fall into their hands.

The following is the account given of the fight at Camden Point by Lieut. CHILD, of Capt. CLAGGETT's company, who was an eye-witness and participant in the affair:

About 2 o'clock P. M., Wednesday, a command composed of the Second Colorado, Fifteenth Kansas, Ninth M. S. M., and several detachments of E. M. M., numbering 500 men, with one piece of artillery, all under command of Col. FORD, of the Second Colorado, took up the line of march from Weston in the direction of Camden Point. When about two miles from that place, the advance guard of eighteen men were fired upon by guerrilla pickets, who then fled, closely followed by our men, who chased them through the brush into the town, firing as they went, and succeeded in killing six guerrillas while on the run. After passing about a mile beyond the town, they met the main force of the enemy, under command of THORNTON, numbering about 140 men, drawn up in line of battle; but, without halting, the eighteen Colorado boys gave a wild yell, dashed right toward the centre of the line, which immediately gave way, and, after firing a few shots, killing one of the attacking party, and wounding another, they fled in wild confusion, with their pursuers close in their rear, and seven of them were killed before they escaped. Having pursued some three or four miles, our men rejoined their command. After getting possession of the town we found two buildings in flames, fired by THORNTON, in which he had stored a large number of arms and ammunition. The explosion of the powder was heard distinctly several miles distant. He had made Camden Point his headquarters, had all his munitions of war there, and was conscripting the able-bodied citizens throughout that section. A few hours previous to the attack he made a speech, returning thanks for a flag that had been presented to him, and which was captured by our forces, in which he stated that it was folly for the Federals to think of attacking him; that he had captured Camden Point and would hold it; that he would fight in every by-road and hog-path in the country. His speech was scarcely ended before the avengers were upon him, and his band in full flight from the town.

A short time after entering town a man named MCCORMICK rode into our lines, and being recognized as a bushwhacker was immediately arrested. He did not know that THORNTON had been driven out, imagined all was right, and tried to pass himself off as one of JENNISON's men.

Once in possession of the town, a sad scene of destruction and pillage commenced, such as we hope never again to witness. Several of the citizens were arrested and taken to headquarters. Houses were burned and pillaged, and the heavens for miles around were lighted with flames. Late into the night the fires continued, and again in the morning were renewed. About two-thirds of the town was destroyed, but the fine Seminary buildings were unharmed when we left.

At the time our forces entered the town they were told that there were a number of men hid in the hemp house, then in flames, having been fired by THORNTON, in which he had a number of guns, and it is supposed that three of them were burnt with the building, and the bodies of two of the dead guerrillas were cast into the flames and also consumed. We hear it estimated that over twenty men were killed belonging to the guerrillas, and only one man killed and one wounded on the part of the attacking forces.

The fine residence of Dr. THOMAS, living at the edge of the town, was a smouldering heap of ashes, as we passed in the morning, and it was reported that the Doctor had been taken out and shot. He was an old man, bore a good character, but it was reported that he had visited a sick guerrilla, hence his fate. Previous to the report of his death, a squad of the Fifteenth Kansas were in possession of his house, which they gutted and then fired; and only waited to get the Doctor to leave a lounge upon which lay his sick wife, to blow his brains out, and we are of the opinion that they accomplished this bloody work before they left. Other citizens in the neighborhood, no doubt shared the same fate.

One OLVIS, formerly of the militia, who had joined the guerrillas at Platte City, was captured, having his leg broken. He recognized one of his captors and called him by name, and received in reply, "OLVIS, you are in d——d bad company." One of the party then held him up, and another placed his carbine close to the prisoner's head, fired, and the soul of OLVIS was in the presence of his Maker.

MCCORMICK, the prisoner named above, was marched into camp and placed under guard. About 8 o'clock a report was circulated that we were attacked, when the guard immediately shot the prisoner, or, as they said, "disposed of him." Col. FORD then addressed the men, and said that, as the guerrillas gave no quarter, he would do the same; that he neither asked any nor gave any, and ordered the men to sleep upon their arms, and not to straggle from their camp.

The loss of Camden Point is the death-blow to the guerrillas. It was the rendezvous where they stored their arms. Among the captures made were several dispatches written by THORNTON, detailing his capture of Camden Point, and his intention of holding it. In looking over the dead, the body of his Adjutant was found, clothed in a new uniform, apparently the first time he had ever worn it. We failed to learn his name.

That this man THORNTON is to blame for the misery brought upon Platte County, no one can doubt, after visiting that section. He came into quite a settlement, murdered and burned, and thus gave a chance for others to retaliate. The blood of the men killed at Camden Point is upon him and his abettors.

The troops engaged in this quick and bloody work needed but this as an incentive to come over. They came, and desolation followed in their track. If our citizens do not want the renewal of the scenes of Camden reënacted here, let them drive the guerrillas from our midst, for if they do not, these troops will be sent here to do for them. We are able to take care of ourselves, and should do it.

The flag captured was a regular Confederate banner, and worked upon it were the words "Protection to Missouri."

On the morning of Thursday, the main portion of the command left in the direction of Platte City, and a detachment of the Fifteenth Kansas and Capt. CLAGGETT's company were detailed as guard to the wounded Colorado men into Weston, and arrived at that place about noon. Capt. C.'s company then came on to this place. It was generally supposed when we left that Platte City would be burned and pillaged.

Operations in the Platte District.

OFFICIAL REPORTS.

HEADQUARTERS DEPARTMENT OF THE MISSOURI,
ST. LOUIS, July 15, 1864.

To Maj.-Gen. Rosecrans:

I have just returned from the District of Northwest Missouri, embracing Platte and Clay Counties. My command is now at Liberty. I shall return to-night. Col. THORNTON's band of rebels is broken up into small bands, and scattered through the country. I shall make my headquarters at Liberty, and scout from there.

I would respectfully suggest that the citizens of those counties should not be armed; nine out of ten are disloyal and have aided THORNTON in recruiting his forces. They take loyalty like gin and sugar, and pass it off just as easy.

I have killed no citizens—none but those in arms fighting us; but any amount of the citizens need killing. Nine-tenths of all the citizens are assisting THORNTON, giving him all the information and keeping everything from me. I would respectfully recommend that troops be sent in this section to remain permanently, or we shall have more trouble. All the arms that are sent in there will go into the hands of bushwhackers.

(Signed,) J. H. FORD, Colonel.

Official: J. LOVELL, A. A. G.

HEADQUARTERS DEPARTMENT OF THE MISSOURI,
ST. LOUIS, Mo., July 16, 1864.

By Telegraph from Kansas City to Gen. Rosecrans:

In passing through the counties I have told all the prominent citizens that from this henceforth I should hold them responsible for every act committed by the rebels; that this passage of mine through the country was only for information, but that I should return, and woe be to those names that I had recorded—names given to me by Union people that have been driven from their homes. I have done some damage in passing through. I alone am responsible for it. I have been careful, and none have suffered but those who richly deserve it.

I have called a meeting of all the prominent rebel sympathizers and citizens to meet me at Liberty on Monday, and I will tell them a course they can pursue that will save their counties. They say they will come and see the handwriting on the wall. They can, if they wish, still save themselves. In my travels through these counties I have found no young men—nothing but old men and women. The negroes say the young massas are in the brush. I shall stay over there until I am ordered back. It is a warfare that I detest, but it is absolutely necessary. Fifteen killed in first skirmish, none wounded, none captured, except two men found armed to the teeth and brought into camp just as I left, one of whom is proven to be an old soldier of PRICE's army, but recently returned to the brush. They will see the last of earth to-night. Total number of killed, found in arms and fighting against us, twenty-four.

I divided up my command to-day in five parties, scouting through the country; heavy firing was heard south of us; no reports when I left; hope to hear good news in the morning. Our loss one killed and one mortally wounded; several of our horses killed. We captured in the first fight about 200 stands of United States arms. We burned one warehouse that had 100 stands United States muskets in it, 12 kegs of powder, lead, caps and buckshot. We captured in the fight a battle flag, and killed the man who carried it. It was made by the ladies of Platte City, and presented by them.

J. H. FORD, Col. Commanding.

J. LOVELL, Asst. Adj.-Gen.

ADDRESS OF GEN. ROSECRANS.

HEADQUARTERS DEPARTMENT OF THE MISSOURI,
ST. LOUIS, July 16, 1864.

To the citizens of Northwest Missouri, whom it may concern:

Your best men have assured me by word and letter that you mean to behave as law-abiding and peaceful citizens. They have assured me of your pledges, and pledged themselves for you. I have intrusted the peace to your keeping. I have supplied you with ammunition, and left arms in your hands. You have given me fair promises, while you allowed rebels and guerrillas to live and recruit among you. You have concealed from our authorities these men and their projects. You have seen robbers and murderers joined by the very men who swore to defend us against them. The arms and ammunition delivered to you for the defence of law and Government, have been used to destroy them. You are guilty of all the blood that will be shed by the use of these arms, and the hands which have basely betrayed both you and the country. You have nothing left before you now but wholly to renounce and help to pursue and exterminate these common enemies of mankind, or your country will become a desolation. I could not save it, and I must tell you as a friend I do not think it would deserve it. Citizens situated as you have been, who will tolerate a species of—I will not call it warfare, but—outrage, which finds no parallel in the annals of our Indian wars—must expect the vengeance due to such moral dereliction among free and professedly Christian people. I implore you, for your own sake, now at once lay the axe at the root of the tree—needful assistance will be given if you do your duty. All loyal and law-abiding citizens must promptly combine with the military authorities, giving all possible aid, assistance and information. Mark those who do not, and regard them as your enemies, whose conduct may ruin yourselves and your families. But while you denounce bushwhacking and private war, remember that the accessories to these crimes are likewise guilty.

Any one who knowingly and willingly advises, counsels, gives consent, food, direction, information or assistance to bushwhackers, is partaker of their crimes, and ought to be of their punishment.

Let not failure to take my advice bring upon the beautiful and now prosperous counties of North Missouri desolation such as reigns along your western borders.

W. S. ROSECRANS,
Major-Gen. Commanding.

J. R. DROUILLARD, Capt. and A. D. C.

MRS. J. W. POLK.

HEADQUARTERS DEPARTMENT OF THE MISSOURI,
ST. LOUIS, Mo., July 16, 1864.

Mrs. ANNA E., wife of JOHN W. POLK, arrested for visiting within our lines without lawful authority, and attempting to leave and carrying letters and articles without permit, by her truthful statement, confirmed by evidence, having satisfied the General Commanding that her intentions were not bad, and that the forbidden letters and articles were imposed upon her care by the selfishness of others less honorable, will be released from custody on taking the oath of allegiance, and permitted to remain within our lines, and, with the consent of the proper military commander, to go beyond them to get her children, and return without unreasonable delay.

By command of Maj.-Gen. ROSECRANS.
O. D. GREENE, A. A. G.

Army Rations.

WASHINGTON, Wednesday, July 20.

Section 2, of the act passed June 20, having modified the army ration, the War Department to-day issued the following regulations:

First—The ration is twelve ounces of pork or bacon, or one pound of salt or fresh beef, eighteen ounces of soft bread or flour, or twelve ounces of hard bread, or one pound and four ounces of corn meal, and to every one hundred rations, fifteen pounds of beans or peas, or ten pounds of rice or hominy, ten pounds of green coffee, or eight pounds of roasted or roasted and ground coffee, or one pound and eight ounces of tea, fifteen pounds of sugar, four quarts of vinegar, one pound and four ounces of adamantine or star candles, four pounds of soap, three pounds and twelve ounces of salt, and four ounces of pepper. The Subsistence Department, as may be most convenient or least expensive to it, and according to the condition and amount of its supplies, shall determine whether soft bread or flour, and what other component parts of the ration as equivalents, shall be issued.

Second—On a campaign, on marches, or on board of transports, the ration of hard bread is one pound.

Third—Desiccated compressed potatoes, or desiccated compressed mixed vegetables, at the rate of one ounce and a half of the former and one ounce of latter to the ration, may be substituted for beans, peas, rice or hominy.

Fourth—Beans, peas, salt and potatoes, fresh, shall be purchased, issued and sold by weight, and the bushel of each shall be estimated at 60 pounds.

Fifth—When deemed necessary, fresh vegetables, dried fruit, molasses, pickles, or any other proper food may be purchased and issued, in lieu of any component part of the ration of equal money value. The Commissary-General of Subsistence is alone authorized to order such purchases.

A new order allows sutlers to supply their respective commands in the Army of the Potomac with such articles as are included in the Wilson bill, and the supplement thereto, in such manner as may be prescribed by the Provost-Marshal-General.

Officers will be permitted to obtain such articles as they may desire, and are not included in the Wilson bill, in the manner provided for by paragraph five, of a circular of Nov. 7, 1862.

Attention is called to order No. 105, of Dec. 11, respecting the delivery of wines and liquors ordered by officers, and to order No. 227, of Aug. 24, regulating the quantity of stores that may be ordered by officers.

Sutlers and traders will at all times hold themselves in readiness to leave the army upon short notice.

From Fortress Monroe.

FORTRESS MONROE, Tuesday, July 19.

The steamers *Parthenia* and *New-Jersey* arrived here to-day from Newbern, N. C., with the Seventeenth Massachusetts Regiment, homeward bound. There is no news from that quarter.

Major-Gen. SMITH arrived in the steamer *Adelaide* this morning from Baltimore, and left for the front in a special boat.

The flag-of-truce steamer *C. W. Thomas*, with Major MULFORD, Assistant Commissioner of Exchange, went up the river this morning with a few prisoners.

Conflicting rumors have been in circulation during the day of an attack on the army gunboat *Charles Chamberlain*, with Gen. BUTLER on board, by a masked battery of four guns, near Wilcox's Landing. Nothing definite, however, has been received.

IMPORTANT FROM MEMPHIS.

The Expedition Under General A. J. Smith.

A Series of Battles With Forrest's and Faulkner's Rebel Forces.

THE REBELS WHIPPED EVERY TIME.

MEMPHIS, Tuesday, July 19.

I am indebted to one of Gen. WASHBURNE's staff officers for the following highly important intelligence:

On the 5th inst. Gen. WASHBURNE sent out a force of infantry, cavalry and artillery from La Grange, under Maj.-Gen. A. J. SMITH and Brig.-Gens. MOWER and GRIERSON, with instructions to move in pursuit of the rebel Gen. FORREST, bring him to bay, fight and whip him.

Gen. SMITH was ordered to pursue him to Columbus, Miss., if he did not overtake him this side.

A dispatch from Gen. SMITH to Gen. WASHBURNE received to-day, says we have met FORREST, LEE and WALKER at Tupelo, and whipped them badly on three different days. Our loss is small compared to that of the rebels. I bring back everything in good order. Not anything is lost.

A scout has since arrived at Lagrange, and reports the enemy's loss at 250, and their defeat overwhelming.

It is also stated by persons who have come in that the rebel Gen. FAULKNER and Col. FORREST were killed, and that Gen. FORREST was wounded in the foot, and his horse and equipments captured.

From other sources I learn that Gen. SMITH met Gen. FORREST at Pontotoc on Wednesday, the 13th inst., fought him on that day, and on Thursday and Friday, driving him below Tupelo, and whipping him badly in five different battles.

Our loss is said to be less than three hundred, while that of the rebels is over two thousand.

Col. WALKER, of the Ninth Minnesota, who commanded a brigade, was killed.

The weather here continues very warm.

The steamer *Mepham* leaves for the White River to-night, laden to her guards.

The steamer *Pauline Cornell* is reported hard aground below.

The steamer *Belle* takes 106 bales of cotton for St. Louis.

Good middling cotton is selling at $1 46 per pound.

FROM THE ARMY OF THE POTOMAC.

All Quiet—The Negro Troops—Deserters—Miscellaneous.

HEADQUARTERS OF THE ARMY OF THE POTOMAC,
Tuesday, July 19, 1864.

The usual quiet along the lines still prevails, and were it not for the sound of an occasional gun and some picket firing at a few points, one would suppose that no enemy was within miles of us.

Gen. BURNSIDE's men make the most of the noise, the enemy taking every opportunity to fire on the colored troops that occupy a portion of his front, and of course the fire is returned with interest, but without much damage on either side.

No deserters come in on this part of the line, as they say they have no chance of getting through without being shot, the negroes being so constantly on the alert.

Deserters, however, are coming into our lines daily at other points in squads.

A rebel sergeant and his squad came in this morning, and all report that thousands are ready to leave as fast as opportunity presents.

The deserters come principally from Georgia, Florida and Alabama regiments, and a rebel officer of a regiment from the former State is said to have gone to his superior a day or two since, and stated that if his company was not soon relieved he would have none to relieve, as they would all be gone over to the enemy.

They state that the rebel army is very short of provisions, particularly of vegetables, and they seem to be glad enough when they get into our lines.

Strict orders have been given that they shall not hold intercourse with our men on the picket line or exchange papers, and one fellow, the other day, who came boldly over and brought a paper with him, taking one back, was caught and made to stand on top of a work in full view, and wave the paper back and forth as a punishment.

An attack from the enemy has been expected for the past two days, and last night from what deserters had said, it was looked for as certain, but no demonstration was made.

It has looked like rain all the afternoon, but none has fallen yet, and dust continues to envelope everything.

Gentlemen of prominence, who have returned from the Army of the Potomac, represent Gen. GRANT to be as hopeful as ever of accomplishing his military purposes.

A FIGHT WITH THE RAIDERS.

The Report Comes via Harrisburgh, and is Important if True.

HARRISBURGH, Penn., Wednesday, July 20.

Important dispatches were received here last night, from which it is indicated that our forces are steadily and successfully pursuing the rebels who recently ravaged the east portion of Maryland, and that the pursuing party are wresting large amounts of plunder from the rebels.

Gen. CROOK, while in the pursuit on Monday last, overtook the enemy at Snicker's Gap, where a sharp and, for a time, terrific encounter took place.

The rebels fought like devils, anxious to save the grain and cattle they had succeeded in carrying that far from Maryland.

Gen. CROOK, however, was as determined that they should not escape. He whipped the rebels thoroughly, capturing over three hundred wagons, heavily laden with grain, and took many prisoners.

As usual the enemy left his dead and wounded on the field to be buried and cared for.

Successful Naval Expedition.

WASHINGTON, Tuesday, July 19.

The Navy Department has received dispatches from Admiral LEE inclosing a communication from Commander MACOMB, of the United States steamer *Shamrock*, dated July 13, in which the latter reports that on the 12th he sent Lieut.-Commander ENGLISH, with the *Ceres* and the *Whitehead*, to ascend the Scuppernong River in coöperation with a detachment of 80 men under command of Lieut.-Col. CLARKE, to burn the bridge at Columbia to prevent the rebels from transporting supplies to their army at Plymouth, N. C. The expedition was entirely successful, effectually destroying the bridge and disabling a large grist-mill. No opposition was encountered.

From Cape Race.

CAPE RACE, Wednesday, July 20—noon.

Weather thick. Wind Southwest. Thermometer 78°.

Refugees moving south from Atlanta

Confederate camp before the Battle of Atlanta

The New-York Times.

VOL. XIII.—NO. 4003. | NEW-YORK, SATURDAY, JULY 23, 1864. | PRICE FOUR CENTS.

ATLANTA.

A BATTLE ON THURSDAY.

THE ENEMY DEFEATED.

Our Forces Steadily Pushing the Rebels.

Railroad Communication with Richmond Completely Severed.

Only Two Routes of Retreat Open to the Rebels.

Telegraphic Communication with Atlanta.

WASHINGTON, Friday, July 22.

Official information from Gen. SHERMAN represents everything to be progressing in a manner highly satisfactory.

All day before yesterday, our army was engaged with the enemy, and the rebels were steadily driven on into their intrenchments.

The city is in plain view of our troops, and our shells can reach it. Our army is in excellent condition.

Five miles of the railroad between Atlanta and Decatur have been destroyed, and thus the road is rendered useless to the rebels.

The *National Republican* has furnished the following, in advance of its publication:

"Official advices from Gen. SHERMAN received this morning, cover the operations down to last night. The work of investing the city was fast going on. There was hard fighting yesterday, which resulted in the repulse of the enemy in his efforts to dislodge our troops. Gen. PALMER advanced his line to a more advantageous position. Our loss during the day was small.

Gen. SHERMAN holds the railroad leading from Atlanta toward Richmond, so that JOHNSTON cannot escape by that route to reinforce LEE. His only means of leaving Atlanta are by two roads leading south to Macon, and southwest to West Point and Mobile. If JOHNSTON escapes with his army by either of these last-named routes, he will be obliged to move quickly. It is a well-settled opinion in military circles that the rebels can better afford to lose Atlanta than JOHNSTON'S army. It may possibly be true that LONGSTREET is already in command of it.

IMPORTANT REPORT.

Telegraphic Communication With Atlanta.

OFFICE ASSOCIATED PRESS, NEW-YORK, Friday, July 22.

The Western Union Telegraph Company are in communication with Atlanta, Ga., to-day, messages from that place, of this date, having been transmitted over their wires.

No official announcement of the capture or occupation of Atlanta has been received at this office up to this hour, 1:30 P. M.

LATER.

WASHINGTON, Friday, July 22.

Dispatches received by the Government this afternoon announce that the rebel Gen. JOHNSTON has been superseded by Gen. HOOD, and that a battle has taken place between the two armies, in which Gen. SHERMAN defeated the enemy.

THE VERY LATEST.

WASHINGTON, Friday, July 22—11 P. M.

Nothing has been received by the Government in relation to the fall of Atlanta.

The Occupation of Decatur—Rebel Desertion.

LOUISVILLE, Ky., Friday, July 22.

The Nashville *Union*, of yesterday morning, states that on Monday morning Decatur, Ga., was occupied by our forces, thus cutting off all rebel communication with South Carolina by way of Macon. Deserters and stragglers had been coming into our lines in great numbers since our crossing the Chattahoochee. They represent that all hopes of saving Atlanta has disappeared.

From Missouri and Kansas.

FORT LEAVENWORTH, Friday, July 22.

A dispatch this morning from Col. FORD, at Liberty, Mo., says the people in the country north and east of that place are joining THORNTON, and his forces were increasing rapidly. Col. FORD has troops well in hand, but his force is too small to effect much, and reinforcements are asked for.

Arms from here to Kansas City and St. Joseph, for arming the loyal men, are called for by Gen. FISK.

A later dispatch from Col. FORD states that THORNTON, with 2,000 men, is moving north, probably with the intention of striking the railroad at Plattsburgh, and Marvin was in their possession last night. Col. FORD left Liberty at 4 o'clock this morning in pursuit.

Gen. CURTIS, with several armed boats, was patroling the Missouri River to prevent the rebels from crossing.

PICKLER and BANKS are reported to have 1,000 men in Southwest Missouri, threatening Fort Scott and our Southern communication.

It is believed that 5,000 of PRICE'S men are now in Missouri. These, joined by THORNTON'S guerrillas and other bands, will make a formidable force.

A portion of our State militia will be called out and the troops are now being concentrated for cooperation.

Gen. BLUNT is here awaiting orders.

The Indians are troublesome on the Western Colorado mail route. Rumors are prevalent of the capture of Lained and the post at Walnut Creek by them.

The Guerrilla War in Missouri.

ST. JOSEPH, Mo., Thursday, July 21.

THORNTON'S guerrillas turned back from Livingston last night, and occupied Caldwell County. On being joined by another band from the West, the combined force, numbering 800 men, marched on Plattsburgh, Clinton County, and demanded the surrender of the garrison, consisting of two companies of militia. Capt. TURNER, commanding the post, refused to surrender, and told his men to escape. A fight followed. Capt. TURNER was killed, but most of his men escaped.

Militia are arriving here in large numbers, Gov. FISK'S appeal being promptly responded to, and a thousand men will be sent into the field at once. BEN LOAN will soon be here.

ARMY OF THE POTOMAC.

Compliments to the Rebels in the Shape of 200-pound Mortar Shells—Important Movements on the Tapis—Gen. Smith Relieved.

From Our Own Correspondent.

HEADQUARTERS ARMY OF THE POTOMAC, Thursday, July 21, 1864—10 A. M.

Yesterday was a day of more than usual activity at the front.

The enemy opened a battery upon our lines, but our Generals and men have not been idle notwithstanding the Maryland raid, and were prepared for them, returning the compliment with a 13-inch mortar, throwing a 200-pound shell, which blew up a rebel caisson, and silenced their most formidable battery. A new depot was discovered on the Weldon Railroad, which was burned by our shells. There were several officers and men wounded during the fight, which lasted four hours, among whom is Gen. WILCOX, slightly in the thigh, by a fragment of a rebel shell.

There are indications of import, and movements at the front which are not yet proper to publish.

Maj.-Gen. W. F. (Baldy) SMITH has been relieved from the command of the Eighteenth Corps and ordered to report for duty at New-York.

The often repeated statement that Gen. SHERIDAN has gone on a raid, is without the slightest foundation in fact.

We had a gentle rain here yesterday, which continued nearly all day, which was gratefully received by thirsty habitants and mother earth.

The Sanders Correspondence.

BUFFALO, Friday, July 22.

The Agent of the Associated Press at Buffalo, learns from the Clifton House, Niagara, this morning, that by an oversight an important letter of HORACE GREELEY'S was omitted in the published correspondence between himself and the Peace Commissioners. It was not handed the Agent of the Associated Press, or it would have appeared with the rest.

Fearful Accident at Niagara Falls—Horace Greeley's Letter.

BUFFALO, Friday, July 22.

An accident occurred on Goat Island, Niagara Falls, this afternoon, near the Biddle Stairs. A carriage containing the wife of Capt. WEBSTER and the wife of Capt HUNT, of the Quartermasters Department, was precipitated over the precipice in consequence of the horses taking fright. Fortunately a shelf in the rock some thirty feet down, broke their fall, and the ladies lodged in the trees. One was severely, and the other slightly, injured.

The omitted letter of HORACE GREELEY, previously spoken of, appears to be simply a letter to W. C. JEWETT, who, fearing that he might be arrested for his connection with the so-called Peace Commissioners, requested Mr. GREELEY to write him a lette stating that what he (JEWETT) had done in the matter was from patriotic motives, and by his (GREELEY'S) desire.

Conflagration in Mexico, Oswego County.

OSWEGO, Friday, July 22.

About one-half of the business portion of the village of Mexico, Oswego County, was destroyed by fire this afternoon. The fire originated in Phenix Block, consuming Parkhurst's dry goods store, Brooks & Huntington's drug-store, Clinton & Eaton's store, Stone & Fuller's hardware store, Holmes & Taylor's shop, Jackson's produce store, Butler's store, the Post-office, Gort's billiard rooms, the Mexico Hotel and barns, and Tickner's house and livery stable. No estimate of the loss has been received. The property was well insured.

Fire in Chicago—Rioters Found Dead.

CHICAGO, Friday, July 22.

The planing-mill of GAGE & SOPER was destroyed by fire this afternoon. Loss $25,000; insurance not known.

Advices from Coles County report that the two O'HAIRS, the instigators and leaders in the riots at Charlestown last March, were found dead, one of them with several bullet holes through the body. Some excitement exists in that county, and fears are entertained of another outbreak.

Arrest of the Editor of the Newark Evening Journal.

NEWARK, N. J., Friday, July 22.

E. N. FULLER, editor of the Newark *Evening Journal*, was arrested at 12 o'clock to-day, on two warrants. The first was for inciting to insurrection, and the second for discouraging enlistments, as provided for by section five of the Enrollment Act. He was released on bail by United States Commissioner MORRIS, he giving bonds in the sum of $7,000.

Indian Hostilities.

OMAHA CITY, Friday, July 22.

Some Indians attacked a train last night 20 miles above Fort Laramie, cut loose 52 horses, and ran them off. A sharp fight ensued, in which about 20 shots were fired, and some of the Indians were wounded. Most of the horses were subsequently recaptured.

The women are reported to be leaving Plum Creek for a place of greater safety. A large party of hostile Indians are reported about 40 miles from that place.

Fire in Boston.

BOSTON, Friday, July 22.

The extensive steam flouring mill, corner of Merrimac and Causeway streets, owned by WILLIAM MARKHAM, and occupied by JOHN F. KEATING, was destroyed by fire this forenoon. Two wooden buildings adjoining were also burnt, one of them occupied by the Boston Union Watch Company. The total loss is $40,000; partly insured.

Naval Captures.

WASHINGTON, Friday, July 22.

The Navy Department has received information of the capture, off Mosquito Inlet, Fla., of the sloop *Sarah Mary* of Nassau, N. P., June 26, with nine bales of cotton. The sloop being unseaworthy, has since sunk, but her cargo was saved.

The United States steamer *Ladona* captured the sloop *Hope*, of Nassau, while attempting to run out of Sapelo July 10, with seventeen bales of cotton and nine boxes of tobacco.

Fire in Philadelphia.

PHILADELPHIA, Friday, July 22.

The Government wagon factory of HENRY SIMONS took fire at 8 o'clock, and will probably be entirely consumed. It is the largest establishment of the kind in the country.

The Weather.

CAPE RACE, Friday, July 22.

Wind southeast: hazy and raining; thermometer 40°.

—The St. Louis *Union* says that Gen. PLEASONTON has been appointed commander of the Department of Missouri, now under Gen. FISK.

LATE SOUTHERN NEWS.

GEN. JOHNSTON RELIEVED FROM COMMAND.

General Hood Appointed to Succeed Him.

Gen. Sherman Cuts Communication Between Atlanta and Montgomery.

From Richmond papers of the 18th and 20th, we obtain the following interesting information:

FROM GEORGIA.

ATLANTA, Monday, July 18, 1864.

The army and public were surprised this morning by the announcement of the change of commanders—Gen. JOHNSTON being relieved, and Gen. HOOD receiving the command. The following is Gen. JOHNSTON'S farewell address to the troops:

HEADQUARTERS ARMY OF TENNESSEE, July 17, 1864.

In obedience to orders of the War Department, I turn over to Gen. HOOD the command of the Army and Department of Tennessee. I cannot leave without expressing my admiration of the high military qualities it has displayed so conspicuously—every soldier's virtue, endurance of toil, obedience to orders, brilliant courage. The enemy move but to be severely repulsed and punished. You, soldiers, have never argued but from your courage, and never counted your fears. No longer your leader, I will still watch your career, and will rejoice in your victories. To one and all I offer assurances of my friendship, and bid an affectionate farewell.

(Signed) J. E. JOHNSTON, General.

Gen. HOOD, on assuming command, issued the following address:

HEADQUARTERS ARMY OF TENNESSEE, July 18, 1864.

SOLDIERS: In obedience to orders from the War Department, I assume command of this army and department. I feel the weight of the responsibility so suddenly and unexpectedly devolved upon me by this position, and shall bend all my energies and employ all my skill to meet its requirements. I look with confidence to your patriotism to stand by me, and rely upon your prowess to wrest your country from the grasp of the invader, entitling yourselves to the proud distinction of being called the deliverers of an oppressed people.

(Signed) J. B. HOOD, General.

Telegraphic communications with Montgomery was suspended last night near Notasulga. The interruption is supposed to have been caused by a portion of that part of the enemy who were reported to be at Talladega on Saturday. No train has arrived to-day from West Point. The main forces of the enemy crossed the Chattahoochee between Isham's Ford and Rosswell, and are slowly pushing forward. Cavalry skirmishing took place this morning at Buck Head, six miles from this place.

THE SITUATION.

From the Richmond Examiner, July 20.

Yesterday was a quiet day. There was no booming of cannon, no heavy masses of smoke on the Southern horizon, and no exciting rumors from any quarter. The fact that the flags of the Yankee shipping in James River were at half-mast on Monday caused many to give credit to the report of GRANT'S death, and this topic and the removal of Gen. J. E. JOHNSTON from the command of the Army of Tennessee, were the topics that chiefly occupied men's minds. Though no one believed his death would be of any great benefit to us, yet every one would have been glad, on general principles, to have been assured of his death. The Yankees think too much of him, and that is sufficient to make us rejoice over any misfortune that might befall him.

We have nothing later from our forces operating in Maryland than the news published yesterday. Other officers and men, wounded at Monocacy, arrived yesterday; but they bring nothing new, except that they estimate the number of horses obtained and secured by us in the raid at seven instead of five thousand.

The only news we have from Georgia is contained in the press dispatch, published in another column. From that it will be seen that affairs at Atlanta begin to wear a serious aspect. SHERMAN and his whole army has crossed to the east bank of the Chattahoochee River, and his cavalry were skirmishing with HOOD'S, within six miles of Atlanta. If Atlanta is to be defended a battle must be delivered within a very brief period. If the enemy is allowed to intrench, having the larger army, he will immediately out-flank Gen. HOOD or oblige him to fall back. The eyes of the country are anxiously turned to this quarter. The dispatch alluded to says, "the army and the public were surprised by the announcement of the change of Commanders." The army and the public in Virginia have seen and experienced such strange things in the last three years, as to have lost the faculty of being surprised at anything done by those in authority.

From the Richmond Examiner.

* * * * The expedition has also shown how easily such things are done against an enemy that attempts enterprises beyond his strength, and strips his own capital of defenders to swell his armies sent against distant cities. Our troops are charmed, on the whole, with the little campaign. They consider that five or six thousand horses, two or three thousand cattle, and eight hundred prisoners, all brought safely across the Potomac (except FRANKLIN and TYLER) was no bad result of a few days' dash into Maryland. They won one small battle, and they lived well; the fighting was good, the eating and especially the drinking was "glorious," and in short, Mr. LINCOLN'S official organ declares that "the rebels are so flattered because they have put Washington and Baltimore in terror, that they will not hesitate to repeat the experiment." We think that extremely likely.

Possibly, too, our Government may at last—but of this we are not sanguine—find out that its duty to its own people does really require it to hurt a little the enemies of that people, when it has the power. And if not, then the people themselves will begin to conclude that the worst enemy they have is the Government which they established for their protection.

HOW TO PROTECT SOUTHERN RAILROADS.

From the Richmond Examiner, July 15.

Of such glorious rumors as those which pervaded the town on yesterday, it is best to decline discourse till we know whether they are truths or only illusions of hope. Let us attend to another report of a different character—that GRANT'S cavalry has started on a fresh raid against the Weldon Railroad.

One of the marked peculiarities of the people with whom we war is, that they publish their military intentions in newspapers before commencing their execution. One of the peculiarities of the singular breed of small politicians set over us at Montgomery, is a resolute disbelief in all information that comes to them through a plain, ordinary public channel. Although the result has a hundred times proven that the plan made public in the New-York paper was really the plan of the enemy's General or Government, they cannot comprehend the fact that the enemy does so give notice of their designs. The publication is to them a perfect proof that they are going to do something else.

They could not believe that this campaign in Virginia was intended, chiefly because the scheme was universally published. They pay as little attention to the plan now ascribed to GRANT by that same press. That plan is simple—to keep a large army close to Petersburgh and LEE, while cavalry raids cut the railroads leading into Richmond as fast as we can mend them.

This plan will be successfully executed if the Confederate authorities do not devise a method of defending the roads. It is useless to repair, if the cavalry can ride in about the time the work is completed and undo it in a couple of hours. They must defend the roads. They must defend the roads by other means than the single method hitherto attempted; because that method has proven utterly and invariably ineffectual—there has not been a solitary exception in the course of the war. The single method yet imagined or tried is, to send our Confederate cavalry in pursuit of the Yankee cavalry. But, as one body of horse will go as fast as another, those who have six hours start are not overtaken before the goal is reached. After the destruction is done and the Yankee raiders have to return, they are sometimes met and sometimes not. When collision occurs, our cavalry sometimes beats them, as they did the other day. But the railroad is broken, and the beating does not mend it.

The object being the salvation of the roads, it is clear that another means should be employed. It would seem to an observer that of all kinds of communication, a railroad should be the easiest to preserve and defend. Steam is stronger than horse flesh; locomotives move faster than cavalry; and a single train can transport a large body of troops to any point on the line in a few hours. But a large body of troops is not necessary to obstruct the advance of cavalry. A few hundred picked and well-mounted men can obstruct roads and bushwack the strongest raid till the pursuing cavalry overtakes and destroys it. Only these few hundred must be before and not behind it —and the railroad can put both them and their horses where they will get before it, if they and the train to convey them are kept in perpetual readiness at a depot. Hitherto the *militia* has been relied on for that work. Is it not time to discover that this expectation is a stupidity? The militia is composed of stiff-limbed old men and little boys, both equally unaccustomed to arms. Yet they are expected to perform the most dangerous as well as the most laborious service that can be demanded of the hardiest and most skillful soldier. To bushwhack is a military duty, requiring more confidence in one's weapon, greater strength of body and a cooler courage than any other whatever. The man, who does it, has to close alone with the enemy, and if caught is killed. For such a service thorough soldiers are required, and this or some other plan must be resorted to, if we would save our roads.

THE MARYLAND RAID.

From the Richmond Enquirer, July 18.

From three to five hundred prisoners have passed through Rockingham from Maryland, captured principally during the first of the invasion by our forces. They are principally Ohians, and nearly all were one hundred day men.

FROM THE INVASION.

Passengers from Staunton last night report that the "invaders" of Maryland were safely south of the Potomac, with a whole country crammed full of all sorts of live and vegetable plunder.

FOREIGN GOODS AT WILMINGTON.

M. CROULY, Auctioneer, advertises that he will sell at auction, July 29, a vast quantity of foreign goods, the cargoes of steamships *Badger* and *Lucy*, and several other vessels, under the heads of dry goods, shoes, leather, &c., cotton cards, clothing, &c., stationery, bagging and rope, groceries, hardware, &c., liquors, &c., drugs, &c.

WESLEYAN UNIVERSITY.

Commencement Exercises—Concert—General News of the Place—Mendelssohn Quintette Club of Boston.

Correspondence of the New-York Times:

MIDDLETOWN, Friday, July 22, 1864.

Unquestionably, the principal object of interest in Middletown, and the one most eagerly inquired after by the stranger visiting this city, is the Wesleyan College. The annual commencement exercises attract crowds of the citizens, and also many strangers, and they certainly go away gratified, or they would not return with such evident eagerness. At the present time, when the country is awaiting, with almost feverish anxiety, for some great movement on the part of our armies, college exercises lose, I am well aware, much of the prestige which usually attends such celebrations; but they never can entirely cease to awaken interest among those who recollect that commencement at any college sends forth to the great field of public life a new set of young men amply qualified to play their *rôle*. Some go to help fill up our armies, others to the judiciary, some to the ministry; and, in fact, nearly all the roads to fame, fortune and glory find many travelers.

The present graduating class has twenty-three members, and a fine-looking set are they, too. Having entered before the commencement of the war, they have been able to follow the course of the rebellion clear up to the present moment, from its very beginning. They go forth, therefore, with a thorough knowledge of the past, a confidence in the future, and the determination to make the most of the present. Among them are many, perhaps more than the usual number, who intend devoting their life to the Gospel ministry, and they bear with them all the evidences of a sure success. Commencement exercises usually last about a week, and Commencement Week is therefore looked forward to as a week of pleasure and amusement by all interested in the college. At the close of the Senior examination, some three weeks ago, when the studies of the class of '64 became things of the past, and all that the Seniors for the next three weeks had to do was to prepare their orations, the class had some exercises of an unusual kind. In the afternoon of the day designated the class had a *campus* on the college green, where the calumet was smoked with evident satisfaction to some and a little "uneasiness below" to others. Songs and long-winded speeches followed, and as the class has a "State-wide" renown for its superior singing, the effect was decidedly agreeable to outsiders. The evening exercises were in the McDonough Hall. The songs were all by members of the graduating class, and were well sung, and one of them, a German song, to the popular tune of "When Johnny Comes Marching Home," was loudly applauded and *encored*. The orator was A. H. WYATT, and he spoke very eloquently and learnedly to his fellow-classmates. His theme was the "Present," and he was succeeded by G. L. THOMPSON, the Class Historian, who took for his theme the "Past," and "well and pleasantly did he discourse thereon." His numerous hits on his mates, puns on their names, descriptions of the many scrapes and scenes through which they had passed, afforded amusement to all who knew anything about the class. His manner of describing the "putting through" of the new Freshmen, and of the numerous deceptions and tricks practiced on them afforded, I am sure, considerable information to the present Junior Class as to several previously mysterious affairs. Next came the Class Prophet, J. D. BEEMAN, who foretold from a vision the *future* of his classmates. For the most part their *aims* were low, but some of them seem destined to reach a good way up the ladder of fame. The evening exercises concluded at an early hour with one of the college songs. The class had a supper in the evening, and broke up in the early hours of the morning only to serenade the President, Professors and fellow students. But Commencement Week really opened last Thursday, July 14, with the "Prize Contest between the Literary Societies." There was a prize debate and prize oration; the two literary societies send some of their members from each class to compete. The successful orator was J. W. H. AMES, Valedictorian of the Graduating Class, the names of the others your correspondent was unable to ascertain. On Friday evening was the prize declamation between the Senior and Sophomore Classes. As on the preceding evening, the Hall was crowded, and the following is a list of the declaimers: L. R. Abbott, C. W. Willard, A. G. Nightingale, S. H. Olin, H. J. Stevens, G. Yager, W. W. Bowdish, A. Clark, W. U. Rice, S. K. Smith, G. L. Westgate, U. F. Whitaker. The young men, almost without exception, showed a thorough appreciation of their subject, and evinced considerable study, doing great credit to their instructor. G. L. WESTGATE took the first prize, and G. YAGER the second. The music was by COLT'S Armory Band, from Hartford, and was very good. On Sunday, the Baccalaureate sermon in the morning, by Rev. JOSEPH CUMMINGS, D. D., President of the College, attracted quite a number to the M. E. Church. The text was from 1 Corinthians, xv. chapter and 29th verse. The Doctor's discourse lasted one hour and a quarter, which, on a hot day, is pretty close work; but his eloquence and earnestness kept the large assembly silent and attentive. Politics, of course, entered largely into the sermon, and, as the Doctor is a thorough Abolitionist, the "rights of man" afforded him a grand chance for reminding the graduating class of the fact that "all men are equal." In the evening, an address before the Missionary Lyceum, composed of those young men mostly who intend becoming ministers, and in which debates on religious subjects are a prominent part of the exercises, was delivered by Rev. ROBERT S. DASKILL, a Methodist divine of considerable repute. J. J. REED, Jr., of the Class of '64, is President of the Lyceum. On Monday evening, the addresses before the United Literary Societies. The orator on this occasion was Hon. SIDNEY DEAN, who delivered a rich and racy discourse on the members of Congress in 1855, of which he was one. Rev. WM. S. STUDLEY delivered the poem on what I should judge to be the follies of the age, though the real subject could with difficulty be discovered by any one. It was quite humorous, however, and was very well received. On Tuesday afternoon took place the meeting of the joint Board of Trustees and Visitors, and in the evening an address before the Phi Beta Kappa Fraternity, by GEORGE THOMPSON, of England. Mr. THOMPSON'S fame as an orator is world-wide, and he fully sustained his reputation. Mr. THOMPSON at first does not impress a person favorably, and it is only when he becomes well warmed up in his discourse that he commands attention, and interests his audience. His comparison between his reception in and departure from this country, thirty years ago, when he was mobbed wherever he attempted to speak, and his reception at the present time, was very amusing. The applause at the mention of the name of GARRISON showed the sympathy of the audience. On Wednesday morning, the business meeting and anniversary of the Alumni Association, and in the afternoon, the address before the Alumni, by Rev. ERASTUS WENTWORTH, D. D. A reunion of the classes of 1839, '40, '54, '57 and '61, took place. The reunion of the classes proved a very interesting occasion, and many and fervent were the welcomings among classmates. The hotels are all crowded, and there is an unusual number of strangers in the place, which gives it a decidedly gay and festive appearance. On Wednesday occurred the grand commencement concert by the celebrated Mendelssohn Quintette Club of Boston. This club is always a favorite in Middletown, and, in fact, everywhere that they go, both by the excellence of their programme and their splendid execution of it. Their performance last evening fully equaled all that was expected of them. Each member of the club is an artist, playing two or three instruments (not at once) as a master, and their combined efforts prove attractive without equal. The names of the performers are: WM. SCHULTZE, CARL WEISEL, ROBERT GOERING, THOMAS RYAN, WOLF GRIES, assisted by the distinguished vocalist, Miss ADDIE S. RYAN. Many of their pieces were deservedly *encored*, and all felt perfectly satisfied with the manner in which they had spent their money.

Thursday, the grand day, at length arrived, and no doubt many a graduate passed a sleepless night, studying and perfecting his morrow's oration. Thursday morning came at last, and with it a thick mist, the sure precursor of either a hot day or a rainy one, neither very agreeable. At an early hour graduates and sub-graduates might have been seen hurrying to and fro across the college green, and many hearty shake of the hand and happy greeting was interchanged among those so soon to part forever. At 9 A. M., Colt's Band, of Hartford, broke forth with martial strains for the procession to form. At 9:30 the procession, headed by the band, with the Provost-Marshal, and followed by the Board of Trustees and visitors, the President, the alumni, distinguished strangers, the graduating class and the college generally, left the University, and proceeded to the church. At the church, the exercises opened with music by the Mendelssohn Club, followed by a prayer by the President, and again music. The salutatory address, in Latin, by THOMAS BOND WOOD, Greencastle, Ind. I will give the orations, as nearly as possible, in the order of merit: Valedictory, by JACOB W. H. AMES, Newport, N. H.; Salutatory—T. B. WOOD, Greencastle, Ind.; Philosophical—GEORGE S. BENNETT, Wilkesbarre, Penn.; Philosophical—JESSE LYMAN HURLBUT, Pennington, N. J.; Ancient Classical, CHARLES WASHBURN CHURCH, Waterbury; Metaphysical—ALBERT HARMON WYATT, Harlem, N. Y.; First-class Orations—CHARLES AMOS MERRILL, Concord, N. H.; B. WHITTEMORE CHASE, Haverhill, Mass.; CHARLES HENRY BUCK, Naponset, Mass.; RICHARD WATSON NEWHALL, Middletown; HENRY BAKER, Pennington, N. J.; COSTELLO LIPPITT, Norwich; HENRY C. M. INGRAHAM, Brooklyn, N. Y.; GEORGE FORSYTH, Armenia, N. Y.; JOHN JOSEPH REED, Jr., Williamsburgh, L. I.; JOHN SWINBURNE WHEDON, Newark, N. J. Orations—WILLIAM SHERIDAN TODD, South Deerfield, Mass.; GEORGE L. THOMPSON, Oiselle, N. Y.; GEORGE NELSON PHELPS, Waterfield; I. DURKEE BEEMAN, North Fairfax, Vt.; STEPHEN AUGUSTUS SNOW, Providence, R. I.; EDWARD HILLER BRECKINRIDGE, Middletown. The degree of "Bachelor of Arts" was given to the graduating class, and that of "A. M." to some nine of the Alumni. The degree of LL.D. was conferred upon Hon. GEO. THOMPSON, of London, amid much applause.

I dislike to speak particularly of any one, but I must say, concerning the valedictorian of the class of 1864 that at eighteen years of age he was a sailor before the mast, not acquainted with much more than his letters, and at twenty-four he graduated head scholar in a class of 23 good scholars all. There is an example for our young men that it is "never too late to mend." By the way, Mr. AMES is to be married this evening. The orations were all very fine and well-delivered; deserving especial mention are those by Messrs. AMES, MERRILL, WYATT, BAKER, WOOD, NEWHALL and INGRAHAM. The exercises were all very pleasantly interspersed with excellent music, and passed off very satisfactory to all concerned. The Alumni, visitors and graduating class, had their festival in the P. M., and in the evening the President held his levee. To-morrow Middletown will relapse into its usual quiet, and the enthusiasm and excitement of Commencement Day with the class of '64, will exist only in the past. The following is a correct and official list of the degrees conferred with which I have at the moment of closing been favored:

The Degree of Bachelor of Arts was conferred on Jacob Worthen Hall Ames, Henry Baker, J. Durkee Beeman, George Slocum Bennett, Edward Hiller Breckinridge, Charles Henry Buck, B. Whittemore Chase, Charles Washburn Church, George Forsyth, Daniel Gould Harriman, Jesse Lyman Hurlbut, Henry C. M. Ingraham, Costello Lippitt, Charles Amos Merrill, Richard Watson Newhall, George Nelson Phelps, John Joseph Reed, Jr., Stephen Augustus Snow, George L. Thompson, Wm. Sheridan Todd, John Swinburne Whedon, Thos. Bond Wood, Albert Harmon Wyatt, Daniel W. Raymond.

The degree of Master of Arts was conferred in course on Edgar Hiram Bancroft, John Wesley Barnhart, James William Brambler, William Dawson Bridge, Edgar Frederick Clark, Roswell Sergeant Douglas, Francis Daniel Edgerton, Christopher Page Flanders, Benjamin Sherwood Gurnee, William Fisk Johnston, Hiram Loammi Leisey, Frank Wilbur Morse, Wilbur Fisk Osborne, Hubbard Bester Payne, George Whitaker, Nathan Willis Wilder, Richard Seaman Williams, William Henry Lee, of the Class of 1860.

The degree of Master of Arts was also conferred on Frederick Wm. Corliss, a graduate of Union College, and on George Lansing Taylor, a graduate of Columbia College.

The honorary degree of Master of Arts was conferred on Rev. Benjamin F. Cocker, Rev. Chas. N. Smith, Rev. Lorenzo White.

The degree of Doctor of Divinity was conferred on Rev. Robert Allyn, Rev. Isaac W. Wiley.

The degree of LL. D. was conferred on George Thompson, of England. H. W. R.

Turf Record.

EXCITING TROT AT THE FASHION COURSE.

SUMMARY.

FRIDAY, July 22—Match for $300.—Mile heats, best 3 in 5, play or pay.

Dan Mace named b. g. Stonewall Jackson, (in harness)........ 2 2 1 1 1

John Lovett named s. m. Lady Tompkins, (in harness)........ 1 1 2 2 2

TIME:

	Quarter.	Half.	Mile.
First heat	0:40¾	1:19	2:40
Second heat	0:41¾	1:20	2:41¾
Third heat	0:39¾	1:18	2:40
Fourth heat	0:40¾	1:19	2:39
Fifth heat	0:39	1:17¾	2:40

First Heat.—From his easy victory over the mare last Friday, under the same conditions as in to-day's trot, *Stonewall* was made the favorite, odds of 100 to 50 and 50 to 20 being laid on him. The partisans of *Lady Tompkins*, however, were sanguine enough to believe that she could beat him. At the third attempt they got off, the mare taking the lead of a length, and the pole from *Stonewall* at the upper turn, and maintaining it to the first quarter; at the old stand the mare was two lengths ahead. There was no alteration subsequently, *Stonewall* being up and down, the mare coming home an easy winner by a length.

Second Heat.—Betting 100 to 40 on *Stonewall*. The mare again took the lead at the turn, and kept it down the back stretch, past the old stand, half-mile pole, to the lower turn, where *Stonewall* tried to close the gap; but in the home stretch he went off his feet, the mare coming home an easy winner by a neck—*Stonewall* running half way up the distance.

Third Heat.—Notwithstanding the mare having put in two heats, the backers of *Stonewall* freely laid 2 to 1 on him. In the start the mare had a slight lead, but in making the turn she broke, and *Stonewall* took a lead of two lengths as he passed the quarter. He in turn broke and ran, but getting down again, he passed the old stand with a length in hand, at the lower turn the mare tried to close up, and succeeding, they came neck-and-neck into the home-stretch, but *Stonewall* outfooting her, had the heat in hand, and won cleverly by a length.

Fourth Heat.—100 to 40 on *Stonewall*. They were wheel-and-wheel to the turn, where *Stonewall* broke and ran, obtaining a lead of a length, increasing it to two at the quarter-pole; he again broke at the old stand but catching quickly, continued to lead past the half mile, and round the turn into the home-stretch, where the mare tried to close, but breaking up at the distance badly, *Stonewall* came home the easiest of winners by eight or ten lengths.

Fifth Heat.—100 to 15 on *Stonewall*, who took a lead of a length at the first turn, and continued past the quarter pole to the old stand, where the mare began to fall off, *Stonewall* leading her two lengths, he here broke, and ran, but was got down again, and passed the half mile with the same advantage, and continued to the home stretch—half way up the mare broke, and *Stonewall* came home the winner of the heat and race by ten lengths.

The Charleston Mercury.

DAILY PAPER—TWENTY DOLLARS FOR SIX MONTHS—PAYABLE IN ADVANCE. | VINDICE NULLO SPONTE SUA SINE LEGE FIDES RECTUMQUE COLLENTUR. | COUNTRY PAPER—THRICE A WEEK—TWELVE DOLLARS FOR SIX MONTHS—PAYABLE IN ADVANCE.

Volume LXXXV. | CHARLESTON, S. C., TUESDAY, JULY 26, 1864. | Number 12,122.

TELEGRAPHIC.

LATEST FROM HOOD'S ARMY.

RICHMOND, July 25.—An official despatch from General Hood, dated July 23, says: "In the engagement of the 22d eighteen stand of colors were captured, instead of five, and thirteen guns, instead of twenty-two, as previously reported. General MERCER was not wounded." Another despatch, dated the 24th, says: "All quiet to-day, except a little picket firing and occasional shells thrown into the city."

ATLANTA, July 25.—There has been continuous skirmishing for the past two days. Many shells from the enemy's batteries have entered the city. A few houses have been struck, but no material damage was done. The enemy's extreme right endeavored, yesterday, to gain possession of a commanding eminence between their lines and ours, but were repulsed by the 11th Texas regiment. All quiet this morning.

THE MERCURY.

TUESDAY, JULY 26, 1864.

The Richmond Sentinel and Gen. Johnston.

The Richmond *Sentinel*, speaking with the air of authority, remarks:

"The people do not *generally* know that all the while that Johnston has been retreating before Sherman, he has had an army approaching nearer in numbers to that of his adversary, than Lee ever had when he has won his great victories. Indeed, at Dalton, and ever since he left there, his army has been large enough to justify and render it his duty to deliver battle."

We agree with the *Sentinel*, that the people *generally*, have not the information the above assertion contains. We go further—we do not know of anybody who does possess it. We go further still—we doubt if the *Sentinel* possesses it. To be sure, we have not access to the back stairs of the War Department, but we are in a pretty good position, to know the truth, as to the condition and numbers of the army lately under General JOHNSTON, and now under General HOOD, and the strength of General SHERMAN'S army opposed to it, and according to the information we have obtained, the *Sentinel* is totally misinformed. We would rejoice to know that the *Sentinel* is correct in its information; but there is no such equality of forces between the two armies as he asserts to exist. But, supposing that its assertions are true, has not General JOHNSTON done exactly what General LEE performed. He, like General LEE, has stood on the defensive; and has fought the enemy, whenever he could do so to advantage, and like GEN. LEE, has retreated when outflanked and he could not fight with advantage. They have both travelled in retreating about the same distance—the one to Richmond—the other to Atlanta, and both have whipped the enemy wherever he has been encountered. But the difference between them has been this. When General LEE reached Richmond, he found reinforcements drawn from other sources, of some thirty thousand men. When General JOHNSTON reached Atlanta, he met no reinforcements, excepting some raw militia reserves called out by the Governor of Georgia. Not even FORREST and MORGAN have been allowed him. The comparison between LEE and JOHNSTON is worth nothing, unless it can be shown that LEE did what JOHNSTON did not do. JOHNSTON is blamed for not assuming the aggressive—but did LEE assume the aggressive? If not—there is notning in LEE'S campaign, from which censure can be deduced against JOHNSTON.

But we notice this animadversion of the *Sentinel*, not to defend General JOHNSTON or General LEE, but for another and more important purpose. If the *Sentinel's* remarks reflects the policy of the Administration, General Hood will receive no reinforcements. He will be expected to fight and drive General SHERMAN out of Georgia and Tennessee with the troops he possesses. Now, this is a most serious and, to us, a very formidable intimation. The consequences of a defeat of the army General HOOD commands, are so vast and important, that he can be no statesman who will allow it, if he can possibly help it, to be put even at hazard. Let that army be defeated, and the thirty five thousand Yankee prisoners now near Americus will be released, and join the Yankee army; and Georgia and South Carolina, Savannah and Augusta, Charleston and Columbia, in all probability fall into their possession. Is it possible, that with such vast interests at stake, the Government of the Confederate States will not speedily concentrate all the troops it can bring together in the west and in Virginia, to strengthen the only bulwark against their destruction—the Army of Western Georgia? Even if they should not be wanted, from the matchless valor of our troops, to save these interests,—are they not wanted to conquer and destroy our foes, and open a highway through Kentucky, to the crowning blessing of peace? With means on all sides to reinforce this army, shall they persistently and desperately be kept away?

FROM THE ARMY OF TENNESSEE.

THE FIGHTING AROUND ATLANTA.

BEHIND THE CHATTAHOOCHEE, July 20.

The great game for the possession of Atlanta is seemingly about to begin, and all indications point to a bloody struggle. I briefly sum up the situation as follows, asking your attention to a map that localities may be properly understood. Flowing from east to west, and emptying into the Chattahoochee River is Peach Tree Creek, forming as it were the base of an inverted triangle, the two sides of which are the Marietta and Augusta Railroads. The enemy's forces consisting of seven corps, crossed the river on the north side of the creek, and subsequently were permitted to fortify and establish themselves on the south side, where they are to-day. The country is broken, thickly covered with forests and undergrowth, and hence admirable positions have been chosen by both armies. Riding along our lines last evening, I found the men busy in building entrenchments after their own notions, and preparing for the battle which appeared about to burst. Some of the commands, more nice than others had even erected bowers of leaves above the works as a shield from sun and rain. Skirmishing was audible in the distance, while from the extreme left, the heavy booming of artillery proclaimed a duel between two rival batteries.

The movements of this morning have been in a measure significant of the events about to follow. At daylight the enemy commenced pressing our cavalry on the right, now covering the Augusta and Atlanta Railroad, several miles of which they destroyed. Heavy skirmishing ensued, during which the enemy planted a battery within range of the city and threw three shells in the vicinity of one of our hospitals, no more than five hundred yards from the heart of the town. Gen. Wheeler, observing this diabolic act, promptly ran a battery into position, and after a half dozen well directed shots, drove the Yankees from their temporary foot-hold. Believing that their demonstration was the beginning of a general attack, I left Wheeler's lines and rode towards headquarters. Troops appeared to be in motion on all sides; Gen. Manigault with three brigades of Hindman's division was throwing up heavy breastworks across the elegant ground which encloses one of the handsomest residences in the vicinity of Atlanta.—Dismounted cavalry were getting into line; wagons pushing to the rear; and couriers dashing by, while far and near there arose about the luxuriant woods heavy clouds of dust, which betokened the manœuvering of troops.

Spurring forward to the headquarters of the Commander-in-Chief, which had been transferred to the edge of town, and nearer the centre of our lines, I found there other signs which added to the perplexity of the moment. The principal officers of the army were in close council—all grave, severe, and apparently deeply impressed with some new responsibility. The consultation concluded, the Generals mounted and, followed by their respective staffs, rode swiftly away in the direction of the army.

At just twelve o'clock, a gathering of General Hood's own military household in front of headquarters announced still another in the chain of mysterious events. But I had not long to wait for the unravelling of the web. The noble Texan, arrayed in full uniform, leaning on his crutch and stick, was standing in the doorway, his manner calm, but his eyes flashing with a strange indescribable light, which gleams in them only in the hour of battle. His first observation as he took my hand, was "Mr. ——, at one I attack the the enemy. He has pressed our lines until he is within a short distance of Atlanta, and I must fight or evacuate. I am going to fight. The odds are against us, but I leave the issue with the God of Battles." We parted, and General Hood with his staff, General Lovell, General Mackall, and escort, then proceeded to the lines. I have remained at headquarters to write these hurried words anticipatory of the battle.

The moments are slipping by, as anxious moments always do, tediously and yet not without a sensation of heart agony that is utterly depressing. One hour more and the mettle of an army opposed by double its numbers, fighting behind breastworks, with diabolic incentive, the spiries of Atlanta in view, and its booty in prospect, will be undergoing an ordeal by fire. One hour more and hundreds of dear friends, whose merry laugh you have answered around their camp fires may be weltering in their blood at these strange hill-sides, or gone forever to their long homes. One hour more and thousands will become widows and orphans, and weary heart cries will ascend to Heaven over the new sacrifice which the cruel struggle demands; while brave men borne to the rear, will linger for a time under the knife and saw of the surgeons, and then perhaps return to their homes maimed for life.

We read of war and its glories, and enthusiasm pervades our nature at every recital of an heroic act; but, when the dreadful reality confronts us, bounded only by the space of an hour or a moment, there is something within us which voluntarily recoils at the repetition of those scenes of suffering and death which, however beneficial in their results to the country, such a fearful price for the good attained, that we remember them only with a shudder. How much more so under circumstances like the present, when the very existence of an army hangs in the balance!

Night—July 20.

A battle, or rather an engagement, has taken place, and the fitful splashes of musketry along the lines, denotes that it has ended without substantial results. I am too weary to enter much into details, and probably it would not be prudent to do so, first, because of the incompleteness of the affair, and secondly, the liability of capture while the letter is *en route* to Macon, it being feared that the enemy will strike our only remaining line of communication to-night. The following, therefore, is only a simple outline of the afternoon's work.

The object of Gen. Hood in planning the attack was two fold, namely, to withdraw if possible from the enemy's left to centre and right a portion of the forces with which he had been so persistently pressing our right, and to defeat and cut up one of his wings.

By examining the map and recalling the preceding description of the situation of Sherman's forces, you will observe that a portion of the line of the latter extended from near the junction of the Chattahoochee and Peach Tree Creek in an easterly direction. Into this angle it was believed that by a proper combination of our forces we could drive the right of Sherman's army, and effect the object in view. Stewart's corps held our left, Hardee the centre. The attack by these two bodies was nearly simultaneous. The advance commenced about two o'clock. Leaving their breastworks, our men slowly but confidently pushed their way towards the front.—Skirmishing began almost immediately.—Strange to say a part of the enemy's line was discovered to be also advancing. Our men charged with a yell and drove it back in disorder. One, two, and in some instances three lines of incipient or temporary breastworks were mounted and left behind, and the battle in our favor appeared to go on swimmingly.—Suddenly Stewart was brought to a stand still. In his front was the main line of Yankee entrenchments and a redoubt manned by a battery. Gathering fresh strength, however, one of his brigades plunged against the work and it yielded. A heavy enfilading fire from a park of artillery on the right drove them back. The Federals reoccupied the redoubts. Our men advanced a second time, and again captured it, but by the same terrible fire poured upon them from the distant artillery, were compelled to abandon the prize. Meanwhile Hardee had also reached the continuation of the same line. His men fighting bravely, had overcome every obstacle thus far, and were prepared to dash yet further on, and drive the enemy into the creek. But here the judgment of the commander and the gallantry of the troops were at variance. Gen. Hardee deemed it imprudent to risk the lives of his men in achieving an object which threatened to cost so much. A halt was ordered, and in brief no further efforts were made to accomplish the end of the expedition.

Of course disappointment prevails throughout the army at the result, for the troops engaged—each one emulating the dash and gallantry of the other—were satisfied of their ability to go on. No blame can, therefore, attach to any one for the negative victory plainly won, and the only regret expressed among the men is that the officers in command were, as they believe, in the present instances, over prudent in pitting probabilities against what seemed a certainty.

Our losses in the affair will doubtless not fall short of a thousand or twelve hundred men. Six hundred and five have been reported in the corps of Gen. Stewart. Our captures are two or three stand of colors, and some three or four hundred prisoners. Hooker's corps is reported by persons to be badly crippled.

While the fight I have recorded was in progress on the left, Wheeler's cavalry successfully held the enemy's infantry in check on our right. With —— small brigades, he contested the ground with two corps—Dodges and Logan's—and after twelve or fourteen hours hard fighting, has prevented them from obtaining any advantage. Cannonading has been constant along the lines all day.

The enemy are evidently endeavoring to manœuvre Hood out of Atlanta, but there is quite as much probability that within thirty-six hours Sherman will be manœuvering to get away from him.—*Correspondence Savannah Republican*

Battle of Atlanta, July 22, 1864

The New-York Times.

VOL. XIII.—NO. 4004. NEW-YORK, MONDAY, JULY 25, 1864. PRICE FOUR CENTS.

ATLANTA.

A Battle Before Atlanta on Friday.

RESULTS THUS FAR FAVORABLE.

Our Siege Guns Bearing on the City.

THE PLACE PARTIALLY AFIRE.

The Contest Still Progressing on Saturday.

A SAD LOSS TO OUR ARMS.

Death of the Great Soldier, Major-Gen. McPherson.

Details of Movements Preliminary to the Battle.

AFFAIRS IN THE ARMY OF THE WEST.

Special Dispatch to the New-York Times.

WASHINGTON, Sunday, July 24—10 P. M.

Official dispatches of another battle before Atlanta, fought on Friday, were received by the authorities last night. At the time of sending the dispatch the contest was still going on, but the results, so far as developed, were favorable. A position had been gained from which SHERMAN was able to bring his siege guns to bear on the city. Extensive fires were raging within its limits as though the rebels were burning stores, &c.

During this engagement Gen. McPHERSON was killed. This sad report it was at first hoped might prove unfounded, but it has been fully confirmed. In this brilliant young officer the country loses one of its ablest Generals. Gen. GRANT has always placed the very highest estimate on his talent, and after the Vicksburgh campaign addressed him a letter, in which he stated that after SHERMAN, no man in his army had rendered him such service, and done so much for the success of the campaign as he.

Gen. McPherson's Death—A Battle on Friday—Fighting Still Going On.

LOUISVILLE, Sunday, July 23.

Major NORCROSS, local Paymaster at Chattanooga, telegraphs Major ALLEN, Chief Paymaster here, that Major-Gen. McPHERSON was killed yesterday before Atlanta. Another correspondent says he was shot fatally through the lungs.

BALTIMORE, Sunday, July 23.

A private dispatch received by a relative of Gen. McPHERSON in this city last night, dated near Atlanta, July 23, announces that that gallant officer was killed in battle the day previous, and that his remains would be sent home in charge of members of his staff.

WASHINGTON, Sunday, July 24.

The latest official dispatches from Gen. SHERMAN represent repeated fighting, and give the circumstances attending the death of Gen. McPHERSON, who fell in battle in the severe contest of Friday.

Gen. Hooker's Corps—Movements of the Army up to July 18—Kenesaw Mountain—Marietta—Chattahoochee River.

CHATTAHOOCHEE RIVER, Ga., Monday, July 18, 1864.

The first act of the grand drama which SHERMAN has been performing this Summer has been played. The Chattahoochee has been reached by the Army of the West. The curtain rests upon the stage, while the actors pause to take breath and arrange their costumes for the inauguration of Act II.—the struggle for Atlanta—which the distant booming of cannon announces is about to begin. That it will be prolific of battle scenes and bloody encounters none can doubt who reflect upon the importance of the position to be wrested from the foe.

Thus far Gen. SHERMAN's campaign has been mainly marked by irregular conflicts, prolonged skirmishing, by arduous marches, flanking operations, and the advance and attack of certain corps to conceal and protect the movements of others. Although the army has frequently been in line of battle and sometimes engaged for a week at a time in heavy skirmishing, if we except "Resaca" of the 14th and 15th of June, no general engagement has been fought between the opposing armies. But our columns have arrived at last at the river behind which the enemy has all along boasted that his main defence would be made. We are now so close to the city of Atlanta that the decisive conflict cannot be delayed much longer. If the army moves at all beyond the river, the north bank of which is now its line, it will be a movement characterized by very heavy fighting.

In a previous letter the prediction was ventured that the most obstinate resistance to be encountered by our army, prior to crossing the Chattahoochee, would be in the vicinity of Kenesaw Mountain. Since that was written the position indicated has been occupied and maintained by JOHNSTON for two weeks against the most determined efforts of our combined armies. It was not without a severe struggle that he was driven from Pine Knob, where, on the 14th, 15th and 16th ults., Gen. HOOKER, with his invincible corps, fought with great bravery. Gen. GEARY's division was chiefly engaged, losing 519 men in killed and wounded. The attack was continued until the desired position was attained, and the enemy retreated. On the 17th other divisions came to the active assistance of the heroic division which Gen. GEARY had handled with so much ability. The enemy was forced back through successive lines of works until the 20th, when Kenesaw and its adjacent ridges presented their stern front, bristling with guns and bayonets, to prevent the further progress of the hitherto triumphant army.

Kenesaw Mountain is a huge, isolated, double hill, rising boldly out of a country of almost uninterrupted forest-covered ridges—themselves of no mean elevation. In these ridges consist the peculiar adaptation of the country for defensive purposes. Aided by military science, they have been made by rebel engineering absolutely impregnable to direct assault. All the works I have seen partake of the same character. They consist of long lines of rifle-pits, elaborately constructed with good revetments of logs or facines, and are well drained. These lines following the crests of the ridges, are occasionally broken by forts constructed on the most commanding elevations. The flanks are always well protected by strong forts. The woods in front of an intrenchment are generally cut down, so as to form an impenetrable abattis. When their lines cross open fields, they are fully guarded by rows of sharpened stakes, driven firmly in the ground, at an angle calculated to impale a horse or man running upon them, and too closely set to permit of passage between. The villainous *chevaux de frise*, is also freely used, particularly on roads where our cavalry are expected to charge. This precaution is altogether unnecessary, as it is a well known fact that we have no cavalry to hurl on rebel works. All we have are required to defend the flanks and rear. Even in the construction of advanced works for skirmishers, the enemy seem to have bestowed time and care. Their forts and lines of intrenchments partake more of the aspect of permanent fortifications than field works for temporary use. The enemy has been driven from them by the flanking process which has been adopted by Gen. SHERMAN with so much success as to earn for him the suggestive appellation of "The Great Flanker."

I will not attempt to record a detailed account of the many assaults and conflicts that occurred between the two armies in the protracted struggle in front of Kenesaw. Suffice it to say that for two weeks Gen. SHERMAN vainly attempted this hill by direct assault. On the 27th of June a general attack was ordered, and in pursuance thereof the Fourteenth and Fourth Corps engaged the enemy's lines near the base of the mountain with great spirit, but could not drive them beyond their breastworks. During the battle, a furious cannonade was kept up on the mountain, enveloping its top and sides in the smoke of exploding shells. The other corps were in readiness to charge the moment the effort should show signs of success. But the attack was not a success, and soon developed the strong position of the foe, proving it to be folly to throw away lives in attempting to dislodge him by assault.

Gen. SHERMAN then turned his attention to other means, and applied to them his never-failing receipt for obstinacy—a flank movement. Supplies were replenished at Big Shanty, the new depot. Preparation was made to pass the entire army to the enemy's rear. As the movement contemplated would, if JOHNSON's lines did not fall back, necessarily leave the railroad at his mercy, the depot was ordered back to Alatoona Bridge. A strong column, SCHOFIELD's I believe, was sent westward on JOHNSTON's left, and on the 2d of July other corps followed. During the night of July 2d the enemy was ascertained to be again in retreat, after having obstinately held out against our assaults for two weeks. We pressed rapidly after them, passing through a series of works more formidable than any before captured. We again overtook them at night on the 3d of July, about two miles south of Marietta.

Marietta deserves more than a passing notice. Prior to the war it was noted throughout the South as one of the centres of Georgian wealth and refinement. Compared with a Northern town its proportions would be diminutive indeed; but in Georgia, with a population of two thousand, it ranked as the sixth town in size in the State. The period of its settlement dates anterior to that of Atlanta, which owes its superiority in size to the fact of its being a centre for several railroads. Marietta, with no commercial aspirations and no manufacturing interest, had, confessedly, a higher social grade than Atlanta, with all its teeming population, workshops and warehouses. It boasted a college of considerable importance—not widely known, but well patronized by those of the South, who preferred educating their sons in their own States to sending them to "Yankee" institutions to be "contaminated" by the enemies of "Southern principles." These watchful guardians of the morality of Southern striplings forgot that their own colleges were almost without exception officered by men of Northern birth and education.

As one might expect, the glory of Marietta College has departed. The buildings are standing gloomily enough upon the hill, from whence they overlook the town and beautiful gardens; but the pupils and teachers are gone; the former to the wars to destroy the Union of their fathers—the latter to their Northern homes to escape the persecution of their former pupils. This picture will answer for all Southern colleges. The war has closed their churches and their schools, with here and there a solitary exception.

Marietta presents a sad spectacle of war's devastating influences. Its fine mansions and lovely gardens, with their shaded walks and arbored seats, still remain, but not as they once were—the abode of a happy people, innocent of war. All these have left, and throngs of soldiers are now roaming over the half-destroyed gardens or strolling through the mutilated mansions, thrumming on the ruined pianos and lolling on the sofas abandoned by their wealthy proprietors. A few matrons—widowed relics of the war—and their half-scared daughters, still remain in the town. These, with a few old men, striplings and decayed servants, are all that are left of the denizens of the place. At one end of the town a half enclosed burial ground, with hundreds of newly made soldiers' graves, side by side, with marble monuments and mausoleums of the past, reveal the fact that Marietta's *dead* are more numerous than Marietta's *living*.

To resume our narrative from which we have digressed. On the 5th of July JOHNSTON moved still further southward, taking position on the railroad about two miles north of the Chattahoochee River. From the tops of the trees on the high hills occupied by the Twentieth Corps, we beheld Atlanta's glittering spires and housetops, seemingly about seven miles south of the river. On the 7th inst. the foe again retrograded and assumed a new position, whose contracted limits were speedily ascertained to be in front of the railroad bridge, the flanks resting on the river on either side of the crossing. It was pretty evident that JOHNSTON was crossing his forces on the pontoons which we knew had been laid in that vicinity. The rebel front was as bold as ever, and no impression was made on their lines. By the morning of the 9th, the last skirmisher had disappeared from our front, and the railroad bridge was discovered to be in flames. We advanced through another series of fortifications to the river-bank, along which our line now rests. The enemy holds the opposite bank, and it is not an uncommon sight to see the soldiers of both armies meet in swimming parties and exchange tobacco and coffee, apparently as good friends as though a shot had never passed between them.

As it was currently reported that JOHNSTON commenced to cross the Chattahoochee on the 4th of July, it can be but a matter of surprise to many who view critically the movements of our armies, that he was not attacked at the time when he would have labored under the misfortune of having a river in his rear in very dangerous proximity. This has been a matter of much comment among officers and men, who still canvass such matters whenever opportunity occurs. A battle was pretty generally expected on the 4th, when it was stated that Gen. SHERMAN, in view of the golden opportunity thus presented by the situation of affairs had ordered a general onslaught to be made by the whole army with a view to drive JOHNSTON in confusion to his crossings. Whether this attack was actually ordered, or the order countermanded, or for some cause rendered inoperative, is a matter for speculation. But one thing all unite in believing—that is—had a fight occurred on that glorious Fourth there would have been but two alternatives accepted by our army—"Victory or death." It would have fought as it never fought before, so eager and expectant for the fray were commanders and soldiers. There are many who regret the postponement of the battle, which they believe would have been decisive of the result of the campaign. They would have attacked at all hazards of life, though the enemy were never so firm and to all appearances secure in their fortifications. Whether these regrets are just or unjust time will develop. No inconsiderable number believe that JOHNSTON was allowed to cross the Chattahoochee in comparative security to insure important results from combined movements, of which we do not at present know, but in which other armies are supposed to be interested. All unite in indorsing the wisdom and generalship of SHERMAN, and willingly abide by any decision he may make, believing his conduct of the campaign to have been masterly, and productive of the most brilliant results.

Although the Chattahoochee River forms the main dividing line between the opposing armies, we have no inconsiderable force on the other side. Firing is occasionally heard from their direction. Supplies are being accumulated at Marietta, from which place they are distributed to the trains of the various corps. No effort is being made to rebuild the railroad bridge, for the reason that a strong fort on the rebel side of the river effectually commands the approaches to the old piers. A general movement to the south side of the river is daily expected. The army is resting and nerving for the severe struggle which will then, in all probability, begin.

Our expectations will be very agreeably disappointed, if the ten miles intervening between our present camp and Atlanta are not more difficult of accomplishment than the one hundred over which Gen. SHERMAN has so successfully led us since we left Chattanooga.

J. G.

Preparing to Cross the Chattahoochee—Skirmishing—The Lines Between Marietta and the Chattahoochee—Interchange of Greeting—The Health of the Army.

HEADQUARTERS FOURTEENTH ARMY CORPS, CHATTAHOOCHEE RIVER, Sunday, July 17, 1864.

As I write—it is a beautiful morning, by the way, made deliciously so by a ten minutes' shower—the entire army is upon the banks of the Chattahoochee River, a turbid, reddish-looking stream, which slices the country eight miles north of Atlanta.

We are on the *qui vive* this morning, as orders were issued last evening to HOOKER and PALMER to have their respective corps in readiness to move across the river at 9 o'clock. It is just 9, and JEFF. C. DAVIS' fine division is passing headquarters. An orderly from department headquarters, however, arrives, and immediately the three Division Commanders of this corps are ordered to halt until further advices. I learn that the particular reason for this "break" is that during the night the rebel force destroyed the pontoon bridge. This was kind on their part, considering there were no soldiers or property of any description upon it. We shall probably get it ready for crossing before noon.

For the first time during the campaign the army has had a little rest. The last skirmish, in which infantry participated, occurred a few miles this side of Marietta, in which the brigade of regulars, under command of Gen. KING, particularly distinguished itself.

Nearly the whole brigade was acting as a grand skirmish line for the First Division. At an extraordinary juncture in the situation Capt. STETSON, of the Fifteenth Infantry, at the head of his company, rushed across an opening in the face of the enemy's infantry and artillery and took up a position in a clump of second growth and opened a handsome fire upon the enemy's cannoniers, compelling the rebel battery, after a couple of shots, to evacuate the premises. The whole brigade witnessed this exhibition of valor upon the part of Capt. STETSON and his men, and felt great concern in regard to the company's safety. As the line advanced the gallant Captain resumed his place in the battalion, with the loss of but one man wounded. It was a decidedly rash performance, but resulting as it did, reflected great credit upon the intrepid Captain and his troops.

During the advance of the army from Marietta to this point, as has, in fact, been the case since the opening of the campaign, the brigade of regulars has been in the advance, and has suffered to a great extent, one company in the Fifteenth losing as high as forty men in killed and wounded. Let me add, too, that during the seventy five days' campaign this brigade has lost but one man as a prisoner, who was wounded upon the skirmish line at the base of Kenesaw, and subsequently captured. In the last skirmish Gen. KING in Gen. JOHNSTON's absence commanded the First Division, and Col. STOUGHTON, of the Eleventh Michigan, commanded the regular brigade.

During the last day of the skirmishing at the mouth of the river, Col. STOUGHTON carried the brigade into the hottest of the contest, succeeding many times in driving the whole of WALKER's division. It was while realizing the glory of the day that a shell severed the left leg from his body, and he was borne from the field. I cannot take my leave of the regulars without speaking a kind word in behalf of the gallant officers in it, all of whom are entitled to praise. I do not know young STETSON, but frequently make mention of him, from the fact that his brother officers, in conversation, dwell at length upon his conduct upon the occasion which I have detailed above. Capt. MULLIGAN, of the Nineteenth, an officer of sterling ability, is still upon Gen. KING's Staff, and has acquitted himself admirably during the grand campaign between Chattanooga and the Chattahoochee.

Gen. JOHNSTON, who had his left side battered in by an ungenerous cannon ball near Kingston, and who was permitted to go home to recuperate, arrived yesterday and resumed command of his division, which is one of the finest in the army. It and JEFF. C. DAVIS' division did the main part of the fighting between Marietta and this place. The latter division takes the advance in the crossing of the river, and will, no doubt, have as much as it can possibly attend to. This division suffered frightfully at Kenesaw, and has experienced an awful ordeal during the last seventy days. Its Commander (JEFF C. DAVIS) is universally admired, and enjoys the reputation of being one of the finest officers and one of the most accomplished gentlemen in the army. I do not believe there is an officer living who can move a division to better advantage than JEFF C. DAVIS. He fights his men, too, superbly, and performs his duties, whether in line of battle, or otherwise, with the coolness, skill, and unostentation characteristic of the true soldier.

During the entire skirmishing between Marietta and this point, we lost less than six hundred men in killed and wounded, and no prisoners. All along the route we picked up the enemy's stragglers and deserters, amounting, in the aggregate, since the occupation of Marietta, to between six and seven hundred.

So soon as the enemy had been thoroughly cleared out upon this side of the river, the respective corps of Gens. SCHOFIELD, BLAIR, LOGAN, DODGE, and HOWARD moved up the river on the left, to the distance of eight miles, and crossed, leaving Gens. HOOKER and PALMER upon this side of the river, with the railroad in the centre. It is immediately in our front that the bulk of the enemy are disposed, within formidable earthworks on all sides. For the past three nights, our forces on this side of the river have been actively engaged in throwing up fortifications; and as I write, a fierce cannonading is being kept up by both parties.

The pickets of the contending armies are in force upon each side of the river, and cease fire upon each other. There is a continual conversation kept up, and temporarily the most friendly feeling exists. Each side allows no officers or groups of men to show themselves without being made a target. This is mutually understood, but I believe there is no official agreement for such proceedings. One of the happiest things that has occurred was told to me yesterday:

REBEL PICKET.—You can't come any farther, boys. We've been reinforced. You'll never cross this river in the world.

FEDERAL PICKET.—O, I guess we'll come when we get ready.

REBEL.—No, Sir; we've been reinforced by LOGAN, and SCHOFIELD, and—

FEDERAL.—We'll send you over HOOKER in a few days.

I have heard several stories related in regard to the performances of the men, but they are of the same tenor, many times published. The above, however, was so good that I thought I would give it a hearing.

As a general thing, the parties upon each side banter each other, and call each other all kinds of names. According to the rebels' statements, they are particularly short of whisky, and, although they are continually begging newspapers, they never have any to give out. They say that there is but one paper published at Atlanta just now—the travelling Memphis *Appeal*.

CHICKAMAUGA.

FROM MEMPHIS.

Important Victories Gained by General Smith.

FORREST OUTMANŒUVRED AND BEATEN.

OUR LOSS FIVE HUNDRED.

REBEL LOSS FOUR THOUSAND.

Particulars of Gen. Smith's Expedition—Forrest Outmaneuvered—The Rebel General Whipped Five Times—The Negroes in the Fight—The Supplies for our Troops Exhausted—Our Loss less than Five Hundred—The Rebel Loss Four Thousand—Two Hundred Prisoners Captured.

CAIRO, Saturday, July 23.

The steamer *Hilman* has arrived here, bringing one day later news from Memphis.

A cavalry officer, who accompanied Gen. SMITH's expedition, gives the following particulars:

Our forces consisted of a division each of infantry and cavalry, together with a brigade of colored troops. Gen. SMITH outmanœuvered FORREST all through, and whipped his forces five times.

The battle at Tupeluci, on the 13th, was a severe one, the enemy being terribly punished by our cavalry and negro troops, who bore the brunt of the engagement.

The same night the rebels assaulted our temporary works and were repulsed.

On the 15th another battle occurred, FORREST making three charges on our line, but was driven back each time with great slaughter.

On the night of the 15th, the last day's rations were distributed, and the next morning the expedition started on its return, followed by BUFORD's cavalry, who retreated, however, with severe loss, after going four miles.

From the night of the 15th to the night of the 19th, when supplies were met at Salem, the troops were obliged to live off the country. On the 20th the expedition reached Lagrange with a loss, all told, of less than 500 men. Not a gun or wagon was lost during the expedition.

Gen. GRIERSON says the rebel loss cannot be less than 4 000. Dispatches captured by Gen. HATCH admit a loss of 2,400. Among the rebels killed at Columbus were FAULKNER, MOWBRAY, NELSON, FORREST, HARRISON and GREEN. Col. WILKINS, Ninth Minnesota, and Lieut. McMAHON, Ninth Illinois, were the only Federal officers known to be killed. The wounded were being brought into Memphis.

The expedition returned solely on account of the exhaustion of supplies. We brought in 2,0.0 prisoners. Rebel dead were buried by our troops on several occasions.

[The steamer *St. Cloud*, from White River, arrived at Memphis on the 21st, bringing the first news received from that river for over one week. She reports the river free of guerrillas, and all boats in the stream safe. Six were on the way down, among them the *Commercial* with 600 bales of cotton.]

Gen. Smith's Expedition.

Special Dispatch to the Chicago Tribune.

MEMPHIS, Tuesday, July 19,
VIA CAIRO, Wednesday, July 20.

There has been nothing additional from Gen. SMITH's vicinity to-day, except that FORREST was wounded in the head in the first day's fight, and was taken to Okolona. The whole of the Seventh Tennessee was captured except portions of three companies. It was conscripted in West Tennessee. A rebel mail carrier named GLENDALE was killed near Germantown by our pickets last Sunday. Important papers were found upon his person. FORREST had 20,000 men that he could command. Three or four small parties were conscripting in West Tennessee, stealing horses and negroes, the latter to take South and sell.

A large section of the Southern country is said to be covered with a cotton crop, which promises an inducement for the people to become loyal, so that trade may be opened. It is said that $150,000,000 worth of cotton would find its way to Memphis the next season if the people were loyal, and the Government open to trade.

ARMY OF THE POTOMAC.

News to Saturday—Skirmishing in Burnside's Front—General Birney to Command the Tenth Army Corps.

WASHINGTON, Sunday, July 24.

A letter from the Army of the Potomac, dated yesterday, says. Nothing of peculiar interest has occurred in the past two days. The skirmishing in BURNSIDE's front Friday afternoon was quite lively, but without injury to our men. This is the only part of the line where it may be said the firing is almost unceasing, scarcely five minutes elapsing in the day or night, without hearing musketry or artillery.

Lieut.-Gen. GRANT has assigned the command of the Tenth Army Corps to Gen. BIRNEY, who proceeded to his new post on Saturday morning. Gen. BIRNEY has well merited this promotion, no division in the army having performed nobler service during the campaign. His personal staff accompany him.

Gen. MOTT succeeds to the command of the Third Division.

Many rumors of other changes are current, but cannot be relied on, and are not, therefore, worth mentioning.

A Correspondent's Troubles—Discomforts of a Summer Night in Virginia—Why the Commissary has a Sentinel—Gens. Martindale and Terry Superseded.

Special Correspondence of the New-York Times.

HEADQUARTERS, DEPARTMENT OF VIRGINIA AND NORTH CAROLINA, IN THE FIELD, Friday Morning, July 21 1864.

I know that the great public read what I write. Convincing proof comes in many a little note of anxious inquiry, redolent of home affection, respecting the welfare of some patriot son, brother or husband, whom the chances of the battle-field and the camp keep silent as regards letter-writing. As far as I am able, where these inquiries are of a strictly personal character, I take pleasure in meeting them individually. But among the questions presented are many which can be answered as well, and with far less labor, by the narration of incidents from the range of one's own experiences, which are necessarily the counterparts of the experiences of many others. Believing and feeling this, I am compelled to overcome all modest scruples about using the single-lettered pronoun, and play reluctantly the unpleasant part of an egotist. Particularly is it necessary so to do when no stirring events are to be recorded, when the vast army holds its active forces in abeyance, and a long period of rest and recuperation follows the exhausting march and the wearying battle. At such times the people are none the less desirous of knowing the *status* of the army, in whose well being their hopes and affections are so deeply rooted. I can understand how eagerly every morning the paper is scanned for information of expected events, and what relief from suspense is experienced by eager minds even by such negative testimony as to affairs here as the correspondence now sent forward implies. Word from the army must be obtained. If there be no news, the fact must be told, and iterated, and reiterated in print as regularly as the day. Such I conceive to be one item of the aggregate of a newspaper's mission; and when I cannot find strong food to serve up, I am fain to content myself with trifles—the last show as plainly as the first how matters are.

I intended to write last night on a subject connected with the well-being of the soldiers, of very great importance and public interest. I went say what it was for two reasons—the first and proper one being that I may find myself incapable of doing it satisfaction, and the second from the selfish consideration that some other correspondent might take the hint before I find opportunity, and thus steal my thunder. The reason of the postponement last night was beyond my control. Bugs were the sole and insuperable cause. Not the sort of midnight marauders which were my pest and abomination in years long ago, when my lot was cast in a respectable New-York boarding-house. There are none such here; but bugs of a larger and less odious kind—Virginia bugs, candle-bugs the native Virginia negroes call them—bugs of every possible variety—bugs with long legs and hard backs—bugs with short legs and sheathed wings—bugs with slender whisk-like antennæ, and bugs with short serrated feelers, yellow bugs, green bugs, red bugs, variegated bugs, bugs with all the colors of the prism, beautiful bugs, and black repulsive, hideous bugs; in fact all the bugs and more besides that were ever seen in the best entomological collection, with a large flickering of broad-winged and narrow winged and stout-bodied moths. Prof. AGASSIS would doubtless like to have secured these demons of the night for his cabinet, but we, having no time to devote to natural history, positively dislike them. Their unruly habits make sitting in the open tent at candle light a most impossible. Without warning, they dash head foremost at our faces, plunge madly into our ink-bottles, drown themselves in the water-pail, bury themselves in our hair, immure themselves between our necks and shirt collars, eclipse the candles, cause more dodging of heads than cannon-balls are apt to do, and make us shrink with a flesh-creeping feeling beneath the shield of our mosquito bars, where we find refuge in sleep from their miserable droning. Last night there was an Egyptian plague of them. They swarmed about our camp in myriads. In the words of JEFF. DAVIS, we beseech them to "let us alone!"

Before I yielded the field to these insects last night I called upon the corporal of the camp guard, requesting him to arouse me this morning at 3 o'clock, when he came to relieve the sentry who is posted before the Commissary's tent. The Commissary is the only man in camp except a General who has a sentinel all to himself, and he will excuse me for making a convenience of this fact. The General has a sentry as a mark of honor to his rank—part of the pomp and panoply of war. The Commissary has one because he is responsible for a barrel of whisky. The inference is plain and unpleasant to the moral sense. Not that there is any violation of the eighth commandment in camp. Far from it. Such an offence would be "unpardonable sin" in a mode of life where locks and keys are unknown, and consequently is rarely heard of. Clothing and cigars are left exposed, and untold gold might be, with little danger of losing it. But some men have strong appetites, and as a measure of precaution against temptation, the Commissary hedges his whisky cask with bayonets. But I wander from my subject. The corporal called me promptly, but I did not feel in the writing mood, and there is no use writing a thing unless it be an imperious necessity, when you are not in the mood, so I have contented myself with sending this instead. I suppose the managing editor won't print it, and he won't if there is not plenty of spare room.

The game of the rebels, played the other day, in firing upon our gunboats from Strawberry Plains, on the James River, has been blocked. An expedition went to the place where the rebels had their guns posted and occupied the premises. The movement was gallantly performed by the Eleventh Maine Regiment, under Lieut. Col. HILL, and a rebel Lieutenant and ten privates were brought in prisoners. Our men had matters their own way and escaped a single casualty.

The rule of Gens. MARTINDALE and TERRY respectively over the Eighteenth and Tenth Corps was brief. Day before yesterday they were temporarily placed in command; to-day I send word that they have been superseded. Gen. E. O. C. ORD, United States Volunteers, is assigned to the Eighteenth Corps, and Major-Gen. D. B. BIRNEY, United States Volunteers, to the Tenth.

Gen. MARTINDALE goes home this evening on sick leave, having suffered greatly from the hardships and exposure of the campaign.

H. J. W.

The Distribution of Vegetables by the Sanitary Commission—Artillery Practice Before Petersburgh—A Mortar on a Railroad Car.

Special Correspondence of the New-York Times.

HEADQUARTERS DEPARTMENT OF VIRGINIA AND NORTH CAROLINA, Wednesday Evening, July 20, 1864.

The pathetic note from GEORGE RODGERS, of SHERIDAN's cavalry, printed in last Sunday's TIMES, has attracted my attention. It is evident that he and his comrades have been "shared out" in the general distribution of onions. That the savory anti-scorbutics did not come their way is certain to be regretted, and without stopping to inquire who was guilty of the oversight, I must correct the false impression this complaint has doubtless left upon the minds of many who read it. I can do this without much trouble, and the kind-hearted public who have subscribed so generously for the purchase of the vegetables, and the little children, who sacrificed their pyrotechnic pleasures on the Fourth of July, for the same worthy object, will be glad to know that their bounty was not misapplied. The Sanitary Commission has been the faithful agent in the distribution. For this assertion I have read the proof in handsome notes of acknowledgment from Major Gens. WARREN, SMITH, BURNSIDE, and a half score more of Division and Brigade Commanders. Quantities of vegetables arrived at City Point about the 20 of July, and through the cheerful exertions of Dr. J. H. DOUGLAS, the Assistant Secretary of the Commission, Drs. MACDONALD, STEVENS and SWALM, Inspectors, Mr. ANDERSON, the transportation agent, and the other employes, without any exception, the onions were apportioned and delivered to the division Commissaries of the respective corps, in time to make part of the Fourth of July dinner.

The Army of the Potomac received 514 barrels.

The Eighteenth Corps received 102 barrels.

The Tenth Corps received 107 barrels.

WILSON's Cavalry division received 12 barrels.

The aggregate number of barrels distributed for that occasion was 743.

On the 6th of July another distribution of 1,153 barrels was made under the direction of Lieut.-Col. MORGAN, Chief Commissary of the armies in the field.

Since that date there have been very large supplies received, not only onions but of potatoes, cabbages, green and dried apples, canned tomatoes and pickles, all of which have been disbursed among the men in the camps and trenches and the patients in the hospitals. The figures show that for the eighteen days, beginning July 1, the commission distributed, 3.353 barrels of potatoes, 2,719 barrels of onions, 1,408 barrels of pickles, 805 barrels of assorted vegetables, 141 barrels of dried apples, — barrels of green apples, and still have a quantity of the less perishable stock on hand to be disposed of among the various hospitals.

From personal investigation, I am able to say that the soldiers appreciate to the full extent the thoughtfulness of their friends, and from a hygienic point of view, the advantages of this liberal supply of fresh vegetables, is inestimable. SHERIDAN's cavalry are the only men in all the army from whom there has been heard a whisper of complaint and that they were overlooked in the distribution, was not the desire, as I am certain it was not the fault, of the agents of the commission. The failure, if traced to its cause, would be found to rest upon the Commissary Department of that organization; or, still more probable, in the miscarriage of the notification to send for the portion assigned for the cavalry.

For a very good reason, the Sanitary Commission at present will send no more vegetables to the army, the Government having a sufficient supply on hand to hold out until the end of this month. After the first of August, however, the Commissaries will no longer issue a ration of fresh vegetables to the soldiers; and, by an order of the War Department, a very general reduction of the entire schedule of rations is to take place from that date. The amount thus far issued during the war has been proved from actual experience to have been extravagantly large—far larger than the men could consume. Now the soldiers, in lieu of the curtailed rations, are to receive $16 per month, instead of $13 as heretofore. The items of potatoes, molasses and, optionally, rice or beans, are to be altogether cut off, and the ration of flour or bread is to be reduced from twenty-two to eighteen ounces per diem. Here then is the opportunity for exercise by the public of a commendable generosity. Let the people promptly step in with their munificent offerings to supply what the Government will not. If fresh vegetables are so highly appreciated now, when an occasional and limited quantity is furnished by the Commissariat Department, will not the appreciation be immeasurably greater under the new order of matters next month? The people have only to understand these things and feel confident that their gifts are properly applied, to insure no lack of these coveted and health-sustaining articles of diet. These vegetables must be furnished to the soldiers, and the Sanitary Commission will doubtless in some way see to that; but how can it add this immense tax upon its means without retrenching its disbursements in other directions? It is the privilege of friends at home to ameliorate by every method the hardships endured by their brave defenders in the field, and the past gives ample proof that they will not fail to exercise it with enthusiasm.

There is scarcely anything new to write respecting affairs at the front. There has been the usual artillery firing on both sides, and occasional skirmishing as well—a desultory and commonplace mode of making a noise. In front of the Ninth Corps a lucky shot exploded one of the enemy's caissons, and in front of the Eighteenth Corps a thirteen-inch mortar, mounted on a platform car, moved up the City Point Railroad track to within two miles of Petersburgh and threw its ponderous missiles into the town. Gen. BUTLER's idea this last, and it works admirably. The facility of moving the mortar from place to place on the track giving us a grand advantage over the enemy, who find it almost impossible to get its range. Doubtless all Richmond, through its blustering journals, will complain of us for taking an unchivalrous and mean advantage, as they did of Capt. WINSLOW for sheathing the boilers of the *Kearsarge* with chain cables.

H. J. W.

List of Wounded in the Eighteenth Army Corps in Field Hospital.

Report from last date, July 21, 1864:

Levi Barrows, F, 2d N H—chest.
Sergt Edwin C Kelly, D, 1st Conn H Art—shoulder.
Corp [illegible], C, 2d Penn Art—head.
Jno Donovan, I, 97th Penn—head.
Corp Thos Costello, D, 8th Conn—killed.
Thos Ford, K, 1[illegible] N Y Art—right hand.
J Mi[illegible], I, 11th New York—[illegible].
Jacob Espernoche, F, 2d P V A—[illegible].
A E Harrington, [illegible], 117th N Y—face and neck, (dead).
Wm A Lewis, A, 8th Maine—head.
Corp [illegible] Robbins, F, 11th N [illegible]—right hand.
Anthony [illegible], M, 2d Penn V Art—left foot.
Andr W C Church, I, 21st Conn—right leg.
Francis Gough, H, 118th N Y—left forearm.
Jacob [illegible], D, 97th Penn—neck and shoulder.
Corp A J Van Horn, K, 13th N Y—left side, hip.
John [illegible]owe, B, 2d Penn A—[illegible].
Thos [illegible], A, 2d Penn V A—contusion, chest.
J Z Brace, A, 2d Penn V A—[illegible].
Chas A Lo[illegible]es, I, 1st Conn—leg.
M V Cuptill, G, 9th Me—temple.
Lu[illegible], E, 27th Mass—small back, dead.
Wm [illegible], [illegible] Art—left side and [illegible].
C B Moore, A, [illegible]—[illegible] leg.
John Coc[illegible], K, 6[illegible]—right [illegible], dead.
John H Norris, [illegible], 1[illegible]th N Y—right thigh and [illegible].
Rob't [illegible], A, 8th Conn—arm and elbow.
Jas [illegible], G, 7th Penn V—left leg.
Corp Wm [illegible], F, 2d [illegible] Conn—left breast & neck.
S W [illegible], [illegible] Mass Cav—right shoulder.
John J B[illegible], B, 11[illegible]th N Y—right arm and side.
Benj [illegible]borne, F, 9th N J—neck.
Sergt Geo Dibble, A, 117th N Y—[illegible].
Joseph [illegible], E, 3d N Y—shoulder.
Sergt [illegible] H Simpson, A, [illegible] Maine—head.
[illegible] Brown, [illegible], 9th Me—shoulder.
[illegible] Dunham, D, 117th New [illegible]—right arm.
Sergt Howard Baker, B, [illegible]th [illegible]—neck and shoulder.
Alfred [illegible], B, [illegible]th Penn—left [illegible] and left thigh.
Geo W [illegible], F, [illegible] N Y A—right foot.
Corp [illegible] Myers, I, [illegible]th Pennsylvania—left leg.
[illegible], [illegible]th Penn—right arm [illegible] and right [illegible].
[illegible], [illegible]1st Conn H A—right shoulder blade.
James McCaffrey, G, 2d [illegible] A—scalp.
[illegible], B, [illegible]th New Hampshire—neck.
[illegible], H, 8th Maryland—through the bowels, dead.
Sergt [illegible] Chapman, F, 4th N H—contusion, side.
Sergt Thos J [illegible]urns, F, 4th N H—hip.
1st Sergt F A Buzzell, I, 4th N H—arm.
[illegible] Shultz, A, [illegible]th N Y—hip and thigh.
John Allen, [illegible], [illegible]th N H—thigh.
[illegible]gert, A, 13th Ind—left shoulder.
Wm [illegible], C, 15th [illegible]—right arm.
[illegible] Myers, F, 115th N Y—[illegible].
[illegible] Smith, E, 27th [illegible].
Corp Samuel Millington, F, 1[illegible]th N Y—contusion.
[illegible] S [illegible], K, 1[illegible]th—contusion right thigh.
[illegible], [illegible]th Wis—left wrist.
T H Swift, I, 40th Mass—nose.
Geo Webster, H, 10th New-York Artillery—right hip, flesh.

The Weldon Railroad.

To the Editor of the New-York Times:

I noticed lately a dispatch from Washington, that thirteen trains had passed over the Petersburgh & Weldon Railroad. That road is of more importance to Gen. LEE's army than all the rest in Virginia, and more easily to be destroyed by Gen. GRANT. With five hundred cavalry he certainly could prevent it being used, and with five thousand cavalry it could be destroyed. At Weldon there is a bridge more than a mile long. Twelve miles up the Roanoke to Gaston, is another bridge across the Roanoke on the Raleigh & Gaston road, that can be reached with ease, and when once destroyed, could not be repaired in six months. There is no force south of the Weldon Railroad to prevent the Union cavalry from operating in that direction.

I am a native of Virginia, and left Petersburgh about four months since. Cause, Union on the brain.

B.

Marine Disaster—Funeral of the Late Col. Chambers—Departure of Troops for Washington.

BOSTON, Sunday, July 24.

The bark *Sicilian*, Capt. LAVENDER, arrived to-day from Georgetown, D C. She picked up, July 16, a boat containing Capt. BEAN, his mate and six seamen, belonging to the steamer *Nare* from New-York for Santa Martha. The steamer sprung a leak July 15, and sank in one hour. The rescued men were landed on the Delaware Breakwater.

Another boat, containing the rest of the crew of the sunken steamer, has not yet been heard from.

The funeral of the brave and lamented Lieut.-Col. JOHN G. CHAMBERS took place at his late home, in Medford, to-day, in the Unitarian Church. He was buried with masonic and military honors. A large attendance was present.

The Forty-second Massachusetts Regiment, of one hundred days volunteers, left this port to-day, for Washington, in the steamers *General McClellan* and *Montauk*.

The Charleston Mercury.

DAILY PAPER—TWENTY DOLLARS FOR SIX MONTHS—PAYABLE IN ADVANCE. | SPONTE SUA SINE LEGE FIDES RECTUMQUE COLLENTUR.—VINDICE NULLO | COUNTRY PAPER—THRICE A WEEK—TWELVE DOLLARS FOR SIX MONTHS—PAYABLE IN ADVANCE.

Volume LXXXV. CHARLESTON, S. C., FRIDAY, JULY 29, 1864. Number 12,125.

FROM THE ARMY OF TENNESSEE.

[Correspondence of Savannah Republican.]

ATLANTA, July 22, night.

A great battle has been fought and splendid successes achieved. But the end is not yet, and for prudential reasons I do not now give you all the details. Yesterday our lines were withdrawn to the entrenchments around the city. The enemy advanced, and planting their guns, commenced to throw shell among the women and children. General Hood, with that energy which is his characteristic, matured his plans at once. Atlanta was to be defended at every hazard and any cost. Evacuated by its citizens—a mere shell of its former self—there was nothing in it as a mere locality which required a sacrifice of life, but the *morale* of the army had to be preserved and the country relieved of the monster pressure bearing so heavily upon its Gate City.

To strike Sherman in front would have been impolitic and disastrous. Gen. Hood, therefore, determined to beat him at his own game—that is, to flank his lines. To this end, he issued orders after nightfall for Hardee to move from his position on the centre, and, with Wheeler's cavalry, proceed to the enemy's right, march quickly, and deal tremendous blows. His instructions were to strike about 12 o'clock noon. The movement was unavoidably delayed until 2. Meanwhile our lines had been extended so as to fill all our works, and skirmishing commenced, interspersed with almost incessant volleys of artillery. Our batteries were massed in such manner that those portions of the fortifications on which they were placed were impregnable.

The morning hours passed slowly and solemnly. Every face wore a look of despondency. Shells were dropping in the streets, and sad groups of women and children, with a temporary supply of provisions, were wending their way to the woods. During the night straggling ruffians had broken into the stores, robbed them of such of their contents as they wanted, and scattered the remainder through the streets. During the morning these demoralizing scenes were repeated. Abandoned women broke into the millinery shops, and men in the uniform of soldiers gutted and pillaged premises from roof to cellar in search of whiskey and tobacco. The office of the Southern Express Company underwent this process before day, and I enjoyed the melancholy privilege of seeing boxes, papers, and everything mentionable thrown, in "confusion worse confounded," on all sides. I dwell on the subject with peculiar dissatisfaction, because of my own losses, which leaves me minus of everything, from toothbrush to blanket, except the clothes in which I stand.—While this indiscriminate pillaging was in progress, wagons, stragglers, citizens and negroes loaded with plunder, were hurrying out of town, fully impressed with the idea that Atlanta was about to be abandoned. Under these circumstances it is no wonder that the officers of the army were in a measure despondent, and regarded the fortunes of the day as decidedly unpromising. Not until evening did this mood change. Then it was ascertained that we had struck the enemy one of the severest blows of the war.

Hardee and Wheeler sweeping silently around the Federal left, pounced upon their flank, and pressed so steadily as to bear down all opposition. Whole batteries with horses and equipments fell into our possession, fortifications with frowning abattis of sharpened pikes were crossed in the teeth of murderous fire, while individual gallantry was conspicuous in the capture of flags and prisoners. Wheeler with his cavalry, co-operating with Hardee, performed deeds of valor that have removed every prejudice which unjustly has attached to their past career. Charging as infantry they drove the enemy from one of his lines of fortifications, captured several hundred prisoners, burned a considerable amount of camp equipage, and galled their antagonists at every step.

Contemporaneous with the superb movement of Hardee, Cheatham with Hoods old corps advanced from the entrenchments they had previously occupied, drove the Yankee skirmishers from their front, and then with a yell commenced one of the greatest charges of the war. Up hill and down, through the woods, across the fields, faltering here and there before the fire of the enemy, but only for a moment, the brave men of Tennessee, Virginia, Georgia, North Carolina, South Carolina, Mississippi, Alabama and Louisiana dashed on, and like their brave competitors for the honors of the field advancing on the right, overcame every obstacle in their path. Thus for a mile and a half, perhaps more, following the Federals over their works, they met with uninterrupted success.

One misstep only wrested from us the completeness of the victory. A brigade is said to have broken—I will not mention names. Into the gap thus created a body of the Yankees rushed, and seizing a strong position held it until a portion of our lines were compelled to retrace their steps to prevent an attack on the flank. In other words, the mishap destroyed that perfect chain of communication designed to be established between Hardee and the corps immediately adjoining. Since nightfall, however, I learn that this desideratum has been accomplished.

Stewart's corps on our left was not exempt from the dangers or the glories of the field, and, although not participating so extensively in the aggressive movements of the day, had occasion during the afternoon to repel the vigorous demonstrations of the enemy.

Such in general terms is the situation to-night. The results of the day have been more than gratifying. While the battle has not been so decisive as was contemplated in the plan of the commander-in-chief, it has nevertheless crippled the enemy, humbled his pride, destroyed his *morale*, nearly annihilated some of his commands, partially destroyed his organization, and reduced his numbers, it is believed to something like an equality with our own. On the other hand, our men have learned that they have a leader on whose judgment they can implicitly rely; that breastworks are not so fearful to encounter as they imagined; that their own strength is yet equal to every emergency, and finally, that by the blessing of God they may yet conquer the Federal army that has so defiantly pushed them back into the heart of the Empire State of the South. The battle has been a benefit. It has proven an inspiration; and if called into the field again to-morrow or the next day, the men of the army will show how more nobly than ever they are determined to crush the hated enemy whose presence stains our soil.

In practical results, few battles of the war have a better showing. Hardee captured from 16 to 20 guns, and Cheatham's corps eight or ten, besides battle flags and regimental colors. In prisoners we cannot have less than from twenty-five hundred to three thousand, among whom are a considerable number of Colonels and subordinate field officers. They are still coming in. The Yankees confess that the flank movement of Generals Hardee and Wheeler was a surprise, and to an entire lack of preparation in consequence. The idea does not appear to have entered a Yankee head that General Hood would have the hardihood to detach a whole corps in the face of the overwhelming numbers by which he was beset, and while the enemy was battering even at the door, send it miles around the rear to strike them on the flank. And they compliment our new commander for his success. It is but a tithe of the tribute which Gen. Hood deserves, when I add that for an officer to assume the command of an army that had retreated nearly one hundred miles in three days, to make himself acquainted with every detail, while the enemy's guns were booming in his ears, and their lines more closely investing his own, and within one week thereafter, fight two important battles—I repeat that for a General to do all this is a mark of genius, judgment, promptness and self-reliance, of which the annals of war furnish but few parallels. I need not tell you that the tide of enthusiasm now runs in his favor with a force that is gathering strength every hour. "Pluck will always win."

Our own loss is yet unknown. In officers I fear it has been heavy. The lion-hearted Major General W. H. T. Walker, of your State, was killed by a ball through the heart, while leading his men. Col. Murray, of an Arkansas regiment, is also among the dead. Generals Gist, James A. Smith (commanding Granbury's Texas Brigade), Colquitt and Strahl, and Col. Pressley, of the 10th S. C. V., are wounded. The latter was in the act of wresting muskets from the hands of the enemy and mounting their breastworks when shot.

The Georgia militia, under General Gustavus W. Smith, held their position like veterans, being exposed to the heavy fire of artillery and musketry, both in the trenches and on the advance. For a long time they lay in front of a Yankee battery, which they were anxious to take, and but for the gap on the right and left, and absence of troops within supporting distance, they would undoubtedly have made the attempt. General Toombs was everywhere along the line, animating the troops in his peculiar style; and with General Smith as their Mentor, they appeared willing to be led anywhere.

A considerable number of Yankee wounded are lying in the depot. Our own wounded are being sent to the various field hospitals and to the rear. The ladies of Atlanta have been kind beyond measure. All that humanity can do is being done for the sufferers, and they lack no comforts. Confidence is generally restored, and few believe that Atlanta will not be saved.

The enemy are still in our front and a portion of our forces in the same position as yesterday; but Hardee is yet on the flank of Sherman, and it is impossible for the latter to move anywhere without again provoking battle, in which event no one doubts the issue.

SATURDAY, July 23, 10 a. m.

Shelling and skirmishing continues along the lines, but without indications of a general engagement. Shells are thrown freely and frequently into the city, and I find it inconvenient to write a letter under their inspiration. Several houses have been badly damaged—many narrow escapes made, but I hear as yet of no loss of life. The Federal General McPherson is undoubtedly killed. Prisoners all report it. He fought Hardee—three corps and part of another, against one. Sherman is apparently on the defensive and digging dirt. Weather cool and favorable for operations.

WHO SHOULD COMMAND THE ARMY IN GEORGIA?

[From the Petersburg Daily Express, July 25.]

We agree with the Richmond Whig, that the "situation in Georgia does not demand rash experiment, but on the contrary, calls for an officer of proved ability of the first order."

From the firing of the first gun through all the long agony of this stupendous struggle, the columns of this journal have steadily upheld every measure of the Government in which we could see even a germ of hope; or the least reasonable prospect of success. With no stinted measure we have lavished praise when praise was due—encouraged the public confidence when it wearied under the pressure of repeated disaster—and chided the impatience which has so often followed hazardous and disastrous experiment. We have even consented to be silent, when it cost some effort to suppress fear and infrequent indignation.

There is a limit to human patience—a limit which may be reached by authority even as potent as that which rules at Richmond, in times as critical as those whose perils now surround the Confederate States. The public judgment did not exhaust its good sense in the election of the President. It is yet entitled to some respect—to some greater consideration, where its voice is quite as unanimous as it ever was in the choice of a Chief Magistrate, than to be asked or commanded to suspend itself, while experiment after experiment with the most vital interests of the country are made, and the men in whom the confidence of the country has settled, after repeated trial, are passed by at the hour of supreme danger, to place tremendous responsibilities in hands certainly inexperienced, and it may be weak.

We agree with the Whig when it says: that Gen. Hood's promotion to the command of the army in Georgia excites much surprise; and while we do not pretend to endorse the motive states, for the blindness which has passed by the most obviously fit man to take command of that army, we shall not hesitate to say that the whole country is stupified with astonishment and roused to no slight indignation at the action of the President.

If the President wished a man whose merit had been assured by success, (and with what disproportionate means no man knows better than the President,) the country does not know where a better man can be found than the first hero of this war—BEAUREGARD! Under the President's own eye, he won the first great historical battle of the war, and with it the highest rank the President could confer.

Bull Run, Manassas, Shiloh, Farmington, Drewry's Bluff, Bermuda Neck, Petersburg, twice—eight battles of more or less importance in the open field, besides the lustre of his splendid and prolonged triumph at Charleston, stand to his credit in the account of service! When we look back at his career, we are amazed that all his record in the field has been accomplished in the brief period when accident has given him command; for less than five months in all has Gen. Beauregard had command of an army in the field and largely of that time his command was due to accident. From the firing of the first gun at Sumter to this day, he has never been off duty, except when he got the furlough to repair his shattered health which was made the opportunity to remove him from the army of the West.

We would like to have some other explanation of the fact that Gen. Beauregard has been passed over at this time, than the hypothesis of the Whig but we are puzzled to find one consistent with the enthusiasm we know his name kindles in the army, and the abiding confidence with which the country looks for success whenever its interests are trusted to his genius, his courage and his patriotism.

THE NEW TARIFF OF THE UNITED STATES.

[From the London Times (city article), July 6.]

The new Tariff Bill just passed by the Senate of the United States makes, as far as intention is concerned, a further considerable stride toward a prohibition of foreign commerce. But the total inadequacy of the manufacturing power of the country to supply the wants of the people and of the army renders it impossible materially to check the demand for European goods, and the chief result, therefore, of each increase of duty is that it enables the home manufacturers to increase to that extent their charges for such goods as they have the means of supplying. The altered scale now about to become law raises the duty on woolen articles from thirty-five per cent., its present rate, to forty per cent. ad valorem, which, as it is payable in gold, is equal, in the existing state of the market, to about ninety per cent. in paper currency. Flannels are increased in rate from eighteen to twenty-four per cent., several classes of cotton goods from fifteen to twenty per cent., steel manufactures from thirty-five to forty per cent., and tea from ten pence per pound to ten pence per pound and ten per cent. ad valorem.

ANDY JOHNSON.—A Yankee paper gives a "Sketch of the Life and Services" of Johnson, the Lincoln candidate for Vice-President. According to this, he was born at Raleigh, N. C., on the 29th December, 1808. He lost his father in his fourth year. His family was very poor, and he was apprenticed to a tailor in his native city, with whom he served seven years. He never attended school a single day in his life; but whilst learning his trade, and by aid of the journeymen, he acquired a familiarity with the alphabet. As soon as he could imperfectly read, he borrowed a few books, from which he amassed all the learning he had until he married, which was in his twentieth year. His wife then taught him to write and cipher. He worked for a short time at Laurens, C. H., South Carolina; then returned to Raleigh. Subsequently, he settled in Greenville, Tennessee, and there was alderman and mayor. In 1835, he was elected to the Legislature. In 1840, he was Democratic Elector of Tennessee. In 1841, he was elected to the State Senate. In 1843, he was sent to Congress, where he served till 1853.—That year he was elected Governor, and re-elected in 1855. In 1857, he was chosen United States Senator, and finished his term last March a year. He is now military Governor of his State, and may be Vice-President of what is left of the United States.

THE SITUATION OF AFFAIRS AROUND ATLANTA—WHAT THE GEORGIA PAPERS SAY.

We gather some interesting paragraphs from our latest Georgia exchanges in regard to the situation of affairs along "the front:"

THE LATE FIGHT—HARDEE'S DASH.

The general impression is that our entire loss in the recent battles will not amount to more than five thousand. The loss of the enemy in killed and wounded has also been overrated, as they fought for the most part behind entrenchments. Our army is unbroken in strength and spirit, and ready to move forward whenever their gallant chief shall give the word. Our wounded are well cared for, and bear their misfortunes like heroes. Seldom is a complaint heard in the hospitals.

The movement of Hardee against the enemy's left wing was one of the most dashing of the war, and a complete surprise. His men dashed upon the enemy as a storm from the clouds, and so panic stricken were the vandals that the first line threw down their arms and ran towards our lines, shouting at the top of their voices: "Don't shoot; we surrender!" The prisoners sent to the rear, Hardee attacked the second line and carried it, but with considerable loss to his corps. He held their works for more than a day, no serious effort being made to molest him, and then moved to a more fruitful portion of the field.

THE ENEMY SUFFERING FOR FOOD.

A gentleman from Atlanta says he was informed by a good many of our soldiers, and the testimony was so concurrent that he could not doubt it, that the Yankee prisoners reported themselves in a famishing condition. They stated they had received no rations for three days. They also reported that no trains had come down for four or five days. As these prisoners were captured on the extreme left of Sherman's line, it may well be that their case was exceptional, and as to the arrival of railroad trains to Sherman, they may well have been entirely ignorant of what was taking place across the river.

THE LAST REPULSE OF THE YANKEES.

On Sunday night the enemy made a heavy demonstration on our centre, with the apparent object of forcing our lines, and to gain a certain advantage of position which would make their operations much more effective. They were repulsed by Gen. Cheatham's corps. The enemy suffered disastrously during the hour that they fought against the impenetrable lines held by that veteran General and his invincible soldiers. After discovering the futility of their operations, Sherman resumed his former position and strengthened his works, especially the wings. We presume he will patiently try the effect of parallels and siege approaches—those offensive operations that have been so eminently characteristic a peculiarity of his plans and very successful hitherto. But we suspect that he will be foiled completely and his strategy overwhelmed by the rapid movements of an active rival whose enterprise is not inferior to his own.

THE BOMBARDMENT OF ATLANTA.

A great many houses in Atlanta have been pierced by Yankee shells. A dozen shells have struck Wesley Chapel and the Parsonage. Two batteries have the range of the Car Shed and the Wesley Chapel, and they peg away night and day, making line shots in the direction of the State R. R. bridge. The women and children fly to the cellars, and the men walk about watching where the shells strike. The Atlanta Relief Committee are busy distributing rations to destitute women and children.

THE GEORGIA MILITIA MOVING TO THE FRONT.

Sixteen hundred of the Georgia militia started from Macon for Atlanta Tuesday. The Telegraph says they made a fine appearance as they marched through the streets; were in the very best spirits and appeared ready to meet the enemy in defence of their homes. The material of this brigade is as good as that of any in the South, and we are certain they will do honor to the State when brought into action. The Telegraph also states that a similar number will go down to Atlanta, each day during the week from this place. There is now a large force of militia at Macon, which, when sent to the front, will prove a valuable accession to our gallant army.

The New-York Times.

VOL. XIII.—NO. 4005. NEW-YORK, TUESDAY, JULY 26, 1864. PRICE FOUR CENTS.

ATLANTA.

The Great Battle of Friday.

Official Statements from General Sherman.

Terrific Slaughter of the Rebels.

The Union Battle Cry, "Remember McPherson."

Sherman Shelling Atlanta, and the City on Fire.

The Rebel Loss Fully Seven Thousand.

General Sherman's Loss Less than Two Thousand.

WASHINGTON, Monday, July 25.

The *Republican*, extra, says:

Dispatches to the Government represent that a great battle was fought in Atlanta on Friday, resulting in a horrible slaughter and a complete repulse of the enemy at every point.

The rebels, holding the largest part of the city, assaulted our works on that day with great fury, evidently expecting to drive our forces out of the city. The Fifteenth Corps, commanded by Gen. FRANK BLAIR, seemed to be the special object of rebel wrath, as they massed against it in overwhelming force. The Fifteenth received the shock gallantly, and held its own until Gen. DODGE, with the Sixteenth Corps, came up, when the rebels were hurled back with great slaughter.

Gen. LOGAN, at the head of the Seventeenth Corps, went into battle with the rallying cry of "Remember MCPHERSON."

This corps, as well as BLAIR's Fifteenth Corps, both constituting the army under Maj.-Gen. MCPHERSON, fought desperately—the news of the death of their brave Commander having been communicated to them just before going into battle.

Gen. MCPHERSON was shot while reconnoitering. He became separated from his staff for a moment, and a rebel sharpshooter shot him from an ambush.

The terrible struggle ended by repulsing the enemy at every point of the line.

It was arranged that on Saturday the dead of both armies should be buried and the wounded removed under a flag of truce.

Our troops buried one thousand rebels left on the field within our lines; besides which the rebels buried many of their own dead themselves near their works. Upon this basis, it is estimated that the rebel killed and wounded, on Friday, will exceed six thousand, the proportion of killed to wounded in battle being about one to seven.

Our loss will reach about 2,500 in killed and wounded. The Fifteenth Corps suffered severely, the enemy's troops having been massed against it. It was this act of the enemy in part that cost him such heavy loss.

While the work of burying the dead and removing the wounded was going on on Saturday, SHERMAN'S heavy artillery was playing upon the city. At the same time large fires were observed in different parts of Atlanta, supposed to be caused by the destruction of supply depots and other rebel property, which the enemy could not carry off, and did not wish to fall into our hands. This is considered as evidence of their intending to evacuate the place.

Several rebel Generals are reported to be killed, but their names are not yet given.

FURTHER DETAILS.

WASHINGTON, Monday, July 25.

The enemy's cavalry at the outset turned our left flank, and the line at that point was driven back. One division retreated in some disorder. The troops were rallied there, however, and the rest of the line repelled the enemy. The enemy suffered seriously, but did not leave so many prisoners and wounded on our hands as on Thursday.

Before the attack was made, Gen. MCPHERSON was killed by a sharpshooter, while reconnoitering alone in front of his lines, and some distance in advance even of his personal staff. Gen. JOHN A. LOGAN succeeded to the command, and exercised it during the day.

Yesterday there was no general engagement, but Gen. THOMAS, who has established himself on the north and northeast, and within a mile and a half of Atlanta, bombarded that city continuously. No news of its positive capture has yet been received. Gen. HOOD's whole army is posted in and about the place.

LATER.

WASHINGTON, July 25, 1864.

A dispatch to-day from General SHERMAN states his loss in the battle of Friday at less than 2,000, while that of the enemy cannot be less than 7,000, owing to the advantage he took of their effort to turn his left column. There is no official information to show that our forces have entered Atlanta.

Special Dispatch to the N. Y. Times.

WASHINGTON, Monday, July 25.

THE BATTLES BEFORE ATLANTA.

Both engagements delivered before Atlanta, namely, that of Wednesday and that of Friday last, have been assaults on the part of the rebels. This is accounted for from the fact that Gen. HOOD, JOHNSTON's successor, has been throughout the campaign one of the most bitter opponents of JOHNSTON's retreating policy; and he felt impelled, the moment he was placed in command, to pitch in. It does not appear that he has gained any other result than to bring upon himself, in each instance, a loss thrice as heavy as that inflicted on the assailed party.

GEN. SHERMAN CONFIDENT OF SUCCESS.

Gen. SHERMAN's latest dispatches show an assured confidence in the capture of Atlanta, though the prize may not be won as speedily as the public had anticipated.

THE DEATH OF GEN. M'PHERSON.

Gen. SHERMAN's dispatches also express the most profound grief at the death of MCPHERSON. That gallant soldier was killed about eleven in the forenoon, while riding in advance of his Staff to form a defensive line to meet the rebel attack. The severe fighting was done after MCPHERSON's death, the engagement continuing until five in the afternoon.

THE LOSSES ON BOTH SIDES.

Gen. SHERMAN estimates the rebel loss at 7,000; our own at 2,000.

Destruction of Railroads—The Siege Progressing.

NASHVILLE, Monday, July 25.

Gen. GARRARD's expedition has been successful, destroying the bridges at Covington, forty miles east of Atlanta. The public stores at Covington and Coneyer were also destroyed, with 2,000 bales of cotton, a locomotive and train of cars. Two hundred prisoners and a number of horses were captured.

Our loss in the recent battle will foot up something less than 2,000.

We have found over 1,000 dead rebels, which, with the usual proportion of wounded, will make their loss over 7,000.

Our army is in good condition, and the situation is favorable.

Official news is in from in front of Atlanta. It is meagre, but no reverses are reported. Gen. SHERMAN still maintains his position, and is vigorously advancing.

Gen. ROUSSEAU has successfully fulfilled his orders, and reports a loss of only 12 of his command.

Gen. McPherson's Remains.

NASHVILLE, Monday, July 25.

The remains of Gen. MCPHERSON reached here at 9 A. M. to-day, and were escorted through to the Louisville depot by the Thirteenth Regulars. Capt. LAMONT, of the Tenth Tennessee Infantry, Col. SCULLY, of the Regular Artillery, Gens. MCELROY and GILLOM, and Gov. JOHNSON and Staff were in the procession, which comprised all the officers of the different departments in the city.

The remains leave by special train, at 12 o'clock at noon, accompanied by a guard of the Thirteenth Regulars, of two officers and fifty men, to Sandusky, Ohio. The streets were thronged with citizens, and all the employes of the departments assembled to honor the remains of Gen. MCPHERSON.

CAVALRY OPERATIONS OF GENERAL SHERMAN'S ARMY.

Important Raid on the Montgomery and West Point Railroad, by Gen. Rousseau—Complete Success of the Expedition.

The following has been received from Gen. ROUSSEAU's expedition:

MARIETTA, GA., July 24, 1864.

To the Assistant Adjutant-General, District of Tennessee:

We arrived here day before yesterday, and have been eminently successful, and have executed the orders of Gen. SHERMAN to the letter. Our loss does not exceed twelve in killed and wounded. I start to-day for Nashville.

On the 22d Gen. SHERMAN announced, in a circular to his army, that Gen. ROUSSEAU had been entirely successful.

The important expedition against the Montgomery and West Point Railroad, the success of which is thus officially announced, was projected by Gen. ROUSSEAU, when Gen. SHERMAN was preparing to depart on his great raid through Mississippi, in the early part of this year; but for various military reasons, its execution was postponed until the present month. On the 30th ult., Gen. SHERMAN revived the project, as an important auxiliary to his grand movement upon Atlanta, his object being to cut the railroad between Columbus, Ga., and Montgomery, Ala., so effectually as to destroy permanently the rebel communications between these points. Abundant preparations were made for the destruction of the ties, rails, bridges, culverts, water-tanks, depot buildings, locomotives, arsenals, Government machine-shops, &c. Gen. ROUSSEAU was also ordered to destroy the town of Opelika, the point of junction of the road from Columbus with Atlanta, West Point and Montgomery road.

Gen. ROUSSEAU received his final orders on the 4th inst., and on the 6th, having completed his preparations, left Nashville with his staff. He was accompanied by Capt. J. C. WILLIAMS, Nineteenth United States Infantry, and Capt. ELKIN, Fifth Kentucky Cavalry, Aides-de-Camp; Capt. RUGER, Topographical Engineer; Capt. MCCONNEL, Inspector, and several other officers. Capt. RUGER had been engaged for several months in preparing maps of the proposed route, and in gathering important information from Union refugees.

The force placed at the disposal of Gen. ROUSSEAU was limited to about 2,760 men, and consisted of the following regiments, which were concentrated at Decatur, Alabama: Fifth Indiana Cavalry, Col. T. J. HARRISON; Fifth Iowa Cavalry, Lieut.-Col. PATRICK; Second Kentucky Cavalry, Maj. EIFORT; Fourth Tennessee Cavalry and the Ninth Ohio Cavalry. The men composing this force were all veterans, well mounted and excellently armed. A thousand SPENCER repeating rifles, firing eight times and invaluable as a cavalry arm, were judiciously distributed among the men. Two light Rodman guns were also taken along.

Gen. ROUSSEAU moved from Decatur with his forces on the 10th inst., taking a southeasterly direction. The details of the expedition have not yet been received, but by referring to a good map of Alabama and Georgia it will be seen that the first important point on the route is Blountsville, about fifty miles from Decatur; the second Ashville, some thirty miles further on. He probably crossed the Coosa River somewhere in the vicinity of Broken Arrow, pushed on to Talladega, and thence to the Tallapoosa River, which he was to cross at the most convenient bridge or ford. This would bring him within thirty miles of the Montgomery road.

Eight important bridges carry this railroad over as many streams, between Opelika and Montgomery; and the thorough destruction of these was one of the principal objects of the raid. Having accomplished this work, and destroyed the workshops and other Government buildings at Opelika, and the bridges between that town and West Point, Gen. ROUSSEAU was ordered to move up on the west side of the Chattahoochee and join Gen. SHERMAN at some point between Marietta, Ga., and that river. That he has done his work effectually we know not only from Gen. SHERMAN's dispatch, but from the rebel acknowledgment that on the 17th inst. telegraphic communication was suspended between Atlanta and Montgomery, and that the railroad between the former place and West Point was not in working order.

THE WAR ON THE MISSISSIPPI.

A Battle Near Grand Gulf—The Rebels Defeated by Gen. Slocum.

CAIRO, Sunday, July 24.

The steamer *Belle*, from Memphis, has arrived here with 97 rebel prisoners, taken in the battle of Tupelo. The officers go to Johnson's Island, and the privates to Alton.

The same steamer also brought up 95 refugees, and a large number of furloughed soldiers, and 25 bales of cotton.

The steamer *Madison* had arrived at Memphis from Vicksburgh. Gen. SLOCUM's expedition had returned to Vicksburgh after defeating 2,000 rebels under WIRT ADAMS, after a short and severe fight at Grand Gulf, on the 17th, in which the rebel loss was severe and the enemy retreated in confusion, leaving a number of dead and wounded on our hands, as well as many prisoners. Our loss was trifling. Among the rebel prisoners are two rebel Colonels of Mississippi cavalry.

When near Napoleon the *Madison* was fired into by musketry, and some soldiers of the Nineteenth Pennsylvania Cavalry were wounded. The fire was effectively returned. Guerrillas were seen at Gainesville and other points.

The *Bulletin* says, on the 19th, 2,500 rebels passed thirty miles from Memphis, on the other side of the river, on the road to Osceola. Other accounts state that three companies of Butternuts, under command of Col. ADAMS, late of Helena, went three days ago northward some distance of Osceola, and that a number of other rebel companies were on the St. Francis and other rivers, moving in a northerly direction. The general impression was that a rebel force was about to concentrate in Missouri.

A train of fifteen cars from Memphis to Lagrange, on the Memphis and Charleston Railroad, ran off the track near Colliersville on the 19th. Some half dozen cars were smashed and a number of persons badly injured. One or two were killed.

FROM WASHINGTON.

MR. FESSENDEN'S FINANCIAL POLICY.

Two Hundred Millions of Seven-Thirties to be Issued.

A Patriotic and Manly Appeal to the People.

Special Dispatches to the New-York Times.

WASHINGTON, Monday, July 25.

THE SPECIAL INCOME TAX.

Further regulations and instructions in regard to the special income tax, imposed under the joint resolution of Congress, approved July 4, will be issued by Commissioner LEWIS, upon his return to his seat. As the law stands now, there is an apparent conflict between it, as it finally passed the House, and the supplementary resolution referred to, which it would be well for all parties concerned to have cleared up.

RAIN AT WASHINGTON.

The long drouth is over. The cool weather of the past three days has culminated in rain. A gentle shower commenced last night, and continued until nearly noon to-day.

MODIFICATIONS IN THE PENSION LAWS.

Several modifications have been made in the Pension Laws of the United States passed by the last Congress. Section fourteen of an act supplementary to the Pension Act of July 14, 1862, provides that the widows and children of colored soldiers who have been, or who may be hereafter killed, or who have died, or may hereafter die of wounds received in battle, or who have died, or may hereafter die of diseases contracted in the military service of the United States, shall be entitled to receive pensions as now provided by law, without other proof of marriage than that the parties had habitually recognized each other as man and wife, and lived together as such for a definite period, not less than two years, next preceding the soldier's enlistment, to be shown by affidavits of witnesses. *Provided further*, That such widow and children are free persons; that if such parties resided in any State in which their marriage may have been legally solemnized, the usual evidence shall be required.

ARRIVAL OF REBEL PRISONERS.

Thirteen rebel prisoners arrived here this morning, having been sent here by Col. HYATT, Provost-Marshal of the Sixth Army Corps. The prisoners belonged to the invading forces, and represent Georgia and North Carolina cavalry regiments. Six of them were committed to the Old Capitol, and the others asked permission to take the oath of allegiance.

SENTENCE OF A BLOCKADE RUNNER.

JOSEPH FEDDERMAN, a blockade runner, was to-day sentenced by Military Commission to imprisonment in the Albany penitentiary during the war.

DEATHS OF NEW-YORK SOLDIERS.

The following are the deaths of New-York soldiers reported from the hospitals to-day: Eugene Smith, F, First Rifles; John H. Rodman, B, Sixth Heavy Artillery; John W. Pews, K, Fiftieth Regulars; George W. Stevens, G, Twenty-fourth Cavalry.

Dispatches to the Associated Press.

WASHINGTON, Monday, July 25.

NEW ASSISTANT TREASURER AT NEW-YORK.

MOSES TAYLOR has been appointed Assistant Treasurer at New-York, to succeed Mr. CISCO, whose continued ill-health compels him to retire from office.

MR. FESSENDEN'S FINANCIAL POLICY—$200,000,000 OF SEVEN-THIRTIES TO BE ISSUED.

Secretary FESSENDEN, under authority of an act of Congress of June last, to issue an amount not exceeding $200,000,000 in Treasury notes, &c., has, to-day, given notice that subscriptions will be received by the Treasurer of the United States, the several Assistant Treasurers and designated depositories, and by the National Banks designated and qualified as depositories and financial agents for Treasury notes, payable three years from Aug. 15, 1864, bearing interest at the rate of seven and three-tenths per cent. per annum, with semi-annual coupons attached, payable in lawful money. These notes will be convertible, at the option of the holder, at maturity, into six per cent. gold-bearing bonds, redeemable after five, and payable twenty years from Aug. 15, 1867. The notes will be issued in denominations of fifty, one hundred, five hundred, one thousand and five thousand dollars, and in blank, or payable to order as may be directed by the subscribers. All subscriptions must be for fifty dollars or some multiple of fifty dollars. Interest will be allowed to August 15 on all deposits made prior to that date, and paid by the Department upon the receipt of the original certificates. As the notes draw interest from August 15, persons making deposits subsequent to that date must pay the interest accrued from the date of the note to the date of the deposit. Parties depositing twenty-five thousand dollars and upward for these notes, at any one time, will be allowed a commission of one quarter of one per cent., which will be paid by the Treasury Department upon the receipt of a bill for the amount, certified to by the officer with whom the deposit was made. No deduction for commissions must be made from the deposits.

AN APPEAL TO THE PEOPLE OF THE UNITED STATES.

Accompanying this advertisement, in a circular form, is Secretary FESSENDEN's appeal to the people of the United States, in which he says: "The circumstances under which this loan is asked for, and your aid invoked, though differing widely from the existing state of affairs three years ago, are such as afford equal encouragement and security. Time, while proving that the struggle for national unity was to exceed in duration and severity our worst anticipations, has tested the national strength and national resources to an extent alike unexpected and remarkable, exciting equal astonishment at home and abroad. Three years of war have burdened you with a debt which but three years since would have seemed beyond your ability to meet. Yet the accumulated wealth and productive energies of the nation have proved to be so vast, that it has been borne with comparative ease, and a peaceful future would hardly feel its weight. As a price paid for national existence and the preservation of free institutions, it does not deserve a moment's consideration. Thus far, the war has been supported and carried on as it only could have been by a people resolved, at whatever cost of blood and treasure, to transmit unimpaired to posterity the system of free government bequeathed to them by the great men who framed it. This deliberate and patriotic resolve has developed a power surprising even to themselves. It has shown that in less than a century a nation has arisen unsurpassed in vigor and exhaustless in resources, able to conduct through a series of years, war on its most gigantic scale, and finding itself when near its close almost unimpaired in all the material elements of power. It has at the present moment great armies in the field, facing an enemy apparently approaching a period of utter exhaustion, but still struggling with a force the greater and more desperate as it sees, and because it sees, the near approach of a final and fatal consummation. Such is my deliberate judgment in the present condition of the great contest for civil liberty in which you are now engaged. Up to the present moment you have readily and cheerfully afforded the means necessary to support your Government in this protracted struggle. It is your war. You proclaimed it and you have sustained it against traitors everywhere with patriotic devotion unsurpassed in the world's history. The securities offered are such as should command your ready confidence. Much effort has been made to shake public faith in our national credit, both at home and abroad. As yet, we have asked no foreign aid. Calm and self-reliant, our own means thus far have proved adequate to our wants. They are yet ample to meet those of the present and future. It still remains for a patriotic people to furnish the needful supply. The brave men who are fighting our battles by land and sea, must be fed and clothed. Munitions of war of all kinds must be furnished, or the war must end in defeat and disgrace. This is not the time for any lover of his country to inquire as to the state of the money market, or ask whether he can so invest his surplus capital as to yield him a larger return. No return and no profit can be desirable, if followed by national dissolution or national disgrace. Present profit thus acquired is but the precursor of future and speedy destruction. No investment can be so surely profitable as that which tends to insure the national existence. I am encouraged in the belief that by the recent legislation of Congress our finances may soon be placed upon a sounder and more stable footing. The present deranged condition of the currency is imputable, in a great degree, to disturbances arising from the withdrawal of necessary checks often inevitable in time war, when the expenditures must largely exceed any possible supply of coin. The opportunities thus presented to acquire sudden wealth, have led to vicious speculation, a consequent increase of prices and violent fluctuations.

The remedy is to be found only in controlling the necessity which begets the evil. Hitherto we have felt the need of more extensive and vigorous taxation. Severe comment has been made upon what seemed to many an undue timidity and tardiness of action on the part of Congress in this regard. I deem it but just to say that a very great misapprehension has existed, and, perhaps, still exists, upon this point. Legislators, like all others, have much to learn in a new condition of affairs. An entirely new system was to be devised, and that system must necessarily be the growth of time and experience. It is not strange that the first efforts should have proved imperfect and inadequate. To lay heavy burdens on a great and patriotic people in such a manner as to be equal, and so as to occasion the least amount of suffering or annoyance, requires time and caution, and vast labor; and, with all these, experience is needful to test the value of the system and correct its errors. Such has been the work that Congress has been called upon to perform. I am happy to say that daily results are proving the Internal Revenue Act to exceed in efficiency the most sanguine expectations of its authors. For the month of June, 1863, it yielded about four and a half millions of dollars, while the corresponding month of this year returned about fifteen millions under the same law. Under the new law which went into operation on the first day of the present month, the Treasury frequently receive one million in a day. As time and experience enable the officers employed in collecting the revenue to enforce the strength of the provisions of the new law, I trust that a million per day will be found the rule, and not the exception. Still much space is undoubtedly left for improvement in the law and in its administration. As a greater amount of necessary information is acquired, the proper sources of revenue, and the most effective mode of obtaining it, are best developed in the execution of the existing laws, and I have caused measures to be initiated which will, it is believed, enable Congress so to improve and enlarge the system as when taken in connection with the revenue from customs and other sources, to afford an ample and secure basis for the national credit. Only on such a basis, and in a steady and vigorous restraint upon the currency can a remedy be found for existing evils. Such a restraint can only be exercised when the Government is furnished with means to provide for its necessities. But without the aid of a patriotic people, the army of the Government is powerless for this or any other desirable end. The denomination of the notes proposed to be issued range from $50 to $5,000. Place these securities within the reach of all who are disposed to aid their country. For their redemption the faith, and honor, and property of that country are solemnly pledged. A successful issue to this contest, now believed to be near at hand, will largely enhance their value to the holders, and peace once restored all burdens can be lightly borne. He who selfishly withholds his aid in the hope of turning his available means to greater immediate profit, is speculating upon his country's misfortunes, and may find what seems to be present gain, leads to future loss. I appeal, therefore, with confidence to a loyal and patriotic people, and invoke the efforts of all who love their country, and desire for it a glorious future, to aid their Government in sustaining its credit, and placing that credit on a stable foundation.

W. P. FESSENDEN,
Secretary of the Treasury.

POST-OFFICE MATTERS—MONEY ORDERS.

Several new and important reforms are being introduced into our National Postal System.

Among the most important of these is the new Money Order System, which has been in process of preparation in the Department for some time past. It is thought it will be fully matured and in operation by the first of October. The necessary blank forms, books, instructions, &c., are now being rapidly prepared. Mr. CHAS. F. MACDONALD, an old and experienced *attaché* of the Department, is placed in charge of the work, and a force of seven clerks detailed to assist him.

Arrangements are also being perfected for the distribution of the mails while *in transitu*, similar to the system so long pursued in Great Britain, France and other European countries.

It has been a matter of surprise to business men why the system of distributing mails for way points and of sorting through letters while en route, so as to facilitate their early and certain delivery, has not been adopted sooner. Traveling Post-offices have constituted an important branch of the postal arrangements of England ever since their railroad system was completed, and even before that period. It has been found to work well, and there is no reason why it should not operate to equal advantage in this country.

Messrs. THOS. CLARK, New-York; GEO. H. LEWIS, Philadelphia; GEO. B. ARMSTRONG, Chicago; and — WHEELER, Cleveland, are now actively engaged in behalf of the Government, in building cars and making all necessary arrangements for putting this system in operation.

The numerous friends of SAYLES J. BOWEN, city Postmaster, in New-York and elsewhere, will be sorry to learn that this gentleman sustained an injury to his knee some time ago, which has required a suspension of duty for the present. He is now at the Elmira Water Cure, slowly recovering.

After the frequent interruptions in mail communication between New-York, Philadelphia and Washington, which have occurred during the past fortnight, it will be pleasing to your readers to know that communications are once more fully restored and the mails dispatched and received regularly.

Rain at Boston.

BOSTON, Monday, July 25.

A welcome rain commenced at noon, and continues falling steadily this evening.

LATER FROM EUROPE.

Arrival of the Belgian off Father Point.

Advices to the 15th of July.

ADVANCE IN THE CONFEDERATE LOAN.

Rumors About the Rebel Cruisers.

PROGRESS OF THE DANISH WAR.

FINANCIAL AND COMMERCIAL INTELLIGENCE

FATHER POINT, Monday, July 25.

The steamship *Belgian*, from Liverpool on the 14th, via Londonderry on the 15th inst., passed this point *en route* to Quebec, at 1 o'clock this afternoon. She was boarded by the news yacht of the Associated Press, and a summary of her news obtained. Her dates are two days later than those already received.

The steamship *North American*, from Quebec, arrived at Londonderry at 10 o'clock on the evening of the 13th inst., and Liverpool same day.

The steamship *Hansa*, from New-York, arrived at Southampton on the 15th inst.

The steamship *Great Eastern* had reached Sheerness, from Liverpool.

GREAT BRITAIN.

The London *Times'* city article says that the advance of the Confederate loan to 74 is partly owing to advices received by speculators.

The London *Daily News* says that the floating supply of Confederate bonds is diminishing, owing to their being absorbed by blockade-runners for the purchase of cotton.

The Atlantic Mail Company Galway Steamship Line have further adjourned their meeting until the 18th of July, to ascertain the definite result of the proposal to the Postmaster-General.

Parliamentary proceedings were unimportant.

The customary Ministerial "White-bait" dinner was fixed for July 23, and Parliament would be prorogued about a week thereafter.

AMERICAN TOPICS.

THE KEARSARGE AND THE FLORIDA.

It was reported that the *Kearsarge* and *Florida* had an engagement off Jersey, July 13; that the *Kearsarge* was disabled, and had to put into Gorey, and that the *Florida* came up and waited off Gorey to renew the engagement. No details are given. [This story is entirely improbable.—Ed. TIMES.]

THE RAPPAHANNOCK.

A letter from Calais says, that the Confederate steamer *Rappahannock*, at that port, lately had judgment pronounced against her by the Boulogne Chambers of Commerce, for commercial debts contracted by her Captain and officers; that the board attempted to fix the notice of sale—but that they were prevented by the Captain, and had to draw up a process verbal.

Capt. SEMMES was traveling *incognito* in Ireland.

DANO-GERMAN AFFAIRS.

The successful passage of the Lynn Fiord by the Prussians is confirmed.

It is also confirmed that Denmark has proposed an armistice with a view to peace negotiations.

The belief is generally entertained that a peace will soon be concluded.

It is reported that King CHRISTIAN proposes in the peace propositions to include the transfer of the Danish Navy on condition of his remaining King of Denmark, under the protection of the German Confederation.

The new Danish Ministry have sent a message to the Rigsraad, of which the following is a summary:

"The King deeming that men unconcerned in late events would be better able to save our Fatherland, has decided upon a change of Ministers.

We hope to obtain the confidence of the Rigsraad and of the people. Otherwise we shall be powerless to lay down a programme at present. It would be impossible to do so. The new Ministers can only give assurance that in taking their stand firmly upon legal ground they will never advise the King to adopt an illegal measure. The message concludes by saying that the Ministers will consider their mission to uphold the independence of Denmark.

The *Indépendance Belge* asserts that the King of Denmark has invoked and obtained the intervention of the Emperor NAPOLEON.

FRANCE.

The Bourse closed firm on the 14th, at 66f. 40c. for the Rentes.

A frightful accident occurred on the Saone River at Lyons. Thirty people were drowned through a lurch of an over-crowded boat.

ITALY.

The National Bank of Italy has reduced its rate of discount to seven per cent.

INDIA.

A Bombay telegram of June 24 reports that AMIER of Cabul completely defeated AFZAL KHAN in a great battle at Bamica.

NEW-ZEALAND.

The London *Times* publishes details of the late disaster to the British troops in New-Zealand. It says it was peculiarly disgraceful and, perhaps, unprecedented. The men were surprised, and fled, while nearly all their officers were killed or wounded in heroic efforts to rally them.

LONDON MONEY MARKET.

In the London money market the funds were improving, under the pacific aspect of affairs. Money was abundant, and the discount rates in the open market were ¼@½ ℔ cent. below the Bank's minimum.

The West India steamer had arrived with nearly two and a quarter millions of dollars in specie.

LATEST VIA LONDONDERRY.

LONDON, Friday, July 15.

Dano-German affairs remain unchanged.

The reported engagement between the *Kearsarge* and *Florida* off Jersey, needs confirmation. It is false as regards the *Kearsarge*, which is cruising off Dover; but it may have been the gunboat *Sacramento*, which has left Cherbourg.

COMMERCIAL PER BELGIAN.

LIVERPOOL COTTON MARKET, 14TH.

The sales of Cotton for four days reach 72,000 bales, including 34,000 bales to speculators and exporters. The market is buoyant, with an advance of ⅛d.@¼d. ℔ lb. since Friday last.

TRADE REPORT.

The Manchester market is excited, with an advancing tendency.

LIVERPOOL BREADSTUFFS MARKETS, 14TH.

The Breadstuffs market is quiet but steady. Messrs. RICHARDSON, SPENCE & Co. report: Flour quiet and steady. Wheat firm: Winter Red, 8s. 6d.@8s. 9d. Corn easier; mixed, 30s. 3d.@30s. 6d.

LIVERPOOL PROVISION MARKET, 14TH.

The Provision market is generally firmer. WAKEFIELD, NASH & Co. and others report: Beef firm. Pork has an upward tendency. Bacon still advancing. Lard firmer at 40s.@43s. Tallow steady. Butter steady.

LIVERPOOL PRODUCE MARKET.

Ashes quiet. Sugar steady. Coffee quiet and steady. Rice quiet. Linseed Oil steady. Rosin, sales small; Spirits Turpentine inactive, at 69s.; Petroleum quiet, quoted 2s. 6d., on spot.

LONDON MARKETS.

Breadstuffs quiet and steady. Sugar easier. Coffee has an upward tendency. Tea dull. Rice quiet. Tallow dull.

LONDON, Thursday, July 14.

CONSOLS close at 90⅛@90¼ for money.

AMERICAN STOCKS—Sales of Illinois Central Railroad at 41½@40½ discount; Erie Railroad at 48@49.

LATEST COMMERCIAL VIA LONDONDERRY.

LIVERPOOL, Friday, July 15.

COTTON—Sales of the week, 115,000 bales, including 34,000 bales to speculators and 24,000 bales to exporters. The market is buoyant, with an advance of ⅛d.@¼d. ℔ lb. on the week. The sales to-day (Friday) were 10,000 bales, including 3,000 to speculators and exporters, the market closing buoyant and unchanged at the following authorized quotations:

	Fair.	Middling.
Orleans	Nominal.	31½d.
Mobile	Nominal.	31¼d.
Uplands	Nominal.	31d.

—Stock in port 211,000 bales, of which 1,750 bales are American.

BREADSTUFFS—The market is quiet and steady. Wheat firmer and upward.

PROVISIONS—The market is firm, with an upward tendency.

LONDON MONEY MARKET.

LONDON, Friday, July 15.

Consols close at 90⅛@90¼ for money.

The bullion in the Bank of England has decreased £230,000.

AMERICAN STOCKS.

The latest sales were: Illinois Central Railroad, 41@40 discount; Erie Railroad, 50@51.

The United States Steamer Connecticut.

BOSTON, Mass., Monday, July 25.

The United States steamer *Connecticut*, Commander ALMY, arrived here to-day from the Wilmington blockade. She has been in commission about a year, and has been very successful in her operations against the blockade-runners having captured within that time four steamers with valuable cargoes. She has also assisted in running ashore and destroying three others. She has not lost a man by sickness during the cruise.

From Cape Race.

ST. JOHNS N. F., Monday, July 25.

A fog came in just as the steamship *Asia*, from Boston for Liverpool, was due off Cape Race, and she was not seen.

The steamship *United Kingdom*, from Glasgow for Quebec, passed Cape Race at 1 o'clock Sunday morning, but was not boarded.

At 10 o'clock this morning the weather at the Cape was thick; thermometer 70.

The Florida—The Reported Engagement a Canard.

NEW-YORK, Monday, July 25.

The reported engagement between the *Kearsarge* or *Sacramento* and the *Florida*, on the 13th inst., off Jersey, in the English Channel, is a canard. The *Florida* was off Cape Henlopen on the 11th inst., and, of course, could not have been in the English Channel on the 13th.

Marine Disaster.

ROCKPORT, Mass., Monday, July 25.

The schooner *Gazelle*, of Provincetown, for Portsmouth, with coal, struck a rock off Thatched Island, on Saturday night, and sank. The vessel was a total loss. The crew were saved.

FROM FORTRESS MONROE.

Rebel Accounts From Atlanta.

FORTRESS MONROE, Saturday, July 23.

The flag-of-truce boat *C. W. Thomas*, Capt. DOANE, arrived here from Aiken's Landing last evening, in charge of Maj. MULFORD. They brought neither news nor passengers. Hon. Secretary SEWARD left here last evening for City Point and Bermuda Hundred on the steamer *City of Hudson*.

The *Cambria*, Capt. BLANCHARD, arrived to-day from New-Orleans 15th inst., with the most of the Thirteenth Connecticut Regiment, whose time have expired. They are going home on furlough, having reënlisted for the war.

The Richmond *Dispatch*, of July 21, contains the following:

PETERSBURGH, Monday, July 25.

There is no change in the situation, and no signs of immediate hostilities on the part of GRANT. Heavy rain yesterday.

The report of GRANT's death is contradicted.

ATLANTA, Wednesday, July 20.

REYNOLD's brigade attacked the enemy's line of skirmishers last evening, at Peach Tree Creek, and took possession of their intrenchments. He then charged the reserve pickets, supported by DILWORTH's corps, and captured 150 prisoners.

The Eightieth Illinois Regiment lost in killed and wounded, 160.

The loss of the Fiftieth Ohio was severe.

SHERMAN evidently intends to rebuild the railroad bridge across the Chattahoochee. HOWARD's Fourth Army Corps, which was on this side of the river, have recrossed, having been relieved by two divisions of DODGE's Sixteenth Corps.

SCHOFIELD's division, Twenty-third Corps, and GIRARD's division of cavalry are on this side, about a mile from the river on Buckhead road, having thrown up breastworks. The enemy are massing troops on our right, with an eye toward Stone Mountain.

Petersburgh to be Blown into the Air.

To the Editor of the Richmond Whig:

PETERSBURGH, Tuesday, July 19.

The editors of the Richmond and Petersburgh papers have been making fun of the declaration of the Northern press that GRANT would soon startle the country with "another brilliant exploit." Do you suppose that GRANT has kept fifty thousand men in complete idleness for six weeks, or fancy that his whole time has been occupied in fortifying himself and organizing raids? If so, you will find yourselves vastly mistaken, and that within a very few days.

In what manner I came into possession of the facts which I am about to narrate is not material. Suffice it to say, they are facts, as time will prove. Perhaps a few hours may bring the dreadful realization. I tremble to think of it.

Know, then, our loved Cockade City will soon be, if it is not at this very moment, thoroughly undermined. GRANT, far from being content to blow up the "rebel fortifications," has determined to destroy the entire city, as by a tremendous blast from the infernal regions. In a single instant every building in the principal streets of Petersburgh will be lifted on high and scattered to the four winds of heaven. You may laugh at this, but it is so. My informant has seen a diagram of the mines, which, when completed, will extend the length of Bollingbrook, Bank, Sycamore and Old streets, and perhaps, as far as the old Fair Grounds, on the south of the City. "This is incredible and impossible on the face of it," you will say. Very well; you are welcome to your opinion. But you will be good enough to tell me what feat ever attempted with the pick and spade the Yankees have failed to execute; and will you explain to me the meaning of GRANT's long inaction? I tell you this is no canard—would that it were—but a plain statement of facts, procured by me from an entirely reliable source.

"Why do I not make my statement to Gen. LEE, or print it in the *Express*?" you will naturally inquire. I answer frankly, because Gen. LEE would rebuff me, (at least I think so,) and because the *Express* refuses positively to admit me to its columns. Many of your readers will fancy that I have been dreaming; but I can assure them that I am in my waking senses—never more so in my life—and sincerely desirous, by this timely warning, of averting one of the most awful catastrophes that ever befel an afflicted people. You can publish this or not, just as you choose.

Respectfully, CHAS. I. BROWNE.

Shipments to Mexico.

CONSULATE GENERAL OF MEXICO IN THE UNITED STATES, No. 33 SOUTH STREET, NEW-YORK July 24, 1864.

The undersigned, Consul-General of the Republic of Mexico for the United States, hereby notifies all merchants and other persons dispatching vessels or shipping merchandise to the ports of Mexico, that they are obliged, under the most strict obligation, to present their manifests and invoices at this office for due consideration, there being no other person recognized as Mexican Consul at this port by the Government of the United States.

J. N. NAVARRO.

Fifth-avenue Evening Stock Exchange.

$20,000 Amer. Gold...	260	100 Cleve & Pitts b[illegible]	109⅝
15,000 do	259	100 do .... btw	1[illegible]⅝
35,000 do	259½	50 Chi. & R. I. R ...	110⅝
5,000 do	258¾	500 do	111
10,000 do	258¾	400 do s3	111
100 Erie Railway .. s3	109½	100 do	110¾
100 do s3	110	100 Cum. Coal b3	69
100 Hud. Riv. R	128¾	200 do	69
200 Reading R	134½	200 Mariposa Min	43
200 Ill. Cen. R	126¼	100 do	43½
100 Chic. & N. W.	61		

THE TWENTY-INCH GUN.—The great 20-inch gun, recently finished at the Fort Pitt Works, has been placed upon the trucks which were built expressly by the Pennsylvania Railroad Company, at their shops in Altoona, to convey it to its destination. It is doubtful whether they are strong enough to bear up its immense weight, 116,497 pounds, or over fifty-eight tons. The 20-inch navy gun, recently cast at the Fort Pitt Works, is now in the turning lathe, and is slowly, but surely coming into shape.—*Pittsburgh Dispatch, July 23.*

The New-York Times.

VOL. XIII.—NO. 4017. NEW-YORK, TUESDAY, AUGUST 9, 1864. PRICE FOUR CENTS.

GOOD NEWS.

Farragut's Attack on Mobile.

A GREAT NAVAL BATTLE

THE REBEL REPORT OF IT.

Our Fleet Passed Fort Morgan and Close to Mobile.

Dreadful Havoc Among the Rebel Gunboats.

The Iron-Clad Ram Tennessee Surrendered.

The Selma Captured, the Gaines Beached. the Morgan Trying to Escape.

The Rebel Admiral Buchanan Maimed and Captured.

Only One Union Monitor Reported Lost.

Official Dispatch from Secretary Stanton.

WAR DEPARTMENT, WASHINGTON, Aug. 8—9 P. M.

To Major-Gen. Dix, New-York:

The following announcement of the successful operations against Mobile, appears in the Richmond *Sentinel* of this date, and is transmitted by Major-Gen. BUTLER to the President.

FROM HEADQUARTERS OF GEN. BUTLER, Monday, Aug. 8—3 P. M.

To His Excellency, A. Lincoln, President:

The following is the official report, taken from the Richmond *Sentinel* of Aug. 8:

B. F. BUTLER, Major-General.

"MOBILE, Aug. 5, 1864.

Hon. J. A. Seddon, Secretary of War:

Seventeen of the enemy's vessels, (fourteen ships and three iron-clads) passed Fort Morgan this morning. The *Tecumseh*, a monitor, was sunk by Fort Morgan. The *Tennessee* surrendered after a desperate engagement with the enemy's fleet. Admiral BUCHANAN lost a leg, and is a prisoner. The *Selma* was captured. The *Gaines* was beached near the hospital. The *Morgan* is safe and will try to run up to-night. The enemy's fleet has approached the city. A monitor has been engaging Fort Powell all day.

(Signed) D. H. MAURY, Maj.-Gen."

Special Dispatch to the New-York Times.

WASHINGTON, Monday, Aug. 8.

Gen. BUTLER telegraphs that Richmond papers of Saturday, 6th inst., announce that our forces had taken possession of Dauphin's Island, at the extremity of which stands Fort Gaines, commanding one of the banks of the entrance to Mobile Bay.

Should FARRAGUT not be willing to risk running the gauntlet of Forts Gaines and Morgan, and the obstructions, the landing on Dauphin's Island will afford a secure *point d'appui* for siege operations against both forts. The analogy between the positions thus gained and that of Gen. GILLMORE on Morris Island will be recognized. Up to the latest advices no naval attack had been made by Admiral FARRAGUT, nor had he attempted to force an entrance with his iron-clad fleet, but the grand *coup* was expected to come off on the 3d inst.

The Attacking Fleet.

We give below a list of the vessels understood to have been the fleet with which Admiral FARRAGUT attacked Mobile. These vessels are provided with the heaviest ordnance.

FLAGSHIP—Hartford, screw sloop, 20 guns.

Iron-clads.

Winnebago.......2 turret monitor.......4 guns
Chickasaw.......2 turret monitor.......4 guns
Tecumseh.......1 turret monitor.......2 guns
Manhattan.......1 turret monitor.......2 guns
Four Mississippi River iron-clads.......10 guns

SCREW SLOOPS.

Richmond, 1st class...20 | Oneida, 2d class.......10
Brooklyn, 1st class...20 | Seminole, 2d class.......13
Monongahela, 2d class...12 | Galena, 3d class.......14
Lackawanna, 2d class...14 | Genesee, 3d class.......8

DOUBLE-ENDERS.

Metacomet.......Side-wheel.......10
Sebago.......Side-wheel.......10
Port Royal.......Side-wheel.......8
Octorara.......Side-wheel.......9

SCREW GUNBOATS.

[illegible].......4
[illegible].......7
[illegible].......5

Besides these, there are five tugs, carrying two guns each.

The Draft to be Enforced.

From the following letter to the Provost-marshal of the Wheeling (Penn.) District, it appears the draft will certainly be enforced in these districts which fail to fill their quota before the 5th of September:

PROVOST-MARSHAL-GENERAL'S OFFICE, WASHINGTON CITY, Aug. 3.

Col. John Ely, A. A. P. M. General, Wheeling, West Virginia:

See that your Enrolling Boards spare no pains in correcting the enrollment lists, and making all necessary preparation for proceeding promptly with the draft in September.

(Signed) J. B. FRY, Provost-Marshal-General.

Preparations for the Defence of Louisville.

LOUISVILLE, Ky., Sunday, Aug. 7.

The Common Council, by request of the military authorities, will furnish 600 men to-morrow to throw up fortifications for the defence of the city against possible contingencies.

GENERAL SHERMAN'S ARMY.

Military Railroads—Farewell of Gen. Jo. Hooker—The Action of the 28th—Our Prospects for Atlanta.

Special Correspondence of the New-York Times.

CHATTANOOGA, Monday, Aug. 1, 1864.

Business of an important nature calling me from the front to this city, alone accounts for the date and place of this letter. I arrived here on Saturday, 30th ult., after a very tiresome ride on one of those modes of conveyance known as a military railroad—a mode of transportation excessively exhausting to feeble constitutions, and a horrible ordeal to men of a small amount of patience. It is the best, however, that Uncle Sam has for the children in this part of his territory; and, like an obedient son of a munificently-disposed parent, we will neither chide him nor find fault with his accommodations.

Thursday morning, the 28th ult., will not be soon forgotten by the Twentieth Army Corps. It was made memorable by the parting salutations of Major-Gen. HOOKER with the officers and men of the corps. The promotion of Major-Gen. HOWARD to the command of the Army of the Tennessee, seems to have been the cause of this change in the relations between Gen. HOOKER and the Western army. It was the ostensible, and, we presume, the substantial cause of Gen. HOOKER's asking to be relieved of his command. His request having been granted, on the morning of the 28th ult. he met the officers of the corps to bid them adieu. He said it had never been his lot to command as good an army as the one he had commanded in the West; and he never expected to command a better. He regretted very much the necessity of his parting with them, and assured them that if it was ever in his power to do anything for them, he would gladly do it. He highly commended the officers of the corps for the urbanity that had uniformly characterized their intercourse with him, and the unfeigned cheerfulness with which they had executed his commands, assuring them that he had never been so attached to any body of men as he was to them. He briefly reviewed the campaign, and the part his own command had taken in it. He said the number of casualties in any army is the measure of service it has rendered, and, during this campaign, they knew, as also did he, that his own command had not failed to render its full measure of service, for one-half of all the casualties in the campaign were in the Twentieth Corps. We have had hard service, and been in many tight places; but in what difficult place have we been put out of which we have not come all right?

These remarks, with many incidental interchanges of sentiment that occurred during the interview, unwound nature's sympathies, and tears were drawn from many eyes. Men in that assembly who could meet the enemy with an unblanching countenance, and a heart that never yields to fear in the presence of the forman, gave up their self-control, or rather had it taken from them in the mutual interchange of feeling that characterized the hour. It was a solemn parting, and one in which the silence was vocal and the nonutterance more pregnant with the meaning of the heart than what was said. Gen. HOOKER was a host in himself. His presence everywhere had something akin to magnetic power over the masses he commanded, and infused the breasts of his men with the same indomitable determination that stood out so boldly as a feature in his own military character. Whenever he passed along the lines he was hailed with the united applause of his whole command, while the men of other commands did not withhold from him kindred honors. He has gone from us, and the blessings of the entire corps are resting on his head, while every heart wishes him long life, a prosperous career and new glory in untried fields.

When I left the front, on Thursday evening, the 28th ult., things were assuming an important aspect. The Army of the Tennessee, under Maj.-Gen. HOWARD, had passed round from our extreme left to our extreme right, on the afternoon of Wednesday, the 27th ult., with the undoubted purpose of making important movements on the enemy's left, and, if possible, intercept his communications on the Macon and Western Railroad. On the day following, namely, 28th ult., these movements were made. The enemy detected the design at an early period of its development, concentrated his force, and made a rapid descent on our lines before, as he supposed, they were in a defensible posture. In this, however, he was egregiously deceived, for the General had been careful before advancing so to make his disposition as that, in the event of the enemy attacking him in the precise manner in which he did, the result should not be doubtful. The end of the engagement showed the wisdom of his plans. It was another victory for the Union arms. The battle lasted from 2½ to 6 o'clock P. M., and the enemy were repulsed, and four stands of colors were taken. There was a demonstration made all along the front. At 4 P. M. the whole front warmed into a perfect fusilade of artillery and musketry, and the whole line was in a sheet of flame and enveloped in smoke. No casualties of consequence occurred along our front, and but few elsewhere, except in the fight with the Army of the Tennessee. How great their loss was I have been unable to learn.

A pile of loose ammunition for BUNDY's battery, Thirteenth New-York Light Artillery, was shot into by a rebel shell, and exploded without personal injury to any one. The battle waned before night came on, and everything became quiet. Nothing but an occasional discharge of a big gun, and now and then a musket discharged, reminded us of the proximate presence of the foe. Hostilities had not been renewed when I left the Quartermaster's Department at the front, on Friday morning, the 29th ult.

Things are moving on steadily, and in the right direction here. The time cannot be distant when the city before which we have now set down will be numbered among the Union towns. A vigorous strike, a united and simultaneous advance of our whole army, while it would place many of our braves *hors du combat*, would result in our occupation of Atlanta, and that, too, in quick order. It has not, however, been the policy of the Commanding-General wantonly to expose his men, or for the sake of achieving for himself the reputation of a dashing and brilliant General to lay his troops on the altar of personal ambition and sacrifice them by thousands to gratify his aspiration. He has studiously sought out the most effectual way of routing the enemy from his stronghold with as little cost in human blood as possible, and how well he has succeeded in accomplishing his purpose, the history of the campaign is a proof.

Very many large fires have been seen in Atlanta since our advent to our present position, caused, it is presumed, by our shells, which are being constantly thrown into it. A citizen from the town who came into our lines to-day, told us that on the night of the 27th ult. one of its prettiest streets was burned. Many large fires, indicating buildings of large proportions, are frequently occurring, and during the night have illuminated the heavens from the horizon to the zenith in their immediate locality, and cast their reflection over our entire camp round about. The right and left wings of our vast army are now within three miles of making the circle complete around the fated city. Thus if the rebels attempt to escape, they are brought under our artillery from both flanks. A little while longer, and the great object of this campaign will be attained, and the nation's heart be gladened.

EPSILON.

Reported Capture of Gen. Stoneman Confirmed.

WASHINGTON, Monday, Aug. 8.

Information from Gen. SHERMAN'S army leaves no doubt of the capture of Gen. STONEMAN with a portion of the forces under his command.

OPERATIONS IN VIRGINIA.

General Averill Overtakes the Enemy.

Reported Attack, and Capture of Rebel Artillery and 500 Prisoners.

Gen. Sheridan in Command on the Upper Potomac.

Official Dispatch from Secretary Stanton.

WASHINGTON, Monday, Aug. 8.

To Gen. John A. Dix, New-York:

Maj.-Gen. SHERIDAN has been assigned temporarily to the command of the forces in the Middle Military Division, consisting of the Department of Washington, the Middle Department and the Department of the Susquehanna and Southwest Virginia. He transmits the following intelligence:

"HEADQUARTERS MIDDLE MILITARY DEPARTMENT, HARPER'S FERRY, Va., Monday, Aug. 8—8:40 P. M.

"*Maj.-Gen. Halleck, Chief-of-Staff:*

"Brig.-Gen. KELLY reports that a scout has just arrived at New Creek, and reports that Gen. AVERILL overtook the enemy near Morefield yesterday, and attacked him, capturing all of his artillery and five hundred prisoners. Nothing official has been received from Gen. AVERILL, however.

(Signed) "P. H. SHERIDAN, Maj.-Gen. Com."

EDWIN M. STANTON, Secretary of War.

PHILADELPHIA, Monday, Aug. 8.

The *Bulletin* of this city has the following special dispatch:

HARRISBURGH, Monday, Aug. 8.

Col. WM. H. BOYD, of the Twenty-first Pennsylvania Cavalry, took possession of Hagerstown yesterday.

The scene of the drama has been transferred from our border to that of rebeldom.

Later intelligence received this morning informs us that the rebels have retreated homeward.

They have again eluded the preparations made for their capture.

It is thought that under the new Commander the rebel inroads into our State will cease.

The members of the Legislature are beginning to make their appearance.

All Quiet on the Potomac.

HARRISBURGH, Penn., Monday, Aug. 8.

A dispatch received at headquarters here, at 9 o'clock this morning, from the military operator at Hagerstown, says:

All is quiet on the Potomac.

Doings of the Rebels at Hagerstown.

WASHINGTON, Monday, Aug. 8.

The *Star* says:

"From a gentleman who arrived here on Saturday, from Hagerstown, where he has been sojourning for two weeks past. we get some interesting particulars of the doings of the rebels in that vicinity.

When the rebels took possession of the town they proceeded to institute a thorough search of the stores. As the merchants had not replenished their stocks since the former visit of the rebels, the latter got but little, with the exception of a small quantity of shoes and hats, mostly taken from SAMUEL RONSEKULP, hatter.

At the grocery-stores they filled their haversacks with sugar and their canteens with molasses, and at one or two stores they turned the molasses out and let it run into the streets.

Seeing that many of the citizens were frightened and anxious to get away, the rebels told them to remain quietly at home and they would not be molested.

The rebels did not keep their promise, however, and amongst other acts of robbery, they compelled several gentlemen to take off their boots and hats and give them up.

DAVID FORD, a printer of this city, who was in Hagerstown at the time, had his hat taken from his head while standing on the street viewing the proceedings of the rebels.

Rebel sympathizers fared worse, if possible, than Union men.

JONAS WINTERS, a confectioner, who refused to open his store, had his doors broken in with an axe and most of his store fixtures destroyed.

Rev. DABNEY BALL, at one time pastor of the Wesley Church in this city, was with this marauding party. He did not take an active part in breaking open the stores, but he looked on and countenanced the doings of the rebels, and no doubt shared in the plunder.

The trains of cars reported to have been burnt by this party when they entered Hagerstown, were destroyed by our own troops in order to prevent them from falling into the hands of the rebels, as the cars contained a valuable cargo of freight, including several thousand dollars' worth of liquor.

The rebels had a list of those merchants who had goods hid away. This list is said to have been furnished them by prominent Secessionists."

From Baltimore.

BALTIMORE, Monday, Aug. 8.

The *American* furnishes the following in advance of its publication here:

"We learn from a gentleman who arrived here this morning from the upper Potomac that the entire rebel force yesterday evacuated the Maryland side of the Potomac, moving off in great haste.

Their rear guard crossed at Shepherdstown at 11 o'clock yesterday morning, and the balance of the invaders crossed at Hancock about the same time.

Previous to leaving, they sent a cavalry force back to Hagerstown yesterday, and arrested and carried off four prominent Union citizens of that town, as hostages for rebel citizens, arrested by order of Gen. HUNTER.

From the south side of the Potomac, we learn that Gen. EARLY has been moving up the valley toward Winchester, with his harvest trains, during the last week, scouring the country for conscripts and grain, consequently making but slow progress.

The information received a week since that the rebels would make a feint movement on Maryland merely to cover his return trains has been verified to the fullest extent, and they are now all moving off toward Staunton. That they will make their escape, however, without interruption, we do not believe."

The Blockade-Runner Falcon.

HALIFAX, N. S., Monday, Aug. 8.

The blockade-runner *Falcon*, with three smoke-stacks and one mast, forward, left on Sunday afternoon, reported for Wilmington direct. She had a cargo on board.

—The PRINCE OF WALES has made the formal application which is preliminary to any person becoming a member of the Masonic body.

FROM PETERSBURGH.

THE BATTLE OF FRIDAY.

Desperate Charge of the Enemy—They Are Repulsed with Slaughter.

FORTRESS MONROE, Sunday, Aug. 7.

A terrific fight took place in front of Petersburgh on Friday afternoon, lasting from 5:30 to 7:30. It commenced by a charge from the enemy, which was repulsed with slaughter. They also exploded a mine, which done no damage to our troops or works, but killed some of the rebels. The fighting on our side was principally by the Ninth Corps, and was most desperate.

The Explosion of the Rebel Mine, &c.

WASHINGTON, Monday, Aug. 8.

A letter from the Army of the Potomac, dated Saturday evening, says:

"It is not generally believed that the purpose of the enemy on Friday was to blow up a fort in front of the Fifth Corps; but their intention was to damage a mine which they suspected was being dug in front of the Eighteenth Corps. Certain it is, there was an explosion, whatever may have been the object of it. Our men were considerably startled, and every one rushed to his post, when a rapid fire commenced from our line in the direction the enemy were supposed to be advancing. As soon as the smoke cleared away, the true state of affairs was discovered, and firing ceased.

A stray ball struck Col. STEADMAN, commanding Second Brigade, Second Division, Eighteenth Corps, inflicting a wound which soon after resulted in death. He was a gallant officer, and his services were highly appreciated."

A party of fifty deserters started to come into our lines yesterday morning at an early hour, when our gunners, not knowing their intention, opened fire upon them, killing and wounding about twenty. Nine of them arrived at headquarters on Saturday forenoon, some of them wounded. They represent the Confederacy as being in a bad way on account of the state of affairs at Atlanta, and tell how their army was frightened on the previous Saturday when the mine was sprung, all leaving their guns and running back some distance, fearing other explosions were going to occur along the line. But they soon regained confidence, and fell back into their former position in time to meet the attack, which, they say, was more than an hour and a half after the explosion.

These men say the reason why the soldiers do not exchange newspapers is, they are ordered not to do so. But this would be of no effect, if they could afford to buy them, the price being 40 cents apiece, and they have not been paid off for a long time.

Very little firing took place on Saturday.

NEWS FROM WASHINGTON.

Special Dispatches to the New-York Times.

WASHINGTON, Monday, Aug. 8.

THE APPOINTMENT OF GEN. SHERIDAN.

Universal satisfaction is expressed here at the appointment of Gen. SHERIDAN to the command of the Middle Military Division. This comprises the four separate departments of Washington, the Susquehanna, Middle Department and Western Virginia. The status of each of these will remain the same as heretofore, but the appointment of Gen. SHERIDAN to the general command gives military unity to the operations in the region named. This of itself would inspire high hopes of efficient work in a direction where that thing has been and is much needed; but this is further insured by the eminent ability of the new Commander. Gen. SHERIDAN is, of all others, precisely the very best that could have been charged with the piece of business he will now have on hand in Maryland, on the Pennsylvania border, and in the Shenandoah Valley. His headquarters are, for the present, at Harper's Ferry.

PAYMENT OF THE TROOPS.

Three millions of dollars are under way to the Army of the Potomac for the payment of the troops.

SENTENCE ON EX-SURGEON GEN. HAMMOND.

Sentence of court-martial on Ex-Surgeon-Gen. HAMMOND, which is known to be in the severest terms, has been approved by Judge-Advocate-Gen. HOLT and the Secretary of War, and now only awaits the final action of the President.

COMMERCIAL INTERCOURSE WITH REBEL STATES.

Rules and regulations concerning commercial intercourse with insurrectionary States, have just been issued from the Treasury Department. To facilitate the execution of these regulations, the several districts of country comprised within the respective special agencies of the department, have been changed, and two new agencies, the sixth and seventh, established. Additional special agencies, if any are established, will be numerically designated in the order of their establishment, and if the boundaries of agencies already established shall be changed, due notice of such change will be given. In most respects these new trade regulations are like those of Sept. 11, 1863. The main points of difference are in the purchase and transportation of products in insurrectionary States, and the method of taking supplies into the same region. These features are made to accord with the provisions of the act of July 2, 1864.

NEW DEPOSITORIES OF PUBLIC MONEY.

The following National Banks have been designated depositories of public moneys from the 6th inst.: National Bank of Newburgh, N. Y., $70,000; Mechanics' National Bank, Chicago, $74,000; First National Bank, Knoxville, Tenn., $50,000; Second National Bank, Ravenna, Ohio, $50,000.

NEW NATIONAL BANKS.

The following National Banks have recently organized, in conformity with the existing law, viz.: The Second National Bank of Glaesburgh, Ill., $60,000; First National Bank, Mount Pleasant, Ohio, $175.000; First National Bank, Decorah, Indiana, $60,000.

THE NEW LOAN.

The subscriptions to the new 7-30 loan to-day amount to $903,360.

A COMMAND FOR GEN. SICKLES.

It is understood that the command of the Veteran Reserve Corps has been tendered to Gen. SICKLES.

Dispatches to the Associated Press.

WASHINGTON, Monday, Aug. 8.

NO PASSES TO VISIT PRISONERS OF WAR.

Provost-Marshal INGRAHAM will hereafter issue no passes to parties desiring to visit prisoners of war confined in the Old Capital Prison, except upon the direct order of the Secretary of War, or the order of Col. HARDIE, acting under the direction of the Secretary.

SENTENCED FOR AIDING A DESERTER.

A hack-driver, tried and found guilty of buying citizens' clothes, to enable a soldier to desert, was sent to the Albany Penitentiary to-day.

SALE OF CONFISCATED PROPERTY.

The United States Marshal of the District of Columbia to-day sold the life interest in the confiscated property of eight persons now in the rebellion. That of Gov. LETCHER was very small. The interest of TRUSTEN POLK and W. T. SMITHSON were not sold, having been withdrawn. The sale netted only $5,000.

TWO DAYS LATER FROM EUROPE

Arrival of the Hibernian off Father Point.

THE PROROGATION OF PARLIAMENT.

The War in Denmark—An Armistice for Nine Months Said to Have Been Agreed Upon.

THE REPORTED SEA-FIGHT EXPLAINED.

FATHER POINT, Monday, Aug. 8.

The steamship *Hibernian*, from Liverpool on the afternoon of the 28th, via Londonderry on the 29th of July, passed Father Point at 6:30 o'clock this morning, en route to Quebec. Her dates are two days later than those already received.

The steamship *Nova Scotian* arrived off Londonderry on the afternoon of the 27th.

The steamship *New-York*, from New-York, arrived at Liverpool on the 28th.

The steamship *City of Baltimore*, from New-York, arrived at Liverpool on the 28th.

The United States steamer *Sacramento* put into Queenstown on the 28th short of coal.

GREAT BRITAIN.

Parliamentary proceedings were unimportant. It was definitely settled that the prorogation would take place on the 30th of July.

The Lord Mayor of London gave a grand banquet to the Ministers on the 27th. The speeches made were of the ordinary routine character.

Earl RUSSELL had made a speech at Hanover in defence of his foreign policy, in which he asserted that England never stood in a prouder position, and that her influence was never greater with all foreign countries than at present.

His remarks were received with perfect coldness.

LARGE ARRIVALS OF COTTON.

The London *News* says that vessels have just arrived at Liverpool with about 15,000 bales of cotton, the proceeds of which are to go towards the sinking fund for redeeming Confederate bonds and paying the dividends of the coming April account, provision having already been made for the September account.

THE YELVERTON CASE.

In the House of Lords, in the famous Yelverton marriage case, the Lord Chancellor pronounced in favor of the validity of the marriage. The other four Lords have not yet given their decision.

THE DANO-GERMAN QUESTION.

A Copenhagen journal of the 26th gives the report that a nine months' armistice has been concluded, during which period the occupation of the Duchies by Austria and Prussia will be continued. If true, this arrangement must have been made by foreign mediation.

It is stated that the Danish Plenipotentiary to Vienna declared, at the preliminary meeting of the conference to conduct negotiations, that his Government would reserve to itself the right of ulterior ratification.

The official Vienna *Journal* denies the rumor that Count RECHBERG had caused the Austrian Ambassadors at London and Paris to declare that the complete separation of the Duchies from Denmark would be the maximum of the German demands, and that the Apenrade and Tondern line of demarcation was still possible.

The Vienna correspondent of the London *Times* gives the alleged programme of the proposed terms of peace, which embrace the complete separation of Schleswig, Holstein and Lunenburg from Denmark, and their ultimate union under the sceptre of a Prince whose claims may be recognized by the Germanic Union.

FRANCE.

The rumor that the Emperor NAPOLEON was preparing an important pamphlet at Vichy, is denied.

The Bourse was dull and drooping. The Rentes closed on the 27th at 66f. 05c.

LATEST VIA LONDONDERRY.

LIVERPOOL, Friday, July 29.

An unknown iron-plated ram, bearing the United States flag, passed the Isle of Wight, to the westward, on the 26th.

It is explained that the reported sea-fight off Bantry Bay, July 11, was mere artillery practice by the coast guardsmen on board an English war vessel.

Capt. SEMMES is still in this city.

LONDON, Friday, July 29.

Parliamentary proceedings are unimportant.

In the House of Lords Earl ELLENBOROUGH again attacked the foreign policy of the Government, and especially in regard to the course it has pursued toward Denmark.

Earl RUSSELL briefly spoke in defence, and reiterated his former arguments, denying that England had in any way forfeited her honor.

The first meeting of the Peace Conference was held at Vienna on the 26th. It was attended by the First and Second Plenipotentiaries of each belligerent Government. Nothing transpired as to the proceedings.

The Chamber of Deputies of Stutgard have adopted a strong protest against the forcible occupation of Rendsburg by Prussia, and called on the other States to resist such violence.

The Prussian garrison at Kiel has been doubled.

PARIS, Thursday, July 28—P. M.

Orders have been given to dispatch the necessary ships to Mexico to take home the troops that are to return to France. The ships are to sail early in August.

The Bourse closed quiet and steady at 66f. 10c.

VERY LATEST PER HIBERNIA.

LONDON, Friday, July 29.

There is no political news of importance.

The House of Lords have finally decided that Mrs. YELVERTON has failed to establish the validity of her marriage.

Commercial per Hibernian.

LIVERPOOL COTTON MARKET, 28TH.

The sales of COTTON for four days was 28,000 bales, including 7,500 bales to speculators and exporters. The market is quiet.

TRADE REPORT.

The Manchester market was dull and easier for cotton goods and yarns.

LIVERPOOL BREADSTUFFS MARKET—28TH.

The BREADSTUFFS market has a declining tendency. Messrs. WAKEFIELD, NASH & Co., report: FLOUR quiet and steady. WHEAT quiet and declined 2d. ℔ cental under heavy arrivals; Winter Red, 8s. 8d.@9s. 10d. CORN inactive and declined 6d.@9d. ℔ quarter; Mixed, 30s.

LIVERPOOL PROVISION MARKET—28TH.

The Provision market is steady; Messrs. GORDON, BRUCE & Co. report—BEEF quiet and steady. PORK firm. BACON steady. BUTTER in active. LARD firm. TALLOW steady.

LIVERPOOL PRODUCE MARKET.

SUGAR very dull. COFFEE—no sales. RICE steady. ASHES quiet and steady. LINSEED OIL steady at 4s. RESIN quiet. SPIRITS OF TURPENTINE steady. PETROLEUM quiet and nominal.

LONDON MARKETS.

BREADSTUFFS dull. SUGAR dull. COFFEE quiet and steady. TEA dull. RICE nominal. TALLOW steady.

LONDON MONEY MARKET.

The demand for money at the Bank of England continued active at the advanced rate of 7 ℔ cent., but the anticipated further advance to 8 had not taken place. In the open market nothing was done below 7½ ℔ cent.

The Stock Exchange was languid, but there were no material variations. [illegible] say: "The extraordinarily rapid rise in Exchange in New-York has so curtailed business for American securities, that transactions now are almost a matter of negotiation, excepting Five-Twenty Bonds and Illinois Shares. The former show a decline of 2 ℔ cent., but are still relatively much above New-York quotations. For the latter there is some inquiry, but holders are unwilling to make the sacrifice which the present price would entail. The quotations for Railway Mortgages are little more than nominal."

LONDON, Thursday, July 28.

Consols closed at 89⅝@90 for Money.

AMERICAN STOCKS.

Illinois Central Railroad, 45½@44½ discount; Erie Railroad, 42@43.

LATEST COMMERCIAL VIA LONDONDERRY.

LIVERPOOL, Friday, July 29.

COTTON—The sales of the week foot up 33,500 bales, including 3,000 bales to speculators and 7,000 bales to exporters. The market has been dull, with a decline of ¼d. for American, and ¼d.@½d. for other descriptions. The sales to-day (Friday) were 6,000 bales, inclusive of 2,000 bales to speculators and exporters, the market closing dull and unchanged, at the following authorized quotations:

	Fair.	Middling.
Orleans	Nominal.	31⅝d.
Mobile	Nominal.	31⅛d.
Uplands	Nominal.	31d.

—Stock in port 238,000 bales, including 12,500 of American.

BREADSTUFFS.—The market is quiet, with a downward tendency.

PROVISIONS.—The market is dull and easier.

LONDON, Friday, July 29.

Consols 89¾@90 for money.

The weekly return of the Bank of England shows a decrease of £175,000 in bullion.

AMERICAN SECURITIES.—The latest sales were: Illinois Central Railroad 45½@44½ discount; Erie Railroad 42@43.

LONDON, Friday, July 29.

Notwithstanding the advance in the rate of discount to 7 ℔ cent. by the Bank of England, the demand for money continues very brisk, and a further advance to 8 ℔ cent. is not unlikely.

INDIA MARKETS.

BOMBAY, Friday, July 8.

COTTON dull and lower. Imports dull, but firm. Freights to Liverpool, 30s. Exchange, 2 1s-1½d.

CALCUTTA, Friday, July 8.

YARN lower. CLOTH dull.

FROM NORTH CAROLINA.

A Fight with the Rebel Ram Expected.

NEWBERN, N. C., Thursday, Aug. 4.

A report from Roanoke Island just received states that our gunboats off Plymouth, in the Albemarle Sound, intend to give battle to-day to the rebel ram *Albemarle* and force her into an engagement. Last Sunday night she attempted a surprise on our fleet, but being discovered in time she went back, not daring to make an attack.

The election for Governor in this State takes place to-day. Gov. VANCE, who is a candidate for reelection, is receiving the hearty support of the authorities at Richmond, and also the aid of the rebel army. The rebel authorities are endeavoring to prevent the Holden men from voting by threats and otherwise. Although HOLDEN's majority in some counties will be heavy, the recent measures resorted to by the rebel authorities to defeat him makes the result doubtful.

Trade With Insurrectionary States.

WASHINGTON, Monday, Aug. 8.

The modified and improved rules and regulations concerning commercial intercourse with, and in, States declared in insurrection, &c., having been approved by the President, are officially declared by the Secretary of the Treasury. From these it appears that commercial intercourse with localities beyond the lines of actual military occupation by the United States forces is absolutely prohibited, and no permit will be granted for the transportation of any property to any place under the control of the insurgents against the United States. Supply stores at places agreed upon by the Commanding-General of the Department, and the proper supervising special agent, may be established by such loyal persons as the supervising special agent, or assistant special agents, shall designate for that purpose. Loyal persons residing in the district, or country contiguous to the place and within the lines of actual occupation by the military forces of the United States may be permitted to procure from any such store, and take to their homes, such family or plantation supplies as may be necessary to their own use. Permits will be granted to sutlers to transport to the regiment or post sutlered by them such articles as they are authorized to sell free of the three per cent. fee; but no permit will be granted to a sutler, excepting on presenting to the proper permit officer the original certificate of his appointment from the commanding officer of his regiment or post, countersigned by the Division Commander, and on application and affidavit in the prescribed form. Transportation is not permitted to any regimental sutler for an amount of goods exceeding two thousand five hundred dollars worth, nor for over two months' supply at one time. The restrictions on carriers and trade in boats on the Western waters, remain as heretofore. Clearances and permits to any point or place affected by the existing blockade will be granted only upon the request of the Department of War or the Department of Navy. All existing authorities to purchase products in the insurrectionary States are revoked, except that products purchased in good faith under such authorities, and paid for prior to the date hereof, may be transported in the same manner and subject to the same conditions as products raised by labor of freedmen, and all authorities to transport goods, wares or merchandise into an insurrectionary State, are revoked. Agents are authorized to purchase for the United States any products of States declared in insurrection at such places as may be designated to the Secretary of the Treasury, at such prices as shall be agreed on with the seller, not exceeding the market value thereof at the place of delivery, nor exceeding three-fourths of the market value in the City of New-York at the latest quotation known to the agent purchasing. The moneys arising from the sale, after the payment of the purchase money and other expenses connected therewith, are required to be paid into the Treasury.

The Secretary of the Treasury has also prepared regulations relative to abandoned, captured and confiscated personal property, which will be carried into effect by the same agents and under the same supervision that are provided under the regulations concerning commercial intercourse. Such property required for public use, is to be appraised and delivered over while provision is made for the sale of the remainder.

The regulations concerning abandoned and confiscated lands, houses and tenements, provide, among other things, for the employment and welfare of freedmen. In each special agency, one or more places, to be known as freedmen's home colonies, are to be established. A Superintendent of Freedmen will be appointed for each of the colonies. The freedmen are classified, and the minimum rate of wages of No. 1 males is to be $25 per month, No. 2, $20; No. 3, $15; No. 1, 2, and 3, females, $18, $14, and $10. These rates shall not restrict mechanics and others from contracting for higher wages, if they can do so. Written agreements may be made between employees and employers on certain conditions, and an interest in the profits of the labor may be given instead of wages. Provision is made for the care of aged and infirm freedmen. Any associations for combinations of associations desiring to improve the condition of freedmen, will have assigned to their care and general charge such freedmen's home colonies as they may desire, and as they can give satisfactory assurance of their ability to provide for, the Secretary of the Treasury reserving the right to revoke or modify the regulation whenever, in his judgment, the public interests will be promoted by such action. Schools are to be established within these Homes, and labor colonies sufficient for the education of all children there under the age of 12 years, and penalties are prescribed for ill usage of freedmen.

The New-York Times.

VOL. XIII.—NO. 4022. NEW-YORK, MONDAY, AUGUST 15, 1864. PRICE FOUR CENTS.

MOBILE.

FARRAGUT'S VICTORY

Full Particulars From Eye-Witnesses.

PASSING THE FORTS.

The Capture of the Confederate Gunboats.

THE SURRENDER OF FORT GAINES.

FARRAGUT ON THE MAIN-TOP.

An Old Sea-Dog Directing the Fight.

Our New-Orleans files received yesterday by the steamship *Creole* contain ample and most interesting particulars of the victory of the gallant FARRAGUT and his fleet at Mobile Bay. The accounts of eye-witnesses, as they appear in the New-Orleans *Times*, *Era* and *Picayune*, are given with admirable clearness.

Farragut's Victories at Mobile.

NEW-ORLEANS, Sunday, Aug. 7.

Intelligence was received at headquarters yesterday, announcing that the fleet under Admiral FARRAGUT passed the forts at the entrance of Mobile Bay at 8 A. M., on the 5th inst.

The monitor *Tecumseh* was blown up by a rebel torpedo.

No other vessels were lost.

The rebel ram *Tennessee* surrendered after an obstinate resistance.

The rebel Admiral BUCHANAN lost a leg in the action, and is now a prisoner.

The land force under Maj.-Gen. GORDON GRANGER invested Fort Gaines, and with light batteries opened simultaneously with the passage of the forts by the fleet, taking the water batteries in reverse, and silencing them.

Our losses are not reported.

LATER.

Later advices from Admiral FARRAGUT's fleet may be summed up as follow:

Fort Gaines has surrendered.

Fort Powell was blown up by the rebels.

[This was at Grant's Pass, at the opposite end of Dauphin Island from where the fight occurred.]

Four monitors went in first, followed by the steam war-vessels *Brooklyn*, *Hartford*, *Metacomet*, and others. The principal fighting was with the ram *Tennessee*, inside the bay.

The *Metacomet*, in attempting to ram the *Tennessee*, struck the *Hartford*, and stove in her side timbers. The *Hartford* will go north for repairs.

The rebel gunboat *Selma* was sunk by the *Metacomet*.

The gunboats *Chickasaw* and *Winnebago* chased two rebel gunboats—the *Gaines* and *Morgan*—into Navy Cove, and they are blockaded there, without a chance of escape.

Only ten persons are known to have survived the destruction of the monitor *Tecumseh* by the torpedo.

The dispatch-boat *Philippi* was burned at sea while the fight was in progress.

Admiral FARRAGUT will push right on for Mobile City.

All the Texas coast, Brownsville included, has been evacuated, with the exception of Brazos Island. A small force is left there under Col. DAY, of the Ninety-third New-York.

Major-Gen. FRANK E. HERRON arrived from there yesterday, and is now at the St. Charles Hotel. His forces are there, and are going into camp above the city.

The rebels here are greatly excited over the Mobile news.

Politics is becoming lively and interesting. The Free State men are organizing for active duty, and the clubs of the last campaign are being revived. There is no doubt about the ratification of the new Constitution by the people. The city is full of people, notwithstanding the large numbers who have left for Northern watering-places.

The Mobile *News* of the 15th ult. boasts of the hanging of two colored soldiers and a cotton speculator, near Vicksburgh, by WHITTAKER'S guerrillas.

A number more of Union prisoners, recently exchanged, have arrived.

The Opening of the Ball.

WEST GULF BLOCKADING SQUADRON, OFF FORT MORGAN, Aug. 3, 1864.

The fleet for the reduction of Mobile, commanded by Admiral FARRAGUT, and composed of the *Winnebago*, *Chickasaw*, *Manhattan* and *Tecumseh* of the monitor fleet, and the *Hartford*, (flagship,) *Brooklyn*, *Oneida*, [illegible], *Tennessee*, and *Metacomet*, of the wooden fleet, will commence to-morrow morning to pour their iron hail into the rebel Fort Morgan.

The ball was opened this afternoon by the monitor *Winnebago*, which steamed defiantly up to the fort and threw in a shell or two to give the rebs a taste of our quality. She is a splendid specimen of monitor naval architecture, and is as buoyant as a cork. On her your correspondent is located, and we expect to be first into the fight to-morrow. Her officers are every one of them gentlemen, and have afforded and will afford me every opportunity to witness the fight.

Capt. THOS. STEVENS is well known as an officer "chock full of fight;" and he is ably seconded by Vol. Lieut. W. F. Shankland, Paymaster Girard, Chief Engineer Simon Shultes, 1st Assistant Engineer John Purdy, Ensigns Morrisey, Murphy and Whitworth, Acting-Master Megathlin, and Robert Sherman, gunner. To the latter gentleman I am indebted for favors to be remembered hereafter.

Of the fighting qualities of this noble vessel I shall speak more fully at some future time. The guns in her forward turret are worked by steam, and that they are terrible in execution the Rebels will bear me witness.

ON BOARD STEAMSHIP WINNEBAGO, August 4, 1864.

This morning opened beautifully. Contrary to expectations, the land forces under Gen. GRANGER failing to co-operate, we did not attempt the reduction of the forts to-day. But Capt. STEVENS, determined not to be baulked of his share of the fight, steamed up in front of Fort Gaines, and at 11:30 o'clock this morning threw his first shell at the transport *Natchez*, which was unloading troops and ammunition at the landing in front of the fort. You should have seen her leave! In less than a minute after the shell burst in her neighborhood, the smoke of burning bacon and resin was plainly visible. We gave and received about a dozen shots, but nobody was hurt on our side.

That you may fully understand the position of affairs, let me explain: As we lay, head up the bay, Fort Morgan stands on our right, by and around the light-house, well known to many of your readers. Immediately opposite, and about five miles off, on the northeast end of Dauphin Island, is Fort Gaines. Running across from Morgan to Gaines is driven a tier of piles, fastened together by a net-work of chains. Opposite each fort a channel is left open, of about fifteen hundred yards in width, for the use of blockade-runners. In the channel, in front of Morgan, *were* placed a lot of buoys, on which the guns of her water battery are trained. I say *were*, for our boys destroyed about half of them last night. Outside of the piles are placed the torpedoes.

Just inside of the obstructions is lying the rebels' pride and hope—the ram *Tennessee*—and three gunboats. Neither of these have dared to show themselves outside while we were firing into their transports, but contented themselves with throwing a shot at us at long range—say about five miles—when they could have no hope of hitting us.

LATER.—Orders have just come aboard for us to go into the fight to-morrow, and from the quantity of fight in the Captain and officers of the *Winnebago*, and of the fleet generally, I can assure you we shall see fun.

Everything now betokens success on our part, and before this reaches you, Mobile, I am convinced, will have fallen.

WEDNESDAY, Aug. 5.

The glory is ours! The victory is with us! I have only time to say that we have passed Fort Morgan, and anchored in the bay.

The rebel ram *Tennessee* is ours, and also one of the gunboats. BUCHANAN, the rebel Commodore, is wounded, and I hear is dying.

The monitor *Tecumseh* was run on a torpedo opposite the obstructions and sunk immediately. All but eighteen of her officers and crew went down with her. Capt. CRAVENS, I believe, was her commander.

The *Chickasaw* is shelling Fort Powell. In the action to-day we have lost about 150 killed and wounded. Yours signally, C.

The bearer of the letter informs us that Fort Powell was blown up, and Fort Gaines taken. We learn from another source that the fleet which passed the forts consisted of fourteen gunboats and four monitors.

Another Account.

The following account is furnished by A. C. STERRETT, who was on board the gunboat *Port Royal* at the time of the fight:

FRIDAY, Aug. 7, 1864.

The fleet, consisting of the *Hartford*, *Brooklyn*, *Richmond*, *Lackawanna*, *Ossipee*, *Monongahela*, *Oneida*, *Galena*, *Port Royal*, *Metacomet*, *Octorora*, *Seminole*, *Itasca*, and the Monitors *Tecumseh*, *Manhattan*, *Chickasaw* and *Winnebago*, and the Admiral's steam barge *Loyal*, got under way at the anchorage off the entrance to Mobile Bay, at sunrise, the monitors in advance and the wooden vessels going together in pairs, the flag-ship taking the lead. When within point blank range of Fort Morgan, the vessels ahead were slowed down to enable the line to close up, and at this time the fort and rebel vessels opened fire on the fleet, which was returned from the 100-pounder Parrotts placed on the bows of our vessels in the advance.

The Admiral waited until directly abreast of Fort Morgan, when he delivered a succession of broadsides from the nine-inch guns of the *Hartford* with such precision and galling effect that the rebels were driven away from their guns, and the water battery and fort were silenced. At this time the monitors engaged the iron-clad ram *Tennessee*, which was discovered, laying in position to advance on our noble Admiral.

At this moment the monitor *Tecumseh* struck a torpedo and was seen to rise and disappear beneath the water almost instantly. The firing now became terrific, and the fleet, although steaming ahead at a full rate of speed, was completely enveloped in flame and smoke. The rebel ram made several attempts to run our passing vessels down, but failed to do so, and in the midst of all this a boat was lowered from the *Metacomet* to pick up the survivors of our ill-fated monitor. It was a beautiful and appalling sight to witness this boat rowing around on its sacred mission to rescue our drowning men, with its beautiful flag flowing to the breeze, and the missiles of death and destruction striking and ricocheting all around it. But the gallant officer (an ensign whose name I forget) heedlessly kept on his way, and succeeded in rescuing the pilot, one of the officers and three men, belonging to the *Tecumseh*.

With the exception of the monitor, our fleet had by this time succeeded in passing Fort Morgan, only to be subject to a galling, raking fire from the three rebel gunboats—*Selma*, *Morgan* and *Gaines*.

Our vessels, which were secured together in pairs, were now cast off, and the engagement became general, which in a short time resulted in driving the ram and two gunboats under the guns of Fort Morgan, whilst the *Selma* steamed up the bay with the evident intention of escaping to Mobile.

After a chase of about forty minutes the *Selma* hauled down her flag to Capt. DRUETT, of the *Metacomet*. On boarding her the cause of her surrender was soon apparent—their decks were covered with the dead and dying, and her scuppers were running with their blood. Among others I recognized the body of Lieut. COMSTOCK, with his bowels torn out and laying across the breach of a gun which he was engaged in sighting at the time of his death. He once belonged to our navy. Language is not adequate to describe the soul stirring cheers which went up from the throats of our brave tars, and was reëchoed from one vessel to another all through this terrible ordeal, and our brave, noble Admiral has exemplified in this fight that his theory of "iron hearts and wooden ships" is a correct one.

At this time, while our fleet, with a few exceptions, had collected together on the west side of the bay, in the direction of Fort Powell, and out of the range of Morgan's guns, the ram *Tennessee* was discovered steaming in the direction.

The monitors closed with her when in range, and one of the most interesting naval engagements of the war succeeded, and we, in the smaller wooden vessels, were the spectators.

A fight of some minutes ensued, when Admiral FARRAGUT, anxious to close the engagement in a summary manner, started toward the *Tennessee* at full speed; at the same time Capt. STRONG, in the *Monongahela*, struck the *Tennessee* amidships, and withdrew in time to give room to our Admiral to grapple his antagonist, BUCHANAN. When the smoke cleared away from the two vessels, a white flag was seen to wave from the *Tennessee's* pilot-house, in token of submission, and Capt. LEROY, who went in as a volunteer on the *Ossippee* as a representative of Admiral FARRAGUT, received the sword of Admiral BUCHANAN, and that terrible engine of destruction was ours, although gained at a great loss of life.

Our loss in this fight is about 240 killed and wounded, including the brave Capt. CRAVAN of the monitor, and 100 of his crew who went down with him. Admiral BUCHANAN of the *Tennessee* was shot through the leg below the knee, and the leg will have to be amputated.

Fort Powell, in Grant's Pass, was blown up last night after dark, and Fort Gaines will soon follow. The rebel gunboats, which sought protection under the guns of Morgan, will be destroyed or captured by our monitors to-day, and the investment and capture of Morgan must follow.

We have, by this great victory, effectually closed the port of Mobile, and its capture is only a question of time; and Admiral FARRAGUT, and the gallant officers and men under his command, have established another claim to the admiration and respect of their countrymen and those who love liberty.

An Officer's Statement.

We are indebted to the courtesy of an officer of the navy, who witnessed the naval engagement in Mobile Bay, on Friday last, for the following interesting particulars:

Between 7 and 8 o'clock on that morning, the fleet moved in the following order: Four monitors and fourteen wooden vessels, the *Tecumseh* leading the former and the *Hartford* (flagship of Admiral FARRAGUT) the latter, advanced. The monitors were the *Tecumseh*, *Manhattan*, *Winnebago* and *Chickasaw*. The wooden vessels followed in pairs.

The rebel ram, the *Tennessee*, and gunboats *Selma*, *Morgan* and *Gaines*, were lying in wait under the guns of Fort Morgan, ready to attack the Federal fleet as it approached. It opened upon them with grape and canister—the *Hartford* and other vessels—with such severity that nothing could withstand the force of the terrific attack. The gunners of Fort Morgan, in the meantime, were driven from their guns, so fierce was the fire from the Federal fleet.

The *Tecumseh*, in passing the forts, was blown up by the explosion of a torpedo. The captain and all on board, with the exception of ten, sank with her. The Confederate ram *Tennessee*, after first attacking the fleet, as it advanced, seemed to return for shelter under the guns of Fort Morgan; but, after the fleet had proceeded some distance up the bay, stood toward them, as if to give battle; whereupon the *Hartford*, the monitors, and the wooden vessels of the fleet, stood for her, and a most terrible engagement commenced. The *Tennessee* was *rammed* by the *Hartford*, the *Lackawanna* and the *Monongahela*—the *Lackawanna* striking her under full headway, and all the vessels delivering a heavy fire at the same instant. The *Manhattan*, meantime, put one solid 15-inch shot at her, which penetrated her armor through and through and lodged on the opposite side.

Admiral FARRAGUT, during the engagement, was stationed in the maintop, where he had lashed himself in case he should receive a wound, communicating his orders below through speaking-tubes. After a most determined and gallant engagement, the *Tennessee* showed a white flag as a token of surrender. An officer of the Federal fleet then boarded the *Tennessee* and demanded the sword of Admiral BUCHANAN, which that officer surrendered, and it was taken on board the flagship. The Confederate Admiral was wounded severely, and will probably have to suffer the amputation of a leg.

The Confederate gunboat *Selma*, in the meanwhile, retreated up the bay, and was followed by the *Metacomet*, Lieut.-Commander JEWETT, and *Port Royal*, Lieut.-Commander GHIRARDI. The *Selma* surrendered to Lieut. JEWETT. The two other rebel gunboats, *Morgan* and *Gaines*, took refuge under the guns of Fort Morgan, and (says our informant) would probably be captured in the course of yesterday.

The U. S. monitor *Chickasaw*, Lieut.-Commander PERKINS, steered gallantly up to Fort Powell, and took in tow a steam barge from immediately under the guns of the fort. After taking the barge out of range, she returned and pelted the fort vigorously for half an hour with 11-inch shell. Fort Powell was finally evacuated, and at 11 o'clock at night was blown up by the rebels.

Of course, as the rebel vessels concentrated their fire principally upon her, she suffered the greatest loss. The total Federal loss, including that of the *Tecumseh*, (which was blown up by the torpedo and sunk,) in killed, wounded and missing, was about 210.

On the *Tennessee* there were twenty officers and about 120 men—Admiral BUCHANAN, commanding. Among the officers beside were Capt. JOHNSTON and Lieuts. BRADFORD and WHARTON.

Farragut's Own Account of the Fight.

From the New-Orleans True Delta.

Since the above was in type, Admiral PALMER has kindly read to us such portions of an official dispatch and private letter from Admiral FARRAGUT as he deems proper to make public. At an early hour on Friday, our fleet, lashed two and two, sailed into the Pass close up under the guns of Fort Morgan, pouring in broadside after broadside of grape and canister—thus driving the gunners of the fort from their pieces and leaving our vessels exposed only to the fire of Forts Gaines and Powell, which were, of course, less effective on account of distance. At the same time Gen. GRANGER'S land batteries enfiladed Gaines and caused the evacuation and blowing up of Powell. In passing the forts the *Oneida* received a shot which temporarily disabled her machinery, but she was safely towed through the fire by her consort.

Our monitor *Tecumseh* was one of the foremost. A torpedo, exploding beneath her bottom, she sunk almost instantaneously, carrying down all her officers, only ten of her crew escaping. She was commanded by Capt. LEWIS CRAVEN. Our loss on this vessel was about one hundred. The gunboats having passed the forts, and being out of their reach, were pursued by the formidable ram *Tennessee*, and three iron-clad gunboats—the *Selma*, *Gaines* and *Morgan*. Our vessels immediately attacked the ram, and battered him so effectually that he surrendered in a few minutes by hanging out the white flag. Admiral BUCHANAN, the Commander, lost a leg, and with all his crew, are prisoners in our hands. There were only 3 killed on the *Tennessee*. She was but slightly damaged, and it is probable that FARRAGUT has her fit for action by this time. We also captured the *Selma*, of which Capt. MURPHY was the commander. Lieut. PRENTISS, of the *Monongahela*, lost both legs. He is a gallant officer, and has a young wife in this city. Capt. MALANEY, of the *Oneida*, lost an arm. All the wounded will be sent to Pensacola. Our loss is two hundred and forty killed and wounded. The two remaining rebel gunboats fled under the guns of Fort Morgan for protection; one of them is aground, and the Admiral is confident that he can destroy them to-day. He has not the slightest doubt of his ability to reduce the forts. But their capture will not give us command of the city, which is extensively fortified at Dog River and elsewhere.

The *Hartford*, FARRAGUT'S flagship, was heavily engaged, losing one officer, HIGGENBOTTOM, Secretary to the Fleet Captain, killed, together with 20 of her crew, and 26 wounded. All our vessels were wooden except three.

Farragut and Granger Before Mobile.

From the New-Orleans Times.

Ever since the capture and occupation of this city by FARRAGUT and BUTLER the possession of Mobile by the Federal Government has been one of the principal objects of the desires of Union men, both here and at the North. Apart from its importance commercially to the Southern States, an importance which has not been lessened during the war, owing to the frequency with which rebel smugglers have evaded the cruisers of the blockading squadron off its harbor. Mobile, from its population and past importance, in a financial point of view, has been considered one of the chief jewels in the possession of the Confederacy. It has always been the opinion of rebels and loyal people that the fall of Mobile would be one of the most disastrous blows possible to the fortunes of the great insurrection which has deluged this country in blood, entailed upon it untold misery and an immense load of debt, diminished its national importance in the eyes of the world, and endangered the progress, the perpetuity even, of liberal principles in politics on the Western hemisphere.

The *Times* of yesterday evening announced the passage of the forts in Mobile harbor by Admiral FARRAGUT and his fleet, the capture of the rebel officer in charge of the Mobile naval defences, the investment of Fort Gaines by Gen. GRANGER, and the surrender of the much famed rebel ram, the *Tennessee*, on the 5th inst. We congratulate our Union population of the Crescent City on this great, glorious and most welcome intelligence. The whole country, outside the limits of rebeldom, and many a man within those hateful bounds, will unite in rejoicing over this magnificent exploit of the thrice-gallant FARRAGUT and the heroic GRANGER. Many a Union man, whose bosom swelled, and pulse beat hard, and eyes filled with tears of joy in New-Orleans on the day when scared rebels whispered the news from ear to ear of the passing of St. Philip and Jackson in April, 1862, felt a jubilant emotion like that which then raised his soul from the depth of despondency to the most delightful hopes and anticipations as he perused yesterday evening's *Times*. They said "God bless him!" of that daring, lion-hearted FARRAGUT, in the hour of their own greatest peril; and they now sympathize, with hearts full of devout thankfulness, with the Union men of Mobile, who have heard similar tidings, and are ready again with their invocations of blessings from on high to rest upon the head of the greatest naval commander of the age.

Perhaps, while we write, Mobile has fallen; but whether this is so or not, Mobile is sure to fall. The wise foresight of CANBY and FARRAGUT, the character of the men to whom the task has been devolved, the ample preparations that have been made, render the fall of the city an absolute certainty. There will be no backward step, no unnecessary delay; nothing but earnest action, guided by consummate skill, hard, telling blows, severely and effectively dealt, until the Stars and Stripes float in triumph over what is left of the metropolis of Alabama. Union men of New-Orleans! remember the feelings which swayed you when the fleet of the United States was forcing its way up the Mississippi, while you were surrounded by foes who would have hung you. Extend your heartiest sympathies to those men of Mobile who may be to-day rejoicing, and stifling their rejoicings, at the progress of the delivering arm of the nation.

With Atlanta partially within our grasp, if not entirely so; with the railroad connection between Atlanta and Mobile effectually severed; with Northern Alabama friendly to the Union cause; with GRANT at Petersburgh, holding before him the main force of the Confederates, tying them hand and foot before Richmond, totally unable to fly to the relief of any other section of the Confederacy; with the attention of the forces held to defend Charleston fully occupied by the gallant little band assailing that city day and night at every vulnerable point, what will prevent the success of the combined naval and land force at Mobile? Truly, "it is thundering all around," and is thundering to excellent purpose.

The brittle Confederacy is assailed at all points by forces that cannot help being successful. The officers in charge of the Union armies have been tried again and again without the discovery of a flaw; they have been winnowed until nothing but the true grain of gold remains. The armies of the United States are composed mainly of men to whom the noise of battle has grown a thing accustomed, and who have for months back carried the inspiring prestige of victory. The navy is cooperating wherever the brave sea-dogs can be of use; and the navy has never known aught but success. Truly, the end seems at hand, and is full of splendid promise.

ROUSSEAU'S raid, and the grand success of FARRAGUT and CANBY, are but the forerunners of the speedy return of Alabama to her place in the Union. A large part of her population did not approve secession. They did not vote for the secession ordinance, nor for the Confederate Constitution. The whole State voted against the immediate secession plan of YANCY. We have few fears for the future of Alabama.

Late Rebel News.

WASHINGTON, Sunday, Aug. 14.

The Richmond *Examiner*, of the 12th, has the following:

MOBILE, Tuesday, Aug. 9.

Hon. S. E. Mallory, Secretary of the Navy:

The enemy steamed in through the main entrance with four monitors and about sixteen heavy vessels of war. The *Tecumseh*, Commander T. A. M. CRAVEN, was sunk with nearly all her crew, and, also, another gunboat, the *Phillippi*, which I subsequently burned.

The *Richmond*, *Hartford* and *Brooklyn*, in line of battle, followed by the remainder of the fleet, pushed by Fort Morgan, under full headway, when they were encountered by the *Tennessee*, the *Morgan*, the *Gaines* and the *Selma*.*

The *Tennessee* and other vessels steamed in close range of the advancing force, and poured a heavy fire into the leading ships. After a desperate struggle between the fleets, the *Gaines* retired to Fort Morgan in a sinking condition.

The *Selma*, cut off, surrendered, and the *Morgan* escaped to Fort Morgan. The *Tennessee*, so far uninjured, steamed toward the whole fleet, and after an obstinate fight surrendered, her rudder disabled, her smoke stack carried away, and, as we suppose, her crew in an exhausted and smothering condition.

On the *Tennessee* Admiral BUCHANAN was severely wounded by a splinter in the leg. Two were killed and several wounded among her crew. On the *Gaines* two were killed and two wounded. On the *Morgan*, one was wounded.

On the *Selma* eight were killed, including her Executive officer, Lieut. J. H. COMSTOCK, and seven were wounded. The enemy suffered severely and requested permission to bury his dead. Respectfully, &c.,

G. W. HARRISON,
Confederate States Navy.

The *Examiner* also gives a list of the 28 Federal vessels engaged, having 212 guns, with the four Confederates, having 32 guns.

"It was a most unequal contest, in which our gallant little navy was engaged, and we lost the battle, but one ensign went down in a blaze of glory."

Up to Thursday night nothing of interest had occurred before Atlanta. Maj.-Gen. BATES received a flesh wound in the leg. The enemy is massing on our right and endeavoring to extend his lines in the direction of the Western Railroad.

A few shots were fired at the city yesterday, (9th.) Brisk shelling commenced at 11 o'clock last night, and continued four hours. No personal casualties are reported.

Prize Cases.

BOSTON, Saturday, Aug. 13.

Since the 28th of June, inclusive, the following decree of distributions has been made in prize cases by the United States District Court in this city:

Steamer *Mary Ann*, captured by the steamer *Grand Gulf*, \$112,356 32; steamer *Scotia*, captured by the steamer *Connecticut*, \$73,459 50, schooner *Alliance*, captured by the steamer *South Carolina*, and schooner *T. A. Ward*, \$23,281 74; steamer *Greyhound*, captured by the steamer *Connecticut*, \$164,632 01; steamer *Young Republic*, captured by the steamer *Grand Gulf*, \$111,519 79. Total, \$1,105,559 36.

This is the greatest distribution ever ordered in this country.

Large Fire at Troy, N. Y.

TROY, N. Y., Saturday, Aug. 13.

The extensive car and coach factory of GILBERT, BUSH & Co., of this city, was destroyed by fire this morning. Loss \$200,000; insurance about \$100,000.

THE PIRATE.

More Captures—Another New-York Pilot-Boat Burned.

BARK SULIOTE CAPTURED AND BONDED.

The Pirate Threatens to Visit New-York Harbor.

Burning of the Passenger Ship Adriatic.

SUFFERINGS OF THE PASSENGERS.

SANDY HOOK, Sunday Noon, Aug. 14.

The boatman of the Associated Press of this point has landed here and furnishes the following report:

I have boarded the bark *Suliote*, of Belfast, Me., from Cow Bay for New-York. She was captured on the 12th inst., off Montauk Point, thirty-five miles distant, by the pirate *Tallahassee*. The pirate bonded the bark for \$5,000, and put on board of her 300 passengers from the ship *Adriatic*, the latter having been burned by the pirate. No water or provisions were given them. The *Suliote* also has on board Mr. CALLAHAN and crew of the pilot-boat *Wm. Bell*, No. 24, which vessel was burned on the 12th, off Mantauk Point by the pirates. Several other persons from destroyed vessels are on board the *Suliote*. The *Suliote* reports seeing a vessel burning on the night of the 12th. The pirate stated to some of the captured persons that he was coming into New-York harbor. When last seen the *Tallahassee* was steering southeast. The pilot-boat *James Funck* is her tender.

The *Suliote* passed the frigate *Susquehanna* Sunday morning, lying still south of Sandy Hook.

The *Suliote* has no provisions or water on board.

More About the Doings of the Privateer—Burning of the Ship Adriatic—Pilot-Boat Wm. Bell—Bonding of the Bark Suliote.

Capt. MOORE, of the ship *Adriatic*, burned by the *Tallahassee*, states: "Left London July 7, with a full cargo of merchandise and 163 passengers, consigned to Messrs. E. E. MORGAN & Co. Nothing of interest occurred during the passage until the 12th inst., at 5 A. M., in latitude 40° 40′, longitude 71° 40′, when we were ordered to heave to by an unknown steamer, and wait until they boarded us, which they immediately did, informing me at the same time that we were a prize to the Confederate steamer *Talahassee*, and that they were going to burn the ship, and telling us to hurry up and get ready to leave. The bark *Suliote*, of Belfast, Me., Capt. PARMO, from Cow Bay (Cape Breton) for New-York, was in sight at the time. They boarded her, and the Captain was compelled to sign bonds for \$5,000, on condition that he would take myself, passengers and crew into New-York. They commenced transferring passengers, and gave them such little time that they were forced to leave almost all their baggage on board, which was burned, together with the ship. In rounding the ship to, we were so close that we carried away the mainmast of the privateer, and had there been a little more wind at the time, the probability is that we would have sunk her.

After myself, crew and passengers, and the crew and two passengers from the pilot boat *Wm. Bell*, No. 24, which she had destroyed the day previous, altogether numbering 201 souls, were put on board the *Suliote*, there was scarcely standing room, and had there been a gale of wind, or even a heavy squall, the lives of two-thirds of those on board would undoubtedly have been sacrificed, as the *Suliote's* decks were even with the water.

13th inst., off Fire Island, spoke and boarded the United States steamer *Susquehanna*, cruising for the privateer, gave them all the information we could, and they supplied us with some provisions; 14th inst., arrived at New-York.

The *Adriatic* was — years old, 989 tons burden, rated A 1, and was owned by R. H. MOORE, the master, Messrs. E. E. MORGAN & SON, and others, of this City."

Capture of Pilot-Boat Wm. Bell.

Mr. JAMES CALLAHAN, of the pilot-boat *Wm. Bell*, No. 24, states that his boat was captured by the privateer *Tallahassee* on the 11th inst., at 1 o'clock P. M., about 90 miles E. S. E. of Sandy Hook, after a chase of half an hour, during which time the privateer fired two solid shot and one shell, the latter exploding about six yards astern, when he hove to, and in an hour she was in flames. They took Mr. CALLAHAN on board the steamer, together with Mr. J. W. HAMBLETT, NICHOLAS COOLE, and a crew of six men, and subsequently transferred them to the bark *Suliote*, which brought them to this City.

The above gentlemen stated that with a full head of steam the privateer can make from fifteen to eighteen knots an hour. The *W. B.*, when captured, was going at the rate of ten knots, and the steamer overhauled her with but nine pounds of steam.

They all speak in high terms of the gentlemanly treatment while on board the privateer.

A Card from the Passengers of the Ship Adriatic.

NEW-YORK HARBOR, Sunday, Aug. 14.

We, the undersigned passengers of the late ship *Adriatic*, burned at sea by the Confederate pirate *Talahassee*, beg publicly to acknowledge and return our sincere thanks to Capt. J. L. PARMO and officers of the bark *Suliote*, of Belfast, Me., (heavily laden with coal,) for the extreme kindness and liberality that they could bestow in this our trying and perilous position, and also the extreme liberal means at their command, having but deck accommodations.

Likewise to Capt. R. H. MOORE's officers for their assistance, also to the crews of the above named vessels, they having rendered all the assistance which human aid could devise.

We also beg further to state that had a storm arisen on our further passage whilst on board the bark, one half or more of those on board would have been sacrificed.

Signed, CHAS. MILNE, RICHARD SANDERS, ED. KIRK, and T. E. EGAN, in behalf of 163 passengers.

THE TALLAHASSEE'S PIRACIES.

Arrival of One of the Captured and Bonded Vessels.

The schooner *Corrall*, of East Machias, Maine, one of the vessels captured day before yesterday by the rebel pirate *Tallahassee*, arrived here yesterday. Her Captain makes the following statement:

"On the 11th instant, in latitude 40° 19′, longitude 72° 27′, was boarded by the Confederate steamer *Tallahassee*, or rather the pilot boat *James Funk*, which was then under command of a Confederate crew, and ordered to heave to until a boat came from the steamer, which was soon effected.

Upon boarding us we were ordered to be in readiness to leave in ten minutes. The Captain was taken on board the privateer, where he signed bonds for the release of the schooner for \$10,000.

We subsequently received on board forty-four persons, being the crews and passengers of the brig *A. Richards*, of Boston, from Glace Bay; bark *Bay State*, of Boston, from Alexandria, for New-York; brig *Carrie Estelle*, of Boston, THURLOW, from Cutler, Me.; and schooner *Atlantic*, of and from Addison for New-York; all of which vessels had been burned. Also, the pilot-boat *James Funk*, No. 22. Sixteen of the above, including the pilots and crew of the *James Funk*, went ashore at Fire Island. Several others were landed at Fort Hamilton this morning.

The Captain of the schooner *Carroll* describes the privateer as about one thousand tons burden, painted a light lead color, no bowsprit, two smoke-stacks (one abaft the other,) and red bottom. The Confederate officer reported having run the blockade at Wilmington, N. C., some ten days previous, and had burned some vessels before falling in with those already reported.

Eight came up to this city to-day in the steam-tug *Stephen E. Babcock*, Capt. BARRETT, all of whom were paroled."

PROVIDENCE, R. I., Saturday, Aug. 13.

Capt. TAYLOR, of the schooner *A. M. Lee*, arrived at this port this afternoon from Philadelphia, and makes the following report:

"On Friday morning my vessel was chased and nearly overtaken by the pilot-boat *James Funk*, recently captured by the Confederate cruiser *Tallahassee*. When six miles westward of Shamrock Point, Long Island, the pilot-boat tacked, and stood for a bark which hove in sight."

Capt. ST. CLAIR, of the British bark *Col. James Scott*, reports that the *Tallahassee* has a tender to her, a Nova Scotian bark, two-thirds loaded with coal.

LATEST.

The pilot-boat *Ezra Nye* arrived here last night, and reports, on the 12th inst., at noon, *Montauk* bearing N. N. E. 25 miles. Saw the pilot-boat *James Funk*, No. 22, leaving a ship on fire, and, soon after, saw a suspicious-looking steamer come up and take the pilot-boat in tow.

The *Nye* then stood to the northward to avoid them, but subsequently returned to the burning ship, which proved to be the *Adriatic*, Capt. MOORE, from London for New-York; took from her a quantity of rigging, &c. Two foreign barks, bound west, were close by at the time, on board of which it is supposed the passengers were transferred. When last seen the privateer was steering southeast. The *Ezra Nye* soon after boarded the ship *Young Mechanic*, who reported seeing the *Tallahassee* to the southeast, near a large ship.

The Crews of the Captured Vessels.

Maj.-Gen. PECK has asked the War Department for authority to give transportation home to the crews of the vessels captured by the steamer *Tallahassee*. They are in a destitute condition, and number forty or fifty persons.

From the Army of the Potomac.

WASHINGTON, Sunday, Aug. 14.

A letter from the Army of the Potomac, dated 13th, says:

The Pennsylvania soldiers in Gen. CRAWFORD'S division of the Fifth Corps, in response to a circular issued by him, have contributed over \$1,000 in aid of the Chambersburgh sufferers. No doubt the other commands will imitate the example.

Gen. CRAWFORD has withdrawn all the guards heretofore detailed from his division to protect families from the annoyances of stragglers in King George County.

A deserter from the Eighth Alabama, who formerly lived in Massachusetts and was conscripted into the rebel army, came into our lines yesterday. He says that KERSHAW'S division of LONGSTREET'S corps passed through Richmond on its way to the valley, accompanied by a large ammunition train, and that he heard a prominent officer say that Gen. LEE had also gone in that direction. He also reports that the enemy are mining on our front, twenty men being detailed at a time to work.

Heavy firing was heard in the direction of Gen. BUTLER'S department this morning.

From Havana.

HAVANA, Wednesday, Aug. 10.

A new censor, Señor CARADA, is to be appointed in place of Señor APOLINAR DEL RATO, and the *Siglo* has resumed publication.

The *Siglo* refutes the recent falsehoods of the *Diario de la Marina* and a New-York correspondent in regard to the war in the United States.

The Rector of the University here has resigned, and Señor DURAN has been appointed his successor.

A fire in Matanzas on Saturday night destroyed SHRINGER'S coopershop. Loss heavy and uninsured.

The heat continues oppressive. Though the yellow fever is decreasing, there are many cases of typhoid fever.

Fires in Coxsackie, N. Y.

ALBANY, Sunday, Aug. 14.

About 10 o'clock Saturday evening a fire broke out in Coxsackie, Green County, destroying three store-houses filled with hay, and a portion of MYGATT'S lumber-yard. The hay was fully insured.

At 12 o'clock to-day another fire destroyed a barn, wagon house, a blacksmith shop and two dwellings.

Both fires were works of an incendiary. A man has been arrested on suspicion. The loss is not known.

Locomotive Boiler Explosion.

POUGHKEEPSIE, N. Y., Sunday, Aug. 14.

The locomotive *Duchess*, attached to the Hudson River Railroad, blew up at Rhinebeck, Saturday morning, at 2 o'clock. The engine-house was completely demolished. The explosion was caused by the watchman leaving the blower on. Nobody hurt.

The Charleston Mercury.

DAILY PAPER—TWENTY DOLLARS PER ANNUM—PAYABLE IN ADVANCE.

SPONTE SUA SINE LEGE FIDES RECTUMQUE COLENTUR —VINDICE NULLO

COUNTRY PAPER—THRICE A WEEK—TWELVE DOLLARS FOR SIX MONTHS—PAYABLE IN ADVANCE.

Volume LXXXV. CHARLESTON, S. C., WEDNESDAY, AUGUST 17, 1864. Number 12,1[illegible]1.

THE MERCURY.

WEDNESDAY, AUGUST 17, 1864.

Spirit of the Northern "Democrats."

The differences of opinion between the leading Democrats of the North, which have heretofore divided them into "War" and "Peace" Democrats, seems to be vanishing. The New York *World* (war) says: "The new President to be nominated at Chicago and elected in November, must be a man ready and willing to meet any and every overture for peace; a man who shall represent truly the dignity and power of the nation, and who will not be unwilling even to tender an armistice suggesting a National Convention of all the States." The New York *News* (peace) agrees to this saying: "The Peace Democracy will endorse a nomination that faithfully represents the sentiments here stated. They are willing to trust to the good sense and patriotism of the people for the realization of a definite peace as the sequel of an Armistice and National Convention."

It thus seems likely that "an Armistice suggesting a National Convention of all the States," will be the main feature of the platform of principles to be put forth by the Democratic Convention which is to assemble at Chicago on the 29th of August.

THE PRESIDENT AND GEN. JOHNSTON.

To the Editor of the Mercury:—Mr. MEMMINGER, at a serenade given to him in Columbia, an evening or two ago, occupied a good deal of time with the removal of Gen. JOHNSTON from the Army of Tennessee. This was in the course of his defence of the President, and was the only topic selected, besides the finances. He did not directly condemn Gen. Johnston, and it is conceded that he handled the subject with delicacy. Still his object was to show that the President was not governed by personal considerations; but the good of the country.

If the President so acted in the case of one of General Johnston's conceded ability, it must have been because General Johnston had failed in his duty. Mr. Memminger's labored effort, therefore, to sustain the President, at a meeting of his friends in the streets, converted into a popular assembly, when nearly a half dozen orators spoke, would, if successful, amount to the condemnation of General Johnston. You will agree with me that his friends should meet an issue thus tendered by so distinguished a source as a late member of the Cabinet, and one of such authority as not only, as he said, to know every act of the Government, but even the *motives* to the President's action. Without authority, and with due regard to the public interest, I shall present to your readers some facts connected with General Johnston's removal, which I shall be quite willing to see subjected to a thorough sifting from any quarter.

The Army of Tennessee, at the commencement of the campaign, was virtually that which had been but recently experienced the disaster at Missionary Ridge. Sherman's army was that which had inflicted it, increased by many recruits and the corps of McPherson and Schofield. The campaign commenced early in May. Our army was reinforced afterwards, but to what extent it would not be prudent, if we knew it, to state. The enemy at a later period in two detachments received 12,000, and frequent small reinforcements—garrisons relieved by the 100 day men. What was the disparity of the force, therefore, with which the campaign commenced your readers may work out for themselves. There never was an assertion wider of its mark than that of the Sentinel, "that Gen. Johnston's army approximated Sherman's more nearly than any Confederate General had fought with." Gen. Bragg knew better, and spoke more accurately.

If General Johnston had given battle on the line from Dalton, under ordinary circumstances, the chances would have been greatly against him. Near Dalton, the enemy held the fortified pass, at Ringgold to fall back into, in case of mishap, and every where else a fortified position in his rear close at hand, so that victory would have been as fruitless as that of Chickamauga, while defeat—if the battle had been between Dalton and the Chattahoochee—would have been ruin. But General Johnston did fight daily, and on such terms as to inflict upon the enemy a loss more than five times as great as he sustained. This is shown by the opinions of experienced officers, reports of prisoners, and the Northern papers, who set down the enemy's loss up to the end of June at forty-five thousand. Ours was comparatively small. A continuation of a system, which was producing such results, would have very soon so reduced the disparity as to have put the chances of battle in our favor. The enemy beaten, with the Chattahoochee behind him, would have been ruined. The consequence of defeat to us on the south of that river, would of course have been less disastrous.

Up to the 18th July, the day General Johnston was deprived of the command, he had marched ninety three miles. His retreat then was at a rate of little more than a mile a day. While beyond the Chattahoochee, the country furnished nothing. It was, therefore, necessary to follow the railroad, and guard against being turned.—Once over the river, there was no such necessity to consider. An army could march in any direction. The turning process, therefore, was no longer to be feared.

But General Johnston is accused of an intention to abandon Atlanta. I have not the power of scrutiny into General Johnston's motives as Mr. Memminger has into the President's (besides not having seen him nor communicated with him on public matters since the war), but judging of his intentions by his actions before the world, I defy the production of any evidence of such intention. The proof is all the other way. He was engaged in mounting siege rifle guns—strengthening its defences. (I have even heard he was in line of battle), and his family and effects were in Atlanta when he was removed.

But again it is said that General Johnston disregarded the wishes and instructions of the Government. This is easier said than proved.—Until it is proved no one who knows General Johnston's thoroughness as a soldier will believe it.

It is further urged that he was removed because he could give no assurances of his ability to hold Atlanta. If he gave the reply he has credit for, it was worthy of a Roman: "No General can say he will hold a position until the battle has been won."

Gen. Johnston's falling back before Sherman was, with the exception of the Wilderness battle, upon the same principle as Gen. Lee's before Grant. Gen. Bragg has asserted, in Richmond, that the odds of numbers were greater against Johnston than against Lee.

Much more could be said if this were the proper time to say it. But Gen. Johnston and his friends could not wish to see him vindicated at the country's expense. The only facts I have used, therefore, are those before the world. He may be content now, giving his utmost aid, as every man should, to the support of the Government for the sake of the country; and relying confidently that in the page of history will be found his vindication, while his friends will look with equal certainty to see him recorded a great captain and a pure patriot. JUSTICE.

DEMORILIZATION IN THE YANKEE ARMY OF THE POTOMAC.

The New York *World* says: "The recent disaster at Petersburg is having a most depressing effect upon the country. Indeed, no defeat of the whole war has created so much dismay." A correspondent of the same paper puts down the Yankee loss on that occasion at "over eight thousand men." From the same journal we copy the following:

The Boston Traveller gives currency to some very extraordinary statements respecting the Army of the Potomac. It says that the private soldiers have given their officers quietly to understand that, they must not expect them to assault impregnable earthworks hereafter; that the campaign so far has been one of useless butchery, in which no regard has been paid to the lives of the troops. This same paper hints, as did the Tribune the other day, that the reason the colored soldiers were given the post of honor at Petersburg was because the white troops were indisposed to make the assault.

The Rochester Democrat, another Republican journal states that there is a great deal of dissatisfaction in the army, and that an unusual number of resignations of officers has been tendered, among whom are five generals. The Boston Advertiser also alludes to rumors it has heard to the same effect. All this is calculated to add to the despondency of the country; but we sincerely hope matters are not so bad as they are represented to be.

EXODUS OF SECESSIONISTS.

CAIRO, August 8.—Several disloyal citizens of Columbus and Paducah, with their families, have arrived here *en route* for Canada. They are banished by General Payne. Amongst them are merchants and leading men, whose property has been confiscated.

AN IMPROBABLE STORY.

NEW YORK, August 8.—The Post publishes a special Washington despatch, to the effect that the War Department has authorized McClellan to raise one hundred thousand men immediately for special service under his command. The report is considered very doubtful.

FROM NOVA SCOTIA.

HALIFAX, August 8.—The blockade runner Falcon, having three smoke stacks and one mast forward, left on Saturday afternoon for Wilmington direct, with a full cargo.

ADDITIONAL FROM THE UNITED STATES.

MOVEMENTS OF GRANT—HIS VISIT TO HUNTER—WHAT HE SAYS ABOUT PETERSBURG—THE MILITARY SITUATION ON THE UPPER POTOMAC

From the Philadelphia *Inquirer* of the 9th we learn the following interesting news. The correspondent of that paper, writing from Monocacy, says:

LIEUT. GEN. GRANT

Has been with us for twelve hours of the last twenty-four. Friday afternoon, at a little before 5 o'clock, the loungers of the Relay House were somewhat astonished to see a small man, wearing three stars and smoking a segar, descend from a car of the Washington 3 p. m. train. Taking a chair on the railroad platform, he talked with the four staff officers accompanying for an hour or more, when a special car from Baltimore hauled up at the Relay House, and in a moment after the Lieutenant General was on his way to hold a conference with General Hunter, whose headquarters then were at Thomas House, about a mile and a half south of the railroad at Monocacy Junction.

The train arrived at the Junction at about o'clock, and a conveyance being in waiting, Gen. Grant was immediately conveyed to Hunter's headquarters, where he remained during the night. Of what transpired there nothing is known, and we can only guess at it, as events slowly develope themselves in the future.

In the course of conversation this morning Grant said of

THE LATE REPULSE AT PETERSBURG,

That there was no earthly reason why it should not have been an entire success if his orders had been obeyed. The springing of the mine, he said, was a complete surprise of the rebels, and it only needed obedience to his orders to have routed the entire rebel army. Further than this, Grant did not say, but, thanks to him, a Court of Inquiry is ordered, through whom the country will soon learn on whose head to visit its vengeance for those five thousand soldiers of the Union slain and maimed in vain, and for that opportunity lost, which may be weeks and months in coming again.

THE SITUATION.

What now of affairs military. Rumor, hundred tongued, as usual, says that Early has again crossed the Potomac in force, being engaged in that work all of yesterday, at Williamsport, and even as high up as Hancock. Whether this is believed at headquarters, our movements, as yet, afford us no clue, but I hope Early has done the very foolish thing of attempting a movement on Pennsylvania.

ONE DAY LATER FROM NEW YORK.

The following extracts from the New York correspondence of the Philadelphia *Inquirer* are interesting:

NEW YORK, August 8.

Governor Seymour, you will see, is out in still another letter, addressed this time "to the various civil and military gentlemen of the State," complaining of the excessive quota of New York under the last call for troops. There is no objection to the Governor's complaint of injustice, if injustice has been done, but it is easy to see by the employment of such language as the following, that his Excellency's motive is to excite such a popular prejudice against the enrollment law as will render its enforcement in September perilous, to say the least of it.

SIR: I send you a copy of a communication which I have addressed to the Secretary of War, with respect to the quotas of your city. You will see, by the facts stated therein, that great injustice has been done. The excessive enrolment falls heavy upon your population, particularly so upon your laborers. They are entitled to the protection of State and city authorities, and of all who can ward off this great wrong. In addition to justice and humanity, there are other considerations well worth your attention. The withdrawal of thirty-six thousand able-bodied men from the first ten districts will disorganize labor, throw a large number of helpless families upon the public for support, and will be injurious alike to the morals and interests of your community.

If this isn't inciting to riot, what is it?

Both branches of the Common Council were in session this afternoon; but no action was taken with reference to additional bounties for volunteer enlistments. It is said that when the Board of Supervisors meet again, to morrow, a resolution will be offered offering the sum of $700 in hand to every man who will enlist.

The day has been an unusually quiet one in financial and commercial circles, and there has been very little activity or animation in any quarter. The gold market has been entirely devoid of the startling and numerous rumors which characterized it during the closing days of last week. It is a noteworthy fact that the rebel raiders, "forty thousand strong," have not been transported, in Wall street, from the Shenandoah to Pennsylvania, thence to Wheeling, Cincinnati, and so on to San Francisco every five minutes during the day. The distance, it is true, is very long, but it is nothing for gold speculators. In the stock market, for a wonder, there has been no "afternoon raid in the Cumberland Valley," by the bears in Harlem and Reading. It is difficult to know what to attribute this want of startling news to, but probably the sultry heat of the day has taken the starch out of speculators.

FROM MOBILE.

In the Mobile *Tribune* we find the annexed particulars in regard to the evacuation of Fort Powell:

On Friday afternoon, one of the enemy's rams carrying four guns, began to reconnoitre in the vicinity of the fort on the bay side, and in a short time opened fire on it. That part of the fort was not completed, though two guns were mounted there, but they were so exposed that they could be of but little service, and one of them was dismounted on the third or fourth shot from the ram. The fort, however, exchanged some few shots, with what effect is not known.

The ram neared the fort to within a few hundred yards, doing great damage to the works—one shot is said to have penetrated the bomb-proof, two of its water tanks were destroyed, and other damage was done. The untenable condition of the place was obvious. Col. Williams, commander, accordingly determined, before his communication with the shore was cut off, to evacuate, so he arranged a fuse to communicate to the magazine at a certain time, and then the men were collected together and quietly landed at Cedar Point. The explosion is said to have taken place at about 8 o'clock at night.

The Tribune also states that it is reported that the members of the Signal Corps that was on little Dauphin Island, were captured by the enemy.

Commodore Farrand has assumed command of the navy in the absence of Admiral Buchanan.

The Mobile *Advertiser* has the following article on the "situation at Mobile."

To persons abroad and unacquainted with the topography of Mobile Bay it will be well to explain that Fort Gaines is twenty-nine miles from the city, on the east end of Dauphin Island, and was intended to be one of the defences of the main entrance to the Bay from the Gulf. Fort Morgan is on the opposite shore. It has always been a matter of query what Fort Gaines was built for. Between it and Fort Morgan there is a water expanse of three and a half miles, but the ship channel is on the Fort Morgan side, and every heavy vessel passing is obliged to run within a mile of the guns of Morgan.

On the Fort Gaines side the water is shallow, and no ship could pass within effective range of its guns. When the fleet ran in on Friday, we do not learn that Fort Gaines fired a gun. Fort Powell lies a little to the west and north of Fort Gaines, and in the direction of the main land of the western shore of the Bay. It is built on an artificial island, directly on Grant's Pass, which it was designed to defend—that pass leading into Pascagoula Sound and the lakes in the direction of New Orleans. Fort Powell is about three quarters of a mile from the main land, at Cedar Point, and at low water is fordable. It was by this easy route that its garrison escaped. If there had been no ford it is probable that Fort Powell would still be in our possession.

Fort Morgan still commands the main ship channel to the Gulf, and by this alone Farragut's fleet can get to sea. He can only bring light vessels and transports through Grant's Pass. Fort Gaines was of no practical value in the defence of the Bay. It adds to the facilities and convenience of the enemy, but was not necessary to his operations. The loss of the garrison is serious, but more serious was the manner of its surrender—the stain upon our arms. That is to be wiped out.

With these explanations the stranger will perceive that the line of our city defences carried by the enemy is from twenty-five to thirty miles distant from Mobile. It has always been a mooted question among military men whether or not it was wise to try to hold these points. Many have been in favor of dismounting all the forts in the lower bay and bringing their guns and garrisons to the inner line nearer the city. The only or the principal reason for a contrary course was found in the importance of keeping possession of the shores of the Bay so as to prevent the enemy from making a water base near the city for the advance of any army.

The loss of Grant's Pass gives the enemy this advantage. That is, he can now sail up the bay with his transports loaded with supplies and troops, thus dispensing with wagon trains, and land within a short distance of the city. But when he does this, he has to encounter the inner line of defences. When he does that, he is no nearer to taking Mobile than Grant is to taking Petersburg, Sherman Atlanta, or Foster Charleston. In other words, this city is a long ways from "going up." Gen. Canby does not command troops enough to take the city by land, nor Farragut ships to break through the guns and obstructions on the water front.

Admiral Farragut's flagship engaging the *Tennessee*

Rear Admiral David G. Farragut

Deck of Admiral Farragut's flagship, the *Hartford*

Farragut's fleet at the entrance to Mobile Bay

The Charleston Mercury.

DAILY PAPER—TWENTY DOLLARS FOR SIX MONTHS—PAYABLE IN ADVANCE.

VINDICE NULLO—SPONTE SUA SINE LEGE FIDES RECTUMQUE COLENTUR.

COUNTRY PAPER—THRICE A WEEK—TWELVE DOLLARS FOR SIX MONTHS—PAYABLE IN ADVANCE.

Volume LXXXV. | CHARLESTON, S. C., THURSDAY, AUGUST 25, 1864. | Number 12,148.

TELEGRAPHIC.

IMPORTANT FROM PETERSBURG.

PETERSBURG, August 21.—About nine o'clock to day our forces again attacked the enemy's position on the Weldon Railroad, in front and flank.

The column assaulting in front pushed the enemy back half a mile, capturing two lines of earthworks and 300 prisoners.

The force assaulting in flank, owing to the presence of a heavy force in the enemy's works and the unaccountable giving way at an important moment of one of our brigades, was repulsed with loss. The flanking force succeeded in capturing the enemy's line of skirmishers, and had reached the enemy's heavy breastworks, when they were compelled to retire. Since then we have had only skirmishing and sharpshooting.

The enemy now has the 2d, 5th and 9th corps holding the railroad, with fortifications of the strongest character. The brave Gen. SAUNDERS, of Alabama, was killed in the action.

The enemy, this morning, made a heavy demonstration on our left with artillery and musketry, firing for half an hour, and accomplished nothing.

PETERSBURG, August 23.—Since the fight of Sunday the enemy has been engaged in extending his lines west of the Railroad, towards the city. The enemy now occupies the ground upon which the battles of the last few days were fought. His pickets have advanced some distance this side.

Vaughn's road, for one mile west of the railroad, is also occupied by the enemy, who is strongly fortified there. The country south of the city is very level, and the enemy's lines are in sight of the corporate limits. Both armies are strongly entrenching.

There has been no offensive movement on either side to-day; consequently everything is very quiet.

CONFIRMATION OF THE CAPTURE OF MEMPHIS.

ATLANTA, August 24.—A despatch from Gen. MAURY, at Mobile, confirms the capture of Memphis by FORREST. Gen. WASHBURNE (the Yankee commandant) and staff were captured with the city.

OXFORD, MISS., August 23.—General FORREST arrived at Panola last night.

He completely surprised Memphis by a night attack. The charge was exciting and terrific. The Yankee loss was 500. After the fight FORREST sent a flag of truce to the enemy offering to exchange prisoners. WASHBURNE refused, saying he would capture him before he could reached Panola.

Gen. SMITH, the Yankee raider, learning FORREST's movements, hastily retreated from Oxford towards Holly Springs, burning the Court House and the principal business portion of the town, as well as many private residences, including the mansion of Colonel JACOB THOMPSON.

Our forces have reoccupied Oxford and are pursuing SMITH.

IMPORTANT FROM MOBILE—FALL OF FORT MORGAN.

MOBILE, August 23.—Several Yankee vessels are cruising below the obstructions in the upper Bay. Our scouts report that yesterday morning the Yankee fleet hauled up close to Fort Morgan and opened fire. The fort replied and crippled two vessels badly.

On the eastern shore the enemy is landing and plundering near Point Clear.

MOBILE, August 24.—Fort Morgan is in the enemy's hands; whether surrendered, evacuated or blown up is unknown. There are conflicting reports, but nothing authentic. A flag of truce boat visited the enemy's upper fleet to-day. The Federal Exchange Agent had not arrived and nothing was accomplished.

A special despatch announces that the enemy burned Abbeville, Miss., last night. Their advance passed through Holly Springs, moving towards Lagrange. A wagon train crossed the Tallahatchie and encamped at Waterford last night.

THE SIEGE OF ATLANTA.

ATLANTA, August 23.—A despatch from Jonesboro' states that the Yankee raiding party had appeard in heavy force at Fayetteville.

Dixon's Bridge, over the Flint river, near Fayetteville, was burned this morning. Our scouts report that another Yankee raiding party, 7000 strong, with nine pieces of artillery, started from Decatur early this morning, in the direction of Covington.

A letter from an officer at Greenville, East Tennessee, states that JOHN MORGAN had left that point for Knoxville. The trains were running regularly from Bristol to Greenville.

The situation around Atlanta is unchanged. The enemy shelled the city at intervals all last night. All was quiet this morning, except an occasional picket skirmish.

A lady was killed near the Express Office last evening by a shell, and a soldier lost a leg.

ATLANTA, August 24.—The enemy shelled the centre of the city steadily all night. MCDANIEL's Warehouse, on Huntel street, between Pryor and Whitehall has been destroyed by fire; 500 bales of cotton were burned at 5 o'clock this morning, but the firemen checked the spread of the flames.

A small frame building near the State Railroad Workshops was also burned last night. Both buildings were fired by shells. The shelling has occasioned no further casualties, and the city is quiet this morning, save the usual skirmishing of artillery and small arms.

The Yankee raid reported by our scouts yesterday is not confirmed by the reports of this morning.

ATLANTA, August 24.—Another large conflagration occurred this evening in Alabama street, destroying a large warehouse and several dwellings. The fire was caused by a shell. During the fire the Yankee batteries shelled that portion of the city with great rapidity.

Prisoners report that SHERMAN's army continues to be well fed. Citizens from Marietta report that the Yankee officers claim that they have twenty days' supplies at that place.

"STARVING OUT THE SOUTH"—WHAT SAY THE STATISTICS.

A correspondent of the Baltimore *Sun* calls attention to some striking and interesting facts, to show that the bugbear of "starving out the South" and "cutting off supplies," &c., may be said with ease, but doing it is another thing. He says:

I will select first, South Carolina, to run the parallel with, for several reasons, the chief of which are that she has been supposed to produce nothing but cotton and rice, and she is the most derided and contemned of all the slaveholding States. Not many persons are aware that this State alone produces five sixths nearly of all the rice grown, but the census of 1850 shows that to be the fact; besides nearly all the rice, she produces wheat to within 3000 bushels of all produced by the six New England States together. She produces almost as much corn as the State of New York, and six millions of bushels of that grain more than all the New England States together, for she produced upwards of 16,000,000 of bushels.

She produced more oats than Maine; more by 1,000,000 bushels than Massachusetts; more than 1,000 000 bushels of potatoes over and above what Maine produced; more beans and peas by 130,000 bushels than all the Northern States together, except New York; more beef cattle than Pennsylvania by 1,740, and almost as many as all the New England States together; more sheep than Iowa and Wisconsin by 10,699; more hogs than New York by 47,251; more than Pennsylvania by [illegible], and 86,000 more than all the New England States, with New Jersey, Michigan, Wisconsin and California in the bargain; more horses and mules by 10,000 than Maine, New Hampshire, Massachusetts and Rhode Island together; besides all which she produces largely of oxen, cows, and a variety of products of the smaller kinds.

Virginia and North Carolina produced jointly 13,363,000 bushels of wheat, or 241,000 bushels more than the great wheat State of New York, or a quantity equal to the whole product of the six New England States, with New Jersey, Michigan, Iowa and Wisconsin, all put together.—Virginia, North Carolina and Tennessee produced 115,471 593 bushels of corn, a quantity exceeding by 300,000 bushels the joint product of New York, Pennsylvania, Ohio, New Jersey, Connecticut, Massachusetts, New Hampshire, Vermont and Maine.

Tennessee alone produced 16,506 more hogs than all the six New England States, with New York, Pennsylvania, New Jersey, Iowa and Michigan; for that State produced 3,104,800 hogs, while the eleven Northern States named produced but 3 088,394. Most of people have thought that the North was really the hog producing section, but such is by no means the fact. The whole number of hogs produced in 1850 was 30,316,608, of which the slaveholding States furnished 20,770,730, or more than two-thirds of the whole swine production.

It will doubtless surprise many persons to be told that the seven gulf or cotton States of South Carolina, Georgia, Alabama, Mississippi, Louisiana and Texas produced 45,137 more beef cattle than the six New England States, New York, Pennsylvania, Ohio, New Jersey, Indiana, Michigan, and Wisconsin, altogether; but such is the fact, for the census of 1850 tells us that these seven cotton States produced 3,354,489 beef cattle, while the thirteen Northern States named produced but 3,312,327.

A single glance at the live stock columns of the seventh census will prove to the inquirer that the slaveholding States produced more beef cattle than the non-slaveholding by 1,782 587.—That while the North produced 3,541,121 cows, the South produced 2 829.810. That the Northern States produced 866,397 work oxen, against 820.340 produced by the Southern States. That while the North produced 2,310 962 horses and mules, the South produced 259 358 more, for the Southern production was 2,570,320.

In conclusion, as people have been so much in the habit of conceding superiority to the North, in these and other points of view, may be the above statements may be doubted; if so, I refer the skeptical to the seventh census of 1850, the last date we have.

THE FIGHTING AT PETERSBURG.

The Petersburg *Express* contains an account of the fight near that city on Friday. It appears that on Thursday our forces, after attacking the Yankees on the Weldon road and driving them one mile, ceased the pursuit, and fell back to a point nearer the city, leaving only a skirmish line in front of the enemy, which was also soon after withdrawn. The *Express* says:

The enemy did not discover our disappearance from their front until yesterday morning, when they immediately threw forward their lines of skirmishers and advanced their left to the battle field of Thursday, in Davis' corn field, throwing up as they advanced, two lines of breastworks. Their right was extended in an oblique direction to the northeast of the railroad, and batteries were placed at favorable points along the whole line.

This occupation of one of our main lines of communication with the South was, of course, not to be permitted without an effort to dislodge the enemy. Accordingly, all arrangements having been completed, Gen. A. P. Hill, commanding Mahone's and Heth's divisions, attacked them between the hours of 3 and 4 o'clock.—Gen. Mahone commanded the troops to the left of the railroad, and Gen. Heth those to the right. The attack was opened by Mahone, and was speedily responed to by Heth on the right, and the battle raged furiously.

On the right, General Heth, with the gallant brigades of his divisions—Davis', Walker's and Archer's—struck the enemy's picket line in the cornfield a short distance beyond Davis' residence. These were quickly forced back upon the first line of breastworks, held by a formidable force. With a cheer, the Confederate troops bounded forward and swept over all obstruction, pressing the Yankees back with severe loss into their second line, and, charging onward, forced them thence with an equal lack of ceremony. Beaten from their works and defeated in their every effort to retain them, the Yankees retreated to their main line of entrenchments, into which they had been driven on the previous evening. This line having been greatly strengthened, proved too strong to be stormed, and our troops were checked in the face of the slaughter which threatened a farther advance.

In the meantime, General Mahone, with Clingman's, Colquitt's, and his own former brigade, had struck the right of the Yankee lines and captured eight hundred prisoners. Pressing forward with his usual energy, he drove the enemy before him, successfully charging them wherever they made a stand. Finding them strongly entrenched, however, in the thick woods opposite Davis' farm, it was determined to dislodge them by a flank movement. Clingman's and Mahone's old brigade engaged them in front, while, by a circuitous route, Colquitt's (Georgia) brigade was thrown on their flank. The movement proved a brilliant success, and caused scarcely any loss to our troops.

Colquitt's men were upon the Yankees almost before they were aware of such close proximity of the rebels, and surrender or fighting under fearful disadvantage was the alternative. Crawford's crack division, of Warren's (Fifth) corps, here fell a helpless victim to rebel strategy, and the greater part of two brigades—numbering over two thousand men—threw down their arms and surrendered. The prisoners were quickly placed under guard and sent to the rear, where they were formed into line and marched to Gen. Hill's headquarters.

The battle still progressed successfully until the enemy was driven back to the position from which he advanced in the morning. At dark, our lines were close up to his works, and occasional volleys of musketry showed still further fighting.

Among the prisoners taken is Brigadier-General Hays, of Massachusetts, several Colonels, and other field officers of less grade. General Hayes was brought into town last night.

During the engagement we left a number of men taken prisoners, but we understand they were afterwards recaptured. The success which followed the attack threw our men into the best spirits, and every soldier wore a smile of satisfaction upon his countenance.

The result of the attack is highly satisfactory to the officers in command, and is viewed in the most favorable light. The enemy has been materially weakened by the loss of three thousand of his best troops taken prisoners and several thousand killed and wounded. He is demoralized by his defeat, and though he may fight hard yet to hold the position he has gained, his prestige is gone, and he will not offer the front he has shown during the last few days.

The weather was rainy during the day, and especially so during the afternoon. The fighting was done amidst a series of heavy showers, which not only incommoded our men, but rendered the ground heavy and slippery. Most of the fighting on our left was done in a dense growth of underbrush and woods.

We can form no estimate of the Yankee loss other than the statement of officers that it was very heavy. Many of their dead and wounded fell into our hands. Nor are we able to form an idea of our own loss, as up to last night but few of the wounded had been brought from the field. The great majority of those we saw were slightly wounded. We shall learn further particulars of the casualties and of the battle to-day. We regret to state, however, that General Clingman was painfully, though not seriously, wounded.

The battle for the possession of the railroad will probably be resumed this morning, and it is believed the enemy will not only be dislodged, but disastrously defeated. This expedition will turn out in the end, to be the greatest disaster that has yet happened to Grant in this department.

Repots from the battle field, late last evening, represent our forces between the enemy and the main army in front of Petersburg. If so, something interesting may occur to-day.

It is also stated that several hundred more prisoners have been taken, thus running the number above three thousand.

As the enemy still hold the railroad, it is impossible to state what damage has been done the track. It is believed, that instead of sending a body of raiders across towards the south side, the enemy's cavalry are operating on the Weldon Road, in the rear of the army.

Interior view of Fort Morgan

The New-York Times.

VOL. XIII.---NO. 4054. NEW-YORK, WEDNESDAY, SEPTEMBER 21, 1864. PRICE FOUR CENTS.

VICTORY!

Great Battle in the Shenandoah Valley.

The Rebels Defeated by General Sheridan.

THE BATTLE OF BUNKER HILL.

The Enemy Thoroughly Whipped.

They are Pursued Beyond Winchester.

Three Thousand Prisoners, Five Guns and Fifteen Battle-Flags Captured.

All the Rebel Dead and Wounded in Our Hands.

The Rebel Generals Gordon, Wharton, Rodes, and Ramsour Killed.

THE UNION GENERAL RUSSELL KILLED.

The Union Generals Chapman, Upton and Mackintosh Wounded.

THE OFFICIAL DISPATCHES.

SECRETARY STANTON TO GEN. DIX.

WAR DEPARTMENT, WASHINGTON, Tuesday, Sept. 20—9:30 A. M.

Maj.-Gen. John A. Dix:

Yesterday, Maj.-Gen. SHERIDAN attacked EARLY, fought a great battle, and won a splendid victory.

Over 2,500 prisoners were captured.

Nine battle-flags and five pieces of artillery were captured.

The rebel Generals Gordon and Rhodes were killed and three other general officers were wounded.

All of the enemy's killed, and most of their wounded, are in our hands.

The details are stated in the following additional telegrams received by this department.

The department learns with deep regret, that we lost General Russell, killed.

GEN. STEVENSON'S FIRST DISPATCH.

HARPER'S FERRY, VA., Monday, Sept. 19—12 M.

Hon. Edwin M. Stanton, Secretary of War:

Gen. SHERIDAN moved on the enemy this morning at daylight. Soon after the movement commenced, there was heavy and continuous firing for two hours. It then ceased, apparently receding. It was resumed about nine o'clock, and has continued to this hour (12 M.,) apparently in the vicinity of Bunker Hill.

JOHN D. STEVENSON, Brig.-Gen.

GEN. STEVENSON'S SECOND DISPATCH.

HARPER'S FERRY, Monday, Sept. 19, 3 P.M.

Hon. E. M. Stanton, Secretary of War:

Just received report from signal officer as follows: Continuous firing between Opequan and near Winchester; very heavy since 10 A.M. Think the engagement is general. Line about 5 miles long.

AVERILL is heavily engaged with the enemy near Darkesville. I have sent a party of scouts and couriers to the front, and shall report promptly all reliable news.

JOHN D. STEVENSON, Brig.-Gen.

GEN. STEVENSON'S THIRD DISPATCH.

HARPER'S FERRY, Monday, Sept. 19—4:30 P. M.

Hon. E. M. Stanton, Secretary of War:

Fighting in the direction of Winchester much heavier. Our forces near Bunker Hill seem to be driving the enemy rapidly.

JOHN D. STEVENSON, Brig.-Gen.

GEN. STEVENSON'S FOURTH DISPATCH.

HARPER'S FERRY, Monday Sept. 19—7 P. M.

Hon. E. M. Stanton, Secretary of War:

Just heard from the front. Our cavalry, under AVERILL and MERRITT engaged BRECKENRIDGE'S corps at Darkesville at daylight, and up to 1 o'clock had driven him beyond Stevenson's Depot, a distance of seven miles, killing and wounding quite a number and capturing two hundred prisoners from GORDON'S division.

On the centre and left the enemy were driven about three miles beyond the Opequan into a line of earthworks, our infantry attacking them in position. Since then, as the officer left, he could distinctly hear heavy musketry fire and continuous and heavy artillery firing as he came in. We have heard here heavy artillery firing, and still continuing to this hour. Every indication is most favorable to us.

JOHN D. STEVENSON, Brig.-Gen.

GEN. STEVENSON'S FIFTH DISPATCH.

HARPER'S FERRY, Tuesday, Sept. 20, 7:40 A.M.

Hon. E. M. Stanton, Secretary of War:

Just heard from the front that SHERIDAN has defeated the enemy, capturing 2,500 prisoners, five pieces of artillery, and five battle-flags. Rebel Generals GORDON and RHODES were killed, and YORK wounded. Our loss was about 2,000. Gen. RUSSELL, of the Sixth Corps, was killed. Gen. MCINTOSH lost a leg. The enemy escaped up the valley under cover of night. SHERIDAN is in Winchester.

J. D. STEVENSON, Brig.-Gen.

Gens. UPTON, MCINTOSH and CHAPMAN are wounded.

GEN. SHERIDAN TO GEN. GRANT.

Gen. SHERIDAN transmits to Gen. GRANT the following official report, which has just been received by the Department:

WINCHESTER, VA., Sept. 19, 7.30 P. M.

Lieut.-Gen. U S Grant:

I have the honor to report that I attacked the forces of Gen. Early, over the Berryville pike, at the crossing of Opequan Creek, and after a most stubborn and sanguinary engagement, which lasted from early in the morning until five o'clock in the evening, completely defeated him, driving him through Winchester, capturing about 2,500 prisoners, five pieces of artillery, nine army flags, and most of their wounded. The Rebel Generals RHODES and GORDON were killed, and three other general officers were wounded. Most of the enemy's wounded and all their killed fell into our hands. Our losses are severe. Among them is Gen. D. A. RUSSELL, commanding a Division in the Sixth Corps, who was killed by a cannon ball. Gens. UPTON, MCINTOSH, and CHAPMAN were wounded. I cannot tell our losses. The conduct of the officers and men was most superb. They charged and carried every position taken up by the rebels from Opequan Creek to Winchester.

The rebels were strong in numbers, and very obstinate in their fighting. I desire to mention to the Lieut.-Gen. Commanding the army, the gallant conduct of Generals WRIGHT, CROOK, EMORY, TORBERT, and the officers and men under their command. To them the country is indebted for this handsome victory. A more detailed report will be forwarded.

P. H. SHERIDAN, Major-General, Commanding.

WAR DEPARTMENT, Tuesday, Sept. 20.

Full details of casualties will be given when received by the Department.

EDWIN M. STANTON, Sec'y of War.

SECRETARY STANTON'S SECOND DISPATCH

WAR DEPARTMENT, WASHINGTON Tuesday, Sept. 20—12 M.

Maj.-Gen. John A. Dix:

The following dispatch has just been received giving further particulars of SHERIDAN'S great victory. A salute of one hundred guns has just been given.

HARPER'S FERRY, Tuesday, Sept. 20—11:40 A. M.

Hon. E. M. Stanton:

Just received the following official from Gen. SHERIDAN, dated 1 A. M. to-day:

GENERAL: We fought EARLY from daylight till between 6 and 7 P. M. We drove him from Opequan Creek through Winchester and beyond the town. We captured 2,500 to 3,000 prisoners, five pieces of artillery, nine battle-flags, and all the rebel wounded and dead.

Their wounded in Winchester amount to some three thousand. We lost in killed Gen. DAVID RUSSELL, commanding a division of the Sixth Army Corps, and wounded Gens. CHAPMAN, MCINTOSH and UPTON. The rebels lost in killed the following General officers:

Gen. RHODES, Gen. WHARTON, Gen. GORDON and Gen. RAMSEUR.

We have just sent them whirling through Winchester, and we are after them to-morrow. This army behaved splendidly. I am sending forward all the medical supplies, subsistence stores and ambulances. (Signed,)

JNO. D. STEVENSON, Brig.-Gen.

EDWIN M. STANTON, *Secretary of War.*

SECRETARY STANTON'S THIRD DISPATCH.

WAR DEPARTMENT, WASHINGTON, Monday, Sept. 20—7 P. M.

To Maj.-Gen. Dix, New York;

The following is the latest intelligence received from Gen. SHERIDAN:

HARPER'S FERRY, VA., Monday, Sept. 20—8 P. M.

Hon. Edwin M. Stanton, Secretary of War:

The body of Gen. RUSSELL has arrived. As soon as it is embalmed, it will be forwarded to New-York. Gen. MCINTOSH, with his leg amputated, has just come in, and is in good spirits.

Several officers from the front report the number of prisoners in excess of 3,000.

The number of battle-flags captured was fifteen, instead of nine.

All concur that it was a complete rout. Our cavalry started in pursuit at daylight this morning. SHERIDAN, when last heard from, was at Kearnstown. I sent forward this morning ample medical supplies. Full subsistence for the entire army goes forward. If you do not hear from me often, it will be because of the distance we are from the scene of action, and because I only send you such information as I esteem reliable.

JOHN B. RICHARDSON, Brig.-Gen.

The President has appointed Gen. SHERIDAN a Brigadier in the regular Army, and assigned him to the permanent command of the Middle Military Division.

Gen. GRANT has ordered the army under his command to fire a salute of one hundred guns at seven o'clock to-morrow morning in honor of SHERIDAN'S great victory.

A dispatch just received from Gen. SHERMAN, at Atlanta, says:

"Everything continues well with us."

The reports of to-day show that the draft is proceeding quietly in all the States. In most of the districts vigorous efforts are continued to fill the quota by volunteers before the drafted men are mustered in.

EDWIN M. STANTON, Secretary of War.

DETAILS OF THE BATTLE.

BALTIMORE, Tuesday, Sept. 20—10 P. M.

The following is the *American's* special account of the great battle in the Shenandoah Valley:

HEADQUARTERS MIDDLE MILITARY DIVISION, WINCHESTER, Va., Monday, Sept. 19—9 P. M.

Gen. SHERIDAN'S army has this day fought one of the most successful and decisive battles of the war. Victory again perched on our banners, and the rebel army which so recently threatened the invasion of the loyal North, has been defeated and utterly routed, with the loss of at least three thousand killed and wounded including five Generals, namely, RHODES, WHARTON, BRADLEY, T. JOHNSON, GORDON, YORK and GODMAN, the first two of whom were killed, and the others badly wounded, and we have captured 2,500 prisoners, nine battle flags, representing nine different regimental organizations, five pieces of artillery with caissons.

The recital of the victory ought to make every loyal heart at the North glow with admiration and gratitude to the brave men and gallant officers who have achieved so signal success.

In order to more thoroughly understand the nature of the battle, with all the surrounding influences, it will be necessary briefly to refer to the operations of Sunday.

Sunday morning EARLY sent GORDON'S division of rebel infantry from Bunker Hill, where it had been stationed for the past few days, to drive AVERILL out of Martinsburg and destroy the bridge on the Baltimore and Ohio R. R. across the Opequan, which they erroneously thought had been repaired. They occupied Martinsburgh for a short time, without doing any damage to the railroad, and were eventually driven by AVERILL as far as Darkesville.

Gen. SHERIDAN, learning their movements, ordered the whole command to break camp and prepare to march. Accordingly, at 3 o'clock on Sunday the tents were all struck and packed in wagons. The different divisions were all under arms, and prepared to move at a moment's notice, and remained in this state for about an hour, when the order came to go into camp for the night, and everything remained perfectly quiet. About 9 o'clock orders were received from SHERIDAN for the Sixth and Nineteenth Corps to be ready to start at 3 o'clock, and the Army of Western Virginia, under CROOK, at 5 the following morning—the order of march to be as follows: The Sixth Corps to move out on the Winchester and Berryville pike, and move in two parallel columns on both sides of the road, with the artillery, ammunition and supply trains on the road; the Nineteenth Corps to follow on the same road and in similar order; the Army of Western Virginia, under CROOK, to move from its camping-ground in the vicinity of Summit Point, and striking across the country in a south-westerly direction, was ordered to form a junction at the crossing of the Opequan, on the Berryville and Winchester pike, and shortly after five o'clock WILSON'S division of cavalry crossed the Opequan at the Berryville and Winchester pike. Moving his command rapidly along the road, driving in the enemy's skirmish line, he gallantly charged the enemy's field works with the first brigade, and carried them at the point of the sabre, capturing thirty prisoners. In this charge, Col. BRINTON, Eighteenth Pennsylvania cavalry, was wounded within a few feet of the enemy's works, whilst gallantly leading his regiment.

These field-works were constructed at the Opequan, and prevent our passage at that point. It will be seen how signally they failed to accomplish the object for which they were constructed.

Our cavalry having secured a safe passage for the infantry, the Sixth corps was moved across the Opequan, and along the pike toward Winchester, (leaving its train in part on the opposite side of the stream,) to a point about a mile and a half distant from the ford, where it formed in line of battle and threw out a strong skirmish line. At the same time the artillery opened on the woods into which the enemy's infantry had retired, and kept up an incessant cannonade, the enemy replying briskly with parts of two batteries.

There was a delay of at least two hours, caused by the non-arrival of the Nineteenth corps, who through misconception of orders, had failed to come up at the proper time. Gen. EMERY had moved his column to the rear of the baggage train of the Sixth corps instead of keeping his command closed up in the rear of the advancing column of the Sixth corps.

Gen. Sheridan having learned on Sunday that the main portion of Early's forces were encamped in the vicinity of Bunker Hill and Stephenson's Depot, resolved to mass his forces on the Winchester and Berryville pike, and by a rapid movement hurl them on Early's rear. There is no doubt but the enemy were surprised and outnumbered by Sheridan.

Whilst his different columns were being marched to the appointed place of rendezvous, a portion of our cavalry under Gen.'s. TORBETT and AVERILL kept up a strong picket line along the Opequan, and by demonstrating in force at Burn's ford kept a large portion of the enemy at that part of the field, which was nearly twelve miles distant from the point where it was intended our infantry should operate, and strike a blow which should result in the signal defeat of EARLY'S army.

The delay in the arrival of the 19th Corps enabled EARLY to move GORDON'S Division at the double quick from Bunker Hill, distant about ten miles, and bring it up in time to form in line of battle with BRECKENRIDGE'S, RAMSEUR'S, and RHODES' commands, who had already arrived, and were formed in a belt of woods skirting Berryville and Winchester.

As soon as the 19th corps arrived, it was formed in four lines of battle, about 300 yards apart, on the right of the 6th corps, and everything being in readiness, the advance was sounded at about 12 o'clock, and the different lines moved forward.

The two corps advanced in splendid style, and just as composedly as though marching at review or on parade, drums beating and colors flying, presenting such an imposing spectacle as has seldom been witnessed in the present war. In fact, some of the oldest and most experienced staff officers present declared they had never before witnessed so truly grand a spectacle.

The first line had not advanced more than two hundred yards before it became warmly engaged with the enemy, who were posted in line about six hundred yards distant. At the same time our artillery opened a furious cannonade, throwing shells and solid shot into the opposite woods, where the enemy could be distinctly seen moving up reinforcements.

Our different lines of battle continued to advance steadily until within nearly two hundred yards of the enemy's line, when the rebels opened a furious canonade with grape and canister, from two batteries which they had previously kept secreted, and which ploughed through our advancing lines, mowing down large numbers of our men.

The first line was obliged to give way under so murderous a fire, and in retreating behind the second line, threw it into momentary confusion, and it also was compelled to fall back behind the third line, which had in the meantime been ordered to lie down, in order to avoid as much as possible the effects of the withring fire which the enemy's battery's were directing against our advancing lines.

The artillery was now brought up and posted on commanding positions, to silence these batteries of the enemy, which had caused us so much annoyance, and our line was reformed, and again moved forward, regaining the advanced position which they had held when they were obliged to fall back. But the success was not gained without the most obstinate resistance on the part of the enemy.

Gen. SHERIDAN had previously ridden along the lines, and was received everywhere by the men with the greatest enthusiasm, and when they advanced, it was with the terrible determination to do or die in the attempt.

Having regained the advanced position which we had previously occupied, the different lines of battle were ordered to lie down and wait the arrival of Gen. CROOK'S Corps which was held in reserve on the eastern side of the Opequan. They were ordered up to take position on the extreme right of our line, and in order to counteract a movement on the part of the enemy who were massing troops on their left flank, with the view of turning our right.

Precisely at 3 o'clock, Gen. CROOK formed on the right of the Nineteenth Corps, his first division on the extreme right of our line, and the second division in the rear supporting a division of the Nineteenth Corps. Gen. CROOK, having formed his men, rode along the lines, and was received with most vociferous cheering, the men promising to go in and wipe out Winchester.

Gen. TORBETT, with MERRITT'S and AVERILL'S divisions of cavalry, having crossed the Opequan about 9 o'clock at BURN'S and KNOX'S Fords, had been hard at work all day, fighting considerable bodies of the enemy's infantry, and having been successful in steadily driving them before them, now arrived on our extreme right, and was prepared to take part in the final struggle which secured us the victory.

Gen. SHERIDAN rode out to where Gen. TORBETT was stationed, and after a consultation with him as to the part the cavalry were to take, ordered the final charge, which was made with an impetuosity which nothing could resist. Our line, extending nearly three miles in length, advanced, amid the cheers and yells, which could be distinctly heard far above the noise caused by the thunder of the artillery and the continuous roar of musketry, which, for its impetuosity, has seldom been exceeded in any battle of this war.

Our men determined to win the day, and nerved themselves accordingly for the coming struggle; and as our lines advanced closer and closer to those of the enemy, the battle became more and more fierce, until in point of desperate and fierce carnage, it will compare favorably with any similar contest of the war.

The slaughter now was truly awful. At every discharge men could be distinctly seen dropping all around, and the two contending lines at some points could not have been over two hundred yards apart.

Just at this critical period, above the roar of artillery, musketry and cheers, and the fiercer yells of the contending armies, could be distinctly heard the shrill notes of the cavalry bugle sounding the charge which was the death knell to EARLY'S army. There could be seen the gallant CUSTER and MERRITT, each with headquarters flag in hand, and conspicuous amongst the advancing squadrons, gallantly leading the charge which in connection with the desperate courage of our infantry, secured us the victory. All honor to these gallant chiefs, who have done so nobly.

Those who have never witnessed a cavalry charge can form no idea of its magnificence, nor of the demoralizing effects when well executed, which it has on an enemy. The stubborn Columns of EARLY'S command were forced to give way and break before the fierce onslaught which our cavalry made upon them, who, with sabre in hand, rode them down, cutting them right and left, capturing 721 privates and non-commissioned offices, with nine battle flags and two guns.

The broken and disorganized divisions comprising EARLY'S command now fled in confusion, throwing away everything which could in any way impede their flight, and strewing the ground with their arms. Some made for the heights above Winchester, but they were speedily dislodged by AVERILL, and forced to beat an hasty and ignominious retreat up the valley, where such of EARLY'S command as are left him are now scattered.

Our victory was a glorious one, and one well calculated to thrill the hearts of every loyal man with the impulses of sincere joy; but it has been well remarked that each joy has its attending amount of sorrow, and it it is for our gallant dead and wounded who poured out their life's blood freely that this great and iniquitous rebellion be put down.

Amongst the killed I regret to announce the gallant RUSSELL, of the First Division, Sixth Corps, commanding. Fearless as was possible for man to be, brave unto rashness, he fell at the post of honor at the head of his division, while leading them in charge.

Gen. MCINTOSH, commanding First Brigade, Third Cavalry Division, was wounded by a pistol ball in the leg, which necessitated amputation. He is doing very well.

Gen. UPTON, commanding division in Sixth Corps was also wounded, but not dangerously.

Of field and line officers I have been able to collect but few names who were killed or wounded. Among them are Col. BABCOCK, Seventy-fifth New-York, wounded in the thigh; Col. E. BRIGHT, One Hundred and Twenty-sixth Ohio. Third Division, Sixth Corps, killed; Capt. WRIGHT, Gen. DEVIN'S Staff, killed; Capt. ROBENBAUGH, Second United States Cavalry, wounded in the arm; Capt. MCGUESTON, Second United States Cavalry, Aid to Gen. MERRITT, killed; Maj. VREDENBURG, Fourteenth New-Jersey, Third Division, Sixth Corps, killed.

Maj. DILLINGHAM, Tenth Vermont, Third Division, Sixth Corps. killed.

Lieut.-Col. BREWER, Seventh Michigan Cavalry, killed.

Lieut. JACKSON, First Michigan Cavalry, arm shot off.

Lieuts. MATHEWS and JOHN ALLEN, First Michigan Cavalry, killed.

The Michigan brigade, Gen. CUSTER'S command, claim the honor of killing Gen. RHODES during the fierce conflict which ensued when they charged a portion of his division.

After the battle had been fought and won and while our troops were passing through the streets of Winchester, among them some of the best ladies residing in the town, came out with Union flags in their hands, and bid our soldiers "Welcome back to Winchester."

The people of Winchester all agree in stating that EARLY'S command is fearfully demoralized, and speak of his defeat as a disgraceful rout, in which both men and officers rushed frantically through the streets, throwing away everything which would in any way encumber them in their flight.

The City Hotel and the adjacent foundries, together with many private houses in Winchester, are full of rebel wounded. It is estimated there are at least 3,000 in Winchester. Allowing for those who were carried away in ambulances, and for those who were able to hobble along, it will be a small estimate to place their wounded at 4,000 and killed at 500, which with the prisoners already captured, numbering 3,000, will make their loss 7,500 in number, equal to one of their corps.

Of the Federal loss, it is impossible, at the time of writing this dispatch, to form any correct estimate; but from information at hand, together with personal observations on the field, I do not think it will exceed 500 killed and 2,500 wounded, if it amounts to that number.

Surely I am correct in stating that this has been one of the most sanguinary and decisive battles of the war, and reflects great credit on Gen. SHERIDAN, who was constantly at the front, exposing himself to the fire of the enemy's sharpshooters, and personally directing the movements of our army.

THE STRATEGY OF THE BATTLE.

Special Dispatch to the New-York Times.

WASHINGTON, Tuesday, Sept. 20,

Gen. SHERIDAN'S grand success near Winchester is noted as the first victory achieved by the national arms in the Shenandoah Valley. But it is so magnificent in its proportions as completely to wipe out the long series of reverses which have given to that region the designation of "The Valley of Humiliation." The loss to the enemy in killed, wounded and prisoners will, it is believed, reach not less than ten thousand, while the circumstances of the enemy's defeat leave EARLY'S army in a condition little short of absolute rout and demoralization.

Popular logic will doubtless associate this brilliant exploit with the recent visit of the Lieutenant-General to the headquarters of Gen. SHERIDAN—an association so far correct, no doubt, that, had not Gen. GRANT authorized Gen. SHERIDAN to assume the offensive, we should not now have this victory to rejoice over. This does not, however, detract from the credit to which that gallant officer is entitled, and all the more so from the modest generosity with which he ascribes all the glory of the splendid achievement to his subordinate commanders.

The bearing of this operation on the greater problem immediately before Gen. GRANT, is of capital importance, and will go far to decide the fate of LEE'S army and Richmond. The tremendous importance of Lynchburgh, as covering the now only remaining line of railroad communication with Richmond, has compelled LEE to retain in the valley full one-half of his entire force; and notwithstanding the terrible straits he has been put to for lack of troops to meet the movements of GRANT, the fatal menace which the presence of SHERIDAN'S army in the Valley constantly held forth, has forced LEE to submit to them, on peril of the loss of Lynchburgh.

The army covering that point has, by SHERIDAN'S splendid success, been disrupted and demoralized, and we may, at length, look for the execution of that movement in the Valley which has always been an integral part of Gen. GRANT'S programme of operations for the capture of Richmond.

Other coöperative moves, not now proper for public mention, may be expected; and those best informed of all the elements of the military situation feel the most assurance that we shall have Richmond before the Presidential election.

Sheridan's Victory at Philadelphia.

PHILADELPHIA, Tuesday, Sept. 20.

The news of SHERIDAN'S victory caused great excitement, and the sudden erection of flags on all the public and many of the private buildings. The whole city is rejoicing over the news, and anxiously awaiting news of a similar character from GRANT.

Salute in Albany for Sheridan's Victory.

ALBANY, Tuesday, Sept. 20.

The Union citizens of Albany fired one hundred guns this evening in honor of SHERIDAN'S victory.

FROM FORTRESS MONROE.

Capture of the Schooner Jane F. Durfee—Rebel Prisoners for Exchange—Lieut.-Gen. Grant Gone to the Front—Accident to the Keystone State.

FORTRESS MONROE, Monday, Sept. 19.

The schooner *Jane F. Durfee*, E. G. DAVIS, master, was captured on Saturday evening last, at 11 o'clock, while at anchor in Warwick River, near James River, by a party of five rebels belonging to the Confederate States navy. It was a complete surprise. The first Capt. DAVIS knew of it, a rebel entered his cabin, and with a pistol directed at his head, demanded the surrender of the schooner, informing him of his crew having been overpowered. The schooner was released by Capt. DAVIS giving bonds for $7,313, the supercargo, WILBUR F. STOCKING, being held as hostage for the payment of the money. The rebels then robbed the schooner, taking $2,709 from the Captain, clothing from the crew, the small boat, colors, papers, compasses, nautical instruments, &c., and bidding the Captain a polite adieu, left at 1 P. M. The Captain of the *Durfee* arrived here with his schooner this morning.

The flag-of-truce steamers *New-York* and *Dictator*, with one thousand rebel prisoners, destined for exchange, arrived last night from Philadelphia, and left at 10 o'clock this morning for Aiken's Landing in charge of Major JOHN E. MULFORD, Commissioner of Exchange of prisoners.

Lieut.-Gen. GRANT arrived this morning from Baltimore and proceeded up the river on the steamer *New-York*.

The steamer *Keyport* ran on an old wreck in Hampton Roads this morning, making a hole in her keel. She was run ashore on Old Point and sunk in shoal water. The wreck had recently floated in and sunk in the channel.

The sloop-of-war *Wyoming* sailed from Hampton Roads this afternoon and went to sea.

From the Army of the Potomac.

WASHINGTON, Tuesday, Sept. 20.

ALL QUIET IN THE ARMY.

A note from the army of the Potomac, dated yesterday, says there is nothing new, and all is quiet with the exception of an occasional shot on the picket lines.

DESTRUCTION OF REBEL SALT WORKS.

Information has been received of the destruction of the extensive salt works on Bonsecours Bay, La., capable of making 20,000 bushels of salt per day, by the U. S. steamer *Trionia*. Two hundred sheds were fired, and the works, which were very substantial and cost over $100,000, were blown up.

The State Fair.

ROCHESTER, N. Y., Tuesday, Sept. 20.

To-day is the opening day of the State Fair. The weather is delightful, but there have not been many visitors. Exhibitors have been busy all day, as things are delayed by an overcrowd on the railroads. The entries are now equal to either of the last ten years. Everything bids fair for a great show of people to-morrow.

The cattle-show is small, but never better. Horses are excellent. Of fine wool sheep, the show is good. Of the better class of machinery, the show is good, and some of it is new and instructive. The fruit exhibition is good. The dairy and vegetables are very poor. The domestic department is small.

Altogether, the exhibition is not what it should be, but it will attract a great crowd of people.

Grain Afloat for Oswego and New-York.

OSWEGO, Tuesday, Sept. 20.

The amount of grain afloat from the upper lakes for Oswego up to the last dates, as near as can be ascertained, is as follows: 122,000 bus. of wheat, and 51,200 bus. of oats.

The amount of flour and grain afloat on the canals for tidewater and New-York, as near as can be ascertained, is as follows: 5,762 bbls. flour. 686,000 bus. wheat, 689,000 bus. corn, 82,000 bus. oats, 81,000 bus. barley, 97,000 bus. rye.

New-Jersey Politics—Union Demonstration at Newark.

NEWARK, Tuesday, Sept. 20.

A large and enthusiastic Union meeting is being addressed by JOHN Y. FOSTER, Esq., of this city. Immense enthusiasm greets the names of Gen. GRANT and our other successful Generals.

Moseby Wounded.

The Alexandria, Va., *Journal* says: We learn through sources, which cannot be discredited, that Moseby received a severe wound in the groin during a recent engagement between our forces and a small portion of his guerilla band in the vicinity of Centreville.

Obituary.

THE LATE GEN. RUSSELL.

Brigadier-General DAVID A. RUSSELL, who fell in the battle of Sept. 19th, near Winchester, was a native of New-York. He graduated at West Point, in 1845. He served in the Mexican war, and was brevetted "for gallant and meritorious conduct in several affairs with guerilleros, at Paso Ovejays, National Bridge and Cerro Gordo." He went into the present war against the rebels as Lieut.-Col. of the Seventh Massachusetts Volunteers, attached to the Sixth Army Corps. He served with distinction through the campaign on the Peninsula, and was commissioned a Brigadier General in December, 1862, just after the battle of Fredericksburg. He afterwards commanded a brigade, in Gen. HOWE'S division, Sixth Army Corps, and subsequently commanded the division. He was a brave and meritorious officer, and his loss will be deeply felt.

LATE SOUTHERN NEWS.

The Situation at Petersburgh—Rebel Fears—How Hood was Whipped at Atlanta.

THE LATEST WAR NEWS.

FROM PETERSBURG.

From the Richmond Enquirer, Sept. 17th.

For three days past the enemy has been manœuvering to effect an expansion of his right wing, and, if possible, seize the Vaughan road. A battle has consequently been expected, and rumors are now current in Petersburg each day anticipating the event. At an early hour on Thursday morning, Warren's 5th corps of Yankees, having left their works in the vicinity of the Weldon railroad, advanced and broke through Gen. Butler's lines at Poplar Spring Church. Col. D. D. Ferrebee, commanding General Dearing's Brigade, met them, and after fighting them for four hours, with varying success, finally repulsed them, inflicting considerable loss. The enemy succeeded in reaching Poplar Spring Church, and threw up breastworks at that point, but were compelled to abandon them. Our loss was small. The enemy left several in killed and wounded, and a number of prisoners. These prisoners stated that this movement was an attempt on their part to advance their lines in the direction of the South Side railroad.

On yesterday morning the enemy made another attempt to extend their picket lines on the left, but were suddenly encountered by a portion of Wilcox's command, suprised, and driven back, losing eighty-nine in prisoners, and several in killed and wounded. We lost none.

The enemy have now a vidette post at the intersection of the Vaughan and Poplar Spring Church roads, which is now their most advanced point of occupation. Poplar Spring Church, from which they were driven, is situated in Dinwiddie county, between the Vaughan and Boydtown roads, about two miles west of the Weldon railroad, and about four from the city.

FROM THE NORTH SIDE.

The city was disturbed with various rumors on yesterday of a fight on the Darbytown road. Official intelligence states that early yesterday morning a strong body of the enemy's cavalry advanced up the road near New Market and drove in our pickets. Later in the day, our forces made a dash upon the enemy, drove them off and re-established our picket lines. No loss on either side is reported.

FINE CONDITION OF THE ARMY OF TENNESSEE.

Official information has been received that the Army of Tennessee is in splendid condition and spirits.

In a dispatch to Gen. BRAGG, dated Sept. 15. 1864, Gen. HOOD says he is very much gratified at the feeling now existing among the officers and men of his army, and that they are in better condition for battle than at any time since they crossed the Chattahoochie.

Official information has also been received that the extra duty list (consisting of detailed men) is being materially decreased.

FROM GEN. EARLY'S ARMY.

Correspondence of the Richmond Enquirer.

FREDERICK COUNTY, VA., Tuesday, Sept., 13.

There was considerable cannonading to-day, seemingly on the Opequon, Southeast of Winchester. Guards, with prisoners, one hundred and eighty who have just passed up the road, say that it seems to be along the line, from Bunker's Hill to Berryville. A force of men yesterday came up from the front and went to work reconstructing the bridge over Cedar Creek, on the Valley turnpike. Constant reacessions to EARLY'S army pass down daily.

The Chicago Platform and its occupants attract but little attention about here. Take the Northern estimate of the Constitution of the old United States, ("a covenant with death and hell,") their valuation of the Bible when it conflicts with an *ism*; their regard for a cartel, or any other obligation, and it is easy to deduce the worth of a political platform, even had there been a single genuine plank of peace in it. Simply *straws*, straws to show which way the wind blows at the moment in *their* country.

THE LATE BATTLE NEAR ATLANTA.

Correspondence of the Richmond Enquirer.

CAMP NEAR LOVEJOY STATION, GA., September 5, 1864.

We have been so constantly in motion for a week, that it has been impossible to write you of the exciting operations in which we have been participating. And such is the fickle fortune of war, that you have scarcely heard that Atlanta has been relieved before we have to announce its fall. The recent movement of Sherman, which, for a time, was enveloped in great mystery, has at last been sufficiently clearly developed. About the 20th ult. he withdrew his troops from our front, and with five corps crossed the Chattahoochee River, moved down about twenty miles, then recrossed at Sandtown and Sweet Water, moved to within a short distance of Jonesboro', on the Western & Macon Railroad, and there threw up a strong line of entrenchments.

On the night of the 30th, Gen. HOOD ordered LEE'S corps, then about five miles south of Atlanta, to move down the railroad, HARDEE'S corps having preceded it. STEWART'S corps and the militia, under Maj.-Gen. G. W. SMITH, were left within the works around the city.

At 3 o'clock the next evening, our line of battle was formed in front of Jonesboro', HARDEE on the right and LEE on the left, and at once moved upon the enemy in his intrenched position. The enemy was massed in front of LEE, while the force opposed to HARDEE'S advance was chiefly cavalry. Our troops advanced steadily and unfalteringly under a galling fire, drove the enemy along the entire line, and from his intrenched picket line. The enemy, in front of HARDEE, retreated to the river. LEE'S corps reached the enemy's principal line of works, but in consequence of their great strength and the greatly superior force of the enemy, was unable to carry them, and was withdrawn in good order, and not followed by the enemy. STEVENSON'S division, of LEE'S corps, suffered more than any other division, although the whole corps fought with great coolness and gallantry. This division advanced under as heavy a fire of shot, shell and musketry as was ever faced by troops. Still it went on under the guidance of its gallant commander, whose coolness and presence of mind under fire have become proverbial. He was soon struck on the head by a ball partially spent, and, although stunned, remained in the saddle, and retained command during the fight. When almost at the enemy's works, Brig.-Gen. CUMMING, commanding a brigade of Georgians, fell severely wounded in the thigh, and wounded also in both hands. Col. CLACK, of the 3d Tennessee Regiment, was killed outright. The loss of this division, in killed and wounded, exceeds five hundred.

On the morning of the 1st LEE'S corps was ordered to Atlanta. It arrived near the city about dark. It had now been determined to evacuate the city, and, after removing a large amount of stores, the troops were withdrawn, and Atlanta was left to be occupied by the enemy. Almost all the commissary stores were saved, though about thirty cars loaded with ammunition, and four engines were destroyed. The enemy did not occupy the place until the following morning.

When it was known to the enemy that Lee's corps had been sent off, he massed his five corps and attacked Hardee. He was again and again repulsed by Hardee's single line; but finally succeeded in entering the works at one point, and captured Brig.-Gen. Govan, and Hewett's and Key's batteries.

Except this small portion of his line, Gen. HARDEE held his position during the whole day, and with comparatively small loss. His loss duing the two days is estimated at eight hundred, while the loss of the enemy on the 1st reaches the almost incredible number of ten thousand. It must be remembered, however, that the enemy charged our position repeatedly with five or six lines.

After leaving Atlanta, the troops marched to McDonald, thence to this place, where they joined HARDEE. We are now in line of battle, and confronted by the enemy, though an attack is not expected, as SHERMAN will, no doubt, be content to rest his army for a time, after having attained the great object of his campaign.

Whilst the fall of Atlanta, in consequence of the moral effect, is regretted, its possession is of no material advantage to SHERMAN. He finds there only empty houses, while our communications from Richmond to the extreme South are still open, and as secure as they have been for some months.

Sept. 6.—The enemy disappeared from our front this morning.

CEDRIC.

The Overland Mail.

FORT KEARNEY, Tuesday, Sept. 20.

The superintendent of the overland mail route with agents, stock, &c., left here this morning to re-open the route. A special mail agent will leave to-morrow to see the mails through.

Fire at St. Louis.

ST. LOUIS, Tuesday, Sept. 20.

The flouring mill of A. W. FAGAN, on Seventh-street, was burned last night. The loss is estimated at $150,000. Insurance unknown.

Congressional Nomination.

MIDDLETON, N. Y., Tuesday, Sept. 20.

Hon. CHARLES H. WINFIELD, M. C., from the Eleventh Congressional District was unanimously renominated to-day.

Sheridan's ride

Major-General Philip H. Sheridan

Cavalry charge at Winchester, Virginia, September 19, 1864

The New-York Times.

VOL. XIII.—NO. 4055. NEW-YORK, THURSDAY, SEPTEMBER 22, 1864. PRICE FOUR CENTS.

THE VICTORY.

THE STRATEGY OF THE BATTLE.

The Magnificent Valor of Our Troops.

Terrific Charge of the Infantry.

The Brilliant Onslaught of the Cavalry.

The Enemy's Loss Nine Thousand.

VIGOROUS PURSUIT OF THE REBELS

Our Forces Crossing Cedar Creek Yesterday Afternoon.

The Number of Prisoners Swelled to Five Thousand.

A Demoralized Retreat up the Valley.

OFFICIAL DISPATCH FROM SEC. STANTON,

[OFFICIAL.]

WAR DEPARTMENT, WASHINGTON, Sept. 21—10:15 A. M.

Maj.-Gen. John A. Dix:

This department has just received the following telegram, announcing the continued pursuit of the rebels by Gen. Sheridan. Cedar Creek, which Gen. Sheridan was crossing yesterday at 3 o'clock in the afternoon, is a short distance this side of Strasburgh. He had pursued the rebels over thirty miles from the point where he attacked them at daylight on Monday.

HARPER'S FERRY, Wednesday, Sept. 21.

Hon. Edwin M. Stanton, Secretary of War:

Reliable news from the front states that our army was crossing Cedar Creek yesterday at 3 P. M. There was no fighting.

The following list of rebel Generals killed and wounded is correct: Gens. Rodes, Ramsour, Gordon, Terry, Goodwin, Bradley Johnson and Fitzhugh Lee.

From all I can learn the number of prisoners will approximate to 5,000.

The indications are that the rebels will not make a stand short of Staunton. They are evidently too much demoralized to make a fight.

JOHN D. STEVENSON, Brig.-Gen,

Gen. Grant transmits the following extract from the Richmond *Sentinel* of yesterday:

"The Richmond *Sentinel*, of the 20th, has the following:

A slight ripple of excitement was produced here yesterday, by the report that a raiding party was advancing on Gordonsville, and were within a few miles of that place. The result of all our inquiries on this head is, that this report originated in the fact that early yesterday morning a party of Yankee raiders, whose numbers are not known, visited Rapidan Bridge, and after destroying it, proceeded to Liberty Mills, five or six miles above, which they also destroyed. From this latter place they are believed to have gone back to Culpepper."

The operation alluded to by the Richmond *Sentinel* was by a force sent out previous to the battle of Monday.

EDWIN M. STANTON, Secretary of War.

Vigorous Pursuit—Five Thousand Prisoners Captured.

WASHINGTON, Wednesday, Sept. 21.

Information received by the Government up to noon to-day makes it certain that Sheridan has secured 5000 prisoners; and every hour more are being sent to the rear.

GRAPHIC DESCRIPTION FROM OUR SPECIAL CORRESPONDENT.

HARPER'S FERRY, Tuesday, Sept. 20, 1864.

Yesterday morning, contrary to all previous expectation, the Army of Western Virginia attacked the rebel position along the line of the Opequan Creek, and after a desperate struggle of over twelve hours duration, succeeded in driving the enemy from his strong entrenchments, totally routing the entire force under Breckenridge and Early, and capturing five pieces of artillery, fifteen stands of colors, 6,000 prisoners, 3,000 of whom are wounded, and killing over 600, all of whom are now lying on the field in our hands. The battle may fairly be considered one of the most desperate and important of this campaign, so successfully prosecuted by Gen. Grant and his Lieutenants. Our troops behaved splendidly, charging fearlessly upon the most formidable positions with the most daring gallantry, carrying before their resistless onslaught, line after line of the rebel positions, and seized with rapidity guns, colors, and prisoners. While the battle lasted, it raged with great fury, and many instances of individual gallantry were observable. Our loss will not exceed 2,500 in killed and wounded, no prisoners being taken by the enemy. Four Generals of Division on the rebel side were killed, and one seriously wounded. Our forces are in possession of Winchester, and Gen. Sheridan is rapidly pushing up the Valley in hot pursuit of the retreating and defeated foe. A glorious success is thus ours.

OPERATIONS OF SUNDAY.

The initiatory steps in this great and successful drama in the theatre of war were taken by Gen. Early, who, seemingly believing that the railroad had been repaired as far as Martinsburgh, sent a heavy force from his main position, at Bunker Hill, subsequently discovered to be Gen. George Gordon's division of Early's corps (formerly Ewell's) with orders to attack our forces occupying that town and drive them out and destroy the Government works and the railroad bridge. Finding that nothing of any importance in the way of destruction could be accomplished they commenced evacuating, and being subsequently attacked by Averill, were driven back with considerable loss to Darkesville, some five miles distant from Martinsburgh. While these movements were in progress the different corps comprising the command of Gen. Sheridan received orders to pack up and prepare for the road at a moment's notice. These orders were obeyed with all due alacrity, the tents were struck, and the army stood to arms at an early hour, but did not continue long so, for countermanding orders soon after arrived, and the corps went again into camp. At this time Gen. Averill's guns could be heard distinctly, and the feeling became general that an engagement was evidently on the *tapis*.

MONDAY'S OPERATIONS.

In accordance with orders received late on Sunday night, the Sixth and Nineteenth Corps and Gen. Crook's command, with the cavalry, were under arms at daylight, and about five o'clock took up their line of march toward Winchester. The order of march was as follows: the Sixth Corps in the advance, moving out on the Berryville pike in two columns, parallel with and flanking the road, upon which they were instructed to keep their ammunition trains and batteries, the Nineteenth Corps followed the Sixth on the same road, and preserving a similar formation in their line of march. The Kanawha Corps, under Gen. Crook, were to strike out simultaneously with the remainder of the army, and pushing through to the Southwest, were ordered to form a junction with the Sixth Corps at the Opequan Creek, near the Berryville turnpike. Our cavalry, consisting of the Third Division, were meanwhile to take the extreme advance and secure a safe crossing for our advancing columns of infantry. Merritt and Averill were to amuse the enemy on our immediate front and conceal our flanking movements.

SHERIDAN'S PLANS.

It will be readily perceived that the intentions of Gen. Sheridan were to turn Early's right flank and so gain his rear, and for this purpose he changed his lines from, in front of Bunker Hill to turn left by massing his troops by a rapid and simultaneous movement on to the Berryville pike, and so threaten Winchester, eventually to gain, as I have said before, the enemy's rear. By one of those unavoidable and inexplicable mistakes so frequently the stumbling-block to all nicely balanced plans, the Commanding General's expectations were not fully realized, and his intentions partially thwarted. Owing to a misconception of orders, Gen. Emory unfortunately failed to connect with the Sixth Corps as soon as intended by Gen. Sheridan, and thus two valuable hours were lost by the entire army not being concentrated at the appointed time. The delay caused by these untoward circumstances enabled Early to reinforce his right, consisting of Breckinridge's, Rodes' and Ramsour's division, by rapidly marching down to their support Gordon's division. All of these divisions suffered terribly in the engagement that afterward ensued, and Breckinridge was the only division commander who was not killed. While our opening movements were going on Gens. Averill and Merritt threw out a heavy force of skirmishers along the line of the Opequan, directly in front of the position of the enemy at Bunker Hill, and by various other movements attracted their attention, and kept them employed. This manœuvre was doubtless the cause of the great success of the day, for it enabled our troops to gain the right flank of the rebel army without serious opposition, and in a measure deceived Early of our ultimate intentions.

OPENING THE BALL.

At precisely 5 o'clock yesterday morning, Gen. Wilson's division of cavalry pushed up the Berryville Pike, and crossed the Opequan without serious opposition. Moving rapidly up the pike toward Winchester, they soon encountered the rebel line of skirmishers, and speedily drove them back into their field-works, thrown up by them in defence of the ford across the creek at that point. Firing in regular line, by brigade, the entire division moved forward in gallant style, and with a wild hurrah, charged the works themselves, and actually carried them at the point of the sabre, capturing some thirty or forty prisoners, and thus securing an undisputed passage of the Opequan for our infantry. This charge is considered one of the most daring on record; for it is not usual for cavalry to charge fortifications, and it reflects great honor upon the famous Third Division.

THE BATTLE.

Immediately after the capture of the lunettes commanding the ford, the Sixth Corps moved forward, leaving the trains in park on this side of the creek, and pushing up the pike toward Winchester some two miles, formed line of battle, throwing out a heavy line of skirmishers, the artillery attached to the corps at the same time taking up position and vigorously shelling the works in which the enemy had taken shelter. Everything was now ready for an onward movement, when it was suddenly discovered that Gen. Emory had failed to connect with Gen. Wright's Corps, but was still on the other side of the creek. Orders were instantly dispatched to correct this error, and as soon as the Nineteenth Corps arrived it was found in four lines of battle by semi-divisions, a few hundred yards apart, on the right of the Sixths Corps, and then the advance began.

Owing to these different manœuvers and connections it was fully noon before the "advance" was sounded, and during this time the enemy's lines had been greatly strengthened, and was formed in a belt of heavy woods skirting the Berryville pike. All this time portions of their artillery kept up a brisk fire, without inflicting any serious loss on our part. When at last everything was ready, the two corps moved slowly but steadily forward.

The advance of our troops was an imposing one. The different lines of battle marched forward with a composure truly gratifying, and almost as cool as on parade. The various Division, Brigade, and Regimental banners floating gaily in the sunlight, with drums beating, enlivened the scene, and gave the spectacle a festive appearance seldom witnessed in the woody wilds of America. On, on, went our gallant boys, to victory and triumph.

The first line of battle had advanced but a few hundred yards when they received a heavy volley from the enemy, and soon became hotly engaged with the rebels, then some six hundred yards distant. Our batteries simultaneously by opening a searching fire, pitching shell and shot into the woods spoken of before with great rapidity, and harassing the rear columns of the enemy, and embarassing the movements of reinforcements, which could be seen moving up.

At this time Gen. Sheridan rode along the lines, and was received with great enthusiasm by the men, and his presence seemed to animate them with renewed determination and an unflinching performance of their perilous duty.

Our troops continuing to move forward, despite the murderous fire of the enemy, they succeeded in getting within two hundred yards of the rebel lines, when a furious cannonade broke out from some batteries hitherto concealed, and by their repeated discharges of grape and cannister mowed down large numbers of our men. So heavy and destructive was the fire from these batteries that our advanced line was compelled to fall back, thus momentarily deranging the formation of the second and third lines of battle. The order was quickly given for the men to lie down, in order to avoid the effects of the showers of grape that were plowing through their ranks.

Our artillery was then rapidly brought up and given commanding positions, from which they soon commenced a withering cannonading of the enemy's advanced position, under the protection of which our lines, now reformed, again advanced, and after a desperate resistance on the part of the rebels, the enemy were compelled to fall back, and we once more gained the position we had lost. After this achievement both corps were ordered to lie down in the lines of battle as they then were, in order to await the arrival of Gen. Crook's command, which was up to this time lying in reserve on the eastern bank of the Opequan Creek. Gen. Crook was ordered to take up a position on the right of the Nineteenth Corps, with a view to check an expected attempt of the enemy to turn our right flank, who could be seen massing his troops on his left for that purpose. It was nearly 3 o'clock when Crook formed his line on our right, his second line being in rear of and supporting the Nineteenth Corps.

ARRIVAL OF THE CAVALRY.

Gen. Torbert, at this juncture, came up very opportunely, bringing with him both Averill's and Merritt's divisions of the cavalry. They had been fighting all day along the Opequan, after crossing that stream at Burns' and Knox's Ford, meeting with strong bodies of the enemy, and succeeded in successfully and steadily driving everything before them. Their presence was greeted with great satisfaction, for now we had our entire force together.

THE GRAND CHARGE.

Gen. Sheridan, having become satisfied with the disposition of his troops, now gave the signal for the grand and final charge that brought victory to our arms and added one more page to the glorious record of our gallant army. As the order was given, our line, now over three miles long, advanced with long continued and hearty cheers, the sound of which rose strong and clear amid all the roar and crash of artillery and the hoarse and continuous rattle of musketry. The charge was made with a headlong impetuosity impossible to resist, and it was one that will compare favorably with any of the famous movements of a like character during the war.

Our men seemed animated by a sublime feeling of victory already in their grasp, and advanced with an eagerness seldom witnessed in even such old and well-tried soldiers. As our lines pushed on, and drew nearer and nearer to the enemy's position, the battle raged still more fierce, and with a fury impossible to describe. The loss of life on both sides during those few fearful moments must have been very great, for the terrible roar of artillery, and the deep, sullen crash of musketry, told but too plainly of the carnage that was in progress. At every volley, men could be seen dropping in every direction, and frequently the opposing lines could not have been many hundred yards apart.

THE CAVALRY CHARGE.

As we stood listening to the fearful roar and convulsion of the two contending armies, anxiously awaiting the result of the splendid charge of the infantry, then in progress, the bugles of the cavalry rang out "the charge," and thus began the closing event of the day. Moving out with the rapidity of an avalanche our gallant knights of the sabre swept on, and thus aiding our invincible infantry by adding their own resistless weight in the furious onslaught then being made upon the enemy's position, succeeded in gaining the splendid victory now in our hands. This last manœuver was too much for the rebels, and they were forced to fall back stubbornly, it is true, but still compelled to give way, and ultimately to break before our continued and determined efforts on their lines. The cavalry claim to have captured nine of the battle-flags and two pieces of artillery. Gens. Custer and Merritt were conspicuous for the daring manner in which they led their commands into the charge. Gen. D. A. Russell, commanding the First Division, was, as usual, with that gallant and fearless officer, foremost in the fight, and, I regret to say, he was killed instantly by a cannon-ball, while urging on his command. In him the country loses one of its bravest generals.

RETREAT OF THE ENEMY.

The shattered and utterly demoralized divisions that go to make up Gen. Early's command, now fled in utter rout and confusion, throwing away in their panic their guns and equipments, and whatever other *impedimenta* they happened to have on their persons. They started in all directions, pushing for the mountains and Winchester, others doggedly giving themselves up as prisoners. Large numbers of the enemy were captured by our forces during this disastrous retreat, and by this means swelled the heavy list of prisoners already in our hands.

TAKING POSSESSION OF WINCHESTER.

As the head of our column reached Winchester, the Union residents, consisting, of course, mostly of ladies, came out joyously and greeted our victorious soldiers with glad smiles and words of warm welcome for the defenders of that flag which they now so triumphantly waved over their heads. You will remember I spoke in a former letter regarding the Union sentiment I found to be existing in that town, and I recognized several of that same little club of loyal ladies I mentioned at that time among those who welcomed our arms. They all agreed in saying that Gen. Early's army is utterly demoralized and routed, and that his men pushed through with haggard faces and discouraged looks, some frantically rushing down the streets, throwing away everything that would impede flight, and seemingly only bent on a safe and speedy retreat.

THE REBEL LOSS

Cannot be much less than *nine thousand, killed, wounded and missing*, as Gen. Sheridan has just sent in to Gen. Stevenson, in command at Harper's Ferry a dispatch saying that he has taken three thousand prisoners, and I know that the wounded now lying in Winchester will not fall far short of four thousand, besides the large number of dead now on the field, and the immense number of wounded not yet attended to, will still more swell our gains. Among the losses of the enemy they have to enumerate *four of their seven division commanders as killed*, three of whom are Major-Generals, Rhodes, Geo. Gordon, and Ramsour, the other is Brig.-Gen. Wharton. General Bradley Johnson is also reported badly wounded.

OUR LOSSES

have been severe, but nothing like an approximate figure to that of the enemy. The total number will not exceed 2,500, in killed and wounded, no prisoners being lost. Amongst our killed stands foremost the gallant old general, D. A. Russell, a fearless soldier and true gentleman. His loss will be severely felt in the glorious old corps to which he had so long been attached. Col. Elright, of the 126th Ohio, of Gen. Upton's Division of the 6th Corps (who was himself wounded), was killed; also another very promising and brave officer, Lieut.-Col. Brewer, of the 7th Michigan, was killed. Owing to the impossibility of gleaning anything like an accurate or full list of casualties when I left Winchester late last night, I am unable to forward you more than the above. Costing as it did so many valuable lives, it must be acknowledged that this battle was one of the most determined during the present campaign, and while we mourn the loss of the brave men who thus offered up their lives on the altar of their country, yet we must rejoice over the signal victory thus achieved over the rebels in this valley, so long their boasted vantage-ground.

G. F. WILLIAMS.

From the Army of the Potomac—No Attack Yet.

WASHINGTON, Wednesday, Sept. 21.

Information from the Army of the Potomac is to the effect that nothing of importance has occurred for the past three or four days.

The attack of the enemy expected on Monday did not take place, although from indications it was believed that the rebels seriously meditated an assault.

Scarcely a shot had been heard along the line for twenty-four hours.

Numbers of deserters were coming in daily, but they brought no news.

SHERMAN VS. HOOD.

THE UNION OCCUPATION OF ATLANTA.

Reply of Gen. Sherman to Gen. Hood.

HOOD VERY BADLY BEATEN ONCE MORE.

Abstract of the Entire Correspondence.

WASHINGTON, Wednesday, Sept. 21.

The following is the reply of Gen. Sherman to Gen. Hood's charge of "studied and ungenerous cruelty," and which was received in Washington to-day:

HEADQUARTERS MILITARY DIVISION OF THE MISSISSIPPI AND IN THE FIELD, ATLANTA, Ga., Sept. 10, 1864.

Gen. J. B. Hood, Commanding Army of the Tennessee Confederate Army.

GENERAL—I have the honor to acknowledge the receipt of your letter of this date at the hands of Messrs. Ball and Crew, consenting to the arrangements I had proposed to facilitate the removal south of the people of Atlanta who prefer to go in that direction. I enclose you a copy of my orders, which will, I am satisfied accomplish my purpose perfectly. You style the measures proposed "unprecedented," and appeal to the dark history of war for a parallel as an act of "studied and ungenerous cruelty." It is not unprecedented, for Gen. Johnston himself very wisely and properly removed the families all the way from Dalton down, and I see no reason why Atlanta should be excepted. Nor is it necessary to appeal to the dark history of war when recent and modern examples are so handy. You, yourself, burned dwelling-houses along your parapet, and I have seen to-day fifty houses that you have rendered uninhabitable because they stood in the way of your forts and men. You defended Atlanta on a line so close to the town that every cannon-shot and many musket shots from our line of investments, that overshot their mark, went into the habitations of women and children. Gen. Hardee did the same at Jonesboro, and Gen. Johnston did the same last Summer at Jackson, Miss. I have not accused you of heartless cruelty, but merely instance these cases of very recent occurrence, and could go on and enumerate hundreds of others, and challenge any fair man to judge which of us has the heart of pity for the families of a "brave people." I say it is a kindness to these families of Atlanta to remove them now at once from scenes that women and children should not be exposed to, and the brave people should scorn to commit their wives and children to the rude barbarians who thus, as you say, violate the laws of war, as illustrated in the pages of its dark history. In the name of common sense, I ask you not to appeal to a just God in such a sacrilegious manner—you, who, in the midst of peace and prosperity, have plunged a nation into civil war, "dark and cruel war," who dared and badgered us to battle, insulted our flag, seized our arsenals and forts that were left in the honorable custody of a peaceful ordnance sergeant, seized and made prisoners of war the very garrisons sent to protect your people against negroes and Indians, long before any overt act was committed by the (to you) hateful Lincoln Government, tried to force Kentucky and Missouri into the rebellion in spite of themselves, falsified the vote of Louisiana, turned loose your privateers to plunder unarmed ships, expelled Union families by the thousand, burned their houses, and declared by an act of your Congress the confiscation of all debts due Northern men for goods had and received. Talk thus to the marines but not to me, who have seen these things, and who will this day make as much sacrifice for the peace and honor of the South, as the best born Southerner among you. If we must be enemies, let us be men, and fight it out as we propose to-day, and not deal in such hypocritical appeals to God and humanity. God will judge us in due time, and he will pronounce whether it be more humane to fight with a town full of women and the families of a "brave people" at our back, or to remove them in time to places of safety among their own friends and people.

I am, very respectfully,
your obedient servant,
(Signed) W. T. SHERMAN,
Major-Gen. Commanding.

Official copy: Signed L. M. Dayton, A. D. C.

CORRESPONDENCE BETWEEN GEN. SHERMAN AND GEN. HOOD.

From the Richmond Examiner, Sept. 19.

The Georgia papers bring us a considerable mass of correspondence which has lately taken place between Gen. Sherman and Gen. Hood. As we have not space to give this correspondence in full, we present an abstract of it, which will serve every purpose.

We have official copies of the correspondence in regard to the truce of ten days recently entered into by Gens. Sherman and Hood. In his letter to Gen. Hood, Sherman says that he "deems it the interest of the United States that the citizens now residing in Atlanta should be removed; those who prefer, to go South, the rest North;" and if Hood consents, he (Sherman) offers to undertake the removal of families in Atlanta who prefer to go South, as far as Rough and Ready. In regard to the slaves, the correspondence mentions as one of its conditions that servants may be permitted to accompany their masters, provided no force be used toward them, one way or the other; if they wish to go with their masters and mistresses, they can do so; otherwise they are sent away or employed by the Quartermasters. To carry out this object Sherman proposes a truce of ten days.

Hood replies, saying that he does not consider that he has any alternative in the matter, and that he accepts the proposition. In closing his letter Gen. Hood protests "in the name of the God of humanity against the expulsion of the people of Atlanta from their firesides," and declares, while he accepts it, that Sherman's position "transcends the studied and ingenious cruelty of all acts ever before brought to the attention of mankind, even in the darkest history of war."

The subject of correspondence number two is in regard to the exchange of prisoners held on both sides. The first letter comes from Hood. He proposes "an exchange of prisoners, officers and men, captured by both armies since the commencement of the present campaign; the exchange to be made man for man, and the equivalents to be allowed as regarded by the stipulations of the cartel." Sherman replies to this, informing Hood that he accepts his offer; the basis of exchange to be the old cartel. This is quickly followed by another letter from Sherman, saying that he cannot recall those prisoners who may have reached beyond Chattanooga; that on arriving at Nashville they properly fall under the jurisdiction of the Commissioner, Col. Hoffman; but proposing to exchange such as he has on hand. He says he holds on the spot twenty-eight officers and seven hundred and eighty-two enlisted men, and en route for Chattanooga ninety-three officers and nine hundred and seven men, making one thousand, eight hundred and ten on hand, that he will exchange for a like number of his own men, captured by Hood in this campaign, who belong to regiments with him, and who can resume their places at once. He takes it for granted Hood will do the same with his. In other words, for these men he (Sherman) is not willing to take equivalents belonging to other armies than his own, or who belong to regiments whose times are out and who have been discharged. Sherman further says that by the laws of the Confederate States all men eligible for service are *ipso facto* soldiers, and if needed for civil duty they are simply detailed soldiers; that he found in Atlanta "about a thousand of these fellows," and that he is satisfied they are fit subjects of exchange, and proposes if Hood will release an equal number of their prisoners at Andersonville, he (Sherman) will gather these together and send them as prisoners, and will take for them men belonging to any part of the United States army, subject to Hood's control.

Hood replies to this, reminding Sherman that he had previously accepted his offer "to exchange prisoners of war in hand at this moment"; that there was no condition attached to the acceptance on Sherman's part of his offer to exchange prisoners, and that he (Hood) regards it as obligatory to the extent of the number of prisonerrs repesented by Sherman to be within his jurisdiction. He says that Sherman's refusal to receive in exchange his soldiers belonging to regiments whose times are out, and who have been discharged, discloses a fixed purpose on the part of his Government to doom to hopeless captivity those prisoners whose term of service has expired or will soon expire; that the new principle which Sherman seeks to interpolate upon the cartel of our respective Governments, as well as upon the laws and customs of war, will not be sanctioned by him; that all captives taken in war who owe no obligation to the captors must stand upon the same equal footing; that the volunteer of a day and the conscript for the war, who may be captured in war, are equally subject to all of the burthens and equally entitled to all of the rights secured by the laws of nations; that this principle is distinctly conceded in the cartel entered into by our respective Governments, and is sanctioned by reason, justice and the public law of all civilized nations. Gen. Hood further says that Sherman's avowal that this class of soldiers (those whose term of service had expired) will not be exchanged is deeply regretted by him, and that he hopes that this declared policy of Sherman's Government will be reconsidered, as it is unjustly oppressive to those whom the hazards of military service has rendered prisoners, and is violative of the well-understood obligations assumed by a Government toward those who are enlisted in its service.

Hood further informs Sherman that his offer to him to effect an exchange of prisoners captured during this campaign, was not only approved, but that the Government placed at his disposal for immediate exchange, man for man, all the prisoners at Andersonville.

Hood renews to Sherman his offer to exchange prisoners as proposed in his first communication, and here the matter ends.

RAILROAD DISASTERS.

Frightful Accident on the Pennsylvania Railroad—Twenty Persons Killed and Injured.

PHILADELPHIA, Wednesday, Sept. 21, 1864.

The fast-line train, going eastward on the Pennsylvania railroad which left Pittsburg last night at 8:40, ran into the rear end of a freight train on the eastward track at Thompsonton station, Juniata county, Pa., at half-past four this morning. The passenger-train was moving at its usual speed when the accident occured. The engine was demolished and the greater portion of the train was badly wrecked. The baggage-car was driven into the front passenger-car, took fire from the over-setting of a stove, and with three passenger-cars was destroyed.

It is supposed that six persons were instantly killed, or held among the ruins of the cars and consumed with them. John Mullison, the conductor of the passenger train is among the lost.

SECOND DISPATCH.

PHILADELPHIA, Wednesday, Sept. 21.

Thirteen of the passengers were taken from the broken cars, all of whom were wounded, and some seriously, and are all now receiving surgical and medical treatment.

The accident is said to have been caused by the neglect of those in charge of the freight train to give the proper notice to the passenger train, which was on its regular time, that the freight train was occupying the road.

One of the tracks was cleared at 10 A. M., and the business of the road was resumed.

Of the six persons supposed to have been killed or buried in the first car, but two have been recognized, viz: John Mullison, the conductor, and L. Imbrie, brakeman.

Thirteen were injured, as follows:

G. H. Abbott, of Chillicothe, Ohio, injured internally.

William Jones, of Downington, both legs broken.

Temple Jones Reeves, of Philadelphia, one leg broken.

Letiman Goldsmith, of Philadelphia, leg broken.

John Bruch, of St. Clair, Schuylkil County, Penn.

Edward M. Williams, of Baltimore, one arm broken.

Catharine Sterndar, of Indianapolis, wounded in the scalp.

W. Notestine, leg broken.

Solomon Brook, mail agent, dangerous internal injuries.

M. Newkirk, of Alleghany City, injured internally.

John Haviland, of Cannansburgh, Pa., slightly injured.

The engineer and fireman of the passenger train both remained at their posts and are not very seriously hurt.

FURTHER PARTICULARS.

PHILADELPHIA, Wednesday, Sept. 21.

The dispatch announcing a very serious accident on the Pennsylvania Central Railroad is not so complete in its details as a statement made to us by Mr. L. Converse, of Bucyrus, Ohio, who was on the train, and escaped without injury.

The train left Pittsburgh at 9 o'clock on Tuesday night, and at 4 A. M. ran into a freight train, demolishing the engine, and forcing the baggage car on top of the first passenger car, which immediately caught fire. Our informant states that the foremost car, in which the loss was greatest, would contain sixty passengers, and but seven or eight are known to have escaped. The doors were locked. The car was crushed, and partly covered with the wreck of the baggage wagon.

Coals from the locomotive fired the baggage-car, which communicated to the passenger-car and caused the explosion of the gas receiver. The car was burned up with all on board, so that only the charred remains could be found, which were beyond identification.

The conductor was recognized by his keys. Six or seven who still lived when Mr. Converse left, were in such physical agony that nothing could be gleaned from them. Passengers in the third and fourth cars were saved without injury, but the cars themselves were burned.

Mr. Converse thinks that more lives might have been saved if the doors of the car had not been locked. The survivors, to the number of eighty-six, subscribed to a statement to that effect.

Accident on the Hudson River Railroad.

POUGHKEEPSIE, Wednesday, Sept. 21.

A serious accident occurred near Breakneck Tunnel, on the Hudson River Railroad to-day, to the train from New-York, at 8 A. M. An axle of the tender broke, throwing the entire train from the track. Two boys in the baggage-car were killed, and a brakeman and one passenger (a lady) injured. The track has been repaired, and trains are now running regularly.

The War in the Southwest.

ST. LOUIS, Wednesday, Sept. 21.

Dispatches to headquarters announce that a fight occurred on the 19th at the Powder Mill on the Little Rock River, in Southeast Missouri, between a detachment of the Third Missouri Militia, under Lieut. Payer, and a portion of Shelby's command. Our loss was 20 killed and wounded. The rebel loss is unknown. Wounded prisoners report Price at Pocahontas, Ark. One thousand rebels are reported at Chalk Bluff, and 400 at Kennett, preparing to attack Bloomfield, Stoddard County. Shelby was reported at Fort Powhattan, Ark., on the 12th, with from 4,000 to 8,000 men.

Sheridan's Grand Victory.

A salute of one hundred guns was fired yesterday in the Park by Capt. George Mawby, under the auspices of the Union Association, of which Hon. Simeon Draper is Chairman.

Sheridan's Victory Celebrated.

BURLINGTON, N. J., Wednesday, Sept. 21.

A salute of thirteen guns was fired here this evening in honor of Sheridan's victory, and an immense concourse gathered at the City Hall, where addresses were made by Col. Fitzgerald and A. G. Cattell, Esq., of Philadelphia. After the meeting adjourned, the whole assembly marched to the residence of Lieut.-Gen. Grant, and cheered enthusiastically for the Generals, the army and navy, and the Union, the band in the meantime playing national airs.

Celebration.

DANBURY, Wednesday, Sept. 21.

The bells were rung and a salute fired here this day in honor of Sheridan's victory.

IMPORTANT INTELLIGENCE.

LATE NEWS FROM THE SOUTH.

A PEACE CONFERENCE AT ATLANTA.

Sherman Corresponding with Leading Rebels.

An Exchange of Prisoners Between Sherman and Hood.

From Richmond papers of Sept. 19, we get the following interesting intelligence:

FROM GEORGIA.

PEACE RUMORS—EXCHANGE OF PRISONERS AGREED ON.

MACON, Sept. 17.—Rumors are rife to-day, that Gen. Sherman has sent an informal request to Governor Brown, Vice-President Stevens, and H. V. Johnson, to come to Atlanta *and confer with him on the subject of peace.*

Gen. Hood has relieved his Chief of Staff, Brig.-Gen. Shoup, from duty. Major Mason is now acting in that capacity.

Five hundred exiled families have arrived in our lines from Atlanta. Their condition is most deplorable.

A special exchange of 2,000 prisoners has been agreed upon by Gens. Hood and Sherman, and 700 Yankees will be sent forward to-night for that purpose.

MACON, Sept. 16.—Parties arrived here from Atlanta say that great numbers of Sherman's army are going home, and that ten thousand are already gone, and more are following, their terms of service being out.

The whole situation here looks well. Yesterday was observed by the people as a day of fasting and prayer.

FROM MOBILE.

MOBILE, Sept. 16—The Yankee gunboat *Selma* (formerly Confederate) anchored on Wednesday night near one of our batteries on the eastern shore. At daylight yesterday morning she was opened on by the battery, struck twice, when she hastily retreated. The three Yankee gunboats that went up Fish River on Sunday last, stole six thousand feet of lumber, a number of cattle, and destroyed the furniture at Milsmith and Pailor.

THE WAR NEWS.

From the Richmond Examiner, Sept. 19.

The following dispatch from General Lee, received on Saturday, contains the most agreeable news since Gen. Hill beat the Yankees at Reams' Station:

"HEADQUARTERS ARMY OF NORTHERN VIRGINIA, September 17, 1864.

"*Hon. J. A. Seddon, Secretary of War:*

"At daylight yesterday the enemy's skirmish line, west of the Jerusalem plank-road, was driven back upon his intrenchments along their whole extent. Ninety prisoners were taken by us in the operation.

At the same hour Gen. Hampton attacked the enemy's position north of the Norfolk Railroad, near Sycamore Church, and captured about three hundred prisoners, some arms and wagons, a large number of horses and twenty-five hundred cattle.

Gen. Gregg attacked Gen. Hampton on his return in the afternoon, at Belcher's Mill, on the Jerusalem Plankroad, but was repulsed and driven back. Everything was brought off savely. Our entire loss does not exceed fifty men.

R. E. LEE."

We are informed that General Hampton started for a point on James river, south of City Point, where he had learned the cattle were on pasture; but while on the march he intercepted a letter addressed to Grant, which contained the information that the cattle had been removed to Sycamore church. The letter also assured Grant that the beeves were of a very superior quality, and expressed apprehensions that the grazing in Prince George would be insufficient. General Hampton changed his route according to the information given by the intercepted epistle.

The affair on Thursday, in which the enemy attempted a reconnoisance in the direction of Poplar Spring church, was much more inconsiderable and insignificant than we had been led to suppose. If any fighting took place on this part of the line—west of the Weldon railroad—it was of so trifling a character as to be beneath General Lee's notice.

This raid of Gen. Hampton's is one of the boldest and most brilliant things of the war. Leaving Reams' Station, on the Weldon Railroad, ten miles south of Petersburgh, passed behind Grant and took his beeves from a position immediately in the rear of the centre of his lines. Sycamore Church, the point at which the captures of cattle, prisoners, &c., was made, is about fifteen miles south by east of Prince George Court-house.

From information received last night we are disposed to believe that Grant has either given up his designs on the Southside Railroad or is pretending to have done so. There is little doubt that he has been transferring his troops from his extreme left.

There was sharp picket firing along the line south of Petersburgh yesterday.

FROM THE VALLEY.

We have no news from the Valley. Well-informed persons from that section say an able and enterprising leader like Hampton is much needed by our cavalry.

FROM GEN. HOOD'S ARMY.

The telegraph informs us that a partial exchange of prisoners has been agreed upon between Gens. Hood and Sherman.

There were rumors in the army on Saturday that Sherman had sent an informal message, requesting Vice-President Stevens, Gov. Brown and Confederate States Senator Johnson to come to Atlanta, and confer with him on the subject of peace. If Sherman sent any such message, he must be deluded into the idea that in capturing Atlanta he has subjugated the State. We trust he will be soon roughly wakened from this delusion.

POLITICAL.

Massachusetts Democratic State Convention.

BOSTON, Tuesday, Sept. 21.

The Democratic State Convention, which met at Worcester to-day, nominated the following ticket: For election at large—Robert C. Winthrop, of Boston, and Erastus D. Beach, of Springfield: for Governor—Henry W. Payne, of Cambridge; Lieut.-Governor—Thomas F. Plunkett, of Pittsfield; Sec. of State, F. O. Prince; Treasurer, Nathan Clark Attorney-General, S. O. Lamb; Auditor, Moses Bates.

Resolutions were adopted, endorsing the nomination of McClellan and Pendleton, and approving the platform of the Chicago Convention, as embodying the only effective way of restoring the Union and securing a permanent peace. The Convention was largely attended, and the proceedings were characterized by much enthusiasm.

Republican Convention in Connecticut—Nomination of Electors.

HARTFORD, Wednesday, Sept. 21.

The Republican State Convention met in this city to-day, and was largely attend d and harmonious. John I. Waite, of Norwich; John P. Elton, of Waterbury; James G. Balterson, of Hartford; Samuel C. Hubbard, of Middletown; Lubin L. Sayles, of Killingly, and F. A. Benjamin, of Stratford, were nominated as Lincoln and Johnson Electors.

Democratic State Convention in Rhode Island.

PROVIDENCE, Wednesday, Sept. 21.

The National Union State Convention met here to-day, Col. Van Zandt, of Newport, presided. The following gentlemen were nominated as Presidential Electors: Messrs. Robert B. Cranston, of Newport; Wm. S. Slater, of Smithfield; Rowe Babcock, of Westerly, and Simeon Henry Greene, of Warwick.

Nomination of Mr. Laflin.

ROME, N. Y., Wednesday, Sept. 21.

Hon. Addison H. Laflin was this afternoon nominated as Union candidate for Congress in the Twentieth Congressional District.

Proposition of the Rebel Col. Scott to "Come Down."

ST. LOUIS, Tuesday, Sept. 20.

An army officer, just from below, brings a report, derived from Gen. Herron's Adjutant, that Col. Scott, commanding rebel troops near Baton Rouge, sent a proposition to Gen. Herron to surrender 4,000 to 6,000 men, provided Gen. Herron would grant an unconditional pardon to the general officers of the command.

The loss by the burning of Fagin's mill last night was $150,000, on which there was no insurance.

The Charleston Mercury.

DAILY PAPER—TWENTY DOLLARS FOR SIX MONTHS—PAYABLE IN ADVANCE. | VINDICE NULLO — SPONTE SUA SINE LEGE FIDES RECTUMQUE COLLENTUR | COUNTRY PAPER—THREE A WEEK—[illegible] DOLLARS FOR SIX MONTHS—PAYABLE IN ADVANCE.

Volume LXXXV. CHARLESTON, S. C., WEDNESDAY, NOVEMBER 2, 1864. Number 12,207.

THE MERCURY.

WEDNESDAY, NOVEMBER 2, 1864.

A Great Defect.

The recent disasters in the Valley of Virginia appear attributable to a want of discipline on the part of our troops, which goes to justify the idea of General SCOTT, that superior discipline in the Northern army would balance against superior material in the Southern army. A want of discipline caused us the disaster that followed the victory of Shiloh. Then, in an army extemporised and commanded by subordinate officers of little knowledge and no experience, it was somewhat excusable. But to discover it at this time of day, and in a crack corps of veterans, is a discreditable and distressing fact. It is useless to conceal that it is the bane of our military organization—a great source of weakness and danger. The inefficient and capricious administration of military law, by officers of every grade and by the government, tempts men to follow their inclinations, undermines the great cardinal principle of subordination, and destroys authority. Hence all these complaints about desertions, absences without leave, and furloughs overstayed by thousands who are needed at the front. Hence the straggling in action and scattered plundering parties before the victory is actually secured. Ought not the privates to be restrained, kept in hand and held accountable for these military offences? Ought not the company officers; the regimental officers and upwards, to the commanders in chief of the armies? Unless the force of the army be directed and controlled, under a rigid system of responsibility, by a real head, it is a most unwieldy and unsafe machine, liable without reason to sudden disorganization and irretrievable destruction. Can we not prevent absences without leave, straggling and plundering, by a sterner enforcement of discipline? It is competent for the heads of armies to establish it by bearing upon their immediate subordinates and so down to company officers and privates.—A little less of personal popularity—hunting and demagogism and a little more scrupulous fulfilment of duty in military life of all ranks would serve the country, and add much to our strength.

THE VIRGINIA CAMPAIGN.

[From the New York World of October 19th.]

REVIEW OF GENERAL GRANT'S OPERATIONS BEFORE RICHMOND—WHERE HE HAS FAILED OF SUCCESS—THE THREE ATTEMPTS TO CAPTURE LYNCHBURG AND THEIR FAILURES—OUR LOSSES IN THE SHENANDOAH—WHAT MOVEMENT OF GENERAL GRANT THE REBELS FEAR THE MOST—WILL THERE BE ANOTHER RAID INTO MARYLAND, ETC.

BALTIMORE, October 17.

THE SEVEN MONTHS' CAMPAIGN AGAINST RICHMOND CONSIDERED AS A WHOLE.

When it is remembered that the present campaign against Richmond has now lasted seven months, and that it has been carried on under the direction of a single military head, without interference or dictation from any quarter whatever; that all the armies in the service except one, with a few trifling exceptions, have been concentrated for this single purpose; that Gen. Grant has had the co-operation of the four armies of Sigel, Hunter, Wright and Sheridan, one after the other, consisting, as will be shown presently, of ninety thousand troops, all operating in the Shenandoah Valley, and all threatening Richmond with imminent and real peril in the rear, while he himself was operating in its front; that Gen. Grant had under his own immediate command, in front of Petersburg and Richmond, as has been proved by Senator Wilson of Massachusetts, and General H. M. Naglee, over 260,000 men, of whom less than 100,000 now survive; that General Grant's army has occupied its present position before Petersburg ever since the 15th of June last, that is to say for a period of four months; that during this long period no progress whatever has been made toward the capture of either Petersburg or Richmond—when these things are remembered, it is worth while to consider the reasons that have enabled the Confederates, with an army that has been notoriously not one third as large as that under General Grant to defend their capital successfully, and to defeat two, and to baffle another, of the first co operating armies above named. And the reasons, thus considered, will not only show what means the rebels have of defending their capital; but they will prove also that Richmond cannot be taken as long as the siege of Petersburg is persisted in.

THREE ATTEMPTS TO CAPTURE LYNCHBURG.

It will be necessary, first, to recur briefly to the four co operating armies above named, because the same strategy which has been used on the part of the Confederates to defeat *them*, will continue to be used against any subsequent army that may attempt to operate in the Shenandoah Valley. Three of these co-operating armies, namely, those of Sigel, Hunter and Sheridan, have had, in succession, the same task assigned to them, namely, the capture of Lynchburg, in order to facilitate the capture of Richmond by Gen. Grant. They have all failed, and the failure of each one, except that of Gen. Sheridan, was attended with great disaster, as the citizens of Maryland, Pennsylvania and Washington well remember.

DETAILS OF THE FORCES WHICH HAVE FAILED TO CAPTURE LYNCHBURG.

Sigel, who started out on the 4th of May with twenty thousand troops, was defeated by General Breckinridge before the 15th of that month, with a loss of five thousand men. General Hunter took command of all the troops in that military department on the 18th of May. By the 25th his command had been so reorganized that it embraced thirty thousand troops, including the fifteen thousand that were left under Sigel. He was ordered to retain General Sigel in command, and he left him in Winchester with ten thousand troops. He commenced his campaign against Lynchburg about the end of May, having in the four divisions of Generals Crook, Sullivan, Averill and Duffie, fully twenty thousand troops. There being no Confederate army to oppose his march, he left Staunton on the 10th of June, and reached Lynchburg on the 17th. He was defeated there on the 18th, and again at Salem, just west of the Blue Ridge, on the 21st. For it will be remembered that he retreated, not to Winchester, as he ought to have done, but to Parkersburg, on the Ohio River, at the extreme western end of Virginia. His losses, by the time he reached that point, on the 1st of July, amounted to fully ten thousand men; for, in addition to the battles that he fought, the country at that time was little better than a desert, as the new crop of wheat, although ripening, was not yet fit to grind, and his men were in a state of destitution.

CONSEQUENCES OF HUNTER'S BLUNDER.

If he had fallen back to Winchester, he would have saved Sigel and prevented the invasion of Maryland and Pennsylvania in July last. As it was, however, no sooner had Hunter's army begun to move westward from Lynchburg than Early's corps was sent into the Valley. Early, with fifteen thousand troops, attacked and defeated Sigel's ten thousand; advanced to the Potomac, crossed the stream, invaded Maryland, frightened Baltimore, burned the town of Chambersburg, and laid siege to Washington.

General Wright, with the Sixth and Nineteenth corps, advanced from Washington to pursue the retreating rebels, about the 15th July. The remnant of the forces of Hunter and Sigel, say ten thousand men, joined him, and he thus had over twenty-five thousand troops, as he superseded Hunter in command. He lost, in various skirmishes before the 5th of August, five thousand men. But his orders did not allow him to uncover the capital, and on the 6th of August he was superseded by General Sheridan.

In my letters soon after that date I enumerated the various bod es of troops that were placed under General Sheridan's orders. They amounted to fifty thousand men. He was reinforced before the 18th of September by ten thousand more troops. His losses between the 6th of August and the 18th of September amounted to fifteen thousand men. It was during this time that he made two "pursuits" of Early; the one to Strasburg, the other to Winchester and the Opequan river. By the 6th of September, it will be remembered, he was safely intrenched at Berryville. No statement of the losses in his recent campaign, from the 10th of September to the 10th instant, has yet been made public. But it is said to have amounted to 20,000 men.

General Sheridan has now 25,000 effective troops, and yet the Confederates in the Valley were strong enough to send a party two days ago to attack and destroy a whole train of cars on the Baltimore and Ohio Railroad, near Martinsburg; and this work they did most thoroughly. No personal injury was done to the passengers. The mail was carried off, and the newspaper bags and the cars were burned; but the track was uninjured, and the trains are running again to-day.

RECAPITULATION OF THE FORCES REPULSED IN THE VALLEY.

Thus there have been sent to operate in the Valley the following bodies of troops: Sigel's corps, 20,000 added by Hunter, May 15 15,000; the 6th and 19th corps added by General Wright, July 15, over 15,000 men; added by Sheridan August 6, 30,000; additional reinforcements before September 18, 10,000 men; total, 90,000 men. The losses have been, under Sigel, 10,000; under Hunter, 15,000; under Wright, 5000; under Sheridan, 35,000; total, 65,000.

HOW THE CONFEDERATES HAVE BAFFLED THE PLANS OF GEN. GRANT.

The successes of the Confederates in baffling the plans of General Grant is owing in a great measure to the accurate knowledge which they possess of the weak points of General Grant's military character, and this was ascertained before the campaign had been in progress two months. By the end of two months, after active operations had commenced, the rebel leaders knew that General Grant was a military dictator, and that he would have the command of men in unlimited number, and of means to an unlimited extent; but they were convinced that he was a General of very ordinary ability; that he had no definite idea of how Richmond was to be taken: that he had formed no fixed plan for the reduction of the city; that he was a man who would try one expedient after another, but without knowing that any one expedient would succeed; and that the only fixed idea he had about the capture of Richmond was, that if he could starve out the rebel capital it must surrender, and that the best way to that was to capture Lynchburg; and that he was a very obstinate man, and that he would never abandon any expedition that he might undertake as long as his Government would continue to furnish him with the men and the means to carry it on.

Such was the view which the rebel leaders entertained of Gen. Grant's military character, and the progress of the campaign has convinced them of its correctness. Ever since the end of June they have been convinced of these three things: 1st. That Gen. Grant regards the capture of Lynchburg as essential to the success of his operations before Richmond, and that, therefore, he will continue his efforts for the capture of the former place, even if he has to employ a portion of his disposable force for the purpose; 2d. That he regards the capture of Petersburg as essential to the success of his operations before Richmond, and, therefore, that he will not commence real operations against Richmond until he has taken Petersburg; and 3d. That he will not commence real operations against Richmond from the north side of the James River—that is, from Harrison's Landing, or from Malvern Hills, or from Birney's present base at Deep Bottom—until all his other expedients are exhausted, until every expedient of which he can think, or which he can devise, shall have been tried, and shall have failed. Then, they think, he may possibly try to take Richmond from that direction.

WHAT THE CONFEDERATES DREAD.

If Richmond is ever taken at all, it must be in that way. And this fact, and the equally important fact that the Confederate leaders are fully aware of it is clearly set forth in my letters of June 11, 15, 18, 21 and 27; and August 2 and 29. Allow me to quote a few sentences. June 15: "After all other expedients have been tried, and have failed, Richmond, when taken, if taken at all, will have to be taken, the rebel leaders believe, by hard and desperate fighting—fighting comes in at the end of a long and protracted siege; and this fighting will have to be done on the north side of the James river." June 21. "So long as General Grant confines his operations to the south side of the James river, the rebels have no fears for the safety of Richmond. What they fear is, that Gen. Grant seeing the helplessness of reaching Richmond from the south, and the impossibility of cutting them off from their supplies, will again cross the James River, and advance on their capital from Malvern Hills. If Richmond is ever taken it will have to be taken in that way." June 27th: "What the rebel leaders fear from our iron-clad fleet is, that it may be used to cover a movement of our army on Richmond from the southeast. The landing of the little force of General Foster at New Market, June 21st, inspired real terror at Richmond, because it was feared that it was only the advance of a much larger force. The movements of General Grant in that direction will be watched by the rebels with anxious solicitude, for on that field they believe the great contest for their capital will terminate." August 29th: "If General Grant should abandon Petersburg, move his whole army to Deep Bottom, and begin a real attack on Richmond from that point as his base, it would be necessary for the rebels to recall every soldier in Virginia for the defence of their capital."

I am sure I need not apologise for the introduction of these extracts. The facts they contain are as true now as when they were written, and events have proved the correctness of the views which they embrace. They afford, besides, the key to the rebel success in defending their capital; and they are particularly worthy of consideration by military men at the present time because we have now, in the positions held by Birney and Ord, such a magnificent base for operations in that direction.

NUMERICAL WEAKNESS OF THE SOUTHERN ARMIES.

I have spoken of the comparatively small force of Confederate troops defending Richmond. It is substantially the same now, in point of numbers, that it was in May and June last, for whatever losses have been sustained, have been made by young men who have recently attained to the proper military age. It has consisted during the whole campaign, and consists now, of the nine divisions of infantry of Generals Anderson, Pickett and Fields, in Longstreet's corps; Heth, Wilcox and Ricketts, in Hill's corps, and Wharton, Rhodes and Gordon, in Early's corps; besides three other divisions until recently under Gen. Beauregard. Each division is 5000 strong. These, with 10,000 cavalry and about three hundred pieces of field artillery, in all seventy-six thousand men, constitute the whole strength of General Lee's army. With this little force, General Lee for several months has baffled and defeated the designs of General Grant, with his two hundred and sixty thousand troops on this line, and the ninety thousand troops operating in the Shenandoah Valley; in all, three hundred and fifty thousand troops. This little force has not only defended both Richmond and Petersburg, but it has also defended Lynchburg, held the Shenandoah Valley for months, and drawn thence vast supplies; invaded Maryland and Pennsylvania; advanced to within twelve miles of Baltimore; isolated Washington from the North, and held it in a state of close siege for twenty four hours.

WHY GRANT HAS BEEN BAFFLED BY LEE'S SMALL ARMY.

The following are the reasons, therefore, why the Confederates, with a force not one-third as large as ours, have been able to defend their capital successfully, and to baffle all of General Grant's attempts for its capture: First. Because our immense force has not been concentrated in front of Richmond, but has been divided. Second. Because the Confederates are not operating on interior lines, and have had, in the railroads between Petersburg and Richmond, and between Richmond and Lynchburg, and between Richmond and Gordonsville, the means of rapidly throwing reinforcements wherever they were needed. In spite of all our efforts, we have never been able to prevent them from having the full and constant use of these railroads.—Third. Because, by means of the railroad from Richmond to Culpeper, and the routes through the Shenandoah Valley, they have been able to threaten Washington and Pennsylvania, and this, too, with peril so imminent that it was absolutely necessary to keep a very large Federal force on the line of the Potomac. Fourth. Because the fortifications defending both Richmond and Petersburg are so strong and extensive that they can be held by a comparatively small force at one place, while the main body of the rebels are employed in repelling attacks elsewhere. Fifth. Because the rebel capital is absolutely inaccessible by water, as I demonstrated months ago, in the face of persistent denials at the time, and as has been abundantly proved since. And sixth. Because Gen. Grant has persisted in frittering away four months before Petersburg, and in dividing his strength between that place and Richmond, instead of concentrating his forces before the latter city.

WE MUST CHANGE OUR PLANS.

These reasons are in full force now. They will continue to operate with equal—even with greater force in the future. And it may safely be said that Richmond can never be taken as long as General Grant persists in his previous policy; never, until all of our land forces are concentrated where Birney is now, and Farragut, or some man like him, takes our fleet up the river, past Fort Darling.

ABSURDITY OF COMPELLING THE EVACUATION OF RICHMOND BY STARVATION.

The idea of starving Richmond into a surrender, or of compelling its evacuation by starvation, with such a country as Virginia at its back, has been proved by the events of the last four months to be as absurd and ridiculous as was the original idea that the whole South could be starved into submission. And yet, for three years, the latter idea was extensively believed at the North. Its means of supplies are ample. Who believes now that Lynchburg can be captured? It might be expected that Sigel and Hunter would have failed to take the place, and yet their armies were large and well appointed, and the rebel force opposed to them was small. But, what shall be said after the failure of Sheridan? Where can there be found a more energetic and more competent General than he? and more competent lieutenants than Wright, Emory, Crook, and Averell? When can we organize, for a campaign in the Shenandoah Valley, a more effective army than the one he started out with on the 19th of September, and the shattered remains of which are now probably at Berryville? When can there be so favorable an opportunity for the capture of Lynchburg as was afforded last month, when the peril to the rebel capital was so great that not a single soldier could be sent away from it; when it was only defended by a brigade of militia under Gen. Colston, and when the whole valley was overflowing with the plenty that has now been destroyed by the orders of General Grant?

THE REBELS EXPECT NOW A CONCENTRATED ATTACK ON RICHMOND.

The result of General Sheridan's campaign will relieve the Confederates of all apprehensions in regard to Lynchburg for many months to come. The rebel leaders will have sense enough to know that what General Sheridan and his splendid army could not do, cannot be done at all, and therefore that Lynchburg is absolutely safe until next summer, at least. What they will look for now will be a concentrated attack on Richmond, to be made by General Grant before winter sets in, by all the troops that can be raised for that purpose. Already the Richmond papers are hinting that Sherman is sending troops to the east to reinforce Grant. I need not say that they are confident of their ability to repel any such attack. But let the government beware that, in whatever they do this fall and winter, the line of the Potomac is not left uncovered. The Confederates have no troops to spare just now for a regular invasion of the North.—But it may be written down as a certainty that, if the line of the Potomac is left unguarded, or guarded by an inadequate force, and the roads remain good till the first or middle of November, a body of 5,000, or 10,000 rebel horsemen will dash through the Shenandoah Valley and visit upon the innocent and helpless people of Pennsylvania the same needless and useless cruelties which the mistaken policy of Grant and Sheridan led them to inflict upon the innocent and helpless women and children in the Shenandoah Valley.

The New-York Times.

VOL. XIII.—NO. 4057. NEW-YORK, SUNDAY, SEPTEMBER 25, 1864. PRICE FOUR CENTS.

SHERIDAN'S GREAT VICTORY.

Additional Official Accounts.

How the Battle of Fisher's Hill was Fought and Won.

Magnificent Gallantry of Our Troops.

The Rebels Throw Down their Arms and Run.

Sixty-two Hundred Prisoners Accounted for by Gen. Stevenson.

REBEL ACCOUNTS OF THE BATTLE.

A Disastrous Defeat Admitted.

OFFICIAL ANNOUNCEMENT FROM GEN. LEE.

WAR DEPARTMENT, WASHINGTON, Sept. 24—10 A. M.

Maj.-Gen. Dix:

The following official dispatch has just been received from Gen. SHERIDAN, detailing some of the particulars of the battle and victory at Fisher's Hill:

HEADQUARTERS MIDDLE DIVISION, WOODSTOCK, Va., Sept. 23—8 A. M.

To Lieut.-Gen. U. S. Grant, City Point:

I cannot as yet give any definite account of the results of the battle of yesterday. Our loss will be light. Gen. CROOK struck the left flank of the enemy, doubled it up, and advanced down their lines. RICKETT's division of the Sixth Army Corps swung in, and joined CROOK. GETTY's and WHEATON's divisions took up the same movement, followed by the whole line, and, attacking beautifully, carried the works of the enemy.

The rebels threw down their arms and fled in the greatest confusion, abandoning most of their artillery. It was dark before the battle ended. I pursued on after the enemy during the night to this point with the Sixth and Nineteenth Corps, and have stopped here to rest the men and issue rations.

If Gen. TORBERT has pushed down the Luray Valley according to my directions, he will achieve great results.

I do not think that there ever was an army so badly routed. The Valley soldiers are hiding away and going to their homes.

I cannot at present give any estimate of prisoners. I pushed on regardless of everything. The number of pieces of artillery reported captured is sixteen.

P. H. SHERIDAN, Major-General.

You are directed to cause a national salute of one hundred great guns to be fired for the victory.

Gen. STEVENSON reports that 3,000 prisoners from the field had reached Winchester last night.

Reinforcements and supplies have been forwarded by Gen. SHERIDAN.

EDWIN M. STANTON, Secretary of War.

Semi-Official Particulars.

WASHINGTON, Saturday, Sept. 24—12:30 P. M.

The *Republican* extra makes the following announcement:—The Government received dispatches from Gen. STEVENSON this A.M., dated Harper's Ferry, announcing that 2,000 Strasburgh prisoners reached Winchester last night. He also states that 1,600 of the prisoners captured on the 19th inst., near Winchester, arrived at Harper's Ferry this morning, and that 1,600 more are yet to come. A later dispatch received from Gen. STEVENSON this forenoon, announces that 1,600 more prisoners, captured at Strasburgh on the 22d, reached Winchester this morning. When last heard from, EARLY's army was flying down the Valley, panic-stricken. SHERIDAN is hot in pursuit, and near Woodstock.

REBEL ACCOUNTS.

A Defeat Admitted—Death of Gens. Rodes and Godwin—Fitz Lee Wounded.

THE WAR NEWS.

From the Richmond Dispatch, Sept. 22.

A report was in circulation at an early hour yesterday morning that a fight occurred near Winchester, in the Valley of Virginia, on Monday last, which resulted disastrously to the Confederate arms. As usual, when any unfavorable news is afloat, the grossest exaggerations prevailed, until the following official dispatch from Gen. LEE was given out by the authorities:

HEADQUARTERS ARMY NORTHERN VIRGINIA, Tuesday, Sept. 20.

Hon. James A. Seddon:

Gen. EARLY reports that on the morning of the 19th, the enemy advanced on Winchester, near which place he met his attack, which was resisted from early in the day till near night, when he was compelled to retire. After night he fell back to Newtown, and this morning to Fisher's Hill.

Our loss reported to be severe.

Major-Gen. RODES and Brig.-Gen. GODWIN were killed, nobly doing their duty.

Three pieces of artillery, of KING's battalion, were lost.

The trains and supplies were brought off safely.

(Signed,) R. E. LEE.

Newton, the point to which our forces fell back on Monday night, is about eight miles this side of Winchester, at the intersection of the Valley turnpike and White Post roads. Fisher's Hill is adjacent to Strasburgh, some eight miles south of Newtown. We have no further particulars of the battle than furnished by the official dispatch, except that Major-Gen. FITZ LEE received a painful, though not dangerous, flesh wound in the thigh.

SHERIDAN, having been reinforced from GRANT's army, was enabled to bring overwhelming numbers against the Confederates, who resisted nearly an entire day before falling back, and the fact that our trains and supplies were brought off safely, shows that it was no rout.

As in all other engagements of magnitude, we have to mourn the loss of many brave officers and men, the most prominent among whom is Maj.-Gen. ROBERT E. RODES, who fell nobly doing his duty. Maj.-Gen. RODES was born in Lynchburgh, Va.; was the son of DAVID RODES, and at the time of his death was about thirty-four years of age. He received a military education, and was for some time an assistant Professor in the Virginia Military Institute. Subsequently, in the capacity of Civil Engineer, he was engaged in the construction of various railroads in the South, and located at Tuskegee, Ala., where he married. On the breaking out of the war, he came to Virginia as Captain of an Alabama company, and, winning distinction by meritorious conduct in the field, rose rapidly from this rank to that of Brigadier. In conformity with a dying request of Gen. T. J. JACKSON, he was subsequently made a Major-General, and appointed to the command of a division, a position which he has filled with honor to himself, and was justly esteemed as one of the most brave and gallant spirits of our army.

Brig.-Gen. ARCHIBALD C. GODWIN was a native of Nansemond County, Va. He was in California at the time of the breaking out of the war, but left for Virginia immediately upon her secession and offered his services to his country. He was assigned to the command of the military prison at Salisbury, N. C., and afterward had charge of the prison in Richmond. Receiving the appointment of Provost-Marshal of this city, he discharged the arduous duties of the position with much credit, but resigned and returned to Salisbury and raised the Fifty-seventh North Carolina Regiment, of which he was appointed Colonel. He led the command through many hard-fought battles, and was finally wounded and taken prisoner. Soon after his exchange he was made a Brigadier, and at once returned to the field, where he had been actively and arduously engaged up to the time of his death. His age was about thirty-six years. It is thought that his remains will be brought to Richmond for interment.

FROM PETERSBURGH.

On some portions of the lines in front of Petersburgh, within the past few days, the picket firing and mortar shelling have been quite brisk, and it is believed that a considerable number of the foe have fallen victims to the unerring aim of our sharpshooters. This was particularly the case on Tuesday, but beyond this nothing of importance occurred, nor was there any change in the general situation. The Yankees have heard of the capture of a large number of cattle by Gen. HAMPTON, and in their accounts are content with the reflection that "a large number of the raiders are reported to have been captured, with some of the cattle." It is said, however, that the Yankee officers are sorely nettled in consequence of the event, as good beef is scarce among them, and the chances of supplying the empty cattle-pens are slim indeed. Meanwhile our boys are enjoying the steaks and roasts, and unanimously vote Gen. HAMPTON a most skillful commissary.

On our extreme right—the enemy's left—both parties continue to watch one another with sleepless vigilance. Each returning day adds strength to the defensive works, and the tug of war, come when it may, will be one of the bloodiest of this very bloody contest.

It is a notorious fact that GRANT has, up to a very recent period, been giving his troops rations of whisky, and has frequently carried them into battle under the inspiration of this "Dutch courage," fearing to trust their natural qualities in this respect. We learn that he has changed his system entirely, and that an order has been issued positively prohibiting the bringing within the lines of the armies operating against Richmond of any spirituous, vinous, or malt liquors, except such as are brought by the commissary or medical departments. Probably GRANT thinks that he, with BUTLER's help, can do drinking enough for the whole army, and hence the withdrawal of the whisky rations from the "rank and file."

We perceive that the army commanded by Beast BUTLER, on the Southside, is now officially recognized by the Yankee War Department as the "Army of the James."

A report was brought over by the ambulance train last evening that the enemy yesterday made a feeble attack upon our advanced works and was repulsed. It is proper to state, however, that persons who arrived at a later hour had heard nothing of it. The usual cannonading took place on the lines yesterday morning.

FROM GEORGIA.

A letter from Lovejoy's Station, dated the 16th instant, gives the latest intelligence from Georgia as follows:

The court of inquiry in relation to the loss of stores at Atlanta has been concluded. There are rumors in camp of several important official changes, transfers, &c., of too visionary a nature to be made the subject of newspaper gossip. Major EUSTIS is temporarily acting chief of staff of this army.

A number of ladies arrived at headquarters, applicants for permits to go through the lines. The inspector-general's office is besieged daily with citizen visitors; and the acknowledged patience and good temper of that energetic official are sorely tried by a thousand and one importunities for personal favors from a thousand and one of the most impracticable and unreasonable sort of people.

The flag-of-truce letters sent forward under the auspices of Major CLAIR, Confederate truce officer, have been permitted to pass. Also, a few telegraphic dispatches have been permitted over the Federal wires to Nashville, and replies received within twelve hours.

An exchange of prisoners, two thousand on each side, has been effected between our Commissioner of Exchange, Col. G. A. HENRY, and Col. WARNER, of SHERMAN's army. After the necessary preliminaries, the two thousand Federal prisoners will be brought forward, and an equal number of Confederates from the other side, for exchange.

Gen. HOOD appears to be in as cheerful a flow of spirits as his brave and patriotic veterans. I saw him to-day surrounded by a group of major-generals and brigadiers, in social converse, under an oak tree. Where the next campaign will be is scarcely ever discussed. At present, there are no evidences of a movement. But I have reason to predict that before many moons have waned, the Federals will hear of HOOD and his army through quite a novel and unexpected channel.

Fourth New-York Cavalry—Mosby's Captures—Union Ladies—Circular No. 61 as Modified by Circular No. 73.

From Our Own Correspondent.

MIDDLE MILITARY DIVISION, Saturday, Sept. 17, 1864.

The army recently lost the services of one of its most active and efficient cavalry officers in the person of Col. DI CESNOLA, of the Fourth New-York Cavalry, whose term of service has expired. At the request of his superior officers he remained in command of a brigade (Second of the First Division) some weeks after his time was out, and during that period participated in several spirited engagements, including that at Front Royal or Crooked River, Leetown and Smithsburgh. The Colonel's conduct in the service stands without reproach. Being a military man by education as well as profession it is to be hoped that he may be again induced to take up arms in defence of the Union. Between May 11 and Aug. 25 the Fourth New-York lost in killed and wounded 111 officers and men out of 290.

In my last letter reference was made to some of our soldiers who were captured by MOSBY, without making any resistance. Another case of a similar kind occurred about the middle of last month, when MOSBY captured a train at Berryville, guarded by some of the one hundred day's men, who ran away without a firing a shot. One of these men, who abandoned his musket at the first alarm, upon arriving at a place of safety, all out of breath, gasped out: "This is the second fight our regiment has been in, and got licked both times!" The remark caused some amusement.

UNION LADIES IN WINCHESTER.

It is pleasant to be able to record the fact that while there are many Secessionists in this valley, occasionally good Union people are to be found—men and women both—who from the first have been true to the Stars and Stripes. These persons are more frequently seen in Winchester than in any other place in the valley—outside of Harper's Ferry—I have visited. Physicians and hospital attendants who have been compelled to remain in Winchester with the sick and wounded when not occupied by our troops, are loud in their praises of many ladies who, despite the gibes and jeers of their rebel sisters, and at the risk of persecution, have come forward freely in aid of Union sufferers in hospitals—furnishing all the little delicacies and attentions so agreeable and useful in a sick room. Long and a happy life to the patriotic women of Winchester is the prayer of every Union soldier in this valley.

A WELL DIRECTED SHOT.

In the fight near Harper's Ferry in July last, a shot fired from one of Col. GRAHAM's guns (Fifth New-York Heavy Artillery) on Maryland Heights, disabled three of the enemy's guns, according to the official report made at the time. The shock struck the muzzle of the first gun, the trunnion of the second, and the coupling-piece of the third. Effective shooting that. I have just received copy of circular (No. 73) issued by the War Department explaining circular No. 61, which was interpreted to mean that all officers who have been mustered for formation would be held to service three years from the time of mustering, reference to which was made in a previous letter. For the benefit of all concerned I annex the circular last issued, No. 73:

WAR DEPARTMENT, ADJUTANT-GENERAL'S OFFICE, WASHINGTON, Sept. 6, 1864.

CIRCULAR, No. 73.—Circular No. 61, current series, from this office, does not impair or modify, in any way, the requirements of Circular No. 36, same series.

When the regiment, company, or other command of a regimental officer is mustered out, it must be distinctly understood that the officer will be considered as mustered out therewith, and at the same "*time and place*" as the command.

An officer "*is held to service*," for the full term of his muster, only when the regulation command is retained in service for him.

Occasion is here taken to remind officers, absent from their commands on detached service, sick, or otherwise, that it is their duty to keep themselves fully advised as to the dates at which their commands go out of service, so that they may be mustered out and discharged therewith. (See Circular No. 36, current series, from this office.) *Officers neglecting this precaution will be held to a strict and rigid accountability.* In cases of doubt, timely application should be made to the Adjt.-General of the Army for information.

E. D. TOWNSEND, Asst. Adjt.-Gen.

This explanatory order will doubtless give general satisfaction in the army.

E. A. PAUL.

THE ARMY OF THE POTOMAC.

Picket Firing—Casualties.

HEADQUARTERS ARMY OF THE POTOMAC, Thursday, Sept. 22—P. M.

The firing between the pickets in front of the Third Division of the Second Corps still continues, and casualties occur daily. To-day a private of the Ninety-third New-York was shot through the eye and instantly killed. A Sergeant of the Fifty-seventh Pennsylvania lost a leg this morning. Yesterday a new recruit, who had been here only three days, belonging to the Twenty-ninth Massachusetts, was killed in front of the Ninth Corps, and his pockets were rifled of $450. It was said he was killed and robbed by a rebel sharpshooter; but many doubt the truth of the statement. Recruits should not bring such large amounts of money with them into the field; as a general thing they are never easy until they have either spent or gambled it away, or had it stolen. One man was seen to offer $100 for a canteen of whisky the other day, but he failed to obtain it even at that price.

To-day the batteries of the Third Division of the Second Corps opened on a barn full of rebel sharpshooters, who had been annoying our men for some time past, and caused them hurriedly to decamp.

FRIDAY, Sept. 23.

All quiet this morning. W. D. McGREGOR.

The Baltimore and Ohio Railroad.

WASHINGTON, Saturday, Sept. 24.

The American Railroad, Phœnix Baltimore and Ohio line, has been redeemed from its three months derangement by the victory of SHERIDAN. The Cumberland coal and gas coals from the Alleghanies, and the heavy produce from West Virginia and the more distant States, can now all come forward again to relieve the consumers and improve the markets. Eight miles of track have been restored, with five bridges and four miles of telegraph poles, beside water stations and sidings. The victory occurred on Monday night last. On Tuesday night preparations for restoring the road begun, and the whole line will be in use again by Tuesday next, the 27th instant. The military authorities are taking such steps by occupying and fortification, as will undoubtedly prevent any further serious interruption to the road.

LETTER FROM A SOLDIER.

Trenches—Fatigue—Skirmish—Sharpshooting—The Necessity of a Whisky Ration.

[Correspondent of the New York Times.]

ON FATIGUE DUTY, BEFORE PETERSBURG, Sept. 16, 1864.

In the trenches, on fatigue, skirmish or vidette line, is now the order of the day. My time for keeping you posted in a private's daily experience is limited enough, and I write this on my knee, whilst relieved on fatigue—one hour on, and one hour off. The great expected attack of LEE's army is hourly looked for night and day. The boom of cannon on our right at Bermuda Hundred is heard every day; but on our left all is silent as the grave—the lull preceding the terrible struggle that is to be made for the possession of that vital road. There is pretty sharp picket-firing each evening on our left, said to be where the one hundred rebel prisoners were recently captured, and that neither party can relieve their pickets until trenches are dug from the main line. Last Saturday, the 10th, the rebel battery killed one man (his arm and side blown off), and wounded ten or twelve at work on fatigue.

Since my last there has not been much mortar shelling, but on Wednesday the 14th, there was the heaviest cannonading on our side yet. It was commenced by the rebels, but they were soon silenced. Towards the conclusion, the Dutch battery fired by volleys, and the voice of its commander giving order to fire could be heard over the rebel lines. Shells burst all along their lines and over their batteries, tearing down a tent. Deserters say they lost a good many, and expecting a charge, were drawn up in two lines of battle. Our loss was two men of the Sixteenth N.Y. Heavy Artillery, (on fatigue) one had his head blown off, the other wounded.

The cars can now be heard passing our lines towards the Weldon road, probably the track is completed partly or in whole in that direction. Four men are said to have been killed last night while felling trees in front of a very important battery; they were volunteers who were to have 60 days furlough.

The weather is cool and occasionally chilly in the night, rendering a blanket and overcoat essential to ones comfort. Over 200 of our men were mustered out on Monday the 12th, and left for home with Col. HAWLEY, who, it is said, is on a short furlough of twenty days. Ninety men for duty in the trenches remain. No more sign of pay-day than there was two months ago. Some of the men have written and received money from their friends at home.

Picket firing is kept up pretty, sharp and accurate on both sides. Yesterday two or three shots struck the sand-bag by my head; about a dozen the bank, and the hole I fired through was partially closed two or three times by the flying dirt. The Johnny's probably, thought they had a green horn they would silence. I never took my gun from the hole until the seven charges in the magazine were exhausted, but kept sighted and ready for my chance. Their distance is from five to six hundred yards, and our bullets, if the gun is kept clean, will nearly every time strike in the same place. The result was that we nearly silenced the rebels by noon, and that a battery that fired one gun was completely silenced the remainder of the day. While writing, this battery has fired three shells without injuring any of us.

Our small whisky ration once a day is to us almost as much as our meat. I am no lover of ardent spirits at home, and would not drink one glass in three months, but I have learned its use and necessity here, to our health and comfort. Coarse food, constant duty, danger and excitement, and no money to purchase any of the little luxuries, a man feels in want of for near seven months. I consider the order of Gen. GRANT giving to men half a gill per day as wise and necessary. L. H. V.

Serious Accident.

PHILADELPHIA, Saturday, Sept. 24.

About 2 o'clock, while a number of workmen were engaged in altering the Philadelphia and Erie Railroad depot, at the corner of Sixteenth and Market streets, the braces gave way and the whole building fell down. Seven men (carpenters) were seriously injured, but none killed outright.

A Base-Ball Match Interfered With.

UTICA, Saturday, Sept. 24.

The match at base-ball between the Atlantics, of Brooklyn, and the Utica Club was called at the end of the Atlantic's fourth innings, on account of the rain. The score stood Atlantics four to Utica two, and Utica had one inning to spare. Over 3,000 people were on the ground.

Internal Revenue Decision.

TREASURY DEPARTMENT, OFFICE OF INTERNAL REVENUE, WASHINGTON, Sept. 17, 1864.

SIR: In answer to your letter of the 12th inst., I have to say, that neither yarn, wire, nor any other material used in the manufacture of hoop-skirts, is exempt from taxation which does not fulfil the condition of the law, viz.: prepared for the manufacture of hoop-skirts *exclusively*, and unfit for other use. Any material not so prepared, or if so prepared, unless it is unfit for other use, is taxable.

Yours, respectfully,

E. A. ROLLINS, Deputy Commissioner.

WM. A. PIERCE, Esq., United States Assessor, Johnston, R. I.

FROM ATLANTA.

The Future of the Place—At what Cost it was Won—Col. Ireland.

Correspondence of the New-York Times.

HEADQUARTERS 2D DIVISION, 20TH CORPS, ATLANTA, GA., Sept. 10, 1864.

After a storm there comes a calm. Now that Atlanta is in our possession, and the famed city having passed through the ordeal of a months' shelling, has ceased to be an object of attack or defense, we may sit quietly within its shady precincts and talk of its value and its cost. The rebel army beaten and pursued thirty miles southward, will be "let alone" for a few days to enjoy its own reflections. We shall pause awhile to rest and estimate our gains. Deep into the central portion of the largest and most populous of the Gulf States the Union Army has penetrated and established itself securely. We have set up our tabernacle and hung out our banners on the outer walls of this city. Henceforth Atlanta shall be a Union city, for all its citizens who acknowledge sympathy for the Confederate cause must emigrate southward within a few days. So says Gen. SHERMAN, and he has excellent notions of what is best.

Four months of steady unremitting pursuit of a single object; of patient, intelligent toil and fighting; of sleepless nights and restless days, by an army of noble men under an able leader, have been crowned with a success of which we may well be proud, and for which our fellow citizens at home should rejoice with thanksgiving. Our losses have been heavy, but are not disproportionate to our gains. It is true that back over the bloody forest-path we have trodden for many leagues, fresh mounds of earth concealing lifeless forms of brave men are thickly scattered. In many a wild and dismal glen rearward,

"Each tree which guards its darkness from the day,
Waves o'er a warrior's tomb."

But the dead warriors are not all of one stripe. Beside the patriot in blue, there lies his traitor foe in garb of gray, all strife between them hushed. These are they to whom no sound of victory or defeat shall come; for whom peace shall bring no earthly blessing, and whose footsteps shall no more be heard on the threshold of home. Turn we then to the brighter side of the picture,—to that view of the "situation" which gives hope and good cheer to loyal, Union-loving citizens everywhere. The right arm of the iniquitous Confederacy is broken, its prospects gulfward are dark and threatening, and its inter-communication is severed. We desire no armistice, we cannot afford it; for the sword which we grasped to maintain our national honor and unity, shall in due time give us a lasting peace. We are ready to negotiate on the basis of submission to the government and laws of the United States. The graves of the dead shall be our shrine for repentance, and we will plant around them the cypress and yew trees, as emblems of our mourning.

Columns of Federal troops are entering the city or passing through hourly, accompanied by soul-stirring music and streaming banners. The ladies of Atlanta look on the war-stained heroes with much apparent interest and curiosity. As in HOMER's account of a bridal procession, so here it may be truthfully said:

"Through the fair streets the matrons in a row
Stand in the porches and enjoy the show."

Passing through one of the principal streets, to-day, I saw an old frame building, bearing a sign, on which, in large letters, were the words, "Auction Sales of Negroes." A shell had passed entirely through the edifice, making a hole into which a man could easily crawl. The spectacle suggested the thought that the Union gun which sent the angry messenger with command of thunder, was but uttering the condemnation of God and the civilized world, against the diabolical traffic. It was like a thunderbolt from Heaven speaking for humanity, and carrying destruction to the accursed tenement wherein the dearest rights of man had often been violated.

In the battle near 'Jonesboro', the gallantry of the Fourteenth Corps was especially marked. They charged upon and carried three lines of the enemy's works successively. After the series of battles at and near Jonesboro', and the surrender of Atlanta, our army was withdrawn from its advanced positions and is now being established in Atlanta and important points contiguous, for rest and recuperation. The rebel papers will doubtless chronicle this action on the part of Gen. SHERMAN, as a retreat from Jonesboro', resulting from a defeat at that place. Nothing could be further from the truth. We had captured Atlanta and had most seriously cri[illegible] army, and these results accomplished, [illegible] manity and the welfare of his army dictated to Gen. SHERMAN the propriety of giving his veterans rest.

Four months of most arduous service have justly entitled them to a few weeks of relaxation, during which their rugged clothing may be put off for garments new and clean; shoeless feet may be comfortably shod, arms and accoutrements put in order for another campaign, and the paymasters have an opportunity to dispense their temporal blessings so well and nobly earned.

Col. DAVID IRELAND, for a long time commanding a brigade in GEARY's division, died of dysentery this morning.

Though much enfeebled, he lived to enter the city in triumph at the head of his brigade, and participate in the success to which he had so worthily contributed. He was formerly an officer in the Seventy-ninth New-York Volunteers, by whom he was much esteemed.

The officers of this corps who were so fortunate as to make the acquaintance of his young and accomplished wife, during her short stay with the command last Winter, take this opportunity to publicly express their condolence and sympathy for her in this bereavement.

The congratulatory orders of President LINCOLN, of Lieut.-Gen. GRANT, and last of all the admirable testimonial of Gen. SHERMAN to the troops of his command, have been most eminently gratifying to the whole army. NICKAJACK.

The Georgia State Troops.

IMPORTANT PROCLAMATION FROM THE GOVERNOR OF GEORGIA.

EXECUTIVE DEPARTMENT, MILLEDGEVILLE, Sept. 10, 1864.

Gen. J. B. Hood, Commanding Army of Tennessee:

GENERAL: As the militia of the State were called out for the defence of Atlanta during the campaign against it, which has terminated by the fall of the city into the hands of the enemy, and as many of them left their homes without preparation, expecting to be gone but a few weeks, who have remained in service over three months, (most of the time in the trenches,) justice requires that they be permitted, while the enemy are preparing for the Winter campaign, to return to their homes and look, for a time, after important interests and prepare themselves for such service as may be required when another campaign commences against other important points in the State. I, therefore, hereby withdraw said organization from your command, in the hope that I shall be able to return it with greater numbers and equal efficiency, when the interests of the public service requires it. In this connection, I beg leave to tender to you, General, my sincere thanks for your impartiality to the State troops, and for your uniform courtesy and kindness to me individually. With assurances of my high consideration and esteem, I am, very respectfully, your obedient servant,

JOSEPH E. BROWN.

Great Ratification Meeting in Boston—Gen. Hooker Invited to be Present.

NEW-YORK, Saturday, Sept. 24.

Gov. ANDREW, of Massachusetts, has, to-day, telegraphed to Col. HOWE, the Massachusetts State Agent, to invite in his name Maj.-Gen. HOOKER to attend the grand ratification meeting in Faneuil Hall, Boston, next Wednesday evening. The Governor assures Gen. HOOKER that his presence would be regarded as a great favor, and his reception will be enthusiastic.

Fatal Accident—Sheridan's Victory.

BOSTON, Saturday, Sept. 24.

A locomotive on the Boston and Eastern Railroad exploded last night at Ipswich Depot, killing the fireman and severely injuring the engineer.

One hundred guns were fired at noon to-day in honor of SHERIDAN's victories.

THE SOUTHERN MILITARY PRISONS.

Inquiry by the United States Sanitary Commission—Confirmatory Account of the Martyrdom of our Soldiers in the South.

From the Philadelphia Press, Sept. 24.

On May 19 last, Dr. VALENTINE MOTT, the eminent savant and medical professor; Dr. ELLERSLIE WALLACE, Professor in Jefferson College of this city; Dr. EDWARD DELAFIELD, President of the New-York College of Physicians; Hon. J. I. CLARK HARE, the distinguished Judge of the District Court; Rev. TREADWELL WALDEN, Rector of St. Clement's Church, of this city; and GOUVERNEUR MORRIS WILKINS, Esq., of New-York, were appointed a Committee of Inquiry by the United States Sanitary Commission to make investigation of the terrible reports of suffering which had reached the public from the prisons of the South, and to furnish to our people and the world an authentic statement of facts. This report is at length ready for the public in the remarkable pamphlet before us. It is the digested narrative of a volume of consistent testimony, which will be appended to the report of the Committee. Let us say here that the character of this body of gentlemen is eminently above reproach. They number three distinguished professors of medicine, one of our most estimable judges, and a well known minister of the Gospel.

THE RETURNED PRISONERS.

The condition of our prisoners at Annapolis has already been reported in these columns in a brief, but very suggestive communication from ELLERSLIE WALLACE, M. D., and by testimony of Miss DELIA DIX, whose noble ministration in our hospitals is well known. The present report intensifies the picture presented with so much feeling by Dr. WALLACE. "It was strange to find a Hercules in bones; to see the immense hands of a young giant pendant from *limbs thinner than a child's*, and that could be spanned with the thumb and finger. * * * Men in one part shriveled to nothing but skin and bones, and in another swollen and misshapen with dropsy or scurvy * * the stomach fallen in, deep as a basin, and the bone protruding through a blood-red hole in the hip." There were many like these, and even worse where all was so horrible and sickening, that the pen almost refuses its duty. The photographs of skeletons lately handed around through the North are only pictures of the hopeful cases. Hundreds died from utter weakness and starvation; scores grew insane or imbecile. There was a fearful amount of this awful misery in the prisoners at Annapolis. In the countenances of some of the best cases there was a "look of utter desolateness, of settled melancholy, as if they had passed through a period of physical agony which had driven the smile from their faces forever." Contrast with this piteous picture the boasted chivalry of the South, and the civilization and Christianity of the age.

LIBBY PRISON.

The rooms are one hundred feet by forty. In six of these twelve hundred United States officers of all grades, from brigadier down, were confined for months. This was the almost incredible space allowed them in which to cook, eat, wash, sleep and take exercise. Ten feet by two claimed by each man for all the purposes of living! At one time they were not allowed benches or stools, or even to fold their blankets and sit upon them, but forced to huddle "like slaves in the middle passage;" at another only allowed to make stools out of the barrels and boxes they received from the North; at all times overrun by vermin, in spite of constant ablutions, no clean blankets ever being issued by the rebels; and lying down at night, according to Libby phrase, "wormed and dove-tailed together like fish in a basket." There were two stoves, and seventy-five windows, all broken, and in Winter the cold was intense. Every prisoner had a cough from the damp or cold. It was among the rules that no prisoner should go within three feet of the window, a rule extremely difficult to observe in the crowded prisons of the South. Often, by accident, or unconsciously, an officer would go near a window, and be instantly shot at. In the Pemberton Buildings, near by, as many as fourteen shots were fired in a single day, and very frequently a prisoner fell killed or wounded. It became a matter of sport to "kill a Yankee." Once the guard caught sight of Lieut. Hammond's hand through a boarded enclosure, where there were no windows, and came within an inch of murdering him. Major Turner, the keeper of Libby, remarked: "The boys are in want of practice." The sentry said "he had made a bet he would kill a d—d Yankee before he came off guard." Almost every prisoner had such an incident to tell. Throughout the Southern prison system it is a regular sport to kill Yankees. The guards were never reproved for their willingness to commit murder.

The daily ration in the officers' quarters of Libby Prison was a small loaf of bread, about the size of a man's fist, made of Indian meal. Sometimes it was made from wheat flour, but of variable quality. It weighed a little over half a pound. With it was given a piece of beef weighing two ounces. "I would gladly," said an officer, "have preferred the horse-feed in my father's stable." The corn bread began to be of the roughest and coarsest description. Portions of the cob and husk were often found ground in with the meal. The crust was so thick and hard that the prisoners called it iron-clad. To render the bread eatable they grated it, and made mush out of it, but the crust they could not grate. Now and then, after long intervals, often of many weeks, a little meat was given them, perhaps two or three mouthfuls. At a later period they received a pint of black peas, with some vinegar, every week. The peas were often full of worms, or maggots in a chrysalis state, which, when they made soup, floated on the surface.

Those who were entirely dependent on the prison fare, and who had no friends at the North to send them boxes of food, began to suffer the horrible agony of craving food, and feeling themselves day by day losing strength. Dreams and delusions began to distract their minds. "I grew so foolish in my mind," said Capt. CALHOUN, "that I used to blame myself for not eating more when at home. The subject of food engrossed my whole thoughts."

But the most unaccountable and shameful act of all was yet to come. Shortly after this general diminution of rations, in the month of January last, the boxes, which before had been regularly delivered, and in good order, were withheld. No reason was given. Three hundred arrived every week, and were received by Col. OULD, Commissioner of Exchange, but instead of being distributed, were retained, and piled up in warehouses near by, and in full sight of the tantalized and hungry captives, to the number of 3,000 at least. At length, five or six were distributed during the week. Scores were stolen.

For offences, trivial or serious, prisoners were consigned to cells beneath the prison, the walls of which were damp, green and slimy. They were never warmed, and often so crowded, that some were obliged to stand up all night. Dead bodies, too, were placed in the cellar, and very often were partly devoured by hogs, dogs, and rats. At the time of KILPATRICK's raid, some negroes pointed to the cellar: "Dug big hole down dar, massa—torpedo in dar, sure!" "Should KILPATRICK succeed in entering Richmond," said RICHARD TURNER, "the prison authorities would blow up the prison and all its inmates." "There is enough there to send every Yankee to hell," LIEUTENANT LATOUCHE was overheard to say. TURNER himself said, in the presence of Col. FARNSWORTH, in answer to the question, "Was the prison mined?" "Yes, and I would have blown you all to Hades before I would have suffered you to be rescued." The remarks of Bishop JOHNS is corroborative as well as curious, in reply to the question, "Whether it was a Christian mode of warfare to blow up defenceless prisoners?" "I suppose the authorities are satisfied on that point, though I do not mean to justify it." This passed comment. It is also well to remember that the Inspector of Libby, RICHARD TURNER, was a negro-whipper by trade.

BELLE ISLE.

Here is an inclosure variously estimated to be from three to six acres in extent, surrounded by an earthwork about three feet high, with a ditch on either side. The interior has something of the look of an encampment, a number of Sibley tents being set in rows, with "streets" between. These tents, rotten, torn, full of holes—poor shelter at any rate—accommodated only a small proportion. From ten to twelve thousand men have been imprisoned in this small space at one time, turned into the inclosure, like so many cattle, to find what resting-place they could. So crowded were they that, at the least, according to the estimated area given them, there could have been but a space two feet by seven, and, at the most, three feet by nine, per man—hardly a generous allotment even for a "hospitable grave."

Some were so fortunate as to find shelter in the tents, but even they were often wet with the rain, and almost frozen when Winter set in. Every day some places were made vacant by diseases or by death, as some were taken to the hospital, and some to burial. But thousands had no tents and no shelter of any kind. Nothing was provided for their accommodation. Lumber was plenty in a country of forests, but not a cabin or shed was built, or allowed to be built. Here thousands lay, with the sand for their beds and the sky for their covering, and fog, rain, cold, snow, hundreds blanketless, coatless and shoeless, others with ragged and rotten clothes. There were few fires and little shelter. A severe Winter came, in which the mercury was down to zero even at Memphis, and water left in buckets on Belle Isle froze two or three inches deep in the night. The snow lay deep on the ground around Richmond. The ice formed in the James and flowed in masses upon the rapids on either side of the island.

The men resorted to every expedient to keep from perishing. They lay in the ditch, as the most protected place, heaped upon one another and lying close together, as one of them expressed it, "like hogs in Winter," taking turns as to who should have the outside of the row. In the morning, the row of the previous night was marked by the motionless forms of those "who were sleeping on in their last sleep"—*frozen to death!*

Every day, during the Winter season, numbers were conveyed away stiff and stark, having fallen asleep in everlasting cold. Some of the men dug holes in the sand in which to take refuge. All through the night crowds of them were heard running up and down, to keep themselves from freezing. And this fate threatened them even more than it would have threatened most men exposed to an equally severe temperature, even with such thin clothing and inadequate shelter—*for they were starving.*

Rock-like husky corn-bread (specimens of which we have seen,) meat often tainted, and suspiciously like mule meat; two or three spoonfuls of rotten beans; soup thin and briny, often with worms floating on the surface, made up their food. None of these were given together, and the whole ration was never one half the quantity necessary for bare life. Hear the words of the prisoners:

"There was no name for our hunger." "I was hungry; pretty nearly starved to death." "I waked up one night and found myself *gnawing my coat sleeve*." "I used to *dream* of having something good to eat." "I walked the *streets* for many a night; I could not sleep for hunger." "I lost flesh and strength for want of food." "*If I were to sit here a week I would not tell you half our sufferings.*" These sentences form the very poem of misery and starvation.

"Lice were in all their quarters." Vermin and dirt incrusted their bodies. They were sore with lying in the sand. None, not even the sufferers with diarrhœa, were allowed to visit the sinks during the night, and in the morning the ground was covered and saturated with filth. The wells were tainted; the air was filled with disgusting odors.

Many were taken sick daily, but were allowed to suffer for days before they were removed to the hospitals; and when this was done, it was often so late that the half of them died before reaching it, or at the very moment their names were being recorded.

There was a hospital tent on the island, which was always full of the sick. It had no floor; the sick and dying were laid on straw, and logs were their only pillows. "If you or I saw a horse dying," said one, "wouldn't we put some straw under his head? Would we let him beat his head on a log in his agony?"

THE HOSPITALS.

The hospitals for our prisoners were virtually worse than the prisons themselves. Dr. FERGUSON testifies that, while the wounded were under treatment, the nourishment and stimulation they received were not sufficient to give them a proper chance for recovery. I am surprised that more do not die. Bedding and covering were very dirty and offensive. In three months, out of 2,800 patients, about 1,400 died. The hospitals were nothing less than hospitals for murder.

PHYSICAL CONDITION OF THE REBELS—THE PRISONS IN THE NORTH.

The investigations of the Commission, based on rebel and general testimony, conclusively show that no excuse can be found in the poverty and sufferings of the rebels for this fearful condition of things. The rebels have uniformly testified that they had, generally, good rations, and were well fed. It must be remembered that the cruelty of the rebel prisons is systematic, incessant and regular, however bad it may be. The rations of the rebel soldier was infinitely superior to that of Libby prison, or how could he have endured the marches, fatigue and hardships of so many severe campaigns? There is no room to doubt that the rebel army itself was fully if not abundantly supplied with the common necessaries.

The prisons of the North were next examined by the committee, and in this connection we have the copious and accurate observations of so respectable a gentleman as Judge HARE. We need not say that our rebel prisoners are well, and even kindly and carefully treated in all the particulars in which the rebel authorities are so barbarously cruel. The rations are better than those usually given to rebel soldiers. They have room to walk, to play and to *live*. Fort Delaware is but a common instance of this. The prisoners are required to be cleanly, and to bathe in squads in the river. They live in good health, and even in good humor, finding amusement in their condition, and a tolerable life among themselves. This part of the committee's inquiry is full and conscientious, and furnishes a strange and marvellous contrast to the treatment of our prisoners in Richmond. We may accept the report as history.

FROM NEWBERN.

Mails Received—Abatement of Fever—Arrival of Refugees—Federal Deserters in North Carolina.

NEW-YORK, Saturday, Sept. 24.

By the arrival of the United States steamer *Albany*, via Fort Monroe, we have North Carolina dates to the 22d inst.

The steamer *Fawn*, which was recently captured and burned by the enemy, contained the Boston mail of the 4th and 5th inst., and the New-York mail of the 5th and 6th inst., a large portion of which has been received from the wreck and brought to Newbern.

A flag of truce recently brought into Newbern a large number of refugees, many of whom belong to the first families of the State, who are on their way North, having lost all confidence in the Confederate cause since the fall of Atlanta. Among the number was the wife of the rebel Gen. MARTIN.

The Wilmington and Weldon Railroad advertise a dividend at 10 per cent.

The Salisbury (N. C.) *Watchman* has the following:

We protest against the inhuman treatment extended to the Yankee deserters, who are subjected to a course of treatment, which makes life far more uncertain than the battle field itself. A general pardon from LINCOLN would doubtless relieve the Confederacy of at least fifty thousand of these miserable beings, provided they have strength enough left to enable them to make their escape North.

"The five Federal officers, consisting of a Colonel, Lieut.-Colonel, Major and two Captains, who were dishonorably expelled by Gen. SHERMAN from the army, and sent into the rebel lines for speaking disrespectfully of the President of the United States in the presence of the enemy, while accompanying a flag of truce, have arrived in Richmond, where they are to be confined during the war, for fighting against their principles."

The sudden appearance of the congestive chills and bilious fever in Newbern, has driven all the transient persons out of the department, including many established business men, who supposed they were fleeing from the yellow fever. Surgeon D. W. HAND, Medical Director, Surgeon H. J. METSINGER, Chairman of the Board of Health, and Dr. DOUGHERTY, Post Surgeon, including the other Surgeons at Newbern, who have been employed night and day, making every exertion possible to subdue the malady, are, through their skill and untiring labors, meeting with gratifying success, and now have the satisfaction of seeing a material abatement of this disease, which had assumed the form of an epidemic.

Union Assembly Nomination.

SING SING, N. Y., Friday, Sept. 23.

Hon. GEORGE A. BRANDRETH was unanimously renominated by the Union Convention to-day for Member of Assembly from the Third District of Westchester County.

Nomination of Roscoe Conkling.

UTICA, N. Y., Friday, Sept. 23.

Hon. ROSCOE CONKLING was yesterday nominated for Congress from the Twenty-first District on the first ballot by a vote of 77 to 18. The convention refused to accept his declination.

The Campaign in Kansas.

A CURIOUS ORDER.

HEADQUARTERS, DISTRICT OF NORTH KANSAS, FORT LEAVENWORTH, Sept. 16, 1864.

SPECIAL ORDERS, No. 103.—It having been represented to the General Commanding District of North Kansas, that the officers, soldiers and employes of the Government at Fort Leavenworth were to be furloughed and sent to Leavenworth City to break up a political meeting to ratify the nomination of MCCLELLAN and PENDLETON, to be held on Saturday evening, Sept. 17, and also, that many of the citizens had put on foot such an understanding, it is ordered—That all officers, soldiers or employes on the Military Reservation shall be present at their various quarters, camp depots, &c., till 11 o'clock P. M., Sept. 17, 1864, and the commanding officer of the post and commanding officers of depots are charged with the execution of this order. There will be ample time for the military authorities to interfere on the commission of acts of disloyalty.

By order of Brig.-Gen. T. A. DAVIES.

SAMUEL G. BEDWELL, Lieut, and A. A. A. G.

The New-York Times.

VOL. XIII---NO. 4080. NEW-YORK, FRIDAY, OCTOBER 21, 1864. PRICE FOUR CENTS.

VICTORY!

Another Great Battle in the Valley.

Longstreet Whipped by Sheridan.

VICTORY WRESTED FROM DEFEAT.

The Rebel Attack at First Successful.

Timely Arrival of Gen. Sheridan.

THE REBELS THEN UTTERLY DEFEATED.

Forty-three Pieces of Artillery Captured.

Many Prisoners and a Large Number of Wagons Taken.

Gen. Bidwell Killed, and Gens. Wright, Ricketts and Grover Wounded.

The Rebel Gen. Ramseur Wounded and a Prisoner.

[OFFICIAL.]

WAR DEPARTMENT, Thursday, Oct. 20—10.45 A. M.

A great battle was fought, and a splendid victory won by SHERIDAN over LONGSTREET, yesterday, at Cedar Creek.

Forty-three pieces of artillery were captured and many prisoners, among them the rebel General RAMSEUR.

On our side Gens. WRIGHT and RICKETTS were wounded, and Gen. BIDWELL killed.

Particulars, so far as received, will be forwarded as fast as the operator can transmit them.

EDWIN M. STANTON, Secretary of War.

SECOND DISPATCH.

[OFFICIAL.]

WAR DEPARTMENT, WASHINGTON, Thursday, Oct. 20—10.45 A. M.

Maj.-Gen. Dix:

Another great battle was fought yesterday at Cedar Creek, threatening at first a great disaster, but finally resulting in a victory for the Union forces under Gen. SHERIDAN, more splendid than any heretofore achieved. The Department was advised yesterday evening of the commencement of the battle by the following telegrams:

RECTORTOWN, Va., Wednesday, Oct. 19—4 P. M.

Maj.-Gen. H. W. Halleck, Chief of Staff:

Heavy cannonading has recommenced in the valley, and is now going on.

(Signed,) C. C. AUGUR, Major-General.

HARPER'S FERRY, Va.—6.40 P. M., Wednesday, Oct. 19.

Hon. E. M. Stanton, Secretary of War:

Firing at the front has been continuous during the day. The direction seemed at intervals to be to the left of Winchester, as if at Berry's Ferry.

No news from the front.

(Signed,) JOHN D. STEVENSON, Brigadier-General.

HARPER'S FERRY, Va.—8.45 P. M., Wednesday, Oct. 19.

Hon. Edwin M. Stanton, Secretary of War:

The enemy attacked our army with great impetuosity this morning at daylight.

The attack was made on the left of the Eighth Corps, and was at first successful, they capturing some guns, prisoners and wagons.

Our line was reformed and heavy fighting continued through the day.

SHERIDAN was reported at Winchester this morning, and went out to the front.

The particulars received are not official, and are not favorable, though no serious disaster could have occurred without direct news from SHERIDAN.

Respectfully,

(Signed) JOHN D. STEVENSON, Brigadier-General.

Matters remain in the doubtful state represented by the foregoing telegrams until this morning, at 9.30, when the following telegram was received, unofficially, reporting the great victory won by SHERIDAN's army:

HARPER'S FERRY, Va., Thursday, Oct. 20—9.30 A. M.

News from SHERIDAN's headquarters at midnight is to the effect that the enemy surprised our forces yesterday morning, driving the command in some confusion this side of Newtown, capturing artillery and prisoners.

SHERIDAN arrived in the field reorganized our forces, drove the enemy beyond Strasburg, capturing, it is reported, forty-three pieces of artillery, one hundred wagons and ambulances, and some two thousand prisoners.

The rout of the enemy is said to be complete.

This is not official, but I think reliable.

(Signed) J. D. STEVENSON, Brigadier-General.

A few minutes later the following official report of his victory was received from Maj. Gen. SHERIDAN:

CEDAR CREEK, Wednesday, Oct. 19, 10 P. M.

To Lieut. Gen. Grant, City Point:

I have the honor to report that my army at Cedar Creek was attacked this morning before daylight and my left was turned and driven in confusion.

In fact most of the line was driven in confusion, with the loss of twenty pieces of artillery.

I hastened from Winchester, where I was, on my return from Washington, and found the armies between Middletown and Newtown, having been driven back about four miles.

I here took the affair in hand, and quickly united the corps, formed a compact line of battle just in time to repulse an attack of the enemy, which was handsomely done at about 1 P. M.

At 3 P. M., after some changes of the cavalry from the left to the right flank, I attacked with great vigor, driving and routing the enemy, capturing, according to the last report, forty-three pieces of artillery and very many prisoners.

I do not know yet the number of my casualties or the losses of the enemy.

Wagons, trains, ambulances and caissons in large numbers are in our possession.

They also burned some of their trains.

Gen. RAMSEUR is a prisoner in our hands, severely, and perhaps mortally wounded.

I have to regret the loss of Gen. BIDWELL killed, and Gens. WRIGHT, GROVER and RICKETTS wounded.

WRIGHT is slightly wounded.

Affairs, at times, looked badly, but by the gallantry of our brave officers and men disaster has been converted into a splendid victory.

Darkness again intervened to shut off greater results.

I now occupy Strasburgh.

As soon as obtained, I will send you further particulars.

(Signed.) P. A. SHERIDAN, Maj. Gen.

The battle was fought on the same day, 19th of the month, that witnessed SHERIDAN's victory in September.

What the numbers were opposed to Gen. SHERIDAN are not yet reported to the Department, but the boldness, vigor and success of the attack strongly indicate that a heavy reinforcement had been sent from Richmond, with the expectation of fulfilling LONGSTREET's boast to smash up SHERIDAN.

LONGSTREET was known to be in the Valley, and had assumed command of the rebel army, and confident hopes of an overwhelming disaster to the Union army were boastfully expressed for several days back by the rebel adherents in Washington and Baltimore.

EDWIN M. STANTON, Secretary of War.

THE LATEST.

BALTIMORE, Thursday, Oct. 20.

We have no additional particulars from the Valley; but all we hear is to the effect that SHERIDAN's victory over LONGSTREET was most complete. The number of guns captured are understood to include the recapture of those which we lost in the morning.

The rebels are said to have continued their retreat rapidly up the Valley, being with their loss of trains and artillery in no condition to make a successful stand against SHERIDAN's victorious troops.

THE WAR IN MISSOURI.

The Whereabouts of Price—Prospects of a Fight—More Guerrilla Depredations.

ST. LOUIS. Mo., Thursday, Oct. 20.

Dispatches from Gen. ROSECRANS say that Gen. PRICE's main force is still east of the Blackwater River. This is regarded as favorable to the disposition of our troops, and increases the chances of Gen. ROSECRANS getting a fight out of the enemy.

Later advices from Danville state that no citizens were burned in the block-house at that place, as previously reported.

A scout from Randolph, Chariton County, returned to Macon yesterday.

The *Republican* has a special dispatch from Jefferson City, which says that the guerrillas, under TODD, entered the German settlement of Lafayette County on Sunday night, killed twenty-eight Germans, fired their houses, compelled the women to remain in them until the roofs were about to fall, when they were allowed to escape.

Gen. CURTIS is concentrating a large force in Kansas City, with which he will move against Gen. PRICE.

Gen. JIM LANE has command of fifteen hundred Kansas Militia.

FROM THE MISSISSIPPI.

No Rebel Force near Memphis—Chalmers Retreating Southward.

CAIRO, Thursday, Oct. 20.

The Steamer *Nannie Berch*, from Memphis, passed this point to-day, with 340 bales of cotton for Cincinnati. Business, which had been entirely suspended at Memphis, was resumed again, and the militia has been discharged, as the danger was believed to have passed. It was the opinion at headquarters that the rebels had no intention of attacking Memphis, that their presence beyond was merely designed to cover the march of troops into Kentucky. There was no rebel force within five miles of the city. When last heard of, CHALMERS was south of Hernando, retreating toward the swamps of Zallahatchie, and FORREST was en route for Meridian with his prisoners.

The Vote in Pennsylvania.

PHILADELPHIA, Thursday, Oct. 20.

Official returns from Clarion County give a Democratic majority of 970. Democratic loss, 10.

PHILADELPHIA, Thursday, Oct. 20.

Adams County—official—Democratic majority, 311; Democratic gain, 13.

York County—official—Democratic majority, 2,505; Democratic gain, 251.

The Campaign in Connecticut.

GREAT MEETING AT NEW-HAVEN.

The Union gathering in New-Haven on Wednesday last was the largest political assembly ever convened in Connecticut. The entire day was given up to it. Early in the morning delegations from all the neighboring towns began to arrive, and at 11 o'clock a grand procession was formed.

Prominent in it were the Faculty of Yale College in carriages, followed by the Yale College Union Club, consisting of some 300 members. They bore numerous banners, among them was one having a picture of JEFF. DAVIS accepting a skeleton for a recruit, and taking children from their cradles for the same purpose, with the words:

"Jeff's Last Recruits."

Also, one banner with the words: "The Nation's Prayer—GRANT us Peace." They also had a large wagon, trimmed with evergreens, on which was a section of rail fence, mounted with a portrait of Old ABE.

The Second Ward Club, with a fine Club banner, made a fine display. They also bore a banner representing a copperhead snake being crushed beneath a large a one, labeled Pennsylvania, Ohio and Indiana, and having this motto—

"The Snake is Scotched."

They also had a wagon, which caused great merriment; and on its sign was a painting of a railroad train, entitled "The Chicago Line," with the following words underneath:

"Passengers are requested not to stand on the platform."—*Geo. B. McClellan.*

After them came a very large delegation from Derby, containing 163 carriages. A very beautiful and attractive feature in this line was a wagon filled with beautiful little girls, with a young lady, representing the Goddess of Liberty, in the centre, holding the flag—all dressed very prettily, and wearing the red, white and blue scarf.

The streets through which the procession passed were profusely and patriotically decorated. After it had completed its circuit, three meetings were organized upon the "Green." Thirty thousand people are estimated to have been in attendance. They were addressed by Hon. H. J. RAYMOND and Hon. W. E. ROBINSON, of this city, Hon. R. H. DANA, of Boston, Col. NOBLE, of the Seventeenth Connecticut Vols., Judge FOSTER, Brig.-Gen. TERRY, Hon. H. C. DEMING, of Hartford, Hon. H. B. HARRISON, and others.

SABBATH SCHOOL CONVENTION AND CELEBRATION.—The annual Convention of the Sabbath School teachers of Essex County, N. J., was held at Bloomfield on Wednesday last. The Sabbath Schools of the township, nine in number, embraced the opportunity to show their strength, and early in the afternoon assembled in the public square to the number of nearly one thousand. After marching in procession around the square, they repaired to the Presbyterian church, which they filled to overflowing, hardly any room being left for outsiders. Spirited addresses were made by Rev. Dr. PORTER, of Williamsburgh, Rev. Mr. PARDEE, of this city, Mr. MOCKA, of Jersey City, and Mr. SWENZEL, of Newark. The singing was under the charge of Prof. W. B. BRADBURY, of this city, and was such as he alone is capable of eliciting from juvenile throats. In the evening the Sabbath school teachers elected the officers of their organization for another year, and listened to an eloquent address from Dr. PORTER upon the importance of their work and its rewards, while Mr. PARDEE gave both superintendents and teachers some practical suggestions regarding the manner in which they might render their labors most effective.

THE ST. ALBANS' RAID.

Capture of a Portion of the Raiders—Recovery of $50,000.

BURLINGTON, Thursday, Oct. 20.

Eight of the raiders who entered St. Albans and robbed the banks and murdered the citizens, have been caught, and $50,000 recovered. They were caught at Stanbridge and Farnham, Canada East. The remainder have been seen on the road and will probably also be arrested.

The Capture of Nine of the Rascals Confirmed—$50,000 Recovered—Death of a British Officer.

ST. ALBAN'S, Thursday, Oct. 20.

Later advices from the parties who are pursuing the raiders, under Capt. NEWTON, Capt. CONGER and Lieut. STRAINHAN, confirm the news of the capture of nine of the freebooters and $50,000 of the stolen bank bills.

Considerable excitement still prevails, though all apprehensions of any further danger at present from the marauders is entirely removed.

Capt. NICKERSON, of the Veteran Reserve Corps, is garrisoning the border with 115 convalescents from the hospitals at Brattleboro.

Judge ALDIS, of the Supreme Court, has just returned from Montreal, where he has had satisfactory interviews with the Canadian authorities, and is now preparing the necessary papers to bring the captured raiders before our courts under the extradition treaty.

Maj. AUSTINE has dispatched Maj. J. L. BARSTOW to St. Johns, C. E., in order, if possible, to secure the arrest of a party of raiders who are approaching that place from St. Austead.

The banks of this place suffered severely, but the St. Alban's Bank announces that they will redeem their bills.

We learn that in a skirmish, last evening, at Freelisburgh, four of the raiders were captured.

WM. HUNT, one of the bailiffs of that municipality, fell mortally wounded while gallantly endeavoring to capture the raiders.

The provincial authorities of the frontier towns did everything in their power to accomplish the arrest of the rascals.

Six of the horses taken by the scoundrels have een recaptured.

Arrest of the Leader of the Bandits and Several of his Followers—A Part of the Booty Recovered—Active Co-operation of the Canadian Authorities in Making the Arrests—Particulars of the Raid by an Eye Witness.

ST. ALBANS, Vt., Thursday, Oct. 20.

Six of the bank robbers were arrested in Stanbridge about midnight, and about $50,000 of their booty was recovered. Three others were arrested at Freleighsburgh. They will be lodged in jail at St. John's, there to await a requisition from the United States authorities.

Major AUSTIN, Provost-Marshal General of the State, arrived here this morning, and has assumed the direction of all military matters.

LATER.

ST. ALBANS, Thursday, Oct. 20—4 P. M.

Capt. CONGER's party have just returned, and report that they caught the leader of the raiders at Stanbridge, and recovered $100,000 in addition to the $50,000 received this morning.

The Canadian authorities are still after villains, and there is a good prospect of the capture of the whole gang.

The Governor-General of Canada has telegraphed that he will respond to a requisition from the United States Government for the surrender of the robbers already arrested, and such as may be hereafter arrested.

The St. Albans' Bank lost $15,000; the Franklin County Bank, $8,500; and the First National Bank, $54,000.

DISPATCH FROM MONTPELIER.

MONTPELIER, Vt., Thursday, Oct. 20.

Immediately after the depredations in St. Albans, by the raiders, Gov. SMITH telegraphed to the Governor-General of Canada, relative thereto, and messengers were sent to points to confer with officers of the Canadian Government.

It is worthy of mention that all communications, oral and written, on the subject, have been treated with great interest and kindness by the British authorities, and so far, every facility and assistance possible has been rendered our pursuing party to hunt down and capture the raiders. The communications of the Governor General to Gov. SMITH are papers worthy of that high official, signifying, as they do, an interest on his part equal to that of our own people, to have the murderers to a speedy retribution.

DISPATCH FROM BURLINGTON.

BURLINGTON, Vt., Thursday, Oct. 20.

The St. Albans Bank and the First National Bank of St. Albans will both redeem their bills, as usual. The recent robbery has not affected their solvency.

The Citizens to Organize for Defence.

BURLINGTON, Vt., Thursday, Oct. 20.

Maj. AUSTIN has ordered the citizens of the frontier towns to organize themselves into home guards. Arms have been distributed to them, and they will shortly be prepared for any emergency.

Account of the Raid by an Eye-Witness.

The Troy *Times* of yesterday contains a graphic account of the raid into St. Alban's, by an eye-witness of the transaction, Mr. BALDWIN, conductor of the sleeping-car train from Rouse's Point to Troy. We make the following extracts:

THE STEALTHY ARRIVAL.

About a week ago, some strangers came to board at the American hotel and the Tremont in St. Alban's. One of them, calling himself Colonel, appeared to be a prominent one among them. He was a man of medium size, about thirty-five years of age, and appeared to have no other name than that of Colonel. Others of the party, who subsequently proved to be thieves and murderers, were habited in the uniform of United States officers, and all wore a sort of wrapper or cape, and each carried a satchel slung by a shoulder strap at the left side, after the manner of English sportsmen. There seemed to be no concert of action between any of these men—they said nothing to each other in public—no conversations ensued that would attract attention—to all appearances, they were substitute brokers, contractors or speculators, such as are often seen in frontier towns—St. Alban's being only sixteen miles from the Canada line. On Tuesday night, the strangers in the village were reinforced by others who arrived in the train from Rouse's Point, and new faces appeared at the breakfast tables of the hotels. On Wednesday morning, a further batch of conspirators arrived, till about thirty raiders had collected. And then the plot was ripe for execution.

HOW THE ATTACK COMMENCED.

At 3 o'clock P. M. on Wednesday, Oct. 19, St. Alban's was in a state of apparent quiet common to New-England towns. Our informant, Conductor BALDWIN, was standing on the steps of the American Hotel, just as the town bell rang out the hour of 3 o'clock, when he saw a man coming out of the door of the First National Bank, and as he did so a citizen on the steps knocked him down. A second was also floored; but the third raider had a pistol in his hand and the citizen retreated. The conductor thought the affair was the freak of some drunken men, but soon he saw symptoms of a disturbance at other points. Several men appeared to be rushing about with pistols, in parties of from five to ten. One of these gangs met a Mr. MORRISON and presented a weapon to him, demanding his surrender. He answered: "You are joking, boys." They fired and he fell, weltering in his blood. Our informant saw him throw up his hands and then sink on the ground, and then he realized for the first time that the village was attacked by an organized body of men, bent on pillage and regardless of human life.

BANKS ROBBED—PEOPLE SHOT.

Meanwhile the attack had been simultaneous on the three banks—the First National, Franklin County and St. Alban's. Parties entered each. When the Teller or Cashier, suspecting no evil, asked what they desired, the leader presented a pistol, with the exclamation, "You are my prisoners. If you move an inch, we'll blow you through." Others of the gang then went to the vault and drawers, and laid violent hands on all the specie, bills and other articles which they could find, and filled the side satchels which each wore, as before described. Of course resistance was useless, for the surprise was complete. At the Franklin County Bank, the raiders pushed the Cashier, Mr. BEARDSLEY, and one of the clerks into the vault and locked them up, and the prisoners were not released until late in the night.

A REIGN OF TERROR.

Then commenced a reign of terror in the village. Plunder had been accomplished, and violence followed. The raid was brief, but the scene must have been terrible while it lasted. The thirty or more marauders rushed up and down the streets firing their pistols in every direction. Whenever they saw a citizen or group of men, they would aim in that direction. They had magnificent arms—seven-shooters—and as fast as one weapon was unloaded, they drew another and kept up the fusilade. Mr. BALDWIN says he can only liken the sounds to the noise of a Fourth of July morning in a large city. There was a continuous bang! bang! bang! Of course this reckless use of fire-arms could not continue long with nobody hurt. The Sheriff of the county soon fell; Mr. HUNTINGTON was shot while resisting the robbery of his store; a woman, whose name we could not learn, fell, and, more dastardly than all, as the guerrillas were leaving the town, they saw a little girl in the street, and wantonly killed her. And the bullets were flying around among the buildings in the Main-street, nearly all of which bear marks of lead. Windows were broken, blinds chipped and people wounded. It was a scene that beggars all description.

THE "CHIVALRY" AS HORSE-THIEVES.

Of course, the entire populace rushed into the streets. They had no idea of the cause of the disturbance—for they were engaged in their usual daily avocations, and the raid was "like thunder from a clear sky." The guerillas, as they rushed through the town, stopped all the citizens they met and gathered them in squads under guard of a few men armed with pistols—retaining them as prisoners on the common. Meanwhile, the remainder of the banditti started to secure horses. They took two from FIELD's livery stable, five from FULLER's, several from the American and Tremont stables, and a $1,200 span from Mr. CLARK, of Rutland—securing about thirty in all. Their adroitness in cutting off harness was marvelous; and the contents of the saddle-makers' shops soon enabled the villains to become cavalry, instead of foot-pads.

THREATS OF THE "CONFEDERATES."

Meanwhile their threats were terrible. "We will burn your d—d town," they said. "*We will treat you as the people of Atlanta were treated.*" They also said: "*We are coming back again, and will burn every town in Vermont.*" Their imprecations were of a blasphemous character. They claimed to be Confederates. Our informant does not think any of the men were Canadians. They all looked like Americans, and Southerners at that. These demons continued their infernal pistol-firing—killing a man named MORSE after they began to "take prisoners."

THE RETREAT.

All this was the work of twenty minutes. Conductor BALDWIN says he can scarcely realize that it all happened, and that so much was done in so short a time. The guerrillas having all secured horses and saddles, commenced their retreat. They abandoned the prisoners and rode off northward, firing their pistols as they proceeded. It appeared to be their intention to make an attack on the Missisquoi Bank at Sheldon.

PURSUIT.

When the villagers became thoroughly aroused to what had happened, they acted in a manner worthy of their Green Mountain sires in the days of the Revolution. Capt. CONGER, with eight men, started in swift pursuit; twenty more followed in half an hour. People seized guns, pistols, cutlasses and clubs, and came out into the streets. Stores were closed—business was suspended. Everybody was wild with excitement. There was a Babel of suggestions, questions, incidents, escapes, comparisons of losses, and speculations as to the future. Telegrams were sent to Montpelier, and the citizens made preparations for home defence.

THE AUTHORITIES AROUSED.

The Legislature, which was in session at Montpelier, and the Governor, received dispatches from St. Alban's at 5 o'clock, announcing the raid. The former appointed a committee; the latter ordered two thousand stand of arms from the arsenal at Vergennes, and sent one hundred veteran reserves from Burlington; Col. BENTON and one hundred volunteers from Burlington and one hundred trusty firemen from Brattleboro. Gen. DIX, at New-York, was communicated with, and gave orders for prompt pursuit.

VERMONT UNDER ARMS.

Conductor BALDWIN left St. Alban's at 8 o'clock last evening—running slowly to keep out of the way of special trains filled with volunteers and arms. At Burlington the citizens were on guard to protect the town. They refused to allow the Lake boat "*Canada*" to land last night, until they found out whether rebels or Capt. FLAGG commanded her. During the afternoon, when the raid was telegraphed, the steamer "fired up" at Rouse's Point, and ran out into the lake, where she anchored, as a measure of precaution. At St. Alban's, "martial law" prevailed last night. It must be garrisoned by several hundred troops by this time, and the frontier is under arms.

Rebel Raid into Vermont—Great Excitement at the Capital of the State—Organizing for Defence—The Legislature Enlist as Soldiers.

Correspondence of the New-York Times.

MONTPELIER, Vt., Wednesday, Oct. 19, 1864—6 P. M.

For the last two hours the most intense excitement has prevailed here, in consequence of news received by telegraph of a rebel raid into the village of St. Albans. St. Albans is about sixty miles north of Montpelier, and connected with it by mail and telegraph. The Legislature, now holding its annual session here, had just adjourned for the day when intelligence of the raid was received. The first appearance of anything unusual was the sight of the messengers, clerks, and various officials connected with the two Houses and the State offices, hurrying with rapid steps from hotel to hotel evidently in great haste and perturbation. The news soon got abroad that the Governor had received dispatches saying that a rebel force was burning and plundering St. Albans, the village, by-the-way, where he has his own residence and home. It was about 4 o'clock, or a little after, when the dispatch was received, and in a very few minutes the two Houses, in obedience to the summons of His Excellency, Gov. SMITH, had assembled in the Representatives Hall. They communicated to the dispatches arrived, which simply states that a party of rebels had robbed the banks of St. Albons, and were murdering its citizens. The Governor furthermore communicated the intelligence that issued orders for two hundred soldiers of the Invalid corps stationed here and at Barlington, to go forward immediately, also that he had directed the citizens of Barlington (about thirty-five miles north of this place, and the largest and finest village of Vermont) to organize for defence. He furthermore added that he had ordered 2,000 stand of arms to be forwarded from Brattleboro, and had given authority for the immediate enlistment of a company here in Montpelia.

Under these circumstances, it may well be supposed there was a good deal of excitement. How great this rebel force might be was unknown. It might be large enough to advance, laying waste the finest portions of the State. The Legislature, considering that Gov. SMITH had taken prompt measures, resolved to do all they could to second his efforts. They adjourned their informal meeting, and I believe nearly all of them at once enlisted in the company gathered hastily here with the intention of moving forward to the scene of conflict. Up to 5 o'clock matters were in this position, and neither the Governor nor the telegraph operator could give any additional intelligence. The railroad trains were detained here, a portion of the soldiers of the Invalid Corps were hastened to the cars, and citizens of the town and members of the Legislature were in line, preparatory to as efficient organization as could be hastily made. The reasonable supposition was, that the wires of the telegraph had been cut by the raiding party near St. Albans, and the dispatches received were all that could be hurried through before the telegraph office was seized by the raiders.

At about 5 o'clock Gov. SMITH received further dispatches, stating that the raiding party was limited to forty men: that they had for some weeks been boarding at the hotels and boarding-houses in St. Albans; that having robbed the banks and murdered several citizens, they had taken horses wherever they could find them and made a hasty retreat. The Governor thereupon gave notice that the services of the citizens would not be required, and the hastily gathered company thereupon disbanded. Some of the soldiers have, I believe, been forwarded. The affair looks more like a robbery than a raid. It has, however, perhaps its origin among the rebel sympathizers gathered along the Northern border. It is still feared that it may be only the precursor of further outrages in northern Vermont, that is connected with a wide-spread conspiracy like that which came so near being successful on the western lakes.

The excitement still continues—7 P. M.—although less intense, by far, than two hours ago. Soldiers of the Invalid Corps are still in the streets, but citizens and members of Legislature, who an hour ago looked forward to doing soldiers' duty, and perhaps feining in a bloody fray, are now gathered in groups talking over the excitement.

It is generally predicted now that an efficient militia law will be enacted by this Legislature in the course of the present session.

The Atlantic Telegraph Cable.

The numerous stockholders and others interested in the success of the Atlantic Telegraph Cable, will read with interest and satisfaction the annexed official report of the progress thus far made in the manufacture of the cable, and other arrangements necessary to insure success to the attempt soon to be made to connect Europe and America by telegraph, via Ireland and Newfoundland:

ATLANTIC TELEGRAPH COMPANY, No. 12 St. HELEN'S-PLACE, BISHOPGATE-STREET-WITHIN, LONDON,

MY DEAR SIR: As our work is now getting fairly under way, a few particulars as to what is going forward here, in addition to my weekly reports, which I trust you receive regularly, will doubtless be of interest to yourself and co-directors in America, as well as to the shareholders.

The covering of the copper conductor, with its four layers of gutta-percha, commenced on the 19th of April, and has since then continued, slowly and with great care, being constantly under electrical tests, by the aid of apparatus, which, if it had been available when our former cable was constructed, would have caused the very best portions of it to have been utterly rejected.

The present core, however, even under these searching tests, shows a perfection of insulation in its worst parts, more than twice that of the high standard prescribed by the specification, and is undoubtedly the finest telegraphic core that has ever been constructed up to this period. Of this about 800 miles have at present been completed, or are in various stages of completion.

The homogeneous iron, which is a new feature in the construction of this cable, is, as you are well aware, provided by Messrs. WEBSTER & HORSFALL, at Birmingham. The total weight contracted for is 1,600 tons. The drawing of it was commenced on the 17th May last, and we have an agent on HORSFALL's premises, who tests nearly every bundle of it for strength and elongation, and transmits his tests weekly to this office for examination. I also occasionally go down to Birmingham personally, and in addition to the contractors, have at Marden Wharf a man whose sole duty it is to retest the wire when delivered in London. I need not say that all the deliveries are fully up to the specifications, as every bundle that is even doubtful, is at once absolutely rejected. It is only fair to the wire-drawers, however, to say that they are striving to the utmost to do their duty, and that the rejections have been very few. Upward of 500 tons have now been delivered.

Large stocks are also now on hand of the Manila yarn, with which the iron wire is to be surrounded, and of the tanned jute, which forms the padding for the protection of the gutta percha core from injury from the compression of the external armor of the Manila-covered wire.

The deliveries of cases from the Gutta Percha Works to the East Greenwich Covering Works, commenced on the 21st of July, but a good deal of delay has necessarily taken place in commencing the last stage of the manufacture (that of covering the core with the external protection,) owing to the fact that a determination to omit no improvements that science and experience have suggested, the contractors have nearly remodeled the works at that place. All the covering machines have been taken down and reconstructed, and every appliance added which forethought and present knowledge can think of, for the security and preservation and testing of the new cable. Eight immense iron tanks have been constructed—one for each machine, so that the cable passes direct out of the manufactory into the water, and twenty-four other iron tanks have been provided for the preservation of the core during its progress through the factory into the covering machines—with special arrangements for applying a severe and special test to every joint before it passes into the covering machine.

Owing to the length of time which these various important matters have occupied, it was not until Thursday the 1st of September, that a machine for turning out the completed cable was started; since then three other machines have got into full work, and a fifth machine will start before the end of the present week; the other three will afterward be speedily set going, and the cable will then be completed at the rate of about eighty miles per week—at present a little over 100 miles have been finished.

The *Great Eastern* steamship left Liverpool on the service of this company on the 11th of July, and arrived at Sheerness on Wednesday, July 13, where she now continues. The contractors commenced on the 16th of September to remove the floor of her upper deck—on the deck below which the iron tanks will have to be erected for storing the cable in water.

These tanks will be three in number, and their dimensions about fifty-nine diameter by twenty feet in depth. The iron plates for them are being rolled and punched by Messrs. WESTWOOD & BAILLE, who rivet them together on board, and who are bound to complete them not later than the middle of December. The first tank is to be ready by the middle of November.

The Government has appropriated two ships to the service of transporting the cable, as it is made, from the works at Marden Wharf, to the *Great Eastern* at Sheerness. These also will each contain three iron tanks, so that the cable will never be out of water for more than a few moments at a time, from its first commencement at the gutta-percha works, to its submersion in the sea. The contractors have in stock the tanks for these ships, and they will therefore only require putting together.

I am happy to tell you that as regards the portion of completed cable nothing can be more satisfactory than the manner in which it can be coiled and handled. It was thought by some that the advantage gained by the great strength of the homogeneous iron would be counteracted by its supposed hardness and springiness; but as regards the portion at present turned out, I can testify that this supposition is quite a fallacy, it lies as dead as a hemp rope in the coil, and has no spring whatever in it.

I trust the above account will be satisfactory to yourself and our Directors and other friends in America. They may be assured of one thing, without any doubt, namely, that we shall have a better cable than has ever hitherto been produced; and, if the opinion of those who should be most competent to judge may be relied upon, the *Great Eastern* is the proper ship for the work.

In the belief, therefore, that every known precaution and appliance in securing success has been and will be made available, we may more safely commit the great and hoped-for final result of our noble undertaking to the protection of that mightiest arm to which even the stormiest waves of the Atlantic are obedient. I am, my dear Sir, very truly yours,

GEO. SAWARD, Secretary and General Superintendent.

CYRUS W. FIELD, Esq.

UNION DEMONSTRATIONS.

Great Meeting at Rochester—Speeches by Govs. Andrew and Brough—Immense Torchlight Procession.

Special Dispatches to the New-York Times.

ROCHESTER, Tuesday, Oct. 18, 1864.

There has been an immense Union mass meeting here to-day, the largest political demonstration I ever seen in Western New-York. A torchlight procession two miles long is now on the streets. There has been not less than fifty thousand people participating, and the eloquent speeches of Govs. ANDREWS and BROUGH and Col. TURNER demonstrates that the people hereabouts are resolved that the rebellion shall be put down, and the old Republic shall live.

Gov. Andrew in New-York.

Correspondence of the New-York Times.

SYRACUSE, Wednesday, Oct. 19, 1864—9 P. M.

Syracuse is alive with bonfires and illuminations, and crowded with people. Gov. ANDREW is electrifying the people by the power and force of his addresses. He spoke an hour this afternoon, and speaks in Hanover square this evening.

Gen. Doblado.

WASHINGTON, Thursday, Oct. 20.

Gen. DOBLADO, the distinguished Mexican commander, arrived in town this morning, and in company with Señor ROMERO, the Mexican Minister, dined with the Secretary of State to-day.

DESPERATION OF THE SOUTH.

ARMING OF THE NEGROES.

Freedom to All who Fight for Slavery.

The Most Significant Sign of Weakness.

The following article, from the Richmond *Enquirer*, and the letter of the rebel Gov. ALLEN, of Louisiana, which is appended, will attract very marked attention throughout the country:

CONSCRIPTING THE SLAVES.

From the Richmond Enquirer, Oct. 18.

The proposition to extend the Conscript Law to the slaves of the States was first formally advanced by the *Enquirer* in the issue of the 6th inst. Since that time we have received many assurances of its popular favor, and none whatever of opposition to it. *We learn that the planters in the extreme Southern States favor the proposition*, and some have signified their readiness to free five, ten or fifteen of their slaves if they will enter the army. The near approach of the time when the Congress meets again, requires that expression be given to the sentiments of the country upon this important measure. We, therefore, earnestly invite its discussion, and open our columns to opponents as well as friends of the proposition.

The result of the late elections is still in doubt, and whether LINCOLN or MCCLELLAN will be elected, it is yet impossible to determine, but there is no uncertainty as to the question of carrying on the war. Whether LINCOLN or MCCLELLAN be the next President, the voice, and the almost unanimous voice, of that people is for a vigorous prosecution of the war. The duty of preparing to meet that issue, will be before the approaching session of the Confederate Congress; that body will have before it, for consideration, the ways and means, as well as of men as of money, for carrying on the war, on our part.

The war cry of the enemy, "*no parley with rebellion in the field—no compromise with slavery in the readjustment,*" fully inform our people that, in plain vernacular, the whites of these States are to be subjugated to slavery, and their slaves reduced to the miserable condition of Yankee free negroes. This is the view of the people, among our enemies, and this will be the result of the war, whether ended by LINCOLN or MCCLELLAN, if the people of these States permit themselves to be conquered.

The conscription of negroes should be accompanied with freedom and the privilege of remaining in the States; this is no part of abolitionism, it is the exercise by the master of the unquestionable right of manumission; it is remunerating those who defend our cause with the privilege of freedom. *Nor should this important subject be predjudiced with questions about putting the negro on an equality with our friends, brothers and fathers. Many of the soldiers in their childhood were fondled and nursed by faithful negro nurses, and yet no question of equality was ever raised.* Many a man has manumitted slaves without ever being subjected to the suspicion of being an abolitionist.

The issues involved in this war are too exalted in their importance and character for us *to permit them to be compromised by being degraded to a question of property.* The liberty and freedom of ourselves and of our children, the nationality of our country, the right of enjoying any kind of property, the houses over our heads, and the very graves of our children and friends, are involved in the struggle. Failure makes slaves of all, white and black; robs all of property, real and personal; divides our lands among our conquerors, who will plow up the very graves of our dead as fertilized ground for making money. *We have in our midst a half million of fighting material which is property*—shall we use that property for the common cause? Justice and sound policy demand that we make freemen of those who fight for freedom. We conscript the master and we impress his horses, cattle, wheat, and every other property except slaves. *This very exception is an imputation that this war is for slavery and not for freedom.* By conscripting the negroes, we show to the world the earnestness that is in our people; we prove to our enemies that at the moment of our supposed exhaustion, in the fifth year of the war, we shall meet them with larger armies than we have before raised; and we explode the false accusation that we are fighting for slavery, or a slave-holder's Confederacy.

There are those who doubt whether sound policy would trust negroes with arms. We are not of those who entertain any fears upon that subject. Drill and discipline makes valuable soldiers of Russian serfs, and no negroes in these States are so ignorant and brutal as those serfs. Between service with the Confederacy and with the Yankees, between living among us, with all their strong local attachments, and going among strangers, who are now openly buying and selling them to recruiting officers, our slaves will find no difficulty in choosing. And, when once it is understood that *freedom and a home in the South are the privileges offered by the Confederate authorities*, while the enemy extend the beggarly hospitalities of Yankee philanthropy, not only will desertion from our ranks be unfrequent, but the drafted negroes of the Yankee armies will exchange services.

This subject addresses itself to the consideration of our people, at this particular time, with great force. The prospect of four more years of war are before our people; the enemy will not even "parley" with us without unconditional surrender, the fruits of which would be confiscation of all property, the deportation of whole communities, the degredation of the people, and the domination and tyranny of Yankee masters. There can be no reconstruction which does not embrace a surrender first, which will not permit confiscation afterwards, which does not insure enslaving the white, without freeing the blacks. If there are any weak-kneed people who imagine they can save their property by reconstruction, let them study the shiboleth of all parties in the United States—"no parley with rebellion in the field; no compromise with slavery in the adjustment." Unconditional surrender is first demanded before even a parley. We are to lay down our arms and submit to the kindness of the BUTLERS, GRANTS, SHERMANS and SHERIDANS; to the fate of New-Orleans, the condition of the Valley, the misery of Atlanta, and, after all that degradation, to give up all our slaves in the adjustment. If there are any reasons against extending the conscription to slaves, we should like to have them stated, *but we are decidedly of opinion that the whole country will agree to the proposition, and that at an early day the next Congress will be called upon to provide for it by law.*

Important Orders by Gen. Canby—The Rebel Governor and the Negroes.

HEADQUARTERS MILITARY DIVISION OF WEST MISSISSIPPI, NEW-ORLEANS, La., Oct. 11, 1864.

The subjoined extract from a dispatch from HENRY W. ALLEN, styling himself Governor of Louisiana, to the rebel Secretary of War, is published for general information:

EXECUTIVE OFFICE, SHREVEPORT, La., Sept. 26, 1864.

To Hon. James A. Seddon, Secretary of War, Richmond, Va.:

MY DEAR SIR—The time has come for us *to put into the army every able-bodied negro man as a soldier.* This should be done immediately. Congress should, at the coming season, take action on this most important question. The negro knows that he cannot escape conscription if he goes to the enemy. He must play an important part in the war. *He caused the fight, and he will have his portion of the burthen to bear.* We have learned from dear-bought experience that negroes can be taught to fight, and that all who leave us are made to fight against us. *I would free all able to bear arms, and put them into the field at once.* They will make much better soldiers with us than against us, and swell the now depleted ranks of our armies.

I beg you to give this your earnest attention.

With assurances of my friendly regards and very high esteem, I remain, very respectfully, your obedient servant, HENRY W. ALLEN, Governor of Louisiana.

The class of persons to whom it refers will not be conscripted into the armies of the United States if they come within our lines. All will be freed, and they will be received and treated as refugees. They will be accepted as volunteers, or will be employed in the public service, and their families will be cared for until they are in a condition to care for themselves. If a draft should become necessary, no discrimination against them will be made on the enrollment or draft. By order of

Maj.-Gen. E. R. S. CANBY.

C. T. CHRISTENSEN, Lieut.-Col. and A. A. G.

GEN. BANKS AT IRVING HALL.—The Union Home School Fair, at Irving Hall, was favored with a visit from Gen. BANKS yesterday, and, after having passed several hours there, in company with his lady, they expressed their satisfaction and gratification at all they saw, as well as with the noble and patriotic purpose for which the institution is founded, and the fair given. In confirmation of which, the General declared it as his intention to be present again this evening, accompanied by his Staff, when, in all probability, the public will have an opportunity of hearing from him in person.

The New-York Times.

VOL. XIV.—NO. 4091. NEW-YORK, THURSDAY, NOVEMBER 3, 1864. PRICE FOUR CENTS

THE REBEL RAM ALBEMARLE.

HOW SHE WAS DESTROYED.

A Bold, Daring and Romantic Feat.

Reports of Com. Macomb and Lieut. Cushing.

Particulars from our Own Correspondent.

WASHINGTON, Wednesday, Nov. 2.

Rear-Admiral PORTER has communicated to the Navy Department a copy of the report of Commander MACOMB, commanding the United States steamer *Shamrock*, dated October 29, from which it appears that on the night of the 27th inst., Lieut. W. B. CUSHING ascended the Roanoke in his torpedo boat, having the second cutter of this vessel in tow, for the purpose of blowing up the ram *Albemarle* at Plymouth. He passed the *Southfield* without being noticed, and arrived within a short distance of the ram before he was discovered, when he cast loose the cutter, ordering it to board the *Southfield* and capture the picket stationed there, while he attacked the ram with his torpedo.

Although the enemy kept up a severe fire of musketry and with howitzers mounted on the wharf, Lieut. CUSHING succeeded in exploding his torpedo under the *Albemarle*, at the same instant that the gun of that vessel, to which they were directly opposite, was fired on the torpedo boat, which immediately filled, and the Lieutenant ordered his officers and men to save themselves, and jumped overboard. He was picked up by the *Valley City* on the night of the 20th.

Report of Lieut. Cushing.

WASHINGTON, Wednesday, Nov. 2.

Admiral PORTER has communicated to the Secretary of the Navy the following interesting particulars from Lieut. CUSHING, in regard to the sinking of the rebel ram *Albemarle* :

ALBEMARLE SOUND, Oct. 30, 1864.

SIR : I have the honor to report that the rebel ironclad *Albemarle* is at the bottom of Roanoke River.

On the night of the 27th, having prepared my steam launch, I proceeded up toward Plymouth, with thirteen officers and men, partly volunteers from the squadron.

The distance from the mouth of the river to the ram was about eight miles, the stream averaging in width some 200 yards, and lined with the enemy's pickets.

A mile below the town was the wreck of the *Southfield*, surrounded by some schooners, and it was understood that a gun was mounted there to command the bend.

I therefore took one of the *Shamrock's* cutters in tow, with orders to cast off and board at that point, if we were hailed.

Our boat succeeded in passing the pickets, and even the *Southfield* within twenty yards, without discovery, and we were not hailed until by the lookouts on the ram.

The cutter was then cast off and ordered below, while we made for our enemy under a full head of steam.

The rebels sprung their rattle, rang the bell, and commenced firing at the same time, repeating their hail and seeming much confused.

The light of a fire ashore showed me the iron-clad made fast to the wharf with logs around her about 30 feet from her side. Passing her closely, we made a complete circle so as to strike her fairly, and went into her bows on.

By this time the enemy's fire was very severe, but a dose of cannister at short range seemed to moderate their zeal and disturb their aim.

Paymaster SWAN, of the *Otsego*, was wounded near me, but how many more I know not.

Three bullets struck my clothing, and the air seemed full of them.

In a moment we had struck the logs just abreast of the quarter-port, breaking them in some feet, our bows resting on them.

The torpedo boom was then lowered, and, by a vigorous pull, I succeeded in diving the torpedo under the over-hang, and exploding it at the same time that the *Albemarle's* gun was fired.

A shot seemed to go crashing through my boat, and a dense mass of water rushed in from the torpedo, filling the launch, and completely disabling her.

The enemy then continued his fire at fifteen feet range, and demanded our surrender, which I twice refused, ordering the men to save themselves, and removing my own coat and shoes.

Springing into the river I swam, with others, into the middle of the stream, the rebels failing to hit us.

The most of our party were captured, some were drowned, and only one escaped beside myself, and he in another direction.

Acting Master's Mate WOODMAN, of the *Commodore Hull*, met him in the water half a mile below the town, and assisted him as best he could, but failed to get him ashore.

Completely exhausted, I managed to reach the shore, but was too weak to crawl out of the water until just at daylight, when I managed to creep into the swamp close to the fort.

While hiding, close to the path, the *Albemarle's* officers passed, and I judged from their conversation that the ship was destroyed.

Some hours' traveling in the swamp served to bring me out well below the town, when I sent a negro in to gain information and found that the ram was truly sunk.

Proceeding through another swamp I came to a creek and captured a skiff belonging to a picket of the enemy, and with this, by 11 o'clock the next night, I made my way out to the *Valley City*.

Acting Master's Mate WM. L. HOWETH, of the *Monticello*, showed, as usual, conspicuous bravery. He is the same officer who has been with me twice in Wilmington harbor. I trust he may be promoted when exchanged, as well as Acting Third Assistant Engineer STOLSBURG, who, being the first time under fire, handled his engine promptly and with coolness.

All the officers and men behaved in the most gallant manner.

The cutter of the *Shamrock* boarded the *Southfield*, but found no guns there. Four prisoners were taken there.

The ram is now completely submerged, and the enemy have sunk three schooners in the river to obstruct the passage of our ships.

I desire to call the attention of the Admiral and Department to the spirit manifested by the sailors in the ships in these sounds. But few hands were wanted, but all hands were eager to go into the action, many offering their chosen shipmates a months pay to resign in their favor.

I am, Sir, respectfully, your obedient servant,
W. B. CUSHING, Lieut., U. S. N.

Rear-Admiral D. D. PORTER, Commanding North Atlantic Squadron.

The name of the man who escaped is WILLIAM HOFFMAN, seaman, on the *Chicopee*. He did his duty well and deserves a medal of honor.

Respectfully.
W. B. CUSHING, U. S. N.

FURTHER PARTICULARS.

The Destruction of the Rebel Ram Albemarle—Full and Authentic Particulars—The Most Daring and Romantic Episode of the War.

From Our Own Correspondent.

FORTRESS MONROE, Va., Tuesday, Nov. 1, 1864.

The most interesting event I have to notice is the sudden appearance among us of Lieut. W. B. CUSHING, Commander of the *Monticello*, whose recent wonderful exploit in the Roanoke River is going to electrify the nation from one end to the other, when they come to learn the particulars. I had the pleasure of being personally introduced to Lieut. CUSHING to-day, in company with Paymaster J. FURZY, also of the *Monticello*, and other naval officers, so that I had the best opportunity of gaining correct information from those who were in a position to know all the circumstances. I make this little prelude respecting authenticity, because there is something so unusual, such marvelous human daring, in the events I am about to narrate, as, very naturally, to draw somewhat largely upon the credulity of the general reader.

It will be remembered how conspicuous a part this rebel monitor—so long the terror of our fleet in the inland waters of North Carolina—played in the desperate fight when Plymouth was taken, and on which occasion she sunk the *Southfield*. When she attacked the *Miami*, a shot from the latter rebounded from the armored side of the monster, killing the *Miami's* gallant commander, CHARLES W. FLUSSER, as brave a man as ever trod the deck of a man-of-war. FLUSSER was CUSHING'S intimate friend, and from that hour he inwardly vowed vengeance against the *Albermarle*, and revenge he has just now so signally gratified.

It was on the night of the 27th inst., that Lieut. CUSHING, acting under orders from Rear-Admiral PORTER, sallied forth with twelve other men in a little boat no longer than an ordinary ship's launch, and with no other armament than one 12-pound howitzer, to destroy the *Albermarle*. On going up the canal he found the lock broken, but discovered a creek, leading he hardly knew where, but which was the only route open to him. Fortunately this creek, after some difficult windings, led back into the canal, by which he managed to find his way to the Roanoke River. Here he discovered that the *Southfield*, which was sunk by the *Albermarle* last Spring, had been converted into a defence, and a rebel picket stationed on her. He, of course, expected to be hailed by them; and had made every preparation for attack, but owing to the darkness of the night he passed them unperceived. He then went unmolested up the river until he arrived at the City of Plymouth about 2:30 A. M.

How he came plump upon the object of his search, securely fastened to the wharf, but surrounded by a number of logs, about thirty feet from her, and denying all approach for the purpose of blowing her up. The rebels, not knowing what to make of their strange visitor, called out frequently : "What boat is that ?" but the only reply was a rattling discharge of grape from the little howitzer, as the dauntless boat's crew went feeling round the logs, to see if there were any means of ingress to the ram, amid a shower of bullets from the now aroused enemy. Finding no possible ingress, and determined not to be baulked in his object, Lieut. CUSHING resolved to put his boat *at and over the logs* to get into the inclosure. In this almost insanely daring effort he very nearly succeeded, but not quite, for the stern of the boat caught and was held fast by the logs in her miraculous leap. Conceive the coolness and determination of men, in such a position, deliberately going to work to plant a torpedo under the *Albermarle*. They did it ! as it struck the bottom and by some mechanical contrivvance, informed Lieut. CUSHING exactly when to pull the string, a ball struck the wrist of his right hand which held the string, fortunately only grazing the skin, for had his hand been disabled the *Albemarle* would be now in existence. The string was pulled—the dead sub-aquerus report took place, knocking a hole clean through the bottom of the enemy, which at the same instant of time, and as she went down, sent a terrific discharge from a large gun and howitzer into the launch, knocking it to pieces and sending its inmates wounded and floundering in the water.

It was now a question of *sauve qui peut*. All that Lieut. CUSHING remembers is taking off his coat and boots, and, being an expert swimmer, striking as best he could for the opposite shore, in the darkness of the night, and under cover of the intense prevailing excitement. Out of the whole thirty, only one other man —— HOFFMAN, a seaman of the *Chicokee*, escaped, but how, I did not learn. The others are supposed to have been either killed, wounded or taken prisoners. Alll this occurred about three A. M., of the 28th.

Once fairly away from the immediate scene of danger, Lieut. CUSHING swam down the river about half a mile, got ashore on the opposite side, and hid himself among the bushes till daylight. Once while there, with a pathway on each side of him, he heard officers passing and talking about the *Albemarle*. He laid flat on his back, and, endeavoring to compress himself into as small a surface as possible, pushed himself along by means of his elbows and heels until he was out of their reach, when he ventured upon his feet and hurried along, but cautiously. After a while he came to a picket-station, where he descried a skiff standing alone. The owners were doubtless at breakfast, comparing notes about the extraordinary events of the night, when our hero quietly took possession of the very accommodating craft, and, after 8 hours' pulling, joined the fleet in Albemarle Sound, amid the rejoicings and congratlations of his comrades.

But this is not the first exploit of Lieut. CUSHING. He seems to have a fancy for adventures of this sort. During the blockade off Wilmington, some time during last month, he went up several times inside the rebel fortifications, in small boats. One night, last March, he landed at Smithville, alongside of a rebel battery, with two boatloads and about thirty men. There he caught a negro and made him him come with him, to show where were the headquarters of Gen. HEBERT, commanding the locality. Arriving at the spot, he took about eight men with him and left the rest with the boats. The negro pointed out the General's headquarters, which proved to be *immediately opposite the garrison*. The sentry must have been asleep, for it was late at night and nobody challenged them. He immediately ranged his men, armed with cutlasses and revolvers, in front of the General's headquarters, in which he was aided by Mr. J. E. JONES, Acting Engineer, also WILLIAM L. HOWARTH, then Acting Master's Mate, now Ensign, the latter of whom was also in the late *Albemarle* exploit. Lieuts. CUSHING and JONES went into the house and proceeded up stairs. The General had that day gone to Wilmington, but they caught Capt. KELLY, Engineer, in charge of the defences, the Adjutant-General and others, very undignifiedly making through the windows and for the woods in their shirt-tails. They evidently must have thought it was a mutiny of the garrison, for had they rushed to the latter instead of the woods our whole party would have been captured. As soon as Capt. KELLY was dressed they started with him as a prisoner for their boats, and just as they reached it and were fairly off, lights flashed along the beach, showing that they were discovered ; but it was too late for the rebels to catch them, and they arrived safely on board the *Monticello*, at about 4 A. M., with their prisoners.

The next day a flag of truce was sent in to the rebel garrison, for Capt. KELLY'S effects, accompanied by a polite note from Lieut. CUSHING to Gen. HEBERT, expressing his regret that he had not had the pleasure of finding him at home the night before. It is said that many mutual pleasantries passed on the occasion, for the whole surprise was so ridiculously complete that even the rebels could not help being good-natured over it, however much chagrined. JONES and HOWARTH were in this adventure also.

In June last Lieut. CUSHING had another bold adventure. He started upon an expedition with one boat and sixteen men, and went to within eight miles of Wilmington, hiding in swamps during the day. On this occasion he captured a rebel courier, with mails from Fort Fisher to Wilmington, containing a large batch of important information—among other things that the rebel rams then being constructed were utterly useless. In coming away he captured a boat containing six soldiers, and being afterward discovered, was chased by several picket boats. Lieut. CUSHING pretended he was going out by the same way he entered—by the western bar—but while they were preparing to dodge and meet him, he suddenly turned off to the left and jumped his boat over the breakers at the new inlet side, where the rebels dared not follow him. He got off safely and was picked up by the *Cherokee*, which brought him to his ship next day with all his prisoners. For this exploit he was complimented by a letter from the Naval Department, in which JONES and HOWARTH were honorably mentioned also, and medals of honor were conferred on WM. WRIGHT, ship's yeoman, and JOHN SULLIVAN, seaman.

The most astounding part of this narrative is that the hero of it is a youth of only 22 YEARS OF AGE, with a record already summed up of which many gray beards would be proud. When introduced to him, I could scarcely reconcile the fact that the unassuming young man before me, with his frank, open countenance and long hair thrown wildly back behind his ears, looking like some student just escaped from college for a little frolic, was the man whose name is already and so justly prominent before the public. Apart from the glory which such episodes as these throw around the character of our navy, this destruction of the rebel ram *Albemarle* is a really important affair. It has, for months past, kept employed in watching and at bay at least five of our double-enders and some five or six other vessels, which will now be released for any other kind of duty.

Lieut. CUSHING was on his way to Washington, and will probably visit New-York shortly, in both of which places he will doubtless receive the attention due to his superior merits. While the navy of the United States can boast of such young and vigorous genius, there is no fear of its ever outliving the grand old stock of its Perrys and its Farraguts.

J. R. HAMILTON.

FROM NORTH CAROLINA.

The Yellow Fever at Beaufort—An arrival from Raleigh—Deserters from the Rebel Army—What they are Doing—Serious Troubles Imminent—Gov. Vance on Grant's Plan.

Business letters from Beaufort, N. C., dated Oct. 28, just received here, state that the recent warm spell of weather had developed eight new cases of the yellow fever in Beaufort on that day. A severe black frost, which must come soon, will eradicate the disease entirely.

Dr. J. W. ROSS, who stands high as a clergyman in North Carolina, arrived here to-day, direct from Raleigh, with important intelligence. He says the entire State of North Carolina, as well as Georgia, is alive with rebel deserters, who in most cases, are armed and organized, and abundantly able to protect themselves.

In the western part of the State they reign supreme. There they not only make repeated raids on the wealthy planters and rebel depots for supplies, but give protection to runaway slaves, who are also armed and accompany these bands of deserters in their raiding expeditions. The rebel authorities, says Dr. ROSS, have given up all hopes of forcing these men back into the rebel ranks, having been repulsed in all their efforts to this end. Every expedition fitted out for this purpose by the rebels has proved a failure, for those who were not killed in battle deserted to the insurgents, whose numbers are continually increasing. JEFF. DAVIS said, when in Raleigh, that the deserters from the Confederate army outnumbered the Confederate soldiers in the field.

The extensive conspiracy recently brought to light at Raleigh, implicates many prominent officers of the conservative party, who now openly threaten to head these deserters and their friends, and take possession of the State Government of North Carolina and all the railroads, in the event Gov. VANCE fails to instigate at once separate State action for peace with President LINCOLN.

The Doctor says that it is now apparent to the rebel authorities that Gen. GRANT has been affording facilities to Gen. LEE to receive his reinforcements, when GRANT, by a sudden spring of his trap, will close up the last gap and oblige LEE to capitulate. This, Gov. VANCE says, is GRANT'S plan, which has given JEFF. DAVIS much concern, who is in favor of evacuating Virginia altogether, having repeatedly implored Gen. LEE to do so and not incur the risk of a capitulation of his army. This was told to Dr. ROSS, just before leaving Raleigh, by an aid on Gov. VANCE'S staff.

THE WAR IN MAINE.

Attempted Rebel Raid on Castine.

BOSTON, Wednesday, Nov. 2.

A dispatch from Augusta, Me., states that an attempt was made on Monday night to surprise the water battery at Castine by a raiding party from the land side. The sentinel there was fired upon, but the garrison rallied, and drove the attacking party off. They escaped by boats, after exchanging a number of shots.

One of the raiders was supposed to be wounded.

None of the garrison were hurt, but bullets came very near some of them.

Castine is defended by two new earthworks, mounting five guns each.

BELFAST, Me., Wednesday, Nov. 2.

A dispatch to the Mayor of this city, from Castine, gives the particulars of the attack upon the battery at that town on Monday at midnight.

A small party of men approached from the rear, and when challenged, immediately fired upon the sentinel, who returned the fire.

Sergeant RAMSDELL was fired upon as he came out of his quarters. Four balls lodged within two feet of him.

The garrison mustered promptly and pursued the raiders for about half a mile, firing upon them, and they replying, when they took to a boat and escaped.

The object, it is supposed, was to capture the United States cutter lying in the harbor.

This city has been put in a state of defence.

By orders from Gov. CONY, the Home Guards are in readiness for duty, and the city government has increased and armed the police.

ANTICIPATED RAIDS FROM CANADA.

Dispatch from the Secretary of State to the Mayor of Buffalo—Rebel Conspiracy to Burn Northern Cities.

BUFFALO, Wednesday, Nov. 2.

The subjoined dispatch was received this afternoon by the Mayor of this city. Mayor FARGO has already taken the matter in hand, and any attempt upon Buffalo will be worse than futile. The following is the dispatch :

WASHINGTON, Nov. 2.

To the Mayor of Buffalo :

This department has received information from the British Provinces, to the effect that there is a conspiracy on foot to set fire to the principal cities in the Northern States on the day of the Presidential election. It is my duty to communicate this information to you. (Signed,) W. H. SEWARD.

Dismasted.

BOSTON, Tuesday, Nov. 1.

The schooner *Harriet*, of Rockland, Me., for Gloucester, put into Provincetown to-day, dismasted.

AN ADDRESS BY BISHOP SIMPSON.—Bishop SIMPSON, of the M. E. Church, will deliver a lecture before the Young Men's Christian Association at the Academy of Music to-night. See advertisement.

KENTUCKY AND TENNESSEE.

Hood Reported to have Crossed the Tennessee River with 30,000 Men.

The Railroad from Louisville to Atlanta in Good Order.

Reported Defeat of Part of Forrest's Forces.

FROM LOUISVILLE.

LOUISVILLE, Ky., Tuesday, Nov. 1.

Rumor says that Gen. HOOD with thirty thousand men crossed the Tennessee River going Northward to-day.

The particulars and locality of the crossing are not stated, and are not attainable at present.

The railroad and telegraph from Louisville to Atlanta are now in good order.

The Henderson, Kentucky, *News* says that the great bulk of the drafted men in Kentucky are going into the Confederate service.

R. A. ALEXANDER'S celebrated horse *Osterer*, valued at $18,000, was captured at Bloomfield, Kentucky, yesterday by the rebels.

SECOND DISPATCH.

LOUISVILLE, Wednesday, Nov. 2.

Reliable dispatches, received this morning, indicate that everything is all right along SHERMAN'S whole line.

FROM CAIRO.

CAIRO, Ill., Tuesday, Nov. 1.

Squads of FORREST'S men, who passed through Dresden yesterday, stated that an engagement had occurred between a portion of FORREST'S force and the forces under Cols. HATCH and SHELBY, last week, in which FORREST'S men were routed, with the loss of their arms, ammunition, baggage and many horses.

The locality of the fight is not stated.

Strong reinforcements of mounted infantry have arrived at Paducah, Ky., which it is believed has caused Gen. FORREST to change his plan of operations. Johnsonville is now thought to be the place where the rebels will make their attack.

The rebel Gens. BUFORD, CHALMERS and LYON held a consultation at Paris, Tennessee, on Friday last.

All of Gen. FORREST'S men furloughed or straggling through the country are ordered to rendezvous at Jackson, Tennessee.

The steamers *Oder Nonghock*, reported captured by the rebels on the Tennessee River, have arrived safely at Paducah.

The steamer captured and burned by the rebels at Fort Herman, on the Tennessee River, on Saturday, was the *Mazeppa*.

She was a new steamer, and making her first trip. She had in tow a barge.

The *Mazeppa* was owned by R. C. LOVELL, of Cincinnati, and was valued at $40,000. Her cargo consisted of Government stores valued at $20,000, and considerable other freight.

Most of the clothing and blankets on board the *Mazeppa*, was taken to Fort Herman, by the rebels, before the boat was burned.

The fire from the gun-boat prevented the rebels from removing all the stores and forage from the river bank.

The fort was shelled by the gun-boat two hours, eliciting no reply, when the ammunition becoming exhausted, the gunboat withdrew, but previously to leaving, sent a party ashore and burned the forage left by the rebels on the river bank.

A rebel force, from Gen. BUFORD'S command, had taken possession of Fort Herman the night previous. This force consisted of about four hundred men, and they had a battery of three guns, 12 and 18 pounders, masked on the river bank, completely commanding the river in each direction.

The officers and crew of the *Mazeppa* escaped to Pine Bluff, with the exception of Capt. PETTIE.

The steamer *Ann* was coming down the river four hours after the *Mazeppa*, and was fired on by another masked battery three miles above Fort Herman, but the *Ann* succeeded in passing the battery with but slight damage.

On passing the fort the *Ann* was again fired upon with shot and shell, completely riddling her uppermost works, and several shells penetrating her hull, but she finally got out of the range of the rebel guns, and was taken in tow by a gunboat.

Forty-four rebel prisoners, including several officers, arrived from below to-day, and were sent to Chicago.

GEN. GRANT'S ARMY.

The Surprise of Our Pickets.

HEADQUARTERS OF THE ARMY OF THE POTOMAC, Tuesday, Nov. 1.

The surprise and capture of a part of our picket line on Tuesday night occurred in front of Fort Davis, and the men taken belonged to the Sixty-ninth and One Hundred and Eleventh New-York regiments.

They were for the greater part new men and somewhat ignorant of their duties, and hence were not so watchful as the older troops, who have been on duty at this point of the line.

This is a place where our men, some time ago, played the rebels a similar trick, and the utmost vigilance has ever since been exercised on both sides to prevent a repetition of the occurrence ; but when the late move commenced every man in the ranks left behind had to take his turn on picket, and some of these men, it is said, had never even loaded a gun.

It seems the rebels did not carry of a single musket belonging to our soldiers.

THE TALLAHASSEE AGAIN.

The Schooner Goodspeed Captured and Scuttled by the Tallahassee—Reported Destruction of Three Other Vessels—A Gunboat in Pursuit of the Pirate.

PROVIDENCE, R. I., Wednesday, Nov. 2.

The schooner *Goodspeed*, Capt. BAXTER, of and from Boston, via Newport, for Philadelphia, was boarded by the *Tallahassee*, seven miles south of Block Island, and scuttled. The Captain and the crew escaped to Block Island in a boat, and have reached Newport. The Captain reports that the *Tallahassee* scuttled another vessel within a short distance. The crew of the privateer said that they had the crews of three other vessels destroyed within a few days. The gunboat *Marblehead* left Newport in pursuit this evening.

From the West Gulf Squadron—Capture of Two Prizes by the United States Steamer Mobile.

PHILADELPHIA, Wednesday, Nov. 2.

The United States steamer *Bermuda* arrived off the Navy-yard last evening from the West Gulf Squadron. She brings 22 officers, and 166 sick and discharged seamen.

The *Bermuda* sailed from Galveston, Texas, on the 20th of October. She reports the capture of two prizes by the United States steamer *Mobile*, formerly the *Tennessee*, one with a cargo of cotton, and the other with an assorted cargo.

There is nothing of importance from Mobile Bay. The following is a list of the vessels at present on that station :

The flagship *Hartford*, Rear-Admiral FARRAGUT ; United States sloop *Richmond*, United States sloop *Lackawanna* ; gunboats *Port Royal*, *Owasco*, *Metacomet*, and monitors *Manhattan*, *Chickasaw*, *Winnebago*, with a number of tugboats as tenders.

The *Bermuda* had as passengers, from Mobile Bay, Brig.-Gen. J. NEWTON and staff, who has been ordered to command the forces at Key West.

The weather during the entire passage of the *Bermuda* has been very fine.

FROM HAVANA.

Southern News—Yellow Fever in Texas—Semmes said to be in Havana under the Name of "Smith."

The blockade-runner *Denbegh* arrived here on the 27th with 350 bales of cotton. She reports from Galveston, but doubtless sailed from Brazos or Velasco. A fleet of United States vessels off Cape Antonio would put a stop to this, as these vessels all put for that point and then creep into port under protection of the land.

The yellow fever is reported to be increasing at Galveston and Houston. Among the deaths is that of Gen. J. M. HAWES.

Dr. SIMS and Rev. J. M. GOSHORN have just arrived from Mobile.

A steamer which had succeeded in getting into Mobile harbor sprung a leak, and partly sunk. Her cargo was much injured and powder destroyed.

It is quite confidently stated that the celebrated pirate SEMMES has arrived here from St. Thomas on the English mail packet *Solent*, under the assumed name of "Smith." I have been unable to establish the truth of this report, though I have received information sufficiently conclusive that he not only came, but is still here incognito.

The news of the capture of the *Roanoke* relieved the anxiety of many persons here who had friends on board, as a report had prevailed that she was wrecked. It is reported here that the authorities of Bermuda have put the pirates in irons, and that they will either be tried or given up to the United States authorities.

SHERIDAN'S recent victories have caused much excitement here and made some Union converts.

The *Diario* to-day labors to prove that Missouri has gone over to the Confederacy, and says the inhabitants are flocking over to the standard of PRICE, basing their statements on the valuable information of their New-York correspondent, the noted PETER HICKS.

THE PENNSYLVANIA ELECTION.

The Official Vote—Union Majority in Forty-one Counties 14,039.

HARRISBURGH, Penn., Wednesday, Nov. 2.

The official vote of forty-one counties has been received at the office of the Secretary of State. The following are the aggregate results, including the soldiers' vote : Union, 190,737 ; Democratic, 176,698 Union majority, 14,039.

An Attack upon a Company of Negro Troops—A Rebel Editor.

WASHINGTON, Wednesday, Nov. 2.

A party of guerrillas made an attack on Monday night on the colored company recently raised by Judge UNDERWOOD, of Alexandria, Va., at their station near Acotink. Quite a spirited fight occurred, which resulted in the rout of the guerrillas.

The Alexandria *Gazette* has been suspended, owing to Mr. SNOWDEN, the proprietor, being among those Southern sympathizers detailed as a safety guard on the Orange and Alexandria Railroad against guerrilla attacks.

THE APPROACHING ELECTION.

A Proclamation by Gov. Seymour.

ALBANY, N. Y., Wednesday, Nov. 2.

Gov. SEYMOUR has issued the following proclamation to the people :

In a few days the citizens of this country are to exercise their constitutional duty of electing a President and Vice-President of the United States, at a time when the condition of our country excites the deepest interest.

The questions of the day not only affect the personal welfare of all, and the happiness of their homes, but are also of a character to arouse the passions, and lead to angry controversies between parties.

The existence of a terrible civil war and the assertion of the right of military commanders in some sections of our country to interfere with elections, have caused painful and exciting doubts in the minds of many with regard to the free and untrammeled exercise of the elective franchise.

I, therefore, appeal to men of all parties to unite with those holding official positions, in their efforts to allay undue excitement, soften the harshness of party prejudices and passions, and avoid all measures and language which tend to strife or disorder.

However we may differ in our views of public policy, we are alike interested in the maintenance of order, in the preservation of the rights and the promotion of the prosperity of our State.

While we do not agree as to the methods by which these ends are to be gained, they are earnestly sought by all.

It is certain they cannot be reached by angry controversies, unreasonable suspicions or disorderly actions.

There are no well-grounded fears that the rights of the citizens of New-York will be trampled upon at the polls.

The power of this State is ample to protect all classes in the free exercise of their political duties.

In doing this, the public authorities will be upheld by good citizens of all parties.

There is no reason to doubt that the coming election will be conducted with the usual quiet and order.

Sheriffs of counties, and all other officers whose duty it is to keep the peace and protect our citizens, will take care that every voter shall have a free ballot in the manner secured to him by the Constitution and laws.

It will be their duty to see that no military or other organized forces shall be allowed to show themselves in the vicinity of the places where the elections are held, with any view of menacing or intimidating citizens in attendance thereon.

Against any such interference they must exercise the full force of law, and call forth if need be, the power of their districts.

In witness whereof I have hereunto signed my name and affixed the privy seal of the State, at the
[L.S.] City of Albany, this second day of November, in the Year of our Lord one thousand eight hundred and sixty-four.
HORATIO SEYMOUR.

By the Governor,
D. WILLERS, Jr., Private Secretary.

THE REGISTRY.

125,000 Votes Registered.

The registry of votes closed last night, and the following list is the complete total in each ward, save some four or five districts. It will be seen that the number is far in excess of any vote heretofore polled in this city :

Wards.	Registry.	Wards.	Registry.
1	2,122	12	4,228
2	603	13	4,625
3	993	14	3,829
4	3,152	15	4,670
5	4,857	16	7,099
6	4,142	17	12,750
7	6,136	18	8,284
8	4,582	19	6,779
9	8,087	20	9,729
10	5,016	21	8,396
11	8,731	22	6,877
Total			124,498

A Political Meeting for the Ladies.

For the purpose of affording the ladies of our city an opportunity to listen to a discussion of the great questions involved in the present canvass, a meeting of the loyal women of New-York will be held under the auspices of the Young Men's Republican Union on Friday evening at the Church of the Messiah, on Broadway opposite the New-York Hotel. Admission will be by tickets, which can be obtained free at the places named in the advertisement, in another column. Addresses may be expected from Rev. Dr. BELLOWS, Senator SUMNER, WM. CURTIS NOYES, Esq., and Gov. PIERPOINT, of Virginia. Tickets should be procured at once, as the number is limited.

UNION RALLY IN THE NINTH WARD.

Speeches by Capt. Geo. F. Noyes, Hon. Wm. A. Cook, and Hon. Geo. Briggs, and Henry J. Raymond.

The series of meeting which have been held under the auspices of the Ninth Ward Union Association at the Bleeker Buildings, were brought to a close last evening by a last grand rally of the citizens of the ward previous to election-day, to ratify the Union nomination for President and for Congress in that District. The building was thronged with Union men and women, and the enthusiasm manifested was a sufficient quarantee of their confidence in the success of the Union ticket on Tuesday next.

The meeting was called to order by A. H. KEECH, Esq., President, and after a couple of excellent campaign songs from the Hudson City Union Glee Club, Capt. GEO. F. NOYES, formerly of the Staff of Gen. WADSWORTH, was introduced as the first speaker. He commenced by saying that it made one's blood beat quicker in his veins to listen to these songs. Such were the songs that were sung by our soldiers in camp. The night after the battle of the Wilderness, while the camp-fires of the army were blazing through the darkness of the battle-field, the soldiers in one of the camps struck up that glorious song, "Rally round the flag, boys," and the boys in the surrounding camps caught up the tune, which rang out in the stillness of the night, and was wafted over the dead bodies of their comrades, filling the air with a holy and patriotic hymn of liberty. Did his hearers ever hear such songs in a Copperhead meeting ? Thank God they did not belong to a party which quakes and turns pale at every Union victory. [Applause.] The hand of Providence was patent and visible in the events of the last two months. At the time of that traitorous gathering, the Chicago Convention, a draft was impending. They said to themselves, "Now is the time to play on the cowardice of the people." So they cooked up as much treason and cowardice as they dared and put it in their platform. Hardly was the ink dry that traced the platform when the thunder tones of victory rang through the land. Atlanta soon fell, and anon gallant PHIL SHERIDAN took up the chorus of victory. The Democrats began to think they had made a mistake, and that they ought to have put more patriotism in their platform. The speaker then gave an amusing imaginary account of the scene at MCCLELLAN'S residence, when he was visited by the committee who announced to him his nomination, and the efforts of the party to manufacture a letter of acceptance which should hoodwink the people. He proceeded to review the military career of MCCLELLAN, criticising it in the severest terms, and making many telling points, which brought down the house. He closed with an eloquent tribute to our brave soldiers, who he said scorned the insulting tender of sympathy offered them by the Chicago Convention. His remarks were frequently applauded.

Hon. WM. A. COOK, of Pennsylvania, was then introduced, and gave an account of the invasion of Pennsylvania by HORATIO SEYMOUR just before the election in that State, and called attention to the remarkable fact that wherever he spoke the vote of the Union party was increased.

[Hon. HENRY J. RAYMOND here entered the hall and was greeted with great applause, followed by three cheers for the candidate for Congress in the Ninth District.]

Mr. COOK proceeded to comment upon the public speeches of Gov. SEYMOUR in Pennsylvania and elsewhere, and his oft repeated complaints about arbitrary arrests. He showed from the annals of the Revolution that the patriots of that day authorized and justified the arrest and arbitrary imprisonment of the tories and enemies of the Revolution, and the proceedings were sanctioned by acts of the Continental Congress. Mr. COOK'S remarks, which were mainly devoted to a scathing review and criticism of Gov. SEYMOUR'S acts and speeches, were received with marked favor by the audience, who repeatedly applauded the telling points.

Mr. BELLIN, the illustrating artist of *Harper's Weekly*, then gave a recitation entitled "Rally Round the Flag, Boys," which was cordially received.

Hon. GEO. BRIGGS, the former representative of the district in Congress, next briefly addressed the meeting. He spoke of the interest he felt in the Ninth District, which was for 30 years his residence, and his hope to see her roll up a heavy majority for the Union candidates. He was sorry to be obliged to confess that he voted for HORATIO SEYMOUR for Governor ; but after his speech to his "friends" on the steps of the City Hall, he dropped him as he would drop a hot potato, and he should never touch him again. [Applause.] He spoke of the feeling in Saratoga, where he now resided, and said that there was only one man there who had ever been for LINCOLN that was now for MCCLELLAN, and he was a Quartermaster who had been dismissed from the army for cheating the soldiers. He closed by congratulating his audience that they were next to listen to their candidate for Congress. Mr. HENRY J. RAYMOND, whom, he was proud to say, he had aided in bringing first before the public as a candidate for the Assembly fifteen years ago. [Applause.]

The President, introducing the speaker, said it was not Mr. RAYMOND'S intention to make a speech, but merely to give a statement of the facts as they now stood relative to the two opposing candidates for Congress in that district.

On taking the stand Mr. RAYMOND was greeted with the most tumultuous applause, which lasted several minutes. After alluding to the flattering prospects of the Union party on the 8th of November, and cautioning his hearers not to remit their exertions between now and next Tuesday by over confidence as to the result, he proceeded to give a detailed history of the efforts made by himself and his friends to bring about a union upon a single candidate for Congress in the Sixth District. As was well known to his hearers he did not desire the nomination, and only accepted it on the assurance of prominent citizens of the District that the interests of the Union cause would thereby be promoted. After his nomination he found to his surprise that another candidate was to be placed in the field. He knew the opposing candidate Col. HAWKINS well, and would say that he was in every respect a gentleman, and every way qualified for the position. He therefore felt willing to withdraw if a union could be effected upon the other candidate. With this view he called on Col. HAWKINS and it was agreed between them that they should each choose a man, and the two should choose a third who, together, should be empowered to decide which of the candidates should withdraw. Col. HAWKINS chose ORISON BLUNT and he chose ERASTUS BENEDICT. After fruitless effort to agree upon a third man, although Mr. BENEDICT offered to accept almost any proposition coming from the other side, the State General Committee took the matter up. They were also unable to induce the friends of Col. HAWKINS to accept any other mode of settling the difficulty than that of choosing by lot which candidate should withdraw—a mode of settling the question which the Committee did not think suitable or proper.

Having thus tried every honorable means of effecting a union upon one candidate in the district, and failing in all, the speaker said he had no course left to him but to continue as their candidate until sundown on the 8th of November. [Tremendous applause, lasting several minutes.] And now, if the people of the District desired him to represent them in the next Congress, and were willing to put forth proper exertions, he thought his chances of being elected were reasonably good. [Applause.] At any rate, he should spare no honorable exertions to that end, for although he did not desire the office, yet as they had seen fit to put him in nomination, he felt bound to do all he could to secure a representation of the loyal and Union sentiment of the Sixth District in the next Congress. [Applause and three cheers for HENRY J. RAYMOND.]

After another song by the Glee Club the meeting adjourned.

A Warning to Voters.

NEW YORK, Tuesday, Nov. 2, 1864.

To the Editor of the New-York Times.

The voters of the Fifth District of the Eighteenth Ward ought to be made aware that there is every probability that many of them will be defrauded of their right of suffrage at the coming election. The poll-books of the District are said to be *lost* (?) or, according to another account, they are in the custody of one of the Aldermen who is conveniently absent from the city ! On calling, yesterday, at the polling place, northeast corner of Seventeenth-street and Third-avenue, I found that my name was not on the registry books, although I voted at the two last elections and have not changed my residence. While I was making inquiry two other voters found that they had been treated in the same way ; and many who have not taken the precaution to examine the register, will make a similar discovery when it is too late. I inclose my card, and remain,

Respectfully yours, J. W. B.

A SUGGESTION ABOUT BALLOTS.

To the Editor of the New-York Times :

Will you not urge on our Ward Committees the propriety of sending round tickets on Monday, to the houses of electors. Much inconvenience is incurred by depending on getting them at the street stands—it shows how you vote, and you may run a chance of being bullied out of it. It is not necessary to point out the advantages of leaving your house with tickets in hand, and then look after your neighbor.

A VOTER OF THIRTY YEARS.

The New-York Times.

VOL. XIV.---NO. 4116. NEW-YORK, FRIDAY, DECEMBER 2, 1864. PRICE FOUR CENTS.

TENNESSEE.

A Severe Battle at Franklin, Tenn.

HOOD DEFEATED BY THOMAS.

The Rebels Desperately Assault Our Works.

They are Repulsed with Fearful Carnage.

Six Thousand Rebels Killed and Wounded.

TWELVE HUNDRED PRISONERS CAPTURED

Our Loss Less than One Thousand.

MAGNIFICENT BEHAVIOR OF OUR TROOPS

Full and Graphic Account from Our Special Correspondent.

OFFICIAL ANNOUNCEMENT.

WASHINGTON, Thursday, Dec. 1.

The following official dispatch concerning the report of the victory in Tennessee, has been received at headquarters:

FRANKLIN, Tenn., Wednesday, Nov. 30.
FRANKLIN, Tenn., Wednesday, Nov. 30.

Major-Gen. Thomas:

The enemy made a heavy and persistent attack with two corps, commencing at 4 P. M., and lasting till after dark. He was repulsed at all points, with heavy loss—probably of five or six thousand men. Our loss is probably not more than one-fourth of that number. We have captured about one thousand prisoners, including one Brigadier-General.

(Signed,) JOHN SCHOFIELD, Major-General.

OUR SPECIAL ACCOUNT.

Special Dispatch to the New-York Times.

FOUR MILES SOUTH OF NASHVILLE, Thursday, Dec. 1.

Gen. SCHOFIELD yesterday fought one of the *prettiest* fights of the war, resulting most disastrously to the rebels, with little loss to ourselves. After three days' skirmishing, the rebels crowded our first line of works yesterday afternoon, and at 4 P. M. made a most desperate attack on our right and centre, forcing our lines to our breastworks, which were thrown up from river to river in an open field on the Cumberland Pike, which ran through the centre of the field.

At least half the rebel force engaged endeavored to pierce our centre, and come down viciously on WAGNER'S Division, which, after desperate fighting, fell back, and MANY'S rebel division, of FRANK CHEATHAM'S corps, got inside our works and captured two guns. Our centre was not broken, however, and, better still, Gen. WAGNER successfully rallied his troops, who charged on the enemy, recaptured the two guns, and *drove the division over the breastworks, capturing one entire brigade and its commander.*

At 4:30 o'clock the battle was waged with unabating vigor, the enemy having made during a half hour several attempts to break our centre.

The Federal position was a magnificent one, and the result of these four days' work were magnificently grand.

All this while the rebels had appeared in front of our right. The plan was to pierce our centre and crush our right wing before dark. A portion of our infantry were engaged three-quarters of an hour firing on the rebel columns who stood their ground like madmen. During every charge made on our right and centre, volleys of grape and canister were hurled into their lines, and only darkness prevented their sacrifice being more awful. It is said that no canister shot was used by the rebels during the day, but fired shot and shell.

After the first break of WAGNER'S division and its recovery, our line never budged a step. All was quiet after 10 P. M. It was not only one of the *prettiest* but *cleanest* battles of the war. The excessive slaughter of the enemy was owing to our wholesale use of canister and grape, and our selection of the ground. The battle was fought in an open field, with no trees or undergrowth, or other interruption. The enemy's loss in killed and wounded approximates 7,000, and we have over 1,200 prisoners, and one general officer and several field officers. The Colonel of the Fifteenth Mississippi, a Northern man, of Illinois, was wounded and taken prisoner. Four-fifths of his regiment were killed, wounded and captured. Our loss does not reach a thousand, *hors du combat.* Gen. BRADLEY, of Illinois, while gallantly leading his troops, was severely wounded in the shoulder. Our loss in field officers is very small. Our troops behaved handsomely. SCHOFIELD commanded on the field, STANLEY on the right, and COX on the left. Gen. STANLEY was wounded slightly in the neck, but remained on the field and is all right to-day.

I have told you all along the programme of Gen. THOMAS would electrify you, and this is but the epilogue of the battle to come off.

After our dead, wounded and prisoners were cared for, our army fell back to this point, and are in line of battle while I write. Up to this time, 3 P. M., the enemy has not made his appearance. The Third Corps of Veterans are in readiness, and a battle is expected before daylight to-morrow. All Government work is suspended, and all are under arms, from Gen. DONALDSON down to the unscientific laborers.

The falling back of our troops was accomplished at 6 o'clock this morning, and bridges burned across Harpeth River to retard the transportation of rebel supplies. The cavalry was handled prettily by Gen. WILSON, between Spring Hill and Triune.

A. J. SMITH'S corps is in line of battle, and the situation is particularly grand. Forts Negley, Morton, Cairo and Houston are alive, and the infantry movements perfectly satisfactory. Something must immediately transpire, as Gen. THOMAS is ready to strike no matter how the rebels move.

BENJ. C. TRUMAN.

ANOTHER ACCOUNT.

NASHVILLE, Tenn., Thursday, Dec. 1—9:30 P. M.

About noon on Wednesday our main army reached Franklin, when Gen. SCHOFIELD prepared to give the enemy battle. There was very little skirmishing, as HOOD'S object was to attack us before we had time to throw up defensive works.

About 4 o'clock the enemy commenced advancing on our lines, when the ball was opened by our batteries shelling their advance, and soon after a regular cannonading opened along the whole line. The rebels, who had been protected by woods, now emerged from cover, and opened with a fierce volley of musketry along the lines and then charged. For a moment part of our line wavered, and fell back before the desperate charge of the enemy. Gens. RUGER and COX, however, rallied their men and charged the enemy, who had crossed over our abandoned line of works.

The rebels were now fighting with the desperation of demons, charging our lines furiously, some leaping our works and fighting hard.

Now was the critical moment, but our Generals, rallying their troops, swung on the rebel flank, doubling them in the centre, where our artillery and musketry mowed them down by hundreds.

The tide was now turned. Our men, inspired with success, gave a wild huzza and swept back on the rebel line like an avalanche, hurling the enemy back in the wildest disorder and confusion.

Night was now setting in, yet we followed up our advantage. What once threatened to be a disastrous defeat was thus turned into a glorious victory. The courage of our officers and the desperate bravery of our men was unexampled.

Our loss is about seven hundred killed and wounded. We captured over one thousand prisoners and eight battle-flags. Two rebel Brigadier-Generals are in our hands. A rebel Division-General was left on the field mortally wounded. The rebel loss in killed and wounded is estimated at three thousand.

The rebel Gens. CHEATHAM and LEE'S corps were engaged. The brunt of the battle on our side fell on the Second Division of the Fourth Corps.

Capt. COUGHLIN, of Gen. COX'S staff, was killed, and several regimental commanders and officers were killed and wounded, whose names have not been ascertained. Gen. STANLEY was slightly wounded in the neck, but did not leave the field.

Gen. COX states that one could walk fifty yards on dead rebels in his front.

The excitement is allayed here by the knowledge of the above facts.

Our troops have taken position in a line of works between Nashville and Franklin.

Further Details.

NASHVILLE, Tenn., Thursday, Dec. 1.

The Federal forces under Gen. THOMAS retired from Franklin last night, and have taken position and formed in line of battle south of Nashville about three miles. Skirmishing has been going on all day about five miles south of here. Heavy cannonading can be distinctly heard in the city. No want of confidence is felt by the citizens in ultimate success by the Federals. The employes of the Quarter-Master's Department are under arms and in the trenches.

One hundred and seven Confederate officers, including one Brigadier-General and one thousand prisoners, arrived in the city this morning. They were captured in the fight last night near Franklin. A great battle may momentarily be expected.

A Most Desperate Attack by the Rebels—The Rebels Charge Our Masked Batteries—Terrible Loss of the Enemy—Forrest Reported Killed—Reinforcements for Schofield.

NASHVILLE, Thursday, Dec. 1.

Parties who have arrived from the front, and who witnessed the battle of yesterday, describe the attack of the rebel forces as desperate. Four charges were made upon the Federal masked batteries in columns four lines deep. Each time the rebels were repulsed with fearful loss.

The fort is on the north bank of the river, opposite the town, extending up the river, and encircling the town was the line of masked batteries. Eye-witnesses say that this engagement, in desperation and furious fighting, was hardly equaled by the battle of Stone River.

FORREST in person was on the field rallying his men. A rumor is in circulation that he was killed, but it lacks confirmation.

About 7 o'clock last night heavy reinforcements reached SCHOFIELD, which caused a complete rout of the rebel forces.

The city to-day is full of fleeing residents of Williamson and other counties south. They state HOOD is gathering up all the horses, hogs and mules that he can find, and sending them south.

There is great panic among the negroes in the counties south of Nashville. Numbers are fleeing to the city for protection.

THE VERY LATEST.

NASHVILLE, Thursday, Dec. 1.

HOOD'S Infantry force crossed the Harpeth River this morning, and he has not advanced that portion of his force since. His cavalry crossed Harpeth River on the fords above Franklin this morning at daybreak, closely following Gen. WILSON, who retired in this direction. Skirmishing with the advance has occurred all day. Gen. WILSON occupies a strong position a few miles south of Nashville, and is able to resist any force the rebels may bring against him.

The rebel General captured yesterday was Col. GORDON, of the Eleventh Tennessee, brevet Brigadier-General.

An officer who witnessed the fight yesterday, describes the battle as one of the most sanguinary of the war. The determined bravery of the rebels exceeded anything before seen. Although slaughtered by hundreds, they still advanced against our batteries. Within five hours, eleven distinct attacks were made against our works, each a failure.

The battle being ended our forces quietly withdrew from the town.

Among the casualties is Maj.-Gen. Stanley, wounded by a shot in the neck. The rebel Gen. Cheatham is reported wounded. Capt. Bissell, of the Twelfth Indiana, and Capt. Staley, One Hundred and Twenty-fourth Indiana, were killed; Capt. Hinton, One Hundred and Twenty-fourth Indiana, mortally wounded; Col. Lowrey, One Hundred and Seventh Illinois, killed; Capt. Coughlin, of Gen. Cox' Staff, was killed; Capt. Dowling, One Hundred and Eleventh Ohio, was wounded; Col. Walters, Third Brigade, First Division, was wounded in the shoulder; Col. Conrad, who commanded a brigade in the Second Division, was wounded.

The following are rebel casualties: Brig.-Gen. Adams, killed; Brig.-Gen. Scott, wounded. The enemy's total killed, wounded and prisoners are estimated at 4,000, 3,000 being either killed or wounded. The Federal loss in killed and wounded was 700. The loss in prisoners is trifling.

Gen. BRADLEY is wounded and in the city.

Col. STOCKTON and Major JAMES, of the Seventy-second Illinois, are also wounded.

It is rumored this evening that HOOD is moving eastward, toward Murfreesboro'.

PRELIMINARY DETAILS.

Dispatches to the Associated Press.

NASHVILLE, Tenn., Wednesday, Nov. 30.

Army movements for the last few days have been simply for position.

The National forces have not retreated except to improve the location, and occupy Franklin to-day; but they will probably select for the battle-field a place much nearer Nashville.

Some skirmishing has occurred, with little or no advantage to either side.

The probabilities are that a great battle will be fought within the next forty-eight hours.

Our forces are in eager and anxious expectation for the fray, while our Generals are hopeful and confident of victory.

Large accessions of Federal troops have reached here, who have been sent to advantageous positions.

Small detachments of rebel cavalry are operating not far from Nashville, doing, however, no real damage to the rail communications, which still remain intact, trains running regularly.

There is much excitement among the citizens of Nashville on account of the near approach of HOOD'S army.

Maj.-Gen. A. J. SMITH'S corps reached here to-night.

Hood's Advance at Spring Hill, Tenn., Thirty-two Miles South of Nashville.

NASHVILLE, Wednesday, Nov. 30—Midnight. RECEIVED Dec. 1—9 A. M.

Heavy skirmishing for the past few days, and still going on between our troops and FORREST.

There was a sharp fight yesterday at Spring Hill, twelve miles south of Franklin. Our cavalry was driven back on our infantry lines which checked the enemy. A squad of rebel prisoners were in charge of these troops, when the rebel cavalry made a dash on them, releasing their men and capturing ours.

A train was attacked near Harpeth River. The engineer detached the locomotive, and both are supposed to be captured. The rest of the train was saved.

A squad of rebel cavalry dashed across the Chattanooga line yesterday, near Cheshire, tearing up the track.

The train was detained all night, but came in next morning.

Our troops have fallen back around Franklin.

The main part of HOOD'S army is across Duck River.

Every indication of a heavy battle in a few days, but we are confident of the result.

Franklin.

Franklin, the scene of the great victory over HOOD on Thursday, is the capital of Williamson County, Tenn., and is situated on the south bank of Big Harpeth River, about 18 miles from Nashville, on the line of the Nashville and Decatur Railroad. Before the war it was a beautiful village, with a population of about 2,000 people. Franklin has changed hands several times during the war. After VAN DORN'S success in capturing a Union brigade at Spring Hill, near Franklin, in March, 1863, that rebel Commander moved upon the latter place, which he attacked on the 10th of April. Major-Gen. GORDON GRANGER was in command of the village. His forces comprised two infantry divisions of 1,600 men, 2,000 cavalry under SMITH and STANLEY, and eighteen guns. The only artificial defence was an uncompleted fort, which mounted two siege guns and two three-inch rifled guns. VAN DORN'S force was estimated at nine thousand infantry and two regiments of cavalry. The rebels were handsomely repulsed, losing three hundred, while GRANGER'S total loss was only thirty-seven.

The town proper is built upon an open, level spot; but circling round to the west and south of it are the Harpeth Hills. Big Harpeth River has its source in Bedford County, and flows northwest through Williamson, past the town of Franklin, enters Davidson County, and falls into the Cumberland River thirty-five miles below this city, after a general comparative course of sixty miles.

Rebel Speculations.

From the Richmond Whig, Nov. 29.

The care which the Yankee newspapers take to represent the movement of HOOD as ineffectual and despicable; the ridicule which they cast upon his present position; their constant declaration that THOMAS is more than a match for him, and that he has entirely failed, prove beyond a doubt that he has not failed. He has succeeded in placing SHERMAN in a most embarrassing situation, from which he could only escape by a desperate plunge, which he has taken, and the effect of which we shall very shortly witness.

The *Whig* of the 29th says Gen. RIPLEY has been placed in command of South Carolina.

FROM NEW-ORLEANS.

An Important Success by Gen. Lee—A Raid Through Mississippi—Capture of Three Guns and a number of Prisoners.

The steamer *Matanzas*, from New-Orleans, Nov. 23 has arrived at this port. She brings the following news:

RAID IN MISSISSIPPI.

The *True Delta*, of Nov. 21, publishes the following:

SIX MILES EAST OF PORT HUDSON, Nov. 21.

Brig.-Gen. Burton:

I am en route home, and shall arrive to-night; have captured 200 prisoners, including 25 commissioned officers. We had a strong fight at Liberty, Miss., in which we whipped the enemy badly. We captured one piece of artillery, and two at Brookhaven, one of them is a siege gun, formerly captured at Port Hudson. I have all of Gen. HODGES staff, from 600 to 800 head of horses and mules, rode by negroes; and destroyed immense stores on the railroad.

(Signed) A. L. LEE, Brig.-Gen.

The above is a copy of a dispatch received by Brig.-Gen. BURTON.

Brig.-Gen. LEE with his whole command, prisoners and captures, as previously reported, has just arrived in Baton Rouge.

IMPORTANT CAPTURE.

LARGE HAUL OF MONEY, ETC.

From the Era, Nov. 20.

The steamer *Grey Eagle* arrived here this morning, having on board Capt. NED MONTGOMERY and twenty-six other rebel prisoners, captured at Choctaw Bend on Wednesday last. The party at the time of the capture were on their way to Texas, where Capt. MONTGOMERY is said to have purchased a rancho, on which he intended to reside for the balance of his days.

On MONTGOMERY was found $250,000 in foreign Exchange, and a quantity of money besides, and all the party were mounted on fine blooded horses.

Capt. MONTGOMERY is well-known here, having been in charge of the construction of the Confederate fleet at the time FARRAGUT passed the forts. He skedaddled at that time, and we believe has since been engaged in guerrilla business, which seems to be profitable, judging from what was found upon him. It is said that he has quit the rebel service, and had determined to become a peaceable citizen, but he may now have cause to change his purpose. "The best laid schemes of mice and men," etc.

THE REBELS DEFEATED AT THIBODAUX.

From the True Delta, Nov. 26.

The talk was current on the streets last evening that an expedition had recently started from Thibodaux, and was successful in defeating a large body of rebels, burning their boats, barracks and baggage. On inquiry, last night, of the proper authority, we found the report to be correct, and that the expedition was under command of Major MILLER. No further particulars had been received by us up to the hour of going to press.

ARRIVAL OF THE MANHATTAN.

From the Era, Nov. 23.

The ocean iron-clad steamer *Manhattan* arrived here on Sunday last from Mobile Bay. She is the first of the monitor class of boats that has made so long a voyage as from New-York to these waters. The *Manhattan* bore a conspicuous part in the great naval and land fight in Mobile Bay last Summer, and still bears the marks of that fearful contest. The following is the list of her officers:

Commander, J. W. A. Nicholson; Acting-Lieut. and Ex. Off., Robert B. Ely, Acting-Ensigns, George B. Mott, J. B. Trott, Chas. H. Sinclair and J. Lewis Harris; Assistant-Paymaster, H. G. Thayer; Surgeon, H. W. Mitchell; Chief-Engineer, Charles L. Carty; First Assistant-Engineer, W. H. Miller; Second Assistant-Engineers, James B. Farrand and Thos. Finnie; Third Assistant-Engineer, William Stollery; Captain's Clerk, A. W. Maxwell.

TORNADO AT RIO JANEIRO.

Terrible Hail Storm—Great Damage to the City and Shipping—Serious Loss of Life.

By the arrival of the bark *Mirago*, Capt. MERRILL, we have advices from Rio Janeiro to Oct. 13th. The ship *Alexander*, Capt. J. BROWN, arrived the night previous from Cardiff, and while off the port Capt. BROWN was washed overboard by a sea and drowned.

A most violent tornado visited that place on the 10th inst., at 6 P. M., accompanied by tremendous large hail stones and torrents of rain. The city for about one quarter of a mile in width suffered severely, many houses being blown down and others completely riddled by the hail. The tornado lasted about 15 minutes.

The shipping has sustained a great deal of damage.

The bark *Leighton*, Capt. BLATCHFORD, was capsized, and his (the Captain's) son, a lad of 10 years, drowned; his wife was saved almost exhausted. The bark *Lapwing* was considerably damaged about the stern. The Brazilian brig *Manuel* was capsized, also several other foreign vessels capsized and a number of lives lost. A boat from the English line-of-battle ship *Bombay*, while going ashore during the tornado, was upset, and all the crew with several officers, lost.

FROM MEMPHIS.

Rebel Incendiaries Caught Firing Government Buildings.

CAIRO, Thursday, Dec. 1.

Memphis papers of yesterday give detailed accounts of a plot by rebel agents to burn the Memphis and Charleston Railroad Depot and Government stores, worth two millions.

The plot was discovered by the United States Detectives, to whom the matter was intrusted by Gen. WASHBURN, and the incendiaries were caught in the act of firing the buildings.

It is alleged that these emissaries were to receive from the rebel Government ten per cent. of the value of the property thus destroyed.

Dr. McMILLAN, proprietor of the Charleston House of Memphis, is among those arrested. He is charged with being the agent of the rebel Government and concocting the plot.

The prisoners have been confined in Irving Block. They will be tried by a military commission, and probably hung.

Major-Gen. Banks.

HE IS TO RESUME HIS COMMAND IN NEW-ORLEANS.

WASHINGTON, Thursday, Dec. 1.

The *Daily Chronicle* of this morning, speaking of Major-Gen. BANKS' preparations to shortly leave here for New-Orleans, to resume his position as head of the Department of the Gulf, including Louisiana, Arkansas and Missouri, says:

"His civil policy has met the approval of the President of the United States, and he returns to his post at the request of the Executive, and it is no less pleasant to announce that the friendliest relations exist between Major-Gen. BANKS and Major-Gen. CANBY, in charge of the military operations in the Division of West Mississippi."

From Port Royal.

The steamer *Melville*, from Port Royal Nov. 27, brings the report that on the 26th inst. Gen FOSTER had issued orders for all citizens to be enrolled at that place, and report for duty on the 29th. These were to be formed in companies for home protection. The United States forces there were to move immediately, destination unknown. The *Melville* reports that after leaving port, at about 6 P. M., heard heavy and quick firing at Port Royal, but could not tell its meaning.

The Lake Erie Raid Case.

TORONTO, C. W., Thursday, Dec. 1.

The case of BURLEIGH, one of the Lake Erie raiders, came before the court to-day, Mr. RUSSELL, District Attorney of Detroit, conducted the case. Witnesses identified the prisoner, and testified to the part taken by him in the raid. The case was then adjourned to next week.

Seizure of Ammunition, &c.

COLLINGWOOD, C. W., Thursday, Dec. 1.

The customs authorities yesterday seized some boxes which, on examination, were found to contain a gun-carriage, with canister, grape, shot, etc., for 18-pounder guns. The *Georgian* is expected daily.

The City Railroads.

DRY DOCK, EAST BROADWAY AND BATTERY RAILROAD COMPANY, OFFICE NO. 282 ELEVENTH-STREET, Dec. 1, 1864.

To the Editor of the New-York Times:

In reply to that portion of the article in your issue of this morning which refers to this road, I desire to state that the drivers in the employ of this company are instructed to drive on a *slow* trot the whole length of the City Hall Park, and to walk their horses around *all* curves, or when crossing the tracks of other roads. The conductor and driver who were on car No. 30 on Tuesday last have been suspended from duty until the charge made against them can be investigated. I have only to add, that every well founded complaint made to me against any employe of this company will receive immediate attention and prompt redress. Very respectfully, your obedient servant.

WM. RICHARDSON, Superintendent.

New-York Historical Society.

The first of a series of three lectures on Egypt and Egyptian Antiquities, was delivered before this society, last evening, by Prof. JOHN WILLIAM DRAPER, LL. D.

The Professor spoke of the position of Ancient Egypt in the family of nations, and what might be learned from their example. He spoke of their antiquities, pyramids, &c., and the peculiar opinions that led to their erection, and more particularly those that induced the people to embalm their dead. He then spoke of the causes which led to the permanence of the Egyptian system, showing that it lasted without material change for about forty centuries. He attributed this durability to the homogeneous character of the people, as arising from the unvariable climate in which they live. He then drew a contrast between that climate and the climate of the United States, showing how the latter produces great differences in the character of man, more especially in those who live in the North, as compared with those who live in the South. He then proposed the inquiry whether it is possible in any manner to compensate for these variations of climate, and to correct the disturbance that perpetually arises through emigration. He showed that, to a great extent, this can be done by public education and intercommunication, and that thus an approach can be made to the condition of things that gave such remarkable permanence to the Egyptian political system.

At the close of the lecture it was announced that Mr. PRIME would give the next lecture, on the Burial-places of Egypt, and that on the following Thursday Dr. ANDERSON would unroll the mummy he had given to the Society.

GEORGIA.

LATER FROM GEN. SHERMAN.

Savannah and Augusta Papers to November 26.

Sherman Still Reported on the Oconee.

A PROBABLE MOVEMENT ON SAVANNAH.

Rebel Troops Concentrating at Augusta.

Bragg Brings Reinforcements from Wilmington.

The Rebels Factories at Augusta Removed,

INTERESTING MISCELLANEOUS INTELLIGENCE.

From Our Special Correspondent.

SAVANNAH RIVER, Georgia, Sunday, Nov. 27, 1864.

We are scarcely less excited here on the question of Gen. SHERMAN'S movement than the rebels themselves, and we know that they are stirred as they never have been before at the boldness of his advance. The Savannah journals are not brought to us now until after they are two days old, for fear that we shall be too highly elated at the strait in which the Confederacy finds itself. The last authentic information from the rebels tells us that SHERMAN is advancing in three columns, with a force estimated at 60,000 men, at least one half of whom are cavalry and mounted infantry. The public buildings of Milledgeville, the capital of Georgia, have been burnt, and the Legislature, being in session at the time of SHERMAN'S advance force entering the town, adjourned in confusion, some of the members paying as high as *one thousand dollars for transportation a distance of eight miles.* You will be able to form an idea of the reign of terror that now obtains in Georgia and South Carolina, from the files of newspapers which I forward. A levy en masse has been ordered, and BEAUREGARD is in command of the troops. There seems to be most perturbation because SHERMAN has shrouded his objective point in mystery, by sending out immense bands of mounted men to ravage the country on the flanks of his main columns. On Monday last he was at Gordon, with artillery, about fifteen miles from Milledgeville, and had fortified the Georgia Central Railroad between Gordon and Griswoldville, cutting off 2,500 of our prisoners that were to have been brought up from Camp Sumter, at Andersonville. To impede his progress, the bridges over the Oconee River have been destroyed and the country devastated in his front, so that he shall be unable to subsist upon it. The roads have been to a great extent rendered impassable by felled trees and pitfalls, and the rebels claim that during the past three days the progress of the Union troops eastward has not exceeded six miles. They also claim that their cavalry are picking up large numbers of our stragglers, by dashing upon our rear and flanks. From all that I can learn, I believe SHERMAN'S main body to be within 125 miles of Savannah, with nothing to oppose him save the militia and such other unorganized forces as the emergency has brought together, and that the chances of his reaching the seaboard are at present altogether in his favor. Should he be delayed, by artificial obstructions of the road, long enough for LEE to detach a part of his army to confront him, GRANT in that case would be able to drive the rebels out of Virginia, and SHERMAN would doubtless find a mode of retreat, from the heart of rebeldom, southwestwardly to Mobile. A tremendously bold game is in progress on the military chess-board, and it is easy to see that the enemy believe it to be in our hands.

H. J. W.

NEWS FROM REBEL SOURCES.

Our correspondent on the fleet in the Savannah River, Mr. H. J. WINSER, has supplied us with full files of Augusta and Savannah papers to the 26th ult., from which we glean the following intelligence about the campaign in Georgia:

SHERMAN'S PROGRESS.

OPERATIONS ON THE OCONEE.

From the Augusta Constitutionalist, Nov. 25.

The latest reliable intelligence from the direction of Macon comes from our scouts sent out from Sparta. These scouts, who came in last evening, *report that a body of from 500 to 1,000 Yankee cavalry had crossed the Oconee,* and were moving slowly and nervously toward Sparta. Beyond some burning and stealing, this small band of troopers has no special significance. We have reason to believe that they will be seriously bushwhacked, and, we trust, cut to pieces.

One of the most encouraging features of this "invasion" is the fact, which we have from the most undoubted testimony, *that hundreds of the enemy are straggling from their main bodies,* and searching for somebody to take them into custody. *They are sprawling all about the country, and those who are not willing to surrender can be beautifully bushwacked.* Let all the old and young folks turn out and give the rascals a taste of Georgia State sovereignty. *The demoralization of our enemy is most providential for us, and ought to stiffen the backbone of the most timid amongst us.*

Three hundred prisoners arrived last evening from up the Georgia Road, and four hundred more are to arrive to-day.

These prisoners report that a division of three thousand of our cavalry had followed them all the way, dashing upon them constantly, picking up stragglers and capturing wagons.

Hampton's invincible cavalry will be with us in a day or two, and hang upon their eastern flank.

Gen. Wayne has whipped Kilpatrick's cavalry division at the Oconee Bridge, driving them headlong and in confusion. He telegraphs that he is perfectly able to take care of himself.

Wheeler, with many thousand men, has intercepted the enemy at a point, at present unmentionable, and is giving them no rest, night or day.

The main body of the enemy is moving down the western side of the Oconee, and has shown no disposition, thus far, to attempt its passage.

The skies are brightening. Everything looks glorious, and ere long Mr. SHERMAN will get a lashing that he little dreamed of when he made his "On to the Gulf." The gulf of perdition be upon him!

From the Savannah News, Nov. 26.

We have no reliable information from the front to-day, of any movements that are going on. We learn that the opinion prevails to some extent in military circles, *that Sherman intends yet to fall upon Macon, and not press on toward the coast at present.*

Our own forces are gathering and going to the proper place. *We are informed that over three thousand rations were issued in this city this morning to newly arrived veteran troops,* and we are also officially informed *that four or five thousand more will pass through here in two or three days.*

LATEST FROM THE FRONT—THE ENEMY REPULSED AT OCONEE.

From the Savannah News, Nov. 24.

Yesterday an official dispatch was received here stating that the enemy, with a large force, *had flanked Gen. Wayne at Oconee Bridge, C. R. R., and compelled him to retire;* and furthermore, that the former had crossed his forces at Ball's Ferry, some four miles below the bridge. This was most unwelcome news, and produced many long faces.

At a late hour last night, however, we were favored with the following dispatch to Gen. HARDEE, who is now in the city, containing the cheering news that the enemy had been repulsed and driven across the river. All honor to our gallant young townsman:

AUGUSTA, Nov. 23—9 P. M.

Lieut.-Gen. Hardee, Savannah:

Major HARTRIDGE has driven the enemy back across the Oconee River. Gen. WAYNE has returned to the Bridge and opened the office there.

J. BRENNER, Supt.

ANOTHER VERSION OF THE ABOVE.

From the Augusta Constitutionalist, Nov. 23.

Gen. WAYNE, having been pressed back by a superior force from Gordon, retired to Oconee Station. At this point he was receiving reinforcements from the proper quarter. His position is an exceedingly strong one, being flanked on either side by impenetrable swamps, and only approachable by the narrow defile of the railroad. This pass is well protected by log forts and stockades, and will baffle the assault of heavy columns.

FROM THE GEORGIA ROAD.

From the Augusta Chronicle and Sentinel Nov. 25.

Trains ran up as far as Greensboro yesterday. Passengers could impart no information concerning the whereabouts of the enemy.

One hundred and forty-six Yankee prisoners were brought down last night from Athens. They were "gobbled up" by GRAHAM'S scouts, Texan Rangers, and squads of other commands.

There was a rumor in town last night *that the main body of Sherman was progressing towards the Altamaha River. Another rumor stated that a body of the Federals was within sixteen miles of Sparta.* We cannot vouch for the truth of either of these rumors. We merely give them as reported to us.

FROM THE CENTRAL RAILROAD

From the Augusta Chronicle and Sentinel, Nov. 25.

Gen. WHEELER with about ten thousand men has crossed the Oconee and effected a junction with Gen. WAYNE. *Gen. Wayne has successfully defended the bridge over the Oconee River.* On this road the cadets of the Georgia Military Institute, who fought under him, have acquitted themselves nobly.

The enemy have left Gen. WAYNE'S front and are supposed to have joined the main body.

There are no Yankees this side of the Oconee River.

WAR RUMORS

From the Savannah News, Nov. 24.

It was reported in the city yesterday, on the authority of a private dispatch, that Milledgeville had not been visited by the Yankees, and the capitol and other public buildings were still safe.

The Augusta *Register* of the 23d says: "The depot at Madison is burned, also all other depots on the road. The column advancing on the Georgia road is composed of SLOCUM'S corps. It is attended by cavalry, variously estimated at from two to five thousand."

Reports from up the Central Railroad indicate that the right wing of the enemy are still advancing, but the exact progress made is not clearly understood. There is a report that they have crossed the Oconee, four miles below the railroad bridge. WHEELER is close on their rear. Our dispatches give some Yankee news of SHERMAN'S intentions.

The Augusta *Constitutionalist* of Wednesday, Nov. 23, has the following:

"It is reported that the enemy has crossed the Oconee in force, near Milledgeville. This rumor, however, is strenuously contradicted by other parties. Milledgeville is reported as burned."

The column operating on the Georgia Road kept the western side, and struck off in the direction of Macon, as though contemplating a junction with the force in that vicinity.

Prisoners captured from the enemy on the Georgia Road state that the intention of SHERMAN was to avoid Augusta, and strike Macon probably—Savannah certainly. Atlanta is now in our possession. A strong force of cavalry is following SHERMAN, and it is not impossible that the invincible FORREST—SHERMAN'S evil genius—may, ere long, hang like a wolf on his rear and flanks.

From the Augusta Register, Nov. 22.

We conversed with an intelligent gentlemen who arrived last night by the passenger train up the Georgia Railroad.

He informed us that on Monday the Federals left the line of the Georgia road, going directly to Eatonton.

The only Yankees who came to Greensboro' were a few stragglers, who were captured.

The trains ran up to Greensboro' and Athens yesterday.

A portion of Maj. GRAHAM'S command reached this city last night. They report that they visited Atlanta several days since and found it completely evacuated and burned. They state that the Federals took all the cattle and forage in their route, but did not molest those who staid at home.

They captured two or three hundred Yankee stragglers, who will probably reach here to-day.

They also corroborate the statement of the Federals leaving the Georgia Railroad and going in the direction of Eatonton.

THE WHEREABOUTS OF THE YANKEES.

From the Augusta Chronicle & Sentinel Nov. 25.

The whereabouts of the main body of the Yankee army is involved in mystery, and there is not a military man in this city that can definitely locate them, in our opinion. We should not be like Micawber, waiting for "something to turn up," but should "turn up something" ourselves.

CHEERING.

From the Augusta Constitutionalist, Nov. 23.

We have intelligence of the most important character, which we deem contraband at present. Suffice it to say, that matters are beginning to assume a comfortable appearance, and Mr. SHERMAN had better keep his weather eye open, or mayhap he will get it closed.

PRISONERS.

Several Yankees, white and black, were captured on this side of the Oconee, and brought to this city.

PREPARATIONS FOR RESISTING SHERMAN.

REINFORCEMENTS FROM WILMINGTON UNDER BRAGG.

From the Augusta Chronicle and Sentinel, Nov. 24.

It will be seen from a dispatch in another column that Gen. Bragg has left Wilmington with reinforcements for this place. These, we are told, number about ten thousand. These, in addition to those who started for Augusta from another section on Saturday, will make quite a formidable array.

The following is the dispatch referred to:

WILMINGTON, Nov. 22.

Hon. R. H. May, Mayor of Augusta:

I leave here to-day with reinforcements for Augusta. Exhort your people to be confident and resolute.

BRAXTON BRAGG.

Reinforcements are constantly arriving in our city. The air resounds with the shriek of the engine whistle day and night. The soldiers appear to be in excellent spirits, and to enjoy the prospect of a fight ahead. The gloom which overspread our city a short time since has disappeared entirely. Everything wears a cheerful aspect.

From the Augusta Constitutionalist, Nov. 23.

Our citizens were gratified last evening by seeing, among the troops arriving in our city, *a portion of Hampton's splendid cavalry from Virginia.*

With the exception of the buzz created by the militia enrolling officers, all remains quiet. The "reliable gentleman" did not have so much to say as usual up to a late hour last night. No one believes that SHERMAN is hard so crazy as to venture on a collision with the forces at this place. *The splendid fortifications that surround the city* would require the expenditure of more ammunition than he can afford to lose without any base of supplies.

He will not risk a battle, but avoid our forces wherever they appear in formidable proportions; destroy

(Continued on the Eighth Page.)

The Charleston Mercury.

DAILY PAPER—Twenty Dollars for Six Months—Payable in Advance. | VINDICE NULLO / SPONTE SUA SINE LEGE FIDES RECTUMQUE COLETUR | COUNTRY PAPER—Three a Week—Twenty Dollars for Six Months—Payable in Advance.

Volume LXXXV. | CHARLESTON, S. C., FRIDAY, DECEMBER 9, 1864. | Number 12,238.

THE MERCURY.

FRIDAY, DECEMBER 9, 1864.

The Fighting Around Savannah.

All the other passing events of the war are, for the moment, subordinate in interest to the operations now progressing on the important lines of railroad which form the main avenues to Savannah.

It is certain that SHERMAN's advance yesterday had encountered our forces, under Gen. HARDEE, at or near Station No. 2½ on the Central railroad, about twenty miles from Savannah. Severe fighting was going on yesterday forenoon; but we have no trustworthy intelligence whatever in regard to the result. Various rumors concerning the engagement—some favorable and some otherwise—were afloat yesterday; but as we are satisfied that they were merely sensation stories, we refrain from repeating them, and await more authentic accounts.

From the line of the Savannah Railroad we have news of a more definite character. On Tuesday, it seems, the enemy advanced to a point about one mile from the railroad, and about five miles from Pocotaligo. Here they were met by our forces, and speedily driven back, with some loss. The movement is believed to have been a reconnaissance merely; for, during Tuesday night, the enemy retired to their entrenchments, and could not be seen next morning.

At an early hour on Wednesday morning a force, consisting of the Citadel Cadets, Captain THOMSON, and the 47th Georgia, the whole commanded by Major J. B. WHITE, of the Cadets, were ordered to advance and reconnoitre the enemy's position. This they did, in gallant style. The Cadets deployed as skirmishers, and the enemy, surprised, apparently, at the vigor and boldness of the attack, retired some distance before our advancing line. Soon, however, the Yankees were heavily reinforced and discovering the numbers that were opposed to them, turned upon our men, who, in turn, were themselves obliged to retire to their works near the railroad. They were pursued till dark to within one mile of the railroad, where the enemy halted and entrenched themselves strongly. They held that position unmolested during Wednesday night and Thursday. It is not unlikely that the fighting may be renewed to-day; but we have confidence in the ability of our forces to hold the railroad in any event.

Amongst our wounded in the fighting on Wednesday were six of our gallant young Citadel Cadets. Their names are as follows: Lieutenant A. COFFIN, A. R. HEYWARD, JOSEPH BARNWELL, A. J. GREEN, W. J. F. PATTERSON and E. C. MCCARTY. They were brought to the city on Wednesday night, and are all tenderly cared for and doing well.

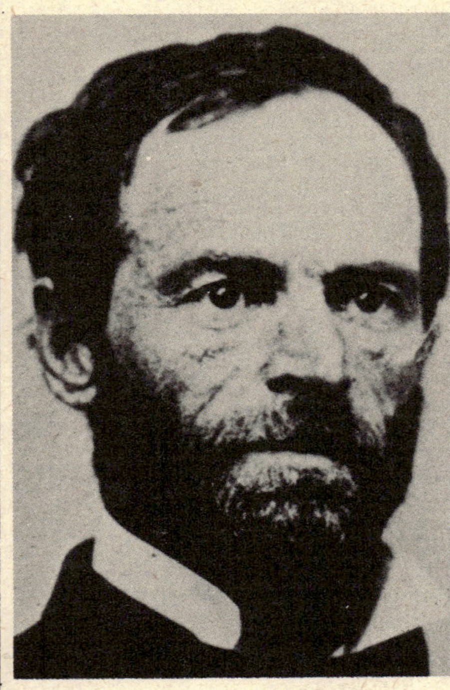

Major General William Tecumseh Sherman

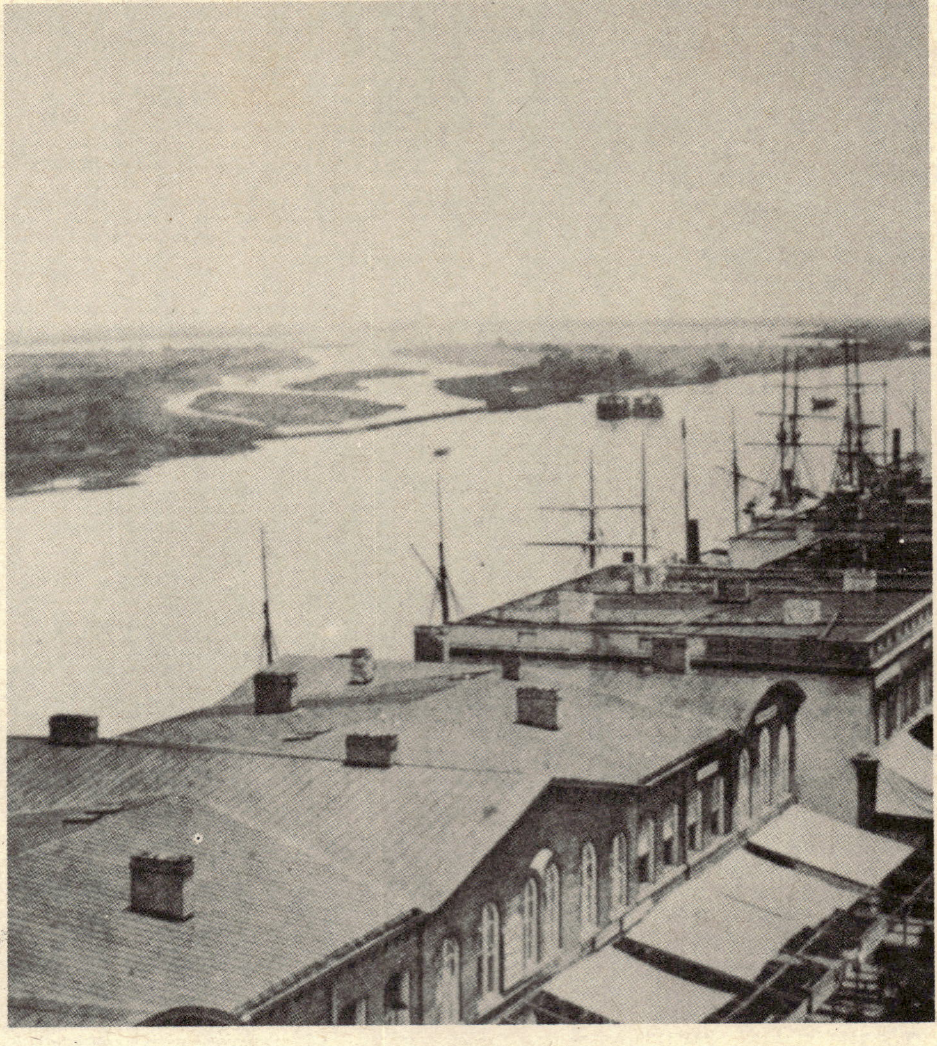

Savannah as seen by Sherman's men

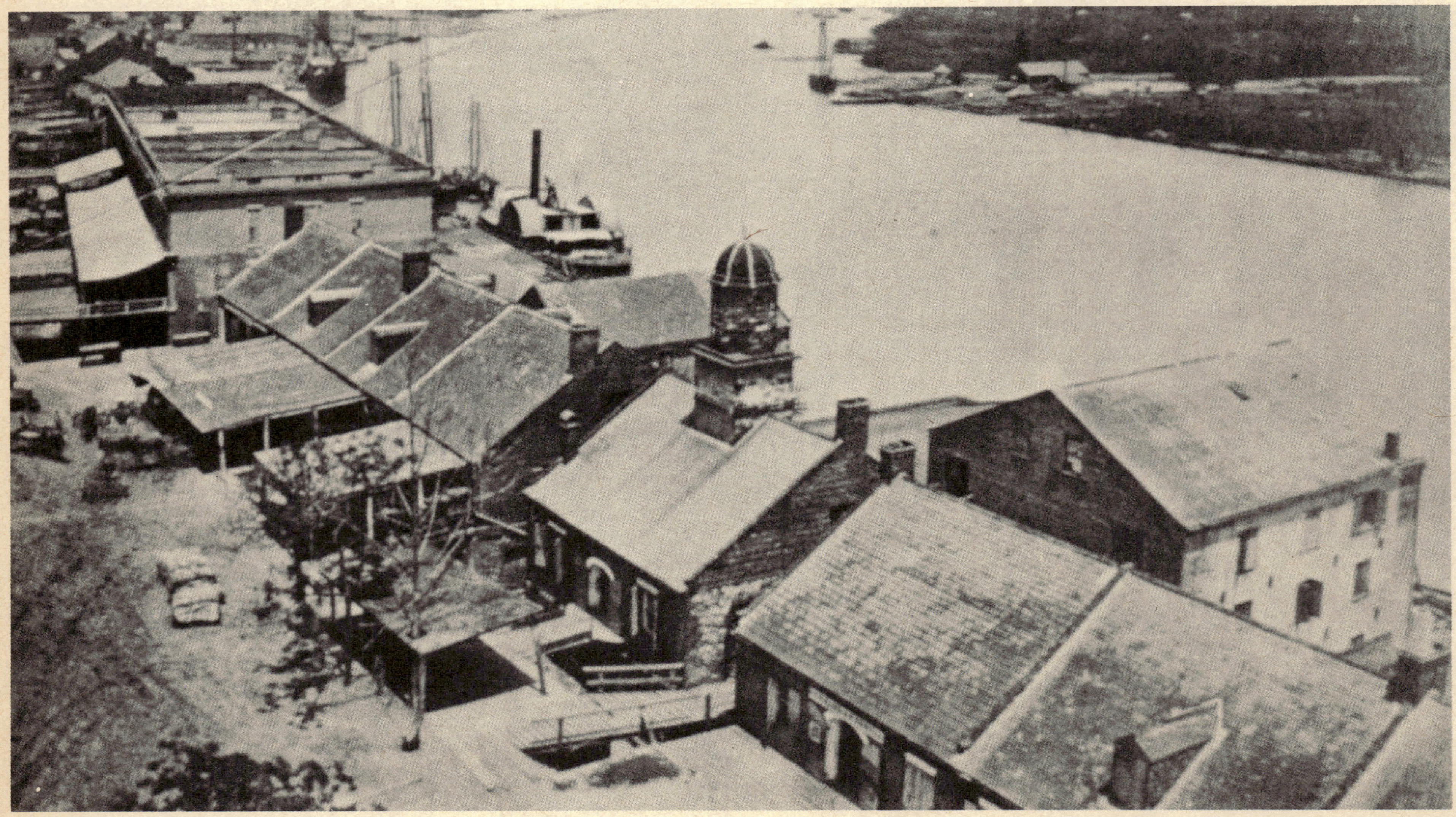

Savannah waterfront

General Sherman's march through central Georgia

The New-York Times.

VOL. XIV.—NO. 4135. NEW-YORK, SATURDAY, DECEMBER 24, 1864. PRICE FOUR CENTS.

GEN. THOMAS' ARMY.

Particulars of Hood's Defeat and Flight.

Eighteen General Officers and Seventeen Thousand Men Disabled.

FIFTY-ONE CANNON CAPTURED.

Hood's Pontoons on the Tennessee Out of Reach of Our Gunboats.

OUR ARMY STILL PURSUING.

The Advance Across Duck River.

HOOD'S ADVANCE AT PULASKI.

Special Dispatch to the New-York Times.

FRANKLIN, TENN., Thursday, Dec. 22.

The rebel retreat from Franklin to Duck River beggars all description. Hood told his Corps Commanders to get off the best way they could with their commands. Frank Cheatham told his aunt, Miss Page, that Hood was ordered to Nashville against his own wishes, but he blames Hood for not attacking Schofield at Spring Hill. Hood ordered Bate to attack at Spring Hill, and he didn't do it.

The rebel army is now beyond Columbia. During the rebel tarry in front of Nashville they captured but two locomotives and ten cars. The railroad is but little injured, and trains are running up to Spring Hill, but two small bridges destroyed. Trains were run to Murfreesboro' on Sunday.

Telegraphic communication is all right with all points. But two small trestles are destroyed on the Johnsonville road. Johnsonville itself was not destroyed.

The rebel loss, during the campaign, was 17,000 men, fifty-one cannon captured and eighteen general officers. The killed, at Franklin, numbered 1,400 the wounded 3,800, and 1,000 prisoners were taken.

In the battles before Nashville and retreat to Columbia there were 3,000 killed (and wounded and 6,000 prisoners. The Federal loss in the battle at Franklin was 2,000, before Nashville not 4,000. The total Federal loss will not reach 7,000, with two generals slightly wounded.

Hood has a pontoon bridge above the shoals on the Tennessee River, where our gunboats can't reach it.

Hood marched on Franklin with 40,000 men, including cavalry, and 65 pieces of artillery. He lost just half his general officers, and counting in deserters which are coming in and stragglers which are being captured, he will lose nearly half his men. The rout is complete, although his army is not quite annihilated.

B. C. TRUMAN.

THE VERY LATEST.

NASHVILLE, Friday, Dec. 23.

The latest accounts from the front locate Gen. Thomas' headquarters at Rutherford Hill, yesterday morning, eight miles this side of Columbia. Since that time our forces have crossed Duck River, and have moved to a point south of Columbia. Our cavalry forces crossed at Hunter's Ford, below Columbia, and dashed into the town, the enemy meanwhile retreating without firing a shot. We captured about fifty stragglers.

The rebel force was, at last accounts, at Pulaski, yesterday morning. They are probably some distance south of that place to-day. They are closely followed by our cavalry. No particular damage was done to the town of Columbia by the passage through it of the two armies.

At least one-third of Hood's army are without arms and equipments, everything which impedes their flight having been thrown away. Rebel deserters and prisoners report the only effective corps of Hood's army to be S. D. Lee's.

Forrest effected a junction with Hood at Columbia on Tuesday evening.

The water on the Shoals is fifteen feet deep, and at a stand-still.

THE BATTLE OF NASHVILLE.

NASHVILLE, Friday, Dec. 16—Midnight.

The readers of newspapers do not know what correspondents suffer sometimes in mind. For instance, imagine a poor fellow taking the chances of a battle all day, then riding several miles in the dark, with mud up to his horse's belly, to find "the wires down east of Louisville." This has been the case with the subscriber, and others, for the past two days. The fighting yesterday and to-day, as I have stated in a telegram which, may be, you have never received, has been grander and more magnificent in detail than anything I have ever witnessed upon a field of battle.

THURSDAY'S FIGHT.

Early in the morning the enemy's line of battle was within musket shot of Nashville, with both flanks resting upon the river, with Gen. Frank Cheatham's corps on the rebel right, crossing the Lebanon, Murfreesboro and Nolensville Pikes; Stephen D. Lee's corps in the centre, crossing the Franklin, Granny White and Hillsboro Pikes, and Stewart on their left, crossing the Harding and Charlotte Pikes, and resting on the river a few miles south of the city, and commanded by Hood in person.

Our forces were commanded by Gen. Thomas, and moved upon the enemy in the following order: A. J. Smith upon the right, Steedman on the left, and Wood in the centre, with Schofield in reserve, and most of our cavalry, under Gens. Johnson, Hatch and Wilson, on the right. Beside, we had gunboats assisting in the protection of our flanks, which rested on the river.

A. J. Smith moved out the Sixteenth Corps about 8 o'clock, and skirmished with the enemy until a little before 1 o'clock, with little or no loss to either side, making about a mile in that time. Wood moved out the celebrated Fourth Corps about the same time, and charged two lines of works and captured them before he took his dinner. Gens. Beatty's and Elliott's divisions charged with great fury and enthusiasm, and were received in gallant manner by the rebels, who fought with their accustomed desperation. But two rebel batteries were brought to bear upon the two divisions, while six batteries of field artillery, and all the big guns on Fort Negley, and guns upon Casino and Confiscation, for more than an hour, were employed in hurling destruction into the rebel ranks. Immediately in front of Mrs. Acklin's house the charge was made with unbounded spirit. Post's brigade and a battery of artillery plied into the lines head over heels, and captured one hundred men and a section of artillery. Gen. Steedman moved out his men, composed of a portion of his own division, detachments of troops belonging to the different corps with Sherman, and two brigades of colored troops respectively commanded by Cols. Thompson and Morgan. Gen. Steedman's orders were to make a vigorous attack, for two reasons: Gen. Thomas desired to get possession of a nasty fort upon our extreme left, which commanded our line for two miles to the right, and further, to deceive Hood, as Smith and Schofield were to turn the enemy's left, had any attempt to crush Steedman taken place. But the rebels did not await the second charge of the two colored brigades, which went right up to the summit of the hill without much wavering, driving the enemy a quarter of a mile, and capturing nearly a hundred prisoners. Up to noon Steedman's troops were pretty actively engaged, the white and the black men, shoulder to shoulder, pitching in like fury, regardless of all considerations of color. At noon Steedman had moved nearly a mile and a half, and had commenced to swing his extreme left in a little from the river. On our extreme right, our cavalry had about all they could conveniently attend to during the forenoon, experiencing slight repulses, owing to the fine positions of the enemy. Our infantry and cavalry got some very rough handling just about this time, but were helped out of their dilemma by the gunboats, which came along in the nick of time. The *Carondelet* threw about fifty 64-pound shells into the rebel left, driving the troops resting on the river in great confusion, and silencing a battery of artillery.

In the afternoon Steedman was not so busily engaged as he had been during the early part of the day. His troops, however, were under fire all the while, and behaved with great gallantry. During all these charges, the colored troops hardly gave way. They were admirably handled by Cols. Thompson and Morgan, both brave young men, and as they tugged up the hill the white soldiers upon either side rent the air with vociferations. The negroes, too, as they dashed inside of the works, shouted, screamed, yelled and threw up their hats, notwithstanding they had left nearly two hundred of their comrades behind, the bleeding victims of rebel shot and shell. As I said above, of the grand charge which I have described, Steedman moved with little opposition, as the rebels, in contracting their lines, necessarily abandoned some strong positions in his front. Wood's corps stood the brunt of the fight in the afternoon, and added new laurels to its well-known and well-earned fame. A little before 3 o'clock, the Second and Third Divisions made two glorious charges upon a long line of rude rifle-pits. An entire battery of brass guns were captured, but most of the troops ran away, and but few prisoners were captured. Before dark another line of works were taken, Wood's corps sustaining a loss of over one hundred men killed and wounded during the charge. He was above an hour from the commencement to the conclusion of this charge, during which time the enemy made very little use of his artillery. At dark the Fourth Corps was four miles from Nashville, having taken half a dozen lines of works, several cannon, and toward four hundred prisoners. Although Wood's corps did the hardest fighting in the afternoon, A. J. Smith, in conjunction with the cavalry and a portion of Schofield's corps, made a multiplicity of brilliant movements, resulting in the capture of two batteries of artillery, nearly a thousand prisoners, a wagon train, and Gens. Lee's and Chalmers's headquarters' trains. This was in a great measure owing to the sagacity and skill of Gen. A. J. Smith, who seems as much at home upon a field of action as one might well imagine. Portions of Schofield's corps were also eminently interested in the taking of the batteries, as were also Hatch's and Johnson's divisions of cavalry. The gunboats kept up their thundering all the latter part of the afternoon, and did considerable execution upon the enemy's left. At dark firing ceased, with the exception that our artillerists threw an occasional shell into the rebel lines. The enemy had been pushed over three miles all round since daylight, although at times the fighting was of the most stubborn character.

The victory was one of the superbest of the war. Our troops drove the enemy at all points, extending our territory three miles south of our position in the morning. Some five distinct lines of rebel works were taken on the left and centre, and the rebel left broken. We captured eighteen guns, with caissons, &c., all in complete order. We also captured 1,600 prisoners, a large amount of small arms, and a number of wagons. It is believed that our own and the enemy's loss in killed and wounded, is about the same, each side losing between 1,200 and 1,500.

The rebels used very little artillery, but used what they did to a purpose. The captured guns were all smooth bores but four, and of excellent workmanship.

On account of the rolling condition of the country and the thinness of the forests, the movements of the troops upon both sides were witnessed to much advantage. At one time the entire front of Steedman's and Wood's troops and two corps of the enemy, could be seen distinctly from a safe position.

Gens. Thomas, Smith, Schofield, Wood, Steedman, Wilson and other general officers, were upon the field all day. No general officer was injured, although Wood like to have lost his head by a cannon ball twice.

FRIDAY'S FIGHT.

In point of splendor and magnificent results, to-day's affair was even more glorious than yesterday's. During the night, Gen. Hood contracted his lines in a remarkable degree, resting his right a short distance east of the Franklin pike, and his left on the Harding pike, making his line of battle less than four miles from flank to flank, although it was double that number of miles in extreme length, owing to its zig-zag order upon and near the Franklin pike. He also retired his army from a naturally weak position and disposed his forces at the base of a range of detached spurs of the Cumberland. It was evident that he intended to make another stand, and it was also evident that the preservation of his rear and his line of retreat upon the Franklin pike, were objects of his particular attention. Gen. Thomas evidently knew what Hood's programme was as well as Hood himself, and at daylight moved Steedman out rapidly upon the left, with orders to swing in and cross the Murfreesboro' and Nolensville pikes. This was done with rapidity, but no captures were made owing to the rebel evacuation of their works on our left during the night. Wood and A. J. Smith moved up to within musket shot of the rebel lines, while Schofield was held partly in reserve on the right and partly in a position to make a rapid dash in conjunction with our cavalry, upon the enemy's left, should the situation suggest such a demonstration. All this transpired before 9 A. M. I went out upon the Granny White pike, a little before night, and watched the movements of our right and the enemy's left until noon.

The enemy had a very fine position at the base of a range of hills, extending from the Granny White to to the Harding pike. He was protected by a line of works which had been hastily constructed near the edge of the woods. Garrard's and McArthur's divisions had to advance through an open field over a mile in length. After getting within four hundred yards of the rebels our column went down upon their bellies, and crawled up some fifty or sixty yards closer. Three batteries followed up these two divisions, and when they halted commenced shelling the woods back of the rebel line and some houses on the pike, from behind which about fifty sharpshooters were banging away. Up to near 11 o'clock this was the order of things in front of Smith. About that time the rebels showed their heads in great numbers above the works, and acted as though they intended to charge the three batteries. They came out of their works shortly after, and our batteries were retired temporarily to a safer position. Just before 12 Smith's whole corps from right to left made a desperate charge, but could not carry the works. About half past 12 the attempt was again made, and a portion of the works were carried. McArthur ordered up two six-gun batteries upon his left, and one battery upon the right of his division, his own and Garrard's men made a charge, the three batteries being advanced so that an enfilading fire could be got in. The whole manœuvre was grand in projection and execution. The artillery did frightful work along the rebel line, our infantry carrying the works during a temporary panic, which was caused by the vigorous hurling of grape and canister into the rebel ranks. In this charge over two hundred of the enemy were captured. Smith's whole line then advanced, his right swinging around a little from off the Hardin pike and a portion of the Twenty-third corps falling and making up the gap between the Sixteenth and Hatch's division of cavalry. It was now quite 1 o'clock, and a most terrible cannonading had opened all along our left and centre. Knowing that Wood and Steedman had a certain amount of work to perform to bring up with Smith, I went over upon the left and centre, where I spent the afternoon until dark, and witnessed, in an unsafe position, more thrilling sights than I have ever seen before.

The rebel bullets were whizzing quite uncomfortably, but their artillery, which is the thing that generally produces the demoralization, remained comparatively quiet, and I, in company with two other correspondents, took the chances of the former.

The Sixth Ohio, and a battery of the Fourth Regular Artillery, took a position upon an open field, about fifty feet in the rear of our infantry; to the right of Beatty's division a Michigan battery and two Ohio batteries, took up a position in an open field, near and upon Wood's extreme right, while two batteries got in on the left. From 1 till 2 o'clock these thirty-six guns shelled the rebel position, which was very strong in Wood's front, and particularly strong in front of Steedman.

At precisely 2 o'clock it commenced to rain, and rained hard during the balance of the day. A little after 2 the Third and First Divisions of Wood's corps made a desperate charge upon the rebel line which was located upon a slight elevation. The firing lasted fully twenty minutes, when the rebels retired in considerable disorder, leaving their dead and wounded and forty odd prisoners in our hands. The rebels had parallel works on this hill, and the two divisions, without orders, with the wildest enthusiasm, charged the other line of works in the face of a deadly volley of musketry and a shower of grape from four Napoleon guns. Really, I discovered no signs of wavering, and the whole drama was in full show. In ten minutes after they rushed into the works, captured three hundred men and the battery, which was a splendid one of four guns. Every member of the battery—the Second Louisiana—was either killed, wounded or captured.

Smith and Wood were now on an even line, and a frowning-looking eminence, topped with strong works, three regiments of Tennessee infantry and Stanford's Mississippi battery lie before Steedman, who, at this juncture, was in conversation with Wood. Capt. Tracy informed me that the two colored brigades would be ordered to storm the hill. I crossed the Franklin pike to see Col. Thompson, commanding one of the colored brigades, who is a particular friend of mine, when I heard the orders given for the assault. Immediately the two brigades of colored men started up the hill. I crossed back to the right of the Franklin pike, where I could see the whole movement, without placing myself in too great danger. When within about a hundred yards of the crest of the hill the four guns and the infantry poured a broadside into the negroes, when a frightful panic took place upon Steedman's right, resting on the pike. The movement ceased for a few moments, when a couple of our batteries commenced an enfilading fire, and the assaulting party, with an additional brigade of white troops, again attempted the ascent. The rebel infantry blazed away at a fearful rate, and the artillery discharged sixteen shots of cannister, which made the assaulting column reel, waver and almost fall back. This was the most exciting picture I had ever seen so close, as I stood, in company with Capt. Both, of Gen. Miller's Staff, about two hundred feet to the right of the assaulting party. After a manly struggle, with the loss of over two hundred men killed and wounded in the colored brigades, including eight officers: the party reached the top, and with a yell, went over the works, captured the entire battery and nearly three hundred prisoners. The guns were of the James pattern, were manufactured at Columbus, Ga., and were quite warm when I arrived. Every caisson had been smashed by our artillery, and most of the horses killed, although the guns were in good order. The men composing this battery stood like men to their post—32 out of 70 being killed and wounded. Every officer was killed. As soon as the hill was taken, the colored troops pitched after the retreating rebels, chasing them through a valley nearly a mile. Firing wholly ceased upon the left, which had swung around nearly a mile and a half in two hours. Wood's corps carried another line of works, without much opposition, however, although Post's and Straight's brigades pitched in like good fellows.

This was a little before 4 o'clock, and, when all was quiet upon the left and centre, a tremendous crash took place upon the right. It only lasted about ten minutes, but the firing was awful during that time. I started to go over to the right, but when half way over, met Capt. Burroughs, of Gen. Thomas' staff, who told me that Smith had made a glorious charge, and with the assistance of Schofield, had taken twelve guns, two general officers, and fifteen hundred prisoners. As I told you in the start, Schofield had a certain plan to carry out if the opportunity presented itself. It did. While Smith was making a charge, Schofield threw his whole corps away round to the right, and shut up toward A. J. Smith's corps in front, the two corps grabbing the number of guns and prisoners stated above in the operation. Darkness came abruptly on, and hostilities ceased. As near as I can judge our loss is about two thousand in killed and wounded. The enemy's loss in killed and wounded is smaller. We captured about four thousand prisoners and two general officers. Gens. Smith and Schofield captured 12 guns, and I saw Wood's and Steedman's corps capture a like number, while Hatch captured a section of artillery on our extreme right. I started for the city a little before 7 o'clock, at which time all was quiet at the front, and all of our dead, and our own and the rebel wounded had been cared for. Our front occupied a position between eight and nine miles from the city.

Rebel prisoners admit their defeat, and deplore their great loss in artillery and prisoners. Orders were issued last night for 5,000 rations for prisoners. Gen. Jackson, captured by Smith, is a Major-General, and is an old man. Smith is a middle-aged man, and pays a high compliment to our troops, who, he says, are brave in a fight and magnanimous after victory.

LOSSES.

The following summing up of the relative losses of both armies during the two days' fight may be considered quite accurate:

Rebel killed and wounded, Thursday	1,500
Rebel killed and wounded, Friday	2,000—3,500
Rebel loss in prisoners, Thursday	1,600
Rebel loss in prisoners, Friday	4,000—5,600
and two general officers.	
Rebel loss of cannon, Thursday	18
Rebel loss of cannon, Friday	26—44

The Federal loss in killed and wounded in the two days' fight, I think, will exceed the enemy's by a thousand. No prisoners are reported taken by the rebels.

Total rebel loss	8,100
Total Federal loss	4,500

Allowing our loss in killed and wounded to be one thousand more than the enemy's even, gives us the advantage of 3,600 men, 2 general officers, 44 cannon, 5,000 small arms, &c., &c.

BENJAMIN C. TRUMAN.

NEWS FROM REBEL SOURCES.

Special Dispatch to the New-York Times.

WASHINGTON, Friday, Dec. 23.

From the Richmond *Examiner* of Wednesday last, received at the office of the Philadelphia *Inquirer*, we extract the following editorial. No later news from Savannah or Wilmington, than that published to-day, is contained in any of the rebel papers of Wednesday:

A BITTER PILL FOR JEFF. DAVIS.

From the Richmond Examiner, Dec. 21.

The news from Tennessee is bad—the situation is bad,—but it is far from being irremediable. The army in Tennessee has been terribly misused, and has suffered awful injury; but it is not lost, and may be restored to full efficiency by the same hand which redeemed it after Missionary Ridge. But to change the fortunes of the country the Executive power and the Legislature must change their character and abandon the road to ruin, hitherto systematically pursued by both. The opening of this campaign found our two best men in real command and in the two principal positions. Lee in Virginia and Johnson in Georgia. The military condition of this country was never so prosperous as it was at Midsummer, for these two men had so done their work that it was then morally certain that the last supreme effort of the enemy was going to fail, and had it failed, it is impossible to doubt that this year would have been the last year of the war. The unexpected freak of the Executive in the removal of Johnston, permitted in silence by the country, has produced fruits such as folly and subserviency never produced before. Although great evils might have been and were apprehended at the time, results have so much surpassed expectations, that they assume the appearance of judgments. But let the past go. The best remedy for the present evil is simply to stop the causes which have caused them. Let the Executive power cease to interfere with the armies; send Johnston to the wreck of that army which he surrendered to Hood in such magnificent conduct; give him *carte blanche* to do what he thinks proper for its salvation and for the defence of the country, and guarantee that neither his commission nor his plans will be any more meddled with. Give to Beauregard complete discretion of action on the coast. Leave to Lee his whole army, and full powers in Virginia, and prosperity will return, good fortune will again befall the army of the South, and the great dangers which now menace the Confederacy will vanish like the clouds of the last rain.

But good sense, moderately and justly used, will never actuate the Executive power while Congress abdicates its functions and public opinion its rights. Nations will suffer just punishment whenever they intrust the power to puny hands, puff up the conceit, and encourage the passions of their rulers by fulsome flattery or silent submission. We have done so. The follies of the Government are manifest to all, but if any one who pays their share of the cost proposes opposition or even remonstrance, the amiable majority cry "Hush! Oh, hush! hush! We can't get rid of him, and he will do thus and so all the more if he is opposed. Don't say anything; we must have concord, unanimity, and there must be no opposition to the Government." Therefore the only voice which is heard at all is the voice of flattery—the voice of those who have neither head nor heart, neither knowledge nor principle. Hence the Executive power is encouraged to pursue its fancies, and although every military misfortune of this country is palpably and confessedly due to the personal interference of Mr. Davis, and the Legislature continued at each session to be his subservient tool, and to furnish new incentives to perversity, new means of mischief. Congress and the Southern public must change their attitude, adopt a more distinct and manly tone, deal with their own affairs with more resolution, keep the Executive power in the path of duty, and curb it with peremptory hands when it interferes with things beyond its capacity.

Great adversity has fallen upon us, but the power of the Southern States is not broken. Their resources are enormous, and on no side is the breach irreparable. Of all external dangers, there is not one that cannot be manfully met. *But greater danger is within.* Folly vested with license, and flattery to encourage folly. No calamity which has happened is in itself ruinous, but what will ruin us is this: that the Government should go on to do and continue the identical acts which have made the calamity by necessary sequence of cause and effect. The more harmony and more concord and more self-abnegation we evince under such circumstances, the more rapid is our progress to destruction. Let us determine that course of the ship shall be altered. *With that determination will be found means to compel change.*

A SUGAR PLUM FOR JEFF. DAVIS.

The Virginia Legislature on Tuesday last adopted a series of resolutions upon the present crisis of affairs in the Confederacy, of which the three following are most significant:

"That it is the imperative and paramount duty of the Confederate Government to continue to devote its utmost energies to the vigorous prosecution of the war, as it is only by the success of our arms that we can hope to obtain honorable peace, and preserve the sovereignty and the liberties of our people from destruction. To that end this Commonwealth will endure every sacrifice, until the freedom which is our heritage shall be securely established in peace, under the protection of a Confederacy of independent and sovereign States.

That the Confederate Government, which is the centre and organ of our united exertions in war, has been also intrusted with the power of concluding peace, by that constitution which binds these States together, and this commonwealth, *believing that the trust has been wisely reposed*, for the common benefit, does not desire either to withdraw the authority which has been delegated by all the States for their common safety, *or to embarrass, by irregular proceedings, the Confederate Government in its delicate and difficult duty of negotiating peace*, and that any proposition from the enemy to any of the States of this Confederacy, to treat for a separate peace, is, in the language of this General Assembly in 1782, insidious and inadmissible.

That unity both in prosecuting the war and in concluding a peace is absolutely essential to our safety, and can be obtained and preserved only by a firm adherence to the constitutional authority established by all the States, and that this General Assembly will not listen to any proposition nor suffer any negotiation inconsistent with their confederate faith and union."

GEN. DAVIDSON'S RAID.

From the Richmond Whig, Dec. 21.

MERIDIAN, Miss., Tuesday, Dec. 20.

Authentic information has been received that the advance of Gen. Davidson's raiding column, from Baton Rouge, passed through Augusta, Perry County, Miss., yesterday, for Mobile. Scott and others are in the right place. Warm work is expected on Monday or Tuesday next.

THE ATTACK ON WILMINGTON.

From the Richmond Whig, Dec. 21.

The dispatches foreshadow warm work off Wilmington. The defences of the place against a naval attack are very strong, and Admiral Porter will doubtless discover that he has undertaken an impracticable job, if he attempts the reduction of Wilmington.

BEAUREGARD'S DEPARTMENT.

From the Richmond Whig, Dec. 21.

By recent orders, the department under Gen. Beauregard has been extended so as to include South Carolina and the Atlantic seaboard of Georgia.

Court-Martial.

INDIANAPOLIS, Friday, Dec. 23.

At a court-martial recently convened here, Chas. Billingsley, John Murray, Thomas Ryan and Thomas Lennow were found guilty of desertion, and sentenced to be shot to-day. The sentence was carried into effect this afternoon, at Camp Burnside, near this city, on the first three. The fourth has been respited by the President for ten days.

PORTER'S EXPEDITION.

A Dispatch from Gen. Bragg to Jeff. Davis.

The Entire Fleet off Wilmington.

The Weather so Bad that it is Unable to Operate.

Bragg says He Can Hold the Place.

Immense Destruction of Rebel Property in Blockade-Runners.

WASHINGTON, Friday, Dec. 23.

The *Republican* says that the Government received a dispatch from Gen. Grant, at City Point, announcing that the Richmond papers of yesterday morning, the 22d inst., contain an official dispatch from Gen. Bragg to Jeff. Davis, dated Fort Fisher, New-Inlet, N. C., Dec. 21, as follows:

"The entire fleet of the enemy is in sight, but cannot operate.

"The weather continues bad.

"We are able to hold Wilmington."

Destruction of the Blockade-runner Petrel—The Work of Admiral Porter's Squadron for the Last Fifty Days.

WASHINGTON, Friday, Dec. 23.

Rear-Admiral Porter, under date of the 15th inst., informs the Navy Department of the destruction of the blockade-runner *Petrel*, driven ashore by the gunboats at New Inlet, Cape Fear River.

The *Petrel* was fired upon and sunk, and finally was destroyed by a northeast gale.

She had on board a large cargo of arms and munitions of war.

Admiral Porter reports that within the last fifty days the fleet has captured and destroyed five millions five hundred thousand dollars' worth of the enemy's property in blockade-runners.

GEN. GRANT'S ARMY.

Bad Weather—Officers Going Home on Furlough—Three Deserters to be Hung.

WASHINGTON, Friday, Dec. 23.

A letter from the Army of the Potomac, dated yesterday, says:

Quiet continues to prevail here.

The weather is such as to prevent any movement, if intended.

A large number of officers are going home on furlough.

Among those who left this morning were Gens. Gregg, Potter, Ayres, Bragg and McAllister, with the members of their staffs.

Gen. Mott went North yesterday to attend the funeral of a brother.

Lieut.-Col Osborne, Division Inspector on Gen. Crawford's Staff, a valuable and efficient officer, goes home this morning, having been mustered out after serving over three years.

Three more deserters are to be hung to-morrow. Their names are: John Smyth, William Miller and George Bradley, all of the Fifth New-Hampshire Volunteers.

NEWS FROM WASHINGTON.

Special Dispatch to the New-York Times.

WASHINGTON, Friday, Dec. 23.

THE TEN-FORTY LOAN.

We are officially informed that Secretary Fessenden has not limited the subscriptions to the ten-forty loan to the 31st of December, but will allow them to continue until after the holidays, when he will communicate his views on the subject to the Finance Committees of both Houses. All reports, therefore, in regard to what he intends to do are wholly unfounded.

VICE-ADMIRAL FARRAGUT.

Vice-Admiral Farragut is expected here to-morrow, when his commission as Vice-Admiral, and the Congressional resolution of thanks inscribed upon parchment, will be presented to him.

Dispatches to the Associated Press.

WASHINGTON, Friday, Dec. 23.

GUERRILLAS CROSSING ON THE ICE.

Early this morning a party of guerrillas, of White's command, attempted a crossing to the Maryland shore, on the ice, about Muddy Branch. They were discovered by the pickets of the First New-Hampshire Cavalry, and were driven back. One guerrilla was shot dead. Maj. Andrews, who commands at the point, is in nightly expectation of raids, now the canal and river are frozen, and has accordingly strengthened his picket line.

DEFEAT OF GUERRILLAS.

Several days ago a portion of our cavalry scouted as far up as White Plains on the Manassas Gap Railroad, and coming up to a large party of guerrillas, a fight ensued. The latter were routed with a loss of one Major, one Lieutenant, mortally wounded, and fifteen prisoners taken by our troops.

ICE IN THE POTOMAC.

The Potomac is covered with ice, and the channel is completely closed up, so that navigation is suspended, and boats do not attempt either to approach or leave Washington. The ice is at most places between two and a half and three inches thick. Several boats with troops, which left yesterday, are ice-bound below Gresboro.

DEATH OF ACTING MASTER THATCHER.

The Navy Department to-day received intelligence of the death of Acting Master Charles Thatcher, of Maine, commanding the *Gazelle*, attached to the Mississippi squadron. He was wounded by guerrillas.

Later from New-Orleans.

CAIRO, Friday, Dec. 23.

The steamer *Pauline Cornell*, from New-Orleans on the 15th inst., has arrived here. She has a few bales of cotton.

The steam transport *Clinton*, from Galveston on the 12th inst., had arrived at New-Orleans with 342 exchanged prisoners from Camp Grace, Texas. The men, who were in the most wretched condition, have been supplied with necessary articles for their comfort by the Sanitary Commission.

Gen. Hamilton and family passed Brazos on the *Clinton*.

A late Matamoras paper states that reinforcements had arrived from Brazos Santiago, swelling our force there to two thousand, fifteen hundred of whom are negroes.

The rebels make frequent sallies from Brownsville, which is not fortified, and have numerous skirmishes with the Federal troops.

We have no change to report in the New-Orleans market.

Pardons by the President.

BALTIMORE, Friday, Dec. 23.

Mrs. Hutchins, recently sentenced to five years' imprisonment in the Fitchburgh, (Mass.,) House of Correction for attempting to send a sword to the rebel Maj. Harry Gilmore, has been released, by order of the President, and she arrived here to-day.

Wm. J. Fish, of the First Connecticut Cavalry, late Provost-Marshal of this city, who was sentenced to the Albany Penitentiary for one year, and to pay a fine of $5,000, has also been released.

HOLIDAY GIFTS.

A Tour in the Wake of Santa Claus.

We noticed in Thursday's Times a few of the places where our readers can find holiday presents suitable for the season, but a want of space compelled us to omit many others to be found in our advertising columns where articles of equal excellence and variety tempt the seeker after the useful, the beautiful, or the curious. In fact the whole business portion of our city seems to be transformed into one grand curiosity shop for the display of holiday gifts; and old Santa Claus variously disguised in pantaloons and petticoats, broadcloth and silks, representing manhood and youth, matron and miss, can be seen hurrying about our streets, peering into the shop-windows, dodging in and out of doorways, in search of gifts suitable to the multitudinous tastes and wants of the legions who delight to call him friend and are anxiously looking for his coming. Alas! that we should so often encounter him dressed in the habiliments of mourning and with a weed upon his hat. The devastating war that has afflicted our dear land for four years past has snatched the protector from many a hearthstone, and the cherubs that gather around those chimney-corners on next Sabbath morning will gaze with tear-dimmed eyes upon the annual gifts which good Santa Claus has brought them. Let our citizens see to it that no dead soldier's home goes unvisited by him, albeit his ruddy and jovial countenance is unused to the sorrowing mood. Following in his wake let us extend our tour in search of Christmas and New-Year's presents, which shall dispel the gloom from all faces and bless alike the giver and the receiver.

Starting in Maiden-lane, the down-town bazaar of the metropolis, let us drop into the store of J. M. Bowen & Co., No. 43, and inspect his brilliant stock of fancy goods and Christmas toys. Here we behold every variety of toy and fancy article which American, English and continental ingenuity has been able to fabricate, for the use or pleasure of man, woman or child. The large assortment of fancy articles at this establishment, and the low prices at which they are offered, render it one of the most desirable places to visit for the selection of holiday presents.

Passing round to Fulton-street we find useful gifts in the way of men's and boys' clothing, of which Evans' extensive establishment at Nos. 66 and 68 is among the most noteworthy.

For presents of slippers, gaiters, boots and shoes for misses' and children, the store of C. C. Richmond, No. 150 Fulton-street, or of Wm. T. Allen, No. 377 Bowery, or of E. A. Brooks, 575 Broadway, or of Cantrell, No. 813 Broadway, or of Lorin Brooks, No. 434 Broadway, affords the most ample assortment.

In the way of head-gear for boys and misses, we have the most tempting specimens presented by Burke, No. 210 Broadway, and Knox, at the corner of Broadway and Fulton-street, and Genin, under the Metropolitan, who also keep the finest articles of ladies' furs, which make a most seasonable holiday present.

Although we have heretofore noticed at some length the holiday gifts of the book-trade, particularly in the higher departments of literature, yet it may not be amiss to mention the large stock of juvenile books and stories for sale by W. T. Pooley, of No. 331 Pearl-street, and of Leggatt Brothers, of No. 119 Nassau-street, and of Hurd & Houghton, No. 401 Broadway. Sheldon & Co. also advertise with good reason their autobiography of Gen. Scott, as a most appropriate holiday gift. James G. Gregory, of No. 540 Broadway, also has on hand a most interesting series of Christmas stories.

Our Brooklyn friends will find at Ovington Bros., Nos. 238 and 240 Fulton-street, an excellent assort- of bronzes, clocks, statuettes, groups and figures, and beautiful dinner and tea services, opening for inspection day and evenings.

The "magic wheel," published by Bradburn, of No. 49 Walker-street, is a new and amusing toy for children, and can be found at all the bookstores.

In the line of perfumery and toilet articles, the most extensive and récherché assortment can be found at the glittering palace of Helmbold, under the Metropolitan Hotel, where the customer will be served with a politeness and attention that make purchasing a pleasure.

Ivory and pearl jewelry of the latest styles and largest variety may be found at Welling's, No. 571 Broadway.

In addition to the sewing machines heretofore noticed, "Barnum's self-sewer" is receiving high praise from all quarters, and can be adapted to any of the different varieties of machines.

One of Foley's gold pens or pencils makes a beautiful holiday present, as any one will admit, after seeing the stock on hand at 169 Broadway.

A fine collection of albums, pictures, busts, &c., &c., can be found at Fowler & Wells' new store, No. 389 Broadway.

Presents of ladies' dress goods for the holidays may be found in untold variety and richness at Strang & Adriance's, No. 355 Broadway; at Paton & Co.'s, No. 341 Broadway; at R. H. Macy's, in Sixth-avenue, near Fourteenth-street; at Kinzey's, No. 343 Eighth-avenue, and at many other houses which our readers will find in our advertising columns. In furnishing goods, Union Adams, of No. 657 Broadway, offers inducements not to be overlooked; and of ladies' cloaks, George Carey, of Broadway and Canal-street, and Percival, of No. 657 Broadway, present a stock unequaled in variety and cheapness.

Of choice wines and brandies for the New-Year's table, J. Marc Martin, of No. 203 Pearl-street, will furnish a supply, warranted pure and of the best quality.

Wherever one turns, whether in Broadway, in the Bowery, or in any of the business streets and avenues of the city, he beholds a glittering array of useful and ornamental goods, toys and nicknacks, from which he can fill a bag, however ample, with presents for all his acquaintances, however numerous. That he may succeed in supplying them all, we earnestly hope, and if any are omitted, it will certainly not be the fault of our shopkeepers, who have so amply provided for every want.

The Unemployed Generals.

To the Editor of the New-York Times:

In your issue of to-day you make some very proper and timely remarks on the bill before Congress, dismissing from the service all Generals who have not been in actual service for three months previous to a certain day; but there are some circumstances connected with this bill which you do not mention, and which are, at least, unfortunate. I allude to the fact that men who have served their country long and ably, and who are now suffering from wounds received in the service, should see their names paraded in the public prints as being dropped from the service. I understand there is a provision in the bill covering such cases, which is all right and proper; the misfortune is, that there was no one whose duty it was to properly classify these Generals off duty, and thereby save the wounded officers the mortification of seeing their names published as "dropped from the rolls," without any comment.

As an evidence of the injustice I refer to, I would cite the case of Brig.-Gen. John B. McIntosh, whose name appears in the list you publish. No officer in the service can show a better record than he. Although born in Florida, he offered his services to the Government during the first month of the rebellion, and was assigned a position as Second Lieutenant in the Second Regular Cavalry, (now the Fifth;) in a short time he was promoted to a First Lieutenantcy, and is now Captain in the Fifth Cavalry. During the Summer of 1863 he was made Colonel of the Third Pennsylvania Cavalry, in which position he served—commanding a brigade most of the time—till he was appointed Brigadier-General last Summer. He has always been connected with the Army of the Potomac, and has made a record which will be as enduring as the name of our noble "Army of the Potomac." Gen. McIntosh's active career terminated, for the present, on the 19th of September last. During the battle of Opequan Creek or Winchester, when our army under Sheridan gained a great victory over Early, he was then shot by a sharpshooter, and had his leg amputated while on the field of battle. He is now in Philadelphia, suffering either from the effects of bad surgery or bad nursing soon after he received his wound.

I have no doubt that what I have written applies with force to other cases, but this coming under my special notice I send it to you, hoping you will publish it, and thereby confer a favor upon Gen. McIntosh's friends.

IRVINGTON.

NEW-YORK, Monday, Dec. 19, 1864.

Major General John M. Schofield

Major General John B. Hood

General James Harrison Wilson

Federal troops charge a Confederate entrenchment, Battle of Nashville, December 15, 1864

The New-York Times.

VOL. XIV—NO. 4140. NEW-YORK, FRIDAY, DECEMBER 30, 1864. PRICE FOUR CENTS.

WILMINGTON.

THE ATTACK ON FORT FISHER.

Official Report from Admiral Porter.

Clear Account of Our Special Correspondent.

THE TERRIFIC FIRE OF THE FLEET

The Guns of the Fort Completely Silenced.

Landing and Reconnoissance of the Troops.

They Approach the Ramparts of the Fort.

Their Unexplained Withdrawal Afterward.

RETURN OF GEN. BUTLER'S FORCES.

The Bombardment Continued by Admiral Porter.

WASHINGTON, Thursday, Dec. 29.

The Secretary of the Navy received this afternoon the following by special messenger:

NORTH ATLANTIC SQUADRON, U. S. FLAG SHIP MALVERN, AT SEA, OFF NEW INLET, Monday, Dec. 26, 1864.

SIR: I was in hopes that I should have been able to present to the nation Fort Fisher and the surrounding works as a Christmas offering, but I am sorry to say it has not been taken yet. I attacked it on the 24th inst. with the Ironsides Canonicus, Mahopac, Monadnock, Minnesota, Colorado, Mohican, Tuscarora, Wabash, Susquehanna, Brooklyn, Powhatan, Juniata, Seneca, Shenandoah, Patuxent, Ticonderoga, Mackinaw, Maumee, Yantic, Kansas, Iasco, Quaker City, Monticello, Rhode Island, Sassacus, Chippewa, Osceola, Tacony, Pontoosuc, Santiago de Cuba, Fort Jackson and Vanderbilt, having a reserve of small vessels, consisting of the Aries, Howqua, Wilderness, Cherokee, A. D. Vance, Anemone, Æolus, Gettysburg, Alabama, Keystone State, Banshee, Emma Lillian, Tristam Shandy, Brittania, Gov. Buckingham and Nansemond. Previous to making the attack, a torpedo on a large scale, with an amount of powder on board supposed to be sufficient to explode the powder magazine of the fort, was prepared with great care, and placed under the command of Commander A. C. RHIND, who had associated with him on this perilous service Lieut. S. W. PRESTON, Second Assistant Engineer A. T. MULLEN, of the United States steamship *Agawam*, and Acting Master's Mate PAUL BAYARD, and seven men. So much had been said and written about the terrible effects of gunpowder in an explosion that happened lately in England, that great results were expected from this novel mode of making war. Everything that ingenuity could devise was adopted to make the experiment a success. The vessel was brought round from Norfolk with great care and without accident, in tow of the United States steamer *Sassacus*, Lieut. Commander J. L. DAVIS, who directed his whole attention to the matter in hand, and though he experienced some bad weather and lost one of his rudders, he took her safely into Beaufort, where we filled her up with powder and perfected all the machinery for blowing her up.

Gen. BUTLER had arrived at the rendezvous before us, and I hastened matters all that I could, so that no unnecessary delay might be laid to my charge.

On the 18th inst. I sailed from Beaufort with all the monitors, the *New Ironsides* and the small vessels, including the *Louisiana*, disguised as a blockade-runner, for the rendezvous, twenty miles east of New Inlet, N. C., and found all the larger vessels and transports assembled there, the wind blowing light from the northeast. On the 20th a heavy gale set in from the southwest, and not being able to make a port without scattering all the vessels, I determined to ride it out, which I did without accident of any kind, except the loss of a few anchors, the monitors all behaving beautifully. Only two vessels went to sea in order to avoid the gale, and fared no better than those at anchor. The transports being short of water put into Beaufort, N. C., and were not suitable for riding out at anchor such heavy weather.

After the southwester, the wind chopped around to the westward and gave us a beautiful spell of weather, which I could not afford to lose, and the transports with the troops not making their appearance, I determined to take advantage of it and attack Fort Fisher and its outworks.

On the 23d, I directed Commander RHIND to proceed and explode the vessel right under the walls of Fort Fisher. Mr. BRADFORD, of the Coast Survey, having gone in at night and ascertained that we could place a vessel of seven feet draught right on the edge of the beach. Lieut. R. H. LAMSON, commanding the *Gettysburgh*, volunteered to go in the *Wilderness*, Acting Master HENRY ARBY in command, and tow the *Louisiana* into position. At 10:30 P. M. the powder vessel started toward the bar, and was towed by the *Wilderness* until the embrasures of Fort Fisher were plainly in sight. The *Wilderness* then cast off, and the *Louisiana* proceeded under steam until within 200 yards of the beach and 500 from the fort. Commander RHIND anchored her securely there, and coolly went to work to make all his arrangements to blow her up. This he was enabled to do, owing to a blockade-runner going in right ahead of him, the forts making the blockade-runner signals, which they also did to the *Louisiana*. The gallant party, after coolly making all their arrangements for the explosion, left the vessel. The last thing they did being to set her on fire under the cabin, and then, taking to their boats, they made their escape off the *Wilderness*, lying close by. The *Wilderness* then put off shore with good speed, to avoid any ill effects that might happen from the explosion.

At 1:45 on the morning of the 24th, the explosion took place. The shock was nothing like so severe as was expected; it shook the vessels some, and broke one or two glasses, but nothing more.

At daylight of the 24th, the fleet got under way, and stood in in line of battle. At 11:30 A. M. the signal was made to engage the forts, the *Ironsides* leading, and the *Monadnock*, *Canonicus* and *Mahopac* following. The *Ironsides* took her position in the most beautiful and seamanlike manner, and opened a deliberate fire on the fort, which was firing at her with all its guns, which did not seem numerous in the northeast face, though we counted what appeared to be seventeen guns. But four or five of these were fired from that direction, and they were silenced as soon as the *Ironsides* opened her terrific battery.

The *Minnesota* then took her position in handsome style, and her guns, after getting the range, were fired with rapidity, while the *Mohican* the *Colorado*, and the large vessels marked on the plan, got to their stations, all firing to cover themselves while anchoring. By the time the last of the large vessels anchored, and got their batteries into play, but one or two guns of the enemy were fired, this *feu d'enfer* driving them all to the bomb-proofs.

The small gunboats *Kansas*, *Unadilla*, *Pequot*, *Seneca*, *Pontoosuc*, *Yantic* and *Huron* took a position on the northward and eastward of the monitors, and enfilading the work. The *Shenandoah*, *Ticonderoga*, *Mackinaw*, *Tacony* and *Vanderbilt* took effective positions, as marked on the chart, and added their fire to that already begun. The *Santiago de Cuba*, *Fort Jackson*, *Osceola*, *Chippewa*, *Sassacus*, *Rhode Island*, *Monticello*, *Quaker City* and *Iasco* dropped into position, according to order, and the battle became general. In one hour and fifteen minutes after the first shot was fired, not a shot came from the fort. Two magazines had been blown up by our shells, and the fort set on fire in several places; and such a torrent of missiles were falling into and bursting over it, that it was impossible for anything human to stand it. Finding that the batteries were silenced completely, I directed the ships to keep up a moderate fire, in the hopes of attracting the attention of the transports and bringing them in. At sunset Gen. BUTLER came in in his flagship with a few transports, the rest not having arrived from Beaufort. Being too late to do anything more, I signaled to the fleet to retire for the night to a safe anchorage, which they did without being molested by the enemy.

There were some mistakes made during the day when the vessels went in to take position. My plan of battle being based on accurate calculations, and made from information to be relied on, was placed in the hands of each Commander, and it seemed impossible to go astray if it was strictly followed. I required those vessels that had not followed it closely to get under way and assume their proper positions, which was done promptly and without confusion. The vessels were placed somewhat nearer to the works, and were able to throw in their shell before falling in the water. One or two leading vessels having made the mistake of anchoring too far off, caused those coming after them to commit a like error, but when they all got into place and commenced work in earnest, the shower of shell (one hundred and fifteen per minute) was irresistible. So quickly were the enemy's guns silenced that not an officer or man was injured.

I regret, however, to have to report some severe casualties by the bursting of six 100-pounder Parrott cannon. One burst on board the *Ticonderoga*, killing six of the crew and wounding seven others; another burst on board the *Yankee*, killing one officer and two men; another on the *Juniata*, killing two officers, and wounding and killing ten others; another on the *Mackinaw*, killing one officer and wounding five men; another on the *Quaker City*, wounding, I believe, two or three; another on the *Susquehanna*, killing and wounding seven. I think the bursting of the guns (six in all) much disconcerted the crews of the vessels where the accidents happened, and gave one and all a great distrust of the Parrott 100-pounders, and as subsequent events proved, they were unfit for service, and calculated to kill more of our men than of those of the enemy. Some of the vessels were struck once or twice. The *Mackinaw* had her boiler perforated with a shell and ten or twelve persons were badly scalded. The *Osceola* was struck with a shell near the magazine, and was at one time in a sinking condition; but her efficient commander stopped up the leak; while the *Mackinaw* fought out the battle notwithstanding the damage she received. The *Yantic* was the only vessel which left the line to report damages.

Commander JOHN GUEST, at the last end of the line, showed unusual intelligence in selecting the position and directing his fire. Twice his guns cut down the flagstaff on the Mound Battery, and he silenced the guns there in a very short time, the *Keystone State* and *Quaker City* coöperating effectively.

Lieut.-Commander J. R. DAVIS, with both rudders disabled, got his vessel, the *Sassacus*, into close action and assisted materially in silencing the works, and the *Santiago de Cuba* and *Fort Jackson* took such positions as they could get, towing other vessels not forming proper lines and throwing them out of place, and fought their guns well. The taking of a new position while under fire, by the *Brooklyn* and *Colorado*, was a beautiful sight, and when they got into place both ships delivered a fire that nothing could withstand. The *Brooklyn* well sustained her proud name under her present commander, Capt. JAMES ALDEN, and the *Colorado* gave evidence that her commander, Commodore H. K. THATCHER, well understood the duties of his position. The *Susquehannah* was most effective in her fire, and was fortunate enough to obtain the right position, though much bothered by a vessel near her that had not found her right place.

The *Mohican* went into battle gallantly, and fired rapidly and with effect, and when the *Powhatan*, *Ticonderoga* and *Shenandoah* got into their positions, they did good service. The *Pawtuxet* fell handsomely into line and did good service with the rest, and the *Vanderbilt* took position near the *Minnesota*, and threw in a splendid fire.

The firing of the monitors was excellent, and when their shells struck great damage was done, and the little gunboats that covered them kept up a fire sufficient to disconcert the enemy's aim.

The rebels fired no more after the vessels all opened on them, except a few shots from the Mound and upper batteries, which the *Iasco* and her consorts soon silenced. Our men were at work at the guns five hours, and glad to get a little rest. They came out of the action with rather a contempt for the rebel batteries, and anxious to renew the battle in the morning.

On the 25th all the transports had arrived, and Gen. BUTLER sent Gen. WEITZEL to see me and arrange the programme for the day. It was decided that we should attack the forts again, while the army landed and assaulted them, if possible, under our heavy fire. I sent seventeen gunboats, under the command of Capt. O. S. GLISSON, to cover the troops and assist with their boats in landing the soldiers. Finding the smaller vessels kept too far from the beach, which was quite bold, I sent in the *Brooklyn*, to set them an example, which that vessel did, relying on every commander should, on the information I gave him in relation to the soundings. To this number was added all the small vessels that were covering the coast along. And finally I sent some eight or nine vessels that were acting under Commander GUEST in endeavoring to find a way across the bar. This gave 100 small boats to land the troops with; beside those, the army were already provided with about 20 more.

At 7 A. M. on the 25th I made signal to get under way and form in line of battle, which was quickly done. The order to attack was given, and the Ironsides took position in her usual handsome style, the monitors following close after her. All the vessels followed according to orders, and took position without a shot being fired at them, excepting a few shots fired at the four last vessels that got into line. The firing this day was slow, only sufficient to answer the enemy while the army landed, which they were doing five miles to the east of the fleet. I suppose about 3,000 men landed, when I was notified they were reëmbarking. I could see our soldiers near the fort reconnoitering and sharpshooting, and was in hopes an assault was deemed practicable.

Gen. WEITZEL, in person, was making observations about 600 yards off, and the troops were in and around the works. One gallant officer, whose name I do not know, went on the parapet and brought away the rebel flag we had knocked down. A soldier went into the works and led out a horse, killing the orderly mounted on him, and taking his dispatches from the body. Another soldier fired his musket into the bombproof among the rebels, and eight or ten others who had ventured near the forts were wounded by our shells.

As the ammunition gave out the vessels retired from action, and the iron-clads and the *Minnesota*, *Colorado and Susquehanna* were ordered to open rapidly, which they did with such effect that it seemed to tear the works to pieces. We drew off at sunset, leaving the iron-clads to fire through the night, expecting the troops would attack in the morning, when we would commence again. I received word from Gen. WEITZEL informing me that it was impracticable to assault, and herewith enclose a letter from Gen. BUTLER, assigning his reasons for withdrawing the troops. I also inclose my answer.

In the bombardment of the 25th the men were engaged firing slowly for seven hours. The rebels kept a couple of guns on the upper batteries firing on the vessels, hitting some of them several times without doing much damage. The *Wabash* and *Powhatan*, being within their range, the object seemed mainly to disable them; but a rapid fire soon closed them up. Everything was cooly and systematically done throughout the day, and witnessed some beautiful practice.

The army commenced landing about 2 o'clock, Capt. GLISSON, in the *Santiago de Cuba*, having shelled Flag Pond Battery to insure a safe landing, and they commenced to reëmbark about 5 o'clock. The weather coming on thick and rainy, about a brigade were left on the beach during the night, covered by the gunboats. As our troops landed, sixty-five rebel soldiers hoisted the white flag, and delivered themselves up, and were taken prisoners by the seamen landing the troops, and conveyed to the *Santiago de Cuba*; and two hundred and eighteen more gave themselves up to the reconnoitering party, all being desirous to quit the war.

I don't pretend to put my opinion in opposition to Gen. WEITZEL, who is a thorough soldier and an able engineer, and whose business it is to know more of assaulting than I do. But I can't help thinking that it was worth while to make the attempt, after arriving so far.

About 12 o'clock I sent in a detachment of double-enders under command of Commander JOHN GUEST, to see if I could effect an entrance through the channel. The great number of wrecks on and about the bar has changed the whole formation, and where the the original channel was, we found a shallow bar. I sent Lieut. W. B. CUSHING in to sound and buoy out the channel if he could find one, with orders to Commander GUEST to drag for torpedoes and be ready to run in by the buoys when ordered. One boat belonging to the *Tacony* was sunk by a shell, and a man had his legs cut off; still they stuck to their work until ordered to withdraw for other duty.

In conclusion, allow me to draw your attention to the conduct of Commander RHIND and Lieut. PRESTON. They engaged in the most perilous adventure that was, perhaps, ever undertaken, and though no material results have taken place from the effects of the explosion that we know of, still it was not their fault. As an incentive to others, I beg leave to recommend them for promotion. Also that of Lieut. R. H. LAMSON, who piloted them in and brought them off. No one in the squadron considered that their lives would be saved, and Capt. RHIND and Lieut. PRESTON had made an arrangement to sacrifice themselves in case the vessel was boarded a thing likely to happen. I inclose herewith the report of Commander RHIND, with the names of the gallant fellows who volunteered for the desperate service.

Allow me to mention, also, the name of Mr. BRADFORD, of the Coast Survey, who has always patiently performed every duty he has been called on to carry out.

My thanks are due to Lieut.-Commander R. R. BREESE, Fleet Captain, for carrying about my orders to the fleet during the action, and for his general usefulness to Lieut-Commander H. A. ADAMS, for promptness in supplying the fleet with ammunition; to Lieut. M. W. SANDERS, Signal Officer, whose whole time was occupied in making signals, and who performed his duty well; and to my Aids, Lieut. S. W. TERRY and Lieut. S. W. PRESTON, who afforded me valuable assistance.

I have not yet received a list of the casualties, but believe they are very few from the enemy's guns. We had killed and wounded about forty-five persons by the bursting of the Parrott guns.

I must not omit to pay a tribute to the officers and crews of the monitors, who rode out the heavy gales on an open coast without murmuring or complaining of the want of comfort, which must have been very serious. They have shown a degree of fortitude and perseverance seldom witnessed. Equally brave in battle, they take the closest work with pleasure, and the effect of their shells is terrific. The following are the names of the commanders, and I hope I shall ever keep them under my command: Commanders E. G. PARROTT, of the *Monadnock*, and E. R. CALHOUN, of the *Saugus*; Lieut.-Commanders GEORGE L. BELKNAP, of the *Canonicus*, and E. E. POTTER, of the *Mahopac*.

There are about 1,000 left on shore by the army, who have not got off yet on account of the surf on the beach. These will be got off in the morning, and then the soldiers will be sent home.

I inclose the general order for the attack.

I am, Sir, very respectfully, your obedient servant,

DAVID D. PORTER, Rear Admiral.

Hon. GIDEON WELLES, Secretary of the Navy, Washington, D. C.

GEN. BUTLER TO ADMIRAL PORTER.

HEADQUARTERS DEPARTMENT OF VIRGINIA AND NORTH CAROLINA, Dec. 25, 1864.

ADMIRAL: Upon landing the troops and making a thorough reconnoissance of Fort Fisher, both Gen. WEITZEL and myself are fully of the opinion that the place could not be carried by assault, as it was left substantially uninjured as a defensive work, by the navy fire. We found 17 guns, protected by traverses, two only of which were dismounted, bearing on the beach and covering a strip of land, the only practicable route, not wide enough for a thousand men in line of battle.

Having captured Flag Pond Battery, the garrison of which, sixty-five men and two commissioned officers, were taken off by the navy, we also captured Half-Moon Battery, and seven officers and two hundred and eight men of the Third North Carolina Junior Reserves, including its Commander, from whom I learned that a portion of HOKE's division, consisting of KIRKLAND's and HAGOOD's brigades, had been sent from the lines before Richmond on Tuesday last, arriving at Wilmington Friday night.

Gen. WEITZEL advanced his skirmish line within fifty yards of the fort, while the garrison was kept in their bomb-proofs by the fire of the navy, and so closely, that three or four men of the picket line ventured upon the parapet, and through the sally-port of the works, capturing a horse, which they brought off, killing the Orderly, who was the bearer of a dispatch from the Chief of Artillery of Gen. WHITING, to bring a light battery within the fort; and also brought away from the parapet the flag of the fort. This was done while the shells of the navy were failing about the heads of the daring men who entered the work; and it was evident, as soon as the fire of the navy ceased because of the darkness, that the fort was fully manned again, and opened with grape and canister upon our picket line.

Finding that nothing but the operations of a regular siege, which did not come within my instructions, would reduce the fort, and in view of the threatening aspect of the weather, the wind arising from the southwest, rendering it impossible to make further landing through the surf, I caused the troops with their prisoners to reëmbark; and I see nothing further that can be done by the land forces. I shall, therefore sail for Hampton Roads as soon as the transport fleet can be got in order.

My engineers and officers report Fort Fisher to me as substantially uninjured as a defensive work.

I have the honor to be, very respectfully, your obedient servant,

BENJ. F. BUTLER, Major-General Commanding.

To Rear-Admiral PORTER.

ADMIRAL PORTER TO GEN. BUTLER.

NORTH-ATLANTIC SQUADRON, U. S. FLAGSHIP MALVERN, OFF NEW-INLET, N. C., Dec. 26, 1864.

GENERAL: I beg leave to acknowledge the receipt of your letter of this date, the substance of which was communicated to me by Gen. WEITZEL last night. I have ordered the largest vessels to proceed off Beaufort to fill up with ammunition, to be ready for another attack in case it is decided to proceed with this matter by making other arrangements. We have not commenced firing rapidly yet, and could keep any rebels inside from moving their head until an assaulting column was within twenty yards of the works. I wish some more of your gallant fellows had followed the officer who took the flag from the parapet, and the brave fellow who brought the horse out from the fort. I think they would have found it an easier conquest than is supposed. I do not, however, pretend to place my opinion in opposition to Gen. WEITZEL, whom I know to be an accomplished soldier and engineer, and whose opinion has great weight with me.

D. D. PORTER, Rear Admiral.

OUR SPECIAL ACCOUNT.

From Our Own Correspondent.

U. S. STEAMER SANTIAGO DE CUBA, Monday, Dec. 26.

The grand naval conflict for the possession of the Wilmington approaches, which, in consequence of the inclement weather and other unavoidable causes, has been postponed for a brief season, was fully inaugurated Friday night by the explosion near Fort Fisher of two hundred and fifteen tons of gunpowder, packed in barrels and bags, on board the steamer *Louisiana*.

THE PREPARATION.

In a previous letter to the TIMES I detailed at length the sailing of the fleet from Hampton Roads, and the arrival of many of the vessels in Beaufort Harbor, N. C. The larger ships of the fleet, including the *Wabash*, *Colorado*, *Minnesota*, *New Ironsides*, and others of like draft, did not rendezvous at Beaufort, but passed on further to the south, keeping out of sight of land. On Friday, the 16th, the *Santiago de Cuba* and the *Fort Jackson* sailed out of Beaufort Harbor, and proceeded on a cruise for blockade-runners, and on the 18th again joined the fleet. On the morning of the 18th all the vessels of the fleet, excepting a few that were still waiting at Beaufort for coal, assembled in latitude 33° 46′ North, and Longitude 27° 20′ West, the rendezvous designated by Admiral PORTER, and communicated by a printed circular to the principal officers in the expedition. This point is twenty-five miles from Fort Fisher, consequently none of the vessels were near enough to be seen from the shore. Conspicuous among the fleet I noticed the *Malvern*, Admiral PORTER's flagship. Also the *Ben Deford*, the flagship of Gen. BUTLER. At 9 A. M. a signal was displayed from the *Malvern* for the vessels to get under way. In a short time paddle-wheels and propellers began to turn, and each ship took her assigned position in regular line and order. Two hours were occupied in manœuvering and inspecting, after which orders were signaled for the fleet to run in toward the shore. At 2 P. M. the fleet dropped anchor sixteen miles from Fort Fisher, and eleven from Masonboro Inlet. The morning of the 20th found the fleet still lying at anchor sixteen miles from Fort Fisher. The day was very clear, but nothing was done toward going into action that day.

TOPOGRAPHY OF THE COUNTRY ABOUT CAPE FEAR.

Doubtless a brief description of the location, character and surroundings of the country at the entrance of the Cape Fear River will, in a measure, assist the reader in obtaining a clear and comprehensive view of the importance and magnitude of the approaching engagement. The river itself is approached from two main inlets, separated by Smith's Island, the southernmost one of which may be termed the mouth of the stream, the other being known as New Inlet. At the north of New Inlet and fronting the ocean, is a narrow strip of land twenty miles in length, which is nearly severed from the main land by a sound, the connection being formed at the southern end. The extreme southern point of this narrow peninsula is called Federal Point, on which Fort Fisher stands. Nearer the inlet is a mound, or earthwork, mounting heavy guns and supporting a lighthouse, the latter being for the special guidance of blockade-runners. Between the Mound and Fisher is a line of water batteries, with guns of moderate calibre. North of Fort Fisher are other water batteries, and five miles distant is the Half-moon Battery. Masonboro Inlet separates the northern end of the peninsula from the island above. Those familiar with the location of the rebel defences in Charleston harbor will readily perceive a resemblance between the military situation on Sullivan's Island and that on the narrow territory north of New Inlet. The soil is sandy and unproductive. According to a coast survey chart, three or four houses formerly stood near the bank of Cape Fear River. Doubtless these houses were owned and inhabited by pilots, some of whom have come into our lines. Near Masonboro Inlet the rebels erected salt works, which gave employment to about 800 men. Expeditions from our fleet have at different times destroyed these works, but on every occasion the rebels would soon rebuild them. One night last Summer a boat's crew from a blockader landed at Masonboro Inlet, and received the most hospitable treatment from the workmen. On returning to the ship fifty of the rebels accompanied the party, and over two hundred others were willing and ready to do likewise, but the boat would not hold them.

Directly opposite Federal Point, across New Inlet, is situated Zekes Island. Two months ago, about the time it began to be whispered that an attack on Wilmington was contemplated, the enemy commenced building an earthwork on that island. Smith's Island is of little account, and is supposed to be free of earthworks, batteries and troops. The ground is low and marshy, and on that portion facing the beach can be observed a sickly growth of pines. On every part of it numerous reptiles abound in alarming numbers. Fort Caswell is situated on a point of the main land on the south side of the principal entrance to Cape Fear River. A short distance above it, on a line with the stream, is Fort Johnson and several smaller works. The distance from Fort Fisher to Fort Caswell, in a direct line, does not exceed nine miles. From Fort Fisher to Wilmington, on the line of the river, the distance is twenty miles. The difficulty of manœuvering ships off the entrance of the river is greatly enhanced by the presence of rocks and dangerous shoals. The Frying Pan Shoals, looked upon by the mariner as the most treacherous and dangerous of any on the coast, extend twenty-three miles seaward from Cape Fear. Thus it will be seen that the vessels doing blockade duty at New Inlet, although within sight of the vessels guarding the main entrance of the river, cannot join them without passing over fifty miles of water besides Frying Pan Shoals. There are others which exist in the vicinity of the forts, and, as a consequence, it requires the utmost care on the part of our officers to keep their vessels from grounding. At the first of the war, blockade-runners chose the South Pass in coming out of the river, but recently they have manifested a preference for New Inlet. Each of the Captains is supplied with an excellent chart of the coast, of English drawing, upon which the depth of water and other particulars are carefully noted.

THE MAMMOTH EXPLOSION.

SATURDAY, Dec. 24.

The marvelous event of the age, the gunpowder explosion, which was to have taken place on the night of the 18th, actually came off at an early hour this morning; but the effect of the same was by no means so serious or astounding as most of us had been led to anticipate. The plan originally laid out for firing the vessel and getting her up to near Fort Fisher was changed in some few minor particulars, and from an interview with the officer who had the matter in charge, I am placed in possession of many interesting facts connected with the event. With the exception of the boat sent out to take aboard the parties who conducted the affair, none of the vessels of the fleet were nearer than twelve or fifteen miles to the scene of the explosion. The *Louisiana*, the steamer used to receive the powder, was a purchased vessel of 296 tons measurement, carried an armament of five heavy guns, and for over a year had been doing duty off Newbern, N. C. Ten days ago she was at Craney Island, taking on board the powder, two hundred and fifteen tons, and at that time I remember meeting some of her officers at Norfolk, who, although aware that the vessel was being filled with an immense and precarious cargo, were greatly puzzled to divine the meaning of it all. They did not dream for a moment that the ship which had been their home for so long a time was to meet with such a novel and tragical end. On the morning of the explosion the ship was commanded by Com. ALEXANDER C. RHIND, of the double-ender steamer *Agawam*, who was assisted in the daring exploit by Lieut. S. W. PRESTON, of Admiral PORTER's Staff; Engineer A. T. E. MULLAN, of the *Agawam*; Master's Mate PAUL BOYDEN, formerly of the *Louisiana*. The crew consisted of seven picked men from the *Agawam*, in whom Commander RHIND could place full trust and implicit confidence. Commander RHIND formerly had command of the monitor *Keokuk*, in Charleston Harbor, and is not unfamiliar with deeds that partake largely of the hazardous. Lieut. PRESTON was attached to Admiral DAHLGREN's staff during the attack on Fort Sumter, and while on a boat expedition that had been sent to seize that work, he was captured, together with a number of the men. Lieut. PRESTON's reconnoissances in Charleston Harbor would naturally tend to give him an appetite to again try his hand at an enterprise which calls for coolness and daring. The night, although not pitchy dark, was not sufficiently light for a vessel to be easily discovered when approaching the shore; and the fact that the moon did not rise till about 3 A. M., added to the chances of the complete success of the scheme. Of course, it was no secret that a gigantic plan had been concocted which had for its object the demolition of the rebel earthworks, and the immediate putting *hors du combat* of all the rebel soldiers in the vicinity of Cape Fear. As a natural consequence the expectations of nearly every one connected with the fleet were raised to an exciting point, and on the night of the 23d all were on tiptoe to watch the phenomena attending the mighty and expeditious mode of opening and closing a battle. It was generally supposed that the terrific concussion would occur at about one A. M., but for fear that they would miss the sublime spectacle or fail to have their ears made forever deaf by the stunning report, hundreds of persons paced the vessels' decks from early in the evening till the hour of the explosion. The first visible intimation or encouragement given that the *Louisiana* was proceeding on her mission was conveyed in the flight of three rockets, followed by a display of constant signals, all of which appeared to originate from a point not remote from Fort Fisher. This was at 12:30 o'clock, and, for one, I began to feel some doubt whether the vessel would escape discovery from the shore, as the signal might possibly create suspicion as to her character, instead of impressing the rebels, as was the intention, that she was a blockade-runner discovered and pursued by our cruisers. As it turned out, the enemy either did not see the vessel, or if he did, mistook the nature of her errand. At one o'clock the watch on deck reported a bright glare in the sky, directly over the place where it was expected the explosion would occur. This glow gradually increased to a bright light, which finally expanded into a brilliant illumination. The illumination did not retain its vividness throughout its appearance, but at intervals would die down to a dull glare, thus giving one the impression that a huge bonfire had been built and was occasionally replenished with fresh fuel. The light continued visible till fifteen minutes of two, when, as if by magic, the heavens were electrified into one vast sheet of vivid flame. This lasted but for a moment, and then the light disappeared altogether. We now breathlessly awaited the fearful shock. The immense concussion came to us in a very meek manner. A deep, heavy report, not unlike that produced by the discharge of a 100-pounder, which communicated a slight trembling motion to the ship, greeted our ears fifteen seconds after the disappearance of the flash of light. Thus ended the exhibition. The officers and men who engineered the experiment—for experiment it certainly was—returned safely to the fleet that night. The next morning, not a vestige of the *Louisiana* was to be seen, and the presumption is that she was blown to atoms. Commander RHIND states that the affair was carried out to the letter. The *Louisiana* was towed by the steamer *Wilderness* to within a short distance of the proposed anchorage, when the line was cast off and her engines put in motion. At a point 300 yards from Fort Fisher the engines were stopped and the steamer was anchored. The rebels on shore discoverd her and made signals, but did not fire on her. Everything being in readiness, a pile of two and a half cords of light dry wood, which had been placed on the stern of the boat for the purpose, and covered with oil, pitch and grease, was fired, when the party jumped into a small boat attached to the *Wilderness* by a rope, and pulled themselves hand over hand to the latter. In a few minutes' time all were on board the *Wilderness*, and away she flew seaward as fast as her machinery would propel her. In about an hour's time, and when the *Wilderness* had crossed a distance of twelve or fifteen miles the explosion occurred. The size of the grains varied, some of the powder having been calculated for cannon and some for rifle use. The effect the explosion had on Fort Fisher or any other of the rebel works is not known, but it is the impression throughout the fleet that it must have been slight, from the fact that the rebels at times during the day, opened their guns in a manner too lively to indicate weakness in material. Major THOMAS CASEY, of the Engineer corps, and stationed at Portland, Missouri, witnessed the explosion, having been ordered to do so by the War Department. In due time he will submit a full and elaborate report of the matter to the authorities.

THE FIRST DAY OF THE BATTLE.

On the morning of the 24th, at 6½ o'clock, a signal was made from the flagship for the vessels of the fleet to prepare for moving. In a short time thereafter all the fleet were steaming toward the shore, which was distant five miles from the anchorage. The day opened favorably for the intended bombardment. The wind was blowing lightly from the southwest, and the rough sea that had been prevailing for two or three days previous had subsided into comparatively smooth water. That the reader may obtain a clear view of the plan of attack, I insert the substance of a general order issued by Admiral PORTER:

"It is first proposed to endeavor to paralyze the garrison by an explosion, all the vessels remaining twelve miles out from the bar, and the troops in transports twelve miles down the coast, ready to steam up and be prepared to take the works by assault, in case the latter are disabled. At a given signal, all the bar vessels will run off shore twelve miles, when the vessel with powder will go in under the forts. When the explosion takes place, all the vessels will stand in shore, in the order marked on the plan. The *New Ironsides* will steam along shore, coming from the eastward, until the flag-staff on Fort Fisher bears southwest by one-half west, and anchor; chain ready to slip, with her broadside bearing on the face of the enemy's works, and open fire without delay. The monitors will come up astern, anchoring not more than one length apart, directly in line along the shore, leaving space only for a gunboat to lie outside of them and fire between them or over them. The *New-Ironsides* and monitors will lie in not less than three and a half fathoms water, which will place them about three-fourths of a mile from Fort Fisher and a little over a quarter of a mile from the beach. In the meantime the large ships will lie formed in line of battle to the east of the iron-clads, and heading parallel with the land south one-half west course in five fathoms of water. When the signal is made to "take position," the frigates and sloops will go ahead slowly and anchor about a mile from Fort Fisher with their cables ready to slip and with not more than fifteen fathoms of chain, the fifteen fathom shackle inside the hawse hole.

"The reserves of each division will form a line out of gun-shot ready to act as occasion may require. Great care and coolness will be required to drop the vessels in their right places, and a too early commencement of fire on the part of those going into position, may create confusion. As we know but little about the calibre and number of rebel guns, the vessels must concentrate their fires on the heaviest batteries, but get the range before firing rapidly. For instance, the large vessels and iron-clads concentrate on Fort Fisher, while the *Vanderbilt*, *Fort Jackson* and the vessels in the line with the *Fort Jackson*, will open on the forts within their reach between Fort Fisher and the mound.

"All the reserved vessels will prepare to attack Zeekes Island Battery, by taking a position where they can enfilade it, which is when the fort bears northwest. Vessels drawing fourteen feet can go within a mile and three-quarters with perfect safety, and use their rifle guns with good effect. They can also reach the forts on Federal Point, and prevent their firing accurately on the other portions of the fleet in closer range.

"As only low steam will be required, those vessels that can move and work handily with half their boilers, will only use those on one side, keeping the boilers on the side near the enemy full of water and without steam; with water warm only, and ready to make steam in case of necessity. Slow, deliberate firing is desirable. There will be smoke enough, anyhow. Rapid and indiscriminate firing will amount to little or nothing. I hope no shot will be thrown away."

The vessels moved up very cautiously, in two columns, and when within five miles of the coast, came to a temporary halt. In a short time the *New Ironsides*, followed by the monitors *Canonicus*, *Monadnock*, and *Mahopac*, left the main columns and advanced toward the rebel works. The first-named vessel crept slowly along the shore until a point three-fourths of a mile from Fort Fisher had been reached, when she came to a stand and gave the rebels the first shot at 1 P. M. This was succeeded by other shots, and by two good broadsides; but they all failed to elicit a response from any of the rebel works. The next vessel to come into action was the *Canonicus*, which took a position a few yards ahead of the *New Ironsides*, and gave Fort Fisher a fifteen-inch shell square in its water face. The *Mahopac* next came into action, so that, by 1½ o'clock, the iron-clads were busily engaged. This amount of metal caused the rebels to throw off their reticence and return the fire, which they did from four pieces, directing it at the *New Ironsides* and then to the monitors. The gunboats *Nyack*, *Unadilla*, *Huron*, and *Pequot* remained near the iron-clads during the engagement. No sooner had the first shot been fired than the frigate *Minnesota*, followed by the *Mohican*, *Colorado*, *Tuscarora*, *Wabash*, *Susquehanna*, *Brooklyn*, *Powhattan*, and *Juniata*, steamed up and took a position on a line south of the iron-clads and distant from Fort Fisher about one mile. Next came the *Senaca*, *Shenandoah*, *Ticonderoga*, *Mackinaw*, *Maumee*, *Yantic* and *Kansas*, which formed in line just in the rear of the line headed by the *Minnesota*, and covered the spaces between those vessels.

Such was the line of battle at two P. M. As soon as each vessel came into position, she threw out her anchor at the bow and kedge at the stern, in order to keep a broadside constantly present to the enemy. The firing now became very heavy and rapid, and was directed principally to Fort Fisher, although the water batteries received considerable attention. While the vessels above enumerated were thus engaged, still another line was formed to the south of the first line of ships and at nearly the same distance from Fort Fisher, consisting of the *Fort Jackson*, *Santiago de Cuba*, *Tacony*, *Osceola*, *Chippewa*, *Sassacus*, *Maratanza*, *Rhode Island*, *Monticello*, *Quaker City*, *Alabama* and *Iasco*. The *Vanderbilt* took a position between the two lines. The vessels in reserve were stationed about one and a half miles from the fort. They were the *Aries*, *Howquah*, *Cherokee*, *A. D. Vance*, *Æolas*, *Gettysburgh*, *Montgomery*, *Keystone State*, *Banshee*, *Emma*, *Lillian*, *Tristam Shandy*, *Britannia*, *Gov. Buckingham* and *Bynonia*. The *Pontoosuc* was in line with the iron-clads. The *Wilderness*, *Nansemond*, *Ada* and *Moccasin* were detailed for special service, and were engaged most of the time conveying dispatches from the *Malvern* to the other vessels. The above list includes all the vessels that were present in the engagement. Many of those classed with the force in reserve took an active part in the fight before the close of the afternoon. At three o'clock all the vessels in battle line were pouring their shots into the enemy's works with astounding rapidity. In fact rapidity rather than precision seemed to characterize the firing. For about an hour the enemy replied in a lively manner from a few guns in Fisher. But after that time he simmered down to an occasional shot. When the vessels moved up to take the position assigned them on the line farthest south from Fisher, the Mound Battery opened with a 100-pounder. This gun was used at long intervals, and apparently only when the cannoniers thought they were pretty sure of hitting the mark. During the afternoon the barracks within the fort and some buildings outside of it took fire several times. At one time three rebel steamers were noticed coming down the Cape Fear River. They arrived as far as the point, and then halted as if to give parties on board an opportunity of watching the progress of the fight. But it so happened the *Keystone State* got a sight at the crowd, and pitched into them with a few rounds of shell, which had the amusing effect of sending the rebel craft up the river as rapidly as their wheels would propel them. During the first part of the fight, I cannot say the accuracy of the firing on the part of the vessels was what we expected, but they improved greatly in that respect later in the day. Far too many missiles fell short. The air was filled with exploding shells, which were intended to be exploded inside the rebel works. The rebels, however, were equally deficient in the accuracy of their range, as may be inferred from the fact that during the day's action, they injured not more than eight or ten of our men. The flagstaff on Fisher was shot away several times. The flag on the mound battery was also struck down three times before sunset. From the number of the vessels engaged in the action, the number of guns brought to bear on the rebel works, and the persistent determination of every men to perform the duty assigned him, the battle could not be otherwise than the most interesting and the grandest that has ever taken place on the sea. From the moment the first shot was fired till nearly dark the terrific roar of the guns was incessant, especially when the monitors sent hurling a fifteen-inch sphere of iron, or the *New-Ironsides* let fly a broadside, the deep, ominous rumbling that followed was almost deafening in its result.

Under the impression that the troops were going to land this day, the *Santiago de Cuba* and the *Fort Jackson* were detailed in the afternoon to proceed up the coast three miles from Fort Fisher, and shell the woods, which they did thoroughly, but failed to elicit a reply. The flagship *Malvern* was constantly moving about the fleet, and was not for a moment

(Continued on the Fourth Page.)

Major General Alfred H. Terry

Rear Admiral David D. Porter

Heavy bombardment falling on Fort Fisher from the Federal ships in the background

Interior of Fort Fisher

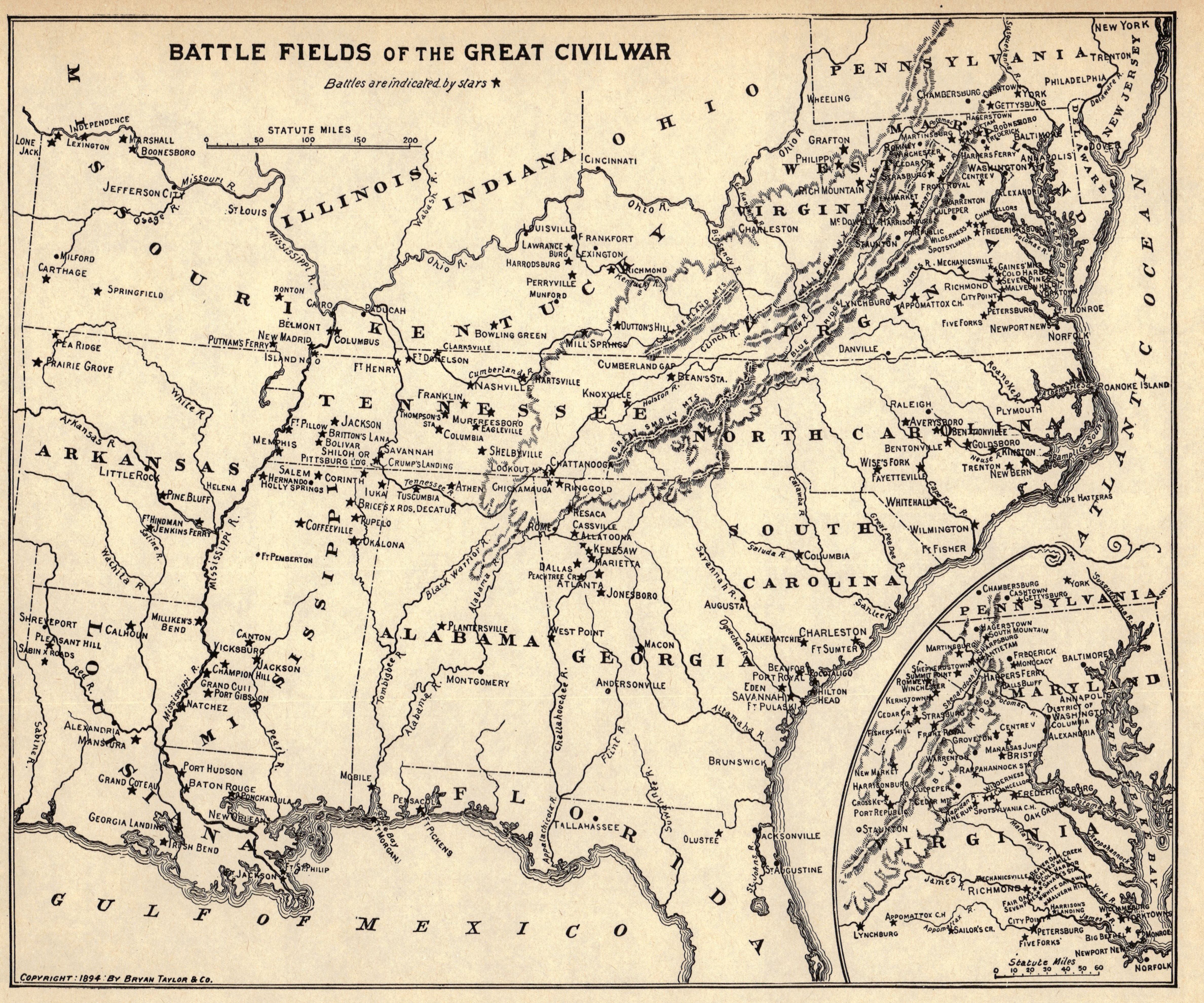

BATTLE FIELDS OF THE GREAT CIVILWAR
Battles are indicated by stars ★
STATUTE MILES
0 50 100 150 200
MISSOURI
ILLINOIS
INDIANA
OHIO
KENTUCKY
WEST VIRGINIA
VIRGINIA
PENNSYLVANIA
MARYLAND
DELAWARE
NEW JERSEY
NEW YORK
TENNESSEE
NORTH CAROLINA
SOUTH CAROLINA
GEORGIA
ALABAMA
MISSISSIPPI
ARKANSAS
LOUISIANA
FLORIDA
ATLANTIC OCEAN
GULF OF MEXICO
LONE JACK
INDEPENDENCE
LEXINGTON
MARSHALL
BOONESBORO
JEFFERSON CITY
ST LOUIS
MILFORD
CARTHAGE
SPRINGFIELD
PEA RIDGE
PRAIRIE GROVE
RONTON
CAIRO
BELMONT
NEW MADRID
PUTNAM'S FERRY
ISLAND NO 10
COLUMBUS
PADUCAH
FT HENRY
FT DONELSON
CLARKSVILLE
BOWLING GREEN
LOUISVILLE
LAWRENCE BURG
HARRODSBURG
PERRYVILLE
MUNFORD
FRANKFORT
LEXINGTON
RICHMOND
CINCINNATI
DUTTON'S HILL
MILL SPRINGS
CUMBERLAND GAP
BEAN'S STA.
KNOXVILLE
NASHVILLE
HARTSVILLE
FRANKLIN
THOMPSON'S STA
MURFREESBORO
EAGLEVILLE
COLUMBIA
SHELBYVILLE
LOOKOUT MT
CHATTANOOGA
CHICKAMAUGA
RINGGOLD
ATHENS
JACKSON
FT PILLOW
BRITTON'S LANE
BOLIVAR
SHILOH OR PITTSBURG LDG
SAVANNAH
CRUMP'S LANDING
MEMPHIS
SALEM
HERNANDO
HOLLY SPRINGS
CORINTH
IUKA
TUSCUMBIA
BRICE'S X RDS.
DECATUR
TUPELO
OKALONA
COFFEEVILLE
FT PEMBERTON
HELENA
LITTLE ROCK
PINE BLUFF
FT HINDMAN
JENKINS FERRY
SHREVEPORT
PLEASANT HILL
SABIN X ROADS
CALHOUN
MILLIKEN'S BEND
CANTON
VICKSBURG
CHAMPION HILL
JACKSON
GRAND GULF
PORT GIBSON
NATCHEZ
ALEXANDRIA
MANSURA
PORT HUDSON
BATON ROUGE
PONCHATOULA
GRAND COTEAU
GEORGIA LANDING
NEW ORLEANS
IRISH BEND
FT JACKSON
FT ST PHILIP
MOBILE
MOBILE BAY
FT MORGAN
PENSACOLA
FT PICKENS
MONTGOMERY
PLANTERSVILLE
ROME
RESACA
CASSVILLE
ALLATOONA
KENESAW
MARIETTA
DALLAS
PEACHTREE CR.
ATLANTA
JONESBORO
WEST POINT
MACON
ANDERSONVILLE
TALLAHASSEE
OLUSTEE
JACKSONVILLE
ST AUGUSTINE
BRUNSWICK
SAVANNAH
FT PULASKI
EDEN
PORT ROYAL
BEAUFORT
POCOTALIGO
HILTON HEAD
SALKEHATCHIE
CHARLESTON
FT SUMTER
AUGUSTA
COLUMBIA
WILMINGTON
FT FISHER
WHITEHALL
FAYETTEVILLE
WISE'S FORK
BENTONVILLE
RALEIGH
AVERYSBORO
GOLDSBORO
KINSTON
TRENTON
NEW BERN
PLYMOUTH
ROANOKE ISLAND
CAPE HATTERAS
DANVILLE
LYNCHBURG
APPOMATTOX CH.
RICHMOND
CITY POINT
PETERSBURG
FIVE FORKS
NEWPORT NEWS
FT MONROE
NORFOLK
CHARLESTON
WHEELING
GRAFTON
PHILIPPI
RICH MOUNTAIN
McDOWELL
STAUNTON
GETTYSBURG
YORK
CHAMBERSBURG
PHILADELPHIA
TRENTON
BALTIMORE
ANNAPOLIS
WASHINGTON
HARPERS FERRY
FREDERICK
FREDERICKSBURG
CHANCELLORSVILLE
SPOTSYLVANIA
MECHANICSVILLE
GAINES' MILL
COLD HARBOR
SEVEN PINES
MALVERN HILL
CULPEPER
FRONT ROYAL
Ohio R.
Mississippi R.
Missouri R.
Tennessee R.
Cumberland R.
White R.
Arkansas R.
Red R.
Sabine R.
Pearl R.
Tombigbee R.
Alabama R.
Black Warrior R.
Chattahoochee R.
Flint R.
Appalachicola R.
Savannah R.
Altamaha R.
Saluda R.
Santee R.
Great Pee Dee R.
Cape Fear R.
Roanoke R.
James R.
GREAT SMOKY MTS.
BLUE RIDGE
Statute Miles
0 10 20 30 40 50 60
COPYRIGHT: 1894 BY BRYAN TAYLOR & CO.

1865

The Charleston Mercury.

DAILY PAPER—Twenty Dollars for Three Months—Payable in Advance. | VINDICE NULLO—SPONTE SUA SINE LEGE FIDES RECTUMQUE COLENTUR. | COUNTRY PAPER—Three a Week—Fifteen Dollars for Three Months—Payable in Advance.

Volume LXXXVI. | CHARLESTON, S. C., FRIDAY, JANUARY 13, 1865. | Number 12,266.

ATTEMPTED ESCAPE OF CONFEDERATES FROM JOHNSON'S ISLAND

The Sandusky (Ohio) *Register* of Wednesday says:

About one o'clock yesterday morning, by a preconcerted arrangement, a rush was made by twenty-four prisoners upon the centre of the guard line, on the northwest side of the prison on Johnson's Island. The prisoners had improvised eight scaling ladders by attaching cleats to boards and strips—very light, easily carried, and just the thing for scaling the high prison fence. The rush upon the guard at once occasioned the proper cry, "Turn out the guard!" accompanied by quite a rattling fire from the guard line; but the rush was so impetuous, and by so many prisoners, that, in spite of the guard, four men out of the twenty four scaled the fence, passed the guard, escaped from the island, crossed the north channel of the bay, and went some distance upon the peninsula. Of the others who did not get through, one received a shot cutting away his coat at the waist, and was knocked down and captured. Another, Lieutenant John B. Bowles, son of the President of the Louisville Bank, Kentucky, was shot twice through the body, about the same instant, and killed. The other eighteen found the work too hot, and retreated to their barracks.

The rush on the guard was immediately followed by the long roll and the proper signal gun. By the way, this is the first "long roll" occasioned by any demonstration of the prisoners since last March; and the only other one was on the night of the 22d of September, when at least one third of the prison fence was swept away in an instant by a tornado.

Under a standing order, all the troops were promptly in position, ready to give proper attention to the rebels should any further efforts be made within the enclosure. To make sure of any who might be lurking on the island awaiting better opportunities to elude observation, three companies of the sixth V. R. C. were ordered out to patrol the island and make a thorough search. At the same time, several detachments of the 128th regiment were ordered off in pursuit of the escaped prisoners, who had passed the picket on the northwest side of the island, receiving a fire from them at long range. The flying rebels made the best time possible, but were hotly pursued; and with soldiers on their rear and both flanks, and the loyal citizens of the Peninsula (who had been aroused by the discharge of the 30-pounder Parrott) in their front, their escape soon terminated in recapture.

The morning roll call and muster of prisoners showed that but four of them had left the prison. They were all back and returned to their home in the "Bull Pen" this morning. The unwilling denizens of that locality are full of their schemes and threats, and seem disposed to make the very most of their opportunities while the ice is practicable as a highway; and it remains to be seen whether the future, with whatever aid they may receive, will be very productive of gratifying results to themselves.

Three of the fugitives were seen running across the peninsula by Mr. G. B. Wright, a gentleman who has a vineyard there. As soon as he heard the firing, he got out with his gun, and seeing the three escaped prisoners, called to them: "Stop, or I'll put a hole through you as big as my hat!" At this they halted, and he marched them back to quarters. Another was brought in by the guard yesterday morning.

FROM THE UNITED STATES.

THE YANKEE RECRUITING, AND WHAT COMES OF IT.

The Yankee papers are often filled with notices of new regiments raised by recruiting large numbers of volunteers, etc. How all this works may be gathered from the following letter from Grant's army, published in the New York *Times*, which is *not* a "Copperhead" paper:

We hear of the President calling for a force of several hundred thousand men. The papers tell us gleefully of the rapidity with which enrollments are taking place; presently we hear every town and village boasting that it has "filled up its quota;" but where are the soldiers? The bounty money has been paid, the men enrolled, we will suppose; but where are they? That is the question—a question, too, fraught with such momentous interest to the nation that it is to be hoped every loyal voice will keep shouting it at Congress until our law givers feel the necessity of looking into it more narrowly. Let people go and inquire of the noble fellows fighting in the field, and they will soon learn what has become of many of these dearly purchased men in buckram—costing something like one thousand dollars each before they have lifted a finger in return.

As an illustration of how some of them disappear, here is the record of one single regiment among those that have come to my notice: Of three detachments of substitutes sent from Concord, New Hampshire, to join the Fifth New Hampshire volunteers, amounting to six hundred and twenty-five men, one hundred and thirty-seven deserted on the passage, leaving only four hundred and eighty-eight to arrive at the regiment. Of the four hundred and eighty-eight who got to the regiment and were assigned to companies, eighty-two deserted to the enemy from picket line; thirty-six deserted to the rear; four have been discharged as utterly worthless, their physical incapacity being so glaring, and of such long standing, that it must have been known at the time of enlistment; five have been sent back to Concord, to have their cases of enlistment investigated, by order of the War Department; and two have been discharged by order of the War Department.

Thus, out of six hundred and twenty-five of these bounty-tempted warriors sent to one regiment only since August last, there are only three hundred and fifty-nine left; and, as these have come to the army through the same venal influences, and probably gone through the same loose or fraudulent examination, it is impossible to tell how many more may follow suit, in spite of the death penalty before them. I use the term fraudulent advisedly; for, out of the four discharged as utterly worthless, one man had one leg several inches shorter than the other; one had hernia; that had made him a cripple for many years past; and the two others were such impracticable imbeciles that any imbecile, without one particle of medical knowledge, must have seen at a glance that they were utterly incapable of any duty whatever, mental or physical. These are shameful revelations, but the sooner the public are made acquainted with the existence of such monstrous abuses, the sooner do we stand a chance of seeing them rectified.

Recruiting in New York

DAILY PAPER—Twenty Dollars for Three Months—Payable in Advance. | VINDICE NULLO—SPONTE SUA SINE LEGE FIDES RECTUMQUE COLENTUR. | COUNTRY PAPER—Three a Week—Fifteen Dollars for Three Months—Payable in Advance.

Volume LXXXVI. | CHARLESTON, S. C., THURSDAY, JANUARY 26, 1865. | Number 12,277.

THE MERCURY.

THURSDAY, JANUARY 26, 1865

Men Run Mad.

The project now agitated by the JEFF. DAVIS devotees, and others carried away from common sense by their influence and the panic of the present situation to which their weakness has brought our affairs, is virtually the abolition of slavery, in order to put two hundred thousand negroes in the army. These negroes are to achieve the independence of white men.

We have said the project is the idea of panic-stricken men—is desperate, destructive, utterly hopeless.

Let us consider this proposition in its three-fold aspect—politically, or economically—socially—and as a war measure.

It was the opinion of Mr. CALHOUN, and is the opinion of the wisest statesmen that South Carolina has produced, that slavery is essential to the existence of a Republican Government. Remove this element of stability and conservatism, and you launch the Government into a mobocracy. We already see to what it has brought the Northern people, in spite of the conservative element of slavery in the South, heretofore acting as a balance wheel to their radical sentiments. And yet the Northern people had the vast and boundless territories of the West, that acted as a huge flood gate to their populace. Yet, in spite of both of these checks, where are they drifting? A few years more, when the territories are stocked by these herding brutes—with the conservative element of slavery removed—and where will they be?—Where are they? Rushing straight into every radicalism, and every other ism—driving into revolution, dyed in blood, sinking into despotism—military rule—empire.

With us the case will be far more desperate, far more hopeless. We have four millions of slaves. By one blow the labor of the Cotton States will be paralyzed. Its products of king cotton and sugar, gone forever. For it is folly to talk of a negro laboring of his own accord.—It has been tried too often all over the world, and always with the same result—*ruin*. The best portions of our whole magnificent country goes to waste—a home for four millions of ignorant idle vagrants and Yankee squatters—and every slaveowner and planter in the land is reduced to poverty. Instead of being the great producers of the world, the Cotton States become its veriest lazzaroni.

But is this all? By no means. It is enough, but it is only the political and the economical view of the proposition.

Socially, the result will be even worse. At a blow, the intelligence, the refinement of the country is reduced to want, and is merged in the general ruin. To the poor man it is still worse. He is reduced to the level of a nigger, and a nigger is raised to his level. Cheek by jowl they must labor together as equals. His wife and his daughter are to be hustled on the street by black wenches, their equals. Swaggering buck niggers are to ogle them, and to elbow him.

Gracious God! is this what our brave soldiery are fighting for?—to reduce themselves to the level and companionship of niggers? No—no—never—not in South Carolina. Let the man who is afraid to fight himself, and wants to send a nigger to fight in his place—heedless of all else, so long as he is out of it—talk of emancipation, and niggers in the ranks. But the brave soldier who is fighting for the supremacy of his race will have none of it—no, none of it. He wants no Hayti here—no St. Domingo—no mongrels in his family—no miscegenation with his blood. Let them not be deceived—this, and nothing else, must be the result. Mobocracy on the one hand—nigger equality and gradual miscegenation the other.

We turn to the negro himself as an element of war, and the project is still more hopeless and desperate.

To hold out any sort of equivalent inducement to the negro to fight in our ranks, you must offer general emancipation. Less will not answer the purpose. For this is what the Yankee holds out to him. He does more, he offers him the soil and perfect equality. To expect the negro then to fight on our side for less is simply absurd. He may not be a creature particularly given to logic or to metaphysical reasoning; but he is not altogether a monkey. There are some simple things that he is able to understand. The project is utterly vain to waste words upon, without this first premise—general emancipation.

But will even this insane measure make the matter better. Not one whit; but, on the contrary, much worse. For it is out of our power to keep up with the Yankee bids. What does the Yankee offer him in the ranks? A large belly full every day, a plenty of meat, grogg, good clothes, shoes and physical comfort, and, at present, an apparently *winning cause*. What have we to offer him when we seize him and put him in our ranks? A lank belly, hard work, a plenty of bullets, scant clothing, and a cause so hard pressed as to require *his* help—a cause so rough that even white men, fighting for their homes, for their wives, and for their independence, fly from the ranks, and leave their standards and their comrades.

Could a proposition be more absolutely absurd?

The negro will *not* fight in the cause, under these circumstances. To one that can be retained in the ranks and will stand fire, ten will break their ranks, and will desert to the enemy. Placed in the line of battle, when pressed by heavy fire he will run, and break the line, and lose the day in consequence. Placed on guard or on picket, he can never be trusted. The countersign will be a farce, and he will lead the enemy into the camp. Out of the two hundred thousand muskets put into their hands, one hundred and fifty thousand at least will be presented by him to the enemy. You will only arm the enemy, and fill his ranks, ten for one.

The whole project is insane, demoralising, destructive, hopeless. The wail of panic, and the cry of despair resounds through every thought connected with it. Away with the folly!

The New-York Times.

VOL. XIV......NO. 4155. NEW-YORK, WEDNESDAY, JANUARY 18, 1865. PRICE FOUR CENTS.

WILMINGTON.

Fort Fisher Carried by Assault.

Official Reports from General Terry and Col. Comstock.

Twenty-five Hundred Prisoners and Seventy-five Guns Captured.

Gen. Whiting and Col. Lamb Taken Prisoners.

OUR LOSS NINE HUNDRED.

ADMIRAL PORTER'S OFFICIAL REPORT.

General Grant Orders a Salute in Honor of the Victory.

REBEL ACCOUNT OF THE FIGHT.

Official Dispatch from General Lee.

[OFFICIAL.]

WASHINGTON, Tuesday, Jan. 17—10:40 A. M.

Maj.-Gen. J. A. Dix:

The following official dispatches have just been received at this department:

HEADQUARTERS UNITED STATES FORCES ON FEDERAL POINT, N. C., Jan. 15, via FORTRESS MONROE, Jan. 17.

Brig.-Gen. J. A. Rawlins:

GENERAL: I have the honor to report that Fort Fisher was carried by assault, this afternoon and evening, by Gen. AMES' division and the Second Brigade of the First Division of the Twenty-fourth Army Corps, gallantly aided by a battalion of marines and seamen from the navy. The assault was preceded by a heavy bombardment from the Federal fleet, and was made at 3:30 P. M., when the First Brigade—CURTISS', of AMES' division—effected a lodgment upon the parapet, but full possession of the work was not obtained until 10 P. M. The behavior of both officers and men was most admirable. All the works south of Fort Fisher are now occupied by our troops. We have not less than 1,200 prisoners, including Gen. WHITING and Col. LAMB, the Commandant of the fort. I regret to say that our loss is severe, especially in officers. I am not yet able to form any estimate of the number of casualties. (Signed,) ALFRED H. TERRY,

Brev. Maj.-Gen., Commanding Expedition.

FORT FISHER, Monday, Jan. 16—2 o'clock A.M.

After a careful reconnoissance on the 14th it was decided to risk an assault on Fort Fisher. PAINE'S division with Col. ABBOTT'S brigade to hold our line, already strong, across the peninsula, and facing Wilmington against HOKE, while AMES' division should assault on the west end. After three hours of heavy navy firing, the assault was made at 3 P. M. on the 15th. CURTIS' brigade led, and as soon as it had made a lodgment on the west end of the land front it was followed by PENNYBACKER'S and the latter by BELL'S. After desperate fighting, gaining foot by foot, and severe loss, by 5 P. M., we had possession of about half the land front. ABBOTT'S Brigade was then taken from our line facing Wilmington, and put into Fort Fisher, and on pushing it forward, at 10 P. M., it took the rest of the work with little resistance—the garrison falling back to the extreme of the peninsular, where they were followed and captured, among others Gen. WHITING and Col. LAMB, both wounded. I think we have quite 1,000 prisoners. I hope our own loss may not exceed 500; but it is impossible to judge in the night. Among the wounded are the Commanders of the three leading brigades; Gen. CURTISS being wounded, not severely; but Cols. PENNYBACKER and BELL dangerously. The land front was a formidable one, the parapet in places, fourteen or fifteen feet high; but the men went at it nobly, under a severe musketry fire. The marines and sailors went up gallantly; but the musketry fire from the east end of the land front was so severe that they did not succeed in entering the work. The navy fire on the work, judging from the holes, must have been terrific. Many of the guns were injured. How many there were on the point I cannot say, perhaps thirty or forty.

(Signed) C. B. COMSTOCK,

Lieutenant-Colonel A. D. C.,

and Chief Engineer.

Another dispatch estimated the number of prisoners captured at 2,500, and the number of guns at 72.

Gen. GRANT telegraphed to his department that in honor of this great triumph, achieved by the united valor of the army and navy, he has ordered a salute of one hundred guns to be fired by each of the armies operating against Richmond.

C. A. DANA,

Assistant Secretary of War.

THE NAVAL DISPATCH.

[OFFICIAL.]

FORTRESS MONROE, Jan. 17.

Hon. Gideon Welles, Secretary of the Navy:

The *Atlantic* is just in from Wilmington.

Fort Fisher and the works on Federal Point are in our possession.

The assault was made by the army and sailors on Sunday afternoon, and by 11 P. M. the works were ours.

The losses are heavy.

Lieuts. S. W. PRESTON and B. H. PORTER, of the navy, are killed.

Our captures were 72 guns and about 2,500 prisoners.

Gens. WHITING and LAMB, (rebels) are prisoners and wounded.

The *Vanderbilt* is on her way North with dispatches.

Two fifteen-inch guns burst on the monitors.

(Signed) E. T. NICHOLS,

Commander.

THE REBEL ACCOUNT.

[OFFICIAL.]

WAR DEPARTMENT, Tuesday, Jan. 17—9 P. M.

Maj.-Gen. Dix, New-York:

The Richmond *Whig* of this morning contains the following account of the capture of Fort Fisher, by the naval and land forces of the United States:

FALL OF FORT FISHER.

The unwelcome news of the fall of Fort Fisher, commanding the entrance to Cape Fear River, was made this morning, and occasioned a sensation of profound regret. *The capture of this fort is equivalent to the closure of the harbor of Wilmington by the enemy's fleet.* It is situated about eighteen miles below the city, but was the main defence of the entrance to the river, and its fall, therefore, will prevent in future the arrival and departure of blockade-runners. How far this reverse may prove injurious to our cause, remains to be seen, but at present we regard it rather as unfortunate than a disastrous event. The following is the official report:

HEADQUARTERS NORTHERN VIRGINIA, Monday, Jan. 16.

Hon. J. H. Seddon:

Gen. BRAGG reports that the enemy bombarded Fort Fisher furiously all day yesterday.

At 4 P. M. their infantry advanced to the assault, a heavy demonstration at the same hour being made against their rear by our troops.

A 6:30 P. M. Gen. WHITING reports that their attack had failed, and the garrison was being strengthened with fresh troops.

At about 10 P. M. the fort was captured with most of the garrison.

No further particulars at this time known.

(Signed,) R. E. LEE.

No dispatches have been received from Gen. TERRY since that of Sunday night announcing the result of the assault. C. A. DANA,

Assistant Secretary of War.

OPERATIONS OF FRIDAY AND SATURDAY.

REPORT OF ADMIRAL PORTER.

The following has been received at the Navy Department from Admiral PORTER:

FLAG SHIP MALVERN, OFF FORT FISHER, N.C., Jan. 14, 1865.

SIR:—I have the honor to inform you that operations have been resumed against the forts at the entrance of Cape Fear River. Since the first attack on that place and the subsequent withdrawal of the troops, I have been employed in filling the ships with ammunition and coal. The difficulties we have encountered no one can conceive, all our work had to be done with the larger vessels, anchored on the coast, exposed, you may almost say at sea, to the violent gales that blow here almost incessantly—on those gales the enemy depended to break up our preparations, we will see. We have gone through the worst of it. Have held on through gales heavy enough to drive any thing to sea, and we have sustained no damage whatever. After the troops arrived the weather set in bad and the gale was very heavy, as soon as it was over I got under way on the 12th instant, and forming the vessels in three lines, with the transports in company, I steamed for Fort Fisher. On the morning of the 13th the fleet took its station in three lines close to the beach, and the boats were sent at once to take off the troops. These were landed with about twelve days' provisions, at about two o'clock P. M. This time I pursued a different plan in attacking the rebel works. I sent in the new *Ironsides*, Commodore RADFORD, leading the monitors *Saugus*, *Canonicus*, *Monadnock* and *Mahopac*. At 7:30 A. M. the forts opened on them as they approached, but they quietly took up their old positions within one thousand yards of Fort Fisher, and when ready they opened their batteries in this way: I tempted the enemy to engage the monitors, that we might see what guns they had; and seeing where they were, be able to dismount them by fire. Quite a spirited engagement went on between the forts and the *Ironsides* and monitors; it was soon apparent that the iron vessels had the best of it. Traverses began to disappear, and the southern angle of Fort Fisher, commenced to look very dilapidated. The guns were silenced one after the other, and only one heavy gun in the southern angle kept up its fire. The fire of this gun was not at all accurate, as it inflicted no damage on the iron vessels. They were hit, though, several times. By way of letting the enemy know we had some shell left on board the wooden ships, and did not intend to take any unfair advantage of him by using the iron vessels alone, I ordered line No. 1, on the plan led by Capt. ALDEN, of the *Brooklyn*, and line No. 2, led by Commodore THATCHER, of the *Colorado*, to go and attack the batteries. This was done in the handsomest manner; not a mistake was committed, except firing too rapidly and making too much smoke.

The heavy fire of the large vessels shut up the enemy's guns at once, and after firing till after dark, the wooden vessels dropped out to their anchorage. The *Ironsides* and Monitors maintained their position through the night, firing a shell now and then. They are now lying within one thousand yards of the fort, and the monitors within seven hundred yards, and the fort does not fire a gun at them, thinking no doubt that it is a waste of powder.

The firing from the fleet will commence as soon as we get breakfast, and will be kept up as long as the Ordnance Department provides us with shells and guns. There is perfect understanding between Gen. TERRY and myself, I believe everything has been done to suit him. I have heard no complaints, and have felt every disposition to help the army along.

A detailed report of our operations here will be sent in when we get through. I see no reason to doubt our success, the forts will be used up so.

We have a respectable force landed on a strip of land which our naval guns completely command, and a place of defence which would enable us to hold on against a very large army.

I will report to you every opportunity.

I have the honor to be, very respectfully, your obedient servant, DAVID D. PORTER,

Rear-Admiral.

To Hon. GIDEON WELLES,

Secretary of the Navy, Washington, D. C.

DETAILS OF OPERATIONS.

BALTIMORE, Tuesday, Jan. 17.

The correspondent of the Baltimore *American* gives the following detailed account of the capture of Fort Fisher:

STEAMER SANTIAGO DE CUBA, Thursday, Jan. 12, 1865.

Yesterday afternoon the steamer *Aries* arrived from Fortress Monroe, bringing dispatches to Admiral PORTER from the President and Secretary of the Navy. As the dispatch steamer crossed the bar into the inner harbor, all eyes were strained to discover some indication that authority had been received to push forward the renewal of the attack on Fort Fisher. The first indication observable outside was smoke from the firing up of the forty gunboats at anchor inside, and heading toward the bar. There could be no mistaking this indication of the character of the dispatches from Washington.

At five o'clock the light-draft gunboats were pouring out in a steady stream, winding their way through the sinuous channel across the bar. It was eight o'clock before the last of these had crossed, the bright moonlight enabling them to thread their way among the buoys. The tide was by this time too low for the monitors to come out, and they remained inside until this morning; and at six o'clock, followed by the *Malvern*, the flag-ship of the Admiral, they were observed moving out. The Admiral threw out the signal "Get under way" to the fleet outside; and in the twinkling of an eye the work of raising anchor was in progress throughout the immense armada. The *Malvern* sailed out majestically through the squadron, and stood out to sea, giving signal to the fleet to "follow the course indicated."

By 8 o'clock the whole of the fleet was in motion, and presented a sight grand beyond description. Frigates, monitors, iron-clads, double-enders, sloops-of-war and gunboats, numbering sixty-two vessels of war, carrying in all five hundred and ninety guns, beside small steamers, tugs, tenders and army transports, were soon formed in four lines on the broad expanse of the ocean, each led by the vessel of its divisional commander. The army transports, including the steamers *Baltic* and *Pacific*, and numbering not less than fifteen steamships, carrying not less than ten thousand troops, led by the flagship of Brevet Maj.-Gen. TERRY, their commander, also formed a fifth line of the great armada. Thus the number of vessels visible from our deck was not less than eighty.

The troops embrace the same that came down with Gen. BUTLER, with one additional brigade and a new commanding officer. The navy are proud of this fact, as it is that the Government has sustained Admiral PORTER, and backed up his opinion, not only that Fort Fisher can be taken, but that it must be taken, and that it can be taken by the same troops under a different commander. The soldiers have had a rough time of it, having laid at anchor for three consecutive days of storm, rain and wind, closely packed in their transports.

Ten o'clock.—We are all fairly under way for New Inlet. The distance is only sixty-eight miles, and we expect to reach our anchorage before sunset, so as to be in readiness for active operations at daylight on Friday morning. The double-turretted *Monadnock* leads the monitor fleet, moving along finely, without any tow, but accompanied by the gunboat *Mohican*. The *Santiago* follows towing the monitor *Canonicus*, the *Fort Jackson* towing the *Mahopac*, the *Alabama* towing the *Saugus*, while the *Vanderbilt* accompanies the *New Ironsides*. The *Dictator* had not arrived when the fleet sailed, though momentarily expected, and hopes are still entertained that she will reach the scene of action before to-morrow morning.

Before the commencement of active operations this morning, the following order, from Admiral PORTER, was read on the quarter-deck of the *Santiago de Cuba* by Lieut. NORMAN H. FARQUHAR, Executive Officer of the flag-ship *Malvern*:

JAN. 4, 1865.

Before going into action, the Commander of each vessel will detail as many of the men as he can spare from the guns as a landing party, that we may have a share in the assault when it takes place. Boats will be kept ready lowered near the water on the off side of the vessels. The sailors will be armed with cutlasses, well sharpened, and with revolvers. When the signal is made to man the boats, the men will get in, but not show themselves. When the signal is made to assault, the boats will pull round the stern of the monitors and land eight abreast of them, and board the fort on the river in a seamanlike way. The marines will form in the rear and cover the sailors. Whilst the soldiers are going over the parapet in front, the sailors will take the sea-face of Fort Fisher. We can land two thousand men from the fleet and not feel it. Two thousand active men from the fleet will carry the day. Two boat-keepers will be kept in each boat.

DAVID D. PORTER, Rear Admiral.

Capt. GLISSON informed the men that he wanted thirty-five blue-jacket volunteers, all that could be spared from the guns, and he wanted only such men as would go willingly, with the determination to plant the flag of the *Santiago* first on the ramparts of Fort Fisher. Those who desired to volunteer were invited to step to the front side of the vessel. There was a pretty general rush, which Capt. GLISSON stopped, as there were some thirty-eight more than were wanted already in the line. Among them were four swarthy, broad-shouldered Sandwich Islanders, and the entire crew of the Captain's gig. At the time I write the grindstones are at work sharpening their sabres, and the storming party exhibit as much gleesome hilarity as a party of children preparing for a picnic. The same spirit has been manifested on all the vessels. If Fort Fisher is not taken, there will at least be some bloody work.

Capt. GLISSON and all the officers of the ship have volunteered to accompany the storming party, which, with the marines, is to consist of fifty-three men. But as only two officers can go, the Admiral will probably decide who shall have that honor. Probably Executive Officer FARQUHAR and Acting Master BOWERS will lead the party.

The *Santiago*, with the *Canonicus* in tow, at 3 o'clock this afternoon had distanced all the vessels of the fleet some ten miles, when a signal from the flag-ship directed us to hold up, and keep in line with the *Brooklyn's* division. In about an hour, the line was closed, and again moved on slowly. The distance from our destination was then twenty-eight miles. The weather continued clear and beautiful, and the sea calm.

At 6 o'clock the flagship joined us and directed the Captain to hoist two white lights and take the lead to the anchorage off Flag Pond Battery, two miles north of Fort Fisher. At 9 o'clock we reached the point indicated, and soon the immense fleet spread over the ocean in our wake closed up, presenting a most magnificent spectacle with its display of innumerable lights. Not a cloud was to be seen overhead, and the moon shone out so brightly that the shore, five miles distant, was distinctly visible. Lights could also be seen on the shore, and rebel eyes were doubtless gazing on the grand panorama.

Friday, Jan. 13.—At eight bells, 4 o'clock this morning, we were aroused from our slumbers by a gun from the flag-ship, and the burning of the preparatory signal of red and green as an indication that it is time to be up and stirring, preparing breakfast and getting through with the routine of morning duty, so as to be in readiness at dawn to commence the serious work of the day. The moon is still shining brightly in a colorless sky, brilliant with stars. The throng of vessels rest calmly on the sea, the wind being too light to stir or even ripple its surface; this, too, it should be remembered, just out of cannon shot of the dreaded coast of North Carolina. Truly, the elements promise to favor this great enterprize. At 5 o'clock the second signal was given by the flag-ship, "Get under way," when the work of weighing anchors commenced, and at 5:30 o'clock the signals of the Divisional Commanders to move forward were given and responded to, causing a brilliant pyrotechnic display. The gunboat *Tacony* was sent ahead last night to anchor off Flagpond Battery, and the day not having yet dawned, her lights can be seen as the steering point of the fleet in shore about three miles ahead of us.

The three frigates *Wabash*, *Minnesota* and *Colorado*, moved off first led by Admiral PORTER'S flagship. They were followed by the *New Ironsides* and monitor fleet. The signals from the army transports added to the scenic display. At the first dawn of day the whole armada was in motion. The wind has changed to due west during the night, and coming off shore, tends to render the landing of the troops comparatively easy.

At a quarter to 7 the Admiral signalled "Form line-of-battle;" whereupon the *Brooklyn*, with her line of vessels, moved along close to the beach in the following order: *Brooklyn*, 26 guns; *Mohican*, 7; *Tacony*, 10; *Kansas*, 8; *Unadilla*, 7; *Huron*, 4; *Maumee*, 5; *Pawtuxent*, 10; *Seneca*, 4; *Pontoosuc*, 10; *Nyack*, 7; *Yantic*, 7; *Nereus*, 11; total 116 guns. This division was ordered to prepare for action and move in close to the beach, to shell the woods, at the point decided upon for the landing of the troops, about three and a half miles from Fort Fisher, near the deserted half-moon battery. In a few minutes the whole division was in position throwing shells into the narrow strip of woods separating the sea shore from Cape Fear River, about a mile inland parallel with the beach.

In the meantime the iron-clads moved into position directly in front of Fisher, the *Ironsides* about three-quarters of a mile, and the monitors about half a mile off, in the following order: *New Ironsides*, Commodore RADFORD, 20 guns; *Monadnock*, Commodore E. G. PARROTT, 4 guns; *Saugus*, Commodore E. R. COLHAM, 2 guns; *Canonicus*, Lieutenant-Commander GEO. S. BELKNAP, 2 guns; *Mahopac*, Lieutenant-Commander E. E. POTTER, 2 guns. Before they got into position the fort opened on them, but they heeded it not until they had secured their anchorage, when, at 8:30, the *Ironsides* opened on the fort and was followed by the monitors with their tremendous shells. Every shot struck in the embrasures and exploding, threw clouds of sand high into the air. The fort occasionally responded, but did not send more than one shot every ten minutes, and at times, so rapid was our firing, they found it impossible to work their guns.

At nine o'clock the boats of the fleet were called away to assist in landing troops. The woods had in the mean time been thoroughly shelled and no enemy had appeared. The transports were enabled to go within half a mile of the shore, and they were soon surrounded by not less than two hundred boats, supplied from all the vessels of the fleet. Several tugs also joined in the work and carried the soldiers to within two hundred yards of the beach, where they were transferred to small boats. The tents and camp equipage were also landed, with several days' provisions for the entire force, which was 8,000 strong.

At 9 o'clock the boats from all the transports moved simultaneously for the shore, and in a few minutes the first five hundred men stepped on the beach and planted their regimental flag on one of the highest sand-hills, amid cheering from the transports and the fleet.

The men were overjoyed to again get from shipboard, and in a few minutes had cut down cedars sufficient to make a rousing fire to dry their clothes, some of them having got wet to their knees in getting through the surf. The bands of music soon commenced playing, while the men could be seen running about and rolling in the warm sand like school-children enjoying a holiday. Not a sign of any enemy could be seen at this time in any direction.

ADVANCE OF SKIRMISHERS.

At 10 o'clock, about 4,000 troops having been landed, a skirmish line was sent forward on the beach.

Admiral PORTER signaled to Capt. GLISSON, commanding the *Saratoga*, to move with his gunboat division inside of the line of the frigate, and shell the beach in advance of the skirmishers. The division moved in the following order:

Santiago de Cuba, 11 guns; Fort Jackson, 7 guns; Oceola, 10 guns; Sassacus, 10 guns; Chippewa, 4 guns; R. R. Cuyler, 10 guns; Maratanza, 6 guns; Rhode Island, 12 guns; Monticello, 7 guns; Alabama, 10 guns; Montgomery, 6 guns; Keystone State, 18 guns; Quaker City, 7 guns; Iasoo, 10 guns—total guns, 128.

The woods in advance of the pickets were thoroughly shelled up to within a mile and a half of Fort Fisher, where we dropped anchor about a mile in the rear of the iron-clad fleet and fully two miles in advance of all the balance of the fleet, which were in the vicinity of the landing of the troops, where they remained up to 4 o'clock in the afternoon.

From our advanced position I had a splendid view of the work of the iron-clads, which was the main business of the day, though some of the shells from Fort Fisher, fired at the monitors, came in rather close proximity. The firing on the fort from the monitors and new Ironsides, was a magnificent sight. From 8 o'clock in the morning up to 4 o'clock in the afternoon, the monitors poured in their ponderous shells at the rate of four per minute, the whole number thrown in that time being not less than two thousand. Every shot struck the embrasures or parapet of the fort, and the gunnery exhibited was never surpassed. During this time the fort probably threw three hundred shells in return, but the difficulty they had in managing their guns, amid the explosion of our shells and the clouds of sand that constantly enveloped the work from our well-directed shots, doubtless marred their gunnery, as most of their shells struck beyond or short of the mark. All of our vessels, however, received honorable scars in the fight, and we could see that several of their smoke-stacks had been perforated and armor bruised. The damage to the fort, by outward appearance, was most distinct. What the internal damage may be is, of course, not yet known. About 4 o'clock a dense and continued smoke from the inside of the fort indicated that some of the rebel huts had been fired.

A GENERAL BOMBARDMENT.

At 4 o'clock the Admiral signaled to the vessels in the line of battle No. 1 to take the positions marked out for them in the chart and join in the bombardment. They moved forward in the order given above, the fourteen vessels, led by the *Brooklyn*, carrying 136 guns. Following rapidly was an order to the line of battle No. 2 to take position and join in the bombardment. It immediately moved forward as follows, presenting an array of the largest vessels in the service, a magnificent spectacle of old wooden walls with their ponderous armaments: *Minnesota*, 52 guns; *Wabash*, 48 guns; *Powhatan*, 21 guns; *Susquehannah*, 16 guns; *Juniata*, 9 guns; *Shenandoah*, 10 guns; *Ticonderoga*, 20 guns. Total—176 guns.

At twenty minutes to 5 o'clock these two immense divisions, carrying 312 guns, in addition to the iron-clads, joined in the grand and awful yet terribly brilliant cannonade—a spectacle that will probably never be witnessed again during the present age. The number of shots fired while this great bombardment lasted, one hour and a-half, closing at ten minutes past 6 o'clock, could not have been less than four per second, broadside after broadside being poured in without the slightest intermission, occasionally interspersed with the dense bass of the fifteen inch guns of the monitors. Four shots per second during this time counts up 21,600 shots—indeed I have no doubt that up to the withdrawal of the wooden walls, this evening, not less than 25,000 shells were fired into Fort Fisher. After the general bombardment commenced but one shot was fired by the fort in return, consequently no one of the wooden vessels were injured.

The *Ironsides* and the monitors did not withdraw when the signal was given for the wooden walls to cease firing, but kept at work throughout the night throwing one shell every ten minutes into the fort, to prevent the repairing of damage by the garrison. The camp-fires of our troops on the shore, together with the burning of signals and the display of white and green lanterns by the fleet, presented a grand spectacle. To-night the troops have advanced up to within a mile and a-half of Fort Fisher, their camp-fires extending down the beach for more than a mile. An order has been received from the Admiral, it being found impossible to bring our division into the fight, the anchoring room being too contracted to proceed in shore to cover the encampments of the troops from any assault by BRAGG from Wilmington.

The troops, as I learn from officers who assisted in landing them, are in high spirits and anxious to be led forward to the assault of the fort. They wish to wipe out the stain cast upon them by the withdrawal of Gen. BUTLER, and prove to the country that they did not believe the fort could not be taken. The announcement received here to-day that Gen. BUTLER had been relieved from the command of the Army of the James, and directed to report at Lowell, Mass., caused great rejoicing throughout the fleet.

I regret to learn that one of the 15-inch guns on the *Mahopac* bursted to-day, but am pleased to add that none of her iron-clad crew were injured by the explosion. She remained in the fight throughout the day. Some good shooting was made by the rebels, and all the iron-clads have numerous indentations of their armor and perforations of their smoke-stacks.

SECOND DAY OF BATTLE.

SATURDAY MORNING, Jan. 14, 1865.

Another bright and beautiful day has dawned, being the third since we left Beaufort, scarcely a cloud dimming the Heavens. The night was magnificently brilliant, the first quarter of a waning moon shedding its silvery rays over land and water, while a light southwestern wind, which seemed hardly to cause a ripple, made everything particularly pleasant. This morning the sun has risen in splendor and beauty. Not a cloud is perceptible in the sky. The cheering rays of Old Sol have already driven off the chilliness of the morning atmosphere. The monitors and the *Ironsides* have continued throughout the night to throw a shell every ten minutes into the fort, discontinuing their work only as daylight approached. The troops on shore are having a fine time and are in the most splendid spirits. A foraging party has just returned to camp with nearly one hundred head of cattle and horses, which they succeeded in picking up during the night. A number of the troops advanced during the night to the abandoned rebel Fort Anderson, and now hold possession of the whole breadth of the peninsula, to Cape Fear River. The advanced pickets are already within a mile of Fort Fisher, preparing to storm it when the proper moment arrives.

The *Santiago*, with the division of Capt. GLISSON, consisting of fourteen gunboats, is anchored this morning close into the beach, with instructions to protect the troops as they advance, and follow them as they move forward. Our position for witnessing operations to-day, is, if possible, more favorable than that of yesterday. The wind is in the right quarter and will drive the smoke off shore and give us an unobstructed view of the effect of the shot of our vessels upon the fort as well as the operations of our storming party.

FLAGSHIP MALVERN, Saturday 11 A. M.

I am just informed that the *Gettysburgh* will start in a few minutes for Fortress Monroe, and I close hastily. Up to this hour nothing has been done this morning. The monitors are lying quietly with the *Ironsides* under the guns of Fort Fisher. Not a shot has been exchanged since four o'clock. A gun burst on the *Mahopac* yesterday, slightly wounding two officers, and one man seriously. These were the only casualties in the fleet. The weather at this moment is not so bright as it has been. The sun is somewhat clouded, though the wind still continues from the westward, giving us a calm sea. We hope to finish the work up to-day or to-morrow by a glorious victory.

ONE O'CLOCK P. M.

The *Ironsides* and monitors have just opened again on Fort Fisher.

TWO O'CLOCK P. M.

The division of wooden vessels are in short range of Fort Fisher, and firing rapidly upon it, but eliciting no reply.

I must close here, as the *R. R. Cuyler* is just about to leave with dispatches for Fortress Monroe.

VERY LATEST FROM FORT FISHER.

The Bloody Nature of the Fight—The Rebel Gen. Whiting and Col. Lamb Both Wounded—Our Loss 900—The Rebel Pirates Chickamauga and Tallahassee Both Driven up the River—Accidental Explosion of Fort Fisher's Magazine.

BALTIMORE, Tuesday, Jan. 17.

The *American* has the following from its special correspondent with the Wilmington expedition, who has just arrived at Fortress Monroe:

FORTRESS MONROE, Tuesday, Jan. 17—6:30 P. M.

After three days and nights of bombardment, Fort Fisher is ours, with all the contiguous works commanding New Inlet. The assault was made by the army and the naval brigade at 3 o'clock on Sunday afternoon. One corner of the fort was secured in half an hour, but we had a hand-to-hand fight with the garrison, which lasted until 9 o'clock at night. It was a very stubborn and bloody resistance, and the fort and the approaches were strewn with dead. The garrison had been heavily reinforced. The number of prisoners taken was over 2,000. The number of guns captured was 72. All the forts, including Mound and Seeks Island batteries, surrendered.

The rebel loss in the assault was 500 dead, beside the wounded. Our loss (army and navy) is about 900 killed and wounded. Fleet-Lieut. PRESTON and Lieut. PORTER, commandant of the flagship, were both killed in the assault. Gen. WHITING and Col. LAMB are both prisoners and wounded.

The rebel pirates *Tallahassee* and *Chicamauga* were both in the fight, and were driven up the river.

Our gunboats went up the river on Monday morning.

Our prisoners will be immediately sent North.

We had several days of delightful weather.

The magazine in the fort exploded by accident on Monday morning, killing and wounding two hundred of our men.

The *Santiago de Cuba* brings the bodies of Lieuts. PRESTON and PORTER, and the wounded of the navy.

Secretary Welles Congratulates Admiral Porter and General Terry—A National Salute Ordered at the Navy-Yards.

WASHINGTON, Tuesday, Jan. 17.

Secretary WELLS has addressed the following congratulatory telegram to Admiral PORTER:

WAR DEPARTMENT, Jan. 17, 1865.

To Rear-Admiral David D. Porter, Commmanding N. A. B. Blockading Squadron, off Wilmington, care of Commandant of the Navy-Yard Washington:

SIR: The Department has just received your brief, but highly-gratifying dispatch, announcing the fall, on the 15th inst., of Fort Fisher, under the combined assault of the navy and army, and hasten to congratulate you and Gen. TERRY, and the brave officers, sailors, and soldiers of your respective commands, on your glorious success. Accept my thanks for your good work.

(Signed,) GIDEON WELLES,

Secretary of the Navy.

Immediately upon receipt of the same the following telegrams was sent to the commandants of each of the Navy-yards:

NAVY DEPARTMENT, Jan. 17, 1865.

Fire a national salute in honor of the capture, on the 15th inst., of the rebel works on Federal Point, near Wilmington, by a combined attack of the army and navy.

(Signed,) GIDEON WELLES.

Secretary of the Navy.

Rejoicings Over the Victory.

A SALUTE IN WASHINGTON.

WASHINGTON, Tuesday, Jan. 17.

A grand salute is now being fired in the northern part of the city in honor of the capture of Fort Fisher by the land and naval forces under Gen. TERRY and Rear-Admiral PORTER.

ALBANY, N. Y., Tuesday, Jan. 17.

A national salute was fired to-day by order of the Adjutant-General, in honor of the capture of Fort Fisher.

MORRISTOWN, Penn., Tuesday, Jan. 17.

A salute of one hundred guns was fired by order of the loyal Union men this evening in honor of the capture of Fort Fisher.

Brevet Major-Gen. Alfred Howe Terry.

Brevet Major-Gen. ALFRED HOWE TERRY, commanding the military branch of the expedition against Fort Fisher, is a native of Connecticut, not more than 35 years of age, an officer in the Volunteer service, and a gentleman famous in the army alike for modesty, culture and gallantry. During many years before the war he devoted most of his leisure, outside the active demands of his profession of the law, to the study of military science, and had served in every capacity—from private to Colonel—in one of the "crack" militia regiments of Hartford. At the first call to arms he organized the Third Regiment of Connecticut Volunteers from among the noblest and best of the patriotic young men in the State, and led his command to the field in time to participate in the first battle of Bull Run, bringing the remnant of the regiment out of the riot and confusion of that adverse day in perfect order and with its *morale* unshaken. Returning home with this regiment after the expiration of its three months' term of service, Gen. TERRY at once took command of the Seventh Connecticut Regiment, which was assigned to the expedition under Brig.-Gen. T. W. SHERMAN, which captured Port Royal, S. C., in November, 1861. Under his command the regiment made a glorious record in the siege operations on Tybee Island, which resulted in the reduction of Fort Pulaski. For his gallant services at this time the President presented Gen. TERRY with a Brigadier's stars, which, *obiter*, it may be remarked, he modestly refused to wear until the Senate confirmed him in his rank. After this he commanded the coast defences from Port Royal to Key West, and was relieved from that duty to lead his brigade at the hard-fought battle of Pocotaligo, S. C., in October, 1862. He subsequently served with great distinction in the capture of Morris Island and the siege of Fort Sumter, and was appointed to the command of the First Division of the Tenth Corps. In April, 1864, when the Tenth Corps was ordered from the Department of the South to report for duty to Gen. BUTLER prior, to the movement up the James River, and the occupation of City Point and Bermuda Hundred, Gen. TERRY came North with his command, and was temporarily placed at the head of the corps, while it was in process of reorganization at Gloucester Point. In all the battles on the James River—at Richmond Turnpike, Drewry's Bluff, Deep Bottom, Petersburgh, and on the Varina, New-Market and Charles City Roads—Gen. TERRY'S division has actively engaged, and in the superb handling of his troops he established for himself a high military reputation for skill and valor, and was repeatedly complimented in general orders. When Gen. GILLMORE was relieved from the command of the Tenth Corps, Gen. TERRY was appointed his successor, and his comrades in arms were at one time very sanguine that he would be retained at the head of the corps, particularly as he had just received the brevet title of Major-General for "gallant and meritorious conduct." But the claims of the late Maj.-Gen. BIRNEY to the position were considered, by the commanding General, to outweigh General TERRY'S, and the former was appointed to the vacancy. During the brief time intervening between Gen. BIRNEY'S assumption of the command and the date of his death—a time marked by active operations, both on the part of the rebels and our own forces, on the north side of the James—Gen. TERRY'S conduct was such as to provoke the admiration of such a tried soldier as BIRNEY, who took every occasion to show his confidence and esteem, especially commending him for the excellent disposition of his division when, early in October last, the enemy surprised and routed KAUTZ' Cavalry, on the Darbytown road, and followed up their success by an impetuous dash upon Gen. BUTLER'S lines, which TERRY met and stayed, sending LEE'S flushed rapscallions staggering back, decimated and discomfited. That was a proud day for the old Tenth Corps—a day in which the indomitable pluck of TERRY'S Division turned a disaster into a victory. A week after this event Gen. BIRNEY was prostrated by the sickness which laid him in his grave, and Gen. TERRY, for the third time was called to the command of the Tenth Corps accepting the honor reluctantly, because it is not pleasant to be the shuttlecock which high military battledores keep in constant transit between a superior and inferior command; but accepting the position, nevertheless, with all proper cheerfulness becoming to an obedient soldier. Here he remained for nearly two months, commanding the old Tenth, now reduced by many a fierce fight, until its aggregate effective force scarcely exceeded a division in numbers, giving satisfaction to his immediate Commander, and beloved by his troops. Late in November, the Tenth and Eighteenth Corps were consolidated, under the name of the Twenty-fourth Corps, and again Gen. TERRY was compelled to give up the command of the corps for the subordinate position of leader of the First Division of the new organization. He was not long in this command, however, before a chance was given him to distinguish himself more highly than ever. The first expedition to Fort Fisher having proved a failure, a second was organized which, under his leadership, has proved a success, the result fully justifying the judgment and sagacity of Gen. GRANT in the selection of its commanding officer.

News from Albany.

ALBANY, Tuesday, Jan. 17.

The State Military Association met here today, and will continue in session to-morrow. The attendance is fair, but no important business has as yet been transacted.

A number of supervisors from the different counties will meet at the Capitol to-morrow, for the purpose of consultation as to the best means to be adopted to bring about the adoption of a uniform State or County bounty.

The Senate will probably arrive at some definite decision to-morrow about the State bounty.

It is expected that the final vote on the Ninth Senatorial contested seat case will be taken to-morrow.

Movements of the Rebel Gens. Vaughn and Breckinridge.

LOUISVILLE, Ky., Tuesday, Jan. 17.

Rebel deserters who came into Knoxville on the 12th inst., state that Gen. VAUGHN, with 700 men, all he had left, was at Bristol on the 4th inst.

Gen. BRECKINRIDGE, with his command, had gone to the Valley of Virginia, and it was thought would not return.

It is reported that the rebels have commenced repairing the damage to the salt-works by STONEMAN, during his late raid into Southwest Virginia.

The most perfect quiet now exists throughout East Tennessee.

Brig.-Gen. AMMEN has resigned, and Brig.-Gen. TILSON is now in command at Knoxville.

The Case of Burleigh.

TORONTO, Tuesday, Jan. 17.

The case of BURLEIGH, the rebel raider, was up again to-day before the Recorder. He announced that the judgement of the court was not ready yet, but that it would be announced on Friday.

The assault and capture of Fort Fisher

The New-York Times.

VOL. XIV......NO. 4156. NEW-YORK, THURSDAY, JANUARY 19, 1865. PRICE FOUR CENTS.

FORT FISHER.

DETAILS OF THE VICTORY.

Official Dispatch from Secretary Stanton.

REPORT OF ADMIRAL PORTER.

Full Particulars of the Assault.

THE BLOODY WORK ON THE RAMPARTS

A Nine Hours Struggle in the Fort.

"From Traverse to Traverse, and from Bomb-proof to Bomb-proof."

Heroic Gallantry of the Soldiers and Sailors.

[OFFICIAL.]

FROM SECRETARY STANTON.

Fortress Monroe, Tuesday, Jan. 17—10 P. M.

To the President:

The rebel flag of Fort Fisher was delivered to me on board the steamer *Spalding*, off that place, yesterday morning, Jan. 16, by Major-Gen. Terry.

An acknowledgment and thanks for their gallant achievement was given in your name to Admiral Porter and Gen. Terry, from whom the following particulars were obtained: The troops arrived off Fort Fisher Thursday night. Friday they were all landed under cover of a heavy fire from the squadron. A reconnoissance was made by Gen. Terry on Saturday. A strong defensive line against any of the enemy's forces coming from Wilmington was established on Saturday, and held by 4,000 men, chiefly colored troops, and an assault was determined on. The assault was made on Sunday afternoon at 3½ o'clock. The sea-front of the fort had been greatly damaged and broken by a continuous and terrible fire of the fleet for three days, and the front was assaulted at the hour mentioned by a column of seamen and marines, 1,800 strong, under command of Capt. Breese. They reached the parapet, but after a short conflict this column was checked, driven back in disorder, and was afterward placed on the defensive line, taking the place of a brigade that was brought up to reinforce the assaulting column of troops. Although the assault on the sea front failed, it performed a useful part in diverting the attention of the enemy, and weakening their resistance to the attack by the troops on the other side. The assault on the other and most difficult side of the fort was made by a column of 3,000 troops of the old Tenth Corps, led by Col. Curtis, under the immediate supervision of Gen. Terry. The enemy's force in the fort was over 2,200. The conflict lasted for seven hours. The works were so constructed that every traverse afforded the enemy a new defensive position from whence they had to be driven. They were seven in number, and the fight was carried on from traverse to traverse, for seven hours, by a skillfully-directed fire thrown into the traverses. One after another they were occupied by the enemy. Admiral Porter contributed to the success of the assaulting column by signals between himself and Gen. Terry at brief intervals. This fire was so well managed as to damage the enemy without injury to our own troops.

At about 10 o'clock at night the enemy were entirely driven from the fort, forced down toward Federal Point, followed by a brigade of our troops; and about 12 o'clock at night Gen. Whiting surrendered himself and his command to Gen. Terry unconditionally as prisoners of war, numbering over 1,800, the remainder of his force being killed and wounded.

Our loss was not accurately ascertained on Monday afternoon, but was estimated at between seven and eight hundred in killed and wounded, beside the naval loss, which was slight, not exceeding one hundred killed and wounded. Not a ship nor a transport was lost.

Col. Curtis was severely but not mortally wounded. Col. Bell died of his wounds Monday morning. Col. J. W. Moore and Lieut.-Col. Lyman were killed. Col. Pennypacker was badly wounded, also Lieut.-Col. Coan. A complete list of the killed and wounded will be forwarded as soon as it can be prepared.

Gen. Leroy reported to Surgeon-Gen. Barnes that he had ample provision of surgeons, nurses and hospital supplies for the wounded. They will be sent North to their respective States as fast as they can be placed on transports, of which there was ample supply.

On Monday morning, between 6 and 7 o'clock, the magazine of Fort Fisher exploded, killing and wounding two or three hundred persons.

After the capture of the fort, all the troops were withdrawn, except one brigade left in charge of the works.

How the explosion occurred was not known, but Gen. Terry believed it was occasioned by accident or neglect.

Gen. Hoke's division, reported as five thousand, was at Wilmington. A portion of it was thrown into the fort not long before the assault, and while that was going on, a demonstration was made by Gen. Hoke against our defensive, but it was found too stronging for anything more than a skirmishing attack.

About 11 o'clock on Monday morning, a heavy cloud of smoke was observed over Fort Smith, on the south side of New Inlet. The naval officer commanding that station reported that the enemy had fired their barracks, and evacuated that fort.

You will be pleased to know that perfect harmony and concert of action existed between the land and naval forces; and their respective Commanders, Admiral Porter and Gen. Terry, vied in their commendation each of the other. Each seemed more anxious to do justice to the other than to claim anything for himself, and they united in the highest commendation of the naval and military officers, and the forces engaged. To this harmony of feeling, and the confident spirit inspired, may, perhaps, be attributed, in some degree, the success of our attack, with nearly equal numbers, against a resolute enemy, in a work unsurpassed, if ever equaled, in strength, and which Gen. Beauregard, a few days before, pronounced impregnable. The armament of the fort was 72 guns, some of large calibre and rifled, and one Armstrong gun. The troops in the fort had rations for sixteen days. Their loss in killed and wounded was between 400 and 500. Gen. Whiting had three wounds in the thigh. Col. Lamb also, who had gone into the fort with reinforcements, and to relieve Gen. Whiting on Sunday, is wounded. On Monday everything was quiet as a Sabbath day. The dead were being buried, and the wounded collected and placed in transports and field hospitals.

EDWIN M. STANTON,
Secretary of War.

REPORT OF ADMIRAL PORTER.

Washington, Wednesday, Jan. 18.

The following was received at the Navy Department this morning:

United States Flagship Malvern,
Off Fort Fisher, Jan. 15, 1865.

Sir: I have the honor to inform you that we have possession of Fort Fisher, and that the fall of the surrounding works will soon follow:

As I informed you in my last, we had commenced operations with the iron vessels, which bombarded while we landed the troops. On the 14th I ordered all the vessels carrying 11-inch guns to bombard with the *Ironsides*, the *Brooklyn* taking the lead. By sunset the fort was reduced to a pulp. Every gun was silenced by being injured or covered up with earth, so that they would not work.

On the 15th Gen. Terry and myself arranged for the assault, and I ordered 1,400 sailors and marines to participate. At daylight the iron vessels, the *Brooklyn* and the 11-inch gunboats commenced battering the works, while the troops made a lodgement within 150 yards of the port. At 10 o'clock all the vessels steamed in and took their stations, opening a heavy fire, which was kept up until 3 P. M., when the signal was made to assault, the soldiers taking the land side, the sailors the sea face, and the ships changing, but not stopping their fire to other works.

The rebels met us with a courage worthy of a better cause, and fought desperately. About thirty of the sailors and officers succeeded in getting to the top of the parapet, amid a murderous fire of grape, cannister and musketry. They had planted the flag there, but were swept away in a moment. Others tried to get up the steep pancopee. The marines could have cleared the parapet by keeping up a steady fire, but they failed to do so, and the sailors were repulsed. Many a gallant fellow fell, trying to emulate their brothers-in-arms who were fighting to obtain an entrance on the northeast angle, as it appears on our charts. The enemy mistook the seamen's attack for that of the main body of troops, and opposed a most vigorous resistance there. But I witnessed it all, and I think the marines could have made the assault successful.

In the meantime our gallant soldiers had gained a foothold on the northeast corner of the fort, fighting like lions, and contesting every inch of the ground. The *Ironsides* and monitors kept storming their shells into the traverses not occupied by our men, but still held by the rebels. In this way our troops fought from traverse to traverse from 3 o'clock in the afternoon until 10 at night, when the joyful tidings were signaled to the fleet. We stopped our fire and gave them three of the heartiest cheers I ever heard.

It has been the most terrific struggle I ever saw, and there was very much hard labor. The troops have covered themselves with glory, and Gen. Terry is my "beau ideal" of a soldier and a General; and his coöperation has been most harmonious, and I think the General will do the navy the justice to say that this time, at least, "we substantially injured the fort as a defensive work." Gen. Terry had only a few more troops than we had on the last occasion, when the enemy had only 150 men in the works. This time the works were fully manned, and contained about 800 men at the time of the assault.

It is a matter of great regret to me to see my gallant officers and men so cut up; but I was unwilling to let the troops undertake the capture of the works without the navy sharing with them the peril all were anxious to undergo, and we should have had the honor of meeting our brothers-in-arms on the works, had the sailors been properly supported.

We have lost about 200 in killed and wounded, among them some gallant officers. I regret to announce the death of Lieut. S. W. Preston and Lieut. B. H. Porter. They were both captured together in the attack on Fort Sumter, and died together in endeavoring to pull down the flag that has so long flaunted in our faces. Lieut. R. H. Lamson was severely wounded. He was lately associated with Lieut. Preston in his perilous adventure on the powder-boat. Lieut. George M. Bache and a number of others were wounded, the former not dangerously.

The assault only took place a few hours ago, and I am unable to inform you of our casualties. They were quite severe from the assault; but we had no casualties from the enemy's cannon.

Knowing the impatience of the Department to receive news from Fort Fisher, I have written these few hurried lines. No one can conceive what the army and navy have gone through to achieve this victory, which should have been ours on Christmas day without the loss of a dozen men. This has been a day of terrific struggle, and is not surpassed by any event of the war. We are all worn out nearly; and you must excuse this brief and unsatisfactory account. I will write fully by the *Santiago de Cuba*, which goes North to-morrow to carry the wounded.

Besides the men in Fort Fisher there were about 500 in the upper forts, and a relief of about 1,500 men was brought down by steamers this morning. So far, I believe, we have only captured the garrison of Fort Fisher. I don't suppose there ever was a work subjected to such a terrific bombardment, or where the approach of a fort was more altered. There is not a spot of earth about the fort that has not been torn up by our shells.

I do not know yet the number of killed and wounded by our fire; but one 15-inch shell alone pierced a bomb-proof, and killed 16 and severely wounded 25.

I presume we are in possession of all the forts, as Fort Fisher commands them all. It is so late now that I can learn nothing more until morning.

I am, Sir, very respectfully, you obedient servant,
DAVID D. PORTER, Rear-Admiral.

Hon. Gideon Welles, Secretary of the Navy, Washington, D. C.

DETAILS OF THE BATTLE.

Baltimore, Wednesday, Jan. 18.

The following is a correspondence of the Baltimore *American*:

Gunboat Santiago, off Fort Fisher,
Monday, Jan. 16, 1865.

After three days of the most fearful and stubborn fighting in the naval or military experience of this war, I have the satisfaction of announcing that Fort Fisher has been compelled to succumb, with all the outlying batteries, and that the flag of the Union now floats from this rebel stronghold.

Our victory is complete.

The bombardment was commenced by the navy on Friday morning, and was continued night and day until 9 o'clock on Sunday night, a period of sixty hours, with little or no cessation. The storming of the fort by the military and naval brigade was a most bloody affair, and it may be doubted whether there has ever been anything equal to it for persistent assault and stubborn resistance. The assault was made on the fort at 3 o'clock on Sunday afternoon, and a lodgment effected on its west angle by the military.

The assault on the north side by the Naval Brigade was repulsed with fearful slaughter, but it served as an important diversion, enabling the military to obtain a foothold. The fight lasted six hours, being a desperate hand-to-hand struggle. Each of the seventeen traverses and embrasures were taken in succession, after the most fierce encounters, in which hecatombs of dead and wounded were added to those that already lined the fort. Suffice it to say, by way of preface to a detailed account, that notwithstanding the fort had been strengthened and reinforced to treble the garrison it had when Gen. Butler decided it could not be taken, it is now in our possession, with seventy-four cannon, 2,000 living prisoners and 700 dead, and that our gunboats have to-day sailed up the Cape Fear River, driving before them the pirates *Chickamauga* and *Tallahassee*, effectually closing it to blockade-running and stopping the only channel the rebels had left for the importation of munitions of war.

The elements seemed to favor us in the great and glorious undertaking. For seven days the wind has blown from the West, giving us a calm and quiet sea. We have had an uninterrupted clear sky, mild weather, and bright and beautiful moonlight nights.

THIRD DAY.

THE GRAND ASSAULT.

Sunday, Jan. 15.

A clear and brilliant moonlight night is succeeded this morning by a cloudless sky and a bright and warm sun, while the ocean is almost as calm as a mill-pond. A combined effort is to be made on the part of Admiral Porter and Gen. Terry to plant our flag on the walls of Fort Fisher at 3 o'clock this afternoon. The monitors and *Ironsides*, together with the *Brooklyn* and several small gunboats, have been steadily at work, since daybreak, shelling the fort. They threw a shell into it every five minutes during the night, and will continue their present task until the balance of the fleet joins them. There has not been a shot fired from the fort since 5 o'clock last evening, although the wooden vessels have been lying under its guns all night. There has been no flag visible at the ramparts for two days, though there is one flying from the Mound Battery, which is a mile south of Fort Fisher. They may possibly be husbanding their energies to resist the assault we are about to make. I learn from the shore, this morning, that Gen. Terry's artillerists have had some warm work, during the night, with the *Chickamauga* and *Tallahassee*, rebel gunboats. Our batteries have been planted to command a wharf to which we have moored a rebel steamer captured by us. The rebel gunboats run up and shell the steamer occasionally, when our artillerists open upon them. Both of them have been struck several times, and any attempt on their part to run up to Wilmington, when the fort falls, will be resisted. We have ten 30-pounder rifles in our batteries. Our storming party, 3,000 strong, are now in the woods within a mile of Fort Fisher. They report that the fort was reinforced last night by 800 men from Fort Caswell. The sailors and marines from the fleet, 2,000 strong, are also to join in the assault, and endeavor to scale the walls of the fort. They are in high glee this morning, and buckling on their armor with the alacrity of veterans.

GRAND BOMBARDMENT AND ASSAULT.

At 10 o'clock the frigates *Wabash*, *Minnesota*, *Powhatan* and *Colorado* took positions in line and joined in the bombardment, which may be regarded as the grand final attempt to take the fort.

10:15 A. M.—The boats from the ships, with marines and sailors to join in the assault, were called away to the flagship—about one hundred boats, with twenty men in each. They started in high spirits, all contending for the opportunity. The little gunboat *Monticello*, commanded by Lieut. Cushing, in close to the fort, has sent out a boat to take soundings. He is getting in position to protect the assaulting party, and has succeeded in shelling the rebel gunboats in Cape Fear River.

10:20 A. M.—The rebel gunboats *Chickamauga* and *Tallahassee* can be seen from the masthead coming down the Cape Fear River and shelling the woods where our soldiers are assembled, preparatory to the assault. Our army battery on the river is engaging the rebel boats, but with what success cannot be ascertained.

10:30 A. M.—The firing of the iron-clads, frigates and gunboats is getting quite brisk. The fort remains silent, except some rifle-shots fired at the daring Cushing, who seems brave to recklessness. The only shots fired by the rebels are from the Mound and water batteries south of the fort. It is believed that the seventeen parapet guns on the north wall of Fisher are disabled.

11 A. M.—The boats' crews are landing on the beach, about a mile from the fort, numbering about 2,000 sailors and marines. Shells are exploding in and around the fort at the rate of sixty per minute, although not more than half of the vessels are yet in position. The firing is deliberate, and the aim most accurate.

11:15 A. M.—The Admiral signals to Capt. Glisson to take his division of gunboats into action, and take position in front of the water batteries and Mound battery south of Fort Fisher. The view of the throngs of boats going to the beach with sailors is most inspiriting. About one-half of the men have already landed, and are forming in four divisions on the beach, their bright sabres glistening in the sun. The bombardment is increasing in volume, and the bursting of shells over Fort Fisher keeps it almost enveloped in smoke and flying sand. It would seem impossible for mortals to exist in it, though its bomb-proofs are said to be most capacious. The Admiral's flagship is moving rapidly from one point to another, in the thickest of the fight, brilliant with flags, giving orders to the various divisions as to their movements.

11:30 A. M.—The sailors and marines have all landed, and are marching along the beach in regular military style. A number of small gunboats are arranged along the beach, throwing shells across the peninsula at the rebel gunboats in Cape Fear River. The men are out on the monitors' decks and turrets, watching the course of their shells.

11:15 A. M.—The naval assaulting party formed in eight lines on the beach, about 250 men in each, now move forward, each boat's crew carrying its flag. Their advance skirmish line are throwing up light rifle-pits about half a mile from the fort. Firing of musketry can be distinctly heard in the woods toward the river, where the military assaulting party are under cover, waiting the signal for the attack.

12:40 P. M.—The bombardment progresses. Capt. Glisson's division of gunboats have just reached the point assigned them south of Fisher. Whilst getting into position the Mound and water batteries opened a furious cannonade on the *Santiago* and gunboat *Fort Jackson*. Several large shells came ricochetting toward us, and the two first bounded over us, one of them passing just over the head of Capt. Glisson and his son, a scale of one slightly injuring Acting Master Wilkes in the eye. The third shell entered the hull just in advance of the wheel-house and exploded on the other side of the vessel, slightly bruising and cutting two of the gunners on the lower deck. The fourth shell passed through the wheel-house, within a few feet of where your correspondent was standing. For about half an hour the heavy guns on Mound Battery continued to rattle shells over and around us, until the *Fort Jackson* got into position, when she divided the honors with us. The double-ender *Sassacus*, which was moving along behind us, caught one of the shells passing over us, which carried away the skylight of the cabin. The other vessels of the division are now in position, and all of them in the fire of the rebel batteries.

1:40 P. M.—The cannonading during the past forty minutes has been most furious, the only response being from the water batteries on Capt. Glisson's division. The Mound continues to pay special attention to the *Santiago*, doubtless recognizing her as the captor of so many blockade-runners.

2:20 P. M.—The line of the Naval Brigade can be seen about half a mile from the fort, lying down, and awaiting the order for the assault. The cannonading by the fleet is still going on quite furiously on Fisher, whilst our division is attending to the Mound and water batteries. We can now see that the Mound and water batteries are changing the positions of their guns, so as to sweep the beach and Fort Fisher.

ANTICIPATED ASSAULT.

2:50 P. M.—There has been no change in the operations during the past half hour. Some of the vessels are moving from the north to the south of Fisher, so as to assist the attack on the Mound, which can rake the storming parties. In a few minutes the hour for the assault will arrive. God grant that it may be successful, and that the lives of our gallant men may not be sacrificed.

3 P. M.—A signal from the Admiral directed the vessels to change their fire from Fort Fisher to the water batteries, and in an instant the Naval Brigade on the beach were observed moving forward toward the fort. They had about a mile to go to reach the abattis. They had scarcely got in motion before shells from the Mound and water batteries were poured upon them. Numbers of them were seen to fall, and scores of others to start back limping or crawling on their hands and knees. Onward, however, the main body pressed at a double-quick, the fire momentarily increasing in its fatal effects, until the whole line of beach over which they had traveled was strewn with dead and wounded. Some had fallen so near the rolling surf that their bodies could be seen tossing up and down the beach with the advancing tide. The ditch and abattis was about one hundred yards from the ramparts, and into this they poured until it was filled to overflowing, when two guns were opened upon them with grape and canister from the ramparts, tearing the abattis in front of them and adding largely to their casualties. The rebel gunboats *Chickamauga* and *Tallahassee* were also shelling them from Cape Fear River, and altogether it was a moment of frightful interest. It soon became evident that these gallant men must retire or all be sacrificed. The abattis and ditch formed a slight protection, but the raising of a head or the slightest exposure was sure to bring a shot from the unerring rifles of sharpshooters, who were seen standing on the ramparts with piles of loaded rifles, taking them up and handing them back to be reloaded. Their whole advance could be noticed from the fort, and it was evident that the greater portion of the garrison had rushed to that side to resist them. We hoped that in resisting the sailors they left the west end of the fort more easy of access to the soldiers. To get through the abattis under the heavy fire was next to impossible, and they were seen to retreat in order, leaving the dead and some of the wounded on the ground, but carrying most of the latter off with them. Those slightly wounded limped or crawled along on the beach out of range, and one gallant fellow was seen to fall dead whilst struggling along after the main body had got out of range, with a wounded officer on his back.

3:30 P. M.—At this moment three American flags greeted our anxious vision on the rear walls of Fisher, showing that the assault by Gen. Terry on that side had been at least partially successful. We could hear the rattle of artillery on the west side of the fort, and the cannonading of our troops by the rebel gunboats; but the whole movement of the men was invisible from the ocean, and the first evidence we had of the character of the struggle going on there was the appearance of "our flag" over the ramparts, with the blue flag of Gen. Terry. It was a glorious and inspiriting sight, though it was evident that we only held one portion of the fort, and that a severe struggle was in progress inside. Rebel reinforcements from the Mound and water batteries, to the number of 600 or 700 could be observed rushing down to Fort Fisher, and climbing over the ramparts, whilst the Mound and water batteries poured shell into one side of the fort, and the *Ironsides* and the monitors rained their ponderous shells in on the other side.

5 P. M.—For the last hour and a half there has been every evidence of a tremendous struggle progressing in Fort Fisher, during which our flags entirely disappeared from the ramparts.

9:30 P. M.—Our ears were greeted a few moments ago by loud and enthusiastic cheering from Fort Fisher. For a few moments we were in doubt as to whether they were rebel cheers or loyal rejoicings, though we imagined they were too hearty and free to come from rebel throats. Our doubts were soon removed by the appearance on the apex of the ramparts of the fort of one of Gen. Terry's signal officers, with his flaming torches, communicating with Admiral Porter's flagship. In a few minutes lights flickered all over the fort, and the cheers were repeated with a heartiness that left no doubt on our minds that it had changed owners.

10 P. M.—The Admiral commenced to throw up the rockets from the flagship, which was instantly understood as evidence of the glorious news that had been communicated to him. Every vessel in the fleet immediately responded by the burning of Roman candles, flashing of Costar's signals, and throwing up of rockets. A regular Fourth of July scene on the ocean. The hearty cheers of the sailors on the ships were responded to by the soldiers in the captured fort.

11 P. M.—All is now silent on land and sea. The signal officers are communicating on the beach.

Monday, Jan. 16.

We retired, last night, overjoyed with the glad tidings of the success of our gallant soldiers.

At the break of day, this morning, we were gratified with the sight of Federal troops, white and colored, strolling on the ramparts of Fort Fisher, examining the guns of the water-batteries, and even exploring the mysteries of the mound, evidently examining the new possession, with "none to molest or make them afraid." Up and down the beach the inevitable Yankee could be seen, and all was peace and quietness, where the storm of war was so lately raging.

AWFUL EXPLOSION.

Whilst looking at Fort Fisher under the federal flag and rejoicing over its downfall, a tremendous explosion took place in its very centre, something louder than the boom of a 15-inch gun. A volume of smoke and sand rose fifty feet in the air, enveloping and hiding from view the whole of the immense work for four or five minutes. It was at once apparent that the magazine had exploded, and that it must have been accompanied with great loss of life.

We soon after learned that the destruction of life was not less than 200, including many sailors from the fleet, who had not yet returned to their ships. It was occasioned by the carelessness of some of the colored troops. Various rumors are afloat as to this terrible catastrophe, some attributing it to the work of a torpedo; but on inquiry I learn that it was undoubtedly the work of carelessness. The loss of life by the explosion, I learn, is about 200, besides quite a number wounded. The magazine that exploded was in the very centre of the parade, and it has scooped out earth to a great depth for fifty feet around, and added to the desolation that reigns in this post monument of engineering ability. Quite a number of sailors from the fleet, and some of the officers also, suffered from the explosion. They had gone ashore to examine the work, and fell victims to their excusable curiosity.

The Paymasters of the *Gettysburgh* and the *Ticonderoga*, and an Ensign from the *Gettysburgh*, are reported among the victims.

Chamber of Commerce.—The Chamber of Commerce will hold a special meeting this day at 1 o'clock, to consider the report of its committee on the operations of the Reciprocity Treaty with Canada; also the memorial of the Boston Board of Trade on the postponement of the Bankrupt Bill now before the United States Senate.

The Fort Fisher Victory.—Yesterday the national flag was displayed on all our public buildings and many private residences in honor of the victory at Fort Fisher.

The Publication of Incomes Forbidden.—Mr. Lewis, United States Commissioner of Internal Revenue, has issued orders to collectors and assessors throughout the country forbidding them to allow the names of tax-payers to be copied from their lists for publication in newspapers.

OUR ALBANY CORRESPONDENCE.

The Contested Seat Case in the Senate Decided in Favor of Henry R. Low—Meeting of Supervisors in Regard to the County Question—The State Military Association—The Railroad Bills—Proposed Amendment of the City School Laws.

Albany, Wednesday Jan. 18, 1865.

The contested seat case, in the Senate, was brought to a conclusion at half-past twelve o'clock. Senators, by a vote of nineteen to ten, awarded the seat to Henry R. Low. In vacating the seat, which he has occupied for more than half the senatorial term, Mr. Niven spoke with much propriety, addressing his associates, and assuring them that he left them with the kindest feelings, and with best wishes for their welfare. Henry R. Low then came forward, took the oath of office and his seat as Senator from the Ninth District. The Committee on Privileges and Elections, in the House, reported, this morning that an extended investigation will be required in regard to the seat contested by Mr. Snook.

A meeting of Supervisors from various parts of the State, to consult in regard to the bounty question, finally took place this morning in the Assembly Chamber. Some of the Supervisors who had come here hoping to have a meeting yesterday, had returned home, but nineteen were present this morning, representing the Counties of Albany, Columbia, Franklin, Lewis, Niagara, Queens, Rensselaer, Steuben, Ulster and Warren. A merely temporary organization was effected, and the meeting then adjourned to meet in convention at the City Hall at 3 o'clock this afternoon. They passed a resolution before adjourning, inviting members of the Legislature to meet with them this afternoon. I do not learn, in conversing with the Supervisors, that they have any definite plans yet as to what they will recommend in reference to the bounty question.

The State Military Association, now in session in this city, have the Assembly Chamber this evening, for the delivery of the annual address before the association, by Col. Gates, of the Twentieth Regiment, New-York Volunteers, of Ulster County. I learn that Col. Gates was a member of the Assembly from Ulster County some ten years since, and is esteemed an able speaker.

The Assembly adopted a resolution this morning providing for the election of Regent on Thursday of next week, to fill the vacancy in the Board of Regent of the University caused by the death of Gen. James S. Wadsworth. The candidates spoken of are J. Meredith Reed, formerly Adjutant General of the State, and Rev. William H. Goodwin, formerly State Senator.

The New-York City railroad bills which have been noticed are most of them now introduced. The Broadway railroad bills, however, are still kept back. Mr. Ingraham gave notice this morning that he would introduce a bill which has a bearing upon the Broadway railroad question. The bill will provide for a railroad parallel to Broadway on the East side. The details of the bill are not yet fully made out. Mr. Van Buren gave notice of an important bill in regard to the schools of New-York City. The proposition is to allow seven instead of five dollars to be reported as the expense for each pupil who shall have actually attended and been taught the preceding year in the schools entitled to participate in the apportionment of money.

STATE LEGISLATURE.

SENATE.

Albany, Wednesday, Jan. 18.

BILLS REPORTED FAVORABLY.

Authorizing the Manufacturers' Bank, Brooklyn, to change its location.

To enable the Trustees of the Seamen's Friend and Retreat to borrow money.

Concerning certain public records in New-York.

To amend the Brooklyn Bounty Act.

To facilitate the organization of lands for croton water purposes.

Fixing the compensation of members of the New-York Common Council at $2,500 per annum.

BILLS INTRODUCED.

Amending the act concerning passengers arriving in vessels at the port of New-York.

Amending the act enabling the New-York Supervisors to raise money by tax.

Confirming the ordinance of the New-York Common Council, authorizing the extension of the Third-avenue Railroad.

The Ninth Senatorial District contested seat case was then taken up and argued by Messrs. Murphy, Bailey and Andrews, when the motion to adopt the majority report, unseating the sitting member, Mr. Niven, and admitting the claims of Mr. Low, was adopted by the following vote:

Ayes—Messrs. Ames, Andrews, Angel, Bailey, Bill, Cole, Cornell, Dutcher, Folger, Hastings, Havens, Hoyt, Hobbs, Julland, Lambeer, Munger, Strong and White.

Nays—Messrs. Allaben, Beach, Christie, Cozans, Fields, Humphrey, Murphy, Shafer, Smith and Woodruff.

The Senate went into Executive Session and afterward took up the State Bounty Bill, which was discussed till the hour of recess.

ASSEMBLY.

Albany, Wednesday, Jan. 18.

The Senate joint resolution relative to the election of a Regent of the University was amended, by fixing the time at next week, Thursday, 12 M.

REPORTS.

To incorporate the Tom Moore Association.

To incorporate the New-York Conservatory of Music.

To incorporate the New-York Yacht Club.

To incorporate the Atlantic Base Ball Club of Brooklyn.

NOTICES OF BILLS.

Relative to district schools in New-York.

By Mr. Stewart—For a railroad in Eighty-sixth-street, New-York.

For the establishment of a one-cent ferry between New-York and Brooklyn.

To incorporate the National Savings Bank of New-York.

By Mr. Ingraham—To incorporate the Broadway Parallel Railroad Company.

To amend the charter of the Emigrant Savings Bank.

BILLS INTRODUCED.

By Mr. McConville—For a railroad in Lexington-avenue, and other streets, New-York.

By Mr. Stewart—For a railroad in Grand-street, New-York.

By Mr. Lyons—To amend the charter of the Washington Insurance Company.

Also, for a railroad in Thirty-fourth and other streets, New-York.

To incorporate a National Savings Bank, relative to the maturity of commissioned paper.

Adjourned.

GEN. GRANT'S ARMY.

An Important Report—Rumored Destruction of the Danville Road by Freshets—Lee's Army Short of Food.

Headquarters Army of the Potomac,
Monday, Jan. 16, 1865—Evening.

A number of deserters came into our lines in front of Petersburgh last night. They bring important news, if it is to be relied on. They say that the Danville Railroad, between Danville and Greensboro, a distance of forty-five miles, has been destroyed by the recent heavy rains, and that every culvert and bridge has been carried away, and that Lee's army is likely to be out of rations altogether very soon. The quantity they issue now is utterly inadequate, they say, to satisfy their wants, and these men were not disposed to remain and suffer almost starvation. Every effort is being made to reconstruct the road, and large gangs of men are detailed for that purpose; but even at that it will take some time to repair it, the destruction of the road being so extensive. As this is the main road by which they get supplies to Richmond, it would not be strange if the state of affairs in this neighborhood should undergo an important change within a few days.

The enemy made a demonstration with a small force on our rear line on Wyatt's farm, near the extreme left, this afternoon, and for a short time it was thought a fight was coming off. A part of the Second Corps were put under arms, but the rebels remained in sight only a short time, evidently having come to that particular place after some forage, which it is believed they carried off. No firing took place, as they did not come within range of our pickets.

Col. Sharpe, so long connected with this army in the capacity of Deputy Provost Marshal General, and lately acting as Deputy Provost Marshal General of the armies operating against Richmond, has been promoted to a Brigadier-General; and Lieut. Stryker, Adjutant of the Signal Corps at Headquarters almost since its organization, has been promoted to a Captaincy. The services rendered by these officers during the past three years have been of the utmost value. Though their promotion has been long in coming, they have the satisfaction of knowing they have worthily earned it.

W. D. McGREGOR.

SOUTH CAROLINA

SHERMAN'S NEW MOVEMENT.

Official Dispatch from Secretary Stanton.

THE CAMPAIGN INAUGURATED.

Advance of General Howard to Pocotaligo.

The Enemy Abandon their Works.

BRANCHVILLE CLOSELY THREATENED.

The Commercial Aspect of Savannah.

[OFFICIAL.]

FROM SECRETARY STANTON.

Fortress Monroe,
Tuesday, Jan. 17—10 P. M.

To the President:

Gen. Sherman renewed the movement of his forces from Savannah, last week. The Fifteenth and Seventeenth Corps went in transports to Beaufort on Saturday, the 14th. The Seventeenth Corps, under Major-Gen. Blair, crossed Port Royal ferry, and, with a portion of Gen. Foster's command, moved on Pocotaligo. Gen. Howard, commanding that wing of the army, reported, on Sunday, 15th, that the enemy abandoned his strong works in our front during Saturday night. Gen. Blair's corps now occupies a strong position across the railroad, covering all approaches eastward to Pocotaligo.

All the sick of Gen. Sherman's army are in good hospitals at Beaufort and Hilton Head, where the genial climate affords advantages for recovery superior to any other place.

The peace and order prevailing at Savannah since its occupation by Gen. Sherman, could not be surpassed. Few male inhabitants are to be seen on the streets. Ladies and children evince a sense of security. No instance of disorder, or personal injury, or insults has occurred. Laboring men and mechanics, white and black, are seeking employment. The troops are cheerful and respectful toward every one, and seem to feel themselves much at home and on good behavior as if in their native towns.

Trade is restricted, for the present, to actual military necessity. Many ships with merchandise from the North are waiting at Hilton Head for permission to go to Savannah, but Gen. Sherman has admitted only a limited quantity of supplies required by his troops.

A mistake prevails at the North as to the present inducement for commerce at Savannah. There is not yet any large population to be supplied, no credit or money, no commodities of exchange, and there can be no great amount for a considerable period.

All the cotton and products now within Savannah belong to the Government, as captured property.

Stringent precautions against supplies that might go to the enemy have been made, and will be enforced by Gen. Sherman.

The cotton captured in Savannah, of which there is a good deal of Sea Island, has been turned over by the Quartermaster to Mr. Draper, Special Agent of the Treasury. The Quartermaster General remains at Savannah, to execute the arrangements for shipping.

EDWIN M. STANTON.
Secretary of War.

Gen. Sherman's Views on the Nature of the Rebellion.

The following letter was written by Gen. Sherman, in reply to certain inquiries from a citizen of Georgia:

Headquarters Military Division of the
Mississippi, in the Field,
Savannah, Ga., Jan. 8, 1865.

N. W——, Esq., —— County, Ga.:

Dear Sir; Yours of the 3d inst. is received, and in answer to your inquiries, I beg to state I am merely a military commander, and act only in that capacity; nor can I give any assurances or pledges affecting civil matters in the future. They will be adjusted by Congress when Georgia is again represented there as of old.

Georgia is not out of the Union, and therefore the talk of "reconstruction" appears to me inappropriate. Some of the people have been and still are in a state of revolt; and as long as they remain armed and organized, the United States must pursue them with armies, and deal with them according to military law. But as soon as they break up their armed organizations and return to their homes, I take it they will be dealt with by the civil courts. Some of the rebels in Georgia, in my judgment, deserve death, because they have committed murder, and other crimes, which are punished with death by all civilized governments on earth. I think this was the course indicated by Gen. Washington, in reference to the Whisky Insurrection, and a like principle seemed to be recognized at the time of the Burr conspiracy.

As to the Union of the States under our Government, we have the high authority of Gen. Washington, who bade us be jealous and careful of it, and the still more emphatic words of Gen. Jackson, "The Federal Union, it must and shall be preserved." Certainly Georgians cannot question the authority of such men, and should not suspect our motives, who are simply fulfilling their commands. Wherever necessary, force has been used to carry out that end; and you may rest assured that the Union will be preserved, cost what it may. And if you are sensible men you will conform to this order of things or else migrate to some other country. There is no other alternative open to the people of Georgia.

My opinion is that no negotiations are necessary, nor commissioners, nor conventions, nor anything of the kind. Whenever the people of Georgia quit rebelling against their Government and elect members of Congress and Senators, and these go and take their seats, then the State of Georgia will have resumed her functions in the Union.

These are merely my opinions, but in confirmation of them, as I think, the people of Georgia may well consider the following words referring to the people of the rebellious States, which I quote from the recent annual message of President Lincoln to Congress at its present session:

They can at any moment have peace simply by laying down their arms and submitting to the national authority under the Constitution. After so much, the Government would not, if it would, maintain war against them. The loyal people would not sustain or allow it. If questions should remain, we would adjust them by the peaceful means of legislation, conference, courts and votes. Operating only in constitutional and lawful channels, some certain and other possible questions are and would be beyond the Executive power to adjust, as, for instance, the admission of members into Congress and whatever might require the appropriation of money.

The President then alludes to the general pardon and amnesty offered for more than a year past, upon specified and more liberal terms, to all except certain designated classes, even these being "still within contemplation of special clemency," and adds:

"It is still so open to all, but the time may come when public duty shall demand that it be closed, and that in lieu more vigorous measures than heretofore shall be adopted."

It seems to me that it is time for the people of

(Continued on the Eighth Page.)

The New-York Times.

VOL. XIV......NO. 4167. NEW-YORK, WEDNESDAY, FEBRUARY 1, 1865. PRICE FOUR CENTS.

THE PEACE QUESTION.

ITS LATEST ASPECT.

Three Commissioners Coming from Richmond.

They Apply for Admission to General Grant's Lines.

A. H. Stephens of Georgia, R. M. T. Hunter of Virginia, and A. J. Campbell of Alabama.

A FLAG OF TRUCE AND A PARLEY.

General Grant in Communication with the Government.

Expected Arrival of the Commissioners at Annapolis.

Special Dispatch to the New-York Times.

WASHINGTON, Tuesday, Jan. 31.

In regard to the rebel Peace Commissioners, the following facts are known:

ALEXANDER H. STEPHENS of Georgia, R. M. T. HUNTER of Virginia, and A. J. CAMPBELL of Alabama, the latter formerly of the United States Supreme Court, arrived at Gen. GRANT'S lines last Sunday afternoon and desired permission to come to Gen. GRANT'S headquarters.

After considerable delay and parley they were allowed to come to Gen. GRANT'S headquarters at City Point. It appears that Gen. GRANT immediately notified the Government of the fact, but up to this time we are not aware of the decision arrived at, though they are expected to reach Washington presently, via Annapolis.

FROM GEN. GRANT'S LINES.

The Commissioners Appear in Front of Petersburgh—Application for a Permit to Come Through—Scenes under the Flag-of-Truce—Excitement among the Soldiers.

From Our Special Correspondent.

HEADQUARTERS FIFTH ARMY CORPS, Sunday, Jan. 29, 1864—10 A. M.

For many days the weather has been intensely cold, and many cases of frost-bitten feet, ears, cheeks, &c., on our picket lines are reported. To-day the intense cold had moderated, and though the sun shone brightly and the air was calm, the roads were solid and travelers many.

In front of Col. HARRIMAN'S brigade, of WILCOX'S division, Ninth Corps, about noon to-day, a flag of truce was displayed on the parapet of the enemy's works, a few rods to the right of the crater. The bearer of the flag stated, that "Hon. ALEXANDER H. STEPHENS, Vice-President of the Southern Confederacy, and Hon. R. M. T. HUNTER, of Virginia, were desirous of proceeding to Gen. GRANT'S headquarters; that they were expected, and would have approached our lines via the James River, but were unable to do so, owing to the ice in the stream."

The message sent by the bearer of the Confederate flag of truce was sent at once to the headquarters of the Ninth Corps.

The news that Messrs. STEPHENS and HUNTER were awaiting permission to enter our lines flew like wild-fire through the camps. They were distinguished men; they had made names for themselves before the war began, before acquiescing in the severance of the Republic, and the Union soldiers, who are reading men, knew it. Curiosity is one of the failings of the Union soldier, and, as the news of the flag passed from camp to camp, tents were evacuated, from bomb-proofs temporarily-buried soldiers emerged, pickets brought their rifled-muskets to an "order," and all, not otherwise engaged, covered the parapets of the works of the main and picket lines. As you know, for many days there has been a tacit understanding along this part of the line that there should be no firing; but, until to-day, the members of the corps did not think it conducive to their health to exhibit themselves prominently.

The white flag, however, brought both Unionists and Confederates within plain, point-blank shooting range of each other, and waiting for a reply to the rebel request, they showed themselves in clouds on the works of the contending armies. "How are you Fort Fisher!" says the Yanks; "Good-bye, European importations;" "Have you heard from HOOD?" "Did you know that your Virginian, THOMAS, had presented to Old ABE a 'worsted Hood'?" and many other remarks of a like nature.

The "Confeds" seemed to take it all in good part, and made, in some instances, quite happy replies, such as, "Fort Fisher may be gone up, but why don't you take Fort Crater?" "GWIN'S a fool, and we don't care a d—n for anything more from Europe;" and "HOOD'S hoodwinked old THOMAS, and you'll hear from him directly, I reckon."

So they passed the time intervening before the reply came. Men who, a few moments later, might be engaged in mortal combat, whiled away the closing hours of the beautiful Sabbath in seemingly friendly intercourse. But does any one dream that, if in the midst of this sort of national gathering, the order had been given, "Prepare for action," any of the soldiers, so jocose and free from care, would have disobeyed the command? No! But, shoulder to shoulder, they would have repeated the lesson they have been endeavoring to teach the foes of their country for these long years. In the soldier's life there is sunshine and shadow, but, alas! the shadow predominates. The Union soldier lives on in the hope that through the shadow will finally break the sun of peace, reflecting amid the black of adversity's clouds a rainbow of victory, telling in unmistakable colors of a "Union" conquered and thereafter indivisible.

As the bright orb of day neared the western horizon, and glanced upon the lofty spires of the yet unconquered "Cockade City," an officer from the headquarters of the Ninth Corps neared our foremost line. All were on the tiptoe of excitement; but, soldierlike, the gallant Colonel kept his own counsel; and, improvising a flag of truce from a white handkerchief, proceeded to scale the works; and, with one companion, advanced to the neutral ground.

After some minutes' waiting, he was met by four officers of the Confederacy, and a conference was held within a stone's throw of the scene of the terrible tragedy of the 30th of July last. What the result of this interview was, was not made public; but, it is believed that no word had been received from Gen. GRANT, and as a consequence, the "distinguished gentlemen" from Georgia and Virginia would have to bide their time, perhaps until to-morrow.

As the flags receded from each other, the thousands who covered the works suddenly disappeared, walking into their tents, crawling into their holes and descending into their bomb-proofs, to speculate upon the meaning of such a seemingly urgent desire on the part of the Vice-President and Ex United States Senator to enter the Union lines. Speculation upon this subject is not only rife among the soldiers, but among other thinking men, and the most extravagant propositions are put forth. Of course it is useless to speculate. It may be that the visit of these noted Southern gentlemen will be productive of good; but time alone will tell.

G. F. WILLIAMS.

REPORTS FROM BALTIMORE.

BALTIMORE, Tuesday, Jan. 31.

The *American*, this afternoon, publishes the following dispatch:

"The report has been current on the street since last evening to the effect that the Richmond *Sentinel* has announced the departure of three Peace Commissioners for Washington.

Up to noon to-day, we have no official confirmation of the rumor, though the assertion has been varied this morning by an equally positive announcement that Peace Commissioners, consisting of the rebel Vice-President ALEXANDER H. STEPHENS, and Ex-Senator R. M. T. HUNTER and Judge CAMPBELL had arrived at City Point and were expected to reach Annapolis to-day.

They are not spoken of as commissioners representing the rebel Government, but as citizens representing the people, on their way to Washington to confer with President LINCOLN on the subject of peace, precisely in the same capacity that Mr. BLAIR visited Richmond.

SECOND DISPATCH.

BALTIMORE, Tuesday, Jan. 31.

The *American* has the following special dispatch from Annapolis this morning:

ANNAPOLIS, Tuesday, Jan. 31.

Col. TYLER, of the Second Maryland Regiment, who arrived here this morning, says that on Sunday, ALEX. H. STEPHENS, R. M. T. HUNTER and two others reached our lines, and requested to come within our lines at Fort Hell, but were refused, and were awaiting permission from Gen. GRANT, who was then absent.

N. B.—I think the Commissioners were admitted nevertheless, and are now on their way to Washington. Hope to have something definite soon.

REPORTS VIA PHILADELPHIA.

PHILADELPHIA, Tuesday, Jan. 31.

A special dispatch to the *Evening Telegraph* says:

WASHINGTON, Tuesday, Jan. 31.

It is known in the best informed circles here that a commission from JEFF. DAVIS, consisting of Vice-President STEPHENS, R. M. T. HUNTER, and Gen. G. W. SMITH, have arrived at Annapolis with full power to arrange a settlement of our national difficulties.

It is believed from the understanding between Mr. BLAIR and Mr. DAVIS that the terms will be entirely satisfactory to the Administration and to Congress, and will chiefly consist of an amnesty to all offenders, and a withdrawal of the confiscation proclamation.

The Departure of the Commissioners from Richmond.

BALTIMORE, Tuesday, Jan. 31.

There is reason to believe that the Richmond papers of Monday contain an explicit statement of departure of commissioners for Washington.

From the Richmond Sentinel, Jan. 28.

It was a matter of pleasurable remark on yesterday that the President and Vice-President *had been engaged in a long consultation on public affairs.*

No Arrival yet from the James at Annapolis.

BALTIMORE, Tuesday, Jan. 31.

A dispatch from Annapolis to-night, says there has been no arrival from the James River, and there is no prospect of one to-night.

The Rebel Peace Commissioners.

The history and personal character of the rebel Vice-President, ALEXANDER H. STEPHENS, as well as his strenuous exertions to preserve the South from the folly and crime of secession, are well known to our readers. A. J. CAMPBELL, of Alabama, formerly occupied a seat on the Bench of the Supreme Court of the United States. It will be remembered that just previous to the capture of Fort Sumter, Mr. CAMPBELL appeared in Washington with Mr. FORSYTHE, of Mobile, CRAWFORD, ex-member of Congress from Georgia, and Mr. STEPHENS, on a mission to obtain the peaceful separation of the South from the Union. Since the commencement of hostilities his name has not been prominently before the public. Mr. R. M. T. HUNTER was formerly United States Senator from Virginia. He served a short time as rebel Secretary of State.

Return of Mr. Singleton.

Special Dispatch to the New-York News.

WASHINGTON, Monday, Jan. 30, 1865.

Gen. SINGLETON arrived in this city this evening, and immediately waited on the President. During his stay at Richmond he had frequent interviews with Mr. DAVIS and other prominent Confederate leaders, including Gen. LEE. Gen. SINGLETON represents those with whom he had intercourse as well disposed toward any movement calculated to restore peace on an honorable basis.

The Southern people remain firm in their determination to resist subjugation. The leaders are not averse to negotiation, provided it is not based on degrading conditions. They will meet us on equal terms, but not otherwise. They will not lay down their arms and accept whatever we choose to give them. There is no despondency in Richmond, but all, from Mr. DAVIS to the least important citizen, are desirous to have the war brought to a close.

FROM WASHINGTON.

ABOLITION OF SLAVERY.

Passage of the Constitutional Amendment.

One Hundred and Nineteen Yeas against Fifty-six Nays.

Exciting Scene in the House.

ENTHUSIASM OVER THE RESULT.

THE PEACE MISSION IN THE SENATE

A Resolution Calling for Information.

Passage of Retaliation Resolutions in the Senate.

Special Dispatches to the New-York Times.

WASHINGTON, Tuesday, Jan. 31.

THE PASSAGE OF THE CONSTITUTIONAL AMENDMENT.

The great feature of the existing rebellion was the passage to-day by the House of Representatives of the resolutions submitting to the Legislatures of the several States an amendment to the Constitution abolishing slavery. It was an epoch in the history of the country, and will be remembered by the members of the House and spectators present as an event in their lives. At 3 o'clock, by general consent, all discussion having ceased, the preliminary votes to reconsider and second the demand for the previous question were agreed to by a vote of 113 yeas, to 58 nays; and amid profound silence the Speaker announced that the yeas and nays would be taken directly upon the pending proposition. During the call, when prominent Democrats voted aye, there was suppressed evidence of applause and gratification exhibited in the galleries, but it was evident that the great interest centered entirely upon the final result, and when the presiding officer announced that the resolution was agreed to by yeas 119, nays 56, the enthusiasm of all present, save a few disappointed politicians, knew no bounds, and for several moments the scene was grand and impressive beyond description. No attempt was made to suppress the applause which came from all sides, every one feeling that the occasion justified the fullest expression of approbation and joy.

PETITIONS OF THE NAVAL CONTRACTORS.

The House Naval Committee having received a reply from the Secretary of the Navy to-day, unanimously instructed their Chairman to report a joint resolution, referring to the Navy Department the petitions of contractors asking for relief for losses in building double-enders, marine engines, &c., to be settled upon the principle of equity and justice. This is all the petitioners for relief ask, and without some such legislation the department cannot act in the matter.

THE TAX BILL.

The Ways and Means Committee to-day nearly finished the amendments to the tax bill. They expect to get through with the bill this week, and will report it at once.

THE NAVAL DEPOT AT CLEVELAND.

The Senate Naval Committee heard the arguments to-day in favor of a naval depot at Cleveland. The committee will not act definitely in regard to the matter until other parties have been heard.

THE TRADE IN COTTON.

The House Committee on Commerce to-day examined a large number of witnesses who are understood to have permits to trade in cotton with rebel States. These gentlemen, however, were very reticent, and the committee failed to elicit the required information as to how and where they got their permits.

Dispatches to the Associated Press.

WASHINGTON, Tuesday, Jan. 31.

THE VOTE ON THE AMENDMENT.

Soon after the passage of the Anti-Slavery Constitutional Amendment this afternoon, a salute was fired in honor of that event. The vote last June, when it was defeated for the want of the requisite two-thirds majority, was yeas, 96; nays, 65; absent, 21. Those who at that time voted against the amendment, but who changed their votes and cast them in the affirmative to-day, are Messrs. Baldwin of Michigan, Coffroth, McAllister, Ganson, Herrick, Radford, Steele, King, Rollins of Missouri, and Hutchins. Those who were absent on the former occasion, and who now voted aye, are as follows: Messrs. Brown of West Virginia, Davis of Maryland, Davis of New-York, Grinnell, McBride, Nelson, Pomeroy, Randall Worthington and Yeaman. The following who were absent or not voting when the June vote was taken, voted nay: Messrs. Hall, Harris of Maryland, Harris of Illinois, Winfield, Ben. Wood and Townsend. Those who voted against the resolution last year, and were to-day absent or not voting, are Messrs. Lazear, Le Blond, McKinney, Marcy, McDowell and Rogers.

MR. WADE ON THE PEACE MISSION.

During the debate on the retaliation resolution, while Mr. WADE was speaking about Mr. BLAIR'S mission to Richmond, Mr. JOHNSON asked how he came to go there. Mr. WADE replied: "I would like to know. Yes, Sir. I intend to know if there is power in the United States Senate to be informed on that subject. I intend to know why it was that any man was permitted to go with impunity through our lines, and confer with the arch traitor of the Confederacy, and come back here and go again." Mr. JOHNSON said he went in a Government vessel the last time. Mr. WADE responded: "Yes, I understand he went on a Government vessel. He had no more right to be on that vessel on a mission to hold communication with this arch traitor and devil, than he had to be on his road to the lower regions in a vehicle furnished by the Government."

THE CIVIL GOVERNMENT OF VIRGINIA.

The Alexandria (Va.) *Journal* says the civil government has been restored on the eastern shore of Virginia, and that in a few days civil government will be restored in every county where it was suppressed by the action of Gen. BUTLER.

THE SUBSCRIPTIONS TO THE SEVEN-THIRTY LOAN.

The financial arrangements just concluded between the Treasury Department and JAY COOKE contemplate the continuance of subscriptions to the seven-thirties through the national banks in New-York, Philadelphia, Boston and elsewhere, as heretofore.

THIRTY-EIGHTH CONGRESS.

SECOND SESSION.

SENATE.

WASHINGTON, Tuesday, Jan. 31.

PROTEST AGAINST THE BANKRUPT BILL.

Mr. WADE, of Ohio, (Union,) presented a joint resolution of the Ohio Legislature protesting against the passage of the bankrupt law, which was ordered to be printed and laid on the table.

THE DUTY ON IMPORTED PAPER.

Mr. WADE also presented a resolution of the Ohio Legislature in favor of the repeal of the duty on printing paper, which was ordered to be printed and laid upon the table.

EMPLOYMENT OF GENERALS.

Mr. WADE—I notice that the Secretary of War, in replying to a communication of the Senate about the employment of Generals, has made a mistake which I wish to correct. He says, among other things, that Gens. BANKS and LEE are before the Committee on the Conduct of the War. This is a mistake, and one which I wish to rectify, because it seems to be a standing one. I think it interferes with the disposition which the Executive wishes to make of these officers. Mr. WADE further stated that on the 14th of December, Gen. BANKS was before the committee for about two hours, to give testimony concerning the Red River expedition. One day in January the committee found him in the city, and called on him for a few minutes to explain some matters. Gen. LEE had not been before the committee since the 13th of January, when he gave testimony for about two hours. He (WADE) wished it to be understood that neither Gen. BANKS nor Gen. LEE were detained here by the Committee on the Conduct of the War.

CLERGYMEN AND THE DRAFT.

Mr. HARRIS, of New-York, (Union,) offered the memorial of certain ministers of the Gospel, asking that they be exempted from the draft. Which was referred to the Committee on Military Affairs.

THE SCHELDT DUES.

Mr. SUMNER, of Massachusetts, (Union,) from the Committee on Foreign Relations, reported a bill for the extinction of the Scheldt Dues. Which was ordered to be printed.

CONGRESSIONAL DIRECTORY.

Mr. ANTHONY, of Rhode Island, (Union,) introduced a resolution that a Congressional Directory be published hereafter, under the superintendence of the Joint Committee on Printing. Mr. ANTHONY explained that this would be more economical than the present arrangement, by which it was published under the auspices of the Postmaster of the House; but its chief benefit would be the appearance of the Directory at an earlier day in the Session than it now appears.

The resolution was adopted.

CALL FOR INFORMATION ON MR. BLAIR'S MISSION.

Mr. SUMNER offered the following resolution:

Resolved, That the President of the United States be requested, if not incompatible with the public interests, to furnish to the Senate any information in his possession, concerning any recent personal communications with the rebel JEFFERSON DAVIS, said to have been under Executive sanction, and also copies of any correspondence relating thereto.

Mr. CONNESS, of California, (Union)—I suggest to the Senator if it would not be better to leave out the verbiage, and make the resolution refer to the message of Mr. BLAIR.

Mr. SUMNER—I beg the Senator's pardon, but I prefer it as it is.

Mr. JOHNSON, of Maryland, (Union,) offered the following as an amendment by way of a substitute for Mr. SUMNER'S proposition:

Resolved, That the President of the United States be requested, if not incompatible with the public interests, to inform the Senate if any person, and if any, who has, with his authority and assent, been to Richmond negotiating with the President of the so-called Confederate States, or with any other person or persons in that place, in relation to the termination of the present war, or with a view to ascertain from such persons upon what terms, if any, they would be willing to have said war terminated; and if so, to inform the Senate, also, what information he has obtained from such agent or person; also, if such person was in Richmond as aforesaid, whether he was authorized or permitted by the President of the United States to represent to the Confederate authorities upon what terms or conditions the President would negotiate in relation to peace, and, if so, what such terms and conditions were.

Mr. SUMNER said that the resolution he offered was much briefer and simpler than that of the Senator from Maryland. There were some words in Mr. JOHNSON'S resolution which he did not like. He did not like to see the Senate adopt such a phrase as the Confederate authorities.

SEVERAL SENATORS—The resolution says "so-called Confederate authorities."

Mr. SUMNER said he preferred to speak of them as rebel authorities.

Mr. DOOLITTLE, of Wisconsin, (Union,) suggested that both resolutions be printed and called up to-morrow.

This was agreed to and it was so ordered.

SECRETARY WELLES INTERROGATED.

Mr. HALE offered a resolution calling upon the Secretary of the Navy for information as to whether the arguments of the Judge-Advocate in the trial of Mr. SMITH, of Boston, had been printed by order of the Navy Department? What edition of the same had been published? What use has been made of the copies thus published? Also, whether any detectives have been employed by the Navy Department since January, 1864, and if so, how many, and how much they have been paid? what instructions they got, either written or verbal, from the Secretary or Assistant Secretary of the Navy? And especially whether any instructions were given to inquire into the conduct and business transactions of any member of either House of Congress? How much expense was incurred in this way? From what sources the funds were drawn, and by what authority?

Mr. CONNESS—I suggest that the resolution of the Senator from New-Hampshire lie over until the return of the chairman of the Committee on Naval Affairs, who is now absent.

Mr. HALE consented to the proposition, and the resolution was ordered to be printed.

NEW-YORK AND PACIFIC MAIL.

Mr. ANTHONY introduced a bill relative to mail service between New-York and the Pacific coast, which authorizes the Postmaster-General to contract for the transportation of the mails upon such lines by steamers on the Atlantic and Pacific coast, and by land transit across the Isthmus, semi-monthly, tri-monthly, or weekly, as in his judgment the public interest may from time to time require; the compensation not to exceed $400,000 for a semi-monthly, $600,000 for a tri-monthly, or $800,000 for a weekly line.

The bill was referred to the Committee on the Post-office and Post Roads.

THE BILL TO BRIDGE THE OHIO.

Mr. POWELL, of Kentucky, (Dem.,) asked that the Senate take up the bill to build a bridge across the River at Louisville.

The motion was disagreed to.

THE PROPOSED COMMITTEE ON CORRUPTIONS.

Mr. HALE then moved that the Senate proceed to the consideration of the resolution of Mr. DAVIS for the appointment of a Standing Committee on Corruptions of the Government.

Mr. DOOLITTLE suggested that as the animadversions of the Senator from New-Hampshire on the conduct of the Navy Department were likely to lead to protracted discussion, it would be well to make this the special order for some day, as there was very little time of the morning hour remaining.

Mr. HALE insisted on his motion.

Mr. HENDERSON desired to take up the bill to reimburse the State of Missouri for the expenses incurred in calling out the militia of that State.

The Senate refused to take up this bill and proceeded to the consideration of the resolution of Mr. DAVIS, upon which Mr. HALE was entitled to the floor.

Mr. HALE said he was opposed to appointing any more committees to investigate corruptions until some action was taken on frauds already discovered. He read at length from a report made by Hon. JOHN SHERMAN, when a member of the House, on the subject of naval contracts, to show that, while Congress had heretofore gone to great trouble and expense to discover frauds, yet none of the guilty parties had ever been punished.

THE QUESTION OF RETALIATION.

The morning hour expired, and the Chair decided that the retaliation resolution was in order on the proposition to recommit the papers on the subject to the Military Committee.

The subject was discussed by Messrs. HENDRICKS, WADE, SUMNER, SPRAGUE and HOWE.

Mr. SAULSBURY, of Delaware, (Dem.,) said that if all the allegations against the rebels as to their treatment of our soldiers be true, it was but another argument for peace. He was not ashamed to stand up in the Senate and advocate peace. He was not in the habit of endorsing what the President did. But if, as he heard, commissioners were on their way here to treat for peace, and this was the result of promises held out to the Confederates by the President, he was willing to endorse him so far.

The question was then taken on the motion to recommit the subject, and the Senate refused so to do. Yeas 10, nays 26.

YEAS—Messrs. Carlile, Davis, Hendricks, Powell, Richardson, Riddle, Saulsbury, Sumner, Van Winkle, Wright.

NAYS—Messrs. Anthony, Chandler, Clark, Collamer, Conness, Cowan, Dixon, Foster, Hale, Harlan, Harris, Henderson, Howard, Howe, Johnson, Lane of Indiana, Morgan, Merrill, Nesmith, Pomeroy, Ramsay, Sherman, Ten Eyck, Wade, Wilkinson, Willey.

The question then recurred on the amendment making retaliation comformable to the law of nations.

Mr. SUMNER moved further to amend by making it conform also to the usages of war as practiced among civilized nations. Mr. SUMNER called for the yeas and nays on the amendment, and it was adopted by a vote of 26 yeas against 13 nays.

YEAS—Messrs. Carlile, Cowan, Davis, Doolittle, Foote, Foster, Harlan, Harris, Henderson, Hendricks, Lane of Indiana, McDougall, Morgan, Nesmith, Pomeroy, Powell, Richardson, Riddle, Saulsbury, Sherman, Sumner, Ten Eyck, Van Winkle, Willey, Wilson, Wright.

NAYS—Messrs. Chandler, Clark, Collamer, Conness, Dixon, Farwell, Hale, Howard, Howe, Ramsay, Trumbull, Wade, Wilkinson.

Mr. SUMNER moved to amend by striking out the following: "Congress does not, however, intend by this to limit or restrict the power of the President to the modes or principles of retaliation herein mentioned; but only advises or requires a resort to them as demanded by the occasion."

Mr. SHERMAN, of Ohio, (Union,) suggested that the amendment be modified so as to strike out the words "to the modes or principles of retaliation herein mentioned."

This was adopted.

Mr. HENDRICKS, of Indiana, (Dem.,) offered as an amendment an additional resolution declaring the sense of the Senate to be in favor of an exchange of prisoners.

Mr. HOWARD, of Michigan, (Union,) thought the subjects were so different that they should not be incorporated in the same resolution.

The amendment was adopted.

Mr. HENDERSON, of Missouri, (Union,) offered an amendment, advising the appointment of Commissioners of Prisoners, to look after the condition of our prisoners in the future.

The yeas and nays were called for, and the amendment was adopted.

YEAS—Messrs. Carlile, Collamer, Cowan, Davis, Doolittle, Foot, Foster, Harris, Henderson, Hendricks, Johnson, Lane of Kansas, McDougall, Morgan, Nesmith, Pomeroy, Powell, Riddle, Sumner, Ten Eyck, Van Winkle, Willey, Wilson, Wright—24.

NAYS—Messrs. Chandler, Clark, Conness, Dixon, Farwell, Hale, Harlan, Howard, Howe, Lane of Indiana, Morrill, Ramsay, Sherman, Trumbull, Wade, Wilkinson—16.

The resolution as amended was then passed and the Senate adjourned.

HOUSE OF REPRESENTATIVES.

WASHINGTON, Tuesday, Jan. 31.

MR. WOOD OFFERS A RESOLUTION.

Mr. FERNANDO WOOD asked leave to offer the following resolution:

Resolved, That it is the duty of the President to maintain, in every constitutional and legal manner, the integrity of the American Union, as formed by the Fathers of the Republic, and in no event, and under no circumstances, to proffer or accept negotiations which shall admit, by the remotest implication, the existence of any other Federal or Confederate Government within the territory of the United States.

Mr. FARNSWORTH, of Illinois, (Union,) objected to the reception of the resolution.

Mr. FERNANDO WOOD gave notice that he would next Monday move a suspension of the rules to introduce the resolution.

THE PRESIDENTIAL VOTE.

The Speaker appointed Mr. Stevens of Pennsylvania, Mr. Washburne of Illinois, Mr. Mallory of Kentucky, Mr. Davis of Maryland, and Mr. Cox of Ohio, as a committee on the part of the House to examine and count the votes for President and Vice-President of the United States, on the second Wednesday of February.

THE ANTI-SLAVERY AMENDMENT.

The House resumed consideration of the Senate joint resolution, proposing amendments to the Constitution of the United States.

Mr. MCALLISTER of Pennsylvania (Dem.) said when this subject was before the House on a former occasion, I voted against the measure. I have been in favor of exhausting all the means of conciliation to restore the Union as our fathers made it. I am for the Union and utterly opposed to secession or dissolution in any way or shape. The result of all the peace missions, and especially that of Mr. BLAIR has satisfied me that nothing short of recognition of their independence will satisfy the Southern Confederacy. It must therefore be destroyed, and in voting for the present measure, I cast my vote against the cornerstone of the Southern Confederacy, and declare eternal war against the enemies of my country.

Mr. COFFROTH, of Pennsylvania, (Dem.,) addressed the House in favor of the amendment, not, however, speaking for or against slavery. He argued the power of Congress to submit the amendment to the Legislatures of the States; that the South could defeat the amendment, that it must be submitted to the seceded States, or it would be recognizing their independence; that if this was done, it would apply only to those which adopted it. He also argued that the South would not remain in the Union under the Constitution as it now is, and that they would not come back after four years' fighting. All relating to slavery should be stricken from our statute books, and then, when the people of the South were tired and sick of this barbarous and inhuman war, and demand a cessation of hostilities, until it be ascertained if peace cannot be obtained, there will be no obstacles in the way of giving new guarantees to every person who shelters himself under the American Constitution. He also argued that slavery was the fruitful theme for the opponents of Democracy. It breathed life and existence into fanaticism, and unless that which sustained and fed fanaticism be removed from the political arena, the country would remain stationary, when all the rest of the world is moving. Change is the universal law of nature. What he had heretofore regarded as impolitic had ceased to operate. Having at the last session voted against the proposed Constitutional amendment, he would now vote for it. He had no doubt of the power to make the amendment in the manner proposed. In amending it three-fourths of the States represent the whole. The time has arrived to exercise the power. He believed that if Democratic policy and measures had been adopted, we should not now be engaged in war; but in the late Presidential election the people had endorsed the anti-slavery issue. He was prepared to follow it. The question had been settled by the verdict of the people, and so far as the National Government was concerned, it was not now a political issue. The adoption of the amendment would tend to restore all that is desirable to the prosperity of the country. He believed the best good of the Democratic party would be enhanced by the passage of the proposition, and it will open up a way to its triumph in the future.

Mr. BROWN, of Wisconsin, (Dem.,) spoke of the dangerous abuse of the power of the amendment. He had never been the apologist for slavery. He never thought it could be entirely destroyed. He was in favor of removing it, and then the people would place in power the Democracy. He gave this vote after much consideration, and as a Democrat, and would consistently stand by the organization of his party. No power on earth should prevent him from voting for the candidates of his party. His desire was the triumph of the party which has made this country great.

Mr. MILLER, of Pennsylvania, (Dem.,) said he owed it to himself and his constituents to reply to the sentiments of his colleagues just uttered on this floor. He wished to so act that when he returned home he would not be found derelict to the duty with which he had been entrusted, having taken an oath to protect, defend and preserve the Constitution of the United States. Long as the matter had been discussed here, it was very strange that no man had answered the question, what was to be done with the freed people, should such an amendment to the Constitution prove effective? Gentlemen on the other side had failed to make out a case. During this Administration the Constitution had been violated in all its important features.

Mr. HERRICK, of New-York, (Dem.,) in the course of his speech, said it was inconsistent that it would be a permanent institution. If he lived in Missouri or Kentucky, he should vote for the abolition of slavery therein; but as to Congressional action on that subject, it might be different. The question of slavery under the Constitution was reserved to the States respectively wherein it exists. In conclusion, he caused to be read a substitute which he desired to submit, providing that hereafter every sale and transfer of slaves shall be void and the slaves shall become free, and from and after 1880 slavery shall cease, and Congress shall give compensation for the actual damage and loss suffered by loyal citizens of the United States.

Mr. HARDING, of Kentucky, (Dem.,) said truth and principle never change, but men change, and from time to time adopt opinions just as readily as they change their garments. But he would rather hold on to the Constitution, which was the only ark of safety. He denied that there was any constitutional power to deprive any State in the Union of its local self-government. Kentucky had been treated in bad faith. Not one of the pledges made to her had been fulfilled. She had been betrayed, and now it was sought suddenly to emancipate all her slaves. The policy would result in the destruction of the slaves, and the men who proposed to carry it out had no more love for the slave than Satan has for sinners.

Mr. KALBFLEISCH, of New-York, (Dem.,) opposed the proposition. He maintained that all our political misfortunes are attributable to a disregard of the Constitution. He had not learned his democracy from his inveterate enemies, and he would not be instructed by them now. This amendment, he contended, if adopted, would stand in the way of peace negotiations and a restoration of the Union. He said he should strive to uphold and carry out the pledges which he had made to protect and defend the Constitution. Apart from the question of power, this was not the time to attempt an amendment of the Constitution in the manner proposed. He denied that the result of the Presidential election was in favor of abolishing slavery everywhere. No such issue was made up in New-York.

The debate having closed, Mr. ASHLEY, of Ohio, (Union,) who had charge of the subject throughout, demanded the previous question, which was on the motion heretofore made by the gentleman, to reconsider the vote of last session, by which the constitutional amendment was lost for the want of the requisite two-thirds majority.

Mr. STILES, of Pennsylvania, (Dem.,) moved that the motion to reconsider be laid on the table.

This was decided in the negative. Yeas, 57; nays, 111.

The question was then taken on the motion to reconsider, and it was decided in the affirmative. Yeas, 112; nays, 57.

Mr. MALLORY, of Kentucky, (Dem.,) raised the question that a vote of two-thirds was requisite to reconsider; but the Speaker overruled the point, saying all motions of this kind were governed by the rules.

Mr. MALLORY suggested a postponement of the vote until to-morrow, saying that several gentlemen who wished to record their names were absent. Let the time for taking the question be fixed so that all could have a fair warning.

Mr. ASHLEY replied that it had been universally understood that the question was to be taken to-day. He had consented to the extension of the debate even against the protest of his friends. It came with a very bad grace to ask for a postponement of the vote, considering the courtesy he had extended to the other side and the fair notice given.

Mr. BROWN, of Wisconsin, (Union,) asked the gentleman to give way in order that he might offer a substitute.

Mr. ASHLEY said he had one himself, which he preferred to the Senate's proposition now before the House.

Mr. ELDRIDGE, of Wisconsin, (Dem.,)—Why do you not offer it?

Mr. ASHLEY—Because I will not protract the proceedings.

The question was then taken on the adoption of the following Senate joint resolution, submitting to the Legislatures of the several States, a proposition to amend the Constitution of the United States:

Be it resolved by the Senate and House of Representatives of the United States of America in Congress assembled, two-thirds of both Houses concurring, that the following articles be proposed to the Legislatures of the several States as an amendment to the Constitution of the United States; when ratified by three-fourths of said Legislatures, shall be valid to all intents and purposes as a part of the said Constitution, namely:

ART. 13.—SECTION 1. Neither slavery nor involuntary servitude, except as a punishment for crime, whereof the party shall have been duly convicted, shall exist within the United States, or any place subject to their jurisdiction.

SEC 2. Congress shall have power to enforce this article by appropriate legislation.

There was much confusion throughout the proceedings, amid which the clerk proceeded to call the roll on the passage of the joint resolution.

The Speaker said, "Call my name as a member of this House."

The name was accordingly called.

When the Speaker answered to the name of SCHUYLER COLFAX, applause followed his response, and also burst out at other parts of the proceedings; which, however, the Speaker checked, and calling the House to order, said he hoped a better example would be set to preserve the decorum of the House.

Several members on the Democratic side of the House said those on the other side were as noisy as the persons in the galleries.

Mr. GANSON, of New-York, (Dem.,) had voted "no" on the question of reconsidering the vote by which the joint resolution was heretofore lost, now voted "aye." and Messrs. RADFORD and STEELE, (Dems.) of New-York, changed their votes in the same manner. These changes gave rise to applause, which was promptly checked.

The utmost interest was manifested throughout the calling of the roll, and there was strict attention on the part of the members to their responses; for, on the previous vote to reconsider, two-thirds of the members present had not voted in the affirmative, but a large majority of the members present had carried that question. It was therefore somewhat doubtful whether the pending joint resolution would be passed.

The votes of Mr. BALDWIN of Michigan (Dem.) and the gentlemen above mentioned however gave additional hopes to the friends of the measure.

When the calling of the roll was completed the Clerk proceeded to read the names, first of those who voted in the affirmative, and next of those who had voted in the negative. The House was now comparatively silent. The result of the vote was noted on a piece of paper and handed by the Clerk to the Speaker, who then announced the passage of the joint resolution by a vote of 119 yeas against 56 nays.

Thereupon rose a general shout of applause. The members on the floor huzzaed in chorus with deafening and equally emphatic cheers of the throng in the galleries. The ladies in the dense assemblage waved their handkerchiefs, and again and again the applause was repeated, intermingled with clapping of hands and exclamations of "Hurrah for freedom!" "Glory enough for one day," &c. The audience were wildly excited, and the friends of the measure jubilant. Never was a scene of such a joyous character before witnessed in the House of Representatives, certainly not within the last quarter of a century.

There was extensive hand-shaking and congratulation in every direction. The proceedings had attracted thousands of persons of both sexes, and having been brought to a close, those on the floor who had been admitted by the favor of the members, and the occupants of the galleries, hastily departed.

The vote on the passage of the joint resolution is as follows:

YEAS (DEMOCRATS IN ITALICS.)

Messrs. Alison, Iowa,	*King*, Missouri.
Ames, Massachusetts,	Knox, Missouri,
Anderson, Kentucky,	Littlejohn, New-York,
Arnold, Illinois,	Loan, Missouri.
Ashley, Ohio,	Longyear, Michigan,
Bailey, Pennsylvania,	Marvin, New-York.
Baldwin, Michigan,	*McAllister*, Pennsylvania,
Baldwin, Massachusetts,	McBride, Oregon.
Baxter, Vermont,	McClurg, Missouri.
Beaman, Michigan,	McIndoe, Wisconsin,
Blaine, Maine,	Miller, New-York,
Blair, West Virginia,	Morehead, Pennsylvania,
Blow, Missouri,	Morrill, Vermont,
Boutwell, Massachusetts,	Morris, New-York,
Boyd, Missouri,	A. Myers, Pennsylvania,
Brandagee, Connecticut,	L. Myers, Pennsylvania,
Broomall, Pennsylvania,	*Nelson*, New-York,
Brown, West Virginia,	Norton, Illinois,
Ambrose W. Clark, New-York,	*Odell*, New-York,
Freeman Clark, New-York,	O'Neill, Pennsylvania,
Cobb, Wisconsin,	Orth, Indiana,
Coffroth, Pennsylvania,	Patterson, New-York,
Colfax, Indiana,	Perham, Maine,
Cole, California,	Pike, Maine,
Creswell, Maryland,	Pomeroy, New-York,
Davis, Indiana,	Price, Iowa,
Davis, New-York,	*Radford*, New-York,
Dawes, Massachusetts,	Randall, Kentucky,
Deming, Connecticut,	Rice, Massachusetts,
Dixon, Rhode Island,	Rice, Maine,
Donnelly, Minnesota,	Rollins, New-Hampshire,
Driggs, Michigan,	*Rollins*, Missouri,
Dumont, Indiana,	Schenck, Ohio,
Eckley, Ohio,	Scofield, Pennsylvania,
Eliot, Massachusetts,	Shannon, California,
English, Connecticut,	Sloan, Wisconsin,
Farnsworth, Illinois,	Smith, Kentucky,
Frank, New-York,	Smithers, Delaware,
Ganson, New-York,	Spalding, Ohio,
Garfield, Ohio,	Starr, New-Jersey,
Gooch, Massachusetts,	*Steele*, New-York,
Grinnell, Iowa,	Stearns, Pennsylvania,
Griswold, New-York,	Thayer, Pennsylvania,
Hale, Pennsylvania,	Thomas, Maryland,
Herrick, New-York,	Tracy, Pennsylvania,
Higby, California,	Upson, Michigan,
Hooper, Massachusetts,	Van Valkenburgh, New-York,
Hotchkiss, New-York,	Washburne, Illinois,
Hubbard, Iowa,	Washburne, Massachusetts,
Hubbard, Connecticut,	Webster, Maryland,
Hubbard, New-York,	Whaley, West Virginia,
Hutchins, Ohio,	*Wheeler*, Wisconsin,
Ingersoll, Illinois,	Williams, Pennsylvania,
Jenckes, Rhode Island,	Wilder, Kansas,
Julian, Indiana,	Wilson, Iowa,
Kasson, Iowa,	Windham, Minnesota,
Kelley, Pennsylvania,	Woodbridge, Vermont,
Kellogg, Michigan,	Worthington, Nevada,
Kellogg, New-York,	*Yeaman*, Kentucky—119.

NAYS (ALL DEMOCRATS EXCEPT CLAY.)

Messrs. J. C. Allen, Illinois,	Law, Indiana,
W. J. Allen, Illinois,	Long, Ohio,
Ancona, Pennsylvania,	Mallory, Kentucky,
Bliss, Ohio,	Miller, Pennsylvania,
Brooks, New-York,	Morris, Ohio,
Brown, Wisconsin,	Morrison, Illinois,
Chanler, New-York,	Noble, Ohio,
Clay, Kentucky,	O'Neil, Ohio,
Cox, Ohio,	Pendleton, Ohio,
Cravens, Indiana,	Perry, New-Jersey,
Dawson, Pennsylvania,	Pruyn, New-York,
Denison, Pennsylvania,	Randall, Pennsylvania,
Eden, Illinois,	Robinson, Illinois,
Edgerton, Indiana,	Ross, Illinois,
Eldridge, Wisconsin,	Scott, Missouri,
Finck, Ohio,	Steele, New-Jersey,
Grider, Kentucky,	Stiles, Pennsylvania,
Hale, Missouri,	Strouse, Pennsylvania,
Harding, Kentucky,	Stuart, Illinois,
Harrington, Indiana,	Sweat, Maine,
Harris, Maryland,	Townsend, New-York,
Harris, Illinois,	Wadsworth, Kentucky,
Holman, Indiana,	Ward, New-York,
Johnson, Pennsylvania,	White, J. W. Ohio,
Johnson, Ohio,	White, C. A. Ohio,
Kalbfleisch, New-York,	Winfield, New-York,
Kernan, New-York,	Ben. Wood, New-York,
Knapp, Illinois,	F. Wood, New-York—56.

ABSENT, OR NOT VOTING.

The absentees, or those not voting, were:

Messrs. Lazear, Penn.,	McKinney, Ohio,
Leblonde, Ohio,	Middleton, New-Jersey,
Marcy, New-Hampshire,	Rogers, New-Jersey,
McDowell, Indiana,	Voorhees, Indiana—8.

All Democrats.

A motion to adjourn was carried amid the greatest confusion, yeas 121, nays 24.

The Charleston Mercury.

DAILY PAPER—Twenty Dollars for [illegible] Months—Payable in Advance. | COUNTRY PAPER—Three [illegible]

Volume LXXXVI. | CHARLESTON, S. C., TUESDAY, FEBRUARY 7, 1865. | Number [illegible]

THE MERCURY.

TUESDAY, FEBRUARY 6, 1865.

A Tandem Team!

The whole country was horrified yesterday to hear by the telegrams from Richmond, that "Commissary General NORTHROP has not resigned, as reported."

We are really so much astonished at this information that we are confounded. We don't know exactly how to begin to express ourselves on the subject. The fact is, the matter is beyond the reach of any words. It is a matter for *action*, not for words. It is a matter, if we comprehend it, for which somebody should be hurt.

Everybody knows that Mr. DAVIS' Cabinet are but his head-clerks of the several Departments, to record his wills and pleasures. Everybody knows that if Mr NORTHROP stays where he is, after the expression of official opinion that has just taken place, it is because he is held there by Mr. DAVIS. It is a maxim in Kingly Governments that the King can do no wrong—(notwithstanding Mr. CHARLES STUART lost his head, because it was thought in England that he *did* wrong) Now, if Mr. DAVIS has already ascended to the title of JEFF. 1st, Autocrat of the Confederate States, in God's name let us hold somebody responsible, as was done in England with STRAFFORD. To what pass have we come, when the people of the Confederate States in Congress assembled, are to be treated with the defiance and the scorn with which Mr. JEFF. DAVIS undertakes to treat them now—What are we all—white negroes, or serfs, or what? What is this little man JEFF. DAVIS? Where did he come from? What authority has he? Where did he get it? Is this man one of the CÆSARS?—or is he one of the Medici?—or perhaps the last of Gothic Amalis?—or is he veritably "the last of the Bourbons?" Can it be so? Or is he indeed that little backwoodman from Mississippi that performed that wonderful and immortal military feat of the figure V,—made the worst and most meddlesome Secretary of War ever known under the old United States Government—and is now making the very [illegible] Executive officer known in the modern world, since the time of his prototype, JAMES 2d, of England. Is this really the man who has the audacity thus to defy the authority of the People of the Confederate States, and to spurn their expressed wishes? Impossible! Surely, surely, the thing is utterly impossible! Has the monomania of this man's egotism utterly overthrown his whole reason, and reduced him to the condition of a mere lunatic? What does the man mean?

And what is Congress after? Have they forgotten the power of the people to impeach? Is there no high toned gentleman in the land, like General LEE, or General JOSEPH E. JOHNSTON who could be raised by Congress to the position now held by this incompetent man, tried now for four long years, and always found equally wanting in capacity and in patriotism? Can not this body, if composed of men too insignificant, individually, to have any respect for themselves, entertain and summon up some respect for the entire people in their official capacity?

Is the mellenium coming or the day of judgment? What is the matter?

The Governor of the State
To the People of South Carolina.

The doubt has been dispelled. The truth is made manifest; and the startling conviction is now forced upon all. The invasion of the State has been commenced; our people driven from their homes; their property plundered and destroyed; the torch and the sword displayed as the fate to which they are destined. The threats of an insolent foe are to be carried into execution, unless that foe is checked and beaten back.

I call now upon the people of South Carolina to rise up and defend, at once, their own rights and the honor of their State. I call upon every man to lay aside selfish considerations, and prepare to do his duty to his State. Let the suggestions of ease and comfort become inglorious and unworthy; let those ends only be honorable which conduce to the defeat of the foe; let all who falter now, or hesitate, be henceforth marked. All who have lived under the protection of the State, who have flourished under its laws, and shared its prosperity, will gladly [illegible] to protect it from subjection. If any seek to escape from duty and danger at this time, let them depart. The hour approaches when all who are true to the State will be found in the ranks of those who arm in its defence. There is no room in the State but for one class of men; they are the men who will fight in her cause.

I give now timely warning to all. The period is near when private business must be for a season suspended. While there is yet time, let all prepare to set their houses in order. Let us hope that the interval may be short in which we will pass from doubt to hope; let us feel that, as we grapple danger, we will pluck safety. In every district of the State the men will be organized. From a portion of these districts only will the militia be drawn. In others, more remote, it will be left for protection to persons and security to property. In such cases, the duty will be as imperative as in others, where the men are called from home.

In every quarter of the State, in every district, village and town, let the men stand with their arms in their hands. When required to move, let them do so with expedition and hope. Until required to move, let them be vigilant and prepared to repress disorder, and put down all violence.

It is the duty of every man to oppose all the resistance he can to the approach of the enemy. It is the command of the State that he shall do so. The foe now upon the soil of the State is here to kill; let him be killed. The foe now upon the soil of the State is here for rapine and lust; let him meet resistance unto death. That foe devotes us to a doom worse than death; let him receive the fate he designs for us.

If any one is so ignorant of the temper with which this war has been waged by the foe, as to suppose that resistance provokes punishment, which unarmed he would not incur, let him be quickly undeceived. He is only safe who is armed; he is only spared who defends himself. The stale, and not unsuccessful practice of the foe, is to [illegible] and threaten punishment. The threat is always executed when he dares; the promise never. Moreover, the State, your country, requires you to arm in its defence. It is not given to any man or any men within its territories to choose whether they will arm or not. When a merciless foe is abroad ravaging the fields, wasting the property, taking the lives of the people, insulting the sovereignty, and impeaching the independence of the State; where the State plants its banner, there will all true men gather. When the State calls, as it now does, to arms, all will echo that call, all must obey that summons.

Remove your property from the reach of the enemy; carry what you can to a place of safety; then quickly rally and return to the field. What you cannot carry, destroy. Whatever you leave that will be of use to your foe, what he will not need, that will be destroy. Indulge no sickly hope that you will be spared by submission; terror will but whet his revenge. Think not that your property will be respected, and afterward recovered. No such feeling prompts him. You leave it but to support and sustain him; you save it but to help him on his course. Destroy what you cannot remove. He will make your return to your homes over a charred and blackened road; prepare you the same way for him as he advances. Let him read everywhere and in everything, that in this State, from one portion of it to the other, there is but one purpose and fixed resolve—that purpose is to meet him at every point; fight him at every road; that resolve is to undergo all suffering, submit to every sacrifice, welcome any fate, sooner than subjection by his army, or submission to his terms.

You have led the way in those acts which united the people of your sister States in this confederation of States, and their secession from the Government of the United States. You first fired the gun at the flag of the United States, and caused that flag to be lowered at your command. As yet, you have suffered less than any other people. You have spoken words of defiance—let your acts be equally significant. In your sister States, with the people of those States, you have a common sympathy in the determination to be free, and in your hatred of the foe: you will not falter in that stronger sympathy which is derived from a common suffering.

You have defied a tyrant: do not apprehend his power. You have dared to do; fear not to die. No worse fate can befall him who has pride in the ancient honor of his State than to see it governed by those who hate it; and insult, with their vices, the virtues we have been taught to cherish.

Once more I say to you your State is invaded. Once more I call upon you to arm in its defence. All who unite with us are more than brothers; all who desert us are as false as the foes which assail us.

It is said there are some who think they are not bound to fight with us, who affect a desire not to forfeit what they call their allegiance to some foreign Power. It may be that there are some who hitherto have been misled. I will not believe that there lives in South Carolina now, any man who, having been under the protection of the State and treated as that State treats its own citizens, will, at this time, attempt to find in this affected zeal for an allegiance he has practically abjured, an excuse for the succor he is bound to render. If there are such, let them depart. They shall not remain here and be the cold witnesses of the sufferings which others endure, while they are secure from danger. If they remain, they will do so with the full knowledge that the State expects and intends that every man shall do his duty.

Be as resolute as your cause is just, and triumphant success awaits you. What right have they to expect success in the sight of God who pursue, with unrelenting hatred, you, who seek nothing more than the privilege of accomplishing the great ends for which your God has given you being? You have not invaded their soil, nor sacked their cities, nor wasted their fields; nor murdered their relatives, nor violated their wives and daughters. They pretend not to the plea of visiting upon you the terrible punishment of retaliation. They claim a right to reduce you to subjection—to hold you in bondage—to strip you of more than life, when they deprive you of the privileges dearer than existence. Rise, then, with the truth before you, that the cause in which you are to arm is the cause of Justice and of Right! Strike, with the belief strong in your hearts, that the cause of Justice and of Right is the cause which a Power superior to the hosts seeking to oppress you will not suffer to be overthrown. And even upon [illegible] of the State in which [illegible] tyranny was first defied [illegible] the fate it deserves, while [illegible] honor will be awarded those who [illegible] that great consummation, in w[illegible] rejoice.

By the Governor:

A. G. MAGRATH.

Official—HENRY BUIST, Lt. Col. and A. D. C.

February 7 [illegible]

A shell bursts in the streets of Charleston, South Carolina

The Charleston Mercury.

DAILY PAPER—Twenty Dollars per Annum—Payable in Advance.

COUNTRY PAPER—Issued Weekly—Payable in Advance.

Volume LXXXVI | CHARLESTON, S. C., WEDNESDAY, FEBRUARY 8, 1865. | Number

The Governor of the State

To the People of South Carolina.

The doubt has been dispelled. The truth is made manifest, and the startling conviction is now forced upon all. The invasion of the State has been commenced; our people driven from their homes, their property plundered and destroyed; the torch and the sword displayed, as the fate to which they are destined. The threats of an insolent foe are to be carried into execution, unless that foe is checked and beaten back.

I call now upon the people of South Carolina to rise up and defend, at once, their own rights and the honor of their State. I call upon every man to lay aside selfish considerations, and prepare to do his duty to his State. Let the suggestions of ease and comfort become inglorious and unworthy; let those ends only be honorable which conduce to the defeat of the foe; let all who falter now, or hesitate, be henceforth marked. All who have lived under the protection of the State, who have flourished under its laws, and shared its prosperity, will gladly arm to protect it from subjection. If any seek escape from duty and danger at this time, let them depart. The hour approaches when all who are true to the State will be found in the ranks of those who arm in its defence. There is no room in the State but for one class of men; they are the men who will fight in her cause.

I give now timely warning to all. The period is near when private business must be for a season suspended. While there is yet time, let all prepare to set their houses in order. Let us hope that the interval may be short in which we will pass from doubt to hope; let us feel that, as we grapple danger, we will pluck safety. In every district of the State the men will be organized. From a portion of these districts only will the militia be drawn. In others, more remote, it will be left for protection to persons and security to property. In such cases, the duty will be as imperative as in others, where the men are called from home.

In every quarter of the State, in every district, village and town, let the men stand with their arms in their hands. When required to move, let them do so with expedition and hope. Until required to move, let them be vigilant, and prepared to repress disorder, and put down all violence.

It is the duty of every man to oppose all the resistance he can to the approach of the enemy. It is the command of the State that he shall do so. The foe now upon the soil of the State is here to kill; let him be killed. The foe now upon the soil of the State is here for rapine and lust; let him meet resistance unto death. That foe devotes us to a doom worse than death; let him receive the fate he designs for us.

If any one is so ignorant of the temper with which this war has been waged by the foe, as to suppose that resistance provokes punishment, which unarmed he would not incur, let him be quickly undeceived. He is only safe who is armed; he is only spared who defends himself. The stale, and not unsuccessful practice of the foe, is to promise pardon and threaten punishment. The threat is always executed when he dares; the promise never. Moreover, the State, your country, requires you to arm in its defence. It is not given to any man or any men within its territories to choose whether they will arm or not. When a merciless foe is abroad ravaging the fields, wasting the property, taking the lives of the people, insulting the sovereignty, and impeaching the independence of the State; where the State plants its banner, there will all true men gather. When the State calls, as it now does, to arms, all will echo that call; all must obey that summons.

Remove your property from the reach of the enemy; carry what you can to a place of safety; then quickly rally and return to the field. What you cannot carry, destroy. Whatever you leave that will be of use to your foe, what he will not need, that will he destroy. Indulge no sickly hope that you will be spared by submission; terror will but whet his revenge. Think not that your property will be respected, and afterward recovered. No such feeling prompts him. You leave it but to support and sustain him; you save it but to help him on his course. Destroy what you cannot remove. He will make your return to your homes over a charred and blackened road; prepare you the same way for him as he advances. Let him read everywhere and in everything, that in this State, from one portion of it to the other, there is but one purpose and fixed resolve—that purpose is to meet him at every point; fight him at every road; that resolve is to undergo all suffering, submit to every sacrifice, welcome any fate, sooner than subjection by his army, or submission to his terms.

You have led the way in those acts which united the people of your sister States in this confederation of States, and their secession from the Government of the United States. You first fired the gun at the flag of the United States, and caused that flag to be lowered at your command. As yet, you have suffered less than any other people. You have spoken words of defiance—let your acts be equally significant. In your sister States, with the people of those States, you have a common sympathy in the determination to be free, and in your hatred of the foe; you will not falter in that stronger sympathy which is derived from a common suffering.

You have defied a tyrant; do not apprehend his power. You have dared to do; fear not to die. No worse fate can befall him who has pride in the ancient honor of his State than to see it governed by those who hate it, and insult, with their vices, the virtues we have been taught to cherish.

Once more I say to you your State is invaded. Once more I call upon you to arm in its defence. All who unite with us are more than brothers; all who desert us are as false as the foes which assail us.

It is said there are some who think they are not bound to fight with us, who affect a desire not to forfeit what they call their allegiance to some foreign Power. It may be that there are some who hitherto have been misled. I will not believe that there lives in South Carolina now, any man who, having been under the protection of the State and treated as that State treats its own citizens, will, at this time, attempt to find in this affected zeal for an allegiance he has practically abjured, an excuse for the succor he is bound to render. If there are such, let them depart. They shall not remain here and be the cold witnesses of the sufferings which others endure, while they are secure from danger. If they remain, they will do so with the full knowledge that the State expects and intends that every man shall do his duty.

Be as resolute as your cause is just, and triumphant success awaits you. What right have they to expect success in the sight of God who pursue, with unrelenting hatred, you, who seek nothing more than the privilege of accomplishing the great ends for which your God has given you being? You have not invaded their soil, nor sacked their cities, nor wasted their fields, nor murdered their relatives, nor violated their wives and daughters. They pretend not to the plea of visiting upon you the terrible punishment of retaliation. They claim a right to reduce you to subjection—to hold you in bondage—to strip you of more than life, when they deprive you of the privileges dearer than existence. Rise, then, with the truth before you, that the cause in which you are to arm is the cause of Justice and of Right. Strike, with the belief strong in your hearts, that the cause of Justice and of Right is the cause which a Power superior to the hosts seeking to oppress you will not suffer to be overthrown. And even upon the soil of the State in which this monstrous tyranny was first defied shall it meet the fate it deserves, while imperishable honor will be awarded those who contributed to that great consummation, in which humanity will rejoice.

By the Governor: A. G. MAGRATH.

Official—HENRY BUIST, Lt. Col. and A. D. C.

February 7 — 2

DAILY PAPER—Twenty Dollars per Annum—Payable in Advance.

COUNTRY PAPER—Issued Weekly—Payable in Advance.

Volume LXXXVI | CHARLESTON, S. C., SATURDAY, FEBRUARY 11, 1865. | Number 12,2[illegible]

The Governor of the State

To the People of South Carolina.

The doubt has been dispelled. The truth is made manifest, and the startling conviction is now forced upon all. The invasion of the State has been commenced; our people driven from their homes, their property plundered and destroyed; the torch and the sword displayed, as the fate to which they are destined. The threats of an insolent foe are to be carried into execution, unless that foe is checked and beaten back.

I call now upon the people of South Carolina to rise up and defend, at once, their own rights and the honor of their State. I call upon every man to lay aside selfish considerations, and prepare to do his duty to his State. Let the suggestions of ease and comfort become inglorious and unworthy; let those ends only be honorable which conduce to the defeat of the foe; let all who falter now, or hesitate, be henceforth marked. All who have lived under the protection of the State, who have flourished under its laws, and shared its prosperity, will gladly arm to protect it from subjection. If any seek escape from duty and danger at this time, let them depart. The hour approaches when all who are true to the State will be found in the ranks of those who arm in its defence. There is no room in the State but for one class of men; they are the men who will fight in her cause.

I give now timely warning to all. The period is near when private business must be for a season suspended. While there is yet time, let all prepare to set their houses in order. Let us hope that the interval may be short in which we will pass from doubt to hope; let us feel that, as we grapple danger, we will pluck safety. In every district of the State the men will be organized. From a portion of these districts only will the militia be drawn. In others, more remote, it will be left for protection to persons and security to property. In such cases, the duty will be as imperative as in others, where the men are called from home.

In every quarter of the State, in every district, village and town, let the men stand with their arms in their hands. When required to move, let them do so with expedition and hope. Until required to move, let them be vigilant, and prepared to repress disorder, and put down all violence.

It is the duty of every man to oppose all the resistance he can to the approach of the enemy. It is the command of the State that he shall do so. The foe now upon the soil of the State is here to kill; let him be killed. The foe now upon the soil of the State is here for rapine and lust; let him meet resistance unto death. That foe devotes us to a doom worse than death; let him receive the fate he designs for us.

If any one is so ignorant of the temper with which this war has been waged by the foe, as to suppose that resistance provokes punishment, which unarmed he would not incur, let him be quickly undeceived. He is only safe who is armed; he is only spared who defends himself. The stale, and not unsuccessful practice of the foe, is to promise pardon and threaten punishment. The threat is always executed when he dares; the promise never. Moreover, the State, your country, requires you to arm in its defence. It is not given to any man or any men within its territories to choose whether they will arm or not. When a merciless foe is abroad ravaging the fields, wasting the property, taking the lives of the people, insulting the sovereignty, and impeaching the independence of the State; where the State plants its banner, there will all true men gather. When the State calls, as it now does, to arms, all will echo that call; all must obey that summons.

Remove your property from the reach of the enemy; carry what you can to a place of safety; then quickly rally and return to the field. What you cannot carry, destroy. Whatever you leave that will be of use to your foe, what he will not need, that will he destroy. Indulge no sickly hope that you will be spared by submission; terror will but whet his revenge. Think not that your property will be respected, and afterward recovered. No such feeling prompts him. You leave it but to support and sustain him; you save it but to help him on his course. Destroy what you cannot remove. He will make your return to your homes over a charred and blackened road; prepare you the same way for him as he advances. Let him read everywhere and in everything, that in this State, from one portion of it to the other, there is but one purpose and fixed resolve—that purpose is to meet him at every point; fight him at every road; that resolve is to undergo all suffering, submit to every sacrifice, welcome any fate, sooner than subjection by his army, or submission to his terms.

You have led the way in those acts which united the people of your sister States in this confederation of States, and their secession from the Government of the United States. You first fired the gun at the flag of the United States, and caused that flag to be lowered at your command. As yet, you have suffered less than any other people. You have spoken words of defiance—let your acts be equally significant. In your sister States, with the people of those States, you have a common sympathy in the determination to be free, and in your hatred of the foe; you will not falter in that stronger sympathy which is derived from a common suffering.

You have defied a tyrant; do not apprehend his power. You have dared to do; fear not to die. No worse fate can befall him who has pride in the ancient honor of his State than to see it governed by those who hate it, and insult, with their vices, the virtues we have been taught to cherish.

Once more I say to you your State is invaded. Once more I call upon you to arm in its defence. All who unite with us are more than brothers; all who desert us are as false as the foes which assail us.

It is said there are some who think they are not bound to fight with us, who affect a desire not to forfeit what they call their allegiance to some foreign Power. It may be that there are some who hitherto have been misled. I will not believe that there lives in South Carolina now, any man who, having been under the protection of the State and treated as that State treats its own citizens, will, at this time, attempt to find in this affected zeal for an allegiance he has practically abjured, an excuse for the succor he is bound to render. If there are such, let them depart. They shall not remain here and be the cold witnesses of the sufferings which others endure, while they are secure from danger. If they remain, they will do so with the full knowledge that the State expects and intends that every man shall do his duty.

Be as resolute as your cause is just, and triumphant success awaits you. What right have they to expect success in the sight of God who pursue, with unrelenting hatred, you, who seek nothing more than the privilege of accomplishing the great ends for which your God has given you being? You have not invaded their soil, nor sacked their cities, nor wasted their fields, nor murdered their relatives, nor violated their wives and daughters. They pretend not to the plea of visiting upon you the terrible punishment of retaliation. They claim a right to reduce you to subjection—to hold you in bondage—to strip you of more than life, when they deprive you of the privileges dearer than existence. Rise, then, with the truth before you, that the cause in which you are to arm is the cause of Justice and of Right. Strike, with the belief strong in your hearts, that the cause of Justice and of Right is the cause which a Power superior to the hosts seeking to oppress you will not suffer to be overthrown. And even upon the soil of the State in which this monstrous tyranny was first defied shall it meet the fate it deserves, while imperishable honor will be awarded those who contributed to that great consummation, in which humanity will rejoice.

By the Governor: A. G. MAGRATH.

Official—HENRY BUIST, Lt. Col. and A. D. C.

February 7

The New-York Times.

VOL. XIV......NO. 4181. NEW-YORK, FRIDAY, FEBRUARY 17, 1865. PRICE FOUR CENTS.

SHERMAN'S MARCH.

Official Dispatches from the Army.

Particulars from Our Own Correspondents.

Interesting Reports from the Rebel Papers.

Branchville Evacuated by the Rebels.

Occupation of Orangeburg by Sherman.

Beauregard's Forces Retreating on Columbia.

THE OPERATIONS ON THE COAST.

Hardee in Command at Charleston.

WASHINGTON, Thursday, Feb. 16.

Maj. STOLBRAND, Chief of Artillery of the Fifteenth Corps, of Gen. SHERMAN's army, has arrived here, bringing dispatches to the Government. He says that Gen. SHERMAN's plans are not generally known in his own army, although he has its entire confidence.

It was Gen. BLAIR's division which defeated the enemy at Rivers' Bridge, the soldiers wading to their waists to make the attack.

It is clear that SHERMAN is moving large columns to the right and left, or east and west, at Branchville.

A little to the northward of that point is a fine, high, fertile and productive section of country, easily traversed with good roads, and abounding in supplies.

If he is aiming at Columbia he will traverse the districts of Orangeburgh and Richland—a region unsurpassed in the whole land for wealth and abundance.

REPORTS VIA PHILADELPHIA.

PHILADELPHIA, Thursday, Feb. 16.

Special dispatches to the *Evening Bulletin*, dated Washington, Feb. 16, says:

Richmond papers of the 15th indicate that SHERMAN's advanced cavalry are actually as far North as Florence, the second important railroad junction on the borders of North Carolina.

They also announce all telegraphic and railroad communication with Charleston destroyed, thus showing SHERMAN's left column must have struck the Northeastern Railroad running from Charleston to Florence.

OPERATIONS BEFORE CHARLESTON.

Preliminary Movements—Our Forces Again on James Island—Gallant Capture of Rebel Works—Position of the Forces under Gen. Hatch.

From Our Own Correspondent.

JAMES ISLAND, S. C., Saturday, Feb. 11, 1865.

The Northern District of the Department of the South, embracing the islands about Charleston harbor, is destined to become once more the scene of active operations. For some time past preparations have been in progress to attack the enemy, and the enemy, noticing the movements, has been busy at work to counteract them. On Friday, the 9th inst., a force of infantry and artillery, under the immediate command of Gen. SCHIMMELFENNIG, crossed over from Folly Island to James Island. This is the first time our troops have visited that locality since the demonstrations made on John's Island a few months ago, under the direction of Gen. FOSTER. It will be remembered that at that time, after having given the enemy a sound thrashing and driven him to his strong defences, our troops withdrew to their former positions on Folly and Morris Islands. The enemy then reoccupied the whole of James Island, and, in order to resist any future assault on our part, threw up additional earthworks at the southern end, and increased his force of men. The late attack was made in the afternoon, the troops having been occupied in the morning in disembarking.

Everything being in readiness, a line of battle was formed on the southern end of the island, and a body of skirmishers sent forward to feel the enemy. They had advanced but about one mile when they discovered just in their front a long line of earthworks, behind which, it was subsequently ascertained, were posted 3,000 rebels. As our skirmishers advanced, fire was opened from a few pieces of light artillery which had been placed in position a short distance at the rear. The gunboat *McDonough* and the mortar schooner *Smith* moved up the Stono River, and joined in the fight by throwing shells into the woods where the rebels had formed their line of battle. The tin-clads *Savannah* and *Augusta*, under the command of Ensign NEIL, also took an important part in the general movement. Late in the day, the howitzers were removed from the tin-clads and placed on shore; but unfortunately, while the men were hauling the pieces to the front, one of them became mired and could not be extricated in time to be brought into service that day. The remaining guns were worked with good effect. The enemy having been shelled pretty thoroughly, a signal was given for our line of battle to advance and seize the outer works of the enemy. Away went the men with a bound and a yell, and in fifteen minutes time they had possession of three redoubts and taken thirty prisoners, including a Major of a South Carolina regiment. The force that defended the redoubts were infantry, nearly all of whom took to flight when our men made the dash upon them. Our loss was fifteen killed and thirty wounded. The enemy's loss in killed and wounded could not be ascertained.

The ground gained by the assault is held by our troops to-day, and it is quite possible that we may see some heavy fighting within a short time. The enemy have erected new and formidable works on the upper portion of James Island, but we believe that by proper management these works can be captured.

Maj.-Gen. GILLMORE came up from Hilton Head early yesterday morning, and remained close to the scene of the fight during the day. This morning he had an interview with Admiral DAHLGREN, when the plan for future operations was discussed and decided upon.

Brig.-Gen. POTTER was also present yesterday. To-day he will take an active command on the shore.

Of course, it is impossible to tell what will be the result of these active movements, but one thing is certain, the enemy must be wary, or he may suddenly find himself without a Charleston.

The forces under Brig.-Gen. HATCH are bivouacked on the Charleston and Savannah Railroad, at the point where it crosses the Combahee River. They are steadily moving forward toward Charleston, the enemy, in the meantime, reluctantly retiring in the same direction. WHIT.

REBEL REPORTS.

From the Richmond Dispatch, Feb. 14.

The following dispatch, received late Sunday night, is the official report of the affair on James Island. It contains also other interesting intelligence.

CHARLESTON, Saturday, Feb. 11.

To Gen. L. Cooper, Adjutant and Inspector-General:

The enemy last evening drove in our pickets on James Island. The lines have been reëstablished to day. The enemy are still in strong force on the island, but the movement is believed to be only a demonstration. There is an increase to-day of eighteen steamers off the Bar. A large attack made to-night upon Battery Tomkins was repulsed.

W. J. HARDEE, Lieutenant-General.

Since the receipt of the above, we are without advices from Charleston.

OPERATIONS IN THE INTERIOR.

From Our Own Correspondent.

SISTER'S FERRY, S. C., Saturday, Feb. 4, 1865.

Cognizant of inability to satisfy your anxious readers—who are eagerly perusing the daily papers for information as to the position and prospects of SHERMAN's army—as to the intention or probable results of the campaign, I can only present in this brief letter, written upon the eve of departure from any line of communication, a short synopsis of events as they have transpired since the forces left Savannah, and our present situation.

LEAVING SAVANNAH.

On the 26th and 27th of January, the last remaining divisions of Gen. SHERMAN's army followed the Fourteenth Corps, which had taken the Augusta turnpike for Sister's Ferry, 35 miles above, on the Savannah River. These divisions were Gen. GEARY's, of the Twentieth Corps, and Gen. CORSE's, of the Fifteenth Corps. Scarcely had the rear guard left the city limits behind them, when a terrific explosion was heard. The rebel arsenal located on the northern edge of town caught fire, and its contents of shell and powder became involved in the conflagration. The sound to the retiring army was as if a furious engagement were progressing in their rear. The continual explosion of shell and the rattle of bursting cartridges, lasting for over an hour, firmly imbued the troops with the idea that GROVER's division in Savannah had been attacked by the enemy. Parties coming up from the city reported the true state of the case, and allayed all apprehension.

SISTER'S FERRY

is the geographical designation of one of the few crossings of the Savannah River, between its mouth and Augusta. The character of this river is such that where one of its banks present a fine bluff, the opposite is almost invariably an impassable swamp, extending from ten to twenty miles into the interior of the country. These swamps afford no footholds for pontoon bridges, or landings for steamers or ferry-boats. The heavy rain which fell about the time the Fifteenth and Seventeenth Corps were moved to Beaufort, submerged the entire country for twenty miles around Savannah, on the Carolina shore, thus frustrating Gen. SHERMAN's original plan of crossing at that point the remaining corps. Hence the left wing, commanded by Gen. SLOCUM, was ordered to seek a crossing further up. Sister's Ferry was the nearest to Savannah, and was selected.

DELAY.

The left wing, excepting the First and Third Divisions of the Twentieth Corps, which had crossed below before the freshet, has remained in camp at Sister's Ferry on the Georgia bank since its arrival. This delay was caused by the necessity of corduroying a road five miles in length over a submerged swamp on the Carolina side. The enemy, well knowing this to be the only open route for this part of the army, had filled the old road with

TORPEDOES.

Some forty of these villainous inventions were discovered in the mud over which our soldiers had to pass, but were exhumed by careful appliances without much accident. Several soldiers of the Twentieth Corps were killed and wounded by the explosion of a torpedo. Had it not been that the enemy had marked the localities where they had planted their destructive engines of—we cannot call it "civilized" warfare—it would have been very difficult to have removed them with safety from our path. As it was, the exact locality of each torpedo was definitely pointed out by a small peg placed directly over it in the road.

This was undoubtedly the means of saving many lives. The enemy wanted to save them in case we selected another ferry to cross at—hence they marked the spot where each was placed.

CROSSING THE FERRY.

The left wing crosses to-day and to-morrow. Gen. GEARY's Second Division of the Twentieth is now entirely over. Gen. KILPATRICK has also crossed. Gen. DAVIS, with the Fourteenth, expects to enter Carolina to-morrow. Gen. CORSE, with the Second Division of the Fifteenth, will accompany the Fourteenth.

THE LEFT WING

is thus in position near the river and advancing northward to threaten Augusta or Branchville as the case may be. It is fairly in motion and may cease all communication with the coast at any moment; but this is not likely to be the case for a few days yet.

THE RIGHT WING

at last accounts received to-day was marching northward from Hickory Hill—a small post-office about thirty miles south of Branchville. The First and Third Divisions of the Twentieth Corps are forty miles north of this point. They must be not far from the Branchville and Augusta Railroad.

THE SITUATION

is at present most encouraging. At Sister's Ferry troops received full supplies, and the trains were loaded to the utmost limit. On the ration question, Gen. SHERMAN is safe. His army can subsist forty days away from all base. Parties from the interior report that the people have not destroyed their crops or driven off their herds. There is no lack for forage or beef. This is most gratifying news, for the army apprehended a scarcity of food. Of the intentions of the General commanding, no one can safely assert knowledge. We can, however, believe that Columbia is aimed at, and, like Milledgeville, the capital of its sister State, South Carolina's Governmental seat is doomed to fall before SHERMAN's prowess.

THE ROADS

give great trouble. Only a spirit of indomitable perseverance would overcome such serious obstacles as the roads present to the movements of an army. But no conditions of weather or of mud deter this army. Pioneer parties are increased from companies to regiments, and even to brigades, and bridges are built miles in extent, on which troops and wagons cross the perilous swamps with safety.

THE ENEMY

has only appeared in small forces of cavalry. A skirmish near Hickory Hill occurred yesterday, but no important movement of the rebel forces has as yet been developed. HUGUENOT.

Additional Particulars of the Movement.

Correspondence of the New-York Times.

SISTER'S FERRY, Ga., Tuesday, Jan. 31, 1865.

The Fourteenth and Twentieth Army Corps, composing the left wing of Gen. SHERMAN's grand army, moved from the City of Savannah on the 22d and 27th, respectively, taking up the same line of march and following each other as closely as the comfort of the troops would allow. Their line of march was back over the road over which they had marched about six weeks before to the conquest of the queen city of the Confederacy. They pursued this line of march as far back as Springfield, an inconsiderable town about twenty-seven miles northwest of the city, and containing from forty to fifty inhabitants. This small place was not improved by the presence of the Federal troops. They rendered it "gloriously less," by taking the weather-boards and shingles of the houses to build cabins for themselves. They did this without compunction or fear, believing the comfort of a Federal soldier of more consequence to the world than a rebel habitation. From this point they took a northeasterly course for the distance of nine miles to this place. Here we have a pontoon bridge over to the South Carolina shore, where, from the high water in the river, we have to enter a swamp overflowed with water, and impassable to an army in its present condition. This difficulty is speedily disappearing before the skill and sturdy efforts of our pioneer corps. The rapidity with which this branch of our army is laying corduroy roads over these natural obstructions, indicates the success with which the present campaign will be prosecuted. Some miles of this kind of road will have to be laid before we can be moved from our present encampment; but as the construction of this kind of road is wrought out in a single day, our detention here will be short. The river has become to this point an important highway for the transportation of commissary and quartermaster's stores, and this is the depot for them. Boats in great numbers, and of *various* sizes and tonnage, are constantly running up and down the river from the city to this place. The village, which a week ago was of no relative value in point of trade, has become of great importance. KILPATRICK's cavalry is with us, on the alert for Mr. WHEELER, who we learn is lurking around us. Troops are on both sides of the river, ready for whatever may come. EPSILON.

REBEL REPORTS.

From the Richmond Dispatch, Feb. 14.

On Saturday a column of SHERMAN's infantry and cavalry crossed the Edisto to the west of and above Branchville, and advanced on the Columbia Branch Railroad. Our troops at Branchville withdrew toward Columbia. According to the last official accounts, received yesterday, the *enemy were at Orangeburgh*, some twenty miles south of Branchville, and on the road to Columbia.

During our retreat, there has been continual skirmishing with the enemy, but no general engagement. It was said here yesterday that BEAUREGARD intended to make a stand on the Salinda, but we think, from present indications, *it is more likely he will fall back beyond the Santee*, and defend the line of that river.

He is said to have an adequate force for either an offensive or defensive policy, whichever he may find it expedient to adopt. Columbia is on the right bank of the Santee, about 50 miles west of north of Orangeburgh.

From the Richmond Enquirer, Feb. 14.

The Columbia *South Carolinian*, of the 9th, received this morning, does not contain one syllable of news from the front. The only scrap of information gleaned from our South Carolina exchanges, is contained in the following paragraph from the Charleston *Courier* of the 8th:

"No official information was received on Tuesday, but reports deemed reliable state that the enemy tapped the South Carolina Railroad yesterday morning in three different places, viz.: Midway, Blackwell and Bamberg.

A passenger who left Augusta, Monday afternoon, on an ordnance train, states that the whooping and shouting of the enemy could be distinctly heard in the distance as the train passed Williston. It is supposed they reached the South Carolina road early on Tuesday morning. The train from Branchville came through all safe on Tuesday evening. Passengers by this train report the road cut at Williston, and state that the enemy had turned off toward Augusta. A number of prisoners, militia principally, are reported captured by the enemy.

The Columbia *Guardian* has the following remarks on 'the situation,' the encouraging tone of which concurs with authentic reports received here yesterday:

'The alarming rumors so industriously circulated through the city on Monday were not as fully followed up on yesterday. Indeed the dearth of sensation reports would almost lead one to suppose that SHERMAN was a myth, or at least if there was such a thing as a Yankee army upon our soil, it occupied a remote and by no means threatening position, so far as the capital of South Carolina is concerned. It is not our intention to treat those alarming rumors with contempt, *for in some instances they were of a character more truthful than pleasant.* Whilst panics are always to be avoided, it is at the same time proper that the people should have a just appreciation of the dangers which threaten them, in order that due preparation may be made to meet those dangers. The hour has come when every man capable of service must take his place in front of the enemy. We have a force sufficient to meet and check SHERMAN, if that force be properly used and all used. A calm determination is all that is requisite, and without it our State may meet with the fate which befell Georgia. SHERMAN, elated by his recent successes, of course feels confident of marching through South Carolina. Doubtless he entertains a conqueror's contempt for the opposition he may meet. We are willing that he should hug the delusion to his heart, as his fall will be the greater when his disgrace comes upon him; for we, too, indulge a feeling of confidence in our strength, based upon far different and much greater grounds.

If croakers and 'peace-on-any-terms' gamblers, who have heretofore been a curse to our cause, fancy the State is to be given up without a struggle that will live in history, they will find themselves disappointed.

SHERMAN's army entered this State with threats openly and defiantly made of the vengeance which should mark his march. South Carolinians are not to be intimidated by the fulminations of a brutal foe, and we are mistaken if South Carolinians have forgotten how to treat the insolence of the hireling.'"

From the Richmond Sentinel, Feb. 14.

The enemy yesterday were at Orangeburgh. There had been no fighting of consequence, our troops falling back in the direction of Columbia. Orangeburgh is about 17 miles above Branchville, which has, no doubt, been evacuated by our troops.

Columbia, the capital of South Carolina, is situated on the left or east bank of the Congaree River, immediately below the confluence of the Saluda and Broad. It is 68 miles north of Branchville, and three or four miles north of the Santee River.

From the Charleston Mercury, Feb. 7.

The following is the substance of the dispatches received yesterday:

NEAR SPRINGTOWN, VIA MIDWAY, Monday, Feb. 6—11:30 A. M.

The enemy crossed a strong force on the left of our works, at Odonis Ford. The enemy can reach the railroad to-day.

LATER.

NEAR SPRINGFIELD, VIA MIDWAY, Monday, Feb. 6—2:15 P. M.

The enemy are skirmishing with us at Odonis Ford. Their strength is not yet ascertained.

The following dispatch was received late Moday night:

NEAR SPRINGTOWN, Feb. 5—12 M.

The enemy demonstrated upon us along the Little Salkahatchie for a distance of seven miles, but on discovering our batteries, after skirmishing with us for some time, commenced building batteries themselves, and have ceased skirmishing. Our scouts report no enemy nearer the Lower Three Runs than last night—(about twelve miles.) The enemy are also moving on the Mathew's Bluff and Orangeburgh River, which crosses the Salkahatchie at Buford's Bridge. Another force, the strength of which has not yet been ascertained, was reported moving on the Buford's Bridge and Blackville Road.

From the Richmond Dispatch, Feb. 14.

The military operations now going on in South Carolina are of the first importance to our cause, and naturally engross the attention of our people to the exclusion of movements reported to be taking place elsewhere. SHERMAN has run through Georgia without meeting with any obstruction, *and it is expected if he is to be checked at all it must be done quickly.* It is only within the past week that his movement against Branchville was clearly developed. Previous to that time it was not known certainly that he would not concentrate against Augusta or Charleston. It is now reported by telegraph that he has a column moving on Augusta, but this must be received as an unconfirmed rumor. We cannot contradict it, though, at the same time, we do not know that it is true, for at present all communication with Augusta is cut off, and we do not know what is going on there or in that neighborhood. As concerns matters at Charleston and in the direction of Columbia, our information is more definite.

NEWS FROM REBEL SOURCES.

WASHINGTON, Thursday, Feb. 16.

From Richmond papers of Tuesday, received at the Washington office of the Philadelphia *Inquirer* to-night, the following is extracted:

AFFAIRS BELOW PETERSBURGH.

From the Dispatch Feb. 13.

All quiet at Petersburgh. There has been no movement of importance since yesterday week. The enemy hold their newly acquired position on Hatcher's Creek, and their pickets are thrown out a short distance to the west of that point. Their new lines take in a very extensive piece of woodland, which will prove great comfort to them. They are building observatories at several points along their lines. With the Yankees the observatory seems completely to have superseded Prof. LOWE and his balloon.

THE REBEL GOVERNMENT GAMBLING IN GOLD.

From the Richmond Enquirer, Feb. 14.

Notwithstanding the sales of gold by the Secretary of the Treasury at one time brought gold from 70 down to 45, it has again gone up to 60 and 65, and that, too, upon sales made on Government account. Notwithstanding the amount of Treasury notes was reduced by the shaving off of one-third, prices went up, and instead of money becoming more valuable by its scarcity, the new notes buy less than the old did. Notwithstanding Mr. TRENHOLM holds six per cent. non-taxable bonds at 136, he cannot sell them for 80. Here we have three important facts which it will do well for Congress to consider.

Gold is still rising and carrying up prices of all other commodities. Shut our eyes as we may, gold is the standard which measures our currency, and daily as gold rises the purchasing value of our notes fall. Notwithstanding the reduction of the currency by shaving one-third, prices have risen, notes have fallen, and *the treasury is empty.* Six per cent. non-taxable bonds would not go, and the treasury has no money to pay its debts.

THE PEACE CONFERENCE.

From the Richmond Sentinel, Feb. 13.

The report of Mr. LINCOLN to his Congress, relative to the late Peace Conference, fills up the space to-day which we had otherwise appropriated, but we defer to the natural wish of our readers to see the Federal version of the late negotiations. The Yankee papers, from which we quote, applaud the part played by the Washington officials, because of the haughtiness of the terms they proposed. In this and in the terms of the correspondence, the reader will see with what sincere efforts our agents sought to give peace to the land, and how Mr. LINCOLN has again written himself guilty of the blood of his own people and of ours.

FROM GEORGIA.

From the Richmond Dispatch, Feb. 14.

We are indebted to the courtesy of Mr. A. WELCH, of the Southern Express Company, for Augusta, Ga., papers of the 8th inst. Instead of peace meetings being held, as reported, in Georgia, we find proceedings of several war meetings published. The Express Company with its usual energy is wagoning over all railroad gaps made by the enemy.

THE REBEL CONGRESS.

NO SPECIE TO PAY THE REBEL SOLDIERS WITH.

In the rebel House, on the 13th, the Appropriation Bill was taken up, Mr. AIKIN, of Georgia, in the chair.

Pending the discussion of the items embraced in it, Mr. SWANN moved that provision be made for the payment of two months' pay to the soldiers in gold. Mr. SWANN said he offered the amendment with no idea that it would pass the House, but, somehow or another, the impression has gained currency among the officers and men of our army, that the Government intended doing this. If it was within its power, he favored it with all his heart. If not, he wanted our brave troops at once to know it. He therefore called upon the Chairman of the Committee of Ways and Means to enlighten him upon the subject.

Mr. LYON, in reply, said that the Secretary of the Treasury had been approached upon this very question by the Legislature of Virginia, and his reply to that body was that it was utterly beyond the ability of the Government to pay the troops even for a single month's service in coin. In fact, without a heavy increase of taxation, he would find it difficult to pay them in Confederate scrip. He therefore urged the House to take prompt action upon the Tax Bill.

ARMING THE NEGROES.

In the Senate, on the 13th, Mr. SPARROW, from the Committee on Military Affairs, reported a bill to amend an act to organize forces to serve during the war; which was read the first time and ordered to be printed.

Mr. SPARROW also reported back bill to provide for raising two hundred thousand negro troops, with the following amendment:

Strike out the fourth section and insert: "All slaves received into the service under the provisions of this act shall be valued and paid for according to existing laws, and that said slaves, or any of them, upon a faithful discharge of their duties, shall be manumitted by general orders from the War Department, if the consent of the State in which the said slaves may be at the time, is given for their manumission."

THE WAR SPIRIT.

The Richmond papers still make feeble efforts to "fire the Southern heart." Some of the regiments, to relieve the monotony of camp life, are holding meetings and passing resolutions breathing the spirit of "dying heroes," the rebel journals say.

From the Richmond Sentinel, Feb. 14.

Mass meetings have been called in Petersburgh and Lynchburgh to express the views of the people on the degrading terms tendered by LINCOLN. Keep the ball rolling.

All our lately received exchanges speak out with one heart and one voice of the Fortress Monroe negotiation, and the duties it has disclosed to us. All, except the Raleigh *Progress* and the Raleigh *Standard*, which are still hanging out the white flag for surrender. The Augusta *Chronicle* will doubtless also take the same ground.

We learn from the Raleigh *Confederate* that one of the happy results of the visit of the North Carolina commissioners to President DAVIS, was the determination that no State should desert her sisters, or enter upon the mad project of separate State action.

MISCELLANEOUS.

From the Richmond Sentinel, Feb. 14.

AFFAIR OF MOSBY'S MEN AT WILLIAMSBURGH.

On Friday night last, Capt. RICHARDSON, of Col. MOSBY's command, with thirteen men, charged into Williamsburgh, which was garrisoned by two hundred infantry and a score or two of cavalry, and run the garrison out of the town. They left fifteen Yankees on the ground, killed and wounded, and retired without the loss of a man.

FROM PRINCE WILLIAM.

The enemy came down on Tuesday last to LAWRENCE COLE's, about six miles below Brentsville, but soon returned. No damage was done by them.

The force at Wolf Run Shoals consisted of the Eighth Illinois, and Thirteenth and Sixteenth New-York Cavalry and one regiment of infantry. They belonged to Gen. SLOAN's command, and returned last Wednesday to their camp at Fairfax Court-house. It is supposed, from their movements in the vicinity of Brentsville, that they contemplate a raid along the Orange and Alexandria Railroad.

RETURN OF CONFEDERATES.

A Yankee flag-of-truce steamer, with 1,080 Confederate prisoners, arrived at Varina on Sunday night. The ice in the river has prevented our steamer from going down.

JOHN MITCHELL.

Maj. JOHN MITCHELL has reported to Gov. MAGRATH, of South Carolina, and has been assigned to duty in that department.

AN ASSIGNMENT.

Brig.-Gen. BRYAN GRIMES, of North Carolina, has been made a Major-General and assigned to the command of RODES' division, EWELL's old corps.

SPECIE IN SOUTH CAROLINA.

The banks of South Carolina have advanced one million of dollars in specie to purchase horses for the cavalry in that State.

NEWS FROM WASHINGTON.

Special Dispatches to the New-York Times.

WASHINGTON, Thursday, Feb. 16.

THE CENSORSHIP OF THE PRESS.

The House Judiciary Committee are investigating the question of the censorship of the press, as exercised by military authorities. The committee having addressed a letter to the Secretary of War upon the subject, that officer sent a reply, stating that they had exercised a sort of censorship in regard to certain matters, but in no instance had they discriminated in favor of any paper, but that they were all treated alike. The Secretary says it may in some cases have worked injuriously to the papers, but he has no doubt it has benefited the military operations of the Government. The committee will report the facts to Congress.

A PIECE OF ENGLISH IMPERTINENCE.

A letter has just been received at the Navy Department from Sir WILLIAM ARMSTRONG, the well known English gunmaker, in which he urges this Government to imitate the example of France and Russia, by manufacturing his guns. To this piece of scientific impertinence, Capt. WISE, of the Ordinance Bureau, has written a caustic reply, in which he tells Sir WILLIAM that the Armstrong guns captured at Fort Fisher afford us the means of testing their supposed efficiency. Upon these guns was found an inscription, setting forth that they were a present from Sir WILLIAM ARMSTRONG to JEFF. DAVIS.

THE RED RIVER EXPEDITION.

Gen. DWIGHT was before the Committee on the Conduct of War this morning, testifying with reference to the Red River expedition.

COLLECTOR AND SURVEYOR OF NEW-YORK.

The Senate Committee on Commerce had another protracted session to-day, for the purpose of considering the nomination of the Collector and Surveyorship of New-York. The committee, without coming to any conclusion, postponed the matter until Saturday.

THE LOAN BILL.

The Ways and Means Committee did not come to any conclusion to-day in regard to the Loan Bill. It will not be reported until the Tax Bill is disposed of.

THE COTTON PERMITS.

The House Committee on Commerce are holding daily sessions for the purpose of investigating the cotton permit business. They have examined a large number of witnesses, most of whom are holding permits. The committee have subpoened several officials who are supposed to know something in regard to this matter.

STEAM COMMUNICATION WITH CHINA.

The House, to-day, passed the Senate bill establishing a line of steamers from San Francisco to China and Japan.

Dispatches to the Associated Press.

WASHINGTON, Thursday, Feb. 16.

THE DEPARTMENT OF ARKANSAS.

Maj.-Gen. HERRON, in his report of the recent investigation at Little Rock, in the Department of Arkansas, transmitted to the Senate to-day, indicates his belief in the existence of corruption and speculation, but exonerates Gen. STEELE from all blame, excepting a too implicit confidence in the integrity of his staff. He seems to regard the Provost-Marshal-General, Lieut.-Col. CHANDLER, of the Seventh Missouri Cavalry, as the principal offender. Fines, licenses, bribes for release from imprisonment, and proceeds of cotton, are the suspected sources of emolument, of which the evidence is not very direct. His dismissal is advised, and Col. T. H. BENTON, of the Twenty-ninth Iowa Infantry, is recommended in his stead. Gen. HERRON also recommends the removal of Col. B. O. CARR, Chief Quartermaster, and the appointment of a more energetic man. It is further stated, that the District of Little Rock is controlled by a combination known as MCDONALD & Co., contractors for supplying Indian stations, with an unlimited license from the Treasury Department, by which they bring in immense stocks of goods relieved from five per cent. tax. One partner is chief clerk in the Quartermaster's Department, and is a brother of a rebel Colonel. HENRY MCKEE conducts the trading store at Fort Gibson for the firm of MCDONALD, and SEYMOUR at Fort Smith. The partners are represented as shrewd and sharp men, with plenty of money, and is a combination which swallows up everything. The officer who cannot be brought into their interest must make way for one who can. Only two or three officers dare oppose them. There have, he says, been brought into that section $500,000 worth of goods, ostensibly for the Indians, but to be sold beyond our lines. It is impossible that one-tenth can be sold within the lines. Other similar cases are mentioned in Gen. HERRON's communication.

THE FRENCH DEFEATED IN SONORA.

Semi-official news from Guaymas, the capital of Sonora, was received to-day. It is stated that a large force of Imperialists, under Gen. VEGA, invaded the State of Sonora, when Gen. PATONI, of the National Army, started to attack him. The French sent some reinforcements on board of the French steamer *Lucifer*, and they landed at Altata. Col. ROSOLIO, of the National Army of Mexico, attacked the reinforcements at the town of San Pedro, and obtained a complete success, defeating the enemy, capturing all their artillery, arms, wagons and ammunition, and many prisoners, among them LASIELLA, the commander of the steamer *Lucifer*, who was commanding the expedition, together with six officers.

Gen. PATONI, at the same time, defeated the Imperialists under VEGA at El Fuirte, and took their artillery and all their ammunition, and a large number of prisoners. Among them was VEGA himself, who was immediately shot as a traitor to his country.]

After this complete failure of the French expedition into Sonora, it is not anticipated that a second one will be attempted.

THE DEPARTMENT OF KENTUCKY.

The following General Order has been promulgated:

WAR DEPARTMENT, ADJUTANT-GENERAL'S OFFICE, WASHINGTON, Feb. 10, 1865.

GENERAL ORDERS No. 21.—1. The State of Kentucky will constitute the Military Department of Kentucky. Maj.-Gen. J. M. PALMER, U. S. Vols., is assigned to the command of the Department of Kentucky.

2. The Department of the Cumberland will include the State of Tennessee and such parts of Northern Georgia, Alabama and Mississippi as may be occupied by the troops under the command of Maj.-Gen. G. H. THOMAS.

3. All troops in the Department of Kentucky and the Cumberland will, in the absence of Major-Gen. SHERMAN, be subject to the orders of Major-Gen. THOMAS, except the posts on the east bank of the Mississippi River, which will be subject to Major-Gen. CANBY's orders, in movements for protecting the navigation of that river. In all other respects they will be under the direct orders of their departments, and whenever time will permit, Gen. CANBY will communicate his orders through such commanders.

4. The Department of Mississippi will embrace so much of that State as may be occupied by troops of the military division of West Mississippi on the river. The Department of the Gulf will embrace the States of Louisiana and Texas. Other military districts on the Gulf of Mexico will report direct to the Commanding-General of the Military Division.

By order of the Secretary of War,

E. D. TOWNSEND, A. A. G.

THIRTY-EIGHTH CONGRESS.

SECOND SESSION.

SENATE.

WASHINGTON, Thursday, Feb. 16.

THE DEPARTMENT OF ARKANSAS.

The Chair laid before the Senate the report of Gen. HERRON as Inspector of the Department of Arkansas.

PETITION FOR INCREASE OF PAY.

Mr. GRIMES, of Iowa, (Union,) presented the petition of naval officers for an increase of pay, which was referred to the Committee on Naval Affairs.

THE AMERICAN COLONIZATION SOCIETY.

Mr. SUMNER, of Massachusetts, (Union,) from the Committee on Foreign Relations, presented a bill to authorize the settlement of claims of the American Colonization Society for the support of recaptured Africans in Liberia, which was passed.

THE LATE SENATOR HICKS.

Mr. JOHNSON, of Maryland, (Democrat,) offered a resolution, which was adopted, requesting the Vice-President to notify the Governor of Maryland of the death of Senator HICKS.

THE PHILADELPHIA PORT OF ENTRY.

Mr. CHANDLER, of Michigan, (Union,) from the Committee on Commerce, reported the bill, extending the boundaries of the port of entry and delivery of Philadelphia, which was passed.

THE ARMY STAFF.

Mr. WILSON, of Massachusetts, (Union,) introduced a bill to increase the efficiency of the staff of the army, as follows:

That officers when assigned to an army, a military department, an army corps or a division, as Chief of the Adjutant General's, of the Inspector General's, of the Quartermaster's and of the Subsistence Departments of Engineers, of Ordnance and of Artillery, shall have respectively, while serving as such, the rank, pay and allowance of the following grades, namely: First, to an army or military department composed of more than one army corps, the rank and pay of a Colonel of cavalry; second, to an army or military department, of not more than one army corps, the rank and pay of Lieutenant-Colonel of cavalry; third, to a division, the rank and pay of a Major of cavalry, and shall be so assigned from the army of the volunteer forces by the President; provided, that nothing herein contained shall prevent officers of higher grade from being thus assigned without loss of rank, and provided further, that no officer so assigned, shall have such increased rank or pay when not actually serving as such chief. This was referred to the Military Committee.

COMMERCE BETWEEN THE STATES.

The bill in relation to the State Courts of Nevada was called up, and discussed until 1 o'clock, when the special order, which was the bill to regulate commerce between the several States, was taken up.

Mr. TEN EYCK, of New-Jersey, (Union,) took the floor in opposition to the measure, which he characterized as unwise, unjust and unnecessary.

At the conclusion of Mr. TEN EYCK's remarks, on motion of Mr. SHERMAN, the bill was postponed till Saturday at 1 o'clock, and the Naval Appropriation Bill for 1866 was taken up.

THE NAVAL APPROPRIATION BILL.

All the amendments of the Finance Committee, affecting appropriations, were concurred in.

The last section of the bill providing for the appointment of an additional midshipman from each Congressional District, to be nominated by the present members of the House, was stricken out.

Mr. WILSON offered an additional section by way of amendment, postponing the time for the restoration of the naval Academy for two years from the first of May, 1865, and repealing an act providing for its restoration in May, 1865. M. WILSON explained the object of this amendment. A portion of the Academy building at Annapolis was being used for a military hospital, and to remove this hospital at the present time and erect one like it elsewhere, would cost thirty thousand dollars. There were nineteen thousand patients under treatment there.

Mr. GRIMES, of Iowa, (Union,) was opposed to the amendment. He regarded it as an objection on the part of medical officers to being removed from comfortable quarters at Annapolis. He was glad to see such a sign of economy in the War Department as to make it anxious about an appropriation of thirty thousand dollars. It was a good sign, and he hoped it would continue. [Laughter.] But he was opposed to keeping naval cadets any longer at Newport, R. I. If we wanted to protect the morals of these young men, the academy must not remain there two years longer.

Mr. ANTHONY, of Rhode Island, (Union,) rose to vindicate the old site of Newport from the foul assertions that had been cast upon it by certain naval officers, writing to the Chairman of the Naval Committee. The society of Newport was as good as that of any city of the Union.

After some remarks by Mr. SPRAGUE in defence of the morals and society of Newport, the amendment of Mr. WILSON was voted down.

Mr. GRIMES offered an amendment, which was adopted, appropriating $100,000 for additions and improvements to the Naval Asylum at Philadelphia.

Also an amendment making appropriations for the expenses of the commission to select a site for a naval station on the Mississippi River.

Mr. WADE, of Ohio, (Union,) offered an amendment similar to that offered in the House a few days since for the appointment of a Board of Admiralty, to consist of a Vice-Admiral, Rear-Admiral, Commodore, Commander and Lieutenant-Commander, who should be advised with on all questions relating to the building, armament, &c., of ships of-war, and other important subjects connected with the Navy Department.

Mr. WADE illustrated the necessity for such a board by what he termed the failure of the light-draft monitors, by which ten millions of dollars were expended.

Mr. SHERMAN, of Ohio, (Union,) hoped his colleague would not press the amendment. It was a matter that should not be put on an appropriation bill, but should come from a committee as an independent proposition. It was a bad practice to offer such amendments to the Appropriation Bill.

Pending the consideration of this question, the Senate adjourned.

HOUSE OF REPRESENTATIVES.

WASHINGTON, Thursday, Feb. 16.

LONGER SESSIONS.

On motion of Mr. STEVENS, of Pennsylvania, (Union,) it was resolved that after to-day the House meet at 11 o'clock A. M., and continue in session until 5½ P. M.

ELECTION CASES.

Mr. DAWES, of Massachusetts, (Union,) said: There are eight cases pending before the Committee on Elections. It is proper they should be speedily disposed of, and I would therefore ask for their consideration on Monday.

ORDER OF BUSINESS FOR NEXT WEEK.

The House arranged the order of business for next week, there being many bills to be acted upon from the Military Committee.

STEAM COMMUNICATION WITH CHINA.

The House proceeded to the consideration of the Senate bill to establish steam mail communication between the United States and China, &c.

Mr. STEVENS, of Pennsylvania, (Union,) desired the bill to be referred to the Committee of the Whole on the State of the Union.

Mr. ALLEY, of Massachusetts, (Union,) replied he did not expect to have the support of the gentleman from Pennsylvania, and while explaining the provisions of the bill he said it contained no private job, but was intended for every body in general. The object of the bill was to establish mail communication between California, Japan and China via the Sandwich Islands. It provides that the Postmaster-General shall advertise for proposals and award the contract to the lowest bidder at a sum not exceeding $500,000 per annum. Its purpose also was to secure commercial advantages. With the Pacific Railroad completed, and this line established, we should bring New-York and China within twenty-six or twenty-seven days of each other, and New-York would be some twelve or fifteen days nearer Hong Kong than London. It would give us vast control over the commerce of the world, and make the City of New-York the greatest commercial city of the world. It would make this city what London is now—the great settling point of the globe. He spoke of the policy of England and France in contradistinction to ours, and showed by facts and figures that both of these countries had exhibited far greater commercial sagacity than the United States. England especially, by the encouragement she had given by Government subsidies, &c., had increased her commerce to gigantic proportions with all those countries she has established ocean mail steam communication with. Ever since Great Britain commenced this system in 1837, she has pursued it with sleepless vigilance and constantly increasing development. The result has shown her far-reaching sagacity; she has in a few years doubled, and in some cases quadrupled her trade with all the countries upon this continent with which she has established this steam communication. He stated that England paid out at the present time, in the shape of subsidies, about five millions of dollars annually, and received in return for postages about half that sum. This amount, although enormous, has been the most profitable investment ever made by her Government. But England has done more to encourage commerce than all other countries combined, and most amply has she been rewarded. He said if this line was established between California and China at the same rate of increase of trade that England had experienced when she established similar lines, the increased duties on imports, added to the postages, would pay the deficiency the first year. If we establish this line of steamers and complete the Pacific Railroad, we shall do all the postal

Continued on Eighth Page.

General Sherman reviewing his army at Savannah

A Massachusetts Colored Regiment singing in the streets of Charleston

The New-York Times.

VOL. XIV......NO. 4182. NEW-YORK, SUNDAY, FEBRUARY 19, 1865. PRICE FOUR CENTS.

GLORIOUS NEWS

Triumphant March of Gen. Sherman.

Columbia, S. C., Occupied on Friday Morning.

Beauregard's Forces Retreat as Our Troops Enter the Town.

Large Quantities of Medical Stores Destroyed by the Rebels.

The "Cradle of Secession" Violently Rocked.

The Evacuation of Charleston a Military Necessity.

Speculations as to where Sherman will Next Strike.

He Lives on the Country and is Unopposed in His Advance.

OFFICIAL REPORTS FROM GENERAL GRANT.

[OFFICIAL.]

War Department, Washington, D. C., Feb. 18, 1865.

Major-Gen. Dix:

The announcement of the occupation of Columbia, S. C., by Gen. SHERMAN, and the probable evacuation of Charleston, has been communicated to the department in the following telegram just received from Lieut.-Gen. GRANT.

EDWIN M. STANTON, Secretary of War.

CITY POINT, 4:45 P. M., Feb. 18, 1865.

Hon. E. M. Stanton, War Department:

The Richmond *Dispatch* of this morning says:—

SHERMAN entered Columbia yesterday morning, and its fall necessitates, it presumes, the fall of Charleston, which it thinks has already been evacuated.

U. S. GRANT, Lieutenant-General.

CITY POINT, Va., Feb. 18, 1865.

Hon. E. M. Stanton, War Department:

The following is taken from to-day's Richmond *Dispatch:*

THE FALL OF COLUMBIA.

Columbia has fallen. SHERMAN marched into and took possession of the city yesterday morning. The intelligence was communicated yesterday by Gen. BEAUREGARD in an official dispatch. Columbia is situated on the north bank of the Congaree River, just below the confluence of the Saluda and Broad Rivers.

From Gen. BEAUREGARD'S dispatch, it appears that on Thursday evening the enemy approached the south bank of the Congaree, and threw a number of shells into the city. During the night they moved up the river, and yesterday morning forded the Saluda and Broad Rivers. Whilst they were crossing these rivers our troops under Gen. BEAUREGARD evacuated Columbia. The enemy soon after took possession.

Through private sources we learn that two days ago, when it was decided not to attempt the defence of Columbia, a large quantity of medical stores, which it was thought it was impossible to remove, were destroyed. The female employes of the Treasury Department had been previously sent off to Charlotte, South Carolina, a hundred miles north of Columbia. We presume the Treasury lithographic establishment was also removed, although as to this we have no positive information.

The fall of Columbia necessitates, we presume, the evacuation of Charleston, which, we think likely, is already in process of evacuation.

It is impossible to say where SHERMAN will next direct his columns. The general opinion is that he will go to Charleston and establish a base there; but we confess that we do not see what need he has of a base. It is to be presumed he is subsisting on the country, and he has had no battle to exhaust his ammunition. Before leaving Savannah he declared his intention to march to Columbia, thence to Augusta, and thence to Charleston. This was uttered as a boast and to hide his designs. We are disposed to believe that he will next strike at Charlotte, which is a hundred miles north of Columbia, on the Charlotte and Columbia Railroad, or at Florence, S. C., the junction of the Columbia and Wilmington and the Charleston and Wilmington Railroads, some ninety miles east of Columbia.

There was a report yesterday that Augusta had been taken by the enemy. This we not believe.

We have reason to feel assured that nearly the whole of SHERMAN'S army is at Columbia, and that the report that SCHOFIELD was advancing on Augusta was untrue.

From the Whig.

The Charleston *Mercury* of Saturday announces a brief suspension of that paper, with a view to its temporary removal to another point. This is rendered necessary by the progress of military events, cutting it off from the mail facilities for distributing its paper to a large portion of its subscribers, while the lack of transportation renders its supply of paper precarious.

SEMMES has been made a Rear-Admiral, and will take command of the James River Squadron.

U. S. GRANT, Lieutenant-General.

Rebel Reports.

From Richmond journals of the 16th, received yesterday at Washington, we get the following:

No official messages were received from any part of South Carolina yesterday.

At last accounts, as we stated in yesterday's paper, the enemy held Orangeburgh, on the Columbia branch railroad, and our forces were falling back toward Columbia.

There was a flying report yesterday, which we could trace to no reliable source, that there had been skirmishing on Tuesday morning, within four miles of Columbus.

Our troops abandoned Branchville last Sunday night.

WHEELER last Friday attacked and whipped KILPATRICK at Aiken, 15 miles northeast of Augusta, and drove him back five miles in the direction of Branchville.

The Augusta papers, of last Wednesday, state that at that time SLOCUM was at Windsor, ten miles east of Arpen, advancing on Augusta, his right flank being protected by the South Edisto, and his left by KILPATRICK'S cavalry.

Two day's after this KILPATRICK was whipped by WHEELER. SLOCUM has with him the Fifteenth and Sixteenth Corps. The Fourteenth and Twentieth Corps comprise the force operating against Columbia and Charleston.

This leaves one corps of SHERMAN'S accounted for. We presume it has been left at Savannah.

By the latest advices through Yankee papers we learn that SHERMAN was still at his headquarters at Beaufort.

Gens. S. D. LEE and WADE HAMPTON, recently appointed Lieut.-Generals, have been confirmed by the Confederate Senate.

The promotion of Gen. HAMPTON makes him rank Gen. WHEELER, and puts him in command of our cavalry now operating against Gen. SHERMAN.

The best events may be expected from this appointment. HAMPTON'S presence will not fail to inspire confidence and enthusiasm.

Table of Distances.

The following table of distances, which have been compiled from reliable sources, will be found valuable to our readers for reference in tracing the various movements now taking place in the Carolinas:

From	Miles.
Charleston to Savannah	104
Charleston to Ashepoo Bridge	35
Charleston to Pocotaligo	55
Charleston to Kingstree	38
Charleston to Florence	102
Charleston to Augusta	137
Charleston to Branchville	62
Charleston to Orangeburgh	79
Charleston to Kingville	105
Charleston to Columbia	130
Charleston to Aiken	128
Charleston to Augusta	137
Charleston to Wilmington (by rail)	209
Charleston to Richmond	457
Charleston to Washington	567
Branchville to Charleston	62
Branchville to Orangeburgh	17
Branchville to Kingville	45
Branchville to Columbia	68
Branchville to Florence	108
Branchville to Augusta	75
Branchville to Wilmington	216
Branchville to Charlotte	174
Kingville to Columbia	25
Kingville to Florence	64
Kingville to Wilmington	171
Columbia to Florence	89
Columbia to Wilmington	196
Columbia to Charlotte	106
Columbia to Salisbury (by inner line)	140
Columbia to Raleigh (by inner line)	261
Columbia to Goldsboro'	329
Columbia to Goldsboro' (by Wilmington route)	270
Columbia to Raleigh (by Wilmington route)	318
Wilmington to Marion	86
Wilmington to Florence	107
Wilmington to Goldsboro'	84
Wilmington to Weldon	162
Wilmington to Raleigh	132
Wilmington to Hillsboro'	172
Wilmington to Greensboro'	214
Wilmington to Salisbury	264
Wilmington to Charlotte	304
Wilmington to Petersburg	226
Wilmington to Richmond	248
Wilmington to Washington	378
Newbern to Beaufort	40
Newbern to Goldsboro'	50

THE CAMPAIGN IN SOUTH CAROLINA.

Interesting Facts Regarding Sherman's Movement—Strength of His Army—Plan of the Campaign—Character and Strength of the Adversary, Etc.

Correspondence of the Chicago Evening Journal.

NASHVILLE, Sunday, Feb. 12.

It would be folly for me here to repeat the statement that preparations are in progress for a grand campaign into Alabama, and that it is about to start, and that it would, ere this, have gone but for the inclemency of the weather; all these things have been told you, over and over; yet there is nothing else transpiring which would in the least interest the readers of the *Journal*, in this immediate locality. I must, therefore, be pardoned for going out of the department for my intelligence; and I am fortunately in possession of numerous facts relative to the situation in an important locality, which will be of interest, not only to every reader of the *Journal*, but to every patriot in the land.

The locality to which I refer is South Carolina, and the operations are those of SHERMAN and his adversary, in that stronghold of rebellion. Our army left Savannah strongly garrisoned with troops belonging to the Nineteenth Corps, so that SHERMAN set out at the head of the following force:

Fourteenth Corps	12,000
Twentieth Corps	19,000
Fifteenth Corps	16,000
Seventeenth Corps	18,000
Foster's army	22,000
Cavalry	16,000
Total	103,000

This may be regarded as a large force; but I am happy to say that it does not exceed, by one man, that number under command of SHERMAN; though in it are included some 10,000 negro troops, who will remain in the vicinity of Port Royal, so that the actual number moving northward is a little over 90,000, including cavalry. Of this number, nearly all the cavalry, and the Fourteenth and Twentieth Corps, in all from 42,000 to 45,000 men, passed through or by Robertsville, with a view to striking the Augusta and Charleston Railroad, some ten miles to the west of the Edisto River, whence they were to march directly upon the bridge over that stream (which is a trestle structure of over seven hundred feet in length,) which is to be destroyed, thereby obviating all necessity for a detour to the west, with a view to the capture of Augusta. That place has lost all importance, since its shops and machinery were removed; and the only possible object SHERMAN could have in paying any attention to it would be to destroy the half mile of trestle-work over the Savannah River. But if he can succeed in cutting the bridge over the Edisto—and from a perfect knowledge of all the facts in the case, so far as developed, I am confident he has done that already—and then those over the Santee and Wateree Rivers, near Kingsville, and between Branchville and Columbia and Florence, then there is no necessity for the destruction of that at Augusta; and the three can be laid in ashes with less marching than would be required to reach the Savannah.

While these two corps and the cavalry are moving into Central South Carolina, the Fifteenth and Seventeenth Corps, and the greater part of FOSTER'S white troops—all infantry, and numbering about 45,000 men—are moving slowly, but surely upon Charleston. They were instructed to cross the Combahee, but to make no haste; but rather, by an appearance of hesitation and indecision, deceive the enemy and make him believe the whole thing a mere feint; and then, when it became apparent that he was concentrating in the vicinity of Branchville, to push rapidly on and invest the cradle of the rebellion, and let it have a taste of a little musketry, as well as artillery.

Some have conjectured that SHERMAN didn't care a fig whether Charleston was captured or not; that he proposed to isolate it, and then let the rebels either hold or evacuate it at their pleasure; but this is a serious mistake, as Charleston is too important a point of support for any such trifling. He wants Branchville first, but he wants, and intends to take, Charleston also; and when once it falls into our hands he will move northward with the assurance that he has done his work well and released another large fleet which will not in the least detract from our moral force in dealing with our neighbors, whether on this Continent or in Europe.

In order to fully understand all these strategic points at which SHERMAN aimed on starting out, the reader should consult a map; without one, he will scarcely be able to fully appreciate the importance of the several movements I have indicated; but he has only to glance at a good atlas to perceive the grandness and magnitude of the present campaign, which cannot be otherwise than successful, with this present large army in the field.

BUT WHAT OF THE REBELS?

Are they idle? Let no one indulge the illusion that they are. What are the preparations which have been made to meet the invincible army of SHERMAN?

In the first place HARDEE, on evacuating Savannah, took with him about 6,000 veterans—the Georgia militia being no longer in the field. There were, in Georgia, at the same time, in scattered garrisons, some 5,000 more, and at Charleston 5,000 more, all of whom are now concentrated under the command of the rebel army of South Carolina, making in all about 16,000. To this must be added the following forces:

From Wilmington	4,000
From Lee's army (5 divisions)	15,000
Add to the above	16,000
Total	35,000

Of this number about five thousand are cavalry; and reinforcements to the number of five thousand more can be had if it is determined to evacuate Wilmington, which will probably be done. This force the rebels must continue to divide, if they propose to try to hold Charleston; but this I think they will scarcely do. In addition, a portion of HOOD'S old army, from eight thousand to ten thousand, have started in the direction of South Carolina. They are under command of CHEATHAM and S. D. LEE, but are not strictly their old corps—they are the picked men of the entire army, and are all of it who are worth the powder and lead it would take to kill them. But they commenced their peregrinations too late in the season. Had they started when HOOD was first driven across the Tennessee they could have been made available. But the first of them left Meridian, on the cars, on the 26th of January last; and the last not till the 4th of February, as transportation was exceedingly scarce; and after going to Talladega on the cars, they will be compelled to march overland 280 miles before they can be of any service, which is a month's journey at the least; so that they will not even set foot upon the "sacred soil" of South Carolina before the first of March; and long before that time SHERMAN will be out of the State and HARDEE'S forces will be scattered.

It is useless to talk about the assistance which the militia will render to the regular rebel troops. The more of these in their army, the worse for the rebels. They are all old men and boys, and only valuable to consume commissaries which might otherwise fall into the hands of the "Yankees." Nor can LEE aid HARDEE, or BEAUREGARD, or whoever has command. He has but 35,000 infantry in the works at Richmond, and the late advance of GRANT evinces that he cannot hold his own, even with his present force; and as for his cavalry, they do not number 8,000 in all Virginia.

This, I repeat, is a correct statement of affairs in South Carolina; but of the results of these grand combinations, you will hear through another channel than Nashville—through Richmond and Washington.

HANDEL.

NEWS FROM REBEL SOURCES.

The Situation on the Appomattox—Reported Evacuation of Wilmington—Union Forces Concentrating at Newbern, &c.

WASHINGTON, Saturday, Feb. 18.

Richmond papers of the 16th inst. have been received here.

The Richmond *Dispatch* contains the following:

There was a cannonade of several hours' duration on our left, near the Appomattox, on Wednesday evening. With this exception, nothing of moment occurred. On the Petersburgh lines picket firing has, by tacit consent of both parties, very much slackened within the past few days. The enemy are quiet in their intrenchments on Hatcher's Run. Throughout Tuesday night the rumbling of wagons and artillery was heard on GRANT'S lines in the neighborhood of Deep Bottom. It was supposed that GRANT was transferring a heavy body of troops to the north side. This may be simply the return of the troops sent over to Petersburgh to participate in the Hatcher's Run affair last Monday.

It was reported yesterday that our troops were evacuating Wilmington. The report is not confirmed, however, by official dispatches. The Yankee papers state that Gen. TERRY is still in the vicinity of Fort Fisher and waiting for Gen. HOKE.

Hitherto the Yankee press have represented Gen. TERRY as about to march toward Wilmington with the confident expectation of taking the place, but Fort Anderson has proved a more effectual obstruction than they had anticipated.

Gen. BAKER is in command of our forces at Goldsboro', and reports to the War Department that he has reason to believe that the enemy are concentrating at Newbern, and that they have with them materials for repairing the railroad from Newbern to Kinston.

Scouts who came into Kingston on the night of the 11th inst., report that Gen. FOSTER is in command at Newbern, and that 2,000 of the Eighteenth Army Corps have arrived there, making the number of troops at the post about 5,000.

It is reported and believed in Kinston that the enemy have landed two locomotives and two cargoes of railroad iron at Morehead City.

It is not apprehended in Kinston that the enemy design an early movement in that direction.

Col. ISAAC M. ST. JOHN, at present Chief of the Nitre and Mining Bureau, has been appointed Commissary-General. He is by profession an engineer.

FROM THE SOUTHWEST.

Orders by Gen. Roberts.

CAIRO, Friday, Feb. 17.

A resolution introduced into the Louisiana Legislature, expressing regret for the assault of Mr. FIELD on Judge KELLY, in Washington, was tabled by a vote of 55 against 7.

Gen. ROBERTS has issued an order in Memphis, requiring owners and holders of real estate in the District of West Tennessee to file with the Provost-Marshal of Memphis a description of their property, its nature source and title; when and where the same was acquired; the consideration paid therefor; by whom occupied and by what authority; and when rent is paid for the same. All agents and attorneys are required to file similar descriptions of the property they control, and if they have money or other effects in their possession, belonging to absentees, to report and make oath to the same property, which, if not reported within thirty days, will be seized by the military authorities.

The steamer *Darling*, from Memphis, passed here for Cincinnati, with 200 bales of cotton.

Boats are again being fired on between here and Memphis.

The Government wharf boat at Memphis, with 11,000 sacks of grain, sank on the 13th. Loss estimated at $50,000.

The City Council of Cairo has passed an ordinance requiring substitute brokers to pay a license of $1,000 for six months.

CAIRO, Ill., Saturday, Feb. 18.

The steamer *Liberty* passed up from Memphis to-day, with 80 bales of cotton for Evansville.

Gen. WASHBURN had arrived at Memphis from Vicksburgh, en route for the Army of the James, but meeting countermanding orders, would return to Vicksburgh.

The draft to fill the quota of the District of Memphis, under Gen. CANBY'S order, passed off quietly. Three hundred and eighty-seven names were drawn.

NEWS FROM WASHINGTON.

Dispatches to the Associated Press.

WASHINGTON, D. C., Saturday, Feb. 18.

INCIDENTS OF SHERMAN'S ADVANCE.

The Richmond *Examiner* of the 16th inst., states that a dispatch was received from an official of the Treasury Department at Columbia, to the effect that SHERMAN'S advance was so near Columbia that the Home Guard and citizens had turned out to aid in resisting the Union forces, and that skirmishing had already commenced not far from the city.

RECONSTRUCTION IN TENNESSEE.

The Select Committee on the Rebellious States, in their amendments to the Reconstruction Bill, as reported to-day, provide for the recognition by the President of the State Government of Tennessee, if such a Government shall be established by the loyal citizens, in conformity with the Constitution, prior to the 1st of May next. The report also provides that the Constitution of Tennessee shall prescribe:

First—That no person shall vote who has held a Confederate military office higher than Colonel, nor a civil office, unless it be ministerial.

Second—That Slavery shall be forever prohibited; and,

Third—That no State, nor Confederate debt, created under the action of a usurping power, shall be recognized or paid by the State, and no rebel law of confiscation shall be binding.

LARGE ARRIVAL OF DESERTERS.

During four days of the present week over 200 rebel deserters came within the lines of the Armies of the Potomac and the James. This morning 46 arrived here, all of whom deserted from rebel picket posts on the night of the 14th inst. Twenty of these belonged to Virginia regiments, and the remainder to Georgia and South Carolina regiments.

GOV. ANDREW'S FRIENDS AND THE PRESIDENT.

The Massachusetts delegation, bearing a petition asking the appointment of Gov. ANDREW to a place in the Cabinet of a reorganization, were introduced to the President to-day by Senator WILSON.

THIRTY-EIGHTH CONGRESS.

SECOND SESSION.

SENATE.

WASHINGTON, Saturday, Feb. 18.

Mr. MORGAN, of New-York, (Union,) introduced a bill to amend "An act to authorize the employment of volunteers to aid in enforcing the laws and protecting public property," approved July 22, 1861.

It authorizes the giving of bounties to honorably discharged soldiers, who have already served two years, the same as are now allowed for three years' service, and entitles the heirs of such soldiers, if dead, to the same bounty. It also gives the same bounty to those who would have been entitled to discharge by reason of wounds, but whose terms of service had expired within two years from the date of enlistment.

RELIEF OF LOYAL TEXANS.

Mr. SPRAGUE, of Rhode Island, (Union,) introduced a bill to check contraband trade and to provide a fund for the relief of indigent loyal refugees from the State of Texas.

It directs the Commercial Agent of the United States at Matamoras, Mexico, pursuant to instructions from the Secretary of State, to charge 1 cent per pound on all cotton, wool and dry hides, and 2 cents per pound on Pecan nuts intended for shipment to any port of the United States, provided such agent shall be satisfied that such shipment is the product of any State or Territory of the United States, and he is further authorized to apply such proceeds or as much as may be needed to the relief of the indigent loyal citizens of the United States, at Matamoras, refugees from Texas. The residue he may retain, provided the sum with his present compensation does not exceed $3,000 per annum.

The bill was referred to the Committee on Finance.

A COMMISSION TO EXAMINE THE REVENUE LAWS.

Mr. SHERMAN, of Ohio, (Union,) offered a joint resolution, providing for the appointment, by the Secretary of the Treasury, of a commission of three persons, to examine into and report upon the subject of raising revenue by taxation, and the articles most fit for taxation.

Mr. CONNESS, of California, (Union,) moved an amendment that one of the commissioners shall be appointed from the Pacific Coast. He explained that it was necessary to make this provision in order to have the interests of the Pacific States represented.

Mr. SHERMAN did not think it wise encumber such a proposition with an amendment proposed by Mr. CONNESS. He had no doubt that the Secretary of the Treasury would see that the interests of the Pacific States were represented in the commission. The Pacific coast only paid one-fiftieth of the revenue, and it would be unjust to ask for it a third of the commission. Mr. SHERMAN then explained the importance of such a commission as he wished to have appointed. The condition of the Tax Bill in the present Congress was an illustration. There were but ten or twelve working days remaining for this Congress, and the bill had yet to be considered in the Finance Committee, and then in the Senate. With the result of the labors of such a commission as he proposed before Congress, both Houses could act understandingly, and with more satisfaction than could attend the deliberations of the closing hours of the session.

Mr. STEWART, of Nevada, (Union,) spoke of the necessity of having the mining interests of the far West represented in such a commission.

The amendment of Mr. CONNESS, of California, (Union,) was subsequently withdrawn.

Mr. CLARK, of New-Hampshire, (Union,) offered an amendment that the commissioners be instructed to inquire also into the past and present mode of collecting the Internal Revenue, which was adopted.

The resolution of Mr. SHERMAN, as amended, was then laid over till Monday.

On motion of Mr. HOWARD, of Michigan, (Union,) a joint resolution was adopted, giving to Mrs. L. WRIGHT, late of Richmond, $1,500 for relief extended by her to prisoners of war in rebel hands.

Mr. ANTHONY, of Rhode Island, (Union,) from the Committee on Printing, recommended the printing of 2,000 copies of the report of the Naval Commission in reference to the establishment of a Naval Depot in the Western waters.

On motion of Mr. JOHNSON, of Maryland, (Dem.,) 2,000 copies of the addresses delivered on the subject of the death of the late Senator HICKS, were ordered to be printed.

Mr. CHANDLER, of Michigan, (Union,) desired to call up the Railroad Bill to regulate commerce between the several States, and have it made the special order for Monday.

Mr. BROWN, of Missouri, (Union,) said this bill was nothing but a cut-throat arrangement between two railroads, to see which would make the most money. He was opposed to postponing important business to give way for such a measure.

Mr. DOOLITTLE, of Wisconsin, (Union,) was opposed to making Mr. CHANDLER'S bill the special order for Monday, as he wished that day to be devoted to the consideration of Indian bills.

Mr. FOSTER, of Connecticut, (Union,) was opposed to making any bill the special order at this late date of the session. It could be set aside by the majority at any time.

After some further discussion Mr. SHERMAN moved to postpone all prior orders and take up the Army Appropriation Bill.

The Army Appropriation Bill was then taken up. The Finance Committee recommended the striking out of a proviso in the House bill that no money shall be paid to land grant railroad for transportation of troops and munitions of war for the United States.

Mr. COWAN, of Pennsylvania, (Union,) moved an amendment, that land-grant railroads shall be paid for transporting troops, etc., but that the subject shall be opened for adjustment hereafter, and that in paying the roads, Congress does not admit the right of the roads to claim compensation.

Mr. WILSON, of Massachusetts, was opposed to the provision proposed to be stricken out. That provision, if not stricken out, he said, would have the effect of ruining all the small land-grant railroads in the country.

Mr. HENDERSON, of Wisconsin, (Union,) spoke of the necessity of striking out the provision of the House bill. If not stricken out, the Pacific Railroad to Kansas City could not be completed, and further work upon it would have to be abandoned.

Mr. COWAN'S amendment was rejected.

The amendment of the committee was adopted, and the provision referred to was stricken out.

Mr. SHERMAN offered an amendment making an appropriation of $7,000,000 to supply deficiencies in the appropriations for the present fiscal year, which was adopted.

On motion of Mr. WILSON, the following provisions were adopted by way of amendment:

"That from and after the 1st of March, 1865, and during the continuance of the present rebellion, the commutation price of officers subsistence shall be fifty cents per ration, providing that the said increase shall not apply to the commutation price of any rations of any officers above the rank of Brevet Brigadier-General, nor of any officer entitled to commutation for fuel or quarters. That all officers of volunteers below the rank of Brigadier-General now in commission, who shall continue in the military service to the close of the war, shall be entitled to receive three months' pay, provided the provisions of this section shall not apply to officers not on duty, or to officers entitled to commutation of fuel and quarters; that commissioned officers serving in the field shall be permitted, hereafter, to purchase rations for their own use on credit from the Commissary Department, and the amount due for rations so purchased shall be reported monthly to the Paymaster General to be deducted from the payment next following such purchase.

Mr. SPRAGUE, of Rhode Island, (Union,) offered an amendment, making it obligatory upon Chaplains to hold religious services once a week, to attend burial services of soldiers who die, &c., which was rejected.

Mr. WILSON offered an amendment that the Secretary of War be directed to furnish, at cost, not exceeding 16 ounces of tobacco per month to each soldier who may deserve it, the cost to be deducted from their pay.

Mr. TRUMBULL of Ill., (Union) offered an amendment providing for the repeal of all laws and regulations of the War Department, giving additional rank or pay to regular officers or volunteers, which was adopted. The bill as amended was then passed.

Mr. TRUMBULL, from the Committee on the Judiciary, reported a resolution recognizing the State Government of Louisiana and the right of that State to Senators in Congress.

Mr. SAULSBURY, of Delaware, (Dem.,) offered the following resolution, which was objected to, and goes over under the rule:

Whereas, In a speech recently delivered by the Hon. ALBERT G. BROWN, late a member of this body, now a member of the Confederate Congress, as reported in the New-York *Herald* of the 4th inst., the following statement is made: "STANTON, the last of this ignoble trio of blatant Democrats alone remained. It seemed that he had no power to disgust LINCOLN; it might be because he was baser than the other two; he rather thought it was, for of all unmitigated falsifiers of sacred pledges and undisguised betrayers of confidence which he himself had created, STANTON was the meanest and basest. He had one consolation in thinking of this, and that was, that he would be certain, sooner or later, to betray LINCOLN. STANTON was incapable of keeping faith. He had a fondness for betraying those who gave him their confidence that has become the charm of his life. Mr. BROWN related an interview which he had with the present Yankee Secretary of War just before he (Mr. BROWN) left Washington the last time. It was under circumstances peculiarly calculated to impress Mr. BROWN. His State had withdrawn from the Union. Mr. BROWN was passing from the Senate and Mr. STANTON from the Supreme Court. They met by accident in front of the Old Capitol, when the conversation turned on "secession," the action of Mississippi on the question, and Mr. BROWN'S withdrawal from the Senate. Mr. BROWN was surprised, and, under the circumstances, delighted to hear Mr. STANTON say that the South was right, and express an earnest hope that 'she would stand firm.' "You are right," said Mr. STANTON, "Go ahead and urge your friends to stand by what they have done, and all will be well. Firmness now will secure you all you ask. Any wavering and you are lost." And

Whereas, in the judgment of the Senate, no person whose patriotism and fidelity to the Constitution and Government of the United States should be a member of the Cabinet of the United States of the present loyal and patriotic Executive, therefore,

Resolved, That a committee of five members of the Senate be appointed by the presiding officer thereof to make inquiry in reference to the truth or falsity of the charges herein, as aforesaid, recited, and in reference to the patriotism and loyalty of the said E. M. STANTON, Secretary of War, past and present, with leave to take testimony, and to make report in writing to the Senate.

Mr. SAULSBURY pledged himself to produce the proof of the above charges against Mr. STANTON, if afforded an opportunity by the Senate to do so.

The Senate then adjourned.

HOUSE OF REPRESENTATIVES.

WASHINGTON, Saturday, Feb. 18.

SOLDIERS' RATIONS.

On motion of Mr. INGERSOLL, the Committee on Military Affairs were instructed to inquire into the expediency of providing in all cases, where less than full rations are issued to soldiers, the difference shall be made up in money.

THE INTERNAL REVENUE BILL.

The House then proceeded to act on the amendments reported yesterday from the Committee of the Whole on the State of the Union, to the Amendatory Internal Revenue Bill.

Nearly all the amendments reported were concurred in, while others were reserved for separate votes.

The House concurred in keeping the tax on ale, beer and porter at $1 a barrel.

Instead of two and a half per centum, as now are the gross receipts of railroads, steamboats, ferryboats, bridges, &c., the law is altered so as to impose a duty of two and a half per centum on the net receipts under $3,000, and five per centum on the excess.

Among the amendments concurred in were the following:

No man not enrolled for military service, cases of physical disability excepted, shall be entitled to take out a license as a pedler.

On all smoking tobacco a tax of 35 cents a pound shall be imposed, excepting on smoking tobacco exclusively made of stems, on which the tax shall be 15 cents a pound. This is the only change in the amendment as reported by the Committee of Ways and Means on that article.

On diamonds, emeralds, precious stones, and imitations thereof, and all other jewelry the duty is reduced to five per centum ad valorum.

All the amendments reported from the Committee of the Whole on the State of the Union were concurred in with the exception of a few reserved for separate votes.

Mr. MORRILL, of Vermont, (Union,) called attention to some of them, including the tax on sales. He said we may put the restriction on foreign trade, but within the vast area of the United States, it is vital that we should leave our trade free. As to the amendment of the gentlemen from Pennsylvania (STEVENS) proposing to tax gold sales, &c., if any other gentleman had offered the proposition he should have regarded it as absurd. He trusted that the vote to-day in the House may show that the vote in the Committee of the Whole yesterday in favor of it was given in mere good nature. The law heretofore passed on that subject was repealed, because it could not be enforced. He expressed his satisfaction that the committee had unanimously agreed upon a bill, which would contribute so materially to the support of the Government.

The House then concurred, by a vote of 72 against 68, in striking out the proposed increase of 50 cents a barrel on ale, beer, lager-bier, porter, and other similar fermented liquors. The tax on these articles therefore remains at $1 a barrel.

The House also concurred in the amendment, that substitute brokers pay a license of $110 (?) for every substitute accepted.

An amendment was made to the 103d section of the present law, by imposing a tax of two and a half per centum on the net instead of the gross receipts of railroads, canals, steamboats, ships, barges, canal-boats, vessels, stage coaches, and vehicles for transporting passengers or property for hire, &c., where the net receipts are under $3,000 per annum, and five per centum on the excess of this amount.

This amendment was concurred in by a vote of 86 against 76.

An amendment was adopted, providing that stamps may be affixed to deeds, instruments, documents, writings or papers, where the same have been omitted, on payment of the stamps and a penalty of $50; but where it is satisfactorily established that the same have been omitted owing to inadvertence or accident, and without willful design, stamps may be affixed merely on payment for the stamp.

The amendment to tax sales one-half of one per centum was non-concurred in by a vote of yeas, 65; nays, 75.

The following is the vote on the amendment to tax sales one-half of one per centum:

YEAS—Messrs. Ames, Ashley, Baldwin of Massachusetts, Beaman, Blow, Boutwell, Boyd, Brandigee, Brown of Wisconsin, Ambrose A. Clark, Freedman Clark, Cobb, Cole, Davis of New-York, Dixon, Driggs, Eckly, Eliot, Farnsworth, Gooch, Higby, Hubbard of Connecticut, Hubbard, Jenckes, Kasson, Kelly, Kellogg of Michigan, Kellogg of New-York, Knox, Littlejohn, Loan, Longyear, McClurg, Miller of New-York, Morehead, Morris of New-York, Leonard, Myers, Nelson, Norton, Odell, O'Neill of Pennsylvania, Perham, Patterson, Pike, Pomeroy, Rice of Massachusetts, Rice of Maine, Rollins of New-Hampshire, Schenck, Shannon, Smith, Smithers, Spalding, Starr, Tracy, Upson, Van Valkenburg, Washburn of Massachusetts, Wheeler, Williams, Wilder, Fernando Wood.

NAYS—Messrs. James C. Allen, Allison, Ancona, Arnold, Bailey, Baldwin of Michigan, Baxter, Blaine, Bliss, Brooks, Broomall, Brown of West Virginia, Chandler, Clay, Coffroth, Cox, Cravens, Cresswell, Dawson, Deming, Dennison, Edin, Edgerton, English, Finck, Ganson, Garfield, Grider, Griswold, Harding, Harrington, Harris of Illinois, Herrick, Hooper, Hubbard of Iowa, Ingersoll, Johnson of Ohio, Kalbfleisch, Kirnan, King, Knapp, Lazear, Leblond, Long, Mallory, Marcy, Marven, McAllister, Miller, Morrill, Morris of Ohio, Pendleton, Pruyn, Randall of Kentucky, Rollins of New-Hampshire, Rollins of New-Jersey, Ross, Schofield, Steele of New-York, Steele of New-Jersey, Stevens, Stuart, Thayer, Wadsworth, Ward, Washburne of Illinois, Whaley, Joseph W. White, Wilson, Winfield, Woodbridge.

The House then voted on Mr. NELSON'S amendment, that every national bank or State bank association shall pay a tax of ten per centum on the amount of notes of any State bank or association paid out by them on and after the first of January next.

The amendment was concurred in by yeas 68; nays, 67.

The following is the vote on Mr. NELSON'S amendment that every National Bank or State Bank shall pay a tax of ten per centum, etc., etc.:

YEAS—Messrs. Allison, Ames, Arnold, Ashley, Baxter, Beaman, Blaine, Blow, Boutwell, Boyd, Brandegee, Broomall, Freeman, Clark, Cobb, Cole, Creswell, Davis of New-York, Dixon, Driggs, Eckley, Farnsworth, Garfield, Gooch, Higby, Hooper, Hubbard of Iowa, Hubbard of Connecticut, Ingersoll, Jencks, Julian, Kasson, Kelly, Kellogg of Michigan, Kellogg of New-York, Knox, Littlejohn, Longyear, Marvin, McClurg, Miller of New-York, Moorhead, Morris of New-York, Amos Myers, Leonard Myers, Norton, O'Neill of Pennsylvania, Patterson, Perham, Pike, Rice of Massachusetts, Rice of Maine, Schenck, Schofield, Shannon, Smith, Smithers, Spalding, Starr, Thayer, Tracy, Upson, Washburne of Illinois, Washburn of Massachusetts, Williams, Wilder, Woodbridge.

NAYS—Messrs. James C. Allen, Ancona, Bailey, Baldwin of Michigan, Brooks, Brown of Wisconsin, Brown of West Virginia, Chandler, Clay, Coffroth, Cox, Cravens, Dawson, Deming, Dennison, Edin, Edgerton, Eldridge, English, Fink, Ganson, Grider, Griswold, Harding, Harris of Illinois, Herrick, Hubbard, Johnson of Ohio, Kalbfleisch, Kernan, King, Knapp, Lazear, Le Blond, Mallory, Marcy, McAllister, Miller of Pennsylvania, Morrill, Morris of Ohio, Morrison, Nelson, Noble, Odell, O'Neil of Ohio, Pendleton, Pomeroy, Pruyn, Radford, Rollins of New-Hampshire, Rollins of Missouri, Ross, Steele of New-York, Steele of New Jersey, Stevens, Stuart, Sweet, Townsend, Wadsworth, Ward, Whaley, Wheeler, Joseph W. White, Winfield, Fernando Wood, Yeaman.

Mr. BROOKS, of New-York, (Dem.,) who first voted in the negative, changed his vote to the affirmative, in order to move a reconsideration of the vote.

A motion was then made to lay the motion to reconsider the vote on the table, which was carried by the casting vote of the Speaker, so the vote adopting the amendment was not reconsidered.

The House next voted on Mr. STEVENS' amendment defining a bullion broker to be one who buys and sells gold at a price above the mint value, unless solely for the purpose of paying duties on imports or for exportation, and requiring every bullion broker to take out a license of one thousand dollars, or otherwise be deemed guilty of a misdemeanor and pay a forfeiture of $5,000, and ten per centum to be paid on each sale and purchase of gold.

The House rejected this amendment by yeas 36, nays 94.

The following is the vote on Mr. STEVENS' amendment defining a bullion broker, etc., etc.:

YEAS.—Messrs. Anderson, Ashley, Bailey, Baxter, Beaman, Blow, Boyd, Brandagee, Cobb, Driggs, Eckley, Higby, Hubbard of Iowa, Hubbard of Connecticut, Ingersoll, Kelly, Kellogg of New York, Knox, Littlejohn, Loan, Longyear, Marvin, McClurg, Moorhead, Morris of New-York, Amos Myers, Leonard Myers, Norton, O'Neil of Pennsylvania, Rice of Maine, Schenck, Shannon, Spalding, Stevens, Upson, Wilder, Wilson.

NAYS—Messrs. Allison, Ames, Ancona, Arnold, Baldwin of Massachusetts, Blaine, Bliss, Boutwell, Brooks, Broomall, Brown of Wisconsin, Brown of West Virginia, Ambrose W. Clarke, Freeman Clarke, Coffroth, Cole, Cravens, J. Davis of New-York, Dawson, Deming, Denison, Dixon, Edin, Edgerton, Eldridge, Eliot, English, Farnsworth, Finck, Ganson, Garfield, Griswold, Harding, Harrington, Harris of Illinois, Herrick, Hooper, Hubbard, Hutchins, Jinks, Johnson of Ohio, Julian, Kalbfleisch, Kasson, Kellogg of Michigan, Kernan, King, Knapp, Law, Leblond, Long, Mallory, Marcy, McAllister, McKinney, Miller of New York, Miller of Pennsylvania, Morrill, Morris of Ohio, Morrison, Nelson, Noble, Odell, Patterson, Pendleton, Perham, Pike, Pomeroy, Pruyn, Rice of Massachusetts, Ross, Rollins of Missouri, Smith, Smithers, Starr, Steele of New-Jersey, Stuart, Sweat, Thayer, Townsend, Tracy, Van Valkenburg, Wadsworth, Ward, Washburne of Illinois, Washburn of Massachusetts, Whaley, Wheeler, Joseph W. White, Williams, Winfield, Fernando Wood, Yeaman.

The Amendatory Internal Revenue Bill was then passed.

SENATE BILLS PASSED.

Mr. SCHENCK, of Ohio, (Union,) from the Committee on Military Affairs, reported the following Senate bills which were passed:

To repeal an act to remove the United States Arsenal from St. Louis.

Authorizing the President to appoint a Second Assistant Secretary of War, at $3,000 per annum.

Providing for the publication of a full army register.

Defining what shall constitute officers' servants.

Mr. SCHENCK also reported a bill providing that any person in the army charged with an offence under the acts calling out the militia, may be brought before the field-officers of his regiment for trial; but nothing in this bill shall be construed to abolish regiment or garrison court-martial.

Also, a bill authorizing the President to make transfers of army officers from the line to staff officers, etc.

Also, a bill for the better organization of the Subsistence Department.

These bills were severally passed.

A REFUGEES AND FREEDMANS BUREAU.

Mr. SCHENCK also reported a bill to establish in the War Department a Bureau for Refugees and Freedmen's affairs.

Mr. SCHENCK said the bill made no distinction on account of color, but was intended to provide for the relief of white refugees.

The bill was passed.

INCREASED PAY FOR THE ARMY.

Mr. YEAMAN, of Kentucky, (Dem.,) from the Committee on Military Affairs, reported a bill to increase the pay of officers of the army below the grade of Brigadier-Generals, and exempting officers from the income and war tax.

On motion of Mr. ROSS, of Illinois, (Dem.,) an amendment was made increasing the pay of privates to twenty dollars per month.

The bill was then re-committed to the Military Committee, who subsequently reported the bill as it was originally introduced, and it was passed.

RANK OF ARMY OFFICERS.

Mr. GARFIELD, of Ohio, (Union,) reported a bill from the Committee on Military Affairs, determining the rank of officers reëntering the military service, and it was passed.

THE AIR-LINE RAILROAD.

Mr. FARNSWORTH, of Illinois, (Union,) from the Committee on Military Affairs, reported a bill authorizing the Northern Central Railroad Company of Pennsylvania and Maryland, or their assigns, to construct a branch railroad between the Borough of York and Baltimore, in an air-line to Washington, in order to facilitate postal and military communication between Washington and New-York.

The company is authorized to increase their capital to the extent of two millions of dollars, the road to be a double track, provided with appliances for the transportation of troops, and to be completed in two years. Three cents are to be charged per mile for passengers, and six cents a ton for freight.

Mr. PENDLETON, of Ohio, (Dem.,) objected to the second reading of the bill.

The question therefore recurred on its rejection.

Mr. FARNSWORTH said it was necessary to have the road proposed. He pointed out the fact that not one cent was appropriated by this bill.

Mr. THOMAS, of Maryland, (Union,) desired a postponement of the bill, and gave among other reasons for this that the Legislature of Maryland, now in session, should have an opportunity of looking into the subject—besides the bill was in conflict with the decision of the Supreme Court of the United States, and in derogation of the rights of the State of Maryland. The legislation proposed was for the benefit of the Northern Central Railroad, and would strike a heavy blow at the Baltimore and Ohio Railroad.

The further consideration of the subject was then postponed for ten days.

Mr. SCHENCK, of Ohio, (Union,) called up the bill amendatory of the Enrollment Act, pending which the House, at 5:30 o'clock, adjourned.

Fire.

ST. LOUIS, Saturday, Feb. 18.

The extensive spoke-factory of WOODBURN & SCOTT, on the corner of Broadway and Colt-street, was burned last night. Loss about $200,000, upon which there is an insurance of $44,000.

Recognized.

WASHINGTON, Saturday, Feb. 18.

The President has recognized HENRY WILLIAM HEMANS as British Consul at Buffalo.

The St. David Outward Bound.

PORTLAND, Me., Saturday, Feb. 18.

The steamship *St. David* will not sail for Liverpool until about 8 o'clock this evening.

The Seven-Thirty Loan.

PHILADELPHIA, Saturday, Feb. 18.

JAY COOKE, Subscription Agent, reports the subscriptions to the 7 30 Loan to-day, $5,082,000, including one from Cincinnati of $300,000; New-York, $600,000, and $2,500 individual subscriptions of $50 and $100 each. The total sales for the week foot up $26,500,000.

ARREST OF BURKE FOR THE ALLEGED MURDER OF HIS WIFE.—MICHAEL BURKE, charged with beating his wife with such severity that she died, was arrested at the house of his uncle, PATRICK BURKE, No. 405 Columbia-street, yesterday morning. When questioned by the officers in regard to the affair, he acknowledged that he had beaten her because he found her drunk when he got home, but that the injury above the left eye was caused by falling upon the edge of the stove. The accused was committed to await the result of the Coroner's investigation.

The New-York Times.

VOL. XIV......NO. 4183. NEW-YORK, MONDAY, FEBRUARY 20, 1865. PRICE FOUR CENTS.

HIGHLY IMPORTANT.

Capture of Columbia by Gen. Sherman.

The Rebels Retreat as Our Troops Enter the City.

Large Quantities of Medical Stores Destroyed by the Enemy.

The "Cradle of Secession" Violently Rocked.

The Evacuation of Charleston a Military Necessity.

Speculations as to where Sherman will Next Strike.

He Lives on the Country and is Unopposed in His Advance.

OFFICIAL REPORTS FROM GENERAL GRANT.

[The following dispatch appeared in our edition of yesterday:]

[OFFICIAL.]

WAR DEPARTMENT,
WASHINGTON, D. C., Feb. 18, 1865.

Major-Gen. Dix:

The announcement of the occupation of Columbia, S. C., by Gen. SHERMAN, and the probable evacuation of Charleston, has been communicated to the department in the following telegram just received from Lieut.-Gen. GRANT.

EDWIN M. STANTON, Secretary of War.

FIRST DISPATCH FROM GEN. GRANT.

CITY POINT, 4:45 P. M., Feb. 18, 1865.

Hon. Edwin M. Stanton, War Department:

The Richmond *Dispatch* of this morning says:

SHERMAN entered Columbia yesterday morning and its fall necessitates, it presumes, the fall of Charleston, which it thinks has already been evacuated.

U. S. GRANT, Lieut.-General.

SECOND DISPATCH FROM GEN. GRANT.

CITY POINT, Va., Feb. 18, 1865.

Hon. E. M. Stanton, War Department:

The following is taken from to-day's Richmond *Dispatch*:

THE FALL OF COLUMBIA.

Columbia has fallen. SHERMAN marched into and took possession of the city yesterday morning. The intelligence was communicated yesterday by Gen. BEAUREGARD in an official dispatch. Columbia is situated on the north bank of the Congaree River, just below the confluence of the Saluda and Broad Rivers.

From Gen. BEAUREGARD's dispatch it appears that on Thursday evening the enemy approached the south bank of the Congaree, and threw a number of shells into the city. During the night they moved up the river, and yesterday morning forded the Saluda and Broad Rivers. Whilst they were crossing these rivers our troops, under Gen. BEAUREGARD, evacuated Columbia. The enemy soon after took possession.

Through private sources we learn that two days ago, when it was decided not to attempt the defence of Columbia, a large quantity of medical stores, which it was thought it was impossible to remove, were destroyed. The female employes of the Treasury Department had been previously sent off to Charlotte, South Carolina, a hundred miles north of Columbia. We presume the Treasury lithographic establishment was also removed, although as to this we have no positive information.

The fall of Columbia necessitates, we presume, the evacuation of Charleston, which, we think likely, is already in process of evacuation.

It is impossible to say where SHERMAN will next direct his columns. The general opinion is that he will go to Charleston and establish a base there; *But we confess that we do not see what need he has of a base.* It is to be presumed he is subsisting on the country, and he has had no battle to exhaust his ammunition. Before leaving Savannah he declared his intention to march to Columbia, thence to Augusta, and thence to Charleston. This was uttered as a boast, and to hide his designs. We are disposed to believe *that he will next strike at Charlotte*, which is a hundred miles north of Columbia, on the Charlotte and Columbia Railroad, or at Florence, S. C., the junction of the Columbia and Wilmington and the Charleston and Wilmington Railroads, some ninety miles east of Columbia.

There was a report yesterday that Augusta had been taken by the enemy. This we do not believe.

We have reason to feel assured that nearly the whole of SHERMAN's army is at Columbia, and that the report that SCHOFIELD was advancing on Augusta was untrue.

From the Richmond Whig, Feb. 18.

The Charleston *Mercury*, of Saturday, announces a brief suspension of that paper, with a view to its temporary removal to another point. This is rendered necessary by the progress of military events, cutting it off from the mail facilities for distributing its paper to a large portion of its subscribers, while the lack of transportation renders its supply of paper precarious.

SEMMES has been made a Rear-Admiral, and will take command of the James River Squadron.

(Signed) U. S. GRANT, Lieutenant-General.

Secretary Stanton to Gov. Fenton—Stimulating Recruiting.

ALBANY, Sunday, Feb. 19.

The following telegram has been received by Gov. FENTON.

WASHINGTON, Sunday, Feb. 19.

Last night this department received the gratifying intelligence of the occupation of Columbia, the capitol of South Carolina, by Gen. SHERMAN, and the probable evacuation of Charleston by the enemy. Hasten on recruiting to fill up the army, and the rebellion must receive the final blow in this Spring's campaign.

(Signed,) E. M. STANTON, Secretary of War.

The News in Washington.

Special Dispatch to the New-York Times.

WASHINGTON, Saturday, Feb. 19.

The splendid progress made by SHERMAN in his campaign through South Carolina inspires the Government and public here with the brightest hopes of a speedy extinction of the armed force of the rebellion. SHERMAN's march demonstrates conclusively the truth of the theory that the Confederacy is but a shell. Notwithstanding the blatant braggadocio of the Richmond papers, it is obvious that the rebels have no adequate force with which they can hope to resist the advance of SHERMAN's conquering host.

SHERMAN'S MOVEMENTS PRIOR TO THE OCCUPATION OF COLUMBIA.

PLEASANT ILLUSIONS RUDELY DISPELLED.

From the Augusta, Ga., Chronicle, Feb. 10.

From a gentleman who arrived on a special train last night, we gather the annexed news.

The Federals, on Thursday morning, were at Windsor, about fifteen miles from Aiken. It is not known in what force. No movements were made by them on Thursday. The cause of this is not ascertained. The troops in the vicinity of Windsor are KILPATRICK's corps. It is reported that Gens. HAMPTON and WHEELER engaged the enemy on the 7th and 8th, repulsing them at all points. Our loss was about seventy killed and wounded, and missing; that of the enemy much greater. The enemy are reported to be moving toward the Congaree River. A gentleman from Columbia states that SLOCUM's corps is moving on that city on the side of the Edisto. His main line, when last heard from, was on the railroad. It is stated in Columbia that KILPATRICK's Corps is protecting SLOCUM's left. It is ascertained that PORTER is again moving on Charleston. When last heard from he was at Green Pond. It is not known where Gen. SHERMAN himself is. Barnwell Court-House was burned on Monday night. The roads are teeming with vehicles, stock, and all kinds of moveable property, fleeing for Georgia and upper Carolina.

From the Charleston Courier, Feb. 10.

Dispatches received Thursday contain very little additional news. A dispatch from Orangeburgh, Feb. 9, says: The enemy are in front of the Edisto line, near New Bridge and Duncan Bridge. The main force is said to be near the railroad. Skirmishing took place to-day near Binniker's Bridge. The enemy show no disposition to force the crossing of Edisto.

A dispatch from Gen. WHEELER, dated Orangeburgh, Feb. 8, says: All the crossings on Edisto, above and below, are fully guarded. A large force of the enemy's infantry struck the railroad at Graham's, and one was moving to strike between Graham's and Blackville. KILPATRICK is at Blackville with three brigades of cavalry.

SOUTH CAROLINIANS TO THE RESCUE.

From the Columbia Guardian, Feb. 12.

Every man capable of bearing arms should march at once to the front, and if there are men in the State, who, after reading the future by the ghastly light of the burning village of Allandale, can expect to save his home in any other way than by shouldering his musket and hurrying to the field, he deserves to be classed with that sagacious quadruped of ÆSOP, who planted his clumsy hoofs upon the shoulder of his master, in hope of being carried like a dog, when, lo! instead of the gentle touches he was looking for, he received such a shower of blows as soon reminded him that he was nothing better than an ass.

Same journal states in its situation article that a portion of the enemy's force have crossed South Edisto at Benneker's Ferry, and are slowly pushing forward toward the north branch of that river. The probabilities briefly are that this movement is made for the double purpose of cutting the Columbia and Charleston road and Wilmington and Manchester road at or near Kingsville. This done SHERMAN will have achieved what he may deem an important object preliminary to the capture of Charleston, namely—the bisection of those important branches of supply. *That he will succeed in doing this we have doubts, very grave doubts, for we know something of the dangerous operations of an army in the hands of Beauregard.* The *Guardian* does not think that the enemy contemplates an immediate advance in that direction, but believes that *long before Columbia falls*, there will be a battle *and a victory*, commensurate in its consequences with the great interests now at stake—one which will prove that *God is fighting by our side*, although with the visor down, and that he has vouchsafed to South Carolina the proud privilege of closing, as she began, this war in triumph.

Gen. BEAUREGARD and staff, consisting of Col. OTEY, Col. RICE, Capt. BEAUREGARD, Capt. FAY and Dr. BRODIE, have arrived in Columbia, and are stopping at NICKERSON's Hotel.

The appointment of Gen. HAMPTON to the command of two such divisions as these of Gens. BUTLER and YOUNG, is an earnest of success. He is once more at the head of the men he has so often led to victory on Virginia fields. Men on whom both the country and himself can depend, and we may, therefore, look for a repetition here of the gallantry which has been bulletined from every battle in which they have had part. The arrival of BEAUREGARD—the thought that HAMPTON is in the saddle—the coöperation of Gen. JOHNSTON, who, a though for the present "behind the scenes," does not withhold his skill and experience whenever demanded—together with a score of other facts of an encouraging character, which should not be published, are events that may well give our people great joy.

SHERMAN IN SOUTH CAROLINA.

From the Columbia Carolinian, Feb. 11.

Whether SHERMAN's objective point is Augusta, Charleston, Columbia, or Richmond, or all four, does not, to unskilled eyes, yet appear. One thing, however, is certain, that every mile of ground the Federal army leaves behind it—provided the latter is promptly met and attacked at the proper time—is so much gained to us. We have troops, our Generals are watchful, and we firmly believe that within twenty days there will be such a concentration of strength and assault as will make the Yankee commander tremble for his safety. He may be permitted to move on our railroads and to penetrate our interior, but these triumphs must be short. The condition of the country will compel him to go forward or back, and that right quickly. If he comes forward, a reception awaits him unlike that which he encountered in his career through Georgia; if he goes to Charleston, he may find himself afflicted in front and rear; if he returns the way he came that will be just what we all desire him to do, and we shall be content to let him alone. On the whole, though some hearts are perturbed with expectations of a sudden appearance of the enemy, we think the aspect not discouraging, especially if our people will but do their duty. By all means, wherever SHERMAN advances, let him find nothing on which to feed man or beast.

From the Richmond Whig, Feb. 16.

Parties who left Columbia on Friday evening last represent as the belief in Columbia that SHERMAN had cut loose entirely from the various points upon which he had demonstrated, and was hastening with all possible rapidity toward Kingsville or Columbia, possibly both. All movements toward Evansville, Charleston and Augusta seem to have been abandoned. From Blacksville and Orangeburg there is an excellent country road, and as SHERMAN appears to have got somewhat the start of our forces, considerable apprehensions were felt at Columbia that he would reach there before he could be overtaken. The Congaree, a considerable stream, has to be crossed before reaching either Kingsville or Columbia; but SHERMAN has pontoon-trains and an efficient engineer corps with him, and crosses streams with surprising facility. Extensive preparations were being made at Columbia to receive the "Great Yankee," and it was hoped that he would be at least held in check until our forces could come up. SHERMAN is said to have a very large army, and he may divide, sending one column to Kingsville, and the other to Columbia.

This would enable him to destroy the Columbia and Charlotte and Wilmington and Manchester Railroads at one and the same time, provided he is not checked. It is also stated that SHERMAN is but little incumbered with commissary and quartermaster's trains. Relying upon his great success in Georgia, he feeds his men and horses off the country as he moves, and all that they do not consume he destroys.

The Columbia *Guardian* learns from persons who have made their escape through the lines that the conduct of the enemy in Barnwell District is characterized by most brutal vandalism. The village of Bufordsbridge has been burned to the ground. The residence of planters on the route which were left unoccupied were invariably destroyed, and where families still remained in their dwellings they were subjected not only to robbery but to various kinds of insults. Pistols were clapped to the bosoms of the women, mothers and wives, the robbers refused to wait until doors and drawers could be unlocked, but broke open ruthlessly the finest cabinets and apartments, destroyed or carried off at pleasure, and to enforce their demands threatened the house with fire over the heads of its inhabitants. They traversed the precinct, it appears, in scattered bands of fifteen or twenty, sometimes with and sometimes without any officer—the officer in general command of these predatory parties being understood to be a Col. ROBBINS.

FLIGHT FROM SOUTH CAROLINA.

From the Augusta Chronicle, 10th.

The roads are teeming with vehicles, stock, and all kinds of movable property, fleeing from Georgia and Upper Carolina.

From the Pacific Coast.

SAN FRANCISCO, Wednesday, Feb. 15.

Advices from Chili say that on and after May 1 the coasting trade of that country will be thrown open to vessels of every nation. This will have the effect to increase commerce with San Francisco.

Arizona papers report that scouting parties have been started out against the Indians, and an exterminating warfare commenced.

SAN FRANCISCO, Thursday, Feb. 16.

Arrived ships *Sea Serpent* and *Great Republic* from New-York.

Gov. BLAISDELL, of Nevada, has presented the message to the Legislature relative to the passage of the constitutional amendment for the abolition of slavery. He recommends action thereon.

The Governors of Idaho and Arizona Territories are on their way hither, en route to Washington.

SAN FRANCISCO, Friday, Feb. 17.

A suit is now pending in the United States District Court to test the validity of various seizures of champagne by the Custom-house authorities, on the ground of an attempt to evade the duties by systematic underrating of values and false invoices. The result of the suit will make a difference of $100,000 annually at this port.

Arrived, mail steamer *Sacramento*, from Panama, with passengers that left New-York Jan. 23.

The opposition steamer *America*, with the passengers that left New-York Jan. 23, has also arrived.

NEWS FROM REBEL SOURCES.

WASHINGTON, Sunday, Feb. 19.

From Richmond papers of Friday, received this morning at the Washington office of the Philadelphia *Enquirer*, we extract the following:

THE REBEL CONGRESS.

THE NEGRO TROOPS.

On Thursday last, the only important proceedings were on the Senate bill to provide for raising 200,000 negro troops, which was taken up.

Mr. JOHNSTON, of Georgia, moved to transfer the bill to the Secret Calendar.

Mr. WIGFALL opposed the motion, but before any decision on the question, the doors were closed, to enabled the Senators to debate on the propriety of transferring the bill to the Secret Calendar.

In the House the same subject was considered.

Mr. BARKSDALE had the floor; but before commencing his speech, on motion of Mr. ATKINS, of Tennessee, the House went into secret session, by a vote of 38 yeas to 35 nays. On the doors being opened, the House adjourned.

During a debate in the rebel Senate, on the 16th inst., on the bill to diminish the number of exemptions, the food question was discussed, during which Mr. HARVY said the difficulty was not the production of food, but the preventing its falling into the hands of the enemy. There was food enough produced in the valley of Virginia last year, but when the harvest was ripe it fell into the hands of the enemy.

Mr. OLDHAM, of Texas, criticised the plan on which the war had been conducted. It had been attempted to defend too much territory. Instead of our armies being combined they were scattered about, and run from one end of the country to the other, to defend some seaport.

Mr. CAPERTON would say to the Senator from Tennessee (Mr. HENRY) that the harvests in the valley had been lost to us by the fact that those who would have gathered them were called into the army by the revocation of all details just at the time when their services were required for securing the crops.

Mr. BURNETT believed there was plenty of food in the country, and if there was not, he did not believe the quantity would be increased by exempting the large farmers. They owned large troops of slaves, and made very little surplus—not as much surplus as did the small farmers. He believed the apparent scarcity of supplies was due to inefficiency in the departments of the Government.

Mr. ORR replied to Mr. BURNETT. The Senator had said there was plenty of food in the country. He would inform him that he knew of hundreds, yes, thousands of soldiers' families who had not tasted meat in the last six months, who were living on bread alone, and a short supply at that.

Mr. GRAHAM said this was the case in his State.

Mr. ORR said the Senator from Tennessee (Mr. HENRY,) seemed to be very anxious to fill up the army. If the Senator should chance to meet with any soldiers from the army he might learn that they had been without meat for a long time. However, as there was to be another and an efficient officer put at the head of the Commissary Department, he hoped matters in this respect would improve.

Mr. BURNETT said it could not be denied there was scarcity in some localities, but it had been brought about by the improper management of the Commissary Department. They had stripped some States and left others where there was a superabundance of food untouched.

From the Richmond Whig, Feb. 19.

We regret to see in the Charleston *Mercury* an article on the subject of arming negroes, which has a tendency to provoke resentment and animosities among our people just at a time when harmony and good feeling are most imperatively needed. We can very well account for the decided differences of opinion on this important question, for without such differences what now appears to be the prevailing sentiment in favor of the proposition could never have been reached. A sudden conversion from unanimous opposition to unanimous support on the part of reflecting people, would be an extraordinary phenomenon in the history of public questions. But the very fact that the question exhibits those phases of transition which seem to indicate an approaching affirmative decision should, we think, have suggested to so candid a journal as the *Mercury* the propriety of abstaining from unqualified impeachment of the integrity and patriotism of those who support the measure. There can be no doubt that the expedient of using the services of negroes in some direct way against the common enemy has grown in popular favor the more thoroughly it has been debated. The highest military authorities recommend it, and people, just as sagacious as any others in the country, urge it upon Congress. The *Mercury* is simply mistaken in assuming that this originated in Virginia, or that it is a reflection of unsound opinion in this State on the subject of slavery—*it was the natural development of the necessities of the crisis*—one among many of the projects and devices to which the uneasiness of the past few weeks has given birth. If most others have fallen still-born, while this one has survived and grown in strength, that fact shows that it possesses superior vitality, and is more congruous with the demands of the times. The *Mercury* does, indeed, limit its denunciations to those who propose to confer emancipation on the negro as compensation for his military services; but it seems to infer that emancipation is the real object of those who favor the measure, thus attributing a kind of abolitionism to a very large number of our people, while, in fact, emancipation is suggested only as an incident by those who imagine that in this way alone could the main expedient be rendered effective. In regard to this point also there may be a latitude of opinion, which does not by any means imply treason or abolitionism, either on one side or the other. People who think that the gift of emancipation would better enable us to utilize the resources presented by our supply of negroes are not, therefore, Abolitionists. The expedient of arming slaves being once adopted, the question might present itself, how best can we render this expedient effective? The question would not be, as it has been asserted, whether freedom or slavery is best for the negro, but whether the negro himself would so consider it. *That large numbers of them do think it a desirable boon* is proven by the fact that they run off to the Yankees in quest of it. That almost all of these would return to us with the same inducement we think unquestionable, but we sincerely hope that we shall not be driven to any such alternative. We may accomplish all that we desire by using negroes simply as slaves, but we do say that *we would not hesitate to use them in any way whatever to get rid of Yankee domination*. We say this in order to meet fully the *Mercury's* assertion that "South Carolina entered into the struggle *for no other purpose than to maintain the institution of slavery*;" that "Southern independence has no other object or meaning;" and that "*independence and slavery must stand together or fall together.*" We do not pretend to dispute the *Mercury's* assertion, but we protest against *applying it to other States*. It is true that to preserve African slavery, menace as it was by an unprincipled and imperious ochlocracy, was the proximate object of secession. So it is true that the stamp act and tea tax were proximate causes of the American Revolution, but we have yet to learn that the patriots of that day would have submitted to England, after declaring their independence, if England had guaranteed to them free tea and unstamped paper forever. Nor do we believe that this people would or ought to return to the Yankee Union, *even if* LINCOLN *could and would guarantee the perpetuity of African slavery*. The *Mercury* will have it that slavery and independence must stand or fall together—that neither of them can stand alone. As to slavery, it is true without independence it must fall. How should we suffer, then, should we, in case of necessity, sacrifice it for the sake of Independence? We hope to preserve it; we believe we can preserve it; so do we hope to preserve a portion at least of our houses and our lands. Would the *Mercury* declare that we should succumb to the Yankees rather than sacrifice any more of our property? or must we be told that it is our duty to give everything for independence—lands, houses, life itself—but not our slaves? These, to be sure, we shall lose at once, should we be conquered; but is it better to be conquered, even to submit to the yoke we so much dread, and against which we have so desperately struggled, *than to make use of the last and it may be the most effective resource.*

From the Richmond Dispatch, Feb. 17.

The bill of the House to abolish the negro clause, to take from the President and Secretary of War the power to make details and exemptions, excepting mechanics and artisans in the employment of the Government, to revoke all exemptions and details heretofore granted by the President and Secretary of War, and to revoke all exemptions of mail contractors not permanently engaged in performing the contracts, was recommitted to the Military Committee, with instructions to inquire into the expediency of bringing in a more liberal bill. There is a strong disposition on the part of the Senate to preserve untouched the present Exemption Law.

GEN. LEE'S ORDER ON ASSUMING CHIEF COMMAND.

The following is a copy of Gen. LEE's general order on assuming command of the land forces of the Confederate States:

HEADQUARTERS CONFEDERATE ARMY, Feb. 9, 1865.

GENERAL ORDER, No. 1.—In obedience to General Order No. 3, Adjutant and Inspector-General's Office, 6th of February, I assume command of the military forces of the Confederate States. Deeply impressed with the difficulties and responsibility of the position, and humbly invoking the guidance of Almighty God, I rely for success upon the courage and fortitude of the army, sustained by the patriotism and firmness of the people, confident that their united efforts, under the blessing of Heaven, will secure peace and independence. The headquarters of the army, to which all special reports and communications will be addressed, will be, for the present, with the Army of Northern Virginia. The stated and regular returns and reports of each army and department will be forwarded, as heretofore, to the office of the Adjutant and Inspector-General.

(Signed,) R. E. LEE, General.

FRANK CONFESSIONS FROM ALABAMA.

From the Mobile Register and Advertiser.

Blue as things now look, or as black as they present themselves to the visions of some, it is nevertheless an undeniable truth that we hold in our hands the means of sudden and perfect deliverance. No one doubts that the cause languishes and suffers, not from a deficiency of resources to maintain a war of defence, but from poverty of spirit to breast reverses, and of fortitude to endure trials. The people are not whipped, *but cowed. Their souls and not their hands are disarmed.* Our strength is not sapped, but *our courage is oozing out at the ends of our fingers.* A lady from Georgia writes in a letter we read this morning: "The people are whipped, but the women are not, and, by the blessing of God, never will be;" and what is wanting to change this leaden aspect and to drive away the clouds which *hang like a pall over the Confederate situation?* Courage! and one more effort. One single flash of that noble warlike enthusiasm, which in 1861 spread its halo of crimson battle-light over this Southern land, now revived and inspiring all hearts to answer with life in hand to the sacred calls of duty and country, and those shadows, now darkening all hearts with gloom, would be lifted like a curtain and unveil a scene of hope, and joy, and deliverance.

VIRGINIA RAILROADS.

THE GREAT DAMAGE DONE BY STONEMAN'S RAID.

From the Lynchburgh Republican.

Virginia and Tennessee Railroad, it is thought, will be open for travel to Bristol by the first of March. Repairs are being pushed forward with their usual energy. Some idea of the magnitude of the work to do may be formed from the statement that *all bridges, some fifty or sixty in number, for a distance of eighty-five miles*, have had to be rebuilt, and much of the track relaid, besides other repairs to be made, of minor consequence.

OPERATIONS BEFORE PETERSBURGH.

The Petersburgh *Express* says that a Yankee force, numbering about five hundred, have again occupied Suffolk, and their pickets extend about three miles from town, in the direction of the Blackwater. A raiding party went out from Suffolk a few days ago, and visited Chuckatuck and Smithfield, doing considerable damage to the country through which they passed. It is not known for what purpose this advance is made.

From the Richmond Enquirer, Feb 17.

The enemy renewed his mortar practice upon the left of our line Wednesday evening, but did no damage. Matters were quiet there yesterday up to the departure of the train. Deserters say that GRANT's army is now receiving only half rations of meat. This accounts in some degree for the frequent incursions made upon the poultry and pigsties of the surrounding country by their dashing cavalry.

THE NEW REBEL COMMISSARY-GENERAL.

From the Richmond Dispatch, Feb 17.

Col. ST. JOHN appointed by the President Commissary General of the Confederate States, was yesterday confirmed by the Confederate Senate. The new Commissary-General will enter at once upon the discharge of his duties.

THE ARMY OF THE JAMES.

Lively Affair at Bermuda Hundred—Deserters—Arrival of Prisoners—Destruction of the Rebel Flag-of-Truce-boat.

WASHINGTON, Sunday, Feb. 19.

Information has been received from the Army of the James, dated 17th.

Deserters from the rebel army, arriving at headquarters, state that this morning, between 12 and 1 o'clock, a company from each of the regiments of STEWART's brigade of PICKET's division, were sent out to advance their picket line about 150 yards, in order to strengthen as well as straighten their line on the Bermuda Hundred front, opposite the position held by the Second Pennsylvania Heavy Artillery. On being discovered they were fired upon by our pickets, and after about twenty shots they retired to their own lines. The party making the attempt are reported as having been supplied with intrenching tools to throw up works for the defence, and when fired upon retreated in the utmost disorder, not waiting to return our fire. Their loss, if any, is unknown.

Nine hundred and eighty-three Union prisoners, including ten officers, mostly from Danville, came down from Richmond on the rebel steamboat *Allison*, to Cox's Landing. They were received and cared for by Lieut. H. S. MERRILL, Acting Assistant Quartermaster, at these headquarters. About 5 o'clock, as the *Allison* was on her return trip to Richmond, and when a short distance above Fort Brady, she struck a torpedo, which, exploding, completely wrecked her. She had on board 213 packages of blankets, and a number of other articles, intended for our prisoners, belonging mostly to the State of Indiana. The loss of life is unknown.

There is no change in the weather. The roads are very bad, owing to the continued rains.

FROM FORT FISHER.

Expected Attack on Fort Anderson—The Fort Believed to be Evacuated—An Arrival from Savannah.

FORTRESS MONROE, Friday, Feb. 7.

The steamer *Ariadne* arrived here to-day from Fort Fisher. The Captain of the steamer reports that our forces had expected to make an attack upon Fort Anderson on the 13th instant, but failed for some cause unknown to him. Before he left Fort Fisher he saw a bright light in the direction of Fort Anderson, and the supposition was that it had been abandoned and burnt by the rebels.

The steamers *Northerner* and *Ellen S. Terry* sailed from here this afternoon for Fort Fisher with colored troops for Gen. TERRY.

The steamer *Louisiana*, of the Bay Line, arrived here this morning from Baltimore, the ice being broken up sufficiently for the resumption of travel.

More coal schooners are anxiously looked for.

The steamer *Blackstone* arrived here this afternoon from Savannah, stopping at Hilton Head, S. C.

The Captain of the *Blackstone* brought dispatches from Gen. SHERMAN, for the authorities at Washington, which were telegraphed from here. The Captain of the *Blackstone* was not informed of the nature of the dispatches, and knew nothing of importance of SHERMAN's contemplated movements.

The War in the Southwest.

CAIRO, Sunday, Feb. 19.

Five hundred and fifty bales and one hundred and fifty bags of cotton have arrived for St. Louis, and three hundred for Cincinnati.

New-Orleans advices to the 13th have been received.

The steamship *Evening Star* had arrived.

The rebel iron-clad *Missouri* and two wooden gunboats, comprising the entire fleet of the enemy in Red River, are below Alexandria, closely watched by our gunboats.

Three hundred and sixty bales of cotton from the prize bark *Science*, were sold at auction at New-Orleans for 59c. for good ordinary, 67c. for middling. There were no private rates. Sugar, 19@20c. Molasses, $1 20@$1 23.

Memphis dates to the 17th have been received.

The steamers *Mercury* and *Grassbeck*, with troops on board, had been attacked by the rebels near Helena. Several soldiers were wounded. The rebels were finally dispersed by the gunboats.

The Memphis *Bulletin* says it is reported upon authority worthy of consideration, that the cotton trade will be closed in this department within twenty days, by order of President LINCOLN, and be reopened upon new principles after his proposed visit South and West, which is looked for soon after the 4th of March.

The Union men of Memphis are preparing a grand reception banquet for W. G. BROWNLOW, who is expected here in a few days.

The rebel Gen. FORREST, commanding the District of Mississippi, West Tennessee and East Louisiana, has established his headquarters at Jackson, Miss., and is conscripting guerrillas and sending them to Richmond, to be put into the Army of Virginia.

The steamer *Dove* was captured and burned, near Helena, by the rebels. The Fifty-sixth —— Regiment were taken prisoners, and Col. DEAN, commanding, killed.

NEWS FROM WASHINGTON.

Special Dispatches to the New-York Times.

WASHINGTON, Sunday, Feb. 19.

THE TREASURY SECRETARYSHIP.

There are no new developments in regard to the Secretaryship of the Treasury. Mr. MCCULLOUGH's friends are sanguine, as are also those of several other gentlemen whose names are prominent. The President will probably settle the matter during the coming week.

THE PERMITS TO TRADE IN COTTON.

A statement in a dispatch last week that the Committee on Commerce in the House had discovered that money had been paid in some instances for the procurement of cotton permits may mislead the public. It is not alleged, I believe, in any quarter, that money has in any case ever been paid to officers of any department of the Government for such permits. But persons acting as counsel for applicants may possibly have been paid for their services. The policy of granting permits for procuring cotton from the rebel States was adopted by the President after a full consultation with the Cabinet officers and the most careful inquiry into all the reasons for and against it. It was decided upon solely on grounds of public policy, which were very clearly and fully stated in a letter from the President to Gen. CANBY, and it has been carried out with all possible precautions against abuse. If the Committee on Commerce expect to convict the President or the Administration of any improper conduct in this matter, they will in due time discover their mistake.

DESERTERS FROM LEE'S ARMY.

Deserters are arriving daily in large squads from City Point, thus showing that the morale of Gen. LEE's army is not improving any faster than his present military position.

THE ENROLLMENT BILL.

The first thing in order to-morrow in the House is the Enrollment Bill. It is necessary that it should be passed at once, in order that it may facilitate matters in the coming draft.

THE LOAN BILL.

The Ways and Means Committee have a special meeting to-morrow to consider the Loan bill. The committee have delayed it for several days, in the hope that a new Secretary of the Treasury would be appointed who might wish to confer with them upon the subject. They have determined to report it at once to the House, leaving it to the Senate to make such alterations as may be thought necessary, in case a new Secretary is appointed during the coming week.

THE NEW-YORK APPOINTMENTS.

The Senate Commerce Committee who have had the nominations of Collectors and Surveyor for New-York under advisement for some time, on Saturday authorized the Chairman to report them to the Senate for confirmation.

THE STATE GOVERNMENT OF LOUISIANA.

The Judiciary Committee of the Senate reported unanimously in favor of the recognition of Louisiana under her present Constitution and admission of the Senators.

THE EXCHANGE OF PRISONERS.

More Arrivals from the James—The Exchange Rapidly Going On.

FORTRESS MONROE, Friday, Feb. 17.

The steamers *New-York* and *George Leary* arrived here last evening, with released Union prisoners from Richmond, and have sailed for Annapolis. Col. MULFORD remained at Varina to effect the exchange of prisoners as fast as they arrive. Other steamers have gone up the James River with rebel prisoners, and the exchange will be made as rapidly as possible.

Arrival of Released Prisoners at Annapolis.

BALTIMORE, Sunday, Feb. 19.

The *American's* special from Annapolis says 926 paroled men have just arrived from the South, many of them in a most horrible condition. The Government building here will soon be all filled with sick and wounded.

The Constitutional Amendment Ratified by Nevada.

CARSON, Thursday, Feb. 16.

The Nevada Legislature has just ratified the amendment to the Constitution of the United States, abolishing slavery. There was only one vote in each House in the negative—both Democrats.

The Dry Goods Sale at Boston.

BOSTON, Sunday, Feb. 19.

The hotels are filling up with merchants from all sections of the country to attend the trade sale commencing on Tuesday. It will be a great event in the dry goods line, and surpass anything of the kind heretofore known. Over 10,000 bales of goods had been entered up to last evening.

The Overland Telegraph Line.

CHICAGO, Sunday, Feb. 19.

The Overland Telegraph line to the Pacific is now fully repaired, and is in perfect working order. Salt Lake City and New-York have been writing direct without repetition all day.

Movements of Gen. Palmer.

LOUISVILLE, Ky., Saturday, Feb. 18.

Major-Gen. PALMER arrived here this morning.

Sailing of the Steamer St. David.

PORTLAND, Sunday, Feb. 19.

The *St. David* sailed at 1:30 this morning for Londonderry and Liverpool.

Arrivals in the City.

Major-Gen. Benjamin F. Butler, accompanied by Capt. Davenport of his staff, arrived at the Hoffman House at an early hour on Saturday morning. They will proceed to Washington this afternoon.

Com. Mervine, of the United States Navy, Col. W. L. Anderson, Cincinnati; and Geo. W. Dana, Boston, are at the Hoffman House.

FROM EUROPE.

THREE DAYS LATER NEWS

Arrival of the Saxonia from Southampton.

THE NEW REBEL IRON-CLAD.

THE MEXICAN QUESTION IN ENGLAND.

Opening of the British Parliament---The Queen's Speech by Commission.

The Peace Rumors---Excitement in Financial Circles.

Large Rise in United States Securities.

The steamship *Saxonia*, from Southampton on Feb. 8, with three days later news from Europe, arrived here yesterday.

The Peruvian war corvettes *Union* and *American* left Plymouth on Sunday last for Peru.

We have also fuller details of the news by the *Europa*—the mails by which arrived here on Saturday at midnight. From the latter we published, exclusively, in our Sunday edition, the opinion of Mr. W. M. EVARTS as to the legal power of English creditors to collect debts due in the United States in specie or the equivalent of specie. We now give fuller comments bearing on the subject.

OUR PARIS CORRESPONDENCE.

The French-Danish Rebel Iron-clad Ram—Disavowal of Responsibility by the French Government—Suspicious Circumstances—How the Vessel Passed from French into Rebel Hands—The Capture of Fort Fisher, and Gloom of the Rebels.

PARIS, Friday, Feb. 3, 1865.

The French Government denies, no doubt with entire sincerity, all complicity in the affair of the *Olinda*. The Minister of Marine, I understand, declares, that before authorizing the departure of this vessel for Denmark, the contract between ARMAN, her builder, and the Danish Government, was shown him; that there was not, and could not have been, the shadow of a doubt on his mind as to the regularity of the contract, and that, as in the case of the two ARMAN frigates sold to Prussia, she was delivered to her purchasers under the French flag. Up to this point everything was regular, and, so far as the French Government was concerned, perfectly fair; but here arises a question for discussion. The vessel, after being examined by the Danish naval commission, was rejected, as not fulfilling the conditions required in the contract. The French flag had been lowered, and the vessel had passed from under French authority before this commission sat upon her. Are the French, therefore, to blame for lowering their flag before they knew whether the vessel was to be accepted or not? This is the question which has come up for discussion. The French minister declares that they acted in good faith; that after seeing the contract, they supposed their mission was finished when they had delivered the vessel in the Danish port, which had been indicated by the Danish Government as the port of delivery, and that when they abandoned the vessel in that port they had no suspicion of what was going to occur. The French Government promised the late American Minister at Paris, Mr. DAYTON, in the most emphatic manner, that none of the vessels built in French ports, on Confederate account, should ever pass from French into Confederate hands; but the *Olinda*, never having been received by the Danish Government, *has* passed from French into Confederate hands, without any intermediary owner; and as Mr. DAYTON declared for his Government, that all damage done on the high seas by vessels which had passed directly from French into Confederate hands, would be charged to the French Government, the latter, if our Government stands up to this point, will probably be made to pay dear for what at present seems only to be an inadvertence and a want of surveillance.

Was the affair a *ruse* on the part of the rebels? There can hardly be a doubt on this point; and what makes the matter more certain, is the fact that the agent employed by M. ARMAN, and by the rebel agents to conduct the vessel to Copenhagen and back again to the high sea, to be delivered into Confederate hands, was M. ARNOUS DE LA RIVIERE, an elder brother of the Lieutenant of Zouaves, who visited the United States five years ago. M. DE LA RIVIERE was formerly the agent of Mr. WEBB, the ship-builder, of New-York, in the affair of the contract between Mr. WEBB and the Italian Government, and has the reputation of being a more than ordinary shrewd business-man. He is also known to be a rebel sympathiser, and to be leagued more or less with the rebel agents in France. There is ground, therefore, for the belief that it was determined before the vessel started to have her refused by Denmark, and then to pass her under the Confederate flag, for M. DE LA RIVIERE not only conducted the vessel to Copenhagen, but he conveyed her afterward into Confederate hands. Moreover, there seems to have been a ship waiting at a concerted point to furnish the *Olinda* with her armament.

As regards the vessel itself, it is the fifth in the list of those built by M. ARMAN for the Confederates, and is a heavily cuirassed ram. But she is known not to possess high speed, and will probably run a short career. It is well enough however to be on the look-out for her.

In fine, the French Government seems to be actuated by the best sentiments in the matter. The Ministers concerned declare that they have acted in good faith, they profess to be deeply surprised and humiliated at the event, and they utter their regret in the most emphatic way. As soon as the official details arrive from Copenhagen the negotiation of the affair will commence, but in view of the sentiments manifested by the French Government there is no doubt but that the affair can be amicably arranged.

The taking of Fort Fisher and the excitement

Continued on Eighth Page.

Columbia, S.C., in flames after occupation by Federal troops

Ruins in Columbia, February, 1865

General Sherman entering Columbia, February, 1865

The New-York Times.

VOL. XIV......NO. 4184. NEW-YORK, TUESDAY, FEBRUARY 21, 1865. PRICE FOUR CENTS.

GOOD NEWS.

CHARLESTON IN OUR POSSESSION.

The City Abandoned by the Rebels on Saturday Last.

Admiral Dahlgren Takes Possession on the Same Day.

SHERMAN'S GRAND TRIUMPH.

His March Still Onward and Victorious.

THE OCCUPATION OF COLUMBIA.

Advance Northward from that City.

News from Other Portions of the Field.

DISPATCH FROM ADMIRAL DAHLGREN.

WASHINGTON, Monday, Feb. 20.

The following dispatch has been received at the Navy Department:

FLAG-SHIP HARVEST MOON, REBELLION ROADS, CHARLESTON HARBOR, Feb. 18, 1865, VIA FORTRESS MONROE, Feb. 20—7 P. M.

Hon. Gideon Welles, Secretary of the Navy:

SIR: *Charleston was abandoned this morning by the rebels. I am now on my way to the city.*

I have the honor to be, very respectfully, your obedient servant,

JOHN A. DAHLGREN, Rear-Admiral.

[OFFICIAL.]

DISPATCH FROM SECRETARY STANTON.

WAR DEPARTMENT, WASHINGTON, Feb. 20—8 P. M.

Maj.-Gen. Dix, New-York:

The following details of military operations and the condition of affairs in the rebel States, taken from the Richmond papers of to-day have been forwarded by Gen. GRANT. This department has received no other intelligence in relation to the operations of our forces against Fort Anderson and Wilmington. A dispatch from Admiral DAHLGREN to the Secretary of the Navy, dated at Charleston Harbor, 18th, says *that the rebels were abandoning Charleston that morning, and he was now on his way to that city.*

EDWIN M. STANTON, Secretary of War.

CITY POINT, Feb. 20.

Hon. Edwin M. Stanton, Secretary of War:

The following paragraphs are extracted from the Richmond papers of to-day:

We now know that Charleston was evacuated on Tuesday last, and that on Friday the enemy took possession of Columbia. It is reported that our forces, under Gen. BEAUREGARD, are moving in the direction of Charlotte. Official intelligence was recived at the War Office last night, that *Sherman was, on yesterday morning, advancing toward and was near Winsboro*, a point on the railroad leading to Charlotte and thirty miles north of Columbia. Charlotte is thronged with refugees from Columbia, who report that some of WHEELER'S cavalry plundered the city before the evacuation. Up to Tuesday last it was uncertain whether Columbia would come within the immediate range of SHERMAN'S purposes, and consequently the public mind was not prepared for such an early solution of the question. The Government had, however, just two weeks ago taken the precaution to remove its specie deposited there amounting to several millions of dollars, and within the past few days all of the dies and plates belonging to the Treasury Department, together with the supplies of Treasury notes on hand, were safely conveyed away. *The enemy being in possession of Branchville, Orangeburgh and Kingsville, precluded movements on the roads leading to Charleston*, and an unfortunate accident upon the Charlotte road from Columbia, prevented the authorities from making use of that avenue to save other valuable materials in the city. A large quantity of medical stores belonging to the Government were there, one-half of which were saved, and the rest, for want of time and transportation, was destroyed. The presses and fixtures for printing Treasury notes, in the establishments of EVANS & COGGSWELL, and KEATING & BALL, were necessarily abandoned, together with the other extensive machinery of those well known firms. The first-named establishment had one hundred and two printing presses, and was unquestionably the largest and best equipped publishing house in the South.

The enemy's forces operating west of Columbia, reached the banks of the Congaree, opposite the city, on Thursday evening, and threw in a number of shells, to which our batteries responded. A portion of this column moved up the river during the night, and crossed the Saluda and Broad Rivers, the main tributaries of the Congaree, which meet near Columbia, a few miles above the city. During the movement Gen. BEAUREGARD evacuated the city, and on Friday morning the enemy entered and took possession without opposition. Our troops were withdrawn to a position some twenty miles from Columbia, where they remained on yesterday.

The enemy's force, entering Columbia, consisted of SHERMAN'S main army, a large portion of which immediately moved up the Charlotte road, *while another portion moved down in the direction of Charleston. The latter city has doubtless ere this been evacuated.*

FROM CHARLESTON.

CHARLESTON, Tuesday, Feb. 14.

The enemy's gunboats and one monitor have been shelling our picket lines on James Island all day. All quiet in our immediate front. Nothing definite from above. The enemy keep up a steady shelling of the city.

CHARLESTON, Wednesday, Feb. 15.

All quiet along our lines. The enemy this morning are reported to be moving in force near Columbia, on the Lexington-road. It is reported that they crossed the Congaree to-day.

OPERATIONS BELOW WILMINGTON.

WILMINGTON, Saturday, Feb. 18.

The enemy shelled Fort Anderson furiously yesterday afternoon, nearly all night, and this morning. It is reported that a land force also attacked our forces at Anderson, but were repulsed. Cannonading is still going on (at 1 P. M.) We have no particulars.

RAID ON THE VIRGINIA AND TENNESSEE RAILROAD.

A dispatch has been received here stating that a force of the enemy, 4,000 strong, 2,000 of it cavalry, are advancing from Knoxville, and had reached Greenville, which is 54 miles from Bristol. This expedition is supposed to be another raid on the Virginia and Tennessee Railroad.

MOVEMENTS IN NORTH CAROLINA.

The telegraph operator at Weldon reported on yesterday that a raid from Washington or Newbern, N. C., was in progress, the supposed destination of the raiders being Rocky Mount Station, on the Wilmington Road, in Edgecomb County. The wires continued to work during yesterday evening through to Wilmington however, from which it would appear that they had not struck the road.

A movement of the enemy was reported yesterday in heavy force upon Kinston, N. C., and it was supposed in official quarters that FOSTER'S forces had been moved up to Newbern.

A cavalry raid was also reported in the direction of Tarboro.' The force moving from Newbern has fifty or sixty pieces of artillery. We shall hear more of these movements in a few days. We are quite certain that they are in progress as we write.

THE EXCHANGE OF PRISONERS.

Col. HATCH, one of our Commissioners of Exchange, has gone to Wilmington, at which place he will, during the week, exchange ten thousand prisoners. We may remark here that the exchange of prisoners on the James River will at the same time go on uninterruptedly.

AFFRAY WITH REBEL DESERTERS.

A desperate affair occurred last Tuesday in Lunenburgh County between some deserters from the Confederate army and some of the Ninth Virginia Cavalry, aided by citizens. Several on both sides were wounded. The deserters were finally captured.

PAROLED PRISONERS ROBBED.

Gen. EWELL, commanding the Department of Henrico, reports a wholesale robbery of nearly one hundred paroled prisoners, on Saturday night, between Camp Lee and the city. Other robberies of returned prisoners are reported as occuring in the streets of Richmond.

U. S. GRANT, Lieut.-General.

SHERMAN'S GRAND MARCH.

From the Richmond Examiner, Feb. 18.

The State Capital of South Carolina has fallen. Columbia is in the hands of SHERMAN. *If the mere overrunning of the country were conquering it, the Yankee enemy might begin to boast of the subjugation of South Carolina*, for so far they have advanced and penetrated to the very heart of the State without serious opposition; but the only value of that advance, for the general purposes of a campaign, consists in its *being a step toward cooperating with Grant in the investment of Richmond. Thus Sherman's enterprise is only beginning* The future plans or present dispositions of BEAUREGARD are unknown here. The little Confederate army however, is safe, and may yet lead SHERMAN such a dance as GREENE led CORNWALLIS over those same rivers and swamps. If the Federal army cannot reach the Danville Railroad, then it had better have staid in Atlanta all this while. But "it is a far cry to Lochow." It is true the Federals can gratify their sense of "poetical justice," or, as we should say, their petty malice by laying waste the unprotected homesteads of that noble State, and wreaking upon the women and children of South Carolinians their noble revenge for the heroic resistance they have encountered on every field at the hands of the men; yet that is not conquering the country. On the contrary, it is making it unconquerable where the breed of men is of the right kind. There is reason to believe that Gen. BEAUREGARD is carrying out a deliberate design, and that SHERMAN is near the end of his triumphs.

We may regard this audacious march of the enemy through the heart of South Carolina as one of the consequences of removing JOHNSTON from the command of our Army of the Tennessee. A large portion of the *Examiner* to-day is occupied by that General's report of his campaign, long since furnished by him, and called for by Congress, but withheld from the public until this moment. It will be read with great interest; and we shall hereafter have somewhat to say by way of comment on it.

FROM NORTH CAROLINA.

Disruption of the Rebel Feeling in the State—What the "Conservatives" Desire—Gen. Sherman to be Gladly Welcomed—Affairs at Newbern.

NEWBERN, N. C., Thursday, Feb. 16.

The fall of Fort Fisher is working a revolution in the minds of the people of this State, which, if there is any meaning in half the threats emanating from the State Capitol, must result in the separation of North Carolina from the Confederacy, soon after Raleigh is garrisoned by the Union forces, which is the necessary protection required by the conservative party, a majority of whom, says a rebel paper, favor a return to the Union, even with emancipation.

The enemy are removing their supplies from Wilmington, with a view, it is thought, of evacuating the city.

It is estimated that there is over one hundred and sixty millions of dollars' worth of cotton, stored from Wilmington, along the line of the railroads reaching into South Carolina and the southern part of North Carolina, which the enemy will order to be burned, as soon as our forces approach.

SHERMAN'S movements are regarded with much alarm by the rebel papers of this State, which predict that he will attempt to hold Goldsboro' and Raleigh.

The Raleigh, N. C., *Standard* and Raleigh *Progress*, and the other conservative papers in this State, are paying high tributes to the military genius of Gen. SHERMAN, whose approach they welcome with open manifestations of joy.

The experiment adopted here last year by the Treasury Department, of leasing abandoned plantations to both white and black persons, who were placed on an equal footing in this respect, has brought forth results highly favorable to the blacks. In the important report just published by Col. HEATON, the Supervising Treasury Agent, he says: "The sanguine expectation, too often indulged in, that legislation may now be exclusively depended upon, as the sovereign antidote for all the temporal ills the freedman is heir to, is fallacious and visionary."

ARMY OF THE JAMES.

An Attempt at a Surprise—Story of a Deserter—The Virginia Soldiers.

From Our Own Correspondent.

HEADQUARTERS ARMY OF THE JAMES, IN THE FIELD, Friday, Feb. 17, 1865.

The enemy made a feeble and spasmodic attempt at about 1 o'clock this morning, which only ended in proving to themselves and to our men—if further proof were needed—the utter demoralization that has overtaken the whole body of LEE'S army now before Richmond. Some 350 of their men, led on by Maj. SHELTON, started to make an attack upon a coveted portion of our right wing, a little to the left of its centre; and doubtless intending to follow up the new movement, if successful, as Gens. STUART and RICKETT were both near the breastworks to witness the proceeding. They came on very slowly and stealthily; but our men being fully prepared, poured a volley into them, at which, after firing but five or six shots, they broke and ran, and all the efforts of their officers could not rally them again. I obtained these particulars from one of the men of PICKETT'S own division, who took part in it, is one of over thirty who have come in to Gen. ORD'S headquarters this morning, and who assured me that it was not cowardice that made them act so, for they have been in many battles, but merely the determination fast rooting itself among the men *not to fight any more for the infernal despotism which they at last discover is closing around them rapidly.*

This man was far above the usual run of rebel deserters who come into our lines. His language and bearing denoted the gentleman of intelligence and culture, in spite of his dirty gray suit; while there was an earnestness and want of affectation about him, that made it impossible to doubt the truth of what he was telling me—even if he could have had any possible inducement for falsifying to the unauthoritative individual with whom he was conversing alone.

This young man assured me that, in spite of all the false statements and loud blustering to be found in the Richmond papers and among the rebel orators, this last peace conference, and still more the action of the rebel authorities respecting it, so far from having roused the army to any new enthusiasm, has only filled them with deeper disgust and despair, by proving not only the utter hopelessness of the cause for which they have been fighting, but the egregious falsehoods by which their leaders are trying to hoodwink them. He says that their Congressmen—among others Messrs. BALDWIN and FLORNOY—have been round to harangue the troops, telling them that the hopes of the Confederacy were never brighter, that the condition of the army was never better, and such a number of "ridiculous lies," (to use his own terms,) that the men had fairly to laugh in spite of their anger. He gave me an account of how such grandiloquent resolutions as are being passed among the army—such proceedings, for instance, as those of the "Louisiana Guard Artillery," (LEE'S provost guard,) and others, are manufactured wholesale. They call the men out in line, when an officer reads out the resolutions, calls upon those who agree to say "aye." and, no matter how few may respond affirmatively, walks off pronouncing the decision *unanimous*. Out of 450 men in his own regiment, drawn up to pronounce upon the resolutions not to give up fighting so long as they had a cartridge left or a foot of ground to stand on, there were not over fifty, including officers, who cried "aye," and yet the resolutions were declared unanimously passed.

One thing, it seems, we may safely count upon, and that is that the Virginian soldiers are determined, *en masse*, not to fight off Virginian soil, and that all those who can will desert to a man, before they will follow LEE out of their own State. Upon this point my informant was as positive and earnest as he was in his assurances of the universal disgust that the soldiers felt at the horrible life they are leading, and, indeed, at everything connected with the so-called Confederacy. He says that he fully believes one-half of PICKETT'S whole division will be voluntarily within our lines during the next few weeks; and certainly facts daily transpiring all along our lines tend to justify this belief. Thirty deserters came in to these headquarters yesterday, twenty-eight to-day up to the present time of writing; and it is a notorious fact that in spite of the order recently issued by LEE to tempt his deserters back—holding sugar in one hand and a lasso in the other—deserters have, since the issue of that order, *become far more frequent, and not one has returned to their lines.*

I send you a batch of orders recently issued by Maj.-Gen. ORD, some of which have not, I believe, been published in the newspapers, and all showing the great amount of interest which this much-respected Commander is taking in the well-being, efficiency and discipline of the army he commands. Another very important order, respecting sutlers and traders in the army, will be issued to-morrow, based upon a similar order already in practice at Fortress Monroe.

The roads along our whole line are in a terrible state, from the effect of the prevailing rains, and so long as they continue so, there does not seem the remotest chance of either side attempting any important movement.

J. R. HAMILTON.

FROM FORTRESS MONROE.

The Exchange of Prisoners—News from Fort Fisher.

FORTRESS MONROE, Sunday, Feb. 19.

The steamers *New-York* and *George Leary* arrived here last night from Annapolis, loaded with rebel prisoners, and sailed early this morning for Varuna.

The steamer *Neures* arrived here this morning from Beaufort, N. C., with twenty-four rebel prisoners.

The steamer *Perit* arrived here this afternoon from Fort Fisher, bringing mails and passengers. When the *Perit* left, Friday 17, fighting had just commenced between our forces and the rebels.

Deaths in United States General Hospital, Fort Monroe, Va., during Week Ending Feb. 18:

Correspondence of the New-York Times.

FORT MONROE, Saturday, Feb. 18, 1865.

The following is a list of the deaths in this hospital during the week ending with this date:

Robt. H. P. Crabb, citizen prisoner.	Squire Blakeley, Co. E, 10th United States.
Sam'l Thornton, Co. C, 6th U. S. Infantry.	James Yeoman, Co. D, 107th United States.
Wm. J. Farra, Co. B, 203d Pennsylvania.	John Rollins, Co. C, 107th United States.
Wm. Disbrow, Co. I, 115th New-York.	Benjamin Reece, Co. K, 29th United States.
Abraham Kaler, Co. E, 203d Pennsylvania.	Lewis Kennard, Co. C, 107th United States.
Abner W. Porter, Co. K, 16th N. Y. Heavy Art.	Samuel Thompson, Co. C, 16th New-York.
Thomas Smith, 32d V. R. Corps.	Aurin T. Prout, Co. G, 12th N. Y. Cavalry.
Geo. M. Dickerson, Co. H, 117th United States.	Michael Smith, Co. E, 10th U. S. Infantry.
Sergt. Robt. Shaw, Co. E, 142d New-York.	James H. Miles, citizen prisoner.
Aaron Dillingham, Co. B, 115th New-York.	Andrew Brown, Co. K, 30th United States.

We have received nearly 700 patients this week from the hospitals at the front, about two-thirds of whom are colored, making the whole number now in the hospital about 3,400. The new camp, containing about 1,100, all colored, is now very full. The late very "*cold snap*" at the first of this week seemed to set hard on some of the patients, which, together with the goodly number of bad cases among the new patients, has *increased* the mortality this week. Much of this week has been damp, heavy, wet weather, and unfavorable for the sick and wounded. We expect to celebrate WASHINGTON'S ensuing Birthday.

A. S. B.

THE POSTAL MONEY-ORDER SYSTEM

Its Adaptation to the Needs of the Armies Before Richmond.

CITY POINT, Va., Monday, Feb. 20.

The Postmaster-General has designated City Point a money-order office, so as to extend to the armies operating against Richmond the privileges of the postal money-order system. Persons who desire to send money away can purchase drafts or orders, payable at money-order post-offices throughout the North, at the following rates, viz.: For an order of $1 and not exceeding $10, ten cents; for an order for more than $10 and not exceeding $20, fifteen cents; for an order for more than $20 and not exceeding $30, twenty cents.

Thirty dollars is the limit of a single order, but more than one order can be obtained by the same person at the same rates.

These orders must be sent in an envelope by themselves, which envelope will not carry any information whatever, so that if the order should by any chance fall into wrong hands, it would be impossible to be collected by the same.

The order itself does not carry any information as to who will present the order for the payment, but a duplicate order, which is sent by the Postmaster here to the Postmaster upon whom the order is drawn, does convey full information as to who will present the order for payment and also who purchased it.

It will thus be seen that if the rules governing the system be observed by the remitter, almost perfect safety in transmission is secured.

These drafts may be indorsed over to second persons by the person in whose favor they are drawn, but more than one indorsement is forbidden by law.

Further information as to the working of the system will be furnished to those who may desire it, upon application.

Officers of the army are requested to give this circular as much publicity as possible.

DAVID B. PARKER,
Special Agent of Post-office Department with the Armies before Richmond.

Approved.

By Command of Lieut.-Gen. GRANT.

T. S. BOWERS, A. A. G.

FROM THE ARMY OF THE POTOMAC.

Stories from Deserters—A Flag of Truce.

WASHINGTON, Monday, Feb. 20.

Information from the Army of the Potomac late as yesterday morning, reports all quiet.

Deserters are constantly coming in, and are more numerous than for a long time. They have averaged over seventy a day for the past week. Among them several officers.

The utmost despondency prevails through their ranks since the late fight, and they seem determined to keep the field no longer, as they claim they can never gain their independence, and see no reason why they should remain and be all killed. They also say that deserting is so general to the rear of their own lines that LEE has issued an order to arrest every man found half a mile away from the camp or post.

One man said his company was thirty strong a week ago, but that fifteen had disappeared since, ten to the United States and five to their homes.

Many of the deserters bring their arms with them.

A flag-of-truce appeared in front of the Second Corps on Saturday, asking for the bodies of some rebel officers killed at the late battle of Hatcher's Run. Their request was finally granted, and their bodies conveyed to the rebel lines.

JOHN HOEPLER, of the One Hundred and Twenty-fourth New-York, was executed on Friday for desertion.

FROM NEW-ORLEANS.

NEW-ORLEANS, Monday, Feb. 13, VIA CAIRO, Monday, Feb. 20.

The rebel Col. GRIFFITH, commanding at Woodville, La., has placed an embargo on the passage of cotton and citizens into the Federal lines.

The annual report of THOMAS W. CONWAY, Superintendent of the Bureau of Free Labor, shows the following result: The number of freedmen now under Mr. CONWAY'S charge, supported by the Government is 14,000; expense to the Government for the year, $113,500. Number of freedmen on plantations in the department, managed by the bureau, 50,000; on plantations under culture by military order, 15,000. Amount of property transferred to treasury, 1,000,240.

The cotton market is poorly supplied. Prices are better; low middling, 72c.@73c.; middlings, 75c.; sugar, 21¾c.@25c.

Escape of the Granite City from Colcasieu—Increase of Blockade-running on the Texas Coast since the Capture of Wilmington—Mobile Evacuated by Gen. Maury—Selma the next Stronghold.

From Our Own Correspondent.

NEW-ORLEANS, Sunday, Feb. 5, 1865.

The *Granite City* has at last escaped to sea with a cargo of cotton. On what particular night she ran the blockade, or to what post she has gone, has not been ascertained.

It will be remembered that both the *Granite City* and *Wave* were captured by the rebels last May in Colcasieu River, not far from Sabine Pass. Since that time both vessels have been watching their opportunity to dodge out and gain the open sea; but so strict has been the blockade, and so narrow and difficult the channel, that before this last month they had not even made the attempt. Refugees have informed us that the guns were removed from the *Granite City* and *Wave* shortly after their capture. The *Wave* is still in the lake.

The *Granite City* is a small gunboat of light draught, and not very fast. She was captured originally while attempting to run the blockade, and was at once bought by the Government.

I do not think there is much danger to be apprehended from her, even were she to obtain armament in some English port. While she is large enough and fast enough to overtake and destroy merchantmen, she is too slow to escape even our blockading gunboats.

Now that Wilmington is closed, Savannah in our possession, Charleston threatened, Galveston is of course the only remaining port of any size or importance that is left to the Confederacy.

Blockade-running is on the increase here all along the coast, but there are very few vessels in this squadron that are fast enough to intercept those elegant Clyde-built swallows that literally *wing* their way from Nassau to Galveston. There is always a Government steamer stationed off the Rio Grande, but of course the officers are powerless to prevent the extensive trade in cotton carried on by vessels in the neutral waters of Mexico.

We are obliged to lie still and witness the loading and unloading of scores of vessels on the Western Coast, all the profits of which trade are as directly beneficial to the rebels as is the blockade-running at Galveston of Velloseo. It is not uncommon for a fleet of a hundred vessels to be anchored off the Rio Grande, waiting for supplies of cotton, or transacting some other kind of traffic for the benefit of the rebellion.

I have just been conversing with an attache of the army who has recently returned from Pascagoula. There is no longer any doubt in regard to the evacuation of Mobile. As a military post it has been abandoned by Gen. MAURY, and Selma is being fortified as rapidly as possible. A severe conscription was ordered about two weeks that sent hundreds of refugees into our ranks. They all confirm the previous account of the horrible destitution of the poorer classes. They are starving, and see no hope for deliverance except from the occupation of the city by the Federal army.

Gen. GRANGER has removed his troops from Pascagoula to the vicinity, probably finding the City of Mobile too easy a prize and too expensive a one also for the Commissary and Quartermaster's department.

Business is dull in the city, owing to the incessant and agitating rumors of fever, and to the severe regulations of Gen. CANBY.

The theatres are now closed on Sunday nights by order of Gen. HURLBURT. This is a new era for New-Orleans, where the Sabbath has always been the grand pleasure day.

G. M. B.

From the Distant West.

ST. LOUIS, Monday, Feb. 20.

Col. LIVINGSTON, commanding on the Plains, reports two fights near Mud Springs, on the 4th and the 9th inst., between nearly two thousand Indians and about two hundred men of the Eleventh Ohio and Seventh Iowa Cavalry, under Lieut. COLLINS. The Indians were driven off with the loss of of forty-five killed. Our loss was two killed and twenty-one wounded. The Indians went north, numbering seven hundred lodges, driving two herds of captured cattle with them.

Gen. EWING telegraphs from Washington that he has made an arrangement for raising thirteen regiments of cavalry in this State for one year's service, which will relieve Missouri from the draft.

Cotton, 74c.@75c. for middling; receipts 725 bales and 166 sacks. Hemp, $1 45@$1 60 for undressed, and $2 65@$2 85 for dressed. Flour dull; single extra $9, and $10 for double extra. Wheat declined 8c.@10c.; quoted at $1 77@$1 95 for prime to choice. Corn steady at $1 05@$1 10. Oats 88c.@91c.

FROM HAVANA.

Movement of the Blockade-runners.

HAVANA, Wednesday, Feb. 15, 1865.

Since my last no items of interest have transpired.

The *Columbia* arrived on the night of the 13th, having stopped off Indian River to furnish mails to some of the Blockading Squadron.

The United States gunboat *Proteus* left on Sunday last, having completed her repairs.

The *Iuka* is nearly ready for sea, and will leave in a day or two.

Several of the blockade runners have started out and returned, reporting in distress, though it is generally supposed to be the fact that they meet our cruisers.

The steamers will probably be sold now, as the blockade-running is broken up.

Galveston is useless. Guns and powder are as cheap there as here, and there is no cotton to bring back.

The coolie-trade is opening again. The French ship *Medoc*, 604 tons, arrived on the 12th inst. with three hundred and five of these poor duped white slaves.

The secesh are now going to purchase small schooners to run to the coast of Florida.

From Cairo.

CAIRO, Monday, Feb. 20.

Two hundred and fifty bales of cotton passed to-day for St. Louis and 160 for Cincinnati. The Mississippi Central Railroad has been repaired by the rebels, and the cars are running to Grenada.

Twelve hundred hogs crossed Pearl River for the Cuba Station, where they are to be slaughtered for the rebel army.

From Memphis.

MEMPHIS, Friday, Feb. 17.

Some thirteen persons are said to have been indicted for treason at the last sitting of the District Court of Tennessee. Several of these persons have been arrested and lodged in military prisons.

Steamers continue to be fired into near Helena.

From California.

SAN FRANCISCO, Saturday, Feb. 18.

Arrived ship *Herald of the Morning* from Boston.

Heavy storms in Oregon had done much damage to roads and bridges.

Rain is falling at intervals in California.

NEWS FROM REBEL SOURCES.

Affairs Below Wilmington—From the Petersburgh Lines—Semmes a Rear-Admiral—Mosby—Gen. Johnson's Report—The Peace Conference.

Special Dispatch to the New-York Times.

WASHINGTON, Monday, Feb. 20.

GEN. JOHNSTON'S REPORT.

The Richmond *Examiner* of Saturday publishes entire the official report of Gen. JOE JOHNSTON, in regard to the operations of the Army of the Tennessee. The document fills four columns of that journal, and is introduced by the following preliminary remarks upon the causes of the delay in the publication of this report:

We give below Gen. JOHNSTON'S report of operations of the Army of Tennessee, the seal of secrecy which has been so long kept upon it having been broken yesterday by the Confederate States Senate. The report is accompanied by certain correspondence on the part of President DAVIS and Secretary SEDDON. The latter, under date of the 3d of January, says that he had delayed forwarding a copy, because, "at first, he doubted whether, from its tendency to induce controversy, it could be communicated without prejudice to the public service." President DAVIS, in his official letter to the Senate of the 4th of January, directs attention to this suggestion of his then Secretary, and adds that it is "not advisable" to publish the report, unless accompanied with certain "correspondence," to "explain events." It is understood that the Senate, having waited in vain for the Executive eclairissement promised in this correspondence, and having applied for it without effect since the 4th of January, yesterday determined that the report should no longer be suppressed from the public.

The report is dated Vineville, Ga., Oct. 20, 1864, and covers the whole series of operations from the time JOE JOHNSTON took command of the army, Dec., 1863, up to the time of his removal from command, the 18th of July, 1864. It is exceedingly interesting, and gives some curious revelations of the distracted policy that has lately ruled the fortunes of the Confederacy. Gen. JOHNSTON makes an elaborate defence of this whole military conduct, especially with reference to his retreating before SHERMAN which was so severely censured at the time.

The Richmond *Dispatch*, alluding to the publication of this report, says that it will give fresh impetus to the great Bragg-Johnston-Hood controversy which, for six months, has engrossed so much of the attention of the press and the country.

FROM NORTH CAROLINA.

THE SITUATION AT WILMINGTON.

From the Richmond Whig, Feb. 18.

The Wilmington *Journal*, of the 13th, says that active skirmishing was going on all day Saturday between the forces at Sugar Loaf and those of the enemy below. Toward night they advanced in force, driving in our skirmishers, and making three attacks on our main line, all of which were handsomely repulsed with considerable, we might say heavy, loss to the enemy. Our casualties were about 20. Finally the lines were resumed pretty nearly as before, and all remained quiet yesterday, with the exception of some shelling by the enemy's fleet. On Saturday one of the monitors in the river threw some of her 15-inch shells at Fort Anderson, with the effect of killing one and wounding another of our men.

THE PETERSBURGH LINES.

From the Richmond Dispatch, Feb. 18.

Several heavy guns were heard in the direction of Dutch Gap yesterday evening. The cause of the firing has not been explained, but probably it was some wet guns which were being fired off.

On Wednesday and Thursday some movement was going on in GRANT'S camp opposite Petersburgh. Deserters state that GRANT has sent eight thousand men to City Point since Saturday, and say it is the impression in the Yankee army that this force is to be sent to Newbern or to reinforce SHERMAN. SHERMAN does not want reinforcements. TERRY, at Wilmington, may require more.

LOSS OF THE FLAG-OF-TRUCE BOAT.

The Richmond *Examiner* of the 18th gives particulars of the blowing-up of the flag-of-truce boat *Schultz* by one of their own torpedoes, which are the same as already published, with the exception that it was thought all on board perished. The *Examiner* says:

Two negro firemen were killed by the explosion, and two soldiers, who had gone down as guards of the Yankee prisoners, were blown into the water and drowned. Two other of the guards were rescued from the water.

There were some seven or eight of the Ambulance Committee on the *Shultz* at the time of the explosion who were saved on the wreck and taken from it by boats of the *Allison*, and Mr. ANDREW JOHNSON was thrown overboard, but swam back to the wreck as it floated past him.

THE JAMES RIVER FLEET.

From the Richmond Whig, Feb. 18.

It is stated that Commander RAPHAEL SEMMES, of the *Alabama*, has been made Rear-Admiral, and will take command of the James River Squadron, in place of Commodore MITCHELL, now commanding.

GEN. JOHNSTON'S REPORT.

From the Richmond Whig, Feb. 18.

Gen. JOHNSTON'S report of his campaign from Dalton to Atlanta was yesterday made public by the Confederate Senate, and ordered to be printed. The publication of this report will give a fresh impetus to the great Bragg-Johnston-Hood controversy, which, for six months, has engrossed so much of the attention of the press and country.

COL. MOSBY.

From the Richmond Sentinel, Feb. 18.

Col. MOSBY was in Lynchburgh on Wednesday. He expects to return to his command in a few days.

BURNING REBEL COTTON.

PEOPLE ADVISED TO RESIST IT.

From the Richmond Whig, Feb. 18.

The Augusta *Chronicle* advises the people of that city to resist the burning of cotton there. It says: "War is to protect the property of citizens, not to destroy it. The same "Yankee" paper praises the late speech of Mr. ECHOLS, and urges him to go ahead. Mr. ECHOLS could not have received a more solemn warning.

THE REBEL FINANCES.

HOW SHALL THE FUNDS BE RAISED.

From the Richmond Examiner, Feb 17.

Although we are arrived at the middle of February, Congress is all at sea in its action and opinions on the subject of taxation. Legislation upon the taxes involves the settlement of the currency; and thus two of the great difficulties of the crisis are as yet untouched.

The wisdom and patriotism of Congress and the country find themselves confronted by four vital and perplexing problems; first, the question of men for the army; second, the question of supplies; third, the question of revenue; and fourth, that of the currency. The first of these great problems is in the rapid process of solution; we shall soon have armies sufficiently strong to meet the enemy on every field. The question of supplies is more difficult, but there is little doubt that supplies will appear from some source or other, as they are required. It is very probable that if Gen. LEE will establish some direct communication between himself and the people, and get rid of the swarm of intermediaries who harry the country and really intercept from the armies the supplies which would be willingly forwarded to them, much of the present restriction in the commissariat would disappear. These subjects lie more within the sphere of the military authority than with Congress.

The great business of this body is with taxation and revenue, and as yet nothing has been done on these important subjects. The demands of the Treasury for the calendar year upon which we have just entered, are very heavy. They may as well be candidly stated, for it is always best to look our liabilities plainly in the face. Shutting one's eyes upon them was never known to diminish or to exorcise them.

The Secretary of the Treasury tells us in his report of the 7th of November last, (page 11,) that he will require, for the expenditures of the Government

for the year 1865	$600 000,000
To this amount must be added, for the redemption of old issue Treasury notes	60,000,000
For the then estimated amount of the floating debt, $114 000,000, since ascertained to amount to	296 000,000
Amount required for 1865	$1 [illegible] 000,000

This is rather an under than an over statement of liabilities; for it must be recollected that since the month of November last the currency has materially depreciated; and that an estimate on that day for $600 000,000 is not likely to embrace the actual cost of the war under the subsequent depreciation.

It is difficult to conjecture at this stage of the debate what precise measure Congress will fall upon to meet this thousand millions of annual expenditure. The majority of the Finance Committee of the House have reported the following scheme of taxation and estimate of receipts from other sources:

Ten per cent. tax on three billions of property supposed now to be held in the Confederate States, within reach of assessors and collectors	$300,000,000	
Tax on incomes, trades, professions, &c., including specific tax	150,000,000	
To be paid in currency and certificates of indebtedness	$150,000,000	
Value to the Government of the tax in kind, credit for which to be repealed	148,000,000	$500,000,000
Deficit		$160,000,000

To be supplied from the following sources:

First.—From sale of six per cent. untaxable bonds.

Second.—From loans on call certificates and use of deposits, in new offices of deposit to be created by law.

Third.—From sale of cotton on hand owned by the Government, for specie or foreign bills.

Whatever may be the demerits of this scheme of revenue, the principal objection urged against it by its opponents is wholly untenable; to wit: that it imposes too heavy a rate of taxation. *Ten dollars in currency upon the ante-war valuation of a hundred dollars in specie, is very far from being a severe tax.* A hundred dollars in specie is equivalent to five thousand in currency; and a tax of ten dollars on the value of five thousand dollars is only at the rate of two mills in the dollar, or one-fifth of one per cent. If to this tax upon valuation be added the tax in kind upon crops, which is estimated to be one per cent. upon the capital employed in production, the total rate of taxation would be only one and one-fifth per cent., or at the rate of a dollar and twenty cents in specie upon the value, under old assessments, of a hundred dollars. To oppose such a tax as too high, in the military emergency which is now upon our country, when all property is at stake, is to sport with the vital interests of society, and to insult the intelligence and patriotism of the people. The people will not only be able to pay so diminutive a tax, but they will be glad to find that so small a contribution will really suffice for a time so serious as the present.

It is not intended in these paragraphs to urge the passage of any particular bill, or to espouse any scheme of finance now before Congress. But really the objection to a measure as too severe because it imposes a rate of taxation amounting only to one and one-fifth per cent., seems too untimely and too unpatriotic to be tolerated with patience.

FOREIGN INTERVENTION.

From the Chattanooga (Selma) Rebel.

We have never had the slightest confidence in foreign intervention as an agency in the termination of the war. That England and France would gladly see our independence established, and the Yankee Government compelled to stop its warfare, we do not doubt. It is so manifestly to their interest that the colossal power of the United States Government, as it existed before the war, should be reduced and divided, and two Governments, hostile to each other, and having no identity of interest, established on its ruins, that there is no room to doubt that they do earnestly desire it. But neither England or France dare interfere alone, and their rival interests will not permit them to act together. They can better afford to maintain a great pauper population, thrown out of employment by the want of cotton, than to incur the risk of the tremendous expenses of a war which might result from interference. They are governed by their interests precisely as we would be under similar circumstances. Their interests lie in another direction, and like prudent people, they follow them, regardless of our sufferings, or that of their own people. *The intervention humbug is now very thoroughly exploded*, and all such reports are received by the mass of the people of the Confederacy with a smile of incredulity.

—The Buffalo Art Gallery was inaugurated Thursday evening. Hon. MILLARD FILLMORE acting as master of ceremonies, the President of the Academy. Mr. S. S. JEWETT made a speech, and was followed by Mr. DORSHEIMER. Rev. Dr. CHESTER delivered a brief o[illegible]

The New-York Times.

VOL. XIV......NO. 4192. NEW-YORK, THURSDAY, MARCH 2, 1865. PRICE FOUR CENTS.

THE SOUTH.

Great Excitement in the Rebel Capital.

THE ABANDONMENT OF RICHMOND

The Removal of Guns and Military Stores in Progress.

CONSTERNATION OF THE CITIZENS.

Unseemly Flight of Rebel Congressmen—Congress Reduced to a Mere Skeleton.

Extraordinary Article from the Richmond Examiner.

The Fall of Richmond the Fall of the Confederacy.

The Prospective Westward Flight of the Rebel Army.

VIRGINIA.

THE PROPOSED ABANDONMENT OF RICHMOND.

Special Dispatch to the New-York Times.

WASHINGTON, Wednesday, March 1.

Richmond papers of Monday contained very important admissions. The *Sentinel* admits that the removal of guns and stores from Richmond is going on, and endeavors to quiet the apprehensions of the people. The *Sentinel* says that the members of the rebel Congress have fled one by one until there is only a quorum left for business. Gen. LEE begs that Congress will not now adjourn, and leave his hands fettered and unprepared for further resistance.

From the Richmond Examiner, Feb. 27.

In the extraordinary message which Mr. DAVIS recently addressed to Congress he declared that "if the campaign against Richmond had resulted in success instead of failure; if we had been compelled to evacuate Richmond as well as Atlanta, the Confederacy would have remained as erect and defiant as ever. Nothing could have been changed in the purpose of its Government, in the indomitable valor of its troops, or in the unquenchable spirit of its people. The baffled and disappointed foe would in vain have scanned the reports of your proceedings at some new legislative seat for any indication that progress had been made in his gigantic task of conquering a free people. There are no vital points, on the preservation of which the continued existence of the Confederacy depends. There is no military success of the enemy which can accomplish its destruction. Not the fall of Richmond, nor Wilmington, nor Charleston, nor Savannah, nor Mobile, nor of all combined, can affect the issue of the present contest." In the African Church, a fortnight ago, he reiterated these extravagant propositions. Mr. BENJAMIN afterward took up the theme on the same rostrum, and spoke of evacuating this city with equal flippancy. Inconsiderate persons and newspapers, we observe with pain, repeat the same ideas; as if they positively desired the country to be taught that the abandonment of this vital position would not only be of no injury to the Confederacy, but of positive advantage.

Let not this fatal error be harbored till it takes root in the imagination. *The evacuation of Richmond would be the loss of all respect and authority toward the Confederate Government, the disintegration of the army, and the abandonment of the scheme of an independent Southern Confederation. The war would, after that, speedily degenerate into an irregular contest, in which passion would have more to do than purpose; which would have no other object than the mere defence or present safety of those immediately persisting in it. The hope of establishing a Confederacy and securing its recognition among nations, would be gone forever. The common sense of the country, the instinct of every man and woman in the land, contradicts the idea that any possibility of an independent South would remain after its capital was abandoned, its Government set adrift, and its army withdrawn into the solitudes of the interior.*

It is idle to pretend that Richmond is of no more importance than Savannah, Atlanta, Mobile or Norfolk, and that its fall would not be fatal to the Confederacy. If it had not been a vital point, why has so much effort been expended for its reduction and in its defence? It has been the great objective point of the enemy through four successive campaigns. The Confederacy has spared no pains or exertions, no cost of blood or treasure to make good its defence. It is the capital of the last of the border States, commanding the entire portion of Virginia east of the Alleghanies, and the most important division of North Carolina. It is situated 140 miles from the sea, yet large ships can unload from its wharves. The occupation of Richmond in strong force by the enemy would necessarily drive the Confederate armies out of Virginia, and render all Eastern North Carolina untenable; and, once gained by a power having command of the water, it could never, under any contingency, be recovered by the Confederacy.

Each contestant in the war has made Richmond the central object of all its plans and all its exertions. *It has become the symbol of the Confederacy. Its loss would be material ruin to the cause, and, in a moral point of view, absolutely destructive, crushing the heart and extinguishing the last hope of the country. Our armies would lose the incentive inspired by a great and worthy object of defence. Our military policy would be totally at sea; we should be without a hope or an object; without civil or military organization; without a treasury or a commissariat; without the means of keeping alive a wholesome and active public sentiment; without any of the appliances for supporting a cause depending upon the popular faith and enthusiasm; without the emblems of the semblance of nationality.*

The withdrawal of the army from Richmond into the interior would so narrow the area of conscription as greatly to reduce our military strength. As the army would dwindle in numbers, *it would move more and more rapidly westward, and before reaching the banks of the Mississippi would have degenerated into a mere body guard for a few officials.* From the hour of giving up the seat of government, our cause would sink into a mere rebellion in the estimation of foreign Powers; who would cease to accord to us the rights of belligerents; while the enemy would be free to treat our officers and soldiers as traitors and criminals; so that every "rebel" would fight thenceforward with a halter round his neck.

Virginia, though slow to come into the Confederacy, has been throughout the contest its main stay and support. It has borne the brunt of every campaign. It has suffered the ravages of war more severely than all the other States together. Every county in the State has felt the hand of the enemy. Its richest and best districts have been utterly desolated. Its sufferings have not only been severe beyond description, but continuous and unceasing. For four years it has been the common campaign and battle ground for the largest armies and bloodiest conflicts of modern times. No country in the world ever sustained as heavy losses or endured as hard a fate, with more heroism or fortitude. The evacuation of Richmond would be the abandonment of Richmond—forever—and without any rational hope of a return. Is it possible that such a desertion could be contemplated after the events of this war? Even if the act were not suicidal in policy, could the Confederacy now consent to cast away this worn and devastated but still powerful Commonwealth as an old shoe that could be put to no further use?

Aside from the disgrace that would attach to such ingratitude, the Confederacy could not afford to put Gen. GRANT into possession of Richmond, a depot and base a hundred and forty miles from the sea, and in the midst of Southern Virginia yet with water carriage to the door, and thus relinquish its last hold upon the last of the border States. It could not expect to continue the struggle with any hope of success, after abandoning States whence its most numerous recruits are obtained, a soil on which its arms have been uniformly victorious, and *withdrawing to States where defeat has constantly attended them.* The abandonment of Virginia would be equivalent to executing a quit claim deed to all the border States, together with Tennessee and North Carolina. Two lines of railways radiate from here into the most populous and influential districts of this latter State, subjecting its best portions to the control of any considerable military power having its base at Richmond. Is the Confederacy's wealth in population and territory now so great that it can afford to make a voluntary donation of all this territory; restricting its jurisdiction to the gulf States, and South Carolina, already overrun?

If Richmond be held but another six months, the fate of the Confederacy will have been favorably decided. The people will cling to the cause as long as the seat of Government is secure. Recent misfortunes will have awakened foreign Powers to the danger which would result to themselves from the restoration of the Union and pacification of this continent, now possessing a trained soldiery more numerous and formidable than any army in Europe. So long as Richmond and Virginia are ours, the very reverses which have been sustained will nerve our people to renewed exertion, and beguile the enemy into a false confidence. The war cannot be carried on much longer against us if we prove but true to ourselves; *and the single test of success will be our determination and ability to hold Richmond.* Other cities may fall, the rest of the Confederacy may succumb; but the cause still remains safe so long as Richmond and Virginia are held.

We have now before Richmond the best army which the Confederacy has ever possessed, impregnably posted, accustomed to victory and success. All its triumphs have been won in the defence of the Confederate capital. It has continued through every trial to make good that defence, and is honored throughout the Confederacy and the world for the prowess which it has exhibited in the successful effort. We have not the slightest belief or expectation that thoughtless friends or eager enemies will ever be gratified by the sight of such a national suicide as the evacuation of Richmond will be, while that noble army exists in any part; but with the hope of putting an end to the fall of the idle and short-sighted on this matter, we throw out these hints as to the consequences of the act of which they speak so lightly.

WILD SKEDADDLE OF THE REBEL CONGRESS.

From the Richmond Examiner, Feb. 27.

During the last four weeks *wild apprehensions of danger have disturbed the minds of the timid. The enemy has lately thrown his forces across lines of easy Congressional retreat to the West, and South, and, since that time, Senators and Representatives have one by one fled the Capitol, leaving the skeleton of the Legislature rapidly diminishing to a minimum number below a quorum.* It is true the President must stand firmer as national danger thickens; it is true the scarred army must bare their breasts to the storm with more heroic courage, as the columns of the enemy converge on the liberty and existence of the country. *Should the President waver and imitate Congressional example there will be no difficulty in finding instances in history to illustrate his disgrace.*

THE RICHMOND AND PETERSBURGH LINES.

From the Richmond Dispatch, Feb. 27.

GRANT has again been massing his troops on Hatcher's Run, on our extreme right, ten miles southwest of Petersburgh, and it *is thought that another attempt by his columns to gain the Southside Railroad was prevented by the rain of Saturday. We think there can be little doubt that he will make this attempt as soon as the state of the roads will permit.* In their present miry condition, the movement of artillery is out of the question. GRANT has enough of the gambler in his character for the disastrous failure of his last advance toward the railroad to make him the more impatient to renew the attempt. At present, the extreme left, which may properly be considered the advance of the Yankee army, occupies a position on the left or north side of Hatcher's Run, between nine and ten miles southwest of Petersburgh, and about five miles in a direct line from the Southside Railroad.

SOUTH CAROLINA.

NOTHING TO TELL.

From the Richmond Examiner, Feb. 27.

In the absence of official information of military affairs in the Carolinas, we take nothing from other sources of intelligence, and omit the usual references to our file of Southern exchanges. We do so at the request of the authorities, and with the understanding that the other city journals have been put under obligations of reticence to the extent indicated above. The public will, no doubt, be properly patient in the interval of silence, and not take it as discouragement; for we are assured that there are good reasons for it, which look to an early official announcement of favorable results.

THE SHELLING OF COLUMBIA.

From the Richmond Examiner, Feb. 27.

One of the most atrocious crimes perpetrated since the beginning of this war, says the Charlotte *Bulletin*, was the shelling of Columbia, S. C., by the enemy, without a moment's warning. We are justified by truth in saying that two batteries were placed at commanding points on the west side of the river, and a bombardment opened upon the city whilst it was filled with women and children. Many of the houses were perforated by the missiles, and the flying of women and children from the terror thus created is said to have been a most heart-rending sight. No demand had been made for the surrender of the city. On the contrary, the enemy's approach was silently and steadily conducted. Some eight or ten persons were killed by the fragments thrown into the midst of helpless non-combatants. We are informed, *also, that after the surrender of the place, squads of the enemy marched about the city shooting down such citizens as they could find, urging as an excuse that they might be stragglers from* BEAUREGARD'S *army.*

From the same Paper, same date.

The news from Columbia corroborates the kind treatment of the inhabitants. The Ursuline Convent was protected by a guard. No public property was allowed to be burned in the city. SHERMAN'S headquarters were at Nicketson's Hotel.

From the best information received here, it appears probable that a considerable conflagration occurred in the western portion of Columbia, occasioned, it is supposed, by the cotton ignited in the streets. It is reported that the fire extended from Main-street to the Charlotte Depot—nearly three-fourths of a mile. The information is positive as to the occurrence of the fire, but doubt is entertained as to its magnitude.

Some of the refugees from Columbia are preparing to return.

The alarm in Charlotte has subsided.

The weather is bad, and the roads heavy, interfering with rapid military movements.

AN UNAUTHENTICATED RUMOR.

From the Richmond Dispatch, Feb. 27.

The usual number of Sunday rumors were in circulation yesterday, the most agreeable of which, though we regret to say not the most authentic, was that SHERMAN had been killed and his army routed and driven into the jungles of South Carolina.

GEN. JOHNSTON.

From the Richmond Despatch, Feb. 27.

Gen. JOSEPH E. JOHNSTON, on Thursday evening last, assumed command of the army in SHERMAN'S front, lately commanded by Gen. BEAUREGARD.

NORTH CAROLINA.

UNION PRISONERS.

From the Richmond Examiner, Feb. 27.

The Raleigh *Confederate* of the 23d says:

"About twelve hundred Yankee prisoners—a dirty, ragged, and as hard-featured a set of men as ever were seen—were sent down from Salisbury, and stopped at the railroad depot, in this place awaiting orders to be sent to Wilmington for exchange. The Yankee authorities below Wilmington refused to receive a lot previously sent, but we understand that GRANT has sent instructions, through our exchange agent, to the officer in command there, ordering their reception at that point, and they were expected to leave last night.

It did not appear that a very strict guard was placed over them, or they were allowed unusual liberty by the officer in command. Many of them were seen straggling through the city during the morning unattended, and in perfect freedom.

A large Government warehouse was destroyed by fire in Fayetteville on Tuesday night last.

AFFAIRS AT CHARLOTTE.

From the Same.

The *Bulletin* of the 22d states that Col. HOKE, commanding post of Charlotte, is displaying the most commendable energy in the regulation of affairs connected with his immediate speciality. He has organized a military police force which occupy every public place, and the preservation of order, when everything is so favorable to confusion, is a task so difficult that its successful accomplishment is worthy al praise.

MISSISSIPPI.

A STATE CONVENTION TO BE CALLED.

From the Richmond Examiner, Feb. 27.

The Legislature of Mississippi is about to convene in extra session, for the purpose, it is said, of calling a State convention.

CHARLESTON.

Official Dispatch from General Gillmore.

The Extent and Importance of Our Captures.

Four Hundred and Fifty Guns Found in the Rebel Works.

Many Pieces of Foreign Manufacture Among Them.

DESTINATION OF HARDEE'S ARMY.

Rebel Apprehensions for Its Safety.

A Portion of Hood's Army Said to be in Front of Sherman.

SECRETARY STANTON TO GEN. DIX.

[OFFICIAL.]

WAR DEPARTMENT, WASHINGTON, March 1, 1865—8:10 P. M.

To Maj.-Gen. Dix, New-York:

The following telegram from Gen. GILLMORE has been transmitted to this department.

EDWIN M. STANTON, Secretary of War.

HEADQUARTERS DEPARTMENT OF THE SOUTH, CHARLESTON, S. C., Feb. 26, 1865.

Lieut.-Gen. U. S. Grant, and Maj.-Gen. H. W. Halleck, Chief of Staff, Washington:

An inspection of the rebel defences of Charleston shows that we have taken *over four hundred and fifty (450) pieces of ordnance*, being more than double what I first reported. The lot includes eight and ten inch Columbiads, a great many 32 and 42 pounder rifles, some seven-inch Brooke rifles, and many pieces of foreign make.

We also captured eight locomotives and a great number of passenger and platform cars, all in good condition.

Deserters report that the last of HARDEE'S army was to have crossed the Santee River yesterday, bound for Charlotte, N. C., and it was feared that SHERMAN had already intercepted their march.

It is reported, on similar authority, that the last of HOOD'S army, 12,000 strong, passed through Augusta last Sunday, the 19th, on the way to BEAUREGARD.

Georgetown has been evacuated by the enemy, and is now in our possession.

Deserters are coming in constantly. We have over 400 already.

(Signed,) Q. A. GILLMORE, Major-General Commanding.

ARRIVAL OF THE ARAGO.

The United States transport *Arago*, HENRY A. GADSDEN commanding, from Port Royal, &c., via Charleston Harbor the 26th inst., arrived at this city yesterday at 3:30 P. M.

When off Charleston Harbor (26th inst.) received the news of the burning of Columbia, South Carolina, on the 24th inst., by Gen. SHERMAN, and *also the report that Augusta had been taken possession of by the Union troops.*

OUR CHARLESTON CORRESPONDENCE.

Feeling Among the Citizens—Ruinous Appearance of the City—Fugitive Citizens Returning—A Union League in Charleston—The Quantity of Cotton Destroyed.

CHARLESTON, S. C., Tuesday, Feb. 21, 1865.

The confused state of affairs which prevailed for the first day or two after the evacuation of the city is rapidly assuming a more quiet and satisfactory condition. The citizens of the place are gradually becoming accustomed and reconciled to the new régime, and do not hesitate to appear on the streets or to visit their places of business. But a few complaints have been made to Provost-Marshal BENNETT, by citizens who have sustained some annoyance in the way of having their premises unceremoniously entered by the soldiers, and by other citizens who have had horses, vehicles, and other property suddenly confiscated. In a few days, however, a guard will be organized throughout the city, and the people will be assured of the safety of themselves and their effects.

The appearance of the city is desolate in the extreme. While on Morris Island I often heard the report that grass was growing in the streets at the lower end of Charleston, and now I am a witness to the truth of the statement. All along the water-front, and, in fact, for a long distance up the city, the buildings are either partially or wholly demolished. The walls of some present great, jagged holes, through which a horse and cart could easily pass, and that is the case not only in one but several streets. No wonder the rebels were solicitous to get beyond the reach of our shells! Such a punishment was never before inflicted upon any city. All of the hotels are closed, the furniture and appointments having been removed by the proprietors to the interior of the State some months ago. The Mills House was struck seventeen times, and at last the guests announced that they would not risk their lives by remaining longer in the building. The Charleston Hotel was also struck several times, so that it became necessary to close it.

While walking through the upper wards this morning, I was astonished to find that shells had even reached as far as the Georgia Railroad depot, thus showing that they had traveled a distance of five and six miles.

The first day of our entry into the city I noticed but few citizens made their appearance. I am told that the more prominent secessionists, and a great many of the Union sympathizers have gone into the country. But within the past few days a number of the latter have returned here, bringing their furniture with them. Unmistakably there is a strong Union feeling in Charleston. There is also a secesh element remaining which in course of time will die a natural death. As to the matter of subsistence the supply is limited, consisting mostly of meal and rice. The entire quantity was seized by our authorities on Saturday, and at noon to-day will be turned over to a committee of the citizens, of which committee Dr. A. G. MACKAY, one of the staunchest Union men in the place, is a member, to be distributed among the poor of the inhabitants. It seems to be inevitable that to prevent suffering, similar measures to those taken by the North in the case of Savannah must be adopted in behalf of the people of Charleston. It is contemplated by the citizens to hold a public meeting for the purpose of choosing delegates to repair to the North and lay before its people, an account of the destitute condition to which the rebellion has reduced them. I have taken special pains to inquire of a number of the inhabitants what general view was entertained in the South as to the results thus far of the war, and in every instance I was informed that the South would do well if it held out two months longer. Gen. HARDEE and other rebel military officers said before they left the city that their armies must concentrate in Virginia, or all would certainly be lost. Perhaps it will surprise many to learn that there was really a Union League established in Charleston. Such was the case, and it received the support of hundreds of the citizens, and many of the members were of such prominent standing that the military authorities dare not make open arrests.

According to the description given, the most inhuman and outrageous acts of cruelty were committed by the rebels when they evacuated. Women and children who had snatched from the flames a few bags of meal or corn, or an apronful of rice, were pursued by the cavalry and cut down with sabres. The rebels were exasperated to the nature of fiends when they approached a man who showed the least desire to share the fate of the city. Had they been allowed to exercise their own will, not a house would have been left standing. The firing of the Northeastern Railroad station together with its contents of rice, meal and flour was a proof of what they designed to do, with all the buildings. The rebels did their work too, regardless of human life and limb. In that railroad station were stored one hundred kegs of powder, which were purposely ignited while a large crowd of half-starved people were within gathering up a little quantity of meal to keep soul and body together. A most terrific explosion followed, the appalling result of which was the killing and mangling of 250 human beings.

The total quantity of cotton destroyed by fire was about 4,000 bales. It is thought that about 10,000 bales are still in the city. It is scattered around in small lots, some of the owners not having over two or three bales. Treasury Agent BROWNE and the Custom-House authorities were here yesterday, and will probably make an early disposition of this property.

In all, eight locomotives and twelve cars were captured. Two of the former are in running order to-day. The remaining six will require more or less repairing before they can be of service. A large force of laborers has been put to work on the railroad leading to Wilmington, thus indicating that we are about to do something in that direction.

The city arsenal contains a considerable quantity of ammunition. Had our troops been five minutes later in reaching the city, the arsenal would have been fired by a party of rebels who were detailed for the purpose. In the open space opposite the citadel are piles of shells suited for the 600-pounder guns which Gen. HARDEE bursted on the morning he took his leave.

Every attention is paid to the wants of the citizens, who flock to the headquarters in vast numbers. Squads of cavalry have been sent out some distance into the interior, and a hundred or more prisoners have been captured.

Maj.-Gen. GILLMORE, Brig.-Gen. WEBSTER, and a large number of staff officers and civilians, including ladies, came up from Hilton Head yesterday morning, on the flag-steamer *W. W. Coit*, Capt. CROWELL.

In a short time measures will be instituted to rid the harbor and rivers of torpedoes. No explosions have yet occurred from that cause, although it is asserted by citizens that a large number of those machines have been sunk between here and Sumter. The monitors are lying off Sumter. Admiral DAHLGREN'S flagship lies a short distance from Vanderhorst Wharf.

WHIT.

FROM BEAUFORT, N. C.

Beaufort to be Made a Depot of Supplies for our Armies in North Carolina.

FORTRESS MONROE Tuesday, Feb. 28.

The steamer *Ariel*, Capt. JONES, arrived this afternoon from Beaufort, N. C., bringing no news of importance.

Extensive preparations were making at Beaufort, N. C., for the purpose of making that place the general depot of supplies for our armies operating in the State of North Carolina; and also with a view to the rapid movement of Major-Gen. SHERMAN'S army northward, when Charleston and Savannah shall be no longer of any value as a basis of supplies of his forces.

The bad weather still continues, with the wind from the northeast, and occasional showers of rain.

NEWS FROM WASHINGTON.

Special Dispatches to the New-York Times.

WASHINGTON, Wednesday, March 1.

ADMIRAL PORTER.

The Committee on the Conduct of the War, having failed to get Admiral PORTER before them, have asked for an extension of twenty days, in order to complete the evidence in the Red River and Fort Fisher expeditions. Their request will be granted.

THE ENLISTMENT OF REBEL PRISONERS.

The Secretary of War sent to the House to-day, in compliance with a resolution of inquiry passed on Saturday, a statement from Provost-Marshal-Gen. FRY relative to the enlistment of rebel prisoners, from which it appears that the total number of such enlistments is 3,800. Nearly 1,500 were enlisted at Point Lookout, and sent to the Department of the Northwest. Four hundred and fifty were enlisted at Fort Delaware into the Third Maryland Cavalry, and sent to the Department of the Gulf. Seventeen hundred and fifty were enlisted at Rock Island and credited to localities in Pennsylvania, which paid them bounty, and sent to the Plains for service on the Overland route. All enlistments were stopped by order of the Secretary of War in September last, and no United States bounty has been paid to such recruits.

THE LOUISIANA QUESTION.

The question of admitting the Senators and Representatives from the State of Louisiana will not be acted on before the adjournment. They had a meeting to-day in regard to the matter, and after a free conference with the friends of the Senate resolution, it was decided that it was useless to press the matter any further.

THE PERMITS TO TRADE IN COTTON.

Mr. WASHBURNE, from the Committee on Commerce, submitted a report to the House, to-day, setting forth that the joint investigating committee had found much corruption and bribery existing under the operations of the act for the purchase of the products of insurrectionary districts, and submitting a bill for the repeal of the eighth section of the act which authorizes the trade. A joint resolution also passed the House, authorizing the continuance of the investigations of the committee after the adjournment of Congress.

MILITARY NOMINATIONS.

The Senate Military Committee at their meeting to-day reported upon all the military nominations recently sent to the Senate. There are now upward of twelve hundred names on the calendar unacted on. They will not be taken up before Monday next for want of time to consider them during the regular session.

THE ARMY APPROPRIATION BILL.

The report of the Conference Committee on the Army Appropriation Bill was presented to the House to-night. The committee having agreed to strike out the appropriation to the Illinois Central Railroad for Government transportation. The proposition was opposed by JAS. C. ALLEN, of Illinois, and warmly advocated by Messrs. WASHBURNE and STEVENS. The report was agreed to. The terms of the land grant to this company, it will be recollected, provide that it shall transport Government stores and troops free of cost.

THE MISSOURI CLAIMS.

The bill to reimburse the State of Missouri for moneys expended in the raising and equipment of troops was taken up in the House, and after a warm contest was finally laid on the table.

THE EXTRA PAY SETTLED.

The Conference Committee on the Executive and Judicial Appropriation Bill made a report to-day, in which the extra compensation of twenty per cent to the House employes, and the appropriation of $160,000 for the extension of the library was adopted.

AT WORK ON THE TAX BILL.

The Senate sat till after midnight last night on the Tax Bill, and have spent the entire day upon it, and will probably finish it to-night. The new section taxing State bank circulation ten per cent. was agreed to in Committee of the Whole. A motion to strike it out was lost by ayes 20, noes 22.

Dispatches to the Associated Press.

WASHINGTON, Wednesday, March 1.

GREAT SUCCESS OF RECRUITING.

The following important and encouraging information has been obtained from an authentic source:

On the 27th day of February, 1865, 6,685 men were enlisted into the service. The average number of men mustered daily for the last three days of February is 3,296. The average number of men mustered for the last ten days of that month was 3,216. (?) If recruiting be kept up, the army will be speedily reinforced to the extent necessary to put an end to the war.

THE PRESIDENT APPRISED OF HIS REELECTION.

Senator TRUMBULL and Representatives WILSON and DAWSON, as the Select Committee of the two houses of Congress, to-day waited upon President LINCOLN, and informed him of his reëlection. To this he responded:

"Having served four years in the depths of a great and yet unended national peril, I can view this call to a second term in no wise more flattering to myself than as an expression of the public judgment that I may better finish a difficult work, in which I have labored from the first, than could any one less severely schooled to the task. In this view, and with increased reliance on that Almighty Ruler who has so graciously sustained us thus far, and with increased gratitude to the generous people for their continued confidence, I accept the renewed trust, with its yet onerous and perplexing duties and responsibilities."

No response has yet been received from the Vice-President elect, who did not arrive here until to-night.

REPORT ON THE PETERSBURGH MINE.

The President sent to the Senate, to-day, a message inclosing the opinion and findings of the Court of Inquiry instituted by him in the Petersburgh mine. The opinion is signed by Maj.-Gen. W. S. HANCOCK, President of the court. After narrating the circumstances of the assault, the failure is ascribed to the following-named officers:

First—Gen. BURNSIDE, in not obeying the orders of the Commanding General in the formation of the assaulting column, in not preparing his parapet and abattis for the passage of his troops, and in not employing engineer officers to lead the columns with the working parties. Yet the court is satisfied that Gen. BURNSIDE believed the measures taken by him would insure success.

Second—Brig.-Gen. LEDLIE, in failing to push forward his troops promptly, and in blocking up the avenue designed for the passage of troops ordered to follow, he being most of the time in a bombproof ten rods in the rear of the main line, where the movement could not be witnessed.

Third—Brig.-Gen. FERRERO, for want of readiness for the assault, not going with his troops, but remaining in a bomb-proof.

Fourth—Col. Z. R. BLISS, of the Seventh Rhode Island, commanding a brigade, in remaining behind with one regiment, in a position where he could not see what was going on.

Fifth—Brig.-Gen. WILCOX, in lack of energy in carrying out Gen. BURNSIDE'S order, to push his troops forward to Cemetery Hill.

The Court concludes the opinion as follows:

"Without intending to convey the impression that there was any disinclination on the part of the commander of the support to heartily coöperate in the attack on the 30th of July, the Court express their opinion that explicit orders should have been given assigning one officer to the command of all the troops intended to engage in the assault, when the Commanding General was not present in person to witness the operations."

THE SEARCH FOR FRAUDS IN THE NAVY.

The Secretary of the Navy, in response to a Senate resolution, submitted by Mr. HALE, says the department has been steadily assailed for abuses which it could not wholly prevent, and that implicated parties have been frequently the most boisterous in complaint. He states that investigations have eventuated in the detection of extensive frauds perpetrated by certain contractors, and that in some instances officers and employes of the Government have been implicated. There being no law officer attached to the department, special counsel was employed. Col. L. C. BAKER and subsequently Col. H. S. OLCOTT conducted these investigations, which embraced inquiries into abuses and malpractices connected with purchases for the Brooklyn, Charlestown, Portsmouth, Philadelphia and Washington Navy-yards. Provost-Marshals, police officers and other agents have been employed.

Mr. FRANKLIN SMITH and his brother, BENJAMIN G. SMITH, both contractors, were summoned before a Committee of Inquiry as witnesses, and were afterward arrested for fraudulent practices, arraigned before a Court-martial in September last, found guilty in January, and sentenced to fine and imprisonment. The testimony in the case covered 2,500 pages of manuscript, which was printed and largely circulated; and 500 copies were ordered by the Department that the Government might not be prejudiced by ex parte statements maliciously and ignorantly made, believing that the publication of the argument on one side justified and rendered necessary the publication of the argument on the other. These copies were distributed to members of Congress and others who were furnished with the argument for the defence. The expense was $500. The Secretary denies that he has given instructions to employes to inquire into the business transactions of any member of either House of Congress. The expenses of these examinations at the navy-yards were $14,894. Restitution to the amount of $47,661 has been made by persons arrested in conseqence of these inquiries who have confessed their guilt. Parties have also been fined to the amount of $75,000.

A communication from Assistant Secretary FOX to Secretary WELLES is also presented, which embodies a personal defence against sundry charges and allegations, and gives the history of his attempt to garrison and provision Fort Sumter in 1861, with the official orders in the case.

THE LOAN BILL PASSED.

The Senate having passed the Six Hundred Million Loan Bill precisely as it went from the House, and as published in the New-York morning papers, it requires only President LINCOLN'S signature to become a law.

THE FORTIFICATION BILL.

The President has approved the Fortification Bill, the appropriations in which were cut down just one-half the amount which was originally reported. He has also approved the bill providing that no part of any ship or vessel shall be admeasured or registered for tonnage that is used for cabins or state-rooms, and constructed entirely above the first deck, which is not a deck to the hull.

POSTMASTER AT PORT ROYAL.

The Senate has confirmed Mr. S. L. BROTTON to be Postmaster at Port Royal, S. C., and Mr. JOHN M. ECKFIELDT to be master and refiner of the branch mint in California.

Atlantic Telegraph Company.

At the annual meeting of the shareholders of the Atlantic Telegraph Company, held in London on the 9th of February, the following gentlemen were elected Directors:

Mr. SAMUEL CUNARD, Bart., of London.
Mr. EDWARD CROPPER, of London.
Mr. GEORGE P. BIDDER, C. E., of London.
Mr. E. M. ARCHIBALD, of New-York.
Mr. PETER COOPER, of New-York.
Mr. WILSON G. HUNT, of New-York.
Mr. HUGH ALLEN, of Montreal.

Up to Friday evening, Feb. 17, 1,269 nautical miles of cable had been completed, and about 100 miles were being manufactured per week, and the *Great Eastern* will be all ready for sea with the entire cable on board by the 1st of June.

ARMY OF THE POTOMAC.

More Rebel Deserters—How they Manage to Escape—Their Stories About Depression in the South.

RIGHT WING ARMY OF THE POTOMAC, Monday, Feb. 27, 1865.

We are beginning to realize the fruits of the policy adopted by Lieut.-Gen. GRANT toward rebel deserters, in the rapid depletion of the army now cooped up in the defences of Richmond. During the week ending on Saturday night last, there were received at Headquarters of the Army of the Potomac, four hundred and ninety-seven deserters from the rebel army; and in the same time there were three hundred and fourteen received in the Army of the James—making an aggregate loss to Gen. LEE'S army on this account, of eight hundred and eight! These deserters arrive in squads of five, ten, or even as many, sometimes, as twenty. On Friday last one hundred and forty-six were received during the day, of whom forty-nine came together, and were members of the same regiment! I am informed that the rebel officers use every means at their command to stop this wholesale depletion of their army. Among other expedients, they send cavalry scouts along between the picket lines to hunt for deserters and bring them back, and within the last week six or eight of these scouts are reported as having come over with horses and equipments. Instead of taking back the others, they preferred to come over themselves.

It is no unusual thing for deserters to notify the pickets, when they reach our lines, that another squad will be over on the succeeding night, and it rarely happens that these predictions are not verified. They seem to have systematized the practice so perfectly that they can escape without difficulty, thus palpably indicating that many of those they leave behind do not regard desertion as a very heinous offence, nor endeavor to prevent it.

As for the stories the deserters tell, as far as they refer to public matters, there is very little dissimilarity, not enough to invalidate any of the statements, nor to make it interesting to publish them. *They all concur in representing that the gloom which pervades the public mind at the South is deepening constantly, and that all hopes of achieving their independence are abandoned* by the great mass of the citizens and soldiers. The only persons who even profess to hope for success now are the leaders. They are compelled to exert themselves to the utmost to continue the war, and are represented to be in imminent danger of being arrested by the citizens and delivered over to our authorities. These statements must be received, however, with considerable allowance. If all they tell were true, the wonder would be that, instead of deserting by tens and twenties, they do not leave by brigades and divisions.

The intelligence of a rumor prevailing at the North that this army had been worsted in an engagement with Gen. LEE'S forces reached here yesterday, and excited considerable merriment. The idea seemed so preposterous, that the originator of it was universally held to be a genius to be able to induce anybody to credit his statement.

HARRY H. YOUNG.

FROM SHERIDAN'S ARMY.

The Late Ashby's Gap Disaster—Names of Killed and Wounded—The Weather.

From Our Own Correspondent.

WINCHESTER, Va., Thursday, Feb. 23, 1865.

Eight men, wounded in the unfortunate affair in the Gap last Sunday, were brought here late last night, and placed in the Taylor Hospital, in care of Surgeon WAGNER. Their names are as follows:

Capt. D. K. Duff, Co. K, 14th Penn. Cavalry, wounded in right arm, head and fingers.
Sergt. James R. Johnson, Co. C., 14th Penn. Cav., wounded in left hip.
Johnson Matthews, Co. G, 14th Penn. Cavalry, wounded in right shoulder.
Elisha Myers, Co. G, 14th Penn. Cavalry, wounded in right arm.
Hugh Townson, Co. B, 14th Penn. Cavalry, wounded in breast.
Samuel Bryson, Co. M., 14th Penn. Cavalry, wounded in left eye.
J. M. Kenner, Co. K, 14th Penn. Cavalry, wounded in left side.
Peter Ingle, Co. F, 14th Penn. Cavalry, wounded in neck and back.

Wounded men left in Ashby's Gap, but who will probably be brought in to-morrow, all belonging to the Fourteenth:

Privates Samuel McCarty, John Morrs, Wm. M. Haney and Daniel Townson.

A number of the slightly wounded are in the regimental camp.

Capt. DUFF knows of seven men who were killed, five of whom were buried by citizens near the church in the Gap, and two at the base of the mountain, near the Shenandoah. He could ascertain the names of only two of the seven:

First Sergt. PHILLIP R. PAUL, Co. D, 14th Penn. Cavalry—killed.

Private WILLIAM COOK, Co. B, 14th Penn. Cavalry—killed.

JAS. MARTIN, of Co. D, was among those captured.

This reduces the number of missing to fifty; most of these are doubtless prisoners, and some of them are slightly wounded. All of the returned wounded were paroled by Major RICHARDS, of MOSBY'S command.

Capt. DUFF commanded the rear guard when the attack was made, and five of the men known to have been killed belonged to his detachment. Had he been properly supported, it is now apparent the result would have been far different. The enemy, eighty strong, charged upon this little band; they emptied their carbines without checking the attacking force, and having neither pistols or sabres, and no support to speak of from the balance of the command, the enemy had everything pretty much their own way.

The capture of GILMOR seems to have aroused the ire of the enemy, and for several days past small forces have been hovering about our lines, without doing any particular harm, however.

The warm rain storm continues, and the snow has nearly disappeared.

E. A. PAUL.

NEW-JERSEY LEGISLATURE.

Rejection of the Constitutional Amendment—Election of Senator Postponed.

TRENTON, N. J., March 1.

The discussion of the Constitutional Amendment continued during the principal part of the day. The vote was taken about five o'clock, and the amendment was defeated by a vote of 30 yeas against 30 nays. The result received cheers and hisses in the lobbies. It was a strict party vote.

The joint meeting of both branches was held. The election of United States Senator was postponed to March 15. JOSEPH B. WALKER was elected prison-keeper.

The Seven-Thirty Loan.

PHILADELPHIA, Wednesday, March 1.

JAY COOKE reports sales of seven-thirties today to the amount of $3,127,000, including one subscription from New-York of over $500,000, and another from Chicago of $92,000, and a large number of individual subscriptions.

Gov. Curtin's Visit South.

HARRISBURGH, Penn., Wednesday, March 1.

Gov. CURTIN leaves next Sunday for Charleston and Savannah, to see the Pennsylvania regiments and benefit his health. He will probably be absent two weeks.

Fire in Newburgh.

NEWBURGH, Wednesday, March 1.

The boiler shop of the Washington Iron Works in this city, was destroyed by fire this morning. Most of the machinery was removed to an adjacent building, and the business of the works will not be seriously interrupted.

The New-York Times.

VOL. XIV......NO. 4195. NEW-YORK, MONDAY, MARCH 6, 1865. PRICE FOUR CENTS

GLORIOUS NEWS

A New Victory for Phil. Sheridan.

Capture of Gen. Early and His Entire Force.

Charlottesville Occupied by Our Troops.

Lieut.-Gen. Grant Co-operating with Sherman.

He Occupies Lee's Attention by Threatening Richmond from the Valley.

Lee Compelled to Send Forces to Defend Lynchburg.

Jeff. Davis' Lines of Retreat in Danger.

Sheridan Knocking at the Back Door to Richmond.

OFFICIAL DISPATCHES.

[OFFICIAL.]

SECRETARY STANTON TO GEN DIX.

WAR DEPARTMENT, WASHINGTON, March 5.

To Maj.-Gen. Dix, New-York:

The following dispatches, in relation to the reported defeat and capture of Gen. EARLY by SHERIDAN, and the capture of Charlottesville, have been received by this department. Gen. SHERIDAN and his force commenced their movement last Monday, and were at Staunton when last heard from. Maj.-Gen. HANCOCK was placed in charge of the Middle Military Division during the absence of Gen. SHERIDAN, with headquarters at Winchester.

(Signed) E. M. STANTON, Secretary of War.

FIRST DISPATCH FROM GEN. GRANT.

CITY POINT, Va., March 5—11 A. M.

Hon. Edwin M. Stanton, Secretary of War:

Deserters in this morning report that SHERIDAN had routed EARLY and captured Charlottesville. They report four regiments having gone from here (Richmond) to reinforce EARLY.

(Signed) U. S. GRANT, Lieut.-General.

SECOND DISPATCH FROM GEN. GRANT.

CITY POINT, Va., Sunday, March 5—2 P. M.

Hon. E. M. Stanton, Secretary of War:

Deserters from every point of the enemy's line confirm the capture of Charlottesville by Gen. SHERIDAN. They say he captured Gen. EARLY and his entire force, consisting of eighteen hundred men. Four brigades were reported as being sent to *Lynchburgh, to get there before Gen. Sheridan, if possible.*

(Signed) U. S. GRANT, Lieut.-Gen.

THIRD DISPATCH FROM GEN. GRANT.

CITY POINT, Va., March 5—4 P. M.

Hon. E. M. Stanton, Secretary of War:

Refugees confirm the statement of deserters as to the capture of Gen. EARLY and nearly his entire force. They say it took place on Thursday last between Staunton and Charlottesville, and that the defeat was total.

(Signed,) U. S. GRANT, Lieut.-General.

ARMY OF THE POTOMAC.

Rebel Deserters Still Coming In—A Curious Incident—Why the Rebels Cheered on Wednesday—A New Whisky Ration.

HEADQUARTERS ARMY OF THE POTOMAC, Friday, March 3.

Nothing of importance is transpiring in this department.

Deserters continue to come into our lines in large numbers, fifty-six having arrived to-day, nearly all bringing their guns and equipments with them, for which they are to be paid. The number of muskets received from deserters, since Feb. 22, is 240, all of them in good order. In addition to the usual stories told by these men, they say that two companies from each regiment of several brigades have been detailed from the army defending Petersburgh, and sent to hunt up deserters, thousands of whom are said to be scattered through the country, endeavoring to reach their homes. This is particularly the case with the North and South Carolina troops, who are sick and tired of the contest, and anxious to join their families, now within our lines. These men are principally veterans of three and four years' service, and many of them are those lately exchanged. All of them being refused furloughs, and not paid for a long time, nor any prospect of getting any soon, they took "French leave."

A few days ago a sergeant was sent out in charge of a team and six men to get wood. The men were unarmed. The sergeant was armed with a revolver and a sword. After getting outside the lines, the mules apparently ran away, but the sergeant guided them straight for our lines, and the whole party arrived safely. They received for the mules $700, which was divided equally.

The cheering among the rebels, on Wednesday evening, was on account of their receiving a ration of whisky, which seems to be quite a rarity in their Commissary Department. Gen. COOK, commanding a brigade in Gen. HETH's division, is said to have harangued his men on the occasion, while grossly intoxicated.

[illegible] RAYMOND, of Company B, and NEWELL J. [illegible], of Company H, of the Sixth New-York Volunteers, were shot, to-day, for attempting to desert to the enemy. Five regiments of the First Division of the Second Corps, to which the criminals belonged, were assembled to witness the execution, the details of which were in charge of the Provost-Marshal of the division.

The Ninety-first New-York Volunteers, a veteran regiment, arrived at the front, to-day, and were assigned to the Third Division of the Fifth Corps. They numbered about 900 men, and present a splendid appearance. W. D. McGREGOR.

Fire in Pittsburgh—The Monitor Manayunk on the Rampage.

PITTSBURGH, Penn., Sunday, March 5.

The tobacco factory of WILSON HAYS & Co., on Irwin-street, was entirely destroyed by fire at 2 o'clock this morning. One fireman, DAVID L. SIMS, was instantly killed by a falling wall, and two others seriously injured. Loss, $12,000. Fully insured.

The new monitor, *Manayunk*, broke from her moorings at 5 o'clock this morning, and drifted down the river. She was overtaken by two tugs three miles below Pittsburgh, and safely returned. The *Manayunk* is nearly completed, and leaves for Cairo in a day or two.

FROM MISSOURI.

Missourian Characteristics—The State Convention—Its Want of Harmony—Military Matters.

Correspondence of the New York Times.

ST. LOUIS, Mo., Tuesday, Feb. 28, 1865.

The disposition and nature of Missourians seem fitly symbolized in the arms of their State—a brace of bears in a fighting hug. The national distinctions between English, Irish and Scotch, and the sub-distinctions of province, burgh, county and shire are not more observable by the traveler in those countries than are the local and State differences in the Great West, only that the language is more uniform, and the idiomatic mean less variable. The great difference, however, lies in the tone and cast of mind and character. In Missouri there exists a bilious doggedness and determination. Perhaps the subject will bear a still further illustration. Missouri character is Samson-like—it will destroy itself with the temple rather than its enemy go unpunished. This is a good trait in a pioneer, for if he does not risk his life amid the miasmas of the unreclaimed territory, and in face of the hostile savage, civilization cannot advance. But another trait of pioneer character is that of opposition to progress. Having taken the initiatory steps, and after attaining a certain stage, the pioneer stands still and beats back the pressure from behind. He belongs to the class who believe "that new truths may have been desirable once, but that we have had enough of them now."

This will all go to explain in a measure the status of the State Convention which has really become contemptible in the eyes of the progressive, loyal people. Too much cookery has spoiled the broth. The delegates have worried themselves into ill-health by venting their spleen on each other, and the cause of their distemper is ignorance of Webster's Dictionary. This may seem ridiculous or unjust, but it is a fact—a fact underlying all the slowness, ill-temper and spirit of anti-progress observable in the Assembly. Mr. CHARLES D. DRAKE, who has an almost national reputation as a public speaker, essays to lead the body, but his inconsistency and vacillation have lost for him the confidence of those who otherwise would yield to his judgment and leadership, and the consequence is that his measures and movements are looked upon with misgiving if not doubt. The fact that before the war, and indeed for some time afterward, he was the most bitter and persistent advocate of slavery, and that up to a short time ago he was the very opposite, and that he now shows some disposition not to go the whole radical idea except it eminate from himself, is the most bitter pill the men associated with him in the cause of human liberty have to swallow.

The *Westliche Post*, edited by EMIL PRETORIUS, is the organ of the German Radicals, who have from the first been the firm friends of freedom and progress in this city and State. Apt to carry their notions to extremes, they have not been as uniformly supported by the same class of Americans, but the present indications are that a better understanding will be established between these two great bodies of citizens. The striking out of the Bill of Rights of the clause making a belief in God incumbent, was done in concession to the Radical Germans, amongst whom, by the way, there are just as many Orthodox Christians as are to be found in any other class of citizens, for, although its retention would have pleased, even gratified, the Puritanic element in the State Convention, that element was not sufficiently strong to resist the powerful influence of the German Radicals, and those who, with them, hold that a perfect freedom in matters of conscience is the best condition for a republic. The Protestant, the Catholic, and the Jew, alike combine with the Radical German against that clause, and hence its elimination.

MILITARY MATTERS.

The collection of forfeited bonds commenced, and for a short time successfully carried on by Maj.-Gen. DODGE, has been stopped by orders from the War Department, or as rumor has it, by orders direct from the President.

The headquarters of the State have this day been removed to Jefferson City, for the better accommodation of the State Government, and the more direct supervision of the State military business by the Governor. The State has been divided into two military divisions, the first constituting that portion lying north of the Missouri, and the second that portion lying south of it. Brig.-Gen. CLINTON B. FISK, recently commissioned Major-General of Militia, will command the First Division, and Brig.-Gen. JOHN MCNEIL, recently commissioned Major-General of Militia, will command the Second Division. these appointments having nothing to do with the military government of the department under the United States authority, as vested in Maj.-Gens. POPE and DODGE. The changes, or rearrangement, is simply to further the objects of the service, by bringing the militia into more direct cooperation with volunteer or national forces.

Gen. DODGE is exercising a questionable clemency toward bushwhackers, found guilty of murder, arson and robbery, by military commission, and sentenced to be hung. But two have been executed since he assumed command here, as many as six having had their sentences commuted to imprisonment during the war.

FROM PANAMA.

The Mission of Gen. Sickles—An Improbable Report—Supposed Scheme to Colonize Negroes from the United States.

The Panama *Mercantile Chronicle*, of Feb. 13, received by the bark *Idaho*, contains the following:

"Our native friends are so greatly exercised in their conjectures relative to the mission of Gen SICKLES to this Government, that we are induced to refer to it again without having any positive data on the subject. It is said that the Generals object is to procure from the Columbian Government a concession of lands on which the United States Government will form a settlement of thirty-thousand of the negroes emancipated by the great secession war.

It is stated that one million of dollars will be given for this privilege, and it is feared that the settlement of 30,000 emancipated slaves will lead to a repetition of Texan history.

We would first state that the American Government will never pay $1,000,000 for this privilege, and in the second place our native friends do not understand the character of the American slaves or the relationship which would exist between them as emigrants, and the United States Government.

The object of the Americans, as disclosed in several of President LINCOLN's speeches and dispatches, is to remove these poor people from a country which has been thrown into a state bordering on destruction, through their presence there in the condition of slaves. To have these people as freed men in the Southern States after the war may have been concluded, would be a constant cause of irritation to the former masters, inducing disaffection and turmoil as successors to a restoration of the Union. It is their wish, therefore, to settle them in one of the neighboring and friendly States where the laws of the country will guarantee them safety, and where it will be easy for the United States Government to extend a protecting hand to them in any hour of extremity. With such laudable motives, we cannot but applaud the object of the United States Government."

Arrival of the Canada at Boston.

BOSTON, Sunday, March 5.

The *Canada* arrived at 2 P. M. The mails go forward to-night, and will be due in New-York early in the morning.

FROM WASHINGTON.

THE INAUGURATION CEREMONIES.

A Fine Display---Enthusiasm Among the People.

Defective Arrangements for the Ceremonies.

SCENES AT THE CAPITOL--A GRAND CRUSH

The Inaugural Address of President Lincoln.

Graphic Account of the Proceedings of the Day.

WASHINGTON, Saturday, March 4.

President LINCOLN was inaugurated for another term of four years at twelve o'clock, noon, to-day.

Overhead the weather was clear and beautiful, and on account of the recent rains the streets were filled with mud. Despite this fact the crowd that assembled was exceedingly large, and thousands proceeded to the capital to witness the inauguration ceremonies.

The procession moved from Sixteenth-street and Pennsylvania-avenue at about 11 o'clock.

President LINCOLN had been at the capital all day, and consequently did not accompany the procession to the scene of the interesting ceremonies.

Several bands of music, two regiments of the Invalid Corps, a squadron of cavalry, a battery of artillery, and four companies of colored troops, formed the military escort.

The Mayor and Councilmen of Washington, visiting Councilmen from Baltimore, the firemen of this city and the visiting firemen from Philadelphia, the Good Will, Franklin and Perseverance companies, each company drawing its engine along, were also in the procession.

Among the benevolent societies present were Lodges of Odd Fellows and Masons, including a colored Lodge of the latter fraternity.

The public and principal private buildings along Pennsylvania-avenue were gaily decorated with flags, and every window was thronged with faces to catch a glimpse of the President elect.

The oath to protect and maintain the Constitution of the United States, was administered to Mr. LINCOLN by Chief-Justice CHASE, in the presence of thousands, who witnessed the interesting ceremony while standing in mud almost knee-deep.

The Inaugural was then read.

THE INAUGURAL ADDRESS.

FELLOW COUNTRYMEN: At this second appearing to take the oath of the Presidential office, there is less occasion for an extended address than there was at the first. Then a statement somewhat in detail of a course to be pursued seemed very fitting and proper. Now, at the expiration of four years, during which public declarations have been constantly called forth on every point and phase of the great contest which still absorbs the attention and engrosses the energies of the nation, little that is new could be presented.

The progress of our arms, upon which all else chiefly depends, is as well known to the public as to myself, and it is, I trust, reasonably satisfactory and encouraging to all. With high hope for the future, no prediction in regard to it is ventured.

On the occasion corresponding to this four years ago, all thoughts were anxiously directed to an impending civil war. All dreaded it; all sought to avoid it. While the inaugural address was being delivered from this place, devoted altogether to saving the Union without war, insurgent agents were in the city seeking to destroy it without war—seeking to dissolve the Union and divide the effects by negotiation. Both parties deprecated war, but one of them would make war rather than let the nation survive, and the other would accept war rather than let it perish, and the war came.

One-eighth of the whole population were colored slaves, not distributed generally over the Union, but localized in the Southern part of it. These slaves constituted a peculiar and powerful interest. All knew that this interest was somehow the cause of the war. To strengthen, perpetuate and extend this interest, was the object for which the insurgents would rend the Union even by war, while the Government claimed no right to do more than to restrict the territorial enlargement of it.

Neither party expected for the war the magnitude or the duration which it has already attained. Neither anticipated that the cause of the conflict might cease with, or even before the conflict itself should cease. Each looked for an easier triumph, and a result less fundamental and astounding.

Both read the same Bible and pray to the same God, and each invokes His aid against the other. It may seem strange that any men should dare to ask a just God's assistance in wringing their bread from the sweat of other men's faces, but let us judge not, that we be not judged. The prayers of both could not be answered. That of neither has been answered fully. The Almighty has his own purposes. "Woe unto the world because of offences, for it must needs be that offences come; but woe to that man by whom the offence cometh." If we shall suppose that American slavery is one of these offences, which in the providence of God must needs come, but which having continued through His appointed time, He now wills to remove, and that He gives to both North and South this terrible war as the woe due to those by whom the offence came, shall we discern therein any departure from those divine attributes which the believers in a living God always ascribe to Him? Fondly do we hope, fervently do we pray, that this mighty scourge of war may soon pass away. Yet, if God wills that it continue until all the wealth piled by the bondman's two hundred and fifty years of unrequited toil shall be sunk, and until every drop of blood drawn with the lash shall be paid with another drawn with the sword, as was said three thousand years ago; so, still it must be said, "The judgments of the Lord are true and righteous altogether."

With malice toward none, with charity for all, with firmness in the right, as God gives us to see the right, let us strive on to finish the work we are in, to bind up the nation's wounds, to care for him who shall have borne the battle and for his widow and his orphans, to do all which may achieve and cherish a just and a lasting peace among ourselves and with all nations.

After the delivery of the address a national salute was fired by a battery stationed east of the Capitol. The procession then again moved up Pennsylvania-avenue, the President being conveyed in an open barouche. Seated with him was his son and Senator FOSTER, of the Committee of Arrangements.

The President was escorted to the White House; after which, the procession separated.

OUR SPECIAL ACCOUNT.

WASHINGTON, Sunday, March 5.

The reinauguration of ABRAHAM LINCOLN has passed, and the chronicle of it may be brief, for it was an event typical in its character of the simplicity of Republican institutions, though it is to be hoped that so far as the nature of some of the arrangements is concerned, they are not to be subjected to a similar comparison if they are, Republican institutions must suffer; but I am not disposed to be captious or over critical and due praise should be accorded in many respects. Yet a regard for truth and the true importance of the occasion demands that it should be known that the pageant and ceremony of yesterday were not, either in detail, or in general, in keeping with the event for which the preparations were made.

The second inauguration of Mr. LINCOLN is a no less significant event than was the same occurrence four years ago. Yet, the affair of yesterday, except that part performed by Mr. LINCOLN himself, was almost insignificant in comparison. No one expected an inaugural address of the same importance, that the occasion did not demand; but the concomitants which attracted hither fifty thousand spectators from every part of the Union should have been of a character to do justice to the occasion. I do not know whose fault it may be, but it was a very faulty affair.

The programme of arrangements for the inaugural ceremony was fixed so as to cause part of it to take place in the Senate Chamber, and part on the east front of the Capitol, in the open air. If the weather proved rainy, then the oath of office to be administered and the inaugural address delivered in the Senate Chamber.

To provide accommodations for ladies, and to prevent the chamber from being crowded by a miscellaneous mass, the entire Senate gallery, except that portion reserved for the press, was set apart for ladies only, and admission was obtained by tickets; the families of Cabinet Ministers, Heads of Bureaus, Members of Congress, the Diplomatic Corps and distinguished Military and Naval officers to have the preference, and these of course were sufficient to fill all the space thus accorded, although I did notice that there were many fair faces there from New-York and Brooklyn, who have not arrived at official political dignity, and have no desire to do so. About eighteen hundred ladies were thus admitted, the only place not crowded being the diplomatic gallery, which was reserved for Mrs. LINCOLN and other distinguished ladies.

The reporters' gallery was reserved for its especial purpose, the representative of each paper being admitted by ticket, and there was a sudden increase of strange faces among that class, to say nothing of the acquisition of ladies, who were sandwiched among the gentlemen of the press. The floor of the Senate was reserved for the Supreme Court, the Diplomatic Corps, members of the Cabinet, the Senators and members of the House, distinguished officers of the army and navy, and a very few others. This filled the floor entirely, save an area of a few feet in front of the presiding officer's chair. By the rules of etiquette, Mr. LINCOLN's Ministers occupied the most prominent place, they being seated immediately on the right of the main isle. The Diplomatic Corps occupied a similar position on the opposite side, so that the two bodies sat nearly facing each other.

The group of the Cabinet attracted great attention, for such a sight is seldom witnessed: the sharp, well-defined features of Mr. SEWARD, the determined, confident and energetic countenance of Mr. STANTON, the serene, placid face of Mr. WELLES, the noble mien of Mr. SPEED, the genial, self-possessed manner of the business-like Mr. DENISON, and the calm dignity of Mr. USHER, were each one a study for the philosopher, and many a beaming eye from the gallery looked upon them with a woman's curiosity.

The diplomatic corps were in full court dress, and attracted much attention and comment. The Senators were seated immediately behind the two bodies just mentioned.

The closing legislative scenes in the Senate were of a very quiet character, the Civil Appropriation Bill suffering the same fate there as in the House; and when the hour of 12 was reached, Mr. FOOTE, the President pro tem. of the Senate, arose, and on behalf of the Senators addressed Vice-President HAMLIN in a feeling and courteous speech, in which he conveyed their thanks to him and their appreciation of the able and impartial manner in which his duties as presiding officer had been discharged. Mr. HAMLIN responded in fitting terms, and in a manner which convinced all the Senators and all others that he severed his official relations with that body with regret.

VICE-PRESIDENT JOHNSON'S ADDRESS.

Mr. HAMLIN then administered the oath of office to Hon. ANDREW JOHNSON, Vice-President elect, who then made a brief address.

Mr. JOHNSON, before taking the oath of office made a short speech, which, as in the case of Mr. HAMLIN, was nearly inaudible, owing to the want of order which prevailed among the women in the galleries. By the choice of the people, he said, he had been made presiding officer of this body, and, in presenting himself here in obedience to the behests of the Constitution of the United States, it would, perhaps, not be out of place to remark just here what a striking thing the Constitution was. It was the Constitution of the people of the country, and under it, here to-day, before the American Senate, he felt that he was a man and an American citizen. He had a proud illustration of the fact that, under the Constitution, a man could rise from the ranks to occupy the second place in the gift of the American people and of the American Government. Those of us who have labored our whole lives for the establishment of a free Government knew how to cherish its great blessings. He would say to Senators and others before him—to the Supreme Court which sat before him, that they all got their power from the people of this country. Turning toward Mr. CHASE, Mr. JOHNSON said, And your exaltation and position depend upon the people. Then turning toward the Cabinet, he said, And I will say to you, Mr. Secretary SEWARD, and to you, Mr. Secretary STANTON, and to you, Mr. Secretary—(to a gentleman near by, sotto voce, Who is Secretary of the Navy? the person addressed replied in a whisper, Mr. WELLES)—and to you, Mr. Secretary WELLES, I would say, you all derive your power from the people. Mr. JOHNSON then remarked that the great element of vitality in this Government was its nearness and proximity to the people. He wanted to say to all who heard him, in the face of the American people, that all power was derived from the people. He would say, in the hearing of the Foreign Ministers, for he was going to tell the truth here to-day, that he was a plebeian—he thanked God for it. It was the popular heart of this nation that was nearing to sustain Cabinet officials and the President of the United States. It was a strange occasion that called forth a plebeian like him to tell such things as these. Mr. JOHNSON next adverted to affairs in Tennessee, and the abolition of slavery there. He thanked God Tennessee was a State in the Union, and had never been cut. The State Government had been discontinued for a time—there had been an interregnum, a hiatus—but she had never been out of the Union. He stood here to-day as her representative. On this day she would elect a Governor and a Legislature, and she would very soon send Senators and members to Congress.

EXTRA SESSION OF SENATE.

The proclamation of the President convening the Senate in Executive session, was then read, and this closed the proceedings of that day.

THE PRESIDENT TAKES THE OATH OF OFFICE.

The President, escorted by Marshal LAMON and the members of the House and Private Secretary NICOLAY, now appeared and entered the Chamber.

The scene at this moment was one of rare brilliancy and great interest. The galleries were radiant with the beautiful faces, eager eyes and elegant apparel of two thousand ladies, the dress of the members of the diplomatic corps was brilliant and conspicuous, the black gowns of the venerable Judges of the Supreme Court seemed invested with additional dignity; the Senators sat in their seats more grave and thoughtful than usual; and interspersed among them could be seen the glorious face of Admiral FARRAGUT, the martial figure of Gen. HOOKER, and many other distinguished officers. For a few moments all is very silent, while a quiet consultation is going on. Up to this time it is supposed that the inaugural will be delivered in the Chamber, but a ray of sunlight is detected penetrating the hall. A movement toward the door is observable on the floor, and a rush takes place from the galleries to the corridors and staircases. It was evident that the inaugural was to be delivered in the open air, and a position to see and hear is the chief thing now to be obtained; and just here was committed one of the great blunders of the arrangements of the day. It was generally announced in the morning that all ingress to the Capitol must be by the main entrance to the Senate on the East front. This was very proper, and all holding tickets were thus admitted; but when the crowd attempted to get out this was the only door open and the crush was terrible, the stair-cases and corridors became a mass of surging humanity, propelled by the pressure from the rear, and moving not where it wanted to; but anywhere it could find any avenue of escape. Ladies were lifted off their feet and carried down staircases. By the immense pressure from behind, crowds went rushing through the building, trying to get out, and getting out finally on every side but the right side, landing in the mud in the streets, to the great loss of time, temper and patience. Not one in fifty of that immense audience got within hearing distance of the President, on account of this blunder, and very many only got on the ground just as he closed the address, and didn't even see him. The procession was a slim affair, the military and the Philadelphia fire companies being the chief feature.

The President, accompanied by his son and Senator FOSTER, of Connecticut, rode in an open barouche, which was followed by several close carriages, containing distinguished individuals of both sexes. The military escort was composed of both white and black troops, and the cavalry body-guard of the President, the Union League car on wheels, and a monitor similarly mounted and manned by a set of jolly tars, were the chief mechanical features of the line. Only two or three civic societies turned out, the streets being in a very bad condition. The citizens of Washington did absolutely nothing toward investing the pageant with interest or attractions, being too much engaged in gorging their own pockets from the pockets of sojourners, but the attendance of visitors was a grand success. Pennsylvania-avenue, for once, rivaled Broadway in its busiest days.

THE PRESIDENT'S RECEPTION.

After the ceremony of the oath and the delivery of the address, the President repaired, at the head of the procession to the White House, and the inauguration was over. The great feature of the evening was the public reception, and there was another repetition of the Senate Chamber jam. From 8 o'clock in the evening until after midnight, the Presidential mansion was densely crowded with a great throng of people. The rush was so great that hundreds of carriages were kept waiting from one to two hours before they could deliver their occupants at the door, and many hundreds after waiting thus long, and hearing of the dreadful crush inside, turned away without entrance. Many distinguished ladies and gentlemen were present, and the President received all with characteristic good nature, and those that had the faculty and patience to squeeze through the crowd seemed to enjoy themselves. The affair was decidedly democratic. Many ladies, who had the bad taste to attend in full toilette, suffered losses amounting to hundreds of dollars, in having valuable laces, dresses, &c., torn to pieces by the pressure.

THE INAUGURATION BALL.

The great feature now is the grand Inauguration Ball, to take place to-morrow night, and, thus far, it promises to be the best-managed affair connected with this occasion. Several thousand tickets have been sold at ten dollars each, and there will be an immense attendance. All the repositories in the Patent Office that can be disturbed have been removed to give room for the promenade, while the grand hall, most elegantly decorated, will afford room for eight hundred dancers on the floor at one time. The supper room is about half as large. A very grand affair is anticipated.

NEWS FROM WASHINGTON.

Special Dispatches to the New-York Times.

WASHINGTON, Sunday, March 5.

A VETO BY THE PRESIDENT.

The President, it is understood, has the Cotton Bill under consideration, and will probably veto it.

THE CABINET.

It is not believed that the President will send to the Senate the name of any Cabinet officer except that of Mr. MCCULLOUGH, to fill the vacancy occasioned by Mr. FESSENDEN's resignation. Mr. USHER will not be disturbed, at least for some weeks to come.

THE FREEDMEN'S BUREAU.

Candidates for the Freedmen's Bureau, just created, are coming out rapidly. Among the names mentioned are those of Gen. BUTLER and Mr. BIRNEY of Missouri.

Dispatches to the Associated Press.

WASHINGTON, Sunday, March 5.

THE EXECUTIVE CALENDAR CLEARED.

The Senate, several hours before its adjournment yesterday, cleared its executive calendar of all the pending Presidential nominations, six hundred in number, nearly all of a military character, which were confirmed.

CONFIRMATION OF MR. DEFREES.

The President, yesterday, sent in the nomination of JOHN D. DEFREES for Superintendent of Public Printing, and the Senate unanimously confirmed it. This is a deserved compliment to the uniform courtesy and ability which have marked this gentleman's management of the Government Letter-press Printing Bureau during the past four years.

LOOKING AFTER PRIVATE INTERESTS.

Many persons are here from a distance, looking after their private interests, and seeking influence to assist them in the procurement of high as well as low positions. They do not seem to be mindful of the fact that there are to be no wholesale removals from place. The terms of about nine-tenths of the commissioned civil officers will very soon expire. This will give the President an opportunity to renew their commissions, or appoint others as he may think proper.

SPEAKER COLFAX AND THE PRESS.

Previous to the adjournment of Congress, the reporters and correspondents occupying the House reporters gallery, united without distinction of party in a letter to Speaker COLFAX, as an honored journalist, expressive of their gratification with the courtesy, dignity and ability which he exhibited in the discharge of the important duties of the Chair, while at the same time they appreciated not less the virtues which adorn his private life. The speaker made a brief reply to those whom he addressed as brethren of the Press, placing a high estimate on their voluntary compliment, especially as they had been impartial and constant observers of his conduct.

HASTY AND CONFUSED LEGISLATION.

The hasty and confused manner in which business was passed through Congress the last two days of the session, is not among the most creditable of the proceedings of Congress. The Senate amendments to the amendatory revenue, the amendatory tariff, and the Indian Appropriation Bills, were not even read to the House, being so numerous, but were all non-concurred in bodily, and forthwith sent to the Conference Committees, on whose reports, and with but brief, and occasionally imperfect explanations, they were adopted; and again, to a bill merely to define the pay of officers' servants, twenty or thirty sections were added in relation to military affairs, including an amendatory Enrollment Bill and kindred objects; and on these there had to be a committee of Conference, and rushed through without an intelligent knowledge of their character. The Civil Appropriation Bill owes its defeat to being loaded down with extraneous amendments and the want of time to adjust the differences between the two Houses.

The Amendatory Tariff Bill imposes an additional duty of $2 a ton on railroad iron.

COLORED PEOPLE AT THE RECEPTION.

The *Chronicle*, of to-day, says, speaking of the reception at the Executive Mansion, last night: "Many colored persons appeared to pay their respects to the President and lady, among whom were FRED. DOUGLASS and wife."

THE EXTRA SESSION OF THE SENATE.

The extra session of the Senate has nothing to do with legislation, but will act upon nominations for office, and probably continue for two weeks.

THE OFFICERS OF BOTH HOUSES.

It is just to say the officers and clerks of the two houses of Congress have been uniformly courteous in their accommodations to the press, for examining and reporting important documents and other public papers. As for the members of Congress, they have received more favors from, than they have conferred upon the press.

CLOSING SCENES.

The closing scenes of Congress were not disgraced by personal quarrels, nor were there any prominent or noisy manifestations of drunkenness as heretofore.

NEW-YORK SUPERINTENDENT OF MILITARY AGENCIES.

The Governor of New-York has appointed D. G. MORGAN Superintendent of Military Agencies.

The agent at Washington is Col. E. R. GOODRICH; at New-York depot, Col. VINCENT COLYER; at Baltimore, Maj. H. S. RICHARDSON; at Alexandria, N. DEDERA; at Philadelphia, Rev. JAMES DE BOIS; at City Point, Mrs. R. H. SPENCER. Agents will soon be appointed at Harper's Ferry, City Point and Annapolis. The object is to visit New-York soldiers in hospitals, to supply their wants, and, as rapidly as possible, procure their transfer to New-York State hospitals, besides receiving contributions for their benefit, and in other respects assist and comfort them.

Rejoicings at Albany.

ALBANY, Saturday, March 4.

A salute of one hundred guns was fired here to day in honor of the recent victories over the enemy, and in the evening the Post-office, the office of the Assistant Provost-Marshal-General, and other public buildings, as well as many private residences were illuminated.

Rejoicings at Providence.

PROVIDENCE, Sunday, March 5.

Notwithstanding the heavy rain, noteworthy demonstrations were made here yesterday. Flags were displayed, national salutes fired, and the First Light Infantry paraded, and had a festival. Gen. PAINE's Second Brigade also made a fine parade, with infantry, cavalry and light artillery.

FROM KENTUCKY.

Gen. Palmer on Compulsory Colored Enlistments and Bounty Brokers—Serious Charges Against Chief Justice J. F. Bullitt.

Correspondence of the New-York Times.

LOUISVILLE, Wednesday, March 1, 1865.

Gen. PALMER announces that the use of force or menaces to compel colored enlistments is unlawful and disgraceful, and any violence or threats toward whites or blacks to compel them to enlist will be severely punished. He forbids any bounty broker to accompany any recruiting party or in any way intermeddle with their operations.

The Legislature, I learn, has provided a $100 State bounty for each one-year Kentucky United States Volunteer.

Guerrillas seem ubiquitous. Even here, in broad daylight, they make off with horses and vehicles of civilians and of officers, and before the alarm is given they are out of sight and scent, and this though Provost patrols are on every block.

A House Committee (of three Conservatives and two Radicals) report that the testimony before them strongly conduces to show that Judge J. F. BULLITT was, last Summer, a prominent officer of the Sons of Liberty, "A treasonable organization, against the suppression of this rebellion, and intended for aiding it in the overthrow of the United States Government, and for encouraging lawlessness and anarchy in the country." The committee recommend that he be summoned to answer before the bar of the House, and to appear within twenty days after the service of the summons. If their recommendations pass, another adjourned session is likely.

On 1st January last, our eight Kentucky banks of issue had an aggregate capital of $9,402,250, and a circulation of $2,343,151. Jan. 1, 1860, the same had $12,660,670 capital, $13,520,207 circulation.

PONTIAC.

Reports from Fortress Monroe.

FORTRESS MONROE, Friday, March 3.

The steamers *Glaucis* and *Neptune* arrived here this afternoon from Smithville, N. C. The Captains of both of these steamers reported having encountered during the trip up the coast very heavy northeast gales. They sailed from Smithville on the 1st inst., at 1 o'clock A. M., and shortly before they left, the steamer *Gen. Meigs* arrived from Wilmington, N. C., bringing the report, which was generally credited by army and navy officers stationed at Smithville, that a portion of Gen. SHERMAN's army had arrived at and was marching through Wilmington, N. C., from which it is conjectured that a junction with Gen. TERRY's army has been effected.

Owing to the thick fog in the bay the mail-boat *James T Brady*, from Washington, D. C., due here at 7 o'clock this morning, did not arrive until 3 o'clock this afternoon.

Sales of Seven-Thirties.

PHILADELPHIA, Saturday, March 4.

JAY COOKE, the subscription agent, reports the sales of the seven-thirty loan to-day at $4,130,000, including a subscription of $234,000 from New-York, and 3,000 individual subscriptions of $50 and $100. Total subscriptions for the week, $20 577,450.

Marine Disaster.

PORTLAND, Me., Sunday, March 5.

The brig *Hattie S. Emery*, from Cardenas, arrived to-day. While coming up through White Head passage, she struck a ledge, but came off—leaking 2,000 strokes per hour.

Sailing of the Nova Scotian.

PORTLAND, Me., Sunday, March 5.

The *Nova Scotian*, Capt. BROWN, sailed at 3 o'clock this morning for Londonderry and Liverpool.

The New-York Times.

VOL. XIV......NO. 4190. NEW-YORK, FRIDAY, MARCH 10, 1865. PRICE FOUR CENTS

FRENZY IN THE SOUTH.

HIGHLY IMPORTANT FROM RICHMOND.

Signs of the Dissolution of the Confederacy.

Strong Submission Party in the Rebel Capital.

CONSPIRACY AGAINST JEFF. DAVIS.

Plot to Overthrow the Rebel Government and Install a Submissionist.

INDIGNANT PROTEST OF THE SENTINEL.

Bitter Reproaches against the Rebel Congress.

It is Pronounced a Wretched Failure.

All Power to be Vested in Davis or Lee.

Is Lee Ready to Consider Terms?

WASHINGTON, Thursday, March 9.

The Richmond *Enquirer* of the 7th has a reply to a correspondent, who inquires:

"*What mean these rumors of Senatorial Committees approaching the President to submit terms of submission?* Is that report true? Are any Senators or Representatives whipped? Have they approached the President, to press upon him any such base propositions? Who were the Senators? What were the propositions? Is there any plan on foot to force the President to compromise with subjugation or resign? Is there any one else ready to volunteer resignation in case he is forced to vacate his place, and if he does, who is proposed to fill that place? *Is any attempt made by rumors to create the impression that Gen. Lee is ready to consider terms for laying down arms under the pretext of preventing the sufferings and sacrifices of a forced surrender?* Who are busy in these plans of surrendering to subjugation? Speak out; the crisis demands boldness and decision, and determined resistance to internal as well as external enemies.

The worst enemies who now depress us are the whipped seceders. This hour of agony is no time for factious opposition or for faltering with peace propositions, which can lead to nothing but despair, relaxation and ruin. *Terms of reconstruction now coming from Congress* are nothing else but subjugation. Let us know the worst, that the summary remedy may be applied."

The *Enquirer*, in response to its correspondent, says *it cannot answer all questions asked, for want of information*, and then goes on in the following remarkable and significant language, showing unmistakably that the rebellion is in its death throes:

"That there is a party of whipped seceders in and about Richmond, cannot be denied. *They are cowed and cowardly, miserable wretches, who brought the war upon the country, and who would now surrender to the enemy. We have no doubt but that there was a plan on foot to force Mr. Davis to resign, and that Mr. Stephens had consented to resign*, so that Mr. HUNTER, as President of the Senate, would become President. The plan, we hope and believe, has miscarried. At any rate, the conspirators may understand that if they should succeed, *they will have placed a barren sceptre in their grasp, thence to be wrenched by an unlineal hand, no son of theirs succeeding.*

ROBERT C. LEE, by and with the consent of the army and the people will grasp the sceptre they may wrench from the hands of Mr. DAVIS, and wield it for the safety and security of his country's liberty and independence. No cabal of whipped seceders shall capitulate this country into slavery and crouch at the footstool of Mr. LINCOLN.

The Congress has utterly failed. It is incompetent and is doing much injury. It has neither capacity nor courage, and is wanting in firmness and resolution. It is unfit for revolution. *The very men who were the foremost to secede are the first to surrender.* a single head and a single arm is now needed, and if Congress would consult its patriotism it would intrust all power with the President and Gen. LEE and go home. The Virginia State banks can furnish one or two millions in gold, and this will secure the supplies now needed. *Let the Legislature promptly act and turn the gold over to Gen. Lee. The Congress is defunct.* The country no longer looks to it for any aid in the struggle. The negroes have been withheld until it is now nearly too late. The currency is beyond their power to help. Those who talk now of compromise mean submission to subjugation.

INDIGNANT PROTEST.

The *Sentinel*, (JEFF. DAVIS' official organ,) in an editorial says:

"This new levy of the Yankees will not avail to overwhelm us. We will surely win the fight, *if we do our duty.* None are more confident of this than those who have had the opportunity of observing things at the North. None are more enthusiastic, none more buoyant with courage and hope—and let no man suppose that such is not the spirit of our people. Let no one imagine that the few poltroons with beards on, who are whipped without even having been in a fight, are a sample of our population. It is a shame indeed that these miserable tremblers are allowed to vex the patience and tire the ear with the exhibitions of their disgraceful cowardice. But we protest against judging others by many. We protest against the judging of Richmond by these whipped croakers, titled or untitled. *We wish our women would take their broomsticks and drive them into the river.* We tell our people that the people are as unconquered and resolved as they, and will stand up to them and sustain them. Let them take care of the Yankees. Those who are to join them in the trenches will take *good care of the whipped men at home. We do not intend to be sold out or betrayed by them.* Let them be sure that such is the temper of the public mind that to attempt this would be as much as the man's life would be worth. *If we cannot find law in the books for such cases, we will be a law unto ourselves.* An ancient people had no law against parricide. We, too, may not have provided for some crimes against our safety, supposing them impossible. But the people will not consent to be destroyed by them nevertheless. We say to our readers, and we say it to stimulate no false hopes and to excite to no useless sacrifices, we say to them in all honesty and sincerity, our success in this contest, God willing, *is sure if we do our duty.* The victory is ours unless we voluntarily forfeit it. The game is in our hands unless we choose to throw it way. It all depends on ourselves. There is nothing in the situation to defeat us. We say this on the highest military authority. If Heaven in its wrath were to curse us with a meanness of soul that would lead us to renounce the price for which we have toiled so long; renounce the liberties for which the noble army of martyrs have died, and fling away the glorious heritage which our fathers gave us; that indeed would be misery, for it would be disgrace, infamy, hopeless ruin, the very blackness of eternal darkness on our country and our names. Proud we are now to claim JACKSON as our compatriot. *The very Turk would kiss us, if shameless, we did it.* We are not yet reduced to the necessity of taking courage from despair. The enemy have, indeed, shut us up to that necessity, if it should ever come. But, thank Heaven, it has not come.

We have bright, natural, certain hopes; hopes big with victory, and radiant with sunlight and glory, if we will bear hardness as a good soldier a little longer. By all that we love, and that are dead; by the fame that attracts, and the shame that urges us, *stand up like men in this time of trial*—the hour of darkness that precedes the day.

SHERIDAN'S RECENT VICTORY.

Official Intelligence of the Battle—Where it Took Place—Our Captures.

WHEELING, Va., Thursday, March 9.

Official information from Cumberland, Md., of the 8th inst., states that Col. THOMPSON, of the First New-Hampshire Cavalry, of Gen. SHERIDAN's command, has just arrived at Winchester with forty officers and 1,300 enlisted men as prisoners, and eight pieces of artillery captured and destroyed.

The principal battle was fought at Fisherville, five miles from Staunton, Va.

TWO RAILROAD DISASTERS.

Accident on the Hudson River Railroad—Train Run into an Open Drawbridge—Two Lives Lost.

POUGHKEEPSIE, Thursday, March 9.

A freight train, bound north on the Hudson River Railroad, about 9 o'clock last evening, ran into the Peekskill drawbridge, smashing several cars and killing the engineer and fireman. At the time of the accident a sloop was passing through the draw, and the necessary signals were visible. The engineer's name was JOHN HEFFERNAN, that of the fireman was WM. LENT. The body of the latter has not been found. The body of the engineer was found on the top of the boiler, four feet under water.

ANOTHER ACCOUNT.

On Wednesday evening, at Peekskill, on the Hudson River Railroad, an accident happened by which, unfortunately, two men lost their lives. Mr. M. BROWN, a passenger on the 4:15 P. M. train from Albany to New-York, has given us the following particulars relating to it:

About 8 o'clock the drawbridge at Peekskill was opened for the purpose of letting a small vessel get through. The Albany evening express had just passed when the draw was opened for the sloop. At this juncture, a special baggage train came along. The signal-man says he showed the usual danger signal, which the engineer on the train did not see, or unheeded.

The train was signaled to "break off" when it was about two hundred feet from the draw. The train came rushing on, when the locomotive and tender were precipitated into the water, the tender being disconnected from the locomotive, and thrown on one side of the bridge, while the engine was on the other. Four of the cars were smashed to pieces, piled one on the other in the water, and completely filling up the chasm, while two other cars lay on top of the whole, but partly on the bridge.

In one of the latter were two boys who were endeavoring to get to Albany without paying the company the usual consideration for the transit. They fortunately escaped being uninjured by the crash and the employes of the line.

No trace could be found of the engineer, JOHN HEFFERNAN, or of the fireman, whose name our informant did not ascertain. A hat and coat were found on the scene of the accident supposed to belong to some one of them. A party of men soon arrived on the spot, and after clearing the debris threw a temporary bridge across the river.

The train from Albany was due at this time but did not come on for a considerable time, about an hour and a half. The cause of the delay was another accident, which took place between Fishkill and Garrison. When the train was on its way between these points a man was observed on the track, the engineer whistled, but he took no notice of it, and before the engineer could stop the train he was struck.

The engineer at once returned and found that the man was badly cut. He appeared to be under the influence of liquor. This delayed the train about an hour and a half, and the supposition is that were it not for this delay the express train would have come right down on the baggage train, and the loss of life which must have ensued would be fearful.

Our informant also heard, at Garrison Station, that a man, an employe of the company, was killed the same evening, on the same line, by falling from the cars. The express was detained at Peekskill about five hours, while a bridge was being constructed to convey the passengers over the river to a train waiting to receive them on the other side. Damage about $50,000.

We understand that the road will be in order, and trains run regularly as usual to-day (Friday.)

Still Another Smash—Train Thrown Off the Track—One Man Injured.

POUGHKEEPSIE, Thursday, March 9.

As the down express train on the Hudson River Railroad, which left Albany this morning, reached a point below Stuyvesant Station, it ran on a broken rail; the tender, express-car and five passenger cars bounding from the track and lodging against the embankment on the east side. The train, at the time of the accident, was going at the rate of 25 miles per hour. Strange to say, but one person was hurt. He was a brakeman named JENKINS. His leg was broken. The track was badly obstructed, delaying all the down trains four or five hours.

FROM HILTON HEAD.

ARRIVAL OF THE FULTON.

Our Forces Advanced to the Santee River.

All Quiet in Charleston.

The United States steam transport *Fulton*, Capt. WOTTON, from Hilton Head, S. C., March 6, at 1:30 P. M., to United States Quartermaster, arrived this afternoon.

The United States steamer *Harvest Moon*, Admiral DAHLGREN's temporary flagship, was blown up by a torpedo on Thursday last, while coming out of Georgetown. The Admiral escaped injury. One man was seriously injured.

Everything is progressing smoothly in Charleston. Traders are beginning to open their stores, and the city is rapidly assuming a business aspect.

Gen. JNO. P. HATCH is in command of the Northern District, Department of the South, and Gen. SCHIMMELFENNIG of the defences about Charleston.

On the N. E. Railroad the cars are running as far as Goose Creek.

Gen. POTTER has advanced to the Santee River without meeting opposition.

News has been received of the total destruction of Columbia by the rebel and our own forces.

OUR CHARLESTON CORRESPONDENCE.

The People Coming to Their Senses—Condition of the Citizens—From Columbia—Sherman's Movements—Rebel Incendiaries—Miscellaneous.

CHARLESTON, S. C., Sunday, March 5, 1865.

Under the new order of things the people of Charleston are gradually coming to their senses, and evince a disposition to make the city once more the leading trading mart for this section of the country. When we first took possession the citizens were shy, and hesitated about making their appearance on the street, but now they come forth in swarms, and of course the majority of them profess to be on the side of the Union. Were it not for Northern enterprise, however, Charleston might remain in the same dormant state in which we found it for years. But happily the new comers have infused a spirit of activity into the old inhabitants, and we shall see the city in a few months' time full of life and gaiety. Some of the citizens still cling to the hope that the rebel Government will eventually succeed in establishing itself on a firm basis, but the same citizens are laughed and jeered at by their more wise neighbors.

For the past week numerous inquiries have been made as to SHERMAN's progress through South Carolina. Many of the citizens here have relatives and friends in Columbia and vicinity, and are very anxious to learn of their fate. A few days ago the news was brought that SHERMAN had entered Columbia. In Columbia was stored an immense quantity of public and private property. To that place fled thousands of people from Charleston at the time SHERMAN was marching from Savannah.

It was not thought by the rebels that SHERMAN would travel so far inland; they had made up their minds that having captured Charleston he would be satisfied to remain on the coast a month, and then proceed in the direction of Wilmington. Acting on this impression, the citizens removed the most of their valuable property to Columbia, and, as a consequence, lost it all. We have not heard direct from SHERMAN since the news came of his being near Charlotte. The impression prevails in Charleston, even among those who sympathize with the rebels, that SHERMAN will succeed in joining his forces with GRANT in Virginia. A few days ago, BEAUREGARD, with eight thousand men, was dancing about somewhere in North Carolina for the purpose of opposing the progress of the Union forces. According to the statements of refugees, he was daily expecting reinforcements from LEE, although it seemed quite evident that LEE had none to spare. The people in Charleston will have to wait a long time before they get good news from rebeldom.

King-street is alive with business. One is astonished to see how some sutlers and other traders have taken stores and exposed goods for sale. The stores are doing an excellent business too. From morning till night they are thronged with customers. The great trouble is that the majority of the citizens have rebel money only. They appreciate the fact that this money is worthless; yet they are very reluctant to part with it without receiving a portion of an equivalent in return. The other day I saw a man who had $10,000 in rebel notes, and who was willing to exchange the entire amount for $500 in greenbacks, and could not find a purchaser. Men, who, before the war, were the wealthiest in the city, are now in the condition of the poorest. Yesterday a man, who, three years ago was worth two millions of dollars, confessed to me that he could not raise twenty dollars in current money if it has demanded of him to save his neck from the gallows. I looked at him, and thought he was just the fellow that the gallows had been waiting for during the past four years. A considerable amount of gold and silver is in circulation. It was the practice of the shrewd ones to turn their rebel rag currency into coin as often as an opportunity offered; hence we see many persons attired in soiled and tattered garments, with the real stuff in their pockets. In accordance with a general order, issued at the Post Headquarters, a premium of one hundred per cent. is allowed on gold, and seventy-five per cent. on silver. So far as subsistence stores are concerned, the citizens of Charleston appear to have been better off than their neighbors in Savannah. To be sure, they did not have a large quantity of meal, but of rice and corn they had an abundant supply. A large quantity of rice and corn, stored in public buildings, was seized by our authorities, and turned over to a committee of the citizens, to be distributed among the most needy.

A change has recently been made in the command of the district. Brig.-Gen. JOHN P. HATCH is in command of the Northern District, Department of the South, his predecessor, Brig.-Gen. SCHIMMELFENNIG, having been assigned to the command of the defences about Charleston. Gen. HATCH is an officer of merit and ability, and has distinguished himself on several occasions on the field. He was in command of the forces that left Pocotaligo to proceed toward Charleston at the time SHERMAN commenced his campaign from Savannah. During that march Gen. HATCH encountered forces of the enemy at different points, but invariably drove them from their positions.

By a recent order, all citizens desiring any favor whatever from the Government, are required to call upon Provost-Marshal [illegible] and take the oath of allegiance. A large number of citizens have, consequently, availed themselves of this opportunity of proving their loyalty to the old Union. Among the number who have taken the oath of allegiance are several ladies; in fact, the first one to take the oath was a lady. Several parties have expressed their apprehension that by taking the oath they would be liable to be forced into the army—not discriminating between the wholesale conscription of the rebels and the system of draft as observed by our own authorities. They do not take into consideration the fact that any one who has served in the rebel ranks cannot, by established law, serve in a military capacity under the United States Government. I am sorry to observe that many persons who profess to be Union, have shown a reluctance to take the oath of allegiance. They proffer all manner of excuses, which simply mean that they are about as much rebel as Union in their composition. Under the present *régime*, the people of Charleston can take their choice—identify themselves as Unionists or rebels.

Maj.-Gen. GILLMORE came up from Hilton Head yesterday. Since his arrival in the department he has been on the constant move. On one day we find him at Savannah, and on the following day at Charleston, or some other point on the coast. By some means the people of Charleston always know when Gen. GILLMORE arrives in town. The moment his flagship touches the pier, a group of citizens are sure to make their appearance and extend him a hearty welcome. It is curious to notice the interest that the people take in informing each other of the fact that Gen. GILLMORE has arrived. When he appears on the street, we are assured of his presence by the remarks that are made by those who espy him. One will say there goes Gen. GILLMORE, the man who gave us so much uneasiness; and another will remark, there passes the officer who destroyed our city. All seem to look upon him as an officer worthy of their particular attention.

The other day we had a skirmish at Monk's Corner, a point on the county road, running nearly parallel with the Northwestern Railroad. The troops on our side engaged in the affair were under the immediate command of Brig.-Gen. POTTER. They advanced in regular order toward the Santee River, intending to make that line their objective, but before they reached the bank a body of rebels made their appearance and disputed the progressive movement. This resulted in a skirmish, in which the rebels were routed. Our loss was only two wounded. The rebels lost a number of killed and wounded. To-day our men hold the line of the Santee River. The cars on the Northwestern Railroad are running as far as Goose Creek. We hold Somerville, which is twenty-two miles north of us; also several points farther to the west, on roads leading to Columbia.

Yesterday, Gen. GILLMORE, accompanied by a party of ladies and gentlemen, among whom I noticed Capt. WOTTON, of the steamship *Fulton*, his wife and daughter, paid a visit to the ruins of Sumter. The party were rowed to the fort in small boats from the steamer *W. W. Coit*, which anchored a short distance from the landing. They walked around the parapet, peered into the magazine, visited the casemates and bombproofs, and wondered at the immense amount of work that had been accomplished by our engineers and artillerists on Morris Island.

The news reached us to-day that the *Harvest Moon*, Admiral DAHLGREN's temporary flagship, was blown up by a torpedo, near Georgetown, on Thursday last. The Admiral himself was aboard, but escaped injury. Only one man was injured by the explosion. The *Harvest Moon* was a sister ship to the *Philadelphia*, the latter having been used as a flagship by the Admiral for a long time.

On Friday last the freedmen of Florida presented a beautiful flag to the Twenty first Regiment, U. S. C. T. The presentation speech was made by Gen. U. S. LITTLEFIELD, and responded to by Lieut.-Col. A. G. BENNETT, of the Twenty-first. The regiment was drawn up in line on Citadel-square, and received the colors from the hands of one of thirteen young girls. A band of music was in attendance, and the whole affair passed off in a most gratifying manner.

Last week Gen. GILLMORE was made the recipient of a beautiful wreath, formed of magnolia leaves. Attached to the wreath was a slip of paper, bearing the following inscription:

"God save the United States.
Long live the United States.
Rule the United States."

The weather for the past week has been damp and disagreeable, but we are looking forward to warmth and sunshine.

WHIT.

GEN. GRANT'S ARMY.

The Freshet in the James—Exchange of Prisoners Resumed—Report that Lynchburgh is in Our Possession.

WASHINGTON, Thursday, March 9.

Information from the Army of the Potomac says:

All is quiet in this department.

The freshet in the James River has nearly subsided, and the exchange of prisoners has been resumed.

A batch of released prisoners are expected down this morning.

Gen. FOSTER's division, of the Twenty-fourth Corps, was reviewed to-day, Tuesday, by Maj.-Gen. ORD. The day being fair the review passed off well. The troops presented a very good appearance, and elicited the highest encomiums from Gen. ORD, as well as from a large concourse of spectators.

A colored division of the Twenty-fifth Corps was also reviewed, and their appearance was equally commended.

A report is in circulation to the effect that Lynchburgh is in our possession, but it cannot be traced to any reliable source.

From Fortress Monroe.

FORTRESS MONROE, Wednesday, March 8.

The steamer *Illinois* arrived this morning from Port Royal, S. C., with the 500 rebel officers who were placed under rebel fire in retaliation for a similar exposure of our officers at Charleston. They will probably be sent to Varina to be exchanged.

The steamers *Weybosset*, *United States* and *Star* arrived to-day from Fort Fisher. They bring no later news from Gen. SCHOFIELD's army, which still maintained its advanced position some ten miles from Wilmington, and until something definite is heard from SHERMAN, it would not hazard too far an advance.

In consequence of the stormy weather for a week past, many vessels have put into the roads for shelter.

The ship *Guy Mannering*, from New-York, arrived here to-day.

EXPEDITION FROM KEY WEST.

Military and Naval Attack on St. Marks—Result of the Expedition Not Known.

PHILADELPHIA, Thursday, March 9.

The *Bulletin* says:

"The United States steamship *Bermuda*, from the East and West Gulf Blockading Squadrons, has arrived at the navy-yard. She was due here on Monday afternoon, but in consequence of rough weather and the breaking of some machinery off Cedar Keys, she was delayed.

She reports that on the 24th of February, an expedition, under the command of Brig.-Gen. NEWTON, consisting of all the troops, both white and colored, stationed at Key West, and the gunboats *Honduras*, *Britannia*, *Magnolia* and *Hendrick Hudson*, started for the purpose of capturing St. Marks.

The result of the expedition had not been heard at the time the *Bermuda* sailed.

The *Bermuda* brings 400 sick and discharged soldiers and sailors."

Seven-Thirties.

PHILADELPHIA, Thursday, March 9.

JAY COOKE reports the sales of 7.30s, to-day, to the amount of $4,065,150, including $135,000 from Chicago, and $1,000,000 from New-York, in single subscriptions, besides 2,843 individual subscriptions for $50 and $100 each.

SHERMAN IN SOUTH CAROLINA.

Sights and Scenes at Columbia on His Arrival.

Grand Flight of the Rebels and Entry of Sherman.

OUTRAGES OF WHEELER'S CAVALRY.

Our Army Singing Union Songs "with Tremendous Energy."

Correspondence of the Richmond Whig.

CHARLOTTE, Feb. 22, 1865.

Time has sufficiently quieted our nerves and restored a healthy circulation, to enable one to narrate a consistent story of the troublous hours through which we of Columbia have been led during the past week.

Sherman's advance on Columbia was unexpected. Sudden as surprising, it found all unprepared for the events which followed, and few cool enough in the crisis to yield to any other than the bent of the first impulse. Hence hundreds are to-day exiles from home who would give almost their all to be safely back. They have learned that being a refugee don't pay.

Orangeburgh and Kingsville were supposed to be the highest points northward on that line at which SHERMAN would strike. The people who planned his campaign thought from thence he would branch off toward Charaw and Fayetteville, leaving Columbia untouched. Four days dispelled the illusion. Our troops fell back until the sounds of cannon reverberated through the city. *Then public officers for the first time began to think of removing the Government stores.* The instructions from Richmond had left many of them no other discretion. Hurry, excitement and some confusion became the order of the day. Everybody, public and private wanted a car. The President of the Charlotte and South Carolina Railroad, Col. WM. JOHNSON, his assistants, Capt. SHARP, the agent of transportation, and his aids, now bent their energies to the Herculean task before them, and accomplished all that men could do. The trains from the South Carolina and Greenville roads were run upon the Charlotte track, filled and hurried away to return and fill again. Engines shrieked their signal notes, morning, noon and night. The activity was ceaseless. The depots were crowded with goods of every description. Passenger trains were thronged, ladies and families in their fright undergoing the most grievous torments of travel to escape from what they believed was a doomed city. The city resounded with the rumble of a thousand wheels, all bearing their freight to the grand funnel out of which it was to be discharged. Horses, wagons, negroes, everything that could aid in the removal of property, was brought into requisition, and between force and persuasion, an immense amount of labor was systematically, rapidly and judiciously employed.

By Wednesday night the tide was at its height. The enemy were within three miles. *The little army in their front* had given back step by step until, flanked out of the fortifications on the opposite side of the Congaree, they retired to the limits of the city itself, where a line of battle again reformed. Three or four shells thrown at the bridge increased the popular agitation until it became a fever. The stores were closed. Militia and detailed men were at the front. Army trains began to move through, and the truth at last flashed upon the minds of all, that Columbia must inevitably be evacuated. Few slept soundly in their beds during the night that followed.

Thursday, the 15th, the enemy opened on the city with shells. Some damage was done, but few casualties are reported. One gentleman only is said to have been killed. The State House, Nickerson's Hotel, *South Carolinian* office, together with some private residences, were paid an iron compliment, and the inmates evacuated without the usual polite formalities of leave-taking. Still the work of removal went bravely forward, and a vast amount was accomplished. The time was too brief, however, to do all, and hundreds of thousands of dollars' worth of public and private property remained in and about the depot, as a prey to the Yankee torch and pilferer.

The worst feature of the entire scene occurred on the day of which I write. A party of WHEELER's cavalry, accompanied by their officers, dashed into town, tied their horses, and as systematically as if they had been bred to the business, proceeded to break into the stores along Main-street and rob them of their contents. A detachment of detailed men fired on one party and drove them out. Capt. HAMILTON, the Provost-Marshal, with another officer, drew swords and pistols on another party, and succeeded in clearing several establishments; but the valiant raiders still swarmed like locusts, and to-day, a hundred miles away from Columbia, you may see men smoking the cigars and wearing on their saddles the elegant cloths stolen from the merchants of that city. It is said that two of the "cavalry" drew pistols on Gen. HAMPTON, who was attempting to protect a store, and threatened his life.

Under these circumstances you may well imagine that our people would rather see the Yankees or old Satan himself than a party of the aforesaid Wheeler's cavalry. The barbarities committed by some of them are represented to be frightful, "life, liberty and the pursuit of happiness" being perfectly incompatible with their presence.

Common rumor says that Sherman's treatment of citizens and private property was uniformly lenient and conciliatory. His headquarters were at Nickerson's Hotel.

The scenes up the railroad may be briefly described. Crowds at every depot seeking temporary shelter; some getting off, more getting on; twenty trains thundering one after the other in quick succession; screaming locomotives, crying babies, tearful women, families traveling in box cars among piles of bacon, salt, bandboxes, trunks and bed clothes; a break down near Winsboro; engine off the track; ten hours delay; enemy reported coming; more consternation; a long night; no wood, no water, no breakfast; ten carloads of ladies of the Treasury Department in most unattractive morning *dishabille*, with hair unkempt, and hollow, deepy eyes, shivering about in the red mucilaginous mud; ten or twelve carloads of Yankee prisoners just ahead, likewise at a dead halt; the guards around their camp fires, *and the individuals of a cerulean aspect singing with tremendous energy Union songs*; still ahead, the section-masters and bricklayers, with a gang of laborers repairing the road and holding post-mortem consultations over the remains of a deserted engine—finally, a run back three miles, a filling of tanks, a fresh start, and an arrival at Charlotte. There an avalanche upon the good people, an appeal to hospitality which is most warmly heeded, and a gradual simmering down of all the elements in agitation. Such, in brief, is the history of our evacuation of Columbia.

F. G. DE F.

Letters and Packages for the North and South Atlantic Blockading Squadrons.

PHILADELPHIA, Thursday, March 9.

All letters and packages for the officers and crews of the several vessels composing the North and South Atlantic Blockading Squadrons of the United States navy, left or forwarded to the office of JOSEPH E. DORITT & Co., No. 427 Walnut-street, Philadelphia, will be forwarded at 10 A. M., on Saturday morning next, by the United States steamer *Massachusetts*, free of any charge.

From Cairo—Acquittal of Gen. Paine—He is Attacked by a Witness.

CAIRO, Thursday, March 9.

It is reported that the court-martial at Paducah has acquitted Gen. PAINE of all charges preferred against him.

Gen. PAINE having accused Mr. ALEXANDER, of Paducah, of giving false testimony before the Military Commission last Fall, the latter individual attacked him on the street yesterday, with a revolver, and he was forced into an encounter. ALEXANDER was arrested and lodged in the guard-house.

New-Jersey Legislature.

TRENTON, N. J., Thursday, March 9.

The General County Bill, after the veto of the Governor, was defeated. A new bill has been introduced.

In the Senate the bill was passed to allow the State bounty to the families of naval recruits and colored volunteers. Mr. SCOVEL, of Camden, and Mr. RANDOLPH, of Hudson, advocated the bill.

THIRTY-NINTH CONGRESS.

SENATE—EXTRA SESSION.

WASHINGTON, Thursday, March 9.

THE COMMITTEES.

Mr. SPRAGUE rose to a question personal to himself. He had been serving as a member of the Committee on Military Affairs—but the caucus which recently remodeled the committees had transferred him from the Military Committee to the Committee on the Public Lands, without any previous knowledge on his part. His State (Rhode Island) had little or no interest in the public lands. She was among the first to offer troops to put down the rebellion, and having himself served with them, and having much interest in legislation pertaining to the military service, he had, with much pleasure, served on the Military Committee. He asked to be excused from serving on the Committee on Public Lands.

Mr. JOHNSON said this involved an unpleasant duty on the part of the Senate, and he appealed to the Senator to withdraw his request.

Mr. WILSON said that when the Senator served on the Military Committee he was always found attentive to his duties. He (WILSON) was surprised when he heard the Senator had been transferred to another committee. He (WILSON) was sure that the change was in no way intended to be disrespectful.

Mr. POMEROY did not presume too much in saying that the Senator would be welcome as a member of committee on Public Lands. As to Rhode Island not being interested in the public lands he would say that she was much concerned in the general question as any other State.

Mr. CONNESS was satisfied that there had been no intention to slight the Senator from Rhode Island.

Mr. SPRAGUE said he had no further remarks to make. He thought the circumstances and justice demanded that the Senate should accede to his request.

Mr. SHERMAN said he could not vote to excuse the Senator. He knew the difficulty in forming committees, and he had no doubt that an entirely satisfactory reason could be given for the change. He was satisfied that no disrespect was intended.

Mr. CLARK said that he, himself, was placed on the Military Committee, and would change with the Senator the Public Lands.

Mr. SPRAGUE thanked the Senator for his kindness, but could not accept of his proposition. He should have been glad to serve on the Committee on Military Affairs, as his heart had been with military matters since the beginning of the war. He had left a command to come to this body.

The Senate refused to excuse Senator SPRAGUE from service on the Committee on Public Lands.

INTERNAL REVENUE BILL.

On motion of Mr. SHERMAN, the Senate ordered the printing of 5,000 copies of the amended Internal Revenue Bill, which is to be properly indexed.

THE ARKANSAS SENATORS.

Mr. TRUMBULL, from the Committee on the Judiciary, made a report on the credentials of Mr. SNOW, Senator elect from Arkansas.

The committee say that in 1861, the constituted authorities of the State of Arkansas, so far as they could succeed, took the State beyond the authority of the United States, and that in pursuance of a law of Congress, the President, by proclamation, declared the inhabitants of that State to be included in the insurrection. Therefore, the committee recommend that the question of admission be postponed until the next Session, and until Congress shall take action in regard to the existing State Government of Arkansas.

The report was adopted.

VIRGINIA SENATORS.

Mr. DOOLITTLE presented the credentials of JOHN C. UNDERWOOD, as Senator elect from the State of Virginia, for six years from the 4th of March, 1865.

Mr. TRUMBULL said the Committee on the Judiciary had just made a report in the case of Arkansas, which was in a similar condition to Virginia, and it was therefore likely the committee would come to a similar conclusion.

Mr. HENDERSON did not indorse the Senator's views. He did not believe that the President's proclamation precluded the Senate from taking action on the subject of admitting Senators. We should encourage the reëstablishment of the local State Governments as a means of putting down the rebellion and guerrilla incursions.

ELECTION OF A CHAPLAIN.

The subject was temporarily laid aside in order to execute the special order, namely: The election of a chaplain for the Thirty-ninth Congress.

Mr. LANE, of Indiana, nominated Rev. Dr. BOWMAN, (Methodist,) the present incumbent.

Mr. HARRIS nominated Rev. Dr. GRAY, a Baptist clergyman, of Washington.

Thirty-nine votes were cast, of which 20 were necessary to a choice.

Rev. Dr. GRAY having received 27 votes, he was declared duly elected Chaplain.

VIRGINIA SENATOR AGAIN.

The consideration of the credentials of Judge UNDERWOOD was then resumed.

Mr. DOOLITTLE said the State of Virginia had been recognized by the Executive and by Congress. The Senate, when West Virginia was set apart as a separate State Government, admitted Senators from the remaining part of Virginia.

The further consideration of the subject was then postponed until the next session.

MORE UNSETTLED SEATS.

On motion, the credentials of JOSEPH SEGAR, of Virginia, and MICHAEL HAHN, of Louisiana, were withdrawn from the file, to be presented and laid over until the next session.

Mr. MORRILL, from the Committee on Contingent Expenses, reported against the resolution referred to them to allow pay and mileage to the Senators from Arkansas and Louisiana, on the ground of a want of jurisdiction, and therefore they asked to be discharged from the further consideration of the subject.

The resolution lies over.

NAVAL CONTRACTS.

Mr. NYE offered the following resolution, which was adopted:

Resolved, That the Secretary of the Navy be requested to organize a board of not less than three competent persons, whose duty it shall be to inquire into and determine how much the vessels of war and steam machinery contracted for by the department in the years 1862 and 1863 cost the contractors over and above the contract price and allowance for extra work, and report the same to the Senate at its next session; none but those that have given satisfaction to the department to be considered.

EXECUTIVE SESSION.

The Senate then went into executive session, and upon the opening of the doors again, at 2:30 P. M., adjourned.

The Philadelphia and Trenton Railroad Accident.

INVESTIGATION BY A CORONER'S JURY—THE VERDICT.

From the Philadelphia Ledger, March 9.

Yesterday morning the Coroner's Jury met at Bristol for the purpose of examining into the cause of the accident on the Philadelphia and Trenton Railroad on Tuesday morning last.

Twenty-four of the soldiers wounded by this sad accident are still at White House Hospital, near Bristol. All of them, with but one or two exceptions, are in a fair way to recover, though a number will be crippled for life.

The Coroner's jury, after hearing the evidence, rendered the following verdict:

BUCKS COUNTY, ss: The Commonwealth of Pennsylvania.—An inquisition taken at Bristol, in the county of Bucks aforesaid, on the 17th and 18th days of March, A. D., 1865, before WM. EARLEY, Coroner for the county of Bucks, upon view of the dead bodies of Joseph Wilds, from Bensalem Township; Wm. Morton, of New-York, Corp., Co. L, 2d Conn., H. Art.; Moses Goddard, of Westfield, Vt., Co. D, 5th Vermont Vols.; Asa Drew, of Georgetown, Massachusetts, Co. C, 28th Massachusetts Vols.; Timothy Leddy, of the City of New-York, then and there lying dead; and upon the solemn oaths and affirmations respectively of Frank Pratt, John Davis, Thomas Callanan, Pugh Dungan, Jacob C. Hamilton, John McDonnell, six good and lawful men aforesaid, charged to inquire (on the part of the Commonwealth of Pennsylvania) when, how and by what means the said Joseph Wilds, William Morton, Moses Goddard, Asa Drew and Timothy Leddy came to their deaths, do, upon their solemn oaths and affirmations, respectfully say, that it appears from the evidence before them, that the said Joseph Wilds, William Morton, Moses Goddard, Asa Drew and Timothy Leddy came to their deaths about 22 minutes past 2 o'clock on Tuesday morning, March 7, 1865, in consequence of an accident on the Philadelphia and Trenton Railroad, in the borough of Bristol:

Said accident resulting from a want of proper caution on the part of the switch-tender at Neshaminy Bridge in not stopping the Washington train according to the orders given him by the conductor of the 12 o'clock P. M. train from Philadelphia, believing, according to the evidence given, that there was a misunderstanding on the part of said switch-tender as to those orders, which, in their opinion, tends to mitigate the censure which otherwise would fall upon said switch-tender; and the jury further exonerates the employes on the trains from all blame.

In witness whereof as well, the said Coroner as the said jurors have to this inquisition set their hands and seals the day and year just mentioned. WILLIAM EARLEY, Coroner; Frank Pratt, Pugh Dungan, John Davis, Jacob C. Hamilton, Thomas Callanan, John McDonnell.

Ruins of the arsenal, Richmond

The Confederate army set fire to Richmond before evacuating the city.

The Union army entering Richmond, April 3, 1865

The New-York Times.

VOL. XIV......NO. 4202. NEW-YORK, TUESDAY, MARCH 14, 1865. PRICE FOUR CENTS.

SHERIDAN'S CIRCUIT.

Occupation of Columbia in the Rear of Richmond.

RICHMOND IN DANGER.

Sweeping Destruction of Lee's Communications.

THE ISOLATION OF LYNCHBURGH.

The Railroad East of that City Torn Up and the Bridges Burned.

THE KANAWHA CANAL DEMOLISHED.

Immense Destruction of Canal Boats and Supplies.

Capture of Fourteen Pieces of Artillery.

[OFFICIAL.]

WAR DEPARTMENT, WASHINGTON, D. C., March 13—10 A. M.

Maj.-Gen. Dix:

The following report of Gen. SHERIDAN'S operations has been received by this department.

EDWIN M. STANTON, Sec. of War.

CITY POINT, Va., March 12, 1865—7 P. M.

Hon. E. M. Stanton, Secretary of War:

The following dispatch is just received.

U. S. GRANT, Lieut.-General.

HEADQUARTERS MIDDLE MILITARY DIVISION, COLUMBIA, Va., Friday, March 10, 1865.

Lieut.-Gen. U. S. Grant, Commanding Armies of the United States:

GENERAL: In my last dispatch, dated Waynesboro, I gave you a brief account of the defeat of EARLY by CUSTER'S division. The same night this division was pushed across the Blue Ridge, and entered Charlottesville at 2 P. M. the next day. The Mayor of the city and the principal inhabitants came out and delivered up the keys of the public buildings.

I had to remain at Charlottesville two days. This time was consumed in bringing over from Waynesboro our ammunition and pontoon trains. The weather was horrible beyond description, and the rain incessant. The two divisions were during this time occupied in destroying the two large iron bridges, one over the Rivanna River, the other over Morse's Creek, near Charlottesville, and the railroad for a distance of eight miles in the direction of Lynchburgh.

On the 6th of March, I sent the First Division, Gen. DEVIN commanding, to Scottsville, on the James River with directions to send out light parties through the country and destroy all merchandise, mills, factories, bridges, etc., on the Rivanna River, the parties to join the division at Scottsville. The division then proceeded along the canal to Duguidsville, fifteen miles from Lynchburgh, destroying every lock, and in many places the bank of the canal. At Duguidsville we hoped to secure the bridge to let us cross the river, as our pontoons were useless on account of the high water. In this, however, we were foiled, as both this bridge and the bridge at Hardwicksville were burned by the enemy upon our approach. MERRITT accompanied this division.

The third division started at the same time from Charlottesville, and proceeded down the Lynchburgh Railroad to Amherst Court-house, destroying every bridge on the road, and in many places miles of the road. The bridges on this road are numerous, and some of them five hundred feet in length.

We have found great abundance in this country for our men and animals; in fact, the canal had been the great feeder of Richmond. At the Rockfish River, the bank of the canal was cut, and at New-Canton, where the dam is across the James, the guard lock was destroyed, and the James River let into the canal, carrying away the banks, and washing out the bottom of the canal.

The dam across the James at this point was also partially destroyed.

I have had no opposition. Everybody is bewildered by our movements. I have had no news of any kind since I left.

The latest Richmond paper was of the 4th, but contained nothing.

I omitted to mention that the bridges on the railroad from Swoop's Depot, on the other side of Staunton, to Charlottesville, were utterly destroyed; also, all bridges for a distance of ten miles on the Gordonsville Railroad.

The weather has been very bad indeed, raining hard every day, with the exception of four days since we started. My wagons have, from the state of the roads, detained me.

Up to the present time we have captured fourteen pieces of artillery, eleven at Waynesboro, and three at Charlottesville.

The party that I sent back from Waynesboro started with six pieces, but they were obliged to destroy two of the six for want of animals. The remaining eight pieces were thoroughly destroyed.

We have captured up to the present time twelve canal boats, laden with supplies, ammunition, rations, medical stores, etc.

I cannot speak in too high terms of Gens. MERRITT, CUSTER and DEVIN and the officers and men of their commands. They have waded through mud and water during this continuous rain, and are all in fine spirits and health.

Commodore HOLLINS, of the rebel navy, was shot near Gordonsville while attempting to make his escape from our advance in that direction. Very respectfully, your obedient servant,

P. H. SHERIDAN, Major-General Commanding.

ARMY OF THE POTOMAC.

LEFT WING.

Nothing New—Bad Weather and Worse Roads—Execution of Deserters, &c.

From Our Own Correspondent.

LEFT WING ARMY OF THE POTOMAC, Saturday, March 11, 1865—8 A. M.

HAIL AND RAIN.

Owing to the continued terrible state of the weather, and the awful condition of the roads and camps, it was almost impossible for any one to ride round our camps. It is almost unnecessary to say, therefore, that there is "no news." Nothing can be done for the present in the shape of active movements, and unless the enemy compels us, there will be no further or speedy resumption of campaigning or of battles.

EXECUTION OF DESERTERS.

Private FERDINAND BLOCK, Company A, Sixty-ninth New-York Volunteers, and private JOHN NICHOLAS, Company A, Sixty-ninth New-York Volunteers, were hanged yesterday at noon, for desertion, in the First Division, Second Army Corps, pursuant to General Court-martial Orders No. 11, Headquarters Army of the Potomac, in the presence of the division to which they belonged. The execution passed off very quietly. GEO. F. WILLIAMS.

A Fine Day—Review in the Second Corps—Visit of Lieut.-Gen. Grant.

From Our Own Correspondent.

LEFT WING ARMY POTOMAC, Sunday, March 12, 1865—8 A. M.

I am again compelled to notice the weather, notwithstanding that I have made it the subject of a paragraph each day for the past week. Out here the weather forms the all-absorbing topic of conversation, for upon it hinges all our movements. A succession of fine days renders a movement probable, if not certain, while rain and storm puts a perfect quietus upon ideas of active operations. Yesterday was a clear, warm and sunshiny day, and much speculation is the result, especially as movements are going on in the rebel army.

Yesterday afternoon Gen. MOTT'S and Gen. HAYS' division of Gen. HUMPHREY'S corps were again reviewed by Gen. MEADE. The reason for a repetition of this ceremony is hard to give, unless, indeed, it was for the gratification of several ladies and gentlemen who were present. The review passed off very satisfactorily, and the appearance of the commands was admirable.

The extreme left of our line was visited yesterday by Lieut.-Gen. GRANT, and he was accompanied by several members of his staff, Mrs. LINCOLN, Mrs. Gen. GRANT and a numerous party of ladies and gentlemen, whose names it was difficult to obtain, owing to the crowd and the rapid movement of the party. The Lieutenant-General and his friends were also on the ground and witnessed the review in the Second Corps. GEO. F. WILLIAMS.

FROM THE RIGHT WING.

Movements of the Enemy—Reported Capture of Lynchburgh—More Lady Visitors—Deserters Still Coming, etc.

From Our Own Correspondent.

RIGHT WING, ARMY OF THE POTOMAC, Saturday, 8 A. M., March 11, 1865.

MOVEMENTS OF THE ENEMY.

It seems to be pretty well established that another considerable portion of Gen. LEE'S army, comprising all of MAHONE'S division, left our front last night. It is supposed they have been sent to arrest the movements of SHERIDAN, who, if reports are true, seems to have had matters pretty much his own way in the vicinity of Charlottesville, notwithstanding the reinforcements previously reported to have been dispatched to EARLY. Of course, the destination of this detachment cannot be positively known here, and the belief that it has gone in the direction indicated arises solely from the fact that deserters state that there is a great deal of apprehension expressed in Richmond relative to SHERIDAN'S movements. The rebels seem to fear him at present even more than SHERMAN.

REPORTED CAPTURE OF LYNCHBURGH.

A rebel corporal who came into our lines night before last, states that it was currently reported in LEE'S army that SHERIDAN has already captured Lynchburgh, after a brief battle, in which he succeeded in taking another large batch of prisoners. There is not much credit attached to this story, however, as it is not confirmed by other deserters who have come in subsequently, and who would certainly have heard the rumor if it had been general. The report that Lynchburgh has been attacked by SHERMAN'S army is, also, brought by deserters, and is probably nearer true than the other more flattering story. It is devoutly to be wished, however, that the corporal's statement may not long remain false, nor even doubtful, and it hardly will be if the latter report is correct.

LADY VISITORS AGAIN.

Another company of lady visitors honored us with their presence yesterday. They reached here on Thursday, but went immediately to the left and spent the time till night in making an inspection of that part of the encampment. Stopping at Army Headquarters all night, they intended yesterday to visit the camps on this wing, but were prevented by the disagreeableness of the weather. I believe they returned to City Point last evening.

STILL THEY COME.

Deserters from the enemy still continue to cross the lines every night. The number is not so large as it was during the season of dark nights, but it will still average from twenty-five to thirty per day. On Thursday night, which was very foggy, there were upwards of sixty reported at headquarters of the army.

AWARDS OF MERIT.

It is understood here that a general order, commending the officers and men who deserved credit by their conduct in the late Hatcher's Run affair, will be issued in a few days by the General commanding. It is stated that about one hundred and fifty persons will be included in the orders.

EXECUTION OF DESERTERS.

Private JOHN KELLY, of the Sixty-seventh Regiment Pennsylvania Volunteers, was shot, to-day, in full view of the Third Division of the Sixth Corps, in pursuance of the sentence of a court-martial, for the crime of desertion. HENRY H. YOUNG.

FROM ATLANTIC CITY.

The Schooner Sea Gull Ashore—Farm Houses Robbed.

ATLANTIC CITY, Monday, March 13.

The *Sea Gull*, with a cargo of oysters, full of water, boat gone and no persons on board, came ashore on the night of the 11th instant, on Brigantine Beach.

A number of farm houses have recently been robbed by a gang of marauders, supposed to be deserters. On Saturday night, the people turned out and pursued the robbers, when a fight ensued. Two of the robbers were killed, and their bodies were found clad in Federal uniform. Their names are unknown. This gang of robbers have been living in caves in the neighborhood.

NORTH CAROLINA.

OFFICIAL DISPATCH FROM SCHOFIELD.

Good News from the Old North State.

Bragg Defeated in Two Engagements with Heavy Loss.

THE REBELS RETIRE TO KINSTON.

Probability of a Severe Fight for the Possession of that Place.

Bragg's Reported Victory on the 8th a Mere Skirmish.

[OFFICIAL.]

WASHINGTON, D. C., March 13, 1865—9:45 P. M.

Maj.-Gen. Jno. A. Dix:

The following dispatch has been received by this department EDWIN M. STANTON, Secretary of War.

CITY POINT, Va., March 13, 1865.

Hon. Edwin M. Stanton, Secretary of War:

The following has just been received:

WISES FORK, NEAR KINSTON, N. C., March 10, 1865.

To Lieut.-Gen. Grant:

The enemy made a heavy attack upon our centre and left, to-day, but were decisively repulsed with heavy loss. His dead and badly wounded were left upon the field. We also took several hundred prisoners. Our loss is small. Gen. COUCH is only 12 miles from here, to-night, and will be up early in the morning. We took prisoners from LEE'S and STEWART'S corps. They say two corps are here, and the rest of JOHNSTON'S army is coming.

J. M. SCHOFIELD, Maj.-Gen.

UNOFFICIAL REPORT.

Desperate Character of the Fighting—The Enemy Make Several Charges, and are Signally Repulsed.

NEWBERN, N. C., Saturday, March 11—9 A. M.

The enemy, elated with the capture of two or three small guns and a line of skirmishers in our front, made several charges yesterday of the most reckless character, in which they were repulsed each time with heavy loss. Our forces were well entrenched, and are now within three miles of Kinston, to which point the railroad is now completed. The enemy continue to receive reinforcements and evidently intend to make a stubborn resistance at Kinston.

Gen. COUCH'S division, from Wilmington, communicated with Major-Gen. Cox last night from Beaver Dam, a point he had just reached, which is eight miles from Gen. Cox's headquarters. Gen. COUCH joins Gen. Cox's forces this morning, which indicates a battle to-day.

The enemy show signs of weakness, and will doubtless fall back to the other side of the Neuse River, and make a stand in Kinston.

The rebel ram is stationed at Kinston to protect the bridge across the Neuse, which is quite an extensive structure.

It is reported by deserters that Gen. ROBERT E. LEE and Major-Gen. BRECKINRIDGE, from Richmond, visited Kinston and gave instructions.

Maj.-Gen. SCHOFIELD remains in the field with Maj.-Gen. Cox, giving every movement his personal attention.

The enemy are much alarmed and mystified in regard to SHERMAN'S movements. We expect to hear from him in a day or two.

Maj.-Gen. Cox has issued an order, congratulating his troops on the heroic manner in which they have met the enemy and successfully sustained themselves, thus far.

Gen. MARKLAND, the military mail agent, has arrived at Morehead City with a large mail for SHERMAN'S army, which he is waiting to deliver by way of Newbern.

BRAGG'S REPORTED VICTORY.

The Rebel Victory Dwindled Down to Nothing—A Few Skirmishers only Captured.

NEWBERN, N. C., Thursday, March 9—10 A. M.

Maj.-Gen. SCHOFIELD and his staff have arrived here, having left Wilmington on Monday last. They bring no news from SHERMAN. The enemy's papers are ignorant of SHERMAN'S whereabouts. The roads are bad, which delays his progress somewhat.

A letter was received here the other day from a young man who has been confined in Salisbury prison for the past two years, stating that he was liberated by the Union forces.

The enemy are in considerable force at Kinston, N. C., having been recently reinforced. LEE'S corps, from HOOD'S army, is reported there (?) Yesterday the *enemy captured some of our skirmishers near Kinston*, belonging to the Fifteenth Connecticut and Seventeenth Massachusetts. Maj. OSBORN, of the Fifteenth Connecticut, is reported wounded and a prisoner. Our captures will offset the enemy's thus far. Gen. BRAGG is reported to be in command of the enemy's forces at Kinston.

Maj.-Gen. J. D. COX, is in command of our forces at that point; he, as well as Gen. SCHOFIELD, is very popular with the troops, who are confident of success when a general move is ordered.

The weather is very warm with an occasional shower of rain.

A SECOND BATTLE—DEFEAT OF BRAGG

Bragg Makes Two Attacks on the 9th Inst., on the Lines of Gen. Cox, and is Twice Repulsed.

PHILADELPHIA, Monday, March 13.

The *Bulletin's* Washington special dispatch says:

"A letter dated near Kinston, March 10, and received here at noon to-day, says that on the day before (the 9th) BRAGG again attacked COX'S forces, making two separate assaults, *which were repulsed with heavy loss to the enemy*.

RUGER'S division of the Twenty-third Corps captured one piece of artillery and two hundred prisoners.

The enemy left the field in confusion, and all of their killed and wounded fell into our hands.

SUSPENSION OF THE DRAFT.

The Draft in the State of New-York Suspended as Long as Volunteers Come in Freely—Men Already Drafted not Required to Report.

EXECUTIVE DEPARTMENT, ALBANY, March 13, 1865.

Assurances are given me by the Provost-Marshal-General, through Lieut.-Gov. ALVORD, who visited Washington at my request, that no draft will be ordered in the State as long as or wherever recruiting is reasonably fast; and where a draft has already taken place, drafted men will not be required to report if volunteers are secured fast enough to give assurance that the quotas will be filled within a brief period. Boards of Enrollment must be kept busy. This indulgence should greatly stimulate to renewed efforts in securing volunteers. Our faith is pledged that such will be the result. I appeal to the people that it be kept.

R. E. FENTON.

FROM HAVANA.

The Blockade-Runner Ruby Captured—Arrival of Coolies—Singular Attempt at Piracy in Havana Harbor.

The steamship *Liberty*, Capt. T. W. WILSON, left Havana on Wednesday, 8th inst., at 4:30 P. M., and has experienced strong winds, and, for a part of the voyage, a heavy head sea. There is nothing of moment to report.

The blockade-runner *Owl*, Capt. MAFFIT, left Havana at noon same day, it was rumored, for Halifax.

The blockade-runner *Ruby* had been captured by Capt. R. W. SHUFELDT, and taken into Key West.

We have nothing of interest from Santo Domingo. The forces there are hourly awaiting orders to abandon the whole undertaking.

On the 4th the Spanish ship *Emigrante* arrived from Macao with 360 coolies, and on the 6th the Belgian ship *Leopold Carteauk*, with 407 coolies.

On the nights of the 4th and 5th our harbor was the scene of an attempt at piracy. The facts, as I am informed, are as follows: About 11 P. M., on the 4th, two boats approached the American steamer *Shooting Star* with muffled oars, one on each side. Only one of the boats was perceived at first, which seemed to contain about twenty men. The other boat had only three men. Finding the crew on the alert the large boat retired, but while attention was being called to it the other boat came alongside, and a man, unperceived by any of the crew, managed to get on board. Shortly afterward, however, he was discovered in the engine-room, when he was seized and handcuffed, but during the night he succeeded in getting the handcuffs off, jumped into the water, and called to the steamer *Leox*, which lowered a boat and picked him up.

On the 5th the Captain learned that another attempt would be made that night, and, in conjunction with friends on shore, applied to the Captain of the port for protection. It was communicated to the Captain-General, who ordered that a barge of armed men should be sent, and that the steamer should be towed under the guns of the Admiral's vessel. This was being done about midnight, when two boats appeared, coming toward the *Shooting Star*. The armed barge started and captured the boat, with 25 men in it, who were taken ashore and, my informants tell me, liberated.

I shall probably learn more, so as to advise per *Corsica* on Saturday. At present I only give the above as a report, not vouching for it.

The *Owl*, which I wrote you of in my last, as having refused to deliver up her "crew list" and other papers, has been detained. She has, I am told, between 60 and 70 men on board, over and above her complement of men.

The *Francis* has been receiving boxes of arms, ammunition, etc., and, I hear, even cannon; but whether to arm her as a corsair, or for transfer to another vessel, I have not heard.

MARCH 6.—Arrived, the English (?) steamer *Asia*, 926 tons, with coal, three and a half days from Nassau.

MARCH 4.—Sailed, English steamer *Evelyn*, for Belize, cleared by Messrs. M. A. HERRARA & Co., of this city.

The English (?) steamer *Ruby*, which left on the 26th ult., for Belize (?) was captured on the 27th by the *Proteus*.

Just as the English steamer was leaving Vera Cruz, news came that the Commandant of that city, Mr. MARSHAL, in the fight with the guerrillas, March 2, was shot dead with quite a number of his men.

FROM THE GULF DEPARTMENT.

Expedition from Baton Rouge—Clinton, La., Occupied—Large Bodies of Troops Moving Toward Mobile—New-York Steamships Taken for Transports.

NEW-ORLEANS, Tuesday March 7, } Via CAIRO, Monday, March 13.

Gen. BAILEY'S expedition from Baton Rouge into the interior of Louisiana and Mississippi consists of 3,000 cavalry, with a strong support of artillery. At last accounts the expedition occupied Clinton, La. This section of the country contains a majority of loyal people, and it is believed that this occupation is designed to be permanent.

Gen. BALDY SMITH accompanied Gen. CANBY on his recent trip to the vicinity of Mobile. He has not yet been assigned to any command.

Large bodies of troops are leaving here for the vicinity of Mobile. There are also indications of movements in other directions. The steamships *Guiding Star* and *George Cromwell* have been taken by the military for the transportation of troops to Mobile.

The steamship *Morning Star* arrived to-day.

Cotton has declined 2c.; low middling, 70c.@72c. Sugar and molasses active. Orders have been received to forward provisions to the North, and 1,000 bbls. Lard are now awaiting shipment. New-York tonnage is scarce. Cotton freights to New-York, ¾c. Bankers' sight checks on New-York at par.

Arrived, brig *Edward H. Kennedy*, from Boston.

West Tennessee Thrown Open to Trade—Arrival of Paroled Prisoners.

CAIRO, Monday, March 13.

Gen. WASHBURNE has thrown the entire District of West Tennessee open to trade. Citizens will be allowed to come freely to Memphis with the products of the country, and take out a limited amount of family supplies. This will continue however, only so long as the people manifest a loyal and friendly feeling toward the Government of the United States, and do not abuse the privileges granted.

Four hundred and fifty paroled prisoners from New-Orleans, belonging to Western regiments, arrived to-day, and will move North as soon as transportation can be furnished.

The Brig Castilian Ashore.

HOLMES' HOLE, Monday, March 16.

The brig *Castilian*, of Portland, from Cardenas for Boston, with a cargo of molasses, dragged ashore, yesterday, on the East Chop. She has received no damage, and will probably be got off to-day.

Escaped from Jail.

PORTLAND, Me., Monday March 13.

HENRY E. CLARKE and ALF. TEELS, confined for running away with the schooner *Blue Bell*, sawed off some bars and escaped from jail yesterday.

REBEL REPORTS.

Whistling to Keep Their Courage Up.

Very Guarded Accounts of a Fight between Hampton and Kilpatrick.

ITS LOCALITY PRUDENTLY CONCEALED.

Kilpatrick Reported to have been Defeated.

Gen. Lee Thinks the Situation Hopeful.

Grant, Sherman, Sheridan, and Schofield Just Where He Wants Them.

[OFFICIAL.]

WASHINGTON, D. C., March 13, 1865—9:45 P. M.

To Maj.-Gen. John A. Dix:

The following dispatches have been received by this Department:

E. M. STANTON, Secretary of War.

CITY POINT, Va., March 13, 1865.

To Hon. Edwin M. Stanton, Secretary of War:

The following items are taken from to-day's Richmond papers:

"We have some good news this morning—news of a victory in South Carolina. It is announced in the following official dispatch from Gen. LEE. Though the dispatch is rather scant in its particulars, enough is given to show that KILPATRICK was badly worsted.

HEADQUARTERS, &c., March 10, 1865.

To Hon. John C. Breckinridge, Secretary of War:

Gen. HAMPTON attacked Gen. KILPATRICK at daylight this morning, and drove him from his camp, taking his guns, wagons, many horses, several hundred prisoners, and relieving *a great number of our own men who had been captured. The guns and wagons could not be brought off for want of horses.* Many of the enemy were killed and wounded. Our loss is not heavy. Lieut.-Col. J. S. KING was killed. Brig.-Gen. HUME, Cols. KAGAN and MORRISON, and Majors DAVIS and FERGUSON, and others, were wounded.

R. E. LEE, General.

It will be observed that the locality of the fight is not named in the dispatch. This is for prudential reasons. SHERMAN has no communication with the North, and it would be imprudent to publish where he was, as it would be giving news to GRANT of his progress.

Matters are beginning to look decidedly better for us in the South. In the last three days we have had news of two victories—one in North Carolina and one in South Carolina.

FROM THE VALLEY.

We alluded in our last issue to a movement that was being made for the purpose of recapturing our prisoners, who were taken from EARLY in the recent fight near Waynesboro, and who were being conducted, under guard, to Winchester. The following official dispatch tells of it:

HEADQUARTERS, March 9, 1865.

Hon. J. C. Breckinridge, Secretary of War:

Gen. ROSSER reports that on the 6th, with a few of his men, he attacked the enemy near Harrisonburgh, who were guarding the prisoners taken at Waynesboro, and captured a few prisoners. On the morning of the 7th he again attacked them near Reid's Hill. Having detained them for a day and a night at the river, he caused them to retire in haste, abandoning the only piece of artillery they had, and their ambulances. He annoyed them a good deal, and enabled a good many of our men to escape.

R. E. LEE, General.

The Northern papers claim to have captured about a thousand prisoners in the fight with EARLY, and report that most of their number had reached Winchester.

CHARLOTTE, Wednesday, March 8.

The Southern Express Company's messenger from Augusta, Ga., brings advices to the 3d inst. No news of interest had transpired west of the Savannah River. The Georgia Senate had passed a resolution declaring that it does not concur in the recommendation of Gov. BROWN for a convention, by a vote of 20 yeas, against 8 nays. Several extensive fires had occurred in Augusta, supposed to be the work of an incendiary.

Four hundred Yankee prisoners will leave Richmond this morning, on their return home, by the flag-of-truce boat. Among them are thirty-three officers, including Gens. KELLEY and CROOK, recently captured. U. S. GRANT, Lieut.-General.

NEWS FROM WASHINGTON.

Special Dispatches to the New-York Times.

WASHINGTON, Monday, March 13.

EARLY PAYMENT OF INTEREST.

The Secretary of the Treasury is considering the question of anticipating the interest on the five-twenties due on the 1st May. It is very probable that he will fix upon the 1st of April. There is disposition manifested to allow the interest to be anticipated at once. This latter idea is not looked upon favorably by the Secretary.

NATIONALIZING NEW-YORK BANKS.

Mr. KITCHEN, President of the Park Bank, is here, for the purpose of effecting arrangements to convert that institution into a National Bank. The President of the Shoe and Leather Bank, and the Tradesmen's Bank, have just left here, having been engaged in the same business. The other New-York Banks are taking steps in the same direction. All the State Banks will take the same course within six months.

ASKING POSTPONEMENT OF THE DRAFT.

There are several delegations here from different localities to urge a postponement of the draft. Neither the President nor the Secretary of War have thus far shown any disposition to interfere with the draft where it has been ordered, and it is not at all likely that they will. Gen. GRANT says that now is the time to strengthen the army.

HEAD OF THE FREEDMEN'S BUREAU.

It is understood that a military man will be designated as the head of the Freedmen's Bureau. There is a strong pressure, however, to put a civilian there. The Secretary of War is said to favor the former rather than the latter.

Dispatches to the Associated Press.

WASHINGTON, Monday, March 13.

THE SINGLETON TOBACCO.

It is known here that Mr. SINGLETON, of Illinois, recently made a contract with a Government agent to sell a certain quantity of tobacco. But it is not so clear that the article recently destroyed at Fredericksburgh was part of his venture. It is a mistake in the rebel papers to say the tobacco was to be exchanged for bacon, for the latter is included in the law contraband of war, as applied to exchanges for products of rebel States. Fredericksburgh was not one of the designated markets or places of purchase, and, therefore, to send the tobacco thence into our lines, would have been a violation of the blockade. Had it been broken foreign ships would have doubtless claimed the privilege to trade at the same port. The Potomac flotilla settled the question by destroying the tobacco. The Executive order based upon the law of Congress, designates New-Orleans, Memphis, Nashville, Pensacola, Port Royal, Beaufort, N. C., Norfolk, and Fernandina, as places of purchase of products of the insurrectionary States. All persons except such as may be in the civil, military or naval service, having in their possession any products of States declared in insurrection, which the treasury agents are authorized to purchase, and all persons owning or controlling such products therein are authorized to convey the products to either of the designated purchasing places. Persons having sold and delivered to a purchasing agent the products of an insurrectionary State in accordance with the regulations, are permitted by the military authority commanding at the place of sale to purchase from any authorized dealer at such place or at any other place in a loyal State, merchandise and other articles not contraband of war nor prohibited by order of the War Department, for coin, bullion, or foreign exchange, to an amount not exceeding in value one-third of the aggregate value of the products sold by them. Had the tobacco been taken to Norfolk instead of Fredericksburgh, the sale could have been made in accordance with the Executive order under the law of Congress without loss to the parties interested.

OUR CONSUL AT MATAMORAS NOT DRIVEN OUT—WE HAVE NO CONSUL THERE.

The report current for a few days past that the United States Consul had been ordered to Matamoras is without foundation in fact. The Consul, Mr. L. PIERCE, resigned his office last year, and the subsequent closing of the Consulate was a matter of course, in view of the complications incident to the war in Mexico, and the blockade of the Rio Grande. The United States Government has, since that time, preferred to be represented at Matamoras by a Commercial Agent instead of a Consul. This class of officers have no political functions and do not require an *exequatur* or official recognition by the Government of the country in which they reside. Mr. E. D. ETCHISON was appointed such commercial agent in September, 1864, and in December, 1864, was recalled for political reasons, and Mr. WOOD, who now holds the position, was appointed in his place. Dispatches have been received from Mr. WOOD within a few days, showing him to be at his post, and in the uninterrupted discharge of his functions.

NEW PAYMASTER-GENERAL.

The President to-day appointed Brig.-Gen. B. W. BRICE, of Ohio, Paymaster-General, U. S. A., to date from the 29th of November, *vice* ANDREWS, retired.

GUERRILLA RAID.

Last night MOSBY'S guerrillas came down to Munson's Hill and Bailey's Cross roads, about seven miles from Washington, and within three or four miles of our fortifications. They stopped at T. B. MUNSON'S house and took six of his horses, leaving but one. An unfortunate contraband was taken back to his master. This is the second night visit Mr. MUNSON has had from these depredators and thieves, but this time they omitted to capture his son, as they did on a former visit. The guerrillas numbered about thirty. They were fresh from a conflict with a squad of our cavalry, which they had defeated, leaving two dead and two wounded on the field, and taken the others, with the exception of the commanding officer, prisoners.

A PLEASURE TRIP TO THE SOUTH.

A party, including Senators Wade, Sherman, Chandler, Ramsey, Morrill, Foot, Grimes, Trumbull and Wilson, and Representatives Pike, Morrill and Baxter, of Vermont, and other Senators and Representatives, together with their families—in all about fifty persons—will leave here to-morrow to take passage for Fort Monroe for a pleasure trip to Charleston and Savannah. They will be gone about two weeks.

Police Station Lodgers.

BARNUM'S temperance drama is very good in its way, but it is all tame recital when compared with our daily morning reports from the police stations. At the Tombs, every morning at 6 o'clock, at the Jefferson Market Police Court, or at the Police Court on the East side, may be seen the real drama, and in it all the actors are up in their parts. But even here in the police courts the story does not fully appear; for among all the prisoners there are no station-house lodgers. This class—a large one, as will presently be shown—includes no felons that policemen drag to the bar of justice; the lodgers find shelter over night in the cells of the police stations, and are dismissed in the morning to go whither they will. Nobody knows them by day; they spring to the surface like mushrooms at night. They are masculine, feminine, of youth, of middle age, and of the sere and yellow leaf; but they are mainly in appearance males of middle age—young men who have grown prematurely old, females of twenty-two, whose haggard or bloated visages are not be described. The aged and very young are seldom of their number; for their vagabond life is not conducive of age, and rum rarely does it work so rapidly as to drag children down to the necessity of seeking lodgings in the police stations. The males are in this time of draft seemingly excellent subjects for army duty in place of men of sedentary habits and comfortable incomes. But ask a Police Captain why he does not enlist them, and the almost invariable reply is, that they have offered to enter the field as substitutes and been rejected by the Surgeons. Theirs is a story of tippling, and they are Satan's own.

Station-house lodgers are not all, however, outcasts. In the Sixth Ward, where in Winter they average a score nightly, (in Summer they sleep under awnings and in the park,) the tale of gin and misery is photographed on every countenance; but in the western half of the First Ward, where the average of lodgers doubles that of the sixth, there is a mixed class of immigrants and seamen, outcasts and tipplers. In the up-town districts, where few lodgers apply, nearly every applicant is a victim of the wine-cup, and their number, throughout the city, as revealed by last year's Police report, was 56,929, distributed among the thirty station-houses thus:

1	845	11	1,713	21	1,504
2	1,398	12	563	22	1,237
3	811	13	1,426	23	165
4	5,119	14	2,273	26	10
5	3,367	15	2,049	27	6,854
6	2,446	16	2,428	28	1,468
7	1,596	17	2,553	29	1,902
8	2,606	18	1,386	30	334
9	3,219	19	998	31	45
10	4,843	20	1,716	32	56

This table tells the story of indulgence in intoxicating beverages completely; but the list of arrests for intoxication does not. The latter list shows only 16,655 prisoners throughout the city during the year, while the total of lodgers is about tripple that of the arrests for drunkenness, and exceeds the total arrests for offences of all kinds, as may be seen by the following: Total arrests in 1864 for intoxication, 16,655; total arrests for intoxication and disorderly conduct, 6,802; for disorderly conduct, 9,368; for assault and battery, 6,591; total arrests for offences of all kinds, 54,751. Verily the policemen read us the most vivid temperance lecture, and BARNUM ought to incorporate in his moral drama a scene from one of the station-houses

VICE-PRESIDENT JOHNSON.—It should stand to Gov. JOHNSON'S credit that before he left Nashville, he telegraphed to Washington that he was not fit to make the trip, and that he would rather remain at home to assist in the regeneration and restoration of Tennessee, than to be Vice-President of the United States. But after a council held among his friends here, it was deemed right that he should be present to participate in the august ceremonies of Mr. LINCOLN'S inauguration for a second term. In obedience to their earnest request, he came, and when he reached Washington was so enfeebled as to be compelled to take to his bed at once. Gov. JOHNSON appeared in the Senate yesterday morning, in company with his friend, Hon. PRESTON KING, of New-York, who is staying with him at the residence of our hospitable fellow-citizen, FRANCIS P. BLAIR, Sr. His health is entirely restored. He was as cheerful as any man could be after having recovered from so severe an indisposition. We have no doubt he will fully justify the warmest anticipations of his countrymen. During his stay in the Vice-President's room a large number of the Senators called to pay their respects, and we observed with much satisfaction that they were pleased to see him well.—*Washington Chronicle.*

The New-York Times.

VOL. XIV......NO. 4210. NEW-YORK, THURSDAY, MARCH 23, 1865. PRICE FOUR CENTS

THE SOUTH.

JEFF. DAVIS AND HIS GOVERNMENT.

The Rebel Senate in Judgment on the Rebel President.

THE REVELATIONS OF DESPAIR.

Scathing Commentary on the Dishonesty, Delays, and Disasters of the Davis Administration.

Conscription, Currency, Tax, and Impressment Bills Rejected by the Gross.

Lee the Forlorn Hope of the Rebels.

Address of the Rebel Congress to the People of the South.

Rodomontade and Misrepresentation.

THE REBEL CONGRESS ON JEFF. DAVIS.

From the Richmond Sentinel, March 20.

The following is the report of the Senate Committee on the recent message of President DAVIS. It was read and adopted in secret session, and the seal of secrecy removed on the 16th instant:

The Select Committee to whom was referred so much of the President's message of the 13th instant, as relates to the action of Congress during the present session, having duly considered the same, respectfully submit the following report:

THE RECOMMENDATIONS OF JEFF. DAVIS.

The attention of Congress is called by the President to the fact that, for carrying on the war successfully, there is urgent need of men and supplies for the army.

The measures passed by Congress during the present session for recruiting the army, are considered by the President inefficient; and it is said that the results of the law authorizing the employment of slaves as soldiers will be less than anticipated, in consequence of the dilatory action of Congress in adopting the measure. That a law so radical in its character, so repugnant to the prejudices of our people, and so intimately affecting the organism of society, should encounter opposition and receive a tardy sanction, ought not to excite our surprise; but if the policy and necessity of the measure had been seriously urged on Congress by an Executive message, legislative action might have been quickened.

THE POLICY OF ARMING SLAVES.

The President, in his official communication to Congress, has recommended the passage of a law putting slaves into the army as soldiers, and the message under consideration is the first official information that such a law would meet his approval. The Executive message transmitted to Congress on the 7th of November last, suggests the propriety of enlarging the sphere of employment of the negro as a laborer, and for this purpose, recommends that the absolute title to slaves be acquired by impressment, and as an incentive to the faithful discharge of duty, that the slaves thus acquired be liberated, with the permission of the States from which they were drawn. In this connection the following language is used:

"If this policy should recommend itself to the judgment of Congress, it is suggested that, in addition to the duties heretofore performed by the slave, he might be advantageously employed as *pioneer and engineer laborers*, and, in that event, that the number should be augmented to forty thousand. *Beyond this limit and these employments it does not seem to me desirable, under existing circumstances to go.*"

In the same message, the President further remarks:

"The subject is to be viewed by us, therefore, solely in the light of policy and our social economy. *When so regarded, I must dissent from those who advise a general levy and arming the slaves for the duty of soldiers.*"

It is manifest that the President, in November last, did not consider that the contingency had then arisen which would justify a resort to the extraordinary policy of arming our slaves. Indeed no other inference can be deduced from the language used by him; for he says:

"These considerations, however, are rather applicable to the *improbable contingency of our need of resorting to this element of resistance than to our present condition.*"

The Secretary of War, in his report, under date of Nov. 3, seemed to concur in the opinion of the President when he said:

"While it is encouraging to know this resource for further and future efforts is at our command, *my own judgment does not yet either perceive the necessity or approve the policy of employing slaves in the higher duties of soldiers.*"

At what period of the session the President or Secretary of War considered the improbable contingency had arisen, which required a resort to slaves as an element of resistance, does not appear by any official document within the knowledge of your committee. Congress [illegible] until the President, whose constitutional duty it is "to give to the Congress information of the state of the Confederacy," has never asked, in any authentic manner, for the passage of a law authorizing the employment of slaves as soldiers. *The Senate, however, did not wait the tardy movements of the President.* On the 29th December, 1864, the following resolution was adopted by the Senate in secret session:

Resolved, That the President be requested to inform the Senate, in secret session, as to the state of the finances, [illegible] means [illegible] and [illegible] the condition of the army and the possibility of enlarging the same, the condition of our foreign relations, and whether any aid or encouragement from abroad is expected, or has been sought, or is proposed; so that the Senate may have a clear and exact view of the condition of our country, of its future prospects, and what measures of legislation are required.

In response to this resolution, the President might well have communicated to the Senate his views as to the necessity and policy of arming the slaves of the Confederacy, as a means of public defence. *No answer whatever has been made to the resolution.* In addition to this, a joint committee was raised by Congress, under a concurrent resolution adopted in secret session on the 30th December, 1864. That committee, by the resolution creating it, was instructed "by conference with the President, and by such other means as they shall deem proper, to ascertain what are our reliable means of public defence, present and prospective."

A written report was made by the committee on Jan. 25, 1865, and, although it had a conference with the President, no allusion is made in the report to any suggestion by him that the necessities of the country required the employment of slaves as soldiers. Under these circumstances, *Congress, influenced no doubt by the opinion of Gen. Lee, determined for itself the propriety, policy and necessity of adopting the measure in question.*

The recommendations of the President to employ 40,000 slaves as cooks, teamsters, and as engineer and pioneer laborers was assented to, and a law has been enacted at the present session for the purpose, without limit as to number.

All the measures recommended by the President, to promote the efficiency of the army, have been adopted except the entire repeal of class exemption; *and some measures not suggested by him—such as the creation of General-in-Chief—were originated and passed by Congress, with a view to the restoration of public confidence and the energetic administration of military affairs.*

THE SUBJECT OF EXEMPTIONS.

On the subject of exemptions, the President, in his message of Nov. 7, uses the following language:

"No pursuit nor position should relieve any one, who is able to do active duty, from enrollment in the army, unless his functions or services are more useful to the defence of his country in another sphere. But it is manifest that this cannot be the case with entire classes. All telegraph operators, workmen in mines, professors, teachers, engineers, editors and employes of newspapers, journeymen printers, shoemakers, tanners, blacksmiths, millers, physicians and numerous other classes mentioned in the laws, cannot in the nature of things, be either equally necessary in their several professions, nor distributed throughout the country in such proportions that only the exact number required are found in each locality."

The casual reader would infer that the laws, as they stood at the date of the message, exempted the classes enumerated by the President, as well as many other classes not mentioned by him. Such is not the fact. The only class exemptions allowed by the laws then in force were the following: Ministers of religion; superintendents and physicians of asylums for the deaf, dumb and blind, and of the insane; one editor for each newspaper, and such employes as the editor may certify on oath as indispensably necessary; the public printers of the Confederate and State Governments, and their journeymen printers; one skilled apothecary in each apothecary store, who was doing business as such on the 10th of October, 1862; physicians over thirty years of age, and for seven years in practice; presidents and teachers of colleges, seminaries and schools, and the superintendents, physicians and nurses in public hospitals; certain mail contractors, and drivers of post-coaches; certain officers and employes of railroad companies; certain agriculturists or overseers.

Officers of the State Government are not properly included among the exempted classes, because it is conceded that Congress has no constitutional power to conscribe them as soldiers. Nor are drunkards, Quakers, or other non-combatants, regarded as belonging to class exemptions, because, under the act of June 7, 1864, the exemption of these persons is subject to the control of the Secretary of War. The exemption of agriculturists or overseers, between the ages of 18 and 45, has been repealed at the present session. Tanners, shoemakers, millers, blacksmiths, telegraph operators, and workmen in mines, enumerated by the President as among the classes exempted, are not now, and have not been, since the passage of the act of 17th February, 1864, exempted as a class. If railroad officers and employes, and State officers who are not constitutionally subject to conscription, be excluded, the classes now exempted east of the Mississippi River embrace about 9,000 men—one-third of whom are physicians, and nearly another third are ministers of the Gospel; the remaining third is principally composed of teachers, professors, printers and employes in newspaper offices, and apothecaries.

DETAILED MEN.

In remarkable contrast to the number of persons relieved from military service by the exemptions above mentioned, the report of the Conscript Bureau exhibits the fact that east of the Mississippi River 22,035 men have been detailed by Executive authority. In consequence of this abuse of the power of detail, Congress, at its present session, passed an act revoking all details, and limiting the exercise of that power in the future. The third section of this act, exempting skilled artisans and mechanics from all military service, which is objected to by the President, and which has since been repealed, was originally adopted in consequence of suggestions contained in the report of the Secretary of War. In alluding to the embarrassments encountered by the administration's bureaus, the Secretary says:

"In addition, they have been constrained, by the stringent legislation of Congress, to relinquish their most active and experienced agents and employes, and substitute them from more infirm and aged classes."

Again:

"Interferences of this kind are inevitably so prejudicial and disturbing, that it is to be hoped a well-devised and permanent system of providing and retaining in continuous employment a sufficient number of artisans, experts and laborers, for all essential operations, may be devised and established."

The truth is, that the bill originally introduced into the Senate, exempting skilled artisans and mechanics, was actually prepared in one of the bureaus of the War Department. Congress, therefore, had reason to suppose that it would meet the sanction of the Executive.

CONSCRIPTION OF MINISTERS AND EDITORS.

To conscribe the ministers of religion, and require them to obtain details to preach the Gospel, would shock the religious sentiment of the country, and inflict a greater injury on our cause than can be described. The conscription of editors and of the printers necessary to the publication of newspapers would destroy the independence of the press, and subject it to the control of the Executive Department of the Government. The railroad officers and employes are as necessary to the prosecution of the war as the soldier in the field. Physicians and apothecaries are essential to the health of the people, and no complaint has reached Congress of abuses in this class of exemptions. If the education of youth be regarded as conducive to the maintenance of society and the preservation of liberty, it is not perceived that the exemption of professors of colleges and teachers of schools can be justly censured. The Senate passed a bill containing a section repealing the exemption allowed to mail contractors and drivers of post coaches; but, at a subsequent stage of proceedings, and on the recommendation of a committee of conference, based on the urgent remonstrances of the Postmaster-General, the section alluded to was stricken out.

CLASS EXEMPTIONS.

The subject of class exemptions was called to the attention of Congress by the Executive message of November last. It was carefully considered, and an act was passed expressive of the views of the legislative department of the Government. The message under consideration recurs to the same subject. It is to be regretted that the views of the legislative department of the Government have not met the favor of the Executive, and that he should deem it both necessary and proper to express dissatisfaction with the matured opinion of Congress.

GENERAL MILITIA LAW.

It is true that Congress has failed to respond to the recommendation of the President to enact a general militia law. The subject was considered, and the failure to act was the result of deliberation. The conscription laws enacted by Congress have placed in the military service of the country all its able-bodied citizens between the ages of seventeen and fifty. *The whole military material of the country, so far as legislation is concerned, is absorbed by the conscription acts. There is none left on which a militia law can operate, except the exempted classes, and the boys under seventeen, and the men over fifty years of age.* It was deemed expedient to allow this material to remain subject to the control of the State authorities for the purposes of local police, to aid in the arrest of deserters, and to enforce the administration of State laws.

THE WRIT OF HABEAS CORPUS.

It is also true that the President has recommended the passage of a law suspending the privilege of the writ of habeas corpus. This recommendation was the subject of a special message, in secret session. It occupied the attention of Congress for four or five weeks. After mature deliberation, the measure was laid aside, as unimportant and inexpedient. Spies can be arrested and tried summarily, without suspending the writ of habeas corpus. Conspiracies, tending in any manner to the injury of our cause, were provided for by a special act, passed at the present session, "to define and punish conspiracy against the Confederate States." The States of North Carolina, Georgia and Mississippi had expressed, through their Legislatures, great repugnance to the past legislation of Congress suspending the writ, and a large portion of the people throughout the country was arrayed against the policy of that legislation. It was deemed wise and prudent to conciliate opposition at a time when dissensions were ruinous; and as the benefits to be derived from the suspension of the writ were conjectural, the deliberate judgment of Congress was expressed by its silence on the subject. It is to be regretted that the Executive does not concur in these views, and again calls on Congress to revise its action, and to suspend the writ of habeas corpus, as a measure "*almost indispensable to the successful conduct of the war.*" If the fact stated in the confidential message, alluded to by the President, be the basis of the opinion that the suspension of the writ "is indispensable to the successful conduct of the war," the Congress does not concur in that opinion. The writ has not been suspended since August last. It is not perceived that the military reverses of the country, since that period, were occasioned by the absence of the legislation asked for.

IMPRESSMENTS.

In regard to Impressments, Congress, at the present session, has passed a bill declaring that the terms "just compensation," as used in the Constitution, entitle the owner whose property is impressed to the market value thereof, at the time and place of impressment. This legislation was considered necessary, in consequence of judicial decisions in some of the States, and because of the difficulty of procuring supplies on any other terms. Indeed it was supposed that the Executive had reached the same conclusion, as the Commissary-General, on the 20th December, 1864, had advertised that he would pay for supplies the price fixed by local appraisement; which is, in fact, the market price. The President, in his annual message of November last, did not call the attention of Congress to any difficulties attendant on the execution of the impressment laws. The present message, for the first time during this session, suggests modifications of those laws; and the recommendations of the President will, doubtless, receive the respectful consideration of Congress. It may well be doubted, however, whether the present specie value, payable in the future, will induce the owner of property to part with it; and whether the passage of such a measure would not result in a general concealment of provisions, and consequent starvation of the army.

FINANCIAL TROUBLES.

It is apprehended by the President that some degree of embarrassment in the management of the finances will be felt in consequence of the inadequate provision made by Congress; and it is intimated that some of the measures recommended by him were so retarded as to lose much of their value; and others, after being matured, were for the same reason abandoned, because no longer applicable to our altered condition. The only financial measure abandoned after being matured was the currency bill, recommended by the Secretary of the Treasury and indorsed by the President in his annual message. It may be remarked that the failure to enact any financial measure which has not sufficient vitality to render it valuable and applicable for the short period of four months, does not deserve much regret.

A VERY TRIFLING DEFICIENCY.

The Currency Bill was recommended to Congress, and based on the condition of the finances presented by the President in his message, and by the Secretary of the Treasury in his report. *It was abandoned without regret, and because at a subsequent period of the Session it was ascertained that the arrears of public debt, constituting cash demands on the Treasury, exceeded—by nearly four hundred millions—the amount originally reported to Congress by the Secretary of the Treasury.* The Currency Bill contemplated the reduction of the currency to one hundred and fifty millions, by a conversion of treasury notes into tithe certificates, payable after the war, and by the annual application of a portion of the taxes in the nature of a sinking fund. The treasury notes received for tithe certificates were to be canceled. *The military reverses which impaired the credit of the Government to such an extent as to destroy the salability of any of its bonds, left little hope that treasury notes would be exchanged for tithe certificates.* As soon as the enormous increase in the arrears of debt was discovered, as above mentioned, all idea of reducing the currency was abandoned as impracticable. For these reasons, the Committee of Conference having charge of the currency bill agreed to abandon it as a useless pledge of future resources without corresponding present advantage. Indeed, if the bill had been passed the first day of the session it would have expired from inanition, on the 9th January, 1865—the day on which the Secretary of the Treasury reported to Congress the deficit of $400,000,000, and recommended an increased taxation to meet it.

THE REBEL TAX BILL.

The Tax Bill is regarded by the President as liberal, though inadequate. No nation on earth ever conducted a protracted war by resources derived from taxation alone. The message intimates a regret that the recommendation by the Secretary of the Treasury of a tax on agricultural income, equal to the augmented tax on other income, payable in Treasury notes, was rejected by Congress. This is evidently a mistake, as it assumes that there has been an increase of taxes on other than agricultural incomes. The present income taxes are those laid by the act of April, 1863, as amended and reënacted on the 17th of February, 1864. To require the agriculturist to pay a tax on the income derived from his farm, in addition to the one-tenth of his gross productions, and the property tax of nine per cent. ad valorem, would be manifestly unjust and oppressive. After the delivery of his tithe, to tax the income of the agriculturist derived from the property producing the tithe, would leave little for family subsistence, for the purchase of supplies necessary for carrying on his agricultural operations, and for the payment of the ad valorem tax on his property. Congress, therefore, did not concur in the recommendation of the Secretary of the Treasury, believing it to be highly inexpedient.

The recommendations of the Secretary of the Treasury have, in the main, received the approbation of Congress, and every disposition has been manifested to coöperate with him. The tax bill adopted very nearly approximates the rate desired by him. He recommended ten per cent. on property. Congress has imposed a tax of nine per cent. A new foreign loan was authorized in secret session, at his request, without any limitation on his authority except as to the amount. A transfer of certain sterling funds abroad was by joint resolution, directed to be made from the navy to the Treasury. Efforts were made to raise specie. A bill was passed in the Senate, in secret session, to accomplish that object by the sale of certain licenses. It is understood the bill was defeated in the House of Representatives by the acquiescence, if not the instigation, of the Secretary of the Treasury. It appears from the correspondence submitted to Congress, that the Secretary of War, as early as the 18th of February, notified the President of the embarrassed condition of his department—and it is to be regretted that the Executive deliberated on, and postponed for so long a period as twenty days, the communication of that information to Congress.

If loss of time be a vice inherent in deliberative assemblies, promptitude is a great virtue in Executive action. There is every disposition on the part of Congress to comply with the requisitions of the President, and some means of raising the coin desired will, no doubt, be devised. It is unfortunate that the necessity for coin in the Commissary Department was not made known until the message under consideration was received. The use of coin in one department of the Government is calculated to superinduce the necessity for its use in all other departments, and hence the policy of the proposed measure, in a financial view, is very questionable. The necessity for supplies, however, overrides all other considerations. If practicable, it would be wiser to employ the specie in the purchase of treasury notes and then use the notes to obtain supplies.

Nothing is more desirable than concord and cordial coöperation between all departments of Government. Hence your committee regret that the Executive deemed it necessary to transmit to Congress a message so well calculated to excite discord and dissension. But for the fact that the success of the great struggle in which the country is now engaged, depends as much on the confidence of the people in the Legislative as in the Executive Departments of the Government, the message would have been received without comment. Your Committee would have preferred silence. It has been induced to an opposite course, because they believe Congress would be derelict in its duty to permit its legitimate and constitutional influence to be destroyed by Executive admonitions, such as those contained in the message under consideration, without some public exposition of its conduct.

Respectfully submitted,

JAMES L. ORR, Chairman,
THOMAS J. SEMMES,
W. A. GRAHAM,
A. T. CAPERTON,
JOHN W. C. WATSON.

ADDRESS OF THE REBEL CONGRESS.

APPEAL TO THE SOUTHERN PEOPLE.

From the Richmond Sentinel, March 20.

FELLOW-CITIZENS: The result of the Peace Commission is known to the country. The hopes of those who have hitherto believed that an honorable termination might be put to the war, by negotiation, have been rudely disappointed. The enemy, after drawing us into a conference, abruptly terminated it by insisting upon terms which they well knew we could never accept. Our absolute surrender and submission to the will of the conqueror are the only conditions vouchsafed by our arrogant foe. We are told that if we will lay down our arms and place our lives, liberty, property and domestic institutions at the feet of President LINCOLN, that he will be merciful to us. Upon his clemency we must rely to save us from universal confiscation and extermination. Yes; these are the conditions upon which the people of the sovereign States composing this Confederacy may be allowed to do—what? To return into the "Union" from which they solemnly and deliberately withdrew themselves, because their interests and their honor required it, and their repugnance to which four years of remorseless and cruel war have served to intensify. Thanks be to God, who controls and overrules the counsels of men, the haughty insolence of our enemies, which they hoped would intimidate and break the spirit of our people, is producing the very contrary effect. From every part of the country there comes up in response a shout of mingled indignation and defiance.

A noble enthusiasm reanimates our gallant army who have been battling so long for freedom and independence! Let us all be united now. Let there be no parties or factions among us. Let us rise to the height of the great occasion. Let us all be willing to spend and be spent in the cause of our country. Let us contribute freely, all that we have, if need be, to carry on the war until our final triumph is secured. Let us take fraternal counsel together, and calmly consider our condition and prospects. Such a survey, we believe, must tend to reassure and encourage even the less sanguine.

SUPPOSED EVILS OF REUNION.

We have, it is true, *recently met with serious disasters. Our fortitude is being severely tried. We have suffered much, and must be prepared to suffer more*, in the cause for which we are struggling. Is the cause worth the sacrifice? To answer correctly, we must constantly keep in mind the end for which we are contending. What is our object in this war? The establishment of our independence, through which alone are to be secured the sovereignty of the States, and the right of self-government. What is the alternative? Our subjugation as a people! Is it possible to over-estimate the horrors of this terrible alternative? Can the imagination over-color the picture which would be presented in the event of our failure? If we fail, not only political degradation, but social humiliation, must be our wretched lot. We would not only be political vassals, but social serfs. An enemy that has shown himself destitute of the ordinary sensibilities of human nature, and whose worst passions are embittered and inflamed against us, would assume the absolute control of our political and social destinies. In vain would a proud though vanquished people look even for that mercy which the conquered receive from a generous foe. Those "State Rights" which we have been taught to prize so dearly as the greatest bulwark of constitutional liberty, and which from the earliest period of our history we have so jealously guarded, would be annihilated. The Confederate States would be held as conquered provinces by the despotic Government at Washington. They would be kept in subjugation by the stern hand of military power, as Venetia and Lombardy have been held by Austria—as Poland is held by the Russian Czar. Not only would we be deprived of every political franchise dear to freedom, but socially we would be degraded to the level of slaves, if, indeed, the refinement or malice in our enemies did not induce them to elevate the negro slave above his former master. Not only would the property and estates of vanquished "rebels" be confiscated, but they would be divided and distributed among our African bondsmen.

DESPAIRING APPEAL TO SOUTHERN MANHOOD.

But why pursue the hideous picture farther? Southern manhood revolts at the bare idea of the spectacle presented. Can you think of it unmoved? Can property—can life itself—be so dear to you as to allow you to weigh them for one moment against degradation so abject—against misery so profound? We do not and cannot believe it. If the proud memories and traditions of our first great revolution do not nerve you to eternal resistance to such a consummation—nor the example of our forefathers, who wrestled for the independence they bequeathed us during seven long years of suffering greater than we have endured—let not the precious blood that has been already shed, by our bravest and best in the present struggle, cry out to us from our yet reeking soil in vain! Fruitlessly, indeed, have these sons and brothers—martyrs of liberty—bled and died, if we falter now in the path which they have illumined before us.

In the revolution of "'76" our armies and our people suffered far more than we have done. Our cities then were almost all in the hands of the British, and we were entirely cut off from all supplies from abroad, while our facilities for producing them were infinitely less than they now are. GREENE tells us that the battle of Eutaw was won by men who had scarcely shoes to their feet, or shirts to their backs. They protected their shoulders from being galled by the bands of their cross-belts, by bunches of moss and tufts of grass. A detachment, marching to GREENE'S assistance, passed through a region so swept by both armies that they were compelled to subsist on green peaches as their only diet. There was scarcely any salt for fifteen months, and when obtained it had to be used sparingly, mixed with hickory ashes. We need but allude to the terrible Winter which WASHINGTON passed at Valley Forge, with an army unpaid, half starved and half naked, and shoeless, to convince us that much as our brave soldiers are now enduring, their forefathers, for a like cause, endured far more.

WASHINGTON did not then despair. LEE does not now despair of the final triumph of a righteous cause. Why should we be doubtful, much less despondent, of our ultimate success?

RESOURCES—A ROSE-COLORED VIEW.

The extent of our territory, the food-producing capacity of our soil, the amount and character of our population, are elements of strength which, carefully husbanded, and wisely employed, are amply sufficient to insure our final triumph. The passage of hostile armies through our country, though productive of cruel suffering to our people, and great pecuniary loss, gives the enemy no permanent advantage or foothold. To subjugate a country, its civil government must be surpressed by a continuing military force, or supplanted by another, to which the inhabitants yield a voluntary or forced obedience. The passage of hostile armies through our territory cannot produce this result. Permanent garrisons would have to be stationed at a sufficient number of points to strangle all civil government before it could be pretended, even by the United States Government itself, that its authority was extended over these States. How many garrisons would it require? How many hundred thousand soldiers would suffice to suppress the civil government of all the States of the Confederacy, and to establish over them, even in name and form, the authority of the United States? In a geographical point of view, therefore, it may be asserted that the conquest of these Confederate States is impracticable.

If we consider the food-producing capacity of our soil, we need feel no apprehension as to our ability to feed the people and any army we may put into the field. It is needless to go into details or adduce statistics in proof of this. It is obvious to every well informed mind. Although the occupation by the enemy, and his ruthless policy of destroying the barns, granaries and agricultural implements of our people, wherever he moves, has, undoubtedly, diminished the amount of our cereals, still, in view of the fact that in every State, without exception, its agricultural labor has been devoted almost exclusively to the raising of breadstuffs, (while before the war it was mainly devoted to the production of cotton, tobacco, and other exports,) it is impossible to doubt that there is an ample supply of food in the country. It is true that the deportation of our slaves by the enemy, and the barbarous policy of arming them against us—a policy reprobated by all authorities on ethics or international law—has considerably diminished our agricultural labor. But when we reflect that, in 1860, our exports, almost entirely the products of slave labor, amounted to ($250,000,000) two hundred and fifty millions of dollars, it may be safely assumed that our slaves, though reduced in number, are fully equal to the task of feeding both the population at home and the army in the field. Our transportation, it is true, is defective and inadequate, but this may be indefinitely improved by more energetic efforts and more thorough and systematic organization. We cannot believe, therefore, that on our bountiful soil, so richly blessed by nature, there is any danger of our failing in this great contest for want of food, of our being starved into submission to the hateful yoke of the conqueror.

ABSENTEES FROM THE REBEL ARMIES.

But if we look to the amount and character of our population, we see especial reasons why we should be encouraged to hope for, nay, to be assured of our ultimate success. No people of our number can be subjugated, unless, false and recreant to themselves, their courage, faith and fortitude fail them. We have upon our rolls a very large army of veteran soldiers. It is true—and it is a sad truth to confess—that the *number present for duty is terribly disproportioned to the entire aggregate. This is too notorious for concealment, and we have no desire to conceal anything.* We wish to speak frankly and truthfully to you of the actual condition of things. The number of absentees from your armies *has been a fruitful cause of disaster.* On many a hard fought field the tide of success which have turned overwhelming in our favor, had all been present whom duty required to participate in the strife. We will not stop to inquire into the causes of an evil which we have so much reason to deplore. The remedy is plainly in the hands of Congress, and it is our province to apply it. But it is partly, also, in your, and we appeal to you to use it. Let every good citizen frown down upon and indignantly discountenance all evasions of military duty—whether temporary or permanent—no matter how plausible the pretext, or palliating the reason.

SKULKERS NOT TO BE TOLERATED.

No duty in this crisis of our affairs can be more imperative than to fight for one's country, family and home. Let no skulker, deserter or absentee without leave from the army be tolerated in any community. Let the reproachful glance of our women, between whose honor and the brutal foe our noble army stands as a flaming sword, drive him back to the field. With proper officers, strict dicipline and an elevated tone of public opinion throughout the country, desertion and absenteeism in the army can be arrested, and all men liable to military duty put into and kept in the ranks of our army. If this be effected we can maintain in the field a force sufficient to defy subjugation. But it is the character of our population, especially, that we find those elements of strength which impress us with the conviction that we never can be conquered. Our people are peculiarly military in their characteristics. Better soldiers than those in our army history has never shown. They have endured extreme hardships and suffered with a fortitude, and fought against constant odds, with a gallantry that has earned the gratitude of their country and extorted the admiration of the world. But in addition to their military attributes, our people are preeminently of a proud and haughty spirit, and deeply imbued with the spirit of constitutional freedom. It belongs to their race and lineage; and, as BURKE long ago remarked, their relation to the servile race in contact with them has intensified the feeling and invested this love of liberty with a sentiment of personal privilege. To suppose that a people with such military, political, and social characteristics will ever voluntarily submit to be ruled by any other Government than one of their own choice, is too insulting to their pride to be entertained for a moment. And to doubt their capacity to achieve independence, and maintain themselves as a separate Power among the nations of the earth, is to close our eyes to all the teachings of history—to ignore the proof which our forefathers have stamped upon its pages—to believe that human nature has changed, or that we are a degenerated race, unworthy descendants of our revolutionary sires.

THE APPOINTMENT OF LEE.

The appointment by the President of LEE as "General-in-Chief" has done much to restore confidence to the country and to reinspire the army. All feel that we may safely repose this weighty trust and responsibility in that great soldier and devoted patriot. All feel that we may lean upon him as our tower of strength. All feel that his calm courage and steadfast purpose, his military skill and wise judgment, will enable him to wield our armies with the maximum efficiency and strength. May God strengthen him for the great task to which a confiding people have called him.

THE BURDENS OF TAXATION.

To provide means for carrying on the war, Congress has been compelled to impose upon the country a heavy burden of taxation. But heavy as it is, it is not too heavy for the country to bear, and not heavier than our wants imperatively demand. It is impossible to maintain the mighty contest in which we are engaged without vast expenditures of money. Money can only be raised by loans or taxation. *Our condition does not enable us to effect the former.* We must of necessity, therefore, resort to the latter. We appeal to you with confidence to submit cheerfully to the burdens which the defence of our country, your homes and your liberties, render necessary. To contribute according to his means to that defence is as much an obligation upon the citizen as it is to peril his life upon the battle-field.

Let us then, fellow-countrymen, tread in the plain path of duty. No nation that has trod it faithfully and fearlessly ever, in the world's history, has stumbled and fallen.

"Nations," says BURKE, "never are murdered; they commit suicide." Let us not be guilty of the folly and crime of self-destruction. Let us show the fortitude, endurance and courage that belong to our race, and neither the brute force of our enemy's arms, nor the subtle poison of his lips, can extinguish the life of this Confederacy, breathed into it by the sovereign States which created it.

WHAT THEY WOULD LIKE TO BELIEVE.

The people of the United States are becoming weary of this war. The foreign material for their armies is beginning to fail them. The mutterings of discontent at the prospect of a further draft upon their home population are beginning to be heard in their large cities. The prospects of a war, indefinitely prolonged, is alarming their capitalists. Public credit must sooner or later collapse under the burden of expenditures, the magnitude of which the most skillful financier cannot venture to predict. The debt of the United States is already equal to the national debt of England, which has been accumulating since the Revolution of 1688. The interest on this debt is six per cent., while the interest on the English debt is only three per cent. It has been computed that the interest on the debt of the United States together with the amount necessary to carry on its Government, (even were the war at an end,) would not fall much short of five hundred millions per annum—a sum affirmed to be greater than the entire annual wealth of the Northern States. While a people in self-defence may submit cheerfully to any privation and suffering, to any sacrifices of treasure and blood, there is a limit beyond which a country waging a war of aggression and conquest will not go. We cannot stop this war without degradation, ruin, dishonor. Our enemies can have peace at any time by abandoning their wicked attempt at our subjugation, and allowing us to govern ourselves in accordance with those great principles for which their fathers and ours fought side by side.

THE SAME OLD COMPLAINTS.

Consider, therefore, in every point of view, is it possible to believe that the people of the Confederate States will ever incur subjugation, or accept submission as the result of the great struggle in which we are engaged. Neither is it possible to believe that these States, compelled by long years of unjust and unconstitutional action toward them by the Northern States, to withdraw from political union with them, can ever be tempted by any promises, or so-called "guarantees," again to unite themselves under a common Government.

Forced into this revolution by their faithless disregard of the obligations of the constitutional compact, and by the selfish and sectional legislation which they fastened upon us, what in the course of this war has occurred to change our opinion as to their character and purpose? The barbarity and unrelenting ferocity which has characterized their conduct of it, has excited the indignant wonder of the world. Falsehood, duplicity and mean cunning marked their course in its inauguration; and, in its progress, every artifice of low diplomacy and persistent misrepresentation has been resorted to by them to lessen us in the estimation of mankind. Our struggle for the right of self-government—which they themselves have always declared to be inalienable—has been held up to the world as a contest for the maintenance of African slavery—a purely State institution, over which neither the Confederate State Government nor the United States Government has any constitutional control.

To prevent foreign nations from according to us that recognition to which we were entitled by public law, and even the very language of existing treaties—a recognition of which they have themselves accorded to other countries on far slenderer grounds—they have deliberately falsified accounts of military operations, and our capacity and resources for continuing the contest.

A war which has been carried on for four years with ever varying fortunes, their Ministers of State have again and again assured foreign Powers could not possibly be waged by us for more than two or three months. And after all their insolent boasts of their power to crush us, they have been compelled to resort to foreign enlistment, and the arming of our captured slaves, in order to fill up the ranks of their armies. In spite of these practices, winked at, if not countenanced by European Powers—they have practically confessed their inability to vanquish us in regular warfare, by the inhuman policy of destroying the dwellings, the food and the agricultural implements of our non-combatant population. Thus endeavoring by the starvation of their wives and children to break the indomitable spirit of our soldiers.

In the invasion of our soil, neither private property, nor age, nor sex, has been spared from the rapacity and brutal passions of their mercenary legions. Wherever they have passed over the surface of our fair land, the blackness of desolation has marked their path, and such barbarous desolation has been their devilish boast. Public records have been destroyed—institutions of learning, public and private libraries—pillaged or burned, and the temples of God sacrilegiously defiled.

Fellow-countrymen, will you, can you ever submit to be ruled by such a people? Can you ever join hands with them in fraternal union? Can you, with all these things freshly before you—daily occurring on your native soil—ever return to political union with these despoilers of your houses—these violators of your wives and daughters. Never! A dark crimson stream divides you, which all the skill of negotiation can never bridge over. The Southern people have determined to be free and independent, and if their fortitude and courage do not fail them, it is impossible to doubt the issue.

But there must be no halting, no hesitation, in the only path that leads to the goal. We must prove to our enemies, and prove to the world, that we cannot be conquered. We must convince them that, though our soil may be overrun, the faith of our people, in the great cause for which they are contending, is unbroken, is unchanged—their will invincible.

WHY WON'T THE REBELS MAKE SACRIFICES?

Let us emulate the example of the Russian people when invaded by the grand army of NAPOLEON. *Let us be willing to make any and every sacrifice*, and consider it but a meet offering on the altar of our country. By the light of the blazing ruin of what had once been a proud palace, NAPOLEON read this inscription, which ROSTOPCHIN had affixed to his gate: "Frenchmen! I have spent eight years in embellishing this residence. Here I have lived happily in the bosom of my family—the inhabitants of this estate, numbering seventeen hundred and twenty persons, have quitted it at your approach, and I have, with my own hands, fired my beloved home to prevent its pollution by your presence!" Shall our patriotism be colder and more calculating than that of the subjects of a despotic ruler? Have we less reason to resist—less reason to detest the invading armies of the North than the Russians had to oppose and hate the French? Our enemies with a boastful insolence, unparalleled in the history of modern civilized warfare, have threatened not only our subjugation, but some of them have announced their determination, if successful in this struggle, to deport our entire white population, and supplant it with a new population drawn from their own territory and European countries! While such a threat may well excite our ridicule and contempt, the devilish spirit which prompts it must provoke in us an indignation that would render the feeblest people invincible! Think of it!

That we, the descendants of a brave ancestry, who wrested from a powerful nation, by force of arms, the country which we inhabit—bequeathed to us by them, and upon which we have been born and reared—that we should be uprooted from it and an alien population planted in our stead, is a thought that should inspire us with undying hostility to an enemy base enough even to have conceived it. Every motive then of honor and of self-interest, of patriotism and of domestic affection, every sentiment of manhood and self-respect, unite in urging us to resist, to the last extremity, our cruel invaders.

FINAL APPEAL.

Success gives us a country and a proud position among the nations of the earth. Failure makes us the vassals of an arrogant people, secretly, if not openly, hated by the most enlightened and elevated portions of mankind. Success records us forever in letters of light upon one of the most glorious pages of history. Failure will compel us to drink the cup of humiliation even to the bitter dregs of having the history of our struggle written by New-England historians! Success is within our reach. We have toiled and panted onward nearly to the goal. We have almost grasped the costly price of independence—never won except through anguish and blood. The crown stands ready to encircle the fair brow of our young republic. The shade of our martyred heroes hover over us and beckon us on. The fearful entreaties of our mothers, wives and daughters to save them from nameless horrors, urge us forward. Will we pause? Can we falter? Will we allow the weapons, which the God of battles has so often directed to the smiting of the despoilers of our homes, now to drop from our nerveless hands! Shall we be discouraged by the superior number of the enemy?

"The battle to the strong
Is not given,
While the Judge of right and wrong
Sits in Heaven!
The God of David still
Guides the pebble at His will,
There are giants yet to kill,
Wrongs unshriven."

But the enemy has already put forth his utmost strength. He has made his most gigantic effort. He has strained his energies to their greatest tension. He has taxed his resources to their utmost limit. He is almost spent and breathless with his tremendous exertions. Let us stand firm. Let us be calm and resolute. Let us show that our faith is in our cause and in His guidance, who shapes the destinies of nations, "is fixed and cannot move." In that faith, and with humble reliance on that guidance, let us hope all things, endure all things; and when we strike the invaders of our country, let religion, patriotism, love, honor, noble pride—every sentiment sacred and dear to the heart of man nerve our arms and give vigor to the blow! Then shall we conquer the peace for which we all so ardently yearn! Thus shall we make the memories of our slaughtered sons and brothers glorious and immortal! Thus shall we compel the nations of the earth to receive and welcome us among them! Thus shall we make the plow and the reaping-hook replace the cannon and the sword, and our ravaged fields smile once more with teeming harvests! Thus shall we return our devoted soldiers to their long-abandoned homes, and enable our people once more to sit each under his own vine and fig tree, with none to make them afraid! Thus shall we make our children, and our children's children to the remotest generations, rise up and call us blessed! Thus, and thus only, shall peace and independence, one and inseparable, spread their broad wings above us, and plenty, prosperity, and happiness reign throughout our native land.

THE REBEL CONGRESS.

CLOSING SCENE OF THE LAST SESSION.

SENATE.

SATURDAY, March 18, 1865.

The Senate met at 10 A. M.

On motion of Mr. WATSON, a resolution was adopted extending the session from 12 M. to 2 P. M.

Mr. WATSON, from the Select Committee on the Treatment and Exchange of Prisoners of War, made a report, which was laid on the table and ordered to be printed.

On motion of Mr. VEST, the Senate resolved into executive session.

When the doors were opened, on motion, by Mr. WATSON, it was resolved that the Chair be authorized to appoint a joint committee, on the part of the Senate, to wait upon the President of the Confederate States, and inform him that, unless he had further communications to Congress, they were ready to adjourn.

The Chair appointed Messrs. WATSON, OLDHAM and HENRY as the committee on the part of the Senate.

The bill to provide for the payment of all arrears now due to the army and navy, returned by the President of the Confederate States to the House, with his objections, was considered. Upon the question, "Shall the bill pass, notwithstanding the objections of the President?" the votes were taken by yeas and nays, as follows:

YEAS—Messrs. Brown, Bennett, Caperton, Henry, Hunter, Johnson of Missouri, Oldham, Simms of Kentucky, Vest, Watson, Wigfall—11.

NAYS—Mr. Semmes of Louisiana.

No quorum voting, the bill was lost.

Mr. WATSON, of Mississippi, then read the following report:

Mr. PRESIDENT: The joint committee charged with that duty, have waited upon the President of the Confederate States, and informed him that, unless he had some further communication to make to Congress, that body was now ready to adjourn. In reply, the President, in substance, stated: That he now had no further communication to make to Congress; that in his recent message he had fully explained his views as to the legislation required by the state of the country; that so far as Congress had not acquiesced in his opinions, he hoped it would turn out that he was mistaken; that, to the full extent of his powers and the resources placed at his disposal, all might feel assured of his purpose faithfully to protect and defend the country. He hoped that the members of the two Houses might all safely reach their homes, and that they and their families and their common country might continue to experience the protection and favor of heaven.

The hour of 2 P. M. having arrived, Mr. HUNTER, President *pro tem.*, rose and said:

"Senators: The hour of 2 P. M. having arrived, it becomes the duty of the Chair to announce the Senate adjourned *sine die.*"

HOUSE OF REPRESENTATIVES.

SATURDAY, March 18, 1865.

The House met at 11 o'clock, and was opened with prayer by Rev. Dr. JETER.

The Chair laid before the House a Senate joint resolution extending the time of adjournment until to-day at 2 o'clock. Agreed to. The House then resumed consideration of the Impressment Bill, and passed the same—yeas 36, nays 18.

Mr. McMULLIN moved to amend the title by substituting the following: "A bill to violate the Constitution of the Confederate States."

The Chair thought the amendment made in good faith, and ruled it out of order.

After the transaction of some further unimportant business, Mr. HOLLIDAY, from Virginia, offered the following resolution, which was adopted:

Resolved, That having acted on all matters of important legislation before us, and being about to adjourn, we pledge ourselves, during the recess, to devote all our energies and influence to the maintenance of our great cause and the prosecution of the war to a successful issue.

The Chair laid before the House the following Senate joint resolution:

Resolved, That a committee be appointed to join such committee as may be appointed by the House of Representatives to wait upon the President of the Confederate States and inform him that if he has no further communication to make, the two Houses are now ready to adjourn.

The resolution was agreed to.

The Chair appointed as the committee on the part of the House Messrs. CONRAD, of Louisiana, CLARK, of Missouri, and GHOLSON, of Virginia.

Mr. CONRAD, on the part of the committee appointed to wait upon the President and inform him that the Congress had completed its business, and was prepared to adjourn, reported that the committee had performed the duty devolving upon it, and that the President had replied that he had no further communication to make to Congress; that in his recent message he had communicated his views in regard to the state of the country, and had recommended certain measures which he had deemed important toward insuring a successful prosecution of the war; that Congress had deliberated, and, no doubt, acted on them conscientiously, but that, in so far as the views of the two Houses were different from his own, all then he had to say was to utter his sincere wish that the result would prove that they were right and he was wrong, and that no evil consequences would result from their actions.

The President reminded the members of Congress that a great deal depended on their individual exertions, in urging their constituents and fellow-citizens

Continued on Eighth Page.

The New-York Times.

VOL. XIV......NO. 4211. NEW-YORK, FRIDAY, MARCH 24, 1865. PRICE FOUR CENTS.

THREE DAYS LATER FROM EUROPE.

ARRIVAL OF THE AUSTRALASIAN.

The British Press Uneasy on American Affairs.

The Question of United States Claims in Parliament.

Mr. Layard Says None Have Yet been Made.

Discussion of the Address in the French Chambers.

DEATH OF THE DUKE DE MORNY.

The Cunard mail steamer *Australasian*, Capt. Cook, which left Liverpool at 9 o'clock on the morning of the 11th, and Queenstown on the 12th March, arrived at this port last evening.

The *Etna* reached Queenstown about noon on the 10th.

GREAT BRITAIN.

COMMENTS ON AMERICAN AFFAIRS.

The news by the *Etna* of the fall of Wilmington was not unexpected, and the effect, therefore, was not so great as it otherwise would have been. Federal securities improved under the news, but the Confederate loan was only a shade lower, having declined in anticipation. At Liverpool and Manchester there was an increased flatness in the cotton trade.

The *Army & Navy Gazette* says the news by the *Etna* is of a character generally to tax the faith of those who believe that the Confederates will maintain their cause in the field. Lee's communications are threatened on all sides. Grant, as if preparing for a rush, has contracted his lines, and is awaiting all Thomas' infantry from the West, Hood and his confeds being quite in *nubibus*.

ENGLAND AND THE UNITED STATES.

The *Daily News* denounces those who cultivate a policy of distrust in regard to America, and says: "It is time to introduce a little reason into the discussion of American affairs. That claims on England by the United States, and on the United States by England, should have grown out of the war, was inevitable. We have seen it stated within these few days, (in the *Times*,) that it is the business of English statesmen to see that we are not placed under the 'penance' of having claims urged upon us that we cannot admit. It is needless to say that no rational Englishman expects such a service from our public men. Our Government has only to persevere in its present course, acting fairly and honorably, and repelling all unjust pretensions. It will then command the support of an united and patriotic people, and we shall not need to disquiet ourselves although our neighbors should become unreasonable."

The *Morning Star* makes the following remarks: "The gossip which is maintained in the city about the probability of a war with America, is probably in some cases assiduously fostered for business purposes, but any genuine alarm appears to be confined to those who were the most scrupulous Confederate partisans. They seem to feel that, having exhibited as much hostility as they possibly could against the United States, a hostile sentiment on the part of that nation may be expected in return. But they may calm their fears. The policy of great nations is not shaped in accordance with the partisanship and animosities of individuals. The course of the British Government during the war has been determined by the policy and interest of the country at large, and not according to the fanatical sympathies of a portion of the people. So will it be with the American Government, should the rebellion be soon put down. The fire-eaters in New-York may utter loud threats, especially if they perceive, from the tone of the journals which supported the South, that a contemptible fear has now taken possession of them; but the Government of the United States, and the vast majority of the nation, will be too heartily glad of peace, when it comes, to think of bolstering up a quarrel against a nation fifty times more formidable than the South."

LETTER FROM CAPT. SEMMES.

Captain, now Admiral, Semmes has written to a friend in England, who has published his letter in the *Morning Herald*. He thus refers to the State of Texas, which, he thinks, has profited rather than suffered from the effects of the war, and will, in all probability, become the great storehouse and manufactory for the supply of the needs of the Confederates:

"The State of Texas alone has within her limits all the materials, and is fast getting the appliances for equipping and maintaining armies; and when you reflect that she has three times as much territory as the empire of France, and that countless herds of horses and beeves wander over her boundless prairies, you can well imagine with what contempt this warlike people regard the insane threat of subjugation. If our armies were driven to-morrow across the Mississippi River, we could still fight the enemy for a century to come in Texas alone."

AFFAIRS IN PARLIAMENT.

In the House of Commons on the 9th inst., Lord Robert Cecil asked whether any demands had been received by the Foreign office from the American Government or the American Ambassador demanding compensation for losses occasioned to American citizens by the *Alabama* or other vessels commissioned by the American Government of the Confederate States.

Mr. Layard said that there had been no demand of the kind made during the last six months.

Mr. Bright asked whether the Government had not received numerous claims from English subjects against the Government of the United States on account of the transactions during the war, and whether they were intended to be forwarded by the Government?

Mr. Layard said the Government had received claims of this character, and they had been forwarded.

Mr. F. Peel, in reply to Mr. Baxter, said that two vessels, not quite seventeen years old, were still employed by the British and North American Royal Mail Company, (Cunard line;) but there had been no complaint as to any delay on that account in the postal service. With respect to the future arrangements the contract would not expire until the end of 1867; but the Select Committee on Postal Contracts had expressed an opinion that no subsidy was now necessary for this line, and that there could be a very efficient postal service without any further subsidy. When the time came, this view of the committee would not be lost sight of.

Mr. White asked whether, with a view to establish friendly relations with Brazil, it was the intention of her Majesty's Government to repeal the act known as the "Aberdeen Act."

Lord Palmerston said it was not the intention of the Government to do so, for he believed that the Brazilian Government, with the best intentions, would not be able to prevent a revival of the slave trade. He might, however, state that negotiations were still going on, through the intervention of the Portuguese Government and that of the Emperor of the Brazils.

Lord Palmerston, in reply to Mr. Maguire, stated that the British Minister had remonstrated against the assumed intention of the Brazilian Admiral and the Commander of the insurgent forces to bombard Monte Video, and had received an assurance that the property of British and foreign subjects should be respected as far as possible.

The naval estimates were further debated and the vote for 69,500 men was agreed to.

The proceedings on the 10th were unimportant in both Houses.

THE LOCK-OUT IN THE IRON TRADE.

There was a prospect of an understanding being come to between the masters and men in the important "lock-out" in the iron trade.

LARGE FAILURE.

The old established bank of Attwood Spooner & Co., of Birmingham, had suspended payment, with liabilities estimated at about £1,000,000 sterling.

THE YELVERTON CASE.

The Court of Sessions at Edinburgh had refused, by a majority of the judges, to sustain the reference of the celebrated Yelverton marriage case to the oath of Major Yelverton.

The *Morning Star* says that Mr. Rumble, the Government Inspector of machinery afloat, who was recently acquitted on the charge of complicity in the case of the rebel steamer *Rappahannock*, has been placed upon half-pay, on the ground of his being no longer deserving of the confidence of the Government.

FRANCE.

DEATH OF THE DUKE DE MORNY.

The Duke de Morny died on the 10th inst.

FRANCE AND THE UNITED STATES.

The Paris correspondent of the *Morning Star* says:

"It is asserted that a remonstrance has been sent to the French Government by the United States Minister in Paris, as to the clandestine shipment of Confederate recruits on board the *Rappahannock*, stationed at Calais. These men had arrived from Liverpool, having been part of the crew of the Southern ship *Florida*."

COMMENTS ON SHERMAN'S CAMPAIGN.

Sherman's successes in South Carolina are thus commented on by the *Opinione Nationale*, of Paris:

"The wild despair which induced the Carolinans to set fire to their metropolis, will not win for them the sympathies of the civilized portion of the world, *for they have never been anything but mere rebels against a just Government. Their cause has never been that of liberty. Their watchword is, "slaves and slavery."* The line of conduct adopted by Sherman is well calculated to force the South to return to the path of duty. The General has baffled the plans of his enemy by the skill of his tactics, and the energy of his movements, whilst by his moderation and justice he has aroused in the insurgent population love of the old Federal flag. The progress of the liberating army (armée liberatrice) toward the north will decide the fate of the rebel capital. Richmond will be the last retreat of Mr. Jefferson Davis, and the last rampart behind which rebel slavery will find a shelter."

THE FRENCH SENATE.

In the French Senate on the 9th the general discussion on the Address was commenced. The Marquis de Boissy expressed a wish that the Ministers should be responsible for the policy of the Government. He pointed out the deplorable conduct pursued by England, which was still the asylum of assassins ready to attempt the life of the Emperor; and continued, "I do not believe that the convention of September will ever be carried out. It is necessary that the Pope should remain in Rome, for, if France is Bonapartist, much more is she Catholic."

Marshal Magnan animadverted in energetic language on the assertion of Marquis de Boissy, that on the day of the Emperor's death, France would fall into a state of anarchy. When this event occurred, the Senate, the Corps Legislatif, the army and the country would proclaim the Prince Imperial, and France would be saved.

The Marquis de Boissy then continued. He condemned the French intervention in Mexico, but strongly expressed a wish that the war between the Federals and Confederates might be carried on to the complete ruin of both belligerents rather than the French army in Mexico should be made prisoners by the conclusion of peace. [Loud expressions of disapprobation.] The Marquis de Boissy hoped, in conclusion, that the Emperor and his dynasty would long continue to reign.

M. Chaix d'Est Ange regretted the impious wishes respecting America, and condemned the expressions of M. de Boissy in reference to England.

On the 10th, after further debate, the general discussion on the address was closed and the first eleven paragraphs were then agreed to.

The announcement of the death of the Duke de Morny, was received with profound expressions of regret in the Senate.

THE BANK OF FRANCE.

The weekly returns of the Bank of France, shows an increase in the specie of over 29,000,000 francs. The Bourse was dull. Rentes on the 10th closed at 67@70.

ELECTION OF M. GUIZOT.

M. Guizot has gained his election for the presbytery of Paris by the measuring cast majority of 10 votes only, the numbers at the close of the poll being: Guizot, 1,298; Barbezat, 1,288. The dissensions among French Protestants may therefore be expected to continue.

ITALY.

M. de Sartiges had had an audience of the Pope, when he requested his Holiness to form an army within two years, with the assistance of France. The Pope declined, ignoring the convention. As regards the departure of the French troops, he would leave it in the hands of Providence.

SPAIN.

The *Official Gazette* of the 9th publishes the encyclical and syllabus, preceded by a declaration which reserves the rights of the crown in ecclesiastical matters, and promises to maintain the liberty of the press in the discussion of these documents.

There had been rumors of another ministerial crisis, but they are said to have been unfounded.

AUSTRIA.

In the Lower House of the Reichsrath, on the 9th, Herr von Schmerling stated that the Emperor had resolved to raise the state of siege in Gallicia on the 18th of April next. The delay is to enable the administrative authorities to take measures for the maintenance of order and tranquillity.

TURKEY.

The Conference of Ambassadors had recommenced its sittings at Constantinople.

It is stated that the Porte had refused to accept the resignation of the Governor-General of Syria; the latter, however, persisted in his resolution to resign on account of the return of Joseph Karam to Syria.

INDIA.

Calcutta journals to Feb. 6 are received. They show that the campaign in Bhooton was by no means at an end. The Bhooteans had attacked Dewangeri in force, but were repulsed with great loss.

The doubts regarding the continued efficiency of the new telegraph line to India were relieved on the 10th, by the receipt of numerous messages from Bombay and Calcutta to the 6th of March. Their contents were private, but one of them acknowledged a London telegram of the 4th. The delays were on the land lines.

FINANCIAL AND COMMERCIAL.

LONDON MARKETS.

The funds on the 10th were without material variation. Consols closed at 88⅞@89⅛ for money, and 88¾@89 for account.

There was a full discount demand at the bank. The current rate was 4½ per cent. There were rumors of gold withdrawals for export to New-York.

The weekly returns of the Bank of England show a decrease in the bullion of £42,700.

AMERICAN SECURITIES.

Baring Brothers & Co.'s Circular says: "United States Five-twenty Bonds are in demand at 54@54¼. Eries have also advanced to 35¼@35½, and Illinois Central to 53¾@54½. In other stocks nothing doing.

LIVERPOOL MARKETS.

Liverpool, Saturday, March 11—A. M.

Cotton.—The Broker's Circular says: "The telegraphic reports announcing the evacuation of Charleston caused, on Saturday, great agitation, and a serious decline in the cotton market, which became very irregular; and though, from time to time during the last few days, more disposition has been manifested both by the trade and speculators to buy, at some decline from the current rates, the week closed heavily on Thursday, at prices considerably below former quotations. American has been in limited demand, and has fallen fully 2d. ⅌ lb., and in most other descriptions, the fall is 2d.@2½d. on the week. The sales of the week add 40,800 bales, including 4,790 on speculation, and 5,130 for export. Middling Orleans is quoted at 16¾d.; Middling Uplands, 16d.; Fair Uplands, 17¼d. Other quotations of American are not given. The sales yesterday (Friday) were about 5,000 bales, including 2,[illegible] for export and speculation, the market closing quietly and partially rather easier, but firm for American.

TRADE AT MANCHESTER

Has exhibited a daily drooping tendency, and although a fair business has been induced by the fall, prices at the close were still in favor of buyers.

Breadstuffs.—Messrs. Richardson, Spence & Co., and Wakefield, Nash & Co. report Flour slow at late rates; Extra State, 20s. 6d.@21s. Wheat in more demand, but without any advance in prices; Red Western, 7s. 9d.@8s. 3d. ⅌ cental. Corn steady at 26s. 3d.@26s. 6d. for Galatz ⅌ quarter.

Provisions.—Messrs. Bigland, Athya & Co., Gordon, Bruce & Co. and others report Beef steady at about late rates. Pork, 2s. 6d. lower. Bacon in fair demand at full prices. Lard in limited demand, but prices steady at 57s. 6d.s for old, and 60s.@61s. for new. Tallow quieter, and generally 6d. easier. Butter dull and still declining.

Produce.—The Broker's Circular reports: Ashes lower. Pots, 29s. 9d., down to 29s. 3d. Pearls, 31s. 6d. Sugars steady. Molasses unchanged. Coffee inactive, but steady. Rice, quiet and unaltered. Bark sells at 8s. 6d. for Philadelphia. Linseed quiet and 2s. easier. Cloverseed, old American red, 63s. 6d. New 70s.@72s. Linseed Cakes, American, £[illegible]. Fish Oils, quiet. Winter bagged Sperm, £86. Linseed Oil steady at 35s. Rosin very flat and almost nominal. Spirits of Turpentine, small sales of French at [illegible].

Petroleum.—Messrs. Bully, English & Brandon report a moderate demand for refined at 1s. 9½d. for inferior up to 2s. for fine. No Crude offering.

LONDON MARKETS.

Messrs. Baring Brothers & Co. report Breadstuffs quiet and unchanged. Iron, Welsh, firm. Rails and bars, £6 5s.; Scotch pigs, 54s. 6d. Sugar steady. Coffee without change. Rice steady. Teas rather lower. Tallow, 3d.@6d. cheaper. New Y. C. 41s. 3d. Spirits of Turpentine, lower; French, 64s. Crude Petroleum, £18; Refined, 1s 11d. Sperm Oil unchanged, at about £[illegible]. Cod, £53 10s. Linseed Oil, 32s. 6d. Linseed Cakes maintain their price.

LATEST COMMERCIAL PER AUSTRALASIAN.

Liverpool, Saturday, March 11—Evening.

Cotton dull and unchanged. Sales to-day 8,000 bales, of which speculators and exporters took 2,000 bales.

Breadstuffs—No sales reported.

Provisions—The Provision market is quiet and steady.

Produce—The Produce market is quiet and steady.

Consols for Money 88⅞@89⅛.

American Stocks are tending upward. Illinois Central, 54¼; Erie, 35¼@35; Five-twenties, 54¼@55.

LATEST VIA LIVERPOOL.

Liverpool, March 11—Evening.

The *Times* (editorial) thinks if the Confederate Government remains firm, and if there is no renewal of the Conference, the Washington Government will endeavor to draw back the States singly by negotiations with each one specially; and that Lincoln may be more conciliatory than to the Richmond Cabinet.

VERY LATEST VIA QUEENSTOWN.

Queenstown, Sunday, March 12.

The *Etna* arrived at Liverpool at noon yesterday.

The *North American* arrived at Londonderry yesterday.

The Paris Bourse is steady, Rentes closed at 67f. 70c.

The European news is unimportant.

Melbourne, Sunday, Feb. 26.

The *Shenandoah* has arrived. She has burnt eleven ships since leaving the Cape.

Affairs in New-Zealand are less peaceable.

NEWS FROM WASHINGTON.

Special Dispatches to the New-York Times.

Washington, Thursday, March 23.

THE STORIES OF DISASTER TO SHERMAN.

The bulletin of Gen. Lee announcing a check to Gen. Sherman's army, creates not the slightest uneasiness here. It is plainly discernable that it was written simply to shed a ray of hope over the fast sinking fortunes of the enemy. The force encountered by Johnston was undoubtedly the advance of the left wing of Sherman's army, as Bentonville lies in the path which that column was pursuing. No information concerning either Sherman or Schofield has been received here to-day, save that obtained from the Richmond papers of Tuesday.

DAVIS AND HIS CONGRESS.

The Richmond *Whig* of Tuesday prints the report made by the Committee on Military Affairs of the rebel House on Jeff Davis' Message. The *Whig* says it was not formally adopted, for want of time and pressure of other business, but it is understood that the report expresses the sentiments of a large majority of the House. The report is similar in tone to that adopted by the Senate, but is couched in more moderate language. The report says that the House objected to giving Davis the sweeping militia law he asked for, simply because it had already placed at his disposal all persons between the ages of 15 and 50; and they further add, "It seems manifest that the extension of the conscription to persons over 45, while it has greatly impaired the productive power of the country, and in other respects prejudiced the public service, has been attended by no compensating advantage." The report raps Davis very hard for asking more conscripts where he had already admitted that more than one-half of the army was absent without leave. It is suggested that as the laws already made for the government of the army cannot be executed, they had better not make any more. The report further says that the Congress has made appropriations on the basis of an army half a million strong, and intimates that this ought to be sufficient. In regard to the delay in passing the negro soldier bill, the report quotes Davis' own message at the adjourning of this session wherein he declared that beyond employing negroes as pioneer and engineer laborers, he did not think it necessary to go. The rebel Secretary of War is also quoted to the same effect. In conclusion, the report says the solemn arrival of deliberate opinion by the President and his own War Minister, communicated to Congress, and never revoked, changed or modified in any subsequent message, left Congress in the position of being compelled to override its judgment of the high functionaries on a subject about which they are presumed to be fully informed, and not likely to fall into error, or to delay action until advised of the happening of the contingencies which would justify a resort to the doubtful policy of arming the slaves.

MOVEMENTS OF THE PRESIDENT.

The departure of President Lincoln for Fortress Monroe and City Point, to-day, has given rise to much rumor and speculation, but there is nothing remarkable in it. The President, with Mrs. Lincoln and young Thaddeus, taking advantage of the fine weather, and being desirous of a little recreation, left at one o'clock in the steamer *River Queen*, on a visit to Gen. Grant. Before leaving, the President was in consultation with the Secretary of War.

Dispatches to the Associated Press.

THE RUMORS ABOUT THE OCCUPATION OF GOLDSBORO.

Washington, Thursday, March 23.

The *Star* says the mail-boat to-day brought up five discharged soldiers, who left Wilmington on Monday morning, on a steamer for Fortress Monroe. At Wilmington it was reported, and generally believed, that a portion of Gen. Sherman's army had entered Goldsboro without any resistance, and that Sherman himself entered the town on Sunday afternoon.

POSTMASTERS CONTINUED.

The President has recently renewed the commission of a large number of postmasters, including those at Pittsburgh, Pennsylvania, and Poughkeepsie, Albany and Auburn, New-York. Charles R. Brayton has been appointed Postmaster at Port Royal, South Carolina.

THE PASSPORT BUSINESS.

The Secretary of State publishes, for the information and guidance of officers of customs, the order dated March 8, rescinding so much of the one issued in December last as required passports from persons entering this country from Canada, and so much of the circular of the Treasury Department, dated Dec. 31, 1864, as relates to the same subject, is rescinded, in order that the action of the two departments may harmonize. The circular of the Treasury Department concludes as follows:

Agreeable also to the suggestion of the Secretary of State on the 13th inst., Collectors of Customs on an arrival from any foreign country except of passengers, other than emigrants, destitute of passports, will refuse them permission to land either their persons or their baggage until notice shall have been given to the military authorities of the United States within the district, who will dispose of the passengers and their baggage, under instructions from the War Department.

MILLS THE SCULPTOR.

Clark Mills is now engaged in a work of art, embracing bronze statues of the President and members of his Cabinet, illustrative of the President's Emancipation Proclamation.

ADMIRAL DAHLGREN.

On inquiry at the Navy Department, it is ascertained there is no truth in the published report that Admiral Dahlgren has asked to be relieved from the command of the South Atlantic Blockading Squadron, and will be succeeded by Commodore Golon.

Reported Failure in St. Louis.

St. Louis, Wednesday, March 22.

It is reported that the banking house of Miller & Karst failed to-day. Their liabilities are not yet ascertained.

SOUTHERN NEWS

A Weak Attempt to Cheer the Southern Heart.

Lee Reports a Doubtful Victory for Johnston.

The Rebel Papers Make the Most of It.

SHERIDAN'S MAGNIFICENT RAID.

The Richmond Press Acknowledges its Destructive Character.

From the Richmond Whig, March 21.

The following official telegram was received at the War Department last evening:

Headquarters Armies C. S., March 20, 1865.

Hon. J. C. Breckinridge, Secretary of War:

Gen. J. E. Johnston reports, that about 5 P. M., on the 19th inst., he attacked the enemy near Bentonville, and routed him, capturing three guns.

A mile in the rear he rallied *upon fresh troops*, but was forced back slowly until 6 P. M., when, *receiving more troops*, he apparently *assumed the offensive*, which was resisted without difficulty until dark.

This morning he is intrenched.

Our loss is small.

The troops behaved admirably well.

Dense thickets prevented rapid operations.

R. E. LEE.

COMMENTS BY THE RICHMOND PRESS.

MAKING THE MOST OF THE REPORT.

From the Richmond Whig, March 21.

The above telegram conveys highly cheering news, as it assures us that *some portion* of the Yankee force which has been striding through the Carolinas without formidable resistance has, at length, met with a decided check. The dispatch does not inform us whether the column encountered *was Sherman's or Schofield's* and our previous information from North Carolina does not enlighten us on this point. Bentonville, near which the conflict occurred, is a small village in Johnson County, three miles west of the Neuse River, and some thirty miles *southeast* of Raleigh. We know that Sherman was at Fayetteville some days ago, and as Fayetteville is a little west of due south of Raleigh, the presumption is that Sherman diverged from the straight line to Raleigh, and moved toward the Neuse for the purpose of forming a junction with Schofield, who was supposed to be marching from Kinston toward Goldsboro, for the purpose of forming a junction with Sherman. Bentonville is fifteen miles west of Goldsboro. *It may, therefore, have been either column*; but the probabilities are that the enemy's main army under Sherman was struck by the Confederate forces, who were concentrated, we suppose, and led against the advancing column under the immediate command of Gen. Johnston.

The attack was evidently bold and vigorous, and in one hour's time the enemy's advance was hurled back in confusion upon the troops in the rear. To *this extent* it was "a rout." The approach of night and the densely wooded character of the country prevented Gen. Johnston from following up the advantage gained as completely as he would otherwise have done. Very little artillery was used on either side, hence only three guns were captured by the Confederates during the flight of the enemy. The effort to change the fortunes of the battle with fresh troops was unavailing. Still the Confederates pressed on, and the Yankees receded before the bayonets of our brave men, until the accessions of additional divisions from the rear enabled the enemy to make some resistance, which does not appear to have been very vigorous or effective. Darkness caused a suspension of hostilities, and our troops remained masters of the field. They fought bravely, and sustained but slight loss. The enemy must have lost heavily. During the night the Yankees threw up intrenchments, which is a sure indication of their discomfiture. One thing is certain: we have gained an important success, and the whole country will award merited praise and honor to Gen. Johnston and his heroic army.

SHERMAN'S PREVIOUS MOVEMENTS.

CONTRADICTORY RUMORS.

From the Richmond Whig, March 21.

The Raleigh *Conservative* of Saturday mentions the currency in that city of various contradictory rumors. Among these reports was one that the Yankees burned no private property in Fayetteville, except the factories. Later in the day there was another, which seemed to be entitled to confidence, that they burned various private residences.

The reports of the movements of Sherman were equally conflicting and uncertain. One statement, apparently reliable, was that he was still remaining in Fayetteville, while another said, with an equal appearance of credibility, that he had left the place with his entire force and proceeded to a considerable distance from there, and that some of the citizens were returning to their old homes in the place. Amid this uncertainty we will only say that we suppose that the military who have us now under their protection, are fully informed on this matter, and hope they are prepared to meet him whatever may be his plans, and checkmate him.

The *Progress*, of same date, says the people of that city are comparatively quiet, and awaiting the issue with the utmost confidence in our army.

SHERIDAN'S RAID.

ACKNOWLEDGMENT OF ITS DESTRUCTIVENESS.

From the Richmond Whig, March 21.

The Lynchburgh *Virginian* learns that Mr. Lemuel Turner, at the mouth of Tye River, lost fifty-one hogsheads of tobacco, burnt by the Yankee raiders. They also destroyed the guard lock at New-Market, and let in the river upon the lands of John Fry, W. D. Cabell, Mayo Cabell and Dr. Horsley, utterly destroying the growing wheat crop. As heretofore reported, they destroyed all the mills on their route, except the Midway Mills, the best on James River, owned by a Northern man named Fazer, supposed to be in sympathy with his section. *The canal is much injured*, but if the Government will assist the company it will soon be put in order.

A complete reconnoissance of the Orange and Alexandria Railroad shows that *all the bridges between Charlottesville and North Garden were destroyed*, including the large structures over North and South Hardware, Rockfish, Tye River, Turner's Creek and Buffalo—aggregating about 1,500 feet in length, with about six miles of railway track more or less injured—and all the depots east of Amherst, with the exception of Lovington and Tye River.

SOUTH CAROLINA AND GEORGIA.

AFFAIRS ABOUT CHARLESTON.

From the Richmond Dispatch, March 21.

From recent advices from South Carolina, we learn that the Yankees posted at Charleston send out daily foraging parties, devastating the plantations on the Santee. All able-bodied negroes are being dragged from their homes to fill the Yankee ranks. The South Carolina Railroad is operating to five miles north of Summerville, twenty-five from Charleston. Dr. A. G. Mackay the famous Masonic author, has been appointed by the Yankees Street Inspector of Charleston. The editors of the *Courier* call him an old and well-tried citizen. Sanitary improvements are progressing in East Bay and Church streets. The Yankees are fearful of the advent of the sickly season, and are purifying, to be prepared. The roads to Charleston are lined with people, white and black, going to Charleston on foot to trade and for protection.

FORT M'ALLISTER.

From the Richmond Whig, March 21.

We learn that about three weeks ago Col. Clinch, of the Fourth Georgia Cavalry, and a party of his men, dashed into Fort McAllister, at Genesis Point, and captured the working force of negroes engaged in dismantling the work. About forty were brought away, together with a number of horses. It will be remembered that this was the first point struck by Sherman on reaching the coast, and that it gave him a commanding base for subsequent operations. The fleet opening fire on Col. Clinch and his party, prevented the work from being held, had it been designed to do so.

NEGRO SOLDIERS.

PARADE OF THE FIRST COMPANY OF SLAVE TROOPS.

From the Richmond Whig, March 21.

A large number of ladies and gentlemen assembled on the Capitol-square, yesterday, to witness the promised parade of the first company of negro troops raised under the recent act of Congress; but owing to the fact that the new recruits have not yet been supplied with their uniforms and equipments, the parade has been postponed. We learn that the recruiting is going on rapidly. A refugee, from Fauquier County, offers to buy ten negroes who are willing to volunteer, and will emancipate them for meritorious service.

The battalion of colored troops from Camps Winder and Jackson, under the command of Dr. Chambliss, including the company under Capt. Grimes, will parade on the Square Wednesday evening at 4½ o'clock.

This is the first company of negro soldiers raised in Virginia. It was organized about a month ago by Dr. Chambliss, from the employes of the hospitals. The men were on the lines during the recent raid.

SLAVE TROOPS IN THE SOUTHWEST.

From the Richmond Dispatch, March 21.

Mobile papers of a recent date have reliable information that Kirby Smith has twenty-five thousand negro troops armed, equipped and organized under their masters, and operating in the Trans-Mississippi Department. The muster-roll of that department contains over one hundred thousand names, of which eighty thousand are effective for service. We should prefer to hear that Gen. Kirby Smith was moving some portion of this immense force to this side of the Mississippi River.

ARMY OF THE POTOMAC.

Reviews and Parades—Rumors from Sheridan—Firing Along the Front, &c.

From Our Own Correspondent.

Right Wing, Army of the Potomac, Monday, March 20—8 A. M.

Yesterday (Sabbath) was a delightful day, and after the usual hours devoted to worship, the Sixth and Ninth Corps were reviewed, partially by brigades, preparatory to a general review to take place some time this week. The reviews were conducted by Division and Brigade Commanders, and all appeared well satisfied with the appearance of their respective commands.

It is stated in this camp, to-day, on the authority of rebel deserters, that part of Gen. Sheridan's command has succeeded in reaching and tearing up sixteen miles of the Richmond and Danville Railroad, somewhere between Richmond and Burkesville. I am unable to gain any further particulars, or to state whether the authority is reliable.

On Saturday night and last night there was considerable firing along our front, between the Appomattox and Fort Sedgewick. No injury ensued to our troops nor to the works, though the fire was pretty heavy at times. HENRY H. YOUNG.

A Quiet Sabbath—Parades and Reviews.

From Our Own Correspondent.

Left Wing Army Potomac, Monday, March 20—A. M.

Yesterday our army lay in quiet repose, and the men enjoyed the beauty and delicious warmth of the day, never caring for any rumors or preparations for a new campaign.

Divine service was held in the different camps, and the customary morning inspections were gone through with.

The First Brigade in Gen. Hay's Division of the Second Corps was formally inspected and reviewed by that officer yesterday afternoon. This brigade is one of the crack organizations in that famous corps, and the command appeared to fine advantage. Col. Olmsted, of the Fifty-ninth New-York, is now in temporary command, in the absence of Gen. West, who is away on leave.

A grand inspection of the entire supply, baggage, ammunition and ambulance trains, of the Second Corps, also took place yesterday morning. One could gain a very good idea of the immense number of wagons and ambulances requisite for the proper supply of a corps. Several acres were required for the entire number to park preparatory to inspection.

I have nothing to send you in the way of news. We are almost stagnated for want of something new. Everybody is speculating and wondering when the new campaign will really commence, and as might be expected, no one agrees with any one else regarding the plans of our commanding General. The sutlers have, I understand, received permission to return, and some are actually coming up from the Point this morning.

GEO. F. WILLIAMS.

FROM CITY POINT.

The Lull in Affairs—How Soon it may be Broken.

From Our Own Correspondent.

City Point, Va., Tuesday, March 21, 1865.

The lull we have had during the past few days—in spite of the fine weather and apparent preparations for active work—is puzzling everybody. I shall be very much surprised, however, if we have to speak of quietude many days longer. Things have come to that pass, just now, that if *we* don't move Lee *must*, or remain and be caught like a hare in its form;—not "foam," by the way, as your Printer's Devil was pleased to make me say, when I used the simile once before.

We heard plenty of heavy distant firing yesterday, which assumed enlarged importance to us at a distance from the front; but, from the testimony of your active correspondent there, it did not amount to much.

I believe our worthy President is to favor us with his ever-welcome presence here to-day.

You will see, by the Richmond papers of yesterday, that the rebel Congress adjourned *sine die* on Saturday. Can they rationally expect ever to meet there again in treasonable conclave? The report of the Senate Committee on Jeff. Davis' last message, which I send in full, is, I think, more important than the message itself. It shows an inherent struggle against the Richmond despotism, quite as fatal to its endurance as even our arms.

J. R. HAMILTON.

FROM SAN FRANCISCO.

Subscriptions to the New Loan—Indian Reports Exaggerated.

San Francisco, Saturday, March 18.

Subscriptions to the 7-30 loan are freely offered here. There have been taken $600,000 since the receipts of the bonds in February.

The statement of the Indian troubles in Nevada are thought to be greatly exaggerated.

The treasure receipts from the interior during the week past amount to $850,000.

The money market is easier than it has ever been. The best mining stocks are ruling high. Trade is dull, but there is a good promise for the Spring, when good roads reduce freight charges to the interior.

San Francisco, Monday, March 19.

The mail steamer *Constitution* arrived from Panama this morning with the passengers that left New-York on the 25th ult.

Destructive Storm at Baltimore.

Baltimore, Thursday, March 23.

Violent storms of wind occurred to-day at 1 in the morning, at 11 o'clock, a. m., and again at 3 and 4 p. m. The force of the wind almost amounted to a tornado. In the western part of the city considerable damage was done. The boiler house of the Vulcan Works of Haglehurst & Wiegand was blown down and one workman was killed, one fatally injured and several severely. The roof of the new Government hospital on Townsend-street was blown off and a colored boy was killed. A chimney of the Eutaw House was prostrated and fell through the attic. Other similar damages are reported.

Maryland Politics.

Baltimore, Thursday, March 23.

The Maryland House of Delegates, to-day, passed a bill appropriating $50,000 to be advanced to the Navy Department to enable it to prepare for the return of the naval school to the academy building at [illegible]. The appropriation made by Congress [illegible] was lost by the failure of the Miscellaneous Appropriation Bill.

IMPORTANT FROM MOBILE.

Gen. Canby's Forces Near the City.

The Grand Attack Expected this Week.

Reconnoissance by our General Officers

They Approach Within Four Miles of the Place.

Heavy Fire Upon Them by the Rebel Batteries.

New-Orleans, Friday, March 17.

Gen. Canby is now near Mobile, and the grand attack by the land and naval forces upon the city will be made within five days.

Gens. Canby, Granger and Smith, and Admiral Thatcher, went within four miles of Mobile on the steamer *Laura*, last week, and drew a heavy fire from many of the rebel batteries that line the harbor.

Important News Expected from Mobile—The Forces Operating Against that City.

Special Dispatch to the New-York Times.

Washington, Thursday, March 23.

Important news is expected here in a short time from the vicinity of Mobile; and it is believed that it will be of the most cheering character. A campaign against the Gulf city has been in preparation since the middle of last January; but on account of the necessity of organizing the Thirteenth and Sixteenth Corps, and the removing of a multiplicity of obstacles, a task which required time, the troops of the Sixteenth Corps were not landed at Fort Gaines until the 12th of this month. The last of Gen. A. J. Smith's command left New-Orleans on the 10th inst.

It was calculated that the blow would be struck between the 25th and 30th of this month. Should our forces attempt to capture Mobile by assault, a sanguinary struggle may ensue, as all the approaches to the place are protected by strong fortifications, and it is supposed that the rebels have a large force in and about the city.

The attacking force is composed of veteran troops, under the chief command of Gen. Canby. Two Generals, whose reputations for fighting energy, skill and determination is well established—Gens. Gordon Granger and A. J. Smith, will command the two wings, respectively.

Beside the Thirteenth and Sixteenth Corps there will be a colored division and a division of cavalry in the field.

The entire force operating near Mobile is without tents or baggage, as the intention is to strike quick and hard.

Rebel Reports of the Operations Against Mobile.

Dispatch to the Associated Press.

Washington, Thursday, March 23.

The latest intelligence from Mobile is a dispatch in the Richmond *Examiner*, of Tuesday, dated 16th, saying there is no change to report in our immediate front. There is great activity among the fleet in the lower bay. All is quiet with a hostile fleet and army below.

FROM FORTRESS MONROE.

News from Newbern—Gen. Schofield's Movements—Condition of Kinston—Arrival of Refugee Negroes.

Fortress Monroe, Wednesday, March 22.

The steamer *Parthenia* arrived here to-day from Newbern, N. C., with mails and dispatches.

Gen. Schofield's army had moved from Kinston, N. C., with a view, it was thought, of joining Terry and Sherman near Goldsboro, where, according to the latest advices, the rebels were assembled in strong force under Bragg and Johnston, with the intention of giving battle and making a desperate resistance before surrendering the town. Affairs in and around Kinston were comparatively quiet. Very little business of any kind was doing. Most of the stores were closed, and the streets presented a deserted and gloomy appearance. When Gen. Schofield moved out of the town he left merely a provost's guard behind to prevent the stragglers of his army from pillaging.

A correspondent, writing from Kinston, says: "The town has changed but little since Gen. Foster was here in 1862, except by ordinary decay. The inhabitants appear somewhat downcast, but are pleasant in their demeanor toward our forces. Several of our wounded, who fell into the hands of the enemy on Wednesday, the 8th instant, are here under the care of the citizens, and have received all possible attention. Some of the inhabitants have admitted that Bragg was badly beaten on Friday, the 10th instant, the day he attacked Schofield's forces, but others deny it. They generally think that the sudden evacuation of the town was caused by orders received by Bragg from his superior."

Two schooners full of negroes arrived here last night from the White House, having followed Gen. Sheridan during his recent raid. They were all sent to Hampton and materials furnished them to build houses.

The steamer *Creole* arrived to-day from New-York. She reports having encountered very heavy weather off the Capes last night, and was compelled to lay-to several hours.

FROM NEW-ORLEANS.

Position of the Rebel Forces in Louisiana—Rebel Cotton Agent—Free Trade on the Mississippi.

New-Orleans, Friday, March 17, 1865.

Gen. Kirby Smith remains at Shreveport. Gen. Buckner is at Natchitoches, and Gen. Thomas at Alexandria. Their respective forces were with them, and they are waiting for an attack from our troops.

Judge Gray, a Texas lawyer, has been sent by the Richmond Government to the Trans-Mississippi Department to take charge of the Rebel cotton trade. He announces that no cotton shall leave his department unless the twenty-five per cent. assessed by the Federal Government is taken off.

Free trade is to be extended along the line of the Mississippi River, and liberal permits granted for supplies.

The steamship *Morning Star* left the bar on the 15th inst., for New-York.

Cotton is quoted at 69c.@72c. for good ordinary to middling. Sugar, molasses, flour and grain are without material change.

The Seven-Thirties.

Philadelphia, Thursday, March 23.

Jay Cooke reports the sales of Seven-Thirties to-day at $3,054,750, including one of $314,000 from Cincinnati, and one of $150,000 from Philadelphia. Also, 2,145 individual subscriptions, of $50 and $100.

The Recent Election.

Utica, Wednesday, March 22.

Oneida County complete, gives a majority of 547 against the Amendment.

The New-York Times.

VOL. XIV......NO. 4223. NEW-YORK, FRIDAY, APRIL 7, 1865. PRICE FOUR CENTS

THE REBEL ROUT.

Lee's Retreat Cut Off by Sheridan.

BURKESVILLE IN OUR POSSESSION

Lee's Army at Amelia Court House, East of Burkesville.

A Junction Between Lee's Forces and Johnston's Now Impossible.

Sheridan Hopes to Capture the Whole Rebel Army.

The Infantry Moving Rapidly to His Support.

General Grant at Sheridan's Headquarters.

[OFFICIAL.]

WAR DEPARTMENT, WASHINGTON, April 6, 1865—12 o'clock noon.

Maj. Gen. Dix:

The following telegram announces the probable speedy destruction of Gen. LEE's army if our troops get up to support SHERIDAN, who has headed off the enemy.

EDWIN M. STANTON, Secretary of War.

JUNCTION SOUTHSIDE AND DANVILLE RAILROAD, BURKESVILLE, VA., April 5—10 o'clock P. M.

Hon. Edwin M. Stanton, Secretary of War:

Lieut. Gen. GRANT received the following dispatch at 6:30 P. M., while on his way to this point, and at once proceeded to Gen. SHERIDAN's headquarters. Gen. GRANT desired me to transmit the dispatch to you, on the opening of the telegraph at this place, and to say that the Sixth Corps, without doubt, reached Gen. SHERIDAN's position within an hour or two after the dispatch was written. Two divisions of the Twenty-fourth Corps will encamp here to-night, and one division of the Twenty-fifth Army Corps at Black's and White's Station, Southside Railroad.

S. WILLIAMS, Brig.-Gen.

DISPATCH FROM GEN. SHERIDAN.

HEADQUARTERS CAVALRY, JETERSVILLE, April 5—3 P. M.

To Lieut. U. S. Grant:

GENERAL: I send you the enclosed letter, which will give you an idea of the condition of the enemy and their whereabouts. I sent Gen. DAVIES' brigade this morning around on my left flank. He captured, at Fame's Cross Roads, five pieces artillery, about two hundred wagons and eight or nine battle-flags, and a number of prisoners. The Second Army Corps is now coming up. I wish you were here yourself. I feel confident of capturing the army of Northern Virginia if we exert ourselves. I see no escape for LEE. I will put all my cavalry out on our left flank, except MCKENZIE, who is now on the right.

(Signed,) P. H. SHERIDAN, Major-General.

THE LETTER.

AMELIA COURT-HOUSE, April 5, 1865.

DEAR MAMMA: Our army is ruined, I fear. We are all safe as yet. SHYRON left us sick; JOHN TAYLOR is well; saw him yesterday. We are in line o battle this evening. Gen. ROBERT LEE is in the field, near us. My trust is still in the justice of our cause and in God. Gen. HILL is killed. I saw MURRAY a few moments since. BERNARD TERRY, it is said, was taken prisoner, but managed to get out. I send this by a negro, I see passing up the railroad o Michlenburgh. Love to all.

Your devoted son,

W. B. TAYLOR, Colonel.

FROM PETERSBURGH.

The Glorious 2d April—Great Struggle along Our Lines—Conflagration—Terrific Explosion—Rebel Flight—Our Entrance Into Petersburgh and Richmond.

From Our Own Correspondent.

PETERSBURGH, Monday, April 3, 1865.

It is really worth any amount of past labor and suffering to go through such glorious excitement as has attended the last 48 eventful and historic hours which have just rolled over us. If we, who have been only lookers-on and chroniclers on the grim outskirts of war, feel so intensely, what must it be, in this hour of consummate victory, for those who have been so long shouldering the musket or wielding the sword in the deadly struggle?—for that great man who, to-day, sees realized and brought to fruition all the sublime calculations upon which he has been so long engaged, and the noble, but formerly ill fated Army of the Potomac, placed, at one majestic bound, and by his doing, upon a pinnacle far beyond the sneers and carpings of those who had hitherto disparagingly contrasted it with other armies of the United States? What feelings must thrill the bosom of that trusty and noble-hearted pilot who has, for four long, dreary years of unceasing and anxious watching, seen the noble ark not only of American, but of all human liberties, struggling against a *Lee*-shore, now safely and unquestionably launched upon the broad and placid waters of unfailing peace and prosperity? ABRAHAM LINCOLN, in person, sitting by GRANT to-day in the "Cockade City," as the latter pensively smokes his cigar, surrounded by his trusty Lieutenants, and watching his conquering legions swarming streets but five or six hours ago held by the enemy! perhaps to-morrow or next day occupying the very chair of the arch-rebel DAVIS, in Richmond itself, (for the telegraph will have long since told you that WEITZEL entered it at 8:15 this morning,) while the latter, with the "unconquerable" LEE and his demoralized and disheartened remnants of an army are flying—God knows where—from the wrath to come! Can the nation require a better picture of overruling and decisive victory? Can the world require any further proofs that the rebellion is now, in reality, crushed, and forever?

The day, evening and night of Sunday, April 2, can never be forgotten by any one who was with this army. From the hour of my arrival at Hancock's Station, near which are the headquarters of the Second Division of the Ninth Army Corps, under Maj.-Gen. R. B. POTTER, then lying prostrate from a painful, but it is hoped not dangerous wound, received while gallantly cheering on his men in the recent great rebel assault, the fighting, which was then and had been long raging furiously along our whole line, and particularly in front of the Ninth Corps, (where are situated Forts Sedgwick and Mahone, so expressively known among the soldiers who occupy them as Forts "Hell" and "Damnation,") became infinitely more virulent as night came on, and was continued uninterruptedly until past midnight. The rebels were determined to regain the forts we had wrested from them, and upon which the fate of Petersburgh, Richmond, indeed the Confederacy itself, depended. Our men were just as determined that they should not regain one foot of lost ground, and the contest was dreadful.

It was about 3 A. M. to-day, the ever-memorable 3d April, when having concluded the long and irksome, but very necessary, task of sending the names of several hundreds of our wounded officers and soldiers, in the division hospitals of the Ninth Corps, I sallied out into the calm starlit night air to watch the progress of events. A dead and ominous silence rested over everything, and seemed almost awful in contrast with the deafening roar of artillery and musketry to which the ear had been so long accustomed. The overtaxed surgeons, fairly worn out by three days and nights of unceasing labor at the operation-table and the crowded wards, had laid down to take an hour or two of fitful sleep; so had the equally tired stewards and other hospital officials. The last ambulance had brought and silently deposited in the hands of the surgeons its sorrowful freight of human agony, and gone away to its quarters. Not a sound could be heard to break the solemn silence, save the occasional suppressed groan of some brave sufferer, whose torture was too great for even his manhood to bear unmurmuringly; the faint call of some other to a nurse to give him a drink of water or help to change his position; or an occasional shell whirled from our batteries, madly shrieking through the blackness of the air, and with such fearful distinctness that the ear could trace with perfect accuracy its curvilinear passage, as it went whirring onward and apparently burst clean over Petersburgh. But that which riveted my attention most, was the magnificent spectacle of the conflagration raging in the town of Petersburgh, and which seemed, at that distance, to envelope a large portion of it in lurid flame. It had been burning during the day, but its appearance now was heightened by its vivid contrast with the darkness of night, and was sublime beyond expression. To my astonishment I saw also, precisely in the direction which Richmond should occupy, another, and seemingly still larger conflagration. Could LEE have committed the cruel and ridiculous trick of converting into miniature Moscows both Richmond and Petersburgh; for both of which—apart from the great moral effect of conquering and possessing them—Uncle Sam would not give the snap of his finger?

Another thing arrested my attention. Loud cheers had, from time to time during the night, been heard proceeding from our lines, and which was construed into the delight of our boys as they succeeded in repelling each successive attack of the rebels. These cheers had now ceased, and not a single musket had been heard for some time previous to that of which I write. What was the meaning of this? Had both parties, fairly exhausted, laid down to rest? or had the enemy, finding his efforts useless, considered the battle over for the present?

While cogitating these matters, I suddenly saw—immediately near the fire which I supposed to be in Richmond—a huge mass of fire dart up, in the shape of an inverted cone, so high that it seemed to reach the clouds, and so intensely vivid as to light up the entire firmament. It was exactly like what I had seen when the grand old *Mississippi* blew up, at the siege of Port Hudson. I knew a magazine had exploded, and waited, with charmed interest, the report that I knew a few seconds would bring. It came, and was so tremendous, though at a distance of not less than twenty-five miles, that it seemed to shake the very earth on which I stood. Some of the doctors and others connected with the hospitals, startled in their slumbers, ran out to see the cause of the noise. When we were considering, just about the hour when night melts into dawn, we suddenly heard vociferous cheers burst from apparently thousands of throats. They evidently came from the honest, hearty lungs of our brave fellows. There was no mistaking that soul-stirring sound for the wild, savage, bitter yell in which the rebels indulge. Again and again the cheers were repeated, at short intervals, quite as vociferous, but apparently getting fainter and fainter. The joyous, suspicious sound found utterance among us, and received confirmation before day had fairly broken. *The rebels had fled!* Our boys had rent the air with cheers, as they entered and found work after work abandoned, which they had for long months been so fearfully struggling for, by day and night. The glorious victory was won! The last faint shouts had proceeded from our men in the heart of the rebellious City of Petersburgh itself, where the stars and stripes were already proudly floating from the summit of the court-house dome, placed there by the First Michigan Sharpshooters, who were the first to enter the city. As to the mysterious explosion, it has since been discovered that it was the blowing up of the rebel ram, or rams, in Richmond.

It is impossible to convey any idea of the joy and excitement that prevailed as the stunning news ran like wildfire among our people. The army moves with a decision and celerity quite inconceivable in any other walk of life. Instantly old quarters, made so comfortable that one would think some of the inmates intended to live there forever, are turned inside out; every man vaults into his saddle and is off, and one short hour will see the most busy military community converted into a lonely desert. One of your correspondents—Mr. YOUNG—had already gone off like a streak of greased lightning, and was one of the first, if not *the* first, who must have dated his letter from Petersburgh. I remained—a fretful prisoner at Hancock's Station—to see our matter of the night and early morning dispatched by the mail-car, which leaves at 8 A. M., immediately after which I started for Petersburgh.

Oh! the delight of that trip, along with the hardy veterans covering the road for miles—most of whom had shared in the desperate work of only a few hours ago—as they made the air ring with their laughter and cheers, while a band would now and then march us along to the air of "Cheer, Boys, Cheer," "Yankee Doodle," &c. The day was most enchanting—the distance scarcely over two and a half miles from where we started—and so I preferred accompanying them on foot, as affording me a better chance of examining the forts at my leisure. Our wounded had been, long since, removed to places of care and comfort, and burying parties had been for some hours engaged in disposing of the dead bodies; but still many lay there—Union and rebel—in all the ghastly variety of contorted faces and limbs, and hideous mutilation—just where death had stricken them down. I came upon a youth, laying flat upon his back, his upturned face exhibiting an expression very like a smile. He had cautiously buttoned to his vest the envelope of an old letter, which gave the following address: "WM. B. ADAIR, Co. K, Two Hundred and Eleventh Pennsylvania Volunteers, Second Brigade, Third Division, Ninth Corps!" Brave boy! he, for one, had died while doing his duty, for I found him close to the very edge of the second line of rebel works.

No one on examining our works can wonder how Gen. GRANT has been so long enabled to keep them like an iron collar around the neck of LEE. The rebel works, although more slovenly in their arrangements, and exhibiting far more traces of damage from our fire than ours do from theirs, are nevertheless, very strong, and it is quite certain that they might have defied us much longer yet if Gen. GRANT had not such a knack of attacking our enemy in half a dozen different plans at once, and bringing him to his senses as much by want as by direct assault.

Long before we reached Petersburgh the colored people, in stray parties of three and four, came to greet us; people that perhaps the day before would not be allowed to stroll out of the confines of the town, lest they should be escaping to the "Yanks." Even free colored people were kept to *unpaid* labor for the government, and they looked like folks just escaped from a prison.

Petersburgh, approached as we came, by the Jerusalem plank road, is hidden from the visitor until fairly arrived at it, by a bluff and deep ravine, at the bottom of which runs a tortuous little stream that joins the Appomattox. Crossing this stream, and mounting the bluff, the whole city bursts full upon the view, and looks very pretty, covering the whole undulating surface sloping down to the Appomattox, and agreeably interspersed with buildings and trees. Sycamore street, the principal street by which we entered, is very pretty, having handsome detached houses on each side, with fine gardens attached, all full of evergreens.

The President is still here, and had almost to run along the City Point wharf yesterday—when returning from Petersburgh—to escape the anxious importunity of the hundreds who were rushing to see him. It would be a glorious thing to meet him in Richmond, and I hope to have the pleasure. Heaven knows that the aspirations of his noble heart have been gratified enough during the last few days to satisfy even *his* longings for the good of his country.

J. R. HAMILTON.

THE PURSUIT OF LEE.

Evidences of the Precipitate Flight of the Enemy—The Roads Strown with Arms, Caissons and Wagons—The Rebels Fighting without Spirit.

From Our Own Correspondent.

AURELIA COUNTY, VA., WINTACOMACK CREEK, ONE AND A HALF MILES SOUTH OF APPOMATTOX, Monday, April 3.

This morning CUSTER's division left camp at a point several miles east of Namozine Creek, and made a rapid movement up what is called the Namozine road, leading into Aurelia County. At the ford on Namozine Creek the rebels were found to be strongly intrenched behind earthworks to cover the crossing. The Eighth New-York, Major BLISS, of WELLS' brigade, had the advance. A part of the First Vermont, under Capt. HAZELTINE, went up the stream a short distance and succeeded in effecting a crossing, flanking the enemy's position. LORD's section of artillery was brought up within easy range to the left of the ford, and simultaneously the ball was opened, firing grape shot at easy range. The enemy were so taken by surprise, they having supposed that the river was not fordable at any other place than where guarded, that they fled in the wildest confusion after a very brief skirmish. Col. WELLS continued the pursuit as rapidly as possible, the enemy endeavoring to obstruct the road by felling trees and piling the rails across, and at several points caissons were emptied, and the contents surrounded by fire, with the devilish hope that some of our daring riders in the advance might be killed.

The road bore abundant evidence of the haste the enemy were in. A number of caissons and wagons were overhauled, disabled, and arms, accoutrements, blankets, clothing and cartridges were to be seen on either hand. When near Namozine Church the enemy made a stand, and the whole Eighth New-York charged and carried the place, without materially interrupting the advance of the column. In this charge Capt. GOODRIDGE was mortally wounded; Capt. C. T. VAN DUZEN received a flesh wound in the thigh; Corp. ELWOOD, Company B, was killed; Corp. GEORGE GRASS, Company H, flesh wound in forehead; H. H. FAIRBANKS, Company G, finger; P. M. BURTON, Company B, wounded in abdomen, dangerous, and OSCAR C. PALMER, Co. E, slightly in shoulder. The First Vermont, Lieut.-Col. HALL, being the advance regiment of the main column, supported the movement, and Sergt. JAS. BOHAN, Co. A, was mortally wounded, having received a ball through his right lung. The Fifteenth New-York, Col. COPPINGER, coming up also in support of the movement, had First Sergt. JOHN MCGOUGH, Co. A, Capt. SKIFF, killed.

From this point the enemy, when once started, fled in confusion again, and WELLS continued the pursuit on toward Bevel's Bridge across the Appomattox, twelves miles distant, having up to this point, besides capturing a flag and recapturing some prisoners, taken from the Second Corps, captured wagons and caissons, and about one hundred prisoners while fighting. The number gathered in during the day I shall give at the close of this letter.

At Namozine Church, CAPEHART's brigade took the road toward the Appomattox, while WELLS pushed forward on a road to the left. In front of WELLS the enemy made several attempts to make a stand after the affair at Namozine Church. They were in every instance dispersed at a dash, until nine miles had been gained, when a large force of infantry was met, and the column rejoined the main column to the right. WELLS' command captured one piece of artillery, about three hundred and fifty prisoners, and a number of caissons and wagons. CAPEHART, on the River Road, moved up to near Deep Creek, capturing nine caissons, fifteen or twenty abandoned wagons, and about one hundred and fifty prisoners. Lieut. CUSTER, who was with WELLS' advance guard, captured a battle-flag. Maj. CUMMINGS, of the First Vermont, rode up to the very side of FITZ LEE, and captured his Adjutant-General. Maj. FERGUSON, of the Eighth New-York, captured Maj. FOOTE, Aid to BUSHROD JOHNSON.

Demoralization of the Enemy—Easy Captures—Narrow Escape of a Rebel Baggage Train.

From Our Own Correspondent.

DEEP CREEK RUN, Tuesday Morning, April 4, via WASHINGTON, April 6.

In the hurry of writing yesterday, I omitted to mention that Gen. BRANIGAN, commanding a brigade of cavalry in W. H. F. LEE's division, was captured. Five hundred of his men are cut off, and if time permits they will be brought in. In a skirmish last evening, after PENNINGTON's brigade had reached the battle-ground, Capt. FAUEL, of the Third New-Jersey, was wounded in three places—arm, neck, and thigh. His wounds, though of a serious character, and received by a less spirited man, might be considered mortal; still he says he does not intend to die yet, and there is hope of his recovery. Last evening Major GOODWIN, of the First Connecticut, went out into the woods and captured thirteen men. Lieut. VANDUL, of the Third New-Jersey Cavalry, was slightly wounded yesterday.

The fact that two brigades of CUSTER's cavalry, as stated in my letter of yesterday, drove six brigades of rebel infantry and two divisions of cavalry, speaks volumes as to the demoralization of the enemy. Three men at one time yesterday brought in a Captain, one Lieutenant, and one hundred and eight privates.

Five pieces of artillery were captured yesterday, instead of one, as stated yesterday. Four pieces were found sheltered in a piece of woods by Major YOUNG, Chief of Scouts, together with a number of loaded wagons.

In our front yesterday was a train of wagons 12 miles in length. This train left Richmond a few days ago, and was going southward when intercepted by our cavalry. It was the main train of the Army of Virginia; and had there been force enough at the front, the whole of the train would have been captured. As it is, the train was forced across the Appomattox at Beverly Bridge, from which place it cannot well get beyond our reach. No more time to write.

E. A. PAUL.

THE ATTACK ON MOBILE.

The Bombardment of the City Opened on March 30.

The Monitor Milwaukee Blown Up by a Torpedo.

Details of the Expedition from Our Own Correspondent.

The steamship *Guiding Star*, from New-Orleans, March 26, and Southwest Pass, the 28th, arrived yesterday.

The United States steamer *Circassian* arrived at Key West, April 2, and reported an attack of Union forces and gun-boats on Mobile, March 30. No particulars were obtained, except that the monitor *Milwaukee* was blown up off Dog River bar, by a torpedo.

The *Guiding Star* brings 2,794 bales cotton, 1,108 barrels flour, 1,000 sacks corn, 73 cases merchandise. The log reports: In consequence of detention by being run aground in Mississippi River by the pilot, had to stop at Key West to coal.

The steamer *Empire City* sailed from Key West, April 2; we passed her off Savannah, on the morning of April 4.

REPORTS FROM NEW-ORLEANS.

NEW-ORLEANS, Friday, March 31, Via CAIRO, Thursday, April 6.

The *Times* and *Delta* say:

"Headquarters have received information that a portion of Gen. CANBY's army was within four miles of Mobile, and siege guns were in position, from which shells could be thrown into the suburbs of the city. The attack on Fort Bradley, the main defence of Mobile, had already commenced. MAURY commanded at Mobile, and Gen. DICK TAYLOR commanded the Spanish Fort. The bombardment of the latter commenced on the 26th. Gens. CANBY, GRANGER and SMITH were five miles up Fishing Creek on the 24th. There was heavy cannonading on the 22d, caused by the gunboats shelling the woods at the mouth of Fishing Creek."

NEW ORLEANS, Saturday, April 1, via CAIRO, April 6.

Gen. STEELE's command, from Pensacola, met with much opposition, but no regular battle was fought until it reached Mitchell's Fork, on the morning of the 27th ult., where the enemy, numbering about 800, made a stand, and, after a severe fight, were repulsed and scattered in the woods, many being captured.

The correspondent of the New-Orleans *Times* writing from the headquarters of the Thirteenth Army Corps, near Blakely, on the 28th ult., says a party of guerrillas made a dash upon a wagon train stuck in the mud near Fish River, and captured ten mules and eight drivers. But all the wagons and stores were brought in yesterday.

There has been much skirmishing, but no regular battle has taken place as yet. The bombardment of the Spanish fort progresses favorably. Torpedoes thickly stud the approaches to the fort. Our skirmishers are within 200 yards, and our artillery within 300 of the fort. We have it encompassed on three sides.

Their only chance of escape is by water, but if a gunboat can get up they cannot escape that way.

Gen. GRANGER and staff narrowly escaped being blown up by a torpedo placed in the road.

Col. BERTRAM's brigade captured a rebel telegraph office and dispatches showing that the rebels are fully posted in relation to all our movements, forces and places. Gen. STEELE captured two railroad supply trains at Pollard.

At last accounts our losses do not exceed 50 killed and 200 or 300 wounded.

Rebel steamers ply regularly between Mobile and the Spanish fort, conveying reinforcements and guns.

Two of our men have been injured by torpedoes near Mobile.

Where Fish River is—Movements of our Troops.

From our Own Correspondent

DONNELLY'S MILLS, NEAR HEAD OF FISH RIVER, ALA., Tuesday, March 21, 1865.

The most complete map of the United States ever published fails to notice the existence of Fish River. As your readers in general may not be posted in this section, geographically, I will tell them where and what Fish River is, and otherwise explain the above date.

Bon Secor Bay is the name of a sort of cove which constitutes the right arm of Mobile Bay. You pass up this arm, or cove, some seven miles to the northeast, and through a little channel pass into another small bay, less than a mile square, turn directly to the east, and you strike the mouth of Fish River, a deep, crooked stream, about fourteen miles in length, running almost due north. Donnelly's Mills, never before known in history, is so called, from the fact that a steam saw-mill, owned by a man named DONNELLY, is located on the left bank of Fish River, about nine miles from its mouth. As I write, over 30,000 national troops are going into camp for the night, and it rains like fury.

THE MOVEMENT AGAINST MOBILE.

Mobile, as I have before informed you, is now next to Richmond the best fortified city in the Southern Confederacy. It has long been an eye sore to us, and some time ago—in fact immediately after the battle of Nashville—the great military eye of the republic was turned this way. Through your correspondents, and otherwise, you have thoroughly kept your readers posted in all the army movements of this section; therefore, suffice it to say, that on Sunday last, Gen. CANBY's army, after six weeks of travel, &c., received marching orders,

FOR MOBILE DIRECT.

The Thirteenth Corps, Gen. GRANGER, started that morning by land, and moved up the right side of Bon Secor Bay, with orders to reach Fish River opposite Donnelly's Mills, before Wednesday noon. The next day A. G. SMITH's Corps, the Sixteenth, embarked on board fourteen transports and six vessels of the Mosquito Fleet, from off Dauphin Island. A portion of the fleet arrived here yesterday. The balance of the boats arrived to-night. Gen. GRANGER's advance is also arriving, and the soldiers of both corps are "going to grass."

THE TRIP UP FISH RIVER.

I arrived at Dauphin Island from New-Orleans just in time to embark upon the *Tarascon*, one of the boats of the fleet. In all there were twenty odd boats, all of which were prepared, long before daylight, for the signal for starting, which was given at 9 A. M. The First Division, Gen. MCARTHUR, took the lead, the Second Division, Gen. GARARD, followed, and the Third Division, Gen. CARR, brought up the rear. Going up the bay nothing occurred, except steamboat races, worthy of passing notice. In rounding into the bay, which leads into Fish River, several of the boats got stuck in the mud, the last of which was lighted and pulled off to-day. We struck the mouth of Fish River at half-past eleven. Here we looked for torpedoes and guerrillas; but, on the contrary, eager multitudes of blacks and whites, of both sexes, of all ages and conditions, flocked to the shores, and rent the very air with their vociferations of joy. In many cases, in all probability, these manifestations were of a bogus character; but on the whole it is my impression they were sincere. This is one of the most curious streams I have ever been upon. The water is deep enough for the largest boats that float, but it is so very narrow that boats over 250 feet in length could not turn around; it is also so very crooked that many of the transports were obliged to run their bow into shore, and then throw a line to the opposite bank, and pull around. The people along the shore actually was wonder-struck; and why shouldn't they have been, to see some of the most gorgeous and luxurious floating-palaces of the the Mississippi wandering such a stream. The condition of the land, upon either side of the river, is of a marshy nature, generally. There were, however, some few pretty farms under a high state of cultivation. Contrabands in great numbers stood along the shores, many of whom jumped upon our boats as they passed along. One of the great peculiarities of the forests upon either side is the great number of eagles and eagle nests, many of the latter being larger than a cart wheel.

THE LANDING.

The boats of the fleet have been arriving ever since 3 P. M. yesterday, those boats which met with no misfortune having all arrived before dark last night. Two boat loads have just come in, which is the last of the Sixteenth Corps. The Thirteenth Corps is also arriving, and is going into camp upon the left, making our line extend from "Donnelly's Mills" on the right, to "Tom Danton's" on the left, a distance of about six miles.

WHERE WE ARE.

Upon the south side of Cow Bend, a branch of Fish River, our left penetrates to within four miles of Mobile Bay, and we are just 27 miles from the mouth of Apalachee River, or 30 miles from Mobile. Sixteen miles up the bay is what is known as the Spanish fort, the last work built by the rebels. This was built to keep our craft from running up the eastern channel; but there were provisions made in its elevation to keep off a land force approaching as ours now does. This force contains sixteen heavy guns, eight of which form water batteries. I understand that to-morrow our monitors and gunboats have orders to assault Spanish Fort, and take it if possible. If they fail to take it, our plans may be materially disarranged. I do not believe, therefore, that we will move again for two or three days, although we were led to believe that we should be within sight of Mobile before the sunset of the 23d inst., and have come thus far without tents and without baggage, all of which were left at Dauphin Island, with a promise that it would soon be brought up.

THE ENEMY.

Opposite us, upon the north side of Cow Bend, is a small brigade of cavalry, under Col. MAURY, a nephew of Gen. DABNEY H., commanding at Mobile. With the exception of the force at Spanish Fort, this body constitutes all the rebel force this side of the defences at the mouth of the Tensaw and Appalachee Rivers. It is quite late as I close, and I hear no picket firing—nothing but the incessant clattering of rain-drops as large as marrowfat peas.

BENJAMIN C. TRUMAN.

Arrival of Gen. Granger's Corps—Difficulties of Campaigning.

THURSDAY NIGHT, March 23.

All is quiet on the banks of Fish. All day yesterday, and a portion of this forenoon the firing in the direction of Spanish Fort was heavy and incessant. It has been quiet, however, in the direction of the bay since 12 o'clock, and it is to be hoped that Spanish Fort has gone up.

Ten rebel cavalrymen, or scouts, made their appearance to-day in front of Gen. MCARTHUR's picket line and fired a volley upon our videttes, which was returned, with no casualties upon either side. This is all the enemy that have been seen as yet.

Nearly all of GRANGER's corps has arrived. Two brigades are back yet. The roads traveled by this corps are pronounced wretchedly bad. Gen. GRANGER himself has arrived. I saw him to-day, the first time for two years. He looks badly, and complains of chills and fever.

Your correspondent is hobbling around himself. I awoke all of Gen. GARRARD's Staff officers last night by a yell. The fact is, there was a young cyclone swept over our camp last night, tearing up trees, blowing down tents, and knocking down things indiscriminately. A pine tree blew down near me, striking me in the leg, and I fear I am badly injured.

I can tell you one thing—we've got mighty little to eat here. The troops are on half rations, and a day behind. The officers fare very badly, and have to pay fabulous sums to the resident merchants for young pigs and old chickens—but plenty of rations are expected.

I have never seen a finer camp—a magnificent pine forest, through which wonder a multiplicity of sparkling streams. Such little pets as snakes, lizzards and scorpions abound; but, then, as they merely crawl over one, when one is asleep, why, one don't mind them much.

BENJAMIN C. TRUMAN.

From the Mississippi.

CAIRO, Thursday, April 6.

The steamer *Olive Branch* from New-Orleans, had 746 bales and 22 bags of cotton for St. Louis.

JOHN MCKINNEY, a rebel sympathizer, confined at Memphis under the military order of Gen. ROBERTS, for the non-payment of a debt of $7,000, due northern parties, was turned over to the civil authorities recently by Gen. WASHBURNE upon habeas corpus, and was released yesterday by the United States District Court upon the payment of costs. It is said he will commence a suit against ROBERTS for false imprisonment.

A hospital steamer has arrived from Vicksburgh, for St. Louis, with 470 exchanged prisoners from Andersonville and Cahawba. Eight hundred remain at Vicksburgh, awaiting transportation North.

The New-Jersey Legislature.

TRENTON, Thursday, April 6.

Ex-Gov. SEYMOUR, of New-York, visited our city to-day, and, accompanied by Gov. PARKER, was introduced to both Houses of the Legislature.

The Hunterdon Farmers' Railroad Bill was defeated for the want of three votes. Objections were made that it would be used as a through route between New-York and Philadelphia.

There was a general illumination in our city yesterday, in honor of the recent victories of the Union arms.

The National Loan.

PHILADELPHIA, Thursday, April 6.

JAY COOKE reports subscriptions to the Seven-thirty loan to-day, to the amount of $2,521,600, including $100,000 from Cleveland and $350,000 from New-York, and 1,769 individual subscriptions for $50 or $100 each.

Reading Triumphant.

READING, Penn., Thursday, April 6.

This place is in a blaze to-night in honor of our recent victories. Every house is illuminated, and the jubilee is general. A large meeting is assembled in the square, and the greatest enthusiasm prevails.

The Christian Commission.

BOSTON, Thursday, April 6.

The subscriptions to the United States Christian Commission in this city up to the present time, amount to over $28,000, and are still going on.

Execution of Guerrillas.

LOUISVILLE, Thursday, April 6.

Two noted guerrillas, JOHN HEDGES and ENOCH DOWNS, were executed here to-day by military order.

THANKSGIVING FOR VICTORY.

Gov. Fenton Recommends Friday, April 14, to be Observed as a Day of Prayer, Thanksgiving and Praise Throughout the State of New-York.

PROCLAMATION BY REUBEN E. FENTON, GOVERNOR OF THE STATE OF NEW-YORK.

Richmond has fallen. The wicked men who governed the so-called Confederate States, have fled their capital, shorn of their power and influence. The rebel armies have been defeated, broken and scattered, and the formidable character of the rebellion is apparently at an end. *Victory* everywhere attends our banners, and our armies, under Providence, are rapidly moving to the closing scenes of the war. Through the self-sacrifice and heroic devotion of our soldiers, the life of the Republic has been saved, and the integrity of the American Union maintained.

In view of these important events of the achievements of our noble armies and their gallant leaders—in view of the progress made in suppressing the rebellion, and the encouraging prospects of the early return of peace, there is great cause for rejoicing thanksgiving and praise. I, REUBEN E. FENTON, Governor of the State of New-York, do, therefore, issue this, my proclamation, designating Friday, the fourteenth of April instant, (the day appointed for the ceremony of raising the United States flag on Fort Sumter) as a day of thanksgiving, prayer and praise, to Almighty God, for the signal blessings we have received at his hands; and I hereby recommend religious societies of all denominations to open their places of worship, and the people, abstaining from their usual avocations, to assemble therein, and with grateful hearts, unite in prayer and praise to Him, who has so mercifully remembered us in the hour of our greatest need and peril.

[L. S.] In witness whereof, I have hereunto set my hand and affixed the privy seal of the State, at the City of Albany, this sixth day of April, in the year of our Lord, one thousand eight hundred and sixty-five.

By the Governor. R. E. FENTON.

GEORGE S. HASTINGS, Private Secretary.

THE STATE LEGISLATURE.

SENATE.

ALBANY, Thursday, April 6.

BILLS PASSED.

Incorporating the Soldiers' Messenger Corps; amending the charter of the Manhattan Gas Company; incorporating the New-York and Point Isabel Navigation Land and Emigration Company; incorporating the Father Mathew Temperance Mutual Benefit Society No. 1 of New-York; incorporating the Father Mathew Total Abstinence Benefit Society No. 6; incorporating the New-York Pier and Warehousing Company.

Mr. STRONG moved to limit the number of piers to this company to six. Mr. LEON moved that the limit be fifteen, which was lost, and Mr. STRONG's motion was adopted.

Mr. SHAFER moved an amendment, requiring the consent of the Commissioners of the Land Office to the sale of a pier, which was carried.

Mr. SHAFER moved to strike out the names of Messrs. MORGAN JONES, J. WILSON GREEN and JOHN C. GUNTHER as corporators, and the names of JOHN ROACH and HENRY MCCADDEN

Mr. STRONG moved to amend by providing that nothing in the bill shall be construed as authorizing any interference with ferry franchises, which was adopted.

The bill was then passed.

To amend the charter of Troy relative to schools.

BILLS REPORTED.

The Bill to amend the Registry Law was ordered to a third reading.

The Broadway Tunnel Railroad Bill.

The bill amending the act relative to the Harlem Bridge was then taken up.

Mr. SMITH moved to reduce the commissioners to three. Carried.

After debate, and on motion of Mr. LAIMBEER, which was carried, JOHN M. DODD and GEO. R. JACKSON were appointed commissioners for New-York.

Mr. LAIMBEER moved that Judge WM. ROBERTSON be commissioner for Westchester County.

Mr. SMITH moved to substitute the name of Gov. MORRIS.

This was lost and Mr. LAIMBEER's motion adopted.

The bill was then ordered to a third reading.

Mr. FIELDS introduced a bill authorizing an increase of the interest of seven per cent on New-York riot bonds.

The bill authorizing the incorporation of clubs and societies for certain social and recreative purposes was passed. Recess.

EVENING SESSION.

The bill authorizing the Second-avenue Railroad Company to construct new tracks was ordered to a third reading. Also a bill establishing the Willard Asylum for home insane poor.

Progress was reported on the Third-avenue Railroad Track Extension Bill, and on the bill relative to Justices and Police Courts in New-York City.

BILLS REPORTED.

To amend the charter of the City Fire Insurance Company of New-York.

To reduce the capital of the Rochester Flour City Bank.

Adjourned.

ASSEMBLY.

The Annual Supply Bill was ordered to a third reading.

The Charity Bill was made the special order for this evening.

The Governor returned the bill to establish a permanent exterior line in the City of New-York for correction.

The bill was reconsidered, corrected and passed.

A resolution to adjourn on the 13th was reconsidered and lost. Recess.

EVENING SESSION.

Mr. GLEASON presented the majority report on the Albany contested seat case, awarding the seat held by Mr. O. M. HUNGERFORD to Mr. JOSEPH SHOOK.

Mr. MCCONVILLE introduced a bill for the appointment of commissioners to examine into the cause of the recent inundation of the City of Rochester from the waters of the Genesee River, the result to be reported to the next Legislature. The rules were suspended and the bill passed.

Mr. LOUTRELL introduced a bill giving control of the fund of the New-York Fire Department to the trustees.

The Senate amendment to the Bounty Bill, making all bounty bonds payable in twelve years, and fixing the rate of interest at 7 per cent., was passed.

Mr. BRANDRETH acting as Speaker *pro tem.*

The State Charity Bill was ordered to a third reading.

Mr. STEWART moved to make the New-York and Brooklyn Railroad Ferry Bill the special order for to-morrow morning. Carried—63 to 21. Adjourned.

The New Surgeon-General.

Special Dispatch to the New-York Times.

ALBANY, Thursday, April 6.

Dr. JAMES E. POMFRET, to-day appointed Surgeon-General on Gov. FENTON's Staff, has served three years as Surgeon in the Seventh New-York Artillery, and as Division Surgeon. He was Professor of Anatomy in the Albany Medical College during the absence of Dr. ORMSBY as Consul to Naples, and is eminent in his profession. He is a straight-out supporter of the Government.

PERSIMMON.

The Canal Board passed a resolution to-day, to open the canals on the 1st of May.

PEOPLE'S CITY CONVENTION IN JERSEY CITY.—A meeting of the men of all parties was held last evening at old Washington Hall, in Montgomery-street, Jersey City, for the purpose of uniting on a People's ticket for city officers. There was a large gathering present. Alderman QUAIFE occupied the chair, and PETER POST acted as Secretary. A Nominating Committee was appointed, who reported the following ticket, which was adopted: For Mayor, Alderman J. M. PANGBORN, (Rep.;) for Water Commissioner, Ex-Mayor JOHN B. ROMAR, (Dem.;) for Chief of Police, JOSEPH MCMANNUS, (Dem.;) for School Superintendent, Rev. Mr. PARMLY, (Rep.) During speeches by Mr. WALKER and Maj. PANGBORN, there was considerable interruption and confusion by the adherents of Mayor CLEVELAND and the other Democratic nominees. Subsequently an adjourned meeting of the delegates to the Republican City Convention was held at the hall corner of Jersey and Newark avenues, and the People's nominees were adopted unanimously.

The New-York Times.

VOL. XIV......NO. 4225. NEW-YORK, MONDAY, APRIL 10, 1865. PRICE FOUR CENTS

HANG OUT YOUR BANNERS

UNION

VICTORY!

PEACE!

Surrender of General Lee and His Whole Army.

THE WORK OF PALM SUNDAY.

Final Triumph of the Army of the Potomac.

The Strategy and Diplomacy of Lieut.-Gen. Grant.

Terms and Conditions of the Surrender.

The Rebel Arms, Artillery, and Public Property Surrendered.

Rebel Officers Retain Their Side Arms and Private Property.

Officers and Men Paroled and Allowed to Return to Their Homes.

The Correspondence Between Grant and Lee.

OFFICIAL.

War Department, Washington, April 9, 1865—9 o'clock P. M.

To Maj.-Gen. Dix:

This department has received the official report of the SURRENDER, THIS DAY, OF GEN. LEE AND HIS ARMY TO LIEUT.-GEN. GRANT, on the terms proposed by Gen. Grant.

Details will be given as speedily as possible.

Edwin M. Stanton,
Secretary of War.

Headquarters Armies of the United States, 4:30 P. M., April 9.

Hon. Edwin M. Stanton, Secretary of War:

GEN. LEE SURRENDERED THE ARMY OF NORTHERN VIRGINIA THIS AFTERNOON, upon the terms proposed by myself. The accompanying additional correspondence will show the conditions fully.

(Signed) U. S. Grant, Lieut.-Gen'l.

Sunday, April 9, 1865.

General—I received your note of this morning, on the picket line, whither I had come to meet you and ascertain definitely what terms were embraced in your proposition of yesterday with reference to the surrender of this army.

I now request an interview in accordance with the offer contained in your letter of yesterday for that purpose.

Very respectfully, your obedient servant,
R. E. Lee, General.

To Lieut.-Gen. Grant, Commanding United States Armies.

Sunday, April 9, 1865.

Gen. R. E. Lee, Commanding Confederate States Armies.

Your note of this date is but this moment, 11:50 A. M., received.

In consequence of my having passed from the Richmond and Lynchburgh road to the Farmville and Lynchburgh road, I am at this writing about four miles West of Walter's church, and will push forward to the front for the purpose of meeting you.

Notice sent to me, on this road, where you wish the interview to take place, will meet me.

Very respectfully, your ob'd't servant,
U. S. Grant,
Lieutenant-General.

Appomattox Court-House, April 9, 1865.

General R. E. Lee, Commanding C. S. A.:

In accordance with the substance of my letters to you of the 8th inst., I propose to receive the surrender of the Army of Northern Virginia on the following terms, to wit:

Rolls of all the officers and men to be made in duplicate, one copy to be given to an officer designated by me, the other to be retained by such officers as you may designate.

The officers to give their individual paroles not to take arms against the Government of the United States until properly exchanged, and each company or regimental commander sign a like parole for the men of their commands.

The arms, artillery and public property to be packed and stacked and turned over to the officers appointed by me to receive them.

This will not embrace the side-arms of the officers, nor their private horses or baggage.

This done, EACH OFFICER AND MAN WILL BE ALLOWED TO RETURN TO THEIR HOMES, not to be disturbed by United States authority so long as they observe their parole and the laws in force where they reside.

Very respectfully,
U. S. Grant, Lieutenant-General.

Headquarters Army of Northern Virginia, April 9, 1865.

Lieut.-Gen. U. S. Grant, Commanding U. S. A.:

General: I have received your letter of this date, CONTAINING THE TERMS OF SURRENDER OF THE ARMY OF NORTHERN VIRGINIA, as proposed by you. As they are substantially the same as those expressed in your letter of the 8th inst., THEY ARE ACCEPTED. I will proceed to designate the proper officers to carry the stipulations into effect.

Very respectfully,
Your obedient servant,
R. E. Lee, General.

THE PRELIMINARY CORRESPONDENCE.

The following is the previous correspondence between Lieut.-Gen. Grant and Gen. Lee, referred to in the foregoing telegram to the Secretary of War:

Clifton House, Va., April 9, 1865.

Hon. Edwin M. Stanton, Secretary of War:

The following correspondence has taken place between Gen. Lee and myself. *There has been no relaxation in the pursuit during its pendency.*

U. S. Grant, Lieutenant-General.

April 7, 1865.

Gen. R. E. Lee, Commanding C. S. A.:

General: The result of the last week must convince you of the hopelessness of further resistance on the part of the Army of Northern Virginia in this struggle. I feel that it is so and regard it as my duty to shift from myself the responsibility of any further effusion of blood, by asking of you the surrender of that portion of the Confederate States Army, known as the Army of Northern Virginia.

Very Respectfully,
Your obedient servant,
U. S. Grant,
Lieutenant-General,
Commanding Armies of the United States.

April 7, 1865.

General: I have received your note of this date.

Though not entirely of the opinion you express of the hopelessness of further resistence on the part of the army of Northern Virginia, I reciprocate your desire to avoid useless effusion of blood, and therefore, before considering your proposition, *ask the terms you will offer, on condition of its surrender.*

R. E. Lee, General.

To Lieut.-Gen. U. S. Grant, Commanding Armies of the United States.

April 8, 1865.

To Gen. R. E. Lee, Commanding C. S. A.:

General: Your note of last evening in reply to mine of same date, asking the conditions on which I will accept the surrender of the Army of Northern Virginia, is just received.

In reply, I would say that *peace being my first desire, there is but one condition that I insist upon*, viz.:

That the men surrendered shall be disqualified for taking up arms again against the Government of the United States until properly exchanged.

I will meet you, or designate officers to meet any officers you may name, for the same purpose, at any point agreeable to you, for the purpose of arranging definitely the terms upon which the surrender of the Army of Northern Virginia will be received.

Very respectfully, your obedient servant,
U. S. GRANT, Lieut.-General,
Commanding armies of the United States.

April 8, 1865.

General: I received, at a late hour, your note of to-day, in answer to mine of yesterday.

I did not intend to propose the surrender of the Army of Northern Virginia, but *to ask the terms of your proposition.* To be frank, I do not think the emergency has arisen to call for the surrender.

But as *the restoration of peace should be the sole object of all*, I desire to know whether your proposals would tend to that end.

I cannot, therefore, meet you with a view to surrender the Army of Northern Virginia, but *as far as your proposition may affect the Confederate States forces under my command, and tend to the restoration of peace*, I should be pleased to meet you at 10 A. M., to-morrow, on the old stage road to Richmond, between the picket lines of the two armies.

Very respectfully, your obedient servant,
R. E. Lee,
General, C. S. A.

To Lieut.-Gen. Grant, Commanding Armies of the United States.

April 9, 1865.

General R. E. Lee, commanding C. S. A.:

General: Your note of yesterday is received. As I have no authority to treat on the subject of peace, the meeting proposed for 10 A. M. to-day could lead to no good. I will state, however, General, that *I am equally anxious for peace with yourself*; and the whole North entertain the same feeling. *The terms upon which peace can be had are well understood. By the South laying down their arms, they will hasten that most desirable event, save thousands of human lives, and hundreds of millions of property not yet destroyed.*

Sincerely hoping that all our difficulties may be settled *without the loss of another life*, I subscribe myself,

Very respectfully,
Your obedient servant,
U. S. Grant,
Lieutenant-General United States Army.

REJOICINGS.

Wilmington, Del., Sunday, April 9.

Wilmington is in an uproar and blaze of glory, rejoicing over the greatest of victories yet achieved by our arms. Guns are firing, bells are ringing, and a large procession is proceeding through the streets. Such an excitement was never before witnessed in this city.

Albany, Monday, April 10—1 A. M.

There is great rejoicing here over the news of the surrender of Gen. Lee and his army.

The news was received at about 10 P. M., and about midnight State and Pearl streets were filled with people anxiously awaiting the particulars.

The bells are ringing, cannon firing, while the multitude are indulging in fireworks.

The Governor was called up and briefly addressed the throng around his residence.

The State House and many private residences are illuminated.

Philadelphia, April 9.

The glorious announcement of Lee's surrender was received here about nine o'clock. It was telegraphed to all sections of the city, and was announced in the several churches. The *Ledger* office was illuminated in five minutes. The bell of Independence Hall was rung by the order of the Mayor. The firemen immediately assembled and blocked up the streets. Salutes were fired, and the whistles of the steam-engines and the cheers of the assembled multitudes made the whole city ring.

Worcester, Mass., Monday, April 9.

The news of the surrender of Lee and his army created an intense excitement here to-night. The bells were rung, guns were fired, bonfires kindled, the fire companies turned out, and many stores and buildings were illuminated.

Pittsburgh, Pa., Sunday, April 9.

The news to-night brought nearly the entire population into the streets. The recruiting booths were turned into bonfires, salutes were fired, speeches were made, and bands played.

Trenton, N. J., Sunday, April 9.

The glorious news was received here with cheering and ringing of bells. The people are turning out *en masse* to receive and rejoice over the glad tidings.

Providence, R. I., Sunday, April 9—Midnight.

Bells are ringing, cannon are firing, and the citizens are out rejoicing over the news of Lee's surrender. A large bonefire is burning on Weybosset bridge.

FROM THE PACIFIC COAST.

Juarez said to be Coming to Washington by way of San Francisco—French Forces in Sinaloa—French War Steamers in California Ports—The Overland Mails.

San Francisco, Friday, April 7.

The steamer *John L. Stephens*, from Mazatlan, brings $93,000 in treasure and a thousand bags of silver ore.

The Mazatlan *Times*, the Imperialist organ, give the report that Juarez was en route for Cape St. Lucas, whence he would sail for San Francisco on his way to Washington.

A French naval expedition had sailed, it was supposed, for Guaymas.

An Imperial force has moved to Sinaloa.

A correspondent of the San Francisco *Bulletin*, writing from Mazatlan, March 4, says that Juarez is still at Chihuahua with his ministers raising troops, though money, arms, and ammunition are scarce.

The French war steamer *Victoria* and transport *Du Rhine* was at Santa Barbara, on the coast of California. They hope to obtain supplies of coal at San Francisco.

The daily Overland Mail, hence to Salt Lake, resumed its trips yesterday. The first mail this way since the interruption arrived last night.

The recent meeting in behalf of the Christian Sanitary Commission, resulted in remittances, by telegraph, within the past few days, of $20,000 in gold.

The scarcity of flour and wheat continues. Extreme prices are obtained, and consequently trade does not improve much.

The Union Convention of Washington Territory have nominated A. A. Denny as Congressional Delegate.

Military celebrations for the national victories were held throughout the State to-day.

A mass meeting in aid of the Soldiers' Relief Association was held here to-night.

THE VICTORY.

Thanks to God, the Giver of Victory.

Honors to Gen. Grant and His Gallant Army.

A NATIONAL SALUTE ORDERED.

Two Hundred Guns to be Fired at the Headquarters of Every Army, Department, Post and Arsenal.

[OFFICIAL.]

War Department, Washington, D. C., April 9, 1865—9:30 P. M.

Lieut.-Gen. Grant:

Thanks be to Almighty God for the great victory with which he has this day crowned you and the gallant armies under your command.

The thanks of this Department and of the Government, and of the People of the United States—their reverence and honor have been deserved—will be rendered to you and the brave and gallant officers and soldiers of your army for all time.

Edwin M. Stanton, Secretary of War.

War Department, Washington, D. C., April 9, 1865—10 o'clock P. M.

Ordered: That a salute of two hundred guns be fired at the headquarters of every army and department, and at every post and arsenal in the United States, and at the Military Academy at West Point on the day of the receipt of this order, in commemoration of the surrender of Gen. Robert E. Lee and the Army of Northern Virginia to Lieut.-Gen. Grant and the army under his command. Report of the receipt and execution of this order to be made to the Adjutant-General at Washington.

Edwin M. Stanton,
Secretary of War.

FROM RICHMOND.

Perils and Excitements of a Voyage Up the James—Scenes and Incidents Along the River.

From Our Own Correspondent.

Richmond, Va., Wednesday, April 5.

The inspiration of the scene and the scope of the theme before us are far beyond the feeble descriptive powers of of the pen of your correspondent. No brilliant rhetoric, no vivid word-painting, no oratorical eloquence can portray the sublimity and immensity of the great victory. It is almost beyond the power of the human mind to comprehend its extent, and when you begin to descend to detail, the task is simply appalling in its magnitude. Think of a line of operations, held defensively and operated from offensively with such success, *thirty-nine miles long from flank to flank, thoroughly fortified throughout its entire length!* Think of the cities captured, of the fortificationss stormed and taken, with their hundreds of guns, great and small, of the material of war now in our hands, yet beyond the possibility of computation of the terrible battles, and the overwhelming defeat, and rout of the chief army of the rebellion of the prisoners captured. Counted by the tens of thousands; of the terrified flight of the arch-traitor and his few desperate minions; of the triumphant entry of Abraham Lincoln into treason's fallen capital. Let every lover of his country depict the vast scene in his own imagination for words to fitly discribe it fails altogether.

Through the courtesy of Provost-Marshal Gen. Patrick, I enjoyed an exceedingly pleasant sail from City Point to the Richmond wharves this morning, on his fleet flag ship, the *Mattino*. Accompanying the General were Hon. C. H. Dana, Assistant Secretary of War, his wife and son, and Hon. Roscoe Conkling, member of Congress from New-York. The snake-like bends of the James between City Point and Varina Landing, were quickly passed, and at the latter place assurance was given that the river was clear for our vessel to the very docks of Richmond; but I can assure you that the navigation of the tortuous channel of the James thence to Richmond, thickly sown with obstructions and supposed torpedoes, was an exceedingly delicate task, and full of excitement. Our pilot knew the channel of old, but he knew not the warlike devices of the enemy.

We were, however, very fortunate, and the approach to the city, especially during the last eight miles from Drewry's Bluff, was full of the intensest interest, for over these waters the Union flag had never before floated during the war. When we leave Dutch Gap and that famous canal, which looks as though it might have been washed out by a billow, we at once enter upon the lines held by the enemy. Howlett House Battery, famous for its determined resistance to our engineering operations on the north side of the river, stands abandoned and gloomy, with its twelve large guns still in the embrasures, but all silent as we steamed rapidly by. Another long and large earthwork appears on the left bank, mounting eight or ten guns, and bearing directly upon the mouth of the canal. This, too, like the rest, is abandoned, with its armament unimpaired. We next pass the wreck of the rebel gunboat, blown up by our batteries during the effort made to run through our fleet some months ago.

The next point of interest is Fort Brady, on the north bank of the river, and the left of the position of our Army of the James. What strikes one as very remarkable here is the fact that owing to the intricate windings of the James there are two rebel batteries, Howlett House and another, absolutely in the rear of this former position of our army. Fort Brady is the point where Gen. Gibbon opened on the retreating rebel rams. Had there been larger guns at his disposal, the range is so good that they would have stood a poor chance of escape.

We are now fairly in that part of the river held solely by the rebels, and a knowledge of the channel and obstructions is absolutely necessary to a safe voyage. The gunboat *Monticello* is therefore hailed, and on asking for information, a pilot who has been up and down is tendered with much politeness. The obstructions sunk by our own fleet are soon passed, likewise the fleet of monitors, and the next object which greets the vision is a gaily dressed tug, with a guard of marines, having in tow Admiral Porter's barge with the President, on his return from Richmond, complacently seated in the stern sheets. It looks very much like a pic-nic. Following a short distance after is the President's handsome flag-ship, the *River Queen*. Not far behind is the beautiful steel gunboat *Bat*, ex-blockade runner, now general convoy to distinguished guests, and one of the fastest vessels in the navy. The *River Queen*, which took the President up the river, proceeded no farther than the obstructions at Drewry's Bluff. We are soon abreast of this historic fortification, and eager eyes scan closely its formidable walls and positions.

Here is the chief line of obstructions sunk by the rebels early in the war, and located as they are, directly under the guns of Fort Darling, subjecting every approaching thing to a terrible plunging fire, it is readily admitted that this was the impassable barrier to the naval advance on Richmond. The river here is very narrow, and the movement of large vessels attended with much danger. The obstructions were placed directly across the river, and filled it completely with the exception of a gap of fifty or sixty feet, left for the passage of the rebel fleet and flag-of-truce boats. They consist of the hulls of two or three old steamships, that formerly plyed between Richmond and New York. The wheel-houses, fast crumbling to decay, still rise above the water, and present the appearance of a melancholy ruin.

We pass so hurriedly under the guns of Fort Darling, that we have no good opportunity to observe its construction. We know it looks very strong, and on the north side it has one or two small outlying works on its flank. Our naval companions tell us that it is a casemated fortification, and with its surrounding field works, all parts of the fort itself, mounts not less than forty guns. All these, like hundreds more, are our trophies without blemish or injury.

Not far above Fort Darling lies the wreck of one of the famous rebel fleet in the James, the iron-clad *Virginia*. Whether she has been blown up or simply scuttled and sunk, cannot be ascertained from looking at her as she lies. She sank in deep water, and is careened over on her side, leaving a portion of her overhang visible above the water-line. Of the other iron-clad, the *Richmond*, we find no trace.

In the immediate vicinity of Fort Darling we pass through a very substantial bridge with a draw, used by Lee for the speedy transfer of troops from the north to the south side of the James. Ere reaching Richmond we pass two more of the same kind, though hardly so well built as the first; but all demonstrating that Lee had no pontoon bridges across the James anywhere—probably, because the rapid current rendered them unsafe, and probably, too, because he had not any pontoons to spare, when something else would answer just as well.

We have now steamed safely by all obstructions and chances of torpedoes, and the very pardonable trepidation which we felt in view of our possible danger, gives way to a feeling that just now is a moment in our lives, the significance, importance and sublimity of which cannot be justly appreciated. The City of Richmond is in view. The spires pointing heavenward; the smoke still rising from the conflagration's awful ruin, and the Stars and Stripes floating from a hundred house-tops and mastheads, all form a picture so sublimely grand and inspiring, that the human mind is simply lost in mute contemplation.

In a few moments we land at the Rockets, and a brisk walk of a mile and a half brings us to the Spotswood House, where we find dinner and a very comfortable room, amid hundreds of loyal guests.

L. L. CROUNSE.

First Impressions of Richmond—The Great Conflagration in the City—Who Was Responsible for it?—The Libby and Castle Thunder—Suffering for Food—Distribution of Supplies—Lee's Family.

From Our Own Correspondent.

Richmond, Thursday, April 6, 1865.

So many thousand facts are presented to the mind of the visitor here in such a very short space of time, that to record them systematically is almost impossible. The great features of the evacuation, the entrance of our troops, the conflagration, the President's visit and reception, have already been forwarded to you in detail by your correspondents who came in with the troops, and I will, therefore, allude to them only in a general way.

Let me say, though, at the outset, that the best part of the city is a ruin. That the awful fire kindled by the enemy, and which at first promised to consume but a few buildings, was so fanned by the rising wind, that before it could be got under subjection, *thirty squares, comprising not less than eight hundred buildings in the very best and most valuable business part of Richmond were in ashes.* What the pecuniary loss is no one can estimate. Nearly all the principal mills, factories, warehouses, stores, banks and insurance offices were destroyed, and the losses being so heavy, the insurance companies, perhaps insolvent already from their countenance of the rebel currency, are now more than bankrupted, and thousands of property owners, computed wealthy in their actual possessions three days ago, are now reduced to beggary. It is among the things easily discernable, that this ruin, wrought by their own friends, to whom they have given all, and to whose tyranny they have submitted, with even cheerfulness, is the cause of far deeper gloom among many than that produced by the loss of the city or the defeat of their army. It is apparent indeed that the transfer of the city to the Union flag was not only *not distasteful to a very large portion of the people, many of them among the best classes, but even highly gratifying.* No captured city, not even Savannah nor Columbia, can present the ruin apparent here in Richmond. It will carry its painful evidences for half a score of years, and the only thing which will speedily alleviate the dire distress that must prevail, and give the city a chance for a speedy recovery from its present stagnation, is immediate peace. It is Richmond's only salvation. The origin of the fire and the incendiaries are so well and positively known that no extended investigation on these points is required. It seems that *Gen. Lee was not responsible for it, but that Jeff. Davis and his Secretary of War, Breckenridge, were.* The destruction of the supplies and the arsenal involved the destruction of the city, and it was so decided by the leading citizens. Gen. Ewell and Maj. Carrington both protested against it in the most earnest manner, as did also a committee of citizens, but Breckinridge, in reply, exclaimed *that he didn't care a d—n if every house in Richmond was consumed, the warehouse must be burned.* Thus this wretched rebel, foisted into a powerful position with no constituents, is responsible for the dreadful ruin, and his master Davis is likewise responsible, because he silently countenanced it.

The fire was started in two places, among the supply warehouses near the wharves, and at the Danville Depot, where there were 1,500 hogsheads of tobacco belonging to the Confederate Government. This consumed the Danville Depot, also the Petersburgh Depot, and the bridge over the James to Manchester. The famous Libby Prison, and Castle Thunder, as I have already informed you, were not burned. They were reserved for a far more appropriate fate. I visited them yesterday, and found Castle Thunder used as a guard-house for factious and thieving negroes, caught in acts of plunder, while the Libby contained 700 rebel prisoners, officers and privates, temporarily shut up together. They looked through the iron gratings with gloomy countenances, while the Union guard outside seemed to richly enjoy the transition that the famous building had undergone, evidently having been there himself. The whirligig of time makes all things even, and the thousands of loyal officers and soldiers who have suffered the tortures and horrors of these dungeons may now contemplate their present uses with serene satisfaction, and yet without resentment.

A close inspection of Castle Thunder reveals one of the most hideous dungeons that can be conceived. We failed to see it, however, in all its filth and nastyness, for a strong force of men had been engaged two days in carrying out the accumulation of the past three years. The corporal of the guard who conducted us through, pointed out a spot on the floor on one of the main halls, not yet cleaned, where the dirt was three inches thick, and alive with vermin, *and yet on this floor, in this condition, prisoners were obliged to sleep either upon the dirt itself or upon palets of decaying straw.*

But I will not descant further upon this vile relic of the rebellion. Its career is too well known. The prisoners confined here, it will be recollected, were those against whom special vengeance was directed, prisoners of State, persons charged with harboring Union prisoners, Union officers charged with being spies, blockade-runners, &c. Well has it been said that a confinement in Castle Thunder is a foretaste of the tortures of the damned.

This building, together with the Libby belongs to the estate of John Enders, and was leased by the rebel Government. They were originally built for stores, but subsequently turned into tabacco manufactories. But their base uses are now at an end.

This is the fourth day of the Union occupation, and the confusion in the city necessarily attendant upon such an evacuation, and such an occupation, is gradually subsiding. Could the ruins of the fire be removed from sight, Richmond would present an attractive appearance, for it is really a handsome city; but, after all, the saddest scenes are at the headquarters of the Provost-Martial, the Commissioners of Subsistence, and the office of Sanitary Commission, the latter being already established here. Gen. Weitzel had no sooner established his headquarters here than thousands of citizens besieged him for rations. And as the city is now shut out from all supplies from the country, the crowd of applicants for subsistence is rapidly increasing. This morning there was nothing in the markets but a few small fish caught by negroes. The Capitol, the City Hall and the Capitol-square are filled with a great throng of all classes, condition, sexes and ages, with basket in hand and an appealing expression of face. What the regulations yet are in regard to the issue of rations to the citizens, I do not know, but a limited quantity is being supplied them at present.

In order to study this peculiar social feature of the rebellion, I mingled with these crowds this morning for a short time, to observe their temper, desires and condition. They were, of course, largely made up of what appeared to be the poorer classes, and many negroes were among them, some for subsistence for themselves and some as servants of families. I found many whose intelligent expression of countenance, fair features and attempted gentility of dress, indicated that they were of the higher classes, on whom the demands of want and hunger were as insatiable as upon those of less position. I noticed several ladies approach the officer in charge at the City Hall, genteelly attired, and with their faces so closely veiled as to defy the gaze of the keenest eye. They spoke in such tremulous tones when giving their names as to cause us to suspect their names were as foreign to them as the hunger they now sought to appease had been in days gone by. Many of the wealthiest families, however, who had the means, have far larger supplies of provisions on hand than was consistent with the repeated appeals of Confederate officials for such to spare from their bounty to feed the army.

The exodus of prominent citizens was confined mainly to those connected with the rebel government, and a few who had made themselves very conspicuous in rebel politics—all the rebel Cabinet and their chief assistants, though not much of their clerical force, got away. The preparations for the evacuation began very quietly among the officials. At noon of Sunday the important records of the departments were boxed up and carted to the depot; but very little suspicion was excited among the citizens as to the real state of the case. A strong guard was stationed at the Danville depot, and four trains were got ready, the first of which left, with Davis on board, at seven o'clock in the evening, and the last at midnight. Davis' family had gone into the country on the Friday preceeding, but not because of any apprehension that the city was to be given up. Very few families left the city, and there are very few vacant houses, the mansions of Jeff. Davis and Gov. Billy Smith being among those now in want of tenants. The family of Gen. Lee, consisting of his wife, who is an invalid, and three daughters, are among those who remain. They occupy a stylish house on Franklin-street, and for their protection a well disciplined guard is placed at the dwelling, and the family are scrupulously protected from annoyance of any character, the staring gaze of the passer-by hardly being allowed. This is the second time that Mrs. Gen. Lee has been in our hands. She was once captured by our cavalry near White House, in 1862, and sent through our lines to Richmond under flag of truce, by order of Gen. McClellan.

L. L. CROUNSE.

Union Sentiment in Richmond—Projects of Reconstruction—Distinguished Visitors—Recruiting Negro Troops—The Truth about Rebel Enlistment of Negroes.

From Our Own Correspondent.

Richmond, Friday, April 7, 1865.

I can give you news, to-day, which will gratify the heart of every loyal American. Virginia will return to the Union, and that right speedily. Desiring to ascertain the exact truth with reference to the alleged existence of a strong Union sentiment in the city, I availed myself of an opportunity to call upon certain gentlemen here whom I had heard alluded to by Secessionists as Union men, and I must say, that I spent two of the happiest hours of my life in full and free conversation with some of the most thorough and radical Union men in the country; men of wealth and position, whose faith has never wavered for an instant, and who, slaveholders, as they are, *demand that Virginia shall be taken back into the Union "under the Emancipation Proclamation;" that no vestige of the rebellion shall be tolerated; that the usurpation State, and Confederate, which has wrecked Virginia, shall not be recognized in a single respect*; that the State Government must be organized anew, by a convention of the people, as soon as that can be properly effected, and the State and its inhabitants thoroughly purged of treason in every shape.

Union sentiments, in this strong form exist here to a far greater extent than has yet been conceived; not alone among the poorer classes,—mechanics and laborers,—*but in wealthy and influential circles, where may be found men who have never lost faith in the Union*; who have confidently anticipated its triumph, and who greeted the old flag with tears of joy. They are men of the John Minor Botts school, and they are the leaven which shall leaven the whole lump here in this venerable old commonwealth of Virginia. They will delight to see the mass of the people treated with magnanimity, but they have felt too deeply the

Continued on Eighth Page.

McClean's house, Appomattox Court-House, Va., where the surrender took place.

Lee at home in Richmond a few days after his surrender. His son Custis (*left*) and Colonel Walter H. Taylor of his staff are with him.

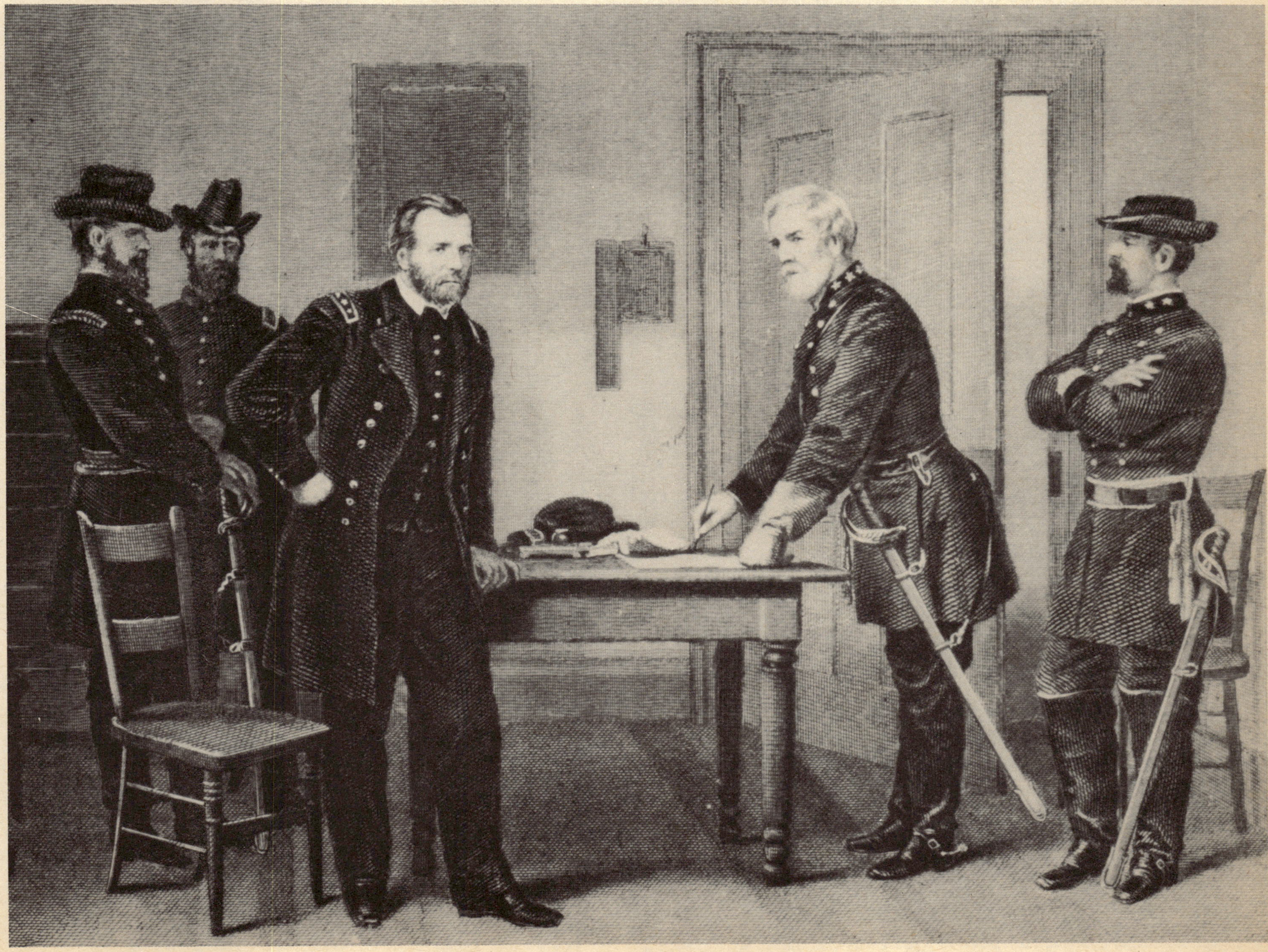

General Lee surrendering to General Grant at Appomattox

The New-York Times.

VOL. XIV......NO. 4226. NEW-YORK, TUESDAY, APRIL 11, 1865. PRICE FOUR CENTS

THE REJOICING.

How the Glorious News is Received.

The Quiet and Reverent Gratitude of the People.

New-York City Preparing to Welcome Peace.

A Widespread Spirit of Charity and Forgiveness.

Meetings at the Post-Office, Custom-House and Produce Exchange.

FLAGS, SALUTES, SPEECHES AND CHIMES.

The Great Jubilee Throughout the Entire Country.

How the American People Bear Their Grand Triumph.

The surrender of LEE and his army was first announced to the people of New-York in an extra TIMES, issued at 11.30, on Sunday night. The premature announcement on Friday had the effect of making the people incredulous; the hour of the real announcement was late, and, as it was on Sunday night, there was not that amount of rejoicing which would naturally have arisen at an earlier hour. Yet the excitement was equaled only by that which followed the attack upon Fort Sumter; the surrender of LEE and his army was anticipated, looked for, and to a great extent discounted in advance. The utter demoralization of the rebel army, the increased esprit of our own forces, the vigorous pursuit of the Union troops and the prophecy of Gen. GRANT had prepared us for the great news which, on Sunday night, was flashed across the wires to an expectant public. Despite this, however, the errand of the mercurial newsboys was successful; with their arms full of extras, they rushed up town and over to the neighboring cities, shouting the glad tidings as they ran, so that before the morning papers disclosed the fact, the great mass of the people were aware that LEE and his army no longer stood in the pathway of the Army of the Potomac. Nevertheless, news extras have been detected ere this in imposing upon a credulous and a hopeful people, and at the hotels it was some little time before the cries of the little fellows were regarded with attention. But the dispatch characteristic of Secretary STANTON settled every doubt, and the wildest delirium of joy seized everybody and held possession for the night.

AT THE POST-OFFICE

the intelligence was received at eleven o'clock. The night clerks immediately organized a meeting, with Mr. THOMAS J. O'BRIEN as Chairman, and Mr. CALEB B. BABCOCK as Secretary. The dispatch of the Secretary was read aloud and the tidings received with hearty cheers. Afterward speeches were made and the following

RESOLUTIONS

unanimously adopted:

Resolved, That we hail with joy the glorious news of the surrender of Gen. LEE and the remnant of his rebel army to Gen. GRANT, and while the news will thrill with gratitude the heart of every loyal man in the nation, we deem it fitting at this moment of honest exultation to render our thanks to the brave rank and file of the army, who through peril and hardship have won for us this glorious victory.

Resolved, That to Gen. GRANT and his subordinate officers who have so skillfully and successfully led our army to victory, we also tender our heartfelt thanks.

Yet while we return thanks to our brave army who have so nobly defended our "old flag," we would not forget those who have fallen in its defence, and whose memory shall be cherished by all lovers of Constitutional Liberty, and be it therefore

Resolved, That to the bereaved friends of those fallen heroes we would tender our most sincere sympathies, and the consolation which points them to Him who doeth all things well.

THOS. J. O'BRIEN, President.

CALEB B. BABCOCK, Secretary.

The interior of the Post-office is gay with the emblems of patriotism and rivals the beautiful display of the Custom-house, in the tasteful arrangement of flags and mottoes. The several departments and tables vie with each other in elaborate adornment, and one would imagine that a sudden eruption of flags had come upon the entire building. Under the superintendence of Mr. S. H. KNAPP, of the Mail and Newspaper Department, the rotunda has been decorated with bunting and placarded with the names of Grant, Sherman, Sheridan, Meade, Humphreys, Warren, Parke, Terry, Foster, Wright, and Ord, presents a beautiful and artistic appearance. In the Box Room, where there are 7,000 boxes and 21,000 regular patrons, it seemed as if every box and every patron had sent in a representative flag, for the apartment was fairly red, white and blue with the star-spangled banner.

The rain fell heavily during the day and seemed determined to keep down the ebullition of natural exultation which every breast contained. Still the display of the national standard was a feature memorable and brilliant. Broadway, Printing House-square, the shipping, all the hotels, the public buildings, and the principal offices and stores down town are glorious with the red flag; with the exception of the *Daily News* and *Day Book*, every newspaper building in the city ran up a broad banner, and hung it out for the recognition of the people; on the City Hall, over the Court-houses, high above the churches and in front of innumerable private dwellings floated the flag of victory, the emblem of successful contest and of coming peace.

THE DETAILS

of the official dispatches are not at first regarded closely. Sufficient it for the present that LEE had surrendered to GRANT upon the latter's own terms—that was the accepted fact, that caused sufficient superabundant joy. With a second reading of the matter came the American desire for details, and to many the details were a cause of dissatisfaction. With all the good-heartedness of our people, and despite the recognized desire for peace and amity, it was very evident that a large number of our citizens would have been better satisfied if GRANT had not allowed LEE and his men their parole. A parole was granted to 14,000 troops at Vicksburg, and those 14,000 very soon found themselves in the rebel army ...

hundred times, yesterday, "I'll bet these men will be back in the ranks in less than three weeks." Toward Gen. LEE there is no such feeling as is manifested toward DAVIS, MASON and the rest ...

Although the news was great and glorious, although it was exactly what the country wanted, its reception failed to excite the public pulse as did the fall of Richmond. ...

PUBLIC SCHOOLS,

by direction, after a reading of the Scriptures and the customary prayer, the glorious news was read and explained, after which the joyous children were dismissed ...

THE CANNON

...

AT THE CUSTOM-HOUSE

...

A GRAND TE DEUM

will be sung at Trinity Church to-day ...

LETTER TO THE PRESIDENT,

...

SIMEON DRAPER, Chairman.

...

DEPARTURE OF THE OCEANUS,

...

hearty huzzas were given for the army, the generals and the victories.

MEETING OF CHAMBER OF COMMERCE—PATRIOTIC RESOLUTIONS.

The Chamber of Commerce held an adjourned meeting yesterday afternoon. JONATHAN STURGES, Esq., in the chair.

On motion of Mr. GEORGE W. BLUNT, the regular business was suspended, and the following communication from the Common Council was read by the Secretary:

OFFICE OF CLERK OF COMMON COUNCIL, NEW-YORK, April 5, 1865.

A. A. Low, Esq., President Chamber of Commerce:

...

ABRAHAM LENT, Chairman Committee of Conference.

...

MEETING OF THE JOINT COMMITTEE OF THE COMMON COUNCIL—A GENERAL ILLUMINATION PROPOSED—NO PARADE AND NO FIREWORKS.

...

MEETING AT THE PRODUCE EXCHANGE.

...

standing on an improvised platform, and beneath a splendid national banner, called the meeting to order. The meeting promptly responded to the call, as far as it was practicable so to do, controlled as it was by such exciting influences. Everybody seemed to outvie everybody else in enthusiastic demonstrations of patriotic pride and satisfaction. The cheering was immense. After the first storm of applause had subsided, Mr. EDWARD CROMWELL proposed a list of officers, which was adopted, as follows: President, Mr. GEORGE D. CRAGIN; Vice-Presidents, Messrs. David Dows, Jesse Hoyt, Lewis Roberts, Josiah M. Fiske, Henry W. Smith, E. W. Coleman, Robert P. Getty, James H. Holcomb, Francis M. French, E. H. Tompkins, John S. Williams, William H. Swan, J. Hobart Herrick, Hiram Walbridge, Ezra Nye. Secretaries, Messrs. Henry Hill, Fredk. Sherwood.

Very appropriate addresses were made by Gen. Hiram Walbridge, and Messrs. James P. Wallace, Henry Hill, Silas B. Dutcher, Henry W. Smith, R. P. Getty and others. Cheers were called for all our national leaders, civil and military, and were given with overwhelming earnestness. All united in fervent thanks to God for the signal favors conferred on our republic.

The hymn commencing "Praise God from whom all Blessings Flow," was chaunted with becoming solemnity. Resolutions, prepared by Mr. JAMES P. WALLACE, and seconded by the whole meeting in reiterated rounds of applause, were adopted unanimously, amidst vociferous cheering. The resolutions were as follows:

Resolved, That we render hearty thanks to Almighty God for the signal success He has vouchsafed to our arms, and that we recognize His hand, and His kind providence, in bringing this nation so near to a triumphant end of this mighty contest for freedom and good government.

Resolved, That we render thanks to President LINCOLN, and all the officers and agents of the Government, for the signal ability they have shown in conducting the affairs of the nation during the past four years of unexampled trial.

Resolved, That we render thanks to Lieut.-Gen. GRANT and the many valiant and true officers and men of the army and navy, for the able and successful manner in which they have conducted the war, and more especially the late campaign.

Resolved, That we highly honor the illustrious dead, and seriously sympathize with the sufferings and trials of the valiant men and their families, brought on by the war, and that we will cheerfully do our part to relieve the survivors in all their wants.

Resolved, That we congratulate each other on the events of the day, and pledge to each other and to the nation that we will ever stand fast by our glorious Union.

Resolved, That we hold out the olive branch to our erring and misguided brethren of the Southern States, and pledge to all of them who are loyal a hearty welcome to all the benefits of our free republic.

Resolved, That the government which has brought this unjustifiable rebellion to a triumphant close, is adequate to the emergency. We leave the terms of the final adjustment of the rebels to that government, in the confident belief that they will be in accordance with the best interests of all the people of the United States.

Cheers were given for THOMAS and CANBY, and other patriot soldiers of Southern birth, who had nobly sacrificed all personal feeling and family pride, and steadfastly adhered to in the country.

A supplementary resolution was read and unanimously adopted by the merchants, to the following purport:

Resolved, That in this hour of exultation we gratefully remember the patriotic services of an illustrious Virginian, who has ever faithfully upheld our government, ever nobly defended its honor; we remember with just pride the illustrious WINFIELD SCOTT, the hero of three wars, and the honored father of the glorious Army of the United States.

The meeting soon after adjourned.

UNITED STATES DISTRICT COURT

At the opening of the Court this morning, Judge Beebe rose and addressed the Court as follows: May it please the Court, since the adjournment of this Court on Saturday, events have transpired to which it seems to me proper that some public reference should be made. For four years this people have been engaged in a struggle for national life—a struggle carried on sometimes in victory, sometimes in defeat—a struggle more ponderous in its character and more important in its results than history has known. And in its progress, out of despondency has come hope, and out of hope has come fruition, and now by the surrender of Gen. Lee and the army of Northern Virginia, that fruition has become a certainty, and our national existence is established as a fact, never more to be disputed; and in this final and crowning issue, I speak I think, the sentiments of all the members of the Bar, in saying that something should stand on the records of this court, in commemoration of this event; that when some antiquarian in long days hereafter shall be going over the musty records of this court, he shall find in them positive evidence that this court and this Bar remained always true to the cause of loyalty and liberty and rejoiced in its success. I move, Sir, the adoption and entry upon the minutes of the court of the following preamble and resolution which I will read.

Whereas, a period has arrived in the history of our national struggle for the maintenance of our unity, the constitution and the laws, when the rebellion has, through the blessing of Divine Providence and the skill, bravery and determination of the government, its officers and soldiers, received its crushing and final blow; and,

Whereas, In order that the court and members of the bar present may, in some degree, express their appreciation of these important events, and the government having recommended that whenever the news shall be received, the day shall be kept as a day of rejoicing,

Resolved, That this court do now adjourn until to-morrow morning at 11 A. M., and that this preamble and resolution be entered upon the minutes of the court.

Mr. E. C. Benedict, rising, said: It seems to me eminently fit and proper that such a movement should proceed from this court, even if it went no further. There may be reasons which will prevent some of the other courts in this city, which do not influence this court, although I believe that all of them will act in harmony with the action of this court. But it is most proper that this movement should proceed from this court, which has always maintained and enforced those rules and principles of national life which have been the sustaining power of the government. This court has proceeded calmly in their enforcement, without change of its rolls, or its rules, whenever that enforcement became necessary, no matter how great, or how strong, or how important the subject affected by that enforcement. I think it is most proper that this Court should adjourn. On such a day anywhere throughout the land, while the flags are floating in the air, while the echoes of two hundred guns and the sounds of rejoicing are coming on the air, it would be unbecoming for any Court of the United States to be calling up witnesses, sitting here upon hard benches, waiting to be examined as to some controversy of every-day lifetime, and such a motion is eminently proper in this Court presided over by a judge, who though of larger previous experience in civil admiralty causes than any judge who has ever lived, will be found to have added largely to his reputation, by the decisions which this Court has been called upon to make during the last four years on questions of prize laws and national law which have been brought before it.

The prospects have not always been as clear for us as now. Many have said that we should fail; that the people would grow weary of the war and its sacrifices and burdens. It has not so proved. From the time when the Old World aristocratic governments said "the Great Republic is no more"—with every year we have grown stronger and more able to bear them—every year has made it easier to go on—every new loan has been more freely taken—and so we should have gone on if necessary to the crack of doom. But from the beginning to the end—from the day when we had but seventy-five thousand men in the field to this day of final triumph—this Court has been unfaltering in its administration of the same great principles, whose success we all this day rejoice over. And in seconding the motion that the resolution and preamble be entered on the minutes of the court, I have desired to allude to the fact of this position of the Court, as making the motion one in every way proper.

There being no further remarks, the Judge said that he heartily concurred in the wishes of the Bar, and without further words requested the members of the Bar present, who were in favor of the motion, to say aye. A unanimous "aye" was given, and the court adjourned.

MEETINGS OF STUDENTS AT NEW-YORK UNIVERSITY AND COLUMBIA COLLEGE.

At the conclusion of the regular morning prayers in the chapel of the University, Chancellor FERRIS made some congratulatory remarks on our recent victories, and was followed by Profs. MARTIN, BAIRD and COAKLEY. The students then sang "America" and the "Doxology," and adjourned to hold a meeting of their own in the large chapel of the University.

The students of Columbia College were addressed at the conclusion of morning prayers by President BARNARD and Prof. PECK, and then, forming in line, marched to the headquarters of the Union League, where they were addressed by Mr. JOHN JAY. At the conclusion of Mr. JAY's remarks, they proceeded to the New-York University, and joined the University members in enthusiastic cheers for LINCOLN, GRANT and victory. A meeting was speedily organized in the University chapel by the election of Mr. W. F. MORGAN as President, and Mr. W. N. MCVICKARS, of Columbia College, as Vice-President. Messrs. DAVID HOPKINS, of the University, and WILLIAM WARD, of Columbia, were appointed Secretaries.

Mr. MORGAN, on taking the chair, made a few brief and stirringly patriotic remarks, and introduced Prof. MARTIN, who was followed by Chancellor FERRIS, both giving the young men good advice, and expressing their sympathy in the rejoicings of the day.

Eloquent speeches, full of vim, wit and enthusiasm, were made by Mr. MCVICKARS, of the Senior Class, and Mr. PUTNAM SMITH, of the Junior Class, Columbia College, and Mr. BENJAMIN H. BAYLISS, of the Senior Class, of the University. The best wishes of each college for the other, and desire for closer friendship in the future were expressed by Messrs. MCVICKARS and BAYLISS.

A committee was appointed who drafted the following resolutions:

Whereas, The armies of the republic have, by the blessing of God, triumphed over the foes of the Union, the constitution and the laws; and

Whereas, In the capture of Richmond and the surrender of Gen. LEE, we see the end of the rebellion and the restoration of the unity of this great people; therefore

Resolved, That the students of Columbia College and the New-York University, while acknowledging the goodness of Almighty God in restoring peace to our beloved country, do at the same time most heartily thank our brave soldiers as the means under His guidance of breaking down the last bulwark of this wicked rebellion.

Resolved, That while remembering with grateful admiration the deeds of the heroic living, the memory of the patriotic dead will always remain enshrined in our hearts.

W. F. Morgan, Chairman; S. Van Nostrand, J. C. Gray, F. Prime, Jr., B. H. Bayliss, Committee.

SALUTE AT UNION-SQUARE.

HEADQUARTERS FIRST DIV. N. Y. S. N. G., NEW-YORK, April 10, 1865.

SPECIAL ORDERS No. 132.—In compliance with orders from general headquarters, Albany, of this date, a salute of one hundred guns will be fired at Union-square, to-morrow, April 11, at noon, to celebrate the national victories at Petersburgh and Richmond, and the surrender of the army of the so-called Confederate States, under the command of Gen. ROBERT E. LEE.

Col. TELLER, commanding Fourth Regiment New-York State National Guard, is charged with the execution of this order, and will make requisitions upon the Commissary-General for the necessary ammunition.

Brig.-Gen. YATES will promulgate the above.

By order of Maj.-Gen. CHAS. W. SANDFORD.

ALEX. HAMILTON, Div. Inspector.

SPECIAL ORDERS.—The above orders are hereby promulgated.

By order of Brig.-Gen. CHAS. YATES.

THE SEVENTH REGIMENT AND OUR VICTORIES.

The following order has been issued by Col. EMMONS CLARK, of the Seventh Regiment:

HEADQUARTERS SEVENTH REGIMENT, NATIONAL GUARD S. N. Y., NEW-YORK, April 10, 1865.

GENERAL ORDER No. 6.—To celebrate the anniversary of the departure of this regiment for Washington on the 19th day of April, 1861, to defend the national capital, then in imminent danger, and in honor of the recent brilliant victories of the Union armies, resulting in the suppression of the great rebellion, it is ordered that the regimental armory be illuminated on the evening of the 19th of April, and that a salute of one hundred guns be fired at 8 o'clock P. M. The Armory, Finance and Music Committees of the Board of Officers will act as a Committee of Arrangements for this celebration. Capt. ROGERS and his command are detailed to fire the salute.

By order of Col. EMMONS CLARK.

J. H. LIEBENAU, Adjutant.

THE SPIRIT OF FORGIVENESS.

NEW-YORK, Monday, April, 10.

To the Editor of the New-York Times:

SIR,—Now that Gen. LEE has surrendered, I would suggest he be sent to New-York city, where he will receive such an ovation as will bring tears to his eyes, in regret that he should ever have taken up arms against a people who would receive him with so much emotion, tender respect, and forgiveness.

Respectfully, J. K.

PRIVATE REJOICINGS.

The employes of BREWSTER & Co.'s carriage manufactory, in Broome-street, fired one hundred guns in honor of the surrender of Gen. LEE.

DEMONSTRATION IN JERSEY CITY LAST NIGHT.

The Mayor of Jersey City issued the following proclamation:

The question of "self-government" is settled forever. The glorious old Union is already restored, and peace and prosperity are already within our grasp. God be praised!

Our citizens are requested to illuminate private and public buildings to night, in honor of the glorious news received this morning.

ORESTES CLEVELAND, Mayor.

MONDAY, April 10, 1865.

In accordance with the above recommendation, the public and private buildings were very generally illuminated last evening, many of them presenting a brilliant and attractive appearance, by means of Chinese lanterns, flags, &c. The City Hall and Police Headquarters presented the most brilliant appearance of all, being lighted with a candle to each pane of glass, and also decorated with innumerable small flags. Bells were rung, salutes were fired, small arms discharged, bonfires kindled and fireworks set off in all parts of the city. Notwithstanding the evening was unfavorable, the streets were thronged by many thousands of people, and in every respect the demonstration was a complete success.

REJOICINGS ELSEWHERE.

Special Dispatch to the New-York Times.

WASHINGTON, Monday, April 10.

THE ENTHUSIASM IN WASHINGTON.

The severe and almost uninterrupted rain storm of the last twenty-four hours has not, apparently, very materially chilled the ardor, nor dampened the enthusiasm of anybody in Washington, and the celebration of victory which begun everywhere in the city with Mr. STANTON's magnificent day-break salute, has been continued all day, and bids fair to continue all night. Thus far it is more imposing and hardly less enthusiastic than that of last Monday.

Willard's Hotel and a few other buildings are illuminated this evening, but the general illumination is put off till to-morrow.

A remarkable instance of the liability of human nature to err in its judgments is found in the fact that, of the thousands of men and women residing here whom everybody has supposed for four years to be arrant Secessionists, every soul of them now declares that he has always been a good Unionist, and never believed the rebellion could or should succeed.

Dispatches to the Associated Press.

WASHINGTON, Monday, April 10.

The intelligence of Gen. LEE's surrender was last night known to only a few persons; but this morning, when the news was generally circulated through the newspapers, scenes of joyous excitement, such as prevailed here last Monday, were everywhere renewed.

The Assistant Secretary of the Treasury, Mr. FIELD, gave a holiday to the clerks of that department, and they immediately started in procession to the President's house, in front of which they sung the "Star-spangled Banner" and "Old Hundred" with electric effect, and then passed on to the War Department, shouting the stirring words and air, "Rally round the flag, boys," &c.

The Secretary of War having been called for, after repeated and urgent demands, appeared before the enthusiastic crowd that thronged the halls and stairways of the War Department building. He was received with cheering, but asked to be excused on account of his health from making any remarks. He, however, begged to introduce Maj.-Gen. HALLECK.

The General was received with hearty cheering, and, although evidently surprised by the strategy of the honorable Secretary, addressed the throng as follows:

"Always ready, as I am, to obey the orders of my superior officer, the honorable Secretary of War, I hardly think he will go so far as to require me to become a stump-speaker. [Laughter, cheers, and cries of 'The people require it;' 'It is a military necessity,' &c.] Stump-speaking, my friends, is something in which I have never indulged. I can only say that our congratulations and thanks are due to Gen. GRANT, and the brave Generals and soldiers in the field, for the great victory announced this morning, and for the blessing of peace of which it is the harbinger."

His Honor Mayor WALLACK was discovered in the crowd, and being loudly called for, replied in a few appropriate words, saying that his heart was too full for utterance, and that he was gratified to observe from their bright looks and happy faces, that they felt as he felt on such an occasion.

The workmen of the Navy-yard, some 1,500 or 2,000 of them, formed in procession, headed by a band of music, and marched up to the city, firing repeatedly a howitzer, and occasionally huzzahing. The line was increased by persons falling in on the way. Their design was to congratulate the President, who last night returned from Richmond. Thousands assembled in front of the Executive mansion. The bands played, and many in the crowd sang in unison with the music. Cannon were fired, and repeated calls were made for the President. When he appeared at the window over the entrance door he was greeted with huzzas, clapping of hands, and waving of hats. He appeared to be calm amid these wild demonstrations before him. Comparative silence having been restored, he said:

"I am very greatly rejoiced that an occasion has occured so pleasurable that the people can't restrain themselves. [Cheers.] I suppose that arrangements are being made for some sort of formal demonstration, perhaps this evening or to-morrow night. [Voices, "We can't wait."] If there should be such a demonstration, I, of course, will have to respond to it, [A voice, "Bully for you,"] and I will have nothing to say, if you dribble it out of me. [Laughter and cries of "We want to hear you now."] I see you have a band. [Voices, "We have three of them.] I propose now closing up by requesting you to play a certain piece of music or a tune. I thought "Dixie" one of the best tunes I ever heard." [Laughter.]

The band began to play "Dixie," but soon ceased, as the President had not concluded his remarks. He continued:

"I had heard that our adversaries over the way had attempted to appropriate it. I insisted yesterday that we had fairly captured it. [Cheers and laughter.] I presented the question to the Attorney-General, and he gave his opinion that it is our lawful prize. I ask the band to give us a good turn upon it!"

The band accordingly played "Dixie" with extraordinary vigor, when three cheers and a tiger were given, followed by the tune of "Yankee Doodle."

The President then proposed three rousing cheers for GRANT and all under his command, and next, three cheers for the navy and all its forces. They were most enthusiastically given.

The President retired amid huzzas, the tune of "Hail Columbia" and the firing of cannon.

The crowd then proceeded to the War Department, and various tunes were played. The Secretary was repeatedly called for, but did not appear.

The immense concourse of persons then separated.

The steam fire-engines were out, decorated with flags, and screamed their joy along Pennsylvania-avenue.

There was a salute of five hundred guns at daylight, and ringing of bells and firing from all the fortifications.

BRIDGEPORT, Monday, April 10.

The heart of Bridgeport is moved by the glorious news of this morning. All the churches are illuminated to-night, and divine service of an hour in each attests the religious tone of our rejoicing. Multitudes are marching through the streets in a torchlight procession, attended by the Fort Trumbull band. The post-office and all other public buildings, the great manufactories, and every principal dwelling-house from East Bridgeport on the east to Barnum's villa on the west are covered with Union banners and sparkling with lights. One hundred and fifty guns and all the bells in the city are sounding the triumph of the Union army, and rockets and fireworks in every shape are blazing in the air. All feel that the great day of jubilee is at hand, and anxiously await the hour when from one extreme of the land to the other we can join the angelic anthem, "Glory to God in the Highest, and on earth peace, good will to men."

ASTORIA, Queens Co., Monday, April 10.

Bells are ringing, banners flying and buildings illuminated this evening in honor of the recent victories. The citizens are now (8 A. M.) gathering in mass meeting.

CLEVELAND, Monday, April 10.

A salute of two hundred guns is now being fired in honor of the surrender of Gen. LEE. The town is frantic with joy. Business is suspended, and processions are marching through the streets, headed by bands of music.

BUFFALO, N. Y., Monday, April 10.

There is great rejoicing here over the surrender of Gen. LEE. The bells are ringing, fire companies parading, meetings being held in the streets, bands of music playing, and joy and gladness everywhere prevails.

The Board of Trade are holding a meeting to do honor to the occasion. The speakers are Rev. Dr. HANCOCK and several members of the board.

SYRACUSE, N. Y., Monday, April 10.

The "glad tidings" of the surrender of Gen. LEE has made the people of this city and the surrounding country perfectly frantic with delight. Joy fills every heart, in gratitude to God that the shedding of fraternal blood is about to cease.

One hundred guns were fired this afternoon, and a grand procession and illumination are in preparation for this evening.

The bells have been ringing and cannon firing since 2 o'clock this morning.

The excitement is intense and universal.

LITTLE VALLEY, N. Y., Monday, April 10.

Two hundred guns were fired here to-day, at noon, in honor of the surrender of Gen. LEE. The church bells are ringing joyfully, and all hearts dancing with exultation, at the prospect of early peace, and the speedy return of the Southern States to the Union.

CINCINNATI, Monday, April 10.

The city is full of joy and excitement to-day, over the surrender of Gen. LEE. Business is entirely laid aside. There is no thought about anything except how best to celebrate the day.

By order of the War Department, 200 guns are being fired.

NORWALK, Conn., Monday, Arpil 10.

The bells here are ringing merry peals, and flags flying in every direction in honor of the surrender of Gen. LEE.

The Mayor has ordered one hundred guns to be fired.

The people pronounce the news most "glorious."

SOUTH NORWALK, Conn., Monday, April 10.

One hundred guns were fired to-night, and the bells rung in honor of the surrender of LEE and his army.

ST. LOUIS, Monday, April 10.

Business was partially suspended, and general joy manifested to-day over the surrender of Gen. LEE.

BOSTON, Monday, April 10.

To-day has been entirely given up to rejoicing. In the Legislature, Speaker BULLECK and others made eloquent and appropriate remarks, after which both houses adjourned. The Supreme Court also adjourned. A great meeting of merchants was held in Franklin-street, and another similar meeting was held in Winthrop-place. Among the speakers were Hon. George S. Boutwell, Samuel H. Walley, Richard H. Dane, William Gray and George S. Hilliard. A severe northeast rain-storm which commenced at noon somewhat interfered with the general street programme. But the military and civic processions were very imposing. The firemen especially, with their engines, whose steam-whistles were screaming in chorus, created a novel sensation. A meeting in the Old South Church was addressed by several of our most eloquent clergymen, while a salute was fired from the belfry of that ancient meeting-house.

The illuminations, both in Boston and Roxbury, to-night, are general, and present brilliant spectacles. It is raining heavily.

BELFAST, Me., Monday, April 10.

Bells were rung, and salutes were fired to-day from the batteries and from the United States steamer *Rhode Island*. Business was suspended, and illuminations to-night are general. Two men of the Invalid Corps were severely injured while firing a salute.

CHICAGO, Monday, April 10.

The stores, courts and public offices were nearly all closed to-day. Business entirely suspended and the day was given up to rejoicing over the glad tidings. There was a procession this afternoon of the Fire Department, benevolent societies and citizens generally, which was over three miles long. The enthusiasm to-night is at fever heat. A number of public buildings and private residences are brilliantly illuminated. A salute of 200 guns was fired during the day.

Dispatches from various cities throughout the West show that the enthusiasm was very great.

INDIANAPOLIS, Monday, April 10.

A salute of two hundred guns was fired to-day. Little business was done, and the citizens are generally celebrating the day.

POUGHKEEPSIE, N. Y., Monday, April 10.

Men, women and children rejoiced here to-day over the good news. The greatest excitement prevailed, and business was partially suspended. A committee of solid men meet to-morrow to make arrangements for a grand country glorification.

TROY, N. Y., Monday, April 10.

Troy is full of excitement and joy to day over the surrender of Gen. LEE and his army and the dawn of peace.

The United States Christian Commission held an meeting last night immense in the new Presbyterian Church in Fifth-street.

The church was crowded by an immense throng of people, and the large chapel connected with the church had to be thrown open, when that also was filled to its utmost capacity, and many persons had to leave, unable to obtain admittance.

The meeting was addressed by Ex-Gov. POLLOCK, of Pennsylvania, who read the news of Gen. LEE's surrender, which caused the most intense enthusiasm.

The audience immediately broke out and sang with glorious effect, the Doxology:

Praise God from whom all blessings flow.

A prayer was then offered up to Almighty God by Gov. POLLOCK for the salvation of the country, which was responded to by an earnest, sincere and heartfelt "Amen."

GEORGE H. STUART, of Philadelphia, also addressed the meeting, saying that his life was saved at the battle of Coal Harbor by the Christian Commission, when the assemblage dispersed.

NEWARK, N. J., Monday, April 10.

The news of the surrender of Gen. LEE and his army creates the most intense excitement.

A salute of 300 guns will be fired this afternoon, and at 5 o'clock, this evening all the church and factory bells will be rung.

To-night a grand jubilee will be held, and there will be grand illuminations to celebrate the glorious event.

HARRISBURGH, Penn., Monday, April 10.

A formal celebration of the surrender of Gen. LEE is to come off here next Saturday, which is to terminate in the evening with a general illumination, including the State Capitol buildings.

The New-York Times.

VOL. XIV......NO. 4226. NEW-YORK, TUESDAY, APRIL 11, 1865. PRICE FOUR CENTS

Editorials

The New Epoch—The Advent of Peace.

This continent quivered yesterday as never since its upheaval from chaos. The lightning flashed peace, and from ocean to ocean, all minds thrilled with the sense of a new order of things. No more deluge of blood. No more whirls of ruin. No more brooding darkness. The republic rested again, and upon foundations as eternal as the hills. The whole heavens were spanned with the rainbow of promise, and every eye saw it.

This tremendous transition has been betokened latterly by many signs, yet its coming was sudden. The terrible trials of the war have weighed so heavily upon the land, and the people have been so often deceived by false appearances, that a confirmed impression existed that the deliverance, if it ever came, would come only with protracted tribulation. Even now, in spite of all we see, it is hard to realize that the rebellion has vanished. But just now it threatened to engulf the nation.

"Glory to the Lord of Hosts, from whom all blessings are." If ever a people under heaven was bound to prostrate itself in gratitude, it is the loyal people of this land. Had it been foretold to them four years ago what trials awaited them, there would have been a universal cry of despairing agony. Human history affords no instance of such a national ordeal. Never could we have endured it but for the strength given from on high, as we had need. The most capacious minds of Europe, schooled to the uttermost limit in all the wisdom of the past, called this war a madness. It was a madness, if estimated by any material standard. Eight millions of Anglo-Saxon rebels, compacted as one man, brave to the last pitch, inhabiting a country peculiarly defensible, having the encouragement of untiring faction beyond their bounds, and a moral alliance with nearly every Power in the Old World, according to all the ordinary rules of judging, would surely prevail. But we had a hidden strength which the world did not understand. It was Faith—a faith that first broke upon us with the first flash of Sumter's guns, and that ever afterward went on widening and deepening. The people came to feel as by an inspiration from heaven, that the moral elements of the national cause made it irresistible. They were penetrated with the feeling, that as sure as there was an Almighty Father, He could not permit the success of a rebellion that was made only for the benefit of human slavery. It was this which carried them through the struggle. Ten times their physical strength would not have kept them up, in the absence of this sovereign faith. The race of Titans could not have maintained this war, if, too, they had been a race of atheists.

That religious faith is fitly followed now by a religious gratitude. It is wonderful to mark the solemn character of the joy that now spreads the land. There are waving flags, ringing bells, booming cannon, and other national tokens of public gladness. But yet it is plain to see that the dominant feeling of the people is no ebullient exhilaration over human achievement, but a profound sense of a Divine blessing. The popular heart relieves itself, not so much in cheers and hurrahs as in doxologies. Never since the hosannas of that Palm Sunday in Jerusalem, has such irrepressible praise rolled up from a city street to the pure vault of heaven as from the great thoroughfare of money-changers in New-York at the tidings that the rebel capital had fallen. Yet that was but the key-note of the universal anthem. The enemies of this republic may talk as they please of its materializing tendencies, may to their heart's content stigmatize our people as worshipers of the "almighty dollar," they but waste their breath. Business activities, strenuous as they are, have not stifled the religious sentiment of the American heart. This has been demonstrated in ways without number, but never so grandly as now.

With this gratitude for deliverance is mingled a fresh assurance that Heaven has reserved our republic for a destiny more glorious than can yet be conceived. Americans now feel that it is less than ever a presumption in them to believe themselves a chosen people, appointed to school the world to new ideas of human capacities and human rights. The monarchs of the Old World are trembling with apprehension lest we shall be moved to repay our injuries by turning against them our arms. They have a thousand times greater reason to fear the moral force of our new position. We stand a living proof of the matchless potency of popular self-government. It rivets the attention of the whole civilized world. It will start new thoughts, will generate new purposes, will nerve to new acts. This is as sure as that the human reason shall continue to exist. It is this that the dynasties have need to fear; it is here that we expect our sweetest revenge.

THE DRAFT.—What are the objects that may be presumed to be sought for by the continuance of a daily bulletin from the Provost-Marshal's office, threatening further and severer drafting measures throughout the city? Major DODGE probably has the commission to write in the following strain to the citizens of a community which is to-day doing ten times as much in recruiting as any other in the Union. But if he has that commission he surely does not exercise it with the utmost discretion. He says.

"I shall exact of New-York City every man of her quota, and the sooner the people make up their minds that the men must be furnished the better it will be for all concerned."

It would be more acceptable to the people at large if Major DODGE would proceed to do what he vows, than continue day after day to *threaten*. We venture, however, to think that the folly of irritating the city with more of this utterly unnecessary business will be promptly put an end to. It is trifling with public intelligence to proclaim the necessity for drafting anywhere. The terms, moreover, in which Major DODGE assumes to address the citizens of New-York might be revised, without a reference to the War Department. New-York is not a military satrapy.

Gen. Johnston's Army.

The most interesting question now is, what will Jo. JOHNSTON do? He commands the only army of any magnitude now left in the Southern Confederacy. It is not a very formidable army in numbers, nor is it coherent in character. In every characteristic of an army, it is vastly inferior to that lately under LEE. It has never, as an army, fought a noteworthy battle. It has no traditions of success. It has no capable leaders. The troops of HARDEE, who fled from Savannah and then from Charleston, form its nucleus, and to these have been added the tail of HOOD's old army, the Wilmington force of BRAGG, the picayune force of BEAUREGARD, various feeble forces and garrisons picked up around, and a cavalry force under WADE HAMPTON and WHEELER. It is a piebald collection. Since its organization—such organization as it has—it has been steadily on the retreat; and the last we hear of it is that it has fled from Raleigh, and it

THE BLESSINGS OF VICTORY.
VICTORY WILL BRING US PEACE.
UNION

must be now somewhere near the Southern border of Virginia. It was supposed that, in the last resort, LEE would try and effect a junction with it; but JOHNSTON and his troops doubtless heard yesterday of the surrender of LEE and his whole army.

Opposed to JOHNSTON is the powerful and magnificent army of Gen. SHERMAN. It is utterly impossible that JOHNSTON should cope with it. He knows it would be ruin for him to try. He knows it would be madness.

In forming a judgment as to the possible course of JOHNSTON in this emergency, we must take into consideration JOHNSTON's hopeless prospect, as well as the great surrender of Sunday. We must take into account, too, the relations of Gen. JOHNSTON to JEFF. DAVIS, and also his relations to Gen. LEE. For nearly two years JOHNSTON and DAVIS have been in a state of bitter animosity with each other. They quarreled at the time of GRANT's operations against Vicksburgh; and the Richmond rebel papers have often given us accounts of the depth of their mutual hatred. Twice has DAVIS removed JOHNSTON from command; and on the last occasion, at Atlanta, it was under circumstances which stung JOHNSTON to the quick. The whole press and people of the South clamored loudly for his reinstatement; but DAVIS was implacable. On the other hand, the relations of JOHNSTON to LEE have always been those of mutual respect and friendliness. One of the first acts of Gen. LEE, when he received from the Confederate Congress the command of all the Confederate armies three months ago, was to put JOHNSTON in command of the only army beside his own that existed in the South.

Now, under these circumstances, leaving out of view the hopeless prospect, it may be doubted whether JOHNSTON will exhibit such devotion to the person and interests of DAVIS as to remain any longer in the field in his service. It is far more likely he will follow the example set him by his chief and friend, the Commander of the Confederate armies. If he does not do it quickly, SHERMAN will presently break him and his army to pieces. Then JEFF. DAVIS will be hardly able to get even a body-guard. This week will doubtless wind up JOHNSTON, one way or another.

REBEL SURRENDERS.—Three rebel armies have surrendered to Gen. GRANT—that under BUCKNER at Fort Donelson, on the 16th of February, 1862; that under PEMBERTON at Vicksburgh, on the 4th of July, 1863; and that under Gen. LEE, on the 9th of April, 1865. He is the only one of our Generals who has ever induced a rebel army to surrender; and he has induced three of them.

The New-York Times.

VOL. XIV......NO. 4228. NEW-YORK, THURSDAY, APRIL 13, 1865. PRICE FOUR CENTS

FOUR DAYS LATER FROM EUROPE.

Arrival of the New-York at this Port and the Moravian at Portland.

The Rebel Ram Stonewall Ordered To Leave Lisbon.

The Niagara and Sacramento Ordered to Remain in Port.

They Attempt to Leave and are Fired On---The Niagara Struck and One Man Killed.

Five-Twenties Advanced Three Per Cent.

THE DISHONORED REBEL DRAFTS PAID.

INTERESTING CONTINENTAL NEWS.

The steamship *New York*, from Southampton on the 30th ult., arrived at this port yesterday afternoon.

The steamship *Moravian*, from Liverpool on the 30th, via Greencastle on the 31st ult., arrived at Portland last evening.

The steamship *City of Limerick*, from Portland, arrived off Liverpool at noon on the 30th ult.

The steamship *City of Baltimore*, from New-York, arrived out on the 29th ult.

The steamship *Belgian*, from Portland, arrived out on the 29th ult.

AMERICAN TOPICS.

THE REBEL RAM STONEWALL.

MORE VICTORIES.

The Rebellion Crumbling to Pieces.

Surrender of Lynchburgh, Va., to a Scouting Party.

SUCCESS OF THE ALABAMA EXPEDITION

CAPTURE OF SELMA BY GEN. WILSON.

Forrest and Roddy with their Entire Command Taken Prisoners.

[OFFICIAL.]

WAR DEPARTMENT, WASHINGTON, D. C.,
April 12—2:30 P. M.

Maj.-Gen. Dix, New-York:

The capture of Selma is reported by Maj.-Gen. GEORGE H. THOMAS.

The surrender of Lynchburgh is also officially reported.

EDWIN M. STANTON,
Secretary of War.

DESPATCH FROM GEN. THOMAS.

HEADQUARTERS, DEPARTMENT OF THE CUMBERLAND,
NASHVILLE, April 11, 1865.

Maj.-Gen. H. W. Halleck, Chief of Staff:

I send the following, just received from Huntsville, Alabama, for the information of the Secretary of War. I am inclined to believe it, although I have received no report direct from Gen. WILSON.

GEO. H. THOMAS, Major General.

HUNTSVILLE, ALA., Tuesday, April 11—9 A. M.

Maj.-Gen. Thomas:

The following is just received from Col. HOOVER at Somerville. Men directly through from Selma report that place captured by Gen. WILSON's forces on the 2d inst. FORREST and RODDY, with their entire command, were captured. Our men dismounted and charged the intrenchments and carried all before them. They also report Montgomery captured.

(Signed) R. S. GRANGER.

SECOND DISPATCH.

CITY POINT, VA., Wednesday, April 12, 1865.

Hon. Edwin M. Stanton, Secretary of War:

Lynchburgh surrendered yesterday to a lieutenant of GRIFFIN's forces at the head of a scouting party. Gen. GRANT has ordered MACKENZIE's' brigade of cavalry to occupy the town and take care of public property.

C. A. DANA, Assistant Secretary of War.

REPORTS VIA NASHVILLE.

NASHVILLE, TENN., Wednesday, April 12.

A dispatch received here from Col. HORNER, of the Eighteenth Michigan, dated Somerville, Tenn., April 10, says:

Two men who have arrived here and came directly through from Selma, Ala., report that place was captured by Gen. WILSON's force on the 2d of April, and with it the rebel Gens. FORREST and RODDY, with their entire commands.

Gen. WILSON dismounted his cavalry and charged the rebel intrenchments, and carried everything before him.

The same parties also report that Montgomery, Ala., has been captured.

CONFIRMATION OF THE REPORT.

CAIRO, Wednesday, April 12.

The Vicksburgh *Herald* confirms the capture and burning of Selma, Ala., and says that Gen. FORREST narrowly escaped being captured.

AFFAIRS IN ALBANY.

The Ninth Election District—The Contested Seat Awarded to Mr. Joseph Shook.

Special Dispatch to the New-York Times.

ALBANY, Wednesday, April 12.

In the Assembly this evening, after a lengthy speech from Mr. VEDDER, in favor of the sitting member, a vote was taken on the resolutions of the Committee on Privileges and Elections, throwing out the

GRANT AND LEE.

Their Anticipated Arrival at City Point.

Gen. Lee Wants to Go to Europe With His Family.

ALL QUIET AT RICHMOND.

Special Dispatch to the New-York Times.

CITY POINT, Va., Tuesday, April 11—10 A. M.
WASHINGTON, Wednesday, April 12.

I arrived here from Richmond this morning, in order to witness the arrival here of Gen. GRANT and staff, who will bring with them Gen. LEE and staff, and are expected this afternoon. A special train left here at midnight last evening for Burkesville to bring them in. Gen. LEE will proceed to Richmond from this point, and I am informed on good authority that he has expressed a desire to depart for Europe with the rest of his family at an early day. He is much affected by late events, and ere leaving Petersburgh, is said to have been deeply moved at the calamity which had overtaken his army. DAVIS has deserted him and is retreating on his own account. Gen. LEE, however, fought as long as there was the least chance, and surrendered only when he could do nothing else.

All is quiet at Richmond. The city is very full of visitors, and presents a lively appearance. The Secessionists admit, without qualification, that they are now completely subjugated, and are already setting to work to let themselves down as gracefully as possible, and to escape, so far as they can, the consequences of their crime.

L. L. CROUNSE.

Rumor About Gen. Lee—He is to Visit this City.

From the Commercial of Yesterday.

Rooms have been engaged at one of our fashionable hotels for Gen. ROBERT E. LEE, late in command of the rebel army in Northern Virginia. The General is expected to arrive either to-day or to-morrow. His visit will be of a strictly private character.

Fort Sumter Anniversary.

CELEBRATION AT THE ACADEMY OF MUSIC.

The anniversary of the attack on Fort Sumter was celebrated last evening by an oratorical and musical entertainment at the Academy of Music, in Fourteenth-street. About five hundred persons were present. After the performance of "William Tell," some selections from "Ernani" and "La Forza del Destino," by Grafulla's Band, Maj.-Gen. JOHN G. PECK made the opening address, in which he referred to the events preceding the attack on Fort Sumter, the defence made by its brave garrison, under the gallant ANDERSON, and the proposed restoration of the old flag to the battered walls of the fort on Friday next. He concluded with an appeal in behalf of the orphans of those who have fallen on the field of battle in defending the country's flag.

A prayer was then offered by Rev. Mr. MITCHELL, after which the band gave "Anderson's March to Sumter."

Hon. CHAUNCEY SHAFFER was then introduced, who delivered a long oration on the "Past, Present and Future of our Country," in which he traced our history from the settlement of the country by our Dutch ancestors up to the breaking out of the rebellion; reviewed the alleged grievances of the Southern people, which he showed to be groundless, and were

The New-York Times.

VOL. XIV......NO. 4230. NEW-YORK, SUNDAY, APRIL 16, 1865. PRICE FOUR CENTS

OUR GREAT LOSS

Death of President Lincoln.

The Songs of Victory Drowned in Sorrow.

CLOSING SCENES OF A NOBLE LIFE.

The Great Sorrow of an Afflicted Nation.

Party Differences Forgotten in Public Grief.

Vice-President Johnson Inaugurated as Chief Executive.

MR. SEWARD WILL RECOVER.

John Wilkes Booth Believed to be the Assassin.

Manifestations of the People Throughout the Country.

OFFICIAL DISPATCHES.

WAR DEPARTMENT, WASHINGTON, April 15—4:10 A. M.

To Major-Gen. Dix:

The President continues insensible and is sinking.

Secretary SEWARD remains without change.

FREDERICK SEWARD's skull is fractured in two places, besides a severe cut upon the head.

The attendant is still alive, but hopeless. Maj. SEWARD's wound is not dangerous.

It is now ascertained with reasonable certainty that two assassins were engaged in the horrible crime, WILKES BOOTH being the one that shot the President, and the other companion of his whose name is not a known, but whose description is so clear that he can hardly escape. It appears from a letter found in BOOTH's trunk that the murder was planned before the 4th of March, but fell through then because the accomplice backed out until "Richmond could be heard from." BOOTH and his accomplice were at the livery stable at six o'clock last evening, and left there with their horses about ten o'clock, or shortly before that hour.

It would seem that they had for several days been seeking their chance, but for some unknown reason it was not carried into effect until last night.

One of them has evidently made his way to Baltimore—the other has not yet been traced.

EDWIN M. STANTON, Secretary of War.

WAR DEPARTMENT, WASHINGTON, April 15.

Major-Gen. Dix:

ABRAHAM LINCOLN died this morning at twenty-two minutes after seven o'clock.

EDWIN M. STANTON, Secretary of War.

WAR DEPARTMENT, WASHINGTON, April 15—3 P. M.

Maj.-Gen. Dix, New-York:

Official notice of the death of the late President, ABRAHAM LINCOLN, was given by the heads of departments this morning to ANDREW JOHNSON, Vice-President, upon whom the constitution devolved the office of President. Mr. JOHNSON, upon receiving this notice, appeared before the Hon. SALMON P. CHASE, Chief Justice of the United States, and took the oath of office, as President of the United States, assumed its duties and functions. At 12 o'clock the President met the heads of departments in cabinet meeting, at the Treasury Building, and among other business the following was transacted:

First—The arrangements for the funeral of the late President were referred to the several Secretaries, as far as relates to their respective departments.

Second—WILLIAM HUNTER, Esq., was appointed Acting Secretary of State during the disability of Mr. SEWARD, and his son, FREDERICK SEWARD, the Assistant Secretary.

Third—The President formally announced that he desired to retain the present Secretaries of departments of his Cabinet, and they would go on and discharge their respective duties in the same manner as before the deplorable event that had changed the head of the government.

All business in the departments was suspended during the day.

The surgeons report that the condition of Mr. SEWARD remains unchanged. He is doing well.

No improvement in Mr. FREDERICK SEWARD.

The murderers have not yet been apprehended.

EDWIN M. STANTON, Secretary of War.

THE ASSASSINATION.

Additional Details of the Lamentable Event.

WASHINGTON, Saturday, April 15.

The assassin of President LINCOLN left behind him his hat and a spur.

The hat was picked up in the President's box and has been identified by parties to whom it has been shown as the one belonging to the suspected man, and accurately described as the one belonging to the suspected man by other parties, not allowed to see it before describing it.

The spur was dropped upon the stage, and that also has been identified as the one procured at a stable where the same man hired a horse in the evening.

Two gentlemen who went to the Secretary of War to apprize him of the attack on Mr. LINCOLN, met at the residence of the former a man muffled in a cloak, who, when accosted by them, hastened away.

It had been Mr. STANTON's intention to accompany Mr. LINCOLN to the theatre, and occupy the same box, but the press of business prevented.

It therefore seems evident that the aim of the plotters was to paralyze the country by at once striking down the head, the heart and the arm of the country.

As soon as the dreadful events were announced in the streets, Superintendent RICHARDS, and his assistants, were at work to discover the assassin.

In a few moments the telegraph had aroused the whole police force of the city.

Maj. WALLACH and several members of the City Government were soon on the spot and every precaution was taken to preserve order and quiet in the city.

Every street in Washington was patrolled at the request of Mr. RICHARDS.

Gen. AUGUR sent horses to mount the police.

Every road leading out of Washington was strongly picketed, and every possible avenue of escape was thoroughly guarded.

Steamboats about to depart down the Potomac were stopped.

The Daily *Chronicle* says:

"As it is suspected that this conspiracy originated in Maryland, the telegraph flashed the mournful news to Baltimore and all the cavalry was immediately put upon active duty. Every road was picketed and every precaution taken to prevent the escape of the assassin. A preliminary examination was made by Messrs. RICHARDS and his assistants. Several persons were called to testify and the evidence as elicited before an informal tribunal, and not under oath, was conclusive to this point. The murderer of President LINCOLN was JOHN WILKES BOOTH. His hat was found in the private box, and identified by several persons who had seen him within the last two days, and the spur which he dropped by accident, after he jumped to the stage, was identified as one of those which he had obtained from the stable where he hired his horse.

This man BOOTH has played more than once at Ford's Theatre, and is, of course, acquainted with its exits and entrances, and the facility with which he escaped behind the scenes is well understood.

The person who assassinated Secretary SEWARD left behind him a slouched hat and an old rusty navy revolver. The chambers were broken loose from the barrel, as if done by striking. The loads were drawn from the chambers, one being but a rough piece of lead, and the other balls smaller than the chambers, wrapped in paper, as if to keep them from falling out.

CLOSING SCENES.

Particulars of His Last Moments—Record of His Condition Before Death—His Death.

WASHINGTON, Saturday, April 15—11 o'clock A. M.

The *Star* extra says:

"At 7:20 o'clock the President breathed his last, closing his eyes as if falling to sleep, and his countenance assuming an expression of perfect serenity. There were no indications of pain, and it was not known that he was dead until the gradually decreasing respiration ceased altogether.

Rev. Dr. GURLEY, of the New-York-avenue Presbyterian Church, immediately on its being ascertained that life was extinct, knelt at the bedside and offered an impressive prayer, which was responded to by all present.

Dr. GURLEY then proceeded to the front parlor, where Mrs. LINCOLN, Capt. ROBERT LINCOLN, Mrs. JOHN HAY, the Private Secretary, and others, were waiting, where he again offered a prayer for the consolation of the family.

The following minutes, taken by Dr. ABBOTT, show the condition of the late President throughout the night:

11 o'clock—Pulse 44.
11:05 o'clock—Pulse 45, and growing weaker.
11:10 o'clock—Pulse 45.
11:15 o'clock—Pulse 42.
11:20 o'clock—Pulse 45; respiration 27 to 29.
11:25 o'clock—Pulse 42.
11:32 o'clock—Pulse 48, and full.
11:40 o'clock—Pulse 45.
11:45 o'clock—Pulse 45; respiration 22.
12 o'clock—Pulse 48; respiration 22.
12:15 o'clock—Pulse 48; respiration 21—echmos both eyes.
12:30 o'clock—Pulse 45.
12:32 o'clock—Pulse 60.
12:35 o'clock—Pulse 66.
12:40 o'clock—Pulse 69; right eye much swollen, and echmoses.
12:45 o'clock—Pulse 70.
12:55 o'clock—Pulse 80; struggling motion of arms.
1 o'clock—Pulse 86; respiration 30.
1:30 o'clock—Pulse 95; appearing easier.
1:45 o'clock—Pulse 86—very quiet, respiration irregular.
Mrs. LINCOLN present.
2:10 o'clock—Mrs. LINCOLN retired with ROBERT LINCOLN to an adjoining room.
2:30 o'clock—President very quiet—pulse 54—respiration 28.
2:52 o'clock—Pulse 48—respiration 30.
3 o'clock—Visited again by Mrs. LINCOLN.
3:25 o'clock—Respiration 24 and regular.
3:35 o'clock—Prayer by Rev. Dr. GURLEY.
4 o'clock—Respiration 26 and regular.
4:15 o'clock—Pulse 60—respiration 25.
5:50 o'clock—Respiration 28—regular—sleeping.
6 o'clock—Pulse failing—respiration 28.
6:30 o'clock—Still failing and labored breathing.
7 o'clock—Symptoms of immediate dissolution.
7:22 o'clock—Death.

Surrounding the death-bed of the President were Secretaries Stanton, Welles, Usher, Attorney-General Speed, Postmaster-General Dennison, M. B. Field, Assistant Secretary of the Treasury; Judge Otto, Assistant Secretary of the Interior; Gen. Halleck, Gen. Meigs, Senator Sumner, R. F. Andrews, of New-York; Gen. Todd, of Dacotah; John Hay, Private Secretary; Gov. Oglesby, of Illinois; Gen. Farnsworth, Mrs. and Miss Kenney, Miss Harris, Capt. Robert Lincoln, son of the President, and Doctors E. W. Abbott, R. K. Stone, C. D. Gatch, Neal Hall, and Mr. Lieberman. Secretary McCulloch remained with the President until about 5 o'clock, and Chief-Justice Chase, after several hours' attendance during the night, returned early this morning.

Immediately after the President's death a Cabinet meeting was called by Secretary STANTON, and held in the room in which the corpse lay. Secretaries STANTON, WELLES and USHER, Postmaster-General DENNISON, and Attorney-General SPEED, were present. The results of the conference are as yet unknown.

Removal of the Remains to the Executive Mansion—Feeling in the City.

WASHINGTON, Saturday, April 15.

The President's body was removed from the private residence opposite Ford's Theatre to the executive mansion this morning at 9:30 o'clock, in a hearse, and wrapped in the American flag. It was escorted by a small guard of cavalry, Gen. AUGUR and other military officers following on foot.

A dense crowd accompanied the remains to the White House, where a military guard excluded the crowd, allowing none but persons of the household and personal friends of the deceased to enter the premises, Senator YATES and Representative FARNSWORTH being among the number admitted.

The body is being embalmed, with a view to its removal to Illinois.

Flags over the department and throughout the city are at half-mast. Scarcely any business is being transacted anywhere either on private or public account.

Our citizens, without any preconcert whatever, are draping their premises with festoons of mourning.

The bells are tolling mournfully. All is the deepest gloom and sadness. Strong men weep in the streets. The grief is wide-spread and deep and in strange contrast to the joy so lately manifested over our recent military victories.

This is indeed a day of gloom.

Reports prevail that Mr. FREDERICK W. SEWARD, who was kindly assisting the nursing of Secretary SEWARD, received a stab in the back. His shoulder blade prevented the knife or dagger from penetrating into his body. The prospects are that he will recover.

A report is circulated, repeated by almost everybody, that BOOTH was captured fifteen miles this side of Baltimore. If it be true, as asserted, that the War Department has received such information, it will doubtless be officially promulgated.

The government departments are closed by order, and will be draped with the usual emblems of mourning.

The roads leading to and from the city are guarded by the military, and the utmost circumspection is observed as to all attempting to enter or leave the city.

AUTOPSY UPON THE BODY OF ABRAHAM LINCOLN.

WASHINGTON, Saturday, April 15.

An autopsy was held this afternoon over the body of President LINCOLN by Surgeon-General BARNES and Dr. STONE, assisted by other eminent medical men.

The coffin is of mahogany, is covered with black cloth, and lined with lead, the latter also being covered white satin.

A silver plate upon the coffin over the breast bears the following inscription:

ABRAHAM LINCOLN,
SIXTEENTH PRESIDENT OF THE UNITED STATES,
Born July 12, 1809.
Died April 15, 1865.

The remains have been embalmed.

A few locks of hair were removed from the President's head for the family previous to the remains being placed in the coffin.

THE ASSASSINS.

Circumstances Tending to Inculpate G. H. Booth—Description of his Confederate in the Crime.

WASHINGTON, Saturday, April 15.

There is no confirmation of the report that the murderer of the President has been arrested.

Among the circumstances tending to fix a participation in the crime on BOOTH, were letters found in his trunk, one of which, apparently from a lady, supplicated him to desist from the perilous undertaking in which he was about to embark, as the time was inauspicious, the mine not yet being ready to be sprung.

The *Extra Intelligencer* says: "From the evidence obtained it is rendered highly probable that the man who stabbed Mr. SEWARD and his sons, is JOHN SURRATT, of Prince George County, Maryland. The horse he rode was hired at NAYLOR's stable, on Fourteenth-street. SURRATT is a young man, with light hair and goatee. His father is said to have been postmaster of Prince George County."

About 11 o'clock last night two men crossed the Anacostia Bridge, one of whom gave his name as BOOTH, and the other as SMITH. The latter is believed to be JOHN SURRATT.

Last night a riderless horse was found, which has been identified by the proprietor of one of the stables previously mentioned as having been hired from his establishment.

Accounts are conflicting as to whether BOOTH crossed the bridge on horseback or on foot; but as it is believed that he rode across it, it is presumed that he had exchanged his horse.

From information in the possession of the authorities it is evident that the scope of the plot was intended to be much more comprehensive.

The Vice-President and other prominent members of the Administration were particularly inquired for by suspected parties, and their precise localities accurately obtained; but providentially, in their cases, the scheme miscarried.

A boat was at once sent down the Potomac to notify the gunboats on the river of the awful crime, in order that all possible means should be taken for the arrest of the perpetrators.

The most ample precautions have been taken, and it is not believed the culprits will long succeed in evading the overtaking arm of justice.

The second extra of the *Evening Star* says:

"Col. INGRAHAM, Provost-Marshal of the defences north of the Potomac, is engaged in taking testimony to-day, all of which fixes the assassination upon J. WILKES BOOTH.

Judge OLIN, of the Supreme Court of the District of Columbia, and Justice MILLER, are also engaged to-day, at the Police Headquarters, on Tenth-street, in taking the testimony of a large number of witnesses.

Lieut. TYRELL, of Col. INGRAHAM's staff, last night proceeded to the National Hotel, where BOOTH had been stopping, and took possession of his trunk, in which was found a Colonel's military dress-coat, two pairs of handcuffs, two boxes of cartridges and a package of letters, all of which are now in the possession of the military authorities.

One of these letters, bearing the date of Hookstown, Md., seems to implicate BOOTH. The writer speaks of "the mysterious affair in which you are engaged," and urges BOOTH to proceed to Richmond, and ascertain the views of the authorities there upon the subject. The writer of the letter endeavors to persuade BOOTH from carrying his designs into execution at that time, for the reason, as the writer alleges, that the government had its suspicions aroused. The writer of the letter seems to have been implicated with BOOTH in "the mysterious affair" referred to, as he informs BOOTH in the letter that he would prefer to express his views verbally; and then goes on to say that he was out of money, had no clothes, and would be compelled to leave home, as his family were desirous that he should dissolve his connection with BOOTH. This letter is written on note paper, in a small, neat hand, and simply bears the signature of "Sam."

At the Cabinet meeting yesterday, which lasted over two hours, the future policy of the government toward Virginia was discussed, the best feeling prevailed. It is stated that it was, determined to adopt a very liberal policy, as was recommended by the President. It is said that this meeting was the most harmonious held for over two years, the President exhibiting throughout that magnanimity and kindness of heart which has ever characterized his treatment of the rebellious States, and which has been so illy requited on their part.

One of the members of the Cabinet remarked to a friend he met at the door, that "The government was to-day stronger than it had been for three years past."

WASHINGTON, Saturday, April 15—3:30 P. M.

To-day no one is allowed to leave the city by rail conveyance, or on foot, and the issuing of passes from the Headquarters of the Department of Washington has been suspended by Gen. AUGUR.

Probable Attempt of the Assassins to Escape into Canada—Order from the War Department.

[CIRCULAR.]

WAR DEPARTMENT, PROVOST MARSHAL GENERAL'S BUREAU, WASHINGTON, D. C.—9.40 A. M., April 15.

It is believed that the assassins of the President and Secretary SEWARD are attempting to escape to Canada. You will make a careful and thorough examination of all persons attempting to cross from the United States into Canada, and will arrest all suspicious persons. The most vigilant scrutiny on your part, and the force at your disposal, is demanded. A description of the parties supposed to be implicated in the murder will be telegraphed you to-day. But in the meantime be active in preventing the crossing of any suspicious persons.

By order of the Secretary of War.

N. L. JEFFERS, Brevet Brig. Gen., Acting Provost-Marshal General.

MR. SEWARD AND SON.

Secretary Seward will Recover—Frederick Seward Still Very Low.

Special Dispatch to the New-York Times.

WASHINGTON, Saturday, April 15.

Mr. SEWARD will recover.

FREDERICK SEWARD is still unconscious. He breathes calmly and has an easy pulse. His head is dreadfully contused and lacerated.

An invalid soldier nurse saved Mr. SEWARD's life.

GEN. GRANT'S MOVEMENTS.

PHILADELPHIA, Saturday, April 15.

Gen. GRANT arrived in this city late last night on his way to Jersey, but was intercepted on his way to Walnut-street wharf, by a dispatch from the office of the Associated Press, and it is supposed he he returned to Washington immediately.

His Return to Washington—Dispatch from Mrs. Grant.

BURLINGTON, N. J., Saturday, April 15.

Lieut.-Gen. GRANT left Burlington for Washington, at 6 o'clock this morning.

MRS. U. S. GRANT.

WASHINGTON, Saturday, April 15.

Gen. GRANT, who left yesterday for New-Jersey, and who was informed of the assassination as he was leaving Philadelphia this morning, arrived here in a special train about noon, and immediately proceeded to the President's house.

The Theatres.

Dispatches from Boston announce that all the theatres in that city will be closed until further notice.

In this city a movement of the same kind has been inaugurated. Fox's Old Bowery Theatre will be closed this evening.

THE SUCCESSION.

Mr. Johnson Inaugurated as President.

The Oath Administered by Secretary Chase.

He Will Perform His Duties Trusting in God.

WASHINGTON, Saturday, April 15—12 A. M.

ANDREW JOHNSON was sworn into office as President of the United States by Chief-Justice CHASE, to-day, at eleven o'clock.

Secretary MCCULLOUGH and Attorney-General SPEED, and others were present.

He remarked:

"The duties are mine. I will perform them, trusting in God.

SECOND DISPATCH.

WASHINGTON, Saturday, April 15.

At an early hour this morning, Hon. EDWIN M. STANTON, Secretary of War, sent an official communication to Hon. ANDREW JOHNSON, Vice-President of the United States, that in consequence of the sudden and unexpected death of the Chief Magistrate, his inauguration should take place as soon as possible, and requesting him to state the place and hour at which the ceremony should be performed.

Mr. JOHNSON immediately replied that it would be agreeable to him to have the proceedings take place at his rooms in the Kirkwood House as soon as the arrangements could be perfected.

Chief Justice CHASE was informed of the fact and repaired to the appointed place in company with Secretary MCCULLOUGH, of the Treasury Department, Attorney-General SPEED, J. P. BLAIR, Sr., Hon. MONTGOMERY BLAIR, Senators FOOT, of Vermont, RAMSAY, of Minnesota, YATES, of Illinois, STEWART, of Nevada, HALE, of New Hampshire, and Gen. FARNSWORTH, of Illinois.

At eleven o'clock the oath of office was administered by the Chief Justice of the United States, in his usual solemn and impressive manner.

Mr. JOHNSON received the kind expressions of the gentlemen by whom he was surrounded in a manner which showed his earnest sense of the great responsibilities so suddenly devolved upon him, and made a brief speech, in which he said:

"The duties of the office are mine. I will perform them. The consequences are with God. Gentlemen, I shall lean upon you. I feel that I shall need your support. I am deeply impressed with the solemnity of the occasion and the responsibility of the duties of the office I am assuming.

Mr. JOHNSON appeared to be in remarkably good health, and has a high and realizing sense of the hopes that are centred upon him. His manner was solemn and dignified, and his whole bearing produced a most gratifying impression upon those who participated in the ceremonies.

It is probable that during the day President JOHNSON will issue his first proclamation to the American People.

It is expected, though nothing has been definitely determined upon, that the funeral of the late President LINCOLN will take place on or about Thursday next. It is supposed that his remains will be temporarily deposited in the Congressional Cemetery.

FROM RICHMOND.

WASHINGTON, Saturday, April 15.

The Richmond *Whig* of yesterday, contains the following:

HEADQUARTERS DEPARTMENT OF VIRGINIA, RICHMOND, Va., April 13, 1865.

Owing to recent events, the permission for the reassembling of the gentlemen recently acting as the Legislature of Virginia, is rescinded. Should any of the gentlemen come to the city under the notice of reassembling already published, they will be furnished passports to return to their homes. Any of the persons named in the call signed by J. A. CAMPBELL and others, who are found in the city, twelve hours after the publication of this notice, will be subject to arrest, unless they are residents of this city.

E. O. C. ORD, Maj.-Gen., Commanding the Department.

HEADQUARTERS DEPARTMENT OF VIRGINIA, ARMY OF THE JAMES, RICHMOND, Va., April 13, 1865.

GENERAL ORDERS No. 37.—Provost-Marshals will grant no passes to citizens from the North or to officers to come to this city, except on orders from the President, the Secretary of War, Lieut.-Gen. GRANT or the Department Commander.

Officers and soldiers now in the city will return to their respective commands at once, or be subject to arrest and confinement.

The Provost-Marshal-General is charged with the execution of this order.

By command of Maj.-Gen. ORD.

E. W. SMITH, Assistant Adjutant-General.

The *Whig* says: Maj.-Gen. GODFREY WEITZEL, commanding the Twenty-fourth Army Corps and Commander of the forces occupying Richmond, has been relieved from his command, and assigned to Petersburgh and vicinity. Maj.-Gen. E. O. C. ORD, commanding the Army of the James, assumes command of this department.

The report that Gen. R. E. LEE arrived in this city on Wednesday evening, was incorrect. The statement originated in the fact that Gen. CURTIS LEE had reached the city on a visit to his mother, Mrs. R. E. LEE. CURTIS LEE is a prisoner in the hands of the Union army, and, being at City Point, was kindly permitted to come to this city to see his mother, who was reported to be in ill-health.

The whereabouts of Gen. ROBERT E. LEE is not known here—at least, not outside of official circles. He is daily expected at Richmond.

Personal.

ST. LOUIS, Friday, April 14.

Maj.-Gen. BANKS and family left this morning for New-Orleans.

THE NATIONAL CALAMITY.

Popular Feeling in New-York and the Country.

REMARKABLE MEETING IN WALL-STREET

Speeches of Representative Men.

Doings of the City Council and Other Public Bodies

Public Expression Throughout the Country.

Sympathy of the Nova Scotia Parliament.

A Rebel Flag Ordered to be Hauled Down.

PROCLAMATION BY GOV. FENTON.

EXECUTIVE CHAMBER, ALBANY, April 15.

The fearful tragedy at Washington has converted an occasion of rejoicing over national victory into one of national mourning. It is fitting, therefore, that the 20th of April, heretofore set apart as a day of thanksgiving, should now be dedicated to services appropriate to a season of national bereavement. Bowing reverently to the Providence of God, let us assemble in our places of worship on that day to acknowledge our dependence on Him who has brought sudden darkness on the land in the very hour of its restoration to Union, Peace and Liberty.

In witness whereof, I have hereunto set my hand and affixed the privy seal of the State, at the City of Albany, this 15th day of April, in the year of our Lord one thousand eight hundred and sixty-five.

(Signed,) R. E. FENTON.

By the Governor,

GEORGE S. HASTINGS, Private Secretary.

The State Legislature.

SENATE.

ALBANY, Saturday, April 15.

After an impressive prayer by Rev. Mr. SELKIRK, Mr. HUMPHREY said:

Mr. President—I understand that His Excellency the Governor is about to send a communication to this body, announcing the terrible calamity that has befallen our country. I move, therefore that no business be transacted until the reception of the communication from the Governor.

Subsequently Col. HASTINGS, the Governor's Private Secretary, appeared within the bar of the Senate and delivered the following message:

STATE OF NEW-YORK, EXECUTIVE CHAMBER, ALBANY, April 15, 1865.

To the Legislature:

It becomes my painful duty to announce to the Legislature the death of ABRAHAM LINCOLN, President of the United States. It is with emotions of profoundest sorrow that I make this announcement to your honorable body. Such an event is a national calamity, and under the circumstances now attending the bereavement, the nation weeps with heightened anguish. To be deprived of his wisdom, experience and counsel at a time when most important to return to the United States peace, fraternity and prosperity—at a time when the gigantic war which confronted him at the threshold of his Administration is about drawing to a close, and a final deliverance obtained from our civil disturbances for which we have sacrificed so much, is a calamity that will cause the deepest sorrow and gloom to the millions of our land, and to the friends of freedom throughout the world.

This is the third time in our history that the Republic has been subjected to this trial, but it is hoped that our good cause and country, watered by a nation's tears and sanctified by its prayers, will pass in safety through the ordeal to a higher life and destiny. I have also to communicate to you the sad intelligence that our noble Secretary of State, and honored, favored son of New-York, WILLIAM H. SEWARD, was likewise a victim of the tragic plot of the assassins, and now lies in an unconscious condition. May God spare his life to this nation.

R. E. FENTON, Governor.

Mr. FOLGER moved the following resolution, which was adopted by consent, in silence:

Resolved, If the Assembly concur, that the message of his Excellency, the Governor, be referred to a joint committee of five from the Senate and seven from the Assembly, which was adopted and transmitted to the Assembly, when a recess was taken until 11:30 o'clock.

The President announced the committee on the part of the Senate: Messrs. Folger, Murphy, Andrews, Cook and Shafer.

Subsequently the committee reported the following through Mr. FOLGER:

The Joint Committee of the two Houses on the message of His Excellency the Governor, this day transmitted to the Legislature, makes the following report:

The Committee having in mind that the funeral ceremonies of the late President of the United States will probably take place on some early day in the next week, and that such day will be observed throughout the whole country as a day of solemn recognition of the tragic and awful event which now fills all thoughts, and that the Legislature will join in that observance, do unanimously recommend that on the day which shall be appointed for such obsequies, the two Houses of the Legislature do meet in their respective chambers, at the hour appointed for such funeral ceremonies, and that then, the two Houses being opened with prayer by clergymen especially selected for that service, resolutions appropriate to the occasion be offered. That the Joint Committee of the two Houses be now empowered to sit again to draft such resolutions, and report them on that day to the respective Houses, and do report the following resolution:

Resolved by the Senate, if the Assembly concur, That, viewing this unexampled and solemn event as demanding a cessation of legislative business, do now adjourn until Tuesday of next week, at 11 o'clock A. M.

CHARLES J. FOLGER, Chairman of the Senate Committee.

THOMAS B. VAN BUREN, Chairman of the Assembly Committee.

The report of the Committee was adopted, and the Senate adjourned until Tuesday morning, at 11 o'clock.

NEW YORK CITY.

Proclamation by the Mayor.

MAYOR'S OFFICE, NEW-YORK, April 15, 1865.

Citizens of New York;

The death of the President of the United States may well excite your profound grief and amazement. I respectfully recommend that business be suspended, and that a public mourning for the departed Chief Magistrate be observed throughout the city.

C. GODFREY GUNTHER, Mayor.

Expressions of Sorrow.

But few words are needed to express the condition of our city since the reception of the news of President LINCOLN's assassination. All men sorrow; all hearts are grieved and sickened at the great calamity which oppresses the nation, and universal gloom attests the sincerity of those who

[Continued on Eighth Page.]

War Department, Washington, April 20, 1865.

$100,000 REWARD!

THE MURDERER

Of our late beloved President, ABRAHAM LINCOLN,

IS STILL AT LARGE.

$50,000 REWARD!

will be paid by this Department for his apprehension, in addition to any reward offered by Municipal Authorities or State Executives.

$25,000 REWARD!

will be paid for the apprehension of JOHN H. SURRATT, one of Booth's accomplices.

$25,000 REWARD!

will be paid for the apprehension of DANIEL C HARROLD, another of Booth's accomplices.

LIBERAL REWARDS will be paid for any information that shall conduce to the arrest of either of the above-named criminals, or their accomplices.

All persons harboring or secreting the said persons, or either of them, or aiding or assisting their concealment or escape, will be treated as accomplices in the murder of the President and the attempted assassination of the Secretary of State, and shall be subject to trial before a Military Commission and the punishment of DEATH.

Let the stain of innocent blood be removed from the land by the arrest and punishment of the murderers.

All good citizens are exhorted to aid public justice on this occasion. Every man should consider his own conscience charged with this solemn duty, and rest neither night nor day until it be accomplished.

EDWIN M. STANTON, ***Secretary of War.***

DESCRIPTIONS.—BOOTH is 5 feet 7 or 8 inches high, slender build, high forehead, black hair, black eyes, and wears a heavy black moustache.

JOHN H. SURRATT is about 5 feet 9 inches. Hair rather thin and dark; eyes rather light; no beard. Would weigh 145 or 150 pounds. Complexion rather pale and clear, with color in his cheeks. Wore light clothes of fine quality. Shoulders square; cheek bones rather prominent; chin narrow; ears projecting at the top; forehead rather low and square, but broad. Parts his hair on the right side; neck rather long. His lips are firmly set. A slim man.

DANIEL C. HARROLD is 23 years of age, 5 feet 6 or 7 inches high, rather broad shouldered, otherwise light built; dark hair, little (if any) moustache; dark eyes, weighs about 140 pounds.

GEO. F NESBITT & CO., Printers and Stationers, cor. Pearl and Pine Streets, N. Y.

John Wilkes Booth

The assassination of President Lincoln at Ford's Theatre, April 14, 1865 as depicted in *Harper's Weekly*

The New-York Times.

VOL. XIV......NO. 4232. NEW-YORK, TUESDAY, APRIL 18, 1865. PRICE FOUR CENTS

CAPTURE OF MOBILE.

The Last of the Coast Cities in Our Possession.

The News Officially Confirmed

The City Surrendered on the 9th inst. to Our Forces.

OVER FIVE THOUSAND PRISONERS.

Large Quantities of Ordnance Stores Taken.

FULL DETAILS OF PREVIOUS OPERATIONS.

NEW-ORLEANS, Monday, April 10, via CAIRO, Sunday, April 16.

The *Times* publishes an official dispatch of the capture of Spanish Fort, and of the town of Blakeley.

The former was captured at 10:30 on the morning of the 9th, with 700 prisoners.

The latter was captured on the same day by assault, with over 5,000 prisoners and a large amount of ordnance stores.

Our gunboats and troops were proceeding unresisted toward Mobile, which place was captured last evening by a portion of Gen. SMITH's command, assisted by the light-draught gunboats, after a short resistance by the enemy.

DETAILS OF THE SIEGE.

Special Dispatch to the New-York Times.

BLAKELY, Ala., Monday, April 10, via CINCINNATI, Monday, April 17.

Gen. CANBY has just achieved a brilliant victory in Mobile Bay, and Gen. WILSON has not only pushed successfully through central Alabama, but has literally smashed up everything in his way.

On Saturday, the 8th inst., all day great preparations were made to get every piece of ordnance in position, which was accomplished about 5 o'clock P. M. Twenty-two heavy Parrotts were got within half a mile of Spanish Fort, and half as many mortars, while the Twelfth Indiana, Seventh Massachusetts and Twenty-first New-York Batteries were advanced to within one-third of a mile of the enemy's works.

At a given time, our entire artillery, assisted by two of our gunboats, blazed away with great fury and alacrity, and at the same time our sappers and skirmishers advanced and killed every rebel artillerist who showed his head. For several hours the roar of artillery was one of the most awful I have ever heard, with the additional vociferations of 20,000 men.

As night progressed there was no abatement of the thunder of our artillery and the racket of our musketry, while the faintness of the enemy's response grew more and more visible, until shortly after midnight, when the firing from Spanish Fort almost entirely ceased. In an hour after the fort surrendered, and at a quarter to 2 on the morning of April 9, our troops were in possession of Spanish Fort and Fort Alexandria, and all they contained, including twenty odd pieces of artillery, a vast amount of ammunition, one general officer, and nearly one thousand prisoners.

The guns of both forts were immediately turned on Forts Tracy and Huger in the harbor, at the mouth of the Blakely and Apalachee Rivers, but failed to elicit a reply. It was subsequently ascertained both works were abandoned by the enemy, after spiking eight heavy guns.

Our monitors and gunboats now went to work, assisted by some prisoners, and in a short time succeeded in removing between thirty and forty torpedoes, and running up almost within shelling distance of Mobile. The gunboat *Cherokee* moved up at night close enough to throw several shells at the enemy's water batteries, but without getting a return fire.

Since the 5th inst. the town of Blakely has been thoroughly invested by land, but the water communication had not been entirely cut off. Before long, however, two vessels of our fleet got close enough to command the mouth of Blakely River, and it was at once resolved to attack the works all round Blakely simultaneously. Gen. STEELE commanded on the right, Gen. SMITH in the centre, and Gen. GRANGER on the left.

Shortly after the capture of Spanish Fort, intelligence of the capture and the fall of Richmond was read to the troops, in connection with orders to attack Fort Blakely. Acclamations rent the air, and immediately almost the entire force moved on the enemy's works. The fire from the rebel batteries was most terrible for a short time, but failed to check the advance of our intrepid troops, who, under a murderous fire of grape and canister overhead, and torpedoes under foot, tore away the elaborately constructed abbattis and chevaux de frieze, swept over the ditches, and at the point of the bayonet, carried the whole line of works.

The success of the assault was manifested by the vociferous shouts of the troops, and for many minutes their demonstrations of joy exhibited no signs of relaxation or discontinuance. Quiet at last prevailed, but was again disturbed when the announcement was made that the results of the assault was the capture of several batteries of artillery, large quantities of ammunition, Gens. GIBSON and TIDDELL, and nearly 4,000 prisoners. Our loss in the whole affair is much less than 2,000 killed and wounded, and none missing.

The national flag floats over all the forts on the eastern shore and in the bay, and will probably float over Mobile before to-morrow night. Boats are working up and meet with no opposition.

The enemy's loss in killed and wounded will amount to about 1,500.

A division of colored troops under Gen. HAWKINS, on our extreme right, behaved handsomely, and, like their white comrades, exhibited unmistakable pluck and intrepidity.

The enemy's works were very strong, and during the assault our lines were enfiladed by one hundred and twenty-four pounder shells from the rebel ironclads *Nashville* and *Huntsville*. During the whole siege our troops exhibited the most remarkable valor and endurance. For two weeks the enemy's forts on shore and in the bay, and four gunboats, kept up an unceasing fire day and night. The Fourteenth Indiana Battery took a position the first day of the siege within a third of a mile of the fort, and held it until its termination, sustaining a loss of fifteen men killed and wounded, and one gun smashed. The First Indiana Heavy Artillery, and Third Indiana, Seventh Massachusetts, Seventeenth Ohio, and Twenty-first New-York Batteries also distinguished themselves. The Iowa and Illinois troops have suffered most during the siege.

In proceeding to the investment of Fort Blakely, many of our troops and horses were killed and injured by torpedoes. The roads were literally lined with them in an attempt to raise the monitor *Milwaukee*, which was sunk, but sustained little injury. It is split in two, and is a total wreck. The monitor *Osage* has had her guns taken out, and, with a little more lightening, it is believed she can be made to float. The other loss sustained by the fleet is two tin-clads and one transport. I have not learned of but six men lost in the fleet during the engagement. Further particulars will be transmitted soon.

Gen. WILSON's cavalry success is certainly brilliant. The rebel papers admit enough to confirm the opinion that he has smashed everything up in central Alabama. He left Eastport about the 20th ult., and advanced in two columns, and struck at Marion and Plantersville simultaneously, respectively situated about twenty miles to the northwest and northeast of Selma. Two brigades of RODDY's division of FORREST's command, under Gen. PATTERSON, were stationed at Marion, and ADAMS' division was at Plantersville. The Mobile *Register* says that the fight at Marion commenced on the morning of the 2d inst., was quite severe and lasted several hours. Ten regiments were armed with Spencer Rifles, which hurled rapid death and destruction into the rebel ranks. The *Register* admits that their loss in killed and wounded is greater than ours, and adds that ultimately PATTERSON's forces were driven in great confusion, with the loss of a considerable number of men and horses, and all their artillery.

The fight at Plantersville was briefer in duration, with about the same results. ADAMS commanded the rebel forces, and three times endeavored to break our lines. The *Register* says that ADAMS fought with distinguished skill and bravery, but was finally overpowered by an overwhelming force and compelled to fly in great disorder, with the loss of all his artillery, many killed and wounded, and a number of prisoners.

The *Register* and *Tribune* both say that in the afternoon of the same day the Federals swarmed in front of Selma, and after a short engagement captured the fortifications, mounting twenty-two guns. Immediately the work of destruction commenced, and in a brief time all the immense government works, arsenal, rolling mills, foundries, factories, munitions of war, ordnance and subsistence stores, and other material, were in ruins.

No rebel papers yet mention the fall of Montgomery, but deserters and prisoners report this, and its capture is believed to have taken place on the 3d inst. The *Register* is desponding in tone, and says that this fall of Selma is a terrible blow. The destruction of property is immense, and Mobile is entirely cut off on all sides. All the Mobile papers say, editorially, that "things look blue," and accuse FORREST, in most vituperative language, of gross mismanagement, and blame his under Generals, saying that they are not only guilty of unharmonious actions, but of playing into the hands of the Federals. The *Tribune* says that the rebel forces in the central section of the State, after a series of quarrels, were distributed injudiciously, and adds that unless concert of action immediately takes place, the whole thing is up in Alabama.

Prisoners and deserters say that Gen. WILSON easily resisted all opposition and swept everything before him. The paper published at Cahawba, in its last issue, says that our forces swept everything in their path, including cities, towns, railroad rolling-stock, manufactories, foundries, cattle, horses and negroes, leaving instead death and desolation.

I am pleased to add that the exact programme that I transmitted just two months ago, has been successfully and handsomely performed.

BENJ. C. TRUMAN.

IMPORTANT FROM GEN. SHERMAN.

Negotiations with Johnston in Progress.

Probable Surrender of the Rebel Army.

WASHINGTON, Monday, April 17.

Information has been received by the government from Gen. SHERMAN that he was in communication with Gen. JOHNSTON, with a view to the surrender of the latter.

Gen. SHERMAN would offer the same terms that Gen. GRANT did to Gen. LEE, and it was supposed they would be accepted.

THE NORTHERN BORDER.

Threatened Raid upon Ogdensburgh and Rochester from Canada.

ROCHESTER, N. Y., Monday, April 17.

A telegram was received, yesterday, by the Mayor, from Maj.-Gen. J. J. PECK, commanding at New-York, stating that information had been received at his headquarters that an organized band of 150 men were in Carolton County, Canada, prepared to make a raid upon Rochester or Ogdensburgh.

The Mayor called a meeting of an advisory committee of citizens to take measures for meeting the raiders.

Gen. WILLIAMS received orders from the Adjutant-General of the State to put the Fifty-fourth Regiment upon duty, and two companies are now under arms.

The raiders will meet with a warm reception if they should come.

FROM HAVANA.

The American News—The Blockade Runners.

HAVANA, Wednesday, April 12.

The prevailing topic of conversation here for the last two days has been the news received by the steamer *Eagle* of the taking of Richmond.

The *Eagle* came into port at about 2 o'clock on Monday afternoon with all her colors flying and machinery decorated as she rounded the *Moro*. She fired thirteen guns. Her gay appearance and the firing of the salute created the greatest excitement, and a general hope was expressed that peace had been declared.

The American Consul hung out his flag, and the Federal commenced rejoicing, and the rebels looked down-cast and sad—but when the news was announced that Richmond was captured, and that LEE and his army were in flight, and the other details were given, the rebels looked still more sorrowful.

Peace would have been preferred by the rebels, for then they would have expected a proclamation of amnesty and a chance to make a living in the United States, for their opinion now is that blockade-running is about "played out."

It was rumored that the act of the American Consul, in hanging out the flag deeply offended them, and that they intended to make an assault on the office on that night, but the police did not allow any groups of men to assemble in that vicinity.

The United States steamer *Santiago de Cuba*, with Assistant Secretary of the Navy FOX, Mr. NICOLAY, and Mr. WALLES, and their party aboard, stopped here for a few days last week, saw Havana and went to Matanzas on Thursday morning.

Sickness has begun to set in in the shape of "Yellow-Jack." One or two cases of small-pox have been reported.

The blockade news is not of much interest. The *Owl* is expected this week from Galveston. Capt. MAFFIT is in command, and there is no truth in the story that he had been put in Moro Castle.

The passport system for the United States is in full sway here now. No one is allowed to embark for the United States unless a passport vised by the American Consul is presented. The Government charge on passports here when delivered to travelers is paid in stamps attached to the passport.

THE ASSASSINATION.

Condition of Secretary Seward Improving.

NEW FACTS ABOUT THE MURDERERS.

Preparations for the President's Funeral.

Official Directions from Heads of Departments.

DESCRIPTION OF THE ASSASSINS.

Reward of Thirty Thousand Dollars Offered for Their Apprehension.

Additional Details of the Conspiracy.

APPEARANCE OF THE CITY.

WASHINGTON, D. C., Tuesday, April 17—9:20 P. M.

The city has to some extent resumed its wonted appearance, though the great grief is still uppermost in all hearts, and its signs are appearent on every hand. Every yard of black fabric in the city on Saturday, was bought up at an early hour on that day, and hundreds of persons who wished to testify their grief by draping the residences were unable to so. This morning, however, further supplies arrived here, and this afternoon many more houses have been draped in morning.

Business has been partially resumed, though large numbers of stores have simply contented themselves with opening their doors and not taking down their shutters. In the Public Departments some work has been done during the day, but business generally will not be resumed therein till after the funeral.

THE NEWS IN RICHMOND.

The news of the murder of the President was received in Richmond during the evening of Saturday, by special telegram to Gen. ORD's headquarters. It created great alarm and consternation, and the first feeling among the officers who learned it Saturday evening was, that swift justice should be meted out to the authors.

THE NEWS AT FORTRESS MONROE.

One of your correspondents with the army, who came up to-day, furnishes the following paragraphs respecting the feeling on the reception of the news at Fortress Monroe, City Point and Norfolk:

"At Fortress Monroe the sad news of the assassination of President LINCOLN, and the attempted murder of Secretary SEWARD and his two sons, was received at first with incredulity; but at length the terrible news was authenticated. One cannot describe the utter feeling of poignant sorrow with which the news was received. The naval vessels in the harbor displayed their colors at half-mast, and the example was followed by nearly all the shipping. For so small a community the excitement was immense, and in the absence of any definite news the most woful forebodings were indulged in. On the arrival of the City Point boat, from up the River James, the passengers were strangely startled by being informed of the awful calamity that had befallen the country. They had at first imagined that the drooping flags, half-masted on the shipping, was indicative of the death of Secretary SEWARD, he being reported injured, but their horror and indignation knew no bounds on learning who it was that the nation's ships thus mourned. Among the passengers the greatest feeling was exhibited, and several ladies on board evinced much distress. Brave men, with wounds received in battle, friends of soldiers, visiting their disabled brethren, all evinced a degree of feeling that has rarely been shown."

FEELING OF PASSENGERS.

The state of suspense among the passengers on their way up to Washington was indeed terrible. Owing to orders to search boats and many often and imperfectly-understood dispatches, progress was somewhat impeded, and one boat had to return to Newport's News to land prisoners of war, and only reached Washington at noon on Monday, having been on the route full forty-eight hours.

TREACHERY AMONG REBEL DESERTERS.

At Norfolk, on Saturday, soon after news of the death of the President arrived, some incipient signs of a rebellion exhibited themselves among two "whitewashed" regiments of rebel deserters, who have taken the oath of allegiance and been enlisted in the service of the United States. The mutinous signs and turbulent acts of the proposed insurgents were quickly quelled and their arms taken from them. On an examination of their cartridge-boxes, ammunition was found therein that had never been issued to them by the government, and it was not at all suited to the arms in their possession. It is currently reported and generally believed that guns were concealed in Norfolk or vicinity for which the mysterious cartridges would come in use. Several paroled rebel prisoners were seized on suspicion of being connected with the mutiny that has been so effectually crushed by the prompt action of the authorities.

ORDERS FOR THE FUNERAL.

Orders have been issued by the heads of the various departments respecting the observance of Wednesday.

The Navy Department will be closed on that day, and work will be suspended in all Navy-yards and naval stations, and on all vessels of the United States. The flags of all vessels and at all the Navy-yards and stations, and marine barracks, will be kept at half-mast during the day; and at 12 o'clock M. twenty-one minute guns will be fired by the Senior officer of each squadron and the Commandants of each of the Navy-yards and stations. Vice-Admiral D. G. FARRAGUT and Rear-Admiral WM. B. SHUBRICK have been designated to make the necessary arrangements on the part of the navy and marine corps for attending the funeral.

The State Department will also be closed, and Acting Secretary HUNTER directs that all persons subject to the orders of the department wear crape for six months upon the left arm.

The Postmaster-General directs that all the post-offices in the United States be closed from 11 till 3 on that day, and that all work therein be suspended.

Secretary USHER directs that the Interior Department be closed, and has sent orders to the various Indian agencies, land offices, pension agencies, &c., in connection with his Department, for a proper observance of the day by a suspension of all business.

The Treasury Department will also remain closed, and Secretary MCCULLOCH has communicated to the various Sub-Treasuries his patriotic wishes and desires.

The Secretary of War and Lieut.-Gen. GRANT direct that the headquarters of every department, post, station, fort, and arsenal, be draped in mourning for thirty days, and appropriate funeral honors be paid by every army in every department, and at every military post, and at the Military Academy at West Point, to the memory of the late illustrious Chief Magistrate of the nation, and Commander-in-Chief of its armies; and that the officers of the armies of the United States wear the badge of mourning on their left arm, and on their swords, and the colors of their commands, and regiments be put in mourning for the period of six months; and further that on Wednesday the national flag be everywhere displayed at half mast, and at dawn thirteen guns be fired at every fort, arsenal, and station, and at West Point, and afterwards at intervals of thirty minutes between the rising and setting of the sun, a single gun, and at the close of the day a national salute of thirty-six guns.

CONDITION OF SECRETARY SEWARD AND SON.

The condition of Secretary SEWARD and son FREDERICK, at the hour of nine o'clock this evening, is so far improved as to encourage the hope of the speedy recovery of both. Secretary SEWARD has slept well to-day, and his condition generally is much easier. The Assistant Secretary is so far improved that the hope of his recovery strengthens with every hour. The others of the injured are doing well.

ARRESTS OF SUSPECTED PERSONS.

Several arrests of parties suspected of being connected with murder of Mr. LINCOLN and the attempted assassination of Secretary SEWARD and sons have been made. Yesterday four men dressed in female attire were arrested in Georgetown and committed to the Old Capitol. Investigations by the civil and military authorities are still in progress, and the testimony of a large number of witnesses has already been taken. These investigations are proceeding quietly, however, as it is deemed best for the ends of justice that no publicity should be given at present to the facts elicited.

EFFECT ON THE FINANCES OF THE COUNTRY.

The effect of the late tragedy upon the finances of the country is most strikingly illustrated by the subscriptions to the popular Seven-thirty loan, which for Fridry and Saturday last amounted to the enormous aggregate of *nine million one hundred and thirty-four thousand seven hundred dollars*. This sum was composed entirely of small subscriptions and does not include those made by heavy holders of government vouchers, who by the Loan Act of the last Congress can receive these bonds in payment of their claims. If any evidence was warted of the determination of the people to sustain the government finances against all attempts of traitors of every dye. This is conclusive.

Dispatches to the Associated Press.

WASHINGTON, Monday, April 17.

The deep interest felt in Secretary SEWARD has thronged his residence with visitors, among them the members of the Cabinet, foreign ministers, and a large number of others.

He was informed yesterday, for the first time, of the assassination of President LINCOLN, and of the attempted assassination of himself and of the Assistant Secretary, and to some extent of the condition in which the latter lay.

Mr. SEWARD, though moved with the most intense sorrow and horror at the recital of the awful facts, nevertheless bore it with considerable firmness and composure, his strength having so far returned as to enable him to undergo the trying ordeal.

Every effort that ingenuity, excited by fervor, can make, is being put forth by all the proper authorities to capture or trace the assassin of Mr. LINCOLN and the would-be assassin of Mr. SEWARD.

The Common Council have offered a reward of $20,000 for the arrest and conviction of the assassins, and to this sum another of $10,000 is added by Col. L. C. BAKER, Agent of the War Department, making a total of $30,000.

To this announcement are added the following descriptions of the individuals accused:

Description of J. WILKES BOOTH, who assassinated the President on the evening of April 14, 1865:

Height, five feet eight inches; weight, 160 pounds; compact built; hair jet black, inclined to curl, of medium length, and parted behind; eyes black, and heavy, dark eyebrows; wears a large seal ring on his little finger; when talking inclines his head forward and looks down.

Description of the person who attempted to assassinate Hon. WM. H. SEWARD, Secretary of State:

Height six feet, one inch; hair black, thick, full and straight; no beard nor appearance of beard; cheeks red on the jaws; face moderately full; twenty-two or twenty-three years of age; eyes large, not prominent, color unknown; brows not heavy but dark; face not large but rather round; complexion healthy; nose straight and well formed, and of medium size; mouth small; lips thin; the upper lip protrudes when he talks; chin pointed and prominent; head medium size; neck short; hands soft and small, fingers tapering, showing no signs of hard labor; broad shoulders; taper waist; straight figure; strong looking man; manner not gentlemanly but vulgar; wears an overcoat with pockets in the side and one on the breast, with lappels or flaps; pants black, and of common stuff; new, heavy boots; voice small and thin, and inclined to tremor.

Meetings are called for this evening of Pennsylvanians, Missourians and Ohioans, who are residents of this city and Georgetown, for the purpose of giving expression to their feelings on the late sad affliction of the country in the death of Mr. LINCOLN, and to make arrangements to attend his funeral.

A meeting of the New-York Club for the same purpose will also be held to-night.

All the theatrical and concert-saloon proprietors announce that their establishments will be closed until further notice.

The *National Intelligencer* says:

"We can state on the highest authority that it has been ascertained that there was a regular conspiracy to assassinate every member of the Cabinet, together with the Vice-President. BOOTH, it is said, sent his card up to the Vice-President at the hotel, but Mr. JOHNSON could not conveniently see him.

We understand from authority, which we deem unquestionable, that a few days ago, after an interview between the late Chief Magistrate and the present one, Mr. LINCOLN expressed himself gratified with their concurrent views, and that he placed implicit confidence in the then Vice-President.

The names of the severally appointed assassins, are, we understand, known, and after the present investigation is concluded and published, the public will be astonished at the developments. From motives of public interest we refrain from mentioning many of them that reach us.

A member of the Cabinet remarked on the day after the murder of Mr. LINCOLN, that the rebels had lost their best friend; that Mr. LINCOLN invariably, at every Cabinet meeting, counselled forbearance, kindness and mercy to these misguided men.

POST-OFFICE DEPARTMENT, WASHINGTON, Monday, April 17.

To Deputy Postmasters:

Business in all the Post-offices of the United States will be suspended, and the offices closed, from 11 A. M. to 3 P. M., on Wednesday, the 19th inst., during the funeral solemnities of ABRAHAM LINCOLN, late President of the United States.

(Signed,) W. DENNISON, Postmaster General.

PROCLAMATION OF GOV. OGLESBY OF ILLINOIS.

To the People of the State of Illinois:

The funeral ceremonies of the late lamented Chief Magistrate are to take place in this city at the Executive Mansion, at 12 M. on Wednesday, the 19th inst. The acting Secretary of the State has invited the various religious denominations throughout the country to meet within their respective places of worship at that hour, for the purpose of solemnizing the occasion with appropriate ceremonies. Responding to the spirit of this announcement, I call upon the people of Illinois, the home of her Martyred Son, to meet in their respective churches and places of worship on that day, to observe in such manner as the painful occasion shall suggest the solemn hour.

(Signed,) J. OGLESBY, Governor.

WASHINGTON, April 17, 1865.

MEETING OF KENTUCKIANS.

A meeting of Kentuckians was held last night. Suitable action was taken in reference to the death of the President.

J. B. STEWART and Cols. SHAFFER and DUNCAN were appointed a committee to carry the arrangements into effect.

REPORTS ABOUT BOOTH'S ARREST.

Report still prevails that BOOTH has been arrested and is on board of a gunboat in the Potomac. The origin of the story was in this wise: A prominent military officer came into the Navy Department on Saturday and said he had just learned that BOOTH was overtaken some miles out on the road leading from Seventh-street, and asked whether the department would consent that he be placed on board of a gunboat. The reply was in the affirmative. Unfortunately the same officer received later information that the report was not true. The military authorities have received no intelligence as to his arrest.

THE FLAG TORN BY THE ASSASSIN.

The National flag draped round the box at the theatre, occupied by the President, belonged to the Treasury Department Regiment. It was torn by the spur of the assassin as he leaped to the stage.

CONDITION OF SECRETARY SEWARD AND SON.

At 10:30 o'clock to-day, Secretary SEWARD was represented to be in an improving condition, though he rested rather uncomfortably last night from mental excitement, caused by conversation with friends in relation to recent events.

His son FREDERICK has partially recovered consciousness, and his symptoms are otherwise somewhat favorable.

MR. HANSELL IS BETTER.

Mr. HANSELL, the Messenger of the State Department, who was stabbed in the back at the same time, is a great sufferer, but believed to be out of danger.

A GRAY COAT STAINED WITH BLOOD FOUND.

WASHINGTON, Monday, April 17.

Yesterday a grey coat stained with blood, and which evidently had been worn as an overcoat, was found near Fort Bunker Hill, just back of Glenwood Cemetery. In the pocket was a false moustache, a pair of riding gloves, and a slip of paper, upon which was "MARY E. GARDNER, 419." The coat is supposed to have been worn by the man who attacked Secretary SEWARD, although the weight of the evidence indicates that all the conspirators took the same route—that of the navy-yard bridge.

BOOTH'S MISTRESS.

This morning, Detective KELLEY and a detail of patrolmen of the Second Ward, by order of Judge OLIN, proceeded to the house of MOLLIE TURNER, on the corner of Thirteenth and Ohio-avenue, and arrested all the inmates, from the mistress to the cook, eight in all, and carried them to the police headquarters, to be held as witnesses. This is the house where BOOTH spent much of his time, ELLA TURNER, the woman who attempted suicide, being his kept mistress.

BOOTH'S RECENT BEHAVIOR.

The *Evening Star* says on Friday last, BOOTH was about the National Hotel, as usual, and strolled up and down the avenue several times. During one of these strolls he stopped at the Kirkwood House, and sent to Vice-President JOHNSON a card, upon which was written:

"I do not wish to disturb you. Are you in?

J. WILKES BOOTH."

A gentleman of BOOTH's acquaintance at this time met him in front of the Kirkwood House, and in the conversation which followed, made some allusion to BOOTH's business, and, in a jesting way, asked: "What makes you so gloomy? Have you lost another thousand in oil?" BOOTH replied he had been hard at work that day, and was about to leave Washington never to return. Just then a boy came out and said to BOOTH: "Yes, he is in his room." Upon which the gentleman walked on, supposing BOOTH would enter the hotel. About 7 o'clock Friday evening he came down from his room at the National, and was spoken to by several concerning his paleness, which, he said, proceeded from indisposition. Just before leaving, he asked the clerk if he was not going to Ford's Theatre, and added: "There will be some very fine acting there to-night." The door-keeper at the theatre noticed BOOTH as he passed in, and shortly after the latter entered the restaurant and in a hurried manner called for "Brandy, brandy, brandy," rapping at the same time on the bar.

The *Star* also contains the following article, headed, "A Clue to the Assailant of Mr. SEWARD:"

About three weeks ago, a man named ATZERARD, represented as being a merchant at Brigantown, Charles Co., Md., went to the stables of THOMPSON NAYLOR, corner of Thirteen and a half and E streets, for the purpose of selling a stallion, and a brown horse blind in one eye. ATZERARD made several attempts to sell the horses to the government, but without success, and finally disposed of the stallion to Mr. THOMPSON NAYLOR, stage contractor to Port Tobacco. He continued to visit Mr. NAYLOR's stables, however, and in a short time reported that he had also sold his brown horse.

On Friday afternoon a man named HARLD, who appeared to be intimate with ATZERARD, came to the stable and hired a roan pacing horse, and shortly afterward ATZERARD appeared with a bay horse, which he left, telling the hostler to have it ready for him at 10 o'clock. Upon calling for the horse at the appointed time, the hostler asked what had become of his friend HARLD and the roan, to which ATZERARD replied: "Has he not returned yet? He'll be here directly." Some time after the hostler heard the pace of the roan coming down from the direction of the Treasury, and went out to meet him, but the rider, apparently to avoid the hostler, turned up Fourteenth and then down F-street. The latter went back to the stable, and fearing HARLD intended to make off with the horse, saddled another, and followed him to the Navy yard bridge, where, in answer to his inquiries, the guard stated that a man riding such a horse had passed over, and was probably about a quarter of a mile in advance. He was told that he might go over, but could not return before morning. He then came back to the stable, and, hearing that a horse had been picked up in the street by the detectives, made inquiries, and, after giving his statement to the Provost-Marshal, was shown a saddle, which he identified beyond doubt as the one used on the brown horse when at NAYLOR's stable, which ATZERARD said he had sold.

This forenoon several prisoners from Prince George's County were brought to Washington. As they were being taken to the Old Capitol from Provost-Marshal INGRAHAM's office a large crowd followed, increasing in numbers at every corner, although, as a precautionary measure, the route taken was down the back streets. The crowd was a motly one, of all ages and colors. It being represented, and the report that the parties were BOOTH and SURRATT gaining credit, as they reached the Baltimore depot, the cry was raised, "Hang them," "kill them," and at the same time the prisoners were attacked with stones, who were struck several times, as were also the guard. Some orderly persons attempted to quiet the crowd by remonstrating with them and assuring them that they were mistaken, but they failed to stop the riotous proceedings, which, however, were soon quieted. After the guard were struck a number of times, they faced about and made ready to defend themselves with their muskets. The prisoners were delivered to the superintendent of the prison, each of them having been somewhat bruised by the flying missiles.

Among other arrests to-day were, it is said, several men in female apparel.

ORDERS CONCERNING THE DEATH OF THE PRESIDENT.

The following were issued to-day:

DEPARTMENT OF STATE, WASHINGTON, April 17, 1865.

It is hereby ordered that, in honor of the memory of our late illustrious Chief Magistrate, all officers and others subject to the orders of the Secretary of State wear crape upon the left arm for the period of six months.

W. HUNTER, Acting Secretary.

WAR DEPARTMENT, ADJUTANT-GENERAL'S OFFICE, WASHINGTON, April 16, 1865.

GENERAL ORDERS, No. 66.—The following order of the Secretary of War, announces to the armies of the United States the untimely and lamentable death of the illustrious ABRAHAM LINCOLN, late President of the United States.

WAR DEPARTMENT, WASHINGTON, April 16, 1865.

The distressing duty has devolved upon the Secretary of War to announce to the armies of the United States that at twenty-two minutes after seven o'clock on the morning of Saturday, the 15th day of April, 1865, ABRAHAM LINCOLN, President of the United States, died of a mortal wound inflicted upon him by an assassin. The armies of the United States will share with their fellow-citizens the feelings of grief and horror inspired by the most atrocious murder of their great and beloved President and Commander-in-Chief with profound sorrow, will mourn his death as a national calamity. The headquarters of every department, post, station, fort and arsenal will be draped in mourning for thirty days, and appropriate funeral honors will be paid by every army, and in every department, and at every military post, and at the Military Academy at West Point, to the memory of the late illustrious Chief Magistrate of the nation, and Commander-in-Chief of its armies. Lieut.-Gen. GRANT will give the necessary instructions for carrying this order into effect.

EDWIN M. STANTON, Secretary of War.

On the day after the receipt of the order at the headquarters of every military division, department, army post, station, fort and arsenal, and at the Military Academy at West Point, the troops and cadets will be paraded at ten o'clock A. M., and the order read to them. After which all labor and operations for the day will cease, and be suspended, as far as practicable in a state of war. The national flag will be displayed at half-staff. At dawn of day thirteen guns will be fired, and afterward at intervals of thirty minutes between the rising and the setting of the sun a single gun, and at the close of the day a national salute of thirty-six guns. The officers of the armies of the United States will wear the badge of mourning on the left arm and on their swords, and the colors of their commands and regiments will be put in mourning for the period of six months.

By command of Lieut.-Gen. GRANT.

(Signed) W. A. NICHOLS, Asst. Adj't-Gen.

WAR DEPARTMENT, WASHINGTON, April 16, 1865.

Lieut.-Gen. Grant, U. S. Army, Commanding Armies of the United States, Washington, D. C.:

GENERAL: You will please announce, by general order to the armies of the United States, that on Saturday, the 15th day of April, 1865, by reason of the death of ABRAHAM LINCOLN, the office of President of the United States devolved upon ANDREW JOHNSON, Vice-President, who on the same day took the official oath prescribed for the President and entered upon the duties of that office.

EDWIN M. STANTON, Secretary of War.

WAR DEPARTMENT, ADJUTANT GENERAL'S OFFICE, WASHINGTON, April 16, 1865.

GENERAL ORDERS, No. 7.—It is hereby announced to the armies of the United States, that on Saturday, the 15th day of April, 1865, by reason of the death of ABRAHAM LINCOLN, the office of President of the United States devolved upon ANDREW JOHNSON, Vice-President, who on the same day took the official oath prescribed for the President, and entered upon the duties of that office. By command of

Lieut.-Gen. GRANT.

W. A. NICHOLS, Asst. Adjt.-General.

NAVY DEPARTMENT, WASHINGTON, April 17, 1865.

SPECIAL ORDER.—Vice-Admiral D. G. FARRAGUT and WILLIAM B. SHUBRICK have been designated to make the necessary arrangements on the part of the Navy and Marine Corps for attending, on Wednesday next, the funeral of the late President of the United States.

GIDEON WELLES, Secretary of the Navy.

NAVY DEPARTMENT, WASHINGTON, April 17, 1865.

SPECIAL ORDER.—Officers of the Navy and Marine will assemble at the Navy Department in uniform, at 10 o'clock A. M. on Wednesday next, for the purpose of attending the funeral of the late President of the United States.

GIDEON WELLES, Secretary of the Navy.

NAVY DEPARTMENT, WASHINGTON, April 17, 1865.

SPECIAL ORDER.—By order of the President of the United States the Navy Department will be closed on Wednesday next, the day of the funeral solemnities of the late President of the United States. Labor will also be suspended on that day at each of the navy-yards and navy stations, and upon all the vessels of the United States. The flags of all vessels and at all navy-yards and stations and marine barracks will be kept at half-mast during the day, and at 12 o'clock, meridian, twenty-one minute guns will be fired by the senior officer of each squadron and the commandants of each of the navy-yards and stations.

GIDEON WELLES, Secretary of the Navy.

The Massachusetts Legislature on the Death of the President—Public Meeting.

BOSTON, Monday, April 17.

Gov. ANDREW delivered a special message to the Legislature this afternoon on the national bereavement, and appropriate resolutions were adopted by both branches. The Governor, accompanied by a special committee appointed by the Legislature will attend the funeral at Washington.

A special meeting of the City Government to-day adopted resolutions and appointed a committee to be present at the funeral.

The public meeting in Faneuil Hall was presided over by Mayor LINCOLN. It was an immense gathering of the people. Among the resolutions adopted were the following:

Resolved, That we now and here avow our determination on this solemn occasion to preserve the Union of our Fathers, to maintain the Constitution of the United States, to inforce the laws of the country, to remove every vestige of barbarism from our borders, to the end that personal freedom, enlightened civilization, pure morality and the sublime principles of the Christian religion may everywhere prevail; and to this we do live, in this temple of liberty where our Fathers have for generations have assembled, pledge our lives, our fortunes and our sacred honor, invoking the aid and guidance of Him in whose hands are the destinies of nations.

From Montreal.

MONTREAL, Monday, April 17.

On Saturday, the flags on the Court-house, City Hall, Custom-house, and other public buildings, were displayed at half-mast.

In all the churches, yesterday, the clergy, in their prayers, referred particularly to the assassination of the President, and expressed their detestation of the crime.

A Union prayer-meeting of all the different denominations of Christians, is to be held to-night in the Wesleyan Chapel, to express sympathy with the people of the United States.

Throughout Canada there is but one feeling—horror at the crime, and the warmest sympathy for the nation.

From Key West.

PHILADELPHIA, Monday, April 17.

An arrival from Key West, April 5, states that Admiral STRIBBLING left here on the 1st inst. to inspect the different vessels of his squadron. He will be absent about ten days. The fleet at Key West is in charge of Commander R. HANDY of the *Dale*.

The gunboat *Sagamore* arrived at Key West on the 4th inst., from Philadelphia.

The following vessels are now in port: the sloops-of-war *Ino* and *Dale*; steamers *Glaucus*, *Clyde*, *Honduras*, *Isonomia*, *Nitra*, *Fort Henry* and *Cherokee*.

The *Cherokee*, *Clyde*, *Honduras* and *Isnomia* were to start on a cruise immediately.

The United States steamer *Iuka* has captured the Confederate schooner *Comus*, with thirty-two bales of Sea Island cotton.

We have received news that some of our vessels on the blockade, near St. Makrs, have destroyed two schooners, which attempted to run the blockade, and were run ashore by their crews.

From Turk's Island.

The Turk's Island *Standard*, of the 1st inst., is received. Of the salt market it states: "The quantity shipped this week is very small, and our market of late has been dull. The opening of the canals in America will no doubt improve the trade. In the meantime we learn that at Salt Cay and East Harbor, as well as at this place, proprietors are increasing their stock. Last sales, 12 cents.

Marion, the Guerrilla, Killed.

LOUISVILLE, Ky., Monday, April 17.

The *Journal* has a special dispatch announcing the killing of MARION, the noted guerrilla leader, by one of Capt. FARREL's men, near Manton, on Saturday.

President Lincoln's funeral procession in Washington